THE
INTERNATIONAL
AUTHORS AND WRITERS
WHO'S WHO

THE INTERNATIONAL AUTHORS AND WRITERS WHO'S WHO

Publisher:
Nicholas S Law

Assistant Publisher:
Christopher Bosman

Consultant Editors:
David Cummings
Tanjam Jacobson

Editorial/Production Manager:
Jocelyn Timothy

Assistant Editors:
Sheryl Rigby
Rebecca Thompson

All communications to: International Authors and Writers Who's Who
International Biographical Centre
Cambridge CB2 3QP, England

THE
INTERNATIONAL
AUTHORS AND WRITERS
WHO'S WHO

FOURTEENTH EDITION

Consultant Editors:
David Cummings
Tanjam Jacobson

LONDON AND NEW YORK

This edition published 2014 by Routledge
2 Park Square, Milton Park, Abingdon, Oxon, OX14 4RN
711 Third Avenue, New York, NY 10017

Routledge is an imprint of the Taylor & Francis Group, an informa business

First published 1934
Second Edition 1935
Third Edition 1948
Fourth Edition 1960
Fifth Edition 1963
Sixth Edition 1972
Reprinted 1972
Seventh Edition 1976
Eighth Edition 1977
Ninth Edition 1982
Tenth Edition 1986
Eleventh Edition 1989
Twelfth Edition 1991
Thirteenth Edition 1993
Fourteenth Edition 1995

ISBN 978-0-948-87581-6 (hbk)

FOREWORD

In this the *Fourteenth Edition* of the **International Authors and Writers Who's Who**, we have been responsible for some 1,000 new or largely new entries, while the remainder have nearly all been revised. The result is a fuller, more accurate and more up-to-date source for those biographees included or for those who use this publication for reference purposes.

Included in the *Fourteenth Edition* are top editors, journalists and columnists in addition to prominent living writers in all of the major genres, fiction, non-fiction, poetry and drama. Entrants are primarily those who write in English and who have had their books published in the UK or the USA but a continuing feature of this edition is that it also includes those writers from non-English speaking countries whose work has received international acclaim. A large proportion of the new entrants in this edition consists of authors living in North America, whether native born or having recently settled there.

The format of the entries includes full biographical details which feature education, appointments and career, together with lists of major publications in date order, any literary honours, awards or prizes and details of membership to any societies.

As before every biographee was sent a typescript of his or her entry for amending and approval and the necessary corrections and updates have been incorporated in the final copy. It should be borne in mind, however, that even in a book with such a wide scope as the **International Authors and Writers Who's Who** it is not possible to include in each case all the information which is submitted. While every care is taken to ensure accuracy, it is inevitable that some detail will have 'fallen under the table'. If errors of this nature have occured we apologize in advance but if we are written to care of the publishers we will endeavour to put matters right in the next edition.

It only remains for us to thank all those who have helped to produce the *Fourteenth Edition*. The Publisher Nicholas Law has kindly allowed us to act as editors and we are particularly grateful to Production Manager Jocelyn Timothy and her staff for their patience, co-operation and efficiency.

David Cummings
Consultant Editor
UK, Commonwealth & Europe

Tanjam Jacobson
Consultant Editor
Canada & USA

March 1995

March 1995

INTERNATIONAL BIOGRAPHICAL CENTRE
RANGE OF REFERENCE TITLES

From one of the widest ranges of contemporary biographical reference works published under any one imprint, some IBC titles date back to the 1930's. Each edition is compiled from information supplied by those listed, who include leading personalities of particular countries or profession. Information offered usually includes date and place of birth; family details; qualification; career histories; awards and honours received; books published or other creative work; other relevant information including postal address. Naturally there is no charge or fee for inclusion.

New editions are freshly compiled and contain on average 80-90% new information. new titles are regularly added to the IBC reference library.

Titles include:

> Dictionary of International Biography
> Who's Who in Australasia and the Far East
> Who's Who in Western Europe
> Dictionary of Scandinavian Biography
> Dictionary of Latin American and Caribbean Biography
> International Who's Who in Art and Antiques
> International Authors and Writers Who's Who
> International Leaders in Achievement
> International Who's Who in Community Service
> International Who's Who in Education
> International Who's Who in Engineering
> International Who's Who in Medicine
> International Who's Who in Music and Musicians' Directory
> Men of Achievement
> The World Who's Who of Women
> The World Who's Who of Women in Education
> International Youth of Achievement
> Foremost Women of the Twentieth Century
> International Who's Who in Poetry and Poets' Encyclopaedia

Enquiries to:
International Biographical Centre
Cambridge, CB2 3QP, England

CONTENTS

CONTENTS

A

AALAVANDAAR. See: **GOPALACHAR Aalavandar.**

AARDEMA Verna Geneva, b. 6 June 1911, New Era, Michigan, USA. Elementary Teacher; Journalist. m. 1) Albert Aardema, 30 May 1936 (dec 1974), 1 son, 1 daughter, 2) Dr Joel Vugteveen, 3 Aug 1975. Education: BA, Michigan State College (now University), 1934. Appointments: Publicity Chairman, Juvenile Writers' Workshop, 1955-69; Staff Correspondent, Muskegon Chronicle. Publications: Why Mosquitoes Buzz in People's Ears, 1975; Who's in Rabbit's House?, 1977; Riddle of the Drum, 1978; Bringing the Rain to Kapiti Plain, 1981; What's So Funny, Ketu?, 1982; The Vingananee & the Tree Toad, 1983; Oh, Kojo! How Could You!, 1984; Bimwili & the Zimwi, 1985; Behind the Back of the Mountain, 1973; Tales for the Third Ear, 1969; A Bookworm Who Hatched, 1993; Sebgugu the Glutton, 1993; Misoso: Tales from Africa, 1993; Forthcoming books: Princess Gorilla and a New Kind of Water, 1988; Rabbit Makes a Monkey of Lion; Pedro and the Padre, 1991; Traveling to Tondo, 1991; Borreguita and the Coyote, 1991; Anansi Finds a Fool, 1992; Forthcoming, The Misoso Storybook, and This For That; books published in Japan, France, South America, England, Canada and USA. Contributions to: Instructor, Cricket and Christian Life. Honours: Caldecott Award, 1976; Lewis Carroll Shelf Award, 1978; Parents' Choice Awards, 1984, 1985; Parents' Choice, 1989, 1991; Junior Library Guild Selection, 1991; Redbook Award, 1991; ALA Notable Book, 1991. Memberships: Juvenile Writers' Workshop; Childrens' Reading Round Table, Chicago; National & Michigan Education Associations; Womens' National Book Association. Literary Agent: Curtis Brown Ltd. Address: 784 Via Del Sol, North Fort Myers, Florida, USA.

AAZIM Muzaffar, b. 29 Apr 1934, Kashmir, India. Poet; Author; Educationist. m. Padshah Jan, 14 Oct 1956, 2 sons. Education: University of Kashmir. Publications: Zolana, poems 1964; Man-i-Kaman, poems 1974; Many poems translated into various European Languages; Author of many plays, articles, papers and translations. Contributions to; Radio, TV, Magazines and Periodicals including Indian Poetry Review, Aaj Kal; Neb Kashmiri Shairi. Honours: Best Book Prize, Jammu & Kashmir Academy of Art, Culture & Languages, 1965, 1976; Soviet Land Nehru Award for the translation of War and Peace, 1978. Memberships: Sahitya Akademi (National Academy of Letters, India); Kashmir Academy of Art, Culture & Languages; The Brontë Society of England; Historical & Cultural Society; Advisory Committee, Kashmir University; The National Authors Registry, USA, 1994. Literary Agent: Dr Akhtar Purvez, Akmich, PO Box 318, Alkhay 11942, Saudi Arabia. Address: 11215 Oak Leaf Drive 802, Silver Springs, MD 20901, USA.

ABBAS (Khwaja) Ahmad, b. 7 June 1914, Panpit, Punjab, India. Novelist. Education: BA, 1933, LLB, 1935, Aligarph Muslim University. Appointments: Proprietor, Naya Sansar film production company, Bombay, 1951-. Publications include: Tomorrow Is Ours!, 1943, as Divided Heart, 1968; Defeat For Death: A Story Without Names, 1944; Blood and Stones, 1947; Inqilab, 1955; When Night Falls, 1968; Mera Naam, Joker, 1970; Maria, 1972; Boy Meets Girl, 1973; Bobby, 1973; Distant Dream, 1975; The World is My Village, 1983; Short stories: Not All Lies!, 1945; Rice and Other Stories, 1947; Cages of Freedom and Other Stories, 1952; One Thousand Nights on a Bed of Stones and Other Stories, 1957; The Black Son and Other Stories, 1963; The Most Beautiful Woman in the World, 1968; The Walls of Glass, 1977; Men and Women, 1977; The Thirteenth Victim, 1986; Several plays, screenplays and non-fiction works. Honours: Padma Shree, 1969. Address: c/o Blitz Publications, Canada Building, 3rd Floor, D N Road, Bombay 400 001, India.

ABBENSETTS Michael, b. 8 June 1938, British Guiana (now Guyana), became British citizen, 1974. Writer. Education: Queen's College, Guyana, 1952-56; Stanstead College, Quebec; Sir George Williams University, Montreal, 1960-61. Appointments: Security Attendant, Tower of London, 1963-67; Staff Member, Sir John Soane Museum, London, 1968-71; Resident playwright, Royal Court Theatre, London, 1974; Visiting Professor of Drama, Carnegie Mellon University, Pittsburgh, 1981. Publications: Plays: Sweet Talk (produced London, 1973, New York, 1974); London, Eyre Methuen, 1976; Alterations (produced London and New York, 1978; revised version produced London 1985); Samba (produced London, 1980), London, Eyre Methuen, 1980; In the Mood (produced London, 1981); Outlaw (produced Leicester and London, 1983); El Dorado (produced London, 1984); Writer for radio and television; Novel: Empire Road (novelization of television series, London, Panther, 1979. Honours: George Devine Award, 1973; Arts Council Bursary, 1977; Afro-Caribbean Award, 1979. Literary Agent: Anthony Sheil Associates, London. Address: Sheil Associates, 43 Doughty Street, London WC1N 2LF, England.

ABBEY Edward, b. 1927. Writer; Farmer. Publications: Jonathon Troy, 1954; The Brave Cowboy, 1958; Fire on the Mountain, 1962; Desert Solitaire (personal history), 1968; Black Sun, 1970 (in United Kingdom as Sunset Canyon); Cactus Country, 1973; Appalachian Wilderness, 1973; The Monkey Wrench Gang, 1975; The Journey Home, 1977; The Hidden Canyon (with J Blaustein), 1977; Back Roads of Arizona (with E Thollander), 1978; Abbey's Road, 1970; Desert Images (with D Muench), 1979; Good News, 1980; Down the River, 1982; Beyond the Wall, 1984; Slumgullion Stew: A Reader, 1985; The Fool's Progress, 1988; One Life at a Time, 1988; Hayduke Lives, 1990; A Voice Crying in the Wilderness, 1990. Address: Box 1690, Oracle, AZ 85623, USA.

ABBOTT John B Jr, b. 25 Feb 1956, Plainfield, New Jersey, USA. Mystery Writer. m. Maria G Di Tommaso, 3 Oct 1992. Education: BA, English, Rutgers University, 1985; Ed M, Rutgers University, 1995. Appointments: Writing Tutor, English Department, Rutgers University, New Brunswick, New Jersey, 1988-; Visiting Professional Lecturer, Rutgers University, 1989-; Instructor Middlesex County College, Edison, NJ; Adjunct Instructor, Mercer County Community College, Trenton, New Jersey, 1993-94; Attending EdM/EdD Program, Rutgers University, Graduate School of Education, New Brunswick, New Jersey; Writing Tutor, Middlesex County College, Edison, NJ, 1994-. Publications: Knight Moves, 1990; Interactive Murder Mystery Scripts: All in the Game; Two for the Money; The Botsford Inn Mystery; The Kris Kringle Kaper; How the West was Fun and Birthdays Can Be Murder; Smithsonian's Knight, 1992. Contributions to: Short stories/Editor in Chief, Untitled, Rutgers University, 1984-85; Cooking with Malice Domestic, 1991. Memberships: Active Member, Mystery Writers of America; Reading Committee Member, Edgar Allan Poe Award, Best Juvenile Mystery, 1994-95. New Jersey College English Association; National Council of Teachers of English; New Jersey Institute for Collegiate Learning & Teaching; New Jersey Association for Developemental Education. Address: 22 Church Street, PO Box 439, Kingston, NJ 08528-0439, USA.

ABISH Walter, b. 24 Dec 1931, Vienna, Austria. Writer. m. Cecile Abish. Literary Appointments: Ingram Marril Foundation, 1977; NEA Fellowship, 1979, 1985; Guggenheim Fellow, 1981; DAAD Berlin, 1987; MacArthur Fellow, 1987, 92; Lila Wallace-Readers Digest Fellow, 1992-95. Publications: Eclipse Fever, 1993; How German Is It, 1980; Alphabetical Africa, 1974; In The Future Perfect, 1977; 99: The New Meaning, 1990; Minds Meet, 1975; Duel Site, 1970. Contributions to: Paris Review; Conjunctions; Granta; Salmgundi; Partisan Review; Antaeus; New Directions Annual; TriQuarterly; Manuskripte. Honours: PEN Faulkner Award, 1980; Merit Medal, The American Academy of Arts and Letters, 1991. Membership: PEN. Literary Agent: Candida Donadio & Associates, 231 West 22nd Str, New York, NY 10011, USA. Address: PO Box 485, Cooper Square, NY 10276, USA.

ABLEMAN Paul, b. 1927. Writer. Publications: Even His Enemy (with Gertrude Macauley), 1948; I Hear Voices, 1958; As Near As I Can Get, 1962; Green Julia (play), 1966; Tests (playlets), 1966; Vac, 1968; Blue Comedy: Madly in Love, Hawk's Night, 1968; The Twilight of the Vilp, 1969; Bits: Some Porse Poems, 1969; Tornado Pratt, 1977; Shoestring (novelization of TV play), 1979; Porridge (novelization of screen play), 1979; Shoestring's Finest House, 1980; County Hall (novelization of TV series), 1981; The Anatomy of Nakedness, 1982; The Doomed Rebellion, 1983. Address: Flat 37, Duncan House, Fellows Road, London NW3, England.

ABRAHAM Claude Kurt, b. 1931. Writer. Literary Appointments: Faculty Member, University of Illinois, 1959-64; Professor of French, University of Florida, Gainesville, 1964-75; Professor of French, University of California, Davis, 1975-. Publications: Gaston d'Orleans et sa Cour, 1963, 1964; Bourgeois Gentilhomme, 1966; The Strangers, 1966; J Mesnard: Pascal (translated with M Abraham), 1969; Enfin Malherbe, 1971 (SAMLA Studies Award); Corneille, 1972; Tristan L'Hermite: Theatre Complet (with J Schweitzer and J van Baelen), 1974; J Racine, 1977; Tristan L'Hermite, 1980; Norman Satrists of the Age of Louis XIII, 1983; Moliere's Comedies - Ballets, 1984, 1985. Address: 1604 Westshore Street, Davis, CA 95616, USA.

ABRAHAM Henry, b. 1921. Appointments: Assistant Professor 1953-57, Associate Professor 1957-62, Professor of Political Science 1962-72, University of Pennsylvania, Philadelphia; James Hart Professor of Government and Foreign Affairs, University of Virginia, Charlottesville, 1971-. Publications: Compulsory Voting, 1955; Government as Entrepreneur and Social Servant, 1956; Courts and Judges: An Introduction to the Judical Process, 1959; Elements of Democratic Government, 4th Edition (with J A Cory), 1964; Essentials of American National Government (with J C Phillips), 1971; Freedom and the Court: Civil Rights and Liberties in the United States, 5th Edition, 1988; The Judiciary: The Supreme Court in the Governmental Process, 6th Edition, 1983, 7th Edition, 1986, 8th Edition, 1991; Justices and Presidents: A Political History of Appointments to the Supreme Court, 1975, 1985, 1992; American Democracy, 3rd Edition (with W E Keefe), 1989; The Judical Process: An Introductory Analysis of the Courts of the United States, England and France, 5th Edition, 1986, 6th Edition, 1992. Address: 906 Fendall Terrace, Charlottesville, VA 22903, USA.

ABRAHAMS Peter (Henry), b. 1919, Vrededorp, near Johannesburg, South Africa. Novelist. m. Daphne Elizabeth Miller, 3 children. Education: Church of England mission schools and colleges. Appointments include: Controller, West Indian News, Jamaica, 1955-64; Chairman, Radio Jamaica, Kingston, 1977-80. Publications: Song of the City, 1945; Mine Boy, 1946; The Path of Thunder, 1948; Wild Conquest, 1950; A Wreath for Undomo, 1956; A Night of Their Own, 1965; This Island Now, 1966; The View from Coyaba, 1985; Short stories: Dark Testament, 1942; Verse: A Black Man Speaks of Freedom, 1938. Address: Red Hills, PO Box 20, St Andrew, Jamaica.

ABRAHAMS Roger David, b. 1933, United States of America. Writer. Appointments: Professor of English and Anthropology, 1969-79, Chairman, Department of English, 1974-79, University of Texas, Austin; Kenan Professor of Humanities and Anthropology, Scripps and Pitzer Colleges, Claremont, 1979-. Publications: Deep Down in the Jungle, 1964, revised edition 1970; Anglo-American Folksong Style (with G W Foss Jr), 1968; Jump Rope Rhymes: A Dictionary, 1968; Positively Black, 1970; A Singer and Her Songs, 1970; Language and Cultural Diversity in American Education (with R C Troike), 1972; Deep the Water, Shallow the Shore, 1974; Talking Black, 1975; Afro-American Folk Culture: An Annotated Bibliography (with J Szwed), 1977; Between the Living and the Dead: Riddles Which Tell Stories, 1980; Counting Out Rhymes: A Dictionary (with Lois Rankin), 1980; And Other Neighborly Names (with Richard Bauman), 1981; Performers, Performances and Enactments, 1983; After Africa (with John Szwed), 1983; African Folktales, 1983; The Man-of-Words in the West Indies, 1983; Afro-American Folktales, 1985.

ABSE Dannie, b. 22 Sept 1923, Cardiff, Glamorgan, Wales. Medical Specialist; Writer. m. Joan Mercer, 1951, 1 son, 2 daughters. Education: St Illtyd's College, Cardiff; University of South Wales and Monmouthshire, Cardiff; King's College, London; Westminster Hospital, London; qualified as physician 1950, MRCS, LRCP; Served in the RAF 1951-54: Squadron Leader. Career: Specialist in charge of chest clinic, Central London Medical Establishment, 1954-; Senior Fellow in Humanities, Princeton University, New Jersey, 1973-74. Publications: Verse includes: Corgi Modern Poets in Focus 4, with others, edited by Jeremy Robson, 1972; Funland and Other Poems, London and New York, 1973; Lunchtime, 1974; Penguin Modern Poets 26, with D J Enright and Michael Longley, 1975; Collected Poems 1948-76, London and Pittsburgh, 1977; Way Out in the Centre, London 1981, as One-Legged on Ice, Athens, University of Georgia Press, 1981; Recordings: Poets of Wales, Argo, 1972; The Poetry of Dannie Avse, McGraw Hill; Dannie Abse, Canto, 1984; Plays include: Gone in January (produced London, 1978), published in Madog, 1981; Various plays for radio; Novels: Ash on a Young Man's Sleeve, London 1954, New York 1955; Some Corner of an English Field, London 1956, New York 1957; O Jones, O Jones, 1970; Voices in the Gallery, 1986; The Music Lover's Literary Companion, 1988; The Hutchinson Book of Post-War British Poets, 1989; Various other published works. Honours: Foyle Award, 1960; Welsh Arts Council Award for verse, 1971, for play 1980. Membership: President, Poetry Society, 1978-. Literary Agent: Anthony Sheil Associates Ltd, 2-3 Morwell Street, London WC1B 3AR. Address: 85 Hodford Road, London NW11 8NH, England.

ACHEBE Chinua, b. 16 Nov 1930, Ogidi, Anambra State. Writer. m. Christie C Okoli, 1961, 2 s, 2 d. Education: University College Ibadan, Appointments include: Producer, Nigerian Broadcsting Corp, Lagos, 1954-58; Regional Controller, Enugu, 1958-61; Director, Voice of Nigeria, Lagos, 1961-66; Senior Research Fellow, University of Nigeria, 1967-72; Founding Editor, Okike, 1971-; Professor, English, University of MA, 1972-75; University of CT, 1975-76; University of Nigeria, 1976-81; Professor Emeritus, 1985-. Publications include: Things Fall Apart, 1958; The Sacrifical Egg and Other Stories, 1962; A Man of the People, 1966; Chike and the River, 1966; Girls at War, 1972; How the Leopard Got His Claws, 1973; The Flute, 1978; The Trouble with Nigeria, 1983. Address: Bard College, Annandale On Hudson, NY 12504, USA.

ACHUGAR Hugo J, b. 9 Feb 1944, Uruguay. m. Marta Del Huerto Diaz, 23 Jan 1967, 1 son, 3 daughters. Education: Professor, Literature, IPA, Uruguay, 1969; PhD, University of Pittsburgh, USA, 1980. Appointments: Editor, Brecha, 1968-69; Editorial Board, Fragmentos, 1976-83; Editorial Board, Revista de Estudios Hispanicos, 1985-; Editorial Board, Cuadernos de Marcha, 1986-. Publications: Poetry: Las Mariposas Tropicales, 1987; Con Bigote Triste, 1971; El Derrumbe, 1969; Textos Para Decir Maria, 1976; Todo Lo Que Es Solido Se Disuelve En El Aire, 1989 (poetry); Forthcoming: Poesia y Sociedad. Contributor to: Marcha; Casa de Las Americas; Eco; Triquarterly. Honours: Literary price, Banda Oriental, 1969; National Literary Award, Poetry, 1969; Feria de Libros, 1973; Jry, Cuba, 1978; National Jury Uruguay, 1986. Memberships: ASESUR; PEN; MMLA; LASA. Address: Hispanic Studies, Northwestern University, Evanston, IL 60208, USA.

ACKERMAN Diane, b. 7 Oct 1948, Waukegan, Illinois, USA. Writer. Education: BA, English, Pennsylvania State University, 1970; MFA Creative Writing 1973, MA English 1976, PhD 1978, Cornell University. Appointments include: Writer-in-residence, College of William & Mary 1982, Ohio University 1983, Washington University 1983; Director, Writers programme, Washington University, St Louis, 1984-86; Visiting Writer, Cooper Union 1984, New York University 1986, Columbia University 1986, Cornell 1987, Columbia 1987. Publications: Poetry: Jaguar of Sweet Laughter, 1990; Lady Faustus, 1984; Wife of Light, 1978; The Planets: A Cosmic Pastoral, 1976; Prose: On Extended Wings, 1985, 1987; Twilight of the Tenderfoot, 1980; Reverse Thunder, 1989; A Natural History of the Senses, 1990; The Moon by Whale Light, 1990; A Natural History of Love, 1994. Contributions to: Newyorker; Life; New York Times; Parade; National Geographic. Honours include: NEA, 1986; Peter I B Lavan Award, Academy of American Poets, 1985; Advisory Board, Planetary Society, 1980-; Board of Directors, Associated Writing Programmes, 1982-85; Poetry Panel, NY Foundation for the Arts, 1985; Poetry judge, various awards & festivals; Panellist, various bodies. Literary Agent: Morton Janklow, 598 Madison Avenue, New York, NY 10022, USA.

ACKROYD Peter, b. 5 Oct 1949, London, England. Writer. Education: MA, Cambridge University, 1971; Mellon Fellowship, Yale University, 1971-73; Hon D Litt, Exeter University, 1992. Appointments: Literary Editor, Spectator, 1973-77; Lead Reviewer, The Times, 1976-. Publications include: The Great Fire of London, 1982; The Last Testament of Oscar Wilde, 1983; Hawksmoor, 1985; Chatterton, 1987; Ezra Pound and His World, 1981; Dickens, 1990; Introduction to Dickens, 1991; English Music, 1992; The House of Doctor Dee, 1993; Dan Leno and the Limehouse Solemn, 1994; Dressing UP: Tranvestism and Drag: The History of an Obsession, 1979. Honours: Somerset Maugham Award, 1984; Whitbread Prize for Biography, 1985; Royal Society of Literatures WE Heinemann Award, 1985; Whitbread Prize for Fiction, 1986; Guardian FictionAward, 1986. Memberships; Royal Society of Literature. Literary agent: Anthony Sheil Associates. Address: c/o Anthony Sheil Ltd, 43 Doughty Str, London wC1N 2LF, England.

ACKROYD Peter (Runham), b. 1917. Appointments include: Samuel Davidson Professor, Old Testament Studies, 1961-82; Professor Emeritus, 1982-; Dean, Faculty of Theology, 1968-69; Fellow, Kings College, University of London, 1969-; Lecturer, Cambridge University, 1952-61; Ordained, Anglican Priest, 1958; President, Society for Old Testament Study, 1972. Publications include: Freedom in Action, 1951; The People of the Old Testament, 1959; Continuity, 1962; The Old Testament Tradition, 1963; Exile and Restoration, 1968; Words and Meanings, 1968; The Cambridge History of the Bible I, 1970; Israel Under Babylon and Persia, 1970; The Age of the Chronicler, 1970; Doors of Perception, 1978, 83; Studies in the Religious Tradition of the Old Testament, 1987; The Chronicler in his Age, 1991. Address: 155 Northumberland Road, North Harrow, HA2 7RB.

ACLAND Alice (Anne Marreco), b. 1912. Author; Freelance Writer. Publications: Caroline Norton, 1948; Templeford Park, 1954; A Stormy Spring, 1955; A Second Choice, 1956; A Person of Discretion, 1958; (As Anne Marreco): The Charmer and the Charmed, 1963; The Boat Boy, 1964; The Rebel Countess, 1967; The Corsican Ladies, 1974; The Secret Wife, 1975; The Ruling Passion, 1976. Address: c/o Curtis Brown Limited, 162-168 Regent Street, London W1, England.

ACZEL Tamas, b. 16 Dec 1921, Budapest, Hungary. Novelist; Professor of English. m. 5 Aug 1959, 1 son, 1 daughter. Education: BA, University of Budapest, 1948; MA, Eotvos Lorant Universit, Budapest, 1950; DLitt, 1992. Appointments: Editor in Chief; Szikra, 1948-59, Csillag, 1950-52; Secretary, Hungarian Writers Association, 1953-54; Editor, Hungarian Literary Gazette, London, 1957-63; Professor, English, University of Massachusetts. Publications: Novels: In the Shadow of Liberty, 1948; Storm and Sunshine, 1950; The Revolt of the Mind, 1959; The Ice Age, 1966; Underground Russian Poetry, 1973; Illuminations, 1980; The Hunt, 1991; Poetry: Song on the Ship, 1941; Vigilance and Faith, 1948; In Lieu of a Report, 1950; Flames and Ashes, 1955; On the Secret, 1956. Contributor to: Preuves; Encounter; Poesie; Monat; Forum; Massachusetts Review. Honours: Kossuth Prize for Literature, 1949; Stalin Prize for Literature, 1952; NEA Award, 1977; Fulbright Scholar, Hungary, 1991-92. Memberships: Vice President, PEN in Exile, American Branch. Literary Address: Department of English, University of Massachusetts, Amherst, MA 01003, USA.

ADAIR Ian (Hugh), b. 1942. Writer. Appointments: Writer; Partner, Supreme Magic Company, Devon, England; President, Ideas Associated; Former Television Announcer and Presenter, STV, Westward Television. Publications: Adair's Ideas, 1958; Magic with Doves, 1958; Dove Magic, Parts 1 and 2, 1959; Dove Magic Finale, 1960; Ideen, 1960; Television Dove Magic, 1961; Television Card Manipulations, 1962; Television Puppet Magic, 1963; Doves in Magic, 1964; Doves from Silks, 1964; New Doves from Silks, 1964; Dove Classics, 1964; More Modern Dove Classics, 1964; Further Dove Classics, 1964; Classical Dove Secrets, 1964; Diary of a Dove Worker, 1964; Magic on the Wing, 1965; Balloon-o-Dove, 1965; Spotlite on Doves, 1965; Watch the Birdie, 1965; Dove Dexterity, 1965; Rainbow Dove Routines, 1965; Heads Off!, 1965; Tricks and Stunts with a Rubber Dove, 1965; Television Dove Steals, 1965; A La Zombie, 1966; Pot Pourri, 1966; Magical Menu (3 vols), 1967; Encyclopedia of Dove Magic, vols 1 and 2, 1968, vol 3, 1973, vol 4, 1977, vol 5, 1980; Magic with Latex Budgies, 1969; Paddle Antics, 1969; Conjuring as a Craft, 1970; Magic Step by Step, 1970; Party Planning and Entertainment, 1972; Oceans of Notions, 1973; Papercraft-Step by Step, 1975; Card Tricks, 1975; Glove Puppetry, 1975; The Know How Book of Jokes and Tricks, 1977; Complete Party Planner, 1978; Complete Guide to Conjuring, 1978; Magic, 1979; Complete Guide to Card Conjuring, 1980; Swindles: The Cheating Game, 1980. Address: 20 Ashley Terrace, Bideford, Devon, England.

ADAIR Jack. See: **PAVEY Don.**

ADAIR James Radford, b. 1923, USA. Writer. Appointments: Editor, Power for Living, Free Way, Teen Power and Counselor weekly churchpapers, 1949-77; Senior Editor, Victor Books Division, Scripture Press Publications Inc, Wheaton, 1970-. Publications: Saints Alive, 1951; Editor, God's Power Within, 1961; We Found Our Way (edited with T Miller), 1964; Editor, Teen with a Future, 1965; Editor, God's Power to Triumph, 1965; The Old Lighthouse, 1966; The Man from Steamhouse, 1967, 1988; Editor, Tom Skinner Top Man of the Lords and Other Stories, 1967; M R DeHaan: The Man and His Ministry, 1969; Editor, Hooked on Jesus, 1971; Escape from Darkness (edited with Ted Miller), 1982; Surgeon on Safari (autobiography, Paul J Jorden MD), 1976, 1985; A Greater Strength (autobiography, Paul Anderson; co-authored W/Jerry Jenkins), 1975, 1990; 101 Days in the Gospels, Oswald Chambers, compiled with Harry Verploegh, 1992; 101 Days in the Epistles with Oswald Chambers, compiled with Harry Verploegh, 1994. Address: 703 Webster Avenue, Wheaton, IL 60187, USA.

ADAM SMITH Patricia (Patsy) Jean, b. 1924, Australia. Author. Appointments: Adult Education Officer, Hobart, Tasmania, 1960-66; Manuscripts Field Officer, State Library of Victoria, 1970-82; President, Federal Fellowship of Australian Writers, 1973-75. Publications: Hear the Train Blow, 1963; Moon Bird People, 1964; There Was a Ship, 1965; Tiger Country, 1966; The Rails Go Westward, 1967; Folklore of Australian Railmen, 1969; No Tribesmen, 1970; Tasmania Sketchbook, 1972; Launceston Sketchbook, 1972; Port Arthur Sketchbook, 1973; Carcoo Salute, 1973; The Desert Railway, 1974; Romance of Australian Railways, 1974; The Anzacs, 1978; Outback Heroes, 1981; The Shearers, 1982; Australian Women at War, 1984; Heart of Exile, 1986; Prisoner of War from Gallipoli to Korea, 1992; Goodbye Girlie, 1994. Honour: OBE AO; Winner, Triennial Award; Order of Australia. Address: 47 Hawksburn Road, South Yarra Vic 3141, Australia.

ADAMS Alice, b. 14 Aug 1926, Fredericksburg, Virginia, USA. Author. m. 1946, divorced 1958, 1 son. Education: BA, Radcliffe College, 1945. Publications: Careless Love (in United Kingdom as The Fall of Daisy Duke), 1966; Families and Survivors, 1975; Listening to Billie, 1978; Beautiful Girl (short stories), 1979; Tich Rewards, 1980; Superior Women, 1984; Return Trips, 1985; Second Chances, 1988; After You're Gone, 1989; Caroline's Daughters, 1991; Mexico, 1991; Roses, Rhododendron. Contributions to: New Yorker; Atlantic Monthly; Redbook; McCalls; Paris Review. Honour: American Academy of Arts & Letters, Literature Award, 1992. Address: 2661 Clay Street, San Francisco, CA 94115, USA.

ADAMS Chuck. See: **TUBB E(dwin) C(harles).**

ADAMS Clifton, (Jonathon Gant, Matt Kinkaid, Clay Randall), b. 1919. Author; Musician; Freelance Writer. Publications: Western Novels: The Desperado, 1950; A Noose for the Desperado, 1951; Six Gun Boss (As Clay Randall), 1952; The Colonel's Lady, 1952; When Oil Ran Red (As Clay Randall), 1953; Two Gun Law, 1954; Gambling Man, 1955; Law of the Trigger, 1956; Outlaw's Son, 1957; Boomer (as Clay Randall), 1957; Killer in Town, 1959; Stranger in Town, 1960; The Legend of Lonnie Hall, 1960; Day of the Gun, 1962; Reckless Men, 1962; The Moonlight War, 1963; The Dangerous Days of Kiowa Jones, 1963; The Oceola Kid (As Clay Randall), 1963; Hardcase for Hire (As Clay Randall), 1963; Amos Flagg Series, 6 vols (As Clay Randall), 1963-69; Doomsday Creek, 1964; The Hottest Fourth of July in the History of Hangtree County, 1964 (in United Kingdom as The Hottest Fourth of July, 1965); The Grabhorn Bounty, 1965; Shorty, 1966; A Partnership with Death, 1967; The Most Dangerous Profession, 1967; Dude Sheriff, 1969; Tragg's Choice, 1969; The Last Days of Wolf Garnett, 1970 (in United Kingdom as Outlaw Destiny, 1972); Biscuit-Shooter, 1971; Rogue Cowboy, 1971; The Badge and Harry Cole, 1972 (in United Kingdom as Lawman's Badge, 1973); Concannon, 1972; Hard Times and Arnie Smith, 1972; Once an Outlaw, 1973; The Hard Time Bunch, 1973; Hasle and the Medicine Man, 1973; Crime Novels: Whom Gods Destroy, 1953; Hardcase (As Matt Kinkaid), 1953; Death's Sweet Song, 1955; The Race of Giants (As Matt Kinkaid), 1956; Never Say No to a Killer (as Jonathon Gant), 1956; The Very Wicked, 1960; The Long Vendetta (as Jonathon Gant), 1963. Address: c/o Ace Books, Berkeley Publishing Group, 200 Madison Avenue, New York, NY 10016, USA.

ADAMS Daniel. See: **NICOLE Christopher Robin.**

ADAMS Deborah, b. 22 Jan 1956, Tennessee, USA. Writer. Publications: Poetry: Propriety, 1976; Looking for Heroies, 1984; Mystery: All the Great Pretenders, 1992; All the Crazy Winters, 1992; All the Dark Disguises, 1993; All the Hungry Mothers, in print. Memberships: Sisters in Crime; MWA; Appalachian Writers' Association. Address: Rt 4, Box 664, Waverly, TN 37185, USA.

ADAMS Douglas (Noel), b. 11 March 1952, Writer; Producer. Education: BA, MA, St Johns College, Cambridge. Appointments: Radio Producer, BBC, London, 1978; Script Editor, Doctor Who, BBC TV, 1978-80. Publications include: The Hitch Hikers Guide to the Galexy, 1978; The Restaurant at the End of the Universe, 1980; The Meaning of Life, 1984; So Long, And Thanks for All the Fish, 1984; The Utterly Itterly Merry, 1986; Comic Relief Christmas Book, 1986; The Long Dark Tea Time of the Soul, 1988; Last Chance to See, 1990; Mostly Harmless, 1991. Address: c/o Ed Victor Ltd, 6 Bayley Str, London WC1B 3HB, England.

ADAMS Harold, b. 20 Feb 1923, Clark, South Dakota, USA. Executive. m. Betty E Skogsberg, 17 Sept 1959, div Apr 1965, 1 daughter. Education: BA, University of Minnesota, 1950. Publications: Murder, 1981; Paint the Town Red, 1982; The Missing Moon, 1983; The Naked Liar, 1985; The Fourth Widow, 1986; When Rich Men Die, 1987; The Barbed Wire Noose, 1987; The Man Who Met the Train, 1988; The Man Who Missed The Party, 1989; The Man Who Was Taller Than God, 1992; A Perfectly Proper Murder, 1993; A Way with Widows, 1994. Honours: Minnesota Book Award, Mystery & Detective,

1993; Shamus Award, Best Private Eye Novel, 1992. Memberships: Author's Guild; Mystery Writers of America. Literary Agent: Ivy Fischer Stone. Address: 12916 Greenwood Road, Hopkins, MN 55343, USA.

ADAMS Hazard, b. 15 Feb 1926, Cleveland, OH, USA. University Professor. m. 17 Sept 1949, 2 sons. Education: BA, Princeton University, 1948; MA 1949, PhD 1953, University of Washington. Appointments: Instructor, Cornell University, 1952-56; Assistant Professor, University of Texas, 1956-59; Associate Professor to Professor, Michigan State University, 1959-64; Professor and Founding Chair of English, University of California, Irvine, 1964-77; Byron W and Alice L Lockwood Professor of Humanities, University of Washington, 1977-; Fulbright Lecturer, Trinity College Dublin, 1961-62; Professor of English, University of California, Irvine, 1990-94. Publications include: (ed) poems by Robert Simeon Adams, 1952; Blake and Yeats: The Contrary Vision, 1955; William Blake - A Reading, 1963; The Contexts of Poetry, 1963; Poetry: An Introductory Anthology, 1968; (ed) Fiction as Process, 1968; The Horses of Instruction (novel), 1968; The Interests of Criticism, 1969; The Truth About Dragons (novel), 1971; (ed) Critical Theory Since Plato, 1972 (reved 1992); Lady Gregory, 1973; Philosophy of the Literary Symbolic, 1983; The Book of Yeats's Poems, 1990; Antithetical Essays on Literary Criticism and Liberal Education, 1990; (ed) Critical Essays on William Blake. Contributor to: Numerous poetry, scholarly and critical journals, 1954-. Membership: American Conference for Irish Studies. Address: 3930 N E 157th Place, Seattle, WA 98155, USA.

ADAMS James MacGregor David, b. 22 Apr 1951, Newcastle, England. Journalist; Author. m. Rene Thatcher Riley, 1 July 1990, 1 daughter. Education: Harrow, 1964-69; Neuchatel University, 1979-71. Publications: The Unnatural Alliance, 1984; The Financing of Terror, 1986; Secret Armies, 1988; Ambush (the War Between the SAS and the IRA) with Robin, Morgan and Anthony Bambridge, 1988; Merchants of Death, 1990; The Final Terror, 1991; Bull's Eye, 1992; Taking the Tunnel, 1993. Contributions to: The Sunday Times; Washington Post; Los Angeles Times; Atlantic. Literary Agent: Janklow Nesbit. Address: c/o The Sunday Times, 1 Pennington Street, London E1 9XW, England.

ADAMS Joanna Z. See: **KOCH Joanne Barbara.**

ADAMS Perseus, b. 11 Mar 1933, Cape Town, South Africa. Writer; Journalist; Teacher; Poet. Education: BA at the University of Cape Town, 1952; Cert Ed, 1961. Appointments: Journalist and English Teacher. Publications: The Land at My Door, 1965; Grass for the Unicorn, 1975. Honours: South Africa State Poetry Prize, 1963; Festival of Rhodesia Prize, 1970; Keats Memorial International Prize, 1971; Bridport Arts Festival Prize, 1984; Runner-Up, Bard of the Year, 1993. Address: 21 Mapesbury Road, Kilburn, London NW2, England.

ADAMS Richard George, b. 9 May 1920, Newbury, Berkshire, England. Author. m. Barbara Elizabeth Acland, 26 Sept 1949, 2 d. Education: MA, Worcester College, Oxford, 1948. Publications: Watership Down, 1972; Shardik, 1974; The Plague Dogs, 1977; The Girl in a Swing, 1980; Nature through the Seasons; The Tyger Voyage, 1976; The Ships Cat, 1977; Nature Day & Night, 1978; The Iron Wolf, 1980; Voyage through the Antarctic, 1982; Maia, 1984; The Bureaucats, 1985; A Nature Diary, 1985; Traveller, 1988; The Day Gone By, 1990. Contributions to: Numerous Journals & Magazines. Honours: Carnegie Medal, 1972; Guardian Award of Childrens Literature, 1972; Medal, CA Young Readers Association, 1977. Memberships: Royal Society of Literature; RSPCA. Literary Agent: David Higham Associates Ltd. Address: Benwells, 26 Church St, Whitchurch, Hants, RG28 7AR, England.

ADAMSON Robert, b. 17 May 1943, Sydney, New South Wales, Australia. Publisher; Designer; Writer. m. Cheryl Adamson, 1973. Appointments: Worked as a pastry cook, fisherman and journalist in the 1960's; Associate Editor, 1968-70, Editor 1970-75 and Assistant Editor 1975-77, New Poetry magazine, Sydney; Editor and Director, Prism Books, Sydney 1970-77; Founding Editor and Director, with Dorothy Hewett, Big Smoke Books, Sydney, 1979-; Designer for Prism Books and New Poetry magazine, 1970-; Designer for Big Smoke Books, 1979-. Publications: Verse: Canticles on the Skin, 1970; The Rumour, 1971; Swamp Riddles, 1974; Theatre I-XIX, 1976; Cross the Border, 1977; Selected Poems, 1977; Where I Came From, 1979; The Law at Heart's Desire, 1982; Novel: Zimmer's Essay, with Bruce Hanford, 1974. Honours: Australia Council Fellowship, 1976, 1977; Grace Leven Prize, 1977. Address: Big Smoke Boks, 1/2 Billyard Avenue, Elizabeth Bay, NSW 2011, Australia.

ADCOCK Fleur, b. 1934, New Zealand. Poet. Publications: The Eye of the Hurricane, 1964; Tigers, 1967; High Tide in the Garden, 1971; The Scenic Route, 1974; The Inner Harbour, 1979; Below Loughrigg, 1979; Selected Poems, 1983; The Virgin and the Nightingale, 1983; The Incident Book, 1986; Time Zones, 1991; Editor: The Oxford Book of Contemporary New Zealand Poetry, 1982; The Faber Book of 20th Century Wowens Poetry, 1987; Memberships: FRSL. Address: 14 Lincoln Road, London N2 9DL, England.

ADDINGTON Larry Holbrook, b. 1932, USA. Writer; Historian. Appointments: Assistant Professor of History 1962-64, San Jose State College; Consultant to the Institute of Advanced Studies, US Army War College, Carlisle, 1968-69; Associate Professor, Professor of History, The Citadel, 1970-; Head, History Department, The Citadel, 1989-94, The Military College of South Carolina, Charleston, 1964-; Visiting Professor, Duke Univerity, 1976-77, Professor Emeritus, 1994. Publications: From Moltke to Hitler: The Evolution of German Military Doctrine 1865-1939, 1967; The Blitzkrieg Era and the German General Staff 1865-1941, 1971; The Patterns of War since the 18th Century, 1984 (2nd edition, 1994); The Patterns of War through the Eighteenth Century, 1990. Address: History Department, The Citadel, Charleston, SC 29409, USA.

ADELBERG Doris. See: **ORGEL Doris.**

ADELI Hojjat, b. 3 June 1950, Southern Shore of Caspian Sea, Iran. Engineering Educator; Author. m. Nahid Dadmehr, Feb 1979, 2 sons, 2 daughters. Education: BS, MS, University of Tehran, 1973; PhD, Stanford University, USA, 1976. Career: Founder, Editor-in-Chief, International Journal of Microcomputers in Civil Engineering, 1986-; Editor-in-Chief, Heuristics, The Journal of Knowledge Engineering, 1991-93; Founder, Editor-in-Chief, Integrated Computer-Aided Engineering, 1993-; Plenary Lecturer, international conferences in Italy, Mexico, Japan, China, USA, Canada, Portugal, Germany, Morocco, Singapore. Publications: Interactive Microcomputer-Aided Structural Design, 1988; Expert Systems for Structural Design (with K V Balasubramanyam), 1988; Parallel Processing in Structural Engineering (with O Kamal), 1993; Machine Learning - Neural Networks, Genetic Algorithms, and Fuzzy Systems (with S L Hung), 1995; Editor, 10 books. Contributions to: Over 250 articles to 40 research journals. Honours: Numerous awards including: Lichtenstein Award for Faculty Excellence, 1990; Lumely Research Award, Ohio State University, 1994. Memberships: Fellow, World Literary Academy; Editorial Board, 22 journals. Address: 1540 Picardae Ct, Powell, OH 43065, USA.

ADHIKARI Santos Kumar, b. 24 Nov 1923, India. Writer; Author; Retired College Principal. m. Sadhona. Education: Calcutta University; Indian Institute of Bankers. Appointments include: Honours Vidyasagar Lectures of the University of Calcutta. Publications include: Clouds on the Horizon, 1960; Novels: Rakta Kamal, 1967; Nirjan Sikhar, 1971; Banking Law & Practice; Lending Banker; Paari Collection of Poems, 1986; Vidyasager and the New National Consciousness, 1990; Netaji Subhas Chandra, 1990. Contributions to: Major Journals, Calcutta; All Indian Radio. Honours include: PRASAD Award, 1986. Memberships: West Bengl Branch PEN; Vidyasagar Research Ctr; Asiatic Society; National Council of Akhil Bharat Bhasha Sahitya Sammelan. Address: Vidyasager Research Ctr, 81 Raja Basanta Roy Road, Calcutta 700 029, India.

ADISA Opal Palmer, b. 6 Nov 1954, Kingston, Jamaica. Teacher. m. V K Tarik Farrar, 12 Aug 1989, 1 son, 2 daughters. Education: BA, Hunter College, City of New York University, 1975; MA, English, San Francisco State University, 1981; MA, Drama, 1986; PhD, University of California, 1992. Appointments: Head Teacher, Booker T Washington Child Development Center, San Francisco, 1978-79; Teacher, Counselor, Lucinda Weeks Center, San Francisco, 1979-81; Instructor, City College of San Francisco, 1980-84; Lecturer, San Francisco State University, 1981-87; Writer, Development Studies Center, San Ramon, CA, 1991; Lecturer, University of California, Berkeley, 1992; Associate Professor and Chair of Ethnic Studies, California College of Arts & Crafts, Fall 1993-. Publications: Tamarind & Other Mango Women; Traveling Women; Bake Face & Other Guava Stories; Pina The Many Eyed Fruit; Essays Inc, Womens Studies International Forum; This Poem Knows You; Book Reviews Inc, The Maidu Indian Myths & Stories of Hanc'ibyim; This Childs Gonna Live; No Telephone to Heaven; Fierce Love (recording with Devorah Major); Poetry & Music. Contributions to: Frontiers; The Berkeley Poetry Review. Honours include: Master Folk Artist; Push Cart Prize;

Affirmative Action Dissertation Year Fellowship; Merit Certificate; Bronze Medal; Feminist Institute & Gender Study Research Grant; Winner, PEN Oakland/Josephine Miles Award for Tamarind and Mango Women. Memberships: Modern Language Association; The Society for the Study of Multi Ethnic Literature of the United States; Diasponic Representative of CAFRA. Address: PO Box 10625, Oakland, CA 94610, USA.

ADKINS Arthur William Hope, b. 1929. Appointments: Assistant, Humanity Department, University of Glasgow, 1954-56; Lecturer in Greek, Bedford College, University of London, 1956-61; Fellow, Classical Languages and Literature, Exeter College, Oxford, 1961-65; Professor of Classics, University of Reading, 1966-74; Visiting Senior Fellow, Society for the Humanities, Cornell University, Ithaca, New York, 1969-70; Edward Olson Professor, Depts of Classical Languages, Literature, Philosophy and Early Christian Literature; Chairman, Committee on Ancient Mediterranean World, University of Chicago, 1974-82. Publications: Merit and Responsibility: A Study in Greek Values, 1960; From the Many to the One: A Study of Personality and Views of Human Nature in the Context of Ancient Greek Society, Values and Beliefs, 1970; Moral Values and Political Behaviour in Ancient Greece, 1972; Poetic Craft in the Early Greek Elegists, 1985; Joint Editor, University of Chicago, Readings in Western Civilization, Vol I, The Greek Polis. Memberships: American Philological Association; Classical Association of Great Britain; Society, Promotion of Hellenic Studies; American Philosophical Association. Address: Department of Classics, University of Chicago, 1050 E 59th Street, Chicago, IL 60637, USA.

ADLER C(arole) S, b. 23 Feb 1932, Long Island, New York, USA. Children's Book Author. m. Arnold R Adler, 22 June 1952, 3 sons. Education: BA 1952, Hunter College; MS 1964, Russell Sage College. Publications: The Magic of the Glits, 1979; The Silver Coach, 1979; In Our House Scott is My Brother, 1980; The Cat That Was Left Behind, 1981; Down By the River, 1981; Shelter on Blue Barns Road, 1981; Footsteps on the Stairs, 1982; The Evidence That Wasn't There, 1982; The Once in a While Hero, 1982; Some Other Summer, 1982; The Shell Lady's Daughter, 1983; Get Lost Little Brother, 1983; Roadside Valentine, 1983; Shadows on Little Reef Bay, 1984; Fly Free, 1984; Binding Ties, 1985; With Westie and the Tin Man, 1985; Good-Bye Pink Pig, 1985; Split Sisters, 1986; Kiss The Clown, 1986; Carly's Buck 1987; Always and Forever Friends, 1988; If You Need Me, 1988; Eddie's Blue Winged Dragon, 1988; One Sister Too Many, 1989; The Lump in the Middle, 1989; Help Pink Pig! 1990; Ghost Brother, 1990; Mismatched Summer, 1991; A Tribe for Lexi, 1991; Tuna Fish Thanksgiving, 1992; Daddy's Climbing Tree, 1993; Willie, the Frog Prince, 1994; That Horse Whiskey, 1994; Youn Hee and Me, 1995; Court Yard Cat, 1995. Honours: William Allen White Award and the Golden Kite Award for the Magic of the Glits; The Shell Lady's Daughter chosen by ALA as Best Young Adult Book of 1984; With Westie and the Tin Man won the Children's Book Award of the Child Study Committee in 1986; That committee has commended several of her books; Split Sisters in 1987 and Ghost Brother in 1991 were IRA Children's Choice selections; One Sister Too Many was on 1991 Young Adults' Choices list; Always and Forever Friends and Eddie's Blue Winged Dragon were on a 1991 IRA 99 Favourite Paperbacks List; Many of her books have been on state lists; She has been widely published in Japan, Germany, England, Denmark, Austria, Sweden and Norway. Memberships: SCBW, Authors Guild. Address: 1350 Ruffner Road, Schenectady, NY 12309, USA.

ADLER Margot Susanna, b. 16 Apr 1946, Little Rock, Arkansas, USA. Journalist; Radio Producer; Talk Show Host; New York Bureau Chief -Correspondent, National Public Radio. Education: BA, University of California, Berkeley, 1968; MS, Columbia School of Journalism, 1970; Nieman Fellow, Harvard University, 1982. Publication: Drawing Down the Moon: Witches, Druids, Goddess-Worshippers & Other Pagans in America Today, 1979, paperback 1981, revised 1986; A 1960's Memoir: Heretics Heart, forthcoming. Memberships: Authors Guild; AFTRA. Literary Agent: Jane Rotrosen. Address: 333 Central Park West, New York, NY 10025, USA.

ADLER Mortimer Jerome, b. 1902, USA. Writer. Education: PhD, Columbia University, 1928; BA Columbia College, 1983. Appointments: Director, Institute for Philosophical Research, Chicago, 1952-; Editor, The Great Ideas Today series, 1962-; Gateway to the Great Books series, 1963-; The Annals of America series, 1968-; Chairman, Board of Editors, 1974-; Editor-in-Chief, Great Books of the Western World (2nd edition), 1990-; Encyclopaedia Britannica,

Chicago; Secretary to Editor, New York Sun, 1915-17. Publications include: Dialectic, 1927; Crime, Law and Social Science (with Jerome Michael), 1933; Art and Prudence: A Study in Practical Philosophy, 1937 revised edition as Poetry and Politics, 1965; What Man Has Made of Man, 1937, 1994; Problems for Thomists: The Problem of Species, 1940; How to Read a Book: The Art of Getting a Liberal Education, 1940, revised edition with Charles Van Doren, 1972; The Difference of Man and the Difference It Makes, 1967, 1993; The Idea of Freedom, 2 vols, 1958, 1961; Some Questions About Language: A Theory of Human Discourse, 1976, 1991; Philosopher at Large: An Intellectual Autobiography, 1977; The Common Sense of Politics, 1971; Aristotle for Everybody, 1978; Six Great Ideas, 1981; Ten Philosophical Mistakes, 1985; A Guidebook to Learning: For the Lifelone Pursuit of Wisdom, 1986; We Hold These Truths: Understanding the Ideas and Ideals of the Constitution, 1987; Reforming Education, 1988; Intellect: Mind over Matter, 1990; Truth in Religion, 1990; Haves Without Have-Nots, 1991; Desires, Right and Wrong, 1991; A Second Look in the Rearview Mirror, 1992; The Great Ideas: A Lexicon of Western Thought, 1992; The Four Dimensions of Philsophy, 1993; Art, the Arts and the Great Ideas, 1994; Adler's Philosophical Dictionary, 1995. Honours: Address: Institute for Philosophical Research, 310 S Michigan Avenue, 7th Floor, Chicago, IL 60604, USA.

ADLER Renata, b. 1938, United States of America. Writer. Appointments: Writer, Reporter, The New Yorker, since 1963. Publications: Toward a Radical Middle: Fourteen Pieces of Reporting and Criticism, 1970; A Year in the Dark: Journal of a Film Critic, 1968-69, 1970; Speedboat, 1976; Pitch Dark (novel), 1984; Reckless Disregard: Westmoreland v CBS et al, Sharon v Time, 1986. Memberships: Member, Editorial Board, American Scholar, 1968-73; PEN, Executive Board, 1964-70; Judge in arts and letters, National Book Awards, 1969; Fellow, Trumbull Coll, Yale University, 1969-72. Address: c/o The New Yorker, 25 West 43rd Street, New York, NY 10036, USA.

ADLER Warren, b. 16 Dec 1927, New York City, USA. Novelist; Playwright; Lyricist; Screenwriter. m. Sonia Kline, 5 May 1951, 3 sons. Education: BA, New York University. Appointments: Chairman of Board, The Adler Group. Publications: The War of the Roses; The Sunset Gang; Trans-Siberian Express; The Housewife Blues; Private Lies; Others inc, Thw Witch of Watergate; Banguest Before Dawn; Twilight Child; Random Hearts; Senator Love; The Ties That Bind, 1994. Contributions to: Rescuing David From the Moonies; Esquire Magazine. Memberships: Authors Guild; Mysters Writers of America. Literary Agent: Peter Lampack. Address: 45 Huckleberry Drive, Jackson Hole, WY 83001, USA.

ADNAN Etel, b. 24 Feb 1925, Bey South, USA. Poet; Writer; Painter. Education: Liecence es Lettres, Lyon University, France, 1949; University of Paris, France, 1950; University of California, Berkeley, USA, 1955-57; Harvard University, USA, 1957-58. Publications: Sitt Marie Role; Ine Indian Never Had a Horse; Journey to Mount Tamalpais; The Arab A Pocalypse; The Spring Flowers Own & The Manifestations of the Voyage; From A to Z; Moonshots; Sitt Marie-Rose, 1992; Of Cities and Women, 1993; Paris, When It's Naked, 1993. Contributions to: Quixate; S B Gazette; Mawakig Karmel; AVEC. Address: 35 Marie Street, Sausalito, CA 94965, USA.

ADOFF Arnold, b. 1935. Writer; Poet. Appointments: Teacher, New York Public Schools, 1957-69; Literary Agent, Yellow Springs, Ohio, 1977-. Publications: Poetry for Children: MAnDA LA, 1971; Black is Brown is Tan, 1973; Make a Circle, Keep Us In: Poems for a Good Day, 1975; My Sister Tells Me That I'm Black, 1976; Tornado, 1977; Under the Early Morning Trees, 1978; Where Wild Willy, 1978; Eats, 1979; I Am the Running Girl, 1979; Friend Dog, 1980; Today We Are Brother and Sister, 1981; OUTside Inside Poems, 1981; Birds, 1982; All the Colors of the Race, 1982; The Cabbages are Chasing the Rabbits, 1985; Sports Pages, 1986; Green: Poems, 1988; Chocolate Dreams, 1989; Hard T Be Six, 1991; In for Winter, Out for Spring, 1991; Malcolm X, 1970; Flamboyan, 1988; Editor: I am the Darker Brother: An Anthology of Modern Poems by Negro Americans, 1968; Black on Black: Commentaries by Negro Americans, 1968; City in All Directions: An Anthology of Modern Poems, 1969; Black Out Loud: An Anthology of Modern Poems by Black Americans, 1970; Brothers and Sisters: Modern Stories by Black Americans, 1970; It Is the Poem Singing into Your Eyes: An Anthology of New Young Poets, 1971; The Poetry of Black America: An Anthology of the 20th Century, 1973; My Black Me: A Beginning Book of Black Poetry, 1974; Celebrations: A New Anthology of Black American Poetry, 1977; Street Music: City Poems,

1992. Address: Box 293, Yellow Springs, OH 45387, USA.

ADORJAN Carol (Kate Kenyon), b. 17 Aug 1934, Chicago, Illinois, USA. Writer; Teacher. m. William W Adorjan, 17 Aug 1957, 2 sons, 2 daughters. Education: BA, English Literature, Magna Cum Laude, Mundelein College, 1956. Appointments: Fellow, Midwest Playwrights Lab, 1977; Writer in Residence, Illinois Arts Council, 1981; Writer in Residence, National Radio Theatre, 1980-81. Publications: Someone I Know, 1968; The Cat Sitter Mystery, 1972; Eighth Grade to the Rescue (as Kate Kenyon), 1987; A Little Princess (abridgment), 1987; Those Crazy Eighth Grade Pictures (as Kate Kenyon), 1987; WKID: Easy Radio Plays (co-author): Yupi Rasovsky, 1988; The Copy Cat Mystery, 1990; Thats What Friends Are For, 1990; Radio & Stage Plays: Julian Theater, BBC, National Radio Theatre, etc. Contributor to: Redbook; Woman's Day; North American Review; Denver Quarterly; Four Quarters; Yankee. Honours: Josephine Lusk Fiction Award, Munderlein, 1955; Earplay, 1972; Illinois Arts Council Completion Grant, 1977-78; Dubuque Fine Arts Society National One-Act Playwriting competition, 1978; Ohio State Award, 1980. Memberships: Dramatists Guild; Society of Midland Authors; Poets & Writers; Children's Reading Roundtable. Literary Agent: Denise Marcil; Shelly Power (Abroad). Address: 812 Rosewood Avenue, Winnetka, IL 60093, USA.

ADRIAN Frances. See: **POLLAND Madelaine Angela.**

ADUNIS (Ali Ahmad Said), b. 1930, Syria. Poet. Education: University of Damascus, 1950-54; PhD, St Joseph University Beirut, 1973. Appointments include: Professor, Lebanese University Beirut, 1971-85; Resident, Paris, 1985. Publications include: Delilah, 1950; The Earth Has Said, 1952; First Poems, 1957; Resurrection and Ashes, 1958; Leaves in the Wind, 1958; The Stage and the Mirrors, 1968; A Time Between Ashes and Roses, 1970; A Tomb for New York, 1971; The Complete Works: Poetry, 1971; The Blood of Adonis, 1971; Mirrors, 1976; Transformations of the Lover, 1982; Victims of a Map, 1984; The Book of the Siege, 1985; An Introduction to Arab Poetics, 1990; Sophism and Surrealism, 1992. Honours include: Jean Malrieu Prize, 1991. Address: c/o Al Saqi Books, 26 Westbourne Grove, London W2 5RH, England.

AFRICANO Lillian, (Nora Ashby, Lila Cook, Jessica March), b. 7 June 1935, USA. Author; Columnist. divorced. 2 sons, 1 daughter. Education: BA, summa cum laude, Barnard College, 1953-57; Columbia University Graduate Schoo, 1958. Literary Appointments: Arts Editor, The Villager, 1971; News Editor, Penthouse/Forum, 1973; Columnist, New York Times Syndicate, 1977; Columnist, Woman's World, 1980. Publications: Businessman's Guide to the Middle East, 1977; Doctor's Walking Book (co-authored), 1980; Something Old, Something New, 1983; Passions, 1985; Gone From Breezy Hill (as Nora Ashby), 1985; Illusions (as Jessica March), 1988; Consenting Adults (as Lila Cook), 1988; Temptations (as Jessica March), 1989; Obsessions, 1990. Contributions to: New York Times; New York News; Reader's Digest; Harper's Bazaar; Woman's Day; Woman's World; National Review; The Nation. Honour: Phi Beta Kappa, 1956. Memberships: Drama Desk, Vice President, Secretary; Outer Critics' Circle; American Society of Journalists & Authors, Authors Guild. Address: 95 West River Rd, Rumson, NJ 07760, USA.

AGEE Jonis, b. 31 May 1943, Omaha, USA. m. Paul McDonough, 1 daughter. Education: BA, University of Iowa, 1966; MA, Suny Binghamton, English, 1969; PhD, 1976. Appointments: Teacher, College of St Catherine, St Paul, Minnesota, 1975-; Literary Consultant, Performing Arts Program, Walker Arts Center, Minneapolis, 1978-84; Chair, Midwestern Writers Festival & Small Press Book Fair, Minnesota, 1976-80; Adjunct Teacher, Macalester College, 1980-88; Literary Post Program, Senior Citizen Writers, 1986-89; Fiction Panel, National Endowment for the Arts, 1993; Fiction Panel, Illinois Arts Council, 1993; Board of Directors, The Loft (Center for Writing), 1994. Publications: Strange Angels; Sweet Eyes; Pretend We've Never Met; Bend This Heart; Two Poems; Mercury; Houses; Anthologies; Stillers Pond; After A While; In the Blood; Salvation Sisters. Contributions to: Resume; Kya; What The Fall Brings; Dead Space; Babylon Dreaming; These are the Footsteps Rising on the Stairs; Stiller's Pond; After A While; A Birthday Poem; Working Their Betrayals To Keep Us Alive. Honours: Loft McKnigh Award of Distinction; Loft McKnight Award in Fiction; National Endowment for the Arts Fellowship; Minnesota State Arts Board Award; Faculty Excellence Award in Teaching. Memberships: Literary Guild; Society of American Poets. Literary

Agent: Ned Leavitt Agency. Address: 634 Montcalm Place, St Paul, MN 55116, USA.

AGUIRRE Eugenio, b. 31 July 1944, Mexico City, Mexico. Writer. m. 6 Aug 1971, 1 son, 1 daughter. Education: BA Law, MA Literature, Universidad Nacional Autonoma de Mexico. Appointments include: Lecturer: University of Lawrence, Kansas, USA; Wabash College, Indianapolis, Indiana, USA; Writers Association of Panama; Several bank & government offices, Mexico. Publications include: Novels: Jesucristo Perez, 1973; Pajar de Imaginacion, 1975; El caballero de las espudas, 1978; Gonzalez Guerrero, 1980; El testamento del diablo, 1981; En el campo, 1982; Cadaver exquisito, 1984; El rumor quillego del mar, 1985; Pajuror de guego, 1986; Un mundo de nino lleno de mar, 1986. Contributions to: Excelsior; Uno & Uno; El Cuento; Plural; Vaso Comunicante; Contenido; El Buho; all Mexico city; Also Angoleta, Venezuela; Paris Atlantic, France. Honours: Great Silver Medal, International Academy of Lutece, Paris, France, 1981; Finalist, 1st crime novel, Plaza de Janes, 1985; Finalist, Fuentes Mares Prize for Literature, 1986; Finalist, 1st International Award, Diana Publishers, 1986. Memberships: Past president, Asociacion de Escritores de Mexico; Board, Sociedad General de Escritores de Mexico; International PEN Club. Address: Buhos no 32, Fracc Loma de Guadalupe, Mexico DF 01720, Mexico.

AHERNE Owen. See: **CASSILL Richard Verlin.**

AHLSEN Leopold, b. 12 Jan 1927, Munich, Germany. Author. m. Ruth Gehwald, 1964, 1 son, 1 daughter. Publications: 13 Plays, 23 radio plays, 42 television plays, 5 novels. Honours: Gerhart Hauptmann Prize; Schiller-Forderungspreis; Golden Bildschirm; Horspielpreis der Kriegsblinden; Silver Nymph of Monaco. Address: Waldschulstrasse 58, 8000 Munich 82, Germany.

AICHINGER Ilse, b. 1 Nov 1921, Vienna, Austria. Novelist; Playwright. Education: University of Vienna, 1945-48. Appointments include: Member of Grupe 47, From 1951-. Publications: Die Grössere Hoffnung, 1948; Rede Unter dem Galgen, 1953; Eliza, Eliza, 1965; Selected Short Stories and Dialogue, 1966; Nachricht und Tag: Erzählungen, 1970; Schlechte Worter, 1976; Meine Sprache und Ich Erzählungen, 1978; Spiegelesichte: Erzählungen und Dialoge, 1979; Plays, Zu Keiner Stunde, 1957, 1980; Besuch im Pfarrhaus, 1961; Auckland: 4 Horspiele, 1969; Knopfe, 1978; Weisse Chrysanthemum, 1979; Radio Plays, Selected Poetry and Prose of Ilse Aichinger, 1983; Collected Works, 8 Volumnes, 1991. Honours include: Belgian Europe Festival Prize, 1987; Town of Solothurn Prize, 1991. Address: c/o Fischer Verlag, Postfach 700480, 6000 Frankfurt, Germany.

AIDOO (Christina) Ama Ata, b. 1942, Ghana. Writer. 1 daughter. Appointments: Lecturer, University of Cape Coast, Ghana, 1970-83; Minister of Education, Ghana, 1982-83; Chair, Africa Regional Panel of Commonwealth Writers Prize, 1990-91. Publications include: Changes, A Love Story; The Dilemma of a Ghost; Anowa; No Sweetness Here; Our Sister Killjoy; Someone Talking to Sometime; The Eagle and The Chickens; Birds and Other Poems; Short Stories inc, To Be a Woman. Contributions to: BBC African Service; MS Magazine; South Magazine; Kumapipi; Rapport; The Chapman Review. Address: PO Box 4930, Harare, Zimbabwe.

AIKEN Joan Delano, b. 4 Sept 1924, Rye, Sussex, England. Writer. m. (1)Ronald George Brown, Dec 1955, 1 s, 1 d. (2)Julius Goldstein, 2 Sept 1976. Appointments include: Librarian, UN London Information Centre, 1945-49; Features Editor, Argosy Magazine, 1955-60; Freelance Writer, Full Time, 1961-. Publications include: 21 Books for adults; Over 50 for Children; Adult Fiction inc. The Fortune Hunters, 1965; Died in a Rainy Sunday, 1972; Deception, 1987; A Harp of Fishbones, Stories, 1972; The Mooncussers Daughter, 1973; The Skin Spinners, 1976; The Teeth of the Gale, 1988; Give Yourself a Fright, 1989; Mortimer and Arabel, 1992; A Creepy company, 1993; Eliza's Daughter, 1994; The Winter Sleepwalker, 1994; Cold Shoulder Road, 1995. Contributions to: New Statesman; Washington Post; good housekeeping; Womans Journal; Childrens Literature in Education; Quarterly Bulletin of Library of Congress. Honours: Guardian Award, 1969; Lewis Carroll Award, 1970. Memberships: Society of Authors; Writers Guild; Mystery Writers of Am; Crime Writers Association. Literary Agent: A M Heath Ltd. Address: The Hermitage, East Str, Petworth, West Sussex GU28 0AB, England.

AITMAYOV Chinglz (Torekulovich), b. 12 Dec 1928, Sheker, Kirghizstan. Novelist. Education: Gorky Literary Institute, Moscow,

1956-58. Appointments include: Deputy, Supreme Soviet, 1966-89; Ambassador, Luxembourg, 1990. Publications include: Dzhamalia, 1960; Melody, 1959; Mother Earth, 1965; Milky Way, 1963; The First Master, 1963; Short Novels, 1964; The Son of a Soldier, 1970; The White Ship, 1972; The Lament of a Migrating Bird, 1973; The Soldier, 1974; Night Dew, 1975; Collected Works, 2 Volumes, 1978; The Legend of the Horned Mother Deer, 1979; Short Stories, 1982; Collected Works, 3 Volumes, 1982-84; Echo of the World, 1985; The Place of the Skull, 1989; Madonna in the Snows, 1987; Mother Earth and Other Stories, 1989; Do The Russians Want War, 1985. Honours include: Lenin Prize, 1963; Hero of Socialist Labour, 1978; Member, World Academy of Art & Science, 1987. Address: Russian Embassy, Luxembourg 1719, EEC.

AJIBADE Adeyemi Olanrewaju (Yemi Ajibade), b. 28 July 1939, Nigeria. Actor; Playwright; Director. m. Gwendoline Augusta Ebonywhite, May 1973, 2 daughters. Education: Diplomas, Dramatic Arts Film Technique; British Drama League Diploma, Theatre Production; Associate of Drama Board; MA, London University, 1985. Appointments: Tutor, Producer, Drama, Panel of Inner London Education Authority; Visiting Director, Actors Workshop, London; Artistic Director, Pan-African Players, Keskidee Centre (London); Assistant Advisor to Earl of Snowdon on Mary Kingsley; Senior Arts Fellow & Artistic Director, Unibadan Masques, Acting Company of Ibadan University, Nigeria; Artist in Residence, Colby College, Waterville, Maine, USA, 1987. Publications: Lagos, Yes Lagos, BBC Radio; Award (Keskidee Centre); The Black Knives (ORTF, Paris); The Big One, Parcel Post (Royal Court, London); Behind the Mountain, Mokai, The Girl from Bulawayo (Arts Theatre, Ibadan University); Fingers Only (Black Theatre Cooperative, London); Para Ginto (black version Peer Gynt), commissioned by Birmingham Repertory Theatre; Waiting for Hannibal (Black Theatre Co-op), 1986. Honours: 4 Times Recipient, British Arts Council Bursary Award for Playwriting, 1976, 1977, 1981, 1984. Memberships: Fellow, Royal Society of Arts; British Kinematographic Society; Theatre Writers Union; Black Writers Association. Literary Agent: Michael Imison Playwrights (London). Address: 29 Seymour House, Churchway, London NW1, England.

AJIBADE Yemi. See: **AJIBADE Adeyemi Olanrewaju.**

AKAVIA Miriam, b. 20 Nov 1927, Krakow, Poland. Novelist; Translator. m. 3 Dec 1946, 2 daughters. Appointments: Co-editor of some bulletins; Hebrew Writers Ass; Pen-Israel; The World Literary Academy; Acum; Ass Intern Trust for Secular Humanistic Judaism; The Israeli Society for the Right to Die with Dignity. Publications: Adolescence of Autumn, 1975; Ha mechir (The Price), 1978; Galia & Miklosh, 1982; Karmi Sheli (My Own Vineyard), 1984; Adventure on a Bus, 1986; Ma Vigne A Moi, 1992; The Other Way, The Story of a Group, in Hebrew, 1992; Written in Hebrew, trans to Polish and other languages. Contributions to: Various literary magazines. Honours: Dvorsecki Prize; Korczak Prize, SEK Prize (Sociéte Européen de Culture); (Amicus Polonie; Cracovians Prize). Literary Agent: Lipman, AG, CG-8044 Zürich. Address: POB 53050, 61530 Tel-Aviv, Israel.

AKEN Paul Van, b. 20 Nov 1948, Reet, Belgium. Teacher; Literary Critic. Education: Free University, Brussels, 1966-70. Publications: Features of the essay; Lettermarker, A History of Dutch Literature; Paul De Wispelaer; About Sugar by Hugo Claus; About Lucifer By Vondel; About the Wall by Jos Vandeloo. Contributions to: Nieuw Vlaams Tydschrift; De Vlaamse Gids; Yang; Kunst & Cultuur; Kruispunt; Ons Erfdeel; Creare; Septentrion. Memberships: PEN; FLANDERS. Address: Dirk Martensstraat 60, 9300 Aalst, Belgium.

AKERS Alan Bert. See: **BULMER Henry Kenneth.**

AKHMADULINA Bella, b. 10 Apr 1937, Moscow, Russia. Poet. m. Boris Messerer, 1974. Education: Gorky Literary Institute, Moscow, 1960. Appointments include: Secretary, Union of Soviet, Russian Writers, 1986-. Publictions include: Fire Tree, 1958; String, 1962; Tale of the Rain, 1963; My Genealogy, 1963; Adventure in an Antique Store, 1967; Fever and Other Poems, 1968; Snowstorm, 1968; Music Lessons, 1969; Candle, 1977; Three Russian Poets, 1979; The Garden, 1987, 1990; Seashore, 1991; Screenplay, Clear Ponds, 1965. Honours include: American Academy of Arts & Letters Member, 1977. Address: Cherniachovskoho Str 4, Apt 37, 125319 Moscow, Russia.

AKSENOV Vasilii (Pavlovich), b. 20 Aug 1932, Kazan, Russia. Novelist. m. Maia Karmen, 1979. Education: Povlov Medical Institute, 1956. Appointments: Exiled to USA, 1980; Writer in Residence,

Universities of MI, Southern CA, George WA, 1981-; Returned Russia, 1992. Publications: Colleagues, 1961; Oranges from Morocco, 1963; Catapult, 1964; Its Time My Friend Its Time, 1969; The Little Wahle, The Varnisher of Reality, 1965; Surplussed Barrelware, 1972; Samson and Samsoness, 1972; Around the Clock Non-Stop, 1976; In Search of a Genre, 1977; The Steel Bird and Other Stories, 1979; Our Golden Ironburg, 1980; The Burn, 1984; The Island of Crimea, 1983; The Paperscape, 1983; Collected Works, from, 1987; The Day of the First Snowfall, 1990; Capital Displacement, 1990; The Yolk of an Egg, 1990; Moscow Saga, 1991; Rendezvous, 1991; Plays, Kollegi, 1962; Always on Sale, 1965; Your Murderer, 1977; The Four Temperaments, 1979; Aristophaniana and the Frogs, 1981; The Heron, 1984; Screenplay, The Blues with a Russian Accent, 1987; In Search of Melancholy Baby, 1987. Address: Krasnoirmeskaia Str 21, Apt 20, 125319 Moscow, Russia.

AL-AZM Sadik J, b. 7 Nov 1934, Syria. University Professor. m. Fawz Touqan, 2 July 1957, 2 s. Education: Gerard Institute Highschool, 1949-53; American University, Beirut, 1953-57; Yale University, CT, 1957-61; Visiting Professor, Near Eastern Studies Department, Princeton University, 1988-90, 1991-92; Visiting Fellow, WissenschaftsKolleg Zu Berlin, 1990-91; Visiting Fellow, Woodrow Wilson International Ctr for Scholars, WA, 1992-93; Chairman, Department of Philosophy and Sociology, Damascus University, 1993-. Publications: Kants Theory of Time: The Origins of Kants Arguments in the Antinomnies; Critique of Religious Thought; Studies in Modern Western Philosophy; Of Love & Arabic Courtly Love; Materialism & History: A Defense; Unbehagen in Der Moderne: Aufklarung im Islam, 1993. Contributions to: Orientalism & Orientalism in Reverse; Sionisme Une Entreprise de Colonisation; Der Palastinensiche Widerstand neu Durchdacht; Palestinian Zionism; The Importance of Being Earnest About Salman Rushdie; South Asia Bulletin. Address: Dept of Philosophy, Faculty of Letters, Damascus University, Damascus, Syria.

AL-KHARRAT Edwar, b. 16 Mar 1926. Writer. 2 s. Education: LLB, Alexandria University, 1946. Appointments include: Editor, Gallery 68 Magazine, 1968; Editor, Afro Asian Writings Magazine, 1968; Edited, Special Issue, Egyptian Literature of AL Karmal Magazine, 1984. Publications: High Walls, 1959; Hours of Pride, 1972; Ramah and the Dragon, 1980; Suffocations of Love & Mornings, 1983; The Other Time, 1985; City of Saffron Arabic, 1986; English, 1989, French, 1990; German, 1991; Spanish, 1992; Girls of Alexandria, 1990; Waves of Nights, 1991; Appollos Ruins, 1992; Penetrations of Love and Perdition, 1993; My Alexandria, 1993; The New Sensibility, 1994; From Silence to Rebellion, 1994; Transgeneric Writing, 1994; Ripples of Salt Dreams, 1994. Contributions to: Many Arab Literary Magazines. Honours: Arts & Letters Medal, 1972; State Prize for Short Story, 1972; Franco Arab Friendship Award, 1989. Memberships: The Egyptian Writers Union; Gezira Sporting Club. Address: 45 Ahmed Hishmat Str, Zamalak 11211, Cairo, Egypt.

AL-SHAROUNI Youssek, b. 14 Oct 1924, Menuf, Egypt. Ministry of Information. m. Nargis S Basta, 2 Oct 1952, 2 s, 1 d. Education: BA, Cairo University. Appointments: Under-Secretary, High Council of Culture, 1978-81; Editorial Board: Al Magalla, 1963-66, (monthlies); Professor for Postgraduate Courses, Cairo University, 1979-81; Editori. Publications: The Five Lovers: A Message to A Woman; The Last Eve; Studies on Love and Friendship in Arabic Tradition; Blood Feud (short stories) 3rd edition, 1991; Complete Short Stories, vol 1, 1992, vol 2, 1993. Contributions to: Al Adib; Al Adab; Al Arabi; Al Muntada; Al Ahram; Abd'a. Honours: Egyptian State Prizes in Short Story, 1970; and Literary studies, 1978, categories: First Grade Order of Science and Arts, Arab Republic of Egypt, 1970; Order of the Republic, 1978; Fellow: German Academic Exchange service, Free University of Berlin, 1976, Netherlands Organisation for Advancement of Pure Research, 1981-82. Memberships: Story Club, Cairo, Board, 1970-73; Writers' Union, Cairo; Pen Club; Fiction Committee at High Council of Culture, 1963-83. Address: 12 El-Sad El Aali Street, El-Maadi, PC 11431, Cairo, Egypt.

ALAMI Ahmad, b. 24 Oct 1939. Librarian. m. 1) Zenat, 1969, 2) Salma, 1980, 3) Samiva, 1988, 1 son, 1 daughter. Education: Sophomore Diploma, 1957; MBBCH, Ain Shams Medical School Cairo, 1966. Appointments: Literary Director, College of Islamic Studies, 1979-. Publicatins include: War of 1948, 1980; War of 1956, 1982; Bloody Days, 1983; Waqt of Saladin, 1981; Waqt of the Moroccans, 1982; Catalogue of Arabic Manuscripts, 1986; The Palestine State (translation), 1984; New Violence (translation), 1987; War of 1967,

1990; numerous contributions to journals and magazines. Address: PO Box 19859, Jerusalem, Israel.

ALBANY James. See: **RAE Hugh Crauford.**

ALBEE Edward Franklin, b. 12 Mar 1928, Virginia, USA. Playwright. Education: Pennsylvania Choale School, Connecticut, 1946; Trinity College, Hartford, Connecticut, 1946-47. Appointments: Radio Writer, WNYC, Office Boy, Warwick & Ledler Record Salesman, Bloomingdales Book Salesman, G Schirmer Counterman, Manhattan Towers Hotel, Messenger, 1955-58; Producer, Richard Barr & Clinton Wilder, Playwrighters University, Alberwild Theatre Arts & Albar Productions, Founder, William Flanagan Center for Creative Persons, 1971. Publications: Plays inc, Who's Afraid of Virginia Woolf; The Zoo Story; The Death of Bessie Smith; The Sandbox; The American Dream; Tiny Alice; Seascape; Everything in the Garden; Screenplay; A Delicate Balance; Marriage Play, Three Tall Women, 1994; Fragments: A Concerto Grosso, 1993. Honours include: London Evening Standard Award; Tony Award; Morgo Jones Award; Pulitzer Prize, 1967, 1975, 1994; American Academy Gold Medal; Brandeis University Creative Arts Award; Obie Award, Sustained Achievement. Memberships: American Academy; International Theatre Institute, USA, President; Dramatists Guild Council; Edward F Albee Foundation, President. Literary Agent: William Morris Agency. Address: 14 Harrison Street, New York, NY 10013, USA.

ALBERT Gabor, b. 30 Oct 1929, Hungary. Writer; Essayist. m. Zuzsanna Marek, 30 Oct 1954, 1 s, 1 d. Education: Eotvos Lorand University, 1955. Appointments: Editor in Chief, Uj Magyarorszag, 1991-92; Editor in Chief, Magyarok Vilaglapja, 1992-; Editor, The Pointer, 1994. Publications: Dragon and Octahedron: Atter Scattering, Essays; Where Are Those Columns; In A Shell; Book of Kings; Heroes of the Failures; Atheist; Final Settlement of a Wedding; Stephen King's Tart Wine, 1993. Memberships: Association of Hungarian Writers; Association of D Berzsenyi. Address: Bimbo ut 3 IV.5, H 1022 Budapest, Hungary.

ALBERT Marvin H (Nick Quarry, Anthony Rome, Tony Rome), b. USA. Author; Freelance Writer. Publications include: Lie Down with Lions, 1955; The Law and Jake Wade, 1956; Apache Rising, 1957; Party Girl (novelization of screenplay), 1958; The Bounty Killer, 1958; The Girl with No Place to Hide (as Nick Quarry), 1959; All the Young Men (novelization of screenplay), 1960; My Kind of Game, 1962; Lover Come Back (novelization of screenplay), 1962; Move Over, Darling (novelization of screenplay), 1963; Palm Springs Weekend, 1963; Honeymoon Hotel, 1964; What's New Pussycat? (novelization of screenplay), 1965; Strange Bedfellows (novelization of screenplay), 1965; The Divorce (non-fiction), 1965; Come September, 1971; Hidden Lives, 1982; Operation Lila, 1983; The Warmakers, 1985; Stone Angel, 1986; Back in the Real World, 1986; Get Off at Babylon, 1987; Long Teeth, 1987; The Untouchables, 1987; Miami Mayhem, 1988; The Man in the Black, 1988; The Riviera Contract, 1992.

ALBEVERIO MANZONI Solvejg, b. 6 Nov 1939, Arogno, Switzerland. Painter; Writer. m. Sergio Albeverio, 7 Feb 1970, 1 d. Education: Textile Designer, Diploma, Como, Italy, 1960; Art Courses, Zurich, 1969; Drawing & Etching Statens, Oslo, 1972-77. Publications: Da stanze chiuse; Il pensatore con il mantello come meteora; Controcanto al chiuso; Il fiore, il frutto, triandro donna; Frange di solitudine. Contributions to: Poems & Drawings in Literary Journals & Reviews; Exhibitions, Many Countries. Honour: Premio Ascona, 1987. Memberships: Swiss Society of Painters, Sculptors & Architects; swiss Society of Womens Painters & Sculptors; PEN; Associazione Scrittori della Svizzera Italiana. Address: Auf dem Aspei 55, D 44801 Bochum, Germany.

ALBRIGHT Daniel, b. 29 Oct 1945, Chicago, IL, USA. Professor. m. Karin Larson, 18 June 1977, 1 daughter. Education: BA, Rice University, 1967; MPhil, Yale University, 1969; PhD, 1970. Appointments: Assistance Professor, University of Virginia, 1970-75; Associate Professor 1975-81, Professor 1981-86; Visiting Professor, University of Munich, 1986-87; Professor, University of Rochester, 1987-. Publications: The Poems: The Music Box & The Nightingale; The Muses; Tug of War; Lyricality in English Literature; Representation & The Imagination; Personality & Impersonality; The Myth Against Myths. Honours: Phi Beta Kappa; NEH Fellow; Guggenheim Fellow. Address: Dept of English, University of Rochester, Rochester, NY 17627, USA.

ALCAIDE CASTRO Jose Antonio, b. 30 May 1963, Cordoba, Spain. Functionario SVA. Education: Graduate Scholar, 1973-75; Monitor de Karate, 3 Dan. Publications: Entre El Silencio Y La Soledad, 1991. Contributions to: Revista Semana Santa Ciudad De Cordoba, 1992. Address: Dulcinea 50, 14014 Cordoba, Spain.

ALCALDE GARRIGA Carmen, b. 5 Aug 1936, Girona, Spain. Journalist. Education: Journalisme and Filosophie. Publications: La Muter en la Guerra Civil Espanola; Feminismo Iberico; Cartas a Lilith; Biografia Federica Montseny; No Huiras; Esta Es Mi Came; Como Escribir un Periodico. Contributions to: Destino; Triofo; La Vanguardia; El Periodico. Memberships: Association Escritores y Traductores. Literary Agent: Ramon Serrano. Address: Avda Mistral 49, 08015 Barcelona, Spain.

ALCOCK (Garfield) Vivien, b. 23 Sept 1924, Worthing, England. Author. m. Leon Garfield, 23 Oct 1948, 1 daughter. Education: Oxford School of Art. Publications: The Haunting of Cassie Palmer, 1980; The Stonewalker, 1981; The Sylvia Game, 1982; Travellers by Night, 1983; Ghostly Companions, 1984; The Cuckoo Sister, 1985; The Mysterious Mr Ross, 1987; The Monster Garden, 1988; The Trial of Anna Cotman, 1989; A Kind of Thief, 1991. Membership: Authors Society. Literary Agent: John Johnson. Address: 59 Wood Lane, London N6 5UD, England.

ALDISS Brian Wilson, b. 18 Aug 1925, East Dereham, England. Writer. m. (1) 1 s, 1 d. (2)Margaret Manson, 11 Dec 1965, 1 s, 1 d. Appointments: Literary Editor, Oxford Mail, 1958-69; Managing Director, Avernus Limited. Publications include: The Brightfount Diaries, 1955; Hothouse, 1962; The Horatio Stubbs Trilogy, 1970, 71, 78; Frankenstein Unbound, 1973; Forgotten Life, 1988; Best SF Stories of Brian W Aldiss, 1965; Cities and Stones, A Travellers Yugoslavia, 1966; This World and Nearer Ones, 1979; The Helliconia Trilogy, 1985; Bury My Heart at W H Smiths, a Writing Life, 1990; Remembrance Day, 1993; Somewhere East of Life, 1994; At The Caligula Hotel, 1995. Address: Woodlands, Foxcombe Road, Boars Hill, Oxford, OX1 5DL, England.

ALDRIDGE James, b. 10 July 1918. Author; Journalist. m. Dina Mitchnik, 1942, 2 s. London School of Economics. Appointments: Herald & Sun, Melbourne, 1937-38; Daily Sketch, Sunday Dispatch, London, 1939; Australian Newspaper Service & North Am Newspaper Alliance, Finland, Norway, Middle East, Greece, USSR, 1939-45; Correspondent, Time and Life, Teheran, 1944. Publications: Signed with their Honour, 1942; The Sea Eagle, 1944; Of Many Men, 1946; The Diplomat, 1950; The Hunter, 1951; Heroes of the Empty View, 1954; Underwater Hunting for Inexperienced Englishmen, 1956; I Wish He Would Not Die, 1958; Gold and Sand, 1960; The Last Exile, 1961; Captive in the Land, 1962; The Statesman's Game, 1966; My Brother Tom, 1966; The Flying 19, 1966; Living Egypt, 1969; Cairo, Biography of a City, 1970; A Sporting Proposition, 1973; The Marvellous Mongolian, 1974; Mockery in Arms, 1974; The Untouchable Juli, 1975; One Last Glimpse, 1977; Goodbye Un America, 1979; The Brokern Saddle, 1982; The True Story of Lilli Stubek, 1984; The True story of Spit MacPhee, 1986. Honours: Rhys Memorial Award, 1945; Lenin Peace Prize, 1972. Address: c/o Curtis Brown, 28/29 Haymarket, London, SW1Y 4SP, England.

ALDRIDGE John Watson, b. 26 Sept 1922, Sioux City, Iowa, USA. Literary Critic; Educator. m. 2) Patricia McGuire Eby, 16 July 1983, 5 sons, previous marriage. Education: BA, University of California, Berkeley, 1947. Appointments include: Lecturer, Christian Gauss seminars in criticism, Princeton University 1953-54; Breadloaf Writers Conference 1966-69; Rockefeller Humanities Fellowship, 1976; Book Critic, MacNeil/Lehrer TV News, 1983-84. Publications include: After the Lost Generation, criticism, 1951; In Search of Heresy, criticism, 1956; The Party at Cranton, novel, 1960; Time to Murder & Create, criticism, 1966; In the Country of the Young, social commentary, 1970; The Devil in the Fire, criticism, 1972; The American Novel & the Way We Live Now, criticism, 1983; Talents and Technicians, criticism, 1992; Classics and Contemporaries, criticism, 1992. Literary Agent: Gerard F McCauley. Address: 1050 Wall Street no 4C, Ann Arbor, MI 48105, USA. MARCHANT Anyda.

ALDYNE Nathan. See: **MCDOWELL Michael.**

ALDRIDGE Sarah. See: **MARCHANT Anyda.**

ALEGRIA Claribel (Flakoll), b. 12 May 1924, Esteli, Nicaragua. Writer. m. Darwin J Flakoll, 29 Dec 1947, 1 son, 3 daughters. Education: BA Philosophy & Letters, George Washington University, Washington DC, USA. Publications include: Cenizas de Izalco, novel, co-author, 1966; Suma y Siqua, poetry, 1982; Nicaragua: la revolucion sandinists, history, 1982; No me agarran viva, testimony, 1983; Woman of the River, poetry, 1989; Y esta poema-rio, poetry, 1989; Family Album, 3 novellas, 1990; Total of 30 books in five languages. Contributions to: Many magazines and journals. Honour: Casa de las Americas poetry prize for Sobrevivo, 1978. Literary Agent: Alexander Taylor, Curbstone Press. Address: Aptdo Postal A-36, Managua, Nicaragua.

ALEX Peter. See: HAINING Peter Alexander.

ALEXANDER Caroline Elizabeth, b. 13 Mar 1956, FL, USA. Writer. Education: BA, FL State University, 1977; BA, Oxford University, 1980; PhD, Columbia University, 1991. Appointments: Editorial Board, Am Oxonian. Publications: One Dry Season; The Way to Xandadu. Contributions to: The New Yorker; The Smithsonian; Outside Magazine; The NY Times; The Independent; The Sunday Telegraph Weekend Magazine; Traveler. Honours: Mellon Fellowship; Rhodes Scholarship. Memberships: Am Philological Society; Royal Geographical Society. Literary Agent: Sheil Land associates. Address: c/o Anthony Sheil, 43 Doughty Str, London WC1 N2LF, England.

ALEXANDER Christine Anne, b. 9 July 1949, Hasting, NZ, Australia. University Lectuer. m. Peter Fraser Alexander, 18 June 1977, 1 s, 1 d. Education: BA, 1970, MA, 1971, University of Canterbury; PhD, University of Cambridge, 1978. Appointments: Assistnt Lectureship, University of Canterbury, 1972; Tutor, 1978-83, Lecturer, 1986-88, Senior Lecturer, 1988-92, Associate Professor, 1993-, University of NSW, Australia. Publications include: Bibliography of the Manuscrips iof Charlotte Bronte, 1982; The Early Writings of Charlotte Bronte, 1983; The Art of the Brontes, 1994. Contributions to: Books, Charlotte Bronte at Roe Head; Search after Love; Articles & Reviews in various Journals; The Authorial Voice, 1990. Address: School of English, University of NSW, PO Box 1, Kensington, NSW 2033, Australia.

ALEXANDER Gary Roy, b. 18 Jan 1941, Bremerton, WA, USA. Writer. m. Shari, 9 Aug 1969, 3 daughters. Publications: Pigeon Blood; Unfunny Money; Kiet and The Golden Peacock; Kiet and the Opium War; Deadly Drought; Kiet Goes West; A Novel Set in Yucatan; Blood Sacrifice; Dead Dinosaurs, 1994. Contributions to: Approx 75 short stories, various magazines. Memberships: Mystery Writers of America. Literary Agents: Gelfman Schneider Agency (Deborah Schneider). Address: 122 SW 104th Street, Seattle, WA 98146, USA.

ALEXANDER Lloyd (Chudley), b. 1924. Publications: Border Hawk: August Bondi, 1958; The Book of Three, 1964; Coll & His White Pig, 1965; The Foundling, and other tales of Pridain, 1973; The King's Fountain, 1971; Westmark, 1981; Time Cat, 1982; The Kestrel, 1982; Drackenberg Adventure, 1988; Jedera Adventure, 1989; Philadelphia Adventure, 1990; Fortune Tellers, 1992; House Gobbaleen, 1995; The Arkadiaus, 1995. Honours: Newbury Medal; Boston Globe; Horn Book Award, 1993.

ALEXANDER Louis George, b. 1932. Writer. Publications include: Sixty Steps, 1962; Poetry and Prose Appreciation, 1963; A First Book in Comprehension, 1965; Essays and Letter Writing, 1965; The Carters of Greenwood, 1966; Detectives from Scotland Yard, 1966; April Fools Day, 1966; New Concept English (4 vols), 1967; Worth a Fortune, 1967; Question and Answer, 1967; For and Against, 1968; Look, Listen and Learn, Sets 1-4, 1968-71; Reading and Writing English, 1969; Car Thieves, 1969; K's First Case, 1975; Good Morning, Mexicol, 1975; Operation Janus, 1976; Clint magee, 1976; Dangerous Game, 1977; Some Methodological Implications of Waystage and Threshold Level, Council of Europe, 1977; Follow Me, 1979; Survive in French/Spanish/German/Italian, 1980; Conversational French/Spanish/German/Italian, 1981; Excel, 1985-87; Plain English, 1987-88; Longman English Grammar, 1988-89; Longman English Grammar Practice, 1990; Step by Step 1-3, 1991; Longman Advanced Grammar, 1993; The Essential English Grammar, 1993. Address: Garden House, Weydown Road, Haslemere, Surrey, England.

ALEXANDER Meena, b. 17 Feb 1951, India. Poet; Professor. m. David Lelyveld, 1 May 1979, 1 s, 1 d. Education: BA, Khartoum University, 1969; PhD, Nottingham University, 1973. Literary Appointments: Professor, Hunter College, CUNY. Publications: Fault Lines, 1993; Nampally Road, 1991; House of a Thousand Doors, 1988; Women in Romanticism, 1989; The Storm, 1991; Night Scene, The Garden, 1992. Contributions to: Grand Street; Poetry Review. Honours: Writer in Residence, 1988; McDowell Fellow, 1993. Memberships: Am PEN; MLA. Literary Agent: Anne Dubuisson, Ellen Levine Agency. Address: English Dept, Hunter College, CUNY, 695 Park Avenue, New York, NY 10021, USA.

ALEXANDER Sue, b. 1933, USA. Writer. Publications: Small Plays for You and A Friend, 1973; Nadir of the Streets, 1975; Peacocks Are Very Special, 1976; Witch, Goblin and Sometimes Ghost, 1976; Smalls Plays for Special Days, 1977; Marc the Magnificent, 1978; More Witch, Goblin and Ghost Stories, 1978; Seymour the Prince, 1979; Finding Your First Job, 1980; Whatever Happened to Uncle Albert? and Other Plays, 1980; Witch, Goblin and Ghost in the Haunted Woods, 1981; Witch, Goblin and Ghost's Book of Things to Do, 1982; Nadia the Willful, 1983; Dear Phoebe, 1984; World Famous Muriel, 1984; Witch, Goblin and Ghost Are Back, 1985; World Famous Muriel and the Scary Dragon, 1985; America's Own Holidays, 1986; Lila on the Landing, 1987; There's More - Much More, 1987; World Famous Muriel and the Magic Mystery, 1990; Who Goes Out on Halloween? 1990. Literary Agent: Marilyn E Marlow/Curtis Brown Ltd. Address: 6846 McLaren, Canoga Park, CA 91307, USA.

ALEXIS Paul. See: HOLLO Anselm.

ALI Agha Shahid, b. 4 Feb 1949, New Delhi, India. Assistant Professor of English; Poet. Education: Universities of Kashmir and Delhi; MA, Pennsylvania State University, 1981; PhD, University of Arizona, 1984. Appointments: Assistant Professor of English, Hamilton College, Clinton, New York, USA, from 1987. Publications: Bone-Sculpture, 1972; In Memory of Begum Akhtar and Other Poems, 1979; The Half-Inch Himalayas, 1987; A Walk Through the Yellow Pages, 1987; T S Eliot as Editor, 1986. Honours: Academy of American Poets Prize, 1983; Ingram Merrill Foundation Fellowship, 1987. Address: Department of English, Hamilton College, Clinton, NY 13323, USA.

ALLABY John Michael, b. 18 Sept 1933, Belper, Derbyshire, England. Author. m. Ailsa Marthe McGregor, 3 Jan 1957 , 1 s, 1 d. Appointments: Editor, The Oxford Dictionary of Natural History, 1980; Co Editor, The Concise Oxford Dictionary of Earth Sciences, 1986; Editor, Series of Official Guides to All the National Trails in England & Wales, 1987. Publications include: Guide to Gaia, 1989; Dictionary of the Environment, 1977, 83, 88, 94; Green Facts, 1989; A Year in the Life of a Field, 1981; The Greening of Mars, 1984; Animal Artisans, 1982; Conservation at Home, 1988; Inventing Tomorrow, 1976; Elements: Air, 1992, Water, 1992, Fire, 1993; Elements: Earth, 1993; Concise Oxford Dictionary of Ecology, 1994. Contributions to: Newspapers and Magazines. Memberships: Society of Authors; NY Academy of Sciences; Association of British Science Writers. Address: Penquite Fernleigh Road, Wadebridge, Cornwall, PL27 7BB England.

ALLAN Elkan, Journalist. Appointments: Writer, Odhams Press, 1950-55; Writer, Producer, Executive and Head of Entertainment, Rediffusion Television, 1955-66; Television Columnist, Sunday Times, 1966-82; Editor, Video Viewer, 1982-83; Columnist, Video Week, 1983-; Listings Editor, The Independent, 1986-88; Senior Editor, 1988-. Publications: Quiz Team, 1945; Editor, Living Opinion, 1946; Good Listening: A Survey of Broadcasting, with D M Robinson, 1948; The Sunday Times Guide to Movies on Television, with A Allan, 1973, 1980; Editor, Video Year Book, 1984, 1985; 10 monographs on Silent Films Makers, 1990-. Contributions to: Senior Editor, The Independent. Honours: Triple Berlin TV Awards, 1966; British Press Awards, 1988. Address: The Independent, 40 City Road, London EC1Y 2DB, England.

ALLAN Mabel Esther, (Jean Estoril, Priscilla Hagon, Anne Pilgrim), b. 11 Feb 1915, Wallasey, Cheshire, England. Author. Publications: A Dream of Hunger Moss, 1983; The Pride of Pine Street, 1985; The Rod to Huntingland, 1986; The Crumble Lane Mystery, 1987; Up the Victorian Staircse, 1987; First Term at Ash Grove, 1988; Drina Ballerina, 1991; Over 150 Other Books. Contributions to: Over 320 Short Stories; Articles; Poetry. Honours: Various Honours & Awards. Literary Agent: Curtis Brown & John Farquharson Ltd. Address: 11 Oldfield Way, Heswall, Wirral L60 6RQ, England.

ALLBEURY Ted. See: ALLBEURY Theo Edward.

ALLBEURY Theo Edward, (Ted Allbeury, Richard Butler, Patrick Kelly), b. 1917. Author. Publications include: A Choice of Enemies, 1973; Snowball, 1974; The Special Collection, 1975; Palomino Blonde, 1975; The Only Good German, 1976; Moscow Quadrille, 1976; The Man with the President's Mind, 1977; The Lantem Network, 1978; Consequence of Fear, 1979; The Alpha List, 1979; The Twentieth Day of January, 1980; The Reaper, 1980; The Other Side of Silence, 1981; The Secret Whispers, 1981; All Our Tomorrows, 1982; Shadow of Shadows, 1982; Pay Any Price, 1983; The Judas Factor, 1984; No Place To Hide, 1984; The Girl from Addis, 1984; Children of Tender Years, 1985; The Choice, 1986; The Seeds of Treason, 1986; The Crossing, 1987; A Wildemess of Mirrors, 1988; Deep Purple, 1989; A Time Without Shadows, 1990; Other Kinds of Treason, 1990; Dangerous Edge, 1991; Show Me a Hero, 1992; The Line Crosser, 1993; As Time Goes By, 1994; As Patrick Kelly: Codeword Cromwell, 1980; As Richard Butler: Where All the Girls are Sweeter, 1975; Italian Assets, 1976. Membership: Society of Authors. Literary Agent: Blake Friedmann Literary Agency. Address: Cheriton House, Furnace Lane, Lamberhurst, Kent, England.

ALLCOT Guy. See: POCOCK Tom.

ALLDRITT Keith, b. 10 Dec 1935, Wolverhampton, England. Professor of English; Writer. m. Joan Hardwick, 10 Apr 1980, 1 son, 1 daughter. Education: BA, MA, St Catherine's College, Cambridge. Publications: The Making of George Orwell, 1969; The Visual Imagination of D H Lawrence, 1970; The Good Pit Man, 1975; The Lover Next Door, 1977; Elgar on the Journey to Hanley, 1978; Poetry as Chamber Music, 1978; Modernism in the Second World War, 1989; Churchill The Writer; His Life as a Man of Letters, 1992. Honour: Fellow, Royal Society of Literature. Memberships: Arnold Bennett Society; Society of Authors; D H Lawrence Society; International Churchill Society; Modern Language Association. Address: 48 Church Street, Lichfield, Staffordshire WS13 6ED, England.

ALLEN Blair H, b. 2 July 1933, Los Angeles, California, USA. Writer; Poet; Artist. m. Juanita Aguilar Raya, 27 Jan 1968, 1 son, 1 daughter. Education: AA, San Diego College, 1964; Studied, University of Washington, 1965-66; BA, San Diego State University, 1970. Appointments: Book Reviewer, Los Angeles Times, 1977-78; Special Feature Editor, Cerulean Press & Kent Publications, 1982-. Publications: Televisual Poums for Bloodshot Eyeballs; Malice in Blunderland; The Atlantis Trilogy; Dreamwish of the Magician; Right through the Silver Lined, 1984; Looking Glass; The Magical World of David Cole; Snow Summits in the Sun; Trapped in a Cold War, Travelogue, 1991; May Burning into August 1992; The Subway Poems, 1992; (Ed) The Cerulan Anthology of Sci-Fi/Outer Space/Fantasy/Poetry and Prose Poems, 1992; 5 Other Small Chapbooks & Poetry. Contributions to: Numerous US Journals, Magazines & Reviews, Los Angeles Times. Honours: Various Honours & Awards. Memberships: Beyond Baroque Foundation, Medina Foundation, California State Poetry Society; Association of Applied Poetry. Address: 9651 Estacia Court, Cucamonga, CA 91730, USA.

ALLEN Diogenes, b. 17 Oct 1932, Lexington, Kentucky, USA. Clergy; Professor. m. Jane Billing, 8 Sept 1958, 3 sons, 1 daughter. Education: BA with high distinction, University of Kentucky, 1954; BA Honours 1957, MA 1961, Oxford University, England; BD 1959, MA 1962, PhD 1965, Yale University. Publications: Reasonableness of Faith, 1968; Finding Our Father, 1974, re-issued as Path of Perfect Love, 1992; Between Two Worlds, 1977, re-issued as Temptation, 1984; Traces of God, 1981; Three Outsiders, 1983; Mechanical Explanations and the Ultimate Origin of the Universe According to Leibniz, 1983; Philosophy for Understanding Theology, 1985; Love, 1987; Christian Belief in a Postmodern World, 1989; Quest, 1990; Spirit, Nature, Community, 1994 (with Eric o Springsted. Contributions to: About 50 magazines and journals. Honours: Phi Beta Kappa, 1953; Rhodes Scholar, 1955-57, 1963-64; Rockefeller Doctoral Fellow, 1962-64; Outstanding Educator of America, 1974; Research Fellowship, Association of Theological Schools, 1975-76; PEW Evangelical Scholar, 1991-92; Research Fellow, Cnter Theological Inquiry, 1984-86, 1994-95. Memberships: Executive Board, Society of Christian Philosophers; Executive Board, American Well Society; Advisory Committee of Center of Theological Inquiry; Leibniz Gesellschaft. Address: Princeton Theological Seminary, Princeton, NJ 08542, USA.

ALLEN John. See: PERRY Ritchie.

ALLEN Oliver E, b. 29 June 1922, Cambridge, Mass, USA. Writer. m. Deborah Hutchison, 8 May 1948, 3 sons, 2 daughters. Education: Harvard, AB, 1943. Publications: New York, New York; Gardening with the New Small Plants; Wildflower Gardening; Decorating With Plants; Pruning & Grafting; Shade Gardens; Winter Gardens; The Windjammers; The Airline Builders; The Pacific Navigators; Building Sound Bones & Muscles; The Atmosphere; Secrets of a Good Digestion; The Vegetable Gardener's Journal; The Tiger, 1993. Contributions to: Horticulture Magazine; American Heritage & Smithsonian. Literary Agent: Curtis Brown Ltd. Address: 42 Hudson Street, New York, NY 10013, USA.

ALLEN Paula Gunn. Publications: Blind Lion: Poems, 1974; Star Child: Poems, 1981; A Cannon between my Knees, 1981; From the Center: A Folio, 1981; Studies in American Indian Literature, 1983; The Sacred Hoop, 1986; The Women Who Owned the Shadows, 1983; Spider Woman's Granddaughters, 1989; Grandmothers of the Light, 1991; Columbus & Beyond, 1992; Voice of the Turtle, 1994. Honours: American Book Award, 1990.

ALLEN Roberta, b. New York City, USA. Writer. Appointments: Creative Writing Instructor, Parsons School of Design, 1986; Guest Lecturer, Murdoch University, Perth, Australia, 1989; Instructor, The Writer's Voice, 1992-95; Instructor, The New School, 1993-95; Instructor, New York University, Continuing Education, 1993-1995. Publications: The Traveling Woman, 1986; The Daughter, 1992; Amazon Dream, 1993; Anthologies: Contemporary American Fiction, 1983; Wild History, 1985; Between C & D, 1988; Mondo Barbie, 1993; Border Lines, 1993; Stories: House Hunting; Certain People. Contributions to: Fiction International, 1993; Chelsea, 1991, 92, 93; Die Reisende, Akzente, Munich, 1992. Honours: LINE (NEA & NYS Council) grant 1985; Yaddo 1987; Yaddo, 1993; VCCA, 1994. Literary Agent: Cindy Kelin, Georges Borchadt Inc. Address: 5 West 16th Street, New York, NY 10011, USA.

ALLEN Stephen Valentine (Steve Allen, William Christopher Stevens), b. 26 Dec 1921, New York, USA. Entertainer. m. Jayne Meadows, 4 sons. Education: First year: Drake University, Des Moines, Iowa; Second year: Anzona University. Publications include: Dumbth, 1989; Meeting of Minds, Vol I 1978, Vol II 1979, Vol II 1989, Vol IV 1989; Murder on the Glitter Box, 1989; Murder in Manhattan, 1990; Passionate Nonsmokers' Bill of Rights, 1989; The Public Hating, 1990; Steve Allen on the Bible, Religion and Morality, 1990; Murder in Vegas, 1991; Hi-Ho, Steverino: My Adventures in the Wonderful Wacky World of TV, 1992; How To Be Funny (re-release), 1992; The Murder Game, 1993; More Steve Allen on the Bible, Religion & Morality, Book Two, 1993; Make 'em Laugh, 1993; Reflections, 1994; Compositions: Written over 4,700 songs. Contributor to: Numerous articles to magazines and newspapers. Address: Meadowlane Ent Inc, 15201 Burbank Boulevard, Suite B, Van Nuys, CA 91411, USA.

ALLEN Steve. See: ALLEN Stephen Valentine.

ALLEN Walter (Ernest), b. 23 Feb 1911, Birmingham, England. Novelist. m. Peggy Yorke Joy, 1944, 2 sons, 2 daughters. Education: BA (Hons), Birmingham University, 1932. Appointments include: Literary Editor, New Statesman, London, 1960-61; Professor of English Studies, New University of Ulster, 1968-73; Berg Professor of English, New York University, USA, 1970-71. Publications: Innocence Is Drowned, 1938; Blind Man's Ditch, 1939; Living Space, 1940; Rouge Elephant, 1946; Dead Man Over All, 1951; All in a Lifetime, 1959; Get Out Early, 1986; Accosting Profiles, 1989; Uncollected short stories: At Aunt Sarah's, 1938; You Hit Me, 1939; Hotel Hudson Potomac, 1941; Other non-fiction and children's works. Honours: Fellowship, Royal Society of Literature, 1960. Address: 4-B Alwyne Road, London N1 2HH, England.

ALLEN Woody. See: KONIGSBERG Allen Stewart.

ALLENDE Isabel, b. 2 Aug 1942, Lima, Peru. Writer. m. William C Gordon, 17 July 1988, 1 son, 1 daughter. Publications: The House of the Spirits; Of Love and Shadows; Eva Luna; Stories of Eva Luna; The Infinite Plan; Several Childrens Stories. Contributions to: Too Numerous. Literary Agents: Carmen Balcells. Address: c/o Carmen Balcells, Diagonal 580, Barcelona 21, Spain.

ALLISON Gaylene Dolores, b. 2 Aug 1948, Saskatchewan, Canada. English and E S L Teacher; Editor; Poet. m. Geoff Hancock, 6 Aug 1983, 1 daughter. Education: BA, BEd, University of British

Columbia; MA, University of Toronto. Appointments: Co-founder, Woman's Writing Collective, 1975; Poetry Editor, Landscape, 1976; Founding Editor, Fireweed Feminist Journal, 1977; Poetry Editor, Waves Literary Journal, 1983; Fiction Editor, The Canadian Forum: Literary and Political Magazine, 1984; Advisory Board: Tiger Lily, 1985. Publications: Women and Their Writing I and II, anthology, 1975, 1976; Landscape, anthology, 1977; Life: Still, poetry, 1981; The Unravelling, 1987; In the Valley of the Butterflies, 1989; Fungus Lady, forthcoming. Contributions to: Landscape; Fireweed; Canadian Literature; Island; The Canadium Forum; Women and Their Writing I/II; PCR; Writers' Quarterly; Femme Plurielle; Prairie Fire; Dandelion; Poetry Toronto; Waves; Room of One's Own; Anthologies: Sp/elles; Women and Words, 1984; Canadian Poetry by Women, 1986; Canadian Women Studies, 1987. Honours: Poetry Award, Ontario Teachers Federation, 1982, 1987; Nominated for Pat Lowther Poetry Award, 1987. Memberships: The League of Canadian Poets; Amnesty International. Address: Fiction Editor, 109 Brunswick Street, Stratford, Ontario N5A 3L9, Canada.

ALLOTT Miriam, b. 16 June 1920, London, England. University Lecturer. m. Kenneth Allott, 2 June 1951 (dec 1973). Education: MA, Liverpool University, 1946; PhD, 1949. Literary Appointments: William Noble Fellowship, English Literature, 1946-48; Lecturer, Senior Lecturer, Reader, English Literature, Liverpool University, 1948-73; Andrew Cecil Bradley Professor, Modern English Literature, 1973-81; Professor of English, Birkbeck College, London University, 1981-85; Honorary Senior Fellow, Liverpool University; Professor Emeritus, London University. Publications: The Art of Graham Green, with Kenneth Allott, 1951; Novelists on the Novel, 1959; Complete Poems of John Keats, 1970; Complete Poems of Matthew Arnold, 2nd edition 1979 (1st edition, Kenneth Allott, 1965); Matthew Arnold, with R H Super, 1986; Numerous essays & articles on 19th & 20th century novelists & poets, notably Keats, Shelley, Arnold, Clough, the Brontes, George Eliot, Henry James, James Joyce, Graham Greene, Iris Murdoch, William Golding; Currently completing: Poems of Matthew Arnold, co-editor with Nicholas Shrimpton; Critical biography of Clough. Membership: Executive Committee, English Association. Address: 21 Mersey Avenue, Liverpool L19 3QU, England.

ALLSOPP Bruce, b. 4 July 1912, Oxford, England. Author; Artist. m. Florence Cyrilla Woodruffe, 29 Dec 1936, Dec 1991, 2 s. Education: BA, 1933, Dip CD, 1935, Liverpool University. Appointments: Senior Lecturer, University of Newcastle Upon Tyne, 1969-73; Reader, 1973-77. Publications include: General History of Architecture, 1955; Art and the Nature of Architecture, 1952; Civilization, The Next Stage, 1969; A Modern Theory of Architecture, 1970; The Country Life Companion to British and European Architecture, 1977; Social Responsibility and the Responsible Society, 1985. Contributions to: Various Journals. Memberships: Athenaeum; Art Workers Guild Master; MRTPI; FSA; Society of Architectural Historians. Address: Woodburn, 3 Batt House Road, Stocksfield, Northumberland NE43 7QZ, England.

ALLWOOD Martin Samuel, b. 13 Apr 1916, Jonkoping, Sweden. Author; Professor. m. Enelia Paz Gomez, 20 Dec 1976, 2 s, 3 d. Education: MA, Cantab; MA, Columbia, 1949; Dr Rer Pol Technische Hochschule Darmstadt, 1953. Appointments: President, Anglo Am Centre, Sweden; Professor, Nordic College of Journalism. Publications include: More than 80 Books in Swedish, English inc. The cemetery of the Cathedrals, 1945; The Swedish Crime, (play), 1976; New English Poems, 1981; Valda Svenska Dikter, 1982; Meet Will Shakespeare, 1985; Indiska Dikter, 1986; Essays on Contemporary Civilization, 1988; The Roots of Western Civilization, 1990; The Empress and Her Lover, 1993; Verona Bratesch, 1993; The Big Book of Humo(u)r From Britain and America, 1993. Contributions to: Numerous articles. Honour: Kaj Munk Society Award, 1992. Memberships: Gothenburg Society of Authors; Swedish Society of Immigrant Authors. Address: Anglo-Am Ctr, 56532 Mullsjo, Sweden, USE

ALMQUIST Gregg Andrew, b. 1 Dec 1948, Minneapolis, Minnesota, USA. Actor; Novelist; Playwright. Education: BA, University of Minnesota, 1971. Publications: Beast Rising, 1988; Pocket Books Inc (published in France under the title L'eveil de la bete); Wolf Kill, 1990; Pocket Books, Inc Plays (produced): The Duke; The Eve of Saint Venus (adapted from Burgess); The Winter That Ended in June; Pavan for a Dead Princess. Literary Agent: Lisa Bankoff, c/o ICM, New York. Address: ICM, 40W 57th Street, New York, NY 10019, USA.

ALONSO ALVAREZ Emilio (Andrenio), b. 2 July 1940, Minera de Luna, Leòn, Spain. Naval Architect. m. Mercedes Pueyo, 29 July 1966, 1 son. Education: Naval Architecture, Escuela Técnica Superior de Ingenieros Navales, 1965. Publications: Coplas de la Transiciòn, De Franco a Tejero, poetry, 1986; Octavas Reales Callejeras sin Ton ni Son, poetry, 1987; An anonymous libel against the Gulf War - El Amor Petrolero es Signo de Mal Agüero, theater, 1991; El Condòn Encantado, theater, not published. Contributions to: El Cocodrilo; El Independiente; El Mundo, all of these are political articles. Honours: Casa Villas Poetry Award, Madrid, 1983. Address: Juan Ramon Jimenez 24, 28036 Madrid, Spain.

ALPERS Antony, b. 1919, New Zealand. Writer. Appointments: Journalist, Editor, New Zealand, 1936-66; Professor of English, Queen's University, Kingston, Ontario, 1966-82 (now Emeritus). Publications: Katherine Mansfield: A Biography, 1953; Dolphins, 1960; Maori Myths and Tribal Legends, 1964; Legends of the South Sea, 1970, as The World of the Polynesians, 1987; The Life of Katherine Mansfield, 1980; The Stories of Katherine Mansfield, 1984. Address: 46 Memorial Avenue, Christchurch 5, New Zealand.

ALPHONSO-KARKALA John B, b. 1923, India. Author: Poet. Appointments: Member, Indian Foreign Missions, Geneva, London, United Nations, New York City, 1953-60; Teaching Fellow, Oriental Studies Programme, Columbia University, New York City, 1962-64; Assistant Professor, 1964-65; Associate Professor, 1965-68, Professor of Literature, 1969-, State University of New York, New Platz. Publications: Indo-English Literature in the Nineteenth Century, 1970; An Anthology of Indian Literature: Selections from Vedas to Tagore, 1972; Passions of the Nightless Nights (novel), 1974; Bibliography of Indo-English Literature 1800-1966 (with Leena Karkala), 1974; Studies in Comparative Literature: Essays, 1974; Jawaharial Nehru: A Literary Portrait, 175; Verdic Vision, 1980; When Night Falls (verse with Leena Karkala), 1980; Joys of Jayamagara (novel), 1981. Memberships: Modern Language Association, USA; American Comparative Literature Association. Address: 20 Millrock Road, New Paltz, NY 12561, USA.

ALTER Robert B, b. 2 Apr 1935, New York City, USA. Professor; Literary Critic. m. Carol Cosman, 17 June 1974, 3 sons, 1 daughter. Education: BA, Columbia College, 1957; MA 1958, PhD 1962, Harvard University. Appointments: Instructor, Assistant Professor, English, Columbia University, 1962-66; Associate Professor, Hebrew & Comparative Literature, University of California, Berkeley, 1967-69; Professor of Hebrew & Comparative Literature, 1969-89; Class of 1937 Professor, 1989-. Publications: Partial Magic, 1975; Defenses of the Imagination, 1978; Stendhal: A Biography, 1979; The Art of Biblical Narrative, 1981; Motives for Fiction, 1984; The Art of Biblical Poetry, 1985; The Pleasures of Reading in an Idealogical Age, 1989; Necessary Angels, 1991; The World of Biblical Literature, 1992; Hebrew and Modernity, 1994. Contributions to: Commentary; New Republic; New York Times Book Review; London Review of Books; Times Literary Supplement. Honours: English Institute Essay Prize, 1965; National Jewish Book Award for Jewish Thought, 1982; Present Tense Award for Religious Thought, 1986; American Academy of Arts and Science, 1986. Memberships: American Comparative Literature Association; Association of Literary Scholars and Critics; Council of Scholars of the Library of Congress; American Academy of Arts and Sciences. Literary Agent: Georges Borchardt. Address: 1475 Le Roy Avenue, Berkeley, CA 94708, USA.

ALTHER Lisa, b. 1944, United States of America. Author. Appointments: Staff Member, Atheneum Publishers, New York City; Lecturer, St Michael's College, Burlington, 1980. Publications: Kinflicks, 1976; Original Sins, 1981; Other Women, 1984; Bedrock, 1990. Contributions to: NY Times Magazine, NY Times Book Review, Natural History, New Society, Arts and Antiques. Memberships: PEN; Authors Guild; National Writers Union. Literary Agent: Gloria Loomis, Watkins-Loomis, 150 E 35th Street, New York, NY 10016, USA. Address: c/o Gloria Loomis, Watkins-Loomis, 150 E 35th Street, New York, NY 10016, USA.

ALTICK Richard Daniel, b. 1915, USA. Writer. Appointments: Faculty 1945, Regent's Professor of English 1968-82, Regent's Professor Emeritus of English 1982-, Ohio State University, Columbus. Publications: Preface to Critical Reading, 1946, 6th revised edition, 1984; The Cowden Clarkes, 1948; The Scholar Adventurers, 1950; The English Common Reader: A Social History of the Mass Reading Public, 1800-1900, 1957; The Art of Literary Research, 1963, 4th revised edition 1992; Lives and Letters: A History of Literary Biography in

England and America, 1965; (ed) Carlyle: Past and Present, 1965; Browning's Roman Murder Story (with J F Loucks), 1968; To Be in England, 1969; Victorian Studies in Scarlet, 1970; (ed) Browning: The Ring and the Book, 1971; Victorian People and Ideas: A Companion for the Modern Reader of Victorian Literature, 1973; The Shows of London, 1978; Paintings from Books: Art and Literature in Britain 1760-1900, 1985; Deadly Encounters: Two Victorian Sensations (as Evil Encounters in UK), 1986; Writers, Readers and Occasions, 1989, (Lit Criticism); The Presence of the Present: Topics of the Day in the Victorian Novel, 1991. Honour: Winner, Phi Beta Kappa's Christian Gauss Award, 1991. Address: Department of English, Ohio State University, 164 West 17th Avenue, Columbus, OH 43210, USA.

ALTMAN Philip, b. 6 Jan 1924, Kansas City, Missouri, USA. Editor; Administrator. m. Lillian Berlinsky, 1 Sept 1946, 1 son, 1 daughter. Education: BA, University of Southern California, 1948; MSc, Western Reserve University, 1949. Appointments: Director, Editor, Office of Biological Handbooks, 1959-79; Executive Editor, Biology Databook Series, 1983-86; Executive Director, Council of Biology Editors, 1981-. Publications: Handbook of Respiration, 1958; Handbook of Circulation, 1959; Blood and Other Body Fluids, 1961; Growth, 1962; Biology Data Book, 1st edition, 1964; Environmental Biology, 1966; Metabolism, 1968; Respiration & Circulation, 1971; Biology Data Book, 2nd edition, Volume 1, 1972, Volume II, 1973, Volume III, 1974; Cell Biology, 1976; Human Health and Disease, 1977; Inbred and Genetically Defined Strains of Laboratory Animals, 1979; Pathology of Laboratory Mice and Rats, 1985. Contributor to: Scientific Journals; Zoology CODATA Director of Data Sources for Science and Technology, in CODATA Bulletin No 38, 1980; Council of Biology Editors: A 25 Year Chronology of Events, in CBE Views, Volume 4, 1981; Publications of the Council of Biology Editors, in CBE Views Volume 6, 1983; The Council of Biology Editors, in Scholarly Publishing, Volume 20, 1989. Address: Council of Biology Editors, 9650 Rockville Pike, Bethesda, MD 20814, USA.

ALUKO Timothy Mofolorunso, b. 14 June 1918, Ilesha, Nigeria. Novelist. m. Janet Adebisi Fajemisin, 1948, 6 children. Education: BSc, University of London, 1950; PhD in Public Health Engineering, University of Lagos, 1976. Appointments: Senior Lecturer, University of Ibadan, 1966; Commissioner of Finance Government of Western Nigeria, 1971-73. Publications: One Man, One Wife, 1959; One Man, One Matchet, 1964; Kinsman and Foreman, 1966; Chief the Honourable Minister, 1970; His Worshipful Majesty, 1973; Wrong Ones in the Dock, 1982; A State of Our Own, 1986; Conduct Unbecoming, 1993; Uncollected short story: The New Engineer, 1968. Honours include: OBE, 1963; OON, 1964. Address: 53 Ladipo Oluwote Road, Apapa, Lagos, Nigeria.

ALVAREZ Alfred, b. 5 Aug 1929, Poet; Author. m. 7 April 1966, 2 sons, 1 daughter. Education: Oundle School; BA, 1952, MA, 1956, Corpus Christi College, Oxford. Appointments: Poetry Critic and Editor, The Observer, 1956-66; Advisory Editor, Penguin Modern European Poets, 1964-76. Publications include: The Shaping Spirit, 1958; The School of Donne, 1961; The New Poetry, 1962; Under Pressure, 1965; Beyond All the Fiddle, 1968; penguin Modern Poets No. 18, 1970; Apparition, 1971; The Savage God, 1971; Beckett, 1973; Hers, 1974; Autumn to Autumn and Selected Poems, 1978; Hunt, 1978; Life After Marriage, 1982; The Bigger Game in Town, 1983; Offshore, 1986; Feeding the Rat, 1988; Rain Forest, 1988; Day of Atonement, 1991; Faber Book of Modern European Poetry, 1992; Night, 1995. Contributions to: Numerous Magazines and Journals. Honours: Vachel Lindsay Prize for Poetry, 1961. Memberships: Climbers; Alpine; Beefsteak. Literary Agent: Gillon Aitken. Address: c/o Aitken & Stone, 29 Fernshaw Road, London SW10 0TG, England.

AMADI Elechi, b. 12 May 1934, Aluu, Nigeria. Novelist. m. Doah Ohlae, 1957, 8 children. Education: BSc in Mathematics and Physics, University College, Ibadan, 1959. Appointments: Writer-in-residence and Dean of the Faculty of Arts, College of Education, Port Harcourt, 1984-87; Commissioner of Education, 1987-89, and Commissioner of Lands and Housing, 1989-90, Rivers State. Publications: The Concubine, 1966; The Great Ponds, 1969; The Slave, 1978; Estrangement, 1986; Plays: Isiburu, 1969; Peppersoup, and The Road to Ibadan, 1977; Dancer of Johannesburg, 1979; Other works including Hymn and Prayer books. Honours: International Writers Program Grant, University of Iowa, 1973. Address: Box 331, Port Harcourt, Nigeria.

AMADO Jorge, b. 10 Aug 1912. Novelist. m. Zelia Gattai, 1945, 1 son, 1 daughter. Publications include: Mar Morto; Jubiaba; The Violent Land; Sao Jorge dos Ilheus; Cacau; Suor; Capitaes da Areia; ABC de Castro Alves; Bahia de Todos os Santos; O Amor do Soldado; Seara Vermelha; O Cavaleiro da Esperanca; O Mundo da Paz; os Subterraneos da Liberdade; Gabriela Cravo e Canela; Os velhos marinheiros; Os pastores da noite; Dona Flor e seus dois maridos!; Tenda dos Milagres; Teresa Bautista Cansada de Guerra; Tieto do Agreste e Farda; Fardao; Camisola de Dormir; O Menino Grapiuna; Tocaia Grande. Honours: Calouste Gulbenkian Prize, Academy du Monde Latin, 1971; National Literary Prize, Brazil; Nonnino Literary Prize, Italy; Commander, Legion d'Honneur, France. Address: Rua Alagoinhas 33, Rio Vermelho-Salvador, Bahia, Brazil.

AMAND Mulk Raj, b. 12 Dec 1905, Peshawar, India. Novelist. m. (2) Shirin Vajifdar, 1950, 1 daughter. Education: BA (Hons), Punjab University, 1924; PhD, University College, University of London, 1929; Cambridge University, 1929-30. Appointments: Director, Kutub publishers, Bombay, 1946-; Taught at the Universities of Punjab, Benares, and Rajasthan, Jaipur, 1948-66. Publications: Untouchable, 1935; The Coolie, 1936; Two Leaves and a Bud, 1937; The Village, 1939; Lament on the Death of a Master of Arts, 1939; Across the Black Waters, 1940; The Sword and the Sickle, 1942; The Big Heart, 1945; Seven Summers: The Story of an Indian Childhood, 1951; Private Life of an Indian Prince, 1953; The Old Woman and the Cow, 1960; The Road, 1961; Morning Face, 1968; Confession of a Lover, 1976; The Bubble, 1984; Death of a Hero, 1995; Also: Various short stories and other works. Honours include: Sahitya Academy Award, 1974. Address: 25 Cuffe Parade, Bombay 400 005, India.

AMANSHAUSER Gerhard, b. 2 Jan 1928, Salzburg, Austria. Writer. Education: Technical University of Graz; Universities of Vienna, Austria & Marburg; Dr H C, 1993. Publications include: Aus der Leben der Quaden, 1968; der Deserteur, 1970; Ärgemisse eines Zauberers, 1973; Schloss mit späten Gâten, 1975; Grenzen Essays, 1977; Gedichte, 1986; Fahrt zur verbotenen Stadt, 1987; Der Ohne Namen See, Chinese Impressions, 1988; Moloch Horridus, 1989; Lektüre, 1991; Gegensätze, 1993; das Erschlagen von Stechmücken, 1993. Contributions to: Literatur und Kritik; Neues Forum; Protokolle; Neue Rundschau. Honours: Georg Trakl Promotion Prize, 1952; Theodor Körner Prize, 1970; Rauriser Literaturpreis, 1973; Förderungspreis der Stadt Salzburg, 1975; Preis der Salzburger Wirtschaft, 1985; Alma Johanna Koenig Preis, 1987. Address: Brunnhausgasse 10, 5020 Salzburg, Austria.

AMB Daniel. See: **ANDERSEN Baltser.**

AMBLER Eric, (Eliot Reed), b. 28 June 1909, London, England. Novelist; Screenwriter. Education: London University. Publications include: A Kind of Anger, 1964; Dirty Story, 1967; The Levanter, 1972; Doctor Frigo, 1974; Send No More Roses, 1977; Here Lies, 1985; Epitapj Fore a Spy, 1938; The Mask of Dimitrois, 1939; The Schirmer Inheritance, 1953; The Night Corners, 1956; Passage of Arms, 1959; The Light of Day, 1962; The Care of Time, 1981. Honours: OBE, 1981; MWA, Grand Master, 1975; CWA Gold & Diamond Daggers. Memberships: Society of Authors; Writers Guild of Am. Literary Agent: Campbell Thomson & MacLaughlin Ltd, 1 Kings Mews, London WC1N 2JA, England.

AMBROSE David Edwin, b. 21 Feb 1943, Chorley, Lancs, England. Playwright; Screenwriter; Novelist. m. Lawrence Huguette Hammerli, 13 Sept 1979. Education: Degree in Law, University of Oxford, Merton College, 1962-1965. Publications: Novels: The Man Who Turned Into Himself, 1993, 1994; Mother of God, 1995; Hollywood Lies; Many TV Plays and Screenplays in Hollywood and Worldwide; also Seige, Cambridge Theatre, London, 1972. Honours: 1st Prize Screenplay, Sitges Film Festival, 1980, for The Survivor. Membership: Dramatists' Club, London. Literary Agent: William Morris Agency, 31 Soho Square, London, WN 5DG, England.

AMBROSE Stephen E, Historian. Appointment: Dir, Eisenhawer Centre, University of New Orleans. Publications include: Upton and the Army, 1964; Ike; Abilene to Berlin, 1973; Crazy Horse and Custer, 1975; Rise to Globalism, 1971; Milton S Eisenhower, Educational Statesman, 1983; Nixon, 1987; Eisenhower: Soldier & President, 1990; Eisenhower and the German POWs, 1992; War Comes Again: The Civil War and World War II, 1995. Address: Department of History, University of New Orleans, New Orleans, LA 70148, USA.

AMERY Carl, b. 9 Apr 1922, Munich, Germany. Writer. m. Marijane Gerth, 10 Apr 1950, 3 sons, 2 daughters. Education: Humanistisches Gymnasium (Abitur 1940); Literary and Language Studies in Munich and Washington 1946-50. Literary Appointments: Director of Munich City Library System, 1967-71; Editor of Bavarian Broadcasting Station, 1950 and 1962 (temporary). Publications include: Die Kapitulation, essay, 1963; Die Grosse Deutsche Tour, novel, 1959; Das Ende der Vorsehung, essay, 1972; Naturals Politik, essay, 1976; Das Koenigsprojekt, novel, 1974; Die Wallfahrer, novel, 1986; Das Geheimnis der Krypta, novel, 1990. Honours: German Federal Cross of Merit, 1988; Honorary Citizen Nr 9 of the village of Granit, South Bulgaria. Memberships: VS (German Writers' Association affiliated to the Media trade union); PEN Center of Germany, President E f Schumachgesellschaft fuer politische Oekologie, Munich, President; ECOROPA member. Address: Draechslstr 7, D-8 Muenchen 90, Germany.

AMERY H Julian (Rt Hon), b. 27 Mar 1919. Member of Parliament, UK (Conservative, Preston North, 1950-66, Brighton Pavilion, 1969; Amery of Lustleigh (Life Baron UK), 1960-92. Education: Eton; Balliol College, University of Oxford, England. Publications: Sons of the Eagle, 1948; The Life of Joseph Chamberlain: Vol IV 1901-03, At the Height of His Power, 1951, Volumes V & VI, Joseph Chamberlain & The Tariff Reform Campaign 1901-14, 1969; Approach March (autobiography), 1973. Contributions to: Various newspapers and journals. Honours include: Privy Councillor, 1960; Knight Commander of the Order of the Phoenix (Greece); Order of Oman (1st Class); Raised to the Peerage as Baron Amery of Lustleigh of Preston in the County of Lancashire & of Brighton in the County of East Sussex, 1992; Grand Cordon of the Order of Skandebeg (Albania); Hon. Dr. of Luog Westminster University Fult Missouri, 1994. Address: 112 Eaton Square, London SW1 9AE, England.

AMES Leslie. See: **RIGONI Orlando Joseph**.

AMES Sarah Rachel, (Sarah Gainham), b. 1 Oct 1922, London, England. Writer. m. Kenneth Robert ames, 14 Apr 1964, Dec 1975. Publications: Time Right Deadly, 1956; Cold Dark Night, 1957; The Mythmaker, 1957; Stone Roses, 1959; Silent Hostage, 1960; Night Falls on the City, 1967; A Place in the Country, 1968; Takeover Bid, 1970; Private Worlds, 1971; Maculan's Daughter, 1973; To The Opera Ball, 1975; The Habsburg Twlight, 1979; The Tiger, Life, 1983. Contributions to: Encounter; Atlantic Monthly; BBC; And others. Address: Altes Forsthaus, Schlosspark, A2404 Petronell, Austria.

AMICHAI Yehuda, b. 1924, Wurzburg, Germany. Istraeli Citizen. Poet. m. Chang Sokolov. Education: Hebrew University, Jerusalem. Appointments include: Visiting Poet, University of Berkeley, CA, 1976, NY University, 1987. Publications include: Now and in Other Days, 1955; Two Hopes Away, 1958; In The Park, 1959; Poetry, 1948-62; Selected Poems, 1968; Now in the Turmoil, 1968; Selected Poems, 1971; And Not in Order to Remember, 1971; Songs of Jerusalem and Myself, 1973; Behind All This Lies Great Happiness, 1974; Amen, 1978; On New Years Day, Next to a House Being Built, 1979; Time, 1979; Love Poems, 1981; Hour of Charity, 1982; Great Tranquility: Questions and Answers, 1983; From Man You Came, and to Men You Will Return, 1985; The Selected Poetry of Yehuda Amichai, 1986; Poems of Jerusalem, 1987; Even a Fist was Once an Open Palm with Fingers, 1991; World is a Room and Other Stories, 1984; Not of This Time, Not of This Place, 1973. Honours include: Honorary Doctorate, Hebrew University, 1990. Address: 26 Malki Street, Yemin Moshe, Jerusalem, Isreal.

AMIN Sayed-Hassan, b. 25 Nov 1948, Persia. University Professor of Law; Author; Advocate. m. 1 son, 2 daughters. Education: LLB, 1970; LLM, 1975; PhD, 1979; Scottish Bar Exams, 1980-82. Appointments: Lecturer, 1979; Senior Lecturer, 1981; Reader, 1984; Professor, 1991, Glasgow Caledonian University; Islamic Institute of International & Comparative Law, President, 1994-. Publications: 36 Books including: International And Legal Problems of the Gulf; Middle East Legal Systems; Law & Justice in Contemporary Yemen; Islamic Law and its Implications for the Modern World; Legal System of Iraq; Legal System of Kuwait; Law of Intellectual Property in Developing Countries. Contributions to: International & Comparative Law Quarterly; Oil & Gas Law & Taxation Review. Memberships: Society of Authors; Executive Council: Scottish Branch; Royal Institute of International Affairs; Faculty of Advocates; Council for National Academic Awards; Patron, Prisoners Abroad, Past Director and Representative, World Development Movement; Fellow, Islamic Academy. Address: Faculty of Advocates, Parliament House, Edinburgh, EH1 1RF, Scotland, England.

AMIS Kingsley (Sir), (Robert Markham), b. 16 Apr 1922, London, England. Author. m. (1) Hilary A Bardwell, 1948, 2 s, 1 d, (2) Elizabeth Jane Howard, 1965, divorced 1983. Education: St Johns College, Oxford, 1941, 1945-49. Appointments: Lecturer, University Coll, Swansea, 1949-61; Fellow, Peterhouse, Cambridge, 1961-63; Visiting Professor, Various Universities, USA. Publications include: A Frame of Mind, 1953; Lucky Jim, 1954; That Uncertain Feeling, 1955; A Case of Samples, 1956; New Maps of Hell, 1960; Take A Girl Like You, 1960; One Fat Englishman, 1963; The James Bond Dossier, 1965; The Egyptologists, 1966; A Look Aroung the Estate, 1967; What Became of Jane Austen?, 1970; On Drink, 1972; The Alteration, 1976; Jake's Thing, 1978; Collected Poems, 1944-79; Russian Hide & Seek, 1980; Stanley and the Women, 1984; How's Your Glass, 1984; The Old Devils, 1986; Difficulties with Girls, 1988; Faber Popular Reciter, 1978; The Golden Age of Science Fiction, 1981; Crime of the Century, 1987; The Folks that Live on the Hill, 1990; We Are All Guilty, 1991; The Russian Girl, 1992; Mr Barrett's Secret, 1993; You Can't Do Both, 1994. Honours: Somerset Maugham Award; John W Campbell Memorial Award; Booker Prize for Fiction; Hon Fellow, University College, Swansea; CBE; Hon Fellow, St Johns Oxford. Address: c/o Jonathan Clowes & Co, 22 Prince Albert Road, London NW1, England.

AMIS Martin Louis, b. 25 Aug 1949, Oxford, England. Author. Education: BA, Exeter College, Oxford. Appointments: Fiction & Poetry Editor, Times Literary Supplement, 1974; Literary Editor, New Statesman, 1977-79; Special Writer, The Observer Newspaper, 1980-. Publications: The Rachel Papers, 1973; Dead Babies, 1975; Success, 1978; Other People: A Mystery Story, 1981; Invasion of the Space Invaders, 1982; Money, 1984; London Fields, 1989; Time's Arrow; Einstein's Monsters: Five Stories, 1987; The Information, 1995. Honours: Somerset Maugham Award, 1974. Address: c/o Peters Fraser & Dunlop, 5th Floor, The Chambers, Chelsea Harbour, Lots Road, London SW10 0xp, England.

AMMONS Archie Randolph, b. 18 Feb 1926, Whiteville, North Carolina, USA. Professor of English; Poet. m. Phyllis Plumbo, 1949, 1 son. Education: BS, Wake Forest College, North Carolina, 1949; University of California, Berkeley, 1950-52; Served in the US Naval Reserve, 1944-46. Appointments: Principal, Hatteras Elementary School, North Carolina, 1949-50; Executive Vice-President, Friedrich and Dimmock Inc, Millville, New Jersey, 1952-62; Assistant Professor 1964-68, Associate Professor 1969-71, Professor of English 1971-, Goldwin Smith Professor of English, Cornell University, Ithaca, New Yorkm 1973-; Visting Professor, Wake Forest University, 1974-75; Poetry Editor, Nation, New York, 1963. Publications: Verse includes: The Snow Poems, 1977; The Selected Poems 1951-1977, 1977; Highgate Road, 1977; For Doyle Fosco, 1977; Poem, 1977; Six-Piece Suite, 1979; Selected Longer Poems, 1980; A Coast of Trees, 1981; Worldly Hopes, 1982; Lake Effect Country, 1983; Marboge, W W Norton, New York, 1993. Address: English Department, Cornell University, Ithaca, NY 14853, USA.

AMOROSO Bruno, b. 11 Dec 1936, Rome, Italy. Associate Professor in Economic Policy. Education: MD, University La Sapienza, Rome, 1966. Publications: Lo Stato Imprenditore, 1978; Rapporto Dalla Scandinavia, 1980; European Industrial Relations, 1990; Macroeconomic Theories & Policies for the 1990s, 1992; Scandinavian Perspectives on European Integration, 1990. Contributions to: Comparative Labour Law Journal; The International Journal of Human Resource Management; Economia Pubblica. Memberships: Vice President, European Inter-University Association on Society, Science & Technology, Brussels; European Culture Association, Venice. Address: Webersgade 28, Copenhagen, DK-2100, Denmark.

ABRAMS Meyer Howard, b. 1912. Publications: The Mirror and The Lamp, 1953; A Glossary of Literary Terms, 1957; English Romatic Poets: Modern Essays in Criticism, 1960; The Norton Anthology of English Literature (editor), 1962 et al; Natural Supernaturalism, 1971; Wordsworth, 1972; The Correspondent Breeze: Essays, 1984; Doing Things With Texts, 1989. Honours: Fellow, American Academy and Institute of Arts & Letters, 1990.

AN Tai Sung, b. 3 Feb 1931, Seoul, Korea. College Professor; Author. m. Sihn Ja Lee, 23 Aug 1969, 2 daughters. Education: Bach of Arts, Indiana University, Bloomington, USA, 1956; Master of Arts, Yale University, New Haven, USA, 1957; PhD, University of Pennsylvania,

USA, 1963. Appointments: Professor of Political Science, Washington College, Chestertown, 1963-73; Everett E Nuttle Professor, Political Science at Washington College, Chestertown, 1973-. Publications: Mao Tse Tung's Cultural Revolution; The Sino Soviet Territorial Dispute; The Lin Piao Affair; North Korea in Transition: From Dictatorship to Dynasty; North Korea: A Political Handbook: The Vietnam War; About 80 articles. Honours: Lindback Award for Distinguished Teaching; Sears Roebuck Foundation Teaching Excellence & Campus Leadership Award. Memberships: American Political Science Association; Association for Asian Studies; Asia Society; Korean Association of Oriental History & Civilization; American Association of University Professors. Address: Dept of Pol Science & Internal Studies, Washington College, 300 Washington Avenue, Chestertown, MD 21620, USA.

ANANIA Michael (Angelo), b. 1938, United States of America. Author; Poet. Literary Appointments: Co-ordinating Council of Literary Magazines, Bibliographer, Lockwood Library, State University of New York, Buffalo, 1963-64; Editor, Audit, 1963-64; Co-editor, Audit/Poetry, Buffalo, 1963-67; Instructor in English, State University of New York, Fredonia, 1964-65, Northwestern University, Evanston, Illinois, 1965-68; Literary Editor, Swallow Press, Chicago, 1968-; Professor of English, University of Illinois, Chicago, 1970-. Publications: New Poetry Anthology I and II, 1969, 1972; The Colour of Dust, 1970; Sets/Sorts, 1974; Riversongs, 1978; The Red Menace, 1984; Constructions/Variations, 1985; The Sky at Ashland, 1986; In Plain Sight, 1991; In Plain Sight: Obsessions, Morals & Domestic Laughter, 1993; Selected Poems, 1965-1994, 1994. Address: Department of English, University of Illinois at Chicago, Chicago, IL 60680, USA.

ANDERSEN Baltser, (Daniel Amb), b. 3 Jan 1956, Ribe, Denmark. Schoolteacher; Author. m. Magdaline Mattak, 26 Dec 1984, 2 daughters. Education: Student, Tonder, 1975; Student, Aarhus, 1976, 1986-88. Appointments: Teacher, Tonder, 1981; Teacher, Greenland, 1982-87; Leader, Greenlandic Peacemovement, Sorsunnata, 1984-87. Publications: Poems: Interlocking Hands, 1973; To Be Awake, 1974; Grey Asphalt, 1979; Travelling Spaceship, 1992; Angantyr and The Black Sword, 1993; Greenland; A Pawn in the Play; Encounter to the Book; Essay, In the name of Democracy. Contributions to: Many articles and essays about political and cultural matters in leftwing danish newspapers: Land & Folk; Socialistisk Weekend. Memberships: Leader, Norse Mythologican Circle, Alfheim; The Danish Writers' Union; Socialistic Peoples Party, 1976-93; The Red-Green Alliance, 1993-; MP Candidate in Denmark. Address: Krusaavej 33 Alslevb, 6240 Logumkloster, Denmark.

ANDERSEN Benny Allan, b. 7 Nov 1929, Copenhagen. Author. m. Cynthia La Touche Andersen, 28 Dec 1981. Publications include: Den Musikalske al, 1960; Den Indre Bowlerhat, 1964; Portraetgaller, 1966; Tykke Olsen M Fl, 1968; Her i Reservatet, 1971; Himmelspraet, 1979; Tiden og Storken, 1985; Chagall & Skorpiondans, 1991; Denne Kommen og Gaen, 1993. Contributions to: Anthologies inc. Niet Noodzakelijk met Insteeming, 1967; Poesia Moderna Danese, 1971; Anthologie de la Poesie Danoise Contemporaine, 1975; Dan Elbeszelok, 1978; Also Malahat Review: Mundus Artium; Contemporry Literature on Translation; Poetry Now; Prism International; West Coast Review; Literary Review; Scandinavian Review; Liberte; svetova Literature; Complete works Translated Kuddama, 1969; Selected Poems, 1975; Livet ar Smalt och Hogt, 1988; Das Leben ist Schmal und hoch, 1977; The Pillows, 1983; Selected Stories, 1983; Ma Velka Doba Byla Mala, 1983; Over Axeln, 1985; Tlustoch Olsen aj, 1989. Address: Kaerparken 11, 2800 Lyngby, Denmark.

ANDERSON Barbara, b. 14 June 1926, New Zealand. Novelist. m. Neil Anderson, 1951, 2 sons. Education: BA, University of Otago, 1946; BA, Victoria University, Wellington, 1983. Publications: Girls High, 1990; Short stories: I Think We Should Go Into the Jungle, 1989; Uncollected short stories: The Peacocks, 1985; I Thought There's Be A Couch, 1990; We Could Celebrate, 1991; Several radio plays. Honours: Victoria University Fellowship, 1991. Address: 36 Beauchamp Street, Karori, Wellington, New Zealand.

ANDERSON David Daniel, b. 1924, United States of America. Writer. Appointments: Distinguished University Professor, Department of American Thought and Language, Michigan State University, East Lansing, 1957-; Editor, Midwestern Miscellany Annual; Executive Secretary, Society for the Study of Midwestern Literature, 1971-73. Publications: Louis Bromfield, 1964; Critical Studies in American Literature, 1964; Sherwood Anderson, 1967; Sherwood Anderson's

Winesburg, Ohio, 1967; Brand Whitlock, 1968; Editor-in-Chief, The Black Experience, 1969; Abraham Lincoln, 1970; The Literary Works of Abraham Lincoln, 1970; The Dark and Tangled Path (with R Wright), 1971; Sunshine and Smoke, 1971; Robert Ingersoll, 1972; Mid-America I-XIV, 1974-87; Sherwood Anderson: Dimensions of His Literary Art (essays), 1976; Woodrow Wilson, 1978; Sherwood Anderson: The Writer at his Craft, 1979; Ignatius Donnelly, 1980; William Jennings Bryan, 1981; Critical Essays on Sherwood Anderson, 1981; Michigan: A State Anthology, 1982; Route Two, Titus, Ohio, 1993. Address: Department of American Thougbt and Language, Michigan State University, East Lansing, MI 48824, USA.

ANDERSON Kenneth Norman, b. 1921, United States of America. Writer. Appointments: Executive Editor, Publishers Editorial Services; President, Editorial Guild; EDitor, Holt Rinehart and Winston Inc, New York, 1965-70; Executive Director, Coffee Information Institute, New York, 1970-. Publications: Co-author, Lawyer's Medical Cyclopedia, 1962; The Family Physician (with Robert Addison), 1963; Today's Health Guide (with William Baver), 1965; Pictorial Medical Guide (with Robert Addison), 1967; Field and Stream Guide to Physical Fitness, 1969; Home Medical Encyclopedia (with Paul Kuhn), 1973; Sterno Guide to the Outdoors, 1977; Eagle Claw Fish Cookbook, 1977; The Newsweek Encyclopedia of Family Health and Fitness, 1980; Banham Medical Dictionary (with Walter Glanze), 1980, 1982; How Long Will You Live, 1981; Dictionary of Dangerous Pollutants, Ecology and Environment (with David Tver), 1981; The Pocket Guide to Coffees and Teas, 1982; Orphan Drugs, 1983; Longman Dictionary of Psychology and Psychiatry (with Walter Glanze and Robert Goldenson), 1984; History of the US Marines (with Jack Murphy), 1984; Prentice-Hall Dictionary of Nutrition and Health (with Lois Harmon Anderson), 1985; Mosby Medical Encyclopedia (with Lois Harman Anderson and Walter Glanze), 1985; The International Dictionary of Food & Nutrition (with Lois Anderson), 1993; International Menu Speller (with Lois Anderson), 1993. Address: Coffee Information Institute, 60 East 42nd Street, New York, NY 10017, USA.

ANDERSON Leone Castell, b. 12 Aug 1923, Los Angeles, California, USA. Free-lance Writer; Owner and Operator of Lee's Booklover's. m. J Eric Anderson, 17 Aug 1946, 3 sons. Education: Attended Austin Academy of Music, 1942-43. Appointments: Copy-writer, Russell Seeds, Advertising, Chicago, Illinois, USA, 1944-46; Free-lance Writer, 1946-49; Member of library staff, Elmhurst Public Library, Elmhurst, Illinois, 1969-74; Free-lance Writer, 1974-; Owner and Operator of Lee's Booklover's, 1979-. Publications: Publications for children include: The Good-By Day, 1984, reprinted as Moving Day, 1987; My Friend Next Door, 1984; Contributor to Christmas Handbook, 1984; Surprise at Muddy Creek, 1984; How Come You're So Shy? 1987; My Own Grandpa, 1987; Other works: Glendenna's Dilemma (readers' theatre), first performed in Chicago, Illinois at Performance Community, 1979; Come-Uppance (readers' theatre) first performed in Stockton, Illinois at Stockton Unitarian-Universalist Church, 1986. Contributions to: Columns in Elmhurst Press and Stockton Herald News (author); Magazines and Newspapers. Memberships: Society of Children's Book Writers (Midwest representative 1981-87); Children's Reading Round Table; Authors Guild; Off-Campus Writer's Workshop. Address: Lee's Booklover's, 127 South Main, Stockton, IL 61085, USA.

ANDERSON Matthew Smith, b. 23 May 1922, Perth, Scotland. Professor; Retired University Teacher. m. Olive Ruth Gee, 10 July 1954, 2 d. Education: Perth Academy, 1929-40; University of Edinburgh, 1940-42, 1945-47. Publications: Europe in the 18th Century, 1713-1783, 1961, 76, 87; The Eastern Question, 1774-1923, 1966; The Ascendency of Europe, 1815-1914, 1972, 85; Peter the Great, 1978; Historian and Eighteenth Century Europe, 1979; Wars and Society in Europe of the Old Regime, 1618-1789, 1988; Britain's Discovery of Russia, 1553-1815, 1958; The Great Powers and the Near East, 1774-1923, 1966. Contributions to: Numerous Articles in Historical Periodicals. Memberships: Royal Historical Soceity; Economic History Society; Past & Present Society. Address: 45 Cholmeley Crescent, Highgate, London N6 5EX, England.

ANDERSON Michael Falconer, b. 16 Jan 1947, Aberdeen. Author; Journalist. m. Hildegarde Becze, 16 Apr 1970, 2 sons. Appointments: Newspaper and Magazine Editor; Chief Sub-Editor of a national weekly; Sub-Editor of a daily newspaper; Showbusiness Writer; Reporter; Correspondent in newspapers, television and radio. Publications: The Woodsmen, 1986; The Unholy, 1987; God of a Thousand Faces, 1987; The Covenant, 1988; Black Trinity, 1989; The

Clan of Golgotha Scalp, 1990; Numerous short stories and plays for radio and television. Contributions to: Feature articles on everything from travel to history, the environment to books, in newspapers and magazines around the world. Memberships: Society of Authors; National Union of Journalists. Address: Portlehen, Aberdeen, Scotland.

ANDERSON Perry, Professor. Publications include: Towards Socialism, 1965; Passages from Antiquity to Feudalism, 1974; Considerations on Western Marxism, 1976; Arguments within British Marxism, 1980; In The Tracks of Historical Materialism, 1984; English Questions, 1992; A Zone of Engagement, 1992; Mapping Europes' Left, 1994. Address: Department of History, University of CA, 405 Hilgard Avenue, Los Angeles, CA 90024 1473, USA.

ANDERSON Poul William, b. 25 Nov 1926, Bristol, Pennsylvania, USA. Writer. m. Karen Kruse, 12 Dec 1953, 1 daughter. Education: BS, University of Minnesota, 1948. Publications: Brain Wave, 1954; The High Crusade, 1960; Guadians of Time, 1961; Three Hearts & Three Lions, 1961; Tau Zero, 1971; The Broken Sword (revised edition), 1971; Hrolf Kraki's Saga, 1973; A Midsummer's Tempest, 1974; The Atavar, 1978; The Merman's Children, 1979; Orion Shall Rise, 1983; The Boat of a Million Years, 1989; Harvest of Stars, 1993; The Stars Are Also Fire, 1994. Contributor to: Analog; Magazine of Fantasy & Science Fiction; Destinies; National Review; Boy's Life and others. Honours: Hugo Awards, 1961, 1964, 1968, 1971, 1973, 1978, 1982; Nebula Awards, 1971, 1972, 1981; Knight of Mark Twain, 1971; Mythopoeic Award, 1975; J R R Tolkien Memorial Award, 1978. Memberships: Science Fiction Writers of America, President 1972-73; Baker Street Iregulars. Literary Agent: Scovil-Chichak-Galen, New York. Address: 3 Las Palomas, Orinda, CA 94563, USA.

ANDERSON Quentin, b. 1912, USA. Writer. Appointments: Columbia University, 1939-82; University of Sussex, 1966-67; University of Barcelona, 1985. Publications: Selected Short Stories by Henry James, 1950; The American Henry James, 1957; The Proper Study: Essays on Western Classics (with Joseph A Mazzeo), 1962; The Imperial Self: An Essay in American Literary and Cultural History, 1971; Art, Politics and Will: Essays in Honor of Lionel Trilling (with others), 1977; Making Americans: An Essay on Individualism and Money, 1992. Honours: National Endowment for the Humanities, Senior Fellow, 1973; Paley Lecturer, Hebrew University of Jerusalem, 1982; Fellow, National Humanities Center, 1979-80; Fellow, New York Institute for the Humanities, 1981-95. Address: 29 Claremont Avenue, New York, NY 10027, USA.

ANDERSON Rachel, b. 1943. Writer: Novels, Short Stories, Plays. m. David Bradby, 4 children. Publications: Books for adults: Pineapple, 1965; The Purple Heart Throbs, A Survey of Popular Romantic Fiction, 1850-1972, 1974; Dream Lovers, 1978; For the Love of Sang, 1990; Books for small children: Tim Walks, 1985; The Cat's Tale, 1985; Wild Goose Chase, 1986; Jessy Runs Away, 1988; Best Friends, 1991; Jessy and The Long-Short Dress, 1992; Tough as Old Boots, 1991; Little Lost Fox, 1992; For older children: Moffatt's Road, 1978; The Poacher's Son, 1982; The War Orphan, 1984; Little Angel Comes to Stay, 1985; Little Angel, Bonjour, 1988; Happy Christmas, Little Angel, 1991; French Lessons, 1988; Renard The Fox (with David Bradby), 1986; The Boy Who Laughed, 1989; The Bus People, 1989; Paper Faces, 1991; When Mum Went to Work, 1992; Forthcoming: The Working Class, 1993; Jessy and the Long Short Dress, 1993. Honours: Medical Journalists Association Award for The Love of Sang, 1990; 25th Anniversary Guardian Children's Fiction Award for Paper Faces, 1992. Address: c/o Oxford University Press, Oxford OX2 6DP, England.

ANDERSON Robert Woodruff, b. 28 Apr 1917, NYC, USA. Playwright; Screenwriter; Novelist. Education: AB, Magna Cum Laude, 1939; MA, Harvard University, 1940. Publications: Plays - Tea and Sympathy, 1953; All Summer Long, 1954; Silent Night Lonely Night, 1959; The Days Between, 1965; You Know I Can't Hear When the Water's Running, 1967; I Never Sang for My Father, 1968; Solitaire/Double Solitaire, 1971; Free and Clear, 1983; Co-author, Elements of Literature, 1988; Novels: After, 1973; Getting Up and Going Home, 1978; Screenplays: Tea And Sympathy, 1956; Until They Sail, 1957; The Nun's Story, 1959; The Sand Pebbles, 1966; I Never Sang For My Father, 1970; Play: The Last Act is A Solo, TV, 1991; Absolute Strangers, TV, 1991. Honours: Recipient Awards for, I Never Sang for My Father, Writer's Guild, 1970; The Ace Award for The Last Act Is A Solo, 1991. Memberships: President, Dramatists Guild, 1971-73; Authors League Council; Writers Guild of America W;

American Playwrights Theatre, Board of Trustees; Theatre Hall of Fame, 1981; PEN. Literary Agent: ICM. Address: Transylvania Road, Roxbury, CT 06783, USA.

ANDRE Robert, b. 30 Aug 1920, Paris. Professor; Writer. m. Marie Thérèse Poirier, 10 Aug 1950, 3 children. Education: Licence, 1945; Master, 1948; PhD, 1950; Doctor, 1980. Publications include: L'Enfant Miroir; L'Amour et la Vie d'une Femme; Les Vertes Feunillantines; L'Amouru a l'Aveugle; A La Belle Saison. Contributions to: La Nouvelle Revue Francaise. Honours: Grand Prix du Roman de la Societé des Gens de Lettres; Prix Mediterranee; Prix de L'Academie Francaise. Memberships: Prsident, International Association of Literary Critics; Societé des Gens de Lettres. Address: 58 Rue Claude Bernard, 75005 Paris, France.

ANDREE Alice. See: **CLUYSENAAR Anne**.

ANDRENIO. See: **ALONSO ALVAREZ Emilo**.

ANDRESKI Stanislav Leonard, b. 18 May 1919, Czestochowa, Poland. Writer. 2 sons, 2 daughters. Education: BSc, 1st Class Honours, 1943, MSc 1947, Economics, PhD 1953. Appointments: Prof Emeritus, University of Reading and Polish University in London, Editorial Board, Journal of Strategic Studies. Publications include: Military Organisation & Society, 1954, 2nd edition 1968; Elements of Comparative Sociology, 1964; The Uses of Comparative Sociology (American Edition of 2), 1965, paperback 1969, Spanish edition, 1973, 1972; Parasitism & Subversion: The Case of Latin America, 1966, 2nd edition 1969; Argentinian Edition in Spanish, 1967; The African Predicament: A Study in Pathology of Modernisation, 1968; Social Sciences as Sorcery, 1972, Spanish translation 1973, German translation 1974, 2nd edition 1977, French translation 1975, Japanese translation 1981, Italian translation 1977, The Prospects of a Revolution in the USA, 1973; Max Weber's Insights & Errors, 1984; Polish Translation, 1992, Syphilis, Puritanism and Witch Hunts: Historical Explanations in the Light of Medicine and Psychoanalysis with a Forecast About Aids, 1989; Wars, Revolutions, Dictatorships, 1992; Editor: Herbert Spencer: Principles of Sociology, 1968; Herbert Spencer: Structure, Function and Evolution, 1971; The Essential Comte, 1974; Max Weber on Capitalism, Bureaucracy and Religion, 1984; Reflection on Inequality, 1975; Co-editor, Class Structure and Social Development, 1964 (in Polish). Contributions to: Approximately 90 articles in learned journals. Memberships: Writers' Guild; Institute of Patentees and Inventors. Address: Farriers, Village Green, Upper Basildon, Berkshire RG8 8LS, England.

ANDREW Prudence, b. 1924. Author. Publications: The Hooded Falcon, 1960; Ordeal by Silence, 1961; Ginger Over the Wall, 1962; A Question of Choice, 1963; Ginger and Batty Billy, 1963; The Earthworms, 1964; Ginger and No 10, 1964; The Constant Star, 1964; A Sparkle from the Coal, novel, 1964; Christmas Card, 1966; Mr Morgan's Marrow, 1967; Mister O'Brien, 1972; Rodge, Sylvie and Munch, 1973; Una and Grubstreet, 1973; Goodbye to the Rat, 1974; The Heroic Deeds of Jason Jones, 1975; Where Are You Going To, My Pretty Maid? 1977; Robinson Daniel Crusoe, 1978 (in United States of America as Close Within My Own Circle, 1980); The Other Side of the Park, 1984. Address: c/o Heinemann Limited, 10 Upper Grosvenor Street, London W1X 9PA, England.

ANDREWS Allen, b. 1913. Author. Publications include: Proud Fortress: Gibralter, 1958; Earthquake (sociology), 1963; The Mad Motorist (exploration), 1964; Those Magnificent Men in Their Flying Machines (humour), 1965; Monte Carlo or Bust (humour), 1969; Quotations for Speakers and Writers, 1969; I Did It My Way (biography as Billy Cotton), 1970; Intensive Inquiries (criminology), 1973; The Follies of King Edward VII, 1975; Kings and Queens of England and Scotland, 1976; The Whisky Barons (biography), 1977; An Illustrated Dictionary of Classical Mythology, 1978; The Cards Can't Lie, 1978; The Royal Coats of Arms of England, 1982; Catle Crespia (novel), 1982; Castle Crespin (novel), 1982; The People of Rome (verse), 1984; Straight Up, 1984; Impossible Loyalties (novel), 1985. Address: 4 Hazelmere Road, London NW6 6PY, England.

ANDREWS Elmer, b. 26 Jan 1948, Northern Ireland. University Lecturer. m. 20 June 1976, 2 daughters. Education: Dalriada School, Ballymoney, 1952-66; Queens University of Belfast, 1966-76; BA,1970; MA, 1976. Appointments: Thessa Loniki University, Greece, 1972-74; Mohammed V University Rabat, Morocco, 1976-80; Queens University Belfast, 1980-81; University of Vister, 1981-88; University of Ulster,

1988-. Publications: The Poetry of Seamus Heaney; All The Realms of Whisper; Seamus Heaney: A Collection of Critical Essays; Contemporary Irish poetry. Contributions to: Many articles, journals & magazines. Honours: Porter Scholarship; Foundation Scholarship. Address: Dept of English, University of Ulster, Coleraine, Northern Ireland.

ANDREWS Lucilla Matthew (Diana Gordon, Joanna Marcus), Writer. Publications: The Print Petticoat, 1954; The Secret Armour, 1955; The Quiet Wards, 1956; The First Year, 1957; A Hospital Summer, 1958; My Friend the Professor, 1960; Nurse Errant, 1961; The Young Doctors Downstairs, 1963; Flowers for the Doctor, 1963; The New Sister Theatre, 1964; The Light in the Ward, 1965; A House for Sister Mary, 1966; Hospital Circles, 1967; A Few Days in Endel (as Diana Gordon), 1968; Highland Interlude, 1968; The Healing Time, 1969; Edinburgh Excursion, 1970; Ring o' Roses, 1972; Silent Song, 1973; In Storm and in Calm, 1975; No Time for Romance: An Autobiographical Account of a Few Moments in British and Personal History (non-fiction), 1977; The Crystal Gull, 1978; One Night in London, 1979; Marsh Blood (as Joanna Marcus), 1980; A Weekend in the Garden, 1981; In an Edinburgh Drawing Room, 1983; After a Famous Victory, 1984; The Lights of London, 1985. Address: c/o Heinemann Limited, 10 Upper Grosvenor Street, London W1X 9PA, England.

ANDREWS Lyman, b. 1938, United States of America. Poet. Appointments: Lecturer, American Literature, University of Leicester, 1965-88; Visiting Professor of English, Indiana University, Bloomington, 1978-79; Poetry Critic, The Sunday Times, London, 1968-79. Publications: Ash Flowers, 1958; Fugitive Visions, 1962; The Death of Mayakovsky and Other Poems, 1968; Kaleidoscope: New and Selected Poems, 1973. Address: Flat 311, 4 Shakespeare Street, Nottingham NG1 4FG, England.

ANDREYEVA Victoria, b. 21 Jan 1942, Omsk, Russia. Writer; Editor. m. Arkady Rovner, 5 Aug 1969, 1 son. Education: MA Russian Philology 1965, Moscow University; Diploma of Literary Editor 1967, Moscow Polygraphic Institute; Completed course work for PhD in Comparative Literature 1981-83, New York University. Appointments: Editor, Gnosis Press 1978-. Publications: Son Tverdii, 1987; Dream of the Firmament, 1989; The Telephone Novel, 1992; P Ya Tschaadaeyen, co-collaborator, 1989; In a Small Circle of Poetry, 1978; Tolstoy and Fet: An Experiment of Life-Building, 1978; Kizeyersky & Tchaadaeyer, 1978; The Time of the Numbers, 1979; Khlopka, 1983; The Meeting of Bely & Blok in Solovyonian Ideas, 1991; The Third Literature, co-collaborator, 1990; Charchoune Whom I Know, 1982; 1000 Russian Verbs, dictionary, 1991; and others. Contributions to: Gnosis Anthology of Contemporary American and Russian Literature; Almanack, Appollo-77; Crossroads; Russian Literary Triquarterly; Spring; Echo; Man and Nature; This and That. Honours: Cummington Community of the Art, 1983; Community of International Writers of Mme Karolgy, Vance, France, 1984. Address: PO Box 42, Prince Street Station, New York, NY 10012, USA.

ANGEL Leonard Jay, b. 20 Sept 1945. Writer; Lecturer. m. Susan, 1 son, 1 daughter, 1 step-daughter. Education: BA Philosophy, McGill University, 1966; MA Philosophy 1968, MA Creative Writing & Theatre 1970, PhD Philosophy 1974, University of British Columbia. Appointments: Department of Creative Writing, University of British Columbia, 1981-82; Department of Creative Writing, University of Victoria, 1984-86. Publications: Antietam, 1975; Isadora and G B, 1976; The Unveiling, 1981; The Silence of the Mystic, 1983; Eleanor Marx, 1985; How to Build a Conscious Machine, 1989; Enlightenment East & West, 1994. Contributions to: Dialogue & Dialectic, Dialogue, 1991; Six of One, 1985. Honours: 1st Prize, Short Fiction, McGill Daily, 1963; 1st Prize (joint) Playhouse Theatre Award, 1971; Canada Council Artist B Grants, 1979, 1982; Nominee Jessie Award, Best New Play, 1982. Memberships: Playwrights Canada 1976-88; Chairman, BC Region, Guild of Canadian Playwrights 1978-79; Regional Representative 1980-81. Address: 865 Durward Avenue, Vancouver, BC, V5V 2Z1, Canada.

ANGELOU Maya, b. 1928, St Louis, MI, USA. University Professor; Writer; Black Activist; Singer. 1 s. Appointments include: Toured Europe and Africa; Night Club Singer & Performer, Genets The Blacks; Involved in Black Struggles in 1960s; Spent Several Years in Ghana, Editor, African Review; Reynolds Professor, Am Studies, Wake Forest University, North Carolina. Publications: 5 Volumns of Autobiography: I Know Why The Caged Bird Sings; Gather Together

In My Name; Singin' and Swingin'; Gettin' Merry Like Christmas; The Heart of a Woman; All Gods Children Need Traveling Shoes; Wouldnt Take Nothing for my Journey Now; Several Collections of Poetry inc. And Still I Rise; Just Give Me A Cool Drink of Water; Fore I Dine; Now Sheba Sings The Song; On The Pulse of Morning. Honour: Inaugural Poet, 1993. Address: 3240 Valley Road, Winston-Salem, NC 27106, USA.

ANGHELAKI-ROOKE Katerina, b. 22 Feb 1939, Athens, Greece. Poet; Translator. Education: Universities, Nice, Athens, Geneva, 1957-63. Appointments include: Freelance Translator, 1962-; Visiting Professor (Fulbright), Harvard, 1980; Visiting Fellow, Princeton University, 1987. Publications: Wolves and Clouds, 1963; Poems, 1963-69, 1971; The Body is the Victory and the Defeat of Dreams, 1975; The Scattered Papers of Penelope, 1977; The Triumph of Constant Loss, 1978; Counter Love, 1982; The Suitors, 1984; Beings and Things on Their Own, 1986; When the Body, 1988; Wind Epilogue, 1990; Empty Nature, 1993; Translations of Works by Shakespeare, Albee, Dylan Thomas, Beckett & Nikos Kazantzakis. Honours include: Greek National Poetry Prize, 1985. Address: Synesiou Kyrenes 4, 114 71 Athens, Greece.

ANGLUND Joan Walsh, b. 1926, United States of America. Children's Writer. Publications: A Friend is Someone Who Likes You, 1958; Look Out the Window, 1959; The Brave Cowboy, 1959; Love is a Special Way of Feeling, 1960; In a Pumpkin Shell: A Mother Goose ABC, 1960; Christmas Is a Time of Giving, 1961; Cowboy and His Friend, 1961; Nibble Nible Mousekin: A Tale of Hansel and Gretel, 1962; Cowboy's Secret Life, 1963; Spring is a New Beginning, 1963; Childhood Is a Time of Innocence, 1964; A Pocketful of Proverbs (verse), 1964; A Book of Good Tidings from the Bible, 1965' What Color is Love? 1966; A Year is Round, 1966; A Cup of Sun: A Book of Poems, 1967; A Is for Always: An ABC Book, 1968; Morning Is a Little Child (verse), 1969; A Slice of Snow: A Book of Poems, 1970; Do You Love Someone? 1971; The Cowboy's Christmas, 1972; A Child's Book of Old Nursery Rhymes, 1973; Goodbye, Yesterday: A Book of Poems, 1974; Storybook, 1978; Emily and Adam, 1979; Almost a Rainbow, 1980; A Gift of Love, 5 volumes, 1980; A Christmas Cookie Book, 1982; Rainbow Love, 1982; Christmas Candy Book, 1983; A Christmas Book, 1983; See the Year, 1984; Coloring Book, 1984; Memories of the Heart, 1984; Teddy Bear Tales, 1985; Baby Brother, 1985; All About Me! 1986; Christmas is Here! 1986; Tubtime for Thaddeus, 1986; A Mother Goose Book, 1991; A Child's Year, 1992; Love is a Baby, 1992; The Way of Love, 1992; Bedtime Book, 1993; The Friend We Have Not Met, 1993; Peace is a Circle of Love, 1993. Address: c/o Random House, 201 E 50th Street, New York, NY 10022, USA.

ANGREMY Jean-Pierre. See: REMY Pierre-Jean.

ANGUS Ian. See: MACKAY James Alexander.

ANGUS Tom. See: POWELL Geoffrey Stewart.

ANIEBO Ifeantichukwu Ndubuisi Chikezie, b. 1939, Nigeria. Novelist. Education: BA, CPhil, MA, University of California, Los Angeles. Appointments: Currently Senior Lecturer in English, University of Port Harcourt. Publications: The Anonymity of Sacrifice, 1974; Short stories: Of Wives, Talismans and the Dead, 1983; Uncollected short stories: The Jealous Goddess, 1963; My Mother, 1963; The Ring, 1964; The Pacemakers, 1965; Shadows, 1966; Mirage, 1966; The Outing, 1972; Happy Survival, Brother, 1977. Address: Department of English, University of Port Harcourt, PMB 5523, Port Harcourt, Rivers State, Nigeria.

ANMAR Frank. See: NOLAN William F(rancis).

ANOUILH Jean, b. 23 June 1910, Bordeaux. Dramatic Writer. m. Nicole Lançon, 1953, 1 son, 2 daughters. Publications: Plays Include: L'Ermine, 1934; Y'avait un prisonnier, 1935; Le Voyageur sans bagages, 1937; Le Bal des Voleurs, 1938; Lev Sauvage, 1938; Cavalcade d'Amour, 1941; Le Rendez-vous de Senlis, 1942; Leocadia, 1942; Eurydice, 1942; Humulus le Niuet, 1945; Oreste, 1945; Antigone, 1946; Jezebel, 1946; Romeo et Jeannette, 1946; L'Invitation au Chateau, 1948; Ardele ou la Marguerite, 1949; Le Repetition ou l'amour puni, 1950; Colombe, 1950; La Valse des toreadors, 1952; L'Alouette, 1953; Ornifle,1955; L'Hurluberlu, 1958; La Foire d'Empigne, 1960; Becket, 1961; Pauvre Bitos, 1963-64; Cher Antoine, 1969; Les Poissons Rouges, 1969; Ne Reveille Pas, Madame, 1970; Tu etais si gentil quand tu etais petit, 1974; Chers Zoiseaux, 1976; Vive Henri IV,

1977; La Culotte, 1978; Le Nombril, 1981; Films include: Monsieur Vincent; Pattes blanches; Caprice de Caroline. Address: c/o Les Editions de la Table Ronde, Rue Huyshans, 75007 Paris, France.

ANSCOMBE Isabelle Mary, b. 4 Oct 1954, Author; Journalist; SCriptwriter; Broadcaster. m. Howar Grey, 17 Dec 1981, 1 d. Education: MA, Newnham College, Cambridge. Publications: Not Another Punk Book, 1978; Arts & Crafts in Britain & America, 1978; Omega And After, 1981; A Womans Touch, 1860 to the Present Day, 1984; Arts & Crafts Style, 1991; Novel Entitled Angel Published under Married Name, Belle Grey, 1990. Contributionst to: Sunday Times; Independent; Daily Telegraph; Cosmopolitan. Memberships: Society of Authors; Romantic Novelists Association. Literary Agent: AM Heath Ltd. Address: c/o AM Heath, 79 St Martins Lane, London WC2N 4AA, England.

ANSELL Jonathan,See:WOLFF Tobias.

ANTHONY James R, b. 1922, United States of America. Professor of Music; Writer. Professor of Musicology, University of Arizona, Tucson, 1952-; Regional Associate of American Council of Learned Societies, 1956-60; Contributor, Grove's Dictionary of Music and Musicians, 1972-; Consultant, National Endowment for the Humanities, 1974-. Publications: French Baroque Music from Beaujoyeulx to Rameau, 1973, 1978; Cantatas, Book III, by Monteclair, 1978; De profundis, by Delalande, 1980; La Musique en France a l'Epoque Baroque, 1981; 40 articles in The New Grove; The New Grove French Baroque Masters, 1986. Address: School of Music, University of Arizona, Tucson, AZ 85721, USA.

ANTHONY Michael, b. 10 Feb 1932, Mayaro, Trinidad. Novelist. m. Yvette Francesca Anthony, 1958, 2 sons, 2 daughters. Education: Junior Technical College, San Fernando, Trinidad. Appointments: Journalist, Reuters News Agency, London, 1964-68; Researcher, National Cultural Council (now Ministry of Culture), Port-of-Spain, 1972-. Publications: The Games Were Coming, 1963; The Year in San Fernando, 1965; Green Days by the River, 1967; Streets of Conflict, 1976; All That Glitters, 1981; Bright Road to El Dorado, 1982; Short stories: Sandra Street and Other Stories, 1973; Cricket in the Road and Other Stories, 1973; Folk Tales and Fantasies, 1976; Various non-fictional works. Address: 99 Long Circular Road, St James, Port-of-Spain, Trinidad.

ANTHONY Piers, See: JACOB Anthony Dillingham.

ANTOINE Yves, b. 12 Dec 1941, Port-au-Prince, Haiti. Professor. 1 daughter. Education: MEd, University of Ottawa, 1972; LittD, University of Ottawa, 1988. Literary Appointments: B. Ped. University of Montréal, 1970. Publications: La Veillée, 1964; Témoin Oculaire, 1970; Au gré des heures, 1972; Les sabots de la nuit, 1974; Alliage, 1979; Libations pour le soleil, 1985; Sémiologie et personnage romanesque chez Jacques S Alexis, 1993; Des mots sans personne, in print. Contributions to: Une affligeante réalité, Le Droit, Ottawa, 1987; L'indélébile, Symbiosis, Ottawa, 1992. Honours: Guest, Harambee Foundation Society, 1988. Memberships: Union of Writers, Quebec; Ligue des Droits et Liberté; Association des auteurs de l'Outaouais québécois. Address: 200 boul Cité des Jeunes, app 403, Hull, Quebec J8Y 6M1, Canada.

ANTOLSKI Zdislaw Henryk, b. 16 Jan 1953, Skallomierz. Educator. Divorced. Education: Pegagogical College, Kielce, 1971-72; Graduate, Culture & Education, Pedagogical College, Kielce, 1976. Appointment: Editorial Assistant, Gossip, 1987-. Publications: Self-Lynch, 1978; Alone in the Crowd, 1980; To Bed I Disguise Myself as my Double, 1981; Joseph's Side, 1984. Contributions to: Poetry; New Books; Creation; New Word; Here and Now. Honours: Red Rose Award, 1982; Bursa's Award, 1986. Membership: Polish Writers' Association. Address: ul Walhelmq Piecka 3m 4, Kielce, 25-001, Poland.

ANTONOV Sergei Petrovich, b. 1915. Soviet Writer; Critic. Publications include: Novels and Stories: Lena, 1948; Rains, 1951; The Penkova Affair, 1956; Empty Journey, 1960; Alenka, 1960; Petrovich, 1964; Torn Rouble Note, 1966; Silver Wedding, 1972; The Three Warrior Knights, 1973; Criticism: Letters about the Short Story, 1964; First-Person Narrative, 1973; The Word, 1974; Vaska, 1987; Ravines, 1988. Honours: State Prize, 1951. Address: 125252 Moscow, Concord of Independent Stats, CIS, Novopeschanaja str N16, ap 72, Russia.

ANTROBUS John, b. 2 July 1933, Woolwich, London. Writer. m. Margaret McCormick, 1958 (divorced 1980), 2 sons, 1 daughter. Education: King Edward VII Nautical College; Royal Military Academy, Sandhurst, Camberley, Surrey. Appointments: Apprentice Deck Officer, Merchant Navy, 1950-52; Served in British Army, East Surrey Regiment, 1952-55; Supply Teacher and Waiter 1953-54; Freelance Writer 1955-. Publications: Plays include: The Bed-Sitting Room, with Spike Milligan (also co-director; produced London, 1963), Walton on Thames, Surrey, Hobbs, 1970, revised version as The Bed-Sitting Room 2 (also director, produced London, 1983), Crete and Sergeant Pepper, 1972, 1974; Captain Oates Left Sock, 1969, 1974; Jonah (also director, produced Cambridge, 1979); Hitler in Liverpool, One Orange for the Baby, Up in the Hide (produced London, 1980), London, Calder and New York; Riverrun Press, 1983; When Did You Last See Your Trousers? with Ray Galton, adaptation of a story by Galton and Alan Simpson (produced Mold, Clwyd, 1986), London 1987, Samuel French, 1988); Screenplays: Carry on Sergeant, with Norman Hudis, 1958; Idol on Parade, 1959; The Wrong Arm of the Law, with others, 1962; The Big Job, with Talbot Rothwell, 1965; The Bed-Sitting Room, with Charles Wood, 1969; Children's Books: The Boy with Illuminating Measles, 1978; Help I'm a Prisoner in a Toothpaste Factory, 1978; Ronnie and the Haunted Rolls Royce, 1982; Ronnie and the Great Knitted Robbery, 1982; Ronnie and the High Rise, 1992; Ronnie and the Flying Fitted Carpet, 1992; Writer for radio and television. Honours: George Devine Award, 1970; Writers Guild Award, 1971; Arts Council Bursary, 1973, 1976, 1980, 1982; Room at the Bottom 1 with Ray Galton, BANFF TV Festival Award, Best Comedy, 1987; Finalist, International Emmy Awards, 1987. Memberships: Writers Guild of Great Britain; Writers Guild of America, West Inc. Literary Agent: c/o Pat White, Rogers Coleridge and White, Address: 20 Powis Mews, London W11 1JN, England.

ANYIDOHO Kofi, b. 1947, Wheta, Ghana. Lecturer in English; Poet. Education: MA in Folklore, Indiana University, Bloomington; PhD in Comparative Literature, University of Texas at Austin. Appointment: Lecturer in English, University of Ghana. Publications: Elegy for the Revolution, 1978; A Harvest of our Dreams, 1984; Earthchild, 1984; Brain Surgery, 1984; Co-editor, Our Soul's Harvest, 1979; Interdisciplinary Dimensions of African Literature, 1985; The Fate of Vultures: New Poetry of Africa, 1989. Honours: Langston Hughes Award (Ghana); Fania Kruger Fellowship. Address: Department of English, University of Ghana, PO Box 25, Legon, Near Accra, Ghana.

APFEL Necia H, b. 31 July 1930, Mt Vernon, New York, USA. Science Writer. m. Donald A Apfel, 7 Sept 1952, dec, 1 son, 1 daughter. Education: BA magna cum laude, Tufts University, 1952; Radcliffe College Graduate School, 1952-53; Northwestern University Graduate School, 1962-69. Publications: Astronomy One (with J Allen Hynek), 1972; Architecture of the Universe (with J Allen Hynek), 1979; It's All Relative; Einstein's Theory of Relativity, 1981; The Moon and Its Exploration, 1982; Stars and Galaxies, 1982; Astronomy and Planetology, 1983; Soft-cover Edition, Astronomy Projects for Young Scientists, 1984; Calendars, 1985; It's All Elementary From Atoms to the Quantum World of Quarks, Leptons, and Gluons, 1985; Space Station, 1987; Space Law, 1988; Nebulae: The Birth and Death of Stars, 1988; Voyager to the Planets, 1991. Contributions to: Various articles to Odyssey magazine; Ask Ulysses, and I/O Port monthly columns. Honours: Phi Beta Kappa, 1952; Nebulae chosen as 1 of 100 Best Children's Books, 1988. Memberships: Society of Midland Authors; Society of Children's Book Writers; Astronomical Society of the Pacific; American Association for the Advancement of Science; Planetary Society. Address: 3461 University Avenue, Highland Park, IL 60035, USA.

APOSTOLOU John L, b. 4 Jan 1930, Brooklyn, New York, USA. Writer. Education: City College, New York, 1948-50; Columbia University, 1950-51; University of Southern California, BA, 1956. Publications: Murder in Japan, 1987; The Best Japanese Science Fiction Stories, 1989. Contributions to: Detective & Mystery Fiction, 1985; Twentieth Century Crime & Mystery Writers, 1991; Armchair Detective; Extrapolation. Address: 425 South Kenmore Avenue, 310 Los Angeles, CA 90020, USA.

APPELFELD Aharon, b. 1932, Czernowitz, Poland, Israeli Citizen. Novelist. Education: Hebrew University, Jerusalem. Appointments include: Lecturer, Be'er Shev'a University, 1984. Publications: In The Wilderness, 1965; Frost in the Land, 1965; At Ground Level, 1968; Five Stories, 1970; The Skin and the Gown, 1971; My Master the River, 1971; Like the Pupil of an Eye, 1972; Years and

Hours, 1975; Lika A Hundred Witnesses: A Selection, 1975; The Age of Wonders, 1978; Badenheim, 1939, 1980; Tzili, The Story of a Life, 1983; The Shirt and the Stripes, 1983; The Retreat, 1985; At One and the Same Time, 1985; To The Land of the Cattails, 1986; The Immortal Bartfuss, 1988; Tongues of Fite, 1988; For Every Sin, 1989; Katerina, 1992; The Rilway, 1991; Essays in First Person, 1979; Writing and the Holocaust, 1988. Honours include: H H Wingate Literary Award, 1989. Address: c/o Keter Publishing House, PO Box 7145, Jerusalem 91071, Israel.

APPIAH Anthony, b. 8 May 1954, London, England. Philosopher; Novelist; Professor. Education: BA, 1975, PhD, 1982, Clare College, Cambridge University. Publications: In My Fathers House, 1992; Necessary Questions, 1989; Avenging Angel, 1990; Nobody Likes Letita, 1994; For Truth in Semantics, Assertion and Conditionals. Contributions to: TLS; NY Times Book Review; WA Post; Book World; New Republic. Honours: Greene Cup, 1975; Annisfield Wolf Book Award, 1993; Herskovitz Book Award, 1993; James Russell Lowell Prize Finalist, 1993. Memberships: African Studies Association; Am Philosophical Association; MLA. Literary Agent: Brandt & Brandt, 1501 Broadway, New York, NY 10036, USA. Address: 1430 Massachusetts Avenue, 4th Floor, Cambridge, MA 02135, USA.

APPIAH Peggy, b. 1921. Children's Writer. Publications: Ananse the Spider, 1966; Tales of an Ashanti Father, 1967; The Pineapple Child and Other Tales from Ashanti, 1969; Children of Ananse, 1969; A Smell of Onions, 1971; Why Are There So Many Roads? 1972; Gift of the Mmoatia, 1973; Ring of Gold, 1976; A Dirge Too Soon, 1976; Why the Hyena Does Not Care for Fish and Other Tales, 1977; Young Readers Afua and The Mouse, Alena and the Python, Kofi and the Crow, The Twins, 1991; Poems of Three Generations, 1978. Literary Agent: David Higham Associates. Address: PO Box 829, Kumasi, Ashanti, Ghana.

APPLE Jacki, b. New York City, USA. Writer; Artist; Producer. Education: Syracuse University; Parsons School of Design. Appointment: Contributing Editor 1984-, Media Arts Editor, High Performance Magazine, 1993-. Publications: Trunk Pieces; Doing it Right in LA; The Mexican Tapes; Swan Lake; Voices in the Dark; The Culture of Disappearance; The Garden Planet Revisited; The Amazon, The Mekong, The Missouri & The Nile. Contributions to: High Performance; Artweek; LA Weekly; Media Arts; Visions; Public Art Review; The Drama Review. Honour: VESTA Award. Memberships: International Association of Art Critics; National Writers Union. Address: 3827 Mentone Avenue, Culver City, CA 90232, USA.

APPLEMAN Philip, b. 8 Feb 1926, Indiana, USA. Distinguished Professor Emeritus of English, Indiana University. m. Marjorie Haberkorn, 19 Aug 1950. Education: PhD, Northwestern University, 1955. Publications: The Silent Explosion, nonfiction, 1965; Kites on a Windy Day, poetry, 1967; Summer Love and Surf, poetry, 1968; In the Twelfth Year of the War, novel, 1970; Open Doorways, poetry, 1976; Shame the Devil, novel, 1981; Darwin's Ark, poetry, 1984; Darwin's Bestiary, poetry, 1986; Apes and Angles, novel, 1989; Let There Be Light, poetry, 1991; Edited: Victorian Studies, founding co-editor and first General Editor 1956-64; 1859: Entering an Age of Crisis, co-editor, 1959; Darwin, 1970, revised ed 1979; The Origin of Species, 1975; Malthus: An Essay on the Principle of Population, 1976. Address: PO Box 39, Sagaponack, NY 11962, USA.

APTHEKER Bettina Fay, b. 2 Sept 1944. Teacher; Writer. 1 son, 1 daughter. Education: BA, University of California, Berkeley, USA, 1967; MA, San Jose State University, 1976, PhD, University of California, Santa Cruz, 1983. Publications: Tapestries of Life: Women's Work, Women's Consciousness and the Meaning of Daily Experience, 1989; Woman's Legacy: Essays on Race, Sex and Class in American History, 1982; The Morning Breaks: The Trial of Angela Davis, 1976; Academic Rebellion in the US: A Marxist Appraisal; With Angela Y Davis: If They Come in the Morning: Voices of Resistance, 1971. Contributor to: Imagining Our Lives: The Novelist as Historian, Woman of Power, Vol 16, 1990; How to Do Meaningful Work in Women's Studies in Women's Studies: An Interdisciplinary Journal 17: 1-2, 1989. Address: Women's Studies, Kresge College, Universityof California, Santa Cruz, CA 95064, USA.

ARCHER Fred, b. 1915. Publications: The Distant Scene, 1967; Under the Parish Lantern, 1969; Hawthorn Hedge Country, 1970; The Secrets of Bredon Hill, 1971; A Lad of Evesham Vale, 1972; Muddy Boots and Sunday Suits, 1973; Golden Sheaves and Black Horses,

1974; The Countryman Cottage Life Book, 1974; When Village Bells were Silent, 1975; Poachers Pie, 1976; By Hook and By Crook, 1978; When Adam was a Boy, 1979; A Hill Called Bredon, 1983; Fred Archer Farmer's Son, 1984; The Village Doctor, 1986; Evesham to Bredon in Old Photographs, 1988; The Village of my Childhood, 1989; Country Sayings, 1990. Address: 54 Stanchester Way, Curry Rivel, Langport, Somerset TA10 0PU, Gloucestershire, England.

ARCHER Jeffrey Howard, b. 15 Apr 1940, Mark, Somerset, England. Author; Politician. m. Mary Weeden, 2 s. Education: Brasenose College, Oxford. Publications: Plays inc. Beyond Reasonable Doubt, 1987; Exclusive, 1990; Not a Penny More, Not a Penny Less, 1975; What Shall We Tell the President?, 1977; Kane & Abel, 1979; A Quiver Full of Arrows, 1980; A Matter of Honour, 1986; The Prodigal Daughter, 1982; First Among Equals, 1984; A Twist in the Tale, 1988; As The Crow Flies, 1991; Honour Among Thieves, 1993; Twelve Red Herrings, 1994; The First Miracle. Contributions to: Numerous Journals & Magazines. Honours: Queen's Birthday Honours, 1992; Lord Archer of Weston Super Mare. Address: Alembic House, 93 Albert Embankment, London SE1 7TY, England.

ARCHIBALD Rupert Douglas, b. 1919, Trinidad and Tobago. Author; Playwright. Appointments: Editor, Progress Magazine, 1952; Member, Editorial Board, Clarion Newspaper, 1954-56. Publications: Junction Village, 1954; Anne Marie, 1958; The Bamboo Clump, 1962; The Rose Slip, 1962; Old Maid's Tale, 1965; Island Tide, 1972; Defeat with Honour, 1973; Isidore and the Turtle (novel), 1973. Address: 7 Stephens Road, Maraval, Trinidad and Tobago, West Indies.

ARDAI Charles, b. 25 Oct 1969, New York City, USA. Author; Editor. Education: BA, English, summa cum laude, Columbia University, 1991. Appointments: Contributing Editor, Computer Entertainment and K-Power, 1985; Editor, Davis Publications, 1990-91. Publications include: Great Tales of Madness & The Macabre, 1990; Kingpins, 1992; Futurecrime, 1992. Contributions to: Alfred Hitchcock's Mystery Magazine; Ellery Queen's Mystery Magazine; Twilight Zone; The Year's Best Horror Stories; Computer Gaming World; and others. Honour: Pearlman Prize for Fiction, Columbia University, 1991. Membership: Active Member, Mystery Writers of America. Address: 350 East 52 Street, New York, NY 10022, USA.

ARDEN John, b. 26 Oct 1930, Playwright. m. Margaratta Ruth D'Arcy, 4 s, 1 dec. Education: Kings College, Cambridge; Edinburgh College of Art. Publications include: Plays Produced, All Fall Down, 1955; The Waters of Babylon, 1957; Live Like Pigs, 1958; Serjeant Musgraves' Dance, 1959; Soldier, Soldier, 1960; The Workhouse Donkey, 1963; Ironhand, 1963; Left Handed Liberty, 1965; The Bagman, 1970; To Put It Frankly, 1979; Garland for a Hoar Head, 1982; The Old Man Sleeps Alone, 1982; The Happy Haven, 1986; The Royal Pardon, 1966; The Hero Rises Up, 1968; Island of the Mighty, 1972; The Non Stop Connolly Cycle, 1975; The Little Gray Home in the West, 1978; Whose is the Kingdom, 1988; Essays, To Present the Pretence, 1977; Novel, Silence Among the Weapons, 1982; Awkward Corners, 1988; Books of Bale, 1988; Cogs Tyrannic, 1991. Address: c/o Casarotto Ramsay Ltd, National House, 60-66 Wardour Str, London W1V 3Hp, England.

ARDEN William. See: **LYNDS Dennis.**

ARDIES Tom, b. 1931, United States of America. Author. Appointments: Reporter, Columnist, Editorial Writer, Vancouver Sun, 1950-64; Telegraph Editor, Honolulu Star Bulletin, 1964-65; Special Assistant to Government of Guam, 1965-67. Publications: Their Man in the White House, 1971; This Suitcase is Going to Explode, 1972; Pandemic, 1973; Kosygi is Coming, 1974 (in United Kingdom paperback as Russian Roulette, 1975); In a Lady's Service, 1976; Palm Springs, 1978.

ARDLEY Neil Richard, b. 26 May 1937, Wellington, Surrey. Writer. m. Bridget Mary Gantley, 3 Sept 1960, Mamhull, Dorset, 1 daughter. Education: BSc Bristol University, 1959. Publications include: How Birds Behave, 1971; Atoms and Energy, 1975; Birds of Towns, 1975; Birds of the Country, 1975; Birds of Coasts, Lakes and Rivers, 1976; Birdwatching, 1978; Man and Space, 1978; Birds, 1978; Birds of Britain and Europe, 1978; Birds and Birdwatching, 1980; 1001 Questions and Answers (with Bridget Ardley), 1981; The World of Tomorrow Series, 1981-82; Transport on Earth, 1981; Out Into Space, 1981; Tomorrow's Home, 1981; School, Work and Play, 1981; Our Future Needs, 1982; Health and Medicine, 1982; Future War and

Weapons, 1982; Fact or Fantasy? 1982; Computers, 1983; Action Science Series, 1983-84; Working with Water, 1983; Using the Computer, 1983; Hot and Cold, 1983; Sun and Light, 1983; Making Measurements, 1983; Exploring Magnetism, 1983; Making Things Move, 1984; Discovering Electricity, 1984; Air and Flight, 1984; Sound and Music, 1984; Simple Chemistry, 1984; Force and Strength, 1984; My Favourite Science Encyclopedia, 1984; Just Look At...Flight, 1984; Sinclair ZX Spectrum User Guide, 1984; Just Look At...The Universe, 1985; The Science of Energy, 1985; Music-An Illustrated Encyclopedia, 1986; My Own Science Encyclopedia, 1987; The Universe - Exploring the Universe, 1987; The Inner Planets; The Outer Planets; The Way Things Work, 1988; The World of the Atom, 1989; Music (Eyewitness Guide), 1989; India, 1989; Greece, 1989; Twentieth Century Science, 1989; The Giant Book of the Human Body, 1989; How We Build Bridges; Dams Oil Rigs, 1989; Language and Communications, 1989; Sound Waves to Music, 1990; Wings and Things, 1990; Snap Happy, 1990; Tune In, 1991; Bits and Chips, 1991; How It Works, 1991; The Way It Works, Light, 1991; The Way It Works, Electricity, 1991; A Series of 15 Science Books, 1991-92; 101 Great Science Experiments, 1993; Dictionary of Science, 1994. Contributions to: Caxton Yearbook: Macmillan Children's Encyclopedia; Collins Music Dictionary; Joy of Knowledge, Children's Illustrated Encyclopedia. Honours: Fellow, Royal Society of Arts, 1982; Science Book Prize (under 16), 1989, shared with David Macauley for The Way Things Work; Times Educational Supplement Senior Information Book Award, 1989 for The Way Things Work with David Macauley. Address: Lathkill House, Youlgrave, Derbyshire DE45 1WL, England.

ARDMORE Jane Kesner, b. 12 Sept 1915, Chicago, Illinois, USA. Author; Journalist. m. Albert Ardmore, 10 Nov 1951, 1 daughter. Education: PhB, University of Chicago. Publications: Novels: Women Inc, 1946; Julie, 1952; To Love Is To Listen, 1967; Biographies: Take My Life, Eddie Cantor, 1957; The Self Enchanted, Mae Murray, 1959; The Dress Doctor, Edith Head, 1959; Portrait of Joan, Joan Crawford, 1962. Contributions to: Good Housekeeping; McCall's; Family Circle, Redbook, Woman, UK; Woman's World, UK; Woman's Own, UK. Honours: Fiction prize, Indiana Writers Conference, 1942; Fiction Award, California Press Women, 1967; Headliner Award, Women in Communications, 1968. Membership: Hollywood Women's Press Club. Literary Agent: McIntosh & Otis, New York; Heath & Company, London, UK. Address: 10469 Dunleer Drive, Los Angeles, CA 90064, USA.

ARGUETA Manilo, b. 24 Nov 1935, San Miguel, El Salvador. Poet; Novelist. Education: Universidad Nacional, San Salvador. Publictions: Fiction, El Valle des Hamacas, 1970; Caperucita en la Zona Rosa, 1977; One Day of Life, 1980, 1983; Cuzcatalan, Where the Southern Sea Beats, 1987; Verse, Poemas, 1967; En el Costado de la Luz, 1979; El Salvador, 1990; Editor, Poesia de El Salvador, 1983. Honours include: University of Central America Prize, 1980. Address: c/o Chatto and Windus, 20 Vauxhall Bridge Road, London SW1N 2SA, England.

ARIDJIS Homero, b. 6 Apr 1940, Mexico. Poet; Novelist. m. Betty Ferber, 1965, 2 d. Education: Autonomous University of Mexico, 1961. Appointments include: Director, Festival Internacional de Poesia, 1981-87. Publictions: Verse: Los Ojos Desdoblados, 1960; Antes del Reino, 1963; La Dificil Ceremonia, 1963; Quemar Las Naves, 1975; Antologa, 1976; Vivir Para Ver, 1977; Construir la Muerte, 1982; Republicia de Poetas, 1985; Obra Poetica, 1960-86, 1987; Imagenes Para el Fin del Milenio, 1990; Fiction: Mirandola Dormir, 1964; Persefone, 1967-86; El Encantador Solitario, 1972; Playa Nudista; El Ultimo Adan, 1982; Memorias del Nuevo Mundo, 1988. Honours include: Novela Novedades Prize, 1988. Address: Sirra Jiutepec 1558, Lomas Barrilaco, Mexico City 11010, Mexico.

ARKOW Philip S, b. 30 Apr 1947, Philadelphia, USA. Education & Publicity Director. m. Melody Meyer, 18 Sept 1982, 1 daughter. Education: BA, University of Pennsylvania, USA, 1969. Publications: The Loving Bond; Pet Therapy; The Luckiest Pets in the World Calendar. Contributions to: Too Numerous. Memberships: Society for the Preservation & Enhancement of the Recognition of Millard Fillmore; Delta Society; American Veterinary Medical Association; Animal Welfare Committee; National Animal Control Association; American Humane Association. Address: PO Box 187, Colorado Springs, CO 80901, USA.

ARLEN Leslie. See: **NICOLE Christopher Robin**.

ARLEN Michael John, b. 9 Dec 1930, London, England. Author. m. Alice Albright, 1972, 4 daughters. Education: BA, Harvard University, USA, 1952. Publications: Exiles, 1970; Passage to Ararat, 1974; Living-Room War, 1969; Thirty Seconds, 1980; The Camera Age, 1982; An American Verdict, 1972; The View from Highway One, 1975; Say Goodbye to Sam, 1984. Contributions to: New Yorker, 1957-. Honours: National Book Award, 1975; Le Prix Bremond, 1976; DLitt, 1984. Memberships: Authors Guild; PEN; Century Association. Literary Agent: Candida Donadio & Associates. Address: 1120 Fifth Avenue, New York, NY 10128, USA.

ARMAH Ayi Kwei, b. 1938, Takoradi, Ghana. Novelist. Education: AB in Social Studies, Harvard University, Massachusetts; Columbia University, New York. Appointments: Scriptwriter for Ghana Television; Teacher at Teacher's College, Dar-es-Salaam, and Universities of Massachusetts, Amherst, Lesotho, and Wisconsin, Madison. Publications: The Beautiful Ones Are Not Yet Born, 1968; Fragments, 1970; Why Are We So Blest?, 1972; Two Thousand Seasons, 1973; The Heales, 1978; Uncollected short stories: A Short Story, 1965; Yaw Manu's Charm, 1968; The Offal Kind, 1969; Doctor Kamikaze, 1989. Address: c/o Heinemann Educational, Ighorado Road, Jericho PMB 5205, Ibadan, Oyo State, Nigeria.

ARMES Roy, b. 1937. Author. Appointments: Reader in Film, Middlesex Polytechnic; Film Critic of London Magazine. Publications: French Cinema since 146 (2 vols), 1966, 1970; The Cinema of Alain Resnais, 1968; French Film, 1970; Patterns of Realism, 1972; Film and Reality, 1974; The Ambiguous Image, 1975; A Critical History of British Cinema, 1978; The Films of Alain Robbe-Grillet, 1981; French Cinema, 1985; Patterns of Realism, 1985. Address: 19 New End, Hampstead, London NW3, England.

ARMITAGE Gary. See: **EDRIC Robert**.

ARMITAGE Ronda (Jacqueline), b. 1943, New Zealand. Children's Writer. Appointments: Infant Teacher, Duvauchelles, 1964-66, Auckland 1968-69; Supply Teacher, London, 1966; Adviser on Children's Books, Dorothy Butler Limited, Booksellers, Auckland, 1970-71; Assistant Librarian, Lewes Priory Comprehensive School, Sussex, 1976-77; Supply Teacher, East Sussex County Council, 1978-81; Family Counsellor - Hastings, 1985-. Publications: The Lighthouse Keeper's Lunch, 1977; The Trouble with Mr Harris, 1978; Don't Forget Matilda, 1979; The Bossing of Josie, 1980, as The Birthday Spell, 1981; Ice Creamss for Rosie, 1981; One Moonlight Night, 1983; Grandma Goes Shopping, 1985; The Lighthouse Keepers Catastrophe, 1986; The Lighthouse Keepers Rescue, 1989; When Dad Did the Washing, 1990; Watch the Baby, 1991; A Quarrel of Koalas, 1992; Looking After Chocolates, 1992. Address: Old Tiles Cottage, Church Lane, Hellingly, East Sussex BN27 4HA, England.

ARMOUR Peter James, b. 19 Nov 1940, Fleetwood, Lancashire, England. University Professor. Education: PhL, English College & Gregorian University, Rome, Italy, 1961; BA (Hons), University of Manchester, 1966; PhD, Leicester, 1980. Publications: The Door of Purgatory, 1983; Dante's Griffin and the History of the World, 1989; Chapters in: G Aquilecchia et al, Collected Essays, K Speight, 1971; D Nolan, Dante Commentaries, 1977 and Dante Soundings, 1981; RA Cardwell & J Hamilton, Virgil in a Cultural Tradition, 1986; G Barblan, Dante e la Bibbia, 1988; T O'Neill, The Shared Horizon, 1990; J R Dashwood & J E Everson, Writers and Performers in Italian Drama, 1991; J C Bames & J Petrie, Word and Drama in Dante, 1993. Contributions to: The Year's Work in Modern Language Studies; Italian Studies, volumes 34 and 38; Lectura Dantis; Dertsches Dante-Jahrbuch, vol 67; Reviews in Italian Studies; Modern Language Review; Medium Aevum; Filologia e Critica; Translations in Journal of Garden History, volumes 1, 3 and 5; The Genius of Venice. Memberships: Societa Dantesca Italiana; Dante Society of America; Society for Italian Studies; Modern Humanities Research Association; London Medieval Society; Middlesex County Cricket Club. Address: Department of Italian, Royal Holloway, University of London, Egham Hill, Egham, Surrey TW20 0EX, England.

ARMSTRONG Alice Catt, b. Fort Scott, Kansas, USA. Author; Editor; Publisher, 1 son. Education: LittD, St Andrews University, England, 1969; St Pauls College & Seminary, Italy, 1970. Publications: 17 books including: California Biographical & Historical Series, 1950-; Dining & Lodging on the North American Continent, 1958; And They Called It Society, 1961-62; Editor, special issue, 200th Anniversary of California, 1968; Also radio skits, travel guides, children's stories including Princess McGuffy & the Little Rebel. Honours: Numerous Honours & Awards including: National Travel Guide Award, National Writers Club, 1958; Dame Grand Cross, Order of St Jaurent; Outstanding Citizen. Memberships include: National Society of Magna Charta Dames; Los Angeles World Affairs Council; National Writers Club; Historical Los Angeles Association; Art Patrons Association of America. Address: Cordell Views 1331, Cordell Place, Los Angeles, California 90069, USA.

ARMSTRONG John Alexander, b. 4 May 1922, Saint Augustine, Florida, USA. Professor Emeritus of Political Science; Author; Consultant. m. Annette Taylor, 14 June 1952, 3 daughters. Education: PhB 1948, MA 1949, University of Chicago; Frankfurt University, West Germany 1949-50 (no degree); PhD, Public Law and Government 1953, Certificate of Russian Institute 1954, Columbia University, New York, USA. Appointments: Research Analyst, War Documentation Project, Alexandria, Virginia, USA, 1951, 1953-54; Assistant Professor, University of Denver, Colorado, 1952; Visiting Assistant Professor, Russian Institute, Columbia University, 1957; Assistant Professor to Philippe de Commynes Professor of Political Science (presently Emeritus), University of Wisconsin, Madison, 1954-86. Publications include: Ukrainian Nationalism, 1955, 1963, 1990; Nations Before Nationalism, 1982; The European Administrative Elite, 1973; Ideology, Politics and Government in the Soviet Union, 1962, 1967, 1974, 1978; The Politics of Totalitarianism, 1961; The Soviet Bureaucratic Elite, 1959; Soviet Partisans in World War II (ed), 1964. Address: 40 Water Street, Saint Augustine, FL 32084, USA.

ARMSTRONG Karen Andersen, b. 14 Nov 1944, Stourbridge, Worcs, England. Writer; Broadcaster. Publications: Through the Narrow Gate, 1981; The Gospel According to Woman, 1986; Holy War: The Crusades and Their Impact on Today's World, 1988; Muhammad: A Western Attempt to Understand Islam, 1991; A History of God, 1993; The First Christian: St Paul's Impact on Christianity, 1984. Contributions to: The Sunday Times; The Daily Telegraph; New Statesman; The Observer. Literary Agent: Felicity Bryan. Address: 2A North Parade, Banbury Road, Oxford, OX2 6PE, England.

ARMSTRONG Patrick Hamilton, b. 10 Oct 1941, Leeds, Yorkshire, England. University Lecturer. m. Moyra E J Irvine, 8 Aug 1964, 2 s. Education: BSc, 1963, Dip Ed, 1964, MA, 1966, University of Durham; PhD, 1970. Publications include: Discovering Ecology, 1973; Discovering Geology, 1974; The Changing Landscape, 1975; A Series of Children's Book for Ladybird Books, 1976-79; Ecology, 1977; Reading & Interpretation of Australian & NZ Maps, 1981; Living in the Environment, 1982; The Earth: Home of Humanity, 1984; Charles Darwin in Western Australia, 1985; A Sketch Map Geography of Australia, 1988; A Sketch Map Physical Geography for Austrlia, 1989; Darwin's Desolate Islands, 1992. Contributions to: New Scientist; Geographical Magazine; East Anglian Magazine; Geography; Cambridgeshire Life; Eastern Daily Press; Work & Travel Abroad; West Australian Newspaper; Weekly Telegraph. Address: Dept of Geography, University of Western Australia, Nedlands, WA 6009, Australia.

ARNOLD Arnold, b. 6 Feb 1928, Germany. m. (1) Eve Arnold, 1942, (2) Alison Pilpel, 1982. Education: St Martins Sch of Art, London, 1937-38; Pratt Institute, NY, 1938-39; NY University, Columbia University, 1939-42. Appointments: Graphic Toy & Industrial Designer, 1946; Director, Workshop School, NY, 1949-52; President, Arnold Arnold Design Inc, 1960-66; President, Manuscript Press Inc, 1963-66; Designer of Childrens Play, Learning Materials & Programs; Consultant Editor, Rutledge Books, NY, 1962-65; Cyberneticist, Writer, Consultant, Systems Analysis & Operational Research, London, 1980-. Publications include: How To Play with Your Child; Your Child's Play; Your Child & You; The World Book of Children's Games; the World Book of Arts & Crafts for Children; The Corrupted Sciences; The I Ching and The Theory of Everything. Contributions to: Several Journals & Newspapers & Reviews. Honour: Fellow, Boston University; Leverhulme Fellow. Address: c/o Andrew Mann Limited, 1 Old Compton Str, London W1V 5PH, England.

ARNOLD Emily. See: **MCCULLY Emily Arnold.**

ARNOLD Heinz Ludwig, b. 29 Mar 1940, Essen, Ruhr, Germany. Writer; Critic; Editor. Education: University of Goettingen. Appointments: Editor, Text & Kritik, 1963; Kritisches Lexikon zur Deutschsprachigen Gegenwartsliteratur, 1978; Kritisches Lexikon zur Fremdespachigan Gegenwartslieteatur, 1983. Publications include:

Brauchen wir noch die Literatur? 1972; Gespraeche mit Schriftstellern, 1975; Gespraech mit F Durrenmatt, 1976; Handbuch der Deutscheaen Arbeiterliteratur, 1977; Als Schriftsteller leben, 1979; Vom Verlust der Scham und Dem Allmaehlichen Verschwinden der Demokratie, 1988; Krieger Waldgaenger, 1990; Querfahrt mit Durrenmatt, 1990; Die Drei Sprunge der Westdeutschen Gegenwartsliteratur, 1993. Contributions to: Die Zeit; Deutsches Allgemeines Sonntagblatt; Various Radio Stations. Memberships: Association of German Writers; PEN; OH Tulip Order. Address: Tuckermannweg 10, 37085 Goettingen, Germany.

ARNOLD Margot. See: **COOK Petronelle Marguerite Mary.**

ARONSON Theo, b. 13 Nov 1930, South Africa. Writer. Education: BA, University of Cape Town, 1950. Publications: The Golden Bees, 1965; Royal Vendetta, 1967; The Coburgs of Belgium, 1968; The Fall of the Third Napoleon, 1970; The Kaisers, 1971; Queen Victoria and the Bonapartes, 1972; Grandmama of Europe, 1973; A Family of Kings, 1975; Victoria and Disraeli, 1977; Kings Over the Water, 1979; Princess Alice, 1981; Royal Family, 1983; Crowns in Conflict, 1986; The King in Love, 1988; Napoleon and Josephine, 1990; Heart of a Queen, 1991; The Royal Family at War, 1993; Prince Eddy, 1994. Contributions to: Various Journals and Magazines. Literary Agent: Andrew Lownie. Address: North Knoll Cottage, 15 Bridge Str, Frome, Somerset, BA11 1BB, England.

ARRABAL Fernando, b. 11 Aug 1932, Melilla, Africa. Writer; Poet. m. Luce Moreau, 1 Feb 1958, 2 children. Publications include: Novels, Baal Babylone, 1959; The Burial of Sardine, 1952; Fêtes et Rites de la Confusion, 1965; La Torre Herida por el Rayo, 1983; Poetry, Pierre de La Folie, 1963; 100 Sonnets, 1966; Un Nuage, 1966; L'Odeur de sainteté, 1975; Les Eveques se noient, 1969; Rêves d'insectes, 1987; Lanzarote, 1988; Le Voyage est le feu, 1985; Sur Les cimes, 1986; Péchés maudits, 1987; La Nature est le Maître, 1976; Anges et taupes, 1979; Cinco Sonetos, 1980; Poèmes, 1982; Numerous Others; Numerous Plays including, The Architect and the Emperor of Assyria; And They Put Handcuffs on the Flowers; Garden of delights; The Automobile Graveyard; Essays, The Panic; The New York of Arrabal; Letter to General Franco; Fischer, 1973; Director, Films; Viva la Muerte; J'irai Comme un Cheval fou; L'Arbre de Guernica; Odyssey of the Pacific; Le Cimètiere Des Voitures; Adieu Babylone!. Honours: Grand Prix du Théâtre, 1967; Grand Prix Humour Noir, 1968; Premio Nadal (novel) 1983; Prix Du Théâtre (Académie Française), 1993; Prix International W.Nabokov (Novel), 1994; Premio Espas De Ensayo, 1994. Memberships: Panique Movement with Topor & Jodorowsky; Political Prisoner, Spain, 1967. Address: 22 Rue Jouffroy d'Abbans, Paris 75017, France.

ARREOLA Juan Jose, b. 12 Sept 1918, Ciudad Guzman, Jalisco, Mexico. Novelist. Education: Paris, 1945. Appointments include: Founding Member, Actor, Poesia en Voz Alta Group. Publications include: Gunther Stapenhorst: Vinetas de Isidoro Ocampo, 1946; Varia Invencion, 1949, 1971; Cinco Cuentes, 1951; Confabulario and Other Inventions, 1952-64; Besitario, 1958; Punta de Plata, 1958; Le Feria, 1963; Cuentos, 1969; Antologia de Juan Jose Arreola, 1969; Palindroma, 1971; Mi Confabulario, 1979; Confabulario Personal, 1980; Imagen Obra Escogida, 1984; Estas Paginas Mias, 1985. Address: Editorial Joaquin Mortiz, Avenue Insurgentes Sur 1162-3, Col del Valle, 03100 Mexico City, Mexico.

ARTHUR Elizabeth Ann, b. 15 Nov 1953, New York, USA. m. Steven Bauer, 19 June 1982. Education: BA, English, University of Victoria, 1978; Diploma, Education, 1979. Appointments: Visiting Instructor, Creative Writing, University of Cincinnati, 1983-84; Assistant Professor, English, Miami University, 1984-85; Assistant Professor, English, IUPUI, Indianapolis, 1985-. Publications: Island Sojourn, 1980; Beyond the Mountain, 1983; Bad Guys, 1986; Binding Spell, 1988; Looking for the Klondike Stone, 1993. Contributor to: New York Times; Outside; Backpacker; Ski-XC; Shenandoah. Honours: William Sloane Fellowship, Bread Loaf Writers' Conference, 1980; Writing Fellowship, Ossabaw Island Project, 1981; Grant in Aid, Vermont Council on the Arts, 1982; Fellowship in Prose, 1988; Fellowship from the National Endowment for the Arts, 1989. Membership: Poets & Writers. Literary Agent: Jean Naggar. Address: Bath, Indiana 47010, USA.

ASCH Frank, b. 6 Aug 1946, Somerville, New Jersey, USA. Education: BA, Cooper Union. Publications: George's Store, Linda, 1969; Elvira Everything, 1970; The Blue Balloon, Yellow Yellow, Rebecka, 1971; I Met a Penguin, 1972; In the Eye of the Teddy, 1973; Gia and the $100 Worth of Bubblegum, 1974; Good Lemonade, 1975;

The Inside Kid, Monkey Face, 1977; Macgoose's Grocery, Moon Bear, Turtle Tale, City Sandwich, 1978; Country Pie, Little Devil's ABC, Popcorn, Sand Cake, Little Devil's One Two Three, Running with Rachel, 1979; The Last Puppy, Starbaby, 1980; Just Like Daddy, Goodnight Horsey, 1981; Happy Birthday Moon, Milk and Cookies, Bread and Honey, 1982; Mooncake, 1983; Moongame, Pearl's Promise, Skyfire, 1984; Baby in the Box, 1990; Journey to Terezor, 1991; Here Comes the Cat, 1991; Little Fish, Big Fish, 1992; Short Train, Long Train, 1992; Dear Brother, 1992; The Flower Faerie, 1993; Moonbear's Books, 1993; Moonbear's Canoe, 1993; Moonbear's Friend, 1993; The Earth & I, 1994. Address: c/o McGraw-Hill Incorporated, 1221 Avenue of the Americas, New York, NY 10020, USA.

ASCHER Sheila (Ascher/Straus), b. New York, USA. Writer. Education: MA, Slavic Literature and Languages, Columbia University. Publications: Letter to an Unknown Woman, 1979; The Menaced Assassin, 1982, revised 1989; Red Moon/Red Lake, 1988; The Other Planet, 1988; Long fictions in anthologies: Pushcart Prize III; Likely Stories; Chelsea: A 25 Year Retrospective; Top Top Stories; Exile: The Fifteen Years. Contributions to: Chicago Review; Paris Review; Epoch; Top Stories; Chelsea; Exile; Calyx; Zone; Central Park; Confrontation; New American Writing; Asylum Annual. Honours: Panache Experimental Fiction Prize, 1973; Pushcart Prize, 1979; CAPS Fellowship, NY State, 1983. Address: Ascher/Straus, PO Box 176, Rockaway Park, NY 11694, USA.

ASH John, b. 29 June 1948, England. Appointments: Primary School Teacher, 1970-71; Research Assistant, 1971-75. Publications: Verse: Casino, 1978; The Bed and Other Poems, 1981; The Goodbyes, 1982; The Branching Stairs, 1984. Address: c/o Carcanet Press Ltd, 208 Corn Exchange Buildings, Manchester M4 3BQ, England.

ASHANTI Baron James, b. 5 Sept 1950, New York, USA. Freelance Writer. m. Brenda Cummings, 11 Sept 1979, 1 son, 1 daughter. Literary Appointments: Literary editor, Impressions Magazine, 1972-75; City editor, Liberation News Service, 1974-79; Contributing editor, The Paper, 1978; Literary editor, New Heat Magazine, 1980-82. Publications: Nova, 1990, nominated for Pulitzer Prize in Poetry; The Candy Marine, novel; The Journeyman, novel. Contributions to: Liberation News Service; Pan African Journal; Presance Africaine; Essence Magazine; Greenfield Review; Maintrend; Race Today; Nethula II & III; Hoodoo VII; Blacks on Paper, III & IV. Honours: Killen Prize, poetry, St Peters College, New York, 1982; PEN Fellowships, 1985, 1987. Memberships: Griots Society; Society of African Poets; Harlem Writers Guild; New Renaissance Writers Guild; John Oliver Killens Writers Workshop, Calabash Poets Workshop. Literary Agent: Mari Brown Associates, New York. Address: 4343 North 9th Street, Philadelphia, Pennsylvania 19140, USA.

ASHBY Nora. See: **AFRICANO Lillian.**

ASHDOWN Dulcie Margaret, b. 24 Feb 1946, London, England. Writer; Editor. Education: BA, Bristol University, 1967. Publications: Christmas Past, 1976; Ladies in Waiting, 1976; Princess of Wales, 1976; Royal Children, 1980; Royal Weddings, 1981; Victoria and the Coburgs, 1981; 4 Other books. Contributions to; Majesty; Heritage; Writers' Monthly; The Lady. Address: c/o National Westminster Bank, 1302 High Road, Whetstone, London N20, England.

ASHE Geoffrey Thomas, b. 29 Mar 1923, London, England. Writer; Lecturer. m. Dorothy Irene Train, 3 May 1946 (dec), 4 sons, 1 daughter. (2) Maxine Lefever, 8 Dec 1992. Education: BA, University of British Columbia, Canada, 1943; BA, Trinity College, Cambridge University, England, 1948. Appointments include: Associate Editor, Arthurian Encyclopaedia, 1986. Publications include: King Arthur's Avalon, 1957; From Caesar to Arthur, 1960; Land to the West, 1962; The Land & The Book, 1965; Gandhi, 1968; The Quest for Arthur's Britain, 1968; Camelot & The Vision of Albion, 1971; The Art of Writing Made Simple, 1972; The Finger & The Moon, 1973; The Ancient Wisdom, 1977; Miracles, 1978; Guidebook to Arthurian Britain, 1980; Kings & Queens of Early Britain, 1982; Avalonian Quest, 1982; The Discovery of King Arthur, 1985; Landscape of King Arthur, 1987; Mythology of the British Isles, 1990; King Arthur: The Dream of a Golden Age, 1990; Dawn Behind the Dawn, 1992; Atlantis, 1992. Contributions to: Associate Editor, The Arthurian Encyclopedia, 1986; Numerous magazines & journals. Honours: Fellow, Royal Society of Literature, 1963. Memberships: Medieval Academy of America;

Secretary, Camelot Research Committee. Address: Chalice Orchard, Well House Lane, Glastonbury, Somerset BA6 8BJ, England.

ASHLEY Bernard, b. 2 Apr 1935, London, England. Teacher. Education: Teachers Certificate; Advanced Diploma, Cambridge Institute of Education. Publications include: The Trouble with Donovan Croft, 1974; Terry on the Fence, 1975; All My Men, 1977; A Kind of Wild Justice, 1978; Break in the Sun, 1980; Dodgem, 1982; High Pavement Blues, 1983; Janey, 1985; Running Scared, 1986; Bad Blood, 1988; The Country Boy, 1989; The Secret of Theodore Brown, 1989; Seeing off Uncle Jack, 1992; Cleversticks, 1993; Three Seven Eleven, 1993, 94. Contributions to: Books for Your Children; Junior Education; Books for Keeps; Times Educational Supplement. Honours: The Other Award, 1976; Runner Up Carnegie Medal, 1979, 86; Royal TV Society Best Childrens Entertainment Programme, 1991. Memberships: Writers Guild. Address: 128 Heathwood Gardens, London SE7 8ER, England.

ASHLEY Leonard Raymond Nelligan, b. 5 Dec 1928, Miami, Florida, USA. Professor of English; Author; Editor. Education: BA, McGill University, 1949; MA, 1950; AM Princeton University, 1953; PhD, 1956. Appointments: Instructor, University of Utah, 1953-56; Assistant to The Air Historian RCAF, 1956-58; Instructor, University of Rochester, 1958-61; Faculty, The New School for Social Research (part-time), 1962-72; Faculty, Brooklyn College of The City University, New York, 1961-. Publications: Whats in a Name?; Elizabethan Popular Culture; Colley Cibber; Nineteenth-Century British Drama; Authorship & Evidence in Renaissance Drama; Mirrors for Man; Other People's Lives; The Wonderful World of Superstition, Prophecy and Luck; The Wonderful World of Magic & Witchcraft; Ripley's Believe It Or Not Book of the Military; The Air Defence of North America, A Military History of Modern China, (collaborator); Shakespeare's Jest Book; George Peele: The Man and His Work; Language in Contemporary Society (co-editor); Geolinguistic Perspectives (co-editor); Phantasms of the Living 2 vols (editor). Contributions to: Great Writers of the English Language; Reference Guide to American Literature; British Women Writers; Encyclopedia of British Humor, Encyclopedia of World Drama, Cyclopedia of Short Fiction; Regular Reviewer for Bibliothèque Humanisme et Renaissance, Names; Encyclopedia, USA; Dictionary of Literary Biography; Dictionary of American Literary Characters. Honours: The Shakespeare Gold Medal; American Name Society Best Article Award; Fellowships & Grants. Memberships include: The American Name Society, past President; International Linguistics Association, former Secretary; American Association of University Professors, former President, Brooklyn College Chapter; American Society of Geolinguistics, President; Princeton Club of New York; Modern Language Association; American Dialect Society. Address: Department of English, Brooklyn College, CUNY, Brooklyn, NY 11230, USA.

ASHTON Christina Julia Allen, b. 16 Sept 1934, Brooklyn, New York. Writer; Teacher. m. 21 Aug 1954, 1 daughter. Education: BA English 1957, Washington State University; MS Special Education 1975, Dominican College. Publications: Words Can Tell, A Book About Our Language, 1988; Codes and Ciphers: Hundreds of Unusual and Secret Ways to Send Messages, 1993; The First Defender of France, article, 1991; The Deer, short story, prize winner, not yet published, 1991. Contributions to: Calliope Magazine. Honours: English Honours, University of Oregon, 1954; Second Prize, California Writers Club, short story, 1991; Second Prize, National Writers Club, short story, 1991; Honorable Mention, National Writers Club, non-fiction book, 1992. Memberships: National Writers Club; California Writers Club, member, Secretary Peninsular Branch. Literary Agent: Norma Lewis Agency, New York. Address: 4009 Kingridge Drive, San Mateo, CA 94403, USA.

ASHTON Robert, b. 21 July 1924, Chester, England. Retired University Professor. m. Margaret Alice Sedgwick, 30 Aug 1946, 2 d. Education: Magdalen College School, Oxford, 1938-40, 1946-49; University College, Southampton, 1949-52; PhD, London School of Economics, 1953. Appointments: Assistant Lecturer, Lecturer, Senior Lecturer, Nottingham University, 1952-63; Visiting Associat Professor, University of CA, 1962-63; Professor, University of East Anglia, 1963-89; Emeritus Professor, 1989-; Visiting Fellow, All Souls College, Oxford, 1974-75, 1987. Publications: The English Civil War: Conservatism & Revolution 1603-49, 1978; The Crown and the Money Market 1603-40, 1960; James I by his Contemporaries, 1969; The City and the Court 1603-1643, 1979; Reformation and Revolution, 1558-1660, 1984; Counter Revolution: The Second Civil War and its

Origins 1646-1648, 1994. Contributions to: Articles in Economic History Review; Bulletin of Institute of Historical Research; Past & Present; Historical Journals. Memberships: Royal Historical Society. Address: The Manor House, Brundall, Norwich NR13 5JY, England.

ASIMOV Janet O Jeppson, b. 6 Aug 1926, Ashland, Pennsylvania, USA. Physician; Writer. m. Isaac Asimov, 30 Nov 1973. Education: BA, Stanford University, 1948; MD, New York University College of Medicine, 1952; Diploma, Psychoanalysis, William Alanson White Institute, 1960. Publications include: The Second Experiment, 1974; The Last Immortal, 1980; The Mysterious Cure, 1985; Mind Transfer, 1988; With Isaac Asimov: How to Enjoy Writing; Laughing Space, 1982; Norby, the Mixed-Up Robot, 1983; Norby's Other Secret, 1984; Norby & the Lost Princess, 1985; Norby & the Invaders, 1985; Norby & the Queen's Necklace, 1986; Norby Finds a Villain, 1987l; The Package in Hypcrspace, 1988; Norby and Yobo's Great Adventure, 1989; Norby & the Oldest Dragon, 1990; Norby Down to Earth, 1991; Norby & the Court Jester, 1991. Contributions to: Several journals. Honour: Phi Beta Kappa, 1948. Memberships: Science Fiction Writers of America; William Alanson White Society; American Academy of Psychoanalysis; American Psychiatric Association. Address: 10 West 66th Street, New York, NY 10023, USA.

ASPENSTROM Werner, b. 13 Nov 1918, Norrbarke, Sweden. Poet; Playwright. m. Signe Lund, 1946. Education: BA, University of Stockholm, 1945. Publications include: Verse: The Scream and the Silence, 1946; Snow Legend, 1949; Litany, 1952; The Dogs, 1954; Poems Under the Trees, 1956; The Stairs, 1964; Within, 1969; Meanwhile, 1972; Earth Cradle Sky Ceiling, 1973; Dictionary, 1976; Early One Morning Late on Earth, 1976-80; You and I and the World, 1980; Murmur, 1983; Beings, 1988; Plays, A Clown Must Have Lost His Way, 1949; The Snare, 1959; Television Plays, Theatre I, 1959; Theatre II, 1963; The Carpet, 1964; The Spiders and a Short Play, 1966; With Ones Own Eyes, 1967; Poor Job, 1969; The Nose, 1971; Not So Young Anymore, 1972; Those Who Wait, 1976; Radio Play, Sidelights: A Selection of Prose, 1989. Honours include: Honorary Doctorate, University of Stockholm, 1976. Address: c/o Bonniers Forlag, Box 3159, 103 63 Stockholm, Sweden.

ASPINWALL Dorothy Brown, b. 21 Oct 1910, Regina, Saskatchewan, Canada. Teacher; University Professor. m. Albion Newton Aspinwall, 10 Jan 1942, 1 son. Education: BA, University of Alberta, 1933; MA, 1939; PhD, University of Washington, 1948. Publications: Translation of PÉguy's Book The Portico of the Mystery of the Second Virtue; French Poems in English Verse; Modern Verse Translations from French; Recitatif Translated under the Title The Party is Over; Choice Poems of Ilarie Voronca. Contributions to: The Atlantic Monthly; Modern Language Journal; PMLA; The Mexico Quarterly; The Explicator; The Husk; The Lantern; Poet Lore; Paradise of the Pacific; Webster Review; Poesie USA. Honours: Carnegie Hero Fund Commission Award; French Government Bursary; Ford Foundation Grant for Research; Danforth Foundation Summer Workshop; NDEA Institute Director. Address: 2003 Kalia Road, 9-1 Honolulu, HI 96815, USA.

ASPLER Tony, b. 12 May 1939, London, England. Writer. m. 11 July 1971, 1 son, 1 daughter. Education: BA, McGill University, Canada, 1959. Publications: With Gordon Page: Chain Reaction, 1978; The Scorpion Sanction, 1980; The Music Wars, 1983; Sole Author: Streets of Askelon, 1972; One of my Marionettes, 1973; Vintage Canada, 1983; The Wine Lover Dines, International Guide to Wine; Titanic, 1989; Vintage Canada (update), 1992; Blood is Thicker than Beaujolais, novel, 1993; Cellar and Silver (with Rose Murray), 1993; Aligote to Zinfandel, 1994. Contributions to: Editor: Wine Tidings; City Food, Toronto Star. Membership: Founding Chairman 1982-84, Crime Writers of Canada. Literary Agent: Livingstone Cooke. Address: 27B Claxton Boulevard, Toronto, Ontario, M6C 1L7, Canada.

ASPREY Robert B, b. 16 Feb 1923, Sioux City, Iowa, USA. Writer. Education: University of Iowa, New College, Oxford University; University of Vienna, Austria, University of Nice, France. Publications: The Panther's Feast; The First Battle of the Marne; Once a Marine; At Belleau Wood; Semper Fidelis; War in the Shadows; Operation Prophet; Frederick the Great - the Magnificent Enigma, 1986; The German High Command at War - Hindenburg and Ludendorff Conduct & World War One, 1991; War in the Shadows, revised and updated, 1994. Contributions to: Marine Corps Gazette; Ency Britannia; New Yorker; Naval Institute Proceedings; Brassey's Annual; Army Quarterly; New York Times; Army (magazine). Honour: Guest Speaker, Western

Front Association, 1993. Memberships include: Authors Guild; Oxford University Society; New College Society; Frilford Heath Golf Club (Oxford); Club de Golf Sotogrande; Army & Navy Club, Washington DC; Special Forces Club, London. Literary Agent: Robert Gottlieb, William Morris Agency, 1350 Avenue of The Americas, New York, NY 10019, USA.

ASSELINEAU Roger Maurice, (Maurice Herra), b. 24 Mar 1915, Orleans, France. Emeritus Professor, American Literature. Education: Licence es Lettres, Agregation, English, 1938, Docteur es Lettres, 1953, Sorbonne. Publications include: L'Evolution de Walt Whitman, 1954; The Literary Reputation of Mark Twain, 1964, USA 1971; Poesies Incompletes, 1959; Evolution of Walt Whitman, 1960-62; E A Poe, 1970; Transcendentalist Constant in American Literature, 1980; Incomplete Poems, 1984; St John de Crevecoeur: The Life of an American Farmer, with Gay Wilson Allen, 1987; Poésies incomplètes (II), 1989; Poètes anglais de la Grande Guerre, 1991; Poèmes de gureere 1939-1944, (under the pseudonym of Maurice Herra), 1991. Contributions to: Etudes Anglaises; Revue de Litterature Comparee; Forum; Dialogue; Calamus; Walt Whitman Review. Honours: Walt Whitman Prize, Poetry Society of America; Honorary doctorate, University of Poznan. Memberships include: Honorary President, French Association for American Studies; Honorary member, Modern Language Association; Hemingway Society; International Association of University Professors of English; Societe des Gens de Lettres. Address: 114 Avenue Leon Blum, 92160 Antony, France.

ASSENSOH Akwasi Bretuo (A Bretuo), b. Ghana, West Africa. Historian; Journalist. m. Dr Yvette Alex-Assensoh, 7 May 1994. Education: University of Stockholm, 1978; School of Journalism, Frilsham, 1968-69; Swedish Language Certification, University of Stockholm, Sweden, 1975-76; BA, Dillard University, 1981; MA, New York University, 1982; PhD, New York University, 1984. Appointments: Writers Society of Liberia, Secretary, 1968-69; Editor, Daily Listener, 1969-71; Associate Editor, The Pioneer, 1971-72; Associate Editor & Head of Research, M L King Jr, Papers Project, Stanford University/King Center, Atlanta, USA, 1988-90; Associate Professor, Southern University, USA, 1991-. Publications: Kwame Nkrumah, Six Years in Exile; Black Woman, Black Woman; Campus Life; Essays on Contemporary International Topics; Martin Luther King Junior and Americas Quest for Racial Integration; Kwame Nkrumah of Africa; Africa in Retrospect; Topics in Socio Historical Studies. Contributions to: PEN International; African Commentary Journal; Journal of Third World Studies; West Africa Magazine of London; African Studies Review; Africa Magazine; African Development. Honours: Dillard University Social Science Plaque for Literary Achievement; Listed Contemporary Authors. Memberships: International PEN; Press Club of Liberia; Press Club of New Orleans; American Historical Association; African Studies Association of America. Address: Department of History, Southern University, PO Box 10281, Baton Rouge, LA 70813, USA.

ASTLEY Thea (Beatrice May), b. 25 Aug 1925, Brisbane, Queensland, Australia. Novelist. m. Edmund John Gregson, 1948, 1 son. Education: BA, University of Brisbane, 1947. Appointments: Senior Tutor, then Fellow in English, Macquarie University, Sydney, New South Wales, 1968-85. Publications: Girl With a Monkey, 1958; A Descant for Gossips, 1960; The Well-Dressed Explorer, 1962; The Slow Natives, 1965; A Boat Load of Home Folk, 1968; The Acolyte, 1972; A Kindness Cup, 1974; An Item from the Late News, 1982; Beachmasters, 1985; It's Raining in Mango, 1987; Reach Tin River, 1990; Short stories: Hunting the Wild Pineapple, 1979; Also various uncollected short stories. Honours include: The Age Book of the Year Award, 1975; Patrick White Award, 1989. Literary Agent: Elise Goodman, Goodman Associates, New York, USA. Address: c/o Elise Goodman, Goodman Associates, 500 West End Avenue, New York, NY 10024, USA.

ASTOR Gerald, b. 6 June 1944, American. Publications: The Charge is Rape, Capitol Hell, A Question of Rape, 1974; Brick Agent (with A Villano), 1978; The Disease Detectives: Deadly Medical Mysteries and the People Who Solve Them, 1983; The Last Nazi: The Life and Times of Dr Joseph Mengele, 1985; The Voices of D-Day, 1994.

ATHANASSIADIS Tassos, b. 1 Nov 1913, Salichli of Asia Minor, Turkey. Author; Novelist; Essayist; Biographer. m. Maria Dimitropoulou, 1979. Education: Law & Foreign Languages, Law School of Athens University, 1931-36. Publications include: The Panthei Saga, 1948-61;

The Guards of Achaia, 1974; The Last Grandchildren, 1981-84; Niobe's Children, 1985-88; Voyage to Loneliness, 19383-42; Three Children of the Century; Essays, Recognitions, 1965; Certainites and Doubts, 1980; From Ourself to Others, 1992; Novels Translated into French, Italian, Swedish, Portuguese, Romanian & German; Holy Youth, 1993. Honours include: Literary State Award, 1955; The Athens Academy Award, 1961; State Literary Award, 1961, 1963; Ipeski Prize of Greek Turkish Friendship, 1989; Doctor Honoris Causa of Athens University, 1994. Memberships: Athens Academy; PEN; Greek Lyric Opera; Greek National Theatre. Literary Agent: Estia Publishing House, Athens. Address: 83 Drossopoulou Str, Athens 112 57, Greece.

ATKINS Stephen E, b. 29 Jan 1941, Columbia, Missouri, USA. Librarian; Professor. m. Susan Starr Jordan, 9 June 1966, 1 son, 1 daughter. Education: BA (Honours), European History, 1963, MA (Honours), French History, 1964, University of Missouri-Columbia; PhD, French History, 1976, MA, Library Science, 1983, University of Iowa. Appointments include: Monograph Cataloguer, University of Iowa Library; Political Science Specialist, Education and Social Science Library, Associate Professor, University of Illinois, Urbana-Champaign, 1983-89, Head of Collection Development, Sterling C Evans Library, 1989-, Professor, 1994-, Texas A&M University, College Station. Publications: Arms Control and Disarmament, Defense and Military, International Security and Peace: An Annotated Guide to Success, 1980-1987, 1989; The Academic Library in the American University, 1991; Terrorism: A Reference Handbook, 1992. Contributions to: Information Sources: Arms Control, Disarmament and International Security, to National Forum, 1986; Subject Trends in Library and Information Science Research, 1975-1984, to Library Trends, 1988; Proceedings of the Western Society for French History; Several others. Honours: Peace Award, American Library Association, 1992. Memberships: Western Society for French History, Executive Board 1984-87; American Library Association, Chairperson, Law and Political Science Section 1989-90; ACCESS: A Security Information Service, Secretary, Board of Directors 1991-94, Chair, Activities Council 1994-95; Association of College and Research Libraries; Social Science History Association; Library Administration and Management Association. Address: 2724 Normand Circle, College Station, TX 77845, USA.

ATKINSON James, b. 27 Apr 1914, Tynemouth, Northumberland. Retired Professor of Theology. m. Laura Jean Nutley, Dec 1967, 1 s, 1 d. Education: BA, 1936, MA, 1938, M Litt, 1950, University of Durham; Dr Theol, University of Muenster, Germany, 1955. Publications: Library of Christian Classics, 1962; Rome and Reformation, 1966; Luther's Works, Vol 44, 1967; Luther and the Birth of Protestantism, 1968; The Reformation, 1968; The Trial of Luther, 1971; Martin Luther, Prophet to Church Catholic, 1983; The Darkness of Faith, 1987. Contributions to: Learned Journals; Part Author of Several Books; Many Articles. Memberships: Society for the Study of Theology; Society of the Study of Ecclesiastical History; L'Academie Internationale des Sciences Religieuses. Address: Leach House, Hathersage, Sheffield, S30 1BA, England.

ATKINSON Mary. See: **HARDWICK Mollie.**

ATLAN Liliane, b. 14 Jan 1932, Montpellier, France. Writer. m. June 1952, div 1976, 1 s, 1 d. Education: Diploma Philosophy; CAPES Modern Literature. Publications include: Plays, Mr Fugue of Earth Sick; The Messiahs, The Carriage of Flames and Voices; Poetry, L'Amour Elementaire; Lapsus, 1971; Videotext, Meme Les oiseaux ne Peuvent pas Toujours Planner, 1979; The Passerby, 1989 (France), 1993 (USA); Many Books and Plays have been broadcast by France Culture. Honours: Prix Habimah, 1972; Prix Wizo, 1989; Chevalier de l'Ordre des Arts et des Lettres, 1984; Prize Villa Medicis Outside the Walls, 1992. Memberships: Writers Union of France; AMOAL. Address: 70 Rude du Javelot, 75645 Paris, Cedex 13, France.

ATTENBOROUGH David Frederick, b. 8 May 1926, London, England. Broadcaster and Naturalist. m. Jane Elizabeth Ebsworth Oriel, 11 Feb 1950, 1 son, 1 daughter. Education: Wyggeston Grammar School, Leicester; Clare College, Cambridge. Publications: Zoo Quest to Guiana, 1956; Zoo Quest for a Dragon, 1957; Zoo Quest in Paraguay, 1959; Quest in Paradise, 1960; Zoo Quest to Madagascar, 1961; Quest Under Capricorn, 1963; The Tribal Eye, 1976; Life on Earth, 1979; The Living Planet, 1984; The First Eden, 1987; Atlas of Living World, 1989; The Trials of Life, 1990. Honours: Silver Medal, Zoological Society of London, 1966; Gold Medal, Royal Geographical Society; Kalinga Prize, UNESCO; Honorary Degrees: Leicester,

London, Birmingham, Liverpool, Heriot-Watt, Sussex, Bath, Ulster, Durham, Bristol, Glasgow, Essex, Cambridge, Oxford. Memberships: Fellow, Royal Society; Honorary Fellow, British Academy of Film and Television Arts. Address: 5 Park Road, Richmond, Surrey, England.

ATWOOD Margaret, b. 18 Nov 1939, Ottawa, Canada. Author; Lecturer. Education: BA, University of Toronto, Canada, 1961; AM, Radcliffe College, Cambridge, Mass, USA, University of BC, Vancouver, USA, 1964-65; Instructor in English, Sir George Williams University, Montreal, 1967-68; University of Alberta, University of Toronto, 1972-73; Tuscaloosa, Alabama, 1985; Berg Professor, New York University, 1986; Macquarie University, Australia, 1987; Holds Honours Degrees from Universities and Colleges. Publications include: Poetry: Double Persephone, 1961; Kaleidoscopes Baroque, 1965; Talismans for Children, 1965; Speeches for Doctor Frankenstein, 1966; The Circle Game, 1966; Two Headed Poems, 1978; Snake Poems, 1983; Selected Poems II, 1986; Selected Poems, 1966-84, 1990; Margaret Atwood Poems, 1991; Fiction: The Edible Woman, 1979; Bodily Harm, 1981; Encounters with the Element Man, 1982; Murder in the Dark, 1983; Cat's Eyes, 1989; The Best American Short Stories, 1989; Wilderness Tips (short stories), 1991; For Children: Up in the Tree, 1978; Anna's Pet, 1980; For the Birds, 1990; Non-fiction: Survival: A Thematic Guide to Canadian Literature, 1972; Days of the Rebels 1815-1840, 1977; TV Scripts: The Servant Girl, 1974; Heaven on Earth, 1986; Radio Scripts: The Trumpets of Summer, 1964. Honours: Recipient of Awards, Medals and Prizes for Writing; Honorary DLitt, Trent University, 1973, Concordia, 1980; LLD, Queen's University. Address: c/o Jonathon Cape, 32 Bedford Square, London WC1B 3EL, England.

AUCHINLOSS Louis Stanton, b. 27 Sept 1917, USA. Lawyer; Author. m. Adele Lawrence, 1957, 3 sons. Education: Yale University; University of Virginia; Admitted, New York Bar, 1941. Publications include: The Indifferent Children, 1947; The Injustice Collectors, 1950; Sybil, 1952; A Law for the Lion, 1953; The Romantic Egoists, 1954; The Great World & Timothy Colt, 1956; Venus in Sparta, 1958; Pursuit of the Prodigal, 1959; House of Five Talents, 1960; Reflections of a Jacobite, 1961; Portrait in Brownstone, 1962; Powers of Attorney, 1963; The Rector of Justin, 1964; Pioneers & Caretakers, 1965; The Embezzler, 1966; Tales of Manhattan, 1967; A World of Profit, 1969; Motiveless Malignity, 1969; Edith Wharton: A Woman in her Time, 1971; I Come as a Thief, 1972; Richelieu, 1972; The Partners, 1974; A Winter's Capital, 1974; Reading Henry James, 1975; The Winthrop Convenant, 1976; The Dark Lady, 1977; The Country Cousin, 1978; Persons of Consequence, 1979; Life, Law & Letters, 1979; The House of the Prophet, 1980; The Cat & the King, 1981; Watchfires, 1982; Exit Lady Masham, 1983; The Book Clan, 1984; Honorable Men, 1985; Diary of a Yuppie, 1987; The Golden Calves, 1989; Fellow Passengers, 1990; J P Morgan, 1990; False Gods, 1992; Family Fortunes: 3 Collected Novels, 1993; Three Lives, 1993; The Style's the Man, 1994. Contributions to: New York Review of Books; New Criterion. Membership: National Institute of Arts & Letters. Address: 67 Wall Street, New York, NY 10005, USA.

AUERBACH Nina, b. 24 May 1943, NY, USA. Education: BA, University of WI; MA, PhD, Columbia University. Appointment: University Professor of English. Publications: Communities of Women, 1978; Private Theatricals: The Lives of the Victorians, 1990; Ellen Terry, 1987; Romantic Imprisonment: Women and Other Glorified Outcasts; Women and the Demon, 1982. Contributions to: Several Collections of Literary Criticism; Numerous Articles & Reviews to Literary Journals. Honours: National Book Critics Circle Nomination, 1982. Address: Department of English, University of Pennsylvania, Philadelphia, PA 19104 6273, USA.

AUGUST Marcus. See: **BANTOCK Gavin.**

AUMBRY Alan. See: **BAYLEY Barrington.**

AUSTER Paul, b. 3 Feb 1947, NJ, USA. m. Siri Hustvedt, 23 Feb 1981, 1 s, 1 d. Education: BA, 1969, MA, 1970, Columbia University. Publications include: The Invention of Solitude, 1982; The New York Trilogy, 1985-86; In The Country of Last Things, 1987; Moon Palace, 1989; The Music of Chance, 1990; Leviathan, 1992; Mr Vertigo, 1994; Disappearances, 1988; The Art of Hunger, 1992. Contributions to: Over 100 inc. Granta; Paris Review; NY Review of Books; NY Times. Honours: Morton Dawen Label Award, 1990; Prix Medicis Etranger, 1993. Membership: PEN. Literary Agent. Carol Mann. Address: c/o Carol Mann Agency, 55 5th Avenue, New York, NY 10003, USA.

AUSTIN Brett. See: **FLOREN Lee.**

AUSTIN William W, b. 1920, American. Appointments: Assistant Professor 1947-50, Associate Professor 1950-60, Professor 1960-69, Goldwin Smith Professor of Musicology 1969-80, Given Foundation Professor of Musicology 1980-90, Professor Emeritus 1990, Cornell University. Publications: Music in the Twentieth Century, 1966; New Looks at Italian Opera (ed), 1968; Debussy's Prelude to the Afternoon of a Faun (ed), 1970; Susanna, Jeanie and the Old Folks at Home: Meanings and Contexts of the Songs of Stephen C Foster from His Time to Ours, 1975, 1987; Esthetics of Music by Carl Dahlhaus (trans), 1982. Address: 205 White Park Road, Ithaca, NY 14850, USA.

AVALLONE Michael Angelo Jr (James Blaine, Nick Carter, Troy Conway, Priscilla Dalton, Mark Dane, Jean-Anne De Pre, Dora Highland, Steve Michaels, Dorothea Nile, Ed Noon, Edwina Noone, John Patrick, Vance Stanton, Sidney Stuart), b. 27 Oct 1924, Manhattan, New York, USA. m. 27 May 1960, 2 sons, 1 daughter. Appointments include: Editor, Republic Features 1956-58, Cape Publications 1958-60, The Third Degree (house organ, Mystery Writers of America) 1961-65; Chairman, Motion Picture Committee 1964-70, TV Committee 1962-64, ibid. Publications: Over 200 books including: The Tall Dolores, 1953; The Man from UNCLE, 1964; Beneath the Planet of the Apes, 1970; Tales of the Frightened, 1963; The Haunted Hall, 1970; Run Spy Run (Nick Carter), 1964; Also: Ed Noon private detective series, 1953-88; Satan Sleuth series, 1973-75; Craghold Hotel series, 1971-73; Hawaii Five-O; Krakatoa East of Java; The Coffin Things; Missing! A Woman Called Golda; The Beast with the Red Hands; All the Way, When Were You Born? Red Roses Forever, Sound of Dying Roses, The Silent Silken Shadows, The Darkening Willows, Treasure Island, The Last of the Mohicans; Articles, short stories. Contributions to: Numerous magazines, films, mystery, general. Honours: Author Award, New Jersey Association of Teachers of English, 1969; Literary Luminary of New Jersey, NJ Literary Hall of Fame, NJ Institute of Technology, 1977; Over 20 scrolls for yearly novels. Memberships: Board Mystery Writers of America, 1958-70; Authors League, 1975-78. Address: 80 Hilltop Boulevard, East Brunswick, NJ 08816, USA.

AVERY Gillian (Elise), b. 1926, British. Writer - children's fiction, literature. Appointments: Junior Reporter, Surrey Mirror, Redhill, Surrey, 1944-47; Staff Member, Chambers Encyclopaedia, London, 1947-50; Assistant Illustrations Editor, Clarendon Press, Oxford, 1950-54. Publications: (ed) A Great Emergency and a Very Ill-Tempered Family, by Juliana Horatia Ewing, 1967; (ed) The Gold of Fairnilee and Other Stories, by Andrew Lang, 1967; (ed) Village Children, by Charlotte Younge, 1967; (ed) Banning and Blessing, by Margaret Roberts, 1967 (ed) The Hole in the Wall and Other Stories, 1968; (ed) Victoria Bess and Others, by Brenda, Mrs Gatty and Frances Hodgson Burnett, 1968; (ed) The Wallypug of Why, by G E Farrow, 1968; (ed) My New Home, by Mary Louisa Molesworth, 1968; (ed) The Life and Adventures of Lady Anne (anonymous), 1969; (ed) Stephanie's Children by Margaret Roberts, 1969; (ed) Annie's Terrible Good Nature and Other Stories for Children, by E V Lucas, 1970; (ed) The Rival Kings, by Annie Keary, 1970; Victorian People in Life and Literature, 1970; A Likely Lad, 1971; Ellen's Birthday, 1971; Jemima and the Welsh Rabbit, 1972; The Echoing Green Memories of Victorian and Regency Youth, 1974; Ellen and the Queen, 1974; Book of Strange and Odd, 1975; Childhood's Pattern A Study of the Heroes and Heroines of Children's Fiction 1770-1750, 1975; Freddie's Feet, 1976; Huck and Her Time Machine, 1977; Mouldy's Orphan, 1978; Sixpence, 1979; The Lost Railway, 1980; Onlookers, 1983; The Best Type of Girl, 1991. Address: 32 Charlbury Road, Oxford OX2 6UU, England.

AVGERINOS Cecily T Grazio, b. 16 Apr 1945, New York, USA. Poet; Novelist. m. Robert T Avgerinos, 24 May 1969, 2 sons, 1 daughter. Education: BA, New York University, 1966. Publications: Poems: My Tatterdemalion, 1985; Sunrises, 1985, 1987; Eternity, 1986; Summer Fantasy, 1986; My Prayer, 1986; Lunch in the Park, 1986; Circle Of Gold, 1986; Lord, I Wonder, 1986; The Fig Tree, 1987; Fishing, 1987; Septecential, 1987; Loss, 1987; Bridge Across Tomorrow, 1987; To My Children, 1987; The Stringless Guitar, 1988; Pink Socks, 1988; My Dogwood-Love's Analogy, 1989; Merry-Go-Round, 1989; Strawsticks, 1989. Contributions to: Numerous anthologies. Honours: 25 Awards of Merit, World of Poetry, 1985-; 4 Golden Poet Awards, 1985-. Memberships: Board, Alumni Association, New York University; Vice President, Parent Organisation. Literary Agent: Scott Meredith. Address: 173 Momar Drive, Ramsey, NJ 07446, USA.

AVI, b. 1937. Publications: Snail Tale, 1972; No More Magic, 1975; Emily Upham's Revenge, 1978; Who Stole the Wizard of Oz?, 1981; Sometimes I Think I Hear My Name: a novel, 1982; Shadrach's Crossing, 1983; The True Confessions of Charlotte Doyle, 1990; Nothing But The Truth: A Documentary Novel, 1991; Blue Heron, 1992; Smuggler's Island, 1994; The Bird, the Frog and the Light: a fable, 1994; History of Helpless Harry, 1995. Honours: Boston Globe; Horn Award, 1991.

AVISON Margaret (Kirkland), b. 23 Apr 1918, Galt, Ontario, Canada. Poet and Translator. Education: BA in English, University of Toronto, 1940. Appointments: Writer-in-residence, University of Western Ontario, 1972-73; Staff member, Mustard Seed Mission, Toronto, from 1978. Publications: Winter Sun, 1960; The Dumbfoundling, 1966; Sunblue, 1978; History of Toronto, 1951; The Research Compendium, 1964; Co-translator, The Plough and the Pen: Writings from Hungary 1930-56, 1963, and Acta Sanctorum and Other Tales, 1970. Honours: Guggenheim Fellowship, 1956; Governor-General's Award, 1961.

AWOONOR Kofi Nyidevu, b. 13 Mar 1935, Wheta, Ghana. Diplomat. 4 sons, 1 daughter. Education: Zion College of West Africa, 1951-54; Achimota Secondary School, 1955-56; University College of Ghana, 1957-60; University of College of London, 1967-68; University of the State of New York at Stony Brook, 1969-72. Publications: Rediscovery, 1964; Night of My Blood, 1971; This Earth My Brother, 1972; Ride Me Memory, 1973; Guardian of the Sacred Word, 1974; Breast of the Earth, essays, 1974; House by the Sea, 1978; Until The Morning After, poetry, 1988; Ghana: A Political History, history, 1990; Comes the Voyager At Last, fiction, 1992; Latin American and Caribbean Notebook, poetry, 1993. Honours: Translation Award, Columbia University, 1972; Ghana Book Award, 1978; Dillons Commonwealth Award, 1989; Ghana Association of Writers Distinguished Authors Award, 1992. Literary Agent: Loretta Barrett Books Inc. Address: Permanent Mission of Ghana to the United Nations, 19 East 47th Street, New York, NY 10017, USA.

AXTON David. See: **KOONTZ Dean R.**

AYCKBOURN Alan, b. 1939, London, England. Theatre Director; Playwright; Artistic Director. Plays: Mr Whatnot, 1963; Relatively Speaking, 1965; How The Other Half Loves, 1969; Time and Time Again, 1971; Absurd Person Singular, 1972; The Norman Conquests, 1973; Absent Friends, 1974; Confusions, 1975; Bedroom Farce, 1975; Just Between Ourselves, 1976; Ten Times Table, 1977; Joking Apart, 1978; Sisterly Feelings, 1979; Taking Steps, 1979; Season's Greetings, 1980; Way Upstream, 1981; Intimate Exchanges, 1982; A Chorus of Disapproval, 1984; Woman in Mind, 1985; A Small Family Business, 1986; Henceforward, 1987; Man of the Moment, 1988; The Revenger's Comedies, 1989; Time of My Life, 1992; Dreams From A Summer House, 1992; Communicating Doors, 1994; Hunting Julia, 1994; Mr A's Amazing Maze Plays, 1989; Invisible Friends, 1991; The Musical Jigsaw Play, 1994. Honours: Hon DLitt, Hull, 1981, Keele, 1987, Leeds, 1987, York, 1992, Bradford, 1994; Cameron Mackintosh Professor of Contemporary Theatre, 1992; CBE, 1987. Membership: Garrick Club; Royal Society of Arts. Literary Agent: Casarotto Ramsay Limited. Address: c/o Casarotto Ramsay Limited, National House, 60-66 Wardour Str, London W1V 3HP.

AYDY Catherine. See: **TENNANT Emma Christina.**

AYERST David (George Ogilvy), b. 1904, British. Appointments: Editorial Staff Member 1929-34, Historian 1964-73, The Guardian, Manchester and London; H M Inspector of Schools, 1947-64. Publications: Europe in the 19th Century, 1940; Understanding Schools, 1967; Records of Christianity (ed with A S T Fisher), 1970, 1977; Guardian: Biography of a Newspaper (in US as The Manchester Guardian), 1971; The Guardian Omnibus (ed), 1973; Garvin of the Observer, 1985. Address: Littlecote, Burford, Oxford, OX18 4SE, England.

AYIM May. See: **OPITZ May.**

AYLEN Leo, b. Vryheid, Zululand, South Africa. Poet; Author; Film director. m. Annette Battam. Education: MA, New College, Oxford University; PhD, Bristol University. Appointment: TV Producer, BBC, 1965-70; Writer. Publications include: Discountinued Design; Return to Zululand; Red Alert: this is a god warning; Jumping Shoes; Rhymoceros; Greek Tragedy and the Modern World; Greece for

Everyone; The Greek Theatre; The Apples of Youth; Films for TV inc, the Drinking Party; Dynamo; Who'll Buy a Bubble; Steel to my Sister; Soul of a Nation. Honours: Nominated British Academy TV Award, 1966; Poet in Residence, Fairleigh Dickinson University, NJ, USA, 1972-74; Cecil Day Lewis Fellowship, 1979-80; Hooker Distinguished Visiting Professor, McMaster University, 1982. Memberships: Poetry Society of Gt Britain; Poetry Society of USA; Britich Actors Equity; Association of Cinema and TV Technicians; Writers Guild of Gt Britain; Writers Guild of USA; British Academy of Film & TV Arts. Address: 13 St Saviours Road, London SW2 5HP, England.

AYLING Stanley Edward, b. 15 Mar 1909, London, England. Biographer. m. 17 Dec 1936, 2 s. Education: Strand Sch, London, 1920-28; Emmanuel College, Cambridge, 1928-31. Publications: George the Third, 1972; The Elder Pitt, Earl of Chatham, 1976; John Wesley, 1979; A Portrait of Sheridan, 1985; Edmund Burke, his Life and Opinions, 1988; Fox: The Life of Charles James Fox, 1991. Honour: Fellow, Royal Society of Literature, 1980. Address: The Beeches, Middle Winterslow, Salisbury, Wilts, England.

AYLMER Gerald Edward, b. 1926, England. Historian.Appointments: J E Proctor Visiting Fellow, Princeton University, NJ, 1950-51; Junior Research Fellow, Balliol College, Oxford, 1951-54; Assistant Lecturer, 1954-57, Lecturer, 1957-62, University of Manchester; Professor and Head of Department, University of York, 1963-78; Master, St Peters College, Oxford, 1978-91; Editorial Board, History of Parliament, 1968-; Chairman, 1989-, Commission on Historical Manuscripts, 1978-,Chairman 1989-94; Vice President, 1973-77, President, 1984-88, Hon Vice President, 1988, Royal Historical Soceity; Hon Vice President, Historical Association, 1992-. Publications: The King's Servants, 1625-1642, 1961; The Diary of William Lawrence, 1961; The Struggle for the Constititution 1603-1689, 1963; The Interregnum 1646-1660, 1972; The State's Servants, 1649-1660, 1973; The Levellers in the English Revolution, 1975; A History of York Minster, 1977; Rebellion or Revolution 1640-1660, 1986. Address: 18 Albert Street, Jericho, Oxford, OX2 6AZ, England.

AYRES Philip James (Diana Lakehurst), b. 28 July 1944, South Australia. University Professor. m. 1) Maruta Sudrabs, 11 Dec 1965, 2) Patricia San Martin, 28 Nov 1981, 1 son. Education: BA, 1965; PhD, 1971; FR Hist S, 1989. Appointments: Tutor, University of Adelaide, Australia, 1969-71; Lecturer, Senior Lecturer, Monash University, 1972-. Publications: Malcolm Fraser, A Biography; Ben Jonson, Sejanus; Cyril Tourneur, The Revengers Tragedy; Anthony Munday, The English Roman Life. Contributions to: Studies in Philology; Modern Philology; Studies in English Literature; Studies in Bibliography; English Literary Renaissance; Short Stories. Honours: Royal Historical Society; Visiting Professor, Vassar College. Address: 13 Harris Avenue, Glen Iris, Victoria 3146, Australia.

B

B Dick. See: **BURNS Richard Gordon.**

B Thomas, See: **JENKINS Dan.**

BABINGTON Anthony Patrick, b. 4 Apr 1920, Cork, Ireland. Education: Reading School: Inns of Court Law School; Called to Bar, 1948; Circuit Judge (London), 1972-90. Publications: For the Sake of Example; No Memorial; Military Intervention in Britain; A House in Bow Street; The Rule of Law in Britain; The Devil to Pay; The Power to Silence; The English Bastille; For the Sake of Example. Memberships: PEN; The Society of Authors; Garrick. Literary Agent: David Fletcher. Address: 3 Gledhow Gardens, Kensington, London SW5 0BL, England.

BABSON Marian, American. Writer. Appointment: Secretary, Crime Writers Association, London, 1976-86. Publications: Cover-up Story, 1971; Murder on Show, 1972; Pretty Lady, 1973; The Stalking Lamb, Unfair Exchange, 1974; Murder Sails at Midnight, There Must Be Some Mistake, 1975; Untimely Guest, 1976; The Lord Mayor Death, Murder Murder Little Star, 1977; Tightrope for Three, 1978; So Soon Done For, The Twelve Deaths of Christmas, 1979; Dangerous to Know, Queue Here for Murder, 1980; Bejewelled Death, 1981; Death Warmed Up, Death Beside the Seaside, 1982; A Fool for Murder, 1983; The Cruise of a Deathtime, A Trail of Ashes, Death Swap, 1984; Death in Fashion, Weekend for Murder, 1985; Reel Murder, 1986; Fatal Fortune, 1987; Guilty Party; Encore Murder, 1989; Past Regret, 1990. Address: c/o William Collins Sons & Co Ltd, 8 Grafton Street, London W1X 3LA, England.

BACHMAN Richard. See: **KING Stephen Edwin.**

BOCOCK Robert James, b. 29 Sept 1940, England. Senior Lecturer in Social Science. Publications: Freud and Modern Society, 1976; Sigmund Freud, 1983; Ritual in Industrial Society, 1974; Hegemony, 1986; Consumption, 1993. Contributor to: British Journal of Sociology; Sociology. Membership: British Sociological Association. Literary Agent: A D Peters, London. Address: Department of Sociology, Faculty of Social Sciences, Crowther Building, The Open University, Walton Hall, Milton Keynes, Buckinghamshire, England.

BADAWI Mohamed Mustafa, b. 1925, England. Lecturer. Appointments: Research Fellow, 1947-54, Lecturer, 1954-60, Assistant Professor, 1960-64, Alexandria University, Egypt; Lecturer, Oxford University, & Brasenose College, 1964-; Fellow, St Antony's College, Oxford, 1967-; Editor, Journal of Arabic Literature, Leiden, 1970; Advisory Board Member, Cambridge History of Arabic Literature. Publications: An Anthology of Modern Arabic Verse, 1970; Coleridge as Critic of Shakespeare, 1973; a Critical Introduction to Modern Arabic Poetry, 1975; Sara, by AM El Aqqad, 1978; Background to Shakespeare, 1981; The Thief and the Dogs by Naguib Mahfouz, 1984; Modern Arabic Literature and the West, 1985; Modern Arabic Drama in Egypt, 1987; Early Arabic Drama, 1988; Cambridge History of Arabic Literature, Modern Arabic literature, 1992; A Short History of Modern Arabic Literature, 1993. Honour: King Faisal International Prize for Arabic Literature. Memberships: Ministry of Culture, Egypt; Unesco Expert on Modern Arabic Culture. Address: St Antonys College, Oxford, England.

BADER-MOLNAR Katarina Elisabeth, b. Berlin, Germany. Retired Teacher, Professor, Freelance Writer. m. Imre Molnar, div. Education: Diploma, Librarian, Berlin, 1934; English Literature Studies, Liverpool, England; MA, French Philology, Kopernikus University, 1950; English Philology Diploma, 1950; DLitt, Albert Einstein International Academy Foundation, 1965. Appointments: Diploma Librarian, Professor & Librarian, Torun, Grudziadz, Dantzig, Zurich, Switzerland; Freelance Writer; Dr h c of Literature, 1993. Publications include: L'idée d'humanité dans l'oeuvre de Voltaire jusqu'en, 1750, 1950; Lyriden, (poems), 1976; Romantisches Gefuege, (poems & stories); 1978; Teufelskreis und Lethequelle, (novel); 1979; Karola contra Isegrim und Reineke (story), 1980; Da waren Träume noch süss, (novel), 1988; Vom Leuchten der Liebe, (novel); 1990; Gehn und Sein (selected poems), 1991; Bruderkriegi Neue Gedichte (new poems), 1994; Various poems, stories for journals, for children and for anthologies in 3 languages. Honours include: Gold Medal, Diploma, Académie

Internationale de Lutèce, Paris, 1984, 1986; Silver Medal, Académie Universelle de Lausanne, 1984; Shield of Valor, ABI, USA, 1992; Diploma of Honour, Life Research Fellow IBC, Cambridge, England, 1993; International Award of Recognition, 1993; International Order of Merit, 1993. Memberships include: Schweizerischer Schriftsteller-Verband Zurich; PEN Zentrum Bern; Zurcher Schriyftsteller-Verband Zurich, Literarischer Club, Zurich; Mozart Gesellschaft; Académie Internationale de Lutèce i Paris, Life Fellow. Address: Tobelhofstr 6, CH-8044, Zurich, Switzerland.

BAERWALD Hans H, b. 1927, American. Professor. Appointments: Assistant Professor 1956-61, Associate Professor of Government 1961-62, Miami University, Oxford, OH; Lecturer 1962-65, Associate Professor 1965-69, Professor of Political Science 1969-, University of California at Los Angeles. Publications: The Purge of Japanese Leaders Under the Occupation, 1959; American Government: Structure, Problems, Policies (with Peter H Odegard), 1962; Chinese Communism: Selected Documents (with Dan N Jacobs), 1963; The American Republic, Its Government and Politics (with P Odegard), 1964, revised edition with William Harvard, 1969; Japan's Parliament: An Introduction, 1974; Party Politics in Japan, 1986. Address: 10538 Edgeley Pl, Los Angeles, CA 90024, USA.

BAI Hua, b. 20 Nov 1930, He Nan, China. Writer. m. Wang pei, 30 Dec 1956, 1 s. Education: Fine Arts Dept, Hsin Yang College of Education. Appointments include: Cultural Propaganda, Peoples Liberation Army, 1947-52; Literary & Creative Activities, General Office of Political Affairs of the Army, 1955-58; Skilled Worker, Shanghai Movies Production Company, 1958-62; Editor, Shanghai Movies Production Company, Army Writer, 1964-66; Writer, Shanghai Writers Association, 1985-. Publications include: Mama, Mama, 1980; Little Birds Cant Understand the Songs Big Tree Sings, 1984; Hometown in the Distance, 1979; Death of a Skilled Fisherman, 1982; The Princess of Peacock, 1957; A Flock of Eagles & The People; Dying Hard Sadder That A Dead Heart, 1993. Contributions to: Numerous Magazines & Journals. Honours: National Best Poems Award, 1981; Taiwan Golden Tripod Award, 1993.Memberships: Shanghai Province Branch, Council of Chinese Writers Association; Chinese Film Artists Association; Beijing Pen Centre, Chinese opera Artists Association. Address: Rm 706, No. 4 Lane 83, Jiangning Road, Shanghai, China.

BAIGELL Matthew, b. 1933, American. Professor. Appointments: Instructor, Assistant Professor, Associate Professor 1961-68, Ohio State University, Columbus; Professor 1968, Distinguished Professor of Art History, Rutgers, 1978-, The State University of NJ, New Brunswick. Publications: A Thomas Hart Benton Miscellany, A History of American Painting, 1971; Thomas Hart Benton, The American Scene: American Painting in the 1930s, 1974; Charles Burchfield, Frederick Remington, 1976; Dictionary of American Art, 1979; Thomas Colel, Albert Bierstadt, 1981; A Concise History of American Painting and Sculpture, 1984; The Papers of the American Artists' Congress (1936), 1985; (ed with Julian Williams): Artists Against War & Facism, 1986. Address: Art History Department, Rutgers University, New Brunswick, NJ 08903, USA.

BAIGENT Beryl, b. 16 Dec 1937. Writer; Teacher. m. Alan H Baigent, 19 Jan 1963, 3 daughters. Education: Grove Park Grammar School, Wrexham, Wales; BA, Physical Education; MA, English Literature, University of Western Ontario, London, Canada. Appointments: Judge, Woodstock Library Contest, 1982, 1985; Judge, United Amateur Press Laureate Awards, 1978; Editor, Pom Seed and Public Works, University of Western Ontario, 1980, 1990; Judge: League of Canadian Poets - Pat Lowther Award, 1992; Canadian Poetry Association - Director, 1993-94; LCP Ontario Representative, 1994-95. Publications include: The Quiet Village, 1972; Pause, 1974; In Counter Point, 1976; Ancestral Dreams, 1981; The Sacred Beech, 1985; Mystic Animals, 1988; Absorbing the Dark, 1990; Undress Stress, 1991; Hiraeth: Poems in Search of Celtic Origins, 1994; Forthcoming: Virgins, Victims and Votives. Contributor to: Poetry Toronto; Poetry Canada Review, CV II; Canadian Author and Bookman; Chester Poetry Anthology; Canadian Humanist; Herspectives; Poet International; Plowman; Pom Seed; Wayzgoose Anthology; Poets Gallery; Public Works; Amethyst Review, Sage Woman. Address: 137 Byron Avenue, Thamesford, Ontario N0M 2M0, Canada.

BAIL Murray, b. 22 Sept 1941, Adelaide, South Australia, Australia. Novelist. m. Margaret Wordsworth, 1965. Education: Norwood Technical High School, Adelaide. Publications:

Homesickness, 1980; Holden's Performance, 1987; Short stories: Contemporary Portraits and Other Stories, 1975; Uncollected short stories: Healing, 1979; Home Ownership, 1981. Membership: Council, Australian National Gallery, Canberra, 1976-81. Honours: The Age Book of the Year Award, 1980; Victorian Premier's Award, 1988. Address: 39/75 Buckland Street, Chippendale, New South Wales 2008, Australia.

BAILEY Anthony Cowper, b. 5 Jan 1933, Portsmouth, England. Author and Journalist, Staff Writer, The New Yorker, 1956-92. Publications include: In the Village, 1971; America, Lost and Found, 1980 (memoir); Rembrandt's House, 1978; Along the Edge of the Forest, 1983; England, First and Last, 1985 (memoir); Major André, 1989 (novel); A Walk Through Wales, 1992; Responses to Rembrandt, 1993. Honour: Overseas Press Club Award, 1974. Literary Agent: Candida Donadio/Abner Stein. Address: c/o Candida Donadio, Donadio and Ashworth, 231 W 22nd Street, New York, NY 10011, USA.

BAILEY David R Shackleton, b. 1917, British. Professor. Education: LittD, Cambridge; Hon DLit, Dublin. Appointments: Fellow 1944-55, Fellow, Deputy Bursar, Senior Bursar, 1964-68, Caius College; Lecturer in Tibetan, Cambridge University, 1948-68; Fellow, Jesus College, 1955-64; Professor of Latin, University of Michigan, Ann Arbor, 1968-74; Visiting Lecturer, 1963, Professor of Greek and Latin 1975-82, Pope Professor of Latin Language and Literature 1982-, Harvard University, Cambridge, MA; Editor, Harvard Studies in Classical Philology, 1980-85. Publications include: The Satapancasatka of Matrceta, Propertiana 1951; Ciceronis Epistulae ad Atticum IX-XVI, 1961; Cicero's Letters to Atticus (7 vols), 1965-70; Cicero, 1971; Two Studies in Roman Nomenclature, 1976; Cicero: Letters to His Friends, 1977; Cicero's Letters to Atticus, 1978; Cicero's Letters to His Friends (2 vols), 1978; Towards a Text of Anthologia Latina, 1979; Cicero: Epistulae ad Q Fratrem et M Brutum, 1981; Profile of Horace, Anthologia Latina I, 1982; Horatius, Cicero: Philippics, 1985; Lucanus, 1988; Martialis, 1990; Back from Exile, 1991. Honours: Recipient, Ch J Goodwin Award of Merit, 1978; Kenyon Medal of British Academy, 1986. Memberships: Fellow, British Academy; American Academy of Arts and Sciences; Member, Philos Society. Address: 303 North Division, Ann Arbor, MI 48104, USA.

BAILEY Fred Arthur, b. 28 Mar 1947, Dumas, Arkansas, USA. Historian. m. Bonnie Pitt, 22 Aug 1968, 2 sons, 1 daughter. Education: BA, Harding University, Searcy, Ark, 1970; MA, University of Tennessee, 1972; PhD, 1979. Publications: Class & Tennessees Confederate Generation. Contributions to: Numerous articles inc: Tennessees Antebellum Culture from the Bottom Up, Journal of Southern Studies; Oliver Perry Temple and the Struggle for Tennessees Agricultural College, Tennessee Historical Quarterly. Honours: E Merton Coulter Award; Outstanding Paper in American History; Tennessee History Book Award; John Trotwood Moore Award; Marshall Wingfield Award. Memberships: Organization of American Historians; Southern Historical Association. Address: 1400 Compere, Abilene, TX 79601, USA.

BAILEY Martin, b. 26 Oct 1947, London, England. Journalist. Education: PhD, London School of Economics, 1974. Appointments: The Observer, 1983-. Publications: Freedom Railway, 1976; Oilgate: The Sanctions Scandal, 1979; A Green Part of the World, 1984; Young Vincent: Van Gogh's Years in England, 1990; Van Gogh: Letters from Provence, 1990; Van Gogh in England: Portrait of the Artist as a Young Man, 1992. Honour: Journalist of the Year, 1979. Literary Agent: A D Peters. Address: The Observer, Chelsea Bridge House, Queenstown Road, London SW8 4NN, England.

BAILEY Paul, b. 16 Feb 1937, London, England. Education: Central School of Speech & Drama, 1953-56. Appointment: Actor, 1953-63. Publications: At The Herusalem, 1967; Trespasses, 1971; A Worthy Guest, A Distant Likeness, 1973; Peters Smarts Confessions, 1977; Old Soldiers, 1980; An English Madam: The Life and Work of Cynthia Payne, 1982; Gabriels Lament, 1986; An Immaculate Mistake, 1990; Hearth and Home, 1990. Honours: Maugham Award, 1968; Arts Council Award, 1968; EM Forster Award, 1974; Orwell Memorial Prize, 1978; Fellow, Royal Society of Literature, 1982. Address: 79 Davisville Road, London W12 9SH, England.

BAILYN Bernard, b. 1922, American. Professor, Assistant Professor 1954-58, Associate Professor 1958-61, Professor 1961-66, Winthrop Professor of History 1966-81, Adams University Professor 1981-, Editor in Chief, John Harvard Library 1962-70, Harvard University; Director, Charles Warren Center for Studies in American History, Harvard University, 1983-; Treelyan Lecturer, Cambridge University, 1971; Pitt Professor, Cambridge University, 1986-87; Trustee, Institute for Advanced Study, Princeton; Co-editor, Perspectives in American History, 1967-76, 1984-86. Publications: The New England Merchants in the Seventeenth Century, 1955; Massachusetts Shipping 1697-1714, 1959; Education in the Forming of American Society, 1960; Pamphlets of the American Revolution, 1965; The Ideological Origin of the American Revolution, 1967; The Origins of American Politics, 1968; The Intellectual Migration, Europe and America 1930-1960 (co-editor), 1969; Law in American History (co-editor), 1972; The Ordeal of Thomas Hutchinson, 1974; The Great Republic (co-author), 1977; The Press and the American Revolution (co-editor), 1980; The Apologia of Robert Keayne: The Self Portrait of a Puritan Merchant (editor), 1965; The Peopling of British North America: An Introduction, 1986; Voyagers to the West, 1986; Faces of Revolution, 1990; Strangers Within the Realm (ed with Philip D Morgan), 1991; The Debate on the Constitution (vols 1 & 2), 1993. Address: 170 Clifton Street, Belmont, MA 02178, USA.

BAINBRIDGE Beryl M, b. 21 Nov 1934, Liverpool, England. Education: Merchant Taylors School, Liverpool. Appointments: Actress, Repertory Theatres in UK, 1949-60; Clerk, Gerald Duckworth & Company Limited, London, 1971-73. Publications: A Weekend with Claude, 1967, 1981; Another Part of the Wood, 1968, 1979; Harriet Said, 1972; The Dressmaker, 1973; The Bottle Factory Outing, 1974; Sweet William, 1975; A Quiet Life, Injury Time, 1976; Young Adolf, 1978; Winter Garden, 1980; English Journey or the Road to Milton Keynes, Watsons Apology, 1984; Mum & Mr Amitage, 1985; Forever England, 1986; Fifthy Lucra, 1986; An Awfully Big Adventure, 1989; The Birthday Boys, 1991. Honours: Whitbread Award, 1977; D Litt University of Liverpool, 1986; Guardian Fiction Award, 1974; Fellow, Royal Society of Literature, 1978. Address: 42 Albert Street, London NW1 7NU, England.

BAINBRIDGE Cyril, b. 15 Nov 1928, Bradford, West Yorkshire, England. Author; Journalist. m. Barbara Hannah Crook, 20 Jan 1953, 1 s, 2 d. Education: Negus College, Bradford. Appointments: Reporter, Bingley Guardian, 1944-45; Reporter, Yorkshire Observer & Bradford Telegraph, 1945-54; The Press Association, 1954-63; Assistant News Editor, 1963-88, News Editor, 1967-69, Regional News Editor, 1969-77, Managing News Editor, 1977-82, Assistant Managing Editor, 1982-88, The Times. Publications: Pavilions on the Sea; Brass Triumphant; The Brontes & Their Country; North Yorkshire & North Humerside; One Hundred Year of Journalism; The News of the World Story, 1993. Contributions to: Various Feature, Travel Articles; Book Reviews. Memberships: The Bronte Society; Chartered Institute of Journalists; Society of Authors. Literary Agent: Laurence Pollinger. Address: 6 Lea Road, Hemingford Grey, Huntingdon, Cambs PE18 9ED, England.

BAITZ Jon Robin, b. 1961. Publications: The Film Society, 1987; The Substance of Fire, and other plays, 1993; Three Hotels, 1993; The End of the Day, 1993. Honours: Fellow, American Academy and Institute of Arts & Letters, 1994.

BAKER Betty (Lou), (Elizabeth Renier), b. 1928, American. Publications: The Sun's Promise, Little Runner of the Longhouse, 1962; Killer-of-Death, The Shaman's Last Raid, 1963; The Treasure of the Padres, 1964; Walk the World's Rim, 1965; The Blood of the Brave, 1966; The Dunderhead War, 1967; Do Not Annoy the Indians, 1968; The Pig War, Arizona, 1969; And One was a Wooden Indian, 1970; A Stranger and Afraid, The Big Push, 1972; At the Center of the World, 1973; The Spirit is Willing, 1974; Three Fools and a Horse, 1975; Settlers and Strangers, 1977; No Help at All, Save Sirrushany!, Partners, 1978; Latki and the Lightning Lizard, 1979; All-by-Herself, Santa Rat, The Great Desert Rat, 1980; Rat is Dead and Ant is Sad, Danby and George, Worthington Botts and the Stream Machine, 1981; Seven Spells to Farewell, And Me Coyote!, 1982; The Turkey Girl, 1983; My Sister Says, The Night Spider Case, 1984. Address: 4127 East Indian School, Apartment 20, Phoenix, AZ 85018, USA.

BAKER David A, b. 27 Dec 1954, Bangor, Maine, USA. Professor; Poet; Editor. m. Ann Townsend, 19 July 1987. Education: BSE, 1976, MA, 1977, Central Missouri State University; PhD, University of Utah, 1983 (all degrees in English). Appointments: Visiting Assistant Professor, Kenyon College, 1983; Assistant Professor, Denison University, 1984; Visiting Professor, Con ell University, 1985; Associate Professor, Denison University, 1989-; Poetry Editor, Kenyon Review, 1989-. Publications: Haunts (poems), 1985; Laws of the Lane (poems), 1981; Sweet Home, Saturday Night (poems), 1991; Poetry Chapbooks: Summer Sleep, 1984; Rivers in the Sea, 1977; Looking Ahead, 1975. Contributor to: Poetry and criticism in: New Yorker, Poetry, Nation, New Republic, Kenyon Review, Southern Review, Sewanee Review, Gettysburg Review, 50 others. Honours: Utah Arts Council Poetry Award, 1981; James Wright Poetry Prize, 1982; Poetry Fellow, National Endowment for the Arts, 1985; Bread Loaf Poetry Fellow, 1989. Memberships: Poets and Writers; Associated Writing Programs; Poetry Society of America; Modern Language Association. Address: 135 Granview Road, Granville, OH 43023, USA.

BAKER Houston Alfred Jr, b. 1943, American. Professor. Appointments: Instructor, Howard University, WA, 1966; Instructor 1968-69, Assistant Professor 1969, Yale University, New Haven, CT; Associate Professor 1970-73, Professor of English 1973, University of Virginia, Charlottesville; Director of Afro-American Studies 1974-77, Professor of English 1977-82, Albert M Greenfield Professor of Human Relations 1982-, University of Pennsylvania, Philadelphia. Publications: Black Literature in America, 1971; Long Black Song: Essays in Black American Literature and Culture, Twentieth Century Interpretations of Native Son, 1972; A Many-Coloured Coat of Dreams: The Poetry of Countee Cullen, Singers of Daybreak; Studies in Black American Literature, 1974; Reading Black: Essays in the Criticism of African, Caribbean and Black American Literature, 1976; No Matter Where You Travel, You Still Be Black, 1979; The Journey Back: Issues in Black Literature and Criticism, 1980; Spirit Run, 1982; Blue, Ideology and Afro-American Literature: A Vernacular Theory, 1984; Blues Journeys Home, 1985; Modernism and the Harlem Renaissance, 1987; Long Black Song; Black Studies, Rap, & the Academy, 1993. Address: Department of English, University of Pennsylvania, Philadelphia, PA 19104, USA.

BAKER Liliane L. See: **BAKER Lillian.**

BAKER Lillian, (Liliane L Baker), b. 12 Dec 1921, New York, USA. Author; Historian. m. Roscoe A Baker, 1 son, 1 daughter. Education: El Camino, California, 1951; UCLA, 1968-77. Appointments: Continuity Writer, WINS, NYC, 1945-46; Columnist, Freelance Writer, Reviewer, Gardena Valley News, 1964-76; Freelance Writer, Editor, Gardena, 1971-; Founder, Editor, International Club for Collectors of Hatpins & Hatpin Holders, 1977-; Conv & Seminar Coordinator, 1979, 82, 84, 87, 90, 92. Publications include: The Common Doom; Collectors Encyclopedia of Hatpins & Hatpin Holders; 100 Years of Collectible Jewelry, 1850-1950; Art Nouveau and Art Deco Jewelry; The Concentration Camp Conspiracy: A Second Pearl Harbor; Hatpins & Hatpin Holders: An Illustrated Value Guide; Creative & Collectible Miniatures; Fifty Years of Collectible Fashion Jewelry: 1925-1975; Dishonoring America: The Collective Guilt of American Japanese; Twentieth Century Fashionable Plastic Jewelry; The Japanning of America: Redress & Reparations Demands by Japanese Americans; American and Japanese Relocation in WWII; Fact, Fiction and Fallacy; Columnist: WWII Times, 1994; The Common Doom; Established The Lillian Baker Collection, Archives Hoover Institution; Poetry, The Coming of Dawn, 1993. Contributions to: Numerous Radio & TV Appearances. Honours: Scholarship Category Award of Merit Conference of California Historical Societies; George Washington Honor Medal; Recipient Award, Freedoms Foundation; Monetary Award, Hoover Institution; Pro-Am Award; Golden Poet Award; Semi-finalist, North American Open Poetry Contest, 1993. Memberships: IBA; National League American Pen Women; National Writers Club; Society Jewelry Historians; National Trust Historic Preservation; Life Member, New York Art Students League. Address: 15237 Chanera Avenue, Gardena,   CA 90249-4042, USA.

BAKER Margaret Joyce, b. 1918, England. Publications include: The Fighting Cocks, 1949; Four Farthings abd a Thimble, 1950; A Castle and Sixpence, 1951; The Family That Grew and Grew, Treasure Trove, 1952; The Young Magicians, Lions in the Potting Shed, 1954; The Wounderful Wellington Boots, 1955; Anna Sewell and Black Beauty, Acorns & Aerials, 1956; The Birds of Thimblepins, 1960; Homer in Orbit, 1961; Into the Castle, The Cats of Honeytown, Away Went Galloper, 1962; Castaway christmas, 1963; Cut off from Crumpets, The Shoe Shop Bears, 1964; Home from the Hill, 1968; Hi Jink Joins the Bears, 1968; Snail's Place, 1970; The Last Straw, 1971; Boots and the Ginger Bears, 1972; The Sand Bird, Prickets Way, 1973; Lock Stock & Barrel, 1974; Sand in Our Shoes, 1976; The Gift Horse, 1982; Catch as Catch Can, 1983; Beware of the Gnomes, 1985; The Waiting Room Doll, 1986; Fresh Fields for Daisy, 1987. Address: Prickets, Old Cleeve, Nr Minehead, Somerset TA24 6HW, England.

BAKER Paul Raymond, b. 1927, American. Professor. Appointments: Professor of History, 1965-, Director of American Civilization Program, 1972-1992, New York University. Publications: Views of Society and Manners in America, by Frances Wright D'Arusmont, 1963; The Fortunate Pilgrims; Americans in Italy 1800-1860, 1964; The Atomic Bomb: The Great Decision, 1968, 1976; (with William Hall); The American Experience (volume I), The American People (volume II), Growth of a Nation, 1976; (volume III) Organizing a Democracy (volume IV), The American Economy (volume V), The United States in World Affairs, 1979; Richard Morris Hunt, 1980, 1986; (Contributor) Around the Square, 1982; Master Builders, 1985; The Architecture of Richard Morris Hunt, 1986; Stanny: The Gilded Life of Stanford White, 1989. Address: c/o Department of History, New York University, 19 University Place, Room 523, New York, NY 10003, USA.

BAKOLAS Nikos, b. 26 July 1927, Thessalonik, Greece. Retired Journalist. m. Helene Issidorou, 6 Sept 1957, 2 sons. Education: University of Thessaloniki; University of Michigan. Appointments: Artistic Manager, National Theatre of Northern Greece, 1980-81, 1990-. Publications: The Big Square; Mythology; The Princes, Garden; Trepass; Don't Cry Darling; Marches; Death Sleep. Contributions to: Numerous. Honours: Plotin Literary Award; National Book Award. Memberships: Greek Literary Society; Journalists Union of Macedonia. Address: 16 Papadiamandi Str, 546 45 Thessaloniki, Greece.

BAKR Salwa, b. June 1949, Elzeton, Cairo. Egypt. Novelist. Education: BA, 1972, BA, 1976, Ayn Shams University, Cairo. Appointments include: Founder of the Hagar journal, 1993. Publications: Zinat at the President's Funeral, 1986; Atiyyah's Shrine, 1986; About the Soul that was Spirited Away, 1989; The Golden Chariot Does Not Ascend to Heaven, 1994; The Wiles of Men and Other Stories, 1992; Monkey Business, 1992; Depicting the Nightingale, 1993; Rabbits; Atijasschrein Die einzige.Address: c/o Atelier of Writers, Karim al-Dawla Street, Talat Harb Square, Cairo, Eygpt.

BALAAM. See: **LAMB Geoffrey Frederick.**

BALABAN John, b. 2 Dec 1943, Philadelphia, Pennsylvania, USA. Professor of English. m. 28 Nov 1970, 1 daughter. Education: BA, 1966, Pennsylvania State University; MA, 1967, Harvard University. Appointments: English Faculty, Pennsylvania State University, 1969; Professor of English and Director of Creative Writing, University of Miami, Florida. Publications: Poetry: After Our War, 1974; Blue Mountain, 1982; Words For My Daughter, 1991; Translation: Ca Dao Vietnam, 1980; Fiction: Coming Down Again, 1985; The Hawk's Tale, 1988; Memoir: Remembering Heaven's Face, 1991; Prose: Vietnam: The Land We Never Knew, 1989; Co-editor, Poets of Bulgaria, 1986. Contributions to: Hudson Review; American Poetry Review; Southern Review; American Scholar. Honours: Lamont Selection, Academy of American Poets, 1974; Nomination, National Book Award, 1975; Fulbright, NEH, NEA Fellowships, 1976, 1971, 1978, 1986; National Poetry Series Selection, 1991. Memberships: American PEN; Poetry Society of America; American Literary Translators Association. Literary Agent: Sanford Greenbuger Associates, New York. Address: University of Miami, Department of English, PO Box 248145, Coral Gables, Florida 33124, USA.

BALFOUR Michael (Leonard Graham), b. 1908, British. Appointments: Lecturer, Politics, Magdalen College, Oxford, 1932-36; Study Group Secretary, Royal Institute of International Affairs, 1936-39; Principal, Ministry of Information, 1939-42; Deputy Director of Intelligence, Political Warfare, Executive, 1942-44; Deputy Chief, Intelligence Section, Psychological Warfare Division, SHAEF, 1944-45; Director of Information Services Control, British Control Commission for Germany, 1945-47; Chief Information Officer, Board of Trade, 1947-64; Professor of European History, University of East Anglia, Norwich, 1966-74. Publications: Nationalism, 1939; States and Mind, 1952; Four-Power Control in Germany 1945-6, 1956; The Kaiser and His Times, 1964; West Germany, 1968; Helmuth von Moltke: A Leader Against Hitler, 1972; Propaganda in War 1939-45, 1979; The Adversaries: America, Russia and the Open World 1941-62, 1981; West Germany: A Contemporary History, 1982; Britain and Joseph Chamberlain, 1985; Withstanding Hitler, 1988. Honours: CBE, 1963. Address: Waine's Cottage, Swan Lane, Burford OX8 4SH, England.

BALL B N. See: **BALL Brian Neville.**

BALL Brian Neville (B N Ball), b. 1932, British. Staff Member, subsequently Senior Lecturer in English, Doncaster College of Education, 1956-; Chairman, Doncaster Prose and Poetry Society, 1968-70. Publications: Mr Tofat's Term, Tales of Science Fiction (as B N Ball), 1964; (as Brian Kinsey Jones) Sundog, 1965; Basic Linguistics for Secondary Schools, 3 vols (as B N Ball), 1966-67; Paris Adventures (as B N Ball), 1967; Timepiece, Timepivot and Timepit, 1968-71; Lay Down Your Wife for Another, Lesson for the Damned, 1971; Night of the Robots (in the US as The Regiments of Night), Devil's Peak, The Probability Man, 1972; Planet Probability, Singularity Station, 1973; Death of a Low Handicap Man, Montenegrin Gold, The Venomous Serpent (in the US as The Night Creature), 1974; The Space Guardians, Keegan: The No-Option Contract, Princess Priscilla (as B N Ball), 1975; Jackson's Friend, Jackson's House, Jackson's Holiday (as B N Ball), 1975-77; Keegan: The One-Way Deal, Witchfinder: The Mark of the Beast, 1976; Witchfinder: The Evil at Monteine, 1977; (as B N Ball), Jackson and the Magpies, 1978; The Witch in Our Attic, Young Person's Guide to UFO's, 1979; Dennis and the Flying Saucer, 1980; The Baker Street Boys, The Starbuggy, 1983; The Doornship of Drax, 1985; Truant from Space, 1985; Look Out, Duggy Dog! 1987; BMX Billy, 1986; Frog Island Summer, 1987; I'm Lost, Duggy Dog! 1987; The Quest for Queenie, 1988; Cat in the Custard, 1988; Stone Age Magic, 1989; Hop It, Duggy Dog! 1989; Bella at the Ballet, 1990; Cat in the Classroom, 1990; Come Back, Duggy Dog, 1991; The Mermaid and the Dolphins, 1991; Mrs Potts' New Pets, in Let's Join In, The 'Jenny' tales, in Here Comes Pob and Pob and Friends and various others in anthologies in the US and the UK; Various reviews and articles for the Guardian and Times Educational Supplement, BBC, Jackanory...televising of The Witch in Our Attic, 1979; Channel 4, in Pob's Programme, televising of the Jenny's stories, 1987-88; BBC Education various playlets in the Let's Join In, programme, 1979. Address: c/o Hamish Hamilton Ltd, 27 Wrights Lane, London W8 5TZ, England.

BALLANTYNE Sheila, b. 26 July 1936, Seattle, Washington, USA. Writer; Teacher. m. Philip Speilman, 22 Dec 1963, 1 son, 1 daughter. Education: Mills College, Oakland, California, USA, BA. Appointments: Dominican College, 1983; Mills College, 1984-; Bay Area Writers Workshop, 1988, 1989. Publications: Norma Jean The Termite Queen; Imaginary Crimes; Life on Earth. Contributions to: The New Yorker; American Review; Prize Stories: The O Henry Awards; Short Story International; Aphra. Honours include: O'Henry award; MacDowell Colony Fellowship; John Simon Guggenheim Fellowship; National Women's Political Caucus Distinguished Achievement Award. Memberships: Authors Guild; National Writers Union; PEN. Address: Department of English, Mills College, 5000 MacArthur Boulevard, Oakland, CA 94613, USA.

BALLARD James Graham, b. 15 Nov 1930, Shanghai, China. Novelist; Short Story Writier. m. Helen Mary Mathews, 1954, Dec 1964, 1 s, 2 d. Education: King's College, Cambridge. Publications include: The Drowned World, 1963; The Terminal Beach, 1964; The Drought, 1965; The Crystal World, 1966; The Disaster Area, 1967; Crash, 1973; Vermilion Sands, 1973; Concrete Island, 1974; High Rise, 1975; Low Flying Aircraft, 1976; The Unlimited Dream Company, 1979; Myths of the Near Future, 1982; Empire of the Sun, 1984; The Day of Creation, 1987; Running Wild, 1988; War Forever, 1990; The Kindness of Women, 1991; The Best Short Stories of J G Ballard, 1978; Myths of the Near Future, 1982; Memories of the Space Age, 1988; War Fever, 1990. Honours: Guardian Fiction Prize, 1984; James Tait Black Prize, 1984. Address: 36 Old Charlton Road, Shepperton, Middlesex, England.

BALLARD Juliet Lyle Brooke, b. 6 Feb 1913. Poet; Editor; Prose Writer. Education: AB, Randolph-Macon Woman's College, 1934; Certificate of Social Case Work, Richmond Professional Institute, 1938. Literary Appointments: Associate Editor, Association for Research and Enlightment Journal, 1966-70; Associate Editor, Association for Research and Enlightenment Children's Magazine, 1970; Editor, Treasure Trove (Association for Research and Enlightenment Children's Quarterly), 1971-73. Publications include: Major works, Under a Tropic Sun, 1945; Winter Has Come, 1945; The Ballad of the Widow's Flag (official poem of the Star-Spangled Banner Flag House Association, Baltimore, Maryland), 1956; Prose Works: The Hidden Laws of Earth, 1979; Treasures from Earth's Storehouse, 1980; The Art of Living, 1982; retitled Unto the Hills, 1987; Research Bulletin, Pilgrimage into the Light, Vols I, II & III, issued by the Edgar Cayce Foundation, 1988, Vol IV, 1989; translation of The Hidden Laws of

Earth into Japanese by Chuo Art Shuppan Sha, 1989. Address: 2217 Wake Forest Street, Virginia Beach, VA 23451, USA.

BALLE Solvej, b. 16 Aug 1962, Denmark. Prose Writer. m. Ole Kiehn, 9 Sept 1990. Education: Studies in Philosophy, Literature, University of Copenhagen, 1984-; The Writers' School, Copenhagen, 1987-89. Literary Appointments: Co-Editor, Den Bla Port, Literary Magazine, 1994-. Publications: Lyrefugl, 1986; Prose Poetry, 1990; According to the Law, short stories, 1993. Memberships: Danish PEN. Literary Agent: L & R, Kristianiagade 14, 2100 Copenhagen, Denmark. Address: Bakkehuset, Rahbeks Allé 23, 1801 Frederiksberg C, Denmark.

BALLEM John Bishop, b. 2 Feb 1925, New Glasgow, Nova Scotia, Canada. Lawyer. m. Grace Louise Flavelle, 31 Aug 1951, 2 sons, 1 daughter. Education: BA 1946, MA 1948, LLB 1949, Dalhousie University, Halifax, Nova Scotia; LLM 1950, Harvard University Law School, Boston, Massachusetts. Publications: The Devil's Lighter, 1973; Dirty Scenario, 1974; Judas Conspiracy, 1976; The Moon Pool, 1978; Sacrifice Play, 1981; Marigot Run, 1983; Oilpatch Empire, 1985; The Oil and Gas Lease in Canada, textbook, 2 ed 1985; Death Spiral, 1989; The Barons, 1991. Contributions to: Numerous legal articles in: The Canadian Bar Review; The Alberta Law Review; and others. Honour: Appointed Queen's Counsel in 1966; Awarded Honorary Doctor of Laws Degree, University of Calgary, 1993. Memberships: Writers Guild of Alberta; Writer's Union of Canada; Crime Writers of Canada; Calgary Writers Association; Member International Bar Association; The Bars of Nova Scotia, Ontario and Alberto; The Law Society of Alberta; Phi Delta Theta. Address: 4000, 150 6th Avenue SW, Calgary, Alberta, T2P 3Y7, Canada.

BALY Elaine Vivienne. See: BROWNING Vivenne.

BANCROFT Anne, b. 17 Apr 1923, London, England. Author. 2 sons, 2 daughters. Publications: Twentieth Century, Mystics and Sages, 1976, Republished 1989; Religions of the East, 1974; Zen: Direct Pointing to Reality, 1980; The Luminous Vision, Republished 1989; Six Medieval Mystics, 1981; Chinse New Year, 1984; Festivals of the Buddha, 1984; The Buddhist World, 1984; The New Religious World, 1985; Origins of the Sacred: The Spiritual Way in Western Tradition, 1987; Weavers of Wisdom, 1989. Contributions to: The Middle Way; Everyman's Encyclopedia; Women in the World's Religions. Memberships: The Society of Authors; Society of Women Writers and Journalists. Address: 1 Grange Villas, The Street, Charmouth, Bridport, Dorset DT6 6QQ, England.

BANCROFT Iris (Julia Barnright, Iris Brent, Andrea Layton), b. 1922, American. Writer. Appointments: Bookeeper then Garment union organizer, Chicago, 1945-50; Teacher, Chicago area, 1957-62; Publishing, CA, 1962-77. Publications: The Sexually Exiting Female, The Sexually Superior Male (both as J Barnright), 1971; Swinger's Diary (as I Brent), 1973; (as A Layton) Love's Gentle Fugitive, So Wild a Rapture, 1978; Midnight Fires, Love's Burning Flame, 1979; Rapture's Rebel, 1980; Rebel's Passion, Dawn of Desire (Iris Bancroft) Whispering Hope, 1981; The Five Minute Phobia Cure (with Roger Callahan), Any Man Can (with William Hartman and Marilyn Fithian), 1984; Sex and Single Parent (with Mary Mattis), Reaching Intimacy (with Jerry DeHaan), 1986. Address: c/o Sandy Watt & Associates, 8033 Sunset Boulevard, Los Angeles, CA 90046, USA.

BANDELE THOMAS Biyi, b. 13 Oct 1967, Kafanchan, Nigeria. Education: Dramatic Arts, Obafemi Awolowo University, ILE IFE, 1987-90. Appointments: Associate Writer, Royal Court Theatre, London, 1992-; Writer in Residence, Talawa Theatre Company, 1993. Publications: The Man Who Came in From the Back of Beyond; The Sympathetic Undertaker and Other Dreams; Incantations On The Eve of An Execution; Plays inc, Rain; Marching for Fausa; Death Catches the Hunter; Screenplay, Not Even God is Wise Enough, 1993; Radio, The Remale God, 1993; The Will of Allah, 1994. Contributions to: West Africa. Honours: International Student Playscript Competition; Arts Council Writers Bursary; LWT plays for Stage Award, 1993. Memberships: Society of Authors; Writers Guild; PEN. Literary Agent: MBA. Address: 45 Fitzroy Str, London W1P 5HR, England.

BANI-SADR Abol-Hassan, b. 22 Mar 1933, Hamadan, Iran. Researcher; Writer; Economist; Politician, Ministry of Economy; Ministry of Foreign Affairs, Iran 1979; President of the Republic, Iran 1980. Education: Degrees in Islamic Law and Economic Sciences, Tehran University. Publications include: The Betrayed Hope; Women and Conjugal Life (in the Koran); The Koran and Human Rights; The Directing Principles of Islam; My Turn to Speak; Petrol and Violence; Which Revolution for Iran? Asian Politics (collective works). Contributions to and founder of the newspaper, Islamic Revolution, 1979-. Address: 5 Rue du General Pershing, 78000 Versailles, France.

BANKOFF George. See: **MILKOMANE George Alexis Milkomanovich.**

BANKS Brian (Robert), b. 4 Oct 1956, Carshalton, Surrey, England. Antiquarian Bookseller. m. Catherine Walton, 28 Sept 1987, 1 son, 2 daughters. Education: Westminister College; Middlesex Polytechnic. Publications: The Image of J-K Huysmans, 1990; Phantoms of the Belle Epoque, 1993 (Introduction by Colin Wilson); Atmosphere and Attitudes (poems), 1993; Contributor to Encyclopaedia of the 1980s, 1993. Contributions to: (Yeats Society); Nuit Iris; Book and Magazine Collector. Memberships: Societe de J K Huysmans, Paris; 1890's Society. Address: c/o 4 Meretune Court, Martin Way, Morden, Surrey SM4 4AN, England.

BANKS James Albert, b. 1941, American. Professor. Appointments: Assistant Professor 1969-71, Associate Professor 1971-73, Professor of Education 1973-, Chairman of the Department of Curriculum and Instruction, 1982-, University of Washington, Seattle; National Council for the Social Studies, 1982. Publications: Teaching the Black Experience: Methods and Materials, March Toward Freedom: A History of Black Americans, 1970, 2nd edition (with Cherry A Banks), 1978; Teaching Social Studies to Culturally Different Children (edition with William W Joyce), Teaching the Language Arts to Culturally Different Children (with W Joyce), 1971; Black Self-Concept (edition with Jean D Grambs), 1972; Teaching Ethnic Studies, Teaching Strategies for the Social Studies, 1973, 3rd edition 1985; Teaching Strategies for Ethnic Studies, 1975, 4th edition 1987; Curriculum Guidelines for Multiethnic Education (with others), 1976; Multiethnic Education: Practices and Promises, 1971; Multiethnic Education: Theory and Practice, 1981, 1988; Education in the 80's: Multiethnic Education, 1981; We Americans: Our History and People, 2 volumes (with Sebesta), 1982; Multicultural Education in Western Societies (with James Lynch), 1986; An Introduction to Multiculture Education, 1993. Address: 115 Miller Hall-DQ-12, University of Washington, Seattle, WA 98195, USA.

BANKS Lynne Reid, b. 31 July 1929, London, England. Writer; Actress. m. Chaim Stephenson, 1965, 3 s. Education: Royal Academy of Dramatic Art, 1947-49. Publications include: The L Shaped Room; An End to Running; Children At the Gate; The Backward Shadow; Two is Lonely; Casualties; Dark Quartet; For children: The Indian in the Cupboard; Return of the Indian; Secret of the Indian; Mystery of the Cupboard and others; For young adults: Writing on the Wall; One More River; Melusine; Broken Bridge and Others; Plays for stage, TV and radio include: Travel of Yoshi and the Tea-Kettle. Contributions to; Sunday Telegraph, Telegraph, Independant, Guardian, Times, Times Educational Supplement, Observer, Jewish Chronicle. Literary Agent: Watson Little Limited. Address: 12 Egbert Str, London NW1 8LJ, England.

BANKS Russell, b. 28 Mar 1940, Newton, Massachusetts, USA. Novelist. 4 daughters. Education: BA, highest honours, English, University of North Carolina. Publications include: Searching for Survivors, 1975; Family Life, 1975; Hamilton Stark, 1978; The New World, 1978; The Book of Jamaica, 1980; Trailerpark, 1982; The Relation of my Imprisonment, 1984; Continental Drift, 1985; Success Stories, 1986; Affliction, 1989; Sweet Hereafter, 1992. Contributions to: New York Times Book Review; Washington Post; American Review; Vanity Fair; Antaeus; Partisan Review; New England Review; Fiction International; Boston Globe Magazine. Honours include: Best American Short Stories, 1971, 1985; Fels Award, fiction, 1974; Prize story, O Henry Awards, 1975; Guggenheim Fellow, 1976; NEA Fellowships, 1977, 1983; St Lawrence Award, fiction, 1976; John dos Passos Award, 1986; Pulitzer Prize nominee, 1986; Award, American Academy of Arts & Letters, 1986. Memberships: Executive, PEN American Centre; Board 1968-71, Secretary 1970-71, Coordinating Council of Literary Magazines. Literary Agent: Ellen Levine. Address: c/o Ellen Levine Literary Agency, 432 Park Avenue South, Suite 1205, New York, NY 10016, USA.

BANNON Paul. See: **DURST Paul.**

BANTOCK Gavin (Marcus August), b. 1939, British. Professor. Appointments: Professor of English, Reitaku University, Japan, 1969-. Publications: Christ: A Poem in Twenty-Six Parts, 1965; Juggernaut, The Last of the Kings: Frederick the Great, 1968; A New Thing Breathing, 1969; Anhaga, 1970; Gleeman, 1972; Eirenikon, 1973; Isles, 1974; Dragons, 1979. Address: c/o Peter Jay, 69 King George Street, London SE10 8PX, England.

BANTOCK Geoffrey Herman, b. 12 Oct 1914, Emeritus Professor of Education. m. Dorothy Jean Pick, 6 Jan 1950. Education: BA, 1936, MA, 1942, Emmanuel College, Cambridge. Publications: Freedom & Authority in Education, 1952; L H Myers, A Critical Study, 1956; Education & Values, 1965; Education, Culture & The Emotions, 1967; Culture, Industrialisation & Education, 1968; Education in an Industrial Society, 1968; T S Eliot & Education, 1970; Dilemmas of the Curriculum, 1980; Studies in the History of Educational Theory, 1980, 84; Parochialism of the Present, 1981. Contributions to: Scrutiny; Cambridge Journal; Essays in Criticism; ELH; TES; Listener and Numerous Other Journals. Honour: Awarded Book Prize of Standing Conference in Education Studies for Best Book on Education Published in 1984. Address: Old Rectory, Melton Road, Rearsby, Leics LE7 4YS, England.

BANTOCK Nick, b. Worcestershire, England. Book jacket illustrator; Writer. Publications include: The Missing Nose Flute, 1991; Wings: A Pop-Up Book of Things that Fly, 1991; Runners, Sliders, Bouncers, Climbers, 1992; The Egyptian Jukebox, 1993. Contributions to: Illustrations for the New York Review of Books.

BANVILLE John, b. 8 Dec 1945, Wexford, Ireland. Author. m. Janet Dunham, 2 s. Education: Christian Brothers Schhol; St Peters College, Wexford. Appointments: Literary Editor, The Irish Times, Dublin, 1988. Publications: Nightspawn, 1971; Birchwood, 1973; Doctor Copernicus, 1976; Kepler, 1983; The Newton Letter: An Interlude, 1985; Mefisto, 1987; The Book of Evidence, 1989; Ghosts, 1993. Contributions to: Reviews for the Observer; NY Review of books; The Irish Times. Literary Agent: Anthony Sheil, Sheil Land Associates Limited. Address: 6 Church Street, Howth, Co Dublin, Ireland.

BARANCZAK Stanislaw, b. 13 Nov 1946, Poznan, Poland. Poet; Professor. Education: MA, 1969, PhD, 1973, Adam Mickiewicz University at Poznan. Appointments include: Professor at Harvard University, Cambridge, Massachusetts, USA, from 1984. Publications : Proofreading of a Face, 1968; In One Breath, 1970; A Morning Diary: Poems 1967-1971; I Know it is Not Right: Poems 1975-76; Artificial Breathing, 1978; A Tryptych of Cement, Exhaustion and Snow, 1980; Poems Almost Collected, 1981; Atlantis and Other Verses, from 1981-85; A Postcard from this World and Other Rhymes, 1986-88; The Weight of the Body: Selected Poems, 1989; 159 wierszy: 1968-88; A Fugitive from Utopia: The Poetry of Zbigniew Herbert, 1987; Breathing Under Water and Other East European Essays, 1990; Editions and translations of poetry, including Donne and Hopkins, and plays by Shakespeare. Honours include: Polish PEN Club Award, 1990. Address: Deaprtment of Slavic Languages, 301 Boylston Hall, Harvard University, Cambridge, MA 02138, USA.

BARBALET Margaret Evelyn Hardy, b. 19 Dec 1949, Adelaide, South Australia. Writer. m. Jack Barbalet, 5 Dec 1970, 3 sons, div 1989. Publications: Adelaide Children's Hospital 1876-1976, 1976; Far From a Low Gutter Girl, 1983; Blood in the Rain, novel, 1986; Various short stories published Canberra Tales, 1988; Steel Beach, novel, 1988; The Wolf, picture, Puffin, 1991; Lady, Baby Gypsy Queen, novel, 1992. Honours: Literature Grant, 1985; New Writers Fellowship, 1986. Memberships: Australian Society of Authors; Amnesty International. Address: c/o Penguin Books, PO Box 257, Ringwood, Victoria 3134, Australia.

BARBER Charles Laurence, b. 20 Apr 1915, Harold Wood, Essex, England. University Teacher. Retired. m. Barbara Best, 27 July 1943, 2 s, 2 d. Education: BA, St Catharines College, Cambridge University, 1937; MA, 1941; Teachers Diploma, University of London, 1938; PhD, University of Gothenburg, Sweden, 1957. Publications: Best Known: The Idea of Honour in the English Drama, 1957; The Story of Language, 1964; Linguistic Change in Present Day English, 1964; Early Modern English, 1976; Poetry in English, An Introduction, 1983; The Theme of Honours Tongue, 1985; The English Language: a Historical Introduction, 1993; Others, Editor of Works by Thomas Middleton, A Trick to Catch the Old One, 1968; Women Beware Women, 1969; A Chaste Maid in Cheapside, 1969; Shakespeare,

Henry V, 1980; As You Like It, 1981; Richard III, 1981; Richard II, 1987. Contributions to: Numerous Articles in Learned Journals. Address: 7 North Parade, Leeds, West Yorkshire, LS16 5AY, England.

BARBER Lynn, b. 22 May 1944, England. Journalist. m. David Cloudesley Cardiff, 1 Sept 1971, 2 daughters. Education: BA Honours, English, Oxford University. Appointments: Assistant Editor, Penthouse Magazine, 1968-73; Staff Feature Writer, Sunday Express Magazine, 1984-89; Feature Writer, Independent on Sunday, 1990-. Publications: How to Improve Your Man in Bed, 1970; The Penthouse Sexindex, 1973; The Single Women's Sexbook, 1975; The Heyday of Natural History, 1980. Honours: British Press Awards as Magazine Writer of the Year, 1986, 1987. Address: Independent on Sunday, 40 City Road, London EC1Y 2DH, England.

BARBER Richard William, b. 30 Oct 1941, Publisher; Author. m. Helen Tolson, 7 May 1970, 1 s, 1 d. Education: Trevelyan Scholar, BA, MA, PhD, 1982; Corpus Christi College, Cambridge University. Publications include: The Knight and Chivalry, 1972; Arthur of Albion, 1961; Edward Prince of Wales & Aquitaine, 1976; Companion Guide to South West France, 1977; Tournaments, 1978; The Penguin Guide to Medieval Europe, 1984; Tournaments: Jousts, Chivalry and Pageants in the Middle Ages, 1989; The Arthurian Legends, 1979; Fuller's Worthies, 1987; The Worlds of John Aubrey, 1988; Pilgrimages, 1991. Contributions to: Arthurian Literature. Honours: Somerset Maugham Award, 1972; Times Higher Educational Supplement Book Award, 1978. Memberships: Royal Society of Literature; Royal Historical Society; Society of Antiquaries. Address: Stangrove Hall, Alderton, Nr Woodbridge, Suffolk IP12 3BL, England.

BARBET Pierre Claude Avice (David Maine, Olivier Sprigel), b. 16 May 1925, Le Mans, France. Science Fiction Writer. m. Marianne, 23 July 1952, 2 sons, 1 daughter. Education: Pharmacist, University of Paris, 1953; Diplomas of Bacteriology and Serology, Parasitology, University of Paris, 1954; PhD, Summa cum laude, Institut Pasteur, Faculte de Pharmacie, University of Paris, 1955. Appointments: Libraries Gallimard, 1962-63; Fleuve Noir, 1966-87; Albin Michel, 1972-82; Champs Elysees, 1976-78. Publications: 72 Novels published; Cosmic Crusaders; Games psybords Play; Napoleon and Emperor of Eridanus; Joan of Arc Replay; Enchanted Planet; Rome doit se detruite and Carthage sera detruite; Survivants de l'apocalypse - Glaciation nucleaire; Cities de l'espace, serial; Venusine - Defense spatiale - Un Reich de 1000 ans; Invasion cosmique - Alex Courville, serial. Contributor to: Horizons de Fantastique; Grande Encyclopedie de Fantastique et de la SF, Italy. Honours: Prix, Ailes d'or du Fantastique, pour son oeuvre de SF; et pour son travail dans l'organisation de la Societe Europeenne de SF, International Institute of SF, Poznana, Poland. Memberships: Co-ordinator, European Society of Science Fiction, 1979-89; Vice President, Francophone Society of SF member of Board, World SF Society; Director, Overseas, The Science Fiction Writers of America; International Association of Critics; Secretary, The French Society of Doctours en Pharmacie; Corresponding Member, the European Academy of Arts, Letters, Science. Address: 4 Square de l'avenue du Bois, 75116 Paris, France.

BARBOSA Miguel, b. 22 Nov 1925, Lisbon, Portugal. Writer; Painter. Education: Economics & Finance, University of Lisbon. Publications: Short Stories: Retalhos de Vida, 1955; Manta de Trapos, 1962; Plays: O Palheiro, 1963; Os Carnivoros, 1964, 1973; O Piquenique, 1964, 1973; O Insecticida, 1965, 1974; A Mulher que Paris a France, 1971; Los profetas de la Paja, 1973; How New York was Destroyed by Rats, 1977; The Materialisation of Love, 1978; Novels: Trineu do Morro, 1972, 1975; Mulher Macumba, 1973; A Pileca no Poleiro, 1976; As Confissoes de Um Cacador de Dinossauros, 1981; Esta Louca Profissao de Escritor, 1983; Cartas a Um Fogo-Fatuo, 1985. Contributor to: various publications. Honours: 1st Prize, Maria Terza Alves Viana Theatre, Sao Paulo, Brazil; Prix Nu, Jubile Mondial d'arts Plastiques, Nice, France, 1984; Honourable Mention, Le Quadriennale Mondiale des Beaux Arts, Lyon, France, 1985; Medaille D'Argent, Academie de Lutece, Paris, 1987; Prix de La Revue D'Art, La Cote des Arts, Cannes, 1990. Address: Avenue Joao Crisostomo 9-12, Lisbon 1000, Portugal.

BARBOUR Douglas, b. 1940, Canadian. Professor. Appointments: Assistant Professor 1969-77, Associate Professor 1977-81, Professor 1982-, University of Alberta, Edmonton; Poetry Editor, Canadium Forum, 1978-80; Former Editor, Quarry Magazine, Kingston, Ontario. Publications: Land Fall, A Poem as Long as the Highway, 1971; White, 1972; Songbook, 1973; He & She &, 1974;

Visions of My Grandfather, 1977; Shore Lines, 1979; Vision/Sounding, 1980; The Pirates of Pen's Chance (with Stephen Scobie), The Maple Laugh Forever: An Anthology of Canadian Comic Poetry, 1981; Writing Right: Poetry by Canadian Women, 1982; Three Times Five: Short Stories by Harris, Sawai, Stenson, 1983; Selected and New Poems by Richard Sommer, The Harbingers, Visible Visions: The Selected Poems of Douglas Barbour, 1984; Tesseracts II, 1987; Story for a Saskatchewan Night, 1990; Beyond Tish, 1991; Michael Ondaatje, 1993. Address: 11655-72 Avenue, Edmonton, Alberta T6G 0B9, Canada.

BARCUCHELLO Gianfranco, b. 29 Aug 1924, Livorno. Publications: Numerous Publications from 1966-92 inc, Dall'archivio dei Cinque Cuori; Al Polo Nord, rotolando. Creative Works: 13 Film & Videos inc, Punto di Fuga; Cinque esercizi di Mesia Difficolta; Numerous One Man Exhibitions, 1963-92. Address: 18 Rue Linne, Paris, France.

BARDIS Panos Demetrios, b. 24 Sept 1924, Arcadia, Greece. Editor; Author; Professor; Poet; Social Philosopher; Historian of Science; Sociologist; Classicist; Linguist. m. Donna Jean Decker, 26 Dec 1964, 2 sons. Education: Diploma, Lyceum, Langadia, Arcadia, 1942; Panteios Supreme School, Athens, 1945-47; BA magna cum laude, Bethany College, West Virginia, USA, 1950; MA, Notre Dame University, Indiana, 1953; PhD, Purdue University, Indiana, 1955. Appointments include: Currently Professor of Sociology, University of Toledo, Ohio; Editor, Book Review Editor, International Social Science Review; Editor-in-Chief, Book Review Editor, International Journal on World Peace; Associate Editor or Book Review Editor, about 40 other journals. Publications include: Ivan and Artemis, novel, 1957; The Family in Changing Civilizations, 1967, 1969; Encyclopedia of Campus Unrest, 1971; History of the Family, 1975; Studies in Marriage and the Family, 1975; 1978; History of Thanatology, 1981; Atlas of Human Reproductive Anatomy, 1983; Evolution of the Family in the West, 1983; Global Marriage and Family Customs, 1983; Marriage and Family, 1988; South Africa and the Marxist Movement, 1989; Nine Oriental Muses, 1983; Ode to Orion: An Epic Poem in Twenty Rhapsodies, 1995. Contributions to: Hundreds of articles, reviews, poems in academic and professional journals, newspapers, magazines. Address: University of Toledo, Toledo, OH 43606, USA.

BAREHAM Terence, b. 17 Oct 1937, Clacton-on-Sea, Essex, England. University Professor. Education: Open Scholar & State Scholar 1959-62, BA (Hons) 1962, MA 1969, Lincoln College, Oxford University, England; DPhil, Ulster University, Northern Ireland, 1977. Publications: George Crabbe: A Critical Study, 1977; George Crabbe: A Bibliography (joint author), 1978; The Art of Anthony Trollope, 1980; Anthony Trollope (Casebook Series), 1982; Tom Stoppard (Casebook Series), 1989; Malcolm Lowry, 1989; Charles Lever: New Evaluations (ed), 1991; York Notes, Monographs on Robert Bolt, T S Eliot, Shakespeare. Contributions to: Numerous on literature of 17th - 20th Century. Address: c/o Dept of English, University of Ulster, Coleraine, Co Derry, Northern Ireland.

BARER Burl, b. 8 Aug 1947, Walla Walla, Washington, USA. Writer. m. Britt Johnsen, 2 Mar 1974, 1 son, 1 daughter. Education: Communications, University of Washington. Publications: Selections from the Holy Quran, 1987; The Saint, 1993; Maverick, 1994; Man Overbaord: The Counterfeit Resurrection of Phil Champagne, 1994. Contributions to: The Epistle; Oxford Companion to Mystery and Detective Fiction. Honours: Edgar Award, 1994. Membership: Mystery Writers of America. Literary Agent: David Hiatt Agency. Address: 1839 Crestline Drive, Walla Walla, WA 99362, USA.

BARKER Audrey Lilian, b. 13 Apr 1918, St Pauls Cray, Kent, England. Author. Appointments: Staff, Amalgamated Press, 1936; Reader, Cresset Press, 1947; Secretary, Sub Editor, BBC, London, 1948-78. Publications include: Innocents, 1947; The Middling, 1967; John Browns Body, 1969; Life Stories, 1981; No Word of Love, 1985; The Gooseboy, 1987; The Woman Who Talked to Herself, 1989; Any Excuse for a Party: Selected Stories, 1991; Zeph, 1991. Contributions: to many short story Anthologies including: Twelve Stories by Famous Women Writers; Tales to Make the Flesh Creep; Magazines including: Harpers; Good Housekeeping; Woman and Beauty. Honours: Atlantic Award in Literature, 1946; Somerset Maugham Award, 1947; Cheltenham Festival Award, 1963; Arts Council Award, 1970; SE Arts Creative Book Award, 1981. Memberships: Fellow Royal Society of Literature; English PEN. Literary Agent: Jennifer Kavanagh. Address: 103 Harrow Road, Carshalton, Surrey, England.

BARKER Dennis, b. 21 June 1929, Lowestoft, England. Journalist; Novelist. m. Sarah Katherine Alwyn, 1 daughter. Education: National Diploma in Journalism, 1959. Appointments: Reporter & Sub-Editor, Suffolk Chronicle & Mercury, Ipswich, 1947-48; Reporter, Feature Writer, Theatre & Film Critic, 1948-58, East Anglian Daily Times; Estates & Property Columnist, 1958-63, Express & Star, Wolverhampton; Midlands Correspondent, 1963-67, Reporter, Feature Writer, Columnist, The Guardian, 1967-91, (contributor). Publications: Novels: Candidate of Promise, 1969; The Scandalisers, 1974; Winston Three Three Three, 1987; Non-fiction: The People of the Forces Trilogy (Soldiering On 1971, Ruling the Waves 1986, Guarding the Skies 1989); One Man's Estate, 1983; Parian Ware, 1985; Fresh Start, 1990. Contributions to: BBC; Punch; East Anglian Architecture & Building Review (editor and editorial director, 1956-58); The Guardian, 1991-. Memberships: National Union of Journalists, secretary Suffolk Branch, 1953-58, Chairman 1958; Chairman, Home Counties District Council, 1956-57; Life Member, 1991; Life Member, Newspaper Press Fund; Writers Guild of Great Britain; Broadcasting Press Guild; The Society of Authors. Address: 67 Speldhurst Road, London W4 1BY, England.

BARKER Howard, b. 1946, British. Appointment: Resident, Dramatist, Open Space Theatre, London, 1974-75. Publications: Stripwell, with Claw, 1977; Fair Slaughter, 1978; That Good Between Us with Credentials of a Sympathiser, The Love of a Good Man with All Bleeding, 1980; The Hand of the Gaol with Heaven, Two Plays for the Right: Birth on a Hard Shoulder and the Loud Boy's Life, No End of Blame: Scenes of Overcoming, 1981; The Castle/Scenes from an Execution, Victory, 1984; Crimes in Hot Countries/Fair Slaughter, The Power of the Dog: Movements in History and Anti-History, A Passion in Six Days/Downchild, 1985; Don't Exaggerate, 1986; The Possibilities, 1987; The Bite of the Night, 1987; The Last Supper, 1988; Women Beware Women, 1988; Seven Lears/Golgo, 1989; The Europeans/Judith, 1990; Collected Plays, Volume I, 1990; Poems - The Breath of the Crowd, 1987; Garry the Thief, 1988; Lullabies for Impatient, 1988; The Ascent of Monte Grappa, 1990. Address: Judy Daish Ass, 83 Eastbourne Mews, Brighton, Sussex, England.

BARKER Nicola, b. 1966, England. Author. Education: Read Philosophy and English, Cambridge University, England. Appointments: BBC Radio 4; Regular reviewer for The Observer. Publications: Short Stories in The Time Out Book of London Short Stories; Story: Food With Feeling, adapted for BBC, Radio 4; Collection of Short Stories: Love Your Enemies, 1992; Reversed Forecast, 1994. Honours: Winner, David Higham Prize for Fiction; Joint Winner Macmillan Silver PEN Award for Fiction.

BARKER Patricia Margaret, b. 8 May 1943, Thornaby on Tees, England. Writer. m. 29 Jan 1977, 1 s, 1 d. Education: BSc, London School of Economics, 1965. Publications: Union Street, 1982; Blow Your House Down, 1984; The Century's Daughter, 1986; The Man Who Wasn't There, 1989; Regeneration, 1991; The Eye in the Door, 1993. Honours: One of Best of Young British Novelists, 1982; Joint Winner, Fawcett Prize, 1982; Hon M Litt University Teesside, 1993; Guardian Fiction Prize, 1994; Northern Electric Special Arts Award, 1994. Memberships: Society of Authors; PEN. Literary Agent: Aitken, Stone & Wylie, England. Address: c/o Aitken, Stone & Wylie, 29 Fernshaw Road, London, SW10 0TG, England.

BARKER Paul, b. 24 Aug 1935, Halifax, Yorkshire, England. Writer; Broadcaster. m. sally Huddleston, 3 s, 1 d. Education: MA, Oxford University. Appointments include: Editor, New Society, 1968-86; Associate Editor, The Independent Magazine, 1988-90; Director, Advisory Editor, Fiction Magazine, 1982-87; Social Policy Editor, Sunday Telegraph, 1986-88; Visiting Fellow, University of Bath, 1986-; Trustee, 1991-, Fellow, 1992; Institute of Community Studies; Fellow, Royal Society of Arts, 1990; Leverhulme Research Fellow, 1993-; Columnist, London Evening Standard, 1987-92. Publications include: A Sociological Portrait, 1972; One for Sorrow Two for Joy, 1972; Social Sciences Today, 1975; Arts in Society, 1977; The Other Britain, 1982; Founders of the Welfare State, 1985; Britain in the Eighties, 1989; Towards a New Landscape, 1993. Address: 15 Dartmouth Park Ave, London NW5 1JL, England.

BARLOW Frank, b. 19 Apr 1911, Wolstanton, England. Emeritus Professor. m. Moira Stella Brigid Garvey, 1 July 1936, 2 s. Education: MA, D Phil, Hon D Litt, Exon; St Johns College, Oxford, 1929-36. Publications include: The Letters of Arnulf of Lisieux, 1939; Durham Annals and Ducouments of the Thirteenth Century, 1945; Durham Jurisdictional Peculiars, 1950; The Feudal Kingdom of England, 1955,

1988; Vita Aedwardl Regis, 1962, 1992; The English Church, 1000-1066, 1963, 1066-1154, 1979; William I and the Norman Conquest, 1965; Edward the Confessor, 1970, 1979; William Rufus, 1983, 1990; Introduction to Devonshire Domesday Book, 1991. Contributions to: Various Professional Journals. Honours: D Litt, 1981, CBE, 1989. Memberships: British Academy; Royal Society of Literature; Royal Historical Society. Address: Middle Court Hall, Kenton, Exeter, EX6 8NA, England.

BARLTROP Robert Arthur Horace, b. 6 Nov 1922, Walthamstow, England. Writer. m. Mary Gleeson, 18 July 1947, 3 sons. Appointments: Editor, Socialist Standard, 1972-78; Editor, Cockney Ancestor, 1983-86. Publications: The Monument, 1974; Jack London: The Man, the Writer, the Rebel, 1977; The Muvver Tongue, 1980; My Mother's Calling Me, 1984; A Funny Age, 1985; Bright Summer, Dark Autumn, 1986; The Bar Tree, 1979; Revolution - Stories and Essays by Jack London (editor), 1981. Contributor to: Weekly columns and features, Recorder Newspapers, 1985-; Guardian Newspapers; Root; Essex Countryside. Membership: National Union of Journalists. Address: 77 Idmiston Road, Stratford, London E15 1RG, England.

BARNABY Charles Frank, b. 27 Sept 1927, Andover, Hampshire, England. Author. m. 12 Dec 1972, 1 s, 1 d. Education: BSc, 1951, MSc, 1954, PhD, 1960, London University. Publications: Man and the Atom, 1970; Nuclear Energy, 1975; Future Warfare, 1983; Prospects for Peace, 1981; The Automated Battlefield, 1986; Star Wars Brought Down to Earth, 1986; The Invisible Bomb, 1989; The Gaia Peace Atlas, 1989; The Role and Control of Arms in the 1990's, 1993; How Nuclear Weapons Spread, 1993. Contributions to: Ambio; New scientist; Technology Review. Honour: Hon Doctorate, Free University, Amsterdam. Literary Agent: June Hall. Address: Brandreth, Station Road, Chilbolton, Stockbridge, Hampshire SO20 6HW, England.

BARNARD Christian (Neething), b. 1922, South African. Professor. Appointments: Professor Emeritus, University of Cape Town, Head of Cardiac Research and Surgery, 1968-83; Developed the Barnard Valve used in open heart surgery; Performed first successful heart transplant, 1967; First double heart transplant, 1974. Publications: Surgery of the Common Congenital Cardiac Malformations, (C N Barnard and V V Schrire), 1968; One Life, (C N Barnard and Bill Pepper), 1970; Heart Attach - All You Have to Know About It, 1971; The Unwanted, (C N Barnard and S Stander), 1974; South Africa - Sharp Dissertion, 1977; In the Night Season, (C N Barnard and S Stander), 1977; The Best Medicine, 1979; Good Life - Good Death, 1980; The Body Machine, 1981; The Junior Body Machine, (with Christopher Fagg), 1983; The Living Body (with Karl Sabbagh), 1984; Christian Barnard's Programme for Living with Arthritis, (with Peter Evans), 1984; The Arthritis Handbook, 1984; The Living Body, (with Karl Sabbagh), 1984; The Faith, (with S Stander), 1984; The Best of Barnard, (with Bob Mooloy), 1984; Your Healthy Heart, (with Peter Evans), 1985. Address: PO Box 6143, Welgemoed, 7538 Cape Town, South Africa.

BARNARD Robert, b. 23 Nov 1936, Burnham On Crouch, Essex, England. Crime Writer. m. Mary Louise Tabor, 7 Feb 1963. Education: Balliol College, Oxford, 1956-59; Dr Philos, Bergen University, Norway, 1972. Publications include: Death of an Old Goat, 1976; Sheer Torture, 1981; A Corpse in a Gilded Cage, 1984; Out of the Blackout, 1985; Skeleton in the Grass, 1987; At Death's Door, 1988; Death and the Chaste Apprentice, 1989; Masters of the House, 1994. Honours: Seven Times Nominated for Edgar Awards. Memberships: Crime Writers Association; Brontë Society; Society of Authors. Literary Agent: Gregory & Radice. Address: Hazeldene, Houghley Lane, Leeds LS13 2DT, England.

BARNES Christopher John, b. 10 Mar 1942, Sheffield, England. University Professor. m. 2 daughters. Education: Cambridge University, 1960-67; Moscow University, 1963-64; MA, 1967; PhD, 1970. Appointments: Lecturer, University of St Andrews, Scotland, 1967-89; Editor, Radio Liberty, 1974-75; Professor, Chairman, University of Toronto, 1989-. Publications: Boris Pasternak: A Literary Biography; Boris Pasternak: The Voice of Prose; Boris Pasternak: Complete Short Prose; Studies in Twentieth Century Literature; Others include: The Blind Beauty; Pasternak & European Literature. Contributions to: Encounter; Scottish Slavonic Review; Irish Slavonic Studies; TLS; Slavica Hierosolymitana; La Pensee Russe; Forum for Modern Language Studies; Performance; Tempo. Memberships: British University Association of Slavists; Canadian Association of Slavists; American Association for Advancement of Slavic Studies; Royal

Musical Association. Address: Dept of Slavic Languages & Literatures, University of Toronto, 21 Sussex Avenue, Toronto, M5S 1A1, Canada.

BARNES Clive Alexander, b. 13 May 1927, London, England. Journalist; Dance & Theatre Critic. m. 2 children. Education: King's College, London; Oxford University. Appointments include: Town planning officer/freelance journalist, 1952-61; Chief dance critic, The Times, London, 1961-65; Executive editor, Dance & Dancers, Music & Musicians, Plays & Players, 1961-65; Dance critic, New York Times, 1965-78, also drama critic (weekdays) 1967-77; Associate editor, chief dance & drama critic, New York Post, 1978-; New York correspondent, Times (London), 1970. Publications: Ballet in Britain Since the War; Fredrick Ashton & His Ballet; Ballet Here & Now; Dance As It Happened; Dance in the 20th Century; Dance Scene USA; Editor, Nureyev, 1983; (ed) Best American Plays 1983-1992, 1993. Honour: CBE, 1975. Address: 825 West End Avenue, New York, NY 10025, USA.

BARNES Jane Ellen, b. 29 Dec 1943, Brooklyn, New York, USA. Poet; Fiction Writer. Education: BA, Georgia State University, 1966; MA, Boston University, 1978. Appointments: Board, Boston First Night Celebration, 1981; Boston Artists Collaborative, 1987. Publications: Blue Giant Mythologies, 1976; They Say I Talk in My Sleep, 1979; Extremes, 1981; Founder, Publisher, Dark Horse, 1974-80; Founder, Quark Pres, and Blue Giant Press. Contributor to: Harvard Magazine; Hanging Loose; Ploughshares; Dark Horse; 13th Moon; Poetry Now. Honours: Honourable Mention, Fiction, Brace Prize, Boston University, 1978. Memberships: Co-ordinating Council, Literary Magazines; New England Small Press Association. Address: 24 Concord Avenue, Apt 308, Cambridge, MA 02138, USA.

BARNES Julian Patrick (Dan Kavanagh, Basil Seal), b. 19 Jan 1946, Leicester, England. Education: Magdalen College, Oxford, 1964-68. Appointments: Lexicographer, Oxford English Dictionary Supplement, 1969-72; TV Critic, 1977-81, Assistant Literary Editor, 1977-79, New Statesman; Contributing Editor, New Review, 1977-78; Deputy Literary Editor, Sunday Times, 1979-81; TV Critic, The Observer, 1982-86. Publications: Metroland Duffy, 1980; Before She Met Me, 1982; Fiddle City, 1983; Flaubert's Parrot, 1984; Putting the Boot In, 1985; Staring at the Sun, 1986; History of the World in Ten & a Half Chapters, 1989; Talking it Over, 1991. Address: The Chambers, Chelsea Harbour, Lots Road, London SW10 0XF, England.

BARNES Peter, b. 10 Jan 1931, London, England. Writer. m. 28 Aug 1963. Publications: Collected Plays (Vol 1), 1989; The Ruling Class, 1969; Red Noses, 1985; Nobody Here But Us Chickens, 1990; The Spirit of Man, 1990; Sunsets and Glories, 1990. Honours: John Whiting Award, 1969; Evening Standard Award, 1969; Giles Cooper Award, 1981; Olivier Award, 1985; Royal Television Award, 1989. Literary Agent: Margaret Ramsay Ltd. Address: 7 Archery Close, Connaught Street, London W2, England.

BARNETT Arthur Doak, b. 1921, American. Professor. Appointments: Associate Professor 1960-64, Professor 1964-69, Head of Contemporary China Program, 1960-69; Columbia University; Senior Fellow, The Brookings Institution, 1969-82, Emeritus 1982; Professor, Johns Hopkins University School of Advanced International Studies, 1982-90, Emeritus 1990. Publications: Turn East Towards Asia, 1958; Communist Economic Strategy: The Rise of Mainland China, 1959; Communist China and Asia: Challenge to American Policy, 1960; Communist China in Perspective, 1962; Communist Strategies in Asia: A Comparative Analysis of Government and Parties (ed), 1963; China on the Eve of Communist Takeover, 1963; Communist China: The Early Years 1959-55, 1964; The United States and China in World Affairs, by Robert Blum (ed), 1966; China After Mao, Cadres Bureaucracy and Political Power in Communist China, 1967; Chinese Communist Politics in Action (ed), 1969; The United States and China: The Next Decade (ed with E O Reischauer), 1970; A New United States Policy Toward China, 1971; Uncertain Passage: China's Transition to the Post-Mao Era, 1974; China Policy: Old Problems and New Challenges, 1977; China and the Major Powers in East Asia, 1977; China's Economy in Global Perspective, 1981; The FX Decision, 1981; US Arms Sales: The China-Taiwan Tangle, 1982; The Making of Foreign Policy in China: Structure and Process, 1985; Modernizing China: Post-Mao Reform and Development (ed with Ralph N Clough), 1986; After Deng, What? Will China Follow the USSR? 1991; China's Far West, 1994. Address: Johns Hopkins University, SAIS, 1740, Massachusetts Avenue NW, Washington, DC 20036, USA.

BARNETT Correlli (Douglas), b. 1927, British. Author. Fellow of the Royal Society of Literature and the Royal Historical Society. Appointments: Keeper of the Churchill Archives Centre and Fellow, Churchill College, 1977-; Defence Lecturer, Cambridge University, 1980-84. Publications: The Hump Organisation, 1957; The Channel Tunnel (co-author), 1958; The Desert Generals, 1960 (new enlarged edition 1984); The Swordbearers, 1963; The Great War (co-author), 1964; The Lost Peace (co-author), 1966; Britain and Her Army, 1970; The Collapse of British Power, 1972; The Commanders, 1973; Marlborough, 1974; Strategy and Society, 1975; Bonaparte, 1978; The Great War, 1979; The Audit of War, 1986; Engage the Enemy More Closely: The Royal Navy in the Second World War, 1991. Honours: Best Television Documentary Script Award, Screenwriter's Guild, for The Great War; Royal Society of Literature Award for Britain and Her Army; Chesney Gold Medal of the Royal United Services Institute for Defence Studies, 1991; Yorkshire Post Book of the Year Award for Engage the Enemy More Closely, 1991. Address: Catbridge House, East Carleton, Norwich NR14 8JX, England.

BARNETT Paul. See: **BARNETT Paul le Page.**

BARNETT Paul le Page (Paul Barnett, Dennis Brezhnev, Eve Devereux, John Grant), b. 22 Nov 1949, Aberdeen, Scotland. Writer; Freelance Editor. m. Catherine Stewart, 7 July 1974, 1 daughter. Education: Kings & University Colleges, London (no degree), 1967-68. Publications include: As John Grant: Ed, Aries 1, 1979; Ed, Book of Discarded Ideas, 1981; Directory of Possibilities, with Colin Wilson, 1981; A Book of Numbers, 1982; Dreamers, 1983; Truth About the Flaming Ghoulies, 1983; Sex Secrets of Ancient Atlantis, 1985; Depths of Cricket, 1986; Encyclopaedia of Walt Disney's Animated Characters, 1987 (2nd edition 1993); Earthdoom, with David Langford, 1987; The Advanced Trivia Quizbook, 1987; Great Mysteries, 1988; Introduction to Viking Mythology, 1989; Great Unsolved Mysteries of Science, 1989; Eclipse of the Kai, with Joe Dever, 1989; Dark Door Opens, with Joe Dever, 1989; Sword of the Sun, with Joe Dever, 1989; Hunting Wolf, with Joe Dever, 1990; Albion, 1991; Unexplained Mysteries of the World, 1991; Claws of Helgedad, with Joe Dever, 1991; Sacrifice of Ruanon, with Joe Dever, 1991; The World, 1992; Monsters, 1992; Birthplace, with Joe Dever, 1992; Book of the Magnakai, with Joe Dever, 1992; Legends of Lone Wolf Omnibus, with Joe Dever, 1992; Tellings, with Joe Dever, 1993; Lorestone of Varetta, with Joe Dever, 1993; Technical Editor, Encyclopaedia of Science Fiction, by John Clute and Peter Nicholls, 1993; As Eve Devereux: Book of World Flags, 1992. Membership: West Country Writers' Association. Literary Agent: Jane C Judd. Address: 17 Polsloe Road, Exter, Devon EX1 2HL, England.

BARNHART Robert K, b. 17 Oct 1933, Chicago, Illinois, USA. Author; Editor. m. Cynthia Ann Rogers, 16 Sept 1955, 3 sons, 2 daughters. Education: University of the South, BA, 1956. Publications: World Book Dictionary; Barnhart Dictionary of Etymology; Barnhart Dictionaries of New English; American Heritage Dictionary of Science. Contributions to: Dictionaries; World Book Ency; Interntional Encyclopedia of Lexicography. Honour: Association of Publishers Award. Memberships: MLA Dict Society of North America Dialect Society. Address: Banhart Books, Box 479, Brewster, NY 10509, USA.

BARNRIGHT Julia. See: **BANCROFT Iris.**

BARNWELL William (Curtis), b. 1943, American. Professor; Writer. Appointments: Assistant Professor of English, University of South Carolina, Columbia, 1971-77; Writer-in-Residence, Columbia College, 1977-. Publications: The Blessing Papers, 1980; Imram, 1981; Writing for a Reason, 1983; The Resourceful Writer, 1987, 1991. Address: c/o Curtis Brown Limited, 575 Madison Avenue, New York, NY 10022, USA.

BARON J W. See: **KRAUZER Steven M.**

BARR Densil, b. Harrogate, Yorkshire, England. Author. Publications: The Man with Only One Hand, novel, 1955; Death of Four, Presidents, novel, 1991; Radio Plays Broadcast; The Clapham Lamp-Post Saga, 1967, 1968, 1969, 1981, 1990; Gladys on the Wardrobe, 1970, 1971, 1972, 1983, 1990; But Petrovsky Goes on for Ever, 1971, 1972, 1973, 1975, 1985; The Last Tramp, 1972, 1973; The Square at Bastogne, 1974; The Battle of Brighton Beach, 1974; To a Green World Far Away, 1975, 1976, 1977; With Puffins for Pawns, 1976, 1979; Anatomy of an Alibi, 1978, 1982; The Speech, 1979; Two Gaps in the Curtain, 1979, 1982; Klemps Diary, 1980; Who Was Karl

Raeder? 1980; The Boy in the Cellar, 1981; The Glory Hallelujah Microchip, 1982; The Dog that was only a Prophet, 1982, 1983; The Mythical Isles, 1983; St Paul Transferred, 1983. Contributor to: Transatlantic Review; International Storyteller; Kolokon. Memberships: Fellow PEN. Address: 15 Churchfields, Broxbourne, Hertfordshire EN10 7JU, England.

BARR Patricia Miriam, b. 25 Apr 1934, Norwich, Norfolk, England. Writer. Education: BA, University of Birmingham; MA, University College, London. Publications include: The Coming of the Barbarians, 1967; The Deer Cry Pavilion, 1968; A Curious Life for a Laby, 1970; To China with Love, 1972; The Memsahibs, 1976; Taming the Jungle, 1978; Chinese Alice, 1981; Uncut Jade, 1983; Kenjiro, 1985; Coromandel, 1988; The Dust in the Balance, 1989. Honour: Winston Churchill Fellowship for Historical Biography, 1972. Membership: Society of Authors. Literary Agent: Murray Pollinger, 222 Old Brompton Road, London. Address: 6 Mount Pleasant, Norwich NR2 2DG, England.

BARRETT Cathlene Gillespie, b. 14 Aug 1962, Utah, USA. Publisher; Editor. m. Kevin Barrett, 29 Aug 1981, 1 son, 1 daughter. Education: Continuing College Education. Appointments: Chairwomen, Utah State Poetry Society Contest, 1991, 1992; Publisher, Editor, Midge Literary Magazine, 1991-; Judge, Pennsylvania Poetry Society, 1991. Publications: American Poetry Anthology; Treasured Poems of America; Bay Area poets Coalition; Utah State Poetry Society Anthology; Fall, Spring, Winter. Contributions to: Poets at Work; Midge Magazine; Archer; Pro Poets of Satem; Review; Portland University. Honours: Golden poet Award; Honorable mention, Utah State Poetry Society, Poet of the year; 3rd Place, Sparrowgrass Annual Contest; Poet Lawveate Contender. Memberships: Utah State Poetry Society; Utah Cavy Breeders Association. Address: 2330 Tierra Rose Drive, West Jordan, UT 84084, USA.

BARRETT Charles Kingsley, b. 4 May 1917, Salford, England. Retired University Professor. m. Margaret E Heap, 16 Aug 1944, 1 son, 1 daughter. Education: BA 1938, MA 1942, BD 1948, DD 1956, Cambridge University, England. Publications: The Holy Spirit and the Gospel Tradition, 1947; The Epistle to the Romans, 1957 (new edition 1991); From First Adam to Last, 1962; The First Epistle to the Corinthians, 1968; The Signs of an Apostle, 1970; The Second Epistle to the Corinthians, 1973; The Gospel according to St John, 1978; Freedom and Obligation, 1985; Paul: An Introduction to His Thought, 1994; The Arts of the Apostles, Volume 1, 1994. Contributions to: Many learned journals. Honours: Fellow, British Academy, 1961; Burkitt Medal for Biblical Studies, 1966; Honorary DD, Hull University, 1970; Aberdeen University, 1972; DTheol, Hamburg University, 1981. Memberships: Studiorum Novi Testamenti Societas, President 1973-74; Society for Old Testament Study; Royal Norwegian Society of Sciences and Letters, 1991. Address: 22 Rosemount, Pity Me, Durham DH1 5GA, England.

BARRETT Judi, b. 1941, American. Appointments: Children's Book Reviewer, New York Times, 1974-; Part-time children's Art Teacher and Free-lance Designer. Publications: Old MacDonald had an Apartment House, 1969; Animals Should Definitely Not wear Clothing, 1970; An Apple a Day, 1973; Benjamin's 365 Birthday, Peter's Pocket, 1974; I Hate to Take a Bath, 1975; I Hate to Go to Bed, The Wind Thief, 1977; Cloudy with a Chance of Meatballs, 1978; I'm Too Small You're Too Big, Animals Should Definitely Not Act Like People, 1981; What's Left, A Snake is Totally Tail, 1983; Pickles Have Pimples, 1986. Address: 230 Garfield Place, Brooklyn, NY 11215, USA.

BARRETT Susan, b. 24 June 1938, England. Writer. m. Peter Barrett, 18 June 1960, 1 son, 1 daughter. Publications: Jam Today, novel, 1969; Travels with a Wildlife Artist, natural history, 1986; The Beacon, novel, 1980; Stephen & Violet, novel, 1988; Private View, novel, 1972; Moses, novel, 1970; Noah's Ark, novel, 1971; Rubbish, novel, 1974. Literary Agent: Toby Eady. Address: c/o Toby Eady Associates Ltd, 3rd Floor Orme Court, London W2 4RL, England.

BARRINGTON Judith Mary, b. 7 July 1944, Brighton, England. Poets; Critic. Education: BA 1978, MA 1980. Appointments: West Coast Editor, Motheroot Journal, 1985-86; Poet in the Schools, Oregon, 1986-87. Publications: Deviation, 1975; Trying to Be an Honest Woman, 1985; History and Geography, 1989; Why Children, co-author, 1980; An Intimate Wilderness, editor, 1991; Anthologies: Work in: One Foot on the Mountain, 1979; Hard Feelings, 1982; Beautiful Barbarians, 1986; The World Between Women, 1987. Contributor to: Contemporary

Literary Criticism; Northwest Magazine; San Francisco Chronicle; Ottawa Citizen; MS Magazine. Honours: Fairlie Place Essay Prize, 1963; Jeanette Rankin Award for Feminist Journalism, 1983; Metropolitan Arts Commission Grant, 1985, 1987; Oregon Institute of Literary Arts Fellowship (Creative Nonfiction), 1989 and Poetry, 1992). Memberships: Poetry Society of America; National Writers; Union; National Book of Critics Circle. Address: 622 SE 29th Avenue, Portland, OR 97214, USA.

BARRON Judith Welch, b. 3 Aug 1939, OH, USA. Lyricist; Author. m. John Ronald Barron, 12 Sept 1959, 1 s, 1 d. Education: Youngstown State University, MBA, 1969; Grove City College, 1961. Publications: Theres A Boy In Here, 1992. Honours: Christopher Award, 1993. Literary Agent: Jed Mattes. Address: 529 West 42nd Street, 7F New York, NY 10036, USA.

BARROS Joseph De, b. 22 July 1921, Goa, History Research; Writer. Education: MA, PhD, DLitt. Appointments: Professor, Principal, National Lyceum Goa; Doctoral Research Teacher, Goa University General Secretary, Institute Menezes, Braganza. Publications: Geography of Goa; History of Goa; Buddhism and World Peace; Francisco Luis Gomes - The Historian; Local Collaborators of Albuquerque, Luis de Camoes; Luis Goan Contribution to Banaglore; Perspectivas do Ensino do Portugues em Goa. Contributions to: The Navhind Times; Herald; Institute Menezea Braganza; Bulletin; R C acau; Gomantak Times. Membership: Indian Academy of Science; Academia Portuguesa da Historia; Academia Canadense de Historia; Geographic Society Lisbon; Royal Asiatic Society of London; Indian History Congress New Delhi; World Academy of Arts & Culture; Institute Menezes Braganza. Honours: Translation of Dr Jose Pizal Poem. Address: PO Box 221, Institute Menezes Braganza, Panaji Gao, India.

BARROW Iris Lena, b. 8 Oct 1933, Auckland, New Zealand. Head of Seminar/Counselling Agency - Psychological Counsellor; Author; Seminar Presenter. m. Robert Barrow, 1 son, 4 daughters. Education: ATCL, Speech and Communications, 1953. Publications: Books: From Strength to Strength, 1988; 15 Steps to Overcome Anxiety and Depression, 1985; Know Your Strengths and Be Confident, 1982; You Can Communicate, 1983; Your Marriage Can Work, 1979; Relax and Come Alive (with Professor Helen Place), 1981; Make Peace with Yourself, 1990; 8 Self-help personal and interpersonal skills-training tapes 1981-89; Children's books 1970-72, Hapi series; Radio plays, 1962-70; Video training tapes, Celebrating Life with Iris Barrow, 1990. Contributor to: Feature Writer (psychological issues) New Zealand; Articles on developing personal skills, New Zealandia; Article on stress, Challenge Weekly; Articles on Self-assertion for Courier Newspaper, contributor to various magazines and journals. Memberships: New Zealand PEN Association; Associate, New Zealand Institute of Management, ex on-air counsellor. Address: 13 Hostel Access Road, Eastern Beach, Auckland, New Zealand.

BARROW Robin (St Clair), b. 1944, British. Professor. Appointments: Assistant Master, City of London School of Boys, 1968-72; Lecturer 1972-80, Reader in Education 1980-, University of Leicester; Professor of Curriculum Theory, Simon Fraser University, Burnaby BC, 1982-. Publications: Athenian Democracy, 1973; Moral Philosophy for Education, Introduction to Philosophy of Education (with R G Woods), Plato Utilitarianism and Education, Sparta, 1975; Common Sense and the Curriculum, Greek and Roman Education, Plato and Education, 1976; Plato: The Apology of Socrates, 1977; Radical Education, 1978; The Canadian Curriculum, 1979; Happiness, 1980; The Philosophy of Schooling, 1981; Injustice Inequality and Ethics, Language and Thought, 1982.

BARRY Mike. See: MALZBERG Barry Norman.

BARRY Sebastian, b. 5 July 1955. Writer. Education: LCC, Newend, London; Catholic University School, Dublin; BA, Trinity College, Dublin, 1977. Appointments: Iowa International Writing Fellowship, 1984; Writer in Association, Abbey Theatre, Dublin, 1989-90; Director of Board, Abbey Theatre, 1989-90. Publications: Boss Grady's Boys, play, 1989; The Engine of Owl-Light, novel, 1987; Fanny Hawke Goes to the Mainland Forever, verse, 1989. Contributor to: Antaeus; London Review of Books; Stand; Observer. Honours: Hawthornden International Fellowships, 1985 and 1988; Arts Council Bursary, 1982; BBC/Stewart Parker Award, 1989. Memberships: Irish Writers' Union; Aosdana; Half Moon Swimming Club. Literary Agent:

Curtis Brown Ltd, 162-168 Regent Street, London. Address: c/o The Abbey Theatre, Abbey Street, Dublin 1, Ireland.

BARSTOW Stan, b. 28 June 1928, Horbury, Yorkshire, England. Novelist; Scriptwriter. m. Constance Mary Kershaw, 8 Sept 1951, 1 son, 1 daughter. Education: Ossett Grammar School. Publications: A Kind of Loving; The Desperadoes; Ask Me Tomorrow; Joby; The Watchers On The Shore; A Raging Calm; A Season With Eros; The Right True End; A Brothers Tale; The Glad Eye; Just You Wait and See; B Movie; Give Us This Day; Next of Kin; Plays: Please Ask Me Tomorrow, 1964; A Kind of Loving, 1965; An Enemy of the People, 1969; Listen for the Trains Love, 1970; Stringer's Last Stand, 1971; We Could Always Fit a Sidecar, 1974; Joby, 1973; The Human Element, and Albert's Part, 1977. Honours: Royal TV Society Writers Award; Honorary MA Open University. Memberships: PEN; Society of Authors; Writers Guild of Great Britain. Literary Agent: Lemon, Jnna & Durbridge. Address: c/o Lemon, Unna & Durbridge Ltd, 24 Pottery Lane, London W11 4LZ, England.

BARTH John, b. 27 May 1930, Cambridge, Maryland, USA. Novelist; Professor of English. m. (1) Harriette Anne Strickland, 1950, 2 sons, 1 daughter, (2) Shelly Rosenberg, 1970. Education: MA, Johns Hopkins University. Appointments include: Professor, State University of New York at Buffalo 1965-73, Johns Hopkins University 1973-. Publications: Novels: The Floating Opera, 1956; The End of the Road, 1958; The Sot-Weed Factor, 1960; Giles Goat-Boy, 1966; Sabbatical, 1982; The Tidewater Tales, 1987; Lost in The Funhouse, stories, 1968; Chimera, 1972; Letters, 1979; The Friday Book, essays, 1984; The Last Voyage of Somebody the Sailor, novel, 1991; Once Upon a Time, novel/memoir, 1994. Honours: National Academy of Arts & Letters Award; National Book Award, 1973; Rockefeller Foundation Grant; Brandeis University Citation in Literature; Honorary DLitt, University of Maryland. Address: Johns Hopkins University, Baltimore, MD 21218, USA.

BARTH John Robert, b. 1931, American. Professor. Appointments: Entered Society of Jesus; Ordained Roman Catholic Priest, 1961; Assistant Professor of English, Canisius College, Buffalo, 1967-70; Assistant Professor, Harvard University, 1970-74; Professor of English, University of Missouri, 1974-88; Dean, College of Arts and Science, Boston College, 1988-. Publications: Coleridge and Christian Doctrine, 1969; Religious Perspectives in Faulkner's Fiction: Yoknapatawpha and Beyond, 1972; The Symbolic Imagination: Coleridge and the Romantic Tradition, 1977; Coleridge and the Power of Love, 1988; Coleridge, Keats and the Imagination: Ramanticism and Adam's Dream (co-ed), 1989. Address: Gasson Hall 103, Boston College, Chestnut Hill, MA 02167, USA.

BARTHELME Frederick, b. 1943, American. Appointments: An Artist, Exhibitions at galleries including Houston, New York City, Seattle, Vancouver, Buenos Aires, 1965-; Architectural draftsman, Jerome Oddo and Associates and Kenneth E Bentsen Associates, Houston, 1965-66; Exhibition Organizer, St Thomas University, 1966-67; Assistant to the Director, Kornblee Gallery, NY, 1967-68; Creative Director, BMA Advertising, 1971-73; Senior Writer, GDL and W Advertising, 1973-76; Professor of English, Director of the Centre for Writers, Editor for Mississippi Review, University of Southern Mississippi, Hattiesburg, 1977-. Publications: Rangoon, 1970; War and War, 1971; Moon Deluxe, 1983; Second Marriage, 1984; Tracer, 1985; Chroma, 1987; Two Against One, 1988; Natural Selection, 1990. Address: 203 Sherwood Drive, Hattiesburg, MI 39401, USA.

BARTKOWIAK Tadeusz Ludwik, b. 19 Aug 1942, Tomaszow Mazowiecki, Poland. Journalist. m. 30 Dec 1968, 1 son. Education: Diploma, Poznan Teachers College, 1962; Diploma, Philosophical & Historical Faculty, Adam Mickiewicz University, Poznan, 1967; Diploma, Evening Univrsity of Marxism - Leninism, 1985. Appointments: Editorial Staff, Poznan Newspaper, 1972-. Publications include: The Western Watch-Tower, 1922-1939; New Materials on the Battle of Poznan, 1945; A Chronicle of Poznan City; The Polish Association of Philatelists in Poznan, 1969-74; The Poznan Newspaper, 2.V.87-9.VI.87; The Union of Poles in Germany, 1922-87; Almanac of Polish Emigrants Society, 1985; 5 awards, Polish Journalists Association, 1976-85. Memberships: Polish Journalists Association; International Union of Philatelic Journalists; Polish Club of Marine Painters & Writers. Address: Osiedle Rzeczypospolitej 14 m 33, 61-397 Poznan, Poland.

BARTLETT Christopher John, b. 12 Oct 1931, Bournemouth, England. University Professor of International History. m. Shirley Maureen Briggs, 7 Aug 1958, 3 sons. Education: University College, Exeter, 1950-53; 1st Class Honours, History (London External), PhD, International History, London School of Economics. Publications: Great Britain and Sea Power 1815-53, 1963; Castlereagh, 1966; The Long Retreat (British Defence Policy 1945-70), 1972; The Rise and Fall of the Pax Americana, 1974; A History of Postwar Britain, 1945-74, 1977; The Global Conflict 1880-1970, 1984; The Global Conflict 1880-90, 1994; British Foreign Policy in the Twentieth Century (1989); The Special Relationship: A political history of Anglo-American relations since 1945, 1992; Defence and Diplomacy, 1993; Britain Pre-eminent, 1969; The Mid-Victorian Reappraisal of Naval Policy in K Bourne and D C Watt Studies in International History, 1967. Contributor to: English Historical Review; History; Annual Register. Memberships: Fellow, Royal Histonal Society; Fellow, Royal Society of Edinburgh. Address: History Department, The University, Dundee DD1 4HN, Scotland.

BARTLETT Elizabeth, b. 28 Apr 1924, Deal, Kent, England. Poet. Education: Dover County School for Girls, 1935-39. Appointment: Lecturer, Workers Education Association, Burgess Hill, 1960-63. Publications: A Lifetime of Dying, 1979; Strange Territory, 1983; The Czar is Dead, 1986; William Scammell and Elizabeth Bartlett (recording), 1984; Look, No Face, 1991; Instead of A Mass, 1991; Two Women Dancing, 1994. Honours: Cheltenham Poetry Competition Prize, 1982; Arts Council Bursary, 1985. Address: 17 St John's Avenue, Burgess Hill, West Sussex RH15 8HJ, England.

BARTLEY William Warren III, b. 1934, American. Professor. Appointments: Lecturer, University of London, 1960-63; Associate Professor, University of California, 1963-67; Fellow, Gonville and Caius College, Cambridge, England, 1966-67; Professor of Philosophy and of History and Philosophy of Science, Associate Director, Senior Research Associate of the Center for Philosophy and Science, University of Pittsburgh, PA, USA, 1967-73; Professor of Philosophy, California State University, Harvard, 1970-; Visiting Scholar 1984, Senior Research Fellow, 1985-, Hoover Institution, Stanford University. Publications: The Retreat to Commitment, 1962; Morality and Religion, 1971; Wittgenstein, 1973; Die Notwendigkeit des Engagements, 1974; Lewis Carroll's Symbolic Logic (author and ed), 1977; Werner Erhard: The Transformation of a Man: The Founding of Est, 1978; Karl Popper's Postscript to the Logic of Scientific Discovery, 1982; Evolutionary Epistemology, Rationality and the Sociology of Knowledge, 1987; Wittgenstein, 1985; The Political Economy of Freedom (ed), 1985; Unfathomed Knowledge, Unmeasured Wealth, 1990. Address: c/o Hoover Institution, Stanford University, Stanford, CA 94305, USA.

BARTOSZEWSKI Wladyslaw, b. 19 Feb 1922, Warsaw, Poland. Writer; Historian. Education: Doctor honoris causa, Polish University in exile, London, 1981; Doctor h.c. Baltimore Hebrew College, USA, 1984. Appointments: Vice President, Institute for Polish Jewish Studies, Oxford, England; Visiting Professor, Munich, Eichstaett, Augsburg, 1983-90; Voted Chairman, International Council of the Museum, Auschwitz, 1990; Appointed to the Council for Polish Jewish Relations by the President of the Republic of Poland, 1991. Publications include: Warsaw Death Ring, 1939-44, 2nd edition, 1970; The Samaritans, Heroes of the Holocaust with Z Lewin, USA, 1970; 1859 Days of Warsaw, 1974; The Warsaw Ghetto As It Really Was, 1983; Days of the Fighting Capital: A Chronicle of the Warsaw Uprising, 1984; On the Road to Independence, 1987; Experiences of My Life, 1989. Contributions to: Various Catholic Magazines and Papers. Honours include: Polish Military Cross, 1944; Medal and Title of The Righteous Among the Nations, The Martyrs and Heroes Remembrance Yad Vashem, Jerusalem, 1963; Prize, Alfred Jurzykowski Foundation, New York, 1967; Prize, Polish Pen, Warsaw, 1975; Herder Prize, Vienna, 1983; Peace Prize, German Publishers' and Booksellers Association, 1986; Commander, Polonia Restituta (with Star), London, 1986; Honorary Citizen of the State of Israel, 1991; Distinguished Service Cross Order of Merit of Germany, 1991; Austrian Cross of Honour for Science and Art, 1st Class, 1992. Memberships: Polish PEN, Secretary General, 1972-83; Board Member, 1988-90; Associate Member, French PEN. Address: ul Karolinki 12, 02 635 Warsaw, Poland.

BARTUSIAK Marcia Frances, b. 30 Jan 1950, Chester, Pennsylvania, USA. Science Writer; Author. m. Stephen A Lowe, 10 Sept 1988. Education: BA, Communications, American University, 1971; MS, Physics, Old Dominion University, Norfolk, 1979. Appointments: Writer, Science News, 1979; Writer, Discover Magazine,

1980-82; Contributing Editor, Discover, 1990-; Contributor, The New York Times Book Review, 1986-. Publications: Thursday's Universe; Through a Jniverse Darkly. Contributions to: Over 100 articles; Discover; Science Digest; Omni; Popular Science; Air & Space; Readers Digest. Honours: American Institute of Physics Science Writing Award; Astronomy Book of the Year; Nasa Journalist in Space Finalist. Memberships: The Authors Guild; National Association of Science Writers; Sigma Xi Honor Society. Literary Agent: Scovil Chichak Galen Literary Agency. Address: c/o Scovil Chichak Galen Literary Agency, 381 Park Avenue South, Suite 1112, New York, NY 10016, USA.

BARZUN Jacques, b. 1907. Publications: Teacher in America, 1945; Of Human Freedom, 1976; Lincoln's Philosophic Vision, 1982; Use & Abuse of Art, 1974; An Essay on French Verse for Readers of English Poetry, 1992; Darwin, Marx, Wagner: critique of a heritage, 1958; The Modern Researcher, 1957; Music in American Life, 1956; The American University, 1968; Race: a Study in Superstition, 1965; Clio & the Doctors, 1974; The Energies of Art, 1975; Interpretation of History, 1983; Begin Here, 1991; A Catalog of Crime, 1989; The Culture We Deserve, 1989. Honours: Melville Cane Award, 1993.

BASINGER Jeanine, b. 3 Feb 1936, Ravenden, Arkansas, USA. Professor; Curator, Founder, Wesleyan Cinema Archives. m. 22 Sept 1967, 1 daughter. Education: BS, 1957, MS, 1959, South Dakota State University. Publications: Anthony Mann, 1979; It's a Wonderful Life Book, 1986; World War II Combat Book, Anatomy of a Genre, 1986; Shirley Temple, 1975; Lana Turner, 1977; Gene Kelly, 1976; Working with Kazan, 1973; The It's A Wonderful Life Book, 1986; A Woman's View: How Hollywood Spoke To Women 1930-1960, 1993; American Cinema: 100 Years of Filmmaking, 1994; A Woman's View, 1994; Silent Stars. Contributions to: American Film Magazine; Bright Lights; Women and the Cinema; Bijou; Great Filmmakers; Great Films; Actors anad Actresses; Numerous contributios to academic journals; the New York Times Book Review, etc. Honours: Anthony Mann nominated as best Film book of year, National Film Society, 1976; Distinguished Alumin Award, South Dakota State University, 1994. Memberships: Trustee, American Film Institute, 1979; Trustee, National Centre for Film and Video Preservation; Board of Advisors, Association of Independent Video and Filmmakers, 1982-; The Connecticut State Film Commission. Address: c/o Wesleyan University Cinema Archives, Wesleyan University, Middltetown, CT 06457, USA.

BASS Jack, b. 1934, American. Appointments: Bureau Chief, Knight Newspapers, Columbia, 1966-73; Visiting Research Fellow, Institute of Policy Sciences and Public Affairs, Duke University, Durham, 1973-75; Writer-in-Residence, South Carolina State College, Orangeburg, 1975-78; Research Fellow, Director of American South Special Projects, University of South Carolina, 1979-85. Publications: The Orangeburg Massacare (with Jack Nelson), 1970; You Can't Eat Magnolias (co-author), Porgy Comes Home, 1972; The Transformation of Southern Politics (with Walter DeVires), 1976; Unlikely Heroes, 1981, 1990; The American South Comes of Age, 1985; Taming the Storm, 1993.

BASS Rick, Publications: Platte River, 1994; The Ninemile Wolves; The Watch; Oil Notes; Winter; The Deer Pasture; Wild to the Heart. Contributions to: Best American Short Stories, 1988,91,92; Paris Review; Esquire; Antaeus; The Quarterly. Honours: Pusheart Prize; O Henry Award; PEN Nelson Award, 1988. Address: 472 Upper Ford Road, Troy, Montana 59935, USA.

BASS Thomas Alden, b. 9 Mar 1951, Chagrin Falls, Ohio, USA. Writer. Education: AB, University of Chicago, 1973; PhD, University of California, 1980. Publications: Camping with the Prince and Other Tales of Science in Africa; The Eudaemonic Pie' The Newtonian Casion; Reinventing the Universe, 1993. Contributions to: Smithsonian; Audubon; The New York Times. Memberships: PEN; Authors Guild. Address: 31 Rue Saint Placide, Paris 75006, France.

BASSANI Giorgio, b. 4 Apr 1916, Bologna, Italy. Novelist; Poet. m. Valeria Sinigallia, 1943. Education: University of Bologna. Appointments include: President of Italia Nostra, from 1966. Publications include: Verse: Te lucis ante, 1947; Un' altra libertà, 1951; L'alba ai vetri: poesie 1942-50; Epitaffio, 1974; In gran segreto, 1979; In rima e senza, 1982; Rolls Royce and Other Poems, 1982; Fiction: Gli ultima anni di Clelia Trotti, 1955; Cinque storie ferraresi, 1956; The Gold-Rimmed Spectacles, 1958, 1960; Una notte del '43, 1960; The Garden of the Finzi-Continis, 1962, 1965; Behind the Door, 1964, 1972;

Due novelle, 1965; The Heron, 1968, 1970; The Smell of Hay, 1972, 1975; Il romanzo de Ferrara, 1984; Di la dal cuore, 1984. Honours include: Bagutta Prize, 1983. Address: Via G B De Rossi 33, Rome, Italy.

BASSETT Ronald Leslie (William Clive), b. 1924, British. Appointments: Served with King's Royal Rifle Corps 1938-1939, Royal Navy 1940-54; Full-time Author, Documentary and medical film scriptwriter, 1958-. Publications: The Carthaginian, 1963; The Pompeians, 1965; Witchfinder General, 1966; Amorous Trooper, 1968; Rebecca's Brat, 1969; Kill the Stuart, 1970; Dando on Delhi Ridge (as W Clive), 1971; Dando and the Summer Palace (as W Clive), 1972; Dando and the Mad Emporer (as W Clive), 1973; The Tune That They Play (as W Clive), 1974; Blood of an Englishman (as W Clive), 1975; Fighting Mac (as W Clive), 1976; Tinfish Run, 1977; Pierhead Jump, 1978; Neptune Landing, 1979; Guns of Evening, 1980; Battle-Cruisers, 1982. Address: 19 Binstead Drive, Blackwater, Camberley, Surrey, England.

BASURTO Luis G, b. 11 Mar 1921, Mexico. Writer; Journalist; Playwright. 1 son. Publications: Cada Quien Suvida, play, 1958, 4th edition 1984; Miercoles De Eniza, play, 1957, 2nd edition 1986; Con La Frente en el Polvo, play, 1986; Asesinato De Una Conciencia, play, 1986; El Escandalo de la Verdad, 1960, 2nd edition 1984; El Candidato de Dios, play, 1986; Los Reyes Del Mundo, 1962; Adaptations for Films and TV. Contributions to: Editor, Excelsior; Columnist; numerous journals and magazines. Honours: National Prize for Theatre, Juan Ruiz De Alarcon, 1956, 1967, 1986; Theatre Prizes in Spain, 1981, Argentina 1962. Memberships: SOGEM, Vice President; Writers of Mexico Association; PEN. Address: Sogem Jose Maria Velasco 59, Mexico 19, DF, Mexico.

BATARDE Eduarde. See: THOMPSON Tom.

BATCHELOR John Barham, b. 15 Mar 1942, England. University Teacher. m. Henrietta Jane Letts, 14 Sept 1968, 2 sons, 1 daughter. Education: MA 1964, PhD 1969, Magdalene College, Cambridge; MA, University of New Brunswick, 1965. Appointments: Lecturer in English, Birmingham University, 1968-76; Fellow and Tutor, New College, Oxford, 1976-90; Joseph Cowen Professor of English Literature, University of Newcastle Upon Tyne, 1990-. Publications: Mervyn Peake, 1974; Breathless Hush (novel), 1974; The Edwardian Novelists, 1982; Lord Jim (World's Classics Edition), 1983; H G Wells, 1985; Victory (World's Classics Edition), 1986; Lord Jim (Unwin Critical Library), 1988; Virginia Woolf, 1991; The Life of Joseph Conrad: A Critical Biography, 1994; Editor, The Art of Literary Biography, 1995. Contributor to: Reviews for: Times Literary Supplement; The Observer; The Economist; Articles in English, The Yearbook of English Studies. Membership: International Association of Professors of English. Literary Agent: Felicity Bryan, 2a North Parade, Oxford. Address: Department of English, University of Newcastle, Newcastle upon Tyne, NE1 7RU, England.

BATES Milton J, b. 4 June 1945, Warrensburg, MO, USA. University Professor. m. 6 May 1972, 1 son, 1 daughter. Education: BA, Classical Literature, English, 1968; MA, English, 1972; PhD, English, 1977. Appointments: Assistant Professor of English, Williams College, 1975-81; Assistant, Associate and Full Professor of English, Marquette University, Milwaukee, Wisconsin, 1981-. Publications: Wallace Stevens: A Mythology of Self, 1985; Sur Plusieurs Beaux Sujects: Wallace Stevens' Commonplace Book (editor), 1989; Opus Posthumous, by Wallace Stevens (editor), 1989. Contributions to: Essays: American Literature; English Literary History; Modern Fiction Studies; The New York Times Book Review; The Southern Review; other periodicals. Honours: Danforth Kent Fellow, 1973; American Council of Learned Societies Fellow, 1980, 1986; Guggenheim Fellow, 1989; Wallace Stevens: A Mythology of Self named a Notable Book of the Year, New York Times Book Review, 1985. Memberships: Executive Committee, Division on 20th Century American Literature and Nominating Committee, American Literature Section, Modern Language Association of America; Editorial Board, The Wallace Stevens Journal; Advisory Board, Wallace Stevens Society. Address: Department of English, Marquette University, Milwaukee, WI 53233, USA.

BATTESTIN Martin Carey, b. 1930, American. Professor. Appointments: Instructor 1956-58, Assistant Professor 1958-61, Wesleyan University, Middleton, CT; Assistant Professor 1961-63, Associate Professor 1963-67, Professor 1967-75, William R Kenan, Jr.,

Professor of English Literature 1975-, Chairman of Department 1983-86, University of Virginia, Charlottesville. Publications: The Moral Basis of Fielding's Art, 1959; Fielding's Joseph Andrews and Shamela, 1961; Fielding's Joseph Andrews, 1967; Twentieth Century Interpretations of Tom Jones, 1968; The Providence of Wit: Aspects of Form in Augustan Literature and the Arts, 1974, 1989 (reissued); Fielding's Tom Jones (co-ed), 1974 (revised paperback edition 1975); Fielding's Amelia, 1983; British Novelists 1660-1800, 1985; New Essays by Henry Fielding: His Contributions to the Craftsman (1734-39) and other early Journalism, 1989; Henry Fielding: A Life, 1989, revised paperback edition 1993 (Biography); The Correspondence of Henry and Sarah Fielding (co-editor), 1993. Address: 1832 Westview Road, Charlottesville, VA 22903, USA.

BATTIN B W (S W Bradford, Alexander Brinton, Warner Lee, Casey McAllister), b. 15 Nov 1941, Ridgewood, New Jersey, USA. Writer. m. Sandra McCraw, 14 Feb 1976, Shreveport, Louisiana. Education: BA, University of New Mexico, 1969. Publications: as B W Battin: Angel of the Night, 1983; The Boogeyman, 1984; Satan's Servant, 1984; Mary, Mary, 1985; Programmed for Terror, 1985; The Attraction, 1985; The Creep, 1987; Smithereens, 1987; Demented 1988; as Warner Lee: Into the Pit, 1989; It's Loose, 1990; Night Sounds, 1992; as S W Bradford: Tender Prey, 1990; Fair Game, 1992; as Alexander Brinton: Serial Blood, 1992; as Casey McAllister: Catch Me if You Can, 1993. Literary Agent: Dominick Abel, New York. Address: 711 North Mesa Road, Belen, NM 87002, USA.

BATTISCOMBE Georgina, b. 21 Nov 1905, London, England. Biographer. m. 1 Oct 1932, Lt Col C F Battiscombe, 1 daughter. Education: St Michael's School, Oxford; BA Honours, History, Lady Margaret Hall, Oxford. Publications include: Charlotte Mary Yonge, 1943; Mrs Gladstone, 1956; John Keble, 1963; Queen Alexandra, 1970; Lord Shaftesbury, 1974; Two on Safari; English Picnics; Reluctant Pioneer, Life of Elizabeth Wordsworth, 1978; Christina Rossetti, 1981; The Spencers of Althorp, 1984; Winter Song, 1992. Contributions: Reviews and articles in, numerous newspapers & magazines including: Times; Sunday Telegraph; Times Literary Supplement; Spectator; Country Life; Books & Bookmen; History Today. Honour: James Tait Black Prize, 1963. Memberships: Fellow, Royal Society of Literature; Society of Authors. Literary Agent: A M Heath & Company. Address: 40 Phyllis Court Drive, Henley-on-Thames, Oxfordshire RG9 2HU, England.

BATTLES Roxy Edith Baker, b. 29 Mar 1921, Spokane, Washington, USA. Novelist; Children's Author; Teacher; Lecturer; Consultant. m. Willis Ralph Battles, 2 May 1941, 1 son, 2 daughters. Education: AA, Bakersfield Junior College, 1940; BA, Californian State University, 1959; MA, University of Pepperdine, 1967. Appointments: Editor, Renegade Rip, 1939-40; Stringer, Bakersfield, California, 1938-40; Long Beach Press Telegramme, 1954-55; Columnist, Manhattan Tide, 1958; Elementary Teacher, Torrance Unified Schools, 1959-85; Instructor, Torrance Adult School, 1968-88; Instructor, Pepperdine University, 1976-79. Publications: Over the Rickety Fence, 1967; The Terrible Trick or Treat, 1970, 1973, Film cassette narrated by Mason Adams, 1975; The Terrible Terrier, 1972, 1973, 501 Balloons Sail east, 1971, 1979; One to Teeter Totter, 1973, 1975, 1982, 1984, 1988, German, Danish, Norwegian, 1976; Eddie Couldn't Find the Elephants, 1974, 1982, 1988; What Does the Rooster Say, Yoshio? 1978, United Nations selection; The Secret of Castle Drai, 1980, adult gothic; The Witch in Room 6, 1987; Harper Trophy 1989 Optioned for television, nominee for Hoosier Award, Garden State Award, 1990; The Chemistry of Whispering Caves, 1989; Mystery with chemistry college text - Texas A & M. Contributor to: Articles, poetry, short stories in 48 American national and regional magazines 1945-60, many educational articles 1960-80. Honours: United Nations Award 1978; Literary Guild Selection, The Terrible Terrier, 1972; National Science Award, 501 Balloons Sail East, 1971; Selected Author-in-Residence, March 1991 (Madrid, Spain)_ American School of Madrid. Memberships: Chaired, Southwest Manuscripters, Shakespeare Study Club and Surfwriters. Address: 560 South Helberta Avenue, Redondo Beach, CA 90277, USA.

BAUER Caroline Feller, b. 12 May 1935, Washington DC, USA. Author; Lecturer. m. 21 Dec 1969, 1 daughter. Education: BA, Sarah Lawrence; MLS Columbia University; PhD, University of Oregon. Publications: Handbook for Storytellers; This Way to Books; Celebrations; Presenting Reader's Theater; My Mom Travels a Lot; Midnight Snowman; Rain day, Snowy Day, Windy Day; Halloween; Valentine's Day: Stories & Poems, 1993; Thanksgiving: Stories &

Poems, 1994; Too Many Books. Contributor to: Cricket. Honours: ERSTED Award for Distinguished Teaching; Christopher Award for My Mom Travels a Lot; Dorothy McKenzie Award for Distinguished Contribution to Children's Literature. Memberships: Society of Children's Book Writers; American Library Association ALSC Chair Notable Books. Address: 10175 Collins Avenue, 201 Miami Beach, FL 33154, USA.

BAUER Steven Albert, b. 10 Sept 1948, Newark, New Jersey, USA. Associate Professor of English, Miami University, Oxford, OH. m. Elizabeth Arthur, 19 June 1982. Education: BA with Honours, Trinity College, 1970; MFA, University of Massachusetts, 1975. Publications: Saturday, a novel, 1980; The River, 1985; Amazing Stories, 1986; Daylight Savings, poems, 1989. Contributions to: Southwest Review; Missouri Review; Indiana Review; Massachusetts Review; The Nation; Prairie Schooner; North American Review; Harrowsmith/Country Life. Honours: Fellowship, Fine Arts Work Center, 1978-79; Fellowship, Bread Loaf Writers' Conference, 1981; Indiana Master Artist Fellowship, 1988; Peregrine Smith Poetry Prize, 1989. Memberships: Poetry Society of America; Associated Writing Programs; Poets & Writers Inc. Literary Agent: Jean V Naggar. Address: 14100 Harmony Road, Bath, IN 47010, USA.

BAUER Yehuda, b. 6 Apr 1926. Historian. 2 daughters. Education: BA Hons 1st Class, Cardiff University, 1950; PhD, Hebrew University, Jerusalem, 1960. Appointments: Jona M Machover Professor of Holocaust Studies, Hebew University; Academic Chairman, Institute of Contemporary Jewry, Hebrew University; Chairman, Vidal Sassoon International Center for the Study of Antisemitism; Editor of Journal of Holocaust and Genocide Studies, Oxford University Press, New York. Publications include: Holocaust in Historical Perspective, 1978; American Jewry and the Holocaust, 1981; A History of the Holocaust, 1982; Flight and Rescue, 1970; Out of the Ashes, 1989; My Brother's Keeper, 1974; From Diplomacy to Resistance, 1970. Contributor to: About 100 articles to newspapers and journals. Honour: Honorary PhD, Hebrew Union College, New York, USA. Memberships: Editorial Board Member, Yad Vashem Studies; Judaism; Moreshet; Scientific Advisory Committee, Yad Vashem. Address: Kibbutz Shoval, Nagev 85320, Israel.

BAUMAN Janina, b. 18 Aug 1926, Warsaw, Poland. Writer. m. Zygmunt Bauman, 18 Aug 1948, 3 daughters. Education: Academy of Social Science, 1951, University of Warsaw, 1959. Appointments: Script Editor, Polish Film, 1948-68. Publications: Winter in the Morning; A Dream of Belonging; Various other publications. Contributions to: The Jewish Quarterly; Oral History; Polin; British Journal of Holocaust Education. Honours: Award by Polityka Polenol Weekly. Address: 1 Lawnswood Gardens, Leeds LS16 6HF, Yorkshire, England.

BAUMAN Zygmunt, b. 19 Nov 1925, Poznan, Poland. Sociologist. m. Janina Bauman, 18 Aug 1948, 3 daughters. Education: MA, 1954; PhD, 1956. Appointments: Warsaw University, 1953-68; Tel Aviv University, 1968-75; University of Leeds, 1971-91. Publications: Modernity & the Holocaust; Legislators & Interpreters; Intimations of Postindermity; Thinking Sociologically; Modernity & Ambivalence; Freedom; Memories of Class; Culture as Praxis; Between Class & Elite; Mortality, Immortality & Other Life Strategies. Contributions to: TLS; The New Statesman; Professional Periodicals. Honours: Amalfi European Prize for Sociology. Memberships: British Sociological Association; Polish Sociological Association. Address: Leeds, England.

BAUMBACH Jonathon, b. 5 July 1933, New York, USA. Writer; Professor. 3 sons, 1 daughter. Education: AB, Brooklyn College, 1955; MFA, Columbia University, 1956; PhD, Stanford University, 1961. Appointments: Instructor, Stanford University, 1958-60; Assistant Professor, Ohio State University, 1961-64; Director of Writing, New York University, 1964-66; Professor, English, Brooklyn College, 1966-; Visiting Professorships, Tufts University, 1970, University of Washington, 1978, 1983. Publications: The Landscape of Nightmare, 1965; A Man to Conjure With, 1965; What Comes Next, 1968; Reruns, 1974; Babble, 1976; Chez Charlotte & Emily, 1979; (Stories): Return of Service, 1979; My Father More or Less, 1984; The Life and Times of Major Fiction, 1987; Separate Hours, 1990. Contributions to: Movie Critic, Partisan Review, 1973-82; Articles, Fiction in Esquire; New American Review; Tri Quarterly; Iowa Review; North American Review; Fiction. Honours: National Endowment of the Arts Fellowship, 1978; Guggenheim Fellowshiop, 1980; O Henry Prize Stories: included 1980, 1984, 1988; Best American Short Stories, included 1978. Memberships: Pen; Teachers & Writers Collaborative, Board of

Directors; National Society of Film Critics, Chairman, 1982-84. Literary Agent: Robert Cornfield. Address: 320 Stratford Road, Brooklyn, NY 11218, USA.

BAUSCH Richard, b. 1945. Publications: Real Prescence, 1980; Tke Me back, 1981; The Last Good Time, 1984; Mr Field's Daughter, 1989; The Fireman's Wife and Other Stories, 1990; Violence, 1992; Rebel Powers, 1993; Rare & Endangered Species, 1994. Contributions to: Altanic Monthly; Esquire; Harpers; New Yorker; Southern Review; New Stories from the South; Best American Short Stories. Honours: Literature Awar; Dottenry Award. Address: Dept of English, George Mason University, 4400 University Drive, Fairfax, VA 22030, USA.

BAWDEN (KARK) Nina Mary, b. 19 Jan 1925. Novelist. m. 1) Henry Walton Bawden, 1946, 2) Austen Steven Kark, 1954, 2 sons, 1 dec, 1 daughter, 2 stepdaughters. Education: MA Oxford 1946, Somerville College. Publications: Main Books: Carrie's War, 1975; Afternoon of a Good Woman, 1976; The Peppermint Pig, 1976; Circles of Deceit; Family Money, 1991; Total 21 novels, 18 children's books, 3 picture books. Contributions to: Reviews for: The Daily Telegraph; Evening Standard. Honours: Guardian Award Children's Books, 1975; Yorkshire Post Novel of the Year, 1976. Memberships: PEN, executive; Council, Royal Society of Literature; President, Society of Women Writers & Journalists; Council, Society of Authors. Literary Agent: Curtis Brown. Address: 22 Noel Road, London N1 8HA, England.

BAXT George, b. 11 June 1923, Brooklyn, New York, USA. Education: City College; Brooklyn College. Publications: Films: Circus of Horrors, The City of the Dead (Horror Hotel), 1960; The Shadow of the Cat, Payroll, 1961; Night of the Eagle (Burn Witch Burn), 1962; Strangler's Webb, Thunder in Dixie, 1965; Books: A Queer Kind of Death, 1966; Swing Low Sweet Harriet, A Parade of Cockeyed Creatures of Did Someone Murder Our Wandering Boys? 1967; Topsy and Evil, 1968; I! Said the Demon, 1969; The Affair of Royalties, 1971; Burning Sappho, 1972; Process of Eliminations, The Dorothy Parker Murder Case, 1984; The Alfred Hitchcock Murder Case: An Unauthorized Novel, 1986; The Tallulah Bankhead Murder Case, 1987; Who's Next? 1988; The Talking Picture Murder Case, 1990; The Greta Garbo Murder Case, 1992; The Noel Coward Murder Case, 1993; The Mae West Murder Case, 1993; The Marlene Dietrich Murder Case, 1993; A Queer Kind of Love; The Bette Davis Murder Case, 1994; 40 short stories, Ellery Queen Mystery Magazine. Honour: Mystery Writers of America (nomination), 1967. Address: c/o St Martin Press, 175 Fifth Avenue, New York, NY 10010, USA.

BAXTER Craig, b. 16 Feb 1929, Elizabeth, New Jersey, USA. Professor; Author; Consultant. m. Barbara T Stevens, 28 May 1984, 1 son, 1 daughter. Education: BS 1951, AM 1954, PhD 1967, University of Pennsylvania, USA. Publications: Bangladesh: A New Nation in an Old Setting, 1984; Co-author: Government and Politics in South Asia, 1987, 1990, 1993; Co-author: Zia's Pakistan: Politics and Stability in a Frontline State, 1985; Co-author: Pakistan Under the Military: Eleven Years of Zia ul-Haq, 1990; The Jana Sangh: Biography of an Indian Political Party, 1969; Co-author: From Martial Law to Martial Law, 1985; Co-author: Historical Dictionary of Bangladesh, 1989; Co-author: Pakistan: Authoritarianism in the 1980s. Contributor to: Publications including: Asian Survey; Journal of Asian Studies; Journal of Asian and African Studies; Current History; World Today; Washington Quarterly. Address: Department of Political Science, Juniata College, Huntingdon, PA 16652, USA.

BAXTER John, b. 1939, Australian. Appointments: Director of Publicity, Australian Commonwealth Film Unit, Sydney, 1968-70; Lecturer in Film and Theatre, Hollins College, 1974-78; Freelance TV Producer and Screenwriter, 1978-87; Visiting Lecturer, Mitchell College, 1987. Publications: The Off Worlders, 1966, in Australia as The God Killers, Adam's Woman (adaptor), Hollywood in the Thirties, 1968; The Pacific Book of Australian Science Fiction, The Australian Cinema, Science Fiction in the Cinema, The Gangster Film, 1970; The Cinema of Josef von Sternburg, The Cinema of John Ford, The Second Pacific Book of Australian Science Fiction, 1971; Hollywood in the Sixties, 1972; Sixty Years of Hollywood, An Appalling Talent: Kent Russell, 1973; Stunt: The Story of the Great Movie Stunt Men, 1974; The Hollywood Exiles, The Fire Came By (with Thomas R Atkins), King Vidor, 1976; The Hermes Fall, 1978; The Bidders (in UK as Bidding), 1979; The Kid, 1981; The Video Handbook) with Brian Norris), The Black Yacht, 1982; Who Burned Australia? The Ash Wednesday Fires, 1984; Filmstruck, 1987; Feature Film Scripts: The Time Guardian, 1988; TV Series: The Cutting Room, 1986; First Take, 1986;

Filmstruck, 1986. Address: c/o MBA Literary Agents, 45 Fitzroy St, London W1P 5HR, England.

BAXTER John, See: **HUNT Everette Howard.**

BAYATI Abdal, b. 1926, Baghdad, Iraq. Poet. Education: Baghdad Teachers Training College. Appointments include: Cultural Adviser at the Ministry of Culture and Fine Arts, Baghdad. Publications: Angels and Devils, 1950; Broken Pitchers, 1954; Glory Be to Children and the Olive Branch, 1956; Poems in Exile, 1957; 15 Poems from Vienna, 1958; 20 Poems from Berlin, 1959; Words that Never Die, 1960; Fire and Words, 1964; The Book of Poverty and Revolution, 1965; That Which Comes and Does Not Come, 1966; Death in Life, 1968; Dead Dogs' Eyes, 1969; The Writing on Clay, 1970; Love Poems on the Seven Gates of the World, 1971; Collected Poems, 1971; Lilies and Death, 1972; The Moon of Shiraz, 1975; The Singer and the Moon, 1976; Eye of the Sun, 1978; Kingdom of the Spike, 1979; Love in the Rain, 1985; Love, Death and Exile, 1990; Play: Trial in Nishapur, 1963. Address: c/o Georgetown University Press, Intercultural Center, Room 111, Washington, DC 20057, USA.

BAYBARS Taner, (Timothy Bayliss), b. 18 June 1936, Cyprus, British. Writer; Winegrower. 1 daughter. Education: Private, Turkish Lycée. Publications: To Catch a Falling Man, 1963; A Trap for the Burglar, 1965; Plucked in a Far-Off Land, 1970; Narcissus in a Dry Pool, 1978; Pregnant Shadows, 1981; A Sad State of Freedom, 1990; Fox and the Cradle Makers, 1995; Many others; Critical Quarterly, Ambit, Orte, Détours d'Ecritures, Hudson Review. Memberships: Club de Vin d'Augoulême; The Poetry Society of London. Literary Agent: MBA Literary Agents. Address: Les Epardeaux, St Amant de Bonnieure, 16230 Mansle, France.

BAYLEY Barrington John, (Alan Aumbry, P F Woods), b. 9 Apr 1937, Birmingham, England. Author. m. Joan Lucy Clarke, 31 Oct 1969, 1 son, 1 daughter. Publications: The Soul of the Robot, 1974; The Rod of Light, 1985; The Knights of the Limits, 1978; The Zen Gun, 1984; The Fall of Chronopolis, 1974; Collision with Chronos, 1973; The Garments of Caean, 1976; The Grand Wheel, 1977; Star Virus, 1970; Annihilation Factor, 1972; Empire of Two Worlds, 1972; Star Winds, 1978; The Pillars of Eternity, 1982; The Seed of Evil, 1979; The Forest of Peldain, 1985. Contributions to: New Worlds, Interzone. Honours: Seiun Award for Best Foreign Science Fiction Novel Published in Japan, 1984-85. Membership: Science Fiction Foundation. Literary Agent: Michael Congdon, Don Congdon Associates Inc. Address: 48 Turreff Avenue, Donnington, Telford, Shropshire TF2 8HE, England.

BAYLEY Peter (Charles), b. 1921, British. Appointments: Fellow, University College, 1947-72; Praelector in English 1949-72, University Lecturer 1952-72, Oxford University; Master, Collingwood College, University of Durham, 1972-78; Berry Professor and Head of English Department 1978-85, Berry Professor Emeritus 1985-, University of St Andrews, Fife. Publications: Editor, The Faerie Queene, by Spenser, Book II 1965, Book 1 1966, 1970; Edmund Spenser, Prince of Poets, 1971; Loves and Deaths, 1972; A Casebook on Spenser's Faerie Queene, 1977; Poems of Milton, 1982; An ABC of Shakespeare, 1985. Address: 63 Oxford Street, Woodstock, Oxford OX20 1TJ, England.

BAYLISS Timothy. See: **BAYBARS Taner.**

BEACHCROFT Ellinor Nina, b. 10 Nov 1931, London, England. Writer. m. Dr Richard Gardner, 7 Aug 1954, 2 daughters. Education: Wimbledon High School, 1942-49; 2nd Class Hons Degree in English Literature, St Hilda's College, Oxford, 1953. Publications: Well Met by Witchlight, 1972; Under the Enchanter, 1974; Cold Christmas, 1974; A Spell of Sleep, 1975; A Vist to Folly Castle, 1976; The Wishing People, 1978; The Genie and Her Bottle, 1983; Beyond World's End, 1985; A Farthing for the Fair, 1977. Memberships: Society of Authors; Children's Writers' Group, twice a Committee Member. Literary Agent: David Highams. Address: 9 Raffin Green Lane, Datchworth, Herts SG3 6RJ, England.

BEALES Derek Edward Dawson, . 1931, British. Appointments: Research Fellow 1955-58, Fellow 1958-, Tutor 1961-70, Vice Master 1973-75, Sidney Sussex College; Assistant Lecturer 1962-65, Lecturer 1965-80, Chairman, Faculty Board of History 1979-81, Professor of Modern History 1980-, Cambridge University; Member of Council, Royal Historical Society, 1984-87; Editor, Historical Journal, 1971-75; British Academy Representative, Standing Committee for Humanities, European Science Foundation, 1993-. Publications: England and Italy

1859-60, 1961; From Castlereagh to Gladstone, 1969; The Risorgimento and the Unification of Italy, 1971; History and Biography, 1981; History, Society and the Churches (ed with G F A Best), 1985; Joseph II: In the Shadow of Maria Theresa 1741-80, 1987; Mozart and the Hapsburgs, 1993. Honours: Doctor of Letters, 1988; Fellow of the British Academy, 1989; Stenton Lecturer, University of Reading, 1992; Birkbeck Lecturer, Trinity College, Cambridge, 1993. Address: Sidney Sussex College, Cambridge CB2 3HU, England.

BEAR Greg(ory Dale), b. 1951, USA. Writer. Literary Appointments: Lecturer, San Diego Aerospace Museum, 1969-72; Writer and Planetarium Operator, Fleet Space Theatre, 1973; Freelance Writer, 1975-. Publications: Hegira, Psychlone, 1979; Beyond Heaven's River, 1980; Strength of Stones, 1981; The Wind From a Burning Woman, 1983; Corona, The Infinity Concerto, 1984; Blood Music, Eon, 1985; The Serpent Mage, 1986; The Forge of God, 1987; Heads, 1991; Hardfought, 1991; Queen of Angels, 1991; Anvil of The Stars, 1992. Address: Lakeview Road, Alderwood Manor, Washington, DC 98036, USA.

BEARDSLEY John Douglas, b. 27 Apr 1941, Montreal, Canada. Writer; Teacher; Editor; Reviewer. 1 d. Education: BA, University of Victoria, 1976; MA, English, 1st Class Honours, York University, Toronto, 1978. Publications: A Dancing Star, 1988; Country on Ice, 1987; Kissing the Body of My Lord, 1982; The Only Country in The World Called Canada, 1976; Going Down into History, 1976; Six Saanich Poems, 1977; Play on the Water, 1978; Premonitions and Gifts, 1979; Poems, 1979; Pacific Sands, 1980; The Rocket, The Flower, The Hammer and Me, 1988. Contributions to: American Poetry Review; Canadian Forum; Canadian Literature; Poetry Canada Review; others. Honours: Canada Council Arts Award; Canada Council Short Term Grants; others. Memberships: League of Canadian Poets; Amnesty International; PEN; International Council of Canadians; Association of Canadians; Association of Canadian University Teachers of English. Address: 1074 Lodge Avenue, Victoria, BC V8X 3A8, Canada.

BEASLEY William Gerald, b. British. Professor. Appointments: Professor of History of the Far East, School of Oriental and African Studies, University of London, 1954-83; now Emeritus. Publications: Great Britain and the Opening of Japan 1833-1858, 1951; Select Documents on Japanese Foreign Policy 1853-1868 (editor and translator), 1955; Historians of China and Japan (ed with E G Pulleyblank), 1961; The Modern History of Japan, 1963, 3rd edition 1981; The Meiji Restoration, 1972; Modern Japan: Aspects of History, Literature and Society, Editor, 1975; Japanese Imperialism 1894-1945, 1987; The Rise of Modern Japan, 1990. Address: Address: 172 Hampton Road, Twickenham TW2 5NJ, England.

BEASLEY-MURRAY George Raymond, b. 10 Oct 1916, London, England. Professor. m. Ruth Weston, 4 Apr 1942, 3 sons, 1 daughter. Education: BD 1941, MTh 1945, PhD 1952, London University; DD, Kings College, 1963; MA 1954, DD 1990, Cambridge University. Appointments: Lecturer, Spurgeons College, London, 1950-56; Professor of Greek New Testament, Ruschlikon Zurich, 1956-58; Principal, Spurgeon's College, London, 1958-73; Professor, Southern Baptist Seminary, Louisville, 1973-80; Senior Professor, 1980-. Publications: Jesus and the Future; A Commentary on Mark Thirteen; Baptism in the New Testament; The Book of Revelation, New Century Bible; Jesus and the Kingdom of God; John, in Word Biblical Commentary; Gospel of Life: Theology in the Fourth Gospel; Jesus and the Last Days. Address: 4 Holland Road, Hove, East Sussex BN3 1JJ, England.

BEATTIE Ann, b. 7 Sept 1947, WA, USA. Education: American University. Publications: Chilly Scenes of Winter, 1976; Distortions, 1976; Secrets and Surprises, 1978; Falling in Place, 1980; The Burning House, 1982; Love Always, 1985; Where You'll Find the Other Stories, 1986; Picturing Will, 1990; What Was Mine, 1991. Contributions to: New Yorker. Address: c/o Janklow & Nesbit, 598 Madison Ave, New York, NY 10022, USA.

BEATTY Warren. See: BEATY Warren.

BEATY Arthur David, b. 28 Mar 1919, Hatton, Ceylon. Author. m. Betty Joan Campbell Smith, 29 Apr 1948, 3 daughters. Education: MA History, Merton College, Oxford University, England, 1940; MPhil Psychology, University College, 1965; Airline Transport Pilot's Licence; Navigation and Radio Licences. Appointments: RAF, 1940-46; British

Overseas Airways Corporation, 1946-53; Foreign Office, 1966-74. Publications: The Take Off, 1948; The Heart of the Storm, 1954; The Proving Flight, 1956; Cone of Silence, 1958; Call Me Captain, 1959; Village of Stars, 1960; The Wind off the Sea, 1962; The Siren Song, 1964; Milk and Honey, 1964; Sword of Honour, 1965; The Human Factor in Aircraft Accidents, 1969; The Temple Tree, 1971; Electric Train, 1974; Excellency, 1977; The Complete Sky Traveller, 1978; The White Sea Bird, 1979; With Betty Beaty Wings of the Morning, 1982; Strange Encounters, 1982; The Stick, 1984; The Blood Brothers, 1987; Eagles, 1990; The Naked Pilot, 1991. Address: Manchester House, Church Hill, Slindon, Near Arundel, West Sussex BN18 0RD, England.

BEATY Betty Smith (Karen Campbell, Catherine Ross), British. Appointments: Former WAAF Officer; Airline Hostess; Medical Social Worker, London. Publications: Maiden Flight, South to The Sea, 1956; Amber Five, The Butternut Tree, 1958; From This Day Forward (as C Ross), 1959; The Colours of The Night (as C Ross), 1962; The Path of The Moonfish, The Trysting Tower (as C Ross), 1964; Miss Miranda's Walk, 1967; Suddenly in The Air (as K Campbell), 1969; Thunder on Sunday (as K Campbell), 1971; Wheel Fortune (as K Campbell), The Swallows of San Fedora, Love and The Kentish Maid, 1973; Head of Chancery, 1974; Master at Arms, 1975; Fly Away Love, Death Descending (as K Campbell), 1976; Exchange of Hearts, 1977; The Bells of St Martin (as K Campbell), Battle Dress (as C Ross), 1979; Wings of The Morning (with David Beaty), 1982; The Missionary's Daughter, Matchmaker Nurse, 1983.

BEATY Warren (Warren Beatty), b. 30 Mar 1937, Richmond, VA, USA. Education: Northwestern University, 1955-56; Stella Adler Theatre School, 1957. Career: Actor, 1957-; Film Producer, 1967-; Screen Writer, 1975-; Film Director, 1978-; Stage Plays include: Compulsion; A Lot of Roses (Broadway Play), 1959; Television programmes include: Studio One; Playhouse 90; Kraft Theatre; Films include: Bonnie and Clyde, 1967; Kaleidoscope, 1968; The Only Game in Town, 1970; McCable and Mrs Miller, 1971; Dollars, 1971; The Parallax View, 1974; The Fortune, 1975; Shampoo, 1975; Heaven Can Wait, 1978; Reds, 1981; Ishtar, 1987. Publications: Screenplays: (with Robert Towne) Shampoo, 1975; (with Elaine May and co-director) Heaven Can Wait, 1978; (with Trevor Griffiths and director) Reds, 1981. Honours: Academy Award nominations from Academy of Motion Picture Arts and Sciences for Best Actor, 1967, for Bonnie and Clyde; for Best Actor, Best Director, Best Screenplay and Best Film, 1978, for Heaven Can Wait; Best Actor, Best Screenplay and Best Film, 1981, for Reds; Academy Award for Best Director, 1981, for Reds. Memberships: Writers Guild of America; Director's Guild of America; Screen Actors Guild. Address: c/o Traubner and Flynn, 1849 Sawtelle, Suite 500, Los Angeles, CA 90025, USA.

BEAVER Bruce (Victor), b. 1928, Australian. Freelance Journalist. Publications: Under The Bridge, 1961; Seawall and Shoreline, 1964; The Hot Spring, 1965; You Can't Come Back, 1966; Open at Random, 1967; Letters to Live Poets, 1969; Lauds and Plaints, 1968-72, 1974; Odes and Days, 1975; Death's Directives, 1978; As It Was, Selected Poems, 1979; Prose Sketches, 1986; Charmed Lives, 1988; New and Selected Poems, 1960-90, 1991. Honours: FAW, Christopher Brennan Award; Patrick White Literary Award, 1982; NSW, State Special Literary Award, 1990; Captain Cook Bi-Centenary Prize; Grace Leven Prize; Poetry Society of Australia Award; AM Award, 1991. Address: 14 Malvern Avenue, Manly, NSW 2095, Australia.

BEAVER Paul Eli, b. 3 Apr 1953, Winchester, England. Journalist; Author; Broadcaster. m. Ann Middleton, 20 May 1978, divorced June 1993. Education: Sheffield City Polytechnic; Henley Management College. Literary Appointments: Editor: IPMS Magazine, 1976-80; Helicopter World, 1981-86; Defence Helicopter World, 1982-86; Jane's Videotape, 1986-87; Assistant Compiler Jane's Fighting Ships, 1987-88; Managing Editor, Jane's Defence Yearbooks, 1988-89; Publisher, Jane's Defence Weekly, 1989-93; Senior Publisher, Jane's SENTINEL, 1993-94. Publications include: Ark Royal - A Pictorial History, 1979; U-Boats in The Atlantic, 1979; German Capital Ships, 1980; German Destroyers and Escorts, 1981; British Aircraft Carrier, 1982; Fleet Command, 1984; Invincible Class, 1984; NATO Navies of the 1980s, 1985; Missile Systems, 1985; Nuclear-Powered Submarines, 1986; Modern British Missiles, 1986; Encyclopaedia of Aviation, 1986; Modern Royal Navy Warships, 1987; British Aircraft Carrier (Third Edition), 1987; Modern Military Helicopters, 1987; Attack Helicopters, 1987; Encyclopaedia of the Fleet Air Arm Since 1945, 1987; Today's Army Air Corps; The Modern Royal Navy; Today's Royal Marines; Jane's World Naval Aviation; The Gulf

States Regional Security Assessment, 1993; The Balkans Regional Security Assessment, 1994; D-DAY: Private Lines, 1994; The South China Sea Regional Security Assessment, 1994; THe CIS Regioanl Security Assessment, 1994; The North Africa Regional Security Assessment, 1994. Address: Poppy Cottage, Barfields, Bletchingley, Surrey RH1 4RD, UK.

BEBB Prudence, b. 20 Mar 1939, Catterick, England. Writer. Education: BA; Dip Ed. Publications: The Eleventh Emerald; The Ridgeway Ruby; The White Swan; The Nabob's Nephew; Life in Regency York; Butcher, Baker, Candlestick Maker. Memberships: English Centre of International PEN. Address: 12 Brackenhills, Upper Poppleton, York YO2 6DH, England.

BECHKO Peggy Anne (Bill Haller), b. 1950, American. Appointments: Former Artist's Model; Legal Secretary; Delivery Person; Gift Wrapper. Publications: Night of The Flaming Guns, Gunman's Justice, 1974; Blown To Hell, Sidewinder's Trail (as B Haller), Dead Man's Feud, 1976; The Winged Warrior, 1977 (in UK as Omaha Jones, 1979); Hawker's Indians, 1979; Dark Side of Love, 1983; Harmonie Mexicaine, 1984. Address: 402B Linda Vista Road, Santa Fe, NM 87501, USA.

BECHMANN Roland Philippe, b. 1 Apr 1919, Paris, France. Architect; Historian; Writer. m. Martine Cohen, 18 July 1942, 6 daughters. Education: Licencié és Lettres, 1938; Architect Diplomé par le Gouvernement, 1944; Docteur (3C) en Géographie, 1978. Publications: Villard de Honnecourt: la pensée technique au XIIIe siécle et sa communication, (technical knowledge in the 13th century and its transmission), Paris, 1991; Les Racines des Cathédrales, L'architecture gothique, expression des conditions du milieu, Paris, 1989, 1984, 1981; Trees and Man: The Forest in the Middle Ages, New York, 1990; Le radici delle cattedrali, pocket book, 1989; Villard de Honnecourt: disegni, 1987 (joint author); Carnet de Villard de Honnecourt XIII e Siecle, 1986 (joint author); Le radici delle cattedrali, Milano, 1984; Des Arbres et des Hommes, La foret au Moyen Age, Paris, 1984. Contributions to: Pour la Science (French Scientific American); Science et Vie; Apollo Historia; BJHS; La Revue des Armes Historama; Chief Editor, Amenagement et Nature, 1966-. Address: 21-23 rue du Conseiller Collignon, 75116 Paris, France.

BECK Tatyana, b. 21 Apr 1949, Moscow, Russia. Poet; Writer. m. div. Education: Diploma of A Literary Editor, Moscow State University, Journalist Department, 1967-72. Appointments: Znamya, 1992 N9, number of poems. Publications: Skvoreshniky, 1974; Snegir, 1980; Zamysel, 1987; Poetry: Mixed Forest, 1993. Contributions to: Poems and Articles in: Novymir; Znamya; Oktyabr; Voprosy; Literatury; Literatyrnoe Obozrenie; Ogoniek; others. Memberships: Writers Union (former USSR), Secretary and Member, Russian PEN Centre. Address: Krasnoarmeiskaya Street, House No 23, Apartment 91, Moscow 125319, Russia.

BECK Warren Albert, b. 1918, American. Professor. Appointments: Professor of History: Augustana College, Sioux Falls SD, 1948-50; Capital University, Columbia, OH, 1950-55; Eastern New Mexico University, Portales, 1955-58; Santa Ana College, CA, 1958-61; California State University, Fullerton, 1961-. Publications: A History of New Mexico, 1962; Historical Atlas of New Mexico (Co-author), 1968; California: A History of The Golden State (Co-author), 1972; Understanding American History Through Fiction (Co-author), Historical Atlas of California (Co-author), 1975; The California Experience 1976: Historical Atlas of The American West (Co-author), 1987. Address: 537 Lee Place, Placentia, CA 92670, USA.

BECKER Gary Stanley, b. 2 Dec 1930, Pottsville, Pennsylvania, USA. Professor of Economics and Sociology. m. (1) Doria Slote, 19 Sept 1954 (dec.), (2) Guity Nashet, 31 Oct 1979, 2 sons, 2 daughters. Education: AB summa cum laude, Princeton University, 1951; AM, 1953, PhD, 1955, University of Chicago. Appointments include: Board of Publications, University of Chicago Press, 1971-75; University Professor, Economics, Sociology, 1983-, Chairman, Department of Economics, 1984-85, University of Chicago, Illinois; Columnist, Business Week, 1985-. Publications: The Economics of Discrimination, 1957, 2nd Edition, 1971; Human Capital, 1964, 3rd edition, 1993; Human Capital and the Personal Distribution of Income: An Analytical Approach, 1967; Economic Theory, 1971; Essays in the Economics of Crime and Punishment (edited with William M Landes), 1974; The Allocation of Time and Goods Over the Life Cycle (with Gilbert Ghez), 1975; Essays in Labor Economics in Honor of H Gregg Lewis (editor),

1976; The Economic Approach to Human Behavior, 1976; A Treatise on the Family, 1981, expanded edition, 1991; Several translated into other languages. Contributions to: American Economic Review; Journal of Political Economy; Quarterly Journal of Economics; Journal of Law and Economics; Journal of Population Economics; Econometrica; Business Economics; Others; Several books. Honours include: Nobel Prize for Economic Science, 1992; 7 honorary doctorates. Memberships include: Phi Beta Kappa, 1950; Economic History Association; National Academy of Sciences; Distinguished Fellow, Past President, American Economic Association; Fellow: American Statistical Association; Econometric Society; American Academy of Arts and Sciences; National Association of Business Econometrics. Address: Department of Economics, University of Chicago, 1126 East 59th Street, Chicago, IL 60637, USA.

BECKER Jurek, b. 30 Sept 1937, Lodz, Poland (German citizen). Novelist. m. Christine Hersch-Niemeyer. Education: Humboldt University, Berlin, 1957-60. Appointments include: Writer-in-residence at Oberlin College, Cornell University and University of Texas, 1978-87. Publications: Jacob the Liar, 1969, 1975; Misleading the Authorities, 1973; The Boxer, 1976; Sleepless Days, 1978; After the Initial Future, 1980; Everybody's Friend, 1982; Bronstein's Children, 1986, 1988; Stories, 1986; Favourite Family Stories, 1991. Honours include: Grimme Prize, 1988; Fallada Prize, 1990. Address: c/o Suhrkamp Verlag, Postfach 101945, 6000 Frankfurt, Germany.

BECKER Lucille Frackman, b. 1929, American. Professor. Appointments: Lecturer in French, Columbia University, 1954-58; Instructor in French, Rutgers University, Newark, 1959-69; Professor of French, Drew University, Madison, 1969-. Publications: Le Maître de Santiago by Henry de Montherlant (edited with A Della Fazia), 1965; Henry de Montherlant, 1970; Louis Aragon, 1971; Georges Simenon, 1978; Françoise Mallet-Joris, 1985; Twentieth Century French Women Novelists, 1988; Chapters in works: Georges Simenon; European Writers; The Twentieth Century, volume 12, 1990; Françoise Mallet-Joris; French Women Writers; A Bio-Biographical Source Book, 1991. Address: Drew University, Madison, NJ 07940, USA.

BECKER Stephen David, b. 31 Mar 1927, Mt Vernon, New York, USA. Novelist; Translator. m. Mary Elizabeth Freeburg, 24 Dec 1947, Beijing, 2 sons, 1 daughter. Education: AB 1947, Harvard College, Yenching University, Beijing, 1947-48. Appointments: Occasional teaching and lecturing at several universities. Publications: Novels: The Season of the Stranger, 1951; Shanghai Incident, 1955; Juice, 1959; A Covenant with Death, 1965; The Outcasts, 1967; When the War is Over, 1970; Dog Tags, 1973, reissue 1987; The Chinese Bandit, 1975; The Last Mandarin, 1979; The Blue-Eyed Shan, 1982; A Rendezvous in Haiti, 1987; Non-fiction: Comic Art in America, 1959; Marshall Field III, 1964; Translations: The Colours of the Day, 1953; Mountains in the Desert, 1954; The Sacred Forest, 1954; Faraway, 1957; Someone Will Die Tonight in the Caribbean, 1958; The Last of the Just, 1961; The Town Beyond the Wall, 1964; The Conquerors, 1976; Diary of My Travels in America, 1977; Ana No, 1980; The Aristotle System, 1985; Cruel April, 1990; Between Tides, 1991; The Forgotten, 1992. Contributions to: Dozens of short stories, essays, reviews, columns, introductions. Honours: Rotary Fellowship to Peking, 1947; Guggenheim Fellowship, fiction, 1954; NEA grant in translation, 1984; Judge, Hopwood Awards, fiction, University of Michigan, 1989. Literary Agent: Russell & Volkening, NY. Address: 1281 NE 85th Street, Miami, FL 33138, USA.

BECKET Henry S A. See: GOULDEN Joseph C.

BECKETT Kenneth Albert, b. 12 Jan 1929, Brighton, Sussex, England. Horticulturalist; Technical Advisor; Editor. m. Gillian Tuck, 1 Aug 1973, 1 s. Education: Diploma, Horticulture, Royal Horticulture Society. Literary Appointments: Technical Editor, Gardener's Chronicle, Readers Digest. Publications: The Love of Trees, 1975; Illustrated Dictionary of Botany, 1977; Concise Encyclopaedia of Garden Plants, 1978; Amateur Greenhouse Gardening, 1979; Growing Under Glass, 1981; Complete Book of Evergreens, 1981; Growing Hardy Perennials, 1981; Climbing Plants, 1983; The Garden Library, 4 volumes: Flowering House Plants, Annuals and Biennials, Roses, Herbs, 1984; The RHS Encyclopaedia of House Plants, 1987; Evergreens, 1990. Contributions to: The Garden; The Plantsman. Membership: Scientific Committee, Royal Horticultural Society. Address: Bramley Cottage, Stanhoe, King's Lynn, Norfolk, PE31 8QF, England.

BECKLES WILLSON Robina Elizabeth, b. 1930, British. Appointments: Teacher, Liverpool School of Art, 1952-56; Ballet Rambert Educational School, 1956-58, London. Publications: Leopards on the Loire, 1961; A Time to Dance, 1962; Musical Instruments, 1964; A Reflection of Rachel, The Leader of the Band, 1967; Roundabout Ride, 1968; Dancing Day, 1971; The Last Harper, The Shell on Your Back, 1972; What a Noise, 1974; The Voice of Music, 1975; Musical Merry-go-Round, 1977; The Beaver Book of Ballet, 1979; Eyes Wide Open, Anna Pavlova: A Legend amond Dancers, 1981; Pocket Book of Ballet, Secret Witch, 1982; Square Bear, Merry Christmas, Holiday Witch, 1983; Sophie and Nicky series, 2 volumes, Hungry Witch, 1984; Music Maker, Sporty Witch, 1986; The Haunting Music, 1987; Mozart's Story, 1991; Just Imagine, 1993. Address: 44 Popes Avenue, Twickenham, Middlesex TW2 5TL, England.

BECKWITH Lillian, b. 25 Apr 1916, Ellesmere Port, England. Author. m. Edward Thornthwaite Comber, 3 June 1937, 1 son, 1 daughter. Education: Onnum College, Birkenhead. Publications: The Hebridean Stories: The Hills is Lonely, 1959; The Sea for Breakfast, 1961; The Loud Halo, 1964; A Rope in Case, 1968; Beautiful Just! 1975; Lightly Poached, 1973; The Spuddy, 1974; Green Hand, 1967; About My Father's Business, 1971; The Lillian Beckwith Hebridean Cookbook (Anecdotes and recipes), 1976; Bruach Blend, 1978; A Shine of Rainbows, 1984; The Bay of Strangers, 1988; A Proper Woman, 1986; The Small Party, 1989; An Island Apart, 1992. Contributions to: The Countryman; Woman's Own and various other magazines for women. Memberships: Society of Authors; Mark Twain Society; Women of the Year Association, Consultative Committee. Literary Agent: Curtis Brown Ltd. Address: c/o Curtis Brown Ltd, 4th Floor Haymarket House, 28/29 Haymarket, London, SW1Y 4SP.

BEDARD Michael, b. 1949; Canadian. Publications: A Darker Magic, 1987; Redwork, 1990; The Nightingale, 1991; Emily, 1992; Painted Devil, 1994. Honours: CLA Book of the Year Award for children, 1991.

BEDAU Hugo Adam, b. 1926, American. Professor. Appointments: Instructor, Dartmouth College, 1953-54; Lecturer, Princeton University, 1954-61; Associate Professor of Philosophy, Reed College, Portland, OR, 1962-66; Professor of Philosophy, Tufts University, Medford, MA, 1966-. Publications: Author: The Courts the Constitution and Capital Punishment, 1977; Death is Different, 1987; Editor: The Death Penalty in America, 1964, 1982; Civil Disobedience: Theory and Practice, 1969; Justice and Equality, 1971; Civil Disobedience in Focus, 1991; Co-author: Nomos VI: Justice, 1963; Nomos IX Equality, 1967; The Concept of Academic Freedom, 1972; Philosophy and Political Action, 1972; Philosophy Morality and International Affairs, Victimless Crimes: Two Views, 1974; Justice and Punishment, 1977; Human Rights and US Foreign Policy, Making Decisions, The Imposition of Law, 1979; Matters of Life and Death, 1980; Ethical Issues in Government, 1981; And Justice for All, 1982; Group Decision Making, 1984; Nomos XXVII: Criminal Justice, 1985; Current Issues and Enduring Questions, 1987, 1990. Address: c/o Department of Philosophy, Tufts University, Medford, MA 02155, USA.

BEDE. See: **JOHNSTON Paul**

BEDFORD Sybille, b. 16 Mar 1911, Carlottenburg, Germany (British). Novelist. m. Walter Bedford, 1935. Education: Private education in Italy, England and France. Appointments: Worked as a Law Reporter for the Observer, London, and the Saturday Evening Post, Philadelphia, Life Magazine, 1963-65. Publications: A Legacy, 1956; A Favourite of the Gods, 1963; A Compass Error, 1968; Official Biography: Aldous Huxley, II Vols, 1973-74; Jigsaw: An Unsentimental Education, 1989; Uncollected short stories: Compassionata at Hyde Park Corner, 1963; Une Vie de Château, 1989; Various non-fiction works. Honours: Society of Authors Travelling Scholarship, 1989; Fellow, Royal Society of Literature, 1964; Vice President, English, PEN; OBE, 1981; Companion of Literature, C.Lit, 1994. Address: Greene & Heaton Ltd, 37 Goldhawk Road, London, W12 8QQ, England.

BEECHING Jack, b. 8 May 1922, Hastings, Sussex, England. Writer. Publications: Poetry: Aspects of Love, 1950; The Polythene Maidenhead, in Penguin Modern Poets, 1969; Twenty Five Short Poems, 1982; The View From The Balloon, 1990; Novels: Let Me See Your Face, 1958; The Dakota Project, 1967; Death of a Terrorist, 1982; Tides of Fortune, 1988; History: The Chinese Opium Wars, 1975; An Open Path: Christian Missionaries 1515-1914, 1979; The Galleys at

Lepanto, 1982. Literary Agent: Tessa Sayle. Address: c/o Tessa Sayle, 11 Jubilee Place, London, SW3 3CE, England.

BEER Patricia, b. 1924, British. Lecturer. Literary Appointments: Lecturer in English, University of Padua, 1946-48, Ministero Aeronautica, Rome, Italy, 1950-53; Senior Lecturer in English, Goldsmiths' College, University of London, 1962-68. Publications: Loss of The Magyar and Other Poems, 1959; New Poems (edited with Ted Hughes and Vernon Scannell), 1962; The Survivors, 1963; Just Like The Resurrection, 1967; Mrs Beer's House (autobiography), 1968; The Estuary, 1971; An Introduction to The Metaphysical Poets, 1972; Spanish Balcony, 1973; Reader, I Married Him, 1974; Driving West, 1975; Moon's Ottery, 1978; Poems 1967-79, Selected Poems, 1979; The Lie Of The Land, 1983; Wessex, 1985. Contributions to: The Listener; London Review of Books. Address: Tiphayes, Up Ottery, Near Honiton, Devon, England.

BEERS Burton Floyd, b. 1927, American. Professor. Appointments: Instructor, 1955-57, Assistant Professor, 1957-61, Associate Professor, 1961-66, Professor of History, 1966-, Alumni Distinguished Professor, 1970-, North Carolina State University, Raleigh. Publications: Vain Endeavour: Robert Lansing's Attempts to End The American-Japanese Rivalry, 1962; The Far East: A History of Western Impacts and Eastern Responses (with P H Clyde), 6th edition, 1976; China in Old Photographs, 1978; World History: Patterns of Civilization (senior writer), 1st-6th editions, 1983-93; N C State: A Pictorial History (with Murray S Downs), 1986; World History: Patterns of Civilizations (senior Writer), 6th revised edition. Memberships: American Historical Association; World History Association. Honour: 1st Recipient of Alexander Quarles Holladay Medal of Excellence, by North Carolina University's Chancellor and Board of Trustees. Address: 629 South Lakeside Drive, Raleigh, NC 27606, USA.

BEEVOR Antony, b. 14 Dec 1946, London, England. Historian; Novelist. m. Artemis Cooper, 2 Feb 1986, 1 son, 1 daughter. Education: Winchester College; Grenoble University; Royal Military Academy, Sandhurst. Publications: Crete, The Battle & The Resistance, 1991; Inside the British Army, 1990; The Spanish Civil War, 1982; The Enchantment of Christina Von Retzen, novel, 1988; The Violent Brink; For Reasons of State; The Faustian Pact; Paris After the Liberation 1944-49, 1994. Contributions to: Times Literary Supplement; Times; Telegraph; Independent, Spectator. Honour: Runciman Award 1992 for Crete - The Battle and the Resistance. Memberships: Society of Authors; Royal Geographical Society; Anglo Hellenic League. Literary Agent: Andrew Nurnberg. Address: 54 Saint Maur Road, London SW6 4DP, England.

BEGLEY Louis, b. 1933, Poland. International Lawyer, Writer. m. 5 children. Education: BA, JD, Harvard University. Publications: Wartime Lies, 1991; The Man Who Was Late; As Max Saw It, 1994. Honours: Ernest Hemingway Foundation Award, 1992; Irish Times/Aer Lingus Book Prize; Prix Medicis Etranger.

BEGUIN Bernard, b. 14 Feb 1923, Sion, Valais, Switzerland. Journalist. m. Antoinette Waelbroeck, 1948, 2 sons, 2 daughters. Education: Les L, Geneva University; Graduate Institute of International Studies. Appointments include: Correspondent, UN European Headquarters, 1946-70; Foreign Editor, 1947; Editor-in-Chief, 1959-70; Journal de Geneve; Diplomatic Commentator, Swiss Broadcasting System, 1954-59; Swiss TV, 1959-70; Head of Programmes, Swiss-French-Speaking TV, 1970-73; Deputy Director, Radio & TV, 1973-86. Honours: Honorary Member, Swiss Press Association, 1974-; Visiting Professor, Professional Ethics, University of Neuchatel, 1984-88. Memberships include: Central President, Swiss Press Council, 1985-90; Federal Commission on Cartels, 1964-80; Board, Swiss Telegraphic Agency, 1968-71; President, Independent Authority on Complaints dealing with Radio and Television, 1991-92; UNESCO Consultant on Media Situation in Belarus, 1994. Address: 41 Avenue de Budé, 1202 Geneva, Switzerland.

BEHLEN Charles William, b. 29 Jan 1949, Slaton, Texas, USA. Poet in Residence. 1 daughter. Education: New Mexico Junior College, 1968-70. Appointments: Literature Fair Coordinator, Texas Circuit, 1979. Publications include: Perdition's Keepsake; Three Texas Poets; Dreaming at the Wheel; Uirsche's First Three Decades; The Voices Under the Floor. Contributions to: The Bloomsbury Review; Cedar Rock; The New Mexico Humanities Review; Poetry Now; Puerto del Sol; The Smith; The Texas Observer. Honours: Pushcart Prize (nominee); Ruth Stephan Reader; Manuscripts Displayed and Placed in Time Capsule by San Antonio Museum of Art. Memberships: Texas Association of Creative Writing Teachers; Texas Circuit. Address: 501 West Industrial Drive, Apt 503-B, Sulphur Springs, TX 75482, USA.

BEHR Edward, b. 7 May 1926, British. m. Christiane Wagrez, 4 Jun 1967. Education: MA, Cambridge, 1953. Literary Appointments: Reuters Correspondent, 1951-54; Correspondent, Time Magazine, 1957-63; Contributing Editor, Saturday Evening Post, 1963-65; Newsweek Bureau Chief, South East Asia, 1966-68; Paris Bureau Chief, 1968-73; European Editor, 1973-83; Newsweek International, 1984-, Paris, France. Publications: The Algerian Problem, 1961; The Thirty Sixth Way (with Sydney Liu), 1969; Bearings, 1978 (in UK as Anyone Here Been Raped - And Speaks English?, 1981); Getting Even, 1980; Roman (with Roman Polanski), 1984; The Last Emperor, 1988; Hirohito - Behind The Myth, 1989; Les Miserables: History in The Making, 1989; Kiss The Hand You Cannot Bite - The Rise and Fall of The Ceausecus; The Making of Miss Saigon. Honours: Gutenberg Prize, 1988 for The Last Emperor. Address: c/o Newsweek, 162 Faubourg Saint Honore, 75008 Paris, France.

BEIM Norman, b. Newark, New Jersey, USA. Playwright; Actor; Director. div. Education: Ohio State University; Hedgerow Theatre School, Philadelphia; Institute of Contemporary Art, Washington DC. Publications: The Deserter, 1979; Theatre includes 11 off-Broadway productions, 1950-70; Success (Holland), 1982, 1983; Pygmalion & Galatea (Holland), 1983; Archie's Comeback (California, 1986); Six Award Winning Plays, 1995. Honours: 1st Prize, Double Image/Samuel French Award; On A Darkling Plain, Winner, David James Ellis Memorial Award, best play of season at Theatre Americana, 1990; Dreams, Winner, new play competition, No Empty Space Theatre, New York, 1992; Shakespeare Revisited, winner Maxim Mazumdar Competition, Alleyway Theatre, New York. Memberships: Dramatists Guild; Actors Equity Association; Literary Managers & Dramatists; Screen Actors Guild; Federation of TV & Radio Artists. Literary Agent: Francis Lonnee, International Drama Agency, Amsterdam, Holland. Address: 425 West 57th Street, Apt 2J, New York, NY 10019, USA.

BEISSEL Henry, b. 12 April 1929, Cologne, Germany. Author. m. Arlette Francière, 3 children. Publications: Poetry including: Witness The Heart, 1963; New Wings for Icarus, 1966; The World Is A Rainbow, A secular cantata based on collection of poems by the same title composed by Wolfgang Bottenberg, 1968; A Different Sun, translation of poems by Walter Bauer, 1976; Season of Blood, 1984; Body of Woman, translation of Pablo Neruda's Veinte Poemas de Amor y Una Cancion Desesperada; Where Shall the Birds Fly? 1988; Stones to Harvest, 1991, 1993; Several Play translations and adaptions including: Sacrifices, adaption of a play by Shie Min, 1988; Improvisations For Mr X, Workshopped by Montreal Playwrights Workshop, 1978; Staged Reading, Actor's Studio, New York, 1979, Dunvegan: revised version, 1989; The Glass Mountain, play, 1990, publication, 1989; Fiction: The Apple Orchard, translation short-story by Walter Bauer, 1960; Munchlaw Maird/The Complete Censor/Honesty in Government, short stories; Forthcoming Juvenile novel, Indian Headband; Non-Fiction: Festschrift Für Werner Berg, 1974; Kanada, 1981; Der Flur, short story, 1985; Raging Like A Fire Festschrift For Irving Layton, 1993. Contributions to: Numerous professional journals. Honours: Epstein Award, 1958; Davidson Award, 1959; DAAD Fellowship, 1977; Walter Bauer Prize, 1994; Recipient of numerous other honours and awards. Memberships: League of Canadian Poets, President 1980-81; International Academy of Poets; Playwrights Canada; Montreal Playwrights Workshop; Theatre Ontario; PEN. Address: c/o PO Box 339, Alexandria, K0C 1A0, Canada.

BEKEDEREMO J P Clark, See: **CLARK John Pepper.**

BELITT Ben, b. 2 May 1911, New York City, USA. Writer. Education: BA, 1932 (Phi Beta Kappa), MA, 1934, University of Virginia, Charlottesville; Served in The US Army Infantry, 1942-44. Literary Appointments include: Editor-Scenarist, Signal Corps Photographic Center Combat Film Section, 1945-46; Assistant Literary Editor, The Nation, NY, 1937-38; Member, English Department, 1938-, currently Professor of Literature and Languages, Bennington College, Vermont. Publications include: Wilderness Stair, 1955; The Enemy Joy: New and Selected Poems, 1964; Nowhere But Light: Poems 1964-69, 1970; The Double Witness: Poems 1970-76, 1977; Possessions: New and Selected Poems, 1985; Other Works: Adam's Dream: A Preface to Translation, 1978; Editor and translator, translator of numerous other works. Honours include: Brandeis University Creative Arts Award, 1962; National Institute of Arts and Letters Award in Poetry, 1965;

William Derwood Award for Poetry, 1986; Bennington College Ben Lectureship Endowment, 1977; Rockerfeller Foundation Grantee Bellagio, Italy, 1984; Fellow, Vermont Academy of Arts and Sciences; Russell Loines Award, 1981; National Endowment For The Arts Grant, 1967. Address: Department of English, Bennington College, Bennington, VT 05201, USA.

BELL Barbara H, b. 7 May 1920. Journalist; Radio Commentator, retired 1983. m. David L Bell, 14 May 1939, Watkins Glen, New York, 1 son, 1 daughter. Appointments include: News Editor, Schuyler County, 1977-78; Feature Writer, Reporter, Photographer, Freelance, 1954-62; Feature Writer, Reporter, Photographer, Ithaca Journal, 1962-78; Editor, Schuyler County Historical Social Journal, 1964-. Publications include: Little Tales from Little Schuyler, 1962; Ballad of Bertie, 1966; More Tales from Little Schuyler, 1967; To My Grandson and Other Poems, 1969; Glance Backward, 1970; Letters to Suzanna, 1992. Contributions to: Mid Western Chaparral Poets; Blue River Poetry Magazine; The American Bard; Hoosier Challenge; Sunday Telegram; Chemung Valley Reporter; Hartford Times; Glance Backward, weekly History column, Ithaca Journal, 1967-78. Honours: B M Heith Award, 1958; Historic Ithaca; New York State Temporary Historic Commission; Retired Senior Volunteer Program. Address: 3460 Co Road, 28 Watkins Glen, NY 14891, USA.

BELL Carolyn. See: **RIGONI Orlando Joseph.**

BELL Charles Greenleaf, b. 31 Oct 1916, Greenville, MS, USA. Author; Educator. Education: BS, University of Virginia, 1936; BA, 1938, MLitt, 1939, University of Oxford, England; MA, 1966. Publications: Verse: Songs For a New America, 1953, revised 1966; Delta Return, 1955, revised 1969; Five Chambered Heart, 1985; Novels: The Married Land, 1962; The Half Gods, 1968; (film) The Spirit of Rome, 1965; Symbolic History (41 slide-tape shows also on video cassettes). Contributions to: Harper's Magazine; New Yorker; Atlantic Monthly. Honours include: Rhodes Scholarship; Ford Foundation Fellowship; Rockerfeller Grant, 1948. Address: 1260 Canyon Road, Santa Fe, NM 87501, USA.

BELL Madison, b. 1 Aug 1957. Education: AB, Princeton University, 1979; MA, Hollins College, 1981. Publications include: The Washington Square Ensemble, 1983; Zero db, 1987; Barking Man, 1990; Save Me, Joe Louis, 1993. Contributions to: Columbia; Crescent Review; Greensboro Review; Northwest Review; Lowlands Review; Poughkeepsie Review; Stories; Witness; Tennessee Illustrated. Honours: Lillian Smith Award, 1989; John Simon Guggenheim Memorial Foundation Fellowship, 1991; Maryland State Arts Council Individual Artist Award, 1991-2; National Endowment for the Art Literature Fellowship, 1992. Literary Agent: Jane Gelfman, 250 West 57th Street, New York, NY 10107, USA.

BELL Marvin Hartley, b. 3 Aug 1937, New York City, USA. Poet; Teacher. m. Dorothy Murphy, 2 sons. Education: BA, Alfred University, 1958; MA, Literature, University of Chicago, 1961; MFA, Literature, University of Iowa, 1963. Appointments: Visiting Lecturer, Goddard College, 1970; Visiting Professor, University of Hawaii, 1981-82; Professor, University of Iowa, 1965; Flannery O'Connor Professor of Letters, 1986-. Publications include: (Poetry): A Probable Volume of Dreams, 1969; The Escape into You, 1971; Residue of Song, 1974; Stars Which See, Stars Which Do Not See, 1977; These Green-Going-To-Yellow, 1981; Segues: A Correspondence in Poetry (with William Stafford), 1983; Old Snow Just Melting; Essays and Interviews, 1983; Drawn by Stones, by Earth, by Things That Have Been in the Fire, 1984; New and Selected Poems, 1987; Iris of Creation, 1990; The Book of the Dead Man, 1994; A Marvin Bell Reader, selected poetry and prose, 1994. Contributor to: Professional journals. Honours include: Lamont Award, Academy of American Poets, 1969; Bess Hokin Award, poetry, 1969; National Book Finalist, 1977; Guggenheim Fellowship, 1977; NEA Fellowships, 1978, 1984; American Poetry Review Prize, 1982; Senior Fulbright Scholar, 1983, 1986; American Academy of Arts and Letters Award, 1994. Address: Writers' Workshop, EPB, The University of Iowa, Iowa City, IA 52242, USA.

BELLAIRS John, b. 17 Jan 1938, Marshall, MI, USA. Writer. Education: AB, Notre Dame University, 1959; AM, University of Chicago, 1960. Publications: The Face in The Frost, 1969; The House With a Clock in Its Walls, 1973; The Figure in The Shadows, 1975; The Letter, The Witch and The Ring, 1976; The Treasure of Alpheus Winterborn, 1978; The Curse of The Blue Figurine, 1983; The Mummy,

The Will and The Crypt, 1983; The Dark Secret of Weatherend, 1984; The Spell of The Sourcerer's Skull, 1984; The Revenge of The Wizard's Ghost, 1985; The Eyes of The Killer Robot, 1986; The Lamp From The Warlock's Tomb, 1987; The Trolley to Yesterday, 1989; The Chessmen of Doom, 1989; The Mansion in The Mist, 1993; The Vengeance of The Witchfinder, 1993. Honour: Recipient, Woodrow Wilson Fellowship, 1959. Memberships: Authors Guild; Authors League. Address: 28 Hamilton Avenue, Haverhill, MA 01830, USA.

BELLAMY David James, b. 18 Jan 1933, England. Botanist; Writer. m. Rosemary Froy, 1959, 2 s, 3 d. Education: Chelsea College of Science and Technology; PhD, Bedford College, London University. Appointments include: Honorary Professor, Adult and Continuing Education, ibid, 1980-88; Special Professor of Botany, University of Nottingham, 1988; Television and radio presenter, scriptwriter of series including: Bellamy's New World, 1983; Seaside Safari, 1985; The End of The Rainbow Show, 1986; Bellamy on Top of The World, 1987; Turning The Tide, 1987; Bellamy's Bulge, 1987-88; Bellamy's Birds Eye View, 1988; Moa's Ark, 1989-90; Visiting Professor, Natural Heritage Studies, Massey University, New Zealand, 1989. Publications include: The Great Seasons, 1981; Discovering The Countryside with David Bellamy, 4 volumes, 1982-83; The Mouse Book, 1983; The Queen's Hidden Garden, 1984; Bellamy's Ireland, 1986; Bellamy's Changing World, 4 volumes, 1988; Englands Last Wilderness, 1989; How Green are You?, 1991; Tomorrow's Earth, 1991; World Medicine, 1992; Various books connected with Television series. Memberships: Fellow, Linnaens Society; Founder Director, Conservation Foundation; President, WATCH, 1982-83; President, Youth Hostels Association, 1983; President, Population Concern; President, National Association Environmental Education; Patron, West Midlands Youth Ballet Siol and Health Association of New Zealand. Address: Mill House, Bedburn, Bishop Auckland, County Durham, DL13 3NW, England.

BELLI Gioconda, b. 1948, Nicaragua. Poet. Education: Studied in Europe and the USA. Appointments include: Barricade newspaper, Ministry of Planning and broadcasting companies, all in Nicaragua. Publications: Sobre la grama, 1974; Linea de fuego, 1978; Truenos y arco iris, 1982; Amor insurrecto, 1984; From Eve's Rib, 1987, 1989; Poesia reunida, 1989; Novels: La Mujer Habitada, 1988, translated into English, German, Italian, Dutch, Danish, Finnish Greek and Turkish; Sofia, 1990; Poems: The Eye of the Woman, collected poems from 1970-90, 1991. Honours include: Casa delas Americas Prize, 1978; Best Political Novel of the Year, Friederich Ebhert Foundation, 1989. Address: c/o Curbstone Press, 321 Jackson Street, Willimantic, CT 06226, USA.

BELLOW Saul, b. 10 Jun 1915, Quebec, Canada. Writer. divorced, 3 s. Education: BS, Northwestern University. Literary Appointments include: Professor, University of Minnesota, 1946-48, Princeton University, 1952-53, University of Chicago, 1964-. Publications include: Dangling Man, 1944; The Victim, 1947; The Adventures of Augie March, 1953; Seize The Day, 1956; Henderson The Rain King, 1959; Great Jewish Short Stories, 1963; Herzog, 1964; The Last Analysis, 1964; Mosby's Memoirs and Other Stories, 1968; Mr Sammler's Planet, 1969; Humboldt's Gift, 1975; To Jerusalem and Back: A Personal Account (non-fiction), 1976; The Dean's December, 1981; Him With His Foot In His Mouth and Other Stories, 1984; The Bellarosa Connection, 1989; Something to Remember Me By, three tales, 1991. Contributions to: Numerous magazines and journals. Honours include: National Book Award, Institute of Arts and Letters, 1953; Ford Foundation Grant, 1959; Prix Internationale de Literature, 1965; US National Book Awards, 1954, 1965, 1971; Pulitzer Prize for Literature, 1976; Fellow, American Academy of Arts and Sciences; Croix de Chevalier des Arts et Lettres, 1968; Malaparte Literary Award, 1984; Commander of The Legion of Honor, 1983. Memberships include: Committee on Social Thought, 1963-. Address: c/o Committee on Social Thought, University of Chicago, 1126 East 59th Street, Chicago, IL 60637, USA.

BELOFF Lord, (Max), b. 2 July 1913, London, England. Historian. m. Helen Dobrin, 20 Mar 1938, 2 sons. Education: St Paul's School, 1926-32; Corpus Christi and Magdalen Colleges, Oxford, 1932-37, MA Oxon 1937, DLitt 1974. Publications include: The Foreign Policy of Soviet Russia, 1947, 1949; The American Federal Government, 1959; New Dimensions in Foreign Policy, 1961; Imperial Sunset - vol 1 Britain's Liberal Empire, 1969; Imperial Sunset - vol 2 Dream of Commonwealth, 1989; The Intellectual in Politics, 1970; Wars and Welfare, Britain 1914-45, 1992; Joint Author: The Government of the UK, 1985; An Historian in the Twentieth Century, 1992; Joint Editor:

L'Europe du XIX siecle et XX siecle (1960-66). Contributions to: The National Interest; The Jewish Journal of Sociology Minerva. Honours: Kt, 1980; Life Peer, 1981; Six honorary doctorates. Memberships: Fellow, British Academy; Fellow, Royal Historical Society; Fellow, Royal Society of Arts. Address: House of Lords, London SW1A 0PW, England.

BELOFF Nora, b. 24 Jan 1919. Author; Journalist. Education: BA Honours, History, Lady Margaret Hall, Oxford, 1940. Appointments: Political Intelligence Department, FO, 1941-44; British Embassy, Paris, 1944-45; Reporter, Reuters News Agency, 1945-46; Paris Correspondent, The Economist, 1946-48; Observer Correspondent, Paris, Washington, Moscow, Brussels and others, 1948-78; Political Correspondent, 1964-76; Roving Correspondent, 1976-78. Publications: The General Says NO, 1963; Le General dit Non, 1965; The Transit of Britain, 1973; Freedom under Foot, 1976; No Travel Like Russian Travel, 1979 (US as Inside the Soviet Empire, Myth and Reality, 1980); Tito's Flawed Legacy: Yugoslavia and the West, 1939-84, 1985; Tito Duori dalla Leggenda Fine di un mito, 1987 translated into Slovene and published in Ljuljana, 1990; Is currently engaged in research on the international responsibilities for the present conflict in ex-Yugoslavia. Address: 11 Belsize Road, London NW6 4RX, England.

BELTRAMETTI Franco, b. 7 Oct 1937. Poet; Writer; Visual Artist. Education: Eth Zurich. Publications: Uno di Quella Gente Condor; Another Earthquake; Quarantuno; Airmail Postcards; Tutto Questo; In Transito; Face to Face; Target; Surprise; Clandestins; Tout Çai Trattato Nanetto Regina di. Contributions to: Coyote's Journal; Tam Tam; Docks; Abracadabra; Il Verri; Mgur; Schreibheft; Grosseteste Review, Mini, Aiou. Memberships: Swiss Society of Writers. Address: PO Box 3, CH 6828 Riva SV, Switzerland.

BEN-RAFAEL Eliezer, b. 3 Oct 1938, Brussels. Professor of Sociology. m. Miriam Neufeld, 3 Aug 1960, 2 daughters. Education: BA, 1966, MA, 1970, PhD, 1973, all at the Hebrew University of Jerusalem. Appointments: Research Fellow, Harvard University, 1974-75; Directeur d'Etudes Associé, Ecole des Hautes Etudes en Sciences Sociales, 1984-85; Visiting Scholar, Oxford Centre for Postgraduate Hebrew Studies, 1989-90; Professor of Sociology, Tel-Aviv University, 1980-. Publications: The Emergence of Ethnicity: Cultural Groups and Social Conflict in Israel, 1982; Le kibboutz, 1983; Status, Power and Conflict in the Kibbutz Gower, 1988; Ethnicity, Religion and Class in Israeli Society, 1991; Language, Identity and Social Division: The Case of Israel, 1994. Contributions to: Co-editor, Israel Social Sciences Review, 1992-; Contributions to, International Sociology; Ethnics Racial Relations; European Journal of Sociology; British Journal of Sociology; International Journal of Comparative Sociology. Memberships: President, Israel Society of Sociology, 1994-. Address: Department of Sociology, Tel-Aviv University, Tel-Aviv 69978, Israel.

BENCE-JONES Mark, b. 29 May 1930, London, England. Writer. m. Gillian Pretyman, 2 Feb 1965, 1 son, 2 daughters. Education: BA 1952, MA 1958, Pembroke College, Cambridge University; MRAC, Royal Agricultural College, Cirencester, 1954. Publications include: Clive of India, 1974; The Viceroys in India, 1982; Twilight of the Ascendancy, 1987; Also: All A Nonsense, 1957; Paradise Escaped, 1958; Nothing in the City, 1965; The Remarkable Irish, 1966; Palaces of the Raj, 1973; The Cavaliers, 1976; Burke's Guide to Irish Country Houses, 1984; The British Aristocracy, co-author, 1979; Ancestral Houses, 1984; A Guide to Irish Country Houses, 1989; The Catholic Families, 1992; Introductory articles, Burke's genealogical publications. Contributions to: Irish Times; Country Life. Memberships: Brooks's; Kildare Street & University Club, Dublin; Royal Irish Automobile Club. Address: Glenville Park, Glenville, County Cork, Ireland.

BENDER Thomas, b. 18 Apr 1944, CA, USA. Writer; Historian; Educator. m. Gwendolyn Wright, 1 son, 1 daughter. Education: BA, University of Santa Clara, 1966; MA, 1967, PhD, 1971, University of CA. Publications include: Toward an Urban Vision, 1975; Community and Social Change in America, 1978; NY Intellect, 1987; Intellect and Public Life, 1993. Contributions to: Nation; Partisan Review; NY Times; Grand Street; Dissent; Newsday. Honours: Frederick Jackson Turner Prize, 1975; American Academy of Arts & Sciences, 1994. Memberships: PEN; Authors Guild; Am Historical Association; Organization of Am Historians. Address: Dept of History, New York University, NY 10003, USA.

BENEDICT Rex, b. 27 June 1920, Jet, Oklahoma, USA. Writer; m. Giusi M Usai, 6 Jan 1966. Education: BA, Northwestern State University, Alva, Oklahoma, 1949; University of Oklahoma, Norman, 1949-50. Appointments: Served with US Navy Air Corps, 1942-45, 1951-53, Lieutenant; Orchestra Director, Alva 1938-41, Orchestra Manager, San Diego, 1945-46; Film Dubber, 1953-57; Film Translator, Rome, Italy, 1957-60; Publisher's Reader, New York, 1960-65; Printer, Corsair Press, New York, 1967-79; Reviewer, New York Times, 1965-79. Publications include: Fiction: Good Luck Arizona Man, New York, 1972, London 1973, Stuttgart 1979; Goodbye to the Purple Sage, New York, 1973, London 1975, Stuttgart 1979; Last Stand at Goodbye Gulch, New York 1974, London 1975; The Ballad of Cactus Jack, New York 1975, London 1976; Run for Your Sweet Life, New York, 1986; Verse: In the Green Grasstime, 1964; Moonwash, 1969; Nights in the Gardens of Glebe, 1970; Epitaph for a Lady, 1970; Haloes for Heroes, 1971; Other: Oh.. Brother Juniper, 1963, illustrated by Joan Berg; Various translations. Literary Agent: McIntosh and Otis Inc, New York. Address: PO Box 176, Jet, OK 73749, USA.

BENEDICT Stewart Hurd, b. 27 Dec 1924, New York, USA. Writer; Editor. Education: AB summa cum laude, Drew University, 1944; MA, The Johns Hopkins University, 1945; Study at New York University, 1946-49, 1961-64. Appointments: Entertainment Editor, Michael's Thing Magazine, New York, 1991. Publications: Tales of Terror and Suspense, ed, 1963; Revision of Harper's English Grammar, ed, 1965; The Crime Solvers, ed, 1966; Teacher's Guide to Senior High School Lit, 1966; Famous American Speeches, ed, 1967; Teacher's Guide to Modern Drama, 1967; Teacher's Guide to Poetry, 1969; Blacklash, ed, 1970; Literary Guide to the US, 1981; Street Beat, 1982. Contributions to: 18 entries to Encyclopedia of World Biography: 20th Century Supplement, vols 13-18, 1982-94; 6 entries to Barron's Student's Concise Encyclopedia, 1988; Book reviews for Publishers Weekly; Play and Book reviews for The Jersey Journal; Play reviews for Michael's Thing. Memberships: Dramatists Guild; The Newspaper Guild. Address: Apt 4A, 27 Washington Square N, New York, NY 10011, USA.

BENEDICTUS David (Henry), b. 16 Sept 1938, London, England. Education: BA, Baliol College, Oxford, 1959. Appointments: Book Reviewer and Theatre Director; Drama Director, 1964-65; Story Editor 1967, BBC Television; Assistant Director, Royal Shakespeare Company, 1970-71; Visiting Fellow, Churchill College, Cambridge, 1981-82; Commissioning Editor, Channel 4 Drama Series, 1984-86; Editor, Readings BBC Radio, 1989-92, Readings and Radio 3 Drama 1992-3, Senior Producer, Serial Readings 1993-1994. Publications: The Fourth of June, 1963; You're a Big Boy Now, 1964; This Animal is Mischievous, 1966; Angels (Over Your Grave) and Geese (Over Mine), 1967; Hump; or Bone by Bone Alive, 1968; Dromedary, 1969; The Guru and the Golf Club, 1970; A World of Windows, What a Way to Run a Revolution, 1972; The Rabbi's Wife, Junk, 1976; Betjemania, 1977; A Twentieth Century Man, 1978; The Antique Collector's Guide, 1980; Lloyd George, 1981; Whose Life Is It Anyway?, The Golden Key, Who Killed the Prince Consort? 1982; Floating Down to Camelot, 1985; Little Sir Nicholas, 1990; Odyssey of a Scientist, 1991; Sunny Intervals and Showers, 1992; The Stamp Collector, 1994; Numerous Radio TV and Stage Credits. Address: 19 Oxford Road, Teddington, Middlesex TW11 0QA, England.

BENEDIKT Michael, b. 26 May 1935, New York City, USA. Writer; Poet; Consultant; Editor; Anthologist; Literary, Art; Theatre & Film Critic. Education: BA, New York Univerity, 1956; MA, Columbia University, 1961. Literary Appointments: The Paris Review, poetry editor, 1974-78; American Poetry Review, contributing editor, 1973-; Professorships in Literature and Poetry, Boston University, 1977-79; Vassar College, 1976-77; Hampshire College, 1973-75; Sarah Lawrence College, 1969-73; Bennington College, 1968-69. Publications: The Badminton at Gt Barrington or Gustave Mahler & The Chattanooga Choo-Choo, poetry, 1980; Night Cries, prose poems, 1976; Mole Notes, prose poems, 1971; Sky, verse, 1970; The Body, verse, 1968; The Prose Poem: An International Anthology, 1976; The Poetry of Surrealism, anthology, 1975; Theatre Experiment, anthology, 1968; Modern Spanish Theatre, anthology (co-edited with George E Wellwarth), 1968; Post-War German Theatre, anthology (co-edited with George E Wellwarth), 1967; in UK, 1968; Modern French Theatre: The Avant-Garde, Dada and Surrealism, anthology (co-edited with George E Wellwarth), 1964; in UK as Modern French Plays: An Anthology from Jarry to Ionesco, 1965. Contributions to: Poetry; Partisan Review; The Paris Review; Massachusetts Review; Ambit; The London Magazine; Poesis (interview); Art International; Art News; Agni Review; New York

Quarterly. Honours: Guggenheim Grant in Poetry, 1968-69; Bess Hokin Prize for Best Poems in Poetry, 1969; National Endowment for the Arts prize for single poem, 1970; Fels award for excellence in magazine editing, 1976; New York State (CAPS) Grant in Poetry, 1975; National Endowment for the Arts Fellowship in Poetry, 1979-80; Subject: Retrospective at The Library of Congress, videotape, 1986; Benedikt: A Profile, critical monograph/festschrift, 1978. Memberships: PEN Club of America; Poetry Society of America. Literary Agent: Georges Borchardt Inc, New York, NY, USA. Address: 315 West 98th Street, New York, NY 10025, USA.

BENFIELD Derek, b. 11 Mar 1926, Bradford, Yorkshire, England. Playwright; Actor. m. Susan Elspeth Lyall Grant, 17 July 1953, 1 son, 1 daughter. Education: Bingley Grammar School; Royal Academy of Dramatic Art. Publications include: Plays: Wild Goose Chase, 1956; Running Riot, 1958; Post Horn Gallop, 1965; Murder for the Asking, 1967; Off the Hook, 1970; Bird in the Hand, 1973; Panic Stations, 1975; Caught on the Hop, 1979; Beyond a Joke, 1980; In for the Kill, 1981; Look Who's Talking, 1984; Touch & Go, 1985; Fish Out of Water, 1986; Flying Feathers, 1987; Bedside Manners, 1988; A Toe in the Water, 1991; Don't Lose the Place, 1992; Anyone for Breakfast? 1994. Membership: Society of Authors. Literary Agent: Lemon Unna & Durbridge Ltd, 24 Pottery Lane, Holland Park, London W11 4LZ, England.

BENFORD Gregory Albert, b. 30 Jan 1941, Mobile, USA. Physicist; Author. m. Joan Abbe, 26 Aug 1967, 1 s, 1 d. Education: BS, University of Oaklahoma, 1963; MS, 1965, PhD, 1967, University of California, San Diego. Appointments include: Professor of Physics, University of California, Irvine, 1971-. Publications include: Find The Changeling, 1980; Timescape, 1980; Against Infinity, 1983; Across The Sea of Suns, 1984; Artifact, 1985; Heart of The Comet, 1986; In Alien Flesh, 1986; Great Sky River, 1988; Tides of Light, 1989; Beyond The Fall of Night, 1990; What Might Have Been, volume 1, 1989, volume 4, 1992; Shiva Descending, 1992; Also research papers on plasma physics, astropysics, solid state physics. Honours: Nebula Awards, Science Fiction Writers of America, 1975, 1981; British Science Fiction Award, 1981; Australian Ditmar Award, 1981; John W Campbell Award, best novel, 1981; Woodrow Wilson Fellow, 1963-64; Various grants, Office of Naval Research, National Science Foundation, Army Research Organisation, Air Force Office for Scientific Research, California Space Office. Memberships: American Physical Society; Royal Astronomical Society; Science Fiction Writers of America; Phi Beta Kappa. Literary Agent: Ralph Vicinanza, 111 8th Avenue, Suite 1501, New York, NY10011, USA. Address: 1105 Skyline Drive, Laguna Beach, California 92651, USA.

BENJAMIN David. See: **SLAVITT David Rytman.**

BENJELLOUN Tahar, b. 1 Dec 1944, Fes, Maroc, France. Ecrivain. m. 1986, 1 son, 1 daughter. Education: Licence de Philosophie, Rabat, 1968; Doctorat den Psychiatrie Sociale, Paris, 1975. Publications: Harrouda; La Reclusion Solitaire; Moha le Fou Moha Le Sage; La priere de l'absent; l'ecuvain public; l'Enfant de Sable; La Nuit Sacree; Jour de Silence á Tanger; Les Yeux Baissis L'Ange aveugle, l'homme rompu, La soudure fraternelle Poesie; Le Amandiers sont morts de leurs blessures; Al'insu de Souvenir' La Remontée des Cendres. Contributions to: Le Monde; La Repubbilca; El Pais. Honours: Prix Goncourt; Prix des Hemyspheres; Docteur Honris Causa de l'université Catholique de Lourain. Memberships: Conseil de la Francophnie. Address: Editor le Sevil, 27 Rue Jacob, 75 Paris 6, France.

BENN Tony (Anthony Neil Wedgwood), b. 3 Apr 1925, London, England. Member of Parliament. m. Caroline Middleton De Camp, 1949, 3 sons, 1 daughter. Education: New College, Oxford, 1941-42, 1946-48, MA Oxon, Hon DPhil, HonDSc, HonDTech, HonDCL. Appointments: Served RAFVR 1943-45, RNVR 1945-46, Joined Labour Party, 1943; Member, NEC 1959-60, 1962-94 (Chairman 1971-72), MP (Lab) Bristol SE, Nov 1950-60 and Aug 1963-83; Postmaster General 1964-66, recommended establishment of GPO as public corporation and founded Giro; Minister of Technology, 1966-70, assumed responsibility for Ministry of Aviation, 1967 and Minister of Power 1969-70; Appointed Privy Councillor 1964. Publications: The Privy Council as a Second Chamber, 1957; The Regeneration of Britain, 1964; The New Politics, 1970; Speeches 1974; Arguments for Socialism, 1979; Arguments for Democracy, 1981; Parliament, People and Power, 1982; (ed), Writings on the Wall; a radical and socialist anthology 1215-1984, 1984; Sizewell Syndrome, 1984; Fighting Back,

1988; A Future for Socialism, 1991; Diaries: Out of the Wilderness - 1963-68, 1987; Office Without Power - 1968-72, 1988; Against the Tide - 1973-76, 1989; Conflicts of Interest, 1977-80, 1990; End of an Era - 1980-90, 1992; Common Sense: A New Constitutor for Britain, 1993; Speaking up in Parliament: Speeches on Video, 1989-93; Years of Hope, 1940-62, 1994, and as an Audiobook; Benn Books, 1994, BBC Enterprises. Contributions to: Various journals in the UK and abroad. Address: House of Commons, London SW1 0AA, England.

BENNETT Alan, b. 9 May 1934, Leeds, England. Dramatist. Education: BA, Modern History, Oxford,1957. Publications: Forty Years On, 1968; Getting on, 1971; Habeas Corpus, 1973; The Old Country, 1977; Enjoy, 1980; Kafka's Dick, 1986; Objects of Affection, 1983; Writer in Disguise, 1984; Talking Heads, 1988; Single Spies, 1989; The Lady in The Van, 1990; Poetry in Motion, 1990; The Wind in The Willows (adaption), 1991; The Madness of George III, 1992; Screenplays: A Private Function, 1984; Prick Up Your Ears, 1987. Contributions to: London Review of Books. Literary Agent: A D Peters. Address: Peter, Fraser and Dunlop, The Chambers, Chelsea Harbour, London, SW10 0XF, England.

BENNETT Bruce Harry, b. 23 Mar 1941, Perth, Australia. University Professor. m. Patricia Ann Staples, 8 July 1967, 1 son, 1 daughter. Education: BA, Western Australia, 1963; MA Oxford, 1972; MA Ed, London, 1974; FACE, 1990. Appointments: Lecturer, University of Western Australia, 1968; Senior Lecturer, 1975; Associate Professor, 1985; Professor, Head of English, University College, Australian Defence Force Academy, 1993-. Publications: Spirit in Exile; An Australian Compass; Myths, Heroes and Anti-heroes; Western Australian Writing; A Sense of Exile; Place, Region and Community; Cross Currents; The Literature of Western Australia; Windows onto Worlds. Address: Department of English, University College, University of NSW, Australian Defence Force Academy, Canberra, ACT 2600, Australia.

BENNETT Dwight. See: **NEWTON D(wight) B(ennett).**

BENNETT Paul, b. 10 Jan 1921, Ohio, USA. Teacher; Writer. m. Jeanne Leonhart, 31 Dec 1941, 2 sons. Education: BA, Ohio University, 1942; AM, Harvard University, 1947. Appointments: Instructor, Samuel Adams School of Social Studies, Boston, 1945-46; Teaching Assistant, Harvard University, 1945-46; Instructor, Professor, Denison University, 1947-86; Poet in Residence, 1986-. Publications: Follow the River, 1987; The Living Things; Robbery on the Highway; A Strange Affinity; The Eye of Reason; Building A House. Contributions to: New York Times Magazine; Centennial Review; Beloit Poetry Journal; College English; Georgia Review; Ohio Journal; America; Christian Science Monitor. Honours include: Denison University, Director of Writing Program; Writing Fellowship, NEA; Significant Achievement Award, Ohio University. Memberships: Ohio Poetry Society; Phi Beta Kappa; Phi Delta Epsilon. Address: 1281 Burg Street, Granville, OH 43023, USA.

BENNETT Louise, b. 7 Sept 1919, Kingston, Jamaica. Lecturer; Poet. m. Eric Coverley. Education: Royal Academy of Dramatic Art, London. Appointments: Resident Artist with the BBC West Indies section, 1950-53; Lecturer and Radio and Television Commentator in Jamaica. Publications: Dialect Verses, 1940; Jamaican Dialect Verses, 1942; Jamaican Humour in Dialect, 1943; Miss Lulu Sez, 1948; Anancy Stories and Dialect Verses, 1950; Laugh with Louise, 1960; Jamaica Labrish, 1966; Anancy and Miss Lou, 1979; Selected Poems, 1982; Various recordings of Jamaican songs and poems. Honours: Norman Manley Award of Excellence; DLitt, University of the West Indies, 1982; MBE; Order of Jamaica. Address: Enfield House, Gordon Town, St Andrew, Jamaica.

BENNIS Warren, b. 8 Mar 1925, NY, USA. Professor; Writer. m. C Williams, 30 Mar 1962, 2 s, 1 d. Education: AB, Antioch College, 1951; London School of Economics, 1952; PhD, Massachusetts Institute of Technology, 1955. Publications include: The Temporary Society (with P E Slater), 1968; Organization Development: Its Nature, Origins and Prospects, 1969; American Bureaucracy, 1970; Today, Tomorrow and The Day After, 1972; Management of Change and Conflict (with J Thomas), 1973; The Leaning Ivory Tower, 1973; Leadership, 1974; The Unconscious Conspiracy: Why Leaders Can't Lead, 1976, 1989; Leaders: Strategies for Taking Charge, 1985; On Becoming a Leader, 1989; Beyond Bureaucracy, 1993; An Invented Life4, 1993; Editor, Leadership in a New Era, 1994. Honours: Edgar D Hayhow Award, 1961; Mackinsey Foundation Awards, 1967, 1969;

Honorary Degrees: Xavier University; Hebrew Union College; George Washington University; Kansas State University. Memberships include: New York Academy of Sciences; American Association for The Advancement of Science. Address: Distinguished Professor of Business Administration, University of Southern California, Los Angeles, CA 90089-1421, USA.

BENOIT Jean-Marie Jules, b. 4 Apr 1942, Paris, France. Author; Academic; Journalist; Senior Fellow, College de France. m. (1) N Breaud, (2) Catherine Dewavrin, 29 Sep 1979, 4 s, 1 d. Education: Licence es Lettres (BA Honours, Arts), 1962, Licence (Honours), Philosophy, 1964, Ecole Normale Superieure; Master of Philosophy, Sorbonne, 1965; Agregation, Philosophy, Paris, 1966. Appointments include: Head, Seris Croisees, Presses Universitaires de France, 1979-; Various editorial appointments. Publications include: Marx is Dead, 1970; Les Outils de la Liberte, 1985; La Revolution Structurale, 1975, 1978; Tyrannie du Logos, 1975; La Generation Sacrifee, 1980; Pavane Pour une Europe Defunte, 1976; Chronique de Decomposition du PCF, 1979; Les Nouveaux Primaires, 1978; Un Singulier Programme, 1978; Le Devoir d'Opposition, 1982. Contributions to: XXth Century Studies; Cambridge Review; Le Figaro; Le Monde; Quotidien de Paris; Connaissance des Arts; La Quinzaine Litteraire; L'Express; Washington Post; Wall Street Journal. Honours: French Academy Awards, 1975, 1979, 1980. Memberships: British Section, PEN Club; Saville Club, London; Travellers Club, Paris; Founder, Chairman, Centre Europeen de Relations Internationales de Strategies. Address: c/o College de France, 11 Place Marcelin Berthelot, 75006, Paris, France.

BENSON Daniel. See: **COOPER Colin Symons.**

BENSON Eugene, b. 1928, Northern Ireland. m. Renate Niklaus, 1968, 2 children. Education: MA, PhD. Appointments: Professor, University of Guelph; President, Director, Guelph Spring Festival; Chair, The Writers Union of Canada; Co President, Vice President, PEN Canada; Co Editor, Routledge Encyclopedia of Post Colonial Literatures in English, 1994. Publications include: Encounter, 1973; The Bulls of Ronda, 1976; Power Game, 1980; J M Synge, 1980; English Canadian Drama, 1987; The Oxford Companion to Canadian Theatre, 1989. Address: 55 Palmer Street, Guelph, Ontario, N1E 2P9, Canada.

BENSON Mary, b. 9 Dec 1919, Pretoria, South Africa. Writer. Publications: Tshekedi Khama, 1960; The African Patriots, 1963, 1964; At the Still Point, 1969, 1986; South Africa: The Struggle for a Birthright, 1969, 1985; Nelson Mandela, 1986, 1994; A Far Cry (autobiography), 1989, 1990; Editor, Athol Fugard Notebooks, 1983. Contributions to: London Magazine; Observer; Yale Theatre; Granta; Botswana Notes & Records; BBC Radio Drama & Documentaries. Literary Agent: Curtis Brown. Address: 34 Langford Court, London NW8 9DN, England.

BENTLEY Eric (Russell), b. 14 Sep 1916, Bolton, Lancashire, England, became US citizen, 1948. Writer. m. (1) Maja Tschernjakow (diss), (2) Joanne Davis, 1953, twin sons. Education: BA, 1938, BLitt, 1939, Oxford University; PhD, Yale University, New Haven, CT, 1941. Appointments include: Professor of Comparative Literature, University of Maryland, College Park, 1982-89; Charles Eliot Norton Professor of Poetry, Harvard University, Cambridge, MA, 1960-61; Fulbright Professor, Belgrade, 1980; Drama Critic, New Republic, NY, 1952-56. Publications include: Plays: The Kleist Variations, Three Plays, 1982; Larry Parks' Day in Court, produced NY, 1979; Lord Alfred's Lover, produced FL, 1979; Toronto, Personal Library, 1981 in Monstrous Martyrdoms, 1985; Monstrous Martyrdoms, Three Plays; Buffalo, Prometheus, 1985; Others include: The Pirandello Commentaries, University of Nebraska, Department of Modern Languages and Literature, 1985; The Brecht Memoir, Performing Arts Journal Publications, NY, 1986; German Requiem, NY, 1990; Round 2 (play), 1991. Contributions to: Translations of many works. Honours include: a Festschrift in his honour entitled, The Critic and The Play, 1986; a Theatre Festival in his name, presenting 3 of his plays and awarded a plaque, Fl, 1992; Honorary Doctorate, New School for Social Research, NY, 1992; Robert Lewis Award for Life Achievement in Theatre, 1992. Memberships: American Academy of Arts and Sciences, 1969; American Academy and Institute of Arts and Letters, 1990. Literary Agent: Jack Tantleff, Suite 700, 375 Greenwich Street, New York, 10013, USA; Joy Westendarp, 22A Aubrey House, Maida Vale, London, W2 1TQ, England. Address: 194 Riverdale Drive, Apartment 4 E, New York, NY 10025, USA.

BENVENISTE Asa, b. 1925, USA. Poet; Playwright. Literary Appointments: Co-editor, Zero-Quarterly, Paris, Tangier, London, 1948-56; Correspondent, Nugget Magazine, London, 1956-57; Copy Editor, Doubleday and Company, New York City, 1957-58; Senior Art Editor, Paul Hamlyn Limited, London, 1959-61; Senior Editor, Studio Vista Limited, London, 1961-63; Executive Editor, Trigram Press Limited. Publications: Tangier For The Traveller (radio play), 1956; Piano Forte (radio play), 1957; Poems of The Month, 1966; A Work in Your Season: A Portfolio of Six Seriagraphs (with Jack Hirschman), 1967; Count Three, 1969; The Atoz Formula, 1969; Free Semantic No 2, 1970; Umbrella, 1972; Time Being (with Ray Di Palma and Tom Raworth), 1972; Blockmakers Black, 1973; Certainly Metaphysics, 1973; It's The Same Old Feeling Again, 1973; Autotypography: A Book of Design Priorities, 1974; Edge, 1975; Poems, 1976; Loose End, 1977; Colour Theory, 1977; Throw Out The Life Line, Lay Out The Corse: Poems 1965-85, 1983. Address: 22 Leverton Street, London, NW5, England.

BERCH Bettina, b. 25 May 1950, Washington DC, USA. Writer. 1 d. Education: BA, Barnard College, 1971; MA, University of Madison, 1973; PhD, 1976. Publications: The Endless Day: The Political Economy of Women and Work; Radical by Design: The Life and Style of Elizabeth Hawes. Contributions to: Early Feminist Fashion; The Resurrection of Out Work; Belles Letters; Paradise of A Kind, Lost. Literary Agent: Malaga Baldi. Address: PO Box 772, Berlize City, Berlize.

BERESFORD Anne Ellen Hamburger, b. 10 Sept 1928, Redhill, Surrey, England. Poet. m. 28 July 1951, 1 son, 2 daughters. Appointments: Poetry Society, General Council 1976-78; Committee Member, Aldeburgh Poetry Festival, 1989; Advisor on Agenda Editorial Board, 1993-. Publications: Walking Without Moving, 1967; The Lair, 1968; The Courtship, 1972; Footsteps on Snow, 1972; The Curving Shore, 1975; Songs Athracian Taught Me, 1980; The Songs of Almut, 1980; The Sele of the Morning, 1988; Landscape With Figures, 1994; Translation, Alexandros Poems of Vera Lungu, 1975; Snapshots From An Album 1884-85, 1992; Co Author of Struck By Apollo, radio play, 1965; Short Story, The Villa, radio, 1968; Duet for 3 voices, Anglia TV, 1984. Contributions to: Agenda; Akzente; The Scotsman; New Statesman; Boston Journal; Hommage a Arp. Address: Marsh Acres, Middleton, Saxmundham, Suffolk IP17 3NH, England.

BERESFORD Elisabeth, b. Paris, France. Writer. 1 s, 1 d. Appointments include: Founder, Alderney Youth Trust. Publications: Historical, romance, gothic, children's fiction including: The Television Mystery, 1957; Trouble at Tullington Castle, 1958; Gappy Goes West, 1959; Two Gold Dolphins, 1961; Paradise Island, 1963; Escape to Happiness, 1964; Game, Set and Match, 1965; The Hidden Mill, 1965; The Black Mountain Mystery, 1967; Sea-Green Magic, 1968; Stephen and The Shaggy Dog, 1970; The Wandering Wombles, 1970; Dangerous Magic, 1972; The Secret Railway, 1973; The Wombles at Work, 1973; The Wombles Annual, yearly, 1975-78; Snuffle to The Rescue, 1975;Orinoco Runs Away, 1975; Bungo Knows Best, 1976; Tobermory's Big Surprise, 1976; Wombling Free, 1978; The Happy Ghost, 1979; Curious Magic, 1980; The Four of Us, 1982; The Animals Nobody Wanted, 1982; The Tovers, 1982; The Adventures of Poon, 1984; One of The Family, 1985; The Ghosts of Lupus Street School, 1986; The Secret Room, 1987; Emily and The Haunted Castle, 1987; The Oscar Puffin Book, 1987; Once Upon a Time Stories, 1988; The Island Railway Armada Adventure, 1989; Rose; Charlie's Ark; The Wooden Gun. Literary Agent: A M Heath; David Higham Associates, 5-8 Lower John Street, London, W1R 4HA, England. Address: Alderney, Channel Islands, UK.

BERESFORD-HOWE Constance, b. 10 Nov 1922. Professor of English; Novelist. m. 31 Dec 1960, 1 s. Education: BA 1945, MA 1946, McGill University; PhD 1950, Brown University. Publications: The Book of Eve, 1973; A Population of One, 1976; The Marriage Bed, 1980; Night Studies, 1984; Prospero's Daughter, 1989; A Serious Widow, 1990. Honours: Dodd Mead Intercollegiate Literary Fellowship, 1948; Canadian Booksellers Award, 1974. Memberships: Canadian Authors Association, past president, Montreal Branch; International PEN, past president, Montreal Branch; Writers Union of Canada; International PEN, Writers in Prison Committee. Literary Agent: Ms Bella Pomer. Address: c/o Macmillan of Canada, 29 Birch Avenue, Toronto, Canada, M4V 1E2.

BERG Leila Rita, b. 12 Nov 1917, Salford, Lancashire, England. Writer. 1 son, 1 daughter. Publications include: Risinghill Death of a

Comprehensive School, 1968; Look at Kids, 1972; The Train Back (with Pat Chapman), 1972; Reading and Loving, 1977; The Adventures of Chunky, 1950; Little Pete, 1952; Trust Chunky, 1954; Fire Engine by Mistake, 1955; The Hidden Road, 1958; Box for Benny, 1958; Folk Tales, 1966; My Dog Sunday, 1968; The Nippers Stories, 1968-76; Snap series, 1977; Chatterbooks series, 1981; Small World series, 1983, 1985; Hannuka, 1985; Christmas, 1985; Time for One More, 1986; Steep Street Stories, 1987 and others; Backwards and Forwards, 1994. Contributions to: In 1960s and 1970s: The Guardian; Anarchy; Times Educational Supplement; Times Literary Supplement. Honours: Eleanor Farjeon Award, 1973 for Services to Children's Literature. Literary Agent: A J Watt. Address: Alice's Cottage, Brook Street, Wivenhoe, Nr Colchester CO7 9DS, England.

BERG Y L. See: **ELBERG Yehuda.**

BERGE Carol, b. 4 Oct 1928, New York City, USA. Writer; Dealer in Arts and Antiques. m. Jack Henry Berge, 1955, 1 s. Literary Appointments include: Visiting Professor, Thomas Jefferson College, 1975; Visiting Professor, University of Southern Mississippi, 1978; Lecturer, SUNY Albany, 1981; Lecturer, University of New Mexico, 1987; Colorado Council, Arts Literary Grants Panel, 1992. Publications include: Editorships: Woodstock Review; Mississippi Review; Wing Bones; Paper Branches; Subterraneans; Fiction and poetry books including: Acts of Love: An American Novel, 1973; Rituals and Gargoyles, 1977; Alba Genesis, 1978; Secrets, Gossip and Slander, 1984; ZEBRAS, Collected Fiction, 1991. Contributions to: Iowa Review; Triquarterly; Center; Fiction International; Measure; Another Chicago Magazine; Poetry Chicago; Fireweed. Honours: NY State Council on The Arts CAPS Grant; National Endowment for The Arts Award in Fiction; Thirteen Grants of Publication for Center Press. Address: 307 Johnson Street, Santa Fe, NM 87501, USA.

BERGE Hans Cornelisten, b. 24 Dec 1938, Netherlands. Writer; poet. Literary Appointments include: Lecturer, Art Academy, Arnhem; Writer in Residence, University of Texas, USA; Editor, Raster, Grid, literary journals, Amsterdam. Publications: Gedichten, collection of 3 poetry books, 1969; White Shaman, 1973; Poetry of The Aztecs, 1972; Va-banque, 1977; Semblance of Reality, 1981; Texas Elegies, 1983; Novels: Zelfportret met witte muts, 1985; Het geheim van een opgewekt humeur, 1986; Songs of Anxiety and Despair, poetry, 1988; The Defence of Poetry, essays, 1988; also numerous poetry translations; 3 prose books; 3 books myths and fables of Arctic peoples, 1 book of essays. Contributions to: Raster; De gids; Vrij Nederland; New Directions in Poetry and Prose; Chicago Review; Plural; Dimension; Les Lettres Nouvelles. Honours include: Prose prize, City of Amsterdam, 1971; Van der Hoogt Prize, 1968. Memberships: Maatschappij der Nederlands Letterkunde (Society of Dutch Literature); PEN. Address: c/o Meulenhoff Publishers, PO Box 100, 1000 AC Amsterdam, Netherlands.

BERGEL Hans, b. 26 Jul 1925, Kronstadt, Romania. Author. Education: History of Arts, University Cluj-Napoca, Bucharest. Publications: Rumanien, Portrait einer Nation, 1969; Ten Southern European Short Stories, 1972; Die Sachsen in Siebenburgen nach dreissig Jahren Kommunismus, 1976; Der Tanz in Ketten, 1977; Siebenburgen, A Picture Book of Transylvania, 1980, 1983; Gestalten und Gewalten, 1982; Hermann Oberth oder Der mythische Traum vom Fliegen, 1984; Der Tod des Hirten, 1985; Literaturgeschichte der Deutschen in Siebenburgen, 1987; Das Venusherz, short novel, 1987; Weihnacht ist uberall, eleven short stories, 1988. Contributions include: Kulturpolotosche Korrespondenz, Bonn; Rhein-Neckar Zeitung, Heidelberg; Sudost-deutsche Vierteljahresblatter, Munchen; Zeitbuhne, Munchen; Der Gemeinsam Weg, Bonn. Honours include: Short Story Prize, Bucharest, 1957, Bonn, 1972; Georg Dehio Prize, Esslingen, 1972; Geothe Foundation Prize, Basel, 1972; Medien Prize, Bavarian Broadcasting Company, 1983, 1989; Bundesverdienstkreuz, 1987; Saxon of Transylvanians Culture Prize, 1988; Geyphius-Prize, 1990. Memberships: Kunstlergilde e V Esslingen; PEN International. Address: Rabensteinstrasse 28, D 8000 Munchen 60, Germany.

BERGER Arthur Asa, b. 1933, USA. Writer. Appointment: Professor, Broadcast Communication Arts Department, San Francisco State University. Publications: Li'L Abner: A Study in American Statire, 1970; The Evangelical Hamburger, 1970; Collaborator, Language in Thought and Action, 3rd edition 1972, 4th edition 1978; Pop Culture, 1973; The Comic-Stripped American, 1974; About Man: An Introduction to Anthropology, 1974; The TV-Guided American, 1976; Television as an Instrument of Terror, 1980; Film in Society, 1980; Media Analysis

Techniques, 1982; Signs in Contemporary Culture: An Introduction to Semiotics, 1984; Television in Society, 1987; Humor, The Psyche and Society, 1987; Visual Sociology & Communication Theory, 1990; Scripts: Writing for Radio & Television, 1990; Media Research Techniques, 1991; Reading Matter: Multidisciplinary Perspective on Material Culture, 1992; Popular Culture Genres, 1992; An Anatomy of Humor, 1993; Cultural Criticism: A Primer of Key Concepts, 1995; Blind Men and Elephants: Perspectives on Humor, 1995. Address: 118 Peralta Avenue, Mill Valley, CA 94941, USA.

BERGER John, b. 5 Nov 1926, Stoke Newington, London, England. Novelist. m. twice, 3 children. Education: Central School of Art and the Chelsea School of Art, London. Appointments: Television Narrator, About Time, 1985, and Another Way of Telling, 1989; Artist, exhibitions at Wildenstein, Redfern, and Leicester galleries, London. Publications: A Painter of Our Time, 1958; The Foot of Clive, 1962; Corker's Freedom, 1964; G., 1972; Into Their Labours: Pig Earth, 1979; Once in Europa, 1987; Lilac and Flag: An Old Wives' Tale of a City, 1990; Plays include: A Question of Geography, 1984; Boris, 1985; Goya's Last Portrait: The Painter Played Today, 1989. Contributions to: Tribune and New Statesman, both London, 1951-60. Honours: Booker Prize, 1972; Guardian Fiction Prize, 1973; New York's Critics Prize, for screenplay, 1976; George Orwell Memorial Prize, 1977; Barcelona Film Festival Europa Award, 1989. Address: Quincy, Mieussy, 74440 Taninges, France.

BERGER Terry, b. 1933, USA. Children's Writer. Publications: Black Fairy Tales (adaptation), 1969; I Have Feelings (psychology), 1971; Lucky, 1974; Being Alone, Being Together, 1974; Big Sister, Little Brother, 1974; A Friend Can Help, 1974; A New Baby, 1974; Not Everything Changes, 1975; The Turtles' Picnic, 1977; How Does it Feel When Your Parents Get Divorced?, 1977; Special Friends, 1979; Stepchild, 1980; Friends, 1981; Co-author: The Haunted Dollhouse, 1982; Ben's ABC Day, 1982; Country Inns: The Rocky Mountains, 1983. Address: 130 Hill Park Avenue, Great Neck, NY 11021, USA.

BERGMAN Ingmar, b. 14 July 1918, Uppsala, Sweden. Film Director and Script Writer. m. Ingrid von Rosen, 1971. Education: University of Stockholm, 1938-40. Publications include: Plays and screenplays: The Day Ends Early, 1947; Moralities, 1948; Summer with Monica, 1953; Sawdust and Tinsel, 1953; Journey into Autumn, 1955; Smiles of a Summer Night, 1955; The Seventh Seal, 1957; Wild Strawberries, 1957; So Close to Life, 1958; The Virgin Spring, 1960; Through a Glass Darkly, 1961; Winter Light, 1963; The Silence, 1963; Persona, 1966; Hour of the Wolf, 1968; The Rite, 1969; The Passion, 1969; The Touch, 1971; Cries and Whispers, 1973; Scenes from a Marriage, 1973; Face to Face, 1973; Autumn Sonata, 1978; From the Life of the Marionettes, 1980; Fanny and Alexander, 1982; Best Intentions, 1992; Sunday's Children, 1992; The Magic Lantern: An Autobiography, 1988. Honours include: Academy Awards, 1961, 1962, 1984; Goethe Prize, 1976; Honorary Professor, Stockholm University, 1985. Address: c/o Norstedts Forlag, Box 2052, 103 12 Stockholm, Sweden.

BERGONZI Bernard, b. 1929. Author; Poet. Appointments: Senior Lecturer 1966-71, Professor of English 1971-92, Emeritus 1992-, University of Warwick, Coventry. Publications: The Early H G Wells, 1961; Heroes' Twilight, 1965, 1980; Innovations: Essays on Art and Ideas, 1968; T S Eliot: Four Quartets: A Casebook, 1969; The Situation of the Novel, 1970, 1979; T S Eliot, 1972, 1978; The Turn of a Century, 1973; H G Wells: A Collection of Critical Essays, 1975; Gerard Manley Hopkins, 1977; Reading the Thirties, 1978; Years: Sixteen Poems, 1979; Poetry 1870-1914, 1980; The Roman Persuasion (novel), 1981; The Myth of Modernism and Twentieth Century Literature, 1986; Exploding English, 1990; Wartime and Aftermath, 1993. Address: 19 St Mary's Crescent, Leamington Spa, CV31 1JL, England.

BERGSON Leo. See: STEBEL Sidney Leo.

BERKELEY Humphry John, b. 1 Feb 1926, Marlow, England. Writer; Author; Former MP. Education: Pembroke College, Cambridge (Exhibitioner), BA 1947, MA 1963. Appointments: Member of Parliament (Conservative) for Lancaster, 1959-66, joined Labour Party 1970; Chairman, United Nations Association of Great Britain and Northern Ireland, 1966-70. Publications: The Power of The Prime Minister, 1968; Crossing The Floor, 1972; The Life and Death of Rochester Sneath, 1974; The Odyssey of Enoch: A Political Memoir, 1977; The Myth That Will Not Die: The Formation of The National

Government, 1978; Faces of The Eighties (with Jeffrey Archer), 1987. Contributions to: Many Articles in The Times; The Sunday Times; The Daily Telegraph; The Financial Times; The Spectator; The New Statesman. Membership: Savile Club. Literary Agent: Mark Hamilton, A M Heath, 79 St Martin's Lane, London, WC2, England. Address: 3 Pages Yard, Church Street, Chiswick, London, W4 2PA, England.

BERKOFF Steven, b. 3 Aug 1937, Stepney, London, England. Writer; Director; Actor. m. Shelley Lee, 1976. Education: Webber-Douglas Academy of Dramatic Art, London, 1958-59; Ecole Jacques Lecoq, Paris, 1965. Career: Actor in repertory in Nottingham, Liverpool, Coventry, and Citizen's Theatre, Glasgow, 6 years. Founding Director, London Theatre Group, 1973-. Publications include: Plays: Kvetch and Acapulco, London, 1986; Los Angeles, 1986 (as Kvetch, NY, 1987, London, 1991); Sink The Belgrano!, London, 1986; With Massage, London, 1987; Metamorphosis, London, 1969; The Trial, London, 1970; In The Penal Colony, London, 1968, 1988; East, Edinburgh, 1975; West, London, 1983; Greek, London, 1980; Decadence, London, 1981; Faber, 1989; The Fall of The House of Usher, Edinburgh, 1985; The Theatre of Steven Berkoff - Photographic Record, Methuen, 1992; Short stories: Gross Intrusion and Other Stories, 1979; Director of plays and actor in many plays and films and for television. Honours: Los Angeles Drama Critics Circle Award for Directing, 1983; Evening Standard Award for Kvetch, Comedy of The Year, 1991. Literary Agent: Joanna Marston. Address: c/o Joanna Marston, Rosica Colin Limited, 1 Clareville Grove Mews, London, SW7 5AH, England.

BERKSON Bill (William Craig), b. 30 Aug 1939, New York City, USA. Poet; Critic; Teacher; Editor. m. Lynn O'Hare, 17 July 1975, 1 son, 1 daughter. Education: Brown University, 1957-59; The New School for Social Research, 1959-60; Columbia College, 1959-60; New York University, Institute of Fine Arts, 1960-61. Appointments: Editor, Best & Company, 1969; Editor, Big Sky magazines & books, 1971-78; Professor, San Francisco Art Institute, 1984-; Contributing Editor, Zyzzyva 1987-92; Corresponding Editor, Art in America, 1988-. Publications: Saturday Night: Poems 1960-61, 1961, 1975; Shining Leaves, 1969; Recent Visitors, 1973; Enigma Variations, 1975; Hymns to St Bridget, (with Frank O'Hara), 1975; Blue is The Hero, 1976; Homage to Frank O'Hara, editor, 1978; Start Over, 1983; Red Devil, 1983; Lush Life, 1983. Contributions to: Paris Review; Poetry (Chicago); This; Sun & Moon; Art Forum; Evergreen Review; O-Blek; Angel Hair; Big Table; The World; New American Writing. Honours: Dylan Thomas Memorial Award, The New School, 1959; Poets Foundation Grant, 1968; Yaddo Fellow, 1968; National Endowment for the Arts Fellowship, 1980; Briarcombe Fellowship, 1983; Marin Arts Council Poetry Award, 1987; Artspace Award for Art Criticism, 1990. Membership: International Association of Art Critics; PEN. Address: 800 Chestnut Street, San Francisco, CA 94133, USA.

BERMAN Claire, b. 1936, USA. Author; Journalist. Appointments: Senior Editor, Cosmopolitan, 1958-63; Contributing Editor, New York Magazine, 1972-78; Former Director of Public Education, Permanent Families for Children, Child Welfare League of America. Publications: A Great City for Kids: A Parent's Guide to a Child's New York, 1969; We Take This Child: A Candid Look at Modern Adoption, 1974; Making It as a Stepparent, 1980, 1986; "What Am I Doing in a Stepfamily?" 1982; A Hole in my Heart: Adult Children of Divorce Speak Out, 1991; Golden Cradle: How The Adoption Establishment Works, 1991. Memberships: Secretary, American Society of Journalists and Authors. Literary Agent: James Levine. Address: 52 Riverside Drive, New York, NY 10024, USA.

BERMAN David, b. 20 Nov 1942, New York, USA. University Teacher. m. Aileen Jill Mitchell, 25 Dec 1970, 1 son, 1 daughter. Education: BA, New School for Social Research, 1965; MA, University of Denver, 1966; PhD, Trinity College, Dublin, 1972. Publications: History of Atheism in Britain; Berkeley's Alciphron in Focus; George Berkeley: Idealism and the Man. Contributions to: Oxford Companion to English Literature; Encyclopaedia of Unbelief; Field Day Anthology of Irish Literature; Irish Mind; George Berkeley; Critical Assessments; Berkeley Newsletter; Dictionaire des Philosophes; Mind; Apollo; Journal of History of Ideas; Journal of History of Philosophy; Book Collector; International Review of Psychoanalysis; Revue International De Philosophie; Idealistic Studies. Address: Philosophy Department, Trinity College, Dublin 2, Ireland.

BERMANT Chaim Icyk, b. 26 Feb 1929, Poland. Author. m. Judith Weil, 16 Dec 1962, 2 sons, 2 daughters. Education: MA

Honours, MLitt, Glasgow University, UK; MSc, London School of Economics. Publications include: Troubled Eden, 1967; The Cousinhood, 1970; Coming Home, 1976; The Jews, 1977; The Patriarch, 1981; House of Women, 1982; Dancing Bear, 1984; What's the Joke, study of Jewish humour, 1986; Titch, 1987; The Companian, 1988; Lord Jakobovits, 1990; Murmurings of a Licenced Heretic, 1990. Contributions to: Innumerable publications. Address: c/o Aitken and Stone Ltd, 29 Fernshaw Road, London SW10 0TG, England.

BERNARD Oliver, b. 6 Dec 1925, Chalfont St Peter, Bucks, England. Writer. 2 s, 2 d. Education: BA, Goldsmiths' College; ACSD, Central School of Speech and Drama. Publications: Rimbaud Collected Poems, 1962; Apollinaire Selection, 1965; Country Matters (poems), 1961; Poems, 1983, Five Peace Poems, 1985; The Finger Points at The Moon, 1989; Moons and Tides, 1989; Getting Over It, 1992. Contributions to: Since 1955: Botteghe Oscure; Times Literary Supplement; The Listener; Poetry (Chicago); Gemini; Spectator; New Statesman; Only Poetry; New Poetry. Honour: Poetry Society Gold Medal for Verse Speaking, 1982. Memberships: William Morris Society; Council Member, Poetry Society; Committee Member, BP Speak-a-Poem. Address: 1 East Church Street, Kenninghall, Norwich, NR16 2EP, England.

BERNARD Robert. See: **MARTIN Robert Bernard.**

BERNAUW Patrick, b. 15 Apr 1962, Alost, Belgium. Writer. m. Elke Van der Elst, 24 Mar 1984, 1 daughter. Appointments: Scenarist Comic Books, Gucky, 1983-84; Producer and Director of Radio Plays, 1988-; Editor, Historische Verhalen (Historical Studies). Publications: Mijn Lieve Spooklidmaat, 1983; De Stillevens Van De Dood, 1985; Mysteries Van Hetlam Gods, 1991; Dromen Van Een Farao, 1991; Landru Bestaat Niet, 1992; Several plays and radio plays. Contributions to: Vlaamse Filmpjes; Kreatief; Bres; Plot; Crime; Ganymedes; short stories and essays. Honours: John Flanders Award, 1987, 1991. Address: Brusselbaan 296, 9320 Erembodegem, Belgium.

BERNE Stanley, b. 8 June 1923, Port Richmond, Staten Island, New York, USA. Research Professor. m. Arlene Zekowski, July 1952. Education: BS, Rutgers University, 1947; MA, New York University, 1950; Graduate Fellow, Louisiana State University, Baton Rouge, 1954-59. Appointments: Associate Professor, English 1960-80, Research Professor, English 1980-, Eastern New Mexico University, Portales; Host, Co-Producer, TV series Future Writing Today, KENW-TV, PBS, 1984-85. Publications: A First Book of the Neo-Narrative, 1954; Cardinals and Saints.. On the aims and purposes of the arts in our time, criticism, 1958; The Dialogues, 1962; The Multiple Modern Gods and Other Stories, 1969; The New Rubaiyat of Stanley Berne, poetry, 1973; Future Language, criticism, 1976; The Great American Empire, 1981; Every Person's Little Book of P-L-U-T-O-N-I-U-M (with Arlene Zekowski), 1992; Alphabet Soup: A Dictionary of Ideas, 1993; The Unconscious Victorious and other Stories, 1969; Anthologies include: Trace, 1965; New World Writing #11; First Person Intense, 1978; Breakthrough Fictioneers, 1979; American Writing Today, 1992; Santa Fe Arts Directory, 1993; Dictionary of the Avant-Gardes, 1993. Honours: Literary research awards, Eastern New Mexico University, 1966-76. Memberships: PEN, COSMEP; New England Small Press Association; Rio Grande Writers Association; Santa Fe Writers. Address: Box 4595 Santa Fe, NM 87502, USA.

BERNER Urs, b. 17 Apr 1944, Schafisheim, Switzerland. Writer. Divorced. Education: Teacher's Training; Studies in History, University of Zurich. Appointments: Editor, then Freelance Journalist. Publications: Friedrichs einsame Traume in der Stadt am Fluss, novel, 1977; Fluchtrouten, novel, 1980; Wunschzeiten, novel, 1985; Das Wunder von Dublin, stories, 1987; die Lottokonige, novel, 1989. Address: Scharerstrasse 9, CH-3014 Berne, Switzerland.

BERNSTEIN Charles, b. 4 Apr 1950, New York, USA. Poet; Essayist; Teacher. m. Susan Bee, 1977, 1 son, 1 daughter. Education: AB, Harvard Coll, 1972. Appointments: David Gray Professor, State University of New York, 1989. Publications: 20 books include: A Poetics; Rough Trades; Content's Dream: Essays; Controlling Interests; Dark City, 1994. Honours: National Endowment for the Arts, Guggenheim; New York Foundation for the Arts. Address: 306 Clemens Hall, English Department, SUNY, Buffalo, NY 14260, USA.

BERNSTEIN Marcelle, See: **CLARK Marcelle Ruth.**

BERRIDGE Elizabeth, b. 3 Dec 1919, London, England. Author; Critic. m. Reginald Moore, 1940, 1 s, 1 d. Literary Appointments: Editor, Peter Owen, 1956-61; Reviewer, Critic: BBC; Spectator; Books and Bookmen; Tribune; Country Life, 1952-74; Fiction Reviewer, Daily Telegraph, 1967-88. Publications: Family Matters, story collection, 1981; People at Play, 1982; Across The Common, 1964, 1985, 1989; Rose Under Glass, 1967, 1985; Sing Me Who You Are, 1972, 1985; Editor and introduction, The Barretts at Hope End, 1974; Run For Home, 1981; That Surprising Summer, (Children's Books), 1973, 1975. Honour: Novel of The Year, Yorkshire Post, 1964. Memberships: PEN; Trustee, Chase Charity. Address: c/o David Higham Association, 5-8 Lower John Street, London, W1R 4HA, England.

BERRY Adrian M, b. 1937. Journalist; Writer. Literary Appointments: Correspondent, Time Magazine, NY, 1965-67; Science Correspondent, Daily Telegraph, London, 1977-. Publications: The Next Ten Thousand Years: A Vision of Man's Future in The Universe, 1974; The Iron Sun: Crossing The Universe Through Black Holes, 1977; From Apes to Astronauts, 1981; The Super Intelligent Machine, 1983; High Skies and Yellow Rain, 1983; Koyama's Diamond (fiction), 1984; Labryinth of Lies (fiction), 1985; Ice With Your Evolution, 1986; Computer Software: The Kings and Queens of England, 1985; Harrap's Book of Scientific Anecdotes, 1989.Honour: Fellow of The Royal Geographic Society, 1984-. Memberships: Fellow, Royal Astronomical Society, London, 1973-; Senior Fellow, British Interplanetary Society, 1986-. Address: 11 Cottesmore Gardens, Kensington, London, W8, England.

BERRY Francis, b. 23 Mar 1915, Ipoh, Malaya. Emeritus Professor. m. 1) Nancy Melloney Graham, 4 Sept 1947, 1 son, 1 daughter, 2) Eileen Marjorie Lear, 9 Apr 1970. Education: BA, University of London, 1947; MA, University of Exeter, 1949. Publications include: Poets' Grammar, 1958; The Iron Christ, 1938; Murdock and Other Poems, 1962; The Galloping Centaur, 1952; Poetry and the Physical Voice, 1962; The Shakespeare Inset, 1966; Morant Bay and Other Poems, 1961; Ghosts of Greenland, 1966; I Tell of Greenland, 1977; From the Red Fort, 1984; Contributions to: BBC; TLS; The Listener; New Statesman; The Observer; Collected poems 1994, Critical Quarterly. Membership: Fellow, Royal Society of Literature. Address: 4 Eastgate Street, Winchester, Hampshire SO23 8EB, England.

BERRY Ila F, b. 9 Jun 1922. Freelance Writer; Poet; Student of Creative Writing. Education: AA, Fullerton College, USA; BA, John F Kennedy University; MA, English and Creative Writing, San Francisco State University, 1985. Appointments: Long Distance Operator and Supervisor, Pacific Telephone Company, Los Angeles, CA; Investigator, International Department, Bank of America, San Francisco, CA. Publications: Poetry: Come Walk With Me, 1979; Re-arranging The Landscape, 1986; Rowing in Eden, 1987; Behold The Bright Demons, 1993. Contributions to: The Los Angeles Times; Oakland Tribune; Blue Unicorns; Attention Please; Ideals; Haiku Highlights; Communicating Through Word and Image; Tunnel Road; The Sandpiper; Torchlight. Honours include: Jessamyn West Creative Award, 1969; Woman of Distinction, Fullerton College, 1969; Grand Prize, Poetry, Poets Dinner, 1974. Memberships: Ina Coolbrith Circle, President, 1977-79; California State Poetry Society; Robert Frost Chapter, Californian Federation of Chaparral Poets; The California Writers Club; The National League of American Pen Women. Address: 761 Sequoia Woods Place, Concord, CA 94518, USA.

BERRY James, b. 1925, Fair Prospect, Jamaica. Editor; Poet. Appointment: Writer-in-residence, Vauxhall Manor School. Publications: Fractured Circles, 1979; Cut-Way Feelins, Loving Lucy's Letters, 1981; Chain of Days, 1985; When I Dance: Poems 1991; Short Stories: The Girls and Yanga Marshall, 1987; A Thief in the Village and Other Stories, 1988; Anancy-Spiderman, 1988; Editor, Bluefoot Traveller: An Anthology of West Indian Poets in Britain, 1976; Bluefoot Traveller: An Anthology of West Indian Poetry, 1976; Dance to a Different Drum: Brixton Poetry Festival, 1983; News for Babylon: The Chatto Book of West Indian-British Poetry, 1984; Don't Leave an Elephant to Go and Chase a Bird, 1990; Ajeema & His Son, 1992. Honours: C Day Lewis Fellowship; Poetry Society Prize, 1981; Boston Globe/Horn Book Award, 1993. Address: c/o Hamish Hamilton Ltd, 27 Wrights Lane, London W8 5TZ, England.

BERRY Paul, b. 1919. Writer. Publications: Daughters of Cain (with Renee Huggett), 1956; By Royal Appointment: A Biography of Mary Ann Clarke, Mistress of The Duke of York 1803-07, 1970; Joint

Editor, The Selected Journalism of Winifred Holtby and Vera Brittain, 1985; Vera Brittain: A Life (with Mark Bostridge), 1993. **Address:** 1 Bridgefoot Cottages, Stedham, Midhurst, Sussex, England.

BERRY Wendell, b. 1934. Poet; Writer; Essayist. m. Appointments: Professor, New York & CA; Writer; Farmer. Publications include: A Place on Earth; The Wild Birds; The Gift of Good Land; Standing By Words; The Unsettling of America; Fidelity; The Memory of Old Jack; A Continuous Harmony; The Wheel; Openings; The Country of Marriage; Clearing; What Are People For?, 1990; Sex, Economy, Freedom & Community, 1992; Entries, 1994; Watch With Me, 1994. Honours: Lannan Foundation Award, 1989; Victory of Spirit of Ethics Award,1992. Address: Lanes Landing Farm, Port Royal, KY 40058, USA.

BERTHA Zoltan, b. 4 June 1955, Szentes, Hungary. Writer; Teacher; Scholar. m. Hajdu Csilla, 5 July 1985, 1 son. Education: University of Debrecen, MA 1978, Doctor's Degree 1982; PhD, 1994. Appointments: Scholar, Debrecen University, 1978-90; Member of Leaders of Society of Young Writers, 1984-88; Editorial Board, Alföld, 1991-93; Holnap, 1990-93; Member of Parliament, 1990-94; Protestant University, Budapest, Professor, 1994-. Publications: Hungarian Literature in Rumania Transylvania in the 70s, 1983, 1985 (with Görömbei, Andras); A Szellem Jelzöfenyei, 1988; Balint Tibor, 1990; Gond es Mu, 1994; Arcvonalban, 1994. Contributions to: Alföld; Tiszataj; Forras; Eletunk; Holnap; Kortars; Lato; Korunk; Helikon; Irodalomtörtenet; Magyar Elet; Magyar Szemle; Hitel; Filologiai Közlöny; Acta Litteraria; Magyar Forum. Honours: Scholarship of Young Critics, 1983; Moricz Zsigmond Literary Scholarship, 1989. Memberships: Association of Hungarian Writers; Society of Young Writers; International Association of Hungarian Studies; Society of Hungarian Literary History; Community of the Hungarian Journalists; Union of Hungarian Artists; Nemeth Laszlo Society; Szabo Dezsö Society; Protestant Cultural Society. Address: Böszörmenyi ut 69, IV 15, H-4032 Debrecen, Hungary.

BERTIN Jack. See: **GERMANO Peter B.**

BERTOLINO James, b. 4 Oct 1942, WI, USA. College Teacher. m. Lois Behling, 29 Nov 1966. Education: BS, University of Wisconsin, Oshkosh, 1970; MFA, Poetry Writing, American Literature, Cornell University, 1973. Literary Appointments: Creative Writing Faculty, Cornell University, 1973; University of Cincinnati, 1974; Western Washington University, 1984; Skagit Valley College, 1985; Djerassi Foundation, 1987; Centrum Arts Foundation, 1989; Edmonds Community College, 1989. Publications: Volumes of poetry: Employed, 1972; Making Space For Our Living, 1975; The Alleged Conception, 1976; New and Selected Poems, 1978; Precinct Kali and The Gertrude Spicer Story, 1982; First Credo, 1986; Others: Drool, 1968; Stone Marrow, 1969; Becoming Human, 1970; Edging Through, 1972; Terminal Placebos, 1975; The Gestures, 1975. Contributions to: Poetry: Gargoyle; International Synergy Journal; In Context; The Amicus Journal; Wilderness; Organic Gardening. Honours: Book of The Month Club, Poetry Fellowship, 1970; National Endowment for The Arts Fellowship, 1974; Ohio Arts Council Award, 1979; International Colladay Book Award for First Credo, 1986. Address: PO Box 1157, Anacortes, WA 98221, USA.

BESS Clayton. See: **LOCKE Robert Howard.**

BETTELINI Lauro, b. 27 Aug 1938, Lugano, Switzerland. Journalist. 1 s, 1 d. Education: Technical Architect, 1957; Journalism Degree, Milan, Italy. Literary Appointments: Gazzetta Ticinese, 1975; Swiss Television, 1979. Publications: Narrative Poetry: Noi Della Piazza, 1987; Lo Zodiaco Del Nonno, 1987; Gli Orti Del Disgelo, 1987; Jl Doppio Allo Specchio, 1988; Television Documentary. Contributions to: Numerous magazines and journals. Honours: Premio Nazionale Narrative, La Spezia Italy, 1985; Premio Letterario L'Autore Poesia, Firenze, 1986; Premio Nazionale Di Poesia, Pisa, 1987; Premio Ascona Finalista Narrativa, Ascona, 1987; Mondo Letterario Finalista Narrative, Milan, 1987. Memberships: Associazione Scrittori della Svizzera Italiana; PEN; Federation of Swiss Journalist. Literary Agent: Lucchini Cristina. Address: Via Crespera 50B, 6932 Breganzona, Switzerland.

BETTERIDGE Anne. See: **POTTER Margaret.**

BETTEX Albert, b. 2 Apr 1906, Basel. Writer; Former Editor; Lecturer. m. Charlotte von Felten, 7 May 1966. Education: Teachers'

Training College & University, 1925-33; PhD, 1933. Appointments: Lecturer, University Extension, Basel, 1933-45; Lektor in German, Cambridge University England, 1936-39; Literary Editor, DU, Zurich, 1945-57; Editor, Librarium, Zurich, 1958-79; Visiting Professor, Universities of Sao Paulo, 1954, Toronto, 1962, Maryland, USA, 1965-66. Publications: Der Kampf um das klassische Weimar, 1788-1798, 1935; Spiegelungen der Schweiz in der deutschen Literatur 1870-1950, 1954; Welten der Entdecker, 1960; Die Entdeckung der Natur, 1965; Europe of the Writers, in preparation. Contributions to: Goethe und die Kunst des Reisens, in Jahrbuch der Goethe-Gesellschaft, 1949; Walter R. Cort ails Mitredaktor des DU, in Schweizer Monatshefte, Mai, 1990. Honours: University of Basel, 1931; Canton & City of Zurich, 1958, 1970, 1961, 1980; Bodmer Foundation, Geneva, 1975. Memberships: PEN Club of Switzerland; Honorary Member, Swiss Society of Bibliophiles, Zurich. Address: Sonnenbergstrasse 47, CH-8800 Thalwil, Switzerland.

BETTS Raymond Frederick, b. 1925, USA. Writer. Publications: Assimilation and Association in French Colonial Theory 1890-1914, 1961; The Scramble of Africa, 1966; Europe Overseas: Phases of Imperialism, 1968; The Ideology of Blackness, 1971; The False Dawn: European Imperialism in The Nineteenth Century, 1975; Tricouleur: The French Colonial Empire, 1978; Europe in Retrospect: A Brief History of The Past Two Hundred Years, 1979; Uncertain Dimensions: Western Overseas Empires in The Twentieth Century, 1985; France and Decolonisation, 1991. Address: 311 Mariemont Drive, Lexington, KY 40505, USA.

BEVAN Alistair. See: **ROBERTS Keith John Kingston.**

BEVAN Gloria, b. New Zealand. Author. Publications: The Distant Trap, 1969; The Hills of Maketu, 1969; Beyond The Ranges, 1970; Make Way for Tomorrow, 1971; It Began in Te Rangi, 1971; Vineyard in A Valley, 1972; Flame in Fiji, 1973; The Frost and The Fire, 1973; Connelly's Castle, 1974; High Country Wife, 1974; Always a Rainbow, 1975; Dolphin Bay, 1976; Bachelor Territory, 1977; Plantation Moon, 1977; Fringe of Heaven, 1978; Kowhai Country, 1979; Half a World Away, 1980; Master of Mahia, 1981; Emerald Cave, 1981; The Rouseabout Girl, 1983; Southern Sunshine, 1985; Golden Bay, 1986. Address: c/o Mills and Boon Limited, 15-16 Brooks Mews, London, W1A 1DR, England.

BEWES Richard Thomas, b. 1 Dec 1934, Nairobi, Kenya. Anglican Rector. m. Elisabeth Ingrid Jaques, 18 Apr 1964, 2 sons, 1 daughter. Education: Marlborough School, 1948-53; MA, Emmanuel College, Cambridge, 1954-57; Ridley Hall Theological College, Cambridge, 1957-59. Publications: Talking About Prayer, 1979; The Pocket Handbook of Christian Truth, 1981; The Church Reaches Out, 1981; John Wesley's England, 1981; The Church Overcomes, 1983; On the Way, 1984; Quest for Life, 1985; The Church Marches On, 1986; When God Suprises, 1986; A New Beginning, 1989; The Resurrection, 1989. Contributor to: The Church of England Newspaper. Membership: The Guild of British Songwriters. Address: 2 All Souls Place, London, W1N 3DB, England.

BEYE Holly, b. 27 Feb1922, Iowa City, IA, USA. Writer; Librarian. Education: BA, Swarthmore College, 1943; MLS, University of New York, Albany, 1967; Graduate, Rutgers University School of Alcoholism, NJ, 1981. Literary Appointments: Performance and Workshop Writer and Director, The Heads, Cafe Theatre political improvisation group, 1960's; WESAW Improvisation for Elementary School students, 1975-85; Holly's Comets Improvisation Group, 1985-. Publications: Do Keep Thee in The Stony Bowes, prose poem, 1951; In The City of Sorrowing Clouds, 1952; XVI Poems, 1953; Stairwells and Marriages, 1954; Monsters in World Folklore, filmstrips, 1970; Lives of the Comets, video, 1989; Refractions, video, 1990; Plays: Afternoon of The Spawn, 1961; Thus, 1963; It's All Yours!, 1963; The Banana Thief, 1965; About The Cast, 1989; Chance, 1989; Dilly, Dawn and Dell, 1990; The Bat Girl, 1992; Sisters, 1993. Contributions to: Quarterly Review of Literature; New Directions Annual. Honours: Prize, Quarterly Review of Literature, 1962. Memberships: Dramatists Guild. PO Box 1043, Woodstock, NY 12498, USA.

BEYFUS Drusilla. Writer. Appointments: Women's Editor, Sunday Express, London, 1952-53; Columnist, Daily Express, London, 1953-56; Associate Editor, Queen Magazine, London, 1959-63; Home Editor, The Observer, London, 1962-64; Associate Editor, Weekend Telegraph Magazine, London, 1963-71; Editor, Brides and Setting Up Home Magazine, London, 1971-79; Associate Editor, Vogue Magazine,

London, 1980-87; Contributing Editor, Telegraph Magazine, 1991-; Visiting Tutor Central St Martins College of Art, 1989-. Publications: Lady Behave (with Anne Edwards), 1956, 1969; The English Marriage, 1968; The Bride's Book, 1981; The Art of Giving, 1987; Modern Manners, 1992; The Move Thing: Courtship, Parties, 1992; Business, Sex, 1993. Contributions to: Sunday Times; Punoh; Sunday Telegraph; New Statesman; Daily Telegraph; The Spectator. Address: 51g Eaton Square, London SW1, England.

BEYNON Huw, b. 1942. Writer; Professor of Sociology. Publications: Perceptions of Work (with R M Blackburn), 1972; Working for Ford, 1973, 1984; Living with Capitalism (with Theo Nichols), 1977; What Happened at Speke? 1978; The Workers Report on Vickers Limited (with Hilary Wainwright), 1979; Born to Work (with Nick Hedges), 1982; Digging Deeper: Issues in the Miners' Strike, 1985; A Tale of Two Industries: The Decline of Coal and Steel in the North of England (with R Hudson and D Sadler), 1991; Master and Servants Class and Patronage in the Making of a Labour Organisation (with T Austrin), 1994; A Place Called Teesside: A Locality in a Global Economy (with R Hudson and D Sadler), 1994. Address: Department of Sociology, University of Manchester, Manchester M13 9PL, England.

BHARGAVA Vicky. See: **BHARGAVA Vishal.**

BHARGAVA Vishal (Vicky Bhargava), b. 9 Feb 1967. Allahabad, India. Journalist. Education: Science Intermediate (Commerce), ISC, 12th Standard, 1985; Diploma in Printing Technology, Northern Indian Institute of Printing Technology, 1987; Bachelor of Commerce, 1988. Appointments: Bhargava and Bhargava Printers (P) Ltd, 1991. Publication: First book, 1994. Contributions to: Mainly to magazines of Bhargava and Bhargava Printers (P) Ltd. Address: 119 Swami Vivekanand Marg, Allahabad 210003, India.

BHARTI Dharmvir, b. 1926, India. Novelist; Poet. Education: MA, University of Allahabad, 1947. Appointments include: Founder, Editor of Charmayug magazine, Bombay; Editor, Alocha quarterly. Publications: Verse: Cold Iron, 1952; The Beloved of Krishna, 1959; Seven Years of Lyrics, 1959; Fiction: The Village of the Dead, 1946; The God of Sins, 1949; The Seventh Horse of the Sun God, 1952; Immortal Son, 1952; The Moon and Broken People, 1965; Heaven and Earth; Plays, The River was Thirsty, 1954; The Blind Age, 1954; Literature and Human Values, 1960. Address: c/o Dharmayug, Bennett, Coleman & Co, Times Building, Dr D B Road, Bombay 400001, India.

BHATNAGAR Om Prakash, b. 30 May 1932, Agra, India. Professor. m. Parvati Bhatnagar, 21 Oct 1959, 1 s, 1 d. Education: MA, 1954; MA, 1956; DLitt, 1959; PhD, 1991. Literary Appointments: Editorial Board, Indian Journal of English Studies, 1979-86. Publications: Poetry, Thought Poems; Angles of Retreat; Oneiric Visions; Shadows in Floodlights; Audible Landscape; Perspectives on Indian Poetry in English; Studies in Indian Drama in English. Contributions to: 69 Literary and Research articles. Honours: Plaque of Honor for Excellence in Poetry; G Ramachandran Award for International Understanding Through Literature. Memberships: Zonal Representative, Indian Association for English Studies; University EnglishTeachers Association. Address: Rituraj, Camp, Amravati 444, 602 India.

BHATTACHARYYA Birendra Kumar, b. 14 Oct 1924, Suffry Sibsagar, Assam, India. Journalist; Writer. m. Binita Bhattacharyya, 1958, 2 s, 1 d. Education: Calcutta University; Gauhati University; BSc, MA, PhD. Appointments include: Science Teacher, Manipur; Editor, Ramdhenu 1951-61, Sadiniya Navayung, 1963-67; Lecturer, journalism, Gauhati University, 1974-85. Publications: Novels: Iyaruingam; Rajpathe Ringiai (Call of The Main Street); Ai (Mother); Satagnai (Killer); Mrityunjay; Pratipad; Nastachandra; Ballari; Kabar Aru Phul; Ranga Megh; Daini; Collections, short stories: Kolongahioboi (Still Flows The Kolong); Satsari (Necklace); Aurobindo, biography; Survey of Assamese Modern Culture (in Assamese). Honours: Sahitya Akademi Award for Assamese Literature, 1961; Jnanpith Award, 1979. Memberships: President, Sahitya Academi, New Delhi; Ex-President, Assam Sahitya Sabha. Address: Kharghuli Development Area, Guwahati 4, Assam, India.

BHYRAPPA Santeshivara Lingannaiah, b. 26 July 1934, Santeshivara, Karnataka, India. m. Saraswati, 13 Dec 1958, 2 sons. Education: BA (Hons), 1957; MA Philosophy, 1958, PhD Aesthetics, 1963. Publications: 17 novels and 4 books on Literary Criticism including: Novels: Vamsha Vriksha, 1966; Grihabhanga, 1970; Daatu,

1974; Parva, 1979; Nele, 1983; Sakshi, 1986; Truth and Beauty, 1964; Story and Its Substance, 1969; Why Do I Write and Other Essays, 1982; Tantu, 1993. Contributions to: Numerous journals. Honours: Best Book of the Year Award, 1967, 1975; Central Sahihya Akademi Award, 1975; Karnataka Government Rajyotsava Day Award. Memberships: Karnataka State Sahitya Akademi; Central Sahitya Akademi; Bharatiya Jnaanapeeth Foundation; Indian Philosophical Congress. Address: 1007 Kuvempunagar, Mysore 570023, India.

BIANCHI Eugene Carl, b. 1930, USA. Writer (Theology/Religion). Publications: John XXIII and American Protestants, 1968; Reconciliation: The Function of the Church, 1969; The Religious Experience of Revolutionaries, 1972; From Machismo to Mutuality (with Rosemary P Ruether), 1975; Aging As a Spiritual Journey, 1982; On Growing Older, 1985; A Democratic Catholic Church, co-ed with Rosemary Ruether, 1992; Elder Wisdom: Crafting Your Elderhood, 1994. Address: Department of Religion, Emory University, Atlanta, GA 30322, USA.

BIBBY Peter Leonard, b. 21 Dec 1940, London, England. Poet; Playwright; Screenwriter. m. 15 Apr 1967, 2 s, 2 d. Education: BA, University of Western Australia; DipEd, Murdoch University. Literary Appointments: Editor, Fellowship of Australian Writers; Editor, Magabala Books, Broome Publishing Project, Australian Bicentennial Authority. Publications: Island Weekend, 1960; Represented in anthologies: Quarry; Breakaway; Summerland; Inprint W A Story; Poetry Australia; Laughing Cry; Broadcast Verse and Drama, ABC. Contributions to: Professional journals including: Bulletin Australia; Outrider; Overland; Poetry Australia. Honours: Tom Collins Literary Awards, Verse, 1978,1982; Lyndall Hadow National Short Story Award, 1983; Donald Stuart , National Short Story Award, 1985. Memberships: Australian Writers Guild; Fellowship of Australian Writers; Australian Film Institute; Computer Graphics Association. Address: c/o PO Box 668, Broome, WA, Australia.

BIBERGER Erich Ludwig, b. 20 July 1927, Passau, Bavaria, Germany. Editor; Writer. Education: Examination Stadt; Wirtschafsaubauschule Passau, 1944; Volkshochschule Passau. Publications include: Dreiklang der Stille (Poems), 1955; Rundgang über dem Nordlicht (Philosophy, Fairy Tales of Atomic Age), 1958; Die Traumwelle (novel), 1962; Denn im Allsein der Welt (poems), 1966; Duadu oder den Mann im Mond (radio plays), 1967; Gar mancher (satirical verses), 1967; Anthology Quer, 1974; Anthology 3 (in 47 languages), 1979; Andere Wege bis Zitterluft (poems), 1982; Was ist hier Schilf, was Reiher (Haiku), 1984; Nichts als das Meer (Poems), 1984; Zwei Pfund Morgenduft (Feuilletons), 1987. Honours: Recipient several honours. Memberships include: Chairman, Regensburger Schriftslellergruppe International, Joint Association of Authors in 25 Countries of the World, 1960-; Founder, Director, Internationale Regensberger Literaturtage, 1967-; Internationale Jungautoren-Wettbewerbe, 1972-; Founder, Editor, Publication series RSG Studio International, 1973-, RSG-Forum 15/2E, 1977-; Member of Humboldt-Gesllschaft für Wissenschaft und Kunst, 1993-. Address: Altmühlstr, D 93059 Regensburg, Germany.

BICKHAM Jack Miles (Jeff Clinton, John Miles), b. 1930, USA. Writer; Professor of Journalism. Literary Appointments: Managing Editor, The Oaklahoma Courier, 1966-69; Professor of Journalism, University of Oaklahoma, Norman, 1969-. Publications include: Wildcat Meets Miss Melody, 1968; Target Charity Ross, 1968; (as Jeff Clinton) Build a Box For Wildcat, 1969; Decker's Campaign (in UK as The Sheriff's Campaign), 1970; (as Jeff Clinton) Wildcat's Claim To Fame, 1970; (as Jeff Clinton) A Stranger Named O'Shea, 1970; Goin', 1971; (as Jeff Clinton) Bounty on Wildcat, 1971; The Apple Dumpling Gang, 1971; Fletcher, 1972; Jilly's Canal, 1972; Dopey Dan, 1972; (as Jeff Clinton) Hang High, O'Shea, 1972; Kate, Kelly and Heck, 1973; (as John Miles) The Night Hunters, 1973; Baker's Hawk, 1974; (as John Miles) The Silver Bullet Gang, 1974; (as John Miles) The Blackmailer, 1974; (as Jeff Clinton) Emerald Canyon, 1974; Hurry Home, Davey Clock, 1974; A Boat Named Death, 1975; (as John Miles with T Morris) Operation Nightfall, 1974; (as Jeff Clinton) Showdown at Emerald Canyon, 1975; (as Jeff Clinton) Kane's Odyssey, 1975; Twister, 1976; The Winemakers, 1977; The Excalibur Disaster, 1978; Dinah, Blow Your Horn, 1979; A Question of Ethics, 1980; The Regensburg Legacy, 1980; All The Days Were Summer, 1981; I Still Dream About Columbus, 1982; Ariel, 1984; Miracleworker, 1987; Breakfast at Wimbledon, 1991; Double Fault, 1993. Address: School of Journalism, University of Oklahoma, Norman, OK 73019, USA.

BIDDISS Michael Denis, b. 15 Apr 1942, Farnborough, Kent, England. University Professor. m. Ruth Margaret Cartwright, 8 Apr 1967, 4 daughters. Education: MA, PhD, Queens' College, Cambridge, 1961-66; Centre des Hautes Etudes Européennes, University of Strasbourg, 1965-66. Appointments: Fellow in History, Downing College, Cambridge, 1966-73; Lecturer/Reader in History, University of Leicester, 1973-79; Professor of History, University of Reading, 1979-. Publications: Father of Racist Ideology, 1970; Gobineau: Selected Political Writings (editor), 1970; Disease and History (co-author), 1972; The Age of the Masses, 1977; Images of Race (editor), 1979; Thatchersim: Personality and Politics (co-editor), 1987; The Nuremberg Trial and the Third Reich, 1992. Address: Department of History, The University of Reading, Whiteknights, Reading RG6 2AA, England.

BIEGEL Paul Johannes, b. 25 Mar 1925, Bussum, The Netherlands. Author. Publications: The King of the Copper Mountains, 1969; The Seven Times Search, 1971; The Little Captain, 1971; The Twelve Robbers, 1974; The Gardens of Dorr, 1975; Far Beyond & Back Again, 1977; The Elephant Party, 1977; Letters from the General, 1979; The Looking-Glass Castle, 1979; The Dwarfs of Nosegay, 1978; Robber Hopsika, 1978; The Fattest Dwarf of Nosegay, 1980; The Tin Can Beast, 1980; The Curse of the Werewolf, 1981; Virgil Nosegay and the Cake Hunt, 1981; Crocodile Man, 1982; Virgil Nosegay and the Wellington Boots, 1984. Honours: Best Children's Book of the Year, 1965; Golden Pencil Award, 1972, 1993; Silver Pencil Award, 1972, 1974, 1981, 1988; Nienke van Hichtum prize for Children's Literature, 1973; State Prize, 1974; Woutertje Pieterse Prize, 1991. Memberships: Vereninging van Letterkudigen; Maatschappij van Letterkunde. Address: Keuzersgracht 227, Amsterdam, The Netherlands.

BIELINSKA Izabela, b. 21 Jan 1925, Lublin, Poland. Writer. Education: Warsaw University. Publications: Margaret, 1960, 1982; The Love Not Will Be, stories, 1963; Don't Beat Your Fathers, 9 short stories, 1976; Le Petit Dejeuner, short story, 1980; Taste of The Wild Strawberry Ice-cream, 1986; Harlequin's Costume, short story, 1990; Polish: Smak lodów poziomkowych, co-author Ewa Otwinowska; Literary, Film and Arts reviews; Radio plays; Film scripts. Contributions to: Literary and Film Magazines; Polish Radio. Memberships: Polish Writers Association; Polish Journalists Association; Film Critics Club. Address: Ul Nowowiejska 4 m 57, 00-649 Warsaw, Poland.

BIELSKI Alison Joy Prosser, b. 24 Nov 1925, Newport, Gwent, Wales. Secretary; Writer; Lecturer. m. 1) D Treverton Jones, 19 June 1948, 2) A E Bielski, 30 Nov 1955, 1 son, 1 daughter. Appointments: Honorary Secretary, Welsh Academy, 10 years. Publications: Across the Burning Sand, 1970; The Story of the Welsh Dragon, 1969; Flower Legends of the Wye Valley, 1974; The Lovetree, 1974; Eagles, 1983; The Story of St Mellons, 1985; Tales and Traditions of Tenby. Contributions to: Anglo-Welsh Review; Poetry Wales; Planet; New Welsh Review; Tribune; Poetry Review; Pembroke Magazine; Acument; Doors; New Poetry; Outposts. Honours: Anglo-Welsh Review Poetry Prize, 1970; Arnold Vincent Bowen Poetry Prize, 1971; Recipient, various other prizes and awards in poetry competitions. Memberships: Society of Women Writers and Journalists; Welsh Union of Writers; Gwent Poetry Society; Welsh Academy. Address: 92 Clifton Road, Paignton, Devon TQ3 3LD, England.

BIERMANN Wolf, b. 15 Nov 1936, Hamburg, Germany. Poet and Songwriter. m. Christine Bark, 2 sons, 1 daughter. Education: Humboldt University, 1959-63. Appointments include: Assistant Director, Berliner Ensemble, 1957-59; Song and guitar performances throughout Germany. Publications include: Die Drahtharfe: Balladen, Gedichte, Lieder, 1965; Mit Marx- und Engelszungen, 1968; Für meine Genossen, 1972; Deutschland: Ein Wintermärchen, 1972; Nachlass I, 1977; Wolf Biermann: Poems and Ballads, 1977; Preussicher Ikarus, 1978; Verdrehte welt- das seh' ich gerne, 1982; Und als ich von Deutschland nach Deutschland; Three Contemporary German Poets (with others), 1985; Affenels und Barrikade, 1986; Alle Lieder, 1991; Vier Neue Lieder, 1992; Play, Der Dra-Dra: Die Grosse Drachentoterschau in 8 akten mit Musik, 1970; Ich hatte viele Bekümmernis: Meditation on Cantata Nr 21 by J S Bach, 1991. Honours include: Möricke Prize, 1991; Buchner Prize, 1991. Address: c/o Verlag Kiepenheuer und Witsch, Rondorfer Strasse 5, 5000 Cologne-Marienburg, Germany.

BIGGLE Lloyd Jr, b. 1923, USA. Author. Publications: The Angry Espers, 1961; All the Colors of Darkness, 1963; The Fury Out of Time, 1965; Watchers of the Dark, 1966; The Rule of the Door and Other Fanciful Regulations (short stories), 1967 (in United Kingdom as The Silent Sky), 1979; The Still Small Voice of Trumpets, 1968; The World Menders, 1971; The Light That Never Was, 1972; Nebula Award Stories 7 (editor), 1972; The Metallic Muse (short stories), 1972; Monument, 1974; This Darkening Universe, 1975; A Galaxy of Strangers (short stories), 1976; Silence is Deadly, 1977; The Whirligig of Time, 1979; Alien Main (with T L Sherred), 1985; The Quallsford Inheritance, A Memoir of Sherlock Holmes, 1986; Interface for Murder, 1987; The Glendower Conspiracy, A Memoir of Sherlock Holmes, 1990; A Hazard of Losers, 1991; Where Dead Soldiers Walk (novel), 1994. Contributions to: Critiques of Science Fiction Quarterly: Science Fiction Goes to College, Riverside Quarterly, vol 6, no 2, 1974; The Morasses of Academe Revisited, Analog, XCVIII, no 9, 1978. Memberships: Founding Secretary Treasurer, 1965-67; Chairman of The Trustees, 1967-73; Science Fiction Writers of America; Founder 1977 and current President, Science Fiction Oral History Association, 1994. Literary Agent: Owlswick Literary Agency. Address: 569 Dubie Avenue, Ypsilanti, MI 48198, USA.

BIGGS Margaret Annette (Margaret Key Bigg), b. 26 Oct 1933, Pike County, Alabama, USA. Writer. m. 1 Mar 1956. Education: BS, Troy State University, 1954; MA, California State University, 1979. Publications: Swampfire, 1980; Sister to the Sun, 1981; Magnolias & Such, 1982; Petals from the Womanflower, 1983; Plumage of the Sun, 1986. Contributions to: Numerous journals including: Panhandler; Earthwise Poetry Journal; Gryphon; International University Poetry Quarterly; Thoreau Journal Quarterly; Echos; Jump River Review; Pipe Dream; Valhalla; Vega; Modern Images; Encore; Black Jack; Unicorn; Taurus; Poetry Monthly; Anthologies include: Peace is Our Profession; Meltdown; Crow Calls; Poets & Peace International; Macomb Fantasy Factory; Best Poems of 1982; Darkness Screams a Yellow Rose; Anthology I, Florida State Poets Association. Literary Agent: Noel S DeLuca. Address: PO Box 551, Port St Joseph, FL 32456, USA.

BIGGS Margaret Key. See: **BIGGS Margaret Annette.**

BIGSBY Christopher William Edgar, b. 27 June 1941, Dundee, Scotland. University Professor; Broadcaster; Novelist. Education: BA, MA, Sheffield University; PhD, Nottingham University. Publications: Confrontation & Commitment: A Study of Contemporary American Drama, 1967; Edward Albee, 1969; Dada & Surealism, 1972; Tom Stoppard, 1976; The Second Black Renaissance, 1980; Joe Orton, 1982, 1984, 1985; David Mamet, 1985; Editor, The Black America Writer, 1969; Three Negro Plays, 1969; Approaches to Popular Culture, 1975; Superculture, 1976; Edward Albee, 1976; Contemporary English Drama, 1981; The Radical Imagination and the Liberal Tradition, 1982; A Critical Introduction to 20th Century American Drama, 3 volumes; Cultural Change in the United States since World War II, 1986; Plays by Susan Glaspell, 1987; File on Miller, 1988; American Drama: 1945-1990, 1992; Hester (novel). Contributor to: Broadcaster, TV and Radio Scriptwriter; Times Literary Supplement; Times Higher Education Supplement; The Sunday Independent; American Quarterly; Modern Drama; Theatre Quarterly; The Guardian. Agent: Richard Scott Simon Ltd. Literary Address: 3 Church Farm, Colney, Norwich, England.

BILLING Graham John, b. 12 Jan 1936, Dunedin, New Zealand. Author. m. Rowan Innes Cunningham, 29 Aug 1978, 1 son, 1 daughter by previous marriage. Education: Otago University, 1955-58. Appointments: Staff, Dunedin Evening Star, 1958-62; Antarctic Division, DSIR, 1962-64; NZ Broadcasting Corporation News Service and TV Service (various appointments), 1964-67; Staff, Dominion Sunday Times, 1967-69; Lecturer, writing, Mitchell College Advanced Education, Bathurst, Australia, 1974-75. Publications: Forbush and the Penguins, 1965; The Slipway, 1973; The Alpha Trip, 1969; Statues, 1971; The Primal Therapy of Tom Purslane, 1980; Changing Countries (poetry), 1980; (Non-Fiction)South: Man and Nature in Antarctica, 1965; New Zealand, the Sunlit Land, 1966; The New Zealanders, 1974; (Radio Plays) Forbush and the Penguins, 1965; Mervyn Gridfem versus the Babsons, 1965; The Slipway, 1976; The Prince of Therapy of Tom Purslane, 1980; Verse, Changing Countries, 1980.

BILLINGTON Michael, b. 16 Nov 1939. Drama Critic. m. Jeanine Bradlaugh, 1978. Education: BA, St Catherine's College, Oxford. Appointments: Trained, as Journalist with Liverpool Daily Post and Echo, 1961-62; Public Liaison Officer, Director, Lincoln Theatre Co, 1962-64; Reviewed Plays, Films and TV for The Times, 1965-71; Film Critic: Birmingham Post, 1968-78, Illustrated London News, 1968-81; Drama Critic, The Guardian, 1971-; London Arts Correspondent, New York Times, 1978-; Drama Critic of Country Life, 1987-. Publications:

The Modern Actor, 1974; How Tickled I Am, 1977I Editor, The Performing Arts, 1980; The Guiness Book of Theatre Facts and Feats, 1982; Alan Ayckbourn, 1983; Stoppard: The Playwright, 1987; Peggy Ashcroft, 1989 (Biography); Twelfth Night, 1990; One Night Stands, 1993. Literary Agent: Curtis Brown. Address: 15 Hearne Road, London W4 3NJ, England.

BILLINGTON Rachel Mary, b. 11 Nov 1942, Oxford, England. Writer. m. 16 Dec 1967, 2 sons, 2 daughters. Education: BA, English, London University. Publications: All Things Nice; The Big Dipper; Beautiful; A Woman's Age; Occasion of Sin; The Garish Day; Lilacs out of the Dead Land; Cock Robin; A Painted Devil; Children's Books; Rosanna and the Wizard-Robot; Star-Time; The First Christmas; The First Easter; Loving Attitudes, 1988; Theo and Matilda, 1990; The First Miracles (for children), 1990; Bodily Harm, 1992; The Family Year, 1992; The Great Umbilical, 1994. Contributions to: Reviewer for Financial Times, New York; Short stories for various publications; 2 plays for BBC TV; 4 plays for Radio. Memberships: PEN; Society of Authors. Literary Agent: David Higham Associates, London. Address: 30 Addison Avenue, London W114QR, England.

BINCHY Maeve, b. 28 May 1940, Dublin, Republic of Ireland. Writer. m. Gordon Snell. Appointments: Joined The Irish Times, 1969. Publications: Maeve's Diary, 1979. Novels: Light A Penny Candle; Echoes; Firefly Summer, 1987; Sliver Wedding, 1989. Collections of short stories: London Transport; Dublin 4; The Lilac Bus. Stage plays: End of Term; Half Promised Land; Deeply Regretted by, TV play. Contributions to: Travel articles. Honours: 2 Jacobs Award and Best Script Award, Prague Film Festival. Address: London, England.

BINGHAM Caroline Margery Conyers, b. 7 Feb 1938. Professional Writer. m. Andrew Bingham, 1958, divorced 1972, 1 daughter. Education: BA Honours, History, University of Bristol. Publications: The Making of a King: The Early Years of James VI and I, 1968; James V, King of Scots, 1971; Contributor, The Scottish Nation: A History of the Scots from Independence to Union, 1972; The Life and Times of Edward II, 1973; The Stewart Kingdom of Scotland 1371-1603, 1974; The Kings and Queens of Scotland, 1976; The Crowned Lions: The Early Plantagenant Kings, 1978; James VI of Scotland, 1979; The Voice of the Lion, verse anthology, 1980; James I of England, 1981; Land of the Scots: A Short History, 1983; The History of Royal Holloway College 1886-1986, 1987; Beyond the Highland Line: Highland History and Culture, 1991. Literary Agent: A M Heath Co Ltd, 79 St Martin's Lane, London WC2N 4AA. Address: 164 Regents Park Road, London NW1 8XN, England.

BINGHAM Charlotte Marie-Therese, b. 29 Jun 1942, Sussex, England. Playwright; Novelist. m. 15 Jan 1964, 1 s, 1 d. Education: Educated in England and France. Publications: Coronet Among The Weeds; Lucinda; Coronet Among The Grass; Belgravia; Country Life; At Home; Television series (with Terence Brady); Upstairs, Downstairs; Nanny; No Honestly; Yes Honestly; Play for Today; Pig in The Middle; Father Matthew's Daughter; Thomas and Sarah; Novels: To Hear a Nightingale; The Business; In Sunshine or In Shadow; Stardust, 1988-1992. Contributions include: Vogue; Tatler; Woman's Journal; Town and Country. Membership: Society of Authors. Literary Agent: Murray Pollinger, c/o 222 Old Brompton Road, London, SW5 OB2, England. Address: c/o 10 Buckingham Street, London, WC1, England.

BINHAM Philip Frank, b. 19 July 1924. Teacher (retired). m. Marja Sola, 21 June 1952, 1 son, 1 daughter. Education: Magdalen College, Oxford, 1935-41; Wadham College, Oxford, 1946-49; BA (Oxon), 1949; MA (Oxon), 1954. Publications: How To Say It, 1965; UK Edition 1968; Executive English I-III, 1968-70; Speak Up, 1975; Snow in May: An Anthology of Finnish Literature 1945-72, 1978; Service with a Smile: Hotel English, Restaurant English 1979, UK Edition 1982; Team 7, 8, 9, 1983-85; Translations: Tamara (Eeva Kilpi), novel, 1972; Compass Rose (Eka Laine), 1985; In Search of Helsinki (Paavo Haavikko), 1986; Five Decades of Social Security (Paavo Haavikko), 1989; The Northeast Passage from the Vikings to Nordenskiöld, 1992. Contributions to: Regularly to World Literature Today (formerly Books Abroad), 1972-. Honours: Order of Finnish Lion, 1972; Finnish State Prize for Foreign Translators, 1990. Memberships: Society of Authors; Finnish Society of Scientific Writers; Honorary Member, Finnish Literature Society. Address: Seunalantie 34A, 04200 Kerava, Finland.

BIRCH Carol, b. 3 Jan 1951, Manchester, England. Writer. m. Martin Lucas Butler, 26 Oct 1990, 2 sons. Education: University of Keele, 1968-72. Publications: Life in the Palace, 1988; The Fog Line,

1989; The Unmaking, 1992; Songs of the West, 1994. Honours: David Higham Prize; Geoffrey Faber Memorial Award. Membership: Society of Authors. Literary Agent: Mic Cheetham, Sheilland Associates. Address: c/o Sheilland Associates, 43 Doughty Street, London WC1N 2LF, England.

BIRDSELL Sandra Louise, b. 22 Apr 1942, Manitoba, Canada. Writer. m. Stanley Vivian Birdsell, 1 Jul 1959, 1 s, 2 d. Literary Appointments: Writer-in-Residence: University of Prince Edward Island; University of Alberta; University of Waterloo, Ontario. Publications: Night Travellers, 1982; Ladies of The House, 1984; The Missing Child, 1989; The Chrome Suite, 1992. Contributions to: Western Living; Canadian Living; Quarry; The New Quarterly; Prairie Fire; Event; Border Crossing; Grain. Honours: Nominated for Governor General Award, English Language Fiction, 1992; Joseph P Stauffler Award, Canada Council; W H Smith, Books in Canada, 1st Novel Award; National Magazine Award; Canada Council Grant; Major Arts Award, Manitoba Arts Council. Memberships: Writers Guild of Canada; Writers Union of Canada; PEN International; Founding Member, President, Manitoba Writers Guild. Literary Agent: Lucinda Vardey Agency, Toronto, Ontario, Canada. Address: 755 Westminster Avenue, Winnipeg, Manitoba, Canada, R3G 1A5.

BIRLEY Julia, b. 13 May 1928, London, England. Writer. m. 12 Sept 1954, 1 son, 3 daughters. Education: BA Classics, Oxon. Publications: Novels, The Children on the Shore; The Time of the Cuckoo; When You Were There; A Serpents Egg; Dr Spicer; Short Stories. Contributions to: Articles in The Guardian. Memberships: PEN; Charlotte Young Society. Literary Agent: Curtis Brown. Address: Upper Bryn, Longtown, Hereford HR2 0NA, England.

BIRNEY Earle, b. 13 May 1904. Education: BA, UBC, 1926; MA, 1927, University of Toronto; Ph.D, Univ of Toronto, 1936. Appointments: English Instructor, University of Utah, 1934; Assistant Professor, University of Toronto, 1936-1942; Professor, UBC; Writer in Residence, University of Toronto, 1965-67, University of Waterloo, 1967-68, University of Western Ontario, 1981-82; Regents Professor, Univ of California, Irvine, 1968; Full Time Writer. Publications: David & other Poems, 1942; Strait of Anian, 1948; Trial of a City, 1952; Down the Long Table, 1955; Selected Poems, 1961; Near False Creek Month, 1964; Rag & Bone Shop, 1970; Bear on the Delhi Road, 1973; What's So Big About Green, 1973; Collected Poems, 1975; The Rugging and the Moving Times, 1976; Turvey, 1976; Ghost in the Wheels, 1977; Big Bird in the Bush, 1978; The Mammoth Corridors, 1980; Alphabeings, 1981; Essays on Chaucerian Irony, 1985; Words on Waves, 1985; Copernican Fix, 1985; Last Makings, 1991. Honours: Governor General's Award for Poetry, 1942-45; Stephen Leacock Medal, 1949; Borestone Mountain Poetry Award, 1951, 53; Lorne Pierce Medal, 1953; Fellow of Royal Society of Canada, 1954; Presidents Medal, 1954; Canada Council Medal, Order of Canada. Address: 1204-130 Carlton Street, Toronto, Ontario, M5A 4K3, Canada.

BISCHOFF David F(rederick), b. 1951, USA. Author. Literary Appointments: Staff member, NBC-TV, Washington DC, 1974-; Associate Editor, Amazing Magazine. Publications: The Seeker (with Christopher Lampton), 1976; Quest (juvenile), 1977; Strange Encounters (juvenile), 1977; The Phantom of The Opera (juvenile), 1977; The Woodman (with Dennis R Bailey), 1979; Nightworld, 1979; Star Fall, 1980; The Vampires of The Nightworld, 1981; Tin Woodman (with Dennis Bailey), 1982; Star Spring, 1982; War Games, 1983; Mandala, 1983; Day of The Dragonstar (with Thomas F Monteleone), 1983; The Crunch Bunch, 1985; Destiny Dice, 1985; Galactic Warriors, 1985; The Infinite Battle, 1985; The Macrocosmic Conflict, 1986; Manhattan Project, 1986; The Unicorn Gambit, 1986; Abduction: The UFO Conspiracy, 1990; Revelation: The UFO Conspiracy, 1991; Deception: The UFO Conspiracy, 1991. Address: c/o Henry Morrison Inc, 320 Mclain Street, Bedford Hill, NY 10705, USA.

BISHER James Furman, b. 4 Nov 1918, Denton, NC, USA. Journalist. Divorced, 3 s. Education: BA, University of North Carolina, 1938; Dartmouth College, 1943. Publications include: With a Southern Exposure, 1961; Miracle in Atlanta, 1966; Strange But True Baseball Stories, 1966; Aaron (with Henry Aaron), 1972-74; Masters-Augusta Revisited, 1976; Arnold Palmer - The Golden Year, 1971; various anthologies including: Grantland Rice Prize Sports Stories; Best Sports Stories of The Year (22 times); Fireside Book of Baseball. Contributions to: Over 600 articles in Saturday Evening Post; Sport; Sports Illustrated; Collier's; Golf Digest; True; Southern Living; GQ; Esquire; Sky Magazine. Honours include: Sportswriter of The Year,

Georgia, 14 times; Furman University Distinguished Alumnus of Year, 1978; University of North Carolina Hall of Fame, 1985; President, Football Writers Association, US, 1959-60; President, National Sportscasters and Sportswriters of America, 1974-76; Sigma Delta Chi Awards for Commentary, 1981-82; Florida Turf Writing Award. Memberships: Turf Writers Association; Baseball Writers Association; Football Writers Association; Tennis Writers Association; National Sportscasters and Sportswriters Association. Address: 3135 Rilman Road NW, Atlanta, GA 30327, USA.

BISHOP Ian Benjamin, b. 18 Apr 1927, Gillingham, Kent, England. University Teacher. m. Pamela Rosemary Haddacks, 14 Dec 1968, 2 d. Education: MA, MLitt, The Quenn's College, Oxford, 1945-51. Literary Appointment: Reader in English, University of Bristol, 1982. Publications: The Narrative Art of The Canterbury Tales, 1988; Pearl in Its Setting, 1968; Chaucer's Troilus and Criseyde: A Critical Study, 1981. Contributions to: The Review of English Studies; Medium Aevum; The Times Higher Education Supplement; Notes and Queries. Address: 8 Benville Avenue, Coombe Dingle, Bristol, BS9 2RX, England.

BISHOP James Drew, b. 18 June 1929, London, England. Journalist. m. 5 June 1959, 2 sons. Education: BA History, Corpus Christi College, Cambridge, 1953. Appointments: Foreign Correspondent, The Times, 1957-64; Foreign News Editor, 1964-66; Features Editor, 1966-70; The Times Editor, 1971-87; Editor-in-Chief, 1987-1994, The Illustrated London News. Publications: Social History of Edwardian Britain, 1977; Social History of the First World War, 1982; The Story of the Times, with Oliver Woods, 1983; Illustrated Counties of England, Editor 1985. Contributions to: USA Chapter in Annual Register, 1960-1988; Articles in many Newspapers and Magazines. Memberships: Association of British Editors, Chairman. Literary Agent: David Higham. Address: 11 Willow Road, London NW3 1TJ, England.

BISHOP Michael Lawson, b. 12 Nov 1945, Lincoln, Nebraska, USA. Writer. m. Jeri Ellis Whitaker, 7 June 1969, 1 son, 1 daughter. Education: BA, English, 1967, MA 1968, University of Georgia. Publications include: Novels: Catacomb Years, 1979; No Enemy But Time, 1982; Ancient of Days, 1985; Transfigurations, 1979; Who Made Stevie Crye? 1983; Unicorn Mountain, 1988; Philip K Dick is Dead Alas, novel, 1987; Count Geiger's Blues, 1992; Brittle Innings, 1994; Short Story Collections: Blooded on Arachne, 1982; Close Encounters with the Deity, 1986; One Winter in Eden, 1984; Also short stories, reviews, criticism, essays, poetry including book, Windows & Mirrors. Contributions to: Various Best of the Year collections; Journals including: Playboy; Interzone; Isaac Asimov's; Analog; Fantasy & Science Fiction; Omni; Galaxy; If; Missouri Review; Georgia Review; Chattahoochee Review; Pulphouse. Honours include: 2 Nebula Awards, best novelette, best novel; Rhysling Award, science fiction poetry; various other regional/speciality awards; Dogs' Lives, appears in The Best American Short Stories, 1985; Mythopoeic Fantasy Award, best novel. Memberships: Science Fiction Writers of America; Science Fiction Poetry Association; Writers Guild of America. Literary Agent: Howard Morhaim. Address: 175 Fifth Avenue, New York, NY 10017, USA.

BISHOP Pike. See: OBSTFELD Raymond.

BISHOP Robert, b. 1938, USA. Antiques, Furnishings, Arts, Crafts. Director, Museum of American Folk Art, New York, 1976-. Appointments: Adjunct Professor, Department of Art and Art Education, New York University, NY, 1980-; Associate Editor, The Gray Letter and Antique Chairman, Museums Council of New York City, 1978-81. Publications include: The American Clock, 1976; The Borden Limner and His Contemporaries, 1976; (with P Coblentz) World Furniture, 1979; Treasures of American Folk Art, 1979; (with P Coblentz) Folk Painters of America, 1979; (with P Coblentz) The World of Antiques, Art and Architecture in Victorian America, 1979; (with P Coblentz) A Gallery of American Weathervanes and Whirligigs, 1980; American Decorative Arts 1620-1980, 1982; Editor, Collectors' Guide to Glass, Tableware, Bowls and Vases, 1982; Editor, Collectors' Guide to Chests, Cupboards, Desks and Other Pieces, 1982; Editor, Collectors' Guide to Chairs, Tables, Sofas and Beds, 1982; (with W Secord and J R Weissman) Collectors' Guide to Quilts, Coverlets, Rugs and Samplers, 1982; (with W Ketchum) Collectors' Guide to Folk Art, 1983; Editor, Collectors; Guide to Toys, 1984; Editor: Collectors' Guide to Silver and Pewter, 1984; (with C Houck) All Flags Flying, 1986; (with J Lipman and E V Warren) Young American, A Folk Art History, 1986;

Hands All Around, 1986; American Quilts, Giftwraps by Artists, 1986. Address: 213 W 22nd Street, New York, NY 10011, USA.

BISHOP Wendy S, b. 13 Jan 1953, Japan. English Professor. m. Marvin E Pollard Jr, 1 son, 1 daughter. Education: BA, English, 1975, BA, Studio Art, 1975, MA, English, 1976, MA, English, 1979, University of California, Davis; PhD, English (Rhetoric and Linguistics), Indian University of Pennsylvania, 1988. Appointments: Bayero University, Kano, Nigeria, 1980-81; Northern Arizona University, USA, 1981-82; Navajo Community College, 1982-85; University of Alaska, Fairbanks, 1985-89; Florida State University, Tallahassee, 1989-. Publications: Released into Language: Options for Teaching Creative Writing, 1990; Something Old, Something New: College Writing Teachers and Classroom Change, 1990; Working Words: The Process of Creative Writing, 1992; The Subject is Writing: Essays by Teachers and Students on Writing, 1993; Co-editor and Contributor to: Colors of a Different Horse: Rethinking Creative Writing, Theory and Pedagogy, National Council of Teachers of English (NCTE), 1994. Contributions to: Poems, fiction, essays to: American Poetry Review; College English; High Plains Literary Review; Prairie Schooner; Western Humanities Review; Many other journals. Address: Department of English, Florida State University, Tallahassee, FL 32302, USA.

BISSET Donald, b. 1910, British. Writer; Actor. Publications: Anytime Stories, 1954; Sometime Stories, 1957; Next Time Stories, 1959; This Time Stories, 1961; Another Time Stories, 1963; Little Bear's Pony, 1966; Hullo Lucy, 1967; Talks With a Tiger, 1967; Kangaroo Tennis, 1968; Nothing, 1969; Upside Down Land, 1969; Benjie The Circus Dog, 1969; Time And Again Stories, 1970; Barcha The Tiger, 1971; Tiger Wants More, 1971; Yak series, 6 volumes, 1971-78; Father Tingtang's Journey, 1973; Jenny Hopalong, 1973; The Happy Horse, 1974; The Aventures of Mandy Duck, 1974; Hazy Mountain, 1974; Oh Dear, Said The Tiger, 1975; Paws With Shapes, 1976; (with Michael Morris) Paws With Numbers, 1976; The Lost Birthday, 1976; The Story of Smokey Horse, 1977; This is Ridiculous, 1977; Jungle Journey, 1977; What Time Is It, When It Isn't, 1980; Cornelia and Other Stories, 1980; Johnny Here and There, 1981; The Hedgehog Who Rolled Uphill, 1982; Snakey Boo Series, 2 volumes, 1982-85; Please Yourself, 1991. Address: 43 Andrewes House, Barbican, London, EC2Y 8AX, England.

BISSETT Bill, b. 1939, Canada. Poet; Artist. Appointments: Editor, Printer, Blewointmentpress, Vancouver, 1962-83. Publications: The Jinx Ship and other Trips: Poems-drawings-collage, 1966; We Sleep Inside Each Other All, 1966; Fires in the Temple, 1967; Where Is Miss Florence Riddle, 1967; What Poetiks, 1967; Gossamer Bed Pan, 1967; Lebanon Voices, 1967; Of the Land/Divine Service Poems, 1968; Awake in the Red Desert! 1968; Killer Whale, 1969; Sunday Work? 1969; Liberating Skies, 1969; The Lost Angel Mining Company, 1969; The Outlaw, 1970; Blew Trewz, 1970; Nobody Owns the Earth, 1971; Air 6, 1971; Dragon Fly, 1971; Four Parts Sand: Concrete Poems, 1972; The Ice Bag, 1972; Poems for Yoshi, 1972, 1977; Drifting into War, 1972; Air 10-11-12, 1973; Pass the Food, Release the Spirit Book, 1973; The First Sufi Line, 1973; Vancouver Mainland Ice and Cold Storage, 1973; Living with the Vishyan, 1974; What, 1974; Drawings, 1974; Medicine My Mouths on Fire, 1974; Space Travel, 1974; You Can Eat it at the Opening, 1974; The Fifth Sun, 1975; The Wind up Tongue, 1975; Stardust, 1975; An Allusyun to Macbeth, 1976; Plutonium Missing, 1976; Sailor, 1978; Beyond Even Faithful Legends, 1979; Soul Arrow, 1980; Northern Birds in Color, 1981; Parlant, 1982; Seagull on Yonge Street, 1983; Canada Gees Mate for Life, 1985; Animal Uproar, 1987; What we Have, 1989; Hard 2 Beleev, 1990; Incorrect Thoughts, 1992; Vocalist with the Luddites, Dreaming of the Night, 1992; The Last Photo of the Human Soul, 1993; th Influenza uv Logik, 1995-. Address: Box 273, 1755 Robson Street, Vancouver BC, V6G 3B7, Canada.

BISSOONDATH Neil (Devindra), b. 19 Apr 1955, Trinidad, West Indies. Education: BA, York University, Toronto, Ontario, Canada. Publications: Digging Up the Mountain, 1985; A Casual Brutality, 1988; On the Eve of Uncertain Tomorrows, 1990; The Innocence of Age, 1992. Honours: Canadian Authors Association Literary Award, 1993.

BISWAS Anil Ranjan (Oneil), b. 1 Feb 1916, Bangladesh. Writer; Former Civil Servant and Teacher. m. Lily Mullick, 15 May 1941, 1 son. Education: BA (Hons), 1937; MA, 1942; LLM, 1968; PhD, 1976. Appointments: Editor, Eastern Law Reports, 1982; Laikhi (writing), 1985. Publications: Footsteps, 1951; Twentieth century Bengali Literature, 1952; Curly Waters, 1961; Shakespeare's Sonnets,

1966; Asutosh's Thoughts on Education, 1968; At Whose Bid the Bell Rings, 1972; Continuum becomes Calcutta, 1973, 1991; On the Shores of Anxiety, 1980; Squaring the Circle, 1985; History of India's Freedom Movement, 1990; Variegated Days, 1991; Bengali Prosody, 1992; Calcutta and Calcuttans, 1992. Address: Gairick, 18 Cooperative Road, Calcutta 700070, India.

BJERG Anne Marie, b. 17 Dec 1937, Copenhagen, Denmark. Translator; Writer. m. Chrenn Bjerg, 29 Dec 1962, divorced, 1 daughter. Education: BA, University of Copenhagen, 1970. Appointments: Regular Reader, Gyldendal's Publishing House, 1971-86. Publications: Love from Signe (novel), 1979; Surviving (short stories), 1985; 65 translations, including: 8 novels by Anita Brookner; Dubliners by James Joyce; The Waves by Virginia Woolf (from English); Live or Die by Anne Sexton; Fear of Flying by Erica Jong; Two Serious Ladies by Jane Bowles (from American); numerous novels by Selma Lagerlöf, Kerstlin Ekman, Göran Tunström, Per Wästberg (from Swedish). Contributions to: BLM. Honours: The Translators Award of the Danish Academy; Honoraly Award of the Danish Translators' Association; Life long grant, Danish State Art Foundation. Memberships: James Joyce Society; Danish Writers Association; Danish PEN; Danish Dramatists Association. Address: Laerdalsgade 6A 1tv, DK-2300 Copenhagen S, Denmark.

BLACK David, b. 21 Apr 1945, Boston, MA, USA. Writer; Producer. m. Deborah Hughes Keehn, 22 Jun 1968, 1 s, 1 d. Education: BA Magna cum Laude, Amherst College, 1967; MFA, Columbia University, 1971. Literary Appointments: Contributing Writer, New Times, 1975-76; Writer-in-Residence, Mt Holyoke College, 1982-86; Contributing Editor, Rolling Stone, 1986-89. Publications include: Minds, 1982; Murder at The Met, 1984; Medicine Man, 1985; Peep Show, 1986; Feature Scripts include: Murder at The Met, 1982; Falling Angel, 1984; Catching It, 1988; Passion, 1990; The Man in The Slouch Hat, 1992; Detectives of The Heart, 1992; Television Scripts: Hill Street Blues, 1987; Send Me, 1987; Alaska, 1988-89; Gideon Oliver, 1988; HELP, 1989; In Your Face, 1989; The Nasty Boys, 1989; Law and Order, 1990; Legacy of Lies, 1992; In The Year 2000, 1992. Contributions include: Over 150 stories and articles to numerous national and international magazines including: The New York Times Magazine; Harper's; Playboy; The Village Voice; The Transatlantic Review; Granta; Cosmopolitan. Honours include: National Magazine Award; National Association of Science Writers Award; Best Article of The Year Award, Playboy; National Endowment for The Arts Grant in Fiction; Firsts Award, short story, Atlantic Monthly; Notable Book of The Year, New York Times (2); Edgar Nominations (2); Pulitzer Prize Nomination. Memberships: PEN; The Writers Guild-East; Mystery Writers of America; International Association of Crime Writers; Century Association; Williams Club. Literary Agent: Dave Wirtschafter. Address: c/o Dave Wirtschafter, ICM, 8899 Beverly Boulevard, Los Angeles, CA 90048, USA.

BLACK David (Macleod), b. 8 Nov 1941, Cape Town, South Africa (British citizen). Lecturer; Poet. Education: MA, Edinburgh University, 1966; MA in Religious Studies, University of Lancaster, 1971. Appointments: Teacher at Chelsea Art School, London, 1966-70; Lecturer and Supervisor, Westminster Pastoral Foundation, London. Publications: Rocklestrakes, 1960; From the Mountain, 1963; Theory of Diet, 1966; With Decorum, 1967; A Dozen Short Poems, 1968; Penguin Modern Poets II, 1968; The Educators, 1969; The Old Hag, 1972; The Happy Crow, 1974; Gravitations, 1979; Collected Poems 1964-87, 1991; A Place for Exploration, 1991. Honours: Scottish Arts Council Prize, 1968; Arts Council of Great Britain Bursary, 1968; Scottish Arts Council Publication Award, 1991. Address: 30 Cholmley Gardens, Aldred Road, London NW6 1AG, England.

BLACK Jim. See: **HAINING Peter Alexander.**

BLACK Veronica. See: **PETERS Maureen.**

BLACKBOURN David Gordon, b. 1 Nov 1949, Spilsby, Lincs. Historian; University Teacher. m. Deborah Frances Langton, 13 Apr 1985, 1 son, 1 daughter. Education: Christs College, Cambridge, England, 1967-70; BA, 1970; MA, 1976; PhD, 1976. Appointments: Research Fellow, Jesus College, Cambridge, 1973-76; Lecturer, Queen Mary College, University of London, England, 1976-79; Lecturer, 1979-85; Reader, 1985-89; Professor, Birkbeck College, University of London, 1989-92; Professor, Harvard University, 1992-. Publications: Class, Religion & Local Politics; The Peculiarities of German History; Populists & Patricians; The German Bourgeoisie; Marpingen:

Apparitions of the Virgin Mary in Bismarckian Germany. Contributions to: New Society; Marxism Today; History Today. Honours: Frequent Guest Lecturer. Memberships: Fellow, Royal Historical Society; Editorial Board, Past & Present; German History Society. Literary Agent: Margaret Hanbury, UK; Robin Straus, USA. Address: Minda De Gunzburg Center for European Studies, Harvard University, 27 Kirkland Street, Cambridge, MA 02138, USA.

BLACKIN Malcolm. See: **CHAMBERS Aidan.**

BLACKWOOD Caroline, b. 16 July 1931, N Ireland. Author. Publications: For All That I Found There (short stories and essays), 1973; The Stepdaughter, 1976; Great Granny Webster, 1977; Darling, You Shouldn't Have Gone To So Much Trouble (cookbook with Anna Haycraft), 1980; The Fate of Mary Rose, 1981; Goodnight Sweet Ladies (stories), 1983; On the Perimeter, 1984; Corrigan, 1984; In the Pink: Caroline Blackwood on Hunting, 1989. Address: c/o Heinemann Limited, 10 Upper Grosvenor Street, London W1X 9PA, England.

BLAINE James. See: **AVALLONE Michael Angelo Jr.**

BLAINEY Geoffrey Norman, b. 1930, Australia. Writer. Publications: The Peaks of Lyell, 1954; A Centenary History of the University of Melbourne, 1957; Gold and Paper, 1958; Mines in the Spinifex, 1960; The Rush That Never Ended, 1963; A History of Camberwell, 1965; If I Remember Rightly: The Memoirs of W S Robinson, 1966; Co-Author and Editor, Wesley College: The First Hundred Years, 1967; The Tyranny of Distance, 1966; Across a Red World, 1968; The Rise of Broken Hill, 1968; The Steel Master, 1971; The Causes of War, 1973; Triumph of the Nomads, 1975; A Land Half Won, 1980; The Blainey View, 1982; Our Side of the Country, 1984; All for Australia, 1984; The Great Seesaw, 1988; A Game of our Own: The Origins of Australian Football, 1990; Eye on Australia, 1991; Jumping over the Wheel, 1993; A Shorter History of Australia, 1994. Memberships: Chairman, Commonwealth Literary Fund, 1971-73; Australia Council, 1977-81. Address: PO Box 257, East Melbourne, Victoria 3002, Australia.

BLAIR Claude, b. 1922. Antiquary and Art Historian. Appointments: Assistant, Tower of London Armouries, 1951-56; Honorary Editor, Journal of Arms and Armour Society, 1953-77; Assistant Keeper 1966-72, Deputy Keeper 1966-72, Keeper 1972-82, Metalwork, Victoria and Albert Museum, London; Consultant, Christie's London, 1982-. Publications: European Armour, 1958; European and American Arms, 1962; Pistols of the World, 1968; Three Presentation Swords in the Victoria and Albert Museum, 1972; The James A de Rothschild Collection at Waddesdon Manor; Arms, Armour and Base-Metalwork, 1974; Pollard's History of Firearms, 1983; A History of Silver, 1987. Address: 90 Links Road, Ashtead, Surrey KT21 2HW, England.

BLAIR Emma. See: **BLAIR Iain John.**

BLAIR Iain John (Emma Blair), b. 12 Aug 1942, Glasgow, Scotland. Novelist. m. 26 Apr 1975, 2 s. Education: Royal Scottish Academy of Music and Dramatic Art. Publications: Where No Man Cries, 1982; Nellie Wildchild, 1983; Hester Dark, 1984; This Side of Heaven, 1985; Jessie Gray, 1985; The Princess of Poor Street, 1986; Street Song, 1986; When Dreams Come True, 1987; A Most Determined Woman, 1988; The Blackbird's Tale, 1989; Maggie Jordan, 1990; Scarlet Ribbons, 1991; The Water Meadows, 1992. Memberships: Romantic Novelists Association; British Actors Equity. Literary Agent: Rogers, Coleridge and White, 20 Powis Mews, London, W11 1JN, England. Address: The Old Vicarage, Stoke Canon, Near Exeter, Devon, EX5 4AS, England.

BLAIR Jessica. See: **SPENCE William John Duncan.**

BLAIR Pauline Hunter, (Helen Clare, Pauline Clarke). Author. m. Peter Hunter Blair, Feb 1969. Education: BA Honours, Somerville College, Oxford. Publications: Works include: As Pauline Clarke: The Pekinese Princess, 1948; The Great Can, 1952; The White Elephant, 1952; Smith's Hoard, 1955; The Boy with the Erpingham Hood, 1956; Sandy the Sailor, 1956; James, the Policeman, 1957; James and the Robbers, 1959; Torolv the Fatherless, 1959, 2nd edition 1974, re-issued 1991; The Lord of the Castle, 1960; The Robin Hooders, 1960; James and the Smugglers, 1961; Keep the Pot Boiling, 1961; The Twelve and the Genii, 1962; Silver Bells and Cockle Shells, 1962; James and the Black Van, 1963; Crowds of Creatures, 1964; The

Bonfire Party, 1966; The Two Faces of Silenus, 1972; As Helen Clare: Five Dolls in a House, 1953; Merlin's Magic, 1953; Bel, the Giant and Other Stories, 1956; Five Dolls and the Monkey, 1956; Five Dolls in the Snow, 1957; Five Dolls and Their Friends, 1959; Seven White Pebbles, 1960; Five Dolls and the Duke, 1963; The Cat and the Fiddle and Other Stories from Bel, the Giant, 1968. Honours: Library Association Carnegie Medal, 1962; Lewis Carroll Shelf Award, 1963; Deutsche Jugend Buchpreis, 1968. Address: Church Farm House, Bottisham, Cambridge CB5 9BA, England.

BLAIS Marie-Claire, b. 5 Oct 1939, Quebec, Canada. Novelist; Playwright. Education: Laval University, Quebec. Publications: Fiction: La Belle Bête, 1960; Tête Blanche, 1961; Le Jour est Noir, 1962; Une Saison dans la vie d'Emmanuel, 1965; Les Voyageurs sacrés, 1966; David Sterne, 1967; The Fugitive, 1967; Manuscrits de Pauline Arhange, 4 volumes, 1969-76; The Wolf, 1972, 1973; St Lawrence Blues, 1974; A Literary Affair, 1975, 1979; Nights in the Underground, 1978, 1979; Deaf to the City, 1979, 1981; Anna's World, 1982, 1985; Pierre, la guerre du printemps 81; The Angel of Solitude, 1989; Plays: The Puppet Caravan, 1962, 1967; Eleonor, 1962; The Execution, 1967; A Clash of Symbols, 1976, 1979; L'Ocean and Murmures, 1976; Sommeil d'hiver, 1984; The Island, 1989; Un jardin dans la tempête, 1990; Radio and Television plays. Honours include: Companion, Order of Canada, 1975; Member, Royal Society of Canada. Address: John C Goodwin and Associates, 839 Sherbrooke Est, Suite 2, Montreal, Quebec, Canada H2L 1K6.

BLAKE Alfred. See: **HARRIS Laurence Mark.**

BLAKE Andrew. See: **HARRIS Laurence Mark.**

BLAKE Jennifer. See: **MAXWELL Patricia Anne.**

BLAKE Ken. See: **BULMER Henry Kenneth.**

BLAKE Norman Francis, b. 1934. Writer. Publications: Editor, Translator, The Saga of The Jomsvikings, 1962; The Phoenix, 1964, 2nd edition 1990; Caxton and His World, 1969; William Caxton's Reynard The Fox, 1970; Middle English Religious Prose, 1972; Selections from William Caxton, 1973; Caxton's Own Prose, 1975; Caxton's Quattnor Sermones, 1973; Caxton: England's First Publisher, 1976; The English Language in Medieval Literature, 1977; Non-Standard Language in English Literature, 1981; Shakespeare's Language, 1983; Textual Tradition of The Canterbury Tales, 1985; William Caxton: A Bibliographical Guide, 1985; Traditional English Grammar and Beyond, 1988; Index of Printed Middle English Prose, 1985; (with R E Lewis and A S G Edwards), The Language of Shakespeare, 1989; An Introduction to The Languages of Literature, 1990. Address: Department of English Language and Linguistics, University of Sheffield, Sheffield, S10 2TN, England.

BLAKE Patrick, See: **EGLETON Clive Frederick William.**

BLAKE Robert (Norman William), (Lord Blake of Braydeston, Norfolk), b. 1916. British History, Politics/Government. Appointments: Lecturer, 1946-47; Student and Tutor in Politics, 1947-68; Christ Church, Oxford; Ford Lecturer in English History, Oxford University, 1967-68; Provost of Queen's College, Oxford, 1968-87; Conservative Member, Oxford City Council, 1957-64. Publications: The Private Papers of Douglas Haig (ed), 1952; The Unknown Prime Minister, The Life and Times of Andrew Bonar Law, 1955; Disraeli, 1966; The Conservative Party from Peel to Churchill, 1970, 2nd ed at The Conservative Party from Peel to Thatcher, 1985; The Office of the Prime Minister, 1975; (ed with John Patten) The Conservative Opportunity, 1976; A History of Rhodesia, 1977; Disraeli's Grand Tour, 1982; The English World (ed), 1982; The Decline of Power, 1985; Churchill, a Major New Assessment of His Life in Peace and War, (ed with Roger Louis), 1993; Joint Editor of the Dictionary of National Biography, 1980-90. Honours: DLitt Oxford; Hon DLitt Glasgow 1972; East Anglia 1983, Buckingham 1988; Life Peer 1971. Memberships: President of the Literary Society; Authors' Society. Address: Riverview House, Brundall, Norwich, Norfolk.

BLAMIRES Harry, b. 6 Nov 1916, Bradford, England. Lecturer in Higher Education; Author. m. Nancy Bowles, 26 Dec 1940, 5 sons. Education: BA 1938, MA 1945, University College, Oxford. Appointments: Head of English Department 1948-72, Dean of Arts and Sciences, retired 1976, King Alfred's College, Winchester. Publications: A Short History of English Literature, 1974, revised 1984; The

Bloomsday Book, Guide to Joyce's Ulysses, 1966, revised 1988; Twentieth-Century English Literature, 1982, revised 1986; The Christian Mind, 1963; Where Do We Stand? 1980; On Christian Truth, 1983; Word Unheard, Guide through Eliot's Four Quartets, 1969; Milton's Creation, 1971; The Victorian Age of Literature, 1988; Guide to 20th Century Literature in English, 1983; Words Made Flesh, 1985 published in UK as The Marks of the Maker, 1987; Meat Not Milk, 1988; The Age of Romantic Literature, 1989; A History of Literary Criticism, 1991; The Queen's English, 1994. Honours: Clyde Kilby Visiting Professor of English, Wheaton College, Illinois, USA, 1987; Hon DLitt, Southampton University, 1993. Membership: Society of Authors. Address: Rough Close, Braithwaite, Keswick, Cumbria CA12 5RY, England.

BLANDIANA Ana (Otila Valeria Rusan), b. 25 Mar 1942, Timisoara, Rumania. Poet. m. Romulus Rusan. Education: Graduated University of Cluj, 1967. Appointments: Columnist of Romania literara magazine, 1974-88; Librarian at the Institute of Fine Arts, Bucharest, from 1975. Publications: First-Person Plural, 1964; The Wounded Heel, 1966; The Third Sacrament, 1969; To be a Witness, 1970; 50 Poems, 1972; October, November, December, 1972; Poems, 1974; The Sleep Within the Sleep, 1977; Four Seasons, 1977; Poems, 1978; The Most Beautiful of All Possible Worlds, 1978; Events in My Garden, 1980; The Cricket's Eye, 1981; Poems, 1982; Projects for the Past, 1982; The Hour of Sand, 1983; Corridor of Mirrors, 1984; Star of Prey, 1985; Poems, 1989; The Hour of Sand: Selected Poems 1969-89. Honours include: Herder Prize, Austria, 1982. Address: c/o Cartea Romaneasca, Str Nuferilor 41, 79721 Bucharest, Rumania.

BLASER Robin (Francis), b. 18 May 1925, Denver, Colorado, USA. Professor of English; Poet. Education: MA & MLS, University of California at Berkeley, 1954-1955. Appointments: Professor of English, Centre for the Arts, Simon Fraser University, British Columbia, Canada, 1972-86. Publications: The Moth Poem, 1964; Les Chimères, 1965; Cups, 1968; The Holy Forest Section, 1970; Image-nations 1-12 and The Stadium of the Mirror, 1974; Image-nations 13-14, 1975; Suddenly, 1976; Syntax, 1983; The Faerie Queene and the Park, 1987; Pell Mell, 1988; The Holy Forest, 1993. Honours: Poetry Society Award, 1965; Canada Council Grant, 1989-90. Address: 1636 Trafalgar Street, Vancouver, British Columbia V6K 3R7, Canada.

BLASHFORD-SNELL John Nicholas, b. 22 Oct 1936, Hereford, England. Soldier; Colonel; Explorer. Education: Victoria College Jersey, Channel Islands; Royal Military Academy, Sandhurst. Publications include: Where the Trail Runs Out; In the Steps of Stanley; Expeditions the Experts Ways, co-author; A Taste for Adventure, 1978; Operation Drake, 1981; In the Wake of Drake, 1982 with M Cable; Mysteries - Encounters with the Unexplained, 1983; Operation Raleigh, The Start of an Adventure, 1985; Operation Raleigh, Adventure Challenge, 1988 with Ann Tweedy; Operation Raleigh Adventure Unlimited, 1990 with Ann Tweedy; Something Lost Behind the Ranges, 1994. Contributions to: Expedition: The Field; British Army Review; Gun Digest; Spectator; Yorks Post; Scotsman; Traveller; Royal Business Journal; Daily Telegraph. Address: c/o The Scientific Exploration Society, Expedition Base, Motcombe, Dorset SP7 9PB, England.

BLAYNE Diana. See: **KYLE Susan Eloise Spaeth.**

BLEAKLEY David Wylie, b. 1925. Writer. Publications: Co-Author, Ulster Since 1800, 1955; Young Ulster and Religion in The Sixties, 1964; Peace in Ulster, 1972; Faulkner: A Biography, 1974; Saidie Patterson, An Irish Peacemaker, 1980; In Place of Work: The Sufficient Society, 1981; The Shadow and Substance, 1983; Beyond Work - Free To Be, 1985; Will The Future Work?, 1988. Honour: CBE, 1984. Address: 8 Thorn Hill, Co Down, BT19 1RD, Northern Ireland.

BLEASDALE Alan, b. 23 Mar 1946. Playwright; Novelist. m. Julia Moses, 1970, 2 s, 1 d. Education: Teachers Certificate, Padgate Teachers Training College. Publications: Scully, 1975; Who's Been Sleeping in My Bed, 1977; No More Sitting on The Old School Bench, 1979; Boys From The Blackstuff (televised), 1982; Are You Lonesome Tonight?, 1985; No Surrender, 1986; Having a Ball, 1986; It's A Madhouse, 1986; The Monocled Mutineer (televised), 1986; GBH (television series), 1992. Honours: BAFTA Writer's Award, 1982; RTS Writer's Award, 1982; Broadcasting Press Guild TV Award for Best Series, 1982; Best Musical, London Standard Drama Awards, 1985. Address: c/o Harvey Unna and Stephen Durbridge Limited, 24 Pottery Lane, Holland Park, London, W11 4LZ, England.

BLIGHT John, b. 1913, Australia. Poet. Publications: The Old Pianist, 1945; The Two Suns Met: Poems, 1954; A Beachcomber's Diary: Ninety Sea Sonnets, 1964; My Beachcombing Days: Ninety Sea Sonnets, 1968; Hart - Poems, 1975; Selected Poems 1939-1975, 1976; Pageantry For a Lost Empire, 1977; The New City Poems, 1979; Holiday Sea Sonnets, 1985. Address: 34 Greenway Street, The Grange, Brisbane, Queensland 4051, Australia.

BLISHEN Edward, b. 29 Apr 1920, Whetstone, Middlesex, England. Author. m. Nancy Smith, 4 Nov 1948, 2 sons. Publications: Roaring Boys, 1955; A Cackhanded War, 1971; Sorry Dad, 1978; A Nest of Teachers, 1979; Lizzie Pye, 1982; The Outside Contributor, 1986; The Disturbance Fee, 1988; Also: This Right Soft Lot, 1969; Uncommon Entrance, 1974; Shaky Relations, 1981; Donkey Work, 1983; A Second Skin, 1984; The Penny World, 1990. Contributions to: Numerous magazines and journals. Honours: Carnegie Medal (with Leon Garfield), 1970; Travelling Scholarship, Society of Authors, 1979; J R Ackerley Prize, autobiography, 1981; Fellow, Royal Society of Literature; Hon Doc, Open University. Memberships: Society of Authors; PEN. Literary Agent: A M Heath. Address: 12 Bartrams Lane, Hadley Wood, Barnet, London EN4 0EH, England.

BLIVEN Bruce, b. 31 Jan 1916, Los Angeles, California, USA. Writer. m. Naomi Horowitz, 26 May 1950, 1 son. Education: AB, Harvard College, 1937. Publications: The Wonderful Writing Machine, 1954; Battle for Manhattan, 1956; The Story of D-Day, 1956, 50th anniversary edition, 1994; The American Revolution, 1958; From Pearl Harbor to Okinawa, 1960; From Casablanca to Berlin, 1965; New York, with Naomi Bliven, 1969; Under the Guns, 1972; Book Traveller, 1975; Volunteers, One and All, 1976; The Finishing Touch, 1978; New York: A History, 1981. Contributions to: The New Yorker; many other national magazines. Memberships: Authors Guild, Council 1970-; Society of American Historians, Board, 1975-; PEN American Centre; American Society of Journalists and Authors. Address: The New Yorker, 20 West 43rd Street, New York, NY 10036, USA.

BLOCH Chana, b. 15 Mar 1940, New York City, USA. Professor; Poet; Critic; Translator. m. Ariel A Bloch, 26 Oct 1969, 2 sons, div. Education: BA, Cornell University, 1961; MA, Brandeis University, 1963; MA, Brandeis University, 1965; PhD, University of California, Berkeley, 1975. Appointments: Hebrew University, Jerusalem, 1964-67; University of California, Berkeley, 1967-69; Mills College, 1973-; Mills College, Professor of English, 1987-. Publications: The Secrets of the Tribe; Spelling the Word; George Herbert and the Bible; Selected Poems of Yehuda Amichai; The Window: New & Selected Poems of Dahlia Ravikovitch; The Past Keeps Changing; The Song of Songs. Literary Agent: Georges Borchardt. Address: 12 Menlo Place, Berkeley, CA 94707, USA.

BLOCH Robert (Tarleton Fiske, Will Folke, Nathan Hindin, Wilson Kane, John Sheldon), b. 5 Apr 1917, Chicago, Illinois, USA. Writer. Publications: Psycho, 1959; The Best of Robert Bloch, 1977; Cold Chills, 1977; The King of Terrors, 1977; Out of the Mouths of Graves, 1979; Such Stuff as Screams Are Made of, 1979; There is a Serpent in Eden, 1979; Psycho II, 1982; Mysteries of the Worm, 1983; The Night of the Ripper, 1984; Unholy Trinity, 1986; Midnight Pleasures, 1987; Lefty Feep, 1987; Selected Short Stories of Robert Bloch, 1987; Lori, 1989; Fear and Trembling, 1989; Psyco House, 1990; Psycho Paths (editor), 1991. Contributions to: Playboy; Penthouse; Gallery; Cosmopolitan; Red Book; Blue Book; Weird Tales; Ellery Queen Mystery Magazine and various others. Literary Agent: The Pimlico Agency, New York; Shapiro Lichtman Talent Agency, Los Angeles. Address: 2111 Sunset Crest Drive, Los Angeles, CA 90046, USA.

BLOCK DE BEHAR Lisa, b. 12 Mar 1937, Montevideo, Uruguay. Professor. m. Isaac Behar, 25 Jun 1957, 2 s. Education: BA, 1961, MS, 1973, Institute of Profesors, Montevideo, Uruguay; PhD, École de Haute Études en Sciences Sociales, Paris, France, 1983. Literary Appointments: Full Professor Literary Theory, Montevideo, 1976; Full Professor Semiotica, Montevideo, 1985. Publications: El Lenguaje de la Publicidad, 1973, 74, 76-92; Al Margen de Borges, 1987; Jules Laforgue, 1987; Dos medios entre dos medios, 1990; Una retórica del silencio, 1984-94; Una palabra propiamente didna, 1994. Contributions to: Jaque; La Republica; Revista Iberoamericana; Semiotica. Honour: Prite Xavier Villurrutia, 1984. Memberships: IASS; ICLA; MLA; IILI. Address: Av. Rivera 6195, Montevideo, Uruguay.

BLOND Anthony, b. 1928. Author; Journalist. Appointments: Trustee LIBERTY; Formerly Director, Blond and Briggs Limited, 1958-90, Publishers, London. Publications: The Publishing Game, 1971; Family Business, 1978; The Book Book, 1985; Blond's Roman Emperors, 1994. Contributor to: Spectator, The Literary Review. Literary Agent: Gillon Aitken. Address: 9 Rue Thiers, 87300 Bellac, France.

BLONDEL Jean Fernand Pierre, b. 26 Oct 1929, Toulon, France. University Professor. m. (1) Michele Hadet, 1954, div, (2) Teresa Ashton, 1982, 2 daughters. Education: Diploma, Institut Etudes Politiques, Paris, 1953; BLitt, Oxford, England, 1955. Publications: Voters, Parties and Leaders, 1963; An Introduction to Conservative Government, 1969; Comparative Legislatures, 1973; World Leaders, 1980; The Discipline of Politics, 1982; Political Leadership, 1987; The Organisation of Governments, 1982; Government Ministers in the Contemporary World, 1985; Political Parties, 1978; Comparative Government, 1990. Contributions to: European Journal of Political Research. Memberships: Royal Swedish Academy of Sciences; American Political Science Association; British Political Studies Association of the UK; Association Francaise de Science Politique. Address: 15 Marloes Road, London W8 6LQ, England.

BLOTNER Joseph, b. 1923, USA. Writer. Literary Appointments: Assistant Professor, 1955-61, Associate Professor of English, 1961-68, University of Virginia, Charlottesville; Professor of English, University of North Carolina, Chapel Hill, 1968-71; Professor of English, University of Michigan, Ann Arbor, 1971-. Publications: The Political Novel, 1955; The Fiction of J D Salinger (with F L Gwynn), 1959; Faulkner in The University (with F L Gwynn), 1959; William Faulkner's Library: A Catalogue, 1964; The Modern American Novel 1900-1960, 1966; Faulkner: A Biography, 2 volumes, 1974, 1984; Selected Letters of William Faulkner, 1977; Uncollected Stories of William Faulkner, 1979; Faulkner: A Biography (revised) 1 volume, 1984; William Faulkner Novels 1930-35, 1986; William Faulkner Manuscripts, 1987; William Faulkner Novels 1936-1940, 1990. Address: 1031 Belmont Road, Ann Arbor, MI 48104, USA.

BLUM Richard A, b. 28 Jul 1943, Brooklyn, NY, USA. Television Programme Development Executive; Writer; Educator. Education: BA, FairleighDickinson University, 1965; MS, Boston University, 1967; PhD, University of Southern California, 1977. Literary Appointments: Professor, Screenwriting, University of Maryland, 1983-; Visiting Professor, Screenwriting, Harvard University Summer School, 1984, 1985, 1986; American Film Institute, 1983, 1984, 1986; The Writers Centre, 1984-88. Publications: Television writing: From Concept to Contract, 1980, 1984; American Film Acting, 1984; Primetime: Network TV Programming (co-author), 1987; Working Actors, 1989; Inside Television Producing, 1991. Contributions to: The Writer; The Scriptwriter; Educational Editor; Journal of Performing Arts Review; Television Writer, Producer, PBS, NBC-TV, Universal Studios, Columbia Pictures-TV. Honours: Best Playwrite, FDU, 1964, 1965; Media Programme Supervisor, NEH, Washington DC, 1978-81; Creative and Performing Arts Award, University of Maryland, 1987; Judge, Nicholl Screenwriting Fellowships, Academy of Motion Pictures Arts and Sciences, 1987, 1988; Judge, Public Television Awards, Corporation for Public Broadcasting, 1988; Ford Foundation Fellowship, 1988. Memberships: Writers Guild of America; Academy of Television Arts and Sciences; University Film and Video Association; Broadcast Education Association; Washington Independent Writers. Address: 2208 Washington Avenue, Silver Spring, MD 20910, USA.

BLUMBERG Stanley, b. 11 Apr 1912, USA. Writer. m. 2 Aug 1952. Education: University of Maryland, 1931; Johns Hopkins University, 1932. Publications: Energy and Conflict - The Life and Times of Edward Teller, 1976; The Survival Factor, Israeli Intelligence from World War I to the Present, 1981; Edward Teller, Giant of the Golden Age of Physics, 1990. Contributions to: The Nation; Baltimore Sun; USA Today; Hopkins Magazine; Human Events. Membership: Literary Guild. Address: 6000 Ivydene Terrace, Baltimore, MD 21209, USA.

BLUME Judy, b. 12 Feb 1938, Elizabeth, New Jersey, USA. Writer. 1 son, 1 daughter. Education: BS, New York University, 1961. Publications: Are You There, God?; It's Me Margaret; Blubber; Deenie; Freckle Juice; Iggie's House; It's Not the End of the World; The One in the Middle is the Green Kangaroo; Otherwise Known as Sheila the Great; Starring Sally J Freedman as Herself; Superfudge; Tales of a Fourth Grade Nothing; Then Again, Maybe I Won't; Tiger Eyes; The

Pain and the Great One; The Judy Blume Diary; Forever; Wifey; Smart Women; Letters to Judy; What Kids Wish They Could Tell You; Just as Long As We're Together; Here's To You, Rachel Robinson, 1993. Honours: Recipient, numerous honours and awards. Memberships: Authors Guild Council; PEN; Board, Society of Children's Book Writers. Address: c/o Claire Smith, Harold Ober Associates Inc, 40 E 49th Street, New York City, NY 10017, USA.

BLYTHE Ronald George, b. 6 Nov 1922, Acton, Suffolk, England. Author. Appointments: Eastern Arts Association Literature Panel, 1975-84; Society of Authors Management Committee, 1979-84; Associate Editor, New Wessex Edition of the Works of Thomas Hardy, 1978. Publications: The Age of Illusion, 1963; Akenfield, 1969; The View in Winter, 1979; From the Headlands, 1982; Each Returning Day, 1989; William Hazlitt: Selected Writings (edited), 1970; The Stories of Ronald Blythe, 1985; Divine Landscapes, 1986; Each Returning Day, 1989; Private Words, 1991; Critical Studies of Jane Austen, Thomas Hardy, Leo Tolstoy, Literature of the Second World War. Contributions to: Observer; Sunday Times; New York Times; The Listener; Atlantic Monthly; London Magazine; Tablet; New Statesman; Bottegue Oscure; Guardian. Memberships: Royal Society of Literature; Society of Authors; President; The John Clare Society; Fabian Society. Literary Agent: Deborah Rogers, London. Address: Bottengoms Farm, Wormingford, Colchester, Essex, England.

BOARDMAN John, b. 1927, United Kingdom. Professor Emeritus of Classical Art and Archaeology. Appointments: Assistant Keeper, Ashmolean Museum, 1955-59; Reader in Classical Archaeology, 1959-78; Lincoln Professor of Classical Art and Archaeology, 1978-94, University of Oxford; Editor, Journal of Hellenic Studies, 1958-65; Co-Editor, Oxford Monographs in Classical Archaeology; Delegate, OUP, 1979-89. Publications: S Marinatos and M Hirmer: Crete and Mycenae (translator), 1960; The Cretan Collection in Oxford, 1961; Island Gems, 1963; The Date of the Knossos Tablets, 1963; The Greek Overseas, 1964, 1974, 1980; Greek Art, 1964, 1973; Excavations at Tocra (with J Dorig, W Fuchs, M Hirmer), 1966; Greek Emporio, 1967; Pre-Classical Style and Civilisation, 1967; Engraved Gems, the Ionides Collection, 1968; Archaic Greek Gems, 1968; Eros in Greece (with E la Rocca), 1978; Greek Sculpture, Archaic Period, 1978; Catalogue of Gems and Finger Rings (with M L Vollenweider), vol I, 1978; Castle Ashby Corpus Vasorum (with M Robertson), 1979; Greek Sculpture, Classical Period, 1985; The Parthenon and its Sculptures, 1985; Athenian Red Figure Vases: Classical Period, 1989; The Diffusion of Classical Art in Antiquity, 1994. Honours: Kt, 1989; Professor of Ancient History, Royal Academy, 1989-; Hon Doctrate: University of Athens, 1990; University of Paris, 1994. Membership: Fellow, British Academy, 1969-. Address: 11 Park Street, Woodstock, Oxford OX20 1SJ, England.

BOAST Philip James, b. 30 Apr 1952, London, England. Writer. m. Rosalind Thorpe, 20 June 1981, 2 sons, 1 daughter. Education: Mill Hill School, 1965-69. Publications: London's Child; London's Millionaire; Watersmeet; Pride; London's Daughter; The Assassinators. Contributions to: Science Fiction Monthly. Literary Agent: Carol Smith. Address: Rhydda Bank Cottage, Trentishoe, Barnstaple, N Devon EX31 4PL, England.

BOCEK Alois. See: **VANICEK Zdenek.**

BODA Laszlo (Ladislas), b. 23 Nov 1929, Dregelypalank, Hungary. Professor. Education includes: Doctor of Theology, Budapest, 1955. Literary Appointments: Professor of Philosophy, Esztergom, 1955-73; Professor Ordinarius, Moral Theology, Budapest, 1973-. Publications: Moral Theology (I-IV), 1980; Moral Theology of The Christian Maturity, 1986; Inner Performance, a postmodern epos adapted from Dante (Hungarian, Belso szinjatek), 1986; To Be Human or To Have?, 1990; Your Way To Marriage, for young people, 1990; Give to God What is God's, 1991; Inkulturation, Church, Europe (first book of the European inkulturation), forthcoming. Contributions include: In Hungarian: Vigilia; Teologia; Diakonia; Articles to: New Man (Uj Ember); about 25 to various journals; about 50 to periodical reviews; In German: Arzt und Christ; Folia Theologica. Memberships: Conferences of European Moral Theology; Societas Ethica; European Theology; Society of Peace and Human Understanding; Society of St Stephen, Hungary; Society of Johannes Messner, Vienna, 1993. Address: David F u 7, Fsz 3, H 1113 Budapest XI, Hungary.

BODELSEN Anders, b. 11 Feb 1937, Copenhagen, Denmark. Novelist. m. Eva Sindahl-Pedersen, 1975. Education: University of Copenhagen, 1956-60. Appointments include: Staff member of Politiken, from 1967. Publications include: Villa Sunset, 1964; The Greenhouse, 1965; Rama Sama, 1967; The Silent Partner, 1968, 1978; Hit and Run, Run, Run, 1968, 1970; Freezing Point, 1969, 1971; Holiday, 1970; Straus, 1971; Help: Seven Stories, 1971; The Girls on the Bridge, 1972; Opposite Number, 1972; Outside Number, 1972; Consider the Verdict, 1973, 1976; Law and Order, 1973; Everything You Wish, 1974; The Wind in the Alley, 1974; Operation Cobra, 1975; Money and the Life, 1976; The Good Times, 1977; Year by Year, 1978; Over the Rainbow, 1982; Domino, 1984; The Shelter, 1984; Revision, 1985; I Must Run, 1987; The Blue Hour, 1987; Blackout, 1988; The Town Without Fires, 1989; Red September, 1991; Radio and Television plays. Honours include: Swedish Crime Writers Academy Prize, 1990. Address: Christiansholms Parkvej 12, 2930 Klampenborg, Denmark.

BODSWORTH Charles Frederick, b. 11 Oct 1918, Port Burwell, Ontario, Canada. Novelist. m. Margaret Neville Banner, 1944, 1 son, 2 daughters. Education: Port Burwell Public and High Schools. Appointments: Staff Writer and Editor, Maclean's Magazine, Toronto, 1947-55; Editor, Natural Science of Canada Series, 1980-81. Publications: Last of the Curlews, 1955; The Strange One, 1959; The Atonement of Ashley Morden, 1965; The Sparrow's Fall, 1967; Other non-fictional works. Honours: Doubleday Canadian Novel Award, 1967. Address: 294 Beech Avenue, Toronto, Ontario, Canada M4E 3J2.

BOECKMAN Charles, b. 9 Nov 1920, San Antonio, Texas, USA. Author. m. Patricia Kennelly, 25 July 1965, 1 daughter. Appointment: Free Lance Writer, 1950-. Publications: Maverick Brand, 1961; Unsolved Riddles of the Ages, 1965; Cool, Hot and Blue, 1968; And the Beat Goes On, 1972; Surviving Your Parent's Divorce, 1980; Remember Our Yesterdays, 1991; House of Secrets, 1992; Our Regional Industries, 1966; Author of over 1000 short stories and articles, and many anthologies. Honours: Mr Banjo, selected for Anthology, Best Detective Stories of the Year, 1979. Membership: American Society of Journalists and Authors. Address: 322 Del Mar Boulevard, Corpus Christi, TX 78404, USA.

BOESCH Hans, b. 13 Mar 1926, Frumsen, Sennwald, Switzerland. Traffic Engineer. m. Mathilde Kerler, 1 July 1950, 3 daughters. Education: HTL Winterthur, 1941-46. Appointments: Hed, Transport Planning, Baudirektion Kanton Aargau; Scientific Collaborator, Dozent, ORL-Institut, ETH Zurich. Publications include: Der junge Os, novel, 1957; Das Gerust, novel, 1960; Die Fliegenfalle, novel, 1968; Menschen im Bau, stories, 1970; Ein David, poems, 1980; Der Mensch im Stadtverkehr, essay, 1975; Der Kiosk, novel, 1978; Unternehmen Normkopf, satire, 1985; Der Sog, novel, 1988. Contributions to: Neue Zurcher Zeitung, Zurich; Tages-Anzeiger, Zurich; Schweizer Monatshefte, Zurich. Honours include: C F Meyer Prize, 1954; Medal of Honour, City of Zurich, 1970, 1978; Prize for Literature, Canton of Aargau, 1983; Prize, Schillerstiftung, 1988; International Bodensee Prize for Literature, 1989; Various, Pro Helvetia and Canton of Zurich. Address: Eichstr 10a, 8712 Stafa, Switzerland.

BOGDANOVICH Peter, b. 30 July 1939, Kingston, New York, USA. Film Director; Writer; Producer; Actor. m. (1) Polly Platt, 1962, div'd 1970, 2 daughters, (2) L B Straten, 1988. Appointments: Film Feature-Writer, Esquire, New York Times, Village Voice, Cahiers du Cinema, Los Angeles Times, New York Magazine, Vogue, Variety and others, 1961-. Publications: The Cinema of Orson Welles, 1961; The Cinema of Howard Hawks, 1962; The Cinema of Alfred Hitchcock, 1963; John Ford, 1968; Fritz Lang in America, 1969; Allan Dwan: The Last Pioneer, 1971; Pieces of Time: Peter Bogdanovich on the Movies (Picture Shows in UK), 1961-85, 1973, enlarged 1985; The Killing of the Unicorn: Dorothy Stratten (1960-1980), 1984; A Year and A Day Calendar (edited with introduction), 1991; This is Orson Wells, 1992; Films: The Wild Angels, 1966; Targets, 1968; The Last Picture Show, 1971; What's Up Doc? 1972; Paper Moon, 1973; Daisy Miller, 1974; At Long Last Love, 1975; Nickelodeon, 1976; Saint Jack, 1979; They All Laughed, 1981; Mask, 1985; Illegally Yours, 1988; Texasville, 1990; Noises Off, 1992; The Thing Called Love, 1993. Honours include: New York Film Critics' Award for Best Screenplay, British Academy Award for Best Screenplay, 1971; Writer's Guild of America Award for Best Screenplay, 1972; Silver Shell, Mar del Plata, Spain, 1973; Best Director, Brussels Festival, 1974; Pasinetti Award, Critics Prize, Venice Festival, 1979. Memberships: Directors Guild of America; Writer's Guild of America; Academy of Motion Picture Arts and Sciences. Address: c/o William Peiffer, 2040 Avenue of the Stars, Century City, CA 90067, USA.

BOISDEFFRE Pierre Jules Marie Raoul (Neraud Le Mouton de), b. 11 July 1926, Paris, France. Writer; Diplomatist; Broadcasting Official. m. Beatrice Wiedemann-Goiran, 1957, 3 sons. Education: Ecole Libre des Sciences Politiques; Ecole Nationale d'Administration; Harvard University, USA. Appointments: Director of Sound Broadcasting, Office de Radiodiffusion et Television Francaise (ORTF), 1963-68; Cultural Counsellor, French Embassy, London, 1968-71; Brussels, 1972-77; Ministry of Foreign Affairs, 1977-78; Minister Plenipotentiary, 1979; Ambassador to Uruguay 1981-84, Colombia 1984-88, Council of Europe, Strasbourg 1988-91. Publications: Metamorphose de la litterature, 2 volumes, 1950; Ou va le Roman? 1962; Les ecrivains francais d'aujourd'hui, 1963; Histoire de la litterature, 1930-85, 2 volumes 1985; Lettre ouverte aux hommes de gauche, 1969; La foi des anciens jours, 1977; Le roman francais depuis 1900, 1979; Les nuits, l'Ile aux livres, Paroles de vie, La Belgique, 1980; Various critical portraits; Souvenirs: Contre fr Vent May'eur, 1994. Honours: Numerous national awards, including Prix de la Critique, 1950; Doctor honoris causa, Universities of Hull (Great Britian) and Bogota (Colombia); Officer de la Legion d'honneur Commandeur de l'ordre national du Merite. Address: 5 Cité Vaneau, 75007 Paris, France.

BOISVERT France (Marguerite de Nevers), b. 10 June 1959, Sherbrooke, Quebec, Canada. French Teacher; Writer; Poet. 1 son. Education: Baccalaureat, 1983; Master in Literature, 1986. Literary Appointments: Salon int du livre de Bruxelles, 1991; York University, Canada, 1991; Speeches, Montreal, Public Lectures, 1991-93. Publications: Les Samourailles, 1987; Li Tsing-tao ou Le grand avoir, prose, 1989; Massawippi, poem, 1992; Comme un vol de gerfauts, poem, 1993; as Marguerite de Nevers: Tableaux et Dictées, editions le Noroît, Poems, 1995. Contributions to: Liberté; La Presse. Honours: Bursery, Minister of Culture, Quebec, 1989, 1990, 1991. Memberships: Union des Ecrivains du Québec; Administration éLue au Conseil d'administration de L'UNEQ. Address: A/S UNEQ Maison des Ecrivains, 3492 Avenue Laval, Montreal H2X 3C8, Canada.

BOLAND Michael John, b. 14 Nov 1950, Kingston, Surrey, England. Poet; Civil Servant. Education: Shene County Grammar School. Appointment: Editor, The Arcadian (Poetry magazine). Publications: The Midnight Circus; The Trout .... Minus One, 1993 (Co-author). Contributions to: Poems in Envoi; Purple Patch; Weyfarers; Firing Squad; Various Anthologies. Honours: Patricia Chown Sonnet Award. Memberships: PEN; Penman Club; Society of Civil Service Authors; Keats Shelley Memorial Association; Wordsworth Trust; Friends of Coleridge; MIAP. Address: 11 Boxtree Lane, Harrow Weald, Middlesex HA3 6JU, England.

BOLD Alan, b. 20 Apr 1943, Edinburgh, Scotland. Writer. m. Alice Howell, 29 June 1963, 1 daughter. Education: Edinburgh University. Publications include: To Find the New, verse, 1967; A Perpetual Motion Machine, verse, 1969; In This Corner: Selected Poems, verse, 1983; The Edge of the Wood, stories, 1984; MacDiarmid, biography, 1988; A Burns Companion, criticism, 1991; East is West, novel, 1991; Rhymer Rab: An Anthology of Poems and Prose by Robert Burns, 1993. Contributions: Weekly Review for Glasgow Herald; Sunday Times; TLS, The Times Higher. Honours: McVitie's Prize for 1989 Scottish Writer of the Year; Arts Award, Royal Philosophical Society of Glasgow, 1990; Honorary President, Auchinieck Boswell Society, 1992. Memberships: Society of Authors; Royal Society of Literature. Address: Balbirnie Burns East Cottage, Nr Markinch, Glenrothes, Fife KY7 6NE, Scotland.

BOLTON, Elizabeth. See: JOHNSTON Norma.

BOMBECK Erma Louise, b. 21 Feb 1927, Dayton, Ohio, USA. Author; Syndicated Columnist. m. William L Bombeck, 13 Aug 1949, 2 sons, 1 daughter. Education: BA, University of Dayton, 1949. Publications: At Wit's End, 1967; Just Wait Till You Have Children of Your Own! (with Bil Keane), 1971; I Lost Everything in the Post-Natal Depression, 1974; The Grass is Always Greener over the Septic Tank, 1976; If Life is a Bowl of Cherries - What am I doing in the Pits, 1978; Aunt Erma's Cope Book, 1979; Motherhood: The Second Oldest Profession, 1983; Family - The Ties that Bind .. And Gag! 1987; I Want to Grow Hair, I Want to Grow Up, I Want to go to Boise, 1989; When You Look Like Your Passport Photo, It's Time to Go Home, 1991; A Marriage Made in Heaven ... Or Too Tired for an Affair, 1993. Honours: Theta Sigma Phi Headliner Award, 1969; Mark Twain Award, 1973; 16 Honorary Doctorates, 1974-90; Golden Plate Award, American Academy of Achievement, 1978; Grand Marshal, Tournament of Roses

Parade, 1986; American Cancer Society Medal of Honour, 1990. Address: Universal Press Syndicate, 4900 Main Street, Kansas City, MO 64112, USA.

BOND Edward, b. 1934, United Kingdom. Playwright; Poet; Director. Publications: Saved, 1966; Three Sisters (Chekov), translator, 1967; Narrow Road to the Deep North, 1968; Early Morning, 1968; The Pope's Wedding and Other Plays, 1971; Lear, 1972; The Sea, 1973; Bingo: Scenes of Money and Death, 1974; Spring's Awakening (translator), 1974; The Fool, 1975; We Come to the River, libretto for Henze, 1976; A-A-America - The Swing and Grandma Faust, 1976; A-A-America, and Stone, 1976; Plays, 4 vols, 1977-92; Theatre Poems & Songs, 1978; Collected Poems, 1978-85; The Woman, 1978; the Bundle, 1980; The Cat, libretto, 1980; The Restoration, 1981; Summer, 1982; Human Cannon, 1985; War Plays (Red, Black and Ignorant; The Tin Can Riots; Great Peace), 1985; Jackets, 1988; In the Company of Men, 1988; Notes on Post-Modernism, 1988; September, 1988; Olly's Prison (3 TV plays), 1992; Tuesday (TV Play), 1993; Selected Letters (4 vols), 1994-95; Coffee, 1995; Lulu: A Monster Tragedy (by Frank Wedekind - Translated). Honours: Hon D Litt (Yale), 1977. Membership: Theatre Writers Union. Literary Agent: Casarotto Ramsay Ltd, National House, 60-66 Wardour Street, London W1V 3HP. Address: c/o Margaret Ramsay Ltd, 14A Goodwin's Court, London WC2N 4LL, England.

BOND Gillian. See: MCEVOY Marjorie.

BOND Michael, b. 1926. Author. Publications: A Bear Called Paddington, 1958; More About Paddington, 1959; Paddington Helps Out, 1960; Paddington Abroad, 1961; Paddington At Large, 1962; Paddington Marches On, 1964; Paddington At Work, 1966; Here Comes Thursday, 1966; Thursday Rides Again, 1968; Paddington Goes to Town, 1968; Thursday Ahoy, 1969; Parsley's Tail, 1969; Parsley's Good Deed, 1969; Parsley's Problem Present, 1970; Parsley's Last Stand, 1970; Paddington Takes the Air, 1970; Thursday in Paris, 1970; Michael Bond's Book of Bears, 1971; Michael Bond's Book of Mice, 1971; The Day the Animales Went on Strike, 1972; Paddington Bear, 1972; Paddington's Garden, 1972; Parsley Parade, 1972; The Tales of Olga de Polga, 1972; Olga Meets Her Match, 1973; Paddington's Blue Peter Story Book, 1973; Paddington at the Circus, 1973; Paddington Goes Shopping, 1973; Paddington at the Seaside, 1974; Paddington at the Tower, 1974; Paddington on Top, 1974; Windmill, 1975; How to Make Flying Things, 1975; Eight Olga Readers, 1975; Paddington's Cartoon Book, 1979; J D Polson and the Dillogate Affair, 1981; Paddington on Screen, 1981; Olga Takes Charge, 1982; The Caravan Puppets, 1983; Paddington at the Zoo, 1984; Paddington's Painting Exhibition, 1985; Elephant, 1985; Paddington Minds the House, 1986; Paddington at the Palace, 1986; Paddington's Busy Day, 1987; Paddington and the Magical Maze, 1987; (Adult Books) Monsieur Pamplemousse, 1983; Monsieur Pamplemousse and the Secret Mission, 1984; Monsieur Pamplemousse Takes the Cure, 1987; The Pleasures of Paris, Guide Book, 1987; Monsieur Pamplemousse Aloft, 1989; Monsieur Pamplemousse Investigates, 1990; Monsieur Pamplemousse Rest's His Case, 1991; Monsieur Pamplemousse Stands Firm, 1992; Monsieur Pamplemousse on Location, 1992; Monsieur Pamplemousse Takes the Train, 1993. Literary Agent: Harvey Unna, London. Address: c/o Lemon Unna & Durbridge Ltd, 24 Pottery Lane, Holland Park, London W11 4LZ, England.

BOND Nancy Barbara, b. 8 Jan 1945, USA. Librarian; Writer. Education: BA, Mount Holyoke College, 1966; Dip Lib Wales, 1972, College of Librarianship Wales. Appointment: Instructor, part-time, Simmons College, Centre for the Study of Children's Literature, 1979-. Publications: A String in the Harp, 1976; The Best of Enemies, 1978; Country of Broken Stone, 1980; The Voyage Begun, 1981; A Place to Come Back to, 1984; Another Shore, 1988; Truth to Tell, 1994. Honours: A String in the Harp, awarded the International Reading Association Award, 1976; Newbery Honour, 1976; Welsh Arts Council Tir na n'Og Award, 1976. Address: 109 The Valley Road, Concord, MA 01742, USA.

BOND Ruskin, b. 1934, India. Author; Journalist; Children's Writer. Appointments: Managing Editor, Imprint, Bombay, 1975-79. Publications: The Room on the Roof, 1956; Grandfather's Private Zoo, 1967; The Last Tiger, 1971; Angry River, 1972; The Blue Umbrella, 1974; Once Upon a Monsoon Time, memoirs, 1974; Man of Destiny: A Biography of Jawaharlal Nehru, 1976; Night of the Leopard, 1979; Big Business, 1979; The Cherry Tree, 1980; The Road to the Bazaar, 1980;

A Flight of Pigeons, 1980; The Young Vagrants, 1981; Flames in the Forest, 1981; The Adventures of Rusty, 1981; Tales and Legends of India, 1982; A Garland of Memories, 1982; To Live in Magic, 1982; Tigers Forever, 1983; Earthquakes, 1984; Getting Granny's Glasses, 1985; The Eyes of the Eagle, 1987; The Night Train at Deoli, short stories; Times Stops at Shamli, short stories, 1989; Ghost Trouble, 1989; Snake Trouble, 1990; Dust on the Mountain, 1990; Our Trees Still Grow in Dehra, 1992; Rain in the Mountains, 1994. Contributions to: The Christian Science Monitor (Boston); Books For Keeps (UK); Cricket (USA); School (NSW, Australia); The Telegraph (Calcutta); Khaleej Times (Dubai); The Weekly Sun (New Delhi). Honours: Sahitya Akademi Award for English writing in India, 1992; John Hewellyn Rhys Prize (British), 1957. Address: Ivy Cottage, Landour, Mussouri, UP 248179, India.

BONE J(esse), b. 1916, USA. Professor of Vetinary Medicine (retired); Science Fiction Writer. Publications: Observations of The Ovaries of Infertile and Reportedly Infertile Dairy Cattle, 1954; Animal Anatomy, 1958, revised edition, Animal Anatomy and Physiology, 1975, 1981, 1988; Canine Medicine (editor), 1959, 2nd edition, 1962; The Lani People, 1962; Equine Medicine and Surgery (co-editor), 1963, 2nd edition, 1972; Legacy, 1976; The Meddlers, 1976; Gift of The Manti (with R Myers), 1977; Confederation Matador, 1978; Animal Anatomy and Physiology, 3rd revised edition, 1988. Address: 3017 Brae Burn, Sierra Vista, AZ 85635, USA.

BONESSIO DI TERZET Ettore, b. Italy. Teacher of Aesthetics, University of Genoa. Education: MA; PhD. Literary Appointments: Editor, Poetry, Art and Aesthetics Magazine, il Cobold. Publications: Solitudine e comunicazione estetica, 1974; Hegel e la poesia moderna, 1975; L'esperienza dell'arte, 1980; Il Principio della Parola (anthology of distinguished poetry after 1974), 1986; Configurazioni, 1990; Del Frammento organico, 1992; Lo Splendore del vuoto, 1993. Contributions to: Sulfur, USA; International Poetry, USA; Tracce; Stilb; Spirali; Symbola; Il Farone; Altri Termini; Nuova Corrente; Artivisive; Studio Marconi; Filosofia Oggi, Italy; Vertice Portugal; XUL, Argentina; Differentia, USA; Anterem; Alfabeta, Italy; Effects, USA. Address: CP 707, 16100 Genova AD, Italy.

BONHAM Frank, b. 1914, USA. Author; Playwright. Publications: Lost Stage Valley, 1948; Bold Passage, 1950; Blood on The Land, 1952; Snaketrack, 1952; The Outcast of Crooked River, 1953; Night Raid, 1954; The Feud at Spanish Fort, 1954; Hardrock, 1956; Border Guns, 1956; Last Stage West, 1957; Tough Country, 1958; The Sound of Gunfire, 1960; One For Sleep, 1960; Burma Rifles: A Story of Merrill's Marauders, 1960; The Skin Game, 1961; Trago..., 1962; Defiance Mountain, 1962; War Beneath The Sea, 1962; By Her Own Hand, 1963; Deepwater Challenge, 1963; Honor Bound, 1963; The Loud, Resounding Sea, 1963; Cast a Long Shadow, 1964; Rawhide Guns, 1964; Logan's Choice, 1964; Speedway Contender, 1964; Durango Street, 1965; Mystery in Little Tokyo, 1966; Mystery of The Red Tide, 1966; The Ghost Front, 1968; Mystery of The Fat Cat, 1968; The Nitty Gritty, 1968; The Vagabundos, 1969; Viva Chicano, 1970; Chief, 1971; Cool Cat, 1971; The Friends of The Loony Lake Monster, 1972; Hey, Big Spender, 1972; A Dream of Ghosts, 1973; The Golden Bees of Tulami, 1974; The Missing Persons League, 1976; The Rascals From Haskell's Gym, 1977; The Forever Formula, 1979; Break for The Border, 1980; Gimme an H Gimme an E gimme an L gimme a P, 1980; Fort Hogan, 1980; Premonitions, 1984; Snaketrack, 1989; That Bloody Bozeman Trail, 1990; Stagecoach West, 1990. Honours: George G Stone Center for Children's Books Award, 1967. Address: Box 130, Skull Valley, AZ 86338, USA.

BONHAM-CARTER Victor, b. 1913, United Kingdom. Author. Appointments: Historian, Records Officer, Dartington Hall Estate, 1951-65; Secretary, Royal Literary Fund, 1966-82; Joint Secretary, Society of Authors, London, 1971-78. Publications: The English Village, 1952; Dartington Hall (with W B Curry), 1958; Exploring Parish Churches, 1959; Farming the Land, 1959; In a Liberal Tradition, 1960; Soldier True, US Edition The Strategy of Victory, 1965; Surgeon in the Crimea (editor), 1968; The Survival of the English Countryside, US Edition Land and Environment, 1971; Authors by Profession, 2 vols, 1978-84; The Essence of Exmoor, 1991. Membership: Fellow, Royal Society of Literature; President, Exmoor Society, 1975-. Literary Agent: Curtis Brown. Address: The Mount, Milverton, Taunton, Somerset TA4 1QZ, England.

BONNEFOY Yves Jean, b. 24 Jun 1923, Tours, France. Writer. m. Lucille Vine, 1968, 1 d. Education: Faculte des Sciences, Poitiers;

Faculte des Lettres, Paris; L es L. Literary Appointments: Professor, College de France, 1981-; Lectures, seminars: Brandeis; Johns Hopkins; Princeton; Geneva; Nive; Yale; others. Publications: Poems: Du mouvement et de l'immobilite de Douve, 1953; Pierre ecrit, 1964; Selected Poems, 1968; Dans le leurre du seuil, 1975; Poems, 1947-1975, 1978; Essays: L'Improbable, 1959; Arthur Rimbaud, 1961; Un reve fait a Mantoue, 1967; Le nuage rouge, 1977; Rue traversiere, 1977; On art: Peintures murales de la France Gothique, 1954; Miro, 1963; Rome 1630, 1969; L'Arriere-Pays, 1972; Entretiens sur la poesie, 1981; La Prescence et l'Image, 1983; Ce qui fut sans lumiere, 1987; Rècits en rève, 1987; other work: Hier regnant desert, 1958; Co-editor, L'Ephemere; translations of Shakespeare; many books also in English. Contributions to: Mercure de France; Critique; Encounter; L'Ephemere. Honours: Prix Montaigne, 1980; Grand Prix de Poesie, Academie Francaise, 1981; Grand Prix Sociètè des bens de Lettres, 1987. Address: c/o College de France, 11 Place Marcelin-Berthelot, 75005 Paris, France.

BONNER Raymond Thomas, b. 11 Apr 1942, USA. Author; Journalist. Education: AB, MacMurray College, 1964; JD, Stanford Law School, 1967. Publications: Weakness and Deceit; US Policy and El Salvador, 1984; Waltzing With a Dictator: The Marcoses and The Making of American Policy, 1987. Contributions to: Numerous professional journals. Honour: Robert F Kennedy Memorial Book Award, 1985. Literary Agent: Gloria Loomis, New York, USA. Address: 110 Riverside Drive, 4C New York, NY 10024, USA.

BONNER Terry Nelson. See: **KRAUZER Steven M.**

BONTLY Thomas John, b. 25 Aug 1939, Madison, Wisconsin, USA. Professor of English. m. Marilyn R Mackie, 25 Aug 1963, 1 son. Education: BA, University of Wisconsin, 1961; Research Student, Corpus Christi College, Cambridge University, 1961-62; PhD, Stanford University, 1966. Appointments: Professor, English, 1966-, Coordinator, Creative Writing, 1975-78, 1968-89, University of Wisconsin, Milwaukee. Publications: The Competitor, 1966; The Adventures of a Young Outlaw, 1974; Celestial Chess, 1979; The Giant's Shadow, 1989. Contributions to: Short stories to Esquire; Redbook; McCall's; Other magazines. Honours: Maxwell Perkins Award, for The Competitor, 1966; Fulbright Lecturer, Germany, 1984. Memberships: Board of Directors, Council for Wisconsin Writers; Milwaukee Literary Society. Literary Agent: Curtis Brown Ltd. Address: Department of English, University of Wisconsin-Milwaukee, PO Box 413, Milwaukee, WI 53201, USA.

BOOHER Dianna Daniels, b. 13 Jan 1948, Hillsboro, TX, USA. Writer; Writing Consultant. 1 s, 1 d. Education: BA, North Texas State University, 1970; MA, University of Houston, 1979. Publications: Would You Put That in Writing?, 1983; Send Me a Memo, 1984; Cutting Paperwork in The Corporate Culture, 1986; Letter Perfect, 1988; Good Grief, Good Grammer, 1988; The New Secretary, 1985; Love, Love, 1985; Making Friends With Yourself and Other Strangers, 1982; Rape: What Would You Do If?..., 1983; Help, We're Moving!, 1978; Coping When Your Family Falls Apart, 1979; Not Yet Free, 1981; Boy Friends and Boyfriends, 1988; They're Playing Our Secret, 1988; That Book's Not in Our Library, 1988; Musical Dramas: For Me, It Was Different, 1984; Christmas of Your Life, 1983. Honours: American Library Association Best Books for Young Adults for Rape: What Would You Do If?..., 1981. Memberships: American Society for Training and Development; National Speakers Association. Literary Agent: Mitch Douglas, International Creative Management. Address: Booher Writing Consultants, 12337 Jones Road, Suite 242, Houston, TX 77070, USA.

BOOKER Christopher John Penrice, b. 7 Oct 1937. Journalist; Author. m. Valerie, 1979, 2 s. Education: Corpus Christi College, Cambridge. Literary Appointments: Liberal News, 1960; Jazz Critic, Sunday Telegraph, 1961; Editor, Private Eye, 1961-63; Regular Contributor, 1965-; Resident Scriptwriter, That Was The Week That Was, 1962-63; Not So Much a Programme, 1963-64. Publications: The Neophiliacs: A Study of The Revolution in English Life in The 50's and 60's, 1969; Goodbye London (with Candida Lycett-Green), 1973; The Booker Quiz, 1976; The Seventies, 1980; The Games War: A Moscow Journal, 1981; The Repatriations from Austria in 1945, 1990; (with Richard Norten) The Mad Officials Know the Bureaucrats Are Strangling Britain, 1994. Contributions to: Spectator, 1962-; Daily Telegraph, 1959-, (Way of The World column, 1987-1990); Sunday Telegraph Columnist, 1990-; Wrote extensively on property development, planning and housing, 1972-77; Private Eye; Anthologies. Honours: Campaigning Journalist of The Year, with Bennie Gray, 1973;

Aims of Industry Free Enterprise Award, 1992. Address: The Old Rectory, Litton, Bath, BA3 4PW, England.

BOORSTIN Daniel Joseph, b. 1 Oct 1914, Atlanta, Georgia, USA. Author; Historian; Librarian of Congress Emeritus. m. Ruth Carolyn Frankel, 9 Apr 1941, 3 sons. Education: AB, summa cum laude, Harvard College, 1934; BA, Jurisprudence, 1st Class Honours, Rhodes Scholar, 1936; BCL, 1st Class Honours, 1937; Bailliol College, Oxford University, England; Student, Inner Temple, London, 1934-37; JSD (Sterling Fellow), Yale, 1940. Publications: The Americans (Triology), 1958, 1965, 1974; The Image, 1971; The Republic of Technology, 1978; The Exploring Spirit, 1976; The Lost World of Thomas Jefferson, 1960, 2nd Edition 1982; The Decline of Radicalism, 1969; America and the Image of Europe, 1960; The Genius of American Politics, 1953; The Mysterious Science of the Law, 1973; Editor, The Chicago History of American Civilization (now 30 volumes); American Civilization, 1972; An American Primer, 2 volumes, 1966; A Lady's Life in the Rocky Mountains, 1960; Textbook for Highschools, A History of the United States, 1980, with Brooks M Kelley; The Discoverers, 1983; The Creators, 1992; Cleopatra's Nose, 1994. Contributions to: Numerous professional journals. Honours: Recipient various honours and awards. Memberships: President, American Studies Association; Colonial Society of Massachusettsp; Antiquarian Society; American Academy of Arts & Sciences; American Historical Society; American Philosophical Society; Royal Historical Society. Address: 3541 Ordway St NW, Washington, DC 20016, USA.

BOOTH Edward, OP b. 16 Aug 1928. Catholic Priest Dominican. Education: Cambridge University, 1949-52, 1971-75; BA, 1952; MA, 1970; PhD, 1975. Publications: St Augustine's Notitia sui, related to Aristotle and the early neo-Platonists (series of articles); Aristotelian Aporetic Ontology in Islamic & Christian Thinkers; St Augustine and the Western Tradition of Self Knowing. Contributions to: Sant' Alberto Magno, l'uomo e il pensatore; La production du livre universitaire au moyen age, Exemplar et pecia; Kategorie und Kategorialitität; Articles in: Angelicum; Augustiniana; Augustinianum; Studia Patristica; The New Grove Dictionary of Music & Musicians; Reviews in Faith; Blackfriars; The Journal of the British Society for Phenomenology. Address: St Anna Stift, Lohstrasse 16-18, D-49074 Osnabrück, Germany.

BOOTH Martin, b. 7 Sept 1944, Lancashire, England. Writer. Publications: Hiroshima Joe, novel, 1985; The Jade Pavilion, 1986; Black Chameleon, novel, 1988; Carpet Sahib: A Life of Jim Corbett, biography and film, 1986; Dreaming of Samarkand, novel, 1989; A Very Private Gentleman, 1991; The Triads: A History of Chinese Secret Societies, 1990; The Humble Disciple, 1992; Rhino Road: The Evolution, natural history and conservation of African rhinos, 1992; The Iron Tree, 1993; Books of verse and other fiction; Screenplays and critical books; The Dragon & The Pearl, 1994 (Non-Fiction). Contributions to: Wide Body of Literary Criticism & Travel Writing since 1990. Honour: Fellow, Royal Society and Literature, 1980. Literary Agent: Murray Pollinger & Co, London. Address: c/o Murray Pollinger & Co, 222 Old Brompton Road, London, SW5 0BZ, England.

BOOTH Philip, b. 8 Oct 1925, Hanover, New Hampshire, USA. Writer. m. Margaret Tillman, 1946, 3 daughters. Education: AB, Dartmouth College, Hanover, 1948 (Phi Beta Kappa); MA, Columbia University, New York, 1949; Served in the United States Army Air Force, 1944-45. Appointments: Associate Professor 1961-65, Professor of English and Poet-in-Residence, 1965-85, Syracuse University, New York. Publications: Verse: Letter from a Distant Land, 1957; The Islanders, 1961; North by East, 1966; Weathers and Edges, 1966; Margins: A Sequence of New and Selected Poems, 1970; Available Light, 1976; Before Sleep, 1980; Relations: Selected Poems, 1950-85; 1986; Selves, 1990; Recordings: Today's Poets 4, with others, Folkways; The Cold Coast, Watershed, 1985; Editor of other works; Pairs, 1994. Address: Main Street, Castine, ME 04421, USA.

BOOTH Rosemary Sutherland, b. 1928, United Kingdon. History Teacher; Author. Publications: The Dear Colleague, 1972; The Burning Lamp, 1973; Ponies on the Heather, for children, 1973; The Heroine's Sister, 1975; Ponies and Parachutes, for children, 1975; Red Rowan Berry, 1976; Castaway, 1978; White Hope, for children, 1978; Payment for the Piper, US Edition Brave Kingdom, 1983; The Belchamber Scandal, 1985; Shadow over the Islands, 1986. Literary Agent: David Highan Associates, England. Address: c/o David Higham Associates, 5-8 Lower John Street, London, W1R 4HA, England.

BORDEN Louise Walker, b. 30 Oct 1949, Cincinnati, OH, USA. Writer. m. Peter a Borden, 4 Sept 1971, 1 s, 2 d. Education: BA, Denison University, 1971. Publications: Caps, Hats, Socks and Mittens, 1989; The Neighborhood Trucker, 1990; The Watching Game, 1991; Albie the Lifeguard, 1993; Just in Time for Christmas, 1994; Paperboy, 1995. Contributions to: Writer, Author, Literacy Poem, to the Reading Teacher, 1992; Christmas in the Stable, 1990. Memberships: Society of Childrens Book Writers; The Authors Guild. Address: 628 Myrtle Avenue, Terrce Park, OH 45174, USA.

BORDEN William Vickers,b. 27 Jan 1938, Indianapolis, Indiana, USA. Writer; Professor. m. Nancy Lee Johnson, 17 Dec 1960, 1 son, 2 daughters. Education: AB, Columbia University, 1960; MA, University of California, Berkeley, 1962. Appointments: Fiction Editor, North Dakota Quarterly, 1986-. Publications: Superstoe, novel, 1968; I Want to be an Indian, play, 1990; Slow Step and Dance, poems, 1991; The Last Prostitute, 1993; Plays produced: Turtle Island Blues; Tap Dancing Across the Universe; Loon Dance; Hangman; Quarks; Jumping; Ledge. Contributions to: Poems and short stories to numerous magazines including: Milkweed Chronicle; Cincinnati Poetry Review; New Orleans Review; Louisville Review; Colorado State Review; Poets On; Zone 3; Dakotah Territory; Loonfeather. Honours: Winner, Playwriting Competitions: Unicorn Theatre, 1983; Towngate Theatre, 983; Humboldt State University, 1985; Deep South, 1992; Great Platte River, 1992. Memberships: Dramatists Guild; American Society of Composers, Authors and Publishers; PEN; Associated Writing Programs. Address: Rt 6 Box 284, Bemidji, MN 56601, USA.

BORENSTEIN Audrey F, b. 7 Oct 1930, Chicago, IL, USA. Freelance Writer. m. Walter Borenstein, 5 Sept 1953, 1 s, 1 d. Education: AB, 1953, M, 1954, University of IL; PhD, LA State University, 1958. Publications include: Custom: An Essay on Social Codes, 1961; Redeeming the Sin, 1978; Older Women in 20th Century America, 1982; Chimes of Change and Hours, 1983; Through the Years: A Chronicle of Cong Ahavath Achim, 1989; Simurgh, 1991. Contributions to: Over 30 Short Fiction Works to Literary Journals. Honours: National Endowment for the Arts Fellowship, 1976; Rockefeller Foundation Humanities Fellowship, 1978; Fiction Prize for NY State, National League of American Pen Womens Annual Competition in Fiction, 1988. Memberships: Poets & Writers. Literary Agent: Bertha Klausner International Literary Agency Inc. Address: Four Henry Court, New Paltz, NY 12561, USA.

BORIS Martin, b. 7 Aug 1930, New York City, New York, USA. Writer. m. Gloria Shanf, 13 June 1952, 1 son, 2 daughters. Education: BA, New York University, University Heights, 1951; MA, New York University, Washington Square, 1953; BA, Lond Island University, Brooklyn College of Pharmacy, 1957. Publications: Two and Two, 1979; Woodridge 1946, 1980; Brief Candle, 1990. Literary Agent: Arthur Pine Literary Agency. Address: 1019 Northfield Road, Woodmere, NY 11598, USA.

BORNSTEIN George, b. 25 Aug 1941. Professor; Author. m. Jane Elizabeth York, 22 June 1982, 2 s, 1 d. Education: BA, Harvard University, 1963; PhD, Princeton University, 1966. Publications: Yeats and Shelley, 1970; Transformations of Romanticism, 1976; Postromantic Consciousness of Ezra Pound, 1977; Ezra Pound Amoung the Poets, 1985; Poetic Remaking: The Art of Browning, Yeats and Pound, 1988; Editor of: Romantic and Modern, 1977; W B Yeats, The Early Poetry, Vol.I, 1987, Vol.II, 1994; Letters to the New Island, 1989; Representing Modernist Texts, 1991; Palimpsest, 1993. Contributions to: Numerous Scholarly Journals. Honours: ACLS Fellowship, 1972; NEH Fellowship, 1982; Guggenheim Fellowship, 1986; Warner Rice Prize for Research in the Humanities, 1988; Julia Lockwood Award, 1993; Distinguished Faculty Achievement Award, 1993. Memberships: Modern Language Association; Society for Textual Scholarship Address: 2020 Vinewood Boulevard, Ann Arbor, MI 48104, USA.

BORODIN George. See: **MILKOMANE George Alexis Milkomanovich.**

BOSLEY Keith Anthony, b. 16 Sept 1937, Bourne End, Buckinghamshire, England. Poet; Translator. m. Satu Salo, 27 Aug 1982, 3 sons. Education: BA Honours, French, Universities of Reading, Paris, Caen. Publications: Mallarmé: The Poems, 1977; Finnish Folk Poetry: Epic, translations, 1977; Stations, poems, 1979; From the Theorems of Master Jean de a Ceppède, 1983; A Chiltern Hundred, poems, 1987; The Kalevala, translation, 1989; I Will Sing of What I

Know, Finnish ballads, 1990; Camoes: Epic & Lyric, translations, 1990; The Kanteletar,translation, 1992; The Great Bear, translations, 1993; Aleksis Kivi: Odes, 1994. Contributions to: Numerous journals and magazines. Honours: Finnish State Prize for Translators, 1978; First Prize, British Comparative Literature Association Translation Competition, 1982; Knighthood First Class, Order of the White Rose of Finland, 1991. Membership: Corresponding Member, Finnish Literature Society, Helsinki. Address: 108 Upton Road, Upton-cum-Chalvey, Slough SL1 2AW, England.

BOSQUET Alain, b. 28 Mar 1919, Odessa, Russia. Writer. Education: Free University of Brussels, Belgium, 1938-49; MA, University of Paris, Sorbonne, France. Publications: Poems: Poèmes Un 1945-67, (Les Testaments) 1979; 100 Notes Pour Une Solitude, 1970; Notes Pour Un Amour, 1972; Notes Pour Un pluriel, 1974; Le Livre du Doute et de la Grâce, 1977; Sonnets Pour Une Fin de Siècle, 1980; Poèms Deux 1970-74, 1982; Un Jour après la Vie, 1985; Le Tourment de Dieu, 1987; Bourreaux et acrobates, 1990; Le Gardien des Rosées (Aphorisms), 1991; Demain Sans Moi, 1994; Novels: Un Besoin de Malheur, 1963; La Confesion Mexicaine, 1965; Les Bonnes Intentions, 1976; Une Mère Russe, 1978; Jean-Louis Trabart, Medicin, 1980; L'Enfant que tu étais, 1982; Ni Guerre Ni Paix, 1983; Les Fêtes Cruelles, 1984; Lettre à mon Père qui aurait eu 100 Ans, 1987; Les Solitudes (trilogy), 1992; Short stories: Un homme pour un autre, 1985; Le Métier d'Otage, 1989; Comme un refus de la planète, 1989; Plays: Un détenu à Auschwitz, 1991. Contributions to: La Revue Des Deux Mondes; Magazine Littéraire; Le Figaro. Honours: Grand Prix de Poésie of French Academy, 1967; Grand Prix du Roman of French Academy, 1978; Royal Academy of Belgium, 1986; Honorary Member, Academy of Letters of Québec, 1993-. Membership: Max Jacob Juries, 1970; Renaudot 1971; President, Mallarmé Academy, 1994-. Address: 32 rue de Laborde, 75008, Paris, France.

BOSTON Raymond Jack (Ray Boston), b. 24 Dec 1927, Manchester, England. Writer; Researcher. m. Elizabeth Isabella Horsfield, 6 Aug 1955, 2 daughters. Education: BA, New College, Oxford, 1951; MA, 1964; MA, University of Wisconsin, USA, 1969. Appointments: Reporter, Manchester Evening News Ltd, 1950-53; Talks Producer, BBC, London, 1953-56; Lecturer, Central London Polytechnic, 1956-67; Writer, Daily Mirror, 1958-60; Sub Editor, The Times, 1960-65; Professor, University of Wisconsin, USA, 1967-69; Professor, University of Sciences, 1970-75; Director, Cardiff, Wales, 1975-85. Publcations: The Essential Fleet Street, Cassell; The Newpaper Press in Britain; British Chartists in America. Contributions to: Journalism Studies Review; British Journalism Review; Journalism Quarterly. Honours: American Studies Fellow; 1st Visiting Fellow, Australia. Memberships: Sigma Delta Chi; The H.A.L. Fisher Society, Founder-President. Address: 85 Severn Grove, Cardiff, CF1 9EQ, Wales.

BOSTWICK Dorothy Lee. See. BOSTWICK Dorothy Vernell Bable.

BOSTWICK Dorothy Vernell Bable, (Dorothy Lee Bostwick), b. 17 June 1927, Freelance Writer. 1 s, 1 d. Education: Practical Nursing, 1959. Publication: Under The Elms; Rose wind; The Great Treasury of World Poems; Twentieth Century Poetry; The Best of Poetry. Contributions to: Tiotes; Reach Out; Invictus; Spafaswap; Aphony; Dusty Road; Must A Poet Conform in Jackson Citizen Patriot. Honours: Merit Awards; Modern Poet Award. Address: 6513 N Lake Road, Clark Lake, Brooklyn, MI 49230, USA.

BOSWELL Robert, b. Sikeston, MI, USA, 1953. Writer. m. Antonya Nelson. Education: University of AR. Appointments: Associate Professor of English. Publications: Dancing In The Movies, 1986; Crooked Hearts, 1987; The Geography of Denver, 1989; Mystery Ride, 1993. Contributions to: Esquire; Best American Short Stories; O Henry Prize Stories; Iowa Review; New Yorker; Ploughshares; Georgia Review. Honours: IA School of Letters Award; O Henry Award. Address: New Mexico State University, English Dept, Box 3E, Las Cruces, NM 88003, USA.

BOSWORTH David, b. 26 Oct 1936, Richmond, Surrey, England. University Lecturer. m. Jenny Lawton, 9 Sept 1961, 1 son, 1 daughter. Education: BA, 1961; B.Phil, 1963, MA, 1968, St John's College, Oxford University. Publications: Logic & Arithmetic, Vol 1, 1974, Vol II, 1979; Plato's Phaedo, 1986; Plato's Theaetetus, 1988. Contributions to: Various Journals. Address: 5-6 Church Street, Twickenham, Middlesex, TW1 3NJ, England.

BOTT George, b. 1920, United Kingdom. Former Educator. Appointments: Formerly Senior English Master and Librarian, Cockermouth Grammar School; Editor, Scholastic Publications, 1960-68. Publications: George Orwell: Selected Writings (editor), 1958; Read and Relate (editor), 1960; Shakespeare: Man and Boy (editor), 1961; Sponsored Talk, 1971; Read and Respond, 1984; Read, Relate, Communicate, 1984; The Mary Hewetson Cottage Hospital, Keswick: Brief History, 1892-1992, 1991; Keswick: The Story of a Lake District Town, 1994. Address: 16 Penrith Road, Keswick, Cumbria CA12 4HF, England.

BOTTING Douglas Scott, b. 22 Feb 1934, London, UK. Author. m. 27 Aug 1964, 2 daughters. Education: MA, St Edmund Hall, Oxford University, 1958. Publications: Nazi Gold, 1984; In the Ruins of the Reich, 1985; Humbolt & the Cosmos, 1973; Wilderness Europe, 1976; Hitler's Last General - The Case Against Wilhelm Mohnke, 1989; Gavin Maxwell: A Life, 1993; Various other books of History, Biography, Travel including: Island of the Dragon's Blood, 1958; The Knights of Bornu, 1961; One Chilly Siberian Morning, 1965; Rio de Janeiro, 1977; The Pirates, 1978; The Second Front, 1978; The Giant Airships, 1980; The Aftermath in Europe, 1945, 1983; The U-Boats, 1979; Wild Britain, 1988. Contributions to: BBC TV & Radio; Sunday Times; Sunday Telegraph; Geographical Magazine; Readers Digest; Time-Life, National Geographic Society. Memberships: Society of Authors; Royal Institute of International Affairs; Royal Geographical Society. Literary Agent: John Johnson Ltd, London. Address: 21 Park Farm Road, Kingston-on-Thames, Surrey, England.

BOUCHER David Ewart George, b. 15 Oct 1951, Wales. Senior Lecturer. m. Clare Mary ffrench Mullen, 8 Sept 1979, 2 daughters. Education: University College, Swansea, 1973-76; BA 1976, London School of Economics, 1976-77; MSc 1977, University of Liverpool, 1977-79; PhD, 1983. Appointments: Advisor, Oxford University Press, 1989; Member, Editorial Board, Australian Journal of Political Science, 1990-92. Publications: Texts in Context; The Political Philosophy of R G Collingwood; Essays in Political Philosophy; The New Leviathan; A Radical Hegelian; Social Contract from Hobbes to Rawls; British Idealist Political Thought. Contributions to: Journal of the History of Ideas; Interpretation; New Literary History; Idealistic Studies; History & Theory; Polity; Political Studies; History of Political Thought; Storia Antropologia E Scienza del Linguagio; Australian Journal of Political Science; Australian Journal of Politics and History. Honours: Tutorial Fellowship; Research Fellowship; Best Special Issue Award; Fellow, Royal Historical Society, elected 1992; Editor, Collingwood Studies. Memberships: Australian Political Science Association; Editorial Board of Association's Journal; Chairman, Trustees of the R G Collingwood Society. Address: Department of Political Theory & Government, University College, Singleton Park, Swansea SA2 8PP, Wales.

BOULTON David, b. 3 Oct 1935, Richmond, Surrey, England. Author and TV Producer. m. Anthea Ingham, 14 Feb 1969, 2 daughters. Education: Hampton Grammar School, 1947-52. Publications: Objection Overruled, 1968; The UVF; Protestant Paramilitary Organizations in Ireland, 1973; The Lockheed Papers (in USA, The Greae Machine), 1980; Jazz in Britain, 1958; The Making of Tania Hearst, 1975; Early Friends in Dent, 1986. Contributor to: Publications including: Tribune; New Statesman; The Listener; The Gaurdian. Honours: Cyril Bennet Awards, Royal Television Society, 1981, for creative services to television. Literary Agent: Curtis Brown. Address: Hobsons Farm, Dent, Cumbria, LA10 5RF, England.

BOULTON James Thompson, b. 17 Feb 1924, Pickering, Yorkshire, England. University Professor, retired. m. Margaret Helen Leary, 6 Aug 1949, 1 son, 1 daughter. Education: BA, University College, University of Durham, 1948; BLitt, Lincoln College, University of Oxford, 1952; PhD, University of Nottingham, 1960. Appointments: Lecturer, Senior Lecturer, Reader in English Literature 1951-63, Professor 1964-75, University of Nottingham; Professor of English Studies and Head of Department 1975-88, Dean of Faculty of Arts 1981-84, Public Orator 1984-88, Emeritus Professor 1989-, University of Birmingham. Publications: Edition of Edmund Burke's Sublime and Beautiful, 1958, 1967, 1987; The Language of Politics in the Age of Wilkes and Burke, 1963; Editor: The Letters of D H Lawrence, volumes 1-7, 1979-93; Samuel Johnson: The Critical Heritage, 1971; Edition: Defoe, Memoirs of a Cavalier, 1972. Address: Institute for Advanced Research in the Humanities, University of Birmingham, Egbaston, Birmingham B15 2TT, England.

BOUMELHA Penny, b. 10 May 1950, London, England. University Professor. 1 daughter. Education: BA, 1972, MA, 1981, DPhil, 1981. Appointments: Researcher, Compiler, Mansell Publishing, 1981-84; Lecturer, University of Western Australia, 1985-90; Jury Professor, University of Adelaide, 1990. Publications: Thomas Hardy & Women: Sexual Ideology & Narrative Form; Charlotte Bronte; Index of English Literary Manuscripts, vol 3. Contributions to: Women Reading Women's Writing; Grafts: Feminist Cultural Criticism; Feminist Criticism: Theory & Practice; The Sense of Sex: Feminist Perspectives on Hardy; Realism, 1992; Constructing Gender, 1994; Southern Review; TLS English; Australian Victorian Studies Association Conference Papers; Review of English Studies; English Australian Feminist Studies; London Review of Books. Address: Department of English, University of Adelaide, South Australia 5005, Australia.

BOUNDY Donna, b. 4 Dec 1949, Framingham, USA. Journalist; Author. Education: BA, University of Connecticut, 1971; MSW, Hunter College, 1981. Publications: When Money is the Drug, 1993; Willpowers Not Enough, 1989; Straight Talk About Cocaine and Crack, 1988; Video Scripts; Parents with Alcholism; Kids with Hope; Maybe I Am; Story of a Teenage Alcholic Sexual Assault Crimes; What Teens Should Know; Setting Your Own Limits; Understanding Suicide, 1986; Crackl, 1986; Sexual Abuse Prevention: A Middle School Primer, 1987; Cocaine and Crack, 1987. Contributions to: NY Times; Womens World Magazine. Literary Agent: Meredith Bernstein, NY, USA. Address: PO Box 1208, Woodstock, NY 12498, USA.

BOURJAILY Vance Nye, b. 17 Sept 1922, Cleveland, Ohio, USA. Publications: The Man Who Knew Kennedy, 1967; Brill Among the Ruins: a novel, 1970; Now Playing at Canterbury, 1976; Country Matters: Collected Reports from the Fields, 1973; The Games Men Play, 1980; The Unnatural Enemy: essays on hunting, 1984; The End of My Life, 1984; The Great Fake Book, 1986; Old Soldier: a novel, 1990; Fishing By Mail, 1993. Honours: Fellow, American Academy & Institute of Arts & Letters, 1993.

BOURKE Vernon J, b. 1907, USA. Emeritus Professor. Appointments: Associate Editor, The Modern Schoolman, 1935-; Speculum, 1948-68; American Journal of Jurisprudence, 1954-; Augustinian Studies, 1969-. Publications include: Augustines Quest of Wisdom, 1945; St Thomas and the Greek Moralists, 1947; Ethics, 1951; St Augustines Confessions, Translation, 1963; St Augustines City of God, 1958; The Pocket Aquinas, 1960; Will in Western Thought, 1964; Augustines View of Reality, 1964; Aquinas Search for Wisdom, 1965; History of Ethics, 1968, translation (French) Histoire de la morale, 1970, (Italian) Storia dell'Etica, 1972, (Polish) Historia Etyki, 1994; Joy in Augustines Love of Wisdom, 1992. Address: 638 Laven Del Lane, St Louis, MO 53122, USA.

BOURNE (Rowland) Richard, Journalist; Author; Director; Commonwealth Human Rights Institute. m. Juliet Mary Attenborough, 1966, 2 sons, 1 daughter. Education: BA, Brasenose College, Oxford. Appointments: Journalist, The Guardian, 1962-72; Assistant Editor, New Society, 1972-77; Evening Standard, Deputy Editor, 1977-78; London Columnist, 1978-79; Founder Editor, Leam Magazine, 1979; Consultant, International Broadcasting Trust, 1980-81; Advisom Council for Adult and Continuing Education, 1982; Deputy Director, Commonwealth Institute, 1983-89; Director, Commonwealth Human Rights Institute, 1990-92; Visiting Fellow, London Institute of Education. Publications: Political Leaders of Latin Americam, 1969; The Struggle for Education, (with Brian MacArthur), 1970; Getulio Vargas of Brazil, 1974; Assault on the Amazon, 1978; Londoners, 1981; Self-Sufficiency, 16-25 (with Jessica Gould), 1983; Lords of Fleet Street, 1990. Literary Agent: Murray Pollinger. Address: 36 Burney Street, London SE10 8EX, England.

BOURNE-JONES Derek, b. 4 Sept 1928, St Leonards-on-Sea, Sussex, England. Director of Studies, B J Tutorials; Writer and Poet. m. Hilary Clare Marsh, 2 Aug 1975. Education: St Edmund Hall, Oxford, 1951-54; BA (Hons) Modern Languages 1954, MA (Oxon) 1958. Appointments: Editor, Downlander Publishing, 1978-. Publications: Senlac, Epic Poem on the Battle of Hastings, 1978; Floating Reefs, Poetry Collection, 1981; The Singing Days, Poetry Collection, 1986; Merrily to Meet (on Sir Thomas More), 1988; Behold The Man, Poetic Sequence, illustrated, on the Stations of the Cross, 1990; Brief Candle, a poetic study of The Lady Jane Grey, illustrated, 1991. Contributions to: Various journals over the years. Memberships: Founder, The Downland Poets Society of Sussex, 1975-90; Fellow, Royal Society of Arts; The Oxford Society. Address: 88 Oxendean Gardens, Lower Willingdon, Eastbourne, East Sussex BN22 0RS, England.

BOUVERIE William. See: **CARPENTER Humphrey.**

BOVA Ben(jamin William), b. 1932, Philadelpia, USA. Writer - Science Fiction, Sciences (general), Social Commentary, Phenomena; Author; Lecturer; Newspaper Reporter. Education: Currently Studying for his PhD, BA in Journalism from Temple University, Philadelphia, 1954, MA, State University of New York at Albany, 1987. Appointments: Former Technical Editor, Project Vanguard, Martin Co, Baltimore, Maryland and with Physics Department, Massachusetts Institute of Technology, Cambridge; Marketing Manager, Avco Everett Research Laboratory, Massachusetts, 1960-71; Editorial Director, Omni Magazine; Editor of Analog Magazine. Publications: (ed) The Analog Science Fact Reader, 1974; (with B Berson) Survival Guide for the Suddenly Single, 1974; The Weather Changes Man, 1974; Workshops in Space, 1974; (with G R Dickson) Gremlins, Go Home!, 1974; End of Exile, 1975; Notes to a Science Fiction Writer, 1975; Through Eyes of Wonder, 1975; Science - Who Needs It? 1975; The Starcrossed, 1975; Millenuium 1976; (ed) Analog Annual, 1976; Multiple Man, 1976; City of Darkness, 1976; The Seeds of Tomorrow, 1977; (with Trudy E Bell) Closeup: New Worlds, 1977; Viewpoint, 1977; Colony, 1978; (ed) Analog Yearbook, 1978; Maxwell's Demons, 1978; Kinsman, 1979; The Weathermakers, 1979; The Exiles Trilogy, 1980; (ed) Best of Omni Science Fiction, 1980-82; Voyagers, 1981; The High Road, 1981; Test of Fire, 1982; Vision of Tomorrow, 1982; Escape Plus Ten, 1984; Assured Survival: How to Stop the Nuclear Arms Race, 1984; The Astral Mirror, 1985; Privateers, 1985; Prometheus, 1986; Voyager Two: The Alien Within, 1986; Best of the Nebulas, (Anthology), 1989; As on a Darkling Plain, 1991; Empire Builders, 1993; Orion and the Conqueror,1994; To Save the Sun, 1993; Death Dream, 1994. Contributions to: Journalism, aerospace and magazine editing, articles, short fiction, opinion pieces and reviews. Various works have appeared in major science fiction magazines, science journals, peridicals: Psychology Today; Modern Bride; The New York Times; Penthouse. Honours: Distinguished Alumnus, 1981, Temple University; Alumni Fellow, 1982. Memberships: President Emeritus of the National Space Society, Fellow of the British Interplanetary Society, Member of Planetary Society American Association for the Advancement of Science, The Nature Conservancy, New York Academy of Sciences, National Space Club, Charter memebr of the Science Fiction Writers of America; Editorial Boards of the World Future Society; PEN Ineternational. Literary Agent: Barbara Bova.

BOVEY John Alden, b. 17 Apr 1913, MN, USA. Retired Diplomat. m. Marcia Peterson, 31 July 1943, 1 d. Education: BA, 1935, MA, 1938, Harvard University. Appointments: Teaching Fellow, Instructor, Harvard, 1938-42; Instructor, US Naval Academy, 1943-45. Publications: Desirable Aliens: The Silent Meteor. Contributions: 35 Short Stories; 27 Articles; VA Quarterly; The Literary Review; Ploughshares; New England Review; Cornhill Magazine; NY Times; London Magazine. Honours: Emily Green Balch Fiction Award; KS Arts Commission Award; Angoff Award; David Bruce Contest, 2nd Prize. Address: 19 Chauncy Street, Cambridge, MA 02138, USA.

BOWDEN Jim. See: **SPENCE William John Duncan.**

BOWDEN Roland Heywood, b. 19 Dec 1916, Lincoln, England. Techer. m. 2 Jan 1946, 1 son, 1 daughter. Education: School of Architecture, Liverpool University, 1934-39. Publications: Peorns From Italy, 1970; Every Season is Another, 1986; Death of Paolini, paly produced Edinburgh, 1980; After Neruda, play produced Hammersmith Riverside, 1984; The Fence, play produced Brighton, Gardner Centre, 1985. Contributions to: Arts Review: London Magazine; Panurge; Words International. Honours: Arts Council Drama Bursary, 1978; Cheltenham Festival Poetry Prize, 1982; 1st Prize All-Sussex Poets, 1983. Membership: National Poetry Secretariat. Address: 2 Roughmere Cottage, lavant, Chichester, West Sussex, PO18 0BG, England.

BOWEN John Griffith, b. 5 Nov 1924, Calcutta, India. Writer; TV Producer. Education: MA, Oxford University. Publications: The Truth Will Not Help Us; After the Rain; The Centre of the Green; Storyboard; The Birdcage; A World Elsewhere; Squeak; The McGuffin; The Girls; Fighting Back; The Precious Gift; No Retreat Plays: I Love You Mrs Patterson; After The Rain; Little Boxes; The Disorderly Women; The Corsican Brothers; Hail Caesar; The Waiting Room; Singles; The Inconstant Couple; Which Way Are You Facing? The Geordie Gentlemen; The Oak Tree Tea-Room Siege; Uncle Jeremy.

Contributions to: London Magazine; Times Literary Supplement; Gambit; Journal of Royal Asiatic Society; Times Educational Supplement; Listener. Honour: Tokyo Prize, 1974. Memberships: Executive Committee, PEN; Committee of Management Society of Authors; Executive Committee, Writers Guild of Great Britain; Board of Management ALCS. Literary Agent: Elaine Greene Ltd. Address: Old Lodge Farm, Sugarswell Lane, Edgehill, Banbury, Oxon OX15 6HP, England.

BOWEN Lynne, b. Saskatchewan, 1940. m. 3 children. Education: Public Health Nursing Degree, University of Alberta; MA, Canadian History, University of Victoria. Publications: Boss Whistle: The Coal Miners of Vancouver Island Remember, 1982; Three Dollar Dreams, 1987; The Dunsmuirs of Nanaimo, 1989; Muddling Through: The Remarkable Story of the Barr Colonists, 1992. Honours: Eatons British Columbia Book Award, 1983; Canadian Historical Association Regional Certificate of Merit, 1984 and 1993; Lieutenant Governors Medal, 1987; Hubert Evans Non-Fiction Prize, 1993. Address: 4982 Fillinger Cr, Nanaimo, British Columbia, V9V 1J1, Canada.

BOWERING George. b. 1 Dec 1936, BC, Canada. Writer. m. Algela Luoma, 14 Dec 1963, 1 daughter. Education: BA, 1960, MA, 1963, Universty of British Columbia. Publications include: Burning Water, 1980; Caprice, 1987; Mirror on the Floor, 1967; A Short Sad Book, 1977; Flycatcher, 1974; A Place to Die, 1983; Harry's Fragments, 1990; Urban S Chow,1992; Likely Stories, 1992; Shoot, 1994. Contributions: to several journals and magazines. Honours: Governor-General's Award, 1969, 1980. Membership: Association of Canadian Television and Radio Artists. Literary Agent: Dinise Bukowski, Toronto. Address: 2499 West 37th Aveune, Vancouver, BC, Canada, V6M 1P4.

BOWERING Marilyn, b. 13 Apr 1949, Winnipeg, Canada. Writer. m. Michael S Elcock, 3 Sept 1982, 1 daughter. Education: BA, First Class, 1971, MA, First Class, 1973, University of Victoria; University of New Brunswick, 1975-78. Literary Appointments: Editor, Noel Collins and Blackwells, Edinburgh, Scotland, 1980-82; Editor and Writer, Gregson/Graham; Full-time Writer, Killin, Scotland, 1977-78; Writer-in-Residence, Aegean School of Fine Arts, Paros, Greece, 1973-74; Script Assistant, film, 1972. Publications: Books: Winter Harbour, forthcoming; To All Appearances A Lady, novel, 1989; Calling All the World, 1989. Poetry: Anyone Can See I Love You, 1987; Grandfather Was a Soldier, 1987; The Sunday Before Winter,1984; Giving Back Diamonds, 1982; Sleeping With Lambs,1980; The Killing Room, 1977; One Who Became Lost, 1976; The Liberation of Newfoundland, 1973; Many Voices (co-edited with D Day), 1977; The Visitors Have All Returned, fiction, 1979. Represented in Anthologies; Readings and/or Workshops; Drama; Radio. Contributons to: The Canadian Forum; Exile; Prospice; Poetry Canada Review; The Moorlands Review; Trends; Toronto Life; Radio 3 Magazine; Canadian Literature; The Malahat Review; Landfall. Honours inlcude: Canada Council Project Award, 1972, 1986; Canada Council Short Term Award, 1977, 1980; Canada Council Arts Award, 1973, 1981, 1984; Ontario Arts Council Award, 1980, 1986; Canada Council Arts Award, 1988; National Magazine Award for Poetry, Silver, 1988. Memberships include: Writers' Union of Canada; Leauge of Canadian Poets; BC Federation of Writers; PEN; CAPAC. Literary Agent: Denise Bukowski, Toronto, Ontario, Canada. Address: c/o 3777 Jennifer Road, Victoria, BC, Canada, V8P 3X1.

BOWKER John Westerdale, b. 1935, United Kingdom. Academic Appointments: Fellow, Corpus Christi College, Cambridge, 1962-74; Lecturer, University of Cambridge, 1965-74; Professor of Religious Studies, University of Lancaster, 1974-85; Fellow, Dean, Trinity College, Cambridge, 1984-93; Gresham Professor, Gresham College, London, 1992-; Honorary Canon, Canterbury Cathedral, 1985-. Publications: The Targums and Rabbinic Literature, 1969; Problems of Suffering in Religions of the World, 1970; Jesus and the Pharisees, 1973; The Sense of God: Sociological, Anthropological and Psychological Approaches to the Origin of the Sense of God, 1973; Uncle Bolpenny Tries Things Out, 1973; The Religious Imagination and the Sense of God, 1978; Worlds of Faith, 1983; Violence and Aggression (editor), 1984; The Meaning of Death, 1991; A Year to Live, 1991; Hallowed Ground, 1993. Honour: Harper Collins Biennial Prize, 1993. Address: 14 Bowers Croft, Cambridge CB1 4RP, England.

BOWLER Peter John, b. 8 Oct 1944, Leicester, England. University Professor. m. Sheila Mary Holt, 24 Sept 1966, 1 son, 1 daughter. Education: Cambridge, BA, 1966; University of Sussex, MSc,

1967; University of Toronto, PhD, 1971. Publications: The Eclipse of Darwinism; Evolution: The History of An Idea; Theories of Human Evolution; The Non Darwinian Revolution; Fossils & progress; The Mendelian Revolution; The Invention of Progress; Charles Darwin: The Man & His Influence; The Fontana History of the Environmental Sciences. Contributions to: Reviews in TLS; THES. Memberships: British Society for the History of Science; History of Science Society. Address: Department of Social Anthropology, Queens University, Belfast BT7 1NN, Northern Ireland.

BOWLING Harry, b. 30 Sept 1931, Bermondsey, London, England. m. Shirley Burgess, 27 July 1957, 1 son, 2 daughters. Publications: Conner Street's War, 1988; Tuppence to Tooley Street, 1989; Ironmonger's Daughter, 1989; Paragon Place, 1990; Gaslight in Page Street, 1991; The Girl From Cotton Lane, 1992; Backstreet Girl, 1993. Literary Agent: Jennifer Kavanagh. Address: Headline Book Publishing plc, Headline House, 79 Great Tichfield St, Lodnon, W1P 7FN, England.

BOWLT John Ellis, b. 6 Dec 1943, London, England. Professor. m. Nicolette Misler, 25 Dec 1981. Education: BA, 1965, MA, 1966, PhD, 1971, University of Birmingham. Appointments: Professor, University of TX, Austin, 1971-88; Visiting Professor, Wellesley College, 1980; Visiting Professor, University of Otago, 1982; Visiting Professor, Hebrew University, 1985; Professor, USC, 1988-. Publications: Russian Avant Garde; Silver Age; Pavel Filonov; On Condition of Soviet Art Criticism; Goncharova and Futurist Theatre; The Thyssen Bornemisza Collection, 1993. Honours: British Cncl Award to Moscow; National Humanities Institute; American Co of Learned Societies to Paris; International Reearch & Exchange Board to Moscow. Memberships: Am Association for Advancement of Slavic Studies. Address: Slavic Dept, University of SO California, Los Angeles, CA 90089, USA.

BOX Edgar. See: VIDAL Gore.

BOYD Brian David, b. 30 July 1952, Belfast, Northern Ireland. University Teacher. m. 1) Janet Bower Eden, 1974, divorced 1980, 2) Bronwen Mary Nicholson, 1983, 3 stepdaughters. Education: BA 1972, MA Hons 1974, University of Canterbury, Christchurch, New Zealand; PhD, University of Toronto, Canada, 1979; Postdoctoral Fellow, University of Auckland, 1979. Appointments: Lecturer 1980, Senior Lecturer 1985, Associate Professor 1992-, University of Auckland, New Zealand; Editorial Board, Nabokov Studies; Visiting Professor, University of Nice-Sophia Antipolis, 1994-95. Publications: Nabokov's Ada: The Place of Consciousness, 1985; Vladimir Nabokov: The Russian Years, 1990; Vladimir Nabokov: The American Years, 1991. Address: Department of English, University of Auckland, Private Bag 92019, Auckland, New Zealand.

BOYD Malcolm, b. 24 May 1932, Newcastle Upon Tyne, England. Retired University Lecturer. m. Beryl Gowen, 3 Apr 1956, 2 sons. Education: Dame Allan's School, Newcastle, 1943-50; BA, Durham University, 1953; MA, 1962. Publications: Bach; Domenico Scarlatti, Master of Music; Palestrina's Style; Harmonizing Bach's Chorales; Bach's Instrumental Counterpoint; Bach: The Brandenburg Concertos; Grace Williams. Contributions to: Musical Times; Music & Letters; Music Review; Early Music. Honours: Yorkshire Post Literary Award for Music. Membership: Royal Musical Association. Address: 211 Fidlas Road, Llanishen, Cardiff, CF4 5NA, Wales.

BOYD William, b. 7 Mar 1952, Ghana. Full-time Writer. Education: Jesus College, Oxford, 1975-80. Appointments: Lecturer in English Literature, St Hilda's College, Oxford, 1980-83; Television Critic, New Statesman, London, 1982-83. Publications: A Good Man in Africa, novel, 1981; On the Yankee Station, short stories, 1981; An Ice-Cream War, novel, 1982; Stars and Bars, novel, 1984; School Ties, screenplay, 1985; The New Confessions, novel, 1987; Brazzaville Beach, 1990; Television Plays Good and Bad at Games, 1985; Dutch Girls, 1985; Scoop, 1987. Honours: Whitbread Prize, 1981; Somerset Maugham Award, 1982; James Tait Black Memorial Prize, 1990; McVitie's Prize, 1991. Address: c/o Harvey Unna and Stephen Durbridge Ltd, 24 Pottery Lane, London W11 4LZ, England.

BOYLE T Coraghessan, b. 2 Dec 1948, Peekshill, New York, USA. Fiction Writer. m. Karen Kvashay, 25 May 1974, 2 s, 1 d. Education: MFA, 1974, PhD, 1977, University of Iowa. Publications: Descent of Man, 1979; Water Music, 1982; Budding Prospects, 1984; Greasy Lake, 1985; World's End, 1987; If the River Was Whiskey,

1989; East Is East, 1990; The Road to Wellville, 1993; Without a Hero,1994. Honours: Faulkner Award, PEN, 1988. Literary Agent: Georges Borchardt, New York, USA. Address: c/o Georges Borchardt, 136 E 57t St, New York, NY 10022, USA.

BOYNTON Sandra, b. 3 Apr 1953, Orange, New Jersey, USA. Company Vice-President; Designer of Greetings Cards; Writer. m. James Patrick McEwan, 18 Oct 1978, 1 d. Education: BA, Yale University, 1974; Graduate study, University of California, Berkely, 1974-75 and Yale University, 1976-77. Appointments: Author and illustrator of children's books; Recycled Paper Products Inc, Chicago, Illinois, Designer of greetings cards, 1974-. Vice-President, 1980-. Publications include: Self-illustrated children's books include: But Not the Hippoppotamus, edited by Klimo, 1982; The Going to Bed Book, edited by Klimo, 1982; Opposites, edited by Klimo, 1982; Sounds, edited by Klimo, 1982; A Is Angry: An Adjective and Animal Alphabet, 1983; Moo Baa La La La, edited by Klimo, 1983; Hey! What's That?, 1985; Chloe and Maude, 1985; Good Night, Good Night, 1985; Christmastime, 1987. Books of Cartoons: Gopher Baroque and Other Beastly Conceits, 1979; The Compleat Turkey, 1980; revised edition published as Don't Let the Turkeys get you Down, 1986; Chocolate: The Consuming Passion, 1982. Other publications. Contributor to: Magazines including Redbook. Honours: Irma Simonton Black Award, 1986, for Cloe and Maude. Membership: Cartoonists Guild.

BOZEMAN Adda Bruemmer, b. 17 Dec 1908, Latvia. Author; Teacher; Consultant. m. (1) Virgil Bozeman, 28 Mar 1937, div, 1 d. (2) Arne Barkhuus, 8 Feb 1951. Education: Ecole Libre des Sciences Politiques, 1934; Middle Temple, 1936; JD, Southern Methodist University, TX, 1937; Hoover Institution, CA, 1938-40. Publications include: Regional Conflicts Around Geneva, 1948; The Future of Law in a Multicultural World, 1971; How to Think About Human Rights, 1978; Numerous Monographs; Politics and Culture in International History, 1994. Contributions to: Expansion of International Society; Hydra of Carnage; Future of International Law; Essays, Reviews to Various Journals. Honours include: Research Grants; Award of Distinction. Memberships include: Am Political Science Association; International Studies Association; Armed Forces Society; Consortium for Study of Civilization. Address: 24 Beale Circle, Bronxville, NY 10708, USA.

BRACEGIRDLE Brian, b. 1933, United Kingdom. Museum Curator. Appointments: Research Consultant in Microscopy, Science Museum. Publications: An Atlas of Embryology (with W H Freeman), 1963; An Atlas of Histology (with W H Freeman), 1966; Photography for Books and Reports, 1970; An Atlas of Invertebrate Structure (with W H Freeman), 1971; An Atlas of Plant Structure (with P H Miles), vol 1, 1971, vol II, 1973; The Archaeology of the Industrial Revolution, 1973; Thomas Telford (with P H Miles), 1973; The Darbys and the Ironbridge Gorge (with P H Miles), 1974; An Advanced Atlas of Histology (with W H Freeman), 1976; An Atlas of Chordate Structure (with P H Miles), 1977; The Evolution of Microtechnique, 1978; Beads of Glass: Leeuwenhoek and the Early Microscope (editor), 1983; The Microscopic Photographs of J S Dancer (with J B McCormick, 1993. Address: Cold Aston Lodge, Cold Aston, Cheltenham, Glos GL54 3BN, England.

BRACKENBURY Alison, b. 20 May 1953, Gainsborough, Lincolnshire, England. Poet. Education: BA English, St Hugh's College, Oxford, 1975. Publications: Journey to a Cornish Wedding, 1977; Two Poems, 1979; Dreams of Power and Other Poems, 1981; Breaking Ground and Other Poems, 1984; Christmas Roses and Other Poems, 1988; Radio play: The Country of Afternoon, 1985. Honours: Eric Gregory Award, 1982. Address: Carcanet Press, 208-212 Corn Exchange Buildings, Manchester M4 3BQ, England.

BRADBROOK Muriel Clara, b. 1909, Unied Kingdom Professor Emeritus; Author. Appointments: Fellow, 1932-35, 1936-, Mistress, 1968-76, Girton College, Cambridge; Lecturer in English, 1945-62, Reader, 1962-65, Professor of English Literature, 1965-76, Professor Emeritus, 1976-, Cambridge University. Publications: Elizabethan Stage Conditions, 1932; Themes and Conventions of Elizabethan Tragedy, 1934; The School of Night, 1936; Andrew Marvell (with M G Lloyd Thomas), 1940; Joseph Conrad, 1941; Ibsen the Norwegian, 1946; T S Eliot, 1950; Shakespeare and Elizabethan Poetry, 1951; The Queen's Garland (complier), 1953; The Growth and Structure of Elizabethan Comedy, 1955; Sir Thomas Malory, 1957; The Rise of the Common Player, 1962; English Deamatic Form, 1965; That Infidel Place: History of Girton College,1969; Shakespeare the Craftsman,

1969; Literature in Action, 1972; T S Eliot: The Making of the Waste Land, 1972; Malcolm Lowry: His Art and Early Life, 1974; Shakespeare, 1978; George Chapman, 1978; John Webster, 1980; Collected Papers, 3 vols, 1982-83; Muriel Bradbrook on Shakespeare, 1984; Collected Papers, vol 1-4, 1982-89. Honours: Litt.D Cantab, 1955; FBA, 1990. Address: 91 Chesterton Road, Cambridge, CB4 3AP, England.

BRADBURY Edward P. See: **MOORCOCK Michael (John).**

BRADBURY Malcolm Stanley, b. 7 Sept 1932, Sheffield, England. Author; Writer; Professor of American Studies. Education: Queen Mary College, University of London, 1953-55; Indiana University, 1955-56. Publications include: Eating People is Wrong, 1959; All Dressed Up and Nowhere To Go, 1962; Evelyn Waugh, 1964; Two Poets (with A Rodway), 1966; The Social Context of Modern English Literature, 1971; The History Man, 1975; The Novel Today, 1977; The After Dinner Game: Stories and Parodies, 1982; Rates of Exchange, 1983; Cuts: A Novella, 1987; Doctor Criminale, 1992; The Modern British Novel, 1993; Dangerous Pilgrimages: Transatlantic Mythologies and the Novel, 1995. Honour: CBE, 1991. Address: University of East Anglia, Norwich, NR4 7TJ, England.

BRADBURY Ray (Douglas), b. 1920, USA. Writer - Novels, Short Stories, Science Fiction, Fantasy, Children's Fiction, Plays, Screenplays, Poetry. Publications include: Tomorrow Midnight, 1966; The Pedestrian (play), 1966; S is for Space, 1966; The Picasso Summer (screenplay), 1968; I sing the Body Electic, 1969; Christus Apollo (play), 1969; Old Ahab's Friend, and Friend to Nosh Speaks His Piece: A Celebration, 1971; The Halloween Tree, 1972; The Wonderful Ice Cream Suit and Other Plays: For Today, Tomorrow and Beyond Tomorrow, 1972; When Elephants Last in the Dooryard Bloomed (poetry), 1972; The Small Assassin, 1973; Zen and the Art of Writing, 1973; Mars and the Mind of Man, 1973; The Son of Richard III, 1974; Long after Midnight (stories), 1976; Pillar of Fire and Other Plays, 1976; Where Robot Mice and Robot Men Run Round in Robot Towns: New Poems Both Light and Dark, 1977; Beyond 1984, 1979; The Stories of Ray Bradbury, 1980; The Ghosts of Forever, 1981; The Haunted Computer and the Android Pope, 1981; The Last Circus, 1981; The Complete Poems of Ray Bradbury, 1982; The Love Affair, 1983; Dinosuar Tales, 1983; A Memory for Murder, 1984; Forever and the Earth, 1984; Death is a Lonely Business, 1985; The Toynbee Convector, 1989; A Graveyeard for Lunatics, 1990; Fahrenheit 451, 1987; The Illustratd Man, 1969. Memberships: President, Science-Fantasy Writers of America, 1951-53; Board of Directors, Screen Workers Guild of America, 1957-61. Address: 10265 Cheviot Drive, Los Angele, CA 90064, USA.

BRADDIN George. See: **MILKOMANE George Alexis Milkomanovich.**

BRADDON Russell Reading, b. 25 Jan 1921, Sydney, Australia. Author; Broadcaster; Scriptwriter. Education: BA, Sydney University, 1940. Publications: The Naked Island, 1952; Cheshire VC, 1954; Joan Sutherland, 1962; The Inseparables, 1968; The Seige, 1968; The Progress of Private Lilyworth, 1971; The Predator, 1977; All the Queen's Men, 1977; End Play, 1977; The Finalists, 1977; The Other Hundred Years War, 1982; Funnelweb, 1990. Contributor to: Many Journals and magazines worldwide; TV documentaries 1980-88, Great River Journeys of the World (BBC); Images of Australia (ABC Australia). Honour: Premier's Literary Award, NSW Scriptwriting, 1985. Literary Agent: Vivienne Schuster, John Farquharson Ltd. Address: c/o John Farquharson Ltd, 162-168 Regent Street, London W1A 5TB, England.

BRADFORD Barbara Taylor, b. 10 May 1933, Leeds, Yorkshire, England. m. Robert Bradford, 1963. Appointments: Editor, Columnist, Periodicals in UK & US. Publications: Complete Encyclopedia of Homemaking Ideas, 1968; How To Be The Perfect Wife, 1969-70; Early Steps to Successful Decorating, 1971; Making Space Grow, 1979; Women of Substance, 1979; Voices of the Heart, 1983; Hold the Dream, 1985; Act of Will, 1986; To Be the Best, 1988; The Women in His Life, 1990; Everything to Gain, 1994; Remember; Angel. Address: c/o Doubleday Publishing, 1540 Broadway, New York, NY 10036, USA.

BRADFORD Karleen, b. 16 Dec 1936, Toronto, Canada. Writer. m. James Creighton Bradford, 22 Aug 1959, 2 s, 1 d. Education: BA, University of Toronto, 1959. Publications: A Year for Growing, 1977; Wrong Again, Robbie, 1983; The Other Elizabeth, 1982; I Wish There Were Unicorns, 1983; The Stone in the Meadow, 1984; The Haunting at Cliff House, 1985; The Nine Days Queen, 1986; Write Now!, 1988; Windward Island, 1989; There Will be Wolves, 1992; Animal Heroes, 1995; Thirteenth Child, 1994. Address: 3005 Linton Road, Ottawa, Ontario, Canada KIV 8H1.

BRADFORD S W. See: **BATTIN B W.**

BRADLEY George, b. 1953. Publications: Terms to be Met, 1986; Of the Knowledge of Good & Evil, 1991. Honour: Lavan Younger Poets Award, 1990.

BRADLEY John Lewis, b. 5 Aug 1917, London, England. University Professor (retired). m. Elizabeth Hilton Pettingell, 4 Nov 1943, 1 d. Education: BA, Yale University, 1940; PhD, Yale University, 1950; MA, Harvard University, 1946. Publications: An Introduction to Ruskin, 1971; Ruskin's Letters from Venice 1851-52, 1955; Ruskin's Letters to Lord and Lady Mount Temple, 1964; Selections From Mayhew's London Labour & The London Poor, 1965; Ruskin's Unto This Last and Traffic, 1967; Ruskin: The Critical Heritage, 1984; Correspondence of John Ruskin and Charles Eliot Norton (with Ian Ousby), 1987; The Cambridge Guide to Literature in English (ed. Ian Ousby), 1988; Editor: A Shelley Chronology, 1993. Contributions to: TLS; THES; Victorian Studies; Essays in Criticism; Studies in English Literature; Journal of English & Germanic Philology; Notes & Queries; Modern Language Review. Honours: Fellow and grantee, American Philosophical Society; Guggenheim Fellow, 1961-62. Address: Church Cottage, Hinton St George, Somerset TA17 8SA, England.

BRADWAY Becky, b. 21 Nov 1957, Phoenix, USA. Writer; Editor. m. Jan 1985, 1d. Education: MA, Sangaman State University; Columbia University, 1985. Appointments: Writer, Editor, Illinois Coalation Against Sexual Assault, 1986-. Publications: Eating Our Hearts Out; American Fiction Number One; American Fiction. Contributions to: Green Mountains Review; Beloit Fiction Journal; South Carolina Review; Sojourner; Other Voices; Ascent; Crescent Review; Greensboro Review; Soundings East; Four Quarters. Honours: 1st Prize, Willow Review; Artist Advancement Awards, American Fiction Competition. Memberships: Illinois Writers Inc; Poets and Writers Inc. Address: 924 Bryn Mawr Boulevard, Springfield, IL 62703, USA.

BRADWELL James. See: **KENT Arthur (William Charles).**

BRADY Anne M (Cannon), b. 23 May 1926, Dublin, Ireland. Writer. m. 2 Feb 1957, 2 s, 2 d. Education: BA, English Literature and Language, University College Dublin; Diploma in Hospital Administration, College of Commerce. Appointments: University Library Assistant, Dublin and Ottawa; Farm Secretary, Co Meath. Publications: The Winds of God, 1985; Honey Off Thorns, 1988; The Biographical Dictionary of Irish writers (with Brian Cleeve), 1985. Contributor to: short stories in women's magazines prior to 1985. Memberships: University College Dublin Graduates Association; Royal Dublin Society. Literary Agent: Eleanor Corey. Address: Rosbeg, 12 Ard Mhuire Park, Dalkey, Co Dublin, Ireland.

BRADY James Winston, b. 15 Nov 1928, NY, USA. Writer; Broadcaster. m. Florence Kelly, 12 Apr 1958, 2 d. Education: AB, Manhattan College, 1950; NY University. Publications: Novels, Paris One, 1977; Nielsen's Children, 1979; Press Lord, 1981; Holy Wars, 1983; Designs, 1986; Non Fiction, The Coldest War, 1990; Fashion Show, 1992; Various UK & Foreign Editions; Books. Contributions to: Parade; Esquire; NY; Advertising Age; TV Guide; People; Harper's Bazaar. Honour: Emmy Award, 1973-74. Literary Agent: Jack Scovil, Chichak, Galen Literary Agency Inc, NY, USA. Address: PO Box 1584, East Hampton, NY 11937, USA.

BRADY Joan, b. 4 Dec 1939, San Francisco, California, USA. Writer. m. Dexter Wright Masters, 23 Sept 1963, dec'd 1989, 1 son. Education: BS, Columbia University, 1965. Publications: The Imposter, 1979; Theory of War, UK and US editions 1993, Germany, Denmark, Sweden, France, Netherlands editions 1994, Norway, Spain and Korea editions 1995; Prologue (published in the US under the title of The Unmaking of a Dancer 1982), 1994. Contributions to: Harpers; MS. Honours: Phi Beta Kappa, 1965; National Endowment for the Arts Grant, 1986; Whitbread Novel, 1993; Whitbread Book of the Year, 1993. Membership: Authors Guild. Literary Agents: Toby Eady, 18 Park Walk, London SW10, England; David Black, Black Inc, 156 5th Avenue, New York, NY 10010, USA.

BRADY John Mary, b. 10 July 1955, Dublin, Ireland. Teacher. m. Johanna Wagner, 1 Aug 1981, 1 s, 1 d. Education: BA, Trinity College, 1980; BEd, University of Toronto, 1981; MEd, 1985. Publications: Kaddish in Dublin; Unholy Ground; A Stone of the Heart; All Souls, 1993. Honours: Arthur Ellis Award; Best First Novel. Literary Agent: Curtis Brown, 10 Astor Place, NY 100003, USA. Address: c/o MGA Agency, 10 St Mary Street, Suite 510, Toronto, Ontario, Canada.

BRADY Nicholas. See: **LEVINSON Leonard.**

BRADY Patricia, b. 20 Jan 1943, Danville, Illinois, USA. Historian. 1 s, 1 d. Education: BA cum laude, with honours, Newcomb College, 1965; MA, History, 1966; PhD, History, 1977, Tulane University. Appointments: Member, Programme Committee, Tennessee Williams-New Orleans Literary Festival, 1991-. Publications: Nelly Custis Lewis's Housekeeping Book, 1982; Introduction, The WPA Guide to New Orleans, 1983; Encyclopaedia of New Orleans Artists, 1718-1918, 1987; George Washington's Beautiful Nelly, 1991; Mollie Moore Davis: A Literary Life, 1992; The Cities of the Dead: Free Men of Color as Tomb Builders, 1993. Contributions to: Black Artists in Antebellum New Orleans, to Loyuisiana History, 1991; Lafcadio Hearn, to Tulanian, 1991; A Woman's Consequence: George Washington's Beautiful Nelly, to Virginia Cavcalcade, 1992. Honours: Scholar, 1961-65, Fellow, 1965-68, Tulane University, Phi Beta Kappa, 1965, Honorary Woodrow Wilson Fellow, 1965; National Defense Foreign Language Fellow, 1965-68; Fulbright-Hays Fellow, 1974. Memberships: Board of Directors, Programme Committee Chair, Tennessee Williams-New Orleans Literary Festival; Board of Directors, Friends of New Orleans Public Library; Board of Directors, Vice-President, New Orleans, Gulf South Booksellers Association, Association for Documentary Editing; Southern Historical Association. Literary Agent: Susan P Urstadt. Address: 1205 Valence St, New Orleans, LA 70115, USA.

BRADY Terence Joseph, b. 13 Mar 1939. Playwright; Novelist; Actor; Columnist. m. Charlotte Mary Therese Bingham, 1s, 1d. Publications: For radio: Lines From My Grandfather's Forehead, 1972; For TV: Broad and Narrow; TWTWTW; With Charlotte Bingham; Boy Meets Girl; Take Three Girls; Upstairs Downstairs; Away From It All; Play For Today; Plays of Marriage; No-Honestly; Yes-Honestly; Thomas and Sarah; Pig In The Middle; The Complete Lack of Charm of the Bourgeoisie; Nanny; Oh Madeline; Father Matthew's Daughter; A View of Meadows Green; Love With a Perfect Stranger; This Magic Moment; for the stage: The Sloane Ranger Revue (contributor), 1985; I Wish I Wish; Novel: Rehearsal, 1972; The Fight Against Slavery, 1976; with Charlotte Bingham: Victoria, 1972; Rose's Story, 1973; Victoria and Company, 1974; Yes-Honestly, 1977; with Michael Felton: Point To Point, 1990; Riders (TV film); Polo (TV film); Oh Madeline! (US TV). Contributions to: Daily Mail; Living; Country Homes and Interiors; Punch; Sunday Express; The Field; Mail on Sunday. Address: c/o Peters Fraser & Dunlop, 5th Floor, The Chambers, Chelsea Harbour, Lots Road, London, SW10 OXF, England

BRAESTRUP Peter, b. 8 June 1929, New York City, USA. Editor. m. Angelica Hollins, divorced. 1 s, 2 d. Education: BA, Yale Unviersity, 1951; Nieman Fellow, Harvard University, 1960. Appointments: Contributing Editor, 1953-55; Correspondent, 1955-57, Time Magazine; Reporter, New York Herald Tribune, 1957-59; Correspondent, New York Times, Algeria, 1962-65; Paris, 1965; Bangkok, Saigon, 1966-68; Saigon Bureau Chief, 1968-69; National Staff Writer, 1969-73, Washington Post; Founding Editor, Wilson Quarterly, 1975-. Publications: Big Story, 1977; Battle Lines, (co-author), 1985; Vietnam as History, 1984, (ed), Contributions to: Marine Coprs Gazette; Atlantic; New Leader; various journals, magazines and newspapers; Honours: Woodrow Wilson International Centre for Scholars Fellow, 1973-75; Sigma Delta Chi Award, for Big Story, 1978. Memberships: Yale Alumni Publications Board, 1977-; Visions Foundation, Board; Yale University Council, 1984-. Address: 600 Maryland Ave, SW, Suite 430, Washington DC 20024, USA.

BRAGG Melvyn, b. 6 Oct 1939, Carlisle, Cumberland, England. Writer; Presenter; Editor. m. (1) Marie-Elizabeth Roche, 1961, deceased, 1 d, (2) Catherine Mary Haste, 1973, 1 s, 1 d. Education: MA, Wadham College, Oxford University. Appointments: Presenter, Editor, The South Bank Show, ITV, 1978-; Head of Arts, LWT, 1982-; Deputy Chairman, Border TV, 1985-; Publications: Plays: Mardi Gras, 1976; Orion, 1977; The Hired Man, 1984. Screenplays: Isadora; Jesus Christ Superstar; Clouds of Glory (with Ken Russell); Speak For England, 1976; Land of The Lakes, 1983; Laurence Olivier, 1984;

Novels; For Want of a Nail, 1965; The Second Inheritance, 1966; Without a City Wall, 1968; The Hired Man, 1969; A Place in England, 1970; The Nerve, 1971; Josh Lawton, Autumn Manoevres, 1978; Kingdom Come, 1980; Love and Glory, 1983; The Life of Richard Burton, 1989; A Time to Dance, 1990, televised 1992; Crystal Rooms, 1992. Contributions to: Punch; other journals. Memberships: Arts Council; Chairman, Literature, Panel of Arts Council; President, Cumbrians for Peace, 1962-; Northern Arts. Address: 12 Hampstead Hill Gardens, London NW3, England.

BRAITHWAITE Max, b. 7 Dec 1911, Saskatchewan. m. Aileen Treleaven, 1935, 5 children. Publications: 25 Books inc. Why Shoot the Teacher?, 1965; The Night We Stole the Mounties' Car, 1971; A Privilege and a Pleasure, 1973; The Hungary Thirties, 1977; The Commodore's Barge is Alongside, 1979; Lusty Winter, 1979; All The Way Home, 1986. Honour: Stephen Leacock Medal, 1972. Address: 45 Elgin Street, Brighton, Ontario, KOK 1HO, Canada.

BRAM Christopher, b. 22 Feb 1952, Buffalo, NY, USA. Novelist. Education: BA, College of William & Mary, VA, 1974. Publications: Surprising Myself, 1987; Hold Tight, 1988; In Memory of Angel Clare, 1989; Almost History, 1992; Father of Frankenstein, 1995. Screenplays: George and Al, 1987; Lost Language of Cranes, 1989. Contribution to: NY Times Book Review; Newsday; Lambda Book Report; Christopher Street; Movie Reviews in NY Times Native & Premiere. Membership: Publishing Triangle. Literary Agent: Donadio & Ashworth Associates. Address: 231 West 22nd Street, New York, NY 10011, USA.

BRANCH Edgar Marquess, b. 21 Mar 1913, Chicago, Illinois, USA. University Professor; Educator; Editor; Author. m. Mary Josephine Emerson, 29 Apr 1939, 1 s, 2 d. Education: Beloit College, Beliot, Wisconsin, 1930-32, 1933-34; University College, University of London, England, 1932-33; BA, Beloit College,1934; Brown University, 1934-35; MA, University of Chicago, 1938; PhD, University of Iowa, 1941. Appointments: Graudate Assistant, University of Iowa, 1938-41; Instructor, 1941-43, Assistant Professor, 1943-49, Associate Professor, 1949-57, Professor, 1957-64; Chairman, Department of English, 1959-64, Research Professor, 1964-78, Miami University, Oxford, Ohio; Visiting Associate Professor, University of Missouri, summer 1950; Independent Author and Editor, Mark Twain Project, University of California, Berkely, 1974-. Publications: The Literary Apprenticeship of Mark Twain, 1950; A Bibliography of the Writings of James T Farrell, 1921-1957, 1959; James T Farrell, University of Minnesota Pamphlets on American Writers, 1963; Clemens of the Call, 1969; James T Garrell, 1971; The Great Landslide Case, 1972; The Grangerford-Shepherdson Fued: Life and Death at Compromse (with Rober H Hirst), 1985; Men Call Me Lucky, 1985; Mark Twain's Early Tales and Sketches, vols 1 and 2 (edited with Robert Hirst); Mark Twain's Letters vol 1 (edited with Michael Frank and Kenneth Sanderson). Contributions to: Numerous articles in 17 magazines and journals; Chapters and sections in books, anthologies. Honours: Bellit Collect Junior Foreign Fellow, 1932-33; Leaves, Research Grants, Miami University, ACLS; Senior Fellow, National Endowment for the Humanities, 1971-72; Literary Executor for James T Farrell, 1975-; Senior Research Fellow, National Endowmenet for the Humanites, 1976-77; Benjamin Harrison medallion, Miami University, 1978; Distinguished Service Citation, Beloit College, 1979; Guggenheim Fellow, 1978-79. Memberships: Phi Beta Kappa; Phi Kappa Psi; Modern Language Association of America; National Council of Teachers of English; Beta Theta Pi. Address: 4810 Bonham Road, Oxford, OH 45456, USA.

BRANCH Taylor, b. 14 Jan 1947, Georgia, USA. m. Christina Macy, 1 s, 1 d. Education: AB, University of North Carolina; Princeton University. Appointments: Staff Member, Washington Monthly, Harpers, Esquire. Publications: Blowing the Whistle, 1972; Second Wind, 1979; The Empire Blues, 1981; Parting the Waters, 1988. Contributions to: New England Monthly; New Republic. Honours: Pulitzer Prize, 1989; National Book Critics Circle Award, 1988; Christopher Award, 1988. Address: c/o Diskant & Associates, Suite 202, 1033 Gayley Avenue, Los Angeles, CA 90024 3417, USA.

BRAND Oscar, b. 1920, Canada. Freelance Writer; Composer and Folk-Singer. Appointments: President, Harlequin Productions; President Gypsy Hill Music; Lecturer on Dramatic Writing, Hofstra University, Hempstead, New York; Coordinator of Folk Music, WNYC; Host, numerous TV folk-songs programmes; Curator, Songwriters Hall of Fame, New York City. Publications: Courting Songs, 1952;

Folksongs for Fun, 1957; The Ballad Mongers, authobiography, 1957; Bawdy Songs, 1958; The Gold Rush (writer, composer), Ballet, 1961; In White America (composer) play 1962; A Joyful Noise (co-writer-composer), musical play, 1966; The Education of Hyman Kaplan (co-writer-composer), musical play, 1967; Celebrate (writer-composer), religious songs, 1968; How to Steal an Election (co-writer-composer), mucial play, 1969; Songs of '76, music history, 1973; When I First Came To This Lane, children, 9754; Thunder Rock (wrtier-composer), musical play, 1974; Party Songs, 1985. Honours: Laureate, Fairfield University, 1972; PhD, University of Winnipeg, 1989; Radio Pioneers of America, 1991; Friends of Old Time Radio, 1991. Memberships: AFTRA; ACTRA, SAG, AFM, Dramatists Guild. Address: 141 Baker Hill, Great Neck, NY 11023, USA.

BRANDER John Morran, b. 26 Jan 1932, San Francisco, California, USA. Lawyer. Education: BSc, 1954; LLB, 1967; LLM, 1971; MA, 1980. Appointments: Editor, Califomia State Poetry Quartlery, 1985-91. Publications: Drawing Dreams; The Trail of the Moon; Black Sun; Dorset Green; Fractured Horizon; Darkness Over Paradise; Blue Silence; Wessex Downs; Ships in the Night; A Time of Geburah. Honours: Golden City Award. Membership: PEN. Address: c/o Davis Alpaugh, Small Poetry Press, 362 Odin Place, Pleasent Hll, VA 94523, USA.

BRANDEWYNE Rebecca, b. 1955, USA. Full-time Writer. Publications: No Gentle Love, 1980; Forever My Love,1982; Love, Cherish Me, 1983; Rose of Rapture, 1984; And Gold Was Ours, 1984; The Outlaw Hearts, 1986; Desire in Disguise,1987; Passion Moon Rising, 1988; Upon a Moon-Dark Moor, 1988; Across a Starlit Sea, 1991; Desparado, 1992; Heatland, 1992; Rainbow's Eng, 1991; Swan Road, 1994. Address: PO Box 780036, Wichita, KS 67206, USA.

BRANDIS Marianne. See: **BRENDER A BRANDIS Marianne.**

BRANDON Joe, See: **DAVIS Robert Prunier.**

BRANDON (Oscar) Henry, b. 1916, United Kingdom. Journalist. Appointments: Joined paper, 1939, War Correspondent, North Africa and Western Europe, 1943-45, Paris Correspondent, 1945-46, Roving Diplomatic Correspondent, 1947-49, Washington Correspondent, 1950-, Associate Editor, Chief American Correspondent, retired, 1983, The Sunday Times newspaper, London; Syndicated Columnist for Washington Star, 1979-81; Syndicated Columnist for New York Times News Service, 1983-. Publications: As We Are, 1961; In the Red, 1966; Conversations with Henry Brandon, 1966; The Anatomy of Error, 1970; Retreat of American Power, 1973; Special Relationships, 1989, (Biography); In Search of a New World Order, 1982. Honour: CBE 1985. Address: 3604 Winfield Lane, NW, Washington DC 20007, USA.

BRANDON Sheila. See: **RAYNER Claire Berenice.**

BRANFIELD John Charles, b. 19 Jan 1931, Burrow Bridge, Somerset, England. Writer; Teacher. m. Kathleen Elizabeth Peplow, 2 s, 2 d. Education: MA, Queens' College, Cambridge University; MEd, University of Exeter. Publications: include: Nancekuke,1972; Sugar Mouse, 1973; The Fox in Winter, 1980; Thin Ice, 1983; The Falklands Sunmmer, 1987; The Day I Shot My Dad, 1989; Llanhydrock Days, 1991. Literary Agent: A P Watt Ltd, 20 John Street, London WC1N 2DR. Address: Mingoose Villa, Mingoose, Mount Hawke, Truro, Cornwall TR4 8BX, England.

BRANIGAN Keith, b. 15 Apr 1940, Slough, England. University Lecturer (Archaeology). m. Kuabrat Sivadith, 20 Jun 1965, 1 s, 2 d. Education: BA (Hons) 1st Class Archaeology & Ancient History, 1963; PhD, University of Birmingham, 1966. Publications: The Foundations of Palatial Crete, 1970; The Tombs of Mesara, 1970; Latimer, 1971; Verulanium & the Roman Chilterns, 1973; Aegean Metalwork of the Early & Middle Bronze Age, 1974; Prehistoric Britain, 1975; Gatcome: A Roman Villa Estate, 1977; The Roman Villa In Southwest England, 1977; Hellas, 1980; Roman Britain, 1980; The Catuvellauni, 1986; Archaeology Explained, 1988; Romano-British Cavemen, 1992; Dancing With Death, 1993; Barra: Archaeological Research on Ben Tangoval, 1994. Contributions to: Over 100 papers in journals. Honour: Elected Fellow, Society of Antiquaries, 1970; Memberships: The Prehistoric Society (Vice- President 1984-86); The Society for Promotion of Roman Studies. Address: Department of Archaeology & Prehistory, University of Sheffield, Sheffield S10 2TN, England.

BRANTENBERG Gerd, b. 27 Oct 1941, Oslo, Norway. Novelist. Education: Graduated University of Oslo, 1971. Appointments include: Teacher until 1982; Founder of Literary Women's Forum, Norway. Publications: What Comes Naturally, 1973, 1986; The Daughters of Egalia, 1977, 1985; Stop Smoking, 1978; The Song of St Croix, 1978; Embraces, 1983; At the Ferry Crossing, 1985; The Four Winds, Oslo 1989, Seattle, US 1994, Children's Book; The Ompadora Place, 1992; Play: Egalia, 1982. Honours include: Sarpsborg Prize, 1989. Address: Nils Bays vei 66, 0855 Oslo, Norway.

BRASHER Christopher William, b. 21 Aug 1928, Guyana. Journalist. m. Shirley Bloomer, 28 Aug 1959, 1 s, 2 d. Education: MA, St John's College, Cambridge. Literary Appointments: Columnist, The Observer, 1961-92; Chairman, Berghaus Ltd, The Brasher Boot Co Ltd and The London Marathon Ltd. Publications: The Red Snows with Sir John Hunt, 1960; Sportsman of Our Time, 1962; A Diary of the XVIIIth Olympiad, 1964; Mexico, 1968; Munich, 1972; Editor, The London Marathon: The First Ten Years, 1991. Contributions to: Numerous professional journals and magazines. Honours: Sportswriter of the Year, 1968, 1976; National Medal of Honour, Finland, 1975. Address: The Navigator's House, River Lane, Richmond, Surrey, TW10 7AG, England.

BRATA Sasthi (Sasthibrata Chakravarti), b. 16 July 1939, Calcutta, India (British). Novelist. m. Pamela Joyce Radcliffe, div. Education: Calcutta University. Appointments: Various part time jobs around Europe; Also worked in New York as a Freelance Journalist, London Columnist, Statesman, 1977-80. Publications: Confessions of an Indian Woman Eater, 1971; She and He, 1973; The Sensuous Guru: The Making of a Mystic President, 1980; Short stories: Encounter, 1978; Verse: Eleven Poems, 1960. Address: 33 Savernake Road, London NW3 2JU, England.

BRATHWAITE Edward Kamau, b. 11 May 1930, Bridgetown, Barbados. Professor in History; Poet. Education: BA, Pembroke College, Cambridge, 1953; DPhil, University of Sussex, at Falmer, 1968. Appointments: Founding Secretary, Caribbean Artists Movement, 1966; Professor of Social and Cultural History of the University of the West Indies at Kingston, from 1982. Publications: The Arrivants: A New World Trilogy, 1973; Penguin Modern Poets 15, 1969; Days and Nights, 1975; Other Exiles, 1975; Poetry '75 International; Black plus Blues, 1976; Mother Poem, 1976; Soweto, 1979; Sun Poem, 1982; Third World Poems, 1983; X-Self, 1987; Folk Culture of the Slaves in Jamaica, 1970; The Development of Creole Society in Jamaica 1770-1820, 1971; Jamaica Poetry: A Checklist 1686-1978, 1979; Barbados Poetry: A Checklist, Slavery to the Present, 1979; The Colonial Encounter: Language, 1984; Jah Music, 1986; Roots (Essays), 1986. Honours: Guggenheim Fellowship, 1972; Fulbright Fellowships, 1987-88; Institute of Jamaica Musgrave Medal, 1983. Address: Department of History, University of the West Indies, Mona, Kingston 7, Jamaica.

BRAUN Volker, b. 7 May 1939, Dresden, Germany. Playwright; Poet. Education: University of Leipzig, 1969-64. Appointments include: Assistant Director, Deutsches Theater Berlin, 1972-77. Publications: Plays: Kipper Paul Bauch, 1967; Hans Furst, 1968; Hinze und Kunze, 1968; Freunde, 1972; Tinka, 1976; Guevara, oder, Der Sonnenstaat, 1977; Grosser Frieden, 1979; Simplex Deutsch, 1980; Dmitri, 1982; Siegfried, 1986; Übergangsgesellschaft, 1987; Transit Europa, 1988; Lenins Tod, 1988; Das Denkmal, 1991; Verse: Vorlaufiges, 1966; Kriegesarklärung, 1967; Wir und nicht sie, 1970, 1979; Gedichte, 1972, 1976; Gegen die symmetrische Welt, 1974; Zeit-Gedichte, 1977; Der Stoff zum Leben, 1977; Gedichte, 1979; Training des aufrechten Gangs, 1979; Rimbaud: ein psalm der aktualität, 1985; Langsamer knirschender Morgen, 1987; Annatomie, 1989; Stories: Drei Berichte, 1972, 1979; Unvollendete Gesichte, 1977; Berichte von Hinze und Kunze, 1983; Bodenloser Satz, 1990. Honours include: Berliner Prize, 1989. Address: Wolfshagener Strasse 68, 1100 Berlin, Germany.

BRAUN Volker, b. 7 May 1939, Dresden, Germany. Playwright; Poet; Author. Education: University of Leipzig, 1960-64. Appointments include: Assistant Director, Deutchen Theater, Berlin, 1972-77; Berlin Ensemble, 1979-90. Publications: Verse/Poems: Provokation für mich, 1965; Wir und nicht sie, 1970; Gegen die symmetrische Welt, 1974; Training des aufrechten Gangs, 1979; Langsamer knirschender Morgen, 1987; Der Stoff zum Leben, 1990; Stories/Novels/Prose: Unvollendete Geschichte, 1977; Hinze-Kunze-Roman, 1985; Bodenloser Satz, 1990; Der Wendehals Eine Unterhaltung, 1995; Plays: Die Kipper, 1965; Hinze und Kunze, 1968; Tinka, 1976;

Guevara, oder Der Sonnenstaat, 1977; Grosser Frieden, 1979; Simplex Deutsch, 1980; Dmitri, 1982; Siegfried, 1986; Die Übergangsgesellschaft, 1987; Lenins Tod, 1988; Transit Europa. Der Ausflug der Toten, 1988; Böhmen am Meer, 1992; Essays: Verheerende Folgen mangelnden Anscheins innerbetrieblicher Demokratie, 1988; Texte in zeitlicher Folge, Band 1-10, 1989-93. Honours include: Heinrich-Mann-Preis, 1980; Bremer Literatur-Preis, 1986; Nationalpreis 1 Klasse, 1988; Berliner Preis, 1989; Schiller-Gedächtnispreis, 1992. Membership: Berliner Akademie der Künste. Address: Wolfshagener Strasse 68, 13187 Berlin, Germany.

BRAXTON Joanne Margaret, (Jodi Braxton), b. 25 May 1950, Washington DC, USA. Cummings Professor of American Studies & English. 1 daughter. Education: BA, Sarah Lawrence College, 1972; MA, Yale University, 1974; PhD, Yale University, 1984. Literary Appointments: Poetry Consultant, Connecticut Commission on the Arts, Director, Poets & Writers in Schools Program, 1975-76. Publications: Sometimes I Think of Maryland, 1977; Black Women Writing Autobiography: A Tradition Within A Tradition, 1989; Editor, The Collected Poetry of Paul Lausenee Dunbar, 1993; Editor, Wild Women in the WhirlWind, 1990. Contributions to: Editorial Board Memberships: African-American Review, Legacy; Autobiography; Numerous Contributions to Journals and Little Magazines. Honours: Danforth Fellow, 1972-76; Michigan Society of Fellows, 1976-79; Outstanding Virginia Faculty Member, 1992. Memberships: Life Member, American Studies Association; Life Member, Modern Language Association; Life Member, College Language Association. Address: Department of English, College of William & Mary, Williamsburg, VA 23185, USA.

BRAXTON Jodi. See: BRAXTON Joanne Margaret.

BRAY John Jefferson, b. 16 Sept 1912, Adelaide, Australia. Retired Chief Justice. Education: St Peter's College, Adelaide, 1925-28; University of Adelaide, 1929-32; LLB (Ord) 1932, LLB (Hons) 1933, LLD 1937, University of Adelaide. Appointments: Chief Justice of South Australia 1967-78; Chancellor, University of Adelaide, 1968-82. Publications: Satura: Selected Poetry and Prose, 1988; Poems, 1962; Poems 1961-1971, 1972; Poems 1972-1979, 1979; The Bay of Salamis and Other Poems, 1986; The Emperor's Doorkeeper (Occasional Addresses), 1988; Seventy Seven (Poems), 1990. Address: 39 Hurtle Square, Adelaide, SA, Australia 5000.

BRAYFIELD Celia Frances, b. 21 Aug 1945, Ealing, England. Writer. 1 d. Education: St Paul's Girls' School; Universitaire de Grenoble. Literary Appointments: TV Critic, The Evening Standard, 1974-82; The Times, 1984-89; London Daily News, 1987; The Sunday Telegraph, 1989. Publications: The Body Show Book, 1981; Glitter, The Truth About Fame, 1985; Pearls, 1987; The Prince, 1990; White Ice, 1993. Contributions to: various journals, magazines and newspapers. Memberships: Society of Authors; Committee of Management, National Council for One Parent Families, 1989-present. Literary Agent: Andrew Hewson, John Johnson Agency. Address: c/o John Johnson Agency, Clerkenwell House, Clerkenwell Green, London EC1R OHT, England.

BREARS Peter Charles David, b. 30 Aug 1944. Writer and Museum Consultant. Education: Dip AD, Leeds College of Art. Publications: English Country Pottery, 1971; The Gentlewoman's Kitchen, 1984; Yorkshire Probate Inventories, 1972; Horse Brasses, 1980; Traditional Food in Yorkshire, 1987; Northcountry Folk Art, 1989; Of Curiosities & Rare Things, 1989; Treasures for the People, 1989; Collector's Book of English Country Pottery, 1974; Images of Leeds, 1992; Leeds Describ'd, 1993; Leeds Waterfront Heritage Trail, 1993. Contributions to: Connoiseur; Folk Life; Post Medieval Archaeology. Memberships: Fellow, Museums Association; Fellow, Society of Antiquities; Vice President, Society for Folklife Studies. Address: 4, Woodbine Terrace, Headingley, Leeds, LS6 4AF.

BRECHER Michael, b. 14 Mar 1925, Montreal, Quebec, Canada. Political Science Educator. m. Eva Danon, 7 Dec 1950, 3 children. Education: BA, McGill University, 1946; MA, 1948, PhD, 1953, Yale University. Appointments: Member, Faculty, McGill University, 1952-; Professor, McGill University, 1963-; R B Angus Professor, McGill University, 1993-; Visiting Professor, University of Chicago, Hebrew University of Jerusalem, University of CA, Berkeley; Stanford University. Publications include: The Struggle for Kashmir, 1953; Nehru: A Political Biography , 1959; The New States of Asia, 1963; Succession in India, 1966; India and World Politics, 1968; Political Leadership in India, 1969; The Foreign Policy System of Israel, 1972; Decisions in Israel's Foreign Policy, 1975; Studies in Crises Behavior,

1979; Decisions in Crisis, 1980; Crises in the Twentieth Century (2 vols), 1988; Crises, Conflict and Istability, 1989; Crises in World Politics, 1993. Contributions to: Over 75 Articles in Field to Professional Journals. Honours include: Canada Council & Social Science and Humanities Research Council of Canada, Research Grantee; Killam Awards; Watamull Wilson Foundation Award, American Political Science Associates; Fieldhouse Teaching Award; Distinguished Scholar Award, International Studies Association. Memberships: Several Professional Organisations. Address: McGill University, 855 Sherbrooke Street W, Montreal, PQ, Canada, H3A 2T7.

BRENDER A BRANDIS Marianne, (Marianne Brandis), b. 5 Oct 1938, Netherlands. Writer. Education: BA, 1960, MA, 1964, McMaster University. Publications: This Spring's Sowing, 1970; A Sense of Dust, 1972; The Tinderbox, 1982; The Quarter Pie Window, 1985; The Sign of the Scales, 1990; Special Nests, 1990; Fire Ship, 1992; Elizabeth, Duchess of Somerset, 1989. Contributions to: Article to Canadian Children's Literature, 1987. Honours: Young Adult Canadian Book Award, 1986; National Chapter IODE Book Award, 1986; Bilson Award, 1991. Membership: Writer's Union of Canada. Address: 10 Lamport Apt 206, Toronto, Ontario, Canada M4W 1S6.

BRENDON Piers George Rundle, b. 21 Dec 1940, Stratton, Cornwall, England. Writer. m. Vyvyen Davis, 1968, 2 s. Education: MA, PhD, Magdelene College, Cambridge. Publications: Hurrell Froude and the Oxford Movement, 1974; Hawker of Morwenstow, 1975; Eminent Edwardians, 1979; The Life and Death of the Press Barons, 1982; Winston Churchill, A Brief Life, 1984; Our Own Dear Queen, 1985; Ike: The Life and Times of Dwight D Eisenhower, 1986; Thomas Cook: 150 Years of Popular Tourism, 1991; The Windsors (with Phillip Whitehead), 1994. Contributions to: Reviews for many papers and journals including: Times; Observer; The Mail on Sunday; New York Times; New Statesman. Literary Agent: Curtis Brown Ltd. Address: 4B Millington Road, Cambridge CB3 9HP, England.

BRENNAN Joseph Payne, b. 20 Dec 1918, Bridgeport, Connecticut, USA. Library Assistant (Retired). m. 20 Oct 1970. Publications include: Heart of Earth, poems, 1950; Nine Horrors and A Dream, 1958; The Wind of Time, Poems, 1962; Nightmare Need, poems, 1964; Stories of Darkness and Dread, 1973; 60 Selected Poems, 1985; The Borders Just Beyond, 1986; Total, 18 books. Contributions to: Esquire; American Scholar; Commonwealth; University Review; Yale Literary Magazine; New York Times; Alfted Hitchcock's Mysterm Magazine; Weird Tales; Georgia Review; Southern Poetry Review. Honours: Leonora Speyer Award, Poetry Society of America, 1961; Clark Ashton Smith Poetry Award, 1978; Life Achievement Award, World Fantasy Convention, 1982. Literary Agent: Kirby McCauley Ltd, 432 Park Avenue South, Suite 1509, New Haven, CT 06515, USA.

BRENNAN Patricia Winifred, (Patricia Daly, Anne Rodway), b. Shaftesbury, Dorset, England. Writer. m. (1) Denis William Reed, 31 Dec 1947, (2) Peter Brennan, 19 Sept 1960. Education: Bristol University; University of London, 1967. Appointments: Production Editor, Pitman Publishing, 1946-48. Publications: Penguin Parade; Writing Today; Albion; A Doctor In Dark Night, novel; Poems: PEN; The Iron Dominion; Arts Council New Poetry; Women Writing. Contributions to: Kimber Anthologies of Ghost Stories, After Midnight Stories; In My Father's House; The Day Trip; Hesperios; Narcissus; Night Driver; Institute of Jewish Affairs; Patterns of Prejudice; Art & Sexual Taboo; Encounter; Our Family Doctors; Swedish Veekojoumalen. Memberships: Society of Authors; PEN; Royal Society of Arts; British Federation of Graduate Women; Richmond & Hampton Association; Bath Association. Address: Iford House, 30 Newbridge Road, Bath BA1 3JZ England.

BRENT Iris. See: BANCROFT Iris.

BRENT Madeleine. See: O'DONNELL Peter.

BRENTON Howard, b. 1942, United Kingdom. Playwright; Poet. Appointments: Resident Dramatist, Royal Court Theatre, London, 1972-73; Resident Writer, University of Warwick, 1978-79. Publications: Notes from a Psychotic Journal and Other Poems, 1969; Revenge, 1969; Scott of the Antartic (or what God didn't see), 1970; Christie in Love and Other Plays, 1970; Lay By (co-author), 1972; Plays for Public Places, 1972; Hitler Diaries, 1972; Brassneck (with David Hare), 1973; Magnificence, 1973; Weapons of Happiness, 1976; The Paradise Run, television play, 1976; Epsom Downs, 1977; Sore

Throats, with Sonnets of Love and Opposition, 1979; The Life of Galileo (adaptor), 1980; The Romans in Britain, 1980; Plays for the Poor Theatre,1980; Thirteenth Night and A Short Sharp Shock, 1981; Danton's Death (adaptor), 1982; The Genius, 1983; Desert of Lies, television play, 1983; Sleeping Policemen (with Tunde Ikoli), 1984; Bloody Poetry, 1984; Pravda (with David Hare),1985; Dead Head, television series, 1987; Greenland, 1988; H.I.D. (Hess is Dead), 1989; Iranian Night, (with Tariq ali), 1989; Diving for Pearls, a novel, 1989; Moscow Gold (with Tariq Ali),1990; Berlin Bertie, 1992; Hot Irons (Essays and Diaries), 1994. Literary Agent: Casarotto Ramsay Ltd, England. Address: c/o Casarotto Ramsay Ltd,National House, 60-66 Wardour Street, London W1V 3HP.

BRESLIN James, b. 1935, Brooklyn, NY, USA. Appointment: Professor, University of CA, Berkeley. Publication include: From Modern to Contemporary: American Poetry 1945-65; William Carlos Williams: An American Artist; Mark Pothko: A Biography, 1993. Address: University of CA Berkeley, Berkeley, CA 94720 0001, USA.

BRETNOR Reginald, (Grendel Briarton), b. 30 July 1911, Vladivostock, Siberia. Writer. m. (1) Helen Harding, deceased 1967, (2) Rosalie Leveille, 1969. Appointments: Writer, Office of War Information (US) later OIICA, 1943-47. Publications: Decisive Warfare, A Study on Military Theory, 1969, 1986; (Fiction) Schimmelhorn's Gold, 1986; Gilpin's Space, 1986; A Killing in Swords, 1978; (Story Collection) The Schimmerlhorn File, 1979; Translator, Moncrif's Cats, 1961; Les Chats by Francois-Angustin Paradis de Moncrif, 1961; Editor, various books including: Modern Science Fiction, Its Meaning and its Future, 1953, 1979; Science Fiction, Today and Tomorrow, 1974; The Craft of Science Fiction, 1976; The Future at War, anthology; I, Thor's Hammer, 1978; II, The Spear of Mars, 1980, III, Orion's Sword 1980; Works of Reginald Bretnor, (bibliography), 1988; Of Force & Violence and Other Imponderables, 1992; One Man's BEM: Thoughts on Science Fiction, 1993. Contributions to: Various journals and magazines. Honour: Easton Award (science fiction criticism), 1988. Memberships: Science Fiction Writers of America; Writers Guild of America; National Rifle Association, Military Conflct Institute. Literary Agent: Owlswick Literary Agency, Philadelphia, USA. Visual Media, All Talent Agency, Pasadena, California, USA. Address: PO Box 1481, Medford, OR 97501, USA.

BRETT Jan Churchill, b. 1 Dec 1949, Bym Mawr, Pennsylvania, USA. Illustrator; Writer. m. Joseph Hearne, 18 Aug 1980, 1 d. Education: Colby Junion College, 196869; Boston Museum School, 1970. Publications: Author and illustrator: Fritz and the Beautiful Horses, 1981; Good Luck Sneakers, 1981; Annie and the Wild Animals, 1985; Goldilocks and the Three Bears, 1987; Illustrator; Wood and Crossings, 1978; Inside a Sand Castle, 1979; Secret Clocks, 1979; St Patrick's Day in the Morning, 1980; Some Birds Have Funny Names, 1981; I Can Fly, 1981; Young Melvin and Bulger, 1981; In the Castle of Cats, 1981; Some Plants Have Funny Names, 1983; Valentine Bears, 1983; Where Are All the Kittens, 1984; Cabbage Patch Kids, The Great Rescue, 1984; Old Devil is Waiting, 1985; Mother's Day Mice, 1986; The Twelve Days of Christmas, 1986; Scary, Scary Halloween, 1986; Noelle of the Nutcracker, 1986; Look at the Kittens, 1987; The Enchanted Book, 1987; Berlioz the Bear, 991; Christmas Trolls, 1993; The Wild Christmas Reindeer, 1990. Contributions to: Cricket Magazine. Honours: Best of Year, Parent's Choice Magazine, 1981; Best of Year for 1983 and 1984 Sunrise Calendar, Gene Shaulit NBC Television, 1983, 1984; Ambassador of Honour, English Speaking Union of the United States, 1983; Outstanding Science trade Book for Chldren, National Science Teachers Association, 1984; Children's Book Award, University of Nebraska, 1984; Top Ten Children's Book Award of the Year, Redbook Magazine, 1985; Booklist Magazine Editor's Choice, American Library Association, 1986. Memberships: Society of Children's Book Writers. Address: 132 Pleasant Street, Norwell, MA 02061, USA.

BRETT John Michael. See: TRIPP Miles Barton.

BRETT Mary Elizabeth (Molly Brett), b. United Kingdon. Freelance Artist and Writer. Publications: The Japanese Garden: Story of a Toy Car; Drummer Boy; Duckling,; Mr Turkey Runs Away; Puppy Schooldays; Tom Tit Moves House; Folow Me Round the Farm; Master Bunny the Baker's Boy, Adventures of Plush and Tatty; A Surprise for Dumpy; The Untidy Little Hedgehog; Robin Finds Christmas; The Forgotten Bear; Two in a Tent; Flip Flop's Secret; Paddy Gets into Mischief; Teddy Flies Away, Midget and the Pet Shop, 1969; Jiggy's Treasure Hunt, 1973 The Party That Grew, 1976; Jumble Bears, 1977;

The Molly Brett Picture Book, 1978; An Alphabet by Molly Brett, 1980; The Runaway Fairy, 1982; Good-Night Time Tales, 1982; Plush and Tatty on the Beach, 1987; The Magic Spectacles, 1987. Address: Chimes Cottage, Horsell Vale, Woking, Surrey, England.

BRETT Michael. See: **TRIPP Miles Barton.**

BRETT Raymond Laurence, b. 1917, United Kingdom. Emeritus Professor. Appointments: Lecturer in English, University of Bristol, 1946-52; G F Grant Professor of English, 1952-82, Dean, Faculty of Arts, 1960-62, Emeritus Professor, 1982-present, University of Hull; General Editor, Writers and Their Background Series. Publications: The Third Earl of Shaftesbury, 1952; George Crabbe, 1956, Revised Edition, 1968; Reason and Imagination, 1960; Lyrical Ballads by Wordsworth and Coleridge, 1798-1805 (edited with A R Jones), 3rd Edition, 1968, 4th Edition, 1991; An Introduction to English Studies, 1965; Poems of Faith and Doubt (editor), 1965; Fancy and Imagination, 1969; S T Coleridge (editor), 1971; William Hazlitt, 1977; Andrew Marvell Tercentenary Essays (editor), 1979; Barclay Fox's Journal (editor), 1979; Coleridge,Writers and Their Work series, 1980. Address: 19 Mill Walk, Cottingham, North Humberside HU16 4RP, England.

BRETT Simon Anthony Lee, b. 28 Oct 1945, Surrey, England. Writer. m. Lucy Victoria McLaren, 27 Nov 1971, 2 s, 1 d. Education: BA Hons, English (1st Class), Wadham College, Oxford, 1963-67. Appointments: Chairman, The Crime Writers' Assocation 1986-87. Publications: 15 Charles Paris Crime Novels, 1975-93; 4 Mrs Pargeter Crime Novels, 1986-92; Editor, Faber Books of Useful Verse, Parodies, Diaries; A Shock To The System, 1984; Dead Romantic, 1985; The Booker Book, 1989; How to Be A Little Sod, 1992; After Henry (Radio and TV Series), 1985-92. Honours: Best Radio Feature, Writers' Guild, 1973; Outstanding Radio Programme, Broadcasting Press Guild, 1987. Memberships: Crime Writers' Association; Detection Club; PEN; Writers Guild; Society of Authors. Litearary Agent: Michael Motley. Address: Frith House, Burpham, Arundel, West Sussex, BN18 9RR, England.

BRETUO A. See: **ASSENSOH Akwasi Bretuo.**

BREW Kwesi, b. 1928, Cape Coast, Ghana. Ambassador; Poet. Education: University College of the Gold Coast, Legon. Appointments: Former Ambassador for Ghana to Britain, India, France, USSR, Germany and Mexico. Publications: The Shadows of Laughter, 1968; Pergamon Poets 2: Poetry from Africa, 1968; African Panorama, 1981; Screenplay: The Harvest. Honours: British Council Prize. Address: c/o Greenfield Review Press, PO Box 80, Greenfield Center, NY 12833, USA.

BREWER Derek Stanley, b. 13 July 1923, Cardiff, Wales. Acedemic; Emeritus Professor. m. Lucie Elisabeth Hoole, 17 Aug 1951, 3 s, 2 d. Education: Magdalen College, Oxford, 1941-42, 1945-48; BA (Oxon), 1948; PhD, Birmingham University, 1956; LittD, Cambridge University, 1980. Appointments: Master Emmanuel College, Cambridge, 1977-90; Editor The Cambridge Review, 1981-86. Publications: Chaucer, 1953; Proteus, 1958; (Editor) The Parlement of Foulys, 1960; Chaucer: The Critical Heritage, 1978; Chaucer and his World, 1978, reprinted, 1992; Symbolic Stories, 1980, reprinted, 1988; English Gothic Literature, 1983; Chaucer: an Introduction, 1984; Books and articles on Chaucer, Malory and other authors, mediaeval to nineteenth century. Address: Emmanuel College, Cambridge, England.

BREWSTER Elizabeth (Winifred), b. 26 Aug 1922, Chipman, New Brunswick, Canada. Professor of English; Poet. Education: University of New Brunswick; Radcliffe College, Cambridge, Massachusetts; King's College, London; PhD, Indiana University, Bloomington, 1962. Appointments: University of Saskatchewan, Saskatoon, from 1972, Professor of English, 1980-1990; Professor Emeritus. Publications: East Coast, 1951; Lilooet, 1954; Roads and Other Poems, 1957; Passage of Summer: Selected Poems, 1969; Sunrise North, 1972; In Search of Eros, 1974; Sometimes I Think of Moving, 1977; The Way Home, 1982; Digging In, 1982; Selected Poems of Elizabeth Brewster 1944-84, 1985; Entertaining Angels, 1988; Spring Again, 1990; Wheel of Change, 1993; Novels: The Sisters, 1974; Junction, 1982. Honours: Canada Council Award, 1985; LittD, University of New Brunswick, 1982. Address: Department of English, University of Saskatchewan, Saskatoon, Saskatchewan, Canada S7N 0W0.

BREWSTER Robin. See: **STAPLES Reginald Thomas.**

BREWSTER Townsend Tyler, b. 23 July 1924, Glen Cove, New York, USA. Playwright; Librettist; Lyricist; Poet; Translator; Critic. Education: BA, Queens College, 1947, MA, Columbia University, 1962. Appointments include: Lecturer, Theatre Department, City College, NY, 1969-73; Translator, adapter, continuity writer, NBC Television Opera, 1950-51; Cpoywriter, Hicks & Greist, 1959-61. Publications include: Translations: Bernard Dadie's Monsieur Thog-gnini, 1976; Maxime N'Debeka's Equatorium, 1987; Various others commissioned & published by Ubu Repertory Theatre. Also: Choreogrpahy of Love, opera libretto, broadcast, 1947; Libretto, The Tower, Santa Fe Opera, 1957; 2 radio lectures, Copenhagen, Denmark, 1972. Plays produced include: Little Girl, Big Town, review, 1953; Please Don't Cry and Say "No", 1972; Though It's Been Said Many Times, Many Ways, 1976; The Girl Beneath the Tulip Tree, 1977; Black-Belt Bertram, 1979; Arthur Ashe & I, 1979; The Liar, translation, Croneille, 1984. Honours include: Playwrights Fellowship, National Theatre Conference, 1947; Story Magazine Playwriting Award, 1968; MCTV Playwriting-in-Residence, Univeristy of Denver, 1969; Louise Bogan Memorial Prize, poetry, 1975; Grant, National Endowment for the Arts, 1977; Jonathan Swift Award, satire, 1979; Various scholarships. Memberships include: ASCAP; Vice President, Harlem Performance Centre; Board, Harlem Culture Council, Centre for Contemporary Opera; Consultant, Apollo Opera & Drama Company,; International Brecht Society. Address: 171-29 103 Road, Jamaica, New York, NY 11433, USA.

BREYTENBACH Breyten, b. 16 Sept 1939, Bonnievale, South Africa. Poet. Education: Graduated University of Cape Town, 1959. Appointments: Founder of the Okhela anti-apartheid group. Publications: The Iron Cow Must Sweat, 1964; House of the Deaf, 1967; Gangrene, 1969; Lotus, 1970; To Paint a Sinking Ship Blue, 1972; In Other Words: Fruits From the Dream of Silence, 1973; Flower Writing, 1977; Sinking Ship Blues, 1977; And Death White as Words: Anthology, 1978; In Africa Even the Flies are Happy: Selected Poems 1964-1977; Fingermoon: Drawings from Pretoria; Eclipse, 1983; Lewendood, 1985; Other writing: Catastrophes, 1980; Memory of Snow and Dust, 1980; Season in Paradise, 1980; Mouroir: Mirrornotes of a Novel, 1984; The True Confession of an Albino Terrorist, 1984; End Papers, 1986; Judas Eye, Self Portrait, Deathwatch, 1988; All One Horse, 1990. Honours include: Rapport Prize, 1986. Address: c/o Faber and Faber Ltd, 3 Queen Square, London WC1N 3AU, England.

BREZHNEV Dennis. See: **BARNETT Paul le Page.**

BRIARTON Grendel. See: **BRETNOR Reginald.**

BRICKLEBANK Peter Noel, b. 19 Oct 1955, Leeds, England. Writer. Education: BA, Communication Studies (Hons), Sheffield Polytechnic, 1977; MA, Literature, City College of New York, USA, 1985. Contributions to: Fiction: The American Voice; Carolina Quarterly; Confrontation; Kansas Quarterly; Mid-American Review; Webster Review; Writers' Forum; The Crescent Review; Descant; Alasaka Quarterly; Queens' Quarterly, Canada. Others, Non-fiction: The American Book Reivew; another Chicago Magazine; Minnesota Review, and others. Honours: Betram D Wolfe Memorial Creative Writing Award, City University of New York, 1985; Nomination, Pushcart Prize, 1989; Fellowship in Fiction, New York Foundation for the Arts, 1990. Address: 1803 Riverside Drive 2J, New York, NY 10034, USA.

BRICKNER Richard P, b. 14 May 1933, New York City, USA. Writer; Teacher. Education: BA, Columbia College, 1957. Publications: My Second Twenty Years; Tickets; The Broken Year; Bringing Down the House; After She Left. Contributions to: NY Times Book Reivew. Honours: National Foundation for the Arts; Guggenheim Fellowship in Fiction. Literary Agent: Joy Harris. Address: c/o Joy Harris, 888 Seventh Avenue, New York, NY 10106, USA.

BRIDGEMAN Harriet (Victoria Lucy) (Viscountess), b. 30 Mar 1942. Director, The Bridgeman Art Library; Author. Education: MA, Trinity College, Dublin. Publications: The Masters, Executive Editor, 1965-68; Discovering Antiques, Editor 1970-71; The British Eccentric, 1974; An Encyclopaedia of Victoriana, 1975; Society Scandals, 1976; Beside the Seaside, 1976; Needlework: An Illustrated History, 1978; A Guide to Gardens of Europe, 1979; The Last Word, 1983. Address: 19 Chepstow Road, London W2 5BP, England.

BRIDWELL Norman Ray, b. 1928, USA. Children's Writer; Freelance Artist. Publications include: Clifford the Big Red Dog, 1962; Bird in the Hat, 1964; The Witch Next Door, 1965; The Country Cat,

1969; What Do They Do When It Rains, 1969; The Witchs Christmas, 1970; Clifford the Small Red Puppy, 1972; Monster Holidays, 1974; Clifford's Good Deeds, 1974; Clifford at the Circus, 1977; The Witch Grows Up, 1979; Clifford Goes to Hollywood, 1980; Clifford's Kitten, 1984; Clifford's Birthday Party, 1988; Where is Clifford?; Clifford We Love You, 1991; Clifford's Animal Noises, 1991; Clifford's Thanksgiving Visit, 1993; Clifford's Happy Easter, 1994; Clifford The Firehouse Dog, 1994; Clifford The Puppy's First Christmas, 1994. Honour: Jeremiah Ludington Memorial Award, 1991. Honorary Degree, Doctor of Humane Letters, Indiana University, 1994. Address: Box 869, Edgartown, MA 02539, USA.

BRIEN Alan, b. 12 Mar 1925. Novelist; Journalist. m. (1) Pamela Mary Jones, 1947, 3d, (2)Nancy Newbold Ryan, 1 s. 1 d, 1961. (3)Jill Sheila Tweedie, 1973. Education: BA, English Literature, Jesus College, Oxford. Appointments: Associate Editor, Mini-Cinema, 1950-52; Courier, 1952-53; Film Critic, Columnist, Truth, 1953-54; TV Critic, Observer, 1954-55; Film Critic, 1954-56, New York Correspondent, 1956-58, Evening Standard; Drama Critic, Features Editor, Spectator, 1958-61; Columnist, Sunday Daily Mail, 1958-62, Sunday Dispatch, 1962-63; Political Columnist, Sunday Pictorial, 1963-64; Drama Critis, Sunday Telegraph, 1964-67; Columnist, Spectator, 1963-65; New Statesman, 1966-72; Punch, 1972-84; Diarist, 1967-75; Film Critic, 1976-84, Sunday Times. Publications: Domes of Fortune, 1979; Lenin the Novel, 1986; Heaven's Will (novel), 1989; And When Rome Falls (novel), 1991. Contributions to: various professional journals. Address: 14 Falkland Road, London, NW5, England.

BRIERLEY David, b. 30 July 1936, Durban, South Africa. Author. m. Caroline Gordon Walker, 23 April 1960, 1 d. Education; BA, Honours, Oxon. Publications: Cold War, 1979; Blood Group O, 1980; Big Bear, Little Bear, 1981; Shooting Star, 1983; Czechmate, 1984; Skorpion's Death, 1985; Snowline, 1986; One Lives, One Dies, 1987; Literary Agent: James Hale. Address: La Vieille Ferme, 24170 St-Germain-de Belvès, France.

BRIGGS Asa (Baron), vb. 7 May 1921, Keighley, Yorkshire, England. m. Susan Anne Banwell, 1955, 2 s, 2 d. Education: 1st Class History Tripos, Parts I and II, Sidney Sussex College, Cambridge, 1941; BSc, 1st Class (Economics), London, 1941; Gerstenberg Studenstship in Economics, London, 1941. Publications: Victorian People, 1954; The Age of Improvement, 1959; History of Broadcasting in the United Kingdom, 4 volumes, 1961-79; Victorian Cities, 1963; A Social History of England, 1983; Victorian Things, 1988. Honours: Life Peerage, 1976; Marconi Medal for Communications History, 1975; Medaille de Vermeil de la Formation, Foundation de l'Academie d'Architecture, 1979; 15 Honorary Degrees. Memberships: Fellow, British Academy; American Academy of Arts and Sciences; President, Social History Society. Address: The Caprons, Keere Street, Lewes, BN7 1TY, England.

BRIGGS Raymond Redvers, b. 18 Jan 1934, Wimbledon, London, England. Illustrator; Writer; Cartoonist. m. Jean T Clark, 1963 (dec 1973). Education: Wimbledon School of Art; Slade School of Fine Art, London, NDD; DFA; FSIAD. Freelance illustrator, 1957-. Children's author, 1961-. Publications: The Strange House, 1961; Midnight Adventure, 1961; Sledges to the Rescue, 1963; Ring-a-Ring o'Roses, 1962; The White Land, 1963; Fee Fi Fo Fum, 1964; The Mother Goose Treasury, 1966; Jim and the Beanstalk, 1970; The Fairy Tale Treausry, 1975; Fungus the Bogeyman, 1977; The Snowman, 1978; Gentleman Jim, 1980; When the Wind Blows, 1982, stage and radio versions, 1983; The Tinpot Foreign General & the Old Iron Woman, 1984; Unlucky Wally, 1987; Unlucky Wally, Twenty Years On, 1989; The Man, 1992. Honours: Awards including: Kate Greenaway Medal, 1966, 1973; BAFTA Award (British Academy of Film & Television Arts). Address: Weston, Underhill Lane, Westmeston, Near Hassocks, Sussex, BN6 8XG, England.

BRIN David, b. 1950, USA. Science Fiction Writer. Publications: Sundiver, 1980; Startide Rising, 1983; The Practice Effect, 1984; The Postman, 1985; Glory Season, 1993; The Uplift War, 1987. Memberships: Secretary, Science Fiction Writers of America. Address: 5081 Baxter Street, San Diego, CA 92117, USA.

BRINGHURST Robert, b. 16 Oct 1946, CA, USA. Poet. Education: BA, Indiana University, 1973; MFA, University of British Columbia, 1975. Appointments: General Editor, Kanchenjunga Poetry Series, 1973-79; Visiting Lecturer, Creative Writing, 1975-77; Lecturer, University of British Columbia, 1979-80; Reviews Editor, Canadian Fiction Magazine, 1974-75; Adjunct Lecturer, Simon Fraser University, 1983-84; Contributing Editor, Fine Print, A Review for the Arts of the Book, 1985-90; Writer-in-Residence, University of Edinburgh, 1989-90; Ashley Fellow, Trent University, Ontario, 1994. Publications include: The Shipwright's Log, 1972; The Stonecutter's Horses, 1979; The Beauty of the Weapons, 1972-82; Tending the Fire, 1985; Ocean, Paper, Stone, 1984; The Blue Roofs of Japan, 1986; The Raven Steals the Light, 1986; Pieces of Map, Pieces of Music, 1987; The Black Canoe, 1991; The Elements of Typographic Style, 1992; The Calling, 1995. Honours: Macmillan Prize, 1975; Canada Council Grants; Ontario Arts Council Literary Grant; Alcuin Society Design Award, 1984, 85; Canadian Broadcasting Corporation Poetry Prize, 1985; Guggenheim Fellowship, 1987-88. Address: Box 357, 1917 West 4th Ave, Vancouver, BC, V6J 1M7, Canada.

BRINK Andre Philippus, b. 29 May 1935, Vrede, South Africa. Professor. Education: DLitt, Rhodes University; DLitt (honoris causa) University of the Witwatersrand. Publications: Lobola vir die Lewe, 1962; File on the diplomat, 1966; Mapmakers (essays), 1983; Looking on Darkness, 1974; An Instant in The Wind, 1976; Rumours of Rain, 1978; A Dry White Season, 1979; A Chain of Voices, 1982; The Wall of the Plague, 1984; The Ambassador, 1985; A Land Apart, 1986; States of Emergency, 1988; An Act of Terror, 1991; The First Life of Adamastor, 1993; On the Contrary, 1993. Contributions to: World Literature Today; Theatre Quartely; Standpunte. Honours: Reina Prinsen Geerlings Prize, 1964; CNA Award, 1965, 1978, 1982; Academy Prize for Prose Translation, 1970; Martin Luther King, Memorial Prize, 1980; Prix Medics Etranger, 1980; Chevalier de la Legion d'Honneur, 1982; Commandeur de l'Ordre des Arts et des Lettres, 1992. Address: University of Cape Town, Randebosch, South Africa.

BRINKLEY Alan, b. 2 June 1949, Washington, District of Columbia, USA. Historian. m. Evangeline Morphos, 3 June 1989. Education: AB, Princeton University, 1971;PhD, Harvard University, 1979. Appointments: Assistant Professor of History, Massachusetts Institute of Technology, Boston, 19780-82; Dunwalke Associate Professor of American History, Harvard University, 1982-88; Professor of History, City University of New York Graduate School, 1988-91; Professor of History, Columbia University, New York City, 1991-. Publications: The Unfinished Nation: A Concise History of the American People, 1993; Voices of Protest; Huey Long, Father Coughlin, and the Great Depression, 1982; America in the Twentieth Century, 1982; American History: A Survey, 1990. Honours: National Book Award for History, 1983; Guggenheim Fellowship, 1984-85; Woodrow Wilson Center Fellowship, 1985; National Humanities Center Fellowship, 1988-89. Memberships: Executive Board, Society of American Historians; Executive Board, Organization of American Historians. Address: 15 West 81st Street, New York, NY 10024, USA.

BRINKLEY Douglas, b. 1950, USA. Education: PhD, Georgetown University. Appointments: Director, Essenhower Centre; Professor, University of New Orleans. Publications: Dean Acheson & The Making of US Foreign Policy, 1991; Dean Acheson: The Cold War Years 1953-71, 1992; Theodore Roosevelt, Many Sided American, 1992; Driven Patriot, 1992; The Magic Bus: An American Odyssey, 1993. Address: Dept of History, University of New Orleans, New Orleans, LA 70148, USA.

BRINNIN John Malcolm, b. 13 Spet 1916, Halifax, Canada. Teacher; Author. Education: BA, University of Michigan; Harvard University. Appointments include: Director, Poetry Centre, New York City, 1949-57; Instructor, English, Vassar College,1942-47; Associate Professor, English, University of Connecticut, 1951-62; Emeritus Professor of English, Boston University. Publications: Dylan Thomas in America, 1955; The Third Rose, Gertrude Stein and Her World, 1958; Selected Poems of John Malcolm Brinnin, 1964; The Sway of the Grand Saloon: A Social History of the North Atlantic, 1971; Sextet: T S Eliot & Truman Capote & Others, 1981; Bean Voyage: Life Aboard Last Great Ships, 1988; Travel & The Sense of Wonder; Selected Operas and Plays of Gertrude Stein. Honours: Award, National Institute of Arts & Letters, 1968; Centennial Medal, Distiction in Literature, Michigan University; Gold Medal, Poetry Society of American. Memberships: National Institute of Arts and Letters. Address: King Caesar Road, Duxbury, MA 02332, USA.

BRINTON Alexander. See: **BATTIN B W**.

BRISCO P A. See: **MATTHEWS Patricia Anne**.

BRISCO Patty. See: **MATTHEWS Patricia Anne.**

BRISKIN Jacqueline, b. 18 Dec 1927, London, England. Novelist; Short Story Writer. m. bert Briskin, 2 s, 1 d. Education: Univerityof California at Los Angeles. Publications: California Generation, 1970; Afterlove, 1974; Rich Friends, 1976; Paloverde, 1978; The Onyx, 1982; Everything and More, 1983; Too Much Too Soon, 1985; Dreams Are Not Engough, 1987; The Naked Heart, 1989; The Other Side of Love, 1991. Memberships: PEN; Author's Guild. Address: Los Angeles, California, USA.

BRISKIN Mae Seidman, b. 20 Oct 1924, Brooklyn, NY, USA. Writer. m. Herbert B Briskin, 1 Dec 1946, 2 s, 1 d. Education: BA, Brooklyn College, 1944; MA, Columbia University, 1946. Publications: A Boy Like Astrid's Mother, 1988; The Tree Still Stands, 1991. Contributions to: Numerous. Honours: Best American Short Stories, 1976; PEN, Syndicated Fiction Awards, 1985, 86, 87, 88; Award for Collection of Short Fiction, 1989. Membership: PEN. Literary Agent: Ellen Levine. Address: 3604 Arbutus Drive, Palo Alto, CA 94303, USA.

BRISTOW Robert O'Neil, b. 17 Nov 1926, St Louis, MI, USA. Author. m. Gaylon Walker, 23 Dec 1950, 2 s, 2 d. Education: BA, 1951, MA, 1965, University of Oklahoma. Appointments: Writer in Residence, Winthrop College, South Carolina, 1961-87. Publications: Time for Glory, 1968; Night Season, 1970; A Faraway Drummer, 1973; Laughter in Darkness, 1974. Contributions to: Approximately 200 Short Stories to Magazines & Journals. Honours: Award for Literary Excellence, 1969; Friends of American Writer's Award, 1974. Address: 613 1/2 Charlotte Avenue, Rock Hill, SC 29730, USA.

BRITTAN Samuel, b. 29 Dec 1933, London, England. Journalist. Education: 1st Class Honours, Economics, Jesus College, Cambridge; Research Fellow, Nuffield College, 1973-74. Literary Appointments: Various posts, 1955-61, Principal Economic Commentator, 1966-, Assistant Editor, 1978-, Financial Times, London; Economics Editor, The Observer, 1961-64. Publications inlcude: Steering the Economy, 3rd Edition, 1971; Left of Right - The Bogus Dilemma, 1968; The Price of Economic Freedom: A Guide to Flexible Rates, 1970; Is There an Economic Consensus? 1973; Capitalism and the Permissive Society, 1973; Second Thoughts on Full Employments Policy, 1975; The Delusion of Incomes Policy (with Peter Lilley) 1977; The Economic Consequences of Democracy, 1977; How British is the British Sickness? 1978; How to End the 'Monetarist' Controversy, 1981; Role and Limits of Government: Essays in Political Economy, 1983; Jobs, Pay Unions and The Ownership of Capital, 1984; Two Cheers for Self-Interest, 1985. Honours: Senior Wincott Award for Financial Journalists, 1971; Elected Visiting Fellow, Nuffield College, 1974; George Orwell Prize for Political Journalism, 1981; Honorary DLtt, Heriot-Watt University, 1985; Member, Peacock Committee on the Finance of the BBC 1985-86; Legion D'Honneur, 1993. Address: The Finacial Times, Number One Southwark Bridge, London SE1 9HL, England.

BROCK Edwin, b. 1927, United Kingdon. Writer; Poet. Appointments: Editorial Assistant, Stonhill and Gillis, London, 1947-51; Poetry Editor, Ambit Magazine, London, 1960-; Advertising Writer, Mather and Crowther, London, 1959-63; Advertising Writer, J Walter Thompson, London, 1963-64; Advertising Writer, Masius Waynne-Williams, London, 1964; Creative Group Head, S H Benson, London, 1964-72; Freelance Writer, Ogilvy Benson and Mather, London, 1972-; Retired from Advertising, 1988. Publications: An Attempt at Exorcism, 1959; Night Duty on Eleven Beat, radio play, 1960; A Family Affair: Two Sonnet Sequences, 1960; The Little White God, novel, 1962, televised, 1964; With Love from Judas, 1963; Penguin Modern Poets 8 (with Geoffrey Hill and Stevie Smith), 1966; Fred's Primer: A Little Girl's Guide to the World Around Her, 1969; A Cold Day at the Zoo, 1970; Invisibility is the Art of Survival: Selected Poems, 1972; The Portraits and the Poses, 1973; Paroxisms, 1974; I Never Saw it Lit, 1974; The Blocked Heart, 1975; Song of Battery Hen, Selected Poems, 1959-75, 1977; Here, Now, Always, autobiography, 1977; The River and the Train, 1979; Five Ways to Kill a Man, (New & Selected Poems), 1990. Address: The Granary, Lower Tharston, Norfolk, NR15 2YN, England.

BROCK Rose,See: **HANSEN Joseph.**

BROCK William Ranulf, b. 16 May 1916, Farnham, Surrey, England. University Teacher (retired). m. Constance Helen Brown, 8 July 1950, 1 s, 1 d. Education: BA, 1937, MA, 1945, PhD, 1941, Tinity College, Cambridge. Appointments: Fellow of Selwyn College, Cambridge; Professor of Modern History, University of Glasgow, 1967-81. Publications: Lord Liverpool and Liberal Toyism, 1941; Character of American History, 1960; An American Crisis, 1963; Conflict and Transformation: USA 1944-77, 1973, USA 1739-1870 (Sources of History), 1975; Parties and Political Conscience (USA 1840-52), 1979; Evolution of American Democracy, 1979; Scotus Americanus (Scotland and American, 15th C), 1981; Investigation and Responsibility (State Agencies in USA), 1984; Welfare, Democracy and the New Deal, 1988. Memberships: Fellow of the British Academy; Fellow, Royal Historical Society; British Association of American Studies (Founder member, Committee 1954-64); Organization of American Historians. Address: 49 Brton Road, Cambridge, CB3 9LG, England.

BROCKHOFF Stefan. See: **PLANT Richard.**

BRODERICK Damien Francis, b. 22 Apr 1944. Writer. Education: BA, Monash University, Australia. 1966; PhD, Deakin University, 1990. Literary Appointments: Writing Fellowships, Literature Board, Australia Council, 1980, 1984, 1990; Writer-in-Reseidence, Deakin University, 1986. Publications: A Man Returned (short stories) 1965; The Dark Between the Stars (stories), 1991; Novels: The Dreaming Dragons, 1980; The Judas Mandala, 1982, revised, 1990; Transmitters, 1984; The Black Grail, 1986; Striped Holes, 1988; The Sea's Furthest Eng, 1993; Valencies (with Rory Barnes), 1983; The Zeitgeist Machine (edited), 1977; Strange Attractors (edited), 1985; Matilda At the Speed of Light (edited), 1988. Contributions to: Melbourne Age, Australian; Australian Book Reivew; New York Review, SF; Foundation; Age Monthly Review; Australian Science Fiction Review. Honours: Ditmar, Australian Science Fiction Achievements Award for The Dreaming Dragons, 1981; Transmitters, 1985, and Striped Holes, 1989; Runner-up John Campbell Memorial Award, 1980. Address: 23 Hutchinson St, Brunswick East, VIC 3057, Australia.

BRODEUR Hélène, b. 13 July 1923, Val Racine, Quebec, Canada. Civil Servant retired; Writer. m. Robert L Nantais, 26 August 1947, 3 sons, 2 daughters. Education: 1st Class Teacher's Certificate, Ottawa University Normal School, 1940; BA, Ottawa University, 1946; Diploma in Senior Management, Canadian Government College, 1974. Appointments: Writer-in-Residence, Ottawa University, 1991; Visiting Professor, French Creative Writing, Ottawa University. Publications: Chroniques du Nouvel-Ontario, Volume 1, La quête d'Alexandre, 1981, Volume 2, Entre l'aube et le jour, 1983, Volume 3, Les routes incertaines, 1986; Alexander, 1983; Rose-Delima, 1987; The Honourable Donald, 1990; Miniseries for Television: Les Ontariens, 1983. Contributions to: Extension Magazine, 1968; A serial, Murder in the Monastery. Honours: Champain Award, 1981; Le Droit Award, 1983; Prix du Nouvel-Ontario, 1984. Memberships: Ontario Authors Association; Union des écrivains; PEN International; Press Club. Address: 1506 160 George Street, Ottawa, K1N 9M2, Canada.

BRODEUR Paul, b. 16 May 1931, Boston, MA, USA. Writer. div, 1 s, 1 d. Education: BA, Harvard College, 1953. Appointments: Lecturer, Columbia University Graduate School of Journalism, 1969-80; Lecturer, Boston University School of Public Communication, 1978-79; Lecturer, University of CA at San Diego, 1989. Publications include: The Sick Fox, 1963; The Stunt Man, 1970; Expendable Americans, 1974; The Zapping of America, 1977; Downstream, 1972; Currents of Death, 1989; Outrageous Misconduct, 1985; Restitution, 1985; The Great Power-Line Cover-up, 1993. Contributions to: Staff Writer; New Yorker; Dozens of Articles. Honours: Sidney Hillman Prize, 1973; Columbia University National Magazine Award, 1973; Am Association for the Advancement of Science Award, 1976; Guggenheim Fellowship, 1976-77; Alicia Patterson Foundation Fellowship, 1978; Am Bar Association Certificate of Merit, 1983; Global 500 Honour Roll, 1989. Address: c/o The New Yorker, 20 West 43rd Street, New York, NY 10036, USA.

BRODKEY Harold, b. 1930, USA. Short Story Writer. Appointments: Associate Professor, Cornell University, Ithaca, 1977-78, 1979, 1981. Publications: First Love and Other Sorrows, 1958; Women and Angels, 1985; Stories in An Almost Classical Mode, 1988; The Abundant Dreamer, 1989; The Runaway Soul, 1991; Profane Friendship, 1994. Contributions to: New Yorker; Esquire; Vanity Fair; Paris Review; Partisan Review. Honours: Prix d Rome, 1959-60; National Magazine Award, 1974; Brandeis University Award, 1975; O Henry First Prize, 1975, 1976; Guggenheim Fellow, 1987; National Endowment Arts Grantee; Present Tense Magazine Award,

1989. Membership: PEN Am. Literary Agent: Anrew Wylie, Wylie, Aitken & Stone. Address: c/o Andrew Wylie, Wylie, Aitken & Stone, 250 W 57th Str, Suite 2106, New York, NY 10107, USA.

BRODSKY Josif Alexsandrovich, b. 24 May 1940, Leningrad, USSR. Russian-Jewish Poet. Education: Secondary School. Began writing poetry, 1955; Sentenced, hard labour, for "social parasitism", 1964; Sentence commuted, 1965; Refused visa to attend Poetry International, London, and Festival of Two Worlds, Spoleto, 1969; Involuntary exile in USA after brief stays in Vienna and London; Appeared at Poetry International, 1972. Poet-in-Residence, Univesity of Michigan, USA, 1972-73, 1974-, Queen's College, New York, 1973-74. Appointments: Andrew MellonProfessor of Literature, Raunt Holyoke College. Publications: A Christmas Ballad, 1962; Elegy for John Donne, 1963; Isaac & Abraham, 1963; New Stanzas to Augusta, 19634; Einem alten Architekten in Rom, 1964; Verses on the Death of T S Eliot, 1965; Verse & Poems, New York, 1965; French & German translations 1966; English traslation, John Donne & Other Poems, New York, 1967, Song Without Music, 1969; A Stop in the Desert: Verse & Poems, 1970; Selected Poems, (Penguin), 1973; A Part of Speech, 1980; Less Than One, 1981; To Urania, 1988; Watermark, 1992. Honours: Nobel Prize for Literature, 1987.

BROGGER Suzanne, b. 18 Nov 1944, Copenhagen, Denmark. Novelist. m. Keld Zeruneith, 1991. Education: University of Copenhagen. Appointments: Journalist in the Middle East and former Soviet Union. Publications: Deliver us from Love, 1973, 1977; Yes, 1984; The Pepper Whistle: Floating Fragments and Fixations, 1986; My World in a Nutshell, 1991; Play: After the Orgy, 1991; Verse: Tone, Epos, 1981; Edward and Elvira: A Ballad, 1988; Also: The Right and Wrong Ways of Love, 1975; Créme Fraiche, 1978; A Pig that's been Fighting Can't be Roasted, 1979; Brew: 1965-80; A Greenland-Essay and Three Other Poems, 1982; Nitrogen: 1980-1990. Honours include: Gabor Prize, 1987. Address: Knudstrup Gl Skole, 4270 Hong, Denmark.

BROME Vincent, Author. Publications: Anthology, 1936; Clement Attlee, 1947; H G Wells, 1951; Aneurin Bevan, 1953; The Ist Surrender, 1954; The Way Back, 1956; Six Studies in Quarrelling, 1958; Sometimes at Night, 1959; Frank Harris, 1959; Acquaintance with Grief, 1961; We Have Come a Long Way, 1962; The Problems of Progress, 1963; Love in our Time, 1964; Four Realist Novelists, 1964; The International Brigades, 1965; The World of Luke Jympson, 1966; Freud and His Early Circle, 1967; The Sugeon, 1967; Dairy of a Revolution, 1968; The Revolution, 1969; The Imaginary Crime, 1969; Confessions of a Writer, 1970; The Brain Operators, 1970; Private Prosecutions, 1971; Reverse Your Verdict, 1971; London Consequences, 1972; The Embassy, 1972; The Day of Destruction, 1975; The Happy Hostage, 1976; Jung - Man and Myth, 1978; Havelock Ellis - Philosopher of Sex, 1981; Ernest Jones: Freud's alter ego,1983; The Day of the Fifth Moon, 1984; J B Priestly, 1988. Contibutions to: The Times; Sunday Times; Observer; Manchester Guardian; New Statesman; New Society; Encounter; Spectator; Times Literary Supplement. Address: 45 Great Ormond Street, London, WC1. England.

BROMIGE David Mansfield, b. 22 Oct 1933, London, England. University Professor. m. Celia Belle, 3 Jan 1981, 1 s, 1 d. Education: BA (Hons), English, University of British Columbia, Canada, 1962; MA, English, 1964, ABD, 1969, University of California, Berkley, USA. Appointments: Editor, Critics' Page, Ubyssey, Vancouver, Canada, 1958-62; Editor, Raven, University of British Columbia, 1960-62; Poetry Editor, Northwest Review, 1962-64; Editor, R C Lion, Berkely, USA, 1966-68; Editor, Open Reading, Cotati, 1970-76; Contributing Editor, Avec, Penngrove, 1987-; Contributing Editor, Kaimana, Honolulu, 1989-; Director, Public Poetry Centre, Sonoma State University, 1970-92. Publications: Desire, 1988; Tight Corners, 1974; My Poetry, 1980; Men, Women & Vehicles, 1990; Tiny Courts, 1991; They Ate, 1992; The Harbor-Master of Hong Kong, 1993; Birds of the West, 1973; The Ends of The Earth, 1968; Threads, 1971; 3 Stories, 1973; Out of My Hands, 1974; Credences of Winter, 1975; Spells & Blessings, 1974; P.E.A.C.E. 1981; You See, 1986; Red Hats, 1986. Contributions include: Caterpillar; Sulfur; Boxcar; This. Honours: Poet Laureate, University of California (all campuses), 1965; Writers Fellowships, Canada Council, 1976-77; and National Endowment for the Arts, 1980-81; Western States Book Award for Poetry, 1988. Memberships: Rimers' Glub, Secretary, University of California, Berkeley, 1966-68; President, Sonoma State University, 1970-76, New Langton Arts SF, 1982-. Address: 461 High Street, Sebastopol, CA 95472, USA.

BRONISLAWSKI Jerzy-Stanislaw Kudas, b. 7 May 1930, Lodz, Poland. Writer. m. Zebina Sobczynska, 18 Dec 1968, 1 s, 1 d. Education: MSc, Faculty of Law, 1970, PhD, Institute of Political Sciences, 1972. Adam Mickiewicz University. Literary Appointments: Editor, Iskry, Warsaw, 1967-74; Mon, Warsaw, 1969-74; Maw, Warsaw, 1974-84; OPZZ, Warsaw, 1985-86; Pojezzierze, Olsztyn, 1987-; Gantaleba -Tbilisi/Georgian. Publications: Sabres and Usurers, 970; The Espionage, Intelligence, Paragraphs, 1974; Life Without Safeguard, 1975; The Master of Empty House, 1978; Without Scruples, 1979; Mazurian Saga, 1980; Duel, 1972; Mr Bailey's Mistake, 1970; The Anatomy of Treason, 1971; The Invisible in the Crowd, 1967, 1968, 1975; Before they Come at Daybreak, 1969, 1970, 1973; The Alienateds, 1972; The Falste Prophetes, 1981, 1984; The Furtively Observed Land, 1987; Polish Dialogue, 1990; 52 Reports, 1 adaptation for film and 3 for television. Contributions to: Kultura; Zeszyty Historyczne/Poznan. Honours: Rafal Urban Award, 1977; Zycie Literackie Award, 1978; Polityka Award, 1983; J Iwaszkiewicz Award, 1990; Polityka Award, 1992. memberships: ZLP; Polish Writers Association; ZAIKS, Societe des Auteurs. Address: ul Powsinska 70m, 48, 02-903 Warsaw, Poland.

BRONK William, b. 1918, USA. Poet; Essayist. Publications: Light & Dark, 1956; The World, The Worldless, 1964; The Empty Hands, 1969; That Tantalus, 1971; To Praise the Music, 1972; Utterances, 1972; Looking at It, 1973; The New World, 1974; A Partial Glossary, 1974; Silence and Metaphor, 1975; The Stance, 1975; My Father Photographed with Friends and Other Pictures, 1976; The Meantime, 1976; Finding Losses, 1976; Twelve Losses Found, 1976; That Beauty Still, 1978; The Force of Desire, 1979; Six Duplicities, 1980; The Brother in Elysium, 1980; Life Supports, 1981; Light in a Dark Sky, 1982; Vectors and Love and Its Apostrophes, 1985; Manifest and Furthermore, 1987; Death is The Place, 1989; Living Instead, 1991; Some Words, 1992; The Mild Day, 1993. Address: 57 Pearl Street, Hudson Falls, NY 12830, USA.

BROOKE, See: JACKMAN Stuart.

BROOKE Michael Zachary, b. 5 Nov 1921, Cambridge, England. Author; Consultant. m. Hilda Gilatt, 25 July 1953, 2 s, 1 d. Education: BA, History, 1st Class Honours, 1943, MA, University of Cambridge, 1945; MA, 1964, PhD, 969, University of Manchester. Publications: Frederic Le Play: Engineer and Social Scientist, 1970; The Strategy of Multinational Enterprise, co-author, 1970, 2nd edition 1978; The Multinational Company in Europe, co-author, 1972; A Bibliogrpahy of International Business, co-author, 1977; The International Firm, co-author, 1977; International Corporate Planning, co-author, 1979; International Financial Management Handbook, co-author, 2 volumes, 1983; Centralization and Autonomy, 1984; Selling Mangement Service Contracts in International Business, 1985; International Travel and Tourism Forecasts, co author, 1985; International Mangement, 1986; South Pennine Escort, 1987; Handbook of International Trade, co-author, 1988; Profits from Abroad,1988 (co-author); International Business Studies (co-author), 1991. Contributions to Numerous professional journals. Honours: Fellow, Academy of Authors, Chairman. Authors North, 1978-80; Independent Publishers' Guild (Chairman North West Region, 1989-91); The Circumnavigator's Club, 1991. Address: 21 barnfield, Urmston, Manchester, M31 1EW, England.

BROOKE Tal, b. USA. Writer; President of Research Think-tank. Education: BA, University of Virginia, 1969; MDiv magna cum laude, Princeton University, 1986. Appointments: President, Chairman, SCP Inc think-tank for research and critique of new religions and cultural trends; Editor, The SCP Journal; TV appearances include ABC Town Meeting, Seattle, Superstation 38, Chicago, Moody Broadcasting; Frequent speaker. Publications: Books: Lord of the Air, 1976, 1990; The Other Side of Death, 1979; Avatar of Night, 1979, 1984; Riders of the Cosmic Circuit, 1986; Harvest (with Chuck Smith), 1988; When the World Will Be As One, 1989. Honours: Spring Arbor National Bestseller List for When the World Will Be As One, 1989; Winner, 1st Place for Critical Review, National EPA Awards, 1991. Membership: Society of the Cincinnati. Address: SCP Inc, Box 4308, Berkeley, CA 94704, USA.

BROOKNER Anita, b. 16 July 1928, London, England. Art Historian. Publications: Jean-Baptiste Grevze, 1972; Genius of the Future, 1971; Jacquest-Louis David, 1980; A Start in Life, 1981; Providence, 1982; Look at Me, 1983; Hotel Du Lac, 1984; Family and Friends, 1985; A Misalliance, 1986; A Friend from England, 1987; Latecomers, 1989; Lewis Percy, 1989; A Closed Eye, 1990; Fraud,

1991. Contributions to: Times Literary Supplement; LRB; Burlington Magazine; Speactator. Honours: Booker Prize, 1984. Literary Agent, A M Heath, London, WC2. Address: 68 Elm park Gardens, London, SW10, England.

BROOKS Andree Nicole Aelion, b. 2 Feb 1937, London, England. Journalist; Author; Lecturer; Columnist. m. Ronald J Brooks, Div, 19 Aug 1959, 1 s, 1 d. Education: Queens College, London, 1952; Journalism Certificate, 1958. Appointments include: Adjunct Professor, Fairfield University, 1982-87; Associate Fellow, Yale University, 1989-; President, Founder, Womens Campaign School on the Campus of Yale University. Contributions to: Over 3000 Articles; Contributing Columnist, NY Times. Honours include: Best Non Fiction Book of Year, 1990; Journalism Awards. Literary Agent: Suzanne Gluck, ICM. Address: 15 Hitchcock Road, Westport, CT 06880, USA.

BROOKS George E, Jr, b. 1933, USA. Professor of History. Appointments: Member, Editorial Advisory Board, International Journal of African Historical Studies, 1968-; Member, Editorial Advisory Board, Liberian Studies Journal, 1968-77. Publications: New England Merchants in Africa: A Histroy Through Documents 1802-1865 (edited with N R Bennett), 1965; Yankee Traders, Old Coasters and Africa Middlemen: In the Nineteenth Century, 1970; The Kru Mariner in the Nineteenth Century: An Historical Compendium, 1972; Themes in African and World History, 1983; Landlords nd Strangers: Ecology, Society and Trade in Western Africa, 1993. Address: Department of History, Indiana Unviersity, Bloomington, IN 47405, USA.

BROOKS Jeremy, b. 1926, United Kingdon. Novelist; Playwright. Reviewer. Appointments: Feature Writer, Pictorial Press, London, 1950-52; Literary Agent, Christy & Moore, London, 1952-53; Fiction and General Reviewer, The Guardian, 1958-60; Play Reader, BBC Television, London, 1959-60; Drama Critic, New Statesman, 1961-62; Literary Manager, 1962-69; Play Adviser, 1969-; Royal Shakespeare Co, Stratford-upon-Avon and London; Reviewer, Sunday Times, 1962-. Publications: The Water Carnival, 1957; Jampot Smith, 1960; Henry's War, 1962; Smith, As Hero, 1965; The Magic Perambulator, 1965; I'll Fight You, 1966; A Value, 1976; Doing The Voices, 1985. Address: 12 Bartholomew Road, London, NW5, England.

BROOKS Mel, b. 1926, Brooklyn, USA. Writer; Director; Actor. m. (1) Florence Baum, 2 s, 1 d, (2) Anne Bancroft, 1964, 1 s. Publications include: TV Script Writer, Your Show of Shows, 1950-54; Caesar's Hour, 1954-57; Get Smart, 1965; Films, The Critic, 1963; Writer, Director, The Producers, 1968; Young Frankenstein, 1974; Writer, Director, Actor, The Twelve Chairs, 1970; Blazing Saddles, 1974; Writer, Director, Actor, Producer, High Anxiety, 1977; Actor Producer, To Be Or Not To Be, 1983. Address: c/o Twentieth Century Fox Film, Corp, Box 900, Beverly Hills, CA 90213, USA.

BROOKS-GUNN Jeanne, b. 9 Dec 1946. Psychologist. m. Robert W Gunn, 1970. Education: BA, Conn College,1969; Wd M, Harvard University, 1970; PhD, University PA, 1975. Appointments include: Associate Dirctor, Institute for the Study of Exceptional Children, Educational Testing Srvice, Princeton, NJ, 1977-82; Assistant Professor of Pediatrics, Columbia University, 1978-85; Senior Research Scientist, Director of Adolescent Study Program, St Lukes Rossevelt Hospital Centre, NYC, 1983-; Adjunct Professor, Univeristy of PA, 1985-91; Visiting Scholar, Russell Sage Foundation, 1989-90; Director, Centre for the Study of Parents & Their Children, Columbia University, 1991; Virginia & Leonard Marx Professor of Child Development, Teachers College, Columbia University; Professor of Pediatrics, College of Physoans and Surgeons, Columbia University, 1992-. Publications: He and She; How Children Develop Their Sex Role Identity; Social Cognition and the Acqusition of Self; Girls at Puberty; Women in Midlife; The Study of Maturational Timing Effects in Adolescence; Adolescent Mothers in Later Life; The Encyclopeida of Adolscence; The Emergence of Depression & Despressive Symptoms During Adolescence; Escape from Poverty; What Makes a Difference for Children. Contributions to: Numerous Articles, Son Child Develpment; Social Psychology. Memberships: Society for Research in Child Development; AAAS; President, Society for Research in Adolescence; National Academy of Science Committees on (Preventing Aids, Child Abuse, Neglect, and Poverty). Address: Province Line Road, Hopewell, NJ 08525, USA.

BROPHY Brigid, b. 12 June 1929, London, England. Writer. m. Sir Michael Levey q.v., 12 June 1954. 1 d. Education: St Hugh's Colldge, Oxford. Literary Appointments: Vice-Chairman, British Copyright Council, 1976-80. Publications include: Hackenfeller's Ape, 1953; The King of a Rainy Country, 1956; Black Ship to Hell, 1962; Flesh, 1962; The Finishing Touch, 1963; The Snow Ball, 1964; Mozart the Dramatist, 1964; Don't Never Forget, 1966; Fifty Works of English Literature We Could Do Without, with Michael Levey and Charles Osborne, 1967; Black and White: A Portrait of Aubrey Beardsley, 1968; In Transit, 1969; Prancing Novelist, 1973; The Adventures of God in his Search for the Black Girl and Other Fables, 1973; Pussy Owl, 1976; Breadsley and His World, 1976; Palace Without Chairs, 1978; The Prince and the Wild Geese, 1983; A Guide to Public Lending Right, 1983; Baroque-N-Roll, 1987; Reads, 1989. Plays include: The Burlgar, 1967; The Waste Disposal Unit, Radio, 1968. Contributions to: London Review of Books; Times Literary Supplement. Honours: Cheltenham Literary Festival, 1st Prize, First Novel, 1954; London Magazine Prize for Pose, 1962. Memberships: Executive Council, 1975-78, Writers Guild of Great Britain; London Magazine Prize for Prose, 1962. Literary Agent: Giles Gordon, Sheil and Associates. Address: Fir Close, 2 Westgage, Louth, Lincolnshire. LN11 9YH, England.

BROSSARD Chandler, (Daniel Harper), b. 1922, USA. Writer; Former Journalist/Editor. Appointments: Reporter, Washington Post, Washington, District of Columbia, 1940-42; Writer, The New Yorker, New York City, 1942-43; Senior Editor, Time Magazine, New York City, 1944; Executive Editor, American Mercury, New York City, 1950-51; Senior Editor, Look Magazine, New York City, 1956-67; Associate Professor, Old Westbury College, Oyster Bay, Long Island, New York, 1968-70. Publications: Who Walk in Darkness, 1952; The Bold Saboteurs, 1953; The Wrong Turn (as Daniel Harper), 1954; All Passion Spent, also as Eipsode with Erika, 1954; The Scene Before You: A New Approach to American Culture (editor), 1955; Harry the Magician, play, 1961; The Double View, 1961; Some Dreams Aren't Real, play, 1962; The Man with Ideas, play, 1962; The Insane World of Adolf Hitler, 1967; The Spanish Scene, 1968; Wake Up, We're Almost There, 1971; Did Christ Make Love, 1973; Raging Joys, Sublime Violation, 1981; As The Wolf Howls atMy Door, 1992. Address; 251 West 89th Street, New York, NY 10024, USA.

BROSSARD Nicole, b. 27 Nov 1943, Montreal, Canada. Poet; Novelist. Education: BA, 1965, MA, 1972, University of Montreal. Appointments include: Co-Founder, The Literary Magazine, La Barre du Jour, 1965-1975; Co-Founder, the Feminist Newspaper, Les Têtes de Pioche, 1976-1979; Co-Director of the Film Some American Feminists, 1976; Founder, L'Intégrale publishing house, 1982; Visiting Professor of French at Queen's University, Kingston, 1982-84. Publications: Verse: Aube à la saison, 1965; Mordre en sa chair, 1966; Suite logique, 1970; Le Centre blanc, 1970; Daydream Mechanics, 1973, 1980; La Partie pour le tout, 1975; D'Arcs de cycle la dérive, 1979; Amantes, 1980; Double Impression: Poems 1967-84; L'aviva, 1985; Mauve, 1985; Under Tongue, 1987; A Tout Regard, 1989; Installations, 1989; Typhon dru, 1990; Langues obscures, 1992; Stories: A Book, 1970, 1976; Sold-Out, 1973; French Kiss, 1974; These Our Mothers, 1977, 1983; Surfaces of Sense, 1980, 1989; Picture Theory, 1982, 1991; The Aerial Letter, 1985, 1988; Le Désert mauve, 1987; Mauve Desert, 1990; Plays and Radio Plays; Le Nuite Verte du parc labyrinthe. Honours include: Governor General 1974 and 1984; Athanase-David Prize, 1991. Address: 34 avenue Robert, Outrement, Quebec, Canada H3S 2P2.

BROUGHTON John Renata, b. 19 Mar 1947, Hastings, New Zealand. University Lecturer in Maori Health. Education: BSc, Massey University, 1971; Bachelor of Dental Surgery, Otago University, 1977. Publications: A Time Journal for Halley's Commet, children's book, 1985; Te Hokinga Mai (The Return Home) stage play, 1990; Te Hara (The Sin), stage play, 1990; Nga Puke (The Hills) stage play, 1990; Nga Mahi Ora, TV documentary on helath career for young Maori people, 1990; Michael James Manaia, stage play, 1991; Maraq, stage play, 1992. Contributions to: Everything you wanted to know about mouthguards, to Te Hau Ora Sports Journal. Honours: Dominion Sunday Times Bruce Mason Playwright Award, 1990. Memberships: PEN New Zealand; Chairman, Araiteura Marae Council Inc; Foundation Member, Maoir Health Workforce Development Group, Department of Health; Otago Branch, New Zealand Dental Association, Committee Member 1979-84. Literary Agent: Playmarket, PO Box 9767, Wellington New Zealand. Address: Te Maraeunui, 176 Queen Street, Dunedin, New Zealand.

BROWN Archibald Haworth, b. 1938, England. Professor. Publications include: Soviet Politics and Political Science, 1974; The Soviet Union since the Fall of Khrushchev, 1975, 1978; Political Culture and Political Change in Communist States, 1977, 1979; The Cambridge Encyclopedia of Russia and the Soviet Union, 1982; Political Culture and Communist Studies, 1984; Political Leadership in the Soviet Union, 1989; New Thinking in Soviet Politics, 1992; The Gorbachev Factor, 1995; The Cambridge Encyclopedia of Russia and the Former Soviet Union, 1994. Contributions to: Various Papers in Academic Journals and Symposia. Honour: Elected Fellow of British Academy, 1991. Address: St Antonys College, Oxford OX2 6JF, England.

BROWN Diana, b. 8 Aug 1928, Twickenham, England. Author; Librarian. m. Ralph Herman Brown, 31 Dec 1964, 2 d. Education: MLS, 1976, MA, Instructional Technology, 1977, San Jose State University. Publications: The Blue Dragon, 1988; The Hand of a Woman, 1984; The Sandalwood Fan, 1983; Come Be My Love, 1982; The Emerald Necklance, 1980; St Martin's Summer, 1981; A Debt of Honour, 1981. Contributions to: San Jose Mercury News; Fresno Bee; Good Housekeeping. Honours: Hand of a Woman, named outstanding title, American Library Association Booklist, 1984. Memberships: Authors Guild; Phi Kappa Phi. Agent: International Creative Management. Address; 1612 Knollwood Avenue, San Jose, CA 95125, USA.

BROWN George McKay, b. 187 Oct 1921, Stromness, Scotlnd. Writer. Education: Newbattle Abbey College, 1951-52; MA, Edinburgh University, 1956-60. Publications: fisherman with Ploughs, 1971; The Wreck of the Archangel, 1989; Greenvoe, 1972; Magnus, 1973; The Golden Bird, 1987; Portrait of Orkney, 1988; The Masked Fisherman, 1989; The Sea King's Daughter, 1991; The Loom of Light, 1987; Beside the Ocean of Time, 1994. Contributions to: New Statesman; Tablet. Honours: OBE, 1974; LLD, 1973; D Litt, 1985. Membership: FRSL. Address: 3 Mayburn Court, Stromness, Orkney KW16 3DH, Scotland.

BROWN Jamie, b. 1945, Canada. Author. Appointments: Consultant, National Film Board of Canada, 1974-77; Lecturer in Creative Writing, Concordia University, Montreal, 1979-85. Publications: The Lively Spirits of Provence, non-fiction, 1974; Stepping Stones, fiction, 1975; So Free We Seem, fiction, 1976; Shrewsbury, fiction, 1977; The War Is Over, screenplay, 1979; Superbike (for children) 1980; Toby McTeague, screenplay, 1986; Keeping Track (also co-produced), screenplay, 1986. Address: 174 Beacon Hill, Beaconsfield, Quebec, Canada, H9W 1T6.

BROWN John Russell, b. 15 Sept 1923, Bristol, England. Writer; Teacher; Theatre Director. m. Hilary Sue Baker, 5 Apr 1961, 1 s, 2 d. Education: BA, 1949, B Litt, 1951, Oxford University; PhD, University of Birmingham, 1960. Appointments: Member, Drama Panel, Arts Council of Great Britain, 1978-82; Chairman, 1980-82, Member, Arts Council. Publications: Shakespeare and His Comedies, 1957, 62; Shakespeare's Plays in Performance, 1966, 69; Effective Theatre, 1969; Shakespeare's Dramatic Style, 1970; Theatre Language, 1972; Free Shakespeare, 1974, 78; Discovering Shakespeare, 1981; Shakespeare and His Theatre, 1982; A Short Guide to Modern British Drama, 1983; Shakespeares, 1991. Contributions to: General Editor, Theatre Production Studies, 1981-83; Editor, Oxford Illustrated History of Theatre, 1995. Address: Court Lodge, Hooe, Battle, Sussex TN33 9HJ, England.

BROWN Marc (Tolon), b. 1946. Publications: D.W. Rides Again, 1993; Arthur's First Sleepover, 1993. Honour: Milner Award, 1991.

BROWN Rita Mae, b. 28 Nov 1944. Education: Broward Junior College, 1965; New York University, BA, 1968; School of the Visual Arts, 1968; Institute for Policy Studies, PhD, 1976. Appointments: Writer in Residence, Womens Writers Centre, Cazenovia College, 1977-78; Review Translations, Attic Greek & Latin, 1978-; President, American Artists Inc. Publications include: Rest In Pieces; Wish You Were Here; Starting From Scratch; A Different Kind of Writers Manual; Six of One; In Her Day; The Hand That Cradles the Rock; Songs to a Handsome Women; Hrotsvitha: Six Medieval Latin Plays; The Plain Brown Wrapper; Rubyfruit Jungle, 1983; Southern Discomfort, 1983; Venus Envy, 1993. Contributions to: Vogue Magazine; Various Anthologies inc: Sisterhood is Powerful; The New Women; Women: The New Voice; Book Reviews. Honours include: Nominated Emmy for Best Mini Series, The Long Hot Summer; Writers Guild of America Award for best Variety Show on Television; Outstanding Young Women of America. Address: c/o American Artists Inc, PO Box 4671, Charlottesville, VA 22905, USA.

BROWN Robert Douglas, b. 17 Aug 1919, Trealaw. Journalist; Publisher. m. Elsie Mary Warner, 17 Aug 1940, 1 s, 2 d. Education: BA,

Open University, 1986. Appointments: Political Staff, News Chronicle, 1951-60; Managing Director, Anglia Echo Newspapers, 1964-80. Publications: The Battle of Crichel Down; The Survival of the Printed Word; The Port of London; East Anglia-The War Years, 7 volumes. Memberships: Fellow PEN; Media Society. Address: Lower Green, Stoke By Clare, Sudbury, Suffolk, England.

BROWN Rosellen, b. 12 May 1939, PA, USA. m. Marvin Hoffman, 16 Mar 1963, 2 d. Education: BA, Barnard College; MA, Brandeis University. Publications: Before and After, 1992; Civil Wars, 1984; Tender Mercies, 1978; Cora Fry, Cora Frys Pillow Book, 1977, 1994. Honours: Guggenheim Fellowship, 1976; Am Academy Institute of Arts & Letters, 1988; Kafka Prize, 1985. Memberships: PEN; Authors Guild; National Writers Union. Literary Agent: Virginia Barber. Address: 1401 Brandard, Houston, TX 77006, USA.

BROWN Stewart, b. 14 Mar 1951, Lymington, England. Lecturer. m. Priscilla M Brant, 1977, 1 s, 1 d. Education: BA, Falmouth School of Art; MA, University of Sussex; PhD, University of Wales. Publications: Lugards Bridge; The Art of Derek Walcott; Zinder; Caribbean Poetry Now; Voiceprint; Carribbean New wave; Heinemann Book of Caribbean Poetry; African Writers; A Reader's Guide. Honours: Eric Gregory Award; South West Arts Literature Award; Elected Member Welsh Academy. Address: Centre of West African Studies, University of Birmingham, Edgbaston, Birmingham B15 2T4, England.

BROWN Terence, b. 1944, Republic of Ireland. Associate Professor. Appointments: Lecturer, 1968-81, Fellow, 1976-, Associate Professor, 1981-, Trinity College; Personal Chair, Anglo Irish Literature, 1993. Publications: Time Was Away; The World of Louis MacNeice, 1974; Louis MacNeice: Sceptical Vision, 1975; Northern Voices, 1975; The Irish Short Story, 1979; Ireland: A Social and Cultural History, 1922-1979, 1981, 1985; Ireland's Literature: Selected Essays, 1988; Tradition and Influence in Anglo Irish Poetry, 1989. Membership: Royal Irish Academy. Literary Agent: Jonathan Williams. Address: Dept of English, Trinity College, Dublin 2, Republic of Ireland.

BROWNE Michael Joseph Dennis, b. 28 May 1940, Walton-on-Thames, England. Teacher. m. Lisa Furlong McLean, 18 July 1981, 1 s, 2 d. Education: BA, Hull University, 1962, MA, University of Iowa, 1967. Publications: The Wife of Winter, London, 1970, New York, 1970; Sun Exercises, 1976; The Sun Fetcher, 1978; Smoke from the Fires, 1985; Over a dozen libretti, music by David Lord, Stephen Paulus, John Foley SJ. Contributor to: Tri-quarterly, The Iowa Review; Virginia Quarterly Review; American Poetry Review; Prairie Schooner. Honours: NEA 1977; Bush Fellowship, 1983. Memberships: American PEN; Poetry Society of America. Address: 2111 E 22nd Street, Minneapolis, MN 55404, USA.

BROWNING Robert, b. 15 Jan 1914, Glasgow, Scotland. Emeritus Professor. Education: MA, University of Glasgow, 1931-35; MA, Balliol College. Appointments: Editorial Board, Past & Present, 1960-78; Reviews Editor, Journal of Hellenic Studies, 1964-74. Publications include: Studies in Byzantine History, Literature and Education, 1977; History, Language and Literacy in the Byzantine World, 1989; The Emperor Julian, 1976; The Byzantine Empire, 1980, 1992; The Greek World; Classical, Byzantine and Modern, 1985; Dated Greek Manuscripts from Cyprus to the Year 1570, 1993. Contributions to: Learned Journals in many Countries. Honours: Fellow, British Academy, 1978; Corresponding Member, Academy of Athens, 1982; Hon DLitt, Birmingham, 1980; Hon Doctor, University of Athens, 1988; Gold Medal, The Alexander S Onassis Center, 199; Gold Medal of City of Athens, 1994. Membership: Society for the Promotion of Hellenic Studies, 1974-77. Address: 17 Belsize Park Gardens, London NW3 4JG, England.

BROWNING Vivenne, (Elaine Vivenne Browning Baly), b. 1 Dec 1922, Sydney, Australia. Writer; Lecturer; Broadcaster. m. W F Baly, 21 Aug 1954, 1 s, 3 d. Education: Mary Datchelor, London, 1942; Hazelhurst College, Melbourne. Appointments: S Sgt Intelligence Corps ATS, 1942-46; Civil Resettlement of Repatriated Prisioners of War, 1945-46; Met Police, CID, London, 1946-50; Board of Directors, International Browning Society, Baylor University. Publications: My Browning Family Album; The Uncommon Medium; BBC Radio; From Stores Detective to Private Eye; Living in Addis Ababa; TV Wednesday Magazine Addis Ababa; Lord Haw Haw. Contributions to: Magazines; The Real Identity of Pauline; From Russia with Love and Plain Speaking. Memberships: Browning Society; New Barnet Literary & Debating Society; Boston Browning Society; Arthur Machen Society;

Intelligence Corps Comrades Association; Metropolitan Police Association; Friend of the Royal Academy of Arts; Sadler's Wells Royal Ballet; Australian Film Society; Keats Shelley Association; Royal Society of Literature; Society of Authors; PEN; Browning Society; New Barnet Lit & Debating Society; Metropolitan Women Police Association. Address: c/o SKOOB Pub, 25 Lowman Road, North London, England.

BROWNJOHN Alan Charles, b. 1931, England. Poet. Appointments: Lecturer, Battersea College of Education, 1965-79; Member Arts Council Literature Panel, 1968-72; Poetry Critic, New Statesman, 1968-76; Encounter, 1978-82; Sunday Times, 1990-. Publications include: (Poems) Travellers Alone, 1954; The Railings, 1961; The Lions' Mouths, 1967; Sandgrains on a Tray, 1969; Penguin Modern Poets 14, 1969; Brownjohn's Beasts, 1970; Warrior's Career, 1972; A Song of Good Life, 1975; The Old Flea-Pit, 1987; To Clear the River (novel), 1964; First I Say This: A Selection of Poems for Reading Aloud, 1969; (criticism) Philip Larkin, 1975; (educational books) Meet and Write, 1985-87; The Way You Tell Them (novel), 1990; The Observation Car (poems), 1990; The Gregory Anthology (ed), 1990; In The Cruel Arcade (poems), 1994. Memberships: Writers' Guild of Great Britain; Poetry Society, London. Literary Agent: Rosica Colin Ltd, London. Address: 2 Belsize Park, London NW3, England.

BROWNJOHN John Nevil Maxwell, b. England. Literary Translator; Screenwriter. Education: MA, Lincoln College, Oxford. Publications: Night of the Generals, 1962; Memories of Teilhard de Chardin, 1964; Klemperer Recollections, 1964; Brothers in Arms, 1965; Goya, 1965; Rodin, 1967; The Interpreter, 1967; Alexander the Great, 1968; The Poisoned Stream, 1969; The Human Animal, 1971; Hero in the Tower, 1972; Strength Through Joy, 1973; Madam Kitty, 1973; A Time for Truth, 1974; The Boat, 1974; A Direct Flight to Allah, 1975; The Manipulation Game, 1976; The Hittites, 1977; Willy Brandt Memoirs, 1978; Canaris, 1979; Life with the Enemy, 1979; A German Love Story, 1980; Richard Wagner, 1983; The Middle Kingdom, 1983; Solo Run, 1984; Momo, 1985; The Last Spring in Paris, 1985; Invisible Walls, 1986; Mirror in the Mirror, 1986; The Battle of Wagram, 1987; Assassin, 1987; Daddy, 1989; The Marquis of Bolibar, 1989; Eunuchs for Heaven, 1990; Little Apple, 1990; Jaguar, 1990; Siberian Transfer, 1992 The Swedish Cavalier, 1992; Infanta, 1992; The Survivor, 1994; Acts, 1994; Love Letters From Cell 92, 1994; Turlupin, 1995; Nostradamus, 1995. Screen Credits; Tess (with Roman Polanski), 1979; The Boat, 1981; Pirates, 1986; The Name of the Rose, 1986; The Bear, 1989; Bitter Moon (with Roman Polanski), 1992. Honours: Schlegel Tieck Special Award, 1979; US Pen Prize, 1981; Schlegel Tieck Prize, 1993. Memberships: Translators Association; Society of Authors. Address: The Vine House, Nether Compton, Sherborne, Dorset, DT9 4QA, England.

BROWNLOW Kevin, b. 1938, England. Author; Film Director; Former Film Editor. Publications: The Parades Gone By, 1968; How It Happened Here, 1968; Adventures with D W Griffith, 1973; Hollywood: The Pioneers, 1979; The War, The West, and the Wilderness, 1979; Napoleon: Abel Gance's Classic Film, 1983; Behind the Mask of Innocence, 1990. Address: c/o Photoplay, 21 Princess Road, London, NW1 8JR, England.

BROXON Mildred Downey, (Sigfriour Skaldaspillir), b. 1944, USA. Freelance Writer; Former Psychiatric Nurse. Publications: A Witch's Welcome (as Sifgriour Skaldaspillir), 1979; The Demon of Scattery (with Poul Anderson), 1979; Too Lond A Sacrifice, 1981; Too Long a Sacrifice, 1984. Memberships: Science Fiction Writers of America, Vice-President 1976-78. Literary Agent: Sharon Jarvis and Co, USA. Address: c/o Sharon Jarvis & Co, 260 Wilard Avenue, Staten Island, NY 10314, USA.

BRUCE George, b. 10 Mar 1909, Fraserburgh, Aberdeenshire, ScotlAnd. Writer; Lecturer; Broadcaster. m. Elizabeth Duncan, 25 July 1935, 1 s, 1 d. Education: MA, Aberdeen University, 1932. Appointments: BBC Producer, 1956-70; First Fellow, Glasgow University, 1971-73; Prescott College, 1974; Lectures at US Colleges, Washington & Lee University, 1975; Visiting Professor, College of Wooster, 1976-77; Extra Mural Lectures, Glasgow University, Edinburgh University, 1970-80. Publications include: Sea Talk, 1944; Landscapes and Figures, 1968; Collected Poems, 1940-70; Perspectives: Poems 1970-1986; Anne Redpath A Monograph of the Scottish Painter, 1975; Some practical Good, The Cockburn Association, 1875-1975; Festival in the North, 1947-75, 1975; Perspectives, 1970-86, 1986; The Land Out There, 1991. Contributions to: A book of Scottish Verse; The Oxford Book of Scottish Verse;

Modern Scottish Poetry; the Penguin Book of Scottish Verse; Scottish Love Poems. Honours: Scottish Arts Council Award, 1967; Honorary Doctor of Letters, 1977; OBE, 1984. Memberships: Scottish Poetry Library; Cockburn Association; Saltire Society. Address: 25 Warriston crescent, Edinburgh, EH3 5LB, Scotland.

BRUCE Lennart, b. 21 Feb 1919, Stockholm, Sweden. Writer. m. Sonja Wiegandt, 22 July 1960, 1 s, 1 d. Education: University Studies. Publications: Agenda (on the works of Wilhelm Ekelund), 1976; Sannsaga, 1982; The Broker, 1983; The Second Light (on the works of Wilhelm Ekelund), 1986; Utan synbar anledning, 1988; Forskingringer, 1989; En Nasares Gang, 1993. Contrinutions to: Over 100 poems, articles to US and Swedish literary magazines. Honours: Swedish Acadmey Award, 1977, 1988. Memberships: PEN American Centre, New York; Swedish Writers Union, Stockholm. Address: 31 Los Cerros Pl, Walnut Creek, CA 94598, USA.

BRUCE Robert Vance, b. 19 Dec 1923, MA, USA. Historian. Education: BS, University of NH, 1945; MA, 1947, PhD, 1953, Boston University. Literary Appointments: Professor, Boston University, 1955-84; Emeritus, 1984-. Publications: Bell: Alexander Graham Bell and the Conquest of Solitude, 1973; The Launching of Modern American Science, 1846-1876, 1987; Lincoln and the Tools of War, 1956; 1877, Year of Violence, 1959. Contributions to: Am Heritage; National Geographic. Honour: Pulitzer Prize, 1988. Address: 28 Evans Road, Madbury, NH 03820, USA.

BRUCHAC Joseph, b. 1942, USA. Author; Poet; Journalist. Appointments: Editor, Greenfield Review, 1970-; Director, Greenfield Review Literary Centre, 1981-. Publications include: Indian Mountain & Other Poems, 1971; Words from the House of the Dead, 1972; Flow, 1975; The Road to Black Mountain, 1976; The Earth is a Drum, 1977; Entering Onondaga, 1978; There Are No Trees in the Prison, 1978; The Good Message of Handsome Lake, 1979; Ancestry, 1980; How to Start and Sustain a Literary Magazine, 1980; The Light from Another Country, 1984; Breaking Silence, 1984; Near the Mountains, 1987; Turtle Meat and Other Stories, 1992; Flying with the Eagle, Racing the Great Bear and Other Native American Stories, 1993; Raven Tells Stories, 1991. Membership: National Association for the Preservation and Perpetuation of Storytelling. Literary Agent: Barbara Kouts, PO Box 558, Bellport, NY 11713, USA. Address: PO Box 308, c/o The Greenfield Review, Greenfield Centre, NY 12833, USA.

BRUIN John. See: **BRUTUS Dennis Vincent.**

BRULOTTE Gaetan, b. 8 Apr 1945, Levis, Canada. Writer. Education: BA, 1966, 1969, MA, 1972, Laval University; Diploma Ecole Normal Superior, Laval University, 1971; PhD, Sorbonne Pris, 1978. Appointments: Professor, Trois Rivieres College, 1970-82; University de Quebec, 1980-81, 1989-90; University of New Mexico, 1981-84, 1993; University of CA, 1982; University of South Florida, 1984-; Director, Book Reviews, Le Nouvelliste, 1980-82. Publications: L'Emprise, 1979; Le Surveillant, 1982; Le Client, 1983; Aspects du Texte Erotique, 1978; L'Imaginaire Et L'Ecriture, 1972; De Dechet in Le Colloque De Tanger, 1976; Ce Qui Nous Tient, 1988; Plages, 1987; Double Exposure, 1988; The Secret Voice, 1900. Contributions to include: Poetique; L'Arc; Etudes Litteraires; The Comparatist; Revue Des Sciences Humaines. Honours: Priz Robert Cliche, 1979; Prix Adrienne Choquette, 1981; Prix France Quebec, 1983; Grand Prize of CBC, 1983; Literary Prize, Trois Rivieres, 1989; Goncourt Prize, 1989; 20 Grants. Memberships: WLA; UNEQ; Mauricies Writers Society; ADELF; International Council on Francophone Studies; Modern Language Association; International Comparative Literature Association; AATF; SARDEC; ACFAS. Address: 82 Rue Des Casernes, Trois Rivieres, Quebec, Canada G9A 1X2.

BRUMARU Emil, b. 1 Jan 1939, Buhmutea, Romania. Physician. m. Tamara Pintile, 4 Feb 1980, 1 s. Education: Faculty of General Medicine. Appointments: Physician, Dolhasch, 1963-75; Unemployed, 1975-83; Corrector, Half Norm, Literary Discussions Review, 1983-90; Vice-Chief Editor, 1990-. Publications: Lyrics; Detective Arthur; Hospitable Julien; Naive Songs; The Wardrobe in Love; Farewell to Robinson Crusoe; The Ruin of a Samovar. Contributions to: Literary Reviews including, Echonox; Steaua; Vatra. Hounours: Eminescu Festival Prize; The Wrtiers Union Prize for Poetry. Memberships: Writers Union of Romania, Bucharest Assocation; PEN; Civil Alliance. Address: Str Cuza Voda No 6, Apt 14, Iassy 6600, Romania.

BRUNNER John Kilian Houston, (John Loxmith, Trevor Staines, Keith Woodcott), b. 24 Sept 1934, Englnd. Author; Company Director. m. (2) LiYi Tan, 1991. Publications include: Age of Miracles, 1973; A Hastily Thrown Together Bit of Zork, 1974; The Book of John Brunner, 1976; Foreign Constellations, 1979; The Infinitive of Go, 1980; The Crucible of Time, 1983; The Complete Traveller in Black, 1986; The Shift Key, 1987; Children of the Thunder, 1989; The Best of John Brunner, 1988; A Maze of Stars, 1991; Muddle Earth, 1993. Contributions to: Numerous Periodicals. Honours include: Hugo Award, 1968; British Fantasy Award; British Science Fiction Award; Bronze Porgie Award; Prix Apollo; Cometa d'Argento. Memberships: European Science Fiction Society; Science Fiction Writers of Am; Society of Authors; British Science Fiction Association. Literary Agent: Jane C Judd, 18 Belitha Vills, London N1 1PD; Am/Asia, William Reiss at John Hawkins & Associates, 71 West 23 Street, NY 10010, USA. Address: c/o Judd Agency.

BRUNSE Niels Henning, b. 24 Aug 1949, Silkeborg Denmark. Translator; Writer. m. Galina Ivashkina, 18 Mar 1977, div. Education: University of Copenhagen & Moscow. Appointments: Co Editor, Literary & Cultural Magazine, Hug, 1974-76; Co Editor, Political Bi Weekly, Politisk Revy, 1978-82; Reviews of Books, Theatre and Film, Daily Newspaper, Information, 1982-94; Politiken, 1994-; Editor, Danish Writers Association Journal, 1983-85. Publications: Everyday Moscow; History Never Stops; But Where Does It Actually Go?; Gommonplaces; The Richest Person in the World; Ramoth-Bezer, 1994; 130 Translations inc 10 Plays by Shakespeare; Complete Short Stories by Heinrich v Kleist; The Aesthetics of Resistance by Peter Weiss; Petersburg by Andrei Bely. Contributions to: Numerous. Honours: Honorary Award of Danish Translators Association; Life Long Grant Danish State Art Foundation; Columbia University Thornton Niven Wilder Award. Memberships: Danish Writers Association; Danish PEN; Chairman, Danish Dramatists Association. Address: Aalandsgade 26, DK 2300 Copenhagen, Denmark.

BRUNSKILL Ronald William, b. 1929, Unived Kingdon. Hon. Fellow in Architecture. Publications: Illustratred Handbook of Vernacular Architecture, 1970, 3rd Edition, 1987; Vernacular Architecture of the Lake Countries, 1974; English Brickwork (with Alec Clifton-Taylor), 1978; Traditional Buildings of Britain, 1981, 2nd edition, 1992; Houses, 1982; Traditional Farm Buildings of Britain, 1982, 2nd edition, 1987; Timber Buildings of Britain, 1985; Brick Buildings in Britain, 1990. Honours: OBE, 1990. Memberships: FSA, 1975, Address: School of Architecture, University of Mancchester, Manchester, M13 9PL, England.

BRUSEWITZ Gunnar (Kurt), b. 7 Oct 1924, Stockholm, Sweden. Author; Artist. m. Ingrid Andersson, 21 Oct 1946, 2 d. Education: Royal Academy of Art. Publications include: Bjornjagare och Fjarilsmalare, 1968; Skissbok, 1970; Nature in Gambia, 1971; Skog, 1974; Strandspegling, 1979; Wings & Seasons, 1980; Sveriges Natur, 1984. Contributions to: Stockholms Tidningen; Svenska Dagbladet; Various Other Swedish Magazines & Publications. Honour include: Stockholm City Presentation Prize, 1970; Dag Hammarskjold Medal, 1975; Die Goldne Blume Von Rheydf Dusseldorf, 1989; Honorary DPhil, 1982. Memberships include: PEN; Swedish Section, World Wildlife Fund; Royal Society of Science. Literary Agent: Wahlstrom & Windstrand Forlag, Stockholm, Address: Lisinge, 762 93 Rimbo, Sweden.

BRUTON Eric (Eric Moore), b. 1915, England. Author; Company Director. Appointments: Managing Director, NAG Press Limited, Colchester, 1963-; Managing Director, Diamond Boutique Limited, 1965-80; Chairman, Things & Ideas Limited, 1970-78. Publications: True Book about Clocks, 1957; Death in Ten Point Bold, 1957; Die Darling Die, 1959; Violent Brothers, 1960; True Book about Diamonds, 1961; The Hold Out, 1961; King Diamond, 1961; The Devil's Pawn, 1962; Automation, 1962; Dictionary of Clocks and Watches, 1962; The Laughing Policeman, 1963; The Longcase Clock, 1964, 2nd edition, 1978; The Finsbury Mob, 1964; The Smithfield Slayer, 1964; The Wicked Saint, 1965; The Fire Bug, 1967; Clocks and Watches 1400-1900, 1967; Clocks and Watches, 1968; Diamonds, 1970, 2nd edition, 1977; Antique Clocks and Clock Collecting, 1974; The History of Clocks, 1978; The Wetherby Collection of Clocks, 1980; Legendary Gems, 1984. Memberships: Council Member, British Horological Institute, 1955-62; Committee Member, Crime Writers Association, 1959-62; Council Member, Gemmological Association of England, 1972-91, President, 1994; President, National Association of Goldsmiths, 1983-95. Address: Pond House, Great Bentley, Colchester CO7 8QG, England.

BRUTUS Dennis Vincent, b. 28 Nov 1924, Salisbury, Southern Rohdesia (now Harare, Zimbabwe). Professor of English and African Literature. m. May Jaggers, 14 May 1950, 4 s, 4 d. Education: BA, Fort Hare University, South Africa, 1944-47; Part LLB, University of Witwatersrand, South Africa, 1962-63. Appointments include: Editorial Boards and Advisory Boards; Africa Today (Denver), Black Lines (Pittsburgh), National Writers Union, American Poetry Centre. Publications include: Sirens, Knuckles, Boots, 1963; Letters to Martha, 1968; Poems from Algeirs, 1979; Thoughts Abroad (John Bruin), 1970; A Simple Lust, 1972; Strains, 1975; China Poems, 1975; Stubborn Hope, 1978, 1983; Salutes and Censures, 1982; Airs & Tributes, 1989; Stubborn Hope: Selected Poems of South Africa and the Wider World, 1991; Still the Sirens, forthcoming. Contributions to: Various anthologies, collections and journals. Honours include: Mbari Prize, Poetry in Africa, 1963; First Recipient, Outstanding Teacher Award, Institute for Policy Studies, 1987; Fellow, African Academy of Arts, 1989; Honorary Degrees, Worcester State College and University of Massachusetts, Amherst, Northeastern University, Boston, USA. Memberships: 1st President, African Literature Association; Vice-President, Union of Writers of the African People; Modern Language Association, President South African Non-Racial Olympic Committee (SAN, ROC). Address: 3812 Bates Street, Bates Hll Apts No 311, Pittsburgh, PA 15213, USA.

BRYANS Robin. See: HARBINSON-BRYANS Robert.

BRYANT Dorothy M(ae), b. 1930, USA. Writer; Publisher. Appointments: English Teacher, San Francisco Public Schools, CA, 1953-56; English Teacher, Lick Wilmerding High School, 1956-61; Instructor, San Francisco State University, 1962; Instructor, Golden Gate College, 1963; Instructor, Contra College, 1964-76; Publisher, Ata Books, 1978-90. Publications: The Comforter, 1971; The Kin of Ata Are Waiting for You, 1976; Ella Princes Journal, 1972; Miss Giardino, 1978; Writing a Novel, 1979; The Garden of Eros, 1979; Prisoners, 1980; Killing Wonder, 1981; A Day in San Francisco, 1983; Myths to Lie Ny, 1984; Confessions of Madame Psyche, 1986; The Test, 1991; Anita, Anita, 1993; Dear Master, 1991; Tea With Mrs Hardy, 1992. Honours: Am Book Award, 1987; Bay Area Drama Critics Award. Address: 1928 Stuart Str, Berkeley, CA 94703, USA.

BRYANT Joseph Allen, b. 1919, USA. Professor. Appointments: Professor, Chairman, University of South Carolina, 1961-68; Professor, Chairman, Syracuse University, 1968-71; Professor, University of KY, 1973-90. Publications: Hippolytas View, 1961; Shakespeare: Romeo and Juliet, 1964; Eudora Welty, 1968; The Compassionate Satirist, 1972; Understanding Randall Jarrell, 1986; Shakespeare and the Uses of Comedy, 1986. Address: 713 Old Dobbin Road, Lexingham, KY 40502, USA.

BRYUCKSTEIN Ludovic, b. 27 July 1920, Mukavevo, Czechoslovakia. Author; Playwright; Journalist. m. Chalotte Czig, 29 Oct 1947 (deceased 1983), 1 s. Education: Graduate in Commerical Studies, 1938; Literature and Literary Criticism, Bucharest, Romania, 1952. Appointments: Lecturer, Theatre and Cinemat Arts Institute. Editor, Literary Monthly Magazine, The Romanina Life, 1952-53. Publications: Night Shift, play, 1949; The Greenwald Family, play, 1953; Generation of the Wildemess, play, 1956; Sleepless Night, 1957; Panopticum 1969; The Confession, 1973; Yaavov Magif's Destiny 1975; The Tinfoil Hallo, 1979; As in Heaven, so on Earth, 1981; The Return of Christopher Columbus, play, 1957; An Unfinished Trail, play, 1962; The Unexpected Guest, play, 1959; Three Histories; 1977; May be Happiness, 1985. Contributions to: Gaseta Literara: Luceafaril Tribuna; Korunk: Ufunk; Numerous other magazines and journals. Honours: Revipient of numerous literary awards and citations in Romania; Brickman Prize for Literature, Israel, 1976; Sion Prize for Literature, Israel, 1977; Creation Prize, World Sionist Organisations and Jewish Agency, Israel, 1986. Memberships: Writers Union of Romania, Secretary, Dramaturgical Department; Chamber of Writers Union of Israel; President, Union of Israeli Writers in Romanian Language; Yiddish Writers Association in Israel; President, Committee for Culture and Arts in Maramuresh, Romania; Member, Chairman, Various cultural literary and Art Associations. Literary Agent: Panopticum, Tel-Aviv, Israel. Address: PO Box 37151, Tel-Aviv 61370, Israel.

BRZEZINSKI Zbigniew, b. 1928, Poland. Appointment: Director, National Security Council Under President Carter. Publications: The Soviet Bloc: Unity & Conflict, 1960; Between Two Ages, 1970; Power & Principle, 1983; Game Plan, 1986; The Grand Failure, 1989; Out of

Control, 1993. Address: 1800 K Street NW, Suite 400, Washington, DC 20006, USA.

BUCH JENSEN Poul, b. 4 Jan 1937, Copenhagen, Denmark. Mechanical Engineer. m. Anna-Lise, 28 July 1962, 1 son, 1 daughter. Education: Bachelor, Engineering; Bachelor, Economics and Marketing. Publications: ISO 9000. A Guide and Commentary, 1991; ISO 9000. Internal Quality Audits, 1992; Service, 1994; Environmental Management and Environmental Certifications, 1994. Contributions to: Numerous magazines and journals. Memberships: Danish Authors Society; American Society for Quality Control; Rotary Club. Address: Alfarvejen 30 - Osted, DK-4000 Roskilde, Denmark.

BUCHANAN Colin Ogilvie, b. 9 Aug 1934, Croydon, Surrey, England. Church of England Clerk in Holy Orders. m. Diana Stephenie Gregory, 14 June 1963, 2 d. Education: BA, 1959, MA, 1962, Lincoln College, Oxford; Tyndale Hall, Bristol, 1959-61; DD, 1993. Appointments: Honorary Assistant Bishop, Diocese of Rochester, 1989-; Vicar of St Marks Gillingham, 1991-. Publications include: Editor, Modern Anglican Liturgies, 1958-68, 1968; Further Anglican Liturgies, 1968-75, 1975; Latest Anglican Liturgies, 1976-84, 1985; Modern Anglican Ordination Rites, 1987; The Bishop in Liturgy, 1988; Open to Others, 1992; Joint Author, Growing into Union, 1970; Anglican Worship Today, 1980; Reforming Infant Batism, 1990; Infant Baptism and the Gospel, 1993; Disestablishment and the Church of England, 1994; Editor, News of Liturgy Monthly, 1975-. Memberships: House of Bishops of General Synod of the Church of England. Address: St Marks Vicarage, 173 Canterbury Street, Gillingham, Kent ME7 5UA, England.

BUCHWALD Art, b. 20 Oct 1924, New York, USA. Journalist; Author; Playwright. m. Ann McGarry, 1952, 1 s, 2 d. Education: University of Southern California, Los Angeles, Appointments: Columnist, Herald Tribune, Paris, 1948-62; Syndicated Columnist to 550 newspapers throughout the world, 1952-. Publications: Paris After Dark; Art Buchwald's Paris; I Chose Caviar; More Caviar; A Gift from the Boys; Don't Forget to Write; How Much is That in Dollars? 1961; Is It Safe to Drink the Water? 1962; I Chose Capitol Pubnishment, 1963; And Then I Told the President, 1965; Son of the Great Society, 1967; Have I Ever Lied to You? 1968; Oh, To Be A Swinger, 1970; Getting High in Government Circles, 1971; I Never Danced at the White House, 1973; I Am Not A Crook, 1974; Washington in Leaking, 1976; Down the Seine & Up the Potomac, 1977; The Buchwald Stops Here, 1978; Laid Back in Washington with Art Buchwald, 1981; While Reagen Slept, 1983; You CAN Fool All of the People All of the Time, 1985; I Think I Don't Remember, 1987; Who's Rose Garden is it Anyway, 1989; Lighten Up, George, 1991; Leaving Home, 1994. Honours: Prix de la Bonne Humeru, Pulitzer Prize, outstanding commentary, 1982. Membership: American Academy of Arts and Letters. Address: 2000 Pennsylvania Avenue, NW, Washington DC 20006, USA.

BUCK Lilli Lee, b. 25 Feb 1950, Butler, Pennsylvania, USA. Teacher; Professional Astrologer. Education: BA, Anthropology, 1972, MEd, Special Education, 1984, College of William and Mary. Publications: Poems in following books: A Vagabond's Sketchbook, 1980; A Lyrical Fiesta, 1985; Poetic Symphony, 1987; Golden Voices, Past and Present, 1989; Voices on the Wind, 1989; Special Poets' Series, 1990; The Poet's Domain, Vol III, 1991, Vol V, 1992. Contribution to: Fate magazine, 1984. Honours: 3rd Place, World of Poetry Contest, 1983; Excellence in Poetry Award, Fine Arts Press, 1985; Editors Choice Award, National Library of Poetry, 1994. Memberships: Poetry Society of Virginia; Association for Research and Enlightenment; Kappa Delta Pi. Address: 7000 Reedy Creek Rd, Bristol, VA 24202, USA.

BUCKERIDGE Anthony Malcolm, b. 20 June 1912, Writer. m (1) Sylvia Brown, 1936, (2) Eileen Norah Selby, 25 Feb 1972, 2 s, 1 d. Education: University College, London, 1932-35. Publications: The Jennings Series of Childrens Book Comprising 24 Titles, 1950-91; The Rex Milligan Series, 4 Titles, 1953-56; A Funny Thing Happened, 1953; Musicals: It Happened in Hamelin, 1980; Jennings A Bounding, 1979; The Cardboard Conspiracy, 1985. Memberships: The Society of Authors; Writers Guild of Great Britain; British Actors Equity. Literary Agent: L R Associates, Aylesbury. Address: East Crink, Barcombe Mills, Lewes, Sussex, BN8 5BL.

BUCKLEY William, b. 1925. Appointment: Editor at Large, National Review. Publications include: Over 30 Books inc. Happy Days Were Here Again; A Very Private Plot; In Search of Anto Semitism; God & Man at Yale; The Jewelers Eye; On The Firing Line: The Public Life. Contributions to: Numerous Periodicals inc. New York Times; National Review. Address: c/o National Review, 150 East 35th Street, New York, NY 10016, USA.

BUCZACKI Stefan Tadeusz, b. 16 Oct 1945, Derby, England. Writer; Broadcaster. m. Beverley Ann Charman, 8 Aug 1970, 2 s. Education: BSc, Southampton University; DPhil, Oxford University. Publications include: Collins Guide to Pests, Diseases and Disorders of Garden Plants, 1981; Collins Gem Guide to Mushrooms & Toadstools, 1982; Zoosporic Plant Pathogens, 1983; Beat Garden Pests & Diseases, 1985; Gardeners Questions Answered, 1985; Garden Warfare, 1988; Understanding Your Garden, 1990; The Essential Gardener, 1991; The Plant Care Manual, 1992; Collins Guide to Mushrooms & Toadstools of Britain & Europe, 1993; The Gardeners Handbook, 1993; Stefan Buczackis Best Gardening Series, 1994. Contributions to: Times; Financial Times; Country; Sunday Mirror; Guardian; The Gardener; Geographical Magazine; Countryman; House & Garden; Numerous Other Journals & Magazines. Memberships: Royal Photographic Society; Fellowships: Institute of Biology; Institute of Horticulture; Linnean Society. Literary Agent: Barbra Levy. Address: c/o Barbara Levy, Literary Agent, 21 Kelly Street, London NW1 8PG, England.

BUDDEE Paul Edgar, b. 12 Mar 1913, Western Australia. Author; Retired School Principal; Lecturer. m. Elizabeth Vere Bremner, 12 Jan 1944, 1 s, 1 d. Publications: Fate of the Artful Dodger, 1984; The Escape of the Fenians, 1972; The Escape of John O'Reilly, 1973; Stand to And Other War Poems, 1943; The Osca and Olga Trilogy, 1943-47; The Unwilling Adventurers, 1967, 1989; The Mystery of Moma Island, 1969; The Air Patrol Series, 1972; The Ann Rankin Series, 1972; The Peter Devlin Series, 1972; The Call of the Sky, 1978; Three Volumns, History of Rotary Club of Thornlue; The First Seven Years. Contributions to: State and Australian Major Papers, Magazines & Journals. Honours: Grants from Australia Commonwealth Literary Board, 1977, 78, 84; Wetstern Australia Citizen of the Year, 1979; OAM, 1989. Memberships: Western Australia Fellowship of Writers; Probus Club of Rossmoyne; Rotary Club of Thornlie. Address: 2 Butson Road, Leeming WA 6149, Australia.

BUDRY Algis, b. 1931, Lithuania. Science Fiction Writer; Publisher; Editor. Appointments: Publisher, Editor, Tomorrow Speculative Fiction Magazine; Assistant Editor, Gnome Press; Assistant Editor, Galaxy Magazine; Staff, Royal Publications; Editor in Chief, Regency Books; Editorial Director, Playboy Press; Operations Manager, Woodall Publishers; President, Unifont Co. Publications: False Night, 1953; Some Will Not Die, 1961; Man of Earth, 1955; Who?, 1958; The Falling Torch, 1959; The Unexpected Dimension, 1960; Rogue Moon, 1960; The Furious Future, 1964; The Iron Thorn, 1968; Michaelmas, 1977; Blood and Burning, 1978; Falling Torch (var), 1990; Hard Landing, 1993. Address: 824 Seward Street, Evanston, IL 60202, USA.

BUERO VALLEJO Antonio, b. 29 Sept 1916, Guadalajara, Spain, Playwright. m. Victoria Rodriguez, 5 Mar 1959, 2 s. Education: ba, 1932, Fine Arts Studies, 1934-36. Publications include: In The Burning Darkness, 1950; Concert at St Ovide, 1962; The Basement Window, 1967; The Sleep of Reason, 1970; The Foundation, 1974; Lazarus in the Labyrinth, 1966; Near Music, 1989; Story of a Stairway, 1949; The Words in the Sand, 1949; Almost a Fairy Tale, 1953; Irene or the Treasure, 1954; A Dreamer for a People, 1958; The Double Case History of Dr Valmy, 1968; Alligator, 1981; Secret Dialogue, 1984. Contributions to: Various Journals. Honours include: Miguel de Cervantes Prize, 1986; Pablo Iglesias Prize, 1986; National Theatre Prize; Mayte Prize; El Espectador y la Critica Prize; Fundacion March Prize; Lope de Vega Prize; Medalla de Oro al Merito en las Bellas Artes, 1993. Memberships include: Real Academia Espanola; Hispanic Society of Am; Ateneo de Madrid; MLA; Am Association of Teachers of Spnish and Portuguese; modern Language Association of Am. Literary Agent: Sociedad General de Autores de España. Address: General Diaz Porlier 36, Madrid 28001, Spain.

BUFALINO Gesualdo, b. 15 Nov 1920, Comiso, Italy. Novelist. m. Giovanna Legion, 1982. Education: Universities of Palermo and Catania, 1939-46. Appointments: Professor at the Instituto Magistrale di Vittoria, 1949-75. Publications include: The Plague Sower, 1981, 1988; Museo d'ombre, 1982; Blind Argus, or, The Fables of the Memory, 1989; Night's Lies, 1988, 1990; Quid pro quo, 1991; Calende greche, 1992; Trittico (play), 1989; Verse: L'amaro miele, 1982, and Rondo della felicità, 1991; Editor and Translator from French. Honours include: Strega Prize, 1988. Address: Via Architetto Mancini 26, 97013 Comiso, Italy.

BUISSERET David Joseph, b. 18 Dec 1934, Isle of Wight, England. History Teacher; Researcher. m. Patricia Connolly, 9 Sept 1961, 3 s, 2 d. Education: BA, 1958, PhD, 1961, Corpus Christi College. Appointments: University of West Indies, 1964-80; The Newberry Library, 1980-. Publications: Sully; Port Royal, Jamaica; Historic Architecture of the Caribbean; Henry IV; Historic Illinois from the Air. Honours: Premiere Medaille, Institute of France; Centennial Medal; J B Jackson Prize. Address: The Newberry Library, 60 West Walton Str, Chicago, IL 60610, USA.

BULLA Clyde Robert, b. 1914, USA. Writer, Novels, Short Stories, Children's Fiction, Translations. Appointments: Farmer until 1943; Linotype Operator and Columnist, Tri-County News, King City, Missouri, 1943-49. Publications include: A Tree is a Plant, 1960; Three-Dollar Mule, 1960; The Sugar Pear Tree, 1961; Benito, 1961; What Makes A Shadow? 1962; The Ring and The Fire: Stories from Wagner's Niebelung Operas, 1962; Viking Adventure, 1963; Indian Hill, 1963; St Valentine's Day, 1965; More Stories of Favorite Operas, 1965; Lincoln's Birthday, 1967; White Bird, 1966; Washington's Bithday, 1967; Flowepot Gardens, 1967; Stories of Gilbert and Sullivan Operas, 1968; The Ghost of Windy Hill, 19678; Mika's Apple Tree: A Story of Finland, 1968; The Moon Singer, 1969; New Boy in Dublin: A Story of Ireland, 1969; Jonah and the Great Fish, 1970; Joseph the Dreamer, 1971; Pocahontas and the Strangers, 1971; (trans), Noah and the Rainbow by Max Bollinger, 1972; Open the Door and See All the People, 1972; Dexter, 1973; The Wish at the Top, 1974; Shoeshine Girl, 1975; Marco Moonlight, 1976; The Beast of Lor, 1977; (with Michael Syson), Conquistal, 1978; Last Look, 1979; The Stubborn Old Woman, 1980; My Friend the Monster, 1980; Daniel's Duck, 1980; A Lion to Guard Us, 1981; Almost a Hero, 1981; Dandelion Hill, 1982; Poor Boy, Rich Boy, 1982; Charlie's House, 1983; The Carboard Crown, 1984; A Grain of Wheat, 1985; The Chalk Box Kid, 1987. Address: 1230 La Flores Drive, Los Angeles, CA 90041, USA.

BULLINS Ed, b. 2 July 1935, PA, USA. Writer; Teacher; Theater Person. Education: Hon DLit, Columbia College, 1975; BA, Antioch University, 1989; MFA, San Francisco University, 1994. Literary Appointments include: Lecturer, Black Studies Dept, San Francisco State University, 1993. Publications: Five Plays by Ed Bullins, 1969; The Duplex, 1971; The Hungered One, 1971; Four Dynamite Plays, 1972; The Theme is Blackness, 1973; The Reluctant Rapist, 1973. Honour: NY Drama Critic Circle Award, 1975. Memberships: Dramatist Guild; MLA. Literary Agent: Helen Merrill Ltd, 435 W 23rd Str, NY 10011, USA.

BULLOCK Kenneth K(en), b. 26 July 1929, Liverpool, England. Canadian Citizen, 1951-66, Australian Citizen, 1966-. Writing Consultant. 2 s, 2 d. Education: Dip Comm, 1961, Royal Canadian Naval College, HMCS, Victoria. Appointments include: British Merchant Navy, 1946-49; Service aircrew, RCN, RAN, 1950-1972; Prime Ministers Deptartment, Office of Information, 1980-83; as Writer, Editor, Teacher, Journalist Counsellor/External Tutor, James Cook University, 1984-95. Publications: Emergency, 1979; Family Guide to Beach and Water Safety, 1980; Silly Billy Learns a Lesson, 1981; Papua New Guinea, 1981; Water Proofing Your Child, 1982; Pelandok, 1986; Port Pirie the Friendly City, 1988; Chopstik, 1993. Contributions to: Papua New Guinea; Post Courier; National Times; Australia; Adelaide Advertiser; Sunshine Coast Daily. Honours: CD, Canadian Military Service Decoration, 1963; Citizen of the Year, 1984; Port Pirie, 1984-88. Memberships: Fellowship of Australian Writers; Australian Society of Authors. Address: 63 Buderim Garden Villge, Mooloolaba Road, Buderim, Queensland 4556, Australia.

BULLOCK Michael, b. 19 Apr 1918, London, England. Professor of Creative Writing; Poet. Education: Stowe School; Hornsey College of Art. Appointments include: Professor of Creative Writing, University of British Columbia at Vancouver, Canada, 1969-83 (now Emeritus). Publications: Transmutations, 1938; Sunday is a Day of Incest, 1961; World Without Beginning, Amen, 1963; A Savage Darkness, 1969; Black Wings, White Dead, 1978; Lines in the Dark Wood, 1981; Prisoner of the Rain: Poems in Prose, 1983; Brambled Heart, 1985; Dark Water, 1987; Poems on Green Paper, 1988; Vancouver Moods, 1989; The Secret Garden, 1990; Labyrinths, 1990; Plays: Not to Hong Kong, 1972; The Island Abode of Bliss, 1972; The Coats, 1975; Biography: A Game (adaption of Max Frisch), 1979; Andorra (adaptation of Max Frisch), 1989; Fiction: Sixteen Stories As They

Happened, 1969; Green Beginning Black Ending, 1971; Randolph Cranstone and the pursuing River, 1975; The Burning Chapel, 1991; The Invulnerable Ovoid Aura and Other Stories, 1993; Voices of the River, 1994; Randolph Cranstone and the Glass Thimble, 1977; Randolph Cranstone and the Veil of Maya, 1986; The Story of Noire, 1987; Randolph Cranstone Takes the Inward Path, 1988; The Walled Garden, 1990; Poetry: Quadriga for Judy, 1982; Avatars of the Moon, 1990; The Sorcerer with Deadly Nightshade Eyes, 1993; The Inflowing River, 1993; Moons and Mirrors, 1994; Dark Roses, 1994; Bilingual Poetry: Zwei Stimmen in meinem Mund/Two Voices in My Mouth (German tr Hedwig Rohde), 1967; Stone and Shadow/Shi Yu Ying (Chinese tr Jin Shen-Hua), 1993. Honours: Schlegel-Tieck German Translation Prize, 1966; Commonwealth Fellowship, 1968; Okanagan Short Fiction Award, 1986. Address: 103-3626 West 26th Avenue, Vancouver, British Columbia, Canada V6S 1S4.

BULMER Henry Kenneth, (Alan Burt Akers, Ken Blake, Kenneth Bulmer, Ernest Corley, Arthur Frazier, Kenneth Johns, Philip Kent, Bruno Krauss, Neil Langholm, Karl Maras, Charles R Pike, Andrew Quiller, Richard Silver, Tully Zetford), b. 14 Jan 1921, London, England. Author. m. Pamela Buckmaster, 7 Mar 1953, 1 s, 2 d. Appointments: Editor, New Writings in SF, 1972-79. Publications: Dray Prescot Saga, Fox Series, 1972-77; Sea Wolf Series, 1978-82; City Under The Sea, 1957; Strike Force Falklands, 1984-86; The Ulcer Culture, 1969; The Odan Trilogy, 1977-80; Roller Coaster World, 1972. Contributions to: New Worlds; Authentic; Nebula; Mag of Fantasy and SF; Infinity; Science Fantasy; Universe. Literary Agent: Carnell Literary Agency. Address: 5/20 Frant Road, Tunbridge Wells, Kent TN2 5SN, England.

BULMER Kenneth. See: **BULMER Henry Kenneth.**

BULPIN Thomas Victor, b. 1918, South Africa. Writer; Publisher. Appointments: Writer and Publisher, Books of South Africa (Pty) Ltd and TV Bulpin Ltd, Cape Town, 1946-. Publications: Lost Trails on the Low Veld, 1950; Shaka's Country, 1952; To the Shores of Natal, 1953; The Golden Republic, 1953; The Ivory Trail, 1954; Storm Over the Transvaal, 1955; Lost Trails of the Transvaal, 1956; Islands in a Forgotten Sea, 1958; Trail of the Copper King, 1959; The White Whirlwind, 1961; The Hunter is Death, 1962; To the Banks of the Zambexi, 1965; Natal and the Zulu Country, 1966; Low Veld Trails, 1968; The Great Trek, 1969; Discovering South Africa, 1970; Treasury of Travel Series, 1973-74; Southern Africa Land of Beauty and Splendour, 1976; Illustrated Guide to Southern Africa, 1978; Scenic Wonders of Southern Africa, 1985. Address: PO Box 1516, Cape Town, South Africa.

BUMGARER Mary, See: **SUBRAMAN Belinda.**

BUNCH Charlotte, (Charlotte Bunch-Weeks), b. 13 Oct 1944, West Jefferson, North Carolina, USA. Director, Centre for Women's Global Leadership, Rutgers University; Writer. m. James L Weeks, 25 Mar 1967 (div 1971). Education: Attended University of California, Berkely, 1965; BA, Magnum cun laude, Duke University, 1966. Appointments: University Christain Movement, New York, Co-Founder and National President, 1966-67; Consultant to Experimental Education groups of fifty college campuses, 1967-68; Case Western Reserve University, Cleveland, Ohio, Member of Campus Ministry Staff, 1968-69; Institute for Policy Studies, Washington DC, Visiting Fellow, 1969-70, Resident Fellow, 1971-75, Tenured Fellow, 1975-77; Public Resource Centre, Washington DC, Founder and Co-Director, 1977-79; Interfem Consultants, New York City, Counder and Director and Consultant to various organizations, 1979-87; Douglass College, Rutgers University, New Brunswick, New Jersey, Laurie New Jersey Chair in Women's Studies, 1987-89. Numerous guest lecturing appointments. Publicatios: Under name Charlotte Bunch-Weeks: The New Women, 1971; Passionate Politics: Feminist Theory in Action-Essays, 1968-86, 987; Editor of many books. Contributions to: Numerous volumes, author or co-author of pamphlets on feminist topics; Numerous Femist, Gay and Christian periodicals; Co-founder and editor of The Furies, 1972-73 and Quest: A Feminist Quarterly, 1974-81; Editor of speical editions of Motive and Off Our Backs. Honours: Community Service awards from Lambda Legal Defense Fund 1982 and National Lesbian and Gay Health Foundation, 1986. Memberships: Numerous profesional memberships. Address: Centre for Women's Global Leadership, PO Box 270, Douglass College, Rutgers University, New Brunsiwck, NJ 08903, USA.

BUNGAY Stephen Francis, b. 2 Sept 1954, Kent, England. Management Consultant. m. Atalanta Armstrong Beaumont, 31 Oct 1987, 2 s. Education: MA, Oxford, 1972-76; D Phil, 1976-81. Publications: Beauty & Truth; Essays in Published Collections inc The Hegelian Project, 1994. Address: The Boston Consulting Group Limited, Devonshire Place, London W1X 5FH England.

BUNSHICHI Niyauchi, b. 1 Dec 1908, Kagoshima, Japan. Professor Emeritus. m. 1 Apr 1935, 3 sons, 2 daughters. Education: Department of English Language & Literature, Hiroshima Normal College, 1930; Litterarum Doctor. Appointments: Professor of English Language & Literature, 1955-74; Professor Emeritus, Kagoshima University, 1974-. Publications: Shakespeare's First Step Abroad, 1972; Immortal Longings: The Structure of Shakespeare's Antony and Cleopatra, 1978; Shakespeare's Structural Poetics, 1979; In and Out of Old Sites, 1985. Contributions to: Tragicality of Dialogue, 1950; Whether an Artificer or Not: a Plea for Shakespeare, 1951; Shakespeare's Drifting Soliloquy, 1953; Desire Named Utopia, 1984. Honours: Decorated The Third Order of Merit with the Sacred Treasure, 1993. Memberships: International John Steinbeck Society; Renaissance Institute of Japan; Japan Society of Shakespeare. Address: 201 Cosmo Kamifukuoka, 57-910 Fujma Kawagoe Shi, Saitama Ken 356, Japan.

BURACK Sylvia Kamerman, b. 16 Dec 1916, Hartford, CT, USA. Editor; Publisher. m. Abraham S Burack, 28 Nov 1940, dec, 3 d. Education: BA, Smith College, 1938. Appointments: Editor, Publisher, The Writer Magazine, The Writer, The Drama Magazine for Young People and Plays, 1978-. Publications include: Editor: Little Plays for Little Players, 1952; Blue Ribbon Plays for Girls, 1955; Blue Ribbon Plays for Graduation, 1957; Fifty Plays for Junior Actors, 1966; Fifty Plays for Holidays, 1969; On Stage for Christmas, 1978; Holidays Plays Round the Year, 1983; Plays of Black Americans, 1987, 1988; Patriotic and Historical Plays for Young People, 1987; Plays from Favorite Folk Tales, 1987; The Big Book of Comedies, 1989; The Bog Book of Holiday Plays, 1990; The Big Book of Folktale Plays, 1991; Plays of Great Achievers, 1992; The Big Book of Dramatized Classics, 1993; The Big Book of Large-Cast Plays, 1995. Adult Books inc. Writing the Short Short Story, 1942; Book Reviewing, 1978; Writing and Selling Fillers, Light Verse, and Short Humor, 1982; Writing & Selling Romance Novels, 1983; Writing Mystery and Crime Fiction, 1985; How to Write and Sell Mystery Fiction, 1990; The Writers Handbook, 1989-95 (an annually). Honours: Honorary Degree, Doctor of Letters, 1985; distinguished Service Award, 1973; Brookline High School Library Named in Honour; Freedoms Foundation Award, 1988; Awarded Smith College Medal, 1995. Memberships: National Book Critics Circle; Friends of the Libraries of Boston University; Phi Beta Kappa; PEN Am. Address: 72 Penniman Road, Brookline, MA 02146, USA.

BURCH Claire R, b. 19 Feb 1925, New York, USA. Writer; Filmmaker. m. Bradley Burch, 24 Apr 1944, 1 s (dec), 3 d. Education: BA, Washington Square College, 1947. Publications: Stranger in the Family, 1972; You Be the Mother Follies; Solid Gold Illusion, 9 Books of images; Goodbye My Coney Island; Baby; Notes of a Survivor; Shredded Millions; Winter Bargains; Homeless In The Nineties - collection of poetry, paintings and photographs, 1964-93; 7 Plays, The Day a Thousand People Went to Jail, non-fiction. Contributions to: Life Magazine; McCalls; Redbook; Saturday Review; Good Housekeeping; Arts and Sciences; New York Times Book Review; Literary Journals and Quarterlies. Hounrous: 2 Carnegie Awards,1978, 1979; Grants from California Arts Council, 1991, 1992; First Prize Historical documentary James Balwin, East Bay Media Centre, People's Choice Alfonia and Entering Oakland, PCTV, Prize Oracle Rising, East Bay Media Centre Festival, 1992. Memberships: Poetry Society of America; Writers' Guild. Literary Agent: Regent Press, Oakland, California. Address: Art and Education Media Inc, 2747 Regent Street, Berkeley, CA 94705, USA.

BURCHFIELD Robert William, b. 27 Jan 1923, Wanganui, New Zealand. Lexicographer; Grammarian. m. (1) Ethel May Yates, 2 July 1949, 1 s, 2 d, div, (2) Elizabeth Austen Knight, 5 Nov, 1976. Education: MA, Victoria University of Wellington, 1948; BA, 1951, MA, 1955, Magdalen College, Oxford. Appointments: Lecturer, Christ Church, Oxford, 1953-57; Lecturer, Tutorial to Fellow, Emeritus Fellow, St Peter's College, 1955-79; Editor, A Supplement to the Oxford English Dictionary, 1957-86. Publications: A Supplement to the Oxford English Dictionary, 1972, 76, 82, 86; The Spoken Word, 1981; The English Language, 1985; The New Zealand Pocket Oxford Dictionary,

1986; Studies in Lexicography, 1987; Unlocking the English Language, 1989; Points of View, 1992; The Cambridge History of the English Language, Vol 4, 1994. Contributions to: The Sunday Times; Encounter; Transactions Philological Society. Honours: CBE, 1975; Hon DLitt, 1978, 83; Freedom of City of Wanganui, 1986; Shakespeare Prize, 1994. Memberships: Early English Text Society; Am Academy of Arts & Science. Address: 14 The Green, Sutton Courtenay, Oxon OX14 4AE, England.

BURFIELD Eva. See: **EBBETT Frances Eva.**

BURGIN Richard Weston, b. 30 June 1947, Boston, USA. Teacher; Writer; Editor. m. Linda K Harris, 7 Sept 1991, 1 step daughter. Education: BA, Brandeis University, 1968; MA, Columbia University, 1969; M.Phil, Columbia University, 1981. Appointments: New York Arts Journal, Founding Member, 1976-83; Critic at Large, Globe Magazine, 1973-74; Boulevard, Founding Editor, 1986-. Publications: Conversations with Jorge Luis Borges; Conversations with Isaac Bashevis Singer; Man Without Memory; Private Fame; The Man With Missing Parts. Contributions to: Partisan Review; Triquarterly; Shenandoah; Southwest Review; Transatlantic Review; The New York Times Book Review; Chicago Review; Hudson Review; Mississippi Review. Honours: Pushcart Prize. Memberships: National Book Critics Circle; YMHA. Literary Agent: Kim Witherspoon. Address: PO Box 30386, Philadelphia, PA 19103, USA.

BURGOYNE Jack. See: **OWEN Warwick.**

BURKE James, b. 22 Dec 1936, Londonderry, Northern Ireland. Writer; Broadcaster. m. Madeline Hamilton, 27 Jan 1967. Education: MA, English Literature, Jesus College, Oxford, 1961. Publications: Tomorrow's World I, 1971; Tomorrow's World II, 1972; Connections, UK, 1978, USA, 1979; Foreign, 1980; The Day The Universe Changed, UK, 1985, USA, 1986; Foreign, 1987; Editor, Weidenfeld an Nicholason Encylcopaedia of World Art, 1964; Editor, Zanichelli Italian-English Dictionary, 1965. Contirunions to: Various publications including: Daily Mail; Listener; Vogue; Vanity Fair; Punch; TV Times; Radio Times. Honours: Gold Medal, 1971, Silver Medal, 1972, Royal Televison Society; Edgar Dale Award for screenwriting, USA, 1986. Memberships: Royal Institution; Savile Club. Literary Agent: Jonathan Clowes Ltd. Address: c/o Jonathan Clowes Ltd, 22 Prince Albert Road, London, NW1 7ST, England.

BURKE James Lee, b. 5 Dec 1936, Houston, TX, USA. Novelist. m. 22 Jan 1960, 1 s, 3 d. Education: BA, MA, University of MI. Publications: A Stained White Radiance: A Morning for Flamingos; Black Cherry Blues; Heaven's Prisoners; The Neon Rain; The Lost Get Back Boogie; The Convict; Two for Texas; Lay Down My Sword and Shield; To the Bright and Shining Sun; Half of Paradise; In The Electric Mist with Confederate Ded, 1993; Dixie City, 1994. Contributions to: Atlantic Monthly; Southern Review; Antioch Review; Best Am Short Stories; New England Review; Epoch; Kenyon Review; Cimmaron Review; New Stories From the South. Honours: Breadloaf Fellowship; Nationl Endowment to the Arts Award; Pulitizer Prize; Guggenheim Fellowship; Edgar Allen Poe Award. Memberships: Amnesty International. Literary Agent: Philip G Spitzer. Address: 11100 Grant Creek, Missoula, MT 59802, USA.

BURKE John Frederick, (Jonthan Burke, Harriet Esmond, Jonathan George, Joanna Jones, Robert Miall, Sara Morris, Martin Sands), b. 8 Mar 1922, Rye, England. Author m. (1) Joan Morris, 13 Sept 1940, 5 d. (2) Jean Williams, 29 June 1963, 2 s. Appointments: Production Manager, Museum Press; Editorial Manager, Paul Hamlyn Books for Pleasure Group: European Story Editor, 20th Century Fox Productions. Publications: Swift Summer, 1949; An Illustrated History of England, 1974; Musical Landscapes, 1983; Illustrated Dictionary of Music, 1988; A Travellers History of Scotland, 1990; DR Caspian Trilogy, 1976, 77, 78; Author of Over 120 Titles including Film And TV Novelisations. Contributions to: The Bookseller; Country Life; Denmark. Honours: Atlantic Award in Literature, 1948-49. Memberships: Society of Authors; The Danish Club. Literary Agent: David Higham Associates. Address: 5 Castle Gardens, Kirkcudbright, Dumfries & Galloway, DG6 4JE, Scotland.

BURKE Jonathan. See: **BURKE John Frederick.**

BURKHOLZ Herbert Laurence, b. 9 Dec 1932, NY, USA. Author. m. Susan Blaine, 1 Nov 1961, 2 s. Education: BA, NY University, 1951. Appointments: Writer in Residence, College of

William & Mary, 1975. Publications: Sister Bear, 1969; Spy, 1969; The Spanish Soldier, 1973; Mulligan's Seed, 1975; The Death Freak, 1978; The Sleeping Spy, 1983; The Snow Gods, 1985; The Sensitives, 1987; Strange Bedfellows, 1988; Brain Damage, 1992; Writer in Residence, 1992; The FDA Follies, 1994. Contributions to: NY Times; Town & Country; Playboy; Penthouse; Longevity. Honours: Distinguished Scholar, 1976. Literary Agent: Georges Borchardt Inc, NY, USA. Address: c/o Georges Borchardt Inc, 136 East 57th Street, New York, NY 10022, USA.

BURLEY Kathleen M, b. 17Jan 1942, Minot, North Dakota, USA. Training; Finance. m. Henry R Burley, 27 Dec 1966. Education: BSc, Music, Education, Minot State University, 1963; MA, Arizona State University, 1966. MBA, University of Phoenix, 1984. Publications include: Looking Back, Book One, 1987; Who You Are, Where You Are, 1988; Poetry in the following collections: Scratchings to a Flea, 1987; Chasing Rainbows, Volume II, 1987; Hearts of Fire, Volume III, 1986; Best New Poets of 1986, 1986; Words of Prasie, Volume II, 1986; American Poetry Anthology, 1985, 1986; Ashes to Ashes, Volume IV, 1985. Honours: One of Best New Poets of 1986, American Poetry Association. Memberships: American Society of Training and Development; Los Angeles Chapter, National Society of Presentation & Instruction; National Association for Female Executives. Address: BCD Enterprises, 1251 W Sepulveda Blvd, No 170, Torrance, CA 90502, USA.

BURLEY William John, b. 1 Aug 1914, Falmouth, Cornwall, England. Retired Teacher. m. Muriel Wolsey, 10 Apr 1938, 2 s. Education: Balliol College, Oxford University, 1950-53. Publications include: Wycliffe and the Beales, 1983; Wycliffe and the Four Jacks, 1985; Wycliffe and the Quiet Virgin, 1986; Wycliffe and the Windsor Blue, 1987; Wycliffe and the Tangled Web, 1988; Wycliffe and the Cycle of Death, 1989; A Taste of Power, 1966; Three Toed Pussy, 1968; Death in Willow Pattern, 1969; Guilt Edged, 1971; Death in a Salubrious place, 1973; Wycliffe and the Schoolgirls, 1976; The Schoolmaster, 1977; Charles and elizabeth, 1979; Wycliffe and a Dead Flautist, 1991; Wycliffe and the Last Rites, 1992; Wycliffe and the Dunes Mystery, 1993. Memberships: Authors Copyright and Lending Society; Crime Writers Association; South West Writers. Literary Agent: Victor Gollancz. Address: St Patricks, Holywell, Newquay, Cornwall, TR8 5PT, England.

BURN Gordon, b. 16 Jan 1948, Newcastle upon Tyne, England. Writer. Education: BA, University of London, 1969. Publications: Somebodys Husband, Somebodys Son: The Story of Peter Sutcliffe, 1984; Pocket Money, 1986; Alma Cogan: A Novel, 1991. Contributions to: Numerous inc The Sunday Times Magazine; The Telegraph; The Face; The Independent. Literary Agent: Gillon Aitken & Stone, 29 Fernshaw Road, London, SW10 0TG. Address: c/o Gillon Aitken & Stone, 29 Fernshaw Road, London, SW10 0TG, England.

BURN Michael Clive, b. 11 Dec 1912, London, England. Writer. m. Mary Walter, 27 Mar 1947. Education: Winchester, 1926-31; Open Scholar, New College, Oxford, 1931; POW, Colditz, 1944. Appointments: Staff, The Times, 1938-39; Correspondent, Vienna, Budapest, Belgrade, 1947-49. Publictions: Yes Farewell, 1946; The Modern Everyman, 1947; Childhood at Oriol, 1951; The Midnight Diary, 1952; The Flying Castle, 1954; Mr Lyward's Answer, 1956; The Trouble with Jack, 1957; The Debatable Land, 1970; Out on a Limb, 1973; Open Day & Night, 1978; Mary and Richard, 1988. Contributions to: Articles and Poems to Encounter; Guardian; Times Literary Supplement. Honours: Keats Poetry First Prize, 1973. Membership: Society of Authors. Address: Beudy Gwyn, Minffordd, Gwynedd, North Wales.

BURNET James William Alexander (Alastair), Sir. b. 1 July 1928, Sheffield, Yorkshire, England. Journalist. m. Maureen Sinclair, 1958. Education: Worcester College, Oxford. Appointments: Sub-Editor, Leader Writer, Glasgow Herald, 1951-58; Leader Writer, The Economist, 1958-62; Political Editor, Independent TV News, 1963-64; rejoined ITN 1976-, Director, 1981-, Associate Editor, 1982-, Editor, The Economist, 1965-74; Editor, Daily Express, 1974-76; Director, The Times, 1982-. Publications: The Time of Our Lives (with Willie Landels), 1981; The Queen Mother, 1985. Contributions include: TV Current Affairs Programmes, This Week, Panorama, News at Ten. Honours: Richard Dimbleby Award, BAFTA, 1966, 1970, 1979; Judges Award, RTS, 1981; Knighthood, 1984. Address: 43 Hornton Court, Campden Hill Road, Lodnon W8 7NT, England.

BURNETT Al. See: BURNETT LEYS Alan Arbuthnott.

BURNETT John, b. 20 Dec 1925, Nottingham, England. Professor of Social History. Education: BA, 1946; MA, 1950, LLB, 1951, Cambridge Unviersity; PhD, London University, 1958. Publications: Plenty & Want - A Social History of Diet in England from 1815 to the Present Day, 1966; Plenty & Want, 1968 3rd ed, Routledge, 1989; A History of the Cost of Living, 1969; The Challenge of the 19th Century, 1970; Useful Toil - Autobiographies of Working Wople form the 1820's to the 1920's, published as The Annals of Labour; A Social History of Housing from 1815 to the Present Day, ; The Autobiography of the Working Class; Bibliography, 3 vols (eds. John Burnett, David Vincent, David Maynell) 1984-89. Contributions to: History Today; Business History; Economic History Review; British Journal of Sociology. Address: Faculty of Social Sciences, Brunel University, Uxbridge, Middlesex. England.

BURNETT LEYS Alan Arbuthnott, (Al Burnett), b. 10 Jan 1921, Natal, South Africa. Author; Screenwriter. m. 4 July 1960, 2 d. Education: BSc, Glasgow University, 1952; D Litt, University of CA, 1969. Appointments: Scenario Writer, MGM, 1954-59; Scenario Writer, Fox, 1960-63; Editor, Sphere International, 1981-84; Managing Editor, Able Publications Co Ltd, 1984-; Freelance Screenwriter; Managing Editor, Able publications & Co, Able Productions Pty Ltd. Publications: Water Wings, 1953; 8 Feature Films; Over 150 Telefilm Series Episodes. Contributions to: Flight International; Rotor and Wing; Yatching Monthly; Motor Boat; Various Travel and Technical Publications. Honour: Croix de Guerre. Memberships: Aviation, Space Writers Association; Australian Writers Guild; The Writers Guild of Great Britain; RNVR Officers Association. Literary Agent: ATP, Western Australia; The Sharland Organisation Ltd, London, England. Address: 8 Seaview Place, Cullen, Banffshire, AB56 2WA, Scotland.

BURNHAM Sophy, b. 12 Dec 1936, MD, USA. Writer. Eduction: BA, Smith College, 1958. Appointments: Manager, Fund For New Am Plays, John F Kennedy Centre, 1992-. Publications include: The Art Crowd, 1973; Threat to Licensed Nuclear Facilities, 1975; Landed Gentry, 1978; Buccaneer, 1977; The Dogwalker, 1979; A Book of Angels, 1990; Plays, Penelope, 1976; The Study, 1979; Films, The Smithsonian's Whale, 1963; The Leaf Thieves; Angel letters, 1991; Revelations, 1992; The Presidents Angel, 1993; For Writers Only, 1994. Contributions to: Town & Country; Esquire; NY Times; New Woman. Honours: Best Magazine Feature, 1974; Best Children's Radio Play, 1980; Award of Excellence, 1980; 1st Prize, Womens Theatre Award, 1981; Public Humanities Award, 1988; NC Festival of New Plays, 1993; VA Duvall Mann Award, 1993. Memberships include: Authors Guild; Daughter, Mark Twain Society; The Cosmos Club. Literary Agent: Anne Edelstein, USA. Address: 1405 31st Street NW, WA, DC 20007, USA.

BURNINGHAM John Mackingtosh, b. 1936, England. Freelance Author; Designer. Publications include: Borka: The Adventures of a Goose with No Feathers, 1963; Chitty Chitty Bang Bang, 1964; Humbert, Mister Firkin and the Lord Mayor of London, 1965; Cannonball Simp, 1966; Storyland: Wall Frieze, 1966; Harquin: The Fox Who Went Down to the Valley, 1967; Jungleland: Wall Frieze, 1968; Mr Gumpy's Outing, 1970; Around the World: Two Wall Friezes, 1972; Mr Gumpy's Motor Car, 1974; Little Book Series: The Blanket, The Cupboard, The Dog, The Friend, 1975; Come Away From the Water, Shirley, 1977; Would You Rather, 1978; Avocado Baby, 1982; The Wind in the Willows (illustrator), 1983; Granpa, 1984; First Words, 1984; Play and Learn Book: abc, 123, Oppersites, Colours, 1985; Where,s Julius, 1986; John Patrick Norman McHennessy - The Boy Who is Always Late, 1987; Rhymetime: A Good Job, The Car Ride, 1988; Rhyme, Animal Chatters, A Grand Band, 1989; Oi Get Off Our Train, 1989; Aldo, 1991; England, 1992; Harvey Slumfenburgers Christmas Present, 1993; Courtney, 1994. Films: Cannonball Simp, 1967; Granpa, 1989. Honours: Kate Greenaway Medal for Borka, 1963; Mr Gumpy's Outing, 1972; W H Smith Award for Harvey Slumfenburgers, 1994. Address: c/o Jonathan Cape Limited, 20 Vauxhall Bridge Road, London SW1V 2FA, England.

BURNS Alan, b. 29 Dec 1929, London, England. Author; Professor. m. (1) Carol Lynn, 1954, (2) Jean Illien, 1980, 1 s, 2 d. Education: Merchant Taylors' School, London. Appointments: C Day Lewis Writing Fellow, Woodberry Down School, 1973; Professor, University of MN, 1977-; Writer in Residence, Associated Colleges of Twin Cities, Minneapolis St Paul, 1980; Bush Foundation of MN Writing Fellow, 1984-85. Publications include: Buster, 1961; Europe After the

Rain, 1965; Celebrations, 1967; Babel, 1969; Dreamerikal, 1972; The Angry Brigade, 1973; The Day Daddy Died, 1981; Revolutions of the Night, 1986; Play, Palach, 1970; To Deprave and Corrupt, 1972; The Imagination on Trial, 1981. Contributions to: Kenyon Review; Books & Bookmen; New Statesman; MN Daily; Times Higher Eduction Supplement. Honours: Arts Council Maintenance Grant, 1967; Arts Council Bursaries, 1969, 73. Memberships: Poets & Writers. Literary Agent: Diana Tyler, MBA Literary Agents, London W1. Address: Creative Writing Dept, Lancaster University, Lancaster, LA1 4YN, England.

BURNS George (Nathan Birnbaum), b. 1896, USA. Comedian. m. Gracie Allen. Career: TV Shows: Burns and Allen Show, 1950-58; George Burns Show, 1959-60; Wendy and Me, 1964. Films include: The Big Broadcast, 1932; International House, 1932; Love in Bloom 1933; Many Happy Returns, 1939; Honolulu, 1939; The Sunshine Boys, 1975; Oh God, 1977; Going in Style, 1979; Just You and Me, Kid, 1979; Oh God, You Devel, 1984. Publications: I Love Her, That's Why, 1955; Living It up, or They Still Love Me in Altoona, 1976; How to Live to Be One Hundred or More, 1983, Dear Geoge: Dr Burns' Prescription for Happiness, 1986. Honours: Academy Award for Best Supporting Actor, The Sunshine Boys, 1975. Address: c/o Putnam, 200 Madison Avenue, New York, NY 10016, USA.

BURNS James MacGregor, b. 1918, USA. Professor of Political Science; Author. Publications: Congress on Trial: The Legislative Process and the Administrative State, 1949; Government by the People: The Dynamics of American National Government (with Jack Walter Peltason), 1952; Government of the People: The Dynamics of American State and Local Government (with Peltason), 1952; Government by the People: The Dynamics of American National State and Local Governement (with Peltason) revision of 2 previous books, 1954, 12 Edition (with Peltason and E Cronin), 1984; 15th edition, 1992; Roosevelt: The Lion and the Fox, 1956; Functions and Policies of American Government (editored with Peltason) 1958; 3rd edition, 1967; John Kennedy: A Political Profile, 1960; The Deadlock of Democracy: Four-Party Politics in America, 1963; Dialogues in Americanism (co-author), 1964; Presidential Government: The Crucible of Leadership, 1966; Our American Government Today (co-author), 1966; Lyndon Baines Johnson: To Heal and to Build (editor) 1968; Roosevelt: The Soldier of Freedom, 1970; Uncommon Sense, 1973; Leadership, 1978; The Vineyard of Liberty, 1982; The Power to Lead, 1984; The Workshop of Democracy, 1985; The Democrats Must Lead, 1992; People's Charter: The Pursuit of Rights in American, 1991. Honours: Recipient, Pulitzer Prize and National Book Award. Address: Department of Political Science, Williams College, Williamstown, MA 01267, USA.

BURNS Rex Raul Stephen Sehler, b. 13 June 1935, San Diego, CA, USA. University Teacher; Writer. m. Terry Fostvedt, 10 Apr 1987, 5 s, 2 d. Education: AB, Stanford University, 1958; MA, 1963, PhD, 1965, University of MN. Appointments include: Regional Editor, Per Se, 1966-68; Editor, People and Policy, 1976-79; Staff Book Reviewer, KS City Star, 1966-68; Mystery Book Columnist, Rocky Mountain News, 1989-. Publications include: The Alvarez Journal, 1975; Success in America, 1976; The Farnsworth Score, 1977; Speak for the Dead, 1978; Angle of Attack, 1979; The Killing Zone, 1988; Parts Unknown, 1990; Body Guard, 1991; Endangered Species, 1993; Body Slam, 1995. Contributions to: Rocky Mountain Social Sciences Journal; TX Studies in Literature and Language; American Literary Realism; Colloquium on Crime; The Writer; Rocky Mountain News. Honours: Fulbright Lecturer, Greece, 1969-70; Edgar Allen Poe Award, 1976; Fulbright Lecturer, Argentina, 1976; Chancellors Achievement Award, 1982; Presidents Teaching Scholar Award, 1990. Memberships: CO Authors League; Mystery Writers of Am; PEN; Writers of Am; International Association of Crime Writers. Literary Agent: Carl D Brandt, 1501 Broadway, New York, NY 10036, USA. Address: 1017 Vivian Circle, Boulder, CO 80303, USA.

BURNS Richard Gordon, (Dick B), b. 15 May 1925, Stockton, California, USA. Author; Retired Attorney. m. Eloise Bell, 23 June 1951, 2 sons. Education: AA with honours, University of California, Berkeley, 1946; AB, Stanford University, 1949; JD, Stanford University Law School, 1951. Publications: Dr Bob's Library, 1994; The Oxford Group and Alcoholics Anonymous, 1992; Anne Smith's Journal, 1994; The Books Early AAs Read for Spiritual Growth, 1994; How It Worked: The Story of Clarence S Snyder and Early Cleveland Alcoholics Anonymous (editor), 1993; New Light on Alcoholism: The AA Legacy from Sam Shoemaker, 1994; The Akron Genesis of Alcoholics

Anonymous, 1994; Courage to Change (with Bill Pittman), 1994. Memberships: American Society of Journalists and Authors; Authors Guild; National Writers Association; American Historical Association; Maui Writers Guild; Phi Beta Kappa. Address: 2747 S Kihei Rd D110, Kihei, HI 96753, USA.

BURNSHAW Stanley, b. 20 June 1906, NY, USA. Writer. m. Lydia Powsner, 1942, dec, 1 d. Education: BA, University of Pittsburgh, 1925; MA, Cornell University, 1933. Publications include: The Poem Itself, 1960; The Seamless Web, 1970; In The Terrified Radiance, 1972; Robert Frost Himself, 1986; A Stanley Burnshaw Reader, 1990. Contributions to: Atlantic Monthly; Sewanee Review; NY Times Book Review; Saturday Review of Literature; Agenda. Honours: National Institute of Arts & Letters Creative Writing Award, 1971; Honorary Doctorate of Humane Letters, 1983. Address: 250 West 89th Street, New York, NY 10024, USA.

BURROUGHS William S(teward), b. 1914, USA. Author; Former Journalist; Private Detective and Bartender. Publications: Junk (as William Lee), 1953, reissued under real name Junkie, 1964; The Nakes Lunch, 1959; The Exterminator, poetry, 1960, The Soft Machine, 1961; The Ticket That Exploded, 1962; Dead Fingers Talk, 1963; The Yage Letters (with Allen Ginsberg), 1963; Towers Open Fire, screenplay, 1963; Nova Express, 1964; Time, poetry, 1965; APO-33: A Metabolic Regulator; A Report on the Synthesis of the Amorphine Formula, 1968; The Third Mind, essays, 1970; The Job: Interviews with William Burroughs, by Daniel Odier, 1970; The Last Words of Dutch Schultz,, play, 1970, novel, 1975; Who's Who (with A Balch), screenplay, 1970; The Wild Boys: A Book of the Dead, 1971; Exterminator! novel, 1973; White Subway, 1974; Port of Saints, 1975; Ah Pook is Here, 1979; Cities of The Red Night, 1981; Blade Runner, screenplay, 1980; The Book of Breathing, 1980; Letters to Allen Ginsberg 1953-57, Letters, 1980; The Place of Dead Roads, 1983; The Burroughs File, 1984; The Adding Machine, 1984; Queer,1985; The Cat Inside, novella, 1986; The Western Lands, novel, 1987; Interzone, 1989; Ghost of Chance, novella, 1991. Honours: Commandeur de l'Ordre des Arts et des Lettres of France, 1984. Memberships: The Authors Guild; PEN Internationa; Dept of Literature, The American Academy and Institute of Arts and Letters. Address: William S Burroughs Communications, PO Box 147, Lawrence, KS 66044, USA.

BURROW John Anthony, b. 1932, United Kingdom. Professor. Appointments: Fellow, Jesus College, Oxford University, 1961-75; Winterstoke Professor, University of Bristol, 1976-. Publications: A Reading of Sir Gawain and the Green Knight, 1965; Geoffrey Chaucer: A Critical Anthology, 1969; Ricardian Poetry: Chaucer, Gower Langland and the Gawain Poet, 1971; Sir Gawain and the Green Knight, 1972; English Verse 1300-1500, 1977; Medieval Writers and Their Work, 1982; Essays on Medieval Literature, 1984; The Ages of Man, 1986; A Book of Middle English, 1992; Langlands Fictions, 1993; Thomas Hoccleve, 1994. Address: 9 The Polygon, Clifton, Bristol, England.

BURROWAY Janet Gay, b. 1936, AZ, USA. McKenzie Professor. m. (1) Walter Eysselinck, 1961, div, 2 s, (2) William Dean Humphries, div, (3) Peter Ruppert. Education: University of AR, 1954-55; AB, Barnard College, 1958; BA, 1960, MA, 1965, Cambridge University; Yale School of Drama, 1960-61. Appointments: Instructor, Lecturer, Professor; McKenzie Professor, 1989. Publications include: Descend Again, 1960; But to the Season, 1961; Eyes, 1966; The Buzzards, 1970; The Giant Jam Sandwich, 1972; Raw Silk, 1977; Material Goods, 1980; Writing Fiction, 1982, 4th edition 1995; Opening Nights, 1985; Cutting Stone, 1992; The Rivals, 1954; Aubade, 1959; James Park, 1961; A Few Particular, 1966; Nuns at Birth, 1970; Separation, 1975; Mother Hood, 1983; Maternal Line, 1985; This is, 1987; Growth, 1990; I'toi, 1991; Pool, 1993; A Certain Age, 1993; Dad Scattered, in anthology The Day My Father Died, 1994. Contributions to include: Numerous Articles in Magazines & Journals. Honours include: Various Scholarships; Elizabeth Janeway Prize; Barnard Phi Beta Kappa; Mount Holyoke Intercollegiate Poetry Prize; Woodrow Wilson Fellowship; Harvard Yale Henry Fellowship; AMOCO Award; FL State University Distinguished Teaching Award; Woodrow Wilson Fellowship. Memberships: Authors Guild; Associated Writing Programs. Literary Agent: Gail Hockman, NY, USA. Address: 240 De Soto Street, Tallahassee, FL 32303, USA.

BURTON Anthony George Graham, b. 24 Dec 1934, Thornaby, England. Writer; Broadcaster. m. 28 Mar 1959, 2 s, 1 d. Education: St James Grammar School. Publications include: A Programmed Guide to Office Warfare, 1969; The Jones Report, 1970; The Reluctant

Musketeer, 1973; Canals in Colour, 1974; Remains of a Revolution, 1975; The Miners, 1976; Back Door Britain, 1977; A Place to Stand, 1977; The Green Bag Travellers, 1978; The Past At Work, 1980; The Shell Book of Curious Britain, 1982; The National Trust Guide to Our Industrial Past, 1983; Walking the Line, 1985; The Shell Book of Undiscovered Britain and Ireland, 1986; Opening Time, 1987; Walking Through History, 1988; Cityscapes, 1990; Astonishing Britain, 1990; The Railway Builders, 1992; The Grand Union Canal Walk, 1993; The Railway Empire, 1994; The Rise & Fall of British Shipbuilding, 1994. Membership: Royal Society of Arts. Address: 25 Cowper Road, Redland, Bristol, BS6 6NZ, England.

BURTON Gabrielle B, b. 21 Feb 1939, USA. Freelance Writer. m. Roger V Burton, 18 Aug 1962, 5 d. Eduction: BA, Marygrove College, MI. Publications: Heartbreak Hotel; I'm Running Away from Home But I'm Not Allowed to Cross the Street. Contributions to: Numerous Essays & Reviews; NY Times; The WA Post; Family Circle; Buffalo News; Spree. Honours: Maxwell Perkins Prize; Great Lakes Colleges Association New Writers Award. Literary Agent: Phyllis Wender, Rosenstone Wender Agency, USA. Address: 211 Le Brun Road, Eggertsville, NY 14226, USA.

BURTON Gregory Keith, b. 12 Feb 1956, Sydney, Australia. Barrister-at-Law; Arbitrator; Mediator; Author. m. Suzanne Brandstater. Education: BA (Hons), University of Sydney, 1978; LLB (Hons), 1980; Bursary to Oxford University; BCL, 1984. Literary Appointments: Editorial Committee, Sydney Law Review, 1978-79; Foundation Editor, Journal of Banking & Finance Law and Practice, from 1990; Co-editor, Weaver & Craigie's Banker & Customer in Australia. Publications: Directions in Finance Law, 1990; Australian Financial Transactions Law, 1991; Trusts, Australian Commentary to Halsbury's Laws of England, 1992; Bills of Exchange & Other Negotiable Instruments, Halsbury's Laws of Australia, 1992; Set-Off, The Laws of Australia, 1993; Arbitration in Australia, 1994. Contributions to: Journal of Banking and Finance Law and Practice; Australian Law Journal; Sydney Law Review. Honours: University Medal in History, 1971. Memberships: NSW Bar Association; Business Law Section, Law Council of Australia; Banking Law Association; Commercial Law Association; LEADR; Australian Institute of Political Law; Australian Institute of Political Science; Australian Institute Administrative Law. Address: 5th Floor, Wentworth Chambers, 180 Phillip Street, Sydney, NSW 2000, Australia.

BURTON John Andrew, b. 2 Apr 1944, London, England. Writer; Wildlife Consultant. m. Vivien Gledhill, 1 Nov 1980. Publications: Over 20 books including: The Naturalist in London, 1975; Nature in the City, 1976; Owls of the World (editor), 1976; Field Guide to Amphibians and Reptiles of Europe, 1978; Gem Guide To Animals, 1980; Gem Guide to Zoo Animals, 1984; Collins Guide to Rare Mammals of the World, 1987. Contributions to: New Scientist; Vole; Oryx. Memberships: Fellow, Linnean Society of London; Executive Secretary, Fauna and Flora Preservation Scoiety, 1975-87; Royal Geographical Society; British Ornithologists Union. Literary Agent: Murray Pollinger.

BUSBEE Shirlee, b. 9 Aug 1941, San Jose, USA. Author. m. Howard Leon Busbee, 22 June 1963. Eductation: Burbank Business College. Publications: Gypsy Lady, 1977; Lady Vixen, 1980; White Passion Sleeps,1983; Deceive Not My Heart, 1984; The Tiger Lily, 1985; Spanish Rose, 1986; Midnight Masquerade,1988; Whisper to Me of Love, 1991; Each Time We Love, 1993; Love a Dark Rider, 1994. Address: c/o Avon Books, 105 Madison Avenue, New York, NY 10016, USA.

BUSBY F M, b. 11 Mar 1921, IN, USA. Communications Engr; Freelance Author. m. Elinor Doub, 28 Apr 1954, 1 d. Education: BSc, WA State University. Publications include: Rissa Kerguelen, 1977; All These Earths, 1978; The Demu Trilogy, 1980; The Breeds of Man, 1988; Zelde M'tana, 1980; Star Rebel, 1984; The Alien Debt, 1984; Rebel's Quest, 1985; Rebel's Seed, 1986; Getting Home, 1987; The Breeds of Man, 1988; Slow Freight, 1991; The Singularity Project, 1993; Islands of Tomorrow, 1994; Arrow From Earth, 1995. Contributions to: Over 40 Short Stories to Magazines and Multi Author Collections. Honours: Three Short Stories included in Best of Year Anthologies; One in Best of New Dimensions. Memberships: Science Fiction and Fantasy Writers of America. Literary Agent: Donald Maass Agency, USA. Address: 2852 14th Avenue West, Seattle, WA 98119, USA.

BUSBY Roger C(harles), b. 1941, England. Writer; Public Relations Officer. Appointments: Journalist, Caters New Agency, Birmingham, 1959-66; Journalist, Birmingham Evening Mail, 1966-73; Head of Public Relations, Devon & Cornwall Police, 1973-. Publications: Main Line Kill, 1968; Robbery Blue, 1969; The Frighteners, 1970; Deadlock, 1971; A Reasonable Man, 1972; Pattern of Violence, 1973; New Face in Hell, 1976; Garvey's Code, 1978; Fading Blue, 1984; The Hunter, 1986; Snow Man, 1987; Crackhot, 1990; High Jump, 1992. Memberships: Crime Writers Association; Institute of Public Relations; National Union of Journalists. Address: Sunnymoor, Bridford, Nr Exeter, Devon, England.

BUSCH Frederick, b. 1 Aug 1941, Writer. m. Judith Burroughs, 29 Nov 1963, 2 s. Education: AB, Muhlenberg College, 1962; MA, Columbia University, 1967; LittD, Muhlenberg, 1981. Appointments: Fairchild Professor of Literature, Colgate University, 1986. Publications include: The Mutual Friend, 1978; Hardwater Country, 1979; Invisible Mending, 1984; Sometimes I Live in the Country, 1986; Absent Friends, 1989; Harry & Catherine, 1990; Closing Arguments, 1991; Long Way From Home, 1993; The Children in the Woods, 1994. Contributions to: New Yorker; Harpers; Esquire. Honours include: National Endowment for the Arts Fellow, 1976; Guggenheim Fellow, 1981; Ingram Merill Fellow, 1982; Jewish Book Award for Fiction, 1986; PEN Malamud Award, 1991. Memberships: PEN; Authors Guild; Writers Guild. Literary Agent: Elaine Markson, USA. Address: RR1 Box 31A, Sherburne, NY 13460, USA.

BUSH Duncan, b. 6 Apr 1946, Cardiff, Wales. Poet; Writer. m. Annette Jane Weaver, 4 June 1981, 2 s. Education: BA (Honours), English & European Literature, Warwick University, 1978; Exchange Scholarship, Duke University, USa, 1976-77; D.Phil, Research in English Literature, Wadham Colldge, Oxford, 1978-81. Appointments: Lecturer, Director, The Word Workshop, Gwent College of Higher Education, 1984-; Writing Tutor, various Bodies. Publcations: The Genre of Silcen, 1988; Salt, 985; Aquarium 1984; Black Faces Red Mouths, 1986; Nostos, 1980; Editor, On Censorship, 1985. Contributions to: Numerous journals and magazines. Honours: Eric Gregory Award for Poetry, 1978; Barbara Campion Memorial Award for Poetry, 1982; Welsh Arts Council Prize for Poetry, 1984, 1986 etc. Memberships: Welsh Academy; Vice Chairman, Welsh Union of Writers, 1982-86. Address: 1 Kemps Covert, St Donats Castle, Llantwit Major, South Glamorgan, CF6 9WF, Wales.

BUSH Ronald, b. 16 June 1946. Professor of English. m. Marilyn Wolin, 14 Dec 1969. 1 s. Education: BA, University of Pennsylvania, 1968; MA, Cambridge University, 1970; PhD, Princeton University, 1974. Appointments: Assistant Professor, 1974-79, Associate Professor, 1979-82; Harvard University; Associate Professor, 1983-85, Professor, 1985-, California Institute of Technology, Pasadena. Publications: The Genesis of Ezra Pound's Cantos, 1976; T S Eliot: The Modernist in History (editor), 1991, Prehistories of the Future Modernism, Primitivism, Politics (editor) forthcoming. Contributions to: The Southern Review; American Literary History; Text; JEGP; Criticism; Yeats: An Annual; The Wallace Stevens Journal; The James Joyce Quarterly; and others. Honours: National Endowment for the Humanities Fellowships, 1977-78, 1992-93. Memberhip: Modern Languag Association Executive committee, Divison of 20th Century English Literature. Address: Division of Humanities, 101-40, Caltech, Pasadena, CA 91125, USA.

BUSS Fran Leeper, b. 1942. Publications: La Partera, Story of a Midwife, 1980; Journey of the Sparrows, 1991. Honour: Jane Addams Childrens Book Award, 1991.

BUTALA Sharon, b. 24 Aug 1940, Saskatchewan. m. 1976, 1 s.Education: University of Saskatchewan. Publications: Country of the Heart, 1984; Queen of the Headaches, 1985; The Gates of the Sun, 1985; Luna, 1988; Fever, 1990; Upstream, 1991; The Fourth Archangel, 1992; The Perfection of the Morning, 1994. Honours: Silver Award, National Magazine Awards, 1991; SWG, Major Drama Award, 1985, 1989; Annual Contributors Prize, 1988; Author's Award, 1992; 1994 Spirit of Saskatchewan & Non-Fiction Awards, Saskatchewan Book Awards. Address: c/o The Writer's Union of Canada, 24 Ryerson Avenue, Toronto, Ontario, M5T 2P3, Canada.

BUTLER Frederick Guy, b. 21 Jan 1918, Cradock, Cape Province, South Africa. Professor; Author. m. Jean Murray Satchwell, 10 Dec 1940, 3 s, 1 d. Education: BA, 1938, MA, 1939, Rhodes University; BA, 1947, MA, 1951, Oxford University. Publications include: Poetry, Stranger to Europe, 1951; South of the Zambezi, 1966; Selected Poems, 1975, 1989; Song and Ballads, 1978; Pilgrimage to Dias Cross, 1987; Selected Poems, 1975, 1989; Pilgrimage to Dias Cross, 1987. Autobiography: Karoo Morning, 1977; Bursting World, 1936-45; A Local Habitation, 1945-90; Plays: The Dam, 1953; A Book of SA Verse, 1959; Richard Gush of Salem, 1982; The Magic Tree, 1989; Demea, 1990; Novel: A Rackety Colt, 1989; Professor, Honorary Research Fellow, Rhodes University. Contributions to: Literary and Academic Journals. Honours include: Cape Tercentenary Foundation Literature Award, 1953; CNA Prize for Literature, 1976; English Academy of SA Gold Medal for Contributions, 1989; Honorary Degrees from Universities of Natal, 1970, Witwatersrand, 1984, South Africa, 1989; Rhodes University, 1994; Lady Usher Award, 1992; Freedom of the City of Grahamstown, 1994. Memberships: Shakespeare Society of SA; English Academy of SA. Address: High Corner, 122 High Street, Grahamstown, South Africa.

BUTLER Gwendoline (Williams), (Jennie Melville). b. United Kingdon. Author. Publications: Receipt for Murder, 1956; Dead in a Row, 1957; The Dull Dead, 1958; The Murdering Kind, 1958; The Interloper, 1959; Death Lives Next Door, US Edition Dine and Be Dead, 1960; Make Me a Murderer, 1961; Series of books featuring John Coffin: Coffin on the Water; Coffin in Oxford, 1962; Coffin for Baby, 1963; Coffin Waiting, 1963; Coffin in Malta, 1964; A Nameless Coffin, 1966; Coffin Following, 1968; Coffin's Dark Number, 1969; A Coffin form the Past, 1970; A Coffin for Pandora, 1973, US Edition Olivia, 1974; A Coffin for the Canary, US Edition Sarsen Place, 1974; The Vesey Inheritance, 1975; Brides of Friedberg, US Edition Meadowsweet, 1977; The Red Staircase, 1979; Albion Walk, 1982; UK Paperback Cavalcade, 1984; As Jennie Melville: Come Home and Be Killed, 1962; Buring Is a Substitute for Loving, 19b3; Murderers' Houses, 1964; There Lies Your Love, 1965; Nell Alone, 1966; A Different Kind of Summer, 1967; The Hunter in the Shadows, 1969; A New Kind of Killer, An Old Kind of Death, 1970, US Edition A New Kind of Killer, 1971; Ironwood, 1972; Nun's Castle, 1973, Raven's Forge, 1975; Dragon's Eye, 1976; Axwater, US Edition Tarot's Tower, 1978; Murder Has a Pretty Face, 1981; The Painted Castle, 1982; The Hand of Glass, 1983; A Series of Charmain Daniels' novels begining with Windsor Red, 1985. Literary Agent: Vanessa Holt. Address: c/o Vanessa Holt Ass, 59 Crescent Road, Leigh-on-Sea, Essex, SS9 2PF, England.

BUTLER Joseph T, b. 25 Jan 1932, Winchester, Virginia, USA. Curator. Education: BS, Univerity of Maryland, 1954; MA, Ohio Univeristy, 1955; MA, University of Delaware, 1975. Publications: American Antiques 1800-1900, A Collector's History and Guide, 1965; Candleholders in America, 1650-1900, 1967; American Furniture, 1973; Sleepy Hollow Restorations, A Cross Section of the Collection, 1983; A Field Guide to American Antique Furnitrue, 1985, 1986; The Family Collections at Van Cortlandt Manor, 1967. Contributions to: Antiques; Antiques Journal; Art & Antiques; The Connoisseur; The Rushlight; Early American Life; Encyclopedia Americana; Encyclopedia Britannica; Encyclopedia of World Biography; House Beautiful. Honours: Winterthur Fellow, University of Delaward, Address: 222 Martling Avenue, Tarrytown, NY 10591, USA.

BUTLER Marilyn, (Speers), b. 1937, England. Professor. Appointments: Current Affairs Producer, BBC, 1960-63; Research Fellow, St Hildas College, Oxford, 1970-73; Fellow, Tutor, St Hughs College, Lecturer, Oxford University, 1973-86; King Edward VII Professor, Cambridge University, 1986-93; Professional Fellow, Kings College, Cambridge, 1988-93; Rector, Exeter College, Oxford, 1993-. Publications: Maria Edgeworth: A Literary Biography, 1972; Jane Austen and the War of Ideas, 1975; Peacock Displayed: A Satirist in His Context, 1979; Romantics, Rebels and Reactionaries, 1760-1830, 1981; Burke, Paine, Godwin and the Revolution Controversy, 1984; Collected Works of Mary Wollstonecraft, 1989; Maria Edgeworth, Castle Recrent and Ennui, 1992. Address: Exeter College, Oxford, England.

BUTLER Muriel Dorothy (Dorothy Butler), b. 24 Apr 1925, Auckland, New Zealand. Teacher; Bookseller; Author. m. Roy Edward Butler, 11 Jan 1947, 2 s, 6 d. Education: BA, University of Auckland, 1940; Diploma in Education, 1976. Publications: Gushla And Her Books; Babies Need books; Five to Eight; Come Back Ginger; A Bundle of Birds; Others inc. My Brown Bear Barney; Higgledy Piddledy Hobbledy Hoy; Good Morning Mrs Martin; Reading Begins at Home; I Will Build You A House. Honours: The Eleanor Faijeon Award; The May Hill Arbuthnot Honour Lectureshop, American Library Citation;

Childrens Literature Association of New Zealand Honour Award; The Margaret Mahy Lecture Award; Awareded OBE, New Years Honours List, 1993. Memberships: PEN; Childrens Literature Association; Reading Associatio, NZ, Childrens Book Foundation of NZ. Literary Agent: Richards Literary Agency. Address: The Old House, Karekare, Auckland West, New Zealand.

BUTLER Nathan. See: **SOHL Gerald A.**

BULTER Octavia E, b. 1947, USA. Science Fiction Writer. Publications: Pattermaster, 1976; Mind of My Mind, 1977; Survivor, 1978; Kindred, 1979; Wild Seed, 1980; Clay's Ark, 1984; Parade of the Sower, 1993; Imago, 1990; Adulthood Rites, 1989; Dawn, 1989. Address: PO Box 6604, Los Angeles, CA 90055, USA.

BUTLER Richard. See: **ALLBEURY Theo Edward.**

BUTLER Robert Olen, b. 1945, IL, USA. m. (4) Elizabeth Dewberry, 1985. Education: BA, Northwestern University; MA, University of IA. Appointments: Professor, McNeese State University. Publications: Alleys of Eden, 1981; Sun Dogs, 1982; Countrymen of Bones, 1983; On Distant Ground, 1985; Wabash, 1987; The Deuce, 1989; A Good Scent from a Strange Mountain, 1992; They Whisper, 1993. Honours: Pulitzer Prize, 1993; Richard & Hinda Rosenthal Prize, 1993; Guggenheim Fellowship, 1993. Address: Dept of Language Arts, McNeese State University, Box 92655, Lake Charles, LA 70609-2655, USA.

BUTLIN Martin, b. 1929, England. Art Consultant. Appointments: Assistant Keeper, 1955-67, Keeper of the Historic British Collection, 1967-89, Tate Gallery, London. Publications include: Catalogue of the Works of William Blake in the Tate Gallery, 1957; Samuel Palmer's Sketch Book of 1824, 1962; Turner Watercolours, 1962; Tate Gallery Catalogues: Modern British Paintings, Drawings and Sculpture, 1964; William Blake, 1966; The Blake Varley Sketchbook of 1819, 1969; The Paintings of J M W Turner, 1977, 1984; The Paintings and Drawings of William Blake, 1981; Turner at Petworth, 1989; William Blake, Exhibition Catalogue, 1990. Honours: Fellow, British Academy , 1984; CBE, 1990. Address: 74c Eccleston Square, London SW1V 1PJ, England.

BUTLIN Ron, b. 17 Nov 1949, Edinburgh, Scotland. Writer. m. Regula Staub, 18 June 1993. Education: MA, Dip CDAE, Edinburgh University. Appointments: Writer in Residence, Edinburgh University, 1983, 85; Scottish Canadian Writing Fellow, 1984; Writer in Residence, Midlothian Region, 1990-91; Writer in Residence, Stirling University, 1993. Publications: Creatures Tamed by Cruelty, 1979; The Exquisite Instrument, 1982; The Tilting Room, 1984; Ragtime in Unfamiliar Bars, 1985; Sound of My Voice, 1987; Several Plays & Opera Libretti; Forthcoming: Histories of Desire; The Sin of Forgiveness.Contributions to: The Scotsman. Honours: Writing Bursary, 1977, 87, 90; Book Awards, 1982, 84, 85, Scottish Arts Council; Poetry Book Society Recommendation, 1985. Literary Agent: Giles Gordon, Sheil Land Association. Address: 7W Newington Place, Edinburgh, EH9 1QT, Scotland.

BUTOR Michel (Marie François), b. 14 Sept 1926, Mons-en-Baroeul, France. Poet; Novelist. m. Marie-Josephe Mas, 1958, 4 daughters. Education: Sorbonne, Paris, 1945-48. Appointments include: Professor at the University of Geneva, from 1975; Visiting Professor at American universities. Publications: Novels: Passage de Milan, 1954; Passing Time, 1956, 1960; Second Thoughts, 1957, 1958; Degrees, 1960; Portrait de l'artiste en jeune singe: capriccio, 1967; Intervalle, 1973; Matière de rêves, 5 volumes, 1975-79; La Rêve d'Irenée, 1979; Vanité: conversation dans les Alpes-Maritimes, 1980; L'Embarquement de la Reine de Saba: d'après le tableau de Claude Lorrain, 1989; Verse: Cycle sur neuf gouaches d'Alexander Calder, 1962; Illustrations 1-4, 4 volumes, 1964-76; Litanie d'Eau, 1964; Comme Shirley, 1966; Tourmente, 1968; Travaux d'approche, 1972; Envois, 1980; Brassée d'Avril; Liminaires et préliminaires: 21 ballades et 7 chansons, 1983; Exprès, 1983; Herbier lunaire, 1984; Victor Hugo écartelé, 1984; Hors d'oeuvre, 1985; Les Jouets du vent, 1985; Ailes, 1987; Zone franche, 1989; La Forme courte. Honours include: Chevalier, National Order of Merit. Address: A l'écart, 74380 Lucinges, France.

BUTORA Martin, b. 7 Oct 1944, Bratislava, Czechoslovakia. Sociologist. m. Zora Butorova, 18 Aug 1978, 3 s, 1 d. Education: Graduated, Philosophy, Sociology minor, 1976; PhD, Sociology, 1980,

Comenius University, Bratislava; Senior Lecturer (Associate Professor), Dozent, Sociology, Charles University, Prague, 1992. Appointments: Editor-in-Chief, Editor; Echo, Reflex, studnet newpspaper, Kultumy Zivot, Bratislava, 1966-69. Publications: Fiction: Lahykym perom, 1987; Posolene v Azii, 1990; Skok a kuk, 1990, Non-fiction: Mne sa to nemoze sta, sociological chapters on alcoholis, 1989; Prekrocit svuj stin, Self-help gourps in health care, 1991; From the Velvet Revolution to the Velvet Divorce? 1993. Contributions to: Slovenske Pohlady; Kulytumy Zivot; Romboid; Frangment K; Lettre Internationale, Journal of Democracy, Europaische Rundschau. Honours: Slovensky Spisovatel Publishing House, 1988; Osveta Publiching House, 1990; Slovak Literary Fund Prize, 1991. Memberships: Obec Spisovatelov Slovenska; PEN Club Bratslava; International Sociological Association; Masarkyova sociologicka spolecnost. Literary Agent: LITA, Bratislava, Slovakia. Address: Lubinska 6, 811 03 Bratislava, Slovakia.

BUTTER Peter Herbert, b. 7 Apr 1921, Scotland. University Professor. m. Bridget Younger, 30 Aug 1958, 1 s, 2 d. Education: MA, Balliol College, 1948. Publications: Shelleys Idols of the Cave, 1954; Francis Thompson, 1961; Edwin Muir, 1962; Edwin Muir: Man & Poet, 1966; Editor, Shelleys Alastor, Prometheus Unbound and Other Poems, 1971; Selected Letters of Edwin Muir, 1974; Selected Poems of William Blake, 1982; The Truth of Imagination: Some Uncollected Essays and Reviews of Edwin Muir, 1988; Complete Poems of Edwin Muir, 1992. Contributions to: Akros; Lines Review; Modern Language Review; Review of English Literature; Review of English Studies; Scottish Literary Journal. Memberships: International Association of University Professors of English. Address: Ashfield, Prieston Road, Bridge of Weir, Renfrewshire, PA11 3AW.

BUTTERS Dorothy Gilman. See: GILMAN Dorothy.

BUTTERWORTH Neil, b. 4 Sept 1934, London, England. Writer. m. Anna Barnes, 23 Apr 1960, 3 d. Education: Nottingham University; London University; Guildhall School of Music. Appointments: Lecturer, Kingston College of Technology, 1960-68; Head of Music Dept, Napier Polytechnic, 1968-87. Publications: Music of Aaron Copland; Dictionary of American Composers; Ralph Vaughan Williams; Neglected Music; Haydn; Dvorák; English for Business & Professional Studies; 400 Aural Exercises. Contributions to: Times Educational Supplement; Classical Music; Classic CD; Library Review; Sunday Standard; Sunday Times; Musical Opinion; Opera. Honours: Conducting Prize; Fellow, London College of Music; Winston Churchill Travelling Fellowship. Memberships: Performing Rights Society; Incorporated Society of Musicians; Scottish Society of Composers. Address: The White House, Inveresk, Mussleburgh, Midlothin EH21 7TG.

BUZO Alexander John, b. 23 July 1944, Sydney, Australia. Playwright. Author. m. Merelyn Johnson, 21 Dec 1968. Education: BA, University of NSW, 1966. Appointments: Resident Dramatist, Melbourne Theatre Company, 1972-73; Writer in Residence, James Cook University, 1985; University of Wollongong, 1989; Writer in Residence, University of Central Queensland, 1991. Publications include: Tavtelogy, 1980; Meet the New Class, 1981; The Search for Harry Allway, 1985; Glancing Blows, 1987; The Young Person's Guide to the Theatre and Almost Everything Else, 1988; Plays, Rooted, 1968; The Front Room Boys, 1969; The Roy Murphey Show, 1970; Big River, 1980; Shellcove Road, 1989; The Longest Game, 1990; Pure Flies North, 1991; Coralie Lausdowne Says No, 1974; Martello Towers, 1976. Contributions to: The Australian Way; The Independent Monthly; Readers Digest; Playboy; Northern Herald; Pacific Island Monthly; New Straits Times; The Australian; The Bulletin; Discovery; Heritage. Honour: Gold Medal, Australian Literature Society, 1972. Memberships: Cen8tre for Australian Language and Literature Studies; Australian Writers Guild. Literary Agent: Margaret Connolly & Associates, Sydney, NSW. Address: 14 Rawson avenue, Bondi Junction, Sydney NSW 2022, Australia.

BYARS Betsy (Cromer), b. 1928, USA. Children's Fiction Writer. Publications: Clementine, 1962; The Dancing Camel, 1965; Rama, The Gypsy Cat, 1966; The Groober, 1967; The Midnight Fox, 1968; Trouble River, 1969; The Summer of the Swans,1970; Go and Hush the Baby, 1971; The House of Wings, 1972; The 18th Emergency, 1973; The Winged Colt of Casa Mia, 1973; After the Goat Man, 1974; The Lace Snail, 1975; The TV Kid, 1976; The Pinballs, 1977; The Cartoonist, 1978; Goodbye, Chicken Little, 1979; Night Swimmers, 1980; The Animal, The Vegetable and Johd D Jones, 1981; The Two Thousand Pound Goldfish, 1981; The Cybil War, 1982; The Glory Girl, 1983; The

Computer Nut, 1984; Cracker Jackson, 1985; Sugar and Other Stories, 1987; McMummy, 1993; Wanted...Mud Blossom, 1993; The Golly Sisters Ride Again, 1994. Address: 4 Riverpoint, Clemson SC 29631, USA.

BYATT Antonia Susan, b. 24 Aug 1936, Sheffield, Yorkshire, England. Author. m. (1) Ian C R Cyatt, 1959, div, 1 s, dec, 1 d. (2) Peter J Duffy, 1969, 2 d. Education: Newnham College, Cambridge; Bryn Mawr College, PA; Sommerville College, Oxford. Appointments: Extra Mural Lecturer, University of London, 1962-71; Lecturer, Literature, Central School of Art & Design, 1965-69; Lecturer, University College, London, 1972-81; Senior Lecturer, 1981-83; Associate, Newnham College, Cambridge, 1977-82; Broadcaster, Reviewer, Judge, Literary Prizes. Publications include: Shadow of a Sun, 1964; Degrees of Freedom, 1965; The Game, 1967; Wordsworth and Coleridge in their Time, 1970; The Virgin in the Garden, 1978; Still Life, 1985; Possession, 1989; Passions of the Mind, 1991; Angels and Insects, 1992; The Matisse Stories, 1994. Honours: FRSL; Hon D Litt, Bradford, 1987, Durham, 1991, York, 1991, Nottingham, 1992, Liverpool, 1993, Portsmouthm, 1994; Macmillan Silver Pen Award, 1990; CBE; Irish Times Aer Lingus International Fiction Prize, 1990; Memberships: Society of Authors. Literary Agent: Peters Fraser & Dumlop, London. Address: 37 Rusholme Road, London SW15, England.

BYLINSKY Gene Michael, b. 30 Dec 1930, Belgrade, Yugoslavia. Science Writer. m. Gwen Gallegos, 14 Aug 1955, 1 s, 1 d. Education: BA, Journalism, Louisiana State University, USA, 1955; Literary Appointments: Staff Writer, Wall Street Journal, 1957-61; Science Writer, National Observer, 1961-62, Newhouse Newpapers 1962-66; Editorial Board, Fortune Magazine, 1966-. Publications include: Life in Darwin's Universe, 1981; High Tech Window on the Future (Story of Silicon Valley), 1985; The Innovation Millionaires, 1976; Mood Control, 1978. Contributons to: New York Times Sunday Magazine, Sunday Book Review; New Republic; American Legion Magazine; Saturday Evening Post; Omni; Science Digest; Science Year, etc. Honours include: Albert Lasker Award, medical journalism, 1970; Deadline Award, Sigma Delta Chi, 1970; Gold Medal, American Chemical Society, 1973; Science writing award, American Medical Association, 1975; Claude Bernard Award, National Association for Medical Research, 1975; Journalism Award, University of Missouri, 1985. Memberships: National Association of Science Writer. Literary Agent: Diane Cleaver, Diane Cleaver Inc, 55 Fifth Ave, New York, NY 10003, Address: c/o Fortune Magazine, Time & Life Building, Rockefeller Centre, New York, NY 10020, USA.

BYRD Odell Richard, Jr, b. 22 Sept 1944, Richmond, Virginia, USA. Educator; Writer. Education: AA, BA, New York University, Albany, 1878. Publications: A Voice Within, 1979; Love Poems, 1980; Richmond Virginia: A City of Monuments & Statues, 1990; Black History of Richmond: Concise and Condense; Black History of Richmond, 1600-1900. Contributions to: New Renaissance; New World Anthology; Black Books Bulletin; International Black Writer. Honours: Outstanding Contribution to Literature, 1981; Fellow, International Academy of Poets, 1981; Human Service Club Award, 1989; Golden Poet Award, 1989, 1990. Address: PO Box 25455, Richmond, VA 23260, USA.

BYRNE John, b. 6 Jan 1940, Paisley, Renfrewshire, Scotland. Writer. m. Alice Simpson, 1964, 1 s, 1 d. Education: St Mirin's Academy and Glasgow School of Art, 1958-63. Appointments: Graphic Designer, Scottish Television, Glasgow, 1964-66; Designer, A F Stoddard, Carpet manufacturers, Elderslie, 1966-68; Writer-in-Residence, Borderline Theatre, Irvine, Ayrshire, 1978-79 and Duncan of Jordanstone College, Dundee, 1981; Associate Director, Haymarket Theatre, Leciester, 1984-85; Theatrical set and costume designer. Publications: Plays include: The Slab Boys Trilogy (originally called Paisley Patterns) London, Penguin, 1987 - The Slab Boys (produced Edinburgh and London 1978, Loisville, 1979, New York, 1980), Cuttin' a Rug (as The Lovliest Night of the Year, produced Edinburgh, 1979, revised version, as Threads, produced London, 1980, as Cuttin' a Rug, produced London, 1982), Still Life (produced Edinburgh 1982); Normal Service (produced London, 1979); Hooray for Hollywood (produced Loouisville, 1980); The London Cuckolds, adaptation of the play by Edward Ravenscroft (produced Leicester and London, 1985). Radio and Television plays. Honours: Evening Standard award, 1978. Litarary Agent: Margaret Ramsey Ltd, London. Address: 3 Castle Brae, Newport-on-Tay, Fife, Scotland.

BYRNE John Keyes. See: LEONARD Hugh.

BYRNE Malcolm M, b. 30 Aug 1955, Newport, Rhode Island, USA. Research Director; Writer. m. Leila J Afzal, 1 Aug 1987, 1 s. Education: BA, Tufts University, 1977; MA, Johns Hopkins University, 1986. Publications: The Chronology; The Documented Day by Day Account of the Secret Military Assistance to Iran and the Contras; the Iran Contra Affair; The Making of a Scandal; A Pattern of Deceit; The Iran Contra Affair. Contributions to: Dissent; The Nation; The WA Monthly. Address: c/o The National Security Archive, Gelman Library, Suite 701, 2130 H Street, NW Washington, DC 20037, USA.

C

CABANIS Jose, b. 24 Mar 1922. Writer. 1 s, 1 d. Education: University de Toulouse. Publications: Novels: L'age ingrat, 1952; Juliette Bonvoilee, 1954; Les mariages de raison, 1958; Le bonheur du jour, 1961; Les cartes du temps, 1962; Les juex de la nuit, 1964; La Bataille de Toulouse, 1966; Les jardins de la nuit, 1973; un essai sur Marcel Journandeau, 1960; Plaisir et lectures, 1964; Plaisir et Lectures II, 1968; Des jardins en Espagne, 1969; Le sacre de Napoleon, 1970; Charles X roi ultra, 1972; Saint-Simon l'Ammirable, 1975; Les profondes annes, 1976; Michelet, le pretre et la femme, 1978; Petit entracte a la guerre, 1981; Lacordaire et quelques autres, 1983. Honours: Prix de Critiques, 1961; Prix des Libraries, 1962; Prix Theophraste Renaudot, 1966; Prix des Ambassadeurs, 1972; Grand Prix de la Critique, 1975. Address: 5 rue Darquie, 31000 Toulouse, Fance.

CABRERA INFANTE G(uillermo), b. 22 Apr 1929, Gibara, Cuba (British citizen). Novelist. m. Miriam Gomez, 1961. Education: University of Havana, 1949-54. Appointments include: Former Chargé d'Affaires in Brussels, Scriptwriter and Porfessor. Publications: Asi en la paz como en la guerra: cuentos, 1960; Three Trapped Tigers, 1965, 1971; A View of Dawn in the Tropics, 1974, 1978; Infante's Inferno, 1979, 1984; Screenplay for Vanishing Point, 1970; Holy Smoke, 1985; A Twentieth-Century Job, 1991. Honours include: Guggenheim Fellowship, 1970. Address: 53 Gloucester Road, London SW7 4QN, England.

CADDEL Richard Ivo, b. 13 July 1949, Bedford, England. Librarian. m. Ann Barker, 31 Aug 1971, 1 s, 1 d. Education: BA, Newcastle University, 1971; Newcastle Polytechnic, 1971-72; ALA, 1974. Appointments: Staff, Durham University Library, 1972-; Director, Pig Press, 1973-; Organiser, Modern Tower Readings, 1974-75; Founder, Colpitts Poetry Readings, 1975; Organiser, Basil Bunting Celebration, Newcastle, 1986; Secretary, Basil Bunting Poetry Achive, 1987; Director, Basil Bunting Poetry Centre, 1989-. Publications: Sweet Cicely, 1983; Uncertain Time, 1990; 26 New British Poets, 1991; Basil Bunting Uncollected Poems, 1991; Basil Bunting Three Essays, 1994; Basil Bunting Complete Poems, 1994; Ground, 1994. Contributions to: Poems & Criticism to numerous Magazines and Periodicals. Honours: Northern Arts Writers Award, 1985, 88, 90; Fund for Poetry Award, 1992. Address: 7 Cross View Terrace, Nevilles Cross, Durham, DH1 4JY, England.

CADE Robin. See: **NICOLE Christopher Robin.**

CADET Maurice, b. 20 June, Jacmel, Haiti. Professor of Literature, College of Alma. div. 2 sons, 3 daughters. Education: Diplomas in Letters & Modern Languages, Audio-visual and BS Law. Publications: Turbulences, poetry, 1989; Chete Pimen, poems, 1990; Haute Dissidence, poetry, 1991; Itinéreires d'un enchantement, poetry, 1992; Réjoissances, poetry, 1994. Contributions to: Text published in a number of Qubec Magazines, including: Focus; Résistonces; Estuaire; Bréves Littéraires; Ruptures. Honours: Haute dissidence finalist, Literary Prize, 1991. Memberships: National Authors Union of Quebec; Language Plus Arts Gallery, Alma, Quebec. Address: 630 Robert Jean App2, Alma, Quebec G8B 7H1, Canada.

CADOGAN Mary (Rose), b. 1928, United Kingdom. Writer; Foundation Secretary; Governor, Educational Centre. Appointments: Secretary, Krishnamurti Writing Inc, London, 1958-68; Secretary, The Krishnamurti Foundation, Beckenham, Kent, 1968-; Governor, Brockwood Park Education Centre, Bramdean, Hants, 1968-. Publications: The Greyfriars Characters (with John Wernham), 1976; You're a Brick, Angela: A New Look at Girls' Fiction from 1839 to 1975 (with Patricia Craig), 1976; Women and Children First: The Fiction of Two World Wars (with patricia Craig), 1978; Charles Hamilton Schoolgirls' Album (with John Wernham), 1978; The Lady Investigates: Women Detectives and Spies in Fiction (with Patricia Craig), 1981; The Morcove Companion (with Tommy Keen), 1981; From Wharton Lodge to Linton Hall; The Charles Hamilton Christmas Companion (with Tommy Keen), 1984; Richmal Crompton: The Woman Behind William, 1986. Address: 46 Overbury Avenue, Beckenham, Kent, BR3 2PY, England.

CADY Jack, b. 20 Mar 1932, OH, USA. Writer. Education: BSc, University of Louisville, KY. Appointments: University of WA, 1968-73; Knox College, 1973-74; Clarion College, 1974; University of Alaska, 1977-78; University of WA Extension, 1978-; Pacific Lutheran University, 1984. Publications: The Burning, 1972; Tattoo, 1978; The Well, 1982; The Jonah Watch, 1982; Singleton, 1982; McDowells Ghost, 1983; The Man Who Could Make Things Vanish, 1984; The Night We Buried Road Dog, 1992; The Sons of Noah and Other Stories, 1992; Inagehi, 1993; Street, 1994. Contributions to: Seattle Post Intellegencer; Daily News; OMNI; Pulphouse; Glimmer Train; Chariton Review; Anthologies; Final Shaows and Prime Evil. Literary Agent: Clyde Taylor, USA. Address: Box 872, Port Townsend, WA 98368, USA.

CAHILL Mike. See: **NOLAN William F(rancis).**

CAIDIN Martin Karl von Strasser, b. 14 Sept 1927, New York, USA. Author; Commerical Professional Pilot; Teacher; Lecturer; Telekinetics Researcher, Instructor; Bionics Development; Radio, TV Broadcaster and War Correspondent; Stunt Pilot and Actor. m. Dee Dee Autry Caidin. Education: Graduated High School and College, 1948; A-2 Advanced Course with US Air Force; Atomic-Biological-Chemical Warfare advanced courses completed with US Army and US Air Force; Maritime School with US Coast Guard; Advanced Flight Training (heavy equipment); Astronautics OJT Air Force Missile Test Centre; Parapsychology at Santa Fe College. Publications: Nearly 200 books including: Cyborg (Six Million Dollar man; Bionic Woman), 1972; Marooned, 1964; Samurai,1955; Saga of Iron Annie, 1978; Hydrospace, 1959; The Mesiah Stone, 1988; Natural or Supernatural? 1993; Thunderbolt: The Fabulous US 56th Fighter Group, 1990; Dark Merriah, 1990. Contributions to: Thousands of articles, short fiction, newspaper stories. Honours include: James Strebig Memorial Award (aviation/space writing) several 1958-; Master Aviator and Pioneer Aviator awarded by Silver Wings, 1987. Memberships: Aviation/Space Writers Association; Science Fiction Writers; Authors' Guild; Authors' League; Knight of Mark Twain; Silver Wings; Ten-Ton Club; Valiant Air Command; Confederate Air Force. Address: 13416 University Station, Gainesville, FL 32604, USA.

CAINE Mark. See: **MASCHLER Thomas Michael.**

CAIRNCROSS Alexander Kirkland, b. 11 Feb 1911, Lesmahagow, Scotland. Economist. m. Mary Frances Glynn, 29 May 1943, 3 s, 2 d. Education: MA, University of Glasgow, 1933; PhD, University of Cambridge, 1936. Publications: Introduction to Economics, 1944, 6th edition, 1982; Home and Foreign Investment, 1870-1913, 1953; Factors in Economic Development, 1962; Control of Long-Term International Capital Movements, 1973; Inflation, Growth and International Finance, 1975; Snatches, 1980; Sterling in Decline, with Barry Eichengreen, 1983; Years of Recovery, 1985; Economics and Economic Policy, 1986; The Price of War, 1986; The Economic Section, 1989, with Nita Watts; Planning in Wartime, 1991; Goodbye Great Britain, 1992, with Kathleen Burk, edited with Frances Cairncross; The Legacy of the Golden Age, 1992; The British Economy Since 1945, 1992. Contributions to: Numerous Journals. Memberships: British Association for Advancement of Science & Technology; Royal Economic Society; Scottish Economic Society. Address: 14 Staverton Road, Oxford, OX2 6XJ, England.

CAIRNCROSS Frances Anne, b. 30 Aug 1944, Otley, Yorkshire, England. Journalist. m. Hamish McRae, 10 Oct 1971, 2 d. Education: Honours Degree in Modern History, Oxford University, 1962-65; MA, Economics, Brown University, Providence, Rhode Island, USA, 1965-66. Appointments: Staff, The Times, 1967-69; Staff,The Banker, 1969; Staff, The Observer, 1969-71; Economics Correspondent, The Guardian, 1971-81; Women's Editor, The Guaridan, 1981-84; Britain Editor, The Economist, 1984-. Publications: Capital City (with Hamish McRae), 1971; The Second Great Crash, 1973; The Guardian Guide to the Economy, 1981; Changing Perceptions of Economic Policy, 1981; Second Guardian Guide to the Economy, 1983; Guide to the Economy, 1987; Costing the Earth, 1991. Address: 6 Canonbury Lane, London, N1 2AP, England.

CAIRNS. See: **DOWLING Basil.**

CALAIS Jean. See: **RODEFER Stephen.**

CALDECOTT Moyra, b. 1 June 1927. Author. m. Oliver Zeriffi Stratford Caldecott, 5 Apr 1951, 2 s, 1 d. Education: BA, English

Literature, Philosophy, 1947; BA Hons, English Literature, 1948; MA, English Literature, 1949, Natal University, Pietermaritizburg, South Africa. Publications: Guardians of the Tall Stones, 1977, 1986, 1987; The Silver Vortex, 1987; Women in Celtic Myth, 1988; Egyptian Triology: Daughter of Amun; Son of the Sun; Daughter of Ra, 1989-90; Crystal Legends, 1990; Ethelreda, 1987.

CALDER Angus, b. 5 Feb 1942, Sutton, Surrey, England. University Teacher. m. (1) Jennifer Daiches, 1 Oct 1963, 1 s, 2 d. (2) Catherine Kyle, 21 Dec 1987, 1 s. Education: MA, Kings College, Cambridge, 1963; D Phil, University of Sussex, 1968. Appointments: Lecturer, University of Nairobi, 1968-71; Staff Tutor, Open University in Scotland, 1979-93; Visiting Professor, University of Zimbabwe, 1992; Joint Convenor, Festival of East African Writing, Nairobi, 1971; Convenor, Scottish Poetry Library, 1983-88; Convenor, Commonwealth Writers Conference, Edinburgh, 1986; Convener, Writing Together, Glasgow, 1990. Publications: The Peoples War, 1969; Revolutionary Empire, 1981; Russia Discovered, 1976; Byron, 1987; T S Eliot, 1987; The Myth of the Blitz, 1991. Contributions to: Editor, Journal of Commonwealth Literature; Articles and Reviews in Cencrastus, London Review of Books, New Statesman, Scotland on Sunday. Honours: John Llewellyn Rhys Memorial prize, 1970; Scottish Arts Council Book Awards, 1981, 1994. Memberships: Society of Authors; Scottish PEN. Literary Agent: Shriel Land Associates. Address: c/o Shriel Land Associates, 43 Doughty St, London, WC1N 2LF, England.

CALDER Nigel David Ritchie, b. 2 Dec 1931, Writer. m. Elisabeth Palmer, 22 May 1954, 2 s, 3 d. Education: Sidney Sussex College, Cambridge University, 1954. Appointments include: Physicist, Mullard Research Lab, 1954-56; Editorial Staff, New Scientist, 1956-62; Editor, New Scientist, 1962-66; Chairman, Association of British Science Writers, 1962-66. Publications include: The Mind of Man, 1970; The Restless Earth, 1972; The Life Game, 1973; The Weather Machine, 1974; The Human Conspiracy, 1976; The Key to the Universe, 1977; Einstein's Universe, 1979; Violent Universe, 1979; Nuclear Nightmare, 1979; The Comet is Coming, 1980; Timescale, 1983; The English Channel, 1986; Scientific Europe, 1990; Spaceship Earth, 1991; Giotto to the Comets, 1992; Out of this World, 1995. Contributions to: Many and Various Magazines & Journals. Honours: UNESCO Kalinga Prize, 1972; AAAS Honorary Fellow, 1986. Memberships: Cruising Association; Royal Astronomical Society; Royal Geographical Society. Literary Agent: Lizzie Calder. Address: 26 Boundary Road, Northgate, Crawley, West Sussex RH10 2BT.

CALDERWOOD James Lee, b. 1930, USA. Appointments: Instructor, MI State University, 1961-63; Assistant Professor, University of CA, 1963-66; Professor, 1966-, Association Dean of Humanitites, 1973-, University of CA. Publications: Forms of Poetry; Perspectives on Poetry; Perspectives on Fiction; Perspectives in Drama; Form of Drama; Essays in Shakespearean Criticism; Love's Labours Lost; Shakespearean Metadrama; Forms of Prose Fiction; Forms of Tragedy; Metadrama in Shakespeares Henriad; To Be of Not to Be, 1983; If It Were Done, 1986; Shakespeare and the Denial of Death, 1987; The Properties of Othello, 1989; A Midsummer Night's Dream, 1992. Address: 1323 Terrace Way, Laguna Beach, CA 92651, USA.

CALHOUN Craig Jackson, b. 16 June 1952, Watseka, Illinois, USA. Education: BA, Unviersity of Southern California, 1972; MA, Columbia University, 1974; MA, 1975, D.Phil, Oxford University, 1980. Appointments include: Research Associate, Columbia University, 1973-74; Visiting Research Association, University of Khartoum, Sudan, 1983; Visiting Lecturer, University of Oslo, 1991; Research Fellow, Research Governing Board, Centre for Psychosocial Studies, Chicago, Illionos, 1991-. Publication: The Anthropological Study of Education: The Question of Class Struggle; Structutes of Power and Constraint; Beijing Spring; Harbermas and the Public Sphere, 1992, Bordieu: Critical Perspectives, 1993. Contributions to: Numerous Articles and Chapters; Review Essays; Translations. Honours: National Merit Scholar; W K Kellogg National Fellowship; Reynolds Fund Award; W R Kenan Fellowship; Order of the Golden Fleece, Honorary Member; P & R Hettleman Faculty Fellowship. Memberships: American Anthropological Association; Royal Anthropological Institute; British Sociological Association; Southern Sociological Society; Social History Society; International Sociological Assocation; International Studies Association; Association of International Education Administrators; Society for the Study of Social Problems. Address: Office of International Programs, University of North Carolina, Chapel Hill, NC 27599, USA.

CALIFANO Joseph A Jr, b. 1931, Ameircan. Appointments: Admitted to New York Bar, 1955; US Naval Reserve, 1955-58; With Law Firm of Dewey, Ballantine, Bushby, Palmer and Wood, NYC, 1958-61; Special Assistant to General Counsel, Department of Defense, 1961-62; General Counsel, Department of the Army, 1963-64; Special Assistant to the Secretary and Deputy Secretary of Defense, 1964-65, and to President Lyndon Johnson, 1965-69; Member of the firm of Arbold and Porter, 1969-171; Partner, Williams, Connolly and Califano, 1971-76; United States Secretary of Health, Education and Welfare, 1977-79; Partner, Dewey Ballantine, 1983-. Publications: The Student Revolution: A Global Confrontation, 1969; A Presidential Nation, 1975; Media and the Law (with H Simons) 1976; The Media and Business (with H Simons), 1978; Governing America: An Insider's Report from the White House and the Cabinet, Report on Drug Abuse and Alcoholism, 1982; America's Health Care Revolution: Who Lives? Who Dies? Who Pays? 1986; The Triumph and Tragedy of Lyndon Johnson, 1992. Address: 1775 Pennsylvania Avenue NW, Washington DC 20006, USA.

CALISHER Hortense (Jack Fenno), b. 20 Dec 1911, NY, USA. Writer. m. 1 son, 1 daughter. Education: BA, Barnard College, Columbia University, 1932. Publications include: The New Yorkers, 1969; In The Palace of the Movie King, 1994; Herself, 1972; Collected Short Stories of Hortense Calisher, 1975; Age, 1987. Contributions to: NY Times; Harpers; Paris Review; Story; New Criterion; Yale Review; Southwest Review; New Yorker. Honours: Two Guggenheim Fellowships, 1952, 55; Kafka Prize, 1987; National Endowment Lifetime Achievement Award, 1989. Memberships: PEN America; American Academy of Arts & Letters. Literary Agent: Donadio & Ashworth. Address: 231 West 22nd St, NY 10011, USA.

CALLAGHAN Barry, b. 5 July 1937, Toronto, Ontario, Canada. Publisher; Poet. Education: MA, University of Toronto, 1963. Appointments: Professor, York Universiy, 1965-; Founder, Publisher, Exile Magazine, 1972-, Exile Editions, Toronto, 1976-. Publications: The Hogg Poems and Drawings, 1978; As Close We Came, 1982; Stone Blind Love, 1988; Novel, The Way the Angel Spreads her Wings, 1989; The Black Queen Stories, 1982; Editor, Lords of Winter and Love: A Book of Canadian Love Poems, English & French, 1983. Honours: Presidents' Medal, For Journalism, 1982, 1985, 1988; Ontario Arts Council Award, 1987. Address: 69 Sullivan Street, Toronto, Ontario M5T 1C2, Canada.

CALLAHAN Steven, b. 6 Feb 1952, USA. Author; Illustrator. Education: BA, Syracuse University, 1974. Appointments: Cont Editor, Sail Magazine, 1982-84; Sailor Magazine, 1984-85. Associate Editor, Cruising World Magazine, 1994-. Publications: Adrift, 76 Days Lost at Sea, 1986; Capsized, 1993. Contributions to include: Sail; Sailor; Cruising World; Sailing; Multihull; NE Offshore; Yankee; NY Times; Ultrasport; International Wildlife; Yachting World; Yachts and Yachting. Honours: Salon Du Libre Maritime, 1986; Best Books for Young Adults, 1986. Address: 804 Newport Green, Newport, RI 02840-6428, USA.

CALLICOTT John Baird, b. 9 May 1941, Memphis, USA. College Professor. m. (1) Ann Nelson Archer, div, 1 s, (2) Frances Moore Lappe, div. Education: BA, Rhodes College; MA, PhD, Syracuse University. Publications: In Defense of the Land Ethic; Nature in Asian Tradition of Thought; Companion to a Sand County Almanac; The River of the Mother of God and Other Essays; Clothed in Fur and Other Tales; Earths Insights, 1994. Contributions to: More than 100, Journals and Book Chapters. Honours: WI Libraries Association Distinguished Achievement Award. Memberships: Am Philosophical ASsociation; Society for Conservation Biology; International Society for Environmental Ethics. Address: Dept of Philosophy, University of WI, SP stevens Point, WI 54481, USA.

CALLISON Brian (Richard), b. 1934, British. Appointments: Deck Officer, British Merchant Navy, 1951-54; Managing Director, Construction Company, 1956-63; General Manager, Entertainment Centre, 1963-67; Freelance Writer, 1967-. Publications: A Flock of Ships, 1970; A Plague of Sailors, 1971; Dawn Attack, 1972; A Web of Salvage, 1973; Trapp's War, 1974; A Ship is Dying, 1976; A Frenzy of Merchantmen, 1977; The Judas Ship, 1978; Trapp's Peace, 1979; The Auriga Madness, 1980; The Sextant, 1981; Spearfish, 192; Bone Collectors, 1984; Thunder of Crude, 1986; Trapp and World War Three, 1988; The Trojan Hearse, 1990. Memberships: Royal Institute of Nagivation (M.R.I.N). Literary Agent: Harper Collins. Address: c/o Harper Collins Publishers, 77-85 Fulham Palace Road, Hammersmith, London, W6 8JB, England.

CALLOW Philip, b. 26 Oct 1924, Birmingham, England. Education: St Lukes College, Exeter, 1968-70. Appointments: Creative Writing Fellow, Open University, 1979. Publications: The Hosanna Man, 1956; Common People, 1958; Native Ground, 1959; Pledge for the Earth, 1960; The Honeymooners, 1960; Turning Point, 1961; Clipped Wings, 1963; The Real life, 1964; In My Own Land, 1965; Going to the Moon, 1968; The Bliss Body, 1969; Flesh of Morning, The Lamb, 1971; Bare Wires, Yours, 1972; Son and Lover: The Young D H Lawrence, 1975; The Story of My Desire, 1976; Janine, 1977; The Subway to NY, 1979; Cave Light, 1981; Woman with a Poet, 1983; NY Insomnia, 1984; Verse, Icons, 1987; Soliloquires of an Eye, 1990; Novels, The Painters Confessions, 1989; Some Love, 1991. Address: Little Thatch, Haselbury, Nr Crewkerne, Somerset, England.

CALLWOOD June, b. 2 June 1924, Chatham, Canada. Writer. m. Trent Frayne, 13 May 1944, 2 sons, 2 daughters. Appointments: Reporter, Brantford Expositor, 1941; Toronto Globe & Mail, 1942; Freelance Journalist, 1945-; Columnist, Globe & Mil, 1983-89; Judge, Governor Generals Non Fiction Award, 1984-86; National Newspaper Award, 1976-83; National Magazine Awards, 1977, 1988-90; Stephen Leacock Award, 1977-80. Publications include: 27 Emma, 1984; Twelve Weeks in Spring, 1986; Emotions, 1986; Jim: A Life with AIDS, 1988; The Sleepwalker, 1990; Trail Without End, 1995. Honours: City of Toronto Award of Merit, 1974; Order of Canada, 1978; Canadian News Hall of Fame, 1984; Windsor Press Club Quill Award, 1987; Order of Ontario, 1989; Udo Award, 1989; Lifetime Achievement Award, 1991; 13 Honorary Degrees; Margaret Lawrence Lecture, 1993. Memberships: The Writers Union of Canada; The Canadian Centre PEN; Toronto Arts Council; Beaver Valley Soaring Club. Address: 21 Hillcroft Drive, Islington, Ontario, Canada M9B 4X4.

CALMAN Mel, b. 19 May 1931, London, England. Free-lance cartoonist. m. (1) Pat McNeill, 1957 (divorced), 2 d. (2)Karen Usborne (divorced 1982). Education: National Diploma in Design, St Martin's School of Art; Art Teachers' Diploma, Goldsmiths College, London. Appointments: Cartoonist, Daily Express, London, 1957-63; Cartoonist for Tonight Programme, British Broadcasting Corporation, London, 1963-64; Cartoonist, Sunday Telegraph, London, 1964-65; Cartoonist, Observer, London, 1965-66; Free-lance Cartoonist for magazines and newspapers, 1966-; Designer of book jackets and advertising campaignes; Illustrator for books; founder of Cartoon Gallery, 1970; Producer of animated caroon The Arrow and syndicated feature Men and Women, 1976-82. Publications: Bed-Sit, 1963; Boxes, 1964; The Penguin Calman, 1968; Contributor, B S Johnson, editor, The Evacuees, 1968; My God, 1970; This Pestered Isle, 1973; Calman at the Movies, 1990; Merry England Plc, 1990; Calman at the Royal Opera House, 1990. Contribnutions to: B S Johnson, editor, All Bull: The National Servicement, 1973; The New Penguin Calman, 1977; DR Calman's Dictionary of Psychoanalysis, 1979; But It's My Turn to Leave You, 1980; How About a Litte Quarrel Before Bed? 1981; Help! and Other Ruminations, 1982; Calman Revisited, 1983; The Big Novel, (radio play; first broadcast by British Broadcasting Corporation_ 1983; It's Only You That's Incompatible, 1984; What Else Do You Do? Sketches From a Cartoonist's Life (Biography), 1986; Sweet Tooth (radio play) first broadcast by British Broadcasting Corporation, 1987; Through the Telephone Directory, 1962; Calman and Women, 1967; Couples, 1972. Memberships: Alliance Graphique Internationale; Royal Society of Art (Fellow), Society of Industrial Artists (Fellow); Society of Artists and Designers (Fellow); Garrick Club. Address: 44 Museum Street, London, WC1A 1LY, England.

CALMENSON Stephanie Lyn, b. Brooklyn, New York, USA. Writer. Education: BA, Brooklyn College; MA, New York University. Publications: Never Take a Pig to Lunch, anthology, 1982; One Little Monkey, 1982, 4th edition 1983, produced by BBC TV, 1984; My Book of the Seasons, 1982; Where Will the Animals Stay? 1983; That's Not Fair! 1983; Where is Grandma Potamus? 1983; The Birthday Hat: A Grandma Potamus Story, 1983; The Kindergarten Book, 1983; Barney's Sand Castle, 1983; Bambi and the Butterfly, 1983; Ten Furry Monsters, 1984; The Afterschool Book, 1984; All Aboard the Goodnight Train, 1984; Waggleby of Fraggle Rock, 1985; Ten Items or Less, 1985; Happy Birthday Buddy Blue, 1985; The Laugh Book, anthology with Joanna Cole, 1986; Gobo and the Prize from Outer Space, 1986; The Sesame Street ABC Book, 1986; The Sesame Street Book of First Times, 1986; Little Duck's Moving Day, 1986; The Little Bunny, 1986; Who Said Moo? 1987; Beginning Sounds Workbook, 1987; The Read-Aloud Treasury, anthology with Joanna Cole, 1987; Tiger's Bedtime, 1987; One Red Shoe (The other One's Blue!), 1987; Spaghetti Manners, 1987; The Giggle Book, 1987; Fido, 19877;

Where's Rufus, 1988; Little Duck and the New Baby, 1988; The Children's Aesop, 1988; The Read-Aloud Treasury with Joanna Cole, 1988; No Stage Fright for Me, 1988; Where is Grandma Rabbit? 1988; 101 Turkey Jokes, 1988; Ho! Ho! Ho!: Christmas Jokes and Riddles, 1988; What Am I! Very First Riddles, 1989; The Principal's New Clothes, 1989; Come To My Party; Zip, Whiz, Zoom, 1992; The Little Witch Sisters, 1993, and many others. Contributor to: numerous journals and magazines. Memberships include: Mystery Writers of America; Society of Children's Book Writers; Authors Guild.

CALVERT Patricia Joyce, b. 22 July 1931, Great Falls, Montana, USA. Editor; Proofreader. m. George J Calvert, 27 Jan 1951, 2 d. Education: BS, Summa Cum Laude, Winona State University, 1976. Publications: The Snowbird, 1980; The Stone Pony, 1982; The Hour of the Wolf, 1983; Hadder MacColl, 1985; Yesterday's Daughter, 1986; Stranger, You and I, 1987; When Morning Comes, 1989; Picking Up the Pieces, 1993. Contributor to: Highlights for Children; Junior Life; The Adventurer; American Farmer; The Friend; Capper's Weekly; Grit; The Writer Magazine; Farmland News; The War Cry. Honours: Society of Children's Book Writers, Work-in-Progress Award, 1978; American Library Society, Best Book Award, 1980; Woman in the Arts Award, YWCA, 1981; Freinds of American Writers Award, 1981; Society of Midland Authors, 1981. Memberships: Society of Children's Book Writers; Childrens Reading Round Table; Minnesota Reading Assocaition; Interantional Reading Assocaition. Literary Agent: Clair M Smith. Address: Foxwood Farm, RR2 Box 91, Chatfield, MN 55923, USA.

CALVERT Peter Anthony Richard, b. 19 Nov 1936, Islandmagee, County Antrim, Northern Ireland. Professor. m. Susan Ann Milbank, 1987. Education: Campbell College, Belfast; Queens College, Cambridge; University of MI. Appointments: Lecturer, 1964-71; Senior Lecturer, 1971-74; Reader, 1974-83; Professor, 1984-; University of Southampton. Publications include: The Mexican Revolution 1910-1914, 1968; A Study of Revolution, 1970; The Falklands Crisis, 1982; Guatemala, 1985; The Foreign Policy of New States, 1986; Argentina: Political Culture and Instability, (with Susan Calvert) 1989; Revolution and Counter Revolution, 1990; Latin America in the 20th Century, (with Susan Calvert) 1993; An Introduction to Comparative Politics, 1993; International Politics of Latin America, 1994; Editor, The Process of Political Succession, 1987; The Central American Security System, 1988; Political and Economic Encyclopedia of South America and the Caribbean. Contributions to: International Affairs Political Studies; World Today. Memberships: Fellow, Royal Historical Society. Address: Dept of Politics, University of Southampton, Southampton, SO17 1BJ, England.

CALVIN Henry. See: HANLEY Clifford.

CALVOCOREI Peter (John Ambrose), b. 1912, British. Author. Appointments: Called to the Bar, 1934; Wing Commander, trial of Major War Criminals, Nuremburg, 1945-46; Member of Staff, 1949-54 and of Council, 1955-72, Royal Institute of International Affairs; Director, Chatto and Windus Limited and The Hogarth Press Limited, publishers, London, 1954-65; Reader, part-time, in International Relations, University of Sussex, Brighton, 1965-71; Editorial Director, 1972-73; Publisher and Chief Executive, 1973-76, Penguin Books Limited, London; Member of the Council, Institute for Strategic Studies, 196-71; Chairman, The Africa Bureau, 1963-71; Chairman, London Library, 1970-73; Chairman, Open University Education Enterprises, 1979-. Publications: Nuremburg: The Facts, the Law and the Consequences, 1947; Survey of International Affairs, 5 volumes, 1947-54; Middle East Crisis (with G Wint), 1957; South Africa and World Opinion, 1961; World Order and New States,1962; World Politics since 1945, 1968, 1975; Total War (with G Wint) 1972; The British Experience 1945-1975, 1978; Top Secret Ultra, 1980; Independent Africa and the World, 1985; A Time for Peace, 1987; Who's Who in the Bible, 1987; Resilient Europe 1870-2000, 1991. Address: 1 Queens Parade, Bath, BA1 2NJ, England.

CAMERON Deborah, b. 10 Nov 1958, Glasgow, Scotland. Lecturer; Writer. Education: BA Hons, University of Newcastle upon Tyne, 1980; M.Litt, Oxford University, 1985. Appointments: Lecturer at Roehampton Institute of Higher Education, Digby Stuart College, London, 1983-; Visiting Professor at College of William and Mary, 1988-90; Worked as teacher of English as a foreign language; Active in British women's movement for more than ten years. Publications: Feminism and Linguistic Theory, 1985; (with T J Taylor) Analysing Converstaiton, 1987; (with Elizabeth Frazer) The Lust to Kill, 1987;

Editor: The Feminist Critique of Language, 1990; Editor with Jennifer Coates: Women in Their Speech Communities, 1989. Contributions to: Articles and reviews to magazines and newspapers, including Language and Communicaiton, City Limits and Cosmopolitan. Address: Digby Stuart College, Roehampton Lane, London, SW25 5PH, England.

CAMERON Donald. See: **HARBINSON-BRYANS Robert.**

CAMERON Dy, See: **COOK Dorothy Mary.**

CAMERON Eleanor, b. 23 Mar 1912, Canada. Writer. m. Ian Stuart Camercon, 24 June 1934, 1 s. Educcation: 2 years at University of California, Los Angeles. Literary Appointments: Editorial Board, Cricket (magazine for children) 1973-. Publications include: Children's Novels: The wonderful Flight to the Mushroom Planet, 1954; A Room Made of Windows, 1971; The Court of the Stone Children, 1973; Julia and the Hand of God, 1977; Julia's Magic, 1984; That Julia Redfern, 1982; For Young Adults: To the Green Mountains, 1975; The Private Worlds of Julia Redfern, 1988. Essays for Adults: The Green and Burning Tree: On the Writing and The Enjoyment of Children's Books, 1969. Contributions to: Various publications. Honours: Distinguied Contribution to Children's Literature Annual Award, 1965; Southern California Council on Literature for Children and Young People; Commonwealth Award, 1969 for the Green and Burning Tree; Boston Globe Horn Book Award, 1971 for A Room Made of Windows; National Book Award 1973 for The Court of the Stone Children; The Kerland Award, University of Minnesota, 1985. Memberships include: The Authors League; Children's Literature, New England; Children's Literature Assocaiation. Address: E P Dutton Children's Books, 375 Hudson Street, New York, NY 10014, USA.

CAMERON Ian. See: **PAYNE Donald Gordon.**

CAMERON Silver Donald, b. 21 June 1937, Toronto, Ontario, Canada. Author. m. (1) Catherine Ann Cahoon, 21 Aug 1959, 3 s, 1 d. (2) Lulu Terrio, 17 May 1980, 1 s. Education: BA, University of British Columbia, 1959; MA, University of California, 1962; PhD, University of London, 1967. Appointments: Associate Professor of English, University of New Brunswick, 1968-71; Fereelance Writer, 1971-; Writer-in-Residence, University College of Cape Breton, 1978-80; University of Prince Edward Island, 1985-86; Nova Scotia College of Art and Design, 1987-88; Founding Executive Director, Centre Bras d'Or, Baddeck, Nova Scotia; President, Novara Software; Owner, Paper Tiger Enterprises Ltd, editorial and consulting sevices. Publications: Faces of Leacock, 1967; Conversations with Canadian Novelists, 1973; The Education of Everett Richardson, 19779; Seasons in the Rain, essays, 1978; Dragon Lady, 1980; paperback 1981; The Baitchopper, children's novel, 1982; Schooner: Bluenose and Bluenoe II, 1984; Outhouses of the West, 1988; Wind, Whales and Whisky: A Cape Breton Voyage, 1991; Lifetime: A Treasury of Uncommon Wisdoms (co-author), 1992; Once Upon a Schooner: An Offshore Voyage In Bluenose II, 1992; Icebouts to Super Ferries: An Illustrated History of Marine Atlantic (co-author). Numerous articles, radio drama, short stories, television scripts and stage plays including The Prophet at Tantramar, 1988. Honours: Several ACTRA Award nominations for radio drama; 4 National Magazine Awards; Best Short film, Canadian Film Celebration; Nominated, Prix Italia for Radio Drama, 1980; City of Dartmouth Book Award, 1992; Atlantic Provinces Booksellers Choice Award, 1992. Memberships: Writers Union, Canada, Vice-Chairman; Periodical Writers Association, Canada; ACTRA; Writers Federation, Nova Scotia. Address: D'Escousse, Nova Scotia, Canada BOE 1KO.

CAMERON WATT Donald, b. 1928, England. Appointments include: Assistant Lecturer, 1954-56, Lecturer, 1956-61, Senior Lecturer, 1962-66, Reader, 1966=72, Professor, 1981-93, Emeritus Professor, 1993-, University of London; Assistant Editor, Documents on German Foreign Policy, 1918-45, 1951-54, 1957-59; Editor, Survey of International Affairs, 1962-71; Chairman, Greenwich Forum, 1974-84. Publications include: Britain and the Suez Canal, 1956; Documents on the Suez Crisis, 1957; Survey of International Affairs, 1961-63, 65, 69, 73; A History of the World in the the 20th Century, 1967; Contemporary History in Europe, 1969; Hitler's Mein Kampf, 1969, new edition 1990; Current British Foreign Policy, 1970-72; Documents on British Foreign Affairs, 1867-1939, 1985 in progress; Succeeeding John Bull, America in Britain's Place 1900-1975, 1983; How War Came, 1989; Argentina Between the Great Powers, 1990. Honour: Fellow, British Academy, DLitt, Oxon; Foreign Member Polish Academy of Arts & Science,

Cracow. Address: c/o London School of Economics & Political Science, Houghton Street, London WC2A 2AE, England.

CAMPBELL Alistair Te Ariki, b. 25 June 1925, Rarotonga. Writer. m. (1) Fleur Adcock, 1952, (2) Meg Andersen, 1958, 3 s, 2 d. Education: BA, Victoria University of Wellington, 1953; Wellington Teacher's College, 1954. Appointments: Editor, School Publications, 1955-72; Senior Editor, New Zealand Council for Educational Research, 1972-87. Publications include: Mine Eyes Dazzle, 1950; Wild Honey, 1964; Stone Rain: The Polynesian Strain, 1992; Island to Island, 1984; The Frigate Bird, 1989; Sidewinder, 1991; Tia, 1993. Contributions to: Poetry New Zealand; Poetry Australia. Honours: Gold Medal for TV Documentary Island of Spirits, 1974; New Zealand Book Award, 1982. Memberships: PEN International New Zealand Centre, Poetry Society. Address: 4 Rawhiti Road, Pukerua Bay, Wellington, New Zealand.

CAMPBELL Ewing, b. 26 Dec 1940, Alice, TX, USA. Novelist. Education: BBA, North TX State University, 1968; MA, University of Southern MS, 1972; PhD, OK State University, 1980. Appointments; Lecturer, 1981-82, Visiting Scholar, 1992, University of TX; Lecturer, OK State University, 1982-83; Instructor, Wharton College, 1983-84; Assistant Professor, 1984-89, Associate Professor, 1990, TX A&M University; Fulbright Lecturer, National University of Cordoba, 1989. Publications: Weave It Like Nighfall, 1977; The Way of Sequentered Places, 1982; The Rincon Triptych, 1984; Piranesi's Dream, 1986; Raymond Carver, 1992. Contributions to: London Magazine; New England Review; Kenyon Review. Honours: Fulbright Fellow, 1989; NEA Fiction Fellowship, 1990; Dobie Paisano Ralph Johnston Memorial Fellowship, 1992. Address: English Dept, TX A&M University, College Station, TX 77843, USA.

CAMPBELL Ian, b. 25 Aug 1942, Lausanne, Switzerland. Reader, English, University of Edinburgh. Education: MA, Aberdeen, 1964; PhD, Edinburgh, 1970; Appointments: Member, English Literature Deparment, University of Edinburgh, 1967-; Guest Appointments, Guelph, Duke, UCLA; British Council Appointments: France, Germany. Publications: Co-Editor, McLellan's Jamie The Saxt; Editor: Carlyle's Reminiscences & Selected Essays, Critical Essays in Nineteenth Century Scottish Fiction; Thomas Carlyle Letters, 15 volumes, 1970-87; Carlyle, 1974, 1975, 1978; Nineteenth Century Scottish Ficton: Critical Esays, 1978; Thomas and Jane, 1980; Kailyard, 1981; Lewis Grassic Gibbon, 1986; Spartacus, 1987. Contributions to: Numerous papers to learned journals. Honours: British Academy Research Fellowship, 1980. Memberships: President, Carlyle Society; Past President Scottish Association for the Speaking of Verse; Council Member, Association for Scottish Literary Studies. Address: Dept of English, University of Edinburgh, David Hume Tower, George Square, Edinburgh EH8 9JX, Scotland.

CAMPBELL James, b. 5 June 1951, Glasgow, Scotland. Writer. Education: Edinburgh University. Appointments: Editor, New Edinburgh Review, 1978-82. Publications: Pains Interzone: Richard Wright and Others On The Left Bank, 1945-60; Talking at the Gates: A Life of James Baldwin; Gate Fever; Invisible Country; The New Edinburgh Review Anthology; The Panther Book of Scottish Short Stories. Literary Agent: Antony Harwood, Curtis Brown. Address: c/o TLS, Priory House, St Johns Lane, London, EC1, England.

CAMPBELL John Malcolm, b. 2 Sept 1947, London, England. Writer. m. Alison McCracken, 5 Aug 1972, 1 s, 1 d. Education: Charterhouse, 1960-65; MA, 1970, PhD, 1975, university of Edinburgh. Publications: Lloyd George: The Goat in the Wilderness, 1977; F E Smith, First Earl of Birkenhead, 1983; Roy Jenkins: A Biography, 1983; Nye Bevan and the Mirage of British Socialism, 1987; The Experience of World War II, 1989; Makers of the Twentieth Century, 1990-; Edward Heath, 1993. Contributions to: Regular Book Reviews, The Times; Times Literary Supplement; New Statesman; London Review of Books. Honours: Yorkshire Post, Best First Book Award; NCR Book Award for non-fiction, 1994. Membership: Society of Authors. Literary Agent: Bruce Hunter, David Higham Associates. Address: 35 Ladbroke Square, London W11 3NB, England.

CAMPBELL Judith, (Anthony Grant), b. 1914, British. Appointments: Journalist; Broadcaster. Publications: Family Pony, 1962; The Queen Rides, 1965; Horses in the Sun, 1966; Police Horse, 1967; Pony Events, World of Horses, 1969; Horses and Ponies, World of Ponies, Anne - Portrait of a Princess, 1970; Family on Horseback (with N Toyne), Princess Anne and Her Horses, Elizabeth and Philip,

1972; The Champions, 1973; Royalty on Horseback, 1974; The World of the Horse, 1975; Eventing, Anne and Mark, 1976; Your own Pony Club, Queen Elizabeth II, 1979; The Mutant (as A Grant), Charles A Prince of His Time, 1980; The Royal Partners, 1982; Royal Horses, 1983; Ponies, People and Palaces, autobiography; Freddy and the Fiddler, Co-author and illustrator Oliver Marland. Address. c/o A M Heath Limited, 79 St Martin's Lane, London, WC2N 4AA, England.

CAMPBELL Karen. See: **BEATY Betty Smith.**

CAMPBELL Martin Crafts, (Marty), b. 24 June 1946, Oakland, CA, USA. Writer. Education: BS, University of Chicago, 1968; MA, Northwestern University, 1972. Appointments: Featured Performer, Poetry, USA & St Croix, 1976-; Publisher, Mar Crafts, 1981-; Editor, SENYA and Companion of Senya, 1989; Editor, Collage Two, 1991; Editor, Poetry Corner, 1991-. Publications: Chapters of Poems, Mesh Up, 1981; Croix These Tears, 1982; Dreem, 1982; Church, 1985; Saint Sea, 1986; Companion to Senya, 1989; Seed, 1994. Contributions to: Hammers; Collage 1, 2 & 3; Caribbean Writer; Verve. Honours: 1st Place, Caribbean Poetry Contest, London, 1981; Black History Monthly Poetry Contest, 1987. Memberships: Performance Poet and Writer; Poets & Writers; Finmen Ocean Swimmers; St Croix Basket Ball Association; Courtyard Players; Island Center for the Performing Arts. Address: 2565 Frederiksted, VI 00841, USA.

CAMPBELL Marty. See: **CAMPBELL Martin Crafts.**

CAMPBELL Ramsey, b. 4 Jan 1946, Liverpool, England. Writer; Film Reviewer. m. Jenny Chandler, 1 Jan 1971, 1 son, 1 daughter. Appointments: Film Reviewer, BBC Radio Merseyside, 1969-; Full-time Writer, 1973-. Publications: Novels: The Doll Who Ate His Mother, 1976, 1985; The Face That Must Die, 1979, 1983; The Parasite, 1980; The Nameless, 1981, 1985; Incarnate, 1983; The Claw, 1983, Night of the Claw, USA; Obsession, 1985; The Hungry Moon, 1986; The Influence, 1988; Ancient Images, 1989; Midnight Sun, 1990; The Count of Eleven, 1991; The Long Lost, 1993; Short stories: The Inhabitant of the Lake and Less Welcome Tenants, 1964; Demons by Daylight, 1973; The Height of the Scream, 1976; Dark Companions, 1982; Cold Print, 1985; Black Wine (with Charles L Grant), 1986; Night Visions 3 (with Clive Barker, Lisa Tuttle), 1986; Scared Stiff, 1987; Dark Feasts: The World of Ramsey Campbell, 1987; Waking Nightmares, 1991;. Alone With The Horrors, 1993; Strange Things and Stranger Places, 1993; Novella: Needing Ghosts, 1990. Contributions to: Ramsey Campbell, Probably, regular column in Necrofile, USA; Anthologies including: Superhorror, 1976; New Terrors, 1980; New Tales of the Cthulhu Mythos, 1980; Fine Frights: Stories That Scared Me, 1988; Uncanny Banquet, 1992. Honours: World Fantasy Awards: Best Short Story, 1978, Best Novel, 1980; British Fantasy Award, Best Short Story, 1978; British Fantasy Awards, Best Novel, 1980, 1985, 1988, 1989, 1991; Bram Stoker Award, 1989; British and World Fantasy Awards, Best Anthology or Collection, for Best New Horror (co-edited with Stephen Jones), 1991; Liverpool Daily Post and Echo Award for Literature, 1993. Memberships; President, British Fantasy Society; Society of Fantastic Films. Literary Agents: Carol Smith, UK; Kirby McCauley, USA; Ralph Vicinanza, foreign. Address: 31 Penkett Road, Wallasey L45 7QE, Merseyside, England.

CAMPS Arnulf. See: **CAMPS Petrus Henricus Johannes Maria.**

CAMPS Petrus Henricus Johannes Maria, (Arnulf Camps), b. 1 Feb 1925, Eindhoven, Netherlands. Emeritus Professor. Education: B Th, University Nijmegen, 1951; DD, University Fribourg, 1957. Appointments include: Professor, Karachi Pakistan, 1957-61; Mission Sec, Netherlands, 1961-63; Ordinary Professor, University of Nijmegen, 1963-90; Consultor, Dialogue Vatican, 1964-79; Board of Directors, World Conf, Religion & Peace, 1979-; Board of Directors, Institute Missiology & Ecumenics, 1981-91. Publications: Partners in Dialogue; The Sanskrit Grammar & Manuscripts of the Father Heinrich Roth; Jerome Xavier S J and the Muslims of the Mogul Empire; Trilogy on Theology of Religions; Het Derde Oog, Van een Theologie in Azie near een Aziatsche Theologie. Contributions to: The Identitity of Europe and Cultural Plurality; Studies in Interreligious Dialogue; For my Bibliography See, Popular Religion. Honours: Knight of the Order of Dutch Lion. Address: Helmkruidstraat 35, NL 6602 CZ Wijchen, Netherlands.

CAMPTON David, b. 1924. British. Playwright; Children's Fiction Writer. Appointments: Clerk: City of Leicester Education Department,

1941-49; East Midlands Gas Board, Leicester, 1949-56; Professional Actor, Director, 1959-. Publications include: On Stage: Containing 17 Sketches and 1 Monologue, 1964; Resting Place, 1964; The Manipulator, 1964; Split Down the Middle, 1965; Little Brother, Little Sister and Out of the Flying Pan, 1966; Two Leaves and a Stalk, 1967; Angel Unwilling, 1967; Ladies Night: 4 Plays for Women, 1967; More Sketches, 1967; Laughter and Fear, 9 One-Act Plays, 1969; The Right Place, 1969; On Stage Again: Containing 14 Sketches and 2 Monologues, 1969; Now and Then, 1970; The Life and Death of Almost Everybody, 1970; Timesneeze, 1970; Gulliver in Lilliput (reader), 1970; Gulliver in The Land of Giants (reader), 1970; The Wooden Horse of Troy (reader), 1970; Johan, 1971; The Cagebirds, 1971; Us and Them, 1972; Carmilla, 1972; In Committee, 1972; Come Back Tomorrow, 1972; In Committee, 1972; Three Gothic Plays, 1973; Modern Aesop (reader), 1976; One Possessed, 1977; What Are You Doing Here?, 1978; The Do-It-Yourself Frankenstein Outfit, 1978; Zodiac, 1978; After Midnight: Before Dawn, 1978; Pieces of Campton, 1979; Parcel, 1979; Everybody's Friend, 1979; Who Calls?, 1980; Attitudes, 1980; Freedom Log, 1980; Dark Wings, 1981; Look-Sea, 1981; Great Whales, 1981; Who's a Hero, Then?, 1981; Dead and Alive, 1983; But Not Here, 1984; Singing in the Wilderness, 1986; Mrs Meadowsweet, 1986; The Vampyre, (children's book), 1986; Our Branch in Brussels, 1986; Cards, Cups and Crystal Ball, 1986; Can You Hear The Music, 1988; The Winter of 1917, 1989; Smile, 1990; Becoming a Playwright, 1992; The Evergreens, 1994. Contributions to: Amateur Stage; Writers News; Drama; Whispers. Memberships: Writers Guild of Great Britain; Society of Authors. Literary Agent: ACTAC (Theatrical and Cinematic) Ltd, Wiltshire, England. Address: 35 Liberty Road, Glenfield, Leicester LE3 8JF, England.

CANAWAY W H (Bill Canaway, William Hamilton Hermes), b. 1925, British. Appointments: Teacher in various education establishments, 1949-662. Publications: A Creel of Willow, 1957; A Snowdon Stream (The Gwyrfai) and How to Fish It, The Ring-Givers, 1958; The Seal, 1959; Sammy Going South (in US as find the Boy), Hose on Fire, 1961; The Hunter and the Horns, 1962; My Feet upon a Rock, 1963; Crows in a Green Tree, The Ipcress File (with J Doran), 1965; The Grey Seas of Jutland, 1966; The Mules of Borgo San Marco, 1967; A Moral Obigation, 1969; A Declaration of Independence, Roll Me Over, 1971; Redezvous in Black,1972; Harry Doing Good, 1973; Glory of the Sea, 1975; The Willow-Pattern War, 1976; The Solid Gold Buddha, 1979; Love of Life, The Race for Number One, 1984; The Helmet and the Cross, 1986. Address 43 Main Street, Repton, Derbyshire, England.

CANNADINE David, b. 1950, England. Professor. m. Linda Colley. Education: D.Phil, Oxford University. Publications: Lords and Landlords, 1980; Patricians, Power & Politics in Nineteenth Century Towns, 1984; The First Modern Society, 1989; The Pleasures of the Past, 1989; The Decline and Fall of the British Aristocracy, 1990; G M Trevelyan, 1992; Aspects of Aristocracy, 1994. Address: Dept of History, Columbia University, New York, NY 10027, USA.

CANNON Curt. See: **LOMBINO Salvatore A.**

CANNON Frank. See: **MAYHAR Ardath.**

CANNON Geoffrey John, b. 12 Apr 1940, Witham, Essex, England. Writer. m. (1)Anthonia Mole, 1961, divorced, (2)Caroline Walker, 1987 (dec) 2 s, 1 d. Education: BA, Philosophy and Psychology, Balliol College, Oxford, 1958-61. Publications: Dieting Makes You Fat (co-author), 1983; The Food Scandal, (co-author), 1984; Additives: Your Complete Survival Guide (contributor), 1986; Fat To Fit, 1986; The Politics of Food, 987; The Good Fight, 1988; The Safe Food Handbook (contributor), 1990; Healthy Eating: The Experts Agree, 1990; Superbug (co-author), 1991. Contributions to: Most leading British newspapers. Honours: Cantor Lecturer, Royal Society of Arts, 1988. Memberships: Secretary, Guild of Food Writers, 1988-91; Secretary, Caroline Walker Trust; Secretary, London Road Runners; Nutrition Society. Literary Agent: Deborah Rogers. Address: 6 Aldridge Road Villas, London W11 1BP, England.

CANNON Steve, b. 10 Apr 1935, New Orleans, Louisiana, USA. Writer; Educator; Publisher. 2 s, 4 d. Education: BA, Literary, University of Nebraska, 1954. Appointments: Professor of Humanities, Medgar Evers College, 1971-92. Publications: Groove, Bang and Jive Around, 1968, 1971; Introduction to Rouzing the Rubble, 1991; Plays: The Set Up, 1992; Chump Change, 1992. Contributions to: Excerpts from novel Looney Tunes under Deep Blue Moon, to Gathering of the Tribes,

1991, Pean Sensible, 1992. Membership: PEN, New York Chapter. Address: 285 East Third Street, New York, NY 10009, USA.

CANTALUPO Charles, b. 17 Oct 1951, Orange, New Jersey, USA. Assistant Professor of English; Writer. m. Catherine Musello, 21 Aug 1976 (died 1983), 1 s. Education: Attended University of Kent at Canterbyry, 1971-72, BA, Washington University, 1973; MA, 1978, PhD, 1980, Rutgers University, New Brunswick. Appointments: Teaching Assistant, 1973-76, Instructor in English, 1977-79; Rutgers University, New Brunswick; Instructor, 1980, Assistant Professor of English, 1981, Pennsylvania State University, University Park, Pennsylavania, affiliated to a number of organisations at Pennsylvania State Univeristy; Director and Chairman of Catherine M Cantalupo Scholarship Foundation at Rutgers University, 1984-; Eucharistic Minister at Pottsville/Warne Hospital Clinic, Pottsville, Pennslyvania. Publications: (Contributor), Seabury in Memorium: A Bicentennial Anthology, 1983; The Art of Hope (poetry), 1983; (Contributor), John H Morgan editor, Fleet Street Poet: A memorial Anthology to Samuel Johnson, 1984; On Common Ground: An Anthology of Poems, 1985; (Contributor), Thomas N Corns editor, The Literature of Controversy, 1986; (Contributing editor), Contemporary Authors, Volume 120 Gale, 1987. Contributions to: Other edited volumes, encyclopedias, periodicals. Honours: American Academy of Poets Prize, 1976 for the Death of Colin Clout; Faculty Organization Teaching Award, 1985-86, Student Government Association Faculty Student Service Award, 1987-88. Memberships: Various professional memberships. Address: Department of English, Pennsylvania State University, Schuylkill Campus, Schuylkill Haven, PA 17972, USA.

CANTOR Norman. Appointment: Professor, New York University. Publications include: Church, Kingship and Lay Investitive in England, 1958; The Medieval World; Medieval History: The Life & Death of a Civilization, 1963; How To Study History, 1967; The English, 1968; Western Civilization: Its Genesis and Destiny, 1969; Perspectives on the European Past, 1971; The Meaning of the Middle Ages, 1973; Twentieth Century Culture; Medieval Lives, 1994. Address: Dept of History, New York University, 19 University Place 5th Floor, New York, NY 10003, USA.

CAPLAN Coren, b. 25 Aug 1944, Federal Republic of Germany. Writer; Academic. 1 d. Education: PhD, 1984. Publications: Seiltanz, 1984. Contributions to: Poetry & Short Stories in Literary Journals, Anthologies and Books. Honours: Short Story Award, 1977; Short Story & Poetry Award, 1987. Memberships: PEN; Australian poets Union; Australian Society of Authors. Address: 12 Bowman Park Estate, New England Highway, Armidale, NSW 2350, Australia.

CAPLAN Paula Joan, b. 7 July 1947, Professor. Education: BA, Harvard University, 1969; MA, Duke University, 1971; PhD, 1973. Appointments include: Postdoctoral Fellow, The Hospital for Sick Children, 1974-76; Lecturer, Women's Studies, University of Toronto, 1979-; Head, Centre for Womens Studies in Education, Ontario Institute for Studies in Education, 1984-85; Full Professor, Ontario Institute for Studies in Education, 1987-. Publications: They Say Your Crazy: How The World's Most Powerful Psychiatrists Decide Who's Normal; You're Smarter Than They Make You Feel: How the Experts Intimidate Us and What We Can Do About It; Thinking Critically About Research on Sex and Gender; Lifting a Ton of Feathers: A Woman's Guide to Surviving in the Academic World; The Myth of Women's Masochism; Between Women: Lowering the Barriers; Barriers Between Women. Contributions to: Numerous Chapters, Monographs, Refereed Journals. Honours: YWCA Women of Distinction Award. Memberships: Fellow, American Orthopsychiatric Association; Canadian Psychological Association.

CAPUTI Jane Elizabeth, b. 27 Oct 1953, Brooklyn, NY, USA. Professor. Education: Boston College, 1974; Simmons College, 1977; Bowling Green State University, 1982. Publications: The Age of Sex Crime; Websters First New Intergalatic Wickedary of the English Language; Gossips, Gorgons and Crones; The Fates of the Earth. Contributions to: MS; Feminist Studies; Womens Studies; Journal of Populat Film & TV; Journal of Am Culture. Honours: Emily Toth Award. Address: Dept of American Studies, University of New Mexico, Albuquerque, NM 87131, USA.

CAPUTO Philip Joseph, b. 10 June 1941, USA. Novelist. m. 21 June 1969, 2 s. Education: BA, English, Loyola University, 1964. Publications: A Rumor of War, 1972; Horn of Africa, 1980; Del Corso's Gallery, 1983; Indian Country, 1987; A Rumor of War, 1987; Means of

Escape, 1992. Contributions to: New York Times; Washington Post, Chicago Tribune; Esquire; Playboy. Honours; Pulitzer Prize (shared) 1972; Sidney Hillman Foundation Award, 1977; Finalist, American Book Award, 1980. Memberships: PEN; Authors Guild; National Writer's Union; Writer's Guild of America. Agent: Aaron M Priest. Address: c/o Aaron Priest Literary Agency, USA.

CARAS Roger Andrew, (Roger Sarac), b. 24 May 1928, MA, USA. Author; TV Correspondent. m. Jill Langdon Barclay, 5 Sept 1954, 1 s, 1 d. Education: BA, Northeastern University, Western Reserve University, University of Southern CA. Appointments: Adjunct Professor, Southampton College; Adjunct Professor, School of Vet Med University of PA. Publications include: Dangerous to Man, 1964; Wings of Gold, 1965; North American Mammals, 1967; Private Lives of Animals, 1974; A Zoo in Your Room, 1975; The Roger Caras Dog Book, 1980; The Endless Migration, 1985; Horse Stories, 1990. Contributions to: Audubon: NY Times; Ladies Home Journal; National Wildlife; Science Digest; National Observer; Finncial Times; Family Health; Physicians World; Family Circles; Numerous Other Journals. Honours include: Honorary Degrees; Numerous Awards. Memberships: Outdoor Writers Association of Am; Dog Writers Association. Literary Agent: Perry Knowlton, c/o Curtis Brown Ltd, USA. Address: Thistle Hill Farm, 21108, Slab Bridge Road, Freeland, MD 21053, USA.

CARD Orson Scott, b. 1951, American. Appointments: Volunteer Mormon Missionary in Brazil, 1971-73; Operated Repertory theatre, Provo, UT, 1974-75; Proofreader, 1974; Editor, 1974-76, Brigham Young University Press, Provo; Editor, Ensign Magazine, Salt Lake City, 1976-78 and Compute Books, Greensborog, NC, 1983. Publications: Listen Mom and Dad, Hot Sleep, Capitol, 1978; A Planet Called Treason, 1979; Songmaster, 1980; Unaccompanied Sonata and Other Stories, Saintspeak, Dragons of Darkness, 1981; Ainge, 1981; Hart's Hope, Dragons of Light (ed), The Worthing Chronicle, 1983; Compute's Guide to IBM PCjr Sound and Graphics, A Woman of Destiny, 1984; Ender's Game, 1985; The Memory of Earth, 1992; The Call of Earth, 1993; The Changed Man, 1992; The Ship's of Earth, 1994; Lovelock, 1994 (with Kathryn H Kidd). Address: 546 Lindley road, Greensboro, NC 27410, USA.

CARDENAL Ernesto, b. 20 Jan 1925, Granada, Nicaragua. Poet. Education: University of Mexico, 1944-48; Columbia University, New York, 1948-49. Appointments include: Roman Catholic Priest, from 1965. Publications: Proclama del conquistador, 1947; Gethsemani, Ky., 1960; La hora O, 1960; Epigramas: poemas, 1961; Gracion por Marilyn Monroe and other poems, 1965; El estrecho dudoso, 1966; Antologia, 1967; Poemas, 1967; Psalms of Struggle and Liberation, 1967, 1971; Mayapan, 1968; Poemas reunidos 1949-69; Homage to the American Indians, 1969; Zero Hour and Other Documentary Poems, 1971, 1980; Antologia, 1971; Poemas, 1971; Antologia, 1972; Canto nacional, 1973; Oraculo sobre Managua, 1973; Poesia escogida, 1975; Canto a un pais que nace, 1978; Apocolypse and Other Poems, 1977; Nueva antologia poetica, 1979; Waslala, 1983; Poesia dela nueva Nicaragua, 1983; Flights of Victory, 1984; With Walker in Nicaragua and Other Early Poems 1949-54, 1985; From Nicaragua with Love: Poems 1976-1986; Golden UFOS: The Indian Poems, 1992; Texts on the Revolution, Editions of poems. Honours include: Premio de la Paz Grant, 1980. Address: Apartado Postal A-252, Managua, Nicaragua.

CARDINAL Marie, b. 9 Mar 1929, Algiers, Algeria. Novelist. m. Jean-Pierre Ronfard, 1953, 1 son, 2 daughters. Education: University of Algiers and Sorbonne, Paris. Appointments include: Teacher of French and Philosophy in Greece, Portugal, Austria. Publications: Ecoutez la mer, 1962; La Mule de Corbillard, 1963; La Souricière, 1965; La Clé sur la porte, 1972; The Words To Say It, 1975, 1983; Une Vie pour Deux, 1978; Le Passé empiété, 1983; Devotion and Disorder, 1987, 1991; Commesi de rien n'était, 1990; Also: Mao (co-author), 1970; Les Pieds-Noirs: Algérie 1920-54; Translator of works by Euripides and Ibsen. Honours include: Prix Littre, 1976. Address: 831 Viger Est, Montreal, Quebec, Canada H2L 2P5.

CARDOSO PIRES Jose (Augusto Neves), b. 2 Oct 1925, Peso, Castelo, Branco, Portugal. Novelist. Education: University of Lisbon. Appointments: Literary Director of various publishing houses in Lisbon. Publications: Historuas de amor, 1952; Estrada 43, 1955; La ancorado, 1958; Jogos de azar, 1963; O hospede de Job, 1963; O delfin, 1968; Dinossauro excelentissimo, 1972; O burro-em-pe, 1978; Ballad of Dogs' Beach: dossier of a crime, 1982, 1986; Alexandra Alpha, 1987; A Republica dos Corvos, 1988; Co-translator of Death of a Salesman, by Arthur Miller, 1963; Plays: O render dos herois, 1960, and

Corpo-delito na sala de espelhos, 1980. Honours include: Grande Premio do Romance e da Novela, 1983. Address: Rua Sao Joao de Brito 7-1, 1700 Lisbon, Portugal.

CAREW Jan (Rynveld), b. 1925, Guyanese. Appointments: Lecturer in Race Relations, University of London Extra-Mural Department, 1953-57; Writer and Editor, BBC Overseas Service, London, 1954-65; Editor, African Review, Ghana, 1965-66; CBC Broadcaster, Toronto, 1966-69; Senior Fellow, Council of Humanities and Lecturer, Department of Afro-American Studies, Princeton University, 1969-72; Professor, Department of African-American Studies, Northwestern University, Evanston IL 1972-87, now Emeritus; Visiting Clarence J Robinson Professor of Caribbean Literature and History, George Mason University 1989-91; Visiting Professor of International Studies, Illinois Wesleyan University, 1992-93; Co-Chairman, Third World Energy Institute, 1978-85; Co-founder Africa Network, 1981-; Chairman, Caribbean Society for Culture and Science, 1979-. Publications: Streets of Eternity, 1952; Black Midas (in US as A Touch of Midas), The Wild Coast, 1958; The Last Barbarian, 1961; Green Winter, 1964; University of Hunger, 1966; The Third Gift, 1975; The Origins of Racism and Resistance in the Americas, Rape of the Sun-people, 1976; Children of the Sun, 1980; Sea Drums in My Blood, 1981; Grenada: The Hour Will Stike Again, 1985; Fulcrums of Change, 1987. Memberships: Co-Chairman, Africa Network, 1981-. Address: Department of African-American Studies, Northwestern University, Evanston, IL 60208, USA.

CAREY Duncan. See: **GARNETT Richard.**

CAREY John, b. 5 Apr 1934, London, England. University Professor. m. Gillian Booth, 13 Aug 1960, 2 s. Education: Lambe Open Scholar, 1954-57; BA, 1957; D Phil, 1960, St John's College, Oxford. Publications: Milton, 1969; The Violent Effigy: A Study of Dickens' Imagination, 1973; Thackerary, Prodigal Genius, 1977; John Donne: Life, Mind and Art, 1981; Original Copy: Selected Reviews and Journalism, 1987; The Faber Book of Reportage, 1989; Donne, 1990; The Intellectuals and the Masses, 1992. Contributions to: Principal Book Reviewer, Sunday Times. Honour: Fellow, Royal Society of Literature; Honorary Fellow, St John's College, 1991, Balliol College, 1992. Membership: Royal Society of Literature. Literary Agent: Xandra Hardie, London. Address: Merton College, Oxford, OX1 4SD, England.

CAREY Peter Philip, b. 7 May 1943, Bacchus Marsh, Australia. Novelist. m. Alison Summers, 16 Mar 1985, 2 s. Education: Dr of letters, University of Queensland, 1989. Appointment: Writer in Residence, NY University, 1990. Publications: The Fat Man in History, 1974, 80; War Crimes, 1979, 1981; Illywhacker, 1985; Oscar & Lucinda, 1989; Until the End of the World, 1990; The Tax Inspector, 1991; The Unusual Life of Triston Smith, 1994. Honours: NSW Premier's Literary Award; Miles Franklin Award; National Book Council Award; The Age Book of Year Award; Victorian Premier's Literary Award; The Booker Prize. Memberships: Royal Society of Literature. Literary Agent: Deborah Rogers, Rogers, Coleridge & White Ltd. Address: c/o Deborah Rogers, Rogers, Coleridge & White Ltd, 20 Powis Mews, London W11 1JN, England.

CARFAX Catherine. See: **FAIRBURN Eleanor M.**

CARKEET David Corydon, b. 15 Nov 1946, Sonora, CA, USA. Writer. m. Barbara Lubin, 16 Aug 1975, 3 d. Education: AB, University of CA, 1968; MA, University of WI, 1970; PhD, IN University, 1973. Publications: The Full Catastrophe: I Been There Before; The Greatest Slump of All Time; Double Negative. Honours: O Henry Award. Literary Agent: Barney M Karpfinger. Address: 23 Ridgemoor Drive, St Louis, MO 63105, USA.

CARLISLE D M, See: **COOK Dorothy Mary.**

CARMI T, b. 31 Dec 1925, New York City, New York, USA (Israeli citizen). Poet. m. Lilach Peled. Education: Sorbonne, Paris, 1946-47; Hebrew University, Jerusalem, 1949-51. Appointments include: Professor of Hebrew Literature at Hebrew Union College and Visiting Professor at universities in the USA. Publications: Blemish and Dream, 1951; There are no Black Flowers, 1953; Snow in Jerusalem, 1956; The Last Sea, 1958; The Brass Serpent, 1961, 1964; The Unicorn Looks in the Mirror, 1967; The Claim, 1967; Another Version Selected Poems and Translations 1951-69; Somebody Like You, 1971; Author's Apology, 1974; Selected Poems, 1976; Into Another Land, 1977; At the Stone of Losses, 1981; One to Me, 1985; Monologues and Other

Poems, 1988; Hebrew versions of plays by Brecht, Shakespeare, Sophocles, and Rostand. Honours include: Bialik Prize, 1990. Address: Hebrew Union College, Jewish Institute of Religion, 13 King David Street, Jerusalem 94101, Israel.

CARMICHAEL Jack B, b. 31 Jan 1938, Ravenswood, USA. Writer; Consultant. m. Julie Ann Carmichael, 2 Oct 1981, 4 daughters. Education: BA, OH Wesleyan University, 1959; PhD, MI State University, 1964; Post-doctored University of OR, 1966-67. Appointments: Editor, Publisher, President, Dynamics Press, Mason. Publications: A New Slain Knight; Black Knight; Tales of the Cousin; Memoirs of the Great Gorgeous; Industrial Water Use & Treatment Practice. Contributions to: Magazines & Journals; Over 30 Articles; 45 Official Reports of the United Nations. Honours: The Am Poetry Association Award Grandpa Outstanding Achievement; Finalist in 1990 Juried Competition of FL Literary Foundation; Merit Awards for Song to Heidi. Memberships: Academy of American Poets; The International Organization for Chemistry in Development; The East West Literary Foundation. Address: Dynamics Press, 519 South Rogers Street, Mason, MI 48854, USA.

CARMICHAEL Joel, b. 1915, USA. Appointments: Editor, Weizmann Letters and Papers, 1968-71, Midstream Magazine, 1975-87, 1990-. Publications include: The Russian Revolution, 19171; A Personal Record, 1955; Anna Karenina by Tolstoy, The Death of Jesus, 1962; Karl Marx: The Passionate Logician, 1964; A Short History of the Russian Revolution, 1965; The Shaping of the Arabs, 1967; Trotsky, 1975; Stalins Masterpiece, 1976; St Pauls Timetable, 1982; The Birth of Christianity: Reality and Myth, 1989; The Satanizing of The Jews, 1992. Address: 302 West 86th Street, New York, NY 10024, USA.

CAROL Bill J. See: **KNOTT William Cecil.**

CARPENTER Allan, b. 11 May 1917, Waterloo, IA, USA. Author; Publisher. Education: BA, University of Northern IA. Publications: Between Two Rivers, 1938; Hi, Neighbor, 1942; Your Guide to Successful Singing, 1945; Popular Mechanics Home Handyman, 1961; Enchantment of Am, 1962-65, 52 vols; Enchantment of Latin Am, 1965-68; Enchantment of Africa, 1968-72, 38 vols; New Enchantment of Am, 1972-79, 52 vols; All About the USA, 1983-86, 7 vols; Encyclopedia of the Regions of the US, 1986; Great Generals, 1987-88; Facts About the Cities, 1990; The World Almanac of the USA, 1993; World Almanac of the USA, 1996; Facts About the Cities, 1995. Contributions to: Monthly to Popular Mechanics and Science Digest; Most Major Magazines. Memberships: Arts Club of Chicago. Literary Agent: Carolyn Kuhn. Address: Suite 4602, 175 East Delaware Place, Chicago, IL 60611, USA.

CARPENTER Bogdana Maria Magdalena, b. 2 June 1941, Poland. Professor. m. John Randell Carpenter, 15 Apr 1963, 1 s, 1 d. Education: Waraw University, 1963; PhD, University of CA, 1974. Appointments: Assistant Professor, University of WA, 1974-83; Assistant Professor, 1983-84, Associate Professor, 1985-91, Professor, 1991-, University of MI. Publications: The Poetic Avant Garde in Poland; Monumenta Polonica: The First Four Centuries of Polish Poetry; Translations, Selected Poems of Zbigniew Herbert; Report from the Besieged City and Other Poems; Still Life with a Bridle. Contributions to: Articles; Reviews; World Literature Today; Translation Review; Malahat Review; Slavic & East European Journal; The Polish Review; Cross Currents. Honours include: Witter Bynner Poetry Translation Prize; Am Council for Polish Culture 1st Prize. Memberships: PEN; AAASS; AATSEEL. Address: Dept of Slvic Languages & Literature, University of MI, 3040 MLB, Ann Arbor, MI 48109, USA.

CARPENTER Humphrey, b. 1946, British. Author; Broadcaster; Musician. Appointments: Staff Producer, BBC, 1968-74; Freelance Boradcaster and reviewer. Publications: A Thames Companion (with M Prichard), 1975; J R R Tolkien, The Joshers, 1977; The Inklings: C S Lewis, J R R Tolkien, Charles Williams and their Friends, 1978; The Captian Hook Affair, 1979; Jesus, 1980; W H Auden, The Letters of J R R Tolkien (ed with C Tolkein), 1981; Mr Majeika, The Oxford Companion to Children's Literature (with M Prichard), 1984; O U D S: A Centenary History of the Oxford University Dramatic Society; Secret Gardens: A Study of the Golden Age of Children's Literature, 1985; Mr Majeika and the Music Teacher, 1986; Mr Majeika and the Haunted Hotel, 1987; A Serious Character: The Life of Ezra pound, 1988; The

Brideshead Generation, 1989; Benjamin Britten, (Biography), 1992. Address: 6 Fardon Road, Oxford, OX2 6R6, England.

CARPENTER Lucas, b. 23 Apr 1947, Elberton, GA, USA. Professor. m. Judith Leidner, 2 Sept 1972, 1 d. Education: BS, College of Charleston, 1968; MA, University of North CA, 1973; PhD, State University of NY, 1982. Appointments: Instr, SUNY, 1973-78; Instructor, Assistant Professor, Associate Professor, Suffolk College, 1978-85; Associate Professor, Oxford College of Emory University, 1985-. Publications: A Year for the Spider, 1972; Selected Poetry of John Gould Fletcher, 1988; Selected Essays of John Gould Fletcher, 1989; John Gould Fletcher and Southern Modernism, 1990. Contributions to: Poetry, Ciritical Essays, Short Fiction in Over 35 Journals, Magazines & Newspapers. Memberships: Poetry Society of America. Address: Oxford College of Emory University, GA 30267, USA.

CARR Glyn. See: **STYLES Frank Showell**.

CARR James Lyod, b. 20 May 1912, Carlton Miniott, Yorkshire, England. Novelist. m. Sally Sexton, 1945, dec'd 1981, 1 son. Education: Castleford Secondary School, Yorkshire. Appointments: Head, Highfields Primary School, Kettering, Northamptonshire, 1951-67; Publisher, 1967-. Publications: A Day in Summer, 1963; A Season in Sinji, 1968; The Harpole Report, 1972; How Steeple Sinderby Wanderers Won the FA Cup, 1975; A Month in the Country, 1980; The Battle of Pollocks Crossing, 1985; What Hetty Did, 1988; Harpole and Foxberrow, Publishers, 1991; Several children's stories and has written and edited numerous non-fiction works. Honours: Guardian Fiction Prize, 1980; MA, Leicester University, 1981. Address: 27 Milldale Road, Kettering, Northamptonshire NN15 6QD, England.

CARR Margaret, (Martin Carroll, Carole Kerr), b. 1935, England. Writer; Local Government Secretary, Retired. Publications include: Begotten Murder, 1967; Spring into Love, 1967; Blood Bengeance, 1968; Goodbye is Forever, 1968; Too Beautiful to Die, 1969; Hear No Evil, 1971; Tread Warily at Midnight, 1971; Sitting Duck, 1972; Whos the Target, 1974; Not for sale, 1975; Shadow of the Hunter, 1975; A Time to Surrender, 1975; Out of the Past, 1976; Twin Tragedy, 1977; Lamb to the Slaughter, 1978; The Wtich of Wykham, 1978; Daggers Drawn, 1980; Stolen Heart, 1981; Deadly Pursuit, 1991; Dark Intruder, 1991. Address: Waverly, Wavering Lane, Gillingham, Dorset SD8 4Nr, England.

CARR Pat Moore, b. 13 Mar 1932, Grass Creek, WY, USA. Writer; Professor. m. (1) Jack Esslinger, 4 June 1955, div, 1970, (2) Duane Carr, 26 Mar 1972, 1 s, 3 d. Education: BA, MA, Rice University; phD, Tulane University. Publications: Bernard Shaw, 1976; The Grass Creek Chronicle, 1976, 1992; The Women in the Mirror, 1977; Mimbres Mythology, 1979, 1988, 1990; Night of the Luminaries, 1985; Sonahchi, 1988; Bluebirds, 1993; Our Brothers War, 1993. Contributions to: Stories and Articles to, Southern Review; Yale Review; Best Am Short Stories; KS Quarterly; AZ Quarterly; Modern Fiction Studies; Modern Drama; Western Humanities Review; Oxford Magazine; Seattle Review; Women Writing; Puetro Del Sol; Florida Review; Cedar Rock. Honours: Phi Beta Kappa, 1955; South & West Fiction Award, 1969; Library of Congress Marc iV, 1970; National Endowment for the Humanities, 1973; IA Fiction Award, 1977; Short Story Award, 1978; Green Mountain Fiction Award, 1985; First State Drama Award, 1991. Memberships: Poets & Writers; International Women Writers Guild. Literary Agent: Barbara Kouts. Address: Dept of English, Western Kentucky University, Bowling Green, NY 42101, USA.

CARR Roberta. See: **ROBERTS Irene**.

CARR Terry (Norman Edwards), b. 1937. America. Freelance Writer; Editor; Lecturer since 1971. Appointments: Associate Editor, Scott Meredith Literary Agency, NYC, 1962-64; Editor, Ace Books, NYC, 1964-71; Editor, SFWA Bulletin, 1967-68; Founder, Science Fiction Writers of America Forum, 1967-68. Publications: Warlord of Kor, 1963, (as Norman Edwards with Ted White); Invation from 2500 (ed with Donald A Wollheim), 1964; World's Best Science Fiction,1965-71; 7 vols 1965-71, first 4 vols as World's Best Science Fiction First (to fouth) Series, 1970; (ed) Science Fiction for People Who Hate Science Fiction, 1966; (ed) New World's of Fantasy 1-3, 3 vols, 1967-71, Vol 1 in UK as Step Outside Your Mind, 1969; (ed) The Others, 1968; (ed) Universe 1-13, 13 vols, 1971-83; (ed) The Best Science Fiction of the Year, 1-13, 1972-84; (ed) This Side of Infinity, 1971; (ed) An Exaltation of Stars, 1973; (ed) Into the Unknown, 1973; (ed) World's Near and Far, 1974; (ed) Creatures from Beyond, 1975;

(ed) The Idea of Tommorrow, (juvenile), 1976; Planets of Wonder: A Treasury of Space Opera (juvenile), 1976; The Light at The End of the Universe, (short stories), 19786; Cirque, 1977; (ed) To Follow a Star, (juvenile), 1977; (ed) Classic Science Fiction: The First Golden Age, 1978; (ed) The Year's Finest Fantasy 1-V, 1978-84; (ed) The Best Science Fiction Novellas of the Year, 1-2, 2 vols, 1979-80; (ed) Beyond Reality, 1979; (ed) Dream's Edge: Science Fiction about the Future of the Planet Earth, 1980; (ed) The Best form Universe, 1984; Spill! The Story of the Exxon Valdez, 1991; Between Two Worlds, 1986; Cirque, 1987.

CARRIER Roch, b. 13 May 1937, Quebec, Canada. m. Diane Gosselin, 1959, 2 d. Education: L'University de Montreal; Sorbonne, University of Paris. Appointments: Professor, Secretary General, Theatre du Nouveau Monde, Quebec, 1970-; Chairman, Salon du Livre, Montreal; Director, Canada Council, 1994-. Publications include: Numerous Fictional Works, Poems, Plays & Screenplays inc.The Ungrateful Land, 1972; The Hockey Sweater, 1980; La Caleste Bicyclette, 1980; No Country Without Grand Fathers, 1983; The End, 1994. Address: c/o Tundra Books Inc, 339 Lansdowne, Westmount, Quebec H3Z 2LS, Canada.

CARRIER Warren, b. 1918, USA. Appointments: Associate Dean, Rutgers University, NJ, 1968-69; Dean, CA State University, San Diego, 1969-72; Vice President, University of Bridgeport, CT, 1972-75; Chancellor, University of WI, 1975-82; Chancellor Emeritus, 1982-; Founder, Editor, Quarterly Review of Literature. Publications: City Stopped in Time, 1949; The Hunt, 1952; The Cost of Love, 1953; Reading Modern Poetry, 1955, 1968; Bay of the Dammed, 1957; Toward Montebello, 1966; Leave Your Sugar for the Cold Morning, 1978; Guide to World Literature, 1980; Literature from the World, 1981; The Diver, 1985; Death of a Chancellor, 1986; An Honorable Spy, 1992; Murder at The Strawberry Festival, 1993. Address: 69 Colony Park Circle, Galveston, TX 77551, USA.

CARROLL Martin. See: **CARR Margaret**.

CARROLL Paul, b. 1927, American. Appointments: Poetry Editor, Chicago Review, 1957-59; Editor, Big Table Magazine, 1959-61; Big Table Books, Follett Publishing Company, 1966-71; Visiting Professor of English, University of Iowa, IA, 1966-67; Professor of English, University of Illinois, 1968-. Publications: Edward Dahlberg Reader (ed), 1966; Odes, The Poem in Its Skin, The Young American Poets, 1968; The Luke Poets, 1971; New and Selected Poems, 1978; The Garden of Earthly Delights, 1986; Poems, 1950-1990, 1990. Address: 1682 North Ada Street, Chicago, IL 60622, USA.

CARROLL Raymond, b. 10 Aug 1924, Brooklyn, New Yorm USA. Writer. m. Anne Starck, 1954, (div 1979) 1 s, 1 d. Education: BA, Hamilton College, 1948; Graduate Study at Johns Hopkins School of Advanced International Studies, 1949-51. Appointments: Owner, Cadmus Book Store, Washsington DC 1953-55; Designer of Promotional Material, Translator from Spanish and Newspaper Columnist, Editors Press Service, New York, 1955-61; Associate Editor, 1961-69; General Editor, 1969-81; also Chief, United Nations Bureau, Newsweek, New York City; Freelance writer, 1981-. Publications: Juvenile publications; Anwas Sadat, 1982; The Palestine Question, 1983; The Caribbean Issues in US Relations, 1984; The Future of the United Nations, 1985. Contributions to: Family Encyclopaedia of American History, 1975; The Story of America, 1975; America's Fascinating Indian Heritage, 1978; Consumer Advisor: An Action Giide to Your Rights, 1984; Funk and Wagnalls New Encyclopaedia Yearbook. Memberships: English-speaking Union; Amnesty International. Address: New York, USA.

CARRUTH Hayden, b. 1921, New England. Poet; Novelist; Essayist. Appointments: Editor, Poetry, Harpers, The Hudson Review. Publications: 1 Novel; 3 Collections of Essays; A Voice That is Great within Us; Tell Me Again How The White Haven Rises, 1991; Collected Shorter Poems 1946-91, 1992; Collected Longer poems, 1994. Honours: Nationl Book Critics Circle Award, 1993; Governor's Medal; Lenore Marshall Nation Poetry Prize; Ruth Lilly Poetry Prize. Address: RD 1 Box 128, Munnsville, NY 13409, USA.

CARRUTHERS Peter Michael, b. 16 June 1952, Manila. Philosopher. m. Susan Levi, 21 Oct 1978, 2 s. Education: University of Leeds, 1971-77; Calliol College, Oxford, 1977-79. Appointments: Lecturer, University of St Andrews, 1979-81; Lecturer, Queens University of Belfast, 1981-83; Lecturer, University of Essex, 1985-91;

Visiting Professor, University of Michigan, 1989-90; Senor Lecturer, University of Sheffield, 1991-92; Professor, University of Sheffield, 1992-. Publications: Introducing Persons; Tractarian Semantics; The Metaphysics of the Tractatus; Human Knowledge and Human Nature; The Animals Issue. Contributions to: Philosophical Quarterly; MIND; Journal of Philosophy; Synthese. Memberships: Aristotelian Society. Address: Department of Philosophy, University of Sheffield, Sheffield, S10 2TN, England.

CARSWELL John Patrick, b. 1918, England. Appointments: Served with Treasury, 1960-64; Assistant Under Secretary of State, Dept of Education and Science 1964-74; Secretary, University Grants Committee, 1974-78; Secretary, British Academy, 1978-83. Publications: Marvellous Campaigns of Baron Munchausen, 1946; The Prospector: The Life of Rudolf Erich Raspe, 1950; The Old Cause: Four Biographical Studies in Whiggism, 1954; The South Sea Bubble, 1960, new enlarged edition 1993; The Civil Servant and His World, 1966; The Descent on England, 1969; From Revolution to Revolution, 1688-1776, 1973; Lives and Letters, 1978; The Exile, 1983; The State and the Universities in Britain, 1966-78, 1985; The Porcupine: The Life of Algernon Sidney, 1989; The Saving of Kenwood and the Northern Heights, 1992. Address: 5 Prince Arthur Road, London, NW3, England.

CARTANO Tony, b. 27 July 1944, Bayonne, France. Author; Editor. m. Francoise Perrin, 10 Nov 1966, 1 s, 1 d. Education: Licence es Lettres, 1964; Diploma d'Etudes Superieures, 1965, University of Paris. Appointments include: Director of Foreign Department, Editions Albin Michel, Paris. Publications include: Novels, Blackbird, 1980; Le Bel Arturo, 1989; Le souffle de Satan, 1991; Le Single Hurleur, 1978; Schmutz, 1987; Malcolm Lowry, (essay) 1979; La Sourde Oreille, 1982; Travel Book: American Boulevard, 1992. Honours: Blackbird and Bocanegra have been Nominated for Prix Goncourt; Chevalier dans l'ordre des Arts et Lettres. Literary Agent: La Nouvelle Agence, 7 Rue de Corneille, 75006, Paris; A M Heath, London. Address: 157 Boulevard Davout, 75020 Paris, France.

CARTENS Jan, b. 25 May 1929, Roosendaal, Netherlands. Writer. Publications: Dat meisje uit Munchen, 1975; De thuiskomst, 1976; Vroege herfst, 1978; Een Roomsche Jeugd, 1980; De verleiding, 1983; Maagdenbruiloft, 1987; Het verraad van Nausikaa, 1989; Een indriger, 1990. Address: Markenland 15, 4871 AM, Etten-Leur, Netherlands.

CARTER Bruce. See: HOUGH Richard Alexander.

CARTER Francis William, b. 4 July 1938, Wednesfield, Staffs, England. m. Krystyna Stephania Tomaszewska, 3 June 1977. Education: BA, Sheffield; MA, PhD, London; D Nat Sc, Prague; D Phil, Cracow. Publications: Dubrovnik: A Classic City State; An Historical Geography of the Balkans: Trade and Urban Development in Poland; Environmental Problems in Eastern Europe. Contributions to: Over 100 Articles. Honour: Croatian Academy of USA. Memberships: Institute of British Geographers; Royal Geographical Society; Royal Asiatic Society; PEN. Address: Dept of Social Sciences, School of Slavonic & East European Studies, University of London, Malet Street, London WC1E 7HU, England.

CARTER Harold Burnell, b. 3 Jan 1910, Mosman, Sydney, NSW, Australia. Scientific Civil Servant, 1939-70. m. Mary Brandon Jones, 21 Sep 1940, 3 s. Education: University of Sydney, BVSC, 1933. Appointments: Walter & Eliza Hall Fellow, University of Sydney, 1936-39; Honorary Fellow, University of Leeds, 1962-70; Director, Banks Archive Project, British Museum, 1989-. Publications: His Majesty's Spanish Flock; The Sheep and wool Correspondence of Sir Joseph Banks; Sir Joseph Banks: A Guide to Biographical and Bibliographical Sources; Sir Joseph Banks 1743-1820. Contributions to: Australian and British Scientific Journals; Bulletin; British Museum; Historical Series. Honours: American Philosophical Society History of Science Grants; Royal Society History of Science Grants; British Academy Major Awards. Memberships: Royal Society of Edinburgh; FLS; FIBiol. Address: Yeo Bank, Congresbury, Nr Bristol, Co Avon, BS19 5JA, England.

CARTER Martin (Wylde), b. 1927, British Guiana. Politician; Poet. Education: Queens College, Georgetown. Appointments: Former Representative for Guyana, United Nations, NY. Publications: The Hill of Fire Glows Red, 1951; To a Dead Slave, 1951; The King Eagle, 1952; The Hidden Man, 1952; Poems of Resistance from British Guiana, 1954; Poems of Succession, 1977; Poems of Affinity, 1978-80,

1980; Man and Making Victim and Vehicle, 1971; Creation: Works of Art, 1977. Address: c/o New Beacon Books, 76 Stroud Green Road, London N4 3EN, England.

CARTER Mary Arkley, b. Oregon, USA. Novelist; Professor. 2 s. Education: Unviersity of Oregon: Pitzer College, Claremont, California. Appointments include: Director, Creative Writing Programme, University of Arizona, 1981-; Lecturer in Fiction, graduate programme, Boston University, 1980-81, 1978-79, 1971-72; Various other university posts. Publications: A Fortune in Dimes, 1963; The Minutes of the Night, 1965; La Maestra, 1973; A member of the Family, 1974; Tell Me My Name, 1975. Numerous Short Stories, reviews, articles, columns. Contributions include: New York Times; Holiday Magazine; Vanity Fair; Kenyon Review; Boston A D Review; column, Connexions. Honours: Fellow, MacDowell, 1973-80; Virginia Centre for Creative Arts, 1972-73; Ossabaw Foundation, 1973; Foundation Karolyi, France, 1973-74, 1977; Fellowship Grant, National Endowment for the Arts, 1986. Memberships: PEN; Authors Guild; Directors Committee, Associated Writing Programmes. Literary Agent: Brandt and Brandt, New York. Address: 169 Fentiman Road, London, SW8 1YJ. England.

CARTER Nick. See: AVALLONE Michael Angelo Jr.

CARTER Nick. See: LYNDS Dennis.

CARTER Nick. See: GARSIDE Jack Clifford.

CARTER Peter, b. 1929, British. Appointments: Apprentice in the Building Trade, 1942-49; Teacher in Birmingham. Publications: The Black Lamp, 1973; The Gates of Paradise, 1974; Madatan, 1975; Mao, 1976; Under Goliath, 1977; The Senntinels, 1980; Children of the Book, 1982; Bury The Dead, 1986. Address: c/o Oxford University Press, Walton Street, Oxford, OX2 6DP, England.

CARTER Robert Ayres, b. 16 Sep 1923, Omaha, NE, USA. Writer; Lecturer. m. 17 Dec 1983, 2 s. Education: AB, New School For Social Research. Publications: Manhattan Primitive, 1972; Written In Blood (USA Casual Slaughters), 1992; Final Edit, 1994; Three Textbooks. Contributions: Publishers Weekly; International Journal Of Book Publishing. Honours: Fulbright Scholar, 1949. Memberships: Poets and Writers; Mystery Writers Of America; International Crime Writers Association; Member, Board Of Directors, 1980-1988, Asst Secretary, 1984-1988, Life Member, The Players. Literary Agent: Regula Noetzli, c/o Charlotte Sheedy Agency. Address: 510 North Meadow Street, Richmond, VA 23220, USA.

CARTER Walter Horace, b. 20 Jan 1921, North CA, USA. Newspaper Publisher; Author; Magazine Writer. m. (1)Lucille Miller Carter, dec, (2)Brenda C Strickland, 29 Oct 1983, 1 s, 2 d. Education: B, University of North CA. Publications: Land That I love, 1978; Creatures and Chronicles from Cross Creek, 1980; Wild and Wonderful Santee Cooper Country, 1982; Natures Masterpiece, 1984; Return to Cross Creek, 1985; Virus of Fear, 1991; Nature Coast Tales & Truths, 1993; Headstart Fishing Handbook, 1994; Over 2000 stories published. Contributions to include: Various Magazines; Over 1000 Stories Published. Honours: Pulitzer Prize, 1953; Sidney Hillman award, 1954. Memberships: Outdoor Writers Association of Am; FL Outdoor Writers Association; Southwestern Outdoor Press Association. Address: Rt3 Box 139A, Hawthorne, FL 32640, USA.

CARTLAND Barbara (Dame). See: MCCORQUODALE Barbara Hamilton.

CARUS Marianne, b. 16 June 1928, Germany. Editor in Chief. m. Milton Blouke Carus, 3 Mar 1951, 1 s, 2 d. Education: Abitur, Gymnasium Gummersbach, 1948; Masters Equivalent, Freiburg University; Additional Studies, Sorbonne, University of Chicago. Appointments: Editor in Chief, Cricket, Ladybug, Spider, Babybug Magazines. Publications: with Clifton Fadiman Editor of Crickets Choice, 1974. Contributions to: Childrens Literature in Education. Memberships: ALSC; ALA; Magazine Publishers Association; Childrens Reading Roundtable; Society of Childrens Book Writers; CCBC; VP; IBBY. Address: The Cricket Magazine Group, PO Box 300, Peru, IL 61354, USA.

CARY Jud. See: TUBB E(dwin) C(harles).

CARY Lorene Emily, b. 29 Nov 1956, PA, USA. Writer. m. R C Cary, 27 Aug 1983, 1 d, 1 stepson. Education: University of PA; University of Sussex. Appointments: Apprentice Writer, Time, 1980; Associate Editor, TV Guide, 1980-82; Contributin Editor, Newsweek Magazine, 1991. Publication: Black Ice. Honour: Doctorate of Letters. Memberships: Authors Guild; Association of Black Journalists. Literary Agent: Jane Dystel, Acton & Dystel Inc. Address: c/o Alfred A Knopf, 201 East 50th Street, NY 10022, USA.

CASEY John D, b. 18 Jan 1939, MA, USA. Writer; Professor. m. Rosamond Pinchot Pittman, 26 June 1982, 4 d. Education: BA, Harvard College, 1962; LLB, Harvard Law School, 1965; MFA, University of IA, 1967. Appointments: Professor, University of VA, 1972-92; Residency, Am Academy of Arts & Letters, 1992-97. Publications: An American Romance, 1977; Testimony and Demeanor, 1979; Sparting, 1989. Contributions to: Stories, Articles, Reviews, 1968-. Honours: Runner Up, Ernest Hemingway Award, 1978; Guggenheim Fellowship, 1979-80; Friends of Am Writers Award, 1980; National Endowment for the Arts Fellowship, 1983; National Book Award, 1989; Ingram Merril Fellowship, 1990. Memberships: PEN. Literary Agent: Michael Carlisle, William Morris Agency. Address: Dept of English, University of VA, Charlottesville, VA 22903, USA.

CASS Joan E, b. England. Appointments: Former Lecturer, Child Development, Institute of Education, University of London. Publications include: The Cat Thief, 1961; The Cat Show, 1962; Blossom Finds a House, 1963; Literature and the Young Child, 1967; The Cats Go to Market, 1969; Chang and the Robber, 1971; The Dragon Who Grew, The Witch of Witchery Wood, 1973; The Role of the Teacher in the Nursery School, Hubert Hippo, Milly Mouse, 1975; Baby Bears Bath, Milly Mouses Measles, The Witch and the Naughty Princess, 1976; Alexanders Magic Quilt, 1978; The Witches Lost Spell Book, 1980; The Four Surprises, 1981; Trouble Among the Witches, 1983; The Persistent Mouse, 1984; The Witches Schhol, Six Mice Too Many, 1985. Address: c/o Abelard Schuman Limited, 14-18 High Holborn, London, WC1V 6BX, England.

CASS Zoe. See: **LOW Lois.**

CASSELLS Cyrus Curtis, b. 16 May 1957, Dover, Delaware, USA. Poet; Teacher; Translator. Education: BA, Stanford University, 1979. Publications: The Mud Actor, 1982; Down from the Houses of Magic; Soul Make a Path Through Shouting, 1994. Contributions to: Southern Review; Callaloo; Translation; The Seneca Review; Quilt; Sequoi. Honours: Academy of American Poets Prize, 1979; National Poetry Series Winner, 1982; Bay Area Book Reviewers Association Award Nominee, 1983; Callaloo Cretive Writing Award, 1983; MA Artists Foundation Fellowship, 1985; NEA Fellowship, 1986; Laven Younger Poets Award, 1992. Memberships: PEN; Poetry Society of Am; Writers League of Boston; North Am Catalan Society. Address: c/o 1142 E Avenue, J1 Lancaster, CA 93535, USA.

CASSIAN Nina, b. 27 Nov 1924, Galati, Rumania. Poet. Education: University of Bucharest and Conservatory of Music. Appointments include: Visiting Professor, New York University, 1985-86. Publications: Verses: Our Soul, 1949; Vital Year 1917, 1949; Youth, 1953; Selected Poems, 1955; Ages of the Year, 1957; The Dialogue of Wind and Sea, 1957; Outdoor Performance, 1961; Everyday Holidays, 1961; Gift Giving, 1963; The Most Beautiful Poems, 1963; The Discipline of the Harp, 1965; Blood, 1966; Parallel Destinies, 1967; Chronophagy 1944-69; The Big Conjugation, 1971; Requiem, 1971; 100 Poems, 1974; Suave, 1977; Orbits, 1978; Mercy, 1981; Lady of Miracles, 1982; Countdown, 1983; Call Yourself Alive?, 1988; Life Sentence: Selected Poems 1900; Cheer Leader for a Funeral, 1993; Verses and plays for children; Translations of Celan, Molière, Brecht, Apollinaire, and Shakespeare. Creative Works: Musical Composition: Songs for the Republic, 1949. Honours include: Fulbright Grant, 1986. Address: 555 Main St #502, Roosevelt Island, New York, NY 10044, USA.

CASSIDY Frederic Gomes, b. 10 Oct 1907, Professor; Lexicographer. m. Hélène Lucile Monod, 26 Dec 1931, 3 s, 1 d. Education: BA, 1930, MA, 1932, Oberlin College; PhD, University of MI. Appointments: Chief Editor, Dictionary of Am Regional English, 1963-. Publications include: The Place Names of Dane County, 1947; A Method for Collecting Dialect, 1953; Development of Modern English, 1954; Dictionary of Jamaican English, 1967; Brights Old English Grammar and Reader, 1971; Dictionary of Am Regional English, 1985, 1991. Contributions to: English Journal; American Speech; Computers and the Humanities; Journal of English Linguistics; Various Other Publications. Honours include: University Fellow, University of MI; First Honorary Fellow, University College of the West Indies; Fulbright Research Fellow to Jamaica; Visiting Fellow, University College of the West Indies; Musgrave Silver Medal; Centenary Medal; Musgrave Gold Medal; IN State University Terre-Haute; Distinguished Service Award. Memberships: President: Am Dialect Society; Society for Caribbean Linguistics; Am Name Society. Address: 207N Spooner Street, Madison, WI 53705, USA.

CASSILL Ronald Verlin, (Owen Aherne, Jesse Webster), b. IA, USA. Author. m. Kay, 2 s, 1 d. Education: BA, University of IA, 1939; MA, 1947. Appointments: Teacher, Writers Workshop, University of IA, 1948-52, 1960-66; Professor, Brown University, 1966-83; Reviewer, NY Times. Publications include: Eagle on the Coin, 1950; Clem Anderson, 1961; The President, 1964; In An iron Time, 1969; Doctor Cobbs Game, 1970; Norton Anthology of Short fiction, 1977; Labors of Love, 1980; Flame, 1980; After Goliath, 1985; Several Short Stories. Contributions to: Atlantic Monthly; Holiday; Saturday Evening Post; Horizon. Honours: Atlantic First Prize, 1947; Rockefeller Grant Fiction Writing, 1954; O Henry Prize Stories, 1956; 3rd Prize, Guggenheim Grant Fiction Writing, 1968. Memberships: Associated Writing Programmes; Phi Beta Kappa. Address: 22 Boylston avenue, Providence, RI 02906, USA.

CASTANEDA Omar S, b. 6 Sept 1954, Guatemala Professor. m. (1) 11 Aug 1984, (2) 26 Feb 1992, 1 s, 1 d. Education: BA, IN University, 1980; MFA, 1983. Publications: Among the Volcanoes Dutton; Cunuman; New Visions: Fiction by Florida Writers; Abuela Weave.; Imagining Isabel, 1994; Remembering to Say Mouth of Face, 1993. Contributions to: Over 40 inc. Keynon Review; Caliban; Mid Americn Review; Left Bank; Latin American Literary Review; Nuestro; Special Report; Fiction; Fiver Fingers Review. Honours: Fulbright Research Award; Critchfield Award; FL Arts Council Award; Critchfield Award; FL Arts Council Award; WA State Arts Council Award; Parents Choice Honoree. Memberships include: AWP; SCBW; Modern Language Association: PEN; AWP; LASA; GSN. Literary Agent: Cine/Lit Representation. Address: MS 9055 Western WA University, Bellingham, WA 98225, USA.

CASTEDO Elena, b. 1 Sept 1937, Spain. Writer. m. A Denny Elleman, 15 Apr 1973, 2 s, 1 d. Education: University of Chile, 1966; University of CA, 1968; Harvard University, 1976. Appointments include: Teacher, English College, Chile, 1954; Mascimiento Institute, Chile, 1966-67; Teaching Fellow, Harvard University, 1969-72; Leacturer, Am University, 1976-77; Editor, Inter American Review, 1987-80. Publications: El Praiso; Paradise; Iquana Dreams; The Sound of Writing; Others inc. El Teato Chileno de Mediados de Sigioxx; Diario. Contributions to: Numeouro inc. Linden Lane Magazine; Phoebe Magazine; The Human Story; Americas Magazine. Honours: UCLA Masters Award; Simon Bolivar Medal; Several Fellowships; Phoebe Award; Nominated, National Book Award, Cervantas Prize. Memberships: PEN; Authors Guild; Modern Language Association; WA Independent Writers Association; Poets & Writers; Bruno Schultz Intrnational Literary Prize. Literary Agent: Elaine Markson, US Carmen Balcells, Spain. Address: c/o Accent Media, 36 Lancaster Street, Cambridge, MA 02140, USA.

CASTEL Albert, b. 11 Nov 1928, KS, USA. Author; Lecturer; Professor. m. George Ann Bennett, 25 June 1959, 1 son, 1 daughter. Education: BA, 1950, MA, 1951, Wichita University; PhD, University of Chicago, 1955. Literary Appointments: University of CA, 1957-58; Western MI University, 1960-81. Publications include: Decision in the West: The Atlanta Campaign of 1864; A Frontier State at War: Kansas, 1861-1865; The President of Andrew Johnson, 1979; The Guerrilla War, 1974. Contributions to: Nearly 100 Published Articles. Address: 66 Westwood Drive, Hillsdale, MI 49242, USA.

CASTELL Megan, See: **WILLIAMS Jeanne.**

CASTLE Barbara Anne, Baroness Castle of Blackburn, b. 6 Oct 1910, Chesterfield, England. Journalist; Author. m. Edward Cyril Castle, 1944. Education: St Hughs College, Oxford. Appointments: Elected to St Pancras Borough Council, 1937; Member, Metropolitan Water Board, 1940-43; Editor, Town and County Councillor, 1936-40; Administrative Officer, Ministry of Food, 1941-44; Housing Correspondent and Affairs Advisor, Daily Mirror, 1940-45; Labour Member, Blackburn, 1945-79; Member, National Executive Committee of the Labour Party, 1950-79; Vice-Chairman, Labour Party, 1957-58;

Chairman, Labour Party, 1958-59; Minister of Overseas Development, 1964-65; Privy Counsellor, 1964; Minister of Transport, 1965-68; First Secretary of State for Employment and Productivity, 1968-70; Secretary of State for Social Services, 1974-76; Member, European Parliament, Greater Manchester North, 1979-84, Greater Manchester West, 1984-89; Leader, British Labour Party, European Parliament, 1979-85; Vice-Chairman, Socialist Group, European Parliament, 1979-86. Publications: Castle Diaries 1964-70, 1984; Sylvia & Christabel Pankhurst, 1987; Castle Diaries 1964-76, 1990; Fighting All the Way, 1993. Honours include: Honorary Fellow of: St Hughs College Oxford, 1966, Bradford & Ilkley Community College, 1985, UMIST, 1991, Humberside Polytechnic, 1991, York University, 1992; Honorary Doctor of: Technology, Bradford University, 1968, Technology, Loughborough, 1969, Laws, Lancaster, 1991; Laws, Manchester University, 1993; Cross of Order of Merit, Germany, 1990; Created Life Peer, 1990. Literary Agent: David Higham Associates Ltd. Address: c/o House of Lords, London SW1A 0PW, England.

CASTLEDEN Rodney, b. 23 Mar 1945, Worthing, Sussex, England. Head of Humanities. m. Sarah Dee, 29 July 1987. Education: BA, MA, Hertford College, Oxford, 1964-67; DipEd, Oxford University, 1967-68; MSc, Oxford, 1970-78. Publications: The Stonehenge People; The Wilmington Giant; The Knossos Labyrinth; Minoans; Book of British Dates; Classic Landforms of the Sussex Coast; Neolithic Britain; The Making of Stonehenge, 1993; World History in Chronological Order, 1994; Knossos, Temple of the Goddess, 1995. Contributions to: The Origin of Chalk Dry Valleys; A General Theory of Fluvial Valley Development. Memberships: FGS; FRGS; Royal Society of Literature; The Quaternary Research Association. Address: 15 Knepp Close, Brighton, Sussex, BN2 4LD, England.

CASTELLIN Philippe, b. 26 June 1948, Isle Sur Sorgnes, Vaucluse, France. Fisherman. 3 s. Education: Arege de Philosophie, ENS; Docteur de Letters, University of Paris, Sorbonne. Appointments: Publisher, Director of Docks. Publications include: Rene Char, Traces, 1988; Paesine, 1989; Livre, 1990; Vers la Poesie Totale, 1992; HPS, 1992. Contributions to: Tam Tam; Lotta Poetica; Texture Press; Others. Honours: Charge de Mission, 1990; Expert Manager, Exhibition of Poetry and Painting. Membership: Societe des Gens de Lettres. Address: c/o Akenaton Docks, 20 Rue Bonaparte, F20000 Ajaccio, France.

CATANACH J N, b. USA. Writer. Publications: White Is the Color of Death, 1988; Brideprice, 1989; The Last Rite of Hugo T, 1992. Address: Box 310, Lenox Hill Station, New York, NY 10021, USA.

CATCHAPAW Dorothy Deane Johnson, (Dorothy Deane), b. 31 Mar 1912, Richmond, Vermont, USA. Former Homemaker; Poet; Songwriter. m. Harley N Catchapaw, 14 Sept 1931, 2 sons (1 dec), 2 daughters. Education: Graduated, Richmond High School, 1931. Publications: Story in Verse and Song Lyrics from Vermont by a Vermonter, 1986; Now I See, poem, 1989; Grandma Fleury's 75th Birthday, 1989-90; Green Mountain, Lovs Songs, Ballads and Lullabies, 1992; Contributions to: I Love Cats, 1993. Honours: Golden Poet Award, 1989.

CATUDAL Honore (Marc), b. 17 Oct 1944, WA, USA. Professor. m. Carol Robinson, 25 July 1987, 3 s, 4 d. Education: Zertifkat, FU of Berlin, 1968; BA, Utica College of Syracuse University, 1969; MIS, 1970; PhD, 1973, American University. Publications include: The Diplomacy of the Quadripartite Agreement on Berlin, 1977; A Balance Sheet of the Quadripartite Agreement on Berlin, 1978; The Exclave Problem of Western Europe, 1979; Nuclear Deterrence: Does It Deter, 1985; Soviet Nuclear Strategy from Stalin to Gorbachev, 1988. Contributions to: Utia College News; Dept of State Newsletter; St Johns Magazine. Honours: Berlin Bear, Mayor Heinrich Albertz, 1965; Scholar Diplomat Seminar, 1974; Seminar, West German President, Gustav Heinemann, 1975. Address: Dept of Government, St Johns University, Collegeville, MN 56321, USA.

CAULDWELL Frank. See: KING Francis Henry.

CAUSLEY Charles (Stanley), b. 24 Aug 1917, Lanceston, Cornwall, England. Editor; Poet. Education: Launceston Colllege. Appointments: Teacher in Cornwall, 1947-76; Member Arts Council Poetry Panel, 1962-66. Publications: Survivors Leave, 1953; Union Street, 1957; Johnny Alleluia, 1961; Pemguin Modern Poets 3, 1962; Ballard of the Breed Man, 1968; Underneath The Water, 1968; Pergamon Poets 10, 1970; Timothy Winters, 1970; Six Women, 1974;

Ward 14, 1974; St Martha and the Dragon, 1978; Collected Poems, 1951-75, 1975; Secret Destinations, 1984; 21 Poems, 1986; A Field of Vision, 1988; Secret Destinations, 1984: Selected Poems, 1986; Plays, Runaway, 1936; The Conquering Hero, 1937; How Pleasant to know Mrs Lear, 1948; The Ballard of Aucassin and Nicolette, 1978; Jonah, Libretto for William Mathias, 1990; Editions of Verse for Children. Honours include: Queen's Gold Medal for Poetry, 1967; D Litt, University of Exeter, 1977; MA, Open University, 1982; CBE, 1986. Address: 2 Cyprus Well, Launceston, Cornwall PL15 8BT, England.

CAUTE (John) David, b. 16 Dec 1936, Alexandia, Egypt. Education: DPhil, Wadham College, Oxford, 1962. Appointments: Fellow, All Souls College Oxford, 1959-65; Visiting Professor New York and Columbia Universities, 1966-67; Reader in Social and Political Theory, Brunel University, 1967-70; Regents Lecturer, University of California, 1974; Literary and Arts Editor, New Statesman, London, 1979-80; Co-Chairman, Writers Guild of Great Britain, 1981-82. Publications: At Fever Pitch, 1959; Comrade Jacob, 1961; Communism and the French Intellectuals 1914-1960, 1964; The Decline of the West, The Left in Europe Since 1789, 1966; Essential Writings of Karl Marx (editor), 1967; The Demonstration, 1969; Fanon, 1970; The Occupation, 1971; The Illusion, 1971; The Fellow-Travellers, 1973 (revised 1988); Collisions: Essays and Reviews. Cuba Yes? 1974; The Great Fear: The Anti-Communist Purge Under Truman and Eisenhower, 1978; The K-Factor, Under the Skin: The Death of White Rhodesia, 1983; The Espionage of The Saints, News From Nowhere, 1986; Sixty-Eight: The Year of the Barricades, 1988; Veronica or the Two Nations, 1989; The Women's Hour, 1991; Joseph Losey: A Revenge on Life, 1994; Dr Orwell and Mr Blair, 1994; radio plays: The Demonstration, 1971; Fallout, 1972; The Zimbabwe Tapes, 1983; Henry and the Dogs, 1986; Sanctions, 1988. Address: 41 Westcroft Square, London W6 0TA, England.

CAUTE David, (John Salisbury), b. 1936, England. Appointments: Fellow, All Souls College, Oxford, 1959-65; Visiting Professor, NY & Columbia Univerisities, 1966-67; Reader, Social & Political Theory, Brunel University, 1967-70; Regents Lecturer, University of CA, 1974; Literary and Arts Editor, New Statesman, London, 1979-80; Co Chairman, Writers Guild of Great Britain, 1981-82. Publications include: At Fever Pitch, 1959; The Decline of the West, The Left in Europe since 1789, 1966; Essential Writings of Karl Marx, 1967; Collisions: Essays and Reviews, Cuba Yes, 1974; The Great Fear: The Anticommunist Purge under Truman and Eisenhower, 1978; The Espionage of the Saints, News from Nowhere, 1986; Veronica or the Two Nations, 1989; The Womens Hour, 1991; Radio Plays, Fallout, 1972; The Zimbabwe Tapes, 1983; Henry and the Dogs, 1986; Sanctions, 1988. Address: 41 Westcroft Square, London W6 0TA, England.

CAWS Mary Ann, b. 1933, Writer; Translator. Appointments include: Faculty Member, Barnard College, Columbia University, 1962-63; Assistant Professor, 1966-70, Associate Professor, 1970-72, Professor, 1972-83, Distinguished Professor, 1972, Hunter College; Distinguished Professor, Graduate School, City University of NY, 1986; Co Director, Henri Peyre Institute for the Humanities, 1981-; Co Editor, Dada Surrealism, University of I; Director, Le Siecle Eclate, Paris; betty Scholar, 1989-90. Publications include: Surrealism and the Literary Imagination, 1966; The Poetry of Dada and Surrealism, 1970; Andre Breton, 1971; The Eye in the Text, 1972; Approximate Man and Other Writings of Tristan Tzara, 1974; Selected Poems of Rene Char, 1976; The Surrealist Voice of Robert Desnos, 1977; Stephane Mallarme: Selected Poetry and Prose, 1981; Reading Frames in Modern Fiction, 1985; Mad Love, 1988; The Art of Interference, 1990; Women & Bloomsbury, 1990; Rockefeller Fellowship, 1994. Memberships: Modern Language Association; Academy of Literary Studies; Am Comparative Literature Association; PEN. Literary Agent: Gloria Loomis. Address: 140 E 81st Street Apt 11D, New York, NY 10028, USA.

CAYTON Andrew Robert Lee, b. 9 May 1954, OH, USA. Historian. m. Mary Alice Kupiec, 23 Aug 1975, 2 d. Education: BA, Universityof VA, 1976; MA, 1977, PhD, 1981, Brown University. Publications: The FRontier Republic: Idelogy and Politics in the Ohio Country 1780-1825, 1986; The Midwest and the Nation: Rethinking the History of An American Region, 1990. Contributions to: Scholarly Articles in, The William and Mary Quarterly; The Journal of the Early Republic; The Historian; OH History. Honours: Phi Beta Kappa, 1976; Ohioana Book Award, 1987. Memberships: Am Historical Association; Organization of Am Historians; Society for Historians of the Early Am

Republic; OH Historical Society; IN Historical Society. Address: DEpt of History, Miami University, Oxford, OH 45056, USA.

CEDERING Siv, b. 5 Feb 1939, Sweden. Writer; Artist. m. David Swickard, 11 Sept 1983, 1 s, 2 d. Publications include: Mother Is, 1975; The Juggler, 1977; The BLue Horse, 1979; Oxen, 1981; Letters from the Floating Worlds, 1984; Cup of Cold Water, 1973; Several Translations. Contributions to: Harpers; Ms; New Republic; Paris Review; Partisan Review; NY Times; Goergia Review; Fiction Interntional Shenandoah; Confrontation; Numerous Other Literary Magazines; over 80 Anthologies & Textbooks. Honours: Best Books of Year, 1980; NY Foundation Fellowship, 1985, 1992. Memberships: PSA; Poets & Writers; Am PEN; CCLM. Literary Agent: Diana Finch, Ellen Levine Agency. Address: Box 800, Amagansett, NY 11930, USA.

CEGIELKA Francis Anthony, b. 16 Mar, Grabow, Poland. Roman Catholic Priest in the Society of the Catholic Apostolate. Education: Collegium Marianum, 1921-27, Wadowice (Krakow); Pontifical Gregorian University, Rome, Italy, 1927-31; Ordained Priest, 1931; Doctorate in Theology (STD) 1931. Appointments: Teacher, Minor Seminary of the Society of the Catholic Apostolate, Chelmno, Poland, 1932-34; Teacher, Major Seminary, SAC, Wadowice, Poland, 1934-36; Rector, Polish Catholic Mission, Paris, France, 1937-47; Prisoner of German Gestapo, held in 9 prisons and 2 concentration camps, 1940-45; Rector, Polish Catholic Mission, Paris, France, 1945-48; Sent to the USA by his Superior General to conduct retreat work; Professor, Felician College, Lodi, New Jersey, 1967-70; Professor, Holy Family College, Philadelphia, USA, 1970-76. Publications include: Reparatory Mysticism of Nazareth, 1951; Holy Mass School of Religious Life, 1953; Life on Rocks (among the Natives of the Union of South Africa), 1957; Spiritual Theology for Novices, 1961; Segregavit nos Dominus, 1963; Three Hearts Meditations, 1963, 2nd volume 1964; Nazareth Spirituality, 1966; All Things New: Radical Reform of Religious Life, 1969; Handbook of Ecclesiology and Christology, 1971; Toward a New Spring of Humankind, 1987; alsopublications in Polish. Honours: Legion d'Honneur Chevalier, French Government, 1945; Nominated as an outstanding Educator of America, 1972, 1974. Memberships: American Association of University Professors; Polish Institute of Arts & Sciences in America. Address: 3452 Niagara Falls Blvd, PO Box 563, North Tonawanda, NY 14120, USA.

CELATI Gianni, b. 1937, Sondrio, Ferrara, Italy. Novelist. Appointments include: Lecturer in Anglo-American Literature at the University of Bologna. Publications: Comiche, 1971; Le avventure di Guizzardi, 1971; Il chiodo in testa, 1975; La banda dei sospiri, 1976; Lunario del paradiso, 1978; Narratori delle pianure, 1985; Quattro novelle sulle apparenze, 1987; Verso la foce, 1989; Also: Finzioni occidentali, 1975; La bottega dei mimi, 1977; Parlamenti buffi, 1989; Profili delle nuvole, 1989; Éditions and translations. Honours include: Mondello Prize, 1990. Address: c/o Feltrinelli, Via Andegari 6, 20121 Milan, Italy.

CESAIRE Aimé (Fernand), b. 25 June 1913, Basse-Pointe, Martinique, West Indies. Poet; Playwright. Education: Ecole Normale Supérieure in Paris, 1935-39. Appointments include: Mayor of Forte-de-France, 1945-84; President, Conseil Régional Martinique, 1983-86. Publications: Les Armes miraculeuses, 1946, 1970; Notebook of a Return to the Native Land, 1947, 1968; Soloeil cou-coupe, 1948, 1961; Lost Body, 1960, 1986; Ferrements, 1960; Cadastre, 1961; State of the Union, 1966; Aimé Cesaire: The Collected Poetry, 1983; Non-Viscious Circle: Twenty Poems, 1984; Lyric and Dramatic Poetry 1946-83, 1990; Plays: Et les Chiens se taisaient, 1956; The Tragedy of King Christophe, 1964; A Season in the Congo, 1966; A Tempest, adaptation of Shakespeare, 1969; Also: Toussaint L'ouverture: la révolution française et le problème colonial, 1960. Honours include: National Grand Prize for poetry, 1982. Address: La Mairie, 97200 Fort-de-France, Martinique, West Indies.

CHACEL Rosa, b. 3 June 1898. Novelist. Education: (F4)Escuela Superior, Madrid. Publications include: Estacion, ida y vuelta, 1930; Teresa, 1941; Memorias de Leticia Valle, 1945; Sobre el pielago, 1952, 1971; La sinrazon, 1960; Barrio de maravillas, 1976; Novelas antes de tiempo, 1981; Acropolis, 1984; Ciencias naturales, 1988; Balaam otros cuentos, 1989; Verse: la orilla de un pozo, 1936; Versos prohibidos, 1978; Poesias 1931-91, 1992; Complete works, 1980, 1989; Translator of works by Camus and Racine. Honours include: National Literature Prize, 1987. Address: Editorial Seix Barral, Corcega 270, 4, 08008 Barcelona, Spain.

CHADWICK (William) Owen, b. 20 May 1916, Bromley, Kent, England. Historian. m. Ruth Hallward, 28 Dec 1949, 2 s, 2 d. Education: BA, 1939, St John's College, Cambridge. Publications: John Cassian, 1950, revised edition 1968; The Founding of Cuddesdon, 1954; From Bossuet to Newman, 1957, 2nd edition 1987; Western Asceticism, 1958; Creighton on Luther, 1959; Mackenzie's Grave, 1959; Victorian Miniature, 1960, 2nd edition 1991; The Mind of the Oxford Movement, 1960; From Uniformity to Unity 1662-1962 (with G Nuttall), 1962; Westcott and the University, 1962; The Reformation, 1964; The Victorian Church, vol 1, 1966, 3rd edition, 1972; vol II, 1970, 2nd edition, 1972; Acton and Gladstone, 1976; The Secularization of the European Mind, 1977; Catholicism and History, 1978; The Popes and European Revolution, 1981; The Oxford History of the Christian Church (editor with Henry Chadwick, brother), 1976-; Newman, 1983; Hensley Henson: A Study in the Friction Between Church and State, 1983; Britain and the Vatican in the Second World War, 1986; Michael Ramsey, 1990, 2nd edition 1991; The Spirit of the Oxford Movement: Tractarian Essays, 1990; the Christian Church in the Cold War, 1992. Contributions to: Times (London); New Statesman; Spectator; Guardian; Sunday Times; Observer; History Journals - esssays in honour of, in G Best and D Beales (editors). Honours: Order of Merit, 1983; KBE, 1982; Wolfson Prize for History (for the Popes and European Revolution), 1981. Memberships: Fellow, British Academy; Fellow, Royal Historical Society. Address: 67 Grantchester Street, Cambridge CB3 9H2, England.

CHADWICK Geoffrey, (Geoffrey Wall), b. 10 July 1950, Cheshire, England. University Lecturer, 3 s, 1 d. Education: BA, University of Sussex, 1972; BPhil, St Edmund Hall, 1975. Publications: Madame Bovary, 1992. Contributions to: Literature and History; Cambridge Quarterly. Memberships: Society of Authors; Association of University Teachers; Translators Association. Address: Dept of English, University of York, Heslington, York, YO1 5D, England.

CHADWICK Whitney, b. 28 July 1943, NY, USA. Art Historian. m. Robert A Bechtle, 6 Nov 1982. Education: BA, Middlebury College, 1965; MA, The PA State University, 1968; PhD, 1975. Publications: Women, Art and Society; Women Artists and the Surealist Movement; Myth in Surealist Paiting; Significant Others: Creativity and Intimate Partnerships, 1993. Contributions to: Art in Am; Artforum; The Art Bulletin; Art International Womens Art Journal. Membership: College Art Association of Am. Literary Agent: Elaine Markson. Address: 8971 DeHaro Street, San Francisco, CA 94107, USA.

CHAGALL David, b. 22 Nov 1930, PA, USA. Author; Journalist. m. Juneau Joan Alsin, 15 Nov 1957. Education: Swarthmore College, 1948-49; BA, PA State University, 1952; Sorbonne, University of Paris. Appointments: Associate Editor, IEE, 1960-61; Investigative Reporter, Nationl Magazine, 1975-; Editor, Publisher, Inside Campaigning, 1984; Contributing Editor, Los Angeles Magazine, 1986-89; Host, TV Series, The Last Hour, 1994-. Publications: The Century God Slept, 1963; Dairy of a Deaf Mute, 1971; The Spieler for the Holy Spirit, 1972; The New Kingmakers, 1981; Television Today, 1981; The Sunshine Road, 1988; The World's Greatest Comebacks, 1989. Contributions to: TV Guide; Time, Life; Family Weekly; Los Angeles Magazine; CA Business; Valley Magazine; Inside Campaigning; New West. Honours include: Carnegie Award, 1964; National Book Award, 1972; Health Journalism Award, 1980; Presidential Achievement Award, 1982. Memberships include: Authors Guild; Ntional Society for the Book; Am Academy of Political Science. Literary Agent: Jay Garon, USA. Address: PO Box 85, Agoura Hills, CA 91376 0085, USA.

CHAKRAVARTI Sasthibrata. See: **BRATA Sasthi**.

CHALFONT Alun Arthur Gwynne Jone, b. 1919, England. Appointments: Served as Regulat Officer, British Army, 1939-61; Defence Correspondent, The Times, 1961-64; Minister of State, Foreign and Commonwealth Office, 1964-70; Representative, Council of Western European Union, 1969-70; Foreign Office Correspondent, New Statesmn, 1970-71; Chairman, UN Association, 1972-73; Director, IBM & /Lazard Brothers Limited; president, Nottingham Building Society; Chairman, All Party Defence Group, 1980. Publictions: The Sword and the Spirit, 1963; The Great Commanders, 1973; Montgomery of Alamein, 1976; Waterloo, 1979; Star Wars: Suicide or Survival, 1985; Defense of the Realm, 1987; By God's Will, 1991. Contributions to: The Times; National and Professional Journals. Address: House of Lord, London SW1A 0PW, England.

CHALKER Jack L, b. 1944, America. Appointments: Founder, Director, Mirage press, 1961-; English, History & Geography Teacher, Baltimore Public High Schools, 1966-78. Publications include: In Memoriam Clark Ashton Smith, 1963; Mirage on Lovecraft, 1964; The Index to the Science Fantasy Publishers, 1966; An Informal Biography of Scrooge McDuck, 1974; A Jungle of Stars, 1976; Midnight in the Well of Souls, 1977; A War of Shadows, And the Devil Will Drag You Under, Dancers in the Afterglow, 1979; Twilight at the Well of Souls, The Devils Voyagem, 1980; A Tiger by the Tail, Four Lords of the Diamond, 1983; The River of Dancing Gods, Spirits of Lux and Anchor, Empires of Flux and Anchor, 1984; The Messiah Choice, The Birth of Flux and Anchor, 1985; Children of Clux and Anchor, 1986.

CHALLIS Chris, b. 11 Feb 1952, Essex, England. Writer; Lecturer. Education: BA, Leicester University, 1973; MA, (Dist) 1974; PhD, 1979. Appointments: ACGB Writer in Residence, Northampton, 1982-83; Four BBC Radio Stateions, 1985; Doncaster Libraries, 1987; WIR Featherstone Library, 1987; WIR Co Durham, 1989-90; WIR West Norfolk, 1991-92. Publications: Quest for Kerouac; Highfields Landscape; William of Cloudeslee; The Wild Thing Went from Side to Side; Four Stout Shoes; Jack Kerouac; Charles Bukowski and Me; A Little Earth for Charity; Ten Plays; Common Ground; A Sense of Place; Wordscan; Together in Eternity; The Place Project Series. Contributions to: Numerous. Honours: Nanda Award; Erna Travel Bursary; Erna Writers Bursary; Judge for Literary Comps; Heinemann Fiction Award. Membership: Writers Guild. Address: 67 Prospect Hill, Leicester, LE5 3RT, England.

CHALMERS Mary Eilleen, b. 16 Mar 1927, Camden, NJ, USA. Author; Artist. Education: Diploma, College of Art, 1945-48; Barnes Foundation, 1948-49. Publications: A Christmas Story, 1956; Throw A Kiss, Harry, 1958; Take A Nap, Harry, 1964; Come to the Doctor, Harry, 1981; 6 Dogs, 23 Cats, 45 Mice and 116 Spiders, 1986; Easter Parade, 1988. Address: 4Q Laurel Hill Road, Greenbelt, MD 20770, USA.

CHALON Jon. See: **CHALONER John.**

CHALONER John, (Jon Chalon), England. Publications include: Three for the Road, 1954; Eager Beaver, 1965; The Flying Steamroller; The House Next Door, 1967; Sir Lance A Little and the Knights of the Kitchen Table, 1971; The Green Bus, 1973; Family Hold Back, 1975; The Dustmans Holiday, 1976; To the Mannor Born, 1978; The Great Balloon Adventure; Will O The Wheels and Speedy Sue, 1990; Occupational Hazard, 1991. Honour: Verbundesdienstkreuz 1st Kt for Services Anglo German Relations, 1990. Address: 4 Warwick Square, London SW1, England.

CHAMBERS Aidan, (Malcolm Blackin), b. 27 Dec 1934, Chester Le Street, County Durham, England. Author; Publisher. m. Nancy Harris Lockwood, 30 Mar 1968. Education: Borough Road College, Isleworth, London University. Publications include: The Reluctant Reader, 1969; Introducing Books to Children, 1973, 1983; Breaktime, 1978; Seal Secret, 1980; The Dream Cage, 1981; Dance on My Grave, 1982; The Present Takers, 1983; Booktalk, 1985; Now I Know, 1987; The Reading Environment, 1991; The Toll Bridge, 1992; Tell Me: Children, Reading & Talk, 1993. Contributions to: Numerous Magazines and Journals. Honours: Childrens Literature Award for Outstanding Criticism, 1978; Eleanor Farjeon Award, 1982; Silver Pencil, 1985, 1986, 1994. Membership: Society of Authors. Address: Lockwood Station Road, Woodchester, Stroud, Gloucs GL5 5EQ, England.

CHAMBERS Catherine E. See: **JOHNSTON Norma.**

CHAMBERS Kate. See: **JOHNSTON Norma.**

CHAMBERS Marjorie Elizabeth, b. 15 May 1938, Northern Ireland. University Lecturer. m. Cyril Weir Chambers, 30 June 1969, 1 s. Education: BA, 1961-62, MA, 1968, Trinity College; Sorbonne, Paris, 1961-62; PGCE Goldsmiths College, London, 1964; University of Thessalonika, 1981. Appointments: Lecturer, Queens University, Belfast. Publications include: Modern Greek Studies Yearbook, volume 7, 1991; My Sisters Song, The March of the Ocean, 1987-88; Poems from Collection, The Big Night and the Window; The Offering; Ongs of Resurrection; The Sequel; Gift in Abeyance. Honours: British Council Grants, Research on Yannis Ritsos, 1987; Research on George Vafopoulos and Nikiforos Vrettakos, 1990. Memberships: Translators Association; Society of Authors; ITI; Dictionary of Translators and Interpreters; Northern Ireland Representative, Examiner in Modern Greek. Address: 3 The Esplanade, Holywood, Co Down, BT18 9JG, Northern Ireland.

CHAMBERS Raymond J, b. 1917, Australian. Appointments: Senior Lecturer, 1953-55, Associate Professor, 1955-59, Professor of Accounting, 1960-82, Emeritus, University of Sydney; Editor, Abacus, 1964-74. Publications include: Financial Management, 1947; Function and Design of Company Annual Reports, 1955; Accounting and Action, 1957; The Accounting Frontier, 1965; Accounting, Evaluation and Economic Behavior, 1966; Accounting Finance and Management, 1969; Securities and Obscurities, 1973; Price Variation and Inflation Accounting, 1980. Address: Dept of Accounting, University of Sydney, Sydney, NSW 2006, Australia.

CHAMPAGNE Maurice (Joseph Pierre), b. 7 May 1936, Montreal, Canada. Philosopher; Human Rights Consultant. m. 1 son, 1 daughter. Education: MA, Montreal, 1956; DES, Nice, 1967; DLitt, Nice, 1968. Literary Appointments: Literature Teaching Coordinator, Quebec Education Department, 1968-69. Publications: La Violewce Au Powvoir, 1971; Lettres D'Amour, 1972; La Famille Et L'Homme A Délivrer Du Pouvoir, 1980; Batir Ou Détruire Le Quebec, 1983; L'Homme-Tetard, 1991. Contributions to: Feature Articles, over one hundred in, Le Devoir and Lapresse. Honours: Governor General of Canada Award, 1980. Memberships: Quebec Writers Union; Quebec Criminology Association; Quebec Human Rights Commission; Past President, Director, Civil Liberties Union, 1970-78. Literary Agent: Louise Myette. Address: 3741 Saint Andre, Montreal, Quebec H2L 3V6, Canada.

CHAMPION Larry Stephen, b. 27 Apr 1932, North CA, USA. University Professor. m. Nancy Ann Blanchard, 22 Dec 1956, 1 s, 2 d. Education: BA, Davidson College, 1954; MA, University of VA, 1955; PhD, University of North CA, 1961. Publications include: Evolution of Shakespeare's Comedy; Perspective in Shakespeare's English Histories; Thomas Dekker & Traditions of English Drama; Quick Springs of Sense: Essays on 18th Century Literature; The Noise of Threatening Drum. Contributions to: Numerous Scholarly Journals. Honours include: Academy of Outstanding Teachers, 1966; SAMLA Studies Awards Committee, 1971;James E Savage Lecturer in Renaissance, 1984; Alumni Distinguished Professor, 1987. Memberships include: Malone Society; Renaissance English Text Society; Phi Beta Kappa; Phi Kappa Phi; American & International Shakespeare Association; Renaissance Society of America; Modern Language Association. Address: 5320 Sendero Drive, Raleigh, North CA 27612 1810, USA.

CHAMPOUX Pierrette, b. 26 Jan 1930, Montréal, Quebec, Canada. Journalist; Radio-Reporter; Singer; Composer. Education: Dramatic School. Literary Appointments: Daily News Reporter, Radio Station CKVL-Verdun; Writer for several newspapers and magazines; Composer, Songs, Music, Numerous public appearances on TV Shows, Radio Programs; Fashion Commentator. Publications: Parle-Moi Du Canada, 1992; Raconte-Moi-Montreal, 1992; Les Pionnieres, 1992; Quebec, en Ballades, 1994; Records: Sur Les Bords Du St-Laurent, 1966, Un Enfant, 1979. Contributions to: Canada Nouveau; Radio-Monde. Honours: Grand Prix, Women's International Year's Contest, 1975; Honorable Mention, The American Song Festival, Hollywood, California, 1976; Honorable Mention, Canadian Committee for the International Year of the Handicapped, 1981; 1st Prize, Le Concours International des Arts et Lettres, France, 1993. Memberships: President, Women's Press Club; Director, United Nations Canadian Association, Montreal Branch; Conseillére, La Société des Ecrivains Canadiens; L'Union des Artistes, Socan. Address: 1770 rue Perrot, Ile Perrot, Quebec, J7V 7P2, Canada.

CHAN Stephen, b. 11 May 1949, New Zealand. Director of University of Kent, London Centre; Research Professor, University of Zambia; Former International Civil Servant; Commonwealth Secretariat. Education: BA, University of Auckland, 1972; MA, 1975; MA, London University Kings College, 1977; PhD, University of Kent, Canterbury, 1992. Publications: Kaunda and Southern Africa; Crimson Rain; Exporting Apartheid; Songs of the Maori King; Ardens Summer; total of nine scholarly books & five volumes of Poetry. Honour: LittD. Memberships: PEN; British Students Karate Federation; Various African Karate Unions. Address: University of Kent, London Centre of International Relations, St Philips Building, Sheffield Street, London WC2A 2EX, England.

CHANCE Stephen. See: **TURNER Philip.**

CHANCELLOR Alexander Surtees, b. 4 Jan 1940, Ware, Hertfordshire, England. Journalist. m. Susanna Elizabeth Debenham, 1964, 2 d. Education: Trinity Hall, Cambridge. Appointments: Reuters News Agency, 1964-74; Chief Correspondent, Italy, 1968-73; ITV News, 1974-75; Editor, The Spectator, 1975-84; Assistant Editor, Sunday Telegraph, 1984-; Editor, Time and Tide, 1984-86; Dep Editor, Sunday Telegraph, 1986; Editor, The Independent Magazine, 1988-92. Address: c/o The Independent, 40 City Road, London, EC1Y 2DB, England.

CHANDLER David (Geoffrey), b. 1934, England. Appointments include: British Army Officer, 1957-60; Lecturer, 1960-64, Senior Lecturer, 1964-69, Deputy Head, 1969-80, Head, 1980-94, Royal Military Academy Sandhurst; president, British Military History Commission, 1967-86; President Emeritus, 1986-; Vice President, International Comission of Military History, 1975-; Editor, David Chanlers Newsletter on the Age of Napoleon, 1987-89; Military Affairs Visiting Professor, Quantico, 1991. Publications include: A Travellers Guide to Battlefields of Europe, 1965; The Campaigns of Napoleon, 1966; Marlborough as Military Commander, 1973; The Art of Warfare on Land, 1975; The Art of Warfare in the Age of Marlborough, 1976; A Journal of Marlboroughs Wars, 1984; Napoleons Military Maxims, 1987; On The Napoleon Wars, 1994; The Oxford Illustrated History of the British Army, 1994. Memberships: Europoen Union of Re Enactment Societies; The Nepoleonic Society of Great Britain. Address: Hindford, Monteagle Lane, Yateley, Camberley, Surrey.

CHANDLER Frank. See: **HARKNETT Terry.**

CHANEY Edward Paul De Gruyter, b. 11 Apr 1951, Historian. m. Lisa Maria Jacka, 2 d. Education: BA, Reading University; M Phil, PhD, London University. Publications: The Grand Tour and the Great Rebellion; Florence: A Travellers Companion; Oxford, China and Haly; England and the Continetal Renaissance; Journal of Anglo Italian Studies; English Architecture; Public And Public. Contributions to include: TLS; Country Life; Apollo; English Histroical Review; Burlington Magazine; Journal of Anglo Italian Studies; Spectator; Daily Telegraph. Honour: Laurea Di Dottore. Literary Agent: Gabriele Pentucci. Membership: FSA. Address: 40 Southfield Road, Oxford, OX4 1NZ, England.

CHANG Lee. See: **LEVINSON Leonard.**

CHAPLIN Jenny, (Tracie Telfer, Wendy Wentworth), b. 22 Dec 1928, Glasgow, Scotland. Head Mistress; Editor; Publisher. m. J McDonald Chaplin, 21 Apr 1951, 1 d. Education; Jordanhill College of Education, 1946-49. Appointments: Editor, Founder, Publisher, International, The Writers Rostrum, 1984-93; Organiser, Lecturer, Writers Workshop, Rarin to Go, 1991. Publications: A Glasgow Childhood; A Glasgow Fair; A Glasgow Hogmanay; One Editors Life; The Puzzle of Parkinsons Disease; Thoughts on Writing; Island Connections; Arthritis News; Book: Tales of A Glasgow Childhood, 1994; In progress: Writers' Workshop Series. Contributions to: Numerous including: Writers News; Sharpen Your Writing Skills; Self Publishing Feature; Article of D C Thomson; You Too Can Be An Editor; The Scotsman Newspaper; Thought for Today; Life on the Lean Side; The Scots Magazine; London Calling; Daily Mail; Scottish Memories; 23 articles to date including: Writing The Haiku; Poetry Today; Writing The Saga; From The Editor's Desk; Scottish Memories; Mammy Was Right; Hell in the Hebrides; See Thon Evacuees; Templeton's Carpet Factory Disaster. Address: Tigh na Mara Cottage, 14 Ardbeg Road, Rothesay, Bute PA20 0NJ, Scotland.

CHAPMAN Elizabeth, b. 5 Jan 1919, Writer. m. Frank Chapman, 22 Nov 1941, 3 s. Education: Barnsley High School for Girls; College of Technology, Barnsley, 1938-39. Publictions: Marmaduke the Lorry, 1953; Marmaduke and Joe, 1954; Riding with Marmaduke, 1955; Merry Marmaduke, 1957; Marmaduke and His Friends, 1958; Marmaduke and the Elephant, 1959; Marmaduke and the Lambs, 1960; Marmaduke Goes to France, 1961; Marmaduke Goes to Holland, 1963; Marmaduke Goes to America, 1965; Marmaduke Goe to Italy, 1970; Marmaduke Goes to Spain, 1978; Marmaduke Goes to Switzerland, 1977; Marmaduke Goes to Morocco, 1979; Marmaduke Goes to Scotland, 1986; Marmaduke Goes to Wales, 1982; Marmaduke Goes to Ireland, 1987. Contributions to: Sunny Stories; Radio Short Stories, Listen With Mother; TV Short Stories, Rainbow. Address: 88 Grange Gardens, Pinner, Middlesex HA5 5QF, England.

CHAPMAN Ivan Douglas, b. 14 Feb 1919, Werris Creek, NSW, Australia. Joumlist; Military Historian. m. Moria Helen Menzies, 12 Sept 1953, 3 d. Education: Sydney Technical College, 1946-47. Appointments: Journalist, ABC News Radio, 1947-52, TV, 1956-76, BBC News, Radio, 1952-54; TV, 1954-56, 1973-74; SBS News Radio, 1979-80. Publications: Details Enclosed; Iven G Mackay; Private Eddie Leonski; Toyko Calling. Contributions to: Australian Dictionary of Biography; Australian Encylopaedia; Weekend Australian; The Bulletin; British History Illustrated; Times Life Books. Memberships: Australian Society of Authors; National Press Club Canberra; Journalists Club Sydney; Ex PoW Association of Australia. Address: c/o Australian Society of Authors, PO Box 1566, Strawberry Hills, NSW 2012, Australia.

CHAPMAN Jean, b. 30 Oct 1929, England. Writer. m. Lionel Alan Chapman, 24 Mar 1951, 1 s, 2 d. Education: BA (Hons), Open University, 1989. Appointments: Creative Writing Tutor for East Midlans Arts 2 Community Colleges. Publications: The Unreasoning Earth, 1981; Tangled Dynasty, 1985; Forbidden Path, 1986; Savage Legacy, 1987; The Bell Makers, 1990; Fortunes Woman, 1992; A World Apart, 1993; The Red Pavilion, 1995; Wide Range of Short Stories. Honours: Romanic Novel of Year, Short Listed, 1981; Kathleen Fidler Award, Short Listed, 1990. Memberships: Society of Authors; Romantic Novelists Association. Literary Agent: Jane Judd. Address: 3 Arnesby Lane, Peatling Magna, Leicester LE8 3UN, England.

CHAPMAN Richard Arnold, b. 15 Aug 1937, Bexleyheath, Kent, England. University Professor. Education: BA, University of Leicester, 1961; MA, Carleton University, 1962; PhD, University of Leicester, 1966; DLitt, 1989. Publications: Decision Making: The Higher Civil Service in Britain; Leaderhip in the British Civil Service; Ethics in the British Cicil Service; The Art of Darkness; Several Other Publications. Contributions to: Public Policy & Administration; Review of Politics; International Review of Administrative Sciences; International Review of History & Political Science. Membership: Joint University Council; Political Studies Association. Address: University of Durham, Dept of Politics, 48 Old Elvet, Durham DH1 3LZ, England.

CHAPMAN Stanley David, b. 1935, England. Appointments: Lecturer, 1968-73, Pasold Reader in Business History, 1973-, Professor, 1993-, University of Nottingham; Editor, Textile History Bi Annual. Publications: The Early Factory Masters, 1967; The Beginnings of Industrial Britain, 1970; The History of Working Class Housing, 1971; The Cotton Industry in the industrial Revolution, 1972; Jesse Boot of Boots the Chemists, 1974; The Devon Cloth Industry in the 18th Century, 1978; Stanton and Staveley, 1971; The Rise of Merchant Banking, 1984; Merchant Enterprise in Britain from the Industrial Revolution to World War I, 1992. Address: Birchlea, Beetham Close, Bingham, Notts NG13 8ED.

CHAPPELL Fred, b. 28 May 1936, Teacher. m. Susan Nicholls, 22 July 1959, 1 s. Education: BA, 1961, MA, 1963, Duke University. Publications: I Am One Of You Forever; Midquest; Brighten The Corner Where You Are; More Shapes Than One; The Fred Chappell Reader; Plow Naked, 1993. Contributions to: Numerous. Honours: National Institute of Arts & Letters Award in Literature; Sir Walter Raleigh Prize; Bollingen Prize. Memberships include: Southern Writers Fellowship. Literary Agent: Rhoda Weyr. Address: 305 Kensington Road, Greensboro, NC 27403, USA.

CHAPPELL Mollie, b. England. Publications include: Little Tom Sparrow, 1950; The Gentle Giant, 1951; The Sugar and Spice, 1952; The Fortunes of Frick, 1953; Cat with No Fiddle, 1954; The Widow Jones, 1956; Endearing Young Charms, 1957; Bachelor Heaven, 1958; A Wreath of holly, 1959; One Little Room, 1960; Come by Chance, 1963; The Wind in the Green Trees, 1969; The Hasting Day, 1970; Summer Story, Valley of Lilacs, 1972; Family Portrait, Cressy, 1972; Loving Heart, Country Air, 1977; Dearest Neighbour, 1981; Cousin Amelia, 1982; The Family at Redburn, 1985. Address: c/o Curtis Brown Limited, 162-168 Regent Street, London W1R 5TA, England.

CHAPPLE John Alfred Victor, b. 1928, England. Appointments: Assistant University College, 1953-55; Research Assistant, Yale University, 1955-58; Assistant Lecture, Aberdeen University, 1958-59; Assistant Lecturer, 1959-61, Lecturer, 1961-67, Senior Lecturer, 1967-71, Manchester University; Professor, Hull University, 1971-92, Emeritus Professor, 1992; Visiting Fellow, Corpus Christi College, 1991. Publications include: The Letters of Mrs Gaskell, 1966; Documenty and Imaginative Lieterature 1880-1920, 1970; Elizabeth

Gaskell: A Portrait in Letters, 1980; Science and Literature in the 19th Century, 1986. Memberships: The Bronte Society; The Gaskell Society; International Association of University Professors of English. Address: 173 Newlanf Park, Hull, HU5 2DX, Yorkshire, England.

CHARBONNEAU Louis H, (Carter Travis Young), b. 1924, America. Writer. Appointments: Instructor, University of Detroit, 1948-52; Copywriter, Mercury Advertising Agency, 1952-56; Staff Writer, Los Angeles Times, 1956-71; Freelance Writer, 1971-74; Editor, Security World Publishing Co, 1974-79. Publications include: No Place on Earth, 1958; Night of Violence, 1959; Nor All Your Tears, 1959; The Savage Plain, 1961; The Bitter Iron, 1964; Long Boots, Hard Boots, 1965; Way Out, 1966; Down to Earth, 1967; The Sensitives, 1968; Down from the Mountain, 1969; Barrier World, 1970; The Captive, 1973; Guns of Darkness, 1974; Embryo, 1976; Inruder, 1979; The Lair, 1979; Writer Drift, 1980; The Brea File, 1983. Address: c/o Scott Mredith Literary Agency, 845 Third Avenue, New York, NY 10022, USA.

CHARD Dorothy Doreen (Judy Chard), b. 8 May 1916, Tuffley, Gloucestershire, England. Author: Freelance Journalist: Broadcaster.m. Maurice Noel Chard, 26 Jul 1941. Appointments: Editor, Devon Life Magazine, 4 years; Tutor, Creative Writing, Devon County Council & WEA; Director of Studies with David and Charles Correspondence College; Critic for Second Opinion on short stories for South West Arts, 1991; Course Leader, Writer's News Home Studies Div Correspondence College, Oct 1992. Broadcaster, BBC and Local radio. Publications: Through the Green Woods, 1974; The Weeping and the Laughter, 1975; Encounter in Berlin, 1976; The Uncertain Heart, 1977; The Other Side of Sorrow, 1978; In the Heart of Love, 1979; Out of the Shadow, 1980; All Passion spent, 1981; Seven Lonely Years, 1982; The Darkening Skies, 1982; When the Journey's Over, 1983; Haunted By the Past, 1984; Sweet Love Remembered, Where the Dream Begins, 1985; Rendevouz With Love, 1986; Hold Me in Your Heart, 1987; Live With Fear, 1987; Wings of the Morning, 1987; A Time to Love, 1987; Encounter in Spain, 1994; The Mysterious Lady of the Moor, 1994; Beatrice Chase, 1994; on audio cassette: For Love's Sake, To Be So Loved, Enchantment, Person Unknown, Appointment With Danger; 7 local books on Devon, The Devon Guide; Traditional Cooking. Contributions to: Columnist, Western Morning News, Plymouth, Heritage Magazine; magazines, national & local newspapers; Regular Broadcaster with BBC and Commercial Radio. Address: Morley Farm, Highweek, Newton Abbot, Devon TQ12 6NA, England.

CHARD Judy. See: CHARD Dorothy Doreen.

CHARLES Francis. See: DE BONO Edward.

CHARLES Gerda, b. 1930, Liverpool, England. Novelist. Education: Liverpool schools. Appointments: Journalist and Reviewer for New Statesman, Daily Telegraphy, New York Times, Jewish Chronicle, and other periodicals; Television Critic, Jewish Observer, London, 1978-79. Publications: The True Voice, 1959; The Crossing Point, 1960; A Slanting Light, 1963; A Logical Girl, 1967; The Destiny Waltz, 1971; Several short stories. Honours: James Tait Black Memorial Prize, 1964; Whitbread Award, 1971. Address: 22 Cunningham Court, London W9 1AE, England.

CHARLES Nicholas. See: KUSKIN Karla Seidman.

CHARLIER Roger Henri, (Henri Rochard), b. 10 Nov 1921, Antwerp, Belgium. University Professor. m. Patricia Mary Simonet, 17 June 1958, 1 s, 1 d. Education: PhD, Erlangen, 1947; LittD, Paris, 1956; ScD, Paris, 1958; Lic Sci, Brussels, 1945; Lic Pol Sci, Brussels, 1941; B Sci, Liège, 1942, Brussels, 1943. Appointments: Contributing Editor, Hexagon, 1962; Consulting Editor, Ocean Abstracts, 1965; Consultant Editor, Foreign Language Quarterly, 1956; Editor-in-Chief, Bull PIANC. Publications: I Was a Male War Bride, 1948; For The Love of Kate, 1962; The Physical Environment, 1964; Pensees, 1965; The World Around Us, 1966; Marine Resources, 1968; Marine Science & Technology, 1970; Economic Oceanography, 1978; Tidal Energy, 1982; Ocean Energies, 1993; Coastal Zone Protection and Management, 1995. Contributions to: Over 600 Literary, Political and Scientific Articles in Magazines & Journals. Honours: Prize Fancois Franck, 1939; National Academy of Arts, Sciences and Fine Letters, 1973; Knight Order of Leopold Belgium, 1973; Knight of the Order of Academic Palms, France, 1973; Grand Medal of Arts Letters and Sciences, 1971; Presidential Award, 1980; Publication Award, 1989; P

H Spaak Memorial Lecture, 1993. Memberships: Geological Society of Am; Am Association of Advancement of Science; NJ Academy of Science. Literary Agent: Hollywood, NY, USA. Address: 4055 North Keystone Avenue, chicago, IL 60641, USA.

CHARLIP Remy, b. 1929, America. Appointments: Choreographer, London Contemporry Dance Theatre, 1972-76; Choreographer, Scottish Theatre Ballet, 1973, Welsh Dance Theatre, 1974; Director, Remy Charlip Dance Company, 1977-; Director, The All Star International Dance Company. Publications include: Dresss Up and Lets Have a Party, 1956; Where is Everybody, 1957; Fortunately, 1964; Mother Mother I Feel Sick Send for the Dictor Quick Quick Quick, 1966; I Love You, 1967, 1981; The Tree Angel; Jumping Beans; Handtalk: An ABC of Finger Spelling and Sign Language, 1974; Thirteen, 1975; Arm in Arm, 1980; I Love You, 1981; First Remy Charlip Reader, 1986; Handtalk Birthday: A Number and Storybook in Sign Language, 1987. Address: 60 East 7th Street, New York, NY 10003, USA.

CHARNAS Suzy McKee, b. 1939, USA. Appointments: Formerly English & History Teacher, Nigeria; Teacher, New Lincoln School; Community Mental Health Organisation Worker; Freelance Writer, 1969-; Judge, James Tiptree Award, 1991. Publications: Walk to the End of the World, 1974; Motherlines, 1979; The Vampire Tapestry, 1980; The Bronze King, 1985; Dorothea Dreams, 1986; The Silver Glove, 1988; The Golden Thread, 1989; The Kingdom of Kevin Malone, 1993; Stage Play, Vampire Dreams, Magic Theatre, 1990; The Furies, 1994. Contributions to: Womens Review of Books. Honours: Nebula Award, 1980; Hugo Award, 1989. Memberships: Authors Guild; SFWA; HWA; Dramatistis Guild. Literary Agent: Jennifer Lyons, Joan Daves Agency, USA. Address: 212 High St NE, Albuquerque, NM 87102, USA.

CHARTERS Samuel Barclay, b. 1 Aug 1929, Pittsburgh, PA, USA. Writer; Music Producer. m. Ann Danberg, 19 Mar 1959, 1 s, 2 d. Education: AB, University of CA. Publications include: The Country Blues, 1959; The Poetry of the Blues, 1963; The Roots of the Blues, 1981; Jelly Roll Mortons Last Night, 1984; Louisiana Black, 1987; Elvis Presley Calls his Mother, 1992; A Country Year, 1992; Several Collections of Poetry; Translations from the Swedish of Tomas Transtromer, Bo Carpelan and Edith Sodergran. Contributions to: Numerous. Honours: Deems Taylor Award for Excellence in Writing on Music, 1984; Artur Lundqvist Translation Award, 1984. Address: c/o Gazell Music, Box 20055, S 16102 Bromm, Sweden.

CHARYN Jerome, b. 1937, USA. Author; Educator. Appointments: English Teacher, High School of Music & Art, School of Performing Arts, NY City, 1962-64; Assistant Professor, Stanford University, 1965-68; Professor, Herbert Lehman College, City University of NY, 1968-80; Founding Editor, The Dutton Review, 1970; Lecturer, Princeton University, 1980-86. Publications include: Once Upon a Droshky, 1964; On The Darkening Green, 1965; Going to Jersualem, 1967; American Scrapbook, 1969; The Single Voice: An Anthology of Contemporary Fiction, 1969; The Troubled Vision, 1970; The Tar Baby, 1973; Blue Eyes, 1975; Marilyn the Wild, 1976; The Franklin Scare, 1977; Secret Isaac, 1978; The Seventh Babe, 1979; Darlin Bill, 1980; Panna Maria, 1982; Pinocchios Nose, 1983; The Isaac Quartet, 1984; Metropolis, 1986; Paradise Man, 1987; Movieland, 1989; The Good Policeman, 1990; Marias Girls, 1992. Memberships: Am PEN; Mystery Writers of Am; International Association of Crime Writers. Literary Agent: George Borchardt. Address: 302 West 12th Street, Apt 10c, New York, NY 10014, USA.

CHASE Elaine Raco, b. 31 Aug 1949, USA. Author. m. Gary Dale Chase, 26 Oct 1969, 1 s, 1 d. Publications include: Rules of the Game, 1980; Tender Yearnings, 1981; A Dream Come True, 1982; Double Occupancy, 1982; Designing Woman, 1982; No Easy Way Out, 1983; Video Vixen, 1983; Best Laid Plans, 1983; Special Delivery, 1984; Lady Be Bad, 1984; Dare the Devil, 1987; Dark Corners, 1988; Rough Edges; Partners in Crime, 1994. Contributions to: Loves Leading Ladies and How to Write a Romance; Lovelines; So You Want a TV Career; Fine Art of Murder; Sex and The Mystery Novel; Who Are All These Sister in Crime. Honours: Walden Book Award, 1985; Top Romantic Supsense Series Award, 1987-88. Memberships: Romance Writers of America; Sisters in Crime National Vice President. Literary Agent: Denise Marcil Agency. Address: 4333 Majestic Lane, Fairfax, VA 22033 3538, USA.

CHASE Glen. See: LEVINSON Leonard.

CHASE Isobel. See: **DE GUISE Elizabeth (Mary Teresa).**

CHATTERTON-NEWMAN Roger. b. 17 Mar 1949, Haslemere, Surrey. England. Author. Appointments: Editorial Staff, Haymarket Publishing, 1970-89. Publications include: A Hampshire Parish, 1976; Brian Boru, King of Ireland, 1983; Murtagh & The Vikings, 1986; Betwixt Petersfield and Midhurst, 1991; Edward Bruce: A Medieval Tragedy, 1992; Polo at Cowdray, 1992. Contributions to: Hampshire Magazine; Cricket World; Horse and Hound; The Countryman; Polo Quarterly International; West Sussex History; Downs Country. Honours: Commendation, Reading Association of Ireland Awards, 1987. Address: Rose Cottage, Rake, West Sussex, GU33 7JA, England.

CHAUDHURI Amit, b. 1962, Calcutta, India. Education: Graduate, University College, London; Doctorate, Balliol College, Oxford, 1993. Appointments: Creative Arts Fellow, Wolfson College, Oxford. Publications: Afternoon Raag; A Strange and Sublime Address. Contributions to: Numerous publications including The London Review of Books and The London Magazine. Honours: Betty Trask Award, 1991; Runner-up, Guardian Fiction Prize, 1991, 1993; Commonwealth Writers Prize for best first work, 1992; Southern Arts Literature Prize, 1993; Arts Council of England Writers' Award, 1993-1994; Encore Award, 1994.

CHAWLA Jasbir, b. 20 June 1953, Etawah, India. Government Servant. m. Ravinder Kaur, 15 Oct 1980, 1 s, 2 d. Education: Diploma, Russian, 1974; BTech, 1976; MBA, 1990; Diploma, French, 1991. Appointments: Member, Editorial Panel Ipat, Vikas, 1984. Publications include: Chernobyl, 1989; Roti Ki Gandh, 1990; Eh Nahin Awaz Khalistan Ki, 1991; Niche Wali Chitkhani, 1992; Punjab: Dararen Aurdalal, 1992; Janta Jaan Gayi, 1992. Contributions to: Dharmyng; Saptahik Hindustan; Pahal; Other Literary Hindi, Bengali, Panjabi, English Magazines; Journal of Institute of Engineers; Avishkar; Ispat Vikas; Other Technical Journals; Regular Programmes with all India Radio and Doordarshan Centres in India. Honours: Award, Central Hindi Dorectorate, 1991; Diploma, Excellence for Poetry. Memberships: Authors Guild of India; PEN; Indian Institute of Metals; Institution of Engineers. Address: 247 Defence Colony, Jalandhar City 144001, India.

CHELEKIS George C, b. 21 Sept 1951, Ithaca, New York, USA. Author; Journalist. m. Gwen Content, 7 July 1979, 1 daughter. Education: BA summa cum laude, English Language and Literature, Ohio University, 1973. Publications: The Complete Guide to US Government Real Estate, 1989; The Action Guide to Government Auctions, 1989; Distress Salel, 1990; The Magic of Credit, 1991; The Official Government Auction Guide, 1992; The Action Guide to Government Grants, Loans and Give-Aways, 1993. Contributions to: Nation's Business; Sky Magazine; Boardroom Reports; Consumer's Digest; Entrepreneur; Business; Bull and Bear. Honours: Gold Charlie, 1993. Memberships: American Society of Journalists and Authors; WISE; International Association of Scientologists. Literary Agent: Jane Gelfman. Address: PO Box 2401, Clearwater, FL 34617, USA.

CHELES Luciano, b. 7 Sept 1948. Lecturer. Education: BA, Reading University, 1973; PGCE, Cardiff University, 1974; M Phil, Essex University, 1980; PhD, Lancaster University, 1992. Publications: The Studiolo of Urbino: An Iconographic Investigation; (ed) Neo Fascism in Europe. Contributions to: Women in Italy; Atlante di Schifanoia; Le Muse E Il Principe; Mots; Artension. Honour: Premio Frontino Montefeltro, 1992. Memberships: Society for Italian Studies; Society for Renaissance Studies; Istituto di Studi Rinascimentali; Association for the Study of Modern Italy. Address: Dept of Italian Studies, Lonsdale College, Lancaster University, Lancaster LA1 4YN, England.

CHELLAPAN Kasiviswanathan, b. 11 Apr 1936, Pagneri, India. Professor of English. Education: MA, English, Annamalai, 1958; Diploma, Teaching of English, Manchester, 1965; PhD, Madurai, 1975. Appointments: Editor, Tamil Language Section, Dakshina, Sahitya Akademi of India Annual, 1990. Publications: Shakespeare and Ilango as Tragedians, 1985; Towards Creative Unity: Tagore Bharathi and T S Eliot, Bharathi, The Visionary Humanist, 1988; translations: History of the Growth and Tamil in Freedom Movement, 1979; History of the Freedom Movement in Tamil, 1988; Kuraloviyom, 1990; in Tamil: Ekenku Kaninum Sakthi, 1981; Ilakkiyathil Pazham Pudumaiyum, Puthup Pazhmaiyum, 1986; Oppival Tamil, 1987; Viduthalai Chittum and Puratchi Kuylum: Studies on Bharathi & Bharathidasan (1993). Contributions to: 60 articles to New Helicon, Indian Literature, New

Comparison and others; 10 articles to Hindustan Times; The Hindu; others. Address: Department of English, Bharathidasan University, Trichy 620 024, Tamil Nadu, India.

CHELTON John. See: **DURST Paul.**

CHEN Jo-Hsi, b. 15 Nov 1938, Taiwan. Novelist. Education: BA, Taiwan National University, 1961; MA, Johns Hopkins University, Baltimore, 1965. Appointments include: Lecturer, University of California at Berkeley, USA, 1983. Publications: Mayor Yin, 1976; Selected works by Jo-Hsi Chen, 1976; The Old Man, 1978; Repatriation, 1978; The Execution of Mayor Yin, and Other Stories from the Great Proletarian Cultural Revolution, 1978; Inside and Outside the Wall, 1981; Tu Wei, 1983; Selected Short Stories by Jo-Hsi Chen, 1983; Foresight, 1984; The Two Hus, 1985; Paper Marriage, 1986; The Old Man and Other Stories, 1986; Also: Reminiscences of the Cultural Revolution, 1979; Random Notes, 1981; Democracy Wall and the Unofficial Journals, 1982; Read to Kill Time, 1983; Flower Grown Naturally, 1987; Trip to Tibet, 1988; Trip to Tibet, 1988; Trip to Inner Mongolia, 1988; Temptation of the Tibetan Plateau. Honours include: Wu Zhuoliu Prize, 1978. Address: 428 Boynton Avenue, Berkeley, CA 94707, USA.

CHENG Tsu-yu, b. 18 Mar 1916, China. Professor (Senior Research Fellow). m. Ting Kwee Choo, 1944, 1 son. Education: Diploma of Rhetoric, Institute of Language Teaching of Waseda University, Tokyo, Japan, 1964-65. Appointments: Visiting Professor, The Graduate Division of Literature, Waseda University, Tokyo, Japan, 1964-65; Full Professor, The Daito Bunka University, 1986-; Senior Research Fellow, The Institute of Chinese Studies, The Chinese University of Hong Kong, 1984-; Visiting Professor, Peking University, 1992-. Publications include: Poetry and Poetics of Lu Xun (Hong Kong), 1951; Criticism of the Works of Huang Zunxian (Hong Kong), 1959; Tokyo Lectures (Singapore), 1963; Evolution of Chinese Rhetoric (Tokyo), 1965; Sinological Research in Japan, (Hong Kong), 1972; The History of Chinese Rhetoric (Shanghai, 1984, Taipei, 1990); Rhetorical Criticism of the Works of the Eight Prose Masters of the Tang and Song Dynasties, 1992. Contributions to: Journal of the Peking University; Journal of the Fudan University, Shanghai; Journal of the Waseda University, Tokyo, Japan; Journal of the South Seas Society, Singapore. Honours: Advisory Professor at Fudan University, Shanghai, 1986-; Advisor, South China Rhetorical Society, Shanghai, 1986-; Honorary Councillor and Academic Consultant, China Rhetorical Society, Peking, 1987. Memberships: China Society, Singapore; Member, Councillor, Hon Secretary, Editor, South Seas Society, 1949-62. Address: Institute of Chinese Studies, The Chinese University of Hong Kong, Shatin, NT Hong Kong.

CHERNOFF Maxine, b. 24 Feb 1952, Chicago, IL, USA. Writer; Professor; Editor. m. Paul Hoover, 5 Oct 1974, 2 s, 1 d. Education: BA, MA, University of IL. Appointments: Creative Writing Instructor, Columbia College, 1979-85; Associate Professor, 1980-; Adjunct Associate Professor, School of the Art Institute of Chicago, 1988-. Publications: Plain Grief; Bop; Leap Year day; New & Selected Poems; New Faces of 1952; Signs of Devotion, 1993; Japan, 1987. Contributions to: The Paris Review; New Directions, Partisan Review; Sulfur; Caliban; Triquarterly; Mississippi Review; New York Times Book Review. Honours: IL Arts Council Literary Fellowship; Carl Sandburg Award; Friends of Am Writers Fiction Award; LSU Southern Review Short Fiction Award. Memberships: Poetry Center, School of the Art Institue; MLA; CCLp; AWP. Literary Agent: Amanda Urban. Address: 2920 W Pratt, Chicago, IL 60645, USA.

CHERNOW Ron, b. 3 Mar 1949, Brooklyn, NY, USA. m. Education: BA, Yale University; M.Phil, Pembroke College, Cambridge University. Publications: House of Morgan, 1990; The Warburgs, 1993. Honours: National Book Awards, 1990; Seymour Prize, Yale University, 1970; Jack London Award, United Steel Workers of America, for Labour Reporting, 1980; Ambassador Book Award, English Speaking Union of the US, 1990.

CHERRY Carolyn Janice, (C J Cherryh), b. 1 Sept 1942, St Louis, MI, USA. Writer. Education: BA, Oklahoma University, 1964; MA, Johns Hopkins University, 1965. Publictions include: Downbelow Station, 1981; Cyteen, 1989; The Faded Sun, 1976; Rusalka, 1989; 40,000 in Gehenna, 1983; Cuckoo Egg, 1985; The Paladin, 1988; Rimrunners, 1989; Chernevog, 1990. Honours: John Campbell Award, 1977; Hugo Award, Short Story, 1979, Novel, 1982, 1989. Memberships: Science Fiction Writers Association; National Space

Society. Literary Agent: Curtis Brown Limited, NY, USA.

CHERRY Gordon Emanuel, b. 6 Feb 1931, Barnsley, England. Town Planning Consultant; Chariman, Bournville Village Trust; President, International Planning History Society; Professor Emeritus. m. Margaret Mary London Cox, 8 June 1957, 1 s, 2 d. Education: BA, London, 1953; DSc, Heriot Watt, 1984. Publications: Town Planning in Its Social Contect; Urban Change and Planning; The Evolution of British Town Planning; Environmental Planning; The Politics of Town planning; Cities and Plans; Birmingham. Contributions to: Planning Perspectives; Studies in History, Planning and the Environment. Memberships: Royal Town Planning Institute; Royal Institute of Chartered Surveyors; Royal Society of Arts. Address: Quaker Ridge, 66 Meriden Road, Hampton in Arden, Solihull, West Midlands, BG2 0BT, England.

CHERRY Kelly, Writer; Professor; Evjue Bascom Professor. m. Jonathan B Silver, 23 Dec 1966, div, 1969. Education: Du Pont Fellow, University of VA, 1961-63; MFA, University of North CA, 1967. Appointments include: Elected, Board of Directors, Associated Writing Programs; Member, Discipline Advisory Committee, Fulbright Awards. Publications: Fiction, Sick and Full of Burning, 1974; Augusta Played, 1979; Conversion, 1979; In The Wink of an Eye, 1983; The Lost Traveller's Dream, 1984; My Life and Dr Joyce Brothers, 1990; Poetry, Lovers and Agnostics, 1975, revised edition 1995; Relativity, 1977; Songs for a Soviet Composer, 1980; Natural Theology, 1988; Benjamin John, 1993; God's Loud Hand, 1993; Time Out of Mind, 1994; Nonfiction: The Exiled Heart, 1991; Writing the World, 1995; Translation: Octavia.Contributions to: Alatantic; Commentary; Ms; Esquire; New Literary History; Am Scholar; VA Quarterly Review; Southern Review; Mademoiselle; Redbook. Honours include: Best Am Short Stories, 1972; Pushcart Prize, 1977; National Endowment for the Arts Fellowship, 1979; WI Arts Board Fellowships, 1984, 89, 94; Hanes Poetry Prize, 1989; Arts Am Speaker Award, 1992; O Henry Prize Stories, 1994; New Work Awards, 1991, 92; Hawthornden Fellowship, 1994. Address: English Dept, University of WI, Madison, WI 53706, USA.

CHERRYH C J. See: **CHERRY Carolyn Janice.**

CHESSEX Jacques, b. 1 Mar 1934, Payerne, France. Novelist; Poet. Education: Graduated University of Lausanne, 1961. Appointments include: Professor of French Literature at the Gymnase Cantonal de la Cité, from 1969. Publications: La Tête ouverte, 1962; La Confession du pasteur Burg, 1967; A Father's Love, 1973, 1975; L'Ardent Royaume, 1975; Le Séjour des morts, 1977; Les Yeux jaunes, 1979; Où vont mourir les oiseaux, 1980; Judas le transparent, 1983; Jonas, 1987; Morgane Madrigal, 1990; Verse: Le Jour proche, 1954; Chant du printemps, 1955; Une Voix la nuit, 1957; Batailles dans l'air, 1959; Le Jeune de huit nuits, 1966; L'Ouvert obscur, 1967; Elégie, soleil du regret, 1976; La Calviniste, 1983; Feux d'orée, 1984; Comme l'os, 1988; Also: Maupassant et les autres, 1981; Mort d'un cimitière, 1989; Flaubert, ou, le désert en abîme, 1991. Honours include: Prix Goncourt, 1973. Address: Editions Grasset, 61 Rue des Sts-Pères, 75006 Paris, France.

CHESTER Tessa Rose, b. 19 Oct 1950, Stanmore, Middlesex, England. Museum Curator. m. (1) Richard James Overy, 18 Apr 1969, 1 s, 2 d. (2) Ronald Albert Chester, 8 Aug 1980. Education: North London Collegiate School, 1957-68; Harrow Art College, 1968-69; Polytechnic of North London, BA, 1977-81. Appointments: Curator of Childrens Books, Bethnal Green Museum of Childhood, London, 1984-. Publications: A History of Chidrens Book Illustration; Childrens Books Research; Sources of Information About Childrens Books. Contributions to: Times Educational Supplement; Phaedrus; International Review of Childrens Literature & Librarianship; Galleries; The Library; Signal; Country Life. Memberships: Childrens Books History Society; Beatrix Potter Society; Poetry Society; British Haiku Society; William Morris Society; Library Association. Address: Bethnal Green Museum of Childhood, Cambridge Heath Road, London E2 9PA, England.

CHEYNEY-COKER Syl, b. 28 June 1945, Freetown, Sierra Leone. Professor; Poet. Education: University of CA, 1970; University of WI, Madison, 1971-72. Appointments: Visiting Professor, University of the Philippines, Quezon City, 1975-77; Senior Lecturer, University of Maiduguri, Nigeria, 1979-. Publications: Concero for an Exile, 1972; The Graveyard Also has Teeth, 1974. Honour: Ford Foundation Grant,

1970. Address: University of Maiduguri, Dept of English, PMB 1069, Maiduguri, Nigeria.

CHILDS David Haslam, b. 25 Sep 1933, Bolton, England. University Professor. m. 13 Jun 1964, 2 s. Education: BSc (Econ) London University, 1956; British Council Scholarship, Hamburg University, 1956-57; PhD, London University, 1962. Appointments: Former Editor PASGAS - Politics and Society in Germany Austria and Switzerland, 1988-92. Publications include: GDR Moscow's German Ally (2nd edition 1988); Britain since 1945 (3rd edition 1992); Germany since 1918 (2nd edition 1980); Marx and the Marxists, 1973; East Germany, 1969; East Germany to the 1990s, 1987; West Germany Politics and Society (2nd edition 1981); Germany on the Road to Unity, 1990; Germany in the 20th Century, 1991; Britain Since 1939: Progress and Decline, 1995. Contributions to: Tablet; Political Studies; Anglo-German Review; Contemporary Review; Current History; Journal of Contemporary History; The Times; THES; TLS; TES; Guardian; Independent; International Affairs; Daily Telegraph; World Today; books. Address: 1 Grange park, West Bridgford, Nottingham NG2 6HW, England.

CHILVER Peter, b. 1933, England. Educator. Appointments: Teacher, Inner London Education Authority, 1964-68; Senior Lecturer, Thomas Hucley College, 1968-77; Head of English Dept, Langdon School, 1977. Publications: Improvised Drama, 1967; Talking Discussion, Improvement and Debate in Schools, 1968; Stories for Improvisation, 1969; Producing the Play, 1974; Teaching Improvised Drama, 1978; Learning and Language in the Classroom, 1982; In the Picture Series, 1985; English Coursework for GCSE, 1987. Contributions to: Perspectives on Small Group Learning, 1990. Address: 27 Cavendish Gardens, Barking, Essex, England.

CHINERY Michael, b. 1938, United Kingdom. Author. Publications: Pictorial Dictionary of the Animal World, 1966; with Michael Gabb: Human Kind, 1966, The World of Plants, 1966, The Life of Animals with Backbones, 1966; Patterns of Living (with David Larkin), 1966; Breeding and Growing, 1966; Pictorial Dictionary of the Plant World, 1967; Visual Biology, 1968; Purnell's Concise Encyclopedia of Nature, 1971; Animal Communities, 1972; Animals in the Zoo, 1973; Field Guide to the Insects of Britain and Northern Europe, 1973; Life In the Zoo, 1976; The Natural History of the Garden, 1977; The Family Naturalist, 1977; Nature All Around, 1978; Discovering Animals, 1978; Killers of the Wild, 1979; Garden Birds (with Maurice Pledger), 1979; Collins Gem Guide to Butterflies and Moths, 1981; The Natural History of Britain and Europe, 1982; Collins Guide to the Insects of Britain and Western Europe, 1986; Garden Creepy Crawlies, 1986; The Living Garden, 1986; Collins Gem Guide to Insects, 1986; Exploring the Countryside, 1987; Butterflies and Day-Flying Moths of Britain and Europe, 1989; All About Baby Animals; Countryside Handbook, 1990; Shark; Butterfly; Ant; Spider; Snake; Frog (6 Children's Books), 1991; All About Wild Animals, 1991; Explore the World of Insects, 1991; Wild World of Animals: Rainforests 1991, Oceans 1991, Deserts 1991, Grasslands and Prairies 1991, Seashores 1992, Forests 1992, Polar Lands 1992, Lakes and Rivers 1992; The Kingfisher Natural History of Britain and Europe, 1992; Spiders, 1993. Address: Mousehole, Mill Road, Hundon, Suffolk C010 8EG, England.

CHISSELL Joan Olive, b. 22 May 1919, Cromer, Norfolk, England. Musicologist. Education: ARCM, GRSM, Royal College of Music, 1937-42. Appointments: Piano Teacher, Royal College of music, 1942-53; Lecturer, Oxford & London Universities, 1942-48; Assistant Music Critic, The Times, 1948-79; Reviewer, The Gramophone, 1968-; Broadcaster, BBC, 1943-; Jury Member, International Piano Competitions, Milan, Leeds, Zwickau, Budapest, Sydney and Dublin. Publications: Robert Schumann, 1948; Brahms, 1977; Clara Schumann: A Dedicated Spirit, 1983. Contributions to: A Compnion to the Concerto, 1988; Numerous Journals and Magazines. Honour: Awarded Robert Schumann Prize, 1991. Memberships: Critics Circle; RCM Union; Royal Life Boat Society. Literary Agent: David Higham Associates. Address: Flat D, 7 Abbey Road, St Johns Wood, London NW8 9AA, England.

CHITHAM Edward Harry Gordon, b. 16 May 1932, Harborne, Birmingham, England. Education Consultant. m. Mary Patricia Tilley, 29 Dec 1962, 1 s, 2 d. Education: BA, MA (Classics), Jesus College, Cambridge, 1952-55; PGCE, University of Birmingham, 1955-56; MA, English, University of Warwick, 1973-77 part-time; PhD, University of Sheffield, 1978-83. Publications: Ghost in the Water, 1972; The Black Country, 1973; The Poems of Anne Brontë, 1979; Brontë Facts and

Brontë Problems (with T J Winnifrith), 1983; Selected Brontë Poems (with T J Winnifrith), 1985; The Brontës' Irish Background, 1986; A Life of Emily Brontë, 1987; Charlotte and Emily Brontë (Macmillans Literary Lives, with T J Winnifrith) 1989; A Life of Anne Brontë, 1991. Contributions to: Byron Journal, Gaskell Society Journal; ISIS Magazine. Memberships: Joint Association of Classics Teachers. Gaskell Society; Brontë Society, Hon Publications Secretary and Editor, Brontë Society Transactions. Address: 11 Victoria Road, Harborne, Birmingham B17 0AG, England.

CHITNIS Anand Chidamber, b. 4 Apr 1942, Birmingham, England. Principal. m. Bernice Anne, 4 July 1970, 2 s, 1 d. Education: Stonyhurst College, Lancashire, 1949-60; University of Birmingham, 1960-63; University of KS, 1963-65; University of Edinburgh, 1965-68. Publications: The Scottish Enlightenment: A Social History and The Scottish Enlightenment & Early Victorian English Society. Contributions to: Annals of Science; Enlightenment Essays; Medical History; Studies in Voltaire and the Eighteenth Century. Honours: Fellowship of Royal Historical Society. Memberships: Catholic Union of Great Britain; British Society for 18th Century Studies; 18th Century Scottish Studies Society. Literary Agent: David Higham Associates. Address: LSU College of Higher Education, The Avenue, Southampton, SO9 5HB, England.

CHITTOCK John Dudley, b. 29 May 1928. Writer; Producer. m. Joyce Kate Winter, 23 Aug 1947. South West Technical College. Appointments: Executive Editor, Focal Press, 1954-58; Part-Time Editor, Industrial Screen, 1962-63; Film and Video Columnist, Financial Times, 1963-87; Founder/Publisher, Screen Digest 1971-, Editor 1971-74; Inaugural Editor of Vision (British Academy of Film and Television Arts), 1976; Founder/Publisher, Training Digest 1978-87; Consultant Editor, Television - Journal of the Royal Television Society 1978-82. Publications: Executive Editor, Focal Encyclopedia of Photography, 1956; Images of Britain, 1986; Film and Effect, 1967; Executive Editor, An International Directory of Stock Shot Libraries, 1969; Editor, A Long Look at Short Films, 1967; How To Produce Magnetic sound For Films, 1962. Honours: Hood Medal of Royal Photographic Society, 1973; Presidential Award of Incorporated Institute of Prefessional Photography, 1983; Video Writer of Year Award, 1983; Queen's Silver Jubilee Medal, 1977; Officer of Order of British Kinematograph, Sound & TV Society; Royal TV Society; Royal Society of Arts. Address: 37, Gower Street, London WC1E 6HH, England.

CHITTY Susan, b. 18 Aug 1929. Freelance Writer, Lecturer and Journalist. Publications: The Diary of Fashion Model, 1958; Editor, The Intelligent Woman's Guide to Good Taste, 1958; White Huntress, 1963; My Life and Horses, 1966; The Woman Who Wrote Black Beauty, 1971; The Beast and the Monk: A Life of Charles Kingsley, 1975; On Next to Nothing (with Thomas Hinde), 1975; Charles Kingsley's Landscape, 1976; (with Thomas Hinde), The Great Donkey Walk, 1977; The Young Rider, 1979; Gwen John, 1981; Now To My Mother, 1985; Edward Lear, 1988; Davies of Antonia White (editor), 1991, 1992. Address: Bow Cottage, West Hoathly, Sussex RH19 4QF, England.

CHITTY Thomas Willes, Sir, (Thomas Hinde), b. 1926. Author. Publications: Mr Nicholas, 1952; Happy as Larry, 1957; For the Good of the Company, 1961; A Place Like Home, 1962; The Cage, 1962; Spain: A Personal Anthology, 1963; Ninety Double Martinis, 1963; The Day the Call Came, 1964; Games of Chance: The Interviewer and the Investigator, 1965; The Village, 1966; High, 1968; Bird, 1970; Generally a Virgin, 1972; Agent, 1974; Our Father, 1975; On Next to Nothing (with Susan Hinde), 1975; The Great Donkey Walk (with Susan Chitty), 1977; The Cottage Book, 1979; Sir Henry and Sons: A Memoir, 1981; Daymare, 1981; Field Guide to the Country Parson, 1983; Stately Gardens of Britain, 1983; Forests of Britain, 1985; Capability Brown: Biography, Courtiers, 1986; Tales from the Pump Room, 1988; Imps of Promise, 1990; Looking-Glass Letters, 1991; Paths of Progress, 1993; Highgate School, 1993. Address: Bow Cottage, West Hoathly, Sussex RH19 4QF, England.

CHIU Hungdah, b. 1936, Chinese. Writer; Professor. Appointments: Assoicate Professor of International Law, National Taiwan University, 1965-66; Research Associate, Harvard Law School, MA, USA, 1966-7, 1972-74; Professor, National Chengchi University, Taiwan, 1970-72; Associate Professor, 1974-77, Professor, 1977-, University of Maryland School of Law; Editor in Chief, Chinese Yearbook of International Law & Affairs, 1981-93. Publications include: The Capacity of International Organization to Conclude Treaties, 1966;

A Calendar, 1968; Law in Chinese Foreign Policy, 1972; China and the Question of Taiwan: Documents and Analysis, 1973; Legal Aspects of US Republic of China Trade and Investment, 1977; Normalizing Relations with the Peoples Republic of China, 1978; China and the Taiwan Issue, 1979; The Chinese Connection and Normalization, 1980; Multi System Nations and International Law, 1981; China 70 Years After the 1911 Hsin Hai Revolution, 1984; Criminal Justice in Post Mao China, 1985; The Future of Hong Kong: Towards, 1997 and Beyond, 1987; International Law of the Sea: Cases, Documents and Readings, 1991. Address: University of Maryland School of Law, 500 West Baltimore Street, Bltimore, MD 21201, USA.

CHODES John Jay, b. 23 Feb 1939, NY, USA. Writer. Education: Germain School of Photography. Appointments: Technical Advisor to Dustin Hoffman, Paramount Pictures Film Marathon Man. Publications: The Myth of Americas Military Power, 1972; Corbitt, 1973; Bruce Jenner, 1977; Chapter, Public Education and Indoctrination, 1993; Chapter Work and Employment in Liberal Democratic Socieities, 1994; Plays, Avenue A Anthology, 1969; Molineaux, 1979; Frederick Two, 1985; The Longboat, 1987; Moileaux (as Musical), 1995. Contributions to: Articles on Education, Politics, Social Issues. Honours: Journalistic Excellence Award, 1974; Outstanding Service Award, 1988. Memberships: Dramatists Guild; Professors World Peace Academy; Road Runners Club of New York; Libertarian Party of NY. Literary Agent: Stephan Rosenberg. Address: 411 East 10th Str, 22G, New York, NY 10009, USA.

CHOI Jin Young, b. 29 Mar 1937, Korea. University Professor. m. Kim Jung Ji, 4 Sept 1963, 1 s, 2 d. Education: BA, College of Lieral Arts, Seoul National University, 1959; MA, University of North Carolina, 1963; PhD, Seoul National University, 1984. Appointments: Columnist, Korea Herald, 1985-91. Publications: Theodore Dreiser: Sister Carrie; The English Novel; One Womens Way; A Study of Theodore Dreiser; The Wind and the River; Nickel Mountain; With God in Russia, Lord of the Files. Memberships: PEN; English Language & Literature Association of Korea; The Hawthorne Society of Korea; The International Steinbeck Society; The Korean Society of Modern British & Am Fiction. Address: 95 503 Banpa Apts, Sucho Ku, Seoul, Korea 137 049.

CHON Kuttikhat Purushothaman, b. 7 May 1932, India. Government Servant. m. Mythily Chon, 27 Apr 1963, 1 s, 2 d. Education: Graduate Philosophy; Diploma, Office Management; Diploma, Materials Management. Publications: Remedy the Frauds in Hinduism, 1991; Nairs Mother Palayi, 1992; Cherumi That of Ezhava, 1992; Simplifying the Alphabetical System in Hindi. Contributions to: On Indology. Memberships: PEN. Literary Agent: Bharatiya Vidhya Bhavan. Address: Kuttikhat House, Peringottukara, Trichur, Kerla, India.

CHOUKRI Mohamed, b. 25 Mar 1935, Beni Chiker, Morocco. Writer. Education: Teacher; Classical Education. Publications: Al Hobs Al Hafi, 1973; Jean Genet in Tangier, 1973; Majnoun Al Guarde, 1978; Tennessee Williamsm in Tangier, 1979; A; Suk Al Dahili, 1985; Al Haima, 1985; Zemen Al Akhtaa, 1992; Translations into 12 languages. Contributions to: Al Adab, Beirut; A; Aqlam; Iraq; Al Alam, Morocco; Harper's, USA; Transatlantic, UK; Antheus, USA; Liberation Al Itihade Al Ichtiraki, Morocco; Many others. Membership: Moroccan Writers Association. Literary Agent: Roberto de Hollanda, Bonn, Germany. Address: BP 179, Tanger, Morocco.

CHOYCE Lesley, b. 21 Mar 1951, NJ, USA. Novelist; Editor; Professor. m. Terry Paul, 19 Aug 1974, 2 d. Education: BA, Rutgers; MA, Monclair; MA, CUNY. Appointments: Editor, Pottersfield Portfolio, 1979-83; Editor, Pottersfield Press, 1979-; professor, Dalhousie University, 1986-. Publications: The Second Season of Jonas MacPherson; Magnificent Obessions; Avalanche of Ocean; Wavewatch; The End of Ice; Numerous Other Publications. Contributions to: McLeans; Harrowsmith; Canadian Literature; Fiddlehead. Honours: Canadian Science Fiction & Fantasy Award, Nova Scotia Literary Competition; Pierian Spring Editors Award; St John Award of Merit; Finalist, The Stephen Leacock Award; Dartmouth Book Award; Event Magazine, Creative Nonfiction Competition. Memberships: Writers Union of Canada; Writers Federation of Nova Scotia; CANSCAIP; Literary Press Group. Address: RR2 Porters Lake, Nova Scota, Canada BOJ 2SO

CHRAIBI Driss, b. 15 July 1926, El Jadida, Morocco. Novelist. m. Sheena McCallion, 1978. Education: Studied in Casablanca and Paris.

Appointments include: Professor at the University of Laval, Quebec, 1969-70. Publications: The Simple Past, 1954, 1990; The Butts, 1955, 1983; L'Ane, 1956; De Tous les Horizons, 1958; La Foule, 1961; Heirs to the Past, 1962, 1971; Un ami viendra vous voir, 1966; La Mother Comes of Age, 1982, 1984; Mort au Canada, 1974; Une Enquête au Pays, 1981; Mother Spring, 1982, 1989; Birth at Dawn, 1986, 1990; L'Homme du livre, 1994; Radio plays. Honours include: Société des Auteurs Prize, 1990. Address: 15 rue Paul Pons, 26400 Crest, France.

CHRISTIAN Carol Cathay, b. 15 Nov 1923, Peking, China. Freelance Writer and Editor. m. John Christian, 23 June 1945, 3 sons, 1 daughter. Education: BA, magna cum laude, Smith College, Northampton, Massachusetts, USA, 1944. Publications: Into Strange Country, 1958; God and One Redhead, Mary Slessor of Calabar, biography with G Plummer, 1970; Editor of In the Spirit of Truth, a reader in the work of Frank Lake, 1991; EFL Readers: Great People of Our Time, 1973; More People of Our Time, 1978; Johnny Ring, 1975 (with Diana Christian) Famous Women of the 20th Century, 1982; Save the Goldfish, 1988, and others. Memberships: Society of Authors; Clinical Theology Association. Address: 20 Pitfold Avenue, Shottermill, Haslemere, Surrey GU27 1PN, England.

CHRISTIAN John. See: **DIXON Roger.**

CHRISTIE Ian Ralph, b. 11 May 1919, Preston, Lancashire, England. Retired University Teacher. Education: Robert Herbert Prize, 1947, BA 1948, MA 1948, Magdalen College, Oxford. Appointments: War Service, RAF, Britain, West Africa and India, 1940-46; Assistant Lecturer in History, University College London, 1948; Lecturer, 1951; Reader, 1960; Professor of Modern British History, 1966-79; Dean of Arts, 1971-73; Chairman, History Department, 1975-79; Astor Professor of British History, 1979-84; Professor Emeritus and Honorary Research Fellow, 1984-. Publications: The End of North's Ministry 1780-1782, 1958; Wilkes, Wyvill and Reform, 1962; Crisis of Empire, 1966; Myth and Reality in late Eighteenth-Century British Politics; 1970; The Correspondence of Jeremy Bentham (Editor), volume 3, 1971; Empire of Independence 1760-1776 (Co-author B W Labaree), 1976; Bibliography of British History 1789-1851 (Co-author Lucy M Brown), 1977; Wars and Revolutions, Britain 1760-1815, 1982; Stress and Stability in Late 18th Century Britain, 1984; The Benthams in Russia 1780-1791, 1993. Contributions to: Various journals. Honour: Elected Fellow, The British Academy, 1977. Memberships: Royal Historical Society, Joint Literary Director 1964-70, Member of Council 1970-74; Editorial Board, History of Parliament Trust, 1973-. Address: 10 Green Lane, Croxley Green, Hertfordshire WD3 3HR, England.

CHRISTIE-MURRAY David Hugh Arthur, b. 12 July 1913, London, England, Retired Schoolmaster. m. (1) Ena Louise Elisabeth Mumford, 11 July 1942, (2) Sheila Mary Blackmore (Watson), 15 Apr 1972, 1 son, 3 daughters, 2 stepdaughters. Education: Diploma in Journalism, University College, University of London, 1932-34; BA 1942, MA 1945, General Ordination Examination 1942, St Peter's Hall, Oxford University and Wyclif Hall, Oxford. Publications: Beckenham Heraldy, 1954; Armorial Bearings of British Schools, series, 1956-66, collected edition, 1966; Illustrated Children's Bible, 1974, 1993; A History of Heresy, 1976, 1989; Voices From the Gods, 1978; My First Prayer Book, 1981, 1985; Reincarnation: Ancient Beliefs and Modern Evidence, Norwegian edition, 1989, Spanish edition 1991; The Practical Astrologer, 1990. Contributions to: Times Literary and Educational Supplements; The Armorial; Christian Parapsychologist; Journal of the Society for Psychical Research; Light. Literary Agent: Watson Little Limited. Address: Imber Court Cottage, Orchard Lane, East Molesey, Surrey KT8 0BN, England.

CHRISTOPHER Matthew F, (Fredric Martin), b. 16 Aug 1917, PA, USA. WRiter. m. Catherine M Krupa, 13 July 1940, 3 s, 1 d. Publications: The Lucky Baseball Bat, 1954, 1991; Catcher With A Glass Arm, 1964; The Year Mom Won The Pennant; The Kid Who Only Hit Homers; Dirt Bike Runaway; The Dog That Pitched A No Hitter, 1989; Diamond Champs; The Hit Away Kid; The Fox Steals Home; Skateboard Tough, 1991; Man Out at First, 1993; Top Wing, 1994; The Winning Stroke, 1994; Pressure Play, 1993; Zero's Slider, 1994; Fighting Tackle, 1995. Contributions to: Approximately About 275 Stories and Articles in Magazines. Honours: Boys Club of America Junior Book Award, 1958; The Milner Award, 1993. Memberships: Society of Childrens Book Writers; SCBWI. Address: 1830 Townes Court, Rock Hill, SC 29730, USA.

CHRISTOPHER Nicholas, b. 1951. Publications: On Tour With Rita, 1982; Desperate Characters: a novella in verse, 1985; A Short History of the Island of Butterflies: Poems, 1986; The Soloists, 1986; Walk on the Wild Side, 1994; Five, & other poems, 1995. Honours: Melville Cane Award, 1994; Lavan Younger Poets Award, 1991

CHRISTOPHERSEN Paul (Hans), b. 1911, Denmark. Emeritus Professor. Appointments: Professor of English, University of Copenhagen, 1946-48; Professor of English, University of Ibadan, Nigeria, 1948-54; Professor of English, University of Oslo, Norway, 1954-68; Reader in English 1969-74, Professor 1974-77, Emeritus Professor 1977-, New University of Ulster, Northern Ireland; Professor of English, University of Qatar, 1977-81. Publications: The Articles, 1939; A Modern English Grammar (with O Jespersen), vol 6, 1942; To Start You Talking (with H Krabbe), 1948; Bilingualism, 1949; The Ballad of Sir Aldingar, 1952; An English Phonetics Course, 1956; Some Thoughts on the Study of English as a Foreign Language, 1957; An Advanced English Grammar (with A Sandved), 1969; Second-Language Learning, 1973; Tina, by Herman Bang, translation, 1984; Contributions to: The Oxford Companion to the English Language, 1992. Address: 1 Corfe Close, Cambridge CB2 2QA, England.

CHARYN Jerome, b. 1937, USA. Author; Educator. Appointments: English Teacher, High School of Music & Art, School of Performing Arts, 1962-64; Assistant Professor, Stanford University, 1965-68; Professor, Herbert Lehman College, City University of NY, 1968-80; Founding Editor, The Dutton Review, 1970; Lecturer, Princeton University, NJ, 1980-86. Publications: Once Upon a Droshky, 1964; On The Darkening Green, 1965; The Man Who Grew Younger and Other Stories, 1967; The Single Voice: An Anthology of Contemporary Fiction, 1969; Going to Jerusalem, 1967; Am Scrapbook, 1969; The Trouble Vision, 1970; Eisenhower, My Eisenhower, 1971; The Tar Baby, 1973; Blue Eyes, 1975; The Education of Patrick Silver, 1976; Marilyn The Wild, 1976; The Franklin Scare, 1977; Secret Isaac, 1978; The Seventh Babe, 1979; The Catfish Man, 1980; Darlin Bill, 1980; Panna Maria, 1982; Pinocchios Nose, 1983; The Isaac Quartet, 1984; War Cries Over Avenue C, 1985; Metropolis, 1986; Paradise Man, 1987; Movieland, 1989; The Good Policeman, 1990; Elsinore, 1991; Maroas Girls, 1992; Montezhmas Man, 1993. Memberships: Am PEN; Mystery Writers of Am; International Association of Crime Writers. Literary Agent: George Borchardt. Address: 302 West 12th Street, Spt 10C, NY 10014, USA.

CHURCH Robert, b. 20 July 1932, London, England. Author. m. Dorothy June Bourton, 15 Apr 1953, 2 daughters. Education: Beaufoy College, London, 1946-48. Appointments: Served Army 1950-52; Metropolitan Police, 1952-78; Probation Service, 1978-88. Publications: Murder in East Anglia, 1987; Accidents of Murder, 1989; More Murder in East Anglia, 1990. Contributions to: The Criminologist and Miscellaneous Journals. Memberships: British Society of Criminology; The Society of Authors; Crime Writers Association. Literary Agent: Don Short, Solo Literary Agency, 49-53 Kensington High Street, London W8 5ED. Address: Woodside, 7 Crome Walk, Gunton Park; Lowestoft, Suffolk NR32 4NF, England.

CHURCHILL Elizabeth. See: **HOUGH Richard Alexander.**

CIANCIOLO Ingrid Mohn, (Pua Kea), b. 17 July 1918, Copenhagen, Denmark. Retired. m. Thomas Cianciolo, 5 March 1991, 1 son. Education: Cand. Mag. 1950; Cand Philol. 1961; University of Oslo, Norway. Literary Appointments: Associate Professor of European Languages & Literature, Univerity of Hawaii, 1968-1980. Publications: Den Hogre Skolen: Go-See-Learn, 1968; The Hawaiian Language Teacher, 1970; Religious Humanist, 1976; In the Shadow of Kohala, 1988; The Sorrows of Womanhood, 1987; Odyssey Beyond 2000, 1991. Memberships: Association of University Women in Norway, 1980-85; Norges Fredslag, 1980-85; American Association of University Women, 1992-1994.

CIEE Grace. See: **CORNISH Gracie.**

CISNEROS Antonio. b. 27 Dec 1942, Lima, Peru. Poet. Education: Catholic and National Universities, Lima; PhD, 1974. Appointments include: Teacher of Literature at the University of San Marcos, from 1972. Publications: Destierro, 1961; David, 1962; Comentarios reales, 1964; The Spider Hangs Too Far from the Ground, 1970; Agua que no has de beber, 1971; Come higuera en un campo de golf, 1972; El libro de Dios y los hungaros, 1978; Cuatro poetas (with others), 1979; Helicopters in the Kingdom of Peru, 1981; La cronica del Nino Jesus de Chilca, 1981; At Night the Cats, 1985; Land of Angels, 1985; Monologo de la casta Susana y otros poemas, 1986; Propios como ajenos poesia 1962088, 1989; El arte de envolver pescado, 1990; Poesia, una historia de locos: 1962-1986, 1990. Honours include: Casa de las Americas Prize, 1968. Address: Department of Literature, Universidad Nacional de San Marcos de Lima, Avda Republica de Chile 295, Of 506, Casilla 454, Lima, Peru.

CIVASAQUI Jose (Shibasaki Sosuke), b. 12 Jan 1916, Saitama-ken. Lecturer; Translator; Poet. m. 18 Sept 1940, 2 sons, 1 daughter. Education: HHD, World University, Tucson, USA, 1977. Appointments: Managing Director, Japan League of Poets, 1972; Japan Guild of Authors & Composers, 1973; President, 1983-85, Honorary President, 1985-, United Poets Laureate International, USA; Deputy Director General, Asia, IBC, 1987; President, Poetry Society of Japan, 1987. Publications: In His Bosom, 1950; In Thy Grace, 1971; Doshin Shien, translation of A Child's Garden of Verses, 1973; Beyond Seeing, 1977; Living Water, 1984; Invitation to the World of Haiku, 1985; Kusa No Tsuyu, translation of Dew of Grass, 1987; Chosuichi Doro No Boken, translation of Reservoir Road Adventure, 1990; Green Pastures, poems, 1993. Contributions to: Japan Times, 1947-48; Mainichi, 1949-50, 1954-55; Study of Current English, 1960-61, 1965-68. Honours: Excellence in Poetry, 3rd World Congress of Poets, 1976; International Poet Laureate, 8th World Congress of Poets, 1985; Knight Commander, Royal Knights of Justice, England, 1986; Premio Speciale, Pelle di Luna, Italy, 1985; Premio Internazional San Valentino d'Oro, Italia, 1989; Senator, International Parliament for Safety & Peace, 1989; Medal for Peace, Albert Einstein International Academy Foundation, 1990; DLit Hon, Albert Einstein International Academy Foundation, 1991; Medallion, Poetry Day Australia & Melbourne Poetry Society Competition, 1991-92; Michael Madhusudan Academy Award, Calcutta, India, 1992; Congress Medallion for Distinguished Participation, IBC & ABI, 1993; Fourth Order of Merit, (Kun Yontoh Zuihosho) Japan, 1993. Memberships: Poetry Society of Japan; United Poets Laureate International; PEN, Tokyo. Address: Honcho 2-12-11, Ikebukuro, Toshima-ku, Tokyo 170, Japan.

CIXOUS Helene, b. 5 June 1937, Oran, Algeria. Professor of English Literature. Writer. m. 1955, divorced 1964, 1 son, 1 daughter. Education: Received Agregation d'Anglais, 1959 and Docteur es Lettres, 1968. Appointments: Assistant, University of Bordeaux, France, 1962-65; Master Assistant, University of Paris (Sorbonne), Paris, France, 1965-67; Master of Conference, University of Paris X, Nanterre, France, 1967-68; University of Paris VIII (Vincennes at St Denis), St Denis, France, helped found the university's experimental branch at St Denis, 1968, Professor of English Literature, 1968-, Founder and Director of Centre de Recherches en Etudes Feminines, 1974-; Visting Professor and Lecturer to many universities in the USA, Austria, Canada, Denmark, England, Spain and Holland. Publications include: Le Livre de Promethea (fiction), 1983, translation by Betsy Wing, published by University of Nebraska Press; Author of Manifesto, La Rire de La Meduse; Co-founder of Revue de Theorie d'Analyse Litteraire: Poetique, 1969; Manna, translation by Catherine MacGillivray, ed by University of Minnesota Press, 1994; The Ladder of Writing, 1993; Work represented in anthologies; Eight Plays. Address: Universite de Paris VIII, 2 Rue de la Liberte, 93526 St Denis, France.

CIZMAR Paula L, b. 30 Aug 1949, Youngstown, OH, USA. Playwright; Screenwriter. Education: OH University, 1967-71. Publications include: Plays, Candy & Shelley to the Desert, 1988; The Death of a Miner, 1983; The Girl Room, 1979; Many Plays Produced. Contributions to: Mother Jones; The Chronicle of Higher Education; Lilith; Detroit Free Press; Others. Honours include: Susn Smith Blackburn Literary Prize, Runner Up, 1981; Jerome Foundation Commission, Fellowship, 1981; NEA Fellowship, 1982; Rockefeller Foundation, International Residency, 1983. Memberships: Dramatists Guild; Writers Guild of Am; League of Professional Theatre Women. Literary Agent: Lynn Pleshette, Pleshette Green Agency. Address: c/o 2700 N Beachwood Drive, Los Angeles, CA 90068, USA.

CLADPOLE Jim. See: RICHARDS James, Sir.

CLAMPITT Amy Kathleen, b. 15 June 1920, IA, USA. Writer. Education: BA, Grinnell College, 1941; Columbia University, 1941-42. Literary Appointments: Writer in Residence, College of William & Mary, 1984-85; Visiting Writer, Amherst College, 1986-87; Grace Mazard Cokling Distinguished Writer, Smith College, 1993. Publications

include: The Kingfisher, 1983; What The Light Was Like, 1985; Archiac Figure, 1987; Westward, 1990; A Silence Opens, 1994. Contributions to: New Yorker; Poetry; Yale Review. Honours: Guggenheim Fellowship, 1982; Fellowship Award Academy of American Poets, 1994; DHL Honoris Causa, Grinnell College, 1984; DHL Honoris Causa, Bowoin College, 1992; MacArthur Fellowship, 1992. Memberships: Academy of American Poets; American Academy of Arts & Letters; PEN; Poetry Society of America; Authors Legue. Address: 160 East 65th Str, New York, NY 10021, USA.

CLANCY Joseph Patrick Thomas, b. 8 Mar 1928, NY, USA. College Teacher. m. gertrude Wiegand, 31 July 1948, 4 s, 4 d. Education: BA, 1947, MA, 1949, PhD, 1957, Fordham University. Appointments: Faculty, 1948, Professor, 1962, Marymount Manhattan College. Publications include: The Odes and Epodes of Horace, 1960; Medieval Welsh Lyrics, 1965; The Earliest Welsh poems, 1970; 20th Century Welsh Poems, 1982; Gwyn Thomas: Living a Life, 1982; The Significance of Flesh: Poems, 1950-83, 1984; Bobi Jones: Selected Poems, 1987. Contributions to include: Poetry Wales; Planet; Anglo Welsh Review; Book News from Wales; Epoch; College English; America. Honours: Am philosophical Society Fellowships, 1963, 68; National Translation Centre Fellowship, 1968; Welsh Arts Council, Literature Award, 1971; Major Bursary, 1972; National Endowment for the Arts Translation Fellowship, 1983; St Davids Society of NY Annual Award, 1986. Memberships: Am Literary Translators Association; Dramatists Guild; Yr Academi Gymreig; Eastern States Celtic Association; St Davids Society of Ny. Address: 1549 Benson Street, New York, NY 10461, USA.

CLANCY Laurence James, b. 2 Dec 1942, Melbourne, Australia. Senior Lecturer. Div, 2 s. Education: BA, Melbourne University, 1964; MA, 1973, La Trobe University. Publications include: A Collapsible Man, 1975; The Wife Specialist, 1978; Xavier Herber, 1981; Perfect Love, 1983; The Novels of Vladimir Nabokov, 1984; City to City, 1989. Contributions to: Regular Contributor, Reviewer to Many Australian Journals & Newspapers. Honours: Co Winner, National Book Council Award, 1975; Winner, Australian Natives Association Award, 1983. Memberships: PEN International. Literary Agent: Curtis Brown Pty Ltd. Address: 227 Westgarth street, Northcote, VA 3070, Australia.

CLANCY Tom, b. 1947, MD, USA. m. Wanda Thomas, Aug 1969, 1 s, 3 d. Education: BA, Loyola College, Baltimore. Appointments: Insurance Agent, 1973; Owner, Insurance Company, 1973-80. Publications: The Hunt for Red October, 1984; Red Storm Rising, 1986; Patriot Games, 1987; The Cardinal of the Kremlin, 1988; Clear & Present Danger, 1989; The Sum of All Fears, 1992; Without Remorse, 1993; Debt of Honor, 1994; Armored Car, 1994; Submarine; Several Non Fiction Books. Address: PO Box 800, Huntingtown, MD 20639 0800, USA.

CLARE Elizabeth. See: COOK Dorothy Mary.

CLARE Ellen. See: SINCLAIR Olga Ellen.

CLARE Helen. See: BLAIR Pauline Hunter.

CLARK Brian Robert, b. 3 June 1932, Playwright. m. (1)Margaret Paling, 1961, 2 s, (2)Anita Modak, 1983, 1 stepson, 1 stepdaughter, (3)Cherry Potter, 1990. Education: Central School of Speech and Drama, London: BA, Nottingham University. Appointments: Teacher, 19550-61, 1964-68; Staff Tutor, Drama, University of Hull, 1968-72; Author, 1971-; Founder, Amber Lane Press, 1978. Publications include: TV Plays, Whose Life is it Anyway; The Saturday Party; TV Series, Telfords Change; Late Starter; Stage plays, Whose Life is it Anyway; Kipling; The Petition, 1986; Hopping to Byzantum, 1990. Address: c/o Judy Daish Associates, 83 Eastbourne Mews, London W2 6LQ, England.

CLARK Bruce (Budge), b. 1918, USA. Professor Emeritus. Appointments: Currently Emeritus Professor of English, Emeritus Dean, College of the Humanities, Brigham Young University, Provo, Utah, USA. Publications: The Longer Carmel Narrative Poems of Robinson Jeffers, 1947; The English Sonnet Sequence 1850 to 1900, 1951; The Spectrum of Faith in Victorian Literature, 1962; The Challenge of Teaching, 1964; Out of the Best Books: A Critical Anthology of Literature, 5 vols, 1964-69; Wisdom and Beauty Through Literature, 1966; Oscar Wilde: A Study in Genius and Tragedy, 1970; Romanticism Through Modern Eyes, 1970; Brigham Young on Education, 1970; Rochard Evans Quote Book, 1971; Idealists in Revolt:

An Introduction to English Romanticism, 1975; Favorite Selections from Out of the Best Books, 1979; Great Short Stories for Discussion and Delight, 1980; The Brigham Young University, College of Humanities 1965-1981, 3 vols, 1985; My Brother Richard L (Editor), 1985. Address: 365 East 1655 Street, Orem, UT 84058, USA.

CLARK Catherine Clifton. See: **CLARK Marie Catherine Audrey.**

CLARK David. See: **HARDCASTLE Michael.**

CLARK David Ridgley, b. 1920, USA. Emeritus Professor. Appointments: Instructor, University of MA, 1951-57; Assistant Prof, 1958, Associate Professor, 1958-65, Professor, 1965-85, Chairman, 1975-76, Emeritus Professor, 1985-, University of MA; Visiting Professor, Chairman, St Marys College, Notre Dame, IN, 1985-87; Visiting Professor, Williams College, MA, 1989-90. Publications include: A Curious Quire, 1962; W B Yeats and the Theatre of Desolate Rality, 1965, expanded, 1993; Irish Renaissance, 1965; Dry Tree, 1966; Riders to the Sea, 1970; A Tower of Polished Black Stones: Early Versions of the Shadowy Waters, 1971; Twentieth Century Interpretations of Murder in the Cathedral, 1971; David Craft, 1971; That Black Day: The Manuscripts of Crazy Jane on the Day of Judgement, 1980; W B Yeats: The Writing of Sophocles King Oedipus, 1989. Memberships: Modern Language Association of Am; Am Conference for Irish Studies; Canadian Association for Irish Studies; International Association for the Support of Anglo Irish Literature; Yeats Association. Address: 481 Holgerson Road, Sequim, WA 98382, USA.

CLARK Douglas, (Malcolm Jackson, Peter Hosier, James Ditton), b. 1919, England. Author; Executive. Publications include: Nobodys Perfect, 1969; Death after Evensong, 1969; Deadly Pattern, 1970; Sick to Death, 1971; The Miracle Makers, 1971; You're Fairly Welcome, 1973; The bigger They Are, 1973; Dread and Water, 1976; Hheberdens Seat, 1979; Roast Eggs, 1981; The Longest Pleasure, 1981; Shelf Life, 1982; The Monday Theory, 1983; Jewelled Eye, 1985; Plain Sailing, 1987; Bitter Water, 1990. Address: c/o Vanessa Holt Associates Limited, 59 Crescent Road, Leigh on Sea, Essex, SS9 2PF, England.

CLARK Eleanor, b. 6 July 1913, Los Angeles, CA, USA. Author. m. Robert Penn Warren, 7 Dec 1952, 1 s, 1 d. Education: BA, Vassar College. Publications include: Bitter Box, 1946; Baldurs Gate, 1974; Gloria Mundi; Camping Out, 1986; Rome and a Villa, 1952; Oysters of Locmariaquer, 1964, 1992; Tamrat, 1982. Contributions to: Partisan Review; The Nation; The New Republic; Kenyon Reivew; Southern Review; Atlantic Monthly. Honours: Guggenheim Fellowship, 1947-48, 1959-60; National Book Award, 1965. Memberships: National Institute of Arts & Letters; Corporation of Yaddo. Address: 2495 Redding Road, Fairfield, CT 06430, USA.

CLARK Eric, b. 29 July 1937, Birmingham, England. Author; Journalist. m. Marcelle Bernstein, 12 Apr 1972, 1 son, 2 daughters. Appointments: Staff of various newspapers including, Daily Mail, The Guardian, The Observer until 1972; Full-time Author, 1972-. Publications: Len Deighton's London Dossier (Part-author), 1967; Everybody's Guide to Survival, 1969; Corps Diplomatique, 1973, USA Edition, Diplomat, 1973; Black Gambit, 1978; The Sleeper, 1979; Send in the Lions, 1981; Chinese Burn, 1984, China Run, USA edition, 1984; The Want Makers (Inside the Hidden World of Advertising), 1988; Hide and Seek, 1994. Contributions to: The Observer; Sunday Times; Daily Mail; Daily Telegraph; Washington Post; Melbourne Age. Memberships: Society of Authors; Fellow, UK Centre International PEN; Crime Writers Association. Literary Agent: A M Heath & Co Ltd, 79 St Martin's Lane, London, WC2N 4AA. Address: c/o Child and Company, 1 Fleet Street, London EC4Y 1BD, England.

CLARK Joan, b. 12 Oct 1934, Nova Scotia. m. Jack, 3 children. Education: Acadia University; University of Alberta. Publications: The Hand of Robin Squires, 1977, 1986, 1994; From a High Thin Wire, 1982; Wild Man of the Woods, 1985; The Moons of Madeleine, 1987; The Victory of Geraldine Gill, 1988, 1994; Swimming Toward the Light, 1990; Eiriksdottir, 1994; The Dream Carvers, 1995. Address: 6 Dover Place, St Johns, Newfoundland, A1B 2P5, Canada.

CLARK John Pepper, (J P Clark Bekederemo), b. 6 Apr 1935, Kiagaboo, Nigeria. Writer. m. Ebun Odutola Clark, 1 s, 3 d. Education: Warri Government College, 1948-54; University of Ibadan, 1955-60; BA, 1960; Princeton University. Appointments: Information Officer,

Government of Nigeria, 1960-61; Head of Features and Editorial Writer, Lagos Daily Express, 1961-62; Research Fellow, 1964-66, Professor, 1966-85, University of Lagos; Founding Editor, Horn Magazine, Ibadan; Co Editor, Black Orpheus, 1968-. Publications include: Plays, The Raft, 1966; Included in Three Plays, 1964; Ozidi, Ibadan, London & New York, 1966; The Bikoroa Plays, The Boat; The Return Home; Screen Play, The Ozidi of Atazi; Radio Play, The Raft, 1966; Verse and Other Publications. Memberships: Society of Nigerian Authors. Literary Agent: Andrew Best, Curtis Brown. Address: c/o Andrew Best, Curtis Brown, 162-168 Regent Street, London W1R 5TB, England.

CLARK John Richard, b. 2 Oct 1930, PHA, USA. Professor. m. Dr Anna Lydia Motto, 7 Nov 1959, 1 s, 1 d. Education: BA, PA State University, 1952; MA, Columbia University, 1956; PhD, University of MI, 1965. Appointments: Member, Editorial Board, Studies in Contemporary Satire, Journal, 1978-. Publications: Form and Frenzy in Swifts Tale of a Tub, 1970; Satire, That Blasted Art, 1973; Senecan Tragedy, 1988; Seneca: A Critical Bibliography 1900-1980, 1989; The Modern Satiric Grotesque and Its Traditions, 1991; Essays on Seneca, 1993. Contributions to: Numerous inc. Guest Editor; Thalia, Seventeenth Century News; Am Notes & Queries; Centennial Review; Mosaic; Explicator; Transaction of the Am Philological Association; Notes & Queries. Honors: Rackham Fellowship, 1962-63; Invited Resident, Institute for Advanced Study, 1979, 80. Memberships: Modern Language Association; South Atlantic Modern Language Association; Am Philological Association; Classical Association of the Middle West & South College English Association. ess: Dept of English, University of South FL, Tampa, FL 33620, USA.

CLARK Jonathan Charles Douglas, b. 28 Feb 1951, London, England. Historian. Education: BA 1972, PhD 1981, Cambridge University. Appointments: Research Fellow, Peterhouse, Cambridge, 1977; Research Fellow, The Leverhulme Trust, 1983; Fellow, All Souls College, Oxford, 1986; Visiting Professor, Committee on Social Thought, University of Chicago, 1993. Publications: The Dynamics of Change, 1982; English Society 1688-1832, 1985; Revolution and Rebellion, 1986; The Memoirs of James 2nd Earl Waldegrave, 1988; Ideas and Politics in Modern Britain, 1990; The Language of Liberty, 1993; Samuel Johnson, 1994. Contributions to: Revolution and Counter-Revolution, 1990; Christianity and Conservatism, 1990; Articles in learned journals; Features and book reviews in: Times Literary Suppliment; The Times; Sunday Times; Sunday Telegraph; Independent on Sunday; Evening Standard; The Specatator. Memberships: Fellow, Royal Historical Society; American Historical Association; North American Conference on British Studies; British Society for Eighteenth Century Studies. Literary Agent: Michael Shaw, Curtis Brown. Address: All Souls College, Oxford OX1 4AL, England.

CLARK LaVerne Harrell, b. 6 June 1929, Smithville, TX, USA. Writer; Photographer; Lecturer. m. L D Clark, 15 Sept 1951. Education: BA, TX Woman's University, 1950; Columbia University, 1951-54; MA, 1962, MFA, 1992, University of AZ. Appointments: Reporter, Librarian, Fort Worth Press, 1950-51; Sales & Advertising Dept, Columbia University Press, 1951-53; Assistant, Promotion News Department, Episcopal Diocese, NY, 1958-59; Founding Director, 1962-66, Photographer, 1966-, Poetry Centre, University of AZ. Publications include: They Sang for Horses, 1966; The Face of Poetry, 1976; Focus 101, 1979; Revisiting the Plains Indians Country of Mari Sandoz, 1979; The Deadly Swarm and Other Stories, 1985, 87; Keepers of the Earth, 1995; The Restoration. Contributions to: Pembroke; Vanderbilt Review; The Pawn Review; Sands; Journal of Popular Culture; AZ Quarterly; AZ and the West; St Andrews Review. Honours include: Am Philosophical Society Grant, 1967-69; Non Fiction Award, Biennial Letters Contest, 1968; Distinguished Alumna Award, 1973; Julian Ocean Literary Prize, 1984. Memberships: PEN; Natl League of Am PEN Women; Western Writers of Am; Society of Southwestern Authors; Mari Sandoz Heritage Society; Honorary Board Member, Westerners International; Kappa Alpha Mu. Address: 4690 N Campbell no. C, Tucson, AZ 85718, USA.

CLARK Marcelle Ruth, (Marcelle Bernstein), b. 14 June 1945, Manchester, England. Writer; Journalist. m. Eric Clark, 12 Apr 1972, 1 s.2 d. Appointments: Staff, The Guardian, Daily Mirror, Observer. Publications: Nuns, 1976; Sadie, 1983; Salka, 1986; Lili, 1988; Body and Soul, 1991. Contributions to: Numerous US & UK Magazines. Honours: Arts Council Bursary, 1986; Helene Heroys Award, 1988. Memberships: Society of Authors. Literary Agent: Caradoc King, AP Watt. Address: c/o AP Watt, 20 John Street, London WC1N 2DR, England.

CLARK Marie Catherine Audrey (Catherine Clifton Clark, Audrey Curling), b. London, England. Writer. m. Clifton Clark, 16 Feb 1938. Publications: Novels: The Running Tide, 1963; Sparrow's Yard, 1964; Historical Novels: The Echoing Silence, 1967; Caste for Comedy, 1970; The Sapphire and the Pearl, 1970; Cry of the Heart, 1971; A Quarter of the Moon, 1972; Shadows on the Grass, 1973; Enthusiasts in Love, 1975; Publisher: Hurst and Blackett; The Lamps in the House, as Catherine Clifton Clark, 1990; The Saturday Treat, 1993; (Biography) The Young Thackeray (Max Parrish), 1966. Contributions to: Homes & Gardens; Womans Own; Woman; Woman's Realm; The Lady. Honours: Theordora Roscoe Award, 1978; 1st Prize, Wandsworth All London Literary Competition, 1982. Memberships: Society of Authors; Romantic Novelists Association; Society of Women Writers and Journalists, Council Member. Address: 35 Hadley Gardens, Chiswick, London W4 4NU, England.

CLARK Mary Higgins, b. 24 Dec 1929, NY, USA. Writer. m. Waren F Clark, 26 Dec 1949, 2 s, 3 d. Education: BA, Fordham University; Villanora University, 1983; Rider COllege, 1986. Publications include: Where Are The Children, 1975; A Stranger is Watching, 1978; The Cradle will Fall, 1980; A Cry in the Night, 1982; Weep No More My Lady, 1987; While My Pretty One Sleeps, 1989; All Around the Town, 1992; Loves Music, Loves to Dance, 1991; Remember Me, 1994. Contributions to include: Ladies Home Journal; Womens Day; Saturday Evening Post. Honours include: Grand Prix de Litteratae Policcere, 1980. Memberships: Mystery Writers of Am; PEN; Am Society of Journalists & Authors. Literary Agent: Eugene Winick.

CLARK Mavis Thorpe (Mavis Latham), b. Australia. Children's Writer. Publications: Hatherly's First Fifteen, 1930; Dark Pool Island, 1949; Missing Gold, 1949; The Twins from Timber Creek, 1949; Home Again at Timber Creek, 1950; Jingaroo, 1951; The Brown Land Was Green, novel, 1956; Gully of Gold, 1958; Pony from Tarella, 1959; John Batman (as Mavis Latham), 1962; Fishing (as Mavis Latham), 1963; They Came South, 1963; Pastor Doug, Biography of Sir Douglas Ralph Nicholls, Aboriginal leader, 1965, 2nd edition, 1972; The Min-Min, novel, 1966; Blue Above the Trees, 1967; Spark of Opal, 1968; A Pack Tracker, 1968; Opal Mining, 1969; Nowhere to Hide, 1969; Iron Mountain, 1970; Strolling Players, 1972; New Golden Mountain, US Edition as If the Earth Falls In, 1973; Wildlife, 1973; The Sky Is Free, 1974; The Hundred Islands, 1976; Spanish Queen, 1977; The Boy from Cumeroogunga, 1979; The Lilly-Pilly, 1979; A Stranger Came to the Mine, 1980; Solomon's Child, 1982; Young and Brave, 1984; No Mean Destiny: History of the War Widows' Guild, Australia, 1986; Soft Shoe, 1988. Honours: Highly Commended for The Brown Land Was Green, Children's Book Council of Australia, 1957; Commended for Blue Above the Trees, Children's Book Council of Australia, 1965; Winner, Book of the Year Award, for The Min-Min, Australian Children's Book Council, 1967; Notable Book, for The Min-Min, Anmerican Library Association List, 1969. Memberships: Past President, International PEN Club, Melbourne Centre; Australian Society of Authors, Member of Committee of Management 15 years; National Book Council, Committee 7 years; Fellowship of Australian Writers, Committee 5 years. Address: Unit I, 22 Rochester Road, Canterbury, Victoria 3126, Australia.

CLARK Patricia Denise (Claire Lorrimer, Patricia Robins, Susan Patrick), b. 1921. British. Writer of Historical/Romance/Gothic, Children's fiction, Poetry; Sub-editor, Woman's Illustrated magazine, London, 1938-40. Publications include: As Claire Lorrimer: A Voice in the Dark, 1967; The Shadow Falls, 1974; Relentless Storm, 1975; The Secret of Quarry House, 1976; Mavreen, 1976; Tamarisk, 1978; Chantal, 1980; The Garden (a cameo), 1980; The Chatelaine, 1981; The Wilderling, 1982; Last Year's Nightingale, 1984; Frost in the Sun, 1986; House of Tomorrow (biography), 1987; Ortolans, 1990; The Spinning Wheel, 1991; Variations (short stories), 1991; The Silver Link, 1993; Fool's Curtain, 1994; As Patricia Robins: To the Stars, 1944; See No Evil, 1945; Three Loves, 1949; Awake My Heart, 1950; Beneath the Moon, 1951; Leave My Heart Alone, 1951; The Fair Deal, 1952; Heart's Desire, 1953; So This is Love, 1953; Heaven in Our Hearts, 1954; One Who Cares, 1954; Love Cannot Die, 1955; The Foolish Heart, 1956; Give All to Love, 1956; Where Duty Lies, 1957; He Is Mine, 1957; Love Must Wait, 1958; Lonely Quest, 1959; Lady Chatterley's Daughter, 1961; The Last Chance, 1961; The Long Wait, 1962; The Runaways, 1962; Seven Loves, 1962; With All My Love, 1963; The Constant Heart, 1964; Second Love, 1964; The Night is Thine, 1964; There Is But One, 1965; No More Loving, 1965; Topaz Island, 1965; Love Me Tomorrow, 1966; The Uncertain Joy, 1966; The Man Behind the Mask, 1967; Forbidden, 1967; Sapphire in the Sand, 1968; Return to Love, 1968;

Laugh on Friday, 1969; No Stone Unturned, 1969; Cinnabar House, 1970; Under the Sky, 1970; The Crimson Tapestry, 1972; Play Fair with Love, 1972; None But He, 1973; Fulfilment, 1993; Forsaken, 1993; Forever, 1993. Membership: Romantic Novelists Association. Address: Chiswell Barn, Marsh Green, Edenbridge, Kent TN8 5PR, England.

CLARKE Anna, b. 28 Apr 1919, Cape Town, South Africa. Author. Education: Schools in Cape Town, Montreal, Canada; BSc Economics, University of London, 1945; BA, Open University, 1971-75; MA, University of Sussex, 1975. Appointments: Private Secretary, Victor Gollancz Publishers, 1947-50; Private Secretary, Eyre and Spottiswoode, Publishers, 1951-53; Administrative Secretary, British Association for American Studies, London, 1956-63. Publications include: The Poisoned Web, 1979; Poison Parsley, 1979; Last Voyage, 1980; Game, Set and Danger, 1981; Desire to Kill, 1982; We the Bereaved, 1982; Soon She Must Die, 1983; Paula Glenning stories: Last Judgement, 1985; Cabin 3033, 1986; The Mystery Lady, 1986; Last Seen in London, 1987; Murder in Writing, 1988; The Whitelands Affair, 1989; The Case of the Paranoid Patient, 1993; The Case of the Ludicrous Letters, 1944. Contributions to: Short stories in Ellery Queen Mystery Magazine, New York. Literary Agent: Wendy Lipkind, New York. Address: c/o Wendy Lipkind, 165 East 66 Street, New York, NY 10021, USA.

CLARKE Arthur C (Charles), b. 16 Dec 1917, Minehead, England. Author. m. Marilyn Mayfield, 1953, div 1964. Education: BSc, 1st Class Honours, King's College, London, 1946-48. Appointments include: Auditor, HM Exchequer and Audit Department, 1936-41; Royal Air Force, 1941-46; Assistant Editor, Science Abstracts, Institution of Electronic Engineers, 1949-50; Diver, Great Barrier Reef and Indian Ocean, 1954-; Lecturer, USA, 1957-70; Played Leonard Woolf in film, Beddegama, 1979; Writer and Host, Television series, Arthur C Clarke's Mysterious World, Yorkshire Television, 1980, and World of Strange Powers, 1984; Host, The Communications Revolution, NVC Television Series, 1983; Chancellor, University of Moratuwa, Sri Lanka, 1979-. Publications include: Author of over 70 books including: Against the Fall of Night; The City and the Stars; The Deep Range; A Fall of Moondust; Glide Path; The Lion of Comarre; The Other Side of the Sky; Prelude to Space; Rendezvous with Rama; The Songs of Distant Earth; Tales from the White Hart; Tales of Ten Worlds; The Wind from the Sun; 2001: A Space Odysse; 2010: Odyssey Two; Ascent to Orbit; The Coast of Coral; The Exploration of Space; Interplanetary Flight. Contributions to: Over 500 articles and short stories. Honours include: Recipient of numerous honours and awards including: Honorary DSc, Beaver College, Pennsylvannia, 1971; Honorary DSc, University of Moratuwa, 1979; International Fantasy Award, 1952; Kalinga Prize, 1961; SF Writers of America Grand Master, 1986; CBE, 1989. Nominated for the Nobel Peace Prize, 1994. Memberships include: Fellow, Royal Astronomical Society; Fellow, International Science Writers Association; Association for the Advancement of Science; Society of Authors. Hobbies: Astronomy; Computers. Literary Agent: c/o David Higham Associates, 5 Lower John Street, Golden Square, London W1R 3PE, England. Address: 25 Barnes Place, Colombo 7, Sri Lanka.

CLARKE Austin Ardinel Chesterfield, b. 26 July 1934, Barbados, West Indies. Author. m. 14 Sept 1957, 2 d. Education: Trinity College, University of Toronto. Appointments: Hoyt Fellow, Yale University, 1968; Margaret Bundy Scott Professor, 1970; Jacob Ziskind Professor, Brandeis University, 1970; Fellow, School of Letters, IN, 1969. Publications: The Meeting Point, 1967; Storm of Fortune, 1972; The Bigger Light, 1973; When He Was Young and Free He Used to Wear Silks, 1972; The Prime Minister, 1977; Growing Up Stupid Under The Union Jack, 1980; When Women Rule, 1985; Nine Men Who Laughed, 1986; Proud Empires, 1986; In This City, 1992; There Are No Eldors, 1993; A Passage Back Home: A Personal Reminiscence of Samuel Selvon, 1994. Contributions to: Tamarack Review; Canadian Literature. Honours: Presidents Medal, 1965; Canada Council Awards, 1968, 72; Casa de las Americas Literary Prize, 1980; Arts Council Award, 1985, 1994; Toronto Arts Award, 1992. Memberships: Arts & Letters CLub. Literary Agent: Harold Ober Associates, David Higham Associates, London. Address: 62 McGill Strret, Toronto, Ontario, Canada M5B 1H2.

CLARKE Brenda (Margaret Lilian), (Brenda Honeyman, Kate Sedley), b. 1926, United Kingdom. Author. Publications: Richard By Grace of God, 1968; The Kingmaker, 1969; Richmond and Elizabeth, 1970; Harry the King, 1971; Brother Bedford, 1972; Good Duke Humphrey, 1973; The King's Minions, 1974; The Queen and Mortimer,

1974; Edward, The Warrior, 1975; All the King's Sons, 1975; The Golden Griffin, 1976; At the King's Court, 1976; The King's Tale, 1977; MacBeth, King of Scots, 1977; Emma, The Queen, 1978; The Glass Island, 1978; The Lofty Banners, 1979; Harold of the English, 1979; The Far Morning, 1982; All Through the Day, 1983; A Rose in May, 1984; Three Women, 1985; Winter Landscape, 1986; Under Heaven, 1988; An Equal Chance, 1989; Sisters and Lovers, 1990; Beyond The World, 1991 as Brenda Clarke; A Durable Fire, as Brenda Clarke, 1993; Death and the Chapman, as Kate Sedley, 1992; The Plymouth Cloak, as Kate Sedley, 1992; The Hanged Man, as Kate Sedley, 1993. Literary Agent: David Grossman Literary Agency, London. Address: 25 Torridge Road, Keynsham, Bristol BS18 1QQ, England.

CLARKE Gillian, b. 8 June 1937, Cardiff, Wales. Lecturer; Poet. Education: BA, University College Cardiff, 1958. Appointments: Lecturer, Gwent College of Art & Design, Newport, 1975-84; Editor, Anglo Welsh Review, 1976-84; President, Ty Nwydd, 1993-. Publications: Snow on the Mountains, 1971; The Sundial, 1978; Letter from a Far Country, 1982; Selected Poems, 1985; Letting in the Rumour, 1989; The King of Britain's Daughter, 1993; Editor, The Poetry Book Society Anthology, 1987-88, 1987. Address: Blaen Cwrt, Talgarreg, Llandysul, Dyfed, Wales.

CLARKE Hugh Vincent, b. 27 Nov 1919, Brisbane, Australia. Journalist; Author. m. Mary Patricia Ryan, 6 June 1961. Education: St Josephs College, Brisbane. Appointments: Director of Information & Publicity, Department of Territories; Director of Information and PR, Department of Aboriginal Affairs. Publications: The Tub; Breakout; To Sydney by Stealth; The Long Arm; Fire One; The Broke and the Broken; Last Stop Nagasaki; Twilight Liberation: A Life for Every Sleeper; Prisoners of War; When the Balloon Went Up. Contributions to: Australian Writes; Australians at War; The Bulletin; Canbera Times; Australasion Past. Memberships: Australian Society for Authors; National Press Club. Address: 14 Chermside Street, Deakin, Canberra 2600, Australia.

CLARKE Joan Lorraine, b. 23 Aug 1920, Sydney, Australia. Author; Freelance Editor. m. R G Clarke, 1946, div, 1 son. Education: Diploma, Secretarial College, 1938. Appointments: Editor, The Australian Author, 1977-81; Editor, Australian Society of Authors, Writers Handbook 2nd edition, 1980. Publications: The Tracks We Travel: Australian Short Stories (contributing author), 1953; Girl Fridays in Revolt (co-author), 1969; Max Herz, Surgeon Extraordinary, 1976; Contributing Author, Australian Political Milestone, 1976; Gold (co-author), 1981; The Doctor Who Dared, 1982; Just Us, 1988; Growing Up With Barnardo's (editor), 1990; All on One Good Dancing Leg (author), 1994. Contributions to: Sydney Morning Herald; Australian Women's Weekly; Flair; Pol; The Australian Author; Overland; Radio talks and features for the Australian Broadcasting Commission and commercial radio. Address: 42/114 Spit Road, Mosman, NSW 2088, Australia.

CLARKE Mary, b. 23 Aug 1923, London, England. Editor; Writer. Literary Appointments: Editor, The Dancing Times, London. Publications: The Sadler's Wells Ballet: A History and an Appreciation, 1955; Six Great Dancers, 1957; Dancers of Mercury; The Story of Ballet Rambert, 1962; Ballet: An Illustrated History (with Clement Crisp), 1973, 1992; recent books with Clement Crisp: Design for Ballet; Making a Ballet; Dancer: Men in Dance; Ballerina; History of Dance. Contributions to: Encyclopedia Britannica; The Guardian; Dance Magazine, New York; Dance News, New York; The Observer; Sunday Times. Honours: 2nd Prize, Cafe Royal Literary Prize for Best Book on Theatre, 1955; Queen Elizabeth II Award, Royal Academy of Dancing, 1990; Knight, Order of Dannebrog (Danish), 1992. Membership: Gautier Club. Address: 54 Ripplevale Grove, London, N1 1HT, England.

CLARKE Pauline. See: BLAIR Pauline Hunter.

CLARKSON Ewan, b. 1929, England. Childrens Writer. Publications include: Break for Freedom, 1967; Halic, The Story of a Grey Seal, 1970; The Running of the Deer, 1972; In The Shadow of the Falcon, 1973; Wolf Country, a Wilderness Pilgrimage, 1975; The Badger of Summercombe, 1977; The Many Forked Branch, 1980; Wolves, 1980; Reindeer, 1981; Eagles, 1981; Beavers, 1981; In the Wake of the Storm, 1984; Ice Trek, 1986. Address: Moss Rose Cottage, Preston, Kingsteignton, Newton Abbot, Devon, England.

CLARKSON J F. See: TUBB E(dwin) C(harles).

CLARKSON Stephen. m. Christin McCall, 3 d. Education: Toronto, Oxford and Sorbonne. Appointments: Professor, Political Economy, University of Toronto, 1964-; Co Founder, Praxis Corp; Former Editor, The Canadian Forum; President, University League for Social Reform. Publications: Many Academic and General Articles; An Independent Foreign Policy for Canada?, 1968; City Lib: Parties and Reform, 1972; The Soviet Theory of Development, 1978; Canada and the Reagan Challenge, 1985; Trudeau and Our Times: The Magnificent Obsession, 1990; Trudeau and Our Times: The Heroic Delusion, 1994. Honours: Rhodes Scholarship, Woodrow Wislon Fellowship; John Porter Award, 1984; Governor General's Award, 1990. Address: 44 Rosedale Road, Toronto, Ontario, M4W 2P6, Canada.

CLARY Sydney Ann, b. 13 Feb 1948, Auburn, AL, USA. Writer. m. Bishop D Clary, 26 Sept 1967, 2 d. Education: Palm Beach Community College. Publications: Double Solitaire; Devil and the Duchess; Eye of the Storm; A Touch of Passion; Her Golden Eyes; Fire in the Night; With a Little Spice; Southern Comfort; This Wildlife Magic. Contributions to: Numerous Articles to Romantic Times; Articles to Romance Writers of Am Magazine. Honours: Reviewers Choice Finalist, 1983, 84, 87, 90; Gold Medallion Finalist, 1988; Reviewers Choice Best All Around Series Author, 1989-90. Memberships: Romance Writers of Am. Literary Agent: Maureen Walters, Curtis Brown Ltd. Address: c/o Curtis Brown Ltd, 10 Astor Place, NEw York, NY 10013, USA.

CLAVELL James, Author; Screenwriter; Film Director; Producer. m. 1953, 2 d. Publications include: The Fly, 1957; The Great Escape, 1960; Satan Bug, 1962; 633 Squadron, 1963; Wheres Jack, 1968; Five Gates to Hell, 1959; Walk Like a Dragon, 1960; Last Valley, 1969; But Not for Children, 1982; King Rat, 1962; Tai Pan, 1966; Noble House, 1980; Thrump o Moto, 1985; Whirlwind, 1986; Gai Jin, 1993. Honours: Emmy; Prabody; Critics; Holden Globe; Golden Eiger, 1972. Address: c/o Foreign Rights inc, 136 E 57th Street, New York, NY 10022, USA.

CLAYDON Duer. See: FINCH Robert.

CLAYPOOL MINER Jane, b. 22 Apr 1933, McAllen, TX, USA. Writer. m. (1)Dennis A Shelley, 1952, dec, 1 d. (2)Richard Yale Miner, 1962, dec. Education: BA, CA State University; University of CA, Los Angeles. Publications include: 60 Books for Teenagers including, Alcohol & You, 1980; Dreams Can Come True, 1981; Joanna, 1985; History of Workers, 1986; Corey, 1987. Contributions to: Numerous Feature Articles, Local & National Publications; Weekly Column, Real Estate. Honour: Member of Year, Society of Childrens Book Writers. Memberships: Society of Childrens Book Writers; Am Society of Authors & Journalists; National Art Club; National Bd of Realtors. Address: 2883 Lone Jack Road, Olivenhain, CA 92024, USA.

CLAYTON Jay. See: CLAYTON John B IV.

CLAYTON John B IV, (Jay Clayton), b. 11 July 1951, Dallas, TS, USA. Professor. m. Ellen Wrigth Clayton, 19 June 1982, 2 s. Education: AB, Yale University, 1974; PhD, University of VA, 1979. Appointments: Associate Professor, CAnderbilt University. Publications: Romantic Vision and the Novel, 1987; Influence and Intertextuality in Literary History, 1991; The Pleasures of Babel, 1993. Contributions to: Southern Review; Southwest Review; Critical Inquiry; Am Literary History; ELH; Contemporary Literature; Denver Quarterly; KS Quarterly; 19th Century Literature. Honours: Fellow, Am Council of Learned Societies, 1981-82; Fellow, Robert Penn Warren Centre for the Humanities, 1988-90; Robert A Partlow Prize, 1988. Memberships: Society of the Study of Narrative Literature; Dickens Society. Address: Dept of English, Vanderbilt University, Nashville, TN 37235, USA.

CLAYTON John J, b. 5 Jan 1935, NY, USA. Writer; Professor, 3 s, 1 d. Education: BA, Columbia college, 1956; MA, NY University, 1959; PhD, IN University, 1966. Publications: Criticism: Saul Bellow: In Defense of Man, 1968, 79; What Are Friends for?, 1979; Bodies of the Rich, 1984; Gestures of Healing, 1991. Contributions to: Esquire; Playboy; VA Quarterly; Agni; Ploughshares; Tri Quarterly; MA Review. Honours: 2nd Prize O. Henry Competition, 1995. Literary Agent: Ellen Levine. Address: English Dept, University of MA, Amherst, MA 01003, USA.

CLAYTON Peter Arthur, b. 27 Apr 1937, London, England. Publishing Consultant; Archaelogical Lecturer. m. Janet Frances Manning, 5 Sept 1964, 2 sons. Education: School of Librarianship; NW Polytechnic, London, 1958; Institute of Archaeology, London University,

1958-62; University College, London University, 1958-62; University College, London, 1968-72. Appointments: Librarian, 1953-67; Archaeological Editor, Thames & Hudson, 1963-73; Humanities Publisher, Longmans, 1973; Managing Editor, British Museums Publications, 1974-79; Publications Director, BA Seaby, 1980-87; Writer, Lecturer, 1987-. Publications: The Rediscovery of Ancient Egypt; Archaeological Sites of Britain; Seven Wonders of the Ancient World; Treasures of Ancient Rome; Companion to Roman Britain; Great Figures of Mythology; Gods and Symbols of Ancient Egypt; Chronicle of the Pharaohs, 1994. Contributions to: Journal of Egyptian Archaeology; Numismatic Chronicle; Coin & Medal Bulletin; Minerva. Address: 41 Cardy Road, Boxmoor, Hemel Hempstead, Herts HP1 1RL, England.

CLEALL Charles, b. 1 June 1927, Heston, Middlesex, England. Writer. m. Mary Turner, 25 July 1953, 2 daughters. Education: Trinity College of Music, London, GTCL; LRAM; ARCO; Jordanhill College of Education, BMus; FRCO; MA, University College of North Wales. Appointments include: Instructor Lieut, Royal Navy, Plymouth Command, 1946-48; Professor, Solo-Singing and Voice Production, TCL, 1949-52; Choral Scholar, Westminster Abbey, 1949-52; Conductor, Morley College Orchestra, 1950-52; BBC Music Assistant, Midland Region, 1954-55; Lecturer in Music, The Froebel Institute, Roehampton, 1967-68; Music Adviser, London Borough of Harrow, 1968-72; Northern Divisional Music Specialist of Her Majesty's Inspectorate of Schools in Scotland, 1972-87; Editor, Journal of The Ernest George White Society, 1983-87. Publications: Voice Production in Choral Technique, 1955, revised 1970; The Selection and Training of Mixed Choirs in Churches, 1960; Sixty Songs from Sankey, 1960, revised 1966; John Merbecke's Music for the Congregation at Holy Communion, 1963; Music and Holiness, 1964; Plainsong for Pleasure, 1969; Authentic Chanting, 1969; A Guide to Vanity Fair, 1982; Walking Round the Church of St James the Great, Stonehaven, 1993. Address: 10 Carronhall, Stonehaven, Aberdeen AB3 2HF.

CLEARE John Silvey, b. 2 May 1936, London, England. Photographer; Writer. m. (2) Jo Jackson, 12 May 1980, 1 daughter. Education: Wycliffe College, 1945-54; Guildford School of Photography, 1957-60. Appointments: Joint Editor, Mountain Life magazine, 1973-75; Editorial Board, Climber and Rambler magazine, 1975-85. Publications: Trekking - Great Walks of the World, 1988; John Cleare's 50 Best Hill Walks in Britain, 1988; World Guide to Mountains, 1979; Mountains, 1975; Rock Climbers in Action in Snowdonia, 1966; Sea-Cliff Climbing in Britain, 1973; Mountaineering, 1980; Scrambles Among the Alps, 1986; Walking the Great Views, 1991; Discovering the English Lowlands, 1991; On Foot in the Pennines, 1994. Contributions to: Times; Sunday Times; Independent; Observer; World; Country Living; Boat International; Intercontinental; Alpine Journal; High; Climber; Great Outdoors. Honours: 35mm Prize, Trento Film Festival, for film The Climbers (as Cameraman), 1971. Literary Agent: Laurel Anderson, Photosynthesis, #20 Issaquah Dock, Sausalito, CA 94965, USA. Address: Hill Cottage, Fonthill Gifford, Salisbury, Wiltshire SP3 6QW, England.

CLEARY Beverly Atlee, b. 12 Apr 1916, McMinnville, OR, USA. Writer. m. Clarence T Cleary, 6 Oct 1940, 1 s, 1 d. Education: BA, University of CA, 1938; BA, University of WA, 1939. Publications include: Henry Huggins, 1950; Fifteen, 1956; The Mouse and the Motorcycle, 1965; Ramona the Pest, 1968; Dear Mr Henshaw, 1983; A Girl From Yamhill: A Memoir, 1988; Strider, 1991; Muggie Maggic, 1992. Contribution to: The Horn Book Magazine. Honours: Laura Ingalls Wilder Award, 1975; Newberry Honor Books, 1978, 82; Newbery Award, 1984; Christopher Award, 1984; Everychild Award, 1985; Doctor of Humane Letters, 1992. Memberships: Authors League of Am. Address: Morrow Junior Books, 1350 Avenue of the Americas, New York, NY 10019, USA.

CLEARY Jon (Stephen), b. 22 Nov 1917, Sydney, New South Wales. Writer of Novels/Short Stories/Screenplays. Appointments: Journalist, Australian News and Information Bureau, London, 1948-49 and New York City 1949-51. Publications: The Small Glories (short stories), 1945; You Can't See Round Corners, 1947; The Long Shadow, 1949; Just Let Me Be, 1950; The Sundowners, 1952, screenplay 1961; The Climate of Courage (in US asNaked in the Night), 1954; Justin Bayard, 1955; The Green Helmet, 1957, screenplay 1960; Back of Sunset, 1959; (with H Watt) The Siege of Pinchgut (screenplay), 1959; North from Thursday, 1960; The Country of Marriage, 1961; Forest of the Night, 1962; Pillar of Salt (short stories), 1963; A Flight of Chariots, 1964; The Fall of an Eagle, 1965; The Pulse of Danger, 1966; The High

Commissioner, 1967; The Long Pursuit, 1968; Season of Doubt, 1969; Remember Jack Hoxie, 1970; Helga's Webb, 1971; The Liberators (in UK as Mask of the Andes), 1971; The Ninth Marquess (in UK as Man's Estate), 1972; Ransom, 1973; Peter's Pence, 1974; Sidecar Boys (screenplay), 1974; The Safe House, 1975; A Sound of Lightning, 1976; High Road to China, 1977; Vortex, 1977; The Beaufort Sisters, 1979; A Very Pirate War, 1980; The Golden Sabre, 1981; The Faraway Drums, 1981; Spearfield's Daughter, 1982; The Phoenix Tree, 1984; The City of Fading Light, 1985; Dragons at the Party, 1987; Now and Then, Amen, 1988; Babylon South, 1989; Murder Song, 1990; Pride's Harvest, 1991; Dark Summer, 1992; Bleak Spring, 1993; Autumn Maze, 1994. Address: c/o Harpers Collins, 77-85 Fulham Palace Road, London W6 8JB, England.

CLEAVER Anastasia N (Natasha Peters). Author. Married. Publications: Savage Surrender, 1977; Dangerous Obsession, 1978; The Masquer, 1979; The Enticers, 1981; The Immortals: A Novel of Shanghai, 1983; Darkness into Light, 1984; Wild Nights, 1986; Stardust, 1992. Address: c/o Ballantine Books, 201 E 50th Street, New York, NY 10022, USA.

CLEESE John (Marwood), b. 1939, United Kingdom. Actor; Frequent stage, TV and film appearances. Publications: Monty Python Books (contributor); Families and How to Survive Them (with Robin Skynner), 1983; The Golden Skits of Muriel Volestrangler FRHS & Bar, 1984; The Complete Fawlty Towers, (with Connie Booth), 1989; Life and How to Survive It (with Robin Skynner), 1993. Honour: Hon LLD, St Andrews. Address: c/o David Wilkinson, 115 Hazlebury Road, London, SW6 2LX, England.

CLEEVE Brian Talbot, b. 22 Nov 1921, Thorpe Bay, Essex, England. Author; Journalist. m. Veronica McAdie, 24 Sept 1945, 2 daughters. Education: BA, University of South Africa, 1954; PhD, University of Ireland, Dublin, 1956. Publications: Cry of Morning, 1970; Sara, 1975; House on the Rock, 1980; The Fourth Mary, 1982; Biographical Dictionary of Irish Writers, 1985; A Woman of Fortune, 1993. Contributions to: Numerous short stories, various magazines. Honours: Award, Mystery Writers of America, 1965 (short story, Foxer); Knight of Mark Twain, 1972-73. Literary Agent: Elaine Markson, 44 Greenwich Avenue, NY, USA. Address: 60 Heytesbury Lane, Ballsbridge, Dublin 4, Ireland.

CLEMENT Richard (Dick), b. 5 Sept 1937, Writer; Director; Producer. m. (1)Jennifer Sheppard, div, 3 s, 1 d. (2)Nancy Campbell, 1 d. Publications include: The Likely Lads, 1964-66; Whatever Happened to the Likely Lads, 1972-73; Porridge, 1974-76; Thock as Thieves, 1974; Going Straight, 1978; Auf Wiedershen Pet, 1984; Freddie and Max, 1990; The Joker, 1967; Otley, 1968; Villain, 1971; Prisoner of Zenda, 1977; Porridge, 1979; Water, 1984; Vice Versa, 1988; Stage: Billy, 1974; Anyone for Dennis, 1981. Honour: Jointly, Peter Sellers Award, 1991. Address: 9700 Yoakum Drive, Beverly Hills, CA 90210, USA.

CLEWELL David, b. 1955. Appointment: Professor of Writing & Literature, Webster University, St Louis, Missouri. Publications: Blessings in Disguise; Now We're Getting Somewhere. Contributions to: New England Review; Poetry/River Styx; Chariton Review; Georgia Review; Kenyon Review; Harpers. Honours: National Poetry Series Winner; Missouri Biennial Writing Award; Felix Pollack Prize, 1994; Lavan Younger Poets Award, 1993.

CLINTON Dorothy Louise Randle, b. 6 Apr 1925, Des Moines, IA, USA. m. Moses S Clinton, 6 June 1950, 1 s. Education: BA, Drake University, 1949. Publications include: The Only Opaque Light, 1989; Memory Lapse, 1983; Ascending Line, 1978; The look and the See, 1979; Snobbery in Nuance, 1978; Black Dignity in Marsh and Haunting Could be Love; Selected Poets of the New Era by American Poetry Association; You Dont Hear the Echo, You Dont Knoe, 1991; Blind Transfer; Stop the Itch Without a Bitch. Honours include: Clover Award, 1974, 1975; Editors Choice Award, 1989. Membership: International Society of Poets. Address: 1530 Maple, Des Moines, IA 50316, USA.

CLINTON Jeff. See: **BICKHAM Jack Miles.**

CLIVE William. See: **BASSETT Ronald Leslie.**

CLOUDSLEY-THOMPSON John Leonard, b. 23 May 1921, Murree, India. Professor of Zoology. m. Jessie Anne Cloudsley, 1944, 3 sons. Education: MA, PhD, Pembroke College, Cambridge; DSc,

London, 1960. Publications include: Spiders, Scorpions, Centipedes and Mites, 1958, 2nd edition 1968; Insects and History, 1976; Tooth and Claw, 1980; Rhythmic Activity in Animal Physiology and Behaviour, 1961; The Desert, 1977; Guide to Woodlands, 1985; Evolution and Adaptation of Terrestrial Arthropods, 1988; Ecophysiology of Desert Arthropods and Reptiles, 1991; (novel) The Nile Quest, 1994; Predation and Defence Amongst Reptiles, 1994; 40 other books including 11 children's books. Contributions to: Encyclopedia Britannica; Encyclopedia Americana. Honours: Honorary DSc, Khartoum and Silver Jubilee Gold Medal, 1981, Foundation for Environmental Conservation (Best Paper Award, 1989). Address: 10 Battishill Street, London N1 1TE, England.

CLOUGH Brenda Wang, b. 13 Nov 1955, WA, USA. Writer. m. Lawrence A Clough, 21 May 1977, 1 d. Education: BA, Carnegie Mellon University, 1977. Appointments: Circulation Dept, United Chapters of Phi Beta Kappa; Associate Editor, Research Institute of America. Publications: Novels, The Crystal Crown, 1984; The Dragon of Mishbil, 1985; The Realm Beneath, 1986; The Name of the Sun, 1988. Membership: Science Fictions Writers Of Am. Address: 1941 Barton Hill Road, Reston, VA 22091, USA>

CLUSTER Richard (Dick) Bruce, b. 17 Jn 1947, MD, USA. Writer, 1 s. Education: BA, Harvard University, 1968; Venceremos Brigade, Cuba, 1970; Auto Mechanics Certificate, Newton MA High School, 1971. Publications: They Should Have Served That Cup of Coffee, 1979; Shrinking Dollars, Vanishing Jobs, 1980; Return to Sender, 1988; Repulse Monkey, 1989; Obligations of the Bone, 1992. Literary Agent: Gina Maccoby, NY, USA; Gregory & Radice, London, England. Address: 33 Jackson Street, Cambridge, MA 02140, USA.

CLUTTERBUCK Richard Lewis, b. 22 Nov 1917, London, England. Security Consultant. m. Angela Muriel Barford, 15 May 1948, 3 sons. Education: MA, Mechanical Sciences, Cambridge University, 1939; PhD, Politics, London University, 1971. Publications: Living with Terrorism, 1975; Guerrillas & Terrorists, 1980; Britain in Agony, 1980; The Media & Political Violence, 1983; Industrial Conflict & Democracy, 1984; Conflict & Violence in Singapore & Malaysia, 1985; Kidnap Hijack & Extortion, 1987; Terrorism Drugs & Crime in Europe After 1992, 1990; Terrorism & Guerrilla Warfare: Forecasts & Remedies, 1990; International Crisis and Conflict, 1993; Terrorism in an Unstable World, 1994; Drugs, Crime and Corruption: Thinking the Unthinkable, 1995. Contributions to: Magazines and journals in UK and USA. Address: Department of Politics, Universityof Exeter, Exeter EX4 4RJ, England.

CLUYSENAAR Anne (Alice Andree), b. 15 Mar 1936, Brussels, Belgium, Irish Citizen. Lecturer; Poet; Song-Writer; Librettist; Painter. m. Walter F Jackson, 1976. Education: BA, Trinity College Dublin, 1957; University of Edinburgh. Appointments: Lecturer, Sheffield Polytechnic, 1976-87; Currently, Part-time Lecturer, University of Wales, Cardiff. Publications: A Fan of Shadows, 1967; Nodes, 1969; Double Helix, 1982; Aspects of Literary Stylistics, 1976; Selected Poems of James Burns Singer (editor), 1977; Poetry Introduction 4, 1978; Time-Slips, New and Selected Poems, 1995. Contributions to: Poetry Wales; Planet; New Welsh Review; Poetry Nation Review. Honours: Chair, Verbal Arts Association, 1983-86; Poetry Society Representative, Gwent, 1994-. Address: Little Wentwood Farm, Llantrisant, Usk, Gwent, NP5 1ND, Wales.

COASE Ronald. Publications: Educational TV: Who Should Pay?, 1968; The Market for Goods and the Market for Ideas, 1975; How Should Economists Choose?, 1982; The Firm, The Market and the Law, 1988; The Nature of the Firm, 1991. Honours include: Nobel Prize for Economics, 1991. Address: University of Chicago, The Law School, 1111 East 60th Street, Chicago, IL 60637, USA.

COATES Ken, b. 16 Sept 1930, Leek. Member European Parliament; Chairman, Human Rights Sub-Committee of European Parliament, 1989-; 94; Special Professor of Adult Education, University of Nottingham. m. Tamara Tura, 21 Aug 1969, 3 sons, 3 daughters. Education: BA, Nottingham University, 1959. Publications: Industrial Democracy in Great Britain (with Tony Topham); Poverty: The Forgotten Englishmen (with Bill Silburn); The Crisis of British Socialism; Essays in Industrial Democracy; The New Unionism (with Tony Topham); Beyond Wage Slavery; The Shop Stewards' Guide to the Bullock Report (with Tony Topham); Democracy in the Labour Party; The Case of Nikolai Bukharin; Work-ins, Sit ins and Industrial Democracy; Trade Unions in Britain (with Tony Topham); Heresies:

The Most Dangerous Decade; Trade Unions and Politics (with Tony Topham); Think Globally; Act Locally; The Making of the Transport & General Workers Union (with Tony Topham); A European Recovery Programme, 1993. Membership: Bertrand Russell Peace Foundation. Address: Bertrand Russell House, Gamble Street, Nottingham NG7 4ET, England.

COBB Vicki, b. 19 Aug 1938, Brooklyn, NY, USA. Writer. Div, 2 s. Education: BA, Barnard College, 1958; MA, Columbia University. Publications include: Science Experiments You Can Eat, 1972; Lots of Rot, 1981; How to Really Fool Yourself, 1981; The Secret Life of School Supplies, 1981; Bet You Can't, Science Impossibilities to Fool You, 1981; Gobs to goo, 1983; The Monsters Who Died, 1983; Chemically Active, 1985; Inspector Bodyguard, 1986; The Science Safari Series; The Imagine Living Here Series; Inventions Series. Contributions to; Numerous Professrional Journals. Honours: Childrens Science Book Award, 1981; Washington Irving Childrens Book Choice Award, 1984; Eva L Gordon Award, 1985; Commended by COPUS and the London Science Museum, 1989. Memberships: Authors Guild; ASJA; Society of Childrens Book Writers; National Writers Union. Literary Agent: Christine Tomasino, RLR Associates Limited. Address: 302 Pondside Drive, White Plains, NY 10607, USA.

COBBAN Helena, b. England. m. (2)William B Quandt, 1 s, 2 d. Education: Oxford University. Appointments: Middle East Correspondent, Christian Science Monitor; Activist, Peace in Middle East. Publications: The Palestinian Liberation Organisation, 1984; The Making of Modern Lebanon, 1985; The Superpowers & The Syrian-Israeli Conflict, 1991. Honour: MacArthur Award. Address: 231844th Street NW, Washington, DC 20007, USA.

COBBETT Richard. See: **PLUCKROSE Henry Arthur.**

COBBING Bob, b. 1920, British. Poet. Appointments: Coordinator, Association of Little Presses, 1971-92; Co-editor, Poetry and Little Press Information, 1980-92. Publications include: Bill Jubobe: Selected Poems, 1942-75, 1976; Cygnet Ring: Collected Poems 1, 1977; A Movie Book, 1978; Two-Leaf Book, 1978 (with Peter Mayer), Concerning Concrete Poetry, 1978; Found: Sound, 1978; Principles of Movement, 1978; Meet Bournemouth, 1978; Fugitive Poem No X, 1978; Game and Set, 1978; Ginetics, 1978; ABC/Wan de Tree: Collected Poems 2, 1978; Sensations of the Retina, 1978; A Peal in Air: Collected Poems 3, 1978; Fiveways, 1978; Niagara, 1978; Grin, 1979; (with Jeremy Adler), A Short History of London, 1979; The Kollekted Kris Kringle: Collected Poems 4, 1979; Pattern of Performance, 1979; The Sacred Mushroom, 1980 (with Jeremy Adler); Notes from the Correspondence, 1980; Voicings 1980; (Soma), Light Song, 1981; Serial Ten (Portraits), 1981; Four Letter Poems, 2 series, 1981; Sound of Jade, 1982; In Line, 1982; Baker's Dozen, 1982; Lightsong Two, 1983; Bob Cobbing's Girlie Poems, Collected Poems 5, 1983; Sockless in Sandals: Collected Poems 6, 1985; Vowels and Consequences, Collected Poems 7, 1985; Lame, Limping, Mangled, Marred and Mutilated: Collected Poems 9, 1986; Metamorphosis, 1986; Variations on a Theme, 1986; Astound and Risible: Collected Poems 8, 1987; Processual, Collected Poems 10, 1987; Entitled: Entitled: Collected Poems 11, 1987; Improvisation is a Dirty Word: Collected Poems 12, 1990; Bob Jubile: Selected Poems 1944-90, 1990; Resonanzas, 1991; Grogram, 1991; Fuerteventura, 1992; Voice Prints: Collected Poems 13, 1993. Address: 89A Petherton Road, London N5 2QT, England.

COBURN Andrew, b. 1 May 1932, Exeter, New Hampshire, USA. Writer. Education: Suffolk University, Boston, 1954-58. Publications: Novels: The Trespassers, 1974; The Babysitter, 1979; Off Duty, 1980; Company Secrets, 1982; Widow's Walk, 1984; Sweetheart, 1985; Love Nest, 1987; Goldilocks, 1989; No Way Home, 1992; Voices in the Dark, 1994. Contributions to: Transatlantic Magazine. Honours: Honorary DLitt, Merrimack College, USA, 1986. Literary Agent: Smith/Skolnik, 23 East 10th Street No 712, New York, NY 10003, USA. Address: 3 Farrwood Drive, Andover, MA 01810, USA.

COCHRAN Jeff. See: **DURST Paul.**

COCKETT Mary, b. 1915, British Childrens Fiction and Non Fiction. Appointments: Editor, National Institute of Industrial Psychology, 1943-48, International Congress of Mental Health, 1948-49. Publications include: The Marvellous Stick, 1972; The Joppy Stories; Boat Girl, 1972; Bells in Our Lives, 1973; Treasure, 1973; The Rainbow Walk, 1973; Look at the Little One, 1974; Dolls and Puppets,

1974; Walls, 1974; Snake in the Camp, 1975; Tower Raven, 1975; Backyard Bird Hospital, 1975; The Story of Cars, 1976; The Drowning Valley, 1978; The Birthday, 1979; Ladybird at the Zoo, Monster in the River, Pig at the Market, 3 Picture Books, 1979; The Christmas Tree, 1979; Money to Spend, 1980; Shadow at Applegarth, 1981; Hoo Mings Discovery, 1982; The Cat and the Castle, 1982; The School Donkey, 1982; At The Tower, 1984; Crab Apples, 1984; Strange Hill, 1984; Zoo Ticket, 1985; Rescue at the Zoo, 1986; Winning All the Way, 1987; Kate of Candlewick, 1987; The Day of the Squirrels, 1987; A Place of his Own, 1987; Mystery on the Farm, 1988; Bridesmaids, 1989. Address: 24 Benville Avenue, Bristol, BS9 2RX, England.

CODRESCU Andrei, b. 20 Dec 1946, Rumania. Writer. m. Alice Henderson, 12 Sept 1969, 2 sons. Appointments: Professor, Louisiana State University, Baton Rouge, USA, 1986. Publications: The Hole in the Flag; Belligerence; The Disappearance of the Outside; Raised by Puppets; License to Carry a Gun; Life and Times of the Involuntary Genius; In America's Shoes; Comrade Past and Mr Present; Monsieur Teste in America; A Craving for Swan; Road Scholar: Coast to Coast Late in the Century, 1993; Zombification: Stories from National Public Radio, 1994. Contributions to: Numerous journals including: Harpers; The New York Times; The Paris Review; New American Writing; New Directions. Honours: Big Table Younger Poets Award; National Endowment for the Arts; Towson University Prize for Literature; Pushcart Prize; General Electric CCLM Poetry Prize. Memberships: Modern Language Association; PEN; Authors League. Literary Agent: Jonathon Lazear Inc, Minneapolis, MN. Address: English Department, Louisiana State University, Baton Rouge, LA 70803, USA.

CODY James. See: ROHRBACH Peter Thomas.

COE Jonathan, b. 19 Aug 1961, Birmingham, England. Novelist. m. Janine McKeown, 28 Jan 1989. Education: Trinity College, Cambridge, 1980-83; Warwick University, 1983-86. Publications: The Accidental Woman; A Touch of Love; The Dwarves of Death; Humphrey Bogart: Take it and Like It; James Stewart: Leading Man; What A Carve Up!. Contributions to: Guardian; London Review of Books; Wire; Spectator; Gegenwart; Sunday Times; Mail on Sunday; Times; Observer. Literary Agent: Tony Peake, Peake Associates. Address: c/o Peake Associates, 14 Grafton Crescent, London NW1 8SL, England.

COEN Ethan, b. 1958, MN, USA. Writer; Producer. m. Hilary, dec1985. Education: Princeton University. Appointments: Statistical Typist, Macys Dept Store, NY, 1979-80; Writer, Producer, Motion Pictures, 1980-. Publications: Screenplays, With Brother, Joel Coen, Blood Simple, Circle Releasing Corporation, 1984; The XYZ Murders, 1986; Raising Arizona, 1987; Millers Crossing, 1990. Honour: Grand Jury Prize from US Film Festival, 1984. Address: c/o Leading Artists, 445 North Bedford Drive, Penthouse, Beverly Hills, CA 90210, USA.

COEN Joel, b. 1955, MN, USA. Div. Education: NY University. Appointments: Writer, Director, Motion Pictures, 1980-; Production Assistant, Assistant Editor, Low Budget Horror Films. Publications: Screenplays, With Brother Ethan Coen, Blood Simple, 1984; The XYZ Murders, 1986; Raising Arizona, 1987; Millers Crossing, 1990. Honours: Grand Jury Prize from the US Film Festival, 1984; Independent Spirit Award, 1986. Address: c/o Leading Artists, 445 North Bedford Drive, Penthouse, Beverly Hills, CA 90210, USA.

COERR Eleanor Beatrice, (Elenor Hicks, Eleanor Page), b. 1922, USA. Writer. Appointments: Reporter, Editor, Edmonton Journal, 1944-49; Editor, Illustrator, Syndicated Weekly Column, Manila Times, 1958-61; Contract Writer, USIS in Taiwan, 1960-62; Voice of Am Special English Division, Washington TC, 1963-65; Librarian, David Library, MD, 1971-72. Publications include: Childrens Non Fiction, Circus Day in Japan, 1953; The Mystery of the Golden Cat, 1968; Twenty Five Dragons, 1971; Biography of Giant Panda, 1975; The Mixed Up Mystery Smell, 1975; Biography of a Red Kangaroo, 1976; Waza at Windy Gulch, 1977; The Big Balloon Race, 1980; The Bell Ringer and the Pirates, 1983; The Josefina Story Quilt, 1986; Lady with a Torch, 1985; Chang's Paper Pony, 1993.

COERS Donald Vernon, b. 2 June 1941, San Marcos, TX, USA. University Professor. m. 30 Dec 1966, 1 s, 1 d. Education: BA, 1963, MA, 1969, University of TX; PhD, TX A&M University, 1974. Appointments: Professor, Sam Houston State University, 1969-; Associate Editor, The TX Review, 1979. Publications: John Steinbeck as Propagandist: The Moon is Down Goes to War, 1991. Honours:

Elizabeth Agee Prize, 1990. Address: 3799 Summer Lane, Huntsville, TX 77340, USA.

COETZE John M, b. 9 Feb 1940, Cape Town, South Africa. Writer; Professor. 1 son, 1 daughter. Education: MA, University of Cape Town; PhD, University of Texas, USA. Appointments: Assistant Professor, English, State University of New York, Buffalo, 1968-71; Lecturer, English, University of Cape Town, 1972-82; Butler Professor of English, State University of New York, Buffalo, 1984, 1986; Professor of General Literature, University of Cape Town, 1984-; Hinkley Professor of English, Johns Hopkins University, 1986, 1989; Visiting Professor, English, Harvard University, 1991. Publications: Dusklands, 1974; In the Heart of the Country, 1977; Waiting for the Barbarians, 1980; Life and Times of Michael K, 1983; Foe, 1986; White Writing, 1988; Age of Iron, 1990; Doubling the Point, 1992; The Master of Petersburg, 1994. Contributions to: Essays in various journals. Honours: CNA Literary Award, 1977, 1980; James Tait Black Prize, 1980; Geoffrey Faber Award, 1980; CNA Literary Award, 1983; Booker McConnell Prize, 1983; Prix Femina Etranger, 1985; Jerusalem Prize, 1987; Sunday Express Award, 1990; Premio Mondello, 1994. Address: PO Box 92, Rondebosch, 7700, South Africa.

COFFEY Brian. See: KOONTZ Dean R.

COFFMAN Virginia, (Victor Cross, Virginia Du Vaul, Jeanne Duval, Anne Stanfield), b. 1914, America. Author. Appointments: Film Reviewer, Oakland Tribune, 1933-40; Secretary, Writer, Carious Film & TV Studios, 1944-56; Secretary, Office Manager, Chich Bennett Inc, 1956-66. Publications include: The Evil at Queens Priory, 1975; Survivor of Darkness, 1973; The Ice Forest, 1975; Marsanne, 1976; The Alpine Coach, 1976; Enemy of Love, 1977; Fire Dawn, 1977; The Gaynor Women, 1978; Looking Glass, 1979; Dinah Faire, 1979; The Lady Serena, 1979; Pacific Cavalcade, 1980; The Golden Marquerite, 1981; The Lombard Cavalcade, 1982; Dynasty of Desire, 1982; The Lombard Heiress, 1983; Dynasty of Dreams, 1984; The Orchid Tree, 1984; Dark Winds, 1985.

COGSWELL Frederick William, b. 1917, Canada. Professor; Author; Poet; Translator. Appointments: Assistant Professor, 1952-57, Associate Professor, 1957-61, Professor, 1961-, University of New Brunswick; Editor, Fiddlehead Magazine, 1952-66; Humanities Association Bulletin, 1967-72. Publications include: The Stunted Strong, 1955; The Haloed Tree, 1956; Testament of Cresseid, 1957; Descent from Eden, 1959; Lost Dimensions, 1960; A Canadian Anthology, 1960; Five New Brunswick Poets, 1962; The Arts in New Brunswick, 1966; Star People, 1968; Immortal Plowman, 1969; In Praise of Chastity, 1970; One Hundred Poems of Modern Quebec, 1971; The Chains of Liliput, 1971; The House Without a Door, 1973; Against Perspective, 1979; A Long Apprenticeship: Collected Poems, 1980; Selected Poems, 1980; Pearls, 1983; The Edge to Life, 1987; The Best Notes Merge, 1988; Unfinished Dreams Contemporary Poetry of Acadie, 1990. Address: Camp A6, Site 6, RR4, Fredericton, New Brunswick, Canada E3B 4X5.

COHAN Anthony Robert, (Tony), b. 28 Dec 1939, NY, USA. Writer. m. 1 June 1974, 1 d. Education: BA, University of CA, 1961. Publications: Nine Ships, 1975; Canary, 1981; The Flame, 1983; Opium, 1984. Honour: Notable Book of the Year, 1981. Memberships: Authors Guild; PEN. Literary Agent: Don Congdon, USA; Anthony Sheil, UK. Address: PO Box 480277 Los Angeles, CA 90048, USA.

COHEN Daniel E, b. 1936, USA. Childrens Non Fiction; Film; Supernatural, Occult Writer. Publications include: Young Adult Books, Southern Fried Rat and other Gruesome Tales, 1983; The Restless Dead, 1983; The Kids Guide to Home Computers, 1983; Teenage Stress, 1984; Masters of Horror, 1984; Henry Stanley and the Quest for the Source of the Nile, 1985; Wrestling Superstars, 1985, 1986; Heroes of the Challenger, 1986; Others Works, Mysterious Places, 1969; Biorhythms in Your Life, 1976; Close Encounters with God, 1979; The Great Airship Mystery, 1981; The Encyclopedia of Ghosts, 1984; Musicals, 1984; Horror Movies, 1984; A History of the Oscars, 1986; When Someone You Know is Gay, 1988; Zoos, 1992; Where to Find Dinosaurs Today, 1992; Ghosts of War, 1989; Railway Ghosts and Highway Horrors, 1991; What Kind of Dog is That, 1989. Membership: Authors Guild. Literary Agent: Henry Morrison Inc. Address: 24 Elizabeth Street, Port Jervis, NY 12771, USA.

COHEN Leonard, b. 21 Sept 1934, Montreal, Quebec, Canada. Novelist; Short Story Writer; Playwright/Screenplay Writer; Poet;

Songwriter/Lyricist; Professional Composer and Singer. Publications: Let Us Compare Mythologies, 1956; The Spice-Box of Earth, 1961; The Favourite Game, novel, 1963; Flowers for Hitler, 1964; Parasites of Heaven, 1966; Beautiful Losers, novel, 1966; Selected Poems, 1956-68, 1968; Leonard Cohen's Song Book, 1969; The Energy of Slaves, 1972; The Next Step, play, 1972; Sisters of Mercy: A Journey to the Worlds and Music of Leonard Cohen, 1973; Death of a Lady's Man, 1979; Two Views, poetry, 1980; Book of Mercy, poetry, 1984. Literary Agent: McClelland and Stewart Ltd, Canada. Address: McClelland and Stewart Ltd, 25 Hollinger Road, Toronto, Ontario, M4B 3G2, Canada.

COHEN Matthew, b. 30 Dec 1942, Kingston, Ontario, Canada. Novelist; Short Story Writer; Poet; Translator; Former Teacher. Publications: Korsoniloff, 1969; Johnny Crackle Sings, 1971; Columbus and the Fat Lady and Other Stories, 1972; Too Bad Galahad, short stories, 1972; The Disinherited, 1974; Peach Melba, poetry, 1975; The Colours of War, 1978; Night Flights: Stories New and Selected, 1978; The Sweet Second Summer of Kitty Malone, 1979; Flowers of Darkness, 1981; The Expatriate: Collected Short Stories, 1982; Cafe Le Dog, short stories, 1983; The Spanish Doctor, novel, 1984; Nadine, novel, 1986; Living on Water, stories, 1988; Emotional Arithmetic, novel, 1990. Membership: Chairman, The Writer's Union of Canada, 1985-86. Literary Agent: Bella Pomer Agency, Canada. Address: Bella Pomer Agency, 22 Shallmar Boulevard, PH2, Toronto, Ontario, M5N 2Z8, Canada.

COHEN Michael Joseph, b. 29 Apr 1940, London, England. Professor of History. Education: BA, History, 1969; PhD, Politics, 1971. Appointments: Professor, Bar Ilan University, Lecturer, 1972; Senior Lecturer, 1976; Professor, 1981. Publications: Palestine & The Great Powers; Churchill & The Jews; Truman & Israel; The Origins & Evolution of the Arab Zionist Conflict; Palestine: Retreat From the Mandate. Contributions to: Middle Eastern Studies; The Historical Journal; Studies in Zionism; Jerusalem Quarterly; The Jerusalem Post; Modern Judaism; Jewish Social Studies; Asian & African Studies. Memberships: The American Historical Association. Address: Department of General History, Bar Ilan University, Ramat Gan, 52100, Israel.

COHEN Morton Norton (John Moreton), b. 27 Feb 1921, Calgary, Canada. Professor; Lecturer; Author. Education: AB, Tufts University, USA; MA, Columbia University, 1950; PhD, 1958. Appointments include: Tutor to Professor, City College, 1952-81, Member, Doctoral Faculty, City College, 1964-81, Deputy Executive Officer, PhD Programme in English, 1976-78, 1979-80, Professor Emeritus, 1981-, City University of New York. Publications: Rider Haggard: His Life and Works, 1960, 2nd Revised Edition, 1968; A Brief Guide to Better Writing (co-author), 1960; Rudyard Kipling to Rider Haggard: The Record of a Friendship, 1965, 1968; Lewis Carroll's Photographs of Nude Children, 1978, republished as Lewis Carroll, Photographer of Children: Four Nude Studies, 1979; The Russian Journal II, 1979; Lewis Carroll and the Kitchins, 1980; Lewis Carroll and Alice 1832-1882, 1982; Lewis Carroll: Interviews and Recollections, 1989; Editor: The Letters of Lewis Carroll, 2 volumes, 1979; The Selected Letters of Lewis Carroll, 1982, 2nd Edition, 1990; Lewis Carroll and the House of Macmillan (co-editor), 1987. Contributions to: Many to numerous magazines, journals, papers and books including: The Times; Independent; New York Times Book Review; Kipling Journal; Dalhousie Review; Jabberwocky; Sundey Telegraph Magazine; Illustrated London News; Sydney Morning Herald; Harper's; Columbia Library Columns; Manuscripts. Honours include: Fulbright Fellow, 1954-55, 1974-75; Guggenheim Fellow, 1966-67; Research Grant, National Endowment for the Humanities, 1974-75; Publication Grant, Guggenheim Foundation, 1979. Memberships: Lewis Carroll Society; Lewis Carroll Society of North America; George MacDonald Society; Tennyson Society; Century Association, New York. Literary Agent: A P Watt Ltd, 20 John Street, London WC1N 2DR, England. Address: 72 Barrow Street, Apartment 3-N, New York, NY 10014, USA.

COHEN Stephen F, b. 25 Nov 1938, IN, USA. Professor; Writer; TV Commentator. Education: BS, 1960, MA, 1962, IN University; PhD, Columbia University, 1969. Publications include: Bukhatin and the Bolshevik Revolution, 1973; An End to Silence, 1982; Rethinking the Soviet Experience, 1985; The Soviet Union Since Stalin, 1980; Voices of Glasnost, 1989. Contributions to: Numerous Journals. Honours: Bukharin and the Bolshevik Revolution Nominated National Book Award, 1974; Newspaper Guild page One Award, 1985. Memberships:

AAASS; APSA; Council on Foreign Relations. Address: Dept of Politics, Princeton University, Princeton, NJ 08544, USA.

COHEN Susan (Elizabeth St Clair), b. 1938, USA. Author; Social Worker. m. Daniel Cohen. Publications include: Stonehaven, 1974; The Singing Harp, 1975; Secret of the Locket, 1975; Mansion in Minature, 1977; Dewitt House, 1977; The Jeweled Secret, 1978; Sandcastle Murder, 1979; With Daniel Cohen, The Kids Guide to Home Computers, 1983; Teenage Stress, 1984; Hollywood Hunks and Heros, 1985; A Six Pack and a Fake ID, 1986; A History of the Oscars, 1986; What Kind of Dog is That, 1989; Where to Find Dinosaurs Today, 1992. Address: 24 Elizabeth Street, Port Jervis, NY 12771, USA.

COHN Ruby, b. 1922, USA. Professor Emeritus. Appointments include: Currently Professor Emeritus of Comparative Drama, University of California, Davis. Publications: Samuel Beckett: The Comic Gamut, 1962; Currents in Contemporary Drama, 1969; Dialogue in American Drama, 1971; Back to Beckett, 1973; Modern Shakespeare Offshoots, 1976; Just Play: Beckett's Theatre, 1980; New American Dramatists, 1982, Revised Edition, 1991; Samuel Beckett Disjecta (editor), 1983; From Desire to Godot, 1987; Retreats from Realism in Recent English Drama, 1990; Anglo-American Interplay in Recent Drama, 1995. Address: Department of Dramatic Art, University of California, Davis, CA 95616, USA.

COHN Samuel Kline, b. 13 Apr 1949, History. Education: Union College, 1971; University of WI, 1972; Harvard University, 1978. Appointments: Harvard University Teacher, 1976-78; Weslayan University, 1978-79; Branders University, Assistance Professor, 1979; Associate Professor, 1985-; Professor, 1988-; Cisiting Professor, Brown University, 1990. Publications: The Laboring Classes in Renaissance Florence; Death and Property in Siena; Strategies for the After Life; The Cult of Remembrence; The Black Death; Six Cities in Central Italy. Honours: The Marraro Award. Memberships: Am Historical Association; Society for Italian Historical Studies. Address: History Dept, Branders University, Walthan, MA 02254, USA.

COLBECK Maurice, b. 21 Sept 1925, Batley, Yorkshire, England. Journalist. m. Brenda Barrowclough, 25 Mar 1950, 1 s, 1 d. Appointments: Reporter, Sub Editor, Various Yorkshire Newspapers; Assistant Editor, E J Arnold and Son Limited; Editor, Yorkshire Life, 1956-. Publications include: White Gods Fury; Four Against Crime; Jungle Rivals; Mosquitoes; How to be a Family Man, 1970; Yorkshire, 1976; Queer Fold, 1977; Yorkshire: The Dales, 1979; Queer Goings On, 1973; The Calendar Year, 1983; Village Yorkshire, 1987. Memberships: Society of Authors; Institute of Journalists. Address: Yorkshire Life, Lensett House, 45 Boroughgate, Otley, LS21 1AG, England.

COLBORN Nigel, b. 20 Feb 1944, England. Journalist; TV Presenter; Author; Gardener. m. Rosamund F M Hewlett, 10 Nov 1972, 2 sons, 2 daughters. Education: King's School, Ely, Cambs, England; BSc, Cornell University, USA. Publications: This Gardening Business (Humour), 1989; Leisurely Gardening (Gardening), 1989; The Classic Horticulturist (Garden History), 1987; Family Piles (Humour), 1990; The Container Garden (Conran Octopus), 1990; Short Cuts to Great Gardens, 1993; Annuals and Bedding Plants, 1994; The Good Old Fashioned Gardener, 1993; The Kirkland Acres (novel), 1994. Contributions to: Gardening and rural press, including New York Times, Country Life, Homes and Gardens, Hortus, The Garden; BBC Gardeners' World Magazine; Sunday Telegraph; Country Homes. Memberships: Society of Authors; Royal Horticultural Society, Member of Standing Committee; Hardy Plant Society; Alpine Garden Society; International PEN. Literary Agent: Laurence Pollinger (Juliet Burton), 18 Maddox Street, London. Address: Careby Manor, Careby, Stamford, Lincolnshire PE9 4EA, England.

COLE Adrian Christopher Synnot, b. 22 July 1949, Plymouth, England. Local Government Officer; Author. m. 25 May 1977, 1 s, 1 d. Publications include: The Dream Lords, 1975; Madness Emerging, 1976; Paths in Darkness, 1977; The Lucifer experiment, 1981; The Sleep of Giants, 1984; A Place Among the Fallen, 1986; The God in Anger, 1988; Mother of Storms, 1989; Thief of Dreams, 1989; Warlord of Heven, 1990; Labyrinth of Worlds, 1990. Contributions to: Numerous Magazines & Journals. Membership: British Fantasy Society. Literary Agent: Abner Stein. Address: The Old Forge, 35 Meddon Street, Bideford, Devon, Ex39 2EF, England.

COLE Barry, b. 13 Nov 1936. Writer. m. Rita Linihan, 1959, 3 daughters. Literary Appointments: Northern Arts Fellow in Literature, Universities of Durham and Newcastle-upon-Tyne, England, 1970-72. Publications: Blood Ties, 1967; Ulysses in the Town of Coloured Glass, 1968; A Run Across the Island, 1968; Moon Search, 1968; Joseph Winter's Patronage, 1969; The Search for Rita, 1970; The Visitors, 1970; The Giver, 1971; Vanessa in the City, 1971; Pathetic Fallacies, 1973; The Rehousing of Scaffardi; Dedications, 1977; The Edge of the Common, 1989. Contributions to: Numerous Publications including: New Statesman; Spectator; The Listener; Times Educational Supplement; Times Higher Educational Supplement; Critical Survey Atlantic Monthly; Tribune; London Magazine; Transatlantic Review; The Observer; The Guardian. Address: 68 Myddelton Square, London EC1R 1XP, England.

COLE Jackson. See: **GERMANO Peter B.**

COLE Joanna, b. 1944. Publications: Cockroaches, 1971; Twins, 1972; A Calf is Born, 1975; A Frog's Body, 1980; A Horse's Body, 1981; Anna Banana: 101 Jump-Rope Rhymes, 1989; Ready, Set, Read!, 1990; Don't Tell the Whole World, 1990; The Magic School Bus, Lost in the Solar System, 1990; Who Put the Pepper in the Pot?, 1992; Gator Girls, 1995; My New Kitten, 1995; Spider's Lunch, 1995. Honour: Milner Award, 1994.

COLE John Morrison, b. 23 Nov 1927, Belfast, Northern Ireland. Journalist; Broadcaster. m. Margaret Isobel Williamson, 4 Sept 1956, 4 s. Eduction: London University, 1952. Publications: The Poor of the Earth, 1976; The Thatcher Years, 1987. Contributions to: Various Books; Observer; Listener. Membership: Athenaeum Club. Address: c/o BBC Office, House of Commons, Westminister, London SW1A 0AA, England.

COLE William, b. 1919. Childrens Non Fiction Writer; Book Reviewer. Publications include: The Best Cartoons from Punch, 1952; the Best Humor from Punch, 1953; Women are Wonderful: A Cartoon History, 1954; Humerous Poetry for Children, 1955; The Poetry Drawing Book, 1956; Poems Old and New, 1957; I Went to the Animal Fair, 1958; Poems of Magic and Spells, 1960; Folk Songs of England, Ireland, Scotland & Wales; The Birds and the Beasts Were there, 1963; A Big Bowl of Punch, 1964; Oh What Nonsense, 1966; D H Lawrence Poems Selected for Young People, 1967; Whats Good for a Four Year Old, 1967; Whats Good for a Five Year Old, 1968; Pith and Vinegar, 1969; Aunt Bella Umbrella, 1970; Pick Me Up, 1971; Poems from Ireland, 1972; A Boy Named Mary Jane: Nonsense Verse, 1975; Knock Knocks You've Never Heard Before, 1977; Im Mad At You, 1978; The Poetry of Horses, 1979; Good Dog Poems, 1980; Poem Stew, 1981. Address: 201 West 54th Street, New York, NY 10019, USA.

COLEGATE Isabel Diana, b. 10 Sept 1931, London, England. Novelist. m. Michael Briggs, 12 Sept 1953, 2 sons, 1 daughter. Education: Runton Hill School, Norfolk, England. Appointment: Literary Agent, Anthony Blond (London) Ltd, 1952-57. Publications: The Blackmailer, 1958; A Man of Power, 1960; The Great Occasion, 1962; Statues in a Garden, 1964; Orlando King, 1968; Orlando at the Brazen Threshold, 1971; Agatha, 1973; News from the City of the Sun, 1979; The Shooting Party, 1980 (filmed 1985); A Glimpse of Sion's Glory, 1985; Deceits of Time, 1988; The Summer of the Royal Visit, 1991; Winter Journey, 1995. Honours: Fellow, Royal Society of Literature, 1981; W H Smith Literary Award, 1981; Honorary MA, University of Bath, 1988. Memberships: Author's Society. Literary Agent: Peters Fraser & Dunlop. Address: Midford Castle, Bath BA1 7BU, England.

COLEMAN Jane (Winthrop) Candia, b. 9 Jan 1939, Pittsburgh, Pennsylvania, USA. Writer. m. (1) Bernard D Coleman, div. 1989, (2) Glenn G Bouer, 1989, 2 sons. Education: BA, University of Pittsburgh, 1961. Appointments: Lecturer, University of Pittsburgh, 1981; Writer-in-Residence, Carlow College, Pittsburgh, 1980-85; Director, Women's Creative Writing Center, Carlow College, 1985-86. Publications: Stories from Mesa Country; No Roof But Sky; Deep In His Heart JR Is Laughing At Us; Discovering Eve; Shadows In My Hands, 1993; Doc Holliday's Woman, 1995. Contributions to: The Christian Science Monitor; Horseman; Puerto Del Sol; South Dakota Review; The Pennsylvania Review; Yankee; The Aqassiz Review; Snowy Egret. Honours: Writing Grant, Pennsylvania Council on the Arts; Western Heritage Award, Poetry, Short Fiction; Grant, Arizona Arts Commission, 1993; Spur Award, Western Writers of America, 1993. Memberships: Western Writers of America; The Authors Guild; PEN.

Literary Agent: Susan Crawford. Address: PO Box 40, Rodeo, NM 88056, USA.

COLEMAN Robert Gordon, b. 17 July 1922, Beechworth, Victoria, Australia. Journalist; Author. m. Lilian Gill, 4 June 1949, 1 daughter. Appointments: Working Journalist (reporter, feature writer, cadet counsellor, columnist, leader writer), 1940-86; Freelance Journalist and Author, 1986-. Publications: Reporting for Work (editor), 1970; The Pyjama Girl, 1978; Above Renown, 1988; Seasons in the Sun, 1993. Honours: Australian Automobile Association National Journalism Award, 1967; Highly Commended, Graham Perkin Award for Journalist of the Year, 1980. Memberships: Australian Journalists Association (Honorary); Victorian Fellowship of Australian Writers. Address: 34 Folkstone Crescent, Beaumaris, Victoria 3193, Australia.

COLEMAN Terry, b. 13 Feb 1931, Bournemouth, England. Reporter and Author. Education: LLB, London University, England. Appointments: Reporter, Poole Herald; Editor, Savoir Faire; Sub-editor, Sunday Mercury; Sub-editor, The Birmingham Post; Reporter, Arts Correspondent and then Chief Feature Writer, The Guardian 1961-74; Special Writer, Daily Mail, 1974-76; Special Correspondent, The Guardian, 1976-79, New York Correspondent, 1980-81, Special Correspondent, 1982-89; Associate Editor, The Independent, 1989-91; Columnist, The Guardian and Mail on Sunday, 1992-. Publications: The Railway Navvies, 1965; Providence and Mr Hardy (with Lois Deacon), 1966; The Only True History, 1969; Passage to America, 1971; The Liners, 1976; Southern Cross, 1979; The Scented Brawl, 1979; Thanksgiving, 1981; Movers and Shakers, 1987; Thatcher's Britain, 1987; Empire, 1994. Honours: Yorkshire Post Prize, Best First Book of Year, 1965; Feature Writer of the Year, British Press Awards, 1982; Journalist of the Year, Granada Awards, 1988. Literary Agent: Peters, Fraser, Dunlop. Address: c/o A D Peters, The Chambers, Chelsea Harbour, London SW10 0XF, England.

COLERIDGE Nicholas David, b. 4 Mar 1957, London, England. Journalist; Author. m. Georgia Elizabeth Metcalfe, 22 July 1989, 2 sons. Education: Trinity College, Cambridge; Eton College. Literary Appointments: Editor, Harpers & Queen Magazine, 1986-89; Managing Director, Conde Nast Publications, 1992-; Editorial Director, 1989-91. Publications: Tunnel Vision, 1981; Around the World in 78 Days, 1984; Shooting Stars, 1984; The Fashion Conspiracy, 1988; How I Met My Wife and Other Stories, 1991; Paper Tigers, 1993. Contributions to: Harpers & Queen; Spectator; Sunday Telegraph; Tatler; Evening Standard (1982-85); GQ; Vanity Fair. Honour: Young Journalist of the Year, 1983. Literary Agent: Leslie Gardner. Address: 24 Chepstow Crescent, London W11 3EB, England.

COLES Donald Langdon, b. 12 Apr 1928, Woodstock, Ontario, Canada. Professor. m. 28 Dec 1958, 1 son, 1 daughter. Education: BA, Victoria College; MA, University of Toronto; MA (Cantab), 1954. Literary appointments: Fiction Editor, The Canadian Forum, 1975-76; Director, Creative Writing Programme, York University, 1979-85; Poetry Editor, May Studio, Banff Centre for the Fine Arts, 1984-93. Publications: Sometimes All Over, 1975; Anniversaries, 1979; The Prinzhorn Collection, 1982; Landslides, 1986; Poetry books: K in Love, 1987; Little Bird, 1991; Forests of the Medieval World, 1993; Someone Has Stayed in Stockholm. Selected and New Poems, 1994. Contributions to: Saturday Night; Canadian Forum; London Review of Books; Poetry (Chicago); Globe and Mail; Arc; Ariel. Honours: CBC Literary Competition, 1980; Gold Medal for Poetry, National Magazine Awards, 1986; Governor General's Award for Poetry, Canada, 1993. Membership: PEN International. Address: 122 Glenview Avenue, Toronto, Ontario, Canada M4R 1P8.

COLES Robert, b. 12 Oct 1929, USA. Physician; Teacher; Writer. m. Jane Hallowell, 3 sons. Education: AB, English, Harvard College, 1950; MD, College of Physicians and Surgeons, Columbia University, 1954; Internship, University of Chicago Clinics, 1954-55; Psychiatric Residency, McLean Hospital, 1956-57. Literary appointments: Contributing Editor: The New Republic, 1966-; American Poetry Review, 1972-; Aperture, 1974-; Literature and Medicine, 1981-; New Oxford Review, 1981-. Publications: Children of Crisis, 5 volumes, 1967, 1972, 1978; The Middle Americans, 1970; The Geography of Faith, 1971; The Old Ones of New Mexico, 1973; William Carlos Williams, 1975; Walker Percy, 1978; Flannery O'Connor's South, 1980; The Moral Life of Children, 1986; The Political Life of Children, 1986; Simone Weil, 1987; Dorothy Day, 1987; The Call of Stories: Teaching and the Moral Imagination, 1989. Contributions to: The Atlantic Monthly; The New Yorker; New York Times Book Review. Honours:

Atlantic Grant, 1966; McAlpin Medal, 1972; Weatherford Prize, 1973; Lillian Smith Award, 1973; Pulitzer Prize, 1973; MacArthur Prize, 1981. Address: 81 Carr Road, Concord, MA 01742, USA.

COLLIER Catrin. See: **WATKINS Karen Christna.**

COLLIER Jane. See: **COLLIER Zena.**

COLLIER Peter (Anthony), b. 1939, USA. Writer; Editor. Appointments: Professor, Dept of English, University of CA, 1963-67; Executive Editor, Ramparts Magzine, CA, 1967-72; Consulting Editor, CA Magazine, 1981-. Publications: Justice Denied, 1971; When Shall They Rest, 1973; The Rockefellers: An American Dynasty, 1976; Downriver, 1978; The Kennedys: An American Drama, 1984; The Fords: Am American Epic, 1988; Second Thoughts: Former Radicals Look Back at the 60's, 1989; Deconstructing the Left: From Vietnam to Persian Gulf, 1991; The Fondas, 1992; Proust & Venice, 1989. Address: 12294 Willow Valley Road, Nevada City, CA 95959, USA.

COLLIER Richard Hughesdon, b. 8 Mar 1924, London, England. Author. m. Patricia Eveline Russell, 24 July 1953. Education: Whitgift School, Croydon, England. Appointments: Associate Editor, Phoenix Magazine for the Forces, SE Asia, 1945-46; Editor, Town and Country Magazine, 1946-48; Features Staff, Daily Mail, 1948-49. Publications: Ten Thousand Eyes, 1958; The Sands of Dunkirk, 1961; The General Next to God, 1965; Eagle Day, 1966; Duce! 1971; Bridge Across the Sky, 1978; The City That Wouldn't Die, 1959; 1940: The World in Flames, 1979; 1941: Armageddon, 1981; The War That Stalin Won, 1983; The Rainbow People, 1984; The Warcos, 1989; The Few (co-author), 1989; D-Day: 6 June 1944, 1992. Contributions to: Reader's Digest; Holiday; The Times. Honour: Knight of Mark Twain, 1972. Memberships: Author's Guild of America; Author's League of America; Society of Theatre Research; Society of Authors. Literary Agent: Curtis Brown. Address: c/o Curtis Brown and John Farquharson, 162/168 Regent Street, London W1R 5TB, England.

COLLIER Zena, (Jane Collier, Zena Shumsky), b. 21 Jan 1926, London, England. Writer. m. (1) Louis Shumsky, 2 sons (1 dec), (2) Thomas M Hampson, 30 Dec 1969. Literary Appointments: Writer-in-Residence: Just Buffalo, 1984-; Southern Tier Library System, Corning, NY, 1985-; Niagara Erie Writers, Buffalo, NY, 1986; Teacher, Writers Workshop, Nazareth College, Rochester, NY. Publications: Novels: A Cooler Climate, 1990; Ghost Note, 1992; Children's books: as Zena Collier: Next Time I'll Know; Seven For The People - Public Interest Groups At Work; as Jane Collier: The Year of the Dream; A Tangled Web; as Zena Shumsky with Lou Shumsky: First Flight; Shutterbug. Contributions to: Southern Humanities Review; Southwest Review; Prairie Schooner; McCalls; Alfred Hitchcock's Mystery Magazine; Literary Review; New Letters; Upstate; Ford Times. Honours: Hoepfner Prize; Citation on Honour Roll of Best American Short Stories; Nomination for Pushcart Prize; Resident Fellow: Yaddo, Macdowell, Virginia Center for the Creative Arts, Alfred University Summer Place. Memberships: Authors Guild; Writers and Books; Poets and Writers. Literary Agent: Harvey Klinger. Address: 83 Berkeley Street, Rochester, NY 14607, USA.

COLLINGS Michael Robert, b. 28 Oct 1947, Ruppert, ID, USA. Professor. m. Judith Lynn Reeve, 21 Dec 1973, 2 s, 2 d. Education: AA, Bakersfield College, 1967; BA, Whittier College, 1969; MA, University of CA, 1973; PhD, 1977. Publications include: A Season of Calm Weather; Stephen King As Richard Bachman; The Films of Stephen King; Piers Anthony; Naked to the Sun; Dark Transformations; In the Image of God; The Work of Orson Scott Card: Annotated Bibliography and Guide, 1993; The Work of Stephen King: Annotated Bibliography and Guide, 1993. Contributions to: Christinity & Literature; Cuyahoga Review; Extrapolation; Expressionists; The Leading Edge; Dialogue; Sunstone; Zarahelma; Wasatch Review; Star Line; Poet; New Era; CA State Poetry Journal. Honours: Triton College Salute to the Arts; Williams Contest, Winner; Rhysling Nominee; Nebula Recommendation; CA State Poetry Contest, 1st Place; Best Winner SPWAO. Memberships: Science Fiction Research Association; Science Fiction Poetry Association. Address: 1089 Sheffield Place, Thousand Oaks, CA 91360 5353, USA.

COLLINS Hunt. See: **LOMBINO Salvatore A.**

COLLINS Jackie, b. England. Novelist; Short Story Writer; Actress. m. Oscar Lerman. Publications: The World is full of Married Men, 1968; The Stud, 1969; Sunday Simmons and Charlie Brick, 1971;

Sinners, 1981; Lovehead, 1974; The Love Killers, 1977; The World is full of Divorced Women, 1975; Lovers & Gamblers, 1977; The Bitch, 1979; Chances, 1981; Hollywood Wives, 1983; Lucky, 1985; Hollywood Husbands, 1986; Rock Star, 1988; Lady Boss, 1990; American Star, 1993; The World is Full of Married Men, 1993. Address: c/o Simon and Schuster, 1230 Avenue of the Americas, New York, NY 10020, USA.

COLLINS James Lee (Jim), b. 30 Dec 1945, Beloit, WI, USA. Author; Editor. m. Joan Hertel, 27 Dec 1974, 2 s. Appointments: Contributing Editor, Encyclopedia USA, 1982. Publications include: Western Writers Handbook, 1987; Sonny, 1987; Spencers Revenge, 1987; Mister Henry, 1986; The Brass Boy, 1987; Gone to Texas, 1984; Comanche Trail, 1984; War Clouds, 1984; Riding Shotgun, 1985; Orphans Preferred, 1985; Campaigning, 1985; Settling the American West, 1993. Contributions to: The Blue and the Gray; Writers Digest Magazine. Memberships: National Writers Club; Western Writers of Am; Colorado Authors League. Literary Agent: Ray Peekner. Address: c/o NWC 194500 S Havana St, Suite 620, Aurora, CO 80014, USA.

COLLINS Larry, b. 1929, USA. Author. Appointments: Correspondent, UPI, Paris, Rome and Beirut, 1957-59; Middle East Correspondent, Newsweek magazine, Beirut, Lebanon, 1959-61; Bureau Chief, Newsweek magazine, Paris, France, 1961-65. Publications: Author with D Lapierre: Is Paris Burning, 1965; Or I'll Dress You im Mourning, 1968; O Jerusalem, 1972; Freedom at Midnight, 1975; The Fifth Horseman, novel, 1980; Fall from Grace, 1985; Maze, 1989. Address: c/o Simon and Schuster, 1230 Avenue of the Americas, New York, NY 10020, USA.

COLLINS Max Allen, b. 3 Mr 1948, Muscatine, IA, USA. Writer. m. Barbara Jane Mull, 1 June 1968, 1 s. Education: AA, Muscatine Community College, 1966-68; BA, 1970, MFA, 1972, University of IA. Appointments: Instructor, Muscatine Community College, 1971-77; Professor, University of IA, 1989-; Workshop Leader, Mississippi Valley Writers Conference, Augustana College, 1973-. Publications include: True Detective, 1983; True Crime, 1984; Neon Mirage, 1988; The Dark City, 1987; A Shroud for Aquarius, 1985; Author of 6 Novels in Nolan Series including, Bait Money, 1973; 5 Novels in Quarry Series; 4 Additional Mallory Mysteries; 3 Additional Eliot Ness Novels. Contributions to: Comic Strip, Dick Tracy, 1977-93; Movie Critic, Mystery Scene Magazine, 1985; Writer, Co Cretor, Ms Tree Comic Book, 1983; Numerous Short Stories and Articles. Honours: Inkpot Award, 1982; Private Eye Writers of Am Shamus for Best Novel of 1983, 1991; Distinguished Alumnus Award, 1984; Edgar Allen Poe Speical Award, 1985. Memberships: Mystery Writers of Am; Private Eye Writers of Am; Am Crime Writers League. Literary Agent: Dominick Abel. Address: 301 Fairview Avenue, Muscatine, IA 52761, USA.

COLLINS Michael. See: **LYNDS Dennis.**

COLLINS Philip Arthur William, b. 1923, United Kingdom. Appointments: Warden, Vaughan College, 1954-62; Senior Lecturer 1962-64, Professor of English 1964-82, University of Leicester; Member, Board of Directors, The National Theatre, 1976-82. Publications: James Boswell, 1956; English Christmas (editor), 1956; Dickens and Crime, 1962; Dickens and Education, 1963; The Impress of the Moving Age, 1965; Thomas Cooper the Chartist: Byron and the Poets of the Poor, 1969; A Dickens Bibliography, 1970; Dickens: A Christmas Carol: The Public Reading Version, 1971; Bleak House: A Commentary, 1971; Dickens: The Critical Heritage (editor), 1971; Reading Aloud: A Victorian Metier, 1972; Charles Dickens: The Public Readings (editor), 1975; Charles Dickens: David Copperfield, 1977; Charles Dickens: Hard Times (editor), 1978; Dickens: Interviews and Recollections (editor), 1981; Thackeray: Interviews and Recollections (editor), 1982; Tennyson, Poet of Lincolnshire, 1985; The Annotated Dickens (edited with Edward Giuliano), 1986; Tennyson: SevenEssays (editor), 1992. Contributions to: Encyclopedia Britannica; Listener; Times Literary Supplement. Address: 26 Knighton Drive, Leicester LE2 3HB, England.

COLLIS Louise Edith, b. 29 Jan 1925, Burma. Writer. Education: BA History, Reading University, England, 1945. Publications: Without a Voice, 1951; A Year Passed, 1952; After the Holiday, 1954; The Angel's Name, 1955; Seven in the Tower, 1958; The Apprentice Saint, 1964; Solider in Paradise, 1965; The Great Flood, 1966; A Private View of Stanley Spencer, 1972; Maurice Collis Diaries (Editor), 1976; Impetuous Heart, the story of Ethel Smyth, 1984. Contributions to: Books and Bookmen; Connoissaur; Art and Artists; Arts Review; Collectors Guide; Art and Antiques; and others. Memberships:

Societyof Authors; International Association of Art Critics. Address: 65 Cornwall Gardens, London SW7, England.

COLLOMS Brenda, (Brenda Cross, Brenda Hughes), b. 1919, United Kingdom. Writer. Appointments: Editor, The Film Star Diary, Cramp Publishers, London, 1948-63. Publications: Happy Ever After (as Brenda Cross), 1947; The Film Hamlet (as Brenda Cross), 1948; New Guinea Folk Tales (as Brenda Hughes), 1959; Folk Tales from Chile (as Brenda Hughes), 1962; Certificate History, Books 1-4: Britain and Europe, 1966-70; Israel, 1971; The Mayflower Pilgrims, 1973; Charles Kingsley, 1975; Victorian Country Parsons, 1977; Victorian Visionaries, 1982; (as Brenda Colloms) The Making of Tottie Fox. Address: 123A Gloucester Avenue, London NW1 8LB, England.

COLMAN E Adrian M, b. 1930, Scotland. Professor Emeritus. Appointments: Lecturer in English 1962-70, Senior Lecturer 1970-74, Associate Professor 1974-78, University of Sydney, New South Wales; Reseach Associate, The Shakespeare Institute, University of Birmingham, England, 1968-69; Professor of English, University of Tasmania, Hobart, 1978-90; Chairman of Board, Australian Theatre for Young People, 1975-78. Publications: Shakespeare's Julius Caesar, 1965; The Structure of Shakespeare's Antony and Cleopatra, 1971; The Dramatic Use of Bawdy in Shakespeare, 1974; Poems of Sir Walter Raleigh (editor), 1977; King Lear (editor), 1982; Henry IV Part I (editor), 1987; Romeo and Juliet (editor), 1993. Address: Department of English, University of Tasmania, Box 252C, GPO, Hobart, Tasmania 7001, Australia.

COLOMBO Furio Marco, b. 1 Jan 1931, Chatillon, Italy. Journalist; Writer. m. Alice Oxman, 16 Aug 1969, 1 daughter. Education: Law Degree, University of Turin. Appointments: Editor, Communicazione Visiva University of Bologna, 1970-77; Communicazioni di Massa Milan, 1979-84; Sanpaolo Chair, International Journalism, Graduate School of Journalism, Columbia University, 1991. Publications include: Nuovo Teatro Americano, 1963; L'America di Kennedy, 1964; Le Donne Matte, 1964; Il Prigioniero della Torre Velasca, Racconti, 1965; Latest publications include: Cosa Faro da Grande, 1986; Giovanni Verga, in European Writers, Essay, 1985; Carriera: Vale Una Vita Rizzoli, 1989; Il Destino Del Libro E Altri Destini, Bollati, 1990; Il Terzo Dopoguerra, Rizzoli, 1990; Scene Da Una Vittoria, Leonardo, 1991; Oer Israele, Rizzoli, 1991; La Citta Profona, Feltrinelli, 1991. Contributions to: Various journals including: Li Mondo, Rome; L'Expresso, Rome; Ulisse, Rome; Il Caffe, Rome; Bianco e Nero, Rome; Il Menabo, Turin; Revista di Estrtica, University of Turin; L'Editore, Turin; New York Review of Books; Enciclopedia Garzanti; Atlante Geografico De Agostini; Enciclopedia Europea Garzanti, 1980; Political Science Quarterly; L'Europeo, 1990-91; Panorama, 1991; La Stampa, 1972. Honours: Trumball Lecturer, Yale University, USA, 1964; Chair, Italian Culture, University of California, Berkeley, 1975; Tevere Prize for Literature, Rome, 1986; Amalfi Prize for Best TV Documentary; Capri Prize for Journalism; Board Director, Agnelli Foundation, Turin, 1991; Board Director, La Stampa Newspaper, Turin, 1991. Memberships include: Scientific Committee, Pio Manzu International Research Centre; Secretary, Friends of Palazzo Grassi Committee, Venice; Board of Visitors, Columbia University, New York. Address: 444 Madison Avenue, Suite 2109, New York, NY 10022, USA.

COLOMBO John Robert, b. 24 Mar 1936, Kitchener, Ontario, Canada. Author; Editor; Communications Consultant. m. Ruth Colombo, 3 children. Appointments: Keynote Speaker, Conference, Russian Academy of Sciences, 1993. Publications: Author, compiler or translator of 82 separate books, quote books, reference books, humour and lore, compilations, including: The Poets of Canada, 1978; Colombo's Names and Nicknames, 1979; Colombo's Hollywood, 1979; Poems of the Inuit, 1981; Colombo's Canadiana Quiz Book, 1983; Great Moments in Canadian History, 1984; We Stand on Guard (co-author), 1985; 1001 Questions About Canada, 1986; Colombo's New Canadian Quotations, 1987; The Dictionary of Canadian Quotations, 1991; Walt Whitman's Canada, 1992; The Little Blue Book of UFO's, 1993; The Canadian Global Almanac; Editor, over 100 books for Canadian publishing houses, 1960-80; Columnist. Contributions to: Canadian Encyclopaedia; Oxford Companion to Canadian Literature; Various journals and radio programmes. Honours include: Best Paperback of the Year, Periodical Distributors of Canada, 1976; Guest, Writers Union, USSR, Rumania, Bulgaria; 1st Writer-in-Residence, Mohawk College, 1979-80; Certificate of Merit, Ontario Library Association; Centennial Medal, Esteeemed Knight of Mark Twain; Order of Cyril and Methodius, 1st Class; Literary Prize, Philips

Informations Systems, 1985. Address: 42 Dell Park Avenue, Toronto, Ontario, Canada M6B 2T6.

COLQUHOUN Keith, b. 5 Aug 1933, London, England. Novelist; Journalist. 3 sons, 3 daughters. Appointments: Asian Affairs Writer, The Economist, 1980-. Publications: The Money Tree, 1958; Point of Stress, 1960; The Sugar Coating, 1973; St Petersburg Rainbow, 1975; Goebbels and Gladys, 1981; Filthy Rich, 1982; Kiss of Life, 1983; Foreign Wars, 1985; Mad Dog, 1992. Address: 8 Meadow Lane, West Mersea, Essex, England.

COLT Clem. See: **NYE Nelson.**

COLTON James. See: **HANSEN Joseph.**

COLVIN Howard Montagu, b. 15 Oct 1919, Sidcup, Kent, England. Historian. m. Christina Edgeworth Butler, 16 Aug 1943, 2 sons. Education: BA, University College, London, 1940; MA, Oxford University, 1948. Publications: A Biographical Dictionary of British Architects 1600-1840, 1978; Unbuilt Oxford, 1983; Calke Abbey, Derbyshire, 1985; The History of the King's Works (General Editor and Part Author), 6 volumes, 1963-82; The White Canons in England, 1951; A History of Deddington, 1963; Catalogue of Architectural Drawings in Worcester College Library, 1964; The Canterbury Quadrangle: St John's College, Oxford, 1988; (With J S G Simmons), All Souls: An Oxford College and its Buildings, 1989; Architecture and the After-Life, 1991. Contributions to: Architectural Review; Archaeological Journal; Country Life. Address: 50 Plantation Road, Oxford OX2 6JE, England.

COLWELL Maxwell Gordon, b. 10 Oct 1926, Brompton, South Australia. Author. m. Betty Joy Holthouse, 27 Nov 1948, 2 sons. Appointments: Journalist, The Young Australian, 1960-62. Publications: Half Days and Patched Pants; Full Days and Pressed Pants; Glorious Days and Khaki Pants; Whaling Around Australia; Voyages of Matthew Flinders; The Journey of Birke Wills; Others in Big Rivers; Lights Vision the City of Adelaide. Contributions to: The Bulletin. Honours: Australian Council Literature Board Senior Fellowship. Membership: Australian Society of Authors. Address: 102 8th Avenue Joslin, South Australia 5070, Australia.

COMAROFF John L, b. 1 Jan 1945, Cape Town, South Africa. Professor. m. Jean Rakoff, 15 Jan 1967, 1 s, 1 d. Education: BA, University of Cape Town, 1966; PhD, University of London, 1973. Appointments: Lecturer, University of Manchester, 1972-78; Professor, University of Chicago, 1987; Director, Ecole des Hautes Studies en Sciences Socials, Paris, 1988; Senior Research Fellow, Am Bar Foundation, 1991; Chairman, University of Chicago, 1991. Publications include: Of Revalation and Revolution; Rules & Process; African Context; The Diary of Sol t Plaatje; An African At Mafekinn; Essays on African Marrige in Southern Africa; Modernity & Its Malcontents: Ritual and Power in Post-Colonial Africa, 1993. Contributions to: Am Ethnologist; Journal of Southern African Studies; Journal of Historical Sociology; Man; Journal of African Law; Thnos; Economy & Society. Memberships: Association of Political & Legal Anthropology; Association of Social Anthropologist; Am Anthropological Association; Royal Anthropological Institute. Address: University of Chicago, Dept of Anthropology, 1126 E 59th Street, Chicago, IL 60637, USA.

COMFORT Alex(ander), b. 10 Feb 1920. Physician; Poet; Novelist. Appointments: Consultant Psychiatrist, Brentwood Veterans Hospital, Los Angeles, California, USA, 1973-89; Lecturer in Psychiatry, Stanford University, California, 1974-81; Fellow, Institute for Higher Studies, Santa Barbara, California, 1975-80; Professor of Pathology, University of California School of Medicine, Irvine, 1976-79; and Adjunct Professor, University of California at Los Angeles, 1979-91; House Physician, London Hospital, 1944; Resident Medical Officer, Royal Waterloo Hospital, 1944-45; Lecturer in Physiology, 1945-51; Honorary Research Associate, Department of Zoology, 1951-73; Director of Medical Research Council Group on the Biology of Ageing, 1966-70, and Director of Research in Gerontology, 1970-73, University College, London. Publications include: The Silver Ring, 1936; The Power House, 1945; On This Side Nothing (novel), 1949; The Right Thing to Do, Together with the Wrong Thing to Do, 1949; Authority and Delinquency in the Modern State: A Criminal Approach to the Problem of Power, 1950; Sexual Behavior in Society, 1950, as Sex in Society, 1963; And All But He Departed (poetry), 1951; Delinquency (lecture), 1951; Art and Social Responsibility, 1952; A Giant's Strength (novel), 1952; The Biology of Senescence, 1953, as Ageing: The Biology of Senescence, 1964, 1979; Darwin and the

Naked Lady: Discursive Essays on Biology and Art, 1961; Come Out to Play (novel), 1964; (translation), The Koka Shastra, 1964; The Nature of Human Nature, 1965; in UK as Nature and Human Nature, 1966; The Anxiety Makers: Some Curious Preoccupations of the Medical Profession, 1967; (ed) History of Erotic Art, vol I 1969; What Rough Beast? and What is a Doctor? (lectures), 1971; The Joy of Sex: A Gourmet's Guide to Love Making, 1973; More Joy: Sequel to the Joy of Sex, 1974; A Good Age, 1976; (ed) Sexual Consequences of Disability, 1978; Tetrarch (novel), 1978; Poems for Jane, 1978; I and That, 1979; A Practise of Geriatric Psychiatry, 1979 (with Jane Comfort), The Facts of Love: Living, Loving and Growing Up (juvenile), 1979; Reality and Empathy, 1984; Imperial Patient (novel), 1987; The Philosophers (novel), 1989; Science, Religion and Scientism (Conway Mem Lecture), 1990; The New Joy of Sex, 1991; Writings Against Power and Death (editor David Goodway) 1993; Mikroko Smos (poems), 1994. Address: 2 Fitzwarren House, Hornsey Lane, N6 5LX, England.

COMFORT Nicholas Alfred Fenner, b. 4 Aug 1946, London, England. Journalist. m. (1) 1970, dissolved 1988, 1 son, 1 daughter, (2) Corinne Reed, 1990, 1 son. Education: MA History (Exhibitioner), Trinity College, Cambridge, England, 1968. Appointments: Morning Telegraph, Sheffield, 1968-74; Daily Telegraph, 1974-89 (Washington 1976-78, Political Staff, 1978-87 Leader Writer, 1987-89); Political Editor, The Independent on Sunday, 1989-90; Political Editor, The European, 1990-92; Political Editor, Daily Record, 1992-. Publications: Mid-Suffolk Light Railway, 1986; The Tunnel - The Channel and Beyond, Contributor, 1987; Brewer's Politics - a Phase and Fable Dictionary, 1993; The Lost City of Dunwich, 1994. Contributions to: Numerous political transport and other journals. Membership: Fellow, Royal Geographical Society. Literary Agent: Patrick Walsh (of Christopher Little). Address: 20 Avenue Road, London N6 5DW, England.

COMINI Alessandra, b. 1934, USA. Professor of Art History. Education includes: PhD. Appointments include: Distinguished Professor of Art History, Southern Methodist University, Dallas, Texas. Publications: Schiele in Prison, 1974; Egon Schiele's Portraits, 1975; Gustav Klimt, 1975; Egon Schiele, 1976; The Fantastic Art of Vienna, 1978; The Changing Image of Beethoven, 1987; Egon Schiele, 1994; Co-author: World Impressionism, 1990; Käthe Kollwitz, 1992. Honours: Grand Decoration of Honour for Services to the Austrian Republic, 1990. Address: 2900 McFarlin, Dallas, TX 75205, USA.

COMPTON David Guy, (Guy Compton, Frances Lynch), b. 1930. Mystery/Crime/Suspense; Historical/Romance/Gothic; Science fiction/Fantasy. Appointments: Worked as stage electrician, furniture maker, salesman, docker and postman; Editor, Reader's Digest Condensed Books, London, 1969-81. Publications: Too Many Murderers, 1962; (as Guy Compton), Medium for Murder, 1963; (as Guy Compton), Dead on Cue, 1964; (as Guy Compton), Disguise for a Dead Gentleman, 1964; (as Guy Compton), High Tide for Hanging, 1965; The Quality of Mercy, 1965, 1970; Farewell Earth's Bliss, 1966; The Silent Multitude, 1966; (as Guy Compton), And Murder Came Too, 1966; Synthajoy, 1968; The Palace, 1969; The Electric Crocodile (in US as The Steel Crocodile), 1970; Chronocules, 1970, in UK as Hot Wireless Sets, Aspirin Tablets, The Sandpaper Sides of Used Matchboxes and Something That Might Have Been Castor Oil, 1971; The Missionaries, 1972; The Unsleeping Eye, 1973, in UK as The Continuous Katherine Mortenhoe, 1974; (as Frances Lynch), Twice Ten Thousand Miles, 1974, as Candle at Midnight, 1977; (as Frances Lynch), The Fine and Handsome Captain, 1975; (as Frances Lynch), Stranger at the Wedding, 1977; (as Frances Lynch), A Dangerous Magic, 1978; A Usual Lunacy, 1978; Windows, 1979; (as Frances Lynch), In the House of Dark Music, 1979; Ascendancies, 1980; Scudder's Game, 1985; Ragnarok, (with John Gribbin), 1991; Stammering, 1993; Nomansland, 1993; Justice City, 1994. Address: c/o Murray Pollinger, 222 Old Brompton Road, London SW5 0BZ, England.

COMPTON Guy. See: **COMPTON David Guy.**

CONDE Maryse, b. 11 Feb 1934, Pointe-à-Pitre, Guadeloupe. Novelist; Playwright. Education: Sorbonne, Paris; PhD, 1976. Appointments include: Editor at Paris Publishers Présence Africaine, from 1972; Chargé de cours at the Sorbonne, 1980-85. Publications: Heremakkonon, 1976, 1982; Une Saison à Rinata, 1981, 1988; Segou: les murailles de terre, 1984, 1987; Pays mêlé; Nanna-ya, 1985; I, Tituba, Black Witch of Salem, 1986, 1992; Tree of Life, 1987, 1992; Traversée de la mangrove, 1989; No Woman No Cry, 1991; Les

Derniers Rois Mages, 1992; Plays: Dieu nous l'a donné, 1973; Mort d'Oluwemi d'Ajumako, 1975; Pension les Alizes, 1989; An Tan Revolisyon, 1989; The Hills of Massabielle, 1991. Honours include: Académie Française Prize, 1988. Address: Montebello, 97190 Petit Bourg, Guadeloupe, French West Indies.

CONDON Richard, b. 18 Mar 1915, New York City, New York, USA. Writer. m. Evelyn Rose Hunt, 14 Jan 1938, 2 daughters. Publications: The Horse Stories, children's record albums, 1947; Men of Distinction, play, 1953; Novels: The Oldest Confession, 1958; The Manchurian Candidate, 1959; Some Angry Angel, 1960; A Talent for Loving, 1961; An Infinity of Mirrors, 1964; Any God Will Do, 1966; The Ecstasy Business, 1967; Mile High, 1969; Vertical Smile, 1971; Arigato, 1972; And Then We Moved to Rossenarra, 1973; The Mexican Stove, 1973; Winter Kills, 1974; The Star Spangled Crunch, 1974; Money is Love, 1975; The Whisper of the Axe, 1976; The Abandoned Woman, 1977; Bandicoot, 1978; Death of a Politician, 1978; The Entwining, 1980; Prizzi's Honor, 1982; A Trembling Upon Rome, 1983; Prizzi's Family, 1986; Prizzi's Glory, 1990; Emperor of America, 1991; The Final Addiction, 1992; The Venerable Bead, 1993; Prizzi's Money, 1994; Screenplays: Prizzi's Honor (with Janet Roach), 1984; Arigato, 1985; Prizzi's Glory, 1988. Contributions to: Over 100 publications, USA and UK. Honours: Chevalier, La Confrérie du Tastevin, 1968; Commanderie de Bontemps, 1969; Chevalier, Chaîne des Rôtisseurs, 1976; Best Screenplay Award, Writers Guild of America, 1986; Best Screenplay Award, British Academy of Film and TV, 1986. Literary Agent: Harold Matson Co, 276 Fifth Avenue, New York, NY 10001, USA. Address: 3436 Asbury Avenue, Dallas, TX 75205, USA.

CONDRY William Moreton, b. 1 Mar 1918, Birmingham, England. Writer. m. Penny Bailey, 17 Apr 1946. Education: BA 1939, DipEd 1940, Birmingham University; BA Hons French, London, 1945; MA, Wales,1951. Publications: The Snowdonia National Park, 1966; Exploring Wales, 1970; Pathway to the Wild, 1975; Woodlands, 1974; The Natural History of Wales, 1981; Snowdonia, 1987; Thoreau, 1954; Birds and Wild Africa, 1967; World of a Mountain, 1977; The National Trust - Wales, 1991; Contributor of the introduction and most of the text in Selborne (Gertrude Hermes Woodgravings), 1988; A Welsh Country Diary, 1993; Contributor of a chapter in The History of Cardiganshire, vol I 1994. Contributions to: Many articles in Country Life, and other magazines; Author, A Country Diary, in the Manchester Guardian, later The Guardian, 1957-. Honour: MSc (Honoris Causa), University of Wales, 1980. Address: Ynys Edwin, Eglwysfach, Machynlleth, Powys SY20 8TA, Wales.

CONE Molly Zelda, b. 3 Oct 1918, Tacoma, Washington, USA. Writer. m. Gerald J Cone, 9 Sept 1939, 1 son, 2 daughters. Education: University of Washington, 1936-38. Publications include: For children: Mishmash; Mishmash and the Substitute Teacher; Mishmash and the Sauerkraut Mystery; Mishmash and the Venus Flytrap; Mishmash and the Big Fat Problem; Come Back, Salmon (with photographs by Sidnee Wheelwright), 1992; Biographies: Hurry Henrietta, 1966; Leonard Bernstein, 1970; The Ringing Brothers, 1971; Non-fiction includes: Stories of Jewish Symbols, 1963; Who Knows Ten, 1965; The Jewish Sabbath, 1966; The Jewish New Year, 1966; Purim, 1967; The Mystery of Being Jewish, 1989; Play: John Bunyan and His Blue Ox, 1966. Honours include: Neveh Shalom Centennial Award for Literary Contribution toward Education of Jewish Children, 1970; Certificate of Recognition, Governor's Festival of Arts, State of Washington, 1970; Washington Press Women: First Place Award for Juvenile Book, for Simon, 1970, Second Place Award for Juvenile Book, for You Can't Make Me If I Don't Want To, 1971, Sugar Plum Award, Field of Communications, 1972, 1st Place Award for Juvenile Book, for Dance Around the Fire, 1974; Second Place Award for Simon, National Federation of Press Women, 1970; Shirley Kravitz Children's Book Award, Association of Jewish Libraries, 1973; For Come Back, Salmon: Washington Governor's Writers Award, 1993, Horn Book Fanfare, 1993, selection by several bodies including International Reading Association. Memberships: Authors League of America; Seattle Free Lancers. Literary Agent: McIntosh and Otis Inc, 310 Madison Avenue, New York, NY 10017, USA. Address: 8003 Sand Point Way NE B-24, Seattle, WA 98115, USA.

CONEY Michael Greatrex, b. 28 Sept 1932, England. Writer. m. Daphne Coney, 14 May 1957, 1 son, 1 daughter. Publications include: King of the Scepter'd Isle; A Judge of Men, 1969; Whatever Became of the McGowans?, 1971; The Snow Princess, 1971; Susanna! Susanna!, 1971; Mirror Image, 1972; The Bridge on the Scraw, 1973; Syzygy, 1973; Friends Come in Boxes, 1973; The Hero of Downways, 1973;

The Hook, the Eye and the Whip, 1974; Winter's Children, 1974; Monitor Found in Orbit, 1974; The Jaws That Bite, The Claws That Catch, 1975; Charisma, 1975; The Hollow Where, 1975; Trading Post, 1976; Hello Summer, Goodbye, 1976; Brontomek!, 1976; Just an Old-Fashioned War Story, 1977; Penny on a Skyhorse, 1979; The Ultimate Jungle, 1979; Neptune's Children, 1981; Cat Karina, 1982; The Celestial Steam Locomotive, 1983; The Byrds, 1983; Gods of the Greataway, 1984; Fang, the Gnome, 1988; No Place for a Sealion; A Tomcat Called Sabrina; Sophie's Spyglass, 1993; Die Lorelie, 1993; The Small Penance of Lady Disdain, 1993; Tea and Hamsters, 1994. Honours: Best British Novel Award for Brontomek!, British Science Fiction Association, 1976. Memberships: Science Fiction Writers of America; Institute of Chartered Accountants. Literary Agents: MBA Literary Agents, England; Virginia Kidd, USA. Address: 2082 Neptune Road, RR3, Sidney, British Columbia, Canada V8L 5J5.

CONLON Kathleen. See: **LLOYD Kathleen Annie.**

CONN Stewart, b. 1936, British. Appointments: Radio Producer, BBC, Glasgow, 1962-77; Head of Radio Drama, BBC Edinburgh, 1977-92; Literary Adviser, Edinburgh Royal Lyceum Theatre, 1972-75. Publications: Thunder in the Air: Poems, The Chinese Tower, Poems, 1967; Stoats in the Sunlight: Poems (in US as Ambush and Other Poems), 1968; The Burning, 1971; In Transit, An Ear to the Ground, Poems, 1972; PEN New Poems, 1973-74 (editor), 1974; Thistlewood, 1975; The Aquarium, The Man in the Green Muffler, I Didn't Always Live Here, 1976; Under the Ice, Poems, 1978; Play Donkey, 1980; In the Kibble Palace, new & selected poems, 1987; The Luncheon of the Boating Party, poems, 1992. Contributions to: Poetry, Chicago; The Observer, London; 12 More Modern Scottish Poets, 1986; The Best of Scottish Poetry, 1989; The Faber Book of Twentieth-Century Scottish Poetry, 1992; Six Poetes Ecossais, 1992; At the Aviary, poems; In the Blood, poems, 1995; The Living Poety (BBC Radio 3), 1990; The Poet Speaks (SABC), 1994. Honours: EC Gregory Award, 1964; Scottish Arts Council awards & poetry prize, 1968, 1978, 1992; Fellow of the Royal Scottish Academy of Music and Drama. Membership: Knight of Mark Twain. Literary Agent: Lemon, Unna & Durbridge, 24 Pottery Lane, London, England. Address: 1 Fettes Row, Edinburgh EH3 6SF, Scotland.

CONNELL Brian Reginald, b. 12 Apr 1916, London, England. Author; Journalist; Broadcaster. m. Esmée Jean Mackenzie, 27 Nov 1944. Education: Brighton Grammar School, 1927-33; Madrid University, 1933-36; Berlin University, 1936-37. Appointments: Reuters 1940-43, Daily Mail 1946-50, News Chronicle 1950-55; ITN 1955-86; Programme Adviser Anglia Television, 1961-86; Chairman, Connell Literary Enterprises/Partner Connell Editors, 1960-. Publications: Regina v Palmerston, 1962; Return of the Tiger, 1960; The Plains of Abraham, 1959; Watcher on the Rhine, 1957; Knight Errant, 1955; Manifest Destiny, 1953; Portrait of a Whig Peer, 1957; The War in the Peninsula, 1973; The Siege of Quebec, 1976; America in the Making, 1977; Editor and compiler of ten autobiographies. Contributions to: European Review; The Economist; The Times 1975-83. Honours: Producers Guild Award, 1963; Cannes Festival International Award, 1965. Memberships: The Pilgrims; National Union of Journalists; Reform Club; Lansdowne Club. Address: B2 Marine Gate, Marine Drive, Brighton, Sussex BN2 5TQ, England.

CONNELLY Karen, b. 1969. Canadian. Writer. Publications: This Brighter Prison: A Book of Journeys, 1993; Touch the Dragon, 1992. Honour: Governor General's Award, 1993.

CONNOLLY Ray, b. 1940, England. Writer. Publications: A Girl Who Came to Stay: That'll Be the Day, 1973; Stardust, 1974; Trick or Teat? James Dean: The First American Teenager, 1975; Newsdeath, 1978; A Sunday Kind of Woman, Honky Tonk Heroes, 1980; John Lennon 1940-1980; The Sun Place, 1981; Stardust Memories (author), 1983; Forever Young, 1984; Lytton's Diary, 1985; Defrosting The Fridge, 1988; Perfect Scoundrels, 1989; Sunday Morning, 1992; Shadows on a Wall, 1994. Contributions to: Columnist for London Evening Standard, 1967-1973, 1983-1984; The Times, 1989-90. Honours: Stardust, Best Original British Screenplay, 1974, Writers Guild of Great Britain. Literary Agent: Gill Coleridge, Rogers, Coleridge and White, London. Address: c/o Rogers, Coleridge and White, 20 Powis Mews, London W11 1JN, England.

CONNOR Fergus. See: **MILLER Karl.**

CONNORS Bruton. See: **ROHEN Edward.**

CONOLEY Gilliam Flavia, b. 29 Mar 1955, Austin, TX, USA. Writer; Professor. m. 22 Mar 1986. Education: BFA, Southern Methodist University, 1977; MFA, University of MA, 1983. Appointments: Staff, Dallas Morning News, 1978-80; Instrutor, University of New Orleans, 1984-87; Visiting Lecturer, Tulane University, 1984-87; Artist in Residence, Eastern Washington University, 1987-; Editor, Willow Springs, 1987-. Publications:Woman Speaking Inside Film Noir, 1984; Some Gangster Pain, 1987; Tall Stranger. Contributions to: American Poetry Review; Ironwood; North Am Review. Honours: Fellowship, MacDowell Colony, 1984; Academy of Am Poets Prize, 1984; Honorable Mention, Great Lakes College Association Award, 1987. Memberships: Associated Writing Programmes; MLA. Address: Eastern Washington University, English Dept M5-25, Pattison Hall, Cheney, WA 99004, USA.

CONOT Robert E, b. 1929, America. Appointments: Journalist, 1952-58; TV Writer, 1958-60; Sepcial Consultant, National Advisory Commission on Civil Disorders, 1967-68; Senior Lecturer, University of South Carolina School of Journalism, 1983-. Publications: Ministers of Vengeance, 1964; Rivers of Blood, Years of Darkness, 1967; Commission on Civil Disorders, 1968; American Odyssey, 1974; Urban Poverty in Historical Perspective: The Case of the United States, 1975; A Steak of Luck: The Life and Legend of Thomas Alva Edison, 1979; Justice at Nuremburg, 1983; The Nuremburg Gift, 1986.

CONQUEST (George) Robert (Acworth), b. 15 July 1917, Malvern, Worcestershire, England. Writer. m. (1) Joan Watkins, 2 sons, (4) Elizabeth Neece, 1 Dec 1979. Education: University of Grenoble, France, 1935-36; Magdalen College, Oxford, 1936-39; MA (Oxon), 1972; DLitt (Oxon), 1975. Literary appointments: Visiting Poet, University of Buffalo, Buffalo, New York, USA, 1959-60; Literary Editor, The Spectator, 1962-63. Publications: Poems, 1955; A World of Difference, 1955; Power and Policy in the USSR, 1961; Between Mars and Venus, 1962; The Egyptologists (with Kingsley Amis), 1965; The Great Terror, 1968, as The Great Terror, A Reassessment, 1990; Arias from a Love Opera, 1969; The Nation Killers, 1970; Lenin, 1972; Kolyma, 1978; Forays, 1979; The Abomination of Moab, 1979; We and They, 1980; Inside Stalin's Secret Police, 1985; The Harvest of Sorrow, 1986; New and Collected Poems, 1988; Tyrants and Typewriters, 1989; Stalin: Breaker of Nations, 1991. Contributions to: London Magazine; Times Literary Supplement; Analog Science Fiction; Soviet Studies; Neva, Leningrad; Novy Mir, Moscow; Poetry, Chicago; The New Republic; The Spectator. Honours: OBE, 1955. Memberships: Fellow, British Academy; Fellow, Royal Society of Literature; Travellers Club; Fellow, British Interplanetary Society; Society for the Promotion of Roman Studies; American Association for the Advancement of Slavic Studies. Literary Agent: Curtis Brown. Address: 52 Peter Coutts Circle, Stanford, CA 94305, USA.

CONRAN Anthony, b. 1931, England. Appointments: Research Fellow, Tutor, University College of North Wales, 1957. Publications include: Formal Poems, 1960; Icons, Asymptotes, A String o Blethers, Sequence of the Blu Flower, The Mountain, For the marriage of Gerald and Linda, 1963; Stalae and Other Poems, 1965; Guernica, 1966; The Penguin Book of Welsh Verse, 1967; Claim, Claim, Claim, A Book of Poems, 1969; Life Fund, On To the Fields of Praise: Essays on the English Poets of Wales, 1979; The Cost of Strangeness, 1982; Welsh Verse, 1987. Address: 1 Frondirion, Glanrafon, Bangor, Carnavanshire, Wales.

CONRAN Shirley, (Ida), b. 1932, England. Appointments: Founder, Co Owner, Conran Fabrics Limited, 1957; Editorial Adviser, Sidgwick and Jackson Limited; Home Editor, Daily Mail, 1962; Womens Editor, 1964, Observer, 1969-70, Daily Mail, 1968; Design & Promotion Consultant, Westinghouse Kitchens, 1969; Columnist, Vanity Fair Magazine, 1970-71; Life ans Styles Editor, Over 21 Magazine, 1972; Handled Publicity for Women in Media Campaigns, 1972-74. Publications: Printed Textile Design for Studio Publication, 1956; Superwoman, 1975; Superwomen Yearbook, 1976; Superwomen 2, 1977; Futures: How to Survive Life After Thirty, 1979; Lace, 1982; The Magic Garden, 1983; Lace 2, 1984; Savages, 1987; Down with Superwoman, 1990; The Amazing Umbrella Shop, 1990; Crimson, 1992. Address: Monaco.

CONROY John, b. 29 Mar 1951, Chicago, IL, USA. Writer. m. Colette Davison, May 1986. Education: BA, University of IL, 1973. Appointments: Senior Editor, Chicago Magazine, 1974-76; Staff Writer, Chicago Reader, 1978. Publications: Belfast Diary: War as a Wy of Life, 1987; UK Edition, War as a Way of Life, A Belfast Diary, 1988.

Contributions to include: NY Times; Boston Globe; Boston Pheonix; Chicago Daily News; Chicago Tribune; Atlanta Constitution; Dallas Morning News; San Diego Union; Village Voice. Honours include: Peter Lisagor Award, 1978; National Award for Magazine Writing, 1978; Alicia Petterson Fellowship, 1987; Society of Midland Authors Award, 1990. Literary Agent: Wendy Weil, Wendy Weil Agency, NY, USA. Address: c/o Chicago Reader, 11E Illinois Street, Chicago, IL 60611, USA.

CONSTABLE Trevor James, b. 17 Sept 1925, Wellington, New Zealand. Radio Electronics Officer. m. Gloria Garcia, 14 Sept 1983, 1 d. Education: Rongotai College, 1936-42. Appointments: Staff Writer, National Commercial Broadcasting Service, 1942-44; Staff Writer, International Broadcasting Company, 1950-52; US Correspondent, NZ Weekly News, 1958-68; Freelance Magazine Writer, 1960-70. Publications: Blond Knight of Germany, 1970; Fighter Aces of the USA, 1977; Fighter Aces of the Luftwaffe, 1978; Horrido, 1968; Fighter Aces, 1966; Hidden Heroes, 1971; The Cosmic Pulse of Life, 1978; Fighter General, the Life of Adolf Galland, 1988. Contributions to: Numerous Military and Aviation Articles. Honour: Aviation, Space Writers Book of the Year Award, 1978. Memberships: Aviation, Space Writers Association; National Maritime Historical Society; Am Radio Association. Address: 3726 Bluff Place, San Pedro, CA 90731, USA.

CONSTANT Clinton, b. 20 Mar 1912, Nelson, British Columbia, Canada. US Citizen. Chemical Engineer; Author. Education: BSc, Alberta University, 1935; Doctorate, Western Reserve University, USA, 1939; Registered Professional Engineer. Publications: The War of the Universe, 1931; The Martian Menace, 1934; O and M Manual for Industrial Waste Treatment Plant, 1975. Contributions to: Numerous Technical publications and reports on Astronomy, Chemistry and Rocketry. Memberships include: American Chemical Society; Royal Astronomical Society, Canada; American Water Works Association; Fellow, New York Academy of Science; American Astronomical Society; Fellow, American Institute of Chemical Engineers; Fellow, American Institute of Chemists; Fellow, American Association for the Advancement of Science; Associate Fellow, American Institute Aeronautics and Astronautics; National Society of Professional Engineers; Air Pollution Control Association; Water Pollution Control Federation; Astronomical Society of the Pacific. Address: PO Box 2529, Victorville, CA 92393, USA.

CONSTANTINE David (John), b. 4 Mar 1944, Salford, Lancashire, England. Lecturer; Poet. m. Helen Best, 1966, 1 s, 1 d. Education: PHD, Wadham College, Oxford, 1971. Appointments: Lecturer, University of Durham, 1969-81; Fellow, Queens College Oxford, 1981-. Publications: A Brightness to Cast Shadows, 1980; Watching for Dolphins, 1983; Talitha Cumi, 1983; Mappa Mundi, 1984; Madder, 1987; Novel, Davies, 1985; Early Greek Travellers and the Hellenic Ideal, 1984; Hölderlin, 1988; Short Stories: Back at the Spike, 1994; Poetry: Selected Poems, 1991; Caspar Hauser, 1994; Translations: Hölderlin, Selected Poems, 1990; Goethe, Elective Affinities, 1994. Honours: Alice Hunt Bartlet Prize, 1984; Southern Arts Literature Prize, 1987; Runciman Prize, 1985. Address: 1 Hilltop road, Oxford OX4 1PB, England.

CONWAY Peter. See: **MILKOMANE George Alexis Milkomanovich.**

CONWAY Troy. See: **AVALLONE Michael Angelo Jr.**

COOK Alistair (Alfred), b, 20 Nov 1908, England. Writer; Broadcaster. m. (1) Ruth Emerson, 1934, (2) Jane White Hawkes, 1 son, 1 daughter. Education: Jesus College, Cambridge; Yale and Harvard Universities. Appointments: Film Critic, BBC, 1934-37; London Correspondent, National Broadcasting Co, 1936-37; Special Correspondent, American Affairs, The Times, 1938-41; Commentator, American Affairs, BBC, 1938-; American Feature Writer, Daily Herald, 1941-44; UN Correspondent, Manchester Guardian (now The Guardian), 1945-48; Chief Correspondent, USA, The Guardian, 1948-72. Publications: Garbo and the Night Watchmen, Editor, 1937; Douglas Fairbanks, 1940; A Generation on Trial: USA v Alger Hiss, 1950; One Man's America (English Title, Letters from America), 1952; Christmas Eve, 1952; A Commencement Address, 1954; The Vintage Mencken, Editor, 1955; Around the World in Fifty Years, 1966; Talk About America, 1968; Alistair Cooke's America, 1973; Six Men, 1977; The Americans: Fifty Letters from America on Our Life and Times, 1979; Above London (with Robert Cameron), Masterpieces, 1982; The Patent Has The Floor, 1986; America Observed, 1988. Honours: Peabody Award, 1952, 1972; Writers Guild Award for Best

Documentary, 1972; Dimbleby Award, 1973; 4 Emmy Awards, 1973; Benjamin Franklin Award, 1973; Hon KBE, 1973; Hon LLD, Edinburgh, Manchester; Hon LittD,St Andrews, 1975; Hon LittD, Cambridge University, 1988. Address: 1150 Fifth Avenue, New York, NY 10128, USA.

COOK Blanche Wiesen, b. 20 Apr 1941, New York City, New York, USA. Writer; Historian. Education: BA. Hunter College, 1962; PhD, Johns Hopkins University, Baltimore, 1970. Literary appointments: Senior Editor, Gailord Library on War and Peace series, 1970-80; Syndicated Journalist. Publications: Past-Imperfect (co-editor), 1973; Crystal Eastman on Women and Revolution, 1978, paperbacks, 1984; The Declassified Eisenhower, 1981; Eleanor Roosevelt, vol I, 1992. Literary Agent: Charlotte Sheedy. Address: John Jay College, City University of New York, New York, NY 10019, USA.

COOK Christopher Piers, b. 20 June 1945, Leicester, England. Writer; Historian. Education: BA (1st Class Honours) History 1967, MA 1970, Cambridge University; DPhil, Modern History, Oxford University, 1974. Appointment: Editor, Pears Cyclopedia, 1976-. Publications: Sources in British Political History, 6 volumes, 1975-84; A Short History of the Liberal Party 1900-92, 1993; The Slump (with John Stevenson), 1976; Dictionary of Historical Terms, 2nd edition 1989; Longman Handbook of Modern British History 1714-1987, 1988; Longman Handbook of Modern European History 1763-1991, 1992; Longman Handbook of World History since 1914, 1991; World Political Almanac, 1989. Contributions to: The Guardian; Times Literary Supplement; THES. Honour: Fellow, Royal Historical Society, 1977. Literary Agent: Derek James, A P Watt & Co, 20 John Street, London WC1. Address: c/o Pears Cyclopedia, Pelham Books, 27 Wrights Lane, Kensington, London W8 5TZ, England.

COOK David, b. 21 Sept 1940, Preston, Lancashire, England. Education: Royal College of Dramatic Art, 1959-61. Appointments: Professional Actor, 1961-; Writer-in-Residence, St Martin's College, Lancaster, England, 1982-83. Publications: Albert's Memorial, 1972; Happy Endings, 1974; Walter, 1978; Winter Doves, 1979; Sunrising, 1983; Missing Persons, 1986; Crying Out Loud, 1988; Walter and June, 1989; Second Best, 1991. Honours: E M Forster Award, 1977; Hawthorn Prize, 1978; Southern Arts Fiction Prize, 1984; Arthur Welton Scholarship, 1991; Oddfellows Social Concern Award, 1992. Membership: Society of Authors. Literary Agents: Elaine Green Ltd. Address: 7 Sydney Place, London SW7 3NL, England.

COOK Dorothy Mary, (Dy Cameron, D M Carlisle, Elizabeth Clare), b. England. Publications include: Chasing Shadows, 1962; The Unreasonable Heart, The Searching Heart, 1964; Love Unfolding, A Land of Stars, 1966; A puzzled Heart, Sunlight Through the Mist, 1967; The Enchanted Tides, Enchanting Adventure, A Song to the Sun, 1969; Magic of Springtime, 1971; Glade in the Woods, 1974; Scent of Jasmin, 1975; Down by the Willows, 1977; A Touch of Spring, By the Golden Waters, 19881; Straws in the Wind, 1983; The Harvest is Sure, 1985; Harvest Issue, 1986. Address: c/o Hale, 45-47 Clerkenwell Green, London, EC1R 0HT, England.

COOK Glen, b. 9 July 1944, New York City, New York, USA. Auto Assembler; Writer. m. 14 June 1971, 3 sons. Publications: The Black Company, series, 1984-89; A Matter of Time, 1985; Pasaage At Arms, 1985; The Garrett Files, series, 1987-; The Dragon Never Sleeps, 1988; The Tower of Fear, 1989. Contributions to: Numerous magazines and journals. Literary Agent: Russell Galen, Scouil-Chichak=Galen, 381 Park Avenue South, Suite 1020, New York, NY 10016, USA. Address: c/o Scott Meredith Inc, 845 Third Avenue, New York, NY 10022, USA.

COOK Lila. See: **AFRICANO Lillian.**

COOK Lyn. See:**WADDELL Evelyn Margaret.**

COOK Michael, b. 1933, Canada. Appointments: Specialist in Drama, 1967-70, Lecturer, 1970-74, Assistant Professor, 1974-78, Associate Professor, 1978-, Memorial University, St Johns Newfoundland; Film & Drama Critic, Evening Telgraph, 1967-82; Member, Editorial Board, Canadian Theatre Review, 1973-; Artistic Director, Newfoundland Summer Festival of the Arts, 1970-74; Director, Newfoundland Arts & Culture Centre Productions, 1971074; One Time Host, Weekly TV Review, Our Man Friday, 1980-81; Govenor, Canadian Conference on the Arts, 1975-79; Vice Chairman, Guild of Canadian Playwrights, 1979; Chairman, Playwrights Canada, 1982-83;

Founding Member, Newfoundland Arts Council, 1980-82. Publications: The Head Guts and Soundbone Dance, 1974; Jacobs Wake, 1975; Not as a Dream, 1976; Three Plays, Tereses Creed, 1977; The Gayden Chronicles, 1979; The Island of Fire, 1980; The Terrible Journey of Frederick Dunglass, 1982; The Fishermans Revenge, 1985. Address: 43 Shrewsbury Street, Stratford, Ontario, N5A 2V4, Canada.

COOK Norman Edgar, b. 4 Mar 1920. Writer; Chief Book Critic, Liverpool Daily Post, 1980-90. m. Mildred Warburton, 1942, 3 sons. Appointments: Ministry of Information, 1943-45; Editor, Northwich Guardian, 1945-47; Liverpool Daily Post, 1947-49; Information Officer, Air Ministry, 1949-53; Night News Editor, Daily Post, 1953-55; Deputy News Editor 1955-59, London Editor 1959-72, Executive News Editor 1972-77, Liverpool Daily Post and Echo; Editor, Liverpool Daily Post, 1978-79; Retired, Sept 1979; Chief Book Critic, Liverpool Daily Post, 1980-91. Publications: Numerous articles and review. Honour: CBE, 1980. Address: 7 Trinity Gardens, Southport, Lancashire PR8 1AU, England.

COOK Petronelle Marguerite Mary, (Margot Arnold), b. 16 May 1925, Plymouth, Devon, England. Writer; Teacher. m. Philip R Cook, 20 July 1949, 2 sons, 1 daughter. Education: BA (Hons), 1946, Diploma in Prehistoric Archaeology and Anthropology, 1947, MA, 1950, Oxford University. Publications: The Officers' Woman, 1972; The Villa on the Palatine, 1975; Marie, 1979; Exit Actors, Dying, 1980, 1988; The Cape Cod Caper, 1980, 1988; Death of a Voodoo Doll, 1981, 1989; Zadok's Treasurer, 1981, 1989; Affairs of State, 1981; Love Among the Allies, 1982; Lament for a Lady Laird, 1982, 1990; Death on the Dragon's Tongue, 1982, 1990; Desperate Measures, 1983; Sinister Purposes, 1985; The Menehune Murders, 1989; Toby's Folly, 1990; The Catacomb Conspiracy, 1991; The Cape Cod Conundrum, 1992; Dirge for a Dorset Druid, 1994; The Midas Murders, 1995; As Petronelle Cook: The Queen Consorts of England, 1993. Contributions to: Numerous short stories to magazines. Honours: Elected President, Oxford University Archaeological Society, 1945; Fiction Prize, National Writers Club, 1983. Memberships: New England Historic and Genealogical Society; Mystery Writers of American, Participant, Mentor programme for fledgling writers. Address: 619 High Street, Bethlehem, PA 18018, USA.

COOK Robin. See: COOK Robert William Arthur.

COOK Robert William Arthur, (Robin Cook, Derek Raymond),b. 1931. England. Author. Publications: The Crust on Its Uppers, 1962; Bombe Surprise, 1963; The Legacy of the Stiff Upper Lip, 1966; Private Paris and Public Places, 1967; A State of Denmark, 1970; Tenants of Dirt Street, 1971; Le soleil quis'eteint, 1983; He Died with His Eyes Open (as Derek Raymond), 1984; The Devil's Home on Leave (as Derek Raymond), 1985; How the Dead Live, 1986; Nightmare in the Street, 1987; Harmful Intent, 1989. Address: Toby Eady Associates, 7 Gledhow Gardens, London SW5 0BL, England.

COOK Stanley, b. 12 Apr 1922, Austerfield, Yorkshire, England. Lecturer; Poet. m. Kathleen Mary Daly, 1 s, 2 d. Education: BA, Christ Church, Oxford, 1943. Appointments: Lecturer, Huddersfield Polytechnic, 1969-81; Editor, Poetry Nottingham, 1981-85. Publications: Form Photograph, 1971; Sign of Life, 1972; Staff Photograph, 1976; Alphabet, 1976; Woods Beyond a Cornfield, 1981; Concrete Poems, 1984; Barnsdale, 1986; Selected Poems, 1972-86, 1986; The Northern Seasons, 1988; Poems for Children. Honours: Cheltenham Festival Competition Prize, 1972. Address: 600 Barnsley Road, Sheffield, South Yorkshire, S5 6UA, England.

COOK Thomas, b. 19 Sept 1947, AL, USA. m. Susan Terner, 17 Mar 1978, 1 d. Education: Georgia State College; MA, Hunter College, NY; M Phil, Columbia University. Publications: Blood Innocents, 1980; The Orchids, 1982; Tabernacle, 1983; Elena, 1986; Sacrificial Ground, 1988; Flesh and Blood, 1989; Streets of Fire, 1989; Night Secrets, 1990; Breakheart Hill, 1994. Contributions to: Atlanta Magazine. Honours: Edgar Allan Poe Award, 1981,88. Address: c/o Russell & Volkening, 50 W 29th Street, New York, NY 10001, USA.

COOKSON Catherine (Ann), (Catherine Fawcett, Catherine Marchant), b. 1906, British. Writer of Historical/Romance/Gothic, Children's Fiction, Autobiography/Memoirs/Personal. Publications include: Mary Ann and Bill, 1967; Katie Mulholland, 1967; The Round Tower, 1968; Joe and the Gladiator (juvenile), 1968; The Glass Virgin, 1969; The Nice Bloke, 1969, in US as The Husband, 1976; Our Kate: An Autobiography, 1969, 1982; The Invitation, 1970; The Nipper

(juvenile), 1970; The Dwelling Place, 1971; Feathers in the Fire, 1971; Pure as the Lily, 1972; Blue Baccy (juvenile), 1972; The Mallen Girl, 1973; The Mallen Steak, 1973; The Mallen Lot (in UK as The Mallen Litter), 1974; (triology) in vol as The Mallen Novels, 1979; Our John Willy (juvenile), 1974; The Invisible Cord, 1975; The Gambling Man, 1975; (as Catherine Marchant) Miss Martha Mary Crawford, 1975; The Tide of Life, 1976; (as Catherine Marchant) The Slow Awakening, 1976; Mrs Flannagan's Trumpet (juvenile), 1976; Go Tell It to Mrs Golightly (juvenile), 1977; The Girl, 1977; The Cinder Path, 1978; The Man Who Cried, 1979; Tilly Trotter (in US as Tilly), 1980; Tilly Trotter Ed (in US as Tilly Wed), 1981; Lanky Jones (juvenile), 1981; Tilly Trotter Widowed (in US as Tilly Alone), 1982; The Whip, 1982; Nancy Nutall and the Mongrel (juvenile), 1982; Hamilton, 1983; The Black Velvet Gown 1984; Goodbye Hamilton, 1984; A Dinner of Herbs, 1985; Harold, 1985; The Moth, 1985; Bill Bailey, 1985; Catherine Cookson Country, 1986; The Parson's Daughter, 1987; Bill Bailey's Lot, 1987; The Cultured Handmaiden, 1988; Bill Bailey's Daughter, 1988; Let Me Make Myself Plain, 1988; The Harrogate Secret, 1989; The Black Candle, 1989; The Windless Bird, 1990; The Gillivors, 1990; My Beloved Son, 1991; The Rag Nymph, 1991; The House of Women, 1992; The Maltese Angel, 1992; The Year of the Virgins, 1993. The Golden Straw, 1993; Justice in a Woman, 1994. Honours: OBE, 1985; Hon D Litt, 1991; DBE, 1993. Address: c/o Anthony Sheil Associates, 43 Doughty Street, London WC1N 2LF, England.

COOLIDGE Clark, b. 1939, USA. Dramatist; Poet. Appointments: Editor, Joglar Magazine, Providence, Rhode Island, 1964-66. Publications: Flag Flutter and US Electric, 1966; Poems, 1967; Ing, 1969; Space, 1970; To Obtain the Value of the Cake Measure from Zero (with T Veitch), play, 1970; The So, 1971; Moroccan Variations, 1971; Clark Coolidge Issue of Big Sky, 1972; Suite V, 1973; The Maintains, 1974; Polaroid, 1975; Quartz Hearts, 1978; Own Face, 1978; Smithsonian Deposition and Subject to a Film (co-author), 1980; American Ones, 1981; Research, 1982; The Book of During, 1991; Odes of Roba, 1991; Sound as Thought, poems, 1982-84, 1990; On the Slates, 1992; Own Face, 1994. Address: c/o Tombouctou Books, PO Box 265, Bolinas, CA 94924, USA.

COOMBS Patricia, b. 23 July 1926, Los Angeles, California, USA. Author; Illustrator of Childrens' Books. m. L James Fox, 13 July 1951, 2 daughters. Education: BA 1947, MA 1950, University of Washington. Publications: Dorrie and the Blue Witch, 1964; Dorrie and the Haunted House, 1970; Dorrie and the Goblin, 1972; Mouse Cafe, 1972; Molly Mullett, 1975; The Magic Pot, 1977; Dorrie and the Screebit Ghost, 1979; The Magician McTree, 1984; Dorrie and the Pin Witch, 1989; Dorrie and the Haunted Schoolhouse, 1992. Contributions to: Partisan Review; The Hudson Review; Poetry. Honours: Dorries Magic, New York Times Ten Best Books of the Year, 1963; Dorrie and the Haunted House, Child Study Association, Childrens Books of the Year, 1970; Mouse Cafe, New York Times 10 Best Illustrated Books of the Year. Memberships: Authors Guild Incorporated. Literary Agent: Dorothy Markinko, McIntosh and Otis, New York, USA; Gerald Pollinger, Laurance Pollinger Ltd, London, England. Address: 178 Oswegatchie Road, Waterford, CT 06385, USA.

COONEY Ray(mond George Alfred), b. 30 May 1932, London, England. Actor; Writer; Director. m. Linda Dixon, 8 Dec 1962, 2 sons. Publications: (Plays): It Runs in the Family? 1987; Two into One, 1985; Run for Your Wife, 1984; (With John Chapman): There Goes the Bride, 1974; Not Now Darling, 1967; Move Over Mrs Markham, 1969; My Giddy Aunt, 1968; (With Tony Hilton): One for the Pot, 1961; Stand By Your Bedouin, 1966; Why Not Stay for Breakfast, (with Gene Stone, 1970); Wife Begins at Forty, with Arne Sultan & Earl Barrett, 1986; Chase Me Conrad, 1964; Charlie Girl (with Hugh & Margaret Williams), 1965; It Runs in the Family, 1989; Out of Order, 1990; Funny Money, 1994. Memberships: Dramatists Club. Agent: H Udwin. Address: Hollowfield Cottage, Littleton, Surrey, GU3 1HN, England.

COONTZ Stephanie, b. 31 Aug 1944, Seattle, Washington, USA. Professor. 1 son. Education: BA, University of California, 1966; MA, University of Washington, 1970. Appointments: Faculty Member, The Evergreen State College, Olympia, Washington, 1975-; Lecturer, Washington Commission for the Humanities, 1989-91; Visiting Scholar, The National Faculty, 1990-. Publications: The Way We Never Were: American Families and the Nostalgia Trap; The Social Origins of Private Life: A History of American Families; Women's Work, Men's Property: On the Origins of Gender and Class. Honours: Woodrow Wilson Fellow; Washington Governor's Writers Award; Dlae Richmond Award, American Academy of Pediatrics. Memberships: Organization of American Historians; American Studies Association; American Historical Association. Address: 3127 Seminar Building, The Evergreen State College, Olympia, WA 98505, USA.

COOPER Bernard, b. 1951. Instructor in English & American Literature, Otis/Parsons Institute of Art & Design, Los Angeles, CA. Publications: Maps to Anywhere, 1990; A Year of Rhymes. Contributions to: Harpers; Grand Street. Honour: Ernest Hemmingway Foundation Award, 1991.

COOPER Brenda Clare, (Clare Cooper), b. 21 Jan 1935, Falmouth, Cornwall, England. Nurse. m. Bill Cooper, 6 Apr 1953, 2 sons, 1 daughter. Publications: Davids Ghost; The Black Horn; Earthchange; Ashar of Qarius; The Skyrifters; Andrews and the Gargoyle; A Wizard Called Jones; Kings of the Mountain; Children of the Camps; The Settlement on Planet B; Miracles and Rubies. Honour: Runner Up Tir Na Nog Award. Memberships: PEN; Society of Authors; Welsh Academy. Literary Agent: Jennifer Luithlen. Address: Tyrhibin Newydd, Newport, Dyfed, SA42 0NT, Wales.

COOPER Bryan, b. 6 Feb 1932, Paris, France. Editor; Author. m. Judith Williams, 7 Apr 1979, 2 sons, 2 daughters (by previous marriage). Appointments: Reporter Kentish Times 1948-50; Feature Writer Flying Review magazine 1950-52; Sub-editor Exchange Telegraph 1953-54; Public Relations Executive British Petroleum in London 1954-58 and New York 1958-64; Editor and Publisher, Petroleum Economist, the International Energy Journal, 1975-89; Energy Writer and Consultant for Energy Research Ltd, Cyprus, 1990-94. Publications: North Sea Oil - The Great Gamble, 1966; The Ironclads of Cambrai, 1967; Battle of the Torpedo Boats, 1970; The Buccaneers, 1970; PT Boats, 1970; Alaska - The Last Frontier, 1972; Tank Battles of World War 1, 1973; Fighter, 1973; Bomber, 1974; Stones of Evil (novel), 1974; The E Boat Threat, 1976; The Wildcatters (novel), 1976; The Adventure of North Sea Oil, 1982. Contributions to: The Times; Financial Times; Numerous magazines. Scriptwriter, over 100 Radio and TV and Film Scripts. Memberships: Writer's Guild of Great Britain; Garrick; London Press Club. Literary Agent: Shelia Watson, Little Ltd, 12 Egbert Street, London NW1 8LJ, England.

COOPER Clare. See: COOPER Brenda Clare.

COOPER Colin Symons, (Daniel Benson), b. 5 July 1926, Birkenhead, England. Journalist; Editor. m. Maureen Elizabeth Goodwin, 6 Sept 1966, 2 sons. Appointments: Features Editor, Guitar Magazine, 1972-73; News Editor 1982-84, General Editor 1984-, Classical Guitar. Publications: The Thunder and Lightning Man, 1968; Outcrop, 1969; Dargason, 1977; The Epping Pyramid, 1978; The Argyll Killings, 1980. Contributions to: Times Literary Supplement; Times Education Supplement; The Guardian; The Independent; Gendai Guitar (Tokyo); Asta Journal (USA); The European. Membership: Writers' Guild of Great Britain. Address: 36 Falkland Road, London N8 0NX, England.

COOPER Derek MacDonand, b. 25 May 1925. Author; Broadcaster; Journalist. m. Janet Marian Feaster, 1953, 1 son, 1 daughter. Education: University College, Cardiff, Wales; Wadham College, Oxford; MA (hons), Oxon. Literary Appointments: Columnist: The Listener; The Guardian; Observer Magazine; World Listener; The Guardian; OBserver Magazine; World Medicine; Scottish Field; Sunday Standard; Homes and Gardens; Saga Magazine; Women's Journal. Publications: The Bad Food Guide, 1967; Skye, 1970, 2nd edition, 1977; The Beverage Report, 1970; The Gullibility Gap, 1974; Hebridean Connection, 1977; Guide to the Whiskies of Scotland, 1978; Road to the Isles, 1979; Enjoying Scotch (wit4h Dione Pattullo), 1980; Wines With Food, 1982, 2nd edition, 1986; The Whisky Roads of Scotland (with Fay Goodwin), 1982; The Century Companion to Whiskies, 1983; Skye Remembered, 1983; The World of Cooking, 1983; The Road to Mingulay, 1985; The Gunge File, 1986; A Taste of Scotch, 1989; Television programmes. Contributions to: In Britain: Signature; Taste; A La Carte; The West Highland Free Press. Honours: Glenfiddich Trophy as Wine and Food Writer, 1973, 1980; Scottish Arts Council Award, 1980; Broadcaster of the Year, 1984; House of Fraser Press Award, 1984. Membership: Founder Member, 1st Chairman, Guild of Food Writers. Address: Seafield House, Portree, Isle of Skye, Scotland.

COOPER Helen, b. 6 Feb 1947, Nottingham, England. University Lecturer. m. M G Cooper, 18 July 1970, 2 daughters. Education: BA, New Hall, Cambridge, 1968; MA, PhD, 1972. Appointments: English Editor, Medium AEvum, 1989. Publications: The Oxford Guides to Chaucer: The Canterbury Tales; The Structure of the Canterbury Tales; Pastoral: Medieval into Renaissance; Great Grand Mother Goose. Contributions to: Numerous. Address: University College, Oxford OX1 4BH, England.

COOPER Jean Campbell, b. 27 Nov 1905, Chefoo, North China. Author; Lecturer. m. Commander V M Cooper DSO, OBE, RN, 21 June 1945. Education: Various boarding schools in China, Australia and England; LLA Hons, 1st Class, Moral Philosophy, St Andrew's University, 1930. Publications: Taoism, the Way of the Mystic, 1972; An Illustrated Encyclopedia of Traditional Symbols, 1978; Yin and Yang, the Harmony of Opposites, 1982; Fairy Tales, Allegories of the Inner Life, 1983; Chinese Alchemy, 1984; Aquarian Dictionary of Festivals, 1990; Symbolic and Mythological Animals, 1993; Brewer's Myth and Legend, 1993. Contributions to: Articles, translations, reviews for Studies in Comparative Religion. Memberships: English PEN; Life Member, Royal Commonwealth Society; Justice of the Peace. Address: Bobbin Mill, Ulpha, Broughton-in-Furness, Cumbria LA20 6DU, England.

COOPER Jilly (Sallitt), b. 1937, England. Writer; Journalist. Appointments: Reporter, Middlesex Independent Newspaper, Brentford, 1957-59; Columnist, The Sunday Times, 1969-85; Columnist, The Mail on Sunday, 1985-; Various other positions including Copywriter and Publishers Reader. Publications: How to Stay Married, 1969; How to Survive from Nine to Five, 1970; Jolly Super, 1971; Men and Super Men, 1972; Jolly Super Too, 1973; Women and Super Women, 1974; Jolly Superlative, 1975; Emily, romance novel, 1975; Super Men and Super Women, omnibus, 1976; Bella, romance novel, 1976; Harriet, romance novel, 1976; Octavia, romance novel, 1977; Work and Wedlock, omnibus, 1977; Superjilly, 1977; Imogen, romance novel, 1978; Prudence, romance novel, 1978; Class: A View from Middle England, 1979; Supercopper, 1980; Little Mabel series, juvenile, 4 vols, 1980-85; Violets and Vinegar: An Anthology of Women's Writings and Savings (edited with Tom Hartman), 1980; The British in Love (editor), 1980; Love and Other Heartaches, 1981; Jolly Marsupial, 1982; Animals in War, 1983; The Common Years, 1984; Leo and Jilly Cooper on Rugby, 1984; Riders, 1985; Hotfoot to Zabriskie Point, 1985; How to Survive Christmas, 1986; Turn Right at The Spotted Dog, 1987; Rivals, 1988; Angels Rush In, 1990; Polo, 1991; The Man Who Made Husbands Jealous, 1993. Address: c/o Desmond Elliot, 15-17 King Street, St James, London SW1, England.

COOPER Kenneth Hardy, b. USA. Physician; Author. Appointments: Served US Air Force, 1957-70; Developed Fitness Regime for US Air Force Training Astronauts; Established The Cooper Aerobics Center, Dallas, Texas. Publications: Aerobics; The New Aerobics; The Aerobics Way: New Data on the World's Most Popular Exercise Program; The Aerobics Program for Total Well-Being: Exercise, Diet, Emotional Balance; Running Without Fear: How to Reduce the Risk of Heart Attack and Sudden Death During Aerobic Exercise; The New Aerobics for Women; Overcoming Hypertension; Kid Fitness: A Complete Shape Up Program from Birth Through High School. Contributions to: Numerous. Honours: Presidential Citation; Inducted into Oklahoma Hall of Fame; Lifetime Achievement Award; Churchman of the Year Award, Religious Heritage of America. Memberships: American Medical Association; Texas Medical Association; Dallas County Medical Scoeity; American Running and Fitness Association; Association for Fitness in Business; American College of Sports Medicine; American Geriatrics Society. Address: The Cooper Aerobics Center, 12200 Preston Road, Dallas, TX 75230, USA.

COOPER Lettice (Ulpha), b. 3 Sept 1897, Eccles, Lancashire, England. Novelist. Education: BA, Lady Margaret Hall, Oxford, 1916-1918. Appointments: President, Robert Louis Stevenson Club, 1958-74; Vice-Chairman, 1975-78, and President, 1979-81, English PEN Club. Publications: The Lighted Room, 1925; The Old Fox, 1927; Good Venture, 1928; Likewise then Lyon, 1928; The Ship of Truth, 1930; Private Enterprise, 1931; Hark to Rover!, 1933; We have come to a Country, 1935; The New House, 1936; National Provincial, 1938; Black Bethlehem, 1947; Penny, 1953; Three Lives, 1957; A Certain Compass, 1960; The Double Heart, 1962; Late in the Afternoon, 1973; Tea on Sunday, 1973; Snow and Roses, 1976; Desirable Residence, 1980; Unusual Behaviour, 1986; Uncollected short stories and other works including children's fiction. Honours: OBE, 1980. Literary Agent: A P Watt Ltd, 20 John Street, London WC1N 2DL, England. Address: 4 Wherry Quayside, Anchor Street, Coltishall, Norwich, Norfolk NR12 7AQ, England.

COOPER Richard Newell, b. 14 June 1934, Seattle, Washington, USA. Economist; Educator. m. Carolyn Caholan, 5 June 1956, 1 son, 1 daughter. Education: AB, Oberlin College, 1956; MSc, London School of Economics, England, 1958; PhD, Harvard University, 1962. Publications: The Economics of Interdependence, 1968; A World Re-Ordered, 1973; Economic Policy in an Interdependent World, 1986; The International Monetary System, 1987; Economic Stabilization and Debt in Developing Countries, 1992; Environmental and Resource Policies for the World Economy, 1994; Co-author: Can Nations Agree?, 1989; Boom, Crisis, and Adjustment, 1993; Macroeconomics Policy and Adjustment in Korea, 1994. Contributions to: The New Republic; The New York Times; The Washington Post; Journal for Political Economy; Quarterly Journal of Ecnomics; Others. Honours: Phi Beta Kappa, 1955; Marshall Scholarship, 1956; LLD, Oberlin College, 1958; Elected Fellow, American Academy of Arts and Sciences, 1974. Memberships: Council on Foreign Relations; American Economic Association; Trilateral Commission. Address: 1737 Cambridge Street, Cambridge, MA 02138, USA.

COOPER Susan, b. 23 May 1935, Burnham, Buckingshire, England. Writer. m. Nicholas J Grant, 1963 (div 1982), 1 son, 1 daughter. Education: MA, Somerville College, Oxford, 1953-56. Publications: Over Sea, Under Stone, 1965; The Dark is Rising, 1973; Greenwitch, 1974; The Grey King, 1975; Silver on the Tree, 1977; Seaward, 1983; Mandrake, 1964; Dawn of Fear, 1970; J B Priestley: Portrait of an Author, 1970; Behind the Golden Curtain: A View of the USA, 1968; Jethro and the Jumbie, 1979; The Silver Cow, 1983; The Selkie Girl, 1986; The Dark is Rising Sequence, 1987; Danny and The Kings, 1993. Contributions to: Many magazines and journals. Honours: Boston Globe-Horn Book Award, 1973; Newberry Medal, 1976; Welsh Arts Council Tir Nan og Award, 1976, 1978; Humanities Award, 1985; Christopher Medal, 1985; Hugo Award, 1984; Writers Guild of America Award, 1984, 1988. Memberships: Society of Authors; Authors Guild; Writers Guild of America. Literary Agent: ICM, New York, (Sam Cohn), USA.

COOPER William. See: **HOFF Harry Summerfield.**

COOPER COHEN Sharleen, b. 11 June 1940, Los Angeles, California, USA. Author. m. Martin L Cohen, 27 Aug 1972, 2 daughters. Education: University of California, Berkeley, 1957-58; University of California, Los Angeles, 1958-60; Los Angeles Valley Film School, 1976-78. Publications: The Day after Tomorrow, 1979; Regina's Song, 1980; The Ladies of Beverly Hills, 1983; Marital Affairs, 1985; Love, Sex and Money, 1988; Lives of Value, 1991; Innocent Gestures, 1994. Contributions to: Santa Barbara Writers Conference, 1978; National Gaucher Foundation Newsletter; Serialisation of novel, Good Housekeeping, 1990. Honours: Honourable Mention, Santa Barbara Writers Conference, 1978; Beverly Hills Hadassah; Women of Achievement, 1989. Memberships: PEN; Authors Guild; Writers Guild of America; National Gaucher Foundation, Board of Directors, Los Angeles Founder and Director; Executive Committee, Women of Distinction, United Jewish Appeal; California State Commission on Humanities. Literary Agent: Elaine Markson Literary Agency, New York City, New York, USA. Address: 16170 Clear Valley Place, Encino, CA 91436, USA.

COOVER Robert, b. 1932, USA. Author. Appointments: Professor, Brown University, Providence, Rhode Island, 1979-. Publications: The Origin of the Brunists, 1966; The Universal Baseball Association, Inc, J Henry Waugh, Prop, 1968; Pricksongs and Descants, short stories, 1969; A Theological Position, plays, 1972; The Public Burning, 1977; Hair o' the Chine, 1989; After Lazarus, 1980; Charlie in the House of Rue, 1980; A Political Fable, 1980; Spanking the Maid, 1982; In Bed One Night and Other Brief Encounters, 1982; Gerald's Party, 1986; Aesop's Forest, 1986; A Night at the Movies, short fictions, 1987; Whatever Happened to Gloomy Gus of the Chicago Bears, 1987; Pinocchio in Venice, 1991. Contributions to: Numerous journals and other publications. Honours: William Faulkner Award, 1966; Rockefeller Foundation Fellowship, 1969; Brandeis Citation for Fiction, 1979; Guggenheim Foundation Fellowship, 1971, 1974; 3 Obie Awards for The Kid, 1973; American Academy of Arts and Letters Award, 1976; National Endowment of the Arts Award, 1985; REA Award for the Short Story, 1987; DAAD Fellowship, 1990. Memberships: PEN; American Academy and Institute of Arts and Letters. Literary Agent: Georges Borchardt, USA. Address: c/o Georges Borchardt, 136 East 57th Street, New York, NY 10022, USA.

COPE Jack Robert Knox, b. 3 June 1914, Mooi River, Natal. Writer; Poet. m. Lesley de Villiers, 4 June 1942, 2 sons. Education: Co-founder and Editor, South African Literary magazine, Contrast, 1960-80. Publications include: The Rain Maker, 1971; The Tame Ox; Lyrics and Diatribes, 1948; Penguin Book of South African Verse, (editor); The Student of Zend, 1972; Selected Poems of Ingrid Jonker, co-translator, 1968, revised 1988; The Adversary Within; Radio broadcasts, stage and TV adaptions; My Son Max, 1977. Contributions to: New Yorker; Harpers; Esquire; Reporter; Short Story International; John Bull; Mademoiselle; Paris Review; Argosy; London Magazine; Leading South African magazines and school textbooks. Honours: British Council Award, 1960; Carnegie Fellowship USA, 1966; CNA Prize, Argus prize and Gold Medallist for Literature, Veld Trust Prize, 1971; DLitt, Rhodes. Literary Agent: Shelley Power. Address: 21 Bearton Road, Hitchin, Herts SG5 1UB, England.

COPE Wendy, b. 21 July 1945, Erith, Kent, England. Teacher; Poet. Education: BA, St Hilds College, Oxford, 1966. Appointments: Teacher in London primary schools, 1967-86; Freelance Writer since 1986. Publications: Across the City, 1980; Hope and the 42, 1984; Making Cocoa for Kingsley Amis, 1986; Poem from a Colour Chart of Housepaints, 1986; Men and Their Boring Arguments, 1988; Does She Like Wordgames?, 1988; The River Girl, 1990; Serious Concerns, 1992; Editor, Is That The New Moon?; Poem by Women Poets, 1989; The Orchard Book of Funny Poems, 1993. Honour: Cholmondeley Award, 1987; FRSL. Address: Peters Fraser and Dunlop, 5th Floor, The Chambers, Chelsea Harbour, Lots Road, London SW10 0XF, England.

COPELAND Ann. See: **FURTWANGLER Virginia Anne.**

CORBEN Beverly Balkum, b. 6 Aug 1926. Artist/Writer; Educator (retired). m. Dr Herbert Charles Corben, 25 Oct 1957, 1 stepson, 2 stepdaughters. Education: AA, Santa Monica College, USA, 1950; BA with honours, University of California, Los Angeles, 1960; MA, Case Western Reserve University, 1972. Appointments: Editorial Associate, Technical Public Relations, The Ramo-Wooldridge Corporation (now TRC Inc), 1954-57; Teaching Assistant, 1972-73; Director of Writing Laboratory, 1973-82 (on leave 1978-80), Scarborough College, University of Toronto, Canada; Visiting Scholar, Harvey Mudd College College, 1978-80, 1982-1988; Scholar-in-Residence, Humanities, 1982-88; Volunteer literary appointments: Chairman, Pascagoula Women's Club May Day (Statewide) Poetry Contests, USA, 1990, 1991; Creative Writing Director, Pascagoula Senior Citizens Center, 1990-. Publications: On Death and Other Reasons for Living (poems), Cleveland State University Poetry Center, 1972, 2nd printing, 1993. Contributor to: Poetic Justice; The Texas Review; Voices International; Prophetic Voices; Modern Haiku; Old Hickory Review; Other journals. Honours: Cleveland State University Honorary Alumna, 1971; More than 60 awards for poetry and fiction nationwide, 1989-; Mississippi Poetry Society (South) Poet of the Year, 1990; Poet of the Year State wide, 1991; Mississippi Jack Scroll of Merit, The Mississippi Press, 1992; WLOX-TV Person-of-the-Week, 11 Mar 1994. Memberships: Mississippi Poetry Society; Gulf Coast Writers Association; Writers Unlimited, President, 1991, 1992; Academy of American Poets. Address: 4304 O'Leary Avenue, Pascagoula, MS 39581, USA.

CORD Barry. See: **GERMANO Peter B.**

CORDELL Alexander, b. 9 Sept 1914, Ceylon. Author. m. 20 Mar 1937, 1 daughter. Education: Partly at Marist Brothers College, Tientsin, N China. Publications include: Welsh Triology: (Rape of the Fair Country, The Hosts of Rebecca, Song of the Earth); Race of the Tiger; This Proud and Savage Land; Land of my Fathers; The Fire People; This Sweet and Bitter Earth; If You Believe the Soldiers; A Thought of Honour; The Bright Cantonese; Tales from Tiger Bay; The Sinews of Love; To Slay the Dreamer; The Dream and the Destiny; Rogue's March; Peerless Jim; Tunnel Tigers; Requiem for a Patriot; Moll; Beloved Exile; The Dreams of Fair Women; Land of Heart's Desire; The Love That God Forgot. For Children: Irish Triology: (The White Cockade; Witch's Sabbath; The Healing Blade); The Traitor Within; Sea Urchin. Address: The Conifers, Railway Road, Rhossdu, Wrexham, Clwyd LLII 2DU, Wales.

COREN Alan, b. 27 June 1938, London, England. Editor of Punch. m. Anne Kasriel, 14 Oct 1963, 1 son, 1 daughter. Education: BA, 1st Class Honours, Wadham College, Oxford, 1961; Harkness Fellowship, Yale, USA, 1961-62; Berkeley, USA, 1962-63. Appointments: Assistant Editor 1963-67, Literary Editor 1967-69,

Deputy Editor 1969-77, Editor 1978-87, Punch Magazine Editor, The Listener, 1988-89. Publications: The Dog It Was That Died, 1965; All Except the Bastard, 1969; The Sanity Inspector, 1974; The Collected Bulletins of Idi Amin, 1974; Golfing for Cats, 1975; The Further Bulletin of Idi Amin, 1975; The Rhinestone As Big as the Ritz, 1977; The Peanut Papers, 1978; The Lady from Stalingrad Mansions, 1979; Tissues for Men, 1980; The Cricklewood Diet, 1982; Bumf, 1984; Something for the Weekend, 1986; Bin Ends, 1987; 12 novels for children (The Arthur Books, 1979-82); The Penguin Book of Modern Humour, Editor, 1983; Seems Like Old Times, 1989, (Autobiography); More Like Old Times, 1990; A Year in Cricklewood, 1991; Toujours Cricklewood? 1993; Sunday Best, 1993. Contributions include: Atlantic Monthly; Tatler; Harpers; Playboy; London Review of Books; The Listener; Sunday Times; Observer; Daily Mail; The Times; The Telegraph; Vogue; Nova; Era; New York Times; Evening Standard. Honour: Editor of the Year, British Society of Magazine Editors, 1986; Hon DLitt, University of Nottingham, 1993. Address: c/o Robson Books, 5 Clipstone Street, London WC1, England.

COREY Deborah Joy, b. 1958, Canadian. Publication: Losing Eddie. Honour: Smith/Books in Canada First Novel Award, 1994.

CORK Richard Graham, b. 25 Mar 1947, Eastbourne, England. Art Critic. m. Vena Jackson, Mar 1970, 2 sons, 2 daughters. Education: Kingswood School, Bath, 1960-64; Trinity Hall, Cambridge, 1965-69. Appointments: Art Critic, Evening Standard, 1969-77, 1980-83; Editor, Studio International, 1975-79; Art Critic, The Listener, 1984-90; Slade Professor of Fine Art, Cambridge, 1989-90; Art Critic, The Times, 1991-; Henry Moore Senior Research Fellow at the Courtauld Institute, London, 1992-. Publications: Vorticism & Abstract in the First Machine Age; The Social Role of Art; Art Beyond the Gallery in Early 20th Century England; David Bomberg; Architect's Choice; A Bitter Truth: Avant-Gorrde Art and the Great War, 1994. Contributions to: The Burlington Magazine; Apollo; Artforum; Art in America; New Statesman; The Independent Magazine. Honours: John Llewelyn Rhys Memorial Prize; Sir Banister Fletcher Award. Memberships: South Bank Board Visual Art Panel; British Council Visual Art Committee; Public Art Development Trust; Contemporary Art Society Trustees. Address: 24 Milman Road, London NW6 6EG, England.

CORKHILL Annette Robyn, (Annette Robyn Vernon), b. 10 Sep 1955, Brisbane, Australia. Translator. m. Alan Corkhill, 18 Mar 1977, 2 sons, 1 daughter. Education: BA(Hon), 1977; DipEd, 1978; MA, 1985; PhD, 1993. Publications: The Jogger, Anthology of Australian Poetry, 1987; Destination, Outrider, 1987; Mangoes Encounter - Queensland Summer, 1987; Age 1, LINQ, 1987; Two Soldiers of Tiananmen, Earth Against Heaven, 1990; Australian Writing: Ethnic Writers 1945-1991, 1994. Contributions to: Outrider; Australian Literary Studies. Honours: Honorary Mention, The Creativity Centre, Harold Kesteven Poetry Prize, 1987. Address: 5 Wattletree Place, The Gap, Queensland 4061, Australia.

CORLETT William, b. 1938, United Kingdom. Children's Author; Dramatist; Repertory and Television Actor. Publications: The Gentle Avalanche, 1962; Another Round, 1962; Return Ticket, 1962; The Scallop Shell, 1963; Flight of a Lone Sparrow, 1965; Dead Set at Dream Boy, 1965; The Scourging of Matthew Barrow, 1965; Tinker's Curse, 1968; We Never Went to Cheddar Gorge, 1968; The Story Teller, 1969; The Illusionist, 1969; National Trust, 1970; The Deliverance of Fanny Blaydon, 1971; A Memory of Two Loves, 1972; Conversations in the Dark, 1972; The Gate of Eden, 1974; The Land Beyond, 1975; The Ideal Tale, 1975; The Once and Forever Christmas (with John Moore), 1975; Return to the Gate, 1975; Mr Oddy, 1975; The Orsini Emeralds, 1975; Emmerdale Farm series, 1975-77; Orlando the Marmalade Cat Buys a Cottage, adaptation of story by Kathleen Hale, 1975; The Dark Side of the Moon, 1976; Orlando's Camping Holiday, adaptation of a story by Kathleen Hale, 1976; Paper Lads, 1978-79; Question series (The Question of Religion, The Christ Story, The Hindu Sound, The Judaic Law, The Buddha Way, The Islamic Space), 1978-79; Kids series, 1979; Going Back, 1979; The Gate of Eden, 1980; Barriers series, 1980; Agatha Christie Hour, adaptation of 4 short stories, 1982; The Machine Gunners, adaptation of Robert Westall book, 1982; Dearly Beloved, 1983; Bloxworth Blue, 1984; Return to the Gate, 1986; The Secret Line, 1988; The Steps up the Chimney, 1990; The Door in the Tree, 1991; The Tunnel Behind the Waterfall, 1991; The Bridge in the Clouds, 1992; The Gondoliers Cat, 1993; Television & Film: The Watchouse, adaptation by Robert Westall book, 1989; Torch, 6 part family adventure series, BBC TV, 1992; Moonacre, 6 part family adventure series, BBC TV, 1994. Memberships: Society of

Authors; Writers Guild of Great Britain. Literary Agent: Shiel Land & Caroline Sheldon. Address: Churchfields, Hope Mansel, Nr Ross-on-Wye, Herefordshire HR9 5TA, England.

CORLEY Ernest. See: **BULMER Henry Kenneth.**

CORMAN Avery, b. 28 Nov 1935, New York City, USA. Writer (Novelist). m. Judith Lishinsky, 5 Nov 1967, 2 sons. Education: BS, New York University, 1952. Publications: Oh God!, 1971; Kramer Vs Kramer, 1977; The Bust-Out King, 1977; The Old Neighborhood, 1980; Fifty, 1987; Prized Possessions, 1991; The Big Hype, 1992. Memberships: PEN American Center; The Writers Guild of America. Literary Agent: Morton L Janklow, Janklow & Nesbit Associates. Address: c/o Janklow & Newbit Associates, 598 Madison Avenue, New York City, NY 10022, USA.

CORMAN Cid, (Sidney Corman),b. 1924, USA. Poet. Appointments: Poetry Broadcaster, WMEX, Boston, Massachusetts, 1949-51; Editor, Origin Magazine and Origin Press, Kyoto, Japan, 1951-. Publications: Subluna, 1945; Thanksgiving Eclogue, 1954; The Precisions, 1955; The Responses, 1956; Stances and Distances, 1957; The Marches, 1957; A Table in Provence, 1958; The Descent from Daimonji, 1959; Clocked Stone, 1959; For Sure, 1959; Cool Melon, by Basjo, translation, 1959; Cool Gong, translation, 1959; For Instance, 1959; For Good, 1961; Sun Rock Man, 1962; Selected Frogs, by Shimpoo Kusano (translated with Kamike Susumu), 1963; In Good Time, 1964; In No Time, 1964; All in All, 1965; Nonce, 1965; For You, 1966; For Granted, 1966; At: Bottom, 1966; Stead, 1966; Words for Each Other, 1967; Back Roads to Far Towns, by Basho, translation, 1967; Frogs and Other Poems, by Shimpeo Kusano (translated with Kamike Susumu), 1968; & Without End, 1968; No Less, 1968; Hearth, 1968; No More, 1969; Plight, 1969; Nigh, 1969; Livingdying, 1970; Of the Breath of, 1970; For Keeps, 1970; For Now, 1971; Things, by Francis Ponge, translation, 1971; Out and Out, 1972; Be Quest, 1972; A Language Without Words, 1973; So Far, 1973; The Gist of Origin: An Anthology (editor), 1973; Leaves of Hypnos, by Rene Char, translation, 1973; Poems: Thanks to Zukerkandi, 1973; Breathing, 1973; Breathings, by Phillippee Jaccottet, translation, 1974; 0/1, 1974; Once and For All, 1976; Auspices, 1978; At Their Word: Essays on the Arts of Language, 2 vols, 1977-78; Aegis: Selected Poems, 1970-1980, 1983; Where We Are Now: Essays and Postscription, 1991. Honour: Lenore Marshall Poetry Prize for 0/1. Address: c/o Black Sparrow Press, Box 3993, Santa Barbara, CA 93130, USA.

CORMAN Sidney. See: **CORMAN Cid.**

CORMANY Michael Eugene, b. 8 Jan 1951, Aurora, USA. Laborer. Publications: Skin Deep Is Fatal; Rich or Dead; Polaroid Man; Red Winter; Lost Daughter; Rich or Dead, 1992; Skin Deep is Fatal, 1992. Honours: Best First Novel; BOMC Mysterious Book Club. Memberships: Mystery Writers of America; Private Eye. Address: 1050 N Farnsworth 315, Aurora, IL 60505, USA.

CORMIER Robert, b. 1925, USA. Writer. Literary appointments: Writer, Radio WTAG, Worcester, Massachusetts, 1946-48; Reporter, Columnist: Worcester Telegram and Gazette, 1948-55; Fitchburg Sentinel and Enterprise, Massachusetts, 1955-78. Publications: For adults: Now and at the Hour, 1960; A Little Raw on Monday Morning, 1963; Take Me Where the Good Times Are, 1965; For young adults: The Chocolate War, 1974; I Am the Cheese, 1977; After the First Death, 1979; Eight Plus One, 1980; The Bumblebee Flies Anyway, 1983; Beyond the Chocolate War, 1985; Fade, 1988; Other Bells For Us To Ring, 1990; We All Fall Down, 1991; I Have Words To Spend, 1991; Tunes For Bears To Dance To, 1992; In The Middle of the Night, 1995. Honours: Alan Award, National Council of Teachers of English, 1982; Margaret Edwards Award, American Library Association, School Library Journal. Address: 1177 Main Street, Leominster, MA 01453, USA.

CORN Alfred, b. 14 Aug 1943, Bainbridge, Georgia, USA. Poet. m. Ann Jones, 1967 (div 1971). Education: Emory University, Atlanta, 1961-65; BA, French, 1965; Columbia University, New York (Woodrow Wilson Fellow; Faculty Fellow) 1965-67; MA 1967; Fulbright Fellow, Paris, 1967-68. Appointments: Preceptor, Columbia University, 1968-70; Associate Editor, University Review, New York, 1970; Staff Writer, DaCapo Press, New York, 1971-72; Assistant Professor, 1978 and Visiting Lecturer, 1980-81, Connecticut College, New London; Visiting Lecturer, Yale University, New Haven, 1977, 1978, 1979, Columbia University 1983, 1985 and City University of New York, 1983,

1985. Publications: Verse: All Roads at Once, 1976; A Call in the Midst of the Crowd, 1978; The Various Light, 1980; Notes from a Child of Paradise, 1984; The West Door, 1989; Antobiographies, 1993. Honours: Ingram Merril Fellowship, 1974; George Dillon Prize, 1975; Oscar Blumenthal Prize, 1977 and Levinson Prize 1982 (Poetry, Chicago); Davidson Prize, 1982; American Academy Award, 1983.

CORNISH Gracie, (Grace Clee), b. 22 Aug 1961, Kingston, Jamaica. Author; Image Consultant. 1 daughter. Education: BA, Social Psychology, 1982. Publications: The Fortune of Being Yourself, 1991; Think and Grow Beautiful, 1992; Radiant Women of Color, 1994. Honours: Certificate of Recognition for Black Women in Literature. Address: c/o Fortune 27 Resources, 610 Fifth Avenue, Box 4739, NY 10185 0040, USA. 6.

CORNISH Sam, (Samuel James), b. 1935, USA. Children's Fiction Writer; Poetry; Consultant (Elementary School Teaching). Appointments: Formerly Editor, Chicory, Enoch Pratt Library Publications, Baltimore, Maryland; Currently Editor, Mimeo Magazine. Publications: In This Corner: Sam Cornish and Verses, 1961; People Under the Window, 1962; Generations, 1964; Angles, 1965; Winters, 1968; Chicory: Young Voices from the Black Ghetto (edited with L W Dixon), 1969; The Living Underground: An Anthology of Contemporary American Poetry (edited with H Fox), 1969; Your Hand in Mine, 1970; Generations: Poem, 1971; Streets, 1973; Sometimes: Ten Poems, 1973; Grandmother's Pictures, children's fiction, 1974; Sam's World, 1978; Songs of Jubilee, 1986; 1935: A Memoir, 1990; Folks Like Me, 1993. Address: c/o Bookstore Press, Box 191, RFDI, Freeport, ME 04032, USA.

CORNWELL David John Moore, (John le Carré), b. 19 Oct 1931. Writer. m. (1) Alison Ann Veronica Sharp, 1954, divorced 1971, 3 sons, (2) Valerie Jane Eustace, 1972, 1 son. Education: Berne University; Lincoln College, Oxford. Appointments: Teacher, Eton College, 1956-58; Foreign Service, 1959-64. Publications: Call for the Dead, 1961 (filmed as The Deadly Affair, 1967); Murder of Quality, 1962; The Spy Who Came in From the Cold, 1963; The Looking Glass War, 1965; A Small Town in Germany, 1968; The Naive and Sentimental Lover, 1971; Tinker Tailor Soldier Spy, 1974; The Honourable Schoolboy, 1977; Smiley's People, 1979; The Quest for Karla (collected edition of previous 3 titles), 1982; The Little Drummer Girl, 1983; A Perfect Spy, 1986; The Russia House, 1989; The Secret Pilgrim, 1991; The Night Manager, 1993; Our Game, 1995. Honours: Somerset Maugham Award, 1963; James Tait Black Award, 1977; Premio Malaparte, 1987; Hon Fellow, Lincoln College, Oxford; Hon Doctor, Exeter University; Edgar Allen Poe Award Mystery Writers Am, 1965; Gold Dagger Crime Writers Association, 1978; Black Memorial Award, 1978; Grand Master Award Mystery Writers Am, 1986; Diamond Dagger Award Crime Writers Association, 1988; Nikos Kasanzakis Prize, 1991. Address: David Higham Associates, 5-8 Lower John Street, Golden Square, London, W1R 4HA, England.

CORRIGAN Robert W(illoughby),b. 1927. American. Theatre; Translations. Appointments: Andrew Mellon Professor and Head of the Department of Drama, Carnegie Institute of Technology, Pittsburgh, 1961-64; Professor of Dramatic Literature, 1964-68 and Dean of School of Arts, 1965-68, New York University; Director, Critics' Programme for National Endowment for the Humanities, 1967-68; President, California Institute of the Arts, Valencia, 1968-74; Dean of School of Fine Arts, University of Wisconsin, Milwaukee, 1974-; Chairman of the Board, SPACE for Innovative Development, New York City. Publications: (ed) The New Theatre of Europe, vol 1, 1962; (trans with M D Dirks), Appia's Music and the Art of the Theatre, 1962; (trans) Chekhov: Six Plays, 1962; The Theatre in the Twentieth Century, 1963; (ed) The New Theatre of Europe, vol II, 1964; (ed with J L Rosenberg), The Art of the Theatre, 1964; (ed with J L Rosenberg), The Context and Craft of Drama, 1964; The Modern Theatre, 1964; (ed) New American Plays, vol I, 1965; (ed) Comedy: Meaning and Form, 1965, 1981; (ed) Tragedy: Vision and Form, 1965, 1981; (ed) Laurel British Drama: 20th Century, 1965; (ed) Laurel British Drama: 19th Century, 1967; (ed) Masterpieces of the Modern Theatre, 9 vols, 1967; (ed) The New Theatre of Europe, vol III, 1968; Arthur Miller, 1969; (ed with G Loney) Tragedy: A Critical Anthology, 1971, 1980; (ed with G Loney) The Forms of Drama, 1972; The Theatre in Search of a Fix, 1973; The World of the Theatre, 1979; The Making of Theatre: From Drama to Performance, 1980; The World of Theatre, 1979; The Making of Theatre: From Drama to Performance, 1980; Classical Comedy: Greek & Roman, 1987. Address: 1037 E Ogden Avenue, Milwaukee, WI 53202, USA.

CORSON Richard, b. 27 Dec, Genoa, Illinois, USA. Teacher; Writer. Education: BA, De Pauw University, 1939; Phi Beta Kappa; MA, Louisiana State University, 1941. Publications: Stage Makeup, 1942, 1960, 1967, 1975, 1981, 1986, 1989; Fashions in Hair, The First 5,000 Years, 1965, 1971, 1980; Fashions in Makeup, From Ancient to Modern Times, 1972, 1981, 1989 (also published in Japanese); Fashions in Eyeglasses, 1967, 1980 (also published in Japanese). Contributions to: Problems in Makeup in Players Magazine, 1943-45 (monthly).

COSGRAVE Patrick, b. 28 Sept 1941. Writer. m. 1) Ruth Dudley Edwards, 1965, divorced, 2) Norma Alice Green, 1974, divored, 1 daughter, 3) Shirley Ward, 1981. Education: BA, MA, University College, NUI, Dublin; PhD, University of Cambridge. Appointments: London Editor, radio Telefis Eireann, 1968-69; Conservative Research Dept, 1969-71; Political Editor, The Spectator, 1971-75; Features Editor, Telegraph Magazine, 1974-76; Special Advisor to Rt Hon Mrs Margaret Thatcher, 1975-79; Managing Editor, Quartet Crime (Quartet Books), 1979-81. Publications: The Public Poetry of Robert Lowell, 1969; Churchill at War: Alone, 1974; Cheyney's Law (novel), 1976; Margaret Thatcher: A Tory and her Party, 1978, end edition as Margaret Thatcher: Prime Minister, 1979; The Three Colonels (novel), 1979; R A Butler: An English Life, 1981; Adventure of State (novel), 1984; Thatcher: The First Term, 1985; Carrington: A Life and a Policy, 1985; The Lives of Enoch Powell, 1989; The Strange Death of Socialist Britain, 1992. Contributions to: Various journals and magazines. Literary Agent: Michael Shaw, Curtis Brown, 162-168 Regent St, London W1R 5TB, England. Address: 21 Thornton Road, London SW12 0JX, England.

COSIC Dobrica, b. 29 Dec 1921, Velika Drenova, Yugoslavia. Novelist. Appointments include: President of the Federal Republic of Serbia, from 1992. Publications: Far Away is the Sun, 1951, 1963; Roots, 1954; D Divisions, 1961; Fairytale, 1966; This Land, This Time, 4 volumes, 1972-79, 1983; Sinner, 1985; Renegade, 1986; Believer, 1990; Also: Seven Days in Budapest, 1957; Action, 1965; Collected Works, 1966; Power and Foreboding, 1972; The Real and the Possible, 1982. Address: c/o Federal Assembly, Belgrade, Serbia.

COSSI Olga, b. St Helena, Napa Valley, California, USA. Freelance Writer. Literary appointments: Staff Correspondent, Columnist, regional newspapers. Publications: Robin Deer; Fire Mate, Revised Edition, 1995; Gus the Bus; The Wonderful Wonderful Donkey; Orlanda and the Contest of Thieves; The Magic Box; Adventure on the Graveyard of the Wrecks; The Great Getaway; Harp Seals; Water Wars, 1993; Edna Hibel, Her Life and Art, 1994; Think Pink, 1994; Amy the Olive Eater, forthcoming; Great Grandma's Cookie Jar, forthcoming. Contributions to: Highlight for Children Magazine. Honours: Parent's Read Aloud Book Club Selection for The Great Getaway; The Magic Box, Books for the Teen Age List, New York Public Library Selection; Harp Seals, Most Outstanding Children's Science Trade Book; Books included in Sonoma County Museum 1992-93 Cover to Cover Exhibition and travelling tour. Membership: Society of Children's Book Writers and Illustrators. Address: 800 H Avenue, Colorado, CA 92118, USA.

COTES Peter, b. 19 Mar 1912. Actor Director; Play Producer and Biographer. m. Joan Miller, 19 May 1948, dec 1988. Education: Italia Conti Stage School. Appointments: Lecturer in Drama, Rose Bruford College; Adjudicator and Public Speaker. Publications: No Star Nonense, 1949; The Little Fellow (co-author Thelma Niklaus), 1951; Handbook for the Amateur Theatre, 1957; George Robey, 1972; JP: The Man Called Mitch, 1976; Elvira Barney, 1977; World Circue (co-author R Croft-Cooke), 1978; Performing (Album of the Arts), 1980; Dickie: The Story of Dickie Henderson, 1988; Sincerely Yours, 1989; Thinking Aloud, 1993. Contributions to: Daily Telegraph; Guardian; The Independent; The Times; The Field; The Stage; Plays and Players; Irish Times; The Spectator. Honours: Fellow, Royal Societyof Arts; Knight of Mark Twain. Memberships: Savage Club; Our Society; Society of Authors. Address: 7 Hill Lawn Court, Chipping Norton, Oxon OX7 5AF, England.

COTTERILL Kenneth Matthew, b. 17 Sept 1950, Sheffield, England. Playwright. m. Marilyn Bokiagon, 6 Oct 1984, 1 son. Education: BA, University of Queensland, 1980; Queensland University of Technology, 1981. Publications: Re Electing Roger; Richard the Third's Revenge; Perfect Murder; Rhinocerus Hides. Contributions to: Australian Jewish Democrat; British Soccer Week; Flashing Blade; International Association of Agricultural Information Specialists, Quarterly Bulletin. Honours: Australias Bicentennial Award; Australia

Day Award for Culture, 1994. Memberships: Australian Writers Guild; Playlab. Address: 44 Martin Avenue, Mareeba, Queensland, Australia.

COTTINGHAM Valery Jean, b. 4 Sept 1934, Kingston-Upon-Hull, Yorkshire, England. m. George Cottingham, 28 Dec 1965, dec'd 1991. Education: Endyke Fifth Avenue High School, Kingston-Upon-Hull. Publications: Memories, A Collection of Poems & Short Stories, Volumes 1, II, III. Contributions to: Modern Poetry, 1981, 1982, 1983, 1984; Winter Gold, 1991; New Beginnings, 1993. Honours: Certificate of Merit, Writer's World Publishers, Australia; Certificate of Merit, California, USA. Address: 58 Colliers Close, Horsell, Woking, Surrey GU21 3AW, England.

COTTON John, b. 7 Mar 1925, Hackney, London, England. m. Peggy Midson, 27 Dec 1948, 2 sons. Education: BA, Hons, English, London University. Literary Appointments: Editor, Priapus, a magazine of poetry and art, 1962-72; Editor, The Private Library, a book collectors' journal, 1969-79; Advisory Editor, Contemporary Poets of the English Language. Publications: Old Movies and other poems, 1971; Kilroy Was Here, 1975; Daybook, 1983; The Storyville Portraits, 1984; The Crystal Zoo, 1984; Oh Those Happy Feet, 1986; The Poetry File, 1989; Two by Two (with Fred Sedgwick), 1990; Here's Looking At You Kid, 1992. Contributions to: Sunday Observer; Poetry Chicago; Times Literary Supplementary; Encounter; The New Review; Outposts; Ambit. Honours: Art Council Publication Award, 1971; Deputy Lieutenant of the County of Hertfordshire, 1989. Memberships: Poetry Society, Chairman 1972-74 and 1977, Treasurer, 1986-89. Address: 37 Lombard Drive, Berkhamstead, Hertfordshire HP4 2LQ, England.

COTTRELL HOULE Mary, b. 1953. Children's Writer. Publications: One City's Wilderness: Portland's Forest Park, 1988; Wings For My Flight: The Peregrine Falcons of Chimney Rock, 1991. Honour: Christopher Award, 1992. Address: c/o Addison Wesley Publishing-Publicity D, 170 Fifth Avenue, New York, NY 10010, USA.

COTTRET Bernard J, b. 23 Apr 1951, Paris, France. Professor British Studies. m. Monique Astruc, 22 Sept 1951, 1 s. Education: Ecole Normale Superieure de Saint-Cloud, 1971-76. Appointments: Prof, University of Versailles; Prof, University of Charleston, SC, 1994. Literary Appointments: Consultant Bibliotheque Nationale, Paris, 1988-1991. Publications: Glorieuse Révolution d'Angleterre, 1988; Le Christ des Lumières, 1990; The Huguenots in England, 1991; Cromwell, 1992; Bolingbroke, 1992; Histoire des îles Britanniques, 1994; Forthcoming: Bolingbroke's Political Writings. Honours: Docteur ès Lettres; Prix Monseigneur Marcel, Académie Francaise, (silver medal), 1993. Address: 1 Res du Lac, 94470 Boissy-St-Léger, France.

COULSON Juanita Ruth, b. 12 Feb 1933, Anderson, Indiana, USA. Freelance Writer. m. Robert Stratton Coulson, 21 Aug 1954, 1 son. Education: BS, 1954, MA, 1961, Ball State University. Publications: The Scent of Magic, in anthology Tales of the Witch World (edited André Norton); Crisis on Cheiron, 1967; The Singing Stones, 1968; Door into Terror, 1972; Dark Priestess, 1976; Space Trap, 1976; Web of Wizardry, 1978; The Death God's Citadel, 1980; Tomorrow's Heritage, 1981, 1989; Outward Bound, 1982, 1989; Legacy of Earth, 1989; The Past of Forever, 1989; Starsister, 1990; Cold, Hard Silver, in anthology Tales of Ravenloft, 1994; A Matter of Faith, in anthology Women At War (edited Lois McMaster Bujold and Roland Green), 1995. Contributions to: Magazine of Fantasy and Science Fiction; Fantastic Science Fiction and Fantasy Science Stories; Goldman Fantasy Foliant III. Honours: Co-winner, Hugo, Best Amateur Publication, World Science Fiction Convention, London, 1965. Membership: Past Member, Science Fiction Writers of America. Literary Agent: James Allen, 538 E Harford Street, Milford, PA 18337, USA. Address: 2677 W 500 N, Hartford City, IN 47348, USA.

COULSON Robert Stratton, b. 12 May 1928, Sullivan, Indiana, USA. Writer. m. 21 Aug 1954, 1 son. Publications: The Invisibility Affair, 1967; The Mind-Twisters Affair, 1967; Now You See It/Him/Them, 1975; Gates of the Universe, 1975; But What of Earth?, 1976; To Renew the Ages, 1976; Charles Fort Never Mentioned Wombats, 1977; Nightmare Universe, 1985. Contributions to: Dictionary of Literary Biography; Fantasy Empire; Amazing Stories; Official Price Guide to Science Fiction and Fantasy Collectibles; Paper Collectors Marketplace; Viking-Penguin Science Fiction Encyclopedia; Review: Comic Buyers Guide. Memberships: Science Fiction Writers of America; Science Fiction Writers of America Forum, Co-editor, 1971, Secretary, 1972-74. Literary Agent: James Allen, 538 E Harford Street,

Milford, PA 18337, USA. Address: 2677 W 500 N, Hartford City, IN 47348, USA.

COULTER Harris Livermore, b. 8 Oct 1932, Baltimore, Maryland, USA. Writer; Translator; Interpreter. m. Catherine Nebolsine, 10 Jan 1960, 2 sons, 2 daughters. Education: BA, Yale University, 1954; PhD, Department of Political Science, Columbia University, 1969. Publications: Divided Legacy: A History of the Schism in Medical Thought, Volume I: The Patterns Emerge, 1975, Volume II: The Origins of Modern Western Medicine, 1977, Volume III: Homeopathy and the American Medical Association, 1973, 1981, Volume IV: Twentieth-Century Medicine: The Bacteriological Era, 1994; Homeopathic Science and Modern Medicine, 1981; DPT: A Shot in the Dark (with Barbara Fisher), 1985; Vaccination, Social Violence, and Criminality, 1990; The Controlled Clinical Trial: An Analysis, 1991. Honours: Hahnemann Prize, Société Royale Belge d'Homéopathie, 1985; La Medalla d'Or del Centenari, Academia Medico-Homepatica de Barcelona, 1990. Membership: American Institute of Homeopathy. Address: Center for Empirical Medicine, 4221 45th Street NW, Washington, DC 20016, USA.

COULTON James. See: **HANSEN Joseph.**

COURLANDER Harold, b. 18 Sept 1908, Indianapolis, Indiana, USA. Author. Education: BA, University of Michigan, 1931; Postgraduate work, Columbia University, 1939-50. Publications include: Haiti Singing, 1939; The Hat Shaking Dance, 1957; Kantchil's Lime Pit, 1950; The Drum and the Hoe, 1960; The King's Drum, 1962; Negro Folk Music USA, 1963; People of the Short Blue Corn, 1970; The Fourth World of the Hopis, 1971; Tales of Yoruba Gods and Heroes, 1973; A Treasury of African Folklore, 1975; A Treasury of Afro-American Folklore, 1976; The Crest and the Hide, 1982; The Heart of the Ngoni, 1982; Hopi Voices, 1982; Novels: The Caballero, 1940; The Big Old World of Richard Creeks, 1962; The African, 1967; The Son of the Leopard, 1974; The Mesa of Flowers, 1977; The Master of the Forge, 1985; The Bordeaux Narrative, 1990; Compiler, Editor, Annotator: Big Falling Snow, 1978. Contributions to: Musical Quarterly; Journal of Negro History; African Arts; Phylon; The American Scholar; Michigan Alumnus; Negro History Bulletin; Resound; Saturday Review; Tomorrow; Bulletin du Bureau National d'Ethnologie; Village Voice; Ethnic Folkways Library; Chronicle, the Quarterly Magazine of the Historical Society of Michigan. Honours: John Simon Guggenheim Fellowships, 1948, 1955; Various awards and academic grants in aid; Outstanding Achievement Award, University of Michigan, 1984. Address: 5512 Brite Drive, Bethesda, MD 20817, USA.

COURTER Gay, b. 1 Oct 1944, Pittsburgh, Pennsylvania, USA. Writer; Film Maker. m. Philip Courter, 18 Aug 1968, 2 sons. Education: AB, Drama, Film, Antioch College, Ohio, 1966. Publications: The Bean Sprout Book, 1974; The Midwife, 1981; River of Dreams, 1984; Code Ezra, 1986; Flowers in the Blood, 1990; The Midwife's Advice, 1992; I Speak ForThis Child, 1995. F3)Contributions to: Parents; Women's Day; Publishers Weekly; Others. Memberships: Authors Guild; Writers Guild of America East; Guardian Ad Litem; International Childbirth Association. Literary Agent: Donald Cutler, Bookmark: The Literary Agency. Address: 121 NW Crystal Street, Crystal River, FL 34428, USA.

COURTNEY Nicholas Piers, b. 20 Dec 1944, England. Author. m. Vanessa Hardwicke, London, 1980. Education: ARICS; MRAC, Royal Agricultural College, Cirencester. Publications: Shopping & Cooking in Europe, 1980; The Tiger, Symbol of Freedom, 1981; Diana, Princess of Wales, 1982; Royal Children, 1982; Prince Andrew, 1983; Sporting Royals, 1983; Diana, Princess of Fashion, 1984; Queen Elizabeth, The Queen Mother, 1984; The Very Best of British, 1985; In Society, The Brideshead Era, 1986; Princess Anne, 1986; Luxury Shopping in London, 1987; Sisters in Law, 1988; A Stratford Kinshall, 1989; The Man, 1990; Winsor Castle, 1991. Contributions to: Times; Redbook. Memberships: Brook's Hurlingham PEN Club. Literary Agent: Sonia Land, Shell Land, 43 Doughty Street, London WC1N 2LF, England. Address: 9 Kemspn Road, London, SW6 4PX, England.

COUZYN Jeni, b. 26 July 1942, South Africa, Canadian Citizen. Lecturer; Poet; Psychotherapist. Education: BA, University of Natal, 1963. Appointments: Freelance Poet, Broadcaster, Lecturer, 1968-; Writer in Residence, University of Victoria, British Columbia, 1976. Publications: Flying, 1970; Monkeys' Wedding, 1972; Christmas in Africa, 1975; House of Changes, 1978; The Happiness Bird, 1978; Life by Drowning, 1983, 1985; In the Skin House, 1993; Poems for Children and Editions of Poetry. Honours: Canada Council Grant, 1977, 1984. Address: c/o Bloodaxe Books, PO Box 1SN, Newcastle Upon Tyne, NE99, England.

COVARRUBIAS ORTIZ Miguel, b. 27 Feb 1940, Monterrey, Mexico. Writer; Professor. m. Silvia Mijares, 18 Mar 1967, 2 daughters. Education: Licenciado en letras, 1973, Maestria en letras espanolas, (pasantia), 1987, Universidad Autonoma de Nuevo Leon, Monterrey. Appointments: Coordinator, Department of Literature, Escuela de Verano, University of Nuevo Leon, 1970; Director, Centre for Literary and Linguistic Research, 1976-79, Coordinator, Creative Writing Workshop, 1981-, Universidad Autonoma de Nuevo Leon, Monterrey. Publications: La raiz ausente, 1962; Custodia de silencios, 1965, 1982; Minusculario, 1966; Poetry: El poeta, 1969; El segundo, 1977, 1981, 1988; Pandora, 1987; Essays: Papeleria, 1970; Olavide o Sade, 1975; Nueva papeleria, 1978; Eidtor: Desde el Cerro de la silla, segundo, 1992. Contributions to: Vide universitaria, 1960-66; Apolodionis, 1959-67; Trabajo y cultura, 1967; Gaceta (Office of Foreign Affairs, Mexico), 1967-68; Suplemento Cultural de El Porvenir, 1968-71, 1982-90; Calendario de Ramon Lopez Velarde (Office of Public Education, Mexico), 1971; Deslinde, 1982-. Honours: 2nd Place, Stgory, Xalapa Arts Festival, 1962; Arts Prize, Literature, Universidad Autonoma de Nuevo Leon, 1989. Membership: Sociedad General de Escritores de Mexico. Address: Kant 2801, Contry-La Silla, Guadalupe, N L, Mexico 67170, Mexico.

COVILLE Bruce Farrington, b. 16 May 1950, Syracuse, New York, USA. Writer. Separated, 2 sons, 1 daughter. Education: Duke University 1968-69, State University of New York at Binghamton, 1969-72, State University College at Oswego, 1973, BA, Elementary Education. Appointments: Teacher 1974-81, specializing in gifted education for last three years. Left teaching for a career in publishing. Publications Include: Books include: Sarah's Unicom, 1979; The Monster's Ring, 1982; Sarah and the Dragon, 1984; Operation Sherlock, 1986; Ghost in the Third Row, 1987; My Teacher is an Alien, 1989; Herds of Thunder, Manes of Gold, 1989; Jennifer Murdley's Toad, 1992; Space Brat, 1993; Aliens Ate My Homework, 1993. Plays: Faculty Room, 1988; It's Midnight, 1983; Out of the Blue, 1982; The Dragonslayers, 1981. Contributions to: Editor, Seniority Magazine, 1983-84. Honours: Second Place Winner of the Colorado Children's Book Award, 1984 for Sarah's Unicom; Winner, South Carolina Children's Choice Award, 1984-85, Nominated for Children's Choice Awards in Arizona, Indiana and Iowa, for The Monster's Ring; IRA Children's Choice List 1985, for Sarah and the Dragon; IRA Children's Choice List 1987 for Operation Sherlock; Nominated for Young Hoosier Book Award for Ghost in the Third Row. Memberships: Society of Children's Book Writers; Science Fiction Writers of America; Dramatists Guild. Address: 14 East 11th Street, New York, NY 10003, USA.

COWAN Peter, b. 4 Nov 1914, Perth, Western Australia. Academic Author. Education: University of Western Australia, BA in English, 1940. Appointments: Senior English Master, Scotch College, Swanbourne, Western Australia, 1950-62; Member of Faculty, 1962-79, Research Fellow, Department of English, 1979-, University of Western Australia, Nedlands. Publications: Drift Stories, 1944; The Unploughed Land: Stories, 1959; Summer, 1964; Short Story Landscape: The Modern Short Story (editor), 1964; The Empty Street: Stories, 1965; Seed, 1966; Spectrum One To Three (co-editor), 1970-79; Today: Contemporary Short Stories (editor), 1971; The Tins and Other Stories, 1973; A Faithful Picture: Letters of Eliza and Thomas Brown, Swan River Colony 1841-1851 (editor), 1977; A Unique Position: A Biography of Edith Dircksey Cowan, 1978; Westerly 21 (editor), 1978; Mobiles, stories, 1979; Perspectives One (editor), short fiction, 1985; A Window in Mrs X's Place, short stories, 1986; The Color of the Sky, novel, 1986; Voices, short fiction, 1988; Maitland Brown: A View of Nineteenth Century Western Australia (biography), 1988; The Hills of Apollo Bay, novel, 1989; Impressions: West Coast Fiction 1829-1988, (editor), 1989; Western Australian Writing: A Bibliography, co-ed, 1990; The Tenants, novel, 1994. Address: English Department, University of Western Australia, Nedlands, WA 6009, Australia.

COWANNA Betty. See: **HARRISON Elizabeth C.**

COWASJEE Saros, b. 12 July 1931, Secundrabad, India. Professor of English. Education includes: MA, Agra University, 1955; PhD, University of Leeds, England. Appointments: Assistant Editor, Times of India Press, Bombay, 1961-63; Teaching, 1963-, Professor of English, 1971-; University of Regina, Regina, Canada; General Editor,

Literature of the Raj series, Arnold Publishers, New Delhi, 1984-. Publications: Sean O'Casey: The Man Behind the Plays, 1963; Sean O'Casey, 1966; Stories and Sketches, 1970; Goodbye to Elsa, novel, 1974; So Many Freedoms: A Study of the Major Fiction of Mulk Raj Anand, 1977; The Last of the Maharajas, screenplay, 1980; Suffer Little Children, novel, 1982; Studies in Indian and Anglo-Indian Fiction, 1993; Others: Editor, several fiction anthologies including: Stories from the Raj, 1982; More Stories from the Raj and After, 1986; Women Writers of the Raj, 1990; The Best Short Stories of Flora Annie Steel, 1994; Orphans of the Storm: Short Fiction on the Partitioning of India, 1994. Contributions to: Encounter; A Review of English Literature; Journal of Commonwealth Literature; The Literary Criterion; World Literature Written in English; Literature East and West; International Fiction Review; Journal of Canadian Fiction. Honours: J N Tata Scholarship, 1957-69; Canada Council and SSHRC Leave Fellowships, 1968-69, 1974-75, 1978-79, 1986-87. Memberships: Cambridge Society; Writers Union of Canada; Authors Guild of India; Association of Commonwealth Literature and Language Studies. Address: Department of English, University of Regina, Regina, Saskatchewan, Canada S4S 0A2.

COWDREY Herbert Edward John, b. 29 Nov 1926, Basingstoke, Hants, England. University Teacher. m. Judith Watson Davis, 14 July 1959, 1 son, 2 daughters. Education: BA, Oxford University, 1949; MA 1951. Appointments: Chaplain & Tutor, St Stephen's House, Oxford, 1952-56; Fellow, St Edmund Hall, Oxford, 1956-94; Emeritus, Fellow, 1994-. Publications: The Cluniacs and the Gregorian Reform; The Epistolae Vagantes of Pope Gregory VII; Two Studies in Cluniac History; The Age of Abbot Desiderius; Popes, Monks and Crusaders. Contributions to: Many articles. Honour: Fellow of the British Academy. Memberships: Royal Historical Society; Henry Bradshaw Society. Address: 30 Oxford Road, Old Marston, Oxford OX3 0PQ, England.

COWIE Leonard Wallace, b. 10 May 1919, Brighton, England. Clerk in Holy Orders. m. Evelyn Elizabeth Trafford, 9 Aug 1949, 1 son. Education: BA 1941, MA 1946, Pembroke College, Oxford; PhD, University of London, 1954. Publications: Seventeenth-Century Europe, 1960; The March of the Cross, 1962; Eighteenth-Century Europe, 1963; Hanoverian England, 1967; The Reformation, 1968; Martin Luther, 1969; Sixteenth-Century Europe, 1977; Life in Britain, 1980; Years of Nationalism (with R Wolfson), 1985; The French Revolution, 1987; Lord Nelson: A Bibliography, 1990; William Wilberforce: A Bibliography, 1992; Edmund Burke: A Bibliography, 1994. Contributions to: History To-Day; History; Church Times. Memberships: Royal Historical Society, Fellow; The Athenaeum. Address: 38 Stratton Road, Merton Park, London SW19 3JG, England.

COWLES Fleur, b. USA. Painter and Writer. Appointments: Associate Editor, Look Magazine, USA, 1949-55; Founder, Editor, Flair Magazine, USA, 1950-51; Editor, Flairbook, USA, 1952. Publications: Bloody Precedent, 1951; The Case of Salvador Dali, 1959; The Hidden World of Hadhramoutt, 1964; I Can Tell It Now, 1965; Treasures of the British Museum, 1966; Tiger Flower, 1969; Lion and Blue, 1974; Friends and Memories, 1975; Romany Free, 1977; The Love of Tiger Flower, 1980; All Too True, 1980; The Flower Game, 1983; Flowers, 1985; People as Animals, 1985; To Be a Unicom, An Artist's Journey, 1986; The Life & Times of the Rose, 1991. Address: A5 Albany, Piccadilly, London W1, England.

COX Charles Brian, b. 1928, United Kingdom. Professor of English Literature. Appointments: Lecturer, Senior Lecturer, University of Hull, 1954-66; Co-editor, Critical Quarterly, 1959-; Professor of English Literature, University of Manchester, 1966-; Director, Manchester Poetry Centre, 1971-; Pro-Vice Chancellor, Manchester University, 1987-91; Visiting Professor, King's College, London, 1994; Honorary Fellow, Westminster College, Oxford, 1994. Publications: The Free Spirit, 1963; Modern Poetry (with A E Dyson), 1963; Conrad's Nostromo, 1964; The Practical Criticism of Poetry (with A E Dyson), 1965; Poems of This Century (edited with A E Dyson), 1968; Word in the Desert (edited with A E Dyson), 1968; The Waste Land: A Casebook (edited with A P Hinchliffe), 1968; The Black Papers on Education (edited with A E Dyson), 1971; The Twentieth Century Mind (edited with A E Dyson), 3 vols, 1972; Conrad: Youth, Heart of Darkness and The End of the Tether (editor), 1974; Joseph Conrad: The Modern Imagination, 1974; Black Paper 1975 (edited with R Boyson), 1975; Black Paper 1977 (edited with R Boyson), 1977; Conrad, 1977; Every Common Sight, verse 1981; Two Headed Monster, verse, 1985; Cox on Cox: AN English Curriculum for the 1990's, 1991; The Great Betrayal: Autobiog, 1992; Collected Poems,

1993. Honours: CBE, 1990; Fellow, Royal Society of Literature, 1993. Membership: Emeritus Professor, Manchester University, 1993-. Address: 20 Park Gates Drive, Cheadle Hulme, Stockport SK8 7DF, England.

COX David Dundas, b. 20June 1933, Goondiwindi. Graphic Artist; Author. m. Elizabeth Beath, 21 Feb 1976, 1 son, 2 daughters. Education: St Martin's School of Art, London, England. Appointments: Head Artist, The Courier Mail, Brisbane. Publications: Tin Lizzie and Little Nell, 1982; Bossyboots, 1985; Ayu and the Perfect Moon, 1984; Spice and Magic, collaboration with Betty Beath, 1983; Miss Bunkle's Umbrella, 1981; (Music Drama for Children) Abigail and the Rainmaker, 1976; Abigail and the Bush Ranger, 1976; The Raja Who Married an Angel, 1981; Frances, 1983; all with Betty Beath. Contributions to: Art Reviews; Childrens Book Reviews. Honours: Walkeley Award (Illustration), 1978; Highly Commended Children's Book of the Year Awards, 1983, 1985. Memberships: Australian Society of Authors; Opera for Youth, USA; Greek Community of St George, Queensland; Playlab, Queensland. Address: 8 St James Street, Highgate Hill, Queensland 4101, Australia.

COX Geoffrey Sandford, (Sir), b. 7 Apr 1910, Writer; Broadcaster. m. Cecily Barbara Talbot, 25 May 1925, 2 s, 2 d. Education: MA, New Zealand, 1931; BA, Oxon, 1934. Appointments: Reporter, News Chronicle, London, 1935; War Correspondent, Spain, 1936; Foreign Correspondent, Daily Express, 1937-40; Political Correspondent, 1945-54; Assistant Editor, 1954-56; Editorial Independent TV News, 1956-58; Deputy Chairman, Yorkshire TV, 1968-71; Chairman Tyne Tees RTV, 1972-74; LBC, 1977-81. Publications: Defence of Madrid, 1937; Race for Trieste, 1977; See It Happen, 1983; A Tale of Two Battles, 1987; Countdown to War, 1988. Honours: MBE, 1945; CBE, 1959; Knighted, 1966; Silver Medal Royal TV Society, 1968; Gold Medal Royal TV Society, 1978; BAFTA Award, 1962. Address: Garrick Club, London WC2, England.

COX (John) Madison IV, b. 23 Sept 1958, Bellingham, Washington, USA. Garden Designer; Author. Education: BFA, Parson's School of Design, Paris, France, 1984. Publications: Private Gardens of Paris, 1989; Gardens of the World (co-author), 1991; Artists' Gardens, 1993. Contributions to: Elle Decor, USA; House and Garden, USA. Literary Agent: Helen Pratt, New York City, USA. Address: c/o Helen Pratt, 1165 Fifth Ave, New York, NY 10029, USA.

COX Richard, b. 8 Mar 1931, Winchester, England. m. 1963, 2 sons, 1 daughter. Education: Stowe School; Honours degree in English, St Catherine's College, Oxford. Publications include: Sam 7, 1976; Operation Sealion, 1974 (paperback 1978); Auction, 1978; Auction, 1978; KGB Directive, 1981; Ground Zero, 1985; An Agent of Influence, 1988; Park Plaza, 1991; Total Eclipse, forthcoming. Contributions include: The Daily Telegraph (Staff Correspondent 1966-72), Travel & Leisure, Traveller, Orient Express Magazine. Honour: Territorial Decoration, 1966. Membership: Army and Navy Club. Literary Agent: William Morris Agency, New York. Address: PO Box 88, Alderney, Channel Islands.

COX William Trevor, (William Trevor), b. 24 May 1928, Co Cork, Ireland. Author. m. Jane Ryan, 1952, 2 sons. Education: Trinity College, Dublin. Publications: The Old Boys, 1964; The Boarding House, 1965; The Love Department, 1966; The Day We Got Drunk on Cake, 1967; Mrs Eckdorf in O'Neill's Hotel, 1968; Miss Gomez and the Brethren, 1969; The Ballroom of Romance, 1970; Elizabeth Alone, 1972; Angels at the Ritz, 1973; The Children of Dynmouth, 1976; Lovers of Their Time, 1979; Other People's Worlds, 1980; Beyond the Pale, 1981; Fools of Fortune, 1983; A Writer's Ireland: Landscape in Literature, 1984; The News from Ireland, 1986; Nights at the Alexandra, 1987; Family Sins and Other Stories, 1989; The Silence in the Garden, 1989; The Oxford Book of Irish Short Stories (editor), 1989; Two Lives, 1991; Reading Turgenev, 1991; My House in Umbria, 1991; Juliet's Story, 1992; Collected Stories, 1992; Felicia's Journey, 1994. Honours: Hawthornden Prize, 1964; Honorary CBE, 1977; Prize, Royal Society of Literature, 1978; Whitbread Prize for Fiction, 1978, 1983; Allied Irish Banks Award for Services to Literature, 1978; Honorary DLitt: Exeter, 1984, Dublin, 1986, Queen's University, Belfast, 1989, Cork, 1990; Winner, Sunday Express Book of the Year Award, 1994; Whitbread Literary Award, 1983, 1994. Membership: Irish Academy of Letters. Address: c/o A D Peters, 5th Floor, The Chambers, Chelsea Harbour, London SW10, England.

COX-JOHNSON Ann. See: SAUNDERS Ann Loreille.

COYLE Harold, b. 6 Feb 1952, New Brunswick, New Jersey, USA. Writer. m. Patricia A Bannon, 5 Oct 1974, 2 sons, 1 daughter. Education: BA, History, Virginia Military Institute, 1974. Appointments: Commissioned Officer, US Army, 1974-91. Publications: Team Yankee, 1987; Sword Point, 1988; Bright Star, 1991; Trial by Fire, 1992; The Ten Thousand, 1993; Code of Honor, 1994. Memberships: Association of Civil War Sites; Reserve Officers Association. Literary Agent: Robert Gottieb, William Morris Agency. Address: c/o Robert Gottieb, William Morris Agency, 1350 Avenue of the Americas, New York, NY 10019, USA.

CRACE Jim, b. 1 Mar 1946, Brocket Hall, Lemsford, Hertfordshire, England. Novelist. m. Pamela Ann Turton, 1975, 1 son, 1 daughter. Education: Birmingham College of Commerce, 1965-68; BA (Hons) in English, University of London (external), 1968. Appointments: Freelance Journalist and Writer, 1972-86; Full-time Novelist, 1986-. Publications: The Gift of Stones, 1988; Continent, 1986; Arcadia, 1992; Signals of Distress, 1994; Uncollected short stories: Refugees, 1977; Annie, California Plates, 1977; Helter Skelter, Hang Sorrow, Care'll Kill a Cat, 1977; Seven Ages, 1980; Radio plays. Honours: David Higham Award, 1986; Whitbread Award, 1986; Guardian Prize for Fiction, 1986; Antico Fattore Prize, Italy, 1988; GAP International Prize for Literature, 1989. Address: c/o Aitken, Stone and Wylie, 29 Fernshaw Road, London, SW10 OT9, England.

CRAFT Robert, b. 20 Oct 1923, Kingston, New York, USA. Orchestral Conductor; Author. Education: Juilliard School, BA 1946. Publications: Le Musiche religiose di Igor Stravinsky con il catalogo analitico completo di tutte le sue opere di Craft, Piovesan, Vlad (with A Piovesan and R Vlad), 1957; Conversations with Igor Stravinsky, 4 vols, 1959; Memories and Commentaries, 1960; Expositions and Developments, 1962; Dialogues and a Diary, 1963; Table Talk, 1965; Themes and Episodes, 1966; Bravo Stravinsky (with A Newman), 1967; Retrospectives and Conclusions, 1969; Stravinsky: The Chronicle of a Friendship 1948-71, 1972; Prejudices in Disguise, 1974; Current Convictions: Views and Reviews, 1977; Stravinsky: Selected Correspondence (editor), 3 vols, 1981-85; A Stravinsky Scrapbook, 1984; Present Perspectives: Critical Writings, 1985.

CRAGGS Robert S, (Jack Creek, Luke Lanside), b. 6 Apr 1920, Manitoba, Canada. Freelance Writer. Publications: Trees for Shade and Beauty, 1961; Sir Adams Archibald, 1967; Ghostwriting for the Mail Order Trade, 1968; Writer Without a By-Line, 1968; Organic Gardening for Profit, 1990; Prophet of the Wheat Fields, in The Almanac for Farmers and City Folk, 1994; Daniel Boone of the Arctic, in Harris' Farmers' Almanac, forthcoming. Contributions to: Hundreds of articles, short stories, cartoon gags to Canadian and US publication; Columnist for various publications. Memberships: National Writers Club, Aurora, Colorado; Friends of Merril Collection. Address: 25 McMillan Avenue, West Hill, Ontario, Canada M1E 4B4.

CRAIG Alisa. See: MACLEOD Charlotte.

CRAIG Gordon, b. 1913, Professor. Education: US and Germany. Publications include: The Diplomats, 1919-39, 1953; The Politics of the Prurrian Army, 1955; From Bismark to Adenauer, 1965; Krieg, Politic und Diplomatie, 1968; Germany, 1866-1945, 1978; Force and Statecraft, 1983; The End of Prurria, 1984; The Politics of the Unpolitical, 1995. Contributions to: New York Review of Books. Honours include: Historian's Prize, City of Muenster, Westphalia, Germany; Gold Medal, Commonwealth Club of California; National Book Award, nominee. Address: Dept of History, Building 200, Stanford University, Stanford, CA 94305 2024, USA.

CRAIG Jasmine. See: CRESSWELL Jasmine Rosemary.

CRAIG Jonathan. See: POSNER Richard.

CRAIG Malcolm McDearmid, b. 1 July 1937, South Shields, County Durham, England. Publisher/Writer. m. Jill Christine Hampson, 31 Jan 1965, 1 son, 2 daughters. Education: BSc Econ (Hons), Dip Cam; Sloan Fellow, London Graduate School of Business. Literary Appointments: Editor, Stockmarket Confidential; Editor, Finance Confidential; Editor and Publisher, Craig's Investment Letter; Craig's Confidential Finance Letter. Publications: The Sterling Money Markets, 1975; Successful Investment, 1977; Investing to Survive the 80's, 1979, 80; Invisible Britain, 1981; Making Money Out of Gold, 1982; Making Money Out of Shares, 1983; Successful Investment Strategy, 1984, 2nd edition 1987. Contributions to: All UK national and leading provincial press, specialist investment and financial publications; BBC Radio; BBC TV. Literary Agent: Dasha Shankman, Ed Victor Literary Agency. Address: 15 Dukes Ride, Gerrards Cross, Buckinghamshire, England.

CRAIG William. See: **BERKSON Bill.**

CRAIK Elizabeth Mary, b. 25 Jan 1939. University Teacher. m. Alexander Craik, 15 July 1964, 1 son, 1 daughter. Education: MA, University of St Andrews, 1960; MLitt, University of Cambridge, 1965. Appointments: University of Birmingham, 1963-64; University of St Andrews, 1964-. Publications: The Dorian Aegean; Marriage and Property; Euripides Phoenician Women; Owls to Athens. Contributions to: Scholarly Journals; Many articles & reviews. Address: Department of Greek, University of St Andrews KY16 9AL, Scotland.

CRAIK Thomas Wallace, b. 17 Apr 1927, Warrington, England. Professor of English (Emeritus 1989). m. Wendy Ann Sowter, 25 Aug 1955, div 1975, 1 son. Education: Boteler Grammar School, Warrington, 1937-45; BA, English Tripos: Part I 1947, Part 2 1948; MA 1952, PhD 1952, Christ's College, Cambridge. Appointments: Assistant Lecturer in English 1953, Lecturer 1954-65, University of Leicester; Lecturer in English 1965-67, Senior Lecturer 1967-73, University of Aberdeen; Professor of English, University of Dundee, 1973-77; Professor of English 1977 until retirement in 1989, University of Durham, now Professor Emeritus. Publications include: The Tudor Interlude, 1958; The Comic Tales of Chaucer, 1964; (ed) Marlowe, The Jew of Malta, 1966; (ed) Shakespeare, Twelfth Night, 1975; (ed) Beaumont and Fletcher, The Maid's Tragedy, 1988; (ed) Shakespeare, The Merry Wives of Windsor, 1989; Editor, Shakespeare's King Henry V, 1995. Contributions to: Articles in Modern Languages Review; Review of English Studies; Scrutiny, Notes and Queries, Stratford-upon-Avon Studies; Renaissance Drama. Membership: International Shakespeare Association. Address: 58 Albert Street, Western Hill, Durham City DH1 4RJ, England.

CRAMER Richard B, b. 12 June 1950, NY, USA. Journalist; Writer. Education: BA, Johns Hopkins University; MS, Columbia University. Publications: Ted Williams: The Season of the Kid, 1991; What It Takes: The Way to the White House, 1992. Contributions to: New York Times; Esquire; Rolling Stone. Honours: Pulitzer Prize, 1979; Ernie Pyle Award, 1980; Hal Boyle Award, 1981; American Society of Newspaper Editors Award. Address: c/o Sterling Lord Literistic Inc, 1 Madison Avenue, New York, NY 10010, USA.

CRANE Richard Arthur, b. 4 Dec 1944, York, England. Writer. m. Faynia Williams, 5 Sept 1975, 2 sons, 2 step-daughters. Education: BA Hons, Classics/English, 1966; MA, 1971, Jesus College, Cambridge. Appointments: Fellow in Theatre, University of Bradford, 1972-74; Resident Dramatist, National Theatre, 1974-75; Fellow in Creative Writing, University of Leicester, 1976; Literary Manager, Royal Court Theatre, 1978-79; Associate Director, Brighton Theatre, 1980-85; Dramaturg, Tron Theatre Glasgow, 1983-84; Visiting Writers Fellowship, University of East Anglia, 1988; Writer-in-Residence, Birmingham Polytechnic, 1990-91; Writer-in-Residence, HM Prison Bedford, 1993. Publications include: Thunder, 1976; Gunslinger, 1979; Crippen, 1993; Under the Stars, 1994; Stage Plays: The Tenant, 1971; Crippen, 1971; Decent Things, 1972; Secrets, 1975; The Quest, 1974; Clownmaker, 1975; Venus and Superkid, 1975; Bloody Neighbours, 1975; Satan's Ball, 1977; Gogol, 1979; Vanity, 1980; Brothers Karamazov, 1981; The Possessed, 1985; Mutiny! (with David Essex), 1985; Soldier Soldier (with Tony Parker) 1986; Envy (with Donald Swann), 1986; Pushkin, 1987; Red Magic, 1988; Rolling the Stone, 1989; Phaedra (with Michael Glenny), 1990; Baggage and Bombshells, 1991; Under the Stars, 1993; TV Plays: Rottingdean, 1980; The Possessed, 1985; Radio Plays: Gogol, 1980; Decent Things, 1984; Optimistic Tragedy, 1986; Anna and Marina, 1991; Understudies, 1992; Vlad the Impaler, 1992; The Sea The Sea (radio serial), 1993. Contributions to: The Edinburgh Fringe; The Guardian; Index on Censorship, Times Literary Supplement. Honours: Edinburgh Fringe First Awards, 1973, 1974, 1975, 1977, 1980, 1986, 1988, 1989. Literary Agent: Casarotto-Ramsay Ltd, Address: c/o Casarotto-Ramsay Ltd, National House, 60-66 Wardour Street, London W1V 3HP, England.

CRANSTON Maurice William, b. 8 May 1920, London, England. Professor. m. Maximiliana, 11 Nov 1958, 2 sons. Education: University of London, St Catherines College, Oxford, BA, 1948; MA, 1951; European University Institute, Florence, 1978-81. Appointments: Teacher, London School of Economics, 1959-85; Vice Chairman,

English Centre of International PEN, 1965-69; Registrar, Royal Literary Fund, 1974-79. Publications Include: Jean Jacques: The Noble Savage; John Locke; Freedom; Political Dialogues; What are Human Rights?. Contributions to: The London Magazine; Encounter; History of European Ideas; The American Spectator. Honours Include: Commandeur de L'Ordre des Palmes Academiques, Paris; Hon Fellow, St Catherines College; LSE. Memberships: International PEN; Society of Authors; Authors Guild of USA. Literary Agent: Peters, Fraser & Dunlop. Address: 1A Kent Terrace, London NW1 4RP, England.

CRAWFORD Linda, b. 2 Aug 1938, Detroit, Michigan, USA. Writer. Education: BA, 1960, MA, 1961, University of Michigan. Publications: In a Class by Herself, 1976; Something to Make Us Happy, 1978; Vanishing Acts, 1981; Ghost of a Chance, 1985. Membership: PEN. Literary Agent: Charlotte Sheedy. Address: 131 Prince Street, New York, NY 10012, USA.

CRAWFORD Robert. See: **RAE Hugh Crauford.**

CRAWFORD Thomas, b. 6 July 1920. University Teacher. m. Jean Rennie McBride, 19 Aug 1946, 1 son, 1 daughter. Education: MA, 1944; MA, 1953. Appointments: Lecturer, Auckland, 1953; Associate Professor, Auckland, 1962; Senior Lecturer, Aberdeen, 1967; Reader, 1973; Hon Reader, 1985. Publications: Burns: A Study of the Poems and Songs; Scott; Love, Labour and Liberty; Society and the Lyric; Boswell, Burns and the French Revolution. Contributions to: Scottish Studies; Studies in Scottish Literature; Scottish Literary Journal; Review of English Studies; Modern Language Review. Memberships: Association for Scottish Literary Studies, Convener of Publications Board; Scottish Text Society. Address: Department of English, University of Aberdeen, Old Aberdeen AB9 2UB, Scotland.

CRAWLEY Anthony Francis, (Tony), b. 26 Mar 1938, Farnham, Surrey, England. Freelance Journalist. m. (1) Jeannette Wild, 1967, (2) Nicole Michelet, 26 Feb 1970, 1 s, 1 d. Publications: The Films of Sophia Loren; Bebe, The Films of Brigitte Bardot; Screen Dreams; The Steven Spielberg Story; Entre Deux Censures; Film Quotes; Brigitte Bardot. Contributions to: Paris Match; Premiere; Photoplay; Variety; Screen International; Nouvel Observateur; Panorama; Cinephage; Starburst; Starfix; Sunday Telegraph Magazine. Address: 6 Allee Claude Monet 78160 Marly Le Roi, France.

CRAY Robert. See: **EMERSON Ru.**

CREASEY Jeanne. See: **WILLIAMS Jeanne.**

CRECY Jeanne. See: **WILLIAMS Jeanne.**

CREEK Jack. See: **CRAGGS Robert S.**

CREELEY Robert White, b. 21 May 1926, Arlington, Massachusetts, USA. Writer; Professor of English. m. (1) Ann McKinnon, 1946, div 1955, 2 sons, 1 daughter, (2) Bobbie Louise Hall, 1957, div 1976, 4 daughters, (3) Penelope Highton, 1977, 1 son, 1 daughter. Education: BA, Black Mountain College, 1954; MA, University of New Mexico, 1960. Appointments include: Professor, 1967-78, David Gray Professor, Poetry, Letters, 1978-989, Samuel P Capen Professor, Poetry, Humanities, 1989, Director, Poetics Programme, 1991-92, State University of New York, Buffalo; Advisory Editor: American Book Review, 1983-, Sagetrieb, 1983-, New York Quarterly, 1984-. Publications: Poetry: For Love, Poems 1950-60, 1962; Words, 1967; Pieces, 1969; A Day Book, 1972; Selected Poems, 1976, revised, 1991; Hello, 1978; Later, 1979; Mirrors, 1983; Collected Poems 1945-75, 1983; Memory Gardens, 1986; Windows, 1990; Echoes, 1994; Prose: The Island, 1963; The Gold Diggers, 1965; Mabel: A Story, 1976; The Collected Prose, 1984; Tales Out Of School, 1993; Criticism: A Quick Graph, 1970; Was That A Real Poem and Other Essays, 1976; Collected Essays, 1989; Autobiography, 1990; Co-editor: New American Story, 1965; The New Writng in the USA, 1967; Editor: Selected Writings of Charles Olson, 1967; Whitman, Selected Poems, 1973; The Essential Burns, 1989; Charles Olson, Selected Poems, 1993. Honours include: Shelley Memorial Award, 1981, Frost Medal, 1987, Poetry Society of America; Berlin Artists Programme Grant, 1983, 1987; Leone d'Oro Premio Speziale, 1984; Distinguished Fulbright Award, Bicentennial Chair of American Studies, University of Helsinki, 1988; Distinguished Professor, State University of New York, 1989; Walt Whitman Citation, State Poet of New York, 1989-91; Horst Bienek Preis für Lyrik, Munich, 1993; Honorary LittD, University of New Mexico, 1993. Memberships: American Academy and Institute of Arts and Letters; PEN American Center. Address: 64 Amherst Street, Buffalo, NY 14207, USA.

CREGAN David (Appleton Quartus), b. 30 Sept 1931, England. m. Ailsa Mary Wynne Willson, 1960, 3 sons, 1 daughter. Author; Dramatist. Education: BA, English Tripos, Cambridge University. Appointments: Worked with Cambridge Footlights, 1953, 1954, The Royal Court Theatre Studio, London, 1964, 1968, Midlands Art Centre, Birmingham, 1971; Head of English Department, Palm Beach Private School, Florida, USA, 1955-57; Assistant English Master, Burnage Boys Grammer School, Manchester, England, 1957; Assistant English Master, Head of Drama Department, 1958-62, Part-time Drama Teacher, 1962-67, Hartfield School Herts; Conducted 3 week studio, Royal Shakespeare Company Memorial Theatre, Stratford-upon-Avon, 1971. Publications: Ronald Rossiter, novel, 1959; Miniatures, 1965; Transcending and The Dancers, 1966; Three Men for Colverton, 1966; The Houses by the Green, 1968; How We Held the Square: A Play for Children, 1973; The Land of Palms and Other Plays, 1973; Poor Tom and Tina, 1976; Play Nine, 1980; Sleeping Beauty, 1984; Red Riding Hood, 1985; Jack and the Beanstalk, 1987. Memberships: Drama Panel, West Midlands Art Association, 1972-75. Address: 76 Wood Close, Hatfield, Herts, England.

CREGIER Don M(esick), b. 28 Mar 1930, Schenectady, NY, USA. Historian; Univ Professor. m. Sharon Kathleen Ellis, 29 June 1965. Education: BA, Union College, NY, 1951; MA, Michigan Univ, 1952. Literary Appointments: Panel of Assessors, International Review of Periodical Literature UK, 1988-89; Abstractor for ABC/Clio Information Services 1978-. Publications: Bounder from Wales: Lloyd George's Career Before the First World War, 1976; Novel Exposures: Victorian Studies Featuring Contemporary Novels, 1979; Chiefs Without Indians: Asquith, Lloyd George, and the Liberal Remnant, 1916-1935, 1982; The Decline of the British Liberal Party: Why and How?, 1985; Freedom and Order: The Growth of British Liberalism Before 1868, 1988; The Rise of The Global Village, 1988 (co-author). Honours: Mark Hopkins Fellow, 1965; Canada Council Fellow, 1972; Social Sciences and Humanities Research Council of Canada Grantee, 1984-85. Memberships: Phi Beta Kappa; Phi Kappa Phi; Mark Twain Society; Canadian Association of University of Teachers; American Historical Association; North American Conference on British Studies; Oxford Club; Phi Sigma Kappa. Address: History Department, University of PEI, Charlottetown, Prince Edward Island, Canada C1A 4P3.

CRERAR. See: REANEY James.

CRESKOFF Ellen Ann Hood, b. 3 Oct 1943, Philadelphia, USA. Translator and Information Analyst. m. Stephen M Creskoff, 11 Aug 1963, 2 sons. Education: BA, magna cum laude, Chemistry, University of Pennsylvania, 1964; Equivalent of Masters: Courses in Biochemistry, Psychology, Scientific and Medical Russian, French and Computer Science. Appointments: Chemist, National Cancer Institute, NIH, Bethesda, Maryland, 1964-68; Translator, College of Physicians, Medical Documentation Service, 1972-74; Editor/Translator/Abstractor, Biosciences Information Service of Biological Abstracts (BIOSIS), 1978-86; Freelance Translator, Abstractor, Indexer, 1968-. Publications: Co-author: Isolation and Characterization of Rat Liver Mitochondrial DNA, Journal of Molecular Biology, 1970; Co-author: Macroion Interactions Involving Components of the Cytochrome System V. Reduction of Cytochrome c by Synthetic Polysaccharides, Journal of Biological Chemistry, 1967; Co-author: Reduction-like effect of carbohydrates on cytochrome c. Science, 1965; Regular contributor to Delaware Valley Translators Association Newsletter, 1979-, Editor, 1982-83; Author, English On-Line Glossaries in Translation, ATA Chronicle, May 1986; Author, Nida Proposes New Classification, ATA Chronicle, June 1990; Translation of Soviet text on Neurophysiology, 1973; Translation of Soviet text on Origin of Life by Oparin, 1969. Honour: Phi Beta Kappa, Association, President 1985-90; Accredited by American Translators Association (Russian to English); Board of Hebrew Immigrant Aid Society; Phi Beta Kappa. Address: 2101 Walnut Street 201, Philadelphia, PA 19103, USA.

CRESSWELL Helen, (Mrs Brian Rowe), b. July 1934. Freelance Author. m. Brian Rowe, 1962, 2 daughters. Education: BA, English, Honours, King's College, London. Publications: TV Series: Lizzie Dripping, 1973-75; Jumbo Spencer, 1976; The Bagthorpe Saga, 1980; The Haunted School, 1987; The Secret World of Polly Flint, 1987; Moondial, 1988; Five Children and It, 1990; The Return of the Psammead, 1993; numerous TV Plays. Books: Sonya-by-the-Shire,

1961; Jumbo Spencer, 1963; The White Sea Horse, 1964; Pietro and the Mule, 1965; Jumbo Back to Nature, 1965; Where the Wind Blows, 1966; Jumbo Afloat, 1966; The Piemakers, 1967; A Tide for the Captain, 1967; The Signposters, 1968; The Sea Piper, 1968; The Barge Children, 1968; The Nightwatchman, 1969; A Game of Catch, 1969; A Gift from Winklesea, 1969; The Outlanders, 1970; The Wilkses, 1970; The Bird Fancier, 1971; At The Stroke of Midnight, 1971; The Beachcombers, 1972; Lizzie Dripping, 1972; Thee Bongleweed, 1972; Lizzie Dripping Again, 1974; Butterfly Chase, 1975; The Winter of the Birds, 1975; My Aunt Polly, 1979; My Aunt Polly By the Sea, 1980; Dear Shrink, 1982; The Secret World of Polly Flint, 1982; Ellie and the Hagwitch, 1984; The Bagthorpe Saga: pt 1, Ordinary Jack, 1977, pt 2, Absolute Zero, 1978, pt 3, Bagthorpes Unlimited, 1978, pt 4, Bagthorpes v the World, 1979, pt 5, Bagthorpes Aborad, 1984, pt 6, Bagthorpes Haunted, 1985, pt 7, Bagthorpes Liberated, 1988; Time Out, 1987; Whodunnit, 1987; Moondial, 1987; Two Hoots, 1988; The Story of Grace Darling, 1988; Dragon Ride, 1988; Trouble, 1988; Rosie and the Boredom Eater, 1989; Whatever Happened in Winlkesea?, 1989; Meet Posy Bates, 1990; Hokey Pokey Did It!, 1990; Posy Bates Again, 1991; Lizzie Dripping and The Witch, 1991; Posy Bates and the Bag Lady, 1992; The Watchers, 1993. Literary Agent: A M Heath, London. Address: Old Church Farm, Eakring, Newark, Notts, NG22 0DA, England.

CRESSWELL Jasmine Rosemary, (Jasmine Craig), b. 14 Jan 1941, Wales. Writer. m. Malcolm Candlish, 15 Apr 1983, 1 son, 3 daughters. Education: BA, Melbourne University, Australia; BA (Honours), Macquarie University; MA, Case Western Reserve University, USA. Publications: More than 40 novels including: Romantic Suspense include: House Guest, 1992; Nowhere to Hide, 1992; Keeping Secrets, 1993; Edge of Eternity, 1994; Historical Romances and Regencies include: The Princess, 1982; Lord Rutherford's Affair, 1984; Traitor's Heir, 1984; The Moreton Scandal, 1986; as Jasmine Craig, Empire of the Heart, 1989; The Devil's Envoy, 1988; Contemporary Romances include: Mixed Doubles, 1984; Hunter's Prey, 1986; Love for Hire, 1992; The Perfect Bride, 1993; as Jasmine Craig, Refuge in his Arms, 1984; Suprised by Love, 1984; Under Cover of Night, 1984; Master Touch, 1985; One Step to Paradise, 1986; For Love of Christy, 1987; Knave of Hearts, 1988; Anthology: Marriage on the Run, 1994; Dutton/NAL: To Catch the Wind, 1993; Timeless, 1994. Honours: Colorado Romance Writer of the Year, 1986, 1987; Top Hand Award for Best Original Paperback published by Colorado Author. Memberships: President, Colorado Authors League; Editor, Writers of America; Authors Guild of America; Novelists Inc, President, 1993. Literary Agent: Curtis Brown, New York, USA. Address: c/o Maureen Walters, 10 Astor Place, New York, NY 10003, USA.

CREW Gary David, b. 23 Sept 1947, Brisbane, Queensland, Australia. Lecturer; Writer. m. Christine Joy Crew, 4 Apr 1970, 1 son, 2 daughters. Education: MA, English (Post-Colonial), University of Queensland. Appointments: Lecturer, Queensland University of Technology, 1987-. Publications: Inner Circle, 1986; The House of Tomorrow, 1988; Strange Objects, 1991; No Such Country, 1992; Tracks, 1992; Lucy's Bay, 1992. Honours: For Strange Objects: Australian Children's Book of the Year, New South Wales Premier's Award and The Alan Marshall Prize, 1991; National Children's Book Award for the Angel's Gate, 1993. Membership: Australian Society of Authors. Address: Green Mansions, 66 Picnic St, Enoggera, Queensland 4051, Australia.

CREWS Frederick, b. 20 Feb 1933, PA, USA. m. Elizabeth Peterson, 9 Sept 1959, 2 daughters. Education: BA, Yale, 1955; PhD, Princeton, 1958. Appointments: Instructor, Professor, University of CA, 1958-1994; Professor Emeritus, 1994-. Publications include: Pooh Perplex, 1963; Skeptical Engagements, 1986; The Critics Bear It Away, 1992. Contributions to: American Literature; ELH; Comparative Literature; PMLA; Am Quarterly; New England Quarterly; Partisan Review; NY Review of Books; London Review of Books; Tri-Quarterly; NY Times Book Review; Book Week; New Republic; Critical Review. Honours include: Various UC Berkeley Research Fellowships; Guggenheim Fellowship, 1970-71; Distinguished Teaching Award, 1985; Nina Mae Kellogg Lecturer, 1989; Spielvogel Diamonstein Pen Award, 1992; Faculty Research Lecturer, UC, 1992-93. Literary Agent: Robert Lescher. Address: Dept of English, University of California Berkeley, Berkeley, CA 94720 1030, USA.

CRICHTON Michael, (John Michael, Jeffrey Hudson, John Lange), b. 23 Oct 1942, Chicago, Illinois, USA. Film Director; Author. Education: AB summa cum laude 1964, MD 1969, Harvard University;

Cambirdge University, England, 1965; Postdoctoral Fellow, Salk Institute for Biological Sciences, California, 1969-70. Publications Include: The Andromeda Strain, 1969; The Terminal Man, 1972; The Great Train Robbery, 1975; Congo, 1980; Sphere, 1987; Five Patients, 1970; Eaters of the Dead, 1976; Jasper Johns, 1977; Electronic Life, 1983; Travels, 1988; Jurassic Park, 1990; Rising Sun, 1992; Disclosure, 1994. Honours: Edgar Awards, Mystery Writers of America, 1968, 1979. Memberships: Authors Guild; Writers Guild of America; Directors Guild; Academy of Motion Picture Arts & Sciences. Literary Agent: Lynn Nesbit, ICM. Address: c/o Lynn Nesbit, ICM, 40 West 57th Street, New York, NY 10025, USA.

CRICHTON Ronald Henry, b. 28 Dec 1913, Scarborough, England. Writer; Music Critic. Education: Radley College, 1927-31; Christ Church, Oxford, 1932-36; BA; MA. Appointments: Programme Organizer, Anglo French Art & Travel Society, London, 1937-39; Army Service, 1940-46; British Council, Greece, Belgium, West Germany, London, 1946-67; Music Critic, Financial Times, 1967; Freelance, 1979; Governing Body, British Institute of Recorded Sound, 1973-77; Arts Council Sub Committees, Dance Theatre, 1973-76; Opera, 1976-80. Publications: Joint editor, A Dictionary of Modern Ballet; Manuel de Falla, A Descriptive Catalogue of His Works; Falla: BBC Music Guide; The Memoirs of Ethel Smyth. Contributions to: The New Grove Dictionary of Music & Musicians and other works of reference; Heritage of Music. Memberships: Critics Circle; Society of Authors. Address: c/o David Higham Associates Ltd, 5-8 Lower Street, London W1R 4HA, England.

CRICK Donald Herbert, b. 16 July 1916, Sydney, Australia. m. 24 Dec 1943, 1 daughter. Publications: Novels: Bikini Girl, 1963; Martin Place, 1964; Period of Adjustment, 1966; A Different Drummer, 1972; The Moon to Play With, 1981; Screenplays: The Veronica, 1983; A Different Drummer, 1985; The Moon to Play With, 1987. Contributions to: Sydney Morning Herald; The Australian; Overland; The Australian Author. Honours: Mary Gilmore Centenary Award, Novel, 1966; Rigby Anniversary Award, Novel, 1980; Awgie Screenplay Award, 1983-85. Memberships: Australian Society of Authors, Board of Management. Literary Agent: Richard Deutch, Sydney. Address: 1/1 Elamang Avenue, Kirribilli, NSW 2061, Australia.

CRISCUOLO Anthony Thomas, (Tony Crisp),b. 10 May 1937, Amersham, Bucks, England. Photographer; Nurse; Driver; Journalist; Plumber; Writer; Therapist. 4 sons, 1 daughter. Publications: Yoga and Relaxation, 1970; Do You Dream?, 1971; Yield, 1974; Yoga and Childbirth, 1975; The Instant Dream Book, 1984; Mind and Movement, 1987; Dream Dictionary, 1989; Liberating The Body, 1992. Contributions to: Dream Columnist for Daily Mail, 1982-84; She; Over 21; Cosmopolitan; 1 to 1; Yoga and Health; Energy and Character; Bio-Energy (Japan); Best; LBC Dream Therapist (Broadcasting Radio); Teletext's Dream Interpreter (TV Channel 4). Address: Ashram, King Street, Combe Martin, Devon EX34 0AG, England.

CRISP Tony. See: **CRISCUOLO Anthony Thomas.**

CRISTOFER Michael. See: **PROCASSION Michael.**

CRITCHFIELD Richard, b. 1931, USA. Freelance Writer. Appointments: Reporter, Cedar Valley Daily Times, 1955-56; Washington Correspondent, Salt Lake City Desert News, 1957-58; Acting Assistant Professor, University of Nagpur, India, 1960-62; Asia and National Correspondent, 1963-72, White House Correspondent, 1968-69, The Washington Star. Publications: The Indian Reporters Guide, 1962; Lore and Legend of Nepal (editor and illustrator), 1962; The Long Charade: Political Subversion in the Vietnam War, 1968; The Golden Bowl Be Broken, 1974; Shahat, 1978; Villages, 1981; Those Days: An American Album, 1986; An American Looks at Britain, 1990; Trees, Why DoYou Wait?, 1991. Contributions to: The Christian Science Monitor; The New York Times; Los Angeles Times; Wall Street Journal; Reader's Digest; The Economist, London. Address: c/o Peggy Ann Trimble, 4532 Airlie Way, Annandale, VA 22003, USA.

CRITCHLEY Julian Michael Gordon, b. 8 Dec 1930, Chelsea, England. 1 son, 3 daughters. Education: MA, Pembroke College, Oxford. Appointments: Editor, Town Magazine, 1966. Publications: Collective Security, 1974; Warning & Response, 1978; The North Atlantic Alliance & The Soviet Union, 1987; Westminster Blues, 1985; Britain: A View from Westminster, Editor, 1986; Heseltine: The Unauthorised Biography, 1987; Palace of Varieties, 1989; Hung Parliament, 1991; Floating Voter, 1992; Some of Us, 1992.

Contributions to: The Conservative Opportunity, 1966. The Complete Imbiber, 1956; The Illustrated Counties of England, 1984; Sunday Times; Times; Daily Telegraph; The Sun; Observer. Honours: Political Journalist of the Year, 1985. Memberships: Various professional organizations. Literary Agent: Curtis Brown. Address: 44 Mill Street, Ludlow, SX81 1BB, England.

CRITTENDEN Toya Cynthia, b. 19 Dec 1958, River Rouge, Michigan, USA. Poetic Author. Education: Speech Pathology, English Literature, Wayne State University, Detroit, Michigan, 1977-80. Publications: World of Poetry Anthology, 1987; Poem, published in Insight Magazine, 1988. Honours: Award Merit Certificate, 1985, 1986, 1987; Golden Poet Award, 1986, 1987; Silver Poet Award, 1989, World of Poetry. Memberships: International Platform Association; The American Biographical Association. Address: 4060 Pasadena, Detroit, MI 48238, USA.

CROCOMBE Ronald Gordon, b. 8 Oct 1929, Auckland, New Zealand. m. Marjorie Tuainekore Crocombe, 7 Apr 1959, 3 sons, 1 daughter. Education: BA, Victoria University, 1955; PhD, Australian National University, 1961. Appointments: Director, Institute of Pacific Studies, University of the South Pacific, 1976-85; Chairman of Judges, Asia/Pacific Region, Commonwealth Writers Prize, 1987, 1988. Publications include: The South Pacific, 1973, 1978, 1983, 1987, 1989, (revised editions); The Pacific Way, 1976 (reprinted many times); Land Tenure in the Pacific, 1971, 1977; Revised edition 1987; Foreign Forces in Pacific Politics, 1983, 1985; Land Tenure in the Cook Islands, 1963, 1971; Pacific Universities, 1988; Pacific Neighbours, 1992. Contributions to: Numerous professional and academic journals. Memberships: South Pacific Social Sciences Association, Past President; Pacific History Association, Past President; South Pacific Creative Arts Society. Address: Box 309, Rarotonga, Cook Islands.

CROFT Julian Charles Basset, b. 31 May 1941, NSW, Australia. University Lecturer. m. (1) Loretta De Plevitz, 23 Oct 1967, 1 son, (2) Caroline Ruming, 12 Dec 1987. Education: BA, University of NSW, 1961; MA, University of Newcastle, NSW, 1966. Appointments: Lecturer, University of Sierra Leone, 1968-70; Associate Professor, University of New England, 1970-94; Professor, UNE, 1994-. Publications: T H Jones; Breakfast in Shanghai; Their Solitary Way; Confessions of a Corinthian; The Life & Opinions of Tom Collins. Memberships: Association for the Study of Australian Literature. Address: Department of English, University of New England, Armidale, 2351, Australia.

CRONE Alla Marguerite, b. 22 Dec 1923, Harbin, Manchuria. Writer. m. Richard I Crone, 27 Mar 1946, 2 sons. Education: San Francisco Conservatory of Music, 1953-57. Publications: Novels: East Lies the Sun, 1982; Winds Over Manchuria, 1983; North of the Moon, 1984; Legacy of Amber, 1985. Contributions to: Christian Scinece Monitor; Michigan Quarterly Review. Honours: Gold Medal, West Coast Review of Books, 1982; Finalist, Gold Medallion Romance Writers, 1983; 2nd Prize, National League of American Penwomen, 1984; Best Book on Russia, Romantic Times, New York, 1985. Memberships: Authors Guild; Romance Writers of America; President 1981, California Writers Club, Redwood Branch. Address: Santa Rosa, CA 95405, USA.

CRONIN Anthony, b. 23 Dec 1928, Enniscorthy, County Wexford, Ireland. Lecturer; Poet. m. Theresa Campbell, 1955, 1 d. Education: BA, University College Dublin, 1948. Appointments: Visiting Lecturer, University of Montana, 1966-68; Columnist, Irish Times, 1973-86; Cultural Adviser, Irish Prime Minister. Publications: Poems, 1957; Collected Poesm, 1950-73, 1973; Reductionist Poem, 1980; RMS Titanic, 1981; 41 Sonnet Poems, 1982; New & Selected Poems, 1982; Letter to an Englishman, 1985; The End of the Modern World, 1989; Play, The Shame of It, 1971; Novels, The Life of Riley, 1964; Identity Papers, 1979; No Laughing Matter: The Life and Times of Flann O'Brian, 1989. Honour: Marten Toonder Award, 1983. Address: Office of the Taoiseach, Government Buildings, Dublin 2, Ireland.

CRONIN Vincent Archibald Patrick, b. 24 May 1924. Author. m. Chantal, 1949, 2 sons, 3 daughters. Education: Trinity College, Oxford. Publications: The Golden Honeycombe, 1954; The Wise Man from The West, 1955; The Last Migration, 1957; A Pear to India, 1959; The Letter after Z, 1960; Louis XIV, 1964; Four Women in Pursuit of an Ideal, 1965; The Florentine Renaissance, 1967; The Flowering of the Renaissance, 1970; Napoleon, 1971; Louis and Antoinette, 1974; Translator, Giscard d'Estaing, Towards a New Democracy, 1977; Catherine Empress of all the Russias, 1978; The View from Planet

Earth, 1981; Paris on the Eve, 1989. Address: Brion, Dragey, 50530 Sarfilly, France.

CRONON William, b. 1954. Professor. m. Nan Fey. Education: University of WI; Oxford University; Yale University. Publications: Nature's Metropolis: Chicago and The Great West, 1991; Changes in the Land: Indians, Colonists, and the Ecology of New England, 1983. Honours: Bancroft Prize; Francis Parkman Prize; MacArthur Fellowship. Address: Dept of History, University of WI, 3211 Humanities Building, 455 North Park Street, Madison, WI 53706, USA.

CROOK Joseph Mordaunt, b. 27 Feb 1937, London, England. Professor of Architectural History, London University; Formerly Slade Professor and Waynflete Lecturer, Oxford University. m. Susan Mayor, 9 July 1975. Education: Wimbledon College; BA, 1st Class, Modern History, 1958, DPhil 1961, Brasenose College, Oxford. Literary Appointments: Editor, Architectural History, 1967-75. Publications: The Dilemma of Style: Architectural Ideas from the Picturesque to the Post Modern, 1987; The Greek Revival, 1972; William Burges and the High Victorian Dream, 1981; The British Museum, 1971. Co-author: The History of the King's Works, vols 5 and 6, 1973-76. Contributions to: Times Literary Supplement; Country Life; Architectural Review; Architectural History. Honours: Fellow, Society of Antiquaries, 1973; Fellow, British Academy, 1987; Public Orator, London University, 1987-90. Memberships: Council, British Academy, 1988-; Historic Buildings Council for England, 1974-80. Address: 55 Gloucester Avenue, London NW1 7BA, England.

CROOK Marion, b. 16 Oct 1941, Canada. Writer. m. Bill Crook, 19 Dec 1964, 2 s, 2 d. Education: BSc; Nursing; MA. Publications include: Looking Good: Teenagers and Eating Disorders, 1992; The Body Image Trap, 1992; Ripetide, 1992; Teenagers Talk About Suicide, 1988. Contributions to: Many. Memberships: Writers Union; ACTRA; Childrens Literature Round Table; Registered Nurses Association. Address: 1680 Cornell Avenue, Coquitlam, V3J 3A1, Canada.

CROSLAND Margaret McQueen, b. Bridgnorth, Shropshire, England. Writer; Translator. Education: BA, London University. Publications: Madame Colette, 1954; Jean Cocteau, 1955; Louise of Stolberg, 1962; Colette: The Difficulty of Loving, 1973; Raymond Radiguet, 1976; Women of Iron and Velvet, 1976; Beyond the Lighthouse, 1981; Piaf, 1985; The Passionate Philosopher, A de Sade Reader, 1991; Simone de Beauvoir, 1992; (ed) Cocteau's World, 1971; many translations. Honours: Prix Bourgogne, France, 1975; Enid McLeod Literary Award, 1992. Literary Agent: Jeffrey Simmons, 10 Lowndes Square, London SW1X 9HA. Address: The Long Croft, Upper Hartfield, Sussex, England.

CROSS (Alan) Beverley, b. 13 Apr 1931, England. Dramatist. m. Dame Maggie Smith, 1975. Education: Balliol College, Oxford, 1952-54. Publications Include: Plays: One More River, 1956; Boeing-Boeing, 1962; Miranda, 1987; Musicals: Half A Sixpence, 1962; Jorrocks, 1965; Hans Andersen, 1972; Opera Libretti: Mines of Sulphur, 1966; The Rising of the Moon, 1972; Screenplays: Jason and the Argonauts; Genghis Khan; Half A Sixpence; Clash of the Titans. Memberships: Garrick Club. Literary Agent: Curtis Brown. Address: c/o Curtis Brown, 162 Regent Street, London, W1R 5TA, England.

CROSS Anthony Glenn, b. 21 Oct 1936, Nottingham, England. Educator. m. Margaret Elson, 11 Aug 1960, 2 daughters. Education: MA 1964, PhD 1966, Cambridge University; MA, Harvard University, USA, 1961; LittD, University of East Anglia, 1981. Appointments: Editor, Newsletter, Study Group 18th Century Russia, 1973-; Review Editor, Journal European Studies, 1971-; Chairman, British Academic Committee for Cooperation with Russian archives, 1981-; Currently, Professor of Slavonic Studies. Publications: N M Karamzin, 1971; Russian Under Western Eyes, 1971; Russian Literature in Age of Catherine the Great, 1976; Russians in 18th Century Britain, 1981; The Russian Theme in English Literature, 1985; Anglo-Russica, 1993; Engraved in the Memory, 1993. Contributions to: Professional journals. Honours: Frank Knox Fellow, Harvard University, 1960-61; Visiting Fellow, University of Illinois, Urbana 1969-70, All Souls College, Oxford 1978-79; Fellow, British Academy, 1989. Memberships: British University Association Slavists, President 1982-84. Address: Department of Slavonic Studies, University of Cambridge, Sidgwick Avenue, Cambridge CB3 9DA, England.

CROSS Brenda. See: **COLLOMS Brenda.**

CROSS Gillian Clare, b. 24 Dec 1945, London, England. Writer. m. Martin Cross, 10 May 1967, 2 sons, 2 daughters. Education: BA (Hons) Class I, Somerville College, Oxford, 1965-69; DPhil, University of Sussex, 1970-73. Publications: The Runaway, 1979; The Iron Way, 1979; Revolt At Ratcliffe's Rags, 1980; Save Our School, 1981; A Whisper of Lace, 1981; The Demon Headmaster, 1982; The Dark Behind the Curtain, 1982; The Mintyglo Kid, 1983; Born of the Sun, 1983; On the Edge, 1984; The Prime Minster's Brain, 1985; Swimathon, 1986; Chartbreak, 1986; Roscoe's Leap, 1987; A Map of Nowhere, 1988; Rescuing Gloria, 1989; The Monster From Underground, 1990; Twin and Super-Twin, 1990; Wolf, 1990; Gobbo The Great, 1991; Rent-A-Genius, 1991; The Great Elephant Chase, 1992; Beware Olga! 1993; Furry Maccaloo, 1993; The Tree House, 1993; Hunky Parker is Watching You, 1994; What Will Emily Do? 1994; New World, 1994. Honours: Wolf, Carnegie Medal, 1990; The Great Elephant Chase, Whitbread Children's Novel Award and Smarties Prize, 1992. Membership: Society of Authors. Address: The Gate House, 39 Main Street, Wolston, Coventry CV8 3HH, England.

CROSS Ian (Robert), b. 1925, Wanganui, New Zealand. Novelist. m. Tui Tunnicliffe, 4 sons. Education: Wanganui Technical College. Appointments: Robert Burns Fellow, University of Otago, Dunedin, 1959; Editor, New Zealand Listener, Wellington, 1973-77; Chairman and Chief Executive, New Zealand on Air, Wellington, from 1977. Publications: The God Boy, 1957; The Backward Sex, 1960; After Anzac Day, 1961; Uncollected short story: Love Affair, 1958; Television play: The City of No, 1970. Honours: Hubert Church Prose Award, 1962.

CROSS Victor. See: **COFFMAN Virginia.**

CROSSLEY-HOLLAND Kevin John William, b. 7 Feb 1941, Buckinghamshire, England. Author; Broadcaster; Teacher. m. 1) 2 sons, 2) Gillian Cook, 2 daughters. Education: MA, Oxford. Appointments include: Editor, Macmillan, 1962-69; Editorial Director, Victor Gollancz, 1972-77; Endowed Chair in Humanities and Fine Arts, St Thomas University, Minnesota, 1991-. Publications: Poetry: The Rain-Giver, 1972; The Dream-House, 1976; Time's Oriel, 1983; Waterslain, 1986; The Painting-Room, 1988; New and Selected Poems, 1991; For Children: Havelok the Dane, 1964; King Horn, 1965; The Green Children, 1966; The Callow Pit Coffer, 1968; Wordhoard (with Jill Paton Walsh), 1969; Pedlar of Swaffham, 1971; Travel: Pieces of Land, 1972; The Sea Stranger, 1973; The Fire-Brother, 1974; Green Blades Rising, 1975; The Earth-Father, 1976; The Wildman, 1976; Mythology: The Norse Myths, 1980; The Dead Moon, 1982; Beowulf, 1982; The Mabinogion (with Gwyn Thomas), 1984; Axe-Age, Wolf-Age, 1985; Storm, 1985; British Folk Tales, 1987; Wulf, 1988; The Quest for Olwen (with Gwyn Thomas), 1988; Piper and Pooka, 1988; Small Tooth Dog, 1988; Boo! 1988; History: The Stones Remain (with Andrew Rafferth), 1989; Dathera Dad, 1989; Under the Sun and Over the Moon (with Ian Penney), 1989; Sleeping Nanna, 1989; Sea Tongue, 1991; Tales From Europe, 1991; Long Tom and the Dead Hand, 1992; Norse Myths, 1993; The Labours of Herekles, 1993; The Green Children, 1994; Opera Libretti: The Green Children, 1990; The Wildman, 1995; (both with Nicola LeFanu). Translations from Old English include: The Battle of Maldon, 1965; Beowulf, 1968; The Exeter Book Riddles, 1978; The Anglo-Saxon Elegies, 1988; Winter's Tales for Children 3, 1967; The Faber Book of Northern Legends, 1977; The Oxford Book of Travel Verse, 1986. Contributions to: Numerous magazines and journals. Honours: Arts Council Award, Best Book for Young Children, The Green Children, 1966-68; Poetry Book Society Choice, The Dream House, 1976; Carnegie Medal, Storm, 1985; Poetry Book Society Recommendation, Waterslain, 1986. Literary Agent: Rogers, Coleridge and White. Address: The Old Vicarage, Walsham-le-Willows, Bury St Edmunds, Suffolk, England.

CROUCH Marcus, b. 12 Feb 1913, Tottenham, Middlesex, England. Chartered Librarian. m. Olive King, 13 Apr 1955, 1 son. Education: BA, Queen Mary College, London University, 1931-34. Appointments: Deputy County Librarian, Kent County Library; retired 1977. Publications: Treasure Seeker and Borrowers, 1962; The Nesbit Tradition, 1972; Kent, 1966; Essex, 1969; The Home Counties, 1975; Canterbury, 1970; Victorian and Edwardian Kent, 1974; Britain in Trust, 1963; Fingerprints of History, 1968; The Ivory City, 1980; The Whole World Story Book, 1985; Ivan, 1989; Kentish Books Kentish Writers, 1989. Contributions to: Times Literary Supplement; Times Educational Supplement; Junior Bookshelf; School Librarian. Memberships: Society of Authors; Library Association, Fellow; LA Youth Library Section,

Chairman; School Library Association, Chairman, Kent Branch. Address: Ty'n Lidiart, Pentrecelyn, Ruthin, Clwyd, Wales.

CROWE John. See: **LYNDS Dennis.**

CROWLEY John, b. 1 Dec 1942, Presque Isle, Maine. Education: BA, Indiana University. Publications: The Deep, 1975; Beasts, 1976; Engine Summer, 1979; Little, Big, 1981; Novelty, 1989; Antiquities: Seven Stories, 1993; Love & Sleep, 1994; Three Novels, 1994; also TV scripts include: America Lost & Found; No Place to Hide. Honour: Fellow, American Academy & Institute of Arts & Letters, 1992.

CROZIER Andrew, b. 1943, England. Lecturer; Poet. Education: MA, Cambridge University; PhD, University of Essex. Appointment: Senior Lecturer, University of Sussex. Publications: Loved Litter of Time Spent, 1967; Train Rides, 1968; Walking on Grass, 1969; In One Side Out The Other, 1970; Neglected Information, 1973; The Veil Poem, 1974; Printed Circuit, 1974; Seven Contemporary Sun Dials, 1975; Pleats, 1975; Duets, 1976; Residing, 1976; High Zero Were There, 1978; Utamoro Variations, 1982; All Where Each Is, 1985; Selected Poems in (with Donald Davie and C H Sisson); Ghosts in the Corridor, 1992. Address; Arts Building, University of Sussex, Brighton, Sussex BN1 9QN, England.

CROZIER Brian Rossiter, (John Rossiter), b. 4 Aug 1918. Writer; Journalist. m. Lillian Samuel, 1940, 1 son, 3 daughters. Education: Peterborough College, Harrow; Trinity College of Music, London. Appointments: Music & Art Critic, London, 1936-39; Reporter, Sub-Editor, Stoke-on-Trent, Stockport, London, 1940-41; Aeronautical Inspection, 1941-43; Sub-Editor, Reuters, 1943-44, News Chronicle 1944-48, Sub-Editor & Correspondent, Reuters-AAP 1951-52; Features Editor, Straits Times, Singapore, 1952-53; Leader Writer, Correspondent, The Economist, 1954-64; BBC Commentator, English French & Spanish Overseas Services, 1954-65; Chairman, Forum World Features, 1965-74; Editor, Conflict Studies, 1970-75; Co-Founder, Director, Institute for the Study of Conflict, 1970-79; Consultant, 1979-; Columnist, National Review, New York, 1978-; Now! London 1980-81, The Times, 1982-84. Publications: The Rebels, 1960; The Morning After, 1963; Neo-Colonialism, 1964; South East Asia in Turmoil, 1965-66-68; The Struggle for the Third World, 1966; Franco, 1967; The Masters of Power, 1969; The Future of Communist Power (in USA, Since Stalin), 1970; De Gaulle, volume I, 1973, volume II, 1974; A Theory of Conflict, 1974; The Man Who Lost China, 1977; Strategy of Survival, 1978; The Minimum State, 1979; Franco: Crepúsculo de un hombre, (Spanish Orig), 1980; The Price of Peace, 1980; Socialism Explained, co-author, 1984; This War Called Peace, co-author, 1984; The Andropov Deception, novel, as John Rossiter, 1984 (under own name, New York 1986); Socialism: Dream and Reality, 1987; The Gorbachev Phenomenon, 1990; Communism: Why prolong its death thrones?, 1990; Free Agent, 1993. Contributions to: Numerous journals. Address: Kulm House, Dollis Avenue, Finchley, London N3 1DA, England.

CROZIER Lorna Jean, b. 24 May 1948, Swift Current, Saskatchewan, Canada. Writer; Teacher. Education: BA Hons 1969, Professional A Teaching Certificate 1970, University of Saskatchewan; MA, University of Alberta, 1980. Appointments: Special Lecturer, University of Saskatchewan, 1986-89. Publications: Inside Is The Sky, 1976; Crows Black Joy: Humans and Other Beasts, 1980; No Longer Two People (with Patrick Lane Turnstone); The Weather, 1983; The Garden Going On Without Us, 1985; Angels of Flesh, Angels of Silence, 1988; Inventing the Hawk, 1992. Contributions to Include: Ariel; Athanos; Event; Grain; Saturday Night; South Dakota Review; Prism International; Fiddlehead; Canadian Forum. Honours: University of Alberta Creative Writing Scholarship, 1978-79; Department of Culture and Youth Poetry Manuscript Award; Saskatchewan Writers;Guild Poetry Manuscript Award, 1983, 1986; Governor General Awards Nominee, 1986. Memberships: Saskatchewan Writers Guild, Vice President, President, Colony Committee; The League of Canadian Poets, Saskatchewan Representative, Chairman of Membership Committee. Address: RR 2, 1886 Cultra Avenue, Saanichton, British Columbia, V0S 1MO, Canada.

CRYSTAL David, b. 1941, British. Writer of Children's Non-Fiction, Linguistics/Language, Medicine/Health, Speech/Rhetoric; Professorial Fellow, University of Wales, Bangor, 1985-; Editor, Child Language Teaching and Therapy, 1985- and Linguistics Abstracts 1985-; Consultant Editor, English Today, 1986-94. Appointments: Assistant Lecturer, University College of North Wales, 1963-65;

Lecturer and Reader, 1965-75, and Professor of Linguistic Science, 1976-85, University of Reading. Publications include: Child Language, Learning and Linguistics, 1976; Working with LARSP, 1979; Eric Partridge: In His Own Words, 1980; A First Dictionary of Linguistics and Phonetics, 1980; Introduction to Language Pathology, 1980; Clinical Linguistics, 1981; Directions in Applied Linguistics, 1981; Linguistic Controversies, 1981; Profiling Linguistic Disability, 1982; Linguistic Encounters with Language Handicap, 1984; Language Handicap in Children, 1984; Who Cares About English Usage? 1984; Listen to Your Child, 1986; (ed with W Bolton), The English Language, 1987; Cambridge Encyclopedia of Language, 1987; Rediscover Grammar, 1988; The English Language, 1988; children's non-fiction: (with J Bevington), Skylarks, 1975; (with John Foster), Heat, Light, Sound, Roads, Railways, Canals, Monasteries, Manors, Castles, Money, Parliament, Newspapers, The Romans, The Greeks, The Ancient Egyptians, Air, Food, Volcanoes, Deserts, Electricity, Motorcycles, Computers, Horses and Ponies, The Normans, The Vikings, The Celts, The Anglo-Saxons, The Stone Age, Fishing, 29 vols, 1979-85; Pilgrimage, 1988; Language A-Z, 1991; Nineties Knowledge, 1992; An Encyclopedic Dictionary of Language and Languages, 1992; The Cambridge Encyclopedia (ed), 2nd edition 1994; The Cambridge Concise Encyclopedia (ed), 1992; The Cambridge Encyclopedia of the English Language, 1995. Address: Akaroa, Gors Avenue, Holyhead, Anglesey, Gwynedd, LL65 1RG, Wales.

CSANDA Endre, b. 14 Mar 1923, Nagyvarad, Hungary. Professor of Neurology. 2 daughters. Education: Medical Degree 1947, PhD 1962, Budapest, 1974; SBE, Neurology, 1951; General Surgery, 1954; Neurosurgery, 1959; Psychiatry, 1974. Appointments: Neuropsychiatric Department, University Medical School, 1947-50; Neurosurgical Institute, 1956-59; Neuropsychiatric and Neurosurgical Department, 1959-61; Neuropsychiatric Department, University Medical School, Szeged, 1971-75; Professor, Chairman, Semmelweis University Medical School, Institute of Neurology, Budapest, 1975-. Publications: Cerebral Oedema as a Consequence of Experimental Cervical Lymphatic Blockage, 1968; Radiation Brain Edema, 1980; Central Nervous System and Lymphatic System, 1983; Adjuvant Drugs in the Treatment of ON-OFF Phenomena in Parkinson's Disease: Some possible histo-pathological correlates of dementia in Parkinsonian patients, 1990. Contributions to: 172 publications or chapters to medical journals and books; Senior author in 105. Honours: Kivalo Award, Finnish Neurological Society, 1985; Apaczai Csere Janos Award, 1986; Honorary Member, Austrian, Czechoslovakian and Polish Neurological Societies. Memberships: President, Hungarian Society for Neurology and Psychiatry; Vice-President, European Federation of Neurological Societies; Past Vice-President, World Federation of Neurology; Past Vice-President, Paneuropean Neurological Society. Address: Balassa u 6, 1083 Budapest, Hungary.

CSERES Tibor, b. 1 Apr 1915, Gyergyoremete, Tras, Hungary. Writer. m. Nora Ulkey, 15 Nov 1944, 1 daughter. Education: University of Economics, Kolozsvar. Publications: Cold Days, 1964; Players and Lovers, 1970; I, Lajos Kossuth, 1980; Pass of Foksany, 1985; Battles of Vizarnua, 1988; Vendeta in Backa, 1991. Honours: Kossuth Prize, 1975; Order of Flag, Hungarian Republic, 1990. Memberships: President, Hungaria Writers Association, 1986-89; President, Hungarian Writers Chamber; Hungarian Academy of Literature and Arts. Address: Orlo 14, 1026 Budapest II, Hungary.

CSOORI Sandor, b. 3 Feb 1930, Zamoly, Transbanubia, Hungary. Poet. Education: Lenin Institute at Papa, from 1951. Appointments include: Dramaturg of the Hungarian Film Studio, from 1971. Publications include: The Bird Takes Wing, 1954; Devil's Moth, 1957; Flight from Solitude, 1962; We Live in Harsh Times, 1967; My Second Birth, 1967; Clowns of a Jam Circus, 1969; Dialogue in the Dark, 1973; The Memories of a Visitor, 1977; Predictions About Your Time, 1979; The 10th Evening, 1980; Wings of Knives amd Nails, 1981; Nightmare Postponed, 1982; Waiting in the Spring, 1983; Memory of Snow, 1983; In My Hand a Green Branch, 1985; Bright Sunshine on Foot, 1987; Breviary, 1988; Monuments of the World, 1989; Selected Poems, 1992; Screenplays; Also: Cuban Diary, 1965; The Poet and the Monkey Face, 1966; From Wall to Wall, 1969; Reassurance, 1973; Journey While Half-Asleep, 1974; The Wanderer's Diary, 1979; Mud-Rain, 1981; The Sea and the Walnut Leaf, 1982; Preparation for the Day of Reckoning, 1987. Honours include: Herder Prize, Austria, 1981. Address: Magveto Konyvkiado, Vorosmartyr ter 1, 1806 Budapest, Hungary.

CUDDON John Anthony Bowden, b. 2 June 1928, Southsea, England. Writer; Teacher. m. Anna-Clare Dale, 17 May 1975, 1 son, 2 daughters. Education: Douai School, 1939-46; Brasenose College, Oxford, 1949-55, MA, BLitt. Publications: The Owl's Watchsong (travel), 1960; A Multitude of Sins (novel), 1961; Testament of Iscariot (novel), 1962; Jugoslavia (travel), 1968; Dictionary of Literary Terms, 1977; Dictionary of Sports and Games, 1981; Acts of Darkness (novel), 1963; The Six Wounds (novel), 1964; The Bride of Battersea (novel), 1967; Penguin Book of Ghost Stories, 1984; Penguin Book of Horror Stories, 1984; Penguin Dictionary of Literary Terms and Literary Theory, 1992. Contributions to: British daily and weekly papers and various journals. Membership: MCC. Address: 43 Alderbrook Road, London SW12, England.

CUMBERLEGE Marcus, b. 23 Dec 1938, Antibes, France. Translator; Poet. m. Maria Lefever, 1973. Appointments: Lecturer, Hilversum & Lugano Universities, 1978-1983. Publications: Oases, 1968; Poems for Quena and Tabla, 1970; Running Towards a New Life, 1973; Firelines, 1977; The Poetry Millionaire, 1977; La Nuit Noire, 1977; Bruges, Brugge, 1978; Northern Lights, 1981; Life is a Flower, 1981; Vlaamse Fables, 1982; Sweet Poor Hobo, 1984; Things I Cannot Change, 1993. Honour: Eric Gregory Award, 1967. Address: Eekhoutstraat 42, 8000 Bruges, Belgium.

CUMMING Peter E, b. 23 Mar 1951, Brampton, Ontario, Canada. Writer; Teacher. m. Mary Shelleen Nelson, 14 Oct 1970. Education: BA, English Literature, 1972; Diploma in Education, 1976; MA, English Literature, 1992. Appointments: Resident Artist in Drama, Wilfrid Laurier University, 1972-73; Executive Director, Atlantic Publishers Association, 1984-85. Publications: Snowdreams, 1982; Ti-Jean, 1983; A Horse Called Farmer, 1984; Mogul and Me, 1989; Out on the Ice in the Middle of the Bay, 1993. Contributions to: Contributing editor, Quill and Quire, 1982-84. Honours: 1st Prize, Children's Prose, 1980, 1st Prize, Adult Fiction, 1981, Writers Federation of Nova Scotia; Toronto Board of Education Canada Day Playwriting Competition, 1981; Our Choice, Children's Book Centre, 1984, 1989, 1993; Hilroy Award for Innovative Teaching, 1990. Memberships: Playwrights Union of Canada; Writers Union of Canada; Canadian Society of Children's Authors, Illustrators, and Performers; Association of Canadian College and University Teachers of English. Address: 201 Front Street, Stratford, Ontario, Canada N5A 4H8.

CUMMINS Walter (Merrill), b. 6 Feb 1936, USA. Professor of English. m. Alison Cunningham, 14 Feb 1981, 2 daughters. Education: BA, Rutgers University, 1957; MA, 1962, MFA, 1962, PhD, 1965, University of Iowa. Literary Appointments: Editor-in-Chief, The Literary Review, Fairleigh Dickinson University, Madison, New Jersey, 1984-; Editorial Committee, Fairleigh Dickinson University Press, 1984-. Publications: Where We Live; Witness; A Stranger to the Deed; Into Temptation. Contributions to: Virginia Quarterly Review; Kansas Quarterly; West Branch; Other Voices; South Carolina Review. Honours: New Jersey State Council Arts Fellowship. Address: The Literary Review, Fairleigh Dickinson University, Madison, NJ 07940, USA.

CUNLIFFE Barrington Windsor, b. 10 Dec 1939, Portsmouth, England. University Teacher. m. Margaret Herdman, 5 Jan 1979, 1 son, 1 daughter. Education: BA 1962, MA 1962, PhD 1966, LittD 1977, Cambridge University. Appointments: Editorial Boards: Oxford Journal of Archaeology, World Archaeology. Series Editor for: Longmans, Routledge, Cambridge University Press. Publications: Iron Age Communities in Britain, 1974, 2nd edition 1978; Rome and Her Empire, 1978; The Celtic World, 1979; Danebury: Anatomy of an Iron Age Hillfort, 1983; The City of Bath, 1986; Greeks Romans and Barbarians, 1988; Roman Bath Discovered, 2nd edition 1984; Heywood Sumners Wessex, 1985. Contributions to: Times Literary Supplement; Encounter; Good Book Review. Honours: Fellow, The British Academy, 1979; Honorary Doctrates: University of Bath, University of Sussex. Literary Agent: Curtis Brown, 162-8 Regent Street, London. Address: Institute of Archaeology, 36 Beaumont Street, Oxford, England.

CURL James Stevens, b. 26 Mar 1937, Belfast, Northern Ireland. Professor of Architectural History, Department Architecture, De Montfort University, Leicester; Architect; Historian. m. (1) Eileen Elizabeth Blackstock, 1 Jan 1960. divorced 1986, 2 daughters. (2) Stanistawa Dorota Iwaniec 1993. Education: Queen's University, Belfast and School of Architecture, 1954-58; DiplArch, Oxford School of Architecture, 1961-63; Oxford Department of Land Use Studies, 1963-67; PhD, University College, London, 1978-81; DipTP; MRTPI;

RIBA; ARIAS; FSA; FSAScot. Publications: The Victorian Celebration of Death, 172; City of London Pubs, 1973; A Celebration of Death, 1980; The Egyptian Revival, 1982; The Life and Work of Henry Roberts (1803-76), Architect, 1983; The Londonderry Plantation 1609-1914, 1986; English Architecture: An Ilustrated Glossary, 1987; Victorian Architecture, 1990; The Art and Architecture of Freemasonry, 1991; Classical Architecture, 1992; Encyclopaedia of Architectural Terms, 1992; Georgian Architecture, 1993. Contributions to: Connaissance des Arts; Country Life; Royal Society of Arts Journal; Architects' Journal; Bauwelt; The World of Interiors; The Literary Review. Honours: Sir Charles Lanyon Prize, 1956 and 1958; Ulster Arts Club Prize, 1958; Stevens Prize for Thesis, 1963; Baroque Prize, 1962; British Academy Research Awards, 1982 and 1983; Society of Antiquaries of London Research Award, 1980, 1981. Address: 2 The Coach House, Burley-on-the-Hill, Rutland LE15 7SU, England.

CURLING Audrey. See: **CLARK Marie Catherine Audrey**.

CURNOW Thomas Allen Monro, b. 17 June 1911, Timaru, New Zealand. Author. m. (1) Elizabeth Jaumaud Le Cren, 1936, 2 sons, 1 daughter, (2) Jenifer Mary Tole, 1965. Education: BA 1934, LittD 1965, Universities of Canterbury and Auckland. Appointments: Staff, The Press, 1935-48, News Chronicle, London, 1949; Associate Professor, University of Auckland, 1967-76. Publications: 17 Volumes of Poems; 1 Play; 1 Criticism; Editor, Anthologies including: Penguin Book of New Zealand Verse; Poetry Titles include: Not in Narrow Seas, 1939; Island and Time, 1941; Sailing or Drowning, 1943; At Dead low Water, 1949; A Small Room with Large Windows, 1962; Trees, Effgies Moving Objects, 1972; Collected Poems, 1933-73, 1974; An Incorrigible Music, 1979; You Will Know When You Get There, 1982; The Loop in Lone Kauri Road, 1986; Continuum, New & Later Poems, 1988; Selected Poems, 1940-89, 1990. Plays Include: The Axe, 1949; The Duke's Miracle, 1968. Contributions to: Encounter; London Magazine; London Review of Books; Partisan Review; Times Literary Supplement; Islands; Landfall. Honours: New Zealand Book Award for Poetry, 5 times, 1958-83; Katherine Mansfield Memorial Fellowship, 1983; LittD, 1975; CBE 1986; Dillons Commonwealth (overall) Poetry Prize, 1989; The Queen's Gold Medal for Poetry, 1989; Cholmondeley Award, 1992. Literary Agent: Curtis Brown. Address: 62 Tohunga Crescent, Parnell, Auckland 1, New Zealand.

CURRAN Colleen, b. 23 Aug 1954, Montreal, Canada. Playwright. Education: BA Hons, English, Loyola College, Concordia University, 1976; Teaching Certificate, McGill University, 1981. Appointment: Playwright in Residence, Centaur Theatre, Montreal, 1984-85. Publications: Major plays produced: El Clavidista, 1 act, Mayor's Council on the Arts, Burlington, 1982; Another Labor Day, 1 act, Montreal, 1984; Cake-Walk, comedy, Blyth Festival, 1984; Maisonneuve, drama series for CBC Radio, 1984; Nuclear Hollywood, performance piece-play, Playwrights' Workshop, Montreal, 1985; Moose County, comedy, Blyth Festival, 1985; Uluru, drama, CBC Radio; Miss Balmoral of the Bayview, Blyth Festival, 1987; Spooks, A haunting comedy, 1987; Cake-Walk in Four New Comedies, 1987; Triple-Play, 3 one-acts: El Clavadista, A Sort of Holiday, Amelia Earhart Was Not A Spy, 1990; Sacred Hearts, play, Alberta Theatre, Projects newplay Rites 1989; adapted CBC Radio Morningside, 1991; Radio Plays, CBC Radio Vanashing Point: Kiss The Bride Goodbye; Lisdoonvarna; A Natural Death (adaptation); Keeping Up With The Smythe-Joneses; Mariana of the Universe (adaptation); for A.T.P. Shorts First Night; Stopping by Woods; Parental Guidance; Whale Watch, premiere 1989 Solar Stage; Senetta Boynton Talent, comedy, Blyth Festival, 1991; Ceili House, comedy, Blyth Festival, 1993; (Ed) Escape Acts: Seven Canadian One Acts, 1992; work included in The Perfect Piece; You're Making A Canadian Comedy. Contributions to: Theatre Writer, Montreal Review and Montreal Calendar; Writer; Loyola News, 1972-76; Book Reviewer, The Gazette, 1985; Travel Writer Contributor, The Gazette, 1993. Honours: Honourable Mention, Ottawa Little Theatre Playwriting Competition, 1982; Dorothy White Playwriting Award, Ottawa Little Theatre Playwriting Competition, 1983; Best New Play, Quebec Drama Festival, 1984; Expo 86 Shorts Competition; Gabriel Radio Award, Texas, 1991. Memberships: Board Member, Playwrights Workshop, Montreal; ACTRA; Playwrights Union of Canada (Editorial Board Chair, National Council 1991-92); Co-Artistic Director, Triumvirate Theatre Company, Montreal, 1992-. Literary Agent: Patricia Ney, Christopher Banks and Associates. Address: 148 Abbott Avenue, Montreal, Quebec, H3Z 2J9, Canada.

CURREY Ralph Nixon, b. 14 Dec 1907, Mafeking, South Africa. Poet. Education: BA, Wadham College, Oxford, 1930. Appointments:

Senior Master for Arts Subjects, Royal Grammar School, Colchester, 1964-72. Publications: Tiresias and Other Poems, 1940; This Other Planet, 1945; Indian Landscape: A Book of Descriptive Poems, 1947; The Africa We Knew, 1973; Radio Plays: Between Two Worlds, 1948; Early Morning in Vaaldorp, 1961; Poets of the 1939-45 War, 1960, 1967. Honours: South Africa Poetry Prize, 1959; Fellow, Royal Society of Literature, 1970. Address: 3 Beverley Road, Colchester, Essex CO3 3NG, England.

CURRY Jane Louise, b. 24 Sept 1932, USA. Writer. Education: Pennsylvania State University, 1950-51; BA, Indiana University of Pennsylvania, 1954; University of California, Los Angeles, 1957-59; London University, England, 1961-62, 1965-66; AM, 1962, PhD, 1969, Stanford University. Appointments: Teaching Assistant, 1959-61, 1963-65, Acting Instructor, 1967-68, Instructor, 1983-84, Lecturer, 1987, English Department, Stanford University, Stanford, California; Freelance Lecturer, Consultant on Children's Books, 1970-. Publications include: Beneath the Hill, 1967; The Sleepers, 1968; The Change-Child, 1969; The Day Breakers, 1970; The Housenapper (also published as Mindy's Mysterious Miniature and The Mysterious Shrinking House), 1970; The Ice Ghosts Mystery, 1972; The Lost Farm, 1974; Poor Tom's Ghost, 1977; The Great Flood Mystery, 1985; The Lotus Cup, 1986; Me, Myself and I, 1986; Little Little Sister, 1989; The Big Smith Snatch, 1989; What the Dickens!, 1991; The Christmas Knight, 1993; The Great Smith House Hustle, 1993; Robin Hood and His Merry Men, 1994. Contributions to: Medium Aevum. Honours: Fulbright Grant, 1961-62; Stanford Leverhulme Fellowship, 1965-66; Book Award, 1971, Special Award, 1979, Southern California Council on Literature for Children; Ohioana Book Award, 1978, 1987. Memberships: The Authors Guild; International Arthurian Society; Southern California Council on Literature for Children and Young People. Address: McElderry Books, Simon & Schuster Children's Publishing Division, 866 Third Avenue, New York, NY 10022, USA.

CURRY Mary Earle Lowry, b. 13 May 1917, Seneca, South Carolina, USA. Writer. m. Reverend Peden Gene Curry, 25 Dec 1941, 1 son, 1 daughter. Education: Furman University, 1944-45. Publications: Looking Up, 1949; Looking Within, 1961, 1980; Hymn: Church in the Heart of the City, 1973. Contributions to: Numerous anthologies and journals including: Yearbook of Modern Poetry; Poets of America; Poetic Voice of America; We, the People; Poetry Digest; Poetry Anthology of Verse; International Anthology on World Brotherhood and Peace; The Greenville News; Inman Times. Honours: World Award for Culture, Centro Studi e Ricerche della Nazioni, Italy, 1985. Memberships: Auxiliary Rotary, Charleston, South Carolina, 1972-74; Centro Studi Scambi Internazionali, Rome; United Methodist Church Women's Organizations; United Methodist Church Ministers; Wives Club, President 1973-74, Charleston; Community clubs. Address: 345 Curry Drive, Seneca, SC 29678, USA.

CURRY Richard Orr, b. 26 Jan 1931, USA. Professor of History. m. 11 Feb 1968, 2 sons, 2 daughters. Education: BA, 1952, MA, 1956, Marshall University; PhD, University of Pennsylvania, 1961; Postdoctoral Fellow, Harvard University, 1965-66. Publications include: The Shaping of America, 1972; Conspiracy: The Fear of Subversion in American History, 1972; Radicalism, Racism and Party Realignment: The Border States During Reconstruction, 1973; The Abolitionists, 1985; Freedom at Risk: Secrecy, Censorship and Repression in the 1980's, 1988; An Uncertain Future: Thought Control and Repression during the Reagan-Bush Era, 1992. Contributions to: Journal of Southern History; Civil War History; Mid-America; Journal of the Early Republic; Ohio History; Others. Honours: Award of Merit, American Association of State and Local History, 1971; Senior Fulbright Lecturer, 1981; Von Mises Postdoctoral Fellow, 1982-83; Distinguished Alumnus Award, 1986; H L Mencken Award, 1989; Outstanding Book Award, 1989; Outstanding Book Award, Gustavus Myers Center for the Study of Human rights in the United States, 1993. Memberships include: Organization of American Historians; Society for the Historians of the Early Republic; American Historical Association; Fulbright Association. Address: 106 Windham Street, Willmantic, CT 06226, USA.

CURTEIS Ian Bayley, b. 1 May 1935, London, England. Playwright. m. (1) Joan Macdonald, 1964 (dissolved), 2 sons; (2) Joanna Trollope, 1985, 2 stepdaughters. Appointments: Director and Actor in Theatres all over Great Britain; BBC TV Script Reader, 1956-63; BBC and ATV Staff Director (drama), 1963-67; Chairman, Committee on Censorship, Writers' Guild of Great Britain, 1981-85. Publications: Television Plays: Beethoven, Sir Alexander Fleming (BBC's entry at 1973 Prague Festival); Mr Rolls and Mr Royce; Long

Voyage Out of War (trilogy); The Folly; The Haunting; Second Time ARound; A Distinct Chill; The Portland Millions; Philby, Burgess and Maclean (British entry 1978 Monte Carlo Festival, BAFTA nomination); Hess; The Atom Spies; Churchill and The Generals (BAFTA nomination, Grand Prize, Best Programme of 1980, NY International Film and TV Festival); Suez 1956 (BAFTA nomination); Miss Morrison's Ghosts (British entry 1982 Monte Carlo Festival, nomination US EMMY); The Mitford Girls; BB and Joe (trilogy); Lost Empires (adapted from J B Priestley); The Trials of Lady Sackville; Eureka (1st Euroserial, simultaneously shown in UK, West Germany, Austria, Switzerland, Italy and France); The Nightmare Years; Also originated and wrote numerous popular drama series; film screenplays; Andre Malraux's La Condition Humaine, 1982; Graham Greene's The Man Within, 1983; Tom Paine (for Sir Richard Attenborough) 1983; Plays: Long Voyage Out of War (trilogy), 1971; Churchill and The Generals, 1979; Suex 1956, 1980; The Falklands Play, 1987. Memberships: Royal Society of Literature; Writers Guild of Great Britain; Garrick Club. Address: The Mill House, Coln St Aldwyns, Cirencester, Glos. GL7 5AJ, England.

CURTEIS Joanna, (Caroline Harvey, Joanna Trollope), b. 9 Dec 1943, Gloucestershire, England. Writer. m. Ian Curteis, 12 Apr 1985, 2 stepsons, 2 daughters. Education: NA English Language & Literature, Oxford University. Publications: 8 Historical Novels; 1 Historical Survey; 6 Modern Novels; Best Known Historical Novels: Eliza Stanhope, 1978; Mistaken Virtues, 1979; Leaves from The Valley, 1980; The City of Gems, 1981; The Steps of The Sun, 1983; The Taverners Place, 1986; The Choir, 1988; A Village Affair, 1989; A Passionate Man, 1990; The Rector's Wife, 1991; The Men and The Girls, 1992; A Spanish Lover, 1992. Contributions to: Books reviews for Books Magazine; Daily Telegraph; Channel Four; Evening Standard; Introductions to reprints of Anthony Trollope; articles for Harpers and Queen, Options. Honours: Romantic Historical Novel of the Year, with Parson Harding's Daughter, 1980. Memberships: PEN; Trollope Society, Committee; Society of Authors. Literary Agent: Pat Kavanagh of A D Peters.

CURTIS Anthony Samuel, b. 12 Mar 1926, London, England. Journalist. m. Sarah, 3 Oct 1960, 3 sons. Education: Midhurst Grammer School, 1940-44; BA (Inter MA) 1st Class Hons, English, Chancellor's Prize for an English Essay, Oxford University, Merton College, 1948-50; US Harkness Fellowship in Journalism, 1958-59. Literary Appointments: Deputy Editor, Times Literary Supplement, 1959-60; Literary Editor, Financial Times, 1970-90. Publications: The Pattern of Maugham, 1974; Somerset Maugham: The Critical Heritage (with John Whitehead), 1987. Contributions to: Times Literary Supplement; Financial Times; BBC Radio 3 and 4. Honour: Fellow, Royal Society of Arts. Memberships: Treasurer, Royal Literary Fund; Trustee, Society of Authors Pension Fund; Garrick Club; Travellers; Beefsteak. Literary Agent: A M Heath. Address: 9 Essex Villas, London W8 7BP, England.

CURTIS Edward. See: PREBBLE John.

CURTIS Jack, b. 4 Jan 1922, Lincoln Center, Kansas, USA. Writer. m. LaVonn Renaas, 7 Sept 1949, 3 sons, 1 daughter. Education: BA, US University, Fresno, California, 1941. Publications: The Kloochman; Banjo; Eagles Over Big Sur; Red Knife Valley; The Sheriff Kill; Texas Rules; Jury on Smoky Hill; Blood Cut; Paradise Valley; Cut and Branded, 1993; The Fight for San Bernardo, 1993; Blood to Burn, 1993; The Mark of Cain, 1993; Quiet Cowboy, 1994; Pepper Tree Rider, 1994; Poetry includes: Cool Of A Kansas; Arctic Circle. Contributions to: Various. Membership: Western Writers of America. Literary Agent: Peekner Literary Agency, 3121 Portage Road, Bethlehem, PA 18017, USA. Address: Apple Pie Ranch Hwy 1, Big Sur, CA 93920, USA.

CURTIS Richard Hale. See: LEVINSON Leonard.

CURTIS Sharon, (Laura London), b. 6 Mar 1951, Dahran, Saudi Arabia. Writer. m. Thomas Dale Curtis, 1970, 2 children. Education: University of Wisconsin-Madison. Publications: A Heart Too Proud; The Bad Baron's Daughter, 1978; Moonlight Mist, 1979; Love's a Stage, 1980; The Gypsy Heiress, 1981; The Windflower, 1984; Sunshine and Shadow, 1986; Keepsake, 1987, (all with Thomas Dale Curtis).

CURTIS Thomas Dale, b. 11 Nov 1952, Antigo, Wisconsin, USA. Writer. m. Sharon, 1970, 2 children. Education: Attended University of Wisconsin-Madison. Appointments: Writer; Worked as a Professional

Musician and Actor. Publications: Romance novels with wife, Sharon Curtis, under joint pseudonym Laura London: A Heart Too Proud, 1978; The Bad Baron's Daughter, 1978; Moonlight Mist, 1979; Love's a Stage, 1980; The Gypsy Heiress, 1981; The Windflower, 1984; Under name Tom Curtis, with Sharon Curtis, Sunshine and Shadow, 1986; Keepsake, 1987.

CURTIS Tony, b. 26 Dec 1946, Carmathen, Wales. Poet. m. Margaret Blundell, 1970, 1 s, 1 d. Education: BA, University College of Swansea, 1968; MFA, Goddard College, Vermont, 1980. Appointments: Professor of Poetry, University of Glamorgan. Publications: Walk Down a Welsh Wind, 1972; Home Movies, 1973; Album, 1974; The Deerslayers, 1978; Carnival, 1978; Preparations: Poems, 1974-79, 1980; Letting Go, 1983; Selected Poems, 1970-85, 1986; The Last Candles, 1989; Taken for Pearls, 1993; Radio Play, Islands, 1975; Out of the Dark Wood: Prose Poems, Stories, 1977; Dannis Abse, 1985; The Art of Seamus Heaney (ed), 1986, 1994; How to Study Modern Poetry, 1990. Honour: National Poetry Competition Winner, 1984; The Dylan Thomas Prize, 1993. Address: Pentwyn, 55 Colcot Road, Barry, South Glamorgan, CF6 8BQ, Wales.

CURZON-BROWN Daniel, b. Litchfield, Illinois, USA. Writer; Professor. 1 son. Education: PhB, University of Detroit, 1960; MA, Kent State University, 1971; PhD, Wayne State University, 1969. Appointments: Currently Bay Area Theatre Critics Circle, San Francisco, California. Publications: Something You Do In The Dark, 1971; The Revolt Of The Perverts, 1978; Human Warmth and Other Stories, 1981; The Joyful Blue Book of Gay Etiquette, 1982; The World Can Break Your Heart, 1984; Curzon in Lov, 1988. Contributions to: Colorado Quarterly; North American Review. Membership: American Association of Composers, Authors and Publishers. Literary Agent: Jeffrey Simmons, London, England. Address: 416 Dorado Terrace, San Francisco, CA 94112, USA.

CUSHMAN Dan, b. 1909, USA. Freelance Writer; Journalist; Former Mining Prospector, Assayer and Geologist. Publications: Montana, Here I Be, 1950; Badlands Justice, 1951; Naked Ebony, 1951; Jewel of the Java Sea, 1951; The Ripper from Rawhide, 1952; Savage Interlude, 1952; Stay Away, Joe, 1953; Timberjack, 1953; Jungle She, 1953; The Fabulous Finn, 1954; Tongking, 1954; Port Orient, 1955; The Fastest Gun, 1955; The Old Copper Collar, 1957; The Silver Mountain, 1957; Tall Wyoming, 1957; The Forbidden Land, 1958; Goodbye, Old Dry, 1959, Paperback Edition as The Con Man, 1960; The Half-Caste, 1960; Brothers in Kickapoo, 1962, UK Edition as Boomtown, US Paperback as On the Make, 1963; 4 for Texas, novelisation of screenplay, 1963; The Grand and the Glorious, 1963; Opium Flower, 1963; North Fork to Hell, 1964; The Long Riders, 1967; The Muskrat Farm, 1977; Rusty Iron, 1984; Non-fiction: The Great North Trail: America's Route of the Ages, non-fiction, 1966; Cow Country Cook Book, 1967; Montana: The Gold Frontier, 1975. Literary Agency: Golden West Literary Agency, 2327 SE Salmon Street, Portland, OR 97214, USA. Address: 1500 Fourth Avenue N, Great Falls, MT 59401, USA.

CUSSLER Clive (eric), b. 15 July 1931, USA. Author. m. Barbara Knight, 28 Aug 1955, 3 children. Appointments: Served in USAF, 1950-54; Owner, Bestgen & Cussler Advertising, Newport Beach, California, 1961-65; Creative Director, Darcy Advertising, Hollywood, California, 1965-67; Advertising Director, Aquatic Marine Corporation, New Port Beach, 1967-69; Vice-President, Creative Director of Boradcast, Mefford, Wolff & Weir Advertising, Denver, Colorado, 1970-. Publications: The Mediterranean Caper, 1973; Iceberg, 1975; Raise the Titanic, 1976; Vixen O-Three, 1978; Night Probe, 1981; Pacific Vortex, 1982; Deep Six, 1984; Cyclops, 1986; Treasure, 1988; Dragon, 1990; Sahara, 1992; Inca Gold, 1994. Honours: Recipient numerous advt awards; Fellow, Explorers Club (Lowell Thomas Explorers award). Memberships: Royal Geog Soc; Chairman, National Underwater & Marine Agency.

CZGANY Lorant Gyorgy, b. 3 June 1935, Hungary. m. Magda Salacz, 28 Sept 1957, 1 daughter. Education: University of Szeged, 1954-56; University of Oxford, 1957-58; University of London, BA, 1958-60; PhD, 1960-64. Appointments: Szepsi Csombor Literary Circle, 1965-88; Editor, Atalier Hongrois, Paris, 1974; Minister, Plenipotentiary for Cultural Affairs, 1990-92. Publications: The Oxford History of Hungarian Literature; The Reception of Hungarian Literature in Victorian England; The Origins of State Control of Hungarian Literature; The Bela Ivanyi Grunwald Collection of Hungarica. Contributions to: The Times; BBC Overseas Service; Outside Contributor. Memberships: Szepsi Csombor Literary Circle; International Association of Hungarian Studies. Address: 15 Temple Fortune Lane, London NW11 7UB, England.

D

D'AGUIAR Fred, b. 2 Feb 1960, London, England. Editor; Poet. Education: BA Hons, University of Kent, 1985. Appointments: Writer in Residence, London Borough of Lewisham, 1986-87, Birmingham Polytechnic, 1988-89; Writing Instructor, The Arvon Foundation week-long residential courses on a once-yearly basis, 1986-; Visiting Writer, Amherst College, 1992-94; Assistant Professor of English, Bates College, 1994-95. Publications: Mama Dot, 1985, 1989; Airy Hall, 1989; British Subjects, 1993; Co-Editor: The New British Poetry, 1988; Novel: The Longest Memory, 1994, (French, Italian, German and Greek Editions, 1995); Play: A Jamaican Airman Forsees His Death, 1995; Television: Sweet Thames (poem/documentary for BBC), 1992; Rain (poem/documentary for BBC), 1994; Radio: 1492 (a long poem commissioned by BBC Radio broadcast), 1992. Honours: T S Eliot Prize for Poetry, University of Kent, 1984; The Malcolm X Prize for Poetry for Mama Dot, 1986; The Guyana Prize for Poetry for Airy Hall, 1989; Sweet Thames won the BBC's Race in the Media Award, 1992 and the British Film Institute's, Most Innovative Film Award in 1993; The Longest Memory won the David Higham Award and the Whitbread Best First Novel Award. Address: c/o Curtis Brown, The Haymarket, 28 Haymarket, London, England.

D'ALFONSO Antonio, b. 6 Aug 1953. Publisher; Writer. m. 8 Sept 1990. Education: BA; MSc. Publications: Fabrizio's Passion (novel), 1995; In Defense of Ethnicity, 1995; Julia; Panick Love; Avril ou l'Anti-passion; L'Amour Panique; L'Autre Rivage; The Other Shore; Black Tongue; Queror; La Chanson du Shaman à Sedna. Contributions to: The Gazette. Memberships: Various. Literary Agent: Guernica Editions, Toronto, Canada. Address: c/o Guernica Editions, PO Box 117, Station P, Toronto, Ontario, Canada M5S 2S6.

DABYDEEN Cyril, b. 15 Oct 1945, Guyana. Writer. m. 6 June 1989, 1 daughter. Education: BA (Hons), Lakehead University, Canada, 1973; MA, 1974, MPA, 1975, Queens University, Ontario. Literary appointments: League of Canadian Poets. Publications: Distances, 1977; Goatsong, 1977; This Planet Earth, 1980; Still Close to the Island, 1980; Islands Lovelier than a Vision, 1988; The Wizard Swami, 1989; Dark Swirl, 1989; Jogging in Havana, 1992; Sometimes Hard, novel, 1994; Stoning the Wind, poetry, 1994; Discussing Columbus, poetry, 1995; Berbice Crossing, stories, 1995; Editor: A Shapely Fire: Changing the Literary Landscape, 1987; Another Way to Dance: Asian-Canadian Poetry, 1992. Contributions to: The Canadian Forum; The Canadian Fiction Magazine; The Fiddlehead; The Dalhousie Review; Quarry; Grain; Waves; The Antigonish Review; Canadian Author and Bookman; The Toronto South Asian Review; Journal of South Asian Literature; Kunapipi; Wascana Review; The Literary Review; The Globe and Mail; Kyk-over-al; The Caribbean Quarterly. Honours: SandbachParker Gold Medal; A J Seymour Lyric Poetry Prize; Poet Laureate of Ottawa. Membership: Canadian Associaiton of Commonwealth Language and Literature Studies. Address: 106 Blackburn, Ottawa, Ontario, Canada K1N 8A7.

DABYDEEN David, b. 9 Dec 1956. Writer; Academic. Education: BA, Cambridge University, 1974-78; PhD, London University, 1978-82. Appointments: Litrature Panel, Arts Council of Great Britain, 1985-89. Publications: The Intended; Slave Song; Coolie Odyssey; Hogarts Blacks; Hogarth; Walpole and Commercial Britain; Disappearance, 1993; Turner, 1994. Contributions to: New Statesman; Guardian. Honours: Sir Arthur Quiller Couch Prize; Commonwealth Poetry Prize; Guyana Literature Prize, 1992. Memberships: Fellow of the Royal Society for the Arts; Member of the Executive Board of UNESCO. Literary Agent: Xandra Hardie. Address: c/o Centre for Carribean Studies, University of Warwick, Coventry, CV4 7AL, England.

DAFTARY Farhad, b. 23 Dec 1938, Brussels, Belgium. Academic. m. Fereshteh Kashanchi, Feb 1980, 1 d. Education: BA, The American University, 1962, MA, 1964; MA, University of California, 1966; PhD, 1971. Appointments: Lecturer, Tehran University, 1972-73; Lecturer, National University, Tehran, 1973-74; Professor, The Institute of Ismaili Studies, London, 1988-; Head, Department of Academic Research and Publications, Institute of Ismaili Studies, London, 1992-. Publications: The Ismailis: Their History & Doctrines; The Assassin Legends; A Short History of the Ismailis; Studies in Ismaili History & Thought. Contributions to: Islamic Culture; Arabica; Iran; Studia Islamica; Encyclopedia Iranica; Encyclopedia of Islam. Memberships:

American Oriental Society; British Institute of Persian Studies; British Society for Middle Eastern Studies; Society for Iranian Studies. Address: 77 Hamilton Terrace, London NW8, England.

DAHL Arlene, b. 11 Aug 1928, USA. Actress; Author; Desinger. m. Marc A Rosen, 30 July 1984, 2 sons, 1 daughter. Education: University of Minnesota; Minneapolis College of Music. Publications: 17 books on Beauty, Health, Fashion and Astrology including: Always Ask a Man, 1965; Your Beautyscope (series of 12), 1968, revised 1978; Arlene Dahls' Secrets of Haircare, 1970; Arlene Dahl's Secrets of Skin Care, 1972; Beyond Beauty, 1980; Lovescopes, 1983; Internationally Syndicated Beauty Column, Lets Be Beautiful, Chicago Tribune/New York News Syndicate, 1950-70. Contributions to: Girl Talk; Woman's World; Good Housekeeping; Woman's Own (England); Family Circle; Parade; The Best (Europe); Jupiter Magazine; Soap Opera Digest; Arlene Dahl's Lucky Stars, Globe Communications, 1988-90; Arlene Dahl's Astrological Forecast, 1990-93, 1994-. Honours: Award, Love's Leading Astrologer (Romantic Times book convention 1985). Memberships: Academy of Motion Picture Arts & Sciences, (New York Screening Committee); Academy of Television Arts & Sciences, (Board of Governors); IPA. Literary Agent: Mitch Douglas, ICM, New York. Address: PO Box 116, Sparkill, New York, NY 10976, USA.

DAICHES David, b. 2 Sep 1912, Sunderland, England. Emeritus Professor; Writer. m. Isobel Janet Mackay, 28 July 1937, 1 s, 2 d. Education: MA, Edinburgh University, 1934; DPhil, Oxford, 1939; Honorary Degrees: Brown University, Sorbonne University, Edinburgh University, Sussex University, Glasgow University, Stirling University, Bologna University, Guelph University. Appointments: Fellow, Balliol College, Oxford, 1936-37; Assistant Professor of English, University of Chicago, 1939-43; Professor, Cornell University, 1946-51; University Lecturer, Cambridge, 1951-61; Fellow, Jesus College, Cambridge, 1957-62; Professor, University of Sussex, 1961-77; Director, Institute Advanced Studies, University of Edinburgh, 1980-86. Publications Include: A Critical Study of English Literature, 1960; Two Worlds, 1956; The Novel and the Modern World, 1960; Robert Burns, 1950; The Paradox of Scottish Culture, 1964; God and the Poets, 1984; Edinburgh: A Travellers Companion, 1986; A Wee Drum, 1990; A Weekly Scotsman and Other Poems, 1994. Honours: FRSL, 1957; Scottish Arts Council Book Award, 1973; FRSE, 1980; Scottish Book of the Year Award, 1984; CBE, 1991. Memberships: Association for Scottish Literary Studies, Honorary President; Saltire Society, Honorary President; Modern Language Society of America, Honorary Member. Literary Agent: David Higham Associates. Address: 22 Belgrave Crescent, Edinburgh EH4 3AL, Scotland.

DALE Celia Marjorie, b. London, England. Author; Literary Consultant. m. Guy Ramsey, 30 Oct 1938, 1 s. Publications: 14 novels, including: A Helping Hand; Act of Love; A Dark Corner; The Innocent Party; Helping With Enquiries; A Personal Call (short stories); Sheeps Clothing. Memberships: Crime Writer's Association. Literary Agent: Curtis Brown, London. Address: 25 Nuffield Lodge, 22 Shepherds Hill, London N6 5UZ, England.

DALE Margaret Jessy, (Margaret J Miller), b. 27 Aug 1911, Edinburgh, Scotland. Writer. m. Clunie Rutherford Dale, 3 Sep 1938, divorced 1954, 1 s, 2 d. Education: 2nd Class Honours BA, English Language and Literature, Lady Margaret Hall, Oxford, 1933. Literary Appointments: Scenario Writer, Associated Screen News, Montreal, Canada, 1935-36; Assisstant Editor, Shell Magazine, London, 1937-39. Publications: The Queen's Music, 1961; The Powers of the Sapphire, 1962; The Far Castles, 1978; Emily, A Life of Emily Brontë, 1969; Knights, Beasts and Wonders, 1969; Mouse Tails, 1967; The Fearsome Road, 1975; The Fearsome Island, 1975; The Fearsome Tide, 1976. Contributions to: 200 scripts for Schools Broadcasting; The Times; The Times Literary Supplement; Scottish Field; The Scots Magazine; Scotland's Magazine. Memberships: PEN; National Book League. Literary Agent: John Johnson. Address: 26 Grey's Hill, Henley, Oxon RG9 1SJ, England.

DALE Peter John, b. 21 Aug 1938, England. Writer. m. Pauline Strouvelle, 29 June 1963, 1 s, 1 d. Education: BA (Hons) English, Oxford University, 1963. Literary Appointments: Co-editor, Agenda, 1972-. Publications include: Selected Poems François Villon (verse translation) 1978-88; One Another Sonnet Sequence, 1978; Poems of Jules Laforgue (verse translation), 1988; Mortal Fire: Selected Poems, 1976; Narrow Straits (verse translation) 19th Century French, 1985; Too Much of Water (poems 1978-82), 1983; Earth Light (poems), 1991; The Divine Comedy (Terza Rima version), 1996; Selected Poems of

François Villon (4th Reprint), 1994. Contributions to: Agenda; Chronicles (USA); Outposts; Acumen: Le Courrier (Brussels); PEN Review; The Use of English; Swansea Review; Poetry Durham; Le Journal Des Poètes. Honour: 1970 Arts Council Bursary. Membership: Society of Authors. Address: 5 Cranbourne Court, Albert Bridge Road, London SW11 4PE, England.

DALESKI H M, b. 1926. Professor of English. Appointments: Assisstant Lecturer to Associate Professor, 1958-76, Professor of English 1976-, Chairman, Department of English, 1968-70, 1984-85, Provost, School of Overseas Students, 1973-76, Hebrew University, Jerusalem. Publications: The Forked Flame: A Study of D H Lawrence, 1965; Dickens and the Art of Analogy, 1970; Joseph Conrad: the Way of Dispossession, 1977; The Divided Heroine: A Recurrent Pattern in Six English Novels, 1984; Unities: Studies in the English Novel, 1985. Honour: Elected Member of Israel Academy of Sciences and Humanities, 1993. Membership: President the Dickens Sociey, 1985. Address: Department of English, The Hebrew University, Jerusalem, Israel.

DALEY Brian Charles (Jack McKinney),b. 22 Dec 1947, Englewood, New Jersey, USA. Writer. Education: Bachelor's Degree (Communications), Jersey City State College, 1974. Publications: The Doomfarers of Coramonde, 1977; The Starfollowers of Coramonde, 1979; The Han Solo Trilogy, 1979-80; A Tapestry of Magics; The Alacrity Fitzhugh & Hobart Floyt Trilogy, 1985-86; The Robotyech Series (1-18) (with James Luceno) under pseudonym Jack McKinney, 1987-89; Novelization: Tron, 1982; Radio serial adaptations: Star Wards, The Empire Strikes Back. TV Scripts: Galaxy Rangers. Membership: Science Fiction Writers of America. Address: c/o Ballantine del Rey Books, 201c 50th Street, New York, NY 10022, USA.

DALMAS John, b. 3 Sept 1926, Chicago, Illinois, USA. Author. m. Gail Hill, 15 Sept 1954, 1 son, 1 daughter. Education: BSc, Michigan State College, 1954; Master of Forestry, University of Minnesota, 1955; PhD, Colorado State University, 1967. Publications: 20 science fiction novels: The Yngling, 1969, 1971, 1977, 1984, 1987; The Varkaus Conspiracy, 1983, 1987; Touch the Stars: Emergence (with Carl Martin), 1983; Homecoming, 1984; The Scroll of Man, 1985; Fanglith, 1985, 1987; The Reality Matrix, 1986; The Walkaway Clause, 1986; The Regiment, 1987, 1989; The Playmasters (with Rodney Martin), 1987; Return to Fanglith, 1987; The Lantern of God, 1987; The General's President, 1988; The Lizard War, 1989; The White Regiment, 1990; The Kalif's War, 1991; Yngling and the Circle of Power, 1992; The Orc Wars, collection, 1992; The Regiment's War, 1993; The Yngling in Yamato, 1994; The Lion of Farside, 1995. Contributions to: Various journals and magazines including: Analog; Saint Magazine; 1985 Annual World's Best Science Fiction; Science Fiction Yearbook, 1985; Far Frontiers III, IV, V, VI; Magazine of Fantasy and Science Fiction. Honours: Xi Sigma Pi Forestry Honorary Society, 1953; Phi Kappa Phi Scholastic Honorary Society, 1954; Sigma Xi Scientific Research Society, 1963. Memberships: Science Fiction Writers of America; Vasa Order of America. Address: 1425 Glass Street, Spokane, WA 99206, USA.

DALTON Annie,b. 18 Jan 1948, Weymouth, England. Writer. div. 1 son, 2 daughters. Education: Upper 2nd, English and American Literature, University of Warwick, 1967-70. Publications: Nightmaze: The After Dark Princess; The Real Tilly Beany; The Alpha Box; Swan Sister; The Witch Rose; Demon Spawn; Out of the Ordinary; Naming the Dark, 1992. Honours: East Midlands Arts Bursary, 1987; Winner, Nottingham Oak Children's Book Award, 1991; Commended for Carnegie, 1992. Literary Agent: Elizabeth Stevens, Curtis Brown. Address: 13 Selbourne Street, Loughborough, Leics LE11 1BS, England.

DALTON Priscilla. See: **AVALLONE Michael Angelo Jr.**

DALY Christopher,b. 7 July 1954, Boston, Massachusetts, USA. England Correspondent for the Washington Post; Freelance Magazine Writer. m. Anne K fishel, 1982, 2 sons. Education: BA magna cum laude, Harvard University, 1976; MA, University of North Carolina at Chapel Hill, 1982. Appointments: Writer and Editor, Associated Press, New York, 1976-80; State House Reporter, 1982-87, State House Bureau Chief, 1987-89, Associated Press, Boston. Publications: With Jacqueline D Hall, Bob Korstad, Lu Ann Jones and others, Like a Family: The Making of a Southern Cotton Mill World, 1987; Author of a Magazine Column on Politics, under a pseudonym. Honours: Shared

Merle Curti Prize from Organization of American Historians, 1988 for Like a Family. Memberships: Wire Service Guild, American Federation of Labor-Congress of Industrial Organizations, Penultimate Society. Address: Associated Press, 184 High Street, Boston, MA 02110, USA.

DALY Maureen (Maureen Daly McGivern), b. USA. Journalist; Writer. Literary appointments: Police Reporter, Columnist, Chicago Tribune, 1946-48; Associate Editor, Ladies' Home Journal, Philadelphia, Pennsylvania, 1948-54; Editorial Consultant, Saturday Evening Post, Philadelphia, 1960-69; Reporter/columns, The Desert Sun, Gannett Newspapers, California, USA. Publications: Seventeenth Summer, 1942; Smarter and Smoother: A Handbook on How to Be That Way, 1944; The Perfect Hostess: Complete Etiquette and Entertainment for the Home, 1948; What's Your PQ (Personality Quotient), 1952; Twelve Around the World, 1957; Patrick series, 4 volumes, 1959-63; Spanish Roundabout, 1961; Sixteen and Other Stories, 1961; The Ginger Horse, 1964; The Small War of Sergeant Donkey, 1966; Rosie: The Dancing Elephant, 1967; Acts of Love, 1986; Promises to Keep, 1987; With William McGivern: Mention My Name in Mombasa: The Unscheduled Adventures of an American Family Abroad, 1958; The Seeing, 1981; Editor: My Favorite Stories, 1948; Profile of Youth, 1951; My Favorite Mystery Stories, 1966; My Favorite Suspense Stories, 1968. Memberships: Authors League; Writers Guild of America; West; Society of Professional Journalists; Mystery Writers of America. Address: 73-305 Ironwood Street, Palm Desert, CA 92260, USA.

DALY Niki, b. 13 June 1946, Cape Town, South Africa. Writer; Illustrator; Editor. m. 7 July 1973, 2 sons. Education: Diploma in Art and Design, 1969, Cape Town Technikon. Literary Appointments: Publisher, Head of Songololo Books (A Division of David Philip Publishers, Cape Town). Publications Include: Not So Fast Songololo; Charlie's House; The Little Girl Who Lived Down The Road; Vim the Rag Mouse; Story Time Series for Walker Books; Joseph's Other Red Sock. Honours: The Litter Girl Who Lived Down The Road, 1978 Provisional Booksellers/British Arts Council Award; Not So Fast Songololo, 1986, USA Parents Choice Award and 1987 (SA) Katrien Harries Award. Literary Agent: Laura Cecil. Address: 36 Strubens Road, Mowbray, 7700 Cape Town, South Africa.

DALY Patricia. See: **BRENNAN Patricia Winifred.**

DALYELL Tam, b. 9 Aug 1932, Edinburgh, Scotland. Member of Parliament. m. Kathleen Wheatley, 26 Dec 1963, 1 son, 1 daughter. Education: Eton, 1945-50; Kings College, Cambridge, 1952-56. Appointments: House of Commons, 1962-. Publications: The Case for Shipp Schools, 1958; Ship School Duhera, 1961; One Man's Falklands, 1982; A Science Policy for Britain, 1983; Misrule: How Mrs Thatcher Deceived Parliament, 1987; Dick Crossman: A Portrait, 1988. Contributions to: Weekly Columnist, New Scientist, 1967-; Many Obituaries, Independent & Daily Newspapers. Honours: Various Awards of Science; Honorary Doctor of Science, University of Edinburgh, 1994. Address: House of Commons, London, SW1 A0AA, England.

DANA Robert Patrick, b. 1929, USA. Professor of English; Poet. Appointments: Assistant Professor, Associate Professor, Professor of English, Cornell College, Mount Vernon, Iowa, 1953-94; Editor, Hillside Press, Mount Vernon, 1957-67; Editor, 1964-68, Contributing Editor, 1991-, The North American Review; Contributing Editor: The American Poetry Review, 1973-88, New Letters, 1980-83. Publications: My Glass Brother and Other Poems, 1957; The Dark Flags of Waking, 1964; Journeys from the Skin: A Poem in Two Parts, 1966; Some Versions of Silence: Poems, 1967; The Power of the Visible, 1971; In a Fugitive Season, 1980; What the Stones Know, 1984; Blood Harvest, 1986; Against the Grain: Interviews with Maverick American Publishers, 1986; Starting Out for the Difficult World, 1987; What I Think I Know: New and Selected Poems, 1990; Wildebeest, 1993; Yes, Everything, 1994. Contributions to: The New Yorker; The New York Times; Poetry; The Georgia Review; Manoa; Many others. Honours: Rainer Maria Rilke Prize, 1984; National Endowment for the Arts Fellowship, 1985, 1993; Delmore Schwartz Memorial Poetry Award, 1989; Carl Sandburg Medal for Poetry, 1994. Memberships: Academy of American Poets; PEN; Associated Writing Programs; Poetry Society of America. Address: 1466 Westview Drive, Coralville, IA 52241, USA.

DANCE Stanley, b. 1910, England. Reviewer. Literary Appointments: Reviewer: Jazz Journal, London, 1948-94; The Saturday Review, New York City, USA, 1962-72; Music Journal, New York City,

1962-79; Jazz Times, Silver Spring, Maryland, 1980-94. Publications: Jazz Era (editor), 1961; The Night People (with D Wells), 1971; The World of Duke Ellington, 1970; The World of Swing, 1974; The World of Earl Hines, 1977; Duke Ellington in Person (with M Ellington), 1978; The World of Count Basie, 1980; Those Swinging Years (with Charlie Barnet), 1984. Honours: Deems Taylor Award for Duke Ellington in Person, American Society of Composers, Authors and Publishers, 1979. Address: 1745 Bittersweet Hill, Vista, CA 92084, USA.

DANE Mark. See: **AVALLONE Michael Angelo**.

DANESHVAR Simin, b. 23 Apr 1921, Shiraz, Iran. Novelist. Education: PhD, University of Teheran, 1949. Appointments include: Professor at the Department of Archaeology, University of Teheran (Emeritus from 1979). Publications: The Extinguished Fire, 1948; A City Like Paradise, 1961; Savushun, 1969, 1991; To Whom Shall I Say Hello?, 1980; Jalal's Sunset, 1981; Daneshvar's Playhouse: A Collection of Stories, 1989; Translations of works by Alan Paton, Hawthorne, Chekhov and Shaw. Address: c/o Mage Books, 1032 29th Street NW, Washington, DC 20007, USA.

DANIEL Colin,See:**WINDSOR Patricia**.

DANIEL Wayne Wendell, b. 14 Feb 1929, Georgia, USA. Statistician. m. Mary Yarbrough, 2 June 1956, 1 son, 2 daughters. Education: BS, University of Georgia, 1951; MPH, University of North Carolina, 1959; PhD, University of Oklahoma, 1965. Publications: Business Statistics; Biostatistics; Applied Nonparametric Statistics; Essentials of Business Statistics; Introductory Statistics with Applications; Pickin On Peachtree; A History of Country Music in Atlanta. Contributions to: More than 100 articles to various publications. Memberships: American Statistical Association; American Public Health Association. Address: 2943 Appling Drive, Chamblee, GA 30341, USA.

DANIELS Dorothy (Danielle Dorsett, Angela Gray, Cynthia Kavanaugh, Helaine Ross, Suzanne Somers, Geraldine Thayer, Helen Gray Weston),b. 1 July 1915, Waterbury, USA. Writer. m. 7 Oct 1937. Publications Include: Numerous Romantic Fiction Books, most recent being: The Magic Ring, 1978; Purple and The Gold, 1978; Yesterday's Evil, 1980; Veil of Treachery, 1980; Legend of Death, 1980; Valley of Shadows, 1980; Monte Carlo, 1981; Saratoga, 1981; Sisters of Valcour, 1981; For Love and Valcous, 1983; Crisis at Valcour, 1985; Illusion of Haven's Edge, 1990. Honours: National Honorary Member, National League of American Pen Women. Memberships: Authors Guild; National League of American Pen Women; Ventura County Writers. Literary Agent: Richard Curtis Associates, New York, USA. Address: 6107 Village 6, Camarillo, CA 93010, USA.

DANIELS Max. See: **GELLIS Roberta Leah**.

DANIELS Molly Ann (Shouri Daniels), b. 2 July 1932, Kerala, India.Writer; Teacher; Editor. 1 son, 1 daughter. Education Includes: PhD, University of Chicago's Committee on Social Thought, 1986. Appointments: Director, The Clothesline School of Writing, Chicago, Illinois, 1984-. Publications: Fiction: The Yellow Fish, 1966; The Prophetic Novel: A Study of A Passage to India, criticism, 1990; The Clotheslines Review, 4 issues of anthology of fiction (editor), 1986-90; Father Gander Rhymes and Other Poems (editor), 1990; The Clothesline Review Manual for Writers, textbook. Contributions to: Indian PEN; Quest; Femina; The Chicago Review; Primavera; The Carleton Miscellany; Tri-Quarterly; Journal of Literary Studies; The Saul Bellow Journal. Honours: Fulbright-Smith Mundt, 1961-62; Illinois Arts Council Fiction, 1978; Illinois Arts Council Criticism, 1982; Syndicated Fiction Award, PEN. Memberships: Midwest Authors. Literary Agent: Jane Jordan Browne. Address: The Clothesline School of Writing, Department of Continuing Education, University of Chicago, 5835 S Kimbark, Chicago, IL 60637, USA.

DANIELS Olga. See: **SINCLAIR Olga Ellen**.

DANIELS Shouri, See: **DANIELS Molly Ann**.

DANIELSON Carl. See: **KRUMMACHER Johann Henrich Karl Daniel**.

DANKOVA Jana. See: **TANSKA Natalie**.

DANN Colin Michael, b. 10 Mar 1943, Richmond, Surrey. Author. m. Janet Elizabeth Stratton, 4 June 1977. Education: Shene County Grammar School. Publications: The Animals of Farthing Wood, 1979; In The Grip of Winter, 1981; Fox's Feud, 1982; The Fox Cub Bold, 1983; The Seige of White Deer Park, 1985; The Ram of Sweetriver, 1986; King of the Vagabonds, 1987; The Beach Dogs, 1988; The Flight from Farthing Wood, 1988; Just Nuffin, 1989; In the Path of the Storm, 1989; A Great Escape, 1990; A Legacy of Ghosts, 1991; The City Cats, 1991; Battle for the Park, 1992. Honour: Arts Council National Award for Children's Literature, 1980. Memberships: Society of Authors. Address: The Old Forge, Whatlington, Battle, East Sussex, England.

DANN Jack, b. 15 Feb 1945, Johnson City, USA. Author. m. Jeanne Van Buren Dann. Education: BA, State University of New York, Binghamton, 1968. Publications: Wandering Stars, editor, 1974; Novels: Starhiker, 1977; Time Tipping, 1980 (Coll); Junction, 1981; The Man Who Melted, 1984; In the Field of Fire, editor with wife, 1987; The Work of Jack Dann, by Jeffrey M Elliot; Unicorns II, 1992; Dragons, 1993; Magicats Two, 1991. Contributions to: New Dimensions; Orbit; New Worlds; Asimov's Science Fiction Magazines; Fiction Writers Handbook; many others. Honours: Nebula Award Finalist, 1973, 1975, 1978, 1979, 1981, (in 2 categories) 1983, 1984, 1985; Esteemed Knight (Hon Member), Mark Twain Society, 1975-; British Science Fiction Association Award Finalist, 1979; World Fantasy Award Finalist, 1981, 1984, 1987; Winner (with Gardner Dozois) Gilgamesh Award 1986, (Spanish Language Award). Memberships: Judge, Nebula Award Rules Committee, 1980; Science Fiction Writers of America; Authors Guild; World Future Society. Literary Agent: John Schaffner Agency, New York. Address: 825 Front Street, Binghamton, NY 13905, USA.

DANTO Arthur C(oleman), b. 1924. Publications: Nietzsche As Philosopher, 1965; Analytical Philosophy of Knowledge, 1968; What Philosophy Is, 1968; Sartre, 1975; Transfiguration of the Commonplace, 1981; Narration & Knowledge, 1985; Philosophical Disenfranchisement of Art, 1986; State of the Art, 1987; Politics of Imagination, 1988; Encounters & Reflections, 1990; Mapplethorpe, 1992; From the Inside Out, 1993; Embodied Meanings, 1994; Playing with the Edge, 1995. Contributor to: Nation. Honour: National Book Critics Circle Awards, 1990.

DARBY (Henry) Clifford, Sir,b. 7 Feb 1909, Resolven, West Glamorgan, Wales. Emeritus Professor of Geography. m. Eva Constance Thomson, 26 Dec 1941, 2 daughters. Education: BA 1928, PhD 1931, MA 1932, St Catharine's College, Cambridge. Literary Appointments: Lecturer in Geography, 1931-45, Professor of Geography, 1966-76, University of Cambridge; Fellow, King's College, Cambridge, 1932-45, 1966-81; Professor of Geography, University of Liverpool, 1945-49; Professor of Geography, University College, London, 1949-66. Publications: An Historical Geography of England, Editor; The Medieval Fenland; The Draining of the Fens; The Changing Fenland: A New Historical Geography of England, Editor; The DomesdayGeography of England, 7 volumes, Editor and Contributor; The University Atlas, (with Harold Fullard); The New Cambridge Modern History Atlas (with Harold Fullard). Contributions to: Geography Journal; Econ History Review; Journal of Historical Geography. Honours: OBE, 1946; CBE, 1978; Kt, 1988; Honorary Doctorates: Chicago 1967; Liverpool 1968; Durham, 1970; Hull, 1975; Ulster, 1977; Wales, 1979; London, 1987; Victoria Medal, Royal Geographical Society, 1963; Honours Award, Association of American Geographers, 1977. Memberships: FBA, 1967. Address: 60 Storey's Way, Cambridge, CB3 0DX, England.

DARBY Catherine. See: **PETERS Maureen**.

DARBY John, b. 18 Nov 1940, Belfast, Northern Ireland. University Professor. m. Marie, 13 Apr 1966, 2 sons. Education: BA, Honours, Modern History, 1962; HDipEd, 1970; DPhil, Ulster, 1985. Appointments: Editorial Board, International Journal of Group Tensions; Editorial Committee, Cahier du Centre Irelandaises, Paris, 1982. Publications: Conflict in Northern Ireland, 1976; Violence and Social Services in Northern Ireland, 1978; Northern Ireland: Background to the Conflict, 1983; Dressed to Kill: Cartoonists and Northern Irish Conflict, 1983; Intimidation and the Control of Conflict in Northern Ireland, 1986; Political Violence: Ireland in a Comparative Perspective, 1990. Address: 17 Lever Road, Portstewart, Co. Derry, Northern Ireland.

DARCY Clare,b. America. Writer of Historical/Romance/Gothic Books. Publications: Georgia, 1971; Cecily, or A Young Lady of Quality, 1972; Lydia, or Love in Town, 1973; Victoire, 1974; Allegra,

1975; Lady Pamela, 1975; Regina, 1976; Elyza, 1976; Cressida, 1977; Eugenia, 1977; Gwendolen, 1978; Rolande, 1978; Letty, 1980; Caroline and Julia, 1982; Eugenia, 1990;Georgia, 1990; Rolande, 1991; Cressida, 1991. Address: c/o Walker & Co, 720 Fifth Avenue, New York, NY 10019, USA.

DARDIS Thomas A,b. 19 Aug 1926, New York, USA. Writer; Teacher. Education: BA 1949; MA 1952; PhD 1980. Publications: Some Time in The Sun, 1976; Keaton, 1979; Harold Lloyd, 1983; The Thirsty Muse, 1989; Keaton, The Man Who Wouldn't Lie Down, 1989. Contributions to: American Film; Journal of Popular Film and Television; Resources for American Literary Study. Membership: PEN. Literary Agent: George Borichardt.

DARKE Marjorie Sheila, b. 25 Jan 1929. Writer. m. 1952, 2 sons, 1 daughter. Education: Worcester Grammar School for Girls, 1938-47; Leicester College of Art, 1947-50; Central School of Art, London, 1950-51; Diploma in Textile Design/Printing, 1949. Publications: For Young Adults: Ride The Iron Horse, 1973; The Star Trap, 1974; A Question of Courage, 1975; The First of Midnight, 1977; A Long Way to Go, 1978; Comeback, 1981, (trilogy); Tom Post's Private Eye, 1982; Messages and Other Shivery Tales, 1984; A Rose From Blighty, 1990. For Beginner Readers: Mike's Bike, 1974; What Can I Do, 1975; The Big Brass Band, 1976; My Uncle Charlie, 1977; Carnival Day, 1979. For Young Children: Kipper's Turn, 1976; Kipper Skips, 1979; Imp, 1985; The Rainbow Sandwich, 1989; Night Windows, 1990; Emma's Monster, 1992. Honours: Runner-up, Guardian Award for Children's Books, 1978, for The First of Midnight. Memberships: Society of Authors, Committee Member, Children's Writers Group, 1980-83; International PEN. Literary Agent: Rogers, Coleridge & White Ltd. Address: c/o Rogers, Coleridge & White, 20 Powis Mews, London, W11 1JN, England.

DARLIN Sergio. See: **JOSÉ Héctor Oscar**.

DARNTON John (Townsend),b. 20 Nov 1941, New York, USA. Metropolitan Editor, New York Times. m. Nina Lieberman, 21 Aug 1966, 1 son, 2 daughters. Education: Attended University of Paris IV, Sorbonne and Alliance Francaise, Paris, 1960-61;BA, University of Wisconsin, 1966. Appointments: New York Times, New York: Copy Boy, News Clerk and News Assistant, 1966-68; City Reporter 1968-69; Connecticut Correspondent, 1970-71; Night Rewriter, 1971-72; Reporter for New York City Fiscal Crisis, 1972-75; Correspondent in Lagos, Nigeria 1976-77 and Nairobi, Kenya 1977-79; Bureau Chief in Warsaw, Poland 1979-82 and Madrid, Spain 1982-84; Deputy Foreign Editor 1984-86; Metropolitan Editor, 1987-; Correspondent and Narrator for Film, Spain: Ten Years After; Member Board of Directors, New York State Associated Press; News Editor/Weekends, New York Times, 1991-. Publications: A Day in the Life of Spain; Contributor to Assignment America; A Collection of Outstanding Writing from the New York Times and About Men: Reflections on the Male Experience. Contributions to: Periodicals including Readers Digest. Honours: George Polk Award from Long Island University 1979 and 1982 for foreign reporting; Pulitzer Prize in International Reporting from Columbia University Graduate School of Journalism, 1982 for Dispatches from Poland. Memberships: Ferris Professor, Princeton University, 1991-92. Address: New York Times, City Desk, 229 West 43rd Street, NY 10036, USA.

DARUWALLA Keki N(asserwanji), b. 24 Jan 1937, Lahore, Pakistan. Poet. Education: MA, University of Punjab, Chandigarh. Publications: Under Orion, 1970; Apparition in April, 1971; Crossing the Rivers, 1976; Winter Poems, 1980; The Keeper of the Dead, 1982; Landscapes, 1987; Stories, Sword and Abyss, 1979; Editor, Two Decades of Indian poetry, 1960-80. Honours: The Sahitya Akademi (National Academy of Letters) Award for Keeper of the Dead, 1984; The Commonwealth Poetry Award (Asia Region) for Landscapes, 1987. Address: OUP, PO Box 43, YMCA Library Building, 1st Floor, Jai Singh Road, New Delhi 100 001, India.

DARVI Andrea. See: **PLATE Andrea**.

DARVILL Timothy Charles, b. 22 Dec 1957, Cheltenham, England. Archaeologist. Education: BA, 1979; PhD, 1983. Appointments: Reviews Editor, Transactions Bristol & Gloucestershire Archaeological Society, 1985-90. Publications: Prehistoric Britain; Ancient Monuments in the Countryside; The Archaeology of the Uplands; Prehistoric Gloucestershire; Glovebox Guide to Ancient Britain; New Approaches to Our Past; Megalithic Chambered Tombs of the Cotswold Severn Region. Contributions to: 40 articles to journals. Memberships: Institute of Field Archaeologists, Chairman 1989-91; Fellow of the Society of Antiquaries of London; Society of Antiquaries of Scotland; Council of the National Trust, 1988. Address: Department of Conservation Science, Bournemouth University, Fern Barrow, Poole, Dorset, England.

DARWISH Adel. See: **DARWISH Ahmed Adel Abed El-Moneim**.

DARWISH Ahmed Adel Abed EL-Moneim (Adel Darwish), b. 8 Dec 1945, Alexandria. Writer; Journalist. m. Elizabeth Catherine Margaret, 6 Apr 1976, div, 1 son, 1 daughter. Education: BSc, Ludda. Literary Appointments: Reporter, Writer on International Affairs, Journalist, Radio & TV Commentator, 1981-. Publications: Unholy Babylon: The Secret History of Saddam's War; Between the Quill and the Sword: The Political Background to the Rushdie Affair; The Muslim Brotherhood and British Secret Diplomacy; Security in the Gulf: Chances of Iraqi Defences; Strategy for the 1990's in the Middle East; Water Wars: Coming Conflict in the Middle East, 1993; The Dawn of Terror, a section in the book, The Persian Gulf War, 1993; Rafsanjani's Iran: Iran's Foreign Policy in the 1990's, 1993; A Bitter Pill: Is Kuwait Defendable?; The Middle East in Post Persian Gulf War. Contributions to: The Sunday Telegraph; The Economist; The Independent; The Evening Standard; Index on Censorship; Defence & Foreign Affairs; American Arab Affairs; Foreign Report; Global Affairs; Gulf Strategy Papers; Global Issues. Memberships: National Union of Journalists; The Writers Guild. Literary Agent: Dianne Coles. Address: The Independent, 40 City Road, London, England.

DAS Kamala, b. 31 Mar 1934, Malabar, South India. Poetry Editor; Poet. m. K Madhava Das, 1949, 3 s. Appointments: Poetry Editor, Illustrated Weekly of India, Bombay, 1971-79. Publications: Summer in Calcutta: Fifty Poems, 1965; The Descendants, 1967; The Old Playhouse and Other Poems, 1973; Tonight This Savage Rite: The Love Poetry of Kamala Das and Pritish Nandy, 1979; Collected Poems, 1987; Novels, Alphabet of Lust, 1977; Manomi, 1987; The Sandalwood Tree, 1988; Short Stores. Honours: Kerala Sahitya Academy Award for Fiction, 1969; Asian World Prize for Literature, 1985. Address: Sthanuvilas Bungalow, Sastgamangalam, Trivndrum 10, Kerala, India.

DASGUPTA Sukamal,b. India. Economist; Poet. Education: MA, Economics, Allahabad University, 1939. Appointments: Lyricist, All India Radio and Doordarshan (Indian Television). Publications: Books of Verse: Gadahar, Life of Sri Ramakrishnan, for children, 1958; Ma Mani, Life of Sarada Devi, wife of Sri Rama Krishna, verse, 1958; Biliti Chhara, Bengali translation of English nursery rhymes, 1960; Saradiya, Chhara, for children, 1962; Chhara Dilam chhariye, for children, 1964; Chharate Ramayan, for children, 1967; K Khelar Chhara, for children, 1969; Bigyaner Chhara, book of elementaryscience in verse for children; Jagrata Bharat, sonmgs, 1978; Purba Negh, book of verse, 1980; Satabdir Aovan, songs, 1985; Bania Bina, songs and poems, 1991; Arati Ajan, songs; 2 unpublished dance dramas. Contributions to: Magazines and journals for children and adults including: Sishusathi; Mauchak; Ramdhanu; Nabakoli; Sandesh. Honours: Prize, Certificate, Critics Council of India, 1982; Bhubaneswari Padak (Medal), Sisha Sahitya Parishad, Bengal, 1985. Memberships: Past Secretary, Sishu Sahitya Parishad; Executive Council, PEN. Address: E-16 Ramgarh, Calcutta 700 047, India.

DASSANOWSKY-HARRIS Robert von, b. 28 Jan 1956, New York City, New York, USA. Writer; Editor; Educator. Education: graduate, BA, 1985, MA, 1988, American Academy of Dramatic Arts, 1977; PhD, University of California, Los Angeles, 1992. Appointments: Founding Editor, Rohwedder, 1986-94; Contributing Editor: Rampike: 1991-94, Osiris, 1991-, PEN Center Magazine, 1992-; Television Writer, The Disney Channel, USA; Assistant Professor of German, University of California, Los Angeles, 1992-93; Assistant Professor of German and Film, University of Colorado, Colorado Springs, 1993-; Managing Editor, Writers' Forum, 1993-. Publications: Phantom Empire(s): The Novels of Alexander Lernet-Holenia, 1995; Telegrams from the Metropole; Collected poems; Numerous play productions and readings. Contributions to: American Book Review; Films in Review; Starlog; East European Quarterly; Germanic Review; Modern Austrian Literature; Germanic Notes; Manhattan Review; Jacaranda Review; Poesie Europe, Germany; Log, Austria; Caractères, France; PEN International, UK; Poetry Australia; Le Guépard, France. Honours: Accademico Honoris Causa, Accademia Culturale d'Europa; BHTG/Julie Harris Playwright Award; Los Angeles Cultural Affairs

Grant, 1991, 1992. Memberships: Board of Directors, PEN USA/West, 1992; President, PEN Colorado Chapter, 1994-; Dramatists Guild; Poets and Writers; Paneuropa Union. Address: 3807 Half Turn Road 324, Colorado Springs, CO 80917, USA.

DATHORNE O(scar) R(onald), b. 19 Nov 1934, Georgetown, Guyana. Professor of English; Writer; Poet. Appointments: Associate Professor, Ahmadu Bello University, Zaria, 1959-63 and University of Ibadan, 1963-66, Nigeria; UNESCO Consultant to the Government of Sierra Leone, 1967-68; Professor of English, Njala University College, University of Sierra Leone, 1968-69; Professor of African Literature, Howard University, 1970; Professor of Afro-American Literature, University of Wisconsin, Madison, 1970-71; Professor of English and Black Literature, Ohio State University, 1975-77; Professor of English, University of Miami, Coral Gables, Florida, 1977-. Publications: Dumplings in the Soup (novel), 1963; The Scholar Man (novel), 1964; Carribean Narrative (editor), 1965; Carribean Verse (editor), 1967; Africa in Prose, 1969; The Black Mind, 1975; African Literature in the Twentieth Century, 1976; Dark Ancestor, 1981; Dele's Child, 1985. Address: Department of English, University of Miami, Coral Gables, FL 33124, USA.

DAUNTON Martin James, b. 7 Feb 1949, Cardiff. University Professor. m. Claire Gobbi, 7 Jan 1984. Education: BA, University of Nottingham, 1970; PhD, University of Kent, 1974. Appointments: Lecturer, University of Durham, 1973-79; Lecturer, University College London, 1979-85; Reader, 1985-89; Professor, 1989-. Publications: Coal Metropolis: Cardiff; House and Home in the Victorian City, 1850-1914; Royal Mail: The Post office Since 1840; A Property Owning Democracy?; Progress and Poverty. Contributions to: Economic History Review; Past & Present; Business History; Historical Research; Journal of Urban History. Memberships: Royal Historical Society; Royal Society of Arts. Address: Department of History, University College London, Gower Street, London WC1E 6BT, England.

DAVEY Frank(land Wilmot), b. 1940, Canada. University Professor; Writer; Poet. Appointments: Lecturer 1963-66 and Assistant Professor 1967-69, Royal Roads Military College, Victoria; Writer-in-Residence, Sir George Williams University, Montreal, 1969-70; Editor, Tish Magazine, Vancouver, 1961-63 and Open Letter Magazine, Toronto, 1965-82; Co-ordinator of Creative Writing Program 1976-79, Associate Professor, Professor 1970-, Chairman, Dept of English, 1985-, York University, Toronto; General Editor, Quebec Translations Series, 1973-; Member of the Editorial Board, Coach House Press, Toronto, 1975-; General Editor, New Canadian Citicism Series, Talonbooks, Vancouver, 1977-. Publications: D-Day and After, 1962; City of the Gulls and Sea, 1964; Bridge Force, 1965; The Scarred Hull, 1966; Four Myths for Sam Perry, 1970; Weeds, 1970; Five Readings of Olson's Maximus (criticism), 1970; Earle Birney (criticism), 1971; Griffon, 1972; King of Swords, 1972; L'An Trentiesme: Selected Poems, 1961-70, 1972; Areana, 1973; The Clallam or, Old Glory in Juan de Fuca, 1973; From There to Here: A Guide to English Canadian Literature since 1960, 1974; (ed) Tish 1-19, 1975; (ed) Mrs Dukes' Million, by Wyndham Lewis, 1977; War Poems, 1979; The Arches: Selected Poems, 1980; Louis Dudek and Raymond Souster (criticism), 1981; The Contemporary Canadian Long Poem, 1981; Capitalistic Affection!, 1982; Surviving the Paraphrase, 1983; Edward and Patricia, 1984; Margaret Atwood: A Feminist Poetics, 1984; The Louis Riel Organ and Piano Company, 1985; Popular Narratives, 1991; Postcard Translations, 1988; Reading Canadian Reading, 1988. Address: 133 Calumet College, York University, Downsview, Ontario, M35 1P3, Canada.

DAVEY Thomas A, b. 2 Jan 1954, Philadelphia, Pennsylvania, USA. Adult and Child Psychologist; Writer. Education: BA, Duke University, 1976; EdD, Harvard University, 1984. Appointments: Teaching Fellow, Harvard University, Cambridge, Massachusetts; Conducts Private Practice in Adult and Child Psychology, Cambridge. Publications: A Generation Divided: German Children and the Berlin Wall, 1987. Contributions to: Articles and reviews to magazines and newspapers, including New Republic, Boston Review, Los Angeles Times Bookreviewer and New Age Journal. Honours: Grants from German Academic Exchange Service, 1981-82 and 1988; Lyndhurst Foundation Prize, 1985, for pursuit of writing and research interests. Memberships: American Psychological Association; Massachusetts Psychological Association. Address: Boston, Massachusetts, USA.

DAVIDSON Basil Risbridger, b. 9 Nov 1914, Bristol, England. Writer. m. Marion Young, 7 Jul 1943, 3 s. Publications include: Old Africa Rediscovered, 1959; The African Slave Trade, 1961; The Africans, 1969; Africa in Modern History, 1978; The Rapids, 1956; Special Operations Europe, 1980; The Fortunate Isles, 1989; African Civilisation Revisited, 1991; The Black Man's Burden; Africa and the Curse of the Nation-State, 1992; The Search for Africa, 1994. Honours: Military Cross, British Army; Bronze Star, US Army; Ansfield Woolf Award, 1959; D. Letters (hc), University of Ibadan, 1975; University of Dar-es-Salaam, 1985; DUniv (hc), Open University of Great Britain, 1980; University of Edinburgh, 1981; Agnelli Visiting Professor, University of Turin, 1990. Address: Old Cider Mill, North Wootton, Somerset BA4 4HA, England.

DAVIDSON Lionel, (David Line). b. 31 Mar 1922, Hull, Yorkshire, England. Author. Publications: The Night of Wenceslas, 1960; The Rose of Tibet, 1962; A Long Way to Shiloh, 1966; Making Good Again, 1968; Smith's Gazelle, 1971; The Sun Chemist, 1976; The Chelsea Murders, 1978; Under Plum Lake, 1980; Run for Your Life, 1966; Mike & Me, 1974; Screaming High, 1985; Kolymsky Heights, 1994. Honours: Most Promising First Novel Award, Authors Club, 1961; Gold Dagger CWA, 1961, 1967, 1979. Literary Agent: Curtis Brown. Address: c/o Curtis Brown, Haymarket House, 28/29 Haymarket, London SW1Y 4SP, England.

DAVIDSON William H, b. 25 Sept 1951, New Mexico. Professor. m. Anneke Rozendaal, 16 June 1973, 3 sons. Education: Harvard College, AB, 1973; Harvard Business School, MA, 1975; Harvard University, DBA, 1979. Publications: 2020 Vision; The Amazing Race; US Competitueness; Managing the Global Corporation, 1989. Contributions to: Numerous. Honours: Academy of International Business Dissertation Award; Fortune Magazine, Best Business Book of the Year. Memberships: Academy of International Business. Literary Agent: Rafoel Sagalyn. Address: 26 Sea Cove Drive, Rancho Palos Verdes, CA 90274, USA.

DAVIE Donald Alfred, b. 17 July 1922, Barnsley, Yorkshire, England. Academic; Literary Critic. m. Doreen John, 1945, 2 sons, 1 daughter. Education: St Catharine's College, Cambridge. Appointments Include: Lecturer, University of Cambridge, 1958-64, Fellow, Gonville and Caius College, Cambridge, 1959-64; Professor, Literature, 1964-68, Pro-Vice-Chancellor, 1965-68, University of Essex; Professor, English, Stanford University, USA, 1968-74; Olive H Palmer Professor in the Humanities, 1974-78; Clark Lecturer, Trinity College, Cambridge, 1976; Andrew W Mellon Professor, Humanities, Vanderbilt University, 1978-88. Publications: Poetry: Brides of Reason, 1955; A Winter Talent, 1957; The Forests of Lituania, 1959; A Sequence for Francis Parkman, 1961; Events and Wisdoms, 1964; Essex Poems, 1969; Six Epistles to Eva Hese, 1970; Collected Poems, 1972; The Shires, 1975; In the Stopping Train, 1977; Collected Poems 1972-83, 1983; Literary Criticism: Purity of Diction in English Verse, 1952; Articulate Energy, 1957; The Heyday of Sir Walter Scott, 1961; Ezra Pound: Poet as Sculptor, 1965; Thomas Hardy and British Poetry, 1972; Pound, 1976; The Poet in Imaginary Museum (essays), 1978; A Gathered Church: The Literature of the English Dissenting Interest 1700-1930, 1978; Dissentient Voice: Enlightenment and Christian Dissent, 1982; Czeslaw Milosz & The Insufficiency of Lyric, 1986; Anthologies: The Late Augustans, 1958, with Angela Livingstone; Modern Judgement: Pasternak, 1969; Augustan Lyric, 1974; The New Oxford Book of Christian Verse, 1981. Honours: Recipient, numerous honours and awards; FBA, 1986. Address: 4 High Street, Silverton, Exeter, EX5 4JB, England.

DAVIE Elspeth, b. 1919, Kilmarnock, Scotland. Teacher; Author. m. George Elder Davie. Education: DA, Edinburgh College of Art. Publications: Novels: Providing, 1965; Creating a Scene, 1971, 1984; Climbers on a Stair, 1978; Short Stories: The Spark and Other Stories, 1968, 1984; The High Tide Talker and Other Stories, 1976; The Night of the Funny Hats, 1980; A Traveller's Room, 1985; Coming to Light, 1989. Honours: Scottish Arts Council Grants, 1971, 1977 and 1979; Katherine Mansfield Prize from English Centre of International PEN, 1978 for short story The High Tide Talker.

DAVIE-MARTIN Hugh. See: MCCUTCHEON Hugh.

DAVIES (Edward) Hunter, b. 7 Jan 1936, Renfrew, Scotland. Writer. m. 11 June 1960, 1 son, 2 daughters. Education: University College, Durham, England, BA, DipEd. Publications: 40 Books including: Here We Go Round The Mulberry Bush, 1965; The Beaties, 1968, 2nd edition, 1985; The Glory Game, 1972, 2nd edition, 1985; A Walk Along The Wall, 1974, 2nd edition, 1986; A Walk Along The

Lakes, 1979; Fit for the Sixth, 1989; In Search of Columbus, 1991. Contributions to: Sunday Times, 1960-84; Punch, 1979-89; Independent, London, 1990-. Literary Agent: Giles Gordon. Address: 11 Boscastle Road, London, NW5, England.

DAVIES James Atterbury, b. 25 Feb 1939, Llandeilo, Dyfed, Wales. University Lecturer. m. Jennifer Hicks, 1 Jan 1966, 1 s, 1 d. Education: BA, 1965; PhD, 1969. Appointments: Senior Lecturer, University College of Swansea, 1990-. Publications: John Forster: A Literary Life; The Textual Life of Dickens's Characters; Leslie Norris; Dylan Thomas's Places. Contributions to: RES; DUJ; DSA; NWR. Memberships: University of Wales Association for the Study of Welsh Writing in English. Address: Department of English, University of Swansea, SA2 8PP, Wales.

DAVIES Pauline (Pauline Fisk), b. 27 Sep 1948, London, England. Writer. m. David Davies, 12 Feb 1972, 2 s, 3 d. Publications: Midnight Blue, 1990; Telling the Sea, 1992. Contributions to: Homes and Gardens, 1989. Honours: For Midnight Blue: Smarties Grand Prix Prize, 1990; Shortlisted, Whitbread Award. Membership: Society of Authors. Literary Agents: Cecily Ware; Comstock Smith. Address: c/o Cecily Ware, 19c John Spencer Square, Canonbury, London N1 2L3, England.

DAVIES Peter Joseph, b. 15 May 1937, Terang, Victoria, Australia. Physician; Writer. m. Clare Loughman, 21 Dec 1960, 1 d. Education: MB, 1961; MRACP, 1968; FRACP, 1974; MRCP, 1970; MD, 1991. Publications: Mozart in Person: His Character and Health, 1989; Mozart's Health in 1790; Bicentenary Collection; Sadie. Contributions to: Some Recent Trends in Mozartiana. Webber's Melbourne, Winter 1990; The Musical Times. Memberships: The Royal Australian College of Physicians; The Gastro-Enterological Society of Australia; The Royal Society of Medicine. Literary Agent: The Greenwood Press. Address: 220 Springvale Road, Glen Waverley, Victoria 3150, Australia.

DAVIES Piers Anthony David, b. 1941, Australia. Barrister and Solicitor; Scriptwriter;Poet. Appointments: Barrister and Solicitor, Jordans, Auckland, New Zealand (qualified 1965); Chairperson, Short Film Fund of NZ Film Commission, 1987-91. Publications: East and Other Gong Songs, 1967; (with Peter Weir), Life and Flight of Rev Buck Shotte (screenplay), 1969; Day Trip from Mount Meru, 1969; (with Peter Weir), Homesdale (screenplay), 1971; (with Peter Weir), The Cars That Ate Paris (screenplay), 1973; Diaspora, 1974;Bourgeois Homage to Dada, 1974; (ed) Central Almanac, 1974; Skin Deep (screenplay), 1978; R V Huckleberry Finn (video documentary), 1979; Olaf's Coast (documentary), 1982; Jetsam, 1984; The Lamb of God (screenplay), 1985; Shipping Law Section of Encyclopaedia of New Zealand Forms & Precedents, 1994. Address: 16 Crocus Place, Remuera, Auckland 5, New Zealand.

DAVIES Robertson (Samuel Marchbanks),b. 1913, Canada. Emeritus Professor; Writer; Playwright. Appointments: Actor and Teacher, Old Vic Theatre Company, London, 1938-40; Literary Editor, Saturday Night, 1940-42; Editor 1942-58 and Publisher 1958-68, Peterborough Examiner; Professor of Eglish and Master of Massey College, University of Toronto, Ontario, 1963-81, now Emeritus Professor. Publications: Shakespeare's Boy Actors, 1939; Shakespeare for Young Players, 1942;The Diary of Samuel Marchbanks, 1947; Eros at Breakfast and Other Plays, 1949; Fortune My Foe (play), 1949; At My Heart's Core (play), 1950;Tempest Tost (novel), 1951; A Masque of Aesop (play), 1952; (with Tyrone Guthrie), Renown at Stratford, 1953; (with Tyrone Guthrie), Twice Have the Trumpets Sounded, 1954; A Jig for the Gypsy (play), 1954; Leaven of Malice (novel), 1954; (with Tyrone Guthrie), Thrice the Brinded Cat Hath Mew'd, 1955; A Mixture of Frailties (novel), 1958; A Voice from the Attic, 1960; The Personal Art, 1961; A Masque of Mr Punch (play), 1963; Samuel Marchbanks' Almanack, 1967; Stephen Leacock, 1970; Feast of Stephen (anthology), 1970; Fifth Business (novel), 1970; Hunting Stuart and Other Plays, 1972; The Manticore (novel), 1972; World of Wonders (novel), 1975; Question Time (play), 1975; One Half of Robertson Davies, 1977; The Enthusiasms of Robertson Davies, 1979; Robertson Davies: The Well-Tempered Critic, 1981; The Rebel Angels (novel), 1981; High Spirits: A Collection of Ghost Stories, 1982; The Mirror of Nature (lectures), 1983; What's Bred in the Bone (novel), 1985; The Papers of Samuel Marchbanks, 1985; The Lyre of Orpheus (novel), 1988; Murther & Walking Spirits (novel), 1991. Honours Include: Lorne Pierce Medal, Royal Society of Canada, 1961; Companion of the Order of Canada, 1972; Lifetime Achievement Award, Toronto Arts Awards, 1986; Molson Prize in the Arts, Canada

Council, 1988; 19 Honorary Degrees in Canada, 3 in USA and DLitt from Trinity College, Dublin and from Oxford; Govenor General's Award for Fiction; American Academy Institute of Arts & Letters, Honorary Member. Literary Agent: Curtis Brown Ltd, Ten Aster Place, New York, NY 10003, USA. Address: Massey College, 4 Devonshire Place, Toronto, Ontario M5S 2E1, Canada.

DAVIES Sumiko,b. 21 Sept 1942, Tokyo, Japan. Illustrator and Writer. m. Derek Davies, 7 Jan 1967, 1 son, 1 daughter. Education: Kuwazawa Design Institute, Diploma in Design and Illustration, 1966. Appointments: Freelance Illustrator, Art Director of Marklin Advertising Agency in Thailand, 1966-67; Work Exhibited at Pinky Gallery, Tokyo, Japan, 1979 and Museum of Modern Art, Oxford, England, 1984. Publications Include: Self-Illustrated Books under name Sumiko: Hans Andersen's Fair Tales, 1979, 1980; My Baby Brother Ned, 1984; My School, 1983; A Kiss on the Nose, 1984; My Holiday, 1987; Peter and Cat, 1989. Membership: Foreign Correspondents Club of Hong Kong. Address: 7C Scenic Villas, Victoria Road, Pokfulam, Hong Kong.

DAVIES William Thomas Pennar,b. 12 Nov 1911, Aberpennar (Mountain Ash), Glamorgan, Wales. m. Rosemarie Wolff, 26 June 1943, 4 sons, 1 daughter. Education: University of Wales, Cardiff, 1929-34; Balliol College, Oxford, 1934-36; Yale University, USA, 1936-38; Mansfield College, Oxford, 1940-43; BA (Wales), 1932; BLitt (Oxon), 1938; PhD (Yale), 1943. Publications Include: Cudd fy Meiau, diary, 1957; Anadl o'r Uchelder, novel, 1958; Yr Efrydd o lyn Cynon, poems, 1961; Caregl Nwyf, short stories, 1966; Meibion Darogan, novel, 1968; Llais y Durtur, short stories, 1985. Also: Cinio'r Cythraul, poems, 1946; Naw Wftt, poems, 1957; Rhwng Chwedl a Chredo, studies, 1966; Y Tlws yn y Lotws, poems, 1971; Y Brenin Alltud, studies; Yr Awen Almaeneg, anthology, German verse in Welsh translation, 1984; Llef, poems, 1987. Contributions to: Articles, reviews, studies, various periodicals, published separately. Honours: Commonwealth Fund Fellow, 1936-38; Fellow, University of Wales, 1938-40; Welsh Academy Prize, 1968; Fellow Honoris Causa, University of Wales, Cardiff, 1986; Honorary DD, ibid, 1987; Honorary Fellow, Yr Academi Gymreig (Welsh Academy), 1989. Memberships: Undeb Awduron Cymru. Address: 10 Heol Grosvenor, Sgeti, Abertawe, Swansea SA2 0SP, Wales.

DAVIS Alan R, b. 30 June 1950, New Orleans, Louisiana, USA. Writer; Professor. m. Catherine Culloden, 4 July 1981, 1 son, 1 daughter. Education: BA, 1973, MA, 1975, University of Louisiana; PhD, University of Denver, 1981. Appointments: Loyola University, 1980-81; University of North Carolina, 1981-85; Chair of English, Director of Creative Writing, Moorhead State University, Moorhead, Minnesota, 1985-; Editor, American Fiction, 1987-. Publications: Rumors From The Lost World; American Fiction. Contributions to: The New York Times Book Review; San Francisco Chronicle; Cleveland Plain Dealer; Chicago Sun Times; Hudson Review; Kansas Quarterly. Honours: Breadloaf Scholarship; State Arts Board Fellow; Minnesota Voices Winner. Memberships: National Book Critics Circle; Associated Writing Programs. Literary Agent: Nat Sobel. Address: PO Box 229, Moorhead State University, Moorhead, MN 56563, USA.

DAVIS Andrew (Wynford),b. 1936, England. Lecturer; Writer; Playwright. Appointments: Teacher, St Clement Danes Grammar School, 1958-61 and Woodberry Down School, 1961-63, both in London; Lecturer, Coventry College of Education and University of Warwick, Coventry College, 1963-. Publications: Plays: Marmalade Atkins in Space, 1982; Also Radio and television plays for children and numerous radio plays for adults. Children's Fiction: The Fantastic Feats of Doctor Box, 1972; Conrad's War, 1978; Marmalade and Rufus, 1979, as Marmalade Atkins Dreadful Deeds, 1982; Marmalade Atkins in Space, 1982; Educating Marmalade, 1983; Danger! Marmalade at Work, 1984; Alfonso Bonzo, 1986; Poonam's Pets, 1990; Fiction Includes: Getting Hurt, 1989; Dirty Foxes, 1990; B Monkey, 1992. Address: c/o Leinon Unna & Durbridge, 24 Pottery Lane, London W11 4LZ, England.

DAVIS Burke,b. 1913, America. Writer; Historian; Biographer. Appointments: Editor, Feature Writer and Sports Editor, Charlotte News, North Carolina, 1937-47; Reporter, Baltimore Evening Sun, Maryland, 1947-52; Reporter, Greensboro News, North Carolina, 1951-60; Writer and Historian, Colonial Williamsburg, Virginia, 1960-78. Publications: Whisper My Name, 1949; The Ragged Ones, 1951; Yorktown, 1952; They Called Him Stonewall, 1954; Gray Fox, 1956; Roberta E Lee, 1956; Jeb Stuart, The Last Cavalier, 1957; To Appomattox, 1959; Our Incredible Civil War, 1960; Marinel, 1961; The

Cowpens-Guilford Courthouse Campaign, 1962; America's First Army, 1962; Appomattox: Closing Struggle of the Civil War, 1963; The Summer Land, 1965; (co-author), A Rebel Raider, 1966; The Billy Mitchell Affair, 1967; A Williamsburg Galaxy, 1967; (co-author) The World of Currier & Ives, 1968; Get Yamamoto, 1969; Yorktown: The Winning of American Independence, 1969; Billy Mitchell Story, 1969; The Campaign that Won America: Yorktown, 1970; Heroes of the American Revolution, 1971; Jamestown, 1971; Thomas Jefferson's Virginia, 1971; Amelia Earhart, 1972; Biography of a Leaf, 1972; Three for Revolution, 1975; Biography of a Kingsnake, 1975; George Washington and the American Revolution, 1975; Newer and Better Organic Gardening, 1976; Biography of a Fish Hawk, 1976; Old Hickory: A Life of Andrew Jackson, 1977; Mr Lincoln's Whiskers, 1978; Sherman's March, 1980; The Long Surrender, 1985; The Southern Railway, 1985; War Bird: The Life and Times of Elliott White Springs, 1986; Civil War: Strange and Fascinating Facts, 1989; Marine: The Life of Chesty Puller, 1991; To Appomattox: 9 April Days 1865, 1989. Address: Rt 1 Box 66, Meadows of Dan, VA 24120, USA.

DAVIS Christopher,b. 23 Oct 1928, Philadelphia, USA. Writer; Teacher. m. Sonia Fogg, 6 June 1953, 4 daughters. Education: BA, University of Pennsylvania, 1955. Appointments: Pennsylvania Council on The Arts, 1981-86. Publications: Lost Summer; A Kind of Darkness; A Peep Into The 20th Century; Suicide Note; Waiting For It; The Producer; Dog Horse Rat; First Family; Belmarch; Ishmael; The Sun in Mid Career. Contributions to: Esquire; Argosy; Der Monat; Travel & Leisure; Holiday; The New York Times; LA Times; The Pennsylvania Gazette; Saturday Evening Post. Honours: O'Henry Prize Story; Best Magazine Articles; National Book Award; Nominee, American Academy & Institute of Arts & Letters Career Award; American Academy of Arts & Letters Literature Award, 1991. Memberships: PEN; Authors Guild. Literary Agent: Curtis Brown. Address: Curtis Brown, 10 Aster Place, New York City, NY 10003, USA.

DAVIS David Brion, b. 1927, USA. Professor of History. Writer. Appointments: Ernest I White Professor of History, Cornell University, Ithaca, New York, 1963-69; Harold Vyvyan Harmsworth Professor, Oxford University, England, 1969-70; Professor, Farnum Professor, 1969-78, Sterling Professor of History, 1978-, Yale University, New Haven, Connecticut, USA; Chair in American Civilisation, Ecole des Hautes Etudes en Sciences Sociales, Paris, France, 1980-81. Publications: Homicide in American Fiction, 1957; The Problem of Slavery in Western Culture, 1967; The Slave Power Conspiracy and the Paranoid Style, 1969; The Problem of Slavery in the Age of Revolution, 1975; The Great Republic (co-author), 1977, 1980, 1992; Slavery and Human Progress, 1984; From Homicide to Slavery: Studies in American Culture, 1986; Revolutions: Reflections on American Equality and Foreign Liberations, 1990; Editor: Ante-Bellum Reform, 1967; The Fear of Conspiracy, 1971; Antebellum American Culture, 1979. Contributions to: Frequent to The New Republic and New York Review of Books. Honours: Pulitzer Prize, 1967; Mass Media Award, National Conference of Christians and Jews, 1967; National Book Award, 1975; Bancroft Prize, 1975; Albert J Beveridge Award, American Historical Association, 1975. Memberships: Corresponding Fellow, British Academy, 1992; American Academy of Arts and Sciences; American Philosophical Society. Address: Department of History, Yale University, New Haven, CT 06520, USA.

DAVIS Dick, b. 18 Apr 1945, Portsmouth, Hampshire, Professor; Poet. m. Afkham Darbandi, 1974, 2 daughters. Education: BA, Kings College, Cambridge, 1966; PhD, University of Manchester, 1988. Appointments: Assistant Professor, 1988, Associate Professor of Persian, 1993-, Ohio State University. Publications: Shade Mariners, 1970; In The Distance, 1975; Seeing the World, 1980; The Covenant, 1984; Visitations, 1983; What the Mind Wants, 1984; Lares, 1986; Devices and Desires: New and Selected Poems, 1967-87, 1989; Editor, The Selected Writing of Thomas Traherne, 1980; Editor, The Rubaiyat of Omar Khayyam, Translated by Edward Fitzgerald, 1989; A Kind of Love, New & Selected Poems, 1991; Epic & Sedition, One Case of Ferdonzi's Shahnameh, 1992; Translations: The Conference of The Birds, 1984; The Legend of Seyavash, 1992. Honour: Royal Society of Literature Heinemann Award, 1981. Address: Dept of Near Eastern Languages, OH State University, 190 North Oval Mall, Columbus, OH 43210, USA.

DAVIS Dorothy Salisbury,b. 26 Apr 1916, Chicago, Illinois, USA. Writer. Education: AB, Barat College, Lake Forest, Illinois. Publications: A Gentle Murderer, 1951; Men of No Property, 1956; The Evening of the Good Samaritan, 1961; Enemy and Brother, 1967;

Where the Dark Streets Go, 1969; The Little Brothers, 1974; A Death in the Life, 1976; Scarlet Night, 1980; Lullaby of Murder, 1984; Tales for a Stormy Night, 1985; The Habit of Fear, 1987; Black Sheep, White Lambs, 1993; A Gentleman Caller, 1989; Old Sinners Never Die, 1991. Contributions to: New Republic. Honours: Grand Master's Award, Mystery Writers of America, 1985; Lifetime Achievement Award, Bouchereon XX, 1989. Memberships: President, Executive Vice President, Mystery Writers of America; Crime Writers Association, England; Authors Guild. Literary Agent: McIntosh & Otis. Address: Palisades, New York, NY 10964, USA.

DAVIS Gordon. See: **LEVINSON Leonard.**

DAVIS Gordon, See: **HUNT Everette Howard.**

DAVIS Jack Leonard,b. 11 Mar 1917, Perth, Western Australia. Writer. m. Madelon Jantine Wilkens, 12 Dec 1987, 1 daughter. Appointments: Writer-in-Residence, Murdoch University, 1982. Publications: The First Born & Other Poems, 1968; No Sugar, play, 1986; Jagardoo-poems from Aboriginal Australia, 1978; John Pat and Other Poems, 1988; The Dreamers & Kullark, plays, 1983; Burungin (Smell the Wind), play, 1989; Honey Spat, 1986; Plays from Black Australia, 1989. Contributions to: Identity. Honours: Human Rights Award, 1987; BHP Award, 1988; Advance Australia, 1987; Awgie, 1986; Australian Artists Creative Fellowship, 1989; Honorary Degrees: DLitt, Murdoch University, DLitt, University of Western Australia. Memberships: Australian Writers Guild; PEN International (Life Member); Aboriginal Writers Oral Literature & Dramatists Association, Chairman. Address: 3 Little Howard Street, Fremantle, Western Australia, Australia.

DAVIS Jon Edward,b. 28 Oct 1952, New Haven, Connecticut, USA. Author. m. Terry Layton, 8 Jan 1978, 1 daughter. Education: BA, English, 1984, MFA, Creative Writing, 1985, University of Montana. Appointments: Writing Programme Co-ordinator, Fine Arts Work Centre, Provincetown, 1987-. Publications: West of New England, 1983; Dangerous Amusements, 1987. Contributions to: Poetry; Georgia Review; Missouri Review; Stand; Malahat Review. Honours: Academy of American Poets Prize, 1985; NEA Fellowship, 1986; Fine Arts Work Centre, Provincetown Creative Writing Fellowship, 1986-87. Memberships: Academy of American Poets; Poets & Writers Inc; Associated Writing Programmes. Address: Fine Arts Work Centre, Box 565, Provincetown, MA 02657, USA.

DAVIS Joy Lynn Edwards, b. 4 Apr 1945, Speedwell, TN. Teacher of English. m. Joe Mac Davis, 22 Jul 1969. Education: BA, Lincoln Memorial University, 1969; MA, Union College, 1974; Stokely Fellow, University of TN, 1984. Publications: Immigrants and First Families of America, 1982; Old Speedwell Families, Revised and Updated, 1983; More Speedwell Families, 1988; American Poetry Anthology, 1990; Great Poets of Our Time, 1993; Distinguished Poets of America, 1993. Honours: Lincoln Memorial University Literary Hall of Fame, 1982; Teacher of the Year, 1991; Delta Kappa Gamma. Memberships: American Federation of Teachers; PETA. Address: Rt, 2, Box 302, LaFollette, TN 37766, USA.

DAVIS Kenneth, b. 29 Sept 1912, KS, USA. m. Florence Marie Olenhouse, 19 Feb 1938, dec. Education: BS, KS State University; MS, University of WI. Appointments: Professional & Academic Career in Journalism; Public Relations, US Commission for UNESCO; Asst to Milton S Eisenhower, 1947-49; Member Adlai Stevenson's Personal Staff, 1955-56. Publications: Over 20 Fictional & Non Fictional Historical Works inc. In The Forests of the Night, 1942; Morning in Kansas, 1952; The Experience of War, 1965; Eisenhower: American Hero, 1969; FDR 4 Vols, 1972-93; Invincible Summer: An Intimate Portrait of the Roosevelts, 1974; A Sense of History, 1985. Honours: Friend of American Writers Award, 1943; Centennial Award, 1963; Francis Parkman Prize, 1973; Achievement Award, KS Authors Club, 1977. Address: 907 East Virginia Terrace, Santa Pauls, CA 93060, USA.

DAVIS Margaret Thomson, b. Bathgate, West Lothian Scotland. Novelist. Divorced, 1 s. Education: Albert Secondary School. Publications include: The Breadmakers Saga; A Very Civilsed Man; The Prisoner; Rag Woman, Rich Woman; Daughters and Mothers; Wounds of War; A Woman of Property, 1991; A Sense of Belonging, 1993; The Making of A Novelist, 1982; Hold Me Forever, 1994; Kiss Me No More, 1995. Contributions to: 200 short stories to women's magazines in Britain and overseas and also newspapers.

Memberships: Committee Member, PEN; Committeee Member, Society of Authors (Scottish branch); Committee Member, Swanwick Writers School; Honorary President, Strathkelvin Writers Club; Strathclyde Writers Group; Scottish Labour History Society; Great Britain USSR Friendship Society. Literary Agent: Heather Jeeves. Address: c/o Heather Jeeves, 9 Dryden Place, Edinburgh, EH9 1RP, Scotland.

DAVIS Nathaniel, b. 12 Apr 1925, Boston, Massachusetts, USA. Professor. m. Elizabeth Kirkbride Creese, 24 Nov 1956, 2 sons, 2 daughters. Education: AB, 1944, PhD, 1960, LLD, 1970, Brown University, 1944; MA, The Fletcher School of Law and Diplomacy, 1947. Appointments: Apprentice Seaman, 1943-44, Ensign, Lieutenant (junior grade), 1944-46, US Naval Reserve; Teacher, Tufts College, 1947; Centro Venezolano Americano, 1961; Howard University, 1962-68; US Naval War College, 1977-83; Salve Regina College, Newport, 1981-82; Harvey Mudd College, 1983-; Various US Foreign Serive appointments including: US Minister to Bulgaria, 1965-66; Senior Staff, The National Security Council (The White House), 1966-68; US Ambassador to Guatemala, 1968-71, Chile, 1971-73, Switzerland, 1975-77; Director General, US Foreign Service, 1973-75; State Department Adviser to the Naval War College, 1977-1983. Publications: The Last Two Years of Salvador Allende; Ambassadors in Foreign Policy; Equity and Equal Security in Soviet Foreign Policy; A Long Walk to Church; A Contemporary History of Russian Orthodoxy. Contributions to: New York Times Magazine; The Washington Post; Foreign Affairs; The Foreign Service Journal; The Department of State Newsletter; The Los Angeles Times; San Diego Union Magazine; Journal of Religious Thought; Naval War College Review. Memberships: National Book Critics Circle; American Association for the Advancement of Slavic Studies; American Foreign Service Association; Council on Foreign Relations; American Historical Association; The Academy of Political Science. Address: 1783 Longwood Avenue, Claremont, CA 91711, USA.

DAVIS Robert Prunier,b. 1929, America. Writer; Playwright. Publications: Day of The Painter (screenplay), 1961; Apes on a Tissue-Paper Bridge, 1963; Good-bye, Bates McGee, 1967; The Dingle War, 1968; (as Joe Brandon), Cock-A-Doodle-Dew, 1972; (as Joe Brandon), Paradise in Flames; The Pilot, 1976; Cate Five, 1977; The Divorce, 1980; Control Tower, 1981; Glass Cockpit, 1991.

DAVIS Sonia. See: **WILLIAMS Alberta Noring.**

DAVIS William,b. 6 Mar 1933. Author; Publisher; Broadcaster. m. Sylvette Jouclas, 1967. Appointments: Staff, Financial Times, 1954-59; Editor, Investor's Guide, 1959-60; City Editor, Evening Standard, 1960-65 (with one years break as City Editor, Sunday Express); Financial Editor, The Guardian, 1965-68; Editor, Punch, 1968-77; Editor, Publisher, High Life, 1973-; Chairman, Headway Publications, 1977-; Editorial Director, Executive World, 1980-, Moneycare, 1983-; Presenter, Money Programme, BBC TV, 1967-69; English Tourist Board, 1990-; Premier Publication Showing since 1992. Publications: Three Years Hard Labour: The Road to Devaluation, 1968; Merger Mania, 1970; Money Talks, 1972; Have Expenses Will Travel, 1975; It's No Sin To Be Rich, 1976; Editor, The Best of Everything, 1980; Money in the 1980's, 1981; The Rich: A Study of the Species, 1982; Fantasy: A Practical Guide to Escapism, 1984; The Corporate Infighter's Handbook, 1984; Editor, The World's Best Business Hotels, 1985; Children of the Rich, 1989, (Non Fiction). Address: British Tourist Authority, Thames Tower, Black's Road, London W6 9EL, England.

DAVIS-FLOYD Robbie Elizabeth, b. 26 Apr 1951, Casper, WY, USA. Anthropologist. m. Robert N Floyd, 30 Jun 1978, 1 s, 1 d. Education: BA, UT, 1972; MA, UT, 1974; PhD, University of TX, 1986. Publications: Birth As An American Rite of Passage, 1992; The Technocratic Body and the Organic Body, in press; Childbirth and Authoritative Knowledge (co-editor Carolyn Sargent), in press. Contributions to: Social Science and Medicine; Medical Anthropology Quarterly; other articles in academic journals. Honours: Phi Beta Kappa; Phi Kappa Phi, 1972. Memberships: AAA; AES; AHMA; APPPAH, Board Member; APHA; CAR; MANA; SAC; SMA; SNN; SSSS; NARM, Board Member. Address: 1301 Capital of TX Highway B128, Austin, TX 778746, USA.

DAVIS-GOFF Annabel Claire, b. 19 Feb 1942. Writer. m. Mike Nichols, 1976, divorced 1987, 1 son, 1 daughter. Publications: Night Tennis, 1978; Tail Spin, 1980; Walled Gardens, 1989. Literary Agent:

Owen Laster, William Morris Agency, New York, USA. Address: 1 West 67th Street, New York, NY 10023, USA.

DAVISON Geoffrey Joseph, b. 10 Aug 1927, Newcastle-upon-Tyne, England. m. Marlene Margaret Wilson, 15 Sept 1956, 2 s. Education: Qualifications: TD (Territorial Decoration); FRICS (Chartered Surveyors). Publications: The Spy Who Swapped Shoes, 1967; Nest of Spies, 1968; The Chessboard Spies, 1969; The Fallen Eagles, 1970; The Honorable Assassins, 1971; Spy Puppets, 1973; The Berlin Spy Trap, 1974; No Name on Their Graves, 1978; The Bloody Legionnaires, 1981. Address: 95 Cheviot View, Ponteland, Newcastle-upon-Tyne, NE20 9BH, England.

DAWE Donald Bruce, b. 15 Feb 1930, Geelong, Australia. Teacher. m. Gloria Desley Blain, 27 Jan 1964, 2 s, 2 d. Education: BA, 1969; MA, 1975; PhD, 1980, Queensland; LittB, UNE, 1973; DLitt, 1995; VSQ, 1995. Appointment: Writer-in-Residence, University of Queensland, 1984. Publications: No Fixed Address, 1962; A Need of Similar Name, 1965; An Eye for a Tooth, 1968; Beyond the Subdivisions, 1969; Condolences of the Season: Selected Poems, 1971; Just a Dugong at Twilight, 1975; Sometimes Gladness: Collected Poems, 1987; Over Here Harv! and Other Stories, 1983; Towards Sunrise, 1986; This Side of Silence, 1990; Bruce Dawe: Essays and Opinions, 1990; Sometimes Gladness: Collected Poems, 1954-92; Mortal Instruments: Poems 1990-95. Contributions to: Journals and magazines. Honours: Myer Poetry Prize, 1966, 1969; Ampol Arts Award for Creative Literature, 1967; Dame Mary Gilmore Medal of Australian Literary Society, 1973; Grace Leven Poetry Prize, 1978; Braille Book of the Year, 1979; Patrick White Literary Award, 1980; Christopher Brennan Award, 1984; Inaugural Institute Award for Excellence in Teaching, 1987, Paul Harris Fellow of Rotary International: Order of Australia (AO), 1992. Memberships: Centre for Australian Studies in Literature, Associate Member; Australian Association for Teaching English, Honorary Life Member; Victorian Association for Teaching of English, Honorary Life Member. Address: 30 Cumming Street, Toowoomba, Queensland 4350, Australia.

DAWSON Clay. See: **LEVINSON Leonard.**

DAWSON Jennifer, (Jenny Sargesson, Jenny Hinton), b. 23 Jan 1929, Hertfordshire, England. m. Michael Hinton, 2 Apr 1964. Education: St Annes College, Oxford; University College, London. Publications: The Ha-Ha, 1961; Fowlers Snare, 1962; The Queen of Trent (with W Mitchell), 1962; The Cold Country, 1965; Strawberry Boy, 1976; Hospital Wedding, 1978; A Field of Scarlet Poppies, 1979; The Upstairs People, 1988; Judasland, 1989; As Jenny Sargesson: The Flying Gardens, 1993. Poems in: Ambit. Honours: James Tait Black Award, 1961; Cheltenham Festival Award, 1962; Fawcett Society Fiction Award, 1990. Address: 6 Fisher Lane, Charlbury, Oxon OX7 3RX, England.

DAWSON Jill Dianne, b. 1962. Writer; Editor. 1 s. Education: BA, American Studies, University of Nottingham, 1980-83. Appointments: Writer in Residence, Doncaster; Fareham College, Hampshire; Tutor of Creative Writing, Au Pair, Yoga Teacher, Market Researcher, Freelance Writer. Publications: Editor of: School Tales, 1990; How Do I Look? (non fiction), 1991; Virago Book of Wicked Verse, 1992; The Virago Book of Love Letters, 1994; White Fish With Painted Nails (poetry), 1994. Contributions to: Virago New Poets, Virago Book of Birth Poetry, In The Gold of Flesh; She; Slow Dancer; Ambit; Envoi; Spectrum; Writing Women; Tears in the Fence; Aurora; Spare Rib; Everywoman; Distaff. Honours: Hackney Poetry Competition; Runner Up KQBX Experimental Poetry Competition; Runner Up Dragon Heart Poetry; Major Eric Gregory Award; Second Prize London Writers Short Story Competition, 1994. Membership: Member of Society of Authors. Address: 38 Lockhurst Street, London, E5 0AP, England.

DAY Robin (Sir),b. 24 Oct 1923, London, England. TV and Radio Journalist. m. Katherine Mary Ainslie, 1965, div 1986, 2 sons. Education: Oxford University. Appointments: President, Oxford Union, 1950; Called to the Bar, 1952; BBC Radio Journalist, 1954-55; Independent TV News Newscaster & Political Correspondent, 1955-59; BBC TV Political Interviewer and Reporter, 1959-89; BBC Radio World at One Presenter, 1979-. Publications: Television - A Personal Report, 1961; The Case for Television Parliament, 1968; Troubled Reflections of a TV Journalist, 1970; Day by Day, 1975; Grand Inquisitor, 1989, (Autobiography); But With Respect, political interviews, 1993. Honours: Richard Dimbleby Award, 1974; Broadcasting Press Guild Award (for Question Time), 1980; Kt, 1981; RTS Judges Award for 30 years TV

Journalism, 1985; Hon LLD, Exeter, 1986 and Keele, 1988; Hon DU, Essex, 1988; Hon Bencher Middle Temple, 1990. Memberships: Phillimore Committee on Law of Contempt, 1971-74; Chairman, Hansard Society for Parliamentary Government, 1981-83. Address: c/o Capron Productions, Gardiner House, Broomhill Road, London SW18 4JQ, England.

DAY Stacey Biswas, b. 31 Dec 1927, London, England. Physician; Educator. m. Ivana Podvalova, 23 Oct 1973, 2 sons. Education: MD, Dublin, Republic of Ireland, 1955; PhD, McGill University, Canada, 1964; DSc, University of Cincinnati, USA, 1970. Appointments: Formerly Editor-in-Chief, Biosciences Communications and Health Communications; Consulting Editor: Plenum Publishing Corporation; Raven Press; Van Nostrand Reinhold; Karger, Basel; Academic Press, University of Minnesota; Editorial Board, Stress Medicine. Publications: Author, over 30 edited medical and scientific books; 15 literary books including verse history and essays; Health Communications, 1978; Cancer, Stress and Death, 2nd Edition, 1986; Life Stress, 1982; Consultant Editor, Dictionary of Scientific Biography; American Lines, 1969; Rosalita, 1968; East of the Navel, poems from Easter Island, 1978; Hagakure-Spirit of Bushido (in Japanese and English), 1993; Wisdom of Hagakure, English and Japanese Edition, 1994. Contributions to: Numerous articles to journals and magazines, 1955-93; Regular radio presentations, USA, Nigeria, Kenya, India. Honours: Various medical distinctions and communications awards, USA; WHO Medal, 1987; First Foreign Honorary Member, Hagakure Society, Japan, 1992. Memberships: Various national and international societies. Address: 6 Lomond Avenue, Spring Valley, NY 10977, USA.

DE ARAUGO Sarah Therese (Tess), b.26 May 1930, Lismore, Victoria, Australia. Writer. m. Maurice De Araugo, 11 Apr 1950, 2 sons, 2 daughters. Education: Notre Dame de Sion College, Warragal, Victoria. Publications: You Are What You Make Yourself To Be, 1980, Revised Edition, 1989; The Kurnai of Gippsland, 1985; Boonorong on the Mornington Peninsula, 1993. Contributions to: Biographies to Encyclopaedia of Aboriginal Australia; Echo of Aboriginal Past, to Weekly Times, 1983; Memories of the Murray River People, to This Australia, 1984-85; Aboriginal Australians and Their Descendants, to Annals Journal, 1990; articles to newspapers; biographies to Australian Dictionary of Evangelical Biography. Honours: New South Wales Premier's Award for Australian Literature, 1985; Banjo Award, Australian Literature, National Book Council, 1985; Fellowship, 1987, Writer's Grant, 1989, Australian Literature Board; Short Story Award, PEN International, Australia, 1991. Memberships: Australian Society of Authors; Fellowship of Australian Writers; Royal Historical Society of Victoria; Women Writers of Australia; Nepean Historical Society. Address: 19 Grenville Grove, Rosebud West, Victoria 3940, Australia.

DE BEER Arnold Stephanus, b. 10 Jun 1942, Standerton, South Africa. Professor & Head, Department of Communication; Director, Institute for Communication Research, Potchefstroom University. m. Professor Nicolette De Beer, 25 Jul 1965, dec, 2 s, 1 d. Education: BA, 1964, BA(Hons), 1965, Potchefstroom University; MA, Rand Afrikaans University, 1977; MIJ, Baylor University, USA, 1979; PhD, Potchefstroom University, 1981. Publications: Nuuswaardes en Nuuswaardigheid, 1977; Joernalistiek Vandag, 1981; Mass Media for the 90's - The South African Handbook of Mass Communication, 1993. Contributions to: Editor: Ecquid Novi, 1980-94; Tydskrif vir Geestewetenskappe; Plural Societies; Communicatie; Journal of Communication Inquiry. Honours: Abe Bailey Fellowship, 1966; Fellow, South African Academy of Arts and Sciences; First recipient, Educator of the Year Award, Public Relations Institute of South Africa; Appointed, Distinguished Visiting Radford Professor, Baylor University, USA, 1992. Memberships: Sacomm, Former President, 1975-; AEJMC 1978-; Society Professional Journalists (USA), Accredited Member, 1978-; PRISA, 1982-; SAAIE, 1982-; SA Committee of University Teacher Associations, Chairperson, 1986. Literary Agent: Juta Publishers, Cape Town, South Africa. Address: Department of Communication, Potchefstroom University, Private Bag X6001, Potchefstroom 2520, South Africa.

DE BELSER Raymond Charles Maria, (Ward Ruyslinck), b. 17 Jun 1929, Antwerp, Belgium. Retired Librarian. m. (1) 1 s, (2) Monika Macken, 18 Dec 1992. Publications: De ontaarde slapers, 1957, as The Deadbeats, 1968; Wierook en tranen, 1958; Het dal van Hinnom, 1961; Het reservaat, 1964 as The Reservation, 1978; Golden Ophelia, 1966, 1975; De heksenkring, 1972; Het ganzenbord, 1974; Wurgtechnieken, 1980; Leegstaande huizen, 1983; De uilen van Minerva, 1985; Stille waters, 1987; Ijlings naar nergens, 1989. Contributions to: Records of

travel, papers on literature and plastic arts to various Belgian and Dutch magazines and journals. Honours: Ark Prize for Free Speech, 1960; Flemish Reader Award, 1964; prize for Literature of the Flemish Provinces, 1967; Europalia Prize for Literature, 1980. Membership: Royal Flemish Academy of Language and Literature, Ex-Chairman. Address: Potaardestraat 25, 1860 Meise, Belgium.

DE BERNIERES Louis, (Henry Piers) Smart, b. 8 Dec 1954, Woowich, London, England. Novelist. Education: Bradfield College, Berkshire; Manchester University, BA; Leicester Polytechnic and University of London (MA). Publications: The War of Don Emmanuels Nether Parts; Senior Vivo & The Coea Lord; The Troublesome Offspring of Cardinal Guzman. Contributions to: Second Thoughts and Granta. Honours: Commonwealth Writers Prize, 1991, 1992; Best of Young British Novelists, 1993. Memberships: PEN. Literary Agent: William Morris Agency UK Ltd. Address: c/o William Morris Agency, 31/32 Soho Square, London W1V 5DG, England.

DE BLASIS Celeste Ninette, b. 8 May 1946, California, USA. Writer. Education: Wellesley College, 1964-65; Oregon State University, 1965-66; BA cum laude, English, Pomona College, 1968. Publications: The Night Child, 1975; Suffer a Sea Change, 1976; The Proud Breed, 1978; The Tiger's Woman, 1981; Wild Swan, 1984; Swan's Chance, 1985; A Season of Swans, 1989; Graveyard Peaches: A California Memoir, 1991. Contributions to: Writers Digest. Memberships: Authors Guild; Novelists Inc; Nature Conservancy; California State Library Foundation. Literary Agent: Kimberly Witherspoon, Witherspoon Associates Inc, New York, USA. Address: c/o Witherspoon Associates Inc, 157 W 57th Street, Suite 700, New York, NY 10019, USA.

DE BOISSIERE Ralph (Anthony Charles), b. 6 Oct 1907, Port-of-Spain, Trinidad (Australian citizen, 1970). Novelist. m. Ivy Alcantara, 1935, 2 daughters. Education: Queen's Royal College, Port-of-Spain, 1916-22. Appointments: Freelance Writer, 1955-60. Publications: Crown Jewel, 1952; Rum and Coca-Cola, 1956; No Saddles for Kangaroos, 1964; Uncollected short stories: Booze and the Goberdaw, 1979; The Woman on the Pavement, 1979; Play: Calypso Isle, 1955. Literary Agent: Reinhard Sander, Department of Black Studies, Amherst College, Amherst, MA 01002, USA. Address: 10 Vega Street, North Balwyn, Victoria 3104, Australia.

DE BONO Edward (Francis Charles),b. 1933, England. Assistant Director of Research; Writer. Appointments: Assistant Director of Research, Department of Investigative Medicine, University of Cambridge, 1964-; Director, Cognitive Research Trust. Publications: The Five Day Course in Thinking, 1967; The Use of Lateral Thinking (in US as New Think), 1967; The Mechanism of Mind, 1969; Lateral Thinking: A Textbook of Creativity (in US as Lateral Thinking: Step by Step Creativity), 1972; (ed) Technology Today, 1972; Lateral Thinking for Management, 1972; The Dog Exercising Machine, 1972; Po: Beyond Yes and No, 1972; Children Solve Problems, 1973; Practical Thinking, 1973; The Case of the Disappearing Elephant, 1974; (ed) Eureka! History of Inventions, 1974; The Greatest Thinkers, 1976; The Happiness Purpose, 1972; Opportunities: A Handbook of Business Opportunity Search, 1978; Future Positive, 1979; Atlas of Management Thinking, 1981; DeBono's Course in Thinking, 1982; Tactics: The Art and Science of Success, 1984; Conflicts: A Better Way to Resolve Them, 1985; Six Thinking Hats, 1985; Masterthinker's Handbook, 1985; I Am Right, You Are Wrong, 1989; Six Action Shoes, 1991; Sur/Petition, 1992; Serious Creativity, 1992; Teach Your Child To Think, 1992. Address: 12 Albany, Piccadilly, London W1V 9RR, England.

DE BRISSAC. See: DOBSON Rosemary.

DE CAMP L(yon) Sprague, b. 27 Nov 1907, New York City, New York, USA. Writer. m. Catherine Adelaide Crook, 12 Aug 1939, 2 sons. Education: BS, Aeronautical Engineering, California Institute of Technology, 1930; MS, Engineering, Economics, Stevens Institute of Technology, 1933. Publications: Fiction: Lest Darkness Fall, 1939; Rogue Queen, 1951; Non-fiction: The Ancient Engineers, 1963; The Great Monkey Trial, 1968; Heroes and Hobgoblins, verse, 1981; About 125 other books including fiction (mostly science fiction and fantasy), historical novels, non-fiction in science, history, biography, juvenile, textbooks, others. Contributions to: About 425 stories and articles to periodicals, anthologies, symposia; Many poems, book reviews, other fugitive pieces. Honours: International Fantasy Award for Non-Fiction, 1953; Athenaeum of Philadelphia Award for Fiction, 1959; Pat Terry

Award, 1973; Grandmaster Fantasy Award, 1976; Nebula Award, Science Fiction Writers of America, 1978; World Fantasy Conference Award, 1984. Memberships: Authors Club, New York, Past Vice-President; Philadelphia Science Fiction Society; Authors Guild; Science Fiction and Fantasy Writers of America; Trap Door Spiders; Smithsonian Associates; Dallas Museum of Natural History; Audubon Society; Dallas Paleontological Society; Heard Natural Science Museum; University Museum, University of Pennsylvania; History of Science Society; Society for the History of Technology. Literary Agent: Eleanor Wood, Spectrum Literary Agency, 111 8th Avenue 1501, New York, NY 10011, USA. Address: 3453 Hearst Castle Way, Plano, TX 75025, USA.

DE CLEMENTS Barthe, b. 1920. Publications: Nothing's fair in 5th Grade, 1981; Seventeen and In-Between: a novel, 1984; 6th Grade Can Really Kill You, 1985; Monkey See, Monkey Do, 1990; Breaking Out, 1991; The Bite of the Gold Bug, 1992; Wake Me at Midnight, 1993; Tough Loser, 1994. Honour: Milner Award, 1992.

DE CRESCENTIS James, b. 29 May 1948, Rochester, New York, USA. Poet; Visual Artist; English Instructor. Education: BA, English, State University of New York, Geneseo, 1971; MFA, Creative Writing, Bowling Green State University, 1984. Appointments: Alternative Literature Programmes in the Schools (ALPS/NY State), 1985, 1986, 1987. Publications: Poetry Chapbooks: The Space Out Back, 1975; Last Minute Notes About Deep Terror, 1984; Poetry Broadside: Pockets of Light, 1981. Contributions Include: The Experimentalist; Cloud Chamber; La Huerta; Ragged Oaks; Clifton Magazine; New Letters; Greenfield Review. Honours: Mary E Thomas Award, Poetry, State University of New York, Geneseo, 1971; Devine Award, Poetry, Bowling Green State University; Theodore Enslin Jude, Summer, 1984. Membership: Poets & Writers Inc. Address: Boston, MA, USA.

DE CRESPIGNY (Richard) Rafe (Champion), b. 1936, Australia. University Reader in Chinese; Historian. Appointments: Lecturer 1964-70, Senior Lecturer 1970-73, Reader in Chinese 1973-, Australian National University, Canberra; Master of University House, 1991-. Publications: The Biography of Sun Chien, 1966; (with H H Dubs) Official Titles of the Former Han Dynasty, 1967; The Last of the Han, 1969; The Records of the Three Kingdoms, 1970; China: The Land and Its People, 1971; China This Century: A History of Modern China, 1975, (2nd ed, 1992); Portents of Protest, 1976; Northern Frontier, 1984; Emperor Huan and Emperor Ling, 1989; Generals of the South, 1990. Memberships: Fellow of the Australian Academy of the Humanities. Address: 5 Rous Crescent, Forrest, ACT 2603, Australia.

DE GRUCHY John Wesley, b. 18 Mar 1939, Pretoria, South Africa. Professor. m. Isobel Dunstan, 2 sons, 1 daughter. Education: BA, Rhodes University, 1959; BD, 1961; M Th Summa Cum Laude, 1964; DD, University of South Africa, 1972. Appointments: Head of Department Religious Studies, 1981-82, 1990-92; Deputy Dean, Faculty of Social Science & Humanities, 1984-86; Acting Dean, 1986-87; Deputy Dean, 1988-89; Member UCT General Purpose Committee, 1986-87; Academic Planning Committtee, 1987-89; University Research Committee, 1990-; University of Cape Town, 1991-. Publications: The Church Struggle in South Africa; Apartheid is a Heresy; Bonhoeffer and South Africa: Theology in Dialogue; Cry Justice; Dietrich Bonhoeffer: Witness to Jesus Christ: Liberating Reformed Theology; Christianity and Democracy; Founding Editor: Journal of Theology for Southern Africa. Honour: Elected Fellow of University of Cape Town, 1991. Memberships: Theological Society of Southern Africa; International Bonhoeffer Society for Archive & Research; HSRC Discipline Oriented Main Committee for Theology. Address: 10 Vredenburg Avenue, Rosebank 7700, South Africa.

DE GUISE Elizabeth (Mary Teresa), (Isobel Chase, Elizabeth Hunter), b. 1934, Nairobi, Kenya. Education: Attended Open University. Appointments: Landholder in Kent, England, 1952-58; English Teacher to Arabic Students in Folkestone, England, 1958-62; Writer 1960-. Publications Include: Romance Novels under the name Elizabeth Hunter: Fountains of Paradise, 1983; London Pride, 1983; Shared Destiny, 1983; A Silver Nutmeg, 1983; Kiss of the Rising Sun, 1984; Rain on the Wind, 1984; Song of Surrender, 1984; A Tower of Strength, 1984; A Time to Wed, 1984; Loving Relations, 1984; Eye of the Wind, 1985; Legend of the Sun, 1985; The Painted Veil, 1986; The Tides of Love, 1988. Romance Novels under pseudonym Isobel Chase include: The House of Scissors, 1972; The Dragon's Cave, 1972; The Edge of Beyond, 1973; A Man of Kent, 1973; The Elban Adventure, 1974; The Cornish Hearth, 1975; A Canopy of Rose Leaves, 1976; The Clouded

Veil, 1976; The Desert Castle, 1976; Singing in the Wilderness, 1976; The Whistling Thorn, 1977; The Mouth of Truth, 1977; Second Best Wife, 1978; Undesirable Wife, 1978. Historical Novels under name Elizabeth De Guise: Dance of the Peacocks, 1988; Flight of the Dragonfly, 90; Came Forth the Sun, 1991; Bridge of Sighs, 92. Contributions to: Women & Home; Woman's Weekly. Memberships: Campaign for Nuclear Disarmament; Pax Christi; Romantic Novelists Association. Literary Agent: June Hall Literary Agents Ltd, 504 The Chambers, Chelsea Harbour, London SW10 0XF. Address: 113 Nun Street, St Davids, Haverfordwest, Dyfed SA62 6BP, Wales.

DE JONGE Alex, b. 1938, England. University Fellow and Tutor; Writer. Appointments: Fellow and Tutor, New College, Oxford, 1965-. Publications: (with others), Nineteenth Century Russian Literature, 1973; Nightmare Culture, Lautreamont and Les Chants de Maldoror, 1973; Dostoevsky and the Age of Intensity, 1975; Prince of Clouds: A Biography of Baudelaire, 1976; The Weimar Chronicle A Prelude to History, 1977; Napoleon's Last Will and Testament, 1977; Fire and Water: A Life of Peter the Great, 1979; The Life and Times of Grigorii Rasputin, 1982; Stalin and the Shaping of the Soviet Union, 1986.

DE LANGE Nicholas, b. 7 Aug 1944, Nottingham, England. Scholar; Translator. Education: Christ Church, Oxford, 1962-70; MA, 1969; DPhil, 1970. Publications: Apocrypha, 1978; Atlas of the Jewish World, 1984; Judaism, 1986; many literary translations incl: My Michael (Amos Oz), 1990; Black Box (Amos Oz), 1990. Contributions to: Contributing Editor, Tel Aviv Review. Honours: George Webber Prize for Translation, 1990. Memberships: Society of Authors; Translators Association; Fellow, Wolfson College, Cambridge; British Association of Jewish Studies, Past President. Address: The Divinity School, St John's St, Cambridge CB2 1TW, England.

DE LINT Charles (Henri Diederick Hoefsmit), b. 22 Dec 1951, Bussum, Netherlands. Canadian citizen, 1961 Editor, Writer. m. Mary Ann Harris, 15 Sept 1980. Literary Appointments: Writer, Ottawa, 1983-; Writer-in-Residence for Ottawa & GoIucester Public Libraries, 1995. Owner, Editor, Triskell Press. Publications include: Contribution, The Annual Review of Fantasy and Science Fiction, 1988; The Valley of Thunder, in Philip José Farmer's The Dungeon: Book 3, 1988; The Hidden City, in The Dungeon: Book 5, 1988; The Fair in Emain Macha, 1990; Drink Down The Moon; A Novel of Urban Faerie, 1990; Ghostwood, 1990; Angel of Darkness, 1990; The Little Country, 1991; Ghosts of Wind and Shadow, 1991; Uncle Dobbin's Parrot Fair, 1991; Death Leaves an Echo, 1991; Hedgework and Guessery, 1991; Paperjack, 1991; Our Lady of the Harbour, 1991; The Harp of the Grey Rose, 1991; Dreaming Place, 1992; Spiritwalk, 1992; Mulengro: a Romany Tale; Yarrow: An Autumn Tale; Ascian in Rose; Merlin Dreams in the Mondream Wood, 1992; From a Whisper to a Scream, 1992; Dreams Underfoot: The Newford Collection, 1993; Into the Green, 1993; The Wild Wood, 1994; Memory and Dream, 1994. Contributions to: Poetry to anthologies; Columns to horror and science fiction magazines; Periodicals. Honours include: William L Crawford Award for Best New Fantasy Author, International Association for the Fantastic in the Arts, 1984; Casper Award for Best Work in English, for Jack the Giant-Killer, 1988; Readercon Small Press Award for Best Short Work, for The Drowned Man's Reel, 1989; Other awards and award nominations. Memberships: Science Fiction Writers of America; Vice-President, Horror Writers of America, 1992-93; Small Press Writers and Artists Organization; Theodore Sturgeon Memorial Short Fiction Award Committee. Literary Agent: Richard Curtis Associates Inc, New York, USA. Address: PO Box 9480, Ottawa, Ontario, Canada K1G 3V2.

DE MARINIS Rick, b. 3 Mar 1934, New York, New York, USA. m. Carole Joyce Bubash, 1 son, 1 daughter. Education: BA, MA, University of Montana. Publications: Scimitar: a novel, 1977; Cinder, 1978; Jack & Jill, 1979. Contributions to: Esquire; Atlantic; Iowa Review; Grand Street; Antioch Review. Honours: Drue Heinz Literary Prize, 1986; Fellow, American Academy & Institute of Arts & Letters, 1990.

DE MILLE Nelson. See: LEVINSON Leonard.

DE MIOMANDRE Marguerite Maria Julia Ghislaine, b. 11 Jun 1925, Belgium. Doctor. m. Emmanuel de Miomandre, 25 Apr 1962. Education: Lycée de Forest, 1942; Brussels University, 1949. Publications: Short stories in Audace; L'ecole des Snobs; Performed Play, En amour comme à la guerre; 5 plays. Contributions to: Audace; Les Cahiers de la Bilogue; Femmes d'Aujourdhui. Honours: Grand

Prize de la Nouvelle de l'Academie Littré; Menthe ou Cassis, 1992. Memberships: PEN; AEB. Address: 151 Avenue Molière, 1060 Brussels, Belgium.

DE NEVERS Marguerite. See: **BOISVERT France.**

DE PAZZI Ellen Eugenia,b. 7 Apr 1915, Elcador, Iowa, USA. Artist; Poet. m. 17 Aug 1940, 2 sons. Education: Indiana University, 1935-38; Atelier Caterina Baratelli in portraiture, Rio de Janrieo, Brazil, 1949-52; Fine Arts Degree, Suffolk Community College, 1988. Contributions to: Poetry and short stories to: Tap Roots Magazine and Annuals, 1973-90; Poetry Anthology, 1974-75; Soundwaves, 1985-90; East End QArts Poetry Corner, 1987-88; Westhampton Chronicle Col9 or and Rhyme. Honours: DAR Essay Prize for History of Frontier Days, 1934; Poetry Prize, Soundwaves, 1985-87; Poetry Bi-annual, for Floodtide and Wildwind. Memberships: Tap Roots for Poets & Writers, 1972-90; Soundwaves Editorial Staff, 1984-80; Southbay Poetry Association, 1987-88; Westhampton Writers Festival, 1986-90; Hampton Centre Gallery Incorporated, Director, 1975-90; South Fork Craftsmen's Guild, Publicity Officer, 1970-88. Address: 5126 Bur Oak Circle, PO Box 31226, Raleigh, NC 27622, USA.

DE PRE Jean-Anne. See: **AVALLONE Michael Angelo.**

DE QUIROS Beltran. See: **ROMEU Jorge Luis.**

DE REGNIERD Beatrice Schenk (Tamara Kitt), b. 1914, America. Writer; Poet; Playwright. Appointments: Director of Educational Materials, American Heart Association, New York City, 1949-61; Editor, Lucky Book Club, Scholastic Inc, New York City, 1961-81. Publications: The Giant Story, 1953; A Little House of Your Own, 1954; What Can You Do With a Shoe?, 1955; Was It A Good Trade?, 1956; A Child's Book of Dreams, 1957; Something Special, 1958; Cats Cats Cats Cats Cats, 1958; The Snow Party, 1959, 1989; What Happens Next?, 1959; The Shadow Book, 1960; Who Likes The Sun?, 1961; The Little Book, Illlustrated by the Author), 1961, reissued as Going For A Walk, 1982, reissued, 1993 with new illustrations by Robert Knox; (as Tamara Kitt), The Adventures of Silly Billy, 1961; (as Tamara Kitt), The Suprising Pets of Billy Brown, 1962; (as Tamara Kitt), Billy Brown: The Baby Sitter, 1962; (as Tamara Kitt), The Boy Who Fooled The Giant, 1963; The Little Girl and Her Mother, 1963; May I Bring A Friend?, 1964; The Abraham Lincoln Joke Book, 1965; David and Goliath, 1965; How Joe The Bear And Sam The Mouse Got Together, 1965, 1990; Penny, 1966, 1987; Circus, 1966; The Giant Book, 1966; (as Tamara Kitt), A Special Birthday Party for Someone Very Special, 1966; (as Tamara Kitt), Sam and The Impossible Thing, 1967; The Day Everybody Cried, 1967; Willy O'Dwyer Jumped in the Fire, 1968; (as Tamara Kitt) Jake, 1968; Catch a Little Fox, 1969; Poems Children Will Sit Still For, 1969; The Boy, The Rat and The Butterfly, 1971; Red Riding Hood Retold in Verse for Boys and Girls to Read Themselves, 1972; It Does Not Say Meow and Other Animal Riddle Rhymes, 1972; The Enchanted Forest, 1974; Little Sister and the Month Brothers, 1976; A Bunch of Poems and Verses, 1977; Laura's Story, 1979; Everyone Is Good for Something, 1979, playscripts and lyrics for musical based on book, 1990; Picture Book Theater, 1982; Waiting for Mama, 1984; So Many Cats, 1985; This Big Cat and Other Cats I've Known, 1985; Jack and The Beanstalk Retold in Verse, 1985; A Week in the Life of Best Friends and Other Poems of Friendship, 1986; Jack The Giant Killer Retold in Verse and Other Useful Information about Giants, 1987; The Way I Feel...Sometimes, 1988; Sing a Song of Popcorn, Every Child's Book of Poems (co-editor), 1988. Memberships: Authors Guild; Dramatists Guild; PEN; Society of Children's Book Writers & Illustrators. Address: 180 West 58th Street, New York, NY 10019, USA.

DE ROO Anne (Louise),b. 1931, New Zealand. Children's Fiction Writer. Appointments: Library Assistant, Dunedin Public Library, 1956; Assistant Librarian, Dunedin Teachers College, 1957-59; Governess, Part-time Gardener, Shropshire, England, 1962-68; Part-time Secretary, Hertfordshire, England, 1969-73. Publications: The Gold Dog, 1969; Moa Valley, 1969; Boy and the Sea Beast, 1971; Cinnamon and Nutmeg, 1972; Mick's Country Cousins, 1974; Scrub Fire, 1977; Traveller, 1979; Because of Rosie, 1980; Jack Nobody, 1984; Friend Troll, Friend Taniwha, 1986; The Bat's Nest, 1986. Address: 38 Joseph Street, Palmerston North, New Zealand.

DE SOUZA Eunice, b. 1 Aug 1940, Poona, India. Lecturer; Poet. Education: BA, University of Bombay, 1960; PhD, 1988. Appointments: Lecturer, Head of Dept of English, St Xaviers College, Bombay, 1990.

Publications: Fix, 1979; Women in Dutch Painting, 1988; Ways of Belonging: Selected Poems, 1990; For Children: All About Birbal, 1969; Himalayan Tales, 1973; More About Birbal; Tales of Birbal; Co Editor, Statements: An Anthology of Indian Prose in English. Address: St Xaviers College, Bombay 400 001 India.

DE VRIES-EVANS Susanna Mary, (Susanna Devries), b. 6 Oct 1935. Author; Lecturer in Art History. m. Jake de Vries, 25 July 1982. Education: Sorbonne, Paris, Cours de Civilisation Francaise, 1953; Universidad Menendez Pelayo, Santander, Spain, 1954; Complutense University Madrid, Bellas Artes. Appointments: Lecturer, Continuing Education Department, University of Queensland, 1991. Publications: Historic Sydney Its Early Artists, 1982, 2nd edition, 1987; Pioneer Women, Pioneer Land, 1988; The Impressionists Revealed: Masterpieces and Collectors, 1982, 2nd Edition 1994; Conrad Martens on the Beagle; Australian Women of Achievement 1788-2000, forthcoming. Contributions to: The Australian Newspaper (Arts Section) Australian Collector Magazine. Honours: Fellowship, Literary Board, Australia Council, 1990; Winston Churchill Fellowship, Arts History, 1994. Memberships: Lyceum Club, Brisbane; Australian Society of Authors. Literary Agent: Selwa Anthony, 10 Loves Avenue, Oyster Bay, NSW 2225, Australia. Address: 10 Matingara Street, Chapel Hill, Brisbane 4069, Australia.

DE WEESE Thomas Eugene (Jean DeWeese, Thomas Stratton, Victoria Thomas), b. 1934. Writer (Romance/Gothic, Science Fiction/Fantasy, Children's Fiction, Crafts). Appointments: Electronic Technician, Delco Radio, Kokomo, Indiana, 1954-59; Technical Writer, Delco Electronics, Milwaukee, Wisconsin, 1959-74. Publications: The Invisibility Affair: Man from UNCLE No 11 (as Thomas Stratton with Robert Coulson), 1967; The Mind-Twisters Affair: Man from UNCLE No 12, 1967; Making American Folk Art Dolls (with Gini Rogowski), 1975; Jeremy Case, 1976; The Wanting Factor, 1980; Something Answered, 1983; Ginger's Wish (as Victoria Thomas with Connie Kugi), 1987; Chain of Attack, Star Trek No 32, 1987; The Peacekeepers, Star Trek: Next Generation No 2, 1988; The Final Nexus, Star Trek No 43, 1988; Renegade, Star Trek No 54, 1991; With Robert Coulson: Now You See It/Him/Them..., 1975; Gates of Universe, 1975; Charles Fort Never Mentioned Wombats, 1977; Nightmare Universe, 1985; As Jean DeWeese: The Reimann Curse, 1975, expanded as A Different Darkness, 1982; The Carnelian Cat, 1975; The Moonstone Spirit, 1975; The Doll With Opal Eyes, 1976; Cave of the Moaning Wind, 1976; Web of Guilt, 1976; Nightmare in Pewter, 1978; Hour of the Cat, 1980; The Backhoe Gothic, 1981; Juvenile fiction, science fiction, non-fiction: Major Corby and the Unidentified Flapping Object, 1979; Nightmares from Space, 1981; The Adventures of a Two-Minute Werewolf, 1983; Computers in Entertainment and the Arts, 1984; Black Suits from Outer Space, 1985; The Dandelion Caper, 1986; The Calvin Nullifier, 1987; Whatever Became of Aunt Margaret?, 1990. Address: 2718 N Prospect, Milwaukee, WI 53211, USA.

DE'ATH Richard. See: **HAINING Peter Alexander.**

DEANE Dorothy. See: **CATCHAPAW Dorothy Deane Johnson.**

DEAR Nick, b. 11 Jun 1955, Portsmouth, England. Playwright. Partner: Penny Downie, 2 s. Education: BA, Hons, European Literature, University of Essex, 1977. Appointments: Playwright in Residence, Essex University, 1985; Playwright in Residence, Royal Exchange Theatre, 1987-88. Publications: Temptation, 1984; The Art of Success, 1986; Food of Love, 1988; A Family Affair (after Ostrovsky), 1988; In The Ruins, 1989; The Last Days of Don Juan (after Tirso), 1990; Le Bourgeois Gentilhomme (after Molière), 1992; Pure Science, 1994; Opera Libretti: A Family Affair, 1993; Siren Song, 1994; several plays for radio; films: The Monkey Parade, 1983; The Ranter, 1988; Persuasion, 1995. Honours: John Whiting Award, 1987; Olivier Award nominations, 1987, 1988. Membership: Writer's Guild of Great Britain. Literary Agent: Rosica Colin Ltd. Address: c/o Rosica Colin Ltd, 1 Clareville Grove Mews, London SW7 5AH, England.

DEARDEN James Shackley, b. 9 Aug 1931, Barrow-in-Furness, England. Curator. Publications include: The Professor; Arthur Severn's Memoir of Ruskin, 1967; A Short History of Brantwood, 1967; Iteriad by John Ruskin (editor), 1969; Facets of Ruskin, 1970; Ruskin and Coniston (with K G Thome), 1971; Turner's Isle of Wight Sketch Book, 1979; John Ruskin, 1981; John Ruskin & Les Alpi, 3 eds, 1989-90; John Ruskin's Camberwell, 1990; A Tour To the Lakes in Cumberland,

John Ruskin's Diary for 1830 (editor), 1990; John Ruskin and Victorian Art, 1993; Ruskin Bembridge and Brantwood, 1994. Contributions to: Book Collector; Connoisseur; Apollo; Burlington; Bulletin of John Rylands Lib; Country Life; Ruskin Newsletter (editor); Ruskin Research Series (general editor); Journal of Pre-Raphaelite Studies (editorial advisory board); Whitehouse Edition of Ruskin's Works (joint general editor). Memberships: Ruskin Association, Secretary and Treasurer; Turner Society; Companion of the Guild of St George; Old Bembridgians Association (Past President); Isle of Wight Foot Beagles, past Chairman and Master. Address: 4 Woodlands, Foreland Road, Bemmbridge, Isle of Wight, England.

DEDERER John Morgan, b. 14 Jan 1951, Fort Meade, Maryland, USA. Historian. m. Melissa G Wetterborg, 22 Jan 1977, 1 son, 2 daughters. Education: BA, 1980, MA, 1982, University of South Florida, Tampa; Visiting Fellow, John Carter Brown Library, Brown University, 1986-87; Dissertation Fellowship, US Army Center for Military History, 1986-87; PhD, University of Alabama, Tuscaloosa, 1988; Olin Postdoctoral Fellow, Yale University, 1988-89. Literary appointments: Editor, Southern Historian, 1984-87. Publications: Making Bricks Without Straw, 1983; War in America to 1775: Before Yankee Doodle, 1990; Contributions to: Essays to: A Guide to Sources in US Military History, Supplements II and III, 1986, 1992; Encyclopedia of the American Military, 1994; Articles to: Military Affairs, 1983, 1986; Virginia Magazine of History and Biography, 1994. Address: 450 Freeman Ave, Stratford, CT 06497, USA.

DEFORD Frank, b. 16 Dec 1938, Baltimore, Maryland, USA. Writer; Editor. m. Carol Penner, 28 Aug 1965, 1 son, 2 daughters. Education: BA, Princeton University, 1962. Appointments: Writer, Sports Illustrated, 1962-89; Commentator: Cable News Network, 1980-86, National Public Radio, 1980-89, 1991-, NBC, 1986-89; ESPN, 1992-; Editor-in-Chief, The National, 1989-91. Publications: Five Strides On The Banked Track, 1969; Cut'N'Run, 1971; There She Is, 1972; The Owner, 1974; Big Bill Tilden: The Triumphs And The Tragedy, 1977; Everybody's All-American, 1981; Alex: The Life Of A Child, 1982; Spy In The Deuce Court, 1987; World's Tallest Midget, 1988; Casey On The Loose, 1989; Love And Infamy, 1993. Contributions to: Numerous magazines; Contributing editor, Vanity Fair, 1993-. Address: Box 1109, Greens Farms, CT 06436, USA.

DEGUY Michel, b. 23 May 1930, Paris, France. Poet. Education: Education: University of Paris. Appointments include: President of the Collège International de Philosophie, at Paris. Publications: Les Meurtrières, 1959; Fragments du cadastre, 1960; Poèmes de la Presqu'île, 1961; Biefs, 1964; Oui-dire, 1966; Figurations, 1969; Poèmes 1960-1970, 1973; Jumelages; Made in USA, 1978; Given Giving: Selected Poems, 1984; Gisants, 1985; Poèmes II: 1970-1980, 1986; Arrêts frequents, 1990; Also: Le Monde de Thomas Mann, 1962; Reliefs, 1975; Brevets, 1986; La poésie n'est pas seule, 1988; Aux Heures d'affluence, 1991; Axiomatique rosace, 1991; Un Poleoscope, 1991. Honours include: Ministry of Culture Poetry Prize, 1989. Address: 48 rue de Vaugirard, 75006 Paris, France.

DEIGHTON Len, b. 18 Feb 1929, London, England. Writer. Education: Marylebone Grammer School; Royal College of Art, 1952-55. Publications: The Ipcress File, 1962; Horse Under Water, 1963; Funeral in Berlin, 1964; Action Cook Book: Len Deighton's Guide To Eating (in US as Cookstrip Cook Book), 1965; Ou est le Garlic: Len Deighton's French Cook Book, revised edition as Basic French Cooking, 1978; The Billion Dollar Brain, 1966; An Expensive Place to Die, 1967; (editor) London Dossier, 1967; The Assassination of President Kennedy, (co-author) 1967; Only When I Larf, 1968; (compiled by Victor and Margaret Pettit), Len Deighton's Continental Dossier: A Collection of Cultural Culinary, Historical, Spooky, Grim and Preposterous Facts, 1968; Bomber, 1970; Declarations of War (stories), 1971; Close-Up, 1972; Spy Story, 1974; Yesterday's Spy, 1975; Twinkle, Twinkle, Little Spy, 1976; Fighter: The True Story of the Battle of Britain, 1977; SS-GB, 1978; (with Arnold Schwartzman), Airshipwreck, 1978; Blitzkrieg: From the Rise of Hitler to the Fall of Dunkirk, 1979; Battle of Britain, 1980; XPD 1981; Goodbye Mickey Mouse, 1982; Berlin Game, 1983; Mexico Set, 1984; London Match, 1985; Spy Hook, 1988; Spy Line, 1989; Spy Sinker, 1990; ABC of French Food, 1989; Basic French Cookery Course, 1990; MAMista, 1991; City of Gold, 1992; Violent Ward, 1993; Blood, Tears & Folly, 1993; Faith, 1994; Hope, forthcoming. Address: c/o Jonathon Clowes Ltd, 10 Iron Bridge House, Bridge Approach, London NW1 8BD, England.

DEIMER Lorena Ruth, b. 11 Jan 1926, Thermopolis, Wyoming, USA. Freelance Writer. m. (1) 1946, (2) Marshall F Deimer, 21 Feb 1959, 1 son, 1 daughter. Education: High School Casper Junior College; International Aurora Community College. Publications: Book: Magnolia Blossoms; Other books in preparation: Roots of Evil; Murder in Church; Elisia. Poetry: Golden Voices Past and Present, 1989; World Treasury of Great Poems, 1989; Great Poems of the Western World, vol 11, 1989; Today's Poets, 1989; Misty and Me, 1991; The Write Technique, 1991. Contributions to: McCall's Ladies Home Journal; Colorado Old Times, 1980-82; Colorado Genealogical; The Denver Post; The Senior Beacon; The Keyboard & Pen Denver Metro Chapter of the National Writers Club; Aurora Community College Newspaper, The National Writers Club Denver Merto Newspaper, 1988-89. Honours Include: Golden Poet Award, 1987, 1988, 1989. Memberships: The National Wirters Club; The Fictional Group, Denver Chapter, The Genealogical Club; Baptist Youth Fellowship Group, President, 1944. Literary Agent: James Lee Young, National Writers Club. Address: 1164 Macon Street, Aurora, CO 80010, USA.

DEJEVSKY Nikolai James, b. 22 Sep 1945, Hanau, Germany. Publishing Consultant. m. Mary Peake, 13 Sep 1975. Education: BA, Cornell University, USA, 1968; MA, University of Pennsylvania, USA, 1971; DPhil, Christ Church, University of Oxford, 1977. Appointments include: Assisstant Editor, Clio Press Ltd, Oxford, 1977-80; Publishing Manager, Pergamon Press ltd, Oxford, 1980-82; Publisher, Professional Publishing Ltd, London, 1982-84; Editorial Director, Gower Publishing Ltd, Aldershot, 1984-85; Publisher, Longman Group Ltd, Harlow, 1985-88; Freelance writer and journalist, 1990-. Publications: Cultural Atlas of Russia and the Soviet Union, 1989; Free-wheeling in Bear Country, 1994. Contributions to: California Slavic Studies; Cambridge Encyclopaedia of Archaeology; Medieval Scandinavia; Solanus; Modern Encyclopaedia of Russian & Soviet History; Year's Work in Modern Language Studies; Business Eastern Europe, 1991; International Automotive Review, 1991-. Address: 37 Ulysses Road, West Hampstead, London NW6 1ED, England.

DEKKER Carl. See: **LYNDS Dennis**.

DEKKER George, b. 1934, USA. Professor of English; Writer. Appointments: Lecturer, University College, Swansea, Wales, 1962-64; Lecturer, 1964-66, Senior Lecturer, 1966-70, Reader in Literature, 1970-72, University of Essex, Colchester, England; Associate Professor, 1972-74, Professor of English, 1974-, Joseph S Atha Professor of Humanities, 1988-, Stanford University, Stanford, California, USA. Publications: Sailing After Knowledge: The Cantos of Ezra Pound, 1963; James Fenimore Cooper: The Novelist, 1967; The American Democrat, by James Fenimore Cooper (editor with Larry Johnston), 1969; James Fenimore Cooper: The Critical Heritage (editor with John McWilliams), 1973; Coleridge and the Literature of Sensibility, 1978; Donald Davie and the Responsibilities of Literature (editor), 1984; The American Historical Romance, 1987. Address: Department of English, Stanford University, Stanford, CA 94305, USA.

DEKKER Rudolf Michel, b. 6 Jun 1951, Amsterdam, Netherlands. m Florence Wilhelmina Johanna Koorn, 2 May 1958, 2 d. Eduxation: University of Amsterdam, 1969-76. Appointments: Lecture, Erasmus University, Rotterdam , 1981-. Publications: Holland in Boering, Oproeren in de 17de en 18de eeeuw; The Tradition of Female Transvestism in Early Modern Europe; De Bredasche Helsinne; Aernout van Overbeke, Anecdota Sive Historiae Jocosae. Contributions to: Theory and Society; History of European Ideas; Women and Politics in the Age of the Democratic Revolution. Memberships: Maatschappÿ der Vaderlandse Letterkunde; Nederlads Historisch Genootschap. Address: Westerhout Straat 28, 2012JS Haarlem, Netherlands.

DEL MAR Norman, b. 31 July 1919, London, England. Orchestral Conductor. m. Pauline Mann, 24 Jan 1947, 2 sons. Education: Royal College of Music. Publications: Richard Strauss, 3 volumes, 1962-72, 1986; Anatomy of the Orchestra, 1981; Mahler's Sixth Symphony - A Study, 1980; Campanion to the Orchestra, 1987; Conducting Beethoven, 1992. Honours: CBE, 1975; Hon DLitt, Sussex, 1977. Literary Agent: David Higham Associates. Address: Clarion/Seven Muses, 47 Whitehall Park, London N19 3TW, England.

DELANEY Shelagh, b. 1939, Salford, Lancashire. England. Playwright. 1 daughter. Publications: Plays: A Taste of Honey, 1958; The Lion in Love, 1960; Films: A Taste of Honey; The White Bus, 1966; Charlie Bubbles, 1968; Dance with a Stranger, 1985; TV Plays: St Martin's Summer, 1974; Find Me First, 1979; TV Series: The House

That Jack Built, 1977 (stage adaptation, New York, 1979); Radio Plays: So Does The Nightingale, 1980; Don't Worry About Matilda, 1983; Sweetly Sings The Donkey, 1963. Honours: Charles Henry Foyle New Play Award, Arts Council Bursary, New York Drama Critics Award, A Taste of Honey; British Film Academy Award, Robert Flaherty Award, A Taste of Honey, 1961; Prix Film Jeunesse Etranger, Cannes, 1985. Address: c/o Tessa Sayle, 11 Jubilee Place, London SW3 3TE, England.

DELANY Samuel R(ay),b. 1942. Sicence Fiction/Fantasy Writer; Professor. m. 24 Aug 1961, div, 1980, 1 son, 1 daughter. Appointments: Editor, Wuark, 1970-71; Senior Fellow, Center for 20th Century Studies, University of Wisconsin, Milwaukee, 1977; Society for the Humanities, Cornell University, 1987; Professor of Comparative Literature, University of Massachusetts, Amherst, 1988-. Publications: The Jewels of Aptor, 1962, unabridged edition, 1968; The Fall of the Towers, vol 1, Captives of the Flames, 1963, as Out of the Dead City, 1968, vol 2, The Towers of Toron, 1964, vol 3, City of a Thousand Suns, 1965; The Ballad of Beta-2, 1965; Empire Star, 1966; Babel-17, 1966; The Einstein Intersection, 1967; Nova, 1968; Driftglass: Ten Tales of Speculative Fiction, 1971; Dhalgren, 1975; Triton, 1976; The Jewel-Hinged Jaw: Notes on the Language of Science Fiction, 1977; The American Shore, 1978; Empire, 1978; (ed) Nebula Award Winners 13, 1979; Distant Stars, 1981; Stars in My Pocket Like Grains of Sand, 1984; Starboard Wine: More Notes on the Language of Science Fiction, 1984; The Splendour and Misery of Bodies, 1985; Flight from Neveryon, 1985; They Fly at Ciron, 1992; Neveryon, 1993; Tales of Neveryon, 1993; The Mad Man, 1994. Literary Agent: Henry Morrison, Box 234, Bedford Hills, NY 10507, USA. Address: c/o Bantam Books, 666 Fifth Avenue, New York, NY 10019, USA.

DELBANCO Andrew, b. 1952. Publications: William Ellery Channing, 1981; The Puritans in America, 1985; The Puritan Ordeal, 1989; The Portable Abraham Lincoln, 1992; The Death of Satan: The Idea of Evil in the American Imagination, 1995. Address: Dept of English, Columbia University, 2960 Columbia University, New York, NY 10027 6902, USA.

DELBANCO Nicholas Franklin,b. 27 Aug 1942, London, England. Writer. m. Elena Carter Greenhouse, 12 Sept 1970, 2 daughters. Education: BA, History & Literature, Harvard College, 1963; MA, English Comparative Literature, Columbia University, 1966. Appointments: Member, Language & Literature Division, Bennington College, 1966-85; Director, Bennington Writing Workshops, 1977-; Visiting Professor, Iowa Writers Programme, University of Iowa, 1979; Adjunct Professor, School of the Arts, Columbia University, 1979; Visiting Artist in Residence, Trinity College, 1980; Visiting Professor, Williams College, 1982; Professor of English, Skidmore College, 1984-85; Professor, English, Director, MFA Programme, University of Michigan, 1985-. Publications: The Martlet's Tale, 1966; Grasse 3/23/66, 1968; Consider Sappho Burning, 1969; News, 1970; In the Middle Distance, 1971; Fathering, 1973; Small Rain, 1975; Possession, 1977; Sherbrooks, 1978; Stillness, 1980; Group Portrait: Conrad Crane Ford James & Wells, 1982; About My Talbe and Other Stories, 1983; The Beaux Arts Trip: A Portrait, 1985; Running in Place: Scenes from the South of France, 1989; The Writers' Trade, and Other Stories, 1990. Contributions to: Atlantic Monthly; Esquire; New York Times Book Reviewer; New Republic, and others. Honours Include: NEA Creative Writing Fellowships, 1973, 1982; Guggenheim Fellowship, 1979. Memberships: Authors League; Authors Guild; Signet Society; Phi Beta Kappa; New York State Writers Institute; PEN. Address: c/o Dept of English, University of Michigan, 7601 Haven Hall, Ann Arbor, MI 48109, USA.

DELDERFIELD Eric Raymond,b. 4 May 1909, London, England. Author; Journalist. m. 1934, 1 daughter. Appointments: Director, David & Charles Publishers, 1962-67. Publications: Lynmouth Flood Disaster, 1953, reprinted 14 times; British Inn Signs and Their Stories, 1965, 1984; West Country Houses and Their Families, 3 vols, 1968, 1970, 1973; Kings and Queens of England, 1966, 1970, 1981; True Animal Stories, 4 vols, 1970-73; Cotswold Villages and Churches, 1961, 1985; Exmoor Wanderings; Kings and Queens Colour, 1990; numerous guides on areas of Britain. Contributions to: Devon Life; This England; and others. Address: 51 Ashleigh Road, Exmouth, Devon EX8 2JY, England.

DELEHANTY Randolph, b. 5 July 1944, Memphis, Tennessee, USA. Writer; Lecturer; Art Curator. Education: BA, Georgetown University, 1966; MA, University of Chicago, 1968; MA, 1969, PhD,

1992, Harvard University. Publications: In The Victorian Style; San Francisco: The Ultimate Guide; Preserving The West; California: A Guidebook; San Francisco: Walks and Tours in the Golden Gate City; New Orleans: Elegance and Decadence, 1993; Classic Natchez, 1995; New Orleans: The Favor of the Crescent City, forthcoming; Art in the American South, forthcoming. Address: The Roger Houston Ogden Collection of Southern Art, 460 Broadway Street, New Orleans, LA 70118, USA.

DELGADO James P,b. 11 Jan 1958, San Jose, California, USA. Historian; Museum Director, Vancouver. m. Mary Jean Bremmer, 7 Oct 1978, 1 son, 1 daughter. Education: BA magna cum laude, American History, San Francisco State University, 1981; MA, Maritime History, Underwater Research, East Carolina University, Greenville, North Carolina, 1985. Appointments: Assistant to Regional Historian, Western Region (Hawaii, Guam, American Samoa, California, Arizona), 1978-79; Chief Historian, Golden Gate National Recreation Area, San Francisco, California, 1979-86; Chief Maritime Historian, National Park Service, Washington, 1987-91; Executive Director, Vancouver Maritime Museum, Canada, 1991-. Publications: Alcatraz Island: The Story Behind the Scenery, 1985; The Log of the Apollo: Joseph Perkins Beach's Log of the Voyage of the Ship Apollo from New York to San Francisco 1849 (editor), 1986; Shipwrecks at the Golden Gate (with Stephen A Haller), 1989; To California By Sea: A Maritime History of the California Gold Rush, 1990; National Parks of America, 1990; Pearl Harbor Recalled: New Images of the Day of Infamy (with Tom Freeman), 1991; Great American Ships (with J Candace Clifford), 1991; Great American Ships (with J Candace Clifford), 1991; Alcatraz Island, 1991; Dauntless St Roch: The Mounties Arctic Schooner, 1992; Shipwrecks of the Northern Shore, forthcoming; Ghost Fleet of the Atomic Age: The Sunken Ships of Bikini Atoll, forthcoming. Contributions to: Professional and popular journals including: The Pacific Historian; The Book Club of California Quarterly; The Point Reyes Historian; The Public Historian; American History Illustrated; CRM Bulletin. Memberships: Society for Historical Archaeology; California Historical Society; Canadian Nautical Research Society; National Maritime Historical Society; Canadian Representative, International Committee on Monuments and Sites; Committee on the International Underwater Heritage; Trustee, Council of American Maritime Museums. Address: 4204 West 10th Avenue, Vancouver, British Columbia V6R 2H4, Canada.

DELIUS Anthony (Ronald Martin), b. 11 June 1916, Simonstown, South Africa. Freelance Writer; Poet. Education: BA, Rhodes University, Grahamstown, 1938. Appointments: Writer, BBC Africa Service, London, 1968-77; Freelance Writer, 1977-. Publications: An Unkown Border, 1954; The Last Division, 1959; A Corner of the World: Thirty Four Poems, 1962; Black South Easter, 1966; Play, The Fall: A Play About Rhodes, 1957; Novels, The Day Natal Took Off: A Satire, 1963; Border, 1963; The Young Traveller in South Africa, 1947; The Long Way Round, 1956; Upsurge in Africa, 1960. Honour: CNA Literary Award, 1977. Address: 30 Graemesdyke Avenue, London SW14 7BJ, England.

DELVIN David George, b. 28 Jan 1939. Doctor; TV Broadcaster; Writer. Education: MB.BS, BS, LRCP, MRCS, King's College Hospital, University of London; D.Obst, RCOG; DCH; Dip Ven; FPA Cert; MRCGP. Appointments include: Associate Editor, New English Encyclopaedia; Consultant Editor, General Practitioner; Consulting Editor, SHE. Publications: The Home Doctor; The Book of Love; You and Your Back; A Patient's Guide to Operations; Your Good Health; Common Childhood Illnesses; Taking the Pill; How to Improve Your Sex Life; Dear Doc; Carefree Love; An A-Z of Your Child's Health. Contributions include: World Medicine; Dr Jekyll Columnist, 1972-82; Columnist, SHE, Weekend, Titbits, Mother & Baby. Honours: Medical Journalist' Association Award of Special Merit, 1974; jointly 1975; American Medical Writer's Association Best Book Award, 1976; Medaille de la Ville de Paris, Echelon Argent, 1983; Consumer Columnist of the Year, 1986. Memberships include: Vice Chairman, Medical Journalist's Association; GMC; Royal Society Medicine; BMA. Literary Agent: A P Watt. Address: c/o Coutts Ltd, 440 Strand, London WC2R OQS, England.

DEMARIA Robert, b. 28 Sept 1928, New York City, New York, USA. Writer; Professor. m. (1) Maddalena Buzeo, (2) Ellen Hope Meyer, 3 sons, 1 daughter. Education: BA, 1948, MA, 1949, PhD, 1959, Columbia University. Appointments: Professor, English, University of Oregon, 1949-52; Professor, English, Hofstra University, 1952-61; Associate Dean, New School for Social Research, New York City,

1961-64; Professor, English, Dowling College, 1965-; Editor, Publisher, The Mediterranean Review, 1969-73. Publications: Carnival of Angels, 1961; Clodia, 1965; Don Juan in Lourdes, 1966; The Satyr, 1972; The Decline and Fall of America, 1973; To Be a King, 1976; Sons and Brothers, 1985. Contributions to: Antaeus; California Quarterly; Southwest Review; Cimarron Review; Beloit Fiction Journal; New Letters; Florida Review. Memberships: Authors Guild; PEN American Center. Literary Agent: Diane Cleaver, 55 Fifth Avenue, New York, NY 10003, USA. Address: 106 Vineyard Place, Port Jefferson, NY 11777, USA.

DEMARIS Ovid, See: **DESMARAIS Ovide E**.

DEMETILLO Ricaredo, b. 1920, Philippines. Professor of Humanities; Writer. Appointments: Assistant Professor 1959-70, Chairman, Department of Humanities 1961-62, Associate Professor 1970-75, Professor of Humanities, University of the Philippines, Diliman, Quezon City. Publications: No Certian Weather: A Collection of Poetry, 1956; La Via: A Spiritual Journey, 1958; Daedalus and Other Poems, 1961; Barter in Panay (poetry), 1961; The Authentic Voice of Poetry, 1962; Masks and Signature (poetry), 1968; The Scare-Crow Christ (poetry), 1973; The Heart of Emptiness is Black (play), 1973; The City and the Thread of Light (poetry), 1974; Lazarus, Troubadour (poetry), 1974; The Genesis of a Troubled Vision (novel), 1976; Major and Monor Keys (criticism), 1986; First and Last Fruits (poetry), 1989. Address: 38 Balacan Street, West Avenue, Quezon City, Philippines.

DEMPSTER Nigel Richard Patton, b. 1 Nov 1941. Editorial Executive. m. (1) Emma de Bendem, 1971, (div 1974), (2) Lady Camilla Godolphin Osborne, 1978, 1 d. Appointments: Broker, Llooyds of London, 1958-59; Stock Exchange, 1959-60; PR Account Executive, Earl of Kimberley Associates, 1960-63; Journalist, Daily Express, 1963-71; Columnist, Daily Mail, 1971-; London Correspondent, Status Magazine, USA, 1965-66. Publications: H.R.H. The Princess Margaret - A Life Unfulfilled, (biography), 1981; Heiress - The Story of Christina Onassis, 1989; Nigel Dempster's Address Book (biography), 1991; Behind Palace Doors (with Peter Evans), 1993. Contributions to: Queen Magazine; Columnist (Grovel) Private Eye Magazine, 1969-85; Broadcaster with ABC, USA and CBC, Canada, 1976- and with TV am 1983-90. Address: c/o Daily Mail, Northcliffe House, 2 Derry Street, London W8 5TT, England.

DENGLER Sandy, b. 8 June 1939. Writer. m. William F Dengler, 11 Jan 1963. Education: BS, Bowling Green State University, Ohio, 1961; MS, Arizona State University, 1967. Publications include: Fanny Crosby, 1985; John Bunyan, 1986; D L Moody, 1987; Susanna Wesley, 1987; Florence Nightingale, 1988; Romance novels, juvenile historical novels including: Barn Social, 1978; Yosemite's Marvellous Creatures, 1979; Summer of the Wild Pig, 1979; Melon Hound, 1980; Horse Who Loved Picnics, 1980; Mystery at McGehan Ranch, 1982; Chain Five Mystery, 1984; Summer Snow, 1984; Winterspring, 1985; This Rolling Land, 1986; Jungle Gold, 1987; Code of Honour, 1988; Power of Pinjarra, 1989; Taste of Victory, 1989; East of Outback, 1990; Death Valley, 1993; Cat Killer, 1993; Dublin Crossing, 1993; Mouse Trapped, 1993; Gila Monster, 1994; Last Dinosaur, 1994; Murder on the Mount, 1994; Shamrock Shore, 1994; Emerald Sea, 1994; The Quick and the Dead, 1995. Contributions to: Numerous articles to journals and magazines. Honours: Writer of the Year, Warm Beach, 1986; Golden Medallion, Romance Writers of America, 1987. Address: 112 Tahoma Woods, Ashford, WA 98304, USA.

DENISON Edward Fulton, b. 18 Dec 1915, Omaha, Nebraska, USA. Economist. m. Elsie Lightbown, 14 June 1941, 1 son, 1 daughter. Education: AB, Oberlin College, 1936; MA 1938, PhD 1941, Brown University; Graduate, National War College, 1951. Appointments: Instructor, Brown University, 1940-41; Economist, US Department of Commerce, 1941-48; Assistant Director, Office of Business Economics, US Department of Commerce, 1949-56; Economist, Associate Director, Committee for Economic Development, 1956-62; Senior Fellow 1962-78, Senior Fellow Emeritus, 1978-, The Brookings Institution, Associate Director, Bureau of Economic Analysis, US Department of Commerce, 1979-82. Publications Include: The Sources of Economic Growth in the United States and the Alternatives Before Us, 1962; Why Growth Rates Differ: Post War Experience in Nine Western Countries, 1967; Accounting for United States Economic Growth, 1929-69, 1974; Accounting for Slower Economic Growth: The United States in the 1970's, 1979; Trends in American Economic Growth 1929-82, 1985; Estimates of Productivity Change by Industry: An Evaluation and an Alternative, 1989; How Japan's Economy Grew So Fast (with William

K Chung), 1976. Contributions to: American Economic Review; Survey of Current Business; Journal of Political Economy; Review of Income and Wealth; Review of Economics and Statistics. Honours: W S Woytinsky Lectureship Award from University of Michigan, 1967; Fellow, American Statistical Association, 1960; Fellow, American Economic Association, 1985; Shiskin Award from Washington Statistical Society, 1982. Memberships: National Academy of Sciences; American Academy of Arts and Sciences; American Economic Association (Vice-President 1978); International Association for Research in Income and Wealth; Conference on Research in Income and Wealth (Former Chairman). Address: Brookings Institution, 1775 Massachusetts Avenue NW, Washington, DC 20036, USA.

DENKER Henry, b. 1912, USA. Writer; Playwright. Publications: I'll Be Right Home, Ma, 1947; My Son, The Lawyer, 1949; Salome: Princess of Galilee, 1951; The First Easter, 1951; The Child is Mine, 1955; The Director, 1970; The Kingmaker, 1972; A Place for the Mighty, 1974; The Physicians, 1975; The Experiment, 1976; The Starmaker, 1977; The Scofield Diagnosis, 1977; The Actress, 1978; Error of Judgement, 1979; Horowitz and Mrs Washington, 1979, as play, 1980; The Warfield Syndrome, 1981; Outrage, 1982, as play, 1983, as film, 1985; The Healers, 1983; Kincaid, 1984; Robert, My Son, 1985; Judge Spence Dissents, 1986; The Choice, 1987; The Retreat, 1988; A Gift of Life, 1989; Payment in Full, 1990; Doctor on Trial, 1991; Mrs Washington and Horowitz, too, 1992; Labyrinth, 1994; Plays: Time Limit, 1957; A Far Country, 1961; A Case of Libel, 1963; What Did We Do Wrong?, 1967; The Headhunters, 1976; The Second Time Around, 1977. Memberships: Dramatists Guild, Council 1970-73; Authors Guild; Authors League, Council; Writers Guild of America East. Literary Agent: Mitch Douglas, ICM, 40 West 57th Street, New York, NY 10019. USA. Address: 241 Central Park W, New York, NY 10024, USA.

DENNING Alfred Thompson, Lord, b. 1899, England. Lawyer; Former Master of the Rolls. Appointments: Called to the Bar, 1923; King's Counsel, 1938; Judge of the High Court of Justice, 1944; A Lord Justice of Appeal, 1948-57; A Lord of Appeal in Ordinary, 1957-62; Master of the Rolls, 1962-82. Publications: (joint editor), Smith's Leading Cases, 1929; (joint editor), Bullen and Leake's Precedents, 1935; Freedom Under The Law (Hamlyn Lectures), 1949; The Changing Law, 1953; The Road to Justice, 1955; The Discipline of Law, 1979; The Due Process of Law, 1980; The Family Story, 1981; What Next in the Law, 1982; The Closing Chapter, 1983; Landmarkes in the Law, 1984; Leaves from My Library, 1986. Address: The Lawn, Whitchurch, Hants, England.

DENNING Mark, See: **STEVENSON John**.

DENNIS Everette Eugene Jr, b. 15 Aug 1942, Seattle, Washington, USA. Foundation Executive; Educator; Author. m. Emily J Smith, 15 June 1988. Education: BS, University of Oregon, 1964; MA, Syracuse University, 1966; PhD, Minnesota University, 1974. Appointments include: Formerly Newspaper Reporter, Communications Officer, Speechwriter; Assistant Professor, Journalism, Mass Communication, Kansas State University, Manhattan, 1968-72; Instructor, Assistant Professor, Associate Professor, School of Journalism and Mass Communication, University of Minnesota, 1972-81; Visiting Professor, Medill School of Journalism, Northwestern University, 1976-77; Dean, Professor, School of Journalism, University of Oregon, 1981-84; Currently: Executive Director, The Freedom Forum Media Studies Center, Columbia University, New York City; Vice-President, The Freedom Forum, Arlington, Virginia; Editor-in-Chief, Media Studies Journal. Publications: 26 books include: Other Voices: The New Journalism in America, 1973; The Media Society, 1978; The Economics of Libel, 1986; Understanding Mass Communication (editor), 1988, 5th edition, 1994; Demystifying Media Technology, 1993; America's Schools and the Mass Media, 1993, 1994. Contributions to: Hundreds of articles to popular, professional and scholarly periodicals. Honours include: 4 fellowships at Harvard University, 1978-79, 1980, 1981; Other fellowships; Various writing prizes and awards. Memberships include: Kappa Tau Alpha; Trustee, International Communication Association; Eastman House International Museum of Photographs; Trustee, American Antiquarian Society; Association for Education in Journalism and Mass Communication; International Press Institute; Society of Professional Journalists. Literary Agent: Jane Dystel, New York City, USA. Address: 420 Riverside Drive, New York, NY 10027, USA.

DENNIS-JONES Harold (Paul Hamilton, Dennis Hessing), b. 2 Dec 1915, Port-Louis, Mauritius. Journalist; Author; Photographer. 2

d. Education: Open Scholar in Classics, St Johns College, Oxford, 1934-38; First Class Honours in Classical Honour Moderations; Second Class Lt Hum. Appointments: Kensley Newspapers 1945-47; Travel Correspondent, Geographical Magazine, 1947-56; London Correspondent, Het Geillustreede Pers, Amsterdam, 1947-52; UK Editor, Guide Kleber, Paris, 1963-72. Publications include: Fifty-six guide books titles/editions, covering all Europe, Morocco, Israel; verse translations from Greek, French, Spanish, Romanian; three language learning titles, French, Spanish, Italian. Contributions to: Most UK Newspapers; many magazines in UK; newspapers and magazines in Europe, USA, etc; Radio and TV Broadcasts. Memberships: British Society of Authors; British Guild of Travel Writers. Address: 53 Sunhill Court, High Street, Pembury, Tunbridge Wells, TN2 4NT, England.

DENOO Joris, b. 6 Jul 1953, Torhout, Belgium. Author; Teacher. m. Lut Vandemeulebroecke, 23 Jul 1976, 1 s, 2 d. Education: Graduate, German Philology, Louvain, 1975; Aggregation PHO, 1976; Specialised in Dutch, Comparative Literature, Poetry. Appointments: Freelance Reporter, Book Reviewer, Flemish Journals, 1986-. Publications: Repelsteel in Bourgondië, novel, 1986; De Bende van de Beeldenaar, story for children, 1986; Binnerscheepvaart, poetry, 1988; Staat van Medewerking, poetry, 1988; Een Paar Kinderen, Graag, story for children, 1992; Voltooid Verwarmde Tijd, poetry, 1992; Taal Is een Aardig Ding, essay, 1993; Verkerde Lieveheer, novel, 1993. Contributions to: Many Flemish and Dutch magazines and journals including: Revisor; Hollands Maandblad; Maatstaf; Brakke Hond. Honours: Vlaamse Klub Prize, Brussels, 1979; Premies West-Vlaanderen, 1983, 1191; Prijs Tielt Boekenstad, 1992. Honours: SABAM, Belgium; Commission Taalen Letterkunde, Province of West Flanders, Bruges. Literary Agent: Lut Vandemeulebroecke. Address: Oude Iepersweg 85, B- Heule, Belgium.

DENVER Drake C. See: **NYE Nelson.**

DEPAOLA Tommie,b. 15 Sept 1934, Meriden, Connecticut, USA. Children's Book Artist; Author. Education: BFA, Pratt Institute, 1956; MFA, California College of Arts & Crafts, 1969; Doctoral Equivalency, Lone Mountain College, 1970. Publications: 200 books from 1964-1992, including: Strega Nona, 1975; The Clown of God, 1978; The Legend Of The Bluebonnet, 1983; Tommie de Paola's Book of Bible Stories, 1990; Jingle, The Christmas Clown, 1992. Honours: Caldecott Honor Book, American Library Association, 1976; Regina Medal, Catholic Library Association, 1983; Doctor of Letters, honoris causa, Colby-Sawyer College, 1985; American Nominee in Illustration for Hans Christian Andersen Award, International Board of Books for Young People, 1990. Memberships: Authors Guild; Society of Children's Book Writers. Address: G P Putnam's Sons, Putnam & Grosset Book Group, 200 Madison Avenue, NY 10016, USA.

DEPESTRE Réné, b. 29 Aug 1926, Jacmel, Haiti (French citizen). Poet. m. Nelly Campano, 1962. Education: Sorbonne and University of Paris, 1946-51. Appointments include: Attaché to the Office of Culture at UNESCO, Paris, 1982-86. Publications include: Etincelles, 1945; Gerbe de Sang, 1946; Vegetations of Splendour, 1951, 1981; Minerai noir, 1956; Journal d'un animal marin, 1964; A Rainbow for the Christian West, 1967, 1972; Poète à Cuba, 1976; En Etat de poésie, 1980; Journal d'un animal marin: choisi de poèmes 1956-1990; Au Matin de la negritude, 1990; Anthologie personnelle, 1992; Fiction: The Festival of the Greasy Pole, 1979, 1990; Alleluia pour une femme-jardin, 1982; Hadriana dans tous mes rêves, 1988; Eros dans un train chinois, 1990; Editor and translator, Poésie Cubaine 1959-1966. Honours include: Prix Goncourt, 1982. Address: 31 bis, Route de Roubia, 11200 Lezignan-Corbieres, France.

DERFLER (Arnold) Leslie, b. 1933, USA. Writer; Historian. Appointments: Faculty, Carnegie Mellon Univerwsity, Pittsburgh, Pennsylvania, 1962-68; Faculty, University of Massachusetts, Amherst, 1968-69; Professor of Hsitory, Florida Atlantic University, Boca Raton, 1969-. Publications: The Dreyfus Affair: Tragedy of Errors, 1963; The Third French Republic 1870-1940, 1966; Socialism since Marx, 1973; Alexandre Millerand: The Socialist Years, 1977; Hindi, 1977; President and Parliament: A Short History of the French Presidency, 1984; An Age of Conflict: Readings in 20th Century European History, 1990; Paul Lafargue and the Founding of French Marxism, 1991. Address: History Department, Florida Atlantic University, Boca Raton, FL 33431, USA.

DERR Mark, b. 20 Jan 1950, Baltimore, Maryland, USA. Writer. m. Gina L Maranto, 11 Sept 1982. Education: AB, 1972, MA, 1973, Johns Hopkins University. Publications: Some Kind of Paradise: Over

Florida; The Frontiersman: The Real Life and the Many Legends of Davy Crockett. Contributions to: The Atlantic; Audubon Society. Literary Agent: Barney Karpfinger, The Karpfinger Agency, New York, USA. Address: 4 245 Sheridan Avenue, Miami Beach, FL 33140, USA.

DERRY John Wesley, b. 1933. Writer. (History, Biography). Publications: William Pitt, 1962; Reaction and Reform, 1963, 3rd Edition, 1970; The Regency Crisis and the Whigs, 1963; Parliamentary Reform, 1966; The Radical Tradition, 1967; Political Parties, 1968; Cobbett's England, 1968; Charles James Fox, 1972; Castlereagh, 1976; Politics in the Age of Fox, Pitt and Liverpool, 1990; Charles, Earl Grey, 1992. Address: Department of History, University of Newcastle upon Tyne, Newcastle, NE1 7RU, England.

DERSHOWITZ Alan, b. 1938, NY, USA. Professor; Writer. m. 2 s, 1 d. Education: Brooklyn College, Yale University. Publications: The Best Defence; Reversal of Fortune: Inside the Von Bulow Case; Taking Liberties: A Decade of Hard Cases, Bad Laws and Bum Raps; Chutzpah, 1991; Contrary to Popular Opinion, 1992; The Abuse Excuse, 1994; The Advocate's Devil, 1994.Address: c/o Helen Rees, 308 Commonwealth Avenue, Boston, MA 02115, USA.

DESAI Anita, b. 24 Jun 1837, Mussoorie, India. Writer. m. Ashvin Desai, 13 Dec 1958, 2 s, 2 d. Education: BA, Honours, Miranda House, University of Delhi. Appointments: Member of Advisory Board for English, Sahitya Akademi, India, 1875-80; Member, Royal Society of Literature, England, 1978-. Publications: Cry, The Peacock; Voices in the City; Fire on the Mountain; Clear Light of Day; In Custody, (also a film, Merchant Ivory Productions, 1994); Baumgartner's Bombay; Where Shall We Go This Summer?; Bye Bye Blackbird; The Peacock Garden; Cat on a Houseboat; The Village by the Sea, (also BBC TV Serial, 1992); Games at Twilight. Contributions to: Writer's Workshop; Quest; Illustrated Weekly of India; The London Magazine; The Literary Review; New York tomes Book review; Washington Post Book World; The New York Review of Books; The New Republic. Honours: Winifred Holtby Award, Royal Society of Literature, 1978; Sahitya Akademi Award for English, 1978; Federation of Indian Publishers Award, 1978; The Padma Shri Award, India, 1989; Hadassah Magazine Award, 1989; Guardian Prize for Children's Fiction, 1983; Literary Lion of New York Public Library, 1993. Memberships: Royal Society of Literature; Sahitya Akademi of India; PEN: Fellow, American Academy of Arts and Letters, 1992; Fellow, Girton College and of Clare Hall, Cambridge. Literary Agent: Deborah Rogers, c/o Rogers, Coleridge & White Ltd. Address: c/o Rogers, Coleridge and White Ltd, 20 Powis Mews, London W11 1JN, England.

DESCHOEMAEKER Frans, b. 8 Sep 1954, Belgium. m. Myriam Blyau. Education: Institute for Psychical and Social Training, Kortryk, 1973-74. Appointments: Editor, Literary Magazine, Diogenes, 1984-. Publications: Stroomafwaarts; In de Spiegelzalen van de Henfst; De Onderhuidse Lach van de Landjonker; Beginselen van Archeologie. Contributions to: The Gensis of a Poem; The Splendid Regions Beyond Words; Bottas Glance, about poetry and Archaeology; The Critical Lexicon of Dutch Literature after 1945. Honours: Poetry Prize Flemish Club Brussels; Poetry Prize of West Flanders; Nominated Hughes C Pernath Prize. Address: Vontstraat 69, 9700 Oudeaarde, Belgium.

DESCOMBES Vincent, b. 4 Dec 1943, Paris, France. Professor. m. Yasuko Ohno, 1981, 1 d. Education: Agregation de Philosophie, 1967; PhD, 1970. Publications: Modern French Philosophy; Objects of All Sorts; Proust; The Barometer of Modern Reason. Contributions to: Critique. Address: 66 Avenue de la Republique, 75011, Paris, France.

DESHPANDE Shashi, b. 19 Aug 1938, Dharwad, India. Novelist. m. D H Deshpande, 1962, 2 sons. Education: BA (Hons) in Economics, 1956, Diploma in Journalism, 1970, MA in English, 1970, University of Bombay; BL, University of Mysore, Karnataka, 1959. Publications: The Dark Holds no Terrors, 1980; If I Die Today, 1982; Roots and Shadows, 1983; Come Up and Be Dead, 1985; That Long Silence, 1988; Short stories: The Legacy and Other Stories, 1978; It Was Dark, 1986; The Miracle and Other Stories, 1986; It Was the Nightingale, 1986; Also a screenplay and children's works. Honours: Rangammal Prize, 1984; Sahitya Academy Award, 1990. Address: 409 41st Cross, Jayanagar V Block, Bangalore 560041, India.

DESJARLAIS John Joseph,b. 19 Mar 1953, Germany. Writer. m. Virginia Louise Wolff, 26 Aug 1978. Education: BA, University of Wisconsin, Madison, 1976; MA, Columbia University, 1984. Appointments: Assistant Editor, Student Leadership Journal, 1992-.

Publications: The Throne of Tara; Relics; Habakkuk; Boutique; God Is Building A City. Contributions to: University Magazine; Student Leadership Journal; STAFF. Honours: Gold Medal, International Multi Image Festival; Christianity Today Readers Choice Award nominee. Memberships: Association for Educational Communications & Technology. Literary Agent: Donald Bradenburgh, Brandenburgh & Associates. Address: PO Box 7895, Madison, WI 53707, USA.

DESMARAIS Ovide E (Ovid Demaris),b. 6 Sept 1919, Biddeford, Maine, USA. Writer; Newspaper Reporter. m. Inez E Frakes, 15 May 1942, 2 daughters. Education: AB, College of Idaho, 1948; Law, Syracuse University; MS, Boston University, 1950. Publications: mystery novels: Ride the Gold Mare, 1956; The Hoods Take Over, 1957; The Long Night, 1957; The Lusting Drive, 1958; The Slasher, 1959; The Enforcer, 1960; The Extortioners, 1960; The Gold-Plated Sewer, 1960; Candyleg, 1961 (as Machine Gun McCanin, 1970); The Parasite, 1963; The Organization, 1965 (as The Contract 1970); The Overlord, 1972; other - Lucky Luciano, 1960; The Linbergh Kidnapping Case, 1961; The Dillinger Story, 1961; (with Edward Reid) The Green Felt Jungle, 1963; (with Garry Wills) Jack Ruby, 1968; Captive City; Chicago in Chains, 1969; American the Violent, 1970; Poso del Mundo: Inside the Mexican-American Border, 1970; Dirty Business: The Corporate-Political Money-Power Game, 1974; The Director: An Oral Biography of J Edgar Hoover, 1975; Brothers in Blood: The International Terrorist Network, 1977; The Last Mafioso: The Treacherous World of Jimmy Fratianno, 1981; The Vegas Legacy, 1983; The Boardwalk Jungle, 1987; J Edgar Hoover: As They Knew Him, 1994. Contributions to: Esquire; Popular Mechanics; Other professional journals and magazines.

DETHIER Vincent G(aston),b. 1915, USA. Appointments: Associate Professor 1947-51, Professor of Biology 1951-58, Johns Hopkins University, Baltimore, MD; Professor of Biology and Psychology, University of Pennsylvania, Philadelphia, 1957-68; Professor of Biology, Princeton University, 1968-75; Professor of Zoology, University of Massachusetts, Amherst, 1975-. Publications: Chemical Insect Attractants and Repellents, 1947; Animal Behavior (co-author), 1961; To Know a Fly, 1962; The Physiology of Insect Senses, 1963; Fairweather Duck, 1970; Biological Principles and Processes, 1971; Buy Me A Volcano, 1972; The Hungry Fly: A Physiological Analysis, 1975; Man's Plague, 1976; The Ant Heap, 1979; The World of the Tent Makers: Natural History of Tent Caterpillars, 1980; Newberry: The Life and Times of a Maine Clam, 1981; The Ecology of a Summer House, 1984; Ten Masses, 1988; Crickets and Katydids, 1992. Address: Department of Zoology, University of Massachusetts, Amherst, MA 01003, USA.

DEUTSCH Andre,b. 15 Nov 1917. Publisher. Education: Budapest, Vienna & Zurich. Appointments: Nicholson & Watson, 1942; Independent Publisher under imprint Allan Wingate (Publrs) Ltd, 1945; Formed Andre Deutsch Ltd, 1951, Chairman & Managing Director 1951-84, President 1989-91; Founder, African University Press, Lagos, 1962, East Africa Publishing House, Nairobi, 1964. Honour: CBE, 1989.

DEVERELL Rex Johnson, b. 17 July 1941, Toronto, Canada. Playwright. m. Rita Joyce Shelton, 24 May 1967, 1 son. Education: BA, 1963; BD, 1966; STM, 1967. Literary Appointments: Resident Playwright, Globe Theatre, Regina, 1975-91; President, Playwrights Union of Canada, 1991-93. Publications: Boiler Room Suite, 1978; Superwheel, 1979; Drift, 1981; Black Powder, 1981; 3 Plays for Children; Various other plays, TV and radio scripts; Anthology, Deverell of the Globe, Opera Libretti, Boiler Room Suite, Land. Contributions to: Canadian Theatre Review; Canadian Children's Literature; Canadian Drama; Prairie Fire; Grain; Others. Honours: McMaster University Honour Society, 1963; Ohio State Award, 1974; Canadian Authors Association Medal, 1978; Major Armstrong Award, 1986; Nominee, Chalmers Award, 1994. Memberships: Saskatchewan Writers Guild; Playwrights Union of Canada; Saskatchewan Playwrights Centre; Amnesty International. Address: 36 Oneida Avenue, RR 4, Coldwater, Ontario, Canada L0K 1E0.

DEVERELL William, b. 1937, Regina. Appointments: Former President, British Columia Civil Liberties Association, Chair, Writers Union of Canada, 1994-95. Publications include: Translations; 5 Screenplays; Needles, 1979; High Crimes, 1981; The Dance of Shiva, 1984; Platinum Blues, 1987; Mindfield, 1989; Fatal Cruise: The Trial of Robert Frisbee, 1990; Kill All THe Lawyers, 1994. Honours: Seal First Novel Award, 1979; Book of Year, 1981. Address: RR1, North Pender Island, British Columbia, VON 2MO, Canada.

DEVEREUX Eve. See: BARNETT Paul le Page.

DEVINE Thomas Martin, b. 30 Jul 1945, Motherwell, Scotland. m. Catherine Mary Lynas, 6 Jul 1971, 2 s, 3 d. Education:BA, University of Strathclyde, 1968; PhD, 1971; D Litt, 1991; Fellow, Royal Society of Edinburgh, 1992. Appointments: Assisstant Lecturer, 1969-71; Lecturer, Senior Lecturer, 1971-83; Reader, 1983-88; Professor, 1988; Dean of Faculty of Arts and Social Studies, 1993. Publications: The Tobacco Lords, Ireland & Scotland 1700-1850; The Great Highland Famine; People & Society in Scotland; Farm Servants and Labour in Lowland Scotland; Irish Immigrants and Scottish Society in the Eighteenth and Nineteenth Centuries; Scottish Emigration and Scottish Society; Clanship to Crofters' War: The Social Transformation of the Scottish Highlands; The Transformation of Rural Scotland: Agrarian & Social Change 1680-1815. Contributions to: Times Literary Supplement; Times Higher Education Supplement; Economic History Review; Social History; Scottish Historical Review; History Today; Scottish Economic & Social History. Honours: Senior Hume Brown Prize; Saltire Prize. Memberships: Economic & Social History Society of Scotland; Scottish Catholic Historical Association; Royal Society; Royal Historical Society. Address: Department of History, University of Strathclyde, McCance Building, 16 Richmond Street, Glasgow, Scotland.

DEVRIES Susanna. See: DE VRIES-EVANS Susanna Mary.

DEW Robb Forman, b. 26 Oct 1946, OH, USA. Writer. m. Charles Burgess Dew, 26 Jan 1968, 2 s. Publications: Dale Loves Sophie to Death, 1982; The Time Of Her Life, 1984; Fortunate Lives, 1991; A Southern Thanksgiving, 1992; The Family Heart, 1994. Honours: Am Book Award. 1st Novel, 1982. Literary Agent: Russell & Volkening, 50 W 29th, Apt 7E, New York, NY 10001, USA.

DEWEESE Jean. See: DE WEESE Thomas Eugene.

DEWEY Jennifer Owings, b. 2 Oct 1941, Chicago, Illinois, USA. Writer, Illustrator. div. 1 daughter. Education: University of New Mexico, 1960-63; Rhode Island School of Design. Publications: CLEM, The Story Of A Raven, 1986; At The Edge Of The Pond, 1987; Birds of Antarctica, The Adelie Penguin, 1989; Can You Find Me, A Book About Animal Camouflage, 1989; Animal Architecture, 1991; Night & Day in the Desert, 1991; About 12 Illustrated Books including: The Sagebrush Ocean; Birds of the Great Basin; Wilderness Sojourn, 1988. Contributions to: Stories to Highlights for Children, 1989. Honours: New York Academy of Science Award for illustration for The Secret Language of Snow; Bookbuilders West, and Bookbuilders East, for Illustration and Design in At The Edge Of The Pond; Bookbuilders West for Illustrations in Idle Weeds. Memberships: San Francisco Society of Illustrators; American Society of Scientific Illustrators; President, Founder, The No Poets Society. Address: 607 Old Taos Highway, Santa Fe, NM 87501, USA.

DEWHIRST Ian, b. 17 Oct 1936, Keighley, Yorkshire, England. Librarian. Education: BA Hons, 1958. Publications: Gleanings From Victorian Yorkshire, 1972; A History of Keighley, 1974; Yorkshire Through the Years, 1975; Gleanings from Edwardian Yorkshire, 1975; The Story of a Nobody, 1980; You Don't Remember Bananas, 1985; Keighley in Old Picture Postcards, 1987; In The Reign of the Peacemaker, 1993; Down Memory Lane, 1993. Contributions to: Yorkshire Ridings Magazine; Lancashire Magazine; The Dalesman; Cumbria; Pennine Magazine; Transactions of the Yorkshire Dialect Society; Yorkshire Journal. Memberships: Yorkshire Dialect Society (Hon General Secretary 1964-74); Brontë Society; The Edward Thomas Fellowship; Associate of the Library Association. Address: 14 Raglan Avenue, Fell Lane, Keighley, West Yorkshire, BD22 6BJ, England.

DEWHURST Eileen Mary, b. 27 May 1929, Liverpool, England. Author. Divorced. Education: BA (Hons) English Language and Literature, St Anne's College, Oxford, 1951. Publications: Crime novels: Death Came Smiling, 1975; After the Ball, 1976; Curtain Fall, 1977; Drink This, 1980; Trio in Three Flats, 1981; Whoever I Am, 1982; The House That Jack Built, 1983; There Was a Little Girl, 1984; Playing Safe, 1985; A Private Prosecution, 1986; A Nice Little Business, 1987; The Sleeper, 1988; Dear Mr Right, 1990; The Innocence of Guilt, 1991; Death in Candie Gardens, 1992; Now You See Her, 1995. Contributions to: Various newspapers and journals. Memberships: Crime Writers Association; The Society of Authors. Literary Agent:

Gregory and Radice, London. Address: c/o Gregory and Radice, 3 Barb Mews, London W6 7PA, England.

DEWHURST Keith, b. 1931, British. Appointments: Sports Writer, Evening Chronicle, 1955-59; Granada Television Presenter, 1968-69; BBC2 Television Presenter, 1972; Witer-on Residence, Western Australia APA Perth, 1984; Publications: Lark Rise To Candleford, 1980; Captain of the Sands, 1981; Don Quixote, 1982; McSullivan's Beach, 1985; Black Snow, 1992. Address: c/o Alexandra Cann Representation, 337 Fulham Road, London SW10 9TW, England.

DEXTER Colin, b. 29 Sep 1930, Stamford, Lincolnshire, England. Educational Administator. Education: Christ's College, Cambridge; MA (Cantab): MA (Oxon). Publications: Last Bus to Woodstock, 1975; Last Seen Wearing, 1976; The Silent World of Nicholas Quinn, 1977; Service of All the Dead, 1979; The Dead of Jericho, 1981; The Riddle of the Third Mile, 1983; The Secret of Annexe 3, 1983; The Wench is Dead, 1989; The Jewel That Was Ours, 1991; The Way Through the Woods, 1992; Morse's Greatest Mystery, 1993; The Daughters of Cain, 1994. Honours: Recipient, Silver Dagger, 1979, 1981, Gold Dagger, 1989, 1992, Crime Writers Association. Memberships: Crime Writers Association; Detection Club. Address: 456 Banbury Road, Oxford OX2 7RG, England.

DI CESARE Mario A, b. 1928, USA. Appointments: Instructor 1959-61, Assistant Professor 1961-64, Associate Professor 1964-68, Master of Newing College, Harpur, 1967-68, Chairman, English Department 1968-73, Professor, 1968-89, Distinguished Professor, 1989-. Publications: Vidas Christiad and Virgilian Epic; The Book of Good Love; Bibliotheca Vidiana; Critical Biography of Marco Girolamo Vida; The Altar and the City; A Reading of Virgil's Aeneid; A Concordance to the Complete Writings of George Herbert; Poetry and Prophecy; George Herbert and the Seventeenth Century Religious Poets; A Concordance to the Nondramatic Poems of Ben Johnson; The Bodleian Manuscript of George Herbert's The Temple; Milton in Italy; Reconsidering the Renaissance. Contributions to: Journal of the American Academy of Religion; English Literary Renaissance; Yearbook of English Studies; The Chaucer Review; Mediavalia. Honours: Samuel S Fels Fellow; Guggenheim Fellow; Robert Frost Library Fellow; National Endowment for the Humanities Senior Fellow. Memberships: Renaissance Society of America; Center for International Scholarly Exchange; Renaissance English Text Society. Address: Tamarack Wood, 1936 Cafferty Hill Road, Owego, NY 13760, USA.

DI CICCO Pier Giorgio, b. 5 July 1949, Erezzo, Italy, Canadian Citizen. Poetry Instructor; Poet. Education: BEd, University of Toronto, 1973. Appointments: Poetry Instructor, Three Schools of Art, Toronto, Humber College & Columbus Centre, 1977-85. Publications: We are The Light Turning, 1975; The Sad Facts, 1977; The Circular Dark, 1977; Dancing in the House of Cards, 1977; A Burning Patience, 1978; Dolce Amaro, 1979; The Tough Romance, 1979; A Straw Hat for Everything, 1981; Flying Deeper into the Century, 1982; Dark to Light: Reasons for Humanness, 1976-79, 1983; Women We Never See Again, 1984; Twenty Poems, 1985; Post Sixties Nocturne, 1985; Virgin Science: Hunting Holistic Paradigms, 1986; Editor, Roman Candles: An Anthology of 17 Italo-Canadian Poets, 1978. Honours: Canada Council Award, 1976, 1980. Address: PO Box 344, King City, Ontario, LOG 1KO, Canada.

DI SCIASCIO Eve Francesca (Alana Thorstensen), b. 3 Aug 1954. Registered Nurse. Education: BSN, 1984. Publications: The Three of Swords, forthcoming; The Scirocco, in progress; Andromeda, forthcoming. Membership: Sigma Theta Tau, National Honour Society of Nursing. Address: 818 South Ellison Drive, San Antonio, TX 78245-3154, USA.

DICK Bernard, b. 25 Nov 1935, Scranton, Pennsylvania, USA. University Professor. m. Katherine M Restaino, 31 July 1965. Education: BA, Classics, Literature, University of Scranton, 1957; MA, Classics, 1960, PhD, Classics, 1962, Fordham University. Publications: The Hellenism of Mary Renault, 1972; The Apostate Angel: A Critical Study of Gore Vidal, 1974; Billy Wilder, 1980; Hellman in Hollywood, 1982; Joseph L Mankiewicz, 1983; The Star-Spangled Screen, 1985; William Golding, Revised Edition, 1987; Radical Innocence: A Critical Study of the Hollywood Ten, 1989; Anatomy of Film, 2nd Edition, 1990; Columbia Pictures: Portrait of a Studio, 1991; The Merchant Prince of Poverty Row: Harry Cohn of Columbia Pictures, 1993. Contributor to: Wall Street Journal; College English; Comparative Literature; World

Literature Today; Modern Drama; Sewanee Review. Honours: Choice Magazine Award, 1 of the Year's Outstanding Scholarly Books, for The Star-Spangled Screen. Address: 580 Wyndham Road, Teaneck, NJ 07666, USA.

DICKENS Eric Anthony, b. 29 Jan 1953, Dewsbury, Yorkshire, England. Translator. Education: BA (Hons), University of East Anglia, 1975; Publications: (Translations) Jan Mårtencon, Drottningholm; Lars & Annika Bäckström, Vadim Sidur; Jaan Kräss, The Peeter Mirk Stories; Piet Vroon, Crocodile Tears. Contributions to : Index on Censorship; Stand; Swedish Book Review; PEN International; Swedish Books; Horisont; Ny Tid; Sirp. Memberships: PEN; Translators Association; SELTA; AITI. Literary Agent: Ann Christine Danielsson, Karlstad, Sweden. Address: Kariekiet 1, 1261 RL Blaricum, Netherlands.

DICKENS Monica (Enid), b. 10 May 1915, London, England. Novelist. m. Roy Olin Stratton, 1951, dec'd 1985, 2 adopted daughters. Education: St Paul's Girls' School, London. Appointments include: Columnist, Woman's Own, London, 1946-65. Publications: Mariana, 1940; The Fancy, 1943; Thursday Afternoons, 1945; The Happy Prisoner, 1946; Joy and Josephine, 1948; Flowers on the Grass, 1949; No More Meadows, 1953; The Winds of Heaven, 1955; The Angel in the Corner, 1956; Man Overboard, 1958; The Heart of London, 1961; Cobbler's Dream, 1963; Kate and Emma, 1964; The Room Upstairs, 1966; The Landlord's Daughter, 1968; The Listeners, 1970; Last Year When I Was Young, 1974; Dear Doctor Lily, 1988; Enchantment, 1989; Closed At Dusk, 1990; Scarred, 1991; Also: Several autobiographical and children's works. Honours: MBE, 1981. Address: Lavender Cottage, Pudding Lane, Brightwalton, Berkshire RG16 0BY, England.

DICKEY Angela Renée, b. 19 Jul 1957, Rome, Georgia, USA. Diplomat; Freelance Writer. Education: BA, Berry College, Georgia, 1979; MSc, Georgetown University, 1981; Postgraduate work, University of Florida, 1983-84. Appointments: Editorial assistant, African Studies Review, 1883-84; Editor, Harcourt Brace Javanovick, Orlando, 1984-86; Reporter, Editor, The Orlando Sentinel, 1986-88; Founding Editor, Pencil Press Quarterly. Contributions to: Orlando Sentinel; Florida Magazine; Pencil Press Quarterly and others. Address: US Embassy Novakchott, BP 222, Navakchott, Mauritania (RIM).

DICKEY James Lafayette III, b. 2 Feb 1923, Atlanta, Georgia, USA. Poet; Novelist. m. (1) Maxine Syerson (dec), 1948, (2) Deborah Dodson, 1976, 2 sons, 1 daughter. Education: BA, 1949, MA, 1950, Vanderbilt University. Literary appointments: Poetry Consultant to Library of Congress, 1966-68; First Carolina Professor and Poet-in-Residence, University of South Carolina, Columbia, 1968-. Publications include: Drowning with Others, 1962; Buckdancer's Choice, verse, 1965; James Dickey: Poems, 1957-1967; Babel to Byzantium: Poets and Poetry Now, 1978; Deliverance, 1970; Jericho: The South Beheld, 1974; Falling, May Day Sermon and Other Poems, 1981; Alnilam, 1987; Wayfarer, 1988; The Whole Motion: Collected Poems, 1992; To The White Sea, novel, 1993. Contributions to: Architectural Digest, Apr 1994; Superbowl XVIII Program, 1994. Address: 4620 Lelia's Court, Columbia, SC 29206, USA.

DICKEY William, b. 1928, American. Appointments: Instructor, Cornell University, Ithica, New York, 1956-59; Assisstant Professor, Denison University, Granville, Ohio, 1960-62; Professor of English and Creative Writing, 1962-, Chairman, Creative Writing Department 1974-77, San Francisco State University, California; Emeirtus Professor, 1991-. Publications: Of The Festivity, 1959; Interpreter's House, 1964; Rivers of the Pacific Northwest, 1969; More Under Saturn, 1971; The Rainbow Grocery, 1978; Sacrifice Consenting, 1981; Six Philosophical Songs, Joy, 1983; Brief Lives, 1985; The King of the Golden River, 1986; Metamorphoses, 1991; Night Journey, 1992. Honour: Phi Beta Kappa. Memberships: PEN American Center; Modern Language Association. Address: Department of Creative Writing, San Francisco State University, 1600 Holloway, San Francisco, CA 94132, USA.

DICKINSON Donald Percy, b. 28 Dec 1947, Prince Albert, Canada. Writer; Teacher. m. Chellie Eaton, 1 May 1970, 2 sons, 1 daughter. Education: BA, University of Saskatchewan, 1977; MFA, University of British Columbia, 1979. Literary appointments: Fiction Editor, Prisim International 1977-79. Publications: Fighting the Upstream; Blue Husbands; The Crew. Contributions to: Best Canadian Short Fiction; Words We Call Home; The New Writers. Honours:

Bankson Award; Governor General of Canada Award Nominee; Ethel Wilson Fiction Prize. Membership: Writers Union of Canada. Address: 554 Victoria Street, Lillooet, British Columbia, Canada V0K 1V0.

DICKINSON Harry Thomas, b. 9 Mar 1939, Gateshead, England. University Professor. m. Jennifer Elizabeth Galtry, 26 Aug 1961, 1 s, 1 d. Education: BA Hons, 1960; Dip Ed, 1961; MA, 1963, Durham University; PhD, Newcastle University, 1968; DLitt, Edinburgh, 1986. Publications: Correspondence of Sir James Clavering, 1967; Bolingbroke, 1970; Walpole and the Whig Supremacy, 1973; Politics and Literature in the 18th Century, 1974; Liberty and Property, 1977; The Political Works of Thomas Spence, 1982; British Radicalism and the French Revolution, 1985; Caricatures and the Constitution, 1987; Britain and the French Revolution, 1989; Editor of History, 1993-; The Politics of the People in Eighteenth Century Britain, 1994. Contributions to: English Historical Review; Transactions of Royal Historical Society; Journal of British Studies; Huntington Library Quarterly; essays in over 30 books. Honours: Earl Grey Fellow, Newcastle University, 1964-66; Fulbright Fellow, 1973; Huntington Library Fellow, 1973; Folgar Shakespeare Library Senior Fellow, 1973; Churchill Fellow, 1980; Leverhulme Award, 1987; Ahmanson Fellow UCLA, 1987; Concurrent Professor, Nanjing University, 1987-; Anstey Memorial Lecturer, Kent University, 1989. Memberships: Royal Historical Society, Council Member, 1986-90; Vice-President, 1991-95; Historical Association, Council Member, 1984-. Address: 44 Viewforth Terrace, Edinburgh EH10 4LJ, Scotland.

DICKINSON Margaret. See: MUGGESON Margaret Elizabeth.

DICKINSON Peter Malcolm (The Honourable), b. 16 Dec 1927, Livingstone, Zambia. Author. m. Mary Rose Barnard, 26 Apr 1953 (dec 1988), 2 s, 2 d. Education: Scholar, Eton College; Exhibitioner, Kings College, Cambridge; 2ndly Robin McKinley, 3 Jan 1992; BA (Cantab) 1951. Appointments: Various editorial posts, Punch, 1952-69; Chairman, Management Committee, Society of Authors, 1978-80. Publications: Children's novels: The Weathermonger, 1968; Heartease, 1969; The Devil's Children, 1970 (trilogy republished as The Changes 1970); Emma Tupper's Diary, 1970; The Dancing Bear, 1972; The Gift, 1973; The Iron Lion, 1973; Chance, Luck and Destiny, 1975; The Blue Hawk, 1976; Annerton Pit, 1977; Hepzibah, 1978; Tulku, 1979; The Flight of Dragons, 1979; City of Gold, 1980; the Seventh Raven, 1981; Healer, 1983; Giant Cold, 1984; editor: Hundreds and Hundreds, 1984; A Box of Nothing, 1985; Eva, 1988; Merlin Dreams, 1988; AK, 1990; A Bone From A Dry Sea, 1992; TV series: Mandog; adult's novels: Skin Deep, 1968; A Pride of Heroes, 1969; The Seals, 1970; Sleep and His Brother, 1971; the Lizard in the Cup, 1972; The Green Gene, 1973; The Poison Oracle, 1974; The Lively Dead, 1975; King and Joker, 1976; Walking Dead, 1977; One Foot in the Grave, 1979; A Summerin the Twenties, 1981; The Last Houseparty, 1982; Hindsight, 1983; Death of A Unicorn, 1984; Tefuga, 1986; Perfect Gallows, 1988; Skeleton-in-Waiting, 1989; Play Dead, 1991. Contributions to: Regular Verse to Punch, 1952-69. Honours: Golden Dagger Award, Crime Writers Association, 1968, 1969; Guardian Award, 1976; Carnegie Medal, 1979, 1980; Whitbread Prize, 1979; Various Awards, USA. Memberships: Society of Authors, Chairman, 1978-80; Crime Writer's Club; Detection Club; PEN. Literary Agent: A P Watt Ltd, 20 John Street, London WC1N 2DL. Address: 61a Ormiston Grove, London WS12 OJP, England.

DICKSON Gordon (Rupert), b. 1923, American. Publications: Alien From Archturus, Mankind on the Run, 1956; Earthman's Burden (with Poul Anderson), 1957; Secret Under the Sea, Time to Teleport, the Genetic General, Delusion World, 1960; Special Delivery, Naked to The Stars, 1961; Necromancer, 1962; Secret Under Antarctica, 1963; Secret Under the Carribean, 1964; Space Winners, The Alien Way, Mission to Universe, 1965; Planet Run, Soldier Ask Not, The Space Swimmers, 1967; None But Man, Spacepaw, Wolfing, 1969; Hour of the Horde, Danger - Human (also known as The Book Of Gordon R Dickson), Mutants, 1970; Sleepwalker's World, The Tactics of Mistake, 1971; The Outposter, The Pritcher Mass, 1972; the Star Road, Alien Art, The R-Master, 1973; Gremlins Go Home! (with Ben Bova), Ancient My Enemy, 1974; Three to Dorsai, Combat SF (editor), Star Prince Charlie (with P Anderson), 1975; The Lifeship (with Harry Harrison), The Dragon and The George, 1976; Time Storm, 1977; Nebula Award Stories Twelve (editor), The Far Call, Home From the Shore, 1978; Spirit of Dorsai, Masters of Everon, Lost Dorsai, 1980; In Iron Years, Love Not Human, 1981; The Soace Swimmers, The Outposter, 1982; The Pitcher Mass, 1983; Dragon At War, Dragon On

The Border, 1992; Blood and War, 1993. Address: PO Box 1569, Twin Cities Airport, MN 55111, USA.

DICKSON Mora Agnes, b. 1918, Britain. Self-employed Author and Artist. Publications: New Nigerians, 1960; Baghdad and Beyond, 1961; A Season in Sarawak, 1962; A World Elsewhere, 1964; Israeli Interlude, 1966; Count Us In, 1968; Longhouse in Sarawak, 1971; Beloved Partner, 1974; A Chance to Serve (editor), The Inseparable Grief, 1977; Assignment in Asia, 1979; The Powerful Bond, 1980; Nannie, 1988. Address: 19 Blenheim Road, London W4, England.

DIDION Joan, b. 5 Dec 1934, CA, USA. Novelist; Reporter; Essayist. Publications: Run River; Slouching Towards Bethleham; Play It as It Lays; A Book of Common Prayer; The White Album; Salvador; Democracy; Miami; After Henry. Contributions to: Best American Essays; New York Review of Books; New Yorker. Address: c/o Janklow & Nesbit Associates, 598 Madison Avenue, New York, NY 10022, USA.

DIETRICH Robert, See: HUNT Everette Howard.

DIGBY Joan (Hildreth), b. 16 Nov 1942, New York City, New York, USA. Professor of English; Writer. m. (1) William Howard Owen, 26 Nov 1965, div, (2) John Michael Digby, 3 Mar 1979. Education: BA summa cum laude, 1963, PhD, 1969, New York University; MA, University of Delaware, 1965. Appointments: Assistant Professor, 1969-73, Associate Professor, 1973-77, Professor of English, Director of Honours Programme and Merit Fellowship, 1977-, Long Island University, C W Post Campus, Brookville, New York. Publications: A Sound of Feathers, prose poems (with collage illustrations by husband John Digby), 1982; Two Presses, nonfiction, 1988; With John Digby: The Collage Handbook, 1985; The Wood Engraving of John de Pol, 1988; Permutations: Readings in Science and Literature (editor with Bob Brier), 1985; Editor with John Digby: Food for Thought, 1987; Inspired By Drink, 1988. Honours: Excellence in Teaching Award, New York State Council of English Teachers, 1987. Memberships: American Society for Eighteenth Century Studies; National Collegiate Honors Council; Phi Beta Kappa. Address: 30 Kellogg Street, Oyster Bay, NY 11771, USA.

DIGBY John (Michael), b. 18 Jan 1938, London, England. Emigrated, USA, 1978. Poet; Collagist. m. (1) Erica Susan Christine Berwick-Stephens, 1963, div, 1 son, (2) Joan Hildreth Weiss, 3 Mar 1979. Publications: The Structure of Biofocal Distance, poems, 1974; Sailing Away From Night, poems, collages, 1978; To Amuse a Shrinking Sun, poems, collages, 1985; The Collage Handbook (with wife, Joan Digby), 1985; Miss Liberty, collages, 1986; Incantation, poems, collages, 1987; A Parliament of Owls, poems, collages, 1989; Editor with Joan Digby: Inspired by Drink, 1988; The Wood Engravings of John de Pol, 1988. Address: 30 Kellogg Street, Oyster Bay, NY 11771, USA.

DIGREGORIO Charlotte Antonia, b. 30 Aug 1953, Portland, OR, USA. Author; Editorial Consultant; Professional Speaker (USA). Education: Bachelor of Arts, Pomona College, 1975; Master of Arts, The University of Chicago, 1979. Publications: Beginners' Guide to Writing and Selling Quality Features, 1990; You Can Be A Columnist, 1993. Contributions to: Magazines and Journals. Memberships: The International Women's Writing Guild; COSMEP; Board Of Directors (1991), Secretary Northwest Association Of Book Publishers; Publishers Marketing Association. Address: 2770 SW Old Orchard Road, Portland, OR 97201, USA.

DILLARD Annie, b. 30 Apr 1945, PA, USA. Adjunct Professor; Writer in Residence. Education: BA, 1967, MA, 1968, Hollins College. Literary Appointments: Scholar in Residence, Western WA University, 1975-79; Visiting Professor, 1979-81, Adjunct Professor, 1983-, Writer in Residence, 1987-, Wesleyan University. Publications: Pilgrim at Tinker Creek, 1974; Holy the Firm, 1977; Teaching a Stone to Talk, 1983, 1988; Encounters with Chinese Writers, 1984; An American Childhood, 1987; The Writing Life, 1989; The Living, 1992; The Annie Dillard Reader, 1994; Tickets for a Prayer Wheel, 1994; Mornings Like This, 1995. Contributions to: Harper's Magazine; Atlantic Monthly; NY Times. Honours include: Pulitzer Prize, 1975; Phi Beta Kappa, 1966; NY Press Club Award, 1975; WA Governor's Award, 1977; CT Governor's Award, 1993; National Endowment for the Arts Grant, 1985; John Simon Guggenheim Foundation Grant, 1986; Middletown Commission on the Arts Award, 1987; Appalachian Gold Medallion, 1989; Ambassador Book Award, 1990; The Campian Award, 1994; The Milton Prize, 1994. Memberships include: PEN International; Poetry

Society of Am; Western Writers of Am; Century Association; NAACP; Society of American Historians.

DILLARD R(ichard) H(enry) W(ilde), b. 1937, American. Appointments: Instructor in English, University of Virginia, Charlottesville, 1961-64; Contribution Editor, The Hollins Critic, 1966-77; Assisstant Professor, 1964-68, Chairman of Graduate Program in Contemporary Literature and Creative Writing, 1971-, Professor in English, 1974-, Hollins College, Virginia; Vice-President, The Film Journal, NYC, 1973-. Publications: The Day I stopped Dreaming About Barbara Steele and Other Poems, Frankenstein Meets the Space Monster (with G Garret and J Rodenbeck) 1966; the Experience of America: A Book of Readings (ed with L D Rubin), 1969; News of the Nile, The Sounder Few; Essays from the Hollins Critic (editor with G Garret and J R Moore), 1971; After Borges, 1972; The Book of Changes, 1974; Horror Films, 1976; The Greeting: New and Selected Poems, 1981; The First Man On the Sun, 1983; Understanding George Garret, 1988. Address: Box 9761, Hollins College, VA 24020, USA.

DILLINGHAM William Byron, b. 7 Mar 1930, Atlanta, Georgia, USA; Writer; Teacher. m. Elizabeth Joiner, 3 July 1952, 1 son, 2 daughters. Education: BA, 1955, MA, 1956, Emory University; PhD, University of Pennsylvania, 1961. Appointments: Instructor, Emory University, 1956-58, Assistant Professor, Associate Professor, Professor, Charles Howard Candler Professor of American Literature, 1959-, Emory University; Editorial Boards: Nineteenth-Century Literature, Frank Norris Society Journal, South Atlantic Bulletin. Publications: Books: Humor of the Old Southwest, 1965, 3rd Edition, 1994; Frank Norris: Instinct and Art, 1969; An Artist in the Rigging: The Early Work of Herman Melville, 1972; Melville's Short Fiction, 1853-1856, 1977; Melville's Later Novels, 1986; Practical English Handbook, 9th Edition, 1992. Contributions to: Many articles and reviews to such journals as Nineteenth Century Literature; American Literature; Philogical Quarterly; College English; English Studies. Address: 1416 Vistaleaf Drive, Decatur, GA 30033, USA.

DILLON Ellis, b. 1920, Irish. Writer of novels/short stories, children's fiction, plays/screenplays. Appointments: Lecturer in Creative Writing, Trinity College Dublin, 1971-72; Writer in Residence, University College Dublin, 1988. Publications: An Choill Bheo (The Live Forest), 1948; Midsummer Magic, 1950; Oscar agus an Coiste Sen Easog (Oscar and the Six Weasel Coach), 1952; The Lost Island, 1952; Death at Crane's Court, 1953; The San Sebastian, 1953; Sent to His Account, 1954; Ceol ne Coille (The Song of the Forest), 1955; The House on the Shore, 1955; The Wild Little House, 1955; Death in the Quadrangle, 1956; The Island of Horses, 1956; Plover Hill, 1957; The Bitter Glass, 1958; Aunt Bedelia's Cats, 1958; The Singing Cave, 1959; Manna (radio play), 1960. The Head of the Family , 1960; King Big-Ears, 1961; A Pony and a Trap, 1962; The Cat's Opera, 1963; The Coriander, 1963; A Family of Foxes, 1964; Bold John Henebry, 1965; The Sea Wall, 1965; The Lion Cub,1966; A Page of History (play), 1966; The Cruise of the Santa Maria, 1967; The Key, 1967; two stories: The Road to Dunmore and the Key, 1968; The Seals, 1968; Under the Orange Grove, 1968; A Herd of Deer, 1969; The Wise Man on the Mountain, 1969; The Voyage of the Mael Duin, 1969; The King's Room, 1970; The Five Hundred, 1972; Across the Bitter Sea, 1973; Living in Imperial Rome, (in US as Rome under the Emperors), 1975; The Hamish Hamilton Book of Wise Animals, 1975; the Shadow of Vesuvius, 1977; Blood Relations, 1977; the Cat's Opera (play), 1981; Wild Geese, 1981; Inside Ireland, 1982; Down in the World, 1983; Citizen Burke, 1984; The Lucky Bag (editor), 1984; The Horse Fancier, 1985; The Islands of Ghost, 1989; The Children of Bach, 1992. Address: 7 Templmore Avenue, Dublin 6 , Ireland.

DILLON Millicent Gerson, b. 24 May 1925. Writer. m. Murray Lesser, 1 June 1948, 2 daughters. Education: BA, Hunter College, 1944; MA, San Francisco State University, 1966. Publications: Baby Perpetua and Other Stories, 1971; The One in the Back is Medea, novel, 1973; A Little Original Sin: The Life and Work of Jane Bowles, 1981; After Egypt, 1990; The Dance of the Mothers, novel. Contributions to: Southwest Review; Witness; Threepenny Review. Honours: 5 O. Henry Short Story Awards; Best American Short Stories, 1992; Guggenheim Fellowship; National Endowment for the Humanities Fellowship. Memberships: PEN; Authors Guild. Literary Agent: Renee Golden. Address: 72 6th Avenue, San Francisco, CA 94118, USA.

DIMBLEBY David, b. 28 Oct 1938, London England. Broadcaster: Newspaper Proprieter. Josceline Gaskell, 1967, 1 s, 2 d.

Education: Christ Church, Oxford; Universities of Paris and Perugia. Appointments: News Reporter, BBC BRistol, 1960-61; Presenter, Interviewer, various scientific, religious and political programmes, BBC TV 1961-63; Foreign Affairs, Film Reporter and Director, 1964-65; Special Correspondent, CBS News, 1966; Reporter, Panorama, BBC TV, 1967-69, Presenter 1974-77; 1980-81; Presenter, 24 Hours, BBC TV 1969-72; Dimbleby Talk-In, 1972-74; People and Power, 1982; General Election Results Programmes, BBC 1979, 1983; Presenter, This Week, Next Week, BBC TV, 1985-87; Managing Director, Dimbleby Newspaper Group, 1966-86, Chairman, 1986-; Reporter, The White Tribe of Africa, BBC TV, 1979. Publication: An Ocean Apart (with David Reynolds), 1988. Honours: Supreme Documentary Award, 1979; Emmy Award, 1991; Golden Nymph Award, 1991. Address: 14 King Street, Richmond, Surrey, TW9 1NF, England.

DIMBLEBY Jonathon, b. 31 Jul 1944. Freelance Broadcaster; Journalist; Author. m. Bel Mooney, 1968, 1 s, 1 d. Education: BA Honours, Philosophy, University College, London. Appointments: TV and Radio Reporter, BBC Bristol, 1969-70; BBC Radio, World at One, 1970-71; for Thames TV: This Week, 1972-78; TV Eye, 1979; Jonathon Dimbleby in South America, 1979; For Yorkshire TV: series, Jonathon Dimbleby in Evidence: The Police, 1980; The Bomb, 1980; The Eagle and the Bear, 1981; The Cold War Games, 1982; The American Dream, 1984; Four Years On - the Bomb, 1984; First Tuesday (Associate Editor, Presenter), 1982-86; TV AM: Jonathon Dimbleby on Sunday (Presenter/Editor), 1985-86; Thames Television: (Presenter/Reporter) This Week, 1986-88, Series Editor, Witness, documentary series, 1986-88; BBC Radio 4, Chairman, Any Questions, 1987-; BBC 1: On The Record, 1988-93; Radio 4: Any Answers, 1988; Election Call, BBC1 & Radio 4; Any Answers, 1987-; Election Call, BBC1 & Radio 4, 1992; Prince Charles, Documentary Profile, ITV, 1994. Publications: Richard Dimbleby Cancer Fund; Trustee, National Aids Trust; President of CPRE, 1992-. Address: c/o David Higham Associates Ltd, 5 Lower John Street, London W1R 4HA, England.

DIMBLEBY Josceline Rose, b. 1 Feb 1943, Oxford, England. m. 20 Jan 1967, 1 s, 2 d. Appointments: Contributor, Daily Mail, 1976-78; Cookery Editor, Sunday Telegraph, 1982-; Regular Contributor to Country Homes and Interiors, 1986-. Publications: A Taste of Dreams, 1976; Party Pieces, 1977; Cooking For Christmas, 1978; Josceline Dimbleby's Book Of Puddings, Desserts & Savouries, 1979; Cooking With Herbs and Spices, 1979; Curries and Oriental Cookery, 1980; Salads for All Seasons, 1981; Festive Food, 1982; Marvellous Meals with Mince, 1982; Sweet Dreams, 1983; The Josceline Dimbleby Collection, 1984 First Impressions, 1984; Main Attractions, 1985; A Traveller's Tastes, 1986; The Josceline Dimbleby Christmas Book, 1987; The Josceline Dimbleby Book of Entertaining, 1988; The Essential Josceline Dimbleby, 1989; The Cook's Companion, 1991; The Almost Vegetarian Cookbook, 1994; The Christmas Book, 1994. Contributions to: Numerous magazines; various TV programmes. Honours: Andre Simon Memorial Award, 1979; Glenfiddich Cookery Writer of the Year, 1993. Literary Agent: Curtis Brown. Address: 14 King Street, Richmond, Surrey, TW9 1NF, England.

DIMITROFF Pashanko, b. 22 Mar 1924, Stanimaka, Bulgaria. Journalist. m. Margaret Greenwood, 18 Jul 1959, 2 s. Education: Law, University of Sofia, 1943-46; Music, Cello, Academy of Music, Sofia, 1943; Doctor of Law, Faculte de Droit, Paris, France, 1959. Publications: Boris III of Bulgaria, 1986; The Silent Bulgarians, in Bulgarian, 1991; King of Mercy, 1993; Princess Clementine, 1994. Address: 49 Church Road, Richmond, Surrey, TW9 1UA, England.

DIMITROVA Blaga, b. 2 Jan 1922, Byala Slatina, Bulgaria. Poet. Education: Graduated University of Sofia, 1945, Gorky Literary Institute, Moscow, 1951. Appointments include: Vice-President of Bulgaria, from 1992. Publications include: Verses about the Leader, 1950; In the Open, 1954; Expedition into Tomorrow, 1964; Condemned to Love: Poems about Vietnam, 1967; Moments, 1968; Impulses, 1972; Forbidden Sea, 1976; Memory: Poems, 1982; Selected Verses, 1985; Selected Poems, 1986; Labyrinth, 1987; Because the Sea is Black, 1989; The Last Rock Eagle, 1992; Fiction: Journey to Oneself, 1965, 1969; Judgement Day, 1968; Black and White Days, 1975; Face, 1981; Digression: Avalanche, 1981; Play: Doctor Faustina, 1971. Honours include: Honoured Cultural Worker, 1974. Address: c/o Bulgarski pisatel, ul Septemvri 35, 1000 Sofia, Bulgaria.

DIMONT Penelope. See: **MORTIMER Penelope (Ruth)**.

DINAN Carolyn, b. England. Writer and Illustrator. Education: Chelsea School of Art; Graduate Study, Royal College of Art. Appointments: Visiting Lecturer in Illustration, Chelsea School of Art, London. Publications: Self-illustrated children's books: The Lunch Box, 1983; Skipper and Sam, 1984; Say Cheese! 1985, 86; Ada and the Magic Basket, 1987; Born Lucky, 1987; illustrator for: Ducks and Dragons: Poems for Children (editor Gene Kemp), 1980; The Clock Tower Ghost (by Gene Kemp), 1981; Nancy Nutall and the Mongrel (by Catherine Cookson), 1982; June Counsel, 1984; Owl and Billy (by Martin Waddell), 1986; Robert Goes To Fetch a Sister (by Dorothy Edwards), 1986; Address: Chelsea School of Art, Manresa Road, London SW3 6LS, England.

DINNERSTEIN Leonard, b. 1934, USA. Writer; Historian. Appointments: Instructor, New York Institute of Technology, New York City, 1960-65; Assistant Professor, Fairleigh Dickinson University, Teaneck, New Jersey, 1967-70; Associate Professor, 1970-72, Professor of American History, Univesity of Arizona, Tucson, 1972-. Publications: The Leo Frank Case, 1968; The Aliens (with F C Jaher), 1970, as Uncertain Americans, 1977; American Vistas (with K T Jackson), 1971, 6th Edition, 1995; Antisemitism in the United States, 1971; Jews in the South (with M D Palsson), 1973; Decisions and Revisions (with J Christie), 1975; Ethnic Americans: A History of Immigration and Assimilation (with D M Reimers), 1975, 3rd Edition, 1988; Natives and Strangers (with R L Nichols and D M Reimers), 1979, 2nd Edition, 1990; America and the Survivors of the Holocaust, 1982; Uneasy at Home, 1987; Antisemitism in America, 1994. Address: 5821 East 7th Street, Tucson, AZ 85711, USA.

DIORIO Mary Ann Lucia (Lucia St John), b. 11 Nov 1945, Norristown, Pennsylvania, USA. Freelance Writer; Businesswoman. m. Dominic A Diorio, 25 Oct 1969, 2 daughters. Education: BA, Immaculata College, 1967; MA, Middlebury College, 1968; MPhil, 1974, PhD, 1977, University of Kansas. Publications: Selling Yourself On You: Balancing Your Budget God's Way; Dating Etiquette for Christian Teens; From Feminism to Freedom. Contributions to: The Saturday Evening Post; The Atlantic City Press; Human Events; Decision; Christian Parenting; Pentecostal Evangel; Moody Magazine. Honours: Poetry Award; AMY Writing Award; 5th Place, Short Story Contest, National Writers Club. Memberships: Lambda Iota Tau; Founder, Director, The New Jersey Society of Christian Writers; National Writers Club; Society of Children's Book Writers. Address: PO Box 748, Millville, NJ 08332, USA.

DISCH Thomas Michael (Leonie Hargrave, Dobbin Thorpe), b. 1940, American. Poet; Librettist; Lyricist; Freelance Writer, Lecturer, 1964-; Theatre Critic, The Nation Magazine, New York City; Former Draftsman, Copywriter. Publications include: The Prisoner, 1969; Highway Sandwiches (poetry with Marilyn Hacker and Charles Platt), 1970; The Right Way to Figure Plumbing (poetry), 1971; The Ruins of Earth: An Anthology of the Immediate Future (editor) 1971; 334, 1972; Bad Moon Rising (editor), 1973; Getting Into Death (short stories), 1973; The New Improved Sun : An Anthology of Utopian Science Fiction (editor), 1975; Clara Reeve (as Leonie Hargrave), 1975; New Constellations (with Charles Naylor), 1976; Strangeness (with C Naylor), 1977; On Wings of Song, 1979; Triplicity (omnibus), 1980; Fundamental Disch (short stories), 1980; Neighboring Lives (historical novel with Chales Naylor), 1981; ABCDEFGHIJKLMNOPQRSTUVWXYZ (poetry) 1981; Orders of the Retina (poetry), 1982; Burn This (poetry), 1982; The Man Who Had No Idea (short stories), 1982; Frankenstein (libretto, Opera by Gregory Sandow), 1982; Ringtime, 1983; The Businessman: A Tale of Terror, 1984; Torturing Mr Amberwell, 1985; The Brave Litle Toaster (children's book), 1986; Amnesia (computer-inter active novel), 1986; The M D , 1992; The Businessman, 1993. Address: 31 Union Square W No 11E, New York, NY 10003, USA.

DITTMERS Manuel, b. 15 Apr 1961, Berlin, Germany. Author; Economist. Education: LSH-Holzminder; Studio School, Cambridge; Mander Portman Woodward, London; Eurocentre Paris; University of Nice; University of Lille; University of Buckingham; BA, MEd, US International University; MSc, London School of Economics. Appointments: Fouder of World Wide Peace, 1984; Founder of World Wide Peace Animal Rights, 1987; Responsible For Middle East Peace Peace Plan, 1986-1991; Amazon and Jahara World Park Project, 1987; Mediterranean Environmental Fund, 1987; World Citizen Passport, 1988. Publications: Charter of World Wide Peace, 1984; The Green Party in West Germany,1986; World and Environment, 1989; Impressions of Fuerteventura, 1990; European Poems, 1990. Honours:

FRSA, 1990; Phi Delta Kappa. Memberships: PEN; British Institute of Management; Fellow, Institute of Directors; Convocation of University of London; Chairman of Board of World Wide Peace; Royal Ocean Racing Club; Silverstone Racing Club. Address: World-Wide-Peace, PO Box 55-10-42, Hamburg 55, Germany.

DITTON James, See: **CLARK Douglas.**

DIVINE Robert A(lexander), b. 1929, USA. Writer; Historian. Appointments: Instructor, 1954-57, Assistant Professor, 1957-61, Associate Professor, 1961-63, Professor of History, 1963-80, George W Littlefield Professor in American History, 1981-, University of Texas, Austin; Fellow, Institute for Advanced Study in Behavioral Sciences, Stanford, California, 1962-63. Publications: American Immigration Policy 1924-52, 1957; American Foreign Policy, 1960; The Illusion of Neutrality, 1962; The Reluctant Belligerent, 1965, 1979; Second Chance, 1967; The Age of Insecurity, 1968; Twentieth Century America (with J A Garraty), 1968; Roosevelt and World War II, 1969; Causes and Consequences of World War II, 1969; American Foreign Policy since 1945, 1969; The Cuban Missile Crisis, 1971, 1988; Foreign Policy and US Presidential Elections 1940-1960, 2 volumes, 1974; Since 1945, 1975, 1979, 1985; Blowing on the Wind, 1978; Eisenhower and the Cold War, 1981; Exploring the Johnson Years, 1981; America: Past and Present (with T H Breen, G M Frederickson, R H Williams), 1984, 1987, 1991, 1995; The Johnson Years: Volume Two, 1987; The Sputnik Challenge, 1993; The Johnson Years: Volume Three, 1994. Address: Department of History, University of Texas, Austin, TX 78712, USA.

DIVINSKY Nathan J, b. 29 Oct 1925, Winnipeg, Canada. Mathematician. 3 daughters. Education: BSc, University of Manitoba, 1946; SM, 1947, PhD, 1950, University of Chicago, USA. Literary appointments: Editor, Canadian Chess Chat, 1959-74. Publications: Around the Chess World in 80 Years, 1963; Rings and Radicals, 1965; Linear Algebra, 1970; Warriors of the Mind (with R Keene), 1988; Chess Encyclopedia, 1990; Life Maps of the GreatChessmasters, 1994. Memberships: Life Master, ACBL (Bridge League); President, Commonwealth Chess Association, 1988-94; Canada's Representative to FIDE (World Chess Federation), 1987-1994. Address: 5689 McMaster Road, Vancouver, British Columbia, Canada V6T 1K1.

DIVOK Mario J, b. 22 Sep 1944, Benus, Czechoslovakia. Real Estate Broker; Author. m. Eva Pytlova, 1990, 1 d. Publications: The Relations, 1975; The Voice, 1975; The Wind of Changes, 1978; Equinox, 1978; The Collection, 1978; I Walk The Earth, 1980; The Blind Man, 1980; Looking For a Road to The Earth, 1983; The Birthday, 1984; Forbidden Island Complete Works: Two, 1986; Selected Work, 1993; MPA, California State University. Honours include: Schlossar Award For Play, Switzerland, 1980; Potpourri International Award, 1980; Winner, One-Act Play Competition, One Way Theatre, San Francisco, 1980; Orange County Poetry Contest, Laguna Poets, 1981; World of Poetry, 1990. Literary Agent: Martin Littlefield. Address: 5 Misty Meadow, Irvine, CA 92715, USA.

DIXON Dougal, b. 1947. Author; Freelance Writer. Appointments: Researcher, Editor, Mitchell-Beazley Ltd, 1973-78; Blandford Press, 1978-80; Part-time Tutor, Earth Sciences, Open University, 1976-78; Chairman, Bournemouth Science Fiction and Fantasy Group, 1981-82; Freelance Writer, 1980-. Publications: Doomsday Planet (comic strip), 1980; After Man: a Zoology for the Future, 1981; Discovering Earth Sciences, 1982; Science World: Geology, 1982; Science World: Geography, 1983; Picture Atlas: Mountains, 1984; Picture Atalas: Forests, 1984; Picture Atlas: Deserts, 1984; Find Out About Prehistoric Reptiles, 1984; Find Out About Jungles, 1984; The Age of Dinosaurs (with Jane Burton), 1984; Nature Detective Serires: Minerals Rocks and Fossils, 1984; Time Machine 7: Ice Age Explorer, 1985; Secrets of the Earth, 1986; Find Out About Dinosaurs, 1986. Address: c/o Hamlyn, 69 London Road, Twickenham, Middlesex TW1 3SB, England.

DIXON Larry, b. Tulsa, Oklahoma, USA. Writer; Artist. m. Mercedes Lackey, 14 Dec 1990. Publications: Arrows of the Queen, 1987; Arrow's Flight, 1987; Arrow's Fall, 1988; Oathbound, Vows and Honor Book One, 1988; Oathbreakers, Vows and Honor Book Two, 1989; Magic's Pawn, The Last Herald-Mage Book One, 1989; Reap the Whirlwind, 1989; Magic's Promise, The Last Herald-Mage Book Two, 1990; Knight of Ghosts and Shadows (with Ellen Guon), 1990; Magic's Price, The Last Herald-Mage Book Three, 1990; By the Sword, 1991; Winds of Fate, 1991; The Elvenbane (with André Norton), 1991; Sacred Ground; Diane Tregarde Investigations series: Burning Water, 1989; Children of the Night, 1990; Jinx High, 1991; Triangle Park; Arcanum

101; Serrated Edge series: Born to Run, 1992; Wheels of Fortune (with Mark Shepherd), 1992; When the Bough Breaks (with Holly Lisle), 1992; The Mage-Wars; The Black Gryphon; The Eric Banyon books: Summoned to Tourney (with Ellen Guon); Beyond World's End (with Ellen Guon); The Mage-Wind books: Winds of Change, 1992; Winds of Fury, 1993; The Bardic Voices series: The Lark and the Wren, 1992; The Robin and the Kestrel; The Eagle and the Nightingale; Numerous short stories, novelettes, novellas. Honours: Arrows of the Queen selected for Best Books for Young Adults, American Library Association. Membership: Science Fiction and Fantasy Writers of America. Address: PO Box 8309, Tulsa, OK 74101, USA.

DIXON Roger, (John Christian, Charles Lewis), b. 1930. Author; Playwright. Publications: over 50 radio plays and series; novels: Noah II, 1970; Christ on Trial, 1973; The Messiah, 1974; Five Gates to Annegeddon (as John Christian), 1975; The Cain Factor (as Charles Lewis), 1975; Going to Jerusalem, 1977; Georgiana, 1984; Return to Nebo, 1991; musical: The Commander of New York (with Phil Medley and Basil Bova), 1987. Adddress: Badgers, Warren Lane, Croos-in-Hand, Heathfield, Sussex, England.

DIXON Stephen, b. 6 June 1936, New York City, New York, USA. Fiction Writer; University Teacher. m. Anne Frydman, 17 Jan 1982, 2 daughters. Education: BA, City College of New York, 1958. Publications: No Relief, 1976; Work, 1977; Too Late, 1978; Quite Contrary, 1979; 14 Stories, 1980; Movies, 1983; Time to Go, 1984; Fall and Rise, 1985; Garbage, 1988; Love and Will, 1989; The Play and Other Stories, 1989; All Gone, 1990; Friends, 1990; Frog, 1991; Long Made Short, 1993; The Stories of Stephen Dixon, 1994; Interstate, 1995. Contributions to: 400 short stories to magazines and journals including Atlantic; Harper's; Esquire; Playboy; Paris Review; Triquarterly; Western Humanities Review; Ambit; Bananas; Boulevard; Glimmer Train; Partisan Review; O. Henry Prize Stories, 1977, 1982, 1993; Best American Stories, 1993. Honours: Stegner Fiction Fellowship, Stanford, 1964-65; National Endowment of the Arts, fiction, 1974-75, 1990-91; Award in Literature, American Academy-Institute of Arts and Letters, 1983; John Train Prize, Paris Review, 1984; John Simon Guggenheim Fellowship, 1985-86; Fiction Finalist for Frog, NBA, 1991; Fiction Finalist for Frog, PEN Faulkner Prize, 1992. Literary Agent: Kim Witherspoon and Associates, 157 W 57th Street, Suite 700, New York, NY 10019, USA. Address: 1315 Boyce Avenue, Baltimore, MD 21204, USA.

DJERASSI Carl, b. 29 Oct 1923, Vienna, Austria. University Professor; Chemist; Writer. m. Diane Wood Middlebrook, 20 June 1985, 1 son. Education: AB summa cum laude, Kenyon College, 1942; PhD, University of Wisconsin, 1945. Publications: Optical Rotatory Dispersion, 1959; Steroid Reactions, 1963; Mass Spectrometry of Organic Compounds (with H Budzikiewicz and D H Williams), 1967; The Politics of Contraception, 1979; The Futurist and Other Stories, 1988; Cantor's Dilemma, novel, 1989, 1991; Steroids Made It Possible, 1990; The Clock Runs Backward, poetry, 1991; The Pill, Pygmy Chimps, and Degas' Horse, autobiography, 1992; The Bourbaki Gambit, novel, 1994; From the Lab into the World, collected essays, 1994; Marx, Verschiedeu (in German), Novel, 1994. Contributions to: Kenyon Review; Southern Review; Grand Street; New Letters; Exquisite Corpse; Michigan Quarterly Review; South Dakota Review; Frank; Midwest Quarterly. Literary Agents: Michael Carlisle, William Morris Agency Inc, 1350 Avenue of the Americas, New York, NY 10019; Andrew Numberg Associates, 45-47 Clerkenwell Green, London EC1R 0HT, England. Address: Department of Chemistry, Stanford University, Stanford, CA 94305, USA.

DJOMIN Andrey A, b. 2 Dec 1925, Moscow, Russia. Economist; Educator. m. Margarita Djemina, 30 Apr 1950, 1 son. Education: Faculty of Economics, St Petersburg University, 1953-58; Candidate of Economics, 1961; Doctor of Economics, 1968. Publications: State Nonopolistic Capitalism, 1983; Federal Republic of Germany Today, 1973; Federal Republic of Germany: Georaphy Population and Economy, 1982; Economies of Different Velosity, 1990; A History of Political Economy of Capitalism, 1992. Contributions to: More than 200 articles in various Magazines and Journals. Honours: Award at St Petersburg University. Address: Faculty of Economics 62, Chaikovskogo str, 191194 St Petersburg, Russia.

DOBAI Peter, b. 12 Aug 1944, Budapest, Hungary. Writer. m. (1) Donatella Failoni, 1972, (2) Maria Mate, 1992. Education: Sailor, Mate, 1963-65; Teacher's Diploma, Philosophy, Italian, Faculty of Humanities, Budapest, 1970. Appointments: Scriptwriter, Dramaturgist, Assisstant

Director, Mafilm, 1970. Publications: Film scripts: Punitive Expedition, 1971; Publications: Film scripts: Punitive Expedition, 1971; Csontvary, The Painter, 1979; Mephisto, 1980; Colonel Redl, 1983; Hanussen, The Prophet, 1984; Consciousness, 1987; Rembrandt van Rijn (Life and Works), 1992; books of poetry: Kilvoglas egy őszi erődből, 1973; Egy arc modosulasai, 1976; Lying on the Back, 1978; Pitfalls of Eden, 1985; Selected Poems, 1989; novels: Csontmolnarok, 1974; Belonging Life, 1975; Avalanche, 1980; Wilderness, 1982; A birodalom ezredese, 1985; Arch, 1988; Fly-Wheel, 1989; short story collections: Jatek a szobakkal, 1976; Chessboard With Two Figures, 1978; 1964 -Island, diary, 1977; Archaic Torso, scripts, essays, 1983. Contributions to: Essays, articles and reviews to magazines and journals. Honours: Joszef Attila Prize, 1976; Several Awards, Hungarian Literary Foundation and Minister of Culture; Best Filmscript for Mephisto, Cannes Film Festival, 1981; Balazs Bela Prize for scripts, 1990. Memberships: Executive Board, Hungarian Writers Association, Leading Member, Prose Committee: Chamber of Writers; Hungarian Academy of Artists; Hungarian PEN Club; Association of Hungarian Film and Television Artists; Professional Feature Film Advisory Board; Hungarian Seaman's Association. Address: Kozraktar u 12 B, 1093 Budapest, Hungary.

DOBEREINER Peter Arthur Bertram, b. 3 Nov 1925, England. Golf Correspondent; Author. m. Betty Evelyn Jacob, 20 Jan 1951, 2 s. 2 d. Education: Lincoln College, Oxford. Appointments: East Sussex Gazette, Oxford Times, News Chronicle, Daily Express, Daily Mail, The Guardian, 1949-65; The Obsrever, 1965-. Publications: The Book of Golf Disasters, 1983; the Game With a Hole in It, 1970, 1973; The Glorious world of Golf, 1973; The World of Golf, 1982; Arnold Palmers Complete Book of Putting, 1986; Golf Ruels Explained, 1980; Down the 19th Fairway, 1982; Tony Jacklin's Golf Secrets, 1982; Stroke Hole or Match, 1976; The Golfers, 1982; the 50 Greatest Post-war Golfers, 1985; Preferred Lies, 1987. Contributions to: Numerous journals and magazines. Honours: Screen Writers Guild Award, 1962; MacGregor Writing Awards, 1977; Donald Ross Award, 1985; Irish Golf Fellowship Award, 1987. Memberships: West Kent Golf Club; Bally Bunion, Ireland; Honorary Member, American Society of Golf Course Architects. Address: Chelsfield Hill House, Pratts Bottom, Nr Orpington, Kent BR6 7SL, England.

DOBSON Andrew Nicholas Howard, b. 15 Apr 1957, Doncaster, England. Politics Lecturer. Education: BA 1st Class, Politics, Reading University, 1979. DPhil Politics, Oxford University, 1983. Appointments: Editorial Board, Environmental Values, 1991-; Editorial Board, Environmental Politics, 1991-; Editorial Board, Anarchist Studies, 1991-. Publications: Introduction to the Politics and Philosophy of José Ortega y Gasset, 1989; Green Political Thought, 1990; The Green Reader, 1991; The Politics of Nature: Explorations in Green Political Theory (edited with Paul Lucardie), 1993; Jean-Paul Sartre and the Politics of Reason: A Theory of History, 1993. Contributions to: Numerous articles and book reviews to magazines and journals. Honours: Spanish Government Scholar, 1983-84; ERSC Postdoctoral Fellow, 1984-87; Appointed to Chair in Politics, Keele University, 1993. Address: Politics Department, Keele University, Keele, Staffs ST5 5BG, England.

DOBSON Julia Lissaant, (Julia Tugendhat), b. 1941, Britain. Publications: The Children of Charles I, 1975; The Smallest Man in England, 1977; Mountbatten Sailor Hero, Children of the Tower, 1978; They Were at Waterloo, 1979; The Ivory Poachers: A Crisp Twins Adventure, The Tomb Robbers, 1981; The Wreck Finders, The Animal Rescuers, 1982; Danger in the Magic Kingdom, 1983; The Chinese Puzzle, 1984; As Julia Tugendhat: What Teenagers Can Tell Us About Divorce and Step Families, 1990; The Adoption Triangle, 1992. Address: 35 Westbourne Park Road, London W2, England.

DOBSON Rosemary (de Brissac), b. 18 June 1920, Sydney, New South Wales, Australia. Poet; Editor; Translator. m. A T Bolton, 1951, 2 s, 1 d. Education: Frensham, Mittagong, NSW. Publications: In A Convex Mirror, 1944; The Ship of Ice & Other Poems, 1948; Child with a Cockatoo and Other Poems, 1955; Poems, 1963; Cock Crow, 1965; Selected Poems, 1973 revised edition, 1980; Greek Coins: A Sequence of Poems, 1977; Over the Frontier, 1978; The Three Fates and Other Poems, 1984; Co Translator, Moscow Trefoil, 1975; Seven Russian Poets, 1979; Collected Poems, 1991; Untold Lives, A Sequence of Poems, 1992. Honours: Patrick White Award, 1984; Officer, Order of Australia, 1987. Address: 61 Stonehaven Crescent, Deakin, Canberra ACT 2600, Australia.

DOBYNS Stephen, b. 1941. Poet; Writer. Publications include: 15 Novels; 7 Volumns of Poetry; Cemetery Nights, 1987; A Boat of the Coast, 1987; Body Traffic, 1990; The Wrestlers Cruel Study, 1993; Saratoga Backtalk, 1994. Honour: Melville Care Award, 1988. Address: Dept of English, Syracuse University, Syracuse, NY 13244, USA.

DOCHERTY John. See: **SILLS-DOCHERTY Jonathon John.**

DOCTOROW Edgar Lawrence, b. 6 Sep 1931, New York, New York, USA. Writer. m. Helen Setzer, 20 Aug 1954, 1 s, 2 d. Education: AB, Kenyon College, 1952; Graduate Study, Columbia University, 1952-53. Appointments: Script Reader, Columbia Pictures, 1959-59; Senior Editor, New American Library, 1960-64; Editor-in-Chief, Dial Press, 1964-69; Publisher, 1969; Writer-in-Residence, University of California, Irvine, 1969-70; Member of Faculty, Sarah Lawrence College, 1971-78; Creative Writing Fellow, Yale school of Drama, 1974-75; Visiting Senior Fellow, Council on the Humanities, Princeton University, 1980; Glucksman Professor of American and English Letters, New York University, 1987-. Publications: Welcome to Hard Times, 1960; Big as Life, 1966; The Book of Daniel, 1971; Ragtime, 1975; Drinks Before dinner (play), 1979; Loon Lake, 1980; Lives of the Poets, 1984; World's Fair, 1985; Billy Bathgate, 1989; Jack London, Hemingway and the Constitution, 1993; The Waterworks, 1994. Honours: Guggenheim Fellowship, 1973; Arts and Letters Award, American Academy and National Institute For Arts and Letters for Ragtime, 1976; National Book Critics Circle Award for Ragtime 1976 and Billy Bathgate, 1989; National Book Award for the World's Fair, 1985; PEN/Faulkner Award for Billy Bathgate, 1990; Howells Medal, American Academy and Institute for Arts and Letters for Most Distinguished Work of Fiction in Five Years, for Billy Bathgate, 1990. Memberships: PEN, American Center; Writers Guild of America; Authors Guild; Century Association. Literary Agent: Arlene Donovan, ICM, 40 West 57th Street, New York, NY 10022, USA. Address: c/o Random House, 201 East 50th Street, New York, NY 10019, USA.

DODD Philip William, b. 24 Nov 1957, Ipswich, Suffolk, England. Publisher. m. Joanna Louise Gibbon, 30 July 1988. Education: Jesus College, Oxford, 1976-80; BA, Modern Languages, 1980; MA (Oxon), 1984. Career: Publisher, Longman Group Limited, 1984; Publisher, Octopus Group Limited, 1989; Publisher, Virgin Publishing Ltd, 1992; Freelance Journalist; Freelance Copywriter. Contributions to: International Musician; Publishing News. Honours: Guardian National Student Press Award for Best Use of Graphics, 1980; Editorial Fellow, Jerusalem Book Fair, 1985. Memberships: Groucho Club, Former Chairman, Society of Young Publishers. Address: 5 Sovereign Mews, Pearson Street, London E2 8ER, England.

DODSON Daniel B, b. 21 Mar 1918, Portland, Oregon, USA. Professor of English (retired). Education: BA, Reed College, 1941; MA, 1947; PhD, 1952, Columbia University. Publications: The Man Who Ran away, 1960; Scala Dei, 1962; On A Darling Plain, 1964; Looking For Zo, 1976; Dancers in the Dark, 1978; The Dance of Love, 1958; The Last Command, 1989; Malcolm Lowry (literary study), 1958. Contributions to: Short Stories in Esquire Story; various scholarly journals. Literary Agent: Harold Ober, New York, USA. Address: Place Jean Aicard, Sollies Ville, 83210 Sollies Point, France.

DOHERTY Berlie, b. 6 Nov 1943, Liverpool, England. Novelist; Playwright; Poet. m. Gerard Doherty, 17 Dec 1966, 1 s, 2 d. (div 1993). Education: BA Hons, English, Durham University, 1964; Post-Graduate Certificate in Social Studies, 1965, Liverpool University; Post-Graduate Certificate of Education, Sheffield University, 1976. Appointments: Member, Literature Panel, Yorkshire Arts Association, 1986-87; Chairperson, Arvon Foundation, Lumb Bank, 1988-1993; Deputy Chairperson, National Association of Writers in Education, 1988. Publications: Requiem, novel, 1991; The Vinegar Jar, novel, 1994; children's books: How Green You Are, 1982; The Making of Fingers Finnigan, 1983; White Peak Farm, 1984; Children of Winter, 1985; Granny Was A Buffer Girl, 1986; Tilly Mint Tales, 1986; Tilly Mint and the Dodo, 1988; Paddiwak and Cosy, 1988; Tough Luck, 1988; Spellhorn, 1989; Dear Nobody, 1990; Snowy, 1992; Big, Bulgy Fat Black Slug, 1993; Old Father Christmas, 1993; Street Child, 1993; Walking on Air, childrens poetry, 1993; Willa and Old Miss Annie, 1994; The Snake-Store, 1995; The Golden Bird, 1995; The Magical Bicycle, 1995. Contributions to: Numerous reviews, some articles to The Times Educational Supplement; reviews, articles to Yorkshire Art Scene. Honours: For Granny Was A Buffer Girl: Carnegie Medal, 1987; Boston Globe Horn Honor, 1987; Burnley Children's Book of the Year Award, 1987; Bronze Award For White Peak Farm, International Film and Television, 1988; Dear Nobody, Carnegie Medal, 1991; Snowy, Children's Award, Picture Book Section, 1993; Dear Nobody, Dramatised Writer's Guild of Great Britain Children's Play Award, 1994; Numerous shortlists for Granny was a Buffer Girl, Paddiwak and Cosy, Snowy, Street Child and Dear Nobody; Numerous short stories published in anthologies and BBC; Numerous plays performed, theatre, BBC, radio, television. Memberships: Arvon Foundation. Literary Agent: Gina Pollinger (Murray Pollinger). Address: 222 Old Brompton Road, London, England.

DOLL Mary Aswell, b. 4 Jun 1940, New York City, New York, USA. Professor of English. m. Willaim Elder Doll Jr, 25 Jun 1966, 1 s. Education: BA, Connecticut College, New London, 1962; MA, Johns Hopkins University, Baltimore, Maryland, 1970; PhD, Syracuse University, Syracuse, New York, 1980. Appointments: Assisstant Professor, State University of New York, Oswego, 1978-84; Lecturer, University of Redlands, California, 1985088; Assisstant Professor, Loyola University, 1988; Visiting Assisstant Professor, Tulane University, 1988; Associate Professor, Our Lady of Holy Cross College, 1989-. Publications: Rites of Story: The Old Man at Play, 1987; Beckett and Myth: An Archetypal Approach, 1988; In The Shadow of the Giant: Thomas Wolfe, 1988; Walking and Rocking, 1989; Joseph Campbell and the Power of the Wilderness, 1992; Stoppard's Theatre of Unknowing, 1993. Contributions to: The Temple Symbol in Scripture, to Soundings, 1987; The Demeter Myth in Beckett, to Journal of Beckett Studies, 1988. Honours: In the Shadow selected as 1 of Choice's Outstanding Books, 1989; Sears-Roebuck Teaching Excellence Award. Memberships: Modern Language Association; Board of Directors, Thomas Wolfe Society; American Academy of English. Address: 69 Belle Grove, Destrehan, LA 70047, USA.

DOMARADZKI Théodore Felix (Felice), b. 27 Oct 1910, Warsaw, Poland. University Professor (retired); Director General of Institute of Comparative Civilization. m. Maria Dobija, 20 Apr 1954. Education: Diploma, Political Science, Warsaw, 1963; MA, Warsaw University, 1939; LittD, Rome University, 1941. Career: Member, Doctoral Examination Commissions, Literature: University of Ottawa, Canada, 1950-53; University of Montreal, 1950-76; Editor-in-Chief, Slavic and East European Studies/Etudes Slaves et Est-Européennes, Montreal-Quebec, 1956-76; Director-General, Institute of Comparative Civilization, Montreal. Publications: Le Culte de la Vierge Marie et le Catholicisme de C K Norwid, 1961; La réalité du mal chez C Baudelaire et C Norwid, 1973; Les post-Romantiques polonais, 1973; Le symbolisme et l'universalisme de C K Norwid, 1974; Personalités ethniques au Québec, 1991; Essays include: Norwid, Poet of Christian Civilization, 1984; Echos romantiques et les musées littéraires et maisons d'auteurs au Canada, 1990. Contributions to: as Felice, Journals and encyclopaedias. Honours: Order of Merit, Polish Literature, University of Lublin, 1969; Order of Canada, 1989; Award of Merit, Canadian Multilingual Press Federation, 1991; Commemorative Medal, Literary Society of Warsaw, 1992. Memberships: PEN Club International, Quebec Section; Société des Ecrivains Canadiens; Polish Scientific Society, London; Société Historique et Littéraire Polonaise, Paris; Former Vice-President, Honorary Life Member: Canadian Association of Slavists; Canadian Society for Comparative Study of Civilizations; Former Vice-President, Quebec Ethnic Press Association; Polish Institute of Arts and Sciences in Canada; Istituto Italiano di Cultura. Address: 6100 Deacon Rd 4E, Montreal, Quebec, Canada H3S 2V6.

DONAGHUE Bernard (Baron), b. 1934. Appointments: Editorial Staff, The Economist, London, 1959-60; Senior Research Officer, Political and Economic Planning (PEP), London, 1960-63; Senior Lecturer, Politics, London School of Economics, 1963-74; Senior Policy Adviser to The Prime Minister 1974-79; Director, Economist Intelligence Unit, London, 1979-81; Assisstant Editor, The Times, London, 1981-82; Head of Research, Kleinworth, Grieveson and Company, 1982-. Publications: Oxford poetry, 1956; British Politics and the American Revolution, 1963; The People into Parliament (co-author), 1964; Herbert Morrison, Portrait of a Politician (co-author), 1973; Prime Minister, 1987. Address: 71 Ebury Mews West, London SW1W 9QA W5, England.

DONAGHUE Denis, b. 1928, Ireland. Writer (literature). Literary Appointments: Henry James Professor of English and American Letters, New York University. Publications: The Third Voice: Modern British and American Verse Drama, 1959; Conoisseurs of Chaos: Ideas of Order in Modern American Literature, 1965; An Honoured Guest: New Essays on W B Yeats (with J R Mulryne), 1965; Swift Revisited,

1968; The Ordinary Universe: Soundings in Modern Literature, 1968; Jonathan Swift: A Critical Introduction, 1969; Emily Dickinson, 1969; William Butler Yeats, 1971; Jonathan Swift: A Critical Anthology, 1971; Memoirs, by W B Yeats, 1973; Thieves of Fire, 1973; The Sovereign Ghost: Studies in Imagination, 1976; Ferocious Alphabets, 1981; The Ants Without Mystery, 1983; Being Modern Together, 1991; The Pure Good of Theory, 1992; The Old Moderns; Warrenpoint, 1993. Contributions to: New York Review of Books. Address: Department of English, New York University, New York, NY 10003, USA.

DONALD David, b. 1 Oct 1920, Goodman, Mississippi, USA. m. Aida Di Pace, 1955, 1 son. Education: AB, Millsaps College; AM, PhD, University of Illinois. Appointment: Professor of History. Publications: Lincoln's Herndon, 1948; Divided We Fought, 1952; The American Civil War & Social Process, 1960; Charles Sumner & The Coming of the Civil War, 1960; The Nation in Crisis 1961-1877, 1969; Gone for a Soldier, 1975; Liberty & Union, 1978; Look Homeward: A Life of Thomas Wolfe, 1987. Honours include: Pulitzer Prize, 1961, 1988. Memberships: Am Historical Association; Society of American Historians; Southern Historical Association, President 1969-70. Address: PO Box 158, Lincoln, Center, MA 01773, USA.

DONALDSON Gordon, b. 1913. Writer (History). Appointments: Assisstant Keeper, Scottish Record Office, 1938-47; Lecturer, 1947-55, Reader, 1955-63, Professor, 1963-79, Emeritus Professor of Scottish History and Palaeography, University of Edinburgh, 1979-. Publications: The Making of the Scottish Prayer Book 1637, 1954; The Register of the Privy Seal of Scotland, Vols V-VIII, 1957-82; Shetland Life Under Earl Patrick, 1958; Scotland: Church and Nation Through Sixteen Centuries, 1960, 1972; The Scottish Reformation, 1960, 1972; Scotland: James V to James VII, 1965, 1978; The Scots Overseas, 1966; Nothwards by Sea, 1966, 1978; Scottish Kings, 1967, 1977; Memoirs of Sir James Melville, 1969; The First Trial of Mary, Queen of Scots, 1969; Scottish Historical Documents, 1970; Who's Who in Scottish History, 1974; Mary, Queen of Scots, 1974; Scotland: The Shaping of a Nation, 1974, 1980; Dictionary of Scottish History, 1977; All the Queen's Men, 1983; Isles of Home, 1983; Scottish Church History, 1985; The Faith of the Scots, 1990; A Northern Commonwealth, Scotland and Norway, 1990. Honour: CBE, 1988. Address: 6 Pan Ha' Dysert, Fife, KY1 2TL, Scotland.

DONALDSON Stephen Reeder (Reed Stephens), b. 13 May 1947, Cleveland, Ohio, USA. Writer. 1 son, 1 daughter. Education: BA, English, Wooster College, 1968; MA, Kent State University, 1971. Literary Appointments: Associate Instructor, Ghost Ranch Writers Workshops, 1973-77; Contributing Editor, Journal of the Fantastic in the Arts. Publications: Lord Foul's Bane, 1977; The IllEarth War, 1977; The Power That Preserves, 1977; The Wounded Land, 1980; The One Tree, 1982; White Gold Wielder, 1983; Daughter of Regals, 1984; The Mirror of Her Dreams, 1986; A Man Rides Through, 1987; The Real Story, 1991; Forbidden Knowledge, 1991; A Dark and Hungry God Arises, 1992; The Gap Into Madness: Chaos and Order, 1994; As Reed Stephens: The Man Who Killed His Brother, 1980; The Man Who Risked His Partner, 1984; The Man Who Tried to Get Away, 1990. Honours: Best Novel, British Fantasy Society, 1979; Best New Writer, John W Campbell, 1979; Honorary DLitt, College of Wooster, 1993. Literary Agent: Howard Morhaim, New York, USA. Address: c/o Howard Morhaim, 175 Fifth Avenue, New York, NY 10010, USA.

DONIGER Wendy, Professor of History of Religions, University of Chicago, USA. Publications include: Asceticism & Eroticism in the Mythology of Siva, 1973; Hindu Myths: A Sourcebook, 1975; Women, Androgynes, & Other Mythical Beasts, 1980; The Critical Study of Sacred Texts (ed), 1981; Tales of Sex & Violence, 1985; Dreams, Illusion & Other Realities, 1984; Other Peoples' Myths, 1988. Contributions to: New York Review of Books. Address: Divinity School, University of Chicago, 1025-35 East 58th Street, Chicago, IL 60637-1577, USA.

DONKIN Nance (CLare), b. 1915, Australia. Children's Fiction Writer; Journalist. Appointments: Journalist, Daily Mercury, Maitland, Morning Herald, Newcastle; President, Children's Book Council, Victoria, 1968-76. Publications: Araluen Adeventures, 1946; No Medals For Meg, 1947; Julie Stands By, 1948; Blue Ribbon Beth, 1951; The Australian's Children's Annual, 1963; Sheep, 1967; Sugar, 1967; An Emancipist, 1968; A Currency Lass, 1969; House By the Water, 1969; An Orphan, 1970; Johnny Neptune, 1971; The Cool Man, 1974; A Friend For Petros, 1974; Margaret Catchpole, 1974; Patchwork Grandmother, 1975; Green Christmas, 1976; Yellowgum Girl, 1976; A

Handful of Ghosts, 1976; The Best of the Bunch, 1978; The Maidens of Pefka, 1979; Nini, 1979; Stranger and Friend, 1983; we of the Never retold for Children, 1983; Two At Sullivan Bay, 1985; Blackout, 1987; A Family Affair, 1988; The Women Were There, 1988; Always a Lady, 1990. Honours: AM, Member of Order, Austalia, 1986; Alice Award, Society Women Writers, Australia, 1990 for Distinguished Contribution to Australian Literature. Memberships: FAW, (Fellowship Australian Writers); ASA, (Australian Society of Authors); Society of Women Writers of Australia; Royal Historical Society; Children's Book Council; Gallery Society; National Trust; Melbourne Theatre Company. Address: 8/8 Mooltan Avenue, Balaclava, Victoria 3183, Australia.

DONLEAVY James Patrick, b. 1926, Brooklyn, New York. Author; Playwright. Publications: The Ginger Man, 1955, Paris, France, UK edition, 1956; The Ginger Man (play), 1959, (in UK as What They Did in Dublin, with the Ginger Man, 1961); Fairy Tales of New York (play), 1961; A Singular Man, 1963; A Singular Man (play), 1965; Meet My Maker the Mad Molecule (short stories), 1964; The Saddest Summer of Samuel S, 1966; The Beastly Beatitudes of Balthazar B, 1968; The Onion Eaters, 1971; The Collected Plays of J P Donleavy, 1972; A Fairy Tale of New York, 1973; The Unexpurgated Code: A Complete Manual Of Survival and Manners, 1975; The Destinies of Darcy Dancer, Gentleman, 1977; Shultz, 1979; Leila, 1983; De Alfonce Tennis, 1984; J P Donleavy's Ireland, 1986; Are You Listening Rabbi Low, 1987; A Singular Country, 1989; That Darcy That Dancer That Gentleman, 1990; The History of the Ginger Man, 1994; The Lady Who Liked Clean Rest Rooms, 1995. Contributions to: Journals, including the Observer, The Times, Guardian and Punch. Address: Levington Park, Mullinger, Co Westmeath, Republic of Ireland.

DONNE Maxim. See: **DUKE Madelaine (Elizabeth).**

DONOSO José (Yanez), b. 5 Oct 1924, Santiago, Chile. Writer. Education: University of Chile and Princeton University. Appointments include: Teacher of English and Literary Critic in Chile. Publications: Coronation, 1957, 1965; Charleston and Other Stories, 1960, 1977; Los mejores cuentos, 1966; Hell Hath No Limits, 1966, 1972; This Sunday, 1967; The Obscene Bird of the Night, 1970, 1973; Cuentos, 1971; Sacred Families, 1973, 1978; A House in the Country, 1978, 1984; The Garden Next Door, 1981, 1992; Cuatro para Delfina, 1982; Curfew, 1986; Taratuta; Still Life with Pipe, 1990, 1993; Verse: Poemas de un novelista. Honours include: National Literature Prize, 1990. Address: Galvarino Gallardo 1747, Santiago, Chile.

DOR Moshe, b. 9 Dec 1932, Tel Aviv, Israel. Poet; Journalist. m. Ziona Dor, 29 Mar 1955, 1 s. Education: Hebrew University of Jerusalem, 1949-52; BA, Political Science, University of Tel Aviv, 1956. Appointments: Counsellor for Cultural Affairs, Embassy of Israel, London, England, 1975-77; Distinguished Writer-In-Residence, American University, Washington, DC, USA, 1987; President, Israel PEN Centre, 1988-90. Publications: From the Outset, 1984; On Top of the Cliff (in Hebrew),1986; Crossing the River, 1989; From the Outset (selected poems in Dutch translation), 1989; Crossing the River (selected poems, English translation), 1989; Love and Other Calamities (poems in Hebrew), 1993; Khamsin (memoirs and poetry in English translation), 1994; some 20 other books of poetry, children's verse, literary essays, interviews with writers. Honours: Honourable Citation, International Hans Christian Andersen Prize for Children's Literature, 1975; Holon prize for Literature, 1981; Prime Minister's Award for Creative Writing, 1986; Balik Prize for Literature, 1987; Memberships: Association of Hebrew Writers, Israel; National Federation of Israel Journalists; Israel Pen Centre. Address: 11 Brodetsky Street, Tel Aviv, Israel 69051.

DORFMAN Ariel, b. 8 May 1942, Buenos Aires, Argentina (Chilean citizen). Novelist; Playwright. Education: Graduated University of Chile at Santiago, 1967; Appointments include: Research Professor of Literature and Latin Studies at Duke University, North Carolina, USA, from 1984. Publications: Fiction: Hard Rain, 1973, 1990; My House is on Fire, 1979, 1990; Widows, 1981, 1983; The Last Song of Manuel Sendero, 1987; Dorando la pildora, 1985; Travesia, 1986; Mascara, 1988; Konfidenz, 1995; Plays: Widows, 1988, 1991; Death and the Maiden, 1991; Reader, 1992; Poems include Last Waltz in Santiago and Other Poems of Exile and Disappearance, 1988; Also: How to Read Donald Duck, 1971, 1984; The Empire's Old Clothes, 1983. Honours include: Olivier Award, London, 1991; Time Out Award, 1991, for best play - Death and the Maiden, Literary Lion, New York Public Library, 1992; also 29th Dong Award, Korea. Address: Center for International Studies, Duke University, Durham, NC 27708-0404, USA.

DORMAN Michael L, b. 9 Oct 1932, New York City, New York, USA. Writer. m. Jeanne Darrin O'Brien, 25 June 1955, 2 daughters. Education: BS, Journalism, New York University, 1953. Literary appointments: Correspondent, The New York Times, 1952-53; Reporter, Editor, The Houston Press, 1953-58; Reporter, Editor, Newsday, Long Island, New York, 1959-64; Freelance Writer, 1965-. Publications include: We Shall Overcome, 1964; The Secret Service Story, 1967; King of the Courtroom, 1969; The Second Man, 1969; Under 21, 1970; Payoff: The Role of Organized Crime in American Politics, 1972; The Making of a Slum, 1972; Confrontation: Politics and Protest, 1974; Vesco: The Infernal Money-Making Machine, 1975; The George Wallace Myth, 1976; Witch Hunt, 1976; Detectives of the Sky, 1976; Dirty Politics, 1979; Blood and Revenge, 1991. Contributions to: Publications such as The New York Times Magazine; Playboy; New York Magazine. Literary Agent: Phillipa Brophy, Sterling Lord Literistic Inc, New York, USA. Address: 7 Lauren Avenue South, Dix Hills, NY 11746, USA.

DORN Ed(ward Merton), b. 1929. Poet; Anthropologist/Ethnologist; Translator. Appointments: Member English Department, University of Colorado, 1977-; Visiting Professor, American Literature, 1965-68, Member English Department, 1974-75, Essex University; Professor, University of Kansas, 1968-69. Publications include: The Newly Fallen, 1962; Hands Up! 1963; By The Sound (novel), 1964, '69, '91; Geography, 1965; The Shoshoneans, 1966; The North Atlantic Turbine, 1967; Our Word: Guerilla Poems from Latin America (translation with G Brotherston), 1968; Gunslinger Book 1, 1968, Gunslinger Book II, 1969, Books 1 & II, 1969; Twenty-Four Love Songs, 1969; Tree Between the Two Walls (translation with G Brotherton), 1969; The Midwest is That Space Between the Buffalo Statlet and The Lawrence Eldridge, 1969; The Cosmology of Finding Your Spot, 1969; Songs Set Two, A Short Count, 1970; Spectrum Breakdown: A Microbook, 1971; A Poem Called Alexander Hamilton, 1971; The Cycle, 1971; Some Business Recently Transacted in the White World (short stories), 1971; The Hamadryas Baboon at the Lincoln Park Zoo, 1972; Gunslinger Book III, 1972; Recollections of Gran Apacheria, 1973; Gunslinger,Bks 1 II III IV, 1975; Collected Poems, 1975; Hello La Jolla, 1978; Views, Interviews, 2 vols, 1978; Captain Jack's Chaps - Houston MLA, 1983; Selected Poems, 1978; Images of the New World (translation), 1979; Yellow Lola, 1981; Abhorrences, 1990; Way West: Essays and Verse Accounts 1963-93, 1993; The Denver Landing, 1993. Address: Campus Box 226, University of Colorado, Boulder, CO 80309, USA.

DORNBERG John Robert, b. 22 Aug 1931, Erfurt, Germany. Journalist; Writer. Education: University of Denver, Denver, Colorado, USA, 1949-52. Appointments: Harry Shubart Co Public Realtions, Denver 1952-54; US Military Service, 1954-56; the Overseas Weekly, Frankfurt, Germany, Managing Editor, 1956-63; Newsweek Magazine, Correspondent, Bureau Chief, Bonn, Vienna, Moscow, Munich, 1963-73; Freelance journalist/writer based in Munich 1973-. Publications: Munich 1923 - The Story of Hitler's First Grab for Power, 1982; Brezhnev - the Masks of Power, 1973; The New Tsars - Russia Under Stalin's Heirs, 1972; The Other Germany, 1968; Schizophrenic Germany, 1961; Berlitz Travellers Guide, Germany 1991-93 (author and consulting editor), 1990; Eastern Europe - The Communist Kaleidoscope, 1980. Contributions to: Reader's Digest; National Geographic Traveller; ARTnews; Conoisseur; Travel and Leisure; The Smithsonian; Institutional Investor; International Management; New York Times; Washington Post. Memberships: Foreign Press Association, Germany (Bonn); Overseas Press Club, New York. Literary Agent: Sterling Lord Literistic Inc, New York. Address: Kreiller Str 3, D-81673, Munich, Germany.

DORNER Majorie, b. 21 Jan 1942, Luxembourg, Wisconsin, USA. University Professor. 2 d. Education: BA, English, St Norbert College, 1964; MA, English, Marquette University, 1965; PhD, English, Purdue University, 1971. Appointments: Professor of English Literature, Winona State University, Winona, Minnesota, 1971-. Publications: Nightmare, 1987; Family Closets, 1989; Freeze Frame, 1990; Winter Roads, Summer Fields, 1992; Blood Kin, 1992. Contributions to: Mass for The Dead, to Great River Review, 1981; Accessory, to Cottonwood Review, 1982; Lee Ann's Little Killing, to Fall Out, 1983; Winter Roads, to Mississippi Valley Review, 1984-85; Pin Money, to Primavera, 1985; Changeling, to New Renaissance, 1988. Honours: Minnesota Book Award for Best Mystery, for Freeze Frame, 1991; Minnesota Book Award for Fiction for Winter Roads, Summer Fields, 1993. Literary Agent: Judith Weber, Sobel Weber Associates, New York, NYC, USA. Address: 777 West Broadway, Winona, MN 55987, USA.

DORRIS Michael, b. 30 Jan 1945, Dayton, Washington, USA. Anthropologist; Writer; Novelist. m. Louise Erdrich, 2 sons, 3 daughters. Education: GA, Georgetown University; MPhil, Yale University. Publications: Native Americans: Five Hundred Years After, 1975; The Broken Cord, 1987; A Yellow Raft in Blue Water, 1987; Working Men, 1993; Paper Trail: Essays, 1994; Guests, 1994; Morning Girl; The Crown of Columbus (with Louise Erdrich). Contributions include: New York Times; Ladies Home Journal; Suntracks; American West; American Indian Culture & Research Journal (on edit board). Honours: Indian Achievement Award, 1985; National Book Critics Circle Award, 1989. Memberships include: Society for Applied Anthropology, Fellow; Society for Values in Higher Education, Fellow; National Congress of American Indians. Address: Department of Native American Studies, Dartmouth College Box 6152, Bartlett Hall Room 306, Hanover, NH 03755, USA.

DORSETT Danielle, See: **DANIELS Dorothy**.

DOSS Margot P(atterson), b. 1922, USA. Writer. Appointments: Performer and Outdoor Editor, KPIX-TV Evening Magazine, 1977-83; Columnist, San Francisco Chronicle, 1961-. Publications: San Francisco at Your Feet, 1964, 3rd edition, 1980; Walks for Children in San Francisco, 1970; Bay Area at Your Feet, 1970, 3rd edition, 1986; Golden Gate Park at Your Feet, 1970, 1978; Paths of Gold, 1974; There, There, 1978; A Walker's Yearbook, 1984. Address: 1331 Greenwich Street, San Francisco, CA 94109, USA.

DOTY Mark, Poet; Writer. Appointments: Former Professor, Goddard College, Vermont College, Sarah Lawrence College. Publications: Turtle, Swan, 1987; Bethlehem in Broad Daylight, 1990; My Alexandria, 1993. Contributions include: Poetry, Yale Review; Ironwood, Azni Review; Crazyhorse. Honour: National Book Critics Circle Award, 1994. Address: 19 Pearl Street, Provincetown, MA 02657-2313, USA.

DOUBTFIRE Dianne Joan, b. 1918. Author; Creative Writer. Appointments: Lecturer, Creative Writing, Isle of Wight County Council Adult Education, 1965-85; Lecturer, Creative Writing, University of Surrey, 1986-. Publications: Lust for Innocence, 1960; Reason for Violence, 1961; Kick a Tin Can, 1964; The Flesh is Strong, 1966; Behind the Screen, 1969; Escape on Monday, 1970; This Jim, 1974; Girl in Cotton Wool, 1975; A Girl Called Rosemary, 1977; Sky Girl, 1978; The Craft of Novel Writing, 1978; Girl in a Gondola, 1980; Sky Lovers, 1981; Teach Yourself Creative Writing, 1983; The Wrong Face, 1985; Overcoming Shyness, 1988; Getting Along With People, 1990. Address: April Cottage, Beech Hill, Headley Down, Hampshire GU35, 8EQ, England.

DOUGALL Robert Neill, b. 27 Nov 1913, Croydon, England. BBC TV Newscaster, retired; Writer. m. N A Byarn, 7 Jun 1947, 1 s, 1 sd. Education: Whitgift School, 1923-31. Publications: In and Out of the Box, 1973; A Celebration of Birds, 1978; Now for the Good News, 1976; British Birds, 1983; Birdwatch Round Britain, 1985; Basil Ede's Birds, text by Robert Dougall, published by Severn House and Van Nostrand Reinhold Co, New York; Years Ahead, 1984. Contributions to: Newspapers and magazines including Sunday Telegraph Magazine; Spectator; Daily Mail; High Life. Honour: MBE 1965. Memberships: Royal Society for Literature, 1975-83; Garrick Club; President, Royal Society for the Protection of Birds, 1970-75, Literary Agent: Curtis Brown. Address: Kendal House, 62 New Street, Woodbridge, Suffolk IP12 1DX, England.

DOVE Rita, b. 28 Aug 1952, Akron, Ohio, USA. Author; Educator. m. Fred Viebahn, 1 d. Education: BA summa cum laude, Miami University, Ohio, 1973; Modern European Literature, University of Turbingen, Germany, 1974-75; MFA, University of Iowa, 1977. Appointments: Professor of English/Creative Writing, Arizona State University, 1981-89; Professor of English/Creative Writing, University of Virginia, 1989-; Poetry Panellist, National Endowment for the Arts (chairperson 1985), 1984-86; Editorial Board, National Forum, 1984; Associate Editor, Callaloo 1986-; Advisory Editor, Gettysburg Review, 1987-; Triquarterly, 1988-; Publications: The Yellow House on the Corner, 1980; Museum, 1983; Fifth Sunday, short stories, 1985; Thomas & Beulah, 1986; Chapbooks: 10 Poems, 1977; The Only Dark Spot in the Sky, 1980; Mandolin, 1982; Grace Notes, 1989; Through the Ivory Gate, 1992; A Darker Face of the Earth, 1994. Contributions to: Numerous Magazines and journals. Honours: Creative Writing Grant, National Endowment for the Arts, 1978; Portia Pitman Fellowship, Tuskagee Institute, 1982; Guggenheim Fellowship, 1983; Lavan

Younger Poet Award, Academy of American Poets, 1986; Pulitzer Prize, poetry, 1987; General Electric Foundation Award, poetry, 1987; Ohio Governor's Award, 1988; Honorary Doctor of Letters, Miami University, 1988; Mellon Senior Fellow, National Humanities Center, 1988-89; Creative Writing Grant National Endowment of the Arts, 1989; Honorary Doctor of Humane Letters, Knox College, 1989; Fellow Centre for Advanced Studies, University of Virginia, 1989-. Memberships: President, 1986-87, Board Member, Associated Writing Program; PEN Club, American Centre. Address: Department of English, Wilson Hall, University of Virginia, Charlottesville, VA 22903, USA.

DOVRING Karin Elsa Ingeborg, b. 5 Dec 1919, Stenstorp, Sweden. American Citizen; Journalist; Author; Communication Analyst. m. Folke Ossiannilsson Dovring, 30 May 1943. Education: Fil.Mag, 1942, Fil.Dr, 1951, Lund University; Fil.Lic, Gothenburg University, 1947. Appointments: Journalist, Swedish Newspapers & Magazines, 1945-60; Foreign Correspondent, Switzerland, France, Germany, Italy, 1953-60; Editor, Journal of Communication, 1965-70; Writer, American Newspapers, 1976-; Writer, Illinois Alliance to Prevent Nuclear War, 1982-; Featured Speaker, Yale Law School, 1992, 1993. Publications: Road to Propaganda, 1959; Songs of Zion, 1-2, 1951; Land Reform as a Propaganda theme, 3rd edition, 1965; Frontiers of Communication, 1975; No Parking This Side of Heaven, 1982; The Optional Society, 1972; Harold Dwight Lasswell: His Communication With A Future, second printing, 1988; If the Bombs Fall: A World of its Own, 1982; Forked Tongue? Body-snatched English in Political Communications, 1990; Heart in Escrow, novel, 1990; Hollywood Songwriter, cassette albums, 1994; America and Light of the World; Songs: IllusionStarvation and Light in the Sky; Film & Television Plays, A Lady of the Jury and Open House, 1994. Contributions to: Numerous professional journals. Honours include: Visiting Professor, Vatican's University for International Studies, Rome, 1956-58. Memberships Include: President, Scandinavian Linguists, 1945-46; National Society of Communications; President, Gerd Literary Society, Sweden, 1938; International Studies Association. Literary Agent: Joseph Nicoletti, Hollywood, USA. Address: 613 West Vermont Avenue, Urbana, IL 61801, USA.

DOWLING Basil (Cairns), b. 29 Apr 1910, Southbridge, Canterbury, New Zealand. Poet. m. Margaret Wilson, 1938, 1 s, 2 d. Education: Canterbury, Otaga & Cambridge Universities; New Zealand Library School, Wellington. Appointments: Head of Dept of English, Raine's Foundation Grammar School, London, 1965-75; Freelance Writer, 1975-. Publications: A Day's Journey, 1941; Signs and Wonders, 1944; Canterbury and Other Poems, 1949; Hatherley: Collective Lyrics, 1968; A Little Gallery of Characters, 1971; Bedlam: A Mid Century Satire, 1972; The Unreturning Native, 1973; The Stream, 1979; Windfalls, 1983. Honour: Jessie Mackay Memorial Prize, 1961. Address: 12 Mill Road, Rye, East Sussex, TN31 7NN, England.

DOWNER Lesley Ann, b. 9 May 1949, London, England. Writer; Journalist; Broadcaster. Education: St Anne's College, Oxford, 1968-71; BA (Hons), MA, English Language and Literature, Oxford University; MA, Area Studies, South Asia, School of Oriental and African Studies, University of London, 1974. Publications: Step-by-Step Japanese Cooking, 1986; Japanese Vegetarian Cookery, 1986; Economist Business Traveller's Guide to Japan (consultant editor, co-author), 1986, 1989; On the Narrow Road to the Deep North, 1989; A Taste of Japan, 1991; The Brothers: The Saga of the Richest Family in Japan, 1994. Contributions to: Independent; Times; Financial Times; Observer; Sunday Times; Correspondent Magazine; Sunday Telegraph Magazine; Vogue. Honours: Glenfiddich Food Book of the Year, 1986. Memberships: Society of Authors; Japan Society; Groucho Club. Literary Agent: Gill Coleridge. Address: 40 Beresford Road, London N5 2HZ, England.

DOWNES David Anthony, b. 17 Aug 1927, Victor, Colorado, USA. Professor of English. m. Audrey Romaine Ernst, 7 Sep 1949, 1 son, 3 daughters. Education: BA cum laude, Regis College, 1949; MA, Marquette College, 1950; PhD, University of Washington, 1956. Appointments include: Assistant Professor, Professor, Chairman of Department, Seattle University, 1953-1968; Professor of English, Dean of Humanities and Fine Arts, 1968-72, Director of Educational Development Projects, 1972-73, Director of Humanities Programme, 1973-74, Director of Graduate English Studies, 1975-78, Chairman of Department, 1978-84, Emeritus Professorship, 1991, California State University, Chico. Publications include: Gerard Manley Hopkins: A Study of His Ignatian Spirit, 1959; Victorian Portraits: Hopkins and

Pater, 1965; The Temper of Victorian Belief: Studies in Victorian Religious Fiction; Pater, Kingsley and Newman, 1972; The Great Sacrifice: Studies in Hopkins, 1983; Ruskin's Landscape of Beatitude, 1984; Hopkins' Sanctifying Imagination, 1985; The Ignatian Personality of Gerard Manley Hopkins, 1990; chapters in: Hopkins, the Man and the City, 1988; The Fine Delight: Centenary Essays, 1989; Gerard Manley Hopkins: New Essays, 1989; Critical Essays on Gerard Manley Hopkins, 1990; Gerard Manley Hopkins & Critical Discourse, 1993; Saving Beauty, 1994. Contributions to: Thought; Victorian Poetry; Hopkins Quarterly; University Journal, Editor, 1974-77; Nineteenth Century Literature; Ultimate Reality & Meaning. Honours include: Andrew Mellon Grant for Summer Seminar, Stanford University, 1982; Senior Scholar International Hopkins Association; Professional Achievement Award, 1984; Exceptional Merit Award for Scholarship, 1984, 88, 90; Exceptional Merit Award for Scholarship, 1992; The Downes Collection placed in the Hopkins Collection, Foley Center, Gonzaga University. Address: 1076 San Ramon Drive, Chico, CA 95926, USA.

DOWNES Mary Raby, b. 31 May 1920, Calcutta, India. Writer. m. (1)Henry May Poade Ashby , 25 Nov 1942, dec, (2) Eric Mytton Downes, 28 Dec 1963, dec, 2 d. Education: Oxford and Cambridge School Certificate, 1938; Countryside Conservation 2 year course, Department of Continuing Education, University of Oxford, 1990-91. Appointments: Currently Village Correspondent, Andover Midweek Advertiser. Publications: Loving is Living, 1965; Out of Evil, novel, 1975; Emma's Family Pony Delight, 1992. Contributions to: Two Worlds; Psychic News; London Calling; Resurgence; Light; Prediction: Game Research; Poem to Scottish Forestry and other publications; Poem to Arrival Press Anthology, 1992. Honours: 1st Prize, national newspaper's competition for The Best Day of My Holiday. Memberships: PEN; The Society of Authors; The College of Psychic Studies; The National Federation of Spiritual Healers; BHS, Dressage Group; Danebury Riding Club; Overseas League; Formerly Council Member of Beauty Without Cruelty; The Poetry Society; Mike Shields Poetry Society. Address: Wheat Cottage, Barton Stacey, Winchester, Hants SO21 3RS, England.

DOWNIE Leonard, b. 1 May 1942, Cleveland, Ohio, USA. Newpaper Editor; Author. m. (1) Barbara Lindsey, 1960 (div 1971), (2) Geraldine Rebach, 1971, 3 s, 1 d. Education: MA, Ohio State University. Appointments: Reporter, Editor, 1964-74, Metropolitan Editor, 1974-79, London Correspondent, 1979-82, National Editor, 1982-84, Managing Editor, 1984-91, Executive Editor, 1991-, Washington Post. Publications: Justice Denied, 1971; Mortgage on America, 1974; The New Muckrakers, 1976. Address: Washington Post, 1150 15th Street NW, Washington DC 20071, USA. ,

DOWNIE Mary Alice Dawe (nee Hunter), b. 12 Feb 1934, USA. Writer. m. John Downie, 27 Jun 1959, 3 d. Education: BA (Hons), English Language & Literature, Trinity College, University of Toronto. Appointments: Book Review Editor, Kingston Whig Standard, 1973-78. Publications: The Wind Has Wings; Poems from Canada, with Barbara Robertson, 1968; Scared Sarah, 1974; Dragon on Parade, 1974; The Last Ship, 1980; Jenny Greenteeth, 1981; A Proper Acadian (with George Rawlyk), 1982; The Wicked Fairy-Wife, 1983; Alison's Ghost (with John Downie), 1984; Stones and Cones (with Jillian Gilliland), 1984; stories: Four short stories, 1973; La Belle et la Laide, 1978; Chapters From Honour Bound, reprinted in Inside and Outside and Measure Me Sky, 1979; Stories From The Witch of the North, reprinted in Story Tellers Rendevouz, 1980; Crossroads 1, 1979 and Out and About, 1981; The Window of Dreams: New Canadian Writing for Children, 1986; The Well-Filled Cupboard (with Barbara Robertson), 1987; How the Devil Got His Cat, 1988; The Buffalo Boy and the Weaver Girl, 1989; Doctor Dwarf & Other Poems for Children, 1990; Cathal the Giant-Killer and the Dun Shaggy Filly, 1991; Written in Stone: A Kingston Reader (with M A Thompso), 1993; The Cat Park, 1993. Contributions to: Hornbook Magazine; Pittsburgh Press; Kingston Whig-Standard; Ottawa Citizen; Globe & Mail; United Church Observer; OWL Magazine; Chickadee; Crackers. Memberships: Writers Union of Canada; PEN. Address: 190 Union Street, Kingston, Ontario, Canada K7L 2P6.

DOWNING Angela, b. 28 Sep 1933, Liverpool, England. Full Professor of English. m. Enrique Hidalgo, 22 Aug 1959, 2 s, 3 d. Education: BA, Modern Languages, University of Oxford, 1956; MA, Oxford, 1962; Liceniatura in English Philology, 1973; PhD, 1976, Universidad Complutense de Madrid. Appointments: Currently Full Professor of English, Universidad Complutense, Madrid, Spain; editor,

Estudios Ingleses de la Universidas Complutense, 1991. Publications: La metáfora gramatical de M A K Halliday y su motivación funcional en el discurso, 1991; An Alternative Approach to Theme: A Systemic Functional Perspective, 1991; A University Course in English Grammer (with Philip Locke), 1992. Contributions to: specialised journals, UK, USA, Spain, with articles on English language discourse and stylistics; The semantics of the get-passive, 1994. Honours: Mary Ewart Scholar, Somerville College, Oxford, 1952-55; The Duke of Edinburgh's Award to A University Course in English Grammer, best Grammer published in 1992. Memberships: The Philological Society. European Society for the Study of English; Sociedad Espanola de Linguistica; Asociación Espanola de Linguistica Aplicada; Asociación Espanola de Estudios Ingleses Medievales; International Association of University Professor of English. Address: Arascues 43 (ant 65), 28023 Madrid, Spain.

DOWNS Donald Alexander, b. 2 Dec 1948, Toronto, Ontario, Canada. Assisstant Professor. m. Susan Yeager Downs, 30 Jan 1971, 1 s, 1 d. Education: BA, Cornell University, 1971; MA, University of Illinois, 1974; PhD, University of California, Berkeley, 1983. Appointment: Assisstant Professor, Political Science, University of Wisconsin, Madison. Publications: Nazis in Skokie: Freedom Community & the First Amendment, 1985; The New Politics of Pornography and the Forms of Democracy, 1988. Contributions to: professional journals, newspapers and magazines. Honours: American Political Science Association; Amnesty International; Southern Poverty Association. Address: 4429 Waite Lane, Madison, WI 53711, USA.

DOYLE Charles (Desmond), b. 18 Oct 1928, Birmingham, Warwickshire, England. Professor Emeritus; Poet; Critic; Biographer. m. (1) Doran Ross Smithells, 1959 (divorced), (2) Rita Jean Brown, 1992; 3 s, 1 d. Education: Diploma of Teaching (NZ), 1956; MA (NZ), 1958; Ph.D (Auckland), 1968. Appointments: Associate Professor, 1968-76, Professor, 1976-93, University of VA, British Columbia. Publications: A Splinter of Glass, 1956; The Night Shift: Poems on Aspects of Love (with others), 1957; Distances, 1963; Messages for Herod, 1965; Earth Meditations, 1971; Earthshot, 1972; Preparing for the Ark, 1973; Plnes (with P K Irwin), 1975; Stonedancer, 1976; A Steady Hand, 1982; The Urge to Raise Hats, 1989; Separate Fidelities, 1991; Intimate Absences: Selected Poems 1954-92, 1993; and James K Baxter (1976); William Carlos Williams and the American Poem, 1982; William Carlos Williams: The Critical Heritage, (editor), 1982; The New Reality (co-editor), 1984; Wallace Stevens: The Critical Heritage (editor), 1985; Richard Aldington: A Biography, 1989; Richard Aldington: Reappraisals (editor), 1990; Periodical: co-editor, Numbers, 1954-59; editor, Tuatara, 1969-74. Address: 641 Oliver Street, Victoria, British Columbia, Canada, V8S 4W2.

DOYRAN Turhan, b. 20 Jun 1926, Ankara, Turkey. Poet; Writer; Photographer. m. Madeleine Doyran, 17 Aug 1953. 1 daughter. Education: Diploma of Filmology, University of Ankara, Grenoble, Paris (Sorbonne) 1957; Ansaldi Academy Theatre, 1953; National Conservatory of Arts and Trades, Paris, 1958; Institut of Advanced International Studies, Paris, 1953. Publications: Plays - Theatre: The Promise, 1946; The Offense, 1947; La Premeditation, 1961; Maree Haute, 1965; Le Mobile, 1967; Les Rois Demeurent, 1984; poetry: Siirler, 1955; Sehir, 1959; Partir, 1962; Gecilmez, 1962; Le Jour, 1962; Il Faut Bien, 1962; Comme Autrefois, 1964; Je ne Suis Pas de Bologne, 1967; The Tree, 1967; The Way, 1975; The Mirror, 1975; Photo-Graphies, 1980; The Rain, 1986. Contributions to: magazines and journals in France, Turkey, Belgium, Italy, Egypt, Switzerland, England, USA. Honours: Prize for Photography, Cannes, 1958; Prize Academy Leonardo da Vinci, Poetry, 1964; Prize Comité Européen Arts and Culture, 1985; Named Artist of Year Plastic Arts, Turkey, 1987. Memberships: Academy Leonardo da Vinci, Rome; Centro Studio et Scambi Internationale, Rome; International High Committee for World Culture and Arts; President, Commission International d'Art Photographique. Address: 8 rue du Cambodge, 75020 Paris, France.

DOZOIS Gardner, b. 1947, USA. Writer. Appointments: Reader, Dell and Award Publishers, Galaxy, If, Worlds of Fantasy, Worlds of Tomorrow, 1970-73; Co-founder and Associate Editor. Isaac Asimov's Science Fiction Magazine, 1976-77. Publications: A Day in the Life, 1972; Beyond the Golden Age; Nightmare Blue (with Geo Alec Effinger), 1975; Future Power (with Jack Dann), 1976; Another World (juvenile), 1977; The Visible Man (short stories), 1977; The Fiction of James Tiptree, Jr, 1977; Best Science Fiction Stories of the Year 6-9, 4 vols, 1977-80; Strangers, 1978; Aliens! (with Jack Dann) 1980; The Year's Best Science Fiction (with Jim Frankell) 1984; Modern Classics

of Science Fiction (editor), 1991; Isaac Asimov's S F Lite (editor), 1993. Address: 401 Quince Street, Philadelphia, PA 19147, USA.

DRABBLE Margaret, b. 5 Jun 1939, Sheffield, England. Author. Education: Newnham College, Cambridge. Publications: A Summer Bird-Cage, 1963; The Garrick Year, 1964; The Millstone, 1965; Wordsworth, 1966; Jerusalem the Golden, 1967; The Waterfall, 1969; A Touch of Love (screenplay), 1969; The Needle's Eye, 1972; Arnold Bennett, 1974; The Realms of Gold, 1975; The Ice Age, 1977; For Queen and Country (juvenile), 1978; A Writer's Britain, 1979; The Middle Ground, 1980; The Oxford Companion to English Literature, 1985; The Radiant Way, 1987; A Natural Curiosity, 1989; Safe as Houses, 1989; The Gates of Ivory, 1991; Angus Wilson: A Biography, 1995. Honours: CBE, 1980. Address: c/o A D Peters, Fifth Floor, The Chambers, Chelsea Harbour, Lots Road, London SW10 OXF, England.

DRACKETT Philip Arthur (Phil), (Paul King), b. 25 Dec 1922, Finchley, Middlesex, UK. Writer; Broadcaster. m. Joan Isobel Davies, 19 Jun 1948. Education: Woodhouse School, 1934-39; Junior County Award, Cambridge University; General Schools, London University. Appointments: News Chronicle; Press Association; Puck Publications: Royal Automobile Club. Publications include: You& Your Car, 1957; Great Moments in Motoring, 1958; Automobiles Work Like This, 1958; Like Father like Son, 1969; Rally of the Forests, 1970; The Classic Mercedes-Benz, 1984; Flashing Blades, 1988; also: Inns & Harbours of North Norfolk; Brabham, Story of a racing Team; Story of RAC International Rally; Encyclopaedia of the Motor Car; Fighting Days; They Call it Courage, The Story of the Segrave Trophy, 1990; Benetton & Ford, A Racing Partnership, 1991. Contributions include: Autoworld; Toyota Today; Yours: Choice; Saga; Ice Hockey World; Mayfair; Sport & Leisure; Titbits; Today; many newspapers. Memberships include: Sports Writers Association; Former committee member, Guild of Motoring Writers; British Ice Hockey Writers Association. Address: 9 Victoria Road, Mundesley, Norfolk NR11 8RG, England.

DRAGONWAGON Crescent, b. 25 Nov 1952, Manhatten, New York, USA. Freelance Writer. m. Ned Shank, 20 Oct 1978. Publications: Always, Always, 1984; The Year it Rained, 1985, also in Swedish, Danish; The Dairy Hollow House Cookbook, 1986; Half A Moon and One Whole Star, 1986; Alligator Arrived with Apples: A Thanksgiving Potluck Alphabet, 1987; Margaret Zeigler, 1988; This is the Bread I Baked For Ned, 1988; Home Place, 1990; The Itch Book, 1990; Winter Holding Spring, 1990; Dairy Hollow House Soup & Bread, A Country Inn Cookbook, 1992; Annie Flies the Birthday Bike, 1993; Alligators and Others, All Year Long: A Book of Months, 1993. Honours include: William Allen White Children's Book Award Master List, 1992-93. Memberships include: Author's Guild; Society of Children's Book Writers. Address: Route 4 Box 1, Eureka Springs, AR 72632, USA.

DRAKE Albert Dee, b. 26 Mar 1935, Portland, Oregon, USA. Professor; Writer. div. 1 s, 2 d. Education: Portland State College, 1956-59; BA, Englaish, 1962, MFA, English, 1966, University of Oregon. Appointments: Research Assisstant, 1965, Teaching Assisstant, 1965-66, English Department, University of Oregon; Assisstant Professor, 1966-70, Associate Professor, 1966-70, Associate Professor, 1970-79, Professor, 1979-, Department of English, Michigan State University, East Lansing. Publications: Michigan Signatures (edited), 1968; Riding Bike, 1973; Roadsalt, 1975; Returning to Oregon, 1975; The Postcard Mysteries, 1976; Tillamook Burn, 1977; In The Time of Surveys, 1978; One Summer, 1979; Garage, 1980; Beyond the Pavement, 1981; The Big Little GTO Book, 1982; Street Was Fun in '51, 1982; I Remember the Day That James Dean Died, 1983; Homesick, 1988; Herding Goats, 1989. Contributions to: over 350 magazines and periodicals including: Redbook; Best American Short Stories; Epoch; December; Northwest Review; Pebble; Arts in Society; Fiction International; Shenandoah; Rod Action. Honours: 1st Ernest Haycox Fiction Award, 1962; 1st Prize, Writer's Digest Fiction Contest, 1979; Grants For Fiction, National Endownment for the Arts, 1974-75, 1983-84; Grant for Fiction, Michigan Council For the Arts, 1982. Address: Department of English, Michigan State University, East Lansing, MI 48824, USA.

DRAKE Walter Raymond, b. 2 Jan 1913, Middlesborough, England. Retired Surveyor, HM Customs & Excise. m. Marjorie Cawthorne, 24 Jun 1944. Publications: Gods or Spacemen? 1964; Gods and Spacemen in the Ancient East, 1968; Gods and Spacemen in the Ancient West, 1974; Gods and Spacemen of the Ancient Past, 1975; Gods and Spacemen Throughout History, 1975; Gods and

Spacemen in Greece and Rome, 1976; Gods and Spacemen in Ancient Israel, 1976; Messengers Form the Stars, 1977; Cosmic Continents, 1986. Contributions include: Flying Saucer Review; Flying Saucer Search; Beyond Science; UFO Nachrichten. Honours: Doctorate in Sacred Philosophy, World University, Tucson, 1985; member l'Academie Europeenne des Sciences des Arts et des Lettres. Memberships: Society of Authors; Sunderland Rotary Club. Address: 2 Peareth Grove, Roker, Sunderland, England.

DRAPER Alfred Ernest, b. 26 Oct 1924. Author. m. Barbara Pilcher, 31 Mar 1951, 2 s. Education: North West London Polytechnic. Publications include: Swansong for a Rare Bird, 1969; The Death Penalty, 1972 (made into a French Film); Smoke Without Fire, 1974; The Prince of Wales, 1975; The Story of the Goons, 1976; Operation Fish, 1978; Amritsar, 1979; Grey Seal, 1981; Grey Seal: the Restless Waves, 1983; The Raging of the Deep, 1985; Storm over Singapore, 1986; The Con Man, 1987; Dawns Like Thunder, 1987; The Great Avenging Day, 1989; a Crimson Splendour, 1991; Operation Midas, 1993. Contributions to: Numerous articles for many national newspapers and magazines. Honours: Runner-up 1969 in Macmillan/Panther First Crime Novel Competition for Swansong for a Rare Bird. Memberships: Society of Authors; Life Member of NUJ. Literary Agent: Juri Gabriel. Address: 31 Oakridge Avenue, Radlett, Herts WD7 8EW, England.

DRAPER Ronald Philip, b. 3 Oct 1928. Regius Chalmers Professor of English. m. Irene Margaret Aldridge, 19 Jun 1950, 3 d. Education: BA, 1950; PhD, 1953. Publications: D H Lawrence, 1964, 3rd edition, 1984; D H Lawrence, The Critical Heritage (editor), 1970; Lyric Tragedy, 1985; The Winter's Tale, Text and Performance, 1985; The Literature of Region and Nation (editor), 1989; Hardy, The Tragic Novels (editor), 1975, 6th edition, 1985; George Eliot, The Mill on the Floss and Silas Marner (editor), 1977; Tragedy, Developments in Criticism (editor), 1980; Hardy, Three Pastoral Novels (editor), 1987; An Annotated Critical Bibliography of Thomas Hardy (co-author M Ray), 1989; The Epic, Developments in Criticism (editor) 1990. Contributor to: Articles and reviews: Critical Quarterly; Essays in Criticism; Etudes Anglaises; English Studies; Journal of D H Lawrence Society; MLR; New Literary History; notes and queries: Revue des Langues Vivantes; Review of English Studies; Shakespeare Quarterly; Studies in Short Fiction; Thomas Hardy Annual; Thomas Hardy Journal. Membership: International Association of University Professors of English, Address: 50 Queen's Road, Aberdeen AB1 6YE, Scotland.

DRECKI Zbigniew Bogdan, b. 20 Nov 1922, Warsaw, Poland. Artist. m. Cynthia Josephine Scott, 22 Feb 1961. Education: Humanistic Gymnasium (High School), Warsaw, 1928-39; Art Diploma, Darmstadt Academy of Art, Federal Republic of Germany, 1952. Publications: Freedom and Justice Spring From the Ashes of Auschwitz, 1992, Polish version in Auschwitz Museum. Contributions to: Polish medical journals; British and US newspapers. Memberships: Life Member, West Country Writers Association; Association of Little Presses. Literary Agent: Self. Address: Winterhaven, 23 Albion Street, Exmouth, Devon EX8 1JJ, England.

DREIER Ole, b. 15 Apr 1946, Nyborg, Denmark. Professor of Social Psychology, University of Copenhagen. m. Dorthe Bukh, 5 Sept 1983, 1 son, 1 daughter. Education: MA, Psychology, 1970; PhD, 1979; DPhil, 1993. Publications: Society and Psychology, 1978; Critical Psychology, 1979; Familiäres Sein und Jamiliäres Bewusstaein, 1980; Psychosocial Treatment, 1993; Contributions in several collected volumes in German and English. Contributions to: Udkast; Nordisk Psykologi; Philosophia; Forum Kritische Psychologie. Honours: Visiting Professor, Mexico City, Berkeley, Leipzig, 1984-86. Memberships: Danish Authors Association; Boards of several journals; Danish Psychological Association; International Society of Theoretical Psychology. Address: Dr Olgas Vej 37, 2000 Frederiksberg, Denmark.

DRENNAN William D, b. 12 Feb 1935, New York City, New York, USA. Writer; Editor; Literary Firm Executive. m. Christina Lavery, 18 Mar 1978, 1 s, 1 d. Education: BA, St John's University, New York City, 1956; St John's University School of Law, New York City, 1956-57. Appointments: Copy Editor, Doubleday & Company, New York City, New York, 1961-67; Chief Copy Editor, L W Singer Company, New York City, 1967-68; Associate Acquisitions and Planning Editor, American Management Association, New York City, 1968-70; Editor, Praeger Publishers, New York City, 1972-72; Consulting Editor, New York City, 1972-80; President, Editorial Director, Drennan

Communications, East Kingston, New Hampshire, 1980-. Publications: The Fourth Strike: Hiring and Training the Disadvantaged (editor), 1970. Contributions to: Take the Local to the Midnight Sun, to Qantas Airways Inflight, 1978. Memberships: National Association of Book Editors, 1967-70, Member-at-Large 1969-70. Address: 6 Robin Lane, East Kingston, NH 03827, USA.

DRENNEN Marcia Simonton, b. 19 July 1915, Columbus, Ohio, USA. Writer; Editor. m. Everett Drennen, 21 Jan 1939, 1 s. Education: BA, English, Ohio State University, 1936; Graduate: Columbia University Adult Education, 1958, New School for Social Research Adult Education, 1964, 1986. Appointments: Staff, Memphis Press-Scimitar, 1941-46; Staff, United Press International, 1946-50; Staff, NBC Television News, 1950-56; Senior Editor, Reader's Digest Condensed books, 1958-80. Publications: American Poetry Association Anthology, 1985; Poetry Showcase, 1986; Best of New Poets, 1986; Art of Poetry Anthology, 1984. Contributions to: Plains Poetry Journal; Poetry Press; Scimitar and Song; The Lyric; International Poetry Review. Honours: 1st Prize, 1985, 5th Prize, 1985, Grant 1987, American Poetry Association; Honourable Mention, Writer's Digest, 1986. Memberships: Browning dramatic Society; President, Chi Delta Phi; Overseas Press Club of America. Address: 11 West 9th Street, New York, NY 10011, USA.

DREWE Robert, b. 9 Jan 1943, Melbourne, Victoria, Australia. Novelist. m. (3) Candida Baker, 4 sons, 2 daughters. Education: Hale School, Perth, Western Australia. Appointments include: Writer-in-residence, University of Western Australia, Nedlands, 1979, and La Trobe University, Bundoora, Victoria, 1986; Columnist, Mode, Sydney, and Sydney City Monthly, 1981-83. Publications: The Savage Crows, 1976; A Cry in the Jungle Bar, 1979; Fortune, 1986; Our Sunshine, 1991; Short stories: The Bodysurfers, 1983; The Bay of Contented Men, 1989; Plays: The Bodysurfers, 1989; South American Barbecue, 1991. Honours include: National Book Award, 1987; Commonwealth Literary Prize, 1990. Literary Agent: Hickson Associates, Wollahra, Australia. Address: Hickson Associates, 128 Queen Street, Wollahra, New South Wales 2025, Australia.

DRISCOLL Peter, b. 1942. Writer; Journalist. Appointments: Reporter, Rand Daily Mail, Johannesburg, South Africa, 1959-67; Sub-editor, Scriptwriter, ITV News, London, 1969-73. Publications: The White Lie Assignment, 1971; The Wilby Conspiracy, 1972; In Connection with Kilshaw, 1974; The Barboza Credentials, 1976; Pangolin, 1979; Heritage, 1982; Spearhead, 1987; Secrets of State, 1991. Address: c/o David Higham Associates, 5-8 Lower John Street, London, W1R 4HA, England.

DRIVER Charles Jonathan (Jonty), b. 19 Aug 1939, Cape Town, South Africa. Headmaster. m. Ann Elizabeth Hoogewerf, 8 Jun 1967, 2 s, 1 d. Education: BA, BEd, University of Cape Town, 1958-62; MPhil, Trinity College, Oxford University, England, 1965-67. Appointments: Literature Panel, 1975-77, Chairman, 1977, Lincolnshire and Humberide Arts; Literature Panel, Arts Council, 1975-77; Editor, Conference & Common Room, 1993-. Publications: Elegy for a Revolutionary, 1968; Send War in Our Time, O Lord, 1970; Death of Fathers, 1972; A Messiah of the Last Days, 1974; Hong Kong Portraits, 1985; I Live Here Now, 1979; Occasional Light (co-author Jack Cope), 1979; Patrick Duncan (biography), 1980; In the Water-Margins (poems), 1994. Contributions to: numerous magazines and journals. Honour: FRSA. Memberships: Headmasters' Conference. Literary Agent: Andrew Hewson, John Johnson Author's Agents. Address: The Master's Lodge, Wellington College, Crowthorne, Berkshire RG11 7PU, England.

DRIVER Paul William, b. 14 Aug 1954, Manchester England. Music Critic; Writer. Education: Oxford University, 1972-79; MA (Hons), 1979. Appointments: Music Critic, The Boston Globe, 1983-84; Music Critic, Sunday Times, 1985-; Member, Editorial Board, Contemporary Music Review. Publications: A Diversity of Creatures (editor), 1987; Music and Text (editor), 1989. Contributions to: Sunday Times; Financial Times; Tempo; London Review of Books; numerous others. Membership: Critics Circle. Address: 15 Victoria Road, London NW6 6SX, England.

DROBOT Eva Joanna, b. 7 Feb 1951, Cracow, Poland. Journalist; Author. m. Jack Kapica, 9 Apr 1983, 1 daughter. Education: Baccalaureat, Universite d'Aix Marseilles, Aix-en-Provence, France, 1971; BA magna cum laude, Tufts University, Medford, Massachussetts, USA, 1973. Appointments: Columnist, The Globe and

Mail, 1980-82, 1990-; Contributing Editor, Saturday Night Magazine, 1988-; Toronto Correspondent, L'Actualite Magazine, 1989-; Board of Directors, Somerville House Publishing, 1994; The Globe & Mail, 1990-93. Publications: Words For Sale (co-editor), 1979, 1983, 1989; Class Acts, 1982, 1984; Zen and Now, 1985; Amazing Investigations: Money, 1987, 1988; Chicken Soup and Other Nostrums, 1987. Contributions to: Hundreds, including book reviews, to magazines and journals. Honours: Gold Medal, Canadian National Magazine Award, 1989; Canadian Authors Award, 1989. Membership: International PEN. Address: 17 Simpson Avenue, Toronto, Ontario, Canada M4K 1A1.

DROWER George, b. 21 Jul 1954, London, England. Feature Writer. Education: BA, (Hons), Politics & Government, City of London Polytechnic, 1979; MA, Area Studies, University of London, 1980; PhD, London School of Economics, 1989. Publications: Neil Kinnock: The Path To Leadership, 1984; Britain's Dependent Territories: A Fistful of Islands, 1992. Contributions to: The Times; The Sunday times; Financial times; Independent Mail on Sunday; Sun; House and Garden; Traditional Homes. Honours: University of London Central Research Fund Travelling Scholarship to Hong Kong; London School of Economics Director's Fund Scholarship. Membership: Inner Temple Rowing Club. Literay Agent: Serafina Clarke, 98 Tunis Road, London W12, England. Address: 480A Church Road, Northolt, Middlesex, UB5 5AU, England.

DRUCKER Henry Matthew, b. 29 Apr 1942, New Jersey, USA. University Development Director. m. Nancy Livia Newman, 29 Mar 1975. Education: BA, Philosophy, Allegheny College, Pennsylvania, 1964; PhD, Political Philosophy, London School of Economics, 1967. Publications: Doctrine and Ethos in the Labour Party, 1979; Developments in British Politics (Series), editor, 1983 and following; Breakaway: The Scottish Labour Party, 1978; The Politics of Nationalism and Devolution (with Gordon Brown); The Scottish Government Yearbook (Series From 1978-88). Membership: Reform Club. Address: Campaign For Oxford, University of Oxford, University Offices, Wellington Square, Oxford OX1 2JD, England.

DRUKS Herbert, b. 1 Apr 1937, Vienna, Austria. Professor. m. 21 Aug 1985, 1 s, 1 d. Education: BA, City College of New York, USA, 1958; MA, Rutgers University, 1959; PhD, New York University, 1964. Appointments: Professor History, Brooklyn College, CUNY, Faculty History and Political Science, The School of Visual Arts; Associate Editor, East Europe Magazine, 1972-75; Editor, R Hecht Papers, published by Garland, New York, 1991. Publications: Truman and the Russians, 1967, 2nd edition, 1981; The Failure to Rescue, 1977; The US and Israel, 1979; From Truman Through Johnson: A Documentary History 1945-68. Contributions to: American Historical Association; Journal of Thought; Midstream; Journal of Church and State; Journal of American History. Honours: Fellowship, Haifa University, 1987, 1988-89. Memberships: American Historical Association; Professional Staff Conference. Address: POB 309, Forest Hills, NY 11375, USA.

DRUMMOND June, b. 15 Nov 1923, Durban, South Africa. Author. Education: BA, English, University of Cape Town. Publications include: Junta, 1989; The Trojan Mule, 1982; The Bluestocking, 1985; The Unsuitable Miss Pelham, 1990; The Patriots, 1979; Slowly the Poison, 1975. Memberships: Writers Circle (Durban), of South Africa; Soroptimist International (Durban); Democratic Party of South Africa. Address: 24 Miller Grove, Durban 4001, South Africa.

DRURY Allen Stuart, b. 2 Sept 1918, Houston, Texas, USA. Writer. Education: BA, Stanford University. Appointments: Editor, Tulare Bee, 1940-41; County Editor, Bakersfield Californian, 1942; senate Staff, United Press, 1943-45; Freelance Correspondent, Washington DC, 1946-47; National Editor, Pathfinder Magazine, 1947-52; National Staff Washington Evening Star, 1952-54; Senate Staff, New York Times, 1954-59. Publications: Advise and Consent, 1959; A Shade of Difference, 1962; A Senate Journal, 1963; That Summer, 1965; Three Kids in a Cart, 1965; Capable of Honour, 1966; A Very Strange Society, 1967; Preserve and Protect, 1968; The Throne of Saturn, 1971; Courage and Hesitation, 1972; Come Ninevah, Come Tyre, 1973; The Promise of Joy, 1975; A God Against the Gods, 1976; Return to Thebes, 1977; Anna Hastings, 1977; Mark Coffin, U S S, 1979; Egypt, the Eternal Smile, 1980; The Hill of Summer, 1981; Decision, 1983; The Roads of Earth, 1984; Pentagon, 1986; Toward What Bright Glory? 1990; Into What Far Harbour? 1993. Contributions to: Readers Digest, 1959-62. Honours: National Editorial Award, Sigma Delta Chi, 1942; Pulitzer prize for novel, Advise and Consent, 1960. Memberships: Authors Guild; Sigma Delta Chi; University and Cosmos,

Washington DC; Bohemian, San Francisco. Literary Agent: Lantz-Harris Agency. Address: c/o Lantz Harris Agency, 888 Seventh Avenue, New York, NY 10106, USA.

DRYDEN Pamela. See: JOHNSTON Norma.

DRYSDALE Helena Claire, b. 6 May 1960, London, England. Writer. m. Richard Pomeroy, 21 May 1987, 1 d. Education: Charterhouse, 1975-77, Trinity College Cambridge, 1978-82; BA Hons, History, Art History, Cambridge. Publications: Alone Through China and Tibet, 1986; Dancing With The Dead, 1991. Contributions to: Vogue; Marie Claire; the Independent; The Independent on Sunday; Harpers and Queen; Cosmopolitan; World; Honours: Exhibitioner, Trinity College. Memberships: PEN Club; Society of Authors: Royal Geographical Society; Globetrotters Club. Literary Agent: A P Watt. Address: 22 Stockwell Park Road, London SW9 OA7, Engalnd.

DU BOURG (Eric) Ross, b. 19 July 1940, Maryborough, Victoria, Australia. Author; Journalist; Columnist; Editor; Critic; Consultant; Research Scientist; Thoroughbred Racehorse Breeder. Education: Partially completed Arts degree and Diploma of Journalism, University of Melbourne, 1960s. Career: Columnist, National Breeding Column, The Australian newspaper, 1966-82; Joint Editor, Bred To Win international magazine, 1970-73. Publications: The Australian and New Zealand Thoroughbred, 3 separate editions, 1980, 1985, 1991. Contributions to: British Bloodstock Breeders' Annual Review, 1970-75; 50 original essays to New Zealand Thoroughbred Breeders' Bulletin, 1969-81. Honours: H A Wolfe Memorial/TAB Award, Racing Writer of the Year, 1976. Address: PO Box 105, Ocean Grove, Victoria 3226, Australia.

DU VAUL Virginia, See: COFFMAN Virginia.

DUBERMAN Martin Bauml, b. 6 Aug 1930, New York City, USA. Professor of History; Writer. Education: BA, Yale University, 1952; MA, Harvard University, 1953; PhD, Harvard University, 1957. Publications: Charles Francis Adams, 1963; In White America, 1964; The Antislavery Vanguard (editor), 1965; James Russell Lowell, 1966; The Uncompleted Past, 1970; The Memory Bank, 1970; Black Mountain, 1972; Male Armor, 1974; Visions of Kerouac, 1977; About Time: Exploring the Gay Past, 1986, 2nd Edition, 1991; Hidden From History: Reclaiming the Gay and Lesbian Past; Paul Robeson, 1989; Mother Earth: An Epic Drama of Emma Goldman's Life, 1991; Cures: A Gay Man's Odyssey, 1991; Stonewall, 1993. Contributions include: New York Times; New Republic; Partisan Review; Harpers; Atlantic Monthly; New York Review; Native; Christopher Street; Radical History Review; Village Voice; Signs; Journal of Homosexuality; Show. Address: History Department, Lehman College, CUNY, Bedford Park Blvd, Bronx, NY 10468, USA.

DUBERSTEIN Larry, b. 18 May 1944, New York City, New York, USA. Writer; Cabinetmaker. 3 d. Education: BA, Wesleyan University, 1966; MA, Harvard University, 1971. Publications: Nobody's Jaw, 1979; The Marriage Hearse, 1983; Carnovsky's Retreat, 1988; Postcards From Pinsk, 1991; Eccentric Circles, 1992; The alibi Breakfast, 1995. Contributions to: Articles, essays, reviews to: The Saturday Review; The Boston Review; The National; The Phoenix; New York Times Book Review; others. Address: Box 609, Cambridge, MA 02139, USA.

DUBIE Norman (Evans Jr), b. 1945, USA. Poet. Appointments: Teaching Assistant, 1969-71, Lecturer, 1971-74, Creative Writing, University of Iowa, Iowa City; Assisstant Professor, Ohio University, Athens, 1974-75; Writer-in-Residence, 1975-76, Director of the Gradual Writing Program, 1976-77, Professor of English, 1980-, Arizona State University, Tempe. Publications: The Horsehair Sofa, 1969; Alehouse Sonnets, 1971; The Prayers of the North American Martyrs, 1975; Popham of the New Song and Other Poems, 1975; In The Dead of The Night, 1975; The Illustrations, 1977; A Thousand Little Things and Other Poems, 1978; Odalisque in White, 1978; The City of The Olesha Fruit, 1979; The Everlastings, 1980; The Selected and New Poems, 1983; The Springhouse, 1986; Groom Falconer, 1989; Radio Sky, 1991; The Clouds of Magellan, 1991. Address: Department of English, Arizona State University, Tempe, AZ 85281, USA.

DUBIE William, b. 24 July 1953, Salem, Massachussetts, USA. Writer; Editor. m. Jo-Ann Trudel, 6 Jun 1987. Education: BA, English, Salem State College, 1977; AA, Liberal Arts, 1981, AA, General Studies, 1984, North Shore Community College; BS, University of the State of New York, 1989; MA, Media Studies, New School of Social

Research. Publications: Closing the Moviehouse (poems), 1981; The Birdhouse Cathedral (poems), 1990. Contributions to: Poems and articles in more than 90 small press and university magazines. Honours: Chapbook Competition winner, for Closing the Moviehouse, 1981; First Prize, Spring Concourse, American Collegiate Press, 1983; Sparrowgrass Poetry Forum, 1990. Membership; Society of Technical Communications, Address: 150A Ayer Road, Shirley, MA 01464, USA.

DUBOIS J E. See: **PARKES Joyce Evelyne.**

DUBOIS M. See: **KENT Arthur (William Charles).**

DUBUS Andre III, b. 11 Sep 1959, Oceanside, California, USA. Writer; Teacher. m. Fontaine Dollas Dubus, 25 Jun 1989. Education: AA, Bradford College, Bradford, Massachusstts, 1979; BA, Sociology, University of Texas, Austin. Appointments: Part-Time Professor of Ceative Writing, Emerson College, Boston, Massachusetts. Publications: Forky, short story, 1984; Last Dance, short story, 1985; The Cage Keeper, novella, 1988; The Cage Keeper and other stories, 1989, soft cover edition, 1990; In the Quiet, short story, 1992; Bluesman, novel, 1993; novel excerpt in Image, 1993. Contributions to: Playboy magazine; Yankee magazine; the Crescent Review; Crazyhorse Quarterly; America Magazine; The Los Angeles Times Book Review. Honours: National Magazine Award in Fiction, 1985; Breadloaf Scholarship, 1986. Membership: Authors Guild. Literary Agent: Philip Spitzer, 50 Talmago Farm Lane, East Hampton, NY 11937, USA. Address: 16 Summit Place, Newburyport, MA 01950, USA.

DUCKWORTH Marilyn, b. 10 Nov 1935, Auckland New Zealand. Writer. m. (1) Harry Duckworth, 28 May 1955, (2) Ian MacFarlane, 2 Oct 1964, (3) Dan Donovan, 9 Dec 1974, (4) John Batstone, 8 Jun 1985, 4 d. Publications: A Gap in the Spectrum, 1959; The Matchbox House, 1960; A Barbarous Tongue, 1963; Over the Fence is Out, 1969; Disorderly Conduct, 1984; Married Alive, 1985; Rest For The Wicked, 1986; Pulling Faces, 1987; A Message From Harpo, 1989; Explosions on the Sun, 1989; Unlawful Entry, 1992; Seeing Red, 1993. Contributions to: stories to: Landfall; New Zealand Listener; Critical Quarterly; Islands; others. Honours: New Zealand Literary Fund Scholarship in Letters, 1961, 1972; Katherine Mansfield Fellowship, 1980; New Zealand Book Award for Fiction, 1985; Shortlisted, Wattie Book of the Award, 1985; OBE for services to literature, 1987; Fulbright Visiting Writers Fellowship, 1987; Australia-New Zealand Writers Exchange Fellowship, 1989; Victoria University of Wellington Writers Fellowship, 1990. Membership: PEN. Literary Agent: Dinah Wiener, London, England. Address: 46 Roxburgh Street, Wellington, New Zealand.

DUCORNET Erica Lynn, (Rikki Ducornet), b. 19 Apr 1943, NY, USA. Writer; Artist; Teacher, 1 s. Education: BA, bard College, 1964. Literary Appointments: Novelist in Residence, University of Denver, 1988-; Visiting Professor, University De Trento, Italy, 1994. Publications: The Butchers Tales, 1994; The Jade Cabinet, 1993; The Fountains of Neptune, 1992, 1989; Entering Fire, 1986; The Stain, 1984, 1986; The Volatilized Ceiling of Baron Munodi. Contributions to: Fiction International; Post Modern Culture; IA Review; Exile; City Lights Review. Honours: Bunting 1987, Eben Demarst, 1990, Lannan, 1993, Nominated National Book Critics Circle Award, 1994. Membership: PEN. Address: English Dept, Denver University, Denver, CO 80208, USA.

DUCORNET Rikki. See: **DUCORNET Erica Lynn.**

DUDEK Louis, b. 6 Feb 1918, Montreal, Quebec, Canada. Professor Emeritus; Poet. m. Aileen Collins, 1970, 1 s. Education: McGill University, Montreal; MA, Columbia University, NY, 1946; PhD, 1955. Appointments: Greenshields Professor, McGill University, 1969-84; Publisher, DC Books, Montreal. Publications: Unit of Five, 1944; East of the City, 1946; The Searching Image, 1952; Cerberus, 1952; Twenty-Four Poems, 1952; Europe, 1954; The Transparent Sea, 1956; En Mexico, 1958; Laughing Stalks, 1958; Atlantis, 1967; Collected Poetry, 1971; Epigrams, 1975; Cross Section: Poems, 1940-80, 1980; Continuation 1, 1981; Zembla's Rocks, 1986; Infinite Worlds, 1988; Editor, DK Some Letters of Ezra Pound, 1974; Editor of Poetry of Our Time. Honours: Quebec Literary Award, 1963; Officer, Order of Canada, 1984. Address: 5 Ingleside Avenue, Montreal, Quebec H3Z 1N4, Canada.

DUDLEY Helen, See: **HOPE-SIMPSON Jacynth (Ann).**

DUFFY Carol, b. 23 Dec 1955, Glasgow, Scotland. Poet. Education: BA, Honours, Philosophy, University of Liverpoool, 1977. Publications include: Standing Female Nude, 1985; Selling Manhatten, 1987; also, Fleshweathercock, Fifth Last Song, Thrown Voices (limited edition poetry), 3 stage plays, 2 radio plays. Contributions to: Numerous magazines and journals. Honours: C Day Lewis Fellowship, 1983; Eric Gregory Award, 1985; Book Award, Scottish Arts Council, 1986. Literary Agent: c/o Liz Graham, 4 Camp View, London, SW19, 4VL, England.

DUFFY Maureen Patricia, b. 21 Oct 1933, Worthing, Sussex, England. Author. Education: BA (Hons) English, King's College, University of London, 1956. Publications include: That's How it Was, 1962; The Microsm, 1966; Wounds, 1969; Love Child, 1971; The Venus Touch, 1971; The Erotic World of Faery, 1972; I Want to Go to Moscow, 1973; Capital, 1975; The Passionate Shepherdess, 1977; Housespy, 1978; poetry: Lyrics For the Dog Hour, 1968; Evensong, 1975; Memorials For the Quick and the Dead, 1979; plays: Rites, 1969; A Nightingale in Bloomsbury Square, 1974; visual art: Prop Art Exhibition (with Brigid Brophy), 1969; Gorsaga, 1981; Londoners, 1983; Change, 1987; A Thousand Capricious Chances, 1989; poetry: Collected Poems, 1985; Illuminations (novel), 1991; Ocean's Razor (novel), 1993. Contributions to: New Statesman. Memberships: Co-founder, Writer's Action Group; President, Witer's Guild of Great Britain; Chair, Author's Licensing and Collecting Society; British Copywright Council. Literary Agent: Jonathon Clowes Ltd, 88D Iron Bridge House, Bridge Approach, London NW1, England. Address: 18 Fabian road, London, SW6 7TZ, England.

DUGAN Alan, b. 1923, USA. Poet. Appointments: Faculty, Sarah Lawrence College, Bronxville, New York 1967-71; Staff Member for Poetry, Fine Arts Work Center, Provincetown, Massachusetts, 1971-. Publications: General Prothalamion in Populous Times, 1961; Poems, 1961; Poems 2, 1962; Poems 3, 1967; Collected Poems, 1969; Poems 4, 1974; Sequence, 1976; Collected Poems 1961-83, 1983; Poems 6, 1989. Address: Box 97, Truro, MA 02666, USA.

DUGGER Ronnie, b. 16 Apr 1930, IL, US. Reporter; Publisher; Writer. m. Patricia Blake Dugger, 29 June 1982; 1 s, 1 d. Education: BA, University of TX, 1950; Oxford University, 1950-51; University of TX, 1951-52, 1954. Literary Appointments: Owner, Publisher, The TX Observer, 1965-1994; Visiting Professor, University of VA, 1977; Visiting Professor, Hampshire College, 1976; Visiting Professor, University of IL, 1976; Research Consultant, Institute of Industrial Relations, UCLA, 1969; TX Correspondent, WA Post, 1960; Stringer, Time, Life, 1956-61. Publications: Books: On Reagan: The Man and His Presidency, 1983; The Politician: The Life and Times of Lyndon Johnson, 1982; Our Invaded Universities, 1974; Dark Star, Hiroshima Reconsidered, 1967; Three Men in TX, 1967. Contributions to: The New Yorker; Atlantic; Harper's; NY Times; TX Observer; Progressive; Life; New Republic. Honours: Alicia Patterson Fellowship, 1994; Fellow, Woodrow Wilson Int'l Center for Scholars, 1983-84; Fellowship, Natural Endowment for the Humanities, 1978; Fellowship, Rockefeller Foundation, 1969-70; other grants and awards. Memberships: PEN; Authors Guild; TX Institute of Letters; Philosophical Society of TX. Literary Agent: Edward J Acton & Jayne Dystel, Acton, Dystel Leone & Jaffe Inc. Address: Box 311, 70A Greenwich Avenue, New York, NY 10011, USA.

DUKE Elizabeth. See: **WALLINGTON Vivienne Elizabeth.**

DUKE Madelaine (Elizabeth) (Maxim Donne, Alex Duncan), b. 1925. Author. Publications: novels: Azael and the Children, 1958; No Margin of Error,1959; A City Built To Music, 1960; Ride the Brooding Wind, 1961; Thirty Pieces of Nickel, 1962; The Sovereign Lords, 1963; Sobaka, 1965; The Lethal Innocents, 1968; Because of Fear in the Night, 1973; novels as Alex Duncan: It's A Vet's Life, 1961; The Vet Has Nine Lives, 1962; Vets in the Belfrey, 1964; Vet Among the Pigeons, 1977; Vets in Congress, 1978; Vet in the Manger, 1978; Vet in a State, 1979; Vet on Vacation, 1979; To Be A Country Doctor, 1980; God and the Doctor, 1981; The Diary of a Country Doctor, 1982; The Doctor's Affairs All Told, 1983; The Women's Specialist, 1988; mystery novels: Claret, Sandwiches and Sin, 1964; This Business of Blumfog, 1967; Death of a Holy Murderer, 1975; Death at the Wedding, 1976; The Bormann Receipt, 1977; Death of A Dandie Dimont, 1978; Flashpoint, 1982; others: The Secret Mission, 1954; Slipstream: The Story of Anthony Duke, 1955; No Passport: The Story of Jan Felix, 1957; Beyond the Pillars of Hercules: A Spanish Journey, 1957; the Secret People (juvenile), 1989; Once in Austria, 1987. Address: c/o

Mondial Books Ltd, Norman Alexander & Co, 5th Floor, Grosvenor Gardens House, 35/37 Grosvenor Gardens, London SW1 0BS, England.

DUKORE Bernard Frank, b. 11 Jul 1931, USA. Professor. m. Barbara, 1 s, 2 d. Education: BA, 1952; MA, 1953; PhD, 1957. Appointments: Professor, University of Hawaii; City University of New York; Stanford University; California State University at LA; University Southern California; Currently University Distinguished Professor of Theatre Arts & Humanities VPI & SU. Publications include: Bernard Shaw Director, 1971; Bernard Shaw, Playwright, 1973; Dramatic Theory and Criticism, 1974; Where Laughter Stops: Pinter's Tragicomedy, 1976; Collected Screenplays of Bernard Shaw, 1980; Money and Politics in Ibsen Shaw and Brecht, 1980; The Theatre of Peter Barnes, 1981; Harold Pinter, 1982; Alan Ayckbourn A Casebook, 1991; Bernard Shaw The Drama Observed, 4 volumes, 1993; 1992: Shaw and the Last Hundred Years, 1994. Contributions to: Modern Drama; Theatre Journal; The World and I; New York Times Book Review; Twentieth Century Literature; Essays in Theatre; Tulane Drama Review. Honours: Guggenheim Fellowship, 1969-70; Fellow American Theatre Association, 1975; NEH Fellowship, 1976-77, 1984-85; Fulbright Research Fellowship, 1991-92; Visiting Fellowship, Humanities Research Centre of the Australian National University, 1979. Memberships: Association for Theatre in Higher Education; Ibsen Society of America; Pinter Society; American Society for Theatre Research. Address: Theatre Arts Department, VPI & SU, Blacksburg, VA 24061, USA.

DUMAS Claudine. See: **MALZBERG Barry Norman.**

DUNANT Peter. See: **DUNANT Sarah.**

DUNANT Sarah (Peter Dunant), b. 8 Aug 1950. Writer; Broadcaster. partner of Ian David Willox, 2 d. Education: Newnham College Cambridge, 1969-72; BA, 2:1 History, Cambridge University, 1972. Publications: as Peter Dunant: Exterminating Angels (co-author), 1983; Intensive Care (co-author), 1986; as Sarah Dunant: Snow Falls in a Hot Climate, 1988; Birth Marks, 1991; Fatlands, 1993; The War of the Words: Essays on Political Correctness (editor), 1994. Contributions to: various London magzines; The Listener; The Guardian. Honours: Shortlisted for Crime Writers Golden Dagger, 1987, 1991. Literary Agent: Gillon Aitken, Aitken and Stone, England. Address: c/o Gillon Aitken, 29 Fernshaw Road, London SW10 OTG, England.

DUNBAR Andrea, b. 22 May 1961, Bradford, Yorkshire, England. Playwright. 1 s, 2 d. Education: Educated at Buttershaw Comprehensive School, Bradford. Publications: plays: The Arbor (produced, London 1980, New York, 1983); 1980; Rite, Sue and Bob Too (produced London 1982), 1982. Shirley (produced London 1986); screenplay, Rite, Sue and Bob Too, 1987. Honours: George Devine Award, 1981. Address: 7 Edge End Gardens, Buttershaw, Bradford, West Yorkshire BD6 2BB, England.

DUNBAR-HALL Peter, b. 15 July 1951, Sydney, Australia. Lecturer. Education: BA, Honours, 1972; MMus, 1989. Publications: Music - A Practical Teaching Guide, 1987; A Guide to Rock'n'Pop, 1988; Music in Perspective, 1990; A Guide to Music Around the World, 1991; Teaching Popular Music, 1992. Contributions to: Many articles in Education Australia; papers in International Review of Aesthetics & Sociology of Music; British Journal of Music Education; International Journal of Music Education. Honours: Frank Albert Prize, Sydney University, 1971; Busby Music Scholarship, Sydney University, 1971; Lady Henley Award for Excellence in Teaching, Sydney Conservatorium of Music, 1993. Literary Agent: Science Press (Sydney), Fitzroy & Chapel Streets, Marrickville, NSW 2204, Australia. Address: 5/198 Kurraba Road, Neutral Bay, NSW 2089, Australia.

DUNCAN Alex. See: **DUKE Madelaine (Elizabeth).**

DUNCAN Lois, b. 28 Apr 1934, Philadelphia, Pennsylvania, USA. Writer. m. Donald W Arquette, 15 Jul 1965, 2 s, 3 d. Publications: 10 children's books; 20 young adult's novels; 2 adult novels; 3 non-fiction books including: Ransom, 1966; A Gift of Magic, 1971; I Know What You Did Last Summer, 1973; Down a Dark Hall, 1974; Summer of Fear, 1976; Killing Mr Griffin, 1978; Daughters of Eve, 1979; Stranger With My Face, 1981; chapters: My Growth as a Writer, 1982; The Third Eye, 1984; Locked in Time, 1985; Horses of Dreamland, 1986; The Twisted Window, 1987; Songs From Dreamland, 1989; The Birthday

Moon, 1989; Don't Look Behind You, 1989; Who Killed My Daughter (non-fiction), 1992. Address: 1112 Dakota NE, Albuquerque, NM 87110, USA.

DUNCAN Paul Edwin, b. 20 Aug 1959, Cape Town, South Africa. Writer; Journalist. Education: University of Edinburgh, 1978-84; MA, (Hons), History of Art. Appointments: London Correspondent, Casa Vogue, 1989-92; Writer, Researcher, The Royal Fine Art Commission, England, 1991-. Publications: Scandal, Georgian London in Decay (co-author), 1986; Insight Guide Tuscany (contributor), 1989; Discovering the Hill Towns of Italy, 1991; AA Tour Guide Italy, 1991; Sicily, A Traveller's Companion, 1991; The Traditional Architecture of Rural Italy, 1993; The Art of Living in London, forthcoming. Contributions to: Italian Vogue; Vogue Glamour; Casa Vogue; GQ; The World of Interiors; the Independent; Sunday Times; Evening Standard; Harpers and Queen, Architect's Journal; Elle; Elle Decoration: L'Uomo Vogue; Country Life. Memberships: Architectural Association. Literary Agent: Anne Engel. Address: 10 The Woodlands Mansions, Clapham Common North Side, London SW4 ORJ, Engalnd.

DUNHAM William Wade, b. 8 Dec 1947, Pittsburgh, PA, USA. Professor of Mathematics. m. Penelope Higgins, 26 Sep 1970, 2 s. Education: BS, University of Pittsburgh, 1969; MS, 1970; PhD, 1974, Ohio State University. Publication: Journey Through Genius: THe Great Theorems of Mathematics, 1990. Contributions to: articles on history of mathematics to: The American Mathematical Monthly; Mathematics Magazine; The College Mathematics Journal; Mathematics Teacher. Honours: Phi Beta Kappa, 1968; M M Culver Award, University of Pittsburgh, 1969; Master Teacher Award, Hanover College, 1981; Director, NEH Summer Seminars on Great Theorems, 1988, 1990, 1992; Humanities Achievement Award for Scholarship, Indiana Humanities Council, 1991; George Pólya Award, Mathematical Association of America, 1993; Truman Koehler Professor of Mathematics, Muhlenberg College, 1992-. Memberships: Mathematical Association of America; National Council of Teachers of Mathematics Civil War Roundtable, (US). Address: Department of Mathematics, Muhlenberg College, Allentown, PA 18104, USA.

DUNKERLEY James, b. 15 Aug 1953, England. University Professor. Education: BA, Modern History, University of York, 1974; MPhil, Latin American Studies, 1977, DPhil, 1979, University of Oxford. Publications: The Long War: Dictatorship and Revolution in El Salvador, 1982; Rebellion in the Veins: Political Struggle in Bolivia, 1984; Los Origines del Podar Militar en Bolivia, 1987; Power in the Isthmus: A History of Central America, 1988; Political Suicide in Latin America, 1992. Address: Department of Political Studies, Queen Mary and Westfield College, Mile End Road, London E1 4NS, England.

DUNKLEY Christopher, b. 22 Jan 1944, Scarborough, Yorkshire, England. Critic; Broadcaster. m. Carolyn Elizabeth Lyons, 18 Feb 1967, 1 son, 1 daughter. Education: Haberdasher's Aske's, 1955-62, expelled. Appointments include: Mass media correspondent, Television critic, the Times, 1968-73; Television critic, Financial Times, 1973-; Presenter, Feedback, BBC Radio 4, 1986-. Publications: Television Today and Tomorrow: Wall to Wall Dallas?, 1985. Contributions to: Telegraph Magazine; Listener; Sunday Times; Stills; Television World; Electronic Media. Honours: Critic of the Year, British Press Awards, 1976, 1986; Broadcaster Journalist of the Year, 1989 & Judges Award, 1990, TV-AM Awards. Memberships: Commodore, Theta Club. Address: 38 Leverton Street, London, NW5 2PG, England.

DUNLAP Leslie W, b. 1911, USA. Writer; Librarian. Appointments: Associate Director, University of Illinois Libraries, 1951-58; Dean of Library Adinistration, 1970-82, Emeritus, 1982-, University of Iowa, Iowa City. Publications: Letter of Willis Gaylord Clark and Lewis Gaylord Clark, 1940; American Historical Societies, 1944; Readings in Library History, 1972; The Wallace Papers: An Index, 1975; The Publication of American Historical Manuscripts, 1976; Your Affectionate Husband, J F Culver, 1978; Our Vice-Presidents and Second Ladies, 1988. Memberships: National Commission on Library and Information Sciences, 1970-74.

DUNLOP Richard, b. 1921, USA. Writer. Publications: The Mississippi River, 1956; St Louis, 1957; Burma, 1958; The Young David (novel), 1959; Rand McNally Vacation Guide, 1964; Doctors of the American Frontier, 1965; Texaco Touring Atlas, 1968; Texaco Touring Atlas (with E Snyder), 1970; Great Trails of the West, 1971; Outdoor Recreation Guide, 1974; Backpacking and Outdoor Guide, 1977, 1978; Wheels West, 1977; Behind Japanese lines: with the OSS in Burma, 1979; Donovan: America's Master Spy, 1982; On the Road in an RV, 1987. Honours: Midland Author's Best Biography Award for Donovan: America's Master Spy, 1982. Memberships: President, Society of American Travel Writers, 1971; Society of Midland Authors, 1980. Address: 1115 Mayfair Road, Arlington Heights, IL 60004, USA.

DUNN Douglas Eaglesham, b. 23 Oct 1942, Inchinnan, Scotland. Writer. m. Lesley Jane Bathgate, 10 Aug 1985, 1 s, 1 d. Education: BA University of Hull, England. Literary Apointments: Writer-in-Residence: University of Hull, 1974-75; University of Dundee, Scotland, 1981-82; Duncan of Jordanstone College of Art, Dundee District Library, 1986-88; Honorary Visiting Professor, University of Dundee, 1987-89; Fellow in Creative Writing, University of ST Andrews, 1989-91; Professorin English, University of St Andrews, 1991-. Publications: Terry Street, 1969; The Happier Life, 1972; Love or Nothing, 1974; Barbarians, 1979; St Kilda's Parliament, 1981; Elegies,1985; Secret Villages,1985; Selected Poems, 1986; Northlight, 1988; New and Selected Poems (USA), 1989; Poll Tax: The Fiscal Fake, 1990; Andromache, 1990; Scotland: an Anthology, 1991; Faber Book of 20th Century Scottish Poetry, 1992; Dante's Drum-Kit, 1993; Boyfriends and Girlfriends, 1994. Contributions to: New Yorker; Punch; Times Literary Supplement; Glasgow Herald. Honours: Fellow, Royal Society of Literature, 1981; Honorary LLD, University of Dundee, 1987; Hon Fellow, Humberside College, 1987; Whitbread Book of the Year Award, 1985. Memberships: Scottish PEN; Society of Authors; Literature Committee, Scottish Arts Council, 1991-; Scottish Arts Council, 1992. Literary Agent: Peters, Fraser and Dunlop, 5th Floor, The Chambers, Chelsea Harbour, Lots Road, London SW10 OXF, England. Address: Dept of English, The University, St Andrews, Fife, Scotland.

DUNN Nell (Mary), b. 1936, London, England. Writer. m. Jeremy Sandford, 1956, 3 children. Publications: plays: Stearning (produced London, 1981, Stamford, Connecticut and New York, 1982), Ambergate, Derbyshire, 1981; New York, Limelight, 1984; Sketches in Variety Night (produced London, 1982); I Want, with Adrian Henri, adaption of their own novel (produced Liverpool, 1983; London, 1986); screenplay: Poor Cow, with Ken Loach, 1967; TV play: Up the Junction, 1965; novels: Poor Cow, 1967; The Incurable, 1971; I Want (with Adrian Henri), 1972; Tear His Head off His Shoulders, London, 1974, New York, 1975; The Only Child: A Simple Story of Heaven and Hell, 1978; short stories: Up the Junction, London, 1963, Philadelphia, Lipincott, 1966. Honours: Rhys Memorial Prize for Fiction, 1964; Susan Blackburn Prize, 1981; Evening Standard Award, 1982; Society of West End Theatres Award, 1982. Literary Agent: Curtis Brown, London. Address: 10 Bell Lane, Twickenham, Middlesex, England.

DUNNETT Dorothy (Dorothy Halliday), b. 25 Aug 1925, Dunfermline, Scotland. Novelist; Portrait Painter. m. Alaistair M Dunnett, 17 Sept 1946, 2 s. Publications include: The Game of Kings, 1961, 7th edition, 1986; Queen's Play, 1964, 8th edition 1986; The Disorderly Knights, 1966, 8th edition, 1987; Dolly and the Singing Bird (also the Photogenic Soprano), 1968, 4th edition, 1984; Pawn in Frankincense, 1969, 8th edition, 1987; Dolly & the Cookie Bird (also Murder in the Round), 1970, 4th edition 1985; The Ringed Castle, 1971, 8th edition 1987; Dolly & the Doctor Bird (also Match For A murdere), 1971, 4th edition 1985; Checkmate, 1975, 8th edition 1987; King Hereafter, 1982, 3rd edition, 1983; Dolly & the Bird of Paradise, 1983, 4th edition 1985; Niccolo Rising, 1986, 4th edition 1987; the Spring of the Ram, 1987, 2 editions; Scottish Short Stories, 1973; Dolly & the Starry Bird, 1973, 4th edition 1985; Dolly and the Nanny Bird, 1976, 4th edition 1985; The Scottish Highlands (with Alastair M Dunnett and David Paterson), 1988; Moroccan Traffic, 1991; Race of Scorpions, 1990; Scales of Gold, 1991; The Unicorn Hunt, 1993. Honours: OBE, 1992; Award Scottish Arts Council, 1976; Fellow, Royal Society of the Arts; Trustee, National Library of Scotland; Board Member, Edinburgh Book Festival. Literary Agent: Curtis Brown. Address: 87 Colinton Road, Edinburgh EH10 5DF, Scotland.

DUNNING Lawrence, b. 8 Aug 1931, Kansas City, Missouri, USA. Writer; Editor. Education: BS, Southern Methodist University, Dallas, Texas. Appointments: Instructor, University of Denver, 1980-83; Instructor, University of Colorado at Denver, 1984-86. Publications: Neutron Two is Critical, 1977; Keller's Bomb, 1978; Taking Liberty, 1980. Contributions to: Denver Post. Honours: Short Story Listed in Best American Short Stories, 1971; Top Hand Award for Best Short Story, Colorado Authors League, 1979. Memberships: Authors Guild Incorporated; Colorado Authors League; MENSA. Literary Agent: Peter

Livingston. Address: c/o Peter Livingston, 143 Collier Street, Toronto, Ontario, Canada, M4W 1M2.

DUO Duo. See: **LI Shizheng.**

DUPIN Jacques, b. 4 Mar 1927, Privas, Ardeche, France. Poet. Education: University of Paris, from 1945. Appointments include: Editor of L'Ephémère review, from 1954. Publications include: Le Nuage en échec, 1956; Les Brisants, 1958; Saccades, 1962; Gravir, 1963; La Nuit grandissante, 1968; L'Embrasure, 1969; Fits and Starts: Selected Poems, 1973; Dehors, 1975; Ballast, 1976; Du Nul Lieu et du Japon, 1981; Une Apparance de soupirail, 1982; L'Espace autrement dit, 1982; De Singes et de Mouches, 1983; Les Mères, 1986; Conturnace, 1986; Chanson troglodytes, 1989; Enchancre, 1991; Rien encours, toujours déjà; Also: Studies of the artists Miro, Giacometti and Chagall. Address: c/o POL Editeur, 8 Villa D'Alesia, 75014 Paris, France.

DUPONT (Jean) Louis, b. 17 Jan 1924, Shawinigan, Canada. School Principal retired. m. Beaulieu Madeleine, 1 Aug 1953, 2 sons, 3 daughters. Education: Superior Diploma, Primary Teaching, 1948; MA, 1952; Master of Public Administration, 1967. Publications: La Guerre du Castor, 1984; La Légende de Thogoruk, 1993. Contributions to: La Presse; Lettres Québécoises. Memberships: La Société Littéraire de Laval; L'Union des Ecrivains Québécois. Address: 1255 Montpellier, Laval, Quebec H7E 3C8, Canada.

DUPUY Arnold C, b. 22 May 1962, Fort Belvoir, VA, USA. Military Historian. 1 s. Education: MA, George Mason University, 1994; Matriculating, George Mason University. Publications: How to Defeat Saddam Hussein (co-author), 1991; Contributing author: The Encyclopedia of Military History: From 3500 BC to the Present, 1986; The Harper Encyclopedia of Military Biography, 1992; International Military and Defense Encyclopedia, 1993. Contributions to: Understanding Wars from Historical Perspective (co-author), Marine Corps Gazette; General Mark Clark - The Man They Called The American Eagle, World War II Review, 1993; War Zone Italy: Incident Along Albano Road, February 1944, World War II Review, 1993; The Bowling Alley, Scenarios for Wargamers, 1994; The Battle for Rome, 1944; Broadhead, England: World War II Review, 1994. Address: 7342 Lee Highway 201, Falls Church, VA 22046, USA.

DUPUY T(revor N(evitt), b. 1916. History/ Military Defence. Appointments: President and Executive Director and Member of the Board, Historical Evaluation and Research Organization, Washington DC, 1962-; President, Data Memory Systems Inc, 1983-; Colonel, US Army, 1938-58; Professor of Military Science and Tactics, Harvard University, Massachussets, 1952-56; Director, Ohio State University, Military History Course, 1956-57; with International Studies Division, Institute of Defence Analyses, 1960-62. Publications include: Civil War Naval Actions, 1961; Military History of World War II, 19 vols, 1962-65; Compact History of the Revolutionary War, 1963; (editor, co-author), Holidays, 1965; Military History of World War I, 12 vols, 1967; The Battle of Austerlitz, 1968; Modem Libraries for Modem Colleges: Research Strategies for Design and Development, 1968; Ferment in Public Libraries: The Impact of Information Technology, 1968; Military History of the Chinese Civil War, 1969; Military Lives Series, 12 vols, 1969-70; (co-author) Encyclopaedia of Military History, 1970, 1977; (co-author) Revolutionary War Land Battles, 1970; (co-author) Revolutionary War Naval Battles, 1970; (editor and co-author) Almanac of World Military Power, 1970, 72, 74, 78; (co-editor) Documentary History of Arms Control and Disarmament, 1973; (co-author) People and Events of the American Revolution, 1974; (co-author) Outline History of the American Revolution, 1975; A Genius of War: The German Army and General Staff, 1977; Numbers, Predictions and War, 1978; Elusive Victory: the Arab-Israeli Wars, 1947-74, 1978; The Evolution of Weapons and Warfare, 1980; (co-author) Great Battles on the Eastern Front, 1982; Options of Command, 1984; (with Paul Martell) Flawed Victory: The 1982 War in Lebanon, 1986; Future Wars: The Worlds Most Dangerous Flashpoints, 1993; (editor) International and Defense Encyclopedia, 6 vols, 1993. Address: 8316 Arlington Boulevard, Fairfax, VA 22031, USA.

DURANTI Francesca. See: **ROSSI Maria Francesca.**

DURAS Marguerite, b. 4 Apr 1914, Gia Dinn, nr Saigon, Vietnam (French citizen). Novelist; Playwright. Education: Graduated Sorbonne, Paris, 1935. Publications include: La Vie Tranquille, 1944; A Sea of Troubles, 1950, 1953; The Sailor from Gibraltar, 1952, 1968; The Little Horse of Tarquinia, 1953, 1960; Whole Days in the Trees, 1954, 1983;

The Square, 1955, 1959; Moderato Cantible, 1958; Ten-Thirty on a Summer Night, 1960; The Ravishing of Lo V Stein, 1964; The Vice Consul, 1966, 1987; L'Amante Anglaise, 1967; Destroy, She Said, 1969; L'Amour, 1971; Ah, Ernesto, 1971; The Malady of Death, 1983; The Lover, 1985; Blue Eyes, Black Hair, 1985; Summer Rain, 1990; L'Amant de la Chine du Nord; Hiroshima mon amour (screenplay), 1960; Une Aussi Longue Absence (screenplay), 1961; Savannah Bay (play), 1983; à musica deuxième (play), 1985; Further screenplays, and French adaptations of plays. Honours include: Prix Goncourt, 1984. Address: c/o Edition Gallimard, 5 rue Sebastien-Bottin, 75007 Paris, France.

DURBAND Alan, b. 1927. Writer (Literature Theatre). Publications: English Workshop books 1-3, 1959; New Directions: Five One-Act Plays in the Modern Idiom, 1961; Contemporary English Books 1-2, 1962; Shorter Contemporary English, 1964; New English Books, 1-4, 1966; Playbill 1-3, 1969; Second Playbill, 1-3, 1973; Prompt 1-3, 1975; Wordplays 1-2, 1982; Shakespeare Made Easy (12 plays), 1984-89. Address: Ty-Nant, Lansilin, Near Oswestry, Salop, SY10 7QQ, England.

DURBRIDGE Francis Henry, (Paul Temple) b. 25 Nov 1912. Playwright; Author. m. Norah Elizabeth Lawley, 1940, 2 s. Education: Birmingham University. Publications: radio plays include: Promotion, 1933; created character of Paul Temple: entered TV with The Broken Horseshoe, 1952 (the first adult TV serial), other serials followed: Portrait of Alison, 1954; My Friend Charles, 1955; the Other Man, 1956; The Scarf, 1960; The World of Tim Frazer (executive producer), 1960-61; Melissa, 1962; Bat Out of Hell, 1964; Stupid Like a Fox, 1971; The Doll, 1971; Breakaway, 1980; films include: 2 for Korda and Romulus, 1954-57; stage plays: Suddenly At Home, 1971; The Gentle Hook, 1974; Murder With love, 1976; House Guest, 1980; Nightcap, 1983; Murder Diary, 1986; The Small Hours, 1989; Sweet Revenge, 1991; Side Effects. Contributions to: various journals, newspapers and magazines. Literary Agent: Lemon, Unna and Durbridge Ltd. Address: c/o Lemon, Unna and Durbridge Ltd, 24 Pottery Lane, Holland Park, London W11 4LZ, England.

DURCAN Paul, b. 16 Oct 1944, Dublin, Ireland. Poet. Education: BA. Publications: Endsville, 1967; O Westport in the Light of Asia Minor, 1975; Teresa's Bar, 1976; Sam's Cross, 1978; Jesus, Break His Fall, 1980; Ark of the North, 1982; The Selected Paul Durcan, 1982, 1985; Jumping the Train Tracks With Angela, 1983; The Berlin Wall Cafe, 1985; Going Home to Russia, 1987; In The Land of Punt, 1988; Jesus and Angela, 1988. Contributions to: Irish Press; Irish Times; Hibernia; Magill; Cyphers; Honest Ulsterman; Gorey Detail; Cork Examiner; Aquarius. Honours: Patrick Kavanagh Poetry Award, 1974; Arts Council of Ireland Bursary for Creative Writing, 1976, 1980-81; Poetry Book Society Choice for the Berlin Wall Cafe, 1985; The Irish American Cultural Institute Poetry Award, 1989. Membership: Aosdána. Address: 14 Cambridge Avenue, Ringsend, Dublin 4, Republic of Ireland.

DURGNAT Raymond Eric (O O Green), b. 1 Sep 1932, London, England. Writer; Lecturer. Education: BA Hons, English Literature, Pembroke College, Cambridge, 1957; MA, 1970. Appointment: Staff Writer, British Picture Corporation, Elstree Studios, 1957-60. Publications include: Durgnat on Film, 1976; Strange Case of Alfred Hitchcock, 1973; Luis Bunuel, 1988; A Mirror For England, 1973; Michael Powell and the English Genius, 1991; The Crazy Mirror; Films and Feelings. Contributions to: British Journal of Aesthetics. Membership: British Society of Aesthetics, Literary Agent: MBA, Campbell Thompson MacLaughlin. Address: 84 Saint Thomas's Road, London N4 2QW, England.

DURKIN Barbara Rae Wernecke, b. 13 Jan 1944, Baltimore, MD, USA. Writer. m. William J Durkin, 20 May 1973, 2 s. Education: AA, Essex Community College, 1964; BS, English, Towson State University, 1966; Graduate Studies, English, Humanities, Morgan State University, John Hopkins University, MD. Publications: Oh You Dundalk Girls Can't You Dance the Polka, 1984; Editor, Visions & Viewpoints, 1993, 1994. Honours: Best of 1984 List, American Library Association, 1984. Memberships: International Women's Writing Guild; American Pen Women; American Society of Training & Development. Literary Agent: Robin Rue, Anita Diament Agency, New York City. Address: 531 Phillips Road, Webster, NY 14580-9760, USA.

DURST Paul, b. 1921, USA. Writer. Appointments: Editorial Writer; Newcaster, St Joseph News-Press, 1946-48; Advertising

Supervisor, Southwestern Bell Telephone Company, Kansas City and St Louis, 1948-50; Advertising Manager, Crofts Engineering, Bradford, 1958-60; J G Graves, Mail Order Firm, Sheffield, 1960-62. Publications: Die! Damn You, 1952; Bloody River, 1953; Trail Herd North, 1953; Guns of Circle 8 (as Jeff Cochran), 1954; Along the Yermo Rim (as John Shane), 1954; My Deadly Angel (crime as John Chelton), 1955; Showdown, 1955; Justice, 1956; Kid From Canadian, 1956; Prairie Reckoning, 1956; Sundown in Sundance (as John Shane), 1956; Six-Gun Thursday (as John Shane), 1956; Gunsmoke Dawn (as John Shane), 1957; John Law, Keep Out, 1957; Ambush at North Platte, 1957; The River Flows West, 1957; If They Want Me Dead (crime as Peter Bannon), 1958; If I Should Die (crime as Peter Bannon), 1958; Kansas Guns, 1958; Dead Man's Range, 1958; The Gun Doctor, 1959; Johnny Nation, 1960; Whisper Murder Softly (crime as Peter Bannon), 1963; Backlash (crime), 1967; Badge of Infamy (crime), 1968; Intended Treason: What Really Happened to the Gunpowder Plot, 1970; A Roomful of Shadows (autobiography), 1975; The Florentine Table (crime), 1980; Paradiso Country (crime), 1985. Address: The Keep, West Wall, Presteigne, Powys, LD8 2BY, Wales.

DUSEK Dusan, b. 4 Jan 1946, Czechslovakia. Writer. m. Nadje Vrabelova, 22 Sep 1973. Education: Magister, University of Komensky, Bratislava, 1970. Appointments: Editor, Smena Daily, 1970-71; Editor, Tip Sports Magazine, 1972-73; Editor, Kamarat Magazine for Young, 1973-78; Freelance Writer, 1978-. Publications include: The Roof of the House, 1972; The Carriage Beside the Heart, 1982; The Calendar, 1983; The Thimble, 1985; Merciful Time, 1992; books for young people including: the Oldest of All Sparrows, 1976; The True Story of Paco, 1980; The Grandma on the Ladder, 1986; Contributions to: Slovenske pohl'ady; Romboid; Kultumy zivot. Honours: Honour List IBBY, 1988. Memberships: Obec spisovatel'ov Slovenska; Slovak Centre PEN. Address: Stare zahrady 10, 821 05 Bratislava, Slovakia.

DUTTON Geoffrey Piers Henry, b. 2 Aug 1922, Anlaby, South Australia. Writer. m. (1) Ninette Trott, 1944, 2 s, 1 d, (2) Robin Lucas, 1985. Education: University of Adelaide; BA, Magdalen College, Oxford, 1949. Literary Appointments: Co-Editor: Australian Letters, 1957-68; Australian Book Review, 1961-70; Editor: The Bulletin Literary Supplement, 1980-85; The Australian Literary Magazine, 1985-88; Editorial Director, Sun Books Limited, 1965-83. Publications: Nightflight and Sunrise, 1945; The Hero as Murderer, 1967; Andy, 1968; Walt Whitman: Patrick White, 1961; Findings and Keepings, 1970; Queen Emma of The South Seas, 1976; Patterns of Australia, 1978; White on Black, 1978; Snow on The Saltbush, 1984; The Innovators, 1986; Kenneth Slessor, 1991; Flying Low, 1992; New & Selected Poems, 1993; Out In The Open, an autobiograhpy, 1994. Contributions to: Numerous journals and magazines and broadcasting services. Honour: Officer, Order of Australia, 1976. Literary Agent: Curtis Brown. Address: c/o Curtis Brown, PO Box 19, Paddington, NSW 2021, Australia.

DUTTON Ninette Clarice Bernadette, b. 24 July 1923, Adelaide, South Australia, Australia. Enameller; Artist; Author. m. Geoffrey Dutton, 31 July 1944, 2 sons, 1 daughter. Education: University of Adelaide. Publications: The Beautiful Art of Enamelling, 1966; Portrait of a Year, 1976; An Australian Wildflower Diary, 1982; Wildflower Journeys, 1985; Probabilities, short stories, 1987; A Passionate Gardener, 1990; Firing, a Memoir, 1994. Contributions to: Weekly column, Adelaide Advertiser, 3 years; Your Garden magazine, 5 years, now occasionally; Regular broadcasts. Honours: Medal, Order of Australia. Memberships: Australian Society of Authors; Fellowship of Australian Writers. Address: PO Box 342, Williamstown, South Australia 5351, Australia.

DUVAL Jeanne, See: COFFMAN Virginia.

DWORKIN Ronald M, b. 1931, Worcester, Massachussetts, USA. Education: AB, LLB, Harvard University; BA Jurisprudence, Oxford University. Career: Lawyer on New York Bar; Professor of Law. Publications: Taking Rights Seriously, 1977; Law's Empire, 1986; A Matter of Principle, 1985; A Bill of Rights for Britain, 1990; Justice & The Good Life, 1990; Life's Dominion, 1993. Contributions include: New York Review of Books. Address: School of Law, New York University, 40 Washington Square South, New York, NY 10012-5499, USA.

DWYER K R. See: KOONTZ Dean R.

DYBECK Stuart, b. 1942. Publications: Brass Knuckles, 1979; Childhood & Other Neighbourhoods, 1980; The Coast of Chicago,

1990. Honours: Fellow, American Academy & Institute of Arts & Letters, 1994

DYER James Frederick, b. 23 Feb 1934, Luton, England. Archaeological Writer. Education: MA, Leicester University, 1964. Publications: Southern England, An Archaeological Guide, 1973; Penguin Guide to Prehistoric England and Wales, 1981; Discovering Archaeology in England and Wales, 1985; Ancient Britain, 1990; Discovering Prehistoric England, 1993. Contributions to: Bedfordshire Magazine; Illustrated London News; Archaeological Journal. Memberships: Society of Authors; Royal Archaeological Institute; Society of Antiquaries. Address: 6 Rogate Road, Luton, Bedfordshire, LU2 8HR, England.

DYLAN Bob (Robert Allen Zimmerman), b. 24 May 1941, Duluth, Minnesota, USA. Poet; Composer; Performer. Appointments: Concert appearances in the United States from 1961, Europe, 1964, Australia, 1964. Publications: Tarantula, 1966; Approximately Complete Works, 1970; Poem to Joanie, 1972; Words, 1973; Writings and Drawings, 1973; The Songs of Bob Dylan, 1966-75, 1976; XI Outlined Epitaphs, and Off the Top of My Head, 1981; Lyrics, 1962-85, 1986. Honours include: DMus, Princeton University, 1970. Address: c/o Jeff Rosen, PO Box 870, Cooper Station, New York, NY 10276, USA.

DYMOKE Juliet, b. 28 Jun 1919, Enfield, England. Writer. m. Hugo de Schanschieff, 9 May 1942, 1 s, 1 d. Publications: The Cloisterman, 1969; Norman Triology, 1970-74; The White Cockade, 1979; Plantagenet Series, 6 books 1978-80; A King of Warfare, 1981; March to Corunna, 1985; The Queens Diamond, 1985; Aboard The Mary Rose, 1985; Two Flags for France, 1986; A Border Knight, 1987; Ride to Glencoe, 1989; Portrait of Jenny, 1990; Hollanders House, 1991; Cry of The Peacock, 1992; Winter's Daughter, 1994. Contribution to: The Lady. Membership: Romantic Novelists Association. Literary Agent: Jane Conway-Gordon, 1 Old Compton Street, London, W1, England. Address: Heronswood, Chapel Lane, Forest Row, East Sussex, RH18 5BS, England.

DYSON Anthony Edward, b. 1928. Writer. Literary Appointments include: Co-Founder, Director, Critical Quarterly Society, 1960-84; Visiting Professor, Concordia University, Montreal, Canada, 1967, 1969; General Editor, Macmillan Casebooks, England, 1968-; Visiting Professor, University of Connecticut, USA, 1976; Director, Norwich Tapes Limited, England, 1979-; Honorary Fellow, former Reader in English, University of East Anglia, Norwich. Publications: Modern Poetry (with C B Cox), 1963; The Crazy Fabric: Essays in Irony, 1965; The Practical Criticism of Poetry, 1965; Modern Judgements on Dickens, 1968; Word in The Desert (with C B Cox), 1968; Casebook on Bleak House, 1969; Black Papers on Education, 3 volumes, 1969-70; The Inimitable Dickens, 1970; Between Two Worlds: Aspects of Literary Form, 1972; Twentieth Century Mind, 3 volumes, (with C B Cox), 1972; English Poetry: Select Bibliographical Guides, 1973; English Novel: Select Bibliographical Guides, 1974; Casebbok on Paradise Lost (with Julian Lovelock), 1974; Masterful Images: Metaphysicals to Romantics (with Julian Lovelock), 1975; Education and Democracy (with Julian Lovelock), 1975; Yeats, Eliot and R S Thomas: Riding The Echo, 1981; Poetry Criticism and Practice, 1986; Thom Gunn, Ted Hughes and R S Thomas, 1990. Contributions to: Over 100 articles in world of English Criticism to various, US, UK and European Community journals; 8 teaching tapes. Address: c/o Lloyds Bank, 3 Sidney Street, Cambridge, CB2 3HQ, England.

DYSON Freeman (John), b. 1923, USA. Writer. Publications: Disturbing The Universe (autobiography), 1979; Weapons and Hope, 1984; Origins of Life, 1986; Infinite in All Directions, 1988; From Eros to Gaia, 1992. Honour: Recipient of National Book Critics Award for Non-Fiction, 1984. Address: 105 Battle Road Circle, Princeton, NJ 08540, USA.

E

EAGLETON Terence Francis, b. 22 Feb 1943, Salford, England. University Teacher, 2 s. Education: MA, Trinity College, 1964; PhD, Jesus College, Cambridge, 1967. Literary Appointments: Poetry Book Society Selector, 1972-74; Sinclair Prize Judge, 1984. Publications: Criticism and Ideology, 1976; Literary Theory: Introduction, 1983; The Ideology of The Aesthetic, 1990; Marzism and Literary Criticism, 1976; The Rape of Clarissa, 1985; The Function of Criticism, 1984; Walter Benjamin, 1981; William Shakespeare, 1986; Against The Grain, 1986; Saint Oscar, a play, 1989; Filmscript: Wittgenstein; Play: The White; The Gold: The Gangrene. Contributions to: Observer; Times Literary Supplement; New York Times Book Review; New Statesman; New Left Review. Honour: Irish Sunday Tribune Arts Award, 1990. Literary Agent: Elaine Steel. Address: St Catherine's College, Oxford, England.

EARLY Gerald, b. 21 Apr 1952, Philadelphia, PA, USA. Professor of English and Afro-American Studies. m. Ida Haynes, 27 Aug 1977, 2 d. Education: BA cum laude, University of Pennsylvania, 1974; MA, English, 1980, PhD, English, 1982, Cornell University. Publications: Tuxedo Junction: Essays on American Culture, 1990; My Soul's High Song, 1991; Lure and Loathing, 1993; Daughters: One Family and Fatherhood, 1994; Culture of Bruising, 1994; How The War in The Streets is Won, 1995. Contributions include: Essays and reviews to many journals; Poetry: The American Poetry Review; Northwest Review; Tar River Poetry; Raccoon; Seneca Review; Obsidian II; Black American Literature Forum. Honours: Cornell University: 1st Year Minority Graduate Fellowship, 1977; Summer Fellowship, Summer Tuition Grant, 1978-80; Creative and Performing Arts Council Creative Writing Award, 1978; 2nd place 1979, 3rd place 1981, Arthur Lynn Andrews Prize for Short Stories; Dissertation Research Award, 1980; Graduate Fellowship and Research Assistantship, 1981; Josephine de Karman Graduate Fellowship, 1981; Washington University Faculty Summer Research Fellowship, 1984; University of Kansas Minority Postdoctoral Fellowship, 1985-87; The Passing of Jazz's Old Guard selected for publication, Ticknor and Early, 1985; The Whiting Foundation Writer's Award, 1988; CCLM-General Electric Foundation Award for Younger Writers, 1988; Her Picture in The Papers: Remembering Some Black Women, selected as Notable Essay, Ticknow and Early, 1989. Address: Washington University, Campus Box 1109, One Brookings Drive, St Louis, MO 63130, USA.

EAST Morris. See: **WEST Morris.**

EASTAUGH Kenneth, b. 1929, Writer. Literary Appointments: Television Critic, 1965-67, Show Business Writer, 1967-70, Daily Mirror, London; Chief Show Business Writer, The Sun, London, 1970-73; TV Columnist, The Times, London, 1977; Chief Show Business Executive, Daily Star, London, 1978-83; Film Critic, Prima Magazine, Music Critic, Classical Music Weekly, 1976-. Publications: The Event (television play), 1968; Better Than A Man (televsion play), 1970; Dapple Downs (radio serial), 1973-74; Awkward Cuss (play), 1976; Havergal Brian: The Making of a Composer (biography), 1976; Coronation Street (television series), 1977-78; The Carry On Book (cinema), 1978; Havergal Who? (television documentary), 1980; Mr Love (novel, screenplay), 1986; Dallas (television serial), 1989; Three film contract with David Puttman/Warner Bros, 1992. Address: David Higham Associates, 5-8 Lower John Street, Golden Square, London, W1R 4HA, England.

EASTHOPE Antony Kelynge Revington, b. 14 Apr 1939, Portsmouth, England. Lecturer. m. Diane Garside, 1 Feb 1972, 1 s, 2 d. Education: Christ's College, Cambridge, 1958-64; BA, 1961; MA, 1965; MLitt, 1967. Literary Appointments: Brown University, Rhode Island, USA, 1964-66; Warwick University, England, 1967-68; Manchester Polytechnic, 1969-. Publications: Poetry as Discourse, 1983; What a Man's Gotta Do, 1986; British Post-Structuralism, 1988; Poetry and Phantasy, 1989; Literary into Cultural Studies, 1991; Wordsworth, Now and Then, 1993. Contributions to: Numerous magazines and journals. Honours: Charter Fellow, Wolfson College, Oxford, 1985-86; Visiting Fellow, University of Virginia, Centre for Literary and Cultural Change, 1990. Address: 27 Victoria Avenue, Didsbury, Manchester, M20 8QX, England.

EASTON Robert Olney, b. 4 Jul 1915, San Francisco, CA, USA. Writer. m. Jane Faust, 24 Sep 1940, 4 d. Education: Stanford University, 1933-34; SB, Harvard University, 1938; MA, University of California, 1960. Publications: The Happy Man, 1943; Lord of Beasts (co-author), 1961; The Book of the American West (co-author), 1963; The Hearing, 1964; Californian Condor (co-author), 1964; Max Brand, 1970; Black Tide, 1972; This Promised Land, 1982; China Caravans, 1982; Life and Work (co-author), 1988; Power and Glory, 1989; Love and War (co-author), 1991. Contributions to: various magazines. Literary Agent: Jon Tuska. Address: 2222 Las Canoas Road, Santa Barbara, CA 93105, USA.

EATON Charles Edward, b. 25 Jun 1916, Winston-Salem, NC, USA. Teacher; Professor; Diplomat; Lecturer. m. Isabel Patterson, 16 Aug 1950. Education: Duke University; AB, University of North Carolina, Chapel Hill, 1936; Princeton University; MA, Harvard University, 1940. Literary Appointments: Instructor on Creative Writing, University of Missouri, Columbia, 1940-42; Professor of Creative Writing, University of North Carolina, Chapel Hill, 1946-52. Publications: The Bright Plain, 1942; The Shadow of The Swimmer, 1951; Greenhouse in The Garden, 1956; Write Mr From Rio, 1959; Countermoves, 1963; The Edge of The Knife, 1970; Karl Knaths, 1971; The Girl From Ipanema, 1972; Karl Knaths: Five Decades of Painting, 1973; The Man in The Green Chair, 1977; The Case of The Missing Photographs, 1978; Colophon of The Rover, 1980; The Thing King, 1983; The Work of The Wrench, 1985; New and Selected Poems, 1942-87, 1987; New and Selected Stories, 1959-89, 1989. Contributions to: many anthologies including: Best Poems of The Year, 1965, 1968, 1969, 1970, 1974, 1975; O Henry Prize Stories, 1972; Contemporary Southern Poetry, 1979. Honours: Ridgley Torrence Award, Poetry Society of America, 1952; Gertrude Boatwright Harris Award, 1954; Arizona Quarterly Award, 1956, 1977, 1979, 1982; Avron Foundation Award, 1980; Brockman Award, 1984. Memberships: Poetry Society of America; New England Poetry Society; North Carolina Art Society.

EATON Trevor Michael William, b. 26 Mar 1934, Harrow, London, England. Professional Performer of Chaucer's Tales. m. Beryl Elizabeth Rose Conley, 29 Sep 1958, 2 s, 2 d. Education: New College, Oxford University, 1955-58; MA, English Language and Literature, Oxford; MA, Applied Linguistics, University of Kent, Canterbury, 1988. Literary Appointments: Section Convenor, Linguistics and Literature Section, Linguistics Association of Great Britain; Founder, International Association of Literary Semantics, 1992. Publications: The Semantics of Language, 1966; Theoretical Semics, 1972; Editor, Essays in Literary Semantics, 1978; Poetries: Their Media and Ends (A I Richards); Commercial recordings: Chaucer's The Canterbury Tales, recited on 18 audio cassettes in Middle English, 1986-93. Contributions to: Linguistics; Cahier Roumains d'Etudes Littéraires; Style; Educational Studies. Honours: Founder, Editor, Journal of Literary Semantics, 1972-. Memberships: International Association of Literary Semantics; International PEN; Linguistics Association of Great Britain; PALA. Address: Honeywood Cottage, 35 Seaton Avenue, Hythe, Kent, CT21 5HH, England.

EBBETT Eve. See: **EBBETT Frances Eva.**

EBBETT Frances Eva (Eva Burfield, Eve Ebbett), b. 6 June 1925, Wellingborough, England. Author. m. Trevor George Ebbett, 22 Oct 1949, 1 daughter. Publications: As Eve Ebbett: In True Colonial Fashion, 1977; Victoria's Daughters, 1981; When The Boys Were Away, 1984; Give Them Swing Bands, 1969; To The Garden Alone, 1970; As Eva Burfield: Yellow Kowhai, 1957; A Chair To Sit On, 1958; The Long Winter, 1964; After Midnight, 1965; Out Of Yesterday, 1965; The White Prison, 1966; The New Mrs Rainier, 1967; The Last Day of Summer, 1968. Contributions to: Short stories New Zealand, Australia, England, France, Italy, Holland, Norway, Sweden and Denmark. Address: 908 Sylvan Road, Hastings, New Zealand.

EBEJER Francis, b. 28 Aug 1925, Malta. Novelist; Playwright (English and Maltese). m. Jane Couch, 5 Sep 1947 (sep 1957), 2 s (1 dec), 1 d. Education: Matriculated, Malta Lyceum, 1939; Fulbright Grant, USA, 1961-62. Literary Appointments: English-Italian Interpreter with British 8th Army Tripolitania, 1943-44; Member, Radio and Television Drama Panel, various periods; Occasional Drama and Literature Lecturer. Publications: A Wreath of Maltese Innocents, London, 1958, Malta, 1981; Evil of The King Cockroach, London, 1960, Malta, 1968; In The Eye of The Sun, London, 1969; Requiem For The Malta Fascist, 1980-; Come Again in Spring, NY, 1980; Leap of Malta

Dolphins, NY, 1982; Plays: Over 40 in Maltese, 7 volumes, 1950-85; 11 in English, 3 volumes, 1950-85; Vacances d'Ete, France, 1985; Vacanze d'Estate, Italy, 1988; For Rozina a Husband, book of 16 short stories. Contributions to: Various, including poetry, essays, to Maltese publications, 1940s-; Short story, Foot-Feet, to PEN Broadsheet; 12 short stories to Short Story, NY, 1980-; 5 short stories for BBC; 3 short stories in Italian translation, to Delta Focus; 1 act play in Polish translation, to Dialog and on Polish Television; Play on WDR Cologne; 4 stories on Radio Free Berlin, Sachsen Radio Leipzig and Radio Basle. Honours: Cheyney Award for Drama, 1964; Malta Literary Award, 4 times, 1972-; Phoenicia Trophy Award for Culture, 1982; Médaille d'Honneur de La Ville d'Avignon, France, 1986; Maltese Academy of Letters, Council Member, 1984-88; Honorary President, Malta Literary Society; Fellow, English PEN; Associate Member, French Academy of Vaucluse, Provence. Address: Apt 3, Nivea Court, Swieqi Valley, Swieqi, Malta, STJ 05.

EBEL Suzanne, (Suzanne Goodwin, Cecily Shelbourne), Writer. Publications include: Love, The Magician, 1956; Journey from Yesterday, 1963; The Half-Enchanted, 1964; The Love Campaign, 1965; The Dangerous Winter, 1965; A Perfect Stranger, 1966; A Name in Lights, 1968; A Most Auspicious Star, 1968; Somersault, 1971; Portrait of Jill, 1972; Dear Kate, 1972; To Seek a Star, 1973; The Family Feeling, 1973; Girl by The Sea, 1974; Music in Winter, 1975; A Grove of Olives, 1976; River Voices, 1976; The Double Rainbow, 1977; A Rose in Heather, 1978; Julia's Sister, 1982; The Provencal Summer, 1982; House of Nightingales, 1986; The Clover Field, 1987; As Suzanne Goodwin: The Winter Spring, 1978 (USA - Stage of Love, as Cecily Shelbourne, 1978); The Winter Sisters, 1980; Emerald, 1980; Floodtide, 1983; Sisters, 1985; Cousins, 1986; Daughters, 1987; Lovers, 1988; To Love A Hero, 1989; A Change of Season, 1990; The Rising Storm, 1992; While the Music Lasts, 1993; Non-fiction: Explore the Cotswolds by Bicycle (with Doreen Impey), 1973; London's Riverside, From Hampton Court in the West to Greenwich Palace in the East (with Doreen Impey), 1975. Address: 52A Digby Mansions, Hammersmith Bridge Road, London W6 9DF, England.

EBERSOHN Wessel (Schalk), b. 1940, South Africa. Author; Writer. Appointments: Technician: Department of Posts and Telecommunications, Pretoria, 1956-62; Gowlett Alpha, Johannesburg, 1962-69; Department of Posts of Telecommunications, Durban, 1970-79; Freelance Writer, 1979-. Publications: A Lonely Place to Die (mystery novel), 1979; The Centurion (mystery novel), 1979; Store up The Anger (novel), 1981; Divide The Night (mystery novel), 1981; Klara's Visitors (novel), 1987. Address: 491 Long Avenue, Ferndale 2194, Transvaal, South Africa.

EBERT Alan, b. 14 Sep 1935, New York, NY, USA. Author. Education: BA, Brooklyn College, 1957; MA, Fordham University, 1975. Publications: The Homosexuals, 1977; Every Body is Beautiful (with Ron Fletcher), 1978; Intimacies, 1979; Traditions (novel), 1981; The Long Way Home (novel), 1984; Marriages (novel), 1987. Contributions to: Family Circle; Essence; Look; Us; Good Housekeeping. Membership: American Society of Journalists and Authors. Address: 353 W 56th Street, New York, NY 10019, USA.

EBERT Tibor, b. 14 Oct 1926, Bratislava, Czechoslovakia. Writer; Poet; Dramatist. m. Eva Gati, 11 Feb 1968, 1 d. Education: BA, Music, Ferenc Liszt Academy of Music, 1952; Law, Philosophy, Literature studies, Department of Law and Philosophy, Eotvos Lorand University, Budapest, 1951-53. Literary Appointments: Dramaturg, Jozsef Attila Theatre, Budapest, Hungary, 1984-85; Editor-in-Chief, Agora Publishers, Budapest, 1989-92; Editor, Hirvivo Literary Magazine, 1990-92. Publications: Mikrodramak, 1971; Rosarium, 1987; Kobayashi, 1989; Legenda egy fuvoszenekarrol, 1990; Job konyve, 1991; Several plays performed on stage including: Les Escaliers; Musique de Chambre; Demosthenes; Esterhazy. Contributions to: numerous short stories, poems, dramas and essays to several leading Hungarian literary journals and magazines. Honours: Honorary Member, Franco-Hungarian Society, 1980-; Bartok Prize, 1987; Commemorative Medal, City of Pozsony-Pressburg-Bratislava, 1991. Membership: PEN Club. Literary Agent: Artisjus Budapest, Hungary. Address: Csevi u 15c, 1025 Budapest, Hungary.

ECHERUO Michael (Joseph Chukwudalu), b. 14 Mar 1937, Umunumo, Mbano Division, Nigeria. Professor of English; Poet. Education: University College, Ibadan, 1955-60; PhD, Cornell University, New York, 1965. Appointments: Professor of English, 1974-80, and Vice-Chancellor, from 1981, Imo State University, Owerri.

Publications: Mortality, 1968; Distanced: New Poems, 1975; Joyce Cary and the Novel of Africa, 1973; Victorian Lagos, 1977; Poets, Prophets and Professors, 1977; The Conditioned Imagination from Shakespeare to Conrad: Studies in the Exo-Cultural Stereotype, 1978; Editor, Shakespeare's The Tempest, 1980. Honours include: All-Africa Poetry Competition Prize, 1963. Address: Vice-Chancellor's Office, Imo State University, Owerri, Nigeria.

ECKARDT Arthur Roy, b. 1918, USA. Writer, Philosophy, Theology, Religion. Appointments: Editor, Journal of the American Academy of Religion, 1961-69; Professor of Religion Studies Emeritus, Lehigh University; Visiting Scholar, Centre for Hebrew Studies, University of Oxford, 1982-88; Senior Associate Fellow, 1990. Publications: Christianity and the Children of Israel, 1948; The Surge of Piety in America, 1965 ; Elder and the Younger Brothers, 1967, 1973; The Theologian at Work, 1968; Encounter With Israel (with Alice Eckardt), 1970; Your People My People, 1974; Long Night's Journey Into Day (with Alice Eckardt), 1982, rev. ed. 1988; Jews and Christians, 1986; For Righteousness' Sake, 1987; Black-Woman-Jew, 1989; Reclaiming the Jesus of History, 1992; Sitting in the Earth and Laughing, 1992; Collecting Myself (ed Alice Eckardt), 1993; How to tell God From the Devil, 1994; No Longer Aliens No Longer Strangers, 1994; On the Way to Death, 1995. Address: 6011 Beverly Hill Road, Coopersburg, PA 18036, USA.

ECO Umberto, b. 5 Jan 1932, Alessandria, Italy. Writer. m. Renate Ramge, 24 Sep 1962, 1 s, 1 d. Education: PhD, University of Turin, 1954. Publications: Diario minimo, 1963, revised edition, 1976; Appunti per una semiologia delle communicazioni visive, 1967; La definizione dell'arte (The Definition of Art), 1968; Le forme del contenuto, 1971; I pampini bugiardi, 1972; Editor, Estetica e teoria dell'informazione, 1972; Storia di una rivoluzione mai esistita l'esperimento Vaduz, 1976; Dalla periferia dell'impero, 1976; Come si fa una tesi di laurea, 1977; Perche continuiamo a fare e a insegnare arte?, 1979; Sette anni di desiderio, 1983; in English: A Theory of Semiotics, 1976; The Role of The Reader: Explorations in the Semotics of Texts, 1979; Semotics and The Philosophy of Language, 1984; Sign of The Three: Dupin, Holmes, Pierce, 1984; The Name of The Rose; Fouccult's Pendulum, 1989. Contributions to: Numerous Encyclopedias including Enciclopedia Filosofica and Encyclopedic Dictionary of Semotics; Essays, Reviews to numerous periodicals including Espreso, Corriere della Sera, Times Literary Supplement, Revue Internationale de Sciences Sociales, Nouvelle Revue Francaise. Honours: Premio Stega and Premio Anghiari, 1981 (for Il nome della rosa); Named Honorary Citizen of Monte Cerignon, Italy, 1982; Prize for Best Foreign Novel, 1982 (for French version of Il nome della rosa); Los Angeles Times Fiction Prize Nomination for The Name of The Rose. Memberships: Secretary General, 1972-1979, Vice President, 1979-, International Association for Semiotic Studies; Honorary Trustee, James Joyce Foundation. Address: Via Melzi d'Eril 23, 20154 Milano, Italy.

EDDINGS David, b. 1931, Washington, USA. Science Fiction Writer. Education: BA, University of Washington. Literary Appointments include: Teacher, College-level English. Publications: High Hunt (adventure story); Belgariad series: Pawn of Prophesy; Queen of Sorcery; Magician's Gambit; Castle of Wizardry; Enchanters' End Game; Mallorean series: Guardians of The West; King of The Murgos; Demon Lord of Karanda; Sorceress of Darshiva, 1989; The Diamond Throne; The Seeress of Kell.

EDELMAN Bernard, b. 14 Dec 1946, Brooklyn, NY, USA. Editor; Consultant. m. Ellen M Leary, 31 May 1985. Education: BA, Brooklyn College, 1968; MA, John Jay College of Criminal Justice, 1983. Publication: Dear America: Letters Home From Vietnam (editor), 1988. Contributions include: Dear America excerpted in several publications including Time magazine; articles to: Police magazine; Daily News Sunday magazine. Honours: Documentary film based on Dear America received 2 Emmy Awards, numerous film festival citations and critical acclaim. Literary Agent: Phillipa Brophy, Sterling Lord Literistic. Address: Mount Joy Road, Finesville, NJ 08865, USA.

EDGAR David, b. 26 Feb 1948, Birmingham, England. Playwright. Education: BA honours, Drama, Manchester University, 1969. Literary Appointments include: Lecturer in Playwriting, Birmingham University, 1974-78; Resident Playwright, Birmingham Repertory Theatre, 1985-; Literary Consultant, Royal Shakespeare Company, 1984-88; Honorary Senior Research Fellow, University of Birmingham, 1988-, Honorary Professor, 1992-. Publications include:

The Second Time as Farce, 1988; Edgar Shorts (Blood Sports with Ball Boys, Baby Love, The National Theatre, The Midas Connection), 1990; Plays include: Maydays, London, 1983, revised edition, 1984; Entertaining Strangers: A Play for Dorchester, produced Dorchester, Dorset, 1985, revised version produced London, 1987; That Summer, London, 1987; Plays I (includes The Jail Diary of Albie Sachs, Mary Barnes, Saigon Rose, O Fair Jerusalem, Destiny), London, 1987; Heartlanders (with Stephen Bill and Anne Devlin), 1989; The Shape of The Table, London, 1990; Dr Jekeyll and Mr Hyde, 1991; Screenplay: Lady Jane, 1986; Radio Plays: Ecclesiastes, 1977; A Movie Starring Me, 1991; Television Plays: The Eagle Has Landed, 1973; Sanctuary From His Play Gangsters, 1973; I Know What I Meant, 1974; The Midas Connection, 1975; Censors (with Hugh Whitemore and Robert Muller), 1975; Voe For Them (with Neil Grant), 1989; Buying a Landslide, 1992. Honours: John Whiting Award, 1976; Bicentennial Exchange Fellowship, 1978; Society of West End Theatre Award, 1980; New York Drama Critics Circle Award, 1982; Tony Award, 1982. Literary Agent: Michael Imison Playwrights, London, England. Address: c/o Michael Imison Playwrights, 28 Almeida Street, London, N1 1TD, England.

EDMOND Lauris Dorothy, b. 2 Apr 1924, Dannevirke, New Zealand. Writer; Editor; University Tutor. m. 16 May 1945, 1 son, 5 daughters. Education: Teaching Diploma, 1943; Speech Therapy Diploma, 1944; BA, Waikato University, 1966; MA, Victoria University, 1971. Appointments: Katherine Mansfield Memorial Fellowship, 1981; Writer in Residence, Deakin University, 1985; Writers Fellowship, Victoria University, 1987. Publications include: In Middle Air, 1975; The Pear Tree, 1977; Salt from the North, 1980; Wellington Letter, 1980; Catching It, 1983; Selected Poems, 1984; Seasons and Creatures, 1986; New & Selected Poems, 1991; Summer Near the Artic Circle, 1988; High Country Weather, 1983; The Mountain Cycle of 4 Plays for Radio, 1981; Between Night and Morning, 1981; Autobiography, Hot October, 1989; Bonfires in the Rain, 1991; The Quick World, 1992; Scenes from a Small City, 1994. Contributions to: Womens Fiction, PB Review; Stand; Planet; The Honest Ulsterman; Verse; Numbers; Poetry Now, UK; Meanjin; Westerly; Overland; Landfall; Poetry New Zealand; The New Zealand Listener; Islands. Honours: Best First book, PEN, 1975; Commonwealth Poetry Prize, 1985; OBE, 1986; Lilian Ida Smith Award, 1987; Honorary DLitt Massey University, 1988. Memberships: PEN; Wellington Poetry Society. Address: 22 Grass Street, Oriental Bay, Wellington, New Zealand.

EDMOND Murray (Donald), b. 1949, New Zealand. Director; Actor; Poet. Appointments: Director and Actor, Town and Country Players, Wellington; Lecturer in Drama, University of Auckland, 1991. Publications: Entering the Eye, 1973; Patchwork, 1978; End Wall, 1981; Letters and Paragraphs, 1987; Co-editor, The New Poets of the 80's: Initiatives in New Zealand Poetry, 1987; From the Word Go, 1992; The Switch, 1994. Address: English Dept, University of Auckland, Private Bag 92019, Auckland, New Zealand.

EDRIC Robert, b. 14 Apr 1956, Sheffield, England. Writer. m. 12 Aug 1978. Education: BA 1st Class Honours, PhD, Hull University. Publications: Winter Garden, 1985; A Season of Peace, 1985; A New Ice Age, 1986; Across The Autumn Grass, 1986. Contributions to: London Magazine; Stand; Critical Quarterly; PEN; New Fiction II; Proof. Honours: James Tait Black Memorial Award, 1985; Trask Award, 1985. Literary Agent: A Harwood, Aitken and Stone Limited. Address: The Lindens, Atwick Road, Hornsea, North Humberside, England.

EDSON Russell, b. 1935, USA. Writer; Poet; Playwright. Publications: Appearances: Fables And Drawings, 1961; A Stone is Nobody's: Fables and Drawings, 1964; The Boundary, 1964; The Very Thing That Happens: Fables and Drawings, 1964; The Brain Kitchen: Writings and Woodcuts, 1965; What a Man Can See, 1969; The Childhood of An Equestrian, 1973; The Clam Theater, 1973; The Falling Sicness (Plays), 1975; The Intuitive Journey, 1976; The Reason Why the Closet-Man is Never Sad, 1977; With Sincerest Regrets, 1980; Wuck Wuck Wuck!, 1984; Gulping' Recital, 1984; The Wounded Breakfast, 1985; The Song of Percival Peacock, 1992; The Tunnel: Selected Poems, 1994. Honours: Guggenheim Fellowship, 1974; NEA, 1981, 1992. Whiting Writers' Award, 1989. Address: 149 Weed Avenue, Stamford, CT 06902, USA.

EDWARDS Anne, b. 1927, USA. Writer. Appointments: Member of Authors Guild, 1978-81, President, 1981-85, The Authors Guild, President Emertus, Board Authors League. Publications: (adaptor) A Child's Bible, 1967; The Survivors, 1968; Miklos Alexandrovitch is

Missing (UK - Alexandrovitch is Missing), 1969; Shadow of a Lion, 1970; The Hesitant Heart, 1974; Judy Garland: A Biography, 1974; Haunted Summer, 1974; The Inn and Us (with Stephen Citron), 1975; Child of Night (UK - Ravenwings), 1975; P T Barnum, 1976; The Great Houdini, 1977; Vivien Leigh: A Biography, 1977; Sonya: The Life of the Countess Tolstoy, 1981; The Road to Tara: The Life of Margaret Mitchell, 1983; Matriarch: Queen Mary and the House of Windsor, 1984; A Remarkable Woman: Katherine Hepburn, 1985; Early Reagan: The Rise to Power, 1986; The Demilles: An American Dynasty, 1987; American Princess: A Biography of Shirley Temple, 1988; Royal Sisters: Queen Elizabeth and Princess Margaret, 1990; Wallis - the Novel, 1991; The Grimaldis of Monaco: Centuries of Scandals Years of Grace, 1992; La Divina, 1994; Throne of Gold: The Lives of the Aga Khans, 1995; Streisand: It Only Happens Once, forthcoming. Contribution to: Architectural Digest. Literary Agent: Rogers Coleridge & White Ltd, 20 Powis Mews, London W11 1JN. Address: c/o International Creative Management Inc, 40 W 57th Street, New York, NY 10019, USA.

EDWARDS F E. See: **NOLAN William F(rancis).**

EDWARDS Josh. See: **LEVINSON Leonard.**

EDWARDS Norman. See: **CARR Terry.**

EDWARDS Page Lawrence Jr, b. 15 Jan 1941. Archivist. m. Diana Selser, 26 Aug 1986, 2 s, 2 d. Education: BA, Stanford University, 1963; MFA, University of Iowa, 1974; MLS, Simmons College, 1982. Literary Appointments: Staff, Breadloaf Writers' Conference, 1982-84; Writer-in-Residence, Flagler College, St Augustine, FL, 1985-. Publications: Mules That Angels Ride, 1972; Touring, 1974; Staking Claims, 1976; Peggy Salte, 1984; Scarface Joe, 1985; The Lake, 1986; American Girl, 1990. Contributions to: Redbook; Woman's World; Bananas; Iowa Review. Literary Agent: Amanda Urban, ICM. Address: c/o Marion Boyars Limited, 26 East 33rd Street, New York, NY 10016, USA.

EDWARDS Philip Walter, b. 7 Feb 1923, Cumbria, England. Professor. m. Sheila Mary Wilkes, 8 May 1952, 3 s, 1 d. Education: BA, 1942, MA, 1946, PhD, 1960, University of Birmingham. Appointments: Lecturer, University of Birmingham, 1946-60; Professor, Trinity College, Dublin, 1960-66; Professor, University of Essex, 1966-74; Professor, University of Liverpool, 1974-90. Publications: Sir Walter Ralegh, 1953; Kyd, The Spanish Tragedy, 1959; Shakespeare and the Confines of Art, 1968; Massinger, Plays and Poems, 1976; Shakespeare's Pericles, 1976; Threshold of a Nation, 1979; Hamlet, 1985; Shakespeare: A Writers Progress, 1986; Last Voyages, 1988; The Story of the Voyage, 1994. Membership: Fellowship; The British Academy, 1986. Address: High Gillinggrove, Gillinggate, Kendal, Cumbria, LA9 4JB.

EDWARDS Rowan (Judith), b. 19 Nov 1945, India. Writer; Former Teacher. m. Martin Brian Edwards, 18 Dec 1965, 1 s, 1 d. Education: BA, Kings College, University of London, 1966. Appointments: Personal Assistant to Labour Member of Parliament and Junior Minister; Teacher, Inner London Education Authority; Freelance Editor, London, West Country; Freelance Writer, Novelist, Journalist; Examiner; Creative Writing Tutoring; Adjudicating Local Competitions; Assessing in MSS for South West Arts. Publications include: 16 Romantic Novels, 1983-94; Trans into 15 Languages in Paperback. Contributions to: Short Stories to Magazines; Articles, Guardian; Bristol Evening Post; Birmingham Post; Travel, Local & Other Specialist Magazines. Honours: Bristol Poetry Competition, 1988; ORBIS, 1989; 1st Prize for Radio Play, 1989. Memberships: Society of Authors; Romantic Novelists Association; Society of Freelance Editors and Proofreaders. Address: 2 Highbury Hall, 22 Highbury Road, Weston Super Mare, BS23 2DN, England.

EDWARDS Ted (Brian), b. 25 Apr 1939, Leigh, Lancashire, England. Explorer; Author; Teacher; Song Writer. Education: BEd, Manchester Polytechnic, 1975-79. Publications include: A Slutchy Brew, 1971; Beyond the Last Oasis, 1985; Fight the Wild Island, 1986; The Empty Quarter, 1984. Contributions to: Expedition Year Book, 1983, 1984, 1985; Readers Digest, 1986; Other Journals & Magazines. Memberships: FBIS; FRGS; PRS; MCPS; BASCA; BAEA. Literary Agent: Watson Little Limited, London. Address: The Garret, 6 Westminster Road, Eccles, Manchester M30 9HF, England.

EFFINGER George Alec, b. 1947, America. Writer of novels, short stories, science fiction, fantasy. Literary Appointment: Teacher of

Science Fiction Course, Tulane University, New Orleans, 1973-74. Publications: What Entropy Means to Me, 1972; Relatives, 1973; Mixed Feelings (short stories), 1974; Nightmare Blue (with G Dozois), 1975; Irrational Numbers (short stories), 1976; Those Gentle Voices, 1976; Felicia, 1976; Death in Florence, 1978, as Utopia Three, 1980; Dirty Tricks (short stories), 1978; Heroics, 1979; The Wolves of Memory, 1981; Idle Pleasures (short stories), 1983; The Nick of Time, 1986; The Birds of Time, 1986; When Gravity Falls, 1987; Exile Kiss, 1991; Maureen Birnbaum, Barbarian Swordsperson, 1993. Address: Box 15183, New Orleans, LA 70175, USA.

EGLETON Clive Frederick William, (Patrick Blake, John Tarrant), b. 25 Nov 1927, Author; Retired Army Officer; Retired Civil Servant. m. Joan Evelyn Lane, 9 Apr 1949, 2 sons. Education: Staff College, Camberley, 1957. Publications include: Seven Days to a Killing, 1988; The October Plot, 1985; The Winter Touch, 1982; Backfire, 1979; Picture of the Year, 1987; Gone Missing, 1988; A Conflict of Interests, 1984; In The Red, 1990; Last Act, 1991; A Double Deception, 1992; Hostile Intent, 1993; A Killing in Moscow, 1994; Death Throes, 1994. Memberships: Crime Writers Association; Society of Authors. Literary Agent: Anthony Goff, David Higham Associates Limited. Address: Dolphin House, Beach House Lane, Bembridge, Isle of Wight, PO35 5TA, England.

EHRENBERG Miriam Colbert, b. 6 Mar 1930, New York City, USA. Psychologist. m. Otto Ehrenberg, 20 Sept 1956, 2 d. Education: BA, Queens College; MA, City University of New York; PhD, New School for Social Research, New York. Publications: The Psychotherapy Maze, 1977, 2nd edition, 1986; Optimum Brain Power, 1985; The Intimate Circle, 1988. Membership: American Psychological Association. Literary Agent: Writers House. Address: 118 Riverside Drive, New York, NY 10024, USA.

EHRENREICH Barbara, b. 26 Aug 1941, Butte, Montana. Feminist; Critic; Novelist. m. (1) John Ehrenreich, 6 Aug 1966, 1 son, 1 daughter, (2) Gary Stevenson, 10 Dec 1983. Education: BA, Reed College, 1963, PhD, Rockefeller University, 1968. Appointments include: Essayist, Time Magazine, 1990-; Columnist, The Guardian (London), 1991-. Publications: Long March, Short Spring, 1969; For Her Own Good, 1978; The Hearts of Men, 1983; Remaking Love, 1986; The Mean Season, 1987; Fear of Falling, 1989; The Worst Years of Our Lives, 1990; Kipper's Game, 1993. Contributions include: New York Times; Mother Jones; The Atlantic, MS; The New Republic; Radical America. Honours: National Magazine Award, 1980; Ford Foundation Award for Humanistic Perspectives on Contemporary Issues, 1981; Guggenheim Fellowship, 1987, Long Island NOW Women's Equality Award, 1988; National Book Critics' Award Nominee; National Magazine Award Finalist for essays, 1992.

EHRLICH Eugene, b. 1922, America. University Faculty Member; Writer. Literary Appointments: Associated with Department of English, Columbia University, New York City, 1948-. Publications: How to Study Better, 1960, 1976; The Art of Technical Writing (with D Murphy), 1962; Researching and Writing Term Papers and Reports (with D Murphy), 1964; College Developmental Reading (with D Murphy and D Pace), 1966; Basic Grammar for Writing (with D Murphy), 1970; Concise Index to English (with D Murphy), 1974; Basic Vocabulary Builder, 1975; English Grammar, 1976; Punctuation, Capitalization and Spelling, 1977; Oxford American Dictionary (with others), 1980; The Oxford Illustrated Literary Guide to The United States (with Gordon Carruth), 1982; Speak for Success, 1984; Amo, Amas, amat and More, 1985; The Bantam Concise Handbook of English, 1986; Harper's Dictionary of Foreign Terms, number 3, 1990. Address: 15 Park Road, Scarsdale, NY 10583, USA.

EHRLICH Paul, b. 1932, USA. Bing Professor of Population Studies, Professor of Biological Sciences. Biologist.Appointments: Assistant Professor, Associate Professor, 1959-66, Professor, 1966-76, Bing Professor of Population Studies, 1976-, Stanford University, CA; Advisor in Biological Sciences, 1966-75, Editor in Population in Biology, 1966-, McGraw Hill Book Co, New York City; President 1969-70, Honorary President 1970-, Zero Population Growth. Publications: How to Know the Butterflies, 1962; Process of Evolution, 1963, 1964; Principles of Modern Biology, 1968; Population Bomb, 1968; Population, Resources, Environment Issues in Human Ecology, 1970; How to be a Survivor, 1971; The Race Bomb, 1977; Ecoscience: Population, Resouces, Environment, 1977; Golden Door: International Migration, Mexico and the United States, 1980; Extinction, 1981; (with others) The Cold and the Dark: The World After Nuclear War, 1984;

The Machinery of Nature, 1986; Earth, 1987; The Science of Ecology, 1987; Birders Handbook, 1988; Population Explosion, 1990: Healing the Plant, 1991; Birds in Jeopardy, 1992. Memberships: National Academy of Sciences; Fellow, American Academy of Arts and Sciences; American Philosophical Society. Address: Department of Biological Sciences, Stanford University, Stanford, CA 94305, USA.

EHRLICHMAN John, b. 20 Mar 1925, Tacoma, WA, USA. Writer. 4 s, 2 d. Education: AB, 1945; JD, 1951. Publications: The Company (Washington Behind Closed Doors), 1976; The Whole Truth, 1978; Witness to Power, 1980; The China Card, 1986; Sketches and Notes, 1987; An Indispensable Guide to Sante Fe, 1987; The Rigby File, 1990. Contributions include: Newsweek; Time; New York Magazine; Travel and Leisure; Parade. Literary Agent: Morton L Janklow and Associates. Address: 795 Hammond Drive, 1607 Atlanta, GA 30328, USA.

EIBEL Deborah, b. 25 Jun 1940, Montreal, Canada. Poet. Education: BA, McGill University, 1960: AM, Radcliffe College, 1962; MA, John Hopkins University, 1971. Publications: Kayak Sickness, 1972; Streets Too Narrow For Parades, 1985; Making Fun of Travellers, 1992. Contributions to: Canadian Literature; The Malahat Review; Moosehead Anthology; Canadian Woman Studies; Canadian Women Writers Issue of Prairie Schooner, Dec 15 1993. Honours: Chester McNaghten Award, 1959; Arthur Davison Ficke Sonnet Award of the Poetry Society of America, 1965; Canada Council Arts Grant 'B.' Memberships: The League of Canadian Poets; The Poetry society of America. Address: 6657 Wilderton Avenue, Montreal, Quebec, Canada, H3S 2L8.

EICHENBAUM Luise Ronni, b. 22 Jul 1952, New York, USA. Psychotherapist; Lecturer; Writer. m. Jeremy Pikser, 1 s, 1 d. Education: BA, highest honours, City University of New York, 1973; MSW, State Univesity of New York at Stony Brook, 1975. Appointments: Women's Therapy Centre, London, England, Co-founder, co-director, psychotherapist, lecturer, 1976-80; Women's Therapy Centre Institute, 1980-; Publications: Understanding Women: A Feminist Psychoanalytic Approach, 1983; What Do Women Want: Exploring the Myth of Dependency, 1983; Between Women: Love Envy and Competition in Women's Friendships, 1989. Memberships: Co-Founder, Women's Therapy Centre, London, England; Co-Founder, Women's Therapy Centre Institute, New York, USA. Literary Agent: Ellen Levine. Address: 562 West End Avenue, New York, NY 10024, USA

EIGNER Larry (Laurence Joel), b. 7 Aug 1927, Swampscott, MA, USA. Writer; Poet. Education: Correspondence courses from University of Chicago. Publications include: some broadsides; Five Poems, Bed Never Self Made, 1964; The Music, The Rooms, 1965; The Memory of Yeats, Blake, DHL, 1965; Six Poems, 1967; Another Time in Fragments, 1967; Towards Autumn, 1967; Air The Trees, 1967; The Breath of Once Live Things, In The Field with Poe, 1968; A Line That May Be Cut, 1968; Valleys, Branches, 1969; Flat and Round, 1969; Over and Over, Ends, As The Wind May Sound, 1970; Poem Nov 1968, 1970; Circuits: A Microbook, 1970; Looks Like Nothing, The Shadow Through The Air, 1972; What You Hear, 1972; Selected Poems, 1972; Words Touching Ground Under, 1972; Shape Shadow Elements Move, 1973; Things Stirring Together or Far Away, 1974; Anything on Its Side, 1974; No Radio, 1974; My God The Proverbial, 1975; Suddenly it Gets Light and Dark in The Streets: Poems, 1961-74, 1975; The Music Variety, 1976; The World and Its Streets, Places, 1977; Watching How or Why, 1977; Cloud, Invisible Air, 1978; Flagpole Riding, 1978; Running Around, 1978; Heat Simmers Cold, 1978; Time, Details of a Tree, 1979; Country-Harbour-Around (prose), 1978; Earth Birds, 1981; Now There's-a-Morning-Holk of The Sky, 1981; Waters-Places-A Time, 1983; Areas, Lights, Heights (essays, reviews, letters), 1989; A Count of Some Things, 1991. Contributions include: Origin; Black Mountain Review; Poetry; Paris Review; Chicago Review. Address: 2338 McGee Avenue, Berkeley, CA 94703, USA.

EINARSSON Sveinn, b. 18 Sept 1934, Reykjavik, Iceland. Writer; Theatre & TV Director; Councellor of Culture. m. Thora Kristjansdottir, 17 Oct 1964, 1 d. Education: Fil kand, Stockholm, 1958; Fil lic, Theatre, 1964. Appointments: Member, Jury, Nordic Price in Literature, 1985-90; Vice President, International Theatre Institute, 1979-81; Pres, Poetry Committee, Council of Europe, 1987-90; Member, European Cultural Centre of Delphi, 1990. Publications include: Gabriella in Portugal, 1985; Dordingull, 1994; Several Plays including, Egg of Life, 1984; Im Gold and Treasures, 1985; Bukolla, 1991; Bandarnannasagh, 1992; Books on the Theatre; Theatre by the

Lake, 1972; My 9 Years Down There, 1987; Icelandic Theatre Vol 1, 1991; Several TV & Radio Plays. Contributions to: Articles on Theatre. Honours: Childrens Book of the Year, 1986; Clara Lachmann Price, 1990. Memberships: Icelandic Writers Union, Pres; Union of Icel Playwrights, 1986-89; Icelandic Theatre Union, 1972-89. Literary Agent: Ormstunga, Reykjavik. Address: Tjarnargata 26, 101 Reykjavik, Iceland.

EINZIG Barbara Ellen, b. 31 May 1951, Michigan, USA. Poet; Fiction Writer. m. 20 Mar 1981, 1 d. Education: BA, High Honours, Literature, University of California, San Diego, 1972. Literary Appointments: Associate Editor, 1977-85, Editor, Special Dreamworks Issue of New Wilderness Letter, 1981. Publications: Color, 1976; Disappearing Work, 1979; Robinson Crusoe: A New Fiction, 1983; Life Moves Outside, 1987. Contributions to: Various magazines and journals. Honours: Chancellor's Prize, Literature, UC San Diego, 1972; Granted MacDowell Colony Residency, 1984; Visiting Scholar, Tisch School of The Arts, 1984-87; Writer in Residence, Rockland Centre for The Arts, 1987. Memberships: Director, Water Street Arts Centre Poetry Series, 1974-75; Participant, Poetry in The Schools Programme, California, 1981-83. Address: 21 Bay Street, Piermont, NY 10968, USA.

EISELE Robert H, b. 9 Jun 1948. Writer. Education: BA,1971; MFA, 1974; UCLA, USA, 1971. Appointments: Playwrighting Fellow, Actor, American Conservatory Theatre, 1975-76; Associate Professor, Theatre Arts, Rio Hondo College, CA, 1976-87. Publications: Plays: Animals are Passing from Our Lives. Productions: A Dark Night of the Soul; A Garden in Los Angeles; Goats; The Green Room; Film; Breach of Contract, 1982; TV: Murder of Einstein, aired on PBS, 1981; Ordinary Hero & Schedule One (episodes of Cagney and Lacey), aired on CBS; 4 episodes of Crime Story, aired on NBC; Suspicion of Innocence; Shadow Play; The Rehearsal; No Place Like Home; Day of the Covenant, The Visitation, Starfire, Prisoners of Conscience, (episodes of The Equalizer aired on CBS), Last Light, Showtime; Lily In Winter, USA Network. Honours include: Samuel Goldwyn Writing Awards, 1973; Oscar Hammerstein Playwrighting Fellowship, 1973-74; Donald Davis Dramatic Writing Awards, 1974; American Conservatory Theatre Playwrighting Fellowship, 1975-76; 1st Prize, Theatre Arts Corporation Contest, 1979; Humanitas Award, 1986; Writers Guild Award Nomination, 1994, (Last Light). Memberships: Screen Actors Guild; Writers Guild of America; Dramatists Guild; Actors Equity Association; Academy of TV Arts & Sciences. Address: Ken Shearman & Associates, 9507 Santa Monica Bld, No. 212, Beverly Hills, CA 90210, USA.

EISEN Sydney, b. 5 Feb 1929, Poland. University Professor. m. Doris Ruth d Ben Kirschbaum, 22 Jan 1957, 2 sons, 2 daughters. Education: Harbord Collegiate Institue, Toronto, 1946; BA, University Toronto, 1950; PhD, Johns Hopkins University, 1957. Appointments: Director, Centre for Jewish Studies, York University, 1989-; University Professor, York University, 1993-. Publications: Co-author, The Human Adventure: Readings in World History, 2 vols, 1964; Victorian Science and Religion: A Bibliography, 1984; General Editor, The West and the World, various books and pamphlets; Victorian Faith in Crisis, 1990. Contributions to: Various articles and reviews in professional journals. Memberships: Victorian Studies Association; Conf on British Studies; History Science Society; American History Association. Address: 5 Renoak Drive, Willowdale, Ont M2R 3E1, Canada.

EISENBERG Gerson G, b. 5 Mar 1909. Author. m. 15 Sept 1967. Education: AB, George Washington University, 1930; Graduate Student, Johns Hopkins University, 1937-38; MBA, New York University, 1944. Publications: Learning Vacations, 6 editions, 1977-86; Marylanders in National Service, 1990. Contribution to: Baltimore Views the Great Depression, to Maryland Historical Society, 1976. Membership: Baltimore Writers Association. Address: 11 Slade Ave 116, Baltimore, MD 21208, USA.

EISENBERG Deborah, b. 20 Nov 1945, Chicago, IL, USA. Writer. Publications: Transactions in a Foreign Currency; Under the 82nd Airborne; Pastorale. Honours: O Henry Story Award; John Simon Guggenheim Fellowship; Mrs Giles Whiting Award; Ingram Merrill Foundation Award; Award in Literature from the American Academy of Arts and Letters. Literary Agent: Lynn Nesbit. Address: c/o Lynn Nesbit, Jarklow & Nesbit Associates, 598 Madison Avenue, New York, NY 10022, USA.

EKINS Paul Whitfield, b. 24 July 1950, Djakarta, Indonesia. Economist. m. Susan Anne Lofthouse, 24 Sept 1979, 1 s. Education: BSC, Imperial College, London, 1971; MSC, Birkbeck College London, 1988; MPhil, University of Bradford, 1990. Publications include: The Living Economy: A New Economy in the Making, 1986; A New World Order, 1992; Wealth Beyond Measure, 1992; Real Life Economics, 1992. Contributions to: The Ecologist; Journal of Environmental Conservation; Development; International Environmental Affairs; Integrated Environmental Management; Science and Public Policy; Resurgence; Ecological Economics; Environmentaland Resource Economics; Medicine and War. Memberships: European Association of Evolutionary Political Economy; International Society for Ecological Economics; Society for the Advancement of Socio Economics; Society for International Development. Address: 42 Warriner Gardens, London SW11 4DU, England.

EKLUND Gordon, b. 24 Jul 1945, Seattle, WA, USA. Writer. 1 d. Publications: The Eclipse of Dawn, 1971; A Trace of Dreams, 1972; Beyond The Resurrection, 1973; All Times Possible, 1974; Serving in Time, 1975; Falling Toward Forever, 1975; If The Stars are Gods, 1976; The Dance of The Apocalypse, 1976; The Grayspace Beast, 1976; Find The Changeling, 1980; The Garden of Winter, 1980; Thunder on Neptune, 1989. Contributions to: Analog; Galaxy; If Science Fiction; Fantasy and Science Fiction; Universe; New Dimensions; Amazing Stories; Fantastic. Honour: Nebula Award, 1975. Membership: Science Fiction Writers of America. Literary Agent: Martha Millard. Address: 6305 East D Street, Tacoma, WA 98404, USA.

EKSTROM Margareta, b. 23 Apr 1930, Stockholm, Sweden. Writer; Translator. 1 s, 1 d. Education: Stockholm University, 1956. Publications: Afternoon in St Petersburg; On Nature at Stora Skuggan; The Foreign Country of Love; Under the Empty Sky; Seperate Fortunes; Screens; Food for Memory, 1993; Olga on Olga, 1994; One alive for dead, 1995. Contributions to: Expressen; Skona Hem; Dagens Nyheter. Honours: Albert Bonniers Foundation; The Swedish Academy; The Swedish Academy Hirsch Foundation. Memberships: Swedish PEN; Lilla Sallskapet. Address: Styrmansg 41, 11454 Stockholm, Sweden.

EKWENSI Cyprian, b. 26 Sep 1921, Minna, Nigeria. Pharmacist; Author. Education: Government College, Ibadam; Achimota College, Ghana; School of Forestry, Ibadan; Chelsea School of Pharmacy, University of London; Iowa University. Appointments include: Lecturer, Igbobi College, Lagos, 1947-49; Lecturer, Pharmacy, Lagos, 1949-56; Pharmacist, Nigerian Medical Service, 1956; Head, Features, Nigerian Broadcasting Corporation, 1956-61; Director of Information, Federal Ministry of Information, Lagos, 1961-66; Director, Information Services, Enugu, 1966; Managing Director, Star Printing and Publishing Company Limited, 1975-79, Niger Eagle Press, 1981-. Publications: When Love Whispers, Ikolo The Wrestler, 1947; The Leopard's Claw, 1950; People of The City, 1954; Passport of Mallam Ilia; The Drummer Boy, 1960; Jagua Nana, 1961; Burning Grass; An African Night's Entertainment; Yaba Round About Murder, 1962; Beautiful Feathers, 1963; Great Elephant Bird; Rainmaker, 1965; Lokotown Juju Rock; Trouble in Form VI; Iska; Boa Suitor, 1966; Coal Camp Boy, 1973; Samankwe in The Strange Forest, 1974; Samankwe and The Highway Robbers; Restless City; Christmas Gold, 1975; Survive The Peace, 1976; Divided We Stand, 1980; Motherless Baby, 1980; Jaguanana's Daughter, 1986; For a Roll of Parchment, 1986. Address: 12 Hillview Crescent, Independence Layout, PO Box 317, Enugu, Nigeria.

ELBERG Yehuda (Y Renas, Y L Berg), b. 15 May 1912, Poland. Novelist. 2 sons, 1 daughter. Education: Rabinical Ordanation, 1929; Textile Engineering, 1932. Literary Appointments: Author in residence, Bar-Ilan University Israel, 1988; Hebrew Studies, Oxford University, 1990 & 1994. Publications: Under Copper Skies, 1951; On the Tip of a Mast, 1974; Scattered Stalks, 1976; Tales, 1980; The Empire of Kalman The Cripple, 1983; In Clay Houses, I and II, 1983; A Man Is But A Man, 1983; Between Morning and Evening, 1983; The Fifteen Powers, 1989. Honours: Feffer Prize, Congress for Jewish Culture, Sao Paulo, Brazil, 1951; J I Segal Prize, Montreal, 1975; Wasjslic-Cymerman Award, Sydney, Australia, 1975; Gonopolsky Prize, Paris, 1977; Manger Prize, Yiddish Literature, Government of Israel, City of Tel Aviv & The Manger Prize Foundation, 1977; Prime Minister's Award, Yiddish Literature, Israel, 1984; I M Wisenberg Prize, Congress for Jewish Culture, New York, 1984; J I Segal Award, Yiddish Hebrew Literature, J I Segal Cultural Foundation, Canada, 1988.

Memberships: PEN International. Address: 1745 Cedar Avenue, Montreal, Quebec H3G 1A7, Canada. 55. 94.

ELDRIDGE Colin Clifford, b. 16 May 1942, University Lecturer. m. Ruth Margaret Evans, 3 Aug 1970, 1 d. Education: BA, 1963, PhD, 1966, Nottingham University. Publications include: England's Mission; The Imperial Idea in the Age of Gladstone and Disraeli, 1973; Victorian Imperialism, 1978; British Imperialism in the 19th Century, 1984; Essays in Honour of C D Chandaman, 1980; Empire, Politics and Popular Culture, 1989. Contributions to: Various Learned Journals. Honour: Fellow, Royal Historical Society. Memberships: Historical Association; Association of History Teachers in Wales; British Association of Canadian Studies; British Australian Studies Association. Address: Tanerdy, Cilau Aeron, Lampeter, Dyfed, SA48 8DL, Wales.

ELEGANT Robert Sampson, b. 7 Mar 1928, NY, USA. Author; Journalist; Novelist. m. Moira Clarissa Brady, 16 Apr 1956, 1 s, 1 d. Education: AB, University of PA, 1946; Japanese Army Language School, 1947-48; Yle University, 1948; MA, 1950, MS, 1951, Columbia University. Appointments: War, Southeast Asia Correspondent, Various Agencies, 1951-61; Central European Bureau, Newsweek, 1962-64; Others, Los Angeles Times, Washington Post, 1965-70; Foreign Affairs Columnist, 1970-76; Speaker, Lecturer, 1964-; Independent Author & Journalist, 1977-. Publications include: Chinas Red Masters, 1951; The Dragon Seed, 1959; The Centre of the World, 1961; The Battle for China, 1972; The Seeking, 1969; The Great Cities, Hong Kong, 1977; Pacific Destiny, 1990; Mandarin, 1983; White Sun, Red Star, 1987; Bianca, 1992; The Everlasting Sorrows, 1994. Contributions to: Numerous Articles, NY Times; Encounter. Honours include: Pulitzer Fellow, 1951-52; Ford Foundation, 1954-55; Edgar Allen Poe Award, 1967; Sigma Delta Chi Award, 1967; Various Other Awards, Recognitions, Honorary Societies; Fellow, Institute for Advanced Study, Berlin, 1993-94. Memberships: Authors League of America; Hong Kong Foreign Correspondents Club. Address: The Manor House, Middle Green, Nr Langley, Bucks, SL3 6BS, England.

ELISH Dan, b. 22 Sep 1960, Washington DC, USA. Writer. Education: BA, Middlebury College, 1983. Publications: The Worldwide Dessert Contest: Jason and The Baseball Bear; The Great Squirrel Uprising; The Transcontinental Railroad, 1993; Harriet Tubman and The Underground Railroad, 1993; James Meredith and School Desegregation, 1994. Contributions to: Sports Illustrated for Kids; 3 2 1 Contest. Honours: National Arts Club, Scholar; The Bread Loaf Writers Conference. Literary Agent: Fran Liebouritz, Writers House. Address: 251 West 97th Street 2H, New York, NY 10025, USA.

ELISHA Ron, b. 19 Dec 1951, Jerusalem. Medical Practitioner; Playwright. m. Bertha Rita Rubin, 6 Dec 1981, 1 son, 1 daughter. Education: BMed, BSurg, Melbourne University, 1975. Publications: In Duty Bound, 1983; Two, 1985; Einstein, 1986; The Levine Comedy, 1987; Pax Americana, 1988; Safe House, 1989; Esterhaz, 1990; Impropriety, 1993; Choice, 1994; Pigtales, 1994. Contributions to: Business Review Weekly; The Age; Vogue Australia; Generation Magazine; Australian Book Review; Centre Stage Magazine; Melbourne Jewish Chronicle. Honours: Best Stage Play, 1982; Major Award, 1982; Best Stage Play, 1984; Gold Award, Best Screenplay, 1990; Best TV Feature, Australian Writers Guild Award, 1992. Memberships: Australian Writers Guild; International PEN; Fellowship of Austrlian Writers. Address: 4 Bruce Ct, Elsternwick Vic 3185, Australia.

ELIZABETH Von S. See: FREEMAN Gillian.

ELKIN Stanley (Lawrence), b. 1930, America. Writer; Playwright. Literary Appointments: Visiting Lecturer, Smith College, Northampton, MA, 1964-65; Joined Faculty of Washington University, St Louis, 1960, Professor of English, 1968-. Publications: Boswell, 1964; Criers and Kibitzers and Criers (short stories), 1966; A Bad Man, 1967; The Six-Year-Old Man (filmscript), 1969; Editor, Stories From The Sixties, 1971; The Dick Gibson Show, 1971; The Making of Ashenden, 1972; Searches and Seizures, 1973, 1974; Eligible Men (short stories), 1974; The Franchiser, 1976; The Living End, 1979; Stanley Elkin's Greatest Hits, 1980; George Mills, 1982, 1990; The Magic Kingdom, 1985; Van Gogh's Room at Arles, 1993. Address: Department of English, Washington University, St Louis, MO 63130, USA.

ELKINS Aaron, b. 24 Jul 1935, Brooklyn, NY, USA. Lecturer; Writer. m. (1) Toby Siev, 1959 (div 1972), 2 s, (2) Charlotte Trangmar, 1972. Education: BA, Hunter College (now City University of New York), 1956; Graduate Study at University of Wisconsin, Madison, 1957-59; MA, University of Arizona, 1960; MA, California State University, Los Angeles, 1962; EdD, University of California, Berkeley, 1976. Literary Appointments include: Management Consultant, Ernst and Whinney, Chicago, IL, 1970-71; Director of Management Development, Government of Contra Costa County, CA, 1971-76, 1980-83; Lecturer in Anthropology, Psychology and Business, University of Maryland, College Park, European Division, 1976-78; Management Analyst, US Office of Personnel Management, San Francisco, CA, 1979-80; Lecturer in Business, University of Maryland, College Park, European Division, 1984-85; Writer, 1984-; Lecturer at California State University, Hayward and Fullerton, and at Golden Gate University, Member of Clallam County Civil Service Commission, 1987-. Publications: Fellowship of Fear, 1982; The Dark Place, 1983; Murder in The Queen's Armes, 1985; A Deceptive Clarity, 1987; Old Bones, 1987; Curses!, in press; Dead Men's Hearts, 1994. Honour: Edgar Allen Poe Award for Best Mystery Novel, Mystery Writers of America, 1988, for Old Bones. Memberships: Authors Guild; Mystery Writers of America. Literary Agent: Karpfinger Agency. Address: c/o Karpfinger Agency, 500 Fifth Avenue, Suite 2800, New York, NY 10110, USA.

ELLEN Margaret. See: OSBORNE Maggie.

ELLERBECK Rosemary Anne L'Estrange (Anna L'Estrange, Nicola Thorne, Katherine Yorke), b. England. Writer. Education: BSc, Sociology, London School of Economics. Literary Appointments include: Former publishers reader and editor. Publications: Numerous historical, contemporary and gothic novels including: Inclination to Murder, 1965; The Girls (as N Thorne), 1967; Bridie Climbing (as N Thorne), 1969; In Love (as N Thorne), 1973; Hammersleigh, 1976; Rose, Rose Where Are You?, 1977; Return to Wuthering Heights (as A L'Estrange), 1978; A Woman Like Us (as N Thorne), 1979; Perfect Wife and Mother (as N Thorne), 1980; Daughters of The House (as N Thorne), 1981; Where The Rivers Meet (as N Thorne), 1982; Affairs of Love (as N Thorne), 1983; A Woman's Place (as K Yorke), 1983; Pair Bond (as K Yorke), 1984; Never Such Innocence (as N Thorne), 1985; Askham Chronicles 1898-1967, 4 titles (as N Thorne), 1985-87; Champagne (as N Throne), 1988; As K Yorke: The Enchantress, 1979; Falcon Gold, 1980; Lady of The Lakes, 1981 (reissued in one volume as, The Enchantress Saga, as N Thorne, 1985). Membership: PEN. Literary Agent: Richard Scott Simon Limited. Address: 96 Townshend Court, Mackennal Street, London, NW8 6LD.

ELLIOT Alistair, b. 13 Oct 1932, Liverpool, Lancashire, England. Librarian; Poet. Education: Fettes College, Edinburgh; BA, Christ Church, Oxford, 1955. Appointments: Special Collections Librarian, Newcastle upon Tyne University Library, 1967-82. Publications: Air in the Wrong Place, 1968; Contentions, 1977; Kisses, 1978; Talking to Bede, 1982; Talking Back, 1982; On the Appian Way, 1984; My Country: Collected Poems, 1989; Turning the Stones, 1993; Editor, Poems by James I and Others, 1970; The Georgics with John Dryden's Translation, 1981; Editor and Translator, French Love Poems (bilingual), 1991; Editor and Translator, Italian Landscape Poems (bilingual), 1993; Translator, Alcestis by Euripides, 1965, and Peace by Aristophanes, 1965; Translator, Medea, by Euripides, 1993. Honours include: Ingram Merril Foundation Fellowship, 1983; Arts Council Grant, 1979; Prudence Farmer award (New Statesman), 1983 and 1991. Address: 27 Hawthorn Road, Newcastle upon Tyne NE3 4DE, England.

ELLIOT Zena Marjorie, b. 13 June 1922, New Zealand. Retired Art Teacher. m. A J Elliot, 10 Aug 1946, div. 1958, 2 sons, 1 daughter. Education: Certified Teacher: New Zealand, 1942; New South Wales, 1960; Diploma, Home Economics, 1969; Diploma, Art Education, 1974. Career: Graduate Assistant, New South Wales, Australia, 1974; Teacher of Art; Retired, 1993. Publications: Concise Coppercraft Book, 1975; Creative Weaving with Art to Wear, 1995. Memberships: Telopea Gallery; Craft at the Rocks; Handweavers and Spinners Guild; National Parks and Wild Life; New South Wales Trust Fund; Blue Mountains Creative Art Centre; Textile Fibre Forum. Address: 15 Hopewell St, Paddington, New South Wales 2021, Australia.

ELLIOTT Janice, b. 14 Oct 1931, Derby, England. Novelist. Education: BA, St Anne's College, Oxford. Publications: Cave With Echoes, 1962; The Somnambulists, 1964; The Godmother, 1966; The

Buttercup Chain, 1967; The Singing Head, 1968; Angels Falling, 1969; The Kindling, 1970; A State of Peace, 1971; Private Life, 1972; Heaven on Earth, 1975; A Loving Eye, 1977; The Honey Tree, 1978; Summer People, 1979; Secret Places, 1981; The Country of Her Dreams, 1982; Magic, 1983; The Italian Lesson, 1985; Dr Gruber's Daughter, 1986; The Sadness of Witches, 1987; Life on The Nile, 1989; Necessary Rites, 1990; The Noise From The Zoo, 1991; City of Gates, 1992; Children's Books: The Birthday Unicorn, 1970; Alexander in The Land of Mog, 1973; The Incompetent Dragon, 1982; The King Awakes, 1987; Life on The Nile, 1989; The Empty Throne, 1988. Contributions to: Numerous magazines and newspapers, short story collections. Honour: Southern Arts Award for Literature, 1981. Memberships: FRSL, PEN; Society of Authors. Literary Agent: Richard Scott Simon Limited. Address: c/o Hodder and Stoughton, 47 Bedford Square, London, WC1B 3DP, England.

ELLIS Alice Thomas. See. HAYCRAFT Anna (Margaret).

ELLIS Bret Easton, b. 7 Mar 1964, CA, USA. Writer. Education: BA, Bennington College, Vermont, 1986. Publications: Less Than Zero, 1985; The Rules of Attraction, 1987; American Psycho, 1993; The Informers, 1994. Contributions to: Rolling Stone; Vanity Fair; Elle; Wall Street Journal; Bennington Review. Membership: Authors Guild. Literary Agent: Amanda Urban. Address: c/o Amanda Urban, ICM, 40 West 57th Street, New York, NY 10019, USA.

ELLIS Ella Thorp, b. 14 July 1928, Los Angeles, CA, USA. Novelist. m. Leo H Ellis, 17 Dec 1949, 3 sons. Education: BA, English, University of California, Los Angeles, 1967; MA, English, San Fransisco State University, 1975. Publications include: Roam the Wild country, 1967; Riptide, 1969; Celebrate the Morning, 1972; Hallelujah, 1974; Hugo and the Princess Nina, 1983; Where the Road Ends; Swimming with the Whales, forthcoming. Contributions To: Mademoiselle. Honours: ALA Honor Books, 1967, 1969, 1972. Memberships: Author's Guild; Society of Children's Book Writers; California Writers' Club; Sierra Club; ACLU; Opera International. Literary Agent: Julie Fallowfield, McIntosh and Otis. Address: 1438 Grizzly Peak , Berkeley, CA 94708, USA.

ELLIS Mark Karl, b. 1 Aug 1945, India. Training Consultant; Author. m. Printha Jane, 30 Aug 1969, 2 s. Education: MA, Cambridge University. Publications: Bannerman; Adoration of the Hanged Man; Fatal Charade; Survivors Beyond Babel; Nelson Counterpoint Series; Nelson Skill of Reading Series; Longman Business Skills Series; Professional English; The Economist; An English Language Guide; Giving Presentations; Teaching Business English; Kiss in the Dark, 1995. Literary Agent: Deborah Rogers. Address: 39 St Martins, Marlborough, Wiltshire, SN8 1AS, England.

ELLIS Richard J, b. 27 Nov 1960, USA. Assistant Professor. m. Juli Takenaka, 18 July 1987, 1 d. Education: BA, with highest honours, University of California, Santa Cruz, 1982; MA, Political Science, 1984; PhD, Politics, 1989, University of California, Berkeley. Appointments: Visiting Lecturer, Univerity of California, Santa Cruz, 1989; Assistant Professor, Williamette University, Salem, OR, 1990-. Publications: Dilemmas of Presidential Leadership (co-author), 1989; Cultural Theory (co-author), 1990; American Political Cultures, 1993. Presidential Lightning Rods: The Politics of Blame Avoidance; Politics Policy and Culture (co-editor). Contributions to: Comparative Studies in Society and History; The Journal of Behavioural Economics; Presidential Studies Quarterly; Journal of Theoretical Politics: Studies in American Political Development; Review of Politics; Polity; Western Political Quarterly; Critical Review. Honours: Regents Fellowship, University of California, 1983-85; I G S Harris Fellowship, 1986-88; Summer Stipend, National Endowment for the Humanities, 1991; Fellowship, George and Eliza Howard Foundation, 1993-94. Memberships: American Political Science Association; Organization of American Historians. Address: Williamette University, Salem, OR 97301, USA.

ELLIS Royston, (Richard Tresillian), b. 10 Feb 1941, Pinner, Middlesex, England. Author; Travel Writer, 1 s. Appointments: Freelance Poet, Travel Writer, 1957-61; Assistant Editor, Jersey News & Features Agency, 1961-63; Associate Editor, Canary Islands Sun, Las Palmas, 1963-66; Editor, The Educator, Director, Dominica Broadcasting Service & Reuter, Cana Correspondent, 1974-76; Managing Editor, Wordsman Features Agency, 1977-86; Editorial Consultant, Explore Sri Lanka, 1990-. Publications include: 30 Books inc, Jiving to Gyp, 1959; The Flesh Merchants, 1966; The Rush at the End, 1967; The Bondmaster Series 1977-83; The Fleshtrader Series,

1984-85; The Bloodheart Series, 1985-87; Rave, 1960; The Rainbow Walking Stick, 1961; The Mattress Flowers, 1963; Burn Up, 1963; The Big Beat Scene, 1961; Rebel, 1962; Giselle, 1987; Guide to Mauritius, 1988; India By Rail, 1989; Sri Lanka By Rail, 1994; With Gemunu Amarasinghe, Guide to Maldives, 1995. Contributions to: The Times; The Guardian; The Sunday Times; Daily & Sunday Telegraphs; Business Traveller Asia, Pacific and Airline and Hotel Magazines in Asia. Honours: Honorary Dukedom of the Caribbean Island Realm of Redonda, 1961; Dominica National Poetry Award, 1967, 71. Memberships: Royal Commonwealth Society; Institute of Rail Transport, India. Address: Royal Cottage, Bentota, Sri Lanka.

ELLISON Harlan Jay, b. 27 May 1934, Cleveland, OH, USA. Author. m. Susan Toth, Sep 1986. Education: OH State University, 1953-55. Appointments: Publisher, Editor, Rogue Magazine, Chicago, IL; 1959-60; Editor, Regency Books, Chicago, 1960-61; Editor, Dangerous Visions, 1967; Editor, Again, Dangerous Vision, 1972; Book Critic, Los Angeles Times, 1969-82; Instructor, Clarion Writer's Workshop, Michigan State University, 1969-77, 1984; Editorial Commentator, Canadian Broadcasting Co, 1972-78; Editorial Commentator,USA Network's Sci-Fi Channel, 1993-; President, The Kilimanjaro Corporation, 1979-. Publications: 64 books including: Demon With a Glass Hand, 1986; Night and the Enemy, 1987; The Essential Ellison, 1987; Angry Candy, 1988; Harlan Ellison's Watching, 1989; The Harlan Ellison Hornbook, Harlan Ellison's Movie, 1990; Dreams With Sharp Teeth, 1991; Run for the Stars, 1991; Mefisto in Onyx, 1993; Mind Fields: 33 stories inspired by the art of Jacek Yerka, 1994. Contributions to: Weekly Columns: Los Angeles Free Press, Los Angeles Weekly. Honours: Numerous including: Most outstanding Scripts Award, Writers Guild of America, 1965, 1967, 1973, 1986; more than 8 Hugo Awards, 1966-86; Nebula Awards, 1965, 1969, 1977. British Fantasy Award, 1978; American Mystery Award, 1987; George Melies Award, Cinematic Achievement, 1972, 1973; Edgar Allen Poe Award, 1974, 1988; Bram Stoker Award, 1988, 1990, 1994; Major Works in American Literature Award, 1988; 1993 Life Achievement Award, World Fantasy Convention. Memberships: Writer's Guild of America, West Council, 1971-72, 1985-87; Vice-Pres, Science Fiction Writers of America, 1965-66; Cleveland Science Fiction Society, Founder 1950. Literary Agent: Richard Curtis Associates, 171 East 74th Street, NY 10021, USA. Address: PO Box 55548, Sherman Oaks, CA 91413, USA.

ELLISON Virginia Howell (Virginia Tier Howell, Leong Gor Yun, Mary A Mapes, Virginia T H Mussey, V H Soskin), b. 1910, USA. Writer for Children and Adults. Appointments: Part Owner, Editor, Howell, Soskin Publications Inc, NYC, 1940-48; Editor, Crown Publishers Inc and Lothrop Lee & Shephard Co, 1948-55; Director of Publications and Promotion, CWU National Council of Churches, NYC, 1961-64. Publications: The Exploits of George Washington (as Virginia T H Mussey), 1933; Chinatown Inside Out (with Y K Chun as Leong Gor Yun), 1936; Falla A President's Dog (as Virginia Howell), 1941; Fun With Your Child (as Mary A Mapes), 1943; Surprise! (as Mary A Mapes), 1944; Who Likes The Dark (as Virginia Howell), 1945; Training Pants (as Virginia Howell), 1946; The Pooh Cook Book, 1969; The Pooh Party Book, 1971; The Pooh Get Well Book, 1973; all as Virginia H Ellison; inventor, Patent no 4,811,747 on Mar 14 1989 to Virginia H Reis (Mrs M J). Address: 92 Mather Road, Stamford, CT 06903, USA.

ELMAN Richard, b. 23 Apr 1934, Brooklyn, NY, USA. Writer. m. Alice Neufeld, 9 Apr 1978, 2 d. Education: BA, Honours, Syracuse University, 1955; MA, Stanford University, 1957. Literary Appointments: Lecturer, Literature, Bennington College, 1967-68; Adjunct Professor, Creative Writing, Columbia University, 1968-74; Lecturer, Sarah Lawrence College, 1971; Visiting Professor, University of Pennsylvania, 1980-82; Visiting Professor, SUNY Stony Brook, 1983; Visiting Professor, University of Arizona, Tucson, 1985; Hopwood Professor, Visiting, University of Michigan, Ann Arbor, 1988; Abrams Professor, Notre Dame University, 1990. Publications include: The Poorhouse State, 1966; The 28th Day of Elul, 1967; Lilo's Diary, 1968; The Reckoning, 1969; An Education in Blood, 1970; Homage to Fats Navarro, 1975; Taxi Driver, 1976; Breadfruit Lotteries, 1980; Cocktails at Somoza's, 1981; The Menu Cypher, 1983; Disco Frito, 1988; Tar Beach, 1991. Contributions to: Reviewer; New York Times; Newsday; National Public Radio; The Nation; Geo; Atlantic; New Republic; Antaeus; LA Daily News; Wall Street Journal; Peace News; Midstream; Partisan Review. Honours: PEN Syndicated Short Story Writers, 3 times; NEA Fiction, 1971; CAPS Fiction, 1974. Memberships: PEN; Author's Guild; National Yiddish Book Centre. Address: PO Box 216, Stony Brook, New York, NY 11790, USA.

ELMORE James B, b. 13 Apr 1949, Buffalo, NY, USA. m. Lorraine J Corbin, 1 Apr 1978, 2 s, 1 d. Education: BA, 1971; MSc, Education, 1972; School Social Studies, 1972; School Counsellor, 1974; Certified Rehabilitation Counsellor, 1977; School Administration, 1987. Publications: A Dream's Fantasy, 1978; The Legacy, 1978; A Special Child, 1980; Lorri, 1980; Jason, David and Kristen, 1980; A Thinker's Treatise, 1981; Essence, 1981; At The Point of A Dream, 1982; Wake Up, 1982; Look at Kristen, 1982; Rememberances, 1983; Canandaigua, 1985; Will There Be A Time, 1985; Armageddon: The Raging War, 1985; A New Tomorrow, 1987. Contributions to: Magic Aura Magazine; Buffalo Evening News; Rochester Art Scene Quarterly; The Chord; Niagara Gazette. Honours: United Nations Citation, 1981; Niagara Falls Chamber of Commerce, Certificate of Appreciation, 1981. Memberships: Various writing and music societies and professional organisations. Address: Elmore Enterprises, 1200 Doebler Drive, North Tonawanda, NY 14120, USA.

ELMSLIE Kenward Gray, b. 27 Apr 1929, New York City, NY, USA. Poet; Librettist; Talespinner; Performer. Education: BA, Harvard University, Cambridge, MA, USA, 1950. Publications: Motor Disturbance, 1971; Circus Nerves, 1971; The Grass Harp (musical play), 1972; The Orchid Stories, 1973; The Seagull, a libretto, 1974; Tropicalism, 1975; 26 Bars (drawings by Donna Dennis), 1987; City Junket, 1987; Sung Sex (drawings by Joe Brainard), 1989; Pay Dirt (drawings by Joe Brainard) 1992; Postcards on Parade, musical play, 1993; Champ Dust (Drawings by Joe Brainard) 1994. Contributions to: The Partisan Review: Paris Review; The Oxford Literary Review; Art & Literature; Big Sky: New American Writing; Locus Solus; Conjunctions; Oblek. Honour: Frank O'Hara Poetry Award, 1971. Membership: American Society of Composers, Authors and Publishers. Address: Box 38, Calais, VT 05648, USA.

ELPHINSTONE Francis. See: POWELL-SMITH Vincent.

ELSEN Albert Edward, b. 1927, America. Professor of Art History. Appointments: Assistant Professor of Art History, Carleton College, Northfield, Mn, 1952-58; Professor of Art History, Indiana University, Bloomington, 1958-68; Professor of Art History, Stanford University, CA since 1968. Publications: Rodin's Gates of Hell, 1960; Purposes of Art, 1962, 4th edition, 1981; Rodin, 1963; Editor, Auguste Rodin: Readings on His Life and Work, 1965; The Partial Figure in Modern Sculpture: From Rodin to 1969, 1969; Seymour Lipton, 1970; Rodin Drawings (with K Varnedoe), 1972; The Scuplture of Henri Matisse, 1972; Paul Jenkins, 1973; Rodin and Balzac (with S McGough and S Wander), 1973; Pioneers of Modern Sculpture, 1973, revised edition as Origins of Modern Sculpture: Pioneers and Premises, 1974; Modern European Sculpture, 1918-1945, 1979; In Rodin's Studio, 1980; Law, Ethics and The Visual Art (with J H Merryman), 2 volumes, 1979, 2nd edition, 1987; Rodin's Thinker and The Dilemmas of Modern Public Sculpture, 1985.

ELSOM John Edward, b. 31 Oct 1934, Leigh on Sea, Essex, England. Author; Journalist; Broadcaster; Lecturer. m. Sally Mays, 3 Dec 1956, 2 s. Education: BA, 1956; PhD, City University, London, 1991. Appointments: Script Advisor, Paramount Pictures, 1960-68; Theatre Critic, London Magazine, 1963-68; The Listener, 1972-82; Correspondent, Contemporary Review, 1978-88; Lecturer, Course Leader, Arts Criticism, City University, London, 1986. Publications include: Theatre Outside London, 1969; Erotic Theatre, 1972; The History of the National Theatre, 1978; Is Shakespeare Still our Contemporary, 1989; Cold War Theatre, 1992; change & Choice, 1978; The Published: How I Coped, 1969; Malone Dies, 1984; The Man of the Future is Dead, 1986. Contributions to: The Observer; The Mail on Sundy; Encounter; Times Literary Supplement; The World and I; Sunday Telegraph; Plays International; Plays & Players; San Diego Union. Memberships: Liberal Party of Great Britains Art and Broadcasting Committee; International Association of Theatre Critics. Address: Stella Maris, Angelsea Road, Kingston Upon Thames, Surrey KT1 2EW, England.

ELSTOB Peter, b. 1915, British. Writer. Literary Appointments: Director, Arts Theatre Club, London, 1946-54; Director, Trade Winds Films, 1958-62; Director, Archive Press Limited, 1965-; Vice President, International PEN, 1982-, Press Officer, 1970-74, Secretary General, 1974-82. Publications: Spanish Prisoner, 1958; Co-author, The Flight of The Small World, 1959; Warriors for The Working Day, 1960; The Armed Rehearsal, 1964; Bastogne, The Road Block, 1968; The Battle of Reichswald, 1970; Hitler's Last Offensive, 1971; Editor, A Register of The Regiments and Corps of The British Army, 1972; Condor Legion,

1973; Editor, The Survival of Literature, 1979; Scoundrel, 1986. Memberships: Vice-President, English PEN; Secretary-General, 1974-82, International Vice-President, 1982, International PEN; Writers Guild; Society of Authors. Address: Burley Lawn House, Burley Lawn, Hampshire, BH24 4AR, England.

ELSY Mary, b. England. Freelance Travel Journalist; Writer. Education: Teaching Diploma, Oakley Training College for Teacher, Cheltenham, 1945. Appointments: Teacher, 1946-51; Realist Film Unit, 1953-55; Editorial Assistant, Childrens Encyclopedia, 1959-62; Editorial Assistant, British Publishing Corporation, 1963; Editorial Assistant, Evans Bros, 1965-66; Childrens Book Editor, Abelard Schuman, 1967-68. Publications: Travels in Belgium and Luxembourg, 1966; Brittany and Normandy, 1972; Travels in Brittany, 1988; Travels in Normandy, 1988; Travels in Alsace and Lorraine, 1989; Travels in Burgundy, 1989. Contributions to: Daily Telegraph; Sunday Telegraph; Observer; Irish Times; Universe; Womans Journal; In Britain; Illustrated London News; Travel; Ham and High; Camping and Walking; My Family; Voyager; Family Life; Christian Herald; Home and Country. Memberships: PEN International; Society of Authors; Institute of Journalists; British Guild of Travel Writers; R Overseas League; Camden History Society. Address: 519c Finchley Road, London NW3 7BB, England.

ELTIS Walter, b. 23 May 1933, Warnsdorf, Czechoslovakia. Economist. m. Shelagh Mary Owne, 5 Sept 1959, 1 s, 2 d. Education: Emmanuel College, Cambridge; BA, Cambridge University; MA, Nuffield College, 1960; DLitt, Oxford University, 1990. Appointments: Fellow, Tutor, Economics, 1963-88, Emeritus Fellow, 1988-, Exeter College, Oxford; Director General, National Economic Development Office, London, 1988-92; Chief Economic Adviser to the President of the Board of Trade, 1992-; Visiting Professor, University of Reading, 1992- Gresham Professor of Commerce, 1993-. Publications: Growth and Distribution, 1973; Britains Economic Problem: Too Few Producers (with Robert Bacon), 1976; The Classical Theory of Economic Growth, 1984; Keynes and Economic Policy (with Peter Sinclair), 1988; Classical Economics, Public Expenditure and Growth, 1993. Contributions to: Many to Economic Journals and Bank Reviews. Honours: Adam Smith Prize. Memberships: Reform Club; Political Economy Club. Address: Danesway, Jam Way, Boars Hill, Oxford OX1 5JF, England.

ELTON Ben, b. 1959. Writer; Comedian. Career: Writer of television series including: The Young Ones; Blackadder; Happy Families; Filthy Rich and Catflap; Writer for British comedians including: Rowan Atkinson; Rik Mayall; Lenny Henry; French and Saunders; Adrian Edmondson; Highly successful stand-up commedian; Host of British television comedy showcase, Friday Night Live; Co-writer and presenter, 30 episodes of South of Watford, documentary series on London art and entertainment, 1984-85. Publications: Regular columnist, The Daily Mirror, 1986, 1987; Bachelor Boys (The Young Ones Book), best selling book, UK, 1984 and topped best seller list, Australia; Stark, 1989; Gridlock, 1992; Recordings: The Young Ones single, gags by Ben Elton, 1986, sold over half a million copies; Album, Motormouth, top selling UK comedy album, 1987; 2 plays: Gasping, 1990; Silly Cow, 1991. Honours: Best Comedy Show of 1984, British Academy Award, for The Young Ones; Blackadder, Best Comedy Show of 1987, British Academy Award, and ACE Award, for Best Comedy of 1987, USA; Friday Night Live was British Independent Television's Light Entertainment entry, Montreux Television Festival, 1986; Awards for South of Watford: Chicago Film Festival; The New York Festival of Film and Television; San Francisco Film and Television Festival, also selected for Input Festival, Granada, Spain, 1987. Address: c/o Phil McIntyre, 15 Riversway, Navigation Way, Preston, Lancashire, PR2 2YP, England.

ELTON Geoffrey Rudolph, b. 17 Aug 1921, Germany. Historian. m. Sheila Lambert, 31 Aug 1952. Education: BA, 1943, PhD, 1949, London; LittD, Cambridge, 1960. Appointments: Assistant in History, University of Glsgow, 1948-49; Assistant Lecturer, 1949-53, Lecturer, 1954-63, Reader, 1963-67, Professor, 1967-83, Regius Professor, 1983-88, Cambridge University. Publications include: The Tudor Revolution in Government, 1953; England Under the Tudors, 1955; Policy and Police, 1972; F W Maitland, 1984; The Parliament of England, 1559-1581, 1986; The Tudor Constitution, 1960; Reformation Europe, 1963; The Parliament of England, 1559-81, 1986; Return to Essentials, 1991; The English, 1992. Contributions to: Collected in STudies in Tudor and Stuart Politics and Government, 4 vols, 1973, 82, 92. Honour: Knighted, 1986. Memberships: The British Academy; Royal

Historical Society; Selden Society; Ecclesiastical History Society. Address: Clare College, Cambridge CB2 1TL, England.

ELYTIS Odysseus, b. 2 Nov 1911, Heraklion, Greece. Poet, Education: Sorbonne, Paris, 1946-52. Appointments include: President of Greek Broadcasting and Television, 1974. Publications include: Orientations, 1939; Heroic and Elegaic Song, 1945; Kindness in the Wolfpasses, 1946; The Axion Esti, 1959, 1974; Six and One Regrets for the Sky, 1960; The Light Tree and the Fourteenth Beauty, 1971; The Sovereign Sun, 1971; The Monogram, 1972; Clear Days, 1972; The Sovereign Sun: Selected Poems, 1974; Maria Nefeli, 1981; Three Poems Under a Flag of Convenience, 1982; Diary of an Invisible April, 1984; The Little Mariner, 1985; What I Love: Selected Poems of Odysseus Elytis, 1986; Krinagoras, 1987; The Elegies of Oxopetras, 1991; Also: The Room of Images, 1985; Public and Private Matters, 1990; Private Way, 1990; In White, 1992. Honours include: Nobel Prize for Literature, 1979. Address: Skoufa Street 23, Athens, Greece.

EMECHET Buchi, b. 21 July 1944, Lagos, Nigeria. Writer; Visiting Professor; Lecturer. m. S Onwordi, 7 May 1960, 2 s, 3 d. Education: BSc, London University, 1974. Appointments: Professional Senior Research Fellow, University of Calabar, Nigeria; Visiting Professor, Many American Universities, 1982-87; Fellow, University of London, 1986-. Publications include: Second Class Citizen, 1975; The Bride Price, 1976; The Slave Girl, 1977; Joys of Motherhood, 1979; In The Ditch, 1972; Double Yoke, 1982; Destination Biafra, 1982; Head Above Water, 1987; Naura Power, 1981; A land of Marriage, 1983; Gwendoline, 1989; Numerous Childrens Books of Essays; Gwendoline Read Gwendolen. Contributions to: New Statesman; New Society; New International Sunday Times Magazine. Honours: One of Best Young British Writers, 1983; Jack Campbell New Statesman Award, 1979; Best Black British Writer, 1978. Memberships: PEN Internationl. Literary Agent: Collins Publishers. Address: Collins Publishers, 8 Grafton Street, London W1X 3LA, England.

EMERSON Ru (Robert Cray), b. 15 Dec 1944, Monterey, CA, USA. Writer. Education: University of Montana, 1963-66. Publications: Princess of Flames, 1986; To The Haunted Mountains, 1987; In The Caves of Exile, 1988; On The Seas of Destiny, 1989; Spell Bound, 1990; Two-Edged Choice, novella in collection of 4 women fantasy writers entitled Spellsingers, 1989; Novelization, at invitation, of TV series Beauty and The Beast (3 episodes, 2nd book in series); Trilogy: Night Threads, 1990, 1991, 1992; The Bard's Tale: Fortress of Frost and Fire (with Mercedes Lackey), 1993; Night Threads: The Craft of Light (first volume of a new trilogy in that world), 1993; As Robert Cray: The Sword and The Lion, 1993. Contributions to: Short story, A Golden Net for Silver Fishes, Argos Magazine; The Werewolf's Gift, Werewolves (a collection); Ali Achmed and The City of Illusion in Arabesques II, 1989; A Spell for Brass Buttons, The Crafters, Book One, 1991; Ironsides and Cottonseed Oil; The Crafters, Book Two, 1992; Of Women and Honor, Tales of Talislanta, 1992. Honours: Year's Best Fantasy, 1989; St Martin's Press for A Golden Net for Silver Fishes; Honorary mention for Werewolf's Gift. Membership: Science Fiction Writers' of America. Literary Agent: Richard Curtis Associates, New York, NY, USA. Address: 2600 Reuben Boise, Dallas, OR 97338, USA.

EMERY Edwin, b. 14 May 1914, CA, USA. Professor; Author. m. Mary M McNevin, 28 Dec 1935, 1 s, 2 d. Education: BA, 1935, PhD, 1943, University of California. Literary Appointments: Reporter, San Francisco Examiner, 1935; Editor, California Monthly, 1936-43; Staff, United Press, 1943-45; Faculty, University of Minnesota, 1945-. Publications: The Press and America, 1954, 7th edition, 1992; Introduction to Mass Communications, 1960, 11th edition, 1993; History of The American Newspaper Publishers Association, 1950; Highlights in The History of The American Press, 1954; Reporting The News, 1959; The Story of America as Reported by Its Newspapers 1690-1965, 1965; America's Front Page News, 1971; Perspectives on Mass Communication, 1982; Reporting and Writing The News, 1983; Maincurrents in Mass Communication, 1985. Contributions include: Editor, Journalism Quarterly, 1964-73; Gazette; Editor and Publisher, Media Asia; Annals of American Academy of Political and Social Science. Honours: Sigma Delta Chi Journalism Research Award, 1950, 1954; Guggenheim Fellowship, 1959-60; Bieyer Award, 1980; Distinguished Scholar, National Academy of Science, 1985; Kobre Research Award, 1992. Memberships include: President, Association for Education in Journalism; Phi Beta Kappa; Kappa Tau Alpha; Society of Professional Journalists; International Press Institute. Address: 2524 Seabury Avenue, Minneapolis, MN 55406, USA.

ENG Stephen Richard (Steve Eng), b. 31 Oct 1940, San Diego, California, USA. Biographer; Poet; Literary Journalist; Scholar. m. Anne Jeanne Kangas, 15 May 1969, 2 s, 2 d. Education: AB English Literature, George Washington University, Washinton, DC, 1963; MS Education (Counseling) Portland State University, Portland, Oregon, 1973. Literary appointments: Amongst these Poetry Editor, The Diversifier, 1977-78; Associate Editor, Triads, 1985; Director and Editor, Nashville House, 1991-; Staff book reviewer, Nashville Banner, 1993-. Publications: Elusive Butterfly and Other Lyrics (Edited), 1971; The Face Of Fear and Other Poems (Edited), 1984; The Hunter of Time: Gnomic Verses (Edited), 1984; Toreros: Poems, (Edited), 1990; Poets of the Fantastic (Co-edited), 1992; A Satisfied Mind: The Country Music Life of Porter Wagoner, 1992. Forthcoming - Biography of Jimmy Buffett. Contributions to: Amongst these The Lyric; Night Cry; The Journal of Country Music; Tennessee Historical Quarterly; Bookpage; Nashville Banner; Music City Blues; Space & Time. Honours: Focus Poet, Bachaet, 1971; First Poetry Prize, The Rufus, 1973; American Poets' Fellowship Society Certificate of Merit, 1973; Co-Winner, Rhysling award for short poem, Science Fiction Poetry Association 1979; 2nd prize, "Narrative Ballad" Chapparal Poets, 1980; "Best Writer, Poetry,Small Press Writers and Artists Organisation, 1979,1983; Special Achievement, Small Press Writers and Artists Organisation 1985; Top Ten nominee, Ralph J. Gleason Music Book of the Year Award, Broadcast Music Inc (BMI); New York University 1993. Memberships: Broadcast Music Inc, 1972-; Small Press Writers and Artists Organization, 1978-93; Syndic, The. F. Marion Crawford Memorial Society, 1978-; Country Music Association, 1990-; Science-Fiction Poetry Association, 1990-; Nashville Songwriters' Association International 1995. Literary Agent: The Ethan Ellenberg Literary Agency. Address: PO Box 111864, Nashville, TN 37222, USA.

ENG Steve. See: **ENG Stephen Richard.**

ENGEL Diana (née Reilly), b. 25 Aug 1947, New York, USA. Writer; Illustrator. m. 23 Aug 1969, 2 d. Education: BFA, Boston University, 1968; MFA, Pratt Institute, 1975. Publications: Josephina the Great Collector; Josephina Hates her Name; The Little Lump of Clay; Gino Badino; Eleanor, Arthur & Claire; Fishing: The Shelf Paper Jungle. Memberships: Society of Childrens Book Writers. Literary Agent: Susan Schulman, 454 West 44th Street, NYC 10036, USA. Address: 245 West 104th Street, New York, NY 10025, USA.

ENGEL Matthew Lewis, b. 11 Jun 1951, Northampton, England. Journalist. Education: BA, Economics, Manchester, 1972. Literary Appointments: Northampton Chronicle and Echo, 1972-75; Reuters, 1977-79; The Guardian, 1979-; Cricket Correspondent, ibid, 1983-87; Future writer and columnist, 1987-. Publications: Ashes '85, 1985; Editor, Guardian Book of Cricket, 1986; Sportswriter's Eye, 1989; Sportspages Almanac, 1989. Honour: Sports Writer of The Year for What The Papers Say, 1985. Literary Agent: Richard Scott Simon Limited. Address: 39 York Rise, London, NW5.

ENGLISH David, Sir, b. 26 May 1931. Editor. m. Irene Mainwood, 1954, 1 s, 2 d. Literary Appointments: Daily Mirror, 1951-53; Feature Editor, Daily Sketch, 1956; Foreign Correspondent: Sunday Dispatch, 1959; Daily Express; 1960; Washington Correspondent, Express, 1961-63; Chief American Correspondent, Express, 1963-65; Foreign Editor, Express, 1965-67; Associate Editor, Express, 1967-69; Editor, Daily Sketch, 1969-72. Publication: Divided They Stand (a British view of the 1968 American Presidential Election), 1969. Honours: Knighted, 1982. Membership: Board, Association of British Editors, 1985-. Address: Daily Mail, London, EC4Y 0JA, England.

ENQUIST Per Olov, b. Bureå, Västerbotten, Sweden. Novelist; Playwright. m. Lone Bastholm. Education: PhD, University of Uppsala, 1964. Appointments include: Critic for Stockholm Expressen, from 1967. Publications include: The Crystal Eye, 1962; The Route, 1963; The Casey Brothers, 1964; The Magnetist's Fifth Winter, 1964, 1989; Hess, 1966; The Legionnaires, 1968, 1973; The Seconder, 1971; Tales from the Age of Cancelled Rebellions, 1974; The March of the Musicians, 1978, 1985; Dr Mabuse's New Will, 1982; Downfall: A Love Story, 1985; Protagora's Theory, 1987; Captain Nemo's Library, 1991; Plays: The Night of the Tribades, 1975; Chez Nous: Pictures from Swedish Community Life, 1976; Man on the Pavement, 1979; To Phaedra, 1980; The Rain Snakes, 1981; The Hour of the Lynx, 1988; Also: Strindberg - A Life, 1984. Honours include: Nordic Council Prize, 1969. Address: c/o Norstedts Forlag, Box 2052, 103 12 Stockholm 2, Sweden.

ENRIGHT Dennis Joseph, b. 11 Mar 1920, Leamington, Warwickshire, England. Writer. m. Madeleine Harders, 3 Nov 1949, 1 d. Education: BA, Cambridge, 1949; MA, 1946; D Litt, University of Alexandria, Egypt, 1949. Appointments: Teacher of English Literature, 1947-70; co Editor, Encounter, 1970-72; Director, Chatto and Windus Publishers, 1974-82. Publications include: Academic Year, 1955; Memoirs of a Mendicant Professor, 1969; The Oxford Book of Death, 1983; A Mania for Sentences, 1983; The Alluring Problem, 1986; Collected Poems, 1987; Fields of Vision, 1988; The Faber Book of Fevers and Frets, 1989; The Oxford Book of Friendship (co-editor with David Rawlinson), 1991; The Way of the Cat, 1992; Old Men and Comets, 1993; The Oxford Book of the Supernatural, 1994; Interplay: A Kind of Commonplace Book, 1995. Contributions to: Scrutiny; TLS; Encounter; Observer; Listener; London Magazine; NY Review of Books. Honours: Cholomondeley Award, 1974; Queen's Gold Medal for Poetry, 1981; Honorary DLitt, , University of Warwick, 1982; Honorary Doctor, University of Surrey, 1985. Memberships: Fellow, Royal Society of Literature. Literary Agent: Watson, Little Limited. Address: 35a Viewfield Road, London SW18 5JD, England.

ENTMAN Robert Mathew, b. 7 Nov 1949, NY, USA. Professor; Consultant. m. Francie Seymour, 1 son, 1 daughter. Education: AB, Duke Univ; PhD, Yale Univ. Literary Appointments: Editorial Boards: Journal of Communication; Political Communication; Communication Law and Policy. Publications: Media Power Politics, 1981; Democracy Without Citizens, 1989; Forthcoming: Media Privatization and Autonomy; Projections of Power; Television, Race and The Urban Community. Contributions to: Journal of Communication; Journalism Quarterly; Journal of Politics. Honours: McGannon Award in Communication Policy Research 1993. Memberships: American Political Science Association; International Communication Association; Speech Communication Association; Association for Education in Journalism and Mass Communication. Address: 108 Colburn Point, Chapel Hill, NC 27516, USA.

ENYEART James L, b. 1943, USA. Photographer, Adjunct Professor, Writer. m. Roxanne Malone, 3 children. Education: BFA, Kansas City Art Institute, 1965; MFA, University of KS, 1972. Appointments: Director, Albrecht Galley of Art, Instructor, Drawing & Design, Missouri Western, University of MO, 1967-68; Curator of Photography, Spencer Museum of Art, Associate Professor, Dept Art History, University of Kansas, 1968-76; Executive Director, Friends of Photography, Carmel, CA, 1976-77; National Conference Chairman, 1976, Member of Board of Directors 1978-82, Nations Society for Photographic Education; Director, Center for Creative Photography, Adjunct Professor of Art, University of Arizona, 1977-89; director, George Eastman House, 1989-. Publications: include: Kansas Album (editor), 1977; Francis Brugiere, 1977; George Fiske Yosemite Photographer, 1980; Photography of the Fifties: An American Perspective, 1980; Heineckan (editor), 1980; W Eugene Smith: Master of the Photographic Essay, 1981; Jerry Uelsmann: Twenty-five Years, a Retrospective, 1982; Aaron Siskind: Terrors and Pleasures 1931-80, 1982; Three Classic American Photographs: Texts and Contexts (with R D Monroe and Philip Stoker) 1982; Edward Weston Omnibus (with others) 1984; Edward Weston's California Landscapes, 1984; Judy Dater: Twenty Years, 1986; Andreas Feininger: A Retrospective (co-editor Henry Holmes Smith) 1986. Honours: include: Photokina Obelisk Award, Cologne, Germany, 1982; John Simon Guggenheim Memorial Fellowship, writing, 1987; Josef Sudek Medal, Ministry of Culture, Prague, Czechoslovakia, 1989. Memberships: American association of Art Museum Directors; American Association of Art Museums; Oracle (Co-Founder). Address: George Eastman House, 900 East Avenue, Rochester, NY 14607, USA.

ENZENSBERGER Hans Magnus, b. 11 Nov 1929, Kaufbeuren, Germany. Poet; Playwright. m. Katharine Bonitz, 1986. Education: University of Hamburg; PhD, Erlangen, 1955. Appointments include: Professor of Poetry at University of Frankfurt, from 1965. Publications: Verteidigung der Wolfe, 1957; Landessprache, 1960; Gedichte, 1962; Blindenschrift, 1964; Poems for People Who Don't Read Poems, 1968; Gedichte 1955-70; Mausoleum, 1975; The Sinking of the Titanic, 1978; Beschreibung eines Dickichts, 1979; Die Furie des Verschwindens: Die Gedichte, 1981; Gedichte 1950-85, 1986; Diderot und das dunkle Ei: eine Mystifikation, 1990; Zukunftsmusik, 1991; Plays: Das Verhör von Habana, 1970; El Cimarron (music by Hans Werner Henze), 1970; La Cubana (music by Henze), 1975; Der Menschenfeind (after Molière), 1979; Die Tochter der Luft, 1992; Also: Critical Essays, 1982; Dreamers of the Absolute: Essays on Politics, Crime, and Culture, 1988; Requiem für eine romantische Frau, 1988; Der fliegende Robert:

Gedichte, Szenen, Essays, 1989. Honours include: Bavarian Academy of Fine Arts Award, 1987. Address: c/o Suhrkamp Verlag, Postfach 101945, 6000 Frankfurt, Germany.

EöRSI István, b. 16 June 1931, Budapest, Hungary. Writer. m. 3 times div, 2 s, 1 d. Education: Eötvös Loránd University, 1949-53. Publications: Prison Memoirs; A Kihallgatás; Nine Plays; Selected Poems; Several Others; Volumes of Essays and Short Stories; My Time With Gombrowicz; Translations. Contributions to: Many Journals. Honours: József Attila Prize; Preis der Frankfurter Autorenstifung. Memberships: Hungarian PEN. Literary Agent: Artisjus Budapest, Verlag der Autoren, Frankfurt. Address: Belgrád rkp 27, H 1056, Budapest, Hungary.

EPP Margaret Agnes, b. 1 Aug 1913, Waldheim, Sakachewan, Canada. Writer. Publications: 39 books including: But God Hath Chosen, biography, 1963; A Fountain Sealed, novel, 1965, reissued 1982; Walk in My Woods, autobiography, 1967, reissued with update, 1990; This Mountain is Mine, biography, 1969, reissued 1990; Into All the World, travel, 1973; Tulpengasse, 1978; Chariots in the Smoke, novel, 1990. Contributions to: Numerous magazines and journals. Address: Box 178, Waldheim, Sakatchewan, Canada SOK 4RO.

EPSTEIN Charlotte, b. 1921, America. Professor Emeritus; Writer. Literary Appointments: Professor Emeritus, Temple University, Philadelphia, 1985-; Assistant Professor of Human Relations and Staff Associate of The Greenfield Center for Human Relations, 1957-61, Associate Professor of Curriculum and Instruction, 1966-69, Professor of Curriculum and Instruction and Adjunct Proprietor of Nursing, 1969-74, Professor of Elementary Education, 1974-85. Publications: Intergroup Relations for Police Officers, 1961; Intergroup Relations for The Classroom Teacher, 1968; Affective Subjects in The Classroom: Exploring Race, Sex and Drugs, 1972; Effective Interaction in Contemporary Nursing, 1974; Nursing The Dying Patient, 1975; Learning to Care for The Aged, 1977; Classroom Management and Teaching: Persistent Problems and Rational Solutions, 1979; Introduction to The Human Services, 1981; The Nurse Leader: Philosophy and Practice, 1982; Special Children in Regular Classrooms: Mainstreaming Skills for Teachers, 1984; Murder in China (mystery novel), 1986. Address: Professor of Elementary Education Emeritus, Temple University, Philadelphia, PA 19122, USA.

EPSTEIN Seymour (Sy), b. 2 Dec 1917, NY, USA. Writer; Retired Professor. m. Miriam Kligman, 5 May 1956, 2 s. Education: College, 2 years. Appointment: Guggenheim Fellow, 1965. Publications: Pillar of Salt, 1960; Leah, 1964; Caught in That Music, 1967; The Dream Museum, 1971; Looking for Fred Schmidt, 1973; A Special Destiny, 1986; September Faces, 1987; Light, 1989. Contributions to: Stories in: Esquire; Harper's; Antioch Review; Redbook; Articles in: The Denver Quarterly; New University Quarterly. Honours: Edward Lewis Wallant Memorial Award, for novel, Leah, 1965; Leah reprinted in Gems of Jewish Literature, 1967; Best Short Stories of 1962. Memberships: PEN; Author's Guild. Literary Agent: Danadio and Ashworth Incorporated. Address: 750 Kappock Street, Appartment 608, Riverdale, Bronx, NY 10463, USA.

ERBA Luciano, b. 18 Sept 1922, Milan, Italy. Poet; Translator. Education: PhD, Catholic University, Milan, 1947. Appointments include: Professor of French Literature at University of Padua, 1973-82, Verona, from 1982. Publications: Linea K, 1951; Il bel paese, 1956; Il prete di Ratana, 1959; Il male minore, 1960; Il prato più verde, 1977; Il nastro di Moebius: The New Italian Poetry (with others), 1981; Il cerche aperto, 1983; L'ippopotamo, 1989; Radio and Television plays; Novel: Françoise, 1982; Translator of works by Thom Gunn, Cyrano de Bergerac, and others. Honours include: Bagutta Prize, 1987. Address: Via Giason del Maino 16, 20146 Milan, Italy.

ERHARD Tom, b. 1923, America. Writer; Playwright; Professor of Drama. Literary Appointments: Information Director, Albuquerque Public Schools, New Mexico, 1953-57; Assistant Director for Press and Radio, National Education Association, Washington DC, 1957-58; Professor of Drama, New Mexico State University, Las Cruces, 1960-. Publications: For The Love of Pete, 1954; The High White Star, 1957; Rocket in His Pocket, 1960, 1964; The Electronovac Gasser, 1963; A Wild Fight for Spring, 1966; In Search of Leaders, 1967; Stress and Campus Response, 1968; The Agony and Promise, 1969; The Cataclysmic Loves of Cooper and Looper and Their Friend Who Was Squashed by a Moving Van, 1969; The Troubled Campus, 1970; Lynn Riggs: Southwestern Playwright, 1970; The New Decade, 1971; 900

Plays: A Synopsis - History of American Theatre, 1978; Pomp and Circumstances, 1982; I Saved a Winter Just For You, 1984; A Merry Medieval Christmas, 1985; Laughing Once More, 1986. Address: 2110 Rosedale Drive, Las Cruces, NM 88005, USA.

ERI Vincent (Serei), b. 12 Sept 1936, Moveave, Papua New Guinea. Novelist. m. Margaret Karulaka, 4 sons, 2 daughters. Education: BA, University of Papua New Guinea, Port Moresby, 1970. Appointments include: With Papua New Guinea Foreign Service: Consul-General in Sydney, 1974-76, and High Commissioner in Canberra, 1976-79; Personnel Director, Harrisons and Crosfield Ltd, 1982-. Publications: The Crocodile, 1970. Address: c/o Longman Paul, Private Bag, Takapuna, Auckland 9, New Zealand.

ERICKSON Donna Mary Hacking, b. 7 May 1940, Tremonton, UT, USA. Writer; Poet; Entertainer. m. Royle Dee Erickson, 21 Aug 1958, 3 s, 8 d. Education: Utah State University, 1962; Institute of Children's Literature, 1987; Writer's Digest School, 1987. Literary Appointments: Instructor, Poetry Workshops, 1987. Publication: Book of Poetry, 1988. Contributions to: Rexburg Standard Journal; Ensign; Country People Magazine. Honours: 3rd place, Local Poetry Contest, 1968; 1st place, Idaho Writer's League Serious Poetry, Open Title, 1986; Golden Poet of The Year, 1985, 1986, 1987. Membership: Idaho Writer's League. Address: 533 East 900 South, Rexburg, ID 83440, USA.

ERICKSON Peter Brown, b. 11 Aug 1945, Worcester, MA, USA. Literary Critic; Librarian. m. Tay Gavin, 30 Jun 1968, 2 s, 1 d. Education: BA, Amherst College 1967; Centre for Contemporary Cultural Studies, University of Birmingham, England, 1967-68; PhD, University of California, Santa Cruz, 1975; MSLS, Simmons College, 1984. Appointments: Assistant Professor, Williams College, 1976-81; Visiting Assistnnt Professor, Wesleyan University, 1982-83; Research Librarian, Clark Art Institute, 1985-. Publications: Patriarchal Structures in Shakespeare's Drama, 1985; Shakespeare's Rough Magic, Renaissance Essays in Honor of C L Barber, 1985; Rewriting Shakespeare, Rewriting Ourselves, 1991, paperback, 1994; Shakespeare's Comedies, in series on Feminist Readings of Shakespeare, 1995. Contributions to: 27 essays in books and journals on Shakespeare and on contemporary African-American literature; 28 book and theatre reviews. Honours: Phi Beta Kappa, 1967; Amherst Memorial Fellowship, 1967-68; Kent Fellowship, Wesleyan University, 1981-82. Memberships: Shakespeare Association of America; Renaissance Society of America; Modern Language Association. Address: Clark Art Institute, PO Box 8, Williamstown, MA 01267, USA.

ERICKSON Stephen (Steve) Michael, b. 20 Apr 1950, Santa Monica, CA, USA. Novelist. Education: BA, 1972, Master of Journalism, 1973, University of California, Los Angeles. Appointments: Arts Editor, LA Weekly, 1989-91; Film Editor, LA Weekly, 1992-93. Publications: Days Between Stations, 1985; Rubicon Beach, 1986; Tours of the Black Clock, 1989; Leap Year, 1989; Arc d'X, 1993. Contributions to: New York Times; Esquire; Rolling Stone; Details; Elle; Los Angeles Times; LA Style; LA Weekly. Honours: Samuel Goldwyn Award, 1972; National Endowment for the Arts Fellowship, 1987. Literary Agent: Melanie Jackson. Address: c/o Melanie Jackson, 250 West 57th Street, Suite 1119, New York 10107, USA.

ERSKINE Barbara, b. 10 Aug 1944, Nottingham, England. Writer. m. 2 s. Education: MA Honours, Edinburgh University, 1967. Publications: Lady of Hay, 1986; Kingdom of Shadows, 1988; Encounters, 1990; Child of The Phoenix, 1992. Contributions to: Numerous short stories to magazines and journals. Membership: Society of Authors. Literary Agent: Blake Friedmann. Address: c/o Blake Friedmann, 37-41 Gower Street, London, WC1E 6HH, England.

ESCANDELL Noemi, b. 27 Sep 1936, Havana, Cuba. Poet; Educator. Education: Bachiller en Letras, Instituto de la Víbora, 1955; BA, Queens College, NY, 1968; MA, 1971, PhD, 1976, Harvard University, USA. Publications: Cuadros; Ciclos; Palabras. Contributions to: Letras Feminas; Third Woman; Dialogue; Peregrine; El Gato Tuerto; Plaza; El Comercio; Verbena; Stone County, CPU Review; Horizontes. Honours: Residencies, Millay Colony for the Arts, 1983, 1990. Membership: Feministas Unidas. Address: 1525 Q St NW #11, Washington DC 20009, USA.

ESMOND Harriet. See: **BURKE John Frederick.**

ESSEX Harry J, b. 1915, America. Writer of novels, short stories, plays and screenplays. Appointment: Teacher, Script Writing. Publications: Something for Nothing, 1937; Dragnet, 1947; He Walked by Night, 1948; Bodyguard (with F Niblo Jr, G W George, R B Altman), 1948; Wyoming Mail (with Leonard Lee, R H Andrews), 1950; Undercover Girl (with F Rosenwald), 1950; The Killer That Stalked New York, 1951; The Fat Man, 1951; It Came From Outer Space (with R Bradbury), 1953; Devil's Canyon, 1953; I Put My Right Foot In (novel), 1954; The Creature From The Black Lagoon, 1954; Raw Edge (with R Hill), 1956; The Lonely Man (with R Smith), 1957; Neighbourhood Affair, 1960; One For The Dame, 1965; The Sons of Katie Elder (with W H Right, A Weiss, T Jennings), 1965; Man and Boy, 1971; Fatty, 1974; Marina, 1981; Terror in The Skies (for television), 1986.

ESSOP Ahmed, b. 1 Sep 1931, Dabhel, India. m. 17 Apr 1960, 1 s, 3 d. Education: BA Honours, English, University of South Africa, 1964. Publications: The Hajji and Other Stories, 1978; The Visitation, 1980; The Emperor, 1984; Noorjehan and Other Stories, 1990. Honour: Olive Schyeiner Award, English Academy of Southern Africa, 1979. Literary Agent: Ravan Press. Address: PO Box 1747, Lenasia 1820, Johannesburg, South Africa.

ESTERHAZY Péter, b. 14 Apr 1950, Hungary. Novelist. m. Gitta Reen. Education: Graduated University of Budapest and Eotvos Lorand University, 1974. Publications: Fancsiko and Pinta, 1976; Don't Be a Pirate on Papal Waters, 1977; Production Novel, 1979; Indirect, 1981; Who Can Guarantee the Lady's Safety?, 1982; Hauliers, 1983; Little Hungarian Pornography, 1984; Helping Verbs of the Heart, 1985, 1991; Seventeen Swans, 1987; Certain Adventure, 1989; Hrabal's Book, 1990; The Glance of Countess Hahn-Hahn, 1991; Also: The Stuffed Swan, 1988; The Wonderful Life of the Little Fish, 1991; From the Ivory Tower, 1991. Honours include: Attila József Prize. Address: c/o Hungarian Writers' Federation, Bajza-utca 18, 1962 Budapest, Hungary.

ESTLEMAN Loren D, b. 15 Sep 1952, Ann Arbor, MI, USA. Writer. Education: BA, English Literature/Journalism, Eastern Michigan University, 1974. Publications: Novels include: The Oklahoma Punk, 1976; The Hider, 1978; Sherlock Holmes vs Dracula, 1978; The High Rocks, 1979; Dr Jekyll and Mr Holmes, 1979; Stamping Ground, 1980; Motor City Blue, 1980; Aces and Eights, 1981; Angel Eyes, 1981; The Wolfer, 1981; Murdock's Law, 1982; The Midnight Man, 1982; Mister St John, 1983; This Old Bill, 1984; Kill Zone, 1984; Sugartown, 1984; Roses are Dead, 1985; Gun Man, 1985; Every Brilliant Eye, 1986; Any Man's Death, 1986; Lady Yesterday, 1987; Downriver, 1988; Bloody Season, 1988; Silent Thunder, 1989; Peeper, 1989; Sweet Women Lie, 1990; Whiskey River, 1990; Sudden Country, 1991; Motown, 1991; King of The Corner, 1992; Non-fiction: The Wister Trace, 1987. Contributions include: numerous professional journals including: Baker Street Journal; Mystery. Honours include: Nominee, American Book Award, for The High Rocks, 1980; WWA Golden Spur Award, 1981, 1987; Michigan Arts Foundation Award, 1987; WWA Stirrup Award, 1983; Nominee, Pulitzer Prize for This Old Bill, 1984. Literary Agent: Ray Peekner Literary Agency. Address: 5695 Walsh Road, Whitmore Lake, MI 48189, USA.

ESTORIL Jean. See: **ALLAN Mabel Esther.**

ETCHEMENDY Nancy Howell, b. 19 Feb 1952, Reno, NV, USA. Writer; Graphic Designer. m. 14 Apr 1973, 1 s. Education: BA, University of Nevada, Reno, 1974. Publications: The Watchers of Space, 1980; Stranger From the Stars, 1983; The Crystal City, 1985. Contributions include: Fantasy & Science Fiction; Shadows 8; Twilight Zone; Year's Best Horror and Fantasy; Various Anthologies. Memberships: Science Fiction Writers of America; Society of Children's Book Writers; Horror Writers Association. Literary Agent: Virginia Knowlton, Curtis Brown Ltd, New York, NY. Address: 410 French Court, Menlo Park, CA 94025, USA.

ETZIONI HALEVY Eva, b. 21 Mar 1934, Vienna, Austria. Political Sociologist. m. Zvi Halevy, 2 s, 1 d. Education includes: PhD, Tel Aviv University, 1971. Appointments: Professor, Bar Ilan University, Israel. Publications: Social Change, 1981; Bureaucracy and Democracy, 1985; The Knowledge Elite and the Failure of Prophecy, 1985; National Broadcasting Under Siege, 1987; Fragile Democracy, 1989; The Elite Connection, 1992. Contributions to: Numerous Magazines & Journals. Honours: Fellow, Academy of Social Sciences in Australia. Address: Dept of Sociology, Bar Ilan University, Ramat Gan 52900, Israel.

EULO Ken, b. 17 Nov 1939, Newark, NJ, USA. Writer. m. 1 s. Education: Attended University of Heidelberg, 1961-64. Literary Appointments: Playwright, director, novelist, Director of Playwrights Forum and O'Neill Playwrights; Artistic Director of Courtyard Playhouse, NY; Member of Actors Studio Playwriting Workshop; Staff Writer for Paramount, 1988-. Publications include: Plays include: Bang?, 1969; Zarf, I Love You, 1969; SRO, 1970; Puritan Night, 1971; Billy Hofer and The Quarterback Sneak, 1971; Black Jesus, 1972; The Elevator, 1972; 48 Spring Street, 1973, published in Off-Broadway Theatre Collection, volume 1, 1977; Final Exams, 1975; The Frankenstein Affair, 1979; Say Hello to Daddy, 1979; Novels: Bloodstone, 1982; The Brownstone, 1982; The Deathstone, 1982; Nocturnal, 1983; The Ghost of Veronica, 1985; House of Caine, 1988; Script writer for television. Contributions to: Magazines and newspapers including: Back Stage; Janus; New York Post; New York Times; Off-Off Broadway; Show Business; Village Voice. Honours: Prize, O'Neill Summer Conference, 1971 for SRO; Grant, Howard P Foster Memorial Fund, 1972; Fellowship, Arken Industries and J and L Tanner, 1973-74; Winner, Children's Theatre Contest sponsored by Children's Theatre of Richmond, 1974 for Aladdin. Memberships: Italian Playwrights of America - The Forum; Writers Guild of America; Dramatists Guild. Literary Agent: Mitch Douglas, International Creative Management, NY, USA. Address: 14633 Valley Vista Boulevard, Sherman Oaks, CA 91403, USA.

EVANS Alan, (Alan Stoker), b. 2 Oct 1930, Sunderland, England. Civil Servant. m. Irene Evans, 30 Apr 1960, 2 s. Education: Grammar School. Publications include: Thunder at Dawn, 1978; Ship of Force, 1979; Dauntless, 1980; Audacity, 1985; Eagle at Taranto, 1987; End of the Running, 1966; Bnnon, 1968; Vicious Circle, 1970; The Big Deal, 1971; Night Action, 1989; Orphans of the Storm, 1990; Sink or Capture, 1993; Sword at Sunrise, 1994; Also Various Books for Children, Short Stories. Contributions to: Various Newspapers & Magazines. Memberships: Society of Authors. Literary Agent: Murray Pollinger. Address: 9 Dale Road, Walton On Thames, Surrey KT12 2PY, England.

EVANS Aled Lewis, b. 9 Aug 1961, Machynlleth, Wales. Teacher; Broadcaster. Education: Joint Honours Degree, Welsh, English, University College of North Wales, Bangor. Publications: Border Town, 1983; Whispers, 1986; Waves, 1989; Can I Have A Patch of Blue Sky, 1991; Between Two September Tides, 1994. Contributions to: Welsh Language Periodicals, Golwg; Barn; Tu Chwith; English Language, Chester Poets Anthologies. Honours: Award, National Eisteddfodof Wales, for a volume of poetry, 1991. Memberships: Gorsedd Bards; Chester Poets. Address: 28 Jubilee Road, Pentrefelin, Wrexham, Clwyd, LL13 7NN, Wales.

EVANS Harold Matthew, b. 28 Jun 1928, England. Editor; Writer. m. 21 Aug 1981, 2 s, 2 d. Education: Durham University, 1949-52; Chicago University, 1956; MA, Durham University, 1962. Literary Appointments: Editor, Northern Echo, 1961-65; Editor, Sunday Times, 1967-81; Editor, The Times, 1981-82; Editor-in-Chief, Atlantic Monthly Press, 1984-86; Editorial Director, US News and World Report, Editor-in-Chief, Conde Nast Traveler, 1986-. Publications: Newsmans English, 1971; Newspaper Design, 1973; Newspaper Headlines, 1974; Newspaper Typography, 1974; Pictures on A Page, 1978; Good Times, Bad Times, 1983; Co-author: We Learned to Ski; Suffer the Children; Eye-Witness; Front Page History. Contributions to: numerous including: Punch; Harpers; US News and World Report; Encyclopaedia Britannica. Honours: Journalist of The Year, British Press Awards, 1967; Editor of The Year, British Press Awards, 1973; Hood Medal, Royal Photographic Society, 1981; Honorary Doctorate, University of Stirling, 1981; Editor of The Year, Granada, 1982. Memberships: International Press Institute; Garrick Club, London; Century, NY. Literary Agent: Michael Sissions, A D Peters, London, England; Mortimer Janklow, New York, USA. Address: c/o Condé Nast's Traveler Magazine, 360 Madison Avenue, New York, NY 10017, USA.

EVANS Julia, (Polly Hobson), b. 1913, England. Writer. Publications: Brought Up in Bloomsbury, 1959; The Mystery House, 1963; Murder Wont Out, 1964; Tittys Dead, 1968; The Three Graces, 1970; Henry Bada bada, 1971; Venus and Her Prey, 1975; Sarahs Story, 1983. Address: 21 The Close, Chequens Park, Wye, Ashford, Kent, England.

EVANS Max, b. 1925, America. Writer; Painter. Appointments: Vice-President, Taos Minerals Incorporated, Taos, New Mexico, 1955-58; President, Solar Metals Incorporated, Taos, New Mexico,

1957-59. Publications: Southwest Wind (short stories), 1958; Long John Dunn of Taos, 1959; The Rounders, 1960; The Hi Lo Country, 1961; Three Short Novels: The Great Wedding, The One-Eyed Sky, My Pardner, 1963; The Mountain of Gold, 1965; Shadow of Thunder, 1969; Three West: Conversations with Vardis Fisher, Max Evans, Michael Straight, 1970; Sam Peckinpah, Master of Violence, 1972; Bobby Jack Smith, You Dirty Coward!, 1974; The White Shadow, 1977; Xavier's Folly and Other Stories, 1984; Super Bull and Other True Escapades, 1985. Address: 1111 Ridgecrest Drive SE, Albuquerque, NM 87108, USA.

EVANS Stuart, b. 20 Oct 1934, Swansea, Wales. Writer. m. Kathleen Bridget Treacy, 31 Dec 1960 (dec 1993). Education: MA, Honours, English Language and Literature, Diploma, Education, Jesus College, Oxford. Publications: Imaginary Gardens With Real Toads, poems, 1972; Meritocrats; 1974; The Gardens of The Casino, 1976; The Caves of Alienation, 1977; The Function of The Fool, 1977; The Windmill Sequence: Centres of Ritual, 1978; Occupational Debris, 1979; Temporary Hearths, 1982; Houses on The Site, 1984; Seasonal Tribal Feasts, 1987. Contributions to: Reviewer: The Times; The Independent. Honours: Newdigate Prize for English Verse, 1955; Welsh Arts Council Prize, 1978. Memberships: Yr Academi Cymreig; Marylebone Cricket Club. Address: 9 Abbey Park Road, Grimsby, DN32 0HJ, England.

EVANS Tabor. See: **KNOTT William Cecil.**

EVELYN John Michael, b. 2 Jun 1916, Worthing, Sussex, England. Retired Lawyer; Writer. Education: MA, Oxford University; Barrister at Law. Publications: 45 Crime novels as Michael Underwood, 1954-90; The Seeds of Murder, 1991; Guilty Conscience, 1992. Honour: CB, 1976. Memberships: Detection Club; Chairman, Crime Writers Association, 1964-65. Literary Agent: A M Heath and Company Limited. Address: 100 Ashdown, Eaton Road, Hove, Sussex, BN3 3AR, England.

EVERS Larry (Lawrence Joseph), b. 15 Aug 1946, Grand Island, NE, USA. Professor of English. m. Barbara Zion Grygutis, 20 Dec 1982, 1 s, 1 d. Education: BA, 1968, MA, 1969, PhD, 1972, University of Nebraska, Lincoln; Postdoctoral Fellow, University of Chicago, 1973-74. Appointments: Assistant to full Professor 1974-86, Full Professor 1986-, English, University of Arizona, Tucson. Publications: Words and Place: Native Literature from the American Southwest, 1979; The South Corner of Time, 1980; With Felipe S Molina: Yaqui Deer Songs - Maso Bwrikam, 1987; Woi Bwikam - Coyote Songs, 1990; Hiakim: the Yaqui Homeland, 1992; Homeplaces, 1995. Honours: National Endowment for the Humanities Fellowship, 1972-73; 1st Place, The Chicago Folklore Prize, 1987; Burlington Foundation Award, 1992. Memberships: Modern Language Association. Address: 273 N Main Avenue, Tucson, AZ 85701, USA.

EWART Gavin Buchanan, b. 4 Feb 1916, London, England. Freelance Writer. m. Margaret Adelaide Bennett, 24 Mar 1956, 1 s, 1 d. Education: Wellington College, 1929-33; Christs College, Cambridge, 1934-37. Appointments: Literary Editor, The Granta, 1936-37; Production Manager, Editions Poetry London, 1946. Publications include: The Collected Ewart, 1933-80; The Gavin Ewart Show, 1971; The Penguin Book of Light Verse, 1980; The Complete Little Ones of Gavin Ewart, 1986; Selected Poems, 1933-88, 1988; Collected Poems, 1980-90, 1991; Like It Ot Not, 1992; 85 Poems, 1993. Contributions to: Times Literary Supplement; New Sttesman; Encounter; London Magazine; Ambit; The Listener; New Verse; Poetry London; New Directions. Honours: Cholmondeley Award for Poetry, 1971; Travelling Scholarship, 1978; The Michael Braude Award for Light Verse, 1991. Memberships: Royal Society of Literature; The Poetry Society; PEN International; Society of Authors. Address: 57 Kenilworth Court, Lower Richmond Road, London SW15 1EN, England.

EWING Jeanne Bunderson, b. 6 May 1933, NE, USA. Editor; Publisher; Teacher. m. Robert Henry Ewing, 19 Mar 1957, 3 d. Education: MA US Hist & Ed, PhD Sociology, Univ of CA, Berkeley. Literary appointments: SF, Chronicle; France Today Magazine; Applied Research Associates; The Owl Press & Editorial. Publications: Resource Handbook on Performance Assessment & Measurement; The Runaway Who Stayed Home; Laura's Dream; Learning To Cope With Chronic Illness; The Reunion; Rural Village in Changing World; When You're Injured. Contributions to: Editor in Chief, Journal of Culture & Society. Honours: Conservatory of Letters. Memberships: Christian Writers; SF Womens Writers Group; NAFE: Commonwealth

Club; Intl Platform Assoc; AAUW; ARA; AERA; SPO. Literary Agent Lindsay Lester Literary. Address: PO Box 3008, Chico, CA 95927-3008, USA.

EXTON Clive, b. 11 Apr 1930, Scriptwriter; Playwright. m. (1) Patricia Fletcher Ferguson, 1951, div (dec'd 1983), 2 d. (2) Margret Josephine Reid, 1 s, 2 d. Education: Christs Hospital. Publications include: TV Plays, No Fixed Abode, 1959; The Silk Purse; Where I Live; Some Talk of Alexander; Hold My Hand; Soldier; Ill Have You to Remember; The Big Eat; The Trial of Doctor Fancy; Land of My Dreams; Are You Ready for the Music; Stigma; Henry Intervenes; The Crezz; Dramatizations of Agatha Christies Poirot for LWT; Jeeves & Wooster; Best Endeavours; Stage Plays, Have You Any Dirty Washing, Mother Dear; Twixt; Murder is Easy; Films, Night Must Fall; Isadora; Entertaining Mr Sloane; Ten Rillington Place; Running Scared; The House in Nightmare Park; The Awakening. Address: c/o Rochell Stevens & Co, 2 Terrets Place, London N1 1QZ, England.

EYRE Peter Gervaise Joseph, b. 11 Mar 1942, NY, USA. Actor. Education: Downside Abbey, Stratton on the Fosse, Bath, Englnd, 1954-59. Publication: Adaptation of the Play Siblings, 1992. Contributions to: Vogue; Tatler; Harpers and Queen; Vanity Fair; The Spactator; The Literary Review; Financial Times. Memberhips: Royal Automobile Club; The Groucho Club. Literary Agent: Antony Harwood, c/o Curtis Brown. Address: c/o ICM, Oxford House, 76 Oxford Street, London W1R 1RB, England.

EYSENCK Hans, b. 4 Mar 1916, Psychologist, 4 s, 1 d. Education: BA, 1938, PhD, 1940, DSc, 1964, University of London. Appointments: Reader in Psychology, 1950; Professor, 1955-83; Professor Emeritus, 1983-. Publications include: Dimensions in Personality, 1947; psychology of Politics, 1954; The Biological Basis of Personality, 1967; Smoking, Health and Personality, 1965; The Inequality of Man, 1973; Genes, Culture and Personality, 1989. Memberships: President, International Society for the Study of Individual Differences; Fellow, British Psychological Society; American Psychological Association; German Psychological Society. Address: 10 Dorchester Drive, London SE24, England.

EZEKIEL Nissim, b. 16 Dec 1924, Bombay, India. Professor; Poet. m. Daisy Jacob, 1952, 1 s, 2 d. Education: M, University of Bombay, 1947. Appointments: Reader, 1972-81, Professor, 1981-85, University of Bombay; Writer in Residence, National University of Singapore, 1988-89. Publications: A Time to Change and Other Poems, 1952; Sixty Poems, 1953; The Third, 1958; The Unfinished Man: 1959, 1960; The Exact Name, 1960-64, 1965; Pergamon Poets 9, 1970; Hymns in Darkness, 1976; Collected Poems, 1952-88, 1990; Three Plays, 1969; Editor, A Martin Luther King Reader, 1969; Editor, All My Sons by Arthur Miller, 1972. Honours include: National Academy Award, 1983; Padma Shree, 1988. Address: 18 Kala Niketan, 6th Floor, 47C, Bhulabhai Desai Road, Bombay 400 026, India.

F

FABEND Firth Haring (Firth Haring), b. 12 Aug 1937, Tappan New York, USA. Writer; Historian. m. Carl Fabend, 12 Feb 1966, 2d. Education: BA, Barnard College, 1959; PhD, New York University, 1988. Publications: As Firth Haring: The Best of Intentions, 1968; Three Women, 1972; A Perfect Stranger, 1973; The Woman Who Went Away, 1981; Greek Revival, 1985; As Firth Haring Fabend; A Dutch Family in the Middle Colonies, 1660-1800. Contributions to: de Halve Maen. Honours: Ms Award, New York State Historical Association, 1989; Hendricks Prize, 1989; Fellow, The Holland Society of New York, 1993. Address: Upper Montclair, NJ 07043, USA.

FABRI Peter, b. 21 Dec 1953, Budapest, Hungary. Writer; Poet; Lyricist. m. (1)1 s, (2)Kriszta Kovats, 7 June 1986, 1 d. Education: Eotvos Lorand University, Budapest, 1973-78. Publications include: Folytatasos Regeny, 1981; Napforduo, 1987; Bameszkodasaim Konyve, 1991; Kolumbusz, Az Orult Spanyol, 1992; 49 Days, 1993; Books and Lyrics for Hungarian Singers LPs; Books and Lyrics for Musicals. Contributions to: Articles to about 12 Hungarian Papers & Monthlies, 1973-89. Honours: Emerton Prize, Best Lyricist of Year, 1990. Memberships: Zenesz Kor; Hungarian PEN. Literary Agent: Dr Szilagyi Istrain, Budapest. Address: Rippl Ronai u 27, 1068 Budapest, Hungary.

FACOS James Francis, b. 28 Jul 1924, Lawrence, MA. USA. Professor. m. 1 Dec 1956, 1 son, 2 daughters. Education: AB, Bates College, 1949; MA, Florida State University, 1958. Publications: The Legacy, 1967; A Day Of Genesis, 1969; The Silver Lady, 1972; Silver Wood, 1977; One Daring Fling, 1978; Morning's Come Singing, 1981; Sara Varn (one act play), 1988; Fugitive's Fair, 1985; Crumpet, 1985. Honours: Bates Prize, 1949; Alden Award, drama, 1956; Walter Peach Award, poetry, 1962; Corinne Davis Award, poetry, 1970; Honory Doctor of Humane Letters Degree, Norwich University, 1989. Membership: New England Poetry Club. Address: 333 Elm Street, Montpelier, VT 05602, USA.

FAGAN Brian Murray, b. 1936, American (born British). Appointments: Keeper of Prehistory, Livingstone Museum, Zambia, 1959-65; Former Director, Bantu Studies Project, British Institute in Eastern Africa; Visiting Associate Professor, University of Illinois, 1965-66; Associate Professor, 1967-69, Professor of Anthropology, 1969-, University of California, Santa Barbara. Publications: Editor, Victoria Falls Handbook, 1964; Editor, Southern Africa During The Iron Age, A Short History of Zambia, 1966, 1968; Iron Age Cultures in Zambia (with S G H Daniels and D W Phillipson), volume 1, 1967, volume II, 1969; The Hunter-Gatherers of Gwisho (with F Van Noten), 1971; In The Beginning, 1972, 7th edition, 1991; People of The Earth, 1974, 7th edition, 1992; The Rape of The Nile, 1975; Elusive Treasure, 1977; Quest for The Past, Archaeology: A Brief Introduction, 1978, 4th edition, 1991; Return to Babylon, 1979; The Aztecs, Clash of Cultures, 1984; Adventures in Archaeology, Bareboating, Anchoring, 1985; The Great Journey, 1987; The Journey From Eden, 1990; Ancient North America, 1991; Kingdoms of Jade, Kingdoms of Gold, 1991. Address: Department of Anthropology, University of California, Santa Barbara, CA 93106, USA.

FAIERS Christopher Fordham, b. 28 Jun 1948, Hamilton, Ontario, Canada. Library Assistant. Education: AA, Miami-Dade Community College. Literary Appointments: Founder, publisher, Unfinished Monument Press; Founder, Main Street Library Poetry Series (6 years, 125 poets). Publications include: Collections: Cricket Formations, Haiku, 1969; Dominion Day in Jail, 1978; Unacknowledged Legislator, 1981; White Rasta in Wintertime, 1982; Island Women, 1983; 5 Minutes Ago They Dropped The Bomb, 1984; Foot Through The Ceiling, 1986; Editor, Unfinished Anthology, volume 1, 1984. Contributions include: Anthologies and textbooks including: Poems for Sale in The Street, 1979; Canadian Haiku Anthology, 1979; Modern English Haiku, 1981; Toronto Collection, 1984; Other Channels, 1984; Anti-War Poems, 1984; Also: Alchemist; Alive; Canadian Book Review Annual, 1983; Haiku Highlights; Poetry Toronto; Various readings, broadcasts. Honour: 1st recipient, Milton Acorn Memorial People's Poetry Award, 1987. Memberships: Haiku Society of Canada; Founding Member, Canadian Poetry Association. Address: c/o Unfinished Monument Press, Box 67, Station H, Toronto, Ontario, Canada, M4C 5H7.

FAINLIGHT Ruth, b. 2 May 1931, NY, USA. Writer. m. Alan Sillitoe, 19 Nov 1959, 1 s, 1 d. Education: Colleges of Arts and Crafts, Birmingham, Brighton. Appointments: Poet in Residence, Vanderbilt University, USA. Publications include: Cages, 1966; To See The Matter Clearly, 1968; The Region's Violence, 1973; Another Full Moon, 1976; Sibyls and Others, 1980; Climates, 1983; Fifteen to Infinity, 1983; Selected Poems, 1987; The Knot, 1990; This Time of Year, 1994; Daylife and Nightlife, 1971 (Dr Clocks Last Case, 1994); Poems: Selected Poems, 1995; Marine Rose, Sophia de Mello Breyner, 1987; Translations: Play, All Citizens Are Soldiers, from Lope de Vega, 1969; Libretti: The Dancer Hotoke, 1991; The European Story, 1993. Contributions to: Atlantic Monthly; Critical Quarterly; English; Hudson Review; Lettre Internationale; London Magazine; London Review of Books; New Yorker; Threepenny Review; TLS; Yale Review. Memberships: PEN; Writers in Prison Committee. Address: 14 Ladbroke Terrace, London, W11 3PG, England.

FAIRBAIRNS Zoe Ann, b. 20 Dec 1948, United Kingdom. Writer. Education: MA, Honours, University of St Andrews, Scotland, 1972. Literary Appointments: C Day Lewis Fellowship, Rutherford School, London, 1977-78; Writer-in-Residence, Deakin University, Australia, 1983; Writer-in-Residence, Sunderland Polytechnic, 1983-85. Publications: Live as Family, 1968; Down, 1969; Benefits, 1979; Stand We At Last, 1983; Here Today, 1984; Closing, 1987; Daddy's Girls, 1991. Contributions to: New Scientist; The Guardian; Women's Studies International Quarterly; Spare Rib; Arts Express. Honour: Fawcett Book Prize, 1985. Membership: Writer's Guild. Literary Agent: A M Heath. Address: c/o A M Heath, 79 St Martins Road, London, WC2N 4AA, England.

FAIRBURN Eleanor M, (Catherine Carfax, Emma Gayle, Elena Lyons), b. 23 Feb 1928, Republic of Ireland. Author. m. Brian Fairburn, 1 d. Appointments: Past Member, Literary Panel for Northern Arts; Tutor, Practical Writing, University of Leeds Adult Education Centre. Publications include: The Golden Hive, 1966; Crowned Ermine, 1968; The Green Popinjays, 1962; A Silence with Voices, 1969, 1971; The Rose in Spring, 1971, 72, 73; White Rose, Dark Summer, 1972, 73; The Rose at Harvest End, 1975, 76; Winter's Rose, 1976; House of the Chestnut Trees, 1977; The Haunting of Abbotsgarth, 1980, 82; A Scent of Lilacs, 1982; The White Seahorse, 1964, 70, 85, 95; To Die a Little, 1972, 73, 79, 86; The Sleeping Salamander, 1973, 81, 86; The Semper Inheritance, 1972-75, 1987; Cousin Caroline, 1981, 87; Frenchmans Harvest, 1982, 87. Contributions to: Brief Biography of Lady Mary for Diver, 1983; Nurse Edith Cavell for This England, 1985; Mary Horneck Glyn, 1987. Memberships: Middlesbrough Writers Group. Literary Agent: Mr Seamus Cashman, Wolfhand Press, Dublin. Address: 27 Minsterley Drive, Acklam, Middlesbrough, Cleveland, TS5 8QU, England.

FAIRFAX John, b. 9 Nov 1930, London, England. Writer, 2 s. Publications: The Fifth Horseman of the Apocalypse, 1969; Adrift on the Star Brow of Taliesin, 1974; Bone Harvest Done, 1980; Wild Children, 1985; The Way to Write, 1981; Creative Writing, 1989; Double Image, 1971; Spindrift Lp, 1981; 100 Poems, 1992. Contributions to: Most Major Literary Magazines. Literary Agent: A D Peters. Address: The Thatched Cottage, Eling, Hermitage, Newbury, Berkshire, RG16 9XR, England.

FAIRFIELD Darrell. See: LARKIN Rochelle.

FAIRLEY John Alexander, b. Liverpool, England. Author; Television Producer. 3 d. Education: The Queen's College, Oxford; MA, Oxon. Appointments include: Formerly Lieutenant, Royal Naval Volunteer Reserve. Publications: The Coup, 1975; The Monocled Mutineer (with Wn Allison), 1976; Arthur C Clarke's World of Strange Powers, 1983; Great Racehorses in Art, 1984; Chronicles of The Strange and Mysterious, 1987; Racing in Art, 1991; Arthur C Clarke's Mysterious World; A Cabinet of Curiosities; A Century of Mysteries, 1993. Contributions to: The Field; Countryweek.

FAIRWEATHER Digby (Richard John Charles), b. 25 Apr 1946, Rochford, Essex, England. Jazz Musician. Education: ALA, Librarianship, Ealing Technical College, 1968; Self-taught in Jazz, professional Jazz musician, 1977-. Publications: How to Play Trumpet, 1985; Jazz: The Essential Companion, 1987; Major contributor to New Grove Dictionary of Jazz, 1988; Short story in, B-Flat, Bebop and Scat (Quartet C 1986), entitled The Killers of '59; Chapter in Blackwell Guide to Recorded Jazz, 1991. Contributions to: Numerous journals including:

Jazz Journal International; Melody Maker; The Jazz Rag. Address: 41 Cobham Road, Westcliff-on-Sea, Essex, SS0 8EG, England.

FALCK Colin, b. 14 July 1934, London. University Teacher, 1 d. Education: BA, 1957, MA, 1986, University of Oxford; PhD, 1988, University of London. Appointments: Associate Editor, The Review, 1962-72; Poetry Editor, The New Review, 1974-78; Associate Professor, York College, 1989-. Publications: Backwards into the Smoke, 1973; In This Dark Light, 1978; With Ian Hamilton, Poems Since 1900, 1975; Robinson Jeffers, Selected Poems, 1987; Myth Truth and Literature, 1989; Edna SC Vincent Millay, Selected Poems, 1991; Memorabilia, 1992; Myth, Truth and Literature (2nd ed), 1994. Contributions to: Many Literary and Philosophical Journals in UK and USA. Literary Agent: John Johnson Ltd, 45-47 Clerkenwell Green, London, EC1R 0HT. Address: 20 Thurlow Road, London, NW3 5PP, England.

FALCONER James. See: **KIRKUP James.**

FALDBAKKEN Knut (Robert), b. 31 Aug 1941, Oslo, Norway. Novelist; Playwright. Appointments include: Literary Reviewer of Dagbladet, Oslo, from 1972. Publications: The Grey Rainbow, 1967; His Mother's House, 1969; Fairytales, 1970; The Sleeping Prince, 1971, 1988; E 18, 1980; The Honeymoon, 1982, 1987; Glahn, 1985; Bad Boy, 1988; Forever Yours, 1990; To the End of the World, 1991; Plays: The Bull and the Virgin, 1976, and Life with Marilyn, 1987. Honours include: Riksmal Prize, 1978. Address: Gyldendal Norsk Forlag, Postboks 6860, St Olavs Plass, 0130 Oslo 1, Norway.

FALKIRK Richard. See: **LAMBERT Derek (William).**

FALKUS Hugh Edward Lance, b. 15 May 1917. Naturalist; Independent Writer; Film Director; Broadcaster. Publications: Films for cinema include: Drake's England, 1950; Shark Island, 1952; Television films include: Salmo - The Leaper; Signals for Survival (with Niko Tinbergen); Highland Story: The Gull Watchers; The Signreaders; The Beachcombers; The Riddle of The Rook; Tender Trap; Self-Portrait of A Happy Man; Sea Trout Fishing, 1962, 2nd edition, 1975, revised 2nd edition, 1981; The Stolen Years, 1965, 2nd edition, 1979; Signals for Survival (with Niko Tinbergen), 1970; Freshwater Fishing (with Fred Buller), 1975, new edition, 1978, revised edition, 1988; Successful Angling (jointly), 1977; Nature Detective, 1978, revised 2nd edition, 1987; From Sydney Cove to Duntroon (with Joan Kerr), 1982; Master of Cape Horn, 1982; Salmon Fishing, 1984; The Sea Trout, 1987. Honours: Italia Prize, 1969; Blue Ribbon, New York Film Festival, 1971; Venice Film Festival, 1972; Royal Geographical Society Cherry Kearton Medal and Award, 1982. Address: Cragg Cottage, Near Ravenglass, Cumbria, CA18 1RT, England.

FALLACI Oriana, b. 29 Jun 1930, Florence, Italy. Writer; Journalist. 2 d. Education: Liceo Classico Galileo Galilei; Faculty Medicine, University of Florence, 1946-48. Appointments: Editor, Special Correspondent, Europeo Magazine, Milan, 1958-77; Currently Special Correspondent, Corriere della Sera, Milan. Publications: The Egotists, 1965; Penelope at War, novel, 1966; If the Sun Dies, 1967; Nothing and So Be It, 1972; Interview With History, 1976; Letter to a Child Never Born, novel, 1977; A Man, novel, 1979; Insciallah, 1990. Contributions to: Collaborated with major publications throughout the world including: Look; Life; Washington Post; New York Times; London Times; Corriere della Sera; Europeo; Der Spiegel; L'Express. Honours: St Vincent Award for Journalism, 1971, 1973; Bancarella Award for, Nothing and So Be It (non-fiction on Vietnam War), 1972; Honorary LittD, Columbia College, Chicago, 1977; 2 Varieggio Prize Awards for, A Man, 1979; Hemingway Prize for Literature and Super Bancarella Prize for, Insciallah, 1991. Address: c/o RCS Rizzoli Corp, 31 West 57th Street New York, NY 10019, USA

FALLON Ivan Gregory, b. 26 June 1944. Deputy Editor. m. Susan Mary Lurring, 1 son, 2 daughters. Education: St Peter's College, Wexford, 1952-62; BBS, Trinity College, Dublin, 1966. Appointments: Irish Times, 1964-66; Thomson Provincial Newspapers, 1966-67; Daily Mirror, 1967-68; Sunday Telegraph, 1968-70; Deputy City Editor, Sunday Express, 1970-71; Sunday Telegraph, 1971-84; Deputy Editor, Sunday Times, 1984-. Publications: DeLorean: The Rise and Fall of a Dream Maker (with James L Srodes), 1983; Takeovers (with James L Srodes), 1987; The Brothers - The Rise of Saatchi and Saatchi, 1988; Billionaire: The Life and Times of Sir James Goldsmith, 1991. Memberships include: Council of Governors, United Medical and Dental Schools of Guy's and St Thomas' Hospitals, 1985-; Trustee,

Project Trust, 1984-; Generation Trust, Guy's Hospital; President, Trinity College, Dublin, Business Alumni, London Chapter, Fellow of The Royal Society of Arts, 1989; Beefsteak and RAC. Literary Agent: Vivienne Schuster, Curtis Brown. Address: Clare Cottage, Mill Street, East Malling, Kent ME19 6BU, England.

FALLON Martin. See: **PATTERSON Harry.**

FALLON Peter, b. 26 Feb 1951, Osnabruck, Germany (Irish citizen). Editor; Poet. Education: BA, Trinity College, Dublin, 1975. Appointments: Editor, Gallery Press, Dublin, from 1970; Fiction Editor, O'Brien Press, Dublin, from 1980. Publications: Among the Walls, 1971; Co-incidence of Flesh, 1972; The First Affair, 1974; Finding the Dead, 1978; The Speaking Stones, 1978; Winter Work, 1983; The News and Weather, 1987; Editor of prose and poems by Irish writers. Honours include: Irish Arts Council Bursary, 1981. Address: Gallery Press, Loughcrew, Oldcastle, County Meath, Ireland.

FANTHORPE Robert Lionel, b. 9 Feb 1935, Dereham, Norfolk, England. Priest; Author; Tutor. m. Patricia Alice Tooke, 7 Sept 1957, 2 d. Education: BA; FIMgt; FCP; Anglican Ordination Certificate. Publications include: The Black Lion, 1979; The Holy Grail Reveled, 1982; Life of St Francis, 1988; Thoughts and Prayers for Troubled Times, 1989; God in All Things, 1988; Birds and Animals of the Bible, 1990; Thoughts and Prayers for Lonely Times, 1990; The First Christmas, 1990; Rennes-le-Château, 1992; The Oak Island Mystery, 1995; The Abbot's Kitchen, 1995. Contributions to: Purnells History of World War 1. Honours: Electrical Development Association Diploma, 1958. Memberships: MENSA; Norwich Science Fiction Society; Cardiff Science Fiction Society. Address: Rivendell, 48 Claude Road, Roath Cardiff, Wales.

FANTHORPE Ursula Askham, b. 22 July 1929, Kent, England. Writer. Education: BA, MA, Oxford University. Literary Appointments: Writer in Residence, St Martin's College, Lancaster, 1983-85; Northern Arts Literary Fellow, Universities of Durham and Newcastle, 1987. Publications: Side Effects, 1978; Standing To, 1982; Voices Off, 1984; Selected Poems, 1986; A Watching Brief, 1987; Neck Verse, 1992. Contributions to: Poems: Times Literary Supplement; Encounter; Outposts; Firebird; Bananas; South West Review; Quarto; Tribune; Country Life; Use of English; Poetry Review; Poetry Book Society Supplement; Writing Women; Spectator; BBC. Honours: Travelling Scholarship, The Society of Authors, 1983; Hawthornden Scholarship, 1987; Fellow, Royal Society of Literature; Arts Council Writers Award, 1994. Memberships: PEN. Address: Culverhay House, Wotton-under-Edge, Gloucestershire GL12 7LS, England.

FARAH Nuruddin, b. 24 Nov 1945, Baidoa, Somalia. Writer. m. (1)1 s, 1 d. (2)Amina Mama, 24 July 1992. Education: Panjab Univerity, 1966-70; Insitite of Education, University of London, 1974-75; Essex University, 1975-76. Appointments: Writer in Residence, University of Jos, Nigeria, 1981-83; Writer in Residence, University of MN, 1989; Professor, Makerere University, Uganda, 1989-91; Writer in Residence, Brown University, 1991. Publications include: Froma Crooked Rib, 1970; A Naked Needle, 1976; Sardines, 1981; Close Sesame, 1983; Maps, 1986; Gifts, 1992. Contributions to: TLS; The Guardian; New African; Transition Magazine; NY Times; The Observer; Times Literary Supplement. Honours: English Speaking Literary Award, 1980; DAAD Prize, 1990; Tycholsky Award, 1991; Premio Cavour Itlian Award, 1992; Zimbabwe Annual Award, 1993. Memberships: Union of Writers of the African People. Literary Agent:Deborah Rogers, c/o Rogers, Caleridge & White, London. Address: c/o Rogers, Coleridge & White, 20 Powis Mews, London W11 1JN, England.

FARELY Alison. See: **POLAND Dorothy Elisabeth Hayward.**

FARIAS Victor, b. 4 May 1940, Chile, Philosopher. m. Teresa Zurita, 31 Dec 1960, 1 s, 2 d. Education: Universidad Catolica, Chile, 1957-60; Dr phil, University of Freiburg, 1967; Dr Hab, Free University, Berlin, 1985. Appointments: La Estetica de la Agresion: Dialogo de J L Borges E Jünger, 1986. Publications include: Sein und Gegenstand, 1967; Los Manuscritos de Melquiades, 1981; Heidegger et le Nazisme, La Grasse, (translated in English, Spanish, Italian, Dutch, German, Portuguese) 1987; Las Actas Secretas, 1994. Contributions to: E Jünger Y El Nazismo; Pablo Neruda Y Stalin; Borges. Honours: Heidegger et le Nazisme Selected as 1 of the Most Important Books of the Decade, 1990; Logica, Lecciones de Verano de Martin Heidegger en el Legado de Helene Weiss, 1991; La Metafisica del Arrabal: El tammaño de mi Esperanza, un Libro Desconocido de Jorge Luis

Borges, 1992. Address: Freie Univeritat, Rudesheimerstr 54-56, 1000 Berlin 49, Germany.

FARLEY Carol, b. 20 Dec 1936, Ludington, MI, USA. Children's Book Writer. m. 21 Jun 1954, 1 s, 3 d. Education: Western Michigan University, 1956; BA, Michigan State University, 1980; MA, Children's Literature, Central Michigan University, 1983. Publications: The Garden is Doing Fine, 1976; Mystery of the Fog Man, 1974; Mystery in the Ravine, 1976; Mystery of the Melted Diamonds, 1985; Case of the Vanishing Villain, 1986; Case of The Lost Look Alike, 1988; Korea, Land of the Morning Calm, 1991; King Sejong's Secret, 1996. Contributions to: The Writer; Society of Children's Book Writer's Bulletin; Cricket. Honours: Best Book of Year, Child Study Association, 1976; Best Juvenile Book by Mid-West Writer, Friends of the Writer, 1978; IRA/CBC Children's Choice Book, 1987. Memberships: Mystery Writers of America; Authors Guild; Children's Book Guild; Society of Children's Book Writers; Chicago Childrens Reading Round Table. Address: 8574 W Higgins Lk Rd, Roscommon, MI 48653, USA.

FARMER Beverley, b. 1941, Australia. Novelist. Publications: Alone, 1980; Short stories: Milk, 1983; Home Time, 1985; A Body of Water: A Year's Notebook, 1990; Place of Birth, 1990; The Seal Woman, 1992; The House in the Light, 1995. Address: c/o University of Queensland Press, PO Box 42, St Lucia, Queensland 4067, Australia.

FARMER David Hugh, b. 30 Jan 1923, Ealing, London, England. Lecturer; Reader. m. Pauline Ann Widgery, 1966, 2 s. Education: Linacre College, Oxford. Appointments: Lecturer, 1967-77, Reader, 1977-88, Reading University. Publications include: Life of St Hugh of Lincoln, 1961, 1985; The Monk of Fame, 1962; The Rule of St Benedict, 1968; The Oxford Dictionary of Saints, 1978, 1992; Dizionario dei Santi, 1989; Benedicts Disciples, 1980, 1995; The Age of Bede, 1983, 1988; St Hugh of Lincoln, 1985, 1992; Bedes Ecclesiastical History, 1990; Christ Crucified and other Meditations, 1994. Contributions to: Dictionnaire D'Histoire Ecclesiastique; New Catholic Encyclopedia; Bibliotheca Sanctorum; Lexikon der Christlichen Ikonographie; Studia Monastica; Studia Anselmiana; Journal of Ecclesistical History; The Tablet; Others. Honours: FSA, 1962; FRHistS, 1967. Address: 26 Swanston Field, Whitchurch, Reading, Berks RG8 7HP, England.

FARMER James b. 12 Jan 1920, Marshall, TX, USA. Distinguished College Professor. 2 d. Education: BS, Wiley College, 1938; BD, Howard University, 1941. Publications: Freedom - When?; Random House; Lay Bare the Heart; Arbor House. Contributions to: Over 100 Articles. Membership: Fund for an Open Society. Address: 3805 Guinea Station Road, Fredericksburg, VA 22408, USA.

FARMER Penelope, b. 1939, British. Appointment: Teacher, London, England, 1961-63. Publications: The China People, 1960; The Summer Birds, 1962; The Magic Stone, 1964; Saturday Shillings, The Seagull, 1965; Emma in Winter, 1966; Charlotte Sometimes, 1969; The Dragonfly Summer, Daedalus and Icarus, Serpent's Teeth: The Story of Cadmus, 1971; A Castle of Bone, 1972; William and Mary, Heracles, August the Fourth, 1974; Year King, The Coal Train, 1977; Beginnings: Creation Myths of the World, 1978; The Runaway Train, 1980; Standing in the Shadow, 1984; Eve: Her Story, 1985; Away from Home, 1987. Address: 39 Mount Ararat Road, Richmond, Surrey, England.

FARR Diana (Diana Pullein Thompson), b. Surrey, England. Author. Publications: Over 30 books, titles include: I Wanted a Pony, 1946; The Boy & The Donkey, 1958; The Secret Dog, 1959; Bindi Must Go, 1962; Ponies in the Valley, 1976; Ponies on the Trail, 1978; Gilbert Cannan: Georgian Prodigy, 1978; Ponies in Peril, 1979; Cassidy in Danger, 1979; Five at Ten, 1985; Choosing, 1988; Many books in foreign editions. Contributions include: Daily Telegraph; Pony; Bookseller; Author; Good Housekeeping. Memberships: Founder Member, Children's Writers Group; PEN; Society of Authors. Address: 35 Esmond Road, Chiswick, London W4 1JG, England.

FARRELL M J. See: **KEANE Molly.**

FARRELL Pamela Barnard, b. 11 Oct 1943, Mt Holly, New Jersey, USA; Writer; Teacher. m. Joseph Donald Farrell, 1 Sept 1968. Education: BA, English, Radford College, 1965; MS, English, Radford University, 1975; MA, Writing, Northeastern University, 1988. Appointments: Editor, The Grapevine, Northeastern University Writing Progam Newsletter, 1986-90; Editorial Board, Computers and Composition, 1987-90; The Writing Center Journal, 1988-; Poetry Teacher/Consultant, Geraldine R Dodge Foundation, 1986-. Publications: Waking Dreams (poetry collection), 1989; The High School Writing Center: Establishing and Maintaining One, 1989; Poetry, in American Poetry Anthology, 1986; Poems in several anthologies and collections, 1985-91; Waking Dreams II, 1990; National Directory of Writing Centres, 1992. Contributions to: Writing with a Word Processor in a Writing Center, 1985; Collaboration: Science Research Writing, 1986; Writer, Peer, Tutor and Computer: A Unique Relationship, 1987; Footprints: Paterson Literary Review, 1990. Honours: Dishonorable Mention, Bulwer Lytton Contest, 1984; Woodrow Wilson National Fellowship Foundation Fellow, 1985; Golden Poet Award, 1986; Invitation to present IFTE Conference, 1986-90; Caldwell Chair of Composition, The McCallie School, 1991-. Memberships: Modern Language Association; National Writing Center Association, President; Assembly of Computer in English, Treasurer; NCTE. Address: The McCallie School, 2850 McCallie Avenue, Chattanooga, TN 37404, USA.

FARRINGTON David Philip, b. 7 Mar 1944, Ormskirk, Lancashire, England. Psychologist; Criminologist. m. Sally Chamberlain, 30 July 1966, 3 d. Education: BA, 1966, MA, 1970, PhD, 1970, Cambridge University. Publications include: Who Becomes Delinquent, 1973; The Delinquent Way of Life, 1977; Psychology, Law and Legal Processes, 1979; Behaviour Modification with Offenders, 1979; Prediction in Criminology, 1985; Reactions to Crime, 1985; Aggression and Dangerousness, 1985; Understanding and Controlling Crime, 1986; Human Development and Criminal Behaviour, 1991; Offenders and Victims, 1992; Integrating Individual and Ecological Aspects of Crime, 1993; Psychological Explanations of Crime, 1994. Contributions to: Over 170 Articles to Journals. Honours: Sellin Glueck Award for International Contributions to Criminology, 1984. Memberships: British Society of Criminology; British Psychological Society; European Association of Psychology and Law. Address: Institute of Criminology, 7 West Road, Cambridge CB3 8DT, England.

FARROW James S. See: **TUBB E(dwin) C(harles).**

FARSON Daniel Negley, b. 8 Jan 1927, London, England. Writer; Journalist; Photographer. Education: BA, Pembroke College, Cambridge, England. Appointments: Stars & Stripes; Panorama, founded & edited; Youngest Lobby Correspondent, House of Commons Central Press; Television Interviewer; Photographer. Publications: Jack the Ripper, 1972; The Man Who Wrote Dracula, 1975; Henry, Biograph of Henry Williamson, 1982; Soho in the Fifties, 1987; Sacred Monsters, 1988; Escapades, 1989; Gallery, 1990; With Gilbert & George in Moscow, 1991; Lime House Days, 1991; The Gilded Gutter Life of Francis Bacon, 1993; A Dry Ship to the Mountains, 1993; Deviser of Art Quiz (Channel 4 TV), Gallery; The Collins Independent Guide to Turkey. Contributions to: Mail on Sunday; Sunday Today; Daily Telegraph. Memberships: The Academy Society; Society of Authors; The London Library. Literary Agent: Bill Hamilton, A M Heath, 79 St Martin's Lane, London WC2, England. Address: 129 Irsha Street, Appledore, North Devon, England.

FAST Julius, b. 17 Apr 1919. Writer. m. 8 June 1946, 1 son, 2 daughters. Education: BS, New York University, 1940. Publications: Fiction: Watchful at Night, 1945; The Bright Face of Danger, 1946; Walk in Shadow, 1947; A Model for Murder, 1956; Street of Fear, 1958; The League of Grey-Eyed Women, 1969; Body Language, 1970; What Should We Do Abnout Davey, 1988; Non-fiction including: The Beatles, 1968; The Incompatibility of Men and Women, 1971; The Pleasure Book, 1975; Bisexual Living, 1975; Creative Coping, 1976; Psyching Up, 1978; Talking Between the Lines, 1979; Body Politics, 1980; Body Language of Sex, Power, Aggression, 1983; Sexual Chemistry, 1983; Ladies' Man, 1985; Omega 3, 1987; Subtext, 1991. Honours: Edgar Allan Poe Award for Best First Mystery, 1945. Literary Agent: Bob Markel. Address: 45 East 85th Street, New York, NY 10028, USA.

FATCHEN Maxwell Edgar, b. 3 Aug 1920, Adelaide, South Australia. Author. m. Jean Wohlers, 15 May 1942, 2 sons, 1 daughter. Appointments: Journalist, Feature Writer, Adelaide News, 1946-55; Special Writer, 1955, 1981-84, Literary Editor, 1971-81, The Advertiser. Publications include: The River Kings, 1966; Conquest of the River, 1970; The Spirit Wind, 1973; Chase Through the Night, 1977; Closer to the Stars, 1981; Wry Rhymes, 1987; A Country Christmas, 1990; Tea for Three, 1994. Contributions to: Denver Post; Sydney Sun; Regional South Australian Histories. Honours: Commendation, 1967; Runner Up, 1974, Australian Childrens Book of Year; Member of the

Order of Australia, 1980; Honour Award, 1988; Advance Australia Award for Literature, 1991. Memberships: Australian Society of Authors; Australian Fellowship of Writers; South Australian Writers Centre; Australian Journalists Association. Literary Agent: John Johnson, London, EC1R 0HT. Address: 15 Jane St Box 6, Smithfield SA 5114, Australia.

FAULK Odie B, b. 26 Aug 1933. Professor of History. m. 22 Aug 1959, 1 s, 1 d. Education: BS, 1958, MA, 1960, PhD, 1962, Texas Tech University. Appointments: Texas A & M, 1962; University of Arizona, 1963; Oklahoma State University, 1968, Emeritus, 1988. Publications: Over 50 publications as author co-author or editor including: Land of Many Frontiers: A History of the American Southwest, 1968; The Geronimo Campaign, 1969; North America Divided: the War with Mexico, 1972; Tombstone: Myth and Reality, 1973; Crimson Desert: Indian Wars of the Southwest, 1975; Dodge City: the Most Western Town Of All, 1977. Contributions to: More than 100 major academic journals of history. Honours: Fellow, Texas State Historical Association, 1965; Best Non-Fiction Book of the Year (Tombstone: Myth and Reality), Southwestern border Library Association, 1973. Memberships: Board of Directors, Westerners International; Oklahoma Historical Society. Address: 5008 Sturbridge Temple, TX 76502, USA.

FAULKNOR (Chauncey) Cliff(ord Vernon), b. 1913, Canada. Appointment: Associate Editor, Country Guide Magazine, Winnipeg, Manitoba, 1954-75. Publications: The White Calf, 1965; The White Peril, the Romance of Beef, 1966; The In-Betweener, 1967; The Smoke Horse, 1968; West To Cattle Country, 1975; Pen and Plow, 1976; Turn Him Loose, 1977; Alberta Hereford Heritage, 1981; Johnny Eagleclaw, 1982. Membership: The Writers Union of Canada. Address: 403-80 Point McKay Crescent NW, Calgary, Alberta, Canada T3B 4W4.

FAUST Naomi, b. Salisbury, North Carolina, USA. Educator; Author; Poet. m. Roy M Faust. Education: AB, Bennet College; MA, University of Michigan; PhD, New York University. Career: Teacher, English; Professor, English; Professor, English Education. Publications: Discipline and the Classroom Teacher, book, 1977; Books of poems: Speaking in Verse, 1974; All Beautiful Things, 1983; And I Travel by Rhythms and Words, 1990; Poems in following anthologies: Adam of Ife; Biennial Anthology of Premier Poets; Dear Dark Faces; A Milestone Sampler, 15th Anniversary Anthology; National Poetry Anthology; Nature Anthology. Contributions to: Black Women in Praise of Black Men; Afro-American newspapers; Bitterroot; Cyclo Flame; Portraits of a People; Essence magazine; Gusto; International Poets; The New York Amsterdam News; The New York Voice; Parnassus Literary Journal; Poems by Blacks; Poet; Poetry Prevue; South and West; Written Word. Honours: Alpha Epsilon; Alpha Kappa Mu; Prize and Certificate of Merit for poem, Poems by Blacks; Prize for poem, Cyclo Flame; International Eminent Poet Award, International Poets Academy. Memberships: New York Poetry Forum; World Poetry Society Intercontinental; National Women's Book Association; American Associatin of University Professors; National Council of Teachers of English. Address: 112-01 175th Street, Jamaica, NY 11433, USA.

FAWCETT Catherine. See: COOKSON Catherine (Ann).

FAWKES Richard Brian, b. 31 July 1944, Camberley, Surrey, England. Writer; Film Director. m. Cherry Elizabeth Cole, 17 Apr 1971, 2 sons. Education: BA, Honours, St David's University College, 1967. Publications: The Last Corner of Arabia, with Michael Darlow, 1976; Fighting for a Laugh, 1978; Dion Boucicault - A Biography, 1979; Notes from a Low Singer, with Michael Langdon, 1982; Welsh National Opera, 1986; Plays for TV, Radio and Stage; Documentary Film Scripts; Book and Lyrics for Musical, The Misfortunes of Elphin, 1988. Contributions to: Classical Music; Sunday Times; Observer; She; Music and Musicians; various other journals & magazines. Honour: West Midlands Arts Association Bursary, 1978. Memberships: Society of Authors; ACTT; Society for Theatre Research. Literary Agent: David Higham. Address: 5-8 Lower John Street, Golden Square, London W1R 4HA, England.

FAYER Steve, b. 11 Mar 1935, Brooklyn, New York, USA. Writer. Education: BA honours in English Literature, University of Pennsylvania, 1956. Appointments: Series Writer, Eyes on the Prize I, 6 1-hour documentaries for Public Broadcasting Service, 1987; Series Writer, Eyes on the Prize II, 8 1-hour documentaries for Public Broadcasting Service, 1990; Series Writer, The Great Depression, 7 1-hour documentaries for Public Broadcasting Service, 1993; Also

Writer, Frederick Douglass - When The Lion Wrote History, 1994; Co-Writer, Malcolm X: Make It Plain, 1994. Publications: Voices of Freedom, 1990. Honours: Emmy Award, National Academy of Television Arts and Sciences, 1987. Membership: Writers Guild of America, New York, USA; International Documentary Association, Los Angeles, CA. Address: 189A Bay State Road, Boston, MA 02215, USA.

FEDERMAN Raymond, b. 15 May 1928, Paris, France. Novelist; Poet. m. Erica Hubscher, 14 Sept 1960, 1 daughter. Education: BA, Columbia University, USA, 1957; MA, 1958, PhD, 1963, University of California, Los Angeles. Appointments: Honorary Trustee, Samuel Beckett Society, 1979. Publications: Novels: Double or Nothing, 1971; Amer Eldorado, 1974; Take It or Leave It, 1976; The Voice in the Closet, 1979; The Twofold Vibration, 1982; Smiles on Washington Square, 1985; To Whom It May Concern, 1990; Criticism: Journey to Chaos, 1965; Samuel Beckett, 1970; Among the Beasts, poetry, 1967l; Surfiction, essays, 1976. Contributions to: Paris Review; Partisan Review; Chicago Review; The Quarterly; Mississippi Review; Fiction International Substance; Caliban. Honours: Guggenheim Fellowship, 1967; Frances Steloff Fiction Prize, 1971; The American Book Award for Smiles on Washington Square, 1986; Distinguished Faculty Professor, State University of New York, 1990. Memberships: PEN American Center; Board of Editors, Fiction Collective. Literary Agent: Erica Hubscher Federman. Address: 46 Four Seasons West, Eggertsville, NY 14226, USA.

FEIFFER Jules, b. 26 Jan 1929, New York, USA. Cartoonist; Writer. m. Judith Sheftel, 1961, 1 daughter. Education: Art Students League; Pratt Institute. Appointments: Assistant to Cartoonist Will Eisner, 1946-51; Cartoonist, Author, syndicated Sunday page, Clifford, engaged in various jobs, 1953-56; contributing cartoonist, Village Voice, New York City, 1956-; cartoons published weeklyin: The Observer (London), 1958-66, 1972-82, regularly in Playboy Magazine; Cartoons nationally syndicated in USA, 1959-. Publications: Books: Sick, Sick, Sick, 1959; Passionella and other Stories, 1960; The Explainers, 1961; Boy, Girl, Boy, Girl, 1962; Hold Me! 1962; Harry, The Rat With Women (novel), 1963; Feiffer's Album, 1963; The Unexpurgated Memoirs of Bernard Mergendeiler, 1965; The Great Comic Book Heroies, 1967; Feiffer's Marriage Manual, 1967; Pictures at a Prosecution, 1971; Ackroyd (novel), 1978; Tantrum, 1980; Jules Feiffer's America: From Eisenhower to Reagan, 1982; Marriage is an Invasion of Privacy, 1984; Feiffer's Children, 1986; Plays: Crawling Arnold, 1961; Little Murders, 1966; God Bless, 1968; The White House Murder Case, 1970; Feiffer on Nixon: The Cartoon Presidency, 1974; Knock Knock, 1975; Grown Ups, 1981; A Think Piece, 1982; Feiffer's America, 1985; Screenplays: Little Murders, 1971; Carnal Knowledge, 1971; Popeye, 1980. Honours: Academy Award for Animated Cartoon, Munro, 1961; Special George Polk Memorial Award, 1962. Membership: Sponsor, National Committee for Sane Nuclear Policy. Address: c/o Universal Press Syndicate, 4400 Johnson Drive, Fairway, KS 66205, USA.

FEIKEMA Feike. See: MANFRED Frederick Feikema.

FEINBERG Barry Vincent, b. 26 Dec 1938, South Africa. Writer; Designer; Film Maker. Education: Slade School of Art, London, 1964-65. Appointments: Editor, Bertrand Russell, The Bertrand Russell Estate, 1966-75; Director, Research, Information, Publications, this International Defence, Aid Fund for Southern Africa, London, 1977-87; Director, University of the Western Cape, 1992-. Publication: Dear Bertrand Russell, 1969; Collected Stories of Russell, 1972; Bertrand Russell's America, 1973, 1984; Poets to the People, 1974; Expanded, 1980; Gardens of Struggle, 1992. Contributions to: Numerous Professional Journals. Honours: Director, Several Prize Winning Documentary Films. Address: 76 Chamberlain Street, Woodstock 7925, Cape Town, South Africa.

FEINBERG David B, b. 25 Nov 1956, Massachusetts, USA. Writer. Education: SB, Mathematics, Massachusetts Institute of Technology, 1977; MA, Linguistics, New York University, 1982. Publications: Eighty-Sixed, 1989; Spontaneous Combustion, 1991. Contributions to: Tribe; Outweek; The Advocate; NYQ-QUU; The New York Times Book Review; Diseased Pariah News; Mandate; Torso. Honours: Lambda Literary Award for Best Gay Male Novel, 1989; Best Fiction, American Library Association Gay and Lesbian Caucus, 1989; Selected by New York Public Library for Books to Remember, 1989. Membership: Act Up, New York. Literary Agent: Norman Lauila. Address: 410 West 23rd Street, 2B, New York, NY 10011, USA.

FEINBERG Joan Miriam (Joan Schuchman), b. 13 Oct 1934, Far Rockaway, New York, USA. Freelance Writer. m. Arnold I Feinberg, 4 Oct 1986, 2 sons. Education: Brooklyn College, 1952-54; BA, 1970, University of Minnesota. Publications: Astrology: Science or Hoax, 1978; Help for Your Hyperactive Child, 1978; Two Places to Sleep, 1979; Broken Dreams, 1992. Contributions to: Carolrhoda Publishing Company; Pamphlet Publications; The Daimandis Corporation; The Institute for Research; Today's Family; Conquest Magazine; Horoscope Guide; World Book and Travel; New York Times Syndicate; International Travel News. Honours: Writer's Digest Article Writing Contests: Depression: The Living Death Disease, 1987, The Diet That Calms Hyperactive Children, 1987. Memberships: Conservatory of American Letters; Women in Communication; Florida Freelance Writers Association; International Women's Writer's Guild. Address: 4725 Excelsior Boulevard Suite 300, Minneapolis, MN 55416, USA.

FEINBERG Leonard, b. 26 Aug 1914, Vitebsk, Russia. Professor. m. Lilian Okner, 26 Nov 1938, 1 daughter. Education: BS 1937, MA 1938, PhD 1946, University of Illinois. Appointments: Instructor in English, University of Illinois, 1938; Assistant Professor 1946, Associate Professor 1950, Professor of English 1957, Iowa State University. Publications: The Satirist, 1963; Introduction to Satire, 1967; Asian Laughter, 1971; The Secret of Humor, 1978. Contributions to: Atlantic; College English; Satire Newsletter. Honours: Fulbright Lecturer, University of Ceylon, 1957-58; Wilton Park Fellow, 1972; Named Distinguished Professor, Iowa State University, 1973. Address: 2404 Loring Street, San Diego, CA 92109, USA.

FEINSTEIN (Allan) David, b. 22 Dec 1946, Brooklyn, New York, USA. Psychologist. m. Donna Eden, 7 Oct 1984. Education: BA, Whittier College, 1968; MA, US International University, 1970; PhD, Union Institute, 1973. Publications: Personal Mythology, 1988; Rituals for Living and Dying, 1990; Serenade at the Doorway, album, 1991. Contributions to: Common Boundary; Magical Blend; Psychotherapy; American Journal of Orthopsychiatry; American Journal of Hypnosis. Honours: William James Award, 1968. Memberships: American Psychological Association; Association for Humanistic Psychology. Address: 777 East Main Street, Ashland, OR 97520, USA.

FEINSTEIN Elaine, b. 24 Oct 1930, Bootle, Lancashire, England. Education: Newnham College, Cambridge, 1952. Appointments: Editorial Staff Member, Cambridg University Press, 1960-62; Lecturer, Bishops Stortford College, 1963-66; Assistant Lecturer, University of Essex, 1967-70. Publications include: In A Green Eye, 1966; The Circle, 1970; The Magic Apple Tree, 1971; At The Edge, 1972; The Celebrants and Other Poems, The Glass Alembic, 1973; The Children of the Rose, 1974; The Ecstasy of Miriam Garner, 1976; Some Unease and Angles, 1977; The Shadow Master, Three Russian Poets, 1978; The Silent Areas, The Feast of Euridice, 1980; The Survivors, 1982; The Border, 1984; Bessie Smith, 1985; A Captive Lion: The Life of Marina Tsvetayeva, 1987; Mothers Girl, 1988; All You Need, 1989; Verse, City Music, 1990. Address: c/o Hutchinson Publishing Group Limited, 62-65 Chandos Place, London, WC2N 4NW, England.

FEKETE John, b. 7 Aug 1946, Budapest, Hungary. Professor of English and Cultural Studies. Education: BA with Honours, English Literature, 1968, MA, English Literature, 1969, McGill University; PhD, Cambridge University, 1973. Appointments: Visiting Assistant Professor, English, McGill University, Montreal, Quebec, Canada, 1973-74; Associate Editor, Telos, 1974-84; Visiting Assistant Professor, Humanities, York University, Toronto, Ontario, 1975-76; Assistant Professor 1976-78, Associate Professor 1978-84, Professor, English, Cultural Studies 1984-, Trent University, Peterborough, Ontario. Publications: The Critical Twilight: Explorations in the Ideology of Anglo-American Literary Theory from Eliot to McLuhan, 1978; The Structural Allegory: Reconstructive Encounters With the New French Thought, 1984; Life After Postmodernism: Essays on Culture and Value, 1987; Moral Panic: Biopolitics Rising, 1994. Contributions to: Editorial contributor to Canadian Journal of Political and Social Theory; Canadian Journal of Communications; Science-Fiction Studies. Address: 181 Wallis Drive, Peterborough, Ontario, K9J 6C4, Canada.

FELD Werner J, b. 1910, American. Appointments: Professor and Chairman, Department of Political Science, University of New Orleans, LA; President, Dixie Speciality Company Incorporated, 1948-61. Publications: Reunification and West German-Soviet Relations, 1963; The Court of the European Communities, 1964; New Dimension in International Adjudication, 1964; The European Common Market and the World, 1967; Transnational Business Collaboration among Common Market Countries, 1970; Nongovernmental Forces and World Politics: A Study of Business, Labor and Political Groups, 1972; The European Community in World Affairs: Economic Power and Political Influence, 1976; Domestic Political Realities and European Unification: A Study of Mass Publics and Elites in the European Community Countries, 1977; The Foreign Policies of West European Socialist Parties, 1978; International Relations: A Transnational Approach, 1979; Multinational Corporations and UN Policies, 1980, Comparative Regional Systems (editor and contributor), Western Europe's Global Reach (ed), 1980; West Germany and the European Community, NATO and the Atlantic Defense: Perceptions and Illusions, 1981; International Organizations: A Comparative Approach, American Foreign Policy: Aspirations and Reality, 1983; Congress and National Defense, 1985; Europe in the Balance (co-author), 1986; Arms Control and the Atlantic Community, 1987. Address: 3743 Blue Merion Court, Colorado Springs, CO 80906, USA.

FELDMAN Alan Grad, b. 16 Mar 1945, New York City, USA. Writer; Teacher. m. Nanette Hass, 22 Oct 1972, 1 son, 1 daughter. Education: AB, Columbia College, 1966; MA, Columbia University, 1969; PhD, State University of New York, Buffalo, 1973. Publications: The Household, 1966; The Happy Genius, 1978; Frank O'Hara, 1978; The Personals, 1982; Lucy Mastermind, 1985; Anniversary, 1992. Contributions to: New Yorker; The Atlantic; Kenyon Review; Mississippi Review; Ploughshares; North American Review; Threepenny Review; Boston Review; Tendril; College English. Honours: Award for Best Short Story in a College Literary Magazine, Saturday Review-National Student Association, 1965; Elliston Book Award for Best Book of Poems by a Small Press in US, for The Happy Genius, 1978. Address: 399 Belknap Road, Framingham, MA 01701, USA.

FELDMAN Gerald D, b. 24 Apr 1937, New York City, USA. Historian. m. Norma von Ragenfeld, 30 Nov 1983, 1 son, 1 daughter (by first marriage). Education: BA, Columbia College, 1958, MA, 1959, PhD, 1964, Harvard University (all degrees in History). Appointments: Assistant Professor 1963-68, Associate Professor 1968-70, Professor 1970-, University of California, Berkeley; Currently member of editorial boards or advisory boards for Geschichte und Gesellschaft, German Yearbook on Business History and Contemporary European History. Publications include: Books: Army, Industry and Labor in Germany, 1914-1918, 1966; Iron and Steel in the German Inflation, 1916-1923, 1977; With Heidrun Homburg, Industrie und Inflation, 1977; Vom Weltkrieg zur Zeltwirtschaftskrise, 1984; With Irmgard Steinisch, Industrie und Gewerkschaften 1918-1924; (with Klaus Tenfelde), Workers, Owners and Politics in Coal Mining, An International Comparison of Industrial Relations, 1990; The Great Disorder: Politics, Economics and Society in the German Inflation, 1914-1923, 1993; Also edited collections of documents and papers, articles and review essays. Honours include: Appointed to Historisches Kolleg Munich for 1982-83; Stephen Allen Kaplan Memorial Lecture at the University of Pennsylvania 1984; Invited Guest, Rockefeller Center at Bellagio, Sept 1987; Appointed to the Wissenschaftskolleg (Institute for Advanced Study) Berlin for 1987-88; Appointed to Woodrow Wilson Center, 1991-92. Memberships include: Corresponding Member, Historische Kommission zu Berlin, 1980-; Chairman, Conference Group for Central European History of the AHA, 1990; Executive Committee, Friends of the German Historical Institute in Washington, 1990-91. Address: Department of History, University of California, Berkeley, CA 94720, USA.

FELDMAN Paula R, b. 4 July 1948, Washington, District of Columbia, USA. University Professor; Writer. m. Robert H Stuart, 28 Jan 1989. Education: BA, Bucknell University, 1970; MA 1971, PhD 1974, Northwestern University. Appointments: Assistant Professor, English 1974-79, Associate Professor, English 1979-89, Professor, English 1989-, Director, Graduate Studies in English 1991-93, University of South Carolina, Columbia. Publications: The Microcomputer and Business Writing (with David Byrd and Phyllis Fleishel), 1986; The Journals of Mary Shelley (edited with Diana Scott-Kilvert), 2 vols, 1987; The Wordworthy Computer; Classroom and Research Applications in Language and Literature (with Buford Norman), 1987; Romantic Women Writers: Voices and Countervoices, ed with Theresa Kelley, 1994. Contributions to: Articles in: Studies in English Literature; Papers of the Bibliographical Society of America; Approaches to Teaching Shelley's Frankenstein, 1990; Blake: An Illustrated Quarterly, 1994. Address: Department of English, University of South Carolina, Columbia, SC 29208, USA.

FELDMAN Ruth (Wasby), b. 21 May 1911, USA. Poet; Translator. m. Moses D Feldman (dec). Education: BA, Wellesley College, 1931; Workshops, Boston University, Radcliffe Institute. Publications include: Books: The Ambition of Ghosts, poetry, 1979; Poesie di Ruth Feldman, poetry, 1981; To Whom It May Concern, poetry, 1986; (Co-editor, translator), Collected Poems of Lucio Piccolo, 1973; Selected Poems of Andrea Zanzotto, 1975; Shema, 1976; Italian Poetry Today, 1979; The Dawn is Always New, 1980; The Hands of the South, 1980; The Dry Air of the Fire, 1981; Collected Poems of Primo Levi, 1988; Sole Translator: Moments of Reprieve, 1986; Liber Fulguralis: Poems by Margherita Guidacci, 1986. Contributions to: Anthologies: New York Times Book of Verse; Anthology of Magazine Verse; Voices Within the Ark; Peter Kaplan's Book; Sotheby's Poetry Competition Prize Anthology; Poesia della Metamorfosi; Poetry Society of America Diamond Anthology; Penguin Book of Women Poets; Barnstone Book of Women Poets; Gates to the New City; In the Pink; Editor's Choice II; Numerous literary magazines & reviews. Honours include: Devil's Advocate Award, 1972; Monthly awards, 1 annual award, Poetry Society of America; Prize, Sotherby's International Poetry Competition, 1982; Co-winner John Florio, 1976; Cire-Sabaudia, 1983. Memberships: Poetry Society of America; New Zealand Poetry Club; American Literary Translators Association. PEN.

FELICE. See: **DOMARADZKI Théodore Felix.**

FELICE Cynthia, b. 10 Oct 1942, Chicago, Illinois, USA. Writer; Technical Manager. m. Robert E Felice Sr, 23 Dec 1961, 2 sons. Publications: Godsfire, 1978; The Sunbound, 1981; Eclipses, 1983; Downtime, 1985; Double Nocturne, 1986; Water Witch, with Connie Willis, 1982; Light Riad, with Connie Willis, 1988; Many novels published in Holland, Germany, Japan. Contributions to: Fiction, non-fiction: Omni; The Writer; Galileo; Various anthologies. Honours: Finalist, Campbell Award nomination, 1979; Outstanding paper, Society for Technical Communication, 1983. Memberships: Science Fiction Writers Association; Society for Technical Communications. Literary Agent: Richard Curtis. Address: 5025 Park Vista Boulevard, Colorado Springs, CO 80918, USA.

FENG Jicai, b. 9 Feb 1942, Tianjin, China. Novelist. Education: Graduate of High School, Tanggu, Tianjin. Appointments include: Writer at Tianjin Federation of Literature and Art Circle, from 1978. Publications: The Boxers, 1977; Flowering Branch Road, 1979; A Letter, 1980; The Magic Lantern, 1981; The Carved Pipe, 1981; Man in the Fog, 1983; Into the Storm, 1983; The Miraculous Pigtail, 1984; The Tall Woman and her Short Husband, 1984; Chrysanthemums, 1985; Thanks to Life, 1985; Three-Inch Golden Lotus, 1986; The Eight Diagrams of Yin and Yang, 1988; Radio and Television plays; also: Voices from the Whirlwind, 1991. Address: 801 Yun-Feng-Lou A, Nanjing Road, Tianjin, China.

FENNARIO David, b. Montreal, 1947. Playwright. m. Elizabeth Fennario, 1976, 1 child. Education: Dawson College, Montreal, 1969-71. Career: Playwright-in-Residence, Centaur Theatre, Montreal, 1973-; Co-founder, Cultural Workers Association. Publications: Plays: On the Job (produced Montreal 1975), Vancouver, Talonbooks, 1976; Nothing to Lose (produced Montreal 1976), Vancouver, Talonbooks, 1977; Toronto (produced Montreal 1978); Without a Parachute, adaptation of his own book produced Toronto, 1978; Balconville (produced Montreal 1979; Bath and London 1981), Vancouver, Talonbooks, 1980; Changes, adaptation of his journal Without a Parachute (produced Ottawa, 1980); Moving (produced Montreal, 1983); Blue Mondays, poems by Daniel Adams, Verdun, Quebec, Black Rock Creations, 1984; Joe Beef, 1991. Honours: Canada Council grant, 1973; Chalmers Award, 1979. Address: c/o Centaur Theatre Company, 453 St Francois Xavier Street, Montreal, Quebec H2Y 2T1, Canada.

FENNELLY Tony (Antonia), b. 25 Nov 1945, Orange, New Jersey, USA. Author. m. James Richard Catoire, 24 Dec 1972. Education: BA, Drama & Communications, University of New Orleans, 1976. Publications: The Glory Hole Murders, 1985; The Closet Hanging, 1987; Kiss Yourself Goodbye, 1989; Der Hippie in Der Wand (Germany), 1992; Hurenglanz (Germany), 1993; The Hippie in the Wall, 1994. Honours: Edgar Allan Poe Special Award, Mystery Writers of America, 1986; Memberships: Mystery Writers of America; Authors Guild; International Association of Crime Writers; Sisters in Crime. Literary Agent: Jim Trupin, Jet Literary Associates Inc, 124 E 84th Street, New York, NY 10028, USA. Address: 921 Clouet St, New Orleans, LA 70117, USA.

FENNER Carol. See: **WILLIAMS Carol Elizabeth.**

FENNER James R. See: **TUBB E(dwin) C(harles).**

FENNO Jack. See: **CALISHER Hortense.**

FENTON James Martin, b. 25 Apr 1949. Writer. Education: MA, Magdalen College, Oxford; FRSL, 1983. Appointments: Assistant Literary Editor, 1971, Editorial Assistant, 1972, New Statesman; Freelance Correspondent, Indo-China, 1973-75; Political Columnist, New Statesman, 1976-78; German Correspondent, The Guardian, 1978-79; Theatre Critic, Sunday Times, 1979-84; Far East Correspondent, The Independent, 1986-88. Publications: Our Western Furniture, 1968; Terminal Moraine, 1972; A Vacant Possession, 1978; A German Requiem, 1980; Dead Soldiers, 1981; The Memory of War, 1982; Translations; Rigoletto, 1982; You Were Marvellous, 1983; Editor, The Original Michael Frayn, 1983; Children in Exile, 1984; Poems 1968-83, 1985; Translation, Simon Boccanegra, 1985; The Fall of Saigon, In Granta 15, 1985; The Snap Revolution in Granta, 1986; Partingtime Hall (with John Fuller), 1987; All the Wrong Places, adrift in the Poltics of Asia, 1989. Address: c/o A D Peters & Co Ltd, 10 Buckingham Street, London WC2N 6BU, England.

FERDINANDY György (Georges), b. 11 Oct 1935, Budapest, Hungary. Professor. m. (1) Colette Peyrethon, 27 May 1958, (2) Maria Teresa Reyes-Cortes, 3 Jan 1981, 3 sons, 1 daughter. Education: Doctorate in Literature, University of Strasbourg, France, 1969. Appointments: Freelance Literary Critic, Radio Free Europe, 1977-86; Professor, University of Puerto Rico, Cayey, Puerto Rico. Publications: In French: L'ile sous l'eau, 1960; Famine au Paradis, 1962; Le seul jour de l'année, 1967; Itinéraires, 1973; Chica, Claudine, Cali, 1973; L'oeuvre hispanoaméricaine de Zs Remenyik, 1975; Fantomes magnétiques, 1979; Youri, 1983; Hors jeu, 1986; Mémoires d'un exil terminé, 1992; In Hungarian: Latoszemueknek, 1962; Tizenharom Töredék, 1964; Futoszalagon, 1965; Nemezio Gonzalex, 1970; Valencianal a tenger, 1975; Mammuttemetö, 1982; A Mosoly Albuma, 1982; Az elveszett gyermek, 1984; A Vadak Utjan, 1986; Szerecsenségem Története, 1988; Furcsa, idegen szerelem, 1990; Uzenöfüzet, 1991; Szomorü Szigetek, 1992; A Francia Völegény, 1993; Saldo a medio camino, Spanish translation, 1976; Book of the Year, 1993. Contributions to: Le Monde; NRF; Europe; Elet és Irodalom; Kortars; Uj Hold; Magyar Naplo. Honours: Del Duca Prix, 1961; St Exupéry Literary Award, 1964. Memberships: Société des Gens de Lettres, France; Hungarian Writers Association; International PEN club. Address: Joaquin Lopez Lopez 1056, Sta Rita, Rio Piedras, PR 00925, USA.

FERGUSON Joseph Francis, b. 11 Feb 1952, Yonkers, New York, USA. Public Relations; Journalist; Critic; Author. m. Janice Robinson, 30 July 1986, 1 son. Education: BA, SUNY, New Paltz, 1979; MS, Pace University (not completed). Publications: Night Image; Duecy and Detour; Priorities; Autumn Road Kill; Autumn Poem; Sky and Stream at Sunset; End of Daylight in a Car Mirror; The Atlar; Jazz; New Orleans; The Glory; Another Damn Dream Poem; Grave Dreams; View From the Graveyard Shift. Contributions to: Hundreds of News and feature articles, wide variety of local, national and international publications. Honours: 1990 World of poetry Golden Poet; American Poetry Association Contest, Honorable Mention; Finalist, San Diego Poets Press. Address: 26 Bank Street, Cold Spring, NY 10516, USA.

FERGUSON Robert Thomas, b. 2 June 1948, Stoke On Trent, England. Writer. m. 3 Apr 1987. Education: BA, University College, London, 1980. Publications: Enigma, The Life of Knut Hamsun, 1987; Henry Miller, A Life, 1991; As Contributor, Best Radio Drama, 1984; Best Radio Drama, 1986. Honours: BBC Methuen Giles Cooper Award, 1984, 86; J G Robertson Prize, 1985-87. Literary Agent: Scott Ferris Associates Limited, London. Address: Steinspranget 7, 1156 Oslo 11, Norway.

FERGUSON William Rotch, b. 14 Feb 1943, Fall River, Massachusetts, USA. Author; Foreign Languages Educator. m. Nancy King, 26 Nov 1983. Education: BA 1965, MA 1970, PhD 1975, Harvard University. Publications: Dream Reader, poems, 1973; La Versificación Imitativa en Fernando de Herrera, scholarly, 1981; Freedom and Other Fictions, stories, 1984. Contributions to: Paris Review; Harper's; Insula; Massachusetts Review; Mississippi Review; Canto; Malahat Review; Reviewer; New York Times Book Review. Memberships: Modern Languages Association; American Association of University Professors; Asociación Internacional "Siglo de Oro". Address: Foreign

Languages Department, Clark University, 950 Main Street, Worcester, MA 01610, USA.

FERLINGHETTI Lawrence, b. 24 Mar 1919, Yonkers, New York, USA. Writer; Editor; Painter. 1 son, 1 daughter. Education: MA, Columbia University; University of Paris. Publications include: Poems: Pictures of the Gone World; A Coney Island of the Mind; Starting of the Gone World; A Coney Island of the Mind; Starting from San Francisco; The Secret Meanings of Things; Tyrannus Nix? Back Roads to Far Places; Open Eye, Open Heart; Landscapes of Living and Dying, 1979; Endless Life: Selected Poems, 1981; Over All the Obscene Boundaries, 1984; These Are My Rivers: New & Selected Poems 1955-1993, 1993; Plays: Unfair Arguments with Existence; Routines; Her (novel); Love in the Days of Rage (E P Dutton), novel, 1988; The Mexican Night (travel journal); We Are We Now? 1976; Literary San Francisco: A Pictorial History from the Beginnings to the Present (with Nancy J Peters), 1980; Leaves of Life: Drawings from the Model, 1983; Editor, City Lights Books; Translations; film-scripts; phonograph records, painter, paintings. Address: c/o City Lights Bookstore, 261 Columbus Avenue, San Francisco, CA 94133, USA.

FERLITA Ernest Charles, b. 1 Dec 1927, Tampa, Florida, USA. Jesuit Priest; Educator; Playwright. Education: BS, Spring Hill College, 1950; STL, St Louis University, 1964; DFA, Yale University, 1969. Publications: The Theatre of Pilgrimage, 1971; Film Odyssey (Co-author), 1976; The Way of the River, 1977; The Parables of Lina Wertmuller (Co-author), 1977; Religion in Film (Contributor), 1982; Gospel Journey, 1983; The Mask of Hiroshima in Best Short Plays, 1989; The Uttermost Mark, 1990. Honours: Play Awards: 1st Prize Christian Theatre Artists Guild, 1971; American Radio Scriptwriting Contest, 1985; Miller Award, 1986. Memberships: Dramatists Guild; Theatre in Higher Education; International Hopkins Society. Address: Loyola University, New Orleans, LA 70118, USA.

FERNANDEZ-ARMESTO Felipe Fermin Ricardo, b. 6 Dec 1950, London, England. Historian. m. Lesley Patricia Hook, 16 July 1977, 2 sons. Education: Magdalen College, Oxford, 1969-72; 1st Class Hons, Modern History, 1972, MA 1976, DPhil, 1977, Oxford University. Appointments: Journalist, The Diplomatist, 1972-74. Publications: The Canary Islands after the Conquest, 1982; Before Columbus, 1987; The Spanish Armada, 1988; Barcelona, 1991; The Times Atlas of World Exploration (general editor), 1991; Columbus, 1991; Edward Gibbon's Atlas of the World, 1992; Others. Contributions to: English Historical Review; History; History Today; Anuarto de Estudios Atlanticos; Other English and Spanish historical periodicals; The Sunday Times Magazines; Other. Honours: Arnold Modern History Prize, 1971; Leverhulme Research Fellowship, 1981; Commendation, Library Association, 1992. Memberships: Council, Hakluyt Society; Society of Authors; PEN; Library Committee, The Athenaeum; Fellow, Royal Historical Society; Historical Association; Association of Hispanists. Literary Agent: Serafina Clarke. Address: River View, Headington Hill, Oxford OX3 0BT, England.

FERRARI Ronald Leslie, b. 3 Feb 1930, Romford, Essex, England. Electrical Engineer. m. Judith Wainwright, 5 Sept 1959, 1 s, 3 d. Education: BSc, DIC, Imperial College, London; MA, ScD. Appointments: Lecturer, Cambridge University, 1965; Fellow, Trinity College, Cambridge, 1966. Publication include; Problems in Physical Electronics, 1973; Introduction to Electromagnetic Fields, 1975; Finite Elements for Electrical Engineers, 1983, 1990. Contributions to: Special Issue of IEE Proceedings. Memberships: Institute of Electrical Engineers. Address: Trinity College, Cambridge CB2 1T, England.

FERRARO Bernadette A, b. 19 Apr 1952, USA. Biomedical Writer. Education: BA, Zoology; Rutgers University, 1974; University of Medicine and Dentistry, New Jersey, 1977. Appointments: Staff, Magazine, Sol '70, 1969-700; Writer, Il Lettere, 1972-73. Publications: (Poetry) Peace, 1972; Journey, 1973; Butterfly, 1986; Multiple Primary Malignancies of Larynx and Lung: Detection by Cytology, 1981, abstracted 1982; Wrote videoscript entitled: 'Room for Us All', 1986; Vincent Van Gough, Did He Suffer from Immotile Celia Syndrome? 1987. Contributions to: Numerous journals and magazines including: Respiration; International Synopses periodical; The Sciences. Honours: Golden Poet Award, 1986; Board of Directors of Nargis Dutt Memorial Foundation, 1986-87; Nominated for position of Executive Committee-At-Large, Nargis Dutt Memorial Foundation, 1987; Judge, Biology & Environmental Sciences Category, 49th Annual School Science Fair, New York City, 1987; Recipient, Grand Ambassador of Achievement, USA Representative, American Biographical Institute,

1987; Fellow, International Biographical Association, 1987. Memberships: American Film Institute, 1976-; American Society of Cytology, 1978; American Society Clinical Pathologists, 1978; New York Academy of Sciences, 1985; American Association for the Advancement of Science, 1985-; Nargis Dutt Memorial Foundation, 1985-. Address: 77 Povershon Road, Nutley, NJ 07110, USA.

FERRERI Marco, b. 11 May 1928, Milan, Italy. Screenwriter and director of motion pictures. m. Jacqueline. Education: Studied veterinary medicine in mid 1940s. Career: Screenwriter and director of motion pictures, worked as liquor salesman and advertising agent in late 1940s; Founder and Promoter of filmed periodical, Documento Mensile, 1950-51; actor and production assistant in Italian film industry in early 1950s; optical instruments salesperson in Spain 1954. Creative Works: Screenplays and director - Films include: (with Fafael Azcona, El cochecito (The Wheelchair), 1960; (with Jean-Claude Carriere), Liza 1972, also released abroad as La Cagna; (with Azcona), La Grande Bouffe (The Big Feast), 1973, also released abroad as Blow-out; (with Azcona), Touochez pas la Femme blanche, 1974; L'ultima donna Productions Jacques Roltfeld/Flaminia Produzioni 1976, released in US as The Last Woman, 1976; Co-author, Bye Bye Monkey, 1978; Chiedo asilo (My Asylum), Gaumont, 1979; (with Sergio Amidei and Anthony Foutz), Tales of Ordinary Madness, 1983; (with Piera Degli Esposti and Dacia Maraini), Storia di Piera, 1983, released in USA as The Story of Piera, 1983; (with Esposti and Maraini), Il futuro e donna (The Future is Woman), 1984; (with Didier Kaminka and Enrico Oldoini), I Love You, 1988. Honours: International Film Critics Award from Venice Film Festival 1960 for El cochecito; International Critics Award from Cannes Film Festival 1973 for La Grande Bouffe. Address: Piazza Mattei 10, Rome, Italy.

FERRIS Paul, b. 1929, England. Freelance Writer. Publications include: A Changed Man, 1958; The City, 1960; Then We Fall, 1960; The Church of England, 1962; A Family Affair, 1963; The Doctors, 1965; The Destroyer, 1965; The Nameless Abortion in Britain Today, 1966; The Dam, 1967; Men and Money: Financial Europe Today, 1968; The House of Northcliffe, 1971; The New Militants, 1972; The Detectives, 1976; Dylan Thomas, 1977; Talk to Me about England, 1979; Richard Burton, 1981; A Distant Country, 1983; Gentlemen of Fortune, 1984; Collected Letters of Dylan Thomas, 1985; Children of Dust, 1988; Sex and the British, 1993; Caitlin, 1993; TV Plays, The Revivalist, 1975; Dylan, 1978; Nye, 1982; The Extremist, 1983; The Fasting Girl, 1984. Literary Agent: Curtis Brown Limited. Address: c/o Curtis Brown Limited, 162-168 Regent Street, London W1R 5TA, England.

FERRON Madeleine, b. 24 July 1922, Louiseville (Quebec), Canada. Writer. m. Robert Cliche, 22 Sept 1945, 2 sons, 1 daughter. Publications: Short Stories: Coeur de Sucre, 1966, rep 1971 & 1988; Le Chemin des Dames, 1977, rep 1993; Histoires Edifiantes, 1981; Un Singulier Amour, 1987; Le Grand Theatre, 1989; Novels: La Fin des Loups-Garous, 1966, reprinted 1982; Le Baron Ecarlate, 1971; Sur le Chemin Craig, 1982; Essays: Quand le Peuple fait la loi, 1972, rep 1982; Les Beaucerons, ces insoumis, 1974, rep 1982; Adrienne, une saga familiale, 1993. Honours: Ordre National du Quebec, Chevalier, 1992; Grand Prix Litteraire de Montreal: Finalist in 1971 & 1987; Prix-Quebec: Finalist in 1966 & 1987; Prix des Editions La Presse, 1982. Literary Agent: Editions Boreal, Montreal, Canada, H2J 2L2. Address: 1130 de la Tour, Quebec, G1R 2W7, Canada.

FICKERT Kurt Jon, b. 19 Dec 1920, Pausa, Germany. Professor. m. Madlyn Barbara Janda, 6 Aug 1946, 2 sons, 1 daughter. Education: BA, Hofstra University, 1941; MA 1947, PhD 1952, New York University, USA. Appointment: President, Ohio Poetry Day Association, 1968-70. Publications: Kafka's Doubles, 1979; Franz Kafka: Life, Work and Criticism, 1984; Hermann Hesse's Quest, 1978; Neither Left Nor Right, 1987; To Heaven and Back: The New Morality in the Plays of Duerrenmatt; Signs and Portents: Myth in Wolfgang Borchert's Work; Johnson: Ansichten, Einsichten, Aussichten (Contributor), 1989; End of a Mission: Kafka's Search for Truth in His Last Stories, 1993. Contributions to: Articles in magazines and journals including: International Fiction Review; The German Quarterly; Monatshefte; Modern Fiction Studies; Journal of Modern Literature. Memberships: Phi Beta Kappa; American Association of Teachers of German; Wolfgang Borchert Gesellschaft. Address: 33 South Kensington Place, Springfield, OH 45504, USA.

FIELD D M. See: **GRANT Neil David Mountfield.**

FIELD Edward, b. 7 June 1924, Brooklyn, New York, USA. Writer. Education: New York University (no degree), 1946-48. Appointments: Guggenheim Fellow, 1963; Fellow, American Academy of Rome, 1980. Publications: Stand Up, Friend, With Me, 1963; Variety Photoplays, 1967; A Full Heart, 1977; A Geography of Poets, editor, 1979; Village (as Bruce Elliott); New and Selected Poems, 1987; Counting Myself Lucky, 1992; The Office (as Bruce Elliott); Eskimo Songs & Stories, 1973; (ed) Head of a Sad Angel: Stories 1953-1966 by Alfred Chester, 1990. Contributions to: New Yorker; New York Review of Books; Partisan Review; Evergreen Review; Botteghe Oscure; Harper's; Kenyon Review; The Listener. Honours: Lamont Award, 1963; Shelley Memorial Award, 1978; Lambda Award, 1993. Membership: Authors Guild. Address: 463 West Street, A323 New York, NY 10014, USA.

FIELD Stanley, b. 20 May 1911, Ukraine. Writer; Professor. m. Joyce Stillman, 7 Dec 1935, 1 son, 1 daughter. Education: BA, Brooklyn College, 1934. Appointments: Writer, National Broadcasting Co, New York City, 1934-40; Script Witer, Radio and TV Programme, US Department of Defense, 1942-75; Adjunct Professor, Creative Writing, The American University, Washington, District of Columbia, 1952-77; Instructor, Creative Writing, Mt Vernon College. Publications: Television and Radio Writing, 1959; Guide to Scholarships, 1967; Bible Stories, 1967; Broadcast Writers Handbook, 1974; The Mini-Documentary, 1975; The Freelancer, 1984. Contributions to: Short stories and poetry to Virginia Country; Adventure; War Cry; Writers Journal; Green's; Omega Chronicles; Minnesota Ink; A Loving Voice; Wellspring Cats; Articles to: Photo; Stag; Woman's Life; Live; Washington Star; Home Life; New York Alive; Poets and Writers; Women's Household; Friar. Honours: YMCA International Script Award, 1945; Fund for the Republic Award, 1952; Freedoms Foundation, 1953, 1954; Writers Digest Fiction Award, 1972; Writers Journal Fiction Award, 1986; Literary Lights Fiction Award, 1988; Wellspring Fiction Award, 1991. Memberships: The Authors Guild; Poets and Fiction Writers; International Society of Dramatists; San Diego Writers Guild; Broadcast Education Association; Associated Writing Programmes. Address: 5196 Middleton Road, San Diego, CA 92109, USA.

FIELDER Mildred, b. 14 Jan 1913, Quinn, South Dakota, USA. Author. m. Ronald G Fielder, 17 Sept 1932, 2 sons. Education: Huron College, 1930-31; University of Colorado, 1946. Publications: Wandering Foot in the West, 1955; Railroads of the Black Hills, 1960; Wild Bill and Deadwood, 1965; Treasure of Homestake Gold, 1970; Guide to Black Hills Ghost Mines, 1972; Chinese in the Black Hills, 1972; Potato Creek Johnny, 1973; Hiking Trails in the Black Hills, 1973; Wild Bill Hickok Gun Man, 1974; Theodore Roosevelt in Dakota Territory, 1974; Deadwood Dick and the Dime Novels, 1974; Sioux Indian Leaders, 1975; Plant Medicine and Folklore, 1975; Lost Gold, 1978; Poker Alice, 1978; Silver is the Fortune, 1978; Preacher Smith of Deadwood, 1981; Fielder's Herbal Helper, 1982; The Legend of Lame Johnny Creek, 1982; Wild Fruits, 1983; Captain Jack Crawford, 1983; Invitation to Fans, 1988. Contributions to: Numerous historical articles and many poems, USA and Canada; 7 prose anthologies; 11 poetry anthologies. Honours: 3 Literary Awards; Certificate of Recognition, South Dakota Historical Society, 1975; Sweepstakes Award, National League of American Pen Women, 1976; Distinguished Service Award, National League of American Pen Women, 1980; Total Awards to date 425, of which 56 were national. Memberships: Life Member, Society of American Historians; South Dakota Poetry Society, 1955-65 (Regional Vice-President); South Dakota Historical Society; National League of American Pen Women, National Historin 1962, National Auditor 1968-70, several National Chairmanships, Book Review Editor, Endowment Fund, in Focus Column for Pen Women Magazine; NLAPW National Letters Board, 1987-88. Address: 264 San Jacinto Drive, Los Osos, CA 93402, USA.

FIENNES Ranulph Twisleton-Wykeham (Sir), b. 7 Mar 1944, England. Travel Writer; Explorer. m. 9 Sept 1971. Education: Eton College, 1956-59; DSc (Hon), Loughborough College. Publications: Talent or Trouble, 1972; Icefall in Norway, 1973; The Headless Valley, 1974; Where Soldiers Fear to Tread, 1975; Hell on Ice, 1977; To the Ends of the Earth, 1983; Bothie - The Polar Dog, 1985; Living Dangerously, 1987; The Feather Men, 1991. Contributions: The Geographical Magazine (UK); The National Geographical Magazine (US); The Smithsonian; Observer Colour Supplement; Sunday Times. Honours: Founders Medal, Royal Geographical Society; Gold Medal, Explorers Club of New York; Polar Medal, awarded by H M The Queen, 1987. Memberships: Antarctic Club; Fellow, Royal Geographical

Society; The Arctic Club. Literary Agent: George Greenfield, John Farquharson Ltd.

FIERSTEIN Harvey, b. 6 June 1954, New York, New York, USA. Dramatist. Education: BFA, Pratt Institute. Career: Actor, Theatre, Film, TV (London debut 1986, Broadway debut 1982, Stage debut New York City 1971); Playwright; Founder, Gallery Players Community Theatre, 1965. Publications: Figure in a Nursery, 1973; Torch Song Triology, 1981; La Cage aux Folles, 1983; Spookhouse, 1984; Safe Sex, 1987. Honours: 1983: Obie Award; Drama Desk Awards (best actor & play); Antoinette Perry Awards (best actor & play); 1984: Los Angeles Drama Critics Circle Award; Antoinette Perry Award; Theatre World Award; Fund for Human Dignity Award; Villager Award (x4); Association of Comedy Artists Award. Memberships: Actors Equity Association; Dramatists Guild; Screen Actors Guild. Address: c/o William Morris Agency, 1350 Avenue of the Americas, New York, NY 10019, USA.

FIFIELD Christopher, b. 4 Sept 1945, Croydon, England. Musician. m. Judith Weyman, 28 Oct 1972. Education: ARCO, 1967; MusB, 1968; GRSM, 1969; ARMCM, 1969. Publications: Max Bruch: His Life and Works, 1988; Wagner in Performance, 1992; Hans Richter, 1993. Contributions to: Musical Times; Strad; Classical Music; Music and Letters; BBC Music Magazine. Address: Coach House, 38 Wrights Road, London SE25 6RY, England.

FIGES Eva, b. 15 Apr 1932, Berlin, Germany. Writer. 1 son, 1 daughter. Education: BA, Honours, English Language & Literature, University of London, 1953. Publications: Patriarchal Attitudes, 1970; Winter Journey, 1967; Waking, 1981; Light, 1983; The Seven Ages, 1986; Nelly's Version, 1977; B, 1972; Little Eden, 1978; Sex & Subterfuge, 1982; Ghosts, 1988; The Tree of Knowledge, 1990; The Tenancy, 1993. Honours: Guardian Fiction Prize, 1967. Memberships: Writers Guild of Great Britain, Chairperson, 1986-87; PEN. Literary Agent: Rogers, Coleridge & White Ltd. Address: 24 Fitzjohns Avenue, London NW3 5NB, England.

FIGUEROA John J(oseph Maria), b. 4 Aug 1920, Kingston, Jamaica. Professor of English; Poet. Education: University of London Institute of Education; University of Indiana at Bloomington. Appointments: Professor of Education, University College of the West Indies, 1957-73; Adviser to Manchester Education Authority, England, 1983-85; General Editor, Caribbean Writers series, Heinemann. Publications: Blue Mountain Peak, 1944; Love Leaps Here, 1962; Ignoring Hurts, 1976; Television plays, St Lucia: Peoples and Celebrations series, from 1983; Society, Schools and Progress in the West Indies, 1971; Editor of poetry from the West Indies. Honours include: Guggenheim Fellowship, 1964; Institute of Jamaica Medal, 1980. Addres: 77 Station Road, Woburn Sands, Buckinghamshire MK17 8SH, England.

FINALE Frank Louis, b. 10 Mar 1942, Brooklyn, New York, USA. Educator. m. Barbara Long, 20 Oct 1973, 3 sons. Education: BS Education, Ohio State University, 1964; MA Human Development, Fairleigh Dickinson University, 1976. Appointment: Editor-in-Chief, Without Halos, helped found 1983, 1985-. Publications: Poems included in anthologies: Life on the Line, 1992; A Loving Voice II, 1994; A Celebration of Cats (Ed Jean Burden), 1974; Anthology of Magazine Verse, 1985, 1986-88; Blood to Remember, 1991; Movie Works, 1991; Peace Is Our Profession, 1981; Dear Winter (Ed Marie Harris), 1984. Contributions to: The Christian Science Monitor; Pig Iron; Georgia Review; New York Quarterly; Kansas Quarterly; The New Renaissance; Negative Capability; Blue Unicorn; Poetry NOW; Poet Lore; Footwork: The Paterson Literary Review; Visions; ELF. Membership: Founding Member, Ocean County Poets Collective, 1983. Address: 19 Quail Run, Bayville, NJ 08721, USA.

FINCH Matthew. See: **FINK Merton.**

FINCH Merton. See: **FINK Merton.**

FINCH Peter, b. 6 Mar 1947, Cardiff, Wales. Bookshop Manager for Welsh Arts Council; Creative Writing Tutor, Experimenter, Literary Entrepreneur. m. 2 sons, 1 daughter. Literary Appointments: Treasurer, Association of Little Presses; Former Executive Member, Poetry Society, and Yr Academy Cymreig; Former Editor, Second Aeon (journal). Publications include: Wanted, 1967; Pieces of the Universe, 1968; How to Learn Welsh, 1977; Between 35 & 42, short stories, 1982; Some Music & A Little War, 1984; How to Publish Your Poetry, 1985; Reds in the Bed, 1986; Selected Poems, 1987; How to Publish

Yourself? 1988; Selected Poems, 1987; Poems for Ghosts, 1991; Make, 1990; The Cheng Man Ch'ing Variations, 1991; Also: Cycle of the Suns; Beyond the Silence; An Alteration in the Way I Breathe; Edge of Tomorrow; End of the Vision; Antarktika; Trowch Eich Radio'mlaen; Connecting Tubes; O Poems; Blues & Heartbreakers; Blats; Big Band Dance Music; Dances Interdites; Visual Texts 1970-1980; Editor, Green Horse. Contributions include: Most major magazines & journals including: PN Review; Ambit; Poetry Review; Stand; Poetry Wales; Planet. Address: 19 Southminster Road, Roath, Cardiff, Wales.

FINCH Robert (Duer Claydon), b. 14 May 1900, Freeport, Long Island, New York, USA. Emeritus Professor; Poet. Education: University of Toronto and Sorbonne, Paris. Appointments: Professor of French, University College, Toronto, Canada, 1952-68. Publications: Poems, 1946; The Strength of the Hills, 1948; Acis in Oxford and Other Poems, 1959; Dover Beach Revisited and Other Poems, 1961; Silverthorn Bush and Other Poems, 1966; Variations and Theme, 1980; Has and Is, 1981; Twelve for Christmas, 1982; The Grand Duke of Moscow's Favourite Solo, 1983; Double Tuning, 1984; For the Back of a Likeness, 1986; Sail-boat and Lake and Other Poems, 1988; Miracle at the Jetty (Poems), 1991; 31 Impromptus (Poems), 1994. Honours include: Fellow, Royal Society of Canada, 1963; LLD, University of Winnipeg, 1984. Address: Massey College, 4 Devonshire Place, Toronto, Ontario, Canada M5S 2E1.

FINCKE Gary W, b. 7 July 1945, Pittsburgh, Pennsylvania, USA. College Educator; Writer. m. Elizabeth Locker, 17 Aug 1968, 2 sons, 1 daughter. Education: BA, Thiel College, 1967; MA, Miami University, 1969; PhD, Kent State University, 1974. Appointments: Writing Program Director, Susquehanna University, 1980-. Publications: Inventing Angels; For Keepsies; The Double Negatives of the Living; Plant Voices; The Public Talk of Death; The Days of Uncertain Health; Handing the Self Back; The Coat in the Heart; Breath; The Inadvertent Scofflaw, 1995. Contributions: Harper's; The Paris Review; Poetry; Yankee; The Georgia Review; The Quarterly; Kenyon Review; Missouri Review; The Gettysburg Review; Poetry Northwest. Honours: Poetry/Fiction Fellowships; PEN Syndicated Fiction Prize; Bess Hokin Prize. Memberships: Poetry Society of America; Associated Writers Program; Poets and Writers. Address: 3 Melody Lane, Selinsgrove, PA 17870, USA.

FINDLEY Timothy Irving Frederick, b. 30 Oct 1930, Toronto, Canada. Writer. Appointments include: Playwright-in-residence, National Arts Centre, Ottawa, Canada, 1974-75; Writer-in-residence, University of Toronto 1979-80, Trent University 1984, University of Winnipeg 1985. Publications include: Last of the Crazy People, 1967; Butterfly Plague, 1969; Can You See Me Yet? play, 1977; The Wars, 1977; Famous Last Words, 1981; Dinner Along the Amazon, collected stories, 1984; Not Wanted on the Voyage, 1984; The Telling of Lies, 1986; Stones (short fiction), 1988; Inside Memory: Pages From a Writer's Workbook, memoir, 1990; Headhunter, 1993; The Stillborn Lover, play, 1993; The Piano Man's Daughter, 1995; The Trials of Erza Pound, 1995. Address: c/o W Whitehead, PO Box 419, Cannington, Ontario, L0E 1E0, Canada.

FINE Anne, b. 7 Dec 1947, Leicester, England. Writer. m. Kit Fine, 3 Aug 1968, 2 d. Education: BA Hons, University of Warwick. Publications include: Novels, The Killjoy, 1986; Taking the Devils Advice, 1990; In Cold Domain, 1994; For Older Children: The Summer House Loon, 1978; The Other Darker Ned, 1979; The Stone Menagerie, 1980; Round Behind the Ice House, 1981; The Granny Project, 1983; Madame Doubtfire, 1987; Goggle Eyes, 1989; The Book of the Banshee, 1991; Flour Babies, 1992; Step by Wicked Step, 1995. Honours: Guardian Children's Award & The Carnegie Medal for Goggle-Eyes, 1989; Smarties Prize, 1990; Library Association Carnegie Medal, 1990, 1993; Guardian Children's Literature Award, 1990; Publishing News, Children's Author of Year, 1990, 1993; Whitbread Children's Novel Award, 1993; Carnegie Medal for Flour Babies, 1993. Memberships: Society of Authors. Literary Agent: Murray Pollinger. Address: 222 Old Brompton Road, London SW5 0BZ, England.

FINER Samuel (Edward), b. 1915, United Kingdom. Emeritus Professor of Politics, Oxford University. Publications: A Primer of Public Administration, 1950; The Life and Times of Sir Edwin Chadwick, 1952; Local Government in England and Wales (with Sir J Maud), 1953; Anonymous Empire: A Study of the Lobby in Britain, 1958, 2nd edition 1966; Private Industry and Political Power, 1958; Backbench Opinion in the House of Commons 1955-59 (with D

Bartholomew and H Berrington), 1961; The Man on Horseback: The Role of the Military in Politics, 1962, 2nd edition 1976; Sieves: What is the Third Estate (editor), 1963; Pareto: Sociological Writings (editor), 1966; Comparative Government, 1970; Adversary Politics and Electoral Reform, 1975; Five Constitutions, 1979; The Changing British Party Systems, 1980; The British Party System, 1986. Address: All Souls College, Oxford OX1 4AL, England.

FINK Merton, (Matthew Finch, Merton Finch), b. 17 Nov 1921, Liverpool, England. Author. m. (1) 15 Mar 1953, 1 s, 1 d. (2) 24 Nov 1981. Education: School of Military Engineers, 1942; School of Military Intelligence, 1943; LDS, Liverpool University, 1947-52. Publications include: 17 Books; 14 Novels; Dentist in the Chair, 1953; Teething Troubles, 1954; The Third Set, 1955; Hang Your Hat on a Pension, 1956; The Empire builder, 1957; Solo Fiddle, 1959; Matchbreakers, 1961; Five Are the Symbols, 1962; Chew this Over, 1965; Eye with Mascara, 1966; Eye Spy, 1967; Simon Bar Cochba, 1971; A Fox Called Flavius, 1973; Open Wide, 1976. Contributions to: Dental Practice, Monthly. Honour: Richard Edwards Scholar, 1950. Memberships: Civil Service Writers; Bath Literary Society; British Dental Association; Admiralty Rifle Club; Bath British Legion; Police Interpreters for German; Bath Arts Association. Literary Agent: laurence Pollinger Limited. Address: 27 Harbutts, Bathampton, Bath BA2 6TA, England.

FINKEL Donald, b. 21 Oct 1929, New York, USA. Poet. m. Constance Urdang, 14 Aug 1956, 1 son, 2 daughters. Education: B Philosophy, 1952, MA English, 1953, Columbia University. Appointment: Poet in Residence, Washington University, 1964-. Publications: The Clothing's New Emperor, 1959; Simeon, 1964; A Joyful Noise, 1966; Answer Back, 1968; The Garbage Wars, 1970; Adequate Earth, 1972; A Mote in Heaven's Eye, 1975; Endurance and Going Under, 1978; What Manner of Beast, 1981; The Detachable Man, 1984; Selected Shorter Poems, 1987; The Wake of the Electron, 1987. Contributions to: Numerous journals and magazines. Honours: Phi Beta Kappa, 1953; Helen Bullis Award, 1964; Guggenheim Fellowship, 1967; Nomination, National Book Award, 1970; Ingram Merrill Foundation Grant, 1972; NEA Grant, 1973; Theodore Roethke Memorial Award, 1974; Morton Dauwen Zabel Award, 1980; Nomination, National Book Critics Circle Award, 1975, 1981. Address: 6943 Columbia Place, St Louis, MO 63130, USA.

FINLAY William. See: **MACKAY James Alexander.**

FINNERAN Richard (John), b. 1943, USA. Professor of English. Appointments: Instructor, University of Florida, 1967-68; Instructor, New York University, 1968-70; Assistant Professor, 1970-74, Associate Professor 1974-77, Professor of English 1977-, Newcomb College, Tulane University; Editor, Yeats Annual, 1982-. Publications: John Sherman and Dhoya by W B Yeats (editor), 1969; William Butler Yeats: The Byzantium Poems (editor), 1970; The Prose Fiction of W B Yeats: The Search for Those Simple Forms, 1973; Letters of James Stephens (editor), 1974; Anglo-Irish Literature: A Review of Research (editor), 1976; The Correspondence of Robert Bridges and W B Yeats (editor), 1977; Letters to W B Yeats (edited with George Mills Harper and William M Murphy), 1977; Recent Research in Anglo-Irish Writers (editor), 1982; Editing Yeat's Poems, 1983; The Poems of W B Yeats (editor), 1983; Critical Essays on W B Yeats, 1986. Address: 89 Versailles Boulevard, New Orleans, LA 70125, USA.

FINNEY Mark. See: **MUIR Kenneth (Arthur).**

FINNIGAN Joan, b. 23 Nov 1925, Ottawa, Canada. Writer. m. Charles Grant Mackenzie, 23 May 1949, 2 sons, 1 daughter. Education: BA, Queens University, 1967. Publications include: Through the Glass, Darkly, 1963; A Dream of Lilies, 1965; Entrance to the Greenhouse, 1968; It Was Warm and Sunny When We Set Out, 1970; In the Brown Cottage on Loughborough Lake, 1970; Living Together, 1976; A Reminder of Familiar Faces, 1978; This Series Has Been Discontinued, 1980; The Watershed Collection, 1988; Wintering Over, 1992; Other Genres: Old Scores: New Goals, History of Ottawa Senators 1891-1992, 1992; Lisgar Collegiate Institute 1843-1993, 1993. Screenplay: The Best Damn Fiddler from Calabogie to Kaladar, 1982; CBC Radio Scripts, Songs for the Bible Belt, May Day Rounds, Children of the Shadows, There's No Good Time Left - None at All, 1976. Address: Hartington, Ontario K0H 1W0, Canada.

FINSTAD Suzanne, b. 14 Sept 1955, Minneapolis, Minnesota, USA. Author; Attorney (non-practising). Education: University of Texas, Austin, 1973-74; BA, French, University of Houston, 1976; University of Grenoble, France, 1979; JD, Bates College of Law, 1980; London School of Economics, 1980. Publications: Heir Not Apparent, 1984; Ulterior Motives, 1987; Sleeping with the Devil, 1991; Biography of Queen Noor of Jordan in progress. Contributions to: Cover profile of Queen Noor for European Travel and Life; Fame; Penthouse; Mademoiselle; Cosmopolitan; Good Housekeeping; Marie Claire (British edition). Honours: American Jurisprudence Award in Criminal Law, Bancroft-Whitney Publishing Co, 1979; Order of the Barons, 1980; Frank Wardlaw for a first work of literary excellence, for Heir Not Apparent. Membership: State Bar of Texas. Literary Agent: Joel Gotler, Los Angeles, USA. Address: c/o Joel Gotler, 152 North La Peer Drive, Beverly Hills, CA 90048, USA.

FIRTH Anne Catherine, (Anne Valery), b. 24 Feb 1926, London, England. Scriptwriter; Autobiographer; Novelist; Theatre Playwright. Education: Matriculation (Hons), Badminton Public School. Publications: The Edge of a Smile, 1974; Baron Von Kodak, Shirley Temple and Me, 1973; The Passing Out Parade (theatre), 1979; Tenko Reunion, 1984; Talking About the War... (non-fiction), 1991; over 50 TV plays. Contributions to: Articles in Radio Times. Honours: Book of the Month, Telegraph; BAFTA Award, Tenko (TV Series), 1984. Memberships: PEN International; Fawcett Society; Executive Committee, Writers' Guild of Great Britain; Chair, Anti-Censorship Committee. Literary Agent: Linda Seifut (plays), Jacintha Alexander (books). Address: 5 Abbot's Place, London NW6 4NP, England.

FISCHER-FABIAN Siegfried, b. 22 Sept 1922, Bad Elmen, Germany. Author. m. Ursula Pauling, 1950, 2 sons. Education: German, History, History of Art, Dramatic Art, Humboldt University and Free University, Berlin; Graduated, Free University, Berlin; Dr phil. Appointments: Journalist, Collaborator with the press and radio; Theatre Critic, Schweizer Monatshefte, BV. Publications: Mit Eva fing d Liebe an, E Kulturgesch d Liebe u Ehe, 11 stories, 1958, 1964; Venus m Herz u Kopfchen, E Liebeserklarung an d Berlinerin, 1959; Mussen Berliner so sein...?, E Bekenntnis in Portraits, 1960; Hurra, wir bauen uns e Haus!, D Gesch e bundesdt Baufamilie, 1962, 1965; Liebe im Schnee, Fast e Tatsachenbericht, 1965, 1968; Das Ratsel in Dir, D Welt d Triebe, Traume u Komplexe, 1966; Deutschland kann lachen..., V Bayern, Berlinern, Sachsen u a Germanen, 1966; Traum ist rings d Welt, E Bericht ub d Liebe gr Dichte, 1967; Europa kann lachen, V Englandern, Franzosen, Schweizern, Russen u a Europiden, 1972; Geliebte Tyrannen, E Brevier f alle Katzenfreunde u solche, d es werden wollen, 1973; Berlin-Evergreen, Bild e Stadt in 16 Portraits, 1973; Aphrodite ist an allem schuld, 1974; D Ersten Deutschen, D Bericht ub d ratselhafte Volk d Germanen, 1975; D deutschen Casaren - Triumph u Tragodie d Kaiser d Mittelalters, 1977; Preussens Gloria, D Aufstieg eines Staates, 1979; Preussens Krieg u Frieden, D Weg ins dt Reich, 1981; Vergesst d Lachen Nicht, D Humor d Deutschen, 1982; Herrliche Zeiten, D Deutschen u ihr Kaiserreich, 1983; D Jungste Tag, D Deutschen im spaten Mittelalter, 1985; Die Macht des Gewissens (Von Sokrates bis Sophie Scholl), 1987; Um Gott und Gold (Columbus entdeckt eine neue Welt), 1991; Columbus, Lebensbilder (Bildband), 1991; F C Piepenburg, SEIN WEG, 1982; WCh Schmitt, Die Auflagenmillonare, 1988. Contributions to: Festschrifts: Prinz Louis Ferdinand, 1982; D Fischer-Dieskau, 1985. Honours: Christophorus Prize, 1988. Address: Sonnenhof, 8137 Aufkirchen, Starnberger See, Germany.

FISH Stanley, b. 19 Apr 1938, Providence, Rhode Island, USA. Professor of English & Law. m. 7 Aug 1982, 1 daughter. Education: BA, University of Pennsylvania, 1959; MA 1960, PhD 1962, Yale University. Appointments include: Full Professor, English, University of California, Berkeley, 1962-74; William Kenan Jr Professor, Humanities, Johns Hopkins University, 1974-85; Arts and Science Distinguished Professor of English, Professor of Law, Duke University; Executive Director, Duke University Press, 1994. Publications include: John Skelton's Poetry, 1965; Surprised by Sin: The Reader in Paradise Lost, 1967; Self-Consuming Artifacts, 1972; Living Temple: George Herbert and Catechizing, 1978; Is There a Text in This Class? 1980; Doing What Comes Naturally, 1989; There's No Such Thing as Free Speech; And It's a Good Thing Too, 1994. Contributions to: Various scholarly journals including Times Literary Supplement, Yale Review. Honours: ACLS Fellowship, 1966; Guggenheim Fellowship, 1969-70; Humanities Research Professorship, UC Berkeley, 1966, 1970; 2nd Place, Explicator Prize, 1968; Nomination, National Book Award, 1972; Honoured Scholar, Milton Society of America, 1991; PEN/Spielvogel-Diamonstein Award for There's No Such Thing as Free Speech, 1994. Memberships: Past President, Milton Society of America; American Academy of Arts & Sciences. Address: Department

of English, 314 Allen Building, Duke University, Box 90015, Durham, NC 27708, USA.

FISHER Allen, b. 1 Nov 1944, Norbury, Surrey, England. Painter; Poet; Art Historian. Education: BA, University of London; MA, University of Essex. Publications: Over 80 Books including Place Book One, 1974; Brixton Fractals, 1985; Unpolished Mirrors, 1985; Stepping Out, 1989; Future Exiles, 1991; Fizz, 1994; Civic Crime, 1994; Breadboard, 1994. Contributions to: Numerous Contributions to Various Magazines and Journals. Honours: Co Winner, Alice Hunt Bartlett Award, 1975. Address: 14 Hopton Road, Hereford HR1 1BE, England.

FISHER Leonard Everett, b. 24 June 1924, New York City, USA. Artist; Author. m. Margery Meskin, 21 Dec 1952, 1 son, 2 daughters. Education: BFA 1949, MFA 1950, Yale University. Appointment: President of Westport (CT) Public Library Board of Trustees, 1986-89. Publications include: 75 books written and illustrated including: Non Fiction: Colonial Americans, 19 volumes, 1964-76; Ellis Island, 1986; Look Around, 1987; The Tower of London, 1987; Galileo, 1992; Tracks Across America, 1992; Stars and Stripes, 1993; Marie Curie, 1994; Fiction: Death of Evening Star, 1972; Across the Sea from Galway, 1975; Sailboat Lost, 1991; Cyclops, 1991; Kinderdike, 1994; Illustrator of more than 250 books for young readers. Contributions to: Five Owls, USa; National Council Teachers of English, USA; Magpies, Australia; North Light, USA; Cricket, USA; Voice of the Narrator. Literary Agent: William B R Reiss, John Hawkins & Associates, New York, USA. Address: 7 Twin Bridge Acres Road, Westport, CT 06880, USA.

FISHER Roy, b. 11 June 1930, Birmingham, England. Poet; Musician. Education: BA 1951, MA 1970, Birmingham University. Literary Appointments include: Various committees. Publications include: City, 1961; The Ship's Orchestra, 1967; Collected Poems, 1968, 1969; Matrix, 1971; The Thing about Joe Sullivan, 1978; Poems 1955-80, 1980; A Furnace, 1986; Poems 1955-87, 1988; Also: Interiors, 1966; The Memorial Fountain, 1968; Metmorphoses, 1971; The Cut Pages, 1971, 1986; Also, 1973; The Left-Handed Punch, 1987. Contributions to: Numerous journals & magazines. Honours: Andrew Kelus Prize, 1979; Cholmondeley Award, 1981. Memberships: Society of Authors; Musicians Union. Address: Four Ways, Earl Sterndale, Buxton, Derbyshire SK17 0EP, England.

FISHLOCK Trevor, b. 21 Feb 1941, Hereford, England. Journalist; Author. m. Penelope Symon, 1978. Appointments: Portsmouth Evening News, 1957-62; Freelance News Agency Reporter, 1962-68; The Times, Wales and West England Staff Correspondent, 1968-78; The Times South Asia Correspondent, 1980-83; The Times New York Correspondent, 1983-86; Roving Foreign Correspondent, The Daily Telegraph, 1986-89; Moscow Correspondent, 1989-91; Roving Foreign Correspondent, The Sunday Telegraph, 1991-. Publications: Wales & The Welsh, 1972; Talking of Wales, 1975; Americans & Nothing Else, 1980; India File, 1983; The State of Ameica, 1986; Discovering Britain - Wales, 1975; Indira Gandhi (For Children), 1986; Out of Red Darkness, 1992. Honours: David Holden Award for Foreign Reporting, British Press Awards, 1983; International Reporter of the Year, British Press Awards, 1986. Memberships: Council for Welsh Language, 1973-77; Fellow, World Press Institute; Society of Authors. Address: The Sunday Telegraph, Peterborough Court at South Quay, 181 Marsh Wall, London E14 9SR, England.

FISHMAN Charles (Adès), b. 10 July 1942, Oceanside, New York, USA. Educator; Writer. m. Ellen Marci Haselkorn, 25 June 1967; Education: BA, MA, Hofstra; Doctor of Arts, State University of New York, Albany, 1982; Permanent Certification, Secondary Education, New York, 1965. Appointments: Poet-in-residence 1970, Director Visiting Writers Program 1979, Director Programs in the Arts 1987, State University of New York, Farmingdale. Publications: Aurora, 1974; Mortal Companions, 1977; Warm-Blooded Animals, 1977; Index to Women's Magazines & Presses, 1977; The Death Mazurka, 1987; Catlives (with Marina Roscher), 1991; Zoom, 1990; Blood to Remember: American Poets on the Holocaust, 1991; As The Sun Goes Down in Fire, 1992; Nineteenth Century Rain, 1994. Contributions to: Prism International; Poetry Canada Review; Cyphers (Ireland); The Abiko Quarterly (Japan); The Tel Aviv Review (Israel); Boulevard (US). Address: Knapp Hall, SUNY Farmingdale, Farmingdale, NY 11735, USA.

FISK Pauline. See: DAVIES Pauline.

FISKE Sharon. See: **HILL Pamela.**

FISKE Tarleton. See: **BLOCH Robert.**

FITTER Richard Sidney Richmond, b. 1 Mar 1913, Author; Naturalist. m. Alice Mary Stewart Park, 1938, 2 s, 1 d. Publications include: London's Natural History, 1945; London's Birds, 1949; Pocket Guide to British Birds, 1952; Pocket Guide to Nests and Eggs, 1954; The Ark in Our Midst, 1959; Guide to Bird Watching, 1963; Wildlife in Britain, 1963; Britain's Wildlife: Rarities and Introductions, 1966; Vanishing Wild Animals of the World, 1968; Finding Wild Flowers, 1972; Flowers of Britain and Northern Europe, 1974; The Penitent Butchers, 1979; Handguide to the Wild Flowers of Britain and Northern Europe, 1979; Gern Guide to Wild Flowers, 1980; Collins Guide to the Countryside, 1984; Grasses, Sedges, Rushes and Ferns of Britain and Northern Europe, 1984; The Wildlife of the Thames Counties, 1985; Wildlife for Man: How and Why we Should Conserve Our Species, 1986; Field Guide to the Freshwater Life of Britain and North West Europe, 1986; Collins Guide to the Countryside in Winter, 1988. Address: Drifts, Chinnor Hill, Chinnor, Oxon OX9 4BS, England.

FITZGERALD Frances, b. 21 Oct 1940, New York, New York, USA. Education: BA, Radcliffe College. Publications: Fire in the Lake: The Vietnamese & Americans in Vietnam, 1972; America Revised: History Schoolbooks in the Twentieth Century, 1979; Cities on a Hill: A Journey Through Contemporary American Culture, 1986. Contributions: The New Yorker; Atlantic Monthly; New York Review of Books; Harpers; Vogue; Look; Nation; New Times. Honours: Pulitzer Prize; National Book Award, 1973; Bancroft Prize, 1973; Overseas Press Club Award, 1967, 1974; Christopher Award, 1973; American Academy of Arts & Letters Award, 1973; National Institute of Arts & Letters Award, 1973. Address: c/o Lescher & Lescher Ltd, 67 Irving Place, New York, NY 10003, USA.

FITZGERALD Maureen Elizabeth, b. 24 Dec 1920, Mumbles, Glamorgan, Wales. Journalist. Education: Pensionnat des Servites, Brussels, Belgium; BSc, Economics, University College, London, England, 1946-49. Appointments: Associate Editor, Local Government Chronicle, 1952-62; Editor, Local Government Chronicle, 1963-73; Director, 1968-77; Managing Editor, 1973-77; Editorial Adviser, 1978-80; Consultant and Profile Writer, 1981-85; Profile Writer, 1985-88. Publication: The Story of a Parish, 1990. Contributions to: Local Government Chronicle; District Council Review; Rating and Valuation; Chamber's Encyclopaedia; Review of the Year; Local Government Review. Honour: MBE, 1979. Memberships: Society of Women Writers and Journalists; Institute of Journalists; Associate Member, United Oxford and Cambridge University Club. Address: 5 Buckingham Court, Chestnut Lane, Amersham, Buckinghamshire HP6 6EL, England.

FITZGERALD Penelope Mary, b. 17 Dec 1916, Lincoln, England. Teacher; Writer. m. Desmond Fitzgerald, 1942, 1 s, 2 d. Education: BA, Somerville College, Oxford. Appointments: English Tutor, Westminister Tutors, London, 1965-. Publications include: The Knox Brothers, 1977; Charlotte Mew and Her Friends, 1984; The Golden Child, 1978; The Bookshop, 1978; Offshore, 1979; Human Voices, 1980; At Freddies, 1982; Innocence, 1986; (Editor & Introduction) William Morris Unpublished Novel on Blue Paper, 1982; The Beginning of Spring, 1989; The Gate of Angels, 1990. Honour: The Booker McConnell Prize, 1979; Fellow, Royal Society of Literature. Address: c/o Harper Collins Publishers, 77-85 Fulham Palace Road, London W6 8BJ, England.

FITZHARDINGE Joan Margaret, (Joan Phipson), b. 1912, Australia. Freelance Writer; Grazier. Publications include: Good Luck to the Rider, 1953; Six and Silver, 1954; It Happened One Summer, 1957; The Boundary Riders, 1962; The Family Conspiracy, 1962; Threat to the Barkers, 1963; Birkin, 1965; The Crew of the Merlin, 1966; A Lamb in the Family, 1966; Peter and Butch, 1969; The Haunted Night, 1970; The Way Home, 1973; Polly's Tiger, 1973; Helping Horse, 1974; Bennelong, 1975; The Cats, 1976; Fly into Danger, 1977, (Australian Edition, The Bird Smugglers, 1979); Hide Till Daytime, 1977; Keep Calm, 1978; No Escape, 1979; Mr Pringle and the Prince, 1979; A Tide Flowing, 1981; The Watcher in the Garden, 1982; Beryl the Rainmaker, 1984; The Grannie Season, 1985; Dinko, 1985; Hit and Run, 1985; Bianca, 1988. Address: Wongalong, Mandurama, NSW 2792, Australia.

FITZSIMMONS Thomas, b. 21 Oct 1926, Lowell, Massachusetts, USA. Poet; Educator. m. Karen Hargreaves, 2 sons. Education: Fresno State College, 1947-49; Sorbonne, Institut de Science Politique, Paris, France, 1949-50; BA, Stanford University, 1951; MA Honours, Columbia University, 1952. Appointments include: Writer, Editor, New Republic magazine, Washington DC, 1952-55; Faculty 1961-, Professor of English 1966-, Oakland University, Michigan, Visiting Lecturer/Professor, various Japanese Universities; Editor/Publisher, Katydid Books, University of Hawaii Press. Publications: Books of poetry: This Time This Place, 1969; Morningdew, 1970; Downinside, 1970; Meditation Seeds, 1970; Mooning, 1971; With the Water: Selected Poems, 1969-70, 1972; Playseeds, 1973; Big Huge, 1975; House of My Friend, 1977; Trip Poems, 1978; Great Hawaiian Conquest, 1979; Nine Seas & Eight Mountains, 1981; Rocking Mirror Daybreak, 1983; Japan Personally, 1985; Translations: Ghazals of Ghalib, 1971; Japanese Poetry Now, 1972; A String Around Autumn, 1982; Editor: A Play of Mirrors: Eight Major Poets of Modern Japan, 1986; Muscle and Machine Dream, 1986; Series Editor: Asian Poetry in Translation; Prospectives on the Arts of Asia; Water Groun Stone, 1994; The Dream Machine, 1994; Editor, The New Poetry of Japan, the 70s and 80s, 1993. Honours: Awards, poetry, 1967, work with Japanese poets, 1982, National Endowment for the Arts; Fulbright Lecturer, 1962-64, 1967-68, 1988-89; National Endowment for the Arts, Belles Lettres, 1990; Fulbright Research Fellowship, 1988-89. Memberships: Poetry Center of New Mexico, Board of Directors; PEN. Address: c/o Department of English, Oakland University, Rochester, MI 48063, USA.

FJELDE Rolf (Gerhard), b. 1926, American. Appointments: Founding Editor, Yale Poetry Review, 1945-49 and Poetry New York, 1949-51; Instructor 1954-58, Assistant Professor 1958-64, Associate Professor 1964-69, Professor of English and Drama 1969-, Pratt Institute, Brooklyn, NY; Teacher of Drama History, Academic Faculty, Juilliard School, NYC, 1973-83; President, Ibsen Society of America, 1979-; Editor, Ibsen News and Comment, 1979-85. Publications: Washington, 1955; The Imaged Word, 1962; Peer Gynt, by Ibsen (trans), 1964, 1980; Four Major Plays, by Ibsen (trans), volume I, 1965, 1992, volume II, 1970; Ibsen: A Collection of Critical Essays (ed), 1965; Washington, 1966; The Rope Walk, 1967; Rafferty One by One, 1975; Complete Major Prose Plays, by Ibsen (trans), 1978; The Bellini Look, 1982. Honours: Royal Medal of St Olar, King of Norway, 1991; Academy Award in Literature, American Academy of Arts and Letters, 1993. Play Agent: Samuel French Inc. Address: 261 Chatterton Parkway, White Plains, NY 10606, USA.

FLAM Jack Donald, b. 2 Apr 1940, USA. Writer; Professor. m. Bonnie Burnham, 7 Oct 1972, 1 daughter. Education: BA, Rutgers University, 1961; MA, Columbia University, 1963; PhD, New York University, 1969. Appointments: Art Critic, The Wall Street Journal, 1984-92. Publications: Matisse on Art; Zoltan Gorency; Robert Motherwell; Matisse: The Man and His Art; Motherwell; Bread & Butter; Richard Diebenkorn: Ocean Park, 1992; Matisse: The Dance, 1993. Contributions to: New York Review of Books; Art News: Art Journal; Art in America; Art International Artforum. Honours: Guggenheim Fellow; NEA Fellow; Manufacturers Hanover - Art World First Prize; Charles Rufus Morey Award. Memberships: PEN; International Association of Art Critics. Literary Agent: Georges Borchardt. Address: c/o Georges Borchardt Inc, 136 East 57th Street, New York, NY 10022, USA.

FLEET Kenneth George, b. 12 Sept 1929, Cheshire, England. Journalist. m. (Alice) Brenda Wilkinson, 28 Mar 1953, 3 sons, 1 daughter. Education: BSc, Economics, London School of Economics. Appointments: Journal of Commerce, Liverpool, 1950-52; Sunday Times, 1955-56; Deputy City Editor, Birmingham Post, 1956-58; Deputy Financial Editor, Guardian, 1958-63; Deputy City Editor 1963, City Editor 1966-77, Daily Telegraph; City Editor, Sunday Telegraph 1963-66; Editor, Business News, 1977-78, Sunday Times; City Editor, Sunday Express, 1978-82; City Editor-in-Chief, Express Newspapers plc, 1982-85; Executive Editor, Finance and Industry, The Times, 1983-87. Honour: Wincott Award, 1974. Memberships: Director: TUS Entertainment plc, 1990-93; Director, Young Vic, 1976-83; Chairman, Chichester Festival Theatre, 1985-; Governor, London Schools of Economics, 1989-. Address: c/o 20 Farrington Road, London EC1M 3NH, England.

FLEISCHMAN Albert Sidney, b. 1920, American. Appointments: Magician in vaudeville and night clubs, 1938-41; Reporter, San Diego Daily Journal, 1949-50; Associate Editor, Point Magazine, San Diego, 1950-51. Publications: The Straw Donkey Case, 1948; Murder's No

Accident, 1949; Shanghai Flame, 1951; Look Behind You, Lady (in UK as Chinese Crimson), 1952; Danger in Paradise, 1953; Counterspy Express, Malay Woman (in UK as Malayan Manhunt), 1954; Blood Alley, 1955; Good-bye My Lady, 1956; Lafayette Escadrille, 1958; Yellowleg, 1960; The Deadly Companions, 1961; Mr Mysterious and Company, 1962; By the Great Horn Spoon! 1963, retitled as Bullwhip Griffin, 1967; The Ghost in the Noonday Sun, 1965; McBroom series, 9 volumes, 1966-80; Chancy and the Grand Rascal, 1966; Longbeard the Wizard, 1970; Jingo Django, 1971; The Wooden Cat Man, 1972; The Ghost on a Saturday Night, 1974; Mr Mysterious' Secret of Magic (in UK as Secrets of Magic), 1975; Me and the Man on the Moon-Eyed Horse, 1977; Humbug Mountain, 1978; The Hey Hey Man, 1979; The Case of the Cackling Ghost (Princess Tomorrow, Flying Clock, Secret Message), 4 volumes, 1981; The Case of the 264-Pound Burglar, 1982; McGroom's Almanac, 1984; The Whipping Boy, 1986. Address: 305 Tenth Street, Santa Monica, CA 90402, USA.

FLEISCHMAN Paul, b. 5 Sept 1952, Monterey, California, USA. Children's Book Writer. m. Becky Mojica, 15 Dec 1978, 2 sons. Education: University of California at Berkeley, USA; BA, University of New Mexico, USA. Publications include: The Birthday Tree, 1979; The Half-a-Moon Inn, 1980; Graven Images, 1982; Path of the Pale Horse, 1983; Finzel the Farsighted, 1983; Coming-and-Going Men, 1985; I Am Phoenix: Poems for Two Voices, 1985; Rondo in C, 1988; Joyful Noise: Poems for Two Voices, 1989; Saturnalia, 1990; Shadow Play, 1990; The Borning Room, 1991; Time Train, 1991. Honours: Newberry Medal, American Library Association, 1983, 1989; Silver Medal, Commonwealth Club of California, 1980; Parents Choice Award, 1983; Numerous citations by Society of Children's Book Writers, American Library Association, New York Times. Memberships: Authors Guild; Society of Children's Book Writers. Address: 855 Marin Pines, Pacific Grove, CA 93950, USA.

FLEISHMAN Lazar, b. 15 May 1944. Professor. m. Irene Strelnikova, 12 Mar 1972, div, 1 son, 1 daughter, (2) Olga Koudriavtseva, 25 July 1994. Education: Latvian State University, 1961-66. Publications: Boris Pasternak: The Poet and His Politics; Boris Pasternak v Tridtsatye Gody; Boris Pasternak v Dvadtsatye Gody; Russkii Berlin; Materialy Po Istorii Russkoi i Sovetskoi Kultury, 1992. Contributions to: Stanford Slavic Studies; Slavica Hierosolymitana; Russian Literature; Izvestiia Akademii Nauk SSSR: Seriia Literary; Iazyka; Druzhba Narodov. Honours: Alexander-von Humboldt Prize; The Pew Foundation Grant; The Guggenheim Foundation Fellowship. Membership: American Association for the Advancement of Slavic Studies. Address: Department of Slavic Languages and Literature, Stanford University, Stanford, CA 94305, USA.

FLEMING Laurence William Howie, b. 8 Sept 1929, Shillong, Assam, India. Author; Artist; Landscape Designer. Education: The New School, Darjeeling, India, 1941-44; Repton School, Derbyshire, 1945-47; Royal Air Force, 1947-49; St Catharine's College, Cambridge, 1949-52. Publications include: A Diet of Crumbs, 1959; The English Garden, 1979; The One Hour Garden, 1985; Old English Villages, 1986. Contributions to: Brazil Journal, A Great Brazilian; Royal Horticultural Society's Journal, Gardens of Burle Marx; Interiors, 1982, Villandry. Memberships: International PEN; The Writers Guild; Anglo Brazilian Society. Address: c/o Lloyds Bank Plc, 112 Kensington High Street, London W8 4SN, England.

FLEMMONS Jerry, b. 14 Jan 1936, Stephenville, Texas, USA. Journalist; Author. div, 1 son. Education: AA, Tarleton State University, 1957; BSc 1959, MSc 1965, East Texas State University. Publications include: Amon: Life of Amon G Carter of Texas, 1978; Texas, 1980, revised 1986; Plowboys, Cowboys & Slanted Pigs, 1984; O Dammit! play, 1985; Also: Fodor's Caribbean Guide, author/editor, 1979. Contributions to: Numerous magazines, national & international. Honours include: Runner-up, Best US Travel Story 1987, winner 1986, Best Newspaper Article on US Travel 1985, Society of American Travel Writers, Lowell Thomas Foundation, University of Missouri School of Journalism; Henry Bradshaw Award, Best Travel Journalism, 1987; 1st runner-up, Grand National prize, Best Travel journalism in America, 1985; 1st recipient, Governor's Award, contributions to Texas tourism, 1985; Pulitzer Prize nomination, 1983. Memberships: Board member 1968-78, Society of American Travel Writers. Address: 3716 Bryce Avenue, Fort Worth, TX 76107, USA.

FLETCHER John Walter James, (Jonathan Fune), b. 23 June 1937, Barking, England. University Teacher. m. Beryl Sibley Connop,

14 Sept 1961, 2 s, 1 d. Education: BA, University of Cambridge, 1959; MA, 1963, M Phil, University of Toulouse, 1961; PhD, 1964. Publications include: The Novels of Samuel Beckeet; Samuel Beckett's Art; Claude Simon and Fiction Now; Novel and Reader; Alain Robbe-Grillet; New Directions in Literature; Samuel Beckett: His Works and His Critics. Contributions to: Spectator; New Statesman; Numerous Academic Journals. Honours: Scott Moncrieff Translation Prize. Memberships: Society of Authors; Translators Association; Society for the Study of French History; Association for the Study of Modern and Contemporary France; Association of University Teachers. Address: School of Modern Languages and European Studies, University of East Anglia, Norwich NR4 7TJ, England.

FLETT Keith Jonquil, b. 30 Nov 1937, Portsmouth, England. Writer. Education: Highbury College, Portsmouth. Publications: Letter Writing: Hobby into Profit; Gold Leaf and Crimson Paper. Contributions to: A Number of Items in the Guardian & Independent. Address: 189 Gladys Avenue, Portsmouth PO2 9BB, England.

FLINN Eugene Christopher, b. 17 July 1924, Jersey City, New Jersey, USA. Writer; College Professor. m. Patricia Pean, 5 June 1971, 4 sons, 4 daughters. Education: BS, Seton Hall University, 1949; MA, 1950, PhD, 1954, St John's University. Appointments: Professor, Jersey State City College; Literary Advisor, Olympia Dukakis's TV Film. Publications: The Literary Guide to the United States; Telling the School Story; Never Mind Who's On First. Contributions to: Numerous including Life; Good Housekeeping. Honours: Winner, National Poetry Contest; Winner: Short Story Contest. Address: PO Box 2, Gillette, NJ 07933, USA.

FLOGSTAD Kjartan, b. 7 June 1944, Sauda, Norway. Novelist. m. Kathrine Norre, 1977. Education: MA, University of Oslo, 1971. Publications: Mooring Lines, 1972; Rasmus, 1974; Not Even Death, 1975; One for All, 1976; Dollar Road, 1977, 1989; Fire and Flame, 1980; U3, 1983; The Seventh Climate: Salim Mahmood in Media Thule, 1986; The Knife at the Throat, 1991; Verse: Pilgrimage, 1968, and Ceremonies, 1969; Also: The Secret Cheering, 1970; The Law West of Pecos and Other Essays on Popular Art and the Culture Industry, 1981; Wording, 1983; Tyrannosaurus Text, 1988; Portrait of a Magic Life: The Poet Claes Gill, 1988; The Light of Work, 1990. Honours include: Melsom Prize, 1980. Address: Gyldendal Norsk Forlag, Postboks 6860, St Olave Plass, 0130 Oslo 1, Norway.

FLORA James Royer, b. 25 Jan 1914, Bellefontaine, Ohio, USA. Artist; Writer. m. Jane Sue Sinnickson, 1 Mar 1941, 2 sons, 3 daughters. Education: Urbana University, 1931-33; Cincinnati Art Academy, 1934-39. Publications: Eighteen children's books including, The Fabulous Firework Family, 1955, complete revision, 1994; The Day The Cow Sneezed, 1957; Leopold, The See-Through Crumbpicker, 1961; My Friend Charlie, 1964; The Great Green Turkey Creek Monster, 1976; Grandpa's Ghost Stories, 1978. Honours: Recipient of numerous awards. Memberships: Art Clubs. Address: 7 St James Place, Rowayton, CT 06853, USA.

FLORA Joseph Martin, b. 9 Feb 1934, Toledo, Ohio, USA. Educator; Professor. m. 30 Jan 1959, 4 sons. Education: BA, 1956, MA, 1957, PhD, 1962, University of Michigan. Publications: Vardis Fisher, 1965; William Ernest Henley, 1970; Frederick Manfred, 1974; Hemingway's Nick Adams, 1982; Ernest Hemingway: The Art of the Short Fiction, 1989; The English Short Story 1880-1945 (editor), 1985; Co-editor: Southern Writers: A Biographical Dictionary; Fifty Southern Writers Before 1900, 1987; Fifty Southern Writers After 1900, 1987; Contemporary Fiction Writers of the South, 1993. Contributions to: Studies in Short Fiction; Dialogue; South Atlantic Review; The Hemingway Review. Address: 505 Caswell Road, Chapel Hill, NC 27514, USA.

FLOREN Lee, (Brett Austin, Lisa Franchon, Claudia Hall, Wade Hamilton, Matt Harding, Matthew Whitman Harding, Felix Lee Horton, Stuart Jason, Grace Lang, Marguerite Nelson, Lew Smith, Maria Sandra Sterling, Lee Thomas, Len Turner, Will Watson, Dave Wilson), b. 1910, USA. Author. Publications: Over 300 novels including most recently: Gambler with a Gun, 1971; Wyoming Showdown, 1972; The Bloodskinners, 1972; War Drum (as Maria Sandra Sterling), 1973; Trail to High Pine, 1974; Long Knife and Musket (as Felix Lee Horton), 1974; Muskets on the Mississippi (as Matthew Whitman), 1974; Valley of Death (as Stuart Jason), 1974; Deadly Doctor (as Stuart Jason), 1974; Boothill Riders, 1979; Renegade Gambler, 1979; Gun Chore, 1979; High Border Riders,

1979; Powdersmoke Attorney, 1979; Edge of Gunsmoke (as Matt Harding), 1979; Nedra (as Grace Lang), 1979; Mercy Nurse (as Marguerite Nelson), 1979; Rope the Wild Wind, 1980; The Bushwhackers, 1980; High Trail to Gunsmoke, 1980; Hard Rock Nurse (as Marguerite Nelson), 1980; Smoky River, 1980; Ride Against the Rifles (as Wade Hamilton), 1980; The High Gun, 1980; North to Powder River, 1981; Cowthief Clanton, 1982; Renegade Rifles, 1983; Buckskin Challenge, 1983; Boothill Brand, 1984; Gun Quick, 1985; West of Barbwire, 1985; Wyoming Gun Law, 1985; The Gringo (as Lee Thomas), 1985; Fighting Ramrod, 1986; Bring Bullets, Texan, 1986; The Tall Texan, 1986; Others as Brett Austin, Claudia Hall, Lew Smith, Len Turner, Will Watson and Dave Wilson. Address: c/o Hale, 45-47 Clerkenwell Green, London EC1R 0HT, England.

FLOURNOY Don Michael, b. 20 Oct 1937, Lufkin, Texas, USA. University Professor. m. Mary Anne Boone, 27 July 1963, 1 son, 1 daughter. Education: BA, Southern Methodist University, 1959; University of London, 1962; MS, Boston University, 1963; MA, PhD, University of Texas, 1964-65. Appointments: Assistant Director, Case Institute of Technology, 1965-66; Assistant Dean, Case Western Reserve University, 1965-69; Associate Dean, University of New York, 1969-71; Dean, 1971-81, Director, Center for International Studies, 1981-84, Professor and Director, Institute for Telecommunication Studies, 1984-, Ohio University, Athens. Publications: CNN World Report; Content Analysis of Indonesian Newspapers; The Rationing of American Higher Education; The New Teachers. Contributions to: Journalism Quarterly; Commdev News; Journal of Development Communications; Satellite Communications; Gazette; Broadcasting and Cable; Via Sat; Electronic Media. Address: Institute for Telecommunications Studies, Ohio University, Athens, OH 45701, USA.

FLYNN Robert (Lopez), b. 1932, USA. Appointments: Assistant Professor, Baylor University, Waco, Texas, 1959-63; Professor, Nevelist-in-Residence, Trinity University, San Antonio, Texas, 1963-. Publications: North to Yesterday, 1967; In the House of the Lord, 1969; The Sounds of Rescue, The Signs of Hope, 1970; Seasonal Rain and Other Stories, 1986; Wanderer Springs, 1987; A Personal War in Vietnam, 1989; When I Was Just Your Age, 1992; The Last Klick, 1994. Address: 101 Cliffside Drive, San Antonio, TX 78231, USA.

FLYNT Candace, b. 12 Mar 1947, Greensboro, North Caroline, USA. Author. m. John Franklin Kime, 29 Jan 1992, 1 son. Education: BA, Greensboro College, 1969; MFA, University of NC, 1974. Publications: Mother Love; Sins of Omission; Chasing Dad. Memberships: Authors Guild; PEN. Literary Agent: Rhoda A Weyr. Address: c/o Rhoda A Weyr, 151 Bergen Street, Brooklyn, NY 11217, USA.

FO Dario, b. 24 Mar 1926, San Giano, Lombardy, Italy. Playwright. Education: Academy of Fine Arts, Milan. Appointments: Founder of La Comune Theatre Collective, Milan, 1970. Publications include: The Virtuous Burglars, One Was Nude and One Wore Tails, Women Undresses and Bodies Ready to be Dispatched, all 1957; Archangels Don't Play Pinball, 1959, 1986; Two Pistols, 1960, 1985; He Who Steals a Foot is Lucky in Love, 1961, 1983; Teatro Comico, 1963; Le Commedie I-IX, 1966-91; The Boss's Funeral, 1969, 1984; Accidental Death of an Anarchist, 1970, 1979; Basta con i fascisti, 1973; We Can't Pay We Won't Pay, 1974, 1978; Female Parts: One Woman Plays, 1977; The Fourth Wall, Waking Up, A Woman and The Same Old Story, all 1984; The Tale of a Tiger, 1978, 1987; Betty, 1980; About Face, 1981; Adaptations of Stravinsky's The Soldier's Tale and Gay's The Beggar's Opera, 1979, 1981; The Mother, 1982; Obscene Fables, 1982; The Open Couple, 1983; Elizabeth: Almost by Chance a Woman, 1984; The History of Masks, 1984; Eve's Diary, 1984; The Whore in the Madhouse and I'm Ulrike, Screaming, 1985; An Ordinary Day, 1986; Il ratto della Francesca, 1986; The Pope and the Witch, 1989; Plays One, 1992; Television plays. Honours include: Soning Award, 1981. Address: c/o CTFR, Viale Piave 11, 20129 Milan, Italy.

FOGEL Robert William, b. 1 July 1926. Economic Historian; Professor. m. 2 children. Education: AB, Cornell University, 1948; AM, Columbia University, 1960; PhD, Johns Hopkins University, 1963; AM, Cambridge University, 1975; AM, Harvard University, 1976; DSc, University of Rochester, 1987. Literary appointments: General Editor: Quantitative Studies in History series, MSSB-Princeton, 1971-76; Interdisciplinary Perspectives in Modern History series, Cambridge University Press, 1979-; Long-Term Factors in Economic Development series, NBER/DAE, 1989-. Publications: About 20 books include: The

Union Pacific Railroad: A Case in Premature Enterprise, 1960; The Reinterpretation of American Economic History (co-author), 1971, Italian edition, 1975; The Dimensions of Quantitative Research in History (co-author), 1972; Time on the Cross: The Economics of American Negro Slavery (with S L Engerman), 1974, several foreign editions; Long-Term Changes in Nutrition and the Standard of Living (editor), 1986; Egalitarianism: The Economic Revolution of the 20th Century, 1994; The Escape from Hunger and Premature Death: Europe, America, and the Third World: 1700-2100, 1995; The Political Realignment of the 1850s: A Socioeconomic Analysis, 1996. Contributions to: Numerous books and journals including: Journal of Economic History; American Economic Review; Journal of Interdisciplinary History. Honours: Many fellowships, grants, prizes, other honours, including: Gilman Fellowship, Johns Hopkins University, 1957-59; Phi Beta Kappa, 1963; Nobel Prize for Economic Sciences, 1993. Memberships: Fellow: American Academy of Arts and Sciences; American Association for the Advancement of Science; Royal Historical Society; British Academy; Several editorial boards. Address: Department of Economics, University of Chicago, 1126 East 59th Street, Chicago, IL 60637-1539, USA.

FOLEY (Mary) Louise Munro, b. 1933, Canada. Now US Citizen. Literaary appointments: Columnist, News-Argus, Goldsboro, North Carolina, USA, 1971-73; Editor of Publications, Institute for Human Service Management, California State University, Sacramento, 1975-80. Publications: The Caper Club, 1969; No Talking, Sammy's Sister, A Job for Joey, 1970; Somebody Stole Second, 1972; Stand Close to the Door (editor), 1976; Tackle, 1978; Women in Skilled Labor (editor), 1980; The Train of Terror, 1982; The Sinister Studies of KESP-TV< 1983; The Lost Tribe, 1983; The Mystery of the Highland Crest, 1984; The Mystery of Echo Lodge, Danger at Anchor Mine, 1985; The Mardi Gras Mystery, 1987; Mystery of the Sacred Stones, 1988; Australia! Find the Flying Foxes, 1988; The Cobra Connection, 1990; Ghost Train, 1991; Poison! Said the Cat, 1992; Blood! said the Cat, 1992; Thief! said the Cat, 1992; In Search of the Hidden Statue, 1993. Memberships: Authors Guild; California Writers Club; National League of American Pen Women. Literary Agent: Ruth Cohen Inc. Address: 5010 Jennings Way, Sacramento, CA 95819, USA.

FOLKE Will. See: BLOCH Robert.

FOLLETT Ken, b. 5 June 1949, Cardiff, Wales. Author. m. 1) 5 Jan 1968, 2) 8 Nov 1985, 1 son, 1 daughter. Education: BA Honours, University College, London; Apprenticeship, Journalism. Publications include: Eye of the Needle, 1978; Triple, 1979; The Key to Rebecca, 1980; The Man from St Petersburg, 1982; On Wings of Eagles, 1983; Lie Down with Lions, 1986; also: The Modigliani Scandal, 1976; The Shakeout, 1975; The Bear Raid, 1976; Secret of Kellerman's Studio, 1976; The Power Twins & the Worm Puzzle, 1976; Paper Money, 1977; The Pillars of the Earth, 1989; Various screenplays. Contributions to: Book reviews, essays, New York Times & other publications. Honour: Edgar Award, Best Novel, Mystery Writers of America, 1979. Memberships: Mystery Writers of America; Crime Writers Association, UK; National Union of Journalists, UK; Writers Guild, USA. Literary Agent: Writers House Inc, 21 West 26th Street, New York, NY 10010, USA. Address: PO Box 708, London SW10 0DH, England.

FONDREN Kervin, b. 3 May 1963, Bessemer, AL, USA. Teacher; News Reporter. Education: BA, University Of Alabama, 1991; Nursing Diploma, Career Institute, AL, 1986; Board Of Directors, American Biographical Institute; CEO, Minority Literary Expo; Publisher, Community Tribune News. Publications: Minority Literary Expo, 1990-1994; Community Tribune, 1990-1994; Pratt City Annual Business Guide, 1992/1994; Pratt City Health Focus, 1994. Contributions to: Newspapers; Magazines; Specialised Publications. Honours: Honourable Mention, Poem Recruit, 1986; Congressional Certificate Of Achievement; Honorary Appointment, Governor Of Alabama Aide-De-Camp; House Of Representatives Resolution Of Recognition; Alabama State Senate Certificates Of Appreciation And Achievement; Birmingham City Council Resolution; Jefferson County Commissioner's Resolution; TRIO Alumni Award And Plaque (UAB Academic Services); Howze-Sanford Recreation Center Community Service Certificate; Good Conduct Medal And Overseas Service Ribbons, US Army; Pratt City Merchants Association Appointment And Award. Memberships: Academy Of American Poets; UAB National Alumni Society; UAB Spanish Club; Health Educators Association; Howze-Sanford Rec-Pac Advisory Board; Pratt Community Neighbourhood Association; Pratt City Merchants' Association. Address: 421 10th Terrace North, Birmingham, AL 35204, USA.

FONER Eric, b. 7 Feb 1943, NY, USA. Historian. m. Lynn Garafola, 1 May 1980, 1 d. Education: BA, Columbia College, 1963; BA, University of Oxford, 1965; PhD, Columbi University, 1969. Publications: Free Soil, Free Labor, Free Men, 1970; Tom Paine and Revolutionary America, 1976; Nothing but Freedom, 1983; Reconstruction: America's Unfinished Revolution, 1988; Freedom's Lawmakers, 1993. Honours: Parkman Prize; Latimes Book Award; Bancroft Prize; Owsley Prize. Memberships: Am Academy of Arts & Science; Organization of Am Historians. Literary Agent: Sandra Dijkstra. Address: 606 West 116th Str, New York, NY 10027, USA.

FONTANA Tom (Thomas Michael), b. 12 Sept 1951, Buffalo, New York, USA. m. Sagan Louis, 18 Dec 1982. Education: BA, State University of New York at Buffalo, USA. Career: Playwright; TV Producer & Director. Appointments: American Writers Theater Foundation, Board of Directors, 1975-. Publications: TV Series: St Elsewhere, 1983; Homicide: Life on the Street, 1992; Plays Include: Johnny Appleseed: A Noh Play, 1971; One/Potato/More, 1975; Nonsense, 1977; The Overcoat; or Clothes Make The Man, 1978; Old Fashioned, 1979; Movin' Mountains, 1981; Mime, 1982; Imagining Lovers, 1982; Also, TV Films & Screenplays. Honours: Emmy Awards, Academy of Television Arts & Sciences, 1984, 1993; Gold Award, New York International Film & Television Festival; People's Choice Award, Bauff Festival; Humanities Prize, Los Angeles Human Family Institute. Address: c/o Rosemary O'Brien, NBC/Channel 4, 30 Rockefeller Plaza, New York, NY 10112, USA.

FOON Dennis, b. 18 Nov 1951, Detroit, USA. Playwright; Screen Writer. 1 daughter. Appointments: Instructor of Playwrighting, University of BC, 1974-79; Playwright, Young People's Theatre, Toronto, 1983-84; Co Founder, Artistic Director, Green Thumb Theatre for Young People, Vancouver, 1975-88; Consultant, Sesame Street Canada, 1988-. Publications: Mirror Game; New Canadian Kid & Invisible Kids; Skin & Liars; The Short Tree and the Bird That Could Not Sing; Am I the Only One?; The Hunchback of Notre Dame; Trummi Kaput; New Canadian Kid; The Windigo; Heracles; Raft Baby; The Last Days of Pual Bunyan. Honours: Scott Newman Award; AYA Award; Chalmers Award; British Theatre Award; Jesse Award; CBC Literary Award; Hopwood Award; Writers Digest Award. Memberships: WGC; PUC; CAPAC; ACTRA; Equity. Address: 647 E 12th Avenue, Vancouver, BC, Canada VJT 2H7.

FOOT Michael Mackintosh (Rt Hon), b. 23 July 1913. Journalist; Politician. m. Jill Craigie, 1949. Education: Wadham College, Oxford. Appointment: Assistant Editor, 1937-38, Joint Editor 1948-52, Editor 1952-59, Managing Director 1952-74, Tribune; Staff Member, Evening Standard, 1938, Acting Editor 1942-44; Political Columnist, Daily Herald, 1944-64; MP. Publications include: Armistice 1918-1939, 1940; Trial of Mussolini, 1943; Brendan and Beverley, 1944; part author, Guilty Men, 1940 and Who Are the Patriots? 1949; Still at Large, 1950; Full Speed Ahead, 1950; The Pen and the Sword, 1957; Parliament in Danger, 1959; Aneurin Bevan Volume I, 1962, Volume II, 1973; Harold Wilson: A Pictorial Biography, 1964; Debts of Honour, 1980; Another Heart and Other Pulses, 1984; Loyalists and Loners, 1986; The Politics of Paradise, 1988. Honours: Hon Fellow, Wadham College, 1969; Hon Member, NUJ, 1985; Hon DLitt, University of Wales, 1985. Address: 308 Gray's Inn Road, London WC1X 8DY, England.

FOOT Michael Richard Daniell, b. 1919, England. Appointments: Professor, Manchester University, 1967-73. Publications include: Gladstone and Liberalism, 1952; British Foreign Policy Since 1898, 1956; Men in Uniform, 1961; SOE in France, 1966, 1968; Gladstone Dairies, Vol 1 & 11, 1825-1839, 1968, vol 111 & IV 1840-55, 1975; War & Society, 1973; Resistance, 1976, 1978; SOE: An Outline History, 1984, 94; Holland at War Against Hilter, 1990; Art & War, 1990. Address: 45 Countess Road, London NW5 2XH, England.

FOOT Paul Mackintosh, b. 8 Nov 1937. Writer; Journalist. m. 3 sons. Appointments: Editor, Isis, 1961; President, Oxford Union, 1961; TUC Delegate, National Union of Journalists, 1967, 1971; Contested (Socialist Workers Party) Birmingham, Stechford, March 1977; Editor, Socialist Worker, 1974-75; Journalist, Daily Mirror, 1979-. Publications: Immigration and Race in British Politics, 1965; The Politics of Harold Wilson, 1968; The Rise of Enoch Powell, 1969; Who Killed Hanratty? 1971; Why You Should be a Socialist, 1977; Red Shelley, 1981; The Helen Smith Story, 1983; Murder at the Farm, 1986; Who Framed Colin Wallace, 1989. Honours: Journalist of the Year, Granada, 1972; Campaigning Journalist of the Year, British Press Awards, 1980. Address: c/o The Daily Mirror, Holborn Circus, London EC1, England.

FOOTE (Albert) Horton (Jr), b. 14 Mar 1916, Wharton, Texas, USA. Playwright. m. Lillian Vallish, 1945, 2 daughters, 2 sons. Education: Educated at Pasadena Playhouse Theatre, California, USA, 1933-35, Tamara Daykarthanova Theatre School, New York, USA, 1937-39. Career: Actor with American Actors Theatre, New York, 1939-42; Theatre Workshop Director and Producer, King-Smith School of Creative Arts, 1944-45 and Manager, Productions Inc, 1945-48, both Washington DC. Publications: Plays include: The Road to the Graveyard (produced New York, 1985); Blind Date (produced New York, 1986); New York, Dramatists Play Service, 1986; Lily Dale (produced New York, 1986); The Widow Claire (produced New York, 1986); Courtship, Valentine's Day 1918, New York, Grove Press, 1987; Screenplays: Storm Fear, 1955; To Kill a Mockingbird, 1962; Baby, The Rain Must Fall, 1964; Hurry Sundown, with Thomas Ryan, 1966; Tomorrow, 1972; Tender Mercies, 1983; 1918, 1984; The Trip to Bountiful, 1985; On Valentine's Day, 1985; Courtship, 1986; Novel: The Chase, New York, Reinhart, 1956; Many television plays. Honours: Oscar, for screenplay, 1963, 1983; DLitt, Austin College, Sherman, Texas, 1987, Drew University, Madison, New Jersey, 1987. Literary Agency: Lucy Kroll Agency, New York. Address: c/o Lucy Kroll Agency, 390 West End Avenue, New York, NY 10024, USA.

FOOTE Shelby, b. Greenville, Mississippi. Education: University of North Carolina, USA. Publications: Novels: Tournament, 1949; Follow Me Down, 1950; Love in a Dry Season, 1951; Shiloh, 1952; Jordan County, 1954; September September, 1977; History: The Civil War: A Narrative: Vol I: Fort Sumter to Perryville, 1958; Vol 2: Fredericksburg to Meridian, 1963; Vol 3: Red River to Appomattox, 1974; Stars in Their Courses, 1994; The Beleaguered City, 1995. Address: 542 East Parkway South, Memphis, TN 38104, USA.

FORBES Bryan, b. 22 July 1926, Stratford, London. England. Film Executive; Director; Screenwriter. m. Nanette Newman, 1955, 2 d. Education: West Ham Secondary School; Royal Academy Dramatic Art. Publications include: Truth Lies Sleeping, 1951; The Distant Laughter, 1972; Notes for a Life, 1974; The Slipper and the Rose, 1976; Neds Girl, 1977; Familiar Strangers, 1979; The Despicable Race, 1980; The Rewrite Man, 1983; The Endless Game, 1986; A Song at Twlight, 1989; A Divided Life, 1992; The Twisted Playground, 1993; Partly Cloudy, 1995. Honours: Best Screenplay Awards; UN Award; Many Film Festival Prizes; Honorary DL London, 1987. Memberships include: Beatrix Potter Society; National Youth Theatre of Great Britain; Writers Guild of Great Britain. Address: c/o The Bookshop, Virginia Water, Surrey, England.

FORBES Colin, b. England. Publications: Tramp in Armour, 1969; The Heights of Zervos, 1970; The Palermo Ambush, 1972; Target Five, 1973; Year of the Golden Ape, 1974; The stone Leopard, 1975; Avalanche Express, 1977; The Stockholm Syndicate, 1981; Double Jeopardy, 1982; The Leader and the Damed, 1983; Terminal, 1984; Cover Story, 1985; The Janus Man, 1987; Deadlock, 1988; The Greek Key, 1989; Shockwave, 1990; Whirlpool, 1991; Cross of Fire, 1992; By Stealth, 1993; The Power, 1994. Literary Agent: Greene & Heaton Limited, London, Address: c/o Greene & Heaton Limited, 37 Goldhawk Road, London W12 8QQ, England.

FORBES DeLoris Stanton, (Stanton Forbes, Forbes Rydell, Tobias Wells), b. 29 July 1923. Writer. m. William James Forbes, 29 Oct 1948, 2 sons, 1 daughter. Appointments: Associate Editor, Wellesley Townsman, Wellesley, Mass, 1960-72. Publications: Over 40 mystery novels, including, Annalisa, 1959; Grieve the Past, 1963; Of Graves, Worms and Epitaphs, 1988; Don't Die on Me, Bille Jean, 1987. Contributions to: several magazines. Honours: Scroll for Grieve for the Past; Best Mystery of the Year, 1963; Best short stories included Quetzalcoat! 1967. Membership: Mystery Writers of America. Address: Sanford, Florida 32771, USA.

FORBES John, b. 1 Sept 1950, Melbourne, Victoria, Australia. Editor; Poet. Education: BA, University of Sydney, 1973. Appointments: Editor, Surfer's Paradise, 1974-83. Publications: Tropical Skiing, 1986; On the Beach, 1977; Drugs, 1980; Stalin's Holidays, 1981; The Stunned Mullet and Other Poems, 1988. Honours include: New Poetry Prize, 1972; Southerly Prize, 1976; Australia Council Literature Board Grants.

FORBES Stanton. See: **FORBES DeLoris Stanton**.

FORCHE Carolyn, b. South Michigan, USA. Poet. Publications: Gathering the Tribes, 1976; The Country Between Us, 1987; The Angel of History, 1994. Contributions: American Poetry Review; Anteus; Atlantic Monthly; New Yorker; Parnassus; Pequod; Virginia Quarterly Review; Womens International Resource Exchange; Poets Choice. Honours: Lamont Poetry Award, American Academy of Poets, 1981; Pusheart Prize. Address: Department of English, George Mason University, 4400 University Drive, Fairfax, VA 22030, USA.

FORD David. See: **HARKNETT Terry.**

FORD George H(arry), b. 1914, USA. Professor of English. Appointments: Professor of English, University of Rochester, Rochester, New York, 1958-. Publications: Keats and the Victorians, 1944; Dickens and His Readers, 1955; Double Measure: The Novels of D H Lawrence, 1965; The Making of a Secret Agent, 1978; Editor: Thackeray, Vanity Fair, 1958; Dickens' David Copperfield, 1958; Selected Poems of John Keats; Dickens Bleak House; Victorian Fiction: A Second Guide to Research; The Dickens Critics (editor with L Lane), 1966; Co-editor: Dickens' Hard Times, 1970; The Norton Anthology of English Literature, 1974. Memberships: American Academy of Arts and Science; International Society for the Study of Time, President 1981-84. Address: Department of English, University of Rochester, Rochester, NY 14627, USA.

FORD Jesse Hill, b. 28 Dec 1928, Troy, Alabama, USA. Author. m. Lillian Shelton Pellettieri, 15 Nov 1975, 2 sons, 2 daughters. Education: BA Classics, Vanderbilt University, 1947-51; MA, University of Florida, 1953-55; Post-graduate, University of Oslo, Norway, 1961-62. Appointments: Staff, The Tennessean, 1950-51; Associate Press, 1953-55; Guest Editorialist, USA Today, 1986-; Writer-in-Residence, Drama, Vanderbilt University, 1987-. Publications: The Liberation of Lord Byron Jones, 1965; Mountains of Gilead, 1961; The Feast of St Barnabas, 1969; The Raider, 1975; Fishes, Birds and Sons of Men, short stories, 1967; Mr Potter and His Bank, 1976; The Conversion of Buster Drumwright, play, 1960; Musical, 1982. Contributions include: Short fiction in Playboy; Esquire; Atlantic; Paris review; Travel essays in major magazines and newspapers. Honours: Best Story, Atlantic First, The Atlantic Monthly, 1959; Atlantic Grant, 1959; O Henry Prize Collection Stories, 1961, 1966, 1967; Best detective stories, 1972-76; Edgar Allen Poe Prize Best Storey for The Jail, 1976; Guggenheim Fellow, fiction, 1966; Visiting Fellow, fiction, Centre for Advanced Study, Middletown, Connecticut, 1965. Memberships: Overseas Press Club of New York; Writers Guild of America, West. Literary Agent: Harold Ober Associates, New York City, USA. Address: Box 43, Bellevue, TN 37221, USA.

FORD Kirk. See: **SPENCE William John Duncan.**

FORD Peter, b. 3 June 1936, Harpenden, Hertfordshire, England. Author; Editorial Consultant, div, 2 s, 1 d. Education: St Georges School, 1948-52. Appointments: Editor, Cassell, 1958-61; Senior Copy Editor, Penguin Books, 1961-64; Senior Editor, Thomas Nelson, 1964-70. Publications: The Fool on the Hill, 1975; Scientists and Inventors, 1979; The True History of the Elephant Man, 1980; The Ghost Disease; The Beetle of Aphrodite; The Picture Buyers Handbook, 1988; A Collectors Guide to Teddy Bears, 1990; Rings and Curtains: Family and Personal Memoirs, 1992; The Monkeys Pair and Other STories by W W Jaciobs, 1994. Memberships: Society of Authors; Society of Freelance Editors and Proofreaders; Am Association for the Advancement of Science; NY Academy of Science. Folklore Society. Literary Agent: David Grossman, London. Address: 42 Friars Street, Sudbury, Suffolk CO10 6AG, England.

FORD R(obert) A(rthur) D(ouglass), b. 8 Jan 1915, Ottawa, Ontario, Canada. Former Ambassador; Poet. Education: MA, Cornell University, New York. Appointments: Ambassador to the Soviet Union, 1964-80; Member of the Palme Commission on Disarmament, from 1980. Publications: A Window on the North, 1956; The Solitary City, 1969; Holes in Space, 1979; Needle in the Eye, 1983; Doors, Words and Silence, 1985; Dostoevsky and Other Poems, 1988; Coming From Afar: Selected Poems, 1990; Our Man in Moscow: A Diplomat's Reflection on the Soviet Union from Stalin to Brezhnev, 1989. Honours include: Governor-General's Medal, 1956; Companion of Canada, 1971; LLD, University of Toronto, 1987. Address: La Poivrière, Saint Sylvestre Pragoulin, 63310 Randan, France.

FORDHAM William. See: **SEARLE Ronald.**

FOREMAN Richard, b. 1937. Publications: Plays & Manifestos, 1976; Theatre of Images, 1977; Reverberation Machines, 1985;

Unbalancing Arts: Foundations for a Theater, 1992; My Head was a Sledgehammer: six plays, 1995. Honours: Fellow, American Academy & Institute of Arts & Letters, 1992.

FORKER Charles Rush, b. 11 Mar 1927, Pittsburgh, Pennsylvania, USA. Professor of English. Education: Bowdoin College, AB, 1951; Merton College, BA, 1953; MA, 1955; Harvard University, PhD, 1957. Appointments include: Resident Tutor, Kirkland House, Harvard University, 1955-57; Instructor, University of Wisconsin, 1957-59; Assistant Professor, Indiana University, 1959-64; Associate Professor, Ind University, 1964-68; Professor, Ind University, 1968-92; Professor Emeritus, Ind University, 1992-. Publications: The Cardinal; Henry V; An Annotated Biblegraphy; Skull Beneath the Skin; Fancy's Images; Edward II. Contributions to: Shakespeare Quarterly; Shakespeare Studies; Medieval and Renaissance Drama. Honours: Phi Beta Kappa; Fulbright Fellowship to England; Shakespeare Prize; ACLS Grant; NEH Senior Research Fellow. Memberships: Guild of Scholars of the Episcopal Church; Shakespeare Society of America; International Shakespeare Society; Malone Society; Marlowe Society. Address: 1219 East Maxwell Lane, Bloomington, IN 47401, USA.

FORREST Leon, b. 1937, American. Appointments: Editor of Community Newspaper, 1965-69; Associate Editor 1969-72 and Managing Editor 1972-73, Muhammad Speaks (Black Muslim Newspaper); Associate Professor 1973-84, Professor 1984-, Chairman of the Department of African-American Studies 1985-, Northwestern University, Evanston. Publications: There is a Tree More Ancient Than Eden, 1973; The Bloodworth Orphans, 1977; Two Wings to Veil My Face, 1984; Relocations of the Spirit: Essays, 1994. Address: Department of African-American Studies, Northwestern University, Arthur Anderson Hall, 2003 Sheridan Road, Evanston, IL 60201, USA.

FORREST Richard Stockton, b. 8 May 1932, Orange, New Jersey, USA. Writer. m. 11 May 1955, 3 sons, 3 daughters. Education: Dramatic Workshop, NYC, 1950; University of South Carolina, 1953-54. Publications: Who Killed Mr Garland's Mistress? 1974; A Child's Garden of Death, 1975; The Wizard of Death, 1977; Death Through the Looking Glass, 1978; The Death in the Willows, 1979; The Killing Edge, 1980; Death at Yew Corner, 1981; Death Under the Lilacs, 1985; Lark's Song, 1986; Under the Name of Stockton Woods: The Laughing Man, 1980; Game Bet, 1981; The Man Who Heard Too Much, 1983; Death on the Mississippi, 1989. Contributions to: Many short stories to numerous magazines. Honour: Special Edgar Allen Poe Award, by MWA, 1976. Membership: Mystery Writers of America. Literary Agent: Phyllis Westberg, Harold Ober Associates, New York City. Address: Box 724, Old Saybrooke, CT 06475, USA.

FORREST Studley. See: **HUGHES Robert.**

FORRESTER Duncan Baillie, Rev Professor. b. 10 Nov 1933, Scotland. Theological Educator. m. Margaret R McDonald, 9 June 1964, 1 s, 1 d. Education: Madras College, St Andrews; University of St Andrews; University of Chicago; University of Edinburgh; University of Sussex. Publications: Caste and Christianity; Christianity and the Future of Welfare; Theology and Politics; Beliefs, Values and Policies; Encounter with God; Studies in the History of Worship in Scotland; Theology and Practice. Memberships: Society for Study of Theology; Society for Study of Christian Ethics. Address: 25 Kingsburgh Road, Edinburgh, EH12 6DZ, Scotland.

FORSHAY-LUNSFORD Cin, b. 2 May 1965, New York City, New York, USA. Author; Lecturer. Education: Queens College, Flushing, New York. Publications: Walk Through Cold Fire, novel, 1985; Saint Agnes Sends the Golden Boy, short story, 1987; Love Potion, short story, 1989; Riding Out the Storm, 1990. Contributions to: Dell Carrousel, 1985; Top of the News, 1986. Honours: Prize for Outstanding First Young Adult Novel, Delacorte Press, 1985; Outstanding Book for Young Adults, College of Education, University of Iowa; Walk Through Cold Fire exhibited at International Children's Book Fair, Bologna, Italy; Named One of the Top 100 Teens in America, Teen Age Magazine; An American Most Likely to Success, Seventeen Magazine. Address: 63 Stevenson Street, Lynbrook, Long Island, NY 11563-1113, USA.

FORSTER Margaret, b. 25 May 1938, Carlisle, Cumberland, England. Writer. m. Hunter Davies, 11 June 1960, 1 s, 2 d. Education: BA, Sommerville College, Oxford, 1960. Appointments: Teacher, Bambury Girls School, London, 1961-63; Chief Non Fiction Reviewer, London Evening Standard, 1977-80. Publications: Georgy Girl, 1963;

The Bogeyman, 1966; The Park, 1968; Mr Bones Retreat, 1971; Mother, Can You Hear Me, 1979; Marital Rites, 1981; Private Papers, 1986; Ladys Maid, 1989; The Battle for Christobel, 1991; 13 Novels, 3 Non Fiction Books. Memberships: Royal Society of Literature. Literary Agent: Tessa Sayle, London. Address: 11 Boscastle Road, London, NW5, England.

FORSYTH Frederick, b. 1938, Ashford, Kent, England. Education: Tonbridge School Kent. Appointment: Former Staff Member, BBC, London. Publications: The Biafra Story, 1969; Day of the Jackal, 1971; The Odessa File, 1972; The Dogs of War, 1974; The Shepherd, 1975; The Devils Alternative, 1979; No Comebacks, 1982; The Fourth Protocol, 1984; The Negotiator, 1990. Honour: Mystery Writers of Am Edgar Allan Poe Award, 1971. Literary Agent: Curtis Brown, London. Address: c/o Curtis Brown, Haymarket House, 4th Floor, 26/28 Haymarket, SW1Y 48P.

FORTINI BROWN Patricia Ann, b. 16 Nov 1936, Oakland, California, USA. University Professor; Art Historian. m. (1) Peter Claus Meyer, May 1957, div 1978, (2) Peter Robert Lamont Brown, Aug 1980, div 1989, 2 sons. Education: AB, University of California, Berkeley, 1959; MA, 1978; PhD, 1983. Appointments: Assistant Professor, 1983-89, Associate Professor, 1989-, Andrew W Mellon Professor, 1991-, Princeton University, Princeton, New Jersey. Publication: Venetian Narrative Painting in the Age of Carpaccio. Contributions to: Art History; Christian Science Monitor; Monitor Book Review; Burlington Magazine; Renaissance Quarterly; Biography. Honours: Premio Salotto Veneto, Italy. Memberships: Renaissance Society of America; American Academy in Rome; College Art Association. Address: Department of Art and Archaeology, Princeton University, Princeton, NJ 08544, USA.

FOSKETT Daphne, b. 23 Dec 1911, Kimpton, Hampshire, England. Author. m. The Rev Reginald Foskett, 7 Apr 1937, late Bishop of Penrith and Holoure, FRSA 1976; RMS 1986, 2 daughters. Education: Private school in Sussex, 1921-27. Publications: Dictionary of British Portrait Miniatures (2 vols), 1972; British Portrait Miniatures, 1963; Samuel Cooper, 1974; John Smart, 1964; John Harden of Brathy Hall, 1974; Collecting Miniatures, 1979; Miniatures, Dictionary and Guide, 1987; Scottish Arts Council Catalogue, 1965 and 1974. Contributions to: Apollo; Antique Collector; Antique Collectors Guide; The Connoiseur. Honours: FRSA, 1976; Theta Sigma Phi, 1964; Commendation for McColvin Medal, 1972. Membership: Royal Overseas League. Address: Flat 55, Riverside Drive, Solihull, West Midlands B91 3HR, England.

FOSTER David (Manning), b. 15 May 1944, Sydney, New South Wales, Australia. Novelist. Education: BSc in Chemistry, University of Sydney, 1967; PhD, Australian National University, Canberra, 1970. Publications: The Pure Land, 1974; The Empathy Experiment, 1977; Moonlite, 1981; Plumbum, 1983; Dog Rock: A Postal Pastoral, 1985; The Adventures of Christian Rosy Cross, 1986; Testostero, 1987; The Pale Blue Crochet Coathanger Cover, 1988; Mates of Mars, 1991; Self Portraits (ed), 1991; A Slab of Fosters, 1994; Short stories: North South West: Three Novellas, 1973; Escape to Reality, 1977; Hitting the Wall: Two Novellas, 1989. Honours include: Australian National Book Council Award, 1981; New South Wales Premier's Fellowship, 1986. Address: PO Box 57, Bundanoon, New South Wales 2578, Australia.

FOSTER Donald Wayne, b. 22 June 1950, Chicago, Illinois, USA. m. Gwen Bell Foster, 29 Dec 1974, 2 sons. Education: BA, Wheaton College, 1972; MA, 1983, PhD, 1985, University of California. Appointments: Visiting Lecturer, University of California, Santa Barbara, 1984-85; Assistant Professor 1986-90, Associate Professor, 1990-, Jean Webster Chair of Dramatic Literature, 1991-, Vassar College, Poughkeepsie, New York. Publications: Eleg, by W S: A Study in Attribution; Women's Works: An Anthology of British Literature; SHAXICON: A lexical database for Shakespeare studies, 1995. Contributions to: The Bible and Narrative Tradition; Privileging Gender in Early Modern England; Philosophy and Literature; PMLA; Shakespeare Quarterly; ELR; Times Literary Supplement. Honours: William Riley Parker Prize; Delaware Shakespeare Prize. Memberships: Modern Language Association; Shakespeare Association of America; Renaissance English Text Society; American Association of University Professors. Address: Box 388, Vassar College, Poughkeepsie, NY 12601, USA.

FOSTER Iris. See: **POSNER Richard.**

FOSTER James Anthony, (Tony Foster), b. 2 Aug 1932, Winnipeg, Canada. Writer. m. 10 Oct 1964, 1 son, 2 daughters. Education: University of Brunswick, 1950. Appointments include: Royal Canadian Air Force, 1950; US Army 10th Special Forces Group, 1952-53; Itinerant Crop Duster Pilot, 1954; Bush Pilot for Saskatchewan, 1957-58; Chief Pilot, 1959; Real Estate Development in Caribbean, 1968; MGm & Wm, 1976. Publications: Zig Zag to Armageddon; The Bush Pilots; By Pass; The Money Burn; Heart of Oak; Sea Wings; Meeting of Generals; Muskets to Missiles; Rue Du Bac; For Love And Glory; Ransom For A God; The Sound and the Silence; Swan Song. Contributions to: Numerous TV movies, documentaries and series scripts. Memberships: Writers Union of Canada; Canadian Authors Association; PEN; Writers Guild of America. Address: 67 Briarwood Crescent, Halifax, Nova Scotia, Canada B3M 1P2.

FOSTER Jeanne. See: **WILLIAMS Jeanne.**

FOSTER Linda Nemec, b. 29 May 1950, Garfield Heights, Ohio, USA. Poet; Teacher of Creative Writing. m. Anthony Jesse Foster, 26 Oct 1974, Maple Heights, Ohio, USA, 1 son, 1 daughter. Education: BA, Aquinas College, Grand Rapids, Michigan; MFA, Creative Writing, Goddard College, Plainfield, Vermont. Literary Appointments: Board Member, Cranbrook Writers Guild, Birmingham, Michigan; Creative Writers in Schools Programme, Michigan Council for the Arts, Detroit; Board Member, Mecosta County Council for the Humanities, Big Rapids, Michigan. Publications: A History of the Body, chapbook of prose poems, 1986; Manhattan Poetry Review; The Penn Review; American Poetry Anthology; Negative Capability; Anthology of Contemporary Michigan Poetry. Contributions to: Poetry Now; Nimrod; Tendril; Invisible City; Chicago Magazine; Croton Review; The Alchemist; University of Windsor Review; Canada; Sierra Madre Review; Room and others. Honours: Poetry manuscript nominated for Anne Sexton Prize, 1979; 2 poems nominated for Pushcart Prize, 1982; Poetry Grant, Michigan Council for the Arts, 1983-84; Prizewinner, Croton Review poetry competition, 1985; Grand Prize, American Poetry Association contest, 1986. Memberships: Detroit Women Writers; Poetry Society of America; Academy of American Poets. Address: 427 W Pere Marquette Big Rapids, MI 49307, USA.

FOSTER Paul, b. 15 Oct 1931, Pennsgrove, New Jersey, USA. Writer. Education: BA, Rutgers University; LLB, New York University Law School. Publications: 25 books of plays including: Tom Paine, 1971, 1975, 1978; Madonna in the Orchard, 1971, 1974; Satyricon, 1972; Elizabeth I, 1972, 1974, 1978; Marcus Brutus, 1976; Silver Queen Saloon, 1976, 1978; Mellon and the National Art Gallery, 1980; A Kiss Is Just A Kiss, 1984; 3 Mystery Comedies, 1985; The Dark and Mr Stone, 1985; Odon von Horvath's Faith, Hope and Charity, translation, 1987; Make Believe (with music by Solt Dome), musical book and lyrics, 1994; Films: Smile, 1980; Cop and the Anthem, 1982; When You're Smiling, 1983; Cinderella, 1984; Home Port, 1984. Contributions to: Off-Off Broadway Book, 1972; Best American Plays of Modern Theatre, 1975; New Stages magazine. Honours: Rockefeller Foundation Fellowship, 1967; British Arts Council Award, 1973; J S Guggenheim Fellowship, 1974; Theatre Heute Award, 1977. Memberships: Dramatists Guild; Society of Composers and Dramatic Authors, France; Players Club, New York City. Address: 44 W 10th Street, New York, NY 10011, USA.

FOSTER Simon. See: **GLEN Duncan Munro.**

FOSTER S(ophia) L, b. 21 Aug 1956, Monroe, LA, USA. Author; Freelance Writer; Journalist. Education: BA, Southern University, 1978; Diploma, Elkins Institute, 1980; Certificate, Atlanta Area Tech, 1985; Certificates, Sears Extensive Institute, 1987, 1990, 1991. Publications: The Southern Palate Cookbook, 1991, (Library Edition, 1992); The Southern Palate Cookbook, Celebrities and Friends, 1994. Contributions to: Jeopardy Game Show; Southernite; Fox Sports Show; Nightline; Falcon's Fever; Oprah Winfrey Show; Newspapers and Magazines including, Jet, Video, People, TV Guide, Time, Newsweek, Southern University Directions, Columbia Journal Review. Memberships: National Writers Association; Executive Member, Southern University Alumni Chapter Council. Literary Agents: Scott Meredith; Abrak- Happy Girl. Address: 2465 Roosevelt Hwy, College Park, GA 30337, USA.

FOSTER Tony. See: **FOSTER James Anthony.**

FOUGERE Jean, b. 5 May 1914, St Amand, Cher, France. Writer. Publications include: Novels: La Pouponniere, 1948; La Cour des Miracles, 1955; La Vie de Chateau, 1958; Les Petis Messieurs, 1963; Nos Tantes d'Avallon, 1968; Les Passagers, 1975; Destinee City, 1983; Un Carnet Du Jour, 1989; Short Stories: Un Cadeau Utile, 1953; La Belle Femme, 1971; Le Faiseur D'or, 1989; Essays, Voulez Vous Voyager Avec Moi, 1957. Contributions to: Le Figaro; Les Nouvelles Litteraires. Honours: Grand Prix de la Nouvelle, Academie Francaise, 1972; Chevalier Legion d'Honneur. Membership: Society of Men of Letters. Address: 22 Quai de Bethune, 75004 Paris, France.

FOURNIS Kate. See: **MURRAY Terry**.

FOWLER Alastair David Shaw, b. 1930. England. Appointments: Junior Research Fellow, Queens College, Oxford, 1955-59; Fellow, Tutor, Brasenose College, 1962-71; Regius Professor, 1971-, Emeritus, University of Edinburgh; Professor, University of Virginia, 1990-. Publications include: Richard Wills De Re Poetica, 1958; Spenser and the Numbers of Time, 1964; The Poems of John Milton, 1968 (with John Carey); Triumphal Forms, 1970; Silent Poetry, 1970; Conceitful Thought, 1975; Spenser, 1978; From the Domain of Arnheim, Kinds of Literature, 1982; A History of English Literature, 1987; The New Oxford Book of 17th Century Verse, 1991; The Country House Poem, 1994. Address: Dept of English, David Hume Tower, University of Edinburgh, George Square, Edinburgh EH8 9JX, Scotland.

FOWLER Don D, b. 1936, USA. Professor of Anthropology. Appointments: Assistant Professor, 1964-67, Associate Research Professor, 1968-72, Research Professor of Anthropology, 1972-78, Mamie Kieberg Professor of Anthropology and Historic Preservation, 1978-, University of Nevada, Reno; Research Associate, Smithsonian Institution, Washington, District of Columbia, 1970. Publications: Down the Colorado: John Wesley Powell's Diary of the First Trip Through the Grand Canyon (editor), 1969; Photographed All the Best Scenery: Jack Hiller's Diary of the Powell Expedition (editor); In a Sacred Manner We Live - Edward S Curtis's Photographs of North American Indians, 1972; The Western Photographs of Jack Hillers, 1989. Memberships: Society for American Archaeology, President 1985-87. Address: Historic Preservation Program, University of Nevada, Reno, NV 89557-0111, USA.

FOWLER Marian Elizabeth, b. 15 Oct 1929, Newmarket, Ontario, Canada. Writer. m. Dr Rodney Singleton Fowler, 19 Sept 1953, Toronto, divorced 1977, 1 son, 1 daughter. Education: BA Hons, English, 1951; MA, English, 1965; PhD, English, 1970, University of Toronto, Canada. Publications: The Embroidered Tent, Five Gentlewomen in Early Canada, 1982; Redney: A Life of Sara Jeannette Duncan, 1983; Below the Peacock Fan: First Ladies of the Raj, 1987; Blenhein: Biography of a Palace, 1989. Contributions to: English Studies in Canada; University of Toronto Quarterly; Dalhousie Review; Ontario History; Dictionary of Canadian Biography; Oxford Companion to Canadian Literature; New Canadian Encyclopaedia. Honours: Governor-General's Gold Medal in English, 1951; Canadian Biography Award, 1979. Memberships: International PEN; Writers' Union of Canada. Literary Agent: Vardey and Brunton. Address: Kilmara, RR2, Lisle, Ontario, L0M 1M0, Canada.

FOWLES John (Robert), b. 31 Mar 1926, Leigh-on-Sea, Essex, England. Novelist. m. Elizabeth Whitton, 1956. Education: Edinburgh University, 1944; BA (Hons) in French, New College, Oxford, 1950. Appointments: Lecturer in English, University of Poitiers, France, 1959-51; Teacher at Anargyrios College, Spetsai, Greece, 1951-52, and in London, 1953-63. Publications: The Collector, 1963; The Magus, 1965; The French Lieutenant's Woman, 1969; Daniel Martin, 1977; Mantissa, 1982; A Maggot, 1985; Short story: The Ebony Tower; Collected Novellas, 1974; Also several plays, verse and non-fiction work. Honours include: W H Smith Literary Award, 1970; Christopher Award, 1981. Literary Agent: Sheil and Associates, London, England. Address: Sheil and Associates, 43 Doughty Street, London WC1N 2LF, England.

FOX Geoffrey Edmund, b. 3 Apr 1941, Chicago, Illinois, USA. Writer; Sociologist; Translator. m. (1) Sylvia Herrera, 8 Aug 1966, (2) Mirtha Quintanales, 15 June 1975, (3) Susana Torre, 5 Oct 1979, 2 sons. Education: BA, Harvard University, 1963; PhD, Northwestern University, 1975. Literary appointments: Editor, Hispanic Monitor, 1983-84; Guest Editor, NACLA Report on the Americas, 1989. Publications: Welcome to My Contri; The Land and People of Argentina; The Land and People of Venezuela; Working Class Emigres from Cuba; Hispanic Nation, in progress. Contributions to: New York Times: The Nation: Village Voice; Yellow Silk; Fiction International; Central Park. Memberships: Authors Guild; National Writers Union; Latin American Studies Association. Literary Agent: Colleen Mohyde. Address: 14 East 4th Street 812, New York, NY 10012, USA.

FOX Levi, b. 1914, United Kingdom. Author. Appointments: Director and Secretary, Shakespeare Birthplace Trust, 1945-89; Director Emeritus of the Trust, 1990; General Editor, Dugdale Society, 1945-80. Publications: Leicester Abbey, 1938; Administration of the Honor of Leicester in the Fourteenth Century, 1940; Leicester Castle, 1943; Leicester Forest (with P Russell), 1945; Coventry's Heritage, 1946; Stratford-upon-Avon, 1949; Shakespeare's Town, 1949; Oxford, 1951; Shakespeare's Stratford-upon-Avon, 1951; Shakespeare's Country, 1953; The Borough Town of Stratford-upon-Avon, 1953; English Historical Scholarship in the 16th and 17th Centuries (editor), 1956; Shakespeare's Town and Country, 1959, 2nd edition 1976, 3rd edition 1990; Stratford-upon-Avon: An Appreciation, 1963, 2nd edition 1976; The 1964 Shakespeare Anniversary Book, 1964; Celebrating Shakespeare, 1965; Correspondence of the Reverend Joseph Greene, 1965; A Country Grammar School, 1967; The Shakespeare Book, 1969; Shakespeare's Sonnets (editor), 1970; Shakespeare's England, 1972; In Honour of Shakespeare, 1972, 2nd edition 1982, The Shakespeare Treasury, compiler, 1972; The Stratford-upon-Avon Shakespeare Anthology, compiler, 1975; Stratford: Past and Present, 1975; Shakespeare's Flowers, 1978, 2nd edition 1990; Shakespeare's Birds, 1978; The Shakespeare's Centre, 1982; Shakespeare in Medallic Art, 1982; Shakespeare's Magic, 1982; The Early History of King Edward VI School, Stratford-upon-Avon, 1984; Coventry Constables' Presentments, 1986; Historic Stratford-upon-Avon, 1986; Shakespeare's Town and Country, 1986, 1990; Minutes and Accounts of the Corporation of Stratford-upon-Avon (1592-96), 1990. Address: The Shakespeare Centre, Stratford-upon Avon, CV37 6QW, England.

FOX Mem, b. 5 Mar 1946, Australia. College Lecturer. m. Malcolm, 2 Jan 1969, 1 son. Education: BA, Flinder University, 1978; B Ed, Sturt College, 1979; Graduate Diploma, Underdale College, 1981. Publications: Possum Magi, 1983; Wilfrid Gordon McDonald Partridge, 1984; A Cat Called Kite, 1985; Zoo-Looking, 1986; Hattie and the Fox, 1986; Sail Away, 1986; How to Teach Drama to Infants, 1984; Arabella, 1986; Just Like That, 1986; A Bedtime Story, 1987; The Straight Line Wonder, 1987. Contributions to: Language Arts. Honours: New South Wales Premier's Literary Award, Best Children's Book, 1984; Koala First Prize, 1987. Memberships: Australian Society of Authors; Australian Children's Book Council. Literary Agent: Caroline Lurie, Victoria Australia. Address: 40 Melton Street, Blackwood, South Australia 5051, Australia.

FOX Paula, b. 22 Apr 1923, New York, New York, USA. Novelist. m. 2) Martin Greenberg, 9 June 1963, 2 sons. Appointments: State University of New York, 1974; University of Pennsylvania, 1980-85; New York University, 1989. Publications: Desperate Characters, 1970; The Slave Dancer, 1974; One-Eyed Cat, 1984; A Servant's Tale, 1983; How Many Miles to Babylon, 1967; The Village by the Sea, 1989; The Western Coast, 1972; The Widow's Children, 1976; The God of Nightmares, 1990. Honours: Guggenheim Fellow, 1972; American Academy of Arts and Letters, 1972; NEA Award, 1973; Brandeis Fiction Citation, 1984; Newbery Medal, 1974; Hans Christian Andersen Medal, 1983; American Book Award, 1980; Rockefeller Foundation Residency Fellow, 1985; Newbery Honour Medal, 1986; Boston Globe/Horn Book Award, 1989. Membership: PEN. Literary Agent: Robert Lescher. Address: c/o Robert Lescher, 67 Irving Place, New York, NY 10003, USA.

FOX Robert R, b. 2 Feb 1943, Brooklyn, New York, USA. Literature Programme Coordinator. m. Susan Fox, 1 son, 1 daughter. Education: BA, Brooklyn College, 1967; MA, Ohio University, Athens, 1970. Publications: Destiny News; TLAR & CODPOL; A Fable; In Buckeye Country (contributor), 1994. Contributions to: Fiction International; Pig Iron; Pulpsmith; American Book Review; Confrontation; Witness; Fiction. Honours: Citation, Ohioana Library Association; PEN Syndicated Fiction Award; Nelson Algren Short Fiction Award. Membership: Associated Writing Program. Address: c/o The Ohio Arts Council, 727 East Main Street, Columbus, OH 43205, USA.

FOX-GENOVESE Elizabeth, b. 28 May 1941, Boston, Massachusetts, USA. Professor of History. m. Eugene D Genovese, 6

June 1969. Education: BA, Bryn Mawr College, 1963; Institut d'Etudes Politiques, Paris, France, 1961-62; MA, 1966, PhD, 1974, Harvard University; Special Candidate, Center for Psychoanalytic Training and Research, Columbia University, 1977-79; Newberry Library, Institute in Quantitative Methods, 1979. Publications: The Origins of Physiocracy: Economic Revolution and Social Order in 18th Century France, 1976; Fruits of Merchant Capital: Slavery and Bourgeois Property in Rise and Expansion of Capitalism (with Eugene Genovese), 1983; Within the Plantation: Black and White Women of Old South, 1988; Feminism without Illusions: A Critique of Individualism, 1991. Contributions to: Washington Post; Boston Globe; First Things; Common Knowledge; New York Times Book Review; Times Literary Supplement; The New Republic. Honours: Doctor of Letters, Millsaps College; C Hugh Holman Prize, Society for Southern Literature; Julia Cherry Spruill Prize, Southern Association of Women Historians. Memberships: Modern Language Association; Society for Study of Southern Literature; South Atlantic Modern Language Association; American Comparative Literature Association; American Antiquarian Society; Society of American Historians; American Political Science Association; American Academy of Religion; Organization of American Historians; Southern Political Science Association. Literary Agent: Kim Witherspoon, Witherspoon & Chernoff Associates Inc, New York City, New York, USA. Address: History Department, Emory University, Atlanta, GA 30322, USA.

FRAGOLA Anthony, b. 22 June 1943, Syracuse, New York, USA. Professor. 1 son, 2 daughters. Education: BA, Columbia University, 1966; MA, University of North Carolina, 1974; Master, Professional Writing, University of Southern California, 1985. Publications: 2 stories by BBC World Service Short Story Series; Author, Adaptor, number of films. Contributions include: Encounter & The Cornhill; Lectures pour tous, France; Dewan Sastra, Malaysia; Chariton Review; St Andrews Review; Sudia Mystica; Greensboro Review. Honours: UNICO National Fiction Award, 1975; Greensboro Review Fiction Award, 1976; Excellence Summer Fellowship, 1978; Recipient, other honours and awards. Memberships: Associated Writing Programme; Poets & Writers; University Film and Video Association. Literary Agent: Mary Jack Wald Agency. Address: 301 Woodlawn Avenue, Greensboro, NC 27401, USA.

FRAILE Medardo, b. 21 Mar 1925, Madrid, Spain. Emeritus Professor in Spanish. Education: DPh, DLitt, University of Madrid, 1968. Publications: Cuentos con Algun Amor, 1954; A La Luz Cambian las Cosas, 1959; Cuentos de Verdad, 1964; Descubridor de Nada y Otros Cuentos, 1970; Con Los Dias Contados, 1972; Hacia una Generacion Sin Critica, 1972; La Penultima Inglaterra, 1973; Poesia y Teatro Espanoles Contemporaneos, 1974; Ejemplario, 1979; Autobiografia, 1986; Cuento Espanol de Posguerra, 1986; El gallo puesto en hora, 1987; Entre parentesis, 1988; Santa Engracia, numero dos o tres, 1989; Teatro Espanol en un Acto, 1989; El rey y el pais con granos, 1991; Cuentos Completos, 1991; Claudina y los, cacos, 1992. Contributions to: Numerous including: Cuadernos de Agora, Sub-editor, Drama Critic, 1957-64; Abside; Revista de Occidente, Caravelle; Clavileno; Cuadernos Hispano-Americanos. Honours include: Critics Book of the Year, 1965; Hucha de Oro Prize, 1971; Research Grant, Carnegie Trust for Universities of Scotland, 1975. Memberships: General Society of Spanish Authors; Working Community of Book Writers, Spain; Association of University Teachers; College of Doctors of Philosophy and Letters, Officer; Membre Correspondent de L'Academie Europeenne des Sciences, des Arts et des Lettres, Paris. Address: 24 Etive Crescent, Bishopbriggs, Glasgow G64 1ES, Scotland.

FRAME Janet, b. 28 Aug 1924, Dunedin, New Zealand. Author. Education: University of Otago Teachers Training College. Publications include: The Lagoon Stories, 1951; Faces in the Water, 1961; The Edge of the Alphabet, 1961; Scented Gardens for the Blind, 1963; The Reservoir Stories and Sketches, Snowman, 1963; The Adaptable Man, 1965; A State of Siege, 1966; The Reservoir and Other Stories, 1966; The Pocket Mirror, 1967; The Rainbirds, 1968; Mona Minim and the Small of the Sun, 1969; Daughter Buffalo, 1972; Living in the Maniototo, 1979; To The Island, 1982; You Are Now Entering the Human Heart, 1984; The Envoy from the Mirror City, 1985; The Carpathians, 1988. Address: 276 Glenfield Road, Auckland 10, New Zealand.

FRANCE (Evelyn) Christine, b. 23 Dec 1939, Sydney, Australia. Art Historian. m. Stephen Robert Bruce France, 22 Dec 1962, 1 daughter. Education: BA, University of Sydney. Publications: Justin

O'Brien: Image and Icon, 1987; Margaret Olley, 1990; Marea Gazzard, Form and Clay, 1994. Contributions to: Art and Australia; Australian Newspapers. Address: 2/89 Ocean St, Woollahra, NSW 2025, Australia.

FRANCHON Lisa. See: **FLOREN Lee**.

FRANCIS Alexander. See: **HEATH-STUBBS John**.

FRANCIS Clare, b. 17 Apr 1946, Surrey, England. Writer. 1 son. Education: Economics Degree, University College, London. Publications: Come Hell or High Water, 1977; Come Wind or Weather, 1978; The Commanding Sea, 1981; Night Sky, 1983; Red Crystal, 1985; Wolf Winter, 1987; Requiem, 1991; Deceit, 1993. Honours: Member, Order of British Empire (MBE); Honorary Fellow, University College, London. Membership: Society of Authors. Literary Agent: John Johnson. Address: c/o John Johnson, Clerkenwell House, 45-47 Clerkenwell Green, London EC1R 0HT, England.

FRANCIS Richard (Dick) Stanley, b. 31 Oct 1920, Pembrokeshire, South Wales. Ex Steeplechase Jockey; Author. m. Mary Margaret Brenchley, 21 June 1947, 2 sons. Appointments: Racing Correspondent, London Sunday Express, 1957-63. Publications: Dead Cert, 1962; Nerve, 1964; For Kicks, 1965; Odds Against, 1965; Flying Finish, 1966; Blood Sport, 1967; Forfeit, 1968; Enquiry, 1969; Rat Race, 1970; Bonecrack, 1971; Smokescreen, 1972; Slay-Ride, 1973; Knock Down, 1974; High Stakes, 1975; In the Frame, 1976; Risk, 1977; Trial Run, 1978; Whip Hand, 1979; Reflex, 1980; Twice Shy, 1981; Banker, 1982; The Danger, 1983; Proof, 1984; Break In, 1985; Bolt, 1986; Hot Money, 1987; The Edge, 1988; Straight, 1989; Longshot, 1990; Comeback, 1991; Driving Force, 1992; Autobiography, The Sport of Queens, 1957; Biography, Lester, 1986. Contributions to: Sunday Express; Daily Express; Sunday Times; Daily Mail; New York Times; Washington Post; The Age, Melbourne; Horse & Hound; Sports Illustrated; Classic. Honours: OBE, 1954; MWA's Edgar Allen Poe Best Novel Award, Forfeit, 1970; Whip Hand, 1981; CWA's Gold Dagger Award, For Kicks, 1966; Whip Hand, 1980; Honorary LHD, Tufts University, MA, USA, 1991. Memberships: Crime Writers Association, Chairman, 1965-66; Mystery Writers of America; Society of Authors; Racecourse Association. Literary Agent: Andrew Hewson, John Johnson Agency, London. Address: c/o John Johnson Agency, 45/47 Clerkenwell Green, London EC1R 0HT, England.

FRANCK Thomas Martin, b. 1931, USA. Professor of Law; Author. Publications: Race and Nationalism, 1960; The Role of the United Nations in the Congo (co-author), 1963; African Law (co-author), 1963; East African Unit Through Law, 1964; Comparative Constitutional Process, 1968; The Structure of Impartiality, 1968; A Free Trade Association (co-author), 1968; Why Federations Fail (co-author), 1968; Word Politics: Verbal Strategy among the Superpowers (co-author), 1971; Secrecy and Foreign Policy (co-editor), 1974; Resignation in Protest (co-author), 1975; Control of Sea Resources by Semi-Autonomous States, 1975; Foreign Policy by Congress (co-author), 1979; United States Foreign Relations Law, vols I-III (co-author), 1981; The Tethered Presidency, 1981; Human Rights in Third World Perspective, 3 vols, 1982; United States Foreign Relations Law, vols IV-V (co-author), 1984; Nation Against Nation, 1985; Judging the World Court, 1986; Foreign Relations and National Security Law (co-author), 1987; The Power of Legitimacy Among Nations, 1990. Address: 15 Charlton Street, New York, NY 10014, USA.

FRANGOPOULOS Theophilos D, b. 15 June 1923, Athens, Greece. Retired University Professor. m. Katy Tsitsekl, 14 Dec 1947, 2 s. Education: Athens University of Law, 1947; University of Surrey, 1967; Boston University, 1978; Queens College, NY, 1979-81; University of Berlin, 1986. Appointments: Secretary General, PEN Club, 1974-89; Treasurer, 1991-; Secretary General, International Theatre Institute, 1975-82; Member, State Literary Price Awards Committee, 1983-85; Columnist, Newspapers. Publications: Collected Poems; Battle Before the Walls Fortitude; The Critique of the Critic. Contributions to: Over 60 Magazines, Newspapers. Honours: Over 10 Awards. Memberships include: Panellenic Cultural Society; Parnassos Society. Address: Skoufa 32, Athens 106-73, Greece.

FRANK Elizabeth, b. 14 Sept 1945, Los Angeles, California, USA. m. Howard Buchwald, 3 Aug 1984, 1 daughter. Education: Bennington College; BA, MA, PhD, University of California at Berkeley, USA. Career: Writer; Professor. Publications: Jackson Pollock, 1984; Louise Brogan: A Portrait, 1985. Honours: Pulitzer Prize, 1986;

National Book Critics Circle Award, nom, 1986. Address: Department of Lang & Lit, Bard College, Annandale on Hudson, NY 12504, USA.

FRANK Joseph Nathaniel, b. 6 Oct 1918, New York, New York, USA. Professor Emeritus of Comparative Literature. m. Marguerite J Straus, 11 May 1953, 2 daughters. Education: Studied, New York University, 1937-38, University of Wisconsin 1941-42, University of Paris 1950-51; PhD University of Chicago, 1960. Literary Appointments include: Editor, Bureau of National Affairs, Washington, 1942-50; Lecturer, Department of English, Princeton University; Associate Professor, Rutgers University, 1961-66; Professor of Comparative Literature, 1966-85; Director of Christain Gauss Seminars, 1966-83, Princeton University; Visiting Member, Institute for Advanced Study, 1984-87; Professor of Slavic & Comparative Literature, Stanford University. Publications: The Widening Gyre, Crisis and Mastery in Modern Literature, 1963; F M Dostoevsky: The Seeds of Revolt, 1821-1849, 1976; F M Dostoevsky: The Years of Ordeal, 1850-1859, 1983; Editor, A Primer of Ignorance, 1967; Dostoevsky: The Stir of Liberation, 1860-1865, 1986; Co-editor, Selected Letters of Fyodor Dostoevsky, 1987; Through The Russian Prisions, 1989. Contributions to: The Southern Review; The Sewannee Review; the Hudson Review; The Partisan Review; Art News; Critique; The Chicago Review; The Minnesota Review; The Russian Review; Le Contract Social; Commentary; Encounter; New York Review, and others. Contributions to various books, numerous book reviews and translations. Honours include: Fulbright Scholar, 1950-51; Rockefeller Fellow, 1952-53, 1953-54; Guggenheim Fellow, 1956-57, 1975-76; Award, National Institute of Arts and Letters, 1958; Fellow, American Academy of Arts and Sciences, 1969; Research Grants; American Council of Learned Societies, 1964-65, 1967-68, 1970-71; James Russell Howell Prize, 1977; Christian Gass Award, 1977; Rockefeller Foundation, 1979-80, 1983-84; National Book Critics Circle Award, 1984; James Russell Howell Prize, 1986. Address: Department of Comparative Literature, 326 East Pyne, Princeton University, Princeton, NJ 08544, USA.

FRANKEL Ellen, b. 22 May 1951, NYC, USA. Editor; Writer; Story Teller. m. Herbert Levine, 3 Aug 1975, 1 son, 1 daughter. Education: BA, University of Michigan, 1973; PhD, Princeton University, 1978. Appointments: Editor in Chief, Jewish Publication Society, 1991-. Publications: Choosing to Be Chosen, Ktav; The Classic Tales: 4000 Years of Jewish Lore; The Encyclopedia of Jewish Symbols; George Washington and the Constitution. Contributions to: Judaism; Jewish Spectator; Moment; Jewish Monthly; Shefer Magazine. Memberships: Association of Jewish Studies; Phi Beta Kappa. Address: 6670 Lincoln Drive, Philadelphia, PA 19119, USA.

FRANKLAND (Anthony) Noble, b. 4 July 1922, Ravenstonedale, England. Historian; Biographer. m. 1) Diana Madeline Fovargue Tavernor, 28 Feb 1944, dec 1981, 1 son, 1 daughter, 2) Sarah Katharine Davies, 7 May 1982. Education: Open Scholar, MA 1948, DPhil 1951, Trinity College, Oxford. Appointments: Official British Military Historian, 1951-60; Deputy Director of Studies, Royal Institute of International Affairs, 1956-60; Director, Imperial War Museum, 1960-82. Publications: Crown of Tragedy: Nicholas II, 1960; The Strategic Air Offensive Against Germany (co-author), 4 volumes, 1961; The Bombing Offensive Against Germany: Outlines and Perspectives, 1965; Bomber Offensive: The Devastation of Europe, 1970; Prince Henry Duke of Gloucester, 1980; Witness of a Century Prince Arthur Duke of Connaught 1850-1942, 1993; Encyclopedia of Twentieth Century Warfare (General Editor and Contributor), 1989; Editor of 3 Volumes, Documents of International Affairs, 1955, 1956, 1957; The Politics and Strategy of the Second World War (Joint Editor), 9 volumes; The Manual of Air Force Law (Contributor), 1956; Decisive battles of the Twentieth century, Land Sea and Air (Contributor), 1976. Contributions: Encyclopedia Britannica; TLS; Times; Daily Telegraph; Observer; Military Journals. Honours: DFC, 1944; CBE, 1976; CB, 1983. Address: Thames House, Eynsham, Witney, Oxford OX8 1DA, England.

FRANKLIN John Hope, b. 2 Jan 1915, Rentiesville, Oklahoma, USA. Writer; University Professor. m. Aurelia E Whittington, 1940, 1 son. Education: AM, Fisk University; PhD, Harvard University. Appointments: Various teaching posts, 1936-64; Professor, American History, 1964-82, Chairman, History, 1967-70, John Matthews Manly Distinguished Service Professor, 1969-, University of Chicago, Illinois; Visiting Professor, various universities. Publications: Free Negro in North Carolina, 1943; From Slavery to Freedom: A History of Negro Americans, 6th Edition, 1987; Militant South, 1956; Reconstruction After the Civil War, 1961; The Emancipation Proclamation, 1963; Land

of the Free (with others), 1966; Illustrated History of Black Americans, 1970; A Southern Odyssey, 1976; Racial Equality in America, 1976; George Washington Williams: A Biography, 1985; The Color Line, 1993; Editor: Civil War Diary of James T Ayers, 1947; A Fool's Errand (Albion Tourgee), 1961; Army Life in a Black Regiment (Thomas Higginson), 1962; Color and Race, 1968; Reminiscences of an Active Life (John R Lynch), 1970. Address: Department of History, Duke University, Durham, NC 27707, USA.

FRANTZ Douglas, b. 29 Sept 1949, North Manchester, Indiana, USA. m. Catherine Ann Collins, 15 Oct 1983, 1 son, 2 daughters. Education: BA, DePauw University, 1971; MS, Columbia University, 1975. Appointments: City Editor, Albuquerque, New Mexico, 1975-78; Reporter, Chicago Tribune, Chicago, Illinois, 1978-87; Reporter, Los Angeles Times, Los Angeles, California, 1987-. Publications: Levine & Co: The Story of Wall Street's Insider Trading Scandal, 1987. Contributions to: Various magazines, including Esquire. Honours: Sigma Delta Chi Award, 1985 for financial reporting; Associated Press-Illinois Award, 1986 and Raymond Clapper Award, 1987, both for investigative reporting; Business Week named Levine & Co one of the best books in 1987. Literary Agent: Dominick Abel, New York. Address: c/o Dominick Abel, 498 West End Avenue, New York, NY 10024, USA.

FRANZKE Andreas, b. 27 Sept 1938, Breslau. Professor of Art History. m. Irmela Franzke, 1969, 1 s, 1 d. Education: University Marboug, Heidelberg, 1969. Appointments: Assistant Professor, 1969, Lecturer, 1972, Professor, 1980, Head of Art History Dept, 1982, President of Academy of Fine arts, Karlsruhe, 1988. Publications: Jean Dubuffet; Antoni Tapies; Christian Boltannski; Georg baselitz; Jean Dubuffet; Antoni Tapies; Skulpturen & Objekte. Contributions to: Pantheon; Das Kunstwerk; Tema Celste; DV. Address: Am Rueppurrer Schloss 3A, 76199 Karlsruhe H, Germany.

FRAPPELL Ruth Meredith, (Ruth Teale), b. 8 Mar 1942, Bathurst, NSW, Australia. Academic; Freelance Writer. m. Leighton Frappell, 15 Aug 1970, 1 son, 2 daughters. Education: BA, 1963; L.Mus.A, Australian Music Exam Board, 1964; MA, 1968; PhD, University of Sydney, 1992. Literary Appointments: Writer, Australian Dictionary of Biography, 1968-; Editor, Journal Royal Australian Historical Society, 1994-. Publications: Thomas Brisbane, 1971; Colonial Eve, 1979. Contributions to: Australian Dictionary of Biography; Journal of Religious History; Journal of Ecclesiastical History; Journal of Royal Australian Historical Society. Honours: Australia Council Literature Board, 1980. Memberships: Life Member, Councillor, Royal Australian Historical Society; Association for Journal of Religious History; President, Macquarie University Library Friends; Australian Historical Association. Address: 22 Ingalara Avenue, Wahroonga 2076, Australia.

FRASER Antonia (Lady), b. 27 Aug 1932, London, England. Author. m. 1) Hugh Fraser, 1956 (div 1977), 3 sons, 3 daughters, 2) Harold Pinter, 1980. Education: MA, Lady Margaret Hall, Oxford, England. Publications: King Arthur, 1954; Robin Hood, 1955; Dolls, 1963; History of Toys 1966; Mary Queen of Scot, 1973; Cromwell: Our Chief of Men, 1973; King James VI and I, 1974; Scottish Love Poems, A Personal Anthology, 1974; Kings and Queens of England, editor, 1975; Love Letters, anthology, 1976; Quiet as a Nun, 1977; The Wild Island, 1978; King Charles II, 1979; Heroies and Heroines, editor, 1980; A Splash of Red, 1981; Cool Repentance, 1982; Oxford in verse, editor, 1982; The Weaker Vessel, 1984; Oxford Blood, 1985; The Warrior Queens, 1989; TV adaptations Quiet as a Nun, 1978; Jemima Shore Investigates, 1983; TV Plays: Charades, 1977; Mister Clay, 1985. Honours: James Tait Black Memorial Prize; Wolfson History Prize; Hon DLitt, Hull, 1986. Memberships: Committee, English PEN, 1979-; Crimewriters Association. Address: c/o Curtis Brown Ltd, 1 Craven Hill, London W2 3EP, England.

FRASER George MacDonald, b. 1925, United Kingdom. Author; Journalist. Appointments: Deputy Editor, Glasgow Herald newspaper, 1964-69. Publications: Flashman, 1969; Royal Flash, 1970, screenplay 1975; The General Danced at Dawn, 1970; Flash for Freedom, 1971; Steel Bonnets, 1971; Flashman at the Charge, 1973; The Three Musketeers, screenplay, 1973; The Four Musketeers, screenplay, 1974; McAuslan in the Rough, 1974; Flashman in the Great Game, 1975; The Prince and the Pauper, screenplay, 1976; Flashman's Lady, 1977; Mr American, 1980; Flashman and the Redskins, 1982; Octopussy, screenplay, 1983; The Pyrates, 1983; Flashman and the Dragon, 1985; Casanova, TV screenplay, 1987; The Hollywood History of the World, 1988; The Sheikh and the Dustbin, 1988; The Return of the Musketeers, screenplay, 1989; Flashman and the Mountain of the Light, 1990. Address: Baldrine, Isle of Man, United Kingdom.

FRASER Jane. See: **PILCHER Rosamunde.**

FRASER Sylvia Lois, b. 8 Mar 1935, Hamilton, Ontario, Canada. Author; Novelist; Journalist. Education: BA, University of Western Ontario, 1957. Appointments: Guest Lecturer, Banff Centre, 1973-79, 1985, 1987, 1988; Arts Advisory Panel to Canada Council, 1978-81; Writer in Residence, University of Western Ontario, 1980; Member, Canadian Cultural Delegation to China, 1985; Instructor, University of New Brunswick, 1986. Publications: The Book of Strange; My Father's House; Berlin Solstice; The Candy Factory; Pandora; A Casual Affair; The Emperor's Virgin. Contributions to: Feature writer, Toronto Star Weekly Magazine. Honours: Women's Press Club Award; President's Medal for Canadian Journalism; Non-Fiction Book Award, Canadian Authors Association. Memberships: Writers Development Trust; PEN; ACTRA. Literary Agent: Sterling Lord Literistic, 1 Madison Avenue, New York, NY 10010, USA. Address: 701 King Street West 302, Toronto, Ontario, Canada M5V 2W7.

FRATTI Mario, b. 5 July 1927, L'Aquila, Italy. US Citizen, 1974. Playwright; Educator. 3 children. Education includes: PhD, Ca Foscari University, 1951. Appointments: Teacher, Adelphi College, USA, 1964-65; Faculty, Columbia University, New York City, 1965-66; Professor of Literature, New School, Hunter College, New York City, 1967-; Faculty, Hofstra University, 1973-74; Drama Critic: Paese, 1963-; Progresso, 1963-; Ridotto, 1963-; Ora Zero, 1963-. Publications: Plays: Cage-Suicide, 1964; Academy-Return, 1967; Mafia, 1971; Bridge, 1971; Races, 1972; Eleven Plays in Spanish, 1977; Refrigerators, 1977; Eleonora Duse-Victim, 1981; Nine, 1982; Biography of Fratti, 1982; AIDS, 1987; VCR, 1988, Encounter, musical, 1989; Family, 1990; Friends, 1991; Lovers, 1992; Leningrad Euthanasia, 1993; Holy Father, 1994. Honours: Tony Award for Nine; Other awards for plays and musicals. Memberships: Drama Desk; American Theatre Critics; Outer Critics Circle, Vice-President. Literary Agent: Susan Schulman, 454 W 44th Street, New York City, NY 10036, USA. Address: 145 W 55th Street, Apt 15D, New York, NY 10019-5355, USA.

FRAYN Michael, b. 3 Sept 1933, London, England. Author; Journalist. Education: BA, Emmanuel College, Cambridge University. Publications: Novels: The Tin Men, 1966; The Russian Interpreter, 1967; Towards the End of the Morning, 1969; A Very Private Life, 1968; Sweet Dreams, 1973; Philosophy: Constructions, 1974; Plays: The Two of Us, 1970; Alphabetical Order and Donkeys Years, 1977; Clouds, 1977; Make and Break, 1980; Noises Off, 1982; Benefactors, 1984; Translations: Chekhov: The Cherry Orchard, 1978; Tolstoy: The Fruits of Enlightenment, 1979; Chekhov: Three Sisters, 1983, Wild Honey, 1984; The Seagull, 1987; Balmoral, 1987; Uncle Vanya, 1989; The Sneeze, 1989; The Trick of It (novel), 1989; A Landing on the Sun (novel), 1991; Now You Know (novel), 1992; Here, 1993; Stage Productions include: Make and Break, lyric, Hammersmith, 1990, Haymarket, 1980; Noises Off, lyric, Hammersmith, 1982, Savoy, 1982, Brooks, Atkinson, New York, 1983; Three Sisters, Royal Exchange, Manchester, 1985; Benefactors, Vaudeville, 1984; Brooks Atkinson, New York, 1985; Uncle Vanya, Vaudeville, 1988; The Sneeze, Aldwych, 1988; TV: Making Faces (6 plays for Eleanor Bron), 1975; Jerusalem, 1984; Screenplay: Clockwise, 1986. Honours: Somerset Maugham Award, 1966; Hawthornden Prize, 1967; National Press Award, 1970; 3 SWET/Olivier Awards; 4 Evening Standard Drama Awards; Sunday Express Book of the Year Award, 1991. Memberships: FRSL; Hon Fellow, Emmanuel College, Cambridge. Literary Agent: Elaine Green Limited; Plays: Fraser and Dunlop (Scripts) Ltd. Address: c/o Elaine Greene Limited, 31 Newington Green, London N16 9PU, England.

FRAZIER Arthur. See: **BULMER Henry Kenneth.**

FREBURGER William Joseph, b. 6 Oct 1940, Baltimore, Maryland, USA. Editor; Author. m. Mary Elizabeth Algeo, 23 Feb 1979, Missouri, 1 son. Education: BA, 1962, St Mary's Seminary, Baltimore, Maryland, USA; STL, 1966, Gregorian University, Rome, Italy. Appointments: Editor, Celebration: A Creative Worship Service, 1978-; Editor, Eucharistic, 1985-87. Publications: Repent and Believe, 1972; This is the Word of the Lord, 1974; Eucharistic Prayers for Children, 1976; The Forgiving Christ, 1977; Liturgy: Work of the People, 1984; Birthday Blessings, 1985. Contributions to: Numerous Theological

Journals including: National Catholic Reporter. Address: 11211 Monticello Avenue, Silverspring, MD 20902, USA.

FREEBORN Richard Harry, b. 19 Oct 1926, South Wales, University Professor (Retired). m. Anne Davis, 14 Feb 1954, 1 son, 3 daughters. Education: MA, PhD, Brasenose College, Oxford University. Appointments: Emeritus Professor of Russian Literature, University of London. Publications: Turgenev, The Novelist's Novelist: A Study, 1960; Two Ways of Life, 1962; The Emigration of Sergev Ivanovich, 1962; A Short History of Modern Russia, 1966; Turgenev: Sketches from a Hunter's Album, 1967; Turgenev: Home of the Gentry, 1970; The Rise of the Russian Novel, 1973; Turgenev: Rudin, 1975; Russian Roulette, 1979; The Ratzian Revolutionary, novel, 1982, p/b 1985; Turgenev: Love and Death, 1983; The Russian Crucifix, 1987; Turgenev: First Love and Other Stories, 1989; Ideology in Russian Literature (ed), 1990; Turgenev: Sketches from a Hunter's Album (ed), 1990; Turgenev: Fathers and Sons, 1991; Turgenev: A Month in the Country, 1991; Chekhov, The Steppe and Other Stories (ed), 1991; Goncharov, Oblomov (ed), 1992. Honour: DLit, University of London, 1984. Membership: Crime Writers Association. Literary Agent: Jon Thurley. Address: 24 Park Road, Surbiton, Surrey KT5 8QD, England.

FREEDMAN Lawrence. Publications: Arms Production in the United Kingdom, 1978; The West & The Modernization of China, 1979; Britain & Nuclear Weapons, 1980; Evolution of Nuclear Strategy, 1981; Atlas of Global Strategy, 1985; Price of Peace: Living with the Nuclear Dilemma, 1986; Britain & The Falklands War, 1988; Europe Transformed, 1990; Signals of War: The Falklands Conflict of 1982, 1991; Population Change & International Strategy (ed), 1992; War, Strategy & International Politics, 1992; The Gulf Conflict 1990-91, 1993; Military Intervention in Europe (ed), 1994; War (ed), 1994. Address: c/o Dept of War Studies, King's College London, The Strand, London, WC2R 2LS, England.

FREEDMAN Russell, b. 11 Oct 1929, San Francisco, California, USA. Children's Book Writer. Education: San Jose State University; BA, University of California at Berkeley. Publications include: Thomas Alva Edison, 1961; 2000 Years of Space Travel, 1963; Scouting with Baden Powell, 1967; The First Days of Life, 1974; How Animals Defend Their Young, 1978; Immigrant Kids, 1980; When Winter Comes, 1981; Dinosaurs & Their Young, 1983; Children of the Wild West, 1984; Lincoln: A Photobiography, 1985; Cowboys of the Wild West, 1985; Sharks, 1985; The First Fifty Years, 1985 (Adult); Indian Chiefs, 1987; The Wright Brothers, 1991; Eleanor Roosevelt, 1993. Contributions to: Columbia Encyclopedia (3rd ed); New Book of Knowledge Annual, 1981-; Cricket; Ranger Rick; other journals. Honours: Notable Book of the Year Citation, American Library Association, 1980, 1983, 1985; Western Heritage Award, 1984; Newberry Medal, 1988; Newberry Honour Citation, American Library Association, 1992; Boston Globe/Horn Book Award, 1994. Memberships: Authors League of America; American Civil Liberties Union. Address: 280 Riverside Drive, New York, NY 10025, USA.

FREELING Nicolas, b. 3 Mar 1927, London, England, Fiction Writer. m. Cornelia Termes, 1954, 4 sons, 1 daughter. Education: Univ of Dublin. Publications include: Author of 30 fiction books most recent including, The Widow, 1979; Castang's City, 1980; Wolfnight, 1982; No Part in Your Death, 1984; A City Solitary, 1985; Cold Iron, 1986; Lady Macbeth, 1988; Sand Castles, 1990; Those in Peril, 1990; The Flanders Sky, 1991; The Pretty How Town, 1992; You Who Know, 1993. Contributions to: Occasional essays and travel articles. Honours: Crimewriters Gold Dagger, London, 1963; Grand Prix de Roman Policier, Paris, 1965; Edgar Allan Poe Prize, New York, 1966. Literary Agent: Curtis Brown, London and New York. Address: 67130 Grandfontaine, France.

FREEMAN Anne Hobson, b. 19 Mar 1934, Richmond, Virginia, USA. Fiction Writer; Essayist. m. George Clemon Freeman Jr, 6 Dec 1958, 2 sons, 1 daughter. Education: AB, Bryn Mawr College, 1956; MA, University of Virginia, 1973. Appointments: Reporter, International News Service, Russia and Eastern Europe, 1957; Editor, Member's Bulletin, Virginia Museum of Fine Arts, 1958-63; Lecturer, English, University of Virginia, 1973-88. Publication: The Style of a Law Firm: Eight Gentlemen from Virginia, 1990; A Hand Well Played, The Life of Jim Wheat, Jr, 1994. Contributions to: Hugh, to Virginia Quarterly Review, 1985; The Girl Who Was No Kin to the Marshalls, to Best American Short Stories, 1982; Miss Julia and the Hurricane, to Mademoiselle Prize Stories; Articles and stories in various journals and magazines, 1951-75. Literary Agent: Virginia Barber. Address: 10 Paxton Road, Richmond, VA 23226, USA.

FREEMAN Gillian, (Von S Elizabeth, Elizabeth Von S), b. 5 Dec 1929, London, England. Writer. m. Edward Thorpe, 12 Sept 1955, 2 daughters. Education: BA, Honours, University of Reading, England, 1951. Publications: The Liberty Man, 1955; The Leather Boys, 1961; The Alabaster Egg, 1970; An Easter Egg Hunt, 1981; The Undergrowth of Literature, 1969; The Schoolgirl Ethic: The Life and Work of Angela Brazil, 1976; Fall of Innocence, 1956; Jack would be a Gentleman, 1959; The Campaign, 1963; The Leader, 1965; The Marriage Machine, 1975; Nazi Lady, 1979; The Story of Albert Einstein, 1960; An Easter Egg Hunt, 1981; As Elaine Jackson, Lovechild, 1984; Ballet Genius (with Edward Thorpe), 1988; Termination Rock, 1989. Contributions to: numerous journals & magazines; many original screenplays & adaptions; Ballet scenarios for Kenneth Macmillans' Mayerling and Isadora. Memberships: Writers Guild of Great Britain, Film Committee, Literature Panel, Arts Council. Literary Agent: Richard Scott Simon. Address: c/o Richard Scott Simon, 48 Doughty Street, London WC1N 2LP, England.

FREEMAN James M(ontague), b. 1 Dec 1936, Chicago, IL, USA. m. Education: BA, Northwestern Univ; MA, PhD, Harvard Univ. Publications: Scarcity & Opportunity in an Indian Village, 1977; Untouchable: An Indian Life Story, 1979; Hearts of Sorrow: Vietnamese-American Lives, 1989. Honour: American Book Award, 1990.

FREEMAN John, Rt Hon. b. 19 Feb 1915. Journalist; Diplomatist; Businessman. m. 1) Elizabeth Johnston, 1938, div 1948, 2) Margaret Kerr, 1948, dec 1957, 3) Catherine Dove, 1962, div 1976, 4) Judith Mitchell, 1976, 2 sons, 3 daughters, 1 adopted daughter. Education: Brasenose College, Oxford. Appointment: Advertising Consultant, 1937-40; Active service, North Africa, Italy and North-West Europe, 1940-45; MP, Labour, Watford, 1945-55; Financial Secretary to War Offic, 1946-47; Under Secretary of State for War, 1947-48; Parliamentary Secretary to Ministry of Supply, 1948-51; Deputy Editor, New Statesman, 1958-61, Editor 1961-65; British High Commissioner in India, 1965-68; Ambassador to USA, 1969-71; Chairman, London Weekend TV, 1971-84, CEO, 1971-76; Chairman and CEO, LWT Holdings, 1977-84; Visiting Professor, International Relations, University of California, Davis, 1985-90. Honours: Gold Medal, Royal Television Society, 1981; Trustee, Reuters, 1984-.

FREEMAN-GRENVILLE Greville Stewart Parker, b. 1918, United Kingdom. Historian; Honorary Fellow, University of York. Publications: The Medieval History of the Coast of Tanganyika, 1962; The East African Coast: Select Documents (editor and translator), 1962, 2nd edition 1975; The Muslim and Christian Calendars, 1963, 2nd edition, 1977; The French at Kilwa Island, 1965; Chronology of African History, 1973; Chronology of World Histoyr, 1975, 1978; A Modern Atlas of African History, 1976; The Queen's Lineage, 1977; Atlas of British History, 1979; The Mombasa Rising Against the Portuguese 1631, 1980; The Beauty of Cairo, 1981; Buzurg ibn Shahriyar: The Book of Wonders of India (c 953) (editor and translator), 1982; Emily Said-Ruete: Memoirs of An Arabian Princess (1888) (editor), 1982, 1993; The Beauty of Jerusalem and the Holy Places of the Gospels, 1982, 2nd edition 1987; The Stations of the Cross, 1982; The Beauty of Rome, 1988; The Swahili Coast; Islam Christianity and Commerce in Eastern Africa, 1988; A New Atlas for African History, 1991; Historical Atlas of the Middle East, 1993. Address: North View House, Sheriff Hutton, York Y06 1PT, England.

FREEMANTLE Brian Harry, b. 10 June 1936, Southampton, England. Author. m. Maureen Hazel Tipney, 8 Dec 1956, 3 daughters. Publications: 33 books in total, 9 books in Charlie Muffin series, including, Comrade Charlie, 1989; KGB, 1983; Cia, 1984. Contributions to: Articles on espionage in London Daily Mail. Honours: Nominated Mystery Writer of America, 1987; Edgar Allan Foe Award. Membership: Mystery Writers of America. Literary Agent: Jonathon Clowes Ltd. Address: 4 Great Minster Street, Winchester, Hampshire SO23 9HA, England.

FREESE Mathias Balogh, b. 23 July 1940, USA. Teacher; Psychotherapist; Writer. m. 15 Feb 1970, 1 son, 2 daughters. Education: BA, 1962, MS, 1966, Queens College; MSW, State University of New York, 1978. Publications: Short stories. Contributions to: Showcase, the Stony Brook Magazine of Fiction; Taboo Magazine; Pig Iron Press; Jewish Currents. Honours: Listed in Distinguished Short Stories of 1974; Awardee, John Warkentin Essay Contest. Address: 9050 Union Turnpike, Glendale, NY 11385, USA.

FRENCH David, b. 18 Jan 1939, Coleys Point, Newfoundland, Canada. m. Leslie Gray, 5 Jan 1978. Playwright. Education: Studied Acting, Pasadena Playhouse, Toronto, Canada; Roy Lawler Acting School, Toronto, Canada. Publications: A Company of Strangers (novel), 1968; Leaving Home, 1972; Of the Fields, Lately, 1973; One Crack Out, 1976; The Seagull, by Anton Chekov, translation, 1978; Jitters, 1980; Salt-Water Moon, 1985; "1949", 1989. Contributions to: Montrealer; Canadian Boy. Honours: Chalmers Award, Best Canadian Play, Ontario Arts Council, 1973; Lieutenant Governors Award, 1974; Canada Council Grants, 1974, 1975. Address: c/o Tarragon Theatre, 30 Bridgman Avenue, Toronto, Ontario M5R 1X3, Canada.

FRENCH Fiona, b. 1944, United Kingdom. Children's Fiction Writer; Illustrator. Publications: Jack of Hearts, 1970; Huni, 1971; The Blue Bird, 1972; King Tree, 1973; City of Gold, 1975; Aio the Rainmaker, 1975; Matteo, 1976; Hunt the Thimble, 1978; Oscar Wilde's Star Child, 1979; The Princess and the Musician, 1981; John Barley Corn, 1982; Future Story, 1983; Fat Cat, 1984; Going to Squintums, 1985; Maid of the Wood, 1985; Snow White in New York, 1986; Song of the Nightingale, 1986; Cinderella, 1987; Rise Shine! 1989; The Magic Vase, 1990. Address: Flat B, 70 Colney Hatch Lane, London N10 1EA, England.

FRENCH Philip (Neville), b. 1933, United Kingdom. Radio Producer; Film Critic. Appointments: Senior Talks and Documentary Producer, BBC Radio, London, 1959-1990; Film Critic, The Observer, London, 1978-. Publications: The Age of Austerity 1945-51 (co-editor), 1963; The Novelist as Innovator (editor), 1966; The Movie Moguls, 1969; Westerns, 1974, 2nd edition, 1977; Three Honest Men: Portraits of Edmund Wilson, F R Leavis, and Lionel Trilling, 1980; The Third Dimension: Voices from Radio 3 (editor), 1983; (ed) Malle on Malle, 1992. Contributions to: Numerous articles and essays in magazines, newspapers and anthologies. Address: 62 Dartmouth Park Road, London NW5 1SN, England.

FRENCH Warren Graham, b. 26 Jan 1922, Philadelphia, Pennsylvania, USA. Retired College Professor. Education: BA, University of Pennsylvania, Philadelphia, USA, 1943; MA 1948, PhD, American Literature 1954, University of Texas. Publications: John Steinbeck, 1961, revised 1974; Frank Norris, 1962; J D Salinger, 1963; The Social Novel at the End of an Era, 1966; Jack Kerouac, 1986; J D Salinger, Revisited, 1988; The San Francisco Poetry Renaissance, 1955-1960, 1991; Editor: The South in Film, 1981; The Thirties, 1967; The Forties, 1969; The Fifties, 1971; The Twenties, 1975. Contributions to: Numerous American Academic Journals. Honour: DHL, Ohio University, 1985. Memberships: President, International John Steinbeck Society; Editorial Board, American Literature; Modern Language Association of America; American Studies Association; Western American Literature Association. Address: 23 Beechwood Road, Uplands, Swansea, West Glamorgan SA2 0HL, Wales.

FREWER Glyn Mervyn Louis, (Mervyn Lewis), b. 4 Sept 1931, Oxford, England. m. Lorna Townsend, 11 Aug 1956, 2 sons, 1 daughter. Education: St Catherine's College, Oxford, 1952-55, MA English Language and Literature. Appointments: Advertising Agency Associate Director, 1974-85 (retired); Proprietor antiquarian/secondhand bookshop, 1985; Author, scriptwriter. Publications include: The Hitch-Hikers (BBC Radio Play), 1957; Adventure in Forgotten Valley, 1962; Adventure in the Barren Lands, 1964; The Last of the Wispies, 1965; Death of Gold (as Mervyn Lewis), 1970; The Tokens of Elkin, 1970; Crossroad, 1970; The Square Peg, 1972; The Raid, 1976; The Trackers, 1976; Tyto: the Odyssey of an Owl, 1978; Bryn of Brockle Hanger, 1980; Fox, 1984; The Call of the Raven, 1987; also scripts for children's TV series, industrial films etc. Contributions to: Birds; Imagery. Honour: Adventure in Forgotten Valley was Junior Literary Guild of America choice in 1964; Made a Freeman of the City of Oxford, 1967. Literary Agent: Watson, Little Ltd. Address: Cottage Farm, Taston, Oxford, OX7 3JN.

FRIEDBERG Maurice, b. 1929, USA. Professor of Slavic Languages and Literatures. Appointments: Associate Professor of Russian, Chairman of Russian Division, Hunter College, City University of New York, 1955-65; Fulbright Professor of Russian Literature, Hebrew University, Jerusalem, Israel, 1965-66; Professor of Slavic Languages and Literatures, 1966-75, Director, Russian and East European Institute, 1967-71, Indiana University, Bloomington, USA;

Professor of Slavic Languages and Literatures, Department Head, University of Illinois, Urbana, 1975-; Directeur d'Etudes Associés, Ecole des Hautes Etudes en Sciences Sociales, Paris, France, 1984-85. Publications: Russian Classics in Soviet Jackets, 1962; A Bilingual Edition of Russian Short Stories, volume II (edited and translated with R A Maguire), 1965, 1966; The Jew in Post Stalin Soviet Literature, 1970; Encyclopedia Judaica (editor, co-author), 16 volumes, 1971-72; The Young Lenin, by Leon Trotsky (editor), 1972; A Decade of Euphoria: Western Literature in Post-Stalin Russia, 1977; Russian Culture in the 1980's, 1986; Soviet Society under Gorbachev (edited with Heyward Isham), 1987; The Red Pencil (edited with Marianna Tax Choldin), 1989; How Things Were Done In Odessa, 1991. Honours include: Two Guggenheim Fellowships; National Endowment for the Humanities Fellowship. Address: 3001 Meadowbrook Court, Champaign, IL 61821, USA.

FRIEDEN Bernard J, b. 1930, USA. Professor of Urban Planning. Appointments: Editor, Journal of the American Institute of Planners, 1962-65; Director, Massachusetts Institute of Technology-Harvard Joint Center for Urban Studies, 1971-75; Chairman, Faculty, 1987-89, Ford Professor of Urban Development, 1989-, Associate Dean of Architecture and Planning, 1993-. Massachusetts Institute of Technology. Publications: The Future of Old Neighborhoods, 1964; Urban Planning and Social Policy (edited with R Morris), 1968; Shaping an Urban Future (edited with W Nash), 1969; The Politics of Neglect (with M Kaplan), 1975, 2nd Edition, 1977; Managing Human Services (edited with W Anderson and M Murphy), 1977; The Environmental Protection Hustle, 1979; Downtown, Inc (with L Sagalyn), 1989. Address: 245 Highland Avenue, West Newton, MA 02165, USA.

FRIEDMAN Alan Howard, b. 4 Jan 1928, New York City, USA. Writer. m. 1) Lenore Ann Helman, 1 Aug 1950, divorced, 1 son, 2) Kate Miler Gilbert, 30 Oct 1977, 1 son. Education: BA, Harvard College, 1949; MA, Columbia University, 1950; PhD, University of California, Berkeley, 1964. Publications: The Turn of the Novel, 1966; Hermaphrodeity: The Autobiography of a Poet (novel, National Book Award Nominee), 1972. Contributions to: (Stories) Hudson Review; Mademoiselle; Partisan Review; New American Review; Paris Review; Fiction International; Kansas Quarterly; Denver Quarterly; Other Voices; Raritan; Formations; Articles, Chapters and Reviews; The Stream of Conscience, Hudson Review, Winter, 1964-65; The Other Lawrence, Partisan Review No 2 1970; The Novel, The Twentieth Century Mind, edited by C B Cox and A E Dyson, 1972; Reviews in New York Times Book Review; The Little Magazine (Poems) Partisan Review; Raritan; Denver Quarterly; Another Chicago Magazine. Honours: D H Lawrence Fellowship, 1974; National Endowment in the Arts Award, 1975; Pen Syndicated Fiction Award, 1987; Illinois Arts Council Award, 1992. Memberships: American PEN; Executive Board, PEN Midwest. Literary Agent: Lynn Nesbit, New York City. Address: 2406 Park Place, Evanston, IL 60201, USA.

FRIEDMAN Bruce Jay, b. 1930, USA. Writer. Appointments: Editorial Director, Magazine Management Co, Publishers, New York City, 1953-64. Publications: Stern, 1962; Far from the City of Class and Other Stories, 1963; A Mother's Kisses, 1964; Black Humor (editor), 1965; Pat O'Brian Movies, 1966; Black Angels, 1966; Scuba Duba: A Tense Comedy, 1967; Steambath, play, 1970; The Dick, 1970; About Harry Towns, 1975; The Lonely Guy's Book of Life, 1979; Let's Hear It for a Beautiful Guy, 1984; Tokyo Woes, 1985; The Current Climate, 1989. Address: PO Box 746, Water Mill, NY 11976, USA.

FRIEDMAN Dennis, b. 23 Feb 1924, London, England. Psychiatrist. m. Rosemary Tibber, 2 Feb 1949, 4 daughters. Education: MRCS, LRCP, London, 1948; MRCPsych, 1972; FRCPsych, 1978. Publications: Chapter in Progress in Behaviour Therapy, 1968; Chapters in Handbook of Sexology, 1977; Chapter in Sex Therapy, 1988; Inheritance: A Psychological History of The Royal Family, 1993. Contributions to: Behaviour Research and Therapy, 1968; Psychiatry, 1972; British Journal of Psychiatry; British Journal of Sexual Medicine. Memberships: Royal Society of Medicine. Address: 2 St Katharine's Precinct, Regent's Park, London NW1 4HH, England.

FRIEDMAN (Eve) Rosemary (Robert Tibber, Rosemary Tibber), b. 5 Feb 1929, London, England. Writer. m. Dennis Friedman, 2 Feb 1949, 4 daughters. Education: Queen's College, Harley Street, London; Law faculty, University College, London University. Publications: An Eligible Man, 1989; To Live in Peace, 1987; A Second Wife, 1986; Rose of Jericho, 1984; A Loving Mistress, 1983; Proofs of

Affection, 1982; The Long Hot Summer, 1980; The Life Situation, 1977; Juvenile: Aristide, Aristide in Paris, 1987; as Robert Tibber: Practice Makes Perfect, 1969; The General Practice, 1967; The Commonplace Day, 1964; The Fraternity, 1963; Patients of a Saint, 1961; We All Fall Down, 1960; Love on My List, 1959; No White Coat, 1957; For Euston Films: Shrinks; For London Weekend Television: An Eligible Man (6 part series); BBC Film, Paris Summer, 1992; Play, Visitor From Seil, 1993. Contributor to: Reviewer: Times Literary Supplement; Articles: The Guardian; The Sunday Times. Memberships: Fellow, PEN; Council and Management Committee Member, Society of Authors. Address: 2 St Katharine's Precint, Regent's Park, London NW1 4HH, England.

FRIEDMAN Lawrence, b. 8 Oct 1940, OH, USA. Professor. m. Sharon Bloom, 3 Apr 1967, 1 daughter. Education: BA, 1962; MA, 1965, PhD, 1967, UCLA. Publications: Menninger: The Family & The Clinic, 1990; Gregarious Saints, 1982; Inventors of the Promised Land, 1975; The White Savage, 1970. Honours: Distinguished University Professor, 1991; OH Literary Association, 1983. Membership: Authors Guild. Literary Agent: Gerald McCauley. Address: Dept of History, IN University, Ballantine Hall Rm 742, Bloomington, IN 47405 6601, USA.

FRIEDMAN Lawrence M, b. 2 Apr 1930, IL, USA. Professor of Law. m. Leah Feigenbaum, 27 Mar 1955, 2 d. Education: AB, JD, LLM, University of Chicago; Hon Degrees, University of Puget Sound; John Jay College; University of Lund. Publications: Crime and Punishment in American History, 1993; A History of American Law, 1985; The Republic of Choice, 1990; Total Justice, 1985; The Legal System: A Social Science Perspective, 1975; Contract Law in America, 1965; Law & Society: An Introduction, 1977. Contributions to: Over 120. Honours: Coif Award, 1976; Hurst Prize, 1982; Harry Kalven Prize, 1992. Memberships: Am Academy of Arts & Science; Law Society Association; Am Society for Legal History. Literary Agent: Gerald McCauley. Address: Stanford Law School, Stanford, CA 94305, USA.

FRIEDMAN Milton, b. 31 July 1912, Brooklyn, New York, USA. Economist. m. Rose Director, 25 June 1938, 1 son, 1 daughter. Education: BA, Rutgers University, 1932; AM, University of Chicago, 1933; PhD, Columbia University, 1946. Literary Appointments: Board of Editors: American Economic Review, 1951-53; Econometrica, 1957-69; Columnist, 1966-84, Contributing Editor, 1974-84, Newsweek; Advisory Board, Journal of Money, Credit and Banking, 1968-94. Publications: Income From Independent Professional Practice (with Simon Kuzbets), 1946; Sampling Inspection (with H A Freeman and others), 1948; Essays in Positive Economics, 1953; A Theory of the Consumption Function, 1957; A Program for Monetary Stability, 1960; Capitalism and Freedom, 1962; A Monetary History of the United States (with A J Schwartz), 1963; Dollars and Deficits, 1968; Monetary Statistics of the United States (with A J Schwartz), 1970; Price Theory, 1976; Free To Choose (with Rose Friedman), 1980; Tyranny of the Status Quo (with Rose Friedman), 1984; Money Mischief, 1992. Contributions to: Numerous magazines and journals. Honours: John Bates Clark Medallist, American Economics Association, 1951; Chicagoan of the Year, Chicago Press Club, 1972; Educator of the Year, Chicago Jewish United Fund, 1973; Nobel Prize for Economic Science, 1976; Tuck Media Award for Economic Understanding, 1980; National Medal of Science, 1988; Presidential Medal of Freedom, 1988; Numerous honorary degrees. Address: Hoover Institution, Stanford, CA 94305, USA.

FRIEDMAN Thomas, b. 1953, Minneapolis, Minnesota, USA. Journalist. m. Ann, 2 daughters. Education: BA, Brandeis University; MPhil, Oxford University. Career: Middle East Correspondent, 1979-88; Diplomatic Correspondent, New York Times, 1989-. Publication: From Beirut to Jerusalem, 1988. Honours: Overseas Press Club Award, 1980; George Polk Award, 1982; Livingston Award, 1982; Pulitzer Prizes for Journalism, 1983, 1988; New York Newspaper Guild Page One Award, 1984; New Israel Fund Award, 1987. Address: New York Times Washington Bureau, 16271 Street NW, Washington, DC 20006, USA.

FRIEL Brian, b. 9 Jan 1929, Killyclogher, County Tyrone. Writer. m. Anne Morrison, 1954, 1 son, 4 daughters. Education: St Columb's College, Derry; St Patrick's College, Maynooth; St Joseph's Training College, Belfast. Appointments: Taught in various schools, 1950-60; Writer, 1960-. Publications: Collected Stories: The Saucer of Larks, 1962; The Gold in the Sea, 1966; Plays: Philadelphia Here I Come! 1965; The Loves of Cass McGuire, 1967; Lovers, 1968; The Mundy Scheme, 1969; Crystal and Fox, 1970; The Gentle Island, 1971; The Freedom of the City, 1973; Volunteers, 1975; Living Quarters, 1976;

Aristocrats, 1979; Faith Healer, 1979; Translations, 1981; Three Sisters, translation, 1981; The Communication Cord, 1983; Fathers and Sons, 1987; Making History, 1988; Dancing at Lughnara, 1990; The London Vertigo, adaptation of a play by Charles Macklin, 1992; A Month in the Country, adaptation of Turgenev, 1992. Honours: Honorary DLitt, NUI, 1983; Ewart Biggs Memorial Prize, British Theatre Association Award. Address: Drumaweir House, Greencastle, Co Donegal, Ireland.

FRITH David Edward John, b. 16 Mar 1937, London, England. Cricket-Writer. m. 11 May 1957, 2 sons, 1 daughter. Education: Canterbury High School, Sydney, 1949-53. Appointments: Editor, The Cricketer, 1973-78; Editor, Wisden Cricket Monthly, 1979-. Publications: England v Australia Pictorial History, 1977; The Fast Men, 1975; The Slow Men, 1984; The Golden Age of Cricket 1890-1914, 1978; The Archie Jackson Story, 1974; A E Stoddart Biography, 1970; Pageant of Cricket, 1987; The Ashes '77, 1977; The Ashes '79, 1979; Runs in the Family, 1969; Cricket's Golden Summer, 1985; Jeff Thomson Biography, 1980; England v Australia Test Match Records, 1986; Cricket Gallery, editor, 1976; By His Own Hand, 1991. Contributions to: Australian Cricket; Cricket Society Journal; Cricketer, Australia; Sportsworld, India; Observer Colour Supplement; Benefit Booklets. Honours: Cricket Society of Jubilee Literary Award, 1970, 1987; Cricket Writer of the Year, Wombwell Cricket-Lovers Society, 1984; British Magazine Sportswriter of the Year, 1988. Memberships: Committee Member, Cricket Writers Club, 1977-; Cricket Society; Association of Cricket Statisticians. Address: 6 Beech Lane, Guildford, Surrey GU2 5ES, England.

FRITZ Jean, b. 16 Nov 1915, Hankow, China. Writer. m. Michael Fritz, 1 Nov 1941, 1 son, 1 daughter. Education: BA, Wheaton College, Norton, Massachusetts. 1937. Publications: The Cabin Faced West, 1957; And Then What Happened, Paul Revere, 1973; Stonewall, 1979; Homesick: My Own Story, 1982; The Double Life of Pocahontas, 1983; The Great Little Madison, 1989; Bully for You, Teddy Roosevelt, 1991. Contributions to: The New Yorker; Redbook; The New York Times; The Washington Post; Seventeen; The Horn Book; Children's Literature in Education. Address: 50 Bellewood Avenue, Dobbs Ferry, NY 10522, USA.

FRITZ Walter Helmut, b. 26 Aug 1929. Writer. Education: Literature & Philosophy, University of Heidelberg. Publications: Achtsam sein, 1956; Veranderte Jahre, 1963; Umwege, 1964; Zwischenbemerkungen, 1965; Abweichung, 1965; Die Zuverlassigkeit der Unruhe, 1966; Bemerkungen zu einer Gegend, 1969; Die Verwechslung, 1970; Aus der Nahe, 1972; Die Beschaffenheit solcher Tage, 1972; Bevor uns Horen und Sehen Vergeht, 1975; Schwierige Uberfahrt, 1976; Auch Jet und morgen, 1979; Gesammelte Gedichte, 1979; Wunschtraum alptraum, 1981; Werkzeuge der Freiheit, 1983; Cornelias Traum und andere Aufzeichnungen, 1985; Immer einfacher, immer schwieriger, 1987; Zeit des Sehens, 1989; Die Schlüssel sind vertauscht, 1992; Gesammelte Gedichte 1979-1994, 1994. Contributions include: Neue Rundschau; Neue Deutsche Hefte; frankfurter Hefte; Jahresring; Ensemble. Honours: Literature Prize, City of Karlsruhe, 1960; Prize, Bavarian Academy of Fine Arts, 1962; heine-Taler, Lyrik Prize, 1966; Prize, Culture Circle, Federation of German Industry, 1971; Stuttgarter Literaturpreis, 1986. Memberships: German Academy for Speech & Poetry; Academy for Sciences & Literature; Bavarian Academy of Fine Arts; PEN; Union of German Writers. Address: Kolbergerstr 2a, 75 Karlsruhe 1, Germany.

FROMMER Harvey, b. 10 Oct 1937, Brooklyn, New York, USA. Professor; Author. m. Myrna Katz, 23 Jan 1960, 2 sons, 1 daughter. Education: BS, Journalism, MA, English, PhD, Communications, New York University. Appointments: Professor, Writing, Speech, New York City Technical College, City University of New York, 1970-; Visiting Professor: Liberal Studies, Dartmouth College, Hanover, New Hampshire, 1992, 1994, Graduate Liberal Studies, Wesleyan University, Middleton, Connecticut, 1994; Reviewer: Yankees Magazine, Library Journal, Choice, Kliatt Paperback Book Guide, Dodger Blue; Frequent Lecturer. Publications include: Growing Up At Bat: 50 Years of Little League Baseball, 1989; Running Tough: The Autobiography of Tony Dorsett, 1989, 1992; Throwing Heat: The Autobiography of Nolan Ryan, 1989; It Happened in the Catskills: An oral history of the Catskill resorts (with Myrna Katz Frommer), 1990; Behind the Lines: The Autobiography of Don Strock, 1991; Holzman On Hoops, 1991; Shoeless Joe and Ragtime Baseball, 1992, Paperback, 1993; Big Apple Baseball, 1995; It Happened in Brooklyn: An oral history of growing up in the borough in the 1940s, 1950s and 1960s,

1993; Growing Up Jewish in America, 1995. Literary Agent: Don Congdon Associates Inc, 156 Fifth Avenue, Suite 625, New York, NY 10010-7002, USA. Address: 791 Oakleigh Road, North Woodmere, NY 11581, USA.

FROST David Paradine, Sir, b. 7 Apr 1939, Beccles, Suffolk, England. TV Personality; Writer. m. (1) Lynne Frederick, 1981, divorced 1982, (2) Lady Carina Fitzalan Howard, 1983, 2 sons. Education: Gonville and Caius College, Cambridge. Publications: That Was The Week That Was; How to Live under Labour; Talking with Frost; To England with Love (with Antony Jay); The Americans; Whitlam and Frost; I Gave them a Sword; I Could Have Kicked Myself, 1982; Who wants to Be a Millionaire? 1983; The Mid-Atlantic Companion (jointly), 1986; The Rich Tide (jointly), 1986; The World's Shortest Books, 1987; TV Programme: Through the Keyhole. Honours: Golden Rose Award, Montreux, 1967; OBE; Richard Dimbleby Award, 1967; Emmy Award, 1970, 1971; Religious Heritage of American Award, 1970; Alber Einstein Award, 1971. Address: David Paradine Ltd, 115-123 Bayham Street, London NW1 0AG, England.

FROST Jason. See: OBSTFELD Raymond.

FRUMKIN Gene, b. 29 Jan 1928, New York City, New York, USA. Poet; Professor. m. Lydia Samuels, 3 July 1955, 1 son, 1 daughter. Education: BA, English, University of California, Los Angeles. Appointments: Professor, University of New Mexico; Editor, Coastlines Literary Magazine, 1958-62; Guest Editor, New Mexico Quarterly, 1969; Visiting Professor, Modern Literature, State University of New York, Buffalo, 1975; Co-Editor, San Marcos Review, 1978-83; Writer-in-Residence, spring 1989, Exchange Professor, 1980-81, 1984-85, University of Hawaii. Publications: Hawk and the Lizard, 1963; Orange Tree, 1965; Rainbow-Walker, 1969; Dosteovsky and Other Nature Poems, 1972; Locust Cry: Poems 1958-65, 1973; Mystic Writing-Pad, 1977; Indian Rio Grande: Recent Poems from 3 Cultures (co-editor), anthology, 1977; Clouds and Red Earth, 1982; Lover's Quarrel With America, 1985; Sweetness in the Air, 1987; Comma in the Ear, 1991; Saturn Is Mostly Weather, 1992. Contributions to: Paris Review; Prairie Schooner; Yankee; Conjunctions; Sulfur; Poetry; Saturday Review; Nation; Evergreen Review; Dacotah Territory; Malahat Review; Minnesota Review; Others. Honours include: 1st Prize for Poetry, Yankee magazine, 1979. Memberships: Past President, Rio Grande Writers Association; Hawaii Literary Arts Council; PEN West. Address: 3721 Mesa Verde NE, Albuquerque, NM 87110, USA.

FRY Christopher, b. 18 Dec 1907. Dramatist. m. Phyllis Marjorie Hart, 1936, dec 1987, 1 son. Education: Bedford Modern School; Actor at Citizen House, Bath, 1927. Publications: The Boy with a Cart, 1939; The Firstborn, 1946; A Phoenix too Frequent, 1946; The Lady's Not for Burning, 1949; Thor, with Angels, 1949; Venus Observed, 1950, revised 1992; Translation: Ring Round the Moon, 1950; A Sleep of Prisoners, 1951; The Dark is Light Enough, 1954; The Lark, 1955; Tiger at the Gates, 1955; Duel of Angels, 1958; Curtmantle, 1961; Judith, 1962; A Yard of Sun, 1970; Peer Gynt, 1970; Television Plays: The Brontes at Haworth, 1973; Sister Dora, 1977; The Best of Enemies, 1977; Cyrano de Bergerac, 1975 (translation); Can You Find Me: A Family History, 1978; Editor and Introduction Charlie Hammond's Sketch Book, 1980; Selected Plays, 1985; Genius, Talent and Failure, 1986 (Adam Lecture); One Thing More of Caedmon Construed, 1987; Looking for a Language (Lecture); A Journey into the Light, 1992; Films: The Queen is Crowned, 1953; The Beggar's Opera, 1953; Ben Hur, 1958; Barabbas, 1960; The Bible: In the Beginning, 1962. Honours: FRSL; Honorary Fellow, Manchester Metropolitan University, 1988; DLitt, Lambeth, 1988; Queen's Gold Medal for Poetry, 1962. Membership: Garrick Club. Address: The Toft, East Dean, Chichester, West Sussex PO18 0JA, England.

FRY Paul Harrison, b. 28 Oct 1944, New York, USA. Professor. m. Brigitte Peucker, 24 Aug 1974, 1 son. Education: BA, University of California, 1965; PhD, Harvard University, 1973. Appointments: Assistant Professor, Yale University, 1972; Associate Professor, 1979; Professor, 1983; William Lampson Professor, 1993. Publications: The Poet's Calling in the English Ode; The Reach of Criticism; William Empson: Prophet Against Sacrifice. Contributions to: Numerous articles. Honours: Melville Caine Award; Best Essay Award. Memberships: Modern Language Association. Address: 509 Boston Post Road, Madison, CT 06443, USA.

FRYE Roland Mushat, b. 3 July 1921, Birmingham, Alabama, USA. Literary and Theological Scholar. m. Jean Elbert Steiner, 11 Jan

1947, 1 son. Education: AB, 1943, PhD, 1952, Princeton University; Special student, Theology, Princeton Theological Seminary, 1950-52. Appointments: Emory University , 1952-61; Folger Shakespeare Library, 1961-65; Faculty, 1965-83, Emeritus Professor, 1983-, National Phi Beta Kappa Visiting Scholar, 1985-86, University of Pennsylvania; L P Stone Foundation Lecturer, Princeton Theological Seminary, 1959; Chairman, Center of Theological Inquiry, Princeton, New Jersey. Publications include: God, Man and Satan: Patterns of Christian Thought and Life, 1960; Shakespeare and Christian Doctrine, 1963; Shakespeare's Life and Times: A Pictorial Record, 1967; Milton's Imagery and the Visual Arts Iconographic Tradition in the Epic Poems, 1978; Is God a Creationist? The Religious Case Against Creation-Science, 1983; The Renaissance Hamlet Issues and Responses in 1600, 1984. Contributions to: The Dissidence of Dissent and the Origins of Religious Freedom in America: John Milton and the Puritans, to Proceedings of the American Philosophical Society, 1989; Numerous other articles in learned journals, literary and theological. Address: 226 West Valley Road, Strafford-Wayne, PA 19087, USA.

FRYER Jonathon, (G L Morton), b. 5 June 1950, Manchester, England. Writer; Broadcaster. Education: Diplome D'Etudes Francaises, Universite de Poitiers (France), 1967; BA Hons (Chinese with Japanese), University of Oxford, 1973; MA, University of Oxford, 1980. Appointment: Visiting Lecturer, School of Journalism, University of Nairobi, Kenya, 1976. Publications: The Great Wall of China, 1975; Isherwood, 1977; Brussels as Seen by Naif Artists (with Rona Dobson), 1979; Food for Thought, 1981; George Fox and the Children of the Light, 1991; Eye of the Camera, 1993; Numerous political pamphlets, mainly on Third World themes. Contributions to: The Economist; The Tablet; The European. Membership: Member of Executive, English PEN. Literary Agent: Jennifer Kavanagh, 39 Camden Park Road, London NW1 9AX, England. Address: 140 Bow Common Lane, London E3 4BH, England.

FUCHS Vivian Ernest (Sir), b. 11 Feb 1908, Freshwater, Isle of Wight. Geologist. m. (1) Joyce Connell, 6 Sept 1933 (dec 1990), 1 son, 2 daughters, (2) Eleanor Honnywill, 8 Aug 1991. Education: BA 1929, MA 1935, PhD 1936. Publications: The Crossing of Antarctica (with Hillary), 1958; Antarctic Adventure, 1959; Forces of Nature (editor), 1977; Of Ice and Men, 1982; A Time to Speak, 1990. Honour: Kt, 1958. Memberships: FRS, 1974; FRGS, Vice President, 1961, President 1982-84; British Association for the Advancement of Science, President 1972; International Giaciological Society, President 1963-66. Address: 106 Barton Road, Cambridge CB3 9LH, England.

FUENTES Carlos, b. 11 Nov 1928, Panama City, Republic of Panama. Writer. Mexican Ambassador to France; University Professor. m. Sylvia Lemus, 24 Jan 1973, 1 son, 2 daughters. Education: Law School, National University of Mexico; Institute de Hautes Etudes Internationales, Geneva, Switzerland. Appointments include: Simon Bolivar Professor, Cambridge, UK; Robert F Kennedy Professor, Harvard, USA; Teaching positions, Columbia, Princeton, Dartmouth College, Washington University, George Mason University, USA; Numerous lecturers, European & North American universities; Lecturer, El Colegio Nacional, Mexico; Mexican Ambassador to France, 1975-77. Publications: La Region Mas Transparente, 1958; La Muerte de Artemio Cruz, 1962; Cambio de Piel, 1967; Terra Nostra, 1975; Gringo Viejo, 1985; Cristobal Nonato, 1987; Also: Las Buenas Conciencias, 1959; Aura, 1962; Cantar de Ciegos, 1964; Zona Sagrada, 1967; Una Familia Lejana, 1980; Agua Quemada, 1983; Myself with Others, essays, 1987; Orchids in the Moonlight, play, 1987; The Campaign, novel, 1991; The Buried Mirror, essay, 1992. Contributions to: New York Times; Guardian; Le Monde; Nouvel Observateur; Washington Post; El Paris. Honours include: Biblioteca Breva Prize, Barcelona, 1967; Romulo Gallegos Prize, Caracas, 1975; Honorary doctorates, Harvard University 1983, Cambridge University 1987, Essex University 1987; National Prize for Literature, Mexico, 1984; Miguel de Cervantes Prize for Literature, Madrid, 1988; HDLL - Miami University, Georgetown University and Warwick University, 1992. Memberships: American Academy of Arts & Sciences; Trustee, New York Public Library. Literary Agent: Carl Brandt, Brandt & Brandt, 1501 Broadway, New York, NY 10036, USA.

FUGARD Athol Harold, b. 11 June 1932, Middelburg Cape, South Africa. Playwright. m. Sheila Meiring, 22 Sept 1956, 1 daughter. Appointments: Playwright; Director; Actor. Publications: Three Port Elizabeth Plays, 1974; Statements, three Plays, co-author, 1974; Sizwi Banzzi is Dead, and The Island, Co-author, 1976; Dimetos and Two Early Plays, 1977; Boesman and Lena and Other Plays, 1978; Tsotsi

(novel), 1980; A Lesson from Aloes, 1981; Master Harold and the Boys, 1982; The Road to Mecca, 1985; Notebooks 1960-1977, 1983; (Film Scripts), The Guest, 1977; Marigolds in August, 1981; My Children! My Africa! 1990; Playland, 1991. Honours: Numerous Prizes and Honorary Doctorates including: New York Drama Critics Circle Award for Best Play, 1980-81 Season; Evening Standard Award, Best Play of the Year, 1984. Memberships: Fellow, Royal Society of Literature; Fellow, Royal Society of Literature; Member, American Academy of Arts and Sciences. Address: PO Box 5090 Walmer, Port Elizabeth 6065, South Africa.

FULLER Jean Violet Overton, b. 7 Mar 1915, Iver Heath, Bucks. Author. Education: Brighton High School, 1927-31; Royal Academy of Dramatic Art, 1931-32; BA, University of London, 1944; University College of London, 1948-50. Publications include: Sickert and the Ripper Crimes, 1990; Dericourt The Chequered Spy, 1989; The Comte de Saint Germain, 1988; Blavatsky and Her Teachers, 1988; Cats and other Immortals, 1992. Honours: Writers Manifold Poems of the Decade, 1968. Membership: Society of Authors. Address: Fuller D'Arch Smith Limited, 37B New Cavendish Street, London, England.

FULLER John L, b. 1 Jan 1937, Ashford, Kent, England. Fellow, Magdalen College, Oxford. m. Cicely Prudence Martin, 20 July 1960, 3 daughters. Education: New College, Oxford, 1957-62; BA, BLitt, MA. Publications include: 12 collections of poetry, criticism, childrens books, 4 novels; Titles include: The Illusionists, 1980; Flying to Nowhere, 1983; Selected Poems 1954-82, 1985; Adventures of Speedfall, 1985; Partingtime Hall, with James Fenton, 1987; The Burning Boys, 1989; Took Twice, 1991; The Mechanical Body, 1991; The Worm and Star, 1993. Honours: Geoffrey Faber Memorial Prize, 1974; Southern Arts Prize, 1980; Whitbread Prize, 1983; Shortlisted, Booker Prize, 1983; Fellow, Royal Society of Literature. Literary Agent: Peters, Fraser & Dunlop. Address: 4 Benson Place, Oxford OX2 6QH, England.

FULLER Roy (Broadbent), b. 11 Feb 1912, Failsworth, Lancashire, England. Professor; Poet. Education: Qualified as Solicitor. Appointments: Professor of Poetry, Oxford University, 1968-73; Chairman of Literature Panel, Arts Council, 1976-77. Publications: Poems, 1939; The Middle of a War, 1942; A Lost Season, 1944; Collected Poems 1938-61, 1962; New Poems, 1968; Pergamon Poets I, 1968; Off Course, 1969; Penguin Modern Poets 18, 1970; To an Unknown Reader, 1970; Tiny Theatres, 1973; An Old War, 1974; Waiting for the Barbarians, 1974; From the Joke Shop, 1975; An Ill-Governed Coast, 1976; Re-treads, 1979; The Reign of Sparrows, 1980; House and Shop, 1982; As From the Thirties, 1983; Mianserin Sonnets, 1984; New and Collected Poems 1934-84, 1985; Subsequent to Summer, 1985; Outside the Canon, 1986; Consolations, 1987; Available for Dreams, 1989; Novels: With My Little Eye, 1948; The Second Curtain, 1953; Fantasy and Fugue, 1954; Image of a Society, 1956; The Ruined Boys, 1959; The Father's Comedy, 1961; The Perfect Fool, 1963; My Child, My Sister, 1965; The Carnal Island, 1970; Stories and verse for children. Honours: Duff Cooper Memorial Prize, 1968; CBE, 1970; Queen's Gold Medal, 1970; Heinemann Prize, 1990. Address: 37 Langron Way, Blackheath, London SE3, England.

FULLERTON Alexander Fergus, b. 20 Sept 1924, Saxmundham, Suffolk, England, Writer. m. Priscilla Mary Edelston, 10 May 1956, 3 sons. Education: Royal Naval College, Dartmouth, 1938-41; Cambridge University, School of Slavonic Studies, 1947. Appointments: Sales Manager, Wm Heinemann, 1959-61; Editorial Director, Peter Davies Limited, 1961-64; General Manager, Arrow Books, 1964-67. Publications: Surface! 1953; A Wren Called Smith, 1957; The White Men Sang, 1958; The Everard Series of Naval Novels: The Blooding of the Guns, 1976; Sixty Minutes for St George, 1977; Patrol to the Golden Horn, 1978; Storm Force to Narvik, 1979; Last Lift from Crete, 1980; All the Drowning Seas, 1981; A Share of Honour, 1982; The Torch Bearers, 1983; The Gatecrashers, 1984; Special Deception, 1988; Bloody Sunset, 1991; Look at the Wolves, 1982; Love for an Enemy, 1993; Not Thinking of Death, 1994. Literary Agent: John Johnson Limited. Address: c/o John Johnson Ltd, 45 Clerkenwell Green, London EC1R 0HT, England.

FULTON Robin, b. 6 May 1937, Arran, Scotland. Writer. Education: MA, Hons, 1959, PhD, 1972, Edinburgh; LittD. Appointments: Editor Literary Quarterly Lines Review, 1967-76. Publications: Poetry: Instances, 1967; Inventories, 1969; The Spaces Between the Stones, 1971; The Man with the Surbahar, 1971; Tree-Lines, 1974; Music and Flight, 1975; Between Flights, 1976; Places to Stay In, 1978; Following a Mirror, 1980; Selected Poems,

1963-78, 1980; Fields of Focus, 1982; Coming Down to Earth and Spring is Soon, 1990; Criticism: Contemporary Scottish Poetry: Individuals and Contexts, 1974; The Way the Words are Taken, Selected Essays, 1989; Editorial Trio; New Poets from Edinburgh, 1971; Iain Crichton Smith: Selected Poems, 1955-80, 1982; Robert Garioch: The Complete Poetical Works with Notes, 1983; Robert Garioch: A Garioch Miscellany, Selected Prose and Letters, 1986; Translations: An Italian Quartet, 1966; Blok's Twelve, 1968; Five Swedish Poets, 1972; Lars Gustafsson, Selected Poems, 1972; Gunnar Harding, They Killed Sitting Bull and Other Poems, 1973; Tomas Tranströmer, Citoyens, 1974; Tomas Tranströmer, Selected Poems, 1974, expanded 1980; Osten Sjöstrand, The Hidden Music & Other Poems, 1975; expanded and with others, Toward the Solitary Star: Selected Poetry and Prose, 1988; Werner Aspenström 37 Poems, 1976; Tomas Tranströmer, Baltics, 1980; Johannes Edfelt, Family Tree, 1981; Werner Aspenström, The Blue Whale and Other Prose Pieces, 1981; Kjell Espmark, Bela Bartok Against the Third Reich and Other Poems, 1985; Olva Hauge, Don't Give Me the Whole Truth and Other Poems, 1985; Tomas Tranströmer, Collected Poems, 1987; Stig Dagerman, German Autumn, 1988; Par Lagervist, Guest of Reality, 1989; Preparations for Clight, and other Swedish Stories, 1990; Four Swedish Poets (Kjell Espmark, Lennart Sjögren, Eva Ström & Tomas Transtromer), 1990; Olva Hauge, Selected Poems, 1990; Hermann Starheimstaeter, Stone-Shadows, 1991. Contributions to: various journals and magazines. Honours include: Gregory Award, 1967; Writers Fellowship, Edinburgh University, 1969; Scottish Arts Council Writers Bursary, 1972; Arthur Lundquist Award for translations from Swedish, 1977; Swedish Academy Award, 1978. Address: Postboks 467, N 4001, Stavanger, Norway.

FUNE Jonathan. See: **FLETCHER John Walter James.**

FURTWANGLER Virginia Anne, (Ann Copeland), b. 16 Dec 1932, Hartford, Connecticut, USA. Fiction Writer; Teacher. m. Albert Furtwangler, 17 Aug 1968, 2 sons. Education: BA, College of New Rochelle, 1954; MA, Catholic University of America, 1959; PhD, Cornell University, Kent, 1970. Appointments: Writer in Residence, College of Idaho, 1980; Linfield College, 1980-81; University of Idaho, 1982, 1986; Bemidji, 1987; Wichita State University, 1988; Mt Allison University, 1990; St Mary's University, 1993. Publications: At Peace; The Back Room; Earthen Vessels; The Golden Thread; The Back Room. Contributions to: The Fiddlehead Matrix; Turnstile; CFM; Southwest Review; The New Quarterly; Wild East; University of Windsor Review; Best American Short Stories; Best Canadian Stories. Honours: Kent Fellowship; Contributor Prize, CFM; Canada Council Grant; NEA Writing Fellowship; Arts Award; Finalist Governor Generals Award; Ingram Merrill Award; Judge, Smith First Novel Competition. Memberships: Authors Guild; Writers Union of Canada; International Womens Writing Guild; AWP; NB Writers Federation. Address: PO Box 1450, Sackville, NB, E0A 3C0, Canada.

G

GAAN Margaret, b. 1914, Shanghai, China. Writer. Appointments: Executive Secretary, China Mercantile Co, Shanghai, 1949-49; Programme Officer, 1950-65, Chief, Asia Desk, 1966-68, Deputy Regional Director for East Asia and Pakistan, 1969-74, United Nations Children's Fund; Now retired. Publications: Last Moments of a World, autobiography, 1978; Novels: Little Sister, 1983; Red Barbarian, 1984; White Poppy, 1985; Blue Mountain, 1987. Address: 967 Commons Drive, Sacramento, CA 95825, USA.

GADGIL Gangadhar, b. Bombay, India. Writer; Economic Adviser. m. Vasanta Gadgil, 12 Dec 1948, 1 son, 2 daughters. Education includes: MA, Bombay University, 1944. Appointments: Honorary Professor, University of Bombay. Publications: Durdamya; Bandoo; Crazy Bombay; Women and Other Stories; Kadu and God. Contributions to: Satyakatha; Hans; Kirloskar; Yugawani; Illustrated Weekly of India; Times of India; Indian Express; Economic Times; Quest; Marg; Evergreen Review; American Review; Western Humanities Review; Quadrant. Honours: R S Jog Award; N C Kelkar Award; State Award, Satahitya Samudra Palikade; State Award, Ole Unha; State Award, Talavatale Chandana; Abhiruchi Award; President, All India Marathi Literary Conference, 1981; President, Marathi Sahitya Mahamandal, 1987; Vice-President, Sahitya Akademi, 1988-93; President, Mumbai Marathi Sahitya Sangh; Vice-President, Mumbai Marathi Grantha Sangrahalay; President, Mumbai Grahak Panchayat; Invited to inaugurate, Marathi Drama Conference; Delivered Presidential addresses, lectures and inaugural addresses at various public functions and seminars. Memberships: Mumbai Marathi Sahitya Sangh; Mumbai Marathi Grantha Sangrahalay; Asiatic Society of Bombay; Vidarbha Sahitya Sangh; Marathwada Sahitya Parishad; Maharashtra Sahitya Parishad; Indian PEN. Address: 4 Abhang, Sahitya Sahawas, Bandra, Bombay 400051, India.

GAGLIANO Frank, b. 1931, USA. Playwright; Screenwriter; Novelist; Professor of Playwriting. Appointments: Playwright-in-Residence, Royal Shakespeare Company, London, England, 1967-69; Assistant Professor of Drama, Playwright-in-Residence, Director of Contemporary Playwrights Center, Florida State University, Tallahassee, USA, 1969-73; Lecturer in Playwriting, Director of Conkie Workshop for Playwrights, University of Texas, Austin, 1973-75; Distinguished Visiting Professor, University of Rhode Island, 1975; Benedum Professor of Theatre, West Virginia University, 1976-; Artistic Director, Carnegie Mellon, Showcase of New Plays, 1986-. Publications: The City Scene, 2 plays, 1966; Night of the Dunce, 1967; Father Uxbridge Wants to Marry, 1968; The Hide-and-Seek Odyssey of Madeleine Gimple, 1970; Big Sur, 1970; The Prince of Peasantmania, 1970; The Private Eye of Hiram Bodoni, TV play, 1971; Quasimodo, musical, 1971; Anywhere the Wind Blows, musical, 1972; In the Voodoo Parlour of Marie Laveau, 1974; The Comedia World of Lafcadio Beau, 1974; The Resurrection of Jackie Cramer, musical, 1974; Congo Square, musical, 1975, revised, 1989; The Total Immersion of Madelaine Favorini, 1981; San Ysidro, dramatic cantata, 1982; From The Bodoni County Songbook Anthology, Book I, 1986, musical version, 1989; Anton's Leap, novel, 1987; Address: c/o Gilbert Parker, William Morris Agency, 1350 Avenue of the Americas, New York, NY 10019, USA.

GAIL. See: KATZ Bobbi.

GAINES Ernest J, b. 1933, Pointe Caipee Parish, Louisiana, USA. Appointment: Writer-in-Residence, University of South West Louisiana. Publications: A Lesson Before Dying, 1993; Gathering of Old Men; In My Father's House; A Long Day in November; The Autobiography of Miss Jane Pitman; Bloodline; Of Love & Dust; Catherine Carnier. Honour: National Book Critics Circle Award, 1994. Address: 932 Divosadero Street, San Francisco, CA 94115, USA.

GAINHAM Sarah. See: AMES Sarah Rachel.

GALBRAITH James Kenneth, b. 29 Jan 1952, Boston, Massachusetts, USA. Professor. m. (1) Lucy Ferguson, 28 July 1979, div, 1 son, 1 daughter, (2) Ying Tang, 17 July 1993. Education: AB, Harvard College, 1974; University of Cambridge, 1974-75; MA, 1976, MPhil, 1977, PhD, 1981, Yale University. Appointments: Professor, LBJ School of Public Affairs, University of Texas at Austin, 1985-.

Publications: Balancing Acts; The Economic Problem; Macroeconomics. Contributions to: Numerous. Honours: Marshall Scholar, University of Cambridge. Memberships: American Economic Association; Association for Public Policy Analysis and Management. Address: LBJ School of Public Affairs, University of Texas at Austin, Austin, TX 78713, USA.

GALIOTO Salvatore, b. 6 June 1925, Italy. Professor of Humanities (retired). m. Nancy Morris, 8 July 1978, 1 son. Education: BA, University of New Mexico, 1952; MA, Denver University, 1955; John Hay Fellow, Yale University, 1959-60; Catskill Area Project Fellow, Columbia University, 1961-62; Mediaeval and Renaissance Doctoral Programme, University of New Haven. Appointments: Member, Judging Jury for Poetry, ASLA Internation Prize for Poetry, Sicily, 1986. Publications: The Humanities: Classical Athens, Renaissance Florence and Contemporary New York, 1970; Bibliographic Materials on Indian Culture, 1972; Let Us Be Modern, poems, English, Italian, 1985; INAGO Newsletter, poems, 1988; Many poems in Snow Summits in the Sun, poetry anthology, 1989; Is Anybody Listening, poems, English, 1990; Flap Your Wings, poems, English, 1992; Rosebushes and the Poor, poems, Italian, 1993. Contributions to: New York Times; Cleveland Plain Dealer; Herald Tribune; Library Journal; Contro Campo; Alla Bottega; Quaderi dell'ASLA; The Poet; California State Quarterly; Midwest Poetry Review Agni Review; Manna Prose Society; American Atheist; San Fernando Poetry Journal; Prophetic Voices; Italian Correspondent, Italian-American Heritage Foundation, San Jose, California; Feelings of Pennsylvania. Honours: Purple Heart, Bronze Star, 1944; John Hay Fellowship, 1958-59; Asian Studies Fellow, 1965-66; Mole of Turin, 1st Prize, Foreign Writer, 1984; 1st Prize, Chapbook Competition, The Poet, 1985, 1986; 1st Prize, Poetry, Gli Etrusci, Italy, 1985; 3rd Prize, Poetry, ASLA, Italy; Trofeo delle Nazioni, Poetry, Italy; Gold Medal for Let Us Be Modern, Istituto Carlo Capodieci, 1987; Poet for 1989, INAGO newspaper. Memberships: Long Island Historians Society; The Asian Society; ASLA, Sicily; California State Poetry Society, San Francisco; Poets and Writers of America, New York City; Representative in Italy, International Society of Poets. Address: Via Bruno Buozzi 15, Montecatini Terme 51016 (Pistoia), Italy.

GALL Henderson Alexander (Sandy), b. 1 Oct 1927, Penang, Malaysia. Television Journalist. m. Aug 1958, 1 son, 3 daughters. Education includes: MA, Aberdeen University, Scotland, 1952. Publications: Gold Scoop, 1977; Chasing the Dragon, 1981; Don't Worry about the Money Now, 1983; Behind Russian Lines: An Afghan Journal, 1983; Afghanistan: Agony of a Nation, 1988; Salang, 1989; George Adamson: Lord of the Lions, 1991; News From the Front: The Life of a Television Reporter, 1994. Honours: Rector, 1978-81, Honorary LLD, 1981, Aberdeen University; Sitara-i-Pakistan, 1986; Lawrence of Arabia Medal, 1987; CBE, 1988. Literary Agent: Peters, Fraser and Dunlop, 503/4 The Chambers, Chelsea Harbour, London SW10 0XF, England.

GALL Sally Moore, b. 28 July 1941, New York City, New York, USA. Librettist. m. William Einar Gall, 8 Dec 1967. Education: BA cum laude, Harvard University, 1963; MAS, 1971, PhD, 1976, New York University. Literary appointments: Poetry Editor, Free Inquiry, 1981-84; Founding Editor, Eidos, The International Prosody Bulletin, 1984-88. Publications: The Modern Poetic Sequence: The Genius of Modern Poetry (co-author), 1983, Paperback, 1986; Ramon Guthrie's Maximum Security Ward: An American Classic, 1984; Maximum Security Ward and Other Poems (editor), 1984; Poetry in English: An Anthology (versification editor), 1987. Contributions to: Reference books, professional journals and literary magazines. Honours: Penfield Fellow, New York University, 1973-74; Academy of American Poets Award, New York University, 1975; Key Pin and Scroll Award, New York University, 1976; Co-winner, Explicator Literary Foundation Award, 1984. Memberships: American Music Center; Dramatists Guild; Lyrica; Modern Language Association; National Opera Association; Opera for Youth, Poets and Writers; Various wildlife societies and community music groups. Address: 5820 Folsom Drive, La Jolla, CA 92037, USA.

GALLAGHER Richard. See: LEVINSON Leonard.

GALLAHER Art Jr, b. 1925, USA. Emeritus Professor of Anthropology and Chancellor; Writer. Appointments: Assistant Professor, Associate Professor, Department of Sociology and Anthropology, University of Houston, Texas, 1956-62; University of Nebraska, 1962-63; Professor of Anthropology, 1963-, Deputy Director, Center for Developmental Change, 1966-70, Chairman, Department of

Anthropology, 1970-72, Dean, College of Arts and Sciences, 1972-80, Chancellor, 1981-89, University of Kentucky, Lexington. Publications: Plainville Fifteen Years Later, 1961; Perspectives in Developmental Change (editor), 1968; The Dying Community (edited with Harland Padfield), 1980. Address: 3167 Roxburg Drive West, Lexington, KY 40503-3439, USA.

GALLAHER John G, n. 28 Dec 1928, St Louis, Missouri, USA. Professor. m. C Maia Hofacker, 2 June 1956, 1 son, 2 daughters. Education: BA, Washington University, 1954; MA, 1957, PhD, 1960, St Louis University. Publications: The Iron Marshal: A Biography of Louis N Davout; The Students of Paris and the Revolution of 1848; Napoleon's Irish Legion. Contributions to: French Historical Studies; Military Affairs; The Irish Sword. Membership: Society for French Historical Studies. Address: History Department, Southern Illinois University of Edwardsville, Edwardsville, IL 62026, USA.

GALLANT Mavis, b. 11 Aug 1922, Montreal, Quebec, Canada. Novelist. Education: Schools in Montreal & NY. Appointments include: Writer in Residence, University of Toronto, 1983-84. Publications include: Green Water, Green Sky, 1959; A Fairly Good Time, 1970; Short Stories, The Other Paris, 1956; My Heart is Broken: Eight Short Stories and a Short Novel, 1964; From the Fifteenth District: A Novel and Eight Short Stories, 1979; Home Truths: Selected Canadian Stories, 1981; In Transit, Twenty Stories, 1988; Numerous Uncollected Short Stories and a Play. Honours include: Governor Generals Award, 1982; Canada Australia Literary Prize, 1984; Honorary Degree, University Sainte Anne, Pointe de Eglise, Nova Scotia, 1984; Officer, Order of Canada, 1981. Literary Agent: Georges Borchardt Inc, 136 East 57th Street, NY 10022, USA. Address: 14 Ruse Jean Ferrandi, 75006 Paris, France.

GALLANT Roy Arthur, b. 17 Apr 1924, Maine, USA. Author; Teacher. m. Kathryn Dale, 1952, 2 sons. Education: BA, 1948, MS, 1949, Bowdoin College; Doctoral work, 1953-59, Columbia University. Appointments: Managing Editor, Scholastic Teachers Magazine, 1954-57; Author-in-Residence, Doubleday, 1957-59; Editorial Director, Aldus Books, London, 1959-62; Editor-in-Chief, The Natural History Press, 1962-65; Consultant for The Edison Project, Israel Arts and Sciences Academy. Publications include: Our Universe, 1986; Private Lives of the Stars, 1986; Rainbows, Mirages and Sundogs, 1987; Before the Sun Dies, 1989; Ancient Indians, 1989; The Peopling of Planet Earth, 1990; Earth's Vanishing Forests, 1991; A Young Person's Guide to Science, 1993; The Day the Sky Split Apart, 1994. Address: PO Box 228, Beaver Mountain Lake, Rengeley, ME 04990, USA.

GALLINER Peter, b. 19 Sept 1920, Berlin, Germany. Publisher. m. (1) Edith Marguerite Goldsmidt, 1948, 1 daughter, (2) Helga Stenschke, 1990. Education: Berlin and London. Appointments: Worked for Reuters, London, England, 1944-47; Foreign Man, Financial Times, London, 1947-60; Chairman of Board, Managing Director, Illstein Publishing Group, Berlin, Germany, 1969-64; Vice-Chairman, Managing Director, British Printing Corporation, 1965-70; International Publishing Consultant, 1965-67, 1970-75; Chairman, Peter Galliner Associates, 1970; Director, Interanational Press Institute, 1975-. Honours: Order of Merit, 1st Class, GFR, 1965; Ecomienda, Orden de Isabel la Catolica, Spain, 1982; Commander's Cross, Order of Merit, GFR, 1990. Address: Untere Zaune 9, 8001 Zurich, Switzerland.

GALLOWAY David Darryl, b. 5 May 1937, Memphis, USA. Journalist; Novelist; Professor; Art Consultant. m. Sally Lee Gantt, dec, 1 son. Education: BA, Harvard College, 1959; PhD, State University of New York, 1962. Appointments: Lecturer, State University of New York, 1962-64; Lecturer, University of Sussex, 1964-67; Chair of American Studies, University of Hamburg, 1967-68; Associate Professor, Case Western Reserve University, 1968-72; Chair of American Studies, Ruhr University, Germany, 1972-. Publications: The Absurd Hero; Lamaar Ransom; Calamus; Artware; A Family Album; Tamsen; The Selected Writings of Edgar Allan Poe; Melody Jones; Editor, Crossroads, since 1989. Contributions to: International Herald Tribune; Art in America; Art News; Editor in Chief, in: German-American Cultural Review, since 1993. Memberships: Royal Society of Arts; The Harvard Club. Address: Band Str 13, 42105 Wuppertal, Germany.

GALLUN Raymond Zinke, b. 22 Mar 1911, Beaver Dam, Wisconsin, USA. Technical Writer. m. (1) Frieda Talmey, 26 Dec 1959 (dec. 1974), (2) Bertha Erickson, 25 Feb 1977 (dec. 1989), 1 stepdaughter. Education: University of Wisconsin-Madison, 1929-30. Publications include: People Minus X, 1957; The Eden Cycle, 1974;

The Best of Raymond Z Gallun, 1977; Sky Climber, 1982; Bioblast, 1985; Star Climber, autobiography, 1990. Contributions to: Science Wonder Stories; Air Wonder Stories; Astounding Stories; Colliers Magazine; The Best of Science Fiction; Adventures in Time and Space. Honours: Hall of Fame Award, Sealon 37th World Science Fiction Convention, Brighton, England, 1979; Lifetime Achievement Award, I-CON IV, New York State University Campus, Stony Brook, 1985. Literary Agent: Forest J Ackerman. Address: 110-20 The Avenue, Forest Hills, NY 11375, USA.

GALTON Herbert, b. 1 Oct 1917, Vienna, Austro-Hungary. University Professor. m. 28 Jan 1992. Education: High School, Vienna, 1935; University of Vienna, 1935-38; PhD, Russian Philology, University of London, 1951; Professor, University of Kansas, 1962-88. Publications: Aorist und Aspekt im Slavischen, 1962; The Main Functions of the Slavic Verbal Aspect, 1976; Reisetagebuch, 1990. Contributions to: The Equality Principle, in anthology, 1974; Freedom - from Illusions, 1984; Lyrische Annalen, 1995. Honours: Gold Medal, Macedonian Academy of Sciences, 1987. Memberships: Austrian Writers' Union; Austrian PEN Club; Societas Linguistica Europaea. Address: Kaiserstrasse 12/18, Vienna 1070, Austria.

GALTON Raymond Percy, b. 17 July 1930. Author; Scriptwriter. m. Tonia Phillips, 1956, 1 son, 2 daughters. Publications: TV - With Alan Simpson: Hancock's Half House, 1954-61; Comedy Playhouse, 1962-63; Steptoe and Son, 1962-74; Galton-Simpson Comedy, 1969; Clochermerle, 1971; Casanova, '74, 1974; Dawson's Weekly, 1975; The Galton and Simpson Playhouse, 1976-77; With Johnny Speight: Tea Ladies, 1979; Spooner's Patch, 1979-80; With John Antrobus: Room at the Bottom, 1986; Films with Alan Simpson: The Rebel, 1960; The Bargee, 1963; The Wrong Arm of the Law, 1963; The Spy with a Cold Nose, 1966; Loot, 1969; Steptoe and Son, 1971; Steptoe and Son Ride Again, 1973; Den Siste Fleksnes, 1974; Die Skraphandlerne, 1975; Theatre with Alan Simpson: Way Out in Piccadilly, 1969; The Wind in the Sassfras Trees, 1968; Albert och Herbert, 1981; Fleksnes, 1983; Mordet pa Skolgatan 15, 1984; With John Antrobus: When Did You Last See Your Trousers? 1986; (Books) With Alan Simpson Hancock, 1961; Steptoe and Son, 1963; The Reunion and Other Plays, 1966; Hancock Scripts, 1974; The Best of Hancock, 1986. Address: The Ivy House, Hampton Court, Middlesex, England.

GALVIN James, b. 8 May 1951, Chicago, Illinois, USA. Poet. Education: BA, Antioch College; MFA, University of Iowa. Career: Professor; Editor of Crazyhorse, 1979-81. Publications: Imagining Timber, 1980; God's Mistress, 1984; Elements, 1988. Contributions include: New Yorker; Nation; Antioch Review; Poetry Now; Antaeus; Sewanee Review. Honours: Discovery Award, Nation/Young Men's Hebrew Association, 1977; National Poetry Series Open Competition, Co-winner, 1984. Address: Iowa Writers Workshop, Univerity of Iowa, 436 EPB, Iowa City, IA 52242, USA.

GALVIN Patrick, b. 1927, Cork, Ireland. Dramatist; Poet. m. Diana Ferrier, 2 sons. Appointments: Resident Dramatist, Lyric Theatre, Belfast, 1974-77; Writer-in-residence, West Midlands Arts Association, 1979-80. Publications: Heart of Grace, 1957; Christ in London, 1960; Two Summers, Parts 1-3, 1970; By Nature Diffident, 1971; Lon Chaney, 1971; The Woodburners, 1973; Man on the Porch, 1980; Collected Poems and Letters, 1985; Let the Seahorse Take Me Home and Other Poems, 1986; Plays: And His Stretched, 1960; Cry the Believers, 1961; Nightfall to Belfast, 1973; The Last Burning, 1974; We Do It For Love, 1976; The Devil's Own People, 1976; Collected Plays and Letters, 1986. Honours include: Leverhulme Fellowship, 1974-76. Address: c/o Martin Brian and O'Keefe, 78 Coleraine Road, Blackheath, London SE3, England.

GALWAY Robert Conington. See: **MCCUTCHAN Philip Donald.**

GAMBARO Griselda, b. 28 July 1928, Buenos Aires, Argentina. Playwright; Novelist. m. Juan Carlos Distefano. Appointments include: Former Drama Teacher and Lecturer. Publications: Matrimonio, 1965; El desatino, 1966; Las paredes, 1966; Los siameses, 1967; The Camp, 1968; Nada que ver, 1972; Solo un aspecto, 1974; El viaje a Bahia Blanca, 1975; El hombre, 1976; Putting Two and Two Together, 1976, 1991; Decir si, 1981; La malasangre, 1982; Real envido, 1983; Del sol naciente, 1984; Teatro, 4 volumes, 1984-90; Information for Foreigners, 1986; The Impenetrable Madam X, 1991; Fiction: Cuentos, 1953; Madrigal en ciudad, 1963; Un Felicidad con menos pena, 1968; Nada que ver con ora historia, 1972; Ganarse la muertel, 1976; Lo impenetrable, 1984. Honours include: Guggenheim Fellowship, 1982. Address: c/o Argentores, Virrey Pacheo De Melo, 1126 Buenos Aires, Argentina.

GAMBONE Philip Arthur, b. 21 July 1948, Melrose, Massachusetts, USA. Teacher; Writer. Education: AB, Harvard University, 1970; MA, Episcopal Divinity School, 1976. Publications: The Language We Use Up Here and Other Stories; Contributing author: Hometowns: Gay Men Write About Where They Belong; A Member of the Family; Men on Men III, 1990; Sister and Brother, 1994. Contributions to: Book reviews to New York Times, Lambda Book Report, Bay Windows. Honours: MacDowell Colony Fellow; Nominee, Lambda Literary Award. Membership: PEN. Address: 47 Waldeck Street, Dorchester, MA 02124, USA.

GANDLEY Kenneth Royce (Oliver Jacks, Kenneth Royce), b. 11 Dec 1920, Croydon, Surrey, England. Novelist. m. Stella Parker, 16 Mar 1946. Publications: My Turn to Die, 1958; The Soft Footed Moor, 1959; The Long Corridor, 1960; No Paradise, 1961; The Night Seekers, 1962; The Angry Island, 1963; The Day the Wind Dropped, 1964; Bones in the Sand, 1967; A Peck of Salt, 1968; A Single to Hong Kong, 1969; The XYY Man (also adapted for TV), 1970; The Concrete Boot (also adapted for TV), 1971; The Miniatures Frame (also adapted for TV), 1972; Spider Underground, 1973; Trapspider, 1974; Man on a Short Leash, 1974; The Woodcutter Operation (also adapted for TV), 1975; Bustillo, 1976; Assassination Day, 1976; Autumn Heroes, 1977; The Satan Touch (also adapted for TV), 1978; The Third Arm, 1980; 10,000 Days, 1981; Channel Assault, 1982; The Stalin Account, 1983; The Crypto Man, 1984; The Mosley Receipt, 1985; Breakout, 1986; No Way Back, 1987; The President is Dead, 1988; Fall-Out, 1989; Exchange of Doves, 1990; Limbo, 1992; Remote Control, 1993; The Ambassador's Son, 1994. Memberships: Society of Authors; Crime Writers Association. Literary Agent: David Higham Associates. Address: 3 Abbotts Close, Abbotts Ann, Andover, Hants SP11 7NP, England.

GANN Lewis Henry, b. 1924, USA. Senior Fellow; Curator, Western European Collection; Writer. Appointments: Senior Fellow, Hoover Institute, Stanford University, California, 19640; Member, Editorial Board, Intercollegiate Review. Publications: The Birth of a Plural Society: The Development of Northern Rhodesia under the British South Africa Company, 1894-1914, 1958; A History of Northern Rhodesia: Early Days to 1953, 1964; Huggins of Rhodesia: The Man and His Country (with M Gelfand), 1964; A History of Southern Rhodesia: Early Days to 1934, 1965; Central Africa: The Former British States, 1971; Guerillas in History, 1971; The Struggle for Zimbabwe (with T Henriksen), 1981; With P Duignan: White Settlers in Tropical Africa, 1962; Burden of Empire: An Appraisal of Western Colonialism in Africa South of the Sahara, 1967; Africa and the World at Large: An Introduction to the History of the Sub-Saharan Africa from Antiquity to 1840, 1972; Colonialism in Africa 1870-1960, 5 vols, 1969-73; The Rulers of German Africa, 1884-1914, 1977; The Rulers of British Africa 1870-1914, 1978; South Africa: War, Revolution or Peace, 1978; The Rulers of Belgian Africa 1884-1914, 1979; Why South Africa Will Survive, 1981; The US and Africa: A History, 1984; The Hispanics in the US, 1986; Hope for South Africa, 1991; The Rebirth of the West, The Americanization of the Democratic World, 1945-1958, 1992. Address: Hoover Institute, Stanford University, Stanford, CA 94305, USA.

GANT Jonathon. See: **ADAMS Clifton**.

GARAFOLA Lynn, b. 12 Dec 1946, New York City, New York, USA. Dance Critic; Historian. m. Eric Foner, 1 May 1980, 1 daughter. Education: AB, Barnard College, 1968; PhD, City University of New York, 1985. Literary Appointments: Editor, Studies in Dance History, 1990-. Publications: Diaghilev's Ballets Russes; André Levinson on Dance: Writings from Paris in the Twenties; The Diaries of Marius Petipa. Contributions to: Dance Magazine; Ballet Review; The Dancing Times; Dance Research Journal; Raritan; The Nation; The Women's Review of Books; The Times Literary Supplement. Honours: Torre de lo Bueno Prize. Memberships: Society of Dance History Scholars; Dance Critics Association; Association Européenne des Historiens de la Danse. Address: 606 West 116th Street, New York, NY 10027, USA.

GARCIA MARQUEZ Gabriel, b. 6 Mar 1928, Aracataca, Colombia. Novelist. Education: Universities of Colombia and Cartegna, 1947-49. Appointments include: Founder-President of Fundacion Habeas, from 1979. Publications: No One Writes to the Colonel, 1957;

Evil Hour, 1962, 1979; Big Mama's Funeral, 1962; One Hundred Years of Solitude, 1967; Leaf Storm and Other Stories, 1972; Innocent Erendira and Other Stories, 1972; Four Stories, 1974; Collected Stories 1947-72; The Autumn of the Patriarch, 1975; Chronicles of a Death Foretold, 1981; Collected Stories, 1984, 1991; Love in the Time of Cholera, 1985; The General in his Labyrinth, 1989; Collected Novellas, 1990; Play: Diatribe of Love Against a Seated Man, 1988; Screenplays; Also: The Fragrance of Guava, 1982; Clandestine in Chile: The Adventures of Miguel Littin, 1986; The Doom of Damocles, 1986. Honours include: Nobel Prize for Literature, 1982. Address: c/o Agencia Carmen Balcella, Diagonal 580, 08031 Barcelona, Spain.

GARDAM Jane Mary, b. 11 July 1928, Yorkshire, England. Writer. m. 20 Apr 1954, 2 sons, 1 daughter. Education: BA, London University, 1949. Publications: A Few Fair Days; A Long Way from Verona; The Summer After the Funeral; God on the Rocks; Bil'gewater; Black Faces White Faces; Crusoe's Daughter; Queen of The Tambourine (novel), 1991; Going in to a Dark House (short stories), 1994; The Iron Coast (non-fiction), 1994; Short Stories, adaptations for TV and film; The Sidmouth Letters; The Pangs of Love; The Hollow Land; Showing the Flag, 1989; Childrens Books: Bridget & William; Kit; Kit in Boots; Swans; Through the Dolls' House Door. Contributions include: Guardian; London Review of Books; Books & Bookmen; Daily Telegraph; Reviewing for The Spectator; The Times; Articles for The Independent Review, The Oldie. Honours: David Higham's Award, 1978; Winifred Holtby Award, 1978; Whitebread Award, 1983, 2nd Whitbread Award, 1991; Katherine Mansfield Award, 1984; The Whitbread Award for Fiction for The Queen of the Tambourine, 1992; PEN, Silver Pen Award, 1995. Memberships: Committee of English Centre of International PEN; Arts Club; University Womens Club; Academy Club; Royal Society of Literature. Literary Agent: David Higham. Address: Haven House, Sandwich, Kent CT13 9TS, England.

GARDAPHE Frederico Luigi, b. Sept 1952, Chicago, Illinois, USA. Professor. m. 18 Sept 1982, 1 son, 1 daughter. Education: Fenwick Prep, 1970; Triton Junior College, 1972; BS, University of Wisconsin, 1976; AM, University of Chicago, 1982; PhD, University of Illinois, 1993. Appointments: Professor, Columbia College, Chicago, 1983-; Arts Editor, Frá Noi, 1987-; Editor, Voices in Italian Americana, 1990-. Publications: From the Margin; Italian American Ways; New Chicago Stories; Italian Ethnics. Contributions to: Melus; Misure Critiche; Italica; Italian Canadiana; Romance Languages Annual; Haymarket; Almanacco; Frá Noi; Il Caffè. Address: Department of English, Columbia College, 600 S Michigan Avenue, Chicago, IL 60605, USA.

GARDEN Bruce. See: **MACKAY James Alexander**.

GARDEN Nancy, b. 15 May 1938, Boston, Massachusetts, USA. Writer; Editor; Teacher. Education: BFA, Columbia University School of Dramatic Art, 1961; MA, Teachers College, Columbia University, 1962. Appointments: Actress, Lighting Designer, 1954-64; Teacher of Speech and Dramatics, 1961-64; Editor, educational materials, textbooks, 1964-76; Teacher of Writing, Adult Education, 1974; Correspondence School, 1974-. Publications: What Happened in Marston, 1971; The Loners, 1972; Maria's Mountain, 1981; Fours Crossing, 1981; Annie on My Mind, 1982; Favourite Tales from Grimm, 1982; Watersmeet, 1983; Prisoner of Vampires, 1984; Peace, O River, 1986; The Door Between, 1987; Lark in the Morning, 1991; My Sister, the Vampire, 1992; Dove and the Sword, 1995; My Brother, the Werewolf, 1995; The Monster Hunter series: Case No 1, Mystery of the Night Raiders, 1987; Case No 2: Mystery of the Midnight Menace; Case No 3: Mystery of the Secret Marks, 1989; Case No 4: Mystery of the Kidnapped Kidnapper, 1994; Case No 5: Mystery of the Watchful Witches, 1995; Non-fiction: Berlin: City Split in Two, 1971; Vampires, 1973; Werewolves, 1973; Witches, 1975; Devils and Demons, 1976; Fun with Forecasting Weather, 1977; The Kids' Code and Cipher Book, 1981. Literary Agent: Dorothy Markinko, McIntosh and Otis Inc, USA. Address: c/o McIntosh and Otis Inc, 310 Madison Avenue, New York, NY 10017, USA.

GARDNER Herbert, b. 1934. Publications include: Plays: Conversations with My Father, 1994; A Thousand Clowns; The Goodbye People; Thieves; I'm Not Rappaport; Who Is Harry Kellerman & Why is He Saying Those Terrible Things About Me? (Screenplay); A Piece of the Action (Novel). Contributions to: Best American Short Stories of 1968. Honours: Antoinette Perry Award, 1986; Outer Critic Circle Award; John Glassner Playwriting Award. Address: c/o Pantheon

Books Publicity Department, 201 East 50th Street, New York, NY 10022, USA.

GARDONS S S. See: **SNODGRASS W D.**

GAREBIAN Keith Stephen, b. 15 July 1943, Bombay, India. Teacher. m. Caryl Taugher, 23 Dec 1972, div., 1 son. Education: BEd, 1964; BA, 1966; MA, 1971; PhD, 1973. Publications include: Hugh Hood; William Hutt: A Theatre Portrait; A Well-Bred Muse: Selected Theatre Writings; Shaw and Newton; Explorations of Shavian Theatre: Leon Rooke and His Works; Hugh Hood and His Works; The Making of 'My Fair Lady'; The Making of 'Gypsy'; George Bernard Shaw and Christopher Newton, 1992; Introducing My Fair Lady, 1992. Contributions to: The Oxford Companion to Canadian Literature; The Oxford Companion to Canadian Theatre; Das Moderne Englische Kanadische Drama; The Bumper Book; Carry On Bumping; The Montreal Story Tellers. Address: 2001 Bonnymede Drive 150, Mississauga, Oontario, Canada L5J 4H8.

GARFIELD Leon, b. 14 July 1921. Author. m. Vivien Dolores Alcock. 1948, 1 daughter. Publications: Jack Holborn, 1964; Devil in the Fog, 1966; Smith, 1967; Black Jack, 1968, filmed, 1979; Mister Corbett's Ghost and Other Stories, 1969; The Boy and the Monkey, 1969; The Drummer Boy, 1970; The God Beneath the Sea (with Edward Blishen), 1970; The Strange Affair of Adelaide Harris, 1971; The Ghost Downstairs, 1972; Child O'War (with David Proctor), 1972; The Captain's Watch, 1972; Lucifer Wilkins, 1973; Baker's Dozen, 1973; The Golden Shadow (with Edward Blishen), 1973; The Sound of Coaches, 1974; The Prisoners of September, 1975; The Pleasure Garden, 1976; The Booklovers, 1976; The House of Hanover, 1976; Mirror Mirror, 1976; The Lamplighter's Funeral, 1976; Moss and Blister, 1976; The Cloak, 1976; The Valentine, 1977; Labour in Vain, 1977; The Fool, 1977; Rosy Starling, 1977; The Dumb Cake, 1977; Tom Titmarsh's Devil, 1977; The Filthy Beast, 1977; The Enemy, 1977; The Confidence Man, 1978; Bostock and Harris, 1978; John Diamond, 1980; The Mystery of Edwin Drood, 1980; Fair's Fair, 1981; The House of Cards, 1982; King Nimrod's Tower, 1982; The Apprentices, 1982; The Writing on the Wall, 1983; The King in the Garden, 1984; The Wedding Ghost, 1984; Guilt and Gingerbread, 1984; Shakespeare Stories, 1985; The December Rose, 1986; The Empty Sleeve, 1988; Blewcoat Boy, 1988; The Saracen Maid, 1991; Shakespeare: The Animated Tales, 1992. Honours: Prix de la Fondation de France, 1984; Swedish Golden Cat, 1985; Fellow, Royal Society of Literature, 1985; Guardian Award for Children's Fiction; Whitbread Award; Carnegie Medal. Address: c/o John Johnson Ltd, Clerkenwell House, 45-47 Clerkenwell Green, London EC1R 0HT, England.

GARFINKEL Patricia Gail, b. 15 Feb 1938, New York City, New York, USA. Writer. 2 sons. Education: BA, New York University. Publications: Ram's Horn, poems, 1980; From the Red Eye of Jupiter, poems, 1990. Contributions to: Numerous publications and anthologies including: Hollin's Critic; Seattle Review; Cedar Rock; Washingtonian Magazine; Black Box City Lights Anthology, 1976; Anthology of Magazine Verse/Yearbook of American Poetry, 1980; Poet Upstairs Anthology; Miller Cabin Anthology, 1984; Montpelier Culture Arts Centre Anthology, 1984; Snow Summits in the Sun Anthology, 1985. Honours: Poetry in Public Places Award for New York State, 1977; Winner, 1st Prize, Lip Service Poetry Competition, 1990; Winner, Book Competition, Washington Writers Publishing House, 1990. Memberships: Poets and Writers Inc; Writers' Center, Glen Echo, Maryland; Elected to Board of Poetry Committee of Greater Washington Area. Address: 2031 Approach Lane, Reston, VA 22091, USA.

GARFITT Roger, b. 12 Apr 1944. Poet and Prose Writer. Education: BA, Hons, Merton College, Oxford, 1968. Literary Appointments: Arts Council Poet in Residence, University College of North Wales, Bangor, 1975-77; Editor, Poetry Review 1978-81; Arts Council Poet in Residence, Sunderland Polytechnic, 1978-80; Member, Literature Panel of Arts Council of Great Britain, 1986-90. Publications: Poetry: Caught on Blue, 1970; West of Elm, Carcanet, 1974; The Broken Road, Northern House, 1982; Rowlstone Haiku, Five Seasons, 1982; Given Ground, 1989. Contributions to: Prose in Granta 27 and 29, 1989. Honours: Guinness International Poetry Prize, 1973; Gregory Award, 1974. Literary Agent: Jane Turnbull. Address: c/o Jane Turnbull, 13 Wendell Road, London W12 9RS, England.

GARLICK Helen Patricia, b. 21 Apr 1958, Doncaster, England; Writer; Solicitor. m. Richard Howard, 1 daughter. Education: LLB Class 2i (Hons), University of Bristol, 1979; Solicitor of Supreme Court, 1983. Career includes: TV and radio appearances. Publications: The Separation Survival Handbook, 1989; The Good Marriage, 1990; The Which? Good Divorce Guide, 1992; Penguin Guide to the Law, 1992. Contributions to: The Independent; The Guardian; Various magazines. Memberships: Chair, National Council for One Parent Families; Family Law Adviser to Consumers Association. Address: c/o Carolyn Brunton, Studio 8, 125 Moore Park Road, London SW6 4PS, England.

GARLICK Raymond, b. 21 Sept 1926. Lecturer; Poet. m. Elin Jane Hughes, 1948, 1 son, 1 daughter. Education: BA, University College of North Wales, Bangor, 1948. Appointments: Principal Lecturer, Trinity College, Carmarthen, 1972-86. Publications: Poems From the Mountain-House, 1950; Requiem for a Poet, 1954; Poems from Pembrokeshire, 1954; The Welsh-Speaking Sea, 1954; Blaenau Observed, 1957; Landscapes and Figures: Selected Poems 1949-63, 1964; A Sense of Europe: Collected Poems 1954-68, 1968; A Sense of Time: Poems and Antipoems, 1969-72, 1972; Incense: Poems 1972-75; Collected Poems 1946-85; Travel Notes: New Poems, 1992; An Introduction to Anglo-Welsh Literature, 1970; Anglo-Welsh Poetry 1480-1900, 1982 (Editor). Honours include: Welsh Arts Council Prizes; Honorary Fellow of Trinity College, Carmarthan; Fellow of the Welsh Academy. Address: 26 Glannant House, College Road, Carmarthen SA31 3EF, Wales.

GARLINSKI Jozef, b. 1913, Poland. Writer. Appointments: Chairman, Executive Committee, Polish Home Army Circle, London, England, 1954-65; Cultural Vice-Chairman, Polish Cultural and Social Centre, London, 1970-79; Chairman, Union of Polish Writers Abroad, 1975-. Publications: Dramat i Opatrznosc, 1961; Matki i zony, 1962; Ziemia, novel, 1964; Miedzy Londynem i Warszawa, 1966; Polish SOE and the Allies, 1969; Fighting Auschwitz, 1975; Hitler's Last Weapons, 1978; Intercept: Secrets of the Enigma War, 1979; The Swiss Corridor, 1981; Polska w Drugiej Wojnie Swiatowej, 1982; Poland in the Second World War, 1985; Szwajcarski Kryterz, 1987; Niezapomniane lata, 1987. Address: 94 Ramillies Road, London W4 1JA, England.

GARNER Alan, b. 17 Oct 1934, Cheshire, England. Author. m. 1) Ann Cook, 1956, div, 1 son, 2 daughters; 2) Griselda Greaves, 1972, 1 son, 1 daughter. Education: Magdalen College, Oxford, 1955-56. Appointments: Member of International Editorial Board, Detskaya Literatura Publishers, Moscow, 1991-. Publications: The Weirdstone of Brisingamen, 1960; The Moon of Gomrath, 1963; Elidor, 1965; Holly from the Bongs, 1966; The Owl Service, 1967; The Book of Goblins, 1969; Red Shift, 1973; The Guizer, 1975; The Stone Book Quartet, 1976-78; Fairy Tales of Gold, 1979; The Lad of the Gad, 1980; British Fairy Tales, 1984; A Bag of Moonshine, 1986; Jack and the Beanstalk, 1992; Once Upon a Time, 1993. Honours: Carnegie Medal, 1967; Guardian Award, 1968; Gold Plaque, Chicago International Film Festival, 1981; Lewis Carroll Shelf Award, USA, 1970. Membership: Portico Library Manchester. Literary Agent: Sheilland Associates. Address: Blackden, Holmes Chapel, Crewe, Cheshire CW4 8BY, England.

GARNER Helen, b. 7 Nov 1942, Geelong, Victoria, Australia. Novelist. m. (2)Jean Jacques Portail, 1980. Education: BA, Lebourne University, 1965. Appointments include: Writer in Residence, Griffith University, Queensland, 1983; University of Western Australia, 1984; Feature Writer, The Age, Melbourne, 1981-. Publications: Monkey Grip, 1977; Moving Out, 1983; The Childrens Bach, 1984; Short Stories, Honour, and Other Peoples Children, Two Stories, 1980; Postcards from Sufers, 1985; A Play and Non Fictional Works. Honours: Australia Council Fellowships; National Book Council Award, 1978; NSW Premiers Award, 1986. Address: c/o McPhee Gribble, 66 Cecil Street, Fitzroy, VA 3065, Australia.

GARNER William, Writer. Education: BSc Hons, University of Birmingham, England. Publications: 13 novels between 1965-90 including: The Morpurgo Trilogy, 1982-86; Zones of Silence, 1986; Paper Chase, 1988; Sleeping Dogs, 1990; The Loud Conspiracy, forthcoming. Contributions to: Numerous national newspapers, magazines. Membership: Writers' Guild of Great Britain. Literary Agent: Heaton Green Ltd. Address: c/o Heaton Green Ltd, 37 Goldhawk Road, London W12 8QQ, England.

GARNETT Michael Pearson, b. 24 Nov 1938, Essex, England. Oil Company Officer; British Petroleum. m. Lyndi Coombe, 1975, divorced, 2 sons. Education: Framlington Coolege, Suffolk; Diploma, Business Management, British Institute of Careers, NSW, Australia.

Appointments: Flight Lieutenant, Royal Air Force in Far East during Malaya emergency, RAAF Reserve. Publications: A History of Royal Tennis in Australia, 1983; Tennis, Rackets and Other Ball Games, 1986; Royal Tennis - For the Record, 1991; The Garnett Family - A History, 1985. Contributions to: Tennis Australia Magazine; Your Sport; In 1985 published a facsimile edition of the rare 1875 edition of, A Treatise on Tennis. Memberships: Melbourne Press Club. Literary Agent: Historical Publications, Melbourne. Address: The Chase, Romsey, Vic 3434, Australia.

GARNETT Richard (Duncan Carey), b. 1923, Britain. Writer; Publisher; Translator. Appointments: Production Manager 1951-59, Director 1954-66, Rupert Hart-Davis Ltd; Director, Adlard Coles Ltd, 1963-66; Editor 1966-82, Director 1972-82, Macmillan, London; Director, Macmillan Publishers, 1982-87. Publications: (ed) Goldsmith: Selected Works, 1950; (trans) Robert Gruss: The Art of the Aqualung, 1955; The Silver Kingdom (in US as The Undersea Treasure), 1956; (trans) Bernard Heuvelmans: On the Track of Unknown Animals, 1958; The White Dragon, 1963; Jack of Dover, 1966; (trans) Bernard Heuvelmans: In the Wake of the Sea-Serpents, 1968; (ed with Reggie Grenfell), Joyce, 1980; Constance Garnett, A Heroic Life, 1991; (ed) Sylvia and David, The Townsend Warner/Garnett Letters, 1994. Literary Agent: A P Watt Ltd, 20 John Street, London WC1N 2DR, England. Address: Hilton Hall, Hilton, Huntingdon, Cambridgeshire PE18 9NE, England.

GARRETT George (Palmer Jr), b. 11 June 1929, Orlando, Florida, USA. Writer. m. Susan Parrish Jackson, 1952, 2 sons, 1 daughter. Education: Columbia University; BA, 1952, MA, 1956, Princeton University. Literary appointments: US Poetry Editor, Transatlantic Review, Rome, then London, 1958-71; Contemporary Poetry Series Editor, University of North Carolina Press, Chapel Hill, 1962-68; Writer-in-Residence: Princeton University, New Jersey, 1964-65, University of South Carolina, Columbia, 1971-73, Bennington College, Vermont, 1979, University of Michigan, Ann Arbor, 1979-84; Co-Editor, Hollins Critic, Virginia, 1965-71; President, Associated Writing Programs, 1971-73; Contributing Editor, Contempora, Atlanta, 1971-; Assistant Editor, Film Journal, Hollins College, 1972-; Co-Editor, Poultry: A Magazine of Voice. Publications: Novels include: In the Briar Patch, 1961; Cold Ground Was My Bed Last Night, 1964; A Wreath for Garibaldi and Other Stories, 1969; The Magic Striptease, 1973; To Recollect a Cloud of Ghosts: Christmas in England, 1979; Plays: Sir Slob and the Princess: A Play for Children, 1962; Garden Spot, 1962; Screen plays: The Young Lovers, 1964; The Playground, 1965; Frankenstein Meets the Space Monster (co-author), 1966; Verse includes: For a Bitter Season and Selected Poems, 1967; Welcome to the Medicine Show: Postcards, Flashcards, Snapshots, 1978; Love's Shining Child: A Miscellany of Poems and Verses, 1981; The Collected Poems of George Garrett, 1984; Fiction includes: Death of the Fox, 1971; The Sucession, 1984; An Evening Performance, 1985; Poison Pen, 1986; Entered From The Sun, 1990; Whistling in the Dark, 1992; The Sorrows of Fat City, 1992; James Jones, 1994; Many edited volumes. Honours: Several grants and fellowships; T S Eliot Award, 1990; Malamud Award, PEN, 1991. Membership: Vice-Chancellor, Fellowship of Southern Writers. Literary Agent: Jane Gelfman/John Farquharson Ltd, USA. Address: 1853 Fendall Avenue, Charlottesville, VA 22903, USA.

GARRETT Leslie, b. 5 July 1932, Philadelphia, Pennsylvania, USA. Writer. m. (1) Jean Collier, 16 June 1951, (2) Linda Kerby, 18 Mar 1973, 1 daughter. Appointments: Director, Fiction Writers Workshop, Knoxville, Tennessee, 1983-84. Publications: The Beasts; In the Country of Desire. Contributions to: New World Writing; Nugget; Escapade; Evergreen Review; Four Quarters; Karamu; Climax; Confrontation; Gallery Magazine; Phoenix; The Crescent Review. Honours: The Maxwell Perkins Commemorative Novel Award; Art Alliance Awasrd; The Alex Halery Literary Fellowship Award. Literary Agent: The Loretta Barret Literary Agency. Address: 1531 Forest Avenue, Knoxville, TN 37916, USA.

GARRETT Richard, b. 15 Jan 1920, London, England. Author; Journalist. m. Margaret Anne Selves, 20 Aug 1945, 2 sons, 1 daughter. Education: Bradfield College. Publications include: Fast and Furious - The Story of the World Championship of Drivers, 1968; Cross Channel, 1972; Scharnhorst and Gneisenau - The Elusive Sisters, 1978; The Raiders, 1980; POW, 1981; Atlantic Disaster - The Titanic and Other Victims, 1986; Flight Into Mystery, 1986; Voyage Into Mystery, 1987; Great Escapes of World War II, 1989; Sky High, 1991; The Final Betrayal - The Armistice, 1918 ... And Afterwards, 1990; Biographies

of Generals Gordon Wolfe and Clive, and a number of children's books. Contributions to: Was Freelance Writer of periodical published by Shell for over 30 years; Sometime broadcaster of talks on Radio 2's John Dunn Show; Latterly regular contributor to County Magazine until its demise in late 1989. Membership: Society of Authors. Literary Agent: Watson, Little Ltd, 12 Egbert Street, London NW1 8LJ, Tunbridge Wells, Kent TN2 5NL, England.

GARRISON Daniel H, b. 24 Dec 1937, Hamilton, New York, USA. Professor. m. Tina Tinkham, 30 May 1991, 1 daughter. Education: AB, Harvard University, 1959; MA, University of North Carolina, 1963; PhD, University of California, 1968. Publications: Mild Frenzy; The Language of Virgil; Who's Who in Wodehouse; The Student's Catullus; Horace Epodes and Odes. Contributions to: 19th Century Fiction; Arion 3; Medical History. Memberships: American Philological Association; American Association for the History of Medicine. Address: 1228 Simpson Street, Evanston, IL 60201, USA.

GARRISON Omar V, b. 2 June 1913. Author. m. Virginia Leah Herrick, 11 Sept 1952. Education includes: PhD, 1938. Publications: Tantra, philosophy, 1964; Balboa Conquistador, biography, 1971; Non-fiction: Spy Government, 1967; Howard Hughes in Las Vegas, 1970; Lost Gems of Secret Knowledge, 1973; Hidden Story of Scientology, 1984; Secret World of Interpol, 1977; Playing Dirty, 1980; The Baby That Laughed All Night, novel, 1989. Membership: Authors Guild. Address: 10 99 Cedar Knolls South, Cedar City, UT 84720, USA.

GARROW David J, b. 11 May 1953, New Bedford, Massachusetts, USA. Author; Professor. m. Susan Foster Newcomer, 18 Dec 1984. Education: BA magna cum laude, Wesleyan University, 1975; MA, 1978, PhD, 1981, Duke University. Appointments: Senior Fellow, The Twentieth Century Fund, 1991-93; Visiting Distinguished Professor, The Cooper Union, 1992-93; James Pinckney Harrison Professor of History, College of William and Mary, 1994-95. Publications: Protest at Selma, 1978; The FBI and Martin Luther King Jr, 1981; Bearing the Cross, 1986; The Montgomery Bus Boycott and the Women Who Started It (editor), 1987; Liberty and Sexuality, 1994. Contributions to: New York Times; Washington Post; Dissent; The Journal of American History; Constitutional Commentary. Honours: Pulitzer Prize in Biography, 1987; Robert F Kennedy Book Award, 1987; Gustavus Myers Human Rights Book Award, 1987. Memberships: Authors Guild; Phi Beta Kappa. Literary Agent: Jane Cushman, JCA Literary Agency, New York City, USA. Address: 200 Cabrini Boulevard PH9, New York, NY 10033, USA.

GARSIDE Jack Clifford (Nick Carter, Jack Hild, Don Pendleton, William K Wells), b. 4 Oct 1924, Montreal, Quebec, Canada. Consultant; Author; Lecturer. m. Mary Wyness Mason, 2 Sept 1944, 2 sons. Education: University of Toronto; Sir George Williams University, Montreal; Princeton University, New Jersey, USA. Appointments: Creative Writing Instructor (voluntary), Venice Library, Florida, USA, 1986-90. Publications: As William K Wells: Chaos, 1986; As Jack Hild: Sakhalin Breakout, 1986; Alaska Deception, 1986; As Nick Carter: East of Hell, 1986; Pressure Point, 1987; Lethal Prey, 1987; Afghan Intercept, 1987; Sukhumi Destruction, 1987; Black Sea Blood Bath, 1987; Sanction to Slaughter, 1988; Deep Sea Death, 1988; Singapore Sling, 1988; Arctic Abduction, 1989; As Don Pendleton: Desert Strike, 1988. Contributions to: Columnist, Friends of the Library, Venice, Florida. Membership: Mystery Writers of America. Literary Agent: Don Cong Don Associates Inc, New York, USA. Address: Coleman Lake, West Guildford, Ontario, Canada K0M 2S0.

GARTNER Chloe Maria, b. 21 Mar 1916, Troy, Kansas, USA. Writer. m. Peter Godfrey Trimble, 22 Jan 1942, div 1957, 1 daughter. Education: University of California; Mesa College, Grand Junction, Colorado; College Marin, Kentfield, California. Publications: The Infidels, 1960; Drums of Khartoum, 1967, 2nd Edition, 1968, German translation as Die Trommeln von Khartoum, 1970; Die Lange Sommer, 1970; Woman From The Glen, 1973; Mistress of the Highlands, 1976; Anne Bonney, 1977; The Image and the Dream, 1980, UK Edition, 1986; Still Falls the Rain, 1983; Dutch translation as Denkend Aan Morgen, Dromen Van Toen; Greenleaf, 1987; Lower Than the Angels, 1989. Contributions to: Cosmopolitan; Good Housekeeping; Others. Honours include: Silver Medal for The Infidels, Commonwealth Club of California, 1960. Memberships include: Authors Guild. Literary Agents: Kidde, Hoyt and Picard, New York City, USA. Address: c/o Kidde, Hoyt and Picard, 355 East 51st Street, New York, NY 10022, USA.

GARTON ASH Timothy John, b. 12 July 1955, England. Writer; Fellow of St Antonys College. m. Danuta Maria, 1982, 2 sons. Education: Sherborne, Oxford. Appointments: Editorial Writer, The Times, 1984-86; Foreign Editor, The Spectator, 1984-90; Columnist, The Independent, 1988-91; Fellow, St Antonys College, Oxford, 1990-. Publications: In Europe's Name; We The People; The Uses of Adversity; The Polish Revolution. Contributions to: New York Review of Books; The Spectator; The Independent; Granta. Honours: Somerset Maugham Award; David Watt Memorial Prize; Prix Européen de Essai. Address: St Antonys College, Oxford OX2 6JF, England.

GASCOIGNE Bamber, b. 24 Jan 1935. Author; Broadcaster; Publisher. m. Christina Ditchburn, 1965. Education: Scholar, Eton; Scholar, Magdalene College, Cambridge; Commonwealth Fund Fellow, Yale, 1958-59. Appointments: Theatre Critic, Spectator 1961-63, Observer 1963-64; Co-editor, Theatre Notebook, 1968-74; Founder, Saint Helena Press, 1977; Chairman, Ackermann Publishing, 1981-85. Publications: Twentieth Century Drama, 1962; World Theatre, 1968; The Great Moghuls (with photographs by Christina Gascoigne), 1971; Murgatreud's Empire, 1972; The Heyday, 1973; The Treasures and Dynasties of China (photographs by Christina Gascoigne), 1973; Ticker Khan, 1974; The Christians (photographs by Christina Gascoigne), 1977; Images of Richmond, 1978; Images of Twickenham, 1981; (Illustrated by Christina Gascoigne), Why the Rope went Tight, 1981; Fearless Freddy's Magic Wish, 1982; Fearless Freddy's Sunken Treasure, 1982; Quest for the Golden Hare, 1983; Cod Streuth, 1986; How to Identify Prints, 1986; Encyclopedia of Britain, 1993; TV Presenter: University Challenge, 1962-87; Connoisseur, 1988-89; Presenter and author of documentary series: The Christians, 1977; Victorian Values, 1987; Man and Music, 1987-89; The Great Moghuls, 1990; Brother Felix and the Virgin Saint, 1992. Address: Saint Helena Terrace, Richmond, Surrey TW9 1NR, England.

GASCOIGNE John, b. 20 Jan 1951. Historian. m. Kathleen May Bock, 6 Apr 1980, 1 son, 1 daughter. Education: BA, Sydney University, 1969-72; MA, Princeton University, 1973-74; PhD, Cambridge University, 1974-80. Appointments: Lecturer, Department of History, University of Papua, 1977-78; Tutor, University of NSW, 1980-84; Lecturer, 1984-89; Senior Lecturer, 1989-. Publications: Cambridge in the Age of the Enlightenment; Joseph Banks and the English Enlightenment; Useful Knowledge and Polite Culture, 1994. Contributions to: Historical Journal; Social Studies of Science; History; Science in Context. Honours: Joint Winner, Australian Historical Association Hancock Prize. Address: School of History, University of New South Wales, Sydney, NSW 2052, Australia.

GASCOYNE David Emery, b. 10 Oct 1916, Harrow, Middlesex, England. Writer; Poet. m. Judy Tyler Lewis, May 1975, 4 stepchildren. Education: Regent Street Polytechnic Secondary, London, 1930-32. Publications include: A Short Survey of Surrealism, 1936, USA, 1982; Night Thoughts, 1956, USA, 1958; Collected Poems, 1965; Collected Verse Translations, 1970; Paris Journal 1937-39, 1978; Journal 1936-37, 1980; Collected Poems, 1988; The Collected Journals 1936-42, 1990. Contributions to: New Verse; The Criterion; Partisan Review; New Writing; Adam International; Horizon; Poetry Nation Review; Cahiers du Sud; Nouvelle Revue Française; Europe; Botteghe Oscure; Temenos; Times Literary Supplement; The Independent. Honours: Atlantic Award, 1946-47; Primo Biella-Poesia Europea, 1982. Memberships: Fellow, Royal Literary Society; Committee Member, World Organization of Poets, Luxembourg; Committee Member, Biennales Internationales de Poésie. Belgium. Literary Agent: Alan Clodd, 22 Huntington Road, London N2 9DU, England. Address: 48 Oxford Street, Northwood, Cowes, Isle of Wight PO31 8PT, England.

GASH Jonathan (Graham Gaunt), b. 30 Sept 1933, Bolton, Lancashire, England. Doctor of Medicine. 3 daughters. Education: Graduated, Faculty of Medicine, London University, 1958; Royal Colleges of Surgeons and Physicians, London; Pathologist, Specialist in Infectious Diseases. Publications: The Judas Pair; Adapted for BBC TV series Lovejoy: Gold from Gemini, 1977, The Grail Tree, 1978, Firefly Gadroon, 1979, The Gondola Scam, 1980, The Vatican Rip, 1981, The Tartan Ringers, 1982, The Sleepers of Erin, 1983, Moonspender, 1984, Pearlhanger, 1985, Spend Game, 1986; Jade Woman, 1987; The Very Last Gambado, 1989; As Graham Gaunt: The Incomer, 1980. Honours: John Creasey Award for Best First Crime Novel, Crime Writers Association, UK, 1976. Membership: Visiting Professor, Royal Society of Medicine Foundation. Address: c/o Desmond Elliott, 38 Bury Street, St James's, London SW1Y 6QU, England.

GASKELL Jane, b. 7 July 1941, Lancashire, England. Writer. Appointments: Feature Writer, Daily Express, 1961-65; Daily Sketch, 1965-71; Daily Mail, 1971-84. Publications: Atlan Books, including The Serpent (fantasy books), 1961 onwards; Strange Evil, 1957; King's Daughter, 1958; All Neat in Black Stockings, 1964 (filmed 1966); A Sweet Sweet Summer, 1970; Attic Summer; The Shiny Narrow Grin; The Fabulous Heroine; Summer Coming; Some Summer Lands, 1977; Sun Bubble, 1990. Honour: Somerset Maugham Award, 1970. Literary Agent: Michael Sharland. Address: Sharland Organisation, 9 Marlborough Crescent, Bedford Park, London W4 1HE, England.

GASKIN Catherine Marjella, b. 2 Apr 1929, Co Louth, Dundalk, Republic of Ireland. Novelist. m. Sol Cornberg, 1 Dec 1955. Education: Holy Cross College, Sydney, Australia; Conservation of Music, Sydney. Appointments: Freelance Writer, 1946-. Publications: This Other Eden, 1946; With Every Year, 1947; Dust in Sunlight, 1950; All Else is Folly, 1951; Daughter of the House, 1952; Sara Dane, 1955; Blake's Reach, 1958; Corporation Wife, 1960; I Know My Love, 1962; The Tilsit Inheritance, 1963; The File on Devlin, 1965; Edge of Glass, 1967; Fiona, 1970; A Falcon for a Queen, 1972; The Property of a Gentleman, 1974; The Lynmara Legacy, 1975; The Summer of the Spanish Woman, 1977; Family Affairs, 1980; Promises, 1982; The Ambassador's Women, 1985; The Charmed Circle, 1988. Memberships: Society of Authors; Author's Guild of America. Address: White Rigg, East Ballaterson, Maughold, Isle of Man IM7 1AR.

GASKIN John Charles Addison, b. 4 Apr 1936, Hitchin, England. Philosopher. m. 20 May 1972, 1 son, 1 daughter. Education: Oxford University, MA, 1956-60. Publications: The Quest for Eternity; Humes Philosophy of Religion; Varieties of Unbelief: Volumes on Hume, 1993;Hobbes, 1994; World's Classics and on the Epicurean Philosopers, 1995;. Contributions to: Philosophy; Ratio; Hibbert Journal; Hermathene; Icarus; Hume Studies; ET Al. Address: Trinity College, Dublin 2, Republic of Ireland.

GASPARIKOVA Viera, b. 15 Apr 1928, Martin-Priekopa, Slovakia. Senior Research Worker of Slovak Academy of Sciences. Education: High School Gymnasium, 1948; Philosophical Faculty, University of Bratislava, 1949-53; University of Prague, 1956-60; PhD, 1953, DSc, 1992, Slovak Academy of Sciences. Publications: Humor and Satire in the Slovak People's Folktales, 1960; Miraculous Tales of the Slovak People, 1984-85; Slovak Folk Prose and its Evolutionary Tendencies, 1987; Catalogue of Slovak Folk Prose I-II, 1991-92; Slovak Folk Tales, 1993; The Sun Horse, 1981; The Singing Linden Tree, 1972. Contributions to: About 300 contributions to Slovak and foreign journals in the fields of ethnology, folklore and literature. Honours: Honorary Fellow, International Society for Folk Narrative Research; Honorary Member, Polish Ethnological Society; Gold Medal, Presidium of the Slovak Academy of Sciences, 1988. Memberships: International Society for Ethnology & Folklore; Slovak Ethnologic Society; Presidium of Slovak Committee of Slavists. Address: Mikoviniho 9, Bratislava 831-02, Slovakia.

GASS William Howard, b. 30 July 1924, Fargo, North Dakota, USA. Professor. m. (1) Mary Pat O'Kelly, 1952, 2 sons, 1 daughter, (2) Mary Henderson, 1969, 2 daughters. Education: AB, Kenyon College, 1947; PhD, Cornell University, 1954; DLitt, Purdue University, 1985. Appointments include: Director, International Writers Center, Washington University, St Louis, Missouri, 1991-. Publications: Omensetters Luck; In the Heart of the Heart of the Country; Fiction and the Figures of Life; On Being Blue; Habitations of the World; Willie Masters' Lonesome Wife; The World Within the Word; The Tunnel, 1995. Contributions to: New York Review of Books; New York Times Book Review; Times Literary Supplement; New Republic; Harpers; The Nation; Esquire; Yale Review; Salmagundi; Iowa Review; River Styx; New Yorker; New American Review. Literary Agent: Lynn Nesbit. Address: International Writers Center, Washington University, Campus Box 1071, St Louis, MO 63130, USA.

GATENBY Greg, b. 5 May 1950, Toronto, Ontario, Canada. Artistic Director; Poet. Education: BA, English Literature, York University, 1972. Appointments: Editor, McClelland and Stewart, Toronto, 1973-75; Artistic Director, Harbourfront Reading Series and concomitant festivals, 1975-. Publications: Imaginative Work: Rondeaus for Erica, 1976; Adrienne's Blessing, 1976; The Brown Stealer, 1977; The Salmon Country, 1978; Growing Still, 1981; Anthologies: 52 Pickup, 1977; Whale Sound, 1977; Whales: A Celebration, 1983; The Definitive Notes, 1991; The Wild Is Always There, 1993; Translator: Selected Poems, by Giorgio Bassani, 1980;

Forthcoming: The Wild Is Always There, vol 2, 1995. Honours include: City of Toronto Arts Award (Literature), 1989; League of Canadian Poets Honorary Lifetime Member, 1991; Jack Award (honouring Lifetime Promotion of Candian Books), 1994. Address: c/o Harbourfront Reading Series, 410 Queen's Quay West, Toronto, Ontario, Canada M5V 2Z3.

GATES Henry Louis Jr, b. 16 Sept 1950. Professor of English; Writer. Education: BA summa cum laude, History, Yale University, 1973; MA, English Language and Literature, 1974, PhD, English Language and Literature, 1979, Clare College, University of Cambridge. Appointments: Lecturer, Director of Undergraduate Studies, 1976-79, Assistant Professor, 1979-84, Associate Professor, 1984-85, English, Afro-American Studies, Yale University, USA; Professor, English, Comparative Literature, Africana Studies, 1985-88, W E B DuBois Professor of Literature, 1988-90, Cornell University; John Spencer Bassett Professor of English, Duke University, Durham, 1990; Currently Chairman, Afro-American Studies Department, Harvard University; Numerous editorial appointments. Publications include: Books: Figures in Black: Words, Signs and the Racial Self, 1987; The Signifying Monkey: Towards A Theory of Afro-American Literary Criticism, 1988; Colored People, 1994; Editor, many books including: Their Eyes Were Watching God, 1989; Jonah's Gourd Vine, 1990; Tell My Horse, 1990; Mules and Men, 1990; Voodoo Gods of Haiti, 1990; Reading Black, Reading Feminist, 1990; Frederick Douglass: Autobiographies, 1994. Contributions to: Numerous essays, articles, book reviews, to magazines and journals. Honours include: Yale Afro-American Cultural Center Faculty Prize, 1983; Award for Cultural Scholarship, Zora Neal Hurston Society, 1986; Honourable Mention, John Hope Franklin Prize, American Studies Association, 1988; Candle Award, Morehouse College, 1989; American Book Award, 1989. Memberships include: Council on Foreign Relations; Union of Writers of the African Peoples; African Roundtable; African Literature Association. Address: Afro-American Studies Department, Harvard University, Cambridge, MA 02138, USA.

GATHORNE-HARDY Jonathon, b. 15 May 1933, Edinburgh, Scotland. Author. m. (1) Sabrina Tennant, 1962, 1 son, 1 daughter, (2) Nicolette Sinclair Loutit, 12 Sept 1985. Education: BA Arts, Trinity College, Cambridge, 1954-57. Publications: One Foot in the Clouds, novel, 1961; Chameleon, novel, 1967; The Office, novel, 1970; The Rise & Fall of the British Nanny, 1972, new editions, 1985-93; The Public School Phenomenon, 1977; Love, Sex, Marriage & Divorce, 1981; Doctors, 1983; The Centre of the Universe is 18 Baedeker Strasse, short stories, 1985; The City Beneath the Skin, novel, 1986; The Interior Castle - A Life of Gerald Brenan, biography, 1992; 10 novels for children. Contributions to: Numerous magazines and journals. Literary Agents: Curtis Brown; For Children's books: Laura Cecil. Address: 31 Blacksmith's Yard, Binham, Fakenham, Norfolk NR21 0AL, England.

GATTELLARI Rocky Vincente, b. 6 Sept 1942, Italy. Finance Broker. m. Emilia Nicosia, 4 Feb 1967, 2 daughters. Appointments: Owner, Finance Broker, Rocky Gattellari Finance Co Pty Ltd, Cabramatta, New South Wales, Australia. Publication: Biography: The Rocky Road. Address: 229 John Street, Cabramatta, New South Wales 2166, Australia.

GATTEY Charles Neilson, b. 3 Sept 1921, London, England. Author; Playwright; Lecturer. Education: London University. Publications include: Books: The Incredible Mrs Van Der Eist (biography), 1972; They Saw Tomorrow, 1977 (Paranormal); Queens of Song, 1979 (opera); The Elephant that Swallowed a Nightingale, 1981 (opera); Peacocks on the Podium, 1982 (music); Foie Gras and Trumpets (foreword by Dame Kiri Te Kanawa), 1984; Excess in Food, Drink and Sex, 1987; Prophecy and Prediction in the 20th Century, 1989; Luisa Tetrazzini (biography), 1995; TV Play: The White Falcon, 1955; Film: The Love Lottery, starring David Niven, 1954. Memberships: Society of Civil Service Authors, President since 1980; The Garrick. Address: 15 St Lawrence Drive, Pinner, Middlesex HA5 2RL, England.

GATTI Armand, b. 26 Jan 1924, Morocco (French citizen). Playwright. Education: Seminary of Saint Paul, near Cannes. Appointments include: Former Journalist. Publications: Le Poisson noir, 1958, 1964; La Crapaud buffle, 1959; Theatre, 3 volumes, 1960-64; L'Enfant - rat, 1961; Le Voyage de Grand Tchou, 1960; Public Performance Before Two Electric Chairs, 1966; Un Homme Seul, 1966; V comme Vietnam, 1967; Le Passion du Général Franco, 1967; La Cigogne, 1968; La Naissance, 1968; Rosa Collective, 1971; La Colonne Durruti, 1972; Le Joint, 1974; Four Schizophrenics in Search of an Unknown Country, 1974; Le Labyrinthe, 1982; Opéra avec titre long, 1986; Le Train, 1987; Oeuvres Théâtrales, 3 volumes, 1991 (Plays produced in Paris, Vienna, Berlin, Marseilles, Lyon, Bremen, Kassel, Genoa, Montreal and Toulouse); Screenplays and television plays. Honours include: Fenon Prize, 1959. Address: La Parole Errante, Esplan a de Benoît, Frachon 931000, Montreuil, France.

GAUNT Graham. See: **GASH Jonathan**.

GAVAC Donna B, b. 16 Sept 1926, Oregon, USA. Educator; Writer. m. Stanley Gavac, 8 June 1979, 2 sons, 2 stepsons, 1 stepdaughter. Education: BA History, George Fox College, 1949; MA, History, University of Michigan, 1949; PhD, Education Administration, University of Portland, 1960. Appointments: Editor, George Fox College, Crescent, 1947; Associate Editor, Northwest Sundial, 1956-59; Abstractor, Clio Press, 1960-65; Academic Dean, University of Alaska, 1970s; Co-Presenter, Employment Workshop, Bad Kissingt-on-Main, Germany, 1983; Researcher, Writer, Western Wordcraft, Anchorage, Alaska, 1985-. Publications include: Homemaker in History, TV series, KLOR-TV, 1957-58; Sources of Educational Controversy, book, 1960; Teaching of High School Social Studies (co-author), 1962; Poems in: American Poetry Anthology; Many Voices, Many Lands; Select Poets of the New Era, 1988-90. Contributions to: Historical Abstracts; His Magazine; America; History and Life; Northwest Sundial; Crescent; Alaska Women; Research in Education. Honours: National Collegiate Press Award, 1947; Gresham Lecturer, Renaissance Institute, 1961; 1-year Ford Foundation Grant, 1962-63; 3-month Grant, Danforth Foundation, 1975; 6-month Research and Travel Grant, University of Alaska, 1977-78; Poetry Award, US and Canada Poetry Center, California, 1989. Memberships: National Writers Club; Vice-President, Treasurer, Northwest Association of Community and Junior Colleges; Director, Board Secretary, Anchorage Civic Opera; Trustee, Commissioner, Northwest Association of Schools and Colleges; Director, Alaska Press Women, 1991; National Federation of Press Women. Address: Western Wordcraft, PO Box 220707, Anchorage, AK 99522, USA.

GAVASKAR Sunil, b. 10 July 1949, Bombay, India. Businessman. m. Mehrotra Marshniel, 23 Sept 1974, 1 son. Education: BA, Bombay University. Publications: Sunny Days; Idols; Ruins; One Day Wonders. Contributions to: Times of India; Hindustan Times; The Hindu; India Today; The Telegraph; Khales Times; Gulf News. Membership: Cricket Club of India. Address: E6 Everest, Tardeo, Bombay 400034, India.

GAVIN Catherine, b. Aberdeen, Scotland. Author. m. John Ashcraft, 1946. Education: MA, PhD, University of Aberdeen; Sorbonne, Paris, France. Publications: Liberated France, 1955; Madeleine, 1957; The Cactus and the Crown, 1962; The Fortress, 1964; The Moon Into Blood, 1966; The Devil in Harbour, 1968; The House Of War, 1970; Give Me The Daggers, 1972; The Snow Mountain, 1973; Traitors' Gate, 1976; None Dare Call It Treason, 1978; How Sleep The Brave, 1980; The Sunset Dream, 1983; A Light Women, 1986; The Glory Road, 1987; A Dawn of Splendour, 1989; The French Fortune, 1991. Contributions to: Time magazine; Kemsley newspapers; Daily Express. Honours: University Medal of Honour, Helsinki, 1970; Honorary DLitt, University of Aberdeen, 1986. Literary Agent: Scott Ferris Associates, London, England. Address: 1201 California Street, San Francisco, CA 94109, USA.

GAVIN Thomas Michael, b. 1 Feb 1941, Newport News, Virginia, USA. Professor. m. Susan Holahan, 5 July 1991, 2 daughters. Education: BA, MA, The University of Toledo. Appointments: Delta College, University Center, Michigan, 1972-75; Middlebury College, Middlebury, Vermont, 1975-80; University of Rochester, Rochester, New York, 1980-. Publications: Breathing Water; Kingkill; The Last Film of Emile Vico; "The Truth Beyond Facts". Contributions to: The Georgia Review; TriQuarterly. Honours: National Endowment for the Arts Fellowship; Andrew W Mellon Fellowship; Lillian Fairchild Award; Nominated for Pushcart Prize; Best of the Small Presses. Literary Agent: Georges Borchardt. Address: English Department, The University of Rochester, Rochester, NY 14627, USA.

GAY Peter (Jack), b. 20 June 1923, Berlin, Germany. Writer. m. Ruth Slotkin, 30 May 1959, 3 stepdaughters. Education: AB, University of Denver, 1946; MA, 1947, PhD, 1951, Columbia University; Psychoanalytic training, Western New England Institute for

Psychoanalysis, 1976-83. Publications: The Dilemma of Democratic Socialism: Eduard Bernstein's Challenge to Marx, 1952; Editor, The Question of Jean Jacques Rousseau, 1954; Voltaire's Politics: The Poet as Realist, 1959; Translated, Voltaire: Philosophical Dictionary, 1962; Translated, Voltaire: Candide, 1963; The Party of Humanity: Essays in the French Enlightenment, 1964; Editor, John Locke on Education, 1964; The Enlightenment: An Interpretation, Volume I: The Rise of Modern Paganism, 1966, Volume II: The Science of Freedom, 1969; A Loss of Mastery: Puritan Historians in Colonial America, 1966; Weimar Culture: The Outsider as Insider, 1968; Deism: An Anthology, 1968; Columbia History of the World (with John A Garraty), 1972; Modern Europe (with R K Webb), 2 volumes, 1973; The Enlightenment: A Comprehensive Anthology, 1973, Revised Edition, 1985; Style in History, 1974; Art and Act: On Causes in History - Manet, Gropius, Mondrian, 1976; The Bourgeois Experience, Victoria to Freud, Volume I, Education of the Senses, 1984, Volume II, The Tender Passion, 1986, Volume III, The Cultivation of Hatred, 1993; Freud: A Life for Our Time, 1989; Reading Freud, 1990. Honours include: Frederic G Melcher Book Award and National Book Award, for The Enlightenment, Volume I, 1967; Guggenheim Fellow, 1967-68, 1977-78; Nomination, Los Angeles Times Book Prize, for The Bourgeois Experience: Victoria to Freud, Volume I, 1990. Memberships: Phi Beta Kappa. Address: 105 Blue Trail, Hamden, CT 06518, USA.

GAYLE Emma, See: **FAIRBURN Eleanor M.**

GE Wujue, b. 12 Sept 1937, Wen-Zhou, Zhejiang, China. Writer. m. Zhao Baotsing, 1 Feb 1962, 1 daughter. Education: Graduated, Chinese Language and Literature Department, Beijing University, 1959. Literary appointments: Vice-Chairman, Ningxia Literature and Art Federation; Vice-Chairman, Chinese Writers Association. Publications: Ma Long's Call, 1980; The Story of Summer, 1982; Melody of the Banquet, 1982; She and Her Girl Friends, 1983; Four Days in Their Lives, 1985; That Strange Feeling, 1987; Contributions to: People's Literature; October. Honours: More than 10 awards for novels, reportages, TV plays, including: October Prize for Literature, 1982; Novel Circles Prize for Works, 1984; Prize for Excellent Plays of Chinese TV Drama, 1985; People's Literature Prize, Readers Most Favourite Work, 1986. Memberships: Chinese Writers Association; Ningxia Calligraphers Association; Chinese Journalists Society. Address: Ningxia Literature and Art Federation, Yingchuan, Ningxia, China.

GEBAUER Phyllis Feltskog, b. 17 Oct 1928, Chicago, Illinois, USA. Writer. m. Frederick A Gebauer, 2 Dec 1950. Education: BA, Northwestern University, Evanston, Illinois, 1950; MA, University of Houston, Texas, 1966; University of California, Los Angeles; University of California, Santa Barbara; Universidad Nacional Autonoma de Mexico. Appointments: Staff, Santa Barbara Writers Conference, 1980-. Instructor, University of California, Los Angeles, Extension, 1989-. Publication: The Pagan Blessing, novel. Contributions: Stories and articles: The Final Murder of Monica Marlowe; The Cottage; Lemuria II; The Canine Manifesto; Criticism: The Art of Give and Take; The Writers LA. Literary Agent: Bobbe Siegel, New York City, USA. Address: 515 W Scenic Drive, Monrovia, CA 91016, USA.

GEDDES Gary, b. Vancouver, British Columbia, Canada, 1940. Writer. Appointments: Visiting Assistant Professor, Trent University, Peterborough, Ontario, Canada, 1968-69; Lecturer, Carleton University, Ottawa, Ontario, 1971-72; Lecturer, University of Victoria, British Columbia, 1972-74; Writer-in-Residence, 1976-77, Visiting Associate Professor, 1977-78, University of Alberta, Edmonton; Visiting Associate Professor, 1978-79, Professor of English, 1979-, Concordia University, Montreal, Quebec; General Editor, Studies in Canadian Literature series. Publications: 20th Century Poetry and Poets, 1969, 3rd edition, 1985; 15 Canadian Poets (edited with Phyllis Bruce), 1970, 3rd edition, 1988; Poems, 1970; Rivers Inlet, verse, 1972; Snakeroot, verse, 1973; Letter of the Master of Horse, verse, 1973; Skookum Wawa: Writings of the Canadian Northwest (editor), 1975; The Inner Ear: an Anthology of New Canadian Poets (editor), 1983; The Terracotta Army, verse, 1984; I Didn't Notice the Mountain Growing Dark (co-translator), 1985; Changes of State, verse, 1986; Vancouver: Soul of a City (editor), 1986; The Unsettling of the West, stories, 1986; Hong Kong, verse, 1987; Letters from Managua, 1990; Light of Burning Towers, vrse, 1990; Girl By The Water, 1994. Honours include: E J Pratt Medal; National Poetry Prize, Canadian Authors Association; America's Best Book Award; Writers Choice Award; National Magazine Award; Archibald Lapman Prize; Milton Acorn Competition. Address: RR 1, Dunvegan, Ontario, Canada K0C 1J0.

GEE Maggie (Mary), b. 2 Nov 1948, Poole, Dorset, England. Novelist. m. Nicholas Rankin, 1983. Education: BA, 1969, M Litt, 1972, PhD, 1980, Somerville College, Oxford. Appointments include: Research Assistant, Wolverhampton Polytechnic, 1975-79; Eastern Arts Writing Fellow, University of East Anglia, 1982. Publications: Dying, In Other Words, 1981; The Burning Book, 1983; Light Years, 1985; Grace, 1988; Several Uncollected Short Shorties and a Play. Literary Agent: Mark Hamilton, A H Heath, 79 St Martins Lane, London WC2N 4AA. Address: c/o Faber & Faber Limited, 3 Queen Square, London WC1N 3AU, England.

GEE Maurice Gough, b. 22 Aug 1931, Whakatane, New Zealand. Writer. Education: MA, University of Auckland, 1954. Appointments: Robert Burns Fellow, University of Otago, 1964; Writing Fellow, Victoria University of Wellington, 1989; Katherine Mansfield Fellow, Menton, France, 1992. Publications: Novels: Plumb, 1978; Meg, 1981; Sole Survivor, 1983; Collected Stories, 1986; Prowlers, 1987; The Burning Boy, 1990; Going West, 1993; Crime Story, 1994; Seven novels for children. Honours: New Zealand Book Award, 1976; 1979, 1981, 1991; New Zealand Book of the Year Award, 1979, 1993; James Tait Black Memorial Prize, 1979; Hon DLitt, Victoria University of Wellington, 1987. Memberships: PEN (New Zealand Centre), National Vice-President, PEN, 1990-91. Literary Agent: Richards Literary Agency, Auckland. Address: 41 Chelmsford Street, Ngaio, Wellington, New Zealand.

GEE Shirley, b. 25 Apr 1932, London, England. Playwright. m. Donald Gee, 30 Jan 1965, 2 sons. Education: Webber-Douglas Academy of Music and Drama. Publications: Plays on radio, TV and Stage; Stones, 1974; Typhoid Mary, 1979; Never in My Lifetime, 1983; Long Live the Babe, 1985; Ask for the Moon, 1986; Warrior, 1989; Bedrock, 1982; Moonshine, 1977; Flights, 1984; Against the Wind, 1988; Adaptations: The Vet's Daughter; Men on White Horses; The Forsyte Saga (co-adapted); Children's poems, stories and songs. Honours: Radio Times Drama Bursary Award, 1974; Giles Cooper Award, 1979; Pye Award, 1979; Jury's Special Commendation Prix Italia, 1979; Giles Cooper Award, 1983; Sony Award, 1983; Samuel Beckett Award, 1984; Susan Smith Blackburn Prize, 1985. Memberships: Broadcasting Committee, Society of Authors, 1983-85; Theatre Committee/Women's Committee, Writers Guild, 1986-88. Literary Agent: John Rush, Shiel Lane Ass Ltd, 43 Doughty Street, London, WC1N 2LF, England.

GEERTZ Clifford, Anthropologist. m. Karen Blu. Publications: The Development of the Javanese Economy, 1956; Religion of Java, 1960; Old Societies & New States, 1963; Agricultural Evolution, 1963; Islam Observed, 1968; The Interpretation of Cultures, 1973; Myth, Symbol & Culture (ed), 1974; Meaning & Order in Moroccan Society, 1979; Negara: The Theater State in Nineteenth Century Bali, 1980; Local Knowledge, 1983; Works & Lives: The Anthropologist as Author, 1988; After the Fact: An Anthropological Retrospective, 1995. Contributions to: New York Review of Books; many articles in scholarly journals. Honour: National Book Critics Circle Award, 1988. Address: Institute for Advanced Study, Olden Lane, Princeton, NJ 08540, USA.

GEISMAR Ludwig Leo, b. 1921, USA. Professor of Social Work and Sociology; Writer. Appointments: Coordinator of Social Research, Ministry of Social Welfare, Israel, 1954-56; Research Director, Family Centred Project, St Paul, Minnesota, USA, 1956-59; Associate Professor, 1959-62, Professor, Social Work and Sociology, Director, Social Work Research Center, Graduate School of Social Work and Department of Sociology, 1963-, Rutgers University, New Brunswick, New Jersey. Publications: Understanding the Multi-Problem Family: A Conceptual Analysis and Exploration in Early Identification (with M A LaSorte), 1964; The Forgotten Neighborhood: Site of an Early Skirmish in the War on Poverty (with J Krisberg), 1967; Preventive Intervention in Social Work, 1969; Family and Community Functioning, 1971, 1980; Early Supports for Family Life (Lagay, Wolock Gerhart and Fink), 1972; 555 Families: A Social Psychological Study of Young Families in Transition, 1973; Families in an Urban Mold (with S Geismar), 1979; A Quarter Century of Social Work Education (edited with M Dinerman), 1984; Family and Delinquency: Resocializing the Young Offender (with K Wood), 1986; Families at Risk (with K Wood), 1989; The Family Functioning Scale: A Guide to Research and Practice (with M Camasso), 1993. Address: 347 Valentine Street, Highland Park, NJ 08904, USA.

GEIST Harold, b. 22 July 1916, Pittsburgh, Pennsylvania, USA. Clinical Psychologist. Education: AB, Cornell University, Ithaca, New

York, 1936; MA, Columbia University, New York City, 1937; PhD, Stanford University, Palo Alto, California, 1951. Publications: The Etiology of Idiopathic Epilepsy, 1962; A Child Goes to the Hospital, 1964; The Psychological Aspects of Diabetes, 1965; The Psychological Aspects of Rheumatoid Arthritis, 1967; The Psychological Aspects of the Aging Process, 1968; From Eminently Disadvantaged to Eminence, 1980; Tennis Psychology, 1981; Emotion Aspects of Heart Disease, 1982; Bahian Adventure, novel, 1982; Migraine, 1983; Manual for Retirement Counsellors, 1988; To Russia With Love, novel, 1990; Commonalities in Psychosomatic Medicine, 1991. Contributions to: 75 articles to magazines and journals. Honours: Doctor of Letters, University of London, 1991. Memberships: Authors Guild of America; Life Member: American Psychological Association; American Association for the Advancement of Science; American Personnel and Guidance Association; International Council of Psychologists. Address: 2255 Hearst Avenue, Berkeley, CA 94709, USA.

GELBART Larry, b. 25 Feb 1928, Chicago, Illinois, USA. Writer. m. Pat Marshall, 25 Nov 1956, 3 sons, 2 daughters. Publications: Co-author: A Funny Thing Happened on the Way to the Forum, musical comedy, 1963; Tootsie, screenplay, 1984; Mastergate, play, 1989; Author: City of Angels, musical, 1989; The Wrong Box, screenplay; Oh, God, screenplay; Movie, Movie, screenplay; Developed and wrote for TV: MASH series; Barbarians at the Gate, 1993. Contributions to: Harper's Bazaar, 1993-94. Address: 9255 Sunset Boulevard, Suite 404, Los Angeles, CA 90069, USA.

GELINAS Gratien, b. 8 Dec 1909, Canada. Actor; Playwright; Producer. m. (1) Simone Lalonde, 1935 (dec. 1967), 4 sons, 1 daughter, (2) Huguette Oligny, 1973. Appointments: Accountant, La Sauvegarde Insurance Co, 1929-37; Actor, casual radio and stage performances including creation of character of Fridolin in series of monologues; Writer, Star: TV serial Les Quat'fers en l'air, 1954-55; Fridolinades, revue, 1956. Publications: Series of 10 topical revues starring Fridolin; Tit-Coq, play, 1949; Bousille et les justes, 1959; Le diable à quatre, satirical revue, 1964; Hier les enfants dansaient, 1966; The Passion of Narcisse Mondoux (translated from French), 1992; Films: La Dame aux Camelias, 1942; Tit-Coq. Honours: Grand Prix, Dramatists Society, 1949; Film of Year Award, for Tit-Coq, 1953; Honorary LLD: Saskatchewan, 1966, McGill, 1968, New Brunswick, 1969, Trent, 1970, Mount Allinson, 1973; Victor Morin Prize, 1967. Memberships: President, Canada Theatre Institute, 1959-60; Founding Member, National Theatre School of Canada, 1960; Royal Society of Canada; Chairman, Canada Film Development Corporation, 1969-78; Other professional organisations. Address: 316 Girouard Street, Box 207, OKA, Quebec, Canada J0N 1E0.

GELLIS Roberta Leah (Max Daniels, Priscilla Hamilton, Leah Jacobs), b. 27 Sept 1927, Brooklyn, New York, USA. Author. m. Charles Gellis, 14 Apr 1947, 1 son. Education: BA, Hunter College, 1947; MS, Brooklyn Polytechnic Institute, 1952. Literary appointments: Copy Editor, McGraw Hill Book Company, 1953-55; Freelance Editor, 1955-. Publications: Knight's Honor, 1964; Bond of Blood, 1965; The Dragon and the Rose, 1977; The Sword and the Swan, 1977; The Space Guardian (as Max Daniels), 1978; Offworld (as Max Daniels), 1979; The Love Token (as Priscilla Hamilton); The Rope Dancer, 1986; Masques of Gold, 1987; A Delicate Balance, 1993; Dazzling Brightness, 1994; The Roselynde Chronicles series: Roselynde, 1978; Alinor, 1978; Joanna, 1979; Gilliane, 1980; Rhiannon, 1982; Sybelle, 1983; The Royal Dynasty series: Siren Song, 1980; Winter Song, 1982; Fire Song, 1984; A Silver Mirror, 1989; The Napoleonic Era series: The English Heiress, 1980; The Cornish Heiress, 1981; The Kent Heiress, 1982; Fortune's Bride, 1983; A Woman's Estate, 1984; Tales of Jernaeve series: Tapestry of Dreams, 1985; Fires of Winter, 1986. Address: PO Box 483, Roslyn Heights, NY 11577, USA.

GELPI Albert, b. 1931, USA. Professor; Writer. Appointments: Assistant Professor, Harvard University, Cambridge, Massachusetts, 1962-68; Associate Professor, 1968-74; Professor, 1974-78, Coe Professor of American Literature, 1978-, Stanford University, Stanford, California. Publications: Emily Dickinson: The Mild of the Poet, 1965; The Poet in America, 1950 to Present, 1973; The Poetry of Adrienne Rich (edited with Barbara Charlesworth Gelpi), 1975; The Tenth Muse: The Psyche of the American Poet, 1975; Wallace Stevens: The Poetics of Modernism (editor), 1986; A Coherent Splendor: The American Poetic Renaissance 1910-1950, 1987; Adrienne Rich's Poetry and Prose (edited with Barbara Charlesworth Gelpi), 1993; Selected Criticism: Denise Levertov (editor), 1993; The Blood of the Poet: Selected Poems of William Everson (edited with introduction), 1994.

Address: Department of English, Stanford University, Stanford, CA 94305, USA.

GENOVESE Eugene D, b. 19 May 1930, NY, USA. Historian. m. Elizabeth Ann Fox, 6 June 1969. Education: BA, Brooklyn College, 1953; MA, 1955, PhD, 1959, Columbia University. Publications include: Roll, Jordan, Roll, 1974; The Political Economy of Slavery, 1965; The World The Slaveholders Made, 1969; From Rebellion to Revolution, 1979; The Slaveholders Dilemma, 1991; The Southern Tradition, 1994. Honours: Am Academy of the Arts Award, 1975; Bancroft Prize, 1994. Memberships: Am Academy of Arts & Science. Address: 1482 Sheridan Walk, Atlanta, GA 30324, USA.

GENSLER Kinereth Dushkin, b. 17 Sept 1922, New York City, New York, USA. Poet; Teacher; Widow, 2 sons, 1 daughter. Education: BA, University of Chicago, 1943; MA, Columbia University, 1946. Literary Appointments: Editor, Alice James Books, 1976-90. Publications: Threesome Poems, 1976; The Poetry Connection (co-author), 1978; Without Roof, 1981; Book chapters: Dream Poems in Broad Daylight, 1975; Poetry and the Impossible, 1988; Poems in anthologies: Best Poems of 1975. Contributions to: Andover Review; Florida Review; Green House; Massachusetts Review; New Renaissance; New York Times; Ploughshares; Poetry; Poetry Northwest; Poets On; Prairie Schooner; Radcliffe Quarterly, including Making of a Cooperative Feminist Press, 1988; Sequoia; Shenandoah; Slant; Sojourner; Virginia Quarterly Review; Women/Poems; Yankee; Yarrow. Honours: Members Award, Poetry Society of America, 1969; Power Dalton Award, New England Poetry Club, 1971; Borestone Mountain Award, 1973; Residency, Ragdale, 1981; Residency, MacDowell Colony, 1982, 1983. Memberships: Academy of American Poets; Alice James Cooperative Society; New England Poetry Club; Poetry Society of America. Address: 221 Mt Auburn St, Cambridge, MA 02138, USA.

GENTLE Mary Rosalyn, b. 29 Mar 1956, Sussex, England. Writer. Education: BA, English, Politics, Geography, 1985, MA, 17th Century Studies, 1988. Literary appointments: Chairperson, Milford Science Fiction Writers Convention, 1989; Guest of Honour, Chronoclasm Convention, Derby, 1990. Publications: A Hawk in Silver, 1977; Golden Witchbreed, 1983; Ancient Light, 1987; Scholars and Soldiers, 1989; Rats and Gargoyles, 1990; The Architecture of Desire, 1991; Gruntsl, 1992; Co-editor, Midnight Rose/Penguin Books anthologies: The Weerde Book 1, 1992; Villainsl, 1992; The Weerde Book 2, The Book of the Ancients, 1993. Contributions to: Review Column, Interzone. Memberships: Society of Authors; British Science Fiction Association; SWFA. Literary Agent: Maggie Noach, The Maggie Noach Literary Agency, 21 Redan Street, London W14 0AB, England. Address: 37 Beane Avenue, Stevenage, Herts SG2 7DL, England.

GENTRY Robert Bryan, b. 21 July 1936, Knoxville, Tennessee, USA. Writer; Educator. m. Mary Sue Koeppel, 31 May 1980, 2 sons. Education: BS, 1958, MA, 1966, University of Tennessee, 1958; US Army Language School, 1959; Graduate work: University of Georgia, 1968-72; University of New Hampshire, 1977. Appointments: Professor of Humanities, Florida Community College, 1972-; Editor, Riverside-Avondale Historic Preservation Publication, 1975-76; College Historian, Florida Community College, 1988-91. Publications: The Rise of the Hump House, novel, 1976; A College Tells Its Story: An Oral History of Florida Community College at Jacksonville, 1963-1991, 1991. Contributions to: A Diarist's Journal; Kalliope: A Journal of Women's Art; Teaching English in the Two-Year College. Honours: Professor of the Year, Florida Community College, 1985; Prize Winner, Quest for Peace Writing Contest, University of California, 1988; Nominated for National Pushcart Award. Memberships: Community College Humanities Association; US English. Address: 3879 Oldfield Trail, Jacksonville, FL 32223, USA.

GEORGE Barbara. See: **KATZ Bobbi.**

GEORGE Elizabeth, Author. Publications: Detective novels: A Great Deliverance; Payment in Blood; Payment Defence, 1990; For the Sake of Elena, 1992; Missing Joseph, 1993; Playing for the Ashes, 1994. Honours: Grand Prix de Littérature Policière, 1990. Address: Huntington Beach, California, USA.

GEORGE Emily. See: **KATZ Bobbi.**

GEORGE Jean Craighead, b. 21 July 1919, Washington, District of Columbia, USA. Author; Illustrator. m. John L George, 28 Jan 1944, div. 1963, 2 sons, 1 daughter. Education: BA, Pennsylvania State University. Literary appointments: Reporter, Washington Post, 1943-46; Roving Editor, Reader's Digest, 1965-84. Publications: My Side of the Mountain, 1959; Summer of the Falcon, 1962; The Thirteen Moons, 1967-69; Julie of the Wolves, 1972; Going to the Sun, 1976; Wounded Wolf, 1978; The American Walk Book, 1978; River Rats, 1979; The Grizzly Bear with the Golden Ears, 1982; The Cry of the Crow, 1982; Journey Inward, 1982; Talking Earth, 1983; How to Talk to Your Animals, 1985; Water Sky, 1987; One Day in the Woods, 1988, as musical, 1989; Shark Beneath the Reef, 1989; On the Far Side of the Mountain, 1990; One Day in a Tropical Rain Forest, 1990; Missing 'Gator of Gumbo Limbo, 1992; The Fire Bug Connection, 1993; Dear Rebecca Winter is Here, 1993; The First Thanksgiving, 1993; Julie, 1994; To Climb a Waterfall, 1995; Animals Who Have Won Our Love, 1994. Address: 20 William Street, Chappaqua, NY 10514, USA.

GEORGE Jonathan. See: **BURKE John Frederick.**

GEORGE Kathleen Elizabeth, b. 7 July 1943, Johnstown, Pennsylvania, USA. Associate Professor. Education: BA, 1964; MA, 1966; PhD, 1975, MFA, 1988. Appointments: Associate Professor, University of Pittsburgh Theatre Department, Pittsburgh, Pennsylvania. Publications: Rhythm in Drama; Playwriting: The First Workshop, 1994. Contributions to: Mademoiselle Magazine; Cimarron Review; Great Stream; Gulf Stream; Alaska Quarterly; West Branch; North American Review; Other Voices. Honours: Louise Laetitia Miele Writing Award; Best American Short Stories: Honours List; Finalist, Pirates Alley Contest. Memberships: Poets and Writers; Association for Theater in Higher Education; Associated Writing Programs; Theater Communication Group; Dramatists Guild. Literary Agent: Kit Ward. Address: 1617 CL, University of Pittsburgh, Pittsburgh, PA 15260, USA.

GEORGEOGLOU Nitsa-Athina, b. 4 Sept 1922, Athens, Greece. Author. m. 9 Nov 1947, 2 sons. Education: Graduate: Greek Gymasium, 1938; Superior Studies, French Institute of Athens. Publications include: 21 novels, 5 books of essays, 1 historical book including: The Wrath of the Earth, 1978; Tom, Tommy and Co, 1971; Vravron, before the Christian Era, 1980; Chronicle of Thyateira, 1981; Seas Afire, 1984; SOS Danger! 1986; Once in Missolonghi, 1971; The Secret Society, 1973; A Ship Called Hope, 1975; Enterprise Archemides, 1977; Toto is My Guest, 1977; Waves and Islands, 1978; Up the Hill, 1979; The Horse Farm, 1981; The Golden Coin, 1982; Saturn Calling, 1984; On Foreign Land, 1985; The Will of Youth, 1987; Uranus Calling, 1987; Walking Through the Centuries, 1987; Difficult Steps, 1988; The Gods of Olympus, 1988; The Three S's, 1989; Adventure in Athens, 1990; Soldiers for Fun, 1991; Sealed Envelopes, 1992; Sunrise, 1993; On the Wings of Youth, 1993; Written on the Waves, 1994; Storm and Lull, 1994. Contributions to: Numerous journals and magazines. Honours include: Award, Woman's Literary Committee of Athens, 1969, 1970, 1971, 1979, 1980, 1981, 1985; Award Circle of Greek Children's Book Authors, 1970, 1977, 1978; Hans Christian Anderson Honour List, 1982; Award of the Woman's Litt Committee, 1992; National Award for the best book for Youth for the year 1989, awarded on 1992. Memberships include: National Society of Greek Authors; Greek IBBY; Vice President, Greek Union, International Soroptimist; Hestia Cultural Club. Address: 83 Plastira Street, 171 21 Nea Smirni, Athens, Greece.

GERGELY Agnes, b. 5 Oct 1933, Endrod, Hungary. Writer. Education: University of Liberal Arts, Budapest, MA 1957; PhD, 1979. Appointments: Teacher, 1957-63; Producer, Radio Budapest, 1963-71; Writer, 1971-74; Editor, 1974-77; Head of Third World Literature Column, 1977-88; Freelance Writer, 1988-; University Lecturer, 1992-. Publications include: Cobalt Country II, Shadow City; The Interpreter; The Chicago Version; Stations of the Cross; A Hungarian of the West, W B Yeats; A Land of King's, Poems; Central Europe Was Promises, essays. Contributions to: Contemporary; Life & Letters; Great World; By the Tisza; 2000; Pompeii. Honours: Attila Jozsef Prize; Tibor Dery Award; Milan Fust Prize; 1995; Honorary Fellow of University of Iowa. Memberships: Hungarian Writers Union; Hungarian Creative Artists Foundation; Hungarian PEN Club; Hungarian Journalists National Union. Literary Agent: Hungarian Copywright Agency, ARTISJUS. Address: Pannonia u 64/B, 1133 Budapest, Hungary.

GERMAIN Jean-Claude, b. 18 June 1939, Montreal, Canada. Author; Director; Actor. Education: Collège Sainte, Université de Montreal. Appointments: Anchorman, Faut Voirca weekly television show; Anchorman, Daily Radio Chronic, CBF Bonjour. Publications:

Les Hauts et les Bas d'la Vie d'une Diva; Un Pays dont la devise est je m'oublie; Les Faux; L'Ecole des reues; A Canadian Play. Contributions to: Le Quebec Littéraire; L'Illettre; Maclean Magazine; Jeu; Canadian Theatre Review. Honours: Prix Victor Morin; Le Salon du Livre de Montréal; Conseil des Arts du Canada. Memberships: Centre d'essai des auteurs dramatiques; L'Association des Directeurs de Théâtre; L'Ecole National du Théâtre du Canada. Literary Agent: Agence Goodwin, Canada. Address: 839 Est, Rue Sherbrooke, MH, PQ, Canada H2L 1K6.

GERMANO Peter B (Jack Bertin, Jackson Cole, Barry Cord, Jim Kane, Jack Slade), b. 1913, USA. Freelance Writer. Publications: Trail Boss from Texas, 1948; The Gunsmoke Trail, 1951; Shadow Valley, 1951; Mesquite Johnny, 1952; Trail to Sundown, 1953; Cain Basin, 1954; The Sagebrush Kid, 1954; Boss of Barbed Wire, 1955; Dry Range, 1955, UK edition The Rustlers of Dry Range, 1956; The Guns of Hammer, 1956; The Gunshy Kid, 1957; Sheriff of Big Hat, 1957; Savage Valley, 1957; The Prodigal Gun, 1957; Concho Valley, 1958; Gun-Proddy Hombre, 1958; The Iron Trail Killers, 1959; Starlight Range, 1959; The Third Rider, 1959; Six Bullets Left, 1959; War in Peaceful Valley, 1959; Maverick Gun, 1959; Last Chance at Devil's Canyon, 1959; Two Guns to Avalon, 1962; The Masked Gun, 1963; Last Stage to Gomorrah, 1966; A Ranger Called Solitary, 1966; Canyon Showdown, 1967; Gallows Ghost, 1967; The Long Wire, 1968; Trouble in Peaceful Valley, 1968; The Interplanetary Adventures (as Jack Bertin), science fiction, 1970; The Coffin Fillers, 1972; Brassado Hill, 1972; Desert Knights, 1973; The Running Iron Samaritans, 1973; Hell in Paradise Valley, 1978; Gun Junction, 1979; Deadly Amigos: Two Graves for a Gunman, 1979; As Jim Kane: Gunman's Choice, 1960; Renegade Rancher, 1961; Spanish Gold, 1963; Tangled Trails, 1963; Lost Canyon, 1964; Red River Sheriff, 1965; Rendezvous at Bitter Wells, 1966; Texas Warrior, 1971.

GERRISH Brian Albert, b. 14 Aug 1931, London, England. University Professor. m. (1) 1 son, 1 daughter, (2) Dawn Ann De Vries, 3 Aug 1990, 1 daughter. Education: BA, 1952, MA, 1956, Queens' College, Cambridge; STM, Union Theological Seminary, New York City, 1956; PhD, Columbia University, 1958. Appointments include: Associate Professor, Historical, Theology, 1965-68, Professor, 1968-85, John Nuveen Professor, 1985-, Divinity School, University of Chicago, Illinois, USA; Co-Editor, Journal of Religion, 1972-85. Publications: Grace and Reason: A Study in the Theology of Luther, 1962, Japanese translation, 1974, reprint, 1979; Tradition and the Modern World: Reformed Theology in the Nineteenth Century, 1978; The Old Protestantism and the New: Essays on the Reformation Heritage, 1982; A Prince of the Church: Schleiermacher and the Beginnings of Modern Theology, 1984, Korean translation, 1988; Grace and Gratitude: The Eucharistic Theology of John Calvin, 1993; Continuing the Reformation: Essays on Modern Religious Thought, 1993; Editor: The Faith of Christendom: A Source Book of Creeds and Confessions, 1963; Reformers in Profile, 1967; Reformatio Perennis: Essays on Calvin and the Reformation in Honor of Ford Lewis Battles, 1981. Address: 1363 E 55th Place, Chicago, IL 60637-1709, USA.

GERROLD David, b. 1944, USA. Writer of Science Fiction and Fantasy; Computer Columnist. Appointments: Story Editor, TV series Land of the Lost, 1974; Computer Columnist, CIT Profiles, 1984-; Columnist, Starlos and Galileo magazines; Freelance Writer, science fiction, short stories, screenplays, TV plays. Publications: The Flying Sorcerers (with Larry Niven), 1971; Generation (editor), 1972; Space Skimmer, 1972; Yesterday's Children, 1972; When Harlie Was One, 1972; With a Finger in My I, short stories, 1972; Battle for the Planet of the Apes, novelisation of screenplay, 1973; The Man Who Folded Himself, 1973; The Trouble with Tribbles, 1973; The World of Star Trek, 1973; Deathbeast, 1978; The Galactic Whirlpool, 1980; The War Against the Chtorr: A Matter for Man, 1983; A Day for Damnation, 1984; When Harlie Was One, 1987; When Harlie Was Two, 1987; Editor with Stephen Goldin: Protostars, 1971; Science Fiction Emphasis I, 1974; Alternities, 1974; Ascents of Wonder, 1977. Address: Box 1190, Hollywood, CA 90028, USA.

GERSTLER Amy, b. 1946. Publications: True Bride, 1986; Primitive Man, 1987; Past Lives, 1989; Bitter Angel, 1990; Nerve Storm, 1993. Honour: National Book Critics Circle Award, 1990.

GERVAIS C(harles) H(enry), b. 20 Oct 1946, Windsor, Ontario, Canada. Journalist; Editor; Poet. Education: BA, University of Guelph, Ontario, 1971; MA, University of Windsor, 1972. Appointments: Book Editor, from 1980, and Entertainment Features, from 1990, Windsor

Star. Publications: Sister Saint Anne, 1968; Something, 1969; Other Marriage Vows, 1969; A Sympathy Orchestra, 1970; Bittersweet, 1972; Poems for American Daughters, 1976; The Believable Body, 1979; Up Country Lines, 1979; Silence Comes with Lake Voices, 1980; Into a Blue Morning: Selected Poems, 1982; Public Fantasy: The Maggie T Poems, 1983; Letters from the Equator, 1986; Autobiographies, 1989; Plays: Baldoon, with James Reaney, 1976; Northern Calamities, 1976; The Fighting Parson, 1979. Honours include: Western Ontario Newspaper Awards.

GEYER Georgie Anne, b. 2 Apr 1935, Chicago, Illinois, USA. Syndicated Columnist; Author; Foreign Correspondent; Speaker; Educator. Education: BS, Journalism, Northwestern University, 1956; Fulbright Scholar, University of Vienna, Austria, 1956-57. Literary appointments include: Reporter, 1959-64, Foreign Correspondent, 1964-75, Chicago Daily News; Syndicated Columnist: Los Angeles Times, 1975-80; Universal Press, 1980-. Publications: Books: New Latins, 1970; The New 100 Years' War, 1972; The Young Russians, 1976; Buying the Night Flight, 1983; Guerrilla Prince, 1991; Waiting for Winter to End, 1994; Chapters in: The Responsibilities of Journalism, 1984; Beyond Reagan: The Politics of Upheaval, 1986. Literary Agent: Richard Curtis, New York City, USA. Address: The Plaza, 800 25th Street NW, Washington, DC 20037, USA.

GHOSE Zulfikar, b. 1935, Pakistan. Author; Poet. Appointments include: Cricket Correspondent, The Observer, London, England, 1960-65; Teacher, London, 1963-69. Publications: Statement Against Corpes (with B S Johnson), 1964; The Loss of India, verse, 1964; Confessions of a Native-Alien, 1965; Jets from Orange, verse, 1967; Penguin Modern Poets 25 (with Gavin Ewart and B S Johnson), 1974; Hamlet, Prufrock and Language, 1978; The Fiction of Reality, criticism, 1983; A Memory of Asia, poetry, 1984; Selected Poems, 1991; The Art of Creating Fiction, criticism, 1991; Shakespeare's Mortal Knowledge, criticism, 1993; Novels: The Contradictions, 1966; The Murder of Aziz Khan, 1967; The Incredible Brazilian Book 1, 1972; Crump's Terms, 1975; The Beautiful Empire, 1975; A Different World, 1978; Hulme's Investigations into the Bogart Script, 1981; A New History of Torments, 1982; Don Bueno, 1983; Figures of Enchantment, 1986; The Triple Mirror of the Self, 1992. Literary Agents: Aitken and Stone, London, England; Wylie, Aitken and Stone, New York City, USA. Address: Department of English, University of Texas, Austin, TX 78712, USA.

GHOSH Ajit Kumar, b. 1 Jan 1919, Shaistanager, Noakhali, India (now Bangladesh). Professor. m. Belarani Ghosh, 20 Apr 1940, 2 sons. Education: Matriculation, 1st Division, 1934; BA, Honours in English, 2nd class, 1938; MA, Bengali, 2nd class, 1940; PHD, 1959; DLitt, 1969. Appointments: Lecturer in Bengali: M M College, Jessore, 1941-47; Surendranath College, Calcutta, 1947-63; Lecturer, Reader, then Professor, 1963-91, Dean, Faculty of Arts, Head, Department of Bengali, 1970-83, Rabindra Bharati University; Editor, Encyclopaedia of Indian Literature, Sahitya Akademi, 1987; Editor, Modern Indian Literature, Sahitya Akademi, 1987; Editor, Modern Indian Literature, Sahitya Akademi, 1992; Editor, Masterpieces of Indian Literature, National Book Trust of India, 1993. Publications: Bangla Nataker Itihas (History of Bengali Drama); Banga Sahitye Hasyaraser Dhara (Humourin Bengali Literature); Saratchandrer Jibani-O-Sahitya Viehar (Life and Literary Arts of Saratchandra Chatterjee); Bangla Natyabhinayer Itihar (History of Stage Acting in Bengal); Nataker Katha (Principles of Drama); Natyatattva Parichay (Theory of Drama); Jibansilpi Saratchandra (Saratchandra: The Artist of Life); Thakurbarir Abhinay (History of Acting in Jorasanko Tagore family); Edited many famous writers' works; Natyatattva O Natyamancha (Theory of Drama and Stage), 1991; Rangamanche Bangla Nataker Prayog (Production of Bengali dramas on the stage), 1994. Contributions to: Over 50 scholarly articles to various magazines and journals. Honours: Appointed Dwijendralal Roy Reader, Rammohan Roy Lecturer, Dineschandra Sen Lecturer, Calcutta University; President, Literary Conferences; Participant, national seminars; Invited by International Congress of Human Sciences, Tokyo and Kyoto, 1983. Memberships: President, Bangiya Sahitya Parishad; Bangla Akademi; Natya Akademi; Senate, Calcutta University; Court, Rabindra Bharati University, Member, Ex Com; President, Calcutta Film Circle; President, Natya Vicharak Samiti; Nominated Member to select Authors, Nobel Prize Committee. Address: AE 510, Salt Lake, Calcutta 700064, India.

GHOSH Oroon Kumar, b. 22 Aug 1917, Calcutta, India. Civil Servant. m. Rekha Majurndar, 29 June 1943. 1 daughter. Education: Bachelor of Science, Rangoon University, 1938; Delhi University, 1953.

Appointments: Editorial Director, Minerva Associates, 1976-90. Publications include: Tales from the Indian Classics; The Dance of Shiva and Other Tales From India; Science, Society and Philosophy; Convergence of Civilizations; How India Won Freedom. Contributions to: Radical Humanist; World History Bulletin; Jijnasa. Memberships: PEN; Royal Asiatic Society; International Society for the Comparative Study of Civilizations; World History Association. Address: CD 6 Sector I, Salt Lake, Calcutta 700064, India.

GIANAKARIS Constantine John, b. 1934, USA. Writer. Appointments include: Co-Founder, Comparative Drama quarterly, 1966-90. Publications: Antony and Cleopatra, 1969; Plutarch, 1970; Foundations of Drama (author, editor), 1974; Co-editor: Drama in the Middle Ages, 1984; Drama in the Twentieth Century, 1985; Drama in the Renaissance, 1985; Peter Shaffer: A Casebook (editor), 1991; Peter Shaffer (author), 1992. Contributions to: Theater Week magazine; Opera News magazine; Theatre and music reviewer for Kalamazoo Gazette Daily. Address: Department of English, Western Michigan University, Kalamazoo, MI 49008, USA.

GIBBS Alonzo Lawrence, b. 17 Feb 1915, Brooklyn, New York, USA. Enginer; Writer. m. (1) Iris H Ebisch, 17 June 1939 (dec. Apr 1983), 1 son, (2) Priscilla Moss, 1986. Education: Hofstra University, 1938; Certificate in Aircraft Structural Layout, Columbia University, 1941. Appointments: Poetry Reviewer, Voices magazine, 1953-64; President, Kinsman Publications, 1961-64; Editor, Kinsman Literary Quarterly; Contributing Editor, Long Island Forum, 1964-. Publications include: Weather-House, 1959; The Fields Breathe Sweet, 1963; Monhegan, 1963; The Least Likely One, 1964; Dolphin Off Hippo, libretto, 1965; A Man's Calling, 1966; By a Sea-Coal Fire, 1969; Drift South, 1969; One More Day, 1971; Sir Urian's Letters Home, 1974; The Rumble of Time thru Town, 1980; Harking Back, 1983; In the Weir of the Marshes, 1990. Contributions to: Poetry and criticism to Voices magazine, 1953-64; Long Island Forum; Essays to Christian Science Monitor. Honours: Section Chief Engineer, Grumman Aerospace Corporation, Bethpage, New York, 1965-73. Membership: Authors Guild. Literary Agent: Curtis Brown. Address: HC 60, Box 20, Waldoboro, ME 04572, USA.

GIBSON Charles E(dmund), b. 1916. Writer (Children's Fiction, History). Publications: The Story of the Ship, 1948; The Secret Tunnel, 1948; Wandering Beauties, 1960; The Clash of Fleets, 1961; Knots and Splices, 1962; Plain Sailing, 1963; Daring Prows, 1963; Be Your Own Weatherman, 1963; The Two Olafs of Norway; With a Cross on Their Shields, 1964; The Ship with Five Names, 1965; Knots and Splices, 1979; Death of a Phantom Raider, 1987. Literary Agent: A M Heath & Co Ltd. Address: 59 Victoria Road, Shoreham-by-Sea, Sussex BN43 5WR, England.

GIBSON Graeme C, b. 9 Aug 1934, Ontario, Canada. Author. m. M Atwood, 2 s, 1 d. Education: MA, University of Western Ontario, 1959. Literary Appointments: Writer in Residence, University of Waterloo, 1982, University of Ottwa, 1985. Publications: Perpetual Motion, 1983; Gentleman Death, 1993; Eleven Canadian Novelists, 1973; Five Legs, 1969; Communion, 1971. Contributions to: Various. Honours: Toronto Arts Award, 1990; Order of Canada, 1992; Harbour Front Festival Prize, 1993. Memberships: The Writers Union of Canada; PEN. Literary Agent: Charlotte Sheedy Agency, 611 Broadway #428, New York, NY 10012, USA. Address: c/o Writers Union, 24 Ryerson Avenue, Toronto, Ontario M5T 2P3, Canada.

GIBSON Josephine. See: **JOSLIN Sesyle.**

GIBSON Margaret, b. 4 June 1948, Ontario, Canada. m. (separated), children. Publications: Lunes: Poems, 1973; On the Cutting Edge, 1976; The Butterfly Ward, 1977; Considering the Condition, 1978; Poem Aaron, 1978; Signs: Poems, 1979; Long Walks in the Afternoon, 1982; Memories of the Future: The Daybooks of Tina Mondotti, 1986; Out in the Open, 1989; The Vigil: a poem in 4 voices, 1993. Honours: Melville Cane Award, 1988; Literary Award from the City of Toronto, 1976.

GIBSON Morgan, b. 6 June 1929, Cleveland, Ohio, USA. Poet; Writer; Professor. m. 1) Barbara Gibson, 1950, div 1972, 2 daughters, 2) Keiko Matsui, 1978, 1 son. Education: BA, Oberlin College, 1950; MA, University of Iowa, USA, 1952; PhD, 1959. Publications: Revolutionary Rexroth: Poet of East West Wisdom; Tantric Poetry of Kukai; Among Buddhas in Japan; The Great Brook Book; Speaking of Light. Memberships: PEN; Academy of American Poets; Poetry Society of America; Buddhist Peace Fellowship. Address: Department of English, Japan Womens University, 2-8-1 Mejiro Dai, Bunkyo-Ku, Tokyo 112, Japan.

GIBSON Walter Samuel, b. 1932, USA. Writer. Publications: Hieronymus Bosch: The Paintings of Cornells Engerbrechsz; Bruegel; Hieronymus Bosch: An Annotated Bibliography; Mirror of the Earth: The World Landscape in Sixteenth Century Flemish Painting; Pieter Bruegel the Elder: Two Studies, 1991, 1993. Address: Department of Art History and Art, Mather House, Case Western Reserve University, Cleveland, OH 44106, USA.

GIBSON William (Ford), b. 1948, Conway, South Carolina, USA. Author. m. Deborah Thompson, June 1972, 1 son, 1 daughter. Education: BA, University of British Columbia, 1977. Publications: Neuromancer, 1984; Count Zero, 1985; Burning Chrome, 1986; Mona Lisa Overdrive, 1987; Dream Jumbo, 1989; The Difference Engine, 1990; Virtual Light, 1993. Contributions to: Omni; Rolling Stone; Science Fiction Review. Honours: Hugo Award, 1983; Nebula Awards, 1984; Philip K Dick Award, 1984; Porgie Award, 1985; Ditmer Award, Australia. Address: 2630 W 7th Avenue, Vancouver, British Columbia, Canada V6K 1Z1.

GIDLEY Charles, 21 Aug 1938, Bristol, England. Writer. m. (1) Felicity Bull, 1962 (div. 1992), 1 son, 1 daughter, (2) Susan Keeble, 1993. Education: Royal Naval College, Dartmouth. Publications include: Novels: The River Running By; The Raging of the Sea; The Believer; Armada; The Fighting Spirit; The Crying of the Wind. Contributions to: Blackwoods Magazine; The Naval Review. Memberships: PEN International. Literary Agent: A M Heath. Address: Winchester, England.

GIFFORD Barry Colby, b. 18 Oct 1946, Illinois, USA. Writer. m. Mary Lou Nelson, 23 Oct 1970, 1 son, 1 daughter. Publications: Jack's Book (co-author), biography, 1978; Port Tropique, 1980; Landscape with Traveler, 1980; The Neighborhood of Baseball, 1981; Devil Thumbs A Ride, 1988; Ghosts No Horse Can Carry, 1989; Wild at Heart, 1990; Sailor's Holiday, 1991; New Mysteries of Paris, 1991; A Good Man to Know, 1992; Night People, 1992; Arise and Walk, 1994; Hotel Room Trilogy, 1995; Baby Cat-Face, 1995. Contributions to: Punch; Esquire; Rolling Stone. Honours: Notable Book Award, American Library Association, 1978, 1988; National Endowment for the Arts Fellowship, 1982; Maxwell Perkins Award, PEN, 1983; Syndicated Fiction Award, PEN, 1987; Premio Brancati, Italy, for Gente di Notte (Night People), 1993. Literary Agent: Peter Ginsberg, President, Curtis Brown Limited, 10 Astor Place, New York, NY 10003, USA. Address: 833 Bancroft Way, Berkeley, CA 94710, USA.

GIFFORD Denis, b. 26 Dec 1927, London, England. Author; Cartoonist. div., 1 daughter. Appointment: Art Assistant, Reynolds News, 1944-45. Publications include: British Film Catalogue 1895-1980; British Comic Catalogue 1874-1974; Pictorial History of Horror Movies, 1973; International Book of Comics, 1984; Golden Age of Radio, 1985; Encyclopaedia of Comic Characters, 1987; Best of Eagle Annual 1951-59, 1989; Comic Art of Charlie Chaplin, 1989; The American Comic Book Catalogue, 1990; Books and Plays in Films, 1991. Contributions include: TV Times; Radio Times; Guardian; Times; Observer; Sunday Times; Independent; Collectors Fayre; Book Collector. Memberships include: Founder, Association of Comics Enthusiasts; Co-Founder, Society of Strip Illustration; Edgar Wallace Society; Old Bill Society; Founder, Savers of Television and Radio Shows; 1940 Society. Address: 80 Silverdale, Sydenham, London SE26 4SJ, England.

GIGGAL Kenneth (Angus Ross), b. 19 Mar 1927, Dewsbury, Yorkshire, England. Publications include: The Manchester Thing, 1970; The Huddersfield Job, 1971; The London Assignment, 1972; The Dunfermline Affair, 1973; The Bradford Business, 1974; The Amsterdam Diversion, 1974; The Leeds Fiasco, 1975; The Edinburgh Exercise, 1975; The Ampurias Exchange, 1976; The Aberdeen Conundrum, 1977; The Congleton Lark, 1979; The Hamburg Switch, 1980; A Bad April, 1980; The Menwith Tangle, 1982; The Darlington Jaunt, 1983; The Luxembourg Run, 1985; Doom Indigo, 1986; The Tyneside Ultimatum, 1988; Classic Sailing Ships, 1988; The Greenham Plot, 1989; The Leipzig Manuscript, 1990; The Last One, 1992; John Worsley's War, 1992; Scripts and Films for TV. Contributions to: Many magazines, national and international. Honour: Truth Prize for Fiction, 1954. Memberships: The Savage Club; The Arms and Armour Society.

Literary Agent: Andrew Mann Ltd. Address: The Old Granary, Bishop Monkton, Near Harrogate, N Yorkshire, England.

GIL David Georg, b. 16 Mar 1924, Vienna, Austria. Professor of Social Policy; Author. m. Eva Breslauer, 2 Aug 1947, 2 sons. Education: Certificate in Psychotherapy with Children, Israeli Society for Child Psychiatry, 1952; Diploma in Social Work, School of Social Work, 1953, BA, 1957, Hebrew University, Jerusalem, Israel; MSW, 1958, DSW, 1963, University of Pennsylvania, USA. Literary appointments: Member, Editorial Boards: American Journal of Orthopsychiatry; Journal of Sociology and Social Welfare; Social Development Issues; Humanity and Society; Evaluation and the Health Professions; Children and Youth Services Review; Victimology; Journal of International and Comparative Social Welfare; Journal of Progressive Human Services; Journal of Teaching in Social Work; Journal of Social Service Research; Changing work; Child Welfare; Our Generation. Publications: Violence Against Children, 1970; Unraveling Social Policy, 1973, 1976, 1981, 1990, 1992; The Challenge of Social Equality, 1976; Beyond the Jungle, 1979; Child Abuse and Violence (editor), 1979; Editor with Eva A Gil: Toward Social and Economic Justice, 1985; The Future of Work, 1987. Contributions to: Over 50 articles to professional journals, book chapters, book reviews. Address: Heller Graduate School, Brandeis University, Waltham, MA 02254-9110, USA.

GILB Dagoberto G, b. 31 July 1950, Los Angeles, California, USA. Writer. m. Rebeca Santos, 1978, 2 sons. Education: BA, MA, University of California. Literary appointments: Visiting Writer, University of Texas, 1988-89; Visiting Writer, University of Arizona, 1992-93; Visiting Writer, University of Wyoming, 1994. Publications: Winners on the Pass Line, 1985; The Magic of Blood, 1993; The Last Known Residence of Mickey Acuña, 1994. Honours: James D Phelan Award; Dobie Paisano Fellowship; Creative Writing Fellowship, National Endowment for the Arts; Whiting Writers Award, 1993; Best Book of Fiction Award, Texas Institute of Letters, 1993; Ernest Hemingway Foundation Award, 1994. Memberships: Texas Institute of Letters; PEN. Literary Agent: Kim Witherspoon. Address: PO Box 31001. El Paso, TX 79931, USA.

GILBERT Anna, b. 1 May 1916, England. Teacher; Writer. m. Jack Lazarus, 3 Apr 1956. Education: BA, Hons, English Language and Literature, 1937, MA 1945, Durham University. Publications: Images of Rose, 1973; The Look of Innocence, 1975; A Family Likeness, 1977; Remembering Louise, 1978; The Leavetaking, 1979; Flowers for Lilian, 1980; Miss Bede is Staying, 1982; The Long Shadow, 1984; A Walk in the Wood, 1989; The Wedding Guest, 1993. Contributions to: Good Housekeeping; Woman; BBC Woman's Hour. Honour: Romantic Novelists' Major Award, 1976 for The Look of Innocence. Literary Agent: Watson Little Ltd, 12 Egbert Street, London NW1 8LJ, England.

GILBERT Bentley Brinkerhoff, b. 1924, USA. Writer; Historian. Publications: The Evolution of National Insurance in Great Britain, 1966; Britain since 1918, 1967; British Social Policy, 1914-1939, 1971; The Heart of the Empire, 1973; David Lloyd George: A Political Life, Volume 1, The Architect of Change, 1987, Volume 2, The Organiser of Victory, 1992. Address: 830-D Forest Avenue, Evanston, IL 60202, USA.

GILBERT Harriett Sarah, b. 25 Aug 1948, London, England. Writer. Education: Diploma, Rose Bruford College of Speech and Drama, 1966-69. Appointments: Co-Books Editor, City Limits magazine, 1981-83; Deputy Literary Editor 1983-86, Literary Editor 1986-88, New Statesman. Publications: The Riding Mistress, 1983; Hotels with Empty Rooms, 1973; A Women's History of Sex, 1987; An Offence Against the Persons, 1974; Tide Race, 1977; I Know Where I've Been, 1972; Running Away, 1979; The Sexual Imagination (editor), 1993. Contributions to: Time Out; City Limits; New Statesman; Guardian; BBC; Australian Broadcasting Corporation; Washington Post; BBC World Service Radio. Memberships: Writers Guild of Great Britain, Ex-chair, Women's Committee. Literary Agent: Richard Scott Simon. Address: 2 Oaktree Court, Valmar Road, London SE5 9NH, England.

GILBERT Ilsa, b. 27 Apr 1933, Brooklyn, New York, USA. Poet; Playwright; Librettist; Lyricist. Education: University of Michigan, 1951-52; BA, Brooklyn College, 1955. Appointments: Editor, Copywriter, Creative Director, various companies, 1955-68; Freelance Copywriter, Vantage Press, 1962-79. Publications include: Pardon the Prisoner, mini-play, 1976; Survivors and Other New York Poems, 1985;

Rooms to Let Live; 45 productions, staged readings, various 1-act plays, verse plays, musicals, concert pieces for theatre, mainly Off-Off Broadway, New York City, titles including: The Bundle Man, 1967; The Dead Dentist, 1968; A Dialogue Between Didey Warbucks and Mama Vaseline, 1969; Little Onion Annie, 1971; The Black Carousel (later called Berlin Blues), 1977; Travellers, 1977; Watering Holes and Garden Paths, 1983; The First Word, 1987; The Bundle Man, opera, 1993. Contributions to: Numerous magazines countrywide. Honours include: Honourable Mention, Atlantic Monthly Nationwide College Poetry Contest, 1955; Best Subjective Poem published in Poet Lore, 1968; Guest Poet and Playwright, Proscenium, Cable TV, 1973; Writers Colony Residencies, Dorset, Vermont, 1982, 1986, 1987. Memberships: Pentangle Literary Society; Women's Salon; PEN American Center; Poets and Writers; Dramatists Guild; Authors League of America. Literary Agent: Claudia Menza. Address: 203 Bleecker Street, Apt 9, New York, NY 10012, USA.

GILBERT Jack, b. 17 Feb 1925, Pittsburgh, Pennsylvania, USA. Writer. Education: BA, University of Pittsburgh, 1954; MA, San Francisco State University, 1962. Appointments: University of California, Berkeley, 1958-59; Faculty, San Francisco State University, California, 1962-63, 1965-67, 1971; Professor, Kyoto University, Tokyo, Japan, 1974-75; Faculty. Syracuse University, Syracuse, New York, USA, 1982-83; Faculty, University of San Francisco, 1985; Chair, Creative Writing, University of Alabama, Tuscaloosa, 1986. Publications: Poems: Views of Jeopardy, 1962; Monolithos, 1982; Kochan, 1984. Contributions to: The New Yorker; The American Poetry Review; Kenyon; Poetry, Chicago; The Atlantic Monthly; The Nation; Ironwood; The Iowa Review; Encounter, England; The Quarterly. Honours: Winner, Yale Younger Poets Award, 1962; Guggenheim Fellowship, 1964; Nominated for Pulitzer Prize, 1962, 1982; National Endowment of the Arts Award, 1974; 1st Prize, American Poetry Review, 1983; Stanley Kunitz Prize, 1983. Address: 919 Oak Street, New Port Richey, FL 33552, USA.

GILBERT John Raphael, b. 1926. Writer (Natural History, Travel, Translations). Publications: Modern World Book of Animals, 1947; Cats, Cats, Cats, 1961; Famous Jewish Lives, 1970; Myths of Ancient Rome, 1970; Pirates and Buccaneers, 1971, 1975; Highwaymen and Outlaws, 1971; Charting the Vast Pacific, 1971; National Costumes of the World, 1972; World of Wildlife, 1972-74; Miracles of Nature, 1975; Knights of the Crusades, 1978; Vikings, 1978; Prehistoric Man, 1978; Leonardo da Vinci, 1978; La Scala, 1979; Dinosaurs Discovered, 1980; Macdonald Guide to Trees, 1983; Macdonald Encyclopedia of House Plants, 1986; Theory and Use of Colour, 1986; Macdonald Encyclopedia of Roses, 1987; Gardens of Britain, 1987; Macdonald Encyclopedia of Butterflies and Moths, 1988; Trekking in the USA, 1989; Macdonald Encyclopedia of Orchids, 1989; Macdonald Encyclopedia of Bulbs, 1989; Trekking in Europe, 1990; Macdonald Encyclopedia of Herbs and Spices, 1990; Macdonald Encyclopedia of Bonsai, 1990; Macdonald Encyclopedia of Amphibians and Reptiles, 1990. Address: 28 Lyndale Avenue, London NW2, England.

GILBERT Martin, b. 25 Oct 1936, London, England. Historian; Official Biographer of Sir Winston Churchill, 1968-. Education: BA, MA, Oxford University, Magdalen, St Antony's & Merton (Fellow 1962-), Colleges, Oxford. Publications include: The Appeasers, with Richard Gott, 1963; The European Powers 1900-45, 1966; Historical Atlases on recent History, British and American History & many aspects of Jewish History; Winston S Churchill, volume III 1914-1916, 1971 (2 pt companion volume 1973), volume IV, 1917-1922, 1975 (3 pt companion volume 1977), volume V, 1922-1939, 1976 (3 pt companion volume 1979-80), volume VI, 1939-1941, 1983 (companion volume September 1939 to May 1940, 1993; May-December, 1940, 1995), volume VII, 1941-1945, 1986, volume VIII, 1945-1965, 1988; Exile & Return, The Emergence of Jewish Statehood, 1978; Children's Illustrated Bible Atlas, 1979; Auschwitz & The Allies, 1980; Churchill's Wilderness Years, 1981; The Holocaust Atlas, 1984; Jerusalem, Rebirth of a City, 1985; The Holocaust, the Jewish Tragedy, 1986; Shcharansky, Portrait of a Hero, 1986; Second World War, 1988; Churchill, A Life, 1990; Atlas of British Charities, 1993; In Search of Churchill, 1994; First World War, 1994; several publications translated into other languages. Contributions to: The Guardian; Sunday Times; Observer; TV Times; Jerusalem Post; New York Review of Books. Honour: CBE, 1990. Membership: FRSL. Literary Agent: A P Watt. Address: Merton College, Oxford University, Oxford, England.

GILBERT Michael, b. 1912. Author; Solicitor. Publications: Close Quarters, 1947; They Never Looked Inside, 1948; The Doors Open,

1949; Smallbone Deceased, 1950; Death has Deep Roots, 1951; Death in Captivity, 1952; Fear to Tread, 1953; Sky High, 1955; Be Shot for Sixpence, 1956; The Tichborn Claimant, 1957; Blood and Judgement, 1958; After the Fine Weather, 1963; The Crack in the Teacup, 1965; The Dust and the Heat, 1967; Game Without Rules (stories), 1967; The Etruscan Net, 1969; The Body of a Girl, 1972; The Ninety Second Tiger, 1973; Amateur in Violence (stories), 1973; Flash Point, 1975; The Night of the Twelfth, 1976; Petrella at Q (stories), 1977; The Empty House, 1978; Death of a Favourite Girl (in United States of America as The Killing of Katie Steelstock), 1980; Mr Calder and Mr Behrens (stories), 1982; The Final Throw (in United States of America as End-Game), 1982; The Black Seraphim, 1983; The Long Journey Home, 1985; The Oxford Book of Legal Anecdotes, 1986; Trouble, 1987; Paint Gold & Blood, 1989; Anything for a Quiet Life, 1991; Prep School, an anthology, 1991; Roller-Coaster, 1993. Honours: Literary honors: Lauréat de Grand Prix de Littérature Policière, 1957; Grand Master, Swedish DeKaradernins, 1981; Grand Master, Mystery Writers of America, 1987; Crime Writers Association Cartier Diamond Dagger, 1994. Memberships: Garrick Club; HAC, Crime Writers Association, 1953. Address: Luddesdown Old Rectory, Gravesend, Kent DA13 0XE, England.

GILBERT Robert Andrew, b. 6 Oct 1942, Bristol, England. Antiquarian Bookseller. m. Patricia Kathleen Linnell, 20 June 1970, 3 sons, 2 daughters. Education: BA (Hons), Philosophy, Psychology, University of Bristol, 1964. Publications: The Golden Dawn: Twilight of the Magicians, 1983; A E Waite, a bibliography, 1983; The Golden Dawn Companion, 1986; A E Waite: Magician of Many Parts, 1987; The Treasure of Montsegur (with W N Birks), 1987; Elements of Mysticism, 1991; World Freemasonry, an Illustrated History, 1992; World Freemasonry: a Celebration of the Craft, 1992; Casting the First Stone, 1993; Editor with M A Cox: The Oxford Book of English Ghost Stories, 1986; Victorian Ghost Stories, an Oxford Anthology, 1991. Contributions to: Ars Quatuor Coronatorum; Avallaunius; Christian Parapsychologist; Gnosis; Hermetic Journal; Cauda Pavonis; Yeats Annual. Memberships: Advisor, Arthur Machen Society; Society of Authors; Antiquarian Booksellers Association; Librarian, Societas Rosicruciana in Anglia. Address: 4 Julius Road, Bishopston, Bristol BS7 8EU, England.

GILCHRIST Ellen, b. 1935. Poet & Writer. Publications: The Anna Papers, 1988; Light Can Be Both Wave & Particle, 1989; Starcarbon: A Meditation on Love, 1994; Anabasis: A Journey into the Interior, 1994; I Cannot Get You Close Enough; In the Land of Dreaming Dreams; The Annunciation; Victory Over Japan; Drunk with Love; Falling Through Space; The Anna Papers. Honour: National Book Award. Membership: Poets & Writers. Address: 834 Eastwood Drive, Fayetteville, AR 72701, USA.

GILES Frank Thomas Robertson, b. 31 July 1919. Retired Editor, Writer. m. Lady Katharine Sackville, 29 June 1946, 1 son, 2 daughters. Education: Wellington College; Brasenose College, Oxford (Open Scholar in History) MA 1946. Appointments: Assistant Correspondent of The Times in Paris, 1947-50; Chief Correspondent of The Times in Rome, 1950-53; Chief Correspondent of The Times in Paris, 1953-61; Foreign Editor of The Sunday Times, 1961-77; Deputy Editor of The Sunday Times, 1967-81; Editor of The Sunday Times, 1981-83; Director, Times Newspapers, 1981-85. Publications: A Prince of Journalists - Life and Times of Henri de Blowitz, 1962; Sunday Times (autobiography), 1986; The Locust Years, story of Fourth French Republic, 1991; 40 Years On (editor), a record of the Anglo-German Königwinter Conferences, 1990; Corfu: The Garden Isle (editor), 1994. Contributions to: DNB, Obituary Notices in The Times, Independent, Sunday Times; Book reviews in various publications. Honour: Winner of Franco-British Society's Prize for Contribution to Franco-British Understanding. Memberships: Brook's Club, London; Beefsteak Club, London. Address: 42 Blomfield Road, London W9 2PF, England.

GILES Kris. See: **NIELSEN Helen Berniece.**

GILES Richard Lawrence, b. 24 May 1937, Petersham, New South Wales, Australia. Teacher. m. Faye Laurel, 3 May 1969. Education: BA, 1957; DipEd, 1969; ATCL, 1971; AMusA, 1973. Literary Appointments: Editor, Good Government, 1980. Publications: Technology, Employment and the Industrial Revolution, 1984; For and Against, 1989, 2nd Edition, 1993; Debating, 1992. Contributions to: Various to: Good Government; Progress; The Individual. Memberships: Director, Australian School for Social Science. Literary Agent: Jacaranda Press. Address: PO Box 443, Enfield, New South Wales

2136, Australia.

GILL Anton, b. 22 Oct 1948, Essex, England. Writer. m. Nicola Susan Browne, 6 Nov 1982. Education: Clare College, Cambridge, 1967-70. Publications: The Journey Back From Hell; Berlin to Bucharest; City of the Horizon; City of Dreams; A Dance Between Flames; City of the Dead; An Honourable Defeat. Honours: HH Wingate Award. Literary Agent: Mark Lucas, PFD Group Limited. Address: c/o Mark Lucas, PFD Group Ltd, 5 The Chambers, Chelsea Harbour SW10 0XF, England.

GILL Bartholomew. See: **McGARRITY Mark.**

GILL Jerry Henry, b. 7 Feb 1933, Lynden, Washington, USA. College Teacher. m. M Sorri, 3 Sept 1982. Education: BA, Westmont College, 1956; MA, University of Washington, 1957; MDiv, New York Theological Seminary, 1960; PhD, Duke University, 1966. Publications: Philosophy Today, Volume 1, 1968, Volume 2, 1969, Volume 3, 1970; Essays on Kierkegaard?, 1969; Possibility of Religious Knowledge, 1971; Wittgenstein and Metaphor, 1980; On Knowing God, 1981; Faith in Dialogue, 1985; Mediated Transcendence, 1989; Post-Modern Epistemology (with M Sorri), 1989; Enduring Questions (with M Rader), 1990; Merleau-Ponty and Metaphor, 1991, Learning to Learn, 1992. Contributions to: Theology Today; Soundings; International Philosophical Quarterly; Mind; Philosophy and Phenomenological Research; Journal of Aesthetics. Honours: Danforth Teacher Grant, 1964-66. Address: 521 W Shadow Place, Tucson, AZ 85737, USA.

GILL Stephen Matthew, b. 25 June 1932, Sialkot, Panjab, India. Writer. m. Sarala Gill, 1 son, 2 daughters. Education: BA, Panjab University, 1956; MA, Agra University, 1963; University of Ottawa, 1967-70; Oxford University, 1971. Appointments: Teacher, India, Ethiopia, Canada; Editor, Canadian World Federalist, 1971-73, 1977-79; President, Vesta Publications Ltd, 1974-90; Editor, Writers Lifeline, 1982-. Publications include: Simon and the Snow King; The Blessing of a Bird; Tales From Canada for Children Everywhere; English Grammar for Beginners; Six Symbolist Plays of Yeats; Anti War Poems; Seaway Valley Poets; Poets of the Capital; Songs for Harmony; Shrine of Social Demons; The Flowers of Thirst, love poems; Life's Vagaries, short stories; The Loyalist Citym, novel; Immigrant, novel; Scientific Romances of H G Wells, critical study; Discovery of Bangladesh, history; Sketches of India, illustrated essays about India. Honours: Ontario Graduate Fellowship; Honorary Doctorate in Literature; Volunteer Service Award; Honorary Life Membership, Texas State Poetry Society, 1991; Pegasus International Poetry for Peace Award, 1991; Certificate of Appreciation, Asian Canada Biological Centre, 1992; Laurel Leaf, 13th World Congress of Poets, 1992; Honourable Mention, 3rd Place, 53rd Annual International Poetry Contest, 1993. Memberships: PEN; World Federalists of Canada. Address: PO Box 32, Cornwall, Ontario, Canada K6H 5R9.

GILLESPIE Robert B, b. 31 Dec 1917, Brooklyn, New York, USA. Writer. m. Marianna Albert, 26 June 1957 (dec), 1 daughter. Education: Brooklyn College, 1935-37; LLB, St John's Law School, 1937-40. Publications: Murder Mysteries: The Crossword Mystery, 1979; Little Sally Does It Again, 1982; Print-Out, 1983; Heads You Lose, 1985; Empress of Coney Island, 1986; The Hell's Kitchen Connections, 1987; The Last of the Honeywells, 1988; Deathstorm, 1990; Many crossword books. Contributions to: St John's Law Review; Discovery 6. Memberships: Authors Guild; Mystery Writers of America. Literary Agent: Albert Zuckerman, Writers House, New York City, USA. Address: 226 Bay Street, Douglaston, NY 11363, USA.

GILLIATT Penelope, b. London, England. Author; Film Critic. m. (1) R W Gilliatt, div., (2) John Osborne, 1963, div., 1 daughter. Education: Queen's College, University of London; Bennington College, Vermont, USA; FRSL. Appointments: Film Critic, 1961-67, Theatre Critic, 1965, The Observer; Guest Film Critic, 1967, Contracted Fiction Writer, 1967-, Regular Film Critic, 1968-79, The New Yorker. Publications: Novels: One by One, 1965; A State of Change, 1968; The Cutting Edge, 1979; Mortal Matters, 1983; A Woman of Singular Occupation, 1988; Short stories: Come Back If It Doesn't Get Better, 1967, UK as What's It Like Out?, 1968; Penguin Modern Short Stories, 1970; Nobody's Business, 1972; Splendid Lives, 1977; Quotations from Other Lives, 1983; They Sleep Without Dreaming, 1985; 22 stories, 1986; Lingo, 1990; Plays, films: Property, 1970; Sunday Bloody Sunday, screenplay, 1971, reprint with new essay, 1986; Cliff Dwellers, 1981; Property, 1983; Nobody's Business, 1983; But When All's Said and Done, 1985; TV plays: Living on the Bos, The Flight Fund, 1974;

In the Unlikely Event of Emergency, 1979; Non-fiction: Unholy Fools; Film and Theatre, 1972; Jean Renoir, Essays, Conversations, Reviews, 1975; Jacques Tati, 1976; Three Quarter Face, 1980; To Wit, 1990; Beach of Aurora, opera libretto, 1973-83; Profiles of Jean Renoir, John Huston, Woody Allen, Jean-Luc Godard, Diane Keaton, John Cleese, Jonathan Miller, Katharine Hepburn, many others. Honours: Awards for Fiction, American Academy, National Institute of Arts and Letters, 1972; Awards for Screenplay, Sunday Bloody Sunday, Oscar nomination, Best Original Screenplay, Winner, Best Original Screenplay. Memberships include: Writers Guild of America; Writers Guild of England; National Society of Film Critics; New York Film Critics Society. Address: c/o The New Yorker, 25 West 43rd Street, New York, NY 10036, USA.

GILLIE Christopher, b. 1914. Writer. Publications: Character in English Literature, 1965; Longman's Companion to English Literature, 1972; Jane Austen: A Preface Book, 1974; English Literature 1900-1939, 1975; E M Forster: A Preface Book, 1983. Address: 1 Barton Close, Cambridge CB3 9LQ, England.

GILLIES Valerie, b. 4 June 1948, Edmonton, Alberta, Canada (British citizen). Writer. m. William Gillies, 1972, 1 son, 1 daughter. Education: University of Edinburgh, 1966-74; MA, 1970; MLitt, 1974. Appointments: Writer-in-residence, Boroughmuir School, Edinburgh, 1978-79. Publications: Trio: New Poets From Edinburgh, 1971; Each Bright Eye: Selected Poems, 1977; Bed of Stone, 1984; The Chanter's Tune, 1990; Radio plays: Rabbits, 1978, Stories of the Mountains, 1979, and Ballad of Tam Lin, 1979. Honours include: Scottish Arts Council Bursary, 1976; Eric Gregory Award, 1976. Address: c/o Canongate Publishing Ltd, 17 Jeffrey Street, Edinburgh EH1 1DR, Scotland.

GILLIS Launa. See: **PARTLETT Launa.**

GILLON Adam, b. 1921. Author; Emeritus Professor. Appointments: Professor, English, Department Head, Acadia University, Nova Scotia, Canada, 1957-62; Faculty, 1962-, currently Emeritus Professor, English, Comparative Literature, State University of New York, New Paltz, USA; Editor, Polish Series, Twayne Publishers Inc, 1963-72; Regional Editor, Conradiana, 1968-72; Editor, Joseph Conrad Today, 1975; Editorial Board, Institute for Textual Studies, Texas Technical University, Lubbock. Publications: The Eternal Solitary: A Study of Joseph Conrad, 1960, 1966; Selected Poems and Translations, 1962; Introduction to Modern Polish Literature (editor, translator, contributor), 1964, 1982; In the Manner of Haiku: Seven Aspects of Man, 1967, 1970; Julian Tuwim's The Dancing Socrates and Other Poems (editor, translator), 1968; Poems of the Ghetto: A Testament of Lost Men (editor, translator, contributor), 1969; Daily New and Old: Poems in the Manner of Haiku, 1971; Strange Mutations in the Manner of Haiku, 1973; Joseph Conrad: Commemorative Essays (editor), 1975; Summer Mom...Winter Weather: Poems 'Twixt Haiku and Senryu, 1975; Conrad and Shakespeare and Other Essays, 1976; Joseph Conrad, 1982; The Withered Leaf: A Medley of Haiku and Senryu, 1982; Joseph Conrad: Comparative Essays, 1994; Novels: A Cup of Fury, 1962; Jared, 1986; Radio plays: Joseph Conrad, 1959; The Bet, 1969; The Solitary, 1969; Screenplays: The Conspirators (co-author), 1985; Dark Country, 1989; Under Western Eyes, 1989; The Bet, 1990; From Russia with Hope, 1990. Literary Agent: Bertha Klausner, International Literary Agency, 71 Park Avenue, New York, NY 10016, USA. Address: Lake Illyria, 490 Rt 299 West, New Paltz, NY 12561, USA.

GILMAN Dorothy (Dorothy Gilman Butters), b. 1923, New Brunswick, New Jersey, USA. Author; Children's Writer. m. Edgar A Butters, 15 Sept 1945, div. 1965, 2 sons. Education: Pennsylvania Academy of Fine Arts, 1940-45; University of Pennsylvania and Art Students League, 1963-64. Publications: Novels: The Unexpected Mrs Pollifax, 1966, in UK as Mrs Pollifax, Spy, 1971; Uncertain Voyage, 1967; The Amazing Mrs Pollifax, 1970; The Elusive Mrs Pollifax, 1971; A Palm for Mrs Pollifax, 1973; A Nun in the Closet, 1975, in UK as A Nun in the Cupboard, 1976; The Clairvoyant Countess, 1975; Mrs Pollifax on Safari, 1977; A New Kind of Country, non-mystery novel, 1978; The Tightrope Walker, 1979; Mrs Pollifax on the China Station, 1983; The Maze in the Heart of the Castle, 1983; Mrs Pollifax and the Hongkong Buddha, 1985; For children: Enchanted Caravan, 1949; Carnival Gypsy, 1950; Ragamuffin Alley, 1951; The Calico Year, 1953; Four-Party Line, 1954; Papa Dolphin's Table, 1955; Girl in Buckskin, 1956; Heartbreak Street, 1958; Witch's Silver, 1959; Masquerade, 1961; Ten Leagues to Boston Town, 1962; The Bells of Freedom, 1963.

Contributions to: Redbook; Goodhousekeeping; Jack and Jill; Ladies Home Journal; Cosmopolitan; Writer; Others. Honours: Catholic Book Award, 1975. Membership: Authors Guild. Address: Portland, Maine, USA.

GILMAN George G. See: **HARKNETT Terry.**

GILMAN Richard, b. 1925, USA, Professor of Drama. Appointments: Professor of Drama, Yale University, New Haven, Connecticut, 1967-. Publications: The Confusion of Realms, 1969; Common and Uncommon Masks, 1970; The Making of Modern Drama, 1974; Decadence, 1979; Faith, Sex, Mystery, autobiography, 1987. Honours: George Jean Nathan Award for Drama Criticism, 1970-71; Morton Dauwen Zable Award, American Academy, 1979. Membership: PEN, New York, President 1981-83, Vice-President 1983-85. Address: 329 W 108th Street 5-D, New York, NY 10025, USA.

GILMAN Sander L, b. 21 Feb 1944, Buffalo, New York, USA. m. Marina von Eckardt, 28 Dec 1969. Education: BA, PhD, Tulane University; University of Munich, Germany; Free University of Berlin, Germany. Career: Professor of German Language & Literature; Professor of Psychiatry. Publications: Nietzschean Parody, 1976; The Face of Madness: Hugh W Diamond & the Origin of Psychiatric Photography, 1976; Bertold Brecht's Berlin, 1976; Seeing the Insane, 1981; Sexuality: An Illustrated History, 1989; The Jew's Body, 1991; Freud, Race & Gender, 1993; The Case of Sigmund Freud: Medicine & Identity at Fin de Siecle, 1994; Re-emerging Jewish Culture in Today's Germany, 1994; Franz Kafka, The Jewish Patient, 1995; Jews in Today's German Culture, 1995; Also scholarly editions of German texts & monographs. F3)Address: Goldwin Smith Pro of Human Studies, Department of Modern Languages, Cornell University 203 Merrill Hall, Ithaca, NY 14853-0001, USA.

GILMOUR Robin, b. 17 June 1943, Hamilton, Scotland. Reader. m. Elizabeth Simpson, 29 Dec 1969, 2 sons, 2 daughters. Education: Loretto School, 1956-61; St John's College, Cambridge, MA, 1961-64; Edinburgh University, PhD, 1964-69. Appointments: Lecturer, University of Ulster, 1969-73; Lecturer, University of Aberdeen, 1973; Senior Lecturer, 1984; Reader, 1990. Publications: The Idea of the Gentleman in the Victorian Novel; The Novel in the Victorian Age. Contributions to: The Gradgrind School, Victorian Studies; Memory in David Copperfield, Dickensian. Address: 9 Brighton Place, Aberdeen, AB1 6RT, Scotland.

GILROY Frank D(aniel), b. 13 Oct 1925, New York City, New York, USA. Writer. m. Ruth Dorothy Gaydos, 1954, 3 sons. Education: BA magna cum laude, Dartmouth College, Hanover, New Hampshire, 1950; Yale University School of Drama, New Haven, Connecticut, 1950-51. Appointments include: US Army, 1943-46. Publications: Plays include: Who'll Save the Plowboy?, 1962; The Subject Was Roses, 1964; That Summer - That Fall, 1966; The Only Game in Town, 1969; The Next Contestant, 1978; Dreams of Glory, 1979; Last Licks, 1979, produced as The Housekeeper, Brighton and London, 1982; Real to Reel, 1987; Match Point, 1990; A Way with Words, 1991; Any Given Day, 1993; Screenplays include: The Fastest Gun Alive, 1956; The Gallant Hours (with Bierne Lay), 1960; The Subject Was Roses, 1978; The Only Game in Town, 1969; Desperate Characters, 1971; From Noon till Three, 1976; Once in Paris, 1978; The Gig, 1985; The Luckiest Man in the World, 1989; Television plays include: Plays for US Steel Hour, Omnibus, Kraft Theater, Studio One, Lux Video Theatre and Playhouse 90, 1952-; Nero Wolfe, from Rex Stout's novel The Doorbell Rang, 1979; Burke's Law series; Private, novel, 1970; Little Ego (with Ruth Gilroy), children's book, 1970; From Noon till Three: The Possibly True and Certainly Tragic Story of an Outlaw and a Lady Whose Love Knew No Bounds, novel, 1973, as For Want of a Horse, 1975; I Wake Up Screening, Everything You Need To Know About Making Independent Films Including A Thousand Reasons Not To, non-fiction, 1993. Address: c/o Dramatists Guild, 234 West 44th Street, New York, NY 10036, USA.

GILSON Estelle, b. 16 June 1926, New York City, New York, USA. Writer. m. Saul B Gilson, 21 Dec 1950, 2 sons. Education: AB, Brooklyn College, 1946; MSSW, Columbia University, 1949. Appointments: Teacher, College of Mt St Vincent Seton Seminars. Publications: Translations: Poetry of Gabriel Preil; Stories and Recollections of Umberto Saba. Contributions to: Columbia Magazine; Present Tense; Congress Monthly. Honours: Case Silver Medal, Best Article of the Year; Italo Calvino Award for Translating; Renato Poggioli Award for Translating, PEN American Center; MLA (Modern Language

Association) first Aldo and Jeanne Scaglione Prize for literary translation, 1994. Memberships: PEN; American Society of Journalists and Authors. Address: 7 Sigma Place, Riverdale, Bronx, NY 10471, USA.

GINDIN James Jack, b. 23 May 1926, Newark, New Jersey, USA. Professor of English. m. Joan Phyllis Frimel, 14 July 1955, 1 son, 1 daughter. Education: BA, Yale University, 1949; MA, 1950, PhD, 1954, Cornell University. Literary Appointments: Checker, New Yorker Magazine, 1954-55. Publications: Postwar British Fiction, 1962; Harvest of A Quiet Eye: The Novel of Compassion, 1971; The English Climate: An Excursion into the Life of John Galsworthy, 1979; John Galsworthy's Life and Art, 1987; William Golding, 1988; British Fiction of the 1930's: The Dispiriting Decade, 1992. Contributions to: Frequent articles on British and American 19th and 20th century fiction, to journals and magazines. Honours: Prize for John Galsworthy's Life and Art, University of Michigan Press, 1988. Membership: Modern Language Association. Address: 1615 Shadford Road, Ann Arbor, MI 48104, USA.

GINSBERG Allen, b. 3 June 1926, Newark, New Jersey, USA. Poet; School Director. Education: Columbia University, 1948. Appointments: Served in Military Sea Transport Service; Book Reviewer, Newsweek, 1950; Market Researcher, New York and San Francisco, 1951-53; Freelance Writer; Participant, many poetry readings and demonstrations; Director, Committee on Poetry Foundation, New York, 1971-; Director, Kerouac School of Poetics, Naropa Institute, Boulder, Colorado. Publications include: Verse including: Poems All Over the Place; Mostly Seventies, 1978; Mostly Sitting Haiku, 1978, revised edition, 1979; Careless Love: Two Rhymes, 1978; Straight Hearts' Delight: Love Poems and Selected Letters 1947-80 with Peter Orlovsky (edited by Winston Leyland), 1980; Plutonian Ode: Poems 1977-1980, 1982; Collected Poems, 1947-1980, 1984; Cosmopolitan Greetings, 1994; White Shroud; Recordings: Howl and Other Poems, Fantasy-Galaxy, 1959; Kaddish, Atlantic Verbum, 1966, produced New York, 1972; William Blake's Songs of Innocence and Experience Tuned by Allen Ginsberg, 1969; First Blues, Folkways, 1982. Honours: National Endowment for the Arts Grant, 1966. Guggenheim Fellowship, 1969; American Academy Grant, 1969; National Book Award, 1974; Gold Medal, National Arts Club, 1979; Los Angeles Times Award, 1982. Membership: American Academy, 1973. Address: PO Box 582 Stuyvesant Station, New York, NY 10009, USA.

GINSBURG Mirra, b. Bobruisk, USSR. Translator; Editor; Author. Appointments: Translation Juries: NBA, 1974, ABA, 1982, PEN 1984, Publications include: Editor, translator: The Fatal Eggs and Other Soviet Satire, 1965, 1968, 1987, 1993; The Dragon: Fifteen Stories by Yevgeny Zamyatin, 1966, 5th edition, 1976; A Soviet Heretic, Essays by Yevgeny Zamyatin, 1970, 1975, 1992; We, 1972, 1983; Mikhail Bulgakov: Heart of a Dog, 1968, 1982, 1987; Flight and Bliss, 2 plays, 1985; The Life of Monsieur de Molière, 1972, 1986, 1988; The Master and Margarita, 1967, 1987; Andrey Platonov: The Foundation Pit, 1975; Yury Tynyanov: Lieutenant Kije and Young Vitushishnikov, 1991, 1992; Children's books: The Master of the Winds, Folk Tales from Siberia, 1970; The Kaha Bird, Tales from Central Asia, 1971; The Lazies, Folk Tales from Russia, 1973; The Twelve Clever Brothers and Other Fools, Tales from Russia, 1979; 25 picture books translated, adapted, written, 1969-89. Honours: National Translation Center Grant, 1967; Lewis Carroll Shelf Award, 1972; Guggenheim Fellowship, 1965-76; Honour List, Austrian National Award for Books for Children, 1985. Memberships: PEN; Dramatists Guild; American Association of Literary Translators; Authors Guild. Address: 150 West 96th Street, Apt 9-G, New York, NY 100025, USA.

GINZBERG Eli, b. 1911, USA. Writer; Director; Consultant. Appointments: Director, Eisenhower Center for the Conservation of Human Resources, 1950-, A Barton Hepburn Professor of Economics, 1967-79, Emeritus A Barton Hepburn Professor, Special Lecturer, 1979-, Columbia University, New York City; Governor, Hebrew University, Jerusalem, 1953-59; Chairman, National Commissions: for Employment Policy, 1974-81, for Manpower Policy, 1978-; Consultant: US Departments of State, Defence, Labour, Health, Education, Welfare. Publications include: American Jews: The Building of a Voluntary Community (in Hebrew), 1980; Home Health Care: Its Role in the Changing Service Market, 1984; Beyond Human Scale: The Large Corporation in Action, 1985; From Health Dollars to Health Services: New York City 1965-1985, 1986; The Financing of Biomedical Research, 1989; Skeptical Economist; My Brother's Keeper, 1989; The Medical Triangle, 1990; Health Reform: Dilemmas and Choices, 1993; The Economics of Medical Education, 1993; The Eye of Illusion, 1993; The Road to Reform: The Future of Health Care in America, 1994; Editor: Corporate Lib: Women's Challenge to Management, 1973; The US Health Care System: A Look to the 1990s, 1985; The Uncertain Future of Medical Practice, 1986; Medicine and Society: Clinical Decisions and Societal Values, 1987; Young People at Risk: Is Prevention Possible?, 1988; Public and Professional Attitudes Toward AIDS Patients, 1989; Health Services Research: Key to Health Policy, 1991. Address: 525 Uris, Columbia University, New York, NY 10027, USA.

GIOSEFFI Daniela, b. 12 Feb 1941, Orange, New Jersey, USA. Actress; Poet; Writer. m. Richard J Kearney, 5 Sept 1965, 1 daughter. Education: BA, Montclair State College; MFA, Catholic University of America. Publications: The Great American Belly Dance, 1977; Earth Dancing: Mother Nature's Oldest Rite, 1980; Women on War, 1989; On Prejudice: A Global Perspective, 1993. Contributions to: Nation; Chelsea; Ambit; Poetry Review; Modern Poetry Studies. Honour: American Book Award, 1990.

GIROUX Joye, b. 31 May 1930. Teacher. Education: BA, Central Michigan University, 1952; Further study: University of Michigan, Michigan State University, Wayne State University, Central Michigan University. Appointments include: Teacher, South Lake Schools, St Clair Shores, 1954-56, 1962-66; Teacher, Big Rapids Public Schools, 1969-87. Publications: A Grain of Sand, No More, 1976; Where Lies the Dream, 1976; Four Women...Getting On With It (co-author), 1977; The Whispering of Leaves, 1978; Draw Me a Morning or Two, 1978; Dust I Cannot Hold, 1978; Whispers Lost in Thunder, 1980; Survivor, 1981; And Who's To Pay Your Passage, 1984; Sunlight I Cannot Capture, 1987; How Fragile the Cobweb Left Behind, 1989. Contributions to: Access to Literature, college literature text, 1981; Various anthologies including: Poetry of Our Time; Notable American Poets; The Lark and the Dawn; Journal of Contemporary Poets; Forty Salutes to Michigan Poets; American Poetry Fellowship Society Bi-Centennial Anthology; Convergence, 1980; Golden Song, 1985; Ezra Pound Memorial Anthology, 1985; Poetry to various journals including: Bardic Echoes; Peninsula Poets; Driftwood E; Gusto; Woods Runner; Adventures in Poetry; American Poet; Jeans's Journal; Wayside Quarterly; Wayside Poetry Quarterly; Wayside Poetry Forum; Kansas Quarterly. Honours: 1st Prize, NFSPS Massachusetts Contest, 1989. Membership: Poetry Society of Michigan, President 1980-84, Editor, Peninsular Poets. Address: 3408 Oak Trail Drive, Clayton, NC 27520, USA.

GITLIN Todd, Professor of Sociology; Writer. Publications: The Murder of Albert Einstein, novel, 1992; Uptown: Poor Whites in Chicago; Busy Being Born; The Whole World in Watching; Inside Prime Time; Watching Television (ed); The Sixties: Years of Hope, Days of Rage. Contributions to: Tikkun; Dissent; New York Times; Harpers; Nation; Mother Jones; New Republic. Address: Sociology Department, University of California at Berkeley, Berkeley, CA 94720, USA.

GLADSTONE William, See: WICKHAM Glynne.

GLAISTER Lesley Gillian, b. 4 Oct 1956, Wellinborough, Northamptonshire, England. Writer. 3 sons. Education: University of Sheffield, MA. Publications: Honour Thy Father; Trick or Treat; Digging to Australia; Limestone and Clay, 1993; Partial Eclipse, 1993. Honours: Somerset Maugham Award; Betty Trask Award; Limestone and Clay won 1993 Yorkshire Author of Year. Membership: Fellow, Royal Society of Literature. Address: 43 Walton Road, Sheffield S11 8RE, England.

GLANVILLE Brian Lester, b. 24 Sept 1931, London, England. Author; Journalist. m. Elizabeth Pamela De Boer, 19 Mar 1959, 2 sons, 2 daughters. Education: Charterhouse, England, 1945-49. Appointments: Literary Adviser to the Bodley Head, 1958-62. Publications include: The Reluctant Dictator, 1952; Henry Sows the Wind, 1954; Along the Arno, 1956; The Bankrupts, 1958; After Rome Africa, 1959; A Bad Streak, 1961; Diamond, 1962; The Director's Wife, 1963; The King of Hackney Marshes, 1965; The Olympian, 1969; A Cry of Crickets, 1970; The Thing He Loves, 1973; The Catacomb, 1988. Contributions to: Sunday Times (as Football correspondent and sports columnist), 1958-; Sports Columnist, The People, 1992-; New Statesman; Spectator and others. Honour: Thomas Y Coward Award, New York, 1969. Address: 160 Holland Park Avenue, London W11 4UH, England.

GLAZEBROOK Philip Kirkland, b. 3 Apr 1937, London, England. Writer. m. Clare Rosemary Gemmell, 5 Oct 1968, 2 sons, 2 daughters. Education: MA, Trinity College, Cambridge. Publications: Try Pleasure, 1968; The Eye of the Beholder, 1975; Byzantine Honeymoon, 1978; Journey to Kars, 1985; Captain Vinegar's Commission, 1988; The Walled Garden, 1989; The Gate at the End of the World, 1989; Journey to Khiva, 1992. Contributions to: The Spectator; Sunday Times; New York Times; Washington Post; Daily Telegraph. Literary Agent: Richard Scott Simon. Address: Strode Manor, Bridport, Dorset, England.

GLEASNER Diana, b. 26 Apr 1936, New Brunswick, New Jersey, USA. Writer. m. G William Gleasner, 12 July 1958, 1 son, 1 daughter. Education: BA cum laude, Ohio Wesleyan University, 1958; MA, University of Buffalo (now State University of New York at Buffalo), 1964. Publications: The Plaid Mouse, 1966; Pete Polar Bear's Trip Down the Erie Canal, 1970; Women in Swimming, 1975; Women in Track and Field, 1977; Hawaiian Gardens, 1978; Kauai Traveler's Guide, 1978; Oahu Traveler's Guide, 1978; Big Island Traveler's Guide, 1978; Maui Traveler's Guide, 1978; Breakthrough: Women in Writing, 1980; Illustrated Dictionary of Surfing, Swimming and Diving, 1980; Sea Islands of the South, 1980; Rock Climbing, 1980; Callaway Gardens, 1981; Inventions That Changed Our Lives: Dynamite, 1982; Inventions That Changed Our Lives: The Movies, 1983; Breakthrough: Women in Science, 1983; Charlotte: A Touch of Gold, 1983; Woodloch Pines - An American Dream, 1984; Windsurfing, 1985; Lake Norman - Our Inland Sea, 1986; Florida Off The Beaten Path, 1986; Governor's Island - From the Beginning, 1988; RVing America's Backroads - Florida, 1989; Touring by Bus at Home and Abroad, 1989. Contributions to: Numerous magazines and newspapers. Memberships: American Society of Journalists and Authors; Society of American Travel Writers; Travel Journalists Guild. Address: 7994 Holly Court, Denver, NC 28037, USA.

GLECKNER Robert F(rancis), b. 1925, USA. Professor of English. Appointments include: Editor, Research Studies Institute, Maxwell Air Force Base, Alabama, 1951-52; Assistant Professor, Associate Professor, Wayne State University, Detroit, Michigan, 1957-62; Professor, English, 1962-78, Chairman, Department of English, 1962-66, Associate Dean, College of Letters and Science, 1966-68, Dean, College of Humanities, 1968-75, University of California, Riverside; Advisory Editor: Criticism, 1962-, Blake Studies, 1970-, Studies in Romanticism, 1977-; Professor, English, 1978-, Acting Department Chairman, 1983, Duke University, Durham, North Carolina; Advisory Editor: Romanticism Past and Present (now Nineteenth Century Contexts), 1980-, The Byron Journal, 1990-. Publications: The Piper and the Bard: A Study of William Blake, 1957; Byron and the Ruins of Paradise, 1967, 2nd Edition, 1982; Blake's Prelude: Poetical Sketches, 1982; Blake and Spenser, 1985; (ed with Mark Greenberg) Approaches to the Teaching of Blake's Songs, 1989; Romanticism: Points of View (edited with G E Enscoe), 1962, Revised Edition (sole editor), 1970, 3rd Edition, 1974; Editor: Selected Writings of William Blake, 1967, 2nd Edition, 1970; Complete Poetical Works of Lord Byron, 1975; Critical Essays on Lord Byron, 1991; (ed with Bernard Beatly) Byron's Plays: Critical Essays, 1995. Contributions to: Bibliographer, Reviewer, Romantic Movement Bibliography, 1989-. Honours: Poetry Society of America Award, The Piper and the Bard, 1957; Elected Faculty Research Lecturer, University of California, Riverside, 1973; Mellon Research Fellow, Huntingdon Library, San Marino, California, 1987, 1991; Distinguished Scholar Award, Keats-Shelley Association of America, 1991. Memberships: Keats-Shelley Association of America; North American Society for the Study of Romanticism; Byron Society. Address: Department of English, Duke University, Box 90015, Durham, NC 27708, USA.

GLEN Duncan Munro (Simon Foster, Ronald Eadie Munro), b. 11 Jan 1933, Lanarkshire, Scotland. Retired Professor; Writer. m. Margaret Eadie, 4 Jan 1958, 1 son, 1 daughter. Publications: Hugh MacDiarmid and the Scottish Renaissance, 1964; Editor, Selected Essays of Hugh MacDiarmid, 1969; In Appearances: A Sequence of Poems, 1971; The Individual and the Twentieth Century Scottish Literary Tradition, 1971; Mr & Mrs J L Stoddard at Home, poems, 1975; Buits and Wellies: A Sequence of Poems, 1976; Gaitherings, poems, 1977; Realities, poems, 1980; On Midsummer Even in Merriest of Nights? 1981; The Turn of the Earth: Sequence of Poems, 1985; The Autobiography of a Poet, 1986; Tales to Be Told, 1987; (ed) European Poetry in Scotland, 1990; Poetry of the Scots, 1991; Selected Poems, 1965-1990, 1991; Hugh MacDiarmid: Out of Langholm and Into the World, 1992. Contributions to: Numerous journals and magazines. Honours: Special Prize, Services to Scottish Literature, Scottish Arts

Council, 1975. Membership: Fellow, Chartered Society of Designers. Address: 18 Warrender Park Terrace, Edinburgh EH9 1EF, Scotland.

GLENDINNING Victoria, b. 23 Apr 1937, Sheffield, England. Author; Journalist. m. (1) O N V Glendinning, 1958, 4 sons, (2) Terence de Vere White, 1981. Education: BA, Honours, Modern Languages, Somerville College, Oxford, 1959; Diploma, Social Administration, 1969. Appointments: Editorial Assistant, Times Literary Supplement, 1970-74. Publications: A Suppressed Cry, Life & Death of a Quaker Daughter, 1969; Elizabeth Bowen: Portrait of a Writer, 1977; Edith Sitwell: A Unicorn Among Lions, 1981; Vita: The Life of V Sackville West, 1983; Rebecca West: A Life, 1987; The Grown-ups, novel, 1989; Hertfordshire, 1989; Trollope, 1992; Electricity (novel), 1995. Contributions to: Various journals, newspapers & magazines. Honours: Duff Cooper Memorial Award & James Tait Black Prize, for Edith Sitwell, 1981; Whitbread Award, for Vita, 1983; Whitbread Award, Trollope, 1992; Hon DLitt, Southampton University, 1994. Memberships: Fellow, Royal Society of Literature; PEN. Literary Agent: David Higham Associates, 5/8 Lower John Street, Golden Square, London W1, England.

GLENDOWER Rose. See: HARRIS Marion Rose.

GLISSANT Edouard, b. 21 Sept 1928, Sainte-Marie, Martinique. Novelist. Education: Sorbonne, and Musée de l'Homme, Paris. Appointments include: Founder and Director, Institute of Martinique Studies, 1967. Publications: The Ripening, 1958, 1985; Le Quatrième Siècle, 1964; Malemort, 1975; La Case du Commandeur, 1981; Mahagony, 1987; Play: Monsieur Toussaint, 1961; Verse: Un Champ d'Iles, 1953; La Terri inquiété, 1954; Les Indes, 1956; Le Sel Noir, 1960; Le Sang rivé, 1961; Selected Poems, 1982; Pays revé, pays réel; Also: Soleil de la conscience, 1955; L'intention poetique, 1969; Carribean Discourse, 1981, 1989; Poetique de la relation, 1990. Honours include: Veillon Prize, 1965.

GLOAG Julian, b. 2 July 1930, London, England. Novelist. 1 son, 1 daughter. Education: Exhibitioner, BA, 1953, MA, 1959, Magdalene College, Cambridge. Publications: Our Mother's House, 1963; A Sentence of Life, 1966; Maundy, 1969; A Woman of Character, 1973; Sleeping Dogs Lie, 1980; Lost and Found, 1981; Blood for Blood, 1985; Only Yesterday, 1986; Love as a Foreign Language, 1991; Ultimate Help; Teleplays: Only Yesterday, 1986; The Dark Room, 1988. Memberships: Fellow, Royal Society of Literature; Authors Guild. Literary Agents: Georges Borchardt Inc, New York, USA; MBA, London, England; Michelle Lapautre, Paris, France. Address: c/o Michelle Lapautre, 6 rue Jean Carriès, 75007 Paris, France.

GLOVER Judith, b. 31 Mar 1943, Wolverhampton, England. Author. 2 daughters. Education: Wolverhampton High School for Girls, 1954-59; Aston Polytechnic, 1960. Publications: Drink Your Own Garden (non-fiction), 1979; The Sussex Quartet: The Stallion Man, 1982; Sisters and Brothers, 1984, To Everything a Season, 1986 and Birds in a Gilded Cage, 1987; The Imagination of the Heart, 1989; Tiger Lilies, 1991; Mirabelle, 1992; Minerva Lane, 1994; Pride of Place, 1995. Literary Agent: Artellus. Address: c/o Artellus Ltd, 30 Dorset House, Gloucester Place, London NW1 5AD, England.

GLÜCK Louise, b. 22 Apr 1943, New York City, New York, USA. Author; Poet. m. John Dranow, 1 Jan 1977, 1 son. Education: Sarah Lawrence College; Columbia University. Publications: Firstborn, 1968, 1981; The House on Marshland, 1975; Descending Figure, 1980; The Triumph of Archilles, 1985; Ararat, 1990; The Wild Iris, 1992; Proofs and Theories: Essays on Poetry, 1994. Honours: National Endowment for the Arts Fellowship, 1969-70, 1979-80, 1988-89; Guggenheim Fellowship, 1975-76, 1987-88; Award in Literature, American Academy of Arts and Letters, 1981; National Book Critics Circle Award, 1985; Melville Cane Award, 1985; Sara Teasdale Memorial Prize, 1986; Phi Beta Kappa Poet, Harvard Commencement, 1990; Bobbitt National Prize for Poetry, 1992; W Carlos Williams Award, 1993; Pulitzer Prize, 1993. Address: Creamery Road, Plainfield, NJ 05667, USA.

GLYN JONES Kenneth, b. 13 Nov 1915, New Tredegar, Wales. Air Navigator. m. Brenda Margaret Thomas, 8 June 1969. Education: RAF Staff Navigation School, 1944; Civil Aviation Flight Navigator's Licence, 1946. Publications: 2 Science Survey Broadcasts on BBC, 1950; Messier's Nebulae, 1975; The Webb Society Deep Sky Observer's Handbook (editor), 8 volumes, 1979-90. Contributions to: The Aeroplane; Sky and Telescope; British Astronomical Association Journal; Journal for the History of Astronomy. Memberships: Fellow,

Royal Astronomical Society, 1969-; President, The Webb Society, 1967-90. Address: Wild Rose, Church Road, Winkfield, Windsor, Berkshire SL4 4SF, England.

GOAD Johnny. See: PHILANDERSON Flavian Titus.

GODBER John (Harry), b. 15 May 1956, Upton, Yorkshire, England. Writer. Education: Bretton Hall College, West Bretton, Yorkshire, 1974-78; Certificate of Education, 1977; BEd (Honours), 1978; MA, Theatre, Leeds University, 1979; Graduate studies, 1979-83. Appointments: Teacher, Minsthorpe High School, 1981-83; Artistic Director, Hull Truck Theatre Company, 1984-; Director: Own plays; Imagine (Stephen Jeffreys), Hedda Gabler (Ibsen), The Dock (Phil Woods), Hull, 1987. Publications: Plays include: A Clockwork Orange, adaptation of novel by Anthony Burgess produced Edinburgh, 1980, London, 1984; Cry Wolf, produced Rotherham, Yorkshire, 1981; Blood, Sweat and Tears, produced Hull and London, 1986; The Ritz, televised, 1987, produced as Putting on the Ritz, Leicester, 1987; Teechers, produced Edinburgh and London, 1987; TV plays: Series scripts for Grange Hill, 1981-83, Brookside, 1983-84, Crown Court, 1983; The Rainbow Coloured Disco Dancer, from work by C P Taylor, 1984; The Ritz series, 1987; The Continental, 1987. Honours: Edinburgh Festival Award, 1981, 1982, 1984; Olivier Award, 1984; Los Angeles Drama Critics Circle Award, 1986. Address: Hull Truck, Spring Street Theatre, Spring Street, Hull, Yorkshire HU2 8RW, England.

GODDARD Hazel Idella Firth, b. 12 Dec 1911, Jordan Ferry, Nova Scotia, Canada. Schoolteacher; Secretary; Nursing Aid. m. Roland Bernard N Goddard, 8 July 1930, 1 son. Education: Business School, Canada. Publications: Prisms in Print, 1966; Hazel Bough, 1972; Chestnuts and Autumn Leaves, 1980; Scattered Stars, 1984, My Loyalist Years; Retracing Steps, 1990; Maritime Christmas, true Christmas stories, 1991; December Daffodils, poetry, short stories, 1992; Starfire, mini poetry, 1993; Profiles, prose, 1993; Arbutus, poetry book, 1994; Reflections, historical book, 1994. Contributions to: Canadian Poets and Friends; Amber; Marsh and Magpie; Harbour Lights; Prophetic Voices; Our World's Best Beloved Poems; The Poet; Parnassus; Quickenings; Poet's Study Club; Haiku Column in Mainichi Daily News, Tokyo; White Wall Review. Address: 404 40 Rose Street, Dartmouth, Nova Scotia, Canada B3A 2T6.

GODDEN (Margaret) Rumer, b 1907, Sussex. Novels/Short stories, Children's fiction, Poetry, Autobiography/Memoirs/Personal, Documentaries/Reportage, Translations. Appointments: Director of a Children's Ballet School in Calcutta in the 1930s. Publications include: Screenplay, The River, with Jean Renoir, 1951; The Greenage Summer (novel), 1958; Candy Floss (juvenile), 1960; Miss Happiness and Miss Flower (juvenile), 1961; China Court: The Hours of a Country House (novel), 1961; St Jerome and the Lion (juvenile poetry), 1961; (translation) Prayers from the Ark (poetry), by Carmen de Gasztold, 1962; Little Plum (juvenile), 1963; The Battle of the Villa Fiorita (novel), 1963; Home is the Sailor (juvenile), 1964; (trans) The Creatures' Choir (poetry), by Carmen de Gasztold, 1965, in US as The Beasts' Choir, 1967; (with Jon Godden), Two under the Indian Sun (autobiography), 1966; (ed) Round the Day, Round the Year, The World Around: Poetry Programmes for Classroom or Library, 6 vols, 1966-67; Swans and Turtles: Stories (in US as Gone: A Thread of Stories), 1968; (ed) A Letter to the World: Poems for Young Readers by Emily Dickinson, 1968; (ed) Mrs Manders' Cookbook by Olga Manders, 1968; The Kitchen Madonna (juvenile), 1969; Operation Sippack (juvenile), 1969; In This House of Brede (novel), 1969; (ed) The Raphael Bible, 1970; The Tale of Tales: The Beatrix Potter Ballet, 1971; (with Jon Godden), Shiva's Pigeons: An Experience of India (autobiography), 1972; The Old Woman Who Lived in a Vinegar Bottle (juvenile), 1972; The Diddakoi (juvenile), 1972; Mr McFadden's Hallowe'en (juvenile), 1975; The Peacock Spring (novel), 1975; The Rocking Horse Secret (juvenile), 1977; The Butterfly Lions: The Story of the Pekingese in History, Legend and Art, 1977; A Kindle of Kittens (juvenile), 1978; Five for Sorrow, Ten for Joy (novel), 1979; Gulbadan: Portrait of a Rose Princess at the Mughal Court, 1981; The Dragon of Og (juvenile), 1981; The Dark Horse (novel), 1981; Thursday's Children, 1984; A House with Four Rooms, 1989; Caromandel Sea Change, 1991; Listen to the Nightingale (juvenile), 1992; Pippa Passes (novel), 1993. Hounour: OBE. Address: Ardnacloich, Moniaive, Thornhill Dumfriesshire D63 4HZ, Scotland.

GODFREY Dave, b. 9 Aug 1938, Winnipeg, Manitoba, Canada. Novelist. m. Ellen swartz, 1963, 2 sons, 1 daughter. Education: BA, 1960, MFA, 1963, PhD, 1966, University of IA; MA, Stanford University,

CA, 1963; University of Chicago, 1965. Appointments: General Editor, Canadin Writers Series, McClelland and Stewart, 1968-72; Co Founding Editor, News Press, Toronto, 1969-73; Editor, Press Porcepic, Erin, Ontario, 1972-; Vice President, Inter Provincial Association for Telematcis and Telidon, 1982-; President, Association of Canadian Publishers, 1972-73. Publications: The New Ancestors, 1970; Short Stories, Death Goes Better with Coca Cola, 1967; New Canadian Writing, 1968, 1969; Dark Must Yield, 1978; Other Non Fiction Works. Honours: University of Western Ontario Presidents Medal, 1965; Canada Council Award, 1969; Governor Generals Award, 1971. Address: Porcepic Books, 4252 Commerce Circle, VA, British Columbia V87 4M2, Canada.

GODFREY Ellen Rachel, b. 15 Sept 1942, Chicago, Illinois, USA. Company President; Author. m. William David Godfrey, 25 Aug 1963, 1 son, 1 daughter. Publications: Georgia Disappeared; Murder Behind Locked Doors; By Reason of Doubt; Murder Among the Well to Do; The Case of the Cold Murderer; Common or Garden Murderer. Honours: Special Award; Edgar Allan Poe Award. Memberships: Canadian Crime Writers Association; Women in Crime Association; British Columbia Trade Development Corporation; Vancouver Island Advanced Technology Centre; The University of Victoria Coop Council; The Premier Advisory Council on Science and Technology. Literary Agent: Lucinda Vardey Agency, Toronto, Ontario, Canada. Address: 4252 Commerce Circle, Victoria, British Columbia, Canada V8Z 4M2.

GODFREY John M, b. 7 July 1945, Massena, New York, USA. Poet. Education: AB, Princeton University, 1967. Publications: 26 Poems, Adventures in Poetry, 1971; Three Poems, Bouwerie Editions, 1973; Music of the Curbs, Adventures in Poetry, 1976; Dabble: Poems 1966-1980, 1982; Where the Weather Suits My Clothes, 1984; Midnight on Your Left, The Figures, 1988. Contributions to: Mother; Paris Review; United Artists; MagCity; Big Sky; ZZZZZ; The World; Oinkl; Broadway; An Anthology of Poets and Painters. Honours: Poetry Fellow, General Electric Foundation/Coordinating Council of Literary Magazines, 1984. Address: 437 E 12th Street, Apt 32, New York, NY 10009, USA.

GODFREY Martyn N, b. 17 Apr 1949, Birmingham, England. Naturalised Canadian Citizen. Writer. m. Carolyn Boswell, 1973, div., 1985, 2 children. Education: BA (Hons), 1973, BEd, 1974, University of Toronto. Appointments: Teacher, elementary schools in Kitchener and Waterloo, Ontario, Canada, 1974-77, Mississauga, Ontario, 1977-80, Assumption, Alberta, 1980-82; Junior High School Teacher, Edson, Alberta, 1983-85; Writer, 1985-. Publications include: For children: The Last War, 1986; It Isn't Easy Being Ms Teeny-Wonderful, 1987; Wild Night, 1987; More Than Weird, 1987; Rebel Yell, 1987; It Seemed Like a Good Idea at the Time, 1987; Baseball Crazy, 1987; Sweat Hog, 1988; Send in Ms Teeny-Wonderful, 1988; In the Time of the Monsters, 1988; The Day the Sky Exploded, 1991; Don't Worry About Me, I'm Just Crazy, 1992; Wally Stutzgummer, 1992. Honours: Award for Best Children's Short Story, for Here She Is, Ms Teeny-Wonderful, Canadian Authors Association, 1985; Award for Best Children's Book, for Here She Is, Ms Teeny-Wonderful, University of Lethbridge, 1987. Memberships: Writers Union of Canada; Canadian Authors Association; Canadian Society of Children's Authors, Illustrators and Performers; Writers Guild of Alberta, Vice-President 1986, President 1987. Literary Agent: Joanne Killock, Edmonton, Canada. Address: c/o Killock and Associates, 11017-80 Avenue, Edmonton, Alberta, Canada T6G 0R2.

GODFREY Peter, b. 8 Sept 1917, Journalist; Author. m. Naomi Cowan, 3 July 1941, 2 sons. Education: BA, Witwatersrand University; University of South Africa. Appointments: Professional Journalist, 1933; Editor, Drum, London, England, 1962; London Times, 1970; Freelance Writer, 1980-. Publications: Death Under the Table; Four O'Clock Noon; Various radio, TV and stage scripts; Over 2000 short stories and articles. Contributions to: The Criminologist. Honours: Ellery Queen Short Story Awards. Memberships: Crime Writers Association; Mystery Writers of America; National Union of Journalists. Address: 3 Ribblesdale, Roman Road, Dorking, Surrey RH4 3EX, England.

GODKIN Celia Marilyn, b. 15 Apr 1948, London, England, Teacher; Illustrator; Children's Author; Biologist. Education: BSc, London University, 1969; MSc, University of Toronto, 1983; AOCA, Ontario College of Art, 1983. Publications: Wolf Island; Ladybug Garden. Contributions to: Bulletin of Marine Science; Environmental Biology of Fishes; Guild of Natural Science Illustrators Newsletter. Honours: Best Information Book Award. Memberships: Guild of Natural Science Illustrators; Canadian Society of Children's Authors, Illustrators and Performers. Address: Division of Biomedical Communications, University of Toronto, Medical Sciences Building, 1 King's College Circle, Toronto, Ontario, Canada M55 1A8.

GODMAN Arthur, b. 10 Oct 1916. Educationalist. m. Jean Barr Morton, 24 June 1950, 2 sons, 1 daughter. Education: BSc, 1937, BSc Hons, Chemistry, 1938, University College, London; Dip Ed, Institute of Education, London, 1939; Malay Government Exam Standards, 1948; CChem. Appointments: Colonial Education Service, 1946-63; Educational Consultant, Longman Group, 1966-77; Honorary Fellow, University of Kent, 1978-; Research Fellow, Department of SE Asian Studies, 1978-. Publications: A New Certificate Approach (with S T Bajah), 1969; Human and Social Biology, 1973; Dictionary of Scientific Usage (with E M F Payne), 1979; Illustrated Science Dictionary, 1981; Illustrated Dictionary of Chemistry, 1981; Illustrated Thesaurus of Computer Sciences, 1984; Energy Supply, 1990. Contributions to: Babel, 1990; Paper read at SOAS, 1988. Memberships: Society of Authors; Royal Society of Chemistry; Royal Asiatic Society. Address: Sondes House, Patrixbourne, Canterbury, Kent CT4 5DD, England.

GODWIN Peter Christopher, b. 4 Dec 1957, Zimbabwe. Journalist. Education: MA, Cambridge University. Literary appointments: East European Correspondent, 1984-86, Africa Correspondent, 1986-, Sunday Times, London, England. Publications: Articles on Eastern Europe and Africa, especially South Africa. Contributions to: Sunday Times; Sunday Times Magazine; Wall Street Journal; Illustrated London News; Economist. Honours: Commended, British Press Awards, 1984. Membership: Foreign Correspondents Association. Address: The Sunday Timesm, Foreign Department, 1 Pennington Street, London E1, England.

GOEDICKE Patricia, b. 21 June 1931, Boston, Massachusetts, USA. Poet. m. Leonard Wallace Robinson, 3 June 1971. Education: BA, Middlebury College, 1953; MA, Ohio University, 1965. Appointments: Editorial Secretary: Harcourt Brace & World Inc, 1953-54, T Y Crowell Co, 1955-56; Lecturer, English: Ohio University, 1963-68, Hunter College, 1969-71; Associate Professor, Creative Writing, Institut o Allende, 1972-79; Visiting Writer in Residence, Kalamazoo College, 1977; Guest Faculty, Writing Programme, Sarah Lawrence College, 1980; Visiting Poet in Residence, 1981-82, 1982-83, Associate Professor, 1983-90, Professor, Creative Writing, 1990-, University of Montana, Missoula. Publications: Between Oceans, 1968; For the Four Corners, 1976; The Trail That Turns On Itself, 1978; The Dog That Was Barking Yesterday, 1980; Crossing the Same River, 1980; The King of Childhood, 1984; The Wind of Our Going, 1985; Listen Love, 1986; The Tongues We Speak, 1989; Paul Bunyan's Bearskin, 1991. Address: 310 McLeod, Missoula, MT 59801, USA.

GOFF James Rudolph Jr, b. 9 Jan 1957, Goldsboro, North Carolina, USA. Historian; Writer. m. Connie Goff, 22 Dec 1978, 1 son, 1 daughter. Education: BA, Wake Forest University, 1978; MDiv, Duke University, 1981; PhD, University of Arkansas, 1987. Appointments: Teaching Assistant, University of Arkansas, 1982-86; Lecturer, 1986-87, 1988-89, Instructor, 1987-88, Assistant Professor, 1989-, Appalachian State University, Boone, North Carolina. Publication: Fields White Unto Harvest. Contributions to: Christianity Today; Kansas History; Ozark Historical Review; Pentecostals From The Inside Out. Honours: Faculty Award; Phi Theta Kappa; Gordon H McNeil Award; Charles Oxford Scholar. Memberships: American Historical Association; Organization of American Historians; Society for Pentecostal Studies; Southern Historical Association. Address: Department of History, Appalachian State History, Boone, NC 28608, USA.

GOGGIN Dan, b. 31 May 1943, Alma, Michigan, USA. Writer; Composer; Playwright; Stage Director. Education: Manhattan School of Music; University of Michigan. Career includes: Lead Singer for musical Luther, first produced on Broadway at St James Theater, New York, 1963; Toured with folk singing duo The Saxons, 5 years; Director, Nunsense musical, produced off-Broadway at Cherry Lane Theater, New York City, 1985. Publications: Nunsense musical (writer); Nunsense greeting cards (creator with Marilyn Farina). Contributions to: Musical scores for Broadway and off-Broadway productions including Hark, Legend and Seven, also for revues Because We're Decadent and Something for Everybody's Mother. Honours: Best Musical, Best Book and Best Music Awards, for All for Nunsense, Outer Critics Circle, 1986. Membership: Dramatists Guild. Literary Agent: Mitch Douglas, International Creative Management, New York,

USA. Address: c/o Mitch Douglas, International Creative Management, 40 West 57th Street, New York, NY 10019, USA.

GOKANI Pushkar Haridas, (Bhikkhoo Sudama, Gopu), b. 23 June 1931, Dwarka, India. m. Jayshree P Mithaiwala, 19 Jan 1955, 2 sons, 1 daughter. Education: BE, 1953; First Aid, 1946. Appointments include: Vice President, Trustee Gujarat Itihas Parishad, 1969-77; President, Astrological Conference, Kutch Bhuj, 1984-86; Research Editor, Sanesh, Almanac, 1983-; Guest of honour/inogarated Guj Astrological Conference, 1987. Publications: Manvi Na Man, (7 editions 1979-94); 47,000 copies. Man Teva Manvi; Sarvapriya Mulla Nasrudin (2nd edition 1993); Gurdief ni Jivankala (5th edition 1994; Yamni Smashan Yatra (1991); Total 26 books - 5 others under print - 2 about Krishnamurthys - Jiddu & UG. Contributions to: Gujarati Magazine; Spiritual Psychology; Gujarat Sama Char; Bombay Samachar; Jansatta; Fulchhaab; Sandesh. Honours: Best Astrological Writer Award; Best Writer Shield; Best Research in Astrology Award. Memberships: PEN; Gujarat Itihas Partshad; Lions Club; Municipal Dwarka; Lohana Maha Jan; Indian Roads Congress; Past President, Rotary Club; Life Member, Gujarat Sahitya Parishad, Sahitya Academy; Marine Archeological Society; Chairman, Vimek Bearings India Limited; Organising Secretary, Shardapeeth Vidyasabha, running 3 collecge faculties & Research Institution; Residential School for Denotified Tribes, 1960-1985; Senate Member, Saurashtra University, 1972-1977; Rural Advisor, Door-Darshan (TV) & all India Radio, Rajot, 1981-85. Literary Agent: Stringer to Times of India. Address: Near Brahmkund, Dwarka 361335, India.

GOLD Ivan, b. 12 May 1932, New York City, New York, USA. Writer. m. Vera Cochran, 22 Oct 1968, 1 son. Education: BA, Columbia College, New York City, 1953; MA, University of London. Literary appointments: Writer in Residence: Austin Peay State University, 1991; University of Massachusetts, Boston, 1992. Publications: Nickel Miseries; Sick Friends; Sams in a Dry Season. Literary Agent: Many Yost Associates, New York, USA. Address: c/o Many Yost Associates, 59 E 54th Street, New York, NY 10022, USA.

GOLDBERG Barbara June, b. 26 Apr 1943, Wilmington, Delaware, USA. Writer; Poet; Editor. m. (1) J Peter Kiers, 1963, div. 1970, (2) Charles Goldberg, 1971, div. 1990, 2 sons. Education: BA, Mount Holyoke College, 1963; MA, Yeshiva University, 1969; MEd, Columbia University, 1971; MFA, American University, 1985. Appointments: Director, Editorial Board, The World Works publishers, 1987-; Executive Editor, Poet Lore, 1990-. Publications: Berta Broad Foot and Pepin the Short; Cautionary Tales; The Stones Remember. Contributions to: The American Scholar; Antioch Review; New England Review; Bread Loaf Quarterly. Honours: Work in Progress Grant; National Endowment for the Arts Fellowship; Armand G Erpf Award; Writter Bynner Foundation Award. Memberships: Poetry Society of America; Poets and Writers; Poetry Committee, Greater Washington Area. Address: 6623 Fairfax Road, Chevy Chase, MD 20815, USA.

GOLDBERG Hillel, b. 10 Jan 1946, Denver, Colorado, USA. Writer; Rabbi. m. Elaine Silberstein, 19 May 1969, 1 son, 1 daughter. Education: BA, Yeshiva University, 1969; MA, 1972, PhD, 1978, Brandeis University; Rabbinical Ordination, Chief Rabbi of Israel, 1976. Appointments: Co-Publisher, Co-Editor, Tempo, 1964; Senior Editor, Editor of Literary Supplement, Intermountain Jewish News, 1966-; Editor, Pulse, 1968-69; Member, Editorial Board, Tradition, 1978-. Publications: Israel Salanter: Text, Structure, Idea, The Ethics and Theology of an Early Psychologist of the Unconscious, 1982; Living Musar: The Face of Torah of Rabbi Yisrael Salanter and His Disciples, 1987; The Fire Within: The Living Heritage of the Musar Movement, 1987; Between Berlin and Slobadka: Jewish Transition Figures from Eastern Europe, 1989. Contributions to: Various journals and newspapers. Honours: Academic Book of the Year Citation, Choice, 1982; Rockower Award for Distinguished Editorial Writing, 1983, 1984, 1986, 1987, for Distinguished News Reportage, 1988. Memberships: Literary Guild; Corresponding Secretary, American Jewish Press Association. Address: 1275 Sherman Street, Denver, CO 80203, USA.

GOLDBERG Lester, b. 3 Feb 1924, Brooklyn, New York, USA. Real Estate Official; Writer. m. Dorothy Weinstein, June 1947, 1 son, 3 daughters. Education: BS, City College (now City University of New York), 1946. Appointments: Worked in Real Estate, affiliated with State Division of Housing, 1988-. Publications: One More River, stories, 1978; In Siberia It Is Very Cold, novel, 1987; Work represented in anthologies including: Best Ammerican Short Stories (edited by Martha Foley), 1974-77; O Henry Prize Stories (edited by William Abrahams),

1979. Contributions to: More than 60 stories to magazines including: Cimarron Review; Sou'Wester; Mid-American Review; Kansas Quarterly; National Jewish Monthly; Transatlantic Review. Honours: Fellow, National Endowment for the Arts, 1979; Grants, New Jersey Arts Council, 1982, 1986; Award for short story Hardware, International PEN Syndicated Fiction Project, 1984. Memberships: Poets and Writers; Metropolitan Association of Housing and Redevelopment Officials. Address: 18 Woods Hole Road, Cranford, NJ 07016, USA.

GOLDEN Mark, b. 6 Aug 1948, Winnipeg, Manitoba, Canada. Professor; Classicist. m. Monica Becker, 1 son. Education: BA, 1970, MA, 1976, PhD, 1981, University of Toronto. Publications: Children and Childhood in Classical Athens. Address: Department of Classics, University of Winnipeg, Winnipeg, Manitoba, Canada R3B 2E9.

GOLDIN Barbara Diamond, b. 4 Oct 1946, New York City, New York, USA. Teacher; Writer. m. Alan Goldin, Mar 1968, div. 1991, 1 son. Education: BA, University of Chicago. Publications: Just Enough Is Plenty; The World's Birthday; A Child's Book of Midrash; Cakes and Miracles; Fire; The Magician's Visit. Contributions to: Cricket Highlights; Jack and Jill; Childlife; Shofan Magazine. Honours: National Jewish Book Award; Anne Izand Storytellers Choice Award; Sydney Taylor Picture Book Award. Membership: Society of Children's Book Writers. Literary Agent: Virginia Knowlton. Address: PO Box 981, Northampton, MA 01061, USA.

GOLDIN Stephen, b. 1947, USA. Freelance Writer. Appointments: Editor: Jaundice Press, Van Nuys, California, 1973-74; San Francisco Ball, 1973-74; Science Fiction Writers of America Bulletin, 1975-77; Currently Director, Merrimont House Creative Consultations. Publications: The Alien Condition (editor), 1973; Herds, 1975; Caravan, 1975; Scavenger Hunt, 1975; Finish Line, 1976; Imperial Stars, 1976; Strangler's Moon, 1976; The Clockwork Traitor, 1976; Assault on the Gods, 1977; Getaway World, 1977; Mindfight, 1978; Appointments at Bloodstar, UK edition The Bloodstar Conspiracy, 1978; The Purity Plot, 1978; Trek to Madworld, 1979; The Eternity Brigade, 1980; A World Called Solitude, 1981; And Not Make Dreams Your Master, 1981; Planet of Treachery, 1982; The Business of Being a Writer (with Kathleen Sky), non-fiction, 1982; Eclipsing Binaries, 1984; The Omicron Invasion, 1984; Revolt of the Galaxy, 1985; Editor with David Gerrold: Protostars, 1971; Science Fiction Emphasis 1, 1974; Alternities, 1974; Ascents of Wonder, 1977. Address: 389 Florin Road No 22, Sacramento, CA 95831, USA.

GOLDMAN Arnold (Melvyn), b. 19 July 1936, Lynn, Massachusetts, USA. Academic. m. Dorothy Joan Shelton, 22 Mar 1963, 2 sons. Education: AB, Harvard University, 1957; AM 1959, PhD 1964, Yale University. Literary Appointments: Advisory Editor, James Joyce Quarterly; Advisory Editor, James Joyce Studies: An Annual; Editorial Adviser, Journal of Modern Literature; Associate Editor, Journal of American Studies, 1977-83; Head of Curriculum Development Services, University of Kent, England. Publications: The Joyce Paradox, 1966; Fitzgerald's Tender is the Night (edition), 1982; Dickens' American Notes (with J S Whitley), edition 1972; Faulkner's Absalom, Absalom! 1971; The Profile Joyce, 1968. Contributions to: Journal of Modern Literature; James Joyce Literary Supplement; Journal of American Studies; James Joyce Quarterly; Times Higher Education Supplement; Yearbook of English Studies; Encounter etc. Honours: Fulbright Fellow, 1957-58; Honorary Woodrow Wilson Fellow, 1957-58; Honorary Professor of American Studies, University of Kent at Canterbury, 1985-. Memberships: British Association for American Studies; Staff and Educational Development Association. Address: 8 St Stephen's Hill, Canterbury, Kent CT2 7AX, England.

GOLDMAN James, b. 30 June 1927, Chicago, Illinois, USA. Playwright; Novelist. Education: PhB, 1947, MA, 1950, University of Chicago; Postgraduate study, Musicology, Columbia University, 1950-52. Publications include: Plays, 1961; Blood, Sweat and Stanley Poole, 1961; The Lion in Winter, 1966; Musicals: A Family Affair (with William Goldman), 1962; Follies (music by Stephen Sondheim), 1972, new book, 1987; Novels: Waldorf, 1965, Penguin, 1968; The Man From Greek And Roman, 1974, Paperbacks, 1975; Myself As Witness, 1980, Penguin, 1981; Fulton County, 1989, Paperbacks, 1990; Screenplays: The Lion in Winter, 1968; They Might Be Giants, 1970; Nicholas and Alexandra, 1971; Robin and Marian, 1976; White Nights (with Eric Hughes), 1985; Television: Evening Primrose (music by Stephen Sondheim), 1967; Oliver Twist, 1982; Anna Karenina, 1985; Anastasia: The Mystery of Anna, 1986. Address: c/o William Morris Agency, 1350 Avenue of the Americas, New York, NY 10019, USA.

GOLDMAN Paul H J, b. 3 Apr 1950, London, England. Museum Curator; Art Historian. m. Corinna Maroulis, 11 July 1987. Education: BA Hons, English, London University, 1971; Postgraduate Diploma in Art Gallery and Museum Studies (Dip AGMS) University of Manchester, 1972; Diploma of the Museums Association in Art (AMA) obtained by examination, 1978. Publications: Sporting Life, An Anthology of British Sporting Prints, 1983; Looking at Prints, Drawings and Watercolours, 1988; Victorian Illustrated Books 1850-1870 - The Heyday of Wood-Engraving, 1994. Contributions to: Connoisseur; Antique Collector; British Library Journal; Antique and New Art; Antiquarian Book Monthly Review; Print Quarterly; Art Bulletin of Tasmania; International Journal of Heritage Studies. Honours: Elected Fellow of the Royal Society of Arts, 1989 (FRSA); Elected Fellow of the Museums association (FMA), 1990. Memberships: Society of Authors; Museums Association; Trustee, Cartoon Art Trust, Elected 1993. Address: c/o Department of Prints and Drawings, The British Museum, Gt Russel Street, London WC1, England.

GOLDREIN Iain Saville, b. 10 Aug 152, Crosby, Liverpool, England. Barrister. m. Margaret de Haas, 18 May 1980, 1 s, 1 d. Education: Pembroke College, Cambridge. Appointments: Visiting Professor, Sir Jack Jacob Chair of Litigation, Nottingham Law School. Publications: Personal Injury Litigation Practice & Precedents, 1985; Ship Sale and Purchase Law and Technique, 1985; Commerical Litigation Pre-Emptive Remedies, 1987 (2nd edition 1991); Butterworths Personal Injury Litigation Service, 1988; Pleadings: Principles and Practice (with Sir Jack Jacob), 1990; Bullen, Leake & Jacob, Precedents of Pleadings, 1990. Contributions to: Law Society Gazette; New Law Journal; Solicitors Journal, Insurance at Re-insurance Research Group. Memberships: Middle Temple; Inner Temple; Northern Circuit; Associate of the Chartered Institute of Arbitrators; British Academy of Experts; Britith Insurance Law Association; Committee of the International Litigation Practitioners Forum; International Union of Lawyers. Address: J Harcourt Buildings, Temple, London, EC4Y 9DA, England.

GOLDSMITH Edward Rene David, b. 8 Nov 1928. Author; Publisher; Editor. m. (1) Gillian Marion Pretty, 1953, 1 s, 2 d, (2) Katherine Victoria James, 1981, 2 s. Education: MA, Magdalen College, Oxford. Appointments: Publisher, Editor, The Ecologist, 1970-; Adjunct Associate Professor, University of Michigan, 1975; Visiting Professor, Sangamon State Univesity, 1984. Publications: Editor, Can Britain Survive? 1971; (with R Allen) A Blueprint for Survival, 1972; The Future of an Affluent Society: the Case of Canada, (report for Env Canada), 1976; The Stable Society, 1977 (Ed with J M Brunetti) La Medecine a la Question, 1981; The Social and Environmental Effects of Large Dams, volume 1 (with N Hildyard), 1984, volume II (editor with N Hildyard), 1986; Green Britain or Industrial Wasteland? (with N Hildyard), 1986; The Earth Report (ed with N Hildyard), 1988; The Great U-Tum, 1988. Address: Whitehay, Witiel, Bodmin, Cornwall, England.

GOLDSTEIN Rebecca, b. 23 Feb 1950, NY, USA. Novelist; Philosopher. m. Sheldon Goldstein, 25 June 1969, 2 d. Education: BA, Barnard College, Columbia University, 1972; PhD, Princeton University, 1976. Publications: The Mind Body Problem, 1983; The Late Summer Passion of a Woman of Mind, 1989; The Dark Sister, 1991; Strange Attractors: Stories, 1993. Honour: Whiting Writers Award, 1991. Membership: PEN. Literary Agent: Harriet Wasserman. Address: 15th N 7th Avenue, Highland Park, NJ 08904, USA.

GOLDSTEIN Robert Justin, b. 28 Mar 1947, Albany, New York, USA. College Professor. Education: BA, University of Illinois, 1969; MA, 1971, PhD, 1976, University of Chicago. Appointments: Research and Administrative Assistant, University of Illinois, 1972-73; Lecturer, San Diego State University, California, 1974-76; Assistant Professor, Associate Professor, Full Professor, Oakland University, Rochester, Michigan, 1976-. Publications: Political Repression in Modern America; Political Repression in Nineteenth Century Europe; Political Censorship of the Press and the Arts in Nineteenth Century Europe; Censorship of Political Caricature in Nineteenth Century France; Limits in the Land of the Free; Saving "Old Glory": The History of the American Flag Desectation Controversy, 1995. Address: Department of Political Science, Oakland University, Rochester, MI 48309, USA.

GOLDSWORTHY Peter, b. 12 Oct 1951, Minlaton, South Australia, Australia. Poet. m. Helen Louise Wharldall, 1972, 1 son, 2 daughters. Education: BMed and BSurg, University of Adelaide. Appointment: Medical Practitioner in Adelaide from 1974. Publications:

Readings from Ecclesiastes, 1982; This Goes With This, 1988; Novel, Maestro, 1989; Short stories: Archipelagoes, 1982; Zooing, 1986; Bleak Rooms, 1988; Co-editor, Number Three Friendly Street: Poetry Reader, 1979. Honours include: Commonwealth Poetry Prize, 1982; Australia Council Fellowships. Address: 8 Rose Street, Prospect, South Australia 5082, Australia.

GOMERY Douglas, b. USA. Professor. Education: BS cum laude, Lehigh University, Bethlehem, Pennsylvania, 1967; MA, Economics, 1970, PhD, Communication, 1975, University of Wisconsin-Madison. Appointments: Instructor, Assistant Professor, Associate Professor, Department of Mass Communication, 1974-81, University of Wisconsin-Milwaukee; Associate Professor, Department of Communication, 1981-86, Professor, Department of Communication Arts and Theatre, 1987-92, College of Journalism, 1992-, University of Maryland; Visiting Professor: Division of Radio-Television-Film, School of Speech, Northwestern University, 1981; Division of Broadcasting and Film, Department of Communication and Theatre Arts, University of Iowa, 1982; University of Utrecht, Netherlands, 1990, 1992. Publications: High Sierra: Screenplay and Analysis, 1979; Film History: Theory and Practice, 1985; The Hollywood Studio System, 1986; The Will Hays Papers, 1987; American Media: The Wilson Quarterly Reader, 1989; The Art of Moving Shadows, 1989; Movie History: A Survey, 1990; Shared Pleasures, 1992; The Future of News, 1992. Address: 4817 Drummond Avenue, Chevy Chase, MD 20815, USA.

GOMEZ Christine, b. 24 Apr 1947, Madras, India. Teacher. m. Patrick Gomez, 21 Oct 1970, 1 son. Education: BSc 1966; MA 1968; PhD, 1982. Appointments: Board of Studies, Bharathidasan University, 1982-84; Ad Hoc Committee, Mother Theresa Womens University, 1984-85; Board of Studies, Bharathi Dasan University, 1984-87. Publications: The Alienated Figure in Drama; Fire Blossoms; The Treasure Hunt; Favourite Stories; Lamplight and Shadows; Love's Triumph; Deiva Dharisanam; Stations of the Cross; Yatra. Contributions to: Hamlet Studies; Indian Journal of Shakespeare Studies. Honours: First Prize, All India Play Writing Competition. Memberships: PEN; Indian Society for Commonwealth Studies; Indian Association of Literary Critics and Theorists; ASRC. Address: Vilma, C91 North East Extension, Thillainagar, Tiruchy 620018, India.

GONCZ Arpad, b. 10 Feb 1922, Budapest, Hungary. President, Republic of Hungary. m. Zsuzsanna Maria Gonter, 2 sons, 2 daughters. Education: Pazmany Peter University, 1938-44; University of Agricultural Sciences, 1952-66. Appointments: Editor, Nemzedek, 1947-48. Publications: Hungarian Medea; Men of God; Iron Bars; Balance; A Pessimistic Comedy; Persephone; Encounters; Homecoming. Contributions to: Regularly in Hungarian Literary Magazines. Honours: Jozsef Attila Award; Wheatland Prize; Premio Mediterraneo. Memberships: Hungarian Writers Association; Hungarian Writers Union; Hungarian PEN Club. Literary Agent: Artisjus, Agency for Literature and Theatre. Address: Parliament, Kossuth ter 1-3, Budapest V, 1055, Hungary.

GONZALEZ-CRUSSI Frank, b. 4 Oct 1936, Mexico City, Mexico. Professor. m. (1) Ana Luz (div) 2 s, 1 d. (2) Wei Hsueh, 7 Oct 1978. Education: BA, 1954, MD, 1961, Universidad Nacional Autonoma de Mexico. Appointments: Intern, Penrose Hospital, Colorado Springs, 1962; Resident in Pathology, St Lawrence Hospital, Lansing, MI, Shands Teaching Hospital, University of Florida, Gainesville, FL 1963-67; Assistant Professor of Pathology, Queens University, Kingston, Ontari, 1967-73; Associate Professor of Pathology, Indiana University-Purdue University at Indianapolis, 1973-78; Professor of Pathology, Northwestern University, Chicago, IL 1978-; Head of Laboratories at Children's Memorial Hospital,, Chicago. Publications: Notes of an Anatomist, 1985; Three Forms of Sudden Death; Other Reflections on the Grandeur and Misery of the Body, 1986; On the Nature of Things Erotic, 1988; Extragonadal Teratomas; Wilm's Tumor and Related Renal Neoplasms of Childhood. Contributions to: Numerous specialized medial journals. Honours: Best Nonfiction Award for the Society of Midland Authors, 1985. Memberships: International Academy of Pathology; Society for Pediatric Patholgy; American Society of Clinical Pathologists; Royal College of Physicians and Surgeons of Canada; Chicago Pathology Society; Authors Guild; Society of Midland Authors. Address: 2626 North Lakeview Avenue, Chicago, IL 60614, USA.

GOOCH John, b. 25 Aug 1945, Weston Favell. Professor. m. Catherine Ann Staley. Education: BA (First Class Honours), 1966, PhD

1969, King's College, London. Appointments: Secretary of the Navy Senior Research Fellow, US Naval War College, Newport, Rhode Island, USA, 1985-86; Reader in History, University of Lancaster, England, 1986-87; Visiting Professor, Yale University, USA, 1988; Professor of History, University of Lancaster, 1987-91; Professor, International History, University of Leeds, England, 1991-. Publications: The Plans of War: The General Staff and British Military Strategy c. 1900-1916, 1974; Armies in Europe, 1980; The Prospect of War: Studies in British Defence Policy 1847-1942, 1981; Strategy and the Social Sciences, 1981; Politicians and Defence: Studies in the Formulation of British Defence Policy (with Ian F W Beckett), Military Deception and Strategic Suprise, Soldati e Borghesi nell'Europa moderna, 1982; Army State and Society in Italy 1870-1915, 1989; Military Misfortunes (with Eliot A Cohen), 1990; Decisive Campaigns of the Second World War, 1990. Contributions to: History Journals. Memberships: Fellow, Royal Historical Society; Chairman, Army Records Society; Vice President, Royal Historical Society. Honours: Premio internazionale di cultura from Citta di Anghiari, 1983; Knight of the Royal Military Order of Vila Viçosa (Portugal), 1991. Address: c/o School of History, University of Leeds, Leeds LS2 9JT, England.

GOOCH Stanley Alfred, b. 13 June 1932, London, England. m. Ruth Senior, 1 Apr 1961. Education: BA (Hons), Modern Languages, King's College, 1955, Diploma in Education, Institute of Education, London, 1957, BSc (Hons), Psychology, Birkbeck College, 1962, London. Publications: Four Years On, 1966; Total Man, 1972; Personality and Evolution, 1973; The Neanderthal Question, 1977; The Paranormal, 1978; Guardians of The Ancient Wisdom, 1979; The Double Helix of the Mind, 1980; The Secret Life of Humans, 1981; Creatures from Inner Space, 1984; The Child with Asthma, 1986; Cities of Dreams, 1989. Contributions to: New Scientist; New Society; British Journal of Psychology; British Journal of Social & Clinical Psychology; British Journal of Educational Psychology; International Journal of Human Development. Honours: Royal Literary Fund Award, 1984, 1987 and 1994. Literary Agent: David Bolt, David Bolt Associates, England. Address: c/o David Bolt, David Bolt Associates, 12 Heath Drive, Send Surrey GU23 7EP, England.

GOOCH Steve, b. 1945, United Kingdom. Playwright. Appointments: Assistant Editor, Plays and Players magazines, London, 1972-73; Resident Dramatist: Half Moon Theatre, London, 1973-74; Greenwich Theatre, London, 1974-75; Solent People's Theatre, Southampton, 1982; Theatre Venture, London, 1983-84; Warehouse Theatre, Croydon, 1986-87; Gate Theatre, Notting Hill, 1990-91. Publications: Big Wolf, translation, 1972; The Mother, translation, 1973; Female Transport, 1974; The Motor Show (with Paul Thompson), 1974; Will Wat, If Not, What Will, 1975; Wolf Biermann's Poems and Ballads, translation, 1977; The Women Pirates, 1978; Wallraff: The Undesirable Journalist, translation, 1978; Fast One, 1982; Landmark, 1982; All Together Now, 1984; Taking Liberties, 1984; Mr Fun, 1986; Writing A Play, 1988 and 1995; Lulu and The Marquis of Keith, translation, 1990; MASSA, 1989. Contributions to: Various contributions to: Time Out; Theatre Quarterly; Drama. Honours: Harper-Wood Scholarship, 1968; Arts Council of Great Britain Bursaries: 1980, 1987, 1992. Literary Agent: Micheline Steinberg Playwrights. Address: c/o Micheline Steinberg Playwrights, 110 Frognal, London NW3, England.

GOODE James Arthur, b. 22 Jan 1924. Editor. Education: AB, Wabash College, 1949. Appointments: Editor, Earth, 1969-71; Correspondent, Life, 1952-61; Executive Editor, Play Girl, 1976; Play Boy, 1975; Editorial Director, Penthouse, 1972-81; Editor, National Times, 1991-92. Publications: The Making of the Misfits; Wiretap. Contributions to: Numerous. Address: 6215 Mulholland Highway, Los Angeles, CA 90068, USA.

GOODFIELD June, b. 1 June 1927, Stratford-on-Avon, England. Author; Clarence J Robinson Professor. Education: BSc (Honours) Zoology, University of London, England, 1949; PhD, History and Philosophy of Science, University of Leeds, 1959. Publications: From the Face of the Earth; An Imagined World; Play God; The Siege of Cancer; Courier to Peking (a novel); A Chance to Live; The Planned Miracle, 1991. Contributions to: London Review of Books; Nature; Scientific American; The American Scholar; Science. Memberships: PEN Club; English Speaking Union; President, United Nations Association (London), 1986-87. Literary Agent: Hilary Rubinstein, A P Watt Ltd, London. Address: The Manor House, Alfriston, East Sussex BN26 5SY, England.

GOODHEART Eugene, b. 26 June 1931, New York City, New York, USA. Professor. m. Joan Bamberger, 1 son, 1 daughter. Education: BA, 1953, PhD, English, 1961, Columbia University; MA, English, University of Virginia, 1954. Publications: The Utopian Vision of D H Lawrence, 1963; The Cult of the Ego, 1968; Cultural and the Radical Conscience, 1973; The Failure of Criticism, 1978; Skeptic Disposition in Contemporary Criticism, 1984; Pieces of Resistance, 1987; Desire and its Discontents, 1991. Contributions to: Partisan Review; Salmagundi; Yale Review; New Literary History; Critical Inquiry; London Review of Books. Honours: ACLS, 1965-66; Guggenheim Fellow, 1970-71; National Endowment for the Humanities Fellow, 1980-81; Numerous other fellowships. Membership: PEN. Address: Department of English, Brandeis University, Waltham, MA 02254, USA.

GOODISON Lorna (Gaye), b. 1 Aug 1947, Kingston, Jamaica. Poet; Painter; Freelance Writer. Education: Art schools in Kingston and New York, 1967-69. Appointments: Teacher of Creative Writing, various schools in the USA and Canada. Publications: Poetry: Tamarind Season, 1980; I Am Becoming My Mother, 1986; Heartease, 1988; Selected Poems, 1992; To Us All Flowers Are Roses, 1990; Short stories: Baby Mother and the King of Swords, 1989. Honours include: Institute of Jamaica Centenary Prize, 1981; Commonwealth Poetry Prize, 1986. Address: 8 Marley Close, Kingston 6, Jamaica, West Indies.

GOODMAN Joan Elizabeth, b. 18 June 1950, Fairfield, Conn, USA. m. Keith A Goldsmith, 12 Sept 1987. Writer; Artist. Education: L'Accademia de Belle Arti, Rome, Italy, 1969-70; Pratt Institute, BFA, 1973. Appointments: Village Voice, New York, type setter, 1968-69; Hallmark Cards, Kansas City, greeting card artist, 1974-76; Freelance writer and illustrator, 1976-. Publications: Self-illustrated Children's Books: Teddy Bear, Teddy Bear, 1979; Bear and His Book, 1982; Right's Animal Farm, 1983; Amanda's First Day at School, 1985; The Secret Life of Walter Kitty, 1986; Good Night, Pippin, 1986; The Bunnies' Get Well Soup, 1987; Edward Hopper's Great Find, 1987; Hillary Squeak's Dreadful Dragon, 1987; The Bear's New Baby, 1988; Time for Bed, 1989. Illustrator: The Gingerbread Boy, 1970; The Grape Jelly Mystery, 1979; The Teddy Bear's Picnic, 1979; Jonny Appleseed, 1980; Yummy, Yummy, 1981; Hocus Pocus, Magis Show! 1981; The Case of the Missing Rattles, 1982; Easter Parade, 19785; The Cat Who Wanted to Fly, 1986.

GOODMAN Jonathan, b. 1933, United Kingdom. Author; Publisher; Editor. Appointments: Theatre Director and Television Producer, various companies, United Kingdom, 1951-64; Director, Anmbar Publications Ltd, London, 1967-; General Editor, Celebrated Trials Series, David & Charles (Publishers) Ltd, Newton Abbott, Devon, 1972-. Publications: Martinee Idylls, poetry, 1954; Instead of Murder, novel, 1961; Criminal Tendencies, novel, 1964; Hello Cruel World Goodbye, novel, 1964; The Killing of Julia Wallace, 1969; Bloody Versicles, 1971; Posts-Mortem, 1971; Trial of Ian Brady and Myra Hindley (editor), 1973; Trial of Ian Ruth Ellis (editor), 1975; The Burning of Evelyn Foster, 1977; The Last Sentence, novel, 1978; The Stabbing of George Harry Storrs, 1982; Pleasure of Murder, 1983; Railway Murders, 1984; Who-He, 1984; Seaside Murders, 1985 The Crippen File (editor) 1985; The Underworld (with I Will), 1985; Christmas Murders (editor) 1986; The Moors Murders, 1986; Acts of Murder, 986; Murder in High Places, 1986; The Slaying of Joseph Bowne Elwell, 1987. Address: 43 Ealing Village, London, W5 2LZ, England.

GOODRICH Norma Lorre, b. 10 May 1917, Huntington, Vermont, USA. Professor. m. (1) Capt. J M A Lorre, 1944; (2) Capt. J H Howard, 1964.1 son. Education: BS, University of Vermont, 1938; Université de Grenoble, 1939; Université de Paris, 1946-53; PhD, Columbia University, 1965. Career: Writer, newspaper articles throughout USA, 1938-59; Encyclopaedia articles: Grolier Corporation and Princeton University Press, 1953-70; Princeton University Press, 1965-70; Author: Franklin Watts Publishers, 1982-; Harper Collins, 1986-. Publications: The Doctor and Maria Theresa, 1962; Charles, Duke of Orleans, 1963; Ways of Love, Medieval Romances, 1965; Charles of Orleans, 1967; Medieval Myths, republished in hardcover, 1994; Ancient Myths, republished in hardcover, 1994; King Arthur; Merlin; Guinevere; Priestesses; Jean Giono, A Study of Themes; The Holy Grail. Contributions to: 50-60 scholarly articles to Etudes Rabelaisiennes; Romanic Review; Revue de Littérature Comparée; French Review. Address: 620 Diablo Drive, Claremont, CA 91711, USA.

GOODRICK-CLARKE Nicholas, b. 15 Jan 1953, Lincoln, England. Author; Historian. m. Clare Radene Badham, 11 May 1985. Education: Lancing College, 1966-70; Jagdschloss Glienicke, Berlin, Germany, 1971; University of Bristol, England, 1971-74; University of Oxford, England, 1975-78. Appointments: Editor, Essential Readings, 1983-; Director, IKON Productions Ltd, 1988-. Publications: The Occult Roots of Nazism; Paracelsus; The Enchanted City; Unholy Relics. Contributions to: Durham University Journal; Theosophical History; Images of War; Decadence and Innovation; Ambix; The Times. Memberships: The Society of Authors; The Scientific & Medical Network; Keston College. Address: Manor Farm House, Manor Road, Wantage OX12 8NE, England.

GOODWIN Jason, b. 1964, London, England. Freelance Travel Writer. Education: Read History, Trinity College, Cambridge. Publications: The Gunpowder Gardens: Travels through India In Search of Tea, 1990; On Foot To The Golden Horn: A Walk To Istanbul, 1993. Honour: Spectator/Sunday Telegraph Young Writer of The Year Award, 1987.

GOODWIN SUZANNE, See: **EBEL Suzanne.**

GOODWIN Trevor Noël, b. 25 Dec 1927, Fowey, Cornwall, England. Writer; Critic. m. Anne Mason Myers, 23 Nov 1963, 1 stepson. Education: BA, London. Appointments: Assistant Music Critic, News Chronicle, 1952-54; Manchester Guardian, 1954-55; Music & Dance Critic, Daily Express, 1956-78; Associate Editor, Dance & Dancers, 1958-; Executive Editor, Music & Musicians, 1963-71; London Dance Critic, International Herald Tribune, 1963-71; International Herald Tribune, Paris, 1978-83; London Correspondent, Opera News, New York, 1980-91; Overseas News Editor, Opera, 1985-91, now member of Editorial Board; planned and presented numerous radio programmes. Publications: London Symphony, Portrait of an Orchestra; A Ballet for Scotland; A Knight at the Opera; Royal Opera and Royal Ballet Yearbooks; Area Editor, Writer, New Grove Dictionary of Music & Musicians; A Portrait of the Royal Ballet. Contributions to: Encyclopaedia Britannica; Encyclopaedia of Opera; Britannica Books of the Year; Cambridge Encyclopaedia of Russia and the Soviet Union; New Oxford Companion to Music; Pipers Enzyklopadie des Musiktheaters; New Grove Dictionary of Opera; Viking Opera Guide; International Dictionary of Ballet; Metropolitan Opera Guide to Recorded Opera. Membership: Critics' Circle of Great Britain, President 1977. Address: 76 Skeena Hill, London SW18 5PN, England.

GOONERATNE Malini Yasmine, b. 22 Dec 1935, Colombo, Sri Lanka. University Professor of English. m. Dr Brendon Gooneratne, 31 Dec 1962, 1 son, 1 daughter. Education: BA, 1st Class Honours, Ceylon, 1959; PhD, English Literature, Cambridge University, England, 1962; DLitt, English and Commonwealth Literature, Macquarie University, Australia, 1981. Appointments include: Editor, Koinonia, 1957; Editor, Thunapaha, 1958; Editor, New Ceylon Writing, 1971-; Editor, Journal of South Asian Literature, Michigan State University, 1976; Judge, Commonwealth Poetry Prize, 1985; Foundation Director, Macquarie University Post-Colonial Literatures and Language Research Centre, 1988-93; National Co-ordinator, Australian Government Commonwealth Visiting Fellowship, 1989; Patron, Jane Austen Society of Australia, 1990-; Vice-President, Federation Internationale des Langues et Litteratures Modernes (FILLM), 1990-; Personal Chair, English Literature, Macquarie University, 1991; Visiting Professor of English, University of Michigan, USA, Edith Cowan University, Western Australia, 1991; External Advisor, Dept of English, University of the South Pacific, 1993. Publications include: Jane Austen, 1970; Relative Merits, 1986; Alexander Pope, 1976; Silence, Exile and Cunning, The Fiction of Ruth Prawer Jhabvala, 1983; Word Bird, Motif, 53 Poems, 1971; Jane Austen: Sense and Sensibility, 1980; The Lizard's Cry and Other Poems, 1972; Diverse Inheritance, A Personal Perspective on Commonwealth Literature, 1980; English Literature in Ceylon 1815-1878: The Development of an Anglo-Ceylonese Literature, 1968; Stories from Sri Lanka (editor), 1979; Poems from India, Sri Lanka, Malaysia and Singapore (editor), 1979; A Change of Skies (novel), 1991; Celebrations & Departures (poems), 1991; 6000 Ft Death Dive (poems), 1981. Contributions to: Literary, critical and bibliographical articles in numerous magazines and journals including: ACLALS Bulletin; Australian Library Journal; Cambridge Historical Journal; Journal of Commonwealth Literature, SPAN. Honours include: Macquarie University Research Grants, 1981, 1985, 1989, 1992; Australian Research Council Grant, 1991; International Rotary Foundation Travel Grant, 1987; Australia Council Literature Board Travel Grant, 1989; National Swiss Foundation for Scientific Research Travel Grant, 1989; Order of Australia, 1990; Eleanor Dark Writers Fellowship, 1991. Marjorie Barnard Literary Award for Fiction, 1992. Memberships include: Australian Society of Authors; 1st Convenor, Macquarie Unit for the Study of the New Literatures in English; Jane Austen Society of Australia, Patron; International Association of University Professors of English (IAUPE); New South Wales Writers Centre, Sydney, Australia; South Pacific Branch of the Association for Commonwealth Literature & Language Studies (SPACLALS); Fulbright Association (NSW); South Asian Studies Association of Australia (SASA). Address: School of English & Linguistics, Macquarie University, North Ryde, NSW 2109, Australia.

GOONETILLEKE Devapriya Chitra Ranjan Alwis, b. 9 Oct 1938, Colombo. Professor of English. m. Chitranganie Lalitha Dalpatadu, 23 Nov 1967, 2 sons. Education: BA, 1961; PhD, 1970. Appointments: Regional Representative, The Journal of Commonwealth Literature, 1978; Associate Editor, Journal of South Asian Literature, 1980; National Editor, The Routledge Encyclopaedia of Commonwealth Literature, 1990; Advisor, Contemporary Novelists, 1990; Advisor, Reference Guide to Short Fiction, 1992. Publications: Developing Countries in British Fiction; Images of the Raj; Joseph Conrad: Beyond Culture and Background; The Penguin New Writing in Sri Lanka; Between Cultures: Essays on Literature, Language & Education. Contributions to: 50 articles. Honours: Commonwealth Scholar; Foundation Visiting Fellow, Clare Hall; Henry Charles Chapman Visiting Fellow, University of London. Memberships: International Chairperson, the Association for Commonwealth Literature and Language Studies; American Studies Association; 1993 Vice-President, Fédération Internationale Des Langues Et Littératures Modernas (FILLM). Address: No 1 Kandewatta Road, Nugegoda, Sri Lanka.

GOPALACHAR Aalavandar (Aalavandaar), b. 1 July 1929, Nanjangud Tq, Karnataka. m. 3 sons, 2 daughters. Appointments: Kannada Language, Novels & Short Stories, Weekly and Monthly Kannada Magazines. Publications: Naadini; Punya Purushartha; Mannu Masana; Tumbida Baduky; Baalondu Nandana; Yeru Peru; Sanjaya Mogilu; Gangaalahari; Sethu Bandhana; Baalina Sanjeyali; Raaja Drohini; Veera Pungava; Rohini Chandra; Jeevana Chakra Bharamana; Bandhamukthi; Jeeva Vahini; Muurudaari - Onde Dharma, 1993; Mareechike, 1994; 32 novels in total; Short Stories: Kallu Sakkare Koliru; Allola Kallola; Antima Icche, published in Kannada Monthly Digest Kasturi, 1993; Muuru Daari - Onde Dharma; Vimukthi, published in weekly magazine of Mangala, 1993. Contributions to: Numerous. Honours: Jnana Jyothi Kala Sangha, Rajajinagar, Bangalore, Yagnananarayana Deekshit Smaraka Memory Award; Award for best Novelist, Short Story Writer by Tarangaranga Associates of Davangere, Chitradurga District, 1984. Memberships: Kannada Sahithya Parishat; Kannada Lekhakara Sangha; Shankara Bhashkara Magazine; Poets International Organisation, Bangalore. Literary Agent: T S Subramanyam. Address: Sahitya Kuteera, No 261/1 Byrappa Block, 2nd Main, Thyagarajanagar Post, Bangalore 560 028, Karnataka, South India.

GOPU. See: **GOKANI Pushkar Haridas.**

GORAK Jan, b. 12 Oct 1952, Black, Professor of English. m. Irene Elizabeth Mannion, 12 Dec 1983. Appointments: Lecturer, Senior Lecturer, University of the Witwatersrand, Johannesburg, 1984-88; Associate, Full Professor, University of Denver. Publications: The Making of the Modern Canon; The Alien Mind of Raymond Williams; God the Artist; Critic of Crisis. Contributions to: Denver Quarterly; English Studies in Africa; Theatre Journal; Cambridge History of Literary Criticis, forthcoming. Honours: Thomas Pringle Prize. Memberships: International Association for the Study of Anglo Irish Literature; Modern Language Association; Society for Theatre Research. Address: Department of English, University of Denver, Denver, CO 80208, USA.

GORBANEVSKAYA Natalia, b. 1936, Moscow, Russia. Poet. Education: Universities of Moscow and Leningrad. Appointments include: Co-founder and Editor of Samizdat journal, 1968-75; Resident in France. Publications: Five Poems, 1968; In the Mad House, 1968; Poems, 1969; Street-Organ Sing, Street-Organ Howl, 1969; Poems, Not Collected in Books, 1971; Selected Poems, 1972; The Littoral, 1973; Don't Sleep in the Sunset, 1974; Three Books of Poetry, 1975; Four Poems, 1976; Wooden Angel, 1982; Poetical Treatise, 1982; Alien Stoves: Poems 1979-82; Occasional Cloudiness, 1985; Where and When, 1985; And a Time to Live, and a Time to Repeat, 1990; From

Various Collections, 1990; From Poetry of the Last Years, 1992; Poems of the Last Years, 1992; Also: Red Square at Noon, 1972. Address: c/o Ardis Publishers, 2901 Heatherway, Ann Arbor, MI 48104, USA.

GORDEY Michel, b. 17 Feb 1913, Berlin, Germany. French Journalist; Writer. m. Beverly Bronstein, 1950, 1 son, 1 daughter. Education: Law Faculty, Sorbonne and Ecole des Sciences Politiques, Paris. Appointments: Lawyer, Paris 1933-37; French Army, 1937-40; US Office of War Information, French Editor, Voice of America, 1941-45, Chief Editor, 1944-45; US Correspondent, Paris-presse, 1945; US and UN Correspondent, agence France-presse, New York & Washington, 1945-46; Roving Foreign and Diplomatic Correspondent, France-Soir, Paris, 1945-56, Chief Foreign Correspondent, 1956-73; Assignments to USSR, USA, Germany, Far East (China, Japan), and most Summit Meetings from 1954-1976; Roving Foreign and Diplomatic Correspondent, L'Express, Paris, 1973-77; Special Correspondent, Europe, Newsday, New York, 1977-. Publication: Visa pour Moscou, 1951. Contributions to: Numerous journals and magazines. Honours: Several journalistic Awards. Address: 16 rue de Savoie, 75006 Paris, France.

GORDIMER Nadine, b. 20 Nov 1923. Writer. m. Reinhold Cassirer, 1954, 1 son, 1 daughter. Publications: The Soft Voice of the Serpent; The Lying Days, 1953; Six Feet of the Country, 1956; A World of Strangers, 1958; Friday's Footprint, 1960; Occasion for Loving, 1963; Not for Publication, 1965; The Late Bourgeois World, 1966; A Guest of Honour, 1970; Livingstone's Companions, 1972; The Black Interpreters (literary criticism), 1973; The Conservationist, 1974; Selected Stories, 1975; Some Monday for Sure, 1976; Burger's Daughter, 1979; A Soldier's Embrace, 1980; July's People, 1981; Something Out There, 1984; Six Feet of Country, 1986; A Sport of Nature, 1987; The Essential Gesture (essays), 1988; Non-fiction: On the Mines (photographs, David Goldblatt); Lifetimes: Under Apartheid (excerpts from W G's novels and stories, photographs, David Goldblatt); My Sons' Story (novel), 1991; Jump (story collection), 1992; None to Accompany Me (novel), 1994. Contributions to: Co-editor, South African Writing Today, 1967. Honours: W H Smith Literary Award, 1961; Thomas Pringle Award, 1969; James Tait Black Memorial Prize, 1971; Booker Prize (co-winner), 1974; Grand Aigle d'Or Prize, France, 1975; Scottish Arts Council Neil M Gun Fellowship, 1981; Modern Language Association Award, USA, 1981; Premio Malaparte, Italy, 1985; Nobel Prize for Literature, 1991; Sachs Prize, Germany, 1985; Bennett Award, USA, 1987; Hon Member American Academy of Arts & Sciences; Hon Fellow Modern Language Association (USA); Fellow Royal Society of Literature; Patron Congress of South African Writers; Novel Prize in Literature, 1991. Memberships: Vice President, International PEN; Hon Member, American Academy, Institute of Arts and Letters. Address: 7 Frere Road, Parktown, Johannesburg 2193, South Africa.

GORDON David M, b. 4 May 1944, Washington, DC, USA. Economist. m. Diana R Gordon, 7 Sept 1967. Education: BA, Harvard College, 1965; PhD 1971. Publications: After the Waste Land; Beyond the Waste Land; Segmented Work, Divided Workers; Problems in Political Economy; Theories of Poverty & Under Employment. Contributions to: Nation; Atlantic; NY Times. Honours: C Wright Mills Award; Guggenheim Fellowship. Memberships: Signet Society; American Economics Association; Union of Radical Political Economics; National Writers Union. Address: 317 E 10th Street, New York, NY 10009, USA.

GORDON Diana. See: ANDREWS Lucilla Matthew.

GORDON Donald. See: PAYNE Donald Gordon.

GORDON Donald Ramsay, b. 14 Sept 1929, Toronto, Ontario, Canada. Writer. m. Helen E Currie, 21 Dec 1952, 3 sons. Education: BA (Hons), Political Science, Economics, Queen's University, Kingston, 1953; MA, Political Economy, University of Toronto, 1955; Predoctoral studies, Political Science, London School of Economics and Political Science, England, 1956-63. Appointments: Writer, Filing Editor, The Canadian Press, Toronto, Montreal, Edmonton, 1955; Assistant Editor, The Financial Post, Toronto, 1955-57; European Correspondent, Canadian Broadcasting Corporation, London, 1957-63; Assistant Professor, Associate Professor, Political Science: University of Calgary, Alberta, 1963-66; University of Waterloo, Ontario, 1966-75; Self-employed Writer, Consultant, 1975-81; Chief Writer, The Image Corporation, Waterloo, 1983-92; Instructor: Conestoga College, Kitchener, Ontario, 1991-; Long Ridge Writers Group, West Redding,

Connecticut, USA, 1992-. Publications: Language, Logic and the Mass Media, 1966; The New Literacy, 1971; The Media, 1972; Fineswine, 1984; The Rock Candy Bandits, 1984; S.P.E.E.D, 1984; The Prosperian Papers, Volume 1, The Rock Candy Bandits, 1989; The Choice, 1990; The Sex Shoppe, 1991. Literary Agent: Morris Talent Management, 33 Nasmith Avenue, Toronto, Ontario, Canada M5A 3J2. Address: 134 Iroquois Place, Waterloo, Ontario, Canada N2L 2S5.

GORDON Gaelyn Mary, b. 26 Nov 1939, Hawera, New Zealand. Writer. m. Peter Gordon, 16 May 1964, 1 son, 1 daughter. Education: BA, University of NZ, 1961; LTCL, 1961. Appointments: Frank Sargeson Fellow, 1992. Publications: Above Suspicion; Prudence M Muggeridge, Damp Rat; Stonelight; Strained Relations; Several Things Are Alive & Well & Living in Alfred Brown's Head; Tales from Another Now; Mindfire; Duckat; Tripswitch; Last Summer.; Take Me to Your Leaders, 1993; Ring Around, 1994; The Hudson Line, 1994. Contributions to: Landfall; NZ Listener; Quote/Unquote. Honours: Choysa Bursary; QE11 Literary Grant; NZ Arts Council Scholarship in Letters. Memberships: Childrens Book Foundation; NZ Book Council; PEN; New Zealand Writers Guild. Literary Agent: Michael Gifkins.

GORDON Giles Alexander Esmé, b. 23 May 1940, Edinburgh, Scotland. Lecturer; Literary Agent; Writer; Theatre Critic. m. (1) Margaret Eastoe, dec, 2 sons (1 dec'd), 1 daughter, (2) Maggie McKernan, 2 daughters. Education: Edinburgh Academy. Appointments: Advertising Manager, Secker & Warburg; Editor, Hutchinson & Co, & Penguin Books; Editorial Director, Victor Gollancz Ltd; Member, Literature Panel, Arts Council of Great Britain; Chairman, Society of Young Publishers; Lecturer, Creative Writing, Tufts University, USA; Lecturer, Theatre Criticism, Hollins College, USA; Fellow, Royal Society of Literature, 1991; Council Member, RSL, 1992-94. Publications: Two & Two Make One, 1966; Two Elegies, 1968; Pictures from an Exhibition, 1970; The Umbrella Man, 1971; Twelve Poems for Callum, 1972; About a Marriage, 1972; Girl with Red Hair, 1974; Farewell Fond Dreams, 1975; Beyond the Words, Editor, 1975; 100 Scenes from Married Life, 1976; Members of the Jury, Editor with Dulan Barber, 1976; Enemies, 1977, Ambroses Vision, 1980; Modern Short Stories, 1940-1980, Editor 1982; Best Short Stories, 1986, 1987, 1988, 1989, 1990, 1991, 1992, 1993, 1994, 1995, Co-editor with David Hughes; Co-editor with David Hughes, Best of Best Short Stories, 1986-1995; Short Stories from 1900-1985, Editor 1988; The Twentieth Century Short Story in English, 1989; Aren't We Due a Royalty Statement? 1993. Contributions to: Theatre Critic, Spectator, 1983-84; Deputy Theatre Critic, Punch, 1985-87; Theatre Critic, London Daily News, 1987; Reviewer of Plays, Observer, Plays & Players, Editor, Drama Magazine; Articles in various journals, magazines & newspapers including, The Scotsman, The Times, Bookseller; London Daily News; Sunday Times, Private Eye, Evening Standard, Forte; Books Columnist, The Times, 1993-. Memberships: Society of Authors; Garrick Club; PEN; Royal Society of Literature. Address: Ann Street, Edinburgh, EH4 1UJ, Scotland.

GORDON Jaimy, b. 1944. Publications: Shame of the City-Solo, 1974; The Bend, the Lip, the Kid: Real Life Stories, 1978; She Drove Without Stopping, 1990. Honour: Fellow, American Academy & Institute of Arts & Letters, 1991.

GORDON John Fraser, b. 1916, United Kingdom. Managing Director; Writer. Appointments: Managing Director, Dongora Mill Co Ltd, London and J F Gordon (London) Ltd, London and J F Gordon (London) Ltd, 1963-. Publications: Staffordshire Bull Terrier Handbook, Bull Terrier Handbook, Bulldog Handbook, Dandie Dinmont Terrier Handbook, 1952-59; Staffordshire Bull Terriers, 1964; Miniature Schnauzers, 1966; Spaniel Owner's Encyclopaedia, 1967; Staffordshire Bull Terrier Owner's Encyclopaedia, 1967; The Beagle Guide, 1968; The Miniature Schnauzer Guide, 1968; All About the Boxer, 1970; The Staffordshire Bull Terrier, 11 editions, 1970; All About the Cocker Spaniel, 1971; The Pug, 1973; The Irish Wolfhound; The Borzoi; Some Rare and Unusual Breeds; The Bull Terrier; The Bulldog; The Dandie Dinmont Terrier; The German Shepherd, 1978; World of Dogs Atlas Pictorials, 1978; The Pyrenean Mountain Dog, 1978; The Alaskan Malamute, 1979; Schnauzers, 1982; All About the Staffordshire Bull Terrier, 1984; All About The Cairn Terrier, 1987. Honours: Freeman of the City of London and Member of the Guild of Freemen, 1938; Horticultural Hybridist of Fuchsia Gordon's China Rose, 1953. Membership: Society of Authors, 1969; Life Vice-President, Southern Counties Staffordshire Terrier Society of London and International and Crufts Judge of SBTs; Member, Antiquarian Horological Society. Address: Forêt, 13 Maypole Drive, Chigwell Row, Essex IG7 6DE, England.

GORDON John William, b. 19 Nov 1925, Jarrow-on-Tyne, England. Writer. m. Sylvia Young, 9 Jan 1954, 1 s, 1 d. Publications: The Giant Under The Snow, 1968, sequel, Ride The Wind, 1989 The House On The Brink, 1970; The Ghost on The Hill, 1976; The Waterfall Box, 1978; The Spitfire Grave, 979; The Edge of The World, 1983; Catch Your Death, 1984; The Quelling Eye, 1986; The Grasshopper, 1987; Secret Corridor, 1990; Blood Brothers, 1991; Ordinary Seaman, autobiography, 1992; The Burning Baby, 1992. Contributions to: Beginnings (Signal 1989). Literary Agent: A P Watt, London, England. Address: 99 George Borrow Road, Norwich, NR4 7HU, England.

GORDON Rex,See:**HOUGH Stanley Bennett.**

GORES Joe, b. 25 Dec 1931, Rochester, Minnesota, USA. Writer; Novelist; Screenwriter. m. Dori Corfitzen, 16 May 1976, 1 son, 1 daughter. Education: BA, University of Notre Dame, 1953; MA, Stanford University, 1961. Literary appointments: Story Editor, B L Stryker Mystery Movie Series, ABC-TV, 1988-89. Publications: A Time of Predators, 1969; Marine Salvage, non-fiction, 1971; Dead Skip, 1972; Final Notice, 1973; Interface, 1974; Hammett, 1975; Gone, No Forwarding, 1978; Come Morning, 1986; Wolf Time, 1989; Mostly Murder, short story collection, 1992; 32 Cadillacs, 1992; Dead Man, 1993; Menaced Assassin, 1994. Contributions to: Numerous magazines and anthologies; 8 film scripts; 25 hours of television drama. Honours: Edgar, Mystery Writers of America: Best First Novel, 1969, Best Short Story, 1969, Edgar, Best Episodic TV Drama, 1975; Falcon, The Maltese Falcon Society of Japan, 1986. Memberships: Mystery Writers of America, President 1986; International Association of Crime Writers; Crime Writers of Association. Literary Agent: Henry Morrison, Henry Morrison Inc, PO Box 235, Bedford Hills, NY 10507, USA. Address: PO Box 446, Fairfax, CA 94978, USA.

GORGEY Gabor, b. 22 Nov 1929, Budapest, Hungary. Writer. m. 1954-84, 1 d. Education: Maturity Examination, 1948; Study of Philosophy, 1948-49; Theology, 1954-55. Appointments: Dramaturgist of Pannonia Film, 9164-72; Art Director, National Theatre of Szeged, Hungary, 1982-88; Columnists of the Daily Magyar Nemet, 1959-. Publications: One Pistol for Five; Encounter with a Half a Dog; Second half of the half a Dog; Anatomy of a Supper; The Hunting Carpet; Book of Temptations; Heads for Ferdinand; Revenge of the Diva; There Was Sometime a Hungary. Honours: Robert Graves Prize; Jozsef Attila Prize; Pro Arts. Memberships: PEN; International Theatre Institute; Literary Agent: Artisjux, Budapest 1054, Vorosmatry ter 1. Address: Jozsa B U 32, Budapest 125, Hungary.

GORMAN Clem, (Brian Gorman), b. 18 Oct 1942, Perth, Western Australia. Writer. m. Sarah Dent, 1967 (div 1986). Education: Louis School Perth, 1955-56; Aquinas College, Perth, 1957-60; BA, Dip Ed, University of Sydney, 1963-67; Diploma in Arts Administation, Polytechnic of Central London, 1875. Career: Freelance Stage Manager and Theatre Administrator, Sydney, 1967-68; Founder, Australian Free Theatre Group; Co-Founder, Masque Theatre Magazine, 1968; Lived in London, 1970-79, Deputy Administrator, Round House Trust, London, 1975-76; Administrator, Moving Being Dance Company, Cardiff, 1976-77; Administrator, Australian National Playwrights Conference, Sydney, 1982; Lecturer in Playwriting, Victoria College of the Arts, Melbourne, 1984 and Adelaide University 1985; Training Officer, Australian Book Publishers Association, Sydney, 1986; Freelance journalist, 1966-. Publications: Plays include: A Fortunate Life, adaptation of the autobiography of A B Facey (produced Meblume 1984); The Journey Home (for children, produced Adelaide, 1985); A Face from the Street (produced Canberra, 1985); The Last Night-Club, Montmorency, Victoria, Yackandandah, 985; Screenplay: The Swans Away (documentary) 1986 and other publications. Honours: Australia Council Literature Board Grant, 1980 and Fellowship 1981. Literary Agent: Anthony Williams, Potts Point, NSW, Australia. Address: 505/3 Greenknowe Avenue, Potts Point, NSW 2011, Australia.

GORMAN Ed, b. 29 Nov 1941, Cedar Rapids, USA. Writer. m. Carol Maxwell, 2 Jan 1982, 1 s. Education: Coe College, 1962-66. Appointments: Editor, Mystery Scene Magazine. Publications: Night Kills; The Autumn Dead; The Night Remembers; Prisoners Collection of Short Stories; A Cry of Shadows; Blood Moon, 1994. Contributions to: Redbook; Ellery Queen; Mayayne of Poetry. Literary Agent: Dominick Abel, 146 West 82nd Street, New York, NY 10024. Address: 3601 Skylark Lane, Cedar Rapids, IA 52403, USA.

GOSLING Paula Louise, b. 12 Oct 1939, Detroit, Michigan, USA. Author. m. Christopher Gosling, 20 July 1968, 2 daughters, div, 2) John Anthony Hare, 17 Sept 1981. Education: BA, Wayne State University. Publications: Running Duck (Fair Game - USA), 1978; Zero Trap, 1979; Loser's Blues (Solo Blues - USA), 1980; Woman in Red, 1983; Monkey Puzzle, 1985; The Wychford Murders, 1986; Hoodwink, 1988; Backlash, 1989; As Ainslie Skinner: Mind's Eye (The Harrowing - USA), 1980; Death Penalties, 1991; The Body in Blackwater Bay, 1992; A Few Dying Words, 1993; The Dead of Winter, 1995. Contributions to: Various Womens Magazines. Honours: John Creasey Award, 1978; Gold Dagger Award, 1986; Arts Achievement Award, Wayne State University, 1994. Memberships: Society of Authors; Crime Writers' Association, Deputy Chairman, 1987, Chairman 1988. Literary Agent: Greene and Heaton. Address: c/o Greene & Heaton, 37 Goldhawk Road, London W12 8QQ, England.

GOTFRYD Bernard, b. 25 May 1924, Poland. Writer. m. 22 Mar 1952, 1 son. Publications: Anton The Dove Fancier and Other Tales Of The Holocaust; Translations: Dutch, Italian, Swedish. Contributions to: Midstream; Jewish Monthly; Forward; Literary Calvacade. Honours: Christopher Award; Martha Albrand Award; American PEN; Nominated for New Visions. Membership: PEN. Literary Agent: Julian Bach. Address: 46 Wendover Road, Forest Hills, NY 11375, USA.

GOTTLIEB Alma, b. 10 July 1954, Queens, NY, USA. Cultural Anthropologist. m. Philip Graham, 7 Aug 1977, 1 son. Education: BA, Sarah Lawrence College, 1975; MA, University of Virginia, 1978; PhD, 1983. Publications: Blood Magic; Under the Kapok Tree; Parallel Worlds; Beng-English Dictionary. Contributions to: Man; Africa; American Anthropologist; American Ethnologist; Anthropology Today; Dialectical Anthropology. Honours: One of Ten best Books in Anthropology, for Blood Magic; Fellowships from National Endowment for the Humanities, Werner-Gren Foundation, Social Science Research Council; Winner (with Philip Graham) of the Victor Turner Prize, 1993 for Parallel Worlds. Memberships: American Anthropological Association; Royal Anthropological Institute of Great Britain & Ireland; International African Institute; MANSA. Literary Agent: Geri Thomas. Address: Department of Anthropology, 109 Davenport Hall, 607S Mathews Avenue, University of Illinois, Urbana, IL 61801, USA.

GOUGH Lawrence, b. Canada. Publications: The Goldfish Bowl, 1987; Silent Knives, 1988; Death on a No 8 Hook, 1988; Serious Crimes, 1990; Hot Shots, 1990; Accidental Deaths, 1991; Sandstorm, 1992; Killers, 1994. Address: c/o McClelland & Stewart, attn Tania Charzewski Publicity, 481 University Avenue Suite 900, Toronto, Ontario, M5G 2E9, Canada.

GOUIN Grace, b. 17 Nov 1918, Manchester, New Hampshire, USA. Nurse; Artist; Writer. Education: College Studies in Music, 1934; Nursing School; University of Montreal, 1939; Co-Founder, Art Centre Exhibitions of Paintings in Montreal, Quebec, USA, Spain. Literary Appointments: Poetry Reading, Aux Poetes, 1993-94; Canadian Writer's Society, 1994; Fra Angelico's Art Center, 1994. Publications: Book of Poems and Drawings, Pendant que la vague, 1993. Contributions to: Articles on cultural events; Le Lys D'Or, 1993. Honours: Honorable Mention for achievement in Art, 1967. Memberships: Canadian Writer's Society; Conseil de la Peinture du Quebec; Friends of the Museum of Fine Arts, Montreal; Friends of Contemporary Art Museum. Address: 10 132 rue Lajeunesse 412, Montreal PQ, H3L 2E2, Canada.

GOULD James L, b. 31 July 1945, Tulsa, Oklahoma, USA. Professor. m. Carol Holly Grant, 6 June 1970, 1 son, 1 daughter. Education: BS, California Institute of Technology, 1970; PhD, Rockefeller University, 1975. Publications: Ethology, 1982; Biological Science, 1986, 1993; Honey Bee, 1988; Life at the Edge, 1988; Sexual Selection, 1989; The Animal Mind, 1994. Contributions to: More than 100 articles to journals and magazines including: Science; Nature; Harper's; Scientific American; The Science; Animal Behaviour. Honours: Fellow, Guggenheim Foundation, 1987; Fellow, American Association for the Advancement of Science, 1989; Fellow, Animal Behavior Society, 1991. Address: Department of Ecology and Evolutionary Biology, Princeton University, Princeton, NJ 08544, USA.

GOULD Stephen Jay, b. 10 Sept 1941, NY, USA. Education: AB, Antioch College, 1963; phD, Columbia University, 1967. Literary Appointments: Assistant Professor, 1967-71, Associate Professor, 1971-73; Professor, 1973-, Harvard University; Alexander Agassiz Professor, 1982-. Honours include: National Magazine Award, 1980;

National Book Critics Circle Award, 1982; Schuchert Award, 1975; J Priestley Award, 1983; Distinguished Service Award, 1984; Westinghouse Science Film Award, 1985; Anthropology in Media Award, 1987; Edinburgh Medal, 1990; James T Shea Award, 1992; J P McGovern Award, 1993. Memberships include: Am Association for the Advancement of Science; Royal Society of Edinburgh; National Academy of Sciences; Society of Systematic Zoology; Society for the Study of Evolution; Sigma Xi; AAAS

GOULDEN Joseph C (Henry S A Becket), b. 23 May 1934, Marshall, Texas, USA. Writer. m. (1) 2 sons, (2) Leslie Cantrell Smith, 23 June 1979. Education: University of Texas, 1952-56. Literary appointments: Staff Writer, Dallas (Texas) Morning News, Philadelphia Inquirer, 1958-68. Publications: The Curtis Caper, 1965; Monopoly, 1968; Truth is the First Casualty, 1969; The Money Givers, 1971; The Superlawyers, 1972; Meany: The Unchallenged Strong Man of American Labor, a biography of Geo Meany, the AFL-CIO President; The Benchwarmers, 1974; Mencken's Last Campaign (editor), 1976; The Best Years, 1976; The Million Dollar Lawyers, 1978; Korea: Untold Story of War, 1982; Myth-Informed (with Paul Dickson), 1983; The News Manipulators (with Reed Irvine and Cliff Kincaid), 1983; Labor's Last Angry Man: a Biography of Public Workers Union President, Jerry Wurf; The Death Merchant, 1984; There Are Alligators in Our Sewers (with Paul Dickson), 1984; Dictionary of Espionage (as Henry S A Becket), 1987; Fit to Print: A M Rosenthal and His Times. Contributions to: Over 200 articles to magazines. Address: 1534 29th Street NW, Washington, DC 20007, USA.

GOYTISOLO Juan, b. 5 Jan 1931, Barcelona, Spain. Novelist. Education: Universities of Madrid and Barcelona, 1948-52. Appointments include: Visiting Professor at universities in the USA. Publications: The Young Assassins, 1954, 1959; Children of Chaos, 1955, 1958; El Circo, 1957; La resaca, 1958; Fiestras, 1958; Para vivir aqui, 1960; Island of Women, 1961; The Party's Over: Four Attempts to Define a Love Story, 1962, 1966; Marks of Identity, 1966, 1969; Count Julian, 1970, 1974; Juan the Landless, 1975; Complete Works, 1977; Makbara, 1980; Landscapes after the Battle, 1987; The Virtues of the Solitary Bird, 1988; La Cuarentena, 1991; Also: The Countryside of Najir, 1960, 1987; Forbidden Territory (autobiography), 1985; Realms of Strife, 1986; Space in Motion, 1987. Honours include: Europalia International Prize, 1985. Address: c/o Editorial Seix Barral, Corcega 270, 4, 08008 Barcelona, Spain.

GRABES Herbert, b. 8 June 1936. Professor. m. Hannelore Koch, 2 Mar 1962, 2 sons, 1 daughter. Education: University of Cologne, 1963; University of Mannheim, 1969. Publications: Der Begriff Des A Priori in Nicolai Hartmann; Fictitious Biographies; The Mutable Glass; Fiktion, Immitation, Asthetik; Das Engusche Pamphlet 1; Editor, Elizabeth Sonnet Sequences; Das Amerikanische Drama der Gegenwart; Text, Leser, Bedeutung; Literatur in Film und Fernsehen; Anglistentag, 1980; Wissenschaft und Neues Weltbild; REAL, volume 1-10. Contributions to: 56 Longer Articles in various German and International Journals. Memberships: Nabokov Society; Dt Shakespeare-Gesellschaft; Gesellschaft für Amerikastudien; Dt Gesellschaft für das Englishsprczhige Theater; IAUPE; ESSE; Angistentag. Address: Sonnenstr 37, 6301 Biebertal 1, Germany.

GRACE Julien, See: **POIRIER Louis.**

GRACE Patricia (Frances), b. 1937, Wellington, New Zealand. Novelist. m. 7 children. Education: St Marys College; Wellington Teachers College. Appointments: Teacher, Primary & Secondary Schools, King Country, Northland & Porirua; Writing Fellow, Victoria University, Wellington, 1985. Publications: Mutuwhenua: The Moon Sleeps, 1978; Potiki, 1986; Cousins, 1992; Short Stories: Waiariki, 1975; The Dream Sleepers and Other Stories, 1980; Electric City and Other Stories, 1980; Selected Stories, 1991; The Sky People, 1994; Collected Stories, 1994; Several Publications for Children including Areta and the Kahawai (picture book in English), 1994; Ko Areta me Nga Kahawai (picture book in Maori), 1994. Honours: New Zealand Fiction Award, 1987; HLD, Victoria University, 1989. Address: c/o Longman Paul Ltd, Private Bag, Takapuna, Auckland 9, New Zealand.

GRAEF Roger Arthur, b. 18 Apr 1936, New York, USA. Writer; Television Producer; Filmmaker. m. Susan Mary Richards, 20 Nov 1985, 1 s, 1 d. Education: BA, Honours, Harvard University; Actors Studio's, New York City. Appointments: Consultant to Collins Publishers, 1982-88. Publications: Talking Blues, 1989; Living Dangerously, 1993; Chairman, Signals International trust: Book Aid (1

million books to Russia); Over 100 films and television programmes for British and International television. Contributions to: Media columns, The Times; The Telegraph; Sunday Telegraph; The Observer; The Guardian; The Independent; The Independent on Sunday; Sunday Times; The Listener; New Society. Hounours: Winner, Royal Televison Society Award, 1979; British Academy of Televison and Film Arts, (BAFTA), 1982; European Television Magazine Award. Memberships: Writers' Guild. Literary Agent: Reogers, Coleridge and White. Address: 72 Westbourne Park Villas, London, W2, England.

GRAFF Gerald Edward, b. 28 June 1937, Chicago, Illinois, USA. Education: AB, University of Chicago; PhD, Stanford University. Career: University Professor. Publications: Poetic Statement & Critical Dogma, 1970; Chicago Letter & Other Parodies, 1978; Literature Against Itself, 1979; Criticism in the University (ed), 1985; Parodies, Etc, & So Forth (ed), 1985; Professing Literature, 1987; The Origins of Literary Studies in America (ed), 1988; Beyond the Culture Wars: How Teaching the Conflicts Can Revitalize American Education, 1992. Contributions to: Numerous academic journals. Honour: American Book Award, 1993. Address: Department of English, Northwestern University, Evanston, IL 60201, USA.

GRAFF Henry Franklin, b. 1921, USA. Historian; Professor Emeritus of History. Publications: Bluejackets with Perry in Japan, 1952; The Modern Researcher (with J Barzun), 1957, 5th edition, 1992; American Themes (with C Lord), 1963; Thomas Jefferson, 1968; The Free and the Brave, 1967, 4th edition, 1980; American Imperialism and the Philippine Insurrection (editor), 1969; The Tuesday Cabinet: Deliberation and Decision on Peace and War under Lyndon B Johnson, 1970; The Adventure of the American People (with J A Krout), 3rd edition, 1973; The Grand Experiment (with P J Bohannan) vol I, The Call of Freedom, vol II, The Promise of Democracy, 1978; This Great Nation, 1983; The Presidents: A Reference History, 1984; America: The Glorious Republic, 1985, 2nd edition, 1990. Address: 47 Andrea Lane, Scarsdale, NY 10583, USA.

GRAFTON Anthony, Professor of History. Publications include: Joseph Scalizer, 1983; From Humanism to the Humanities, 1986; Forgers & Critics, 1990; Defenders of the Text, 1991; New Worlds & Ancient Texts, 1992. Address: Department of History, Princeton University, Dickinson Hall, Princeton, NT 08544-1017, USA.

GRAHAM Ada, b. 1931,USA. Author. Appointments: Vice-Chairman, Maine State Commissionon the Arts, 1975-80; Board Memebr, New England Foundation for the Arts, 1977-80; Developer, Writer, Audobon Adventures, National Audobon Society, 1984-. Publications: The Great American Shopping Cart (with Frank Graham), 1969; Wildlife Rescue (with Frank Graham) 1970; Puffin Island (with Frank Graham), 1971; The Mystery of the Everglades, 1972; Dooryard Garden, 1974; Let's Discover the Winter Woods, 1974; Discover Changes Everywhere, 1974; Let's Discover Birds in Our World, 1974; The Careless Animal, 1974; The Milkweed and Its World of Animals (wth F Graham), 1976; Foxtails, Ferns and Fishscales: A Handbook of Art and Narute Projects, 1976; Whale Watch, 1978; Bug Hunters, 1978; Coyote Song, 1978; Falcon Flight, 1978; Audobon Readers (with F Graham) 6 vols, 1978-81; Alligators (with F Graham), 1979; Careers in Conservation (with F Graham) 1980; Birds of the Northern Seas (with F Graham) 1980; Bears, 1981; The Changing Desert (with F Graham), 1981; Jacob and the Owl (with F Graham) 1981; Three Million Mice (with F Graham), 1981; Six Little Chicadees, 1982; Busy Bugs (with F Graham), 1983; The Big Stretch (with F Graham) 1985; We Watch Squirrels (with F Graham), 1985. Honours: First Prize, Annual Children's Science Book Award, New York Academy of Sciences, 1986; Eva L Gordon Award of the American Nature Study Society, 1989. Memberships: Board of Directors, Maine Family Planning Association, 1973-80. Address: Milbridge, ME 04658, USA.

GRAHAM Charles S. See: **TUBB E(dwin) C(harles).**

GRAHAM Frank Jr, b. 1925, USA. Author; Editor. Appointments: Field Editor, Audubon magazine, 1968-. Publications: It Takes Heart (with M Allen), 1959; Disaster by Default, 1966; The Great American Shopping Cart (with Ada Graham), 1969; Since Silent Spring, 1970; Wildlife Rescue, (with A Graham), 1970; Puffin Island (with A Graham), 1971; Man's Dominion, 1971; The Mystery of the Everglades (with A Graham), 1972; Where the Place called Morning Lies, 1973; Audubon Primers (with A Graham, 4 vols, 1974; The Careless Animal (with A Graham), 1975; Gulls: A Social History, 1975; Potomac: The Nation's River, 1976; The Milkweed and its Wrold of Animals (with A Graham),

1976; The Adirondack Park: A Political History, 1978; Audubon Readers (with A Graham) 6 vols, 1978-81; Careers in Conservation (with A Graham) 1980; Birds of the Northern Seas (with A Graham), 1981; A Farewell to Heroes, 1981; The Changing Desert (with A Graham), 1981; Jacob and Owl (with A Graham), 1981; Three Millino Mice (with A Graham) 1981; Busy Bugs (with A Graham) 1983; The Dragon Hunters, 1984; The Big Stretch (with A Graham), 1985; We Watch Squirrels, (with A Graham), 1985; The Audubon Ark, 1990. Address: Milbridge, ME 04658, USA.

GRAHAM Henry, b. 1 Dec 1930, Liverpool, England. Lecturer. Education: Liverpool College of Art, 1950-52. Appointments: Poetry Editor, Literary Magazine, Ambit, London, 1969-90. Publications: Good Luck to You Kafka/You'll Need It Boss, 1969; Soup City Zoo, 1969; Passport to Earth, 1971; Poker in Paradise Lost, 1977; Europe After Rain, 1981; Bomb, 1985; The Very Fragrant Death of Paul Gauguin, 1987; Jardin Gobe Avions, 1991. Contributions to: Ambit; Transatlantic Review; Prism International Review; Evergreen Review; Numerous anthologies worldwide. Honours: Arts Council Literature Awards, 1969, 1971, 1975. Address: Flat 5, 23 Marmion Road, Liverpool L17 8TT, England.

GRAHAM James. See: **PATTERSON Harry**.

GRAHAM Jorie, b. 1951, Italy. Poet; Creative Writing Instructor. m. 1 daughter. Publications: Hybrids of Plants & Ghosts; Erosion; Region of Unlikeness. Honours: Lavan Younger Poets Award, 1990; MacArthur Fellowship; Morton Dauwen Zabel Award, American Institute for Arts & Letters.

GRAHAM Leonard. See: **BALFOUR Michael**.

GRAHAM Sonia. See: **SINCLAIR Sonia Elizabeth**.

GRAHAM Winston Mawdsley, b. 30 June 1910, Victoria Park, Manchester, England. m. Jean Mary Williamson, 1939 (dec'd 1992), 1 son, 1 daughter. Publications: Books translated into 17 languages: some early novels (designedly out of print) and: Night Journey, 1941 (revised edition 1966); The Merciless Ladies, 1944 (revised edition 1979); The Forgotton Story, 1945 (ITV production 1983); Ross Poldark, 1945; Demelza, 1946; Take My Life, 1947 (filmed 1947); Cordelia, 1949; Night Without Stars, 1950 (filmed 1950); Jeremy Poldark, 1950; Fortune is a Woman, 1953 (filmed 1956); Warleggan, 1953; The Little Walls, 1955; The Sleeping Partner, 1956 (filmed 1958); Greek Fire, 1957; The Tumbled House, 1959; Marnie, 1961 (filmed 1963); The Grove of Eagles, 1963; After the Act, 1965; The Walking Stick, 1967 (filmed 1970); The Spanish Armadas, 1972; The Black Moon, 1973; Woman in the Mirror, 1975; The Four Swans, 1976; The Angry Tide, 1977; The Stranger from the Sea, 1981; The Millers Dance, 1982; Poldark's Cornwall, 1983; The Loving Cup, 1984; The Green Flash, 1986; Cameo, 1988; The Twisted Sword, 1990; Stephanie, 1992; Tremor, 1995; BBC TV Series Poldark (the first 4 Poldark novels), 1975-76, second series (the next 3 Poldark novels), 1977; Circumstantial Evidence, play, 1979. Honours: OBE, 1983; FRSL. Address: Abbotswood House, Buxted, East Sussex TN22 4PB, England.

GRAHAM-YOOLL Andrew Michael, b. 5 Jan 1944, Buenos Aires, Argentina. Journalist; Writer. m. 17 Jan 1966, 1 son, 2 daughters. Appointments include: News Editor & Political Columnist, Buenos Aires Herald, 1966-76; Freelance Writer, San Francisco Chronicle, 1967-70 & 1976, Baltimore Sun, 1967-69, & 1976, The Miami Herald, 1969, Kansas City Star, 1969-73, New York Times, 1970, Newsweek, 1970, others; Broadcaster, BBC World Service, London, 1976; Occasional News Commentary, London Broadcasting Company; Sub Editor, Foreign News, Daily Telegraph, London, 1976-77; Foreign Correspondent, The Guardian, London, 1977-84; Editor, Writers News, London, 1983-85; Deputy Editor, 1984-85, Editor, 1985-88, South Magazine, London; Editor, Index on Censorship, 1989-93; Senior Visiting Fellow, Queen Mary and Westfield College, London, 1990-; Press Fellow, Wolfson College, University of Cambridge, 1994; Editor-in-Chief, Buenos Aires Herald, 1994-. Publications: The Press in Argentina, 1973-78, 1979; Portrait of an Exile, 1981; The Forgotten Colony, 1981; Small Wars You May Have Missed (in South America), 1983; A State of Fear, 1986; Argentina, Peron to Videla 1955-1976, 1989; Point of Arrival, 1992; Short Stories: The Date Might Be Forgotten, 1967; The Premonition, 1968; Twenty Pages of Garcia, 1974; Money Cures Melancholy, 1974; Sirens, 1980; After the Despots, 1991; Poetry in Spanish. Honours: Poetry Prize, El

Vidente Ciego Magazine Rosario, Argentina, 1975; British Council Visitorship to Britain, 1976; Nicholas Tomalin Memorial Award for Journalists, 1977. Memberships: PEN; Press Officer, 1979-87; Writers Guild of Great Britain, Executive Council, 1983; Argentine Writers Society; Anglo-Argentine Society, Committee Member, 1989-90; The Royal Literary Fund, Life Member, 1987; Association of British Editors, Member of the Board, 1990-93; Arts Council Literature Touring Panel, 1992-. Address: c/o Buenos Aires Herald, Azopardo 455, 1107 Buenos Aires, Argentina.

GRANADOS Paul. See: **KENT Arthur (William Charles)**.

GRANDOWER Elissa, See: **WAUGH Hillary Baldwin**.

GRANGE Peter. See: **NICOLE Christopher Robin**.

GRANT Anthony. See: **CAMPBELL Judith**.

GRANT Charles L, b. 1942, USA. Freelance Writer; Former Teacher. Appointments: English Teacher, Toms River High School, New Jersey, 1964-70; Chester High School, New Jersey, 1970-72; Mt Olive High School, New Jersey, 1972-73; English and History Teacher, Roxbury High School, New Jersey, 1974-75. Publications: The Shadow of Alpha, science fiction novel, 1976; The Curse, 1976; The Hour of the Oxrun Dead, 1977; Writing and Selling Science Fiction (editor), 1977; The Ravens of the Moon, science fiction novel, 1978; The Sound of Midnight, 1978; Shadows 1-9 (editor), 9 vols, 1978-86; Nightmares (editor) 1979; The Last Call of Mournng, 1979; Legion, science fiction novel, 1979; Tales from the Nightside, 1981; Glow of Candles and Other Stories, 1981; Nightmare Seasons, science fiction novel, 1982; Night Songs, science fiction novel, 1984; The Tea Party, 1985; The Pet, 1986; The Orchards, 19786; Something Stirs, 1992.

GRANT Ellen Catherine Gardner, b. 29 Sept 1934, Scotland. Medical Practitioner. m. David Norman Grant, 12 Sept 1959, 1 son, 2 daughters. Education: MB ChB (Commend), St Andrews University, 1958; DRCOG, London, England, 1959. Publications: The Bitter Pill, 1985, 1986; L'Aer Pillule (France), 1988; Den Bitre Pillen (Norway), 1987; De Bitre Pille (Denmark), 1986; De Bittere Pil (Holland), 1986; The Bitter Pill (Japan), 1992; Sexual Chemistry, 1994; Chapters in: Smoking and Migraine, 1981; Biological Aspects of Schizophrenia and Addiction, 1982. Contributions to: Lancet; British Medical Journal; Clinical Oncology; The Ecologist; Journal of Obstetrics & Gynaecology of the British Commonwealth; Headache; International Journal of Environmental Studies; Nutrition & Health; The Case Against the Pill, 1994; Journal of Nutritional Medicine. Memberships: British Society for Nutritional Medicine; British Society for Allergy & Environmental Medicine; Foresight (Association for the Promotion of Preconception Care); The Dyslexia Institute. Literary Agent: Deborah Rodgers. Address: 20 Coombe Ridings, Kingston-upon-Thames, Surrey KT2 7JU, England.

GRANT John. See: **BARNETT Paul le Page**.

GRANT Maxwell. See: **LYNDS Dennis**.

GRANT Michael, b. 21 Nov 1914, London, England. Writer; Former University Professor & Vice Chancellor. m. Rut Anne Sophie Beskow, 2 Aug 1944, 2 sons. Education: BA, MA, LittD, Trinity College, Cambridge. Publications include: From Imperium to Auctoritas, 1946; Roman Imperial Money, 1954; The World of Rome, 1960; Myths of the Greeks & Romans, 1962; The Civilizations of Europe, 1965; The Climax of Rome, 1968; The Ancient Mediterranean, 1969; Julius Caesar, 1969; The Ancient Historians, 1970; The Roman Forum, 1970; Herod the Great, 1971; The Jews in the Roman World, 1973; Cleopatra, 1972; The Fall of the Roman Empire, 1976; Greek and Latin Authors 800BC - AD 1000, 1980; The Dawn of the Middle Ages, 1981; From Alexander to Cleopatra, 1982, reprinted as The Hellenistic Greeks, 1990; History of Ancient Israel, 1984; The Roman Emperors, 31BC - AD476, 1985; A Guide to the Ancient World, 1986; The Rise of the Greeks, 1987; The Classical Greeks, 1989; The Visible Past, 1990; Short History of Classical Civilization (Founder of the Western World in USA), 1991; Greeks and Romans: A Social History (A Social History of Greece and Rome in USA), 1992, Readings in the Classical Historians, 1992; The Emperor Constantine, 1993; Saint Peter, 1994; My First Eighty Years, 1994. Contributions to: Various journals. Honours: OBE, 1946; CBE, 1958; Honorary LittD Dublin, 1961; Honorary LLD, Belfast, 1967; Gold Medal, Education, Sudan, 1977; Premio del Mediterraneo Mazara del Vallo, 1983; Premio Latina, 1986;

Premio Internazionale delle Muse (Florence), 1989. Memberships: Medallist, Honorary Fellow, former President, Royal Numismatic Society; Huntingdon Medalist, American Numismatic Society; former President, Virgil Society; former President, Classical Association. Address: Le Pitturacce, 381 Via della Chiesa, Gattaiola, 55050 Lucca, Italy.

GRANT Neil David Mountfield (David Mountfield, D M Field and Gail Trenton), b. 9 June 1938, England. Writer. m. Vera Steiner, 23 Sept 1979. 2 daughters. Education: MA (Hons), St Johns College, Cambridge, 1958-61. Publications include: Children's History of Britain, 1977; Greek and Roman Erotica, 1982; A History of Polar Exploration, 1974; A History of African Exploration, 1976; American Folktales & Legends, 1988; The White Bear (fiction), 1983; Neil Grant's Book of Spies & Spying, 1975; London's Villages, 1990. Membership: Royal Geographical Society. Literary Agent: Laurence Pollinger. Address: 2 Avenue Road, Teddington, Middlesex TW11 0BT, England.

GRANT Nicholas. See: NICOLE Christopher Robin.

GRANT Roderick, b. 1941, United Kingdom. Author. Appointments: Sub Editor, Weekly Scotsman, 1965-67. Publications: Adventure in My Veins, 1968; Seek Out the Guilty, 1969; Where No Angels Dwell, 1969; Gorbals Doctor, 1970; The Dark Horizon (with Alexander Highlands), 1971; The Lone Voyage of Betty Mouat, 1973; The Stalking of Adrian Lawford, 1974; The Clutch of Caution, 1975, 2nd edition, 1985; The 51st Highland Division at War, 1976; Strathalder: A Highland Estate 1978 (2nd edition, with illustrations, 1989); A Savage Freedom, 1978; The Great Canal,1978; A Private Vendetta, 1978; But Not in Anger (with C Cole), 1979; Clap Hands for the Singing Molecatcher, 1989. Address: 3 Back Lane Cottages, Bucks Horn Oak, Farmham, Surrey, England.

GRASS Gunter, b. 16 Oct 1927, Danzig, Poland (German citizen). Novelist; Playwright. Education: State Academy of Fine Arts, Berlin, 1953-55. Appointments include: Co-editor, Verlages L'80 publishing house, from 1980. Publications: The Tin Drum, 1959; Cat and Mouse, 1961; Dog Years, 1963; Local Anaesthetic, 1969; From the Diary of a Snail, 1972; The Flounder, 1977; The Meeting at Telgte, 1979; Headbirths: or, The Germans are Dying Out, 1980; The Rat, 1986; Tierschutz, 1990; The Call of the Toad, 1992; Plays: Flood, 1957; Uncle, Uncle, 1958; Only Ten Minutes to Buffalo, 1959; The Wicked Cooks, 1961; The Plebians Rehearse the Uprising, 1966; Davor, 1969; Screenplay for The Tin Drum, 1979; Ballet scenarios; Radio plays; Verse: Selected Poems, 1966; New Poems, 1967; Collected Poems, 1971; Inmarypraise, 1973; Mit Sophie in die Pilze gegangen, 1976; In the Egg and Other Poems, 1977; Kinderlied: Verse and Etchings, 1982; Nachruf auf einen Handschuh, 1982; Poems, 1985; The Poems 1955-86, 1988; Also: Show Your Tongue (travel), 1988; Two States - One Nation? The Case Against German Reunification, 1990; Other political texts. Honours include: International Literature Award, 1976; Honorary Doctorate, Harvard University, 1976. Address: Niedstrasse 13, 1000 Berlin 41, Germany.

GRAU Shirley Ann, b. 8 July 1930, New Orleans, Louisiana, USA. Writer. m. James Feibleman, 4 Aug 1955, 2 sons, 2 daughters. Education: BA, Tulane University, New Orleans. Publications: The Black Prince, 1955; The Hard Blue Sky, 1958; The House on Coleseum Street, 1961; The Keepers of the House, 1964; The Condor Passes, 1971; The Wind Shifting West, 1973; Evidence of Love, 1977; Nine Women, 1985; Roadwalkers, 1994. Contributions to: New Yorker; Saturday Evening Post; Others. Honours: Pulitzer Prize for Fiction, 1965. Literary Agent: Brandt and Brandt, New York City, USA. Address: 210 Baronne Street, Suite 1120, New Orleans, LA 70112, USA.

GRAVER Elizabeth, b. 2 July 1964, Los Angeles, California, USA. Writer; Teacher. Education: BA, Wesleyan University, 1986; MFA, Washington University, 1990; MA, Cornell University, 1992. Appointment: Visiting Professor of English and Creative Writing, Boston College, Massachusetts, 1993-95. Publication: Have You Seen Me?. Contributions to: Best American Short Stories; Story; Southern Review; Antaeus; Seventeen; Southwest Review; O Henry Prize Stories, 1994; Louder Than Words; Ploughshares. Honours: Fulbright Fellowship; Drue Heinz Literature Prize; National Endowment for the Arts Fellowship; Writers Exchange Winner. Membership: Phi Beta Kappa. Literary Agent: Richard Parks, USA. Address: c/o Richard Parks Agency, 138 E 16th Street 58, New York, NY 10003, USA.

GRAVER Lawrence Stanley, b. 6 Dec 1931, New York, New York, USA. Professor of English. m. Suzanne Levy Graver, 28 Jan 1960, 2 d. Education: BA, City College of New York, 1954: PhD, University of California, Berkeley, 1961. Appointments: Assistant Professor, University of California, Los Angeles, 1961-64; Associate Professor, 1964-71; Professor, 1971-; Williams College, 1964-; Publications: Conrad's Short Fiction, 1968; Carson McCullers, 1969; Beckett: The Critical Heritage, 1979; Mastering the Film, 1974; Beckett: Waiting for Godot, 1989; An Obsession with Anne Frank: Meyer Levin and The Diary, 1995. Contributions to: New York Times Book Review; Saturday Review: New Republic; New Leader; 19th Century Fiction. Membership: Modern Language Association. Address: Department of English, Williams College, Williamstown, MA 01267, USA.

GRAY Alasdair, b. 28 Dec 1934, Glasgow, Scotland. 1 son. Education: Diploma, Glasgow Art School, 1957, Awarded Bellahouston Travelling Scholarship. Appointments: Part time art teacher 1958-62; Theatrical scene painter 1962-63, Free-lance playwright and painter 1963-75, Artist-recorder, People's Palace (local history museum) 1977, Writer in residence, University of Glasgow, 1977-79, Free-lance painter and maker of books 1979-. Publications: Lanark: a novel, 1981, revised 1985; Unlikely Stories, 1983, revised 1984; 1982 Janine, a novel, 1984, revised 1985; The Fall of Kelvin Walker: A Fable of the Sixties; Lean Tales (with James Kelman and Agnes Owens), 1985; Saltire Self-Portrait 4, 1988; Old Negatives, four verse sequences; McGrotty and Ludmilla, or The Harbinger Report: A Romance of the Eighties, 1989; Something Leather, 1990; Why Scots Should Rule Scotland, 1992; Poor Things, 1992; Ten Tales Tall and True, 1993; The History Maker, 1994. Contributions to: Periodicals including Chapman and The Edinburgh Review. Honours: Three grants Scottish Arts Council, between 1968 and 1981; Saltire Society, 1982; Cheltenham Literary Festival, 1983; Scottish branch of PEN, 1986; Whitbread Award, Poor Things, 1992. Memberships: Society of Authors; Scottish Society of Playwrights; Glasgow Print Workshop; Various organizations supporting coal miners and nuclear disarmament. Literary Agent: Xandra Hardie.

GRAY Alice Wirth, b. 29 Apr 1934, Chicago, Illinois, USA. Writer. m. Ralph Gareth Gray, 16 July 1954, 2 d. Education: BA, University of California, 1958; MA, 1960. Publication: What the Poor Eat, 1993. Contributions to: The Atlantic; The American Scholar; Poetry; Breakfast Without Meat; The Little Magazine; Helicon Nine; Primavera; Sequoia. Honours: Illinois Arts Council Literary Award; Gordon Barber Memorial Award; Duncan Lawrie Award. Memberships: Poetry Society of America; PEN Center USA West. Address: 1001 Merced Street, Berkeley, CA 94707, USA.

GRAY Angela,See:DANIELS Dorothy.

GRAY Caroline. See: NICOLE Christopher Robin.

GRAY Dorothy Randall, b. Davisboro, GA, USA. Executive Director. m. Ronald K Gray. Education: BS, City College. Appointments: Poet in Residence, Hunter College, 1989; Skidmore, Writing Facilitator, 1990-92; Columbia University, Writing Consultant, 1991; Anges Scott College, Writing Facilitator, 1992. Publications: Gaptooth Girlfriends; Muse Blues; The Passion Collection; A Rock Against The Wind; Glowchold; 360 Degrees of Blackness; Women Writing. Contributions to: The New York Times; Blacks on Black; The Paper. Memberships: International Womens Writers Guild; Poets and Writers; Associated Writing Programs. Address: 162 Underhill Avenue, Brooklyn, NY 11231, USA.

GRAY Douglas, b. 17 Feb 1930, Melbourne. University Teacher. m. 3 Sept 1959, 1 son. Education: MA, Victoria University of Wellington, New Zealand, 1952; BA, 1956; MA, 1960, Merton College, Oxford. Publications: Oxford Book of Late Medieval Verse and Prose, 1985; Robert Henryson, 1979; Themes and Images in the Medieval English Religious Lyric, 1972; Articles in medieval literature. Honour: FBA, 1989. Memberships: President, Society for Study of Medieval Languages and Literatures, 1982-86; Council, Early English Text Society. Address: Lady Margaret Hall, Oxford OX2 6QA, England.

GRAY Dulcie Winifred, b. 20 Nov 1920. m. Michael Denison 29 Apr 1939. Publicatios: Murder on the Stairs, 1957; Baby Face, 1959; For Richer for Richer, 1970; Ride on Tiger, 1975; Butterflies on my Mind, 1978; Dark Calypo, 1979; The Glanvill Women, 1982; Mirror Image, 1987; Looking Forward, Looking Back, autobiography, 1991. Contributions to: Daily Express; Evening Standard; Womans Own;

Vogue. Honours: Queens Silver Jubilee Medal, 1977; The Times Educational Supplement Senior Information Award, 1978; CBE, 1983. Memberships: Society of Authors; Royal Society of Arts, Fellow; Linnean Soceity; British Actors Equity. Literary Agent: Doulgas Rae. Address: 28 Charring Cross Road, London, WC2, England.

GRAY Francine du Plessix, b. 1930, USA. Author. Appointments: Reporter, United Press International, New York City, 1952-54; Assistant Editor, Realites Magazine, Paris, France, 1954-55; Book Editor, Art in America, New York City, 1962-64; Visiting Professor, City University of New York, 1975; Yale University, New Haven, Connecticut, 1981; Columbia University, New York City, 1983; Ferris Professor, Princeton University, New Jersey, 1986. Publications: Divine Disobedience: Profiles in Catholic Radicalism, 1970; Hawai: The Sugar-Coated Fortress, 1972; Lovers and Tyrants, 1976; World Without End, 1981; October Blood, 1985; Adam and Eve and the City, 1987; Soviet Women: Walking the Tightrope, 1991; Rage and Fire: A Life of Louise Colet, 1994. Memberships: American Academy of Arts and Letters. Literary Agent: Georges Borchardt Inc, USA. Address: c/o Georges Borchardt Inc, 145 East 57th Street, New York, NY 10022, USA.

GRAY Marianne Claire, b. 1947, Cape Town, South Africa. Journalist; Biographer. Education: University Aix Marseille, 1965-66; Cambridge Polytechnic, 1967; BA, UNISA, 1972. Appointments: Reporter, Argus Group, South Africa, 1968-70; Reporter, Cape Times, 1970-73; Editor, Athens News, 1974; Syndication Assistant, South African National Mags, London, 1975-77; Freelance Journalist, 1977-. Publications: Depardieu; La Moreau, 1994; Freelance Alternative; The Other Arf; Working from Home; Thoughts About Architecture. Contributions include: Sky; Cosmopolitan; Arena; Options; Empire; Company; The Face; You; New Women; Womens Journal. Memberships: Women in Publishing; Critics Circle; Lawrence Durrell Research Centre; Women in Film International. Literary Agent: Blake Friedmann. Address: 32 Eburne Road, London N7 6AU, England; 20 Rue du Caminol, St Jean de Fos, 34150 France.

GRAY (John) Richard, b. 1929, United Kingdom. Professor Emeritus of African History, University of London. Appointments: Editor, Journal of African History, 1968-71. Publications: The Two Nations: Aspects of the Development of Race Relations in the Rhodesias and Nyasaland, 1960; A History of the Southern Sudan, 1839-1889, 1961; Materials for West African History in Italian Archives (with D Chambers), 1965; Pre-Colonial African Trade (edited with D Birmingham), 1970; Cambridge History of Africa, vol IV (editor), 1975; Christianity in Independent Africa (edited with E Fasholé-Luke and others), 1978; Black Christians & White Missionaries, 1990. Membership: Britain-Zimbabwe Society, Chairman 1981-85. Address: 39 Rotherwick Road, London NW11 7DD, England.

GRAY Richard Butler, b. 29 May 1922, Ft Atkinson, Wisconsin, USA. Professor Emeritus of Political Science. Education: BA, Hispanic Studies, University of Wisconsin, 1947; MA, International Relations, Fletcher School of Law and Diplomacy, 1949; Diploma, Cuban Politics, University of Havana, 1957; PhD, Political Science, University of Wisconsin, 1957. Publications: José Martí, Cuban Patriot, 1962; International Security Systems, Concepts and Models of World Order (editor), 1969; Security in a World of Change, Readings and Notes in International Relations, (edited with Lee W Farnsworth) 1969; Latin America and the United States in the 1970's, (editor), 1971; A Dictionary of Political Science (contributor), 1964; Handbook of World History (contributor), 1967; An Encyclopedia of Latin America, 1975; World Encyclopedia of Peace (contributor), 1986. Contributions to: The Americas; Hispanic American Historical Review; Inter-American Review of Bibliography; Journal of Developing Areas; Journal of Inter-American Studies; Journal of Southeastern Latin American Studies. Honours: Sigma Delta Pi, 1943; Pi Gamma Mu, 1958; Pi Sigma Alpha, 1959; Pi Gamma Mu National Merit Award, 1981; Award Premio Periodistico José Martí, 1966. Memberships: Honorary Member, Dobro Slovo, 1985; Southeastern Conference of Latin American Studies, President, 1974-75; Southern Political Science Association. Address: 1502 Mitchell Avenue, Tallahassee, FL 32303, USA.

GRAY Robert, b. 23 Feb 1945, Australia. Poet. Appointment: Writer-in-residence, Tokyo, 1985. Publications: Introspect, Retrospect, 1970; Creekwater Journal, 1974; Grass Script, 1978; The Skylight, 1983; Selected Poems 1963-83, 1985, 1990; Piano, 1988; Co-editor, The Young Australian Poets, 1983; Co-author, Alun Leach-Jones,

1988. Honours include: Adelaide Arts Festival National Poetry Award, 1985; New South Wales Premier's Award, 1986. Address: c/o Angus and Robertson, PO Box 290, North Ryde, New South Wales 2113, Australia.

GRAY Simon John Halliday, (Hamish Reade), b. 21 Oct 1936, Hayling Island, Hants, England. Playwright. m. Beryl Mary Kevern, 1966, 1 son, 1 daughter. Education: BA, Honours, Cambridge. Publications: Fiction: Colmain; Simple People; Little Portia; A Comeback for Stark; Non-Fiction: An Unnatural Pursuit, 1985; How's That For Telling 'em, Fat Lady?, 1988; Stage Plays: Wise Child, 1967; Dutch Uncle, 1969; The Idiot; Spoiled, 1971; Butley, 1971; Otherwise Engaged; Dog Days, 1976; Molly, 1977; The Rear Column, 1978; Close of Play, 1979; Stage Struck, 1979; Quartermaine's Terms, 1981; Chapter Seventeen; The Common Pursuit, 1984; Melon, 1987; Hidden Laughter, 1990; The Holy Terror; Cell Mates; Television Plays: The Caramel Crisis; Death of a Teddy Bear; A Way With The Ladies; Sleeping Dog; Spoiled; Pig in a Poke; The Dirt on Lucy Lane; The Princess; Man in a Side-Car; Plaintiffs and Defendents; Two Sundays; Radio Plays: The Holy Terror; The Rector's Daughter; Suffer The Little Children; With a Nod and a Bow; Television Films: After Pilkington; Quartermaine's Terms; Old Flames; They Never Slept; The Common Pursuit; Running Late; Unnatural Pursuits; Femme Fatale; Films: Butley; A Month in the Country. Honours: Writers' Guild Award; Evening Standard & Plays & Players Best Play Awards, 1975. Memberships: Fellow, Royal Society of Literature; Dramatists Society. Literary Agent: Judy Daish Associates. Address: c/o Judy Daish Associates, 2 St Charles Place, London W10 6EG, England.

GRAY Spalding, b. 5 June 1941, Providence, Rhode Island, USA. Playwright. Eduction: Fryeburg Academy, Maine; BA, Emerson College, Boston, 1965. Career: Actor in summer stock, Cape Cod, Massachusetts and in Saratoga, New York, 1965-67; with Performance group, New York, 1969-75; Founder, with Elizabeth LeCompte, the Wooster Group, New York, 1975. Publications: Plays include: Travels Through New England (produced Cambridge, Massachusetts, 1984); Rivkala's Ring, adaptation of a story by Chekhov in Orchards, (produced Urbana, Illinois, 1985, New York, 1986); Knopf, 1986; Terrors of Pleasure: The House (produced Cambridge, Massachusetts, 1985, New York, 1986, London, 1987); Included in Sex and Death at the Age 14, 1986; Sex and Death at the Age 14, New York, Random House, 1986, augmented edition, including Swimming to Cambodia, parts 1 and 2, as Swimming to Cambodia: The Collected Works, London, 1987. Screenplay: Swimming to Cambodia, 1987; Television Play: Bedtime Story with Renee Shafransky, 1987. Honours: National Endowment for the Arts, Fellowship, 1977; Rockefeller Grant, 1980; Guggenheim Fellowship, 1985; Obie Award, 1985. Literary Agent: Suzanne Gluck, International Creative Management, New York. Address: c/o The Wooster Group, Box 654, Canal Street Sation, New York, NY 10013, USA.

GRAY Tony (George Hugh), b. 1922, Irish. Writer. Appointments: Former Features Editor, Daily Mirror, London. Publications: Starting from Tomorrow, 1965; The Real Professionals, 1966; Gone the Time,1967; The Irish Answer, 1967; (adaptor) Interlude, 1968; (with L Villa) The Record Breakers, 1970; The Last Laugh, 1972; The Orange Order, 1972; Psalms and Slaughter, 1972; (with C McBride) The White Lions of Timbavati, 1977; (with T Murphy) Some of My Best Friends Are Animals, 1979; (with C McBride) Operation White Lion, 1981; The Irish Times Book of the 20th Century, 1985; The Road to Success: Alfred McAlpine, 1935-85, 1987.

GREAVES Margaret, b. 1914, United Kingdom. Lecturer in English (retired); Children's Fiction Writer. Appointments: Principal Lecturer in English, 1946-70; Head of Department, 1960-70, St Mary's College of Education, Cheltenham. Publications: The Blazon of Honour, 1964; Regency Patron, 1966; Gallery, 1968; Gallimaufry, 1971; The Dagger and the Bird, 971; The Grandmother Stone, US Edition Stone of Terror, 1972; Little Jacko, 1973; The Gryphon Quest, 1974; Curfew, 1975; Nothing Even Happens on Sundays, 1976; The Night of the Goat, 1976; A Net to Catch the Wind, 1979; The Abbottsbury Ring, 1979; Charlie and Emma Series, 4 vols, 1980-87; Cat's Magic, 1980; The Snake Whistle, 1980; Once There Were No Pandas, 1985; Nicky's Knitting Granny, 1986; The Mouse of Nibbling Village, 1986; Hetty Pegler, 1987; Mouse Mischeif, 1989; Juniper's Journey, 1990; Magic from the Ground, 19990; Henry's Wild Morning, 1990. Address: 8 Greenways, Winchcombe, GL54 5LG, England.

GREELEY Andrew, b. 1928. Professor of Sociology; Catholic Minister; Novelist. Publications include: Over 19 mystery novels include: Happy Are the Poor in Spirit, 1994; Irish Gold, 1994; Virgin & Martyr; Thy Brother's Wife; The Cardinal Sins; God Game; The Final Planet; Lord of the Dance; All About Women; Non-fiction: The Catholic Myth, 1990; Sacraments of Love, 1994. Address: 1012 East 47th Street, Chicago, IL 60653, USA.

GREEN O O. See: **DURGNAT Raymond Eric.**

GREEN Benjamin, b. 17 Jul 1956, San Bernardino, California, USA. Writer. Education: BA, Humboldt State University, Arcata, 1985. Publications: The Field Notes of A Madman, The Lost Coast; From a Greyhound Bus; Monologs from the Realm of Silence; Green Grace, 1993; This Coast of Many Colors, 1993. Honours: Ucross Fellow. Address: 3415 Patricks Point Drive 3, Trinidad, CA 95570, USA.

GREEN Benny, b. 9 Dec 1927. Freelance Writer. m. Antoinette Kanal, 1962, 3 s, 1 d. Appointments: Saxophonist, 1947-60; Jazz Critic, Observer, 1958-77; Literary Critic, Spectator, 1970-; Film Critic, Punch, 1972-77; TV Critic, 1977-. Publications: Books and Lyrics: Boots with Strawberry Jam 1968; Co-Deviser, Cole, 1974; Oh Mr Porter, 1977; D D Lambeth, 1985; (Books) The Reluctant Art, 1962; Blame it on My Youth, 1967; 58 Minutes to London, 1969; Drums in my Ears, 1973; I've Lost My Little Willie, 1976; Swingtime in Tottenham 1976; Editor, Cricket Addict's Archive, 1977; Shaw's Champions, 1978; Fred Astaire, 1979; Editor, Wisden Anthology, volume 1 1864-1900, 1979, volume II, 1900-1940, 1983; P G Woodhouse: a literary Biography, 1981; Wisden Book of Obituaries, 1986; A Histroy of Cricket, 1988; Let's Face the Music,1989. Address: c/o BBC Broadcasting House, Portland Place, London, W1, England.

GREEN Clifford, b. 6 Dec 1934, Melbourne, Victoria, Australia. Author; Screenwriter. m. Judith Irene Painter, 16 May 1959, 1 son, 3 daughters. Education: Primary Teachers Certificate, Toorak Teachers' College, 1959. Publications: Marion, 1974; The Incredible Steam-Driven Adventures of Riverboat Bill, 1975; Picnic at Hanging Rock: A Film, 1975; Break of Day, 1976; The Sun is Up, 1978; Four Scripts, 1978; Burn the Butterflies, 1979; Lawson's Mates, 1980; The Further Adventures of Riverboat Bill, 1981; Plays for Kids, 1981; Cop Out! Riverboat Bill Steams Again, 1985; Boy Soldiers, 1990. Honours: Australian Writers Guild Awards, 1973, 1974, 1976, 1978, 1979; Television Society of Australia Awards, 1974, 1976, 1978, 1980; Variet Club of Australia Award, 1978; Australian Writers Guild Awards, 1990, 1992. Memberships: Australian Writers Guild, former Vice-President. Address: c/o Rick Raftos Management, PO Box 445, Paddington, NSW 2021, Australia.

GREEN Hannah. See: **GREENBERG Joanne.**

GREEN John F, b. 5 June 1943, Saskatoon, Saskatchewan, Canada. Teacher. m. Maureen Anne Horne, 1 Feb 1969, 3 s, 1 d. Education: Ryerson Institute, 1964-67; Teachers Certificate, Red River Community College, 1976. Appointments: Professor, Arts and Sciences, Durham College, Oshawa, Ontario, 1976-; Writer and producer for western Canadian broadcasting companies. Publications: There are Trolls, The Bargain, 1974; The House on Geoffrey Street, 1981; The Gadfly, 1983; There's a Dragon in My Closet, 1986; Alice and The Birthday Giant, 1989; Junk-Pile Jennifer, 1991; The House That Max Built, 1991. Honours: Canadian Children's Book Centre Gold Seal Award for Alice and The Birthday Giant, awarded 1990. Literary Agent: Denise Anderson, Scholastic Publishers, 123 Newkirk Road, Richmond Hill, Ontario, Canada, L4C 365. Address: 966 Adelaide Street East, No 70 Oshawa, Ontario, Canada, L1K 1L2.

GREEN Jonathon, b. 20 Apr 1948, Kidderminster, Worcs, England. Writer; Broadcaster. 2 sons. Education: Brasenose College, Oxford, BA, 1966-69. Publications: Dictionary of Contemporary Slang; Dictionary of Contemporary Quotations; Dictionaryu of Jargon; Days in the Life; Them; Others inc. Famous Last Words, Slang Down The Ages. Literary Agent: Jacintha Alexander Assoc. Address: c/o Jacintha Alexander Assoc, 57 Emperor's Gate, London SW7 4HJ, England.

GREEN Martin (Burgess), b. 1927, United Kingdom. Professor of English; Writer. Apppointments: Instructor, Wellesley College, Massachusetts, USA, 1957-61; Lecturer, Birmingham University, England, 1965-68; Professor of English, Tufts University, Medford, Massachusetts, 1968-. Publications: Mirror for Anglo-Saxons, 1960; Reappraisals, 1965; Science and the Shabby Curate of Poetry, 1965;

The Problem of Boston 16; Yeat's Blessings on von Hugel, 1968; Cities of Light and Sons of the Morning, 1972; The von Richthofen Sisters, 1974; Children of the Sun, 1975; The Earth Again Redeemed, novel, 1976; Transatlantic Patterns, 1977; The Challenge of the Mahatmas,1978; Dreams of Adventure, Deeds of Empire, 1970; The Old English Elegies, 1983; Tolstoy and Gandhi, 1983; The Great American Adventure, 1984; Montains of Truth, 1986; The Triumph of Pierrot (with J Swan), 1986. Address: 8 Boylston Terrace, Medford, MA 02144, USA.

GREEN Melissa. Publications: Squanicook Eclogues, 1987; Color is the Suffering of Light: a memoir, 1995. Honour: Lavan Younger Poets Award, 1989.

GREEN Michael Frederick, b. 2 Jan 1927, Leicester, England. Writer. Education: BA, Honours, Open University. Publications: The Art of Coarse Rugby, 1960; The Art of Coarse Sailing, 1962; Even Coarser Rugby, 1963; The Art of Coarse Acting, 1964; The Art of Coarse Golf, 1967; The Art of Coarse Moving, 1969 (TV Serial 1977); The Art of Coarse Drinking, 1973; Squire Haggard's Journal, 1976, television series, 1990 and 1992; Tonight Josephine, 1981; The Art of Coarse Sex, 1981; Don't Swing from the Balcony Romeo, 1983; The Art of Coarse Office Life, 1985; The Boy Who Shot Down an Airship, 1988; Nobody Hurt in Small Earthquake, 1990. Memberships: Society of Authors; Equity; National Union of Journalists. Literary Agent: Anthony Sheil Associates. Address: 78 Sandall Road, Ealing, London W5 1JB, England.

GREEN Sharon, b. 6 July 1942, Brooklyn, New York, USA. Novelist. Divorced, 3 s. Education: BA, New York University, 1963. Publications: The Warrior Within, 1982; The Crystals of Mida, 1982; The Warrior Enchained, 1983; An Oath to Mida, 1983; The Warrior Rearmed, 1984; Chosen of Mida, 1984; Mind Guest, 1984; The Will of the Gods, 1985; Gateway to Xanadu, 1985; To Battle the Gods, 1986; The Warrior Challenged, 1986; The Rebel Prince, 1987; TheFar Side of Forever, 1987; Lady Blade, Lord Fighter, 1987; The Warrior Victorious, 1988; Mists of the Ages, 1988; Dawn Song, 1988. Contributions to: various journals and magazines. Memberships: Science Fiction Writers of America; The Planetary Society; Literary Agent: Richard Curtis, New York, USA. Address: c/o Richard Curtis Associates Inc, 163 E 64th Street, New York, NY 10021, USA.

GREEN Timothy (S), b. 1936, United Kingdom. Writer. Appointments: London Correspondent, Horizon, and American Heritage, 1959-62; London Correspondent, Life, 1962-64; Editor, Illustrated London News, 1964-66. Publications: The World of Gold, 1968; The Smugglers, 1969; Restless Spirit, UK Edition The Adventurers, 1970; The Universal Eye, 1972; World of Gold Today, 1973; How to Buy Gold, 1975; The Smuggling Business, 1977; The World of Diamonds, 1981; The New World of Gold, 1982, 2nd edition 1985; The Prospect for Gold, 1987; The World of Gold, 1993. Address: Suite 515, Premier House, 10 Greycoat Place, London SW1P 1SB, England.

GREEN Vivian Hubert Howard, b. 18 Nov 1915. Honorary Fellow, Lincoln College, Oxford. Education: BA 1937, BD 1941, Cambridge University; DD (Oxford and Cambridge) 1957. Publications include: Renaissance and Reformation, 1952; Oxford Common Room, 1957; The Young Mr Wesley, 1961; Religion at Oxford and Cambridge, 1964; The Commonwealth of Lincoln College 1427-1977, 1979; Love in a Cool Climate: The Letters of Mark Pattison and Meta Bradley, 1985; The Madness of Kings, 1993. Honours: Thirlwall Prize and Medal, Cambridge University, 1940. Membership: Fellow of the Royal Historical Society. Address: Calendars, Sheep Street, Burford, Oxford OX8 4LS, England.

GREENBAUM Sidney, b. 31 Dec 1929, London, England. Education: BA Honours, 1951, MA 1953, Postgraduate Certificate in Education, 1954, BA, Honours, 1957, PhD, 1967, London University. Appointments: Visiting Assistant Professor, University of Oregon, USA, 1968-69; Associate Professor, University of Wisconsin, Milwaukee, 1969-72; Visiting Professor, Hebrew University, 1972-73; Professor, University of Wisconsin-Milwaukee, 1972-83. Quain Professor of English Language and Literature, University College London, England, 1983-90; Director of Survey of English Usage, University College, London, 1983-; Visiting Professor, University College, London, 1991-. Publications include: Studies in English Adverbial Usage, 1969; Verb-Intensifier Collocations in English, 1970; Elicitation Experiments in English (co-author), 1970; A Grammar of Contemporary English (co-author), 1972; A University Grammar of English (co-author), 1973; A Comprehensive Grammar of the English Language (co-author), 1985; Good English and the Grammarian, 1988; The Longman Guide to English Usage (co-author), 1988; A College Grammar of English, 1989; A Student's Grammar of the English Language (co-author), 1990; An Introduction to English Grammar, 1991; The Oxford Companion to the English Language (associate editor), 1992. Contributions to: About 50 articles in magazines and journals. Honours: 1st prize for A Comprehensive Grammar of the English Language, Duke of Edinburgh Language award, 1985; Honorary Doctor of Humanities, University of Wisconsin-Milwaukee, 1989. Memberships: International Association of University Professors of English; Linguistic Society of America; Linguistic Association of Great Britain; Reform Club. Address: 73 Highfield Avenue, London NW11 9UB, England.

GREENBERG Alvin David, b. 10 May 1932. Author; Teacher. Education: BA, MA, University of Cinncinnati, USA; PhD, University of Washington. Appointments: University of Kentucky, 1963-65; Professor, English, Macalester College, St Paul, 1965-. Publications: The Metaphysical Giraffe, 1968; Going Nowhere, 1971; House of the Would-Be Gardener, 1972; Dark Lands, 1973; Metaform, 1975; The Invention of the West, 1976; In Direction, 1978; The Discovery of America and Other Tales, 1980; And Yet, 1981; Delta Q, 1983; The Man in the Cardboard Mask, 1985; Heavy Wings (poetry), 1988; Why We Live With Animals (poetry), 1990. Contributions to: American Review; Antioch Review; Ploughshares; Poetry North-West; American Poetry Review; Mississippi Review; Georgia Review; Gettysburg Review; Ohio Review. Honours: Bush Foundation Artist Fellowships, 1976, 1980; NEA Fellowship, 1972, 1992; Short Fiction Award, Associated Writing Programmes, 1982; Pablo Neruda Poetry Prize, 1988; Loft-Mi Knight Poetry, 1991; Chelsea Poetry Award, 1994; Luft McKnight Award of Distinction in Poetry, 1994. Address: Dept of English, Macalester College, St Paul, MN 55105, USA.

GREENBERG Joanne, (Hannah Green), b. 24 Sep 1932, Brooklyn, New York, USA. Author; Teacher. m. Albert Greenberg, 4 Sep 1955, 2 sons. Education: BA, American University. Publications: The Kings Persons, 1963; I Never Promised You A Rose Garden, 1964; The Monday Voices, 1965; Summering: A Book of Short Stories, 1966; In This Sign, 1970; Rites of Passage, 1972; Founder's Praise, 1976; High Crimes and Misdemeanors, 1979; A Season of Delight, 1981; The Far Side of Victory, 1983; Simple Gifts, 1986; Age of Consent, 1987; Of Such Small Differences, 1988; With The Snow Queen (Short Stories), 1991; No Reck'ning Made, 1993. Contributions to: Articles, reviews, short stories to numerous periodicals including: Hudson Review, Virginia Quarterly, Chatelaine; Saturday Review. Honours: Harry and Ethel Daroff Memorial Fiction Award, 1963; William and Janice Epstein Fiction Award, 1964; Marcus L Kenner Awards, 1971; Christopher Book Award, 1971; Freida Fromm Reichman Memorial Award, 1971; Honory Doctorates from: Western Maryland College, 1997, Gallaudet College, 1979; University of Colorado, 1987; Rocky Mountain Women's Institute Award, 1983; Denver Public Library Bookplate Award, 1990; Colorado Author of the Year. Memberships: Authors Guild; PEN: Colorado Authors League; National Association of the Deaf; Ladies Tuesday Skiing and Terrorist Society. Literary Agent: Lois Wallace. Address: 29221 Rainbow Hill Road, Golden, CO 80401, USA.

GREENBERG Martin, b. 3 Feb 1918, Norfolk, Virginia, USA. Writer; Translator. m. Paula Fox, 9 June 1962, 1 son. Education: BA, University of Michigan. Career: Editor; Professor. Publications: The Terror of Art: Kafka & Modern Literature, 1968; The Hamlet Vocation of Coleridge & Wordsworth, 1986; Translations: The Diaries of Franz Kafka 1914-23, 1948-49; The Marquise of O & Other Stories, 1960; Five Plays (von Kleist), 1988; Faust, Part One, 1992; Faust, Part Two, 1994. Honours: Literature Award, American Academy & Institute of Arts & Letters, 1989; Harold Morton Lansdon Translation Award, 1989. Membership: Academy of American Poets. Address: 306 Clinton Street, Brooklyn, NY 11201, USA.

GREENBERGER Howard, b. 4 Sep 1924, New York City, USA. Writer. Education: BBA, City College of New York; Postgraduate Theatre Studies, Columbia University. Appointments include: TV & Radio Producer, 1955-65. Publications: Shadow on the Moon, play, 1944; Gay Masqurade, musical, 1945; Birthday of Eternity, 1946; The End of the Circle, play, 1948; Turning Points, radio series; Once Upon a Tune, TV series, 1955; A Celebration for Emily, TV play, 1968, Our Play on the Future Has No Name, musical, with Robert Rheingold, 1970; Everything's the Same, Only Different, musical, 1971; The Off-

Broadway Experience, history, 1971; Bogey's Baby, biography, 1976; Grow With Me, play, with R Rheingold, 1980; Getting Your Foot in the Door, book with Dr Kenneth S L Brownlie. Contributions to: Book Digest. Address: 404 East 55th Street, New York, NY 10022, USA.

GREENBLATT Stephen J, b. 7 Nov 1943, MA, USA. Professor; Writer. m. Ellen Schmidt, 27 Apr 1969, 2 s. Education: BA, 1964, MA, 1968, PhD, 1969, Yale; BA, Cantab, 1966. Publications: Marvellous Possessions, 1991; Learning to Curse, 1990; Shakespearean Negotiations, 1988; Renaissance Self Fashioning, 1980; Sir Walter Raleigh, 1973. Contributions to: Representations. Honours: Guggenheim Fellowship, 1978, 1984; British Council Prize, 1981; James Russell Lowell Prize, 1989. Memberships: Am Academy of Arts & Science; Modern Language Association. Address: Dept of English, UC Berkeley, Berkeley, CA 94720, USA.

GREENE A C, B. 4 Nov 1923, Texas, USA. Professor; Historian; Author. m. Judy Dalton, 20 Jan 1990, 3 s, 1 d. Education: BA, Abilene Christian Unviersity, Texas; Co-Director, Centre for Texas Studies, University of North Texas. Publications: A Personal Country, 1969; The Santa Claus Bank Robbery, non-fiction, 1972; The Last Captive, 1972; Dallas: The Deciding Years, 1972; The Highland Park Woman, fiction, 1984; Taking Heart, 1990. Contributions to: Atlantic; McCalls; Southwestern History Quarterly; New York Times Book Review. Honours: National Conference of Christians and Jews, 1964; Dobie-Paisano Fellow, 1968; Fellow, Texas State History Association, 1990. Memberships: Texas Institute of Letters, President, 1969-71, Fellow 1981-; Writers Guild of America, West; PEN International. Literary Agent: Jan Miller, 5518 Dyer, Dallas, TX 75206, USA. Address: 4359 Shirley Drive, Dallas, TX 75229, USA.

GREENE Constance C(larke), b. 1924, USA. Writer. Publications: A Girl Called Al, 1969; Leo the Lioness, 1970; Good Luck Bogie Hat, 1971; Unmaking of Rabbit, 1972; Isabelle the Itch, 1973; The Ears of Louis, 1974; I Know You, Al, 1975; Beat the Turtle Drum, 1976; Getting Nowhere, 1977; I and Sproggy, 1978; Your Old Pal, Al, 1979; Dotty's Suitcase, 1980; Double-Dare O'Toole, 1981; A(lexandra) the Great, 1982; Ask Anybody, 1983; Isabelle Shows Her Stuff, 1984; Star Shine, 1985; Other Plans, for adults, 1985; Just Plain Al, 1986; The Love Letters of J Timothy Owen, 1986. Address: c/o Viking Press Inc, 40 W 23rd Street, New York, NY 10010, USA.

GREENE Jonathon (Edward), b. 1943, USA. Editor; Poet. Appointments: Founding Editor, Director, Gnomon Press, Frankfort, Kentucky, 1965-; Editor, Kentucky Renaissance, 1976. Publications: The Reckoning, 1966; Instance, 1968; The Lapidary, 1969; A 17th Century Gamer, 1969; An Unspoken Complaint, 1970; The Poor in Church, by Arthur Rimbaud, translation, 1973; Scaling the Walls, 1974; Glossary of the Everyday, 1974; Peripatetics, 1978; Jonathan Williams: A 50th Birthday Celebration (editor), 1979; Once a Kingdom Again, 1979; Quiet Goods, 1980; Idylls, 1983; Small Change for the Long Haul, 1984; Trickster Tales, 1985; Idylls, Second edition, revised & enlarged, 1990; Les Chambre des Poètes, 1990. Address: PO Box 475, Frankfort, KY 40602, USA.

GREENER Michael John, b. 28 Nov 1931, Barry, Wales. Chartered Accountant Company Director. m. May 1964, div 1972, 1 son. Education: BA, University of South Wales and Monmouthshire, 1949-53; Articled, Deloitte Plender Griffiths, Cardiff, Wales, 1949-57; Qualified as Chartered Accountant, 1957; FCA, 1967; BA Open University, 1991. Publications: Between the Lines of the Balance Sheet, 1968, revised 1980; Penguin Dictionary of Commerce, 1970, revised 1980, revised and reissued as Penguin Business Dictionary, 1987, revised 1994; Problems for Discussion in Mercantile Law, 1970; The Red Bus, 1973. Contributions to: Many articles in business and professional journals. Membership: Fellow, Institute of Chartered Accountants, 1967. Address: 33 Glan Hafren, The Knap, Barry, South Glamorgan CF6 8TA, Wales.

GREENFIELD Harry Isaac, b. 8 Sep 1922, NYC, USA. Professor. m. Gladys Frohlinger, 23 Jun 1946, 2 s, 1 d. Education: Bachelor of Social Science, City College, NY, 1942; MA, 1948; PhD, Columbia University, 1959. Publications: Manpower and Growth of Producer Services; Allied Health Manpower; Hospital Efficiency & Public Policy; Accountability in Health Facilities; Principal Editor of Theory for Economic Efficiency; Invisible Outlawed and Untaxed: America's Underground Economy, 1993. Address: 11205 Watermill Lane, Wheaton, MD 20902, USA.

GREENHILL Basil Jack, b. 26 Feb 1920, Great Britain; Author; Company Director. m. Ann Giffard, 2 June 1961, 2 sons. Education: BA 1946, PhD 1980, University of Bristol, England. Publications: The Merchant Schooners, 1951, 1968, 1978, 1988; The British Assault on Finland (co-author Ann Giffard), 1988; The Grain Races (co-author John Hackman), 1986; Westcountrymen in Prince Edward's Isle, 1967, 1975 (co-author Ann Giffard), 1991; The Evolution of the Wooden Ship, 1988; The Last Tall Ships, 1978, 1990; The Archaeology of the Boat, 1976; The Life and Death of the Sailing Ship, 1980; The British Seafarer, 1980; The Herzogin Cecilie, 1991; (Joint Editor), The Maritime History of Devon, 1993; Steam, Politics & Patronage (co-author Ann Giffard), 1994; Consultant Editor, Conways History of the Ship (12 vols), 1994. Contributions to: The Times; The Observer; Radio Times; The Listener; Country Life; Daily Telegraph; Christian Science Monitor; Guardian; Antiquity; Classic Boat; Wooden Boat. Honours: CMG, 1967; CB, 1981; Knight Commander of the White Rose of Finland, 1980; Award of Merit, American Association for State and Local History, 1968. Memberships: Vice-President, Society for Nautical Research; Honorary Member, The Arts Club, London; President, Devon History Society, 1993-. Address: West Boetheric Farmhouse, St Dominic, Saltash, Cornwall PL12 6SZ, England.

GREENLAND Colin, b. 17 May 1954, Dover, Kent, England. Freelance Writer. Education: MA 1978, DPhil 1981, Pembroke College, Oxford, England. Appointments: Writer-in-residence, NE London Polytechnic, 1980-82. Publications: The Entropy Exhibition, 1983; Daybreak on a Different Mountain, 1984; The Hour of the Thin Ox, 1987; With Roger and Martyn Dean: Magnetic Storm, 1984; With Paul Kerton: The Freelance Writer's Handbook, 1986; Co-editor, Interzone: The First Anthology, 1985; Storm Warnings, 1987; Other Voices, 1988; Take Back Plenty, 1990; Michael Moorcock: Death is No Obstacle, 1992; Harm's Way; 1993. Contributions to: Book Reviews etc for Foundation: The Review of Science Fiction; Times Literary Supplement; New Statesman; British Book News; City Limits; Time Out; Sunday Times; The Face; Other Edens II, 1988; Zenith: The Best in New British SF, 1989; Zenith 2: The Best in New British S F, 1990; More Tales From the Forbidden Planet, 1990; Journal Wired, 1990; Temps, 1991; Final Shadows, 1991; The Weerde, 1992; In Dreams, 1992; R.E.M. 1992; Eurotemps, 1992; The Weerde Book 2, 1993; Touch Wood, 1993. Honours: Eaton Award for Science Fiction Criticism, 1985; Arthur C Clarke Award and BSFA Award, Best S F Novel, 1992; Eastercon Award, 1992. Memberships: Chair, Milford S F Writers' Conference, 1986; Council Member, Science Fiction Foundation, 1989-. Literary Agent: Maggie Noach, 21 Redan Street, London W14 0AB, England. Address: 2A Ortygia House, 6 Lower Road, Harrow, Middlesex HA2 0DA, England.

GREENLEAF Stephen (Howell), b. 1942, USA. Attorney; Novelist (Mystery, Crime, Suspense). Education: JD; Bar Admissions: California, 1968; Iowa, 1977. Publications: Grave Error, 1979; Death Bed, 1980; State's Evidence, 1982; Fatal Obsession, 1983; The Ditto List, 1985; Beyond Blame, 1986; Toll Call, 1987; Impact, 1989; Book Case, 1991; Blood Type, 1992; Southern Cross, 1993; False Conception, 1994. Honour: Maltese Falcon Award, Japan, 1993. Address: c/o Esther Newberg, ICM, 40 W 57th Street, New York, NY 10019, USA.

GREENLEAF William, b. USA. Science Fiction Writer. Publications: Time Jumper, 1981; The Tartarus Incident, 1983; The Pandora Stone, 1984; Starjacked, 1987. Address: c/o Ace Books, 220 Madison Avenue, New York, NY 10016, USA.

GREENWOOD Ted (Edward Alister Greenwood), b. 1930, Australia. Children's Fiction Writer; Former Lecturer in Art Education. Publications: Obstreperous, 1969; Alfred, 1970; VIP: Very Important Plant, 1971; Joseph and Lulu and the Prindiville House Pigeons, 1972; Terry's Brrrmmm GT, 1974; The Pochetto Coat, 1978; Ginnie, 1979; Curious Eddie 1970; The Boy Who Saw God, 1980; Everlasting Circle, 1981; Flora's Treasurers, 1982; Marley and Friends, 1983; Warts and All (with S Fennessy), 1984; Ship Rock, 1985; I Don't Want to know (with S Fennessy), 1986; Windows, 1989; Uncle Theo is a Number Nine, 1990. Address: 50 Hilton Road, Ferny Creek, Victoria, 3786, Australia.

GREER Germaine. b. 29 Jan 1939, Melbourne, Australia. Writer; Broadcaster. Education: BA Hons, Melbourne University, 1959; MA Hons, Sydney University, 1962; PhD, Cambridge University, 1967. Appointments: Senior English Tutor, Sydney University, 1963-64; Assistant Lecturer & Lecturer, English, University of Warwick, 1967-72;

Lecturer, N America, American Program Bureau, 1973-78; Visiting Professor, Graduate Faculty of Modern Letters, 1979, Professor of Modern Letters, 1980-83, University of Tulsa; Founder-Director, Tulsa Centre for Study of Woman's Literature, Tulsa Studies in Women's Literature, 1981; Director. Stump Cross Books, 1988-; Special Lecturer and Unofficial Fellow, Newnham College, Cambridge, 1989-. Publications: The Female Eunuch, 1969; The Obstacle Race: The Fortunes of Women Painters and Their Work, 1979; Sex and Destiny: The Politics Of Human Fertility, 1984; editor: Shakespeare, 1986; The Madwoman's Underclothes, selected journalism, 1986; Kissing the Rod: an Anthology of Seventeenth Century Verse, 1988; Daddy, We Hardly Knew You, 1989; Editor: The Uncollected Verse of Aphra Benn, 1989; The Change: Women, Ageing and the Menopause, 1991. Contributions to: Journalist, columnist, reviewer, 1972-79. Honours: Scholarships, 1952, 1956; Commonwealth Scholarship, 1964; J R Ackerly Prize & Premio Internazionale Mondello, 1989. Address: c/o Aitken and Stone Ltd, 29 Fernshaw Road, London, SW10 0TG, England.

GREGER Deborah, b. 1949. Publications: Winter Poems, 1977; Movable Islands, 1980; Cartography: Poems, 1980; Normal Street, 1983; And: Poems, 1985; Blank Country, 1985; The 1002nd Night, 1990; Off-Season at the Edge of the World, 1994. Honour: Fellow, American Academy & Institute of Arts & Letters, 1990.

GREGORIOU Gregory, b. 20 May 1929, Athens, Greece. Physician; Psychiatrist. Education: Diploma, Psychiatry, McGill University, 1965; Specialist Certificate, Royal College of Physicians & Surgeons of Canada, 1965; Specialist Certificate, College of Physicians & Surgeons of the Province of Quebec, 1968. Appointments: Faculty Lecturer, Department of Psychiatry, McGill University, 1968-; Psychiatrist, Queen Elizabeth Hospital, Montreal; Co-ordinator, Continuing Medical Education Program, Department of Psychiatry, Queen Elizabeth Hospital, Montreal; Director, Creativity Clinic, Department of Psychiatry, Queen Elizabeth Hospital, Montreal. Publications: Le Devin du Village - Un coté peu connu de l'oeuvre de Jean-Jacques Rousseau, 1984; Le livret de l'opéra de Jean-Jacques Rousseau, Le Devin du Village une expression lyrique de sa philosophie, 1989; Musicothérapie, 1992; La Renaissance de la Psychiatrie, 1992; Le Danger Des Paranoiaques et Des Sociopathes Pour La Société, 1993; Le Passé Et L'Avenir De L'Humanisme Medical, 1994. Honours: Cesare Pavese Prize, 1990. Memberships: Include: Fellow, Royal College of Physicians & Surgeons of Canada; Professional Corporation of Physicians of Quebec; Quebec Medical Association; Quebec Psychiatric Association; Federation of Medical Specialists of Quebec; Medical Association of Athens, Greece; Association of Doctors Writers of France; Hellenic Doctors Writers Association; World Association of Doctors Writers; American Physicians Poetry Association. Address: 5025 Rue Sherbrooke 0, Westmount QC, H4A 1S9, Canada.

GREGORY Richard L, b. 1923, United Kingdom. Emeritus Professor of Neuropsychology. Publications: Eye and Brain, 1966, 4th edition, 1990; The Intelligent Eye, 1970; Illusions in Nature and Art (edited with E H Gombrich), 1973; Concepts and Mechanisms of Perception, 1974; Mind in Science, 1981; Odd Perceptions, 1986; Oxford Companion to the Mind, 1987; Evolution of the Eye and Visual System, Vol 2 of Vision and Visual Dysfunction, 1991; Even Odder Perceptions, 1994. Honours: CBE, 1989; FRS, 1992; LLD (Bristol), 1993. Literary Agent: Mr Derek Johns, A P Watt Ltd, 20 John Street, London WC1N 2DR, England. Address: University of Bristol, Department of Psychology, 8 Woodland Road, Bristol BS8 1TN, England.

GREIDER William B, Career: Political Journalist; Former Managing Editor, Washington Post. Publications: Who Will Tell the People, 1992; The Trouble with Money; Secrets of the Temple; The Education of David Stockman & Other Americans. Address: c/o Rolling Stone Magazine, 1290 Avenue of the Americas, New York, NY 10104, USA.

GRENDEL Lajos, b. 6 Apr 1948, Levice, CSFR. Writer. m. Agota Sebok, 6 July 1974, 1 s, 1 d. Education: University Komens Keho. Appointments: Editor, Publishing House, Medech Brehsleva; Editor in Chief, Lit Monthly, Kalligram, Chairman, Publishing House Kalligram, 1992. Publications: Elesloveszet; Attetelil; Borondok Tartalma; Theszevz es a Pekete ozvegy; Einstien harangjai; Galeir, Hutleneck. Contributions to: Hungarian and Slovak magazines. Honours: Dery Prize; Jozsef Attila Prize; Cryslal Vilenica. Memberships: Union of

Hungarian Writers. Address: Vazovova 15, 81107 Bratislava, Czech Republic.

GRENNAN Eamon, b. 13 Nov 1941, Dublin, Ireland. Teacher. 1 s, 2 d. Education: BA, University College, Dublin, 1963; MA, 1964; PhD, Harvard University, 1972; Publications: Wildly for Days; What Light There is; What Light There Is and Other Poems; As If It Matters. Contributions to: Ireland & America; Poetry Ireland; Irish Times; The New Yorker; Poetry; The Nation. Honours: NEA Award; Guggenheim Fellowship, 1994. Address: Box 352 Vassar College, Poughkeepsie, NY 12601, USA.

GRENVILLE John A S, b. 1928, United Kingdom. Professor of Modern History. Publications: The Coming of the Europeans (with Joan Fuller), 1962; Lord Salisbury and Foreign Policy, 1964; Politics Strategy and American Diplomacy 1873-1917 (with G B Young), 1966; The Munich Crisis (with Nicholas Pronay), film, 1968; The End of Illusions, from Munich to Dunkirk (with N Pronay), film, 1970; The Major International Treaties 1914-1973: A History and Guide with Texts, 1974, revised edition in 2 vols, 1987; Europe Reshaped 1948-1974, 1976 and subsequent editions; Film as Evidence: Tomorrow the World, film, 1977; World History of the Twentieth Century, vol I 1900-1945, 1980; Collins History of the World in the Twentieth Century, 1994. Literary Agent: David Highams. Address: PO Box 363, Birmingham B15 2TT, England.

GRESSER Seymour Gerald, b. 9 May 1926, Baltimore, Maryland, USA. Sculptor; Writer. m. (1) 1 Jul 1950, (2) 9 Jul 1976, div, 3 s, 1 d. Education: BS, 1949, MA, 1972, Maryland University; Stone Carving, Institute of Contemporary Arts, Washington DC, 1949-52. Appointments: Sculptor Residency, Mt Rushmore, South Dakota, 1980; Colgate University, 1989; Yale University, 1969. Publications: Stone Elegies, 1955; Coming of Atom, 1957; Poems from Mexico, 1964; Voyages, 1969; A Garland for Stephen, 1971; A Departure for Sons, 1973; Fragments and Others, 1982; Hagar and her Elders, 1989. Contributor to: Numerous literary quarterlies worldwide including: Gargoyle Magazine, Washington DC. Address: 1015 Ruatan Street, Silver Spring, MD 20903, USA.

GREY Anthony Keith, b. 5 July 1938, Norwich, England. Author. m. Shirley McGuinn, 4 Apr 1970, 2 d. Appointments: Journalist, Eastern Daily Press, 1960-64; Foreign Correspondent, Reuter, East Berlin and Prague, 1965-67, Peking, 1967-69. Publications: Hostage in Peking, 1970; Saigon, 1982; A Man Alone, 1971; Some Put Their Trust in Chariots, 1973; The Bulgarian Exclusive, 1976; The Chinese Assasin, 1978; The Prime Minister was a Spy, 1983; Peking, 1988; The Naked Angels, 1990; The Bangkok Secret, 1990; Himself (radio play). Contributor of short stories and feature articles to various publications. Honours: OBE, 1969; UK Journalist of the year, 1970. Memberships: Society of Authors; Royal Institute of International Affairs. Literary Agent: Michael Sissons. Address: A D Peters & Co Ltd, 5th Floor, The Chambers, Chelsea Harbour, Lots Road, London, SW10 0XF, England.

GREY Belinda. See: **PETERS Maureen.**

GREY Charles. See: **TUBB E(dwin) C(harles).**

GREY Ian, b. 5 May 1918, Wellington, New Zealand. Author; Editor. Education: LLB, University of Sydney, Australia. Major Publications: Peter the Great, 1960; Catherine the Great, 1961; Ivan the Terrible, 1964; The First Fifty Years: Soviet Russia 1917-67; The Romanovs: Rise & Fall of the Dynasty, 1970; A History of Russia, 1970; Boris Godunov, 1973; Stalin: Man of History, 1979; Parliamentarians, The History of the Commonwealth Parliamentary Association 1911-1985, 1986. Address: 10 Alwyn Avenue, Chiswick, London W4, England.

GRIDBAN Volsted. See: **TUBB E(dwin) C(harles).**

GRIFFIN Keith B(roadwell), b. 1938, UK. Economist; Professor, Department of Economics, University of California, Riverside. Publications: Underdevelopment in Spanish America, 1969; Planning Development (with John Enos), 1970; Financing Development in Latin America (editor), 1971; Growth and Inequality in Pakistan (edited with A R Khan), 1972; The Political Economy of Agrarian Change, 1974; Land Concentration and Rural Poverty, 1976; International Inequality and National Poverty, 1978; The Transition to Egalitarian Development (with J James), 1981; Growth and Equality in Rural China, (with A Saith), 1981; Institutional Reform and Economic Development in the

Chinese Countryside (editor), 1984; World Hunger and the World Economy, 1987; Alternative Strategies for Economic Development, 1989; Human Development and the International Development Strategy for the 1990 (edited with J Knight), 1990; (Editor) The Economy of Ethiopia, 1992; Globalisation and the Developing World (with A R Khan), 1992; The Distribution of Income in China (edited with Zhao Renwei), 1993; Implementing a Human Development Strategy (with Terry McKinsley), 1994. Address: Department of Economics, University of California, Riverside, CA 92521, USA.

GRIFFITH Arthur Leonard, b. 1920, England. Retired Minister of Religion. Publications: The Roman Letter Today, 19509; God and His People, 1960; Beneath the Cross of Jesus, 1961; What is a Christian, 1962; Barriers to Christian Belief, 1962; A Pilgrimage to the Holy Lnd, 1962; The Eternal Legacy, 1963; Pathways to Happiness, 1964; God's Time and Ours, 1964; The Crucial Encounter, 1965; This is Living, 1966; God is Man's Experience, 1968; Illusions of Our Culture, 1969; The Need to Preach, 1971; Hang on to the Lord's Prayer, 1973; We Have This Ministry, 1973; Ephesians: A Positive Affirmation, 1975; Gospel Characters, 1976; Reactions to God, 1979; Take Hold of the Treasure, 1981; From Sunday to Sunday, 1987. Address: 71 Old Mill Road, 105 Etobicoke, Ontario, M8X 1G9, Canada.

GRIFFITHS Helen, (Helen Santos), b. 8 may 1939, London, England. Writer. Publications: Horse in the Clouds, 1957; Wild and Free, 1958; Moonlight, 1959; Africano, 1960; The Wild Heart, 1962; The Greyhound, 1963; Wild Horse of Santander (award), 1965; Dark Swallows, 1965; Leon, 1966; Stallion of the Sands, 1967; Monshie Cat, 1968; Patch, 1969; Federico, 1970; Russian Blue, 1973; Just a Dog, 1974; Witch Fear (award), 1975; Pablo, 1976; Kershaw Dogs, 1978; The Last Summer, 1979; Blackface Stallion, 1980; Dancing Horses, 1981; Hari's Pigeon, 1982; Rafa's Fog, 1983; Jesus, As Told By Mark, 1983; Dog at the Window, 1984; Also, as Helen Santos: Caleb's Lamb, 1984; If Only, 1987; Scripture Union. Honours: Daughter of Mark Twain, 1966; Highly Commended, Carnegie Medal award, 1966; Silver Pencil Award, best children's book, Netherlands, 1978. Address: 9 Ashley Terrace, Bath, Avon, BA1 3JZ, England.

GRIFFITHS Ormhaugh Ella, b. 22 Mar 1926, Oslo, Norway. Author; Copywriter; Radio Reporter; Journalist; Columnist; Translator. Education: Oslo University; Conservatory of Music, Oslo; Mass Media Studies, American University, Salzburg Seminar in American Studies, Salzburg, Austria; Certificate, proficiency, English, University of Cambridge; Film/Video Seminar, Norwegian Film Industries. Publications: Some 25 adult books including the police procedurals: The Water Widow; Unknown Partner; Murder on Page 3; Five to Twelve; 12 Childrens and Youth Novels including: Pia, Kim and Tiny, 1979; Tiny and Bombastus, the Cat, 1981; Tiny and Pepper, the Tortoise, 1983; Fiddle Diddle Grasshopper and other Fairytales, 1984; Thrusday, January 32 (science fiction), 1985; Short Stories in The John Creasey Crime Collections, 1980, 1983, 1984, 1986, several of her works are published in Sweden, Denmark, Finland, UK, USA and Unknown Partner in USSR, 1986-87. Honours include: US Information Agency (Washington) Award for Meritorious Service, 1962; Department of State AID-USUAS (Washington) Outstanding Service Award, 1977. Literary Agent: Ulla Lohren, Nordic Countries; Laurence Pollineger Limited, London. Address: Kirkeveien 99a, 1344 Haslum, Norway.

GRIFFITHS Trevor, b. 4 Apr 1935, Manchester, Lancashire, England. Playwright. m. 1) Janice Elaine Stansfield, 1960, dec 1977, 1 son, 2 daughters, 2) Gillian Cliff, 1992. Education: St Bede's College, Manchester 1945-52; BA, English, Manchester University, 1955. Appointments: Teacher of English, Oldham, Lancashire, 1957-61; Lecturer in Liberal Studies, Stockport Technical College, Cheshire, 1962-65; Further Education Officer, BBC Leeds, 1965-72; Co-editor, Labour's Northern Voice, 1962-65 and series editor for Workers Northern Publishing Society. Publications: Plays include: Apricots (produced London 1971), and Thermidor, London, 1978, (prod. Edinburgh 1971); Lay By, with others (produced Edinburgh and London, 1971), London, 1972; Sam, Sam (produced London 1972, revised version produced London, 1978), published in Plays and Players (London), April 1972; The Party (produced London 1973, revised version produced 1974), London, 1974; Occupations, 1980; All Good Men and Absolute Beginners (both produced BBC TV, 1974), London, 1977; Comedians, 1976; Through the Night (produced BBC TV, 1975), London, 1977; Bill Brand (produced Thames TV), 1976; The Cherry Orchard, London, 1989; Deeds (with others), 1978; Sons and Lovers (version for TV, produced BBC TV 1981), Nottingham, 1982; Country (produced BBC TV 1981), London, 1981; Reds, 1981; Oi for

England, 1982; The Last Place on Earth (produced Central TV 1985), published as Judgement Over the Dead), 1986; Real Dreams (produced Williamstown, 1984, also director); London, 1986, 1987; Fatherland (film released 1986), London, 1987; Collected plays for Television, 1988; Piano London, 1990; The Gulf Between Us (produced Leeds, 1992, also director, published London, 1992); Thatcher's Children (produced Bristol 1993); Hope in the Year Two (produced BBC TV 1994), London 1994. Honour: BAFTA Writer's Award, 1982. Literary Agent: c/o Peters Fraser and Dunlop Group Ltd, London. Address: c/o Peters Fraser and Dunlop Group Ltd 503/4, The Chambers, Chelsea Harbour, Lots Road, London SW10 0XF, England.

GRIFO Lionello. See: **VAGGE Ornello.**

GRIGG John (Edward Poynder), b. 15 Apr 1924. Writer. m. Patricia, 1958, 2 sons. Education: Exhibitioner, MA Modern History, Gladstone Memorial Prize, New College, Oxford. Appointments: Grenadier Guards, 1943-45; Editor, National and English Review, 1954-60; Columnist, The Guardian, 1960-70. Publications: Two Anglican Essays, 1958; The Young Lloyd George, 1973; Lloyd George: The People's Champion, 1978, 1943; The Victory That Never Was, 1980; Nancy Astor: Portrait of a Pioneer, 1980; Lloyd George: From Peace to War 1912-1916, 1985; The Thomson Years (vol VI in The History of the Times), 1993. Contributions to: various books of essays, magazines and journals. Honours: Whitbread Award, 1978; Wolfson Literary Prize, 1985. Memberships: Chairman, the London Library, 1985-91; President, Blackheath Society; FRSL. Address: 32 Dartmouth Row, London SE10, England.

GRIMM Barbara Lockett, (Cherry Wilder), b. 3 Sept 1930. Auckland, New Zealand. Science Fiction and Fantasy Writer. m. Horst Grimm, 1963, 2 d. Education: BA, Cabnterbury University College, Christchurch, NZ, 1952. Publications: Novels: The Luck of Brin's Five, 1977; The Nearest Fire, 1979; The Tapestry Warrior's 1982; (Torin Trilogy)I Second Nature, 1982; A Princess of the Chameln, 1983; Yorath the Wolf, 1984; The Summer's King, 1985 (Rulers of Hylor Trilogy); Cruel Designs, 1988. Contributions: Short Stories: Various anthologies; journals including Meanjin (Australia), Prism Interantional (Canada) Omni, Calileo, Issac Asimov's SF Magazine, Interzone (UK), Reviews: Sydney Morning Herald; The Australian, 1966-75; Various science fiction journals, UK and Australia. Honours: Literary Grants, Australia Council, 1973, 1975; Dimar, Australian Science Fiction award, 1978. Memberships: Women Writers of Australia; Science Fiction Writers of America; British Science Fiction Association; Science Fiction Club of Germany. Literary Agents: Virginia Kidd, 538 East Harford, Milford, PA 19337, USA; Maggie Noach, 21 Redan Street, London, W14 0AB, UK; Thomas Schluck, hiter der Worth 12, 3008 Garbsen 9 Germany. Address: 19 Egelsbacherstrasse, 6070 Langen/Hesseh, Germany.

GRINSELL Leslie Valentine, b. 14 Feb 1907, Hornsey, North London, England. Retired, Curatorship, Bristol City Museum. Education: Highgate School, 1921-23. Appointments: Clerk, Barclays Bank, 1925-49; Staff, Victoria County History of Wiltshire, 1949-52; Curator in Archaeology, Bristol City Museum, 1952-72. Publications: Ancient Burial Mounds of England, 1936, 1953, 1975; Egyptian Pyramids, 1947; Archaeology of Wessex, 1958; Archaeology of Exmoor, 1970; Barrow, Pyramid & Tomb, 1975. Contributions: mostly on barrows, to the proceedings of societies (in counties south of the Severn and the Thames, except Cornwall, now in progress). Honours: MA, Bristol University, 1971; OBE, 1972; Treasurer, Prehistoric Society, 1947-70; Memberships: County Archaeological Societies in Southern England; Society of Antiquaries, London. 32 Queens Court, Clifton, Bristol BS8 1ND, England.

GRISHAM John, b. 8 Feb 1938, Jonesboro, Arkansas, USA. Career: Former Lawyer. Publications: The Firm, 1991; The Pelican Brief, 1992; The Client, 1993; The Chamber, 1994; A Time to Kill. Address: c/o Jay Garon-Brooke Associates, Attn Jean Free, 101 W 55th St Ate 5K, New York, NY 10019, USA.

GROSS John. Literary/Theatrical Critic. Appointments: Editor, Times Literary Supplement, 1973-81; Staff Writer, New York Times; Currently, Theatre Critic, Sunday Telegraph. Publications: The Rise and Fall of the Man of Letters; Editor: The Oxford Book of Aphorisms; The Oxford Book of Essays.

GROSS Natan, b. 16 Nov 1919, Poland. Film Director; Poet; Translator; Journalist. m. Shulamit Lifszyc, 1 son, 1 daughter.

Education: Dip Film Directing, Polish Film Institute, 1946. Appointments: Editor, Youth Monthly Stowo Mtodych (Youth's Word), 1946-1949, Poland; Film Critic, Daily Al Hamishmar, 1962-82. Publications include: Selection of New Hebrew Poetry, 1947; Song of Israel, 1948; What is Left of it All, 1971; Holocaust in Hebrew Poetry (anthology), with J Kest and R Klinow 1974; Songs of Holocaust and Rebellion, 1975; Crumbs of Youth, 1976; Children in the Ghetto (with Sarah Nishmith), 1978; Palukst (art monography), 1982; Homage to Janusz Korczak (anthology of poetry), 1986 (co-editor); This was the Hebrew School in Krakow (editor), Who Are You Mr Grymek? 1989; History of Jewish Film in Poland, 1989; History of Hebrew Film (with Jacob Gross), 1991; Meir Bossak - Historian - Writer - Poet (editor), 1993; Poets and Holocaust, 1994. Contributions to: Arts Lexicon; Polish Jews Art and Culture, Photo Album; many other professional journals and magazines. Honours: Ben-Dor Prize, Davar Newspaper, 1960; Jugendpreis, Film Festival Berlin, 1964; Israeli and International Film Festival Awards; Leon Lustig Prize, 1986; IUPA Award, 1988; Israel, Film Academy Award, 1991; Echo Krakowa Prize (for the best book of year about Krakow). Memberships include: Israeli Film Union, Secretary 1951-71; Film Critics Sec; Film and TV Directors Guild of Israel; Israel Journalists Association; Israel Federation of Writers Union. Address: 14 Herzog Street, Givatayim 53586, Israel.

GROSS Robert A, b. 1945. m. 1 son. Education: BA, University of Pennsylvania; MA, PhD, Columbia University. Career: Formerly Assistant Editor, Newsweek; Professor of History. Publications: The Minutemen & Their World, 1976. Contributions to: Newsweek; New York Times; Harpers; Esquire; Saturday Review. Honour: Bancroft Prize, 1977. Address: American Studies Program, College of William & Mary, PO Box 8795, Williamsburg, VA 23186-8795, USA.

GROSSKURTH Phyllis, Publications include: John Addington Symonds: A Biography, 1964; Havelock Ellis: A Biography, 1980; Melanie Klein: Her World and Her Work, 1986; Margaret Mead: A Life of Controversy, 1989; The Secret Ring: Freud's Inner Circle and the Politics of Psychoanalysis, 1991. Honours: Governer General's Award for Non-fiction, 1965; University of British Columbia Award for Biography, 1965. Address: 147 Spruce Street, Toronto, Ontario, M5A 2L6, Canada.

GROSSMAN David, b. 1954, Jerusalem, Israel. Novelist. Publications: Jogger, 1983; See Under: Love, 1986, 1989; The Smile of the Lamb, 1990; Book of Intimate Grammar, 1991; Play: Riki's Kindergarten, 1988; Also: Itamar Walks on Walls, 1986; The Yellow Wind, 1987; Itamar of the Letter, 1988; Itmar Meets a Rabbit (for children), 1988; War Diaries, 1991; Sleeping on a Wire, 1992; The ZigZag Boy, 1994. Honours include: Israel Publishers Association Prize, 1985. Address: Hakibuts Publishing House, PO Box 16040, 34 Hayetzirah Street, Tel Aviv 61160, Israel.

GROVE Fred(erick Herridge), b. 1913, USA. Author; Former Journalist. Appointments: Reporter, Sports Editor, Daily Citizen, Cushing, Oklahoma, 1937-40; Reporter, Morningin News, Shawnee, Oklahoma, 1940-42; Sports Editor, Star, Harlingen, Texas, 1942; Reporter, 1943-44, Managing Editor, 1944-45, Morning News and Star, Shawneee; On copy desk, Times and Daily Okalhoma, Oklahoma City, 1946-47; Senior Assistant, University of Oklahoma Public Relations Officer, 1947-53; Part-time Instructor of Journalism, University of Oklahoma, 1964-68; Director of Public Information, Oklahoma Educational Television Authority, Norman, 1969-74. Publications: Flame of the Osage, 1958; Sun Dance, 1958; No Bugles, No Glory, 1959; Comanche Captives, 1961; The Land Seekers, 1963; Buffalo Spring, 1967; The Buffalo Runnrs, 1968; War Journey, 1971; The Child Stealers, 1973; Warrior Road, 1974; Drums Without Warriors, 1976; The Great Horse Race, 1977; Bush Track, 1978; The Running Hoses, 1980; Phantom Warrior, 1981; Match Race, 19782; A Far Trumpet, 1985; Search for the Breed, 1986; Deception Trail, 1988; Bitter Trumpet, 1989; Trail of Roguees, 1993. Address: PO Box 1248, Sivler City, NM 898062, USA.

GRUFFYDD Peter, b. 12 Apr 1935. Freelance Actor/Writer; Poet/Translator. m. Susan Soar, 28 Dec 1974, 3 sons, 1 daughter (1 son, 1 daughter by previous marriage). Education: BA, Honours, University of Wales, Bangor. Publications: Triad, 1963; The Shivering Seed, 1972; Anthologies: Anglo Welsh Poetry, 1984; Glas-Nos, 1987; On Censorship, 1985; Welsh Voices, 1967; The Lilting House, 1970; Poems, 1969; Poems, 1972; Damned Braces (long extract from autobiography of childhood), 1993; Environmental Teletext - for Centre for Performance Research, Cardiff, 1989. Contributions to: Sunday

Observer; Western Mail; Critical Quarterly; Poetry Wales; Transatlantic Review; Anglo-Welsh Review; Planet; The Golden Blade; The London Welshman; Decal; Mabon; London Magazine; New Welsh Review; Social Care Education; Momentum; Resurgence; Radical Wales; Wales on Sunday; Nouvelle Manonier (Paris); 2nd Aeon; Honest Ulsterman. Honours include: Eric Gregory Trust, 1963; 2nd, Young Poets Competition, Welsh Arts Council, 1969; Welsh Arts Council, 1969, 1970; The Arts Council of Great Britain, 1972; Aberystwyth Open Poetry Competition, 1984 (1st), 1986, 1991, 1993 (3rd in all 3); Arvon/Observer International Poetry Competition, 1993, 3rd, Duncan Jawrie Prize. Memberships: Yr Academi Gymraeg; Welsh Union of Writers; PEN International, Founder-member Welsh Branch, 1993; Equity. Address: 21 Beech Road, Norton, Stourbridge, West Midlands DY8 2AS, England.

GRUMBACH Doris, b. 1918, USA. Writer; Former Professor of English; Radio Critic; Bookstore Owner. Appointments: Title-Writer, MGM 1940; Associate Editor, Architectural Forum ,1941; Professor of English, College of St Rose, Albany, New York, 1952-70; Literary Editor, New Republic, 1973-75; Columnist, Saturday Review, 1975-76; Professor of English, American University, Washington, District of Columbia, 1976-85; Columnist, New York Times Book Review, 1977-80. Publications: The Spoil of the Flowers, 1962; The Short Throat, the Tender Mouth, 1964; The Company She Kept, biography of Mary McCarthy, 1967; Chamber Music, 1979; The Missing Person, 1981; The Ladies, 1984; The Magician's Girl, 1987; Coming Into the End of the Zone, 1992; Extra Innings, 1993, Fifty Days of Solitude, 1994. Address: Sargentville, Mairne 04673, USA.

GRUMLEY Michael, b. 1941, USA. Author. Publications: Atlantis: The Auto-biography of a Search (with R Ferro), 1970; There Are Giants in the Earth, 1974; Hard Corps, 1977; After Midnight, 1978; Life Drawing, novel, 1988.

GUARE John, b. 5 Feb 1938, New York, USA. Dramatist. m. Adele Chatfield-Taylor, 20 May 1981. Education: AB, Georgetown University, 1961, MFA, Yale University, 1963. Appointments: Playwright-in-Residence, New York Shakespeare Festival, 1977; Ajunct Professor of Playwriting, Yale University, 1878-81; Member of Board of Directors, New York Municipal Arts Society. Publications: The Loveliest Afternoon of the Year, and Something I'll Tell You Tuesdayu, 1968; Muzeeka, and Other Plays, 1969; Kissing Sweet, and A Day for Surprises, 1970; Taking Off (with Milos Forman), screenplay, 1970; Two Gentlement of Verona, (with Mel Shapiro), adaptation, 1973; Marco Polo Sings and Solo, 1977; The Landscape of the Body, 1978; The House of Blue Leaves, 1968; Blooms and Neglect, 1980; Three Exposures, 1982; Lydie Breeze, 1982; Gardenia, 1982; Atlantic City (screenplay), 1981; Hey, Stay a While, 1984; Orchards, 1986. Honours: Obie Awards, 1968, 1968-69; New York Drama Critics Circle, 1971, 1971-72; Tony Award, 1972; American Academy of Arts and Letters, Merit Award, 1981; National Society of Film Critics Award, 1981; Venice Film Festival Grand Prize, 1981. Memberships: Authors League of America; Dramatists Guild, Eugene o'Neill Playwrights Conference (founding member). Literary Agent: Dramatists Play Services, USA. Address: c/o Dramatists Play Services, 440 Park Avenue S, New York, NY 10016, USA.

GUEST Henry Bayly (Harry), b. 6 Oct 1932, Penarth, Glamorgan, Wales. Schoolmaster. m. Lynn Doremus Dunbar, 28 Dec 1963, 1 son, 1 daughter. Education: BA, Trinity Hall, Cambridge, 1951-54; DES, Sorbonne, 1954-55. Publications: Arrangements, 1968; The Cutting Room, 1970; Post-War Japanese Poetry, editor and translator, 1972; A House Against the Night, 1976; Days, 1978; The Distance, The Shadows, 1981; Lost and Found, 1983; The Emperor of Outer Space, radio play, broadcast 1976, published 1983; Lost Pictures, 1991; Coming To Terms, 1994; Traveller's Literary Companion To Japan, 1994. Contributions to: Agenda; Ambit; Atlantic Review; Outposts; Pacific Quarterly; Poetry Australia; Poetry Review; Times Educational Supplement. Honour: Honorary Research Fellow, Exeter University, 1994-. Memberships: General Council, Poetry Society, 1972-75. Address: 1 Alexandra Terrace, Exeter, Devon EX4 6SY, England.

GUEST Lynn Doremus, b. 6 Oct 1939, MO, USA. Writer. m. Harry Guest, 28 Dec 1963, 1 s, 1 d. Education: BA, Sarah Lawrence College, Edinburgh University. Publications: Post-War Japanese Poetry, 1972; Novels: Children of Hachiman ,1980; Yedo, 1985. Honour: Georgette Heyer Historical Novel Prize for Children of Hachiman, 1980. Literary Agent: Campbell Thomson and McLaughlin,

London, England. Address: 1 Alexandra Terrace, Exeter, EX4 6SY, Devon, England.

GUGLIELMO Dolores, b. 29 Aug 1928, Corona, Long Island, New York, USA. Writer (poetry). Education: BA, English, St John's University, Jamaica, New York, 1983; currently working on Mater's Degree in English. Publications: Premier Poets: Down By the Bearch, 1985-86; Christ Was a Hod Carrier, 1987-88, Poet International: Autumn 1986; Sea Shells, 1987; Woman at Window, 1987; Jazz Man, 1987; A Prayer for Tolerance, 1988; Love's Prayer, 1988; Wild Horses, 1989; The Tolling, 1989; The Sitters, 1989; Alma Mater, 1989; Conversations, 1989; Tree By Side of Road, 1989; Old Dog, 1990; Brownstone Window Box, 1990; Hi-Rise Spring Song, 1992; Daylight Savings Time, 1992; City Street, 1991; The Station Master, 1992; Forthcoming Poet International: Dead of Night, 1992; Beginning, 1993. Contributions to: World Poetry, Wroxton Abbey, 1993, Poetic Symphony 1987, Summer Nights; A Galazy of Verse; Midwest Poetry Review; Soundings East; Poems of the Century; Reflections; Images; American Poetry Anthology; River Run; Drum Magazine; Ripples. Honors: Winner, International Poetry Contest, Seven Magazine, 1967; Poetry Recital on David Frost Show, 1970; The Writers Club Award, Excellence in Poetry, 1992; Queen's College, English Honours Award. Memberships: World Poetry Society; Fine Arts Society, Mishawaka, Indianna; The Writers Club. Address: 43-44 Kissena Boulevard, Flushing, NY 11355, USA.

GUILES Fred Lawrence, b. 1922, USA. Author. Publications: Norma Jean: The Life of Marilyn Monroe, 1969; Marion Davies, 1973; Hanging on in Paradise, 1975; Tyrone Power: The Last Idol, 1979; Stan: The Life of Stan Laurel, 1981; Jane Fonda: The Actress in Her Time, 1982; Legend: The Life and Death of Marilyn Monroe, 1984; Loner At the Ball, 1989.

GUNN James Edwin, b. 12 Jul 1923, Kansas City, USA. Professor; Writer. m. Jane Frances Anderson, 6 Feb 1947, 2 s. Education: BS, Journalism, 1947, MA, English, 1951, University of Kansas, USA. Appointments: Assistant Instructor, 1950-51, 1955, Instructor, English, 1958-70, Lecturer, 1970-74; Professor, 1974-93, Emeritus Professor, 1993-; University of Kansas; Administrative Assistant to the Chancellor for University Relations, 1959-70. Publications: This Fortress World, 1955; Star Bridge (co-author Jack Williamson), 1955; Station in Space, 1958; The Joy Makers, 1961; The Immortals, 1962; Future Imperfect, 1964; The Witching Hour, 1970; The Burning, 1972; Breaking Point, 1972; The Listeners, 1972; The Magicians, 1976; Kampus, 1977; The Dreamers, 1981; Alternate Worlds: The Illustrated History of Science Fiction, 1975; Isaac Asimov: The Foundations of Science Fiction, 1982; The Road To Science Fiction (editor), Nos 1-4 1977, 1979, 1979, 1982; Crisisl, 1986; (editor) The New Encyclopedia of Science Fiction, 1988; (Editor) The Best of Astounding: Classic Short Novels from the Golden Age of Science Fiction, 1992; Forthcoming: The Road to Science Fiction Number 5: the British Way; Catastrophel. Contributions to: over 80 science fiction stories and over 100 articles in magazines and journals, many reprinted in Australia, England, France, Germany, Greece, Hungary, Italy, Japan, Netherlands, Poland, Romania, Scandinavia, South America, Spain, Russia, Ukraine and Yugoslavia. Honours: Byron Caldwell Smith Prize, 1971; SFRA Pilgrim Award, 1976; Hugo Awards, 1976, 1983; Edward Grier Award, 1989; Eaton Award, for Lifetime Achievement, 1992. Memberships: Science Fiction Research Association, President, 1980-82; Science Fiction Writers of America, President, 1971-72; Authors Guild. Literary Agent: Dorris Halsey; Maggie Noach. Address: 2215 Orchard lane, Lawrence, KS 66049, USA.

GUNN Thom(son William), b. 29 Aug 1929, Gravesend, England. Poet. Education: Trinity College, Cambridge. Appointments: Taught English, 1958-66; Lecturer, English, 1977-, Senior Lecturer, 1988-, University of California, Berkeley, USA. Publications: Fighting Terms, 1954; The Sense of Movement, 1957; My Sad Captains, 1961; Positives (with Ander Gunn), 1966; Touch, 1967; Moly, 1971; Jack Straw's Castle, 1976; Selected Poems, 1979; The Passages of Joy, 1982; The Occasions of Poetry (prose), 1982 (expanded edition 1985); The Man with Night Sweats, 1992; Collected Poems, 1993; Shelf Life (prose), 1993; Honours: Levinson Prize, 1955; Somerset Maugham Prize, 1959; Grant, National Institute of Arts and Letters, 1964; Rockefeller Foundation, 1966; Guggenheim Foundation, 1972; Lila Wallace/ Reader's Digest Fund Award, 1991; Forward Poetry Prize, 1992; MacArthur Fellowship, 1993; Lenore Marshall Prize, 1993. Address: 1216 Cole Street, San Francisco, CA 94117, USA.

GUNSTON William (Bill) (Tudor), b. 1 Mar 1927, London, England. Author. m. Margaret Anne, 10 Oct 1964, 2 daughters. Education: University College, Durham, 1945-46; RAF Pilot, 1946-48; City University, London, 1948-51. Literary Appointments: Editorial Staff, Flight, 1951-55; Technical Editor, Flight, 1955-64; Technology Editor, Science Journal, 1964-70; Freelance author 1970-; Director, So Few Limited. Publications: Total of 323 hardback titles including: Aircraft of The Soviet Union, 1983; Jane's Aerospace Dictionary, 1980, 1986, 1988; Encyclopaedia of World Aero Engines, 1986, 1989, 1995; Avionics, 1990; Airbus, 1988; Encyclopaedia of Aircraft Armament, 1987; Giants of The Sky, 1991; Faster Than Sound, 1992; World Encyclopaedia of Aircraft Manufacturers, 1993; Jet Bombers, 1993; Piston Areo Engines, 1994; Encyclopaedia of Russian Aircraft, 1995; Jet and Turbine Aero Engines, 1995. Contributions to: 188 periodicals; 18 partworks; 75 video scripts. Honours: FRAeS. Address: High Beech, Kingsley Green, Haslemere, Surrey, GU27 3LL, England.

GUNTRUM Suzanne Simmons, (Sizanne Simms), b. 29 Aug 1946, Storm Lake, Iowa, USA. Writer. m. Robert Ray Guntrum, 9 Sept 1967, 1 s. Education: BA, English Literature, 1967, Pennsylvania State University. Publications: Made in Heaven, 1988; The Genuine Article, 1987; Christmas in April, 1986; (As Suzanne Simms): Moment of Truth, 1986; Nothing Ventured, 1986; Dream within a Dream, 1984; Only This Night, 1984; So Sweet a Madness, 1983; All the Night Long, 1983; A Wild Sweet Magic, 1983; Of Passion Born, 1982; Moment in Time, 1982; 8 other books. Contributions to: Numerous Regional magazinnes. Honour: Silhouette Desire of the Year, 1982-83. Memberships: Romance Writers of America; Authors Guild; Mensa. Agent: Curtis Brown Ltd, New York, USA. Address; 5245 Willowview Road, Racine, WI 53402, USA.

GURGANUS Allan, b. 1947, Rocky Mount, North Carolina, USA. Education: University of Pennsylvania; Pennsylvania Academy of Fine Arts; Sarah Lawrence College; Iowa Writers' Workshop. Career: Professor of Writing. Publications: Oldest Living Confederate Widow Tells All, 1989; Blessed Assurance, 1990; White People, 1991. Contributions to: Harpers; Interview; Granta. Honours: PEN Syndicated Fiction Prizes; Ingram Merrill Award; Sue Kaufman Award; American Academy & Institute of Arts & Letters, 1989. Address: c/o Amanda Urban, ICM 40 West 57th Street, New York, NY 10019, USA.

GURI Haim, b. 9 Oct 1923, Tel Aviv, Palestine. Poet. Education: Hebrew University, Jerusalem, and Sorbonne, Paris. Appointments include: Writer for Davar newspaper, from 1970. Publications: Flowers of Fire, 1949; Till Dawn Rises, 1950; Seal Poems, 1954; Rose of the Winds, 1960; Movement to Contact, 1968; Visions of Gebazi, 1974; Pages from the Cycle of the Eagle, 1974; To the Eagle Line, 1975; Selected Poems, 1975; Terrible, 1979; And Still He Wants Her, 1987; Notebooks of Elul, 1988; Selected Poems 1945-1987; Stories: The Chocolate Deal, 1968; The Crazy Book, 1971; Who Knows Joseph G.?, 1980; The Interrogation: Reuel's Story, 1981; Also: Facing the Glass Cell, 1963; Jerusalem Years, 1968; The Family of the Palmach: A Collection of Songs and Deeds, 1976. Honours include: Israel Prize, 1987. Address: c/o Hakibuts Publishing House, PO Box 16040, 34 Hayetzirah STreet, Tel Aviv 61160, Israel.

GURNEY A(lbert) R(amsdell), b. 1 Nov 1930, Buffalo, New York, USA. Professor of Literature; Writer. m. Mary Goodyear, 1957, 2 s, 2 d. Education: St Paul's School, New Hampshire, 1944-48; BA, Williams College, Williamstown, MA, 1952; MFA, Yale University School of Drama, 1958. Served in US Naval Reserve 1952-55. Appointments: Member of Faculty 1960-, Professor of Literature 1970-, MIT, Cambridge. Publications: Plays include: Children, London, 1974, New York, 1976; The Dining Room (produced New York 1982, London 1983); London, French 1982; included in Four Plays 1985; Four Plays, New York, Avon, 1985; The Perfect Party (produced New York 1986; London 1987) New York Dramatists Play service, 1986; Another Antigone (produced San Diego 1986, New York 1987); Sweet Sue (produced Williamstown, MA, 1986, New York 1987); Screenplay: The House of Mirth, 1972; TV Play: O Youth and Beauty, from a story by John Cheever, 1979; Novels: The Gospel According to Joe, 1974; The Snow Ball, 1985; The Cocktail Hour, play, 1988, New York, 1989; Love Letters, play, New York, 1989; The Old Boy, play, New York, 1991; The Fourth Wall, play, 1992; Later Life, play, New York, 1993; A Cheever Evening, play, New York, 1994; Sylvia, play, New York, 1995; Overtime, play, 1995. Honours: Drama Desk Award, 1971; Rockefeller Grant, 1977; National Endowment for the Arts Award, 1982; DDL, Williams College, 1984; DDL, State University, Buffalo, New York; Theatre Award, American Academy of Arts And Sciences, 1990.

Literary Agent: Gilbert Parker, Willaim Morris Agency, New York. Address: 40 Wellers Bridge Road, Roxbury, CT 06783, USA.

GURR Andrew, b. 23 Dec 1936, Leicester, England. University Teacher. m. Elizabeth Gordon, 1 Jul 1961, 3 s. Education: BA, 1957, MA 1958, University of Auckland, New Zealand; PhD, University of Cambridge, 1963. Appointments: Lecturer, Leeds University, 1962; Professor, University of Nairobi, 1969; Professor, University of Reading, 1976-. Publications: The Shakespeare Stage 1574-1642, 1970, 1980, 1992; Writers In Exile, 1982; Katherine Mansfield, 1982; Playgoing in Shakespeare's London, 1987; Studying Shakespeare, 1988; Rebuilding Shakespeare's Globe, 1989; editor, Shakespeare, Richard II, Henry V; editor, Beaumont and Fletcher, Philaster, The Maid's Tragedy, Knight of The Burning Pestle. Contributions to: Articles in magazines and journals on Shakespeare and Elizabethan drama and on Commonwealth Literature. Memberships: International Shakespeare Association; Association of Commonwealth Literature and Language Studies; Society for Theatre Research; Malone Society. Address: English Department, University of Reading, PO Box 218, Reading, Berkshire, RG6 2AA, England.

GURR David, b. 5 Feb 1936, London, England. Publications include: Troika, 1979; A Woman Called Scylla, 1981; An American Spy Story, 1984; The Ring Master, 1987; The Voice of the Crane, 1989; Arcadia West: The Novel, 1994. Honours: Commonwealth Writers Prize, shortlisted, for The Voice of the Crane, 1989; Governer General's Award for Fiction, shortlisted, for The Ring Master; Creasey Prize, shortlisted, for Troika. Address: 239 E Argyle Avenue, Ottawa, Ontario, K2P 1B8, Canada.

GURT Elizabeth, b. 19 May 1917, Vienna, Austria. Freelance Writer. Education: Examination as School Teacher; Studies of Languages. Publications: Author of over 40 novels, childrens books and short stories including: Eine Frau fur drei Tage, 1942; Es gehort dir nichts, 1947; Bis dass der Tod euch scheidet, 1953, 1979; Ein Stern namens Julia, 1955; Kein Mann fur alle Tage, 1961, 1975; Verzaubert con Tuju, 1980; Vierzig Jahre und ein Sommer, 1981; Denkst du noch an Korfu? 1982; Hinter Weissen Turen, 1984; Manchmaltraumich von Venedig, 1986; Komm Doch Mitnach ischia, 1987; Young Peoples Novels: Vor uns das Lebe; Wolken in Sommer; Du bist kein Kind mehr, Gundula, 198; Erwachsen wirst du ober Nacht, 1984; Short Stories: Wunsche sind wie Sommerwolken; Flammen in Schnee; Die Stunde zeischen act und neun; Immer werde ich dich liebe. Contributions to: Various journals and magazines. Honours: Silver Honorary Award of Merit, Republic of Austria, 1981. Memberships: Austrian Writers Association; Der Erieis; Austrian Womens Club; Association of Female Wrtiers and Artists; Landtannkreis. Address: Schaumburger Gasse 16, A-1040 Vienna, Austria.

GUSTAFSON David A, b. 2 Sept 1946, Superior, Wisconsin, USA. Writer; Consultant; Executive. Education: BS, Information Systems Management, University of San Francisco. Publications: Points, 1992 Address: 28405 Faircrest Way, Hidden Meadows, CA 92026, USA.

GUSTAFSON Ralph, b. 1909, Eastern Townships, Quebec, Canada. m. Elisabeth Renniger, 1958. Education: MA, DCL, Bishop's University; MA, Oxford University. Career: Professor; Poet; Music Critic. Publications: 30 books of poetry include: The Moment in All, 1983; Collected Poems, 1987; Plummets & Other Partialities, 1987; Shadows in the Grass, 1991; Penguin Book of Canadian Verse (ed). Honour: Governor General's Award, 1974. Membership: League of Canadian Poets, Life Member. Address: PO Box 172, North Hatley, Quebec, J0B 2C0, Canada.

GUSTAFSON Thane, Consultant; Professor of Government. Appointment: Professor of Government at Georgetown University, Washington DC. Publications: Reform in Soviet Politics, 1981; Selling the Russians the Rope, 1981; Russia At the Crossroads, 1982; The Soviet Economy in the 1980s, 1982; The Soviet Gas Campaign, 1983; Soviet Negotiating Strategy: The East-West Gas Pipeline, 1985; Crisis amid Plenty, 1989; Soldiers & The Soviet State, 1990; Russia 2010: And What It Means for the World, 1993 (with Daniel Vergin). Address: Cambridge Energy Research Associate, Charles Square, 20 University Road, Cambridge, MA 02138, USA.

GUSTAFSSON Lars, b. 17 May 1936, Västerås, Sweden. Novelist; Poet. m. Dena Chasnoff, 1982. Education: Graduated University of Uppsala, 1961; PhD, 1978. Appointments include: Adjunct

Professor at the University of Texas at Austin, from 1983. Publications: The Last Days and Death of the Poet Brumberg, 1959; The Brothers: An Allegorical Story, 1960; The Travel Company, 1962; The Essential Story of Mr Arenander, 1966; Preparations for Flight and Other Tales, 1967; Cracks in the Wall, 5 volumes, 1971-78; Summer Stories: Six Swedish Novellas, 1973; The Tennis Players, 1977, 1983; The Small World, 1977; Stories of Happy People, 1981; Funeral Music for Freemasons; Bernard Foy's Third Castling, 1986; Collected Stories, 1987; The Strange Animal from the North and Other Science-Fiction Stories, 1989; Verse: The Balloonists, 1962; A Morning in Sweden, 1963; A Journey to the Centre of the Earth and Other Poems, 1966; The Poems of a Private Man, 1967; Declaration of Love to a Sephardic Lady, 1970; Selected Poems, 1972; Warm Rooms and Cold, 1972; The Native Country Under the Earth, 1973; Sonnets, 1977; Artesian Wells Cartesian Dreams, 1980; Out of the Picture, in the Picture: Collected Poems 1950-80; The Stillness of the World Before Bach, 1982, 1988; The Creative Impulse, 1989; Preparations for the Winter Season: Elegies and Other Poems, 1990; Plays and broadcast plays; Essays and political texts. Address: Akademie der Kunste, Hanseatenweg 10, 1000 Berlin 21, Germany.

GUTHRIE Alan. See: **TUBB E(dwin) C(harles).**

GUTTERIDGE Don(ald George), b. 30 Sept 1937, Sarnia, Ontario, Canada. Professor of English; Poet. m. Anne Barnett, 1961, 1 son, 1 daughter. Appointments: Professor of English Methods, University of Western Ontario, from 1977. Publications: The Brooding Sky, 1960; New Poems, 1964; Intimations of Winter, 1967; Riel: A Poem for Voices, 1968; The Village Within: Poems Towards a Biography, 1970; Death at Quebec and Other Poems, 1971; Perspectives, 1971; Saying Grace: An Elegy, 1972; Coppermine: The Quest for North, 1973; Borderlands, 1975; Tecumseh, 1976; A True History of Lambton County, 1977; God's Geography, 1982; The Exiled Heart: Selected Narratives 1968-82, 1986; Novels: Bus-Ride, 1974; All in Good Time, 1980; St Vitus Dance, 1987; Shaman's Ground, 1988; Editor, Rites of Passage, 1979; Poetry: Love in the Wintertime, 1990; Fiction: How the World Began, 1991; Summer's Idyll, 1993. Honours include: President's Medal, University of Western Ontario, 1971. Address: 114 Victoria Street, London, Ontario, Canada N6A 2B5.

GUTTMANN Allen, b. 1932, USA. Professor of English and American Studies. Appointments; Professor of English and American Studies, Amherst College, Amherst, Massachusetts, 1959-. Publications: The Wound in the Heart: America and the Spanish Civil War, 1962; The Conservative Tradition in America, 1967; The Jewish Writer in America, 18971; From Ritual to Record: The Nature of Modern Sports, 1978; Life of George Washington, by Washington Irving (co-editor), 5 vols, 1981; The Games Must Go On: Avery Brundage and the Oplympic Movement, 1984; Sports Spectators, 1986.

GUY Rosa, b. 9 Jan 1928, Trinidad, West Indies. Professor, Writer-in Residence. Appointment: Writer-in-Residence, Michigan Technical University. Publications: The Friends, 1973; Edith Jackson, 1978; Ruby, 1976; The Disappearance, 1979; A Measure of Time, 1983; New Guys Around the Block, 1983; My Love My Love; The Ups and Downs of Carl Davis III: Bird at My Window, 1966, 1989; Pee Wee and Big Dog, 1984; I Heard a Bird Sing, 1986; Music of Summer, 1992; Once on This Island - adapted from My Love My Love for stage, 1990. Contributions to: New York Times Sunday Magazine; Red Book; Cosmopolitan. Honours: The Other Award, England; Best of the Best, New York Times. Memberships: Harlem Writers Guild, President; PEN. Literary Agent: Ellen Levine. Address: 20 West 72nd Street, New York, NY 10023, USA.

GWYN Sandra, b. St John's, Newfoundland. m. Richard Gwyn, 1958. Appointments: Long Apprenticeship as a Writer-Researcher with CBC, Time Canada and various federal task forces and royal commissions. Began writing in earnest, for Saturday Night under Robert Fulford's editorship, early 1970s; Ottawa editor, 1975-80; Book-writing, early 1980s. Publications include: The Private Capital: Ambition and Love in the Age of Macdonald and Laurier, 1984; Mary Pratt, 1989; Tapestry of War: Private View of Canadians in the Great War, 1992. Honours: Governer General's Award for Non-fiction, 1984; Canadian Authors' Association Award, Non-fiction, 1984; National Magazine Awards, Silver Medal, Gold Medal, 1979; Gold Medal, with Richard Gwyn, 1984. Address: 300 Carlton Street, Toronto, Ontario, M5A 2L5, Canada.

GYARFAS Endre, b. 6 May 1936, Szeged, Hungary. Poet; Novelist; Playwright. m. Edit Kincses, 7 Dec 1963, 1 s. Education: Hungarian: English Literature, Elte University of Budapest, 1961. Literary Appointments: Editor, Publisher Europa, 1960-63; Editor, Hung Television, 1964-66. Publications: Partkozelben, poems, 1964; Pazarlo Skotok, travel book, 1970; Apaczai, novel, 1978; Varazslasok, poems, 1984; Hosszu Utnak Pora, novel, 1988; Zsuzsanna Kertje, novel, 1989; Zoldag-Parittya, poems, 1990; Cowboyok, Aranyasok, Csavargok, Folk Poetry of North America, 1992. Honours: Gold Medal for Children's Literature, 1976; Fulbright Grant, 1988. Memberships: PEN Club of Hungary; Union of Hungarian Writers. Literary Agent: Artisjus, Budapest. Address: 1 Attila ut 133, Budapest 1012, Hungary.

GYLLENSTEN Lars Johan Wictor, b. 12 Nov 1921, Stockholm, Sweden. Former Professor of Histology; Author. Education: MD. Publications include: Barnabok, 1952; Senilia, 1956; Sokratod, 1960; Desparados (short stories), 1962; Juvenilia, 1965; Palatset i parken, 1970; Ur min offentliga sektor (essays), 1971; Grottan i oknen, 1973; I skuggan av Don Juan, 1975; Baklangesminnen, 1978; Skuggans aterkomst, 1985; Sju vise mastare om karlek (short stories), 1986; Just sa elle kahske det (short stories), 1989; Det himmelska gästabudet, 1991; Anteckningar fån en vindskupa, 1993. Memberships: Royal Swedish Academy of Sciences; Royal Swedish Academy of Letters, History and Antiquities. Address: Karlavagen 121, 115 26 Stockholm, Sweden.

GYORE Balazs, b. 8 May 1951, Hungary, Writer. m. Adrienn Scheer, 25 Sept 1980, 1 d. Education: Eotvos Lorand University in Budapest, 1971-76; Studies Hungarian and Russian. Publications: The Hand of Humble Abbot Paphnutius (poems), 1982; I Can Safely Asleep on The 91 Bus (novel), 1989; One Has to Search For His Own Death (short novels), 1993; To Call Somebody is Illusion (short stories), 1994. Contributions to: Ujhold; Liget; Elet es Irodalom. Memberships: Association of Hungarian Writers; Hungarian PEN Club. Address: Bartok B 52, 1111 Budapest, Hungary.

H

HAAKANA Anna-Liisa, b. 20 Jan 1937, Rovaniemi, Finland. Author. m. Veikko Olavi Haakana, 24 Feb 1963, 1 s, 1 d. Education: Literature studies, University of Tapere. Publications include: 3 children's books, 1978-84; 4 books for young people, Ykä All Alone, 1980; Top Girl, 1981; A Flower, Nevertheless, 1983; The Black Sheep of The Family, 1986; The Love of an Ugly Girl, 1989; Bird, Little Bird, 1991; Sticks in The Heart, 1993. Honours: National Award for Literature, 1981; Anni Swan Medal, 1982; H C Andersen's Certificate of Honour, 1982; Church's Award for Literature, 1982; Arvid Lydecken Award, 1984. Memberships: Association of Finnish Writers for Children and Youth; Finnish Society of Authors. Literary Agent: Werner Söderström Oy/Gummerus Oy. Address: 99600 Sodankylä, Finland.

HAAS Carolyn Buhal, b. 1 Jan 1926, Chicago, USA. Author; Publisher; Consultant. m. Robert Green Haas, 29 June 1947, 2 s, 3 d. Education: BEd, Smith College,1947. Appointments: Co-Founder Parents As Resource, 1968-81; President, CBH Publishing Inc, 1979-. Publications: Co-author, I Saw a Purple Cow, 1972; A Pumpkin in a Pear Tree, 1976; Children are Children, 1978; Bakyard Vacation, 1980; Purple Cow to the Rescue, 1982; Fun and Learning, 1982; Recipes for Fun Series, 1979-85; Author: The Big Fun Book, 1980; Look at Me, Activities for Babies and Toddlers, 1985. Contributions include: Parents' Magazine; McCalls; Day Care and Early Education; My Own Magazeine; CRRT Newsletter; Family Lesiure. Memberships include: Childrens Reading Roundtable; The Writer; Society of Childrens Book Writers; International Reading Association; Phi Delta Kappa; President, Friends of the Glencoe Public Library; American Library Association. Literary Agent: Curtis Brown Ltd. New York City. Address: 400 E Ohio Street, N 2302, Chicago, IL 60611, USA.

HAAVIKKO Paavo, b. 25 Jan 1931, Helsinki, Finland. Poet; Playwright. Education: University of Helsinki, 1951. Appointments include: Director, Arthouse Publishing Group, Helsinki, from 1983. Publications include: Verse: Roads to Far Away, 1951; On Windy Nights, 1953; Land of Birth, 1955; Leaves, Leaves, 1958; Winter Palace, 1959; Poems 1951-61; The Trees, All their Green, 1966; Selected Poems, 1968; Poems from a Voyage Across the Sound, 1973; Poems 1949-74; Longer Poems, 1975; May, Eternal, 1975; Kullervo's Story, 1975; Wine, Writing, 1976; Bridges: Selected Poems, 1984; Five Sequences from Fast-Flowing Life, 1987; Of Love and Death, 1989; Winter Poems, 1990; Poems, Poems, 1992; Plays: Munchhausen, 1958; The Dolls, 1960; Agricola and the Fox, 1968; The Brotterus Family, 1969; The Feather, 1973; The Horseman (libretto for opera by Aulis Sallinen), 1975; The Strongest Men Don't Remain Unscathed, 1976; Kaisa and Otto, 1977; Radio and Television plays; Stories: Private Affairs, 1960; Another Heaven and Earth, 1961; Years, 1962; A Man Named Barr, 1976; Novels and Short Stories, 1981; Fleur's Autumn Term, 1993. Honours include: Knight First Class of the White Rose of Finland, 1978. Address: c/o Arthouse Group, Bulevardi 19C, 00120 Helsinki, Finland.

HABECK Fritz, b. 8 Sept 1916, Neulengbach. Writer. m. Gerda Vilsmeiere, 1951, 2 s, 2 d. Education: University of Vienna. Publications: Novels: Der Scholar vom linken Gaigen, 1941; Der Tanz der sieben Teufel, 1950; Das Boot kommt nach Mitternacht, 1951; Das zerbrochene Dreieck, 1953; Ronoan Gobain, 1956; Der Ritt auf dem Tiger, 1958; Der Kampf um die Barbacane, 1960; Die Stadt der grauen Gesichter, 1961; Der verliebt Oesterreicher, 1961; Der einaugige Reiter, 1963; In eigenem Auftrag (Selections), 1963; Der Piber 1965; Die Insel Oer den Wolken, 1965; Konig Artus, 1965; Aufstand der Salzknechte, 1967; Salzburg-Spiegel, 1967; Marianne und der wilde Mann, 1968; Francoi Villon, 1969; Doktor Faustus, 1970l Johannes Gutenberg, 1971; Schwarzer Hund in goldenen Feld, 1973; Der schwarze Mantel meines Vaters, 1976; Wind von Sudost, 1979; Der Gobelin, 1982; DerGeneral unddie Distel, 1985; Plays: Swei und zwei ist vier, 1948; Baiser mit Schlag, 1950; Marschall Ney, 1954. Honours: Goehe Award City of Vienna; City Prize of Vienna; Austrian State Prize; Handel-Mazzetti Prize; Vienna Children's Book Prize, 1960, 1961, 1963; 1967; 1970, 1973; State Children's Book Prize, 1963, 1967, 1973; Prize City of Vienna. Memberships: PEN; President, Austrian Centre, 1978. Address: Grillparzerstrasse 6, A-2500 Baden, Austria.

HABGOOD John Stapylton (Archbishop of York), b. 23 June 1927, England. m. Rosalie Mary Ann Boston, 7 June 1961, 2 s, 2 d.

Education: MA, PhD, King's College, Cambridge. Cuddesdon College, Oxford. Publications: Religion and Science, 1964; A Working Faith: Essays and Addresses on science, Medicine and Ethics, 1980; Church and Nation in a Secular Age, 1983; Confessions of a Conservative Liberal, 1988. Contributions include: many symposia including Soundings,1962; numerous essays and review in: Journal of Physiology; Nature; New Scientist; Theology; Expository Times; Frontier; Journal of Theological Studies; Crucible; Times Supplements. Honours: Hon.DD, Durham, 1975, Cambridge, 1984, Hon.DD, Aberdeen, 1988, Huron 1990, Hull, 1991; Hon Fellow, King's College, Cambridge, 1985. Address: Bishopthorpe, York, YO2 1QE, England.

HACKER Marlyn, b. 27 Nov 1942, New York, USA. Writer; Editor; Critic; Teacher. 1 d. Education: BA, Washington Square College, New York University, 1963. Appointments: Jenny McKean Moore Fellow in Writing, George Washington University, 1976-77; Writer-in-Residence, American Studies Institute, Columbia University, 1988; George Elliston Poet-in-Residence, University of Cincinnati, 1988; Distinguished Writer in Residence, The American University, 1989. Publications: Presentation Piece, 1974; Separations, 1976; Taking Notice, 1980; Assumptions, 1985; Love, Death and the Changing of the Seasons, 1986, 1987; Going Back to the River, 1990; The Hang-Glider's Daughter, 1990; Forthcoming: New and Selected Poems; Editor, The Kenyon Review; Contributions to: The Nation; Grand Street; The Paris Review; Boulevard; The Women's Review of Books; Ambit. Honours: Lamont National Book Award, 1975; Guggenehim Fellowship, 1980; Lambda Literary Award, 1991. Memberships: PEN; The Authors' Guild; Poetry Society of America. Literary Agent: Frances Collin. Address: The Kenyon Review, Kenyon College, Gambier, OH 43022, USA.

HACKETT John Winthrop, (General, Sir), b. 5 Nov 1910, Perth, Australia. Soldier; Academic; Author. m. Margaret Frena, 21 Mar 1942, 1 d (dec), 2 adopted stepdaughters. Education: MA, B.Litt, New College, Oxford, 1929-33. Appointments: Commissioned 8th King's Royal Hussars, 1931; Service before, throgunt, after World War II; Deputy Chief General Staff, Commander in Chief, British Army of the Rhine; Commander, Northern Army Group, NATO; Principal, University of London, King's College, 1968-75; President, UK English Association; President, UK Classical Association; Fellow, Royal Society of Literature; Visiting Professor, Classics, King's College, London, 1977-. Publications include: I Was a Stranger, 1977; The Third World War (jointly),1978; The Untold Story, 1982; The Profession of Arms, 1983; Warfare in the Ancient World (ed), 1989; Chapters and forewords in a number of books. Contributions include: Articles, reviews, lecturers. Honours include: MBE, 1938; MC, 1941; DSO, 1942, Bar, 1945; CBE, 1953; CB, 1958; KCB, 1962; GCB, 1967; Honorary Degrees: LLd Queen's University, Belfast, 1967, University of Western Austalia, 1963, Exeter University, 1977, Buckingham University, 1987; Honorary Fellow, St George's College, Perth, New College Oxford, 1972; Fellow, King's College, London. Memberships: Principal, Council of International Institute of Strategic Studies, 1968-77; Lord Chancellor's Committee on the Reform of the law of Contempt of Court, 1971-74; Disciplinary Committee, Senate of the Inns of Court and Bar, 1972-83. Literary Agent: David Higham Associates, London. Address: Coberley Mill, Cheltenham, Gloucestershire, GL53 9NH, England.

HADAS Rachel, b. 8 Nov 1948, New York, NY, USA. m. George Edwards, 22 July 1978. Education: BA, Harvard University; MA, Johns Hopkins University; PhD, Princeton University. Publications: Starting From Troy, 1975; Slow Transparency, 1982; Form, Cycle, Infinity, 1985; A Son for Sleep, 1987; Pass It On, 1989; Unending Dialogue: Voices for AIDS Poetry Work, 1991; Mirror of Astonishment, 1992; The Empty Bed, 1994. Honour: Fellow, American Academy & Institute of Arts & Letters, 1990.

HAGGARD William, b. 11 Aug 1907, Croydon, Surrey, England. Novelist. m. Barbara Myfanwy Sant, 1936, 1 son, 1 daughter. Education: BA, Christ Church, Oxford, 1929; MA, Oxford University, 1947. Publications: Slow Burner, 1958; The Telemann Touch, 1958; Venetian Blind, 1959; Closed Circuit, 1960; The Arena, 1961; The Unquiet Sleep, 1962; The High Wire, 1963; The Antagonists, 1964; The Powder Barrel, 1965; The Hard Sell, 1965; The Power House, 1966; The Conspirators, 1967; A Cool Day for Killing, 1968; The Doubtful Disciple, 1969; The Hardliners, 1970; The Bitter Harvest, 1971; The Protectors, 1972; The Old Masters, 1973; The Kinsmen, 1974; The Scorpion's Tail, 1975; Yesterday's Enemy, 1976; The Poison People, 1978; Visa to Limbo, 1978; The Median Line, 1979; The Money Men, 1981; The Mischief-Makers, 1983; The Heirloom, 1983; The Need to

Know, 1984; The Meritocrats, 1985; The Martello Tower, 1986; The Diplomatist, 1987; The Expatriates, 1989; The Vendettists, 1990. Literary Agent: John Farquharson, 162-168 Regent Street, London W1R 5TB, England. Address: 3 Linkside, Holland Road, Frinton-on-Sea, Essex CO13 9EN, England.

HAGON Priscilla. See: **ALLAN Mabel Esther.**

HAIDA. See: **NAGARAJA RAO C K.**

HAIDAR Qurratulain, b. 1927, Aligarh, India. Novelist. Education: MA, Lucknow University, 1947. Appointments include: Visiting Professor at New Delhi and at Aligarh Muslim University, 1979. Publications: Before the Stars, 1947; My Temples Too, 1949; Safina's Woeful Heart, 1952; Houses of Glass, 1952; The Exiles: A Novelette, 1955; River of Fire, 1959; Autumn's Voice, 1967; An Instrument, 1976; The Task of Life is Long, 2 volumes, 1977-79; Last Night's Travellers, 1979; Four Novellettes, 1981; The Light's Speed, 1982; Circling the Colours of the Garden, 1987; Candi Begum, 1990; The Fireflies' World, 1990; Also: Ghalib and His Poetry, 1970; Picture Gallery, 1983. Honours include: Jnanpith Award, 1989. Address: c/o Sterling Publishers, L-10 Green Park Extension, New Delhi 110016, India.

HAIGH Christopher, b. 28 Aug 1944, Birkenhead, England. Lecturer. 2 d. Education: BA, Cambridge University, 1966; PhD, Victoria University of Manchester, 1969. Appointments: Lecturer in History, Victoria University of Manchester, 1969-79; Lecturer in Modern History, Oxford University, Christ Church, Oxford, 1979-. Publications: The Last Days of The Lancashire Monasteries, 1969; Reformation and Resistance in Tudor Lancashire, 1975; The Cambridge Historical Encyclopaedia of Great Britain and Ireland, 1984; The Reign of Elizabeth I, 1985; The English Reformation Revised, 1987; Elizabeth I: A Profile in Power, 1988; English Reformations: Religion, Politics and Society Under The Tudors, 1993; The Church of England and Its People, 1559-1642, forthcoming. Membership: Fellow, Royal Historical Society. Address: c/o Christ Church, Oxford University, Oxford, OX1 1DP, England.

HAIGH Jack, b. 21 Feb 1910, West Hartlepool, England. Journalist. m. Josephine Agnes Mary McLoughlin, 7 July 1949, London. Appointments: Script Writer, The Rascals, official soldiers' concert party for Palestine, 1939-41; Editor, Jerusalem Services Magazine, 1941-42; Staff, The Racing Calendar, 1956-68; Sport Sub Editor, The Daily Mail, 1972-84; Proprietor, Greenfriar Press. Publications: Theory of Genius, 1972; Constellation of Genius, 1982; Phillimore: The Postcard Art of R P Phillimore, 1985; Psychology of Genius, 1991. Contributions to: 30 Children's Radio play broadcasts from Jerusalem, 1941-44; Special Feature Programme introduced by Prince Peter of Greece and Denmark, 1944; 116 Radio Programmes broadcast, Forces Broadcasting Service, 1945-47. Memberships: Honorary Secretary, Freelance Specialist Panel, Institute of Journalists, 1951-53, 1964-72. Address: 28 Manville Road, London, SW17 8JN, England.

HAILBLUM Isidore, b. 1935, USA. Freelance Writer; Former Interviewer; Scriptwriter and Folk-Singer's Agent. Publications: The Tsaddik of the Seven Wonders, 1971; The Return, 1973; Transfer to Yesterday, 1973; The Wilk Are Among Us, 1975; Interworld,1977; Nightmare Express, 1979; Outerworld, 1979; Faster Than a Speeding Bullet: An Informal History of Radio's Golden Age, (with Stuart Silver), 1980; The Mutants Are Coming, 1984; The Identity Plunderers, 1984; The Hand of Ganz, 1985; Murder in Yiddish, 1988. Contributions to: Book reviews. Address: 160 West 77th Street, New York, NY 10024, USA.

HAILEY Arthur, b. 5 Apr 1920, Luton, England. Novelist. British & Canadian Citizen. m. Shelia Dunlop, 38 Jul 1951, 4 sons, 2 daughters. Appointments: Pilot\Flight Lieutenant, Royal Air Force, 1939-47; Editor, Bus & Truck Transport, Toronto, 1949-53; Freelance Writer, 1956-. Publications: Novels: Runway-Zero Eight, 1958 (with John Castle); The Final Diagnosis, 1959; In High Places, 1962; Hotel, 1965; Airport, 1968; Wheels, 1971; The Moneychangers, 1975; Overload, 1979; Strong Medicine, 1984; The Evening News, 1990; Author novels published in 38 languages; Collected Plays Close-up on Writing for Television, 1960; Motion Picture includes: Zero Hour, 1956; Time Lock 1957; The Young Doctors, 1961; Hotel, 1966; Airport, 1970; The Moneychangers, 1976; Wheels, 1978; Strong Medicine, 1986; Poem: A Last Request; Screenplays and Television Plays. Honours include: Air Efficiency Award RAF; Canadian Council of Artists and Authors Award, 1956; Best Canadian TV Playwright Award, 1957, 59;

Doubleday Prize Novel Award, 1962. Memberships: Writers Guild of America (Life); Authors League of America; Alliance of Canadian Cinema, Television and Radio Artists (Hon Life). Address: Lyford Cay, PO Box 7776, Nassau, Bahamas.

HAILEY Elizabeth Forsythe, b. 31 Aug 1938, Dallas, Texas, USA. Novelist. m. Oliver Hailey, 25 Jun 1960, 2 d. Education: BA, Hollins College, Virginia, 1960; Diplome d'Etudes (Mention Tres Bien), Sorbonne, Paris, France, 1959. Publications: A Woman of Independent Means, 1978; Life Sentences, 1982; Joanna's Husband and David's Wife, 1986; Home Free, 1991; Her Work (anthology of Stories by Texas Women); New Growth (anthology). Literary Agent: Molly Friedrich, Aaron M Priest Literary Agency, New York, USA. Address: 11747 Canton Place, Studio City, CA 91604, USA.

HAILSHAM OF ST MARYLEBONE, Quintin McGarel (Hogg), Baron, b. 9 Oct 1907, London, England. Law; Politics. m. Mary Evelyn Martin, 18 Apr 1944, dec 1978, 2 s, 3 d. Education: 1st Class Honour Moderatous, 1928, 1st Class Literae Humaniores, 1930. Appointments: Fellow, All Souls, 1931, Oxford University; Barrister at Law, 1932; QC, 1953; Bencher, Lincoln's Inn, 1956. Publications: The Law of Arbitration, 1935; The Left Was Never Right, 1945; The Case For Conservatism, 1947, 1959; The Devils Own Song and Other Verses, 1968; The Door Wherein I Went, 1975; The Dilemma of Democracy, 1978; A Sparrow's Flight, 1990; On The Constitution, 1992; Values, Collapse & Cure, 1994. Contributions to: numerous articles in journals and magazines. Honours include: Fellow, Royal Society, 1973; Honorary Degrees: DCL, Oxford, 1974; LLD, Cambridge; Knight of The Garter, 1988. Memberships: Royal Society of Arts; Royal Institute of Arbitrators. Literary Agent: Curtis Brown Limited. Address: The Corner House, Heath View Gardens, London, SW15 3SZ, England.

HAINES John Meade, b. 29 Jun 1924, Norfolk, VA, USA. Poet; Essayist; Teacher. 1 ss, 2 sd. Education: American University, 1948-49; Hans Hofman School of Fine Art, NYC, 1950-52. Appointments: Writer in Residence, University of Alaska, 1972-73; Visiting Professor, University of Washington, 1974; Visiting Lecturer, University of Montana, 1974-75; Visiting Writer, Montalvo Centre, 1986; Visiting Lecturer, UC Santa Cruz, 1986; Writer in Residence, Ucross Foundation, 1987; Visiting Writer, The Loft, 1987; Visiting Professor, Ohio University, 1989-90; Visiting Writer, George Washington University, Washington DC, 1991-92. Publications: The Stars The Snow, The Fire, 1989; News From the Glacier, 1982; Living Off The Country, 1981; The Stone Harp, 1971; Winter News, 1966; New Poems, 1980-88, 1990; Stories We Listened To, 1986; Other Days, 1982; Of Traps and Snares, 1983; Cicada, 1977; In A Dusty Light, 1977; Meditation on a Skull Carved in Crystal, 1989; Rain Country, 1990; The Owl in the Mask of a Dreamer, 1993. Contributions to: Hudson Review; Ohio Review; New Virginia Review; Gettysburg Review; Nothwest Review; AWP Chronicle; Triquarterly; Graywolf Annual; New England/ Breadloaf Quarterly; ZYZZYVA; Pushcart Annual; The New Criterion. Honours: Guggenheim Fellowship, 1965-66, 1984-85; NEA Fellowship, !967-68; Amy Lowell Scholarship, 1976-77; Alaska State Council on the Arts Fellowship 1979-80; Hon Doctor of Letters, University of Alaska, 1983; Western States Federation Award, 1990; Elliston Fellow in Poetry, University of Cinncinnati, 1992; Lenore Marshall, Nation Award for New Poems, 1991; Poets Prize for New Poems, 1992; Chair of Excellence in the Arts, Austin Peay State University, Tennessee, 1993. Memberships: Poetry Society of America; Academy of American Poets; PEN American Centre; Wilderness Society; Sierra Club; Alaska Conservation Society; Natural Resources Defence Council. Address: PO Box 73961, Fairbanks, AK 99707, USA.

HAINES Pamela Mary, b. 4 Nov 1929, Harrogate, England. Writer. m. Anthony Haines, 24 June 1955, 2 s, 3 d. Education: Honours degree, English Literature, Newnham College, Cambridge University, 1949-52. Publications: Tea at Gunters, 1974; A Kind ow War, 1976; Men on White Horses, 1978; The Kissing Gate, 1981; The Diamond Waterfall, 1984; The Golden Lion, 1986; Daughter of the Northern Fields, 1987. Honours: Spectator New Writing Prize, 1971; Yorkshire Arts Young Writers Award, 1975. Memberships: Society of Authors; PEN, Committee, 981-86; Royal Commonwealth Institute; Academy Club. Literary Agent: Peters Fraser Dunlop, London, SW10. Address: 57 Middle Lane, London, N8 8PE, England.

HAINING Peter Alexander (William Pattrick, Richard Peyton, Sean Richards, Peter Alex, Jim Black, Richard De'ath, Richard Peters), b. 1940, Great Britain. Writer: Novels; Short Stories;

Supernatural/Occult Topics. Appointments: Editorial Director, New English Library, publishers, London, 1970-73. Publications include: The Ghost Ship, 1985; Great Irish Stories of The Supernatural, 1992; Irish Tales of Terror, 1988; Masters of The Macabre, 1993; Movie Monsters, 1988; The Mummy, 1988; Poltergeist, 1987; Stories of The Walking Dead, 1986; Supernatural Sleuths, 1986; Tales of Dungeons and Dragons, 1986; The Television Late Night Horror Omnibus, 1993; Tune in for Fear, 1985; Vampire, 1985; Stories of The Walking Dead, 1986; Eyewitness to The Galaxy, 1985; Race for Mars, 1986; Werewolf, 1987; Mysterious Motoring Stories, 1987; Sinister Gambits, 1991; The Scarecrow: Fact and Fable, 1988; The Supernatural Coast, 1992; The Dracula Scrapbook, 1992; Great Irish Detective Stories, 1993; The Armchair Detectives, 1993; Great Racing Stories, 1993; Bob Hope: Thanks for The Memory, 1989; Charlie Chaplin: A Centenary Celebration, 1989; The Day War Broke Out, 1989; The Elvis Presley Scrapbook, 1991; The English Highwayman, 1991; Hook, Line and Laughter, 1989; The Legend of Garbo, 1990; Spitfire Summer, 1990; The Legend That is Buddy Holly, 1990; Tombstone Humour, 1993; numerous others. Honour: Nominated for Edgar Allan Poe Award, 1992. Membership: PEN International. Address: Peyton House, Boxford, Suffolk, England.

HAKIM Seymour (Sy), b. 23 Jan 1933, New York City, USA. Poet; Writer; Artist; Educator. m. Odetta Roverso, 18 Aug 1970. Education: AB, Eastern New Mexico University, 1954; MA, New York University, 1960; Postgraduate work, various universities. Appointments include: Consultant Editor, Poet Gallery Press, New York, 1970; Editor, Overseas Teacher, 1977. Publications: The Sacred Family, 1970; Manhattan Goodbye, poems, 1970; Under Moon, 1971; Museum of the Mind, 1971; Wine Theorem, 1972; Substituting Memories, 1976; Iris Elegy, 1979; Balancing Act, 1981; Birth of a Poet, 1985; Elanor, Goodbye, 1988. Contributions to: Overseas Educator; California State Poetry Quarterly; American Writing; Dan River Anthology; It's On My Wall; Older Eyes. Honours: Exhibits with accompanying writings: 1970, 1973, 1982-83, 1985; Art works in public collections in various countries, prints in collections in Taiwan, Korea and Japan. Memberships: Association of Poets and Writers; National Photo Instructors Association; Italo-Brittanica Association, 1972-80. Address: Via Chiesanuova No 1, 36023 Longare, VI 36023, Itlay.

HAKIMZADEH. See: ZAND Roxane.

HALBERSTAM David, b. 10 Apr 1934, New York, New York, USA. m. (1) Elizabeth Tchizerska, 13 June 1965 (div), (2) Jean Sanders, 29 June 1979, 1 daughter. Education: AB, Harvard University. Career: Journalist; Writer, 1971-. Publications: The Noblest Roman, 1961; The Making of Quaguire, 1965; The Unfinished Odyssey of Robert Kennedy, 1969; The Best & The Brightest, 1972; The Powers That Be, 1979; The Breaks of the Game, 1981; The Amateurs, 1986; The Reckoning, 1986; Summer of '49, 1989; The Next Century, 1991; The Fifties, 1993; October 1964, 1994. Contributions to: Esquire; Atlantic Monthly; McCall's; Harpers. Honours: Page One Award, Newspaper Guild of America, 1962; George Polk Award, 1964; Louis M Lyons Award, 1964; Pulitzer Prize for Vietnam Reporting, 1964; Overseas Press Club Award, 1973; National Book Award, nominee (twice). Address: c/o Random House, 201 East 50th Street, 12th Floor Reception, New York, NY 100022, USA.

HALDEMAN Joe William, b. 9 Jun 1943, Oklahoma City, USA. Novelist. m. Mary Gay Potter, 21 Aug 1965. Education: BS, Physics & Astronomy, University of Maryland, 1967; MFA, English, University of Iowa, 1975. Appointment: Associate Professor, writing programme, Massachusetts Institute of Technology, 1983-. Publications: War Year, 1972; Cosmic Laughter, editor, 1974; The Forever Year, 1975; Mindbridge, 1976; Planet of Judgement, 1977; All My Sins Remembered, 1977; Study War No More, editor, 1977; Infinite Dreams, 1978; World Without End, 1979; Worlds, 1981; There is No Darkness (co-author), 1983; Worlds Apart, 1983; Nebula Awards 17, 1983; Dealing in Futures, 1985; Tool of the Trade, 1987; Body Armour 2000, 1986; Supertanks(co-editor), 1987; Starfighters (co-editor), 1988; The Long Habit of Living (called Buying Time, in US), 1989; The Hemingway Hoax, 1990; Worlds Enough and Time, 1992; 1968, 1994 in Britain. Honours: Purple Heart, US Army, 1969; Hugo Award, 1976, 1977, 1991; Nebula Award, 1975, 1990, 1993. Rhysling Award, 1984, 1990; World Fantasy Award, 1993. Memberships: President, Science Fiction and Fantasy Writers of America; Author's Guild; Poets & Writers Inc; National Space Institute; Writers Guild. Literary Agent: Ralph Vicinanza. Address: 5412 NW 14th Avenue, Gainesville, FL 32605, USA.

HALE A Dean, b. 28 Aug 1929, Blackwell, OK, USA. Writer; Editor; Engineer; Historian; Photographer. m. Barbara Dean Chambers, 12 Oct 1952, 1s. Education: BS Engineering & Management, OK State University, 1953. Literary Appointments: Editor, Pipeline & Gas Journal, 1953-88; Director of Communications, Southern Gas Association, 1988-present. Publications: 21 Technical and Historical books. Contributions to: More than 500 Journal articles, Honours: Neal award, 1979; 2 Dallas Press Club Katie awards; 6 Western Publishers Association Maggies; Sigma Delta Chi. Memberships: SGA; AGA; MGA; ASHE; AITE. Address: 3412 High Bluff, Dallas, TX 75234, USA.

HALE Keith, b. 3 July 1955, Little Rock, AR, USA. Writer. Eudcation: BSE, University of Texas at Austin, 1980. Appointments: Schoolteacher, Austin, Texas, 1981-82; Publicity Office, University of Texas, Performing Arts Centre, 1982-84; Editor, English Language Book Editors, Amsterdam, Holland, 1984; Editor, Arkansas Writers; Project, Little Rock, 1984-87; Copy Editor, Arkansas Gazette, Little Rock, 1987-. Publications: Clicking Beat on the Brink of Nada, 1983; Cody, 1987.

HALEY Kenneth Harold Dobson, b. 19 Apr 1920. Historian. m. Iris Houghton, 22 Mar 1948, 1 s, 2 d. Education: MA; BLitt, Balliol College, 1938-40, 1945-47. Publications: William of Orange and The English Opposition 1672-74, 1953; The First Earl of Shaftesbury, 1968; The Dutch in The Seventeenth Century, 1972; Politics in The Reign of Charles II, 1985; An English Diplomat in The Low Countries: Sir William Temple and John de Witt, 1986; The British and The Dutch, 1988. Contributions to: Articles to various historical journals. Honour: FBA, 1987. Membership: Honorary Vice-President, Historical Association, 1994. Address: 15 Haugh Lane, Sheffield, S11 9SA, England.

HALL Angus, b. 1932, United Kingdom. Author; Editor. Appointments: Film and Theatre critic, London Daily Sketch, 1958-1; Editor, IPC Publishers, London, 1971-; Editor, BPC Publishers, London, 1972-. Publications: London in Smoky Region, 1962, High-Bouncing Lover, 1966; Live Like a Hero, 1967; Comeuppance of Arthur Hearne, 1967; Qualtrough, 1968; Late Boy Wonder, 1969; Devilday, 1970; To Play the Devil, 1971; Scars of Dracula, 1971; Long Way to Fall, 1971; On the Run, 1974; Signs of Things to Come: A History of Divination, 1975; Monsters and Mythic Beasts, 1976; Strange Cults, 1977; The Rigoletto Murder, 1978; Self-Destruct, 1985. Address: 96 High Street, Old Town, Hastings, Sussex, England.

HALL Carl William, b. 16 Nov 1924, Tiffin, Ohio, USA. Engineer. m. Mildred E Wagner, 5 Sep 1949, 1 d. Education: SB, BAE summa cum laude, Ohio State University, 1948; MME, University of Delaware, 1950; PhD, Michigan State University, 1952; Certificate, SMG, JFK School of Government, Harvard University, 1983. Publications: Agricultural Engineers Handbook, 1961; Biomass Handbook, 1988, 1989; Encyclopedia of Food Engineering, 1971, 1986; Dictionary of Drying, 1979; Food and Natural Resources, 1984, author 26 books. Contributions to: 34 books, 175 articles in technical journals, 250 articles in general media; Founding Editor, Editor Emeritus, columnist, Drying Technology: An International Journal. Honours: Max Eyth Medal, 1979; Massey-Ferguson Gold Medal, 1976; Cyrus Hall McCormick Gold Medal, 1984; Food Engineer Award, 1993. Memberships: Vice President, ASME; National Academy of Engineers; National Society of Professional Engineers; International Club of Washington. Address: 2454 N Rockingham St, Arlington, VA 22207, USA.

HALL Claudia. See: FLOREN Lee.

HALL Donald, b. 20 Sept 1928, New Haven, Connecticut, USA. Poet & Writer. m. (1) Kirby Thompson, 13 Sept 1952, 1 son, 1 daughter, (2) Jane Kenyon, 17 April 1972. Education: BA, Harvard University; BLitt, Oxford University; Stanford University. Career: Professor; Broadcaster, BBC & US; Lecturer. Publications: Poetry, Prose, Plays, Editor of Anthologies include: To The Loud Wind & Other Poems, 1955; Exiles & Marriages, 1955; String Too Short to Be Saved, 1961 (autobiog); An Evening's Frost, 1965; Henry Moore, 1966; The Yellow Room: Love Poems, 1971; Writing Well, 1974; Bread & Roses, 1975; Remembering Poets, 1978; The Ox-Cart Man, 1979; To Read Literature, 1980; The One Day, 1987; Old & New Poems, 1990; Here At Eagle Pond, 1990; Life Work, 1993; Editor: Faber Book of Modern Verse; Concise Encyclopedia of English & American Poets & Poetry; Oxford Book of American Literary Anecdotes. Contributions include: Iowa Review; American Poetry Review; Yankee; Playboy. Address: Eagle Pond Farm, Danbury, NH 03230, USA.

HALL Gimone, b. 30 Apr 1940, Highland Park, Illinois, US. Novelist. m. Lawrence C Hall, 13 July 1963, 2 s, 1 d. Education: BA, University of Texas. Publications include: Raptures' Mistress, 1979; Rules of the Heart, 1983; Fury's Sun, Passion's Moon, 1980; The Kiss Flower, 1985; The Jasmine Veil, 1987; Esctasy's Empire, 1981. Contributions to: Fiction in Red Book, Good Housekeeping, Woman's Own. Honours: Best Romantic Fiction of the Year, West Coast Review of Weeks, 1980. Literary Agent: Donald MacCampbell. Address: Million Wishes Farm, PO Box 485, Ottsville, PA 18942, USA.

HALL Hugh Gaston, b. 7 Nov 1931, Jackson, MS, USA. Emeritus Reader, University of Warwick. m. Gillian Gladys Lund, 16 Jul 1955, 1 s, 2 d. Education: BA, Millsaps College, 1952; Diplome pour l'Enseignement, University of Toulouse, 1953; MA Oxon, 1959; PhD, Yale, 1959. Appointments: Yale University, 1958-60; University of Glasgow, Lecturer, 1960-64; University of California, Berkeley, Assistant Professor, 1963; Monash University, Senior Lecturer, 1965; University of Warwick, Senior Lecturer, 1966-74; Reader, 1974-89; City University of New York, Professor of Romance Languages, 1970-72; Fellow, Humanities Research Centre, Canberra, 1984; Camargo Foundation, Cassis, 1987, 1990. Publications: Moliere: Tartuffe, 1960; Quadruped Octaves, 1983; Comedy in Context, 1984; Alphabet Aviary, 1987; Richelieu's Desmarets and The Century of Louis XIV, 1990; Moliere's Le Bourgeois Gentilhomme, 1990. Contributions to: Numerous professional humanities journals and reference books. Address: 18 Abbey End, Kenilworth, Warwickshire, England.

HALL James Byron, b. 21 July 1918, Midland, Ohio, USA. Writer. Professor. m. Elizabeth Cushman, 14 Feb 1946, 1 s, 4 d. Education: Miami University, Ohio, 1938-39; University of Hawaii, 1938-40; BA 1947; MA, 1948, PhD, 1953, State University of Iowa. Appointments include: Writer-in-Residence, various universities; Faculty 1958-68, Professor, 1960-68, Director, Writing Centre, 1965-68, University of California, Irvine; Provost, 1968-75, Emeritus, 1983-, University of California, Santa Cruz. Publications include: Not By The Door, 1954; The Short Story, 1955, 1957; Racers fo the Sun, 1960; Us He Devours, 1964; Realm of Fiction, 1965, 1977; Moem Culture and Arts, 1967, 1975; Mayo Sergeant, 1967; The Hunt Within, 1973; Short Hall, stories, 1981; Squall Line, 1989. Contributions to: Stories, poetry, various anthologies; Literary archive, Miami University, Oxford, Ohio. Honours inlcude: Numerous prizes and awards, poetry and fiction; Rockefeller grantee, 1955; James B Hall Gallery named, University of California Regents, 1985; Jams B Hall Travelling Fellowships founded, University of California, Santa Cruz, 1985. Memberships include: American Association of University Professors; Past Local President, National Writers Union. Literary Agent: Gerard McCauley Agency, PO Box AE, Katona NY. Address: 1670 East 27th Avenue, Eugene, OR 97403, USA.

HALL J(ohn) C(live), b. 12 Sept 1920, London, England. Poet. Education: Oriel College, Oxford. Publications: Selected Poems, 1943; The Summer Dance and Other Poems, 1951; The Burning Hare, 1966; A House of Voices, 1973; Selected and New Poems 1939-84, 1985; Edwin Muir, 1956; Editor, Collected Poems of Edwin Muir, 1921-51, 1952; Co-editor, New Poems, 1955. Address: 9 Warwick Road, Mount Sion, Tunbridge Wells, Kent TN1 1YL, England.

HALL Oakley Maxwell (Jason Manor), b. 1 Jul 1920, San Diego, CA, USA. Author. m. Barbara Erdinger, 28 Jun 1945, 1 s, 3 d. Education: BA, University of California, Berkeley, 1943; MFA, University of Iowa, 1950. Appointments: Director, Programs in Writing, University of California, Irvine, 1969-89; Director, Squaw Valley Community of Writers, 1969-. Publications: So Many Doors, 1950; Corpus of Joe Bailey, 1953; Mardios Beach, 1955; Warlock, 1958; The Downhill Racers, 1962; The Pleasure Garden, 1962; A Game for Eagles, 1970; Report from Beau Harbor, 1971; The Adelita, 1975; The Badlands, 1978; Lullaby, 1982; The Children of the Sun, 1983; The Coming of the Kid, 1985; Apaches, 1986; The Art and Craft of Novel Writing, 1989; (as O M Hall) Murder City, 1949; (as Jason Manor) Too Dead to Run, 1953; The Red Jaguar, 1954; The Pawns of Fear, 1955; The Tramplers, 1956. Honours: Nomination for Pulitzer Prize, 1953; Commonwealth Club of California Silver Medal, 1954; Western Writers of America Golden Spur Award, 1984; Cowboy Hall of Fame Wrangler Award, 1989. Literary Agent: Virginia Barber Literary Agency. Address: Department of English, University of California, Irvine, CA 92717, USA.

HALL Peter (Geoffrey), b. 1932, United Kingdom. Professor of Geography; Professor of City and Regional Planning. Publications: The Industries of London,1962; London 2000, 1963, revised 1969; Labour's New Frontiers (editor), 1964; Land Values (editor), 1965; The World Cities, 1966, 3rd edition 1984; Von Thunen's Isolated State (editor), 1966; An Advanced Geography of North West Europe (co-author), 1967; Theory and Practice of Regional Planning, 1970; Containment of Urban England: Urban and Metropolitan Growth Processes or Megalopolis Denied (co-author), 1973; Containment of Urban England: The Planning System: Objectives, Operations, Impacts (co-author), 1973; Planning and Urban Growth: An Anglo-American Comparison (with M Clawson), 1973; Urban and Regional Planning: An Introduction, 1974, 2nd edition 1982; Europe 2000, 1977; Great Planning Disasters, 1980; Growth Centres in The European Urban System, 1980; Transport and Public Policy Planning (edited with D Banister), 1980; The Inner City in Context (editor), 1981; Silicon Landscapes (editor), 1985; Can Rail Save The City? (co-author), 1985; High-Tech America (co-author), 1986; Western Sunrise (co-author), 1987; The Carrier Wave (co-author), 1988; Cities of Tomorrow, 1988; London 2001, 1989; The Rise of The Gunbelt, 1991; Technopoles of The World, 1994. Address: The Bartlett School of Planning, University College London, Wates House, 22 Gordon Street, London, WC1H 0QB, England.

HALL Rand, b. 17 Jul 1945, New Jersey, USA. Writer; Editor; Publisher - Shadowood Publications. 1 s, 1 d. Education: Hofstra University, New York; New York University, Agricultural & Technical Institute, Farmingdale, NY; St Petersburg Jr College, St Petersburg, Florida, USA. Literary Appointments: Editor-in-Chief, The Gazette, Florida's Gay & Lesbian News. Publications: Voices in the Night, Clies Press McNarron & Morgan editors, 1984; The Alternative Papers, Temple University Press, 1984; Lavenderblue, Shadowood Publications, 1988. Contributions to: Poetry, essays in : Sinister Wisdom; Common Lives: Feminary; Oblisk. Honour: World of Poetry, Silver Poet Award. 1986. Memberships: Womonwrites (Register - Southeastern Lesbian Writers Conf. 1981-89); National Board for Certifcation - CDT; Tampa Bay Business Guild. Address: 7134 5th Avenue N, St Petersburg, FL 33710, USA.

HALL Rodney, b. 18 Nov 1935, Solihull, England. Writer. m. Bet MacPhail, 3 d. Education: BA, Queensland University, Australia. Literary Appointments: Poetry Editor, The Australian, 1967-78; Creative Arts Fellow, Australian National University, 1968-69; Chairman, The Australia Council, 1991-1994. Publications: Poetry: Penniless Till Doomsday, 1962; Selected Poems, 1975; Black Bagatelles, 1978; Novels: The Ship on The Coin, 1972; A Place Among People, 1975, 2nd edition 1984; Just Relations, 1982, 4th edition 1985; Kisses of The Enemy, 1987; Captivity Captive, 1988; The Second Bridegroom, 1991; The Grisly Wife, 1993. Contributions to: Hundreds of poems and several short stories in Australian Literary Magazines, Newspapers, Journals; Book Reviews, The Australian; Sydney Morning Herald; The Bulletin. Honours: Grace Leven Prize for Poetry, 1973; Australia Council, Senior Fellowships, 1973, 1976, 1983, 1985; Miles Franklin Award, for novel, 1982 and 1994. Memberships: The Order of Australia, 1990. Literary Agent: Elaine Markson, 44 Greenwich Avenue, New York, NY 10011, USA. Address: PO Box 7, Bermagui South NSW 2546, Australia.

HALL Roger Leighton, b. 17 Jan 1939, Woodford, Wells, Essex, England. Writer. m. Dianne Sturm, 20 Jan 1968, 1 son, 1 daughter. Education: BA, 1966; MA, 1968, Victoria University, Wellington, New Zealand; Diploma of Teaching. Publications: Plays: Glide Time, 1976; Middle Age Spread, 1977; State of The Play, 1978; Prisoners of Mother England, 1979; The Rose, 1981; Hot Water, 1982; Fifty-Fifty, 1982; Multiple Choice, 1984; Dream of Sussex Downs, 1986; The Hansard Show, 1986; The Share Club, 1987; After The Crash, 1988; Conjugal Rites, 1990; By Degrees, 1993; Musicals with Philip Norman and A K Grant; many plays for TV, Radio and for children; Television: Conjugal Rites, 1993, 1994. Honours: Robert Burns Fellow, Otago University, 1977, 1978; Fulbright Travel Award, 1982; QSO, 1987; Turnovsky Award, Outstanding Contribution to The Arts, 1987. Memberships: PEN; NZ Scriptwriters Guild. Literary Agents: Playmarket, Box 9767, Wellington, New Zealand; The Casarotto Company Ltd, 60-66 Wardour Street, London, W1V 3HP, England. Address: c/o Playmarket, PO Box 9767, Wellington, New Zealand.

HALL Willis, b. 6 Apr 1929. Writer. m. Valerie Shute, 1973, 1 s (3 s by previous marriages). Publications include: The Villa Maroc; They Don't Open Men's Boutiques; Song at Twilight; The Road to 1984; TV series: Stan's Last Game, 1983; The Bright Side, 1985; The Return of The Antelope, 1986; Books: (with Michael Parkinson) Football Classified, 1974; My Sporting Life, Football Final, 1975; Children's Books: The Last Vampire, 1982; The Inflatable Shop, 1984; The Return of The Antelope, 1985; Dragon Days, 1986; The Antelope Company Ashore, Spooky Rhymes, The Antelope Company at Large, 1987; Doctor Jekyll and Mr Hollins, 1988; The Vampire's Holiday, 1992; The Vampire's Christmas, 1994; Plays: England Our England, 1962; Squat Betty and The Sponge Room, 1963; Say Who You Are, 1965; Whoops A Daisy, 1968; Children's Day, 1969; Who's Who, 1972; Saturday, Sunday, Monday (adapation from de Filippo), 1973; Filumena (adaptation from de Filippo), 1977; Jane Eyre (adaptation from Charlotte Bronte), 1992; Mansfield Park (adaptation from Jane Austen), 1993; The Three Musketeers (adaptation from Alexandre Dumas), 1994; Musicals: (with Keith Waterhouse) The Card, 1973; (with Denis King): Treasure Island, 1985; The Wind in The Willows (adaptation from A A Milne), 1985; (with John Cooper) The Water Babies (adaptation from Charles Kingsley), 1987. Address: c/o Alexander Cann Representation, 337 Fulham Road, London, SW10 9TW, England.

HALLAHAN William H(enry), b. USA. Author. Publications: The Dead of Winter, 1972; The Ross Forgery, 1973; The Search for Joseph Tully, 1974; Catch Me, Kill Me, 1977; Keeper of the Children, 1978; The Trade, 1981; The Monk, 1983. Address: c/o William Morrow Inc, Madison Avenue, New York, NY 10016, USA.

HALLER Bill. See: BECHKO Peggy Anne.

HALLIDAY Dorothy. See: DUNNETT Dorothy.

HALLIN Emily W, b. Arkansas, USA. Writer. m. Clark Ossell Hallin, 16 Aug 1952, 2 s, 1 d. Education: AB, University of Missour, 1948. Appointments: Editor; Publicist, United Aircraft Corp, Chance Vought Division, 1948-52. Publications: Wild White Wings, 1962; Follow the Honey Bird, 1964; Moya and the Flamingoes, 1966; Blossom Valley Series (19 books) 1980-88; Wanted: Tony Roston, 1988; A Dark Horse, 1989; Queen Bee, 1989; The Meg and Stanley Series (3 books), 1990. Contributions to: Various children's magazines, journals. Memberships: Mystery Writers of America; California Writers Club; Society of Childrens Book Writers. Literary Agent: Ruth Cohen. Address: 1350 Castro Way, Monterey, CA 93940, USA.

HALLMUNDSSON Hallberg, b. 29 Oct 1930, Iceland. Poet; Translator; Editor. m. May Newman, 29 Jul 1960. Education: BA, University of Iceland, 1954; University of Barcelona, 1955-56; New York University, 1961. Appointments: Columnist, Frjals Thjod, 1954-60; Stringer, Newsweek 1960; Assistant, Associate Senior Editor, Encyclopedia International, 1961-76; Senior Editor, Americana Annual, 1977-78; Senior Editor, Funk & Wagnells New Encyclopedia, 1979-82; Production Copy Editor, Business Week, 1984-. Publications: Anthology of Scandinavian Literature, 1966; Poetry, Haustmal, 1968; Neikvaeda 1977; Spjaldvisur, 1985; Thraetubók, 1990; Spjaldvisur II, 1991; Skyggnur, 1993; Short Stories: Eg kalla mig Ofeig, 1970; Icelandic Folk and Fairy Tales, with May Hallmundsson,1987; Translator various books. Contributions include: Americana Annual; Icelandic Canadian; Iceland Review; Visions International; Grand Street 1993. Honours include: 1st Prize, short story contest, Rejkjavik, 1953; 1st prize, Translation of Norwegian Poetry, Minneapolis, 1966; Grant, Translation Centre, New York, 1975; Grant, government of Iceland, 1976-79; Grant, American Scandinavian Society, 1991; Grant, Translation Fund (Iceland), 1994. Memberships: Writers Union of Iceland; American Literary Translators Association; Reykjavik Drama Critics' Society, Treasurer 1957-59. Address: 30 5th Avenue, New York, NY 10011, USA.

HALLS Geraldine. See: JAY Geraldine Mary.

HALLUM Rosemary, b. 2 Oct, Oakland, California, USA. Writer. Education: BA, UC Berkeley; MA, San Jose State University; PhD, Walden University. General Elementary and Secondary Teaching Credentials. Publications: Action Reading Kit Series, 1973-77; I Like to Read Series, 1982; 30 children's Records including Mother Goose Favorites, Fingerplay Fun, Fingerplays and Footplays, and Square Dancing Made Easy, 1971-95; Multicultural Folktales, Filmstrip set, 1977; Beginnings (book), 1982. Contributions to: Contributing Editor, Iron Man, Muscular Development, Muscle Mag, Total Fitness, Body Fitness, Muscle Training Illustrated, 1982-; Former Columnist: Teacher Magazine; Contributor: Walking, Grand Slam, Black Beat, Clavier, Childhood Education, Flex. Honours: Best of the Year, Filmstrip Award in Language Arts, Previews Magazine; National Educational Film Festival Finalist Award. Memberships: International Food Wine and Travel Writers Association; California Writers Association; National Writers Association; ASCAP; AFM; AFT. Literary Agent: Florence Feiler. Address: 1021 Otis Drive, Alameda, CA 94501, USA.

HALLWORTH Grace Norma Leonie, b. 4 Jan 1928, Trinidad, West Indies. Ex-Librarian; Author; Storyteller. m. Trevor David Hallworth, 31 Oct 1964. Education: Exemptions from Matriculation, 1946; Associate of Library Association, 1956; Diploma in Education, London University, 1976. Literary Appointments: Member of Library Advisory Council for England, 1977-79; Panel Member for Other Award, 1977-80. Publications: Listen to this Story, 1977; Mouth Open Story Jump Out, 1984; Web of Stories, 1990; Cric Crac, 1990; Buy A Penny Ginger, 1994; Essay on Children's Reviewing Journals in A J Walford's Reviews & Reviewing: A Guide. Contributions to: Signal, 1981; Child Education, 1987; International Review of Children's Literature & Librarianship, 1991; Bookmark No 7, First Impressions, Language Matters Special Issue No 3, 1993. Memberships: Chairperson, Society for Storytelling, 1993-94. Address: 18 Mayflower Avenue, Hemel Hempstead, Hertfordshire, HP2 4AE, England.

HALPERIN Mark W, b. 19 Feb 1940, New York City, USA. Professor of English; Writer. m. Barbara Scot, 1 s. Education: BA Physics, Bard College, 1960; MFA, Poetry, University of Iowa, 1966. Publications: Backroads, 1976; A Place Made Fast, 1982; The Measure of Islands, 1990. Contributions to: Poetry, Iowa Review; Shenandom, Senica, Seattle Review. Honours: Glasscock Award, Undergrad Poetry, 1960; US Award, International Poetry Forum, 1976. Address: Rt 4 Box 279A, Ellensburg, WA 98926, USA.

HAM Wayne Albert, b. 1938, USAl. Author. Publications: Enriching Your New Testament Studies, 1965; Man's Living Religion, 1965; Faith and the Arts, 1968; The Call to Covenant, 1969; Publish Glad Tidings, 1970; The First Century Church, 1971; Where Faith and World Meet, 1972; Listening for God's Voice, 1973; On the Growing Edge, 1973; Yesterday's Horizons, 1975; More Than Burnt Offerings, 1978; My Million Faces, 1985. Address: PO Box 1059, Independence, MO 64051, USA.

HAMBRICK-STOWE Charles Edwin, b. 4 Feb 1948, Worcester, Massachusetts, USA. m. Elizabeth Anne Hambrick-Stowe, 11 Sept 1971, 2 s, 1 d. Education: BA, Hamilton College, 1970; MA and MDiv, Pacific School of Religion, 1973; PhD, Boston University Graduate School, 1980. Appointments: Religion Columnist, Evening Sun Newspaper, Carrol County, MD, 1982-85. Publications: The Practice of Piety: Puritan Devotional Disciplines in 17th C New England, 1982; Early New England Meditative Poetry: Anne Bradstreet and Edward Taylor, 1988; Theology and Identity: Traditions Movements and Issues in the United Church of Christ, 1990; A Living Theological Heritage: American Beginnings, 1995; Massachusetts, Militia Companies and Officers of the Lexington Alarm, 1976; Charles G Finney and the Spirit of American Evangelicalism, forthcoming. Contributions to: Church History Christian Century, Japan Christian Quarterly, Lutheran Quarterly, Bulletin of The Congregational Library; Journal of Presbyterian Church History; Book Chapters: Encyclopaedia of Religion in America; Encyclopaedia of the Reformed Faith; Dictionary of Christianity in America. Honours: Jamestown Prize for Early American History, 1980. Memberships: American Historical Association; American Society of Church History; American Academy of Religion; Cliosophic Society (Lancaster, PA). Address: 1101 Davis Drive, Lancaster, PA 17603, USA.

HAMBURGER Michael (Peter Leopold), b. 22 Mar 1924, Berlin, Germany (British citizen). Poet. Education: MA, Christ Church, Oxford, 1948. Appointments: Visiting Professor at American Universities from 1969, University of Essex at Wivenhoe from 1978. Publications: Later Hogarth, 1945; Flowering Cactus: Poems 1942-49, 1950; Poems 1950-51, 1952; The Dual Site, 1957; Weather and Seasons: New Poems, 1963; In Flashlight, 1965; In Massachusetts, 1967; Feeding the Chickadees, 1968; Travelling: Poems 1963-68, 1969; Penguin Modern Poets 14, 1969; Home, 1969; In Memoriam: Friedrich Holderlin, 1970; Travelling I-V, 1972; Ownerless Earth: New and Selected Poems 1950-72, 1973; Conversations with Charwomen, 1973; Babes in the Wood, 1974; Real Estate, 1977; Palinode: A Poet's Progress, 1977; Moralities, 1977; Variations in Suffolk IV, 1980; Variations, 1981; In Suffolk, 1982; Collected Poems 1941-83, 1987; Selected Poems, 1988; Trees, 1988; Roots in The Air, 1991; Collected Poems 1941-1994, 1994; Editions, translations and studies of German literature. Honours include: Institute of Linguists Gold Medal, 1977; DLitt, University of East Anglia at Norwich, 1988; OBE, 1992. Address: c/o John Johnson Ltd,

Clerkenwell House, 45-47 Clerkenwell Green, London, EC1R 0HT, England.

HAMEL-MICHAUD Susanne, b. 10 Aug 1928, Ancienne Lorette, Canada. Former Educator, Nursing School; Writer. m. 19 Dec 1974, 2 sons. Education: Classical, Collge Ursulines Québec, 1947; BSD, Laval University, 1951; Study of the Harp,, Conservatoire Music, Ballet Company, 1944-58; Perfecting, Charity Hospital, USA, 1959-60. Publications: Poetry: Reseda et Capucine, 1986; Hublots, 1987; La Chambre Aux Miroirs, 1989; L'Innommable érectile Voltigeant, 1991; Chant, Echo Du Coeur De Pablo, 1994; 4 essays. Contributions to: Fed Des Femmes, Quebec; Canadian Campus; National Federation of Canadian University Students. Honours: Laureate Winner, Essay, International Competition, Women's Year, 1975. Memberships: SEC; UNEQ; Pour Corporation des diététistes du Qué Québec; Artistes Pour Lapaix. Address: 1585 St Michel, Ancienne Lorette QC, G2E 2V4, Canada.

HAMELIN Claude, b. 25 Aug 1943, Montreal, Quebec, Canada. Poet; Scientist. m. Renée Artinian, 11 Sept 1970, 1 son, 1 daughter. Education: BPed, 1965; BSc, 1970; MSc, 1972; PhD, 1975. Literary Appointments: 40 Recitals done inside and outside Quebec. Publications: Fables des quatre-temps, poetry, 1990; Lueurs froides, poetry, 1991; Nef des fous, poetry, 1992; Roman d'un quartier, novel, 1993; Néant bleu/Nada azul/Blue Nothingness, poetry, 1994; Contributions to: Numerous poems have appeared in various journals, reviews and anthologies inside and outside Quebec. Honours: Jaycee's Five Outstanding Young Canadians, 1983. Memberships: UNEQ; PEN; SEC; SLL; Pres, CSM; Officer, GSC; President, SBM; President, ESM; ASM; NYAS; GSA. Address: 4630 ave Lacombe, Montreal, Quebec, H3W 1R3, Canada.

HAMILL Pete, b. 1935, Brooklyn, New York, USA. m. (1) 2 daughters, (2) Fukiko Aoki. Career: Journalist; Novelist. Publications: A Killing for Christ, 1968; Irrational Ravings, 1971 (Essays); The Drinking Life: A Memoir, 1994; Novels 1973-79: The Gift; Dirty Laundry; Flesh & Blood; The Deadly Piece; Guns of Heaven; Loving Women; Short Stories: The Invisible City; Tokyo Sketches. Contributions to: New York Magazine; Esquire; New York Daily News. Address: c/o New York Magazine, 755 Second Avenue, New York, NY 10017, USA.

HAMILTON Charles, b. 1913, USA. Author; President Hamilton Galleries, New York City. Publications: Cry of the Thunderbird: The American Indian's Own Story, 1950; Men of the Underworld: The Professional Criminal's Own Story, 1952; Braddock's Defeat, 1959; Collecting Autographs and Manuscripts, 1961; Lincoln in Photographs (with L Ostendorf), 1963; The Robot that Helped Make A President, 1965; Scribblers and Scoundrels, 1968; Big Name Hunting (with D Hamilton) , 1973; Collecting Autographs and Manuscripts, 1974; the Book of Autographs, 1978; The Signature of America, 1979; Great Forgers and Famous Fakes, 1980; Auction Madness, 1981; American Autographs, 1983; Leaders of The Third Reich, 1984; In Search of Shakespeare, 1985; The Hitler Diaries: Fakes That Fooled the World. Address: c/o Harvard University Press, 79 Garden Street, Cambridge, MA 02138, USA.

HAMILTON Donald B, b. 24 Mar 1916, Uppsala, Sweden. Writer. m. Kathleen Stick, 12 Sep 1941, dec'd Oct 1989, 2 s, 2 d. Education: BS, University of Chicago, 1938. Publications: Author of 25 novels featuring agent Matt Helm, 1960-93; The Big Country, 1958; 4 western novels 1954-60; 5 mystery novels, 1947-56; On Guns and Hunting, 1970; Cruises with Kathleen, 1980. Contributions to: Articles on photography, guns, hunting, yachting, writing. Honour: WWA Spur, 1967. Memberships: Author's Guild; Mystery Writers of America; Western Writers of America; Outdoor Writer's Association of America. Literary Agent: Brandt and Brandt. Address: PO Box 1141, Old Saybrook, CT 06475, USA.

HAMILTON Eleanor, b. 6 Oct 1909, Portland, Oregon, USA. Marriage Counsellor; Sex Therapist. m. A E Hamilton, 11 Aug 1932, 1 s, 3 d. Education: AB, University of Oregon, 1930; MA, Teachers College, Columbia University, 1939; PhD, Columbia University, 1955. Publications: Partners in Love, 1969; Sex Before Marriage; Sex With Love: A Guide for Young People, 1979; Pleasure Anxiety, 1983; Love and Sex in Old Age, in progress. Contributions to: Modern Bride Magazine; Living and Loving; Science; several newspapers. Honours: American Library Award, 1979; Woman of the Year, Society for Scientific Study of Sex; American Society of Sex Education Counsellors and Therapists; American Society of Journalists &

Authors. Address: 60E Robert Drive, PO Box 765, Inverness, CA 99937, USA.

HAMILTON (Robert) Ian, b. 24 Mar 1938, King's Lynn, Norfolk, England. Lecturer; Poet. Education: BA, Keble College, Oxford, 1962. Appointments: Poetry and Fiction Editor, Times Literary Supplement, 1965-73; Presenter, Bookmark, BBC Television, 1984-87. Publications: Pretending Not to Sleep, 1964; The Visit, 1970; Anniversary and Vigil, 1971; Returning, 1976; Fifty Poems, 1988; A Poetry Chronicle: Essays and Reviews, 1973; The Little Magazines: A Study of Six Editors, 1976; Robert Lowell: A Biography, 1983; In Search of J D Salinger, 1988; Writers in Hollywood 1915-51; Editions of contemporary poetry. Honours include: Eric Gregory Award, 1963; English-Speaking Union Award, 1984. Address: 54 Queen's Road, London SW19, England.

HAMILTON John Maxwell, b. 28 Mar 1947, Evanston, Illinois, USA. Journalist; Lecturer. m. Regina N, 19 Aug 1975, 1 s. Education: BA, Journalism, Marquette University, 1969; MS, Journalism, Boston University, 1974; PhD, American Civilization, George Washington University, 1983. Appointments: The Milwaukee Journal, 1967-69; Marine Corps, 1969-73; Freelance Writer, ABC Radio correspondent, 1973-78; Agency for International Development (political appointee) 1979-81; House Foreign Affairs Committee, 1981-83; World Bank, 1983-84 and 1988-92; Society of Professional Journalists, 1985-87; Visiting Professor, Journalism, Northwestern University, 1985-87; Director, Manship School of Mass Communication, Louisiana State University. Publications: Main Street America and the Third World, 1986, revised, enlarged edition, 1988; Edgar Snow: A Biography, 1988; Entangling Alliances, 1990. Contributions include: Numerous book chapters in: The Nonproliferation Predicament; From Parachialism to Globalism; Numerous newpapers and magazines including: Christian Science Monitor; New York Times; Washington Post; Boston Globe. Honours: Ford Fondation, Germon Marshall Fund, Carnegie Corporation and Benton Foundation Grants, 1985-88; Frank Luther Mott Journalism Research Award, (for Snow Biography), 1989; By-line Award, Marguette University, 1993. Memberships: Society of Professional Journalists; Society of International Development; Director, Board of Directors, Centre for Foreign Journalists. Literary Agent: Peter Shepherd, Harold Ober Associates. Address: 567 LSU Avenue, Baton Rouge, LA 70808, USA.

HAMILTON Mollie. See: **KAY Mary Margaret.**

HAMILTON Morse, b. 16 Aug 1943, Detroit, Michigan, USA. Teacher. m. Sharon Saros, 20 Aug 1966, 3 d. Education: BA, University of Michigan, 1967; MA, 1968; PhD, Columbia University, 1974. Publications: Children's books: My Name is Emily, 1979; Big Sisters are Bad Witches, 1980; Who's Afraid of the Dark?, 1983; How do You Do Mr Birdsteps?, 1983; Effie's House (novel), 1990; Little Sister for Sale, 1992; The Black Hen, 1994; Yellow Blue Bus Means I Love You (novel), 1994. Honours: Hopwood Award, 1967; Woodrow Wilson Dissertation Fellow, 1971; George Bennet Memorial Fellow, 1973. Address: c/o English Department, Tufts University, Medford, MA 02155, USA.

HAMILTON Paul. See: **DENNIS-JONES Harold.**

HAMILTON Priscilla. See: **GELLIS Roberta Leah.**

HAMILTON Virginia, b. 1936. Publications: Zeely, 1967; Time-Ago Tales of Jadhu, 1969; House of Dies Drear, 1969; Illusion & Reality, 1974; Justice & Her Brothers, 1978; W.E.B. DuBois: A Biography, 1982; Anthony Burns, 1987; Dustland, 1989; Bells of Christmas, 1989; Dark Way: Stories from the Spirit World, 1990; Drylongso, 1992; Many Thousand Gone, 1993; Her Stories: African American Folktales, 1995. Honour: Boston Globe/Horn Book Award, 1988.

HAMILTON Wade. See: **FLOREN Lee.**

HAMMICK Georgina, b. 24 May 1939, Hampshire, England. m. 24 Oct 1961, 1 s, 2 d. Education: Educated boarding schools, England and Kenya, Studied Fine Art at Academie Julian, Paris, 1956-57; Salisbury Art School, 1957-59. Publications: People for Lunch, 1987; A Poetry Quintet (poems) 1976; Spoilt, short stories, 1992; Editor, The Virago Book of Love and Loss, 1992. Contributor to: Critical Quarterly; The Listener; Woman's Journal; Ficton magazine etc. Memberships: The Writers Guild. Literary Agent: Rachel Calder, Tessa Sayle Agency.

Address: Bridgewalk House, Brixton Deverill, Warminster, Wiltshire, BA12 7EJ, England.

HAMMOND Jane. See: **POLAND Dorothy Elizabeth Hayward.**

HAMMOND Ralph. See: **HAMMOND INNES Ralph.**

HAMMOND INNES Ralph (Ralph Hammond, Hammond Innes), b. 15 Jul 1913, Horsham, Sussex, England. Author. m. Dorothy Mary Lang, 21 Aug 1937 (dec 3 Feb 1989). Education: Feltonfleet and Cranbrook School. Publications include: Wreckers Must Breathe, 1940; The Trojan Horse, 1940; Attack Alarm, 1941; Dead and Alive, 1946; The Lonely Skier, 1947; The Killer Mine, 1947; Maddon's Rock, 1948; The Blue Ice, 1948; The White South (Book Society Choice), 1949; The Angry Mountain, 1950; Air Bridge, 1951; Campbell's Kingdom (Book Society Choice), 1952; The Strange Land, 1954; The Mary Deare (Book Society Choice), 1956; The Land God Gave to Cain, 1958;Harvest of Journeys (Book Society Choice), 1959; The Doomed Oasis (Book Society Choice), 1960; Atlantic Fury (Book Society Choice), 1962; Scandinavia, 1963; The Strode Venturer, 1965; Sea and Islands (Book Society Choice), 1967; The Conquistadors (Book of The Month and Literary Guild), 1969; Levkas Man, 1971; Golden Soak, 1973; North Star, 1974; The Big Footprints, 1977; The Last Voyage (Cook), 1978; Solomons Seal, 1980; The Black Tide, 1982; High Stand, 1985; Hammond Inne's East Anglia, 1986; Medusa, 1988; Isvik, 1991; Target Antarctica, 1993. Contributions to: Fiction and travel articles in numerous journals. Honours: CBE, 1978; Hon D Litt, Bristol University, 1985. Memberships: PEN; Society of Authors; The Garrick Club. Literary Agent: Curtis Brown. Address: Ayres End, Kersey, Suffolk, IP7 6EB, England.

HAMPSHIRE Susan, b. 12 May 1942. m. 1981, 1 s, 1 d dec. Education: Hampshire School, Knightsbridge. Publications: Susan's Story, 1981; The Maternal Instinct, 1984; Lucy Jane at The Ballet, 1985; Lucy Jane on Television, 1989; Trouble Free Gardening, 1989; Every Letter Counts, 1990; Lucy Jane and The Dancing Competition, 1990; Easy Gardening, 1992; Lucy Jane and The Russian Ballet, 1993. Honours: Hon D, London University, 1984; Hon DLitt, St Andrew's University, 1986; Hon D Ed, Kingston University, 1994. Memberships: Royal Society of Authors. Address: c/o Chatto and Linnit Ltd, Prince of Wales Theatre, Coventry Street, London, W1V 7FE, England.

HAMPSON Norman, b. 8 Apr 1922, Leyland, Lancashire, England. Retired University Professor. m. Jacqueline Gardin, 22 Apr 1948, 2 d. Education: University College Oxford, 1940-41, 1945-47. Publications: La Marine de l'An II, 1959; A Social History of The French Revolution, 1963; The Enlightenment, 1968; The Life and Opinions of Maximilien Robespierre, 1974; Will and Circumstance: Montesquieu, Rousseau and The French Revolution, 1983; Prelude to Terror, 1988; The First European Revolution, 1963; A Concise History of The French Revolution, 1975; Danton, 1978; Saint-Just, 1991. Contributions to: Numerous magazines and journals. Honour: D Litt (Edinburgh), 1989. Memberships: Fellow of The British Academy; Fellow of The Royal Historical Society. Address: 305 Hull Road, York, YO1 3LB, England.

HAMPTON Angeline Agnes (A A Kelly), b. 28 Feb 1924, London, England. Writer. m. George Hughan Hampton, 31 Dec 1944, 1 s, 3 d. Education: BA (Ext) English Honours, University of London, 1965; L Es- L, 1969, D Es- L, 1973, University of Geneva, Switzerland. Publications: Liam O'Flaherty the Storyteller, 1976; Mary Lavin Quiet Rebel, 1980; Joseph Campbell, 1879-1944, Poet and Nationalist, 1988; Editor, The Pillars of The House, 1987; Editor, The Letters of Liam O'Flaherty, 1994; The Wandering Foot, 1994. Contributions to: English Studies: Comparative Education; Eire, Ireland; Hibernia; Linen Hall Review; Geneva News and International Report; Christian. Honours: British Academy Grant, 1987. Memberships: International Association for The Study of Anglo-Irish Literature; Society of Authors; PEN International. Literary Agent: Gregory and Radice, London. Address: Gate Cottage, Pilley Green, Lymington, Hampshire, SO41 5QQ, England.

HAMPTON Christopher (James), b. 26 Jan 1946, Fayal, The Azores. Playwright. m. Laura de Holesch, 1971, 2 d. Education: Schools in Aden and Alexandria, Egypt; Lancing College, Sussex, 1959-63; BA Modern Languages (French and German), 1968; MA, New College, Oxford. Appointment: Resident dramatist, Royal Court Theatre, London, 1968-70. Tales From Hollywood (produced Los Angeles, 1982, London, 1983) London, Faber, 1983; Tartuffe or The Imposter, adaptation of the play by Moliere (produced London, 1983)

London, Faber, 1984; Les Liaisons Dangereuses, adaptation of the novel by Choderlos de Laclos (produced Stratford on Avon, 1985, London, 1986, New York, 1987) London, Faber, 1985; Dangerous Liaisons (film) Faber, 1989; Hedda Gabler and A Doll's House (translations) Faber, 1989; Faith Hope and Charity (translation) Faber, 1989; The Ginger Tree (adaptation of novel by Oswald Wynd) Faber, 1989; White Chameleon, Faber, 1991; The Philanthropist and Other Plays, Faber, 1991; Screenplays include: Beyond The Limit (The Honorary Consul), 1983; The Good Father, 1986; Wolf at The Door, 1986; Dangerous Liaisons, 1988; Various radio and television plays. Membership: Fellow, Royal Society of Literature. Literary Agent: Casarotto Ramsay Limited. Address: National House, 60-66 Wardour Street, London, W1V 3HP, England.

HAMLYN Paul Bertrand, b. 12 Feb 1926, Berlin, Germany. Publisher. m. (1)Eileen Margaret Watson, 1952, divorced 1969, (2)Helen Guest, 1970, 1 s, 1 d. Appointments: Founder, Hamlyn Publishing Group; Formed Books for Pleasure, 1949; Prints for Pleasure, 1960; Records for Pleasure; Golden Pleasure Books, 1961; Music for Pleasure (EMI) 1965; Paul Hamlyn Group acquired by IPC, 1964; joined IPC Board with speical responsibility for all book publishing activities, acquired Butterworth and Co, 1968; Director IPC 1965-70, Chairman, IPC Books, 1965-70; Joint Managing Director, News International Ltd, 1970-71; Founder, Chairman, Octopus Publishing Group, 1971-; Chairman, Octopus Books Ltd 1971-, Mandarin Publishers, Hong Kong, 1971-; Co-founder (with David Frost), and Director, Sundial Publications, 1973-; Co-founder (with Doubleday and Co, New York), and Director, Octopus Books International BV, Netherlands, 1973-; Director, News America, Tigerprint Ltd, News International etc, TV AM, 1981-83; Co-Chairman Conran Octopus Ltd, 1983-; Chairman, Heinemann Group of Publishers Lltd, 1985-; Hamlyn Publishing Group, 1986-; Board Director, International Plc, Chairman, Reed International Books, 1987-; Chancellor of Thames Valley University, 1993-; Chairman, Book Club Associates, 1993; Director, Reed Elsevier PLC, 1993-. Honours: University of Keele, 1988; University of Warwick, 1991. Address: Michelin House, 81 Fulham Road, London, SW3 56RB, England.

HAN Suyin, b. 12 Sept 1917, Sinyang Honan Province, China. Novelist; Medical Doctor. Education: Yenching University, Beijing, China; Brussels University, Belgium; London University, Royal Free Hospital, London. Publications: A Many Splendoured Thing, 1952; The Mountain is Young, 1958; The Crippled Tree, 1965; My House Has Two Doors,1980; Till Morning Comes, 1982; A Share of Loving, 1987; Lhassa The Open City, 1977; The Enchantress, 1985; Wind in the Tower; Les Cent Fleurs; Chinese Painting Today; La Chine Aux Mille Visages (Photography); Chine Terre, Eau et Hommes (Photography); Han Suyin's China, 1987; Film Scripts: Man's Fate; The Marvellous Mongolian; Cast the Same Shadow, 1963. Contributions inlcude: New York Times; Life Holiday; New Yorker; Medical Journals. Honours: Bancaralla Prize, Italy, 1956; McGill Beatty Prize, Canada, 1968; Nutting Prize, Canada, 1980; Woman Reader Prize, Italy, 1983. Address: c/o Jonathan Cape, 32 Bedford Square, London, WC1, England.

HANBURY-TENISON Robin, b. 1936, United Kingdom. Writer; Farmer. Publications: The Rough and The Smooth, exploration, 1969; A Question of Survival for The Indians of Brazil, 1973; A Pattern of Peoples: A Journey Among The Tribes of the Outer Indonesian Islands, 1975; Mulu: The Rain Forest, 1980; The Aborigines of The Amazon Rain Forest: The Yanomami, 1982; Worlds Apart, autobiography, 1984; White Horses Over France, 1985; A Ride Along the Great Wall, 1987; Fragile Eden: A Ride Through New Zealand, 1989; Spanish Pilgrimage: A Canter to St James, 1990; The Oxford Book of Exploration, 1993. Honours: OBE, 1981; DRE, 1992. Memberships: President, Survival International, 1969-; Council Member, Royal Geographical Society, 1968-82; Gold Medalist, Royal Geographical Society, 1979; Vice President, Royal Geographical Society, 1982-86. Address: Cabilla Manor, Cardinham, Bodmin, Cornwall, PL30 4DW, England.

HANCOCK Geoffrey White, b. 14 Apr 1946, New Westminster, Canada. Writer; Literary Journalist. m. Gay Allison, 6 Aug 1983, 1 daughter. Education: BFA, 1973; MFA, University of British Columbia, 1975. Literary Appointments: Editor in Chief, Canadian Fiction Magazine, 1975; Consulting editor, Canadian Author and Bookman, 1978; Fiction editor, Cross-Canada Writers Quarterly, 1980; Literary consultant, CBC Radio, 1980. Publications: Magic Realism, 1980; Illusion: fables fantasies and metafictions, 1983; Metavisions, 1983; Shoes and Shit: Stories for Pedestrians, 1984, published in Canada,

1990; Moving Off the Map: From Story to fiction, 1986; Invisible Fictions: Contemporary Stories from Quebec, 1987; Canadian Writers at Work: Interviews, 1987; Singularities, 1990; Fast Travelling, 1995. Contributions to: Toronto Star; Writer's Quarterly; Canadian Author and Bookman; Books In Canada; Canadian Forum. Honour: Fiona Mee Award for Literary Journalism, 1979. Memberships: Periodical Writers of Canada; Director Candian Fiction Magazine, Box No 1061, Kingston, Ontario K7L 4Y5, Canada.

HANDKE Peter, b. 6 Dec 1942, Griffen, Carinthia (Austrian citizen). Playwright; Novelist. Education: University of Graz, 1961-65. Publications: Offending the Audience, 1966, 1970; Self-Accusation, 1966, 1970; Prophecy, 1966, 1972; Calling for Help, 1967, 1972; Kaspar, 1968; My Foot My Tutor, 1969; Quodlibet, 1970; The Ride Across Lake Constance, 1971; They Are Dying Out, 1974; Über die Dorfer, 1982; The Long Way Round, 1989; Das Spiel vom Fragen, 1989; Screenplays; Stories: The Goalkeeper's Fear of the Penalty Kick, 1970; Short Letter, Long Farewell, 1974; Sorrow Beyond Dreams, 1975; A Moment of True Feeling, 1975; The Left-Handed Woman, 1976; Slow Homecoming, 1979; The Lesson of Mont Sainte Victoire, 1980; Across, 1983, 1986; Repetition, 1986; Absence, 1987, 1990; The Afternoon of a Writer, 1987; Also: The Innerworld of the Outerworld of the Innerworld (verse), 1974; Nonsense and Happiness, 1974; The Weight of the World, 1977, 1984; Versuch über die Jukebox, 1990; Translations include A Winter's Tale by Shakespeare. Honours include: Salzburg Literary Prize, 1986.

HANDLEY Graham Roderick, b. 1926, England. Writer. Appointments: Head of English Department, Borehamwood Grammar School, Hertfordshire, 1957-62, and Hatfield School, Hertfordshire, 1962-67; Senior Lecturer, 1967-76 and Principal Lecturer in English, 1967-80, College of All Saints, Tottenham, London; Research Officer in English,Birbeck College, University of London, 1981-83. Publications Include: An Informal History of the College of All Saints, 1978; Dickens' Little Dorrit, 1979; (with Stanley King) O'Casey's Shadow of a Gunman and The Plough and the Stars, 1980; (with Stanley King) Graham Greene's The Quiet American, 1980; (with Barbara Handley) Wilkie Collins' The Woman in White, 1980; (ed) Short Stories on Sport, 1980; The Metaphysical Poets, 1981; (ed) Wuthering Heights, 1982; (ed) Daniel Deronda by George Eliot, 1984; Thackeray's Vanity Fair, 1985; Harper Lee's To Kill A Mockingbird, 1985; (ed) The Mill on The Floss by George Eliot, 1985; Shakespeare's Macbeth, 1985; Shakespeare's Twelfth Night, 1985; George Eliot's Silas Marner, 1985; George Eliot's Middlemarch, 1985; Shakespeare's As You Like It, 1985; Hardy's Tess of the D'Urbervilles, 1986; Wycherley's The Country Wife, 1986; Chaucer's The Pardoner's Tale, 1986; Trollope's Barchester Towers, 1987; Hartley's The Go-Between, 1987; Hardy's The Woodlanders, 1987; Fielding's Tome Jones, 1987. Address: Glasgow Stud Farm, Crews Hill, Enfield, Middlesex, England.

HANDLIN Oscar, b. 1915. m. Lilian. Appointments: Professor Emeritus of History, Harvard University. Publications include: Over 2 dozen books including: Boston's Immigrants, 1940; The Uprooted, 1951; Truth in History, 1979; Liberty & Equality, 1920-1994 (with Lilian Handlin), 1994. Honours: J H Dunning Prize, American Historical Association, 1941; Pulitzer Prize, 1951. Address: 18 Agassiz Street, Cambridge, MA 02140, USA.

HANKIN Cherry Anne, b. 30 Sep 1937, Nelson, New Zealand. University Professor. m. John Charles Garrett, 18 May 1981. Education: MA, University of New Zealand, 1959; PhD, University of California, Berkeley, 1971. Appointments: The University of Canterbury, Christchurch, New Zealand, 1971-; Chief Fiction Judge, New Zealand Department of Internal Affairs Literary Awards, 1975; Judge, Katherine Mansfield Centennial Award, 1988. Publications: Katherine Mansfield and Her Confessional Stories; The Letters of John Middleton Murray to Katherine Mansfield; Letters Between John Middleton Murray and Katherine Mansfield; Critical Essays on The New Zealand Novel; Life in A Young Colony: Selections from Early New Zealand Writing; Critical Essays on The New Zealand Short Story. Contributions to: Language as Theme in Janet Frame's, Owls Do Cry; New Zealand Women Novelists: Their Attitudes towards Life in A Developing Society; Fantasy and The Sense of An Ending in The Work of Katherine Mansfield. Honours: Advanced Graduate Travelling Fellowship in English, University of California, Berkeley, 1969. Memberships: Board of Trustees, Christchurch Theatre Trust. Address: 5 Stratford Street, Christchurch 1, New Zealand.

HANKINSON Alan, b. 25 May 1926, Gatley, Cheshire, England. Freelance Writer. m. Roberta Lorna Gibson, 15 Dec 1951, div 1985, 1 s. Education: MA History, Magdalen College, Oxford, 1949. Publications: The First Tigers, 1972; Camera on The Crags, 1975; The Mountain Men, 1977; Man of Wars, 1982; The Blue Box, 1983; The Regatta Men, 1988; A Century on The Crags, 1988; Coleridge Walks The Fells, 1991. Contributions to: Cumbria Life. Honours: BP Arts Journalism, runner up, 1991; Portico Prize, 1991; Cumbria Book of The Year, 1992. Address: 30 Skiddaw Street, Keswick, Cumbria, CA12 4BY, England.

HANKLA (Bonnie) Susan, b. 22 Sept 1951, Roanoke, Virginia, USA. Writer; Teacher; Poet-in-the-Schools. m. Jack Glover, 22 Apr 1981. Education: BA, Hollins College; MA, Creative Writing, Brown University. Appointments: Fellow, Virginia Centre for the Creative Arts, Sweet Briar, 1985. Publications: Mistral for Daddy and Van Gogh, 1976; I Am Running Home, 1979; Co-editor, Sermons in Paint, 1985. Contributions to: Permanent Press; Artemis; Boys and Girls Grow Up; The Burning Deck Anthology; Film Journal; Gargoyle; Hollins Critic; Intro 5; Laurel Review; New Virginia Review; Open Places; Poetry Northwest; Richmond Arts Magazine; Richmond Quarterly Review; Southern Poetry Review; Fiction; Commonwealth; Michigan Quarterly Review; American Signatures. Honours: Nancy Thorpe Memorial Prize for Poetry, Hollins College, 1973; Finalist, Virginia Prize for Fiction, 1985, 1987. Address: 1109 West Avenue, Richmond, VA 23220, USA.

HANKLA Cathy, b. 20 Mar 1958, Richlands, Virginia, USA. Professor. Education: BA, 1980, MA, Hollius College, 1982. Appointments: Hollius College, 1982-; Lecturer, Theatre Arts, 1982-83; Lecturer, English, 1983-86; Assistant Professor, 1986-; Associate Professor, 1993-; Washington & Lee University, 1989-91. Publications: A Blue Moon in Poorwater, 1988; Afterimages, 1991; Learning the Mother Tongue, 1987; Phenomena, 1983: Cool Water, 1992. Contributions to: poetry in New Virginia Review; stories in Mondo Barbie, That's What I like About the South, Mondo Elvis; College English; The World and I; Chicago Tribune Magazine. Honours: PEN Syndicated Fiction Prize. Memberships: Authors Guild: Associated Writing Programs: Academy of American Poets; PEN America. Address: Box 9673, Hollins College, VA 24020, USA

HANLEY Clifford (Henry Calvin), b. 28 Oct 1922, Glasgow, Scotland. Writer. m. Anna Clark, 10 Jan 1948, 1 s, 2 d. Education: Eastbank Academy, Glasgow. Appointments: Professor of Creative Writing, York University, Toronto, 1979. Publications include: Dancing in The Streets, 1958; The Taste of Too Much, 1960; Nothing But The Best, 1964; Prissy, 1978; The Scots, 1980; Another Street Another Dance, 1983; Plays: The Durable Element, 1961; Oh For an Island, 1966; Dick McWhittie, 1967; Jack O'The Cudgel, 1969; Oh Glorious Jubilee, 1970; The Clyde Moralities, 1972. Contributions to: Numerous articles in magazines and journals. Honour: Hollywood Oscar for Best Foriegn Documentary, Seawards The Great Ships, of which Mr Hanley wrote the commentary, 1960. Memberships: Ours Club, Glasgow, President; PEN, Scottish President, 1975. Address: 35 Hamilton Drive, Glasgow, Scotland.

HANLEY Gerald (Anthony), b. 17 Feb 1916, Ireland. Author; Playwright. Publications: Monsoon Victory, 1946; The Consul at Sunset, 1951; The Year of The Lion, 1954; Drinkers of Darkness, 1955; Without Love, 1957; The Journey Homeward, 1961; Gilligan's Last Elephant, 1962; A Voice From The Top (radio play), 1962; Gandhi (screenplay), 1964; The Blue Max (screenplay), 1966; See You in Yasukuni, 1970; Warriors and Strangers (travel), 1971; Noble Descents, 1982. Address: c/o Gillon Aitken, 17 S Eaton Place, London, WC1W 9ER, England.

HANNAH Barry, b. 1942, USA. Author. Appointments Include: Writer-in-Residence, Middlebury College, Vermont, 1974-75; Writer for Director Robert Altman, Hollywood, 1980; Writer-in-Residence, University of Iowa, 1981, University of Mississippi, Oxford, 1982, 1984, 1985. Publications: Geronimo Rex (novel), 1972; Nightwatchmen (novel), 1973; Airships (short stories), 1978; Ray (novel), 1981; Black Butterfly (short stories), 1982; The Tennis Handsome (novel) 1983; Power and Light (novel), 1983; Captain Maximus (short stories), 1985.

HANNON Brian Owens, b. 20 Apr 1959, Florida, USA. Administrative Co-Ordinator of Contemporary Arts Center. Education: BA, Florida State University, 1982; MA, Creative Writing, University of Southern Mississippi, 1984. Appointments: Served, Advisory Panel, Louisiana Division of the Arts, Literature Panel, 1987. Publication: The

Deep End of Dogtown, 1986. Honours: Story Dogs in Texas, nominated, Pushcart Prize XII, Best of the Small Presses. Memberships: President, Tallahassee Writers Guild, 1982; Associated Writing Programmes. Address: 1231 Decatur St, 3rd Floor, New Orleans, LA 70116, USA.

HANNON Ezra. See: **LOMBINO Salvatore A.**

HANSEN Ann Natalie, b. 15 Sep 1927, Newark, Ohio, USA. Historian. Education: BA, College of St Mary of the Springs, 1948; MA, Ohio State University, 1950; BLitt, Somerville College, Oxford University, 1963. Appointments: Editor, Martha Kinney Cooper Ohiana Library Association, 1951-53; Staff, The Columbus Dispatch, 1954-58. Publications: Westward the Winds: Being Some of the Main Currents of Life in Ohio 1788-1873, 1974; So You're Going Abroad, How to Do it, 1984; The English Origins of the "Mary & John" Passengers, 1985; The Dorchester Group: Puritanism and Revolution, 1987; Etienne Francois Duc de Choseul, New Catholic Encyclopedia. Contributions to: American Neptune; New England Quarterly; Wisconsin Magazine of History: Timeline; Silver Magazine. Honours: Honourable Mention, Lyrics, National League of American Pen Women, 1976; Recipient, First Distinguished Alumni Award, Ohio Dominican College (formerly College of St Mary of The Springs), 1981. Memberships: National League of American Pen Women, Past President, Columbus Branch. Address: 2341 Brixton Road, Columbus, OH 43221, USA.

HANSEN Joseph (Rose Brock, Hames Colton, James Coulton), b. 1923, USA. Author. Publications: Lost on Twilight Road (as James Colton), 1964; Strange Marriage (as James Colton), 1965; The Corrupter and Other Stories (as James Colton), 1968; Known Homosexual (as James Colton), 1968, (as Stranger to Himself, 1978 and Pretty Boy Dead, 1984); Cocksure (as James Colton), 1969; Hang-up (as James Colton), 1969; Gard (as James Colton), 1969; Fadeout (mystery), 1970; Tarn House (as Rose Brock), 1971; The Outward Side (as James Colton), 1971; Todd (as James Colton), 1971; Death Claims (mystery), 1973; Longleaf (as Rose Brock, 1974; Troublemaker (mystery), 1975; One Foot in The Boat (verse), 1977; The Man Everybody Was Afraid Of (mystery), 1978; Skinflick (mystery), 1979; The Dog and Other Stories, 1979; A Smile in His Lifetime (novel), 1981; Gravedigger (mystery), 1982; Backtrack (mystery), 1982; Job's Year (novel), 1983; Brandsetter and Other (short stories), 1984; Steps Going Down (mystery), 1985; The Little Dog Laughed, 1986; Early Graves, 1987; Bohannon's Book (five mysteries), 1988; Obedience (mystery), 1988; The Boy Who Was Buried This Morning (mystery), 1990; A Country of Old Men (mystery), 1991. Address: 2638 Cullen Street, Los Angeles, CA 90034, USA.

HANSON William Stewart, b. 22 Jan 1950, Doncaster, Yorkshire, England. University Lecturer; Archaeologist. m. Lesley Macinnes. Education: BA Ancient History/Archaeology, 1972, PhD Archaeology, 1982, Manchester. Publications: Rome's North-West Frontier: The Antonine Wall, 1983; Agricola and The Conquest of The North, 1987; Scottish Archaeology: New Perceptions (co-editor), 1991. Contributions to: Major academic archaeological and antiquarian journals. Memberships: President, Council for Scottish Archaeology; Fellow, Societies of Antiquaries of London and Scotland; Executive Committee, Council for British Archaeology. Address: 4 Victoria Road, Stirling, Scotland.

HARBINSON Robert. See: **HARBINSON-BRYANS Robert.**

HARBINSON William Allen, b. 9 Sep 1941, Belfast, Northern Ireland. Writer. m. Ursula Elizabeth Mayer, 3 Nov 1969, 1 s, 1 d. Education: Belfast College of Technology, 1956-57; Liverpool College of Building, 1958-61. Publications: Genesis; Inception; Revelation; Otherworld; The Lodestone; Dream Maker; The Light of Eden; None But The Damned; Knock; Strykers Kingdom; Elvis Presley: An Illustrated Biography; Charles Bronson; George C Scott; Evita Peron; Fiction: Projekt Saucer: Book 1, Inception, Book 2, Phoenix, Book 3, Genesis, Book 4, Millennium, 1994-95; Biography: Growing Up With The Memphis Flash, 1994. Contributions to: Books and Bookmen; The Lady; 19; Lookout; The Unexplained; Disc; Goldmine; Club International; Mayfair. Memberships: PEN; Society of Authors; Institute of Journalists; British Film Institute. Literary Agent: MBA, London; Writers House, New York, USA. Address: 44 Rosebery Road, Muswell Hill, London, N10 2LJ, England.

HARBINSON-BRYANS Robert (Robin Bryans, Donald Cameron, Robert Harbinson), b. 1928, United Kingdom. Author.

Publications: Gateway to The Khyber, 1959; Madeira, 1959; Summer Saga, 1960; No Surrender (as Robert Harbinson), 1960; Song of Erne (as R Harbinson), 1960; Up Spake the Cabin Boy (as R Harbinson), 1961; Danish Episode, 1961; Tattoo Lily (as R Harbinson), 1962; Fanfare for Brazil, 1962; The Protégé (as R Harbinson), 1963; The Azores, 1963; Ulster, 1964; Lucio, 1964; Malta and Gozo, 1966; The Field of Sighing (as Donald Cameron), 1966; Trinidad and Tobago, 1967; Faber Best True Adventure Stories (editor), 1967; Sons of El Dorado, 1968; Crete,1969; Songs Out of Oriel (as R Harbinson); The Dust Has Never Settled, 1992; Let The Petals Fall, 1993; Checkmate, 1994. Address: 58 Argyle Road, London, W13 8AA, England.

HARBOTTLE Michael Neale, b. 7 Feb 1917, Littlehampton, Sussex, England. Army. m. (1) 1 Aug 1940, div 1 s, 1 d, (2) Eirwen Helen Simonds, 5 Aug 1972. Publications: The Impartial Soldier, 1970; Blue Berets, 1971; Knaves of Diamonds, 1976; The Thin Blue Line (co-author), 1974; The Peace Keepers Handbook (compiler), 1978; Ten Questions Answered, 1983; Reflections on Security in The Nuclear Age, 1988; What is Proper Soldiering, 1991. Contributions to: Building and Social Housing Foundation; Columbia University Press; Princeton University Press; Massachusetts Institute of Technology Press; Books: Building Peace in The Middle East; Challenge for Stakes and Civil Society; Voices on The Threshold of Tomorrow. Honours: OBE, 1960; Doctor of Philosophy, The Open International University for Complementary Medicines, 1994. Memberships: Royal Institute for International Affairs, United Kingdom; International Council, Center for Conflict Analysis and Resolution, George Mason University, Washington DC, USA. Address: 9 West Street, Chipping Norton, Oxon, OX7 5LH, England.

HARCOURT Geoffrey Colin, b. 27 Jun 1931, Australia. University Teacher. m. Joan Margaret Bartrop, 30 Jul 1955, 2 s, 2 d. Education: B Com, Hons, 1954, M Com, 1956, University of Melbourne; PhD, 1960, Litt D, Cambridge University, 1988. Publications include: Some Cambridge Controversies in The Theory of Capital, 1972 (Italy, 1973, Poland, 1975, Spain, 1975, Japan, 1980); The Social Science Imperialists, Selected Essays G C Harcourt, 1982; Controversies in Political Economy, Selected Essays by G C Harcourt, 1986; With R H Parker and G Whittington, editors, Readings in The Concept and Measurement of Income, 2nd edition, 1986; Editor, Keynes and His Contemporaries: The Sixth and Centennial Keynes Seminar held in the University of Kent at Canterbury 1983, 1985; Editor, The Microeconomic Foundations of Macroeconomics, 1977; On Political Economists and Modern Political Economy, Selected Essays of G C Harcourt, 1992; Post-Keynesian Essays in Biography, Portraits of Twentieth Century Political Economists, 1993; With Mauro Baranzini, editors, The Dynamics of The Wealth of Nations, Essays in Honour of Luigi Pasinetti, 1993; With Alessandro Ronlaglia and Robin Rowley, editors, Income and Employment in Theory and Practice, 1994. Contributor to: Over 130 articles in learned journals and/or chapters in books. Honours: Fellow of the Academy of The Social Sciences in Australia (FASSA), 1971; Professor Emeritus, University of Adelaide, 1988; Reader in The History of Economic Theory, Cambridge University, 1990; President, Jesus College, Cambridge, 1988-89, 1990-92. Memberships: Royal Economic Society, Council Member, 1990; Economic Society of Australia and New Zealand, President, 1974-77; Officer in the General Division of the Order of Australia, 1994. Address: Jesus College, Cambridge, CB5 8BL, England.

HARCOURT Palma. Author. Publications: Climate for Conspiracy, 1974; A Fair Exchange, 1975; Dance for Diplomats, 1976; At High Risk, 1977; Agents of Influence, 1978; A Sleep of Spies, 1979; Tomorrow's Treason, 1980; A Turn of Traitors, 1981; The Twisted Tree, 1982; Shadows of Doubt, 1983; The Distant Stranger, 1984; A Cloud of Doves, 1985; A Matter of Conscience, 1986; Limited Options, 1987; Clash of Loyalties, 1988; Cover for A Traitor, 1989; Double Deceit, 1990; The Reluctant Defector, 1991; Cue For Conspiracy, 1992; Bitter Betrayal, 1993; The Vermont Myth, 1994. Address: c/o Murray Pollinger, Literary Agent, 222 Old Brompton Road, London, SW5 0BZ, England.

HARDCASTLE Michael (David Clark), b. 6 Feb 1933, Huddersfield, England. Author. m. Barbara Ellis Shepherd, 30 Aug 1979, 4 d. Literary Appointment: Literary Editor, Bristol Evening Post, 1960-65. Publications: Author of over 100 children's books, 1966-; One Kick, 1986; James and The TV Star, 1986; Mascot, 1987; Quake, 1988; The Green Machine, 1989; Walking The Goldfish, 1990; Penalty, 1990; Advantage Miss Jackson, 1991; Dog Bites Goalie, 1993; One Good Horse, 1993; Soccer Captain, 1994; Puzzle, 1995; Please Come Home,

1995. Contributions to: Numerous articles in magazines and journals. Honour: MBE, 1988. Memberships: Federation of Children's Book Groups, National Chair, 1989-90, Vice-Chair, 1988-89, Newsletter Editor, 1985-89; Society of Authors. Address: 17 Molescroft Park, Beverley, East Yorkshire, HU17 7EB, England.

HARDEN Blaine, b. 4 Apr 1952, Washington State, USA. Journalist. Education: BA, Philosophy and Political Science, Gonzaga University, Spokane, WA, 1974; MA, Journalism, Syracuse University, NY, 1976. Appointments: East Europe Correspondent, Washington Post, 1989-93; Africa Correspondent, Washington Post, 1985-89. Publications: Africa: Dispatches from a Fragile Continent, 1990. Contributions to: Washington Post. Honours: Livingston Award for Young Journalists, 1986; America Society for Newspaper Editors, Feature Writing, 1987; Pen's Martha Albrand Citation for First Book of Non-fiction, 1991; Ernie Pyle Award for Human Interest Reporting, 1993. Literary Agent: Raphael Sagalyn. Address: c/o Foreign Desk, The Washington Post, 1150 15th St NW, Washington DC 20071, USA.

HARDIE Katherine Melissa, (Melissa Hardie), b. 20 Apr 1939, Houston, Texas, USA. Writer; Publisher; Collector. m.(1) J W Woelfel, 1958, 2 daughters; (2)M C Hardie, 1974; (3) Philip Graham Budden, 8 Jan 1986. Education: BA, English Language & Litterature, Boston University, 1961; SRN, St Thomas Hospital, England, 1969; PhD, Social Science, Edinburgh University, 1980. Literary Appointments: Publisher, The Patten Press, 1981-; Director, The Jamieson Library of Women's History, 1986-. Publications: Understanding Ageing, Facing Common Family Problems, 1978; Nursing Auxiliaries in Health Care, 1978; In Time & Place, Lamorna, Life of E Lamorna Kerr, 1990; Editor, A Mere Interlude, Some Literary Visitors to Lyonnesse, 1992; One Hundred Years at Newlyn, Diary of a Gallery (editor), 1995. Contributions to: Nursing Times; International Hospitals; Social Work Today; Health & Society Service Journal. Honours: Winston Churchill Travelling Fellow, 1975; YWCA Woman of the West, 1994. Memberships: Thomas Hardy Society; West Country Writers Association; Private Libraries Association. Address: The Old Post Office, New Mill, Penzance, TR29 4XN, England.

HARDIE Melissa. See: **HARDIE Katherine Melissa.**

HARDIN Clement. See: **NEWTON D(wight) B(ennett).**

HARDING Christopher Philip, b. 4 Aug 1944, Somerset, England. Retired. Education: SFPE, 1977; DPhE, 1978; FIBA, 1985; AAABI, 1986; MCC, 1988; PhD, 1988; SRFP, 1990; Honorary Doctor of Commercial Science, London Institute of Applied Research, 1990; MP, The International Pariament for Safety & Peace, 1991; Diplome de membre d'honneur, International Fine Arts Council, 1991; Doctorate, International University, Institute of Management, Bombay, India, 1991. Appointments: CIAE, 1969-83; Good News, 1983-86; Eltran, 1985-87; Computer Consultants, 1987-88; Point One Advisory Group Inc, 1988-90. Publications: Co-author, The Ultimate IQ Book. Contributions to: Buros Mental Measurements Yearbook, 1978, 1985; Tests in Print, 1983, 1994; Tests of the Test Corporation of America, 1983, 1984; Tests Supplement, 1984, 1987; Test Critiques, 1985. Honours include: Certificate, Poetic Achievement, American Poetry Association, 1989; Awarded, International Biographical Centre Medal, England, 1990; Commemorative Medal of Honour, Am Biographical Institute, 1991; Medal, Largest Fund Raiser, Foundation Ethiopia Economia, 1991; Twenty Five Year Achievement Award, American Biographical Institute, 1992; Decree of Merit, International Biographical Centre, England, 1993; 20th Century Achievement Award, American Biographical Institute, 1993. Memberships include: International & Australian MENSA, 1966-; INTERTEL, 1971-; International Society for Philosophical Enquiry, 1974-; The Mega Society, 1982-; Rockhampton Leagues Club, 1985-; The Triple Nine Society, 1992-; Frenchville Sports Club Ltd, 1993-; M E Syndrome Society, Queensland, 1994-. Address: PO Box 5271, The Mail Centre, North Rockhampton, Queensland 4702, Australia.

HARDING Cole. See: **KRAUZER Steven M.**

HARDING George. See: **RAUBENHEIMER George H.**

HARDING Karl Gunnar, b. 11 June 1940, Sundsvalla, Sweden. Poet; Translator; Critic; Editor. m. Ann Charlotte Jending, September 1966, 1 son, 3 daughters. Education: BA, University of Uppsala, 1967. Appointments: Editor, FIB: Lyrikklabb and Magazine, Lyrikvannen, 1971-74; Poetry Critic, Expressen, Daily Paper, 1970-88; Editor, Artes Magazine, 1989. Publications: Blommortil James Dean, 1969; Ballander, 1975; Starnberger See, 1977; Stjarndykaren, 1987; Mitt Vinterland, 1991; Vortex, 1990; Kreol, 1991. Contributions to: Evergreen Review; Ambit. Honours: Lifetime Scholarship, Swedish Writer's Union; Several Poetry Prizes. Memberships: Vice President, Swedish PEN, 1975-78; Swedish Writer's Union; Swedish Bunk Johnson Society. Address: Vasterled 206, S-16142, Bromma, Sweden.

HARDING Lee (John), b. 1937, Australia. Writer of Science Fiction and Children's Fiction. Appointments: Freelance Writer, SF Novels, Short Stories, Radio Plays, Freelance Photographer, 1953-70. Publications: The Fallen Spacemen (juvenile), 1973, 1980; A World of Shadows, 1975; Future Sanctuary, 1976; The Children of Atlantis (juvenile), 1976; The Frozen Sky (juvenile), 1976; Return to Tomorrow (juvenile), 1976; Beyond Tomorrow: An Anthology of Modern Science Fiction, 1976; The Altered I: An Encounter with Science Fiction, 1976, 1978; The Weeping Sky, 1977; Rooms of Paradise, 1978; Displaced Person (in United States of America as Misplaced Persons), 1979; The Web of Time (juvenile), 1979; Waiting for the End of the World (juvenile), 1983; Born a Number: Autobiography, 1986.

HARDING Matt. See: **FLOREN Lee.**

HARDING Matthew Whitman. See: **FLOREN Lee.**

HARDWICK Elizabeth, Novelist; Essayist; Co-Founder & Advisory Editor, New York Review of Books. Publications include: Sleepless Nights; Bartleby in Manhattan & Other Essays; Seduction & Betrayal. Contributions include: New York Review of Books. Honour: Gold Medal, American Academy & Institute of Arts & Letters, 1993. Address: 15 West 67th Street, New York, NY 10027, USA.

HARDWICK Mollie (Mary Atkinson), British. Writer; Author. Appointments: Announcer, 1943-46; Producer and Script Editor, Drama Department. Publications Include: (with Michael Hardwick), The Sherlock Holmes Companion, 1962; (with M Hardwick), The Man Who Was Sherlock Holmes, 1964; (with M Hardwick), Four Sherlock Holmes Plays, 1964; (with M Hardwick), The Charles Dickens Companion, 1965; (compiler), Stories from Dickens, 1967; (with M Hardwick), Alfred Deller: A Singularity of Voice, 1968, 1980; (with M Hardwick) Writers' Houses, 1968; Emma, Lady Hamilton, 1969; (with M Hardwick), Dickens's England, 1970; (with M Hardwick), Plays from Dickens, 1970; Mrs Dizzy, 1972; (with M Hardwick), The Charles Dickens Encyclopedia, 1973; Upstairs Downstairs: Sarah's Story, 1973; (with M Hardwick), The Bernard Shaw Companion, 1974; (with M Hardwick), The Charles Dickens Quiz Book, 1974; Upstairs Downstairs: The War to End Wars, 1975; (with M Hardwick), The Upstairs, Downstairs Omnibus, 1975; World of Upstairs Downstairs, 1976; Beauty's Daughter, 1976; The Duchess of Duke Street: The Golden Years, 1976; (with M Hardwick), The Turning, 1977; Charlie Is My Darling, 1977; The Atkinson Heritage, 1978; The Atkinson Heritage: Sisters in Love, 1979; Thomas and Sarah, 1979; Lovers Meeting, 1979; Willowood, 1980; The Atkinson Heritage: Dove's Nest, 1980; Juliet Bravo 1, 1980; Juliet Bravo 2, 1980; The Shakespeare Girl, 1983; By the Sword Divided, 1983; The Merrymaid, 1984; Girl With A Crystal Dove, 1985; Malice Domestic, 1986; Parson's Pleasure, 1987.

HARDY Barbara (Gladys). Writer (Literature); Lecturer. Appointments: Emeritus Professor, University of London, Birkbeck College; Honorary Professor, University College of Wales, Swansea. Publications: The Novels of George Eliot: A Study in Form, 1959; Wuthering Heights, 1963; The Appropriate Form: An Essay on the Novel, 1964; Jane Eyre, 1964; Middlemarch: Critical Approaches to the Novel, 1967; Daniel Deronda, by George Eliot (ed), 1967; Charles Dickens: The Later Novels, 1968; Critical Essays on George Eliot, 1970; The Moral Art of Dickens, 1970; The Exposure of Luxury: Radical Themes in Thackeray, 1972; The Trumpet Major by Thomas Hardy (ed), 1974; Tellers and Listeners: The Narrative Imagination, 1975; A Laodicean by Hardy (ed), 1975; A Reading of Jane Austen, 1976; The Advantage of Lyric: Essays on Feeling in Poetry, 1976; Particularities: Readings in George Eliot, 1983; Forms of Feeling in Victorian Fiction, 1985; Narrators and Novelists, 1989. Memberships: Hon Member, MLA; Fellow, Welsh Academy; Vice President, George Eliot Fellowship, Thomas Hardy Society. Address: Birkbeck College, Malet Street, London, WC1E 7HX, England.

HARDY Frank, b. 21 Mar 1917, Southern Cross, Victoria, Australia. Novelist. Appointments: President, Realist Writers Group, Melbourne, Sydney, 1954-74; Co Founder, Australian Society of

Authors, Sydney, 1968-74; President, Carringbush Writers, Melbourne, 1980-83. Publications: Power Without Glory, 1962; The Four Legged Lottery, 1958; The Outcasts of Follgarah, 1971; Who Shot George Kirkland? 1981; Warrant of Distress, 1983; The Obsession of Oscar Oswald, 1983; Short Stories The Loser Now Will be Later to Win, 1985; Hardys People, 1986; Plays, Black Diamonds, 1956; The Ringbolter, 1964; Who Was Harry Larsen, 1985; Faces in the Street: An Epic Drama, 1990; You Nearly Had That time and Other Cricket Stories, with Fred Trueman, 1978. Address: 9/76 Elizabeth Bay Road, Elizabeth Bay, NSW 2011, Australia.

HARDY Laura. See: **HOLLAND Sheila.**

HARE David, b. 1947. Playwright. Appointments Include: Literary Manager, 1969-70, Resident Dramatist, 1970-71, Royal Court Theatre, London; Resident Dramatist, Nottingham Playhouse, 1973; Associate Director, National Theatre, 1984-. Publications: Slag, 1970; Lay By (with Others), 1971; The Great Exhibition, 1972; Brassneck (with Howard Brenton), 1974; Knuckle, 1974, 1978; Teeth'n'Smiles, 1976; Fanshen, 1976; Licking Hitler, 1978; Plenty, 1978; Dreams of Leaving, 1980; Saigon, 1981; A Map of the World, 1982; The History Plays, 1984; Wetherby (screenplay), 1985; Pravda (with Howard Brenton), 1985; The Asian Plays, 1986; The Bay at Nice, 1986; Paris By Night (screenplay), 1988; The Secret Rapture, 1988; Strapless (screenplay), 1990; Racing Demon, 1990; Writing Lefthanded (collected essays), 1991; The Early Plays, 1991. Address: c/o Margaret Ramsay Ltd, 14a Goodwins Ct, St Martins Lane, London WC2, England.

HARFIELD Alan, b. 12 Dec 1926, Gosport, Hampshire, England. Freelance Author. m. June Bowler, 6 June 1966, 1 daughter. Publications include: A History of the Village of Chilmark, 1961; The Royal Brunei Malay Regiment, English and Malay, 1977; Headdress and Badges of the Royal Signals, 1982; British & Indian Armies in the East Indies, 1984; Blandford and the Military, 1984; Fort Canning Cemetary, 1981; Christian Cemeteries and Memorials in Malacca, 1984; Bencoolen, the Christian Cemetary and the Fort Marlborough Monuments, 1986; Early Signalling Equipment, 1986; Christian Cemeteries of Penang and Perak, 1987; Early Cemeteries in Singapore, 1988; Pigeon to Packhorse, 1989; British and Indian Armies on the China Coast 1785-1985, 1990; Indian Army of the Empress 1861-1903, 1990; Meerut, The First Sixty Years 1815-1875, 1992; Bencoolen, A History of the East India Company's Garrison on the West Coast of Sumatra 1685-1825, 1994. Contributions to: Crown Imperial; Hamilton's Medal Journal Despatch; The Military Chest; Military Historical Society Journal; Society for Army Research; Orders & Medals Research Society Journal; Journal of the Company of Military Historians; Durbar, The Journal of Indian Military Historical Society; Special Publications of the Gosport Society. Honours: Fellow, Royal Historical Society; Fellow, Company of Military Historians (of USA, Class of 89); Military, British Empire Medal, 1953; Most Blessed Order of the Setia Negara Brunei 3rd Class. Memberships: Royal Asiatic Society; Company of Military Historians; The Military Historical Society, Hon Editor, 1978-90; Society for Army Historical Research, Hon Treasurer, 1990-93; Hon Editor & Membership Secretary, 1994-; Orders & Medals Research Society; Indian Military Historical Society, Hon Auditor. Address: Plum Tree Cottage, Royston Place, Barton-on-Sea, Hampshire BH25 7AJ, England.

HARGITAI Peter, b. 28 Jan 1947, Budapest, Hungary. Writer. m. Dianne Kress, 24 Jul 1967, 1 s, 1 d. Education: MFA, University of Massachusetts, 1988. Appointments: Lecturer in English, University of Miami, 1980-85, University of Massachusetts, 1987-88; Professor and Writing Specialist, Florida International University, 1990-. Publications: Perched on Nothings Branch, 1986; Budapest to Bellevue, 1989; Budapesttöl New Yorkig és tovább..., 1991; Magyar Tales, 1989; Forum: Ten Poets of The Western Reserve, 1976; Fodois Budget Zion, 1991; The Traveler, 1994; Attila: A Barbarian's Bedtime Story, 1994. Contributions to: North Atlantic Review; Colorado Quarterly; Nimrod; College English; California Quarterly; Spirit; Prairie Schooner; Poetry East; Cornfield Review; Blue Unicorn. Honours: Academy of American Poets Translation Award, 1988; Fulbright Grant, 1988; Florida Arts Council Fellowship, 1990; Fust Milan Award from Hungarian Academy of Sciences, 1994. Memberships: PEN International; Literary Network, New York. Address: Katalin Katai, Artisjus, Budapest, Hungary.

HARGRAVE Leonie. See: **DISCH Thomas Michael.**

HARING Firth. See: **FABEND Firth Haring.**

HARITAS. See: **NAGARAJA RAO C K.**

HARKEY Ira Brown Jr, b. 1918, USA. Writer. Appointments: Reporter, Rewriter, Magazine Writer, New Orleans Times-Picayune, 1940-49, 1946-49; Editor, Pascagoula, Mississippi Chronicle, 1949-66. Publications: The Smell of Burning Crosses, 1967; Pioneer Bush Pilot: The Story of Noel Wien, 1974; Alton Ochsner (co-author), 1990. Honour: Pulitzer Prize for Distinguished Editorial Writing, 1963. Address: HCR 5, Box 574-540, Kerrville, TX 78028, USA.

HARKNETT Terry (George G Gilman, Frank Chandler, David Ford, William M James, Charles R Pike, James Russell, William Terry), b. 1936, British. Writer of Mystery/crime/suspense, westerns/adventure, travel/exploration/adventure; Freelance Writer since 1972. Appointments: Copyboy, Reuters, 1952; Clerk, Newspaper Features Ltd, 1952-54; Typist, Reuters, Comtelburo, 1956-57; Publicity Assistant, 20th-Century Fox, 1957-58; Editor, Newspaper Features Ltd, 1958-61; Reporter and Features Editor, National Newsagent, 1961-72, all London. Publications include: Edge series include: Arapaho Revenge, 1983; The Blind Side, 1983; House of the Range, 1983; The Godforsaken, 1982; Edge Meets Steele No 3 Double Action, 1984; The Moving Cage, 1984; School for Slaughter, 1985; Revenge Ride, 1985; Shadow of the Gallows, 1985; A Time for Killing, 1986; Brutal Border, 1986; Hitting Paydirt, 1986; Backshort, 1987; Uneasy Riders, 1987; Adam Steele series includes: Canyon of Death, 1985; High Stakes, 1985; Rough Justice, 1985; The Sunset Ride, 1986; The Killing Strain, 1986; The Big Gunfight, 1987; The Hunted, 1987; Code of the West, 1987; The Undertaker series includes: Three Graves to a Showdown, 1982; Back from the Dead, 1982; Death in the Desert, 1982; As William Terry: Red Sun (novelization of screenplay), 1972; As Frank Chandler: A Fistful of Dollars (novelization of screenplay), 1972; As Charles R Pike: Jubal Cade series, The Killing Trail, 1974; Double Cross, 1974; The Hungary Gun, 1975; As William M James: Apache series - The First Death, 1974; Duel to the Death, 1974; Fort Treachery, 1975; As Terry Harknett: The Caribbean, 1972; As James Russell: The Balearic Islands, 1972; As David Ford: Cyprus, 1973; Ghostwriter: The Hero by Peter Haining, 1973; The Savage and Doomsday Island, both by Alex Peters, 1979. Address: Spring Acre, Springhead Road, Uplyme, Lyme Regis, Dorset DT7 3RS, England.

HARLAN Elizabeth, b. 11 Nov 1945, New York City, USA. Writer. m. Leonard Harlan, 27 Aug 1969, 2 sons. Education: BA, Barnard College, 1967; MPhil, Yale Graduate School, 1971; MFA, Columbia University, 1987. Publications: Footfalls, novel, 1982; Watershed, 1986. Contributions to: New York Times; Harpers. Literary Agent: Rosalie Siegel. Address: Windmill Farm, Cranbury, NJ 08512, USA.

HARLAN Louis R. Publications: Separate & Unequal, 1958; The Negro in American History, 1965; Booker T Washington: The Making of a Black Leader, 1972; Book T Washington: The Wizard of Tuskegee, 1983; Booker T Washington in Pespective, 1988; Editor, The Booker T Washington Papers, 14 vols, 1972-89. Honour: Bancroft Prize, 1973, 1984; Pulitzer Prize, 1984. Address: Department of History, University of Maryland at College Park, College Park, MD 20742, USA.

HARLE Elizabeth. See: **ROBERTS Irene.**

HARLEMAN Ann, b. 28 Oct 1945, Youngstown, Ohio, USA. Writer; Educator. m. Bruce A Rosenberg, 20 Jun 1981, 1 daughter. Education: BA, English Literature, Rutgers University, 1967; PhD, Linguistics, Princeton University, 1972; MFA, Creative Writing, Brown University, 1988. Literary Appointments: Assistant Professor of English, Rutgers University, 1973-74; Assistant Professor of English, 1974-79, Associate Professor,1979-84, University of Washington; Visiting Professor of Rhetoric, MIT, 1984-86; Visiting Scholar, Programme in American Civilisation, Brown University, 1986-. Publications: Graphic Representation of Models in Linguistic Theory, 1976; Ian Fleming: a Critical Biography (with Bruce A Rosenberg), 1989; Mute Phone Calls, a translation of fiction by Ruth Zernova, 1992; Happiness, 1994. Honours: Numerous awards including: Guggenheim Fellowship, 1976 Fulbright Fellowship, 1980; Winner Raymond Carver Contest, 1986 Runner-up, Nelson Algren Competition, Chicago Tribune, 1987 Finalist, PEN/Algren Competition, Chicago Tribune, 1987 and 1988 MacDowell Colony Fellow, 1988; National Endowment for the Humanities (NEH) Fellowship, 1989; Rhode Island State Council on the Arts Fellowship, 1990; Rockefeller Foundation Grant; Winner Iowa Short Fiction Prize, 1993; PEN Syndicated Fiction Award, 1991; Senic Fellow, American Council of Learned Societies, 1993. Memberships

Modern Language Association, Chair, General Linguistics Executive Committee; Poets & Writers Inc; PEN American Center. Address: 55 Summit Avenue, Providence, RI 02906, USA.

HARLOW Michael, b. 1937, New Zealand. Lecturer; Poet. Appointments include: Lecturer, Christchurch Teachers Training College. Publications: Poems, 1965; The Book of Quiet, 1974; Edges, 1974; The Identikit, 1978; Text, Identities, 1978; Nothing But Switzerland and Lemonade, 1980; Today Is the Piano's Birthday, 1981; Vlaminck's Tie, 1985; Take a Risk, Trust Your Language, Make a Poem, 1985. Address: c/o University of Auckland Press, Private Bag, Auckland, New Zealand.

HARMON Maurice, b. 1930, Ireland. Associate Professor. Appointments include: Lecturer in English, 1964-76; Associate Professor of Anglo-Irish Literature and Drama, 1976-; Professor Emeritus, 1990, University College, Dublin; Editor, University Review, 1964-68; Editor, Irish University Review, 1970-. Publications include: Romeo and Juliet, by Shakespeare (editor), 1970; J M Synge Centenary papers 1971 (editor), 1971; King Richard II, by Shakespeare (editor), 1971; Coriolanus, by Shakespeare (editor), 1972; The Poetry of Thomas Kinsella, 1974; The Irish Novel in Our Time (edited with Patrick Rafroidi), 1976; Select Bibliography for The Study of Anglo-Irish Literature and Its Backgrounds, 1976; Richard Murphy: Poet of Two Traditions (editor), 1978; Irish Poetry After Yeats: Seven Poets (editor), 1979; Image and Illusion: Anglo-Irish Literature and Its Contexts (editor), 1979; A Short History of Anglo-Irish Literature From Its Origins to The Present (with Roger McHugh), 1982; The Irish Writer and The City (editor), 1985; James Joyce: The Centennial Symposium (with Morris Beja et al), 1986; Austin Clarke: A Critical Introduction, 1989; The Book of Precedence (poems), 1994; Sean O'Faolan, A Life, 1994. Address: 20 Sycamore Road, Mount Merrion, Blackrock, Co Dublin, Ireland.

HARMS Valerie, b. 17 Jul 1940, Chicago, Illinois, USA. Writer. m. Laurence Sheehan, 12 Jan 1962, div, 1 son, 1 daughter. Education: Smith College, 1962. Publications: The Inner Lover; Trying to Get to You; Celebration with Anais Nin; Unmasking; Frolics Dance; Stars in My Sky; The National Audobon Society Almanac of the Environment, 1994. Contributions to: Humanic Arts; Audubon Activist; Westport News; Pilgramage; Anais Journal; MBI Inc; School Library Journal; Profiles; Womens Diaries; County Magazine; Connecticut Woman; New Age; Book Forum; Parents Choice; Womanspirit; Chrysalis; MS Magazine; Camera 35; Harpers Magazine; New York Times; Mens Journal; Advocate. Honours: UN Award. Memberships: PEN; Authors Guild. Address: 10 Hyde Ridge, Weston, CT 06883, USA.

HARNESS Charles L(eonard), b. 1915, USA. Writer (Science Fiction/Fantasy, Earth Sciences, Marketing). Publications: Marketing Magnesite and Allied Products (with Nan C Jensen), 1943; Mining and Marketing of Barite (with F M Barsigian), 1946; Flight into Yesterday, 1953 (as The Paradox of Men, 1955, in England with Dome Around America, 1964); The Rose, short stories, 1966; The Ring of Ritornel, 1968; Wolfhead, 1978; The Catalyst, 1980; Firebird, 1981; The Venetian Court, 1984; Redworld, 1986. Address: 6705 White Gate Road, Clarksville, MD 21029, USA.

HARONITIS G Vassilios, b. 24 Aug 1933, Anogia Rethimnon, Greece. Teacher. m. Klio Koutoulaki, 26 Apr 1965, 1 s, 1 d. Education: Diploma, Pedagogical Academy of Heraklion, 1954; University of Athens, 1964. Appointments: Spokesman, 6th International Cretological Congress; Spokesman, 7th International Cretological Congress, 1991. Publications: Haroumenes Strofes, 1960; Parthenios Peridis, 1966; Drosostalides, 1975; Titivismata, 1975; Kalimera stin Anixi, 1977; Asterakia, 1978; Theatrikes Scholikes Parastasis, 1978; Nicon, 1978; To Pedi mou ki Ego, 1979; Ola gia ti Lefteria, 1980; I Kriti ton Thrilon, 1986; I Kriti ton Thrilon (2), 1988; I Kriti ton Thrilon (1) second edition, 1989; I Storiki topi tis kritis, 1990. Contributions to: Kretan Estia; We; Amalthia; Intellectual Deletion. Honours: Award, Group of Women Writers; 1st Laudation, Circle of Greek Children's Books; 1st Award, Greek Association of The Journalists and Writers of Tourism. Memberships: Literary Association of Hania Chrysostomos; Union of Intellectual Creators of Hania; Historical and Cultural Association of Crete; Teachers Association of Hania; Christian Union of Teachers; Society of Greek Writers; Board Member, Greek Red Cross of Hania. Address: Parados Meletiou Piga 5, 73100 Hania, Crete, Greece.

HARPER Daniel. See: **BROSSARD Chandler.**

HARPER Marjory-Ann Denoon, b. 6 Apr 1956, Blackpool, Lancashire, England. University Lecturer. m. Andrew J Shere, 22 Aug 1991. Education: MA Hons History, 1978, PhD, 1984, University of Aberdeen. Publications: Emigration from N E Scotland: Willing Exiles, 1988; Emigration from N E Scotland: Beyond the Broad Atlantic, 1988. Contributions to: History Today; British Journal of Canadian Studies; Northern Scotland; Southwestern Historical Quarterly; Aberdeen Leopard; The Weekend Scotsman; The Glasgow Herald; The Highlander. Memberships: Fellow, Royal Historical Society; British Association of Canadian Studies. Address: Department of History, University of Aberdeen, Old Aberdeen, AB9 2UB, Scotland.

HARPER Michael S(teven), b. 1938, USA. Poet. Publications: Dear John, Dear Coltrance, 1970; History is Your Own Heartbeat, 1971; Photographs: Negatives: History as Apple Tree, 1972; Song: I Want a Witness, 1972; Debridement, 1973; Nightmare Begins Responsibility, 1974; Heartblow: Black Veils, 1974; Images of Kin: New and Selected Poems, 1977; Chant of Saints: A Gathering of Afro-American Literature, Art and Scholarship (with Robert B Stepto), 1970; The Collected Poems of Sterling A Brown, 1980; Rhode Island: Eight Poems, 1981; Healing Song for the Inner Ear, 1986. Address: Box 1852 Brown University, Providence, RI 02912, USA.

HARPER Stephen, b. 15 Sep 1924, Newport, Monmouthshire, England. Journalist. Publications: Novels: A Necessary End, 1975; Mirror Image, 1976; Live Till Tomorrow, 1977; Non-Fiction: Last Sunset, 1978; Miracle of Deliverance, 1985, 1987. Membership: Society of Authors. Address: Green Dene Lodge, Greene Dene, East Horsley, Surrey, England.

HARRINGTON Alan Stewart, b. 16 Jan 1919, Newton, Massachusetts, USA. Writer. m. (1) Virginia Hannah Luba Petrova, 28 Nov 1941, (2) Margaret Young, 18 Jan 1968, 2 sons, 1 daughter. Education: AB, English Literature, Harvard University, 1939. Appointments: Adjunct Lecturer, Creative Writing Programme, University of Arizona, 1983-92; Lecturer in Creative Writing, University of Arizona Extended University, 1990-92. Publications: The Revelations of Dr Modesto; Life in The Crystal Palace, 1959; The Secret Swinger, 1966; The Immortalist, 1969; Psychopaths... 1972; Love and Evil: From a Probation Officers Casebook, 1974; Paridise I, 1978; The White Rainbow, 1981. Contributions to: Harper's Atlantic; Saturday Review; The Nation; The New Republic; Playboy; Penthouse; The Chicago Review. Memberships: PEN; Author's Guild, President. Address: 2831 North Orlando Avenue, Tucson, AZ 85712, USA.

HARRIS Aurand, b. 1915, USA. Dramatist; Educator. Appointments include: Drama Teacher, Grace Church School, New York City, 1946-77; Teacher of Playwriting and Directing: University of Texas, 1977-87, University of Kansas City, 1979; California State University, 1981; Purdue University, Indiana University, Indianapolis, 1985; University of Hawaii, 1989; New York University, 1990. Publications: Plays for children: Pinnochio and the Fire-Eater, 1949; Once Upon a Clothesline, 1944; The Doughnut Hole, 1947; The Moon Makes Three, 1947; Seven League Boots, 1947; Circus Days, 1948; revised edition, Circus in the Wind, 1960; Pinocchio and the Indians, 1949; Simple Simon: Or Simon Big Ears, 1952; Buffalo Bill, 1953; We Were Young That Year, 1954; The Plain Princess, 1954; The Flying Prince, 1958, 1985; Junket (No Dogs Allowed), 1959; The Brave Little Tailor, 1960; Pocohontas, 1961; Androcles and the Lion, 1964; Rags to Riches, 1965; The Comical Tragedy or Tragical Comedy of Punch and Judy, 1969; Just So Stories, 1971; Ming Lee and the Magic Tree, 1971; Steal Away Home, 1972; Peck's Bad Boy, 1973; Robin Goodfellow, 1974; Yankee Doodle, 1975; Star Spangled Minstrel, 1975; Six Plays for Children, 1977; A Toby Show, 1978; Plays Children Love: An Anthology (co-editor), 1979; The Arkansaw (sic) Bear, 1980; The Magician's Nephew, 1984; Ride a Blue Horse, 1986; Huck Finn's Story, 1988; Plays Children Love vol 2; An Anthology, 1988; Monkey Magic, 1990; The Pinballs, 1992; Peter Rabbit and Me, 1994; The Prince and the Pauper, 1995; Adult plays: Ladies of the Mop, 1945; Madame Ada, 1948; And Never Been Kissed, 1950; Romancers, adaptions, 1978; Short Plays of Theatre Classics, an Anthology, 1991. Honours include: AATE Distinguished Pay Award, 1991, 1993; Children's Theatre Foundation's Medallion Award, 1993. Address: c/o Anchorage Press, Box 8067, New Orleans, LA 70182, USA.

HARRIS Christie Lucy, b. 21 Nov 1907, New Jersey, USA. Writer. m. Thomas A Harris, 13 Feb 1932, 3 sons, 2 daughters. Education: BC Teachers Diploma, 1924. Publications: 20 books including: Once Upon a Totem; Ravens Cry; Secret in the Stlalakum

Wild; Mouse Woman and the Vanished Princesses; The Trouble with Princesses; You Have to Draw the Line Somewhere. Contributions to: Canadian Broadcasting Corporation; Juvenile Musical Fantasies; Adult Plays & Humour Sketches; Womens Talk; Something Weird is Going On; School Broadcasts; Adventure Serial for Children. Honours include: CACL Medal, Book of the Year for Children; BC Library Commissions Award; Vicky Metcalf Award; Canada Council Childrens Literature Prize; Order of Canada. Memberships: Writers Union of Canada; BC Federation of Writers; CANSCAIP. Address: 430 Arnold Avenue, Victoria, BC, Canda V8S 3M2.

HARRIS Jana N, b. 21 Sep 1947. Writer. m. Mark Allen Bothwell. Education: BS, University of Oregon, 1969; MA, San Francisco State University, 1972. Appointments: Poet-in-Residence, Alameda County Neighbourhood Arts; Instructor, California poetry in Schools; Instructor, Creative Writing, Modesto Junior College, California; Instructor, Creative Writng, New York University, 1980; Director, Writers in Performance, Manhatten Theatre Club, New York, 1981; Instructor, Creative Writing, University of Washington, 1986-, Pacific Luteran University, 1988. Publications include: This House That Rocks with Every Truck on the Road, 1976; Pin Money, 1977; The Clackamas, 1980; Alaska, novel, 1980; Who's That Pushy Bitch, 1981; Running Scared, 1981; Manhatten as a Second Language, 1982; The Sourlands, Poems by Jana Harris (Ontario Review Press, Princeton, NJ), 1989; Oh How Can I Keep on Singing, Voices of Pioneer Women, Poems 1993. Contributions to: Congressional Record; New Letters Berkeley Monthly; Berkeley Poetry Review; Sunbury; Black Maria; Napa College Catalogue; East Bay Review; Performing Arts; San Fransisco Bay Guardian; Room; Beatitudes. Honours: Berkeley Civic Arts Commemoration Grant 1974; Washington State Arts Council Fellowship, 1993. Memberships: Poets & Writers, New Jersey; Feminist Writers Guild; Associated Writing Programs; Women's Salon; New Jersey State Arts Council, 1982; PEN: Poetry Society of America; National Book Critics Club. Address: 32814 120th St SE Sultan, WA 98294, USA.

HARRIS Jocelyn Margaret, b. 10 Sep 1939, Dunedin, New Zealand. University Teacher (Personal Chair). 1 s, 1 d. Education: MA (Otago), 1961; PhD (London), 1969. Publications: Editor, Samuel Richardson, Sir Charles Grandison, 1972; Samuel Richardson, 1987, 1989; Jane Austen's Art of Memory, 1989. Contributions to: Studies in Bibliography; Bulletin of Research in The Humanities; British Journal of 18th Century Studies; 18th Century Fiction. Memberships: Past President, Australian and South Pacific 18th Century Society. Address: English Department, University of Otago, Box 56, Dunedin, New Zealand.

HARRIS Joseph Herbert, b. 18 Aug 1918, Birmingham, Alabama, USA. Headmaster Emeritus. m. Rosa Mary Stewart, 19 Apr 1946, 1 son, 1 daughter. Education: BA, Birmingham-Southern College, 1941; Graduate work, University of Alabama and Fairleigh Dickinson University. Contributions to: Poetry and/or short stories to 300 literary journals and other magazines including: The Literary Review; The Georgia Review; New Voices; Folio; The Roanoke Review; Prairie Schooner; Poetry Venture; Fantasy and Science Fiction; Contemporary Poets; Voices International; Black Buzzard Review; Poet Lore; South Carolina Review; Christian Science Monitor; Saturday Evening Post; Poet; Bitterroot; Christian Herald; The Poet; Icarus; Northwest Magazine; Epos; New Earth Review; Front Street Trolley; Kansas Quarterly; Pulp: Fiction and Poetry; Emily Dickinson Bulletin; Notable American Poets; Z Miscellaneous; DeKalb Literary Arts Journal; Scholia Satyrica; Prophetic Voices; International Poetry Review; Piedmont Literary Review; Nit and Wit; The Spectator; Midwest Poetry Review; The Small Pond Magazine; Salome: A Literary Dance Magazine; Negative Capability; Earthwise Poetry Journal; Black Willow; The Texas Review; Orphic Lute; Poetry Today; Studia Mystica; Poet and Critic; Nebo: A Literary Journal; Kaleidoscope; Parnassus Literary Journal; Carolina Literary Companion; Ellipsis; The American Scholar; The Lyric; Appalachian Heritage; The Davidson Miscellany; America; 12 anthologies. Memberships: Academy of American Poets; Poets and Writers; The South Carolinian Historical Society. Address: 194 Dogwood Road, Aiken, SC 29803, USA.

HARRIS Kenneth, b. 11 Nov 1919. Journalist; Author; Business Executive. m. (1) Doris Young-Smith, 1949 (dec 1970). (2) Jocelyn Rymer, 1987. Education: Wadham College, Oxford. Appointments: War Service, RA, 1940-45; Washington Correspondent, 1950-53, Associate Editor, 1976-, Director 1978, The Observer; Radio and TV work (mainly for BBC), 1957-; Chairman, George Outram Ltd, The Observer Group,

1981-. Publications: Travelling Tongues: Debating Across America, 1949; About Britain, 1967; Conversations, 1968; Life of Attlee, 1982; The Wildcatter: The Life of Robert O Anderson; David Owen, 1987; Thatcher, 1988. Address: The Observer, Chelsea Bridge House, Queenstown Road, London SW8, England.

HARRIS Larry Mark. See: HARRIS Laurence Mark.

HARRIS Laurence Mark (Alfred Blake, Andrew Blake, Larry Mark Harris, Laurence M Janifer, Barbara Wilson), b. 1933, USA. Writer of Crime; Suspense; Historical; Romance; Gothic; Science Fiction; Fantasy. Professional Comedian, 1957-; Editor, Scott-Meredeth, 1985-. Appointments: Pianist and Arranger, New York City, 1950-59; Editor, Scott Meredith Literary Agency, New York City, 1952-57; Editor and Art Director, Detective and Science Fiction Magazines, 1953-57; Carnival Fire-Eater, 1960-69. Publications Include: Slave Planet (science fiction), 1963; The Impossibles (as Mark Phillips), 1963; Supermind (as Mark Phillips), 1963; Faithful for 8 Hours (as Alfred Blake), 1963; Sex Swinger (as Andrew Blake), 1963; Love Hostess (as Andrew Blake), 1963; The Wonder War (science fiction), 1964; The Pleasure We Know (as Barbara Wilson), 1964; You Sane Men (science fiction), 1964, as Bloodworld, 1968; The Velvet Embrace (as Barbara Wilson), 1965; The Woman Without a Name, 1966; (ed) Master's Choice, 1966, as 18 Great Science Fiction Stories, 1971; The Final Fear, 1967; You Can't Escape, 1967; A Piece of Martin Cann (science fiction), 1968; (with S J Treibich), Target: Terra (science fiction), 1968; Impossible? (SF short fiction), 1968; (with S J Treibich), The High Sex (science fiction), 1969; (with S J Treibich), The Wagered World (science fiction), 1969; (ghostwriter), Tracerl by Ed Goldfader, 1970; Power (science fiction), 1974; Survivor (science fiction), 1977; Knave in Hand, 1979; Reel, 1983. Address: c/o Doubleday, 245 Park Avenue, New York, NY 10167, USA.

HARRIS Lavinia. See: JOHNSTON Norma.

HARRIS Marilyn, b. 1931, USA. Author. Publications: King's Ex (short stories), 1967; In The Midst of Earth, 1969; The Peppersalt Land (juvenile), 1970; The Runaway's Diary (juvenile), 1971; Hatter Fox, 1973; The Conjurers, 1974; Bledding Sorrow (romance), 1976; Eden Series (romance): This Other Eden, 1977, The Prince of Eden, 1978, The Eden Passion, 1979, The Woman of Eden, 1980, Eden Rising, 1982; The Last Great Love, 1982; The Portent, 1982; The Diviner, 1984; Warrick, 1985. Address: 1846 Rolling Hills, Norman, OK 73069, USA.

HARRIS Marion Rose (Rose Glendower, Rose Young), b. 12 July 1925, Cardiff, South Wales. Author. m. Kenneth Mackenzie Harris, 18 Aug 1943, 2 s, 1 d. Literary Appointments: Freelance, 1953-63; Editor/Owner, Regional Feature Service, 1964-74; Editorial Controller, W Foulsham and Company Limited, 1974-82; Authorship, 1982-. Publications: Soldiers' Wives, 1986; Officers' Ladies, 1987; Nesta, 1988; Amelda, 1989; The Queen's Windsor, 1985; Captain of Her Heart, 1976; Just a Handsome Stranger, 1983; Sighing for The Moon (as Rose Glendower), 1991; To Love and Love Again (as Rose Young), 1993. Memberships: Society of Authors; Romantic Novelists Association; The Welsh Academy. Literary Agent: International Scripts, 1 Norland Square, Holland Park, London, W1 4PX, England. Address: Walpole Cottage, Long Drive, Burnham, Slough, SL1 8AJ, England.

HARRIS Philip Robert, b. 1926, USA. Writer, Administration/ Management, Education. Appointments include: Co-author, Insight Series, Harcourt Brace Jovanovitch, New York City, 1957-65; Co-author, Challenge Series, St Paul Publishers, Alallabad, India, 1962-63; Book Review Editor, Behavioral Science, Journal of the International Society of Systems Sciences, 1993-95; Editorial Board, European Business Review, 1990-. Publications: Regents Study Guide to State Scholarships, 1949, 1965; Official Guide to Catholic Educational Institutions, editor, 1959; Author: Impact (textbook), 1965; Organizational Dynamics, 1973; Effective Management of Change, 1976; Improving Management Communication Skills (with D Harris), 1978; Managing Cultural Differences (with R Moran), 1979, 1987, 1991, 1995; Innovations in Global Consultation (with G Malin), 1980; Managing Cultural Synergy (with R T Moran), 1982; New Worlds, New Ways, New Management, 1983; Global Strategies for Human Resource Development, 1984; Innovations in Global Consutation, 1984; Management in Transition, 1985; High Performance Leadership, 1987-1994; Co-editor, Managing Cultural Differences Series (8 vols) & Gulf Publishing Co, 1993-95; co-author, Transcultural Leadership (with G M Simmons & C Vaquez), 1993; co-author, Multicultural

Management (with F Elashmarie), 1993; Developing Global Organisations (with R T Moran and W G Stripp) 1993; Author: The New Work Culture Series, 1994-95: High Performance Leader, 1994; HRD Reproducible Assessment Instruments, 1995; New Work Culture and HRD Transformational Management, 1995; Social Concerns, vol 4 of Space Resources (edited by M F & D S McKay & M B Duke), 1992; Co-author, Multicultural Law Enforcement, 1994; Author, Living and Working in Space, 1992. Honours: Associate Fellow, American Institute of Aeronautics and Astronautics; Faculty Fellow NASA; Fulbright Professor to India. Memberships: Vice President, United Societies in Space. Address: 2702 Costobelle Drive CA 92037, USA.

HARRIS Randy Allen, b. 6 Sept 1956, Kitimat, Canada. Professor; Author. m. Indira Naidoo-Harris, 4 Aug 1984. Education: BA, honours, English Literature, Queen's University, 1980; MA, English Literature, Dalhousie University, 1982; MSc, Linguistics, University of Alberta, 1985; MS, Technical Communication, 1986; PhD, Communication & Rhetoric, 1990, Rensselaer Polytechnic Institute. Publications: Acoustic Dimensions of Functor Comprehension in Broca's Aphasia, 1988; Linguistics Wars, 1993; Landmark Essays in Rhetoric of Science, 1995. Contributions to: College English; Perspectives on Science; Rhetoric Review; Historiographia Linguistica; Rhetoric Society Quarterly; Neuropsychologia. Honours: Heritage Scholar; Rensselaer Scholar; Killam Scholar; Killam Fellow. Memberships: Authors Guild; Linguistic Society of America. Address: Department of English, University of Waterloo, Waterloo Ontario, N2L 3G1, Canada.

HARRIS Rosemary (Jeanne), b. 1923. Author. Appointments: Formerly picture restorer, Reader for Metro-Goldwyn-Mayer, 1951-52; Children's Book Reviewer, The Times, London, 1970-73. Publications: The Summer-House, 1956; Voyage to Cythera, 1958; Venus with Sparrows, 1961; All My Enemies, 1967; The Nice Girl's Story, 1968 (in USA as Nor Evil Dreams, 1974); The Moon in The Cloud, 1968; A Wicked Pack of Cards, 1969; The Shadow on The Sun, 1970; The Seal-Singing, 1971; The Child in The Bamboo Grove, 1972; The Bright and Morning Star, 1972; The King's White Elephant, 1973; The Double Snare, 1974; The Lotus and The Grail: Legends from East to West (abridged edition in USA as Sea Magic and Other Stories of Enchantment), 1974; The Flying Ship, 1975; The Little Dog of Fo, 1976; Three Candles for The Dark, 1976; I Want to Be A Fish, 1977; A Quest for Orion, 1978; Beauty and The Beast (folklore), 1979; Green Finger House, 1980; Tower of The Stars, 1980; The Enchanted Horse, 1981; Janni's Stork, 1981; Zed, 1982; Summers of The Wild Rose, 1987; Editor, Poetry Anthology, Love and The Merry-Go-Round, 1988; Ticket to Freedom, 1991. Honour: Awarded Library Association Carnegie Medal for The Moon In The Cloud. Membership: Society of Authors. Address: c/o A P Watt Limited, 20 John Street, London, WC1N 2DR, England.

HARRIS Sheldon H, b. 1928, USA. Writer. Appointments: Professor Emeritus of History, California State University. Publications: Paul Cuffe: Black America and the African Return, 1972; Intervention: President Johnson's Decision to Intervene in Vietnam, 1972; The Prohibition Era: A Study of Law and Private Morality, 1974; Blues Who's Who, 1979; I Remember (with Clyde Berhardt), 1986; Factories of Death: Japanese Biological Warfare 1932-1945 & The American Cover-up, 1994. Address: 17144 Nanette Street, Granada Hills, CA 91344, USA.

HARRIS Thomas, b. 1940. Writer of Novels. Publications: Black Sunday, 1975; Red Dragon, 1981; Silence of the Lambs, 1988 (all adapted for films). Address: c/o St Martins Press, Attn Author Mail Department, 175th Fifth Avenue, New York, NY 10010, USA.

HARRIS William M, b. 20 Oct 1941, Richmond, Virginia, USA. College Professor. 3 daughters. Education: BSc Physics, Howard University, 1964; Master of Urban Planning, 1972, PhD Urban Planning, 1974; University of Washington. Appointments: Western Washington State University, 1973; Portland State, 1974-76; Adjunct, Virginia State University, 1979-85; Visiting, Cornell University, 1986; University of Virginia, 1976-92. Publications: Black Community Development, 1976; Perspectives of Black Studies, 1977; The Chesapeake Bay: A Black Perspective, 1982; Black Congretational Economic Development, 1985; A Conceptual Scheme for Analysis of the Social Planning Process, 1987; Race and Ethical Issues in the Academy, 1992; Mortgage Disclosure and Redlining in Central Virginia, 1992; What Else to Look for When Choosing a College, 1990; Black Community Development in Charlottesville, 1982. Contributions to:

Business and Professional Ethics Journal; College Digest; Thoughtlines; Urban League Review; Western Journal of Black Studies; Northwest Journal of African and Black American Studies; Journal of the National Technical Association; Housing and Society Journal; Negro Educational Review; Planning Magazine. Honours: NDEA Fellow, University of Washington, 1992-94; Visiting Associate, Battelle Seattle Research Centre, 1970-74; Danforth Associate, 1980; Ethics and the Professions Workshop, 1989. Memberships: Association for the Study of Afro- American Life and History; American Planning Association; National Council for Black Studies. Address: Department of Urban and Environmental Planning, School of Architecture, Campbell Hall, University of Virginia, Charlottesville, VA 22903, USA.

HARRIS (Theodore) Wilson, b. 24 Mar 1921, New Amsterdam, British Guiana. Poet; Novelist. m. (1) Cecily Carew, 1945, (2) Margaret Whitaker, 1959. Education: Queen's College, Georgetown. Appointments include: Visiting Lecturer, State University of New York, Buffalo, 1970; Writer-in-Residence, University of West Indies, Kingston, Jamaica, Scarborough College, University of Toronto, 1970, University of Newcastle, New South Wales, 1979; Commonwealth Fellow in Caribbean Literature, Leeds University, Yorkshire, 1971; Visiting Professor, University of Texas, Austin, 1972, 1981-82, University of Mysore, 1978; Yale University, New Haven, Connecticut, 1979; Regents Lecturer, University of California, Santa Cruz, 1983. Publications include: Verse: Fetish, 1951; The Well and The Land, 1952; Eternity to Season, 1954, revised edition, 1979; Novels include: The Guyana Quartet, 1960-63; Tumatumari, 1968; Black Marsden, 1972; Companions of The Day and Night, 1975; Da Silva's Cultivated Wilderness, 1977; Genesis of The Clowns, 1977; The Tree of The Sun, 1978; The Angel at The Gate, 1982; The Carnival Trilogy, 1985-90; Resurrection at Sorrow Hill, 1993-; short stories and other publications. Address: c/o Faber and Faber Limited, 3 Queen Square, London, WC1N 3AU, England.

HARRISON Edward Hardy (Ted), b. 28 Aug 1926, Wingate, Co Durham, England. Artist; Writer. m. Robina McNicol, 12 Nov 1960, 1 son. Education: Hartlepool College of Art, 1943-45, 1948-50; National Diploma, Design, Kings College, Newcastle-upon-Tyne, 1951; BEd, University of Alberta, Canada, 1977. Publications: Children of the Yukon, 1977; The Last Horizon, 1980; A Northern Alphabet, 1982; The Cremation of Sam McGee, by R W Service, Illustrator, 1986; The Blue Raven, Story for television, 1987; O Canada, 1992 (1993 USA). Honours: Best Childrens Book, A Child Study Association of Canada, 1977; Choice Book, Childrens Book Centre, Toronto, 1978; Ibby - Certificate of Honour for Illustration, 1984. Memberships: Writers Union of Canada; The Order of Canada; PEN, Canada; Honorary Doctorate, Athabasca University, 1991. Literary Agent: Barry Bergh, 1350 - 13th Ave SE, Salmon Arm, BC, Canada, VIE 267. Address: 2029 Romney Place, Victoria BC, Canada V8S 4J6.

HARRISON Elizabeth C, (Betty Cowanna, Elizabeth Headley), b. 24 Jun 1909, Camden, New Jersey. Author. m. (1) Edward Headley, 5 Aug 1940, (dec 1952), 1 son, (2) George Russell Harrison, 9 Mar 1957. Education: AB, 1929. Publications include: All juvenile or young adult books: Puppy Stakes, 1943; The Black Spaniel Mystery, 1945; Secret Passage, 1946; Going on Sixteen, 1946; Spurs for Suzanna, 1947; A Girl Can Dream, 1948; Paintbox Summer, 1949; Spring Comes Riding, 1950; Twos Company, 1951; Lasso Your Heart, 1952; Love Laurie, 1953; Six on Easy Street, 1954; The Boy Next Door, 1956; Angel on Skis, 1957; Stars in her Eyes, 1958; The Scarlet Sail, 1959; Accent on April, 1960; A Touch of Magic, 1961; Fancy Free, 1961; The First Book of Wildflowers, 1961; A Breath of Fresh Air, 1966; The First Book of Fiji, 1969; The First Book of Morocco, 1970; Mystery on Safari, 1971; Around the World Today series; Connie Blair mystery series; The Surfer and the City Girl, 1981; Stamp Twice for Murder, 1981; Wanted: A Girl for the Horses, 1984; Romance on Trial, 1984; Banner Year, 1987. Honours: Honorary Phi Beta Kappa, Douglas College, 1935; Hall of Distinguished Alumni, Rutgers University, 1990. Address: 45 Pasture Lane, Bryn Mawr, PA 19010, USA.

HARRISON Elizabeth Fancourt, b. 12 Jan 1921, Watford, Hertfordshire, England. Author. Publications include: Coffee at Dobree's, 1965; The Physicians. 1966; The Ravelston Affair, 1967; Corridors of Healing, 1968; Emergency Call, 1970; Accident Call, 1971; Ambulance Call, 1972; Surgeon's Call, 1973; On Call, 1974; Hospital Call, 1975; Dangerous Call, 1976; To Mend a Heart, 1977; Young Dr Goddard, 1978; A Doctor Called Caroline, 1979; A Surgeon Called Amanda, 1982; A Surgeon's Life, 1983; Marrying A Doctor, 1984; Surgeon's Affair, 1985; A Surgeon at St Mark's, 1986; The Surgeon

She Married, 1988; The Faithful Type, 1993; The Senior Partner's Daughter, 1994; Paperback editions throughout the world. Honours: Runner-up 1970, shortlisted 1971, 1972, 1973, major award, Romantics Novelists Association. Memberships: Society of Authors; Vice-President, Romantic Novelists Association. Literary Agent: Mary Irvine. Address: 71 Wingfield Road, Kingston on Thames, Surrey, KT2 5LR, England.

HARRISON Jim, b. 1937, USA. Author; Poet. Publications: Plain Song, 1965; Locations, 1968; Walking, 1969; Outlyers and Ghazals, 1971; Wolf (novel), 1971; A Good day to Die (novel), 1973; Letters to Yesenin, 1973; Farmer (novella), 1976; Legends of the Fall (novella), 1979; Warlock (novel), 1981; New and Selected Poems, 1982; Natural World (with Diana Guest) 1983; Sundog (novel), 1984; The Woman Lit By Fireflies (novella), 1990; Just Before Dark (non-fiction), 1991; Julip (novella), 1994. Address: Box 135, Lake Leelanau, MI 49653, USA.

HARRISON M(ichael) John, b. 1945. Writer (science fiction/fantasy). Appointments: Literary Editor and Reviewer, New Worlds Magazine. Publications: The Committed Men, 1971; The Pastel City, 1971; The Centauri Device, 1974; The Machine in Shaft Ten and Other Stories, 1975; A Storm of Wings, 1980; In Viriconium, 1982; The Floating Gods, 1983; The Ice Monkey and Other Stories, 1983; Viriconium Nights, 1984; Climbed, 1989. Address: c/o Anthony Sheil Associates, 43 Doughty Street, London, WC1N 2LF, England.

HARRISON Raymond Vincent, b. 28 Oct 1928, Chorley, Lancashire, England. Inspector of Taxes; Financial Consultant. m. 7 Apr 1977. Education: BA Hons, 1952; MA, 1954, Magdalene College, Cambridge. Publications: French Ordinary Murder, UK 1983, USA 1984; Death of An Honourable Member, UK 1984, USA 1985; Deathwatch, UK 1985, USA 1986; Death of A Dancing Lady, UK 1985, USA 1986; Counterfeit of Murder, UK 1986, USA 1987; A Season for Death, UK 1987, USA 1987; Harvest of Death, UK 1988, USA 1988; Tincture of Death, UK 1989, USA 1990; Sphere of Death, UK 1990, USA 1990; Patently Murder, UK 1991, USA 1992; Akin to Murder, UK 1992; Murder in Petticoat Square, UK 1993. Address: Forthill, Kinsale, Co Cork, Eire.

HARRISON Sarah, b. 1946. Author. Appointments: Journalist, IPC Magazines, London, 1969-72. Publications: The Flowers of The Field, 1980; In Granny's Garden (children's book), 1980; A Flower That's Free, 1984; Hot Breath, 1985; Laura From Lark Rise, series (children's books), 4 volumes, 1986; An Imperfect Lady, 1987; Cold Feet, 1989; Foreign Parts, 1991; The Forests of The Night, 1992; Be An Angel, 1993. Literary Agent: Carol Smith. Address: 17 Station Road, Steeple Morden, Royston, Hertfordshire, England.

HARRISON Sue Ann McHaney (Sue Harrison), b. 29 Aug 1950, Lansing, Michigan, USA. Novelist. m. Neil Douglas Harrison, 22 Aug 1969, 1 son, 2 daughters (1 dec). Education: BA, English, 1971. Publications: Mother Earth Father Sky, 1990; My Sister the Moon, 1992; Brother Wind, 1994. Literary Agent: Rhoda Weyr. Address: PO Box 6, 18 Mile Road, Pickford, MI 49774, USA.

HARRISON Tony, b. 1937, England. Publications: Earthworks, 1964; Aitkin Mata (with J Simmons), play, 1965; Newcastle is Peru, 1969; The Loiners, 1970; Voortrekker, 1972; The Misanthrope, 1973; Poems of Palladas of Alexandria, (editor and translator), 1973; Phaedra Britannica, play, 1975; Bow Down, music theatre, 1977; The Passion, play, 1977; The Bartered Bride, libretto, 1978; The School of Eloquence, poems, 1978; Oresteia, adaptation, 1981; Continuous, 1981; A Kumquat for John Keats, 1981; US Martial, 1981; Selected Poems, 1984, revised 1985; The Fire Gap, 1985; Dramatic Verse 1973-1985, 1985; The Mysteries, 1985; Theatre Works 1973-1985, 1986; The Trackers of Oxyrhynchus, 1990; A Cold Coming: Gulf War Poems, 1991; The Common Chorus, 1992; The Gaze of The Gorgon, 1992; Square Rounds, 1992; Black Daisies for The Bride, 1993; Poetry or Bust, 1993; A Maybe Day in Kazakhstan (TV film-poem), Channel Four. Honours: Cholmondley Award for Poetry, 1969; Geoffrey Faber Memorial Prize, 1972; European Poetry Translatin Prize, 1983; Whitbread Award (for poetry), 1992; Prix d'Italia:- Black Daisies for the Bride, Mental Health Award: Best Drama, 1994. Address: c/o 2 Crescent Grove, London, SW4 7AH, England.

HARROWER Elizabeth, b. 8 Feb 1928, Sydney, NSW, Australia. Novelist. Appointments: Australian Broadcasting Commission, Sydney, 1959-60; Reviewer, Sydney Morning Herald, 1960; MacMillan and Company Ltd, Sydney, 1961-67. Publications: Down in the City, 1957;

The Long Prospect, 1958; The Catherine Wheel, 1960; The Watch Tower, 1966; Stories, The Cost of Things, 1964; English Lesson, 1965; The Beautiful Climate, 1966; Lance Harper, His Story, 1968; The Retrospective Grandmother, 1976; A Few Days in the Country, 1977. Honours include: Commonwealth Literary Fund Fellowship, 1968; Australian Council for the Arts Fellowship, 1974. Address: 5 Stanley Avenue, Mosman, NSW 2088, Australia.

HARRY J S, b. 1939, Adelaide, South Australia, Australia. Poet. Appointments include: Writer-in-residence, Australian National University, Canberra, 1989. Publications: The Deer Under the Skin, 1970; Hold for a Little While, and Turn Gently, 1979; A Dandelion for Van Gogh, 1985. Honours include: Harri Jones Memorial Prize, 1971; PEN International Lynne Phillips Prize, 1987. Address: PO Box 184, Randwick, New South Wales 2031, Australia.

HARSENT David, b. 9 Dec 1942, Devonshire, England. Writer. m. (1) div, 2 s, 1 d, (2) 1 d. Appointments: Bookseller, Aylesbury, then worked for publishers Eyre Methuen, Arrow Books and Deutsch, all London; ran own imprint, Enigma; Fiction Critic, Times Literary Supplement, London, 1965-73; Poetry Critic, Spectator, London, 1970-73. Publications: Verse: Tonight's Lover, 1968; A Violent Country, 1969; Ashridge, 1970; After Dark, 1973; Truce, 1973; Dreams of The Dead, 1977; Mister Punch, 1984; Selected Poems, 1989; Novel: From an Inland Sea, 1985; Editor: New Poetry 7, 1981; Poetry Book Society Supplement, 1983; Savremena Britanska Poezija: a selection of British and Irish poetry made for Writers Union, Sarajevo, 1988; Gawain (libretto), 1991, for an opera by Birtwistle commissioned by, and first performed at, The Royal Opera House, London; Storybook Hero (limited edition), 1992; News From The Front (verse), 1993. Honours: Eric Gregory Award, 1967; Cheltenham Festival Prize, 1968; Arts Council Bursary, 1969, 1984; Faber Memorial Award, 1978; Society of Authors Travel Fellowship, 1989. Address: c/o Oxford University Press, Walton Street, Oxford, OX2 6DP, England.

HART John, b. 18 June 1948, Berkeley, California, USA. Writer. Education: AB, Princeton University, 1970. Publications Include: Walking Softly in the Wilderness; The Climbers, poems; San Francisco's Wilderness Next Door; The New Book of California Tomorrow; Hiking the Great Basin; Hiking the Bigfoot Country; Booklength reports for various organizations, titles include: Endangered Harvest; Eroding Choices/Emerging Issues; California 2000; Democracy in the Space Age. Contributions Include: Numerous publications, including: Sierra; Outside; Cry California; Poetry Letter; Interim; Southern Poetry Review; Works. Honours Include: James D Phelan Award, poetry, 1970; Merit Award, California Chapter, American Institute of Planners, 1972. Organizational Awards: Outstanding Planning Programme Award, American Planning Association, 1982; Conservation Community Award, Natural Resources Council of America, 1987. Memberships: Secretary, Lawrence Hart Institute for Study of Excellence in Poetry; Amercan Alpine Club; Sierra Club; Wilderness Society. Address: Box 556, San Anselmo, CA 94960, USA.

HART Kevin, b. 5 July 1954, London, England (Australian citizen). Lecturer; Poet. Education: Stanford University, California, and University of Melbourne; PhD, 1987. Appointments include: Lecturer in English, Melbourne University, Australia, 1986-87; Lecturer in Literary Studies at Deakin University, Victoria, from 1987. Publications: Nebuchadnezzar, 1976; The Departure, 1978; The Lines of the Hand: Poems 1976-79; Your Shadow, 1984; Peniel, 1990; The Buried Harbour, 1990; The Trespass of the Sign: Deconstruction, Theology and Philosophy, 1989; Editor, Shifting Frames: English/Literature/Writing, 1988. Honours include: Australian Literature Board Fellowship, 1977; New South Wales Premier's Award, 1985. Address: 247 Richardson Street, North Carlton, Victoria 3054, Australia.

HART-DAVIS Duff, b. 1936. Author. Appointments: Feature Writer, 1972-76, Literary Editor, 1976-77, Assistant Editor, 1977-78, Sunday Telegraph, London; Country Columnist, Independent, 1986-. Publications: The Megacull, 1968; The Gold of St Matthew (in USA as The Gold Trackers), 1968; Spider in the Morning, 1972; Ascension: The Story of a South Atlantic Island, 1972; Peter Fleming (biography), 1974; Monarchs of the Glen, 1978; The Heights of Rimring, 1980; Fighter Pilot (with C Strong), 1981; Level Five, 1982; Fire Falcon, 1984; The Man-Eater of Jassapur, 1985; Hitler's Games, 1986; Armada, 1988; The House the Berrys Built, 1990; Horses at War, 1991; Country Matters, 1991; Wildings: The Secret Garden of Eileen Soper, 1992;

Further Country Matters, 1993. Address: Owlpen Farm, Uley, Dursley, Gloucestershire, England.

HART-DAVIS Rupert (Charles) Sir, b. 28 Aug 1907. Author; Editor; Former Publisher. m. (1) Peggy Ashcroft, 1929, (div), (2) Catherine Comfort Borden-Turner, 1933, 2 sons, 1 daughter (div), (3) Winifred Ruth Simon, 1964, (dec 1967), (4) June Clifford, 1968. Education: Eton; Balliol College, Oxford; Student, Old Vic, 1927-28; DLitt, Reading University, 1964; DLitt, Durham University, 1981. Appointments: Actor, Lyric Theatre, Hammersmith, 1928-29; Office Boy, William Heinemann Ltd., 1929-31; Manager, Book Society, 1932; Director, Jonathan Cape Ltd., 1933-40; Served in Coldstream Guards, 1940-45; Founder, Rupert Hart-Davis Ltd., 1946, Director, 1946-64; Vice President, Committee of the London Library, 1971-, Chairman, 1957-69. Publications: Hugh Walpole, a Biography, 1952; The Arms of Time, a memoir, 1979; The Power of Chance, 1991; Editor: the Essential Neville Cardus, 1949; E.V. Lucas: Cricket all his Life, 1950; George Moore: Letters to Lady Cunard, 1957; The Letters of Oscar Wilde, 1962; Max Beerbohm: Letters to Reggie Turner, 1964; Max Beerbohm: More Theatres, 1969; Max Beerbohm: Last Theatres, 1970; Max Beerbohm: A Peep into the Past, 1972; A Catalogue of the Caricatures of Max Beerbohm, 1972; The Autobiography of Arthur Ransome, 1976; William Plomer: Electric Delights, 1978; The Lyttelton Hart-Davis Letters, volume 1, 1978, volume II, 1979, volume III, 1981, volume IV, 1982, volume V, 1983, volume VI, 1984; Selected Letters of Oscar Wilde, 1979; Two Men of Letters, 1979; Siegfried Sassoon Diaries: 1920-1922, 1981, 1915-1918, 1983, 1923-1925, 1985; The War Poems of Siegfried Sassoon, 1983; A Beggar in Purple: a Commonplace Book, 1983; More Letters of Oscar Wilde, 1985; Siegfried Sassoon: Letters to Max Beerbohm, 1988; Letters of Max Berrbohm 1892-1956, 1989; The Power of Chance, 1991. Address: The Old Rectory, Marske-in-Swaledale, Richmond, North Yorkshire, DL11 7NA, England.

HARTCUP Adeline, b. 26 Apr 1918, Isle of Wight, England. Writer. m. John Hartcup, 11 Feb 1950, 2 sons. Education: MA, Oxon, Classics and English Literature. Appointments: Editorial Staff, Times Educational Supplement; Honorary Press Officer, Kent Voluntary Service Council. Publications: Angelica, 1954; Morning Faces, 1963; Below Stairs in the Great Country Houses, 1980; Children of the Great Country Houses, 1982; Love and Marriage in the Great Country Houses, 1984; Spello: Life Today in Ancient Umbria, 1985. Contributions to: Times Educational Supplement; Harpers; Queen; Times Higher Educational Supplement, etc. Address: Swanton Court, Sevington, Ashford, Kent, TN24 0LL, England.

HARTE Marjorie. See: MCEVOY Marjorie.

HARTFIELD Hermann, b. 14 Nov 1942, Yagodnoye, USSR. Pastor; Guest Lecturer; Author. m. 16 July 1970. Education: English Language, at Cambridge University, 1978-79; MMin, Winnipeg Theological Seminary, 1980-81; MDiv, Mennonite Brethren Biblical Seminary, 1981-83. Docs. Theol, Facultatis Theological Reformatorie Brussels, 1985-87; PhD, Pacific Western University, 1988-89. Publications include: Faith Despite KGB, 1976; Irina, Wuppertal: Brockhaus, 1980; Faith Despite KGB; Evangelistiche Strategie; Homosexulität im Kontext von Bible, Theologie und Seelsorge; Faith Despite the KGB, translated by Henry Wagner, Christian Herald Books, 1980 & Pickering & Inglis, 1981; Irina's Story, translated by Henry Wagner, 1983; Aufstehen. Das Gericht Kommt; Heimkehr In Ein Fremdes Land, 1986; Evangelistische Strategie, 1987; Homosexualität im Kontext von Bibel, Theologie und Seelsorge, 1991. Address: Freiherr-vom-Stein Str 30, 47475 Kamp-Lintfort, Germany.

HARTILL Rosemary Jane, b. 11 Aug 1949, Oswestry, England. Writer; Broadcaster. Education: BA Hons, English, University of Bristol, 1970. Appointments: BBC Religious Affairs Correspondent, 1982-88; Presenter of BBC World Service's Meridian Books Programme, 1990-92, 94; Presenter of Writers Revealed (Radio 4, 18 part, BBC Series); and Immortal Diamonds (Radio 4, 12 part, Series on Poets). Publications: Emily Brontë: Poems (editor), 1973; Wild Animals, 1976; In Perspective, 1988; Writers Revealed, 1989; Were You There?, 1995. Honours: Nominated for Sony Award for Radio Reporter of the Year, 1988 and Best Arts Radio Feature, 1990; Sandford St Martin Trust Personal Award, 1994. Address: Old Post Office, 24 Eglingham Village, Alnwick, Northumberland, NE66 2TX, England.

HARTLAND Michael, b. 1941, Cornwall, England. Writer. m. 1975, 2 daughters. Education: Christs College, Cambridge, 1960-63.

Appointments: British Diplomatic and Civil Service, 1963-78; United Nations, 1978-83; Full-time Writer, 1983-; Regular Book Reviewer and Feature Writer: The Sunday Times, The Times, Guardian and Daily Telegraph; Resident Thriller Critic: The Times, 1989-90; Daily Telegraph, 1993-; Chairman, Wade Hartland Films Limited; Radio and Television include: Sonja's Report, (ITV Channel 3), 1990; Masterspy, interviews with Oleg Gordievsky (BBC Radio 4), 1991. Publications: Down Among The Dead Men; Seven Steps to Treason (dramatized for BBC Radio 4, 1990); The Third Betrayal; Frontier of Fear; The Year of the Scorpion (adapted as feature film, 1995). Honours: Fellow of the Royal Society of Arts; Hon Fellow, University of Exeter; South West Arts Literary Award. Memberships: Crime Writers Association; Mystery Writers of America; Society of Authors. Address: Cotte Barton, Branscombe, Devon, EX12 3BH, England.

HARTLE Mary Jean McCoy, b. 21 Jan 1938, Montrose, South Dakota, USA. Secretary; Housewife. m. Kenneth A Hartle, 28 Dec 1957, 3 sons, 1 daughter. Education: Office Procedures, 1978; Medical Secretary Course, 1984-85; Writers Seminar, 1986, Sioux Falls Community College, South Dakota. Publications: Humboldt Centennial Book - The Pioneers, 1989; Book on handicapped children and book of poems, in progress; Poems in anthologies: Spring's Rebirth, 1986; The Challenger Crew, 1987; A Doll is a Special One, 1988; Liberty the Spirit of America, 1988; Our Lady Liberty (as Mary J McCoy), 1988; Life's Keepsakes, 1988; Work and Prayer, 1989; Apple Orchard Memories, 1989; The Party Line, 1989; The Founding of the Constitution - To Our Modern Day (Phillip Morris Writers Competition entry), 1986; Sarajevo, Sarajevo, 1994; The Heart Of The Little Bird; In The Garden of My Heart, 1991; Evening Wine, 1993; Flying Home At Sunset, 1993. Contributions to: South Dakota Pasque Petals; Phillip Morris Magazine; Montrose Herald; Humboldt Journal. Honours: Honourable Mention, Golden Poet Award, Silver Poet Award for Our Lady Liberty and Liberty - the Spirit of America, Great American Poetry Anthology, 1988; Golden Poet, World of Poetry, 1991. Memberships: South Dakota State Poetry Society; Pasque Petals; National Federation of State Poetry Societies; Former Member, Officers Wives Club; Randolph AF Base, Texas, Reese AF Base, Texas, Moody AF Base, Georgia, Ramstein AF Base, Germany; Past Treasurer, Catholic Daughters of America; Sioux Vocational Auxiliary for the Handicapped; St Ann's Altar Society; Life Member, National Poetry Society, 1994; Air Force Association; Disabled American Veterans Auxilliary. Address: 412 S Jefferson, Humboldt, SD 57035, USA.

HARTMAN Geoffrey H, b. 1929, Germany. Writer. Publications: The Unmediated Vision: An Interpretation of Wordsworth, Hopkins, Rilke and Valery, 1954; Andre Malraux, 1960; Wordsworth's Poetry, 1787-1814; , 1964; Hopkins: A Collection of Critical Essays, 1966; Beyond Formalism: Literary Essays 1958-70, 1970; Selected Poetry and Prose of William Wordsworth, 1970; New Perspectives on Coleridge and Wordsworth, 1972; Romanticism: Vistas, Instances, Continuities, 1973; The Fate of Reading and Other Essays, 1975; Criticism in the Wilderness, 1980; Saving the Text, 1981; Easy Pieces, 1985; Midrash and Literature, 1986; Bitburg in Moral and Political Perspective, 1986; The Unremarkable Wordsworth, 1987; Minor Prophecies: The Literary Essay in the Culture Wars, 1991; Holocaust Remembrance: The Shapes of Memory, 1994. Address: 260 Everit Street, New Haven, CT 06511, USA.

HARTMAN Jan, b. 23 May 1936, Stockholm, Sweden. Writer-Dramatist. m. 9 June 1960, 2 daughters. Education: Phillips Andover Academy, 1956; BA, Harvard College, 1960. Literary Appointments: Resident Playwright, The Theatre of The Living Arts, Philadelphia, 1964-65; Instructor in Theatre, 1969; Teacher of Political Theatre, 1975; New School; Contributing Editor, Religious Theatre Magazine; Director, Founder, Playwrights Theatre Project Circle in the Square, 1967-69, and Eleventh Hour Productions, 1977; Resident Playwright, Theatre St Clements, 1977-78; Visiting Professor, Syracuse University, Fall Semester, 1985-86; Resident Playwright, Co-artistic Director, The Performance Theatre Centre; Professor of Dramatic Writing and Shakespeare, New York University, 1981-. Publications: Television: Felling Good; Alfred Running Wild; The Long Conversation; A Memory of Autumn; The Survivor; Alexander, 1963-75; Board For Freedom; With All Deliberate Speed; Song of Myself, 1976; Follow The North Star; Hewitt's Just Different; The Great Wallendas, 1977-78; His First Love; Second Sight, 1978-79; The Herman Graebe Story; The Late Great Me; Ethics in The Professions; The Maimie Papers, 1979-80; A Lasting Love, 1980-81; Killing The Goose; Sticks and Stones; The Next War, 1982-83; The Manor and The Estate, 1983-84; The Campbells; Muir: Earth, Planet, Universe, 1984-85; Pigeon

Feathers, 1985-86; The Presidents; Ganesh; The Story of Mother Teresa of Calcutta; A Winter Visitor; The James Family, 1986-87; The Last Weapon; Les Egare's, 1987-88. Theatre Productions: Samuel Hoopes Reading From His Own Works, 1963; The Shadow of The Valley, 1964; Legend of Daniel Boone, 1986; Antique Masks, 1966; Freeman, Freeman; Final Solutions, 1968; Fragment of A Last Judgment, 1967; The American War Crimes Trial, 1973; Flight 981, 1977; Abelard and Heloise; To The Ninth Circle, 1983; K, 1987. Feature Films-Screenplays, Prior to 1983: Hail to the Chief; The Kastner Affair; Emily; The Cursed Medallion; Jelly Roll; The Bauhaus, 1982-83. Publications: Samuel Hoopes Reading from His Own Works, 1978; Political Theatre, An Anthology; Elements of Film Writing; Joshua; The Shadow of The Valley; 4 Contemporary Religious Plays: Flatboatment; Every Year A St Carnival. Contributions to: Articles in The Dramatists Guild Quarterly. Honours: Many Awards and Fellowships given in recognition of work commissioned. Memberships Include: PEN; Writers Guild of America; Eugene O'Neill Memorial Theatre Foundation; American National Theatre and Academy; Dramatists Guild; Chairman, Committee On Censorship WGA, East. Address: c/o Robert A Freeman Dramatic Agency Inc, 1501 Broadway, Suite 2310, NY 10036, USA.

HARTMANN Betsy. See: HARTMANN Elizabeth.

HARTMANN Elizabeth (Betsy Hartmann), b. 20 July 1951, Princeton, NJ, USA. Lecturer; Writer. m. James Kenneth Boyce, 17 Nov 1976, 2 sons. Education: BA magna cum laude, Yale University, 1974. Appointments: Project Manager at Economic Development Bureau, New Haven; Visiting Lecturer in Economics at Yale University; Public Speaker on issues of international development and reproductive rights; Fellow, Institute for Food and Development Policy, 1978-79; Writer, 1980-. Publications: Needless Hunger: Voices From A Bangladesh Village (with James Boyce), 1979; A Quiet Violence: View From A Bangladesh Village (with James Boyce), 1983; Food, Saris and Sterilization: Population Control in Bangladesh (with Hilary Standing), 1985; Reproductive Rights and Wrongs: The Global Politics of Population Control and Contraceptive Choice, 1987. Contributions to: Magazines and newspapers in the USA and Abroad, including Nation, New Internationalist, South. Honours: Howland Fellowship, 1974. Memberships: Women's Global Network on Reproductive Rights; Bangladesh International Action Group; National Worr en's Health Network; National Writers Union; New England Women & Development Group.

HARTNACK Jostus, b. 29 May 1912, Copenhagen, Denmark. Professor. m. Ing Benedicte, 12 Mar 1937, 1 son, 1 daughter. Education: MA, Philosophy, 1976; DPhil, 1976. Appointments: Professor of Philosophy, at various American Universities, 1946-77; Professor, University of New York, 1972-77. Publications: History of Philosophy, 1969; Human Rights; Several Textbooks in Danish, some of which have been translated into other Languages. Contributions to: Several articles in International Journals. Honours: First Prize, Competition, 1954; Outstanding Educator in America, 1974-75; The Rosinkjaer Prize, 1983. Memberships: Various societies and associations. Address: 16 Woodstock Close, Oxford OX2 8DB, England.

HARTNETT David William, b. 4 Sept 1952, London, England. Writer. m. Margaret R N Thomas, 26 Aug 1976, 1 son, 1 daughter. Education: Scholarship to read English Language and Literature at Exeter College, Oxford, 1971, First Class Honour Moderations, 1973, First Class BA in English Language and Literature, 1975, MA, 1981, D Phil, 1987. Literary Appointment: Editor (with Michael O'Neill and Gareth Reeves) of the literary magazine Poetry Durham (founded 1982). Publications: Collections of poetry: A Signalled Love, 1985; House of Moon, 1988; Dark Ages, 1992; Novel: Black Milk, 1994. Contributor to: Reviews in Times Literary Supplement. Honour: Winner of the 1989 Times Literary Supplement/Cheltenham Festival Poetry Competition. Address: c/o Jonathan Cape, 20 Vauxhall Bridge Road, London, SW1V 2SA, England.

HARTNETT Michael, b. 18 Sept 1941, County Limerick, Ireland. Poet. Education: University and Trinity College, Dublin. Appointments include: Teacher of Physical Education, National College, Limerick. Publications: Anatomy of a Cliche, 1968; Selected Poems, 1971; Culuide, The Retreat of Ita Cagney, 1975; A Farewell to English and Other Poems, 1975; Poems in English, 1977; Prisoners, 1978; Collected Poems, Volumes 1 and 2, 1985-87; A Necklace of Wrens: Poems in English and Irish, 1987; House of Moon, 1989; Editor and

Translator. Honours include: c/o Gallery Press, Loughcrew, Oldcastle, County Meath, Ireland.

HARTSHORNE Charles, b. 5 Jun 1897, Kittanning, USA. University Professor; Writer. m. Dorothy E Cooper, 22 Dec 1928, 1 d. Education: BA, 1921, MA, 1922, PhD, 1923, Harvard; Postdoctoral Study in Europe, 1923-25. Appointments: Consulting Editor, Journal of Philosophy & Phenomenological Research, many years; Contributor to many Encylopedias including Britannica, and Encyclopedia of Religion. Publications: The Divine Relativity, 1947; Philosophers Speak of God, with W Reese, 1953; The Logic of Perfection, 1962; Creative Synthesis and Philosophic Method, 1970; Insights and Oversights of Great thinkers, 1983; Omnipotence and Other Theological Mistakes, 1984; The Philosophy and Psychology of Sensation, 1934; Beyond Humanism: Essays in the New Philosophy of Nature, 1937; Anselm's Discovery, 1965; A Natural Theology for our time, 1967; Creativity in American Philosophy,1 984, Wisdom and Moderation, 1987; Born to Sing: An Interpretation and World Survey of Bird Song, 1973, 1992. Contributor to: over 400 articles and reviews in journals and magazines. Address: 724 Sparks Ave, Austin, TX 78705, USA.

HARTSTON William Roland, b. 1947. Writer. Appointments Include: Chess Columnist, The Mail on Sunday. Publications: The King's Indian Defence (with L Barden and R Keene), 1969, 1973; The Benoni, 1969, 1973; The Grunfeld Defence, 1971, 1973; Karpov-Korchnoi (with R Keene), 1974; The Best Games of C H O'D Alexander (with H Golombek), 1975; How to Cheat at Chess, 1976; The Battle of Baguio City, 1978; Soft Pawn, 1979; The Penguin Book of Chess Openings, 1980; Play Chess 1 and 2, 2 vols, 1980-81; London (with S Reuben), 1980; The Master Game Book Two (with J James), 1981; Karpov v Korchnoi, 1981; The Psychology of Chess (with P C Wason), 1983; The Ultimate Irrelevant Encyclopaedia (with J Dawson), 1984; Teach Yourself Chess, 1985; Kings of Chess, 1985; Chess: The Making of a Musical, 1986. Address: 48 Sotheby Road, London N5 2UR, England.

HARVEY Anne Berenice, b. 27 Apr 1933, London, England. Actress; Freelance Writer; Editor. m. Alan Harvey, 13 Apr 1957, 1 son, 1 daughter. Education: Guildhall School of Music & Drama, 1950-54; AGSM; LGSM. Literary Appointments: Series Editor for Poetry Originals (Blackie). Publications: A Present for Nellie, 1981; Poets in Hand, Editor, 1985; Of Caterpillars, Cats & Cattle, Editor, 1987; In Time of War: War Poetry, Editor, 1987; Something I Remember, Selection of Eleanor Farjeon Poetry, Editor, 1987; A Picnic of Poetry, Editor, 1988; The Language of Love, Editor, 1989; Six of the Best, Editor, 1989; Faces in a Crowd, Editor, 1990; Headlines from the Jungle, Editor with Virginia McKenna, 1990; Occasions, Editor, 1990; Shades of Green, Editor, 1991; Elected Friends, (Poems for & About Edward Thomas), Editor, 1991; Solo Audition Speeches For Young Actors, 1993; He Said, She Said, They Said (Bothas Editor), 1993; Flora's Red Socks, 1991; Criminal Records, 1994; Scenes for 2 books, Solo and Take Two; numerous radio scripts. Contributions to: various journals and magazines. Memberships: Poetry Society; Edward Thomas Fellowship; Childrens Books History Society; Friends of the Dymock Poets; Childrens Book Circle; Eighteen Nineties Society. Honour: Winner of the Signal Poetry Award for Shades of Green. Address, 1992. Address: 37 St Stephen's Road, Ealing, London, W13 8HJ, England.

HARVEY Brett, b. 28 Apr 1936, NY. Writer. 1 s, 1 d. Appointments: Drama and Literature Director, WBAI-FM, 1971-74; Publicity and Promotion Director, The Feminist Press, Old Westbury, 1974-80, NY; Free-lance journalist, book critic and children's book author, 1980-. Publications: My Prairie Year, 1986; Immigrant Girl, 1987; Cassie's Journey, Various Gifts: Brooklyn Fiction, 1988; My Prairie Christmas, 1990; The Fifties: A Women's Oral History, 1993. Contributions to: Articles in periodicals, including Village Voice, New York Times Book Review, Psychology Today, Voice Literary Supplement, Mirabella, Mother Jones, Mademoiselle. Address: 305 8th Ave, Brooklyn, NY 11215, USA.

HARVEY Caroline. See: TROLLOPE Joanna.

HARVEY John Barton, b. 21 Dec 1938, London, England. Writer. Education: Goldsmith College, University of London; Hatfield Polytechnic; University of Nottingham. Publications: What about it, Sharon, 1979; Ghosts of a Chance (collected poems), 1992; Lonely Hearts, 1989; Rough Treatment, 1990; Cutting Edge, 1991; Off minor, 1992; Wasted Years, 1993; Cold Light, 1994; Living Proof, 1995;

Numerous Scripts for Radio & Television. Literary Agent: Blake Friedmann. Address: 37-41 Gower Street, London, WC1E 6HH, England.

HARVEY John Robert, b. 25 June 1942, Bishops Stortford, Hertfordshire, England. University Lecturer, Cambridge English Faculty. m. Julietta Chloe Papadopoulou, 1968, 1 daughter. Education: BA, Honours Class 1, English, 1964, MA, 1967, PhD, 1969, University of Cambridge. Appointments: Editor, Cambridge Quarterly, 1978-86. Publications: Victorian Novelists and Their Illustrators, 1970, Novels: The Plate Shop, 1979; Coup d'Etat, 1985; The Legend of Captain Space, 1990. Contributions to: London Review of Books; Sunday Times; Sunday Telegraph; Listener; Encounter; Cambridge Quarterley; Essays in Criticism. Honour: David Higham Prize, 1979. Literary Agent: Curtis Brown. Address: Emmanuel College, Cambridge, England.

HARWOOD Lee, b. 1939. Poet; Translator. Publications: Verse: Title Illegible, 1965; The Man With Blue Eyes, 1966; The White Room, 1968; The Beautiful Atlas, 1969; Landscapes, 1969; The Sinking Colony, 1970; Penguin Modern Poets 19 (with John Ashbery and Tom Raworth), 1971; The First Poem, 1971; New Year, 1971; Captain Harwood's Log of Stern Statements and Stout Sayings, 1973; Freighters, 1975; H.M.S Little Fox, 1976; Boston - Brighton, 1977; Old Bosham Bird Watch and Other Stories, 1977, 1978; Wish You Were Here (with A Lopez), 1979; All the Wrong Notes, 1981; Faded Ribbons, 1982; Wine Tales (with Richard Caddel), 1984; Crossing the Frozen River: Selected Poems 1965-1980, 19840 Monster Masks, 1986; Translations of the works of Tristan Tzara: A Poem Sequence, 1969, revised edition as Cosmic Realities Vanilla Tobacco Drawings, 1975; Destroyed Days, 1971; Selected Poems, 1975. Address: c/o 9 Highfield Road, Chertsey, Surrey, England.

HARWOOD Ronald, b. 1934, Cape Town, South Africa. Writer. Publications Include: Novels: All The Same Shadows; The Guilt Merchants; The Girl in Melanie Klein; Articles of Faith; The Genoa Ferry; Cesar and Augusta; And a Selection of Short Stories, One Interior Day, adventures in the film trade. Biography: Sir Donald Wolfit, CBE. Plays Include: Country Matters; A Family; The Ordeal of Gilbert Pinfold (from Evelyn Waugh); The Dresser; After the Lions, 1982; Tramway Road, 1984; Another Time, 1989; Reflected Glory, 1992. Films: One Day in the Life of Ivan Denisovich; Operation Daybreak; The Dresser. Television: Mandela; Breakthrough at Reykjavik; Countdown to War, 1989. Memberships: President, English PEN, 1990. Address: 83 Eastbourne Views, London W2 6LQ, England.

HASHMI (Aurangzeb) Alamgir, b. 15 Nov 1951, Lahore, Pakistan. Professor; Editor; Broadcaster. 2 sons, 1 daughter. Education: MA, 1972; MA, 1977; Litt D, 1984. Appointments: Assistant Editor, The Ravi, 1970-71; Faculty Adviser, Folio, 1973-74; Editor, Broadcaster, English Magazine, 1973-74; Guest Editor, The New Quarterly, 1978; Foreign Editor, Explorations, 1978-88; Corresponding Editor, Associate Editor, Helix, 1978-85; Correspondent, Regional Representative, The Journal of Commonwealth Literature, 1979-; Member, Editorial Board, Crosscurrent, 1980s; Staff Reviewer, World Literature Today, 1981-; Editorial Adviser, Kunapipi, 1981-; Member, Editorial Board, Poetry Europe, 1982; Associate Editor, Member, Editorial Board, Commonwealth Novel in English, 1982-; Member, Editorial Board, Pacific Quarterly, 1982-85; Guest Editor, Pakistani Literature, 1993; Co-Editor, Encyclopedia of Post-Colonial Literatures, 1994. Publications: The Oath and Amen; America Is a Punjabi Word; An Old Chair; Pakistani Literature; My Second in Kentucky; This Time in Lahore; Commonwealth Literature; Ezra Pound in Melbourne; Neither This Time/Nor That Place; The Worlds of Muslim Imagination; The Commonwealth, Comparative Literature and the World; Inland and Other Poems; The Poems of Alamgir Hashmi; Sun and Moon and Other Poems. Address: c/o Indus Books, PO Box 2905, Islamabad GPO, Pakistan.

HASKINS Hames, b. 19 Sept 1941, Alabama, USA. Professor; Writer. Education: BA, Georgetown University, 1960; BA, Alabama State University, 1962; MA, University of New Mexico, 1963. Publications Include: The Cotton Club, 1977, 2nd edition 1984; Diary of a Harlem Schoolteacher, 1969; Resistance: Profiles in Nonviolence, 1970; The War and the Protest: Vietnam, 1970; Jokes from Black Folks, 1973; Street Gangs, Yesterday and Today, 1974; Witchcraft, Mysticism & Magic in the Black World, 1974; Jobs in Business and Office, 1974; The Picture Life of Malcolm X, 1975; Dr J: A Biography of Julius Erving, 1975; A New Kind of Joy: The Story of the Special Olympics, 1976; Pele: A Biography, 1976; The Life and Death of Martin Luther King, Jr, 1977; Barbara Jordan, 1977; Voodoo & Hoodo: Their Tradition and Craft, 1978; Scott Joplin: The Man Who Made Ragtime, 1978; Scott Joplin: The Man Who Made Ragtime, 1978; The New Americans Vietnamese Boat People, 1980; Werewolves, 1981; The New Americans: Cuban Boat People, 1982; Sugar Ray Leonard, 1982; Black Theatre in America, 1982; Lena Horne, 1983; Bricktop with Bircktop, 1983; About Michael Jackson, 1985; Breakdancing, 1985; Ella Fitzgerald: A Life Through Jazz, several languages, 1992; I Have a Dream: The Life of Martin Luther King Jr, 1992; The March on Washington, 1992; Diana Ross: Star Supreme, 1985; Queen of the Blues: A Biography of Dinah Washington, 1987; Black Music in America, 1987. Contributions to: Numerous journals, magazines and newspapers. Honours: Recipient, many honours and awards. Memberships: Authors Guild; National Book Critics Circle, 1975-79. Address: 325 West End Avenue, 7D, New York, NY 10023, USA.

HASLAM Gerald William, b. 18 Mar 1937, Bakersfield, California, USA. Writer; Educator. m. Janice E Pettichord, 1 July 1961, 3 s, 2 d. Education: BA, 1963; MA, 1965, San Francisco State University; PhD, Union Graduate School, 1980. Appointments: Associate Editor, ETC; A Review of General Semantics, 1967-69; Editor, Ecolit, 1971-73; General Editor, Western American, 1973-76; Columnist, California English, 1987-93; Columnist, San Francisco Chronicle, 1992-93. Publications: Snapshots, 1985; Okies, 1973; The Wages of Sin, 1980; Voices of a Place, 1987, Hawk Flights, 1983; Masks, 1976; The Man Who Cultivated Fire, 1987; Forgotten Pages of American Literature, Editor, 1970; Western Writing, Editor, 1974; California Heartland, Editor, with James D Houston, 1978; Coming of Age in California, 1990; That Constant Coyote, 1990; The Other California, 1990; Many Californias, Editor, 1992; The Great Central Valley: California's Heartland, 1993; Condor Dreams and Other Fictions, 1994; The Other California (second, englarged edition), 1994. Address: Box 969, Penngrove, CA 94951, USA.

HASLIP Joan, b. 27 Feb 1912. Author. Appointments: Sub-Editor, London Mercury, 1929-39; Broadcast and Contributed Articles to BBC; Lectured for British Council, Italy and Middle East. Publications: (several translated): Out of Focus, 1931; Grandfather Steps, 1932 (USA 1933); Lady Hester Stanhope, 1934; Parnell, 1936 (USA 1937); Portrait of Pamela, 1940; Lucrezia Borgia, 1953 (USA 1954); The Sultan, Life of Abdul Hamid, 1958, reprinted 1973; The Lonely Empress, a Life of Elizabeth of Austria, 1965 (translated into 10 languages); Imperial Adventurer, 1971; Catherine the Great, 1976; The Emperor and the Actress, 1982; Marie Antoinette, 1987 (translated into 10 languages); Madame DuBarry, 1991. Contributions to: Various magazines and journals. Honours: Book of Month Choice, USA, 1972. Address: 8 Via Piana, Bellosguardo, 50124 Florence, Italy.

HASLUCK Nicholas (Paul), b. 17 Oct 1942, Canberra, Australia. Novelist. Education: University of Western Australia, 1960-63; Oxford University, 1964-66. Appointments: Barrister, Solicitor, Supreme Court of Western Australia, 1968; Deputy Chairman, Australia Council, 1978-82. Publications: Quarantine, 1978; The Blue Guitar, 1980; The Hand that Feeds You: A Satiric Nightmare, 1982; The Bellarmine Jug, 1984; Truant Stte, 1988; The Country without Music, 1990; The Blosseville File, 1992; Offcuts From a Legal Literary Life, 1993; A Grain of Truth, 1994; The Hat on the Letter O and Other Stories, 1978; Verse, Anchor and Other Poems, 1976; On The Edge, 1980; Chinese Journey, 1985. Honours: The Age Book of Year Award, 1984; Member, Order of Australia, 1986. Address: 14 Reserve Street, Claremont, Western Australia 6010, Australia.

HASSEL R Chris Jr, b. 16 Nov 1939, Richmond, Virginia, USA. Professor of English. m. Sedley Hotchkiss, 16 June 1962. 2 s. Education: BA, University of Richmond, 1961; MA, Univesity of North Carolina, 1962; PhD, Emory University, 1968. Appointments: Instructor in English, Mercer University, 1962-65; Professor of English, Vanderbilt University 1968-. Publications: Faith and Folly in Shakespeare's Romantic Comedies, 1980; Renaissance Drama and the English Church Year, 1979; Songs of Death, 1987; Context and Charisma: The Sher-Alexander Richard 3 SQ, 1985; Military Oratory in Richard 3, SQ, 1984; Love Versus Charity in Love's Labour's Lost Shakespeare Studies: Donne... and the New Astronomy MP, 1971; Shakespeare's Comic Epilogues, Shakespeare Jahrbuch, 1970. Address: Box 129 B, Vanderbilt University, Nashville, TN 37235, USA.

HASTINGS March. See: **LEVINSON Leonard.**

HASTINGS Max Macdonald, b. 28 Dec 1945, London, England. Author; Broadcaster; Journalist. m. Patricia Edmondson, 27 May 1972, 2 sons, 1 daughter. Education: Exhibitioner, University College, Oxford, 1964-65; Fellow, World Press Institute, St Paul, Minnesota, USA, 1967-68. Appointments: Researcher, BBC TV, 1963-64; Reporter, London Evening Standard, 1965-67, BBC TV Current Affairs, 1970-73; Editor, Evening Standard Londoner's Diary, 1976-77; Columnist, Daily Express, 1981-83, Sunday Times, 1985-86; Editor, Daily Telegraph, 1986-; Editor-in-Chief and a Director of The Daily Telegraph Plc, 1989-. Publications: The Fire This Time, 1968; Ulster, 1969; The Struggle for Civil Rights in Northern Ireland, 1970; Montrose: The King's Champion, 1977; Yoni: The Hero of Entebbe, 1979; Bomber Command, 1979; The Battle of Britain (with Lee Deighton), 1980; Das Reich, 1981; Battle for the Falklands, with Simon Jenkins, 1983; Overlord: D-Day & the Battle for Normandy, 1984; Oxford Book of Military Anecdotes, editor, 1985; Victory in Europe, 1985; The Korean War, 1987; Outside Days, 1989. Honours: Somerset Maugham Prize, non-fiction, 1979; Yorkshire Post Book of the Year, 1983, 1984; British Press Awards, Journalist of the Year, 1982 (cited 1973, 1980); Granada TV Reporter of the Year, 1982; Editor of the Year, 1988. Literary Agent: The Peters Fraser and Dunlop Group Ltd. Address: c/o The Daily Telegraph, 1 Canada Square, London, E14 5DT, England.

HASTINGS Michael, b. 2 Sept 1938. Playwright. m. Victoria Hardie, 1975, 2 sons, 1 daughter by previous marriage. Education: Various South London Schools; Bespoke Tailoring Apprenticeship, London, 1953-56; FRGS. Publications: Plays: Don't Destroy Me, 1956; Yes and After, 1957; The World's Baby, 1962; Lee Harvey Oswald: A Far Mean Streak of Independence Brought on by Neglect, 1966; The Cutting of the Cloth, 1969; The Silence of Saint-Just, 1971; For The West (Uganda), 1977; Gloo Joo, 1978; Full Frontal, 1979; Carnival War a Go Hot, 1980; Midnite at the Starlite, 1980; Moliere's The Miser (adaptation), 1982; Tom and Viv, 1984; The Emperor (with Jonathan Miller), 1987; Novels: The Game, 1957; The Frauds, 1960; Tussy is Me, 1968; The Nightcomers, 1971; And In The Forest The Indians, 1975; Poems: Love Me Lambeth, 1959; Stories: Bart's Mornings and Other Tales of Modern Brazil, 1975; Criticism: Rupert Brooke, The Handsomest Young Man in England, 1967; Sir Richard Burton, a biography, 1978; Films and TV: For the West (Congo), 1963; Blue as His Eyes The Tin Helmet He Wore, 1966; The Search for the Nile, 1972; The Nightcomers, 1972; Auntie Kathleen's Old Clothes, 1977; Murder Rap, 1980; Midnight at the Starlight, 1980; Michael Hastings in Brixton, 1980; Stars of the Roller State Disco, 1984; The Emperor (Michael Hastings/Jonathan Miller-Miller co-wrote and directed), 1988; Three Political Plays with introductory essay, (Penguin Books), 1990. Address: 2 Helix Gardens, Brixton Hill, London, SW2, England.

HASTREITER Marge Thielman, (Sally West), b. 26 April 1934, Buffalo, NY, USA. Author. m. 17 Nov 1956, 2 sons (1 deceased), 3 daughters. Education: Regents Diploma, Bishop Colton HS. Publications: Lovejoy Memories, Book 1, 1989; Lovejoy Memories, Book 11, 1990; Sketchbook Summer and Other Short Stories, 1990; Family Charms, 1991; Don't Talk About It, Son, 1991. Contribution to: Center Stage Publication. Honours: Award from Common Council of Buffalo, 1989; Award from Buffalo Veterans Medical Center. Memberships: Buffalo Literary Society; Vice-President, Iron Island Preservation Society of Lovejoy; Buffalo and Erie County Historical Society; Buffalo Friends of Olmstead Parks; Charter Member, Upsilon Sigma Chi. Address: 230 Longnecker Street, Buffalo, NY 14206, USA.

HASWELL Chetwynd John Drake, b. 18 July 1919, Penn Buckinghamshire, England. Soldier; Author. m. Charlotte Annette Petter, 25 Oct 1947, 2 sons, 1 daughter. Education: Winchester College, 1933-37; Royal Military College, Sandhurst, 1938-39. Appointments: Soldier, 1939-60; Appointed Author, Service Intelligence, Intelligence Centre, Ashford, 1966-84. Publications: (Under the name of George Foster) Indian File, 1960; Soldier on Loan, 1961; (Under the name Jock Haswell) The Queen's Royal Regiment, 1967; The First Respectable Spy, 1969; James II, Soldier and Sailor, 1972; British Military Intelligence, 1973; Citizen Armies, 1973; The British Army, 1975; The Ardent Queen, Margaret of Anjou, 1976; The Battle for Empire, 1976; Spies and Spymasters, 1977; The Intelligence and Deception of the D Day Landings, 1979; The Tangled Web, 1985; The Queen's Regiment, 1986; Spies and Spying, 1986. Memberships: Regimental Historian for the Queen's Regiment. Address: The Grey House, Lyminge, Folkestone, Kent, CT18 8ED, England.

HATCHER Robin Lee, b. 10 May 1951, Payette, Idaho, USA. Novelist. m. Jerrold W Neu, 6 May 1989, 2 d. Education: General High School Diploma, 1969. Publications: Stormy Surrender, 1984; Heart's Landing, 1984; Thorn of Love, 1985; Passion's Gamble, 1986; Heart Storm, 1986; Pirate's Lady, 1987; Gemfire, 1988; The Wager, 1989; Dream Tide, 1990; Promised Sunrise, 1990; Promise Me Spring, 1991; Rugged Splendor (as Robin Leigh), 1991; The Hawk and the Heather, 1992 (as Robin Leigh) Devlin's Promise, 1992; Midnight Rose, 1992; A Frontier Christmas, 1992; The Magic, 1993; Where The Heart Is, 1993; Forever, Rose, 1994; Remember When, 1994. Contributions to: Assembling Your Press Kit, to Fiction Writers Magazine, 1987; Full Time Writer, to Affaire de Coeur, 1988; The Stuff that Dreams are made of, to Romantic Times Magazine, 1989; Go the Distance, to Romance Writers Report, 1990; Have We Learned So Much We've Lost The Passion, to Romance Writer's Report, 1992. Literary Agent: Natasha Kern. Address: PO Box 4722, Boise, ID 83711, USA.

HATHAWAY Michael Jerry, b. 20 Sept 1961, El Paso, Texas, USA. Typesetter. Appointments: Chairman, Poetry Rendezvous (Great Bend, KS), 1988-89. Publications: Shadows of Myself, 1980; Puddle of Stars, 1984; Founder & Edito, The Kindred Spirit, 1982-; Inconspicuous, 1988; Excerpt, 1989; Come Winter and Other Poems, 1989. Contributions Include: New Voices; WOP; APA; Explorer; Baltimore Vegetarian; Manna; Wheels; Alchemist Review; Cat Fancy. Honours: Featured Editor: The Forum for Universal Spokesmen, 1987; Featured Poet, Keith Publications Newsletter, 1987; 1st Place, Jubilee Press Contest, 1987; Judge, Various Poetry Contests. Memberships: Forthwriters (Treasurer), 1985. Address: Rt 2, Box 111, St John, KS 67567, USA.

HATTENDORF John Brewster, b. 22 Dec 1941, Hinsdale, Illinois, USA. Naval and Maritime Historian. m. Berit Sundell, 15 Apr 1978, 3 d. Education: AB Kenyon College, 1964; AM Brown University, 1971; DPhil, University of Oxford, 1979. Appointments: Serving Officer, US Navy, 1964-73; Professor, Military History, National University of Singapore, 1981-83; Ernest J King Professor of Maritime History, US Naval War College, 1984-. Publications: The Writings of Stephen B Luce, 1975; On His Majesty's Service, 1983; Sailors and Scholars, 1984; England in the War of the Spanish Succession, 1987; Maritime Strategy and the Balance of Power, 1989; The Limitations of Military Power, 1990; A Bibliography of the Works of A T Mahan, 1986; Mahan on Naval Strategy, 1991; The Influence of History on Mahan, 1991; Mahan is Not Enough, 1993; Ubi Sumnus: The State of Maritime and Naval History, 1994; Co-Editor, British Naval Documents, 1993. Address: 28 John Street, Newport, RI 02840-3106, USA.

HATTERSLEY Roy (Sydney George), b. 1932, British. Appointments: Journalist and Health Service Executive, 1956-64; Member of City Council, Sheffield, 1957-65; Labour Member of Parliament (UK) for Sparkbrook Division of Birmingham, 1964-, Parliamentary Private Secretary, Minister of Pensions and National Insurance, 1964-67, Parliamentary Secretary, Ministry of Labour, 1967-68, Department of Employment and Productivity, 1968-69, Minister of Defence for Administration, 1969-70, Labour Party Spokesman on Defence, 1972 and on Education, 1972-74, Minister of State, Foreign and Commonwealth Office, 1974-76, Secretary of State for Prices and Consumer Protection, 1976-79, Opposition Spokesman on Home Affairs, 1980-83, on Treasury Affairs, 1983-, Deputy Leader of the Labour Party, 1983-; Director, Campaign for a European Political Community, 1966-67; Columnist for the Guardian, 1981-, Punch, 1982-87. Publications: Nelson: A Biography, 1974; Goodbye to Yorkshire, 1976; Politics Apart, 1982; A Yorkshire Boyhood, Press Gang, 1983; Endpiece Revisited, 1984; Choose Freedom, 1987; Economic Priorities for a Labour Government, 1987; The Maker's Mark (novel), 1991; In That Quiet Earth, 1991; Skylark's Story, 1994; Between Ourselves (Essays), 1994. Address: House of Commons, London, SW1A DAA, England.

HAUCK Dennis William, b. 8 Apr 1945, Hammond, Indiana, USA. Writer. Education: Indiana University, 1963-66; University of Vienna, Austria, 1969-72. Appointments: Editor, Infor Services Inc, 1973-76; Countrywide Publications, NY, 1976-79; Writer, Oldenberg Group Inc, Sacramento, 1983-91; Columnist, Today's Supervisor, Sacramento, 1991-; The Long Island Journal, Long Beach, NY, 1977-78. Publications: The UFO Handbook, 1974; Ufology, 1975; The Secret of the Emerald Tablet, 1991; The Haunted Places Guidebook, 1991; William Shatner: A Biography, 1992; Jewish Alchemy, 1992. Contributions to: Suttertown News, Sacramento Magazine, Highway Patrol Magazine, The City, San Francisco Magazine; Articles in Sign of the Times, Poet, In the Company of Poets, Journal of Occult Studies, Approche, Accept, Omega Magazine. Honours: Appeared in and wrote script for theatrical release, Mysteries of the Gods, 1976. Memberships: Authors Guild; National Writers Union; Society for Technical Communication; California Writers Club. Literary Agent: Michael Larsen, Elizabeth Pomada, San Francisco. Address: PO 22201, Sacremanto, CA 95822, USA.

HAUGAARD Erik Christian,b. 13 Apr 1923, Copenhagen, Denmark. Author. m. (1) Myra Seld, 23 Dec 1949, deceased 1981. (2) Masako Taira, 27 July 1986, 1 son, 1 daughter. Publications Include: The Little Fishes, 1967; Orphas Of The Wind, 1969; The Untold Tale, 1972; Translated all Hans Christian Andersen's Fairy Tales, 1973; Chase Me Catch Nobody, 1980; Leif The Unlucky, 1982; The Samurai's Tale, 1984; Princess Horrid, 1990; The Boy and The Samurai, 1991. Honours: Herald Tribune Award; Boston Globe-Horn Book Award; Jane Addams Award; Danish Cultural Ministry Award; 1988 Phoenix Award. Memberships: The Authors Guild; The Society of Authors; British PEN; Danish Authors Union. Literary Agent: McIntosh and Otis Inc, 310 Madison Avenue, New York, USA. Address: Toad Hall, Ballydehob, West Cork, Ireland.

HAUGEN Einar Ingvald, b. 19 Apr 1906, Sioux City, Iowa, USA. m. 18 June 1932, 2 d. Education: BA 1928; PhD 1931. Appointments: University of Wisconsin, 1931; Harvard University, 1964. Publications include: Fire and Ice (translated), 1970; First Grammatical Treatise, 1972; The Scandinavian Languages, 1976; The Ecology of Language, 1977; The Land of the Free, 1978; Scandinavian Structures, 1982; Oppdalsmalet, 1982; Ole E Rolvaag, 1983; Han Ola og han Per, 1984; Blessings of Babel, 1987; Immigrant Idealist, 1989; Ole Bull: Romantisk musiker o kosmopolitisk Nordmann, 1992 (co-author); Studies by Einar Haugen, 1971; Studies for Einar Haugen, 1972; Linguistics in North America: Current Trends in Linguistics, 1971; Die Skandinavisches Sprache, 1984; Norwegian Language in America: A Study in Bilingual Behaviour, 1953, new edit 1969; Bilingualism in the Americas: A Guide to Research, 1957, 2nd edit 1964; Norwegian-English Dictionary, 1965, 3rd edit 1983; Language Conflict and Language Planning, 1966; The Norwegians in America, 1967. Address: 45 Larch Circle, Belmont, MA 02178, USA.

HAUGEN Paal-Helge, b. 26 Apr 1945, Valle, Norway. Author. Education: Studied medicine, film and theatre, Norway and USA. Appointments: Chairman, Board of Literary Advisors, Association of Norwegian Authors, 1984-88; Chairman, International Pegasus Prize Committee, 1988. Publications: Poetry: På botnen av ein mork sommar, 1967; Sangbok, 1969; Det synlege menneske, 1975; Fram i lyset, tydeleg, 1978; Steingjerde, 1979; Spor, Selected and new poems, 1981; I dette huset, 1984; Det overvintra lyset, 1985; Anne, novel, 1968; Herr Tidemann reiser, 1980, Childrens book. Inga anna tid, ingen annan stad, stage play, 1986; Horisont (poems, with lithographies by Kjell Nupen), 1986; Verden open, selected poems, 1988; Vårfuglen, Children's book, 1989; translations in German: Das überwinterte Licht, Münster, 1988; Anne, Münster, 1989; Meditasjonar over Georges de La tour, (poems), 1990; Vidde (a poem with images by Gunnar Torvund), 1991; Sone O (poems), 1992; A., (a monodrama for music, with Iannis Xenakis), 1993; Poesi - Collected Poems 1965-1995, 1995; German transl. (cont), 1993; Meditationen über Georges de La Tour, Münster, 1993; English Translation: Wintering With the light, Los Angeles, 1995. Contributions to: Various professional journals; Plays for radio, television and stage; Several opera libretti. Literary Agent: Pip Hallén, J. W. Cappelen, P. O. Box 350 Sentrum, 0101 Oslo, Norway. Address: Skrefjellv 5, 4645 Nodeland, Norway.

HAUPTMAN William (Thornton), b. 26 Nov 1942, Wichita Falls, Texas, USA. Playwright. m. (1) Barbara Barbat, 1968 (div 1977), 1 daughter; (2) Marjorie Endreich, 1985, 1 son. Education: Graduate, Whichita Falls Senior High School, 1961;BFA, Drama, 1966, University of Texas, Austin; MFA, Playwrighting, Yale University School of Drama, New Haven, Connecticut, 1973. Publications: Plays Include: Hear (produced NYC, 1974) New York, Samuel French, 1977; Domino Courts/Comanche Cafe (produced NYC, 1975) New York, Samuel French, 1977; New York, Performing Arts Journal Publications, 1980; Big River, music and lyrics by Roger Miller, adaptation of the novel Adventures of Huckleberry Finn by Mark Twain (produced Cambridge, Massachusetts, 1984, MY, 1985) New York, Grove Press, 1986; Gillette (produced Cambridge Massachusetts, 1985; revised version produced La Jola, California, 1986) New York,Samuel French, 1989. Television Play: A House Divided series (3 episodes), 1981. Fiction: Good Rockin Tonight and Other Stories, New York, Bantam, 1988; The Storm Season, Bantam, 1992. Honours: CBS Grant, 1976; National Endowment for the Arts Grant, 1977; Boston Theatre Critics Circle

Award, 1984; Tony Award, 1985; Drama-Lounge Award, 1986; Jesse Jones Award (best work of fiction), Texas Institute of Letters, 1989. Literary Agent: Gloria Loomis, Watkins-Loomis, NYC. Address: 240 Warren Street, Apartment E, Brooklyn, NY 11201, USA.

HAUTZIG Esther Rudomin, b. 18 Oct 1930, Vilna, Poland. American. Publications: Let's Cook Without Cooking (as E Rudomin), 1955; Let's Make Presents, 1961; Redecorating Your Room for Practically Nothing, 1967; The Endless Steppe, In the Park, 1968; At Home 1969; In School, 1971; Let's Make More Presents, 1973; Cool Cooking, 1974; I L Peretz: The Case Against the Wind and Other Stories (trans and adaptor), 1975; Life with Working Parents, 1976; A Gift for Mama, 1981; Holiday Treats, 1983; I L Peretz: The Seven Good Years and Other Stories (trans and adaptor), 1984; Make It Special, 1986; Christmas Goodies, 1989; Remember Who You Are, 1990; On the Air, 1991; Riches, 1992; New Introduction to a fascimile edition of Vilna by Israel Cohen, 1992. Contributions to: Publishers Weekly, 1969; Horn Book, 1970; The Five Owls, 1986; Something About The Author Authobiographical Series, 1992. Memberships: Authors Guild; Authors League of America. Address: 505 West End Avenue, New York, NY 10024, USA.

HAVEL Václav, b. 5 Oct 1936, Prague, Czechoslovakia. President of the Czech Republic; Writer. m. Ölga Splichová, 1964. Education: Faculty of Economy, 1955-57; Drama Department, Academy of Arts, Prague, 1966. Appointments: ABC Theatre Prague, 1959-68, Resident Playwright, 1968; Editorial board of: Tvár, 1965; Lidové noviny, 1987-89; Co-founder of: Charter 77, 1977; VONS, 1978; Civic Forum, 1989; President, Czech Republic, 1993. Publications: 13 Plays; 10 Books: Many Essays; English translations include: The Garden Party, 1969; The Increased Difficulty of Concentration, 1972; Václav Havel or Living in Truth, 1986; Letters to Olga, 1988; Disturbing the Peace, 1990; Open Letters: Selected Writings 1965-90, 1991; Selected Plays by Václav Havel, 1991; Summer Meditations, 1992; Toward a Civil Society, 1994. Honours: Many awards for writing, and work for human rights, including: The Olof Palme Prize, 1989; Simon Bolívar Prize UNESCO, 1990; Political Book of the Year 1990. Memberships: Honorary member: PEN-centre, Germany; PEN, Sweden; Hamburg Academy of Liberal Arts; Austrian PEN club committee; Royal British Legion, 1991; Member, Czech PEN, 1989; Associé éntranger Académie des sciences morales et politiques Institut de France, 1992. Literary Agent: Aura Pont Agency, Prague. Address: Kancelár prezidenta republiky, 119 08 Praha-Hrad, Czech Republic.

HAWK Alex. See: **KELTON Elmer Stephen.**

HAWKES Jacquetta, b. 5 Aug 1910, Cambridge, England. Author; Archaeologist. m. (1) Christopher Hawkes, 1933, 1 son (div. 1953), (2) J. B. Priestly, 1953. Education: MA, Newnham College, Cambridge, 1951. Research & Excavation, UK, Eire, France, Palestine, 1931-40. Literary Appointments: John Danz Visiting Professor, University of Washington, USA, 1971; Governor, British Film Institute, 1950-55; Member, UNESCO Cultural Advisory Committee, 1966-79; Life Trustee, Shakespeare Birthplace Trust, 1985-. Publications include: A Land, 1951; Guide to Prehistoric & Roman Monuments in England & Wales, 1951; Man on Earth, 1954; The Dawn of the Gods, 1968; The First Great Civilizations, 1973; Mortimer Wheeler: Adventurer in Archaeology, 1982; Shell Guide to British Archaeology, 1986; Also poetry, plays, fiction. Contributions to: Many leading journals & national periodicals. Honours: OBE, 1952; 100 Kemsley Award (A Land), 1951; Honorary DLitt, Warwick University, 1986. Memberships: Society of Authors; PEN; Fellow Society of Antiquaries, 1940-; Antiquity Trustee. Literary Agent: A.D. Peters. Address: Littlecote, Leysbourne, Chipping Campden, Gloucestershire, GL55 6HL, England.

HAWKES John, b. 17 Aug 1925, Stamford, Connecticut, USA. Writer; Professor Emeritus of English. m. Sophie Parks Goode Tazewell, 5 Sept 1947, 3 s, 1 d. Education: AB Harvard University, 1949. Publications: Novels: The Cannibal, 1949; The Lime Twig, 1961; Second Skin, 1964; The Blood Oranges, 1971; Adventures in the Alaskan Skin Trade, 1985; Whistlejacket, 1988; The Beetle Leg, 1951; The Goose on the Grave and The Owl, 1954; Death, Sleep and the Traveller, 1974; Travesty, 1976; The Passion Artist, 1979; Virgine: Her Two Lives, 1983; Sweet William: A Memoir of Old Horse, 1993. Address: 18 Everett Ave, Providence, RI 02906, USA.

HAWKESWORTH John, b. 1920, London, England. Film & TV Producer & Writer. Education: BA, Oxford University. Publications: Film and TV Scripts: Tiger Bay; The Conan Doyle Series; The Million Pound

Bank Note, adaptation; The Elusive Pimpernel; The Goldrobbers; Upstairs, Downstairs, TV Series 1-5; Novels: Upstairs: Secrets of an Edwardian Household, 1972; Upstairs Downstairs in My Lady's Chamber, 1973; The Duchess of Duke Street, 2 TV Series; Danger UXB; Creator and Scriptwriter (TV): The Flame Trees of Thika; The Tale of Beatrix Potter; By the Sword Divided, 2 series; Oscar; Campion; Chelworth; The Adventures of Sherlock Holmes; The Sign of Four; Mrs Arris Goes To Paris. Literary Agent: Casarotto Co Limited. Address: Fishponds House, Knossington, Oakham, Leics, LE15 8LX, England.

HAWKING Stephen William, b. 8 Jan 1942, Oxford, England. British Physicist; Educator; Editor; Author. Publications: The Large Scale Structure of Space-time (co-author), 1973; Is the End in Sight for Theoretical Physics? An Inaugural Lecture, 1980; Superspace and Supergravity: Proceedings of the Nuffield Workshop (co-editor), 1981; The Very Early Universe: Proceedings of the Nuffield Workshop, 1983; Three Hundred Years of Gravitation, 1987; A Brief History of Time: From the Big Bang to Black Holes, 1988; Black Holes and Baby Universes and Other Essays, 1993. Honours: Pius XI Gold Medal from the Pontifical Academy of Sciences, 1975; Dannie Heineman Prize for Mathematical Physics from the American Physical Society and the American Institute of Physics, 1976; Royal Astronomical Society Gold Medal, 1985; Paul Dirac Medal and Prize from the Institute of Physics, 1987. Address: Department of Applied Mathematics and Theoretical Physics, University of Cambridge, Silver Street, Cambrdige, CB3 9EW, England.

HAWKINS Aileen Daisy Doreen, b. 24 Feb 1916, Dorchester, England. Housewife. m. Edgar Hawkins, 16 Oct 1943, dec 1990. Education: Dorset County School. Publications: A Patchwork Book of Poems, 1974; Peace, 1984; The World of Verse, 1971; Poetry International, 1971; World Poets, 1971; Book of Poems - 'To Dorset With Love', 1993. Author of 3,275 poetic works. Contributions to: Sensibility Magazine; The Dorset Year Book; Poetry Now Magazine. Memberships: West Country Writers Association; Thomas Hardy Society; William Barnes Society. Address: Craigaras, Wavering Lane, Gillingham, Dorset, SP8 4NR, England.

HAWKINS Angus Brian, b. 12 Apr 1953, Portsmouth, England. Historian. m. Esther Armstrong, 20 May 1980, 2 daughters. Education: BA Hons, Reading University, 1975; PhD, London School of Economics, 1980. Publications: Parliament, Party and the Art of Politics in Britain, 1987; Victorian Britain: An Encyclopaedia, 1989. Contributions to: English Historical Review, Parliamentary History, Journal of British Studies, Victorian Studies; Nineteenth Century Prose, Archive. Honours: McCann Award, 1972; Gladstone Memorial Prize, 1978. Memberships: Reform Club. Address: Rewley House, University of Oxford, 1 Wellington Square, Oxford, England.

HAWORTH-BOOTH Mark, b. 20 Aug 1944, Westow, Yorks, England. m. Rosemary Joanna Miles, 19 July 1979, 2 daughters. Education: English Tripos, parts I & II, Cambridge University, 1963-66; Postgraduate Diploma in Fine Art, Edinburgh University, 1967-69. Publications: E McKnight Kauffer: A Designer and his Public, 1979; The Golden Age of British Photography 1839-1900, 1983; Bill Brandt's Literary Britain, 1984; Photography Now, 1989; Camille Silvy: River Scene, France, 1992. Contributions to: Times Literary Supplement; London Magazine; The Spectator; New Statesman; Aperture. Honours: Hood Medal, 1988; Sudek Medal, 1989. Address: Victoria & Albert Museum, London, SW7 2RL, England.

HAWTHORNE Douglas Bruce, b. 12 Aug 1948, Mineola, Long Island, NY, USA. m. Marjorie Jo Rheinscheld, 21 Dec 1979. Education: AA, Pima Community College, 1981; BA, 1983, MA, 1985, University of Arizona, 1985. Publications: Men and Women of Space, 1992; Men and Women of Space, 2nd ed, forthcoming 1995. Contributions to: The Daily Territorial; The Weekly Territorial; The Oro Valley Territorial 1986-. Memberships: Fellow of The British Interplanetary Soc; National Space Soc; Phi Kappa Phi; Phi Theta Kappa. Address: 5946 North Camino Del Conde, Tucson, AZ 85718-4312, USA.

HAWTHORNE Susan, b. 30 Nov 1951, Wagga Wagga, New South Wales, Australia. Writer; Publisher. Education: DipT, 1972, MA (Prelim), 1981, University of Melbourne; BA Hons, La Trobe University, 1976. Appointments: Coordinator, New Moods Womes Writers' Festival, 1985; Editor, Commissioning Editor, Penguin Boods Australia, 1987-91; Chair, Australian Feminist Book Fortnight Management Committee, 1989-91; Chair, 6th International Feminist Book Fair, 1992-1994; Publisher, Spinifex Press, 1991-; Chair, Board of Australian

Womens' Book Review, 1993. Publications: The Falling Women, 1992; The Language in my Tongue, 1993; The Spinifex Book of Women's Answers, 1991; The Spinifex Quiz Book, 1993; Co-editor: Australia for Women, 1994; Angels of Power, 1991; Moments of Desire, 1989; The Exploding Frangipani, 1990; Editor, Difference, 1985; 807 Fragen und Frauen, 1994; (Co-editor) Australia for Women, 1994; Australien der Frauen, 1994. Address: c/o Spinifex Press, 504 Queensbury Street, North Melbourne, Victoria 3051, Australia.

HAYCRAFT Anna (Margaret), (Alice Thomas Ellis, Brenda O'Casey). Writer. Appointment: Director, Duckworth, publishers, London; Columnist (Home life), The Spectator, 1984-90, London, also The Universe, 1989-90, The Catholic Herald, 1990-. Publications: Natural Baby Food: A Cookery Book (as Brenda O'Casey), 1977; The Sin Eater (novel), 1977; Darling You Shouldn't Have Gone to So Much Trouble (cookery) (as Anna Haycraft with Caroline Blackwood), 1980; The Birds of the Air (novel), 1980; The 27th Kingdom (novel), 1982; (ed) Mrs Donald by Mary Keene, 1983; The Other Side of the Fire (novel), 1983; Unexplained Laughter (novel), 1985; Home Life (collected columns from the Spectator), 1986; Secrets of Strangers (with Tom Pitt Aikens) (psychiatry), 1986; The Clothes in the Wardrobe (novel), 1987; More Home Life (collection), 1987; The Skeleton in the Cupboard (novel), 1988; Home Life III (collection), 1988; The Loss of the Good Authority (with Tom Pitt Aikens), (psychiatry), 1989; Wales: An Anthology, 1989; The Fly in the Ointment (novel), 1989; Home Life IV (collection), 1989; The Inn at the Edge of the World (novel), 1990; A Welsh Childhood (autobiography), 1990; Pillars of Gold, 1992; The Serpent on The Rocks, 1994; The Evening of Adam, 1994. Literary Agent: Giles Gordon (Sheilland). Address: 22 Gloucester Crescent, London, NW1 7DS, England.

HAYDEN Dolores, b. 15 Mar 1945, New York, USA. Professor; Author. m. Peter Marris, 18 May 1975, 1 d. Education: BA Mount Holyoke College, 1966; Dipl English Studies, Girton College, Cambridge, 1967; M.Arch, Harvard Graduate School of Design, 1972. Publications: Seven American Utopias, 1976; The Grand Domestic Revolution, 1981; Redesigning the American Dream, 1984; The Power of Place, 1995. Contributions to: Poetry in numerous journals including: Electrum; Witness. Honours: NEH Fellowship, 1976; NEA, 1980; Guggenheim, 1981; Rockefeller, 1981; ACLS/Ford, 1988. Memberships: American Studies Association; Organization of American Historians. Address: School of Architecture, Yale University, PO Box 208242, New Haven, CT 06520, USA.

HAYDEN Donald E, b. 1915, USA. Appointments: Instructor, Syracuse University, 1937-42; Head of English, Westbrook Junior College, Portland, 1942-47; Assistant Professor of English, 1947-56, Professor 1956-85, Dean of Liberal Arts 1956-70, Professor Emeritus of English 1985-, University of Tulsa. Publications: After Conflict, Quiet - A Study ofWordsworth, 1951; A Semantics Workbook (with E P Alworth), 1956; Classics in Semantics (ed), 1965; Classics in Linguistics (co-author), His Firm Estate (ed), 1967; Classics in Composition (ed), 1969; Introspection - The Artist Looks at Himself, 1971; Literary Studies: The Poetic Process, 1978; Wordsworth's Walking Tour of 1790, 1983; Wordsworth's Travels in Scotland (Wales and Ireland, Europe), 3 volumes, 1985-88.Address: 3626 South Birmingham Avenue, Tulsa, OK 74105, USA.

HAYES Charles Langley. See: **HOLMES Bryan John.**

HAYLOCK John Mervyn, b. 22 Sept 1918, Bournemouth, England. Writer. Education: Diploma francais, Institut de Touraine, Tours, France, 1937; Certificat d'Immatriculation, Grenoble University, France, 1938; Pembroke College, Cambridge, England, 1938-40, 1946-47, BA Hons, 1940; MA Hons, 1946. Publications: New Babylon, A Portrait of Iraq (with Desmond Stewart), 1956; See You Again, 1963; It's All Your Fault, 1964; Choice and Other Stories, 1979; One Hot Summer in Kyoto, 1980; Tokyo Sketch Book, 1980; Japanese Excersions, 1981; Japanese Memories, 1987; Romance Trip and Other Stories, 1988; A Touch of the Orient, 1990; Uneasy Relations, 1993; Translation from French of Philippe Jullian's Flight into Egypt, 1970. Contributions to: Regularly to Blackwoods Magazine (1975-80); London Magazine; Short Story International, New York; The Japan Times; Winter's Tales. Membership: Orient Club, London. Literary Agent: Rivens Scott, 15 Gledhow Gardens, London, SW5 0AY, England. Address: 5 Powis Grove, Brighton, BN1 3HF, England.

HAYMAN Daivd,b. 7 Jan 1927, New York, USA. University Professor. m. Loni Goldschmidt, 28 June 1951, 2 daughters. Education:

BA, New York University, 1948; Doctorat d'Universite de Paris, 1955. Appointments: Instructor of English, 1955-57, Assistant Professor, 1957-58, Associate Professor, 1958-65, University of Texas; Professor of English and Comparative Literature, University of Iowa, 1965-73; Professor of Comparative Literature, University of Wisconsin, 1973-; Evjue-Baslom Professor, 1990-. Publications: Joyce et Mallarme, 1956; A First Draft Version of Finnegans Wake, 1963; Configuration Critique de James Joyce (ed), 1965; Ulysses: The Mechanics of Meaning, 1970; Form in Fiction (with Eric Rabkin), 1974; The James Joyce Archive (ed 25 Finnegans Wake vols), 1978; Philippe Sollers: Writing and the Experience of Limits (ed and co-translator), 1980; Re-forming the Narrative, 1987; The Wake in Transit, 1990; James Joyce's Ulysses: Critical Essays (ed with Clive Hart), 1974; In the Wake of the Wake (ed), 1978. Contributions to: Novel, PMLA, ELH, Comparative Literature Studies, James Joyce Quarterly, Joyce Studies Annual, Art Forum, Art and Antiques, Poétique, Tel Quel, TriQuarterly, Orbis Litterarum, Quimera, Diario 16, Contemporary Literature; Beckett Studies; Changes; Contemporary Literature; ELH; Espiral; Etudes Anglaises; Europe; European Joyce Studies; Iowa Review;James Joyce LiterarySupplement; Joyce Studies Annual; Ligua y Stile; La Revue des Lettres Modernes; The Review of Contemporary Fiction; Substance; Texas Studies in English; Texas Quarterly. Honours: Guggenheim Fellowship 1958-59; National Endowment for the Humanities 1979-80; Harry Levin Prize (American Comparative Literature Association), 1989. Memberships: MLA; ACLA. Address: 2913 Columbia Road, Madison, WI 53705, USA.

HAYMAN Ronald, b. 1932, British. Appointment: Assistant Producer, Northampton Repertory Company, 1962-63. Publications: Harold Pinter, Samuel Beckett, John Osborne, John Arden, 1968; Robert Bolt, John Whiting, Collected Plays of John Whiting (ed) 2 volumes, Techniques of Acting, 1969; The Art of the Dramatist and Other Pieces (ed), Arthur Miller, Tolstoy, Arnold Wesker, 1970; John Gielgud, Edward Albee, 1971; Eugène Ionesceo, 1972; Playback, 1973; The Set-Up, Playback 2, 1974; The First Thrust, The German Theatre (ed), 1975; The Novel Today 1967-75, 1976; My Cambridge (ed), Tom Stoppard, How to Read a Play, Artaud and After, 1977; De Sade, 1978; Theatre and Anti-Theatre, British Theatre since 1955: A Reassessment, 1979; Nietzsche: A Critical Life, 1980; K: A Biography of Kafka, 1981; Brecht: A Biography, 1983; Fassbinder: Film Maker, Brecht: The Plays, 1984; Günter Grass, Secrets: Boyhood in a Jewish Hotel 1932-54, 1985; Writing Against: A Biography of Sartre, 1986; Proust; A Biography, 1990; The Death and Life of Sylvia Plath, 1991; Tennessee Williams: Everyone Else is an Audience, 1994; Thomas Mann, 1995. Membership: Society of Authors. Literary Agent: Aitken Stone & Wylie. Address: Flat 2, 119 Westbourne Terrace, London, W2 6QT, England.

HAYTER Alethea Catharine, b. 1911, Cairo, Egypt. Former British Council Representative and Cultural Attache. Education: MA, University of Oxford. Publications: Mrs Browning: A Poet's Work and Its Setting, 1962; A Sultry Month: Scenes of London Literary Life in 1846, 1965; Elizabeth Barrett Browning, 1965; Opium and the Romantic Imagination, 1968; Horatio's Version, 1972; A Voyage in Vain, 1973; Fitzgerald to His Friends: Selected Letters of Edward Fitzgerald, 1979; Portrait of a Friendship, Drawn From New Letters of James Russell Lonell to Sybella Lady Lyttelton 1881-1891, 1990; The Backbone: Diaries of a Military Family in The Napoleonic Wars, 1993. Contributions to: Oxford Companion to English Literature; Sunday Times; Times Literary Supplement; New Statesman; History Today; Ariel; London Review of Books; The Longman Encyclopedia. Honours: W.H. Heinemann Prize, RSL for Mrs Browning: A Poet's Work and Its Setting; Rose Mary Crawshay Prize, British Academy, for Opium and the Romantic Imagination; OBE. Memberships: FRSL; Society of Authors, Committee of Management, 1975-79; PEN. Address: 22 Aldebert Terrace, London, SW8 1BJ, England.

HAYWARD Lana Janes, b. 9 Oct 1943, Ft Worth, Texas, USA. Writer. m. John Edward Hayward, 1 Dec 1961, 1 daughter. Education: English and Psychology, University of Texas, San Antonio, 1981-86. Publications: Of Hobos and Rainbows, 1992; House Cleaning, 1992; Cat's in Cradle, 1993; Ink on the Trees, 1987; Son of Man, 1987; Nickels and Dimes, 1985; Clean,1992. Contributions to: Denver Post; Air Force Times; Colorado Woman's News; San Antonio Light; Alamagordo Daily News; Aurora Sentinel; Lowry Airman; Journal of University of Texas. Honours: 3rd Place, National League of American Pen Women, 1992; National Writers Club Award, 1992; Denver Woman's Press Club Award, 1990. Memberships: National Writers Club, President, Denver Chapter, 1992. Address: Aurora, CO 80013, USA.

HAZEN Robert M, b. 1 Nov 1948, NY, USA. Scientist; Musician. m. Margaret Hindle, 1 s, 1 d. Education: BS, SM, 1971; PhD, 1975. Literary Appointments: Clarence Robinson Prof, George Mason University; Geophysical Laboratory, Carnegie Institution of Washington. Publications include: Science Matters, 1991; The Breakthrough, 1988; The New Alchemists, 1994; The Music Men, 1994; Keepers of the Flame, 1993; Poetry of Geology; The Science. Contributions to: Smithsonian; Newsweek; Scientific American; New York Times Mag; Washington Post; Science; Nature. Honours: MSA Award, 1981; Ipatief Prize, 1984; Deans Taylor Award, 1988; Education Pras Award, 1991. Memberships: AAAS; ACS; GSA; MSA; AGU; Sigma Xi. Literary Agent: Gabriele Pantucci, Artellu Ltd, London. Address: 5251 Broad Branch Road NW, WA 20015, USA.

HAZLETON Lesley, b. 20 Sept 1945, Reading, England. Writer. Education: BA Hons, Psychology, Manchester University, England, 1963-66; MA, Psychology, Hebrew University of Jerusalem, Israel, 1970-72. Literary Appointments: Visiting Professor, Penn State University, USA. Publications: England, Bloody England, 1989; Jerusalem, Jerusalem, 1986; In Defence of Depression, 1984; Where Mountains Roar, 1980; Israeli Women, 1978. Contributions to: New York Times; Harper's Tikkun; The Nation; New York Review of Books; Vanity Fair and many others; Automotive Columnist for Fame and Lear's Magazines. Memberships: PEN American Center; IMPA (International Motor Press Association). Literary Agent: Watkins-Loomis Inc. Address: c/o Watkins-Loomis Inc, 150 East 35, New York, NY 10016, USA.

HAZO Samuel (John), b. 1928, USA. Appointments: Joined Faculty 1955, Dean, College of Arts and Science 1961-66, Professor of English 1965-, Duquesne University, Pittsburgh; Director, International Forum, 1966-. Publications: Discovery and Other Poems, 1959; The Quiet Wars, 1962; Hart Crane: An Introduction and Interpretation, 1963, as Smithereened Apart: A Critique of Hart Crane, 1978; The Christian Intellectual Studies in the Relation of Catholicism to the Human Sciences (ed), 1963; A Selection of Contemporary Religious Poetry (ed), 1963; Listen with the Eye, 1964; My Sons in God: Selected and New Poems, 1965; Blood Rights, 1968; The Blood of Adonis (with Ali Ahmed Said), 1971; Twelve Poems (with George Nama), Seascript: A Mediterranean Logbook, Once for the Last Bandit: New and Previous Poems, 1972; Quartered, 1974; Inscripts, 1975; The Very Fall of the Sun, 1978; To Paris, 1981; The Wanton Summer Air, 1982; Thank a Bored Angel, 1983; The Feast of Icarus, 1984; The Color of Reluctance, The Pittsburgh that Starts Within You, 1986; Silence Spoken Here, 1988; STILLS, 1989; The Restis Prose, 1989; Lebanon, 1990; Picks, 1990; The Past Won't Stay Behind You, 1993. Address: 785 Somerville Drive, Pittsburgh, PA 15243, USA.

HAZZARD Shirley, b. 30 Jan 1931, Sydney, Australia. Writer. m. Francis Steegmuller, 22 Dec 1963. Publications: Novels: The Transit of Venus, 1980; The Evening of the Holiday, 1966; The Bay of Noon, 1970; Stories: Cliffs of Fall, 1963; People in Glass Houses, 1967; History: Defeat of An Ideal, 1973; Contenance of Truth,1990. Contributions to: The New Yorker; Times Literary Supplement. Honours: Award in Literature, National Institute of Arts and Letters, USA, 1966; Guggenheim Fellow, 1974; First Prize, O Henry Short Story Awards, 1976; National Book Critics Circle Award for Fiction, 1981. Memberships: Trustee, New York Society Library; Member, American Academy of Arts and Letters, 1982. Literary Agents: McIntosh and Otis, 310 Madison Ave, New York, NY 10017, USA. and A M Heath, London, England. Address: 200 East 66th St, New York, NY 10021, USA.

HEADLEY Elizabeth. See: HARRISON Elizabeth C.

HEADLEY John Miles, b. 23 Oct 1929, New York, USA. Educator; Historian. m. Anne Renouf, 27 July 1965, div. Education: BA, Princeton University, 1951; MA, 1952; PhD, 1960, Yale University; Publications: Luther's View of Church History, 1963; The Emperor and his Chancellor, 1983.; Co-author, San Carlo Borromeo: Catholic Reform and Ecclesiastical Politics, 1988; Editor, Responsio ad Lutherum, Complete works of St Thomas More, 1969. Contributions to: Several journals including, Journal of the History of Ideas. Honours: Guggenheim Fellow, 1974; Selma V Forkosch Prize, 1988. Memberships: American Society for Reformation Research, President,

1978-80; Renaissance Society of America. Address: Deptartment of History, University of North Carolina, Chapel Hll, NC 27599-3195, USA.

HEALD Timothy Villiers, (David Lancaster), b. 28 Jan 1944, Dorset, England. Writer. m. Alison Martina Leslie, 30 Mar 1968, 2 sons, 2 daughters. Education: MA, Honours, Balliol College, Oxford, 1962-65. Appointments: Chairman, Crime Writers Association, 1987-88; International Co-ordinator, Writers in Prison Committee, PEN, 1986-89; Council of Management, Society of Authors, 1988-91. Publications Include: Unbecoming Habits; HRH The Man Who Would Be King; The Character of Cricket; Networks; Class Distinctions; Murder at Moosejaw; Blue Blood Will Out: Deadline; Let Sleeping Dogs Die; Masterstroke; Red Herrings; Brought to Book; Business Unusual; The Rigby File (Editor); Its a Dog's Life; Making of Space 1999; John Steed (The Authorised Biography) volume 1; The Newest London Spy (Editor); By Appointments: 150 Years of the Royal Warrant and Its Holders; My Lord's (Editor); A Classic English Crime (Editor), 1990; The Duke: A Portrait of Prince Philip, 1991; Honourable Estates, 1992; Barbara Cartland - A Life of Love, 1994; Denis - The Authorised Biography of The Incomparable Compton, 1994. Literary Agent: Vivien Green, c/o Richard Scott Simon Ltd, 43 Doughty Street, London, WC1N 2LF. Address: 305 Sheen Road, Richmond, Surrey, TW10 5AW, England.

HEALEY Denis (Winston), b. 1917, British. Appointments: Member, Labour Party National Executive Committee; Secretary, Labour Party International Department, 1946-52; Member of Council, Royal Institute of International Affairs, London, 1948-60; Member of the Executive Fabian Society, 1954-61; Member of the Council, Institute of Strategic Studies, 1958-61; MP for SE Leeds, 1952-55; Labour MP for Leeds East, 1955-1992; Secretary of State for Defence, 1964-70; Shadow Foreign Secretary, 1970-74, 1980; Chancellor of the Exchequer, 1974-79; Baron Healy of Riddlesden, 1992. Publications: The Curtain Falls, 1951; New Fabian Essays, 1952; Neutralism, 1955; Fabian International Essays, 1956; A Neutral Belt in Europe, 1958; NATO and American Security, 1959; The Race Against the H Bomb, 1960; Labour Britain and the World, 1963; Managing the Economy, 1979; Healey's Eye, 1980; Labour and World Society, 1985; Beyond Nuclear Deterrence, 1986; The Time of My Life, 1989; (essays) When Shrimps Learn to Whistle, 1990; My Secret Planet, 1992. Address: House of Commons, London, SW1A 0AA, England.

HEANEY Seamus, b. 13 Apr 1939, Northern Ireland. Author; Poet. m. Marie Devlin, 1965, 2 sons, 1 daughter. Education: Queen's University of Belfast. Appointments: Lecturer St Joseph's College, Belfast, 1963-66, Queen's University, Belfast, 1966-72; Freelance Writer, 1972-75; Lecturer, Carysfort College, 1975-81; Senior Visiting Lecturer, Harvard University, 1982-; Bolyston Professor, Rhetoric and Oratory, 1984; Professor of Poetry, Oxford, 1989-94. Publications: Poetry: Death of a Naturalist, 1966; Door into the Dark, 1969; Wintering Out, 1972; North, 1975; Field Work, 1979; Sweeney Astray, 1984; Station Island, 1984; The Haw Lantern, 1987; Prose: Preoccupations, 1980; New Selected Poems, 1966-1987, 1990; Seeing Things, 1991; Sweeney's Flight, 1992 (with photographs by Rachel Giese). Honours: W.H. Smith Prize, 1975; Bennet Award, 1982; Mondello Prize, 1993. Address: c/o Faber and Faber, 3 Queen Square, London, WC1N 3AU, England.

HEARLE Kevin James, b. 17 Mar 1958. Poet; Scholar. m. Elizabeth Henderson, 26 Nov 1983. Education: AB English, (dist) Stanford, 1980; MFA English, University of Iowa, 1983; PhD, Literature, University of California, Santa Cruz, 1990. MA, Literature, University of California, Santa Cruz, 1991; Appointments: Poetry Co-Editor, Quarry West, 1988-91; Assistant, National Endowment for the Humanities Summer Institutes on Literary Translation, 1988-89; Lecturer in English, San Jose State University, 1992; Lecturer in American Literature, University of California, Santa Cruz, 1993; Lecturer in English, San Jose State University, 1993-94. Publications: Each Thing We Know is Changed Because We Know It, 1994; (Dissertation) Regions of Discourse: Steinbeck, Cather, Jewett and the Pastoral Tradition of American Regionalism, 1991. Address: 320 N Palm Drive #304, Beverly Hills, CA 90210, USA.

HEARNE Vicki, b. 1946. Publications: Nervous Horses, 1980; In the Absence of Horses, 1983; Adam's Task: Calling Animals by Name, 1986; The White German Shepherd: a novel, 1988; Bandit: dossier of a dangerous dog, 1991; Animal Happiness, 1994; The Parts of Light: Poems, 1994. Honour: Fellow, American Academy & Institute of Arts & Letters, 1992.

HEATER Derek Benjamin, b. 28 Nov 1931, Sydenham, England. Writer. m. Gwyneth Mary Owen, 12 Mar 1982, 1 son, 1 daughter. Education: BA, Honours, History, University College London, 1950-53; Postgraduate Certificate in Education, Institute of Education, University of London, 1953-54. Appointments: Editor, Teaching Politics, 1973-79; British member, Editorial Board, International Journal of Political Education, 1977-84; Co-editor, with Bernard Crick, Political Realities Series, 1974-93. Publications: Political Ideas in the Modern World, 1960; Order and Rebellion, 1964; Contemporary Political Ideas, 1974; Britain and the Outside World, 1976; Essays in Political Education, (Co-author Bernard Crick), 1977; World Studies, 1980; Our World This Century, 1982; Our World Today, 1985; World Affairs, (Co-author Gwyneth Owen), 1972; World Studies, 1980; Peace Through Education, 1984; Reform and Revolution, 1987; Refugees, 1988; Case Studies in Twentieth-Century World History, 1988; Citizenship: The Civic Ideal in World History, Politics and Education, 1990; The Idea of European Unity, 1992; The Remarkable History of Rottingdean, 1993; Introduction to International Politics, (with G.R. Berridge), 1993; Foundations of Citizenship, (with Dawn Oliver), 1994; National Self-Determination, 1994. Contributions to: Over 70 articles in learned journals, educational press and contributions to symposia; Approximately 100 entries for encyclopaedias. Honours: Children's Book of the Year Award for Refugees, 1988; Fellow of the Politics Association, 1994. Membership: Founder-Chairman, The Politics Association, 1969-73. Address: 3 The Rotyngs, Rottingdean, Brighton, BN2 7DX, England.

HEATH Roy A K, b. 13 Aug 1926, British Guiana. Appointments: Teacher in London, 1959-; Barrister, 1964-. Publications: A Man Come Home, 1974; The Murderer, 1978; From the Heat of the Day, 1979; One Generation, 1980; Genetha, 1981; Kwaku, 1982; Orealla, 1984. Address: c/o Harper/Collins, 77 Fulham Palace Road, London, W6 8J, England.

HEATH-STUBBS John (Francis Alexander), b. 9 July 1918, London, England. Education: Worcester College for the Blind; Queen's College, Oxford. Appointments: English Tutor, 1944-45; Editorial Assistant, Hutchinsons, 1945-46; Gregory Fellow, Poetry, University of Leeds, 1952-55; Visiting Professor English, University of Alexandria, 1955-58, University of Michigan, 1960-61; Lecturer, English Literature, College of St Mark and St John, Chelsea, 1963-73; President, Poetry Society, 1992-. Publications: Poetry: Wounded Thammuz, 1942; Beauty and the Beast, 1943; The Divided Ways, 1946; The Swarming of the Bees, 1950; A Charm Against the Toothache, 1954; The Triumph of the Muse, 1958; The Blue Fly in his Head, 1962; Selected Poems, 1965; Satires and Epigrams, 1968; Artorius, 1973; A Parliament of Birds, 1975; The Watchman's Flute, 1978; Birds Reconvened, 1980; Buzz Buzz, 1981; Naming of the Best, 1982; The Immolation of Aleph, 1985; Cats Parnassus, 1987; Time Pieces, 1988; Partridge in a Pear Tree, 1988; Ninefold of Charms, 1989; The Parson's Cat, 1991; Collected Poems, 1990; Drama: Helen in Egypt, 1958; Crticism: The Darkling Plain, 1950; Charles Williams, 1955; The Pastoral, 1969; The Ode, 1969; The Verse Satire, 1969; Translantions: Hafir of Shiraz, 1952; The Rubiyyat of Omar Khayyam (both with Peter Avery), 1979; Leopardi: Selected Prose and Poetry (with Iris Origo), 1960; the Poems of Anyte with Carol A. Whiteside), 1974; Editor, Selected Poems of Jonathan Swift, 1948; of Tennyson; of Alexander Pope, 1964; In the Shadows, (with David Gray), 1991;, Sweet Apple Earth, 1993; Hindsights (autobiography), 1993; Chimeras, 1994. Honours: Queen's Gold Medal for Poetry, 1973; OBE, 1989. Address: 22 Artesian Road, London, W2, England.

HEATHCOTT Mary. See: KEEGAN Mary Constance.

HEBALD Carol, b. 6 July 1934, New York City, USA. Writer. Education: MFA, University of Iowa, 1971; BA, City College of City University of New York, 1969. Publications: Three Blind Mice, 1989; Clara Kleinschmidt, 1989 (two short novels); Martha, (play), 1991. Contributions to: Antioch Review; Massachusetts Review; The Humanist; New Letters; Confrontation; North American Review; New York Tribune. Honours: McGraw Hill Nomination; Editors' Book Award Pushcart Prize, 1987; PEN American Fund, 1985, 1986; Harper Collins Nomination of the novel A Warsaw Chronicle, Editors' Book Award Pushcart Prize, 1994. Memberships: PEN American Centre; Authors Guild of America; Poet and Writers Inc; Phi Beta Kappa. Address: 463 West Street, No 353, New York, NY 10014, USA.

HEBEBER Thomas, b. 13 Nov 1947, Offenbach, Germany. Professor; Political Science, East Asia and China, University of Trier.

m. Jing Wang, 24 Aug 1979, 1 son, 1 daughter. Education: University of Heidelberg, 1973; Doctor's Degree, University of Bremen; Qualifications for Professorship, 1989. Publications: et al. Corruption in China, 1991; The Functions of the Individual Sector in China for Labour market and urban development, 1989; Xiandaihua: The Modernization Process of China, 1990; Nationalities Policy and Development Policy in China's Minority Areas, 1984; China and its National Minorities: Autonomy or Assimilation, 1989; Editor: Ethnic Minorities in China: Tradition and Transformation, 1989; Problems and Strategies in German-Chinese Trade, 1992; Economic Reform in China, 1985; China on its way to the year 2000, 1989; China's Economic Policy after Mao, 1989; Transformation of the Chinese System or Social Change, 1993; Is the Chinese Empire Threatened with Discintegration? The Peril of Growing Nationalities Unrest, 1991; (ed) Mao Zedong - the Immortal Revolutionary?; A Reassessment on the Occassion of his 100th birthday, 1995 (ed) Yaogun Yinyue: Youth-, Sub-culture and Rockmusic in China, political and social background of a new phenomenon, 1995. Address: Universitât Trier, Fachbereich III, Politikwissenschaft, Schwerpunkt Ostasien, 54286 Trier, Germany.

HEBERT Anne, b. 1 Aug 1916, Sainte-Catherine-de-Fossambault, Quebec, Canada. Novelist; Poet. Education: Collège Notre Dame, Bellevue, Quebec. Publications: The Torrent: Novellas and Short Stories, 1950, 1973; The Silent Rooms, 1958, 1974; Kamouraska, 1970; Children of the Black Sabbath, 1975; Heloise, 1980; In the Shadow of the Wind, 1982; The First Garden, 1988; The Dreaming Child, 1992; Verse: Les Songes en équilibre, 1942; The Tomb of the Kings, 1953, 1967; Poems, 1960, 1975; Selected Poetry, in translation, 1978; Eve: Poems, 1980; Selected Poems, 1987; Plays: Le Temps sauvage, La Mercière assassinée and Les Invités au procès, all 1966; La Cage and L'Ile de la demoiselle, 1990. Honours include: Académie Française Award, 1975; DLitt, Universities of Toronto and Quebec. Address: 24 rue de Pontoise, 75005 Paris, France.

HECHT Anthony Evan, b. 16 Jan 1923, New York, USA. Poet; Professor of English. m. (1) Patricia Harris, 1954 (div 1961), 2 sons, (2) Helen d'Alessandro, 1971, 1 son. Education: Bard College; MA, Columbia University. Appointments: Teacher, Kenyon College, 1947-48, State University, Iowa, 1948-49, New York University, 1949-56, Smith College, 1955-59; Associate Professor, English, Bard College, 1961-67; Faculty, 1967, John H Deane Professor, Rhetoric and Poetry, 1968, University of Rochester; Hurst Professor, Washington University, 1971; Professor Graduate School, Georgetown University, 1987-. Publications: Poetry: A Summoning of Stones, 1954; The Seven Deadly Sins, 1958; A Bestiary, 1960; The Hard Hours, 1968; Million of Strange Shadows, 1977; Jiggery Pokery (co-author and co-editor), 1967; Seven Against Thebes (translated with Helen Bacon), 1973; The Venetian Vespers, 1979; Obbligati: Essays in Criticism, 1986. Honours: Guggenheim Fellow, 1954, 1959; Ford Foundation Fellow, 1967; Rockefeller Foundation Fellow, 1967; Fellow, Academy of American Poets, Chancellor, 1971-; Prix de Rome, 1950; Brandeis University Creative Arts Award, 1965; Pulitzer Prize, 1968; Bollingen Prize, 1983; Eugenio Montale Prize for Poetry, 1985. Memberships: Trustee, American Academy, Rome; National Institute of Arts and Letters; American Academy of Arts and Science. Address: 4256 Nebraska Avenue NW, Washington, DC 20016, USA.

HECKELMANN Charles N, b. 25 Oct 1913, Brooklyn, New York, USA. Book Publisher (Retired); Author. m. 17 Apr 1937, 1 s, 1 d. Education: BA, maxima cum laude, University of Note Dame, 1934. Appointments include: Various editorial, administrative positions with: Cupples & Leon Company, 1937-41; Popular Library, 1941-58; Monarch Books, 1958-65; David McKay Company, 1965-68; Cowles Book Company, 1968-71; Hawthom Books, 1971-75; National Enquirer, 1975-78. Publications include: Guns of Arizona, 1949; Two-Bit Rancher, 1950; Fighting Ramrod, 1951; Hard Man with A Gun, 1954; Rawhider, 1952; Bullet Law, 1955; Trumpets in the Dawn, 1958; Big Valley, 1966; The Glory Riders, 1967; Writing Fiction for Profit, 1968; Stranger From Durango, 1971; Return to Arapahoe, 1980; Wagons to Wind River, 1982. Also: Vengeance Trail, 1944; Lawless Range, 1945; Six-Gun Outcast, 1946; Deputy Marshall, 1947 (also filmed); Let the Guns Roar, 1950. Contributions to: 200 short stories, novels, newsletter, various magazines. Honours: Valedictorian, senior class, Meyers Burse Award, University of Notre Dame. Memberships: Past president, Catholic Writers Guild; Western Writers of America; Life Member, National Cowboy Hall of Fame. Address: 10634 Green Trail Drive South, Boynton Beach, FL 33436, USA.

HECKLER Jonellen, b. 28 Oct 1943, Pittsburgh, Pennsylvania, USA. Writer. m. Lou Heckler, 17 Aug 1968, 1 son. Education: BA, English Literature, University of Pittsburgh, 1965. Publications: Safekeeping, 1983; A Fragile Peace, 1986; White Lies, 1989; Circumstances Unknown, 1993. Contributions to: Numerous poems and short stories in Ladies Home Journal Magazine between 1975-83. Memberships: The Authors Guild. Literary Agent: Janklow & Nesbit Associates. Address: 5562 Pernod Drive SW, Ft Myers, FL 33919, USA.

HECKSCHER William S(ebastian), b. 14 Dec 1904, Hamburg, Germany. Professor of Art History; Painter; Freelance Writer. m. Roxanne Sanossian, 15 Feb 1973, 3 daughters. Education: Palaeography, Corpus Christi College, Oxford, England; New York University; PhD, Hamburg University, 1936; Diploma in Teaching. Appointments: Linguistic Intelligence Work, Canadian Government; Professor of German Language and Literature: Carleton College, Ottawa, Ontario, Canada, Universities of Saskatchewan and Manitoba; Art History Teacher (especially mediaeval art): State University of Iowa, Utrecht University (keeper of 2 libaries); Duke University (founder and director Museum of Art); Member Advisory Council to the Minister of Education, The Netherlands. Publications Include: Sixtvs IIII aeneas Statvas restitvendas censvit, 1955; Rembrandt's Anatomy of Dr. Tulp, 1956; Art and Literature, 1986; The Human Form in Contemporary Art, 1971. Contributions to: Over 100 articles to literature and art history journals. Honours: Hon Doctorate, McGill University; Carey Award (Society of Indexers), 1987; Bronze Medal, College de France, Paris, 1981. Memberships Include: Fellow, Royal Society of Art; National Gallery Washington DC; Six Times Member of the Princeton Institute of Advanced Study; Consultant, Rare Books, Princeton University Library. Address: 32 Wilton Street, Princeton, NJ 08540, USA.

HEDIN Mary Ann, b. 3 Aug 1929, Minneapolis, Minnesota, USA. Professor. m. Roger Willard Hedin, 3 sons, 1 daughter. Education: BS, University of Minnesota; MA, University of California. Appointments: Fellow, Yaddo, 1974; Writer in Residence, Robinson Jeffers Tor House Foundation, 1984-85. Publications: Fly Away Home, 1980; Direction, 1983. Contributions to: McCalls; Red Book; Southwest Review; South Dakota Review; Descant; O Henry Prize Short Stories; Best American Short Stories; Poems in: Shenandoah; South; Perspective World Order. Honours: John H McGinnis Memorial Award, 1979; Iowa School of Letters Award for Short Fiction, 1979. Memberships: Authors Guild; PEN; American Poetry Society. Address: 182 Oak Avenue, San Anselmo, CA 94960, USA.

HEDLEY Annie. See: HUNT Fay Ann.

HEFFERNAN Thomas (Carroll), b. 19 Aug 1939, Hyannis, USA. Lecturer. m. Nancy Eiler, 15 July 1972, (div 1978). Education: AB, Boston College, 1961; MA, English Literature, University of Manchester, England, 1963; Universita per-Stranieri, Perugia, Italy, summer 1965; PhD English Literature, Sophia University, Tokyo, 1990. Appointments: Poet in Schools, North Carolina Department of Public Instruction, Raleigh, 1973-77; Visiting Artist, Poetry, North Carolina Department of Community Colleges, 1977-81; Visiting Artist, Poetry, South Carolina Arts Commission, 1981-82; Co-editor, The Plover (Chidori), bi-lingual haiku journal, Japan, 1989 to present; Professor of English, Kagoshima Prefectura 1 University, Japan. Publications: Mobiles, 1973; A Poem is A Smile You Can Hear, Editor, 1976; A Narrative of Jeremy Bentham, 1978; The Liam Poems, 1981; City Renewing Itself, 1983; Art and Emblem: Early Seventeenth Century English Poetry of Devotion, Renaissance Institute, 1991. Contributions to: Essays in Renaissance Monographs; Yearbook of Interdisciplinary Studies in the Fine Arts; Mainichi Daily News. Poems in: Modern Haiku; Mainichi Daily News; Frog Pond, Red Pagoda; Wind Chimes. Reviews in: The Plover (Chidori). Address: Kagoshima Prefectural University, 44-2 Shimo-ishiki-cho, Kagoshima-shi, Japan 890.

HEFFRON Dorris M, b. 18 Oct 1944, Canada. Novelist. m. D L Gauer, 29 Oct 1980, 1 s, 3 d. Education: BA, MA. Appointments: Tutor, Lecturer, Oxford University, 1970-80; Tutor, The Open University, 1972-78. Publications: A Nice Fire and Some Moonpennies; Crusty Crossed; Rain and I; The Saving Note. Contributions to: Queens Quarterly. Honours: Canada Council Arts Grant. Memberships: Authors Society; Writers Union of Canada, PEN. Literary Agent: Sheila Watson, Watson Little Limited. Address: 202 Riverside Drive, Toronto, Ontario, Canda, M6S 4A9.

HEGI Ursula Johanna, b. 23 May 1946, West Germany. Writer and Professor, 2 s. Education: BA, 1978; MA, 1979, UNH. Appointments: Currently: Associate Professor of English, Eastern Washington University; Board, NBCC, 1992, 1993. Publications: Instrusions, 1981; Unearned Pleasures and Other Stories, 1988; Floating in My Mother's Palm, 1990; Stones from the River, 1994; Salt Dancers, 1995. Contributions to: Los Angeles Times Book Reivew. Honours: PEN Syndicated Fiction - six years; NEA, 1990; Artists Trust, 1988. Literary Agent: Gail Hochman, Brandt and Brandt. Address: Eastern Washington University, Cheney, WA 99004, USA.

HEIDE Florence Parry, b. 1919, USA. Writer of Children's Fiction. Appointments: Currently Full-time Writer. Formerly worked for RKO and in Public Relations and Advertising, New York; Former Public Relations Director, Pittsburgh Playhouse. Publications Include: God and Mr (non-fiction), 1975; You and Me (non-fiction), 1975; (with Roxanne Heide), Mystery of the Vanishing Visitor, 1975; (with Roxanne Heide), Mystery of the Bewitched Bookmobile, 1975; When the Sad One Comes to Stay, 1975; Growing Anyway Up, 1976; (with Roxanne Heide), Mystery of the Lonely Lantern, 1976; (with Roxanne Heide), Mystery at Keyhole Carnival, 1977; (with Roxanne Heide), Brillstone Break-In, 1977; (with Roxanne Heide), Mystery of the Midnight Message, 1977; (with Sylvia W Van Clief), Fables You Shouldn't Pay Any Attention To, 1978; Banana Twist, 1978; Secret Dreamer, Secret Dreams, 1978; (with Roxanne Heide), Mystery at Southport Cinema, 1978; (with Roxanne Heide), I Love Every-People, 1978; Changes (non-fiction), 1978; Who Taught Me? Was It You, God? (non-fiction), 1978; By The Time You Count To Ten (non-fiction), 1979; (with Roxanne Heide), Face at the Brillstone Window, 1979; (with Roxanne Heide), Mystery of the Mummy's Mask, 1979; (with Roxanne Heide), Body in the Brillstone Garage, 1980; (with Roxanne Heide), Mystery of the Forgotten Island, 1980; (with Roxanne Heide), A Monster is Coming! A Monster is Coming!, 1980; (with Roxanne Heide), Black Magic at Brillstone, 1981; Treehom's Treasure, 1981; Time's Up!, 1982; The Problem with Pulcifer, 1982; The Wendy Puzzle, 1982; (with Roxanne Heide), Time Bomb at Brillstone, 1982; (with Roxanne Heide), Mystery On Danger Road, 1983; Banana Blitz, 1983; Treehom's Wish, 1984; Time Flies, 1984; Tales for the Perfect Child, 1985; The Day of Ahmed's Secret (with Judith Heide Gilliland), 1990. Address: 6910 Third Avenue, Kenosha, WI 53143, USA.

HEIDELBERGER Michael, b. 9 Aug 1947, Karisruhe, Germany. University Professor. m. Nicole Jeannet, 16 Sept 1978, 1 son, 1 daughter. Education: PhD, Philosophy, History of Science, University of Munich, 1978; Habilitation, Philosophy of Science, University of Goettingen, 1989. Publications: Co-editor: The Probabilistic Revolution, 1987; Natur und Erfahrung, 1981; Die innere Seite der Natur: Gustav Theodor Fechners Wissenschaftlich- philosophische Weltauffassung, a study on G T Fechner (1801-87), 1993; Many articles in professional journals, editions of anthologies. Contributions to: Studies in history and philosophy of science; Erkenntnis; Philosophia Naturalis; British Journal for the Philosophy of Science; Corpus; Behavioural and Brain Sciences, 1993; Annals of Theoretical Psychology, 1993. Address: Philosophisches Seminar, Universität Freiburg, 79085 Freiburg, Germany.

HEIGERT Hans A, b. 21 Mar 1925, Mainz, Germany. Journalist. m. Hildegard Straub, 1951, 3 sons, 2 daughters. Education: PhD, Universities of Stuttgart, Heidelberg and Oklahoma. Appointments: Journalist, Newspapers, Radio and TV, 1950-; Chief Editor, Suddeutsche Zeitung, 1970-85. Publications: Statten der Jugend, 1958; Sehnsucht nach der Nation, 1966; Deutschlands falsche Traume, 1968. Honours: Winner, Theodor Heuss Preis, 1969; Bayersicher Verdienstorden, 1974; Bundesverdienstrkreuz, 1979. Membership: Goethe Institute, Munich, 1984-93, President, 1989-93. Address: Eichenstr. 12, 82110 Germering, Germany.

HEILBRONER Robert, b. USA. m. Education: BA, Harvard University; PhD, New School for Social Research. Appointments: Currently Professor of Economics, Emeritus, New School for Social Research. Publications: The Worldly Philosophers, 1953; The Future And History, 1959; An Inquiry into the Human Prospect, 1975; Marxism: The For & Against, 1980; Nature & Logic of Capitalism, 1985; Behind The Veil of Economics, 1988; 21st Century Capitalism, 1993; Visions of the Future. Memberships include: American Economic Association, Formerly Vice President. Address: 830 Park Avenue, New York, NY 10021, USA.

HEILBRUN Carolyn, b. 1926. Professor; Feminist. Publications: In the Last Analysis, 1964; Christopher Isherwood, 1970; Toward A Recognition of Androgyny, 1973; Lady Ottoline's Album, 1976; Reinventing Womanhood, 1979; Representation of Women in Fiction (ed), 1983; Writing a Women's Life, 1988; Hamlet's Mother & Other Women, 1990. Address: Department of English Columbia University, 2960 Columbia University, New York, NY 10027-6902, USA.

HEIN Christoph, b. 8 Apr 1944, Heinzendorf/Schlesien, Germany. Novelist; Playwright. Education: University of Leipzig and Humboldt University, Berlin. Appointments include: Dramaturg and Playwright at the Deutsches Theater, East Berlin, 1971-79. Publications: Nachfahrt und früher Morgen, 1980; The Distant Lover, 1982, 1989; Homs Ende, 1985; Der Tangospieler, 1989; Plays: Cromwell, 1977; Lassalle fragt Herm Herbert nach Sonja, 1981; Der neue Mendoza, 1981; Schlotel, oder was solls, 1981; The True Story of Ah Q, 1983; Passage, 1987; Die Ritter der Tafelrunde, 1989; Also: Jamie and his Friends (for children), 1984; I Saw Stalin as a Child, 1990. Honours include: City of Hamburg Prize, 1986; Lessing Prize, 1989. Address: c/o Aufbau-Verlag, Postfach 1217, 1086 Berlin, Germany.

HEINESEN Jens Pauli, b. 12 Nov 1932, Torshavn, Faroe Islands. Novelist. Education: University of Copenhagen, 1953-54. Appointments include: Teacher at Torshavn, 1957-70. Publications: The Dawn Shower, 1953; The Beautiful Calm, 1959; You, World of Origin, 3 volumes, 1962-64; The Waves Play on the Shore, 1969; In the Garden of Eden, 1971; The Serpent's Name is Fraenir, 1973; The Beachcomber, 1977; Drops in the Ocean of Life, 1978; They Carve Their Idols, 1979; Now You are a Child of Man on Earth, 1980; The World Now Shines Before You, 1981; Your Playing is Like the Bright Day, 1982; The World Now Stretches Boundless Before You, 1983; A Depth of Precious Time, 1984; The Mysteries of Love, 1986; Exposed to the Wind, 1986; Blue Mountain, 1992; Stories, Gestur, and Little Frants Vilhelm, 1972. Honours include: Nordic Council Prize, 1987. Address: Stoffalag 18, Torshavn, The Faroe Islands, via Denmark.

HELDRETH Leonard Guy, b. 8 Apr 1939, Shinnston, West Virginia, USA. Associate Dean, University Professor and Department Head. m. Lillian R Marks, 18 June 1964, 2 s. Eduation: BS, 1962, MA, English, 1964, West Virginia University; PhD, English, University of Illinois, 1973. Appointments: Interim Dean, College of Arts and Sciences, 1991-92; Associate Dean, College of Arts and Sciences, Northem Michigan University, 1994-; Film Reviewer, WNMU-FM Radio, Marquette, Michigan; Video Reviewer, Marquette Monthly newspaper, 1987-. Publications: Book chapters: In Search of the Ultimate Weapon: The Fighting Machine in Science Fiction Novels and Films, 1982; Ascending the Depths: Wordsworth on Mt Snowdon, 1982; Clockwork Reels: Mechanical Environments in Science Fiction Films, 1983; The Ultimate Horror: The Image of the Dead Child in King's Stories and Novels, 1985; Close Encounters of the Carnal Kind; Sex with Aliens in Science Fiction, 1986; The Beast Within: Sexuality and Metamorphosis in Horror Films, 1986; Viewing The Body: Stephen King's Portrait of the Artist as Survivor, 1987; The Dead Child as Fantasy in Albee's Plays, 1988; From Reality to Fantasy in Albee's The Zoo Story, 1988-89; Fantasy in Forster's Short Fiction, 1990; The Supernatural Short Fiction of Henry James, 1990; The Cutting Edges of Blade Runner, 1991; The Ghost and the Self in Henry James, 1992; Re-Retrofitting Blade Runner, 1994; Architecture as Fantasy in Tim Burton's Films, 1995. Address: 376 East Hewitt Avenue, Marquette, MI 49855, USA.

HELLER Joseph, b. 1 May 1923, Brooklyn, USA. Writer. m. (1) Shirley Held, 1945, 1 son, 1 daughter, (2) Valerie Humphries, 1987. Education: New York University; Columbia University; University of Oxford; MA. Appointments: Instructor, Pennsylvania State University, 1950-52; Advertisement Writer, Time Magazine, 1952-56, Look Magazine, 1956-58; Promotion Manager, McCall's Magazine, 1958-61; Former Teacher of Writing, Yale University, University of Pennsylvania, City University, New York. Publications: Novels: Catch 22, 1961; Something Happened, 1974; Good As Gold, 1979; God Knows, 1984; Poetics, 1987; Plays: We Bombed in New Haven, 1968; Clevinger's Trial, 1974; No Laughing Matter (with Speed Vogel), 1985. Honours: National Institute of Arts and Letters Grand for Literature, 1963; Prix Medicis Etranger, 1985. Address: c/o General Publishing Co, PO Box 429, Dayton, OH 45449, USA.

HELLER Marlene Ann, b. 31 Aug 1953, Brooklyn, New York, USA. Freelance Writer; Editor; Personal Poet. m. Gary Robert Heller, 27 July 1985, 1 son, 1 daughter. Education: BA, Monmouth College,

1975. Appointments: Associate Editor, Craft Model & Hobby Industry Magazine, 1975; Production Editor,Bell Labs, 1976; Marketing Editor, Gifts & Decorative Accessories Magazine, 1977-80; Business Correspondent, North Brunswick Post, 1987. Contributions to: Model Retailer; Home Fashions-Textiles; Retail Week; Flowers; Stringer, Princeton Packet Newspapers. Memberships: National Writers Club; Writers Data Bank.

HELLER Ruth. See:**HELLER GROSS Ruth Myrtle.**

HELLER GROSS Ruth Myrtle (Ruth Heller), b. 2 Apr 1923, Winnipeg, Canada. m. (1) Henry David Heller, 21 Dec 1951; (2) Richard Philip Gross, 21 Feb 1987, 2 sons. Education: BA Fine Arts, University of California, 1946; California College of Arts and Crafts, 1963-65. Publications: Chickens Are'nt The Only Ones, 1981; The Reason For A Flower, 1983; A Cache of Jewels, 1987; Kites Sail High, 1988; Many Luscious Lollipops, 1989; Animals Born Alive and Well, 1982; Plants that Never Ever Bloom, 1984; How To Hide A Butterfly, How To Hide A Polar Bear, How To Hide An Octopus, 1984; How To Hide A Crocodile, How To Hide A Grey Tree Frog, How To Hide Whip Pool Will, 1986; Merry Go Round, 1990; Up Up and Away, 1991. Honours: Chickens Aren't The Only Ones won a honorable mention from the New York Academy of Science, 1983. Address: 150 Lombard Street, San Francisco, CA 94111, USA.

HELMINEN Jussi, b. 7 Oct 1947, Turku, Finland. Dramatist; Theatre Director. m. Tellervo Helminen, 1972, 3 sons. Education: Finnish Theatre Academy. Publications: Up to the Stage!, 1989; Cortex, 1990. Plays: The Drugstory, 1972; Hello World, 1973; The Numskulls, 1975; Yellowcloth, 1985; Mutjo, 1987; 'Try With Water' answered the firechief, 1977; TV Plays: Mother Gets Married, 1973; Bigboy and the Boot, 1975; Hands, 1975; Mother's Difficult Age, 1983; Reflection, 1984; Smiley, 1984; Impossibles, 1986; Musical: "Maja of the Stormy Island", composer Matti Puurtinen. Honours: Finnish State Drama Award, 1971, 1972; TV (Eurovision) Prix Jeunesse in Munich, 1974; TV (Intervision) Prix Donau Bratislava, 1975; Tampere Theatre Summer Award, 1972, 1973. Membership: Finnish Dramatists Union; Board of the Finnish Theatre Federation; Board of the Nordic Theatre Union. Agent: Finnish Dramatists Union. Address: TTT, PI 139, 33201 Tampere, Finland.

HELWIG David (Gordon), b. 5 April 1938, Toronto, Canada. Author; Poet. Publications: Figures in a Landscape, 1967; A Time in Winter (play), 1967; The Sign of Gunman, 1969; The Streets of Summer (short stories), 1969; The Day Before Tomorrow (novel), 1971; Fourteen Stories High: Best Canadian Stories of 71 (with T. Marshall), 1971; The Best Name of Silence, 1972; A Book about Billie, 1972; 72, 73 and 74 (with J. Harcourt); New Canadian Stories, 3 vols, 1972-74; The Glass Knight (novel), 1976; The Human Elements, 1978; A Book of the Hours (poetry), 1979; Jennifer (novel), 1979; The King's Evil (novel), 1981; It Is Always Summer (novel), 1982; The Rain Falls Like Rain (verse), 1982; Catchpenny Poems, 1983; A Sound Like Laughter (novel), 1983; The Only Son (novel), 1984; The Bishop, 1986; A Postcard from Rome (novel), 1988; Old Wars (novel), 1989; The Hundred Old Names (verse), 1988; Of Desire (novel), 1990.

HELYAR Jane Penelope Josephine (Josephine Poole), b. 12 Feb 1933, London, England. Writer. m. (1) T R Poole, 1956, (2) V J H Helyar, 1975, 1 s, 5 d. Publications: A Dream in The House, 1961; Moon Eyes, 1965; The Lilywhite Boys, 1967; Catch as Catch Can, 1969; Yokeham, 1970; Billy Buck, 1972; Touch and Go, 1976; When Fishes Flew, 1978; The Open Grave, The Forbidden Room (remedial readers), 1979; Hannah Chance, 1980; Diamond Jack, 1983; The Country Dairy Companion (to accompany Central TV series), 1983; Three For Luck, 1986; Wildlife Tales, 1986; The Loving Ghosts, 1988; Angel, 1989; This is Me Speaking, 1990; Paul Loves Amy Loves Christo, 1992; Puss in Boots, 1988; The Sleeping Beauty, 1989; Snow White, 1991; TV scripts: The Harbourer, 1975; The Sabbatical, 1981; The Breakdown, 1981; Miss Constantine, 1981; Ring A Ring A Rosie, 1983; With Love; Belinda, 1983; The Wit to Woo, 1983; in West Country Stories Series: Fox, 1984; Buzzard, 1984; Dartmoor Pony, 1984; Pinocchio (re-written), 1994; Scared to Death, 1994. Literary Agent: Gina Pollinger. Address: Poundisford Lodge, Poundisford, Taunton, Somerset, TA3 7AE, England.

HEMLEY Robin, b. 28 May 1958, New York City, USA. Associate Professor of English. m. Beverly Bertling Hemley, 18 July 1987, 2 d. Education: BA, Comparative Literature, Indiana University, 1990; MFA, University of Iowa, 1982. Appointments: Association Professor of

English, University of North Carolina at Charlotte, 1986-94; Assistant Professor of English, Western Washington University, Bellingham 1994-. Publications: The Last Studebaker, 1992; All you can Eat, 1988, 1989; The Mouse Town, 1987; Stadt Der Maus, 1992; Tabehodai (translation of All You Can Eat, Hakusui-sha, Tokyo Japan, 1990); Turning Life into Fiction, 1994. Address: 2021 Thomas Avenue, Charlotte, NC 28205, USA.

HEMMING John Henry, b. 5 Jan 1935, Vancouver, Canada. Author; Publisher. m. Sukie Babington-Smith, 1979, 1 son, 1 daughter. Education: McGill and Oxford Universities; MA; D.Litt. Appointments: Director, Secretary, Royal Geographical Society, 1975-; Joint Chairman, Hemming Publishing Ltd, 1976-; Chair, Brintex Ltd., Newman Books Ltd; Explorations in Peru and Brazil, 1960, 1961, 1971, 1972, 1986-87. Publications: The Conquest of the Incas, 1970; Tribes of the Amazon Basin in Brazil (with others), 1973; Red Gold: The Conquest of the Brazilian Indians, 1978; The Search for El Dorado, 1978; Machu Picchu, 1982; Monuments of the Incas, 1983; Change in the Amazon Basin, 2 volumes (Editor), 1985; Amazon Frontier: The Defeat of the Brazilian Indians, 1987; Maracá, 1988; Roraima: Brazil's Northernmost Frontier, 1990; The Rainforest Edge (Editor), 1994. Address: Hemming Publishing Ltd, 32 Vauxhall Bridge Road, London, SW1V 2SS, England.

HENDERSON Hamish, b. 11 Nov 1919, Blairgowrie, Perthshire, Scotland. Poet; Lecturer. Education: MA, Downing College, Cambridge. Appointments include: Senior Lecturer and Research Fellow, School of Scottish Studies, University of Edinburgh, from 1951. Publications: Elegies for the Dead in Cyrenaica, 1948; Freedom Come-All-Ye, 1967; Alias MacAlias, 1990; Collected Essays, 1990; Editor and contributor, Ballads of World War II Collected Seumas Mor Maceanruig. Honours include: Somerset Maugham Award, 1949. Address: School of Scottish Studies, University of Edinburgh, Old College, South Bridge, Edinburgh EH8 9YL, England.

HENDERSON Kathy Caecilia,b. 22 Apr 1949, Oxford, England. Writer; Illustrator; Editor. 2 sons, 1 daughter. Education: BA Hons, English Language and Literature, Oxford, 1969. Publications: My Song is My Own, 1979; Sam and the Big Machines, 1985; 15 Ways to go to Bed, 1986; Series, Where does it come from? Water, 1986, Sweater, 1986, Lego, 1986, Banana, 1986, Bread, 1987, Letter, 1987; Sam and the Box, 1987; The Babysitter, 1988; Don't Interrupt, 1988; The Baby's Book of Babies, 1988; 15 Ways to get Dressed, 1989; Sam, Lizzie and the Bonfire, 1989; Baby Knows Best, 1991; Annie and the Birds, 1991; Second Time Charley, 1991; In the Middle of the Night, 1992; Pappy Mashy, 1992; Annie and the Tiger, 1992; Jim's Winter, 1992. Honours: 15 Ways to go to Bed, Shortlisted for the Smarties Prize, 1986; Sam and the Big Machines, Selected by Parents Magazine for its Best Books for Babies, 1987; Selected for the Book Trust's Childrens Book of the Year, 1987, 1989, 1990, 1993. Address: Muswell Hill, London N1O 3UN, England.

HENDERSON Kent William, b. 29 Jan 1954, Geelong, Victoria, Australia. Author; Teacher. m. Marise de Quadros, 19 Dec 1993, 1 daughter. Education: Deakin University and Victoria University of Technology; Diploma of Teaching; BEd; Graduate Certificate of Education; Graduate Diploma of Education; MEd. Publications: Masonic World Guide, 1984; Naracoorte Caves - South Australia, 1986; Masonic Grand Masters of Australia, 1989; Jenolan Caves, 1989; Buchan and Murrindal Caves, 1992. Contributions to: Australasian Cave and Karst Management Association Journal (editor); Transactions, Victorian Lodge of Masonic Research Annual Book; Numerous to journals and magazines. Membership: Fellowship of Australian Writers. Address: PO Box 332, Williamstown, Victoria 3016, Australia.

HENDERSON Maurice Brian, b. 1 Jan 1961, Philadelphia, Pennsylvania, USA. Professional Writer; Teacher. Education: BBA, Adelphi University, New York, 1983; New York Institute of Technology, 1984. Appointments Include: Associate Editor, Umoja National News Magazine, 1983-85; Theatre Critic, Scoop USA Newspaper. Publications Include: When I Stopped To Think, 1983; Images, 1984; When The Walls Come Tumbling Down, 1986; Voices Around Me, 1987; A Collectors Item, 1987. Also various plays: Ghettoland; No Where to Run; Color Me Black. Nationally syndicated column. Contributions to: Black American; Norfolk Journal; Final Call; Scoop USA; Black Masks. Honours Include: Langston Hughes Award, 1983; Black Arts Award, 1984; Alpha Phi Alpha Literary Award, 1985. Membership: NYC Critics Association. Literary Agent: New Arts

Productions. Address: 2340 Tasker Street, Philadelphia, PA 19145, USA.

HENDERSON Richard, b. 20 Oct 1924, Baltimore, Maryland, USA. Commerical Artist; Writer. m. Sarah L Symington, 28 June 1947, 1 s, 1 d. Publications include: First Sail for Skipper, 1960; Hand, Reef and Steer, 1965; Dangerous Voyages of Capt William Andrews (ed), 1966; Sail and Power, 1967; The Racing-Cruiser, 1970; Encyclopedia of Sailing, (co-author), 1971; Sea Sense, 1972; The Cruisers Compendium 1973; Singlehanded Sailing, 1976; Better Sailing, 1977; Choice Yacht Design, 1979; Philip L Rhodes and His Yacht Designs, 1981; 53 Boats you can Build, 1985; John G Alden and His Yacht Designs, (co-author Robert Carrick), 1983; Heavy Weather Guide (co-author William J Kotsch), 1984; Understanding Rigs and Rigging, 1985; Sailing at Night, 1987; Sailing in Windy Weather, 1987; East to the Azores, 1978. Contributions to: Yachting; Telltale Compass; Rudder; Cruising World; Ocean Navigator; Yachting Monthly; Motor Boating and Sailing. Memberships: American Boat and Yacht Council, Seaworthiness Technical Committee; Cruising Club of America; Ocean Cruising Club, Slocum Society. Address: Box 185, Gibson Island, MD 21056, USA.

HENDERSON-HOWAT Gerald. See:HOWAT Gerald Malcolm David.

HENDON Donald W, b. USA. University Professor; Author. Education: MBA, Univeristy of California, Berkeley; BBA, PhD, University of Texas, Austin. Appointments: Professor, Marketing, University of North Alabama; President, Business Consultants International; Adviser to firms in USA and Worldwide. Publications: Author, 335 separate works including: Battling for Profits; How to Negotiate Worldwide; World Class Negotiating; Classic Failures in Product Marketing; 4 monographs; 50 journal articles. Contributions to: numerous journals and magazines including: Journal of Marketing; Journal of Applied Psychology; Business Horizons; 8 journals in the UK, Singapore, Hong Kong, Mexico, Philippines, Peru and 5 in Australia. Memberships: 16 professional associations including: Academy of Internatonal Business; Academy of Management; MENSA; American Marketing Association. Address: Dept of Marketing, University of North Alabama, Florence, AL 35632, USA.

HENDRICKS Kathleen, b. 28 July 1939, Salem, Virginia, USA. Author. m. Robert F Hendricks, 26 Apr 1958, 1 son, 1 daughter. Education: National Business College, 1957-58; Writer's Institute of America, 1968-70. Publications: Man's Zeal, 1986; Freedom, 1986; To Bob, My Love, 1987; Coming of Age, 1987; Clan-Destined, 1987; Destiny, 1987. Contributions to: Columnist, Solon, Iowa Newspaper; Organization Reporter, Iowa City; Contributor, numerous articles to professional journals. Honours: Honourable Mention, Lyrical Iowa, 1987, World of Poetry, 1987; Golden Poet Award, World of Poetry, 1987. Memberships: Chairperson, numerous community and national Charities in Virginia, Michigan and Iowa; Active, Community activities and Improvement Plans. Address: 261 Hillcrest Court, Central City, IA 52214, USA.

HENDRIKS A(rthur) L(emiere) , b. 1922, Jamaica. Poet; Freelance Writer. Publications: The Independence Anthology of Jamaican Literature (with C Lindo), 1962; On This Mountain and Other Poems, 1965; These Green Islands, 1971; Muet, 1971; Madonna of the Unknown Nation, 1974; The Islanders and Other Poems, 1983; Archie and the Princess and the Everythingest Horse (for children), 1983; The Naked Ghost and Other Poems, 1984; Great Families of Jamaica, 1984; To Speak Slowly: Selected Poems, 1986. Address: Box 265, Constant Spring, Kingston 8, Jamaica.

HENDRY Diana, Writer. Education: BA, University of Bristol; M Litt. Appointments include: Part Time English Teacher, Clifton College, 1984-87; Part Time Lecturer, Bristol Polytechnic, 1987; WEA, Modern Poets Course, 1987-; Tutor, Open University, 1991-92. Publications: Midnight Pirate; Fiona Finds Her Tongue; Hettys First Fling; The Not Anywhere House; The Rainbow Watchers; The Carey Street Cat; Christmas in Exeter Street; Sam Sticks and Delilah; A Camel Called April; Double Vision; A Moment for Joe; Harvey Angell; Kid Kibble; The Thing-in-a Box, 1992; Harvey Angell, 1991; Wonderful Robert & Sweetie-Pie Nell, 1992; Back Soon, 1993. Contributions to: Bananas Magazine; The Guardian; TES; THEs; Poetry Review; The Spectator; Critical Survey; Peterloo Preview 3. Honours: Stroud International Poetry Competition, 1st Prize; Runner Up, Manchester Open Poetry Competition; 2nd Prize, Peterloo Poetry Competition, 1993; 3rd Prize,

Peterloo Poetry Competition; Whitbread Award; 5th Prize, Cardiff International Poetry. Memberships: Society of Authors; PEN; West Country Writers Association. Address: 52 York Road, Montpelier, Bristol, BS6 5QF, England.

HENDRY Joy McLaggan, b. 3 Feb 1953, Perth, Scotland. Writer; Broadcaster. m. Ian Montgomery, 25 July 1986. Education: MA, Honours, Edinburgh University, 1970-76; Diploma in Education, Moray House College, Edinburgh University, 1976-77. Appointments: Editor, Chapman Magazine; General Editor, Scottish Critics Series, Edinburgh University Press; Director, Chapman Publications; Radio critic, Scotsman newspaper. Publications: (Editor) Poems and Pictures by Wendy Wood, 1985; Critical Essays on Sorley MacLean, (Co-editor Raymond J Ross), 1986; Critical Essays on Norman MacCraig, (Co-editor Raymond Ross), 1991; The Land for the People, (Co-editor Irene Tait); Sang down wi' a Sang, Play on Perth poet William Soutar, Produced at Perth Theatre, 1990; The Wa' at the Warld's End - on William Sontar (play), Broadcast on Radio 3, 1993. Contributions to: Cencrastus; Oxford Poetry; Agenda; Lallans; Scottish Literary Journal; The Scots Magazine; The Scotsman; Glasgow Herald; Scotland on Sunday; Der Spiegel; Poetry Ireland; BBC Scotland, Radio 3, Radio 4 and STV; Temenos. Address: 4 Broughton Place, Edinburgh, EH1 3RX, Scotland.

HENLEY Elizabeth Becker, b. 8 May 1952, Jackson, Mississippi, USA. Playwright. Education: BFA, Southern Methodist University. Publications: Crimes of the Heart, 1981; The Wake of Jamey Foster, 1982; Am I Blue, 1982; The Miss Firecracker Contest, 1984; The Lucky Spot, 1987; The Debutante Ball, 1988; Abundance, 1990; Control Freaks, 1993. Honours: Pulitzer Prize for Drama, 1981; New York Drama Critics Circle Best Play Award, 1981; George Oppenheimer/Newsday Playwriting Award, 1981. Address: c/o Gilbert Parker, The William Morris Agency, 1350 Avenue of the Americas, New York, NY 10019,USA.

HENNESSY Helen,See:VENDLER Helen.

HENNESSY Peter John, b. 28 Mar 1947, London, England. Author; Professor; Journalist; Broadcaster. m. Enid Mary Candler, 14 June 1969, 2 daughters. Education: BA, 1969, PhD, 1990, Cambridge; London School of Economics, 1969-71; Harvard, Kennedy Memorial Scholar, 1971-72. Appointments: Times Higher Educational Supplement, 1972-74; The Times, 1974-76; Lobby Correspondent, Financial Times, 1976; Whitehall Correspondent, The Times, 1976-82; The Economist, 1982; Leader Writer, The Times, 1982-84; Columnist, New Statesman, 1986-87; Columnist, The Independent, 1987-91; Professor of Contemporary History, Queen Mary and Westfield College, University of London, 1992-; Gresham Progress of Rhetoric College, 1994-. Publications: Never Again: Britain, 1945-51, Duff Cooper Prize, 1993; NCR Prize, 1993; Whitehall, 1989; Cabinet, 1986; Sources Close to the Prime Minister, 1984, co-author: States of Emergency, 1983, co-author: What the Papers Never Said, 1985. Contributions to: Columnist, Director Magazine, 1990-. Membership: Fellow of the Royal Historical Society, 1993. Literary Agent: Giles Gordon, Shieland Associates. Address: Department of History, Queen Mary and Westfield College, Mile End Road, London, E14 N5O, England.

HENNING Ann Margareta Maria (Countess of Roden), b. 5 Aug 1948, Goteborg, Sweden. Author; Translator. m. Earl of Roden, 13 Feb 1986, 1 son. Education: BA, Lund University, Sweden, 1975. Publications: The Connemara Whirlwind, 1990; The Connemara Stallion, 1991; The Connemara Champion, 1994; Modern Astrology, 1985. Contributions to: Vogue Magazine. Memberships: Translators Association; Society of Authors; Irish Writer's Union; SWEA; SELTA. Address: 4 The Boltons, London, SW10 9TB, England.

HENRI Adrian (Maurice), b. 10 Apr 1932, Birkenhead, Cheshire, England. Painter; Poet. Education: BA Fine Art, King's College, Newcastle, 1955. Appointments include: Lecturer, Manchester Coll of Art, 1961-64, Liverpool Coll of Art, 1964-1967; Member of the Liverpool Scene, poetry-rock group, 1967-70; Visiting Lecturer, Bradford College, 1973-76, Trent Polytechnic, 1989. Publications: The Mersey Sound: Penguin Modern Poets 10, 1967, 1983; Tonight at Noon, 1968; City, 1969; Talking After Christmas Blues, 1969; Poems for Wales and Six Landscapes for Susan, 1970; Autobiography, 1971; America, 1972; The Best of Henri: Selected Poems 1968-70; One Year, 1976; City Hedges: Poems 1970-76; Words without a Story, 1979; From the Loveless Motel: Poems 1976-79, 1980; Harbour, 1982; Penny Arcade

1978-82; New Volume, with Roger McGough and Brian Patten, 1983; Holiday Snaps 1967-85; Wish You Were Here, 1990; Not Fade Away, 1994; Verse for children; Plays; Novel: I Want, with Nell Dunn, 1972. Honours include: DLitt, Liverpool Polytechnic, 1990. Address: 21 Mount Street, Liverpool L1 9HD, England.

HENRY Desmond Paul, b. 5 July 1921, Almondbury, Yorks, England. Philosopher; Artist. m. Louise H J Bayen, 19 May 1945, 3 daughters. Education: BA Hons, Philosophy, University of Leeds, 1949; PhD, University of Manchester, 1960. Appointments: Philosophy Teacher, University of Manchester, 1949-82; Visiting Professor: Brown University, 1966; University of Pennsylvania, 1970. Publications: The Logic of St Anselm, 1967; Medieval Logic and Metaphysics, 1972; Commentary on De Grammatico, 1974; That Most Subtle Question, 1984; Medieval Merology, 1991; The De Grammatco of St Anselm. 1964; Teaching and Study Companion, 1977. Contributions: The Proslogion Proofs, 1955; St Anselm's Nonsense, 1963 and dozens of others. Memberships: Société Internationale pour L'Etude de la Philosophie Médiévale; Past President, Manchester Medieval Society. Address: 4 Burford Drive, Whalley Range, Manchester, M16 8FJ, England.

HENSHAW James Ene, b. 29 Aug 1924, Calabar, Nigeria. Medical Practitioner. m. Caroline Womadi, 15 Feb 1958, 5 sons, 3 daughters. Education: Christ the King College, Onitsha, Nigeria, 1938-41; MB,BCh, BAO(NUI), University College, Dublin, Ireland, 1949; TDD, Cardiff, Wales, 1954. Literary Appointments: Editor, Eastern Nigeria Medical Circular, special publication, Nigerian Independence, 1960-61; Chairman, Cultural Centre Board, Cross River State, Nigeria, 1975-78. Publications: This Is Our Chance: Plays from West Africa, London, 1957; Children of the Goddess, 1964; Medicine for Love, London, 1964; Dinner for Promotion, London, 1967; Enough is Enough, Nigeria, 1976; A Song to Mary Charles, Irish Sister of Charity, Nigeria, 1985. Contributions to: Medical Journals, West Africa, England. Honours: Henry Carr Memorial Cup, 1st Prize, Playwriting, All Nigeria Festival of Arts, 1952; Knight, Order of Niger, for medical services & contributions to literature, 1979. Memberships Include: Association of Nigerian Authors; Nigerian Medical Association; Nigerian Medical Council, 1970-72. Address: Itiaba House, 4 Calabar Road, Calabar, Nigeria.

HENSTELL Bruce Michael, b. 3 Oct 1945, Los Angeles, California, USA. Writer; Producer. m. 4 Aug 1983, 1 son. Education: BA, University of California, Berkeley; MA, University of Michigan; MLS, University of California, Los Angeles. Appointments: Freelance Writer, 1967-; Film Writer, 1972-; Writer, Producer: KCBS TV, 1981-86, Los Angeles History Project, KCTV, 1989, 1990; Chief Librarian, Curator of Photographic Collections, California Historical Society, 1979-80; Director of Research, LA Daily News Project, UCLA University Research Library, 1981-82. Publications: American Film Criticism, 1967; Los Angeles: An Illustrated History, 1981; Sunshine and Wealth: Los Angeles in the 20s and 30s, 1985; The Home Front: Los Angeles in the 1940s. Contributions to: Los Angeles Times; Los Angeles Magazine; New York Times; Westways. Honours: Southern California Radio and TV News Editors Golden Mike, 1981; Academy of Television Arts and Sciences Emmy Nominations, 1982, 1983, 1984, 1989; Academy of Television Emmy, 1984; Silver Medal, NY International Film and Video Festival, 1984; WAVE Award, 1991; Southern California Cable Association Diamond Award. Memberships: Society of Los Angeles Chronologers (past President). Literary Agent: Mitchell Hamilburg. Address: Santa Monica, CA 90405, USA.

HERALD Kathleen. See: PEYTON Kathleen Wendy.

HERBERT Brian Patrick, b. 29 June 1947, Seattle, USA. Author. Education: BA, Sociology, University of California at Berkeley, 1968. Publications: Songs of Muad' Dib, (editor) 1992; The Race for God, 1990; Memorymakers, (co-author Marie Landis), 1990; The Notebooks of Dune (editor), 1988; Prisoners of Arionn, 1987; Man of Two Worlds, (co-author Frank Herbert), 1986; Sudanna, Sudanna, 1985; The Garbage Chronicles, 1984; Sidney's Comet, 1983; Incredible Insurance Claims, 1982, Classic Comebacks, 1981; Never As It Seems (editor), 1992. Contributions to: The Contract (co-author Marie Landis) forthcoming; The Bone Lady (co-author Marie Landis) published in Dark Destiny, 1994; When Bad Things Happen, 1993; In Celebration of Sidney, 1987. Honours: Guest of Honour, Dragon Con SF-Fantasy Convention, 1987. Memberships: Science Fiction Writers of America; National Writers Club; L-5 Society. Literary Agent: Cine/Lit Representation, Edmonds, WA, USA. Address: PO Box 10164,

Bainbridge Island, WA 98110, USA.

HERBERT Ivor, b. 1925. Author; Journalist; Scriptwriter. Appointments: Travel Editor, Racing Editor, The Mail on Sunday, 1982-. Publications: Eastern Windows, 1953; Point to Point, 1964; Arkel: The Story of a Champion, 1966, 1975; The Great St Trinian's Train Robbery, screenplay, 1966; The Queen Mother's Horses, 1967; The Winter Kings, co- author, 1968, enlarged, 1989; The Way to the Top, 1969; Night of the Blue Demands, play, co-author, 1971; Over Our Dead Bodies, 1972; The Diamond Diggers, 1972; Scarlet Fever, co-author, 1972; Winter's Tale, 1974; Red Rum: Story of a Horse of Courage, 1974; Television scripts: Hyperion: The Millionaire Horse, Odds Against?, The Queens Horses: The Filly, novel, 1977; Six at the Top, 1977; Classic Touch, TV documentary, 1985; Spot the Winner, 1978, updated, 1990; Longacre, 1978; Horse Racing, 1980; Vincent O'Brien's Great Horses, co-author, 1984; Revolting Behaviour, 1987; Herbert's Travels, 1987; Reflections on Racing, co-author, 1990; Riding Through My Life (with HRH The Princess Royal), 1991; Partner in : Equus Productions Ltd (video) and Bradenham Wines. Address: c/o David Higham Associates Ltd, 5-8 Lower John Street, London, W1R 4HA, England.

HERBERT James (John), b. 1943. Author. Publications: The Rats, 1974; The Fog, 1975; The Survivor, 1976; Fluke, 1977; The Spear, 1978; Lair, 1979; The Dark, 1980; The Jonah, 1981; Shrine, 1983; Domain, 1984; Moon, 1985; The Magic Cottage, 1986; Sepulchre, 1987; Haunted, 1988; Creed, 1990; Portent, 1992; James Herbert: By Horror Haunted, Edited by Stephen Jones, 1992; James Herbert's Dark Places, 1993; The City, graphic novel, 1994; The Ghosts of Sleath, 1994; Films: Fluke, 1995; Haunted, 1995. Address: c/o Bruce Hunter, David Higham Associates, 5-8 Lower John Street, London, W1R 4HA, England.

HERBST Phillip H, b. 1 June 1944, Peoria, IL, USA. Editor; Writer; Researcher. Education: BA, IL Univ, 1966; Phd, Cornell Univ, 1976. Publications: A Multicultural Dictionary: A Guide to Ethnic and Racial Words, 1993; Speaking of People: An Encyclopedic Dictionary of Ethnic Bias in the United States, 1995. Contributions to: Oceans; Booklist: Contemporary Times; Book Jacket. Honours: Visiting Scholar, Northwestern University 1989-92. Address: 2415 Central Street, Evanston, IL 60201, USA.

HEREN Louis Philip, b. 6 Feb 1919, London, England. Journalist; Author. m. Patricia Cecilia O'Regan, 2 June 1948, 1 son, 3 daughters. Education: St George's School, London. Publications: New American Commonwealth, 1968; No Hail, No Farewell, 1970; Growing Up Poor in London, 1973; The Story of America, 1976; Growing Up On The Thames, 1978; Alas, Alas For England, 1981; Power of the Press?, 1985; Memories of Times Past, 1988. Contributions to: UK and USA newspapers and magazines. Honour: John F Kennedy Memorial Award, 1968. Memberships: Fellow, Royal Society of Literature; Garrick Club. Literary Agent: David Higham Associates. Address: Fleet House, Vale of Health, London NW3 1AZ, England.

HERMODSSON Elisabet, b. 20 Sept 1927, Gothenburg. Writer; Artist; Songwriter. m. (1) Ingemar Olsson, 1951; (2) Olof Hellstrom, 1956, 2 daughters. Publications Include: Poem-things, 1966; Human Landscape Unfairly, 1968; Rite and Revolution, 1968; Swedish Soul-life, 1970; Culture at the Bottom, 1971; Voices in the Human Landscape, 1971; What Shall We Do With The Summer, Comrades? (songs), 1973; Disa Nilsons Songs, 1974; Through The Red Waist Coat Of The Ground 75; Visional Turning Point, 1975; Words in Human Time, 1979; Wake Up With A Summer Soul, 1979; Make Yourself Visible, 1980; Discourses Meanwhile, 1983; Stones, Shards, Layers of Earth, 1985; Creation Betrayed, 1986; Streams of Mist, 1990; Creation Betrayed, 1988; Only Fools and Dreamers, 1992 (songs); The Dumb in the Word, 1993. Contributions to: Journals, Magazines and the Editor of Several Anthologies. Memberships: PEN Club. Address: Ostra Agatan 67, 75322 Uppsala, Sweden.

HERR Pamela (Staley), b. 24 July 1939, Cambridge, MA, USA. Writer. 2 d. Education: BA, magna cum laude, Harvard University, 1961; MA, George Washington University, 1971. Appointments: Writer and Editor, Field Educational Publications, 1973; Editor, Sullivan Associates, 1973-74; Project Manager, Sanford Associates, Education Development Corporation, Menlo Park, 1974-76; Managing Editor, American West, Cupertino, CA, 1976-79; Historian and Writer, 1980-. Publications: The Women Who Made the West (Contributor), 1980; Jessie Benton Fremont: A Biography, 1987; Selected Letters of Jessie

Benton Fremont (with Mary Lee Spence), 1993. Address: 559 Seale Ave, Palo Alto, CA 94301, USA.

HERRA Maurice. See: **ASSELINEAU Roger Maurice.**

HERSEY April (Maeve), b. 4 Apr 1924. Writer; Editor. Literary Appointments: Consultant Scriptwriter, Pilgrim International; Editor: Craft Australia, 1974-81; POL, 1976; Oz Arts Magazine, 1990-. Publications: Australian Style, 1968; New Zealand, 1969; Hooked On God, 1970; 4 novels in progress. Contributions to: Bulletin; Sun Herald; Women's Day; Home and Family; Home; House and Garden; Life; Sunday Times; Readers Digest. Memberships: Australian Society of Authors; Fellowship of Australian Writers. Hobbies: Garden design; Studying languages. Literary Agent: William Morris, Anthony Williams Management, 50 Oxford St, Paddington, New South Wales 2021, Australia. Address: 12 Wright St, Glenbrook, New South Wales 2772, Australia.

HERSEY John Richard, b. 17 June 1914, Tientsin, China. Writer. m. (1) Frances Ann Cannon, 1940, divorced 1958, (2) Barbara Day Kaufman, 1958, 3 sons, 2 daughters. Education: BA, Yale University; Clare College, Cambridge, England. Appointments Include: Editor, Time, 1937-42; War and Foreign Correspondent, Time, Life, New Yorker, 1942-46; Master, Pierson College, 1965-70, Fellow, 1965-, Lecturer, 1971-75, Visiting Professor, 1976-77, Adjunct Professor, 1977-84, Adjunct Professor Emeritus, 1984-, Yale University. Publications: Men on Bataan, 1942; Into the Valley, 1943; A Bell for Adano, 1944; Hiroshima, 1946; The Wall, 1950; The Marmot Drive, 1953; A Single Pebble, 1956; The War Lover, 1959; The Child Buyer, 1960; Her to Stay, 1962; White Lotus, 1965; Too Far ToWalk, 1966; Under the Eye of the Storm, 1967; The Algiers Motel Incident, 1968; Letter to the Alumni, 1970; The Conspiracy, 1972; The Writers' Craft, 1974; My Petition for More Space, 1974; The President, 1975; The Walnut Door, 1977; Aspects of the Presidency, 1980; The Call, 1985; Blues, 1987; Life Sketches, 1989; Fling and Other Stories, 1990. Honours: Recipient, numerous honours and awards including Honorary Degrees; Pulitzer Prize for Fiction, 1945; Sidney Hillman Foundation Award, 1951; Howland Medal, Yale, 1952. Memberships Include: American Academy Arts and Letters, Secretary, 1961-75, Chancellor, 1981-84; National Institute of Arts and Letters; Authors Guild; Authors League, Vice President, 1949-55, President, 1975-80; American Academy of Arts and Sciences; Honorary Fellow, Clare College, Cambridge University, 1967. Address: 719 Windsor Lane, Key West, FL 33040, USA.

HERSH Burton David,b. 18 Sept 1933, Chicago, Illinois, USA. Author; Biographer. m. Ellen Eiseman, 3 Aug 1957, 1 son, 1 daughter. Education: BA magna cum laude, Harvard College, 1955; Fulbright Scholar, 1955-56. Publications: The Ski People, 1968; The Education of Edward Kennedy, 1972; The Mellon Family, 1978; The Old Boys, 1992. Contributions to: Many major American magazines including Holiday; Esquire; The Washingtonian, etc. Honours: History and Literature Prize, Harvard College, 1954; Bowdoin Prize, Harvard College, 1955; Senior Phi Beta Kappa, Harvard College, 1955; Book Find Selection, 1972; Book-of-the-Month Club Section, 1978. Memberships: Authors Guild; American Society of Journalists and Authors; PEN. Literary Agent: Jonathan Matson, Harold Matson Comapny Inc, 276 Fifth Avenue, New York, NY 10001, USA. Address: PO Box 433, Bradford, New Hampshire 03221, USA.

HERZBERG Judith, b. 4 Nov 1934, Amsterdam, Netherlands. Poet; Playwright. Education: Graduated Montessori Lyceum, 1952. Appointments include: Teacher at film schools in Netherlands and Israel. Publications: Slow Boat, 1964; Meadow Grass, 1968; Flies, 1970; Grazing Light, 1971; 27 Love Songs, 1973; Botshol, 1980; Remains of the Day, 1984; Twenty Poems, 1984; But What: Selected Poems, 1988; Plays: Near Archangel, 1971; It Is Not A Dog, 1973; That Day May Dawn, 1974, 1977; Lea's Wedding, 1982; The Fall of Icarus, 1983; And/Or, 1984; The Little Mermaid, 1986; Scratch, 1989; Lulu, adaptation of Wedekind, 1989; A Good Head, 1991; Texts for the Stage and Film, 1972-1988; Screenplays and Television plays; Translations, including The Trojan Women by Euripides, and Ghosts, by Ibsen. Honours include: Netherlands-Vlaamse drama prize, 1989. Address: c/o De Harmonie, Postbus 3547, 1001 AH Amsterdam, Netherlands.

HESKETH Phoebe, b. 29 Jan 1909, Preston, Lancashire, England. Lecturer (Emeritus); Poet. Education: Cheltenham Ladies' College, 1924-26. Appointments include: Lecturer, Bolton Women's College, 1967-69; Teacher of Creative Writing, Bolton School, 1977-79.

Publications include: Poems, 1939; Lean Forward, Spring, 1948; No Time for Cowards, 1952; Out of the Dark, 1954; Between Wheels and Stars, 1956; The Buttercup Children, 1958; Prayer for Sun, 1966; A Song of Sunlight, 1974; A Ring of Leaves, 1985; Brook, 1985; Netting the Sun: New Selected Poems, 1989; Sundowner, 1992; The Leave Train, New Poems, 1994; Prose: My Aunt Edith, 1966; Rivington: The Story of a Vcillage, 1972; What Can the Matter Be?, 1985; Rivington: Village of the Mountain Ash, 1989. Honours include: Fellow, Royal Society of Literature, 1950's; Member PEN 1950's-1960's; Honorary Fellow, University of Central Lancashire, 1992. Address: 10 The Green, Heath Charnock, Chorley, Lancashire PR6 9JH, England.

HESSAYON David Gerald, b. 13 Feb 1928, Manchester, England. Author; Publisher. m. Joan Parker Gray, 2 Apr 1951, 2 daughters. Education: BSC, Leeds University, 1950; PhD, Manchester University, 1954; Hon Doctorate of Science, 1990. Publications: The House Plant Expert, 1980; The Tree and Shrub Expert, 1983; The Flower Expert, 1984; The Garden Expert, 1986; The Bedding Plant Expert, 1991; The Rose Expert, 1988; The Lawn Expert, 1982; The Armchair Book of the Garden, 1983; The Vegetable Expert, 1985; The Indoor Plant Spotter, 1985; The Home Expert, 1987; The Fruit Expert, 1990; Be Your Own Greenhouse Expert, 1990; The New House Plant Expert, 1991; The Garden DIY Expert, 1992; The Rock & Water Garden Expert, 1993; The Flowering Shrub Expert, 1994; The Greenhouse Expert, 1994. Honours: Lifetime Achievement Trophy, National British Book Awards, 1992; Gold Veitch Memorial Medal, Royal Horticultural Society, 1992. Memberships: Member, Royal Society of Arts, Society of Authors. Address: Hilgay, Mill Lane, Broxbourne, Herts, EN10 7AX, England.

HESSAYON Joan Parker, b. 21 Jan 1932, Louisville, Kentucky, USA. Author. m. David Hessayon, 2 Apr 1951, 2 daughters. Publications: All Kinds of Courage, 1983; For All Good Men, 1984; Little Maid All Unwary, 1985; Sylbilla, 1986; Thorsby, 1987; Lady from St Louis, 1989; Belle's Daughter, 1990; Roxanne's War, 1991; House on Pine Street, 1992. Memberships: Vice Chairman, The Society of Women Writers and Journalists; The Romantic Novelists Association, former Council member. Address: Hilgay, Mill Lane, Broxbourne, Herts, EN10 7AX, England.

HESSING Dennis. See: **DENNIS-JONES Harold.**

HESTER William, b. 6 June 1933, Detroit, Michigan, USA. Author; Lyricist. div, 1 daughter. Education: Brown University, 1951-52; University of Detroit, 1956; BA, Mesa College, 1970; MA, Special Studies, UCLA/NYU; Currently PhD Candidate. Literary Appointments: Staff, Warner Brothers Pictures, 1961-62; Creative Staff, Sierra Productions, 1962-65; Staff, Playboy Magazine, 1966-68; Associate Director, Vance Publications, 1970-73. Publications: Please Don't Die In My House, 1965; Selections, 1967; Running Off, 1970; Not The Right Season, 1984; Another Town, 1984; Still Not The Right Season, 1985; Our Place, 1986; Sleeping Neighbours, 1986, 1992; Tyranny/2000, 1988. Also music. Contributions to: Pulpsmith; Confrontation; Amelia; Easy Riders; The Poet; Playboy; Witness; Golf Magazine; Fortune News; Wind. Honours Include: EMMY nominee, 1974; Eisner Fellowship, 1984; 1st & 2nd Awards, fiction & non-fiction, PEN American Centre, 1985, 1986; Various awards, American Song Festival. Memberships: Authors Guild; Conservatory of American Letters; Broadcast Music Inc (lyricist); ASCAP (publisher). Literary Agent: Al Hart, Fox Chase Agency, Public Ledger Building, Philadelphia, PA 19106, USA. Address: c/o James McDonald Inc, 1130-20th St, 5 Santa Monica, CA 90403, USA.

HETHERINGTON (Hector) Alastair, b. 31 Oct 1919, Llanishen, Galmorganshire, Wales. Journalist. m. (1) Helen Miranda Oliver, 1957, (div 1978), 2 sons, 2 daughters, (2) Sheila Cameron, 1979. Education: MA, Corpus Christi College, Oxford. Appointments: Staff, Glasgow Herald, 1946-50; Joined Manchester Guardian, 1950; Foreign Editor, 1953, Editor, 1956-75, Director, Guardian Newspapers Ltd., 1967-75; with BBC 1975-80, Controller BBC Scotland, 1975-78; Manager, BBC Highland, 1979-80; Research Professor, Stirling University, 1982-88, Emeritus since 1988. Publications: Guardian Years, 1981; News, Newspapers and Television, 1985; Perthshire in Trust, 1988; News in the Regions, 1989; Highlands and Islands, a generation of progress, 1990; Cameras in the Commons, 1990; Inside BBC Scotland, 1975-1980, 1992; A Walker's Guide to Arran, 1994. Address: High Corrie, Isle of Arran, KA27 8GB, Scotland.

HETHERINGTON Norriss Swigart, b. 30 Jan 1942, Berkeley, CA, USA. Professor. m. Edith Wiley White, 10 Dec 1966, 1 s, 1 d. Education: BA, 1963; MA, 1965; MA, 1967, University of California, Berkeley; PhD, Indiana University, Bloomington, 1970. Appointments: Lecturer in Physics and Astronomy, Agnes Scott College, Decatur, GA 1967-68; Assistant Professor of Mathematics and Science, York University, Toronto, Ontario, 1970-72; Administrative Specialist National Aeronautics and Space Aministration, WA 1972; Assistant Professor of History, University of Kansas, 1972-76; Chairman of Program in History and Philosophy of Science, 1973-74; Assistant Professor of Science, Technology and Society, Razi University, Sanandaj, Iran, 1976-77; Visiting Scholar, Cambridge University, England, 1977-78; Associate Professor of History of Science, Oklahoma University, Norman, 1981; Research Associate at Office for History of Science and Technology, University of Calfornia, Berkeley, 1978-; Director, Institute for the History of Astronomy, 1988-. Publications: Ancient Astronomy and Civilization, 1987; Science and Objectivity: Episodes in the History of Astronomy, 1988; The Edwin Hubble Papers, 1990; Encyclopedia of Cosmology, 1993; Cosmology: Historical, Literary, Philosophical, Religious and Scientific Perspectives, 1993. Address: 1742 Spruce, Apartment 201, Berkeley, CA 94709, USA.

HEWETT Dorothy (Coade), b. 1923, Australia. Author; Playwright; Poet. Appointments Include: Advertising Copywriter, Sydney, 1956-58; Poetry Editor, Westerly Magazine, Perth, 1972-73; Editorial Committee, Overland Magazine, Melbourne, 1970-; Writer in Residence, Monash University, Melbourne, 1975; Editor, Director, Big Smoke Books, Review Editor, Poetry, Sydney, 1975-. Publications: Bobbin Up (novel), 1959; What about the People (poetry with Merv Lilly), 1962; The Australians have a Word for It (stories), 1964; The Old Man Comes Rolling Home, 1968; Windmill Country (poetry), 1968; The Hidden Journey (poetry), 1969; Late Night Bulletin (poetry), 1970; The Chapel Perilous, or The Perilous Adventures of Sally Bonner, 1971; Sandgropers: A Western Australian Anthology, 1973; Rapunzel in Surburbia (poetry), 1975; Miss Hewett's Shenanigans, 1975; Bon-Bons and Roses for Dolly, and The Tatty Hollow Story, 1976; Greenhouse (poetry), 1979; The Man from Mukinupin (play), 1979; Susannah's Dreaming, and The Golden Oldies (plays), 1981; Joan, 1984; Golden Valley, Song of the Seals, 1985. Address: 49 Jersey Road, Woollahra, NSW 2025, Australia.

HEYEN William H, b. 1 Nov 1940, New York, USA. Professor. m. Hannelore Greiner, 1962, 2 children. Education: BS.Ed, SUNY College, Brockport, 1961; MA, 1963; PhD, 1967 English, Ohio University. Publications: Depth of Field, 1970; A Profile of Theodore Roethke, editor, 1971; Noise in the Trees: Poems and a Memoir, 1974; American Poets in 1976, editor, 1976; The Swastika Poems, 1977; Long Island Light, 1979; The City Parables, 1980; Lord Dragonfly: Five Sequences, 1981; Erika: Poems of the Holocaust, 1984; The Generation of 2000: Contemporary American Poets, editor, 1984; Vic Holyfield and the Class of 1957: A Romance, 1986; The Chestnut Rain: A Poem, 1986; Pterodactyl Rose: Poems of Ecology, 1991; Ribbons: The Gulf War, 1991; The Host: Selected Poems 1965-1990, 1994; With me Far Away: A Memoir, 1994. Address: 142 Frazier Street, Brockport, NY 14420, USA.

HEYERDAHL Thor, b. 6 Oct 1914. Author; Anthropologist. m. (1) Liv Coucheron Torp, 1936 (dec 1969), 2 sons, (2) Yvonne Dedekam-Simonsen, 1949, 3 daughters. Education: University of Oslo, 1933-36. Appointments Include: Organised and Led, Kon-Tiki Expedition, 1947; Made Crossing from Safi, Morocco to West Indies in Papyrus Boat, RAII, 1970. Publications: Paa Jakt efter Paradiset, 1938; The Kon-Tiki Expedition, 1948; American Indians in the Pacific: The theory behind to Kon-Tiki Expedition, 1952; (with A Skjolsvold) Archaeological Evidence of pre-Spanish Visits to the Galapagos Islands, 1956; Aku-Aku: The Secrets of Easter Island, 1961, vol II Miscellaneous Papers, 1965; Naval of the World (Chapter XIV) in Vanished Civilizations, 1963; Indianer und Alt-Asiaten im Pazifik: Das Abenteuer einer heorie, 1965 (Vienna); Sea Routes to Polynesia, 1968; The Ra Expeditions, 1970; Chapters in Quest for America, 1971; Fatu-Hiva Back to Nature, 1974; Art of Easter Island, 1975; Zwischen den Kontinenten, 1975; Early Man and the Ocean, 1978; The Tigris Expedition, 1980; The Mystery of the Maldives, 1986; Easter Island, 1990. Contributions to: Numerous professional journals. Honours: Recipient, numerous honours and awards including: Royal Gold Medal, Royal Geographical Society, London, 1964; Commander with Star, Order of St Olav, Norway, 1970; Order of Merit, Egypt, 1971; Grand Officer, Royal Alaouites Order, Morocco, 1971; Hon Citizen, Larvik,

Norway, 1971; International Pahlavi Environment Prize, UN, 1978; Order of Golden Ark, Netherlands, 1980. Address: Kan-Tiki Museum, Oslo, Norway.

HEYLIN Clinton Manson, b. 8 Apr 1960, Urmston, England. Writer. Education: BA Hons, History, University of London, 1978-81; MA, History, University of Sussex, 1982-83. Publications: Dylan: Behind the Shades, 1991; The Penguin Book of Rock and Roll Writing, 1992; From the Velvets to the Voidoids, 1993; Rise/Fall, 1989; Stolen Moments, 1988; Form and Substance: Gypsy Love Songs and Sad Refrains, 1989. Contributions to: Spiral Scratch; Dirty Linen; The Telegraph; Q; Goldmine; Record Collector; Music Collector. Address: 203 Northenden Road, Sale, Cheshire M33 2JB, England.

HEYM Stefan, b. 10 Apr 1913, Chemnitz, Germany. Novelist. Education: Universities of Berlin and Chicago; MA, 1935. Career: Resident in Berlin from 1952. Publications: Hostages, 1942; Of Smiling Peace, 1944; The Crusaders, 1948; The Eye of Reason, 1951; Goldsborough, 1953; The Cannibals and Other Stories, 1953; Shadows and Light: Eight Short Stories, 1960; The Lenz Papers, 1964; Uncertain Friend, 1969; The Queen Against Defoe and Other Stories, 1972; Five Days in June, 1974; Collin, 1980; The Wandering Jew, 1984; Schwarzenberg, 1984; Collected Stories, 1984; Built on Sand, 1990; Play: Tom Sawyer's Great Adventure, 1952; Also: Nazis in USA: An Exposé of Hitler's Aims and Agents in the USA, 1938; A Visit to Soviet Science, 1959; Nachruf (autobiography), 1988; Selected Prose, 1990. Honours include: DLitt, University of Cambridge, 1991; Jerusalem Prize, 1993. Address: Rabindranath-Tagore Strasse 9, 1180 Berlin-Grunau, Germany.

HIBBERD Jean (J O McDonald), b. 11 Oct 1931, London, England. Coordinator; Creative Writing Teacher. m. Reginald George Hibberd, 8 Mar 1952, 2 sons, 2 daughters. Education: Diploma, Short Story Writing, 1980. Appointments include: Coordinator, Nepean Community College; Editor, Compiler, Nepean Community College Annual Anthology, 1985-; Holiday and Travel Writer for Western Weekender, 1991-93. Publications: The Adventures of Peter Possum and His Friends, 1985; Further Adventures of Peter Possum and His Friends, 1987; Duty to My God, 1989; In progress: On the Sea of the Moon, romance; Ordeal by Love; The Artist and the Gypsy; Poetry of the Sun; Short Stories from Aound the World. Contributor to: Sydney Morning Herald; Western Weekender; New Idea; Travel; Blue Mountains Gazette; The Land; Penrith Press; New England Advertiser; School magazines; Scout magazine, Australia. Honours: Medal of Merit, Scout Association, 1971; Gold Sheaffer Pen for Story of the Week, New Idea, 1993, 1994; Order of Australia Medal, 1994. Memberships: Fellowship of Australian Writers; Australian Society of Authors; Order of Australia Society. Address: 7 Rusden Rd, Blaxland, New South Wales 2774, Australia.

HIBBERT Christopher, b. 5 Mar 1924, Author. m. Susan Piggford, 1948, 2 sons, 1 daughter. Education: MA, Oriel College, Oxford. Appointments: Served in Italy, 1944-45; Captain, London Irish Rifles; Partner, firm of land agents, auctioneers and surveyors, 1948-59. Publications include: The Road to Tyburn, 1957; King Mob, 1958; Wolfe at Quebec, 1959; The Destruction of Lord Raglan, 1961; Corunna, 1961; Benito Mussolini 1962; The Battle of Arnhem, 1962; The Roots of Evil, 1963; The Court at Windsor, 1964; Agincourt, 1964; The Wheatley Diary, (Editor), 1964; Garibaldi and His Enemies, 1965; The Making of Charles Dickens, 1967; Waterloo: Napoleon's Last Campaign, (Editor), 1967; An American in Regency England: The Journal of Louis Simond, (Editor), 1968; Charles I, 1968; The Grand Tour, 1969; London: Biography of a City, 1969; The Search for King Arthur, 1970; Anzio: The Bid for Rome, 1970; The Dragon Wakes: China and the West, 1793-1911, 1970; The Personal History of Samuel Johnson, 1971; George IV, Prince of Wales 1762-1811, 1972; George IV, Regent and King 1812-1830, 1973; The Rise and Fall of the House of Medici, 1974; Edward VII: A Portrait, 1976; The Great Mutiny: India, 1857, 1978; The French Revolution, 1981; Africa Explored: Europeans in the Dark Continent, 1796-1889, 1982; The London Encyclopaedia, (editor), 1983; Queen Victoria in Her Letters and Journals, 1984; Rome: The Biography of a City, 1985; Critics and Civilizations, 1985; The English: A Social History, 1987; Venice: Biography of a City, 1988; The Encyclopaedia of Oxford, (Editor), 1988; Redcoats and Rebels: The War for America 1760-1781, 1990; The Virgin Queen: The Personal History of Elizabeth I, 1990; Captain Gronow: His Reminiscences of Regency and Victorian Life (ed), 1991; Cavaliers and Roundheads: The English at War 1642-1649, 1993; Florence: Biography of a City, 1993; Nelson: A Personal History, 1994. Honours: Heinemann Award for

Literature, 1962; McColvin Medal, 1989. Address: c/o David Higham Associates, 5-8 Lower John Street, Golden Square, London, W1R 4HA, England.

HICKEY Marie Frances, b. 27 Apr 1939, Melbourne, Victoria, Australia. Chemist Assistant. m. 15 Apr 1963, 5 sons, 1 daughter. Publications: Making Crepe Paper Flowers, 1980. Contributions to: Home Beautiful; Waverley Women. Address: 16 Pamay Road, Mt Waverley, Victoria 3149, Australia.

HICKMAN Tracy Raye, b. 26 Nov 1955, Salt Lake City, USA. m. Laura Curtis, 17 June 1977, 2 sons, 2 daughters. Appointments: Projectionist, Mann Theatres, 1974-78, Assistant Director of KBYU-TV 1976-77, Theatre Manager in Provo and Logan 1978-81; Game Designer, TSR Incorporated, Lake Geneva, 1981-86; Consultant,1986-; Missionary in Java and Indonesia. Publications: Dragons of Autumn Twilight, 1984; Dragons of Winter Night, Dragons of Spring Dawning, 1985; Time of the Twins, War of the Twins, Test of the Twins, Magic of Krynn, 1986; Kender Gnomes and Gully Dwarves, Love and War, 1987 (all with Margaret Weis); Forging the Darksword, Doom in the Darksword, Triumph of the Darksword, 1988; Rose of the Prophet, 1989; Dragonwing, 1990; Elvenstar. Address: 453 Forest Highlands, Flagstaff, AZ 86001, USA.

HICKS Eleanor. See: **COERR Eleanor Beatrice.**

HIGDON Hal, b. 1931, USA. Writer. Appointments: Assistant Editor, The Kiwanis Magazine, 1957-59. Publications: The Union vs Dr Mudd, 1964; Heroes of the Olympics, 1965; Pro Football USA, 1967; The Horse That Played Center Field, 1967; The Business Healers, 1968; Stars of the Tennis Courts, 1969; 30 Days in May, 1969; The Electronic Olympics, 1969; On The Run from Dogs and People, 1969; Finding the Groove, 1973; Find the Key Man, 1974; The Last Series, 1974; Six Seconds to Glory, 1974; The Crime of the Century, 1976; Summer of Triumph, 1977; Fitness after Forty, 1977; Beginner's Running Guide, 1978; Runner's Cookbook, 1979; Johnny Rutherford, 1980; The Marathoners, 1980; The Team That Played in the Space Bowl, 1981; The Masters Running Guide, 1990; Run Fast, 1992; Marathon: The Ultimate Training and Racing Guide, 1993; Falconara: A Family Odyssey, 1993; Ideas For Rent, The VOP Story, 1994; Boston: A Century of Running, 1995. Memberships: American Society of Journalists and Authors; The Authors Guild; North American Ski Journalists Association. Address: Box 1034, Michigan City, IN 46360, USA.

HIGGINBOTHAM Prieur Jay, b. 16 July 1937, Pascagoula, Mississippi, USA. Archivist. m. Louisa Martin, 27 June 1970, 2 s, 1 d. Education: BA, University of Mississippi; Graudate Study, City College of New York, American Univesity Washington DC. Publications: Discovering Russia, 1989; Autumn in Petrishcnevo, 1987; Fast Train Russia, 1983; Old Mobile, 1977; Voyage to Dauphin Island, 1974; Brother Holyfield, 1972; Fort Maurepas, 1968; Mauvila, 1990. Contributions to: Library Journal; Alabama Riview; Foreign Literature: Literaturnaya Gazeta; Louisiana Studies; Encyclopaedia Britannica; Dictionary of Louisiana Biography; Funk and Wagnalls Encyclopedia. Address: 60 North Monterey Street, Mobile, AL 36604, USA.

HIGGINS Aidan, b. 3 Mar 1927, Celbridge, County Kildare, Ireland. Novelist. Education: Clongowes Wood College, County Kildare. Publications: Stories Felo De Se, 1960; Langrishe, Go Down, 1966; Balcony of Europe, 1972; Scenes from a Receding Past, 1977; Bornholm Night Ferry, 1983; Helsingor Station & Other Departures, 1989; Ronda Gorge & Other Precipices: Travel Writings, 1959-89; Lions of the Grunewald, novel, 1993. Honours: British Arts Council Grant; James Tait Black Memorial Prize, 1967; Irish Academy of Letters Award, 1970. Address: c/o Secker and Warburg, Michelin house, 91 Fulham Road, London SW3 6RB, England.

HIGGINS George V(incent), b. 13 Nov 1939, Brockton, Massachussets, USA. Writer; Journalist. m. (1) Elizabeth Mulkerin, 4 Sept 1965 (div), 1 son, 1 daughter, (2) Loretta Lucas Cubberley, 23 Aug 1979. Education: BA, 1961, JD, 1967, Boston College; MA, Stanford University, 1965. Appointments: Reporter, Journal and Evening Bulletin, Providence, Rhode Island, 1962-63; Newsman, Boston, Massachussets, 1964; Writer, Instructor in Law Enforcement Programs, Northeastern University, Boston, 1969-71; Consultant, National Institute of Law Enforcement and Criminal Justice, Washington DC, 1970-71. Publications: The Friends of Eddie Coyle, 1972; The Digger's Game, 1973; Cogan's Trade, 1974; A City on a Hill, 1975; The Judgement of

Deke Hunter, 1976; Dreamland, 1977; A Year or So with Edgar, 1979; Kennedy for the Defense, 1980; The Rat on Fire, 1981; The Patriot Game, 1982; A Choice of Enemies, 1984; Penance for Jerry Kennedy, 1985; Imposters, 1986; Wonderful Years, Wonderful Years, 1989; Trust, 1989. Contributions to: Columnist, Boston Herald American, 1977-79; Author of Magazine Criticism Column, Boston Globe, 1979-85; Biweekly Television Column, Wall Street Journal, 1984-; Contributor of Essays and Short Fiction to Journals and Magazines including Arizona Quarterly, Cimarron Review, Esquire, Atlantic, Playboy, GQ, New Republic, Newsweek. Honours: The Friends of Eddie Coyle, chosen as one of the top twenty postwar American novels by Book Marketing Council, 1985. Membership: Writers Guild of America. Address: 15 Brush Hill Lane, Milton, MA 02186, USA.

HIGGINS Jack. See: **PATTERSON Harry.**

HIGGINS John Dalby, b. 7 Jan 1934, Hong Kong. Editorial Executive. m. Linda Christmas, 3 Sept 1977. Education: MA, Worcester College, Oxford, 1957. Appointments: Literary/Arts Editor, Financial Times, 1966-69; Arts Editor, The Times, 1970-88; Chief Opera Critic/Obituaries Editor, The Times, 1988-. Publications: Don Giovanni - The Making of an Opera, 1977; Glyndebourne - A Celebration, Editor, 1984; Travels in the Balkans, 1969; British Theatre Design, (contributor) 1978-88. Honours: Chevalier des Arts et des Lettres; Ehrenkreuz fur Kunst und Wissenschaft, Austria; Goldenes Verdienstzeichnis. Memberships: Royal Literary Fund, Committee, 1970-. Address: The Times, London, England.

HIGGINS Richard C (Dick), b. 15 Mar 1938, Cambridge, England. Writer. m. 30 Jan 1960, 2 d. Education: BS, English, Columbia University, 1960 Manhattan School of Printing. Publications: 38 books including: Intermedia, 1985; Poems, Plain and Fancy, 1986; Pattern Poems: Guide to an Unkown Literature, 1987; Fluxis: Theory and Reception, 1986; 5 Hear-Plays, 1987; On the Composition of Images, Signs and Ideas, 1987; The Journey, 1991; The Autobiography of the Moon, 1992; Happytime the Medicine Man, 1992. Contributions to: Numerous journals and magazines including: Fluxhoe; The Beat Scene, WIN magazine; West Coast Poetry Review. Honours: Grants for pattern poetry projects. Purchase College Foundation, 1984-86 1988-; Bill C Davis Drama Award for The Journey, 1988; New York State Council on the Arts: Collaborations Grant from Visual Arts Program to build The Hanging Gardens of Lexington at Art Awareness in Lexinton, NY, 1989-; Pollock Krasher Grant in Painting, 1993. Recipient of various other awards. Address> PO Box 27, Barrytown, NY 12507, USA.

HIGHAM Robin (David Stewart), b. 20 June 1925, London, England. Professor of History. m. Barbara Jane Davies, 5 Aug 1950, 3 daughters. Education: AB cum laude, Harvard, 1950; MA, Claremont Graduate School, 1953; PhD, Harvard University, 1957. Appointments: Editor, Military Affairs; Editor, Aerospace Historian; Editor, Journal of the West; President, Sunflower University Press. Publications Include: Britain's Imperial Air Routes, 1960; The British Rigid Airship, 1961, 1982; Armed Forces in Peacetime, 1963; The Military Intellectuals in Britain, 1966; Air Power: A Concise History, 1973, 1984; The Diary of a Disaster, 1986. Contributions to: American Neptune; Balkan Studies; Business History Review; Airpower Historian; Military Affairs; Naval War College Review. Honours: Aviation and Space Writers Award, 1973; History Book Club Selection, 1973; Samuel Eliot Morison Prize, American Military Institute, 1986-87. Memberships: Publications Committee, Conference on British Studies; Editorial Advisory Board, Technology and Culture. Literary Agent: Bruce Hunter, David Higham, Claire Smith, Harold Ober. Address: 2961 Nevada Street, Manhattan, KS 66502, USA.

HIGHLAND Dora. See: **AVALLONE Michael Angelo.**

HIGHLAND Monica. See: **SEE Carolyn.**

HIGHSMITH (Mary) Patricia (Claire Morgan), b. 19 Jan 1921, Ft Worth, Texas, USA. Education: BA, Barnard College, 1942. Publications: Author, numerous books including Ripley Under Water, 1992. Honours: Recipient, Grand Prix de Litterature Policiere, 1957; Crime Writers Association Silver Dagger, 1964; Le Prix Litteraire (Deauville), 1987. Literary Agent: Digenes Verlag. Address: c/o Diogenes Verlag, Sprecherstrasse 8, CH 8032, Zurich, Switzerland.

HILD Jack. See: **GARSIDE Jack Clifford.**

HILDICK (Edmund) Wallace, b. 29 Dec 1925, Bradford, England. Author. m. Doris Clayton, 9 Dec 1950. Appointments: Visiting Critic and Associate Editor, Kenyon Review, Gambier, Ohio, USA, 1966-67. Publications: The Boy at the Window, 1960; Jim Starling Series, 1958-63; Birdy Jones Series, 1969-74; McGurk Series, 1974-90. Contributions to: Various journals. Honours: Tom Gallon Short Story Award, 1957; Edgar Allan Poe Special Award, 1979; Best Translated Works Award (Japan), 1979. Memberships: Authors Guild, USA; Society of Authors, England. Address: c/o Coutts & Co, 440 Strand, London WC2R 0QS, England.

HILL (John Edward) Christopher (K E Holme), b. 1912. Writer (History). Publications: The English Revolution 1640, 1940; As K.E. Holme: Two Commonwealths, 1945; Lenin and the Russian Revolution, 1947; The Good Old Cause (with E Dell), 1949; Economic Problems of the Church, 1956; Puritanism and Revolution, 1958; The Century of Revolution, 1961; Society and Puritanism, 1964; Intellectural Origins of the English Revolution, 1965; Reformation to Industrial Revolution, 1967; God's Englishman, 1970; Antichrist in Seventeenth Century England, 1971; The World Turned Upside Down, 1972; The Law of Freedom and Other Writings by Gerrard Winstanley, 1973; Change and Continuity in Seventeenth Century England, 1975; Milton and the English Revolution, 1978; Some Intellectual Consequences of the English Revolution, 1980; The Experience of Defeat, 1983; Writing and Revolution, 1985; Religion and Politics in 17th Century England, 1986; People and Ideas in 17th Century England, 1986; A Turbulent 5 Editions & Factives People: John Bunyan and his Church, 1988; A Nation of Change and Novelty, 1990; The English Bible and The 17th Century Revolution, 1993. Address: Woodway House, Sibford Ferris, Oxon, England.

HILL Douglas Arthur, (Martin Hillman), b. 6 Apr 1935, Canada. Author. m. Gail Robinson, 8 Apr 1958, div, 1 s. Education: BA, University of Saskatchewan, 1957. Appointments: Literary Editor, Tribune, London, 1971-84. Publications include: The Supernatural, 1965; The Opening of the Canadian West, 1967; John Keats, 1969; The Scots to Canada, 1972; Galactic Warlord, 1980; The Huntsman, 1982; The Last Legionary Quartet, 1985; Penelope's Pendant, 1990; The Unicorn Dream, 1992; The Lightless Dome, 1993; The Voyage of Mudjack, 1993; World of the Stiks, 1994; The Leafless Forest, 1994. Memberships: Society of Authors; Children's Book Circle. Literary Agent: Sheila Watson of Watson, Little Limited, London. Address: 3 Hillfield Avenue, London, N8 7DU, England.

HILL Elizabeth Starr, b. 4 Nov 1925, USA. Author. m. Russell Gibson Hill, 28 May 1949, 1 s, 1 d. Publications: The Wonderful Visit to Miss Liberty, 1961; The Window Tulip, 1967; Evan's Corner, 1967; Master Mike and the Miracle Maid, 1967; Pardon My Fangs, 1968; Bells: A Book to Begin On, 1970; Ever After Island, 1977; Fangs Aren't Everything, 1985; When Christmas Comes, 1989; Evan's Corner, (new edition), 1991; The Street Dancers, 1991; Broadway Chances, 1992; The Banjo Player, 1993; Curtain Going Up!, 1995. Contributions to: New Yorker; Reader's Digest; Harper's Seventeen; Cricket. Literary Agent: Harold Ober Ass Inc. Address: c/o Harold Ober Ass Inc, 425 Madison Ave, New York, NY 10017, USA.

HILL Errol Gaston, b. 5 Aug 1921, Trinidad, West Indies. College Professor Emeritus. m. Grace Lucille Eunice Hope, 11 Aug 1956, 1 son, 3 daughters. Education: Graduate Diploma, Royal Academy of Dramatic Art, London, England, 1951; Diploma in Dramatic Art with distinction, London University, 1951; BA summa cum laude, 1962, MFA, Playwriting, 1962, DFA, Theatre History, 1966, Yale University, USA. Publications: Man Better Man: A Musical Comedy, 1964, reprinted, 1985; The Trinidad Carnival, 1972; The Theatre of Black Americans, 1980, reprinted, 1987; Shakespeare in Sable: A History of Black Shakespearean Actors, 1984; The Jamaican State, 1655-1900, 1992; Editor: Caribbean Plays, vol 1, 1958, vol 2, 1965; A Time and a Season: 8 Caribbean Plays, 1976; Plays for Today, 1985; Black Heroes: Seven Plays, 1989. Contributions to: McGraw Encyclopaedia of World Drama, 1984; Theatre Journal; Theatre History Studies; American Literature Forum; Caribbean Quarterly; Cambridge Guide to World Theatre; Many others. Honours: British Council Scholarship, 1949-51; Rockefeller Foundation Fellowship, 1958-60, 1965; Theatre Guild of America Fellowship, 1961; Guggenheim Foundation Fellowship, 1985-86; Barnard Hewitt Award for Theatre History, 1985; Fulbright Fellowship, 1988. Memberships Include: Executive Committee, American Society for Theatre Research; Executive Committee, American Theatre and Drama Society; Association of Commonwealth Language and Literature Studies; Phi Beta Kappa, President of Alpha of New Hampshire, 1982-85; International Federation for Theatre Research. Literary Agent: Lucy Kroll Agency, New York City, USA. Address: 3 Haskins Road, Hanover, NH 03755, USA.

HILL Geoffrey, b. 18 June 1932, Bromsgrove, Worcestershire, England. Professor; Poet. Education: BA, Keble College, Oxford, 1953. Appointments include: Professor, University of Leeds, 1976-80; University Lecturer in English, Cambridge, 1980-88, Clark Lecturer, Trinity College, Cambridge, 1986; University Professor, Professor of Literature and Religion, Boston University, 1988-; Visiting Lecturer, USA & Nigeria. Publications include: Poems, 1952; For the Unfallen: Poems, 1952-58; Preghiere, 1964; King Log, 1968; Mercian hymns, 1971; Tenebrae, 1978; The Mystery of the Charity of Charles Peguy, 1983; The Lords of Limit, 1984; Collected Poems, 1985; Brand, Adaptation of Ibsen, Produced London, 1978; The Enemy's Country, 1991; New and Collected Poems 1952-1992, 1994. Honours include: Duff Cooper Memorial Prize, 1979; D Litt, University of Leeds, 1988; Honorary Fellow, Keble College, Oxford, 1981; Honorary Fellow, Emmanuel College, Cambridge, 1990. Address: The University Professors, Boston University, 745 Commonwealth Avenue, Boston, MA 02215, USA.

HILL Jane, b. 17 Oct 1950, Seneca, South Carolina, USA. Teacher; Editor; Writer. m. Robert W Hill, 16 Aug 1980, 1 daughter. Education: BA 1972, MA 1978, Clemson University; PhD, University of Illinois, 1985. Appointments: Associate Editor, Peachtree Publishers, 1986-88; Senior Editor, Longstreet Press, 1988-91; Director, Kennesaw Summer Writers Workshop, 1988-92; Assistant Professor, West Georgia College, 1992-. Publications: Gail Godwin, 1992; Editor: Street Songs: New Voices in Fiction, 1990; Our Mutual Room: Modern Literary Portraits of the Opposite Sex, 1987; An American Christmas: A Sampler of Contemporary Stories and Poems, 1986; You Haven't to Deserve: A Gift to the Homeless/Fiction by 21 Writers, 1991; Author, Cobb County: At the Heart of Change, 1991. Contributions to: Numerous stories, poems, essays and reviews since 1978. Honours: Frank O'Connor Prize for Fiction, 1989; Syvenna Foundation Fellow, 1991; Monticello Fellowship for Female Writers, 1992. Memberships: Modern Language Association. Address: 1419 Arden Drive, Marietta, GA 30060, USA.

HILL Pamela, (Sharon Fiske), b. 26 Nov 1920, Kenya. Writer. Publications include: Flaming Janet, 1954; The Devil of Aske, 1972; The Malvie Inheritance, 1973; Homage to a Rose, 1979; Fire Opal, 1980; This Rough Beginning, 1981; My Lady Glamis, 1981; The House of Cray, 1982; The Governess, 1985; Glamis, 1981; Summer Cypress, 1981; Venables, 1988; The Sutburys, 1987; The Brocken, 1991; The Sword and the Flame, 1991; Mercer, 1992; The Silver Runaways, 1992; O Madcap Duchess (forthcoming); The Parson's Children (forthcoming). Contributions to: Argosy; Chambers Journal. Memberships: Society of Authors; PEN. Address: 89a Winchester Street, Pimlico, London SW1V 4NU, England.

HILL Reginald (Charles), (Dick Morland, Patrick Ruell, Charles Underhill), b. 1936, Author; Playwright. Publications include: A Clubbable Woman, 1970; Fell of Dark, 1971; As Dick Morland: Heart Clock, 1973; A Very Good Hater, 1974; Albion! Albion!, 1974; As Patrick Ruell: The Castle of Demon, 1971; An Advancement of Learning, 1972; A Fairly Dangerous Thing, 1972; Red Christmas, 1972; An Affair of Honour (play), 1972; Ruling Passion, 1973; Death Takes the Low Road, 1974; An April Shroud, 1975; Urn Burial, 1976; Another Death in Venice, 1976; The Long Kill, 1986; Child's Play, 1987; Death of a Dormouse, 1987; The Collaborators, 1987; There are no Ghosts in the Soviet Union, 1987; Under World, 1988; Dream of Darkness, 1989; Bones and Silence, 1990; One Small Step (novella). 1990; The Only Game, 1991; Recalled to Life, 1992; Blood Sympathy, 1993; As Charles Underhill: Captain Fantom, 1978; A Pinch of Snuff, 1978; The Forging of Fantom, 1979; Pascoe's Ghost (stories), 1979; A Killing Kindness, 1980; The Spy's Wife, 1980; Who Guards a Prince, 1981; Traitor's Blood, 1983; Deadheads, 1983; Exit Lines, 1984; No Man's Land, 1984; Honours: Gold Dagger Award, 1990. Literary Agent: Caradol King, A P Watt Limited. Address: c/o A P Watt Limited, 20 John Street, London WC1N 2DR, England.

HILL Selima (Wood), b. 13 Oct 1945, London. Poet. m. Roderic Hill, 1968, 2 s, 2 d. Education: New Hall College, Cambridge. Publications: Saying Hello at the Station, 1984; My Darling Camel, 1988; The Accumulation of Small Acts of Kindness, 1989; A Little Book of Meat, 1993; Trembling Hearts in The Bodies of Dogs, 1994.

Honours: Cholmondeley Prize, 1986; Arvon Observer Poetry Competition Prize, 1988; Arts Council Writers Bursary, 1993; H K Travel Scholarship to Mongolia, 1994; Judge, Observer Prize, 1990, Bridport Prize, 1995. Address: c/o Bloodaxe Books, PO Box 1SN, Newcastle Upon Tyne, NE99 1SN, England.

HILL Susan Elizabeth, b. 5 Feb 1942, Scarborough, Yorkshire, England. Novelist; Playwright. m. Stanley W Wells, 3 d, 1 dec. Education: BA, University of London, 1963. Appointments: Literary Critic, Various Journals, 1963; Numerous Plays for BBC, 1970-. Publications include: The Enclosure, 1961; Do Me a Favour, 1963; Gentleman and Ladies, 1969; A Change for the Better, 1969; I'm the King of the Castle, 1970; Strange Meeting, 1971; The Bird of Night, 1972; The Cold Country and Other Plays fior Radio, 1975; The Magic Apple Tree, 1982; The Woman in Black, 1983; Through the Garden Gate, 1986; Mothers Magic, 1986; Lanterns Across the Snow, 1987; Can It Be True?, 1988. Memberships: FRSL. Address: Midsummer Cottage, Church Lane, Beckley, Oxon, England.

HILLARD Darla, b. 7 July 1946, Illinois, USA. Publications: Vanishing Tracks: Four Years Among the Snow Leopards of Nepal, 1989. Contributions to: National Geographic, 1986; French Geographic, 1988; Airone, 1987. Address: International Snow Leopard Trust, 4649 Sunnyside Avenue, North Seattle, WA 98103, USA.

HILLERMAN Tony, b. 27 May 1925. Writer of Fiction & Nonfiction. m. Marie Unzer, 3 sons, 3 daughters. Education: BA, University of Oklahoma; MA, University of New Mexico, USA. Career: Journalist; Professor of Journalism; Writer, 1985-. Publications include: The Bleming Way, 1970; The Fly on the Wall, 1971; Coyote Waits; Talking to God; Hillerman Country; The Great Taos Bank Robbery, 1973; The Spell of New Mexico, 1976; The People of Darkness, 1978; Ghostway, 1984; Skinwalkers, 1986; The Best of the West (ed), 1991; Sacred Clowns, 1993. Contributions to: True; New Mexico Quarterly; Natinal Geographic; Popular Psychology; Readers Digest. Honours: Edgar Award; Grand Master Award; Mystery Writers of America; Public Service Award; US Dept of the Interior. Address: 2729 Texas NE, Albuquerque, NM 87110, USA.

HILLERT Margaret, b. 22 Jan 1920. Teacher. Education: RN, University of Michgan School of Nursing; AB, Wayne University College of Education. Appointments include: Registered Nurse, 3 years; Primary Teacher, 34 years. Publications: Farther Than Far, 1969; I Like to Live in the City, 1970; Who Comes to Your House, 1973; Come Play With Me, 1975; The Sleeptime Book, 1975; What Is It? 1978; I'm Special...So Are You!, 1979; Action Verse for the Primary Classroom, 1980; Doing Things, 1980; Let's Take a Break, 1981; Rabbits and Rainbows, 1985; 55 juvenile books, 12 included in Dear Dragon Series; various translations into Swedish, Danish, German, Portuguese. Poetry: Seasons, Holidays, Anytime, 1987; Dandelions and Daydreams, 1987; Lightning Bugs and Lullabies (poetry), 1988; God's Big Book, 1988; Guess, Guess, 1988; The Birth of Jesus, 1988; Jesus Grows Up, 1988; Sing a Song of Christmas (poetry), 1989; The Sky is Not So Far Away, 1994. Contributions to: Numerous literary magazines and journals; numerous anthologies. Address: 31262 Huntley Square East, Birmingham, MI 48025, USA.

HILLIS Rick L, b. 3 Feb 1956, Canada. Writer. m. Patricia Appelgren, 29 Aug 1988, 1 s, 1 d. Education: BEd, University of Saskatchewan, 1979; MFA, University of Iowa, 1974. Appointments: Stegner Fellow, Stanford University, 1988-90; Jones Lecturer in Fiction, Stanford, 1990-92; Chesterfield Film Writer's Fellowship, 1991-92; Visiting Assistant Professor of English, Reed College, 1994-96. Publications: Limbo River, 1990. The Blue Machines of Night, 1988. Honours: Drue Heinz Literature Prize, 1990; Commonwealth Club of California Silver Medal, 1990. Memberships: PEN; ACTRA. Address: 499A Thompson Avenue, Mountain View, VA 94040, USA.

HILLMAN Ellis Simon, b. 17 Nov 1928, London, England. University Lecturer. m. Louise, 10 Dec 1967, 1 s. Education: University College School, 1942-46; RAF Instructor, Ground Wireless, 1947-49; Chelsea College of Advanced Technology, 1971. Appointments: Local Government Correspondent, The Tribune, 1963-67; Editorial Advisory Board, Underground Services, 1975-79; Editorial Board, Underground Services, 1975-79; Editorial Board, Colson News, 1986-. Publications include: London Under London, 1985; Earthquakes in London, 1967; The Built Environment, 1984. Contributions to: Underground Services; Architect and Surveyor; Architects Journal; Structural Survey; The Environmentalist; Municipal Journal. Honours: The London Visitors and Convention Bureau Best Known Book, 1985; National Book Legue Prize, 1986. Memberships: Science Fiction Foundation; Lewis Carroll Society; LCC; GLC; ILEA. Address: 29 Haslemere Avenue, Hendon, NW4 2PU.

HILLMAN Martin. See: Hill Douglas Arthur.

HILLS Charles Albert Reis, b. 21 Aug 1955, London, England. Report Writer, BBC Monitoring. Publications: The Facist Dictatorships, 1979; The Hitler File, 1980; World Trade, 1981; Modern Industry, 1982; Growing Up in The 1950s, 1983; The Second World War, 1985; The Destruction of Pompeii and Herculaneum, 1987. Contributions to: The Guardian; The Daily Telegraph; Encounter; Books; Jennings Magazine; The Lady. Memberships: English Centre PEN. Address: 3 Lucas House, Albion Avenue, London SW8 2AD, England.

HILLS Geraldine. See: JAY Geraldine Mary.

HILTON Margot Pamela,b. 18 Aug 1947, London, England. Arts Administrator; Writer; Journalist. m. Graeme Blundell, 3 Oct 1979, 1 son, 1 daughter. Education: BA, English, Honours, 1971, MA, Drama & Theatre Arts, 1972, Leeds University, England. Appointments: Drama Adviser, Victorian Ministry for the Arts, 1974-79; Storyliner & Scriptwriter with Grundy Organization, 1980; Executive Officer, Australian Society of Authors, 1981-84; Playwright in Residence, Australian National Playwrights Conference, 1983; Executive Secretary, Victorian Premier's Inaugural Literary Awards, 1984-85; Publicity Manager, Angus & Robertson Publishers, 1985-87. Publications: (Performer Plays): Potiphar's Wife, 1979, 1980, 1981; Marmalade File, 1983; Squealing Pips, 1983. Books: Women on Men, 1987; Potiphar's Wife, 1987. Contributions to: Theatre Australia; Playboy; New Review; Australian Author; Bulletin; Architecture Australia; National Times; Times on Sunday; Sydney Morning Herald; Sun-Herald. Literary Agent: Hickson Assocs. Address: 84 Surrey Street, Potts Point, NSW 2011, Australia.

HILTON Suzanne McLean, b. 3 Sept 1922, Pittsburgh, Pennslyvania, USA. Writer. m. Warren Mitchell Hilton, 15 June 1946, 1 s, 1 d. Education: BA, Beaver College, 1946. Appointments: Editor, Bulletin of Old York Road Historical Society, 1976-92; Associate Editor, Montgomery County History, 1983; Editor, Bulletin of Historical Society of Montomery County, 1987-89. Publications: 18 books including: How Do They Get Rid of It?, 1970; How Do They Cope with It?, 1970; Beat It, Burn It and Drown It, 1974; The Way It Was - 1976, 1975; Who Do You Think You Are?, 1976; Yesterday's People, 1976; Here Today and Gone Tomorrow, 1978; Faster than a Horse: Moving West with Engine Power, 1983; Montomery County, The Second Hundred Years, 1983; The World of Young Tom Jefferson, 1986; The World of Young George Washsington, 1986; The World of Young Herbert Hoover, 1987; The World of Young Andrew Jackson, 1988; A Capital Capitol City, 1991; Miners, Merchants and Maids, 1995. Contributions to: Historical journals. Honours: Legion of Honour, Chapel of the Four Chaplains, 1978; Award for Excellence in Non Fiction, Drexel University, 1979; Golden Supur, Western Writers of America, 980; Gold Disc, Beaver College, 1981. Memberships: Society of Children's Book Writers and Illustrators; Philadelphia Childrens Reading Round Table. Address: 3320 108th St NW, Gig Harbour, WA 98332, USA.

HIMMELFARB Gertrude, b. USA. Career: Professor; Essayist. Publications include: Lord Acton: A Study in Conscience & Politics, 1952; Darwin & The Darwinian Revolution, 1962; Victorian Minds, 1968; On Liberty & Liberation: The Case of John Stuart Mill, 1974; The Idea of Poverty: England in the Early Industrial Revolution, 1984; Marriage & Morals Among the Victorians, 1986; The New History & The Old, 1987; Poverty & Compassion, 1992; On Looking Into the Abyss: Untimely Thoughts on Culture and Society, 1994; The De-Moralization of Society, 1995. Contributions to: Commentary; American Scholar; New York Times Book Review. Address: c/o Knopf Publishers 201 E 50th Street, 20th Floor Reception, New York, NY 10022, USA.

HINDE Thomas. See: CHITTY Thomas Willes, Sir.

HINDIN Nathan. See: BLOCH Robert.

HINE Daryl, b. 1931, Canada. Author; Playwright; Poet. Publications: Five Poems, 1955; The Carnal and the Crane, 1957; The Devil's Picture Book: Poems, 1960; The Prince of Darkness and Co (novel), 1961; Heroics: Five Poems, 1961; Polish Subtitles: Impressions of a Journey, 1962; The Wooden Horse: Poems, 1965;

Minutes: Poems, 1968; The Death of Seneca (play), 1968; The Homeric Hymns and the Battle of the Frogs and the Mice, 1972; Resident Alien: Poems, 1975; In and Out: Poems, 1975; Daylight Saving: Poems, 1978; The Poetry Anthology 1912-1977, 1978; Selected Poems, 1981; Theocritus: Idyllis and Epigrams, 1982; Academic Festival Overtures, 1985; In and Out (revised), 1989; Arrondissements, 1989; Ovid's Heroines, 1991; Postscripts, 1991. Honours: MacArthur Fellowship, 1986-91. Address: 2740 Ridge Avenue, Evanston, IL 60201, USA.

HINES Barry Melvin, b. 30 June 1939, Barnsley, Yorkshire, England. Writer, div, 1 s, 1 d. Education: Loughborough College of Education, 1958-60, 1962-63. Appointments: Yorkshire Arts Association Fellow, Sheffield University, 1972-74; East Midlands Art Association Fellow, Matlock College of High Education, 1975-77; Arts Council of Great Britain Fellow, Sheffield City Polytechnic, 1982-84. Publications include: The Blinder, 1966; First Signs, 1972; The Price of Coal, 1979; Unfinished Business, 1983; The Game Keeper, 1979; A Question of Leadership, 1981; The Heart of It, 1994. Literary Agent: Sheila Lemon, Lemon and Durbridge Limited, London. Address: 323 Fulwood Road, Sheffield, S10 3BJ, England.

HINES Donald Merrill, b. 23 Jan 1931, Minnesota, USA. Writer; Publisher. m. Linda Marie Arnold, 10 June 1961, 3 s. Education: BS, English and Speech Arts, Lewis and Clark College, Portland, Oregon, 1953; MAT, English and Education, Reed College, 1960; PhD, Folklore and American Studies, Indiana University, 1969. Appointments: Associate Professor, Departments of English, Washington State University, 1968-77; College of Education, King Saud University-Abha, Saudi Arabia, 1982-90; Blue Mountain Community College, Pendleton, OR, 1990-91. Publications: Ghost Voices, Yakima Indian Myths, Legends, Humour and Hunting Stories, 1992; Tales of the Okanogans, 1976; Cultural History of the Inland Pacific Northwest Frontier, 1976; Frontier Folksay: Proverbial Lore of the Inland Pacific Northwest Frontier, 1977; Tales of the Nez Perce, 1984; The Forgotten Tribes, Oral Tales of the Tenino and Adjacent Mid-Columbia River Indian Nations, 1991; Magic in the Mountains, The Yakima Shaman: Power and Practice. Contributions to: Southern Folklore Quarterly; Western Review; Pennsylvania Folklife; American Speech; Journal of Folklore Institute; The Folklore Historian. Honours: Ford Foundation Fellowship, Indiana University, 1965; Third Prize, Chicago Folklore Contest, University of Chicago, 1970. Memberships: American Folklore Society. Address: 3623 219th Place SE, Issaquah, WA 98027, USA.

HINOJOSA-SMITH R Roland, b. 21 Jan 1929, Mercedes, Texas, USA. English Professor; Writer. m. Patricia Sorensen, 1 Sept 1963, 1 s, 2 d. Education: BS University of Texas at Austin, 1953; Highlands University, New Mexico, 1963; PhD, University of Illinois, 1969. Appointments: University of Minnesota, 1977-81; University of Texas, 1981-. Publications: The Valley, 1983; Klail City, 1986; Dear Rafe, 1985; Partners in Crime, 1987; Korean Love Songs, 1978; Rites and Witnesses, 1984; Estampas del Valle, 1973; Klail City y sus alrededores, 1976; Claros varones du Belken, 1987; Becky and her Friends, 1989; The Useless Servants, 1993. Contributions to: Texas Monthly; Southwest Airlines Spirit; Latin American Review Magazine; Southwest Review. Honours: Best Novel, 1973, 1976, 1981; Qinto Sol Prize, Case de Las Americas Prize; Best Writing in the Humanities Prize, 1981; Alumnus of the University of Illinois, 1989. Memberships: Modern Language Association; Board of Directors, Texas Committee on the Humanities. Address: Dept of English, University of Texas, Austin, TX 78712, USA.

HINTON Jenny. See: **DAWSON Jennifer.**

HIPPOPOTAMUS Eugene H. See: **KRAUS Robert.**

HIRO Dilip, Writer. Education include: MS, State University of Virginia, USA, 1962. Publications: A Triangular View, 1969; Black British, White British, 1971; To Anchor A Cloud, 1972; The Untouchables of India, 1975; Inside India Today, 1976; Clean Break, play, 1978; Apply, Apply, No Reply, play, 1978; Interior, Exchange, Exterior, 1980; Inside the Middle East, 1982; Iran Under the Ayatollahs, 1985; Three Plays, 1987; Iran: The Revolution Within, 1988; Islamic Fundamentalism, 1988; The Longest War: The Iran-Iraq Military Conflict, 1989; Desert Shield To Desert Storm: The Second Gulf War, 1992; Black British, White British: A History of Race Relations in Britain, 1992; Lebanon, Fire and Embers: A History of the Lebanese Civil War, 1993; Between Marx and Muhammed: The Changing Face of Central Asia, 1994. Contributions to: Washington Post; Wall Street Journal; Los Angeles Times; Boston Globe; Sunday Times; Observer; Guardian; New Statesman and Society; Nation; Atlantic; Community Journal; Middle East Report; Toronto Star; Times Literary Supplement. Honours: Silver Hugo, Chicago Film Festival for A Private Enterprise, British Feature Film, as co-scriptwriter, 1975. Memberships: Middle East Studies Association of North America; Centre for Iranian Research and Analysis. Literary Agent: David Higham Associates, London, England. Address: 31 Waldegrave Road, Ealing, London W5 3HT, England.

HIRSCH Edward Mark, b. 20 Jan 1950, IL, USA. Poet. m. Janet Landay, 29 May 1977, 1 s. Education: BA, Grinnell College, 1968; PhD, University of PA, 1979. Publications: Earthly Measures, 1994; The Night Parade, 1989; Wild Gratitude, 1986; For the Sleepwalkers, 1981. Contributions to: New Yorker; New Republic; Nation; NY Times Book Review; Paris Review. Honours: Lyndhurst Prize, 1994; Rome Prize, 1988; National Book Critics Circle Award, 1987. Literary Agent: Liz Darhansoff. Address: Dept of English, University of Houston, TX 77204, USA.

HIRSCHHORN Clive Errol, b. 20 Feb 1940, Johannesburg, South Africa. Critic. Education: BA, University of Witwatersrand, Johannesburg, South Africa. Publications: Gene Kelly - A Biography, 1974; Films of James Mason, 1976; The Warner Bors' Story, 1978; The Hollywood Musical, 1981; The Universal Story, 1983; The Columbia Story, 1989. Contributions to: Film and Theatre Critic of the London Sunday Express, 1966-. Literary Agent: Tony Peake. Address: 42a South Audley Street, Mayfair, London W1, England.

HISSEY Jane Elizabeth, b. 1 Sept 1952, Norwich, Norfolk, England. Author; Illustrator. m. Ivan James Hissey, 1 Aug 1979, 2 s, 1 d. Education: Art Foundation Course, Great Yarmouth College of Art & Design, 1970; BA, Brighton Polytechnic, 1974, Art Teachers Certificate, Brighton Polytechnic, 1975. Publications: Old Bear, 1986; Little Bears Trousers, 1987; Little Bear Lost, 1989; Jolly Tall, 1990; Jolly Snow, 1991; Old Bear Tales, 1991; Little Bear's Day, Little Bear's Bedtime, 1992; Ruff, 1994. Honours: BAFTA, 1993. Address: c/o Hutchinson Childrens Books, Random House, 20 Vauxhall Bridge Road, London SW1V 2SA, England.

HITCHENS Christopher, b. UK. Journalist; Writer. Publications: Hostage to History: Cyprus from the Ottomaus to Kissinger, 1984; Prepared for the Worst, 1989; Blood, Class & Nostalgia: Anglo-American Ironics; Imperical Spoils; Blaming the Victims; James Callaghan: The Road to Number 10; Karl Marx & The Paris Commune; The Monarchy: A Critique of Britain's Favourite Fetish. Contributions: Vanity Fair; The Nation; Harpers; Grand Street; Z; New Left Review; TLS; London Review of Books. Address: The Nation, 72 Fifth Avenue, New York, NY 10011, USA.

HJORTSBERG William Reinhold, b. 23 Feb 1941, New York City, USA. Author. Education: BA, Dartmouth College, 1962; Postraduate, Yale Drama School, 1962-63; Stanford University, 1967-68. Publications: Alp, 1969; Gray Matters, 1971; Symbiography, 1973; Torol Torol Torol, 1974; Falling Angel, 1978; Tales and Fables, 1985; Nevermore, 1994. Films, Thunder and Lightning, 1977; Legend, 1986; Georgia Peaches (co-author), 1980. Contributions to: various journals, magazines and newspapers. Literary Agent: Robert Dattila, Phoenix Literary Agents. Address: Main Boulder Route, McLeod, MT 59052, USA.

HOAGLAND Edward, b. 21 Dec 1932, NY, USA. 1 child. Education: AB, Harvard. Literary Appointments include: Teacher, New School for Social Research, 1963-64; Teacher, University of IA Writers Workshop, 1978; Teacher, Bennington, 1987-97; University of CA, Davis, 1990, 1992. Publications include: Cat Man, 1984; Walking the Dead Diamond River, 1993; City Tales, 1986; The Final Fate of the Alligators, 1992; Balancing Acts, 1992. Contributions to: The Noble Savage; Esquire; Paris Review; New Am Review; Transatlantic Review; New Yorker; NY Times Book Review; Harpers; Science Digest; Backpacker. Honours: Houghton Mifflin Literary Fellowship, 1954; Longview Foundation Award, 1961; Prix de Rome, 1964; Guggenheim Fellowship, 1965; NY State Arts Council Grant, 1972; Harold Vursell Award, 1981; Lannan Foundation Award, 1993; National Book Critics Circle Award, 1980; Am Book Award, 1982; National Magazine Award, 1989. Address: PO Box 51, Barton, VT 05822, USA.

HOBAN Russell Conwell, b. 4 Feb 1925, Lansdale, USA. Author. m. (1) Lillian Aberman, 1944, (div 1975), 1 son, 3 daughters, (2)

Gundula Ahl, 1975, 3 sons. Education: Philadelphia Museum School of Industrial Art. Publications: Novels: The Mouse and His Child, 1967; The Lion of Boaz-Jachin and Jachin-Boaz, 1973; Kleinzeit, 1974; Turtle Diary, 1975; Riddley Walker, 1980; Pilgermann, 1983; 51 children's picture books and 2 books of verse for children, 1959-; Text for The Carrier Frequency (theatre piece, Impact Theatre Co-operative), 1984; Stage version of Riddley Walker (Manchester Royal Exchange Theatre Co), 1986; Various essays and pieces for Granta and The Fiction Magazine. Honours: Whitbread Prize for How Tom Beat Captain Najork and His Hired Sportsmen, 1974; John W Campbell Memorial Award and Australian Science Fiction Achievement Award for Riddley Walker, 1983. Address: David Higham Associates Ltd, 5-8 Lower John Street, Golden Square, London W1R 4HA, England.

HOBBS Anne Stevenson. Museum Curator, Victoria and Albert Museum; Frederick Warne Curator of Children's Literature. Education: BA, 1964; MA Hons, 1967, Newham College, Cambridge. Publications: Fables: 500 years of illustration and text, 1986; Beatrix Potter: The V & A Collection, 1985; Beatrix Potter, 1866-1943: The Artist and Her World, 1987; Beatrix Potter's Art, 1990; A Victorian Naturalist: Beatrix Potter's Drawings in the Armitt Collection, 1992. Contributions to: Beatrix Potters Writings; Some Literary and Linguistic Influences a major article in Beatrix Potter Studies III, 1989. Honours: Committee, Beatrix Potter Society; European String Teachers Association; Lewis Carroll Society; Arthur Rackham Society. Address: c/o Archive of Art and Design, 23 Blythe Road, London W14 O9F, England.

HOBFOLL Stevan E, b. 25 Sept 1951, Chicago, Illinois, USA. Professor of Psychology. m. Ivonne H Hobfoll, 18 May 1972, 2 sons, 1 daughter. Education: London Kings College, 1971-72; BS, Psychology, University of Illinois, 1973; MA, 1975; PhD, 1977, Psychology, University of South Florida. Publications: The Ecology of Stress, 1988; Stress, Social Support and Women, 1986; War-Related Stress, 1991; Conservation of Resources, 1989. Contributions to: Over 60 journal articles and 25 book chapters; Editor, Anxiety, Stress and Coping; An International Journal, 1992-. Honours: Ecology of Stress judged significant contribution to learning and understanding by Encyclopaedia Britannica, 1989 yearbook; Peer recognition award for work with HIV/AIDS on Ohio's racial and ethnic communities, 1990. Memberships: Fellow, American Psychological Association; Stress and Test Anxiety Research Society; International Society for the Study of Personal Relationships. Address: Applied Psychology Centre, 106 Kent Hall, Kent State University, OH 44242, USA.

HOBHOUSE Hermione, b. 1934. Urban Historian and Writer, since 1983 General Editor, Survey of London, RCHME. Appointments Include: Researcher, Scriptwriter, Associated-Rediffusion Television, 1956-58; Researcher, Scriptwriter, Granada Television, 1958-63; General Editor, Survey of London, 1983-. Publications: The Ward of Cheap in the City of London: A Short History, 1963; Thomas Cubitt: Master Builder, 1971; Lost London, 1971; History of Regent Street, 1975; Oxford and Cambridge, 1980; Prince Albert: His Life and Work, 1983; (ed) Southern Kensington, Earl's Court, 1986. Honour: MBE, 1981. Address: 61 Dunstan's Road, London, W6 8RE, England.

HOBHOUSE Penelope. See: MALINS Penelope.

HOBSBAUM Philip Dennis, b. 29 June 1932. Writer. University Professor. m. Rosemary Phillips, 20 July 1976. Education: BA, 1955, MA, 1961, Downing College, Cambridge; LRAM, Royal Academy of Music, 1956; PhD, University of Sheffield, 1968. Appointments: Lecturer in English, Queen's University, Belfast, Northern Ireland, 1962-66; Lecturer in English Literature, 1966-72, Senior Lecturer, 1972-79, Reader, 1979-85, Titular Professor, 1985-, Glasgow University, Scotland. Publications: The Place's Fault and Other Poems, 1964; In Retreat and Other Poems, 1966; Coming Out Fighting: Poems, 1969; A Theory of Communication, 1970; Women and Animals: Poems, 1972; A Reader's Guide to Charles Dickens, 1972, 1982, 1989; Tradition and Experiment in English Poetry, 1979; A Reader's Guide to D H Lawrence, 1981, 1989; Essentials of Literary Criticism, 1982, 1989. Contributions to: Times Literary Supplement; Spectator; Listener; Poetry Review; Outposts; The Hudson Review; Encounter; Modern Language Review. Memberships: Chairman, Sheffield University Arts Society, 1960-61; Scottish Association for Literary Studies; BBC Club; Association of University Teachers. Address: c/o Department of English Literature, University of Glasgow, Glasgow G20 6BS, Scotland.

HOBSON Fred Colby Jr, b. 23 Apr 1943, Winston-Salem, NS, USA. Professor of Literature; Writer. m. 17 June 1967, (div), 1 d.

Education: AB, English, University of North Carolina, 1965; MA, History, Duke University, 1967; PhD, English, University of North Carolina, 1972. Appointments: Professor of English, University of Alabama, 1972-86; Professor of English and Co-editor, Southern Review, Louisiana State University, 1986-89; Professor of English and Co-editor, Southern Literary Journal, University of North Carolina. Publications: Tell About the South: The Southern Rage to Explain, 1984; Serpent in Eden: H L Mencken and the South, 1974; South-Watching: Selected Essays of Gerald W Johnson (editor), 1984; Literature at the Barricades: The American Writer in the 1930's (co-editor), 1983l; The Southern Writer in the Post-Modern World, 1990; Mencken: A Life, 1994; Thirty-Five Years of Newspaper Work by H L Mencken (co-editor), 1994. Contributions to: Virginia Quarterly Review; Sewanee Review; Kenyon Review; New York Times Book Review; Commonwealth; American Literature; Times Literary Supplement. Address: Department of English, University of North Carolina, Chapel Hill, NC 27514, USA.

HOBSON Polly. See: EVANS Julia.

HOCH Edward D, b. 22 Feb 1930, Rochester, New York, USA. Author. m. Patricia A McMahon, 5 June 1957. Education: University of Rochester, 1947-49. Publications: The Thefts of Nick Velvet, 1978; The Quests of Simon Ark, 1984; Leopold's Way, 1985; The Night My Friend, 1991; The Shattered Raven, 1969; The Transvection Machine, 1971; The Spy and the Thief, 1971; Best Detective Stories of the Year, (Editor), 1976-81; Year's Best Mystery and Suspense Stories, (Editor), 1982-95; All But Impossible, (Editor), 1981. Contributions to: Over 800 stories in mystry magazines and anthologies, including a story in every issue of Ellery Queen's Mystery Magazine since 1973. Honours: Mystery Writers of America Edgar Award for best short story, The Oblong Room, 1967; Edgar Nominee for The Most Dangerous Man, 1980. Memberships: President, Mystery Writers of America, 1982-83; Author's Guild; Crime Association, England; Science Fiction Writers of America. Literary Agent: Larry Sternig, 742 Robertison Street, Milwaukee, WI. Address: 2941 Lake Avenue, Rochester, NY 14612, USA.

HOCHHUTH Rolf, b. 1 Apr 1931, Germany; Playwright. m. 3 s. Education: Universities of Heidelberg & Munich, 1952-55. Appointments: Former Publishers Reader, President Municipal Playwright, Basel, 1963. Publications: The Representative, 1962; The Employer, 1965; The Soldiers, 1966; Anatomy of Revolution, 1969; The Guerillas, 1970; The Midwife, 1972; Lysistrata and the NATO, 1973; A German Love Story, 1980; Judith, 1984. Membership: PEN. Address: PO Box 661, 4002 Basel, Switzerland.

HOCHSCHILD Adam, b. 5 Oct 1942, New York City, USA. Writer. m. Arlie Russell, 26 June 1965, 2 s. Education: AB cum laude, Harvard University, 1963. Appointments include: Reporter, San Francisco Chronicle, 1965-66; Editor and Writer, Ramparts Magazine, 1966-68, 1973-74; Commentator, National Public Radio, 1982-83; Commentator, Public Interest Radio, 1987-88; Co-founder, Editor, Now Writer, Mother Jones Magazine, 1974-; Regents Lecturer, University of California at Santa Cruz, 1987; Lecturer, Graduate School of Journalism, University of California at Berkeley, 1992, 1995-. Publications include: Half the Way Home: A Memoir of Father and Son, 1986; The Mirror at Midnight: A South African Journey, 1990; The Unquiet Ghost: Russians Remember Stalin, 1994. Contributions to: Harpers; New York Times; Los Angeles Times; The Washington Post; Progressive; Village Voice; New York Review of Books; Mother Jones. Literary Agent: Georges Borchardt Inc, NYC. Address: 84 Seward St, San Francisco, CA 94114, USA.

HOCKING Mary E, b. 1921. England. Appointments: Local Government Officer, 1946-70. Publications include: The Winter City, 1961; Visitors to the Crescent, 1962; The Sparrow, 1964; The Young Spaniard, 1965; A Time of War, 1968; The Hopeful Traveller, 1970; Family Circle, 1972; Daniel Come to Judgement, 1974; Look Stranger, 1979; He Who Plays the King, 1980; March House, 1981; Trilogy: Good Daughters, 1984, Indifferant Heroes, 1985, Welcome Strangers, 1986; An Irrelevant Woman, 1987; A Particular Place, 1989; Letters from Constance, 1991; The Very Dead of Winter, 1993. Address: 3 Church Row, Lewes, Sussex, England.

HODGE Jane Aiken, b. 4 Dec 1917, Author. m. Alan Hodge, 3 Jan 1949, 2 d. Education: BA, Somerville College, Oxford, 1935-38; AM, Radcliffe College, Cambridge, MA, 1938-39. Publications include: Lives of Jane Austen, 1972, Georgette Heyer, 1984; Leading Lady,

1990; First Night, 1989; Polonaise, 1987; Secret Island, 1985; The Private World of Georgette Heyer, 1984; The Lost Garden, 1982; Windover, 1992; Escapade, 1993; Whispering, 1995. Contributions to: Various Short Stories Reviews in History Today, Sunday Telegraph, Evening Standard. Membership: Lewes Monday Literary Club. Literary Agent: David Higham Associates. Address: 23 Eastport Lane, Lewes, East Sussex, BN7 1TL, England.

HODGE Paul William, b. 8 Nov 1934, Seattle, Uashington, USA. Astronomer. m. Ann Uran, 14 June 1962, 2 sons, 1 daughter. Education: BS, Yale University, 1956; PhD, Harvard University, 1960. Appointments: Editor, Astronomical Journal, 1984-. Publications: Concepts of the Universe, 1969; Revolution in Astronomy, 1970; Contemporary Astronomy, 1979; Interplanetary Dust, 1981; Atlas of the Andromeda Galaxy, 1981; Galaxies, 1986; Solar System Astrophysics; Atlas of the Small Magellanic Cloud; Atlas of the Large Magellanic Cloud. Contributions to: 300 technical articles to astronomical journals. Honours: Beckwith Prize in Astronomy, 1956; Bart Bok Prize in Astronomy, 1962; Award for Best Physical Science Book for Galaxies, 1986. Memberships: American Astronomical Society; Vice President, Astronomical Society of the Pacific, Board of Directors, Vice President. Address: Astronomy, FM-20, University of Washington, Seattle, WA 98195, USA.

HODGINS Jack Stanley, b. 3 Oct 1938, Vancouver Island, Canada. Novelist; Teacher. m. Dianne Child, 17 Dec 1960, 2 s, 1 d. Education: BEd, University of British Columbia. Publications: Spit Delaney's Island, 1976; The Invention of the World, 1977; The Resurrection of Joseph Bourne, 1979; The Honorary Patron, 1987; Innocent Cities, 1990; Over Forty in Broken Hill, 1992; A Passion for Narrative, 1993. Honours: Gibson First Novel Award, 1978; Governor General's Award for Fiction, 1980; Canada-Australia Literature Prize, 1986; Commonwealth Literature Prize, 1988. Memberships: PEN; The Writers Union of Canada. Literary Agent: Bella Pomer. Address: c/o Bella Pomer Agency, 22 Shallmar Blvd, Toronto, Ontario, Canada.

HOEFSMIT Henri Diederick. See: DE LINT Charles.

HOERR John Peter III, b. 12 Dec 1930, Pennsylvania, USA. Writer. m. Joanne Lillig, 24 Nov 1960, 2 sons. Education: AB, Penn State University, 1953. Appointments: Reporter, United Press International, 1956-57, 1958-60; The Daily Tribune, Royal Oak, Mich, 1957-58; Reporter, Business Week, 1960-63, 1964-69; Labour Editor, Senior Writer, Business Week, 1975-91; Reporter and Commentator, WQED-TV, public television, Pittsburgh, 1969-74. Publications: And The Wolf Finally Came: The Decline of the American Steel Industry, 1988; Co-author, The Reindustrialization of America, 1981. Contributions to: The Atlantic; The American Prospect; Pittsburgh Magazine; Harvard Business Review. Honours: Richard A Lester Award, Princeton University, Outstanding Book in Industrial Relations and Labour Economics, 1988; Page One Award, Best Labour Story, Magazine, 1985, 1988, New York Newspaper Guild. Memberships: National Writers Union; Industrial Relations Research Association. Address: 12 Parker Lane, Teaneck, NJ 07666, USA.

HOFF Harry Summerfield, (Willim Cooper), b. 1910, Novelist. m. Joyce Barbara Harris, 1951, 2 d. Education: Christs College, Cambridge. Appointments: Assistant Commissioner, Civil Service Commission, 1945-56; Personnel Consultant to UKAEA, 1958-72; CEGB, 1958-72; Commission of European Communities, 1972-73; Assistant Director, Civil Service Selection Board, 1973-76; Member, Board of Crown Agents, 1975-77; Personnel Advisor, Millbank Technical Services, 1975-77; Adjunct Professor, Syracuse University, 1977-90. Publications include: Rhea, 1935; Three Marriages, 1946; Scenes from Provincial Life, 1950; The Struggles of Albert Woods, 1952; Young People, 1958; Scenes from Married Life, 1961; Memoirs of a New Man, 1966; Shall We Ever Know?, 1971; Love on the Coast, 1973; Scences From Metropolitan Life, 1982; Scences From Later Life, 1983; From Early Life, 1990; Immortality At Any Price, 1991. Memberships: Royal Society of Literature; International PEN. Literary Agent: Gillon Aitken, Aitken & Stone, London. Address: 22 Kenilworth Court, Lower Richmond Road, London SW15 1EW, England.

HOFFMAN Alice, b. 16 Mar 1952, New York, USA. Freelance Writer. m. Tom Martin, 2 sons. Education: BA, Adelphi University, 1973; MA, Stanford University, 1975. Publications: Property Of, 1977; The Drowning Season, 1979; Angel Landing, 1980; White Horses, 1982; Fortune's Daughter, 1985; Illumination Night, 1987; At Risk, 1988; Seventh Heaven, 1990; Second Nature, 1993; Also various

screenplays. Contributions to: Redbook; American Review; Playgirl. Address: c/o Putnam, 200 Madison Avenue, New York, NY 10016, USA.

HOFFMAN Daniel, b. 3 Apr 923, New York City, USA. Professor of English; Writer. m. Elizabeth McFarland, 1948, 2 children. Education: AB, 1947; MA, 1949; PhD, 1956, Columbia University, New York. Appointments: Instructor in English, Columbia University, 1962-56; Visiting Professor, University of Dijon, 1956-57; Assistant Professor, 1957-60; Associate Professor, 1960-65, and Professor of English, 1965-66, Swarthmore College, Pennsylvania; Professor of English, 1966-. Poet-in-Residence, 1978-; Felix E Schelling Professor of English, Emeritus, 1993-, University of Pennsylvania, Philadelphia; Visiting Professor, King's College London, 1991-92. Publicatons: Verse includes: An Armada of Thirty Whales, 1954; Striking the Stones, 1968; Broken Laws, 1970; Corgi Modern Poets in Focus 4, with others, 1971; The Center of Attention, 1974; Able Was I Ere I Saw Elba: Selected Poems 1954-1974, 1977; Brotherly Love, 1981; Hang-Gliding from Helicon, 1988; Middens of the Tribe, 1995; Prose: Barbarous Knowledge, 1967; Poe Poe Poe Poe Poe Poe Poe, 1972; Words to Create a World, 1993. Address: Department of English, University of Pennsylvania, Philadelphia, PA 19104-6273, USA.

HOFFMAN Eva Alfreda, b. 1 July 1945, Cracow, Poland. Writer. Literary Appointments: Editor, The NY Times Book Review, 1987-90. Publications: Lost in Translation: A Life in a New Language, 1989; Exit Into History: A Journey Through The New Eastern Europe, 1993. Contributions to: Many inc. The NY Times. Honours: Am Academy of Arts & Letters Award, 1990; Whiting Award, 1992; Guggenheim Fellowship, 1993. Memberships: PEN; NY University Institute for the Humanities. Literary Agent: Georges Borchardt. Address: c/o Georges Barchardt, 136 East 57th Str, New York, NY 10022, USA.

HOFFMAN Lee (Georgia York), b. 1932, American. Appointments: Formely in Printing Production; Assistant Editor, Infinity and Science Fiction Adventures, both 1956-58; Freelance Writer, 1965-. Publications: Gunfight at Laramie, The Legend of Blackjack Sam, 1966; Bred to Kill, The Valdez Horses, Telepower, 1967; Dead Man's Gold, The Yarborough Brand, 1968; Wild Riders, Loco, Return to Broken Crossing, West of Cheyenne, 1969; Always the Black Knight, 1970; The Caves of Karst, Change Song, 1972; Wiley's Move, The Truth about the Cannonball Kid, 1975; Fox, Nothing but a Drifter, Trouble Valley, 1976; The Sheriff of Jack Hollow, 1977; The Land Killer, 1978; Savage Key (as Georgia York), 1979; Savannah Grey (as Georgia York), 1981; In and Out of the Quandry, 1982; Savage Conquest (as Georgia York), 1983. Address: 3290 Sunrise Trail NW, Port Charlotte, FL 33952, USA.

HOFFMAN Mary Margaret Lassiter, b. 20 Apr 1945, Eastleigh, Hants, Englnd. Writer; Journalist. m. Stephen James Barber, 22 Dec 1972, 3 d. Education: James Allen's Girls School; BA, 1967, MA, 1973, Newnham College, Cambridge; University College, London, 1970. Appointments: Children's Books Award Judge, 1981-87; Judge, Ibby Hans Anderson Award British Panel; Research Associate, University of Exeter. Publications include: 50 Children's Books including, My Grandma Has Black Hair, 1989; Amazing Grace, 1991; Henry's Baby, 1993. Contributions to: Daily Telegraph; Guardian; Independent; Sunday Times; Specialist Children's Book Press. Honours: Waldenbooks Best Children's Book Honor Award, 1991. Memberships: Society of Authors; CENTRAL. Literary Agent: Pat White, Rogers, Coleridge & White. Address: c/o Rogers, Coleridge & White, 20 Powis Mews, London, W11 1JN, England.

HOFFMAN William M, b. 12 Apr 1939, New York City, USA. Writer. Education: BA, cum laude, City College of New York. Publications: The Ghosts of Versailles (libre Ho), 1991; As Is, 1985; Gay Plays (Editor), 1977; New American Plays 2, 3, 4, Editor, 1968, 1970, 1971. Contributions to: Numerous jounals and magazines. Honours: Erwin Piscator, 1994; International Classical Music Award, 1991, Emmy, 1992, WGA Award, 1992; Obie, 1985; Drama Desk, 1985; Tony Nomination, 1985. Memberships: ASCAP; Writers Guild of America; Dramatists Guild; PEN; Circle Repertory Company. Literary Agent: Mitch Douglas ICM, New York. Address: c/o Mitch Douglas ICM, 40 W 57th St, New York, NY 10019, USA.

HOFFMANN Ann Marie, b. 6 May 1930, Abingdon, Berks, England. Author; Researcher. Education: Tunbridge Wells County Grammar School, 1940-46; St Godrics College, London, 1947-48. Appointments: Various, Publishing, International Conference

Organising, London, 1948-51, 1962-66; United Nations, Geneva, Paris, The Hague, 1952-58; PA to Author, Robert Henriques, 1959-61; Principal, Author's Research Services, 1966-87. Publications: Research for Writers, 1975, 1979, 1986, 1992; Majorca, 1978; Lives of the Tudors, 1977; Bocking Deanery, 1976; The Dutch: How They Live and Work, 1971, 1973. Memberships: Society of Authors; PEN; Society of Women Writers and Journalists; Society of Sussex Authors.

HOFFMANN Donald, b. 24 June 1933, Illinois, USA. Architectural Critic; Hisorian. m. Theresa McGrath, 12 Apr 1958, 4 s, 1 d. Education: University of Chicago, University of Kansas City. Appointments: General Assignment Reporter, 1956-65; Art Critic, 1965-90, Kansas City Star; Assistant Editor, Journal of the Society of Architectural Historians, 1970-72. Publications: The Meanings of Architecture: Buildings and Writings by John Wellborn Root (ed), 1967; The Architecture of John Wellborn Root, 1973; Frank Lloyd Wright's Fallingwater, 1978 (2nd edit 1993); Frank Lloyd Wright's Robie House, 1984; Frank Lloyd Wright's Hollyhock House, 1992. Honours: Fellow, National Endowment for the Humanities, 1970-71; Fellow, National Ednwoment for the Arts, 1974; Graham Foundation Grant, 1981. Memberships: Life Member, The Art Institute of Chicago. Address: 6441 Holmes St, Kansas City, MO 64131-1110, USA.

HOFMAN David, b. 26 Sept 1908, Poona, India. Author; Publisher, 1 s, 1 d. Appointments: Editor, New World Order, 1937-39; Editor, The Bahá'í World, 1963-88; Founder, George Ronald publishers, 1984. Publications: The Renewal of Civilization, 1946; God and His Messengers; George Townshend, 1983; A Commentary on the Will & Testament of Abdul Baha, 1950; Bahá' u' lláh, The Prince of Peace, A Portrait, 1992. Memberships: Publishers Association. Address: 28 Kirk Close, N Oxford, OX2 8JN, England.

HOFMANN Michael, b. 25 Aug 1957, Freiburg, Germany. Poet. Education: BA, Magadalene College, Cambridge, 1979. Appointments include: Teacher in Creative Writing, University of Florida, Gainesville, 1990-94; University of Michigan, Ann Arbor, 1994. Publications: Nights in the Iron Hotel, 1983; Acrimony, 1986; K S in Lakeland: New and Selected Poems, 1990; Corona, Corona, 1993; Plays, The Double Bass, Adaptation of a Play by Patrick Suskind, 1987; The Good Person of Sichuan, Adaptation of a Play by Brecht, 1989; Translations. Honours include: Cholmondeley Award, 1984; Geoffrey Faber Memorial Rrize, 1988; Schlegel Tieck Prize, 1988. Address: c/o Faber and Faber, 3 Queen Square, London WC1N 3AU, England.

HOGAN Desmond, b. 10 Dec 1950, Ballinasloe, Ireland. Teacher; Writer. Education: BA, 1972, MA, 1973, University College, Dublin. Appointments: Strode Fellow, University of Alabama, 1989. Publications: The Ikon Maker, 1976; The Leaves on Grey, 1980; A Curious Street, 1984; A New Shirt, 1986; A Link with the River, 1989; The Edge of the City, 1993. Honours: John Llewellyn Memorial Prize, 1980; Irish Post Award, 1985; Strode Fellow, University of Alabama, 1989; DAAD Fellowship Berlin, 1991. Literary Agent: Deborah Rogers.

HOGAN James P(atrick), b. 1941, England. Full-time Writer; Former Electronics Engineer and Sales Executive. Publications: Inherit the Stars, 1977; The Genesis Machine, 1977; the Gentle Giants of Ganymede, 1978; The Two Faces of Tomorrow, 1979; Thrice upon a Time, 1980; Giants' Star, 1981; Voyage from Yesteryear, 1982; Lode of the Lifemaker, 1983; The Proteus Operation, 1985; Minds, Machines and No-Nuke Neanderthals, short stories, 1986.

HOGAN Kathleen Margaret, (Kay Hogan), b. 13 Feb 1935, Bronx, New York, USA. Writer; Lab Technician; Housewife. m. James P Hogan, 4 s, 1 d. Education: High School Graduate, 1952. Publications: The El Train, 1882; The Silent Men, 1984; Widow Women, 1985; Little Green Girl, 1986; Of Saints and Other Things, 1992; The Women Wore Black, 1993. Contributions to: Descant; Long Pond Review; Journal of Irish Literature; North Country Anthology; Catholic Girls Antholgoy; Glens Falls Review. Address: 154 East Avenue, Saratoga Springs, NY 12866, USA.

HOGAN Kay. See: **HOGAN Kathleen Margaret.**

HOGAN Robert (Goode), b. 1930, USA. Professor of English. Appointments: Publisher, Proscenium Press, 1964-; Professor of English, University of Delaware, 1970-; Editor, Journal of Irish Literature, 1972-; Editor, George Spelvin's Theatre Book, 1978-85. Publications: Experiments of Sean O'Casey, 1960; Feathers from the Green Crow, 1962; Drama: The Major Genres (edited with S Molin),

1962; Arthur Miller, 1964; Independence of Elmer Rice, 1965; Joseph Holloway's Abbey Theatre (edited with M J O'Neill), 1967; The Plain Style (with H Bogart), 1967; After the Irish Renaissance, 1967; Seven Irish Plays (editor), 1967; Joseph Holloway's Irish Theatre (edited with M J O'Neill), 3 vols, 1968-70; Dion Boucicault, 1969; The Fan Club, 1969; Betty and the Beast, 1969; Lost Plays of the Irish Renaissance (with J Kilroy), 1970; Crows of Mephistopheles (editor), 1970; Towards a National Theatre (editor), 1970; Eimar O'Duffy, 1972; Mervyn Wall, 1972; Conor Cruise O'Brien (with E Young-Bruehl), 1974; A History of the Modern Irish Drama, vol 1, The Irish Literary Theatre (with J Kilroy), 1975, vol II, Laying the Foundation (with J Kilroy), 1976, vol III, The Abbey Theatre 1905-09 (with J Kilroy), 1978, vol IV, The Rise of the Realists, 1910-1915 (with R Burnham and D P Poteet), 1979, vol V, The Art of the Amateur 1916-1920 (with R Burnham), 1984, vol V1, The Years of O'Casey (with R Burnham), 1992; The Dictionary of Irish Literature (editor), 1979; Since O'Casey, 1983; The Plays of Frances Sheridan (edited with J C Beasley), 1984; Guarini's The Faithful Shepherd, translated by Thomas Sheridan (edited and completed with E Nickerson), 1990; Murder At The Abbey (with J Douglas), 1993. Address: PO Box 361, Newark, DE 19711, USA.

HOGGARD James Martin, b. 21 June 1941, Wichita Falls, Texas, USA. Professor of English. m. Lynn Taylor, 23 May 1976, 1 s, 1 d. Education: BA, Southern Methodist Univeristy, MA, University of Kansas. Appointments: Newspaper Reporter; University Professor, English; President, Texas Institute of Letters, 1994. Publications: Eyesigns, 1977; Trotter Ross, 1981; The Shaper Poems, 1983; Elevator Man, 1983; Two Gulls, One Hawk, 1983; Breaking an Indelicate Statue, 1986; The Art of Dying (translations), 1988; Love Breaks (translations), 1991; Chronicle of My Worst Years, (translations), 1994. Address: 111 Pembroke Lane, Wichita Falls, TX 76301, USA.

HOGGART Simon David, b. 26 May 1946. United States Correspondent, The Observer, 1985-89; Political Editor, 1992-. m. Alyson Clare Corner, 1983, 1 son, 1 daughter. Education: BA, King's College, Cambridge. Appointments: Reporter, 1968-71, The Guardian, Northern Ireland Correspondent, 1971-73, Political Correspondent, 1973-81; Feature Writer, 1981-85, The Observer; Political Columnist, Punch, 1979-85. Publications: The Pact (with Alistair Michie), 1978; Michael Foot: A Portrait (with David Leigh), 1981; On The House, 1981; Back On The House, 1982; House of Ill Fame, 1985; America, A Users Guide, 1990. Contributions to: New Society; Presenter, BBC Forth Column. Honours: David Holden Award for Resident Foreign Correspondent, British Press Awards, 1987. Literary Agent: Curtis Brown, London. Address: The Observer, Chelsea Bridge House, Queenstown Road, London SW8 4NN, England.

HOGWOOD Christopher Jarvis Haley, b. 10 Sept 1941, Nottingham, England. Musicologist; Writer; Editor; Broadcaster. Education: MA, Pembroke College, Cambridge. Appointments: Editor of Books & Music. Publications: Music at Court, 1977; The Trio Sonata, 1979; Haydn's Visits to England, 1980; Music in 18th Century England (ed), 1983; Handel, 1984; Holmes' Life of Mozart (ed), 1991. Honours: Honorary D Mus, 1991; Honorary Professor of Music, University of Keele, 1986-90; Honorary Fellow, Jesus College, Cambridge, 1989, Pembroke College, Cambridge, 1992; FRSA, 1982; Cobbett Medal, 1986. Address: 10 Brookside, Cambridge, CB2 1JE, England.

HOLBROOK David Kenneth, b. 9 Jan 1923, Norwich, England. Author; Emeritus Fellow, Downing College. m. 23 Apr 1949, 2 s, 2 d. Education: MA, Downing College, 1945. Appointments: Fellow, Kings College, Cambridge, 1961-65; Writer in Residence, Dartington Hall, 1972-73; Fellow, Director of English Studies, Downing College, 1981-88; Senior Leverhulme Research Fellow, 1965; Leverhulme Emeritus Research Fellow, 1988-90. Publications include: English for the Rejected, 1964; Flesh Wounds, 1966; A Play of Passion, 1978; Nothing Larger than Life, 1987; English for Maturity, 1961; Imaginings, 1961; Against the Cruel Frost, 1963; Object Relations, 1967; Old World New World, 1969; Chance of a Lifetime, 1978; The Secret Places, 1964; The Exploring Word, 1967; Children's Writing, 1967; English in Australia Now, 1972; English for Meaning, 1980; The Novel and Authenticity, 1987; Edith Wharton and the Unsatisfactory Man, 1991; Where D H Lawrence Was Wrong About Women, 1992; A Little Athens, 1990; Jennifer, 1991; Creativity and Popular Culture, 1994; The Gold in Father's Heart, 1992; Even if They Fail, 1994. Contributions to: Numerous Professional Journals. Memberships: Society of Authors. Literary Agent: Vernon Futerman, 159 Goldhurst Terrace, London,

NW6 3EU. Address: Denmore Lodge, Brunswick Gardens, Cambridge, CB5 8DQ, England.

HOLDEN Joan, b. 18 Jan 1939, Berkeley, California, USA. Playwright. m. (1) Arthur Holden, 1958, (div), (2) Daniel Chumley, 1968, 3 d. Education: BA, Reed College, Portland Oregon, 1960; MA, University of California, Berkeley, 1964; Career: Waitress, Claremont Hotel, Berkeley, 1960-62; Copywriter, Librairie Larousse, Paris, 1964-66; Research Aassistant, University of California, Berkeley, 1966-67; Playwright, 1967-; Publicist, 1967-69; Business Manager, 1978-79; San Francisco Mime Troupe; Editor, Pacific News Service, 1973-75; Instructor in Playwriting, University of California, Davis, 1975, 1977, 1979, 1983, 1985, 1987. Publications include: Americans; or, Last Tango in Huahuatenango, with Daniel Chumley (produced Dayton, Ohio and London, 1981, New York, 1982); Factwino Meets the Moral Majority, with others (produced San Francisco, 1981, New York, 1982), Published in West Coast Plays 15-16 (Berkeley, California) Spring, 1983; Factwino vs Armaggedonman (produced San Fransicso, 1982), Published in West Coast Plays 15-16 (Berkeley, California) Spring, 1983; Steeltown, music by Bruce Barthol (produced San Francisco, 1984; New York, 1985), 1985 with others (produced San Francisco, 1985, Spain /36, music by Bruce Barthol, produced Los Angeles, 1986); The Mozamgola Caper, with others (produced San Fancicso, 1986); Seeing Double, 1989; Back to Normal, 1990; Offshore, 1993. Contributions to: Melodrama, 1990; Collaborating Offshore, 1994. Honours: Obie Award, 1973, 1990; Rockefeller Grant, 1985; Edward G Robbins Playwriting Award, 1992. Address: San Francisco Mime Troupe, 855 Treat Street, San Francisco, CA 94110, USA.

HOLDEN William Melville, b. 25 Apr 1923, Richmond, California, USA. Writer. m. (1) Bertha Audrey Jones, 26 Jan 1956 (div), (2) Patricia E Mayer, 24 Nov 1974, 4 d. Education: AB, Economics, 1950; Postgraduate study in Philosophy, 1951, New York University. Appointments: Newspaper Reporter, Northern Carlifornia Newspapers including San Francisco Examiner, 1953-62. Publications: Sacramento, Excursions Into Its History and Natural World, 1988. Contributions to: Saturday Evening Post; Popular Science; Science News; Oceans; Boats; Rudder; Westways; American Legion; Southwest; Sacramento. Honours: Award for Sacramento Book, Sacramento County Historical Society, 1988; Merit award in Regional History, California Historical Society, 1989. Memberships: California Writers Club; Vice President, Sacramento County Historical Soceity. Address: PO Box 2384, Fair Oaks, CA 95628, USA.

HOLDSTOCK Robert, b. 1948. England. Freelance Writer. Publications include: Eye Among the Blind, 1976; Earthwind, 1977; Octopus Encyclopaedia of Science Fiction, 1978; Stars of Albion, 1979; Alien Landscapes, 1979; Tour of the Universe, 1980; Where Time Winds Blow, 1981; Mythago Wood, Emerald Forest, 1985; The Labyrinth, 1987; Other Edens, 1987; Lavondyss, 1988; The Fetch, 1991; The Bone Forest, 1992; The Hollowing, 1993; Merlin's Wood, 1994. Honours: World Fantasy Award, 1985, 1993. Literary Agent: AP Watt Limited, WC1, London. Address: 54 Raleigh Road, London, N8, England.

HOLLAND Cecelia (Anastasia), b. 31 Dec 1943, Henderson, Nevada, USA. Author. Education: Pennsylvania State University; BA, Connecticut College, 1965. Publications: The Firedrake, 1966; Rakosy, 1967; Kings in Winter, 1968; Until the Sun Falls, 1969; Ghost on the Steppe, 1969; The King's Road, 1970; Cold Iron, 1970; Antichrist, 1970; Wonder of the World, 1970; The Earl, 1971; The Death of Attila, 1973; The Great Maria, 1975; Floating Worlds, 1976; Two Ravens, 1977; The Earl, 1979; Home Ground, 1981; The Sea Beggars, 1982; The Belt of Gold, 1984; Pillar of the Sky, 1985. Honours: Guggenheim Fellowship, 1981-82. Address: c/o Knopf, 201 East 50th Street, New York, NY 10022, USA.

HOLLAND Isabelle, b. 1920, USA. Author. Appointments: Publicity Director, Lippincott Dell, and Putnam Publishing Companies, New York City, 1960-68. Publications: Cecily, 1967; Amanda's Choice, 1970; The Man Without A Face, 1972; The Mystery of Castle Renaldi (as Francesca Hunt), 1972; Heads You Win, Tails I Lose, 1973; Kilgaren, romance, 1974; Trelawny, romance, UK Editionrn, Trelawny's Fell, 1976; Moncrieff, romance, 1975, UK Edition, The Standish Place, 1976; Of Love and Death and Other Journeys, 1975; Journey for Three, 1975; Darcourt, romance, 1976; Grenelle, romance, 1976; Alan and the Animal Kingdom, 1977; Dinah and the Green Fat Kingdom, 1978; Ask No Questions, 1978; Tower Abbey, romance, 1978; The Marchington Inheritance, romance, 1979; Counterpoint, romance, 1980; Now Is Not

Too Late, 1980; Summer of My First Love, 1981; The Lost Madonna, romance, 1981; A House Named Peaceable, 1982; Abbie's God Book, 1982; Perdita, 1983; God, Mrs Musket and Aunt Dot, 1983; The Empty House, 1983; Kevin's Hut, 1984; Green Andrew Green, 1984; A Death at St Anselm's, 1984; Flight of the Archangel, 1985; The Island, 1985; Jennie Kiss'd Me, 1985; Love Scorned, 1986; Henry and Grudge, 1986. Address: c/o JCA, 242 West 27th Street, New York, NY 10010, USA.

HOLLAND Norman N, b. 1927, USA. Professor. Appointments: Instructor to Associate Professor, Massachusetts Institute of Technology, Cambridge, 1955-66; Professor, 1966-79; Chairman of English Department, 966-68; NcNulty Professor, 1979-83, State University of New York, Buffalo; Milbauer Professor, University of Florida, Gainesville, 1983-. Publications: The First Modern Comedies, 1959, 2nd Edition 1967; The Shakespearean Imagination, 1964, 2nd edition 1968; Psychoanalysis and Shakespeare, 1966, 2nd edition 1975; The Dynamics of Literary Response, 1968, 2nd edition 1989; Poems in Persons, 1973, 2nd edition 1989; 5 Readers Reading, 1975; Laughing, 1982; The I, 1985; The Brain of Robert Frost, 1988; Holland's Guide to Psychoanalytic Psychology and Literature-and-Pscychology, 1990; The Critical I, 1992. Literary Agent: Sterling Lord Literistics. Address: Department of English, University of Florida, Gainesville, FL 32611, USA.

HOLLAND Tom, b. 11 July 1947, Poughkeepsie, New York, USA. Screenwriter. Education: BA, summa cum laude, 1970, JD, 1973, University of California, Los Angeles. Appointments: Actor in plays and motion pictures, director of plays, and director of motion pictures, including Fright Night, 1985. Publications: The Beast Within, 1981; Psycho II, 1983; Class of 1984, Scream for Help, Cloak and Dagger, 1984; Fright Night, 1985. Honours: Nominated for Edgar Allan Poe Award from Mystery Writers of America for Psycho II. Memberships: Phi Beta Kappa. Address: c/o Columbia Pictures, Producers Eight, Room 247, Burbank, CA 91505, USA.

HOLLANDER John. Poetry; Criticism; Children's Books. Education: Columbia University; Indiana University, USA. Career: Professor of English. Publications include: Poetry: A Crackling of Thorns, 1958; Types of Shape, 1969; Tales Told of Fathers, 1975; Blue Wine & Other Poems, 1979; Harp Lake, 1989; American Poetry, vol I & II (ed), 1993; Terserae & Other Poems, 1993; Criticism: The Untuning of the Sky, 1961; Vision & Resonance, 1975; The Figure of Echo, 1981; Melodious Guide: Fictive Pattern in Poetic Language, 1988; Children's: The Quest of the Gole, 1966; The Immense Parade on Supererogation Day & What Happened to It, 1972. Honours: Melville Cane Award, 1990; Yale Series of Younger Poets Selection, 1958; Bollingen Prize, 1983; MacArthur Foundation, Fellowship. Memberships: American Academy of Arts and Letters; American Academy of Arts and Sciences. Address: English Department, Yale University, Box 208302, Yale Station, New Haven, CT 06520-8302, USA.

HOLLANDER Paul, b. 3 Oct 1932, Budapest, Hungary. Professor. m. Mina Harrison, 1976, 1 d. Education: BA LSE, 1959; MA, University of Illinois, 1960; MA, 1962; PhD, 1963, Princeton University, all in Sociology. Publications: Editor, American and Soviet Society, 1969; Soviet and American Society: A Comparison, 1973, 1978; Many Faces of Socialism, 1984; Survivial of the Adversary Culture, 1988; Political Pilgrims, 1981, 1983, 1990; Anti-Americanism, 1992; Decline and Discontent, 1992. Contributions to: Commentary; Encounter; Partisan; Review; Policy Review; American Scoiological Review; Problems of Communism; Society; Wall Street Journal; New York Times. Honours: Guggenheim Fellowship, 1973-74; Ford Foundation Fellow, 1963; Visiting Scholar, Hoover Institue, summers of 1985, 1986 and Spring 1993. Memberships: National Association of Scholars, Advisory Panel. Address: 35 Vernon Street, Northampton, MA 01060, USA.

HOLLANEK Adam Michal Franciszek, b. 4 Oct 1922, Lwow, Poland. Writer; Journalist. m. Anna Eva Owsianka, 24 Dec 1970, 1 son, 2 daughters (1 child from 1st marriage). Publications: About 40 books including: (Fiction) Plaza w Europie, 1967; Bandyci i Policjanci, 1982; Ksiezna z Florencji, 1988; Topless, 1988; (Science Fiction) Katastrofa na Sloncu Antarktydy, 1958; Zbrodnia wielkiego czlowieka, 1960; Muzyka dla was, chlopcy, 1975; Ukochany z ksiezyca, 1979; Jeszcze troche pozyc, 1980; Olsnienie, 1982; Kochac bez skory, 1983; (Poetry) Pokuty, 1986; (Non-fiction) Niewidzialne armie kapituluja, 1954; Sprzedam smierc, 1961; Skora jaszczurcza, 1965; Lewooki cyklop, 1966. Contributions to: Numerous papers and magazines. Honours:

Polish Academy of Sciences Award, 1978; Prix Europeenne de Science Fiction, 1986; Special W-SF Presidents Award, 1987. Memberships: ZAIKS; World Science Fiction Professional Association, President, Polish Section, 1983-85; Societe Europeenne de Science Fiction, General Secretary, 1987-. Literary Agent: Authors Agency, Warsaw, Hipoteczna 2. Address: Warsaw, Poland.

HOLLES Robert, b. 11 Oct 1926, Author; Playwright. m. Philippa Elmer, 12 July 1952, 2 sons, 1 daughter. Appointments: Former Member, Broadcasting Commission, Society of Authors; Artist in Residence, Central State University of Oklahoma, 1981-82. Publications include: Now Thrive the Armourers, 1952; The Bribe Scorners, 1956; Captain Cat, 1960; The Siege of Battersea, 1962; The Nature of the Beast, 1965; Spawn, 1978; I'll Walk Beside You, 1979; Sunblight, 1981; Humour: The Guide to Real Village Cricket, 1983; The Guide to Real Subversive Soldiering, 1985; Some 30 Plays in TV Series including Armchair Theatre, Play For To-day. Contributions to: Various Magazines & Journals. Literary Agent: David Higham Associates. Address: Crown Cottage, 14 Crown Street, Castle Hedingham, Essex, England.

HOLLINGDALE Reginald John, b. 1930, England. Appointments: Sub Editor, The Guardian Newspaper, 1968-91. Publications include: Thus Spoke Zarathustra, 1961; One Summer on Majorca, 1961; The Voyage to Africa, 1964; Nietzsche, The Man and His Philosophy, 1965; Western Philosophy, An Introduction, 1966, 1979; The Will to Power, On The Genealogy of Morals, 1967; Twilight of the Idols and the Anti Christ, 1968; Essays and Aphorisms of Schopenhauer, 1970; Elective Affinities, 1971; Thomas Mann, 1971; Beyond Good and Evil, 1973; A Nietzsche Reader, 1977; Ecce Homo by Nietzsche, 1979; Otto Dix, 1981; Daybreak, 1982; Dithyrambs of Dionysus, 1984; Before the Storm, 1985; Human, All Too Human, 1987; Between Literature and Science, 1988; Aphorisms of Lichtenberg, 1990; The Rise of Neo Kantianism by Klaus Christian Köhnke, 1991. Contributions to: Three Essays by Wolfgang Müller-Lauter, 1993. Honour: Visiting Fellow, Trinity College, Melbourne, 1991. Memberships: Hon President, B Nietzsche Society; National Union of Journalists. Address: 32 Warrington Crescent, London W9 1EL, England.

HOLLINGHURST Alan, b. 26 May 1954, Stroud, Gloucestershire. Novelist. Education: BA, Magdalen College, Oxford, 1975, M.Litt, 1979. Appointments: Assistant Editor, 1982-84, Deputy Editor, 1985-90, Poetry Editor, 1991-, Times Literary Supplement, London. Publications: Novels, The Swimming-Pool Library, 1988; The Folding Star, 1994; Verse, Confidential Chats with Boys, 1982; Translator, Bajazet, By Jean Racine, 1991. Address: c/o Times Literary Supplement, Admiral House, 66-68 East Smithfield, London E1 9XY, England.

HOLLIS Carolyn Sloan, b. 15 Apr 1937, London, England. Freelance Journalist and Children's Author. m. David Hollis, 15 May 1961, 2 sons. Education: Harrogate College; Tutorial Schools in Newcastle and Guilford. Appointments: Editorial Secretary, Features Assistant, Queen Magazine, 1956-60; Press Officer, Yvonne Arnaud Theatre, Guilford, 1976-80. Publications: The Sea Child, 1987; Victoria and the Crowded Pocket, 1973; Helen Keller, 1984; Don't Go Near The Water, 1988; Shakespeare Theatre Cat: Carter is a Painter's Cat, 1971; The Penguin and The Vacuum Cleaner, 1974; Sam Snake, 1975; Mr Cogg and His Computer, 1979; Further Inventions of Mr Cogg, 1981; Skewer's Garden, 1983; Mr Cogg and the Exploding Easter Eggs, 1984; The Friendly Robot, 1986; An Elephant for Muthu, 1986; T-Boys Weekend, 1988; The Mall Series, 4 books, 1989; Nine Lives, 1991; Working Dogs, 1991; Working Elephants, 1991; Working Horses, 1992. Contributions to: Features contributed to Daily Telegraph, Sunday Telegraph and Radio Times. Memberships: Society of Authors; New Playwrights Trust. Literary Agent: Murray Pollinger. Address: 7 Dapdune Road, Guilford, Surrey GU1 4NY, England.

HOLLO Anselm, (Paul Alexis), b. 1934, Finland. Poetry; Translations. Career: Programme Assistant and Co-ordinator, BBC, London, 1958-66; Visiting Lecuter, 1968-69; Lecturer in English and Music, 1970-71; and Head, Translation Workship, 1971-72, University of Iowa; Poetry Editor, Iowa Review, Iowa City, 1971-72; Associate and Visiting Professor, Bowling Green University, Ohio, 1972-73; Poet-in-Residence, Hobart and William Smith College, Geneva, New York, 1973-74; Writer-in-Residence, Sweet Briar College, Virginia, 1978-80; Associate Professor, Writing and Poetics, The Naropa Institute, Boulder, CO, 1989-. Publications include: The Twelve and Other Poems by Aleksandr Blok, 1971; (with Jack Marshall and Sam

Hamod), Surviving in America, 1972; Sensation 27, 1972; Some Worlds, 1974; Lingering Tangos, 1976; Sojourner Microcosms: New and Selected Poems, 1959-1977, 1977; Heavy Jars, 1977; Curious Data,1978; (ed and trans with Gunnar Harding), Recent Swedish Poetry in Translation, 1979; With Ruth in Mind, 1979; Finite Continued, 1980; No Complaints, 1983; (ed and trans), Pentti Saarikoski, Poems 1958-80, 1983; Pick Up the House, 1986; Egon Schiele: The Poems, 1988; Peter Stephan Jungk: Franz Werfel: The Story of a Life, 1990; Outlying Districts: New Poems, 1990; Near Miss Haiku, 1990; Space Baltic: The science fiction poems, 1962-1987, 1991; Paavo Haavikko: Selected Poems, 1949-1989, 1991; Blue Ceiling (a poem), 1992; Jaan Kross: The Czar's Madman (a novel), 1993; High Beam: 12 Poems, 1993; West Is Left of the Map (a poem sequence), 1993. Address: 3336 14th Street, Boulder, CO 80304, USA.

HOLLOWAY David Richard, b. 3 June 1924. Literary Editor. m. Sylvia Eileen, (Sally), Gray, 1952, 2 sons, 1 daughter. Education: Birbeck College, London; Magdalen College, Oxford. Appointments: Reporter, Middlesex County Times, 1940-41; Daily Sketch. 1941-42; Daily Mirror, 1949; News Chronicle: Reporter and Leader Writer, 1950-53; Assistant Literary Editor, Novel Reviewer, 1953-58; Book Page Editor, 1958-60; Deputy Literary Editor, 1960-68; Literary Editor, 1968-88, The Daily Telegraph. Publications: John Glasworthy, 1968; Lewis and Clark and the Crossing of America, 1971; Derby Day, 1975; Playing the Empire, 1979; Nothing So Became Them...(with Michael Geare), 1987; Editor, Telegraph Year 1-3, 1977-79. Contributions to: Folio Magazine and Book Trade Journals. Memberships: Committee of Royal Literary Fund, 1976-, Registrar, 1981-. Literary Agent: Scott Ferris. Address: 95 Lonsdale Road, London SW13 9DA, England.

HOLLOWAY (Percival) Geoffrey, b. 23 May 1918, Birmingham Warwickshire, England. Poet. Education: University of Southampton, 1946-48. Appointments include: Social Worker, Mental health Worker. Publications: To Have Eyes, 1972; Rhine Jump, 1974; All I Can Say, 1979; The Crones of Aphrodite, 1985; Salt, Roses, Vinegar, 1986; Precepts Without Deference, 1987; My Ghost in Your Eye, 1988; The Strangest Thing, 1990; The Leaping Pool, 1993; A Sheaf of Flowers, 1994; Editor, Trio 2. Memberships include: Brewery Poets. Address: 4 Gowan Crescent, Staveley, Nr Kendal, Cumbria LA8 9NF, England.

HOLLOWAY Glenna Rose, b. 7 Feb 1928, Nashville, Tennessee, USA. Silversmith; Enamelist. m. Robert Wesley Holloway. Contributions to: Western Humanities Review; Georgia Reivew; Poet Lore; Christian Science Monitor; Modern Maturity; Manhattan Poetry Review; Orbis; Voices International; Poetry International; Northwest Magazine; The Lyric; Connecticut River Review; McCall's; Louisiana Literature; Saturday Review; Chicago Tribune; Illinois Magazine; Miami Magazine; Crazy Quilt Quarterly; Light Year 87; Icon; Christian Single; Cornerstone; America; The New Renaissance; Shorelines; Moody Monthly; Chicago Sun Times; Anhinga Press; The Formalist; The Retired Officer; Amelia; Hammers; Wisconsin Review; Pikestaff Forum; Airel ; The Hollins Critic; Good Housekeeping; Christian Century; South Coast Poetry Journal; St Anthony Messenger; Rurual Heritage; Poet; Webster Review; Inside Chicago Magazine, Daily Herald; Dallas Review; Verve; Blue Unicorn, Buffalo Spree, Saturday Evening Post. Address: 913 East Bailey Road, Naperville, IL60565, USA.5, USA.

HOLLOWAY John, b. 1920, Croydon, Surrey, England. University Professor; Author. Education: MA, DPhil, New College, All Souls College, Oxford; D.Litt, University of Aberdeen; LittD, University of Cambridge. Publications include: The Victorian Sge, 1953; The Minute, 1956; The Fugue, 1960; The Landfallers, 1962; The Story of the Night, 1962; The Lion Hunt, 1964; Blake, The Lyric Poetry, 1968; Planet of Winds, 1977; The Proud Knowledge, 1977; Narrative and Structure, 1979; The Slumber of Apollo, 1983; The Oxford Book of Local Verses, 1987; Civitatula: Cambridge, the Little City, 1993. Contributions to: Hudson Review; Burlington Magazine; London Magazine; Encounter; Art International; Essays in Criticism; Critical Inquiry; Kenyon Review; P N Review. Membership: FRSL; BRONZS. Address: Queen's College, Cambridge, England.

HOLLY David C, b. 17 Oct 1915, Baltimore, Maryland, USA. Retired Naval Officer; University Professor. m. Carolyn King, 15 June 1949, 3 sons. Education: BS, John Hopkins University, 1938; MA, University of Maryland, 1939; PhD, American University, 1964. Publications: Exodus 1947, 1969; Steamboat on the Chesapeake, 1987; Tidewater by Steamboat, 1991; Chesapeake Steamboats: Vanished Fleet, 1994. Contributions to: Numerous articles to professional journals. Honours: Phi Kappa Phi; Pi Sigma Alpha; Pi

Gamma Mu; Legion of Merit; Bronze Star; Order of Merit. Address: 918 Schooner Circle, Annapolis, MD 21401, USA. 7.

HOLME K E. See:HILL (John Edward) Christopher.

HOLMES Bryan John, (Ethan Wall, Charles Langley Hayes), b. 18 May 1939, Birmingham, England. Lecturer. m. 1962, 2 s. Education: BA, University of keele, 1968. Publications include: The Avenging Four, 1978; Hazard, 1979; Blood, Sweat and Gold, 1980; Gunfall, 1980; A Noose for Yanqui, 1981; Shard, 1982; Bad Times at Backwheel, 1982; Guns of the Reaper, 1983; Another Day, Another Dollar, 1984; Dark Rider, 1987; Dollars for the Reaper, 1990; A Legend Called Shatterhand, 1990; Loco, 1991; The Last Days of Billy Patch, 1992; Blood on the Reaper, 1992; All Trails Leads to Dodge, 1993; Montana Hit, 1993; A Coffin for the Reaper, 1994; Dakota Hit, 1995. Contributions to: Miscellaneous Short Stories in Magazines, Scholarly Articles in Academic and Professional Journals. Address: c/o Robert Hale Limited, Clerkenwell Green, London EC1R 0HT, England.

HOLMES Charlotte Amalie, b. 26 Apr 1956, Georgia, USA. University Professor. m. James Brasfield, 7 Mar 1983, 1 son. Education: MFA, Writing, Columbia University, 1977; BA, English, Louisiana State University, 1980. Appointments: Editorial Assistant, Paris Review, 1979; Associate and Managing Editor, The Ecco Press, 1980; Instructor, Western Carolina University, 1984; Assistant Professor, Pennsylvania State University, 1987. Publications: Gifts and Other Stories, 1993. Contributions to: The Antioch Review; Carolina Quarterly; Epoch; Grand Street; The New Yorker; The Southern Review; Story Magazine. Honours: Stegner Fellowship, Stanford University, 1982; Bread Loaf Writer's Conference National Arts Club Scholarship, 1990; North Carolina Arts Council Grant, 1986; Pennsylvania Council on the Arts Fellowship, 1988 and 1993; Poets & Writers, Inc, Writers Exchange Award, 1993. Memberships: Associated Writing Programs. Literary Agent: Neil Olson, Donadio & Ashworth Inc. Address: Dept of English, Pennsylvania State University, University Park, PA 16802, USA.

HOLMES Geoffrey Shorter, b. 17 July 1928, Sheffield, England. Emeritus Professor of History. m. Ella Scott, 16 Sept 1955, 1 son, 1 daughter. Education: Pembroke College, Oxford, 1945-48, 1950-51; BA, (Oxon) 1948; MA (Oxon), 1952; BLitt (Oxon), 1952; DLitt (Oxon), 1978. Publications: British Politics in the Age of Anne, 1967, revised edition, 1987; The Divided Society (with W A Speck), 1967; Britain After The Glorious Revolution (editor, co-author), 1969; The Trial of Doctor Sacheverell, 1973; The Prime Ministers (co-author), 1974; The Electorate and the National Will in the First Age of Party, 1976; The Whig Ascendency (co-author), 1981; Augustan England: Professions, State and Society 1680-1730, 1982; The London Diaries of William Nicolson, Bishop of Carlisle 1702-1718 (edited with Clyve Jones), 1985; Politics, Religion and Society in England 1679-1742, 1986; Stuart England (co-author), 1986; The Making of a Great Power: Late Stuart and Early Georgian Britain 1660-1722, 1993; The Age of Oligarchy: Pre-industrial Britain 1722-1783, 1993; General Editor, Longman's Foundations of Modern Britain series, 1983-93. Contributions to: History; English Historical Review; Bulletin of the Institute of Historical Research; The Times; Times Literary Supplement; Transactions of the Royal Historical Society; British Journal for the History of Science; Parliamentary History; Proceedings of the British Academy. Honours: Fellow, British Academy, 1983. Memberships: Fellow, Royal Historical Society, Vice President, 1985-89. Literary Agent: London Management. Address: Tatham Lodge, Burton-in-Lonsdale, Carnforth, Lancs LA6 3LF, England.

HOLMES John. See: SOUSTER Raymond.

HOLMES John, b. 12 May 1913, Bishopton, Renfrewshire, Scotland. Farmer; Dog Breeder/Trainer. m. Kathleen Mary Trevethick, 6 Dec 1955. Education: Edinburgh and East of Scotland College of Agriculture, 1929-30. Publications: The Family Dog, 1957, 13 editions; The Farmers Dog, 1960, 13 editions; The Obedient Dog, 1975, 6 editions; Looking After Your Dog (co-author, Mary Holmes), 1985; The Complete Australian Cattle Dog (co-author Mary Holmes), 1993. Contributions to: The Kennel Gazette; Dog World; Our Dogs; The Field; Carriage Driving; Horse and Hound; Pedigree Digest. Memberships: Society of Authors; British Actors Equity Association; UK Registry of Canine Behaviourists. Address: Formakin Farm, Cranbourne, Dorset BH21 5QY, England.

HOLMES Marjorie Rose, b. Storm Lake, Iowa, USA. Author. m. (1) Lynn Mighell, 9 Apr 1932, 1 s, 2 d, (2) George Schmieler, 4 July 1981. Publications: World by the Tail, 1943; Ten O'Clock Scholar, 1946; Saturday Night, 1959; Cherry Blossom Princess,1960; Follow Your Dream, 1961; Love is a Hopscotch thing; 1963; Senior Trip, 1962; Love and Laughter, 1967; I've got to talk to Somebody, God, 1969; Writing the Creative Article, 1969; Who Am I, God? 1969; To Treasure our Days, 1971; Two from Galilee, 1972; Nobody Else Will Listen, 1973; You and I and Yesterday, 1973; As Tall as My Heart, 1974; How Can I Find You God: 1975; Beauty in Your Own Back Yard, 1976; Hold Me Up a Little Longer, Lord, 1977; Lord, Let Me Love, 1978; God and Vitamisn, 1980; To Help You Through the Hurting, 1983; Three from Galilee, 1985; Secrets of Health, Energy and Staying Young, 1987l; The Messiah, 1987; At Christmas the Heart Goes Home, 1991; The Inspriational Writings of Marjorie Holmes, 1991; Gifts Freely Given, 1992; Second Wife, Second Life, 1993; Writing Articles from the Heart, 1993. Contributions to: numerous journals and magazines. Address: 8681 Cobb Road, Lake Jackson Hill, Manassas, VA 22110, USA.

HOLMES Raymond. See: SOUSTER Raymond.

HOLMES Richard, b. 5 Nov 1945, London, England. Poet; Biographer. Publications: One for Sorrow, Two for Joy, 1970; Shelley: The Pursuit, 1975; Inside the Tower, 1977; Shelley on Love: An Anthology, 1980; Coleridge, 1982; Footsteps: Adventures of a Romantic Biographer, 1985; Coleridge: Early Visions, 1989; Dr Johnson and Me Savage, 1992. Honours: Somerset Maugham Award, 1974, for Shelley: The Pursuit; Whitbread Book of the Year Prize, 1989. Address: c/o Hodden & Stoughton, 47 Bedford Square, London WC1B 3DP, England.

HOLMES Sherlock S, b. 25 Oct 1962, Massachusetts, USA. Author; Freelance Journalist; Indexer. Education: Ordained Minister, 1983; Emergency Medical Technician Certificate, 1980; Doctor of Divinity, 1983; Doctor of Psychology Degree, 1985; Certificate of Journalism Arts, 1991. Appointments: Assistant News Director, Radio Station WNEB, 1982; Corresponding Journalist, CNS News Internationa, 1991-; Freelance Contributor, Modern Maturity Magazine, 1993-. Publications: Many News Pieces with Associated Press Wire Service, 1981-; Personality Profile of an Assassin: John Wilkes Booth, co-author, 1991; Currently working on: Sherlock Holmes and the Word of God: Did the Master Believe in God?; Various Medical Journal Articles, 1991-; NESN Magazine, two monthly columns, 1991-; American History Illustrated, magazine article, 1991; Various brochures, manuals, handouts, speeches; Hundred of news stories while employed as Assistant News Director for radio station. Contributions to: RCMA Journal; NESN Magazine; Modern Maturity Magazine Articles, 6 in 1993, 5 in 1994; CGT Newsletter; New England Journal of Medicine; Journal of America Medical Association; Medical Ghostwriter for Client Authors to Appear in: New England Journal of Medicine, 2 articles in 1993. Honours: Worcester County News Broadcaster Excellence Award, 1983; McGraw Hill Highest Honours Achievement Award, 1991; NESN Editor's Award, 1991. Memberships: British Homeopathic Society, 1980-; Sherlock Holmes Society of London, 1986-; Titanic Historical Society, 1987-; Certified Teacher, Evangelical Training Association, Wheaton, USA, 1987-; Associate Instructor, Emmaus Bible College, Chicago, USA, 1987-; Association of Bible Teachers, 1994-; San Francisco Literary Society, Founding Member & Past President; National Writers Union, Local Steering Committee; American Medical Writers Association; American Society of Indexers; National Writers Club. Address: PO Box 3, Worcester, MA 01613, USA.

HOLMES Stewart Quentin, b. 25 Dec 1929, London, England. Journalist; Actor. Education: Hendon College, Kings Lynn Technical Institute; Hong Kong University. Appointments: Telephone Reporter, Reuters Limited, 1952-58; Reporter, Chief Film and Drama Critic, Harrow Observer, 1958-61; Sub Editor, Diary Writer, Hendon Times, 1961-63; Reporter, The Daily Telegraph, 1963-66; Sub Editor, Exchange Telegraph, 1966-68; Script Writer, British Movietone News, 1968-70; Press Officer, Decimal Currency Board, 1970; Correspondent to BBC and Numerous British Papers in Persia, Hong Kong, Toyko, Hawaii; Freelance for Journals, Magazines, 1970-89. Publications: Odes and Ends, 1985; Once Upon a Rhyme, 1986; London Correspondent, International Press Bureau, USA; London Life Columnist, Union Jack Newspapers; Other UK Publications. Memberships: Poetry Society; Chartered Institute of Journalists; Foreign Press Association; British Actors Equity; British MENSA.

Address: 146 Clarence Gate Gardens, Baker Street, London NW1 6AN, England.

HOLMGREN Lavinia Stella (Venie Holmgren), b. 15 Sept 1922, York, Western Australia, Australia. Poet. m. John Wraymond Holmgren, 20 May 1946, 2 sons, 1 daughter. Appointment: Honorary Tutor, Poetry, Bega West Primary School, Bega, New South Wales. Publications: The Sun Collection, poetry, 1989; The Sun Collection, cassette, 1990. Contributions to: Eling; Scarp; Redoubt; New England Review; Up From Below; Lamama Poetica; Poetry of Canberra; Other anthologies. Honours: 1st Prize, FSC FAW Poetry Competition, 1980. Memberships; FSC; FAW, New South Wales. Address: Burragate RSD, via Bega, New South Wales 2550, Australia.

HOLMGREN Venie. See: **HOLMGREN Lavinia Stella.**

HOLROYD Michael, b. 27 Aug 1935, London, England. Author. m. Margaret Drabble, 1982. Appointments: Chairman, Society of Authors, 1973-74, National Book League, 1976-78; Chairman, Arts Council Literature Panel, 1992-; President, English Centre of PEN, 1985-88. Publications: Hugh Kingsmill, 1964; Lytton Strachey, 1967-68; Unreceived Opinions, 1973; Augustus John, 1974-75; Bernard Shaw: The Search for Love, 1988; The Pursuit of power, 1989; The Lure of Fantasy, 1991; The Last Laugh, 1992; The Shaw Companion, 1992. Honour: CBE, 1989. Literary Agent: AP Watt Limited. Address: c/o A P Watt Limited, 20 John Street, London WC1N 2DI, England.

HOLT George. See: **TUBB E(dwin) C(harles).**

HOLUB Miroslav, b. 13 Sept 1923, Pilsen, Czechoslovakia. Scientific Worker; Writer. m. Jitka Langrova, 6 July 1969, 2 s, 1 d. Education: MD, Charles University, Prague, 1953; PhD, Czechoslovak Academy of Science, 1958; Dr of Humanities & Letters, Oberlin College, 1985. Appointments: Scientist; Member, Editorial Boards of Literary Magazines. Publications include: Selected Poems, 1967; Notes of a Clay Pigeon, 1977; Vanishing Lung Syndrome, 1990; The dimension of the Present Moment, 1990; Jingle Bell Principle, 1992. Contributions to: Most European and Many US Magazines, Newspapers. Honours: Publishers Awards, 1963, 65, 67, 69, 87; J E Purkynje Medal, 1988; G Theiner Award, 1991. Memberships: Czech PEN; European Society for the Promotion of Poetry; Czech Writers Union; Bavarian Academy of Arts; British Poetry Society. Literary Agent: Dila, Prague. Address: Svepomocna 107 Hrncire, CS 149 00 Prague 4, Czechoslovakia.

HOLYER Erna Maria, b.15 Mar 1925, Germany. Author; Freelance Writer. m. Gene Wallace Holyer, 24 Aug 1957. Education: AA, San Jose Evening College, 1964; College of San Mateo, San Jose State University, University of California at Santa Cruz, 1965-74; Creative Writing instruction under Louise Boggess, Duane Newcomb and Norma Youngberg, 1959-68; Lifetime California Teaching Credential in Creative Writing and Journalism 1971; Doctor of Literature, World University, 1984; Diploma, Writing to sell Fiction, Writer's Digest School, 1987. Appointments: Instructor, Creative and nonfiction writing, San Jose Metropolitan Adult Education, 1968-; Seminar Leader, Writer's Connection. Publications: Reservoir Road adventure, 1982; Sigi's Fire Helmet, 1975; The Southern Sea Otter, 1975; Shoes for Daniel, 1974; Lone Brown Gull, 1971; Song of Courage, 1970; At the Forest's Edge, 1969; A Cow for Hansel, 1967; Steve's Night of Silence, 1966; Rescue at Sunrise, 1965. Contributions to: Reader's Digest; Encylopaedia Britannica; Advent Verlag Zurich; The 1993 Writer's Yearbook; Articles to The Writer, Woman's World, and eighty other publications. Address: 1314 Rimrock Drive, San Jose, CA 95120, USA.

HOMBERGER Eric (Ross), b. 1942, USA. Appointments: Lecturer in American Literature, University of East Anglia, Norwich, 1970-; Reader in American Literature, 1988; Visiting Professor of American Literature, University of New Hampshire, 1991-92. Publications: The Cambridge Mind: Ninety Years of the Cambridge Review 1879-1969 (ed with William Janeway and Simon Schamal), 1970; Ezra Pound: The Critical Heritage (ed), 1972; The Art of the Real: Poetry in England and America since 1939, 1977; The Second World War in Fiction (ed with H Klein and J Flower), 1984; American Writers and Radical Politics 1900-1939; Equivocal Commitments, John le Carre, 1986; The Troubled Face of Biography (ed with J Charmley), 1987; John Reed, 1990; John Reed and the Russian Revolution: Uncollected Articles, Letters, Speeches on Russia 1917-1920 (ed with

John Biggart), 1992. Address: 74 Clarendon Road, Norwich NR2 2PN, England.

HOME William Douglas, b. 3 June 1912. Playwright. m. Rachael Brand, 26 July 1951, 1 son, 3 daughters. Education: Eton College; Oxford University; 4th Degree in History. Publications: Half Term Report, autobiography, 1954; Mr Home Pronounced Hume, autobiography, 1979; Sins of Commission, 1985; Letters to Parents 1939-45 War; Old Men Remember, 1991; Plays include: The Chiltern Hundreds; Now Barrabas; The Reluctant Debutante; The Secretary Bird; Lloyd George Knew My Father; The Kingfisher Master of Arts; The Dame of Sark, 1974; Portraits, 1987; A Christmas Truce, 1989. Honours: ITV Writer of the Year (Playwright), 1973. Memberships: The Literary Society; Traveller's Club; Beefsteak Club; Garrick Club. Literary Agent: Eric Glass. Address: Derry House, Kilmeston, Nr Alresford, Hampshire SO24 0NR, England.

HOMES A M, b. Washington DC, UA. Writer. Education: MFA, University of Iowa, 1988; BA, Sarah Lawrence College, 1985. Appointments: Creative Writing Lecturer, New York Universty, 1988; Columbus Universty, 1991-;. Publications: In a Contry of Mothers, 1993; The Safety of Objects, 1990; Jack, 1989; Film Scripts: Hi I'm Bob, and Boonie Ted and Me.Contributions to: ARt Forum; Bomb; Christopher Street; Mirabella; Cosmopolitain; UK; Der Alttag, Between Co D; The Village Voice; The Quarterly; Story; New York Woman; Newspaper Reviews for The Washington Post, Miami Harald, Boston Globe, Philadelphia Inquirer, the Loss Angeles Times. Honours: Helfield Transatlantic Review Award, 988; James Michener Felowship, 1988-89; New York Foundation Arts Fellowship, 1988; Helena Rubenstein Fellowship, Whitney Museum of Art, 1988;Deutscher Jugendliteraturpreis, 1993. Memberships: PEN. Liteary Agent: Wyle, Aiken and Stone, 250 West 57th St, New York, 10107, USA.

HONAN Park, b. 1928. Appointments: Dumptruck Driver, Oregon Lumber Mills, 1950's; Professor of English and American Literature, University of Leeds, 1984-; British Editor, Novel: A Forum on Fiction; Co-editor, Ohio and Baylor Presses Browning Edition. Publications: Browning's Characters: A Study in Poetic Technique, 1961; Shelley (ed), 1963; Bulwer Lytton's Falkland (ed), 1967; The Complete Works of Robert Browning (co-ed), 9 vols, 1969-; The Book, The Ring and The Poet: A Biography of Robert Browning (co-author), 1975; Matthew Arnold: A Life, 1981; Jane Austen: Her Life, 1987; The Beats: An Anthology of "Beat" Writing (ed), 1987; Authors' Lives: On Literary Biography and the Arts of Language, 1990. Literary Agent: Gerald J Pollinger. Address: School of English, University of Leeds, Leeds LS2 9JT, England.

HONAN William Holmes, b. 11 May 1930, New York City, USA. Journalist. m. Nancy Burton, 22 June 1975, 2 s, 1 d. Education: BA, Oberlin College, 1952; MA, University of Virginia, 1955. Appointments: Editor, The Villager, New York, 1957-60; Assistant Editor, New Yorker Magazine, 1960-64; Freelance writer, National Magazines, 1964-68; Associate editor, Newsweek, New York City, 1969; Assistant Editor, New York Times Magazine, 1969-70; Travel Editor 1970-72, 1973-74; Arts and Leisure Editor, 1974-82; Culture Editor, 1982-88; Chief Cultural Correspondent, 1988-93, National Higher Education Correspondent, 1993-; New York Times; Managing Editor, Saturday Review, 1972-73. Publications: Greenwich Village Guide, 1959; Ted Kennedy: Profile of a Survivor, 1972; Bywater: The Man Who Invented the Pacific War, British edition, 1990; Visions of Infamy: The Untold Story of How Journalist Hector C Bywater Devised the Plans that Led to Pearl Harbour, 1991; Fire When Ready, Grindley! - Great Naval Stories from Manila Bay to Vietnam, editor, 1992; Pamphlet, Another LaGuardia, 1960. Contributions to: Numerous magazines. Literary Agent: Roslyn Tarqu, Roslyn Targ Literary Agency. Address: c/o New York Times, 229 West 43rd St, New York, NY 109036. USA.

HONE Joseph, b. 25 Feb 1937, London, England. Writer; Broadcaster. m. Jacqueline Mary Yeend, 5 Mar 1963, 1 s, 1 d. Education: Kilkenny College, Sandford Park School, Dublin; St Columba's College, Dublin. Publications: The Flowers of the Forest, 1982; Children of the Country, 1986; Duck Soup in the Black Sea, 1988; Summer Hill, 1990. Contributions to: Radio and TV Critic in the Listener, 1975-80; Book Reviewers for TLS, Spectator. Membership: Upton House Cricket Club. Literary Agent: Gillon Aitken, Aitken & Stone Limited. Address: c/o Aitken & Stone Limited, 29 Fernshaw Road, London SW10, England.

HONEYCOMBE Gordon, b. 27 Sept 1936, Karachi, India. Writer; TV Presenter; Actor. Education: The Edinburgh Academy, 1946-55; University College, Oxford, 1957-61. Publications include: Neither the Sea Nor the Sand, 1969; Dragon under the Hill, 1972; The Edge of Heaven, 1981; The Redemption, 1964; Red Watch, 1976; Royal Wedding, 1981; The Murders of the Black Museum, 1982; The Year of the Princess, 1982; TV ams Official Celebration of the Royal Wedding, 1986; More Murders of the Black Museum, 1993; Siren Song, 1992; TV Plays, Stage Plays. Literary Agent: Bill Hamilton, A M Heath & Co, London WC2N 4AA. Address: c/o Martyn Smith, Stephenson & Co, 43 Poole Road, Bournemouth, BH4 9DN, England.

HONEYMAN Brenda. See: **CLARKE Brenda**.

HONIG Edwin, b. 3 Sept 1919, New York City, USA. Poet; Playwright; Author. m. (1) Charlotte Gilchrist, 1940 (died 1963); (2) Margot S Dennes, 1963 (div 1978); 2 s. Education: Educated in public schools, New York, BA, 1941, MA, 1947, University of Wisconsin, Madison. Served in the US Army 1943-46. Appointments: Library Assistant, Library of Congress, Washington DC, 1941-42; Instructor in English, Purdue University, Lafayette, Indiana, 1942-43; New York University and Illinois Institute of Technology, Chicago, 1946-47; University of New Mexico, Albuquerque, 1947-48; Instructor, 1949-52, Assistant Professor, 1952-57, Harvard University, Cambridge, MA; Professor of Comparative Literature, Brown University, 1957-82; Visiting Professor, University of California, Davis, 1964-65; Mellon Professor, Boston University, 1977; Poetry Editor, New Mexico Quarterly, 1948-52; Director, Rhode Island Poetry in the Schools Program, 1968-72. Publications include: Poetry: Survival, 1964; Spring Journal, 1968; Four Springs, 1972; At Sixes, 1974; Selected Poems 1955-1976, 1979; Interrupted Praise: New and Selected poems,1983; Gifts of Light, 1983; The Imminence of Love, 1993 - Poems 1963-1993; Plays: Cervantes: Eight Interludes, translations by Honig, 1964; Calisto and Melibea (produced Stanford, University of California), 1966; published, 1972; opera version (produced Davis, California, 1979); Ends of the World and Other Plays, 1983; Radio Play: Life is a Dream, 1970 (UK); Four Plays by Calderon de la Barca (translation) 1961; Calderon, Six plays, 1993. Honours: Guggenheim Fellowship, 1948, 1962; Saturday Review Prize 1957; New England Poetry Club Golden Rose, 1961; Bollingen grant for translation, 1962; American Academy and Institute of Arts and Letters grant, 1966; Amy Lowell Travelling Poetry Fellowship, 1968; National Endowment for the Arts Grants, 1975, 1977; Honorary MA, Brown University, 1958. Address: Box 1852, Brown University, Providence, RI 02912, USA.

HOOD Ann, b. 9 Dec 1956, Rhode Island, USA. Writer. Education: BA, University of Rhode Island, 1978; MA, New York University, 1985. Publications: Somewhere Off The Coast of Maine; Waiting to Canish; Three Legged Horse; Something Blue; Places To Stay; The Night. Contributions to: Glamour; Cosmopolitan; Mademoiselle; New Women; Redbook; Seventeen; Washington Post. Memberships: PEN; Authors Guild. Literary Agent: Gail Hochman.

HOOD Hugh, b. 30 Apr 1928, Toronto, Canada. Writer;Teacher. m. Noreen Mallory, 22 Apr 1957, 2 sons. Education: BA 1952, MA 1952, PhD 1955, University of Toronto. Appointments: Professor Titulaire, Department of English Studies, University of Montreal, 1961-. Publications: The Swing in the Garden, 1975; Black and White Keys, 1982; Be Sure To Close Your Eyes, 1993; Flying A Red Kite, 1962; You'll Catch Your Death, 1992. Honours: City of Toronto Literary Award, 1975; SQPELL Literary Award, 1988; Officer of the Order of Canada, 1988. Memberships: The Arts and Letters Club of Toronto. Address: 4242 Hampton Avenue, Montreal, Quebec, H4A 2K9, Canada.

HOOKER Jeremy, b. 23 Mar 1941, Warsash, Hampshire, England. College Lecturer. Education: BA 1963, MA 1965,Southampton University. Appointments: Arts Council Creative Writing Fellow, Wincester School of Art, 1981-83. Publications Include: Soliloquies of a Chalk Giant, 1974; Solent Shore, 1978; Poetry of Place, 1982;A View from the Source: Selected Poems, 1982; The Presence of the Past, 1987; Master of the Leaping Figures, 1987. Contributions to: Anglo-Welsh Review; New Welsh Review; PN Review; Planet; The Green Book; Poetry Wales. Honours: Welsh Arts Council Literature Prize for Soliloquies of a Chalk Giant, 1975. Memberships: Academi Gymreig, English Language Section; Powys Scoeity; Richard Jefferies Society. Address: Old School House, 7 Sunnyside Frome, Somerset, BA11 1LD, England.

HOOPES Lyn Littlefield, b. 14 July 1953, New York City, USA. Writer. m. Claude B Hoopes, 20 May 1978, 1 s. Eduction: AB, English Literature, Stanford University, 1975. Appointments: Editorial Assistant, Harper and Row, 1975-77; Assistant Editor, Atlantic Monthly Press, 1977-80; Editor, Childrens Books, Houghton Mifflin Co, 1980-82. Publications: Childrens Books: Nana, 1981; When I Was Little, 1983; Daddy's Coming Home, 1984; Mommy, Daddy, Me, 1988; Half a Button, 1989; Wing-a-Ding!,1990; My Own Home, 1991; Forthcoming: The Unbeatable Bread. Contributions to: Childrens Book Reviewer; Christian Science Monitor, Parents Choice. Honours: Nana, Children's Choice, Children's Book Council. Address: 91 Piney Point Road, Marion, MA 02738, USA.

HOOVER Dwight, b. 15 Sept 1926, Oskaloosa, Iowa, USA. College Professor. m. Janet Holmes, 20 July 1983, 3 daughters. Education: BA, William Penn College, 1948; MA, Harverford College, 1949; PhD, University of Iowa, 1953. Appointments: Co-editor, Conspectus on History, 1972-82; Member, Editorial Advisory Board, Indiana Magazine of History, 1978-82; Associate Editor, Social Change Newsletter, 1986-; Associate Editor, Historical Journal of Film, Radio and Television, 1986-89. Publications: The Red and the Black, 1976; A Pictorial History of Indiana, 1980; Magic Middletown, 1986; Understanding Negro History, 1968; Henry James Sr and the Religion of Community, 1969; Cities, 1976; A Teacher's Guide to American Urban History, 1971. Contributions to: Changing View of Community Studies; Middletown as a Case Study, 1989; The Return of the Narrative, 1989; The Sporting Live in Middletown, 1990; The Long Ordeal of Modernization Theory, 1987; Censorship or Bad Judgement, 1987; The Diverging Paths of American Urban History, 1968. Memberships: American Historical Association; Organization of American Historians; American Studies Association; American Association of University Professors; Indiana Association of Historians. Address: 705 N Forest, Muncie, IN 47304, USA.

HOOVER Helen Mary (Jennifer Price), b. 5 Apr 1935, Stark County, Ohio, USA. Writer. Publications: Children of Morrow, 1973; The Lion Cub, 1974; Treasures of Morrow, 1976; The Delikon, 1977; The Rains of Eridan, 1977; The Lost Star, 1979; Return to Earth, 1980; The Time of Darkness, 1980; Another Heaven, Another Earth, 1981; The Bell Tree, 1982; The Shepherd Moon, 1984; Orvis, 1987; The Dawn Palace, 1988; Away Is A Strange Place To Be, 1989. Contributions to: Language Arts; Top of the News; Journal of American Library Association. Honours: Best Book List, for Another Heaven, Another Earth, American Library Association, 1981; Ohioana Award, 1982; Award, Outstanding Contribution to Children's Literature, Central Missouri State University, 1984; Parents Choice Award (Orvis), 1987, and (The Dawn Palace), 1988; Library of Congress Best Book of 1988; American Library Association, Best Y.A. Book of 1988. Memberships: Authors Guild. Address: c/o Viking Penguin Children's Books, 40 West 23rd Street, New York City, NY 10010, USA.

HOOVER Paul, b. 30 Apr 1946, Harrisonburg, Virginia, USA. Writer and Teacher. m. Maxine Chernoff, 5 Oct 1974, 2 sons, 1 daughter. Education: BA cum laude, Manchester College, 1968; MA, University of Illinois, 1973. Appointments: Poet in Residence, Columbia College, 1974-; Editor, New American Writing (journal). Publications: Saigon, Illinois, 1988; Editor, Postmodern American Poetry, 1993; Poetry: The Novel, 1990; Idea, 1987. Contributions to: The Paris Review; The New Yorker; Partisan Review; Sulfur; New Directions; and others. Honours: NEA Fellowship in Poetry, 1980; GE Foundation Award for Younger Writers, 1984; Carl Sandburg Award for Poetry, 1987. Memberships: The Poetry Centre at Museum of Contemporary Art, Chicago, 1974-88; President of Org, 1977-80; MLA; Associated Writing Programmes. Literary Agent: Irene Skolnick of Curtis Brown. Address: 2920 W Pratt, Chicago, IL 60645, USA.

HOPCRAFT Arthur Edward, b. 29 Nov 1932, Essex, England. Writer. Appointments: Staff, The Daily Mirror, 1956-59; The Guardian, 1959-64. Publications include: The Football Man, 1968; The Great Apple Raid, 1970; Mid-Century Men, 1982; Major TV Dramatisations & Original Screenplays, 1971-92 include, Hard Times; Bleak House; The Nearly Man; The Reporters; Baa Baa Blacksheep; A Tale of Two Cities; Hostage; Tinker, Tailor, Soldier, Spy; A Perfect Spy. Contributions to: The Observer; Sunday Times; Nova; New Statesman; The Listener. Honours: Broadcasting Press Guild TV Award; Best Single Play; Best Drama Series; British Academy of Film & TV Arts Writers Award. Memberships: Writers Guild of Great Britain. Literary Agent: A P Watt Limited. Address: c/o 20 John Street, London WC1N 2DL, England.

HOPE Catherine (Cathy) Jane Margaret, b. 15 Sept 1945, Waikari, South Island, New Zealand. Primary School Teacher; Educational Author. m. Terry Hope, 30 Dec 1966, 2 daughters. Education: Trained Infant School Teacher, Coburg Teachers College, Victoria, 1965. Publications: Thematic Approach To Tadpoles 'N' Things, 1978; Themes Through The Year, 1980, 6 reprints; Ideas For Excursions, 1981; Everyone's Different, 1981; Seasons-Themes Through The Year, 1982; Everyone Ages, 1983; Themes From The Playground, 1984, reprint, 1985; All Australian Themes, 1987, reprint, 1987; Ideas For Multicultural Education, 1992; Fundraising For Schools, 1994, reprint, 1994; 5 others. Membership: Fellowship of Australian Writers. Address: c/- Thomas Nelson, 102 Dodds St, South Melbourne, Victoria 3205, Australia.

HOPE Christopher David Tully, b. 26 Feb 1944, Johannesburg, South Africa. Writer. m. Eleanor Marilyn Margaret Klein, 1967, 2 s. Education: BA, Natal University, 1969; MA, University of Witwatersrand, 1972. Publications include: A Separate Development, 1981; My Chocolate Redeemer, 1989; White Boy Running, 1988; Serenity House, 1992; Cape Drives, 1974; In The Country of the Black Pig, 1981; The King, The Cat and the Fiddle, 1983; The Dragon Wore Pink, 1985; The Love Songs of Nathan J Swirsky, 1993. Contributions include: Times Literary Supplement; London Magazine; Les Temps Modernes. Honours: Cholmondely Award, 1974; David Higham Prize, 1981; International PEN Award, 1983; Whitbread Prize, 1985; FRSL. Memberships: Society of Authors. Literary Agent: Deborah Rogers, Rogers, Coleridge & White Limited. Address: c/o Rogers, Coleridge & White Limited, 20 Powis Mews, London W11 1JN, England.

HOPE Ronald, b. 1921. England. Appointments: Fellow, Brasenose College, Oxford, 1945-47; Director, Seafarer's Education Service, London, 1947-76; Director, The Marine Society, 1976-86. Publications include: Spare Time at Sea, 1954; Economic Geography, 1956; Dick Small in the Half Deck, Ships, 1958; The British Shipping Industry, 1959; The Shoregoer's Guide to World ports, 1963; Seamen and the Sea, 1965; Introduction to the Merchant Navy, 1965; Retirement from the Sea, 1967; In Cabined Ships at Sea, 1969; Twenty Singing Seamen, 1979; The Seamens World, 1982; A New History of British Shipping, 1990. Address: 2 Park Place, Dollar, FK14 7AA.

HOPE-SIMPSON Jacynth (Ann) (Helen Dudley), b. 1930, England. Publications: Anne Young, Swimmer, 1959; The Stranger in the Train, 1960; The Bishop of Kenelminster, Young Netball Player, 1961; The Man Who Came Back, Danger on the Line, The Bishop's Picture, 1962; The Unravished Bride, 1963; The Witch's Cave, The Ninepenny, 1964; Hamish Hamilton Book of Myths and Legends, The Ice Fair, 1965; The High Toby, The Edge of the World, Hamish Hamilton Book of Witches, 1966; Escape to the Castle, 1967; The Unknown Island, 1968; They Sailed from Plymouth, 1970; Elizabeth I, Tales in School (ed), 1971; The Gunner's Boy, 1973; Save Tarranmoor!, 1974; Always on the Move, The Hijacked Hovercraft, 1975; Black Madonna, Vote for Victoria, 1976; The Making of the Machine Age, 1978; The Hooded Falcon (as Helen Dudley), 1979; Island of Perfumes, 1985; Cottage Dreams, 1986. Address: Franchise Cottage, Newtown, Milborne Port Sherborne, Dorset, England.

HOPKINS Antony, b. 21 Mar 1921, London, England. Composer; Conductor. Appointments: Former Professor, Royal College of Music, London; Presenter, Talking about Music, BBC, 1955-90. Publications: Talking about Symphonies, 1961; Talking about Concertos, 1964; Music All Around Me, 1967; Music Face to Face, 1971; Talking About Sonatas, 1971; Downbeat Guide, 1977; Understanding Music, 1979; The Nine Symphonies of Beethoven, 1980; Songs for Swinging Golfers, 1981; Sounds of Music, Beating Time, 1982; Musicamusing's, Pathway to Music, 1983; The Concertgoer's Companion, 1984, 1985, reprinted as single Vol, 1994. Address: Woodyard, Ashridge, Berkhamsted, Herts, England.

HOPKINS Harry, b. 26 Mar 1913, Preston, Lancashire, England. Journalist; Author. m. Endla Kustlov, 26 Jan 1948. Education: BA, Merton College, 1935. Appointments: Assistant Editor, Birmingham Gazette, 1936-38; Diplomatic Correspondent, Manchester Evening News, 1946-47; Feature Writer, John Bull Magazine, 1947-60. Publications: New World Arising: A Journey Through the New Nations of SE Asia, 1952; England is Rich, 1957; The New Look: A Social History, 1963; Egypt the Crucible, 1969; The Numbers Game, 1972; The Strange Death of Private White, 1977; The Long Affray, 1985. Memberships: National Union of Journalists; Society of Authors. Address: 61 Clifton Hill, St Johns Wood, London NW8 0JN, England.

HOPKINS Lee Bennett, b. 1938, USA. Author, novels/short stories, children's fiction, poetry and children's non-fiction; Freelance Writer; Educational Consultant. Publications Include: (ed) Beat the Drum! Independence Day Has Come, 1977; (ed) A-Haunting We Will Go, 1977; (ed) Witching Time, 1977; Poetry to Hear, Read, Write and Love, 1978; (ed) To Look at Any Time, 1978; (ed) Merrily Comes Our Harvest In, 1978; (ed) Kits, Cats, Lions and Tigers, 1978; (ed) Go to Bed, 1979; Wonder Wheels (novel), 1979; (ed) Merely Players, 1979; (ed) Easter Buds Are Springing, 1979; (ed) My Mane Catches the Wind: Poems About Horses, 1979; (ed) Pups, Dogs, Foxes and Wolves, 1979; (ed) Elves, Faires and Gnomes: A Book of Poems, 1980; The Best of Book Bonanza, 1980; (ed) Moments: Poems about the Seasons, 1980; (ed) By Myself, 1980; (ed) Morning, Noon and Nightime, Too!!, 1980; Mama and Her Boys (novel), 1981; (ed) An God Bless Me, Prayers, Lullabies and Dream-Poems, 1982; (ed) Circus! Curcus!, 1982; (ed) The Sky Is Full of Song, 1983; (ed) A Song in Stone, 1981; (ed) A Dog's Life, 1983; (ed) Crickets and Bullfrogs and Whispers of Thunder: Poems by Harry Behn, 1984; (ed) Surprises: An I Can Read Book, 1984; (ed) Creatures, 1985; (ed) Munching: Poems About Food and Eating, 1985; (ed) Love and Kisses, 1984; (ed) Best Friends, 1986; (ed) The Sea Is Calling Me, 1986; (ed) Dinosaurs, 1987; (ed) Click, Rumble, Roar: Poems about Machines, 1987; (ed) More Surprises, 1987. Address: Kemey's Cove (3-7), Scarborough, NY 10510, USA.

HOPPE Arthur Watterson, b. 23 Apr 1925, Honolulu, USA. Journalist. m. Gloria Nichols, 27 Apr 1946, 1 s, 3 d. Education: AB cum laude, Harvard, 1949. Publications: The Love Everybody Crusade, 1960; Dreamboat, 1962; The Perfect Solution to Absolutely Everything, 1968; Mr Nixon and My Other Problems, 1971; Miss Lollipop and the Doom Machine, 1973; The Tiddling Tennis Theorum 1977; The Marital Arts, 1985. Contributions to: Esquire; The New Yorker; The Atlantic Monthly. Literary Agent: Don Congdon. Address: The San Francisco Chronicle, 901 Mission St, San Francisco, CA 94103, USA.

HORNE Alister Allan, b. 9 Nov 1925, Author; Journalist; Lecturer. m. (1) Renira Margaret Hawkins, 3 d, (2) The Hon Mrs Sheelin Eccles, 1987. Education: MA, Jesus College, Cambridge. Appointments: Foreign Correspondent, Daily Telegraph, 1952-55; Official Biographer, Prime Minister Harold MacMillan, 1979. Publications include: Back into Power, 1955; The Land is Bright, 1958; Canada and the Canadians, 1961; The Fall of Paris 1870-1871, 1965; To Lose a Battle: France 1940, 1969; Death of a Generation, 1970; The Paris Commune, 1971; Small Earthquake in Chile, 1972; Napoleon, Master of Europe 1805-1807, 1979; The French Army and Politics 1870-1970, 1984; MacMillan Vol I, 1894-1956, 1988; Vol II, 1957-1986, 1989; A Bundle from Britain, 1993; The Lonely Leader: Monty 1944-45, 1994. Contributions to: Various Periodicals. Honours: Hawthorden Prize, 1963; Yorkshire Post Book of Year Prize, 1978; Wolfson Literary Award, 1978; Enid Macleod Prize, 1985; CBE, 1992; Chevalier Legion d'Honneur, 1993; LittD. Memberships: Society of Authors; Royal Society of Literature. Address: The Old Vicarage, Turville, Nr Henley on Thames, Oxon RG9 6QU, England.

HORNE Donald Richmond, b. 26 Dec 1921, Sydney, Australia. Author; Lecturer; Professor Emeritus. m. 22 Mar 1960, 1 s, 1 d. Education: Sydney University, Canberra University College, 1944-45. Appointments: Editor, The Observer, 1958-61, The Bulletin, 1961-62, 1967-72, Quadrant, 1963-66; Contributin Editor, Newsweek International, 1973-76; Chancellor, University of Canberra, 1992-. Publications include: The Lucky Country, 1964; The Permit, 1965; The Education of Young Donald, 1967; god is an Englishman, 1969; Money Medus, 1976; Death of the Lucky Country, 1976; His Excellencys Pleasure, 1977; Right Away Dont Go Back, 1978; In Search of Billy Hughes, 1979; Time of Hope, 1980; Story of the Austrlian People, 1988; Ideas for a Nation, 1989; The Intelligent Tourist, 1993. Contibutions to: Numerous Professional Journals. Honours: AO, 1982; Honorary DLitt, University of NSW, 1986; D Univ, Griffits Univ, 1991. Memberships: Australian society of Authors; Copyright Agency Limited. Address: 53 Grosvenor Street, Woollahra, Sydney, NSW 2025, Australia.

HOROVITZ Michael, b. 1935, England. Appointments: Editor and Publisher, New Departures International Review, 1959-; Founder, Co-ordinator and Torchbearer, Poetry Olympics Festivals, 1980-. Publications: Europa (trans), 1961; Alan Davie, 1963; Declaration, 1963; Strangers: Poems, 1965; Poetry for the People: An Essay in Bop Prosody, 1966; Bank Holiday: A New Testament for the Love Generation, 1967; Children of Albion (ed), 1969; The Wolverhampton

Wanderer: An Epic of Football, Fate and Fun, 1970; Love Poems, 1971; A Contemplation, 1978; Growing Up: Selected Poems and Pictures 1951-1979,The Egghead Republic (trans), 1983; A Celebration of and for Frances Horovitz, 1984; Midsummer Morning Jog Log, 1986; Bop Paintings, Collages and Drawings, 1989; Grandchildren of Albion (ed), 1992. Address: New Departures, Mullions, Bisley, Stroud, Gloucestershire GL6 7BU, England.

HOROWITZ Donald Leonard, b. 27 June 1939, New York City, USA. Professor. m. Judith Anne Present, 4 Sept 1960, 2 s, 1 d. Education: AB, 1959; LL.B, 1961, Syracase University; LLM, 1962, MA, 1965, PhD, 1968, Harvard University. Appointments include: Charles S Murphy Professor of Law and Professor of Political Science, 1980-& James B Duke Professor of Law and Political Science, Duke University. Publications: The Courts and Social Policy, 1977; The Jurocracy, 1977; Coup Theories and Officers' Motives, 1980; Ethnic Groups in Conflict, 1985; A Democratic South Africa, 1991. Contributions to: Articles to: Le Monde; The New Republic; Commentary; The Washington Post; The New Leader; The Los Angeles Times; The Wall Street Journal; Also to scholarly jounals including: World Politics; Comparative Politics; Policy Sciences. Third World Quarterly. Memberships: American Bar Assocaition; American Political Science Association. Address: Duke Univerity, School of Law, Durham, NC 27708-0360, USA.

HOROWITZ Irving Louis, b. 25 Sept 1929, Harlem, New York, USA. Social Scientist; Publisher. m. Mary Ellen Curtis, 9 Oct 1979. Education: BSS, City Univeristy of New York, 1951; MA, Columbia University, 1952; PhD, Buenos Aires University, 1957; Post-doctoral research in Philosophy, Brandeis University. Appointments: Social Science Editor, Oxford Unversity Press, 1965-73; Editor-in-Cheif, Society, 1962-94; President, Transaction Publishers,1966-94; Senior Editor, Book Research Quarterly, 1984-; Senior Editor, Academic Questions, 1988-. Publications: Three worlds of Development, 1965, 1972; Beyond Empire and Revolution, 1982; The War Game, 1963; Foundations of Political Sociology, 1972 Radicalism and Revolt Against Reason, 1961; Ideology and Utopia in The United States, 1976; Communicating Ideas, 1986, 1991; Daydreams and Nightmares: Reflections of a Harlem Childhood, authobiography, 1990; Delivered The Bacardi lectures for 1992, published under the title The Conscience of Worms and the Cowadice of Lions; The Decomposition of Sociology, 1993, 1994. Address: 1247 State Road, Route 206, Blanwenburg Road, Rocky Hill Intersection, Princeton, NJ 08540, USA.

HORSFORD Howard C, b. 26 Nov 1921, Montezuma, Iowa, USA. Education: BA magna cum laude, Ripon Colige, 1943; University of Iowa, 1947; MA, 1951;PhD, 1952, Princeton University. Appointments: Instructor, Assistant Professor, Princeton University, 1951-60; Assistant to Full Professor, Rochester University, 1960-87; Bread Loaf School of English, 1980, 1961, 1963, 1964. Publications: Melville's Journal of a Voyage to Europe and the Levant, 1956-57, 1955; Melville's Journals, 1989; Editor, An Oxford Anthology of English Poetry, 1956; The Southern Mandarins: Letters of Caroline Gordon to Sally Wood, 1984. Contributions to: Irving, Hawthorne, Melville, Crane, C Gordon, Faulkner. Honours: Phi Beta Kappa, 1955; Bicentennial Preceptor, Princeton University, 1957-60. Memberships: Melville Society, President 1957. Address: Department of English, University of Rochester, NY 14627, USA.

HORTON Felix Lee. See: **FLOREN Lee.**

HORTON Michael Scott, b. 11 May 1964, California, USA. President of a Theological Think Tank. Education: BA, Humanities, History, Biola Unviersity; MAR Theoemphais, Westminster Theological Seminary; Certificate, International Inst of Human Rights, Strasbourg, France; History Studies, University of Cambridge; PhD Candidate, Wycliffe Hall, Oxford. Publications: The Agony of Deceit,1990; Made in America, 1991; Putting Amazing Back into Grace,1991; Power Religion, 1992; Mission Accomplished, 1986; Christ The Lord, 1993; The Law of Perfect Freedom, 1993; Beyond Culture Wars, 1994. Honours: Book of the Year for Contemporary Issues; Christianity Today; First Runner Up, Book of the year, 1992. Memberships: Royal Institute of Philosophy,; Oxford Union Society; Phi Alpha Theta. Address: 2568 E Riles Circle, Anaheim, CA 92806, USA.

HORWOOD Harold Andrew, b. 2 Nov 1923, St John's Newfoundland, Canada. Appointments: Creative Writing Teacher, Memorial University, 1974; Writer in Residence, University of Western Ontario, 1976; University of Waterloo, 1980, 1982. Publications:

Tomorrow will be Sunday, 1966; The Foxes of Beachy Cove, 1967; Newfoundland, 1969; White Eskimo, 1972; Death on Ice, 1972; Voices Underground, 1972; Beyond the Road, 1976; Bartlett, 1977; Only the Gods Speak, 1979; Tales of the Labrador Indians, 1981; The Colonial Dream, 1981; A History of Canada, 1983; Pirates and Outlaws of Canada, 1984; Corner Brook, 1986; A History of Newfoundland Ranger Force, 1986; Bandits and Privateers, 1987; Dancing on the shore, 1987; Joey: The Life and Political Times of Joey Smallwood, 1989. Contributions to: Numerous publicatins. Honours: Beta Sigma Phi first Novel, 1966; Best Scientific Book of the Year, 1967; Canada Council Senior Arts Award, 1975; Order of Canada, 1980. Memberships: Writers Union of Canada, Vice Chairman and Chairman. Literary Agent: Bella Pomer Inc, 22 Shallmar Blvd, Toronto. Address: PO Box 489, Annapolis Royal, Nova Scotia, Canada BOS 1A0.

HOSIER Peter. See: **CLARK Douglas.**

HOSILLO Lucila V, b. 29 June 1931, Tanza, Iloilo City, Philippines. Education: AB, English, Far Eastern University, Manila, 1958; AM, Comparative Literature, 1962, PhD 1964, Indiana University, USA. Appointments: Instructor, State University of New York at Buffalo, 1963-64; Assistant Professor, Full Professor of Comparative Literature, University of Philippines, 1966-85; Visiting Professor, National University of Singapore, 1983-84; Cultural Consultant, Freelance, 1985-. Publications: The Concentric Sphere and Other Essays in Comparative Literature, 1968; Philippine American Literary Relations 1898-1942, 1969, 1976; Philippine Literature and Contemporary Events, 1970; Anthology of Third World Poetry, 1978; Originality as Vengeance in Philippine Literature, 1984; Perempuam (Woman), editor, 1987; Hiligaynon Literature: Texts and Contexts, 1992; Participation in International Congress: Plenary Speaker at XIIIth Triennial International Congress, FILLM, Sydney, Australia, 1975; XIVth Congress Association of Asian Institutions of Higher Learning, Hong Kong, 1982; XVI FILLM Congress, Budapest, Hungary, 1984 (Federation International des Langues et Litteratures). Contributions to: Encyclopaedia Universalis; Cooperator; International Dictionary of Literary Terms; A Comparative History of Literature in European Languages; International Directory of Comparative Literature Studies. Honours Include: 1st Prize, Hiligaynon Short Story Writing Contest, Liwayway Publications, 1969; 1st Prize, ASEAN Literary Contest, Manila, 1977; Grand Prize, Literary Criticism in English, Cultural Centre of the Philippines 10th Anniversary Literary Contest, 1979; 2nd Prize, UNESCO Contest on Least Developed Countries, 1981. Memberships: Federation Internationale des Langues et Literatures Modernes; Association Internationale de Litterature Comparée; American Comparative Literature Association; ASEAN Writers Association; Founder, Chairman and President, Illonggo Language and Literature Foundation Inc. Address: 5 Peace Street, East Fairview 1121, Quezon City, Philippines.

HOSPITAL Janette Turner, b. 12 Nov 1942, Melbourne, Victoria, Australia. Novelist. Education: BA, University of Queensland, Brisbane, 1965; MA, Queen's University, Canada, 1973. Appointments: Lecturer, Queens University, St Lawrence College, Kingston, Ontario, 1971-82; Writer in Residence, Massachusetts Institute of Technology, 1985-89; Adjunct Professor, La Trobe University, 1991-93. Publications: The Ivory Swing, 1983; The Tiger in the Tiger Pit, 1983; Boderline, 1985; Charades, 1988; A Very Proper Death, 1990; Novel: The Last Magician, 1992; Short Stories Dislocations, 1988, Isobars, 1990. Honours: Seal Award, 1982; Fellowship of Australian Writers Award, 1988. Literary Agent: c/o Mic Cheetham, 138 Buckingham Palace Road, London, SW1W 9SA, England.

HOSTE Pol, b. 25 Mar 1947, Lokeren, Belgium. Writer. Education: Licentiate Germanic Philology, State University of Ghent, 1970. Publications: De Veranderingen, 1979; Vrouwelijk Enkelvoud, 1987; Een Schoon Bestaan, 1989; Brieven Aan Mozart, 1991; Ontroeringen van een Forens, 1993. Address: Kortedagsteeg 31, B-9000 Gent, Belgium.

HOSTRUP-JESSEN Paula Eugenie, b. 16 Jan 1930, London, England. Danish-English Translator. m. Carl Hostrup-Jessen, 24 Jan 1953, 2 s, 1 d. Education: Royal Free Hospital School of Medicine, 1947-53; University of Copenhagen, 1969-90. Appointments: Chief Editor, Tordenskjold, Literary Magazine, 1988-90; Publishers Reader, 1990-. Publications include: Villy Sorensen: Tutelary Tales, 1988; The Downfall of the Gods, 1989; Harmless Tales, 1991; Steen Steensen Blicher: The Dairy of a Parish Clerk, 1968, 1991; Hans Christian Anderson: Brothers Very Far Away and Other Poems, 1988, 1991.

Contributions to: Encounter; Stand; Scandinavian Review; Seattle Review; Translation; Cimarron Review; Sprint; World Literature Today. Honours: Christian Wilster Prize, 1990. Memberships: Danish Writers Association; Am Literary Translators Association; International PEN; British Society of Authors. Address: Sortemosen 48, PO Box 122, DK 3450 Allerd, Denmark.

HOTCHNER Aaron Edward, b. 1920, USA. Author. Career: Articles Editor, Cosmopolitan Magazine, 1948-50. Publications: The Dangerous American, 1958; For Whom the Bell Tolls, by Hemingway (adaptor), television play, 1958; The Killers, by Hemingway (adaptor), television play, 1959; Adventures of a Young Man, by Hemingway (adaptor), screenplay, 1961; The White House, play, 1964; Papa Hemingway: A Personal Memoir, 1966; The Hemingway Hero, play, 1967; Treasure, 1970; Do You Take this Man, play, 1970; King of the Hill, 1972; Looking for Miracles, 1974; Doris Day: Her Own Story, 1976; Sophia: Living and Loving, 1979; Sweet Prince, play, 1980; The Man Who Lived at the Ritz, 1982; Choice People, 1984; Hemingway and His World, 1988; Welcome to The Club, Broadway Musical, 1989; Blown Away, 1990. Contributions to: Esquire; New York Times; New Yonker; Readers Digest, New York; Redbook. Honours: Honorary degree Doctor Humane Letters, Washington University, 1992; Distinguished Alumni Award, Washington University Law School, 1992. Memberships: PEN; Dramatist Guild; Author's League; Century Club. Literary Agent: Andrew Wykie, 259 W 57th St, NYC 10107, USA. Address: 14 Hillandale Road, Westport, CT 06880, USA.

HOUGH Charlotte, b. 24 May 1924, Hampshire, England. Writer. m. Richard Hough, 17 July, 1941, div, 1973, 4 d. Publications include: The Bassington Murder, 1980; Red Biddy, 1966; Sir Frog, 1968; Three Little Funny Ones, 1962; Jim Tiger, 1956; Mortons Pony, 1957; The Homemakers, 1959; The Story of Mr Pinks, 1958; The Hampshire Pig, 1958; The Animal Game, 1959; The Trackers, 1960; Algernon, 1962; Anna Minnie, 1967; The owl in the Barn, 1964; More Funny Ones, 1965; My Aunts Alphabet, 1969; A Bad Child's Book of Moral Verse, 1970. Memberships: PEN Society of Authors; Crime Writers Association. Address: 1A Ivor Street, London NW1 9PL, England.

HOUGH Julia Marie. See: TAYLOR Judy.

HOUGH Richard Alexander, (Bruce Carter, Elizabeth Churchill, Pat Strong), b. 15 May 1922, Writer. m. (1) Helen Charlotte, 1943, div, 4 d. (2) Judy Taylor, 1980. Appointments include: Publisher, 1947-70; Bodley Head, 1955; Director, Managing Director, Hamish Hamilton Childrens Books, 1955-70. Publications include: The Fleet that Had to Die, 1958; Admirals in Collison, 1959; The Potemkin Mutiny, 1960; The Big Battleship, 1966; First Sea Lord: An Authorised Life of Admiral Lord Fisher, 1969; The Pursuit of Admiral von Spee, 1969; The Blind Horns Hate, 1971; Captain Bligh and Mr Christian, 1972; One Boys War, 1975; Advice to a Grand Daughter, 1975; The Great Admirals, 1977; The Murder of Captain James Cook, 1979; Man O War, 1979; Nelson, 1980; Mountbatten, 1980; The Great Wat at Sea, 1914-1918, 1983; Former Naval Person: Churchill and the Wars at Sea, 1985; The Longest Battle: The War at Sea, 1986; Born Royal: The Lives and Loves of the Young Windors, 1988; Bless Our Ship: Mountbatten & the Kelly, 1982; The Fight to the Finish, 1979; Bullers Guns, 1981; Razor Eyes, 1981; Bullers Dreadnought, 1982; Bullers Victory, 1984; Edward and Alexandra, 1992; Numerous Books on Motoring History and Books for Children under Pseudonym Bruce Carter; Captain James Cook, 1994. Address: 31 Meadowbank, Primrose Hill, London NW3, England.

HOUGH Stanley Bennett (Rex Gordon, Bennett Stanley), b. 25 Feb 1917, Preston, Lancashire, England. Author. m. Justa E C Wodschow, 1938. Appointments: Radio Operator, Marconi Company, 1936-38; Radio Officer, International Marine Radio, 1939-45; Professional Yachtsman, 1946-51. Publications Include: Frontier Incident, 1951; Moment of Decision, 1952; Mission in Guemo, 1953; The Seas South, 1953; The Primitives, 1954; The Bronze Perseus, 1959; The Tender Killer, 1962; Sea to Eden, 1954; Extinction Bomber, 1956; A Pound A Day Inclusive, 1957; Expedition Everyman, 1959; Beyond The Eleventh Hour, 1961; Where?, 1965; Dear Daughter Dead, 1965; Sweet Sister Seduced, 1968; Fear Fortune Father, 1974; No Man Friday (as Rex Gordon), 1956; Government Contract (as Bennett Stanley), 1956. Honours: Infinity Award for Science Fiction, 1957. Memberships: Chairman, Workers Education Association, South West District; Chairman, Secondary School Boards; President, Royal Cornwall Polytechnic Society, 1985-88. Literary Agent: A M Heath &

Company Ltd. Address: 21 St Michael's Road, Ponsanooth, Truro TR3 7ED, England.

HOUGHTON Eric, b. 4 Jan 1930, West Yorkshire, England. Teacher; Author. m. Cecile Wolffe, 4 June 1954, 1 s, 1 d. Education: Sheffield City College of Education, 1952. Publications include: The White Wall, 1961; Summer Silver, 1963; They Marched with Spartacus, 1963; A Giant Can Do Anything, 1975; The Mouse and the Magician, 1976; The Remarkable Feat of King Caboodle, 1978; Steps Out of Time, 1979; Gate of Glass, 1987; Walters Wand, 1989; The Magic Cheese, 1991; The Backwards Watch, 1991; Vincent the Invisible, 1993. Contribution to: Review. Honour: Junior Book Award, 1964. Memberships: Society of Authors; Childrens Writers Group. Address: The Crest, 42 Collier Road, Hastings, East Sussex, TN34 3JR, England.

HOUSTON Douglas Norman, b. 18 Mar 1947, Cardiff, Wales. Writer; Lecturer. m. Karen Mary Pearce, 5 July 1986, 3 sons, 1 daughter. Education: BA, English, 1969, PhD, English, 1986, University of Hull. Appointments: Freelance Reviewer, articles, poems etc. in various journals, industrial copywriter; Visiting Lecturer, Trinity College, Dublin University College, Dublin; Staff of English Department, University College of Wales, Aberystwyth. Publications: With the Offal Eaters, 1986; A Rumoured Cty, ed Meic Stephens, 1982; The Bright Field, ed, Douglas Dunn, 1991; Casting a Spell, ed, Angela Huth, 1992. Contributions to: Poetry Review; London Magazine; Oxford Guide to Twentieth Century Literature in English. Honours: Welsh Arts Council Book Prize, 1987; Welsh Arts Council Bursary, 1990; Elected to Welsh Academy, 1987. Address: Brynheulog, Cumbrwyno, Aberystwyth, Dyfed, Wales.

HOUSTON James Archibald, b. 1921, Canada. Author; Artist. Career: Associate Director of Design, 1962-72; Master Designer, 1972-, Steuben Glass. Publications: Tikta-likta, 1965; Eagle Mask, 1966; The White Archer, 967; Eskimo Prints, 1967; Akavak, 1968; Wolf Fun, 1971; The White Dawn, for adults, 1971; Ghost Paddle, 1972; Ojibwa Summer, 1972; Kiviok's Magic Journey, 1973; Frozen Fire, 1977; Ghost Fox, for adults, 1977; River Runners, 1979; Spirit Wrestler, for adults, 1980; Long Claws, 1981; Black Diamonds, 1982; Eagle Song, 1983; Ice Swords, 1985; The Falcon Bow, 1986; Whiteout, 1988; Running West, for adults, 1989; Drifting Snow, 1992. Address: 24 Main Street, Stonington, CT 06378, USA.

HOUSTON R B. See: RAE Hugh Craurford.

HOVANNISIAN Richard G, b. 1932, USA. Professor of Armenian and Near Eastern History; Director, Near Eastern Center, UCLA; Holder, Armenian Educational Foundation Chair in Modern Armenian History since 1987. Appointments: Member, Editorial Board: Armenian Review; International Journal of Middle East Studies, Ararat; Haigazian Armenological Review, Beirut. Publications: Armenia on the Road to Independence, 1967, 4th edition, 1984; The Republic of Armenia, vol I, 1971, 3rd edition, 1984, vil II, 1982; The Armenian Holocaust, 1978, 2nd edition, 1980; The Armenian Image in History and Literature, 1982; Ethics in Islam, 1985; The Armenian Genocide in Perspective, 1986; The Armenian Genocide: History, Politics, Ethics, 1992. Contributions to: Read More About It; Armenian Review. Honours: Elected Armenian Academy of Sciences, 1990. Memberships: Society for Armenian Studies, Chairman 1974-75, 1976-77, 1990-91, 1991-92; Middle East Studies Association; American Association for Advancement of Slavic Studies; Oral History Association; American Historical Association. Address: Department of History, University of California, Los Angeles, CA 90024, USA.

HOWARD Anthony Michell, b. 12 Feb 1934, London, England. Obituaries Editor, The Times. m. 26 May 1965. Education: BA, Oxford University, 1955; Called to Bar, Inner Temple, 1956. Appointments: Editor, New Statesman, 1972-78, Listener, 1979-81; Deputy Editor, Observer, 1981-88. Publications: The Making of the Prime Minister, 1965; The Crossman Diaries: Selections from the Diaries of a Cabinet Minister, 1979; Rab: The Life of R A Butler, 1987; Crossman: The Pursuit of Power, 1990; Lives Remembered, 1993. Contributions to: The Baldwin Age, 1960; The Age of Austerity, 1963; Sunday Times; Times Literary Supplement; NY Times Book Review; The Independent; London Review of Books; Spectator. Literary Agent: Peters, Fraser and Dunlop. Address: 17 Addison Avenue, London W11 4QS, England.

HOWARD Clark, b. 1934, USA. Author. Publications: The Arm, novel, 1967; Mystery novels: A Movement Toward Eden, 1969; The

Doomsday Squad, 1970; The Killings, 1973; Last Contract, 1973; Summit Kill, 1975; Mark the Sparrow, 1975; The Hunters, 1976; The last Great Death Stunt; Other: Six Againt the Rock, 1977; The Wardens, 1979; Zebra: The True Account of the 179 Days of Terror in San Francisco, 1979, UK Edition The Zebra Killings, 1980; American Saturday, 1981; Brothers in Blood, 1983; Dirt Rich, 1986; Hard City, 1990; Love's Blood, 1993; City Blood, 1994. Honours: Edgar Allan Poe Award, 1980; Ellery Queen Award, 1985, 1986, 1988, 1990. Memberships: Board of Directors, Mystery Writers of America. Literary Agent: Ms Roslyn Targ. Address: The Roslyn Targ Agency, 105 W 13 St, Suite 15-E, New York, NY 10011, USA.

HOWARD Deborah Janet, b. 26 Feb 1946, Westminister, London, England. University Lecturer. m. Malcolm S Longair, 26 Sept 1975, 1 s, 1 d. Education: BA, Newnham College, Cambridge, 1960; MA, PhD, University of London, 1968-72. Publications: Jacopo Sansovino: Architecture and Patronage in Renaissance Venice, 1975, 87; The Architectural History of Venice, 1980, 81, 87. Contributions to: Numerous Articles and Book Reviews. Honours: Fellow, Society of Antiquaries, since 1984; Society of Antiquarians of Scotland since, 1991. Memberships: Royal Commission on the Ancient & Historical Monuments of Scotland; Royal Fine Art Commission for Scotland. Address: St Johns College, Cambridge, CB2 1TP, England.

HOWARD Elizabeth Jane, b. 26 Mar 1923, London, England. Author. m. Kingsley Amis, 1965, div 1983. 1 d. Education: Trained as Actress, London Mask Theatre School, Scott Thorndike Student Repertory. Appointments: Honorary Director, Cheltenham Literary Festival, 1962; Co Director, Salisbury Festival, 1973. Publications include: The Beautiful Visit, 1950; The Long View, 1956; The Sea Change, 1959; After Julius, 1965; Odd Girl Out, 1972; The Lovers Companion; Howard and Maschler on Food, 1987; Bettina; The Light Years, 1990; Making Time, 1991; Confussion, 1993; Collection of Short Stories; 14 TV Plays; 3 Film Scripts. Contributions to: The Times; Sunday Times; Telegraph; Encounter; Vogue; Harpers; Queen. Honours: Yorkshire Post Novel of the Year, 1982. Memberships: Fellow of Royal Society of Literature; Authors Lending and Copyright Society. Literary Agent: Jonathan Clowes, London, England. Address: c/o Jonathan Clowes, Ivan Bridge house, Bridge Approach, London, NW1 8BD, England.

HOWARD Lynette Desley (Lynsey Stevens), b. 28 Sept 1947, Sherwood, Queensland, Australia. Writer; Ex-Librarian. Publications: Ryan's Return, 1981; Terebori's Gold, 1981; Race for Revenge, 1981; Play Our Song Again, 1981; Tropical Knight, 1982; Starting Over, 1982; Man of Vengeance, 1982; Closest Place to Heaven, 1983; Forbidden Wine, 1983; The Ashby Affair, 1983; Lingering Embers, 1984; Leave Yesterday Behind, 1986; But Never Love, 1988; A Rising Passion, 1990; Touched by Desire, 1993; A Physical Affair, 1994. Honours: Arty, Romantic Times, Worldwide Romance, 1984. Memberships: Romantic Novelists Association, UK; Queensland Writers Centre; Australian Society of Authors; Romance Writers of America; Romance Writers of Australia. Address: PO Box 264, Runaway Bay, Queensland 4216, Australia.

HOWARD Maureen, b. 1930, USA. University Educator. Appointments: Worked in advertising and publishing, 1953-54; Lecturer in English: New School for Social Research, New York City, 1967-68, 1970-71, 1974-; University of California, Santa Barbara, 1968-69; Amherst College, Amherst, Massachusetts; Brooklyn College, New York; Currently Member, English Department, Columbia University, New York City. Publications: Not A Word About Nightingales, novel, 1960; Bridgeport Bus, novel, 1965; Before My Time, novel, 1975; Facts of Life, autobiography, 1978; Grace Abounding, novel, 1982; Expensive Habits, novel, 1986. Address: c/o Summit Books, Simon & Schuster, 1230 Sixth Avenue, New York, NY 10020, USA.

HOWARD Philip Nicholas Charles, b. 2 Nov 1933, London, England. Writer; Literary Editor. m. Myrtle Janet Mary Houldsworth, 17 Oct 1959, 2 sons, 1 daughter. Education: MA, Major Scholar, Trinity College, Oxford, 1953-57. Appointments: Reporter, Feature Writer, Leader Writer, Parliamentary Correspondent, The Glasgow Herald, 1960-64; Reporter, Feature Writer, Columnist, Leader Writer, 1964-, Literary Editor, 1978-, The Times. Publications: The State of the Language, 1984; We Thundered Out, 200 Years of The Times, 1985; Winged Words, 1988; A Word in Time, 1990; Word-Watching, 1988; London's River, 1975; The Royal Palaces; The Black Watch; New Words for Old; Weasel Words; Words Fail Me; A Word in Your Ear; The Book of London. Contributions to: Diverse magazines and journals.

Honours: Fellow, Royal Society of Literature, 1985; IPC Press Awards. Memberships: The Literary Society; The Society of Bookment; Council, The Classical Association; International PEN; Society of Authors; National Union of Journalists. Address: Flat 1, 47 Ladbroke Grove, London W11 3AR, England.

HOWARD Richard (Joseph), b. 13 Oct 1929, Cleveland, Ohio, USA. Freelance Literary and Art Critic; Translator; Writer. Education: Educated at Shaker Heights High School, Ohio; BA 1951, MA 1952, Columbia University, New York; The Sorbonne, Paris, 1952-53. Appointments: Lexicographer, World Publishing Company, Cleveland, 1954-56 and in New York, 1956-58; Freelance Literary and Art Critic and Translator, 1958-; Poetry Editor, American Review, New York; Director, Braziller Poetry Series. Publications: Verses Includes: Findings, 1971; Two-Part Inventions (includes radio plplay The Lesson of the Master), 1974; Fellow Feelings, 1976; Misgivings, 1978; Lining Up, 1984; Plays: The Automobile Graveyard, adaptation of a play by Fernando Arrabal (produced New York, 1961); Wildflowers (produced New York, 1976); Natures (produced New York, 1977); Two-Part Inventions (produced Chicago, 1979); Like Most Revelations, 1994. Honours: Guggenheim Fellowship, 1966; Harriet Monroe Memorial Prize, 1969; Levinson Prize, 1973; American Academy Grant, 1970; Award of Merit Medal, 1980; Pulitzer Prize, 1970; American Book Award for translation, 1983; Fellow, Morse College, Yale University, New Haven, Connecticut, Member, American Academy, 1983; Fellowship, American Academy of Poets, 1989.

HOWARD Roger, b. 19 June 1938, Warwick, England. Theatre Writer; Poet; Lecturer. Education: MA, Drama. Appointments: Writing Fellow, York University, 1976-78, East Anglia University, 1979-; Lecturer, University of Essex; Senior Lecturer, University of Essex, 1993-. Publications include: Slaughter Night and Other Plays, 1971; A Break in Berlin, 1979; Contemporary Chinese Theatre, 1978; The Siege, 1981; Senile Poems, 1988; The Tragedy of Mao, 1989; Britannia & Other Plays, 1990. Contributions to: Transatlantic Review; Stand; Bananas; Times Literary Supplement; Double Space; New Society; Times Education Supplement; Minnesota Review; New Comparison; History of European Ideas; Theatre Quarterly; Plays & Players; Theatre Research International; Journal of American Studies. Address: c/o Theatre Underground, Dept of Literature, University of Essex, Wivenhoe Park, Colchester, Essex CO4 3SQ, England.

HOWARTH David Armine, b. 18 July 1912. Author. Education: Trinity College, Cambridge. Appointments: Talks Assistant, etc, BBC, 1934-39; War Correspondent, 1939-40; RNVR, 1940-45. Publications: The Shetland Bus, 1951; We Die Alone (also under title Escape Alone), 1955; The Sledge Patrol, 1957; Dawn of D-Day, 1959; The Shadow of the Dam, 1961; The Desert King, A Biography of Ibn Saud, 1964; The Golden Isthmus, 1966; A Near Run Thing: The Day of Waterloo, 1968; Trafalgar: The Nelson Touch, 1969; Sovereign of the Seas, 1974; The Greek Adventure, 1976; 1066 The Year of the Conquest, 1977; The Voyage of the Armada: The Spanish Story, 1981; Tahiti, 1983; Pursued by a Bear (autobiography), 1986; (with S Howarth) The Story of P & O; (fiction) Group Flashing Two, 1952; One Night in Styria, 1953; (for children) Heroes of Nowadays, 1957; Great Escapes, 1969; Editor, My Land and My People (by HH The Dalai Lama), 1962. Address: Wildings Wood, Blackboys, Sussex, England.

HOWATCH Susan, b. 14 July 1940, Leatherhead, Surrey, England. Writer. Education: LLB, Kings College, University of London, 1958-61. Publications include: The Dark Shore, 1965; The Waiting Sands, 1966; Call in the Night, 1967; The Shrouded Walls, 1968; April's Grave, 1969; The Devil on Lammas Night, 1970; Penmarric, 1971; The Rich are Different, 1977; Sins of the Fathers, 1980; The Wheel of Fortune, 1984; Glittering Images, 1987; Glamorous Powers, 1988; Ultimate Prizes, 1989; Scandalous Risks, 1991; Mystical Paths, 1992; Absolute Truths, 1994. Contributions to: The Writer; The Church Times; The Tablet. Honour: Winifred Mary Stanford Memorial Prize, 1992. Memberships: PEN; Society of Authors; Authors League; Royal Overseas League. Literary Agent: Brian Stone, Aitken, Stone & Wiley, UK; Claire Smith, Harold Ober Associates Inc, USA. Address: c/o Aitken, Stone & Wiley, 29 Fernshaw Road, London SW10 0T6, England.

HOWCROFT Wilbur Gordon, b. 28 Aug 1917, Kerang, Australia. Wheat & Sheep Farmer. m. Barbara Innes McLennan, 17 Aug 1942. Publications: Outback Observations, 1970; This Side of the Rabbit Proof Fence, 1971; The Clancy That Overflowed, 1971; Random Ramblings, 1972; The Farm that Blew Away, 1973; Facts, Fables &

Foolery, 1973; Sand in the Stew, 1974; The Old Working Hat, 1975; The Eucalypt Trail, 1975; Black with White Cockatoos, 1977; Dungarees & Dust, 1978; Nonsery Rhymes, 1978; Bush Ballads & Buffoonery, 1979; Bush Ballads & Buldust, 1982; Hello Cocky, 1982; The Bushman Who Laughed, 1982; The Bushman Who Laughed Again, 1983; The Wilbur Howcroft Omnibus, 1985; Bush Characters, 1986; Aussie Odes, 1988; Billabongs and Billy Tea, 1989; Mopokes and Mallee Roots, 1989; Whimsical Wanderings. Contributions to: Frequent Radio and TV appearances; Professional journals, newspapers and magazines. Memberships: Australian Society of Authors. Literary Agent: Caroline Lurie, Australian Literary Management. Address: PO Box 36, Culgoa, Vic 3530, Australia.

HOWE James, b. 2 Aug 1946, Oneida, New York, USA. m. Betsy Imershein, 5 Apr 1981, 1 d. Education: BFA, Boston University, 1968; MA, Hunter College, 1977. Publications: Bunnicula, 1979; Teddy Bear's Scrapbook, 1980; The Hospital Book, 1981; Howliday Inn, 1982; A Night Without Stars, 1983; The Celery Stalks at Midnight, 1983; Morgan's Zoo, 1984; The Day the Teacher Went Bananas, 1984; What Eric Knew, 1985; Stage Fright, 1986; When You Go to the Kindergarten, 1986; There's A Monster Under My bed, 1986; Babes in Toyland, 1986; Eat Your Poison, Dear, 1987; Nighty-Nightmare, 1987; I Wish I Were a Butterfly, 1987; The Fright Before Christmas, 1988; Scared Silly, 1989; Hot Fudge, 1990; Dew Drop Dead, 1990; Pinky and Rex, 1990; Pinky and Rex Get Married, 1990; Pinky and Rex and the Spelling Bee, 1991; Pinky and Red and the Mean Old Witch, 1991; Greepy-Crawly Birthday, 1991; Dances With Wolves: A Story for Children, 1991; Return to Howliday Inn, 1992; Pinky and Rex Go To Camp, 1992; Pinky and Rex and the New Baby, 1993; Rabbit-Cadabral, 1993; Bunnicula Fun Book, 1993; Bunnicula Escapes! A Pop-up Adventure, 1994; There's a Dragon in My Sleeping Bag, 1994; Playing With Words, 1994; Pinky and Rex and the Double-Dad Weekend, 1995. Contributions to: Writing for the Hidden Child in The Horn Book Magazine, 1985; School Library Journal; Writing Mysteries for Children - The Horn Book Magazine, 1990. Literary Agent: Amy Berkower, New York, USA. Address: Writers House, 21 West 26 Street, New York, NY 10010, USA.

HOWE Tina, b. 21 Nov 1937, New York City, USA. Playwright; Professor. m. Norman Levy, 1961, 1 s, 1 d. Education: BA, Sarah Lawrence College, Bronxville, New York, 1959. Career: Adjunct Professor, New York University, 1983-; Visiting Professor, Hunter College, New York, 1990-. Publications: Productions: The Nest, (Provincetown, Massachusetts, 1969; New York, 1970); Museum (Los Angeles, 1976, New York, 1977), New York, Samuel French, 1979; The Art of Dining (Washington DC and New York, 1979-80), New York, Samuel French, 1980; Painting Churches (New York, 1983), New York, Samuel French, 1984; Coastal Disturbances (New York, 1986) New York, Samuel French, 1987; Approaching Zanzibar (New York, 1989), New York, Samuel French, 1993; Books: Coastal Disturbances: Four plays by Tina Howe (include Museum, The Art of Dining, Painting Churches, Coastal Disturbances), Theatre Communications Group, 1989; Approaching Zanzibar, Theatre Communications Group, 1990. Literary Agent: Flora Roberts Inc, 157 West 57th St, New York, NY 10019, USA.

HOWELL Anthony, b. 20 Apr 1945, London. Poet. Education: Leighton Park School; Royal Ballet School, London. Appointments include: Lecturer, Grenoble University, 1969-70; Editor, Softly Loudly Books, London; Currently: Lecturer (Time based studies), Cardiff School of Art; Editor, Grey Suit, video for Art and Literature. Publications: Inside the Castle, 1969; Femina Deserta, 1971; Oslo; A Tantric Ode, 1975; The Mekon, 1976; Notions of a Mirror: Poems, 1964-82, 1983; Winter's Not Gone, 1984; Why I May Never See the Walls of China, 1986; Howell's Law, 1990; Novel, In the Company of Others, 1986; First Time in Japan, 1995. Honours include: Welsh Arts Council Bursary, 1989. Address: 21 Augusta Street, Adamsdown, Cardiff CF2 1EN, Wales.

HOWELL Virginia Tier. See: ELLISON Virginia Howell.

HOWES Barbara, b. 1 May 1914, New York, USA. Poet; Anthologist. m. William Jay Smith, 1 Oct 1947. 2 s. Education: Graduated from Bennington College, 1937. Publications: Books of Poetry: The Undersea Farmer, 1948; In the Cold Country, 1954; Light and Dark, 1959; Looking up at Leaves, 1966; The Blue Garden, 1972; A Private Signal: Poems New and Selected, 1977; Moving, 1983; Collected Poems, 1995; Short Stories: The Road Commissioner and Other Stories, 1983. Edited Anthologies: 23 Modern Stories, 1963;

From the Green Antilles: writings of the Caribbean, 1966; The Sea-Green Horse, with Gregory Jay Smith, 1970; The Eye of the Heart: stories from Latin America, 1973, paperback, 1974. Contribution to: Accent; Antaeus; The Atlantic; Berkshire Review; Partisan Review; Poetry; The New York Times; The Souhtern Review; The Sewanee Review; Stand; The Virginia Quarterly Review; Yale Review and others. Address: RR1 Box 175, North Pownal, VT 05260, USA.

HOWLAND Bette, b. 28 Jan 1937, Chicago, IL, USA. Writer, 2 s. Education: AB, University of Chicago, 1955. Appointments: Visiting Professor, University of Chicago, 1993-; Committe on Social Thought, Literature. Publications: W3, 1974; Blue in Chicago, 1978; Things to Come and Go, 1983; German Lessons, 1993. Contributions to; Various Newspapers, Journals & Magazines. Honours: Rockefeller Foundation, 1969; Marsden Foundation, 1973; Guggenheim Foundation, 1978; MacArthur Foundation, 1984-89. Address: 102 Mulbarger Lane, Bellefonte, PA 16823, USA.

HOWLETT John Reginald, b. 4 Apr 1940, Leeds, England. Author; Scriptwriter. m. Ada Finocchiaro, 10 June 1967, 2 d. Education: BA, Jesus College, Oxford. Publications: James Dean, 1974; Christmas Spy, 1975; Tango November, 1976; Maxiumum Credible Accident, 1980; Orange, 1982; Murder of a Moderate Man, 1985; Frank Sinatra, Biography. Literary Agent: Elaine Green, Alan Brodie. Address: Orchard House, Stone in Oxney, Tenterden, Kent TN30 7JR, England.

HOYLAND Michael (David), b. 1 Apr 1925, Nagpur, India. Retired Art Lecturer; Author. m. Marette Nicol Fraser, 21 July 1948, 2 s, 2 d. Appointments: School Teacher, 1951-63; Lecturer, 1963-65, Senior Lecturer in Art, 1963-80, Kesteven College of Education. Publications include: Introduction Three, 1967; Art for Children, 1970; Variations: An Integrated Approach to Art, 1975; A Love Affair with War, 1981; The Bright Way In, 1984; 139 Poems in Journals and a Collection; 6 Short Stories. Contributions to: Reviewing for Ore; Jade. Memberships: Stamford Writers Group; PEN; Welland Valley Art Society; East Anglian Potters Association. Address: Foxfoot House, South Luffenham, Nr Oakham Rutland, Leics LE15 8NP, England.

HOYLE Fred, b. 1915, Science Fiction, Fantasy Astronomy, Physics, Autobiography. Appointments: Honorary Fellow, St Johns College, Cambridge, 1973, Emmanuel College, Cambridge, 1984, Lecturer, 1945-58, Plumian Professor, 1958-72, Director, Institute of Theoretical Astronomy, 1966-72, Cambridge University; Staff Member, Mount Wilson & Palomar Observatories, 1956-62; Professor, Royal Institute, London, 1969-72; White Professor, Cornell University, NY, 1972-78. Publications include: Into Deepest Space, 1976; The Incandescent Ones, 1977; Ten Faces of the Universe, 1977; Lifecloud, 1978; The Westminister Disaster, 1978; Diseases from Space, 1979; Commonsense in Nuclear Energy, 1979; Evolution from Space, 1981; Facts and Dogms in Cosmology and Elsewhere, 1982; The Giants of Universl Park, 1982; The Intelligent Universe: A New View of Creation and Evolution, 1983; Home is Where the Wind Blows, 1994. Honour: KT, 1972. Address: St Johns College, Cambridge.

HOYLE Geoffrey, b. 1942, England. Author. Appointments: Worked in Documentary Films, 1963-67. Publications include: Fifth Planet, 1963; Seven Steps to the Sun, 1970; Molecule Men, 1971; The Inferno, 1973; Into Deepest Space, 1976; The Incandescent Ones, 1977; The Westminister Disasters, 1978; commonsense in Nuclear Energy, 1979; The Energy pirate, 1982; The Giants of Universal park, 1982; The Frozen Planet of Azuron, 1982; The Planet of Death, 1982; Flight, 1984. Address: West Wissett, 8 Milner Road, Bournemouth, BH4 8AD, England.

HOYLE Peter, b. 25 Oct 1939, Accrington, Lancashire. Retired Librarian. m. Barbara Croop, 22 Oct 1983, 1 s, 1 d. Education: BA, Liverpool University, 1959-62. Publications: The Man in the Iron Mask, 1984; Brantwood, 1986. Contributions to: Stories in Stand, P N Review. Honours: Bursary NW Arts, 1986. Memberships: Associate of Library Association. Address: 19 Hexham Avenue, Bolton, Lancs BL1 5PP, England.

HOYT Erich, b. 28 Sept 1950, Akron, Ohio, USA. Writer. m. Sarah Elizabeth Wedden, 4 Mar 1989, 1 son, 1 daughter. Education: Vannevar Bush Fellow in Science Journalism, Massachusetts Institute of Technology, 1985-86. Appointments: Contributing Editor, Equinox Magazine, Canada, 1982-; Field Correspondent, Defenders Magazine, USA,, 1985-; Visiting Lecturer: Massachusetts Institute of Technology, Cambridge, 1986-87, Ohio State University, 1992-; Consultant for science and botanical museums, 1987-; Gave opening plenary lecture, European Cetacean Society Annual General Meeting, 1994. Publications: Orca: The Whale Called Killer, 1981, 3rd edition, 1990; The Whale Watcher's Handbook, 1984, German edition, 1987; Conserving the Wild Relatives of Crops, 1988, French, Chinese, Portuguese and Spanish editions, 1992; Seasons of the Whale, 1990, French edition, 1993; Extinction A-Z, 1991; Meeting the Whales, 1991; Riding with the Dolphins, 1992. Contributions to: Anthologies and textbooks; National Geographic; The New York Times; The Globe and Mail, Toronto; Discover; The Guardian; Over 100 other journals. Honours: Francis H Kortwright Award, 1st place, Magazines, 1983; Environment Canada Award for Best Magazine Article, 1986; BBC Wildlife Award for Nature Writing, 2nd place for Essay, 1988; James Thurber Writer-in-Residence, Thurber House, 1992. Memberships: The Writers Guild; American Society of Journalists and Authors; International Science Writers Association; National Association of Science Writers; Outdoor Writers of Canada; Society for Marine Mammalogy; Association of British Science Writers; Society for Economic Botany; Xerces Society. Address: 29 Dirleton Avenue No 11, North Berwick EH39 4BE, Scotland.

HRABAL Bohumil, b. 28 Mar 1914, Brno, Czechoslovakia. Novelist. Education: Graduated Charles University, Prague, 1946. Publications: People's Conversations, 1956; A Pearl at the Bottom, 1963; Closely Observed Trains, 1965; The Death of Mr Balitsberger, 1966; Fair Songs and Legends, 1968; The Haircut, 1970, 1992; I Served the King of England, 1971, 1989; Tender Barbarian, 1973; Too Loud a Solitude, 1976, 1990; Lovely Wistfulness, 1977; The Town Where Time Stood Still, 1978; A Miracle Every Day, 1979; The Poetry Club, 1981; The Harlequin's Millions, 1981; Weddings in the House, 1984; Selected Stories, 1984; Vacant Sites, 1986; My World, 1988; Magic Flute, 1990; Screenplay, Closely Observed Trains, 1967, and others. Honours include: Artist of Merit, 1989. Address: Na Hrazi 24 Prague 8-Liben, Czech Republic.

HSIA Hsiao. See: LIU Wu-chi.

HUBLER Richard G, b. 1912, USA. Appointments: Public Relations Consultnt, 1938-60; Associate Book Reviewer, 1960-; Former Teacher, Ventura College, University of CA, Assistant to President, San Fernando Valley State College, 1964. Publications include: Lou Gehrig, 1941; I Flew for China, 1942; Flying Leathernecks, 1944; Ive Got Mine, 1945; The Brass God, The Chase, 1952; The Pass, 1955; SAC; Strategic Air Command, 1958; St Louis Woman, The Shattering of the Image, True Love True love, 1959; The Blue and Gold Man, The Worlds Shorest Stories, 1961; Trial and Triumph, Wheres the Rest of Me, The Cole Porter Story, 1965; South of the Moon, Soldier and Sage, The Christianis, 1966; Wheeler, 1967; In All His Glory, 1968; The Earthmaker Drinks Blood, 1975. Address: Box 793, Ojai, CA 93023, USA.

HUDDLE David, b. 1942, Ivanhoe, Virginia, USA. m. Lindsey M Huddle, 2 daughters. Education: BA, Foreign Affairs, University of Virginia, 1968; MA, English, Hollins College, 1969; MFA, Writing, Columbia Unversity, 1971. Career inlcudes: Faculty, Warren Wilson College, MFA Programme for Writers, 1981-85; Goddard College, 1980, Bread Loaf School of English, 1979, 1975-; Professor of English, University of Vermont, 1982-; Editor, New england Review, 1993-94. Publications: A Dream With No Stump Roots In It, 1975; Paper Boy, 1979; Only the Little Bone, 1986; Stopping by Home, 1988; The High Spirits, 1992; The Writing Habit; Essays on Writing, 1992; The Nature of Yearning, 1992; Intimates, 1993; Tenormen, 1995. Contributions to: Esquire; Harper's; The New York Times Book Review; Kentucky Poetry Review; Texas Quarterly; Poetry; Shenandoah; American Poetry Review. Honours include: Honorary Doctorate of Humanities, Shenandoah College and Conservatory, Virginia, 1989; Bread Loaf School of English Commencement Speaker, 1989; Robert Frost Professor of American Literature, 1991. Address: Department of English, University of Vermont, Burlington, VT 05405, USA.

HUDSON Christopher, b. 29 Sept 1946, England. Writer. m. Kirsty McLeod, 10 Mar 1978, 1 s. Education: Scholar, Jesus College, Cambridge. Appointments: Editor, Faber & Faber, 1968; Literary Editor, The Spectator, 1971; The Standard, 1981. Publications: Overlord, 1975; The Final Act, 1980; Insider Out, 1982; The Killing Fields, 1984; Colombo Heat, 1986; Playing in the Sand, 1989. Literary Agent: Gill Coleridge. Address: 64 Westbourne Park Road, London W2, England.

HUDSON Helen. See: LANE Helen.

HUDSON Jeffrey. See:CRICHTON Michael.

HUDSON Liam, b. 20 July 1933, London, England. Visiting Professor, Tavistock and Portman Clinics. m. Bernadine Jacot de Boinod, 2 July 1965, 3 s, 1 d. Education: MA, Exeter College, 1954-57; PhD, Cambridge University, 1957-61. Publications: Contrary Imaginations, 1966; Frames of Mind, 1968; The Ecology of Human Intelligence, 1970; The Cult of the Fact, 1972; Human Beings, 1975; The Nympholepts, 1978; Bodies of Knowledge, 1982; Night Life, 1985; The Way Men Think, 1991; Intimate Relations, 1995. Contributions to: Times Literary Supplement. Membership: British Psychological Society. Address: Balas Copartnership, 34 North Park, Gerrards Cross, Bucks, England.

HUDSON Michael. See: KUBE-MCDOWELL Michael Paul.

HUFANA Alejandrino G, b. 1926, Filipino. Appointments: Research Assistant, 1954-56; English Dept, 1956, Principle Research, Iloko Literature, 1972, Professor, 1975, University of Philippines; Co Founding Editor, Signatures Magazine, 1955, Comment Magazine, 1956-67, Heritage Magazine, 1967-68, University College, 1961-72; Editor, Panorama Magazine, 1959-61; Managing Editor, University of the Philippines Press, 1965-66; Director, 1970, Editor, Pamana Magazine, 1971, Cultural Centre of the Philippines; Associate, University of Philippines, 1979-82; Director, 1982, 85; Editor, College of Arts & Letters, 1985; Literary Editor, Heritage Magazine, 1987-. Publications include: 13 Kalisud, 1955; Man in the Moon, 1956; Sickle Season, 1948-58, 1959; Poro Print, 1955-1960, 1961; Curtain Raisers: First Five Plays, 1964; A Philippine Cultural Miscellany, 1970; The Wife of Lot and Other New Poems, The Unicorn, Salidomay, 1971; Notes on Poetry, 1973; Philippine Writing, 1977; Shining On, 1985; Dumanon, 1994; No Facetious Claim: Notes on Writers and Writing, 1995. Address: c/o Heritage, 20218 Tajauta Avenue, Carson, CA 90746, USA.

HUFF Robert, b. 3 Apr 1924, Evanston, IL, USA. Professor; Poet. 1 s, 2 d. Education: AB, 1949, AM, 1952, Wayne State University. Appointments: Instructor, University of Oregon, Fresno State College, Oregon State University; Poet in Residence, University of Delaware, 1960-64; Associate Professor, Modem Poetry Humanities, Western WA State College, 1964-66; Writer in Residence, University of Arkansas, 1966-67; Professor, Modern Poetry, Western WA University, 1967-. Publications include: Colonel Johnsons Ride, 1959; The Course, 1966; The Ventriloquist, 1977; Shore Guide to Flocking Names, 1985; Numerous Poems Recoded, Books in Progress, Taking Her Sides on Immortality; Beginning in Winter. Contributions to: Numerous Magazines, Journals and Newspapers. Honours include: Robert Huff Manuscript Collections at University of KY, Wayne State University, Carnegie Library, Syracuse University; Student Fellowship, IN University, 1957; Writing Scholarship, 1961; Writing Fellowship, 1963. Memberships include: Northwest Poetry Circuit. Address: Dept of English, Western WA University, Bellingham, WA 98225, USA.

HUGGETT Frank Edward, b. 1924, England. Appointments: Sub Editor, Daily Telegraph, 1951-53; Editor, Look and Listen, 1956-57; Visiting Lecturer, Polytechnic of Central London, 1957-65, Ministry of Defence, 1965-72. Publications include: South of Lisbon, 1960; Farming, 1963; Modern Belgium, 1969; A Short History of Farming, 1970; The Battle for Reform, 1815-1832, A Day in the Life of a Victorian Factory Worker, Factory Life and Work, 1973; The Dutch Today, 1974; A Dictionary of British History 1815-1973, The Land Question and European Society, Life and Work at Sea, Slavery and the Slave Trade, 1975; Goodnight Sweetheart, Carriages at Eight, 1979; Cartoonists at War, 1981; The Dutch Connection, 1982; Teachers, 1986.

HUGGETT Joyce, b. 16 Sept 1937, Exeter, England. Teacher. m. David John Huggett, 16 July 1960, 1 s, 1 d. Appointments: Teacher, Nuffield Priory School, 1960-62; Peripatetic Teacher, Health Centre, Croydon, 1963-65, Cambridge, 1971-73; Director of Pastoral Care and Counselor, St Nicholas Church, 1973-; Regular Broadcaster on TV and Radio. Publications include: Two into One: Relating in Christian Marriage, 1981; Growing into Love; We Believe in Marriage, 1982; Growing into Freedom, 1984; Conflict: Friend or Foe, 1984; Just Good Friends, 1985; The Joy of Listening to God, 1986; Writer of Scripture Notes: Open to God, 1989; The Smile of Love: Scripture Notes for Scripture Union and Bible Reading Fellowship. Contributions to: Magazines, Newspapers. Address: 18 Lenton Road, The Park, Nottingham, NG7 1DU, England.

HUGHES Brenda. See: **COLLOMS Brenda.**

HUGHES Colin Anfield, b. 4 May 1930, Bahamas. Professor of Political Science. m. Gwen Glover, 6 Aug 1955, 1 son. Eduction: BA, 1949, MA, 1950, Columbia; PhD, London School of Economics, 1952. Publications: Readings in Australian Government, 1968; Images and Issues, 1969; Mr Prime Minister, 1976; The Government of Queensland, 1980; Race and Politics in the Bahamas, 1981; Handbook of Australian Government and Politics, 1975-84, 1986. Address: Dept of Government, University of Queensland, St Lucia 4072, Australia.

HUGHES David (John), b. 27 July 1930, England. Eduction: BA, Christ Church, Oxford, 1953. Appointments: Assistant Editor, London Magazine, 1953-54; Editor, Town Magazine, 1960-61; Film Writer, 1961-68; Lived in France, 1970-74; Editor, New Fiction Society, 1975-77, 1981-82; Film Critic, Sunday Times Newspaper, 1982-83. Publications include: A Feeling in the Air, 1957; Sealed with a Loving Kiss, 1959; The Forsehair Sofa, 1961; The Major, The Road to Stockholm and Lapland, 1964; The Cats Tale, 1965; The Seven Ages of England, 1966; Flickoma, The Man Who Invented Tomorrow, 1968; The Rosewater Revolution, 1971; Memories of Dying, 1976; Evergreens, 1977; A Genoese Fancy, 1979; The Imperial German Dinner Service, 1983; The Pork Butcher, 1984; But for Bunter, 1985; The Stories of Ernest Hemingway, 1986. Address: c/o Anthony Sheil Associates, 43 Doughty Street, London WC1N 2LF, England.

HUGHES Glyn, b. 25 May 1935, Author. m. Jane Mackay, 5 Mar 1990, 1 s. Education: College of Art, Manchester, 1952-56; ATD, 1959. Appointments: Teaching, Lancaster & Yorkshire, 1956-72; Art Council Fellow, Bishop Grosseteste College, Lincoln, 1979-81; Southern Arts Writer in Residence, Farnborough, 1982-84; Arts Council Writer in Residence, D H Lawrence Centenary Festival, 1985. Publications include: Novels, Where I Used to play on the Green, 1982; The Hawthorn Goddess, 1984; The Antique Collector, 1990; Authobiography: Fair Prospects, 1976; Verse: Neighbours, 1970; Best of Neighbours, 1979; plays, Mary Hepton's Heaven, 1984; Various Plays for BBC School Broadcasts on tv and Radio. Honours: Welsh Arts Council Poets Prize, 1970; Guardian Fiction Prize, 1982; David Higham Fiction Prize, 1982. Literary Agents: Shiel Land, 43 Doughty Street London; MIC Cheetham, MIC Chestham Agency, London. Address: Mors House, 1 Mill Bank Road, Mill Bank, Sowerby Bridge, West Yorkshire HX6 3DY, England.

HUGHES H Stuart, b. 7 May 1916, New York, USA. Historian. m. Judith Markham, 26 Mar 1964, 2 s, 1 d. Education: BA, Amherst College, 1937; MA, 1938; PhD, 1940, Harvard University. Publications: Consciousness and Society, 1958; History as Art and as Science, 1964; The Obstructed Path, 1968; The Sea Change, 1975; Prisoners of Hope, 1983; Sophisticated Rebels, 1988; Gentleman Rebel, 1990; An Essay for Our Times, 1950; Oswald Spengler, 1952; The US and Italy, 1953; Contemporary Europe, 1961; An Approach to Peace, 1962. Contributions to: Commentary; The American Scholar; New York Review of Books; Times Literary Supplement; American Historical Review; Revista Storica Italiana. Memberships: American Academy of Arts and Sciences; Accademia Nazionale dei Lincei, Rome; American Historical Association. Address: 8531 Avenida de las Ondas, La Jolla, CA 92037, USA.

HUGHES Ian. See: **PATERSON Alistair.**

HUGHES Jon Christopher, b. 30 Jan 1945, Elkhart, IN, USA. Professor. m. Susan Elaine Zavodny, 15 Jan 1968, 1 s, 1 d. Education: BS, 1967, MA, 1972. Appointments: Writing Programme Director, University of Cincinnati; Journalism Programme Coordinator, 1975; President, Radio Repertory Comapny, 1988; Executive Producer, Dimention Radio Thearer, 1988-90; Writing Programme Director, University of Cincinnati, 1991-93. Publications include: The Tanyard Murder, 1982; The Jolly Book, 1984; Period of the Gruesome, 1990; Dismal Man, 1990; Numerous Radio Plays, Screenplays; Script Editor, Bill Monroe: Father of Bluegrass Music, 1993. Contributions to: North Am Union List of Victorian Serials; Am Humour Magazines and Comic Papers; Over 200 Articles to Journals, Newspapers. Honours: Award of Distinction, Am Association of Museums, 1984; OBIE, 1989, 1990; Emmy, 1990; Distinguished Alumnus, 1992. Memberships: Am Association of University Professors; Lafcadio Hearn Society.

HUGHES Matilda. See: **MACLEOD Charlotte.**

HUGHES Monica, b. 3 Nov 1925, Liverpool, England. Writer. m. Glen Hughes, 22 Apr 1957, 2 s, 2 d. Publications: The Keeper of the Isis Light, 1980; Hunter in the Dark, 1982; Ring-Rise, Ring-Set, 1982; Crisis on Conshelf Ten, 1975; Invitation to the Game, 1991; The Crystal Drop, 1992; The Golden Aquarians, 1994. Contributions to: Short Stories in: Take your Knee off my Heart, 1990; Mother's Day, 1992; Owl Summer Fun. Articles: Creating Books for Children; Perception of Society through Children's Literature; Writing Science Fiction and Fantasy; My Search for Somewhere; What is a Child After All?; Behind the Mask. Address: 13816-110A Avenue, Edmonton, BA, Canada, T5M 2M9.

HUGHES Robert (Studley Forrest), b. 28 July 1938, Sydney, Australia. m. 1 son. Education: BA, Sydney University. Career: Freelance Writer; Art Critic; Maker of TV documentaries. Publications include: Books, Essays, Exhibition Catalogues, TV documentaries include: Donald Friend, 1965; The Art of Australia: A Critical Survey, 1966; Heaven & Hell in Western Art, 1968; The Shock of the New, 1980; Art of the Real, 1983; Nothing If Not Critical, 1987; The Culture of Complaint: The Fraying of America, 1993. Address: Time Magazine, Rm 2673, Time-Life Building, Rockefeller Center, New York, NY 10020, USA.

HUGHES Shirley, b. 1927, England. Childrens Fiction Writer, Illustrator. Appointments: Public Lending Right Registrars Advisory Committee, 1984-88; Library & Information Services Council, 1989-92. Publications include: Lucy & Tom Series, 6 vols, 1960-87; The Trouble with Jack, 1970; Sallys Secret, 1973; Its too Frightening for Me, 1977; Moving Molly, 1978; Up and Up, 1979; Charlie Moon and the Big Bonanza Bust Up, 1982; An Evening at Alfies, 1984; The Nursery Collection, 6 vols, 1985-86; Another Helping of Chips, 1986; The Big Alfie and Annie Rose Story Book, 1988; Out and About, 1989; The Big Alfie Out of doors Story Book, 1992. Honours: Kate Greenaway Medal for Dogger, 1977; Eleanor Farjeon Award, 1984. Membership: Society of Authors.

HUGHES Ted, b. 17 Aug 1930, Yorkshire, England. Childrens Fiction,Plays, Screenplays, Poetry, Literature Editor. m. (1)Sylvia Plath, 1956, (2)Carol Orchard, 1970. Education: BA, 1954, Pembroke College, Cambridge. Publications include: Sean, The Fool, The Devil and the Cats, 1971; A Choice of Emily Dickinson's Verse, 1968; A Choice of Shakespeare's Verse, 1971; Selected Poems by Yehuda Amichai, 1971; Selected Poems 1957-67, 1982; In The Little Girls Angel Gaze, 1972; The Iron Man, 1968; The Story of Vasco, 1974; Season Songs, 1976; Cave Birds, 1978; Chaismadon, 1977; Moortown Elegies, 1978; A Solstice, 1978; Orts, 1978; Adam and the Sacred Nine, 1979; Moortown, 1979; Remains of Elmet, 1979; Collected Poems by Sylvia Plath, 1981; Under the North Star, 1981; The Journals of Sylvia Plath, 1985; Flowers and Insects, 1986; Wolfwatching, 1989; The Cat and the Cuckoo, 1991; Rain-Charm for the Duchy, 1992. Honour: OBE, 1977; Signal Award, 1978, 1981; Guardian Children's Fiction Award, 1985. Address: c/o Faber & Faber Limited, 3 Queen Square, London WC1N 3AU, England.

HUHNE Christopher Murray Paul, b. 2 July 1954, London, England. Economist. m. Vasiliki Courmouzis, 19 May 1984, 1 s, 1 d. Education: BA, Oxford University, 1975; University de la Sorbonne, Paris, 1972. Publications: Debt and Danger, 1985, 1987; Real World Economics, 1990; The ECU Report, 1991. Contributions to: New Statesman; Spectator; Political Quarterly; London Review of Books. Honours: Wincott Awards for Financial Journalism, 1981, 1990. Memberships: Royal Economics Society. Literary Agent: Michael Sissons, Peters Fraser & Dunlop. Address: 8 Crescent Grove, London SW4 7AH, England.

HULME Keri, b. 9 Mar 1947, Christchurch, New Zealand. Writer; Fisher; Dreamer. Education: Canterbury University, Christchurch. Appointments: New Zealand State Literary Fund Advisory Committee, 1985; Literature Committee, Arts Council, 1986-89. Publications: The Bone People, 1984; Te Kaihau, The Windeater, 1986; BAIT, 1993; The Silences Between, 1982; Lost Possessions, 1986; Homeplaces, 1989; Strands. Contributions to: Many and Varied. Honours: NZ Writing Nursary, 1983; NZ Book of the Year, 1984; Mobil Pegasus Prize, 1984; Booker McConnell Award, 1985; The Special 1990 Scholarship in Letters. Memberships: Nga Puna Waihanga; NZ PEN. Address: Okarito Private Bag, Hokitika PO, Westland, New Zealand.

HULSE Michael William, b. 12 June 1955, Stoke on Trent, England. Freelance Translator; Critic; Poet. Education: MA, University of St Andrews, 1977. Appointments: English Editor, Benedikt Taschen Verlag, 1988. Publications: Monochrome Bloood, 1980; Dole Queue, 1981; Knowing and Forgetting, 1981; Propaganda, 1985; Translations of German Literature for Catcanet, Penguin, Farrar Straus & Giroux, Anvil Press, Macmillan.Contributions to: About 200 Essays and Reviews. Honours: 1st Prize, Nationl Poetry Competition, 1979; Eric Gregory Award, 1980; 3rd Prize, Tate Gallery Poetry Competition, 1985; 2nd Prize, Times Literary Supplement, Cheltenham Literature Festival Poetry Competition, 1987. Address: c/o Secker & Warburg Limited, 54 Poland Street, London W1V 3DF, England.

HUME A(Lexander) Brit(ton), b. 22 June 1943, WA, USA. Reporter; Author. m. Clare Jacobs Stoner, 10 Feb 1965, 2 s, 1 d. Education: BA, University of VA, 1965. Appointments: Reporter, Hartford Times, 1965-66; Reporter, United Press International, 1967; Evening Sun, 1968; Freelance Reporter, 1969; Investigative Reporter, 1970-72; Editor, More Magazine, 1973-75; Consultant, ABC News Closeup Documentary Series, 1973-79; General Correspondent, 1976-77, Principal Correspondent, US House of Representatives, 1977-80, Chief Senate Correspondent, 1981-, Anchor of World News Tonight, 1985-, Author, Column The Computer Report; Host, Brit Hume. Publications include: Death and the Mines: Rebellion and Murder in the United Mine Workers, 1971; Inside Story, 1974; News closeup including Arson: Fire for hire, 1978; The Killing Ground, Nobodys Children, Battleground Washington: The Politics of Pressure, 1979; St Albans: An Illustrated History of St Albans School, 1981. Contributions to: Articles Periodicals including New York Times Magazine; Harpers; Atlantic Monthly; New Republic. Honour: Fellow, WA Journalism Ctr, 1969. Membership: Radio TV Correspondents Association. Address: 5409 Blackistone Road, Bethesda, MD 20816, USA.

HUME Basil. See: **HUME George Hailburton.**

HUME George Hailburton, (Basil Hume), b. 2 Mar 1923, Newcastle Upon Tyne, England. Education: M, St Benets Hall, 1947; STL, University of Fribourg, 1951; University of Surrey, 1992; Newcastle upon Tyne Polytechnic, 1992. Appointments include: Entered Ordo Sancti Benedicti, 1941; Assistant Priest, Village Church, Teacher, Monasterys Secondary School for Boys, 1950-63; Chairman of Benedictine Ecumenical Commission, 1972-76; President, Bishops Conference of European Episcopal Conferences, 1978-87; Member, Vatican Secretariat for Christian Unity and Council of Synod on the Family; Vice President, Council of Christians and Jews; President, Catholic Institute for International Relations and European Committee of Bishops Conferences, 1979-87; Co Founder, Benedictine Monastery. publications: Searching for God, 1977; In Praise of Benedict, 1981; To BE a Pilgrim: A Spiritual Notebook, 1984; Towards a Civilisation of Love, 1988; Light in the Lord, 1991. Contributions to: British Periodicals. Honours: Honorary Degrees include DD, University of Newcastle Upon Tyne; Honorary Bencher of Inner Temple, 1976; Honorary Freeman of London and Newcastle upon Tyne, 1980. Address: Archbishops House, Ambrosden Avenue, Westminster, London SW1P 1QJ, England.

HUME John Robert, b. 1939, England. Appointments: Lecturer, 1964-82, Ensior Lecturer, University of Strathclyde, 1982-; Chairman, SCottish Rilway Preservation Society, 1966-75; Treasurer, 1968-71, Editor, 1971-79, Scottish Society for Industrial Archaeology; member, Inland Waterways Amenity Advisory Council, 1974; Director, Scottish Industrial Archaeology Survey, 1978-85; Seconded to Historic Scotland as Principal Inspector of Ancient Monuments, 1984-91; Principal Inspector, Historic Buildings, 1991-. Publications include: Industrial History in Pictures: SCotland, 1968; Glasgow as it Was, 3 vols, 1975-76; A Plumbers Pastime, 1975; The Workshop of the British Empire, The Industrial Archaeology of Scotland: The Highlands and the Islands, 1977; Beardmore: History of a Scottish Industrial Giant, 1979; A Bed of Nails, 1983; Shipbuilders to the World: A History of Harland Wolff, Belfast, 1986; Various Guidebooks to Historic Scotland Monuments in Cars. Honour: Andre Simon Prize, 1981; Memberships: Society of Antiquaries: Society of Antiquarie of Scotland. Address: Historic Scotland, 20 Brandon Street, Edinburgh, EH3 5KA, Scotland.

HUMPHREYS Emyr Owen, b. 15 Apr 1919, Clwyd, Wales. Author. m. Elinor Myfanwy, 1946, 3 sons, 1 daughter. Education: University College, Aberystwyth; University College Bangor. Publications include: The Little Kingdom, 1945; The Voice of a Stranger, 1949; A Change of Heart, 1951; Hear and Forgive, 1952; A Mans Estate, 1955; The Italian Wife, 1957; A Toy Epic, 1958; The Gift,

1963; Outside the House of Baal, 1965; Natives, 1968; Ancestor Worship, 1970; National Winner, 1971; Flesh and Blood, 1974; Landscapes, 1976; The Best of Friends, 1978; The Kingdon of Bran, 1979; The Anchor Tree, 1980; Pwyll a Riannon, 1980; Miscellany Two, 1981; The Taliesin Tradition, 1983; Salt of the Earth, 1985; An Absolute Hero, 1986; Open Secrets, 1988; The Triple Net, 1988; Bonds of Attachment, 1990; Outside Time, 1991. Honours: Somerset Maugham Award, 1953; Hawthornden Prize, 1959; Society of Authors Travel Award, 1978; Welsh Arts Council Prize, 1983; Honorary DLitt, University of Wales, 1990 L1; Welsh Book of the Year, 1992; Honorary Professor of English, UCNW Bagnor. Literary Agent: Richard Scott Simon. Address: Llinon, Penyberth, Llanfairpwll, Ynys Môn, Gwynedd LL61 5YT, Wales.

HUMPHRYES Josephine, b. 2 Feb 1945, Charleston, South Carolina, USA. Novelist. m. Thomas A Hutcheson, 30 Nov 1968, 2 s. Education: AB, Duke University, 1967; MA, Yale University, 1968. Publications: Dreams of Sleep, 1984; Rich in Love, 1987; The Firemans Fair, 1991. Contributions to: Occasional Reviews; Travel Articles for NY Times. Honours: PEN, Erners Hemingway Foundation, 1985; Guggenheim Foundation Fellowship, 1985; Lyndhurst Prize, 1986. Literary Agent: Harriet Wasserman. Address: c/o Harriet Wasserman, 137 E 36 Street, New York, NY 10016, USA.

HUMPHRY Derek John, b. 29 Apr 1930, Bath, England. Journalist; Author; Broadcaster. Appointments: Messenger Boy, Yorkshire Post, London, 1945-56; Cub Reporter, Evening World, Bristol, 1946-51; Junior Reporter, Evening News, Manchester, 1951-55; Reporter, Daily Mail, 1955-61; Deputy Editor, The Luton News, 1961-63; Editor, Havering Recorder, 1963-67; Home Affairs Correspondent,The Sunday Times, London, 1967-78; Special Writer, Los Angeles Times, 1978-79; Roving Correspondent in North America, The Sunday Times, London, 1979-81; Editor, Hemlock Quarterly, 1983-92; Editor, Euthanasia Review, 1986-88; Editor, World Right to Die Newsletter, 1992-94. Publications: Because They're Black, 1971; Police Power and Black People, 1972; Passports and Politics, 1974; False Messiah, 1977; The Cricket Conpiracy, 1976; Jean's Way, 1978; Let Me Die Before I Wake, 1982; The Right to Die! Understanding Euthanasia, 1986; Final Exit (bestseller), 1991; Dying with Dignity, 1992; Lawful Exit, 1993. Contributions to: New Statesman; The Independent, London; USA Today; Joint Editor, The Euthanasia Review, New York. Literary Agent: Robert I Ducas, 350 Hudson St, New York, NY 10014, Address: 24829 Norris Lane, Junction City, OR 97448-9559, USA.

HUNNICUTT Benjamin Kline, b. 16 Nov 1943, Releigh, North Carolina, USA. University Professor. m. Francine Marderello, 8 June 1963, 2 s, 1 d. Education: BA, 1967, MA, 1972, PhD, 1976, University of North Carolina. Publications include: Work Without End, 1988; The New Deal: The Salvation of Work and the end of the Shorter Hour Movement, 1988; Monsignor John A Ryan and the Shorter Hours of Labour: A Forgotten Vision of Genuine Progress, 1983. Contributions to: Labour History; The Wall Street Journal. Honours: Old Gold Fellowship, 1979, 80; Historian for the Society of Park and Recreation Educators, 1980-81. Memberships: Low Parks and Recreation Association; National Recretion and Park Association; Society of Parks and Recreation Eductors. Address: 1610 College Street, IA 52240, USA.

HUNT Bruce J, b. 23 June 1956. Historian. m. Elizabeth Hedrick. Education: BA, History, BS, Physics, University of Washington, 1979; PhD, History of Science, Johns Hopkins University, 1984. Publications: The Maxwellians, 1991. Contributions to: Isis; Historical Studies in the Physical Sciences; The British Journal for the History of Science. Honours: Schuman Prize, History of Science Society, 1980; Visiting Fellow, Clare Hall, Cambridge, 1989-90. Memberships: History of Science Society; British Society for the History of Science; Society for the History of Technology; Lone Star History of Science Group. Address: Dept of History, University of Texas, Austin, TX 78712, USA.

HUNT E(verette) Howard, (John Baxter, Gordon Davis, Robert Dietrich, David St John), b. 1918, America. Writer. Appointments: Scriptwriter, Editor, March of Time, 1942-43; War Correspondent, Life Mag, 1943; Screenwriter, 1947-48; Attache, Am Embassy, Paris, 1948-49, Vienna, 1949-50, Mexico City, 1950-53; Political Officer, Far East Command, 1954-56; First Secretary, Am Embassy, 1957-60; Consultant, Dept of Defence, WA, 1960-65, Dept of State, WA, 1965-70; Vice President, Creative Director, Robert R Mullen, 1970-72; Consultant to President Richard M Nixon, 1971-72;

Served Terms in Federal Prison for Watergate Scandal, 1973-74, 1975-77. Publications include: The Hargrave Deception, 1980; The Gaza Intercept, 1981; The Kremlin Conspiracy, 1985; I Cam to Kill, 1953; Washington Payoff, 1975; Counterfeit Kill, 1963; Where Murder Waits, 1965; The Cheat, 1954; The House on Q Street, 1960; Murder on Her Mind, 1960; Angel Eyes, 1961; Curtains for a Lover, 1961; Return from Vorkuta, 1965; The Venus Proble, 1966; One of Our Agents is Missing, 1967; The Coven, 1972; Give Us This Day, 1973; Undercover Memoirs of an American Secret Agent, 1974.

HUNT Fay Ann, (Annie Hedley), b. 18 July 1935, Cornwall, England. Farmer; Teacher; Writer. div, 3 s. Education: Redland College of Education. Publications: Listen Lets Mke Music, 1980; Look at Home before you Look Away, 1983; Creative Activities for the Mentally Handicapped, 1986; Motherin Sunday, 1990. Contributions to: TES; Lancet; Special Education; Cornish Scene; Observer; Correspondent; Western Morning News; Cornish Times. Honours: 1st Prize, Ian S James Award, 1990. Memberships: West Country Writers Association. Literary Agent: Gill Coleridge, Coleridge, White & Taylor. Address: Clift Farmhouse, Anthony, Torpoint, Cornwall, PL11 2PH, England.

HUNT Francesca. See:HOLLAND Isabelle.

HUNT Gill. See: TUBB E(dwin) C(harles).

HUNT Joyce, b. 31 Oct 1927, NY, USA. Writer. m. Irwin Hunt, 25 June 1950, 2 s. Education: BA, Brooklyn College; MA, Hunter College. Publications include: Watching Orangutans, 1983; A First Look at L Leaves, 1972; Fish, 1972; Mammals, 1973; Birds, 1973; Insects, 1974; Frogs and Toads, 1976; Animals without Backbones, 1976; Flowers, 1977; Snakes, Lizards and Other Reptiles, 1977; Animals with Backbones, 1978; The World of Plants, 1978; Monkeys and Apes, 1979; Sharks, 1979; Wahels, 1980; Cats, 1981; Dogs, 1981; Horses, 1981; Dinosaurs, 1982; Spiders, 1983; Seashells, 1983; Rocks, 1984; Bird Nests, 1984; Poisonous Snakes, 1986; Caterpillars, 1987; Seals and Walruses, 1987; Keep Looking, 1989; A First Look at Animals with Horns, 1989. Honours: Outstanding Science Books for Children Award, 1977, 1979. Address: 131 Riverside Drive, New York, NY 10024, USA.

HUNT Morton, b. 20 Feb 1920, PA, USA. Writer. m. (3)Bernice Weinick, 10 Sept 1951. Education: AB, Temple University, 1941. Appointments: Freelance Writer, 1949-. Publications include: The Natural History of Love, 1959; Her Infinate Variety: The American Woman as Lovers, Mate and Tival, 1962; The Affair: A Portrait of Extramarital Love in Contemporary American, 1969; The Mugging, 1972; Sexual Behaviour in the 1970's, 1974; Prime Time: A Guide to the Plesures and Opportunities of the New Middle Age, 1975; The Divorce Experience, 1977; Profiles of Social Research: The Scientific Study of Human Interaction, 1985; The Compassionate Beast: What Science is Discovering About the Humane Side of Humankind, 1990; The Story of Psychology, 1993. Contributions to: About 400 Articles in The New Yorker; NY Times Magazine; Readers Digest. Honours: Am Association for the Advancement of Science Westinghouse Award, 1952; Claude Bernard Award, 1971; am Society of Journalists and Authors, 1983. Literary Agent: Goerges Borchardt Incorporated, USA. Address: 15 Kingstown Avenue, East Hampton, NY 11937, USA.

HUNT Sam, b. 1946, New Zealand. Poet. Publications: Between Islands, 1964; A Fat Flat Blues, 1969; Selected Poems, 1965-69, 1970; A Song About Her, 1970; Postcard of a Cabbage Tree, 1970; Bracken Country, 1971; Letter to Jerusalem, 1971; Bottle Creek Blues, 1971; Bottle Creek, 1972; Beware the Man, 1972; Birth on Bottle Creek, 1972; South into Winter, 1973; Roadsong Paekakariki, 1973; Time to Ride, 1976; Drunkards Garden, 1978; Collected Poems, 1963-80, 1980; Three Poems of Seperation, 1981; Running Scared, 1982; Approaches to Paremata, 1985; Selected Poems, 1987. Address: PO Box 1, Mana, Wellington, New Zealand.

HUNT Tim(othy Arthur), b. 22 Dec 1949, California, USA. College Teacher. m. Susan D Spurlock, 1 s, 1 d. Education: AB cum laude, 1970; MA, 1974; PhD, 1975, Cornell University. Career: Assistant, Associate Professor, English Department, Indiana-Purdue University, Fort Wayne, 1985-87; Academic Dean, Deep Springs College, California, 1987-90; Associate Professor· of English, Coordinator for Humanities, Washington State University, Vancouver, 1990-. Publications include: The Collected Poetry of Robison Jeffers: Volume 1, 1920-28; 1988; Volume II, 1928-38, 1989; Volume III, 1938-62, 1991; Kerouac's Crooked Road: Development of a Fiction,

1981; Various articles and essays, papers and poems. Address 323 NW 74th Street, Vancouver, WA 98665, USA.

HUNTER Alan James Herbert, b. 25 June 1922, Hoveton St John, Norwich, England. Author. m. Adelaide Elizabeth Cecily Cubitt, 6 Mar 1944, 1 d. Education: RAF, 1940-46. Appointments: Crime Reviewer, Eastern Daily Press, 1955-71. Publications: Gently Go Man, 1961; Vivienne: Gently Where She Lay, 1972; The Honfleur Decision, 1980; Gabrielles Way, 1981; The Unhung Man, 1984; Traitors End, 1988; Bomber's Moon, 1994; The Norwich Poems, 1945; Author of 42 Crime Novels. Contributions to: Magazines & Journals. Memberships: Society of Authors; Crime Writers Association; Authors Licensing & Collecting Society. Address: 3 St Laurence Avenue, Brundall, Norwich NR13 5QH, England.

HUNTER Elizabeth. See: DE GUISE Elizabeth (Mary Teresa).

HUNTER Evan. See: LOMBINO Salvatore A.

HUNTER Kristin, b. 1931, USA. Author; University Educator. Career: Copywriter, Lavenson Bureau of Advertising, Philadelphia, Pennsylvania, 1952-59; Copywriter, Wermen and Schorr, Philadelphia, 1962-63; Senior Lecturer in English, Univesity of Pennsylvania, Philadelphia, 1972-. Publications: God Bless the Child, 1964; The Double Edge, play, 1965; The Landlord, 1966; The Soul Brothers and Sister Lou, 1968; Boss Cat, 1971; The Pool Table War, 1972; Uncle Daniel and the Racoon, 1972; Guests in the Promised Land: Stories, 1973; The Survivors, 1975; The Lakestown Rebellion, 1978; Lou in the Limelight, 1981. Literary Agent: Jane Dystel Literary Management, 1 Union Square West, New York, NY 10003, USA.

HUNTINGTON Samuel Philips, b. 1927, America. Military/Defence, Politics/Government. Career: Eaton Professor of Science of Government, Harvard University, Cambridge, 1982- (joined faculty 1950; Dillon Professor of International Affairs, 1981-82); Director for International Affairs, Harvard University, 1978-89; Director, John M Olin Institute for Stategic Studies, 1989-; Vice President, 1984-85 and President, 1986-87, American Policitcal Science Association; Assistant Director, 1958-59, Associate Director, 1959-62, Institute of War and Peace Studies and Associate Professor of Government, 1959-62, Columbia University, New York City; Member of Council, American Political Science Assocaition, 1969-71; member, Presidential Task Force on International Development, 1969-70; Member, Commission on US/Latin American Relations, 1974-75; Member, Commission on Integrated Long Term Strategy, 1986-88; Co-ordinator of Security Planning, National Security Council, 1977-78; Co-editor, Foreign Policy Journal, 1970-77. Publications: The Soldier and the State: The Theory and Politics of Civil-Military Relations, 1957; The Common Defence Strategic Programs in National Politics, 1961; (co-editor) Changing Patterns of Military Politics, 1962; (co-author) Political Power, USA/USSR, 1964; Political Order in Changing Societies, 1968; (co-editor) Authoritarian Politics in Modem Society: The Dynamics of Established One-Party Systems, 1970; (co-author) The Crisis of Democracy, 1975; (with J M Nelson) No Easy Choice: Political Participation in Developing Countries, 1976; American Politics: The Promise of Disharmony, 1981; (editor) The Strategic Imperative: New Policies for American Security, 1982; (co-author) Living with Nuclear Weapons, 1983; (co-editor) Global Dilemmas, 1985; (co-editor) Reorganizing America's Defence, 1985; (co-editor) Understanding Political Development, 1987; The Third Wave: Democratization in The Late Twentieth Century, 1991. Address: 1737 Cambridge Street, Cambridge, MA 02138, USA.

HUOT Cécile, b. 2 May 1919, Boischatel, Quebec, Canada. Teacher. Education: BA, Laval University, 1958; Licence, Laval University, 1965; B Pedogogie, Licence, Montreal University, 1959-61; Doctorat, Lettres, Toulouse, France, 1973. Publications: Une Symphonie inachevée, Wilfrid Pelletier's Mémoirs, 1972; Entretiens avec Omer Létourneau, 1979; More than 70 items for The Encyclopédie de la Musique au Canaca Fides, 1983, new edition, 1993; Dictionnaire des Genres, 1983, new edition, 1991; Simon Violon m'etait conté, 1988. Contributions to: Les Cahiers Canadiens de la Musique. Memberships: L'Union des Ecrivains Québécois; Conseil International d'Etudes Francophones. Address: 5025 ave Notre Dame de Grace. Montreal, Quebec H4A 1K2, Canada.

HURD Douglas, (Richard) Rt Hon, b. 8 Mar 1930. Politician: Writer. m. (1) Tatiana Elizabeth Michelle. 1960. 3 s. (2) Judy. 1982. 1 s, 1 d. Education: Eton; Trinity College, Cambridge. Appointments include: H M Diplomatic Service, 1952-66; Joined Conservative Research Department, 1966, Head of Foreign Affairs Section, 1968, Private Secretary to Leader of Opposition, 1968-70, Political Secretary to Prime Minister, 1970-74; Member of Parliament, Mid Oxon, 1974083, for Witney, 1983-; Minister of State FCO, 1979-83; Secretary of State for Northern Ireland, 1984-85; Visiting Fellow, Nuffield College, Oxford, 1978-86. Publications: The Arrow War, 1967; Truth Game, 1972; Vote to Kill, 1975; An End to Promises, 1979; Send Him Victorious, 1968; The Smile on the Face of the Tiger, 1969, 1982; Scotch on the Rocks, 1971; War Without Frontiers, 1982; Palace of Enchantments, 1985. Honours: CBE, 1974; PC, 1982. Address: House of Commons, London SW1, England.

HURD Michael John, b. 19 Dec 1928, Gloucester, England. Composer; Author. Education: BA, 1953, MA, 1957, Pembroke College, Oxford. Publications include: Immortal Hour, 1962; The Ordeal of Ivor Gurney, 1978; The Oxford Junior Companion to Music, 1979; The Orchestra, 1981; Sailor's Songs and Shanties, 1965; Soldier's Songs and Marches, 1966; The Composer, 1968; Vaughan Williams, 1970; The Orchestra, 1981; Vincent Novello - and Company, 1981; Rutland Boughton and the Glastonbury Festivals, 1993. Contributions to: The New Grove Dictionary of Music & Musicians; The New Oxford Companion to Music; The Oxford Illustrated Encyclopedia; The Oxford Children's Encyclopedia; The Athlone History of Music in Britain. Address: 4 Church Street, West Liss, Hants, GU33 6JX.

HUS Andre George Paul, b. 14 Oct 1955, Paris, France. Chef; Historiographer. Education: Archeological Works of Gallo Roman Escavations, Saint Malo, France, 1971-72; BEP, Hotel Management, High School, Le Touquet, France, 1974; The National Archives of France, Paris, 1978-82. Publications: Louis XVII La Véritable Clé L'énigme, 1982; La Petite Histoire De La Gastronomie En Nouvelle, France 1992. Contributions: Gault et Millaut, 1984; Le Courier Français, 1991-92; Cahiers Louis XVII, Paris, France, 1992; Société Des Gensde Lettres de France, 1992; Union des écrivains, Quebec, Canada. Memberships: Foundation Napoléon, Paris, France; Circle Historique Louis XVII; Société des Cuisiniers de France, Paris, 1974; Société des Chefs Cuisiniers et Patessiers du Quebec, 1987. Address: 2038 rue Lavallee 2, Longueuil, Quebec J4J 4E5, Canada.

HUSTON Nancy Louise, b. 16 Sept 1953, Alberta, Canada. Writer. m. Tzvetan Todorov, 18 May 1981, 1 s, 1 d. Education: BA, Sarah Lawrence College, 1975; Diploma, The Ecole Des Hautes Etudes, 1977. Literary Appointments: Writer in Residence, American University, Paris, 1989; Facilitator, South African Writers Workshop, France, 1994. Publications include: La Virevolte, 1994; Cantique Des Plaines, 1993; Les Variations Goldberg, 1991; Journal De La Creation, 1990; Jover Aopapa Et A L'Amant; Dire & Interdire; Lettres Parisiennes; A L'Amour Comme A La Guerre; Trois Fois Septembre. Honours include: Prix, Binet Sangle de l'Acaderue, 1980; Prix Contrepoint, 1981; Prix du Gouverneur, 1993. Literary Agent: Mary Kling, La Nouvelle Agence, 7 Rue Corneille 75006, Paris.

HUTCHEON Linda Ann Marie, b. 24 Aug 1947, Toronto, Canada. m. Michael Alexander Hutcheon, 30 May 1970. Education: BA, Modern Language and Literature, 1969; PhD, Comparative Literature, 1975, University of Toronto, MA, Romance Studies, Cornell University, 1971. Career: Assistant, Associate and full Professor of English, McMaster, 1976-88; Professor of English and Comparative Literature, University of Toronto, 1988-. Publications: Books: Narcisisstic Narrative, 1980, 1984; Formalism and the Freudian Aesthetic, 1984; A Theory of Parody, 1985; A Poetics of Postmodernism, 1988; The Canadian Postmodern 1988; The Politics of Postmodernisms, 1989; Splitting Images, 1991 Editor: Other Solitudes, 1990; Double-Talking, 1992; Likely Stories, 1992; A Postmodern Reader, 1993. Contributions to: Articles in Diacritics; Textual Practice; Cultural Critique and other journals. Address: University of Toronto, Ontario, Canada, M5S 1A1.

HUTCHINS Hazel Jean, b. 9 Aug 1952, Canada. Writer. m. James E Hutchins, 13 Jan 1973, 2 s, 1 d. Publications: The Three and Many Wishes of Jason Reid, 1983; Anastasia, Morningstar, 1984; Leanna Builds a Genie Trap, 1986; Ben's Snow Song, 1987; Casey Webber and the Great, 1988; Norman's Snowball, 1989; Nicholas at the Library, 1990; Katie's Babbling Brother, 1991; A Cat of Artimus Pride, 1991; And You Can Be the Cat, 1992; The Best of Arlie Zack, 1993; The Catfish Palace, 1993; Within a Painted Past, 1994. Honours: Parenting Magazine Reading Magic Awards List, 1988; White Raven Collection of Interantional Youth Library, 1987; Alberta Writers Guild

Award for Children's Literature, 1992. Address: c/o Annick Press, 15 Patricia Avenue, Ontario, Canada, M2M 1H9.

HUTCHINS Pat, b. 18 June 1942, Yorkshire, England. Writer; Illustrator. m. 20 Aug 1966, 2 s. Education: Darlington School of Art, 1958-61; Leeds College of Art, 1961-63; National Diploma in Design. Publications include: Rosies Walk, 1968; Titch, 1971; Goodnight Owl, 1972; The Wind Blew, 1974; The Very Worst Monster, 1985; Tom and Sam, 1968; The Surprise Party, 1969; Clocks and More Clocks, 1970; Changes, Changes, 1971; The House That Sailed Away, 1975; The Tale of Thomas Mead, 1980; King Henrys Palace, 1983; One Hunter, 1982; Youll Soon Grow into them Titch, 1983; The Curse of the Egyptian Mummy, 1983; The Doorbell Rang, 1986; Where's the Baby?, 1988; Which Witch is Which?, 1989; Rats, 1989; What Game Shall We Play, 1990; Tidy Titch, 1991; Silly Billy, 1992; My Best Friend, 1992. Honour: Kate Greenaway Medal, 1975. Address: 75 Flask Walk, London NW3 1ET, England.

HUNTINSON Ron, b. Near Lisbon, Northern Ireland. Education: Schools in Coventry. Appointments: Worked at Various Jobs including Fish Gutter, Carpet Salesman, Scene Shifter and Bookseller; Clerk, Ministry of Defence and Ministry of Labour; Social Worker, Claims Investigator; Resident Writer, Royal Shakespeare Company, 1978-79. Publications include: Plays, The Dillen, 1983; Rat in the Skull, 1984; London Methuen, 1984; Mary, After the Queen, 1985; Curse of the Baskervilles, 1987; Novels, Connie, 1985; Radio Plays include, Murphy Unchained, 1978; The Winkler, 1979; Bull Week, 1980; The Marksman, 1987. Honours: George Devine Award, 1978; John Whiting Award, 1984. Literary Agent: Judy Daish Associates, London. Address: c/o Judy Daish Associates, Eastbourne Mews, London, W2 6LQ, England.

HUTTON John Harwood, b. 21 Nov 1928, Manchester, England. Retired Teacher. m. Gladys May Lloyd, 31 July 1965. Education: BA, 1949, teaching Diploma, 1950, MA, 1952, University College of North Wales. Publications: 29 Herriott Street, 1979; Accidental Crimes, 1983. Honour: Gold Dagger Award, 1983. Memberships: Crime Writers Association; The Society of Authors. Address: Gwylfa, Old Holyhead Road, Berwyn, Llangollen, Wales.

HUTTON Ronald Edmund, b. 19 Dec 1953, Ootacamund, India. Historian. m. Lisa Radulovic, 5 Aug 1988. Education: BA, Cantab, 1976; MA, 1980; DPhil, 1980. Publications: The Royalist War Effort, 1981; The Restoration, 1985; Charles II, 1989; The British Republic, 1990; The Pagen Religions of the Ancient British Isles, 1991; The Rise and Fall of Merry England, 1994. Contributions to: Essays in Seven Journals. Honours: FRHistS, 1981; Benjamin Franklin Prize, 1993; FSA, 1994. Memberships: Royal Historical Society; Folklore Society. Address: 13 Woodland Road, Bristol, BS8 1TB, England.

HUXLEY Anthony Julian, b. 2 Dec 1920, Oxford, England. Writer; Editor; Phiotographer. Eduction: MA, Cambridge University. Publications include: Flowers of the Mediterranean, 1965; Mountain Flowers, 1967, 1986; House Plants, Cacti and Succulents, 1972; Plant and Planet, 1974; Flowers of Grece and the Aegean, 1977; An Illustrated History of Gardening, 1978; Success with House Plants, 1979; Penguin Encycleopaedia of Gardening, 1981; The Macmillan World Guide to House Plants, 1983; Green Inheritance, 1985; The Painted Garden, 1988; Royal Horticultural Societys Dictionary of Gardening, 1988. Contributions to: Country Life; The Garden. Honour: Award, Victoria Medal of Honour. Memberships: Horticultural Club; Royal Horticultural Society. Address: 50 Villiers Avenue, Surbiton, Surrey KT5 8BD, England.

HUXLEY Elspeth Josceline, b. 23 July 1907, London. Writer. m. Gervas Huxley, 12 Dec 1931, 1 s. Education: Reading University, 1925-27; Cornell University, 1927-28. Appointments: Assistant Press Officer, Empire Marketing Board, 1929-32; News Dept, BBC, 1941-43. Publications include: The Flame Trees of Thika, 1959; The Mottled Lizard, 1961; Out in the Midday Sun, 1985; White Mans Country, 1935; The African Poison Murders, 1938; Murder on Safari, 1937; Nine Faces of Kenya, 1990; Peter Scott, Painter and Naturalist, 1993. Contributions to: Many Articles to New York Times Magazine; Daily Telegraph; Encounter; Times and Tide. Honour: CBE, 1962. Membership: Society of Authors. Literary Agent: Heather Jeeves, 9 Dryden Plance, Edinburgh, Scotland, EH9 1RP. Address: Green End, Oaksey, Malmesbury, Wilts SW16 9TL, England.

HUYLER Jean Wiley, b. 30 Mar 1935, Seattle, Washington, USA. Communications Management Consultant; Author-Writer; Editor;

Photojournalist. divorced, 1 s, 1 d. Education includes: Business Administration, University of Washington, 1953-55; BA, Maryhurst College, 1979; MA, Pacific Lutheran University, 1979; D Litt, Fairfax University, 1989. Literary Appointments: Various newspaper and magazine editorships, 1963-75; Editor, books for Education System Managers, Washington School Directors Association, 1977-81; Designer and Editor, For The Record, A History of Tacoma Public Schools, Tacoma School District 1985-. Publications: Demystifying the Media, 1980, 1981; Crisis Communications, 1983; Campaign Savvy - School Support, 2nd Edition, 1981; Communications is a People Process, 1981; How to Get Competent Communications Help, 1983; Sharing A Vision for Gifted Education with Business and Education Leaders, 1988; Lifespan Learning on Centerstage of the Future, 1988; Learning to Learn - New Techniques for Corporate Education, 1989. Address: 5407 64th St CT NW, Gig Harbor, WA 98335-7449, USA.

HWANG David Henry, b. 11 Aug 1957, Los Angeles, CA, USA. Playwright; Director. m. Ophelia Y M Chong, 1985. Education: AB, Stanford University, 1979; Yale University, School of Drama, 1980-81. Appointments: Director, Plays, A Song for a Nisel Fisherman, 1980; The Dream of Kitamura, 1982. Publications include: Family Devotions, 1981; Sound and Beauty, 1983; The House of Sleeping Beauties in Broken Promises, 1987; The Sound of A Voice, Dramatists Play Service, 1984; Broken Promises, 1983; Rich Relations, 1986; As the Crow Flies, 1986. Honours: Drama Logue Award, 1980-86; Obie Award, 1981; Rockefeller Fellowship, 1983; Guggenheim Fellowship, 1984; National Endowment for the Arts Fellowship, 1985. Literary Agent: Paul Yamamoto and William Craver, Writers and Artists Agency. Address: c/o Pual Yamamoto and William Craver, Writers and Artists agency, 70 West 36th Street, New York, NY 10018, USA.

HYKISCH Anton, b. 23 Feb 1932, Ban Stiavnica, Slovakia. Economist Manager; Diplomat; Journalist. m. Eva Suchonova, 19 Oct 1957, 1 s, 1 d. Education: Economical University, Bratislava, 1956. Appointments: Managing Director, Mlada Leta Publishers, 199-92; Ambassador of Slovakia to Canada. Publications include: A Step in the Unknown, 1959; The Square in the Town Mahring, 1965; The Time of Masters, 1977; Lets Love the Queen, 1984; Defending Mysteries, 1990; I've Met You, 1963; Canada in Not a Fun, 1968; Atomic Summers, 1988; My Little Chippy, 1989. Contributions to: Slovak and Czech Literary Magazines and Weeklies. Honours: Award for Fiction, 1988; Childrens Book Award, 1989. Memberships: Union of Slovak Centre; Committee for Education and Culture; Pan Europa Union; Christian Social Union. Literary Agent: Lita Slovak Literary Agency, Address: Lachova 18, 851 03 Bratislava, Slovakia.

HYLAND Paul, b. 15 Sept 1947, Poole, England. Author. m. Maggie Ware, 8 Dec 1990. Education: BSc, Bristol University, 1968. Publications: Purbeck: the Ingrained Island, 1978; Poems of Z, 1982; Wight: Biography of an Island, 1984; The Stubborn Forest, 1984; The Black Heart: A Voyage into Central Africa, 1988; Getting into Poetry, 1992; Indian Balm: Travels in The Southern Subcontinent, 1994; Kicking Sawdust, 1995; Poetry, Drama, Features for Radio. Contributions to: Poems in Many Magazines. Honours: Alice Hunt Bartlett Award, 1985; Eric Gregory Award, 1976. Memberships: Poetry Society; Society of Authors; Orchard Theatre Company; Company of Poets; Dorset Natural History & Archaeological Society. Literary Agent: David Higham Associates Limited. Address: 2 Mays Leary Cottages, Filleigh, Barnstple, Devon EX32 0TJ.

HYMAN Harold Melvin, b. 1924, America. History. Career: William P Hobby Professor of History, Rice University, Houston, Texas, 1968-; (Chairman of Department, 1968-70. Member of Board of Editors, Reviews in American History, 1964-; Ulysses S Grant Association, 1968-; and the American Journal of Legal History, 1970-; Assistant Professor of History, Earlham College, Richmond, Indiana, 1952-55; Visiting Professor, 1955-56; and Professor of History, 1957-63, University of California, Los Angeles; Associate Professor, Arizona State University, Tempe, 1956-67; Member, Board of Editors, Journal of American History, 1970-74. Publications include: (ed) Heard, Round the World: The Impact of the Civil War and Reconstruction, 1968; (ed with F B Hyman) The Circuit Court Opinions of Salmon Portland Chase, 1972; (ed) Sidney George Fisher: The Trial of the Consitution, 1972; (ed with H K Trefousse) The Political History of the United States During the Great Rebellion 1860-1865; The Political History of the United States of America During the Period of Reconstruction, Apr 15 1865-July 15 1870, and the Handbook of Politics, 6 vols, 1972-72; A More Perfect Union: The Impact of the Civil War and Reconstruction on the Constitution, 1973; Crisis and Confidence 1860-1870, 1975; (with

N Wiecek) Equal Justice under Law Constitutuional Development, 1935-1875, 1982; American Singularity, 1987; Oleander Odyssey: The Kempners of Galveston, 1870-1980, 1990. Address: Department of History, Rice University, PO Box 1892, Houston, TX 77251, USA.

I

ICHIKAWA Satomi, b. 15 Jan 1949, Gifu, Japan. Author. Appointments: Author, Illustrator, Childrens Books, 1974-. Publications include: A Childs Book of Seasons, 1975; Friends, Sophie and Nicky Go to Market, 1976; From Mornto Midnight, 1977; Keep Running, Allenl, Sophie and Nicky and the Four Seasons, 1978; Suzette et Nicolas and the Sunijudi Circus, 1979; Lets Play, Children Through Four Seasons, 1981; Angels Descending from the Sky, The Wonderful Rainy Week: A Book of Indoor Games, Merry Christmas, Children at Christmastime Around the World, 1983; Here a Little Child iStand, 1985; Noras Castle, 1986; Happy Birthday, 1988. Honour: Sepcial Mention for Prix Critici in Erba, Bologna Childrens Book Fair, 1978.

ICHIMURA Shinichi, b. 30 Mar 1925, Kyoto, Japan. Professor. m. Yukiko Kondo, 2 May 1956, 2 s, 1 d. Education: BA, Kyoto University, 1949; PhD, MIT, USA, 1953; DEcon, Osaka University, 1961. Publications: The Str of Japanese Economy, 1957; The Development of Southeast Asia, 1980; Challenge of Asian Developing Countries, 1988; Econometric Models of Asian LINK, 1988; Japanese Management in Asia, 1990; Economietric Models of Asian Pacific Countries, 1993; The Role of Japan in Asia, 1993. Contributions to: Regional Integration Issues in Asia. Honours: Fellow, Econometrics Society; President, East Asian Economic Association; Dr of Economics. Memberships: East Asian Economic Association; Econometric Society; Association of Asian Politics & Economics. Address: 2-40 Minami Kasugaoka, 4 Ibaraki, Osaka 567, Japan.

IDDINGS Kathleen, b. west Milton, OH, USA. Writer; Publisher, div, 1 s, 3 d. Education: BS, Miami University, 1968; UCSD, Napa College, Mira costa College, San Diego City College. Appointments: Editor, Publisher, Originator of San Diego Poets Press, 1981; La Jolla Poets Press, 1985; Poetry Consultant, GATE Programme; Poetry Editor, San Diego Writers Monthly. Publications: The Way of Things, 1984; Selected and New Poems, 1980-90. Contributions to: McGraw Hill College Text, Literature; Over 250 in Anthologies and Quarterlies. Honours: Nationl Endowment for the Arts, COMBO Fellowship, 1986; 2 Carnegie and 2 PEN Writers Grants, 1988-92; Djerassi Artists Colony Residency, 1992. Memberships: Poetry Society of America; PeN; AWP; Academy of AM Poets; San Diego Independent Scholars. Address: PO Box 8638, La Jolla, CA 92038, USA.

IGGERS Georg Gerson, b. 7 Dec 1926, Hamburg, Germany. Historian. m. Wilma Abeles, 23 Dec 1948, 3 s. Education includes: BA, University of Richmond, 1944; AM, 1945; PhD, 1951, University of Chicago; Graduate Student, New School For Social Research, 1945-46; Instructor, University of Akron, 1948-50; Associate Professor, Philander Smith College, 1950-56; Visiting Professor, University of Arkansas, 1956-57 & 1964; Associate Professor, Dillard University, 1957-63; Visiting Associate Professor Tulane University, 1957-60, 1962-63; Associate Professor, Roosevelt University, 1963-1965; Professor State University of New York at Buffalo, 1965-; Since 1978, Distinguished Professor; Visiting Professor University of Rochester, 1970-71; Visiting School, Technische Hochschule Darmstadt, 1971; Visiting Professor, University of Leipzig, 1992; Visiting Scholar, Forschungsschwerpunkt zeithistorische Studien, Potsdam, Germany, 1993. Publications: German Conception of History, 1968; New Directions in European Historiography, 1975; Cult of Authority, Political Philosophy of the Saint Simonians, 1958; Social History of Politics, (Editor), 1985; Leopold von Ranke, The Shaping of History, 1990; Aufklarung und Geschichte, (co-editor), 1986; International Handbook of Historical Studies, (co-editor), 1979; Leopold von Ranke, The Theory and Practice of History (co-editor), 1973; Leopold von Ranke and the Shaping of the Historical Discipline (co-editor), 1990; Marxist Historiography in Transition: Historical Writings in East Germany in the 1980's (editor), 1991; Geschichtswissenschaft 20, Jahrhundert, 1993. Contributions to History and Theory; American Historical Review; Journal of Modern History; Geschichte und Gesellschaft; Historische Zeitschrift. Address: Department of History, Park Hall, SUNY/Buffalo, Buffalo, NY 14260, USA.

IGIGUERE Diane Liliane, b. 6 Dec 1937, Montreal, Canada. Education: College Marie de France, 1941; Conservatory of Dramatic Arts, 1954-56. Publications: Le Temps Des Jeux, 1961; L'eau Est Profonde, 1965; Dans Les Ailes du vent, 1976; L'Abandon, 1993. Honours: 1st Prize in Modern Drama, Conservatory of Dramatic Arts,

1956; Pri du Cercle du Livre de France for Innocence, a novel, 1961; Guggenheim Fellowship Award, New York, 1969; France Quebec Prize for Dans Les Ailesz de vent, 1977. Memberships: Writers' Union, Quebec; Association of French Speaking Writers at Home and Overseas. Address: 60 rue William Paul 304, Ile des Soeurs, Quebec H3E 1M6, Canada.

IHIMAERA Witi, b. 7 Feb 1944, Gisborne, New Zealand. Author. Education: University of Auckland, 1963-66; Victoria University, 1968-72. Publications: Pounamu, Pounamy, 1972; Tangi, 1973; Whanau, 1974; Maori, 1975; The New Net Goes Fishing, 1977; Into the World of Light, 1980; The Matriarch, 1986; The Whale Rider, 1987; Dear Miss Mansfield, 1989. Address: c/o Ministry of Foreign Affairs, Private Bag, Wellington 1, New Zealand.

IMPEY Rose(mary June), b. 7 June 1947, Northwich, Cheshire, England. 2 d. Education: Teachers Certificate, 1970. Publications include: Whos A Clever Girl, Then, 1985; The Baked Bean Queen, 1986; Desperate for a Dog, 1988; The Flat Man, 1988; The Girls Gang, 1986; Letter to Father Christmas, 1988; Joe's Cafe, 1990; First Class, 1992; Trouble with the Tucker Twins, 1992; Revenge of the Rabbit, 1990; Instant Sisters, 1989; Orchard Book of Fairytales, 1992; Animal Crackers, 1993. Honours: 100 Most Borrowed Library Books award; Shortlisted, Smarties Childrens Books Prize. Literary Agent: Caroline Sheldon. Address: 6 The Homestead, Mountsorrel, Loughborough, Leicestershire, LE12 7HS, England.

INCHBALD Peter Bingham, b. 1919, London, England. 2 s. Education: MA, Oxon; Diploma, Royal Academy School of Painting. Publications: Tondo for Short, 1981; The Sweet Short Gras, 1982; Short Break in Venice, 1983; Or the Bambino Dies, 1985. Memberships: Society of Authors; Crime Writers Association; Cheltenham Writers Circle. Literary Agent: Curtis Brown.

INDICK Benjamin Philip, b. 11 Aug 1923, New Jersey, USA. Pharmacist; Writer. m. 23 Aug 1953, 1 s, 1 d. Education: BS, Biology, Rutgers University, New Brunswick, NJ, 1947; BS, Pharmacy, Ohio State University, Columbus, Ohio, 1951; The New School, New York, 1960-61, no degree. Publications include: Plays: He, She and the End of the World, 1982; Incident at Cross Plains, 1976; The Children of King, 1989; Books: A Gentleman from Providence Pens a Letter, 1975; The Drama of Ray Bradbury, 1976; Ray Bradbury: Dramatist, 1989; Non Fiction: Exploring Fantasy Worlds, 1985; Discovering Modern Horror Fiction, 1, 1985, II, 1988; Kingdon of Fear, 1986; Discovering H P Lovecraft, 1987; Reign of Fear, 1988; Penguin Encyclopaedia of Horror and the Supernatural, 1986; George Alec Effinger: From Entropy to Budayeen, 1993. Contributions to: Eldritch Tales; Etchings and Odysseys; Twilight Zone Magazine; Lone Star Fictioneer; Castle Rock; The Stephen King Newsletter; The Scream Factory; Reign of Fear, 1988; Das Stephen King Buch (German), 1989. Honours: First Prizes, Playwright Contests, 1962, 1964, 1965. Memberships: The Dramatists Guild; Horror Writers of America; Rho Chi; Phi Lambada Epsilon. Address: 428 Sagamore Ave, Teaneck, NJ 07666-2626, USA.

ING Dean, b. 1931, America. Freelance Writer; Engineer. Appointments: Engineer, Aerojet General, Sacramento, CA, 1957-62, Lockheed, San Jose, 1962, 1965-70; Assistant Professor, Missouri State University, 1974-77. Publications: Soft Targets, 1979; Anasazi, 1980; Systemic Shock, 1981; High Tension, 1982; Pulling Through, 1983; The Lagrangists by Mack Reynolds, 1983; Single Combat, 1983; Home Sweet Home 2010 AD, 1984; Eternity, 1984; The Other Time, 1984; Wild Country, 1985; Trojan Orbit, 1985.

INGALLS Jeremy, b. 2 Apr 1911. Poet; Retired University Professor Emerita; Translator. Education: BA, MA; LittD, Tufts University; University of Chicago. Career: Assistant Professor, English Literature, Western College, 1941-43; Professor, Head, English and American Literature, Director, Asian Studies, Rockford College, 1950's; Rockefeller Foundation Lecturer, American Poetry; Ford Foundation Fellowship, Asian Studies; Fulbright Professor, American Liteature, Japan, 1957, 1958. Publications: A Book of Legends, 1941; The Metaphysical Sword, 1941; Tahl, 1945; The Galilean Way, 1953; The Woman from the Island, 1958; These Islands Also, 1959; Nakagawa's Tenno Yugao, 1975; The Malice of Empire, 1970; This Stubborn Quantum, 1983; Summer Liturgy, 1985; The Epic Tradition and Related Essays, 1989. Contributions to: Poetry Now; Michigan Quarterly Review; Christianity and Crisis; Religion in Life; The Classical Journal; Yearbook of General and Comparative Literature; Literature East and West; East-West Review; Poetry, New Republic; Saturday Review;

Accent; American Mercury; American Prefaces; Atlantic Monthly; Beloit Poetry Journal; Chicago Review; Common Sense; Maryland Quarterly; Studia Mystica. Address: 6269 East Rosewood, Tucson, AZ 85711, USA.

INGALLS Rachel, b. 13 May 1940, Boston, MA, USA. Education: BA, Radcliffe College. Publications: Mediterranean Cruise, 1974; Mrs Caliban, 1983; I See a Long Journey, 1985; The Pearlkillers, 1986; Binstead's Safari, 1988; The End of the Tragedy, 1989; Something to Write Home About, 1990; Be My Guest, 1992. Honours: First Novel Award, Author's Club, UK, 1971; Fellow, American Academy & Institute of Arts & Letters, 1991.

INGHAM Daniel. See: **LAMBOT Isobel Mary.**

INGHAM Kenneth, b. 9 Aug 1921, Emeritus Professor. m. Elizabeth Mary Southall, 18 June 1949, 1 s, 1 d. Education: BA, 1941, MA, 1947, DPhil, 1950, University of Oxford. Publications include: A History of East Africa, 1962; The Making of Modern Uganda, 1958; Reformers in India, 1956; The Kingdom of Toro in Uganda, 1975; Jan Christian Smuts, 1986; Politics in Modern Africa, 1990; Obote: A Political Biography, 1994. Contributions to: Britannica Book of Year. Honour: Military Cross, 1946; OBE, 1961. Memberships: Royal Historical Society; Royal African Society; British Institute in Eastern Africa. Address: The Woodlands, 94 West Town Lane, Bristol, BS4 5DZ, England.

INGLE Stephen James, b. 6 Nov 1940, Ripon, Yorkshire, England. University Professor. m. Margaret Anne Farmer, 5 Aug 1964, 2 s, 1 d. Education: BA, 1962, DipEd, 1963, MA, 1965, University of Sheffield; PhD, Victoria University, NZ, 1967. Publications: Socialist thought in Imaginative Literature, 1979; Parliament and Health Policy, 1981; British Patry System, 1989; George Orwell: A Political Life, 1993. Contributions to: Many in Fields of Politics and Literature. Honours: Commonwealth Scholar, 1964-67; Erasmus Scholar, 1989; Visiting Research Fellow, Victoria University & Wellington, NZ, 1993. Memberships: Political Studies Association. Address: Dept of Political Studies, University of Stirling, Scotland, FK9 4LA.

INGLIS Brian, b. 31 July 1916, Dublin, Ireland. Journalist. m. Ruth Langdon, div, 1 s, 1 d. Education: BA, Oxon; PhD, Dublin. Publications include: The Story of Ireland, 1956; Revolution in Medicine, 1958; Abdication, 1966; Poverty and the Industrial Revolution, 1971; Roger Casement, 1973; The Forbidden Game, 1975; Natural and Supernatural, 1977; Natural Medicine, 1978; The Alternative Health Guide, 1983; Science and Parascience, 1984; The Hidden Power, 1986; The Unkown Guest, 1987; The Power of Dreams, 1987; Trance, 1989; Downstart, 1989. Contributions to: The Lancet; World Medicine; The Guardian; The Times; Spectator; Punch; Encounter; Vogue. Memberships: Royal Society of Literature. Literary Agent: Curtis Brown. Address: Garden flat, 23 Lambolle Road, London NW3 4HS, England.

INGRAMS Richard Reid, (Philip Reid), b. 11 Aug 1937, London, England. Journalist. m. 1962, 2 s, 1 d. Education: University College, Oxford. Appointments: Private Eye, 1962, Editor, 1963-86, Chairman, 1974-; TV Critic, The Spectator, 1976-84; Editor, The Oldie, 1993-94. Publications include: Private Eye on London, 1962; Private Eye's Romantic England, 1963; Mrs Wilson Diary, 1966; The Tale of Driver Grope, 1968; The Life and Times of Private Eye, Editor, 1971; Harris in Wonderland, 1973; Cobbets's Country Book, 1974; The Best of Private Eye, 1974; God's Apology, 1977; Goldenballs, 1979; The Other Hald, 1981; Piper's Places, 1983; Down the Hatch, 1985; Just the One, 1986; John Stewart Collis: A Memoir, 1986; The Best of Dear Bill, 1986; Mud in Your Eye, 1987; You Might as Well Be Dead, 1988; Number 10, 1989; On and On, 1990. Address: c/o Private Eye, 6 Carlisle Street, London W1, England.

INNAURATO Albert, b. 2 June 1947, PA, USA. Playwright; Director. Education: BA, Temple University; BFA, CA Institute of the Arts, 1972; MFA, Yale University School of Drama, 1975. Appointments: Playwright in Residence, Playwrights Horizons, NY, 1983; Adjunct Professor, Columbia University, Princeton University, 1987; Director of Plays. Publications include: Plays include, The Transfiguration of Benno Blimpie, 1973; The Idiots Karamazov, 1974; Earth Worms; Gemini; Ulysses in Traction; Passione. Honours: Guggenheim Grant, 1975; Rockefeller Grant, 1977; Obie Award, 1977; National Endowment for the Arts Grant, 1986. Literary Agent: George

Lane, William Morris Agency, NY. Address: 325 22nd Street, New York, NY 10011, USA.

INNES Brian, b. 4 May 1928, Croydon, Surrey, England. Writer; Publisher. m. (1) Felicity McNair Wilson, 5 Oct 1956, (2) Eunice Lynch, 2 Apr 1971, 3 s. Education: Whitgift School, Croydon, 1938-46; BSc, Kings College, London, 1946-49. Appointments include: Assistant Editor, Chemical Age, 1953-55; Associate Editor, The British Printer, 1955-60; Art Director, Hamlyn Group, 1960-62; Director, Temperance Seven Limited, 1961-; Director, Innes Promotions Limited; Proprietor, Brian Innes Agency, 1964-66; Proprietor, Immediate Books, 1966-70; FOT Library, 1970-; Creative Director, Deputy Chairman, Orbis Publishing Limited, 1970-86; Editorial Director, Mirror Publishing, 1986-88. Publications include: Book of Pirates, 1966; Book of Spies, 1967; Book of Revolutions, 1967; Book of Outlaws, 1968; Flight, 1970; Saga of the Railways, 1972; Horoscopes, 1976; The Tarot, 1977; Book of Change, 1979; The Red Baron Lives, 1981; Red Red Baron, 1983; The Havana Cigar, 1983; Crooks and Conmen, 1993. Contributions to: Man Myth & Magic; Take Off; Real Life Crimes; Fire Power; The Story of Scotland; Discover Scotland; Made Numerous Recordings, Films, Radio & TV Broadcasts; Many Photographs Published; Honours: Royal Variety Command Performance, 1961. Memberships: Chartered Society of Designers; Royal Society of Arts; Institute of Printing; Crime Writers Association. Address: Les Forges de Montgaillard, 11330 Mouthoumet, France.

INNES Hammond. See: **HAMMOND INNES Ralph.**

INOUE Kenji, b. 15 Feb 1929, Toyko, Japan. Professor. m. Midori Yoshiura, 10 May 1956, 1 s. Education: University of Toyko, 1951; Graduate, School of University of Toyko, 1953; Oberlin College, 1956-60. Publications include: Winner Take Nothing, 1982; Works of Frank Norris, 1984; A Month of Sundays, 1988; Nyumon Dokushno Note, 1991; Rabbit Redux, 1993. Contributions to: Eigo Seinen; Kaoen; Dokushojin; Tosho Shinbun; Teinbeck Quarterly. Honours: Recognition Award, International John Steinbeck Society, 1991. Memberships: Am Literature Society of Japan; Am Studies Association of Japan Nihon Bungeika Kyokai; international John Steinbeck Society. Address: 1-3-8 Sekimae, Mushashino-Shi, Toyko 180, Japan.

INSINGEL Mark, b. 3 May 1935, Lier, Antwerp. Belgium. Author. 1 s. Education: MA, Koninklijk Vlaams Muziek Conservatorium, 1959; French Literature, Sorbonne Paris, 1960-62. Publications: Reflections, 1970; A Course of Time, 1977; When a Lady, 1982; That is to Say, 1986; My Territory, 1987; Perpetuum Mobile, 1969; Modellen, 1970; Posters, 1984. Contributions to: Major Literary Journals and Magazines in Holland, Belgium. Memberships: PEN; Maatschappij voor Nederlandse Letterkunde te Leiden. Address: Rucaplein 205, B 2610 Antwerpen, Belgium.

IOANNIDES I D, b. 25 Nov 1931, Kavala, Greece. Professor. m. Rita Kalodemou, 30 Aug 1970, 1 daughter. Education: University of Athens, 1963; American University, 1959; University of Thessaloniki, 1961; Temple University, 1965. Appointments: Teacher, Elementary School, 1952; Professor, Teachers College, 1965. Publications include: The White Horse, 1968; Secret Journeys, 1970; Radiography, 1971; The Golden Bow, 1975; Educational Psychology, 1977; A Ship in the Shop Window, 1979; The Three Boys, 1980; A Girl with Two Mothers, 1984; Without a Stem, 1984; A Story in a Blue Pencil, 1985; The Whip & The Umbrella, 1985; Zaza: Elephant Dreams, 1986. Contributions to: Nea Estia; Nea Poria; Erevn; Skpti Lli; The Athenian; To Rhodi. Honours: 2 Award, Womens Literary Association; Award, Greek Literary Association of Athens. Memberships: Greek Literary Association of Thessaliniki; Circle of Greek Childrens Book Writers; Greek Educational Society. Literary Agent: Kedros, A S E Kastaniotis. Address: 2 Arist, Stani Street, Kavala 65403, Greece.

IOANNOU Noris, b. 22 Feb 1947, Larnaca, Cyprus. Historian; Critic; Writer. Education: BSc (Hons), 1969, DipEd, 1971, University of Adelaide; PhD, Visual Arts, Archaeology, Flinders University, South Australia, 1989. Publications: Ceramics in South Australia 1836-1986, 1986; The Culture Brokers, 1989; Craft in Society (editor), 1992; Australian Studio Glass, 1995; The Barossa Folk: The Story of Germanic furniture and other traditions in Australia, 1995; Contributing author: The Australian Dictionary of Biography, 1988; The Barossa. A Vision Realised. Contributions to: Regularly to: Oz Arts; Object; Art and Australia; Country Style; Ceramics Art and Perception. Honours: Australian Heritage Award, 1987; Writing Fellowship, Australian Council, 1989. Memberships: Executive, Association of Professional

Historians; Australiana Society; Australian Society of Authors. Address: 28 Osmond Terrace, Norwood, Adelaide, South Australia 5067, Australia.

IOANNOU Susan, b. 4 Oct 1944, Toronto, Canada. Writer; Editor. m. Lazaros Ioannou, 28 Aug 1967, 1 s, 1 d. Education: BA, 1966; MA, 1967, University of Toronto. Career: Managing Editor, Coiffure du Canada, 1979-80; Associate Editor, Cross-Canada Writers' Magazine, 1980-89; Poetry Editor, Arts Scarborough Newsletter, 1980-85; Poetry Instructor, Toronto Board of Education, 1982-94; Poetry Instructor, University of Toronto, 1989-90. Publications: Spare Words, 1984; Motherpoems, 1985; The Crafted Poem, 1985; Familiar Faces, Private Griefs, 1986; Ten Ways To Tighten Your Prose, 1988; Writing Reader-Friendly Poems, 1989; Clarity Between Clouds, 1991; Read-Aloud Poems: For Students from Elementary through Senior High School, 1993; Polly's Punctuation Primer, 1994. Address: PO Box 456, Station O, Toronto, Ontario, Canada, M4A 2P1.

IPSEN David Carl, b. 15 Feb 1921, Schenectady, New York, USA. Frelance Writer. m. Heather Marian Zoccola, 28 Aug 1949, 2 s. Education: BS, Engineering, University of Michigan, 1942; PhD, Mechanical Engineering, University of California, 1953. Publications: Units, Dimensions, and Dimensionless Numbers, 1960; The Riddle of the Stegosaurus, 1969; Rattlesnakes and Scientists, 1970; What Does a Bee See? 1971; The Elusive Zebra, 1971; Eye of the Whirlwind: The Story of John Scopes, 1973; Isaac Newton: Reluctant Genius, 1985; Archimedes: Greatest Scientist of the Ancient World, 1988. Memberships: The Authors Guild. Address: 655 Vistamont Ave, Berkeley, CA 94708, USA.

IRBY Kenneth, b. 18 Nov 1936, Bowie, Texas, USA. Writer; Teacher. Education: BA, Univerity of Kansas; MA, 1960, PhD, Studies, 1962-63, Harvard University; MLS, University of California, 1968. Publications: The Roadrunner Poem, 1964; Kansas-New Mexico, 1965; Movements/Sequences,1965; The Flower of Having Passed Through Paradise in a Dream, 1968; Relation,1970; T Max Douglas, 1971; Archipelago, 1976; Catalpa, 1977; Orexis, 1981; Riding the Dog, 1982; A Set, 1983; Call Steps, 1992. Contributions to: Anthologies and magazines including: Chicago Review; Paris Review; Poetry; Poetry Review; Parnassus; Conjunctions (contributing editor). Address: N-311 Regency Pl, Lawrence, KS 66049, USA.

IRELAND David, b. 24 Aug 1927, Lakemba, NSW, Australia. Novelist. Education: State Schools, NSW. Publications: The Chantic Bird, 1968; The Unknown Industrial Prisoner, 1971; The Flesheaters, 1972; Burn, 1974; The Glass Canoe, 1976; A Woman of the Future, 1979; City of Women, 1981; Archimedes and the Eagle, 1984; Bloodfather, 1987; Short Story The Wild Colonial Boy, 1979; Play, Image in the Clay, 1962. Honours: Adelaide Advertiser Award, 1966; The Age Book of Year Award, 1980; Member, Order of Australia, 1981. Address: Curtis Brown Pty Limited, 27 Union Street, Paddington, NSW 2021, Australia.

IRELAND Kevin Mark, b. 18 July 1933, Auckland, New Zealand. Writer. m. Phoebe Caroline Dalwood, 2 s. Appointments: Writer in Residence, Canterbury University, 1986; Sargeson Fellow, 1987, Literary Fellow, 1989, Auckland University. Publications include: Poetry, Face to Face, 1964; Educating the Body, 1967; A Letter From Amsterdam, 1972; A Grammar of Dreams, 1975; Literary Cartoons, 1978; The Dangers of Art, 1980; Practice Night in the Drill Hall, 1984; The Year of the Comet, 1986; Selected Poems, 1987; Tiberius at the Beehive, 1990. Honour: New Zealand National Book Award, 1979. Membership: PEN. Address: 1 Anne Street, Devonport, Auckland 9, New Zealand.

IRVING Clifford, (John Luckless), b. 1930, USA. Author; Screen Playwright. Publications: On A Darkling Plain, 1956; The Losers, 1957; The Valley, 1962; The 38th Floor, 1965; Spy, 1969; The Battle of Jerusalem, 1970; Fake, 1970; Global Village Idiot, 1973; Project Octavio, 1978; The Death Freak, 1979; The Hoax, 1981; Tom Mix and Pancho Villa, 1982; The Sleeping Spy, 1983; The Angel of Zin, 1984; Daddys Girl, 1988; Trial, 1990; Final Argument, 1993. Literary Agent: Frank Cooper. Address: c/o Frank Cooper, 10100 Santa Monica Bldg, Los Angeles, CA 90067, USA.

IRVING John Winslow, b. 2 Mar 1942, New Hampshire, USA. Novelist. m. (1) Shyla Leary, 1964, div, 1981, 2 sons, (2) Janet Turnbull, 1987, 1 son. Education: BA, University of New Hampshire; MFA, University of Iowa, 1967. Publications: Setting Free the Bears,

1969; The Water-Method Man, 1972; The 158 Pound Marriage, 1974; The World According to Garp, 1978; The Hotel New Hampshire, 1981; The Cider House Rules, 1985; A Prayer for Owen Meany, 1989; A Son of the Circus, 1994. Contributions to: New York Times Book Review; The New Yorker; Rolling Stone; Esquire; Playboy. Honours: O'Henry Prize, Best Short Stories, 1981; Pushcart Prize, Best of the Small Presses, 1978; The American Book Award, 1979. Membership: Executive Board, PEN American Centre. Literary Agent: Janet Turnbull, The Turnbull Agency, USA. Address: c/o The Turnbull Agency, PO Box 757, Dorset, VT 05251, USA.

ISAACS Alan, (Alec Valentine), b. 14 Jan 1925, London, England. Writer; Lexicographer. m. Alison Coster, 1 s, 3 d. Education: St Pauls School, 1938-42; Imperial College, 1942-50. Publications include: Penguin Dictionary of Science, 1964; Introducing Science, 1965; Survival of God in the Scientific Age, 1967; Macmillan Encylopedia, 1981; Collins English Dictionary, 1978; Longman Dictionary of Physics, 1975; Brewer's Twenthieth Century Phrase and Fable, 1991; Sex and Sexuality, A Thematic Dictionary of Quotations, 1993. Contributions to: Nature; New Scientist. Address: 74 West Street, Harrow on the Hill, HA1 3ER, England.

ISAACS Susan, b. 7 Dec 1943, Novelist; Screenwriter. m. 11 Aug 1968, 1 s, 1 d. Education: Queens College, NY. Publications include: Compromising Positions, 1978; Close Relations, 1980; Almost Paradise, 1984; Shining Through, 1988; Magic Hour, 1991; Film Scripts, Compromising Positions, 1985; Hello Again, 1987. Contributions to: Book Reviews to NY Times; Washington Post; Newsday; Detroit News; Essays to NY Times Art & Leisure; Am Film. Memberships: National Book Critics Circle; PEN; Poets and Writers; Authors Guild; Mystery Writers of Am; International Crime Writers Association. Literary Agent: Owen Laster, William Morris Agency. Address: c/o Harper Collins, 10 East 53rd Street, New York, NY 10022, USA.

ISHIGURO Kazuo, b. 8 Nov 1954, Nagasaki, Japan. Writer; Resettlement Worker. Education: BA, University of Kent, 1978; MA, University of East Anglia. Appointments: Grouse Beater the Queen Mother, Balmoral, Scotland, 1973; Community Worker, Glasgow, 1976; Residential Social Worker, London, 1970-. Publications include: A Pale View of Hills, 1982; An Artist of the Floating World, 1986; The Remains of the Day, 1989; The Summer After the War Appeared in Granta, 1980; Family Supper Appeared in Quarto and has Also been Published in Firebird and in the Pengiun Collection of Modern Short Stories; A Profile of Arthur J Mason, 1985; The Gourmet, 1987. Honours: Winifred Holtby Prize; Whitbread Book of Year Award; Booker Prie, 1989; Honorary Doctor of Letters, 1990; Fellow, Royal Society of Literature, 1989; Fellow, Royal Society of Arts, 1990. Address: c/o Faber & Faber Limited, 3 Queen Square, London, WC1N 3AU, England.

ISLER Ursula, b. 26 Mar 1923, Zürich. Writer; Doctor; Critic. Education: Gymnasium and University of Zürich. Publications: Nadine - eine Reise Artemis Verlag Zürich, 1967; Landschaft mit Regenbogen Classen Verlag, 1975; Madame Schweizer Artemis Verlag, 1982; Die Ruinen von Zürich pendo Verlag, 1985; Frauen aus Zürich NZZ Buchverlag, 1991; Der Künstler und sein Fälscher pendo Verlag, 1992. Contributions to: Staff, Neue Zürcher Zeitung, 1950-. Honours: Numerous literary awards, including: Schweiz Schillerstiftung, Honorary Gifts Stadt u Kanton Zürich. Literary Agent: Pendo Verlag, Wolfbachstr 9, 8032 Zürich, Switzerland. Address: Homweg 14, 8700 Küsnacht, Switzerland.

ITALIANO Joseph, b. 21 Mar 1957, Ringwood, Victoria, Australia. Graphic Designer; Retailer; Writer. m. 29 Apr 1984, 1 son, 1 daughter. Education: Diploma of Art (Graphic Arts), 1979. Publications: Super Squadron, 1983; TOME, 1985; Super Science, 1986. Contributions to: TACC; Disney Adventures (Australian edition); Multiveres. Membership: Australian Writers Guild. Address: PO Box 1278, Windsor, Victoria 3181, Australia.

IWASE Tsuneko, b. 26 Jan 1940, Toyko, Japan. University Professor. Education: BA, 1966, Ma, 1967, Western Michigan University; Certified General Travel Service Supervisor, 1986. Publications: English for the Hospitality Industry, 1987; How to Road Materials for the Travel Business, 1990; English for Tour Operators Tomorrow, 1989; An English Dictionary of Travel Business, 1990; Enjoyment of Classroom Reading, 1977. Contributions to: Journal of Transportation World. Memberships: International Steinbeck Society;

Japan AMerican Literary Society; Japan English Literary Society. Address: 14-9 Schome Suginami-Ku, Toyko 166, Japan.

IYAYI Festus, b. 1947, Nigeria. Novelist. Education: PhD, University of Bradford, Yorkshire, 1980. Appointments: Lecturer, University of Benin. Publications: Violence, 1979; The Contract, 1982; Heroes, 1986. Honours: Association of Nigerian Authors Prize, 1987; Commonwealth Writers Prize, 1988. Address: Dept of Business Administration, University of Benin, PMB 1145, Ugbowo Campus, Benin City, Nigeria.

J

J J. See: **JUNOR John Donald Brown, Sir.**

JACCOTTET Philippe, b. 30 June 1925, Moudon, Switzerland. Poet. Education: Graduated University of Lausanne, 1946. Publications include: Requiem, i947; L'Effraie et autres poésies, 1953; L'ignorant: poèmes 1952-56; Airs: poèmes 1961-64; Leçons, 1969; Poésie 1946-67; Chants d'en bas, 1974; Breathings, 1974; Pensées sous les nuages, 1983; Selected poems, 1987; Cahier de verdure, 1990; Libretto, 1990; Also: Through the Orchard, 1975, 1978; Des Histoires de passage: prose 1948-78: Autres Journées, 1987; Translator of works by Robert Musil, Thomas Mann, Leopardi, Homer and Holderlin. Honours include: Larbaud Prize, 1978. Address: c/o Editions Gallimard, 5 rue Sebastien-Bottin, 75007 Paris, France.

JACK Ian, (Robert James), b. 1923, England. Appointments: Lecturer, Fellow, Brasenose College, 1950-61; Visiting Professor, University of Alexandria, 1960; de Carle Lecturer, University of Otago, 1964; Warton Lecturer, British Academy, 1967; Visiting Professor, University of Chicago, 1968-69, University of CA, 1968-69, University of BC, 1975, University of VA, 1980-81, Tsuda College, 1981; Fellow, 1961-, Librarian, 1965-75, Pembroke College; Lecturer, 1961-73, Reader, 1973-76, Professor, 1976-, Cambridge University. Publications include: Augustan Satire, 1952; Keats and the Mirror of Art, 1967; Brownings Major Poetry, 1973; E Brontes Wuthering Heights, 1976; Oxford English Text Edition of Brownings Poetical Works, 5 vols. Address: Highfiel House, High Street, Fen Ditton, Cambs CB5 8ST, England.

JACKMAN Brian, b. 25 Apr 1935, Epsom, Surrey, England. Journalist. m. 14 Feb 1964, 1 d. Education: Grammar School. Appointment: Staff, Sunday Times, 1970-. Publications: The Marsh Lions, 1982; The Countryside in Winter, 1986; We Learned to Ski, 1974; Dorset Coast Path, 1977; My Serengeti Years, 1987. Contributions to: Country Living; Country Life; BBC Wildlife; Script Consultant; Survival; Anglia TV. Honours: TTG Travel Writer of Year, 1982; Wildscreen 1982 Award. Memberships: Royal Geographical Society; Fauna and Flora Preservation Society. Literary Agent: Curtis Brown. Address: Way Cottage, Powerstock, Nr Bridport, Dorset DT6 3TF, England.

JACKMAN Stuart, (Brooke), b. 1922, England. Appointments: Congregational Minister, Barnstaple Devon, 1948-52, Pretoria, 1952-55, Caterham, Surrey, 1955-61, Auckland, 1961-65, Upminster, Essex, 1965-67, Oxford, Surrey, 1969-; Editor, Council for World Mission, 1967-71, Oxted, Surrey, 1969-81, Melbourne, Cambs, 1981-87. Publications include: Portrait in Two Colours, 1948; But They Wont Lie Down; Three Plays, The Numbered Days, 1954; Angels Unawares, 1956; One Finger for God, 1957; The Waters of Dinyanti, 1959; The Daybreak Boys, 1961; The Desiable Property, The Davidson Affair, 1966; The Golden Orphans, 1968; Guns covered with Flowers, 1973; Slingshot, 1975; The Burning Men, 1976; Operation Catcher, 1980; A Game of Soldiers, The Davidson File, 1981. Address: c/o Curtis Brown, 162-168 Regent Street, London W1R 5Tb, England.

JACKONT Amnon, b. 3 Oct 1948, Israel. Insurance Underwriter; Broker; Analyst; Editor. m. Varda Rasiel Jackont, 30 Sep 1990, 1 s. Education: Hebrew University of Jerusalem; Israel Insurance Academy; Bar Ilan University. Literary Appointments: Editor, Keter Publishing House, Jerusalem. Publications: Borrowed Time, 1982; The Rainy Day Man, 1987; The Last of The Wise Lovers, 1991; Honey Trap, 1994. Contributions to: Magazines and Journals including Iton 77, Ha'ir, Kol Israel, Yediot Aharonot. Memberships: Israel Authors Association; Israel's Chamber of Insurance Brokers. Address: 20 Manne Street, Tel Aviv 64363, Israel.

JACKOWSKA Nicki, b. 6 Aug 1942, Brighton, Sussex, England. Writer; Tutor, 1 d. Education: BA, 1977, MA, 1978, University of Sussex. Appointments: Freelance Writer; Writer in Residence, Tutor to Numerous Workshops, Weekend and Residential Courses Throughout Britain; Founder, Tutor, The Brigton Writing School; Writer in Residence, Brighton Festival, 1987, 1988, 1989; Readings, Forums, TV & Radio Appearances. Publications include: Doctor Marbles and Marianne, 1982; The Road to Orc, 1985; The Islanders, 1987; The House that Manda Built, 1981; Earthwalks, 1982; Letters to Superman,

1984; Gates to the City, 1985; News from the Brighton Front, 1993. Contributions to: Poetry and Fiction; Ambit; Resurgence; Poetry Review; Outposts; Bananas; Poetry Wales; New Statesman; Tribune; Writing Women; Poetry Durham; Stand; the Rialto. Honours: Winner, Stroud Festival Poetry Competition, 1972; Continental Bursary South East Arts, 1978; C Day Lewis Fellowship, 1982; Arts Council Writers Fellowship, 1984-85; Prizewinner Stand International Short Story Competition, 1986; Arts Council Writer's Busary, 1994. Memberships: The Poetry Society. Literary Agent: Judy Martin, 138 Buckingham Palace Road, London. Address: 98 Ewart Street, Brighton, BN2 2UQ, England.

JACKS Oliver. See: **GANDLEY Kenneth Royce.**

JACKSON Alan, b. 6 Sept 1938, Liverpool, Lancashire, England. Poet. m. Margaret Dickson, 1963, 2 s. Education: Edinburgh University, 1956-59, 1964-65. Appointments include: Founding Director, Kevin Press, Edinburgh; Director, Live Readings, Scotland, 1967-. Publications: Under Water Wedding, 1961; Sixpenny Poems, 1962; Well Ye Ken Noo, 1963; All Fall Down, 1965; The Worstest Beast, 1967; Penguin Modern Poets, 1968; The Grim Wayfarer, 1969; Idiots are Freelance, 1973; Heart of the Sun, 1986; Salutations: Collected Poems, 1960-89, 1990. Honours include: Scottish Arts Council Bursaries. Address: c/o Polygon, 22 George Square, Edinburgh EH8 9LF, England.

JACKSON E F. See: **TUBB E(dwin) C(harles).**

JACKSON Everatt. See: **MUGGESON Margaret Elizabeth.**

JACKSON Gulda. See: **JACKSON-LAUFER Gulda Myrl Miller.**

JACKSON Keith. See: **KELLY Tim.**

JACKSON Kenneth T(erry), b. 1939, USA. Professor of History. Appointments: Assistant Professor of History, 1968-71, Director of Urban Studies, 1970-77, Associate Professor, 1971-76, Professor of History, 1976-, Barzun Professor of History and Social Sciences, 1990-, Chairman, Department of History, 1994-, Columbia University, New York City; General Editor, Columbia History of Urban Life series, 1980-; Chairman, Bradley Commission on History in Schools, 1987-90; Chairman, National Council for History Education, 1990-92; Vice President, Society of American Historians Incorporated, 1991-; President, Urban History Association, 1994. Publications: The Ku Klux Klan in the City 1915-1930, 1967; American Vistas, 2 volumes (edited with L Dinnerstein), 1971, 7th Edition, 1987; 1995; Cities in American History (edited with S K Schultz), 1972; Atlas of American History, 1978; Crabgrass Frontier: The Suburbanization of the United States, 1985; Silent Cities: The Evolution of the American Cemetery, 1989. Honours: Bancroft Prize, 1986; Francis Parkman Prize, 1986; Mark Van Doren Prize, 1989. Address: Department of History, Columbia University, New York, NY 10027, USA.

JACKSON MacDonald Pairman, b. 13 Oct 1938, Auckland, New Zealand. University Professor. m. Nicole Philippa Lovett, 2 Sept 1964, 1 s, 2 d. Education: MA, University of New Zealand, 1960; BLitt, Oxford, 1964. Appointments: Lecturer, University of Auckland, 1964; Professor, 1989-. Publications include: Studies in Attribution: Middleton and Shakespeare, 1979; The Revenger's Tragedy, 1983; The Oxford Book of New Zealing Writing Since 1945, 1983; The Selected Plays of John Marston, 1986. Contributions to: Chapters in Cambridge Companion to Shakespeare Studies, 1986; The Oxford History of New Zealand Literature in English, 1991; Academic & Literary Journals. Honours: Folger Shakespeare Library Fellowship, 1989; Huntingdon Library Fellowship, 1993. Memberships: International Shakespeare Association. Address: 21 Te Kowhai Pl, Remuera, Auckland 5, New Zealand.

JACKSON Malcolm, See: **CLARK Douglas.**

JACKSON Michael (Derek), b. 1940, Nelson, New Zealand. Lecturer; Poet. Education: MA, University of Auckland; PhD, Cambridge University. Appointments: Senior Lecturer, Massey University, Palmerston North. Publications: Latitudes of Exile: Poems, 1965-75, 1976; Wall, 1980; Going On, 1985; Rainshadow, 1987; Duty Free; Selected Poems, 1965-88, 1989; Novels, Barawa and the Birds Fly in the Sky, 1986; Rainshadow, 1987. Honours include: New Zealand Book Award, 1981; Katherine Mansfield Writing Fellowship, 1982.

JACKSON Richard Paul, b. 17 Nov 1946, Lawrence, MA, USA. Writer; College Professor; Editor. m. Margaret McCarthy, 28 Jun 1970, 1 d. Education: BA, Merrimack College, 1969; MA, Middlebury College, 1972; PhD, Yale University, 1976. Literary Appointments: Journal Editor, UT-Chattanooga Faculty; Journal Editor, Mala Revija. Publications: Part of The Story, 1983; Acts of Mind, 1983; Worlds Apart, 1987; Dismantling Time In Contemporary Poetry, 1989; Alive All Day, 1993. Contributions to: Georgia Review; Antioch Review; North American Review; New England Review. Honours: NEH Fellowship, 1980; NEA Fellowship, 1985; Fulbright Exchange Fellowship, 1986 and 1987; Agee Prize, 1989; CSU Poetry Award, 1992. Memberships: Sarajevo Committee of Slovene; PEN; AWP. Address: 3413 Alta Vista Drive, Chattanooga, TN 37411, USA.

JACKSON Robert Louis, b. 10 Nov 1923, New York City, New York, USA. B E Bensinger Professor, Languages and Literature. m. Elizabeth Mann Gillette, 18 July 1951, 2 daughters. Education: BA, Cornell University, 1944; MA, 1949, Certificate, Russian Institute, 1949, Columbia University; PhD, University of California, Berkeley, 1956. Appointments: Instructor, 1954, Assistant Professor, 1958, Professor, Russian Literature, 1967, B E Bensinger Professor, Slavic Languages and Literatures, 1991, Yale University. Publications: Dostoevsky's Underground Man in Russian Literature, 1958; Dostoevsky's Quest for Form: Study of his Philosophy of Art, 1966; The Art of Dostoevsky, 1981; Dialogues with Dostoevsky: The Overwhelming Questions, 1993; Editor: Chekhov: Collected Critical Essays, 1967; Crime and Punishment, Collected Critical Essays, 1974; Dostoevsky: Collected Critical Essays, 1984; Reading Chekhov's Text, 1993. Contributions to: Yale Review; Yale French Studies; Russian Literature; Slavica Hierosolymitana; Comparative Literature; Slavic Review; Slavic and East European Journal; Scando-Slavica; Richerche Slavistiche; Sewanee Review; Dostoevsky Studies; Voprosy Literatury. Address: Box 3, Hall of Graduate Studies, Yale University, New Haven, CT 06520, USA.

JACKSON William Godfrey Fothergill, b. 28 Aug 1917, Lancashire, England. Retired General, British Army. m. Joan Mary Buesden, 7 Sept 1946, 1 s, 1 d. Education: MA, Kings College, Cambridge; Staff College, Camberley; Imperial Defence College. Publications include: British Official History of the Mediterranean and Middle East Campaigs, 1940-45, Vol VI, 1986-88; Attack in the West, 1953; Seven Roads to Moscow, 1957; Batle for Italy, 1967; Battle for Rome, 1968; North African Campaigns, 1975; Overlord: Normandy, 1944, 1978; Rock of the Gibraltarians, 1986; Withdrawal From Empire, 1986; The Alternative Third World War, 1987; Britains Defence Dilemmas, 1990; The Chiefs, 1992; The Pomp of Yesterday, 1994; As Ninevah and Tyre, 1995. Honours: GBE, 1975; KCB, 1971; OBE, 1958; MC, 1940; Bar to MC, 1944; Kings Medal, 1937; Rusi Gold Medals, 1953, 1964. Address: West Stowell, Marlborough, Wilts, SN8 4JU.

JACKSON William Keith, b. 5 Sept 1928, Colchester, Essex, England. University Emeritus Professor, 3 s. Education: BA, University of Nottingham; PhD, University of Otago. Publications include: NZ Politics in Action, 1962; New Zealand, 1969; The NZ Legislative Council, 1972; NZ Politics of Change, 1973; Beyond NZ, 1980; The Dilemma of Parliament, 1987; Fight for Life: NZ, Britain & The EEC, 1971. Contributions to: Various Popular and Academic Journals, Radio & TV Current Affairs Commentaries. Honours: Mobil Award, 1979; Henry Chapman Fellow, 1963; Canterbury Fellowship, 1986. Memberships: Editorial Advisory Boards; Journal of Commonwealth & Comparative Studies; Political Science; Politics; Electoral Studies; NZ Journalism Review. Address: 92A Hinau Street, Christchurch, New Zealand.

JACKSON-LAUFER Guida Myrl Miller (Guida Jackson), b. Clarendon, Texas, USA. Author; University Lecturer; Editor. m. (1) Prentice Lamar Jackson, 3 sons, 1 daughter, 1954, (2) William Hervey Laufer, 1986. Education: BA, Texas Tech University, 1954; MA, California State University, 1986; PhD, Greenwich University International Institute of Advanced Studies, 1989. Literary Appointments: Managing Editor, Touchstone Literary Journal, 1976-; Lecturer in Writing, 1986-. Publications: Passing Through, 1979; The Lamentable Affair of the Vicar's Wife, 1981; The Three Ingredients (co-author), 1981; New Growth: Contemporary Fiction by Texas Writers (contributor), 1988; Heart to Heart, 1988; Women Who Ruled, 1990; African Women Write (compiler), 1990; Virginia Diaspora, 1992; Encyclopaedia of Traditional Epic, 1994; Legacy of the Texas Plains, 1994; Texas Short Fiction (contributor), 1994. Contributions to: University of North Texas Press New Texas, 1991, 1992; Texas

Country; Thema; Town and Country; Conjunto; North American Mentor. Address: c/o Touchstone, PO Box 8308, Spring, TX 77387-8308, USA.

JACOB Anthony Dillingham, (Piers Anthony), b. 1934, Author. Publications include: Chthon, 1967; Om, 1971; Ox, 1976; The Ring, 1968; The ESP Worm, 1970; Rings of Ice, 1974; Martial Arts Adventure Series, 1974; Mistress of Death, 1974; Bamboo Bloodbath, 1974; Hasan, 1977; Cluster, 1977; Chaining the Lady, 1978; Viscous Circle, 1982; The Source of Mgic, 1979; Castle Roogna, 1979; Centaur Aisle, 1982; Ogre Orge, 1982; Crewel Lye, 1985; Battle Circle, 1978; Var The Stick, 1973; The Pretender, 1979; God of Tarot, 1979; Vision of Tarot, 1980; Faith of Tarot, 1980; The Apprentice Adept, 1982; Juxtaposition, 1982; Bearing an Hourglass, 1984; With a Tangled Skein, 1985; Weilding a Red Sword, 1986; Bio of a Space Tyrant Quintology, Refugee, 1983; Mecenary, 1984; Polition, 1985; Executive, 1985; statesman, 1986; Anthology, 1985; Ghost, 1986; Shade of the Tree, 1986. Address: 7140 E Entwood Court, Inverness, FL 32650, USA.

JACOB John, b. 27 Aug 1950, Chicago, IL, USA. 1 s, 1 d. Education: AB, University of MI, 1972; MA, 1973, PhD, 1989, University of IL. Appointments: Instructor, 1974-79, 1984-, Northwestern University; Chief Writer, IL Legislative Investigating Commission, 1979-82; Development Director, Community Advancement Programs, 1973-77; Lecturer, Roosevelt University, 1975-; Assistant Professor, North Central College, 1987-; Member Board of Directors, Domestic and Violence Support Group; Consultant to IL Arts Council. Publications: Scatter: Selected Poems, 1979; Hawk Spin, 1983; Wooden Indian, 1987; Long Ride Bakc, The Light Fandango, 1988. Contributions to: Margins; ALB Booklist. Honours: Carl Sandburg Award, 1980; Grants from IL Arts Council, 1985, 87. Memberships: International PEN; Modern Languages Association of Am; Associated Writing Programs; Authors Guild; Multi Ethnic Literature Society of the US. Address: 527 Lyman Street, Oak Park, IL 60304, USA.

JACOBS Arthur David, b. 14 June 1922, British Musicologist; Critic. Education: Manchester Grammer School; Merton College, Oxford. Appointments: Deputy Editor, 1962-71; Member, Editorial Board, Opera, 1972-; Critic and Columnist, Hi Fi News & Record Review, 1964-89; Opera Record Reviewer, Sunday Times, London, 1964-89; Editor, British Music Yearbook, 1971-79; Professor, Royal Academy of Music, 1964-79; Professor, Head of Dept of Music, Huddersfield Polytechnic, 1979-84; Member, Advisory Board, New Grove Dictionary of Opera, 1988-; Visiting Scholar, Wolfson College, Oxford, 1991-92. Publications include: Gilbert and Sullivan, 1951; A New Dictionary of Music, 1958; Choral Music, 1963; Pan Book of Opera, 1966; Music Education Handbook, 1976; Arthur Sullivan: A Victorian Musician, 1984; Penguin Dictionary of Musical Performers, 1990; Henry J Wood: Maker of the Proms, 1994. Contributions to: The New Grove Dictionary of Music, 1980; The New Grove Dictionary of Opera, 1992; The Viking Opera Guide, 1993. Address: 7 Southdale Road, Oxford, OX2 7SE England.

JACOBS Barbara, b. 6 Feb 1945, St Helens, England. Writer. m. Mark Jacobs, 26 Feb 1968, div, 1 s. Education: BA, 1966, PGCE, 1967, Leicester University. Appointments: Freelance Journalist, 1978-. Publications: Two Times Tow, 1984; Stick, 1988; Just How Far, 1989; Not Really Working, 1990; Loves A Pain, 1990; Ridby Graham, 1982; The Fire Proof Hero, 1986; Desperadoes, 1987; Listen to My Heartbeat, 1988; Goodbye my Love, 1989. Contributions to: My Guy; Just Seventeen; Girl; Jackie; Patches; Blue Jeans; Me; Catch; Mizz. Address: 29 Gotham Street, Leicester, LE2 0NA, England.

JACOBS Leah. See: GELLIS Roberta Leah.

JACOBSON Dan, b. 7 Mar 1929, Johannesburg, South Africa. Writer. m. Margaret Pye, 3 s, 1 d. Education: BA, University of Witwatersrand. Appointments include: Professor, Syracuse University, NY, 1965-66; Fellow, State University of NY, 1972; Fellow, Royal Society of Literature, 1974; Lecturer, 1975-80, Reader, 1980-87, Fellow, Humanities Research Centre, Australian National University, 1981. Professor, 1988-94, University College, London; Professor Emeritus University College, London, 1994-; Fellow, Humanities Research Centre, Australian National University, 1981. Publications include: The Trap, 1955; A Dance in the Sun, 1956; The Price of Diamonds, 1957; The Evidence of Love, 1960; The Beginners, 1965; The Rape of Tamar, 1970; The Confessions of Josef Baisz, 1979; The Story of the Stories, 1982; Time and Time Again, 1985; Adult Pleasures, 1988; Hidden in the Heart, 1991; The God Fearer, 1992; The Electronic Elephant, 1994. Contributions to: New Yorker;

Commentary; Grand Street; London Magazine; London Review of Books; TLS; The Guardian. Honours: John Llewelyn Rhys Memorial Award, 1958; W Somerset Maugham Award, 1964; H H Wingate Award, 1979; J R Ackerley Award, 1986; Mary Elinore Smith Prize, 1992. Literary Agent: A M Heath & Co Limited, London. Address: c/o A M Heath & Co Limited, 79 St Martins Lane, London WC2, England.

JACOBSON Howard, b. 25 Aug 1942, Manchester, England. Novelist. m. Rosalin Sadler, 1978, 1 son. Education: BA, Downing College, Cambridge. Appointments: Lecturer, University of Sydney, 1965-68; Supervisor, Selwyn College, Cambridge, 1969-72; Senior Lecturer, Wolverhampton Polytechnic, 1974-80; Presenter, Travellers Tales TV Series, 1990; TV Critic, The Sunday Correspondent, 1989-90; Book Reviewer, The Independent, London; Writer/Presenter, Roots Schmoots (Channel 4 TV), 1993, Yo, Mrs Askew! (BBC2), 1991, Sorry, Judas (Channel 4 TV), 1993. Publications: Coming From Behind, 1983; Peeping Tom, 1984; Redback, 1986; Shakespeare's Magnanimity: Four Tragic Heroes, Their Friends and Families, 1978; Travel, In The Land of Oz, 1987; The Very Model of a Man, 1992; Roots Schmoots, 1993; Seeing With The Eye: The Peter Fuller Memorial Lecture, 1993; Forthcoming: From the Ridiculous to the Sublime: The Progress of Comedy; Editor: The Picador Book of Spleen. Memberships: Editorial Board, Modern Painters. Address: Peter Fraser & Dunlop, 503-4 The Chambers, Chelsea Harbour, Lots Road, London SW10 0XF.

JACOBUS Lee A, b. 20 Aug 1935, Orange, New Jersey, USA. Professor of English. m. Joanna Jacobus, 1958, 2 children. Education: BA, 1957, MA, 1959, Brown University; PhD, Claremont Graduate School, 1968. Appointments: Faculty, Western Connecticut State University, 1960-86; Assistant Professor, 1968-71, Associate Professor, 1971-76, Professor, English, 1976-, University of Connecticut; Visiting Professor, Brown University, 1981; Visiting Fellow, Yale University, 1983. Publications: Improving College Reading, 1967, 6th Edition, 1993; Issues and Responses, 1968, Revised Edition, 1972; Developing College Reading, 1970, 1979, 5th edition 1995; Humanities Through the Arts (with F David Martin), 1974, 4th Edition, 1990; John Cleveland: A Critical Study, 1975; Sudden Apprehension: Aspects of Knowledge in Paradise Lost, 1976; The Paragraph and Essay Book, 1977; The Sentence Book, 1980; Humanities: The Evolution of Values, 1986; Writing As Thinking, 1989; Shakespeare and the Dialectic of Certainty, 1993; Editor: Aesthetics and the Arts, 1968; 17 From Everywhere: Short Stories from Around the World, 1971; Poems in Context (edited with William T Moynihan), 1974; Longman Anthology of American Drama, 1982; The Bedford Introduction to Drama, 2nd Edition, 1992; A World of Ideas, 4th Edition, 1994; Enjoying Literature, 1995. Contributions to: Scholarly articles to: Several books and proceedings; Huntington Library Quarterly; Bucknell Review; Children's Literature; Milton Studies; James Joyce Quarterly; Stories and poems to literary magazines, 1962-. Address: Dept of English U-25, University of Connecticut, Storrs, CT 06269, USA.

JACOBUS Mary, b. 1944, England. Professor of English. Appointments: Lecturer, Department of English, Manchester University, 1970-71; Fellow, Tutor in English, Lady Margaret Hall, Oxford, 1971-80; Lecturer in English, Oxford University, 1971-80; Associate Professor, 1980-82, Professor, 1982-, John Wendell Anderson Professor of English, 1989, Department of English, Cornell University, Ithaca, New York, USA. Publications: Tradition and Experiment in Wordsworth's Lyrical Ballads (1798), 1976; Women Writing and Women about Women (editor), 1979; Reading Women, 1986; Romanticism, Writing, and Sexual Difference: Essays on The Prelude, 1989; Body/Politics: Women and the Discourses of Science (co-editor); First Things: Thinking The Maternal Body, 1995. Contribution to: Numerous magazines and journals. Honours: Guggenheim Fellowship, 1988-89. Membership: Modern Language Association. Address: Department of English, Cornell University, Ithaca, NY 14853, USA.

JADAV Kishore, b. 15 Apr 1938, Gujarat, India. Government Service. m. Smt Kumsangkola Ao, 4 Mar 1967, 2 s, 3 d. Education: BCom, 1960, MCom, 1963. Appointments: General Secretary, 1976, Vice President, 1986, North Eastern Writers Academy. Publications include: Suryarohan, 1972; Chhadmavesh, 1982; Kishore Jadavni Vartao, 1984; Nishachakra, 1979; Riktaraag, 1989; Aatash, 1993; Novels, Critical Essays, Contemporary Gujarati Short Stories. Contributions to: Kishore Jadav Sathe Vartalap; Kishore Jadavni; Sahityik Goshthi; Kishore Jadav Sathe Cartakala Vishe Vartalap. Honours: Awards from Gujarat Goverment, 1972; Gujarati Sahitya Parishad Award, 1988; Critics Sandham Award, 1988. Memberships:

Gujarati Sahitya Parishad; Indian PEN; Lions Club. Address: PO Box 19 Nagaland, PO Kohima 797 001, India.

JAFFE Rona, b. 12 June 1932, NY, USA. Freelance Writer; TV Personality. Education: AB, Radcliffe College, 1951. Publications: The Best of Everything, 1958; Away from Home, 1960; The Last of the Wizards, 1961; Mr Right is Dead, 1965; The Cherry in the Martini, 1966; The Fame Game, 1969; The Other Woman, 1972; Family Secrets, 1974; The Last Chance, 1976; Class Reunion, 1979; Mazes and Monsters, 1981; After the Reunion, 1985. Address: c/o Delacorte Press, 1 Dag Hammarskjold Plaza, New York, NY 10017, USA.

JAFFEE Annette Williams, b. 10 Jan 1945, Abilene, TX, USA. Novelist. div, 1 s, 1 d. Education: BS, Boston University, 1966. Publications: Adult Education, 1981; Recent History, 1988. Contributions to: Ploughshares; Missouri Reviews; The Ontario Review. Honours: NJ Arts Council Grant, 1986; Dodge Fellow at Yaddo, 1991. Memberships: Authors Guild; PEN. Literary Agent: Liz Darhansoff. Address: PO Box 26, River Road, Lumberville, PA 18933, USA.

JAGLOM Henry David, b. 26 Jan 1943, London, England. Film Writer; Film Director; Actor. m. Victoria Foyt Jaglom, 22 Oct 1991, 1 son, 1 daughter. Education: University of Pennsylvania; Actors Studio. Publications: Writer, Director, films: A Safe Place, 1971; Tracks, 1976; Sitting Ducks, 1980; Can She Bake a Cherry Pie, 1983; Always But Not Forever, 1985; Someone to Love, 1987; New Year's Day, 1989; Eating, 1990; Venice/Venice, 1992; Babyfever, 1994; Last Summer In The Hamptons, 1995; Books: Eating (A Very Serious Comedy about Women and Food), 1992; Babyfever (For Those Who Hear Their Clock Ticking), 1994. Address: Rainbow Film Company, 9165 Sunset Boulevard, The Penthouse, Los Angeles, CA 90069, USA.

JAIN Girilal, b. 21 Sept 1923, Pipli Khere, Haryana. Journalist. m. Sudarshan Jain, 1951, 1 s, 3 d. Education: Delhi University. Appointments: Entered Journalism, 1945, Sub Editor, Times of India, Delhi, 1950, Reporter, 1951, Chief Reporter, 1958, Foreign Correspondent, Pakistn, 1961, London, 1962, Assistant Editor, Delhi, 1964, Resident Editor, 1970, Editor, 1976, Editor in Chief, 1978-. Publications: What Mao Really Means, 1957; India Meets China in Nepal, 1959; Panchsila and After, 1960. Address: 22 Ashoka Apt, Napean Sea Road, Bombay 6, India.

JAKIMOW Françoise, b. 14 Jan 1940, Troyes, France. Teacher; Translator. m. Manuel Barrera, 26 Oct 1975, divorced, 1 daughter. Education: BA, 1960; Licence es Lettres, 1965; MA, French Literature, 1973; CEC, Education, 1974. Appointments: Symposium on Contemporary Ukrainian Poetry, Ottawa University, 1985; Salon du livre de l'Outaouais, Ottawa, 1991. Publications: Les autres, lui, toi, 1972; Ukraine, ma terre absente, 1974; Les chevaux des Scythes, 1986. Contributions to: Echanges, Paris, 1972. Honours: Troisieme Medaille du Prix Marie-Stuart, Concours International de Poesie, France, 1963. Memberships: Union des ecrivaines et ecrivains quebecois. Address: 316, 40th Avenue, Lachine, Quebec H8T 2E8, Canada.

JAMES Alan, b. 1943, England. Appointments: Master, Junior School, Royal Grammar School, Newcastle Upon Tyne, 1968-78; Deputy Head, Runnymede First School, Ponteland, 1979-. Publications include: Animals, Hospital, 1969; Buses and Coaches, 1971; Tunnels, Sir Rowland Hilland the Post Office, Living Light Book Two, 1972; Clock and Watches, Zoos, 1974; Keeping Pets, Newspapers, Buildings, Living Light Book Five, 1975; Spiders and Scorpions, The Telephone Operator, The Vet, 1976; Stocks and Shares, 1977; Circuses, 1978; Lets Visit Finland, 1979; Lets Visit Austria, Lets Visit Denmark, 1984; Homes in Hot Places, 1987; Homes in Cold Places, 1987; Castles and Mansions, 1988; Homes on Water, 1988; Gilbert and Sullivan; Their Lives and Time, 1990. Address; The Stable, Market Square, Holy Island, Northumberland, TF15 2RU, England.

JAMES Andrew. See: KIRKUP James.

JAMES Anthony Stephen, b. 27 Oct 1956, South Wales. Freelance Writer. m. Penny Windsor, 24 May 1987, divorced 1994, 1 daughter. Education: BA, University College of Swansea, 1991. Publications include: Author of Novel, A House with Blunt Knives, Poetry Published in Acumen; Anglo Welsh Review; Collection of Poems; All That The City Has to Offer; Celtic Dawn; Envoi; Foolscap; Hybrid; Krax; Nutshell; Orbis; Poetry Nottingham; Poetry Wales;

Radical Wales; Social Care Education; Tears in the Fence; The White Rose Literary Magazine; Bradford Poetry Quarterly; New Welsh Review; Passport; Social Care Education; Western Mail; Wish You Were Here, 1994. Contributions to: Contemporary Review; Ore. Honours: Eileen Illtyd David Award, 1983. Membership: The Literature for More Than One Year Group. Address: 16 Buckingham Road, Bonymaen, Swansea, SA1 7AL, Wales.

JAMES Clive Vivian Leopold, b. 7 Oct 1939, Writer; Broadcaster; Journalist. Education: Sydney University; Pembroke College, Cambridge. Appointments include: Record Albums as Lyricist for Pete Atkin; TV Series include, Cinema; Up Sunday; So It Goes; A Question of Sex; Saturday Night People; TV Documentaries include, Shakespeare in Perspective, Hamlet, 1981; The Return of the Flash of Lightening, 1982; Clive James Live in Las Vagas, 1982; The Clive James Great American Beauty Pageant, 1984; Clive James on Safari, 1986; Feature Writer, The Observer, 1972-; TV Critic, 1972-82. Publications include: The Fate of Felicity Frk in the Land of the Media, 1975; Peregrine Prykkes Pilgramage Through the London Literary World, 1976; Visions Before Midnight, 1977; The Crystal Bucket, 1981; Charles Charmings Challenges on the Pathway to the Throne, 1981; From the Land of Shadows, 1982; Snakecharmers in Texas, 1988; Brilliant Creatures, 1983; Poem of the Year, 1983;Falling Towards England: Unreliable Memoirs II, 1985; May Week was in June, Unreliable Memoirs III, 1990.

JAMES Dana. See: POLLARD Jane.

JAMES Irene, See: JAMES Robin.

JAMES Noel David Glaves, b. 16 Sept 1911, Author; Retired Land Agent. m. Laura Cecilia livingstone, 29 Dec 1949, dec, 3 s, 1 dec. Education: Haileybury College, 1925-28; Diploma, Royal Agricultural College, Cirencester, 1932. Publications include:Before the Echoes Die Away, 1980; A History of English Forestry, 1981; The Foresters Companion, 1989; The Arboriculturist, 1990; An Historical Dictionary of Forestry and Woodland Terms, 1991. Honours: Military Cross, 1945; Territorial Decoration, 1946; OBE, 1964; Gold Medal for Distinguished Service to Foresty; Bledisloe Gold Medal. Memberships: Chartered Land Agents Society; Royal Forestry Society of England, Wales and Northern Ireland. Address: Blackemore House, Kersbrook, Budleigh Salterton, Devon EX9 7AB, England.

JAMES P(hyllis) D(orothy), (Baroness of Holland Park). b. 3 Aug 1920, Oxford, England. Writer, (as P D James); Former Civil Servant. 2 d. Appointments: Member BBC General Advisory Council, 1987-88, Arts Council, 1988-92, British Council, 1988-93; Chairman Booker Prize Panel of Judges, 1987; Governor of BBC, 1988-93. Publications include: Cover Her Face, 1962; A Mind to Murder, 1963; Unnatural Causes, 1967; Shroud for a Nightingale, 1971; The Maul and the Pear Tree, (with T A Critchley) 1971; An Unsuitable Job for a Woman, 1972; Innocent Blood, 1980; The Skull Beneath the Skin, 1982; A Taste for Death, 1986; Devices and Desires, 1989; The Children of Men, 1992; Original Sin, 1994. Literary Agent: Greene & Heaton Limited, London. Address: c/o Greene & Heaton Limited, 37 Goldhawk Road, London W12 8QQ.

JAMES Robert. See: JACK Ian.

JAMES R(obert) V(idal) Rhodes Sir, b. 1933, England. Appointments: Assistant Clerk, 1955-61, senior Clerk, 1961-64, House of Commons; Fellow, All Souls College, Oxford, 1964-68, 1979-81; Kratter Professor, Stanford University, 1968; Director, Institute for the Study of International Organisation, University of Sussex, 1968-73; Principal Officer, Executive Office of the Secretary, General of the UN, 1973-76; Conservative Member of Parliament for Cambridge, 1976-92; Parliamentry Private Secretary, Foreign And Commonwealth Office, 1979-81; Chairman, Parliament Trust, 1983; Member, Speakers Panel of Chairman of the House of Commons, 1987-92. Publications include: Lord Randolph Churchill, 1959; Memoirs of a Conservative: The Memoirs and Papers of J C C Davidson, 1968; Chirchill: A Study in Failure 1900-1939, 1970; Britains Role in the UN, 1970; Ambitions and Realities: British Politics, 1964-1970, 1971; Victor Cazalet: A Portrait, 1976; Albert, Prince Consort, 1983; Anthony Eden, 1986; Bob Boothby: A Portrait, 1991. Address: The Stone Horse, Great Gransden, Nr SAndy, Bedfordshire, SA19 3AF, England.

JAMES Robin, (Irene James), b. 24 Sept 1953, Seattle, WA, USA. Artist. m. Michael George Cosgrove, 1 July 1980. Appointment:

Freelance Artist, 1971-. Publications include: Wheedle on the Needle, Muffin Muncher, The Dream Tree, 1974; Little Mouse on the Praire, 1975; Bangalee, Creole, 1976; Gabby, Leo the Lop, leo the Lop: Tail Two, Leo the Lop: Tail Three, 1977; Snaffles, 1978; Grampa Lop, 1979; Nitter Pitter, 1980; Maui Mauj, Ming Ling, Tee Tee, 1981; Morgan and Yew, 1982; Morgan Morning, 1983; Baby Puppies, Baby Kittens, Crabby Gabby, 1985; Buttermilt, Mumkin, Baby Horses, 1986; Misty Morgan, 1986; Pernickity, 1988; Any McClark the Aardverk, 1989. Memberships: International Wildlife Federation; American Humane Society of US; National Wildlife Federation; People for the Ethnical Treatment of Animals; Delt Society. Address: Snohomish, WA, USA.

JAMES Tegan. See: ODGERS Sally Farrell.

JAMES William M. See: HARKNETT Terry.

JAMIE Kathleen, b. 13 May 1962, Johnston, Renfrewshire, Scotland. Poet. Education: MA, University of Edinburgh. Appointments include: Write in Residence, Midlothian District Libraries, 1987-89. Publications: Black Spiders, 1982; A Flame in Your Heart, 1986; The Way We Live, 1987; Radio Play, Rumours of Guns, 1985. Honours include: Scottish Arts Council Awards; Compton Fund Grant, 1989. Address: c/o David Fletcher Associates, 58 John Street, Peniciuk, Midlothian, Scotland.

JANDL Ernst, b. 1 Aug 1925, Vienna, Austria. Writer. Education: Teachers Diploma, 1949, PhD, 1950, University of Vienna. Publications include: Laut und Luise, 1966; Funt Mann Menschen, 1968; Aus der Fremde, 1980; Der Kunstliche Baum, 1970; Idyllen, 1989; Gesammelte Werke 3 vols, 1985; Stanzen, 1992. Honours: Horspielpreis der Kriegsblinden, 1968; Georg Trakl Prize, 1974; Prize of the City of Vienna, 1976; Mulhelmer Dramatiker Preis, 1980; Austrian State Prize, 1984; Georg Buchner Preis, 1984; Medal of Honour in Gold of the City of Vienna, 1986; Peter Huchel Preis, 1990; Heinrich Von Kleist Preis, 1993. Memberships: Academy of Arts, West Berlin; Academy of Arts of GDR; Deutsche Akademie fur Sprache und Dichtung; Academy of Fine Arts, Munich; Forum Stadtpark, Graz; Grazer Autorenversammlung; Osterreichischer Luchterhand Literaturverlag, Hamburg, Kiepenheuer & Witsch Theaterverlag, Cologne. Address: PO Box 227, A 1041 Vienna, Austria.

JANES Joseph Robert, b. 23 May 1935, Toronto, Ontario, Canada. Writer. m. Gracia Joyce Lind, 16 May 1958, 2 sons, 2 daughters. Education: BSc, Mining Engineering, 1958, MEng, Geology, 1967, University of Toronto. Publications: Children's books: The Tree-Fort War, 1976; Theft of Gold, 1980; Danger on the River, 1982; Spies for Dinner, 1984; Murder in the Market, 1985; Adult books: The Toy Shop, 1981; The Watcher, 1982; The Third Story, 1983; The Hiding Place, 1984; The Alice Factor, 1991; Mayhem, 1992; Carousel, 1992; Kaleidoscope, 1993; Salamander, 1994; Mannequin, 1994; Dollmaker, 1995; Stonekiller, 1995, The Great Canadian Outback, non-fiction, 1978; Textbooks: Holt Geophoto Resource Kits, 1972; Rocks, Minerals and Fossils, 1973; Earth Science, 1974; Geology and the New Global Tectonics, 1976; Searching for Structure (co-author), 1977; Teachers Guide: Searching for Structure (co-author), 1977; Airphoto Interpretation and the Canadian Landscape (with J D Mollard), 1984. Contributions to: Toronto Star; Toronto Globe and Mail; The Canadian; The Winnipeg Free Press; The Canadian Children's Annual. Honours: Grants: The Canada Council; Ontario Arts Council; J P Bickell Foundation; Thesis Award, Canadian Institute of Mining and Metallurgy; Works-in-progress Grant, Ontario Arts Council, 1991. Memberships: Association of Professional Engineers of Ontario; Crime Writers of Canada. Address: PO Box 1590, Niagara-On-The-Lake, Ontario, L05 1J0, Canada.

JANET Lillian. See: O'DANIEL Janet.

JANICKI Jerzy, b. 10 Aug 1928, Czortkow, Poland. Writer. m. Krystyna Czechowicz Janicka, 20 June 1964, 2 d. Education: MA, University of Wroclaw, 1948. Publications include: 6 Novels, 5 Selections of Reportages; 4 Selections of Radio Plays; 3 Dramas; 18 Film Screenplays; Over 40 TV Screenplays; 3 TV Serials; Radio Novel, Over 1600 Episodes, Running Since, 1956-. Contributions to: Numerous Journals and Magazines. Honours: 2 State Awards. Memberships: Society of Polish Writers; Society of Polish Filmmakers; Society of Polish Journalists; Society of Stage Authors and Composers. Address: 02 928 Warsaw, Zelwerowicza 36, Poland.

JANIFER Laurence M. See: HARRIS Laurence Mark.

JANOSY Istvan Laszlo, b. 18 May 1919, Besztencebanya, Slovensko. Poet; Writer. m. Katalin Nylkos, 18 Dec 1953, 1 son. Education: Arts Dept, University of Sciences, Budapest, 1937-44. Publications: Prometheus, 1948; The Godess of Maize; The Depth of Well of Dreams in Fathomless, - all poems: Experience and Rememberances; Vanishing Faces; Translations include: Tragedies by Aeschylus by Sophocles; The State of Plato; Odes of Pindar; Works of Lukian; Ramayana; Paradise Lost; Der Grune Heirich; Die Leute Von Seldvila; The Angloamerican Poetry of XX Century; Poems of John Berryman. Honours: Jozsef Attila Award, 1973; Dery Tibor Award, 1986. Memberships: Hungarian Pen Club; Association of Hungarian Writers; Ecumenical Society. Address: Mogyorodi ut 64B, H-1148 Budapest, Hungary.

JANOWITZ Phyllis, b. 3 Mar 1940, New York City, New York, USA. Poet. div., 1 son, 1 daughter. Education: BA, Queens College; MFA, University of Massachusetts, Amherst, 1970; Appointments: Hodder Fellow in Poetry, Princeton University, 1979-80; Associate Professor in English, then Professor, Cornell University, Ithaca, New York, 1980-; National Endowment for the Arts Fellow, 1989. Publications: Rites of Strangers, 1978; Visiting Rites, 1982; Temporary Dwellings, 1988. Contributions to: Poems to The New Yorker; Atlantic; The Nation; The New Republic; Paris Review; Ploughshares; Radcliffe Quarterly; Prairie Schooner; Esquire; Andover Review; Harvard Magazine Backbone; The Literary Review; The Mid-Atlantic Review. Address: Department of English, Cornell University, Ithaca, NY 14853, USA.

JANOWITZ Tama, b. USA. Publications: Slaves of New York; A Cannibal in Manhattan; American Dad; The Male Cross-Dresser Support Group. Contributions include: New Yorker; Paris Review; Spin; Bomb; Interview. Address: c/o Amanda Urban, ICM 40 West 57th Street, New York, NY 10019, USA.

JANSEN Michael Elin, b. 16 Dec 1940, By City, MI, USA. Writer. m. Godfrey Henry Jansen, 31 Oct 1967, 1 d. Education: BA, Mount Holyoke College, MA; MA, Am University of Beirut. Publications: The Battle of Beirut, 1982; Dissonance in Zion, 1987; The Aphrodite Plot, 1983; The US and the Palestinian People, 1970. Contributions to: The Irish Times; Middle East International; Gemini News Service. Literary Agent: Jacqueline Korn of David Higham, London. Address: 5 Metaxas Street, Aylos Dhometios, Nicosia 164, Cyprus.

JANUS Ludwig, b. 21 Aug 1939, Essen, Germany. Psychoanalyst, Psychotherapist. m. Brigitte Janus-Stanek, 17 Nov 1972, 3 s, 3 d. Education: Dr Med, 1969, Psychoanalyst, 1974. Publications: Wie die Seele entsteht.dtv, Muenchen 1993; Die Psychoanalyse der vorgeburtlichen Lebenszeit und der Geburt, Centaurus, Pfaffenweiler, 1991; (with Helga Haesing) Ungewollte Kinder, Rowohlt, Reinbek, 1994; editor several books on prenatal psychology. Contributions: About 50 articles in scientific journals eg Psyche, Pre-and Perinatal Psychology Journal, International Journal of Prenatal Psychology and Medicine. Memberships: German Psychoanalytical Society, International Society of Prenatal and Perinatal Psychology and Medicine, a.o. Literary Agent: Hoffman und Campe, Hamburg. Address: 69118 Heidelberg, Koepfelweg 52, Germany.

JARMAN Mark Foster, b. 5 June 1952, Mt Sterling, Kentucky, USA. Poet; Teacher. m. Amy Kane Jarman, 28 Dec 1974, 2 daughters. Education: BA, University of California, Santa Cruz; MFA, University of Iowa. Publications: Tonight is the Night of the Prom, a Chapbook of Verse, 1974; North Sea, 1978; The Rote Walker, 1981; Far and Away, 1985; The Black Riviera 1990; Iris, 1992. Contributions to: American Poetry Review; Hudson Review; New Yorker; Ohio Review; Partisan Review; Poetry; Prairie Schooner; The Reaper. Address: Department of English, Vanderbilt University, Nashville, TN 37235, USA.

JAROS Peter, b. 22 Jan 1940, Hybe, Slovakia. Writer. m. Maria Zuzana Kristova, 5 July 1980. 2 sons, 1 daughter. Education: Philosophical Faculty, Komensky University Bratislava, 1962. Literary Appointments: Editor, Kultumy Zivot, 1964-66; Editor, Literary Department, Slovak Radio, 1967-71; Slovak Film, 1972-91. Publications: Popoludnie na Terase (Afternoon of the Terrace), 1963; Zdesenie (Anxiety), 1965; Menuet, 1967; Krvaviny (Stories of Blood), 1970; Orechy (Nuts), 1972; Tisicrocna Vcela (1000 year old Bee), 1979; Neme Ucho, Hluche Oko (Dumb Ear, Deaf Eye), 1984; Lasky Hrnat (A Clutch of Love), 1988. Contributions to: Kultumy Zivot; Slovenske Pohlady; Romboid; Nove Slovo; Mlada Tvorba; Inostrannaja

Literatura (USSR): Literatura na Swiece (Poland). Honours: Ivan Krasko's Award for Popoludnie Na Terase, 1963; Award, Publishing House Smena, for Menuet, 1967; Award, Publishing House Slovensky spisovatel for Krvaviny, 1968; Award of the Slovak Union of Writers, for Tisicrocna Vcela, 1979. Membership: Slovak Union of Writers; Slovak PEN Club. Literary Agent: LITA, Slovak Literary Agency, Bratislava. Address: Klzava 11, 83101 Bratislava, Slovakia.

JARVIS Martin, b. 4 Aug 1941, Cheltenham, Gloucestershire, England. Actor; Writer. m. (2) Rosalind Ayres, 23 Nov 1974. 2 sons (from previous marriage). Education: Diploma (Hons), Royal Academy of Dramatic Art, 1962. Appointments: Numerous acting roles on stage, film and television productions, starred in Alan Ayckbourn's Woman in Mind, Vaudeville Theatre, London, 1987; Co-star, feature film, "Buster", 1988; Alan Ayckbourn's Henceforward, Vaudeville Theatre, London, 1989; British Première of Yuri Trifonov's Exchange, 1989; Literary Consultant, Countdown, 1990; Co-produced, own adaptation of Frayn's Make and Break, Los Angeles, 1993; Co-produced, Directed, Tales From Shakespeare, Los Angeles, 1993; Co-produced, Best of Second World War Poetry, spoken word cassette, 1993; Co-starred as M de Renal in Scarlet and Black, BBC TV, 1993. Major Publications: Play; Bright Boy, 1977; Short stories: Name out of a Hat, 1967; Alphonse, 1972; Late Burst, 1976; adapted over 60 Just William stories of Richmal Crompton for BBC Radio and TV, 1972-76; adapted, Goodbye Mr Chips, by James Hilton for BBC Radio & Television, 1973; Founded Jarvis and Ayres Productions, 1986; Created Jarvis's Frayn for BBC Radio 4, 1986; Adapted, William at Easter, for BBC, 1987; William Stories: Personal Selection, (book), 1992; Spoken Word Cassettes; Co-produced with CSA: Home for the Holidays; His Last Bow; Stage: Starred in Los Angeles in Man of the Moment, 1994. Contributions to: Scripted various TV and Radio Shows: "The Listener" and "Punch", 1988; Comic Relief and Children In Need, 1988-89; Solo reading on cassette taps including: Just William, 1, 2, 3 & 4; Plain Tales from the Hills, by Kipling and Classic Love Stories; regular contributor to Fourth Column, BBC Radio 4. Honours: Vanbrugh Award, Silver Medal, Royal Academy of Dramatic Art, 1968; National Theatre Player, 1982-84; Emmy Award, 1991; Sony Silver Award for Radio, 1992. Membership: Council member, National Youth Theatre; Board Member, Children's Film Unit. Literary Agent: I.C.M. Address: 76 Oxford Street, W1, England.

JARVIS Sharon, b. 1 Oct 1943, Brooklyn, New York, USA. Literary Agent; Editor; Writer. Education: BFA, Hunter College, 1964. Literary appointments: Copy Editor, Ace Books, 1969; Assistant Managing Editor, Popular Library, 1971; Editor, Ballantine Books, 1972; Editor, Doubleday and Co, 1975; Senior Editor, Playboy Books, 1978. Publications: The Alien Trace (with K Buckley), 1984; Time Twister, 1984; Inside Outer Space, 1985; True Tales of the Unknown, 1985; True Tales of the Unknown: The Uninvited, 1989; True Tales of the Unknown: Beyond Reality, 1991; Dead Zones, Dark Zones, 1992. Memberships: International Fortean Organization; Association of Authors Representatives; American Booksellers Association; Endless Mountains Council of the Arts. Address: RR2 Box 16B, Laceyville, PA 18623, USA.

JASON Katherine, b. 9 Feb 1953, NY< USA. Instructor. m. Peter Rondinone, 23 Apr 1984. Education: AB, Bard College, 1975; MF, Columbia University, 1978; Doctural Study, Graduate Center of the City University of NY, 1980-81. Appointments: Instructor, Hunter College, City University of NY, 1981-. Publications: Racers, What People, 1984; Words in Commotion and Other Stories, 1986; Name and Tears: Forty Years of Italian Fiction, 1990. Contributions to include: Omni; New Yorker; The Phoenix; Folio; The Northern Review; Armenian Poetry Through the Ages; The New Directions Anthology, 1982. Honours; Fulbright Fellow, 1978-79; Finalist for Renato Poggioli Award, 1984; Finalist, Nation Award for Unstringing, 1985. Address: 348 West 11th Street, no. 38 New York, NY 10014, USA.

JASON Stuart. See: **FLOREN Lee.**

JASPER David, b. 1 Aug 1951, Stockton on Tees, England. University Teacher; Clergyman. m. Alison Elizabeth Collins, 29 Oct 1976, 3 daughters. Education: Dulwich College, 1959-69; Jesus College, Cambridge, 1969-72. BA, MA, 1976; BD, Keble College, Oxford, 1976-80; PhD, Hatfield College, Durham, 1979-83. Appointments: Director, Centre for the Study of Literature and Theology, Durham University, 1986-91, Glasgow University, 1991-; Editor, Literature and Theology. Publications: Coleridge as Poet and Religious Thinker, 1985; The New Testament and the Literatry

Imagination, 1987; The Study of Literature and Religion, 1989; General Editor of Macmillan Series, Studies in Literature and Translation. Contributions to: Rhetoric Power and Community, 1992. Honours: Dana Fellow, Emory University, Atlanta, 1991; Hon Fellow, Research Foundation, Durham University, 1991. Memberships: Sec, European Society for Literature and Religion; American Academy of Religion; Modern Language Association. Address: Netherwood, 124 Old Manse Road, Wishaw, Lanarkshire, ML2 0EP, Scotland.

JAY Antony Rupert, b. 20 Apr 1930, London, England. Writer; Producer. m. Rosemary Jill Watkins, 15 June 1957, 2 s, 2 d. Education: Open Major Classical Scholarship, 1948-52, BA, 1952, MA, 1955, Magdalene College, Cambridge. Publications include: Corporation Man, 1972; Yes Minister, 3 vols; The Complete Yes, Prime Minister, 1989; Management & Machiavelli, 1967, 1987; To England with Love, 1967; Corporation Man, 1971. Honours: Knighthood, 1989; Honorary MA, 1978; Honorary DBA, 1988; CVO, 1992; FRSA, 1992; CIM, 1992. Literary Agent: Curtis Brown & Michael Imison Playwrights. Address: c/o Video Arts Limited, Dumbarton House, 68 Oxford Street, London W1N 9LA, England.

JAY Charlotte, See: JAY Geraldine Mary.

JAY Geraldine Mary, (Geraldine Hills, Charlotte Jay), b. 1919, Australia. Appointments: Operates Oriental Antiques Business, Somerset, England, 1958-71, Adelaide, 1971-. Publications: The Knife is Feminine, 1951; Beat Not the Bones, The Fugitive Eye, 1953; The Yellow Turbn, 1955; The Feast of the Dead, 1956; The Silk Project, 1956; The Man Who Walked Away, 1958; Arms for Adonis, 1960; A Hank of Hair, 1964; The Cats of Benares, 1967; The Cobra Kite, 1971; The Voice of the Crab, 1974; The Last of the Men Shortage, 1976; The Felling of Thawle, 1979; The Last Inheritor, 1980; Talking to Strangers, 1982. Address: 21 Commercial Road, Hyde Park, SA 5061, Australia.

JAY Martin Evan, b. 4 May 1944, NY, USA. Historian. m. Catherine Gallagher, 6 July 1974, 2 d. Education: BA, Union College, 1965; PhD, Harvard University, 1971. Publications: The Dialectical Imagination: A History of the Frankfurt School and The Institute of Social Research, 1923-1950, 1973; Marxism and Totality, 1984; Downcast Eyes, 1993; Adorno, 1984; Permanent Exiles, 1985; Fin de Siecle Socialism, 1989; Force Fields, 1993. Contributions to: Salmagundi. Honour: Herbert Baxter Adams Award, 1973. Memberships: Am Historical Association; Society for Exile Studies. Address: 718 Contra Costa Avenue, Berkeley, CA 94707, USA.

JAY Peter, b. 7 Feb 1937, England. Editor; Writer; Broadcaster. m. (1) Margaret Ann Callaghan, 1961, 1 son, 2 daughters, (2) Emma Thornton, 1985, 3 sons. Education: Winchester College; Christ Church, Oxford; MA Oxon 1st Class Honours, 1960; Nuffield College, 1960. Literary Appointments: Economics Editor, The Times, 1967-77; Associate Editor, Times Business News, 1969-77; Director, The Economist Intelligence Unit, 1979-83; Consultant Economist Group, 1979-81; Director, Landen Press Limited, 1982-; Editor, Banking World, 1986; Chief of Staff to Robert Maxwell, Publisher of Mirror Group Newspapers and Chairman of BPCC plc and Pergamon, 1986-89; Economics Editor, BBC, 1990-. Publications: The Budget, 1972; The Crisis for Western Political Economy and Other Essays, 1984; Apocalypse 2000, 1987. Contributions to: Numerous newpapers and magazine articles; Foreign Affairs - America and the World, 1979. Address: Hensington Farmhouse, Woodstock, Oxon, OX20 1LH, England.

JEAL Tim, b. 27 Jan 1945, London, England. Author. m. Joyce Timewell, 11 Oct 1969, 3 d. Education: MA, Christ Church, Oxford. Publications include: For Love of Money, 1967; Livingstone, 1973; Cushings Crusade, 1974; Until the Colours Fade, 1976; A Marriage of Convenience, 1979; Baden Powell, 1989. Honours: Joint Winner, Llewelyn Rhys Memorial Prize, 1974; Writers Guilds Laurel Award. Membership: Writers Guild of Great Britain; Society of Authors. Literary Agent: Toby Eady Associates. Address: 29 Willow Road, London, NW3 1TL, England.

JEFFERSON Alan, b. 1921, England. Appointments: Visiting Professor of Vocal Interpretation, Guildhall School of Music and Drama, London, 1967-74; Administrator, London Symphony Orchestra, 1967-68; Manager, BBC Concert Orchestra, 1968-73. Publications: The Operas of Richard Strauss in Great Britain, 1910-1963; The Lieder of Richard Strauss, 1971; Delius, 1972; The Life of Richard Strauss, 1973; Inside the Orchestra, 1973; Strauss, (The Musicians), 1975; The Glory of Opera, 1976; The Complete Gilbert and Sullivan Opera Guide, 1984; Richard Strauss: Der Rosenkavalier, 1986; Lotte Lehmann, 1988; Elisabeth Schwarzkopf, 1995. Address: c/o Watson Little Ltd, 12 Egbert Street, London, NW1 8LJ, England.

JELLICOE P(atricia) Ann. b. 15 July 1927, Playwright; Director. m. (1)C E Knight Clark, 1950, div, (2)Roger Mayne, 1962, 1 s, 1 d. Publications include: The Sport of My Mad Mother, 1958; Shelley, 1965; The Rising Generation, 1967; Flora and the Bandits, 1976; The Bargain, 1979; The Tide, 1980; The Western Women, 1984; You'll Never Guess, 1973; A Good Thing or a Bad Thing, 1974; Rosmersholm, 1960; The Seagull, 1963; Some Unconscious Influences in the Theatre, 1967; Shell Guide to Devon, 1975; Har to Put Them In, 1988. Honours: OBE, 1984. Address: c/o Margaret Ramsey Limited, 14a Goodwins Court, St Martins Lane, London WC2.

JENCKS Charles Alexander, b. 21 June 1939, Baltimore, MD, USA. Writer; Architect; Professor. m. Margaret Keswick, 3 s, 1 d. Education: BA, 1961, BA, MA, 1965, Harvrd University; PHP, London University. Appointments: Editor, Connection, Harvard USA, 1963; Editorial Advisor, Architectural Design, London, 1979. Publication include: The Language of Post Modern Architecture, 1977; Modern Movements in Architecture, 1973, 1984; Architecture Today, 1982, 1988; Le Corvisier and the Tragic View of Architecture, 1974; Ad Hocism, 1972; Daydream Houses of LA, 1978; Late Modern Architecture, 1980. Contributions to: Architectural Design; Times Literary Supplement; Encounter. Honours: Melbourne Oration, 1974; Boston Lectures, Royal Society of Arts. Literary Agent: Ed Victor. Address: Architectural Association, 36 Bedford Square, London WC1, England.

JENKIN Len (Leonard), b. 2 Apr 1941, NY, USA. 1 d. Education: Columbia University, 1958-64, 1969-71. Appointments: Lecturer, Brooklyn College, 1965-66; Associate Professor, Manhattan Community College, 1967-79; Associate Professor, Tisch School of Arts, NY University, 1980; Associate Artistic Director, River Arts Repertory Company, 1983-. Publications include: Plays, A Country Doctor, 1983; Madrigal Opera, 1985; American Notes, 1986; A Soldiers Tale, 1986; Screenplays, Merlin and Melinda, 1977; Blame It on The Night, 1985; Novel, New Jerusalem, 1986; Various TV Plays. Honours include: Yaddo Fellowship, 1975; National Endowment for the Arts Fellowship, 1979, 1982; Rockefeller Fellowship, 1980; Christopher Award, 1981; Creative Artists Public Service Grant, 1981; Obie Award, 1981; MacDowell Fellowship, 1984; Guggenheim Fellowship, 1987. Literary Agent: Flora Roberts Inc, NY, USA. Address: c/o Flora Roberts Inc, 157 West 57th Street, NY 10019, USA.

JENKINS Alan, b. 5 Sept 1914, Carshalton, Surrey, England. Journalism; Public Relations. m. Margaret Elizabeth Hoskin, 15 Dec 1956, 1 d. Education: BA, 1935, MA, 1948, St Edmund Hall, Oxford. Appointments: Fiction Editor, Nashs Magazine, 1936-37; Assistant Editor, Argosy Magazine, 1938-39; Editor, Army Illustrated Magazine, 1941-46; Assistnt Editor, World Review, Lilliput, Leader. Publictions include: The Twenties, 1974; The Thirties, 1976; The Forties, 1977; STephen Potter, 1978; The Book of the Thames, 1983; Various Company Histories: Taylor Woodrow; Knight Frank & Rutley; The Stock Exchange Story. Contributions to: Most Leading Magazines and Newspapers in USA and England. Honours: The Twenties, First, BCA Choice; The Thirties, BCA Choice; The Forties, BCA Choice. Literary Agent: David Higham Associates Limited. Address: 7 Beech Close, Effingham, Surrey KT24 5PQ, England.

JENKINS Dan, (Thomas B), b. 2 Dec 1929, Fort Worht, TX, USA. Writer. m. (3)June Burrage, 2 s. 1 d. Education: TX Christian University. Appointments: Affiliated with Forth Worth Press, Fort Worth, 1948-60; Affiliated with Dallas Times Herald, 1960-62; affiliated with Sports Illustrated, NY, 1962-84; Affiliated with Playboy, IL, 1985-; Writer. Publications include: Sports Illustrateds the Best Eighteen Golf Holes in America, 1966; The Dogged Victims of Inexorable Fate, 1970; Dead Solid Perfect, 1974; Limo, 1976; Life Its Ownself: The Semi Thougher Adventures of Billy Clyde Puckett and Them, 1984; Football, 1986; Fast Copy, 1988. Contributions to: Author of Film and TV Screenplays.

JENKINS Daniel Thomas, b. 9 June 1914, Merthyr Tydfil, Wales. Minister and Professor of Theology. m. Agatha Helen Mary Cree, 15 Aug 1942, 2 sons, 3 daughters. Education: Edinburgh University, MA 1935, BD 1938; Yorkshire United College 1935-37; Mansfield College, Oxford, BA (Oxon) 1939. Appointments: Assistant Editor, Christian

News-Letter, 1945-48; Commonwealth Fund Fellow, New York, 1948-49; Professor (part-time) University of Chicago, 1950-62; Reader and University Chaplain, University of Sussex, 1963-73; Professor, Princeton Theological Seminary, New Jersey, 1981-84; Also Minister of various United Reformed Churches. Publications: The Nature of Catholicity, 1942; The Gift of Ministry, 1947; The Strangeness of the Church, 1955; Beyond Religion, 1962; Equality and Excellence, 1961; The Christian Belief in God, 1964; The British, Their Identity and Their Religion, 1975; and twelve others. Contributions to: Numerous journals in Britain and the USA; London Times and Times Literary Supplement. Honours: DD, Knox College, Toronto, 1957; DD, Edinburgh University, 1964. Memberships: Athenaeum, London. Address: 301 Willoughby House, Barbican, London, EC2Y 8BL, England.

JENKINS Elizabeth, b. England. Writer. Education: Newnham College, Cambridge. Publications include: The Winters, 1931; Lady Caroline Lamb: A Biography, 1932; Harriet, 1934; The Phoenix Nest, 1936; Jane Austen, A Biography, 1938; Young Enthusiasts, 1946; Henry Fielding, 1947; Six Criminal Women, 1949; The Tortoise and the Hare, 1954; Ten Fascinating Women, 1955; Elizabeth & Leicester, 1961; Brightness, 1963; Honey, 1968; The Mystery of King Arthur, 1975; The Princes in the Tower, 1978; The Shadow and the Light, 1983. Honour: OBE, 1981; Femina Vie Heureuse Prize, 1934. Address: 8 Downshire Hill, Hampstead, London NW3, England.

JENKINS John Geraint, b. 4 Jan 1929, Llangnrannog, Dyfed, Wales. Museum Curator. m. 8 Jan 1954, 3 s. Education: BA, 1952, MA, 1953, DSc, 1980, University of Wales, Swansea and Aberystwyth. Appointments: Editor, Folk Life, 1963-78; President, Society for Folk Life Studies, 1983-86; Chairman, Society for the Interpretation of Britains Heritage, 1975-81. Publications: The English Farm Wagon, 1963; Traditional Country Craftsmen, 1965; Nets and Coracles, 1974; The Welsh Woolen Industry, 1969; Life and Tradition in Rural Wales, 1973; The Coracle, 1985; Agricultural Transport in Wales, 1966; Exploring Museums, Wales, 1990; Interpreting the Heritage of Wales, 1990. Contributions to: Country Life; Folk Life; Agricultural History Review; Home and Country. Honour: Druid Eoredd of Bards, National Eiseddfod of Wales, 1969. Address: The Garden House, St Fagans, Cardiff, CF5 6DS, Wales.

JENKINS Peter George James, b. 11 May 1934, Amersham, Buckinghamshire, England. Journalist. m. Polly Toynbee, 28 Dec 1970, 1 s, 3 d. Education: BA, Trinity Hall, Cambridge, 1957; University of WI, 1957. Appointments: Financial Times, 1958-60; Reporter, 1960, Labour Correspondent, 1963-67, Political Columnist, 1967-72, Washington Correspondent, 1972-74, Policy Editor, Chief Political Commentator, 1974-85, The Guardian; Columnist, Sunday Times, 1985-87; Associate Editor, Political Commenttor, The Independent, 1987-. Publications: The Battle of Downing Street, 1970; Mrs Thatchers Revolution: The Ending of the Socialist Era, 1987; Play, Illuminations, 1980. Contributions to: Numerous Professional Journals. Honours: Visiting Fellow, Nuffield, 1980-87. Literary Agent: A D Peters & Co, London. Address: The Independent, 40 City Road, London EC4, England.

JENKINS Robin, b. 11 Sept 1912, Cambusland, Lanarkshire, England. Education: BA, 1935, Glasgow University. Appointments: Teacher, Gjazi College, Khabul, 1957-59; British Institute, Barcelona, 1959-61, Gaya School, Sabah, 1963-68. Publications. Go Gaily Sings the Lark, 1951; Happy for the Child, 1953; The Thistle and the Grail, 1954; The Cone-Gatherers, 1955; Guests of War, 1956; The Missionaries, 1957; The Changeling, 1958; Love is a Fervent Fire, 1959; Some Kind of Grace, 1960; Dust on the Paw, 1961; The Tiger of Gold, 1962; A Love of Innocence, 1963; The Sardana Dancers, 1964; A Very Scotch Affair, 1968; The Holly Tree, 1969; The Expatriates, 1971; A Toast to the Lord, 1972; A Figure of Fun,, 1974; A Would-Be-Saint, 1978; Fergus Lamont, 1979; The Awakening of George Darroch, 1985; Poverty Castle, 1991. Address: Fairhaven, Toward by Dunoon, Argyll, PA23 7UE, Scotland.

JENKINS Roy Harris, Rt. Hon., Lord Jenkins of Hillhead, b. 11 Nov 1920. Politician; Writer; Chancellor of Oxford University, 1987-; Former President, European Commission. m. Jennifer Morris, 2 sons, 1 daughter. Education: Balliol College, Oxford. Appointments include: MP, Labour, Central Southwark, London, 1948-50, Stetchford, Birmingham, 1950-77; Home Secretary, 1965-67, 1974-76; Chancellor of the Exchequer, 1967-70; Co-Founder, Social Democratic Party, 1981, Leader 1982-83; MP, SDP, Hillhead, Glasgow, 1982-87. Publications: Purpose and Policy, Editor, 1947; Mr Attlee: An Interim Biography, 1948; New Fabian Essays (contributor), 1952; Pursuit of

Progress, 1953; Mr Balfour's Poodle, 1954; Sir Charles Dilke: A Victorian Tragedy, 1958; The Labour Case, 1959; Asquith, 1964; Essays and Speeches, 1967; Afternoon on the Potomac?, 1972; What Matters Now, 1973; Nine Mem of Power, 1974; Partnership of Principle, 1985; Truman, 1986; Baldwin, 1987; Twentieth Century Portraits, 1988; European Diary, 1989; A Life at the Centre, 1991; Portraits & Miniatures, 1993. Honours: Order of Merit, 1993; Life Peer, cr. 1987; Recipient, numerous honours and awards including: Hon. Fellow, Berkeley College, Yale, Balliol College, Oxford, Loughborough, University College, Cardiff; Honorary LL.D., Leeds 1971, Harvard 1972, Pennsylvania 1973, Dundee 1973, Oxford 1973; Bath 1978, Michigan 1978, Essex 1978, Wales 1978, Reading 1979, Bristol 1980; Numerous other honorary degrees; Charlemagne Prize, 1972; Robert Schumann Prize, 1972. Address: 2 Kensington Park Gardens, London, W11, England.

JENKINS Simon David, b. 10 June 1943, Birmingham, England. Times Columnist, Editor. m. Gayle Hunnicutt, 1978. Education: BA, St John's College, Oxford. Appointments: Staff, Country Life Magazine, 1965; News Editor, Times Educational Supplement, 1966-68; Leader Writer, Columnist, Features Editor, 1968-74, Editor, 1977-78, Evening Standard; Insight Editor, Sunday Times, 1974-76; Political Editor, The Economist, 1979-86; Director, Faber and Faber (Publishers) Ltd., 1981-90. Publications: A City at Risk, 1971; Landlords to London, 1974; Newspapers: The Power and the Money, 1979; The Companion Guide to Outer London, 1981; Images of Hampstead, 1982; The Battle for the Falklands, 1983; With Respect, Ambassador, 1985; Market for Glory, 1986; The Selling of Mary Davies, 1993. Memberships: Board, Old Vic Co., 1979-81; Part-time Member, British Rail Board, 1979-90; London Regional Transport Board, 1984-86; Museum of London, 1984-88; Vice Chairman, Thirties Society, 1979-90; Director, The Municipal Journal, 1980-90; Historic Buildings and Monuments Commission, 1985-90; South Bank Board, 1985-90. Address: 174 Regents Park Road, London, NW1, England.

JENNINGS Elizabeth (Joan), b. 18 July 1926, Boston, England. Education: Oxford High School, MA, St Annes College, Oxford. Appointments: Assistant, Oxford City Library, 1950-58; Reader, Chatto and Windus Limited, Publishers, 1958-60; Freelance Writer, 1961-; Guildersleeve Lecturer, Barnard College, NY, 1974-. Publications include: Verse, Relationships, 1972; Growing Points, 1975; After the Ark, 1978; Moments of Grace, 1979; Selected Poems, 1979; A Dream of Spring, 1980; Celebrations and Elegies, 1982; Author or Edition of Many Other Publications. Honours: Arts Council Award, 1953; Bursary, 1965, 68, 81; Grant, 1972; Somerset Maugham Award, 1956; Richard Hillary Memorial Prize, 1966; WH Smith Award, 1987. Literary Agent: David Higham Associated Limited. Address: 11 Winchester Rod, Oxford, OX2 6Na, England.

JENNINGS Phillip C, b. 5 Mar 1946, Seattle, WA, USA. m. Deborah Louise McCarl, 6 Sept 1969, 1 s, 1 d. Education: BA, Macalester College, 1968. Appointments: Programmer, Analyst, State of MN, St Paul, 1969-78; Programmer and Analyst, Control Data Corporation, Arden Hills, MN, 1978-79; Programmer, Analyst, United Information Services, MO, 1979-83; Writer, 1983-; Member of St Johns Episcopal Chirch Choir. Publications: Tower to the Sky, 1988; The Bug Life Chronicles, 1989. Contributions to: Stories in Magazines; Work Represented in Anthologies. Memberships: Science Fiction Writers of AM; Planetary Society; National Organization for Women. Address: 32130 County Road 1, St Cloud, MN 56303, USA.

JENOFF Marvyne Shael, b. 10 Mar 1942, Winnipeg, Manitoba, Canada. Teacher. Education: BA, University of Manitoba, 1964; Teacher Training. Publications: The Emperor's Body, adult fables, 1995; Poetry: No Lingering Peace, 1972; Hollandsong, 1975; The Orphan and the Stranger, 1985; New Poet's Handbook (editor), 1984-85. Contributions to: Prism International; The Fiddlehead; The Antigonish Review; Matrix; The Canadian Forum. Memberships: League of Canadian Poets; The Writers Union of Canada. Address: c/o The Writers' Union of Canada, 24 Ryerson Avenue, Toronto, Ontario, Canada M5T 2P3.

JENSEN De Lamar, b. 1925, USA. Appointments: Instructor in History, New York University, New York City, 1954-57; Professor of History, Brigham Young University, Provo, Utah, 1957-. Publications: Machiavelli: Cynic, Patriot or Political Scientist? (compiler, editor), 1960; Diplomacy and Dogmatism: Bernardino de Mendoza and the French Catholic League, 1964; The Expansion of Europe: Motives, Methods and Meanings (compiler, editor), 1967; The World of Europe:

The Sixteenth Century; Confrontation at Worms: Martin Luther and the Diet of Worms, 1973; Renaissance Europe, 1980, 2nd Edition, 1991; Reformation Europe, 1981, 2nd Edition, 1991. Address: 1079 Briar Avenue, Provo, UT 84604, USA.

JENSEN Laura Linnea, b. 16 Nov 1948, Tacoma, WA, USA. Poet; Occasional Teacher. Education: BA, University of WA, 1972; MFA, University of IA, 1974. Appointments: Manuscript Judge, NEA, 1977; Panel Member, NEA, 1981; Prize Judge, Poetry Society of Am, 1982, 85; Hopwood Awards, University of MI, 1986; Visiting Poet, Oklahoma State University, 1978. Publications include: Shelter, 1985; Memory, 1982; Bad Boats, 1977; Anxiety & Ashes, 1976; Also Chapbooks & Pamphlets; A Sky Empty of Orion, 1985; Tapwater, 1978; The Story Makes Them Whole, 1979; After I Have Voted, 1972. Contributions to: American Poetry Review; Antaeus; Field; IA Review; Ironwood; New Yorker; Northwest Review; Poetry Northwest; Pushcart Prize. Honours: Honours Award, 1978; Fellowship Grant, 1985-87; WA State Arts Commission; Fellowship, National Endowment for the Arts, 1980-81; Grant, Ingram Merrill Foundation, 1983; Theodore Roethke Award, 1986; Guggenheim Fellowship, 1989-90; Lila Wallace Readers Digest Writers Award, 1993. Memberships: Poets & Writers; Associated Writing Programmes; Academy of Am Poets. Address: 302 North Yakima C3, Tacoma, WA 98403, USA.

JENSEN Ruby Jean, b. 1 Mar 1930, Author. m. Vaughn Jenson, 1 d. Publications: Novels, House of Illusions, 1988; Chain Letter, 1987; Such a Good Baby, 1982; Pendulum, 1989; Jump Rope, 1988; Death Stone, 1989; Annabelle, 1987; The House That Samael Built, 1974; The Lake, 1983; The Seventh All Hallows Eve, 1974; Dark Angel, 1978; Hear the Children Cry, 1981; Mama, 1983; Home sweet Home, 1985; Celia, 1991; Baby Dolly, 1991. Literary Agent: Marcia Amsterdam. Address: 41 West 82nd Street, New York, NY 10024, USA.

JENZER Louis Romain, b. 8 June 1945, Melchnau, Switzerland. Publisher; Writer. Education: Business Studies Diploma, 1961-64; Liceum Latin, 1975-81; Philosophy, Marketing Management, 1972-73. Publications: The real Jaccob, 1981; The Birth of the Roadseller, 1982; Aphorism, by Professor Kurz Göttingen, 1982; Foundation of Minerva, 1985; Fabula rasa, 1987; The Bird of the Roadseller, 1991. Contributions to: Columne Newspaper of Culture, Switzerland. Memberships: Swiss Writer Association; Bern Writer Association; German Dramatic Society; Editor Association Swiss SBVV; PEN, 1987. Address: Postcase 6849, 3001 CH Bern, Switzerland.

JERINA Carol, b. 2 Sept 1947, TX, USA. Writer. m. Drew Jerina, 20 Dec 1968, 4 s. Appointments: Sales Clerk, Sanger Harris, 1964-66; Tax and Data Processing Clerk, City of Dallas, 1966-68. Publications: Lady Raine, Gallaghers Lady, 1984; Fox Hunt, 1985; Brighter Than Gold, Embrace An Angel, 1987; Tropic Gold, The Tall Dark Alibi, Sweet Jeopardy, 1988. Honours: Reviewers Choice Awards from Romantic Times for Best Humourous Historical Romance, for Fox Hunt, 1985; Nomination for Best Post Civil War Romance, For Embrace an Angel, 1987. Memberships: Romance Writers Of Am; Greater Dallas Writers Association. Address: 3109 Bluffview Drive, Garland, TX 75043, USA.

JERSILD Per Christian, b. 14 Mar 1935, Katrineholm, Sweden. Writer. m. Ulla J, 1960, 2 sons. Education: MD. Publications: The Animal Doctor, 1975, 1988; After the Flood, 1986; Childrens Island, 1987; The House of Babel, 1987; A Living Soul, 1988; also 29 books published in Sweden. Honours: Swedish Grand Novel Prize, 1981; Swedish Academy Award, 1982. Memberships: Swedish PEN, Board. Address: Rosensdalsv. 20, 5-19454 Uppl. Vasby, Sweden.

JESSUP Frances, b. 29 July 1936, England. Author. m. Clive Turner, 2 Jan 1960, 1 son, 3 daughters. Education: BA Hons Philosophy, King's College, London University, 1955-58. Appointments: Organiser of Theatre Writing in Halesmere, UNA, 1992. Publications: The Fifth Child's Conception, 1970, 1972. Contributions to: New Poetry, 1980; New Stories, 1981; Hard Lines, 1987; Words Etcetera, 1973; Words Broadsheet, Pen Broadsheet, 1986; Weyfarers; Overspill; MTD Journal. Honours: First Prize for Fiction and Poetry, Moor Park College, 1972; UNA Trust Award (for Peace Play Festival), 1988; University of Surrey Arts Committee Literary Festival Award, 1991. Memberships: PEN; TWU. Literary Agent: Patricia Robertson. Address: Strone Grove Road, Hindhead, Surrey, GU26 6QP, England.

JHABVALA Ruth Prawer, b. 7 May 1927, Cologne, Germany. Writer. m. 16 June 1951, 3 d. Education: BA, 1948, MA, 1951, DLitt, London. Publications: The Householder, 1960; A New Dominion, 1971;

Heat & Dust, 1975; Out of India, 1986; Three Continents, 1987; Poet and Dancer, 1993. Honours: Booker Prize, 1975; Neil Gunn International Fellowship, 1979; MacArthur Foundation Fellowship, 1984-89; Academy Award, 1987, 1993; Am Academy of Arts & Letters, Literature Award, 1992. Memberships: Fellow Royal Society of Literature; Authors Guild; Writers Guild of Am. Literary Agent: Harriet Wasserman. Address: 400 East 52nd Street, New York, NY 10022, USA.

JIMENEZ Francisco, b. 29 June 1943, Mexico. University Professor and Administrator. m. Laura Facchini Jimenez, 17 Aug 1968, 3 sons. Education: BA, Santa Clara University, USA, 1966; MA, 1969, PhD, 1972, Columbia University; Management Development Programme Certificate, Harvard University, 1989. Literary appointments: Editorial Board, 1973-, West Coast Editor, 1974-, The Bilingual Review; Board of Directors, Asociacion Literaria de Bellas Artes, 1978-; President, Chicano Literature Executive Committee, Modern Language Association of America. Publications: The Circuit; Cajas de Carton; Prosa chicana cubana puertorriquena; Los Episodios Nacionales de Victoriano Salado Alvarez, 1974; Identification and Analysis of Chicano Literature; Hispanics in the US: An Anthology of Creative Literature; Viva La Lengua; Poverty and Social Justice; Critical Perspectives; Introduction, Voices from the Fields by Beth Atkin, 1993. Contributions to: Cuadernos Americanos; Hispania; The Bilingual Review; La Luz; El Grito; Lector; Mensaje; Revista de Cultura y Arte; Arizona Quarterly; El regalo de Alma, to Journal of the Association of Mexican American Educators, 1989; The Circuit, to Literary Cavalcade, 1992. Address: 624 Enos Court, Santa Clara, CA 95051, USA.

JOEL Laurence. See: EIGNER Larry.

JOHANSSON-BACKE Karl Erik, b. 24 Nov 1914, Stockholm, Sweden. Teacher (Retired 1963); Author; Playwright. m. Kerstin Gunhild Bergquist, (childrens author), 21 Nov 1943, 1 son, 3 daughters. Education: Degree, High School Teacher. Publications: A Pole in the River, (novel), 1950; Daybreak, (novel), 1954; Lust and Flame, (poetry), 1981; The Mountain of Temptation, (novel), 1983; The Ghost Aviator (documentary), 1985; The Tree and the Bread, (novel), 1987; King of Mountains (novel), 1993; Author, 30 books and 10 plays, amongst them: Just Old Pearl, 1965; The Wolf, 1974. Honours: Many literary awards from 1961-93. Memberships: Swedish Authors Federation; Honorary Member of the Swedish Playwrights Federation, 1986. Literary Agent: Arbetarkultur, Stockholm; Bonniers, Stockholm; Proprius, Stockholm. Address: Kopmangstan 56, 83133, Ostersund, Sweden.

JOHN Katherine, See: WATKINS Karen Christna.

JOHN Nicholas, See: VIDOR Miklos Janos.

JOHNS Kenneth. See: BULMER Henry Kenneth.

JOHNSON A E. See: JOHNSON Annabel (Jones).

JOHNSON Alison Findlay, b. 19 Nov 1947, Stafford, England. Author. m. Andrew J D Johnson, 1973, 1 d. Education: MA, Aberdeen University, 1968; BPhil, Oxford, 1970. Publications: A House by the Shore, 1986; Scarista Style, 1987; Children of Disobedience, 1989; Islands in the Sound, 1989; The Wicked Generation, 1992. Contributions to: West Highland Press; The Times. Literary Agent: Vivien Green. Address: c/o Vivien Green, 43 Goughty Street, London wC1N 2LF, England.

JOHNSON Annabel (Jones) (A E Johnson), b. 1921, USA. Publications: As A Speckled Bird, 1956; The Big Rock Candy (with Edgar Johnson), 1957; The Black Symbol, 1959; Torrie, The Bearcat, 1960; Pickpocket Run, 1961; Wilderness Bride, 1962; A Golden Touch, 1963; The Grizzly, 1964; A Peculiar Magic, 1965; The Burning Glass, 1966; Count Me Gone, 1968; The Last Knife, 1971; Finders Keepers, 1981; An Alien Music, 1982; The Danger Quotient, 1984; Prisoner of PSI, 1985; A Memory of Dragons, 1986; Gamebuster, 1990; I Am Leaper, 1990; As A E Johnson: The Rescued Heart, The Secret Gift, 1961; A Blues I Can Whistle, 1969. Address: 2925 S Teller, Denver, CO 80227, USA.

JOHNSON Barbara Ferry, b. 1923, America. Appointments: Association Editor, Am Lumberman Magazine, 1945-48; High School English Teacher, Myrtle Beach, 1960-62; MEmber of The English Dept, Columbia College, 1964-. Publications: Lioners, 1975; Delta Blood,

1977; Taras Song, 1978; Homeward Winds the River, 1979; The Heirs of Love, 1980; Echoes from the Hills, 1982. Address: c/o Warner Books, 660 Fifth Avenue, New York, NY 10103, USA.

JOHNSON Carlos Alberto, b. 26 June 1943, Lima, Peru. Writer. Education: BS, Education & Spanish, Buffalo State College, 1971-72; MA, Spanish, Brooklyn College, 1972-74; Completed 60 Credits Toward PhD, Spanish, CUNY Graduate Centre, 1974-76. Appointments: Correspondent and Reporter for El Dominical of the Peruvian Newspaper El Diario El Comercio, 1981-88. Publications: El Ojo-Cara del Professor, 1983; Adivina quien es?, 1976; El monologo del vendedor ambulante, 1984; Cuando me muera que me arrojen al Rimac en un cajon blanco, 1990. Contributions to: Centerpoint; Revista Chicano-Riquena; Revista Casa de las Americas; Chasqui, Revista de Literatura Latinoamericana; Inti Rev de Lit Hispanica; Linden Lane Magazine; New Delhi Magazine; Sunday Sketch; El Dominical; El Guacamayo y la Serpiente; Rev de la Casa de la Cult; Ecuatoriana. Honours: Creative Writing Fellowship, National Endowment for the Arts, 1989. Address: 30-98 Crescent Street Apt 1C, Astoria, NY 11102, USA.

JOHNSON Colin, b. 1939, Beverley, Western Australia. Novelist. Appointments include: Lecturer, University of Queensland, St Lucia. Publications: Wild Cat Falling, 1965; Long Live Sandawara, 1979; Doctor Wooreddys Prescription for Enduring the End of the World, 1983; Doin' Wildcat, 1988; Dalwurra: The Black Bittern, 1988; Before the Invasion: Aboriginl Life to 1788, 1980; Writing from the Fringe, 1990. Honours: Wieckhard Prize, 1979; Western Australia Literary Award, 1989. Address: c/o Dept of English, University of Queensland, St Lucia, Queensland 4067, Australia.

JOHNSON David, b. 26 Aug 1927, Meir, Staffs, England. Education: Repton; Sandhurst. Publications: Sabre General, 1959; Promenade in Champagne, 1960; Lanterns in Gascony, 1965; A Candle in Aragon, 1970; Regency Revolution, 1974; Napoleon's Cavalry and its Leaders, 1978; The French Cavalry 1792-1815, 1989. Contributions to: Military History, USA. Address: 16 Belgrave Gardens, London, NW8 0RB, England.

JOHNSON Denis, b. 1949, America. Publications: The Man Among the Seals, 1969; Inner Weather, 1976; The Incognito Lounge and Other Poems, 1982; Angels, 1983; Fiskadoro, 1985; The Stars at Noon, 1986; Jesus' Son, 1993. Honours include: American Academy of Arts, Letters, Literature Award, 1993. Address: c/o Knopf Incorporated, 201 E 50th Street, New York, NY 10022, USA.

JOHNSON Diane Lain, b. 28 Apr 1934, IL, USA. m. John Frederick Murray, 9 Nov 1969, 4 children. Education: AA, Stephens College, 1953; BA, University Utah, 1957; MA, PhD, UCLA, 1968. Appointments: Faculty, Dept of English, University of CA, 1968-87. Publications include: Fair Game, 1965; Loving Hands at Home, 1968; The Shadow Knows, 1975; Lesser Lives, 1972; Terrorists and Novelists, 1982; Dashiell Hammett, 1983; Perian Nights, 1987; Health and Happiness, 1990; Natural Opium, 1993. Contributions to: New York Review of Books; NY Times Book Reviews; New yorker; WA Post; Los Angeles Times. Honours: Nominee, National Book Award, 1973, 79; Recipient, Rosenthal Award Am Academy of Arts & letters, 1979; Mildred and Harold Strauss Living Am Academy and Institute of Arts & Letters, 1988. Memberships: PEN; Writers Guild of Am. Literary Agent: Lynn Nesbit.

JOHNSON E(mil) Richard, b. 1938, Am. Inmate at Stillwater, MN State Prison, 1964-. Publications: Silver Street, 1968; The Inside Man, Monogos Back in Town, 1969; Cage Five is Going To Break, The God Keepers, 1970; Case Lord, Maxiumum, The Judas, 1971; The Cardinalli Contract, 1975; Blind Mans Bluff, Fur: Food and Survival, 1987; The Hands of Eddy Loyd, 1988; Dead Flowers, 1990. Address: Box 55, Stillwater, MN 55082, USA.

JOHNSON George, b. 20 Jan 1952, Fayetteville, AK, USA. Writer. Education: MA, Am University, 1979; BA, University of New Mexicos, 1975. Appointments: Alicia Patterson Journalism Fellow, 1984. Publications: Architects of Fear, 1984; Machinery of the Mind, 1986; In the Places of Memory, 1991. Contributions to: NY Times Book Review; The Sciences; PM Magazine; NY Times Magazine. Literary Agent: Esther Newbery ICM. Address: c/o Esther Newbery ICM, 40 West 57th Street, NY 10019, USA.

JOHNSON Hugh Eric Allan, b. 10 Mar 1939, London, England. Author; Editor. m. Judith Eve Grinling, 1965, 1 son, 2 daughters.

Education: MA, King's College, Cambridge. Appointments: Feature Writer, Conde Nast Magazines, 1960-63; Editor, Wine and Food Magazine, 1963-65; Wine Correspondent, Sunday Times, 1965-67; Travel Editor, 1967; Editor, Queen Magazine, 1968-70; Wine Editor, Cuisine Magazine, New York, 1983-84; Editorial Consultant, The Garden, 1975-. Publications: Wine, 1966; The World Atlas of Wine, 1971, 1977, 1985, 1994; The International Book of Trees, 1973, 1994; The California Wine Book (with Bob Thompson), 1975; Hugh Johnson's Pocket Wine Book, annually, 1977; The Principles of Gardening, 1979; Hugh Johnson's Wine Companion, 1983; How to Handle a Wine (video), 1984; Hugh Johnson's Cellar Book, 1986; The Atlas of German Wines, 1986; Understanding Wine (A Sainsbury Guide), 1986; Atlas of the Wines of France (with Hubrecht Duijker), 1987; A History of Wine, Channel 4 TV series, 1989; The Story of Wine, 1989; The Art and Science of Wine, 1992; Hugh Johnson on Gardening, 1993. Address: Saling Hall, Great Saling, Essex, CM7 5DT, England.

JOHNSON James Henry, b. 19 Nov 1930, University Professor. m. Jean McKane, 31 Mar 1956, 2 sons, 2 daughters. Education: BA, Belfast, Northern Ireland, 1953; MA, Wisconsin, USA, 1954; PhD, London, England, 1962. Appointments: Editor, Aspects of Geography Series, Macmillan, 1980-. Publications: Urban Geography: An Introductory Analysis, 1967; Trends in Geography, (Editor), 1969; Geographical Mobility of Labour in England and Wales, (Co-author), 1974; Surburban Growth, (Editor), 1974; Urbanisation, 1980; The Structure of Nineteenth Century Cities, (Co-editor), 1982; Labour Migration, (co-editor), 1990; Population Migration, (co-author), 1990; The Human Geography of Ireland (Wiley), 1994. Contributions to: Geographical journals, 1956-93. Address: The Coach-house, Wyreside Hall, Dolphinholme, Lancaster, LA2 9DH, England.

JOHNSON James Ralph, b. 20 May 1922, Fort Payne, Alabama, USA. Writer; Artist. m. (1) 2 sons, 1 daughter, (2) Burdetta F Beebe, 11 Oct 1961. Education: BS, Economics, Howard College, Birmingham, Alabama; US Navy Intelligence School, Anacostia, Maryland, 1951; Armed Forces Staff College, Norfolk, Virginia, 1960. Publications: Mountain Bobcat, 1953; Lost on Hawk Mountain, 1954; The Last Passenger, 1956; Big Cypress Buck, 1957; Horsemen Blue and Gray, 1960; Anyone Can Live Off the Land, 1961; Best Photos of the Civil War, 1961; Wild Venture, 1961; Utah Lion, 1962; Anyone Can Camp in Comfort, 1964; American Wild Horses, 1964; Camels West, 1964; Anyone Can Backpack in Comfort, 1965; The Wolf Cub, 1966; Advanced Camping Techniques, 1967; Pepper, 1967; Ringtail, 1968; Blackie the Gorilla, 1968; Animal Paradise, 1969; Moses Band of Chimpanzees, 1969; Everglades Adventure, 1970; Southern Swamps of America, 1970; Zoos of Today, 1971; Photography for Young People, 1971; Animals and Their Food, 1972. Contributions to: Marine Corps Gazette; Leatherneck; Saga; Boys' Life; Field and Stream. Honours: Best Like of Year Selection, for Anyone Can Camp in Comfort, Boys' Clubs of America, 1965. Memberships: Western Writers of America; Outdoor Writers of America; Santa Fe Society of Artists Incorporated. Address: Box 5295, Santa Fe, NM 87502, USA.

JOHNSON (John) Stephen, b. 1947, British. Publications: The Roman Fort of the Saxon Shore, 1976, 1979; Later Roman Britain, 1980; Late Roman Fortifications, 1983; Hadrian's Wall, 1989; Rome and its Empire, 1989; Address: 50 Holmdere Avenue, London SE24 9LF, England.

JOHNSON Linton Kwesi, b. 1952, Chapeltown, Jamaica. Editor; Poet. Education: BA, University of London, 1973. Appointments include: Arts Editor, Race Today Magazine; Writer in Residence, London Borough of Lambeth; Producer, BBC Series on Jamaican Music. Publications: Voices of the Living and the Dead, 1974; Dread, Beat, and Blood, 1975; Ingian is a Bitch, 1980; Record Albums Featuring Poems & Lyrics. Honours include: C Day Lewis Fellowship, 1977. Address: c/o Island Records Limited, 22 St Peters Square, London W6 9NW, England.

JOHNSON Louis Albert, b. 27 Sept 1924, Wellington, New Zealand. Teacher; Journalist. m. Cecilia Wilson, 14 Nov 1970, 1 s, 1 d. Education: Wellington Teachers College. Appointments: Lecturer, Senior Lecturer, Mitchell College Advanced Education, NSW, 1970-79; OIC Bureau Literature, PNG, 1968-69; Writer-in-Residence, Victoria University, Wellington, 1980; Member, New Zealand Literary Fund Advisory Board, 1982-. Publications: True Confessions Of the Last Cannibal, 1986; Coming & Going, 1982; Fires & Patterns, 1975; Land Like a Lizard, 1970; Bread and a Pension, 1964; New Worlds For Old, 1956; Founder, Editor, Numbers, 1953-60; Founder Editor, New

Zealand Poetry Yearbook, 1951-64. Contributions to: Poetry Australia; The Bulletin; Quadrant; Poetry London; London Magazine; Landfall. Honours: New Zealand Book Award, Poetry, 1975; Writers Fellowship, Victoria University, 1980; OBE, 1987. Memberships: PEN, New Zealand Centre, Secretary, 1955-59, President, 1986-87. Address: 4 Te Motu Road, Pukera Bay, New Zealand.

JOHNSON Mel. See: **MALZBERG Barry Norman.**

JOHNSON Nora, b. 31 Jan 1933, Hollywood, California, USA. Author. m. (1) Leonard Siwek, 1955; (2) John A Milici, 1965, 2 s, 2 d. Education: BA, Smith College, 1954. Publications: The World of Henry Orient, 1958; A Step Beyond Innocence, 1961; Love Letter in the Dead Letter Office, 1966; Flashback, 1979; You Can Go Home Again, 1982; The Two of Us, 1984; Tender Offer, 1985; Uncharted Places, 1988; Perfect Together, 1991. Contributions to: New York Times Book Review; LA Times Magazine; LA Times Book Review; New Yorker; Seventeen; McCall's Sport Illustrated; Atlantic Monthly; Cosmopolitan. Honours: McCall's Short Story Prize, 1962; Nomination, Screen Writer's Award, 1964; O Henry Award Story, 1982; NU Times Best Book 1982, 1984. Memberships: Author's Guild; PEN. Literary Agent: Helen Brann, 94 Curtis Road, Bridewater, CT 06752, USA. Address: 1385, York Avenue 8G, New York City, NY 10021, USA.

JOHNSON Owen Verne, b. 22 Feb 1946, Madison, Wisconsin, USA. Historian; Associate Professor. m. Marta Kucerova, 17 July 1969, 2 daughters. Education: BA, Washington State University, 1968; MA, 1970, Certificate, 1978, PhD, 1978, University of Michigan. Appointments: Sports Editor, General Assignment Reporter, Pullman Washington Herald, 1961-67; Reporter, Editor, Producer, WUOM, Ann Arbor, Michigan, 1969-77; Administrative Assistant, Russian and East European Center, University of Michigan, 1978-79; Assistant Professor, Journalism, Southern Illinois University, 1979-80; Assistant Professor, Journalism, 1980-87, Associate Professor, Journalism, 1987-, Acting Director, Polish Studies Center, 1989-90, Director, Russian and East European Institute, 1991-, Indiana University, Bloomington. Publications: Slovakia 1918-1938: Education and the Making of a Nation, 1985; Mobilizing and Mobilized: The Roles and Functions of the Mass Media in Eastern Europe, forthcoming; Editor: Czech Marks, 1982-84; Clio Among the Media, 1983-84. Address: School of Journalism, Indiana University, Bloomington, IN 47405, USA.

JOHNSON Paul (Bede), b. 2 Nov 1928, Barton, England. Historian; Journalist; Broadcaster. m. Marigold Hunt, 1957, 3 sons, 1 daughter. Education: BA, Magdalen College, Oxford. Appointments: Assistant Executive Editor, Realites, Paris, 1952-55; Assistant Editor, New Statesman, 1955-60, Deputy Editor, 1960-64, Editor, 1965-70, Director, 1965-75; DeWitt Wallace Professor of Communications, American Enterprise Institute, Washington DC, 1980; Freelance Writer; Daily Mail Columnist. Publications: The Offshore Islanders, 1972; Elizabeth I: A Study in Power and Intellect, 1974; Pope John XXIII, 1975; A History of Christianity, 1976; Enemies of Society, 1977; The National Trust Book of British Castles, 1978; The Civilization of Ancient Egypt, 1978; Civilizations of the Holy Land, 1979; British Cathedrals, 1980; Ireland: Land of Troubles, 1980; The Recovery of Freedom, 1980; Pope John Paul II and the Catholic Restoration, 1982; History of the Modern World: From 1917 to the 1980s, 1984; The Pick of Paul Johnson, 1985; A History of the Jews, 1986; The Oxford Book of Political Anecdotes, Editor, 1986; The Intellectuals, 1989; The Birth of the Modern World Society, 1815-30, 1991. Honours: Book of the Year Prize, Yorkshire Post, 1975; Francis Boyer Award for Services to Public Policy, 1979; Krag Award for Excellence, Literature, 1980. Memberships: Royal Commission on the Press, 1974-77; Cable Authority 1984-. Address: 29 Newton Road, London, W2, England.

JOHNSON Stowers, British. Appointments: Principal, Dagenham Literary Institute, 1936-39; Headmaster, Aveley School, 1939-68; Editor, Anglo-Soviet Journal, 1966-68; Art Curator, National Liberal Club, London, 1974-79. Publications: Branches Green and Branches Black, 1944; London Saga, 1946; The Mundane Tree, 1947; Mountains and No Mules, Sonntes They say, 1949; Before and After Puck, 1953; When Fountains Fall, 1961; Gay Bulgaria, 1964; Yugoslav Summer, 1967; Collector's Luck, 1968; Turkish Panorama, The Two Faces of Russia, 1969; Agents Extraordinary, 1975; Headmastering Man, 1986; Hearthstones in the Hills, 1987; Collector's World, 1989. Address: Corbiere, 45 Rayleigh Road, Hutton, Brentwood, Essex, England.

JOHNSON Terry, b. 20 Dec 1955. Playwright. Education: Queens School, Bushey, Hertfordshire, England; BA, Drama,

University of Birmingham, 1976. Career: Actor in late 1970's and Director. Publications: plays: Amabel (produced London 1979); Days Here so Dark (produced London, Edinburgh, 1981); Insignificance (produced London 1982, New York, 1986); Bellevue (toured 1982); The Idea (produced Bristol 1983); Unsuitable For Adults (produced London 1984, Costa Mesa, California, 1986); Cries From the Mammal House (produced London and Leicester, 1984); Tuesdays Child, with Kate Lock (televised 1985, produced London 1986); screenplays: Insignificance, 1985; Killing Time, 1985; Way Upstream, 1987; TV plays: Time Trouble, 1985; Tuesdays Child with Kate Lock, 1985. Honour: Evening Standard Award, 1983. Literary Agent: Goodwin Associates, London. Address: c/o Phil Kelvin, Goodwin Associates, 12 Rabbit Row, London W8 4DX, England.

JOHNSON Wendell Stacy, b. 27 Dec 1927, Jackson County, Missouri, USA. Writer; University Professor. Education: BA, University of Missouri, 1948; MA, 1949; PhD, 1952, Ohio State University. Publications: The Voices of Matthew Arnold, 1961; An Introduction to Literary Criticism, 1962; Gerard Manley Hopkins, 1968; A Poetry Anthology with M Danziger, 1968; Words Things And Celebrations, 1972; Sex and Marriage in Victorian Poetry, 1975; Living in Sin, 1979; Charles Dickens - New Perspectives (editor), 1982; Browning Institute Annual (editor), 1983; Sons and Fathers, 1985; W H Auden, 1989. Contributions to: various journals and magazines. Honours: Fulbright Fellowship, 1952; Howald Postdoctora; Fellowship, 1962; ACLS Grants, 1964, 1967; Guggenheim Fellowship, 1965; NEH Senior Research Fellowship, 1979; Huntington Library Grants, 1968, 1980. Memberships: MLA, Chairman Victorian Group; Golier Club; American Association of University Professors. Literary Agent: Charlotte Sheedy. Address: 65 Hampton Street, Southampton, NY 11968, USA.

JOHNSTON George Benson, b. 7 Oct 1913, Hamilton, Ontario, Canada. Poet, Translator. m. Jeanne McRae, 1944, 3 sons, 3 daughters. Education: BA, 1936, MA, 1945, University of Toronto; LLD, Queen's University, Kingston, Ontario, 1971; LitD, Carleton University, 1979. Appointments: Assistant Professor of English, Mount Allison University, Sackville, 1946-48; Staff, English Department, Carleton University, Ottawa, 1950-79; Now retired. Publications: Verse: The Cruising Auk, 1959; Home Free, 1966; Happy Enough, 1972; Between, 1976; Taking a Grip, 1979; Auk Redivivus: Selected Poems, 1981; Ask Again, 1984; Endeared by Dark (Collected Poems), 1990; Editor-Translator: Rocky Shores: An Anthology of Faroese Poetry, 1981; George Whalley: Collected Poems, 1986; Translator: The Saga of Gisli, 1963; The Faroe Islanders' Saga, 1975; The Greenlanders' Saga; Wind over Romsdal: Selected Poems (Odegard), 1982; Bee-Buzz, Salmon-Leap (Odegard), verse, 1988; Seeing and Remembering (Matras), verse, 1988; Barbara, novel in translation, 1993; Thrand of Goth, sagas in translation. Address: PO Box 788, Huntingdon, Quebec, Canada J0S 1H0.

JOHNSTON Jennifer, 12 Jan 1930. Author. m. (1) Ian Smyth, 1951, 2 s, 2 d, (2) David Gilliland, 1976. Publications: The Captains and the Kings, 1972; The Gates, 1973; How Many Miles to Babylon? 1974; Shadows on our Skin, 1978 (dramatised for TV, 1979); The Old Jest, 1979; play: The Nightingale and Not the Lark, 1980; The Christmas Tree, 1981; The Railway Station Man, 1984; Fools Sanctuary, 1987; plays: Indian Summer, Belfast, 1983; The Porch, Dublin, 1986; The Invisible Man, Dublin, 1986; The Invisible Worm (novel), 1991; BBC radio: O Ananais, Azarais and Misael, 1990; Billy, 1990; Triptych, Dublin, 1989. Honours: Hon D Litt, NUU, 1984; Hon D Litt, TCD. Membership: AOSDANA. Address: Brook Hall, Culmore Road, Derry, Norhtern Ireland, BT48 8JE.

JOHNSTON Julia Ann, b. 21 Jan 1941, Ontario, Canada. Writer. m. Basil W Johnston, 12 Oct 1963, 4 d. Education: SFDCI Honour Grad Diploma, 1960; University of Toronto, 1963; Trent University, 1984. Publications include: Adam and Eve And Pinch Me, 1994; Hero of Lesser Causes, 1992; The Interiors of Pots, 1992; After 30 Years of Law, Ken Jarvis Sculpts New Career, 1990; Tasting The Alternative, 1982; Don't Give Up The Ghosts, 1981; Theres Going to be a Frost, 1979. Honours: Governor Generals Literary Award, 1992; Canadian Childrens Book Centre, 1992 Our Choice List; National Chapter of Canada Violet Downey Book Award, 1993; Nominated for Mister Christies Book Award, 1993; A School Library Journal Best Book, 1993; Joan Fassler Memorial Book Award, 1994. Memberships: Writers Union of Canada; Canadaian Society of Childrens Authors. Address: 463 Hunter Street W, Peterborough, Canada, K9H 2M7.

JOHNSTON Norma (Elizabeth Bolton, Catherine E Chambers, Kate Chambers, Pamela Dryden, Lavinia Harris, Adrian Robert, Nicole St John), American. Writer, fiction, children's fiction, children's non-fiction, mythology & folklore. Has worked as retailer, producer, director, actress, teacher and businesswoman. Appointments: President, St John Institute of Arts and Letters. Publications include: Pride of Lions, 1972; A Nice Girl Like You, 1980; Myself and I, 1981; The Days of the Dragon's Seed, 1982; Timewarp Summer, 1982; Gabriel's Girl, 1983; The Carlisle Chronicles, 3 vol series, 1986; Shadow on Unicorn Farms, 1986; Watcher in the Mist, 1986; as Nicole St John: Wychwood, 1976; Gueniver's Gift, 1977; as Pamela Dryden: Mask For My Heart, 1982; as Lavinia Harris: Dreams and Memories, 1982; The Great Rip-Off, 1984; A Touch of Madness, 1985; Soaps in the Afternoon, 1985; Cover-Up, 1986; The Packaging of Hank and Celia, 1986; as Kate Chambers: Secrets on Beacon Hill, 1984; The Legacy of Lucian Van Zandt, 1984; The Threat of the Pirate Ship, 1984; as Catherine Chambers: Indian Days: Life in a Frontier Town, 1984; Texas Roundup: Life on The Range, 1984; Wagons West: Off to Oregon, 1984; as Elizabeth Bolton: The Secret of the Ghost Piano, 1985; The Secret of the Magic Potion, 1985; The Tree House Detective Club, 1985; as Adrain Robert: My Grandma The Witch, 1985; The Secret of the Haunted Chimney,1985; The Secret of the Old Barn, 1985.

JOHNSTON Ronald, b. 1926, British. Appointments: Associate, Chartered Insurance Institute; with Manufacturers Life Insurance of Canada, 1947-51; Salesman, General Manager, Director, Anglo-Dutch Cigar Company Limited, 1959-68. Publications: Disaster at Dungeness (in US as Collision Ahead), 1964; Red Sky in the Morning (in US as Danger at Bravo Key), 1965; The Stowaway, 1966; The Wrecking of Offshore Five, 1967; The Angry Ocean, 1968; The Black Camels (in US as as the Black Camels of Qahran), 1969; Paradise Smith, 1972; The Eye of the Needle, 1975; Sea Story, 1980; Flying Dutchman, 1983. Memberships: Council Member, Scottish Arts Council, 1973-; Management Committee, Society of Authors, 1975-.

JOHNSTON Ronald John, b. 30 Mar 1941, Swindon, England. University Professor. m. Rita Brennan, 16 Apr 1963, 1 son, 1 daughter. Education: BA, 1962, MA, 1964, University of Manchester, England; PhD, Monash University, Australia, 1967. Publications: Geography and Geographers, 1979, 1983, 1987, 1991; City and Society, 1984; A World in Crisis?, 1986, 1989; Dictionary of Human Geography, 1981, 1986, 1993; The New Zealanders, 1976; Bell-Ringing, 1986; On Human Geography; Environmental Problems; Geography of Elections; The Geography of English Politics; A Nation Dividing?; Geography and The State. Contributions to: Over 300. Honours: Murchison Award, 1984, Victoria Medal, 1990, Royal Geographical Society. Memberships: Institute of British Geographers, Secretary, 1982-85, President, 1990. Address: Vice-Chancellor, University of Essex, Wivenhoe Park, Colchester, C04 3SQ, England.

JOHNSTON William, b. 1925, Irish. Appointments: Ordained Catholic Priest, 1957; Professor of Theology, Sophia University, 1960-. Publications: The Mysticism of the Cloud of Unknowing, 1967, 1975; Silence by S Endo (translation), 1969; The Still Point: On Zen and Christian Mysticism, 1970; Christian Zen, 1971; The Cloud of Unknowing and the Book of Privy Counselling (editor), 1973; Silent Music: The Science of Meditation: The Inner Eye of Love: Mysticism and Religion, 1978; The Mirror Mind: Spirituality and Transformation, 1981; The Wounded Stag, The Bells of Nagasaki by T Nagai (translation), 1984; Being in Love: the Practice of Christian Prayer, 1988; Letters to Contemplatives, 1991; Lord, Teach Us To Pray, 1992. Address: Sophia University, 7 Kioi-Cho, Chiyodaku, Tokyo 102, Japan.

JOHNSTONE Iain Gilmour, b. 8 Apr 1943, England. Film Critic. m. Maureen Hammond, 1957, 1 son, 2 daughters. Education: LLB Honours; Distinction, Solicitor's finals. Literary Appointments: Film Critic, The Sunday Times. Publications: The Arnhem Report, 1977; The Men With No Name, 1980; Dustin Hoffman, 1984; Cannes: The Novel, 1990; Wimbledon 2000, 1992. Address: 16 Tournay Road, London, SW6, England.

JOKOSTRA Peter, b. 5 May 1912. Literary Critic; Novelist; Poet. m. Annemarisa Hintz, 16 July 1965, 2 sons, 3 daughters. Education: Universities of Frankfurt, Munich, Berlin. Literary Appointments: Publishers Reader, 1951; Press Officer, 1958; Publicity Officer, 1962. Publications include: Herzinfarkt, Roman, 1960; Die Gewendete Haut, Lyrik, 1967; Als die Tuilerien brannten, History, 1971; Sudfrankreich fur Kenner, autobiography, 1979; Heimweh nach Masuren, autobiography,

1982; Damals in Mecklenburg, Roman, 1990. Contributions to: Die Welt, Rheinische Post, Akzente, Sinn und Form, Neue deursche Literatur; Voix des Poetes, Suddeutscher Rundfunk, Stuttgart; RIAS Berlin. Honours: Poetry Prize, Ministry of Culture, 1956, 1958; Andreas Gryphius Prize, 1965; Maj Art Prize Rheinland Pfalz, 1979; Ehrengast der Villa Massimo, Rom, 1990. Memberships: PEN - Zentrum der BRD; Verband deutscher Schriftsteller; Gesellschaft Amicus Poloniae. Address: In der Stehle 38, D-53547 Kasbach-Ohlenberg, Germany.

JOLL James, b. 1918, British. Appointments: Fellow and Tutor in Modern History and Politics, New College, 1946-50; Fellow and Sub-Warden of St Antony's College, Lecturer in Modern History, Oxford University, 1951-67; Visiting Membe, Institute for Advanced Study, Princeton, New Jersey, 1953, 1971; Stevenson Professor of International History 1967-81, Emeritus 1981-, London School of Economics. Publications: Britain and Europe from Pitt to Churchill (editor), 1950, 1961; The Second International 1889-1914, 1955, 1975; The Decline of the Third Republic (editor), 1959; Three Intellectuals in Politics, 1960; The Anarchists, 1964, 1979; Anarchism Today (editor with D Apter), 1971; Europe Since 1870, 1973, 83, 90; Gramsci, 1977; The Origins of The First World War, 1984, 2nd edition 1992. Membership: Fellow of the British Academy. Literary Agent: Peters, Fraser and Dunlop. Addrss: 24 Ashchurch park Villas, London W12 9SP, England.

JOLLEY Elizabeth, b. 4 June 1923, Birmingham, England. Writer; Tutor. m. Leonard Jolley, 1 son, 2 daughters. Education: Nursing Training, 1940-46; Honorary Doctorate, Technology, Western Australian Institute of Technology, 1986. Appointments: Writer in Residence, Western Australian Institute of Technology, now Curtin University of Technology, Perth, 1980-; Citizen of the Year Arts Culture and Entertainment, 1987; Officer of the Order of Australia (AO) for Services to Australian Literature, 1988. Publications: Five Acre Virgin & Other Stories, 1976; The Travelling Entertainer, 1979; Woman in a Lampshade, 1983; (Novels) Palomino, 1980: The Newspaper of Claremont Street, 1981; Mr Scobie's Riddle, 1983; Miss Peabody's Inheritance, 1983; Foxbybaby, 1985; Milk and Honey, 1984; The Well, 1986; The Sugar Mother, 1988; My Father's Moon, 1989; Cabin Fever, 1990; Central Mischief, 1992; The Georges' Wife, 1993, (novel); Diary of a Weekend Farmer, 1993 (poetry). Literary Agent: Australian Literary Management, Victoria, Australia. Address: 28 Agett Road, Claremont, WA 6010, Western Australia.

JONAS Ann, b. 15 July 1919, Joplin, Missouri, USA. Poet. m. 30 Mar 1944, 1 daughter. Education: Graduate, Goodman Theatre, Chicago, Illinois. Publications: Anthologies: Dark Unsleeping Land, 1960; Deep Summer, 1963; Kentucky Contemporary Poetry, 1964, 1967; Kentucky Harvest, 1968; The Diamond Anthology, 1971; Ipso Facto, 1975; Peopled Parables, 1975; Barbeque Planet Sampler, 1977; Friendship Bridge/Anthology of World Poetry, 1979; The Kentucky Book, 1979; A Merton Concelebration, 1981; Dan River Anthology, 1985; Lawrence of Nottingham, 1985. Contributions to: Adena; Approaches; Bitterroot; Carolina Quarterly; Colorado Quarterly; Kentucky Poetry Review; The Poetry Review; The Southern Review; The Quest; Prism International, Canada. Address: 2425 Ashwood Drive, Louisville, KY 40205, USA.

JONAS Manfred, b. 9 Apr 1927, Mannheim, Germany. Historian. m. Mancy Jane Greene, 19 July 1952, 2 sons, 2 daughters. Education: BS, City College of New York, 1949; AM, 1951, PhD, 1959, Harvard University. Appointments: Visiting Professor for North American History, Free University of Berlin, 1959-62; Assistant Professor to Professor of History, 1963-81, Washington Irving Professor in Modern Literary and Historical Studies, 1981-86, John Bigelow Professor of History, 1986-, Union College, Schenectady, New York, USA; Dr Otto Salgo Visiting Professor of American Studies, Eötvös Lorand University, Budapest, Hungary, 1983-84. Publications: Die Unabhängigkeitserklärung der Vereingten Staaten, 1964; Isolationism in America 1935-1941, 1966, 1990; American Foreign Relations in the 20th Century, 1967; Roosevelt and Churchill: Their Secret Wartime Correspondence, 1975, 1990; New Opportunities in the New Nation, 1982; The United States and Germany: A Diplomatic History, 1984. Contributions to: The Historian; Mid-America; American Studies; Maryland Historical Magazine; Essex County Historical Collections; Jahrbuch für Amerikastudien. Address: Department of History, Union College, Schenectady, NY 12308, USA.

JONES Ann Maret, b. 3 Sept 1937, USA. Author. Education include: MA, University of Michigan, 1961; PhD, University of

Wisconsin, 1970. Appointments include: Writing Faculty, Mount Holyoke College, 1986-. Publications: Uncle Tom's Campus, 1973; Women Who Kill, 1980; Everyday Death: Case of Bernadette Powell, 1985; When Love Goes Wrong (with Susan Schechter), 1992; Next Time, She'll Be Dead, 1994. Contributions to: Nation; Ms; Vogue; American Heritage; New York Times; Newsday; Women's Rights Law Reporter; National Geographic Traveler; Condé Nast Traveler; Women's Sports. Honours: Author/Journalist of the Year, National Prisoners Rights Union, 1986. Memberships: PEN American Center; Authors Guild; National Writers Union; National Book Critics Circle. Literary Agent: Charlotte Sheedy. Address: 229 Sullivan Street, New York, NY 10012, USA.

JONES Brian, b. 1938, British. Publications: The Lady With The Little Dog, 1962; Poems, 1966; A Family Album, 1968; Interior, 1969; The Mantis Hand and Other Poems, 1970; For Mad Mary, 1974; The Spitfire on the Northern Line, 1975; The Island Normal, 1980; Children of Separation, 1985; Freeborn John, 1990. Address: c/o Caranet Press, 208 Corn Exchange Buildings, Manchester, M4 3BQ, England.

JONES Brian Kinsey. See: BALL Brian Neville.

JONES Christopher Dennis, b. 13 Dec 1949, New York, USA. Playwright. m. Gwendoline Shirley Rose, 18 Aug 1979, London, England. Education: BA, English Literature, University of Pittsburgh. Literary Appointments: Resident Playwright, Carnaby Street Theatre, London, England, 1975-76; Resident Playwright, New Hope Theatre Company, London, 1977- 78. Publications: plays: Passing Strangers, 1975; Nasty Corners, 1977; New Signals, 1978; In Flight Reunion, 1979; Sterile Landscape, 1982; Ralph Bird's River Race, 1985; Dying Hairless With A Rash, 1985; Bitter Chalice, 1987; Begging the Ring, 1989; Burning Youth, 1989. Contributions to: Country Life; Arts Review. Membership: Writer's Guild of Great Britain. Literary Agent: Fraser & Dunlop. Address: c/o Richard Wakeley, Fraser and Dunlop, 91 Regent Street, London W1R 8RU, England.

JONES D(ennis) F(eltham), British. Appointments: Bricklayer; Market Gardener. Publications: Colossus, 1966; Implosion, 1967; Don't Pick the Flowers (in US as Denver is Missing), 1971; The Fall of Colossus, 1974; Earth Has Been Found (in UK as Xenos), 1979. Address: c/o Sedgewick and Jackson Limited, 1 Tavistock Chambers, Bloomsbury Way, London, WC1A 2SG, England.

JONES Diana Wynne, b. 16 Aug 1934, London, England. Writer. m. J A Burrow, 23 Dec 1956, 3 sons. Education: BA, Oxford University, 1956. Appointments: Panelist on Guardian Award, 1979-82; Panelist on Whitbread Award, Children's Book Section, 1988. Publications: Charmed Life, 1977; Archer's Goon, 1984; The Ogre Downstairs, 1974; Witch Week, 1974; Power of Three, 1976; Fire and Hemlock, 1985; Dogsbody, 1975; Eight Days of Luke, 1975; Cart and Cwidder, 1975; Wilkin's Tooth, 1973; Drowned Ammet, 1977; Who Got Rid of Angus Flint?, 1978; The Magicians of Caprona, 1979; The Spellcoats, 1980; Howl's Moving Castle, 1986; The Lives of Christopher Chant, 1988; A Tale of Time City, 1987; Wild Robert, 1989; Chair Person, 1989; The Homeward Bounders, 1981; The Four Grannies, 1980; Castle in the Air, 1990; Warlock at the Wheel, 1984; Black Maria, 1991; Yes Dear, 1992; A Sudden Wild Magic, 1992; The Crown of Dalemark, 1993; Hexwood, 1993. Contributions to: Reviews in The Guardian, The Daily Telegraph. Honours: Guardian Award for Children's Books, 1978; Honour Book, Boston Globe, Horn Book Award, 1984, 1986; Runner-up for Carnegie Award, 3 times. Membership: Society of Authors. Literary Agent: Laura Cecil. Address: 9 The Polygon, Bristol, BS8 4PW, England.

JONES Douglas Gordon, b. 1 Jan 1929, Bancroft, Ontario, Canada. Professor; Poet. Education: MA, Queens University, Kingston, Ontario, 1954. Appointments include: Professor, University of Sherbrooke, Quebec, 1963-1994; Retired. Publications include: Frost on the Sun, 1957; The Is Axeman, 1961; Phrases from Orpheus, 1967; Under the Thunder the Flowers Light Up the Earth, 1977; A Throw of Particles: Selected and New Poems, 1983; Balthazar and Other Poems, 1988; Butterfly on Rock: A Study of Themes and Images in Canadian Literature, 1970; Editor, Translator. Honours include: President's Medal, University of Western Ontario, 1976; D Litt, Guelph University, 1982; Governor General's Award for Poetry, 1977; Governor General's Award for Translation, 1993. Address: PO Box 356, North Hatley, Quebec, J0B 2CO, Canada.

JONES Elwyn Ashford, b. 7 Mar 1941, Cynwyd, Wales. Teacher. Education: BEd, University of Wales, Bangor. Publications: Y Baal Barfog, 1971; Picell Mewn Cefn, 1978; Nain Ar Goll, 1986; Cicio Nyth Cacwn, 1987; Straeon Hanner Nos, 1989; Heb El Fai, 1992. Contributions to: Short Stories, Essays and Children's Stories for various magazines. Address: Pen y Ddol, Cynwyd, Corwen, Clwyd LL21 0ET, Wales.

JONES Evan (Lloyd), b. 20 Nov 1931, Melbourne, VA, Australia. Lecturer; Poet. m. Margot Jones, 1966, 4 children. Education: MA, University of Melbourne, 1957; MA, Stanford University, CA. Appointments include: Senior Lecturer, University of Melbourne, 1965-89. Publications: Inside The Whale, 1960; Undertandings, 1967; Recognitions, 1978; Left at the Post, 1984; Kenneth MacKenzie, 1969; Co Editor, The Poems of Kenneth MacKenzie, 1972. Address: Dept of English, University of Melbourne, Parkville, VA 3052, Australia.

JONES Glyn, b. 28 Feb 1905, Merthyr Tydfil, Wales, retired Schoolmaster. m. Phyllis Doreen Jones, Aug 1935. Education: St Paul's College, Cheltenham. Appointments: First Chairman, English Section, The Welsh Academy, 1968. Publications: Fiction: The Blue Bed, 1937; The Water Music, 1944; Selected Short Stories, 1971; Welsh Heirs, 1977; The Learning Lark, 1960; The Valley the City the Village, 1956; The Island of Apples, 1965; Criticism; The Dragon has Two Tongues, 1968; Profiles, (co-author John Rowlands), 1980; Goodbye, What Were You? (selections), Gomer, 1994; Translation from Welsh Heledd, (with Dr T J Morgan) Gregynog, 1994. Poems: Poems, 1939; The Dream of Jake Hopkins, 1954; Selected Poems, 1975; Selected Poems, Fragments and Fictions, 1988 (Translations); The Saga of Llywarch the Old (with T J Morgan), 1955; When the Rosebush Brings Forth Apples, 1980; Honeydew on the Wormwood, 1984. Contributions to: Poetry Chicago; Wales; Welsh Review; Life and Letters Today; News Chronicle; Western Mail; London Welshman; Anglo-Welsh Review; Poetry Wales. Honours: DLitt, University of Wales, 1974; Fellow, The Welsh Academy, 1989; Honorary Fellow, Trinity College, Carmarthen, 1993; Fellow, The Welsh Academy, 1990. Membership: Welsh Academy, English Language Section. Literary Agent: Laurence Pollinger, Maddox Street, Mayfair, London, England. Address: 158 Manor Way, Whitchurch, Cardiff, CF4 1RN, England.

JONES Gwyn, b. 24 May 1907, Blackwood, Monmouthshire, Wales. Novelist. Education: MA, University College Cardiff, 1929. Appointments: Professor, University College of Wales, 1940-65; Ida Beam Visiting Professor, University of IA, 1982; Chairman, Welsh Arts Council, 1957-67. Publications include: Richard Savage, 1935; Times Like These, 1936; The Nine Days Wonder, 1937; The Green Island, 1946; The Flowers Beneath the Scythe: The Walk Home, 1963; The Still Waters and Other Stories, 1949; Shepherds Hey and Other Stories, 1953; Selected Short Stories, 1974; A Prospect of Wales, 1948; Kings, Beasts and Heroes, 1972; The Novel and Society, 1981; Editor, Volumes of Verse and Stories; Translator, Sagas and Sir Gawain and the Green Knight. Honours include: D Litt, University of Wales, 1977; Fellow, University College Cardiff, 1980, University College of Wales, 1987; CBE, 1965. Address: Castle Cottage, Sea View Place, Aberystwyth, Dyfed, Wales.

JONES Hettie, b. 16 Jul 1934, Brooklyn New York, USA. Writer. div. 2 d. Education: BA, Washington College, University of Virginia, 1955; Graduate Study, Columbia University. Appointments: Associate Professor, Writing; Hunter College, 1984; State University of New York, 1989-91; The New School, 1991; University of Wyoming, 1993. Publications: How I Became Hettie Jones, 1991; Big Star Fallin' Mama, 1975; The Tees Stand Shining, 1971; Longhouse Winter, 1974; Coyote Tales, 1976; How to Eat Your ABCs, 1978; I Hate To Talk About Your Mother, 1980. Contributions to: Stories and poems in the Village Voice, Ikon and others. Honours: Best Books for Young Adults Award, New York Public Library, 1975; New York Times Recommended Reading List, Best Books Of the Year, 1991; Phi Beta Kappa. Memberships: PEN (Prison Writing Committee). Literary Agent: Berenice Hoffman. Address: c/o Berenice Hoffman Literary Agency, 215 West 75th Street, New York, NY 10022, USA.

JONES J Farragut. See: LEVINSON Leonard.

JONES Joanna. See: BURKE John Frederick.

JONES John Philip, b. 3 July 1930, Caernarvon, Wales. University Professor. m. Wendy Maudlayne Hoblyn, 4 Oct 1958, 1 son, 1 daughter. Education: BA (Hons), 1953, MA, 1957, Cambridge

University. Publications: The Great Gray Spire, 1985; What's in a Name? Advertising and the Concept of Brands, 1986; Does It Pay to Advertise? Cases Illustrating Sucessful Brand Advertising, 1989; How Much is Enough? Getting the Most From Your Advertising Dollar, 1992; When Ads Work, New Proof that Advertising Triggers Sales, 1995. Contributions to: International Journal of Advertising; Admap; Harvard Business Review; New York Times; Marketing Management; Others. Honours: Distinguished Advertising Educator of the Year, American Advertising Federation, 1991; Member, National Advertising Review Board, 1994. Address: 122 Edgehill Road, Syracuse, NY 13224, USA.

JONES Julia, b. 27 Mar 1923, Liverpool, England. Writer. m. Edmund Bennett, 10 Oct 1950, 1 s, 1 d. Education: Royal Academy of Dramatic Art, 1946-48. Publications include: The Navigators, 1986; over 50 plays for theatre, television and radio, films; numerous dramatisations. Honour: The Golden Prague, 1st Prize Drama, Prague TV Festival, 1970. Memberships: Dramatists Club; Green Room Club; TV Committee, Writers Guild of Great Britain. Literary Agent: Jill Foster Ltd. Address: c/o Jill Foster Ltd, 35 Brompton Road, London SW3 1DE, England.

JONES Kenneth Westcott, b. 11 Nov 1921, London, England. Travel Writer & Author. Literary Appointments: Travel Editor, East Anglian Daily Times, 1951-93; Group Travel Correspondent, United Newspapers, 1960-83; Travel Contributor to The Bulletin, Scotland, 1953-60; Travel World & Business Travel, Focus Correspondent, 1962-83. Publications: New York, 1958; America Beyond the Bronx, 1961; Great Railway Journeys of the World, 1964; Exciting Railway Journeys of the World, 1967; To the Polar Sunrise, 1957; By Rail to the Ends of the Earth, 1968; Business Air Travellers Guide, 1970; Romantic Railways, 1971; Steam in the Landscape, 1972; Railways for Pleasure, 1981; Scenic America, 1984; Where To Go in America, 1991; Rail Tales of the Unexpected, 1992. Contributions to: Go Magazine, Railway Magazine; Going Places; The Universe. Honours: Canton of Valais Award, 1964; Thomson Travel Award, Travel Writer of the Year, 1971. Memberships: Croydon Writers Circle, 1954-61; British Guild of Travel Writers, Chairman 1975-76, Secretary 1959-62; Fellow Royal Geographical Society. Address: Hillswick, Michael Road, London, SE25 6RN, England.

JONES Le Roi, b. 7 Oct 1934, Newark, New Jersey, USA. Assissatnat Professor of African Studies; Writer. m. (1) Hettie Cohen, 1958 (div 1965), 2 d; (2) Sylvia Robinson, 1966, 2 sd, 1 d. Education: Central Avenue School; Barringer High, Newark; Howard University, Washington, DC; US Air Force, 1954-56. Appointments: New School for Social Research, New York, 1961-64, summers of 77-79; State University of New York, Buffalo, summer, 1964; Columbia University, New York, 1964, spring 1980; Visiting Professor, San Francisco State College, 1966-67; Yale University, Connecticut, 1977-78; George Washington University, Washington DC, 19978-79; Assisstant Professor, African Studies, State University of New York, Stony Brook, 1980-; Founder, Yugen Magazine and Totem Press, New York, 1958; Editor (with Diana de Prima), Floating Bear Magazine, New York, 1961-63; Founding Director, Black Arts Repertory Theatre, Harlem, 1964-66; Founding Director, Spirit House, Newark, 1966-; Member, United Brothers, 1968, Committee for United Newark, 1969-75; Chaiman, Congress of Afrikan People, 1972-75. Publications include: verse: It's Nation Time, 1970; In Our Terribleness: Some Elements and Meaning in Black Style, with Fundi (Billy Abernathy), 1970; Spirit Reach, 1972; Afrikan Revolution, 1973; Hard Facts, 1976; Selected Poetry, 1979; AM/TRAK, 1979; Reggae or Not!, 1982; plays: The Motion of History (directed, produced, New York 1977); The Motion of History and Other Plays, 1978; What Was The Relationship of the Lone Ranger to the Means of Production? (produced New York, 1979); At The Dim'cracker Convention (produced New York, 1980); Boy and Tarzan Appear in A Clearing (New York 1981); screenplays: Dutchman, 1967; A Fable, 1971; novel: The System of Dante's Hell, 1965 (UK, 1966); short stories and other publications. Honours: Whitney Fellowship, 1961; Obie Award for Drama, 1964; Guggenheim Fellowship, 1965; Dakar Festival Prize, 1966; Rockefeller Grant, 1981; DHL, Malcolm X University, Chicago, 1972. Memberships: Black Academy of Arts and Letters. Address: 808 South 10th Street, Newark, NJ 07108, USA.

JONES Madison Percy, b. 21 Mar 1925, Nashville, Tennesseee, USA. Author; Retired Professor of English. m. Shailah McEvilley, 5 Feb 1951, 3 s, 2 d. Education: BA, Vanderbilt University, 1949; MA, University of Florida, 1953. Appointments: Instructor in English, Miami University of Ohio, 1953-54; Instructor in English, University of Tennessee, 1955-56; Professor and Writer-in-Residence, Auburn University, 1956-87. Publications: novels: A Cry of Absence, 1971; A Buried Land, 1963; An Exile, 1967; Last Things, 1989; The Innocent, 1957; Passage Through Gehenna, 1978; Season of the Strangler, 1983; Forest of the Night, 1960; To the Winds (novel), Forthcoming. Contributions to: Short stories, essays, reviews: Sewanee Review, Southern Review, South Atlantic Quarterly, Studies in Short Fiction, New York Times Book Review, Washington Post Book World. Honours: Sewanee Review Writing Fellowship, 1954-55; Rockefeller Foundation Fellowship, 1968; Book Award of Alabama Library Association, 1968; Guggenheim Foundation Fellowship, 1973-74. Memberships: Member, Fellowship of Southern Writers, 1988-; Member Alabama Academy of Distinguished Authors. Literary Agent: Elizabeth McKee, McIntosh, McKee and Dodds, New York. Address: 800 Kuderna Acres, Auburn, AL 36830, USA.

JONES Malcolm Vince, b. 7 Jan 1940, Professor of Slavonic Studies. m. Jennifer Rosemary Durrant, 27 July 1963, 1 son, 1 daughter. Education: Cotham Grammer School, Bristol, 1950-58; University of Nottingham, 1958-62; Postgraduate at University of Nottingham, 1962-65. Literary Appointment: General Editor, Cambridge Studies in Russian Literature. Publications: Dostoyevsky, The Novel of Discord, Paul Elek, London, 1976; Barnes and Noble, New York, 1976; New Essays on Tolstoy, ed. Cambridge University Press, Cambridge, London, New York and Melbourne, 1978; New Essays on Dostoyevsky, ed. with Garth M Terry, Cambridge University Press, Cambridge, London, New York and Melbourne, 1983; Dostoyevsky after Bakhtin, Cambridge University Press, Cambridge, London, New York and Melbourne, 1990. Contributions to: Various academic journals in Slavonic Studies. Memberships: Secretary, British Universities' Association of Slavists, 1966-68; President, 1986-88; President, Association of Teachers of Russian, 1985-86; Vice-President, International Dostoyevsky Society, 1983-86; Chairman of Co-ordinating Council for Area Studies Association, 1993; Vice-President, British Association for Soviet Slavonic and East European Studies, 1988-91. Address: Department of Slavonic Studies, University of Nottingham, University Park, Nottingham, NG7 2RD, England.

JONES Mervyn, b. 27 Feb 1922, London, England. Education: New York University, 1939-41. Appointments: Assistant Editor, 1955-60, Drama Critic 1958-66, Tribune; Assistant Editor, New Statesman, 1966-68, London. Publications: No Time to Be Young, 1952; The New Town, The Last Barricade, 1953; Helen Blake, 1955; Guilty Men (with Michael Foot), Suez and Cyprus, 1957; On the Last Day, 1958; Potbank, 1961; Big Two (in US as The Antagonists), 1962; Two Ears of Corn: Oxfam in Action (in US as In Famine's Shadow: A Private War on Hunger), A Set of Wives, 1965; John and Mary, 1966; A Survivor, 1968; Joseph, 1970; Mr Armitage Isn't Back Yet, 1971; Life on the Dole, 1972; Holding On (in US as Twilight of the Day), The Revolving Door, 1973; Lord Richard's Passion, Strangers, K S Karol: The Second Chinese Revolution (trans), 1974; The Pursuit of Happiness, 1975; The Oil Rush (with Fay Godwin), Scenes from Bourgeois Life, 1976; Nobody's Fault, 1977; Today the Struggle, 1978; The Beautiful Words, 1979; A Short Time to Live, 1980; Two Women and Their Men, 1982; Joanna's Luck, 1985; Coming Home, 1986; Chances, 1987; That Year in Paris, 1988; A Radical Life, 1991; Michael Foot, 1994. Address: 1 Evelyn Mansions, Carlisle Place, London, SW1P 1NH, England.

JONES Owen Marshall, b. 17 Aug 1941, Te Kuiti, New Zealand. Write. m. Jacqueline Hill, Dec 1965, 2 d. Education: MA Hons, University of Canterbury, 1964; Diploma in Teaching, Christchurch Teachers College, 1965. Publications: The Master of Big Jingles, 1982; The Day Hemingway Died, 1984; The Lynx Hunter, 1987; The Divided World, 1989; Tomorrow We Save the Orphans, 1991; Supper Waltz Wilson, 1979. Contributions to: numerous magazines and journals. Honours: NZ Literary Fund Scholarship in Letters, 1988. Literary Agent: Glenys Bean. Address: 10 Morgans Road, Timaru, New Zealand.

JONES Peter (Austin), b. 1929, British. Appointments: Managing Director, Carcanet Press Limited, Manchester, 1970-. Publications: Rain, 1970; Seagarden for Julius, Tribute to Freud, by Hilda Doolittle (editor), 1971; The Peace and the Hook, Imagist Poetry (editor), 1972; Shakespeare - The Sonnets: A Casebook, The Garden End: New and Selected Poems, 1977; An Introduction to Fifty American Poets: Critical Essays, 1979; British Poetry Since 1970: A Critical Survey (editor), 1980. Membership: English Faculty, Christ's Hospital, Horsham, Sussex, 1954-69. Address: Carcanet Press, 208 Corn Exchange Building, Manchester M4 3BQ, England.

JONES Phyllis Marjory, b. 12 Mar 1923, Truro, Cornwall. Nursing Officer. m. (1) Cecil Vernon Arthur, dec'd 1958, (2) Ivor Gordon Jones, 27 June 1959, dec'd 1994. Education: State Registered Nurse; OHNC, Occupational Health. Publications: They Gave Me A Lamp, 1992; Volumes of Poetry; The Grass Is Not Yet Grown; Song of Gower; The Bells of Truro, 1994. Contributions to: Nursing Times; Occupational Health; Contry Quest; Anglo Welsh Review; New Welsh Review; Cornish Review; Cornish Scene; Athena. Honours: Runner up, Theodora Doorae Award Novel of Literary Merit, 1972; Winner, Cornish Gorsedd, Poetry Rose Bowl, 1972. Memberships: Society of Women Writers and Journalists; Welsh Academy; West Country Writers; Society of Authors. Address: Pen-y-Bont, Hoel Sylen, Pontyberem, Dyfed, SA15 5NW, Wales.

JONES Rhydderch Thomas, b. 25 Dec 1935, North Wales. Television Producer. m. 3 Mar 1980. Education: Diploma Education, Normal College, Bangor. Appointments: Teacher, English Literature & Dramatic Art, Croydon and Llanrwst; BBC, Light Entertainment Dept, 1973-. Publications: Roedd Catarinao Gwmpas Ddoe, 1974; Mewn Tri Chyfrwng, 1979; Cofiant Ryan, 1979; Ryan, 1980 (English); TV drama: Mr Lolipop MA; Man a Lle; Broc môr; Gwenoliaid (Swallows); Lliwiau (Colours); radio plays: Edau Frau; Charlie's Aunt, Brandon Thomas: trans Madam Siarli, 1962; Offshore Island, Marganita Laski; Trans A Oes Heddwch; co-writer, Sit-Com with G Parry, Fo a Fe, Hafod Henri. Honours: Pye Award, Best Regional Drama, 1987; Royal TV Society Award for Outstanding Contribution to Creative Writing, 1987. Membership: Yr Academi Gymraeg. Address: 39 Heol Hir, Llanishen, Cardiff, Wales.

JONES Richard Andrew III, b. 8 Aug 1953, London, England. Poet. Education: BA, 1975, MA, 1976, University of Virginia, USA. Publications: Country of Air, 1986; At Last We Enter Pradise, 1991; A Perfect Time, 1994. Contributions to: American Poetry Review; Poetry; Tri Quarterly. Honours: The Posner Prize, 1986; Illinois Arts Council Award, 1991; Literary Award, 1991. Address: Department of English, DePaul University, Chicago, IL 60614, USA.

JONES Robert Gerallt Hamlet, b. 11 Sept 1934, Nefyn, Gwynedd, Wales. University Administrator. m. Susan Lloyd Griffith, 15 Sept 1962, 2 sons, 1 daughter. Education: BA, 1954; MA, 1956, University College of North Wales. Appointments: Creative Writing Fellow, University of Wales, 1976-78; Senior Lecturer in Welsh Studies, University College, Aberystwyth, 1979-89; Editor of Taliesin, Welsh Academy Quarterly, 1988-; Chairman, Wales Film Council, 1992-; Editor, Books From Wales, 1992-; Chairman, Mid-Wales Arts Trust, 1993-. Publications: Triptych, 1977; Jamaican Landscape, 1969; Cerddi 1955-89, (poems), 1991; Cafflogion, 1979; Tair Drama, 1988; 30 volumes of poetry, novels and critism in Welsh language. Honours: Prose Medal, National Eisteddfod of Wales, 1977, 1979; Hugh McDiarmid Award, 1984; Welsh Arts Council Poetry Award, 1990. Memberships: Welsh Academy, Chairman, 1982-87; Welsh Arts Council, Chairman, Film Committee, 1987-; Welsh Fourth Channel Authority (S4C), 1990-. Address: Gregynog, University of Wales, Newtown, Powys, SY16 3PW, Wales.

JONES Rodney, b. 1950. Poet. Publications: Story They Told Us of Light, 1980; Unborn, 1985; Transparent Gestures, 1989; Apocalyptic Narrative & other poems, 1993. Honour: National Book Critics Circle Award, 1990.

JONES Sally Roberts, b. 1935, United Kingdom. Author; Publisher. Appointments: Senior Assistant, Reference Library, London Borough of Havering, 1964-67; Reference Librarian, Borough of Port Talbot, Wales, 1967-70; Publisher, Alun Books, 1977-. Publications: Turning Away, 1969; Elen and the Goblin, 1977; The Forgotten Country, 1977; Books of Welsh Interest, 1977; Allen Raine (Writers of Wales), 1979; Relative Values, 1985; The History of Port Talbot, 1991; Pendaruis, 1992. Honours: Welsh Arts Council Literature Prize, 1970. Memberships: The Welsh Academy, (Founder Member), Chairman, 1994-; Afan Poetry Society, President; Welsh Union of Writers; Associate of The Library Association; Port Talbot Historical Society, (General Secretary). Address: 3 Crown Street, Port Talbot, SA13 1BG, Wales.

JONES Virgil Carrington, b. 7 June 1906, Charlottesville, Virginia, USA. Journalist. m, Geneva Carolyn Peyton, 30 June 1934, 1 son, 1 daughter. Education: BA, Journalism, Washington and Lee University, Lexington, Virginia, 1930. Publications: Ranger Mosby, 1944; The Hatfields and the McCoys, 1956; Gray Ghosts and Rebel

Raiders, 1956; Eight Hours Before Richmond, 1957; The Civil War at Sea, 3 vols, 1962; The Birth of Liberty, 1964; Roosevelt's Rough Riders, 1971; Author, Log of Apollo 11, official report of the Moon Landing. Address: 13905 Deviar Drive, Centreville, VA 22020, USA.

JONES-EVANS Eric (John Llewllyn), b. 2 Oct 1898, West Coker, Somerset, England. General Medical Practitioner (retired); Former Actor; Theatre Historian. m. Agnes Maude Edwards, 27 Feb 1922, 1 s (dec). Education: Qualified in Medicne, St Thomas' Hospital, London, 1921; LRCP; MRCS. Literary Appointments: Theatre Historian, Hampshire Magazine, Southern Evening Echo, Kent Life, Bygone Kent. Publications include: Henry Irving & The Bells, memoir, edited by Dr David Mayer, 1980; Character Sketches from Dickens, In the Footsteps of Barnaby Rudge, 1947; John Jasper's Secret, stage Version of Dickens' Edwin Drood; Suicide Isn't Murder, 1951; The Black Bag, 1957; plays published: Death on the Line; Lucky Venture; Death of a Lawyer; Scrooge the Miser, 1962; The Haunted Man, 1962; The Weaver of Raveloe, 1963; The Murder of Nancy, 1963; The Jackal, 1964; The Blue Cockade, 1951; (award winner) Mr Crummles Presents... 1966; David Copperfield, 1970; Footlight Fever, autobiography; Death on the Line, radio play, 1971; the Dream Woman, 1973; The Music of Melodrama, Markheim, The Body Snatchers, radio plays. Honours: 1st Prize, Festival of Britain playwriting competition, 1951. Literary Agent (Plays): Samuel French Ltd, Fitzroy Street, London W1P 6JR. Address: The Treshams, Fawley, Nr Southampton, Hampshire, England.

JONG Erica Mann, b. 26 Mar 1942, New York City, USA. Author; Poet. 1 d. Education: BA, Barnard College, 1963; MA, Columbia University, 1965. Literary Appointments: Faculty, English Department, City University of New York, 1964-65, 1969-70; Member, Literary Panel, New York State Council on Arts, 1972-74. Publications include: Fruits and Vegetables, poems, 1971; Half-Lives, poems, 1973; Fear of Flying, novel, 1973; Loveroot, poems, 1975; How To save Your Own Life, novel, 1977; At The Edge of the Body, poems, 1979; Fanny: Being the True Story of Fanny Hackabout-Jones, novel, 1980; Witches, 1981; Ordinary Miracles, poems, 1983; Parachutes and Kisses, novel, 1984. Honours: Bess Hokin Prize, Poetry Magazine, 1971; Alice Faye di Castagnola Award, Poetry Society of America, 1972; Grant, National Endowment for Arts, 1973. Memberships: Director 1975, Authors Guild; Writers Guild of America; PEN; Phi Beta Kappa. Literary Agent: Ed Victor Ltd. Address: 162 Wardour Street, London, IV 3AT, England.

JORDAN June, b. 1936, American. Appointments: Instructor, City College, City University of New York, 1967-69, Sarah Lawrence College, Bronxville, 1969-70, 1973-74; Columnist, The Black Poet Speaks of Poetry, American Poetry Review, 1974-; Professor of English, 1981-; Director of the Poetry Center, 1986-. Publications: Who Look at Me, 1969; Soulscript, Some Changes, His Own Where, The Voice of the Children (co-ed), 1971; Dry Victories; Fannie Lou Hamer, 1972; New Days, 1974; I Love You, New Life: New Room, 1975; Things I Do in the Dark: Selected Poetry, 1977; Passion: New Poems, 1980; Civil Wars, Kimako's Story, 1981; Living Room, 1985; On Call, 1986; Naming Our Destiny: Haruko/Love Poems, 1994. Address: Department of English, State University of New York, Stny Brook, NY 11790, USA.

JORDAN Leonard. See: **LEVINSON Leonard.**

JORDAN Neil Patrick, b. 25 Feb 1950, Sligo, Republic of Ireland. Author; Director. 3 sons, 2 daughters. Education: BA, 1st Class Honours, History/English Literature, University College, Dublin, 1969-72. Appointments: Co-Founder, Irish Writers Co-operative, Dublin, 1974. Publications: Night in Tunisia, 1976; The Dream of a Beast, 1983; The Past, 1979; Sunrise with Sea Monster, 1995; Films as a Director: Angel, 1982; Company of Wolves, 1984; Mona Lisa, 1986; High Spirits, 1988; We're No Angels, 1989; The Miracle, 1990; The Crying Game, 1992; Interview With The Vampire, 1994 (Feature Film). Honours: Guardian Fiction Prize for Night in Tunisia, 1979; Film Awards: Los Angeles Film Critics Award; New York Film Critics Award, 1986; London Critic Circle Award, 1986; Best Original Script - The Crying Game - Acadamy of Motion Pictures Arts & Sciences (Oscar). Literary Agent: Jenne Casarotto, Casarotto Comp Limited, UK; Suzanne Gluck, ICM, USA. Address: c/o Jenne Casarotto Co Ltd, National House, 60-66 Wardour St, London, W1V 3HP, England.

JOSÉ Héctor Oscar (Sergio Darlin), b. 14 Feb 1936, Córdoba, Argentina. Writer. m. Soltero José, 1 daughter. Literary Appointments: One of the creators and theorists of signist (typewriter signi) poetry, international movement of poetry and advanced narrative, 1961.

Publications: After Hiroshima, 1965, 1975; Reports for an operating theater history, 1980; Growth of the Apocalypsis, 1987; New reports for an operating theater history, 1991; The Madness Starts at the Steps, 1991; After Hiroshima III, 1993. Contributions to: Magazines and journals. Honours: Ribbon of Honour, SADE, 1976; Statue of Victory for Personality of 1984; Italian Word Award for Culture, ALPI Biennale Award; Honorary Member, Argentine Writers Association. Address: Pringles 3230, 1605 Florida, Prov Buenos Aires, Argentina.

JOSEPH Jenny, b. 7 May 1932, Birmingham, England. Writer; Lecturer. m. C A Coles, 29 Apr 1961, 1 son, 2 daughters. Education: BA, Honours, English, St Hilda's College, Oxford University, 1950-53. Publications: The Unlooked-for Season, 1960; Warning, poem, 1961; Boots, 1966; Rose in the Afternoon, 1974; The Thinking Heart, 1978; Beyond Descartes, 1983; Persephone, 1986; The Inland Sea, 1989; Beached Boats, folio and book, with photographer Robert Mitchell, 1991; Selected Poems, 1992; Author of 6 books for children. Contributions to: Contributor of poems, articles and prose in various magazines and anthologies. Honours: Gregory Award, 1962; Cholmondely Award, 1974; Arts Council of Great Britain Award, 1975; James Tait Black Award for Fiction for Persephone, 1986. Memberships: National Poetry Society of Great Britain, Council, 1975-78. Membership: Founder Member, Director & Judge for BP Spoken Poetry Competition. Literary Agent: John Johnson Limited, London. Address: 17 Windwill Road, Minchinhampton, Gloucestershire, GL6 9DX, England.

JOSEPH Stephen M, b. 1938, American. Appointments: Teacher, NYC Board of Education, 1960-70, Lecturer, The Cooper Union and New York University, 1970-71; Lecturer, Wyoming State Arts Council, 1973-; Writer-in-Residence, New York State Arts Council. Publications: The Me Nobody Knows (editor), 1969; The Shark Bites Back, Meditations (editor), 1970; Children in Fear, 1974; Mommy, Daddy, I'm Afraid, 1979. Address: 270 First Avenue, New York, NY 10009, USA.

JOSEPHY Alvin M, b. 1915, American. Appointments: Director and Senior Editor, American Heritage Publishing Company Incorporated, NYC, 1960-79. Publications: The Long and the Short and the Tall, 1946; The Patriot Chiefs, The American Heritage Book of Indians (editor), 1961; The American Heritage Book of Natural Wonders (editor), 1963; Chief Joseph's People and Their War, 1964; The American Heritage History of the Great West, The Nez Perce Indians and the Opening of the NorthWest, 1965; RFK, His Life and Death, The Indian Heritage of America, 1968; The Artist Was a Young Man, 1970; Red Power, The Horizon History of Africa (editor), 1971; American Heritage History of Business and Industry (editor), 1972; The Pictorial History of the American Indians, by Oliver La Farge (reviser), The Law in America (editor), 1974; History of the US Congress, 1975; Black Hills, White Sky, 1978; On the Hill: A History of the American Congress, 1979; Now That the Buffalo's Gone, 1982; War on the Frontier, 1986; The Civil War in the American West, 1991; America in 1492, 1992. Honour: Doctor of Humanities, College of Idaho, 1987. Memberships: Society of American Historians; American Antiquarian Soviety; Western History Association. Literary Agent: Julian Bach, New York. Address: 4 Kinsman Lane, Greenwich, CT 06830, USA.

JOSIPOVICI Gabriel David, b. 8 Oct 1940, Nice, France. Professor of English. Education: BA, Hons 1st Class, St Edmund Hall, Oxford, 1958-61. Publications: Novels: Migrations, 1977; The Air We Breath, 1981; Contre-Jour, 1986; The Big Glass, 1990; In a Hotel Garden, 1993; Moo Pak, 1994; The Inventory; Words; The Present; The Echo Chamber; Conversations in Another Room. Stories: Mobius the Striper, 1974; In the Fertile Land. Essays: The World and the Book, 1971; The Lessons of Modernism; Writing and the Body; The Book of God: A Response to the Bible, 1988; Text and Voice, 1992. Contributions to: Encounter; New York Review of Books; London Review of Books; Times Literary Supplement. Honours: AG 1977 and Mr Vee 1989, radio plays, both BBC nominations for Italia Prize; Invited to give the 1981 Lord Northcliffe Lectures, University of London. Invited to be Lord Weidenfeld visiting professor of comparative literature, University of Oxford. Literary Agent: John Johnson. Address: 60 Prince Edwards Road, Lewes, Sussex, England.

JOSLIN Sesyle, b. 1929, USA. Writer, novels, short stories, children's fiction, poetry. Appointments: Editorial Assisstant, Holiday magazine, 1947-49; assisstant Fiction Editor, Westminster Press, 1950-52, Book Editor, Countrty Gentleman Magazine, 1950-52; Production Assisstant, film, Lord of the Flies, Peter Brook, Puerto Rico,

1963. Publications: What Do You Say Dear? 1958; Brave Baby Elephant, 1960; Baby Elephant's Trunk, 1961; What Do You Do Dear? 1961; There is a Dragon in My Bed (French Primer), 1961; (with Al Hind as G b Kirtland) One Day in Elizabethan England, 1962; Dear Dragon...and Other Useful Letter Forms for Young Ladies and Gentlemen Engaged in Everyday Correspondence, 1962; Senor Baby Elephant, The Pirate, 1962; Baby Elephant and the Secret Wishes, 1962; Baby Elephant Goes to China, 1963; (with Al Hind as G B Kirtland) One Day in Aztec, Mexico, 1963; La Petite Famille (reader),1964; Baby Elephant's Baby Book, 1964; Please Share That Peanut! 1965; Spaghetti for Breakfast (Italian Primer), 1965; (with Al Hine as Josephine Gibson) Is There A Mouse in the House? (verse), 1965; There is a Bull on My Balcony (Spanish Primer), 1966; Pinkety, Pinkety, A Practical Guide to Wishing, 1966; La Fiesta (reader), 1967; The Night They Stole The Alphabet, 1968; Doctor George Owl, 1970; The Spy Lady and the Muffin Man, 1971; Last Summer's Smugglers, 1973; The Gentle Savages, 1979.

JOY David (Anthony Welton), b. 1942, British. Appointments: General Reporter, Yorkshire Post Newspapers, 1962-65, Editorial Assisstant, 1965-70, Books Editor, 1970-88, Dalesman Publishing Company Limited, Editor 1988-. Publications: Settle-Carlisle Railway (with W R Mitchell), 1966; Main Line Over Shap, 1967; Cumbrain Coast Railways, 1968; Whitby-Pickering Railway, 1969; Railways in the North, Traction Engines in the North, 1970; George Hudson of York (with A J Peacock), 1971; Railways of the Lake Countries, 1973; Regional History of the Railways of Great Britain: South and West Yorkshire, Railways in Lancashire, Settle-Carlisle Centenary, 1975; Railways of Yorkshire, The west Riding, 1976; North Yorkshire Moors Railway (with P Williams), 1977; Steam on the North York Moors, 1978; Yorkshire Railways (with A Haigh), 1979; Steam on the Settle and Carlisle, 1981; Yorkshire Dales Railway, Settle- Carlisle in Colour, 1983; Regional History of the Railways of Great Britain: The Lake Counties, 1984; Portrait of the Settle: Carlisle, 1984; Yorkshire dales in Colour, 1985; The Dalesman - A Celebration of 50 Years, 1989; Life in the Yorkshire Coalfield, 1989; Settle-Carlisle Celebration, 1990; Best Yorkshire Tales, 1991, 1991. Address: Hole Bottom, Hebden, Skipton, North Yorkshire, BD23 5D1, England.

JOY P K, b. 25 Sept 1940, Kerala, India. Business Manager and Consultant. m. Saramma (Dolly), 10 June 1965, 2 s. Education: PhD, Management Studies. Publications: Handbook of Construction Management, 1990; Total Project Management - The Indian Context, 1993; The Final Goal, 1986, reprinted 1988; For A More Beautiful World, 1988; Forced Smiles, 1988; Convener of Indian Writers Club; Indian Editor for several foreign journals. Contributions to: Numerous Indian English newspapers and journals including: the Hindu, Financial Express, The Indian Management, Fortune India. Honours: DLitt, several universities and academies. Memberships: Director, International Liason, World Poetry Society; British Institute of Management; American Management Association; Indian Society for Tech Education; Indian Council of Arbitration; Project Management Institute (USA). Address: C-23 Annanagar East, Madras 600 106, India.

JUDD Cyril. See: MERRILL (Josephine) Judith Grossman.

JUDD Denis, b. 28 Oct 1938, Byfield, Northants, England. Historian; Writer. m. Dorothy Woolf, 10 July 1964. 3 sons, 1 daughter. Education: BA Hons, Modern History, Oxford University, 1961; PGCEd, 1962, PhD, 1967, London University. Publications: Balfour & the British Empire, 1968; The Boer War, 1977; Radical Joe: Joseph Chamberlain, 1977; Prince Philip, 1981; Lord Reading, 1982; Alison Uttley, 1986; Jawaharlal Nehru, 1993; 2 novels/books and stories for children; Other history books and biographies. Contributions to: History Today; History; Journal of Imperial & Commonwealth History; Times Literary Supplement; Financial Times: New Statesman and Society. Honours: Fellow, Royal Historical Society, 1977; Awarded Professorship, 1990. Literary Agent: Bruce Hunter, David Highams, London. Address: 20 Mount Pleasant Road, London, NW10 3EL, England.

JUDSON John, b. 1930, USA. Educator; Editor; Writer. Appointments: Editor, Juniper Press, Northeast/Juniper Books, literary magazine and chapbook series, 1961-; Professor of English, University of Wisconsin, La Crosse, 1965-1993. Publications: Two from Where It Snows (co-author), 1963; Surreal Songs, 1968; Within Seasons, 1970; Voyages to the Inland Sea, 6 volumes, 1971-76; Finding Worlds in Winter: West of Burnam South of Troy, 1973; Ash Is the Candle's Wick, 1974; Roots from the Onion's Dark, A Purple Tale, 1978; North of Athens, Letters to Jirac II, 1980; Reasons Why I Am Not Perfect, 1982;

The Carrabassett Sweet William Was My River, 1982; Suite for Drury Pond, 1989; Muse(sic), 1992. Address: 1310 Shorewood Drive, La Crosse, WI 54601, USA.

JUERGENSEN Hans, b. 17 Dec 1919, Myslowitz, Germany (now Poland). Professor Emeritus. m. Ilse Dina Loebenberg, 27 Oct 1945, 1 daughter. Education: BA, Upsala College, New Jersey, USA, 1942; PhD, Johns Hopkins University, 1951. Appointments include: Associate Professor, English, Chairman, Quinnipiac College, Hamden, Connecticut, 1953-61; Assistant Professor, Associate Professor, 1961-68, Professor, Humanities, 1968-92, Professor Emeritus, 1992-, University of South Florida, Tampa; Poetry in Schools Coordinator, Hillsborough County, Florida, 1972-76; Nominating Committee, Nobel Prize in Literature, 1975-. Publications: Poetry: I Feed You From My Cup, 1958; In Need for Names, 1961; Existential Cannon and Other Poems, 1965; Florida Montage, 1966; Sermons from the Ammunition Hatch of the Ship of Fools, 1968; From the Divide, 1970; Hebraic Modes, 1972; Journey toward the Roots, 1976; The Broken Jug, 1977; California Frescoes, 1980; General George H Thomas: A Summary in Perspective, 1980; The Record of a Green Planet, 1982; Fire Tested, 1983; Beachheads and Mountains, 1984; The Ambivalent Journey, 1986; Roma, 1987; Testimony, 1989; Editor: Gryphon, 1974-89; Ipso Facto, 1975; For Neruda, For Chile, 1975; Children's Poetry Anthology, 1975; The Anthology of American Magazine Verse, 1981; Co-editor: Orange Street Poetry Journal, 1958-62; University of South Florida Language Quarterly, 1961-74. Contributions to: Over 200 to New York Times; Herald Tribune; PM; Bitterroot; Apalachee Poetry Journal; Pulpsmith; Cantilevers; Others. Address: 7815 Pine Hill Drive, Tampa, FL 33617.

JULIAN Jane. See: **WISEMAN David.**

JULL COSTA Margaret Elisabeth, b. 2 May 1949, England. Literary Translator. Education: BA First Class Hons, Hispanic Studies, Bristol University, 1977; MA Spanish and Portuguese, Stanford University, California, 1978; Post Graduate Diploma in English as a Second Language, Leeds University, 1982. Publications: Translations: All Souls by Javier Marias, 1992; Obabakoak by Bernardo Atxaga, 1992; The Book of Disquiet by Fernando Pessoa, 1991; The Witness by Juan Jose Saer, 1990; The Last Days of William Shakespeare, by Vlady Kociancich, 1990; The Resemblance by Alvaro Pombo, 1989; The Hero of the Big House by Alvaro Pombo, 1988; Lúcio's Confession by Mário de Sá-Carneiro, . Honours: Joint Winner, Portuguese Translation Prize, 1992. Memberships: Translators Association. Address: 13 Mickleton Drive, Leicester, LE5 6GE, England.

JUNKINS Donald (Arthur), b. 1931, American. Appointments: Assisstant Professor, Emerson College, Boston, 1961; Assisstant Professor, California State College, Chico, 1963-66; Assisstant Professor, 1966-69, Associate Professor 1969-74, Director, Master of Fine Arts Program in English, 1970-78, Professor of English, 1974-, University of Massachussetts, Amherst. Publications: The Sunfish and the Partridge, 1965; The Graves of Scotland Parish, Walden 100 Years after Thoreau, 1968; And Sandpipers She Said, 1970; The Contemporary World Poets (editor), 1976; The Uncle Harry Poems and Other Maine Reminiscences, 1977; Crossing By Ferry, 1978; The Agamenticus Poems, 1984; Playing For Keeps, 1991. Contributions to: poems in New Yorker; Atlantic; Sewanee Review; American Poetry Review; articles in Hemingway Review. Honours: NEA Fellowship Grants, 1974, 1979; John Masefield Award, 1973. Memberships: PEN; Hemingway Society. Address: Hawks Road, Deerfield, MA 01342, USA.

JUNOR John Donald Brown, Sir, (J.J.), b. 15 Jan 1919, Glasgow, Scotland. Journalist. m. Pamela Welsh, 1942, 1 son, 1 daughter. Education: MA, Glasgow University. Appointments: Political Columnist, Sunday Express, 1948-50; Assistant Editor, Daily Express, 1951-53; Deputy Editor, Evening Standard, 1953-54; Editor, Sunday Express, 1954-86, Director, 1956-, Chairman, 1968-; Director, Express Newspapers, 1960-86, Fleet Holdings PLC, 1982-. Publications: Proletariat of Westminster, 1949; Equal Shares, 1950; The Best of J.J., 1981; Listening For a Midnight Tram (memoirs), 1990. Honours: Hon. Dr. Law, New Brunswick, 1973; Kt, 1980. Address: c/o Bank Scotland, 16 Picadilly, London, W1, England.

JURGENSEN Manfred, b. 26 Mar 1940, Flensburg, Germany. Professor. m. Uschi Fischer, 1986. Education: Ba, 1964; MA, 1966; PhD, 1968. Appointments: Editor, Outrider, Journal of Multicultural Literature; Co Editor, Seminar; Director, Phoenix Publications.

Publications: Stations; Places; Signs & Voices; A Kind of Dying; A Winters Journey; South Africa Transit; State Security; The Skin Trade; Waiting For Cancer; First Presence; Break Out; Experimental Man; A Difficult Love; Other inc On Gunter Grass; Thomas Bernhard; Boell; Frisch; Intruders. Contributions to: numerous. Memberships: Australian Fellowship of Writers; Australian Society of Authors; National Book Council of Australia; International PEN; Deutscher Achriftstellerverband; Humboldt Fellowship; AULLA. Literary Agent: Michael Meller, Munich. Address: c/o Department of German, University of Queensland, St Lucia, Brisbane 4072, Australia.

JUSSAWALLA Adil (Jehangir), b. 8 Apr 1940, Bombay, India. Lectuer; Poet. Education: MA, University College, Oxford, 1964. Appointments include: Lecturer, St Xavier's College, Bombay, 1972-75; Editor, Debonair, Bombay, 1989. Publications: Lands End, 1962; Missing Person, 1976; Television Plays Train to Calcutta, 1970; War, 1989; Editor, New Writing in India, 1974; Co Editor, Statements: An Anthology of Indian Prose in English, 1976. Address: Palm Springs, Flat R2, Cuffe Parade, Bombay 400 005, India.

JUST Ward, b. USA. Publications include: 10 novels & nonfiction include: To What End: Report from Vietnam, 1968; A Soldier of the Revolution, 1970; The Congressman who Loved Flanbert, 1973; Nicholson At Large, 1975; A Family Trust, 1978; In the City of Fear, 1982; The American Blues, 1984; Jack Grace, 1989; Twenty-One: Selected Stories, 1990; The Translator, 1991; Ambition & Love, 1994. Address: c/o Vineyard Haven PO, Vineyard Haven, MA 02568, USA.

JUSTICE Donald Rodney, b. 12 Aug 1925, Miami, Florida, USA. m. Jean Ross, 22 Aug 1947, 1 s. Education: BA, University of Miami, 1945; Ma, Univwersity of North Carolina, 1947; PhD, University of Iowa, 1954. Appointments: University of Iowa, 1957-66, 1971-82; Syracuse University, 1966-70; University of California, Irvine, 1971; University of Florida, 1982-92. Publications: The Summer Anniveraries, 1960; Night Light, 1967; Departures, 1973; selected Poems, 1979; The Sunset Maker, 1987; Platonic Scripts, Criticism, 1984; A Donald Justice Reader, 1992; The Collected Poems of Weldon Kees, editor, 1960. Contributions to: numerous journals and magzines. Honours: Lamont Award, 1959; NEA Fellowships, 1967, 1973, 1980, 1989; Guggenheim Fellowship, 1976; Pulitzer Prize Poetry, 1980; Academy of American Poets Fellow, 1988; NEA Fellowship, 1989; Co-Winner of Bollingen Prize, 1991. Membership: American Academy and Institute of Arts and Letters. Address: 338 Rocky Shore Drive, Iowa City, IA 52246, USA.

JUSTICIAR. See: **POWELL-SMITH Vincent.**

K

KADOHATA Cynthia Lynn, b. 7 Feb 1956, Chicago, USA. Novelist. m. 30 Aug 1992. Publications: In The Heart of the Valley of Love, 1992; The Floating World, 1989. Contributions to: Grand Street; New Yorker; Mississippi Review; PA Review; NY Times. Honours: National Endowment for the Arts, 1991; Whiting Writers Award, 1991. Literary Agent: Richard Curtis.

KAEL Pauline, b. 19 June 1919, Sonoma County, California, USA. Movie Critic. Education: University of California, Berkeley, 1936-40. Appointment: Movie Critic, The New Yorker, 1968-91. Publications: Books: I Lost it at the Movies, 1965; Kiss Kiss Bang Bang, 1968; Going Steady, 1970; Raising Kane in The Citizen Kane Book, 1971; Deeper into Movies, 1973; Reeling, 1976; When the Lights Go Down, 1980; 5001 Nights at the Movies, 1982; Taking It All In, 1984; State of the Art, 1985; Hooked, 1989; Move Love, 1991; For Keeps, 1994. Contributions to: Partisan Review; Vogue; The New Republic; McCall's; The Atlantic; Harper's. Honours: Guggenheim Fellow, 1964; George Polk Memorial Award for Criticism, 1970; The National Book Award, Arts and Letters, for Deeper into Movies, 1974; Front Page Awards: Newswomen's Club of New York: Best Magazine Column of 1974, Distinguished Journalism, 1983; Recipient of 8 honorary degrees. Address: c/o The New Yorker, 20 West 43rd Street, New York, NY 10036, USA.

KAGAN Andrew Aaron, b. 22 Sept 1947, St Louis, Missouri, USA. Art Historian; Art Adviser, m. Jayne Wilner, 17 May 1987. Education: BA, Washington University; MA, 1971, PhD, 1977, Harvard University. Appointments: Advisory Editor, Arts Magazine, 1975-89; Critic of Art, Music, Architecture, St Louis Globe Democrat, 1978-81. Publications: Paul Klee/Art and Music, 1983; Rothko, 1987; Trova, 1988; Marc Chagall, 1989; Absolute Art, 1995; Paul Klee at the Guggenheim, 1993. Contributions to: McMillan Dictionary of Art; Arts Magazine; Burlington Magazine; Others. Honours: Phi Beta Kappa, 1969; Harvard Prize Fellowship, 1970-77; Kingsbury Fellowship, 1977-78; Goldman Prize, 1985. Membership: Founder, Director, Wednesday Night Society. Address: 232 N Kingshighway No 1709, St Louis, MO 63108, USA.

KAHN James, b. 1947, American. Appointments: Resident, Los Angeles County Hospital, 1976-77; University of California at Los Angeles, 1978-79; Physician, Emergency Room Physician, Rancho Encino Hospital, Los Angeles, 1978-. Publications: Diagnosis Murder, Nerves in Patterns (with Jerome McGann), 1978; World Enough and Time, Time's Dark Laughter, Poltergeist, 1982; Return of the Jedi, 1983; Indiana Jones and the Temple of Doom, 1984; Goonies, 1985; Timefall, Poltergeist II, 1986. Address: c/o Jane Jordan Browne, 410 S Michigan Avenue, Suite 724, Chicago, IL 60605, USA.

KAHN Michele Anne, b. 1 Dec 1940, Nice, France. Writer. m. Pierre-Michel Kahn, 8 Jan 1961, 1 s. Education: Diploma In Social Sciences, University of Paris, 1976. Publications include: Contes du jardin d'Eden, 1983; Un Ordinateur pas Ordinaire, 1983; Juges et Rois, 1984; de l'autre cote de brouillard, 1985; Hotel Riviera, 1986; Rue du Roi-dore, 1989; La vague noire, 1990; Boucles d'Or et Bebe Ours (serie), 1990. Contributions to: Magzine Litteraire. Honours: Diplomes Loisirs Jeunes, 1971; Diplome Loisirs Jeunes, 1983; Liste d'Honnoeur, Osterreichen und Jugenbuchpriesen, 1977. Memberships: International PEN Club; Secretaire Generale dela Societe des Gens de Lettres De France, 1982-86; Vice Presidente de la Societe des Gens Des Lettres de France, 1986-91; Vice President de la Societe Civile des Auteurs Multimedia. Literary Agent: Claudia Vincent. Address: Residence Belloni, 192A Rue de Vaugirard, Paris 75015, France.

KAHN Peggy. See: KATZ Bobbi.

KALB Jonathan, b. 30 Oct 1959, New Jersey, USA. Theatre Critic; Assistant Professor of Theatre. m. Julie Heffernan, 18 June 1988, 1 son. Education: BA, English, Wesleyan University; MFA, Dramaturgy, Dramatic Criticism, 1985, DFA, Dramaturgy, Dramatic Criticism, 1987, Yale School of Drama. Appointments: Theatre Critic, The Village Voice, 1987-; Assistant Professor of Performance Studies, New York City, 1990-92; Assistant Professor of Theatre, Hunter College, City University of New York, 1992-. Publications: Beckett in Performance, 1989; Free Admissions: Collected Theater Writings,

1993. Contributions to: American Theatre; Michigan Quarterly Review; Theatre Three; The Threepenny Review; Performing Arts Journal; Modern Drama; Theatre Journal; High Performance; Theater; Theater Heute; Theatre Forum; The Annual of Bernard Shaw Studies; Theatre reviews, book reviews, feature articles for The Village Voice and other newspapers. Honours: Fulbright Hays Grant, 1988-89; T C G Jerome Fellowship, 1989-90; George Jean Nathan Award for Dramatic Criticism, 1990-91. Memberships: Modern Language Association; PEN American Centre. Address: Hunter College of CUNY, Department of Theatre, 695 Park Avenue, New York, NY 10021, USA.

KALECHOFSKY Roberta, b. 11 May 1931, New York City, New York, USA. Writer; Publisher. m. Robert Kalechofsky, 7 June 1953, 2 sons. Education: BA, Brooklyn College, 1952; MA, 1957, PhD, 1970, English, New York University. Literary appointments: Literary Editor, Branching Out feminist journal, Canada, 1973-74; Contributing Editor: Margins, 1974-77; On The Issues, feminist journal, 1987-94. Publications: Stephen's Passion, 1975; La Hoya, 1976; Orestes in Progress, 1976; Solomon's Wisdom, 1978; Rejected Essays and Other Matters, 1980; The 6th Day of Creation, 1986; Bodmin 1349, 1988; Haggadah For the Liberated Lamb, 1988; Autobiography of a Revolutionary: Essays on Animals and Human Rights, 1991; Justice, My Brother, re-issued, 1993; Haggadah For the Vegetarian Family, 1993; K'tia, A Savior of the Jewish People, 1995; A Boy, A Chicken and The Lion of Judah - How Ari Became a Vegetarian, (a children's book), 1995. Contributions to: Confrontation; Works; Ball State University Forum; Western Humanities Review; Rocky Mountain Review; Between the Species; So'western; Response; Reconstructionist. Address: 255 Humphrey Street, Marblehead, MA 01945, USA.

KALLEN Lucille Eve, b. Los Angeles, California, USA. Writer; Author. m. Herbert Engel, 22 Aug 1952, 1 son, 1 daughter. Education: Harbord Collegiate, Toronto, Canada; Toronto Conservatory of Music. Publications: Outside There, Somewhere, 1964; Introducing C B Greenfield, 1979; C B Greenfield: The Tanglewood Murder, 1980; C B Greenfield: No Lady in the House, 1982; C B Greenfield: The Piano Bird, 1984; C B Greenfield: A Little Madness, 1986; Television work includes Your Show of Shows, 1949-54; Maybe Tuesday, play, 1958. Honours: Introducing C B Greenfield nominated for American Book Award, 1980. Memberships: Mystery Writers of America; Authors Guild; Dramatists Guild; Writers Guild of America, East. Literary Agent: Arnold Goodman, USA. Address: c/o Arnold Goodman, 500 WestEnd Avenue, New York, NY 10024, USA.

KALOKERINOS Archie, b. 28 Sept 1927, Glen Innes, New South Wales, Australia. Medical Practitioner. m. Catherine Hunter, 17 Dec 1977, 1 son, 1 daughter. Education: MB BS, University of Sydney, 1951; Fellow, Royal Society of Tropical Medicine. Publications: In Search of Opal, 1967; Australian Precious Opal; Every Second Child, 1971; God Knows Why But It Works, biographical film, 1973. Contributions: Articles on Australian opal, aboriginal health, sudden infant death, vitamin and mineral supplements. Honours: Australian Medal of Merit, 1980. Address: RMB 218ZA, Bournes Lane, Tamworth, New South Wales 2340, Australia.

KAMINSKI Ireneusz Gwidon, b. 1 Mar 1925, Gniezno, Poland. Writer. m. Alicja Gardocka, 26 Aug 1960, 2 sons, 2 daughters. Education: MA, Liberal Arts, Mickiewicz University, Poznan, 1952. Literary Appointments: Journalist, Teacher, Librarian, 1950-70; War Correspondent, Vietnam, 1968, 1972; 2nd editor-in-chief, Morze (Sea) monthly, 1971-85. Publications: 10 novels, 25 short stories, 1 reportage, 3 radio plays, numerous essays, etc; First published (poetry), 1950; Titles include: Wegierska opowiesc, 1954; Czerwony sokol, 1957; Msciciel przyplywa z Rugii, 1958; Czas slonca, 1960; Biale wrony, 1963; Anastazja, 1969; Paszcza smoka, 1970; Krystyna i rapier, 1971; Odro, rzeko poganska, 1975; Swiety Ateusz, 1987; Kontredans, 1988; Retrospekcja, 1990; Diabelska ballada, 1992; Dziesiata planeta, 1994; Powracajaca fala, 1994. Honours: Literary Awards, City of Szczecin, 1958, 1975, 1985. Memberships: Executive, Polish Writers Union; Sea Yacht Club, Szczecin. Address: 70-791 Szczecin, ul Kozia 16, Poland.

KAMINSKY Stuart, b. 1934, USA. Author; Professor. Appointments: Science Writer, University of Illinois, Champaign, 1962-64; Editor, News Service, University of Michigan, Ann Arbor, 1965-66; Director of Public Relations, Assisstant to Vice-President for Public Affairs, University of Chicago, 1969; Joined Faculty, 1972, currently Professor of Radio, Television and Film, Northwestern University, Evanston, Illinois. Publications: Don Siegal: Director, 1973;

Clint Eastwood, 1974; American Film Genres: Approaches to a Critical Theory of Popular Film, 1974; Ingmar Bergman: essays in Criticism (edited with Joseph Hill), 1975; John Huston: Maker of Magic, 1978; Bullet For A Star, novel, 1977; Murder on the Yellow Brick Road, novel, 1978; You Bet Your Life, novel, 1979; The Howard Hughes Affair, novel, 1979; Never Cross a Vampire, novel, 1980; Basic Filmaking, (with Dana Hodgdon), 1981; Death of a Dissident, novel, 1981; High Midnight, novel, 1981; Catch a Falling Clown, novel, 1982; He Done Her Wrong, novel, 1983; Whenthe Dark man Calls, novel, 1983; Black Knight on Red Square, novel, 1983; American Television Genres (with Jeffrey Mahan), textbook, 1984; Down for the Count, novel, 1985; Red Chameleon, novel, 1985; Exercise in Terror, novel, 1985; Smart Moves, novel, 1987; A Fine Red Rain, novel, 1987; Lieberman's Day, 1994. Address: School of Speech, Northwestern University, Evanston, IL 60201, USA.

KAN Sergei, b. 1953. Publications: Wrap Your Father's Brothers in Kind Words, 1982; Symbolic Immortality: the Tlingit Pottatch, 1989. Honour: American Book Award, 1990.

KANAME Hiroshi, b. 15 Dec 1940, Osaka, Japan. Professor. m. Motoko Nakata, 29 Apr 1976, 1 s. Education: BA, Kobe City University of Foreign Studies, 1964; MA, Osaka City University, 1969. Appointments: Lecturer, 1973, Associate Professor, 1976, Professor, 1991-, University of Osaka Prefecture. Publications: American Novels: Study and Appreciation, 1977; Alienation and American Novels, 1982; The Dream and Its Collapse in American Literature, 1988. Memberships: American Literature Society of Japan; The International John Steinbeck Society; John Steinbeck Society of Japan. Address: 1-10-14-741, Imafuku-Higashi, Joto-Ku, Osaka-shi, Japan 536.

KANAVA Zoe, b. 6 Jan 1933, Greece. Writer. m. John Kanavas, 2 s. Publications include: Liontaria ston Hippodrome, 1977; Na Sas Po Mia Historia? 1978; To Stichima, 1979; O Glaros Tou Aigiogiou, 1980; Ta Genethlia Tis Chelonas, 1981; O Saligaros Vgainei Amaxada, 1982; Me Tis Alyssides tis Eleftherias, 1982; Paschalia Me Autostop, 1983; Apo Kei Vgainei O Helios, 1985; O Polemistis Tou Megalou Kastrou, 1987. Contributions to: numerous magazines and journals, radio & TV programmes. Honours: Literary Awards, Society of Christian Letters, Circle of Greek Children's Books, Youth Literature Honour of the University of Padova. Memberships: National Society of Greek Literature Authors; Awards Jury, Womens Literary Circle of Greek Children's Books. Address: Xenias 45, GR 15771 Athens, Greece.

KANDELL Alice S, b. 1938, USA. Children's Author. Publications: Sikkim: The Hidden Kingdom, 1971; Mountaintop Kingdom: Sikkim (With Charlotte Y Salisbury), 1971; Max the Music Maker (with Miriam Stecher), 1980; Daddy and Ben Together (with Miriam Stecher), 1981; Friends (with Terry Berger), 1981; Ben's ABC Day (with Terry Berger), 1982. Address: 11 East 68th Street, New York, NY 10021, USA.

KANE Jim. See: **GERMANO Peter B.**

KANE Penny. See: **RUZICKA Penelope Susan.**

KANE Wilson. See: **BLOCH Robert.**

KANIGEL Robert, b. 28 May 1946, Brooklyn, New York, USA. Writer. m. Judith Schiff Pearl, 28 June 1981, 1 son. Education: BS, Rensselaer Polytechnic Institute, Troy, New York. Appointments: Freelance Writer, 1970-; Instructor, Johns Hopkins University School of Continuing Studies, 1985-91; Visiting Professor of English, University of Baltimore, Maryland, and Senior Fellow, Institute of Publications Design, 1991-. Publications: The Man Who Knew Infinity: A Life of the Genius Ramanujan, 1991, 2nd Edition, 1992; Apprentice to Genius: The Making of a Scientific Dynasty, 1986, 2nd Edition, 1993. Contributions to: New York Times Magazine; The Sciences; Health; Psychology Today; Science 85; Johns Hopkins Magazine; Washington Post. Address: 202 Dunkirk Road, Baltimore, MD 21212, USA.

KANN Mark E, b. 24 Feb 1947. Professor of Political Science. m. Kathy Michael, 13 Feb 1969, 1 son. Education: BA, 1968, MA, 1972, PhD, 1975, University of Wisconsin, Madison, USA. Publications: Thinking About Politics: Two Political Sciences, 1980; The American Left: Failures and Fortunes, 1983; Middle Class Radicals in Santa Monica, 1986; On the Man in Question: Gender and Civic Virtue in America, 1991. Contributions to: Numerous newspapers, journals and magazines. Honours: Various research and teaching awards.

Membership: Vice-President, Thomas Jefferson Center. Address: Department of Political Science, University of Southern California, Los Angeles, CA 90089-0044, USA.

KANNAN Lakshmi (Kaaveri), b. 13 Aug 1947, Mysore, India. Writer. m. L V Kannan, 2 sons. Education: BA Hons, MA, PhD, all in English. Appointments: Writer-in-Residence, University of Kent at Canterbury, Canterbury, UK, on a Charles Wallace Trust Fellowship, 1993; British Council Visitor & Participant, Cambridge Seminar on Contemporary British Writing, Summer 1992; 1992 Delegate, 5th International Feminist Book Fair at Amsterdam, The Netherlands; 1990 Delegate, First World Summit For Women, Monteal, Canada; 1988 Delegate, Third International Feminist Book Fair at Montreal, Canada. Publications: Rhythms, 1986; Parijata, 1992; Exiled Gods, 1985; Glow and the Grey, 1976; Laya Baddh (Hindu), 1990 (translation); Wooden Cow, 1979 (translation); As Kaaveri: Osaigal, (Tamil), 1985; Athukku Poganum (Tamil), 1986, 1989; Venmai Porthiyathu (Tamil), 1992; India Gate (English), 1993; Inru Malai, Ennudan (Tamil), 1994. Address: B-11/8193, Vasant Kunj, New Delhi, 110030, India.

KANTARIS Sylvia, b. 9 Jan 1936. Poet. m. Emmanuel Kantaris, 11 Jan 1958, 1 son, 1 daughter. Education: BA Hons, 1957, CertEd, 1958, Bristol University; Diplome d'Etudes de Civilisation Francaise, Sorbonne, Paris, France, 1955; MA 1967, PhD 1972, Queensland University, Australia, 1964-71. Appointments: Member of Literature Panel, South West Arts, 1983-87; Literary Consultant, SWA, 1990-. Publications: Time and Motion, 1975, 1986; The Tenth Muse, 1983, 1986; The Sea at the Door, 1985; The Air Mines of Mistila, 1988; Dirty Washing: New and Selected Poems, 1989; Stocking Up, 1981; News from the Front, 1983; Lad's Love, 1993. Contributions to: Essays in French Literature; Australian Journal of French Studies; New Poetry; Prospice; Stand; Poetry Review; Outposts Poetry Quarterly; The Observer; Times Literary Supplement; London Magazine; London Review of Books. Honours: Hon DLitt, University of Exeter, 1989; Major Arts Council Literature Award, 1991; Society of Authors Award, 1992. Memberships: Poetry Society of Great Britain. Address: 14 Osborne Parc, Helston, Cornwall TR13 8PB, England.

KANTOR Peter, b. 5 Nov 1949, Budapest, Hungary. Poet. Education: MA English and Russian Literature, 1973, MA Hungarian Literature, 1980, Budapest NLTE University. Appointments: Literary Editor of Kortars (literary magazine), 1984-86. Publications: Naplo, 1987-89, 1991; Hogy no az eg, 1988; Gradicsok, 1985; Halmadar, 1981; Kavics, 1976; Sebbel Lobbal, 1982; Font lomb, lent avar, 1994; Mentafü (selected poems), 1994. Contributions to: Holmi, Kortars, Es, Agni; Raster 42, de Tweede Ronde, Storm. Honours: George Soros Fellowship, 1988-89; Wessely Laszlo Award, 1990; Dery Tibor Award, 1991; Fulbright Fellowship, 1991-92; Fust Milan Award, 1992; Jozsef Attila Award, 1994. Memberships: Hungarian Writers Union; International PEN Club. Address: Stollar Bela u 3/a, Budapest 1055, Hungary.

KAPLAN Harold, b. 3 Jan 1916, Chicago, Illinois, USA. Professor Emeritus. m. Isabelle M Ollier, 29 July 1962, 1 son, 2 daughters. Education: BA, 1937, MA, 1938, University of Chicago. Appointments: Instructor of English, Rutgers University, 1946-49; Professor of English, Bennington College, 1950-72; Professor of English, 1972-86, Professor Emeritus, 1986-, Northwestern University. Publications: The Passive Voice, 1966; Democratic Humanism and American Literature, 1972; Power and Order, 1981; Conscience and Memory: Meditations in a Museum of the Holocaust, 1994. Contributions to: Commentary; Nation; Partisan Review; Sewanee Review; Poetry Magazine; The New Leader; The Hudson Review. Honours: Fulbright Lecturer, 1967, 1981; Rockefeller Foundation Humanities Fellowship, 1982. Memberships: Northwestern University: Chairman, American Culture Programme, Chairman, Department of English. Address: Turnabout Lane, Bennington, VT 05201, USA.

KAPLAN Morton A, b. 9 May 1921, Pennsylvania, USA. Professor Political Science. m. Azie Mortimer Kaplan, 22 Jul 1967. Education: BS Temple University, 1943; PhD, Columbia University, 1951. Appointments: Associate Editor, Journal of Conflict Resolution, 1961-72; Board Of Editors, World Politics, 1956-71; Orbis, 1967-90; Member Advisory Board, Washington Times, 1982-; Editor, Publisher, World and I, 1985-. Publications include: System and Process in International Politics, 1965; Political Foundation of International Law, 1961; Justice, Human Nature and Political Obligation, 1976; Science, Language and the Human Condition, 1989; Law in a Democratic Society, 1939. Memeberships include: American Political Science

Association; International Political Science Association; International Institute for Strategic Studies; Hon Member, International Cultural Society of Korea. Address: The University of Chicago, Dept of Political Science; 5828 South University Avenue, Chicago, IL 60637, USA.

KAPLAN Robert David, b. 23 June 1952, NY, USA. Author; Journalist. m. Maria Cabral, 26 Aug 1983, 1 s. Education: BA, University of CT, 1973. Publications: The Arabists, The Romance of an American Elite, 1993; Balkan Ghosts, A Journey Through History, 1993; Soldiers of God: with the Mujahidin in Afghanistan, 1990; Surrender or Starve: The Wars Behind The Famine, 1988. Contributions to: The Atlantic Monthly (as a Contributing Editor); The New Republic; Conde Nast Traveler; NY Times; Wall Street Journal; International Herald Tribune. Honour: nominated for the Pulitzer Prize, 1993, for Balkan Ghosts. Memberships: Authors Guild; Authors League of Am. Literary Agent: Carl D Brandt. Address: Washington DC, USA.

KAPUR Rajiv Alochan, b. 26 Nov 1951, New Delhi, India. International Civil Servant. 1 daughter. Education: BA, cum laude, Cornell University, USA, 1972; DPhil, Oxford University, England, 1979. Appointments: Senior Fellow, Centre for Policy Research, New Delhi, India, 1987-88. Publications: Sikh Separatism: The Politics of Faith, 1985. Contributions to: Khalistan: India's Punjab Problem; Third World Quarterly; The Sikh Community: Encyclopaedia Britannica. Memberships: Fellow, Royal Asiatic Society. Address: c/o United Nations High Commission for Refugees, Palais des Nations 1211, Geneva 10, Switzerland.

KAPUSCINSKI Ryszard, b. 4 Mar 1932, Pinsk, Poland. Journalist; Writer. m. Alicija Mielczarek, 6 Oct 1952, 1 d. Education: MA Faculty of History, Warsaw University. Appointments: Sztander Mlodych, daily, 1951; Polityka, weekly, 1957-61; Correspondent, Polish Press Agency (PAP) in Africa, Latin America, 1962-72; Kutura, weekly, 1974-81. Publications: The Emperor; The Soccer War; Another Day of Life; The Shah of Shahs; Bush Polish Style; Lapidarium; Notes; Imperium, 1993. Contributions to: Vanity Fair; Tempo; The Independent; The Guardian; Frankfurter Augemeine Zeitung. Honours: Gold Cross of Merit; Knight's Croos Order Polonia Restituta; Prize of International Journalists Organisation, 1976; State Prize. Memberships: PEN; Polish Centre Club; Board of Advisors, NPQ; Polish Association of Artistic Photographers; the Natural Council of Culture. Literary Agent: Ms Eva Koranile, Liepman Ag, Meienburgweg 32, CH-8044, Zürich, Switzerland. Address: ul Prokuratorska 11 m2, 02-074 Warsaw, Poland.

KARAVIA Lia Headzopoulou, b. 27 June 1932, Athens Greece. Writer. Philologue; Actress. m. Vassilis Caravias, 20 Sept 1953, 2 s.Education: Diploma, English Literatur, Pierce College, Athens, 1953; Diploma French Literature, Institute of France, Athens, 1954; Diploma, Acting, Acting School, Athens. 1962; Classical Literature, University of Athens, 1972; Doctorat Nouveau Regime, Comparative Literature, Paris, 1991. Appointments: Teacher, Acting, History of The Theatre, Public Schools, 1984-90. Publications include: Hypermesia, 1979; Riki, 1980; The Silent Piano Keys, 1969; Trilingual Edition of the Lion - Riki-The Silent Piano Keys, 1984; The Censor, 1986; Our Neighbourhood, 1986; Oldsters and Youngsters, 1992; 10 Collections of Poetry; 1 collection Short Stories; 10 novels; 4 short plays; 5 long plys; scripts for Greek TV; radio plays for Greek radio. Contributions to: numerous journals, magzines; Romanian Poetry Anthology, 1987; French Poetry Anthologies; short story: Die Schwägerinnen in Frauen in Griecherland, dtv editions in Germany, 1991; essays in US publications. Honours including: Memlaos Loudemis Prize, 1980; Michaela Averof's Prize, 1981; League of Philologue's Prize, 1986; Women's Literary Club Prizes, 1986 and 1988; National Prize,Best Play For the Young, 1989; National Playwrights Prize for "Generation Gaps", 1990; National Playwrights Prize for "Bench in a Public Garden", 1991. Memberships include: World Academy of Arts and Culture; Founding Member, Maison Internationale de Poeses, Liege; Society of Greek Writers; International Theatre Centre; Actors League of Greece; Society of Greek Translators; Union of Greek Playwrights; Society of Greek Women Scientists. Address: 51 Aghiou Polycarpou Str, Nea Smyrni 17124, Athens, Greece.

KARINTHY Ferenc, b. 2 June 1921, Budapest, Hungary. Writer. m. Agnes Boross, 1 s, 1 d. Education: Budapest University of Arts & Sciences. Appointments: Lecturer, History of Literature & Theatre, MIT, Columbia University, New York, University of California at Los Angeles and Chicago State University; Drama Adviser, National Theatre of Budapest, 1949-50, Madach Theatre, 1952-53, Hungarian TV 1965-70.

Publications: novels: DOn Juan ejszakaja, 1943; Szellemidezes, 1946; Kentaur, 1947; Budapesti tavasz, 1953; Epepe, 1970; Ösbemutato, 1972; Alvilagi naplo, 1979; Budapesti Ösz, 1982; Uncle Joe, 1987; short stories: Irodalmi tortenek, 1956; Ferencvarosi Sziv, 1960; Kek-zold Florida, 1962; Hatorzag, 1965; Viz folott, viz alatt, 1966; Vegtelen szonyeg, 1974; Harmincharom, 1977; Marich Geza utolso kalandja, 1979; Mi van a Dunaban, 1980; Zenebona, 1986; plays: Ezer ev, 1956; Bosendorfer, 1966; Goz, 1967; Dunakanyar, 1967; Het jatek, 1969; Gellerthegyi almok, 1972; Pesten esBudean, 1972; Korallzatony, 1976; sketches: Hazai tudositasok, 1954; Teli furdo, 1964; Leanyfalu es videke, 1973; studies: Olasz joveveny szavaink, 1947; Nyeveles, 1964; Dialogus, 1978; Ovilag es Ujvilag, 1985. Honours: Recipient various oprizes including: Baumgarten Prize for Literature, 1947; Jozsef Attila Prize, 3 times; Kossuth Prize, 1955. Memberships: PEN; International Theatre Institute. Address: Menesi ut 71, 1118 Budapest, Hungary.

KARL Frederick Robert, b. 10 Apr 1927, Brooklyn, New York, USA. Professor; Writer. m. Dolores Mary Oristaglio, 8 June 1951, 3 daughters. Education: BA, 1948, Columbia College, 1948; MA, Stanford University, 1949; PhD, Columbia University, 1957. Appointments include: Professor, City College of New York, 1957-80; Professor, New York University, New York City, 1981-. Publications: Joseph Conrad: The Three Lives, biography; American Fictions: 1940-1980; Modern and Modernism: Sovereignty of the Artist 1885-1925; The Quest, novel; The Adversary Literary; Collected Letters of Joseph Conrad, Volumes I, II, III, IV (editor); William Faulkner: American Writer, 1989; Franz Kafka: Representative Man, 1991; Reader's Guide to Joseph Conrad; An Age of Fiction; The Contemporary English Novel. Contributions to: Yale Review; Sewanee Review; Criticism; The Nation; New Republic; 20th Century Literature; 19th Century Fiction; Midway; Mosaic; Comparative Literature; Journal of Modern Literature; Numerous essays in books, on various subjects. Literary Agent: Melanie Jackson. Address: 2 Settlers Landing Lane, East Hampton, NY 11937, USA.

KARLIN Wayne Stephen, b. 13 June 1945, Los Angeles, California, USA. Writer; Teacher. m. Ohnmar Thein, 27 Oct 1977, 1 son. Education: BA, American College, Jerusalem, 1972; MA, Goddard College, 1976. Literary appointments: President, Co-Editor, First Casualty Press, 1972-73; Visiting Writer, William Joiner Center for the Study of War and Social Consequences, University of Massachusetts, Boston, 1989-. Publications: Free Fire Zone (co-editor, contributor), 1973; Crossover, 1984; Lost Armies, 1988; The Extras, 1989; US, 1993. Contributions to: Prairie Schooner; Glimmer Train; Indiana Review; Swords and Ploughshares: An Anthology; Antietam Review; New Outlook; New Fiction from the South; The Best of 1993, anthology. Honours: Fellowship in Fiction and Individual Artist Award, Maryland State Arts Council, 1988, 1991, 1993; National Endowment for the Arts Fellowship, 1993. Membership: Associated Writing Programs. Literary Agent: Phyllis Westberg, Harold Ober Associates Inc, 425 Madison Avenue, New York, NY 10017, USA. Address: Post Office Box 239, St Mary's City, MD 20686, USA.

KARNOW Stanley, b. 4 Feb 1925, New York City, New York, USA. Writer. m. Annette Kline, 21 Apr 1959, 2 sons, 1 daughter. Education: BA, Harvard University; Sorbonne, Paris, France; Ecole des Sciences Politiques; Nieman Fellow; Fellow, Kennedy School of Government and East Asia Research Center, Harvard University. Publications: Southeast Asia, 1963, 1965; Mao and China: From Revolution to Revolution, 1972; Vietnam: A History, 1983; In Our Image: America's Empire in the Philippines, 1989. Contributions to: New York Times; GEO; Atlantic; Foreign Affairs; Foreign Policy; Esquire. Honours: Overseas Press Club, 1967, 1978, 1983; Dupont Polk Award, 1984; Emmy Award, 1984; Pulitzer Prize in History, 1990. Memberships: Century Association; Authors Guild; Council on Foreign Relations; PEN; Society of American Historians. Address: 10850 Springknoll Drive, Potomac, MD 20854, USA.

KAROL Alexander. See: KENT Arthur (William Charles).

KARP David, (Adam Singer, Wallace Ware), b. 5 May 1922, New York City, New York, USA. Writer. m. (1) Lilian Klass, 25 Dec 1944 (dec 1987), 2 sons, (2) Claire Leighton, 23 June 1988, 1 son, 1 daughter. Education: BS, Social Sciences, City College of New York, 1948. Literary appointment: Guggenheim Fellow in Creative Writing, 1956-57. Publications: One, 1953; The Day of the Monkey, 1955; All Honorable Men, 1956; Leave Me Alone, 1957; Enter, Sleeping, 1960; Vice President in charge of Revolution (with M D Lincoln), 1960; Hardman, 1952; The Brotherhood of Velvet, 1952; Platoon, 1953; The

Charka Memorial, 1956; Non-fiction: The Last Believers, 1964. Contributions to: New York Times; National Saturday Review; Los Angeles Times; Others. Honours: Guggenheim Fellow, 1956; Look Magazine Award for Best TV Play, 1958; Edgar Award, 1959; Emmy Award, 1965. Memberships: PEN; Writers Guild of America, President, TV-Radio Branch, various other offices. Address: 300 East 56th Street, Apt 3C, New York, NY 10022, USA.

KARSEN Sonja Petra, b. 11 Apr 1919, Berlin, Germany. US Citizen. Professor of Spanish Emerita. Education: BA, Carleton College, USA, 1939; MA, Bryn Mawr College, 1941; PhD, Columbia University, 1950. Literary appointments: Reviewer, World Literature Today, 1959-92; Editor, Language Association Bulletin, 1980-82; Publications include: Guillermo Valencia, Colombian Poet, 1873-1943, 1951; Educational Development in Costa Rica with UNESCO's Technical Assistance, 1951-54, 1954; Jaime Torres Bodet: A Poet in a Changing World, 1963; Selected Poems of Jaime Torres Bodet, 1964; Versos y prosas de Jaime Torres Bodet, 1966; Jaime Torres Bodet, 1971; Essays on Iberoamerican Literature and History, Peter Lang, 1988; Bericht über den Vater: Fritz Karsen (1885-1951), 1993; Papers on Foreign Languages, Literature and Culture, 1982-88; The Role of the Americas in History (América en la Historia), by Leopoldo Zea, translation, 1992. Contributions to: Over 100 articles and book reviews to professional journals including Texas Quarterly; Revista Interamericana de Bibliografia. Address: 1755 York Avenue, New York, NY 10128-6875, USA.

KARVAS Peter, b. 25 Apr 1920, Banska Bystrica, CSFR. Writer; Professor. m. Eva Ruhmnn, 15 May 1969, 1 s. Education: PhD, 1946; Professor, 1989. Publications include: Prose: Night in My Town, 1979; Humoresques, 1984, 86; The Seven Witnesses, 1969; Absolute Prohibition, 1970; Private Party, 1972; Visit by Night, 1973; Back Entrance, 1976; The 20th Night, 1971; A Kingdom for a Murderer, 1988; Prose: The Mitigating Circumstance, 1991; Us, Who Do Not Want to Be Named, 1992; The Colossus, 1993; Wigs, 1990; Te Art of Drama and the Phenomenon of Television, 1992; The Radio in the Age of Television, 1993. Contributions to: Numerous Studies and Articles. Honours: Czechoslovak State Prize, 1960; Czechoslovak Writers Union Prizes, 1991. Memberships include: Slovak Writers Union; Czechoslovak Writers Union; Slovak Pen Centre; Club of Independent Writers; Slovak Writers Association. Address: Vickova 7, 81106 Bratislava, Czech Republic.

KASDAGLIS Nikos, b. 10 Mar 1928. Retired Bank Manager. m. Irene Athanasiadou, 1 May 1957, 1 son, 1 daughter. Education: High School Graduate, 1946. Publications: The Cogs of the Millstone, 1955; Shaved Heads, 1959; Maria Wandering Over the Metropolis of the Waters, 1982; Highways of the Land and the Sea, 1988; Blessed are the Merciful, 1991; Squalls; I am the Lord Thy God, 1961; Thirst, 1970; Mythology, 1977; The Bowstring, 1985; The Swamp, 1988. Contributions to: Both Greek and Foreign Press. Honours: Greek Novel National Prize, 1955; Society of Writers, Greece. Memberships: Greek Section of Amenesty International. Address: End of Stockholm St, 85100 Rhodes, Greece.

KASSEM Lou(ise Sutton Morrell), b. 10 Nov 1931, Tennessee, USA. Author. m. Shakeep Kassem, 17 June 1951, 4 daughters. Education: East Tennessee State University, 1949-51; Short courses: University of Virginia, 1982, Vassar College, 1985. Publications: Dance of Death, 1984; Middle School Blues, 1986; Listen for Rachel, 1986; Secret Wishes, 1989; A Summer for Secrets, 1989; A Haunting in Williamsburg, 1990; The Treasures of Witch Hat Mountain, 1992; Odd One Out, 1994; The Druid Curse, 1994. Contributions to: The Alan Review; Signal. Honours: Notable Book in Social Studies, American Library Association, 1986. Memberships: Society of Children's Book Writers; Writers in Virginia; Appalachian Writers; The National League of American Pen Women. Literary Agent: Ruth Cohen. Address: 715 Burruss Drive NW, Blacksburg, VA 24060, USA.

KATKO István, b. 17 June 1923, Jászjakohalma. Writer. m. (1) Zsuzsa Kalmár, 1949, (2) Anna-Maria Fridrich, 1979, 1 son, 1 daughter. Education: Literature Degree; Teacher's Diploma. Appointments: TV Editor of Hungarian Literatura Pensioner. Publications: Novels: Kokárda, 1993; A hohér, 1992; Háziörizet, 1981; Vadhajtas, 1973; Félszívú apostolok, 1958; Nap adja az árnyékot is, 1962; Öt férfi komoly szándékkal. Contributions to: Élet es Irodalom, Népszabaság, Vasarnapi Hirek. Honours: Andor Gábor Prize, 1970; SZOT Trade Union Prize, 1983. Memberships: Union of Hungarian Writers; PEN:

Union of Film and Television Artists of Hungary. Address: Farkas Biró u 8, Budapest 1011, Hungary.

KATO Shuichi, b. 19 Sept 1919, Tokyo, Japan. Writer; Professor. Education: Graduate, Faculty of Medicine 1943, MD 1950, Tokyo University. Publications: Form, Style, Tradition, Reflexions on Japanese Art and Society, 1969; Japan-China Phenomenon, 1973; Six Lives/Six Deaths, Portraits from Modern Japan (co-authors Robert Lifton & Michael Reich), 1979; A History of Japanese Literature, 3 volumes, 1979-1983; Chosakushu (Collected works), 15 volumes, 1978-80. Contributions to: Asahi Shimbun; Many Japanese, French and American periodicals. Honours: Osaragi Jiro Prize for A History of Japanese Literature, 1980; Ordre des Arts et des Lettres, 1985. Membership: PEN Club, Japanese Branch. Address: Kaminage 1-8-16, Setagaya-ku, Tokyo 158, Japan.

KATTAN Naim, b. 26 Aug 1928. Writer. m. 21 July 1961, 1 son. Education: Law College, Baghdad, 1945-47; Sorbonne, Paris, 1947-52. Appointments include: Head of Writing and Publishing, Associate Director, Canada Council, Ottawa, Canada, 1990-91; Writer in Residence, 1991-93, Associate Professor, 1993-, University of Quebec, Montreal. Publications: Reality and Theatre, 1970; Farewell Babylon, 1974; La Memoire de la Promesse, 1980; Le Père, 1988; Farida, 1989; La Réconciliation, 1993; Portraits d'un Pays, 1994; A M Klein, 1994; La distraction, 1994. Contributions to: Critique; Quaizaire; Nouvelle Revue Française; Passages; Le Devoir; Canadian Literature. Honours: Prix France, Canada, 1971; Segal Awards, 1975; Order of Canada, 1987; Order of Arts and Letters, France, 1989; Order of Quebec, 1990. Memberships: Royal Society of Canada; Académie des Lettres, Montreal; Union des Ecrivains du Quebec. Address: 3463 Rue Ste Famille 2114, Montreal, Quebec, Canada H2X 2K7.

KATZ Bobbi, (Gail, Barbara George, Emily George, Peggy Kahn, Don E Plumme, Ali Reichi), b. 2 May 1933. Writer; Editor. m. H D Katz, 1956, div. 1979, 1 son, 1 daughter. Education: BA with special honours, Fine Arts, Goucher College, Phi Beta Kappa, Maryland, USA, 1954. Literary appointments: Editor, Books for Young Readers, Random House, New York City, 1982-. Publications: Over 90 books for children; Over 100 poems; Upside Down and Inside Out: Poems for All Your Pockets, collection of own poems, 1976; Poems for Small Friends, 1988; Anthologies: Birthday Bear's Book of Birthday Poems, 1983; Bedtime Bear's Book of Bedtime Poems, 1984; A Popple in Your Pocket and Other Funny Poems, 1986; Ghosts and Goosebumps: Poems to Make You Shiver, 1991; Puddle Wonderful: Poems to Welcome Spring; Novels include: The Manifesto and Me, Meg, 1978; Non-fiction: The Creepy, Crawly Book, 1988; A Family Hanukkah, 1992; I Meet Nelson Mandeal, 1995. Contributions to: The Cousteau Almanac; First Teacher; Highlights for Children; Ladybug Magazine; Various textbooks. Membership: Authors Guild, PEN. Address: 65 W 96th Street 21H, New York, NY 10025, USA.

KAUFMAN Amy Rebecca, b. 8 Oct 1951, Long Beach, California, USA. Editor; Publisher. Education: BA, University of California, Berkeley. Publications: Founder, Editor, Publisher, Stories Magazine, 1982-. Honours: Selections from stories in Best American Short Stories, 1984, and Prize Stories, 1985: The O Henry Awards. Membership: Magazine Publishers of America. Address: 14 Beacon Street, Boston, MA 02108, USA.

KAUFMAN Bel, b. Berlin, Germany. Writer; Lecturer; Educator; div, 1 son, 1 daughter. Education: BA magna cum laude, Hunter College, New York City; MA, Columbia University; DLett, Nasson College. Appointments: Teacher of English, New York City High Schools, USA; Creative Writing workshops, seminars, various universities; Lecturer, 18th Century English, New School for Social Research, New York City; Assistant Professor, Adjunct Professor, English, City University of New York; Keystone Speaker, education conventions, USA. Publications: Up the Down Staircase, 1964, 57 editions, latest, 1991; Love Etc, 1979; Translations of Russian poetry. Contributions to: Numerous short stories and articles to Saturday Review; McCall's; Esquire; Today's Education; Ladies Home Journal; The English Journal; New York Times; Collier's; Today's Health; Fifty Plus; New Choices; A Joy Observed, article, Commonwealth, 1994. Literary Agent: Maurice Greenbaum, 575 Madison Avenue, New York, USA. Address: 1020 Park Avenue, New York, NY 10028, USA.

KAUFMANN Myron S, b. 27 Aug 1921, Boston, Massachusetts, USA. Novelist. m. Paula Goldberg, 6 Feb 1960, div 1980, 1 son, 2 daughters. Education: AB, Harvard University, 1943. Publications:

Novels: Remember Me To God, 1957; Thy Daughter's Nakedness, 1968; The Love of Elspeth Baker, 1982. Literary Agent: Sterling Lord, New York City, USA. Address: 111 Pond Street, Sharon, MA 02067, USA.

KAUFMANN Thomas DaCosta, b. 7 May 1948, New York, USA. University Professor. m. Virginia Burns Roehrig, 1 Jun 1974, 1 d. Education: BA, MA, 1970, Yale University; MPhil, Warburg Institute, University of London, 1972; P hD, Harvard University, 1977. Publications: The School of Prague: Painting at the Court of Rudolf II, 1988; Drawings From the Holy Roman Empire 1540-1650, 1982; Variations on the Imperial Theme, 1978; Central European Drawings, 1680-1800, 1989; Art and Architecture in Central Europe, 1550-1620, 1985; The Mastery of Nature, 1993. Contributions to: Art Journal; Journal of the Warburg and Courtauld Institutes and other Scholarly journals. Honours: Finley Fellowship; American Council of Learned Societies Dissertation Prize; Alexander Van Humboldt Senior Fellowship; Jan Mitchell Prize for the Best Book on Art History, 1988. Memberships: College Art Association of America; Renaissance Society of America. Address: Dept of Art and Archeology, McCormick Hall, Princeton University, Princeton, NJ 08544, USA.

KAUFMANN William J, b. 1942, USA. Astronomer; Writer. Publications: Relativity and Cosmology, 1973, 2nd Edition, 1977; Astronomy: The Structure of the Universe, 1977; The Cosmic Frontiers of General Relativity, 1977; Exploration of the Solar System, 1978; Stars and Nebulas, 1978; Planets and Moons, 1979; Galaxies and Quasars, 1979; Black Holes and Warped Spacetime, 1979; Particles and Fields (editor), 1980; Universe, 1985, 1988, 1991, 1994; Discovering the Universe, 1987, 1990, 1993; Supercomputing and the Transformation of Science, 1993. Address: 385 Paraiso Drive, Danville, CA 94526, USA.

KAVALER Lucy Estrin, b. 29 Aug 1930, New York City, New York, USA. Author. m. 9 Nov 1948, 1 son, 1 daughter. Education: BA magna cum laude, Oberlin College, Ohio; Fellowship, Advanced Science Writing, Columbia University Graduate School. Literary appointments: Associate Editorial Director, PW Communications International, 1976-89; Vice President, Editorial, Editorial Director, AJN Company, 1989-. Publications: Major works: Private World of High Society, 1960; Mushrooms, Molds and Miracles, 1965; The Astors, 1966; Freezing Point, 1970; Noise the New Menace, 1975; A Matter of Degree, 1981; The Secret Lives of the Edmonts, 1989; Heroes and Lovers, 1995; Others: Green Magic; Cold Against Disease; Life Battles Cold; The Wonders of Fungi; Artificial World Around Us; The Dangers of Noise; The Astors (for children); Wonders of Algae. Contributions to: Smithsonian; Natural History; McCall's; Reader's Digest; Redbook; Primary Cardiology; Woman's Day (and encyclopaedia); The Skin Cancer Foundation Journal; Memories; Female Patient. Address: c/o Claire Smith, Harold Ober Associates, 425 Madison Avenue, New York, NY 10017, USA.

KAVALER Rebecca, b. 26 July 1930, Atlanta, Georgia, USA. Writer. m. Frederic Kavaler, 1955, 2 sons. Education: AB, University of Georgia. Publications: Further Adventures of Brunhild, 1978; Doubting Castle, 1984; Tigers in the Woods, 1986. Honours: Short stories included in Best of Nimrod, 1957-69; Best American Short Stories, 1972; Award for Short Fiction, Association of Writers and Poets, 1978; National Endowment for the Arts Fellowships, 1979, 1985. Membership: PEN. Literary Agent: Lisa Bankoff, ICM Agency. Address: 425 Riverside Drive, New York, NY 10025, USA.

KAVANAGH Dan. See: **BARNES Julian Patrick.**

KAVANAGH Patrick Joseph Gregory, b. 6 Jan 1931, Worthing, Sussex, England. Writer. m. (1) Sally Philipps, (2) Catherine Ward, 2 sons. Education: Merton College, Oxford. Literary Appointments: Columnist, The Spectator, 1983-. Publications: The Perfect Stranger (memoir), 1966; Editor: Poems of Ivor Gurney, 1982; The Oxford Book of Short Poems (with James Michie), 1985; G K Chesterton (The Bodley Head Edition), 1985; A Book of Consolations, 1992; Poems: One and One, 1959; On the Way to the Depot, 1968; About Time, 1970; Edward Thomas in Heaven, 1974; Life Before Death, 1979; Selected Poems, 1982, 2nd edition 1987; Presences, 1987; Novels: A Song and Dance, 1968; A Happy Man, 1972; People and Weather, 1978; Scarf Jack (The Irish Captain), 1978; Only By Mistake, 1986; Rebel for Good, 1980; People and Places (essays), 1988; Finding Connections (travel), 1990; Selected Poems of Ivor Gurney, 1990; An Enchantment, 1990; Voices in Ireland: A Traveller's Literary Companion, 1994; Collected

Poems, 1992. Honours: Richard Hillary Prize, 1966; Guardian Fiction Prize, 1968; Cholmondely Prize for Poetry, 1993. Membership: Fellow, Royal Society of Literature. Literary Agent: The Peters Fraser and Dunlop Group Ltd.

KAVANAUGH Cynthia. See: **DANIELS Dorothy.**

KAWALEC Julian, b. 11 Oct 1916, Wrzawy, Poland. Writer. m. Irene Wierzbanowska, 2 June 1948, 1 daughter. Education: Graduate, Jagellonian University, Cracow. Publications: Paths Among Streets, 1957; Scars, 1960; Bound to the Land, 1962; Overthrown Elms, 1963; The Dancing Hawk, 1964; Black Light, 1965; Wedding March, 1966; Appeal, 1968; Searching for Home, 1968; Praise of Hands, 1969; To Cross the River, 1973; Gray-Aureole, 1974; Great Feast, 1974; To Steal the Brother, 1982; Among the Gates, 1989; Dear Sadness (poems), 1992. Contributions to: Literary Life, Cracow; Literary Monthly, Warsaw. Honours: Prize Polish Editors, 1962; Prize of Minister of Culture and Art, 1967, 1985; Prize of State, 1975. Memberships: Polish Pen Club; Polish Writers Association; Society European Culture. Address: 39 Zaleskiego, 31-525 Krakow, Poland.

KAWIN Bruce Frederick, b. 6 Nov 1945, Los Angeles, California, USA. Professor of English and Film Studies; Poet; Critic; Screenwriter. Education: AB cum laude, English, Comparative Literature, Columbia University, 1967; MFA, Creative Writing (Poetry), Filmmaking, 1969, PhD, Modern Literature, Film Aesthetics, 1970, Cornell University. Publications: Telling It Again and Again: Repetition in Literature and Film; Mindscreen: Bergman, Godard, and First-Person Film; The Mind of the Novel: Reflexive Fiction and the Ineffable; How Movies Work; Faulkner and Film; Faulkner's MGM Screenplays; Breakwater and Slides, poetry chapbooks; Editor: To Have and Have Not; Gerald Mast, A Short History of the Movies, Editor 5th edition, Co-Author 6th edition; Several screenplays. Contributions to: Film Quarterly; Dreamworks; Paris Review; Rolling Stone. Honours: University of Colorado Faculty Book Prize, for Mindscreen, 1978. Memberships: Modern Language Association; Executive Council, Society for Cinema Studies. Literary Agent: Rick Balkin, PO Box 222, Amherst, MA 01004, USA. Address: 915 15th Street, Boulder, CO 80302, USA.

KAWINSKI Wojciech, b. 22 May 1939, Poland. Poet. m. Helena Lorenz, 17 Apr 1964, 1 s, 1 d. Education: MA, 1964. Appointments: Pismo Literacko-Artystyczne, Sub-Director, 1985-90. Publications: Odleglosci Posluzne, 1964; Narysowane We Wnetrzu, 1965; Ziarno Rzeki, 1967; Pole Widzewnia, 1970; Spiew Bezimienny, 1978; Pod Okiem Slonca, 1980; Listy Do Ciebie, 1982; Milosc Nienawistna, 1985; Ciemna strona jasnosci, 1989; Wieczorne sniegi, 1989; Czysty zmierzch, 1990; Pamiec zywa, 1990; Zwierciadlo sekund, 1991. Contributions to: numerous journals and magzines including: Wiez; Echo Krakowa. Honours: Prize, City of Cracow, 1985; Red Rose for Poetry, Gdansk, 1985. Membership: Polish Writers Association. Address: ul Stachiewicza 22a, 31-303 Krakow, Poland.

KAY Guy Gavriel, b. 7 Nov 1954, Weyburn, Canada. Author. m. Laura Beth Cohen, 15 Jul 1984, 1 s. Education: BA Philosophy, University of Manitoba, 1975; LLB, University of Toronto, 1978. Appointments: Principal Writer and Associate Producer, The Scales of Justice, CBC Radio Drama, 1981-90. Publications: A Song for Arbonne, 1992; Tigana, 1990; The Summer Tree, 1984; The Wandering Fire, 1986; The Darkest Road, 1986. Contributions to: Malahat Review; MacLean's. Honours: Aurora Prize, Best Work Of Speculative Fiction, Canada, 1986, 1990; Award, Best Dramatic Treatment of a Legal Issue, 1986. Memberships: Law Society of Upper Canada; Association of Canadian Radio and TV Artists. Literary Agents: (1) MGA, 10 St Mary St, Toronto, Canada; (2) Curtis Brown. Address: c/o Curtis Brown Agency, 162-168 Regent Street, London W1R 5TB, Engalnd.

KAYE Geraldine, b. 14 Jan 1925, Watford, Herts, England. Writer. m. 1948, div 1975, 1 son, 2 daughters. Education: BSc Economics, London School of Economics, 1946-49. Publications: Comfort Herself, 1985; A Breath of Fresh Air, 1986; A Piece of Cake, 1991; Someone Else's Baby, 1990; Snowgirl, 1991; Stone Boy, 1991; Summer in Small Street, 1989; Hands Off My Sister, 1993. Honours: The Other Award, 1986. Memberships: PEN; West Country Writers; Society of Authors; Women Writers and Journalists. Literary Agent: A M Heath. Address: 39 High Kingsdown, Bristol BS2 8EW, England.

KAYE Marvin Nathan, b. 10 Mar 1938, Philadelphia, Pennsylvania, USA. Writer. m. Saralee Bransdorf, 4 Aug 1963, 1 daughter. Education: BA, MA, Pennsylvania State University; Graduate study, University of Denver, Colorado. Appointments: Senior Editor, Harcourt Brace Jovanovich; Adjunct Professor, 1994-, Creative Writing, New York University. Publications: The Histrionic Holmes, 1971; A Lively Game of Death, 1972; A Toy is Born, The Stein and Day Handbook of Magic, 1973; The Grand Ole Opry Murders, The Handbook of Mental Magic, 1974; Catalog of Magic, My Son the Druggist, The Laurel and Hardy Murders, 1977; The Incredible Umbrella, My Brother the Druggist, 1979; The Amorous Umbrella, The Possession of Immanuel Wolf, 1981; The Soap Opera Slaughters, 1982; Fantastique, novel, 1993; With Parke Godwin: The Masters of Solitude, 1978; Wintermind, 1982; A Cold Blue Light, 1983; Editor, anthologies: Bullets for Macbeth, Fiends and Creatures, 1975; Brother Theodore's Chamber of Horrors, 1975; Ghosts, 1981; Masterpieces of Terror and the Supernatural, 1985; Ghosts of Night and Morning, Devils and Demons, 1987; Weird Tales, the Magazine That Never Dies, 1988; Witches and Warlocks, 1989; 13 Plays of Ghosts and the Supernatural, 1990; Haunted America, 1991; Lovers and Other Monsters, 1991; Sweet Revenge, 1992; Masterpieces of Terror and the Unknown, 1993; Frantic Comedy, 1993; The Game is Afoot, 1994; Angels of Darkness, 1995. Contributions to: Amazing; Fantastic; Galileo; Family Digest; Columnist, Science Fiction Chronicle. Honours include: 1st runner-up, Best Novelist, British Fantasy Awards, 1978. Memberships; Several professional organisations. Literary Agent: Donald C Maass, 157 West 57 Street, Ste 1003, New York, NY 10019, USA.

KAYE Mary Margaret, b. 1911, UK. Author. Publications: Six Bars at Seven, 1940; Death Walks in Kashmir, 1984; Death Walks in Berlin, 1955; Death Walks in Cyprus, 1956, as Death in Cyprus, 1984; Shadow of the Moon, revised edition 1979; Later Than You Think, 1958, as Death in Kenya, 1983; House of Shade, 1959, as Death in Zanzibar, 1983; Night on the Island, 1960; Trade Wind, 1963, revised edition, 1981; The Far Pavilions, 1978; The Ordinary Princess, for children, 1980; The Golden Calm (editor), 1980; Thistledown, for children, 1981; Autobiography; vol 1, The Sun in the Morning, 1990. Address: c/o St Martin's Press, 175 Fifth Avenue, New York, NY 10010, USA.

KAZAN Elia, b. 7 Sept 1909. Writer/Director. m. (1) Moly Day Thacher, 12 Dec 1932 (dec) 2 s, 2 d; (2) Barbara Loden, 5 Jun 1967 (dec) 1s; (3) Frances Rudge, 28 Jun, 1982. Education: Williams College, 1930; Yale University, Postgraduate School of Drama, 1932; Honoray Degrees: Wesleyan University, DLitt, 1955; Yale University, MFA, 1959; Carnegie Institute of Technology, DLitt, 1962; Williams College, DLitt, 1964; Katholieka Universitait, Luuven, Belgium Doctor Honoris Causa, 1978. Publications: America, America, 1962; The Arrangement, 1967; The Assassins, 1972; The Understudy, 1975; Acts of Love, 1978; The Anatolian, 1982; Elia Kazan: A Life, 1988; Beyond the Aegean, 1994. Contributions to: The Writer and Motion Pictures, in Sight and Sound, 1957; Theatre, New Stages, New Plays, New Actors, in New York Times Magazine, 1962; Mr Kazan Finds a Find, New York Herald Tribune, 1963; On What Makes a Director, Directors Guild of America, 1973; Inside a Turkish Prison, New York Times Magazine, 1979. Literary Agent: Irving Paul Lazar.

KAZANTZIS Judith, b. 14 Aug 1940, Oxford, England. Poet. 1 d, 1 s. Education: BA, Somerville College, Oxford. Appointments include: Former Poetry Reviewer, Spare Rib Magazine; Poetry Editor, PEN Broadsheet. Publications: Poetry Collections: Minefield, 1977; The Wicked Queen, 1980; Touch Papers, 1982; Let's Pretend, 1984; A Poem from Guatemala, 1988; Flame Tree, 1988; The Rabbit Magician Plate, 1992; Selected Poems, 1977-1992, 1995; Editor, The Gordon Riots: A Collection of Contemporary Documents, 1966; Editor, Women in Revolt: The Fight for Emancipation, 1968. Address: 9 Avondale Park Gardens, London W11, England.

KEA Pua. See: CIANCIOLO Ingrid Mohn.

KEANE John B(rendan), b. 1928, Ireland. Author; Pub Owner. publications: Sive, 1959; Sharon's Grave, 1960; The Highest House on the Mountain, 1961; Many Young Men of Twenty, 1961; the Street and Other Poems, verse, 1961; Hut 42, 1963; the Man From Clare, 1963; Strong Tea, 1963; The Year of theHiker, 1964; self-Portrait, 1964; The Field, 1965; The Rain at the End of the Summer, 1967; Letters of a Successful T D, 1967; Big Maggie, 1969; The Change in Marne Fadden, 1971; Moll, 1971; Letters of An Irish Parish Priest, 1972; letters of an Irish Publican, 1973; Values, 1973; The Crazy Wall, 1973; The Gentle Art of Matchmaking, 1973; Letters of a Love-Hungry Farmer, 1974; letters of a Matcmaker, 1975; Death Be Not Proud, stories, 1976; letters of a Civic Guard, 1976; Is the Holy Ghost Really

a Kerryman, 1976; The Good Thing, play, 1976; Letters of a Country Postman, 1977; Unlawful Sex and other Testy Matters, 1978; The Buds of Ballybunion, 1979; Stories From a Kerry Fireside, 1980; The Chastitute, 1981; More Irish Short Stories, 1981; Letters of Irish Minister of State, 1982; Man of the Triple Name, 1984; Owl Sandwiches, 1985; The Bodhran Makers, 1986; Love Bites, 1991; Duraneo, 1992; the Ram of God, 1992. Honours: Hon D Litt, Trinity College, Dublin, 1984; Hon Doc of Fine Arts, Marymount Manhatten College, 1984; Independent Irish Life Award, 1986; Sunday Tribune Award, 1986; Irish American Literary Award, 1988; Person of the Year Award, 1991. Memberships: Irish PEN, President 1973-74; Hon Life Membership, Royal Dublin Society, 1991. Address: 37 William Street, Listowel, Co Kerry, Republic of Ireland

KEANE Molly, (M J Farrell), b. 4 July 1904, County Kildare, Eire. Novelist. m. Robert Lumley Keane, 1938, Dec 1947. Publications: Good Behaviour, 1981; Time After Time, 1984; Loving and Giving, 1989; Novels, as M J Farrell, The Knight of Cheerful Countenance, 1928; Young Entry, 1929; taking Chances, 1929; Mad Puppetstown, 1931; Conversation Piece, 1932; Devotes Ladies, 1934; Full House, 1935; The Rising Tide, 1938; Two Days in Aragon, 1941; Loving Without Tears, 1951; Tresure Hunt, 1952; Plays as M J Farrell, Spring Meeting, 1939; Ducks and Drakes, 1941; Guardian Angel, 1944; Treasure Hunt, 1949; Dazzling Prospect, 1961; Good Behaviour, Time after Time, Loving & Giving, 1980's. Address: Dysert, Ardmore, County Waterford, Ireland.

KEATING Bern, b. 1915, USA. Author. Publications: The Mosquito Fleet, 1963; The Grand Banks, 1968; Alaska, 1969; Famous American Explorers; Northwest Passage, 1970; Mighty Mississippi, 1971; Florida, 1972; Gulf of Mexico, 1973; Famous American Cowboys, 1977; The Flamboyant Mr Colt and His Deadly Six-Shooter, 1978; Mississippi, 1984; Legend of the Delta Queen, 1986. Address: 141 Bayou Road, Greenville, MS 38701, USA.

KEATING Frank, b. 4 Oct 1937, Hereford, England. Journalist. m. Jane Anne Sinclair, 8 Aug 1987. Appointments: Editor, Outside Broadcasts, ITV, 1964-70; Columnist, The Guardian, 1975-; Punch, 1980-. Publications: Bowled Over, 1979; Up and Under, 1980; Another Bloody Day in Paradise, 1981; High, Wide, & Handsome, 1985; Long Days, Late Nights, 1986; Gents & Players; Half-Time Whistle, 1992. Contributions include: Punch; New Statesman; Listener; Cricketer. Honours: Sportswriter of the Year, 1978, 1980, 1989; Magazine Writer of the Year, 1987; Sports Journalist of the Year, British Press Awards, 1988. Address: Church House Marden, Hereford, HR1 3EN, England.

KEATING Henry Reymond Fitzwalter, b. 31 Oct 1926, St Leonards-on-Sea, Sussex, England. Author. m. 1953, 3 sons, 1 daughter. Education: BA, Trinity College, Dublin, Republic of Ireland. Publications: The Perfect Murder, 1964; Inspector Ghote Trusts the Heart, 1972; The Lucky Alphonse, 1982; Under A Monsoon Cloud, 1986; Dead on Time, 1989; The Iciest Sin, 1990; Crime Wave (ed), 1991; Cheating Death, 1992; The Man Who (ed), 1992; The Rich Detective, 1993; Doing Wrong, 1994; The Good Detective, 1995. Contributions to: Crime books reviews, The Times, 1967-83. Honours: Gold Dagger, Crime Writers Association, 1964, 1980. Memberships: Crime Writers Association (Chairman 1970-71); Society of Authors (Chairman 1982-84); The Detection Club (President 1986); Fellow, Royal Society of Literature, 1990. Literary Agent: The Peters Fraser and Dunlop Group Ltd. Address: 35 Northumberland Place, London W2 5AS, England.

KEAY John, b. 1941, United Kingdom. Author. Publications: Into India, 1973; When Men and Mountains Meet, 1977; The Gilgit Game, 1979; India Discovered, 1981; Eccentric Travellers, 1982; Highland Drove, 1984; Explorers Extraordinary, 1985; The Royal Geographical Society's History of World Exploration, 1991; The Honourable Company, 1991; Collins Encyclopaedia of Scotland, 1994. Literary Agent: David Higham and Assoc, 5-8 Lower John Street, London W1, England. Address: Succoth, Dalmally, Argyll, Scotland.

KEE Robert, b. 5 Oct 1919, Calcutta, India. Journalist; Author; Broadcaster. m. (1) Janetta Woolley, 1948, (2) Cynthia Judah, 1960, 1 s (1 s dec), 2 d. Education: Magdalen College, Oxford. Appointments: Journalist, Picture Post 1948-51; Picture Editor, WHO, 1952; Foreign Correspondent, Observer, 1956-57, Sunday Times 1957-58; Literary Editor, The Spectator, 1957; with BBC 1958-62, 1979-82, ITV, 1962-79, 1984; now Freelance Broadcaster, Presenter, 7 Days (Channel 4), TV series include: Ireland: a Television History (13 parts); The Writing on the Wall. Publications: A Crowd is Not Company, 1947; The Impossible Shore; A Sign of the Times; Broadstrop in Season; Refugee World; The Green Flag, 1972; Ireland: A History, 1980; The World We Left Behind, 1939, 1984; 1945: The World We Fought For, 1985; Trial and Error, 1986; Munich: the Eleventh Hour, 1988; The Picture Post Album, 1989. Address: c/o Lloyds Bank, 112 Kensington High Street, London W8, England.

KEEBLE Neil Howard, b. 7 Aug 1944, London, England. University Reader in English Literature. m. Jenny Bowers, 20 July 1968, 2 sons, 1 daughter. Education: BA Lampeter, 1966; DPhil, Oxford; 1974; D Litt, Stirling, 1994. Publications: Richard Baxter: Puritan Man of Letters, 1982; The Literary Culture of Nonconformity, 1987; Calendar of the Correspondence of Richard Baxter, 1991, co-author; Editor: The Autobiography of Richard Baxter, 1974; The Pilgrim's Progress, 1984. John Bunyan: Conventicle and Parnassus, 1988; The Cultural Identity of Seventeenth-century Women, a reader, 1994; Lucy Hutchinson, Memoirs of the Life of Colonel Hutchinson, 1995. Contributions to: Numerous articles on cultural history 1500-1700, in academic journals. Honour: Fellow, Royal Historical Society, 1990. Address: Duncraggan House, Airthrey Road, Stirling FK9 5JS, Scotland.

KEEFFE Barrie (Colin), b. 31 Oct 1945, London, England. Playwright; Editor. m. 1) Dee Truman, 1969, div 1979, 2) Verity Bargate, 1981, dec 1981, 2 stepsons, 3) Julia Lindsay, 1983, div 1993. Appointments: Actor at Theatre Royal Stratford East, London, 1964 and National Youth Theatre, 3 years; Reporter, Stratford and Newham Express, London to 1969 and for news agency to 1975; Dramatist-in-Residence, Shaw Theatre, London (Thames TV Playwright Scheme) 1977, and Royal Shakespeare Company, 1978; Since 1986, Associate Writer, Theatre Royal Stratford East until 1991; Since 1877 member of Council, National Youth Theatre; Since 1978 Member of the Board of Directors, Soho Poly Theatre, London. Publications: Plays include: A Mad World, My Masters (produced London 1977; San Francisco 1978, revised version produced London 1984) London; Eyre Methuen, 1977; Gimme Shelter, 1977; Frozen Assets (produced London and New York, 1978 revised version produced London 1987), London, Eyre Methuen, 1978; Sus (produced London 1979, New York 1983) London; Eyre Museum, 1979; Heaven Scent (broadcast 1979), published in Best Radio Plays of 1979, London, Eyre Methuen, 1980; Bastard Angel (produced London 1980) London, Eyre Methuen, 1980; Black Lear (produced Sheffield), 1980); She's So Modern (produced Hornchurch, Essex, 1980); Chorus Girls, music by Ray Davies (produced London 1981); A Gentle Spirit, with Jules Croiset, adaptation of a story by Dostoevsky (also director: produced Amsterdam, 1981; London 1982); The Long Good Friday (screenplay) London, Methuen, 1984; Better Times (produced London 1985) London, Methuen, 1985; King of England, 1986; My Girl, 1989; Not Fade Away, 1990; Wild Justice, 1990; Gimme Shelter, 1990; Radio Plays: Good Old Uncle Jack, 1975; Pigeon Skyline, 1975; Self Portrait, 1977; Heaven Scent, 1979; Paradise, 1990; My Girl, 1992; Television Plays include: Gotcha 1977, Champions, 1978; Hanging Around, 1978; Waterloo Sunset, 1979; No Excuses series, 1983; King 1984. Honours: French Critics prize, 1978; Mystery Writers of America Edgar Allan Poe Award, for screenplay, 1982. Literary Agent: Lemon Unna & Durbridge Ltd. Address: 110 Annandale Road, London SE10 0JZ, England.

KEEGAN Mary Constance, (Mary Heathcott, Mary Raymond), b. 1914, United Kingdom. Author. Appointments: Editorial positions: London Evening News, 1934-40; Straits Times and Singapore Free Press, 1940-42; MOI All-India Radio, 1944; Time and Tide, 1945; John Herling's Labor Letter, 1951-54. Publications: As Mary Keegan, Mary Heathcott or Mary Raymond: If Today Be Sweet, 1956; Island of the Heart, 1957; Love Be Wary, 1958; Her Part of the House, 1960; Hide My Heart, 1961; Thief of My Heart, 1962; Never Doubt Me, 1963; Shadow of a Star, 1963; Take-Over, 1965; Girl in a Mask, 1965; The Divided House, 1966; The Long Journey Home, 1967; I Have Three Sons, 1968; That Summer, 1970; Surety for a Stranger, 1971; The Pimpernel Project, 1972; The Silver Girl, 1973; Villa of Flowers, 1976; April Promise, 1980; Grandma Tyson's Legacy, 1982. Address: Cockenskell, Blawith, Ulverston, Cumbria, England.

KEEGAN William James, b. 3 July 1938, London, England. Journalist. m. (1) Tessa Ashton, 7 Feb 1967, div 1982, 2 sons, 2 daughters, (2) Hilary Stonefrost, 1992. Education: Economics Editor 1977, Associate Editor 1983-, The Observer; Visiting Professor of Journalism, Sheffield University, 1989-. Publications: Consulting Father Wintergreen, novel, 1974; A Real Killing, novel, 1976; Who Runs the

Economy? 1979; Mrs Thatcher's Economic Experiment, 1984; Britain Without Oil, 1985; Mr Lawson's Gamble, 1989; The Spectre of Capitalism, 1992. Contributions to: The Tablet; Frequent Broadcaster. Memberships: Advisory Board, Department of Applied Economics, Cambridge, 1988-93. Address: c/o Garrick Club, London WC2, England.

KEEN Geraldine. See: **NORMAN Geraldine.**

KEENAN Brian, b. Sept 1949, Ireland. Appointments: Former Teacher; Writer-in-Residence, University of Dublin, 1993-94. Publication: An Evil Cradling, 1992. Literary Agent: Hutchinson, Random Century House, 20 Vauxhall Bridge Road, London, SW1V 2SA, England.

KEENE Dennis, b. 10 July 1934, London, England. University Professor; Poet; Translator. m. Keiko Keene, 5 May 1962, 1 daughter. Education: BA, 1957, MA, 1961, DPhil, 1973, St John's College, Oxford. Publications: Yokomitsu Riichi, Modernist, 1980; The Modern Japanese Prose Poem, 1980; Surviving, poems, 1980; Universe and other poems, 1993; Translations: The House of Nire (Kita Morio), 1984; Rain in the Wind (Saiichi Maruya), 1989; Ghosts (Kita Morio), 1991. Contributions to: PN Review book reviews; Various academic publications elsewhere. Honours: Independent Foreign Fiction Special Award, 1990; Noma Translation Prize, 1992. Address: 77 Staunton Road, Headington, Oxford OX3 7TL.

KEENE Donald, b. 1922, USA. Writer; Translator; Professor of Japanese. Appointments include: Lecturer, Cambridge University, England, 1948-53; Former Guest Editor, Asahi Shimbun, Tokyo, Japan; Currently Shincho Professor Emeritus of Japanese, Columbia University, New York City, USA. Publications: The Battles of Coxinga, 1951; The Japanese Discovery of Europe, 1952, 2nd Edition, 1969; Japanese Literature: An Introduction for Western Readers, 1953; Living Japan, 1957; Bunraku, the Puppet Theater of Japan, 1965; No: The Classical Theater of Japan, 1966; Landscapes and Portraits, 1971; Some Japanese Portraits, 1978; World Within Walls, 1978; Meeting with Japan, 1978; Travels in Japan, 1981; Dawn to the West, 1984; Travellers of a Hundred Ages, 1990; Seeds in the Heart, 1993; On Familiar Terms, 1994; Editor: Modern Japanese Literature, 1956; Sources of Japanese Tradition, 1958; Twenty Plays of the No Theater, 1970; Translations: The Setting Sun, 1956; Five Modern No Plays, 1957; No Longer Human, 1958; Major Plays of Chikamatsu, 1961; The Old Woman, the Wife and the Archer, 1961; After the Banquet, 1965; Essays in Idleness, 1967; Madame de Sade, 1967; Friends, 1969; The Man Who Turned into a Stick, 1972; Three Plays of Kobo Abe, 1993. Memberships: Japan Society, New York, Director 1979-82; American Academy of Arts and Letters; Foreign Member, Japan Academy, 1990. Address: 407 Kent Hall, Columbia University, New York, NY 10027, USA.

KEESING Nancy Florence, b. 7 Sep 1923, Sydney, Australia. Writer. m. Dr A M (Mark) Hertzberg, 2 Feb 1955, 1 s, 1 d. education: Diploma of Social Studies, University of Sydney. Literary Appointments: Member, Literature Board, 1973-74, Chairman Literature Board, 1974-77, Australia Council. Publications include: poetry: Imminent Summer, 1951; Three Men and Sydney, 1955; Showground Sketchbook, 1968; Hails and Farewells, 1977; Garden Island People (memoirs), 1975; anthologies: editor, with Douglas Stewart, Australian Bush Ballads, 1955, Old Bush Songs, 1957; John Lang and the Forger's Wife, Biography, 1979; Lily and the Dustbin/Slang of Australian Women and Families, 198, reprinted 1985; Riding the Elephant, 1988, reissued 1989. Contributions to: Sydney Morning Herald; Australian; Bulletin; Overland; Southerly; Westerly. Honour: Member, Order of Australia (AM), 1979. Memberships include: Vice President, English Association (New South Wales); International PEN; Board Member, Overland Magazine; Committee of Management, Australian Society of Authors; Royal Australian Historical Society; Australian Jewish Historical Society. Literary Agent: Curtis Brown Australia Ltd. Address: c/o Australian Society of Authors Ltd, PO Box 315, Redfern, NSW 2016, Australia.

KEIGER John Frederick Victor, b. 7 Dec 1952, Wembley, England. University Reader. Education: Institut d'etudes Politiques d'Aix-en Provence, University of Aix Marseille III, France, 1971-74; PhD, University of Cambridge, 1975-78. Publications: France and the Origins of the First World War; Europe 1848-1914 (19 volumes in British Documents on Foreign Affairs, Reports and papers from the Foreign Office Confidential Print, 1988-92. Contributions to: Reviews for the Times Higher Education Supplement; History; International History Review. Address: Department of Modern Languages, Salford University, Manchester M5 4WT, England.

KEILLOR Garrison, b. 1942, Minnesota, USA. Writer. m. Ulla Skaerved, 4 children. Education: Graduated, University of Minnesota, 1966. Appointments: Worked on campus radio station, University of Minnesota; Presenter of live radio show, A Prairie Home Companion, 1974-87, by 1980 was being broadcast nationwide by satellite; Followed by The American Radio Company, 1989-; On both shows Garrison Keillor tells the story of the inhabitants of a mythical mid-Western town, Lake Wobegon. Publications: Lake Wobegon Days, novel derived from radio monologues, bestseller in United States in UK, 1986, published in paperback 1987; Collection of short stories Happy To Be Here; Leaving Home, Short Stories based on tales from Lake Wobegon published 1988, paperback 1989; We Are Still Married, collection of stories, essays and reflections, 1990; Radio Romance, 1992; The Book of Guys, 1994. Honour: Lake Wobegon Days, No 1 in Sunday Times Bestseller List, remained in list for over 20 weeks. Address: c/o Kay Gornick, Minnesota Public Radio, 45 East 7th Street, St Paul, MN 55101, USA.

KEITH William John, b. 9 May 1934, London, England. University Teacher; Critic. m. Hiroko Teresa Sato, 26 Dec 1965. Education: BA (Cantab), 1958; MA, 1959, PhD, 1961, Toronto. Publications: Richard Jefferies: A Critical Study, 1965; The Rural Tradition, 1974; The Poetry of Nature, 1980; Epic Fiction: The Art of Rudy Wiebe, 1981; Canadian Literature in English, 1985; Regions of the Imagination, 1988; A Sense of Style, 1989; An Independent Stance, 1991; Echoes in Silence, poems, 1992; Literary Images of Ontario, 1992. Contributions to: Frequent articles on Canadian literature to such journals as: Canadian Literature; Essays on Canadian Writing. Honours: Editor, University of Toronto Quarterly, 1976-85; Fellow, Royal Society of Canada, 1979-. Address: University College, University of Toronto, Toronto, Ontario, Canada M5S 1A1.

KELL Richard (Alexander), b. 1 Nov 1927, Youghal, County Cork, Irelnd. Lecturer; Poet. Education: BA, Trinity College, Dublin, 1952. Appointments include: Senior Lecturer, Newcastle upon Tyne Polytechnic, 1970-83. Publications: Poems, 1957; Control Tower, 1962; Six Irish Poets, 1962; Differences, 1969; Humours, 1978; Heartwood, 1978; The Broken Circle, 1981; Wall, With Others, 1981; In Praise of Warmth, 1987; Rock and Water, 1993. Address: 18 Rectory Grove, Gosforth, Newcastle upon Tyne, NE3 1AL, England.

KELLEHER Victor, (Michael Kitchener), b. 19 July 1939, London, England. Lecturer; Writer. m. Alison Lyle, 2 Jan 1962, 1 son, 1 daughter. Education: BA, University of Natal, 1961; Diploma in Education, University of St Andrews, 1963; BA (with Honours), University of the Witwatersrand, 1969; MA 1970, DLitt et Phil 1973, University of South Africa. Appointments: Junior Lecturer in English, University of Witwatersrand, Johannesburg, 1969; Lecturer 1970-71, Senior Lecturer in English 1972-73, University of South Africa, Pretoria; Lecturer in English, Massey University, Palmerston North, New Zealand, 1973-76; Lecturer 1976-79, Senior Lecturer 1980-83, Associate Professor of English 1984-87, University of New England, Armidale, Australia. Publications: Voices from the River, Forbidden Paths of Thual, 1979; The Hunting of Shadroth, 1981; Master of the Grove, 1982; Africa and After, 1983; The Beast of Heaven, Papio; The Green Piper, 1984; Taronga, 1986; The Makers, 1987; Em's Story, 1988; Baily's Bones, 1988; The Red King, 1989; Wintering, 1990; Brother Night, 1990; Del-Del, 1991; To the Dark Tower, 1992; Micky Darlin, 1992; Where The Whales Sing, 1994; Parkland, 1994; Double God (as Veronica Hart), 1994; The House That Jack Built (as Veronica Hart), 1994. Contributions to: Articles and stories to magazines; Work represented in anthologies, including Introduction 6, 1977. Address: 1 Avenue Road, Glebe, NSW 2037, Australia.

KELLER Evelyn Fox, b. 20 Mar 1936. Professor of History and Philosophy of Science. 1 son, 1 daughter. Education: BA, Brandeis University, 1957; MA, Radcliffe College, 1959; PhD, Department of Physics, Harvard University, 1963. Publications: A Feeling for the Organism: The Life and Work of Barbara McClintock, 1983; Reflections on Gender and Science, 1985; Secrets of Life, Secrets of Death: Essays on Language, Gender and Science, 1992; Refiguring Life, 1995; Editor: Body/Politics, 1989; Conflicts in Feminism, 1990; Keywords in Evolutionary Biology, 1992; Feminist Philosophy of Science, 1995. Contributions to: Animals, Humans, Machines; Models of Scientific Practice; History of the Human Sciences; Journal of

History of Biology; Social Studies of Science; Great Ideas Today; Perspective in Biology and Medicine; The Human Genome Initiative; The Annals of Scholarship. Address: Program in Science Technology and Society, Massachusetts Institute of Technology, Cambridge, MA 02139, USA.

KELLER Mark, b. 21 Feb 1907, Austria. Editor; University Professor. m. 30 Dec 1930, 1 d. Appointments: Managing Director, Editor, Quarterly Journal of Studies on Alchohol, Yale University, 1941-61; Editor, Journal of Studies on Alchohol, Rutgers University, 1962-77; Emeritus Professor, Documentation, Rutgers University, 1977-; Editor, Data (Johnson Institute), 1984-86. Publications: The Alchohol Language, with J R Seeley, 1958; CAAAL Manual, with V Efron & E M Jellinek, 1965; A Dictionary of Words about Alchohol, with M McCormick and V Efron, 1982. Contributions include: British Journal of Addiction; Encyclopaedia Britannica; Contemporary Psychology; Canaer Research; Medical Communications: Medical Tribune; Alkohologia, Budapest; Mercurio, Milan; Japanese Journal of Studies on Alchohol; Annals of the American Academy of Political and Social Science. Honours: Hammond Award for Distinguished Medical Journalism, American Medical Writers Association, 1976; Jellinek Memorial Award, 1977. Memberships: American Medical Writers Association; Council of Biology Editors; American Association for the Advancement of Science; American Professors for Peace in the Middle East; British Society for the Study of Addiction; American Public Health Association. Address: Centre of Alchohol Studies, Rutgers University, POB 969, Piscataway, NJ 08855, USA.

KELLERMAN Jonathan Seth, b. 9 Aug 1949, NY, USA. Novelist;Clinical Child Psychologist; Medical School Professor. m. Fate Marder, 23 July 1972, 1 s, 3 d. Education: AB, UCLA, 1971; AM, 1973, PhD, 1974, Univ S CA. Publications: When The Bough Breaks, 1985; Blood Test, 1986; Over The Edge, 1987; The Butchers Theater, 1988; Silent Partner, 1989; Time Bomb, 1990; Private Eyes, 1992; Devils Waltz, 1993; Bad Love, 1994; Self Defense, 1995; Helping The Fearful Child; Daddy, Daddy Can You Touch the Sky. Contributions to: Numerous Articles in Medical & Psychological Journals. Honours: Edgar Allan POE, 1985; Anthony Bouchal, 1986; Samuel Goldwyn Literary Award, 1972. Membership: Mystery Writers of Am. Literary Agent: Barney Karrfinger. Address: 505 S Beverly Drive, Ste 170, Beverly Hills, CA 90212, USA.

KELLEY Leo P(atrick), b. 1928, USA. Freelance Novelist and Short Story Writer. Publications: The Counterfeits, 1967; Odyssey to Earthdeath, 1968; Time Rogue, 1970; The Coins of Murph, 1971; Brother John, novelisation of screenplay, 1971; Mindmix, 1972; Time: 110100, 1972, UK edition the Man From Maybe, 1974; Themes in Science Fiction: A Journey Into Wonder (editor), 1972; The Supernatural in Fiction, (editor), 1973; Deadlocked, novel, 1973; The Earth Tripper, 1973; Fantasy: The Literature of the Marvellous (editor), 1974; science fiction novels for children: The Time Trap, 1977; Backward in Time, 1979; Death Sentence, 1979; Earth Two, 1979; Prison Satellite, 1979; Sunworld, 1979; Worlds Apart, 1979; Dead Moon, 1979; King of the Stars, 1979; On the Red World, 1979; Night of Fire and Blood, 1979; Where No Star Shines, 1979; Vacation in Space, 1979; Star Gold, 1979; Goodbye to Earth, 1979; Western novels: Luke Sutton series: 9 vols, 1981-90; Cimarron series, 20 vols, 1983-86; Morgan, 1986; A Man Named Dundee, 1988; Thunder Gods Gold, 1988. Address: 702, Long Boulevard, Long Beach, NY 11561, USA.

KELLMAN Steven G, b. 15 Nov 1947, Brooklyn, New York, USA. Critic; Professor. Education: BA, State University of New York, 1967; MA, 1969, PhD, 1972, University of California, Berkeley. Appointments: Editor in Chief, Occident, 1969-70; Assistant Professor, Bemidji State Univesity, Minnesota, 1972-73; Lecturer, Tel-Aviv University, Israel, 1973-75; Visiting Lecturer, University of California, Irvine, 1975-76; Assistant Professor, 1976-80, Associate Professor, 1980-85, Professor, 1985-, University of Texas, San Antonio; Fulbright Senior Lecturer, USSR, 1980; Visiting Associate Professor, University of California, Berkeley, 1982; Literary Scene Editor, USA Today; Partners of the Americas Lecturer, Peru, 1988-95. Publications: The Self-Begetting Novel, 1980; Approaches to Teaching Camus's The Plague (editor), 1985; Loving Reading: Erotics of the Text, 1985; The Modern American Novel, 1991; The Plague: Fiction and Resistance, 1993; Perspectives on Raging Bull, 1994. Contributions to: San Antonio Light; Village Voice; The Nation; Georgia Review; Moment; Newsweek; Modern Fiction Studies; Midstream; New York Times Book Review; The Washington Post Book World; The Gettysburg Review; Film Critic, The

Texas Observer. Address: 302 Fawn Drive, San Antonio, TX 78231, USA.

KELLOGG Steven, b. 1941, USA. Children's Fiction Writer. Publications: The Wicked Kings of Bloon, 1970; Can I Keep Him, 1971; The Mystery Beast of Ostergeest, 1971; The Orchard Cat, 1972; Won't Somebody Play With Me, 1972; The Island of the Skog, 1973; The Mystery of the Missing Red Mitten, 1974; There was an Old Woman, 1974; Much Bigger Than Martin, 1976; Steven Kellogg's Yankee Doodle, 1976; The Mysterious Tadpole, 1977; The Mystery of the Magic Green Ball, 1978; Pinkerton Behave, 1979; The Mystery of the Flying Orange Pumpkin, 1980; A Rose for Pinkerton, 1981; The Mystery of the Stolen Blue paint, 1982; Tallyho Pinkerton, 1982; Ralph's Secret Weapon, 1983; Paul Bunyan, 1984; Chicken Little, 1985; Best Friends, 1986; Pecos Bill, 1986; Aster Aardvark's Alphabet Adventure, 1987; Prehistoric Pinkerton, 1987; Johnny Appleseed, 1990; Mike Fink, 1992; The Christmas Witch, 1992. Address: Bennett's Bridge Road, Sandy Hook, CT 06482, USA.

KELLY A A. See: **HAMPTON Angeline Agnes.**

KELLY James Plunkett, b. 21 May 1920, Dublin, Ireland. Author. m. Valerie Koblitz, 4 Sept 1945, 3 sons, 1 daughter. Education: Synge Street Christian Brothers' School, Dublin Municipal College of Music, Dublin. Appointments: Assistant Head, Drama, Radio Eireann, 1955-61; Head, Features, Telefis Eireann, 1969-72. Publications: Strumpet City, 1969; Farewell Companions, 1977; The Gems She Wore, 1972; The Trusting and the Maimed, 1959; Collected Short Stories, 1977; The Risen People, 1958; The Boy on the Back Wall - and other Essays, 1987; The Circus Animals, 1990. Contributions to: The Bell; Irish Writing; Bookman; Writing Today. Agent: The Peters Fraser and Dunlop Group Ltd, London. Address: 29 Parnell Road, Bray, Co Wicklow, Ireland.

KELLY M T(erry), Author. m. 2 sons. Education: BA, English, Glendon College, 1970; BEd, University of Toronto, 1976. Appointment: Contributing Interviewer, TVO's Imprint, Public Television. Publications: I Do Remember the Fall, 1979; County You Can't Walk In, 1979; The More Loving One, 1980; The Ruined Season, 1982; The Green Dolphin, 1982; County You Can't Walk In and Other Poems, 1984; A Dream Like Mine, 1987; Arctic Argonauts (editor), 1990; Breath Dances Between Them, Stories by M T Kelly, 1991. Contributions to: Toronto Life; The Globe and Mail; Canadian Forum; Antigonish Review; Many other professional journals and magazines. Address: 60 Kendal Avenue, Toronto, Ontario M5R 1L9, Canada.

KELLY Patrick. See: **ALLBEURY Theo Edward.**

KELLY Tim, (Robert Swift, J Moriarity, Vera Morris, Keith Jackson), b. 2 Oct 1937, Massachusetts, USA. Playwright; Screenwriter. Education: BA, 1956, MA, 1957, Emerson College; American Broadcasting Co Fellow, Yale University, 1965, Publications include: Over 300 plays in print, including: The Uninvited; MASH; Crimes At The Old Brewery; Wagon Wheels West; Don't Be Afraid Of Dark. Honours: Numerous award and grants including 7 major university awards, National Endowment for the Arts, Office of Advance Drama Research; Fellow, College of Fellow of the American Theatre; Tim Kelly Theatre Collection established at University of Wyoming. Memberships: Dramatist Guild; Authors League; Writers Guild of America. Literary Agent: William Talbot, Samuel French Inc, New York City, USA. Address: 8730 Lookout Mountain Avenue, Hollywood, CA 90046, USA.

KELMAN James, b. 9 June 1946, Glasgow, Scotland. Novelist. m. Marie Connors, 2 daughters. Education: University of Strathclyde, 1975-78, 1981-82. Publications: The Busconductor Hines, 1984; A Chancer, 1985; A Disaffection, 1989; Short Stories, An Old Pub Near the Angel, 1973; Short Tales from the Nightshift, 1978; Not Not While the Giro and Other Stores, 1983; Lran Tales, 1985; Greyhound for Breakfast, 1987; The Burn, 1991; The Busconductor Hines; A Chancer; Greyhound for Breakfast; How Late it Was, How Late, 1994; Plays, The Busker, 1985; Le Rodeur, 1987; In The Night, 1988; Hardie and Baird, The Last, 1990; Screenplay, The Return, 1990. Honours: Scottish Arts Council Fellowships; Scottish Arts Council Bursaries, Book Awards, 1983, 87, 89; Cheltenham Prize, 1987; James Tait Black Memorial Prize, 1989; Winner, Booker Prize, 1994. Address: 244 West Princess Street, Glasgow G4 9DP, Scotland.

KELTON Elmer Stephen, (Alex Hawk, Lee McElroy), b. 29 Apr 1926. Novelist; Agricultural Journalist. m. Anna Lipp, 3 July 1948, 2 sons, 1 daughter. Education: BA, Journalism, University of Texas. Publications include: The Day the Cowboys Quit, 1971; The Time It Never Rained, 1973; The Good Old Boys, 1978; The Wolf and the Buffalo, 1980; Stand Proud, 1984; The Man Who Rode Midnight, 1987; Honour At Daybreak, 1991; Slaughter, 1992; The Far Canyon, 1994. Contributions to: Numerous articles to magazines and newspapers. Honours: 5 Spur Awards, Western Writers of America; 4 Western Heritage Awards, National Cowboy Hall of Fame; Tinkle-McCombs Achievement Award, Texas Institute of Letters. Memberships: Western Writers of America, President 1963-64; Texas Institute of Letters, former Counsellor; Sigma Delta Chi. Literary Agent: Sobel Weber & Associates, New York City, USA. Address: 2460 Oxford, San Angelo, TX 76904, USA.

KEMAL Yashar, b. 1923. Writer; Journalist. m. Thilda Serrero, 1952, 1 s. Education: Self-educated. Publications: (in English) Memed, My Hawk, 1961; The Wind From the Plain, 1963; Anatolian Tales, 1968; They Burn The Thistles, 1973; Iron Earth, Copper Sky, 1974; The Legend of Ararat, 1975; The Legend of a Thousand Bulls, 1976; The Undying Grass, 1977; The Lords of Akchasaz, Part I, Murder in the Ironsmiths Market, 1979; The Saga of a Seagull, 1981; The Sea-Crossed Fisherman, 1985; The Birds Have Also Gone, 1987; To Crush the Serpent, 1991; novels, short stories, plays and essays in Turkish. Honours: Commander, Legion d'honneur, 1984; Prix Mondial cino del Duca, 1982; Doctor Honoris Causa, Universite de Sciences Humaines, Strasburg, 1991. Address: PK 14, Basinkoy, Istanbul, Turkey.

KEMP Gene, b. 1926, United Kingdom. Children's Fiction Writer; Educator. Appointments: Teacher, St Sidwell's School, Exeter, 1962-74; Lecturer, Rolle College, 1963-79. Publications: Tamworth Pig series, 4 vols, 1972-78; The Turbulent Term of Tyke Tiler, 1977; Gowie Corby Plays Chicken, 1979; Ducks and Dragons (editor), 1980; Dog Days and Cat Naps, 1980; The Clock Tower Ghost, 1981; No Place Like, 1983; Charlie Lewis Plays For Time, 1984; The Well, 1984; Jason Bodger and the Priory Ghost, 1985; McMagus is Waiting For You, 1986; Juniper, 1986; I Can't Stand Losing, 1987; Room With No Windows; Matty's Midnight Monster; Just Ferret; The Mink War. Honours: Children's Awards, 1977; Carnegie Medal, 1978; Hon MA, Exeter University, 1984; Runner-up Whitbread, 1985. Literary Agent: Laurence Pollinger Ltd, England. Address: c/o Laurence Pollinger Ltd, 18 Maddox Street, London W1R OEU, England.

KEMP (Patricia) Penn. 1 s, 1d. Education: MEduc, University of Toronto, 1988; Honours in English Language and Literature, 1966; Appointments: Writer in Residence: Flesherton Library, 1988-89; Women and Words, University of Victoria, 1983; Niagara Eue Writers, New York State, 1984; Labrador, 1986. Publications: Binding Twine, 1984; Throo, 1990; Some Talk Magic, 1986; Eidolons, 1990; Bearing Down, 1972; The Universe is One Poem, 1990. Contributions to: Tessara, Prism. Honours: Arts Grants, Canada Council, 1979-80, 1981-82, 1991-92; Ontario's Graduate Scholarship, 1987-88. Memberships: Writer's Union; Playwright's Union; League of Canadian Poets; CAPAC. Address: 136 Stephenson Ave, Toronto, Ontario, Canada M4C 1G4, England.

KEMPER Troxey, b. 29 Apr 1915, Oklahoma, USA. Editor; Novelist; Poet. m. Jeanne Doty, 31 July 1954, div. 1964, 2 daughters. Education: BA, University of New Mexico, Albuquerque, 1951. Appointments: Newspaper Reporter, Albuquerque Journal, 1951-69; Editor, Tucumcari Literary Review, 1988-. Publications: Mainly on the Plain, 1982; Whence and Whither, 1983; Folio and Signature, 1983; Part Comanche, 1991; Comanche Warbonnet, 1991; Under a Sky of Azure, 1993. Contributions to: Poets and Writers Magazine; Small Press Review; Amarillo News Globe; Los Angeles Daily News; Los Angeles Times; American Film Magazine. Honours: Honourable Mention, National Writers Club, 1990. Memberships: National Writers Union; Sigma Delta Chi. Address: 3108 W Bellevue Avenue, Los Angeles, CA 90026, USA.

KEMSKE Floyd, b. 11 Mar 1947, Wilmington, Delaware, USA. Writer. m. Alice Geraldine Morse, 21 Dec 1968. Education: BA, University of Delaware, 1970; MA, Michigan State University, 1971. Publications: Novels: Lifetime Employment, 1992; The Virtual Boss, 1993. Membership: National Writers Union. Address: PO Box 841, Melrose, MA 02176, USA.

KENDALL Carol, b. 13 Sept 1917, Bucyrus, Ohio, USA. Writer. m. Paul Murray Kendall, 15 June 1939, 2 daughters. Education: AB, Ohio University, 1939. Publications: The Black Seven, 1946, 1950; The Baby Snatcher, 1952; The Other Side of the Tunnel, 1956, 1957; The Gammage Cup, 1959, as The Minnipins, 1960; The Big Splash, 1960; The Whisper of Glocken, 1965, 1967; Sweet and Sour Tales, retold by Carol Kendall and Yao-Wen Li, 1978, 1979; The Firelings, 1981, 1982; Haunting Tales from Japan, 1985; The Wedding of the Rat Family, 1988. Contributions to: Something About the Author Autobiography Series, Volume 7. Honours: Ohioana Award, 1960; Newbery Honour Book, 1960; American Library Association Notable Book, 1960; Parents Choice Award, 1982; Aslan Award, Mythopoeic Society, 1983. Memberships: PEN American Center; Authors League of America; Authors Guild. Address: 928 Holiday Drive, Lawrence, KS 66049, USA.

KENEALLY Thomas Michael, b. 7 Oct 1935, Sydney, Australia. Author. m. Judith Mary Martin, 1965, 2 daughters. Education: St Patrick's College, Strathfield, New South Wales, Australia. Appointments: Lecturer, Drama, University of New England, 1968-70; Visiting Professor, University California, Irvine, 1985; Berg Professor, New York University, 1988; District Professor, Department of English, University California, Irvine, 1991-. Publications: Bring Larks and Heroes, 1967; Three Cheers for the Paraclete, 1968; The Survivor, 1969; A Dutiful Daughter, 1970; The Chant of Jimmie Blacksmith, 1972; Blood Read, Sister Rose, 1974; Gossip from the Forest, 1975; Season in Purgatory, 1976; A Victim of the Aurora, 1977; Passenger, 1978; Confederates, 1979; Schindler's Ark, 1982; Outback, 1983; The Cut-Rate Kingdom, 1984; A Family Madness, 1985; The Playmaker, 1987; Towards Asmara, 1989; Flying Hero Class, 1991; The Place, Where Souls are born, 1992; Now and In Time to be Woman of the Inner Sea, 1992; Our Republic, 1993; Jacko (novel), 1993. Honours: Booker Prize, 1983, Royal Society of Literature, 1983; Los Angeles Times Fiction Prize, 1983. Memberships: President, National Book Council of Australia, 1985-; Australia-China Council, Inaugural Member, 1978-83; Chairman, Australian Society Authors, 1987-; Council, Australian Society Authors, 1985-; Literary Art Board Australia 1985-88. Literary Agent: Deborah Rogers. Address: c/o Deborah Rogers, 20 Powis Mews, London W11 1JN, England.

KENNAN George (Frost), b. 1904, USA. Professor Emeritus; Former Diplomat. Appointments: US Foreign Service, 1927-63: Various postings, Hamburg, Tallinn, Riga Kovno and Tallinn (USSR), Berlin, Riga, Moscow, Vienna, US Department of State, Washington DC, Prague, Berlin Lisbon, 1927-42; Counsellor to US Delegation, European Advisory Committee, London, 1944; Minister-Counsellor, 1945; Deputy for Foreign Affairs, National War College, Washington, 1946; Director, Policy Planning, US Department of State, 1947-50; Ambassador to USSR, 1952, to Yugoslavia, 1961-63; Numerous Visiting Professorships, 1954-60; Professor, 1955, now Professor Emeritus, Institute for Advanced Study; President: National Institute of Arts and Letters, 1965-68, American Academy of Arts and Letters, 1967-71; University Fellow, History, Slavic Civilisations, Harvard University, 1966-70; Fellow, All Souls College, Oxford, England, 1969. Publications include: Realities of American Foreign Policy, 1954; Soviet-American Relations 1917-1920, vol 1 Russia Leaves the War, 1956, vol 2 The Decision to Intervene, 1958; Russia, The Atom and the West (Reith Lectures), 1958; Soviet Foreign Policy, 1917-1945, 1960; Russia and the West under Lenin and Stalin, 1961; On Dealing with the Communist World, 1963; Memoirs 1925-50, 1967; Democracy and the Student Left, 1968; From Prague after Munich: Diplomatic Papers 1938-40, 1968; The Marquis de Custine and His Russia in 1939, 1971; Memoirs 1950-63, 1972; Cloud of Danger, 1978; The Decline of Bismarck's European Order: Franco-Russian Relations, 1875-1890, 1979; The Nuclear Delusion, 1982; The Fateful Alliance, 1984; Sketches From A Life, 1989; Around The Cragged Hill, 1993. Honours: Numerous honorary academic degrees including Oxford University, 1969; Numerous literary prizes and distinctions; German Order of the Pour le Mérite for Arts and Sciences of the German Federal Republic, 1979; Albert Einstein Peace Prize, 1981; German Peace Prize, 1982; Toynbee Prize, 1988; British Academy; Presidential Medal of Freedom, 1989; Distinguished Service Award, Dept of State, 1994. Address: 146 Hodge Road, Princeton, NJ 08540, USA.

KENNEDY Adrienne (Lita), b. 1931, Pittsburgh, PA, USA. m. Joseph C Kennedy, 15 May 1953, 2 sons. Education: BA, Ohio State University; Columbia University, New School, for Social Research, American Theater Wing, Circle in the Square Theater School, Edward Albee's Workshop. Publications: Cities in Bezique: 2 one-act plays, 1969; People Who Led to my Plays: a Memoir, 1989; Deadly Triplets:

A Theater Mystery & Journal, 1990; The Alexander Plays, 1992. Honours: American Book Award, 1990, Obie Award, 1964, Yale Fellowship 1974-75, Stanley Award; American Academy & Institute of Arts & Letters, 1990.

KENNEDY Beryl, b. 2 Feb 1917, Tamworth, New South Wales, Australia. Physiotherapist; Feldenkrais Practitioner. m. Kenneth Robert Kennedy, 15 Feb 1949, 3 sons. Education: Diploma in Physiotherapy, Sydney, 1937; Continuing postgraduate education, Feldenkrais Training, Sydney, 1986-90. Publications: Dynamic Back Care Through Body Awareness, 1982; Dynamic Back Care Training Program, 1987. Contributions to: Australian Journal of Physiotherapy, 1965, 1973, 1977; Proceedings of the World Confederation for Physical Therapy, 1967, 1987; New Zealand Journal of Physiotherapy, 1978; Physiotherapy Journal, UK, 1980. Memberships: Australian Society of Authors; Australian Feldenkrais Guild; Australian Feldenkrais Interest Group; Australian War Widows Guild. Address: 110 Belmont Road, Mosman, New South Wales 2088, Australia.

KENNEDY John Hines, b. 1 Nov 1925, Washington DC, USA. Cardiothoracic Surgeon (retired); Physiologist, Cambridge and Paris. m. Shirley Angela Josephine Watson, 2 s, 2 d, (from previous marriage). Education: Princeton University, 1943-45; MD, Harvard Medical School, 1945-49; MPhil, Imperial College, London, 1990; FACS, 1957. Publications: French poetry: Carnet Parisien, 1987; Vieux Colombier, Promethee, Paris, 1987-88; Les Images, 1991. Contributions to: 148 in health care field; 5 chapters in books on health; Review, Houston Post. Honours: Medal of Vishnevsky, Moscow, 1962; Medal, Un Liège, Belgium, 1978. Memberships: PEN club; Chevy Chase Club, MD, USA; Cercle de l'Union Intersiliée, Paris. Address: Old Court, Clare, Sudbury, Suffolk CO1O 8NP, England.

KENNEDY Joseph Charles, (X J Kennedy), b. 21 Aug 1929, NJ, USA. Writer. m. Dorothy Mintzlaff, 31 Jan 1962, 4 sons, 1 daughter. Education: BSc, Seton Hall University, 1950; MA, Columbia University, 1951; University of Paris, 1955; LHD, Lawrence University, 1988. Literary Appointments: Poetry Editor, The Paris Review, 1961-64. Publications: Nude Descending A Staircase, 1961; Cross Ties, 1985; Dark Horses, 1992; An Introduction to Poetry, 1968, 8th Ed, co-author Dana Gioia, 1994; The Bedford Reader, 1982, 5th Ed, with Dorothy M Kennedy & Jane A Aarron, 1994; 13 Children's Books. Contributions to: New Yorker; Atlantic; The Cornhill; New Statesman; TLS; NY Times Book Review; Poetry; Sewanee Review. Honours: Lamont Award, 1961; Los Angeles Times Book Award, 1985. Memberships: PEN; Authors Guild; Modern Language Association; John Barton Wolgamot Society. Literary Agent: Curtis Brown Ltd, 10 Astor Place, New York, NY 10003, USA. Address: 4 Fern Way, Bedford, MA 01730, USA.

KENNEDY Ludovic Henry Coverley, b. 3 Nov 1919, Edinburgh, Scotland. Writer; Broadcaster. m. Moira Shearer King, 1950, 1 s, 3 d. Education: Christ Church, Oxford. Appointments include: Editor, Feature, First Reading, BBC Third Programme, 1953-54; Lecturer, British Council, Sweden, Finland, Denmark, 1955, Belgium, Luxembourg, 1956; Introduced Profile, ATV 1955-56; Newscaster, ITV 1956-58; Introducer on Stage, Associated Rediffusion, 1957, This Week, 1958-59; Chairman BBC Features: Your Verdict1962, Your Witness, 1967-70; Commentator, BBC Panorama, 1960-63; Election TV Broadcasts, 1966; Presenter, 24 Hours, BBC 1969-72, AD Lib, BBC 1970-72, Midweek, BBC 1973-75, Newsday, BBC 1975-76; Interviewer, Tonight, BBC 1976-80; Presenter, Lord Mountbatten Remembers, 1980, Changes of Direction, 1980, Did You See, 1980-, Great Railway Journeys of the World, 1980. Publications: Sub-Lieutenant, 1942; Nelson's Band of Brothers, 1951; One Man's Meat, 1953; Murder Story, 1956; Ten Rillington Place, 1961; The Trial of Stephen Ward, 1964; Very Lovely People, 1969; Pursuit: The Chase and Sinking of the Bismarck, 1974; A Presumption of Innocence: the Amazing Case of Patrick Meehan, 1975; The Portland Spy Case, 1978; Wicked Beyond Belief: The Luton Post Office Murder Case, 1980; A Book of Railway Journeys, 1980; A Book Of Sea Journeys, 1981; A Book of Air Journeys, 1982; General Editor, The British at War, 1973-; Menace: The Life and Death of the Tirpitz, 1979; The Airman and the Carpenter: The Lindbergh Case and the Framing of Richard Hauptmann, 1985; On My Way to the Club (autobiography), 1989; Euthanasia, 1990; Truth to Tell (collected writings), 1991. Honours: Recipient, various honours and awards. Literary Agent: Rogers, Coleridge and White. Address: c/o 20 Powis Mews, London W11 1JN, England.

KENNEDY Michael, b. 19 Feb 1926, Manchester, England. Journalist; Critic. m. Eslyn Durdle, 1947. Appointments: Staff Music

Critic, The Daily Telegraph, 1950-; Chief Music Critic, Sunday Telegraph, 1989-; Northern Editor 1960-86. Publications: The Hallé Tradition, 1960; The Works of Ralph Vaughan Williams, 1964; Portrait of Elgar, 1968; History of Royal Manchester College of Music, 1971; Barbirolli, 1971; Portrait of Manchester, 1971; Mahler, 1974; Strauss, 1976; Britten, 1980; Concise Oxford Dictionary of Music, 1980, 4th edition, 1995; Oxford Dictionary of Music, 1985, 2nd edition 1994; Adrian Boult, 1987; Portrait of Walton, 1989; Music Enriches All: 21 Years of Royal Northern College of Music, Manchester. Address: 3 Moorwood Drive, Sale, Cheshire, England.

KENNEDY Moorhead, b. 5 Nov 1930, New York, USA. Educator; Retired Foreign Service Officer. m. Louisa Livingston, 8 Jun 1955, 4 s. Education: AB, Princeton University, 1952; JD, Harvard Law School, 1959; National War College, 1974-75. Appointments: Public Lecturer and Frequent Guest on network TV. Publications: the Ayatollah in the Cathedral, 1986; co-author: (Think About) Terrorism, The New Warfare; Hostage Crisis; Death of a Dissident; Fire in the Forest; Na-Tel 1995; Hinomaru; Metalfabriken. Contributions to: Criminal and Civil Investigation Handbook, 1993; Collier's Encyclopaedia, all editions since 1962. Honours: LLD, Middlebury College, 1983; DPS, University of Pittsburgh, 1983; DPS, North Adams State College, 1991; Medal for Valor, Department of State, 1981; Gold Medal of National Institute of Social Sciences, 1991. Memberships: Church Club of NY; American Foreign Service Association; Board of Managers, International Programme Branch, YMCA of Greater New York; National Council, America for Middle East Understanding. Address: 55 Liberty Street Apt 7A, New York, NY 10005, USA.

KENNEDY Paul, b. 1945, Wallsend-on-Tyne, England. Professor of History. m. Catherine, 3 sons. Education: BA, University of Newcastle, England; DPhil, Oxford University, England. Publications: Preparing for the Twenty-First Century, 1993; The Rise & Fall of the Great Powers. Contributions to: New York Times; New York Review of Books; New Republic; Washington Post; The Atlantic; The Economist. Membership: Royal Historical Society, Fellow. Address: Department of History, Yale University, PO Box 1504a, New Haven, CT 06520-7425, USA.

KENNEDY Thomas Eugene, b. 9 Mar 1944, New York, USA. Writer; Editor; Translator; Teacher; Administrator. m. Monique M Brun, 28 Dec 1974, 1 son, 1 daughter. Education: BA (summa cum laude), Fordham University, New York, USA; MFA, Vermont College, Norwich University, USA, 1985; PhD, Copenhagen University, 1988. Literary Appointments: Guest Editor, Nordic Section, Frank magazine, 1987; European Editor, Rohwedder, 1988-89; European Editor, Cimarron Review, 1989-; Contributing Editor, Pushcart Prize, 1990-; Advisory Editor, Short Story, 1990-; International Editor, Potpourri, 1993-; Editorial Board International Review, 1994. Publications include: Andre Dubus: A Study, 1988; Crossing Borders (novel), 1990; The American Short Story Today, 1991; Robert Coover: A Study, 1992; Index, American Award Stories, 1993; A Weather of the Eye (novel), 1995; Unreal City (stories) 1995; (ed) New Danish Fiction, 1995. Address: Fragariavej 12, DK-2900 Hellerup, Denmark.

KENNEDY William Joseph, b. 16 Jan 1928, Albany, USA. Educator; Novelist. m. Ana Daisy Segarra, 31 Jan 1957, 1 s, 2 d. Education: BA, Siena, College, 1949; LHD, Hon, Russell sage College, 1980; DLit, Hon, 1984, DLetters, Hon, Russell Sage College, 1980; DLit, Hon, 1984, DLetters, Hon, College St Rose, 1985; Hon ArtsD, Hon LHD, Rensselaer Poly Inst, 1987; Hon Degree, Long Island University, 1989. Appointments: Assisstant Sports Editor, Columnist, Glens Falls Post Star, 1949-50; Reporter, Albany Times-Union, 1952-56; Special Writer, 1963-70; Assisstant Managing Editor, Columnist, PR, World Journal, San Juan, 1956; Reporter, Miami Herald, Florida, 1957; Correspondent, Time Life Publishers, in PR, 1957-59; Reporter, Knight Newpapers, 1957-59; Founding Managing Editor, San Juan Star, 1959-61; Lecturer, SUNY, 1974-82, Professor, English, 1983-. Publications: The Ink Truck, 1969; Legs, 1975; Billy Phelan's Greatest Game, 1978; Ironweed, 1983; non-fiction, O Albany! with Francis Ford Coppola, 1983; The Cotton Club, 1983; Charlie Malarkey and the Belly Button Machine, 1986. Contributions to: various journals and newspapers. Address: Writers Institute, SUNY, 1400 Washington Ave, Albany, NY 12222, USA.

KENNEDY William S, b. 23 Jan 1926, South Norfolk, Virginia, USA. Journal Editor and Publisher; Short Fiction Genre Founder and Promoter. Career: Founder, Editor, Publisher, Reflect literary journal; Founder, The Spiral Mode (spiral fiction), 1982. Publications: Johnny Mowbrough, spiral novel, published as serial in Puck and Pluck, 1994-; Manuals: Paranormal Writing; Music Writing. Contributions to: Spiral fiction to Reflect and other literary journals. Honours: Reflect included in Top 60 Poetry Magazines in USA and Canada, Writer's Digest, June 1993. Memberships: Norfolk Musicians Union; AFM. Literary Agent: Fred C Pugarelli, Director, Rhodes Literary Agency. Address: 3306 Argonne Ave, Norfolk, VA 23509, USA.

KENNEDY X J. See: **KENNEDY Joseph Charles.**

KENNELLY Brendan, b. 17 Apr 1936, Ballylongfoed, Co Kerry, Ireland. Professor of Modern Literature. Education: BA (1st Class Honours, English and French), 1961, MA 1963, PhD (Trinity College and Leeds University, Yorkshire England), 1966, Trinity College, Dublin. Publications include: Poetry: Good Souls to Survive, 1967; Dream of a Black Fox, 1968; Selected Poems, 1969, enlarged edition 1971; A Drinking Cup: Poems from the Irish, 1970; Bread, 1971; Love Cry, 1972; Salvation, the Stranger, 1972; The Voices, 1973; Shelley in Dublin, 1974, 2nd edition 1982; A Kind of Trust, 1975; New and Selected Poems, 1976, 1978; Islandman, 1977; The Visitor, 1978; A Small Light, 1979; The Boats Are Home, 1980; The House That Jack Didn't Build, 1982; Cromwell, 1983, reprinted 1984, 1986; Moloney Up and At It, 1984, reprinted 1987; Selected Poems, 1985; Mary, 1987; Love of Ireland, 1989; Novels: The Crooked Cross, 1963; The Florentines, 1967; Editor, The Penguin Book of Irish Verse, 1970, 1972, 1974, 1976, enlarged edition 1981, 1988. Contributions to: International magazines. Honours: AE Memorial Prize for Poetry, 1967; Fellow, Trinity College, 1967; Critics' Special Harveys Award, 1988. Address: Department of English, Arts Building, Trinity College, Dublin 2, Republic of Ireland.

KENNER Hugh, b. USA. Publications: Paradox in Chesterton, 1948; Poetry of Ezra Pound, 1951; Seventeenth Century Poetry, 1964; Bucky: A Guided Tour of Buckminster Fuller, 1973; A Homemade World: American Modernist Writers, 1974; Joyce's Voices, 1978; A Colder Eye: The Modern Irish Writers, 1983; The Mechanic Muse, 1987; A Sinking Island: The Modern English Writers, 1988; Mazes: Essays, 1989; Historical Fictions: Essays, 1990; Chuck Jones: A Flurry of Drawings, 1995. Address: Department of English, University of Georgia, Athens, GA 30602, USA.

KENNET Wayland Hilton Young, (2nd Baron cr 1935), (Wayland Young), b. 2 Aug 1923. Author; Politician. m. Elizabeth Ann, 1948, 1 son, 5 daughters. Education: Stowe, Trinity College, Cambridge. Publications: (as Wayland Young): The Italian Left, 1949; The Deadweight, 1952; Now or Never, 1953; Old London Churches (with Elizabeth Young), 1956; The Montesi Scandal, 1957; Still Alive Tomorrow, 1958; Strategy for Survival, 1959; The Profumo Affair, 1963; Eros Denied, 1965; Thirty Four Articles, 1965; (ed) Existing Mechanisms of Arms Control, 1965; (as Wayland Kennet) Preservation, 1972; The Futures of Europe, 1976; Editor, The Rebirth of Britain, 1982; (with Elizabeth Young) London's Churches, 1986; Northern Lazio, 1990; Fabian and SDP pamphlets on defence, disarmament, environment, multinational companies, etc. Address: House of Lords, SW1A 0PW, England.

KENNEY Catherine, b. 3 Oct 1948, Memphis, Tennessee, USA. Writer; Professor. m. John Patrick Kenney, 1 June 1968, 1 son. Education: BA, English, Siena College, 1968; MA, English, 1970, PhD, English, 1974, Loyola University, Chicago. Publications: Thurber's Anatomy of Confusion, 1984; The Remarkable Case of Dorothy L Sayers, 1990; Dorothy L - A Matter of Life and Death, play, 1993. Contributions to: Dorothy L Sayers: A Centenary Celebration; Old Maids to Radical Women; 100 Great Detectives; Scholarly journals; Chicago Tribune; Christian Century; Chicago Sun Times; Arkansas Times. Address: 228 Stanley Avenue, Park Ridge, IL 60068, USA.

KENNEY Susan McIlvaine, b. 28 Apr 1941, Summit, New Jersey, USA. Novelist; Professor of English and Creative Writing. m. Edwin J Kenney Jr, 28 Nov 1964 (dec.), 1 son, 1 daughter. Education: BA with distinction, honours in English, Northwestern University, 1963; MA, 1965, PhD, English and American Literature, 1968, Cornell University. Appointments include: Dana Professor of Creative Writing, Colby College, Waterville, Maine, 1992-. Publications: Garden of Malice, 1983; In Another Country, 1984; Graves in Academe, 1985; Sailing, 1988; One Fell Step, 1990. Honours: Phi Beta Kappa, 1962; O Henry Prize Stories, 1982; QPB New Voices Award, 1985. Memberships: Authors Guild; PEN American Center. Literary Agent:

Maxine Groffsky. Address: Department of English, Colby College, Waterville, ME 04901-4799, USA.

KENNY Adele, b. 28 Nov 1948. Poet; Teacher; Writing Consutant. Education: BA, English, 1970; MS, Education, 1982. Appointments: Poetry/Writing Consultant, 1980-; Artist-in-Residence, Middlesex County Arts Council, 1979-80; Poetry Editor, NJ Art Form, 1981-83; Grants Review Panelist, NJ State Council of the Arts, 1985; Henderson Award Judge, 1985; Japan Airlines Haiku Competition Judge, 1988; associate Editor, Muse-Pie Press, 1988-. Publications include: Migrating Geese, 1987; Between Hail Marys, 1986; The Roses Open, 1984; Counseling Gifted, Creative and Talented Youth Through the Arts, 1989; The Crystal Keepers handbook, 1988; Illegal Entries, 1984; An Archeology of Ruins, 1982; Starship Earth, 1990; Questi Momenti, 1990; Castles and Dragons, 1990. Contributions to: The Alchemist; Black Swan Review; Brussels Sprout; Home Planet News; Mirrors; journal of NJ Poets, and others. Honours: Fellowships in Poetry, NJ State Council on the Arts, 1982, 1987; Merit Book Award, 1983, 1987; Writer Digest Award, 1981; Roselip Award, 1988; Haiku Quarterly Award, 1989. Memberships: The Poetry Society of America; The Haiku Society of America, President 1987, 1988, 1990. Address: 207 Coriell Avenue, Fanwood, NJ 07023, USA.

KENRICK Tony, b. 1935, Australia, Author. Appointments: Advertising Copywriter, Sydney, Toronto, San Francisco, New York, London, 1953-72. Publications: The Only Good Body is a dead One, 1970; A Tough One To Lose, 1972; Two for the Price of One, 1974; Stealing Lillian, 1975, UK paperback, The Kidnap Kid, 1976; The Seven Day Soldiers, 1976; The Chicago Girl, 1976; Two Lucky People, 1978; The Nighttime Guy, 1979; The 1st Site, 1980; Blast, 1983; Faraday's Flowers, 1985; US Paperback Shanghai Surprise; China White, 1986; Neon Tough, 1988; Glitterbug, 1991. Literary Agent: Jean Naggar. Address: c/o 216 E 75th Street, New York, NY 10021, USA.

KENT Alexander. See: REEMAN Douglas Edward.

KENT Arthur (William Charles), (James Bradwell, M DuBois, Paul Granados, Alexander Karol, Alex Stamper, Brett Vane), b. 1925, United Kingdom; Author; Former Journalist. Appointments: Journalist: News Chronicle, London, 1943-46; Australian Daily Mirrors, 1947-53; Beaverbook Newspapers, UK, 1957-69; BBC, London, 1970-71. Publications: Sunny (as Bret Vane), 1953; Gardenia (as Bret Vane), 1953; Broadway Contraband (as Paul Granados), 1954; El Tafile (as M DuBois), 1954; Legion Etrangere (as M DuBois), 1954; March and Die (as M DuBois), 1954; Revolt at Zaluig (as Alex Stamper), 1954; Inclining to Crime, 1957; Special Edition Murder, 1957; Kansas Fast Gun, 1958; Stairway to Murder, 1958; Wake Up Screaming, 1958; The Camp on Blood Island (with G Thomas), 1958; Last Action, 1959; Broken Doll, 1961; Action of the Tiger, 1961; The Weak and the Strong, 1962; The Counterfeiters, 1962; Long Horn, Long Grass, 1964; Black Sunday, 1965; Corpse to Cuba; Plant Poppies on My Grave, 1966; Red Red Red, 1966; Fall of Singapore (with I Simon), 1970; The Mean City (as James Bradwell), 1971; A Life in the Wind (with Z de Tyras), 1971; Sword of Vengeance (as Alexander Karol), 1973; Dark Lady (as Alexander Karol), 1974; The King's Witchfinder (as Alexander Karol), 1975; The Death Doctors; Maverick Squadron, 1975; The Nowhere War, 1975. Address: 26 Verulam Avenue, London E17, England.

KENT Helen. See: POLLEY Judith Anne.

KENT Philip. See: BULMER Henry Kenneth.

KENTON Maxwell. See: SOUTHERN Terry.

KENWARD Jean, b. 10 May 1920, Pangbourne, Berkshire, England. Writer. m. David Chesterman, 5 Sept 1945, 2 sons, 1 daughter. Education: Diploma, Speech & Drama, Central School. Appointments include: Lecturer, Complementary Studies, Harrow School of Art. Publications: A Flight of Words, 1971; The Forest, 1971; Old Mr Hotchpotch, 1974; Ragdolly Anna, 1979; Clutterby Hogg, 1980; Theme & Variations, 1981; 3 Cheers for Ragdolly Anna, 1985; Aesop's Fables, 1986; Ragdolly Anna's Circus, 1987; The Hotchpotch Horse, 1987; A Kettle Full of Magic, 1988; Ragdolly Anna's Treasure Hunt, 1989; Seasons, 1989. Contributions to: Country Life; Countryman; Script; Poetry Review; Middle Way; Child Education; Liberal Education; Over 70 Anthologies; Regular Broadcasts on BBC schools. Honours: Premium Prize, Poetry Review, 3 times, 1940. Address: 15 Shire Lane, Chorleywood, Hertfordshire, England.

KENYON Bruce Guy, b. 16 Aug 1929, Cadillac, Michigan, USA. Bookseller. m. Marian Long, 1950 (div 1954). Publications: as Daisy Vivian: Rose White, Rose Red, 1983; Fair Game, 1986; A Marriage of Inconvenience, 1986; The Counterfeit Lady, 1987; as Meredith Leigh: A Lady of Qualities, 1987; An Elegant Education, 1987; also: The Forrester Inheritance, 1985; Wild Rose, 1986; Return to Cheyne Spa, 1988; A Certain Reputation, 1990. Contributions to: New Leaves; Harvest; Hidden Path; Manscape. Memberships: Authors Guild Inc; Authors League of America Inc. Literary Agent: Kearns and Orr. Address: c/o Kearns and Orr, 686 Lexington Avenue, New York, NY 10022, USA.

KENYON John (Phillips), b. 1927, UK. Professor of Modern History, St Andrews University. Publications: Robert Spencer, Earl of Sunderland, 1958; The Stuarts, 1958, 2nd edition, 1970; The Stuart Constitution, 1966; The Popish Plot, 1972; Revolution Principles, 1977; Stuart England, 1978; The History Men, 1983. Address: 82 Hepburn Gardens, St Andrews, Fife KY16 9LN, Scotland.

KENYON Kate. See: ADORJAN Carol.

KENYON Michael, b. 26 June 1931, England. Author. 3 daughters. Education: Wadham College, Oxford, 1951-54; MA (Oxon), History. Publications: May You Die in Ireland, 1965; The 100,000 Welcomes, 1970; Mr Big, 1973; The Rapist, 1976; A Healthy Way to Die, 1986; Peckover Holds the Baby, 1988; Kill the Butler!, 1991; Peckover Joins the Choir, 1992; A French Affair, 1992. Contributions to: 35 articles to Gourmet Magazine. Membership: Detection Club. Literary Agents: R S Simon, UK; Geo Borchardt, USA. Address: 164 Halsey Street, Southampton, NY 11968, USA.

KEOGH Dermot Francis, b. 12 May 1945. Academic. m. Ann, 22 Aug 1973, 2 s, 2 d. Education: BA, 1970, MA, 1974, University College, Dublin; PhD, 1980, European University Institute, Florence. Appointments: Lecturer, Department of Modern History, 1970-90, Jean Monnet Professor of Modern Integration, 1990-, University College, Cork. Publications: The Vatican, the Bishops and Irish Politics 1919-1939, 1985; The Rise of the Irish Working Class 1890-1914, 1983; Ireland and Europe 1919-1989, 1989; Ireland, 1922-1993, (editor) Church and Politics in Latin America, 1990. Contributions to: Academic journals and national press. Honour: Fellow, Woodrow Wilson Centre for Scholars, Washington DC, 1988. Address: Department of Modern History, University College, Cork, Ireland.

KERMODE John Frank, (Sir), b. 29 Nov 1919, Douglas, Isle of Man. Literary Critic. Education: BA 1940, MA 1947, Liverpool University; MA, Cambridge, 1974. Publications include: Romantic Image, 1957; The Sense of an Ending, 1967; The Classic, 1975; The Genesis of Secrecy, 1979; History and Value, 1988; An Appetite for Poetry, 1989; The Uses of Error, 1991. Contributions to: The Guardian; NY Times; London Review of Books; New York Review of Books; New Republic, and others. Honours: Hon Doctorates, Chicago University, 1975; Liverpool University, 1981; Amsterdam University, 1987; Newcastle University,1993; Knighted, 1991. Memberships: FRSL; FBA; American Academy of Arts and Sciences. Literary Agent: The Peters Fraser and Dunlop Group Ltd. Address: 27 Luard Road, Cambridge CB2 2PJ, England.

KERN Gregory. See: TUBB E(dwin) C(harles).

KERNAGHAN Eileen Shirley, b. 6 Jan 1939, Enderby, British Columbia, Canada. Writer. m. Patrick Walter Kernaghan, 22 Aug 1959, Enderby. 2 s, 1 d. Education: Elementary Teaching Certificate, University of British Columbia. Publications: The Upper Left-Hand Corner: A Writer's Guide for the Northwest, co-author, 1975, revised, 1986; Journey to Aprilioth, 1980; Songs for the Drowned Lands, 1983; Sarsen Witch, 1988; Walking After Midnight, 1991. Contributions to: Galaxy, USA; Room of One's Own, Canada; Northern Journey; Branching Out; Canadian Review; Origins; Nimbus; Tesseracts; Prism International, and others. Honours: Siver Porgy Award for original paperback (Journey to Aprilioth), West Coast Review for Books, 1981; Canadian Science Fiction and Fantasy Award (for Songs from the Drowned Lands), 1985. Memberships: Witers Union of Canada; Federation of British Columbian Writers; Secretary, Treasurer, Newsletter editor, Burnaby Writers Society. Literary Agent: Jane Butler. Address: 5512 Neville Street, Burnaby, British Columbia, Canada, V5J 2H7.

KERR Carole. See: CARR Margaret.

KERR (Anne) Judith, b. 1923, Germany. Children's Fiction Writer. Appointments: Secretary, Red Cross, London, England, 1941-45; Teacher and Textile Designer, 1948-53; Script Editor, Script Writer, BBC-TV, London, 1953-58. Publications: The Tiger Who Came to Tea, 1968; Mog the Forgetful Cat, 1970; When Hitler Stole Pink Rabbit, 1971; When Willy Went to the Wedding, 1972; The Other Way Round, 1975; Mog's Christmas, 1976; A Small Person Far Away, 1978; Mog and the Baby, 1980; Mog in the Dark, 1983; Mog and Me, 1984; Mog's Family of Cats, 1985; Mog's Amazing Birthday Caper, 1986; Mog and Bunny, 1988; Mog and Barnaby, 1990; How Mrs Monkey Missed the Ark, 1992; The Adventures of Mog, 1993; Mog on Fox Night, 1993; Mog in The Garden, 1994; Mog's Kittens, 1994. Address: c/o Harper Collins Publishers, 77-85 Fulham Palace Road, London W6 8JB, England.

KERSH Cyril, b. 24 Feb 1925. Author; Journalist. m. Suzanne Fajner, 1956. Appointments: Worked variously for newsagent, baker, woollen merchant, toy manufacturer, 1939-43; reporter, then News and Features Editor, The People, 1943-54; Features Editor, Illustrated, 1954-59; Features Staff, London Evening Standard, 1959-60; Editor, Men Only, 1960-63; Daily Express (one day), 1963; Features Editor, then Senior Features Executive, 1963-76, Sunday Mirror; Editor, Reveille, 1976-79 (Fleet Street's First Photocomposition Editor); Assisstant Editor, Features 1979-84, Managing Editor, 1984-86, Sunday Mirror. Publications: The Aggravations of Minnie Ashe, 1970; The Diabolical Liberties of Uncle Max, 1973; The Soho Summer of Mr Green, 1974; The Shepherd's Bush Connection, 1975; Minnie Ashe at War, 1979; A Few Gross Words, 1990. Address: 14 Ossington Street, London W2 4LZ, England.

KERSHAW Peter. See: **LUCIE-SMITH John Edward McKenzie.**

KESSELMAN Wendy (Ann), b. America. Appointments: Teaching Fellow, Bryn Mawr College, Pennsylvania, 1987; Writer, Composer; Songwiter. Publications: plays: Becca (for children) music and lyrics by Kesselman (produced New York, 1977); Maggie Magalita (produced Washington DC, 1980, New York, 1986); My Sister in This House, music by Kesselman (Louisville and London, 1987) Merry-Go-Round (Louisville 1981, New York, 1983); I Love You, I Love You Not (1-act version, Louisville, 1982, New York, 1983, Full-length version, St Paul, 1986, New York, 1987); The Juniper Tree: A Tragic Household Tale, music and lyrics by Kesselman (Stockbridge, Massachussetts, 1982, New York, 1983); children's fiction includes: Time for Jody, 1975; Emma, 1980; There's a Train Going by My Window, US, 1982, UK 1983; Flick, 1983. Honours: Meet the Composer Grant, 1978, 1982; National Endowment for the Arts Fellowship, 1979; Sharfman Award, 1980; Susan Smith Blackburn Prize, 1980; Playbill Award, 1980; Guggenheim Fellowship, 1982; McKnight Fellowship, 1985. Literary Agent: George Lane, William Morris Agency, 1350 Ave of the Americas, NY 10019 or Jane Annakin, William Morris Agency Ltd, 31-32 Soho Square, London W1V 6AP. Address: PO Box 680, Wellfleet, MA 02667, USA.

KESSLER Jascha, b. 27 Nov 1929, New York, USA. Writer; Professor of English & Modern Literature. m. 17 July 1950, 2 sons, 1 daughter. Appointments: Professor of English and Modern Literature, University of California at Los Angeles, 1961-. Publications: American Poems: A Contemporary Collection, 1964; An Egyptian Bondage, 1967; Death Comes for the Behaviorist, 1983; Transmigrations: 18 stories, 1985; Classical Illusions: 28 Stories, 1985; Siren Songs: 50 Stories, 1992; Whatever Love Declares, 1969; After the Armies have Passed, 1970; In Memory of the Future, 1976; Bride of Acacias: The Poetry of Forough Farrokhzad, 1983; The Magician's Garden: 24 Stories by Geza Csáth (with Charlotte Rogers), 1980; Opium, 1983; Under Gemini: The Selected Poetry of Miklós Radnóti, 1985; Medusa: The Selected Poetry of Nicolai Kantchev, 1986; The Face of Creation: 23 Contemporary Hungarian Poets, 1987; To Kolonos, 1988; Catullan Games, 1989; Writer of several plays and full length opera, The Cave. Honours: Recipient, various research grants and prizes, writing fellowships, 1952-; Major Hopwood Award for Poetry, University of Michigan, 1952; 2 Senior Fulbright Awards to Italy; Fellowship, National Endowment of the Arts, 1974; Rockefeller Fellow, 1979; Hungarian PEN Club Memorial Medal, 1979; George Soros Foundation Prize, 1989; Fellow in Fiction Writing, 1993-94, California Arts Council. Memberships: Poetry Society of America; ASCAP; American Literary Translators Association. Address: English Department, University of California at Los Angeles, 405 Hilgard Avenue, Los Angeles, CA 90095-1530, USA.

KESSLER Lauren Jeanne, b. 4 Apr 1950, New York City, USA. Author; Professor. m. Thomas Hager, 7 Jul 1984, 2 s. Education: BS Northwestern University, 1971; MS University of Oregon, 1975; PhD, University of Washington, 1980. Publications: The Stubborn Twig: A Japanese Family in America, 1993; After All These Years: Sixties Ideals in a Different World, 1990; Aging Well, 1990, 1987; The Dissident Press: Alternative Journ in American History, 1984; When Worlds Collide, 1984, 1988, 1992; The Search, 1991; Mastering the Message, 1989. Contributions to: Self, Working Mother, Modern Maturity, Us, Spring, Northwest Magazine, Oregon Magzine, Journalism Quarterly; Journalism History; American Journalism; Oregon Historical Quarterly. Honours: Council for the Advancement of Secondary Education, Excellence in Periodical Writing, 1987; Sigma Delta Chi for Excellence in Journalism, 1987. Memberships: Association for Education in Journalism and Mass Communications; American Journalism Historians Association; Union for Democratic Communication. Literary Agent: Nat Sobel. Address: School of Communications, Allen Hall, University of Oregon, Eugene, OR 97405, USA.

KETTELKAMP Larry Dale, b. 1933, American. Writer of children's fiction, Music, Psychology, Sciences, Supernatural/Occult topics; freelance writer, editor, composer, lecturer Institute of Graphic Design, Rider College, Lawrenceville, New Jersey, 1986-; Director, Bookarts Associates, Cranbury, New Jersey, 1986-. Appointments: Art Director, Garrard Publishing Co, Champaign, Illinois, 1959-60; Layout and Staff Artist, Highlights for Children magazine, Honesdale, Pennsylvania, 1962-67; Director of Publications, Summy-Birchard Music, Princeton, New Jersey, 1981-82. Publications: Magic Made Easy, 1954, 1981; Spooky Magic, 1955; The Magic Sound, 1956, 1982; Shadows, 1957; Singing Strings, 1958; Kites, 1959; Drums, Rattles and Bells, 2960; Gliders, 1961; Flutes, Whistles and Reeds, 1962; Puzzle Patterns, 1963; Spirals, 1964; Horns, 1964; Spinning Tops, 1966; Song, Speech and Ventriloquism, 1967; Dreams, 1968; Haunted Houses, 1969; Sixth Sense, 1970; Investigating UFOs, 1971; Religions East and West, 1972; Astrology, Wisdom of the Stars, 1973; Tricks of Eye and Mind, 1976; Hypnosis, 1975; The Dreaming Mind, 1975; A Partnership of Mind and Body, Biofeedback, 1976; Investigating Psychics, 1977; The Healing Arts, 1978; Lasers: The Miracle Light, 1979; Mischevious Ghosts: The Poltergeist and PK, 1980; Your Marvelous Mind, 1980; Electronic Musical Instruments: What They Do, How They Work, 1984; Starter Solos For Classical Guitar, 1984; Intermediate Etudes for Classical Guitar, 1984; The Human Brain, 1986; Modern Sports Science, 1986; Bill Cosby: Family Funny Man, 1987. Address: 2 Wynnewood Drive, Cranbury, NJ 08512, USA.

KEYES Daniel, b. 9 Aug 1927, New York City, New York, USA. Author. m. Aurea Georgina Vazquez, 14 Oct 1952, 2 daughters. Education: BA, 1950; MA, 1962. Appointments: Lecturer, Wayne State University, 1962-66; Professor, English, Ohio University, 1966-. Publications: Flowers for Algernon, 1966, filmed as Charly; The Touch, 1968; The Fifth Sally, 1980; The Minds of Billy Milligan, non-fiction, 1986; Daniel Keyes Short Stories (Japan), 1993; Daniel Keyes Reader (Japan), 1994; The Milligan Wars, 1995. Literary Agent: c/o William Morris Agency, 1350 Avenue of the Americas, New York, NY 10019, USA.

KHATCHADOURIAN Haig, b. 22 July 1925, Old City, Jerusalem, Palestine. Professor of Philosophy. m. Arpine Yaghlian, 10 Sept 1950, 2 sons, 1 daughter. Education: BA, MA, American University of Beirut, Lebanon; PhD, Duke University, USA. Appointments: American University of Beirut, Lebanon, 1948-49, 1951-67; Professor of Philosophy, University of Southern California, USA, 1968-69; Professor of Philosophy, University of Wisconsin-Milwaukee, 1969-. Publications: The Coherence Theory of Truth: A Critical Evaluation, 1961; Traffic with Time (co-author), poetry, 1963; A Critical Study in Method, 1967; The Concept of Art, 1971; Shadows of Time, poetry, 1983; Music, Film and Art, 1985. Contributions to: Numerous professional and literary journals. Address: Department of Philosophy, University of Wisconsin, Milwaukee, WI 53201, USA.

KHATENA Joe, b. 25 Oct 1925, Singapore. University Professor. m. 17 Dec 1950, 2 s, 2 d. Education: Normal Trained Certificate, Education, Singapore Teachers Training College, 1953; Certificate of Education, University of Malaya, 1957; BA (General) 1960; BA (Honours) English, 1961, University of Malaya; MEd, Education, University of Singapore, 1965; PhD, Psychology, University of Georgia, 1969. Literary Appointments: Member of Editorial Boards of Gifted Children Quarterly, 1975, and Journal of Mental Imagery, 1982; Guest

Editor of Gifted Child Quarterly, 1975, 79; Publications: Thinking Creatively with Sounds and Words (co-author Torrance), 1973; Khatena-Torrance Creative Perception Inventory, 1976; The Creatively Gifted Child, 1978; Educating the Ablest, 2nd edition (co-editors Gowan and Torrance), 1979; Teaching Gifted Children to Use Creative Imag. Imagery, 1979; Images of the Inward Eye: Poems, 1981; Creative Imag Imagery Actionbook, 1981; Creativity: Its Educational Implications, 2nd Edition (co-editors Gowan and Torrance), 1981; Educational Psychology of the Gifted, 1982; Imagery and Creative Imagination, 1984; Khatena-Morse Multitalent Perception Inventory, 1987. Contributions include: Journal of Educational Psychology; Gifted Child Quarterly; Journal of Creative Behaviour; Sociology and Social Research; Art Psychotherapy; Educational Trends; Indian Journal of Psychology; Journal of Mental Imagery; APA Proceedings. Honours: Book Award 1957, Scholarship 1956-61, University of Malaya; Fellow of APA, 1975; Marshall University research Award, 1976; USOE Office of Gifted Certificate of Recognition, 1976; Distinguished Scholar Award, 1982, Distinguished Service Award, 1983, Life Member, 1982, National Association for Gifted Children; Distinguished Lecturer, Texas Women's University, 1985; Fulbright Senior Lecturer Award to India, 1985. Memberships: National Association for Gifted Children, President, 1977-79; American Psychological Association, Fellow 1975; Creative Education Foundation, Colleague, 1983; American Education Research Association, 1972; New York Academy of Sciences, 1985; Kappa Delta Phi, 1968; Phi Kappa Ohi, 1984. Address: Department of Educational Psychology, Drawer EP, Mississippi State University, Mississippi State, MS 39762, USA.

KHAYAM Massoud, b. 5 May 1947, Tehran, Iran. Consultant Engineer. m. T Z Ganji, 7 Oct 1976, 2 s, 1 d. Education: Diploma, 1966; MSc, Engineering, 1975; BSc Engineering, 1971; research Officer, 1976-79. Appointments: Lecturer, Tehran University of Science, 1990; Assisstant Editor, Safar Quarterly, 1991; Assisstant Editor in Chief, Doya Sokhan monthly magazine, 1988; In Charge of Homa University, 1986; Lecturer, Navy University, 1978. Publications: Human Zoo, novel, 1991; Shanameh in Land Rover (humour), 1990; Universal Construction of Knowledge, 1982; Earthly (collected essays), 1988; Black Hole, 1982; Omar Khayam and the Golden Age of Mathematics, 1990; Mama and Nima, novel, in press; On War, Collection of Short Stories; Narrow Stream; further five books - mostly banned in Iran. Contributions to: Most of the Private Journals in Iran. Honours: Best Lecturer Award. Memberships: Informatic Society. Literary Agent: Pary Ganji Tehran. Address: PO Box 15875, Tehran 3168, Iran.

KHEIRABADI Masoud, b. 28 Feb 1951, Sabzevar, Iran. Teacher; Researcher. Education: BS, Geography, University of Tehran, 1973; MS, Agricultural Mechanization, Texas A & I University, 1978; MA, PhD, (Geography) University of Oregon, 1983, 1987, respectively. Appointments: Lecturer, University of Oregon, 1987-89; Lecturer, Lewis & Clark College, 1989-; Lecturer, Portland State University, 1989-; Lecturer, Clackamas C College, 1990-. Publications: Iranian Cities: Formation and Development, 1991, 1993. Contributions to: Encyclopedia Iranica, Columbia University Press; Articles on the Middle Eastern Studies to Scholary Journals, Periodicals and Popular Newspapers. Memberships: Middle East Association of North America; National Geographic Society; Association of American Geographers. Address: 67 SW Oswego Summit, Lake Oswego, OR 97035, USA.

KHERDIAN David, b. 1931, American. Writer, Poetry, Literature, Biography; Director, Two Rivers Press, 1978-. Appointments: Literary Consultant, Northwestern University, Evanston, Illinois, 1965; publisher, Giligia Press, 1967-73; Poetry Judge, Institute of American Indian Arts, Santa Fe, New Mexico, 1968; editor, Ararat Magazine, 1970; Poet-in-the-Schools, State of New Hampshire, 1971. Publications include: (with G Hausman) Eight Poems, 1968; Six San Francisco Poets, 1969; On the Death of My Father and Other Poems, 1970; (editor with J Baloian) Down at the Santa Fe Depot: Twenty Fresno Poets, 1970; Homage to Adana, 1970; Looking Over Hills, 1972; (editor) Visions of America; By the Poets of Our Time, 1973; A David Kherdian Sampler, 1974; The Nonny poems, 1974; (editor) Settling Smerica: The Ethnic Expression of Fourteen Contemporary Poets, 1974; Any Day of Your Life, 1975; (editor) Poems Here and Now, 1976; (editor) The Dog Writes on the Window with His Nose and other Poems, 1977; (editor) Travelling America with Today's Poets, 1977; (editor) If Dragon Flies Made Honey, 1977; Country Cat, City Cat, 1978; I Remember Root River, 1978; (editor) I Sing The Story of Myself, 1978; The Road From Home: The Story of An Armenian Girl, 1979; The Farm, 1979; (trans) The Pearl: Hymn of the Robe of Glory, 1979; It Started with the Old Man Bean, 1980; Finding Home, 1981; Beyond

Two Rivers, 1981; Taking the Soundings on Third Avenue, 1981; The Farm, Book Two, 1981; (trans) Pigs Never See the Stars: Proverbs From the Armenian, 1982; The Song in the Walnut Grove, 1983; The Mystery of the Diamond in the Wood, 1983; Right Now, 1983; The Animal, 1984; Root River Run, 1984; Threads of Light, 1985.

KHOSLA Gurdial Singh, b. 15 Jan 1912, Lahore. Writer. m. Manorama, 16 Oct 1941, 1 son, 1 daughter. Education: BA Hons, 1931, MA 1933, English, Punjab University, Lahore. Appointments: Lecturer in English, Khalsa College, Amritsar, 1934-35; General Manager, Western Railway, 1967-70; Adviser and Head, Department of Dramatic Arts, Punjab University, 1970-72. Publications: Plays: The Daughter at the Doorstep; The Homeless and other one-act plays; Mar Milthn Wale; Before Doomsday; Railway Management in India, 1972; A History of Indian Railways, 1988; The Auction of a City; Literary and Other Essays, 1951; Road to Nowhere, a novel in English, 1993. Contributions to: Punjabi Duniya, Punjabi Sahit, The Indian Express, Sun; Observer; The Statesman; Hundustan Times; Times of India; YOJNA, Journal of the Planning Commission, India. Honours: Eminent Theatreman, By Delhi Natya Sangh, 1980 and By President of India at World Punjabi Conference, 1983; Drama Award, Punjabi Academy, Delhi, 1988 and Sahitya Academy Pubjab, 1989. Memberships: PEN International: President, Pubjabi Theatre; Founder Member and Treasurer, Authors Guild of India, 1974-81; Founder Member and President, Conservation Society Delhi, 1983-86; Hon Secretary, General Indian Heritage Society, 1987-93. Address: D103 Defence Colony, New Delhi 110-024, India.

KHRUSHCHEV Sergei Nikitich, b. 2 July 1935, Moscow, Russia. Control Systems Engineer. m. Valentina N Golenko, 3 Aug 1985, 3 sons. Education: Moscow Electrical Institute, 1952-68; PhD Engineering, 1967, Assistant Professor, 1968, Moscow Technical University; Doctorate, Ukrainian Academy of Sciences, 1988. Appointments: Professor, Control Computer Institute, 1989; Senior Scholar, Thomas J Watson Jr Institute for International Studies, Brown University Providence, RI, USA, 1991; Columnist, Asia Inc, business magazine for Pacific region, 1992-. Publications: Khrushchev on Khrushchev, 1990, in Japan, Germany, France, Norway, Netherlands, South Korea, Hungary, Czechoslovakia, 1991-93; Pensioner Sousnogo Znachenia, 1991; Nikita Khrushchev: Crises and Missiles, 1994, Moscow. Contributions to: Magazines in USSR and Russia including Ogonck; 150 articles to international publications. Honours: Lenin Prize for Engineering, 1959; Hero of Soviet Labour, 1963; Council of Ministers Prize, USSR, 1985. Memberships: International Informatization Academy; Russian Computer Society. Address: 3 Laurelhurst Road, Cranston, RI 02920, USA.

KHUE Danh. See: LUU Van Lang.

KIDD Ian Gray, b. 6 Mar 1922, Chandernagore, India. University Professor Emeritus. m. Sheila Elizabeth Dow, 17 Dec 1949, 3 sons. Education: MA, St Andrews University, 1947; BA, MA, Lit Humaniores, Queen's College, Oxford, 1947-49. Publications: Posidonius I (with L Edelstein), The Fragments, 1972, 1989; Posidonius II, A-B, The Commentary, 1988; (with R Waterfield) Plutarch, Essays, 1992. Contributions to: Concise Encyclopedia of Western Philosophy and Philosophers, 1960; The Encyclopedia of Philosophy, 1967; Problems in Stoicism, 1971; Literature and Western Civilisation, Vol I, 1972; The Stoics, 1978; Les Stoiciens et leur Logique, 1978; Stoic and Peripatetic Ethics, 1983; Aspects de la Philosophie Hellenistique, 1986; The Criterion of Truth, 1989; Philosophia Togata, 1989; Theophrastus, 1993; Articles and Reviews in learned journals including: Classical Quarterly; Classical Review; Journal of Hellenic Studies; Philosophical Quarterly; Philosophical Books. Honours: Member, Institute for Advanced Study, Princeton, 1971-72, 1979-80; Fellow of the British Academy. Honorary Fellow: St Leonard's College, St Andrews, and Institute for Research in Classical Philosophy and Science, Princeton. Address: Ladebury, Lade Braes Lane, St Andrews, Fife KY16 9EP, Scotland.

KIDD Virginia, b. 2 June 1921, Germantown, Philadelphia, Pennsylvania, USA. Literary Agent. m. (1) Jack Emden, 17 Apr 1943, div 1947, 1 daughter, (2) James Blish, 23 May 1947, div 1964, 2 sons, 2 daughters. Publications: Saving Worlds, also known as The Wounded Planet (edited with Roger Elwood), 1973; The Best of Judith Merril (editor), 1976; Millennial Women, 1978; Edited with Ursula K Le Guin, 1980: Edges; Interfaces. Contributions to various journals and magazines including: The Mad River Review; Just Friends; Accent; Speculative Poetry Review; Short stories to: Orbit; Galaxy; Venus;

Quark. Memberships: Science Fiction and Fantasy Writers of America; Science Fiction Research Association; Science Fiction Poetry Association; Academy of American Poets; Authors Guild. Address: 538 E Harford Street, PO Box 278, Milford, PA 18337, USA.

KIDDER Tracy, b. 12 Nov 1945, New York, New York, USA. m. Frances T Toland, 2 Jan 1971. Education: AB, Harvard University; MFA, University of Iowa. Publications: The Road to Yuba City: A Journey into the Juan Corona Murders, 1974; The Soul of a New Medicine, 1981; Old Friends, 1994; Among Schoolchildren; House. Contributions: Atlantic Monthly; Science 1983; Country Journal. Honours: Pulitzer Prize, 1982; Altantic First Award (short story); Sidney Hillerman Foundation Prize; American Book Award, 1982. Address: c/o George Borchardt Inc, 136 East 47th Street, New York, NY 10019, USA.

KIDMAN Fiona Judith, b. 26 Mar 1940, Hawera, New Zealand. Writer. m. Ernest I R Kidman, 20 Aug 1960, 1 son, 1 daughter. Publications: A Breed of Women, 1979; Mandarin Summer, 1981; Mrs Dixon and Friends, 1982; Paddy's Puzzle, 1983; Going to the Chathams, 1985; The Book of Secrets, 1987; Unsuitable Friends, 1988; True Stars, 1990 (novels); Wakeful Nights (poems), 1991; The Foreign Woman (short stories), 1993. Contributions to: Numerous. Honours: Scholarship in Letters, 1981, 1985, 1991, 1995; QE II Arts Council Award for Achievement, 1988; OBE, 1988; New Zealand Book Award for Fiction, 1988. Memberships: Secretary 1972-75, President 1980-82, PEN International NZ Centre; Secretary Organiser, 1972-75, President 1992-, New Zealand Book Council; New Zealand Writer's Guild; Media Women. Literary Agent: Ray Richards, Richards Literary Agency, PO Box 31-240 Milford Auckland, New Zealand. Address: 28 Rakau Road, Hataitai, Wellington 3, New Zealand.

KIELY Benedict, b. 15 Aug 1919, Dromore, Co Tyrone, Ireland. Writer. Education: Christian Brothers' School, Omagh and National University of Ireland; Visiting Professor & Writer in Residence at several US Universities. Appointments: Journalist in Dublin, 1940-65. Publications include: Novels: Land Without Stars, 1946; In a Harbour Green, 1949; Call for a Miracle, 1950; Honey Seems Bitter, 1952; The Cards of the Gambler: A Folktale, 1953; There was an Ancient House, 1955; The Captain with the Whiskers, 1960; Dogs Enjoy the Morning, 1968; Proxopera: A Novella, 1977; Nothing Happens in Carmincross, 1985; Drink to The Bird - Memoir, 1991; Short story collections, Non-fiction and edited works: Selected stories, 1993. Honours: American Irish Foundation Award, 1980; Irish Academy of Letters Award, 1980; Irish Independent Literary Award, 1985; DLitt (hc), National University of Ireland and of Queen's University, Belfast. Address: 119 Morehampton Road, Donnybrook, Dublin 4, Eire.

KIENZLE William X, b. 11 Sept 1928, Detroit, Michigan, USA. Author. m. Javan Herman Andrews, Nov 1974. Education: BA, Sacred Heart Seminary College, 1950; St John's Seminary, 1950-54. Literary appointments: Editor: The Michigan Catholic, 1962-74; MPLS Magazine, 1974-76. Publications: The Rosary Murders, 1979; Death Wears a Red Hat, 1980; Mind Over Murder, 1981; Assault with Intent, 1982; Shadow of Death, 1983; Kill and Tell, 1984; Sudden Death, 1985; Deathbed, 1986; Deadline for a Critic, 1987; Marked for Murder, 1988; Eminence, 1989; Masquerade, 1990; Chameleon, 1991; Body Count, 1992; Dead Wrong, 1993; Bishop as Pawn, 1994; Call No Man Father, 1995. Honours: Journalism Award for General Excellence, Michigan Knights of Columbus, 1963; Honourable Mention for Editorial Writing, Catholic Press Association, 1974. Membership: Authors Guild. Address: PO Box 645, Keego Harbor, MI 48320, USA.

KILBRACKEN John Godley, Lord, b. 17 Oct 1920, London, England; Nationality: Irish. Writer/Journalist. m. 1) Penelope Reyne, 22 May 1943, div, 2 sons (1 dec); 2) Susan Heazlewood, 15 May 1981, div, 1 son. Education: Eton, 1934-39 (won Hervey English Verse Prize); Balliol, Oxford 1939-40 and 1945-47; BA and MA 1948. Literary Appointments: Reporter: Daily Mirror, 1947-49, Sunday Express 1949-51; Foreign Correspondent for Evening Standard, 1960-65. Editorial Director of Worldwatch, 1984-85; Publications: Even For An Hour (poems), 1940; Tell Me The Next One, 1950; The Master Forger, 1951; Letters From Early New Zealand (editor), 1951; Living Like A Lord, 1955; A Peer Behind The Curtain, 1959; Shamrocks and Unicorns, 1962; Van Meegeren, 1967; Bring Back My Stringbag, 1979; The Easy Way to Bird Recognition, 1982; The Easy Way to Tree Recognition, 1983; The Easy Way to Wild Flower Recognition, 1984. Contributions to: many UK and foreign newspapers and magazines. Honours:DSC, for service as naval pilot in World War II, 1945; Times

Ed Supp Senior Information Book Award, 1982 (for book The Easy Way to Bird Recognition). Literary Agent: Curtis Brown, London and New York. Address: Killegar, Co Leitrim, Ireland.

KILGORE James C, b. 2 May 1928. Professor. Education: BA, Wiley College, 1952; MA, English, University of Missouri, 1963; various other courses, workshops. Publications: The Big Buffalo, 1969; Midnight Blast, 1970; A Time of Black Devotion, 1971; Night Song, 1974; Let It Pass, 1976; A Black Bicentennial, 1976; Until I Met You, 1978; African Violet, 1982; I've Been in the Storm So Long, 1983; During Arabica Lunch, 1986. Contributions to: various magazines and journals. Honours include: Ohio Poet of the Year, 1982; Ralph Besse Award for Teaching Excellence, 1983. Memberships: National Council of Teachers of English; MLA; Renaissance Society of America; Ohio Poets' Association; Phi Beta Sigma; many others. Address: 2531 Richmond Road, Beachwood, OH 44122, USA.

KILJUNEN Kimmo Roobert, b. 13 June 1951, Rauha, Finland. Development Researcher; Director, Institute of Development Studies, Helsinki University. m. Marja Liisa Kiljunen, 17 Jan 1972, 2 sons, 2 daughters. Education: MA, Helsinki University, 1973; MPhil 1977, DPhil 1985, Sussex University, England. Publications: Editor: Kampuchea, Decade of the Genocide, 1984; Namibia, the Last Colony, 1981; Region to Region Cooperation between Developed and Developing Countries, 1990; Author, Finland and the New International Division of Labour, 1992; Books published in Finland in Finish: Author: The Underdeveloped world, 1976; Premises for Regional Policy in the 1980s, 1979; Three Worlds, 1989; You and the World Poor, 1991; World States and Flags, 1995. Honour: President, Urho Kekkonen Foundation Literary Award, 1992. Memberships: European Association of Development Research and Training Institutes, Executive Committee, 1987-. Address: Linnoittajanpolku 3 g 15, 01280 Vantaa, Finland.

KILLANIN The Lord (Michael Morris), b. 30 Jul 1914, London, England. Writer; Film Producer; Company Director. m. Mary Sheila Dunlop, MBE, 17 Dec 1945, 3 s, 1 d. Education: Eton 1928-31; Sorbonne, Paris, 1931-32; Magdelene College, Cambridge, 1932-35; BA, 1935; MA, 1939. Literary Appointments: Reporter: Daily Express, 1935; Daily Mail, 1936; Sunday Dispatch, 1938. Publications: Four Days, 1938; Sir Godfrey Knelier, 1947; Shell Guide to Ireland, with M V Duigan, 1956; The Olympic Games, with John Rodda, 1976, 1980, 1984; My Ireland - A Personal Impression, 1987; films produced include: The Rising of the Moon; The Playboy of the Western World; Gideon's Day; film Commentary for Connemara and Its Pony. Honours include: MBE; Olympic Order (Gold), 1980; Honorary LLD, National University of Ireland, 1975, LLD (NUI); Honorary DLitt (NUU), New University of Ulster, 1977; Chubb Fellowship, Yale, 1981; Chubb Scholar, 1981; numerous foreign honours. Memberships include: President, Olympic Council of Ireland, 1950-73, Honorary Life President, 1981-; MRIA, 1954; Elected Member, International Olympic Committee, 1952, Executive Board 1967, Vice President, 1968, President, 1972-80, Honorary Life President, 1980-; Member French Academy of Sports, 1984; Honorary Life Member, Royal Dublin Sociert, 1981; Fellow, Royal Society of Arts, Royal Society of Antiquaries of Ireland, 1984; Hon Life Member, National Union of Journalists and of the Association of Cinema and Television Technicians, 1985; Hon Life Member, Chambers of Commerce of Ireland; Hon Member, Marketing Institute of Ireland; Honorary Consul General for the Principality of Monaco in Ireland 1961-84; Chairman National Heritage Council, 1988-; Chairman, Dublin Theatre Festival, 1958-70, Patron, 1971. Literary Agent: Scott Ferris Associates. Address: 9 Lower Mount Pleasant Avenue, Dublin 6, Ireland.

KILLDEER John. See: **MAYHAR Ardath.**

KILLOUGH (Karen) Lee, b. 1942, USA. Science Fiction Writer; Radiological Technologist. Publications: A Voice Out of Ramah, 1979; The Doppelganger Gambit, 1979; The Monitor, the Miners, and the Shree, 1980; Aventine, 1981; Deadly Silents, 1982; Liberty's World, 1985; Spider Play, 1986; Blood Hunt, 1987; The Leopard's Daughter, 1987; Bloodlinks, 1988; Dragon's Teeth, 1990. Address: Box 422, Manhattan, KS 66502, USA.

KILMARTIN Terence Kevin, b. 10 Jan 1922. Literary editor. m. Joanna Pearce, 1952, 1 s, 1 d. Appointments: Private Tutor, France, 1938-39; Special Operations Executive, 1940-45; Assisstant Editor, World Review, 1946-47; Freelance Journalist, Middle East, 1947-48; Assisstant Editor, Observer Foreign News Service, 1949-50; Assisstant

Literary Editor, 195052, Literary Editor, 1952-86, The Observer. Publications: A Guide to Proust, 1983; Translations of Henry de Montherlant: The Bachelors, 1960; The Dream, 1962; Chaos and Night, 1964; The Girls, 1968; The Boys, 1974; André Malraux: Anti-Memoirs, 1968; Lazarus, 1977; Charles De Gaulle, Memoirs of Hope, 1971; Marcel Proust, rev trans of Remembrance of Things Past, 1981. Address: 44 North Side, Clapham Common, London SW4, England.

KILROY Thomas, b. 23 Sept 1934, Ireland. Writer; University Teacher. m. Julia Lowell Carlson, 9 Dec 1981, 1 d. 3 sons by first marriage. Education: BA 1956, MA 1959, University College, Dublin, Ireland. Publications: Death and Resurrection of Mr Roche (Play), 1968 The Big Chapel (novel), 1971; Talbots' Box (play), 1977; The Seagull (play adaptation), 1981; Double Cross (play), 1986; Ghosts, 1989; The Madame McAdam Travelling Theatre (play), 1990; Gold in the Streets, TV, 1993. Contributions to: Radio; TV Drama; Numerous journals & magazines. Honours: Guardian Fiction Prize, 1971; Heinnmann Award for Literature, 1971; Irish Academy of Letters Prize, 1972; American-Irish Foundation Award for Literature, 1974. Memberships: Fellow, Royal Society of Literature, 1971; Irish Academy of Letters, 1973. Literary Agent: Casarotto Ramsay Ltd, National House, 60-66 Wardour Street, London W1V 3HP, England. Address:Kilmaine, County Mayo, Ireland.

KILWORTH Garry, b. 5 Jul 1941, York, England. Writer. m. Annette Jill Bailey, 30 Jun 1962, 1 s, 1 d. Education: Business Studies, 1974; Honours Degree in English, 1985. Publications: Hunter's Moon, 1989; In The Hollow of the Deep- Sea Wave, 1989; Songbirds of Pain, 1984; Standing on Samshan, 1992; Spiral Winds, 1987; The Drowners; Midnight's Sun; Abandonati; Cloudrock; Witchwater Country; In Solitary; The Electric Kids; The Rain Ghost; Frost Dancers. Contributions to: Omni Magazine; Isaac Asimov's Magazine; F & SF Magazine; Interzone; Sunday Times Review. Honours: Sunday Times, Gollancz Short Story Award Winner, 1974; Librarian Association's Carnegie Medal Commendation, 1991. Memberships: PEN. Literary Agent: Maggie Noach, 21 Redan Street, London, England. Address: Wychwater, The Chase, Ashingdon, Essex, England.

KIM Unsong William, b. 1 Sept 1924, North Korea. Retired Professor, Molecular Biology. m. Sue Kim, 18 Jan 1948, 4 s. Education: BS, Biology, Seoul University, 1949; MS, 1956, PhD 1958, Virology, University of Wisconsin, USA. Publications: 100 Classical Korean Poems (Sijo) selected, translated, 1986; Classical Korean Poems, Translated in English, 1986; Search for Life, Poems by Kim Unsong, 1987; Poems by Mao Tsetung, Translated by Kim Unsong, 1988; Generfa Biology, 1950; Introduction to Molecular Biology, 1975; Philosophy of Science, 1980; Lao Tza's Tao-Te-Ching, Lyrical trans in English and Korean, 1990; poetry Kim Unsong, International Poet's Book V, 1991. Contributions to: Over 30 scientific papers in various journals including: Scince; Biochim.; Biophys.; Acta; other interantional journals; poems in Poet: Korean - American Journal; American Anthology; New York Federal Anthology. Honours: Essay Award, Governor General, 1937; 1st Prize, Essay, Korea Times, 1975; 1st Prize, World Poetry International, 1987; Hon DLitt, World Academy of Arts and Culture, 1991; many other awards and honours. Memberships: Daly City Creative Writers Group; California Federation of Chapparal Poets; President, World Poetry International; Editor of Poetry Journal, Poet 1990; Vice President, International Poets Academy. Address: PO Box No 1131, san Bruno, CA 94066, USA.

KIM Yong-ik, b. 15 May 1920, Korea. Writer. m. 11 Feb 1972, 3 d. Education: BA, Aoyama Jakuin College, Tokyo, 1942; BA Florida Southern College, 1951; MA, University of Kentucky, 1952. Publications: Moons of Korea, 1959; The Happy Days, 1960; The Diving Gourd, 1962; Blue in the Seed, 1964; The Wedding Shoes, 1984; Love in Winter, 1970; The Shoes From Yang San Valley, 1981. Contributions to: Harpers Bazaar; The New Yorker; Mademoiselle; Korea Journal; Hudson review; The Yankee Magazine; Prism International. Honours include: First Overseas Korean Literature Prize, Korean Literary and Writers Association, 1990; Main Stream America Award for Excellence in Literature, Asian Pacific Council, 1991. Memberships; Korean American Literature Society. Address: 1030 Macon Avenue, Pittsburgh, PA 15218, USA.

KIMBALL Penn Townsend, b. 12 Oct 1915, New Britain, Connecticut, USA. Journalist; Professor Emeritus. m. (1) (dec.), 1 daughter, (2) Julie M Ellis, 27 July 1985. Education: BA, Princeton University School of Public and International Affairs, 1937; BA, MA, Balliol College, Oxford University, England, 1939; PhD, Columbia

University, 1988. Appointments include: Editor, Writer, US News, 1939; Newspaper PM, 1940; Time Magazine, 1946; New Republic, 1947; New York Times, 1951-54; Omnibus TV, CBS, 1954-55; Colliers, 1955-56; Columbia Journalism Review, 1960-85; Consulting Editor, Harris Survey, 1963-74; Currently Professor Emeritus, Graduate School of Journalism, Columbia University. Publications include: Chapter in The Professions in America, 1965; Bobby Kennedy and the New Politics, 1968; The Disconnected, 1972; The File, 1982, UK Edition, 1984; Keep Hope Alive, 1991; Downsizing The News, 1994. Contributions to: Various journals; Life Magazine; Saturday Review; Public Opinion Quarterly; Washington Journalism Review. Literary Agent: Berenice Hoffman. Address: Box 240, Chilmark, MA 02535, USA.

KIMBALL Roger, b. 13 Aug 1953, Ohio, USA. Writer; Editor. m. Alexandra Mullen, 1993. Education: BA, Bennington College, 1975; MA, 1977, MPhil, 1978, Yale University. Publications: Tenured Radicals: How Politics has Corrupted our Higher Education, 1990. Contributions to: The New Criterion; The Wall Street Journal; The Times Literary Supplement; Commentary; the American Scholar; Architectural Record. Literary Agent: Writers Representatives, 25W 19th Street, NYC 10011, Usa. Address: 850 7th Avenue, New York City, NY 10019, USA.

KIMBROUGH Robert (Alexander III), b. 1929, USA. Professor of English. Appointments: Instructor to Associate Professor, 1959-68, Professor of English, 1968; Chair, Integrated Liberal Studies Department, 1970-75, University of Wisconsin, Madison. Publications: Joseph Conrad, Heart of Darkness: An Authoritative Text, Backgrounds and Sources, Essays in Criticism (editor), 1963, 3rd edition, 1987; Dhakespeare's Troilus and Cressida and its setting, 1964; Henry James, The Turn of the Screw: An Authoritative Text, Backgrounds and Sources, essays in Criticism (editor), 1966; Troilus and Cressida: A Scene by Scene Analysis with Critical Commentary, 1966; Sir Philip Sydney, Selected Prose and Poetry, 1969, 2nd edition, 1982; Sir Philip Sidney, 1971; Christopher Marlowe, 1972; The Nigger of the Narcissus, by Joseph Conrad (editor), 1984; Shakespeare and the Art of Human Kindness: the essay toward androgyny, 1990. Address: 3206 Gregory Street, Madison, WI 53711, USA.

KIMES Beverly Rae, b. 17 Aug 1939, Aurora, Illinois, USa. Writer; Editor. m. James H Cox, 6 Jul 1984. Education: BS, Journalsim, University of Illinois; MA, Journalism, Pennsylvania State University. Publications: The Classic Tradition of the Lincoln Motor Car, 1968; Oldsmobile: The First Seventy-Five Years, 1972 (co-author); The Cars That Henry Ford Built, 1978; Editor, Great Cars and Grand Marques, 1976; Editor, Packard: A History of the Motor Car and the Company, 1979; Editor, Automobile Quarterly's Handbbok of Automotive Hobbies, 1981; My Two Lives: Race Car to Restauranteur (co-author), 1983; Chevrolet: A History From 1911 (co-author), 1984; Standard Catalog of American Cars, 1805-1942, 1985; The Star and the Laurel, 1986. Contributions to: American Heritage; Automobile Quarterly; The Classic Car; Automobiles Classiques; Wheels; Car and Driver; Road and Track. Honours: Cugnot Award, Society of Automotive Historians, 1978, 1979, 1984-86; McKean Trophy, Antique Automobile Club of America, 1984-86; Moto Award, National Automotive Journalism Association, 1984-86; many other honours and awards. Membership: Society of Automotive Historians, President, 1987-. Address: 215 East 80th Street, New York, NY 10021, USA.

KIMPEL Benjamin Franklin, b. 1905, USA. Emeritus Professor of Philosophy; Author. Publications: Principle of Contradiction in Idealistic Metaphysic, 1934; Religious Faith, Language and Knowledge, 1952; Faith and Moral Authority, 1953; Symbols of Religious Faith, 1954; Moral Principles in the Bible, 1956; Language and Religion, 1957; Principles of Moral Philosophy, 1960; Kant's Critical Philosophy, 1964; Hegel's Philosophy of History, 1964; Schopenhauer's Philosophy, 1964; Nietzsche's Beyond Good and Evil, 1965; A Philosophy of Zen Buddhism, 1966; Philosophies of Life of Ancient Greeks and Israelites: An Analysis of Their Parallels, 1980; Emily Dickinson as Philosopher, 1981; A Philosophy of the Religion of Ancient Israelites and Greeks, 1982; Stoic Moral Philosophies: Their Counsel for Today, 1985; Moral Philosophies in Shakespeare's Plays, 1987. Address: 65 West Street, North Bennington, VT 05257-9705, USA.

KINCAID Jamaica, b. 1949, St John's, Antigua, West Indies. writer. Appointments: Contributor, currently Staff Writer, The New Yorker Magazine, New York City, 1974-. Publications: At The Bottom of the River, short stories, 1984; Annie John, novel, 1985; A Small Place, non-fiction, 1988; Lucy, novel, 1990. Address: c/o The New Yorker magazine, 25 West 43rd Street, New York, NY 10036, USA.

KING Betty Alice, b. 17 June 1919, Historical Novelist. m. D James King, 14 June 1941, 2 sons, 1 daughter. Education: Queenswood School, Hertfordshire; Open University. Publications include: The Lady Margaret, 1965; The Lord Jasper, 1967; The King's Mother, 1969; Margaret of Anjou, 1974; Emma Hamilton, 1976; Nell Gwyn, 1979; Claybourn, 1980; The French Countess, 1982; We Are Tomorrow's Past, 1984; Large Print: We Are Tomorrow's Past; The French Countess; White Unicorn. Contributions to: Hertfordshire Countryside; Enfield Gazette. Memberships: The Society of Authors; Samuel Pepys Association. Literary Agent: A M Heath, London, England. Address: Crescent House, 31 North Road, Hertford, Herts SG14 1LN, England.

KING Clive, b. 28 Apr 1924, Richmond, Surrey, England. Author. m. (1) Jane Tuke, 1948, 1 s, 1 d, (2) Penny Timmins, 1974, 1 d. Education: Downing College, 1947. Publications: The Town That Went South, 1959; Stig of the Dump, 1963; The Twenty-Two Letters, 1966; The Night the Water Came, 1973; Snakes and Snakes, 1975; Me and My Million, 1976; Ninny's Boat, 1980; the Sound of Propellers, 1986; The Seashore People, 1987; 7 other books. Honours: Boston Globe-Horn Book Award, Honour Book, 1980. Memberships: Chairman, Children's Writers Group, Society of Authors, 1980-82.Literary Agent: Murray Pollinger. Address: Pond Cottage, Low Road, Thurlton, Norwich NR14 6PZ, England.

KING Cynthia, b. 27 Aug 1925, USA. Writer. m. Jonathan King, 26 July 1944, 3 sons. Education: Bryn Mawr College, 1943-44; University of Chicago, 1944-45; New York University Writers Workshop, 1964-67. Literary appointments: Associate Editor, Hillman Periodicals, 1945-50; Managing Editor, Fawcett Publications, 1950-55. Publications: In the Morning of Time, 1970; The Year of Mr Nobody, 1978; Beggars and Choosers, 1980; Sailing Home, 1982. Contributions to: The New York Times Book Review; The Detroit News; Los Angeles Daily News; Short Stories; Good Housekeeping; Texas Stories and Poems; Encore. Honours: Artists Grant, Michigan Council for the Arts, 1986. Memberships: Authors Guild; Detroit Women Writers, President 1979-81, Treasurer 1978; Poets and Writers. Literary Agent: Philippa Brophy, Sterling Lord Literistic Inc, USA. Address: 5306 Institute Lane, Houston, TX 77005, USA.

KING Francis Henry, (Frank Cauldwell), b. 4 Mar 1923. Author; Drama Critic. Education: Balliol College, Oxford. Appointments: Drama Critic, Sunday Telegraph, 1978-88. Publications: Novels: To the Dark Tower, 1946; Never Again, 1947; An Air That Kills, 1948; The Dividing Stream, 1951; The Dark Glasses, 1954; The Firewalkers (under pseudonym Frank Cauldwell), 1956; The Widow, 1957; The Man on the Rock, 1957; The Custom House, 1961; The Last of the Pleasure Gardens, 1965; The Waves Behind the Boat, 1967; A Domestic Animal, 1970; Flights, 1973; A Game of Patience, 1974; The Needle, 1975; Danny Hill, 1977; The Action, 1978; Act of Darkness, 1983; Voices in an Empty Room, 1984; Frozen Music, 1987; The Woman Who Was God, 1988; Punishments, 1989; Visiting Cards, 1990; The Ant Colony, 1991; (with Tom Wakefield and Patrick Gale), Secret Lives, 1991; The One and Only, 1994; Short Stories: So Hurt and Humiliated, 1959; The Japanese Umbrella, 1964; The Brighton Belle, 1968; Hard Feelings, 1976; Indirect Method, 1980; One is a Wanderer, 1985; (Poetry) Rod of Incantation, 1952; Biography: E M Forster and His World, 1978; Editor, My Sister and Myself: The Diaries of J R Ackerley, 1982; General: (Editor) Introducing Greece, 1956; Japan, 1970; Florence, 1982; Editor, Lafcadio Hearne: Writings from Japan, 1984; A Literary Companion to Florence, 1991; Autobiography: Yesterday Came Suddenly, 1993. Honours: OBE, 1979; CBE, 1985; FRSL; Somerset Maugham Award, 1952; Katherine Mansfield Short Story Prize, 1965. Memberships: International President, PEN, 1986-89; International Vice-President, PEN, 1989-; President, English Pen, 1978-86. Literary Agent: A M Heath & Co. Address: 19 Gordon Place, London W8 4JE, England.

KING Larry L, b. 1 Jan 1929. Playwright; Author; Actor. m. Barbara S Blaine, 2 sons, 3 daughters. Education: Texas Technical University, 1949-50; Nieman Fellow, Harvard University, 1969-70; Duke Fellow of Communications, Duke University, 1975-76. Appointments: Visiting Ferris Professor of Journalism and Political Science, Princeton University, 1973-74; Poet Laureate (life), Monahans (Texas) Sandhills Literary Society, 1977-. Publications: Plays: The Kingfish, 1979; The

Best Little Whorehouse in Texas, 1978; Christmas: 1933, 1986; The Night Hank Williams Died, 1988; The Golden Shadows Old West Museum, 1989; The Best Little Whorehouse Goes Public, 1994; Books: The One-Eyed Man, novel, 1966; ...And Other Dirty Stories, 1968; Confessions of a White Racist, 1971; The Old Man and Lesser Mortals, 1974; Of Outlaws, Whores, Conmen, Politicians and Other Artists, 1980; Warning: Writer at Work, 1985; None But a Blockhead, 1986; Because of Lozo Brown, 1988. Contributions to: Harper's; Atlantic Monthly; Life; New Republic; Texas Monthly; Texas Observer; New York; Playboy; Parade; Esquire; Saturday Evening Post; National Geographic; Many others. Literary Agent: Barbara S Blaine, 700 13th Street NW, 7th Floor, NW Washington, DC 20005, USA. Address: 3025 Woodland Drive, NW Washington, DC 20008, USA.

KING Laurie R, b. 19 Sept 1952, Oakland, California, USA. Writer. m. Noel Q King, Nov 1977, 1 son, 1 daughter. Education: BA, University of California, Santa Cruz, 1977; MA, Graduate Theological Union, Berkeley, 1984. Publications: A Grave Talent, 1993; The Beekeeper's Apprentice, 1994; To Play the Fool, 1995. Honours: Grave Talent won Edgar Award for Best First Novel of 1993. Memberships: Mystery Writers of America; Sisters in Crime, Literary Agent: Linda Allen, 1949 Green Street 5, San Francisco, CA 94123, USA. Address: PO Box 1152, Freedom, CA 95019, USA.

KING Michael, b. 15 Dec 1945, Wellington, New Zealand; Writer. m. 17 Oct 1987, 1 son, 1 daughter. Education: BA, Victoria University, 1967; MA 1968, DPhil 1978, Waikato University. Appointments: Katherine Mansfield Fellow, 1976; Writing Fellow, Victoria University, 1983; National Library Fellow, 1990; Fellowship in Humanities, Waikato University, 1991-. Publications: Te Puea, 1977; Maori, 1983; Being Pakeha, 1985; Death of the Rainbow Warrior, 1986; Moriori, 1989. Contributions to: Columnist, and feature writer for variety of newspapers and magazines including New Zealand Listener, New Zealand Sunday Times, Metro. Honours: Feltex Award, 1975; Cowan Prize, 1976; NZ Book Award, 1978; Wattie Book of the Year Prize, 1984, 1990; OBE, 1988; Literary Fund Achievement Award, 1989. Memberships: PEN, New Zealand President, 1979-80; New Zealand Authors Fund Advisory Committee, 1980-92; Frank Sargeson Trust, 1982-; Auckland Institute Museum Council, 1986-91; Chatham Islands Conservation Board, 1990-. Address: PO Box 109, Whangamata, New Zealand.

KING Paul. See: DRACKETT, Philip Arthur (Phil).

KING Ronald, b. 1914, UK. Author. Appointments: Secretary, Royal Botanical Gardens, Kew, London, 1959-76. Publications: World of Kew, 1976; Botanical Illustration, 1978; Quest for Paradise, history of the world's gardens, 1979; Temple of Flora, 1981; Tresco: England's Island of Flowers, 1985; Royal Kew, 1985. Address: Kuranda, Northfield Place, Weybridge, Surrey KT13 ORF, England.

KING Stephen Edwin, (Richard Bachman), b. 21 Sep 1947, Portland, Maine, USA. Author. m. Tabitha J Spruce, 1971, 2 s, 1 d. Education: University of Maine. Appointments: Teacher of English, Hampden Academy, Maine, 1971-73; Writer-in-Residence, University of Maine, Orono, 1978-79. Publications include: Carrie, 1974; Salem's Lot, 1975; The Shining, 1977; The Stand, 1978; The Dead Zone, 1979; Firestarter, 1980; Danse Macabre, 1981; Cujo, 1981; Christine, 1983; Pet Sematery, 1983; The Talisman (with Peter Straub), 1984; Cycle of the Werewolf, 1985; It, 1986; The Eyes of the Dragon, 1987; Misery, 1987; The Tommyknockers, 1987; The Dark Half, 1989; Four Past Midnight, 1990; Needful Things, 1991; Gerald's Game, 1992; Dolores Claiborne, 1993; Insomnia, 1994; The Dark Tower Stories: Volume 1: the Gunslinger, 1982, Volume 2: the Drawing of the Three, 1984; Short story collections: Night Shift, 1978; Different Seasons, 1982; Skeleton Crew, 1985; Nightmares & Dreamscapes, 1993; As Richard Bachman: Thinner, 1984; The Bachman Books: Rage, the Long Walk, Roadwork, The Running Man, 1985; numerous other short stories. Memberships: Authors Guild of America; Screen Artists Guild; Screen Writers of America; Writers Guild. Address: c/o Press Relations, Viking Press, 625 Madison Avenue, New York, NY 10022, USA.

KING Thomas, b. 1943, California, USA. Publications: The Native in Literature, 1987; Medicine River, 1990; All My Relations, ed, 1992; Green Grass, Running Water, 1993; One Good Story, That One: Stories, 1993. Address: c/o Denise Bukowski Agency, 182 Avenue Road Suite 3, Toronto, Ontario, M5K 2J1, Canada.

KING-HELE Desmond George, b. 3 Nov 1927, Seaford, England. Author. Education: BA (Hons) 1948, MA 1952, Trinity College, Cambridge. Appointments: Editor, Notes and Records of the Royal Society, 1989-. Publications include: Shelley: His Thought and Work, 1960, 3rd edition 1984; Satellites and Scientific Research, 1962; Erasmus Darwin, 1963; Satellite Orbits in an Atmosphere, 1964, new edition 1987; Observing Earth Satellites, 1966, new edition 1983; Essential Writings of Erasmus Darwin, 1968; The End of the Twentieth Century? 1970; Poems and Trixies, 1972; Doctor of Revolution, 1977; The Letters of Erasmus Darwin, 1981; Animal Spirits, 1983; Erasmus Darwin and the Romantic Poets, 1986; A Tapestry of Orbits, 1992. Contributions to: Over 400 papers to various journals. Honours: Fellow, Royal Society, 1966; Honorary Degrees: DSc, University of Aston, 1979, D Univ, University of Surrey, 1986; Several Scientific awards. Memberships: Fellow, Institute of Mathematics and Its Applications, since 1964; Fellow, Royal Astronomical Society, since 1966. Address: 7 Hilltops Court, 65 North Lane, Buriton, Hampshire GU31 5RS, England.

KING-SMITH Dick, b. 1922, UK. Freelance Writer; Former Farmer and Teacher. Publications: The Fox Busters, 1978; Daggie Dogfoot, 1980, Us Edition, Pigs Might Fly, 1982; The Mouse Butcher, 1981; Magnus Powermouse, 1982; the Queen's Nose, 1983; the Sheeep-Pig, 1985; Harry's Mad, 1984; Lightning Fred, 1985; Saddlebottom, 1985; Noah's Brother, 1986; Dumpling, 1986; Yob, 1986; Pets For keeps, 1986; E S P, 1986; H Prince, 1986; The Hedgehog, 1987; Tumbleweed, 1987; Friends and Brothers, 1987; Dodos are Forever, 1987; Sophie's Snail, 1988; Emily's Legs, 1988; the Trouble With Edward, 1988; George Speaks, 1988; Martin's Mice, 1988; The Jenius, 1988; The Water Horse, 1990; Ace, 1990; Paddy's Pot of Gold, 1990; Alphabeasts, 1992; The Hodgeheg, 1992; Martin's Mice, 1992. Address: Diamond's Cottage, Queen Charlton, Near Keynsham, Avon BS18 2SJ, England.

KING-SMITH Ronald Gordon, b. 27 Mar 1922, Bitton, Gloucestershire, England. Children's Author. m. Myrle England, 6 Feb, 1943, 1 s, 2 d. Education: Marlborough; BEd, Bristol University. Publications: The Fox Busters, 1978; Daggie Dogfoot, 1980; The Mouse Butcher, 1981; Magnus Powermouse, 1982; The Queen's Nose, 1983; The Sheep-Pig, 1984; Harry's Mad, 1984; Saddlebottom, 1985; Lightning fred, 1985; Pets For Keeps, 1986; Noah's Brother, 1986; ESP, 1986; Yob, 1986; Dumpling, 1986; H Prince, 1986; Tumbleweed, 1987; The Hodgeheg, 1987; Farmer Bungle Forgets, 1987; Friends and Brothers, 1987; Cuckoobush Farm, 1987; Country Watch, 1987; Town Watch, 1987. Honour: the Guardian Award for Children's Fiction, The Sheep-Pig, 1984. Literary Agent: Pamela Todd, A P Watt, London. Address: Diamond's Cottage, Queen Charlton, Keynsham, Avon, England.

KINGDON Robert McCune, b. 1927, USA. Professor; Historian. Appointments include: Professor of History, University of Wisconsin, Madison. Publications: Geneva and the Coming of the Wars of Religion in France, 1956; Registres de la Compagnie des Pasteurs de Génève au temps de Calvin (edited with J-F Bergier), 2 volumes, 1962, 1964; William Cecil: Execution of Justice in England, and William Allen: A True, Sincere and Modest Defence of English Catholics (editor), 1965; Geneva and the Consolidation of the French Protestant Movement, 1967; Calvin and Calvinism: Sources of Democracy (edited with R D Linder), 1970; Théodore de Béze: du droit des magistrats (editor), 1971; Transition and Revolution: Problems and Issues of European Renaissance and Reformation History (editor, contributor), 1974; The Political Thought of Peter Martyr Vermigli, 1980; Church and Society in Reformation Europe, 1985; Myths about the St Bartholomew's Day Massacres, 1988; Jean de Coras, Question politique: s'il est licite aux subjects de capituler avec leur prince (editor), 1989; A Biography of the Works of Peter Vermigli (compiled with John Patrick Donnelly), 1990; Adultery and Divorce in Calvin's Geneva, 1995. Address: Institute for Research in the Humanities, University of Wisconsin, 1401 Observatory Drive, Madison, WI 53706, USA.

KINGMAN Lee, b. 1919, USA. Freelance Writer and Editor. Literary appointment: Children's Book Editor, Houghton Mifflin Co, Boston, Massachusetts, 1944-46. Publications: Pierre Pidgeon, 1943; Ilenka, 1945; The Rocky Summer, 1948; The Best Christmas, 1949; Philippe's Hill, 1950; The Quarry Adventure,, 1951, UK Edition as Lauri's Surprising Summer; Kathy and the Mysterious Statue, 1953; Peter's Long Walk, 1953; Mikko's Fortune, 1955; The Magic Christmas Tree, 1956; The Village Band Mystery, 1956; Flivver, the Heroic Horse, 1958; The House of the Blue Horse, 1960; The Saturday Gang, 1961;

Peter's Pony, 1963; Sheep Ahoy, 1963; Private Eyes, 1964; Newbery and Caldecott Medal Books: 1956-1965 (editor), 1965; The Year of the Raccoon, 1966; The Secret of the Silver Reindeer, 1968; Illustrators of Children's Books: 1957-1966 (edited with J Foster and R G Lontoft), 1968; The Peter Pan Bag, 1970; Georgina and the Dragon, 1971; The Meeting Post: A Story of Lapland, 1972; Escape from the Evil Prophecy, 1973; Newbery and Caldecott Medal Books: 1966-1975 (editor), 1975; Break a Leg, Betsy Maybe, 1976; The Illustrator's Notebook, 1978; Head over Wheels, 1978; Illustrators of Children's Books: 1967-1976 (edited with G Hogarth and H Quimby), 1978; The Refiner's Fire, 1981; The Luck of the Miss L, 1986; Newbery and Caldecott Medal Books: 1976-1985 (editor), 1986; Catch the Baby!, 1990. Address: PO Box 7126, Lanesville, Gloucester, MA 01930, USA.

KINGSTON Maxine Hong, b. 27 Oct 1940, Stockton, California, USA. Writer. m. 23 Nov 1962, 1 s. Education: AB, University of California, Berkeley, 1962, Secondary Teaching Credaential, UC, Berkeley, 1965. Appointments: Variou teaching positions; currently at University of California, Berkeley, 1990. Publications: The Woman Warrior, 1976; China Men, 1980; Hawaii One Summer, 1987; Tripmaster Monkey - His Fake Book, 1989. Contributions to: numerous including: The Iowa Review; American Heritage; English Journal; The Michigan Quarterly; Mother Jones; new York Times; Los Angeles Times. Honours: The National Book Critics Circle Award, 1977; Mademoiselle Magazine Award, 1977; Anisfield-Wolf Race realtions Book Award, 1978; National Endowment for the Arts Writing Fellowship, 1980; Living Treasure of Hawaii, The National Book Award, 1981; Pulitzer Prize Runner-up, 1981; The National Book Critics Circle nominee, 1981; Guggenheim Fellowship, 1981; Stockton Arts Commission Award, 1981; Asian/Pacific Women's Network Woman of the Year, 1981; Hawaii Award for Literature, 1982; The California Council for the Humanities Award, 1985; Honorary DEd, Eastern Michigan University, 1988; Governor's Award for the Arts, California, 1989; PEN USA West Award in Fiction, 1990; American Academy and Institute of Arts and Letters Award, 1990; DHL, honoris causa, Colby College, 1990; Bradeis University National Women's Committee Major Book Collection Award, 1992. Memberships: Authors Guild; PEN American Centre; PEN West; American Academy of Arts & Sciences. Literary Agent: Timothy Schaffer.

KINGTON Miles Beresford, b. 13 May 1941. Humerous Columnist. m. (1) Sarah Paine, 1964, div 1987, 1 s, 1 d, (2) Caroline Maynard, 1987, 1 s. Education: BA, Modern Languages, Trinity College, Oxford. Appointments: Freelance Writer, 1963-; Part-Time Gardener, 1964; Jazz Reviewer, The Times, 1965; joined staff of Punch, 1967, literary editor, 1973-80; Freelance Writer, 1980-; Regular Let's Parler Franglais Column in Punch and Daily Moreover Column in the Times, 1981-87; Member, Musical Group, Instant Sunshine; jazz player, 1970; Daily Columnist, The Independent, 1987-. Publications: World of Alphonse Allais, 1977, reprinted as A Wolf in Frog's Clothing, 1983; 4 Franglais Books, 1979-82; Moreover, Too... 1985; The Franglais Lieutenant's Woman, 1986; Welcome to Kington, 1985; Steaming Through Britain, 1990; Anthology of Jazz (editor), 1992. Address: Lower Hayze, Limpley Stoke, Bath BA3 6HR, England.

KINKAID Matt. See: **ADAMS Clifton**.

KINKLEY Jeffrey Carroll, b. 13 July 1948, Urbana, Illinois, USA. Professor of History. m. Chuchu Kang, 16 May 1981. Education: BA, University of Chicago, 1969; MA, 1971, PhD, 1977, Harvard University. Publications: The Odyssey of Shen Congwen, 1997; After Mao (editor), 1985; Hsio Ch'ien, Traveller Without a Map (translator), 1990; Chen Xuezhao, Surviving the Storm (editor), 1990; Modern Chinese Writers (co-editor), 1992. Memberships: Assistant Editor, China, Journal of Asian Studies; Editorial Board, Clear, Republican China. Address: 8 Laurel Lane, Bernardsville, NJ 07924, USA.

KINNELL Galway, b. 1 Feb 1927, Providence, Rhode Island, USA. Writer. m. Ines Delgado de Torres, 1965, 1 son, 1 daughter. Education: Princeton University. Publications: Poetry: What a Kingdom It Was, 1960; Flower Herding on Mount Monadnock, 1963; Body Rags, 1966; The Book of Nightmares, 1971; The Avenue Bearing the Initial of Christ into the New World, 1974; Mortal Acts, Mortal Words, 1980; Selected Poems, 1982; The Past, 1985; When One Has Lived A Long Time Alone, 1990; Imperfect Thirst, 1994; The Poems of François Villon, translation, 1965; Black Light, novel, 1966; On the Motion and Immobility of Douve, 1968; The Lackawanna Elegy, 1970; Interviews: Walking Down the Stairs, 1977; How the Alligator Missed His Breakfast, children's story, 1982; The Essential Whitman (editor), 1987.

Honours: Award, National Institute of Arts and Letters, 1962; Cecil Hemley Poetry Prize, 1969; Medal of Merit, 1975; Pulitzer Prize, 1983; American Book Award, 1983; MacArthur Fellowship, 1984. Memberships: PEN; Poetry Society of America; Modern Language Association. Address: RFD, Sheffield, VT 05866, USA.

KINNEY Arthur F(rederick), b. 5 Sept 1933, Courtland, New York, USA. Author; Editor; Teacher. Education: AB magna cum laude, Syracuse University, 1955; MA, Columbia University, 1956; PhD, University of Michigan, 1963. Appointments: Editor, English Literary Renaissance, 1971-; Editor, Twayne English Authors Series in the Renaissance, 1973-; President, Renaissance English Text Society, 1985-; Editor, Massachusetts Studies in Early Modern Culture; Thomas W Copeland Professor of Literary History, University of Massachusetts, Amherst. Publications include: Humanist Poetics, 1986; John Skelton, Priest as Poet, 1987; Continental Humanist Poetics, 1989; Renaissance Historicism, 1989; Elizabethan Backgrounds, 1990; Rogues, Vagabonds, and Sturdy Beggars, 1990. Contributions to: Renaissance Quarterly; Huntington Library Quarterly; Shakespeare Quarterly; Southern Review; Southern Quarterly; English Literary History; Modern Philology, Journal of English and Germanic Philology; Shakespeare Studies; Shakespeare Survey; Others. Honours: Avery and Jules Hopwood Major Award in Criticism; Bread Loaf Scholar in Fiction and Criticism; Fulbright-Hays Scholar; Senior Fellow: National Endowment for the Humanities, twice; Huntington Library, 3 times; Folger Shakespeare Library, twice. Memberships: Conference of Editors of Learned Journals, President 1971-73, 1980-82; Board Member and Consultant to many journals and publishers. Literary Agent: Elizabeth McKee. Address: 25 Hunter Hill Drive, Amherst, MA 01002, USA.

KINSELLA Thomas, b. 4 May 1928, Dublin, Ireland. Professor; Poet. Appointments include: Professor, Temple University, PA, 1970; Artistic Director, Lyric Players Theatre, Belfast. Publications include: The Starlit Eye, 1952; Three Legendary Sonnets, 1952; Another September, 1958; Downstream, 1962; Wormwood, 1966; Nightwalker, 1967; Tear, 1969; A Selected Life, 1972; Notes from the Land of the Dead and Other Poems, 1972; New Poems, 1973; Vertical Man, 1973; The Good Fight, 1973; The Messenger, 1978; Fifteen Dead, 1979; Peppercanister Poems, 1972-78, 1979; One Fond Embrace, 1981; Her Vertical Smile, 1985; Out of Ireland, 1987; St Catherine's Clock, 1987; Blood and Family, 1988; Personal Places, 1990; Madonna and other poems, 1991; Open Court, 1991; From Centre City, poems, 1990-1994, 1994; Editor and Translator. Honours include: D Litt, National University of Ireland, Dublin, 1984. Address: Killalane, Laragh, County wicklow, Ireland.

KINZIE Mary, b. 30 Sep 1944, Montgomery, Alabama, USA. Poet; Teacher. Education: MA, 1972, PhD, 1980, English, MA, Writing Seminars, 1970, Johns Hopkins University; Ba, German, Northwestern University, 1967. Appointments: Executive Editor, Triquarterly Magazine, 1975-78; Instructor, 1975-78, Lecturer, English, 1978-85, Director, English Major in Writing, 1979-, Associate Professor, English, 1985-, Professor, 1990-, Northwestern University. The Threshold of the Year (original verse), 1982; Masked Women and Summers of Vietnam, verse, 1990; Qutumn Eros, verse, 1992; essays, Poems, articles and reviews in literary periodicals. Honours: Fulbright Scholarship, 1967-68; Illinois Arts Council Award in Poetry, 1981; Devins Award, University of Missouri Press, 1982; IAC Essay Award in Poetry, 1984; Guggenheim Fellowship in Poetry, 1986. Memberships: PEN; Poetry Society of America; Society of Midland Authors. Address: English Dept, University Hall 102, Northwestern University, Evanston, IL 60201, USA.

KIPPENHAHN Rudolf, b. 24 May 1926, Barringen, Czechoslovakia. Astronomer. m. 19 Sept 1955, 3 daughters. Education: Studies in mathematics in Halle and Erlangen, 1945-51, Diploma, 1950, PhD, 1951. Publications: 100 Billion Suns, 1983; Light from the Depth of Time, 1987; Bound to the Sund, 1990; Stellar Structure and Evolution, 1990; Der Stern von dem wir leben, 1990; Abenteuer Weltall, 1991; Elementare Plasmaphysik, 1975. Contributions to: Artronomy and Astrophysics; Bild der Wissenschaft, among others. Honours: Carus Preis der Stadt Schweinfurt Lorenz Oken Medaille. Memberships: International Astron Union, Vice President 1991; Royal Astron Society, Associate. Address: Rautenbreite 2, 37077 Gottingen, Germany.

KIRK Geoffrey Stephen, b. 1921, United Kingdom. Classicist; Professor Emeritus. Appointments: Reader, 1958-64, Regius Professor

of Greek, 1973-; Currently Regius Emeritus Professor of Greek, Cambridge University; Professor of Classics: Yale University, New Haven, Connecticut, USA, 1965-71; University of Bristol, England, 1971-73. Publications: Heraclitus: The Cosmic Fragments (editor), 1952; The Presocratic Philosophers (with J E Raven), 1956; The Songs of Homer, 1962; The Language and Background of Homer (editor), 1964; Euripides: Bacchae (editor and translator), 1970; Myth, 1970; The Nature of Greek Myths, 1974; Homer and the Oral Tradition, 1977; The Ilad: A Commentary, vol I 1985, vol II 1990. Honour: Corresponding Fellow, Academy of Athens, 1993. Address: 12 Sion Hill, Bath, Avon BA1 2UH, England.

KIRK Michael. See: KNOX William.

KIRK Philip. See: LEVINSON Leonard.

KIRK Russell, b. 19 Oct 1918, Plymouth, Michigan, USA. Writer; Editor. m. Annette Courtemanche, 19 Sep 1964, 4 d. Education: BA, Michigan State University, 1940; MA, Duke University, 1941; DLH, St Andrews University, Scotland, 1952. Appointments: Editor, Modern Age, 1957-59; Editor, The University Bookman, 1960-; Director, Social Science Programme, Educational Research Council of America, 1979-84. Publications: The Conservative Mind, 1953; Eliot and His Age, 1971; The Roots of American Order, 1974; Edmund Burke, 1967; Old House of Fear, 1961; the Conservative Constitution, 1990; Randolph of Roanoke; St Andrews; Prospects for Conservatives; Enemies of the Permanent Things; the Intemperate Professor. Contributions to: Fortune; Yale Review; Modern Age; National Review; Chronicles; Sewanee Review; Kenyon Review; Society; Contemporary Review; Fortnightly. Honours: Christopher Award, 1971; Weaver Prize of Ingersoll Awards, 1983; Constitutional Fellowship, National Endowment For The Humanities, 1985; Presidential Citizens Medal, 1989. Literary Agent: Kirby Macauley, 432 Park Avenue South, New York, NY 10016, USa. Address: PO Box 4, Mecosta, MI 49332, USA.

KIRK-GREENE Anthony (Hamilton Millard), b. 16 May 1925 United Kingdom. University Lecturer in Modern African History; Fellow, St Antony's College, Oxford. Literary Appointments: Editorial Advisor, Journal of African Administration, 1960-70; Editorial Advisor, Cultures & Development, 1970-80; Editor Advisor, African Affairs, 1980-; Series Editor, Africana (Holmes & Meier), 1970-80; Co-Editor, Hoover Colonial Series, 1975-80; General Editor, Studies in African History, 1970-75; General Editor, Africana Revivals, 1990-; Series Editor, Radcliffe Press, 1990-. Appointments: Director, Foreign Service Programme, Oxford University, 1986-90. Publications: Adamawa Past and Present, 1958; The Cattle People of Nigeria (with Caroline Sassoon), 1959; The River Niger (with Caroline Sassoon), 1961; Barth's Travels in Nigeria, 1962; Principles of Native Administration in Nigeria, 1965; The Making of Northern Nigeria (editor), 1965; The Emirates of Northern Nigeria (with S J Hogben), 1966; Hausa Proverbs, 1966; A Modern Hausa Reader (with Y Aliyu), 1967; Lugard and the Amalgamation of Nigeria, 1968; Language and People of Bornu (editor), 1968; Crisis and Conflict in Nigeria, 1971; West African Narratives (with P Newman), 1972; Gazetteers of Northern Nigeria (editor), 1972; Teach Yourself Hausa (with C H Kraft), 1973; The Concept of the Good Man in Hausa, 1974; Nigeria Faces North (with Pauline Ryan), 1975; The Transfer of Power in Africa (editor), 1978; Stand by Your Radios: The Military in Tropical Africa, 1980; Biographical Dictionary of the British Colonial Governor, 1981; Nigeria since 1970 (with D Rimmer), 1981; The Sudan Political Service: A Profile, 1982; Margery Perham: West African Passage (editor), 1983; Pastoralists of the Western Savanna (with Mahdi Adamu), 1986; Margery Perham: Pacific Prelude (editor), 1988; The Sudan Political Service: A Preliminary Register of Second Careers (with Sir Gawain Bell), 1989; A Biographical Dictionary of the British Colonial Service, 1939-66, 1991. Contributions to: Dictionary of National Biography; Encyclopaedia Brit; numerous journals. Honours: MBE, 1963; Hans Wolff Memorial Lecturer, 1973; FRHist, 1985. Memberships: Royal African Society; International African Institute; African Studies Association of England, President, 1989-91; Festschrift: Essays in Honour of Anthony Kirk-Greene, 1993. Address: c/o St Antony's College, Oxford, OX2 6JF, England.

KIRKPATRICK Sidney Dale, b. 4 Oct 1955. Writer; Film Maker. m. 26 Nov 1983, 2 sons. Education: BA, Hampshire College, Amherst, 1978; MFA, New York University, 1982. Appointment: Reader, Huntington Library. 1992. Publications: A Cast of Killers, 1986; Turning the Tide, 1991; Lords of Sipan, 1992. Contributions to: Los Angeles Times; American Film. Honours: Winner, American Film Festival, 1982. Membership: PEN Center West, Board of Directors 1991-92. Literary

Agent: Tim Seldes, Russell and Volkening, New York City, USA. Address: c/o Tim Seldes, Russell and Volkening, 50 W 29th Street, New York, NY 10001, USA.

KIRKUP James, (James Falconer, Andrew James, Ivy B Summerforest, Jun Terehata, Shig eru Tsuyuki), b. 23 Apr 1918, South Shields, England. Writer; Playwright; Broadcaster. Education: BA, FRSL; Durham University; Gregory Fellow, Poetry, Leeds University, 1950-52. Publications include: The Cosmic Shape, 1947; The Droned Sailor, 1948; The Creation, 1950; The Submerged Village, 1951; A Correct Compassion, 1952; A Spring Journey, 1954; Upon This Rock, The Dark Child, The Trump of Harmony, 1955; the True Mystery of the Nativity, Ancestral Voices, The Radiance of the King, 1956; The Descent Into The Cave, The Only Child (autobiography), 1957; The Peach Garden, Two Pigeons Flying High (TV Plays), Sorrows, Passions and Alarms (autobiography), 1960; the Love of Others (novel), 1962; Tropic Temper (travel), 1963; Refusal to Conform, Last and First Poems, 1963; The Heavenly Mandate, 1964; Japan Industrial Volumes 1 and II, 1964-65; Tokyo, 1966; Bangkok, 1967; Filipinescas, 1968; One Man's Russia, 1968; Streets of Asia, 1969; Hong Kong, 1969; Japan Behind the Fan, 1970; Insect Summer (novel), 1971; Brand (Ibsen), 1972; Peer Gynt, 1973; Play Strindberg, 1974; The Conformer, 1975; Don Carlos, 1975; Scenes From Sutcliffe, 1981; Ecce Homo: My Pasolini, 1981; To The Unknown God, 1982; The Bush Toads, 1982; Folktales Japanesque, 1982; The Glory That Was Greece, 1984; Hearn in My Heart, 1984; operas: An Actor's Revenge, 1979; Friends in Arms, Shunkinsho, 1980; No More Hiroshimas, 1982; The Damask Drum, 1984; The Sense of the Visit: New Poems, 1984; Trends and Traditions, 1985; Dictionary of Body Language, 1985; English With a Smile, 1986; Fellow Feelings (poems), 1986; Portraits and Souvenirs, 1987; The Mystery and the Magic of Symbols, 1987; The Cry of the Owl: Native American Folktales and Legends, 1987; I of All People: An Autobiography of Youth, 1988; The Best of Britain: Essays, 1989; First Fireworks, 1992; A Room in The Woods, 1991; Shooting Stars, 1992; Notes for an Autobiography, 1992; A Poet Could Not But Be Gay, autobiography, 1992; Gaijin on the Ginza, novel, 1992; Queens have Died Young and Fair, novel, 1993; Me All Over: Memoirs of a Misfit, autobiography, 1993; Words for Contemplation; Mantras, Poems, 1993; Look at This Way, poems for children, 1993; others; numerous poems, plays and essays and translations from French, German, Japanese, Italian and Norwegian. Honours: Numerous awards including: Scott-Moncrieff Prize for Translation, 1992; JAI Foudation Grant, 1993. Memberships: numerous professional organisations; President The British Haiku Society. Address: c/o British Monomarks, Box 2780, London, WC1N 3XX, England.

KIRTLAND G T. See: JOSLIN Sesyle.

KISS Iren, b. 25 Sept 1947, Budapest, Hungary. Writer; University Professor. m. Laszlo Tabori, 10 June 1988. Education: PhD, History of Literature, Budapest University, 1992. Publications: Szelcsend, poems, 1977; Allokep, novel, 1978; Arkadiat Tatarozxzak, poems, 1979; Maganrecept (cycle), 1982; Kemopera, plays, 1988. Contributions to: Elet es Irodalom; Nagyvilag; Kortars; Hitel Eletunk; In Italy - Bollettario; Invarianti; per Approssimazione. Honours: Yeats Club Award, 1987; Golden Medal of the Brianza World Competition of Poetry, Italy, 1988. Memberships: Association of the Hungarian Writers; Hungarian PEN. Literary Agent: Anita Kenedi, Hungarian Artis Jus. Address: Somloi ut 60/B, Budapest 1118, Hungary.

KISS Karoly, b. 22 Aug 1930, Mako, Budapest, Hungary. Writer; Poet; Columnist. m. 27 Aug 1982, 2 sons. Education: BA Economics, Karoly Marx Economics University, 1969. Appointments: Staff, Daily Magyar Nemzet, 1973-87; Editor, Budapest (monthly), 1987-89, Hid (quarterly), 1989-. Publications: Songs about Zrinyi, 1956; Songs about Hunyadi, 1956; Girl of Kosovo, 1957; Memory of Mohacs, 1976; Prey of Destruction, 1982. Memberships: Hungarian Writers Association; PEN Club. Literary Agent: Magyar Irodalmi Lexikon, Budapest. Address: Lajos u 116, Budapest 1036, Hungary.

KISSINGER Henry Alfred, b. 27 May 1923, Furth, Germany. US Citizen. Company Director. m. (1) Anne Fleischer, 1949, 1 son, 1 daughter, (2) Nancy Maginnes, 30 Mar 1974. Education: BA summa cum laude, Harvard College, 1950; MA, 1952, PhD, 1954, Harvard University. Appointments: US Secretary of State, 1973-77; Assistant to US President, for National Security Affairs, 1969-75; Chairman, National Bipartisan Commission on Central America, 1983-85; Member: President's Foreign Intelligence Advisory Board, 1984-90; Commission on Integrated Long-Term Strategy, National Security Council and Defence Department, 1986-88; Currently: Chairman, Kissinger Associates Inc; Counsellor to Chase Manhattan Bank and Center for Strategic and International Studies; Chairman, International Advisory Board, American International Group Inc; Member, Board of Directors, several companies. Publications: A World Restored: Castlereagh, Metternich and the Restoration of Peace 1812-1822, 1957; Nuclear Weapons and Foreign Policy, 1957; The Necessity for Choice: Prospects of American Foreign Policy, 1961; The Troubled Partnership: An Reappraisal of the Atlantic Alliance, 1965; Problems of National Strategy: A Book of Readings (editor), 1965; American Foreign Policy, Three Essays, 1969; White House Years, 1979; For the Record: Selected Statements 1977-1980, 1981; Years of Upheaval, 1982; Observations: Selected Speeches and Essays 1982-1984, 1985; Diplomacy, 1994. Contributions to: Numerous publications including Los Angeles Times Syndicate; National and international newspapers. Honours: Nobel Peace Prize, 1973; Presidential Medal of Freedom, 1977; Medal of Liberty, 1986. Memberships include: Honorary Governor, Foreign Policy Association. Literary Agent: International Creative Management, 40 W 57th Street, New York, NY 10019, USA. Address: 1800 K Street NW, Suite 400, Washington DC, USA.

KITCHEN Herbert (Bert) Thomas, b. 24 Apr 1940, Liverpool, England. Artist; Illustrator; Author. m. Muriel Chown, 2 Apr 1960, 2 daughters. Education: London Central School of Arts & Craft, 1958-61. Publications: Mythical Creatures; Tenrecs Twigs; Somewhere Today; Animal Alphabet; Animal Numbers; Gorilla/Chinchilla; Pig in a Barrow; And So They Build, 1993; When Hunger Calls, 1994. Memberships: The Society of Authors. Literary Agent: Gina Pollinger. Address: 222 Old Brompton Road, London SW5 0BZ, England.

KITCHEN Martin, b. 21 Dec 1936, Nottingham, England. University Professor. Education: BA, Hons, 1963; PhD, 1966, School of Slavonic and East European Studies, University of London. Publications include: British Policy towards the Soviet Union during the Second World War, 1986; Europe Between the Wars, 1988; The Political Econmy of Germany 1815-1914, 1978; Fascism, 1976; The Silent Dictatorship, 1976; The German Officer Corps 1890-1914, 1968. Contributions to: International History Review; Central European History; Journal of the History of Ireas; Military Affairs; Slavonic Review; others. Honours: Fellow, Royal Society of Canada; Royal Historical Society; Moncado Prize, American Military Academy, 1978. Address: Department of History, Simon Fraser University, Burnaby, BC, Canada.

KITCHENER Michael. See: KELLEHER Victor.

KITEL Patricia, b. 2 Feb 1940, New York, USA. Writer. 4 d. Education: BA, Rehabilitation Science, 1961; Biology Certificate, 1972; MS, Mass Communication and Journalism, 1982. Appointments: Staff, California State University, Journalism Department, 1983-84; Staff, Ohlone College, Journalism Department, 1984-87. Publications include: How to be Successfully Interviewed By the Press, 1982; Interview Tips and Tricks, 1983; How to Self-Promote Your Book, 1983; Writing Fast Fun-Money Fillers, 1985; Controlling Lawn and Garden Insects, 1987; Syndicating Your Column, 1987. Contributions to: Over 1000 articles, short stories etc in numerous publications including: Highlights for Children, Bronx Botanical Garden Magazine, San Francisco Chronicle, San Jose Mercury, Writer's Digest. Honours: Stanford CWC Short Story Award, 1977; Romance Writers Award, 1984; Garden Writers of America Merit Award, 1988, 1989. Memberships: Sigma Delta Chi; Society of Children's Book Writers; Writer's Connection; Vice President, National Society of Newspaper Columnists, 1986-88; Entomological Society of America; Pacific Coast Entomological Society; Garden Writers Association; Northern California Science Writers Association. Address: PO Box 8318, Fremont, CA 94537, USA.

KITT Tamara. See: DE REGNIERS Beatrice Schenk.

KITTEREDGE William Alfred, b. 14 Aug 1932, Portland, Oregon, USA. Professor, 1 s, 1 d. Education: BS Agriculture, Oregon State University, 1953; MFA, University of Iowa, 1969. Appointments: Professor of English, University of Montana, 1969-. Publications: The Van Gogh Field, 1979; We Are Not in This Together, 1984; Owning It All, 1984; Hole in the Sky, 1992. Contributions to: Harpers; Atlantic; Esquire; Paris Review; Triquarterly; others. Honours: Governor's Award for Literature, Montana, 1987; Humanist of the Year, Montana, 1988. Address: English University of Montana, Missoula, MT 59801, USA.

KIZER Carolyn, b. Spokane, Washington, USA. Poet. Career: Founder of Poetry Northwest, 1959; First Literature Program Director, National Endowment for the Arts; Poet-in-Residence at numerous universities. Publications: Yin, 1984; Mermaids in the Basement, 1984; The Nearness of You, 1986; Prozes, 1993. Contributions to: Quarry West; Denver Quarterly; Willow Springs. Honours: Pulitzer Prize, 1985; Theodore Roetuke Prize, 1988. Address: 19722 Eighth St East, Sonoma, CA 95476, USA.

KLAPPERT Peter, b. 14 Nov 1942, Rockville Center, New York, USA. Poet; Educator. Education: BA, Cornell University, 1964; MA, 1967, MFA, 1968, University of Iowa. Appointments: Instructor, Rollins College, 1968-71; Briggs-Copeland Lecturer, Harvard University, Cambridge, Massachusetts, 1971-74; Visiting Lecturer, New College, Florida, 1972; Writer in Residence, 1976-77, Assistant Professor, 1977-81, Director, Graduate Writing Programme, 1979-80, College of William and Mary; Associate Professor, 1981-91, Director, Graduate Writing Programme, 1985-88, Professor, 1991-, George Mason University, Fairfax, Virginia. Publications: Lugging Vegetables to Nantucket, 1971; Circular Stairs, Distress in the Mirrors, 1975; Non Sequitur O'Connor, 1977; The Idiot Princess of the Last Dynasty, 1984; 52 Pick-up; Scenes from The Conspiracy, A Documentary, 1984; Internal Foreigner, audio-cassette, 1984. Contributions to: Antaeus; The Atlantic Monthly; Harper's; American Poetry Review; Agni Review; Ploughshares; Missouri Review; Paris Review; Parnassus; Poetry in Review. Address: MS 3E4, Department of English, George Mason University, Fairfax, VA 22030, USA.

KLASS Perri Elizabeth, b. 29 Apr 1958, Trinidad. Pediatrician; Writer. 1 s, 1 d. Education: AB, magna cum laude, Biology, Radcliffe College, Harvard University, 1979; MD, Harvard Medical School, 1986. Publications: Recombinations (novel), 1985; I Am Having An Adventure (short stories), 1986; A Not Entirely Benign Procedure (essays), 1987; Other Women's Children (novel), 1990. Contributions to: Numerous magazines and journals including: The New York Times Magazine; Massachusetts Medicine; Discover; Vogue; Glamour; Esquire; Boston Globe Magazine; Mademoiselle; Triquarterly; North American Review. Memberships: PEN; Media Spokesperson; American Academy of Pediatrics; American Medical Women's Association; Massachusetts Medical Society; Tilling Society. Literary Agent: Maxine Groffsky. Address: Department of Pediatric Infectious Diseases, Maxwell Finland Building, Boston City Hospital, Boston, MA 02118, USA.

KLEIN Alexander, b. 1923, Hungary. US Citizen. Writer. Appointments: Consultant, Theatre for Ideas and Common Cause; Co-Founder, Arden House Annual Convocations on Foreign Policy, 1947-; Adjunct Professor, History, Political Science, Sociology, Fordham University, New York, 1970-77; Director of Public Relations, CARE World Headquarters, 1972-82. Publications: Armies for Peace, 1950; Courage is the Key, 1953; The Empire City, Grand Deception, 1955; The Counterfeit Traitor, 1958; The Double Dealers, 1959; The Fabulous Rogues, 1960; The Magnificent Scoundrels, 1961; Rebels, Rogues, Rascals, 1962; That Pellett Woman!, 1965; Natural Enemies? Youth and the Clash of Generations, 1969; Dissent, Power and Confrontation, 1972; Black Banana (co-author), 1974, filmed as Shalom, Baby!, 1975; The Savage, 1975. Address: 75 Bank Street, Apartment 3A, New York, NY 10014, USA.

KLEIN Theodore Eibon Donald, b. 15 July 1947, New York City, New York, USA. Writer; Editor. Education: AB, Brown University, 1969; MFA, Columbia University, 1972. Literary appointments: Editor-in-chief: Brown Daily Herald, 1968, Twilight Zone magazine, 1981-85, Crime Beat magazine, 1991-93. Publications: The Ceremonies, novel, 1984; Dark Gods, story collection, 1985. Contributions to: Sunday features, New York Times; New York Daily News; Washington Post Book World; Film column, Night Cry Magazine; Writer's Digest. Honours: Phi Beta Kappa, 1969; Award for Best Novel, British Fantasy Society, 1985; Award for Best Novella, World Fantasy, 1986. Membership: Arthur Machen Society. Literary Agents: Kirby McCauley, USA; Leslier Gardner, UK. Address: 210 West 89th Street, New York, NY 10024, USA.

KLEIN Zachary, b. 6 July 1948, New Jersey, USA. Writer. 2 sons. Education: Hillel Academy, Jewish Educational Centre, Mirrer Yeshia; University of Wisconsin. Publications: Still Among the Living, 1990; Two Way Toll, 1991; No Saving Grace, 1994. Honours: Notable Book of 1990, New York Times; Editors Choice, Drood Review. Literary Agent: Herb Katz and Nancy Katz. Address: 5 Oakview Terace, Boston, MA 02130, USA.

KLIAFA Maroula, b. 24 Mar 1937, Trikala, Greece. Author. m. Constantine Kliafas, 20 May 1961, 2 s. Education: Diplome d'Etudes Superieures, French Institute, Athens, 1976; Diploma, Journalism, 1970. Publications: The Ray of The Sun, 1974; Storks Will Come Again, 1976; Tales of Thessaly, 1977; Let's Play Again, 1979; A Tree in Our Yard, 1980; Thessaly 1881-1981: A Hundred Years' Life, 1983; People Are Bored With Reading Sad Stories, 1986; Translations from French into Greek. Contributions to: Numerous magazines and journals. Honours: Award, Greek Children's Book Circle, 1974; Michaela Averof Award, Greek Authors Society, 1982; List of Honour, IX Premio Europeo di Litteratura Giovanile, Provinica di Trenton, 1983; Greek Academy Award, 1983. Memberships: Greek Children's Book Circle; Film Club of Trikala. Address: 10 Omirou Street, GR 42100 Trikala, Greece.

KLIMA Ivan, b. 14 Sep 1931, Prague, Czechoslovakia. Writer. m. Helena Mala-Klimova, 24 Sep 1958, 1 s, 1 d. Education: Master's Degree, Czech Language and Esthetics, Philosophy Faculty, Chales University, Prague, 1956. Literary Appointments: Editor, Ceskoslovensky spisorvatel, Publishing House, 1958-63; Editor, Literary Weeklies: Literarni noviny, 1963-67; Literarni Listy, 1968; Listy, 1968-69; Visiting Professor, Slavic Department, Ann Arbor, MI, USA, 1969-70; Freelance Author publishing abroad, 1970-89. Publications include: Laska a Smeti (English: Love and Garbage, 1990), 1987; Soudce z milosti (English: Judge on Trial), 1987; Plays: Zamek (English: The Castle), 1964; The Master (English version, 1970), 1967; The Sweetshop Myriam (English version, 1969), 1968; President and The Angel, English version, 1975; Klara and The Two Men (English version, 1969), 1968; Bridegroom for Marcela (English version, 1969), 1968; The Games (English version, 1985), 1975; Kafka and Felice, 1986; Moje Zlata Remesla (English: My Golden Trades), 1992. Contributions to: Various magazines in various countries including: New York Review of Books; National; Granta; Index on Censorship. Honours: Hostovsky Award, NY, 1985. Memberships: Union of Czechoslovak Writers, Central Committee, 1963-70; Executive President, Czech PEN Centre, 1990-; Council Member, Czech Writers, 1989-. Literary Agents: Adam Bromberg, Stockholm, Sweden; Theatre Agent: Projeklt Köln Brd.

KLINE Suzy Weaver, b. 27 Aug 1943, Berkeley, California, USA. Teacher; Children's Author. m. Rufus Kline, 12 Oct 1968, 2 daughters. Education: BA, University of California, Berkeley; Standard Teachers Credential, California State University. Publications: Shhhh!, 1984; Don't Touch, 1985; Herbie Jones, 1985; What's the Matter with Herbie Jones, 1986; Herbie Jones and the Monster Ball, 1988; Horrible Harry in Room 2B, 1988; Ooops, 1988; The Hole Book, 1989; Horrible Harry and the Green Slime, 1989; Horrible Harry and the Ant Invasion, 1989; Herbie Jones and the Hamburger head, 1989; Orp, 1989; Orp and the Chop Suey Burgers, 1990; Horrible Harry's Secret, 1990; Horrible Harry's Christmas Surprise, 1991; Orp Goes to the Hoop, 1991; Herbie Jones and the Dark Attic, 1992; Herbie Jones Reader's Theater, 1992; Horrible Harry and the Kickball Wedding, 1992; Mary Marony and the Snake, 1992; Mary Marony Hides Out, 1993; Herbie Jones and the Birthday Showdown, 1993; Song Lee in Room 2B, 1993; Who's Orp's Girlfriend?, 1993; Mary Marony, Mummy Girl, 1994. Address: 124 Hoffman Street, Torrington, CT 06790, USA.

KLINKOWITZ Jerome, b. 24 Dec 1943, Milwaukee, Wisconsin, USA. Author. m. (1) Elaine Plaszynski, 29 Jan 1966, (2) Julie Huffman, 27 May 1978, 1 son, 1 daughter. Education: BA, 1966, MA, 1967, Marquette University; University Fellow, 1968-69, PhD, 1970, University of Wisconsin. Appointments: Assistant Professor, English, Northern Illinois University, 1969-70; Associate Professor, English, 1972-75, Professor, 1975-, University Distinguished Scholar, 1985-, University of Northern Iowa. Publications: Literary Disruptions, 1975; The Life of Fiction, 1977; The American 1960s, 1980; Kurt Vonnegut, 1982; Peter Handke and the postmodern Transformation, 1983; The Self Apparent Word, 1984; Literary Subversions, 1985; The New American Novel of Manners, 1986; Rosenberg/Barthes/Hassan: The Postmodern Habit of Thought, 1988; Short Season and Other Stories, 1988; Their Finest Hours: Narratives of the RAF and Luftwaffe in World War II, 1989; Slaughterhouse-Five: Reinventing the Novel and the World, 1990; Listen: Gerry Mulligan/An Aural Narrative in Jazz, 1991; Donald Barthelme: An Exhibition, 1991; Writing Baseball, 1991; Structuring the Void, 1992; Basepaths, 1995. Contributions to: Over 250 essays to Partisan Review, New Republic, The Nation, American Literature; Short stories to North American Review, Chicago Tribune, The San Francisco Chronicle. Honours: National Endowment for the Arts/PEN Syndicated Fiction Prizes, 1984, 1985. Memberships: PEN

American Center; Modern Language Association. Literary Agent: Nat Sobel, 146 East 19th Street, New York, NY 10003-2404, USA. Address: 1904 Clay Street, Cedar Falls, IA 50613, USA.

KLOTER Eduard J, b. 21 July 1926, Basle, Switzerland. Physician; Medical Doctor. m. Cornelia Vogt, 1 Aug 1956, 3 sons, 2 daughters. Education: Matura Basle, 1945; Studies, Vienna & Basle University, MD, 1951; Dr.med, 1951; Postgraduate, Thun-Bern-London-Basle; FHM Allgem Med; Private Surgery, 1956-85; District Medical Health Officer, temporary medical delegate of ICRC. Publications: Mit Den Menschen Sein - Texte Eines Ikrk-Arztes, 1985; Dabei-dazwischen-daneben, 1988; Skizzen aus Kabul, 1989; Befindlichkeiten - empfindlichkeiten, 1992; Glost und Gluegt, 1993; Die Verkehrskranke Stadt und ihre Kinder, 1991. Contributions to: Die Region; Nebelspalter; Entlebucher Brattig, ASEM-Almanach. Honours: Gold Medal ASEM, 1986; Premio Cesare Pavese, 1988; Medaille du Centre Mondial de la Paix et des Droits de l'Homme, 1990. Memberships: ISDE; IPPNW; Lions; Innerschweizer Schriftsteller Verein; PEN Schweiz; Aerzte Schriftsteller Verein Schweiz; UMEM (Union Mondiale des Ecrivains Médecins); Address: Kreuzbühlweg 18, CH-6045 Meggen, Lucerne, Switzerland.

KNAAK Richard Allen, b. 28 May 1961, Chicago, Illinois, USA. Author. Education: Bachelor's degree (LAS), Rhetoric, University of Illinois. Publications: The Legend of Huma, 1988; Firedrake, 1989; Ice Dragon, 1989; Kaz the Minotaur, 1990; Wolfhelm, 1990; Shadow Steed, 1990; The Shrouded Realm, 1991; Children of the Drake, 1991; Dragon Tome, 1992; The Crystal Dragon, 1993; King of the Grey, 1993; The Dragon Crown, 1994; Frostwing, 1995. Membership: Science Fiction and Fantasy Writers of America. Literary Agent: Peekner Literary Agency. Address: PO Box 8158, Bartlett, IL 60103, USA.

KNECHT Robert Jean, b. 20 Sept 1926, London, England. Emeritus Professor of French History. m. (1) Sonia Hodge, 8 Aug 1956, (2) Maureen White, 28 July 1986. Education: BA 1948, MA 1953, Kings College, London; DLitt, Birmingham, 1984. Publications: The Voyage of Sir Nicholas Carewe, 1959; Francis I, 1982; French Renaissance Monarchy, 1984; The French Wars of Religion, 1989; Francis I and Absolute Monarchy, 1969; The Fronde, 1975; Richelieu, 1991; Renaissance Warrior and Patron, 1994. Contributions to: Times Literary Supplement; English Historical Review; History; Journal of Ecclesiastical History; Bulletin Monumental; and others. Memberships: Society of Renaissance Studies, Chairman 1989-92; FR Historical Society; Societe de l'Histoire de France. Address: 79 Reddings Road, Moseley, Birmingham B13 8LP, England.

KNEVITT Charles Philip Paul, b. 10 Aug 1952, Dayton, OH, USA, British. Journalist. m. Lucy Joan Isaacs, 4 Jun 1981, 1 d. Education: BA, Honours, School of Architecture, University of Manchester. Literary Appointments: Freelance Journalist, 1974-; Editor, What's New in Building, 1978-80; Architecture Correspondent, Sunday Telegraph, 1980-84; The Times, 1984-; Architecture and Planning Consultant, Thames News, Thames Television, 1983-86. Publications: Manikata, 1980; Editor, Connections, 1984; Editor, Monstrous Carbuncles, 1985; Space on Earth, 1985; Perspectives, 1986; Community Architecture (with Nick Wates), 1987; Co-editor, Architectural Anecdotes, 1988. Contributions to: Guardian; Daily Telegraph; Architects' Journal; Architectural Review; Building; Building Design. Honours: Architectural Journalist of The Year, IBP, 1984; Special Commendation for Manikata (Interarch), 1983; Commendation, Young Writer of The Year, IBP, 1978; Student Travel Award, Manchester Society of Architects, 1974. Memberships: Fellow, Royal Society of Arts, 1987; Architecture Club, 1985, Honorary Treasurer, 1986-; International Building Press, 1977, Executive Committee, 1977-80, Honorary Treasurer, 1978-80. Address: Crest House, 102-104 Church Road, Teddington, Middlesex, TW11 8PY, England.

KNIGHT Alanna, b. South Shields, Tyne and Wear, England. Novelist; Biographer. m. Alexander Harrow Knight, 2 s. Education: Fellow, Royal Society of Antiquaries, Scotland. Literary Appointments include: Founder, Chairman, Aberdeen Writers Workshop, 1967; Lecturer, Creative Writing, Workers Educational Association, and Andrews' University Summer School, 1971-75; Tutor, Arvon Foundation, 1982. Publications include: Legend of The Loch (award), 1969; This Outward Angel, 1971; October Witch, 1971; Castle Clodha, 1972; Lament for Lost Lovers, 1972; White Rose, 1974; A Stranger Came By, 1974; Passionate Kindness, 1974; A Drink for The Bridge, 1976; Black Duchess, 1980; Castle of Foxes, 1981; Colla's Children, 1982; Robert Louis Stevenson Treasury, 1985; The Clan, 1985; RLS

in The South Seas, 1986; Estella, 1986. Contributions include: Scottish Field; Highlander; Aberdeen Leopard; Radio documentaries, short stories, plays; Features and short stories with world syndication. Honour: 1st Novel Award, Romantic Novelists Association, 1969. Memberships include: Former Committees, Society of Authors, Scottish PEN; Crime Writers Association; Radiowriters Association; Romantic Novelists Association. Literary Agent: Giles Gordon, Anthony Shiel Associates, 43 Doughty Street, London, WC1N 2LF, England. Address: 9 Dryden Place, Edinburgh, EH9 1RP, Scotland.

KNIGHT Andrew Stephen Bower, b. 1 Nov 1939. Journalist; Newspaper Executive. m. (1) Victoria Catherine Brittain, 1966, (div), 1 s, (2) Begum Sabiha Rumani Malik, 1975, 2 d. Literary Appointments: Editor, The Economist, 1974-85; Chief Executive, Daily Telegraph, 1985-. Memberships: Director, Tandem Computers Inc, 1984-; Advisory Board, Centre for Economic Policy Research, Stanford University, USA, 1981-; Council Royal Institute of International Affairs, 1976-; Council, Templeton College, Oxford, 1984-; Governor and member, Council of Man, Ditchley Foundation, 1982-; Atlantic Institute, 1985-; Steering Committee, Bilderberg Meetings, 1980; Council of Friends of Covent Garden, 1981; Trustee, Harlech Scholars Trust, 1985; Director of Hollinger Inc, 1987; Director of Reuters, 1988. Address: The Daily Telegraph, Peterborough Court, South Quay, 181 Marsh Wall, London, E14 9SR, England.

KNIGHT Arthur Winfield, b. 29 Dec 1937, San Francisco, California, USA. Writer. m. 25 Aug 1976, 1 daughter. Education: AA, Santa Rosa Junior College, 1958; BA, English, 1960, MA, Creative Writing, 1962, San Francisco State University. Appointments: Professor of English, California University of Pennsylvania, 1966-93; Film Critic: Russian River News, Guerneville, 1991-92, Anderson Valley Advertiser, Boonville, California, 1992-, Potpourri, Prairie Village, Kansas, 1993-. Publications: A Marriage of Poets, 1984; King of the Beatniks, 1986; The Beat Vision (co-editor), 1987; Wanted!, 1988; Basically Tender, 1991; Cowboy Poems, 1993, retitled Outlaws, Lawmen and Bad Women. Contributions to: New York Quarterly; Poet Lore; Oui; The Cape Rock; College English; The Massachusetts Review; The Redneck Review of Literature; New Frontiers, Volume II. Honours: Winner, 1st Place, 3rd Annual Poetry Competition, Joycean Lively Arts Guild, 1982. Memberships: Western Writers of America. Address: PO Box 2580, Petaluma, CA 94953, USA.

KNIGHT Bernard, (Bernard Picton), b. 1931, British. Appointments: Lecturer in Forensic Medicine, University of London, 1959-65; Medical Editor, Medicine, Science and the Law, 1960-63; Lecturer 1962-65, Senior Lecturer 1965-76, Reader 1976, Professor and Consultant in Forensic Pathology, University of Wales, College of Medicine; Senior Lecturer in Forensic Pathology, University of Newcastle, 1965-68. Literary Appointments: Managing Editor, Forensic Science International (Elsevier), 1980-92; Pathology Editor, Forensic Science International (Elsevier), 1992-. Publications: The Lately Deceased (as Bernard Picton), 1963; Thread of Evidence (as Bernard Picton), 1965; Mistress Murder (as Bernard Picton), 1968; Policeman's Progress (as Bernard Picton), 1969; Tiger at Bay (as Bernard Picton), 1970; Murder, Suicide or Accident, 1971; Deg Y Dragwyddoldeb, 1972; Legal Aspects of Medical Practise, 1972, 3rd edition 1982; In the Dead, Behold the Quick, Edfyn Brau, 1973; Discovering the Human Body, 1980; Forensic Radiology, 1981; Lawyer's Guide to Forensic Medicine, 1982; Sudden Death in Infancy, Coroner's Autopsy, 1983; Post-Modern Technicians Handbooks, 1984; Pocket Guide to Forensic Medicine, 1985; Simpson's Forensic Medicine, 10th edition 1991; Forensic Pathology, 1991; Editor: The Estimation of the Time Since Death (Book), 1995. Honour: CBE (Commander of British Empire), 1993. Memberships: Crime Writers Association; Welsh Union of Writers; Academi Gymraeg. Address: Wales Institute of Forensic Medicine, Royal Infirmary, Cardiff CF2 1SZ, Wales.

KNIGHT Cranston Sedrick, b. 10 Sept 1950, Chicago, Illinois, USA. Poet. m. Dolores Anderson, 5 Aug 1978, 2 sons, 1 daughter. Education: BA, History, Southern Illinois University, 1977; MA, East Asian and American History, Northeastern Illinois University, 1990. Literary appointments: Poetry Editor, Eclipses magazine, University of Illinois, 1971; Editor, C'est la Vie magazine, Northwestern University, 1983-86; Literary Consultant, Mystic Voyage, 1978-79; B.O.L.T., Southern Illinois University, 1979-80. Publications include: Tour of Duty, 1986; Cadence Magazine, 1986; Samisdat Literary Anthology, 1987; Freedom Song, poetry, 1988; Garden of the Beast, poetry, 1989; Pearl Magazine Spring, poem, 1989; Wide Open Magazine, poem, 1989. Contributions to: The Otherwise Room Anthology; American

Poetry Association; Walking Point; Black American Literature Forum; Deros Poetry Magazine; AIM Magazine; Prospective column, Chicago Daily Defender newspaper. Address: 55935 N Magnolia, Apt 1, Chicago, IL 60660, USA.

KNIGHT David. See: **PRATHER Richard.**

KNIGHT David Marcus, b. 30 Nov 1936, Exeter, England. University Professor. m. Sarah Prideaux, 21 July 1962, 2 sons, 4 daughters. Education: BA Chemistry, 1960, Keble College; Diploma, History and Philosophy of Science, 1962; DPhil, 1964, Oxford University. Appointments: Editor, British Journal of History of Science 1982-88; General Editor, Blackwell Science Biographies, 1989-. Publications: Zoological Illustration, 1977; The Transcendental Part of Chemistry, 1978; Ordering the World, 1981; Sources for the History of Science, 1984; The Age of Science, 1988; Natural Science Books in English 1600-1900, 1989; A Companion to the Physical Sciences, 1989; Humphry Davy, 1992; Ideas in Chemistry, 1992; Contributions to: Isis; British Journal for the History of Science; Annals of Science; Ambix; Studies in Romanticism. Literary Agent: The Peters, Fraser and Dunlop Group Ltd. Address: Department of Philosophy, Durham University, 50 Old Elvet, Durham DH1 3HN, England.

KNIGHT Gareth. See: **WILBY Basil Leslie.**

KNIGHT William Edwards, b. 1 Feb 1922, Tarrytown, New York, USA. US Foreign Service Officer. m. Ruth L Lee, 14 Aug 1946, 2 sons. Education: BA, Yale College, 1942; Pilot Training, US Army Air Force, 1943-44; B-24 Co-Pilot, 1944-45; MA, Yale University, 1946; Industrial College of the Armed Forces, 1961-62; State Department Senior Seminar in Foreign Policy, 1971-72. Appointments: Foreign Service Officer, US Department of State, 1946-75. Publications: Mystery and Suspense: The Tiger Game, 1986; The Bamboo Game, 1993; Screenplays in progress: Plague of Locusts; The Byte Fairy. Contributions to: Articles to journals of foreign policy and diplomatic affairs; President and Chief Executive Officer, The Araluen Press, 1992-. Memberships: Washington Independent Writers; Diplomatic and Consular Officers Retired; Army Navy Country Club of Washington; Army Navy Club of Manila, Treasurer, 1970; Yale Club of Washington; Randolph Mountain Club, Pres, 1985-87. Literary Agent: Bookworld Services Inc, 1933 Whitfield Loop, Sarasota, FL 34243, USA. Address: Araluen Press, 5000 Park Place, Suite 300, Bethesda, MD 20816, USA.

KNIGHT William Nicholas, b. 18 Apr 1939, Mount Vernon, NY, USA. Professor of English. m. 2 Sep 1961, 1 s, 3 d. Education: BA, cum laude, Amherst College, 1961; MA, University of California, Berkeley, 1963; PhD, Indiana University, 1968; Postdoctoral, Institute of Advanced Legal Studies, University of London, 1969-70. Appointments include: Wesleyan University, 1966-75; Chairman, Humanities, University of Missouri, Rolla, 1975-. Publications include: Death of J K, play, 1969; Shakespeare's Hidden Life, 1974; Law in Spenser, in Spenser Encyclopaedia, Toronto, 1988. Contributions to: Numerous journals, USA, Europe, Japan, including: Christian Science Monitor; USA Today; Avalon to Camelot; Shakespeare Translation; Review of English Studies; Shakespeare Survey; Erasmus Review; Costerus Essays; American Legal Studies Association; Reviews, poems, short stories, various small magazines. Honours include: Scholar, Warburg Institute, University of London, 1969-70; Fellow, Wesleyan Centre for Humanities, 1971; Ford Foundation Fellow, 1972; Newberry Fellow, 1983; Numerous Teaching Awards, Research Grants. Memberships include: International Shakespeare Association; Shakespeare Association of America; Spenser Society; Modern Language Association; Missouri Philogical Association. Literary Agents: Arthur C Pine Associates; NYC, USA; Sterling Lord Associates, NYC, USA. Address: 1313 Whitney Lane, Rolla, MO 65401, USA.

KNIGHTLEY Phillip George, b. 23 Jan 1929, Sydney, Australia. Author; Journalist. m. Yvonne Fernandes, 13 Jul 1964, 1 s, 2 d. Publications: The First Casualty, 1975; The Vestey Affair, 1980; The Second Oldest Profession, 1986; An Affair of State, 1988; Philby: KGB Masterspy, 1989. Honours: British Journalist of The Year, 1980, 1988. Memberships: Society of Authors; NUJ. Literary Agent: Tessa Sayle Agency. Address: 4 Northumberland Place, London, W2 5BS, England.

KNOLL Erwin, b. 17 July 1931, Vienna, Austria. Editor; Writer. m. Doris E Ricksteen, 1 Mar 1954, 2 sons. Education: BA, New York University, 1953. Literary appointments: Staff, Editor and Publisher

Magazine, 1948-53, 1955-56; Associate Editor, Better Schools Magazine, 1756-57; Reporter, Assistant World Editor, Washington Post, 1957-62; Washington Editor, Los Angeles Times-Washington Post News Service, 1962-63; Washington Correspondent, Newhouse National News Service, 1963-68; Washington Editor, 1968-73, Editor, 1973-, The Progressive, Madison, Wisconsin. Publications: Anything But the Truth, 1968; Scandal in the Pentagon, 1969; American Militarism, 1970; War Crimes and the American Conscience, 1970; No Comment, 1984. Contributions to: Many periodicals. Address: c/o The Progressive, 409 East Street, Madison, WI 53703, USA.

KNOTT Bill. See: **KNOTT William Cecil.**

KNOTT Will C. See: **KNOTT William Cecil.**

KNOTT William Cecil, (Will C Knott, Bill Knott), b. 7 Aug 1927, Boston, MA, USA. Professor of English. Education: AA, 1949; BA, 1951, Boston University; MA, State University of New York, Oswego, 1966. Publications include: Circus Catch, 1963; Scatback, 1964; Long Pass, 1966; Night Pursuit, 1966; Junk Pitcher, 1967; Lefty's Long Throw, 1967; High Fly to Center, 1972; Fullback Fury, 1974; The Craft of Fiction, 1974; Taste of Vengeance, 1975; Lyncher's Moon, 1980; Longarm and The Railroaders, 1980; Longarm on The Yellowstone, 1980; Mission Code: King's Pawn, 1981; The Trailsman Series (15 books), 1984-86; The Golden Hawk Series (9 books), 1986-88; The Texan, 1987; Longarm and The Outlaws of Skull Canyon, 1990; Longarm and The Tattoed Lady, 1990. Memberships: Western Writers of America, President, 1980-81. Address: 216 Falls of Venice, South Venice, FL 34292, USA.

KNOWLING Michael John, b. 26 Apr 1953, Edinburgh, Scotland. College Principal; Journalist, Editor of Northern Newspapers Ltd, NSW, 1981-88.. Education: MA, with honours, University of Glasgow, 1975; Master of Letters, University of New England, 1987. Publications: Collins Concise Encyclopaedia, 1977; Race Relations in Australia: A History, 1982; University of New England Gazette, 1990-92. Honours: Association of Rhodes Scholars in Australia Scholarship, England-Australia, 1977. Memberships: Media, Entertainment & Arts Alliance; International Federation of Journalists; Australian & New Zealand Communication Association; Australian Rhodes Scholars Association. Address: PO Box 503, Armidale, NSW 2350, Australia.

KNOX Bill. See: **KNOX William.**

KNOX Elizabeth, b. 15 Feb 1959, Wellington, New Zealand. Novelist. m. Fergus Barrowman, 1989. Education: BA, Victoria University, Wellington, 1986. Appointment: Lecturer, Film Studies, Victoria University, 1989. Publications: After Z Hour, 1987; Paremata, 1989; Short Stories, The Sword, 1990; After Images, 1990; Post Mortem, 1990; Afraid, 1991; Take as Prescribed, 1991. Honours: ICI Bursary, 1988; Penn Award, 1988, Fellowship, 1991. Address: PO Box 11-806 Wellington, New Zealand.

KNOX William, (Michael Kirk, Bill Knox, Robert MacLeod, Noah Webster), b. 20 Feb 1928, Glasgow, Scotland. Author; Journalist. m. Myra Ann Mackill, 31 Mar 1950, 1 son, 2 daughters. Appointments: Deputy News Editor, Evening News, 1957; Scottish Editor, Kemsley Newspapers, 1957-60; News Editor, Scottish Television, 1960-62; Freelance author and broadcaster 1962-; Presenter STV Crimedesk 1977-89; Editor, RNLI Scottish Lifeboat, 1984-. Publications: Over 60 novels of crime, sea and adventure; also radio and TV adaptations of own work. Honours: William Knox Collection established, Boston University, 1969; Police Review Award, 1986; Paul Harris Fellow, Rotary International, 1989. Memberships include: Association of Scottish Motoring Writers, past President, Hon Member; Scottish Committee, Society of Authors; Crime Writers Association; Mystery Writers Association. Literary Agent: Random-Century Publishing, London and Heather Jeeves Literary Agency, Edinburgh EH9 1RP. Address: 55 Newtonlea Avenue, Newton Mearns, Glasgow G77 5QF, Scotland.

KNOX-JOHNSTON Robin, b. 17 Mar 1939, Putney, London, England. Master Mariner; Author. m. 6 Jan 1962, 1 daughter. Education: Master's Certificate, 1965. Publications: A World of My Own, 1969; Sailing, 1974; Twilight of Sail, 1978; Last But Not Least, 1978; Seamanship, 1986; The BOC Challenge 1986-87, in 1987; The Cape of Good Hope, 1989; The History of Yachting, 1990; The Colombus Venture, 1991; Sea Ice Rock (with Chris Bonington), 1992. Contributions to: Yachting World, UK; Yachting Monthly, UK; Cruising

World, USA; The Guardian. Honours: Commander, Order of British Empire (CBE), 1969; Hon DSc, Maine Maritime Academy. Memberships: Younger Brother, Trinity House; Honourable Company of Master Mariners; FRGS (Fellow of the Royal Geographical Society); Hon Doctor of Technology, Nottingham Trent University, 1993. Memberships: Trustee National Maritime Museum Greenwich, 1993; Chairman, Sail Training Association, 1993. Literary Agent: Curtis Brown & John Farquarson. Address: St Francis Cottage, Torbryan, Newton Abbot, Devon TQ12 5UR.

KNOX-MAWER June Ellis, b. 10 May 1930, Wrexham, North Wales. Writer; Broadcaster. m. Ronald Knox-Mawer, 30 June 1951, 1 son, 1 daughter. Education: Grove Park Girls Grammar School, Wrexham, 1941-47. Appointments: Trained as Journalist, Chester Chronicle, 1948-50; Aden Correspondent, Daily Express, 1952-56; Presenter and Author, various literary and feature programmes Womans House (BBC Radio 4), 1970-. Publications: The Sultans Came to Tea, 1961; A Gift of Islands, 1965; A World of Islands, 1968; Marama, novel of 19th century Fiji, 1972; A South Sea Spell, 1975; Tales from Paradise, 1986; Marama of the Islands, 1986; Sandstorm (novel set in South Arabia), 1991. Contributions to: The Guardian; Various women's magazines. Honours: Sandstorm, Romantic Novel of the Year Award, 1992. Memberships: Council, Royal Commonwealth Society; Library Committee, Commonwealth Trust. Literary Agent: Bruce Hunter, David Higham Associates, England. Address: c/o David Higham Associates, 5-8 Lower John Street, Golden Square, London W1, England.

KNUDSON R(ozanne) R, b. 1932, USA. Writer. Publications: Selected Objectives in the English Language Arts (with Arnold Lazarus), 1967; Sports Poems (edited with P K Ebert), 1971; Zanballer, 1972; Jesus Song, 1973; You Are the Rain, 1974; Fox Running, 1974; Zanbanger, 1977; Zanboomer, 1978; Weight Training for the Young Athlete (with F Colombo), 1978; Starbodies (with F Comombo), 1978; Rinehart Lifts, 1980; Just Another Love Story, 1982; Speed, 1982; Muscles, 1982; Punch, 1982; Zan Hagen's Marathon, 1984; Babe Didrikson, 1985; Frankenstein's 10 K, 1985; Martina Navratilova, 1986; Rinehart Shouts, 1986; Julie Brown, 1987; American Sports Poems (edited with May Swenson), 1987; The Wonderful Pen of May Swenson, 1993. Address: 73 Boulevard, Sea Cliff, NY 11579, USA.

KOCH Christopher John, b. 16 July 1932, Hobart, Tasmania. Author. m. Irene Vilnonis, 23 Apr 1960, 1 son. Education: BA Hons; DLitt, University of Tasmania. Publications: The Boys in the Island, 1958; Across the Sea Wall, 1965; The Year of Living Dangerously, 1978; The Doubleman, 1965; Essays: Crossing the Gap, 1987. Honours: National Book Council Award for Australian Literature, 1979; Miles Franklin Prize, 1985. Literary Agent: Curtis Brown Ltd. Address: PO Box 19, Paddington, NSW 2021, Australia.

KOCH Claude Francis, b. 28 Nov 1918, Philadelphia, Pennsylvania, USA. Emeritus Professor. m. Mary P Kane, 7 Sept 1941, 5 sons, 1 daughter. Education: BS, La Salle University; MA, University of Florida. Publications: Island Interlude; Light in Silence; The Kite in the Sea; A Casual Company; Mother; Anne Askewe. Contributions to: Sewanee Review; Southern Review; Antioch Review; Kansas Quarterly; Four Quarters; Northwest Review; Ave Maria; Delta Review. Honours: Dodd, Mead Intercollegiate Literary Fellowship; Sewanee Review Fellowship in Fiction; La Salle College Centenary Award; Rockefeller Foundation Fellowship in Fiction; Lindback Award for Distinguished Teaching. Literary Agent: Russell and Volkening. Address: 128 West Highland Avenue, Philadelphia, PA 19118, USA.

KOCH Joanne Barbara, (Joanna Z Adams), b. 28 Mar 1941, Chicago, IL, USA. Author; Playwright. m. Lewis Z Kock, 30 May 1964, 1 s, 2 d. Education: BA, Honours, Cornell University; MA (Woodrow Wilson Fellowship), Columbia University. Literary Appointments: Guest Lecturer: Loyola University; DePaul University; Writer-in-Residence, Lake Forest College, Southern Illinois University. Publications: The Marriage Savers (with Lewis Koch), 1976; Contributor: Readings in Psychology Today, 1978; Children: Development Through Adolescence, 1983; Marriage and The Family, 1983; Child Development: Topical Approach, 1985; Novels as Joanna Z Adams: Makeovers, 1987; Rushes, 1988; Plays: Haymarket: Footnote to a Bombing; Teeth; Nesting Dolls; XX-XY; Grant 5742; Danceland (musical with Julie Shannon); Teleplays: Today I Am a Person; The Price of Daffodils. Contributions to: Parade; Psychology Today; Newsday; MaCalls; Washington; others; Syndicated Columnist, Newspaper Enterprise Association. Honours include: First place, Media

Award, Family Service Association; Harris Media Award, American Psychoanalytic Association; Grants from Illinois Arts Council for Playwriting; First place, International Playwriting Contest, Southern Illinois University and Piscator Foundation. Memberships include: Phi Beta Kappa; Phi Kappa Phi; Society of Midland Authors, President, 1978-80; Chairperson, Drama Award, Society of Midland Authors, 1980-84; Dramatists Guild; Women in Theatre; Board of Directors, Women in Film. Literary Agent: Timothy Seldes, Russell and Volkening, NY, USA. Address: 343 Dodge Avenue, Evanston, IL 60202, USA.

KOCH Kenneth, b. 27 Feb 1925, Cincinnati, Ohio, USA. Professor of English; Writer. m. Mary Janice Elwood, 1955, 1 daughter. m. Karen Steinbrink, 1994. Education: AB, Harvard University, 1948; MA, 1953, PhD, 1959, Columbia University. Appointments: US Army, 1943-46; Lecturer, English, Rutgers University, New Brunswick, New Jersey, 1953-54, 1955-56, 1957-58; Lecturer, English, Brooklyn College, 1957-59; Director, Poetry Workshop, New School for Social Research, New York City, 1958-66; Lecturer, 1959-61, Assistant Professor, 1962-66, Associate Professor, 1966-71, Professor of English, 1971, Columbia University, New York City; Associated with magazine Locus Solus, 1960-62. Publications: Verse includes: The Art of Love, 1975; The Duplications, 1977; The Burning Mystery of Anna in 1951, 1979; From the Air, 1979; Days and Nights, 1982; Selected Poems, 1985; On The Edge, 1986; Seasons on Earth, 1987; Selected Poems, 1991; One Train, 1994: On the Great Atlantic Rainway, Poems 1950-1988, 1994; Other plays include: Rooster Redivivus, 1975; The New Diana, 1984; A Change of Hearts, 1986; Popeye Among The Polar Bears, 1987; One Thousand Avant-Garde Plays, 1988; Screenplays: The Scotty Dog, 1967; The Apple, 1968; Other works include: The Red Robins, novel, 1975, as play, 1978; Hotel Lambosa, short stories, 1993. Literary Agent: Maxine Groffsky, 2 Fifth Avenue, New York, NY 10011, USA. Address: 25 Claremont Avenue, Apt 2-B, New York, NY 10027, USA.

KOCH Klaus, b. 4 Oct 1926, Sulzbach, Thueringen, Germany. University Professor. m. Eva-Maria Koch, 28 Mar 1978. Education: Universities of Heidelberg, Mainz and Tuebingen, 1945-50; Dr theol, University of Heidelberg, 1953; Habilitation, University of Erlangen, 1956. Appointments: Assistant, University of Heidelberg, 1950; Pastor, Lutheran Church, Jena, 1954; Dozent, Old Testament, University of Erlangen, 1956; Dozent, University of Hamburg, 1957; Professor, Old Testament, Kirchliche Hochschule, Wuppertal, 1960; Professor, Old Testament, History of Ancient Near Eastern Religions, University of Hamburg, 1962-. Publications: Was ist Formgeschichte? 1964, 5th edition 1989; Ratlos vor der Apokalyptik, 1970; English Edition: The Rediscovery of Apocalyptic, 1972; Die Profeten I, Assyrische Zeit, 1978, 3rd edition, 1995; English Edition: The Prophets I, 1982; Die Profeten II, Babylonisch-Persische Zeit, 1980, 2nd edition 1988; English Edition: The Prophets II, 1984; Spuren des hebraeischen Denkens, Gesammelte Aufsaetze I, 1991; Geschichte der aegyptischen Religion, 1993. Contributions to: 80 scholarly journals. Memberships: Joachim-Jurgius Gesellschaft der Wissenschaften, Hamburg; Wissenschaftliche Gesellschaft fur Theologie. Address: Diekbarg 13 A, D 22397 Hamburg, Germany.

KOCHAN Miriam Louise, b. 5 Oct 1929, London, England. Freelance Writer; Translator. m. Lionel Kochan, 23 Dec 1951, 2 s, 1 d. Education: BSc, Economics, Honours, London University, 1950. Literary Appointments: Sub-Editor, Reuters Economic Services, 1950-54; Assistant Sub-Editor, Past and Present, a journal of historical research, 1977-81; General Editor, Berg Women's Series, 1985-88. Publications: Life in Russia Under Catherine The Great, 1969; The Last Days of Imperial Russia, 1976; Prisoners of England, 1980; Britain's Internees in The Second World War, 1983; Numerous translations. Contributions to: Reviews to Jewish Quarterly. Address: 237 Woodstock Road, Oxford, OX2 7AD, England.

KOELB Clayton, b. 12 Nov 1942, New York City, NY, USA. Educator. m. Susan J Noakes, 1 Jan 1979, 1 s, 1 d. Education: BA, 1964, MA, 1966, PhD, 1970, Harvard University. Literary Appointments: Assistant Professor, Associate Professor, Professor of German and Comparative Literature, 1969-91, Chairman, Department of Germanic Languages, 1978-82, University of Chicago, IL; Visiting Professor, Purdue University, 1984-85; Visiting Professor, Princeton University, 1985-86; Visiting Eugene Falk Professor, 1990, Guy B Johnson Professor, 1991-, University of North Carolina, Chapel Hill. Publications: The Incredulous Reader, 1984; Thomas Mann's Goethe and Tolstoy, 1984; The Current in Criticism, 1987; Inventions of

Reading, 1988; The Comparative Perspective on Literature, 1988; Kafka's Rhetoric, 1989; Nietzsche as Postmodernist, 1990. Contributions to: About 40 articles to literary and critical journals. Honours: Germanistic Society of America, Fellow, 1964-65; Danforth Foundation Fellow, 1965-69; Woodrow Wilson Foundation Fellow, 1965; Susan Anthony Potter Prize, Harvard University, 1970. Memberships: Modern Language Association of America; International Association for Philosophy and Literature; Semiotics Society of America; Vice-President, President-Elect, Kafka Society of America. Address: University of North Carolina, 434 Dey Hall, Chapel Hill, NC 27599, USA.

KOEPPEL Mary Sue, b. 12 Dec 1939, Phlox, Wisconsin, USA. Educator; Writer. m. Robert B Gentry, 31 May 1980. Education: BA, English, Alverno College, Milwaukee; MA, English, Loyola University. Appointments: Co-Editor, Instructional Network News, 1983-85; Co-Editor, Tips for Teachers, 1985; Editor: Kalliope journal, 1988-; New Lit on the Block, 1990; Lollipops, Lizards and Literature, 1994. Publication: Writing Resources for Conferencing and Collaboration, 1989. Contributions include: Clockwatch Review; Christian Science Monitor; Bittersweet; Poets for Liveable Planet; Single Parent; Florida Times Union. Address: 3879 Oldfield Trail, Jacksonville, FL 32223, USA.

KOESTENBAUM Wayne, b. 20 Sept 1958, CA, USA. Professor. Education: BA, Harvard, 1980; MA, Johns Hopkins, 1981; PhD, Princeton, 1988. Publications: The Queen's Throat, 1993; Rhapsodies of a Repeat Offender, 1994; Ode to Anna Moffo and Other Poems, 1990; Double Talk, 1990. Literary Agent: Faith Hamlin, c/o Sanford J Greenburger, 55 Fifth Avenue, NY 10003, USA. Address: English Dept, Yale University, New Haven, CT 06520, USA.

KOGAN Norman, b. 15 June 1919, Chicago, Illinois, USA. Professor Emeritus of Political Science. m. Meryl Reich, 18 May 1946, 2 sons. Education: BA, 1940, PhD, 1949, University of Chicago. Appointments: University of Connecticut, 1949-88; Visiting Professorships, University of Rome, Italy, 1973, 1979, 1987. Publications: Italy and the Allies, 1956; The Government of Italy, 1962; The Politics of Italian Foreign Policy, 1963; A Political History of Postwar Italy, 1966; Storia Politica dell' Italia Repubblicana, 1982, 2nd Edition, revised and expanded, 1990; A Political History of Italy: The Postwar Years, 1983. Contributions to: Yale Law Journal; Il Ponte; Western Political Quarterly; Journal of Politics; Comparative Politics; Indiana Law Journal. Address: 7 Eastwood Road, Storrs, CT 06268, USA.

KOGAWA Joy, b. 6 Jun 1935, Vancouver, BC, Canada. Writer. 1 s, 1 d. Literary Appointments: Writer-in-Residence, University of Ottawa, 1977. Publications include: Poetry: The Splintered Moon, 1967; A Choice of Dreams, 1974; Jericho Road, 1977; Woman in The Woods, 1985; Novels: Obasan, 1981; Naomi's Road, 1986; Itsuka, 1992. Honours: First Novel Award, Books in Canada; Book of The Year Award, Canadian Authors Association; Best Paperback Fiction Award, Periodical Distributors of Canada; The American Book Award, Before Columbus Foundation; Notable Book, American Library Association; Member of The Order of Canada. Memberships: Director, Canadian Civil Liberties Association; Patron, Canadian Tribute to Human Rights; Writers Union of Canada; PEN International. Address: c/o Writers Union of Canada, 24 Ryerson, Toronto, Ontario, Canada, M5T 2P3.

KOGER Lisa Jan, b. 9 Jun 1953, Elyria, OH, USA. Writer. m. Jerry Lynn Koger, 28 Dec 1974, 2 s. Education: BSW, West Virginia University, 1974; MS, Communications (Journalism), University of Tennessee, 1979; MFA, Creative Writing, Iowa Writers Workshop, University of Iowa, 1989. Literary Appointments: Iowa Teaching and Writing Fellow, Writers Workshop, University of Iowa, 1988-89; Writing Instructor, Graduate Studies Center, Rock Island, IL, summer 1989; Visiting Lecturer, Creative Writing, Mississippi State University, 1990-91. Publications: Farlanburg Stories, 1990; Writing in The Smokehouse, essay in The Confidence Woman, 1991. Contributions include: Book reviews to: The New York Times Book Review; Atlanta Journal Constitution; Fiction to: Seventeen Magazine; Ploughshares; The American Voice; New Myths-MSS; The Chattahoochee Review; Highlights for Children. Honours: Writing Grant, Kentucky Foundation for Women, 1987; Teaching and Writing Fellowship, Iowa Writers Workshop, 1988; James Michener Award, 1989. Memberships: Authors Guild; Authors League of America; Kappa Tau Alpha; Phi Kappa Phi; Mortar Board. Literary Agent: Jane Gelfman, John Farquharson Limited, USA.

KOLAKOWSKI Leszek, b. 23 Oct 1927, Radom, Poland. Academic. m. Tamera Dynenson, 19 Nov 1949, 1 d. Education: MA, Lodz University, 1950; PhD, Warsaw University, 1953. Publications: Individual and Infinity, 1959; Chrietieus sans eglise, 1969; Main Currents of Marxism, 1978; Religion, 1982; Metaphysical Horror, 1988. Contributions to: Many magazines, newspapers and journals in Britain, Poland, France, Germany and Italy. Honours: Friedenpreis des Deutschen Bouchhandels, 1977; Erasmus Prize, 1982; Prix Europa d'Essai; Jefferson Award, 1985; McArthur Fellowship, 1985. Memberships include: Polish Writers Association; PEN Club; British Academy; International Institute of Philosophy; American Academy of Arts and Sciences; Philosophical Societies in Oxford and in Poland. Address: 77 Hamilton Road, Oxford, OX2 7QA, England.

KOLLER James, b. 30 May 1936, Oak Park, Illinois, USA. Writer; Artist. div, 2 sons, 4 daughters. Education: BA, North Central College, Naperville, Illinois, 1958. Publications: Poetry: Two Hands, 1965; Brainard and Washington Street Poems, 1965; The Dogs and Other Dark Woods, 1966; Some Cows, 1966; I Went To See My True Love, 1967; California Poems, 1971; Bureau Creek, 1975; Poems for the Blue Sky, 1976; Messages-Botschaften, 1977; Andiamo, 1978; O Didn't He Ramble-O ware er nicht unhergezogen, 1981; Back River, 1981; One Day at a Time, 1981; Great Things Are Happening-Grossartoge Dige passieren, 1984; Give The Dog A Bone, 1986; Graffiti Lyriques (with Franco Beltrametti), graphics and texts, 1987; Openings, 1987; Fortune, 1987; Roses Love Sunshine, 1989; This Is What He Said, graphics and texts, 1991; Prose: Messages, 1972; Working Notes 1960-82, 1985; Gebt dem alten Hund'nen Knochen (Essays, Gedichte and Prosa 1959-85), 1986; The Natural Order, essay and graphics, 1990; Fiction: If You Don't Like Me You Can Leave Me Alone, UK Edition, 1974, US Edition, 1976; Shannon Who Was Lost Before, 1975. Address: PO Box 629, Brunswick, ME 04011, USA.

KOLLER Marvin Robert, b. 24 Feb 1919, Cleveland, Ohio, USA. Professor of Sociology. m. Pauline Esther Steinfeld, 27 Jan 1945, 1 son. Education: BS, Education, Kent State University, 1940; MA, Sociology, 1947, PhD, Sociology, 1950, Ohio State University. Publications: Sociology of Childhood, 1964, 2nd Edition, 1978; Modern Sociology, 1965, 3rd Edition, 1974; Social Gerontology, 1968; Families, 1974; Foundations of Sociology, 1975; Humor and Society, 1988; 5-4-3-2-1-0, A Docudrama on the May 4, 1970 Shootings at Kent State University, presented at Ripon College, Wisconsin, 1981. Contributions to: Residential Propinquity of White Mates at Marriage in Relation to Age and Occupations of Males, Columbus, Ohio, to American Sociological Review, 1938, 1946; Some Changes in Courtship Behavior in Three Generations of Ohio Women, to American Sociological Review, 1951. Honours: Fellowship in Social Gerontology, 1959; National Science Foundation Grant in Anthropology, 1962; National Endowment for the Humanities in Tragi-Comedy, 1980. Memberships: American Sociology Association; National Council on Family Relations; American Gerontological Society; American Association of University Professors. Address: Sociology Department, Kent State Department, Kent, OH 44242, USA.

KOLM Ronald Akerson, b. 21 May 1947, Pittsburgh, Pennsylvania, USA. Writer; Editor; Publisher. m. Donna Sterling, 5 Sept 1984, 2 sons. Education: BA, Albright College, 1970. Publications: Plastic Factory, 1989; Welcome to the Barbecue, 1990; Suburban Ambush, 1991; Rank Cologne, 1991. Contributions to: Cover Magazine; Appearances Magazine; New Observations; Semiotext(e); Red Tape. Address: 30-73 47th Street, Long Island City, NY 11103, USA.

KOMUNYAKKA Yusef, b. 1947. Poet. Publication: Neon Vernacular, 1993. Honours: Pulitzer Prize, 1994; Kingsley Tufts Poetry Award, 1994.

KONDOLEON Harry, b. 1955, American. Literary Appointment: Taught Playwriting, New School for Social Research, NYC, 1983-84. Publications: Slacks and Tops, Christmas on Mars, 1983; The Vampires, Self Torture and Strenuous Exercise (in The Short Plays, 1984), 1984; Linda Her and The Fairy Garden, The Cote d'Azur Triangle, Anteroom, 1985; The Brides (in Wordplays 2), The Death of Understanding, 1986; Andrea Rescued, The Whore of Tjampuan, 1987. Address: c/o George Lane, William Morris Agency, 1350 Avenue of The Americas, New York, NY 10019, USA.

KONER Pauline, b. 26 June 1912, New York City, New York, USA. Choreographer; Writer; Lecturer; Teacher. m. 23 May 1939.

Education: Columbia University, 1928; Professional Training with Michel Fokine, Michio Ito and Angel Cansino. Publications: Solitary Song - An Autobiography, 1989; Elements of Performance, 1993; Essays: The Truth about The Moor's Pavane, 1966; Intrinsic Dance, 1966; Pauline Koner Speaking, 1966. Contributions to: Dance Magazine; Ballet Review; Dance Chronicle. Honours: Dance Magazine Award, 1963; Honorary Doctorate of Fine Arts, Rhode Island College, 1985; Special Citation, De La Torre Bueno Award, 1989. Membership: American Dance Guild. Address: 263 West End Avenue, 9F, New York, NY 10023, USA.

KONIGSBERG Allen Stewart, (Woody Allen), b. 1 Dec 1935, Brooklyn, NY, USA. Actor; Writer; Producer; Director. m. (1) Harlene Rosen (div), (2) Louise Lasser, 1966 (div 1969). Education: City College of New York. Appointments: Actor in numerous films, stage and Television productions. Publications: Plays: Play It Again Sam; The Floating Light Bulb, 1981; Films: What's New Pussycat?, 1965; Casino Royale, 1967; What's Up, Tiger Lily?, 1967; Take The Money and Run, 1969; Bananas, 1971; Everything You Always Wanted to Know About Sex, 1972; Play It Again Sam, 1972; Sleeper, 1973; Love and Death, 1976; The Front, 1976; Annie Hall, 1977; Interiors, 1978; Manhattan, 1979; Stardust Memories, 1980; A Midsummer Night's Sex Comedy, 1982; Zelig, 1983; Broadway Danny Rose, 1984; The Purple Rose of Cairo, 1985; Hannah and Her Sisters, 1985; Husbands and Wives, 1992; Shadows and Fog, 1992; Books: Getting Even, 1971; Without Feathers, 1975; Side Effects, 1980; Written for Television performer: Herb Shriner; Sid Caesar; Art Carney; Jack Parr; Carol Channing; Writer for The Tonight Show and Gary Moore Show. Honours: Academy Award, Best Director and Best Writer for Annie Hall. Address: 930 Fifth Avenue, New York, NY 10021, USA.

KONING Hans, b. 12 Jul 1924, Amsterdam, Netherlands. Writer. m. Kathleen Scanlon, 1 s, 3 d. Education: Universities of Amsterdam, Zurich and Paris-Sorbonne. Publications: The Affair, 1958; A Walk With Love and Death, 1960; The Revolutionary, 1967; Death of a Schoolboy, 1974; A New Yorker in Egypt, 1976; The Kleber Flight, 1981; America Made Me, 1983; DeWitt's War, 1983; Acts of Faith, 1986; Nineteen Sixty-Eight, A Report, 1987. Contributions to: New Yorker; Nation; Atlantic Monthly; others. Honours: NEA Award, 1978; Connecticut Arts Award, 1980; Literary Agent: Lantz Office, New York, USA. Address: c/o The Lantz Office, 888 Seventh Avenue, New York, NY 10106, USA.

KONOPINSKI Lech Kazimierz, b. 16 Mar 1931, Poznan, Poland. Writer; Journalist; Doctor of Economics. m. Hanna Zapytowska, 26 Jul 1956, 1 s, 1 d. Education: Master's Degree, Higher School of Economics, 1955; Doctorate, University of Lodz, 1973. Literary Appointments include: Columnist, Szpilki (Needles), 1954-; Kaktus (Cactus), 1957-60; Karuzela, 1958-; satirical weekly journals. Publications: 17 books, 3 plays, over 300 songs. Titles include: Actions and Reactions, 1960; Devil's Dodges, 1968; Paradise Apples, 1971; Eyes of A Peacock's Tail, 1975; Amor Alphabet, 1977, 1989; Jocular Leaflets, 1980; Funny Resentments, 1981; Jokes From Warta River, 1983; Prince Lech and The Three Friends, 1984; Children's Books include: Fabulous Stories, 1970; What Creeps and Frisks in The Woods and Fields, 1979; From Flower to Flower, 1983; From Pole to Pole, 1986; What Flies and Walks in Our Farm, 1988; What Jumps and Runs Among Trees and Flowers, 1989; The Mysterious Signs, 1989. Contributions to: Szpilki; Karuzela; Plomyczek; Swierszczyk; Mis; Gazeta Poznanska; Express Poznanski. Honours include: Golden Book, 1971; Golden Ring, 1973, 1980; Awards of Honour, Poznan; Golden Order of Merit; Chivalry Order of Merit; Prize in Reward for Universalize of Culture. Memberships include: Various offices, Polish Writers Association, Polish Authors and Composers Association; Association of Authors; Polish Philatelists Association; Officer, Association International des Journalistes Philateliques. Literary Agent: Wydawnictwo Poznanskie, Poznan, ul, Frefry 8. Address: ul Michalowska 18 m 3, PL 60 645 Poznan, Poland.

KOONTS Jones Calvin, b. 19 Sept 1924. Educator. m. 1 son, 1 daughter. Education: AB 1945, LittD 1979, Catawba College, North Carolina; MA 1949, PhD 1958, George Peabody College, Nashville; Postdoctoral study: Harvard University 1960, Smithsonian/Oxford Seminar, Oxford University, England. Publications: I'm Living in a Dream, song, 1947; You Know, Love, song, 1989; Since Promontory, 1967; Under the Umbrella, book of poetry, 1971; Editor, Green Leaves in January, 1972; A Slice of the Sun, 1976; Poems represented in National Poetry Anthology, 1957, 1959, 1960, 1962; Editor, Inklings, 1983; A Stone's Throw, book of poetry, 1986; Straws in the Wind, book of poetry, 1968; Lines: Opus 8, book of poetry, 1994. Honours:

Fulbright Grantee, 1964; Winner, William Gilmore Simms Poetry Prize, South Carolina, 1973; Unicom Poetry Prize, 1974; Lyric Poetry Size, 1975; Elizabeth B Coker Poetry Award, 1977. Memberships include: NEA; Academy of American Poets; AACTE; ATE; Phi Delta Kappa. Address: Box 163, Erskine College, Due West, SC 29639, USA.

KOONTZ Dean R, (David Axton, Brian Coffey, K R Dwyer), b. 9 July 1945, Everett, PA, USA. Novelist; Screenwriter. m. Gerda Ann Cerra, 15 Oct 1966. Education: BS, Shippensburg University, 1966. Publications include: Whispers, 1980; Phantoms, 1983; Darkness Comes, (in USA as Darkfall), 1984; Strangers, 1986; Watchers, 1987; Twilight Eyes, 1987; Lightning, 1988; Midnight, 1989; The Bad Place, 1990; Mr Murder, 1993; Dark Rivers of the Heart, 1994; Strange Highways, 1995; plus over 40 others; numerous contributions to journals and magazines. Honours: Doctor of Letters, Shippensburg University, PA, 1989; Daedalus Award for Twilight Eyes, 1988. Literary Agent: Robert Gottlieb, William Morris Agency, New York. Address: PO Box 9529, Newport Beach, California 92658, USA.

KOONZ Claudia, American. Author; Educator. Literary Appointments: Professor of History, College of The Holy Cross, Worcester, MA; Associate Professor, History Department, Duke University, Durham, NC. Publications: Women in European History, 1977; Co-editor, Becoming Visible, revised edition, 1987; Mothers in The Fatherland: Women, Politics and The Family in Nazi Germany, translated into Dutch, French, Japanese, 1987, revised German edition as Mütter im Vaterland, 1991; Forthcoming: The Biopolitics of Race and Gender in Nazi Germany. Contributions to: Periodicals: New York Times Book Review, 1988; SIGNS; Women's Review of Books; American Journal of Sociology; Journal of Oral History; Feministische Studien; Geisichichte und Gesellschaft. Honours: Nomination for National Book Award for Mothers in The Fatherland: Women, The Family and Nazi Politics, 1987; Winship Prize, Berkshire Conference Prize; Feminist Fortnightly Prize; US Library Association Prize; National Association Jesuit Colleges Prize. Memberships: American History Association (Research Division); Berkshire Conference, Executive Committee; German Studies Association; PEN International. Literary Agent: Charlotte Sheedy Inc, 41 King Street, New York, NY 10014, USA. Address: Department of History, Duke University, Durham, NC 27705, USA.

KOOSER Theodore (Ted) John, b. 25 Apr 1939, Ames Iowa, USA. Insurance Executive. m. 14 Sep 1977, 1 s. Education: BA, Iowa State University, 1962; MA, University of Nebraska, 1968. Publications: Sure Signs (poems), 1980; One World At A Time (poems), 1985. Contributions to: Poems published in many literary magazines including: The Nation; Poetry; The New Yorker. Honours: National Endowment Fellowships, 1976, 1984; Midlands Poetry Prize for Best Book of Poetry published that year, 1980. Membership: PEN. Address: Rt 1 Box 10, Garland, NE 68360, USA.

KOPS Bernard, b. 28 Nov 1926, London. Novelist. m. Erica Gordon, 1956. Appointments: Lecturer, Spiro Institute, 1985-86; Surrey, Ealing, Inner London Education Authorities, 1989-90; City Literary Institute, London, 1991. Publications include: Awake for Mourning, 1958; Motorbike, 1962; Yes Fron No Man's Land, 1965; By the Waters of Whitechapel, 1970; The Passionate Past of Gloria Gaye, 1971; Settle Down Simon Katz, 1973; Partners, 1975; On Margate Sands, 1978; Plays: The Hamlet of Stepney Green, 1958; Goodbye World, 1959; Change for the Angel, 1960; Stray Cats and Empty Bottles, 1961; Enter Solly Gold, 1962; The Boy Who Wouldn't Play Jesus, 1965; More Out than In, 1980; Ezra, 1981; Simon at Midnight, 1982; Some of these Days, 1990; Sophie, Last of Red Hot Mamas; Playing Sinatra, 1991; Androcles and the Lion, 1992; Dreams of Anne Frank, 1992; Who Shall I be Tomorrow? 1992; Call in the Night, 1995; Radio & TV Plays; Verse Collections. Honours: Arts Council Bursaries; C Day Lewis Fellowship, 1981-83. Address: 35 Canfield Gardens, Flat 1, London NW6, England.

KORBAR Marcia M, b. 20 Nov 1955, Gowanda, NY, USA. Mental Health Therapist. Education: Jamestown Community College, 1978. Publications: Poetry, various anthologies. Contributions to: World Poetry Anthology; American Collegiate Poets; Young American Poets. Honours: Special Award, American Collegiate Poets; Golden Poets Awards, 1985, 1986; Award of Merit, Honourable Mention, 1985. Address: 106 Chestnut Street, Gowanda, NY 14070, USA.

KORDA Michael Vincent, b. 8 Oct 1933, London, England. Writer. m. (1) Carolyn Keese, 1 s, (2) Margaret Mogford. Education: BA, Magdalen College, Oxford University, 1958. Literary Appointments include: Publishing Entrepreneur; Editor-in-Chief, Simon and Schuster Publishing House; Bestselling Author. Publications: Male Chauvinism! How It Works, 1973; Power! How To Get It, How To Use It, 1975; Success!, 1977; Charmed Lives: A Family Romance, 1979; Worldly Goods, 1982; Queenie, 1985; The Fortune. Honours: Pulitzer Prize; The National Book Award; National Book Critics Circle Award for editing Richard Rhodes, The Making of The Atomic Bomb; The Fortune on The New York Times Bestsellers List, 1989 10 weeks; The Fortune main selection of The Literary Guild.

KORFIS Tasos. See: **ROMBOTIS Anastasios.**

KORG Jacob, b. 1922, American. Appointments: Assistant and Associate Professor 1955-65, Professor of English 1965-, University of Washington, Seattle; Former Staff Member, English Department, Bard College, Annandale-on-Hudson, University of Maryland, College Park and City College of New York; Visiting Professor, 1960, National Taiwan University, 1959-61, University of Washington; Professor, 1965-91, Professor Emeritus, 1991-. Publications: Westward to Oregon (ed with S F Anderson), Thought in Prose (ed with R S Beal), 1958, 3rd edition, 1966; An Introduction to Poetry, 1959; London in Dickens's Day (ed), 1960; The Complete Reader (ed with R S Beal), 1961; George Gissing's Commonplace Book (ed), 1962; George Gissing: A Critical Biography, 1963; Dylan Thomas, 1965, updated edition, 1991; The Force of Few Words (author and ed), 1966; Twentieth Century Interpretations of Bleak House (ed), 1968; The Poetry of Robert Browning (ed), 1971; Thyrza, by George Gissing (ed), 1974; The Unclassed, by George Gissing (ed), 1976; George Gissing on Fiction (ed with C Korg), 1978; Language in Modern Literature, 1979; Browning and Italy, 1983. Memberships: Modern Language Association; International Association of University Professors of English. Address: 6530 51st Avenue NE, Seattle, WA 98115, USA.

KORMONDY Edward John, b. 1926, American. Appointments: Assistant Professor, Associate Professor and Professor of Biology, 1957-68, Oberlin College, OH; Director, Commission on Undergraduate Education in the Biological Sciences and Director Office of Biological Education, American Institute of Biological Sciences, WA, 1968-71; Member of the Faculty 1971-79, Interim Acting Dean, 1972-73, Vice-President and Provost 1973-78, Evergreen State College, Olympia, WA; Senior Professional Associate, National Science Foundation, 1979; Provost and Professor of Biology, University of Southern Maine, Portland, 1979-82; Vice-President, Academic Affairs and Professor of Biology, California State University, Los Angeles, 1982-86; Senior Vice-President and Chancellor and Professor of Biology, University of Hawaii, Hilo and University of Hawaii-West Oahu, 1986-93. Publications: Introduction to Genetics, 1964; Readings in Ecology (ed), 1965; Readings in General Biology (ed), 2 volumes, 1966; Concepts of Ecology, 1969, 1976, 1983; Population and Food (ed with Robert Leisner), Pollution (ed with R Leisner), Ecology (ed with R Leisner), 1971; General Biology: The Natural History and Integrity of Organisms (with T Sherman et al), 1977; Handbook of Contemporary Developments in World Ecology (with F McCormick), 1981; Environmental Science: The Way the World Works (with B Nebel), 1981, 1987; Biology (with B Essenfield), 1984, 1988; International Handbook of Pollution Control, 1989. Address: 1388 Lucile Avenue, Los Angeles, CA 90026, USA.

KORNFELD Robert Jonathan, b. 3 Mar 1919, Newtonville, Massaachusetts, USA. Author; Playwright. m. Celia Seiferth, 23 Aug 1945, 1 son. Education: AB, Harvard University, 1941; Also attended Columbia, Tulane, New York University, The New School, Circle-in-the-Square School of Theatre; Playwrights Horizons Theatre School & Laboratory. Literary Appointments: Founder, Chair, Riverdale Contemporary Theatre, 1965; Director, Broadway Drama Guild, 1979-81. Publications: Great Southern Mansions, 1977; Two plays written in summer stock at Hangar Theatre, Ithaca, New York, 1979; Libretto, A Dream Within a Dream, 1987; Acting Out at Samuel Beckett Theatre, New York City, Fall, 1989; Southern Repertory Theatre, Spring, 1990; Landmarks of the Bronx, 1990; Music for Saint Nicholas, performed at Lincoln Center, New York, 1992. Contributions to: Many travel articles in New York Times, Poems in French in Cahiers d'Art et D'Amitié, in English in Botteghe Oscure, Rome. Honours: Many early National Drama Awards; Best New Play, San Francisco Playwrights Center, 1988; BRIO Award for playwrighting, Bronx Council on the Arts, 1989. Memberships: Dramatists Guild; Authors League; Co-Chair, Literary Committee & Chair, Literary Scholarship Committee, The National Arts Club; Vice President, Bronx Society of Science & Letters; Vice President, Historic Districts Council; Victorian Society; Freedom to Write Committee, PEN. Address: 5286 Sycamore Avenue, Riverdale, NY 10471, USA.

KORNHAUSER Julian, b. 20 Sep 1946, Gliwice, Poland. Writer. m. Alicja Wojna, 1971, 1 s, 1 d. Education: Slavic Philology, Jagiellonian University, 1965-70; PhD, 1975; Habilitation, 1982. Literary Appointments: Institute of Slavic Philology, University of Cracow, 1970-; Member, Editorial Staff, Pismo, 1981-83. Publications: And The Lazy Will Have Their Feast, 1972; In Factories We Pretend To Be Sad Revolutionaries, 1973; The Unportrayed World (with Adam Zagajewski), 1974; A Few Moments, 1975; The Potato Eaters, 1978; Exceptional Conditions, 1978; Basic Difficulties, 1979; The Procurer of Ideas, 1980; Hurrraaa!, 1981; 148 poems (selection), 1982; Internal Light, 1984; For Us, With Us, 1985; Another Order, 1985; Poems of The 80-ies, 1991; Six books on Serbian and Croatian Literatures, 1978, 1980, 1981, 1983, 1991, 1993. Contributions to: Kultura, Tworczosc; Pismo; Student; Naglos; Arka; Zeszyty Literackie. Honours: Koscielski Foundation, 1975; Andrzej Bursa Award, 1981; DAAD Fellowship, West Berlin, 1986; European Literary Award, Yugoslavia, 1989. Membership: SPP, Poland. Address: Boleslawa Chrobrego 29 3, Cracow, Poland.

KORZENIK Diana, b. 15 Mar 1941, New York City, New York, USA. College Educator. Education: Oberlin College; BA, Vassar College; Master's Programme, Columbia University; EdD, Graduate School of Education, Harvard University. Appointments: Professor, Massachusetts College of Art, Boston, Massachusetts. Publications: Art and Cognition, 1977; Drawn to Art, 1986; Art Making and Education (co-authored with, Maurice Brown), 1993; Chapter in Framing the Past. Contributions to: Studies in Art Education; Art Education Magazine; Boston Magazine; Manchester Magazine; Arnheim & the Diversity of American Art, Journal of Aesthetic Education, 1994. Address: Massachusetts College of Art, 621 Huntington Avenue, Boston, MA 02115, USA.

KOSSOFF David, b. 24 Nov 1919 (Russian parentage). Actor; Designer; Illustrator. Publications: Bible Stories retold by David Kossoff, 1968; The Book of Witnesses, 1971; The Three Donkeys, 1972; The Voices of Masada, 1973; You Have a Minute Lord? 1975; The Little Book of Sylvanus, 1975; A Small Town is a World, 1979; Sweet Nutcracker, 1985; Own Bible Storytelling programmes (writer & teller) on radio & TV; Appeared, many plays & films & on radio & TV; since 1972, one-man performances: As According to Kossoff, A Funny Kind of Evening, The Kossoff Storytellings (to children). Honours: British Academy Award, 1956; Elected Member, Society Industrial Artists, 1958; FRSA, 1969; Hon DLitt, 1990. Membership: Society of Authors. Address: 45 Roe Green Close, Hatfield, Hertfordshire, England.

KOSTELANETZ Richard, b. 14 May 1940, New York City, New York, USA. Writer. Education: AB, honours in American Civilisation, Brown University, 1962; Foreign Scholar, King's College, London, 1964-65; MA, American History, Columbia University, 1966; Further study, Music, Theatre, Morley College London and New School, New York. Career: Co-Founder, President, Assembling Press, 1970-82; Literary Director, The Future Press, Cultural Council Foundation, 1976-; Senior Staff, Indiana University Writers Conference, July 1976; Co-Editor, Publisher, Precisely: A Critical Magazine, 1977-; Sole Proprietor, Archae Editions, 1978-; Coordinator, Interviewer, American Writing Today, Voice of America Forum Series, 1979-81; Guest residencies: Mishkenot Sha'ananim, Jerusalem, 1979, 1986; DAAD Berliner Kunstlerprogramm, 1981-83. Publications: The New American Arts collection (co-author, editor), 1965, Paperback, 1967, in Spanish, 1967, in Portuguese, 1968; The End of Intelligent Writing: Literary Politics in America, 1974; Numbers: Poems and Stories, 1976; Metamorphosis in the Arts, 1981; The Grants-Fix, 1987; Wordworks: Poetry Selected and New, 1993; A Dictionary of the Avant-Gardes, 1993; On Innovative Performance(s), 1994; Poems in anthologies; Many others. Contributions to: Interdisciplinary and International Review; Contemporary Dramatists; New York Arts Journal; The Humanist; Arts in Society; Performing Arts Journal; Lotta Poetica; AvantGarde; Black River Review; American Poetry Review; Poets On; Many others. Honours: Fellowships, grants, including: Pulitzer Fellowship in Critical Writing, 1965; 1 of Best Books, American Institute of Graphic Arts, 1976. Address: PO Box 444, Prince St, Station, New York, NY 10012-0008, USA.

KOT Jozef, b. 1 Sept 1936, Bratislava, Slovakia. Writer. m. Dagmar Krivdova, 13 Feb 1965, 1 son, 1 daughter. Education: University of Comenius, Bratislava, 1958. Literary Appointments:

Editor, Mlada tvorba, 1956-59; Editor, Slovenske pohlady, 1961-66; Editor, Revue avetovej literatury, 1966-67; Editor-in-Chief, Publishing House, Tatran, 1968-71. Publications: The Last Ones, 1963; The Ascension of the Centre-Forward, 1965; Welcoming of the Spring, 1968; The Fever, 1973; The Birthday, 1978; The Skittle-ground, 1983; The Foot-race without End, 1986; Film adaptation of the Fever, 1975; Translations from English into Slovak: William Shakespeare, James Joyce, Carl Sandburg, E L Masters, Eugene O'Neill, William Faulkner, E Hemingway, H Miller, J Updike. Contributions to: Numerous literary magazines and journals. Honours: Honour, for the Eminent Work, 1975; The Slovak National Prize, 1976; Honourable title, Meritorious Writer, 1980; Honour, for the Merits, 1987; Literary Awards of the publishing houses; Literary Award of Slovensky Spisovatel Publishing House for Translation of James Joyce's Ulysses, 1994. Membership: Society of Slovak Writers. Literary Agent: Slovak Literary Agency, Bratislava. Address: Hrdlickova 1, 831 01 Bratislava, Slovakia.

KOTLOWITZ Alex, b. 31 Mar 1955, NY, USA. Journalist; Author. m. Maria Woltjen, 3 Oct 1993. Education: BA, Wesleyan University. Appointments: Staff Writer The Wall Street Journal, 1984-93.Publications: There Are No Children Here, 1991. Contributions to: NY Times; National Public Radio. Honours: Helen B Bernstein Award; Christopher Award; Carl Sandburg Award; Robert F Kennedy Journalism Award; George Polk Award. Literary Agent: David Black, Black Literary Agency.

KOTOW Piotr, b. 25 Aug 1919, Pokrowka, USSR. Teacher. m. Anna Kremzo, 14 Mar 1953, 2 d. Education: Masters Degree, Russian Philology Department, Warsaw University, 1963. Publications: Poetry: Z Tamtego Brzegu, 1980; Slady, 1986; Stara Piesn, 1988; Widziakczem Kotlas, 1989; Za Kregiem Polarnym, 1990; Wecnyj Ogon, 1973; Sledy, 1986; Weczernij Zwol, 1989. Contributions to: Numerous poems, scholarly articles and book reviews in professional magazines in Russian and Polish. Memberships: Polish Writers Association; Stage Authors and Composers Association. Address: Ul Siennicka 11m 37, 80 703, Gdansk-Przerölka, Poland.

KOTSIRAS Georgis, b. 9 Jun 1921, Athens, Greece. Lawyer; Poet; Writer; Essayist; Translator. m. Despina Mikhailidi, 22 Aug 1954, 1 d. Education: Political Sciences and Law, University of Athens, 1939-45. Appointments: Self-employed Lawyer and Notary Public. Publications: The Home, fiction, 1947; Herostratus, tragedy, 1970; Poetry: I Hora ton Lotofagon, 1948; Frouri tis Siopis, 1949; Poliorkia tou Hronou, 1955; Sinomilia me ton sisifo, 1958; Aftognosia, 1959; Anatomia Englimatos, 1964; Mythologia ton Pragmaton, 1968; Metallages, 1974; To 'Alfa' tou Kentarpou, 1975; Aftopsia Englimatos, 1978; Ta poiimata, 1980-87; I Lampas kai to Teras Engomio, 1983; Translations: Don Camilo (Giovanni Guareschi), 1954; The Stranger (Albert Camus), 1955, later editions; The Home of Bernarda Alba (F G Lorca), 1957, 2nd edition, 1959; The Sacred Comedy (Dante Alighieri), rhymed translation, Hell, Purgatory, Havens, 3 columns, 1987. Contributions include: Kathemerini; Vradeni; Ethnos; Acropolis; Nea Estia; Eflhini. Honours: 2 State Awards for poetry, 1958, 1975; Award of The Twelve for poetry, 1964; 2 Awards for poetry, Academy of Athens, 1980, 1989; Award, Greek Association of Translators of Literature, 1988. Memberships: Association of Greek Writers; PEN Club of Greece, former Vice-President, former President; Bar Association of Greece. Address: 22 Adrianou, GR 145 61 Kifissia, Greece.

KOTT Jan, b. 27 Oct 1914, Warsaw, Poland. University Professor. m. Lidia Steihaus, 17 Jun 1939, 1 s, 1 d. Education: LLM, University of Warsaw, 1936; PhD, Lodz University, Poland, 1947. Literary Appointments: Professor of Polish Literature, University of Warsaw, 1952-59; Professor of Drama and Slavic Literature, 1969-73; Professor of Comparative Literature and English, 1985. Publications: Shakespeare Our Contemporary, 1961; The Eating of The Gods, 1973; The Theatre of Essence, 1984; The Bottom Translation, 1987; Four Decades of Polish Essays, 1990; Przyczynek do bigrafii, 1990; Pisma Wybrane, 1991; La Vie en Sursis, 1991; The Memory of The Body, 1992; The Gender of Rosalind, 1992; Leben auf Raten, 1993; Still Alive, 1994. Contributions to: NY Review; NYT; Formations; New Theatre Quarterly, England; Lettre Internationale; Zeszyty Literackie, Paris-Warsaw; Theatre Yale. Honours: Haerder Award, Vienna, 1964; Alfred Jurzykowski Award, NY, 1976; George G Nathan Award, 1985; Guggenheim Fellow, 1972-73; Getty Scholar, 1985; Officier Ordre des Arts et des Lettres, 1991; Robert Levis Medal, 1993. Memberships: Polish PEN Club; Centre for Medieval and Renaissance Studies, UCLA. Address: 29 Quaker Path, Stony Brook, NY 11790, USA.

KOTZ Nathan K (Nick), b. 16 Sept 1932, San Antonio, Texas, USA. Journalist; Author; Educator. m. Mary Lynn Booth, 7 Aug 1960, 1 son. Education: BA magna cum laude, International Relations, Dartmouth College, 1955; London School of Economics, England, 1955-56. Appointments: Reporter, Des Moines Register, 1958-64; Washington Correspondent, Des Moines Register and Minneapolis Tribune, 1964-70; National Correspondent, The Washington Post, 1970-73; Author, Freelance Journalist, 1973-; Adjunct Professor, The American University School of Communication, 1978-87; Senior Journalist in Residence, Duke University, 1983. Publications: Let Them Eat Promises: The Politics of Hunger in America, 1970; The Unions (co-author), 1972; A Passion for Equality: George Wileyand the Movement (co-author), 1977; Wild Blue Yonder: Money, Politics and the B-1 Bomber, 1988. Literary Agent: Arnold Goodman, Goodman Associates, 500 West End Avenue, New York, NY 10024, USA. Address: Galemont Farm, Broad Run, VA 22014, USA.

KOTZIAS Alexandros, b. 27 Jan 1926, Athens, Greece. Writer; Journalist; Translator. m. Eleni Apostolou, 25 Feb 1954, 1 s, 1 d. Education: Law School, University of Athens. Literary Appointments: Literary Editor and Book Reviewer, Mesimvrini newspaper, 1961-67; Book Reviewer, Vma, newspaper, 1971-72; Co-editor, Synechid, magazine, 1973; Literary Editor and Book Reviewer, Kathmerini, newspaper, 1976-82. Publications: Novels: Siege, 1953; The Attempt, 1964; The Usurpation of Authority, 1979; Imaginary Adventure, 1955; Jaguar, 1987. Contributions to: Ikoner; Tachydzomos; Nex Pozia; Synechia; Tzam; Haztis; Anti; Gzammata ke Technes. Honours: Prose Prize of The 12, 1965; Ford Foundation Grant, 1970; State Prose Prize, 1986. Memberships: Founding Member, Society of Greek Writers, 1981; VP, 1982-84, Board Member, 1984-, Journalists Union of The Athens Daily Newspaper. Address: 162, Papadiamontopoulou Street, 15773 Athens, Greece.

KOTZWINKLE William, b. 1938, American. Freelance Writer. Publications: The Fireman, 1969; The Ship That Came Down The Gutter, Elephant Boy: A Story of The Stone Age, The Day The Gang Got Rich, 1970; The Oldest Man and Other Timeless Stories, Return of Crazy Horses, 1971; Hermes 3000, 1972; The Supreme, Superb, Exalted and Delightful, One and Only Magic Building, 1973; The Fan Man, Night-Book, Up The Alley with Jack and Joe, 1974; Swimmer in The Secret Sea, 1975; Doctor Rat, The Leopard's Tooth, 1976; Fata Margana, 1977; Herr Nightingale and The Satin Woman, The Ant Who Took Away Time, 1978; Dream of Dark Harbor, The Nap Master, Jack in The Box, 1980; Christmas at Fountaine's, E T: The Extra-Terrestrial, The Extra Terrestrial Storybook, 1982; Superman III, Great World Circus, Trouble in Bugland; A Collection of Inspector Mantis Mysteries, 1983; Queen of Swords, 1984; E T: The Book of The Green Planet, Seduction in Berlin, The Book of The Green Plant, 1985; Hearts of Wood, The World is Big and I'm So Small, 1986; The Game of Thirty, 1994. Address: c/o Putnam's, 200 Madison Avenue, New York, NY 10016, USA.

KOURKOV Andrei, b. 23 Apr 1961, Leningrad. Writer. m. Elizabeth Sharp, 25 Jun 1988. Education: BA, Kiev Institute; Moscow Culture Institute. Literary Appointments: Editor, Dnipro; Senior Lecturer, Film Script Writing; Theatre Institute, Kiev. Publications: Napadenie; DeKlassirovannie; Don't Take Me to Kengaraks; The Cosmopolitans Favorite Song; Bickfords World; Goshas Stories; The School for Flying Cats; Flying South; Eleven Odd Stories. Honours: Ukranian Literary Fund Prize; Renaissance Short Story Competition, 2nd Prize. Memberships: PEN; Cinematographer's Union of The Ukraine. Address: Drive Mayakovskovo 46 K17, 253232 Kiev, Ukraine.

KOURTOVIK Dimosthenis, b. 15 July 1948, Athens, Greece. Author; Literary Critic; Translator; Anthropologist. m. Vibeke Espholm, 10 Aug 1988. Education: Doctor, University of Wroclaw. Appointments: Literary Critic, O Scholiastis; Eleftherotypia; Ta Nea. Publications: Three Thousand Kilometres; The Last Earthquake; The Greek Autumn of Eva Anita Bengtsson; The Dust of the Milky Way; Doct Thesis on the Evolution of Human Sexuality; Greek Intellectuals and the Greek Movie; Domestic Exile; Antilexicon of Modern Greek Chrestomathy. Contributions to: Numerous. Honour: Greek Publishers Award. Memberships: European Anthropological Association. Address: 23 Amynandrou Street, 117 41, Athens, Greece.

KOURVETARIS George A, b. 21 Nov 1933, Greece. Professor of Sociology; Author; Editor. m. Toula Savas, 22 Nov 1966, div 1987, 2 sons, 1 daughter. Education: Teacher's Diploma, Tripolis, Greece, 1955; BS, Loyola University, Chicago, USA, 1963; MA with honours,

Roosevelt University, Chicago, 1965; PhD, Northwestern University, Evanston, Illinois, 1969. Publications: First and Second Generation Greeks in Chicago: An Inquiry Into Their Stratification and Mobility Patterns, 1971; Co-author: Social Origins and Political Orientations of Officer Corps in a World Perspective, 1973; Society and Politics: An Overview and Reappraisal of Political Sociology, 1980; A Profile of Modern Greece: In Search of Identity, 1987; Co-editor: World Perspectives in the Sociology of the Military, 1977; Political Sociology: Readings in Research and Theory, 1980; A Book of poetry in Greek and in part English, 1992; Social Thought, 1994. Memberships include: Delta Tau Kappa, International Social Science Honor Society; American Sociological Association; Modern Greek Studies Association; American Humanist Association; American Association of European Union. Address: 109 Andresen Ct, DeKalb, IL 60115, USA.

KOVEL Ralph, Author; Company President. m. 1 s, 1 d. Publications: Dictionary of Marks, Pottery and Porcelain, 1953; A Directory of American Silver, Pewter and Silver Plate, 1958; American Country Furniture 1780-1875, 1963; Kovel's Know Your Antiques, 1967, 3rd edition, 1981; Kovel's Antiques and Collectibles Price List, annually 1968-; Kovel's Bottles Price List, biennially, 1971-; Kovel's Collector's Guide for Collector Plates, Figurines, Paperweights and Other Limited Edition Items, 1974, 1978; Kovel's Collector's Guide to American Art Pottery, 1974; Kovel's Organizer for Collectors, 1978, 1983; Kovel's Illustrated Price Guide to Royal Doulton, 1980, 1984; Kovel's Illustrated Price Guide to Depression Glass and American Dinnerware, 1980, 1983; Kovel's Know Your Collectibles, 1981; Kovel's Book of Antique Labels, 1982; Kovel's Collectors Source Book, 1983; Kovel's New Dictionary of Marks, Pottery and Porcelain, 1850-Present, 1985; Kovel's Advertising Collectibles Price List, 1986; Kovel's Guide to Selling Your Antiques and Collectibles, 1987; Kovel's American Silver Marks, 1650 to the Present, 1989; Kovel's Collectibles, 1990 Calender, 1989. Contributions to: Monthly column, House Beautiful, 1979-; Newspaper column, Kovels Antiques and Collecting; Editor, Publisher, Kovels on Antiques and Collectibles, Newsletter, 1974-. Honours: Recipient of numerous honours and awards. Address: 9090 Bank Street, Valley View, OH 44125, USA.

KOWALCZYK David Theodore, b. 22 Nov 1952, New York, USA. Teacher. Education: BA 1974, MA English Creative Writing 1988, State University of New York, USA. Appointments: English Instructor: Arizona State University, 1983-84; Genesee Community College, 1987-93. Publications: A Gentle Metamorphosis, 1993; Sinner, short story in anthology, Bless Me, Father, 1994. Contributions to: Albany Review; Maryland Review; Oxalis; Entelechy. Honours: First Prize, Poetry Competition, City Magazine, 1984; First Prize, Fiction, Chatauqua Council on Arts Awards, NY, 1990. Membership: Phi Beta Kappa. Address: 4641 East Alta Vista Road, Phoenix, AZ 85040, USA.

KOWALSKI Kazimierz Maria, b. 18 Aug 1926, Chelmno, Poland. Writer. m. Stanislawa Nowak, 12 Jun 1948, 1 s, 1 d. Education: University of Wroclaw. Appointment: Polish Radio, Opole, 1954-92. Publications: Fighter Will Never Give Up, 1964, 1969; Strip Tease Without Fun, 1977; Both Our Hearts, 1977, 1978; Crazy With Love, 1984; Escape to The Green Meadows, 1985; The One Whom I Love, 1989; Long Odysses Return (collection of the radio performances), 1989; Neither Too Early, Nor Too Late, 1992; 27 books; Radio Plays include: Not Far From a Dead Forest; Ophelia, Hamlet's Lover; Daddy in Some Other Clothes; Call Controlled; La Mort on The Marat's bath; Dramas: To Dearest Catherine; Screenplay: It Was a Beautiful Funeral, People Cried; Numerous translations. Contributions to: Kwartalnik Opolski; Tak i nie; Osnowa; Zycie Literackie; Opole. Honours: Voivodship Literary Awards, 1959, 1984, 1991; Jan Langowski Award, 1981; Main Award, President of Polish Radio and Television, 1982. Memberships: Society of Polish Writers; National Council of Culture. Literary Agent: Authors Agency Limited, Warsaw, Poland. Address: ul Strzelcow Bytomskich 5 m 6, 45 084 Opole, Poland.

KOWALSKI Marian, b. 8 Sept 1936, Szymonki, near Rawicz, Poland. Writer. m. Jadwiga Abrahamow, 13 Jan 1961, 1 daughter. Education: MA, Literature, Department of Polish Philology, Wroclaw University. Publications: Novels, short stories, screen plays, theatrical plays: Chtopiec z ortem, 1971; Ktos obecy, 1974; Sydonia, 1984; Titles include: Koty, 1958; Jesienna, 1964; Odnajdywanie siebie, 1965; Blinda, 1973; Wszedzie i Nigdzie, 1973; Junga, 1977; Wszedzie i Donikad, 1980; Moj przyjaciel Delfin, 1981; Skarb Morza Sargassowego, 1983; Galapagos, 1982; W Oczekiwaniu, 1984; Przed Kurtyna, 1984; Karczowiska, 1985; Dom na Klifie, 1986; Moj najwiekszy nieprzyjaciel, 1987; Cecylia i Eryk, 1990; Wiatraki na

birekicie, 1990. Contributions to: Odra; Nowe Sygnaly; Teatr; Scena, Student; Kurier Szczecinski; Glos Szczecinski; Morze i Ziemia. Honours: Award, J Czechowicz competition, 1970; 1st Prize for play, 1971; Grand Prix for film screenplay, Joseph Conrad Prize for novel, 1971. Memberships: Polish Writers Union; Polish Marine Writers Association. Address: ul Szafera 130 m 12, 71-245 Szczecin, Poland.

KOZAK Henryk Jozef, b. 15 Jul 1945, Krasna, Poland. Writer, Poetry and Prose. m. Maria Tomasiewicz, 1 Jul 1967, 2 s. Education: MA History, University of Maria Curie-Sklodowskiej, 1969. Publications: First Poems published, Lublin local press, 1968; Titles include: W krajobrazie lagodnych slow, poem, 1973; Podroze do zrodel, poem, 1978; Chwila, poem, 1979; W cieniu ciszy, poem, 1982; Coraz cichsze lata, poem, 1985; Kupic smierc, novel, 1985; Kiedy konczy sie milosc, detective novel, 1987; Nie dokonczona powiesc o milosci, detective novel, 1990; Participant, numerous literary events, 1968-. Contributions include: Numerous journals and magazines including: Kamena; Tygodnik Kulturalny; Poezja; Akcent; Kierunki. Honours: Josef Czechowicz Literary Awards, selections of poems (1st prize), 1980, 1987. Membership: Society of Polish Writers. Address: 20 854 Lublin, ul Paryska 7 m 6, Poland.

KOZBELT Laurie, b. 11 Nov 1963, Greensburg, Pennsylvania, USA. Writer; Editor; Designer. Education: BA magna cum laude, Journalism, Indiana University of Pennsylvania, Indiana, Pennsylvania, 1985; MA summa cum laude, Journalism, Communications, Point Park College, Pittsburgh, 1991. Career: Editor, Designer, 2 bi-monthly newsletters, quarterly corporate publications to readerships of 10,000, Allegheny Ludlum Corporation, 1988- Contributing Editor, Out Publishing Company, Pittsburgh, Pennsylvania, 1991. Publications: Book of short stories in progress. Contributions: Hundreds of news and feature articles in various publications, 1983-; News and features articles, Out monthly magazine, 1988-. Honours: Winner's Circle Award for Best Newsletter, International Association of Business Communicators, 1985; Best in the East Award for Best Internal Publication, Virginia Society for Hospital Public Relations and Marketing, 1985; Gold Quill, International Association of Business Communicators, 1986; 3 EFfie Awards, 1986, 4 EFfie Awards, 1987, Editors Forum; Honourable Mention, 1987, Award of Excellence, 1991, Matrix Award, Women in Communications; Design Finalist, International Mercury Award, MerComm Inc, 1990; Honourable Mention, 1992, 1993, Best of Category, 1992, 26th Annual Exhibition, Printing Industry of Western Pennsylvania. Memberships: International Association of Business Communicators; Women in Communications Inc. Address: 3004 Greenridge Drive, Verona, PA 15147-2222, USA.

KOZOL Jonathan, b. 5 Sep 1936, Boston, USA. Author. Education: Harvard College; Magdalen College, Oxford, England. Literary Appointments: Teacher Boston area, 1964-72; Lecturer, numerous Universities, 1973-85. Publications: Death At An Early Age, 1967; Free Schools, 1972; The Night is Dark, 1975; Children of The Revolution, 1978; On Being a Teacher, 1979; Prisoners of Silence, 1980; Illiterate America, 1985; Rachel and Her Children, 1988; Savage Inequalities, 1991. Honours: Rhodes Scholar, 1954; National Book Award, 1968; Guggenheim Fellow, 1972, 1984, 1985; Field Foundation Fellow, 1973, 1974; Rockefeller Fellow, 1978; Senior Fellow, 1983; Robert F Kennedy Memorial Book Award, 1989. Address: PO Box 145, Byfield, MA 01922, USA.

KRAFT Joseph, American. Literary Appointments: Staff Writer, New York Times, 1951-57; Washington Correspondent, Harpers Magazine, NYC, 1961-66; Syndicated Columnist, Los Angeles Times Syndicate. Publications: The Struggle for Algeria, 1961; The Grand Design, 1962; Profiles in Power, 1966; The Chinese Difference, 1973; The Mexican Debt Rescue, 1985. Address: 2101 Connecticut Avenue, NW Washington DC 20008, USA.

KRAMER Aaron, b. 13 Dec 1921, Brooklyn, New York, USA. Professor of English; Poet. m. Katherine Kolodny, 10 Mar 1942, 2 daughters. Education: BA 1941, MA 1951, Brooklyn College; PhD, New York University, 1966. Publications: The Glass Mountain, 1948; The Poetry and Prose of Heinrich Heine, 1948; Roll The Forbidden Drums! 1954; The Tune of the Calliope, 1958; Rumshinsky's Hat, 1964; Rilke, Visions of Christ, 1967; The Prophetic Tradition in American Poetry, 1968; Melville's Poetry, 1972; On Freedom's Side, 1972; On the Way to Palermo, 1973; Carousel Parkway, 1980; The Burning Bush: Poems and Other Writings 1940-1980, 1983; A Century of Yiddish Poetry, 1988; Indigo, 1991. Contributions to: Numerous magazines and journals including: West Hills Review Co-Editor, 1978-85; American

Annals of the Deaf; Massachusetts Review; Midstream; Modern Poetry Review; New York Times; Village Voice; Kenyon, Missouri and New England Reviews; Writers Forum; Journal of Poetry Therapy. Memberships: PEN; International Academy of Poets; NE MLA; Association for Poetry Therapy, Executive Board, 1969-84; ASCAP. Literary Agent: John K Payne Literary Agency Inc. Address: English Department, Dowling College, Oakdale, NY 11769, USA.

KRAMER Dale, b. 1936, American. Appointments: Instructor 1962-63, Assistant Professor of English 1963-65, Ohio University, Athens; Assistant Professor 1965-67, Associate Professor 1967-71, Professor of English 1971-, Associate Dean, College of Liberal Arts and Sciences, 1992-, University of Illinois, Urbana; Associate Vice Provost, 1990, University of Oregon, Eugene; Editor, Journal of English and German Philology. Publications: Charles Maturin, 1973; Thomas Hardy: The Forms of Tragedy, 1975; Critical Approaches to the Fiction of Thomas Hardy (ed), 1979; The Woodlanders by Thomas Hardy (ed), 1981, 1985; The Mayor of Casterbridge, by Thomas Hardy (ed), 1987; Critical Essays on Thomas Hardy, 1990; Thomas Hardy: Tess of the d'Urbervilles, 1991. Address: Department of English, University of Illinois, Urbana, IL 61801, USA.

KRAMER Larry, b. 25 Jun 1935, Bridgeport, CT, USA. Screenwriter; Playwright; Novelist. Education: BA, Yale University, 1957. Literary Appointments: Associated with training programs, NY, for William Morris Agency, 1958 and Columbia Pictures, 1958-59; Assistant Story Editor, Columbia Pictures, 1960-61; Production Executive, London, England, 1961-65; Assistant to The President of United Artists, 1965; Associate Producer of motion picture, Here We Go Round The Mulberry Bush, 1967; Producer of motion picture Women in Love, 1969; Co-founder of Gay Men's Health Crisis in NY, 1981; Founder of ACT UP (AIDS Coalition to Unleash Power), 1988. Publications: Women in Love, 1969; Faggots, 1978; The Normal Heart, 1985; Just Say No, 1988; Reports from The Holocaust: The Making of an AIDS Activist, Sissies' Scrapbook, The Furniture of Home, 1989. Contributions to: Political writings to periodicals including: New York Times; Village Voice. Honours: Academy Award Nomination for Best Screenplay, Academy of Motion Picture Arts and Sciences, British Film Academy for Best Screenplay, 1970, for Women in Love; Dramatists Guild Matron Award, City Lights Award, Sarah Siddons Award, all for Best Play of The Year, Olivier Award for Best Play, 1986, for Normal Heart; Arts and Communication Award, Human Rights Campaign Fund, 1987. Address: New York, USA.

KRAMER Leonie Judith (Professor Dame), b. 1 Oct 1924, Melbourne, Australia. Professor. m. Dr Harold Kramer, 2 Apr 1952 (dec), 2 d. Education: BA, University of Melbourne, 1945; DPhil, University of Oxford, UK, 1953. Literary Appointments include: Director, Quadrant Magazine Company; Chairman, Board of Directors, National Institute of Dramatic Art (NIDA), 1987-92; Deputy Chairman, Senior Fellow, Institute of Public Affairs (IPA), 1988-; Deputy Chancellor, University of Sydney, 1989-91, Chancellor, 1991-. Publications include: Author of Henry Handel Richardson and Some of Her Sources, 1954; Companion to Australia Felix, 1962; Myself When Laura: Fact and Fiction in Henry Handel Richardson's School Career, 1966; Henry Handel Richardson, 1967; Language and Literature: A Synthesis (with R D Eagleson), 1976; Guide to Language and Literature (with R D Eagleson), 1977; Co-editor, A D Hope, 1979; Coast to Coast, 1963-64, 1965; Hal Porter, Selected Stories, 1971; Oxford History of Australian Literature, 1981; Oxford Anthology of Australian Literature, 1985; My Country: Australian Poetry and Short Stories, 200 years, 2 volumes, 1985; James McAuley: Poetry, Essays and Personal Commentary, 1988; David Campbell: Collected Poems, 1989. Contributions to: Numerous journals. Honours: Dame of British Empire, 1982; AC, 1993; Inaugural Britannica Award, 1986; Honorary Doctorates, Tasmania, Melbourne, Australian National University, Queensland, New South Wales. Memberships include: Fellow, Australian Academy of Humanities, College of Education; Vice President, Australian Council for Educational Standards. Address: 12 Vaucluse Road, Vaucluse, NSW 2030, Australia.

KRAMER Lotte Karoline, b. 22 Oct 1923, Mainz, Germany. Poet; Painter. m. Frederic Kramer, 20 Feb 1943, 1 son. Education: Mainz, 1930-38; Evening classes, Richmond, England, 1958-68. Publications: Scrolls, 1979; Ice Break, 1980; Family Arrivals, 1981; A Lifelong House, 1983; The Shoemaker's Wife, 1987. Poetry: The Desecration of Trees, 1994; Earthquake and Other Poems, 1994. Poetry in anthologies including: PEN New Poetry; Writers of East Anglia; Chaos of the Night; Poetry of Chess; Shades of Green;

Contemporary Women Poets; In the Gold of the Flesh;Desecration of Trees, 1994; Earthquake, 1994. Contributions to: Agenda; Ambit; Ariel; Chapman; The Christian Science Monitor; The New York Times; The Spectator; The New Statesman; Encounter; The Jewish Chronicle; The Jewish Quarterly; Stand; Literary Review; The Observer; The PEN; Outposts; The Month; The Rialto; Passport; Others. Honours: 2nd Prize, York Poetry Competition, 1972. Memberships: PEN; Ver Poets; Writers in Schools; Poetry Society, Peterborough Museum Society; Decorative and Fine Arts Society. Address: 4 Apsley Way, Longthorpe, Peterborough PE3 9NE, England.

KRAMER-BADONI Rudolf, b. 22 Dec 1913, Rudesheim, Germany. Freelance Writer. Education: PhD. Publications: 8 novels including: Jacobs Jahr, 1943, 1978; Bewegliche Ziele (French translation, Les realites mouvantes), 1962; Gleichung mit einer Unbekannten, 1977; Political works including: Anarchismus, 1970; Die niedliche revolution, 1973; Religious works including: Revolution in der Kirche-Lefebvre und Rom, 1980; also: Galileo Galilei, biography, 1983; Zwischen allen Stuhlen, autobiography, 1985. Contributions to: Die Welt, Bonn. Honour: Konrad Adenauer Literature Prize, 1979. Memberships include: Past German Secretary, PEN Club, Switzerland. Address: Brunnenstrasse 6, D 6200 Wiesbaden, Germany.

KRANTZ Hazel Newman, b. Brooklyn, New York, USA. Writer; Teacher. m. Michael Krantz, 7 June 1942, 2 sons, 1 daughter. Education: BS Journalism, New York University; MS Elementary Education, Hofstra University. Appointments: Classroom Teacher, Nassau County, New York; Copy Editor, DB, The Sound Engineering Magazine; Editor, True Frontier Magazine. Publications: 100 Pounds of Popcorn; Freestyle for Michael; The Secret Raft; Tippy; A Pad of Your Own; Pink and White Striped Summer; None But The Brave; Daughter of My People; The Story of Henrietta Szold; For Love of Jeremy; Space Doctor; Look to the Hills, 1995. Contributions to: Numerous magazines and journals. Membership: Society of Children's Book Writers. Address: 1306 Stoney Hill Drive, Ft Collins, CO 80525, USA.

KRANTZ Judith, American. Literary Appointments: Contributor, Good Housekeeping, 1948-54, McCalls, 1954-59, Ladies Home Journal, 1959-71; Contributing Editor, Cosmopolitan, 1971-79. Publications: Scruples, 1978; Princess Daisy, 1980; Mistral's Daughter, 1982; I'll Take Manhattan, 1986; Till We Meet Again, 1989; Dazzle, 1990; Scruples Two, 1992; Lovers, 1994. Membership: PEN. Literary Agent: Morton Janklow. Address: c/o Morton Janklow, Lyn Nesbitt Associates, 598 Madison Avenue, New York, NY 10022, USA.

KRAPF Norbert, b. 14 Nov 1943, Jasper, Indiana, USA. Professor of English. m. 13 June 1970, 1 son, 1 daughter. Education: BA English, magna cum laude, St Joseph's College, Indiana, 1965; MA English 1966, PhD English and American Literature 1971, University of Notre Dame. Literary Appointment: Professor of English, Long Island University, joined 1970, appointed Full Professor, 1984. Publications include: Lines Drawn from Dürer, 1981; A Dream of Plum Blossoms, 1985; Ed: Under Open Sky: Poets on William Cullen Bryant, 1986; Trans and ed: Beneath the Cherry Sapling: Legends from Franconia, 1988; Arriving on Paumanok, 1979; Circus Songs, 1983; Trans and ed: Shadows on the Sundial: Selected Early Poems of Rainer Maria Rilke, 1990; Somewhere in Southern Indiana: Poems of Midwestern Origins, 1993; Blue-Eyed Grass: Poems of Germany, in progress. Contributions to: American Scholar; Poetry; New Letters; Kansas Quarterly; Confrontation; Beloit Poetry Journal; Ontario Review. Address: English Department, Long Island University, Brookville, NY 11548, USA.

KRASILOVSKY Phyllis, b. 1926, American. Publications: The Man Who Didn't Wash His Dishes, 1950; The Very Little Girl, 1953; The Cow Who Fell in The Canal, 1957; Scaredy Cat, 1959; Benny's Flag, 1960; The Very Little Boy, 1961; Susan Sometimes, 1962; The Girl Who Was A Cowboy, 1965; The Very Tall Little Girl, 1969; The Shy Little Girl, 1970; The Popular Girls Club, 1972; LC Is The Greatest, 1975; The Man Who Tried to Save Time, 1979; The Man Who Entered a Contest, 1980; The First Tulips in Holland, The Man Who Cooked for Himself, 1982; The Happy Times Story Book, 1987. Address: 1177 Hardscrabble Road, Chappaqua, NY 10514, USA.

KRASNER William, b. 8 June 1917, St Louis, Missouri, USA. Writer, semi-retired. m. Juanita Frances Frazier, 12 Oct 1956, 4 sons. Education: Washington University, St Louis, 1935-36; Army Air Force Meteorology Schools, 1942-46; BS Psychology, Columbia University, 1948. Appointments: Writer-producer, CBS St Louis, Radio-TV,

1957-59; Development Staff Writer, Washington University, 1962; Articles Editor, Trans-Action magazine, 1963-69; Senior Assistant Editor, Psychiatric Reporter, 1969; Staff Writer-Editor, University of Pennsylvania, 1970-74; Staff Writer, Temple University, 1977; Writer (contract), NIMH, 1977-78; Freelance, 1946-. Publications: Novels: Walk the Dark Streets, 1949, 1950, 1986; The Gambler, 1950, 1951, 1987; North of Welfare, 1954; The Stag Party, 1957, 1958; Francis Parkman, Dakota Legend, 1983; Death of a Minor Poet, 1984; Resort to Murder, 1985; Drug Trip Abroad (non-fiction, collaboration), 1972; Look For the Dancer (German), 1993. Literary Agent: Curtis Brown, 10 Astor Place, New York, NY 10003, USA. Address: 538 Berwyn Avenue, Berwyn, PA 19312, USA.

KRAUS Robert, (Eugene H Hippopotamus), b. 1925, America. Writer of Children's Fiction; Cartoonist; Illustrator. Literary Appointments: Founding President, Windmill Books, 1966-, and Springfellow Books, 1972-. Publications include: The Tree That Stayed up Until Next Christmas, 1972; Good Night, Little A B C, 1972; Good Night, Little One, 1972; Good Night, Richard Rabbit, 1972; Milton, The Early Riser, 1972; Big Brother, 1973; How Spider Saved Halloween, 1973; Poor Mister Splinterfitzi, 1973; Herman The Helper, 1974; The Night-Lite Story Book, 1974; Rebecca Hatpin, 1974; Owliver, 1974; Pinchpenny Mouse, 1974; I'm a Monkey, 1975; Three Friends, 1975; The Gondolier of Venice, 1976; Kittens for Nothing, 1976; Boris Bad Enough, 1976; The Good Mousekeeper, 1977; The Detective of London, 1977; Noel The Coward, 1977; Springfellow, 1978; Another Mouse to Feed, 1979; Meet The Blunt, 1980; Box of Brownies, 1980; The King's Trousers, 1981; See The Christmas Lights, 1981; Tubby Books, 6 volumes, 1981-82; Leo The Late Bloomer Takes a Bath, 1981; Herman The Helper Cleans Up, 1981; Squeaky Books, 2 volumes, 1982; Tony The Tow Truck, 1985; Freddy The Fire Engine, 1985; How Spider Saved Valentine's Day, 1986; Mrs Elmo of Elephant House, 1986; Where are You Going Little Mouse?, 1986; Come Out and Play, Little Mouse, 1987. Address: c/o Greenwillow Books, 105 Madison Avenue, New York, NY 10016, USA.

KRAUSS Bruno. See: BULMER Henry Kenneth.

KRAUSS Clifford, b. 30 Jul 1953, NY, USA. Journalist. Education: BA, Vassar College, 1975; MA History, University of Chicago, 1976; MS Journalism, Columbia University, 1977. Publications: Inside Central America: Its People, Politics and History, 1991. Contributions to: The Nation; Foreign Affairs; The Wilson Quarterly; Times Literary Supplement. Literary Agent: Gloria Loomis. Address: 1305 Corcoran Street NW, Washington DC 20009, USA.

KRAUSS Rosalind, b. 30 Nov 1940, Washington, DC, USA. m. Richard I Krauss, 17 Sept 1962 (div). Education: AB, Wellesley College; MA, PhD, Harvard University. Career: Professor; Guest Curator. Publications: Terminal Iron Works: The Sculpture of David Smith, 1971; Joan Miro: Magnetic Fields, 1972; Line as Language, 1974; Passages in Modern Sculpture, 1977; Cindy Sherman: 1975-1993, 1993. Contributions to: Art in America; October; Partisan Review; Artforum (editor). Honour: Mather Award for Criticism, College Art Association, 1973. Address: Department of Art History, Columbia University, 2960 Columbia University, New York, NY 10027-6902, USA.

KRAUZER Steven M, b. 9 Jun 1948, Jersey City, USA. Writer. m. Dorri T Karasek, 2 Nov 1992, 2 d. Education: BA, Yale University, 1970; MA English Literature, University of New Hampshire, 1974. Publications include: The Cord Series, 1982-86; The Executioner Series, 1982-83; Blaze, 1983; The Diggers, 1983; The Dennison's War Series, 1984-86; Framework, 1989; Brainstorm, 1991; Rojak's Rule, 1992; Anthologies: Great Action Stories, 1977; The Great American Detective, 1978; Stories into Film, 1979; Triquarterly 48: Western Stories, 1980. Contributions to: American West; Montana: The Magazine of Western History; Outside. Memberships: Writers Guild of America West Inc; Authors Guild; Authors League; Mystery Writers of America. Literary Agent: Ginger Barber, Virginia Barber Literary Agency. Address: c/o Virginia Barber Literary Agency, 101 5th Avenue, New York, NY 10003, USA.

KREMP Herbert, b. 12 Aug 1928, Munich, Germany. Journalist. m. Brigitte Steffal, 1956, 2 d. Education: Munich University. Literary Appointments: Reporter, Frankfurter Neue Presse, 1965-67; Political Editor, 1957-59, Bonn Correspondent, 1961-63, Editor in Chief, 1963-68, Rheinische Post; Director, Political Department, Der Tag, Berlin, 1959-61; Editor in Chief, 1969-77, 1981-85, Publisher, 1985-87,

Die Welt; Chief Correspondent, Peking, 1977-81, Chief Correspondent, Brüssal, 1987-, Die Welt, Springer Group Newspapers. Publications: Am Ufer der Rubikon: Eine Politische Anthropologie, 1972; Die Bambusbrucke: Ein Asiatisches Tagebuch, 1982. Honour: Konrad Adenauer Prize, 1984; Theodor-Wolff Prize, 1980. Address: St Hubertusdreef 24, 1900 Overyse, Belgium.

KRESS Nancy, b. 20 Jan 1948, Buffalo, NY, USA. Teacher. m. (1) Michael Kress, (div) 2 s, (2) Mark P Donnelly, 19 Aug 1988. Education: BS, State University of NY College, Plattsburgh, 1969; MS Education, 1978, MA English, 1979, State University of NY College, Brockport. Literary Appointments: Elementary School Teacher, Penn Yan, 1970-73; Adjunct Instructor, State University of NY College, Brockport, 1980-; Senior Copywriter, Stanton and Hucko, Rochester, 1984-. Publications: The Prince of Morning Bells, 1981; The Golden Grove, 1984; The White Pipes, 1985; Trinity and Other Stories, 1985; An Alien Light, 1988; Brain Rose, 1990. Contributions to: Periodicals including: Isaac Astimov's Science Fiction; Omni; Fantasy and Science Fiction; Twilight Zone; Work represented in anthologies including: The Best Science Fiction of The Year 12; Universe 12; Full Spectrum, 1982. Honours: Nebula Award, Science Fiction Writers of America, 1985, for Out of All Them Bright Stars. Memberships: Science Fiction Writers of America (director of Speakers Bureau). Address: 50 Sweden Hill Road, Brockport, NY 14420, USA.

KRETZMER Herbert, b. 5 Oct 1925, South Africa. Journalist; Lyric Writer. m. Elisabeth Margaret Wilson, 1961 (div), 1 s, 1 d. Literary Appointments: Entered journalism, 1946; Reporter, Entertainment Columnist, Sunday Express, Johannesburg, 1951-54; Feature Writer, Columnist, Daily Sketch, London, 1954-59; Columnist, Sunday Dispatch, London, 1959-61; Theatre Critic, Daily Express, 1962-78; Television Critic, Daily Mail, 1979-87. Publications: Our Man Crichton, 1965; Co-author, Every Home Should Have One, 1970; Lyricist, Ivor Novello Award Song, Goodness Gracious Me, 1960; Lyricist, contributed to weekly songs to That Was The Week...; Not So Much a Programme...BBC3, That's Life. Honours: ASCAP Award, 1969; Gold Record for She, 1974; Tony Award for lyrics of RSC's, Les Miserables, 1987; Grammy Award, 1988; Television Critic of The Year, Philips Industries Award, 1980; Commended British Press Awards, 1981. Address: c/o London Management, 235-241 Regent Street, London, W1A 2JT, England.

KRIEGER Murray, b. 27 Nov 1923, Newark, New Jersey, USA. Professor; Literary Critic. m. Joan Alice Stone, 15 June 1947, 1 son, 1 daughter. Education: MA, University of Chicago, 1948; PhD, Ohio State University, 1952. Appointments: Assistant, Associate Professor, English, University of Minnesota, 1952-58; Professor, English, University of Illinois, 1958-63; Carpenter Professor, Literary Criticism, University of Iowa, 1963-66; Professor, English, University of California, Irvine, 1966-, Los Angeles, 1973-82; University Professor, University of California, 1974-; Director, School of Criticism and Theory, U C Irvine and Northwestern University, 1976-81; Honorary Senior Fellow, 1982-; Director, University of California Humanities Research Institute, 1987-89. Publications: New Apologists for Poetry, 1956; The Tragic Vision, 1960; A Window to Criticism: Shakespeare's Sonnets and Modern Poetics, 1964; The Play and Place of Criticism, 1967; The Classic Vision, 1971; Theory of Criticism, 1976; Poetic Presence & Illusion, 1979; Arts on the Level: The Fall of the Elite Object, 1981; Words About Words About Words: Theory Criticism and the Literary Text, 1988; A Reopening of Closure: Organism Against Itself, 1989; Ekphrasis: The Illusion of the Natural Sign, 1992; The Ideological Imperative: Repression and Resistance in Recent American Theory, 1993; The Institution of Theory, 1994. Address: Dept of English & Comparative Literature, University of California, Irvine, CA 92717-2650, USA.

KRIEGLER-ELLIOTT Carolyn Patricia, b. 14 Apr 1949, Niagara Falls, NY, USA. Author and Illustrator of Children's Books. m. Tom Elliott, 8 Apr 1983. Education: BFA Honours, Illustration, Virginia Commonwealth University; Early Childhood Education, St Petersburg Junior College, Tarpon Springs, FL, 1987. Literary Appointments: Children's Book Agent, Richards Literary Agency, 1990; Guest, Aim Children's Book Week, National Library Service, Whangarei, New Zealand, 1992. Publications include: Rosie Moonshine (with Anthony Holcroft), 1989; A Lollipop, Please, 1989; Good Night, Little Brother, 1989; Pins and Needles, 1989; Rain, 1990; Chen Li and The River Spirit (with Anthony Holcroft), 1990; Lulu, 1990; Lucky for Some, 1990; Cat Concert, 1990; A Present for Anna, 1990; Higgledy Piggledy Hobbledy Hoy, 1991; Woodsmoke, 1991; The Cave, 1991; Googer in

Space, 1991; Night Cat, 1991; By Jingo!, 1992; What Peculiar People, 1992; Good Night, Alice, 1992; Island in The Lagoon (with Anthony Holcroft), 1992; A Dog for Keeps (with Pauline Cartwright), 1992. Contributions include: Time Magazine; Reader's Digest; New Zealand Listener, 1978-79. Honours include: Guest Promotion Art Director, award, Mademoiselle Magazine, 1971; Legend of The Kiwi presented to HRH Prince Charles and HRH Princess Diana, RNZAF, 1983. Memberships include: New Zealand Book Council; PEN; Writers in Schools, New Zealand Book Council; Sathya Sai Organization of New Zealand. Literary Agent: Ray Richards, Richards Literary Agency. Address: c/o Richards Literary Agency, PO Box 31240, Milford, Auckland 9, New Zealand.

KRISTENSEN Lise Lotte, b. 13 May 1961, Frederiksberg, Denmark. Writer; Poet. Education: University of Copenhagen, for 5 years. Literary Appointments: Borgen Publishers, 1989; Borgen Publishers, 1990; Borgen Publishers, 1993. Publications: Immediately but Flowing, 1989; The Time it Takes Being God, 1991; Southern Balm, 1994. Contributions to: Studiekamraten; Ildfisken; Hojskolebladet. Honours: Madam Hollatz Grant. Memberships: The Danish Writers Union; Committee for World Peace; Buddhist Forum. Literary Agent: Borgen Publishers, Valbygårdsvej 33, 2500 Valby-Kbh, Denmark. Address: Toldbodgade 14B 1 Tv, 1253 Kobenhavn K, Denmark.

KROETSCH Robert, b. 26 June 1927, Canada. Writer; Professor. Education: BA, University of Alberta, 1948; MA, Middlebury College, Vermont, USA, 1956; PhD, University of Iowa, 1961. Appointments: Assistant Professor 1961, Professor 1967, State University of New York at Binghamton; Professor, University of Manitoba, 1978. Publications: The Studhorse Man, 1969; Badlands, 1975; What the Cow Said, 1978; Alibi, 1983; Completed Field Notes, poetry, 1989; The Lovely Treachery of Words, essays, 1989; But We Are Exiles; The Words of My Roaring; Gone Indian; Alberta, travel; The Puppeteer, 1992. Address: Department of English, University of Manitoba, Winnipeg, R3T 2N2, Canada.

KROPP Lloyd, American. Literary Appointments: Teacher, University of North Carolina, Greenboro, 1970-75; Teacher, Southern Illinois University, Edwardsville, 1975-. Publications: The Drift, 1969; Who Is Mary Stark?, 1974; One Hundred Times to China, 1979; Greencastle, 1987. Address: 32 South Meadow Lane, Edwardsville, IL 62025, USA.

KRUKOWSKI Lucian Wladyslaw, b. 22 Nov 1929, New York City, NY, USA. Professor of Philosophy. m. Marilyn Denmark, 17 Jan 1955, 1 d. Education: BA, Brooklyn College, 1952; BFA, Yale University, 1955; MS, Pratt Institute, 1958; PhD, Washington University, 1977. Publications: Art and Concept, 1987; Aesthetic Legacies, 1992; Anthologies: The Arts, Society, and Literature, 1984; The Reasons of Art, 1985; Cultural Literacy and Arts Education, 1990; Ethics and Architecture, 1990; The Future of Art, 1990. Contributions to: Over 25 articles to professional philsophical journals. Memberships: American Society for Aesthetics; American Philosophical Association. Address: 24 Washington Terrace, St Louis, MO 63112, USA.

KRUMMACHER Jo(hann Henrich Karl Daniel), (Carl Danielson), b. 27 Dec 1946, Heidelberg, Germany. Writer; Minister. m. Ingrid Elisabeth Weng, 17 July 1986, 6 sons. Education: University Heidelberg; University Tübingen, 1972; Ordained to Ministry, Lutheran Church, 1972. Literary Appointments: Author of numerous books and radio essays on Ethics and Culture. Publications: Frieden im Klartext, 1980; Motivationen, 1982; Ratgeber für Kriegsdienstverweigerer, 1987; Übergänge, 1987; Wachzweige, 1991. Contributions to: Deutsches Allgemeines Sonntagsblatt; Junge Kirche; Radius; Das Plateau. Memberships: Chairman, Collegium Artium Stuttgart, 1990; President, Verein für Kirche und Kunst, 1993; Vice Chairman, Radius Pub Corp, Stuttgart. Address: Im Städtle 20, D-75385 Bad Teinach-Zavelstein 2, Germany.

KRUPAT Arnold, b. 22 Oct 1941, New York City, NY, USA. Professor. 1 s, 1 d. Education: BA, New York University, 1962; MA, 1965, PhD, 1967, Columbia University. Publications: For Those Who Come After, 1985; I Tell You Now (edited with Brian Swann), 1987; Recovering The Word (edited with Brian Swann), 1987; The Voice in The Margin, 1989; Ethnocriticism: Ethnography, History, Literature, 1992; Editor, New Voices: Essays on Native American Literature, 1993; Editor, Native American Autobiography, 1993. Contributions to: Numerous to critical journals. Address: Sarah Lawrence College, Bronxville, NY 10708, USA.

KRZYZAGORSKI Klemens, b. 1 Oct 1930, Zduny. Journalist. m. Education: Academy of Political Sciences, Warsaw. Appointments: Head, Artistic Programmes, Section of TV Wroclaw, 1965-67; Editor in Chief, Odra, Wroclaw, 1967-72, Kontrasty, Bialystok, 1974-79; Editor in Chief, Prasa Polska, 1981-85; Editor in Chief, Kultura, 1985-86, Literatura, 1986-89. Publications: Collected Journalism Klopoty z cialem, 1969; Co-author, Co-editor, 10 volumes of prose, essays in literary and socio-cultural journals, theatre scenarios: Albertus Return, 1966, Long Live the King, 1966. Address: ul Dobra m 10, 00-344 Warsaw, Poland.

KUBE-MCDOWELL Michael Paul, (Michael Hudson), b. 29 Aug 1954, Philadelphia, PA, USA. Freelance Writer; Novelist. m. Karla Jane Kube, 12 Dec 1975 (div 7 Oct 1987), 1 s. Education: BA Honours, Michigan State University, 1976; MS Education, Indiana University, 1981. Literary Appointments: Writing Instructor, Miles Laboratories, 1978-80, Goshen College, 1984-85; Correspondent, Elkhart Truth, 1982-84; Jurist, Nebula Award, 1989; Instructor, Clarion Workshop, 1990. Publications: Emprise, 1985; After The Flames, 1985; Enigma, 1986; Empery, 1987; Thieves of Light (as Michael Hudson), 1987; Odyssey (Isaac Asimov's Robot City), 1987; Alternities, 1988; The Quiet Pools, 1990; Teleplays for Tales From The Darkside: Lifebomb; Effect and Cause; The Bitterest Pill, 1985-86. Contributions to: Numerous fiction and non-fiction in various magazines. Honours: National Merit Scholar, 1972; Courier-Post Journalism Award, 1972; Hoosier State Press Association Honourable Mention, 1983; Presidential Scholar Distinguished Teacher, 1985; Philip K Dick Award Finalist, 1986. Memberships: Science Fiction Writers of America; Writers Guild of America; National Space Society; Planetary Society. Literary Agent: Scott Meredith Literary Agency. Address: PO Box 706, Okemos, MI 48805 0706, USA.

KUBLY Herbert Oswald, b. New Glarus, WI, USA. Novelist; Author; Retired Educator. (div), 1 s. Education: BA, University of Wisconsin. Literary Appointments: Professor Emeritus of English, University of Wisconsin, Parkside, Kenosha; Fellow, Wisconsin Academy of Science, Arts and Letters, 1989. Publications: American in Italy, 1955; Easter in Sicily, 1956; Varieties of Love, short stories, 1958; Italy, 1961; The Whistling Zone, novel, 1963; Switzerland, 1964; At Large, essays, 1964; Gods and Heroes, 1969; The Duchess of Glover, novel, 1975; The Native's Return, 1981; The Parkside Stories, 1985; Amazing Grace, 1990; Plays: Men to The Sea, National Theater, NY; The Cocoon, Playhouse Theater, London; The Virus, University of Wisconsin Parkside Theater; Perpetual Care, University of Wisconsin Parkside Theater. Contributions to: Esquire; Atlantic; Saturday Review and other magazines; Editor: Time Magazine; Writer For Life; Holiday magazines; Gourmet and Travel writer, Sunday Magazine of Milwaukee Journal, 1969-84. Honours: Rockefeller Grants, 1947, 1948; Fulbright Research Grant, Italy, 1950; National Book Award, 1956; First Award, Wisconsin Council for Writers, 1970, 1976; Citations for Distinguished Service in Letters, Wisconsin State Legislature and Wisconsin Academy of Science, Arts and Letters, 1982. Memberships: Authors League of America; Dramatists Guild of America, National Secretary, 1947-49; Council of Wisconsin Writers; Wisconsin Academy of Science, Arts and Letters; Poetry Society of America. Literary Agent: Harold Ober Associates, New York, USA. Address: W4970 Kubly Road, New Glarus, WI 53574, USA.

KUBRICK Stanley, b. 26 Jul 1928, NY, USA. Film Writer; Producer; Director. m. Suzanne Harlan, 1958, 3 d. Education: City College of New York. Appointments: Staff Photographer, Look, 1946-50; Produced, directed and photographed documentaries for RKO, 1951; Produced, written and directed feature films, 1952-. Publications: Co-writer, Paths of Glory, 1948; Fear and Desire, 1953; Killer's Kiss, 1955; Dr Strangelove, 1963; The Killing, 1965; Co-author, 2001: A Space Odyssey, 1968; A Clockwork Orange, 1971; Barry Lyndon, 1975; The Shining, 1978; Full Metal Jacket, 1987. Honours: New York Critics' Best Film Award, Dr Strangelove, 1964; Oscar, 1968; Best Director Award, 1971. Address: c/o Loeb and Loeb, 10100 Santa Monica Boulevard Suite 2200, Los Angeles, CA 90067, USA.

KULICKI Krzysztof Bogdan, b. 7 Feb 1938, Warsaw, Poland. Chemist. m. Danuta Kulicka, 10 Jul 1973. Education: BS Chemistry, 1961; Doctor of Technical Sciences, 1966. Publications: Straight Ahead, 1972; These Few People, 1974; Welcome The Second Year, 1975; Bad Streets, 1978; Escapers From The Street of Dreams, 1979; After Storm, 1979; Square of Harmony, 1982; Kif, 1989. Contributions to: Life of Warsaw , 1978-; Polityka, 1975-. Honours: Prize of The Publishing House of Ministry of National Defence, 1974; Competition of The Ministry of Culture, 1975. Memberships: The Union of Polish Writers, 1976-; Vice-President, Polish Section of AIEP. Literary Agent: Publishing House of Bellona, Grzybowska 77, Warsaw, Poland. Address: Sanocka 11a 26, 02 110 Warsaw, Poland.

KULTERMANN Udo, b. 1927, American (b. German). Appointments: Director, Museum Schloss Morsbroich, Leverkusen, West Germany, 1959-84; Professor of Architecture 1967-86, Ruth and Norman Moore Professor of Architecture 1986-94, Washington University, St Louis; Member, National Faculty of Humanities, Arts and Sciences, Atlanta, Georgia, 1986-; Member, Architecture Committee, Venice, Biennale, 1979-82. Publications: Architecture of Today, Hans and Wassili Luckhardt: Bauten und Entwuere, 1958; Dynamische Architektur, 1959; New Japanese Architecture, 1960; Der Schluessel zur Architektur von heute; Junge deutsche Bildhauer; New Architecture in Africa, 1963; New Architecture in the World, 1965; History of Art History, 1966; Architektur der Gegenwart: Kunst der Welt; The New Sculpture, 1967; Gabriel Grupello, 1968; The New Painting; New Directions in African Architecture, 1969; Modern Architecture in Color (with Werner Hofmann); Kenzo Tange: Architecture and Urban Design; Art and Life, 1970; New Realism, 1972; Ernest Trova, 1977; Die Architektur im 20 Jahrhundert, 1978; I Contemporanei (volume XIV of Storia della Scultura del Mondo), 1979; Architecture of the Seventies; Architekten der Dritten Welt, 1980; Zeitgenoessische Architektur in Osteuropa, 1985; Kleine Geschichte der Kunsttheorie, 1987; Visible Cities - Invisible Cities, 1988; Kunst und Wirklichkeit von Fiedler Gis Derrida, Zehn Annaeherungen, 1991. Address: 300 Mercer, Apt 17B, New York, NY 10003, USA.

KUMAR Satish, b. 27 May 1933, Moga, India. University Professor. m. Manjari, 7 May 1963, 2 daughters. Education: MA, Political Science, Delhi University; PhD, Indian School of International Studies, Delhi University, 1962. Appointments: Assistant Professor, South Asian Studies, Indian School of International Studies, 1961-67, Senior Research Officer (Pakistan), Ministry of External Affairs, 1967-72; Associate Professor, 1972-83, Professor of Diplomacy, School of International Studies, Jawaharlal Nehru University, 1983-; Visiting Professor, University of Torino, Italy, May-June 1990. Publications: Rana Polity in Napal, 1967; The New Pakistan, 1978; CIA and the Third World: A Study in Crypto Diplomacy, 1981; Bangladesh Documents, two volumes, 1971, 1972; Documents on India's Foreign Policy, 3 volumes, 1975, 1976, 1977; Yearbook on India's Foreign Policy, 1982-83, 1983-84, 1984-85, 1985-86, 1987-88, 1989, 1990-91. Contributions to: About 50 research articles in Indian and foreign journals. Address: 66 Dakshinapuram, New Campus, Jawaharlal, Nehru University, New Dehli 110067, India.

KUMIN Maxine Winokur, b. 6 Jun 1925, Philadelphia, PA, USA. Writer. m. Victor M Kumin, 29 Jun 1946, 1 s, 2 d. Education: AB, 1946, AM, 1948, Radcliffe College. Literary Appointments: Brandeis University, 1975; Hurst Professor, Literature, Washington University, 1977; Woodrow Wilson Visiting Fellow, 1979; Consultant in Poetry, Library of Congress, 1981-82; Poet-in-Residence, Bucknell University, 1983; Master Artist, Atlantic Centre for The Arts, FL, 1984. Publications include: Poetry: Halfway, 1961; The Privilege, 1965; The Nightmare Factory, 1970; Up Country, 1972; The Retrieval System, 1978; Our Ground Time Here Will Be Brief, 1982; Closing The Ring, 1984; The Long Approach, 1985; Nurture, 1988; Novels; Through Dooms of Love, 1965; The Passions of Uxport, 1968; The Abduction, 1971; The Designated Heir, 1974; In Deep: Country Essays, 1987; Women, Animals and Vegetables: Essays and Stories, 1994; short stories, essays, children's books. Contributions to: Numerous magazines and journals. Honours include: Various honorary degrees; Eunice Tietjens Memorial Prize, Poetry Magazine, 1972; Pulitzer Prize, Poetry, 1973; 1st Prize, Borestone Mountain, 1976; Recognition Award, Radcliffe College Alumnae, 1978; Award, American Academy and Institute, Arts and Letters, 1980; Academy of American Poets Fellowship, 1985; Levinson Award, Poetry Magazine, 1986; Poet Laureate, State of New Hampshire, 1989; Fellowships; Scholarships. Memberships: Poetry Society of America; PEN; Writers Union. Literary Agent: Emilie Jacobson, Curtis Brown Limited. Address: c/o Curtis Brown Limited, 10 Astor Place, New York, NY 10003, USA.

KUNDERA Milan, b. 1 Apr 1929, Brno, Czechoslovakia. Writer. m. Vera Hrabankova, 1967. Education: Film Faculty, Academy of Music and Dramatic Arts, Prague. Literary Appointments: Assistant, Assistant Professor, Film Faculty, Academy of Music and Dramatic Arts, Prague, 1958-69; Professor, University of Rennes, 1975-80; Professor, Ecole des hautes etudes en sciences sociales, Paris, 1980-. Publications: Drama: Jacques et son maitre, 1971-81; Short stories: Laughable Loves, 1970; Novels: The Joke, 1967; Life is Elsewhere, 1973; La Valse aux adieux, 1976; Livre du rire et de l'oubli, 1979; Essays: L'art Du Rohan, 1986; The Unbearable Lightness of Being, 1984. Honours: Union of Czechoslovak Writers' Prize, 1968; Czechoslovak Writers' Publishing House Prize, 1969; Prix Medicis, 1973; Premio Letterario Mondello, 1978; Commonwealth Award, 1981; Prix Europa-Litterature, 1982; Los Angeles Times Prize, 1984; Jerusalem Prize, 1985; Prix de la Critique de l'Academie Française, 1987; Prix Nelly Sachs, 1987; Ostereichischere staatspreis für europeische litterateur, 1987. Memberships: Editorial Board, Literami noviny, 1963-67, 1968; Editorial Board, Listy, 1968-69. Address: Ecole des hautes etudes en sciences sociales, 54 boulevard Raspail, Paris 75006, France.

KUNITZ Stanley (Jasspon), b. 1905, America. Poet; Writer of Literary Essays. Literary Appointments include: Director, YM-YWHA Poetry Workshop, NY, 1958-62; Danforth Visiting Lecturer, US, 1961-63; Lecturer, 1963-67, Adjunct Professor of Writing, 1967-85, Columbia University, NY; Editor, Yale Series of Younger Poets, Yale University Press, New Haven, CT, 1969-77; Visiting Professor, Yale University, New Haven, CT, 1970 and Rutgers University, Camden, NJ, 1974; Consultant in Poetry, Library of Congress, WA, 1974-75; Visiting Professor and Senior Fellow in Humanities, Princton University, NJ, 1978; Visiting Professor, Vassar College, Ploughkeepsie, NY, 1981; Montgomery Fellow, Dartmouth College, Hanover, NH, 1991. Publications include: On Intellectual Things (verse), 1930; Passport to The War: A Selection of Poems, 1944; Edited with H Haycraft, British Authors Before 1800: A Biographical Dictionary, 1952; Selected Poems 1928-1958, 1958; Editor, Poems by John Keats, 1964; Edited with V Colby, European Authors 1000-1900: A Biographical Dictionary of European Literature, 1967; The Testing-Tree Poems, 1971; Editor and translator with M Hayward, Poems of Akhmatova, 1973; The Terrible Threshold: Selected Poems 1940-70, 1974; Translation, Under Full Sail by A Voznesensky, 1974; A Kind of Order, A Kind of Folly, essays, 1975; Editor and co-translator, Orchard Lamps by Ivan Drach, 1978; The Poems of Stanley Kunitz, 1928-1978, 1979; The Wellfleet Whale and Companion Poems, 1983; Next-to-Last Things, poems and essays, 1985; Editor, The Essential Blake, 1987. Address: 37 West 12th Street, New York, NY 10011, USA.

KUNSTLER William M, b. 1919, American. Appointments: Partner, Kunstler and Kuby, lawyers, 1949-; Associate Professor of Law, New York Law School, 1950-, and Pace College, 1951-; Lecturer, New School for Social Research, 1966-. Publications: Our Pleasant Vices, 1941; The Law of Accidents, 1954; First Degree, 1960; Beyond a Reasonable Doubt, 1961; The Case for Courage, 1962; ... And Justice for All, 1963; The Minister and the Choir Singer, 1964; Deep in My Heart, 1966; The Hall-Mills Murder Case, 1980; Trials and Tribulations, 1985; Hints & Allegations, 1994; My Life As a Radical Lawyer, 1994. Contributions to: The Nation; The New York Times; Covert Action; The Champion; The Los Angeles Times; The St John's Law Review; The Creighton Law Review; The Gonzaga Law Review; The New York University Journal of Social Change; Others. Memberships: PEN; Phi Delta Phi; Phi Beta Kappa. Literary Agent: Richard Curtis' Associates Inc. Address: 13 Gay Street, New York, NY 10014, USA.

KUNZE Reiner Alexander, b. 16 Aug 1933, Oelsnitz, Germany. Writer. Education: Studies on philosophy & journalism, literary history, art history, music history, University of Leipzig, 1951-55; MA; DPhil. Publications: Poetry, Prose, Translations, Films; Sensible Wege, 1969; Der Loewe Leopold, 1970; Zimmerlautstaerke, 1972; Brief mit blauem Siegel, 1973; Die wunderbaren Jahre, 1976; Film Script, Die wunderbaren Jahre, 1979; Auf eigene Hoffnung, 1981; Eine stadtbekannte Geschichte, 1982; In Deutschland zuhaus, 1984; Gespraech mit der Amsel, 1984; Eines jeden einziges Leben, 1986; Zurueckgeworfen auf sich selbst, 1989; Das weisse Gedicht, 1989; Deckname Lyrik, 1990; Wohin der Schlaf sich schlafen legt, 1991; Mensch ohne Macht, 1991; Am Sonnenhang, 1993; Begehrte, unbequeme Freiheit, 1993. Honours: Translation Prize, Czech Writers Association, 1968; German Young People's Book Prize, 1970; Moelle Literary Prize, Sweden, 1973; Literary Prize, Bavarian Academy of Fine Arts, 1973; Georg Trakl Prize, Austria, 1977; Andreas Gryphius Prize, 1977; Georg Buechner Prize, 1977; Bavarian Film Prize, 1979; Geschwister Scholl Prize, 1981; Eichendorff Prize, 1984; Bundesverdienstkreuz 1 Klasse, 1984; Bayerischer Verdienstorden, 1988; Kulturpreis Ostbayern, 1989; Herbert und Elsbeth Weichmann Preis, 1990; Hanns Martn Schleyer Preis, 1990; Grossest Verdienstkreuz der Bundesrepublik Deutschland, 1993;

Ehrendoktorwürde der Technischen Universität Dresden, 1993. Memberships: Bavarian Academy of Fine Arts; Academy of Arts, Berlin, 1975-92; German Academy for Language & Literature, Darmstadt; Freie Akademie der Künste Mannheim; Ehrenmitglied des Collegium europaeum Jenense der Friedrich Schiller Universität Jena; des Ungarischen Schriftstellerverbandes und des Tschechischen PEN-Zentrums. Address: Am Sonnenhang 19, D-94130 Obernzell-Erlau, Germany.

KUO Gloria Liang-Hui, b. 10 Jul 1926, Kaifeng, Henan, China. Author. m. 1949, 2 s. Education: BA, National Szechuan University, Chengtu, 1948. Literary Appointment: Journalist, Hsin Ming Evening News, Shanghai, 1948-49. Publications: 34 novels, 20 novelettes, 2 non-fiction books, some in English including: Debt of Emotion, 1959; The Lock of A Heart, 1962; Far Far Way to Go, 1962; Stranger in Calcutta, 1973; Taipei Women, 1980; Appreciating Chinese Art, non-fiction, 1985; Untold Tales of Chinese Art, 1987. Contributions to: Major newspapers: China Times; United Daily News, Taiwan; World Journal, NY; Sing Tao Daily News; Sing Tao Evening News; Sing Tao Express, Hong Kong; Morning Post; Sabah Times, Malaysia; Major magazines include: Artist, Taiwan; Art of China Monthly, Hong Kong and Taiwan. Memberships: Chinese Literature Association, Taiwan; Executive Director, 1978-, Chinese Antique Collectors Association. Literary Agent: International Art Promotions Centre, 906 Eastern Centre, 1065 King's Road, Quarry Bay, Hong Kong. Address: 11F, 126-23 Chung Hsiao East Road, Sec 4, Taipei, China.

KUO Nancy (Nany Kuo, Nanse, Ssujen), b. 8 Apr 1921, Shanghai, China. Writer; Artist; Designer; Director; Dancer. m. Guy Davis, 1 Oct 1949, 1 daughter. Education: Diplomas, Xin Hua Art Academy, Shanghai, 1936. Appointments: Editor, Suixi Weekly, 1937; Member, Editorial Board, Jun Zhi You, 1946; Art Critic, Arts Review, London, England, 1967-70; Honorary President, Voice of Qing Yuan, 1989. Publications: Chinese Paper-Cut Pictures, 1964, paperback 1965; Chinese Painting, 1967-70; The Mount Trust Collection of Chinese Art, 1970; The Harari Collection, 1970; The Fantastic Landscape, of Kweilin, 1973; Chinese Acrobats, Past and Present in China, 1973; Chinese Exhibition in London, 1974; Chinese Way, 1975-76; I Tai-P'ing, I Protagonisti della Rivoluzione, 1975; The Magic of Chinse Gardens, 1980; Japanese Ceramics Today Exhibition, 1983; Chinese Cinema Past and Present, 1984; The Sky is Singing and Other Poems, 1984; Rolling and Folding, 1985; The Amazing Chinese Puppet Theatre, 1987; Art Reviews on Courbet, Leonardo and other exhibitions. Address: 35 Artillery Road, Ramsgate, Kent CT11 8PT, England.

KUO Nany. See: KUO Nancy.

KUPFERBERG Herbert, b. 1918, American. Literary Appointments: With New York Herald Tribune, 1942-66; Senior Editor, Parade Magazine, 1967-. Publications: Those Fabulous Philadelphians, 1969; The Mendelssohns, 1971; Felix Mendelssohn, 1972; A Rainbow of Sound, 1969; Opera, 1975; Tanglewood, 1976; Basically Bach, The Book of Classical Music Lists, 1985; Amadeus: A Mozart Mosaic, 1986. Address: 113-114 72 Road, Forest Hills, New York, NY 11375, USA.

KUPPNER Frank, b. 1951, Glasgow, Scotland. Poet. Education: University of Glasgow. Publications: A Bad Day for the Sung Dynasty, 1984; The Intelligent Observation of Naked Women, 1987; Ridiculous Absurd Disgusting, 1989. Address: c/o Carcanet Press Ltd, 208-212 Corn Exchange Buildings, Manchester M4 3BQ, England.

KURAPEL Alberto, b. 5 Feb 1946, Santiago. Playwright; Poet; Essayist; Performer. m. Susana Cáceres, 5 Jan 1968. Education: Graduate, School of Theatre, University of Chile, 1969. Literary Appointments: Artistic Director, Compagnie des Arts Exilio, 1981-94; Playwright in residence. Publications: Correo de Exilio/Courrier de'exil, 1986; 3 Performances, Theatrales de Alberto Kurapel, 1987; Prométhée Enchainé selon Alberto Kurapel, 1988; Carta de Ajuste ou Nous N'avons Plus Besoin de Calendrier, 1991; Pasarelas/Passerelles, 1991; Berri-UQAM, 1992; Des marches sur le dos de la neige/Peldaños en la espalda de la nieve, 1993. Contributions to: Canadian Theatre Review; Revue Possibles; La Escena Latinoamericana; Revue Humanitas; Ellipse. Honours: Gold Medal, International Competition, Verso il Futuro, Italy, 1976; Special Prize, F de Santis per la Poesia, Italy, 1976; Honorary Mention, contribution for knowledge and diffussion of Latin American Theatre, University of Santiago and Instituto Internacional de Teoría y Crítica de Teatro Latinoamericano, 1992. Memberships: PEN Club; Playwrights Union of Canada; Union

des écrivains et écrivaines québécois; Association des poètes du Québec. Address: La Compagnie des Arts Exilio, 6865 Christophe Colomb 313, Montréal, Québec, H2S 2H3, Canada.

KUREISHI Hanif, b. 5 Dec 1954, London, England. Education: BA Philosophy, King's College, University of London. Literary Appointment: Writer-in-Residence, Royal Court Theatre, London, 1981, 1985-86. Publications: Plays: Soaking The Heat (produced London), 1976; The Mother Country (produced London), 1980; The King and Me (produced London), 1980; Outskirts (produced London), 1981; Cinders, from a play by Janusz Glowacki (produced London), 1981; Borderline (produced London), 1981; Artists and Admirers, with David Leveaux, from a play by Alexander Ostrovsky (produced London), 1981; Birds of Passage, 1983; Included in Outskirts, The King and Me, Tomorrow-Today!, London and New York, 1983; Mother Courage, adaptation of a play by Brecht (produced London), 1984; The Buddha of Suburbia; My Beautiful Launderette (screenplay) includes essay The Rainbow Sign, London, 1986; Sammy and Rosie Get Laid (screenplay), London, 1988; Radio Plays: You Can't Go Home, 1980; The Trial, from a novel by Kafka, 1982. Honours: George Devine Award, 1981; Evening Standard Award for Screenplay, 1985. Literary Agent: Sheila Lemon. Address: c/o Sheila Lemon, Lemon and Durbridge Limited, 24 Pottery Lane, London, W11 4LZ, England.

KURTZ Katherine Irene, b. 18 Oct 1944, Florida, USA. Author. m. Scott Roderick MacMillan, 9 Apr 1983, 1 son. Education: BS, University of Miami, 1966; MA, University of California, Los Angeles, 1971. Publications: Deryni Rising, 1970; Deryni Checkmate, 1972; High Deryni, 1973; Camber of Culdi, 1976; Saint Camber, 1978; Camber the Heretic, 1981; The Bishop's Heir, 1984; The King's Justice, 1985; The Quest for Saint Camber, 1986; Lammas Night, 1983; The Legacy of Lehr, 1986; The Deryni Archives, 1986; The Harrowing of Gwynedd, 1989; Deryni Magic: A Grimoire, 1990; King Javan's Year, 1992; The Bastard Prince, 1994; With Deborah Turner Harris: The Adept, 1991; Lodge of The Lynx, 1992; The Templar Treasure, 1993; Dagger Magic, 1994; Edited Anthology, Tales of The Knights Templar, 1995; Various short stories. Honours: The Edmund Hamilton Memorial Award, 1977; The Balrog Award, 1982. Memberships: Authors Guild; Science Fiction Writers of America. Literary Agent: Russell Galen, Scovil, Chichak, Galen Literary Agency. Address: Holybrooke Hall, Kilmacanogue, Bray, Co Wicklow, Ireland.

KURUP O N V, b. 27 May 1931, India. University Teacher, Professor Emeritus. m. Sarojini, 5 Jun 1958, 1 s, 1 d. Education: BA Economics and History; MA Malayan Literature and Kerala History. Literary Appointments: Sahitya Akademi, Delhi; Professor Emeritus, Calicut University. Publications: Porutunna Soundariam, 1950; Dahikkunna Pana Patram, 1956; Mayilppeeli, 1964; Oru Tulli Velicham, 1966; Agni Salabhangal, 1971; Aksharam, 1974; Karutha Pakshiyude Pattu, 1977; Uppu, 1980; Bhoomikkoru Charamageetam, 1984; Sarngaka pakshikal, 1987. Contributions to: Various magazines and journals. Honours: Kerala State Sahitya Akademi Award for Poetry, 1971; National Sahitya Akademi Award, 1975; Soviet Land Nehru Award, 1982; Vayalar Literary Award, 1981. Memberships: Executive Board: State Sahitya Akademi, 1972-84, National Sahitya Akademi, New Delhi, 1982-87; Kerala Sahitya Parishad. Address: Indeevaram, Cotton Hill, Trivandrum 695014, India.

KURZMAN Dan, b. 1929, American. m. Florence Knopf. Appointments: Correspondent, International News Service, 1948; Feature Writer, Marshall Plan Information Office, 1948-49, Paris; Correspondent, National Broadcasting Company, Middle East, 1950-53; Bureau Chief, McGraw Hill World News Service, Tokyo, 1954-59; Correspondent, Washington Post, 1962-69; Contributor, Washington Star, 1975-80, Independent News Alliance, 1979-84, San Francisco Chronicle, 1991-92. Publications: Kishi and Japan: The Search for the Sun, 1960; Subversion of the Innocents, 1963; Santo Domingo: Revolt of the Damned, 1965; Genesis 1948: The First Arab-Israeli War, 1970; The Race for Rome, 1975; The Bravest Battle: The Twenty-Eight Days of the Warsaw Ghetto Uprising, 1976; Miracle of November: Madrid's Epic Stand 1936, 1980; Ben-Gurion: Prophet of Fire, 1983; Day of the Bomb: Countdown to Hiroshima, 1985; A Killing Wind: Inside Union Carbide and The Bhopal Catastrophe, 1987; Fatal Voyage: The Sinking of the USS Indianapolis, 1990; Left to Die: The Tragedy of the USS Juneau, 1994; Blood and Water: Sabotaging Hitler's Bomb, 1995. Contributions to: New York Times Op-Ed Page, 1988-; Washington Post (Book Reviewer), 1988-; Los Angeles Times (Book Reviewer), 1988-. Literary Agent: Julian Bach Literary Agency,

New York, USA. Address: c/o H Knopf, 187 Boulevard, Apartment 9-H, Passaic, NJ 07055, USA.

KUSCHE Lothar, b. 2 May 1929, Berlin, Germany. Author. Publications: Satirical novels and essays including: Das bombastische Windei, 1958; Nanu wer schiesst denn da?, 1960; Ueberall ist Zwergenland, 1960; Quer durch England in anderthalb Stunden, 1961; Kaese und Loecher, 1963; Kein Wodka fur den Staatsanwalt, 1967; Wie man einen Haushalt aushaelt, 1969; Patientenfibel, 1971; Kusches Drucksachen, 1974; Kellner Willi serviert, 1978; Knoten im Taschentuch, 1980; Donald Duck siehe unter Greta Garbo, 1981; Leute im Hinterkopf, 1983; Der Mann auf dem Kleiderschrank, 1985; Nasen die man nicht vergisst, 1986. Contributions to: Die Weltbuehne; Eulenspiegel, Berlin. Honours: Heinrich Heine Prize, 1960; Heinrich Greif Prize, 1973; National Prize, DDR, 1984. Memberships: International PEN; Writers Association of Germany; Association of Journalists of Germany. Address: Woelckpromenade 5, DDR 1120, Berlin, Germany.

KUSHNER Aleksandr Semyonovich, b. 14 Sep 1936, Leningrad, Russia. Poet. m. Elena Vsevolodovna Nevzgliadova, 21 Jul 1984, 1 s. Education: Graduate, Pedagogical Institute, 1959. Literary Appointments: Editor in Chief, Publishing House, Biblioteka Poeta. Publications: First Impression, 1962; Omens, 1969; Letter, 1974; Voice, 1978; The Tavrichesky Garden, 1984; The Hedgerow, 1988; A Night Melody, 1991; Apollo in The Snow, essays on Russian Poetry and personal memoirs, 1991. Contributions to: Novii Mir; Znamya; Zvezda; Unost; Voprosi Literaturi. Memberships: Union of Writers; PEN Club. Address: Kaluzhsky Pereulok 9, Apt 48, St Petersburg 193015, Russia.

KUSHNER Tony, Dramatist. Publications: The Illusion (adaptation of Corneille); A Bright Room Called Day, 1987. Creative works: Plays: Angels in America: Millenium Approaches & Perestroika; Slavs!, 1994; A Bright Room Called Day. Honours: Pulitzer Prize, 1993; Literature Award, American Academy & Institute of Arts & Letters, 1994; Perry Award, Best Play, 1993, 1994. Address: c/o Joyce Ketay Agency, 1501 Broadway Suite 1910, New York, NY 10036, USA.

KUSKIN Karla Seidman, (Nicholas Charles), b. 1932, American. Writer and Illustrator of children's fiction and verse. Publications include: James and Rain, verse, 1957; In the Middle of the Trees, verse, 1958; Just Like Everyone Else, fiction, 1959; Square as a House, verse, 1960; The Bear Who Saw the Spring, verse, 1961; All Sizes of Noises, verse, 1962; (as Nicholas Charles), How Do You Get From Here to There? verse, 1962; Sand and Snow, verse, 1965; (as Nicholas Charles), Jane Ann June Spoon and Her Very Adventurous Trip to the Moon, verse, 1966; The Walk the Mouse Girls Took, fiction, 1967; Watson, The Smartest Dog in the USA, fiction, 1968; What Did You Bring Me? fiction, 1973; What Do You Mean by Design? screenplay, 1973; An Electric Talking Picture, screenplay, 1973; Near the Window Tree: Poems and Notes, 1975; A Boy Had a Mother Who Brought Him a Hat, verse, 1976; A Space Story, 1978; Herbert Hated Being Small, verse, 1979; (contributing Author), The State of the Language, 1980; Night Again, verse, 1981; Something Sleeping in the Hall, verse, 1985; Jerusalem, Shining Still, 1987; Soap Soup, 1992; A Great Miracle Happened There (illustrated by Robert Andrew Parker), 1993; City Dog, 1994; Patchwork Island (illustrated by Petra Mathers), 1994; Paul (illustrated by Milton Avery), 1994; City Noise (illustrated by Renee Flower), 1994. Contributions to: New York Mag; House and Garden; Horizon Magazine; Wilson Lib Bulletin; New York Times Book Section; Contributing Editor, Saturday Review, 1973. Address: 96 Joralemon Street, Brooklyn, NY 11201, USA.

KUSTOW Michael (David), b. 1939, British. Literary Appointments: Director, Institute of Contemporary Arts, 1967-71; Associate Director, National Theatre of Great Britain, 1973-81; Lecturer in Dramatic Arts, Harvard University, Cambridge, MA, 1980-82; Commissioning Editor, Channel 4 TV, 1981-. Publications: Productions: Editor, The Book of Us, Jose Triana; Night of The Assassins, translation, 1968; Tank, Roger Planchon and People's Theatre, 1975; Stravinsky: The Soldier's Story, 1980; Charles Wood's Has Washington Legs, Harold Pinter's Family Voices, 1981; The Manhabbaraten, 1989; The War That Never Ends, 1991. Address: c/o Tom Corrie, The Peters Fraser and Dunlop Group Limited, The Chambers, Chelsea Harbour, Lots Road, London, SW10 0XF, England.

KWITNY Jonathon, Journalist; Writer. Publications: The Fountain Pen Conspiracy, 1973; The Mullendove Murder Case, 1974; Shakedown, 1977; Vicious Circles: The Mafia in the Marketplace, 1979;

Endless Enemies, 1984; The Crimes of Patriots, 1987; Acceptable Risks, 1992. Work in Progress: Biography of Pope John Paul II (Karol Wojtyla). Address: Box 7333, James A Farley Station, New York, NY 10116, USA.

KYLE Duncan (Michael Meldrum), Author. Publications: A Cage of Ice, 1970; Flight into Fear, 1972; A Raft of Swords, 1974; The Semonov Impulse (as James Meldrum), 1975; Terror's Cradle, 1975; In Deep, 1976; Black Camelot, 1978; Green River High, 1979; Stalking Point, 1981; The King's Commissar, 1983; The Dancing Men, 1985. Address: c/o William Collins Limited, 8 Grafton Street, London, W1X 3LA, England.

KYLE Susan (Eloise Spaeth), (Diana Palmer, Diana Blayne), b. 12 Dec 1946, Cuthbert, Randolph County, Georgia, USA. Author. m. James Edward Kyle, 9 Oct 1972, 1 son. Education: BA, History, Piedmont College, 1995. Publications: Heather's Song, 1982; Amelia, 1993; Diamond Spur, 1988; Nora, 1994; All That Glitters, 1995; 79 others, including 1 science fiction novel. Contributions to: Poetry in several small Journals; Various Non-fiction articles in Magazines. Honours: Alpha Chi; Torch Club; 7 Walden Books Bestseller Awards; 4 Dalton Bestseller Awards; Numerous Others. Memberships: The Authors Guild, New York. Literary Agent: Maureen Walters/Curtis Brown Ltd, New York, USA. Address: PO Box 844, Cornelia, GA 30531, USA.

L

L'ENGLE Madeleine, b. 29 Nov 1918, New York City, USA. Author. m. Hugh Franklin, 26 Jan 1946, 1 son, 2 daughters. Education: AB, Smith College, 1941. Appointments: Writer-in-residence, Cathedral St John the Divine, New York City, 1965-. Publications: A Wrinkle in Time; A Wind in the Door; A Swiftly Tilting Planet; Circle of Quiet; A Severed Wasp; A Ring of Endless Light; (for Younger Readers) Many Waters; A House Like A Lotus; The Sphinx at Dawn; Prayers for Sunday; Prayers for Everyday; Dragons in the Waters; Dance in the Desert; The Young Unicorns; The Arm of the Starfish; The Moon by Night; A Wrinkle in Time; The Anti-Muffins; Meet the Austins; Camilla; And Both Were Young. Literary Agent: Robert Lescher, Lescher & Lescher, 67 Irving Place, NYC, NY 10003, USA. Address: 924 West End Avenue, Apt 95, New York, NY 10025, USA.

L'ESTRANGE Anna. See: **ELLERBECK Rosemary Anne L'Estrange.**

L'HEUREUX John. Publications: Family Affairs, 1974; Desires, 1981; A Woman Run Mad, 1988; Comedians, 1990; An Honorable Profession, 1991; A Shrine to Altamira, 1992. Address: Dept of English, Stanford University, Stanford, CA 94305-2087, USA.

LA FRENAIS Ian, b. 7 Jan 1937. Writer; Screenwriter; Producer. m. Doris Vartan, 1984, 1 stepson. Publications include: Writer or Co-Writer (with Dick Clement) Television: The Likely Lads, 1965-68; The Adventures of Lucky Jim, 1968; Whatever Happened to The Likely Lads, 1971-73; Seven of One, 1973; Thick as Thieves, 1974; Comedy Playhouse, 1975; Porridge, 1974-77; Going Straight, 1978; Further Adventure of Lucky Jim, 1983; Auf Wiedershen Pet, 1983-84; Mog, 1985; Lovejoy, 1986; Freddy and Max, 1989; Spender, 1990; Old Boy Network, 1992; Full Stretch, 1992; The Rainbow, 1993; US Television: On The Rocks, 1976-77; Billy, 1979; Sunset Limousine, 1983; Films: Writer or Co-Writer (with Dick Clement): The Jokers, 1967; The Touchables, 1968; Otley, 1968; Hannibal Brooks, 1969; The Virgin Soldiers, 1969; Villain, 1971; The Likely Lads, 1974; Porridge, 1979; To Russia with Elton, co-produced and co-directed, 1979; Prisoner of Zenda, 1981; Bullshot, produced, 1983; Water, 1984; Vice Versa, co-written, co-produced, 1988; The Commitments, 1991; Stage: Billy, writer, 1974; Anyone for Denis?, co-producer, 1982; Partner (with Dick Clement and Allan McKeown), Witzend Productions. Honours: Awards from BAFTA, Broadcasting Guild, Evening News, Pye, Screen Writers' Guild, Society of TV Critics, London Film Critics, Evening Standard Film Awards, Writers Guild of America. Address: 2557 Hutton Drive, Beverley Hills, CA 90211, USA.

LA TOURETTE Jacqueline, b. 1926, USA. Novelist. Publications: The Joseph Stone, 1971; A Matter of Sixpence, 1972; The Madonna Creek Witch, 1973; The Previous Lady, 1974; The Pompeii Scroll, 1975; Shadows in Umbria, 1979; The Wild Harp, 1981; Patarran, 1983; The House on Octavia Street, 1984; The Incense Tree, 1986. Address: c/o Raines and Raines, 71 Park Avenue, New York, NY 10016, USA.

LACEY Robert, b. 1944. Author. Literary Appointments: Assistant Editor, Sunday Times Magazine, London, 1969-73; Editor, Look! pages, Sunday Times, 1973-74. Publications: The French Revolution, 2 volumes (author, editor), 1968; The Rise of Napolean (author, editor), 1969; The Peninsular War (author, editor), 1969; 1812: The Retreat From Moscow (author, editor), 1969; Robert, Earl of Essex: An Elizabethan Icarus, 1971; The Life and Times of Henry VIII, 1972; The Queens of The North Atlantic, 1973; Sir Walter Raleigh, 1973; Sir Francis Drake and The Golden Hinde (author, editor), 1975; Heritage of Britain (editor, contributor), 1975; Majesty: Elizabeth II and The House of Windsor, 1977; The Kingdom: Arabia and The House of Saud, 1981; Princess, 1982; Aristocrats, 1983; Ford: The Men and The Machine, 1986; God Bless Her: Her Majesty Queen Elizabeth The Queen Mother, 1987; Little Man: Meyer Lansky and The Gangster Life, 1991; Grace, 1994. Address: 12783 E West Forest Hill Boulevard, Suite 105, West Palm Beach, FL 33414, USA.

LACKEY Mercedes, b. South Bend, IN, USA. Writer. m. 14 Dec 1990. Education: BSci Biology, Purdue University, 1972. Appointments: Artist's model, 1975-81; Computer Programmer, Associates Data Processing, 1979-82; Surveyor, Layout Designer, Analyst, CAIRS (survey and data processing firm), 1981-82, South Bend, IN; Computer Programmer, American Airlines, Tulsa, OK, 1982-. Publications: Arrows of The Queen, 1987; Arrow's Flight, 1987; Arrow's Fall, 1988; Oathbound, 1988; Oathbreakers, 1989; Reap The Whirlwind, 1989; Magic's Pawn, 1989; Burning Water, 1989; Magic's Promise, 1990; The Magic-Winds Books: Winds of Change, 1992; Winds of Fury, 1993; The Bard's Tale Series: Fortress of Frost and Fire, 1993; Prison of Souls, 1993; Forthcoming: Oathbound; Oathbreakers; Freedom, Flight and Fantasy; Written lyrics for and recorded nearly 50 songs for Off-Centaur. Honour: Best Books, American Library Association, 1987 for Arrows of The Queen. Membership: Science Fiction and Fantasy Writers of America. Literary Agent: Scott Meredith, New York, USA. Address: PO Box 8309, Tulsa, OK 74101 8309, USA.

LADERO QUESADA Miguel-Angel, b. 14 Jan 1943, Valladolid, Spain. Professor of Mediaeval History. m. Isabel Galan Parra, 22 June 1968, 2 sons, 1 daughter. Education: Doctorate in History, University of Valladolid, 1967. Appointments: Professor of Mediaeval History, La Laguna University, Canary Islands, 1970; Professor of Mediaeval History, University of Seville, 1974; Professor of Mediaeval History 1978-, Director, Mediaeval History Department, 1980-95, University Vice-Rector, 1986-87, Complutensian University, Madrid. Publications: Castilla y la conquista del reino de Granada, 1967, 3rd edition 1993; Granada Historia de un pais islamico, 1969, 3rd edition, 1988; La Hacienda Real de Castilla en el siglo XV, 1973; Historia de Sevilla La ciudad Medieval, 1976, 3rd edition 1988; Historia Universal Edad Media, 1987, 2nd edition 1992; Los mudejares de Castilla y otros estudios, 1988; Los Reyes Catolicos, La Corona y la unidad de Espana, 1988; Andalusia en tomo a 1492, 1992; Fiscalidad y Poder Real en Castilla (1252-1369), Madrid, 1993. Contributions to: Hispania; Anuario de Estudios Medievales; En la Espana Medieval, Madrid; Historia Instituciones, Documentos, Sevilla; Annales ESC, Paris; Sefarad, Madrid; Cuadernos de Historia de Espana, Buenos Aires. Honours: National Prize for History, 1994; Officer, Ordre des Palmes Academiques, 1987. Memberships: Full Member, Royal Historical Academy of Spain; International Commission of Urban History; International Commission of Representative and Parliamentary Institutions; Society for Spanish and Portuguese Historical Studies, USA. Address: Departamento de Historia Medieval, Facultad de Geografia e Historia, Universidad Complutense, 28040 Madrid, Spain.

LADIA Eleni, b. 13 Aug 1945, Athens, Greece. Writer. Education: Graduated, Archaeology, University of Athens, 1970. Publications: Figures on a Krater, short stories, 1973; The Fragmentary Relationship, novel, 1974, 3rd edition, 1983; Articles on the poetry of Kavafis, 1974, 1975; The Black Hermes, short stories, 1977; The Copper Sleep, short stories, 1980; The Schizophrenic God, short stories, 1983; Poets and Ancient Greece, essay, 1983; X, The Lion-Faced, novel, 1986; Horography, short stories, 1990; Frederic and John, narrative, 1991. Contributions to: Short stories, essays and archaeological articles to various journals and magazines, Athens and abroad. Honours: 2nd State Prize for Copper Sleep, 1981; Prize, Academy of Athens-Uranis Foundation, for Horography, 1991. Memberships: National Greek Literary Society; PEN Club. Address: 44 Kavatha Street, 157 73 Athens, Greece.

LADY BALOGH. See: **STORR Catherine.**

LAFFERTY R(aphael) A(loysius), b. 1914, USA. Freelance Writer; Former Buyer. Publications: Past Master, 1968; The Reefs of Earth, 1968; Space Chantey, 1968; Fourth Mansions, 1969; Nine Hundred Grandmothers, short stories, 1970; The Devil is Dead, 1971; Arrive at Easterwine, 1971; The Fall of Rome, historical novel, 1971; The Flame is Green, historical novel, 1971; Okla Hannali, historical novel, 1972; Strange Doings, short stories, 1972; Does Anyone Else Have Something Further to Add, short stories, 1974; Funnyfingers, and Cabrito, short stories, 1976; Horns on Their Heads, short stories, 1976; Not to Mention Camels, 1976; Apocalypses, 1977; Archipelago, 1979; Aurelia, 1982; The Annals of Klepsis, 1983; Golden Gate and Other Stories, 1983; Four Stories, 1983; Heart of Stone Dear and Other Stories, 1983; Snake in His Bosom and Other Stories, 1983; Through Elegant Eyes, stories, 1983; Ringing Changes, stories, 1984; The Man Who Made Models and Other Stories, 1984; Half a Sky, 1984; Slippery and Other Stories, 1985. Address: 1715 South Trenton Avenue, Tulsa, OK 74120, USA.

LAFFIN John, b. 21 Sept 1922, Sydney, Australia. Author; Journalist; Lecturer. m. Hazelle Stonham, 6 Oct 1943, 1 son, 2 daughters. Education: MA; DLitt. Appointments: Battlefield

Archaeologist; Advisor/Consultant, War, Military History and Islam. Publications: 116 books including: Digger - Story of Australian Soldier, 1958, 1990; The Hunger to Come, 1966; Devils Goad, 1970; The Arab Mind, 1974; Dagger of Islam, 2979; Damn the Dardanelles! 1980, 2nd edition 1985; Fight for the Falklands, 1982; Man the Nazis Couldn't Catch, 1984; On the Western Front, 1985; Know the Middle East, 1985; Brassey's Battles, 1986; War Annual 1, 1986; War Annual 2, 1987; Battlefield Archaeology, 1987; Western Front, 1916-17: The Price of Honour, 1988; Western Front, 1917-18: The Cost of Victory, 1988 (both Time/Life books); Holy War - Islam Fights, Collins; War Annual 3, 1987; War Annual 4, 1988; British Butchers and Bunglers of World War I, 1989; War Annual 5, 1991; The Western Front Illustrated, 1991; Dictionary of Africa Since 1960, 1991; Guidebook to Australian Battlefields of France and Flanders 1916-18, 1992; Digging up the Digger's War, 1993; Panorama of the Western Front, 1993; A Western Front Companion, 1994; Forever Forward, 1994; War Annual 6, 1994; Aussie Guide to Britain, 1995; Hitler Warned Us, 1995; Contributions to: Magazines and Journals: Special Correspondent for the Daily Mail, London, on Islam, Arab World and Middle East; The Australian, Military History. Memberships: Society of Authors, UK; Australian Society of Authors; Founder, 1988, John Laffin Australian Battlefield Museum. Address: Oxford House, Church St, Knighton, Powys LD7 1AG, Wales: Oxford House, Sundown Village, Narrabundah, ACT 2604, Australia.

LAHTINEN Anni, b. 2 Feb 1914, Kuhmalahti, Finland. Writer. Publications: Ystavani Elvirra, Mustalaistytto, 1973; Hiiret, 1974; Kakstoista Meren Rannalla, 1976; Jattilaisen Tasku, 1980; Voi Elaman J Kevat, 1981; Sinappia, Olkaa Hyva, 1982; Tuku Tuku Lampaitani, 1983; Tunturikurmitsa Kutsuu, 1984; Kyynelia Joulupuurossa, 1985; Tukikohdan Mirja, 1987; Kylla, herra tohtori, 1988; Vetehisen kutsu, 1989. Contributions to: Various publications and broadcasting productios: Rivien Välistä and Heitä luetaan, 1992. Honours: Country Award for Literature, 1980; Finnish State Prize for Literature, 1981; City Prize, 1981; Publishing Company's Prize, 1983. Memberships: Finnish Writers' Society; Finnish Provincial Writers' Society; Finnish Dramatists' Society; Local Literary Society. Address: Yrjönkatu 3-5 A 7, 33100 Tampere, Finland.

LAIRD Elizabeth Mary Risk, b. 21 Oct 1943, New Zealand. Writer. m. David Buchanan McDowall, 19 Apr 1975, 2 s. Education: BA, Bristol University; MLitt, Edinburgh University. Publications: The Miracle Child, 1985; The Road to Bethlehem, 1987; Red Sky in The Morning, 1988; Crackers, 1989; Arcadia, 1990; Kiss The Dust, 1991; Toucan Tecs, 1992. Honours: Children's Book Award, The Burnley Express. Membership: Society of Authors. Literary Agent: Gill Coleridge, Rogers Coleridge and White. Address: 31 Cambrian Road, Richmond, Surrey, TW10 6JQ, England.

LAKATOS Menyhert, b. 11 Apr 1926, Budapest, Hungary. Writer. div, 2 daughters. Education: Matriculation Diploma; Technical University. Appointments: Chief Editor. Publications: Smoked Faces, novel, 1975; Angarka-Buslodorfi, tales, 1977; Seven bearded wolves, tales, 1978; Paramisches' descendants, novel, 1980; The Secret of the Old Pot, tales, 1981; Those who wanted to live, novel, 1982; Csandra's Caravan, short stories, 1984; Various plays and scripts including: Curse and Love; Nationality is Unwanted; Those who wanted to Live. Contributions to: Hundreds of articles to newspapers. Honours: Milan First Literary Prize, 1977; Order of Magnitude with Gold Wreath, Hungarian Republic, 1991. Memberships: Society of Hungarian Writers; Literary Foundation of the Hungarian Republic; Club of Gipsy Intelligentsia; Vice-President, Auswitz Foundation. Address: Fust Milan u 22, 1039 Budapest, Hungary.

LAKE David John, b. 26 Mar 1929, Bangalore, India. University Professor. m. Marguerite Ivy Ferris, 30 Dec 1964, 1 daughter, 3 stepchildren. Education: BA, MA, DipEd, Trinity College, Cambridge, 1949-53; Diploma of Linguistics, University of Wales (Bangor), 1964-65; PhD, University of Queensland, Australia, 1974. Publications: The Canon of Thomas Middleton's Plays, 1975; The Gods of Xuma, 1978; The Man who Loved Morlocks, 1981; The Changelings of Chaan, 1985; Hornpipes and Funerals, poems, 1973; Walkers on the Sky, 1976; The Right Hand of Dextra, 1977; The Wildings of Westron, 1977; The Fourth Hemisphere, Warlords of Xuma, The Ring of Truth, West of the Moon. Contributions to: Extrapolation; Science Fiction Studies; Foundation; Notes and Queries; The Explicator; The Ring Bearer. Honours: Ditmar Awards for best Australian Science Fiction Novel, 1977 (for Walkers on the Sky) and 1982 (for The Man Who Loved Morlocks). Literary Agent: Pamela Buckmaster. Address: 7 8th Avenue, St Lucia, Queensland 4067, Australia.

LAKEHURST Diana. See: **AYRES Philip James**.

LAM Truong Buu, b. 1933, Vietnam. Associate Professor of History. Publications: Patterns of Vietnamese Response to Foreign Intervention, 1967; New Lamps for Old, 1983; Resistance, Rebellion, Revolution in Vietnamese History, 1984. Address: History Department, University of Hawaii, 2530 Dole Street, Honolulu, HI 96822, USA.

LAMANTIA Philip, b. 1927, USA. Poet. Literary Appointments: Assistant Editor, View Magazine, NY, 1944. Publications: Erotic Poems, 1946; Narcotica: I Demand Extinction of Laws Prohibiting Narcotic Drugs, 1959; Ekstasis, 1959; Destroyed Works, 1962; Touch of The Marvelous, 1966; Selected Poems, 1943-1966, 1967; Penguin Modern Poets 13 (with Charles Bukowski and Harold Norse), 1969; The Blood of The Air, 1970; Becoming Visible, 1981; Meadowlark West, 1986. Address: c/o City Lights Books, 261 Columbus Avenue, San Francisco, CA 94133, USA.

LAMB Andrew Martin, b. 23 Sept 1942. Writer on Music. m. Wendy Ann Davies, 1 Apr 1970, 1 son, 2 daughters. Education: Corpus Christi College, Oxford, England, 1960-63; MA (Hons), Oxford. Publications: Jerome Kern in Edwardian London, 1985; Ganzl's Book of the Musical Theatre (with Kurt Ganzl), 1988; Skaters' Waltz: The Story of the Waldteufels, 1995; Editor: The Moulin Rouge, 1990; Light Music from Austria, 1992; Substantial contributions to: The New Grove Dictionary of Music and Musicians; The New Grove Dictionary of American Music; The New Grove Dictionary of Opera; Others. Contributions to: Gramophone; The Musical Times; Classic CD; American Music; Music and Letters; Wisden Cricket Monthly; The Cricketer; The Listener; Others. Memberships: Fellow, Institute of Actuaries; Associate Member, Institute of Investment Management & Research; Lancashire County Cricket Club. Address: 12 Fullers Wood, Croydon CR0 8HZ, England.

LAMB Elizabeth Searle (K L Mitchell), b. 22 Jan 1917, Topeka, Kansas, USA. Writer; Editor. m. F Bruce Lamb, 11 Dec 1941, 1 d. Education: BA 1939, BMus 1940, University of Kansas. Literary Appointments: Editor, Frogpond, Haiku Quarterly, 1984-91; Co-Editor, Haiku Southwest, 1993-. Publications: Co-Author, Pelican Tree and Other Panama Adventures, 1953; Today and Every Day, 1970; Inside Me, Outside Me, 1974; In This Blaze of Sun, 1975; Picasso's Bust of Sylvette, 1977; 39 Blossoms, 1982; Casting Into a Cloud Southwest Haiku, 1985; Lines For My Mother, Dying, 1988. Contributions include: Numerous to magazines and journals in USA and abroad; Juvenile journals include: Jack and Jill; The Children's Friend; Wee Wisdom; Poetry journals include: Frogpond; Cicada; Haiku; Bonsai. Honours include: Ruth Mason Rice Awards, 5 times; National League of American Pen Women Awards, 4 times; Henderson Awards, 1978, 1981, 1991; Dellbrook Poetry Award, 1979; Yuki Teikei, 1981; Poetry Society of Japan, 1987; World Haiku Contest, Japan, 1989. Memberships: Past President and Vice-President, Haiku Society of America; Past Vice-President, New York Women Poets; National League of American Pen Women; Poetry Society of America. Literary Agent: Bertha Klausner, NY, USA. Address: 970 Acequia Madre, Sante Fe, NM 87501, USA.

LAMB Geoffrey Frederick (Balaam), b. London, England. Author. Education: BA (Hons), Teacher's Diploma, MA (English) 1939, King's College, London. Publications: English for General Certificate, 1954; Chalk in My Hair (under pseudonym Balaam), 1953; Victorian Magic, 1976; Magic, Witchcraft, & The Occult, 1977; Pocket Companion Quotation Guide, 1983; Harrap Book of Humorous Quotations, 1990; Franklin - Happy Voyager, 1956; The Happiest Days, 1959; Modern Adventures at Sea, 1970; One Hundred Good Stories, 1969-70; Animal Quotations, 1985; Shakespeare Quotations, 1992. Memberships: Society of Authors (Honorary Secretary Children's Writers Group 1962-67); Magic Circle. Address: Penfold, Legion Lane, Kings Worthy, Winchester, England.

LAMB Larry (Sir), b. 15 Jul 1929, Fitzwilliam, Yorkshire, England. Editor. m. Joan Mary Denise Grogan, 2 s, 1 d. Literary Appointments: Journalist: Brighouse Echo; Shields Gazette; Newcastle Journal; London Evening Standard; Sub-Editor, Daily Mirror; Editor: Daily Mail, Manchester, 1968-69; The Sun, 1969-72, 1975-81; Director, 1970-81, Editorial Director, 1971-81, News International Limited; Deputy Chairman, News Group, 1979-81; Director, The News Corporation (Australia) Limited, 1980-81; Deputy Chairman, Editor in Chief, Western Mail Limited, Perth, Australia, 1981-82; Editor in Chief, The Australian, 1982-83; Editor, Daily Express, 1983-86; Chairman,

Larry Lamb Associates, 1986-. Publication: Sunrise, 1989. Address: Bracken Cottage, Bratton Fleming, North Devon, EX31 4TG, England.

LAMB Patricia Frazer, b. 15 Jan 1931, CA, USA. Writer. Divorced, 2 s. Education: BA, Boston University, 1966; MA, Brandeis University, 1968; PhD, Cornell University, 1977. Literary Appointments: Assistant Professor of English, University of Kentucky, 1974-76; Professor of English, 1978-90, currently Emeritus Professor of English, Westminster College, PA. Publications include: Touchstones: Letters Between Two Women 1953-64, 1983; Erotic Universe Sexuality and Fantastic Literature, 1986, 2 essays in number 2; Write This Way: A Classical Rhetoric Handbook, 1980. Contributions to: Essays in: College English Association Forum; Westminster Magazine; Women's Review of Books; Bulletin of The PCTE. Honours: Bunting Fellowship, Radcliffe College, 1984-85; Distinguished Visiting Scholar, Sacramento State University, CA, 1983; Jane Bakerman Award, Best Published Essay, Popular Culture Association, 1986. Literary Agent: Martha Casselman, San Francisco, CA, USA. Address: 1718 N Decatur, Number 5, Las Vegas, NV 89108, USA.

LAMBERT Derek (William) (Richard Falkirk), b. 1929, United Kingdom. Novelist. Literary Appointments: Journalist for Devon, Norfolk, Yorkshire and National newspapers, 1950-68. Publications: Novels: For Infamous Conduct, 1970; Grans Slam, 1971; The Great Land, 1977; The Lottery, 1983; Mystery Novels: Angels in The Snow, 1969; The Kites of War, 1970; The Red House, 1972; The Yermakov Transfer, 1974; Touch The Lion's Paw (US paperback edition, Rough Cut, 1980), 1975; The Saint Peter's Plot, 1978; The Memory Man, 1979; I, Said The Spy, 1980; Trance, 1981; The Red Dove, 1982; The Judas Code, 1983; The Golden Express, 1984; The Man Who Was Saturday, 1985; Chase, 1987; Triad, 1988; Mystery novels as Richard Falkirk: The Chill Factor, 1971; The Twisted Wire, 1971; Blackstone, 1972; Beau Blackstone, 1973; Blackstone's Fancy, 1973; Blackstone and The Scourge of Europe, 1974; Blackstone Underground, 1976; Blackstone on Broadway, 1977; Other: The Sheltered Days: Growing Up in The War, 1965; Don't Quote Me - But, 1979; And I Quote, 1980; Unquote, 1981; Just Like The Blitz: A Reporter's Notebook, 1987; The Night and The City, 1989; The Gate of The Sun, 1990. Literary Agent: Robert I Ducas. Address: 350 Hudson Street, New York, NY 10014, USA.

LAMBOT Isobel Mary, (Daniel Ingham, Mary Turner), b. 21 July 1926, Birmingham, England. Novelist. m. Maurice Edouard Lambot, 19 Dec 1959 (dec). Education: BA, Liverpool University; Teaching Certificate, Birmingham University. Appointments: Tutor in Creative Writing, Lichfield Evening Institute, 1973-80. Publications: Under Isobel Lambot: Taste of Murder, 1966; Deadly Return, 1966; Shroud of Canvas, 1967; Dangerous Refuge, 1967; Danger Merchant, 1968; The Queen Dies First, 1968; Killer's Laughter, 1968; Let the Witness Die, 1969; Point of Death, 1969; Watcher on the Shore, 1971; Come Back and Die, 1972; Grip of Fear, 1974; The Identity Trap, 1978; Past Tense, 1979; Rooney's Gold, 1984; Still Waters Run Deadly, 1987; Blood Ties, 1987; Bloody Festival, 1991; The Flower of Violence, 1992; The Craft of Writing Crime Novels, 1992. Under Daniel Ingham: Contract for Death, 1972. Under Mary Turner: The Justice Hunt, 1975; So bright a Lady, 1977; Runaway Lady, 1980. Contributions to: Women's journals. Memberships: Crime Writers' Association; Society of Authors; Writers' Guild of Great Britain. Literary Agent: Mrs Mary Irvine, 11 Upland Park Road, Oxford, OX2 7RU. Address: 45 Bridge Street, Kington, Herefordshire, NR5 3DW, England.

LAMMING George (Eric), b. 8 June 1927, Carrington Village, Barbados. Novelist. Appointments: Writer in Residence, University of the West Indies, Kingston, 1967-68. Publications include: In The Castle of My Skin, 1953; The Emigrants, 1955; Of Age and Innocence, 1958; Water with Berries, 1971; Natives of my Person, 1972; Short Stories, David's walk, 1948; A Wedding in Spring, 1960; Birds of a Feather, 1970; Birthday Weather, 1966. Honours: Guggenheim Fellowship, 1954; Maugham Award, 1957; Canada Council Fellowship, 1962; D Litt, University of West Indies, 1980. Address: 14a Highbury Place, London N5, England.

LAMONT Marianne. See: RUNDLE Anne.

LAMONT-BROWN Raymond, b. 20 Sept 1939, Horsforth, England. Author; Broadcaster. m. (2) Dr Elizabeth Moira McGregor, 6 Sept 1985. Education: MA; AMIET; FSA (Scot). Appointment: Managing Editor, Writers Monthly, 1984-86. Publications: Discovering Fife, 1988; The Life & Times of Berwick-upon-Tweed, 1988; The Life

& Times of St Andrews, 1989; Royal Murder Mysteries, 1990; Scottish Epitaphs, 1990; Scottish Superstitions, 1990; 50 volumes including Scottish Witchcraft, 1994. Contributions to: Magazines and newspapers. Memberships: Society of Authors, Secretary in Scotland, 1982-89; Rotary International, Past President, St Andrews Branch, 1984-85. Literary Agent: David Bolt Associates, 12 Heath Drive, Send, Surrey GU23 7EP, England. Address: 3 Crawford House, 132 North Street, St Andrews, Fife KY16 9AF, Scotland.

LAMPARD Dulcie Irene, b. 30 May 1923, Albany, Western Australia. Retired. Publications: Ride! 1985, Saddle Up!, 1994. Honours: Bookshop of the Year Award, 1980, 1984, 1988. Literary Agent: Openbook Publishers. Address: Lot 4, Mayo Road, Wooroloo, West Australia 6558.

LAMPITT Dinah, b. 6 Mar 1937. Author. m. L F Lampitt, 28 Nov 1959, dec, 1 son, 1 daughter. Education: Regent Street Polytechnic, London, England, 1950s. Appointments: Worked on Fleet Street for the Times, The Evening News and various magazines, 1950s. Publications: Sutton Place Trilogy: Sutton Place, 1983; The Silver Swan, 1984; Fortune's Soldier, 1985; To Sleep No More, 1987; Pour the Dark Wine, 1989; The King's Women, 1992; As Shadows Haunting, 1993; Banishment, 1994. Serials: The Moonlit Door; The Gemini Syndrome; The Staircase; The Anklets; The Wardrobe. Contributions to: Numerous short stories to women's magazines. Membership: The Society of Authors; Romantic Novelists' Association. Literary Agent: Rupert Crew Ltd, London, England. Address: c/o Rupert Crew Ltd, 1A King's Mews, London WC1N 2JA, England.

LAMPLUGH Lois Violet, b. 9 Jun 1921, Barnstaple, Devon, England. Author. m. Lawrence Carlile Davis, 24 Sep 1955, 1 s, 1 d. Education: BA Honours, Open University, 1980. Literary Appointments include: Editorial Staff, Jonathan Cape Publishers, 1946-56. Publications include: The Pigeongram Puzzle, 1955; Nine Bright Shiners, 1955; Vagabond's Castle, 1957; Rockets in The Dunes, 1958; Sixpenny Runner, 1960; Midsummer Mountains, 1961; Rifle House Friends, 1965; Linhay on Hunter's Hill, 1966; Fur Princess and Fir Prince, 1969; Mandog, 1972; Sean's Leap, 1979; Winter Donkey, 1980; Falcon's Tor, 1984; Barnstaple: Town on The Taw, 1983; History of Ilfracombe, 1984; Minehead and Dunster, 1987; A Shadowed Man: Henry Williamson, 1990; Take Off From Chivenor, 1990; Sandrabbit, 1991; Lundy: Island Without Equal, 1993. Contributions to: Western Morning News. Memberships: Society of Authors; West Country Writers Association. Address: Springside, Bydown, Swimbridge, Devon, EX32 0QB, England.

LAN David Mark, b. 1 June 1952, Cape Town, South Africa. Writer; Social Anthropologist. Education: BA, University of Cape Town, 1972; BSc 1976, PhD 1983, London School of Economics, UK. Publications include: Book: Guns & Rain, Guerrillas & Spirit Mediums in Zimbabwe, 1985; Plays: Painting a Wall, 1974; Bird Child, 1974; Homage to Been Soup, 1975; Paradise, 1975; The Winter Dancers, 1977; Not in Norwich, 1977; Red Earth, 1977; Sergeant Ola & His Followers, 1979; Flight, 1986; A Mouthful of Birds, with Caryl Churchill, 1986; Desire, 1990; Television films: The Sunday Judge, 1985; The Crossing, 1988; Welcome Home Comrades, 1990; Dark City, 1990; Radio Plays: Charley Tango, 1995; Adaptations: Ghetto, 1989; Hippolytos, 1991; Ion, 1993. Honours: John Whiting Award, 1977; George Orwell Memorial Award, 1983; Zurich International Television Prize, 1990. Literary Agent: Judy Daish Associates, 83 Eastbourne Mews, London W2, England.

LANCASTER David. See: HEALD Timothy Villiers.

LANCASTER-BROWN Peter, b. 13 Apr 1927, Cue, Western Australia. Author. m. Johanne Nyrerod, 15 Aug 1953, 1 son. Education: Astronomy; Surveying; Mining Engineering; Civil Engineering. Appointments include: Full-time Author, 1970-. Publications include: Skywatch, 1993; Halley's Comet & The Principia, 1986; Halley & His Comet, 1985; Megaliths & Masterminds, 1979; Megaliths, Myths & Men, 1976; Fjord of Silent Men, 1983; Astronomy in Colour, 1972; Comets, Meteorites & Men, 1973; Planet Earth in Colour, 1976; What Star is That? 1971; Australia's Coast of Coral & Pearl, 1972; Call of the Outback, 1970; Twelve Came Back, 1957; Astronomy, 1984; etc. Contributions to: Blackwood's; Nature; New Scientist; Sky & Telescope. Membership: Society of Authors. Address: 10A St Peter's Road, Aldeburgh, Suffolk IP15 BG, England.

LANCE Betty Rita Gomez, b. 28 Aug 1923, Costa Rica. Professor of Romance Languages and Literatures; Writer. 2 s. Education: Teaching Diploma, Universidad Nacional, Costa Rica, 1941; BS, Central Missouri State University, 1944; MA, University of Missouri, 1947; PhD, Washington University, 1959. Publications: La Actitud Picaresca en la Novela Espanola del Siglo XX, 1969; Poetry: Vivencias, 1981; Bebiendo Luna, 1983; Vendimia del Tiempo, 1984; Alas en el Alba, 1987; Hoy Hacen Corro las Ardillas (short story), 1985. Contributions to: Americas; Letras Femeninas; Caprice. Memberships: Poets and Writers of America; Asociacion de Escritores de Costa Rica; Asociacion Prometeo de Poesia, Madrid; Asociacion Iberoamericana de Poesia, Madrid; American Association of University Professors; American Association of University Women; American Association of Teachers of Spanish and Portuguese. Address: 1562 Spruce Drive, Kalamazoo, MI 49008, USA.

LANDERT Walter, b. 3 Jan 1929, Zurich, Switzerland. Merchant. Education: Higher School of Commerce, Neuchatel; Merchant Apprentice w diploma; Diploma, Swiss Mercantile School, London; Student Trainee, Westminster Bank, London. Publications: Manager auf Zeit (novel), 1968; Selbstbefragung (poems), 1969; Entwurf Schweiz (literary essay), 1970; Koitzsch (novel), 1971; Traum einer besseren Welt (short stories & poems), 1980; UnKraut im helvetischen Kulturgartchen (literary essays), 1981; Meine Frau baut einen Bahnhof (short stories), 1982; S huus us Pilatusholz (monodrama), 1st performance, 1985; Klemms Memorabilien - Ein Vorspiel (novel), 1989; Umwerfende Zeiten - Ein Prozess (novel), 1990; Treffpunkt: Fondue Bourguignonne (novel), 1993. Contributions to: Various newspapers. Honours: Artemis Jubilee Prize, 1969; Poetry Prize, Literary Union, Saabrucken, 1977. Memberships: Swiss Authors; Olten Group. Address: Lendikonerstrasse 54, CH 8484 Weisslingen/ZH Switzerland.

LANDES David S, b. USA. Publications: The Rise of Capitalism (ed), 1966; The Unbound Promethens: Technological Change & Innovation, 1968; Bankers & Pashas, 1969; History As Social Science (ed), 1971; Revolution in Time: Clocks & The Making of the Modern World, 1983; Favorites of Fortune: Technology, Growth & Economics, 1991. Address: Harvard University, Littauer Building, Cambridge, MA 02138-3800, USA.

LANDESMAN Jay, b. 15 Jul 1919, St Louis, MO, USA. Publisher; Author; Playwright; Producer. m. Frances Deitsch, 15 Jul 1950, 2 s. Education: University of Missouri, 1938-40; Rice Institute, Houston, 1940-42. Publications: Editor: Neurotica; The Complete, 1981; Rebel Without Applause (memoir), 1987; The Nervous Set (novel), 1954, Broadway Musical, 1959; A Walk on The Wild Side (musical), 1960; Molly Darling (musical), 1963; The Babies (play), 1969; Small Day Tomorrow (major film in production, 1990); Bad Nipple (novel), 1970; Nobody Knows The Trouble I've Been (play). Memberships: Dramatists Guild; AFTRA; Groucho Club, London. Address: 8 Duncan Terrace, London, N1 8BZ, England.

LANDIS J(ames) D(avid), b. 30 June 1942, Springfield, MA, USA. m. (1) Patricia Lawrence Straus, 15 Aug 1964, div, 1 daughter, (2) Denise Evelyn Tillar, 20 July 1983, 2 sons. Education: BA (magna cum laude), Yale College, 1964. Appointments: Assistant Editor, Abelard Schuman, 1966-67; Editor, Senior Editor, William Morrow & Co, 1967-80; Editorial Director, Senior Vice-President, Publisher, Quill Trade paperbacks, 1980-85; Senior Vice-President, William Morrow & Co, 1985-91; Publisher, Editor-in-Chief, Beech Tree Books, 1985-87; Publisher, Editor-in-Chief, William Morrow & Co, 1988-91. Publications: The Sisters Impossible, 1979; Love's Detective, 1984; Daddy's Girl, 1984; Joey and the Girls, 1987; The Band Never Dances, 1989; Looks Aren't Everything, 1990. Contributions to: American Review; The Bennington Review; The New York Times Book Review. Honours: Roger Klein Award for Editing, 1973; Advocate Humanitarian Award, 1977. Memberships: Phi Beta Kappa; PEN. Literary Agent: Phyllis Wender, Rosenstone/Wender. Address: 19 Gill Street, Exeter, NH 03833, USA.

LANDON Howard Chandler Robbins, b. 1926, USA. Professor of Music. Publications: The Symphonies of Joseph Haydn, 1955; The Mozart Companion (co-editor), 1956, 2nd edition 1970; The Collected Correspondence and London Notebooks of Joseph Haydn, 1959; Complete Symphonies by Haydn (editor), 1965-68; Complete String Quartets, by Haydn (co-editor), 1968-83; Beethoven, 1970; Complete Piano Trios, by Haydn (editor), 1970-78; Haydn: Chronicle and Works, biography, 5 vols, 1976-80; Mozart and the Masons, 1982; Handel and his World, 1984; 1791: Mozart's Last Year, 1987; Mozart: The Golden

Years, 1989; The Mozart Compendium (ed), 1990; Mozart and Vienna, 1991; Five Centuries of Music in Venice, 1991; Une Journée Particulière De Mozart, 1993; Vivaldi, Voice of the Baroque, 1993; The Mozart Essays, 1995. Address: Chateau de Foncoussières, 81800 Rabastens (Tarn), France.

LANDRY Yves, b. 23 Dec 1952, St Jean sur Richelieu, Quebec, Canada. Historian; Demographer. m. Manon Pomerleau, 17 Aug 1974, 2 sons. Education: BA History, Université de Montreal, 1974; MA History, Université de Montreal, 1977; Doctorate, Historical Demography, Ecole des hautes études en sciences sociales, Paris, 1990. Publications: Inventaire des registres paroissiaux catholiques du Quebec 1621-1876, 1990, co-author; Pour le Christ et le Roi La vie au temps des premiers Montréalais, 1992, editor; Orphelines en France, pionnières au Canada: les Filles du roi au XVII siècle, 1992; The First French Canadians, Pioneers in the St Lawrence Valley, 1993, co-author. Contributions to: Revue d'histoire de l'Amérique française; Histoire sociale-Social History; Annales de Démographie Historique; Journal of Family History; Social Science History; Cahiers Québécois de Démographie; Histoire, Economie et Société. Honours: Queen's Fellowship, Canada Council, 1975; Jean Charles Falardeau Prize, for book, 1993; Percy W Foy Prize, for book, 1993. Memberships: International Union for the Scientific Study of Population, 1985-; Contributor, International Bibliography of Historical Bibliography, 1987-; Treasurer, Institut d'histoire de l'Amérique Française, 1993-95; Société de Démographie Historique; Union des écrivains du Quebec. Address: Départment d'Histoire, Université de Montreal, CP 6128, Succursale Centreville, Montreal, Quebec H3C 3J7, Canada.

LANE Helen (Helen Hudson), b. 31 Jan 1920, New York City, New York, USA. Writer. m. Robert Lane, 15 Nov 1944, 2 sons. Education: BA, Bryn Mawr College, 1941; MA 1943, PhD 1950, Columbia University. Publications: Tell The Time To None, 1966; Meyer Meyer, 1967; The Listener, 1968; Famsbee South, 1971; Criminal Trespass, 1986; A Temporary Residence, 1987. Contributions to: Short stories to: Antioch Review; Sewannee Review; Virginia Quarterly; Northwest Review; Mademoiselle; Quarterly Review of Literature; Red Book; Ellery Queen; Mid-Stream; Best American Short Stories; O Henry Prize Stories; Others. Honour: Virginia Quarterly Prize Story, 1963. Memberships: Authors Guild; Authors League; American PEN. Literary Agent: Candida Donadio. Address: 558 Chapel Street, New Haven, CT 06511, USA.

LANE M Travis (Millicent Elizabeth Travis), b. 23 Sept 1934, USA. Writer. m. Lauriat Lane, 26 Aug 1957, 1 son, 1 daughter. Education: MA, PhD, Cornell University. Appointments: Assistantships, Cornell University, University of New Brunswick; Honorary Research Associate, University of New Brunswick. Publications: Five Poets: Cornell, 1960; An Inch or So of Garden, 1969; Poems 1968-72, 1973; Homecomings, 1977; Divinations and Shorter Poems 1973-78, 1980; Reckonings, Poems 1979-85, 1988; Solid Things: Poems New and Selected, 1989; Temporary Shelter, 1993; Night Physics, 1994. Contributions to: Canadian Literature; Dalhousie Review; Ariel; Essays on Canadian Writing; University of Toronto Quarterly; Fiddlehead Magazine; Essays on Canadian Writing. Honour: Pat Lowther Prize, League of Canadian Poets, 1980. Address: 807 Windsor Street, Fredericton, New Brunswick, E3B 4G7, Canada.

LANE Patrick, b. 26 Mar 1939, Nelson, Canada. Writer; Poet. 4 s, 1 d. Literary Appointments: Editor, Very Stone House, Publishers, Vancouver, 1966-72; Writer-in-Residence, University of Manitoba, Winnepeg, 1978-79; University of Ottawa, 1980; University of Alberta, Edmonton, 1981-82; Saskatoon Public Library, 1982-83; Concordia University, 1985; The Globe Theatre Company, Regina, Saskatchewan, 1985-. Publications: Letters From The Savage Mind, 1966; For Rita - In Asylum, 1969; Calgary City Jail, 1969; Separations, 1969; Sunflower Seeds, 1969; On The Street, 1970; Mountain Oysters, 1971; Hiway 401 Rhapsody, 1972; The Sun Has Begun to Eat The Mountain, 1972; Passing into Storm, 1973; Beware The Months of Fire, 1974; Certs, 1974; Unborn Things: South American Poems, 1975; For Riel in That Gawdam Prison, 1975; Albino Pheasants, 1977; If, 1977; Poems, New and Selected, 1978; No Longer Two People (with Lorna Uher), 1979; The Measure, 1980; Old Mother, 1982; Woman in The Dust, 1983; A Linen Crow, A Caftan Magpie, 1985; Selected Poems, 1987; Milford and Me, 1989; Winter, 1990; Mortal Remains, 1992; How Do You Spell Beautiful, 1992. Contributions to: Most major Canadian magazines, American and English journals. Honour: Governor-General's Award for Poetry, 1979. Memberships: League of Canadian Poets; Writer's Union of Canada. Address: c/o Writer's Union of Canada, 24 Ryerson Avenue, Toronto, Ontario, Canada, M5T 2P3.

LANE Roumelia, b. 31 Dec 1927, Bradford, West Yorkshire, England. Writer.m. Gavin Green, 1 Oct 1949, 1 s, 1 d. Literary Appointment: Writer, Bournemouth Echo, mid 1950's. Publications: Sea of Sanj, 1969; Cafe Mimosa, 1971; Stormy Encounter, 1974; Second Spring, 1980; Dream Island, 1981; Night of The Beguine, 1986; Hideaway Heart; A Summer to Love; House of The Winds; Summer of Conflict; Desert Haven; The Fires of Heaven; Hidden Rapture; The Brightest Star; 30 books, Television and film scripts: Phantom of The Oscar; Icebound; Tender Saboteur; Chantico; Turn of The Tide. Contributions to: Various journals and magazines including: Bournemouth Echo. Honours: Featured Writer, Writers of Distinction, Harlequin, USA and Canada, 1970's; Featured Writer, Coast to Coast Press Promotion for Coca Cola (Books), USA; Featured Writer, Coast to Coast Promotion of Books, Avon Cosmetics, USA, 1970's. Memberships: Society of Authors of Great Britain; Writers Guild of Great Britain; Affiliate Member, Writers Guild of America (East and West); ALCS. Address: Casa Mimosa, Santa Eugenia, Majorca, Beleares, Spain.

LANG Grace. See: **FLOREN Lee.**

LANG King. See: **TUBB E(dwin) C(harles).**

LANGDALE Cecily, b. 27 Jul 1939, USA. Art Dealer; Art Historian. m. Roy Davis, 24 Jul 1972. Education: Swarthmore College, 1961. Publications: Gwen John: Paintings and Drawings from The Collection of John Quinn and Others (with Betsy G Fryberger), 1982; Monotypes by Maurice Prendergast in The Terra Museum of Art, 1984; Gwen John: An Interior Life (with David Fraser Jenkins), 1985, 1986; Gwen John: With a Catalogue Raisonne of The Paintings and a Selection of The Drawings, 1987, paperback edition, 1989; Maurice Brazil Prendergast, Charles Prendergast: A Catalogue Raisonne (contributor), 1990. Contributions to: The Connoisseur, 1979; Antiques, 1987; Drawing, 1990, 1992; Dictionary of National Biography: Supplementary Volume: From The Beginnings to 1985. Membership: Cosmopolitan Club, NY. Address: 231 East 60 Street, New York, NY 10022, USA.

LANGDON Philip Alan, b. 6 Jan 1947, Greenville, Pennsylvania, USA. Journalist; Author. m. Maryann Dunkle, 12 June 1971. Education: BA, Allegheny College, 1969; Certificate in American Studies, 1973, MA History, 1977, Utah State University. Appointments: Reporter, The Patriot, Harrisburg, Pennsylvania, 1969-71; Reporter, Columnist, Architecture Critic, The Buffalo Evening News, Buffalo, New York, 1973-82; Journalist-in-residence, University of Michigan, 1979-80; Writer, Home column, Design column, The Atlantic Monthly, 1987-90; Senior Editor, Progressive Architecture Magazine, 1994-. Publications: Orange Roofs, Golden Arches, 1986; American Houses, 1987; Urban Excellence, 1990; This Old House Kitchens (with Steve Thomas), 1992; This Old House Bathrooms (with Steve Thomas), 1993; A Better Place to Live, 1994. Contributions to: Many articles to The Atlantic Monthly, 1984-, including 2 cover articles; The American House, 1984; A Good Place to Live, 1988; Planning; Landscape Architecture; Others. Literary Agent: Christina Ward (North Scituate, Mass). Address: 178 East Rock Road, New Haven, CT 06511, USA.

LANGE John,See:**CRICHTON Michael.**

LANGER Lawrence L, 20 June 1929, NY, USA. College Professor. m. Sondra Weinstein, 21 Feb 1951, 1 s, 1 d. Education: BA, City College of NY, 1951; AM, 1952, PhD, 1961, Harvard. Literary Appointments: Instructor, University of CT, 1957-58; Instructor, Simmons College, 1956-61; Assistant Professor, 1961-66, Associate Professor, 1966-72; Professor, 1972-76, Alumnae Chair Professor, 1976-92, Emeritus, 1992-. Publications: Holocaust Testimonies: The Ruins of Memory, 1991; The Holocaust and the Literary Imagination, 1975; The Age of Atrocity: Death in Modern Literature, 1978; Versions of Survival: The Holocaust and the Human Spirit, 1982; Art from the Ashes: A Holocaust Anthology, 1994; Admitting the Holocaust: Collected Essays, 1994. Honour: National Book Critic Circle Award, 1991. Memberships: PEN Am; PMLA; NEMLA; AJS. Address: 249 Adams Avenue, West Newton, MA 02165, USA.

LANGFORD Gary, b. 21 Aug 1947, Christchurch. Writer; Senior Lecturer. 1 daughter. Education: BA 1969, MA (Hons) History 1971, MA (Hons) English 1973, University of Canterbury; Diploma of Teaching

Drama, Christchurch Sec Teachers College, 1973. Appointments: Senior Lecturer, Creative Writing, University of Western Sydney, 1986; Writer in Residence, University of Canterbury (part), 1989. Publications: 20 Books, including 8 novels such as Death of the Early Morning Hero, 1975; Players in the Ballgame, 1979; Vanities, 1984; Pillbox, 1986; Newlands, 1990 and 7 books of poetry such as Four Ships, 1982; The Pest Exterminator's Shakespeare, 1984; Bushido, 1987; Love at the Traffic Lights, 1990; Poetry and Anthologies: 150-200 performances of scripts and plays on stage, television and radio. Honours: Young Writers Fellowship, Australia Council, 1976; Alan Marshall Award, 1983. Address: c/o Curtis Brown (Aust) Pty Ltd, Box 19, Paddington, NSW 2021, Australia.

LANGHOLM Neil. See: **BULMER Henry Kenneth.**

LANGTON Jane, b. 30 Dec 1922, Boston, Massachusetts, USA. Writer. m. William Langton, 10 June 1943, 3 sons. Education: BS 1944, MA 1945, University of Michigan; MA 1948, Radcliffe College. Publications: Adult Suspense Novels: The Transcendental Murder, 1964; The Memorial Hall Murder, 1978; Emily Dickinson is Dead, 1984; Murder at the Gardner, 1988; Dark Nantucket Noon, 1975; Natural Enemy, 1982; Good and Dead, 1986; The Dante Game, 1991; God in Concord, 1992; Divine Inspiration, 1993For Children: Diamond in the Window, 1962; Paper Chains, 1977; The Fledgling, 1980; The Fragile Flag, 1984; Her Majesty, Grace Jones, 1961; The Swing in The Summerhouse, 1967; The Astonishing Stereoscope, 1971; The Boyhood of Grace Jones, 1972. Honours: Newbery Honor Book, 1981 for The Fledgling; Nero Wolfe Award for Emily Dickinson is Dead. Literary Agent: Meg Ruley Inc for adult books: McIntosh & Otis for children's books. Address: Baker Farm Road, Lincoln, MA 01773, USA.

LANIER Sterling E(dmund), b. 1927, USA. Writer; Sculptor. Literary Appointments: Research Historian, Winterhur Museum, Switzerland, 1958-60; Editor, John C Winston Company, 1961; Chilton Books, 1961-62, 1965-67; Macrae-Smith Company, 1963-64; Full-time Writer and Sculptor, 1967-. Publications: The War For The Lot (juvenile), 1969; The Peculiar Exploits of Brigadier Ffellowes (short stories), 1972; Hiero's Journey, 1973; The Unforsaken Hiero, 1983; Menace Under Marwood, 1983; The Curious Quest of Brig Ffellowes, 1986. Literary Agent: Curtis Brown Limited. Address: c/o Curtis Brown Limited, 575 Madison Avenue, New York, NY 10022, USA.

LANSIDE Luke. See: **CRAGGS Robert S.**

LANTRY Mike. See: **TUBB E(dwin) C(harles).**

LAPINSKI Susan, b. 27 May 1948, Baltimore, MD, USA. Magazine Writer; Author. m. 31 Dec 1973, 2 d. Education: BA, College of Notre Dame, MD, 1970; MA, Communications, University of North Carolina, Chapel Hill, 1977. Literary Appointments: Editor in Chief, Lady's Circle, 1979-80; Senior Editor, Family Weekly, 1980; Columnist, American Baby, 1985-. Publications: In a Family Way, 1982. Contributions to: Numerous magazines and journals including: Family Circle; Glamour; Ladies Home Journal; McCall's; Redbook. Honours: Honourable Mention, Atlantic Monthly Poetry Competition, 1970; Runner up, Front Page Award, 1987. Memberships: American Society of Journalists and Authors; Newswomen's Club; Writers' Network. Literary Agent: Aaron Priest Literary Agency. Address: 152 Remsen Street, Brooklyn Heights, NY 11201, USA.

LAPPE Frances Moore, b. 10 Feb 1944, Pendleton, Oregon, USA. Educator. m. Paul Martin Du Bois, 19 Aug 1991, 1 son, 1 daughter. Education: BA, Earlham College, Indiana. Publications: Diet for a Small Planet, 1971; Food First: Beyond the Myth of Scarcity, co-author, 1977; World Hunger, Ten Myths (co-author), 1979; Aid as Obstacle, 1980; World Hunger: Twelve Myths, 1986; Betraying the National Interest (co-author), 1987; Mozambique and Tanzania: Asking the Big Questions and Casting New Molds: First Steps Toward Worker Control in a Mozambique Factory (co-author), 1980; What To Do After You Turn Off the TV: Fresh Ideas for Enjoying Family Time, 1985; Rediscovering America's Values, 1989; Taking Population Seriously, co-author, 1989; The Quickening of America (co-author), 1994. Contributions to: New York Times; Harper's; Readers Digest; Journal of Nutrition Education; War on Hunger. Address: Center for Living Democracy, Black Fox Road, Brattleboro, Vermont 05301, USA.

LAPPING Brian (Michael), b. 1937, United Kingdom. Television Producer; Journalist; Editor. Appointments: Reporter, Daily Mirror, London, England, 1959-61; Reporter and Deputy Commonwealth

Correspondent, The Guardian, London, 1961-67; Editor, Venture, Fabian Society monthly journal, 1965-69; Feature Writer, Financial Times, London, 1967-68; Deputy Editor, New Society, London, 1968-70; Television Producer, Granada Television Ltd, 1970-88; Executive Producer, World in Action 1976-78, The State of the Nation 1978-80, End of Empire 1980-85; Chief Executive of Brian Lapping Associates, 1988-; Executive Producer, Countdown to War, 1989; Hypotheticals (three programmes annually for BBC2); Question Time (weekly for BBC1), 1991-94; The Second Russian Revolution (for BBC2), 1991; The Washington Version (for BBC2), 1992; Watergate (for BBC2), 1994; Fall of the Wall (for BBC2), 1994. Publications: More Power to the People (co-editor), 1968; The Labour Government 1964-70, 1970; The State of the Nation: Parliament (editor), 1973; The State of the Nation: The Bounds of Freedom, 1980; End of Empire, 1985; Apartheid: A History, 1986. Address: 61 Eton Avenue, London NW3, England.

LAQUEUR Walter, b. 26 May 1921, Breslau, Germany. History Educator. m. Barbara Koch, 29 May 1941, 2 d. Literary Appointments: Journalist, Freelance Author, 1944-55; Editor of Survey, 1955-65; Co-editor, Journal of Contemporary History, 1966-. Publications: Communism and Nationalism in The Middle East, 1956; Young Germany, 1961; Russia and Germany, 1965; The Road to War, 1968; Europe since Hitler, 1970; Out of The Ruins of Europe, 1971; Zionism, a History, 1972; Confrontation: The Middle East and World Politics, 1974; Weimar: A Cultural History 1918-1933, 1974; Guerrilla, 1976; Terrorism, 1977; The Missing Years, 1980; A Reader's Guide to Contemporary History (edited jointly), 1972; Fascism: A Reader's Guide (editor), 1978; The Terrible Secret, 1980; Farewell to Europe, 1981; Germany Today: A Personal Report, 1985; World of Secrets: The Uses and Limits of Intelligence, 1986; The Long Road to Freedom: Russia and Glasnost, 1989; Thursday's Child Has Far To Go, 1993. Honours: Recipient, 1st Distinguished Writer's Award, Center Strategic and International Studies, 1969; Inter Nations Award, 1985. Address: Center for Strategic and International Studies, 1800 K Street NW, Washington DC 20006, USA.

LARDNER Ring W (Jr), b. 19 Aug 1915, Chicago, IL, USA. Writer. m. Frances Chaney, 28 Sep 1946. Education: Phillips Academy, Andover, MA; Princeton University, 2 years. Publications: The Ecstasy of Owen Muir, UK 1954, USA 1955; The Lardners: My Family Remembered, 1976; All for Love, 1985. Honours: Best Original Screenplay for Woman of The Year (with Michael Kanin), Academy of Motion Pictures, 1942; Best Screenplay Based on Material from Another Medium for M A S H, Academy of Motion Picture Arts and Sciences, 1970; Best Comedy Award for M A S H, Writers Guild of America, 1970; Laurel Award for Lifetime Achievement in Screenwriting, Writers Guild of America, West, 1989. Memberships: Vice-President, Screen Writers Guild, 1945; Writers Guild of America, East; PEN. Literary Agent: Jim Preminger Agency. Address: c/o Jim Preminger Agency, 1650 Westwood Boulevard, Los Angeles, CA 90024, USA.

LARKIN Rochelle, b. 1935, USA. Author. Literary Appointments: Editor, Countrywide Publications, NY, 1963; Editor, Kanrom Inc, NY, 1964-70; Editor, Pinnacle Books, NY, 1970; Editor-in-Chief, Lancer Books, NY, 1973-74; Editor-in-Chief, Female Bodybuilding Magazine, 1986-89; Editor-in-Chief, Bodybuilding Lifestyles Magazine, 1990-91; Editor, Waldman Publishing, 1992-. Publications: Soul Music, 1970; Supermarket Superman, 1970; Teen Scene (with Milburn Smith), 1971; The Godmother, 1971; Honour Thy Godmother, 1972; For Godmother and Country, 1972; 365 Ways to Say I Want To Be Your Friend (with M Smith), 1973; Black Magic, 1974; The Beatles: Yesterday, Today, Tomorrow, 1974; The Greek Goddess, 1975; Call Me Anytime, 1975; International Joke Book, 1975; The Raging Flood, 1976; Hail Columbia, 1976; The First One, 1976; Valency Girl (with Robin Moore), 1976; Pusher, 1976; Sexual Superstars, 1976; Harvest of Desire, 1976; Kitty, 1977; Mafia Wife (with Robin Moore), 1977; Mistress of Desire, 1978; Instant Beauty (with Pablo Manzoni), 1978; Tri (with Robin Moore), 1978; Torches of Desire, 1979; Glitterball, 1980; Beverly Johnson's Guide to a Life of Health and Beauty (with Julie Davis), 1981; Only Perfect, 1981; Golden Days, Silver Nights, 1982; Amber series (as Darrell Fairfield), 6 volumes, 1982; The Crystal Heart, 1983; Angels Never Sleep, 1984. Address: 351 East 84th Street, New York, NY 10028, USA.

LARSEN Eric Everett, b. 29 Nov 1941, USA. College Educator; Writer; m. Anne Schnare, 5 June 1965, 2 daughters. Education: BA, Carleton College, 1963; MA 1964, PhD 1971, University of Iowa.

Appointments: Professor of English, John Jay College of Criminal Justice, City University of New York, 1971-. Publications: Novels: An American Memory, 1988; I Am Zoe Handke, 1992. Contributions to: Harper's; The New Republic; The Nation; Los Angeles Times Book Review; The North American Review; The New England Review; Others. Honours: The Heartland Prize for An American Memory, Chicago Tribune, 1988. Literary Agent: Brandt and Brandt, Literary Agents Inc, 1501 Broadway, New York, NY 10036, USA.

LASKA Vera, b. 21 July 1928, Kosice, Czechoslovakia. Professor; Lecturer; Columnist; Author. m. Andrew J Laska, 5 Nov 1949, 2 sons. Education: MA History, 1946, MA Philosophy, 1946, Charles University, Prague; PhD History, University of Chicago, 1959. Appointments: Professor of History, Regis College, Weston, Massachusetts, USA, 1966-; Fulbright Professor, Charles University, Prague, Czech Republic, 1993. Publications: Remember the Ladies, Outstanding Women of the American Revolution, 1976; Franklin and Women, 1978; Czechs in America 1633-1977, 1978; Benjamin Franklin the Diplomat, 1982; Nazism, Resistance and Holocaust: A Bibliography, 1985; Women in the Resistance and in the Holocaust, 1983, 1988. Contributions to: Over 200 articles and book reviews in newspapers and professional journals. Address: 50 Woodchester Drive, Weston, MA 02193, USA.

LASKER David Raymond, b. 21 Apr 1950, NY, USA. Writer; Musician, Double-Bassist. Education: BA, 1972, MMus, 1974, Yale University; studies, Juilliard School of Music, NY, 2 years. Literary Appointment: Editor, Contract Magazine, Toronto, Canada, 1989. Publication: The Boy Who Loved Music, 1979. Contributions to: Interior Design; Progressive Architecture; Architectural Digest; Los Angeles Times; ID; House and Home; Canadian Interiors; Ontario Living; City and Country Home; Toronto Life; Maclean's. Honours: Notable Book, for Boy Who Loved Music, American Library Association, 1980. Memberships: Fees Committee, Periodical Writers Association of Canada. Address: Contract Magazine, Victor Publishing Company Limited, 7777 Keele Street, Unit 8, Concord, Ontario, Canada, L4K 1Y7.

LASKOWSKI Jacek Andrzej, b. 4 June 1946, Edinburgh, Scotland. Author; Translator. m. Anne Grant Howieson, 8 July 1978, 2 daughters. Education: MagPhil, Jagiellonian University, Krakow, Poland, 1973. Appointments: Literary Manager, Haymarket Theatre, Leicester, 1984-87. Publications: Plays Produced: Dreams to Damnation, BBC Radio 3, 1977; Pawn Takes Pawn, BBC Radio 4, 1978; The Secret Agent, BBC Radio 4, 1980; Nostromo, BBC Radio 4, 1985; Phoney Physician (after Moliere), 1986; Orestes/Electra (with Nancy Meckler), 1987; Wiseguy Scapino (after Moliere), 1993. Memberships: Theatre Writers Union, General Secretary, 1981-82; Society of Authors, Vice-Chairman, Broadcasting Committee, 1982-83. Literary Agent: Michael Imison Playwrights. Address: c/o Michael Imison Playwrights, 28 Almeida Street, London N1 1TD, England.

LASSITER Adam. See: **KRAUZER Steven M.**

LATHAM Mavis. See: **CLARK Mavis Thorpe.**

LATOW Roberta, b. 27 Sep 1931, Springfield, MA, USA. Author. Education: Whitney School of Interior Design, NY. Appointments: International Interior Designer, USA, The Middle East, Europe, Africa, United Kingdom, 1952-81; Art Dealer, owning galleries in Springfield, MA and NY, 1954-62. Publications: Three Rivers, 1981; Tidal Wave, 1983; Soft Warm Rain, 1985; This Stream of Dreams, 1986. Honour: The Romantic Erotica Award, USA, 1984. Membership: Authors Guild. Address: Wiltshire, England.

LAU Evelyn, b. 1971, Canadian. Poet; Writer. Publications: You Are Not Who You Claim, 1990; Oedipal Dreams, 1992; In the House of Slaves, 1994; Fresh Girls, & Other Stories, 1995. Honour: Governor General's Award, Nominee. Address: c/o Coach House Press, Attn Pblcty Department, 50 Prince Arthur A, Suite 107, Toronto, Ontario, M5R 1B5, Canada.

LAUMER Keith, b. 1925, American. Writer of Mystery, Crime, Suspense, Science Fiction, Fantasy, Recreation, Leisure, Hobbies. Literary Appointments: Freelance Writer since 1964; Staff Member, University of Illinois, Urbana, 1952; Foreign Service Vice-Consul and Third Secretary, Rangoon, 1956-59. Publications include: It's a Mad, Mad, Mad Galaxy (short stories), 1968; The Afrit Affair (suspense, novelization of Television series), 1968; The Drowned Queen (suspense, novelization of Television series), 1968; The Gold Bomb (suspense, novelization of Television series), 1969; The World Shuffler, 1970; The House in November, 1970; Time Trap, 1970; Editor, Five Fates, 1970; Retief's Ransom, 1971; The Star Treasure, 1971; Deadfall, 1971, as Fat Chance, 1975; Dinosaur Beach, 1971; Retief of The CDT (short stories), 1971; Once There Was a Giant (short stories), 1971; The Infinite Cage, 1972; Night of Delusions, 1972; The Shape Changer, 1972; The Big Show (short stories), 1972; Timetracks (short stories), 1972; The Glory Game, 1973; The Undefeated (short stories), 1974; Retief, Emissary to The Stars (short stories), 1975; Bolo: The Annals of The Dinochrome Brigade, 1976; The Best of Keith Laumer (short stories), 1976; The Ultimax Man, 1978; Retief Unbound (short story omnibus), 1979; Retief at Large (short stories), 1979; The Star Colony, 1981; The Breaking Earth (short stories), 1981; Worlds of The Imperium (short stories), 1982; The Other Sky, 1982; Retief to The Rescue (short stories), 1983; The Galaxy Builder (short stories), 1984; The Return of Retief, 1985; Rogue Bolo, 1985; End as a Hero, 1985. Address: Box 972, Brooksville, FL 33512, USA.

LAURIE Rona, b. 16 Sept 1916, Derby, England. Actress; Writer; Drama Lecturer; Professor of Speech and Drama, Guildhall School of Music and Drama. m. Edward Lewis Neilson, 1961. Education: Derby High School; Penrhos College; University of Birmingham; Royal Academy of Dramatic Art; BA (Hons), FGSM LRAM, LGSM, FRSA. Literary Appointments: Dramatic Critic Teachers' World; Dramatic Critic, On Stage (Australia). Publications: Festivals and Adjudication, 1975; A Hundred Speeches from the Theatre, 1966; Adventures in Group Speaking, 1967; Speaking Together I & II, 1966; Scenes and Ideas, 1967; Children's Plays from Beatrix Potter, 1980; Mrs Tiggywinkle and Friends, 1986; Auditioning, 1985; The Actors' Art and Craft, 1994. Contributions to: Speaking Shakespeare Today (Speech and Drama); Speaking the Sonnet (Speech and Drama). Memberships: Guild of Drama Adjudicators, Ex-Chairman, Council Member; Society of Teachers of Speech and Drama, Ex-Chairman; Gold Medal Examiner for The Poetry Society; Adjudicator, British Federation of Music Festivals. Address: 21 New Quebec Street, London W1H 7DE, England.

LAURO Shirley (Shapiro) Mezvinsky, b. 18 Nov 1933, Des Moines, IA, USA. m. (1) Norton Mezvinsky (div), 1 d, (2) Louis Paul Lauro, 18 Aug 1973. Education: BS cum laude, Northwestern University, 1955; MS, University of Wisconsin-Madison, 1957. Literary Appointments include: Professional film, television and stage actress, NY, Boston, MA, Detroit, MI, Chicago, IL, Wisconsin, 1959-; Writer, 1961-; Instructor in speech and theatre, City College of The City University of NY, 1967-71; Instructor in speech theatre and playwriting, Yeshiva University, 1971-76; Literary Consultant, 1975-80, Production Critic, 1975-, Member's Council, 1975-, Resident Playwright, 1976-, Ensemble Studio Theatre; Instructor in speech, Manhattan Community College, 1978; Instructor in English and Creative Writing, Marymount Manhattan College, 1978-79; Resident Playwright, Alley Theatre, Houston, 1987; Adjunct Professor Playwriting, Tisch School of The Arts, New York University, 1989-; Actress and Free-lance Editor; Afiliated with American Place Theatre Women's Project. Publications : The Edge, 1965; The Contest, 1975; Open Admissions, Nothing Immediate, I Don't Know Where You're Coming From At All!, The Coal Diamond, Margaret and Kit, 1979; In The Garden of Eden, 1982; Sunday Go To Meetin', 1986; Pearls on the Moon, 1987; A Piece of My Heart, 1992. Contributions to: Short stories in periodicals including: Jewish Horizon; New Idea; The Christian Science Monitor. Honours: Recipient of numerous honours and awards for professional services including The John Simon Guggenheim. Memberships: Writers Guild of America; PEN; League of Professional Theatre Women (Vice-President); Authors League; Authors Guild; Dramatists Guild. Address: 275 Central Park West, New York, NY 10024, USA.

LAVERS Norman, b. 21 Apr 1935, USA. Teacher. m. Cheryl Dicks, 20 July 1967, 1 son. Education: BA 1960, MA 1963, San Francisco State University; PhD, University of Iowa, 1969. Publications: Mark Harris (criticism) 1978; Selected Short Stories, 1979; Jerzy Kosinski (criticism) 1982; The Northwest Passage (novel), 1984; Pop Culture Into Art: The Novels of Manuel Puig (criticism), 1988. Contributions to: Contributing Editor, Bird Watcher's Digest. Honours: National Endowment for the Arts Fellowship in Creative Writing, 1982, 1991; O Henry Award, 1987; Editor's Choice Award, 1986; Hohenberg Award, 1986; Pushcart Award, 1992; William Peden Prize, 1992. Literary Agent: Sobel Weber Associates Incorporated, 146E 19th Street, New York, NY 100003, USA. Address: Rt 5 Box 203, Jonesboro, AR 72401, USA.

LAVIN Mary, b. 12 Jun 1912, East Walpole, MA, USA. Writer. m. (1) William Walsh, 1942 (dec 1954), (2) Michael MacDonald Scott, 1969, 3 d. Education: University College, Dublin. Publications: Tales From Bective Bridge, 1942; The Long Ago, 1944; The House in Clewe Street, 1945; The Becker Wives, 1946; At Sallygap, 1947; Mary O'Grady, 1950; A Single Lady, 1956; The Patriot Son, 1956; A Likely Story, 1957; Selected Stories, 1959; The Great Wave, 1961; The Stories of Mary Lavin, Volume 1, 1964, Volume II, 1973, Volume III, 1985; The Middle of the Fields, 1967; Happiness, 1969; Collected Stories, 1971; The Second Best Children in The World (illustrated by Edward Ardizzone), 1972; A Memory, 1972; The Shrine, 1977; A Family Likeness, 1985. Honours: James Tait Black Memorial Prize, 1943; Guggenheim Fellowship, 1959-60; Katherine Mansfield Prize, 1961; Ella Lyman Cabot Award, 1972; Eire Society Gold Medal, 1974; Gregory Medal, Supreme Literary Award of The Irish Nation, 1975; American Irish Foundation Literary Award, 1979; Allied Irish Banks Literary Award, 1981; Honorary DLitt, University College Dublin. Memberships include: President, Irish PEN, 1964-65, 1985-86; President, Irish Academy of Letters, 1972-73; Board of Governors, School of Irish Studies, Dublin, 1974-. Address: The Abbey Farm, Bective, Co Meath, Ireland.

LAVRENTIEV Alexander Nikolaevich, b. 12 May 1954, Moscow, Russia. Designer; Art Historian. m. Presnetsova irina Sergeevna, 6 Nov 1974, 1 daughter. Education: Grad, Faculty of Industrial Art, Moscow Institute of Industrial and Applied Arts, 1976; PhD, Art History, 1983. Appointments: Freelance Critic, Soviet Photo, 1977; Freelance Author, Sovetsky Khudosznik, 1982. Publications: Varvara Stepanova: A Constructivist Life, 1988; Rodchenko Photography, 1982; Rodchenko Stepanova Family Workshop, 1989; Rodtschenko Stepanova, Die Zukunft ist unser einziges Ziel; Exhibition Catalogue, 1991. Contributions to: Soviet Photo; Tehnicheskaya Estetica; DAPA, Journal of Agitational and Propaganda Art; Art and Design; Interpressgraphic. Membership: Union of Journalists; Union of Designers; Union of Photo-Artists. Address: Society Designers of Russia, Arbatskaya Square 1/2, Moscow 121019, Russia.

LAWRENCE Clifford Hugh, b. 28 Dec 1921, London, England. Professor of Mediaeval History. m. Helen Maud Curran, 11 July 1953, 1 son, 5 daughters. Education: Lincoln College, Oxford, 1946-51; BA Hons, Class I, History, 1948; MA, 1953; DPhil (Oxon), 1955. Publications: St Edmund of Abingdon: A Study of Hagiography and History, 1960; The English Church and the Papacy, 1965; Medieval Monasticism, Forms of Religious Life in Western Europe in the Middle Ages, 1984, 2nd edition 1989; The University in State and Church, History of the University of Oxford, Vol I, 1984; The Friars: The Impact of the Early Mendicant Movement on Medieval Society, 1994. Contributions of articles and reviews to: English Historical Review; History; Journal of Ecclesiastical History; The Month; The Tablet; Times Literary Supplement; Times Higher Education Supplement; The Spectator; Others. Memberships: Fellow, Royal Historical Society; Society of Antiquaries; Reform Club. Address: 11 Durham Road, London SW20 0QH, England.

LAWRENCE Jerome, b. 1915, USA. Playwright; Lyricist; Biographer. Literary Appointments: Partner, 1942-, President, 1955, Lawrence and Lee Inc, New York City and Los Angeles; Professor of Playwriting: University of Southern California, New York University, Baylor University, Ohio State University; Member, Board of Directors: American Conservatory Theatre, National Repertory Theatre, American Playwrights' Theatre. Publications: Look, Ma, I'm Dancin' (Co-author), musical, 1948; Inherit The Wind (with Robert E Lee), 1955; Auntie Mame (with Lee), 1957; The Gang's All Here (with Lee), 1960; Only in America (with Lee), 1960; Checkmate (with Lee), 1961; Mame (Co-author), musical, 1967; Dear World, musical, 1969; Sparks Fly Upward (Co-author), 1969; The Night Thoreau Spent in Jail (with Lee), 1970; Live Spelled Backwards, 1970; The Incomparable Max (with Lee), 1972; The Crocodile Smile (with Lee), 1972; Actor: The Life and Times of Paul Muni, 1974; Jabberwock (with Lee), 1974; First Monday in October (with Lee), 1975; Whisper in The Mind (with Lee and Norman Cousins), 1987. Memberships: Board of Directors, Dramatists Guild; Board of Directors, Authors League. Address: 21056 Las Flores Mesa Drive, Malibu, CA 90265, USA.

LAWRENCE Karen Ann, b. 5 Feb 1951, Windsor, Ontario, Canada. Writer. m. Robert Gabhart, 18 Dec 1982, 1 son. Education: BA (Hons), University of Windsor, 1973; MA, University of Alberta, 1977. Publications: The Life of Helen Alone, 1986; Springs of Living Water, 1990; The Life of Helen Alone, Screenplay, 1987; Nekuia: The Inanna

Poems, 1980. Honours: W H Smith/Books in Canada First Novel Award, 1987; Best First Novel Award, PEN, Los Angeles Center, 1987. Memberships: Authors Guild; Writers' Union of Canada; ACTRA (Canada). Literary Agent: Esther Newberg, ICM Inc, 40W 57th Street, New York, NY 10019, USA. Address: 2153 Pine Street, San Diego, CA 92103-1522, USA.

LAWRENCE Louise, b. 5 June 1943, Surrey, England. Novelist. m. Graham Mace, 28 Aug 1987, 1 son, 2 daughters. Education: Leatherhead Poplar Road Primary School, 1948-56; Lydney Grammar School, Gloucestershire, 1956-61. Publications: Andra, 1971; Power of Stars, 1972; Wyndcliffe, 1974; Sing and Scatter Daisies, 1977; Star Lord, 1978; Cat Call, 1980; Earth Witch, 1981; Calling B for Butterfly, 1982; Dram Road, 1983; Children of the Dust, 1985; Moonwind, 1986; Warriors of Taan, 1986; Extinction is Forever, 1990; Ben-Harran's Castle, 1992; The Disinherited, 1994. Address: 22 Church Road, Cinderford, Gloucestershire GL14 2EA, England.

LAWRENCE P. See: **TUBB E(dwin) C(harles).**

LAWRENCE Steven C. See: **MURPHY Lawrence Agustus.**

LAWSON Chet. See: **TUBB E(dwin) C(harles).**

LAWSON James, b. 1938, USA. Author; Company Vice-President. Literary Appointments: Copywriter, McCann-Marschalk Advertising, 1961-62; Reporter, Aspen Times, Colorado, 1962; Copywriter, J Walker Thompson Advertising, NY, 1963-64; Copywriter, Al Paul Lefton Advertising, Philadelphia, PA, 1964-66; Vice-President, Copy Supervisor, Doyle Dane Bernbach Advertising, NY, 1966-78; Senior Vice-President, Director of Creative Services, Doremus and Company, NY, 1978-80; Senior Vice-President, Creative Director, DDB Needham Worldwide, NY, 1982-. Publications: XXX, 1963; Disconnections, 1972; The American Book of The Dead, 1974; Crimes of The Unconcious, 1975; The Girl Watcher, 1976; The Copley Chronicles, 1980; The Fanatic, 1981; Forgeries of The Heart, 1981; The Madman's Kiss, 1987; Frederick Law Olmsted (teleplay), 1990. Address: 756 Greenwich Street, New York, NY 10014, USA.

LAYTON Andrea. See: **BANCROFT Iris.**

LAYTON Irving (Peter), b. 1912, Canadian. Poet; Professor of English Literature, York University, Toronto, 1968-78. Literary Appointments include: Part-Time Lecturer, 1949-68, Poet-in-Residence, 1965-69, Sir George Williams University, Montreal; Writer-in-Residence, University of Guelph, Ontario, 1969-70; Writer-in-Residence, University of Toronto, 1981; Adjunct Professor of Writer-in-Residence, Concordia University, 1988-89. Publications include: Periods of The Moon: Poems, 1967; The Shattered Plinths, 1968; The Whole Bloody Bird, 1969; Selected Poems, 1969; Editor, Poems to Colour: A Selection of Workshop Poems, 1970; Collected Poems, 1971; Nail Polish, 1971; Engagements: The Prose of Irving Layton, 1972; Lovers and Lesser Men, 1973; Editor, Anvil Blood: A Selection of Workshop Poems, 1973; The Pole-Vaulter, 1974; Seventy-Five Greek Poems, 1974; Selected Poems, 2 volumes, 1975; For My Brother Jesus, 1976; The Uncollected Poems, 1936-59, 1976; The Poems of Irving Layton, 1977; The Covenant, 1977; Taking Sides: The Collected Social and Political Writings, 1977; The Tightrope Dancer, 1978; Droppings From Heaven, 1979; The Love Poems of Irving Layton, 1979; There Were No Signs, 1979; An Unlikely Affair: The Correspondence of Irving Layton and Dorothy Rath, 1979; For My Neighbours in Hell, 1980; Europe and Other Bad News, 1981; A Wild Peculiar Joy, 1982; The Gucci Bag, 1983; With Reverence and Delight: The Love Poems, 1984; A Spider Danced a Cozy Jig, 1984; Fortunate Exile, 1987; The Complete Correspondence 1953-78 (with Robert Creeley), 1990; The Improved Binoculars, 1991; Fornalutx, Selected Poems, 1928-1990, 1992. Address: 6879 Monkland Avenue, Montreal, Quebec, Canada, H4B 1J5.

LAZARUS Arnold Leslie, b. 20 Feb 1914, Revere, MA, USA. Writer. m. Keo Felker, 24 Jul 1938, 2 s, 2 d. Education: BA English and Classics, University of Michigan, 1935; BS, Middlesex Medical School, 1937; MA, 1939; PhD, 1957, UCLA. Literary Appointments: English and Drama Teacher, Santa Monica, CA, 1945-53; Literature Teacher, Technical Director, Theatre, Santa Monica City College, 1953-58. Publications: Harbrace Adventures in Literature (with R Lowell and E Hardwick), 1970; Modern English (with others), 1970; The Indiana Experience, 1977; Best of George Ade, 1985; Some Light, new and selected verse, 1988; A George Jean Nathan Reader, 1990;

Entertainments and Valedictions, 1970; A Suit of Four, 1973; Beyond Graustark (with Victor H Jones), 1981; Glossary of Literature and Composition (with H Wendell Smith), 1983. Contributions to: Over 200 poems and reviews in various periodicals. Honours: Ford Foundation Fellow, 1954; Purdue University, Best Teacher Award, 1974; Kemper McComb Award, 1976; US Office of Education Grant, 1963; Chief Midwest Judge, Book of The Month Club Writing Fellowships, 1967-70. Memberships: Phi Beta Kappa; Academy of American Poets; Poetry Society of America; American Society for Theatre Research; Comparative Literature Association; Screenwriters Association of Santa Barbara; Modern Language Association of America; National Council of Teachers of English; College English Association. Literary Agent: Andrea Brown, 319 East 52nd Street, New York, NY 10022, USA. Address: 709 Chopin Drive, Sunnyvale, CA 94087, USA.

LAZARUS Henry. See: **SLAVITT David Rytman.**

LE CARRE John. See: **CORNWELL David John Moore.**

LE GUIN Ursula K(roeber), b. 1929, USA. Fiction Writer; Poet; Essayist. Publications include: Wild Angels, poetry, 1975; A Very Long Way From Anywhere Else, 1976; The Word for World is Forest, 1976; Orsinian Tales (short stories), 1976; Editor, Nebula Award Stories 11, 1977; The Language of The Night (essays), 1978; Leese Webster, 1979; Malafrena, 1979; The Beginning Place (UK edition, Threshold), 1980; Interfaces (edited with Virginia Kidd), 1980; Edges (edited with Virginia Kidd), 1981; Hard Words and Other Poems (poetry), 1981; The Compass Rose (short stories), 1982; The Eye Of The Heron, 1983; In The Red Zone (poetry), 1983; The Visionary, 1984; Always Coming Home, 1985; Buffalo Gals and Other Animal Presences (short stories), 1987; Solomon Leviathan's 931st Trip Around The World, 1988; A Visit From Dr Katz, 1988; Wild Oats and Fireweed (poetry), 1988; Catwings, 1988; Catwings Return, 1989; Fire and Stone, 1989; Dancing at The Edge Of The World (essays), 1989; Tehanu: The Last Book to Earthsea, 1990; Searoad, 1991; A Ride on The Red Mare's Back, 1992; Fish Soup, 1992. Honours: Boston Globe-Hornbook Award, 1968; Hugo Award, 1969, 1972, 1973, 1975, 1988; Nebula Award, 1969, 1975, 1991; Newbery Honor Medal, 1972; National Book Award, 1972; Gandalf Award, 1979; Janet Heidinger Kafka Award, 1986; Prix Lectures-Jeunesse, 1987; International Fantasy Award, 1988; Pushcart Prize Story, 1991; Harold D Vursell Award, American Academy and Institute of Letters, 1991; Writers of Distinction Award, National Council for Research on Women, 1992. Literary Agent: (All Rights) Virginia Kidd. Address: c/o Virginia Kidd, Box 278, Milford, PA 18337, USA.

LE PLASTRIER Robert, See: **WARNER Francis.**

LE ROY Claude, b. 13 Mar 1937, Orne, France. Headmaster. Literary Appointment: Director of magazine NOREAL founded in 1972. Publications: Anthologies of Norman Poets, 1971, 1972, 1980; Picking, Drinking and Eating, 1981; The Memory of the Streets, 1982; In the Shady Corner of the Mirror, 1985; Poems from a 50 Years Old Man, 1987; Fingers of Light for Gloomy Ways, 1989; The Templar's Cry, 1969 (all in French except Fingers of Light for Gloomy Ways, which was written in English); Gens De Chez Nous (People From Here), 1991. Contributions to: International Poetry (USA); World Poetry 1989 (COREA), several magazines in Italy and France. Membership: Societe des Gens de Lettres, Paris. Address: College Jean Moulin, Rue de Broceliande, 14000 Caen, France.

LEA-JONES Julian, b. 2 Dec 1940, Bristol, England. Avionics Researcher; Writer; Presenter. m. Diane Susan Parsons, 22 Dec 1962, 1 son, 1 daughter. Education: College Certificates; Diplomas for Telecommunications & Business Management Studies. Literary Appointments: Contributing Author, Editor, The Templar, 1980-; Past Joint Editor, Alha Journal, Avon Past, 1986. Publications: St John's Conduit: An Account of Bristol's Medieval Water Supply, 1985; Survey of Parish Boundary Markers and Stones for Eleven of the Ancient Bristol Parishes, 1986; Yesterdays Temple, 1987; Bristol Past Revisited, 1989, 1990; Bristol Faces & Places, 1992. Contributions to: AvoIndustrial Archeological Trust, Journal; Newspapers, Radio & TV; Trust, Journal; Also short pieces on Local History. Memberships: West of England Writers Association; Founder, Life Member, Temple Local History Group; Archivist, Bristol History Research Exchange. Address: 33 Springfield Grove, Henleaze, Bristol BS6 7XE, England.

LEACH Penelope, b. 19 Nov 1937, London, England. Psychologist. m. Gerald Leach, 23 Mar 1963, 1 s, 1 d. Education: BA, Cantab, 1959; Graduate Diploma in Social Sciences, LSE, 1961; PhD,

Psychology, London, 1964. Publications include: Baby and Child (in US as Your Baby and Child), 1977, 1989; The Parents' A-Z (in US as Your Growing Child), 1985; Babyhood, revised edition, 1983; The First Six Months: Coming to Terms With Your Baby, 1986; The Babypack (in US as The Babykit), 1990; Videos: England: Becoming a Family; Baby to Toddler; Toddler to Child, Virgin Video, 1988; USA: Your Baby, 1990; Your Baby and Child With Penelope Leach. Contributions to: Numerous magazines and journals; Year-long series in Parenting Magazine, 1990-91; Year-long series in Redbook Magazine, 1992-93. Honours: Fellow, British Psychological Society, 1989; Cable Ace Award, Best Informational Television Presentation, 1993. Membership: Society of Authors. Address: 3 Tanza Road, London, NW3 2UA, England.

LEALE B C, b. 1 Sep 1930, Ashford, Middlesex, England. Bookseller; Poet. Publications: Under a Glass Sky, 1975; Preludes, 1977; Leviathan and Other Poems, 1984; The Colours of Ancient Dreams, 1984. Contributions to: Magazines and journals including: Ambit; Encounter; The Fiction Magazine; Kayak; The Listener; The Literary Review; London Review of Books; Montana Gothic; The Observer; Pacific Quarterly; Poetry Review; A Review of English Literature; Second Aeon; The Spectator; The Times Literary Supplement; Tribune; Anthologies: Best of The Poetry Year 6; A Group Anthology; New Poems 1963 and 1977-78; New Poetry 1, 2, 4, 6, 7, 9; New Writing and Writers 16 and 18; PEN New Poetry 1; The Poetry Book Society Anthology 1986-87; Voices in The Gallery; Double Vision. Address: Flat E10, Peabody Estate, Wild Street, London, WC2B 4AH, England.

LEAPMAN Michael Henry, b. 24 Apr 1938, London, England. Writer; Journalist. m. Olga Mason, 15 July 1965, 1 son. Appointments: Journalist, The Times, 1969-81. Publications: One Man and His Plot, 1976; Yankee Doodles, 1982; Companion Guide to New York, 1983; Barefaced Cheek, 1983; Treachery, 1984; The Last Days of the Beeb, 1986; Kinnock, 1987; The Book of London (Editor), 1989; London's River, 1991; Treacherous Estate, 1992; Eyewitness Guide to London, 1993. Contributions to: Numerous magazines & journals. Honours: Campaigning Journalist of the Year, British Press Award, 1968; Thomas Cook Travel Book Award, Best Guide Book of 1983. Memberships: Society of Authors; National Union of Journalists. Literary Agent: Felicity Bryan. Address: 13 Aldebert Terrace, London SW8 1BH, England.

LEAR Peter. See: **LOVESEY Peter.**

LEASOR (Thomas) James, b. 20 Dec 1923, Erith, Kent, England. Author. m. Joan Margaret Bevan (LLB, Barrister-at-Law), 1 Dec 1951, 3 sons. Education: City of London School; Oriel College, Oxford, BA Honours, 1948, MA Honours 1952. Literary Appointments: Feature Writer, Foreign Correspondent, Daily Express, London, 1948-55; Editorial Advisor, Publishing Company, Newnes and Pearson, Later IPC, 1955-69; Director, Publishing Company, Elm Tree Books, 1970-73. Publications: novels and works of non-fiction; several have been filmed and many published in up to 19 foreign editions; Most recent publications include, Boarding Party, 1977; The Unknown Warrior, 1980; Who Killed Sir Harry Oakes, 1983; The Marine from Mandalay, 1988. Memberships: FRSA (Fellow of Royal Society of Arts); O St J (Order of St John). Address: Swallowcliffe Manor, Salisbury, Wiltshire SP3 5PB, England.

LEBIODA Dariusz Thomas, b. 23 Apr 1958, Bydgoszcz, Poland. University Teacher. m. Danuta Mary Futyma, 25 Jun 1983, 1 s. Education: MA, Higher Pedagogical School, 1984. Literary Appointments: Teacher, 1983-84, Grammar School Teacher, 1984-85, University Teacher, Higher Pedagogical School, 1985-; Editor, quarterly magazine, Metorfora, 1989-. Publications: Poems: Suicides from Under The Charles' Wain, 1980; Mary, 1982; The Newest Testament, 1983; A Moment Before The End of The World, 1988; The Ground Dying European Roller, 1988; Cry My Generation (selected poems 1980-1990), 1990; Stories: Pilots of The Ultra-Violet Distances, 1987, 1990; The Wounded of The Childhood, in preparation; Novels: Trilogy, in preparation. Contributions include: The Art; Miesiecznik Literacki; Literature Life; Culture, Poetry. Honours: Andrzej Bursa Prize for Poetry, 1984; Red Rose Prize, 1984; Klemens Janicki Prize, 1988; Stanislav Wyspianski Artistic Prize for Literature, 1989. Memberships: Adam Mickiewicz Literary Society; Henryk Sienkieicz Literary Society; Polish Writers Union. Address: Osiedlowa 18 m 16, 85 792 Bydgoszcz, Poland.

LEBOW Jeanne, b. 29 Jan 1951, Richmond, Virginia, USA. Writer; Teacher. m. (1) Howard Lebow, (2) Steve Shepard, 5 July 1985. Education: AB, College of William and Mary, 1973; MA, Hollins College, 1982; PhD, University of Southern Mississippi, 1989. Appointments: Instructor, Memphis State University, 1982-84; Graduate Teaching Assistant, University of Southern Mississippi, 1984-87; Fulbright Professor, University of Ouagadougou, West Africa, 1987-88; Assistant Professor, Northeast Missouri State University, 1988-92; Currently Adjunct Professor, University of Southern Mississippi, Gulf Coast. Publications: The Outlaw James Copeland and the Champion-Belted Empress, 1991. Contributions to: Poems to: New Virginia Review; South Florida Poetry Review; Nimrod; Chariton Review; Poems and essays to various anthologies. Honours: National Award, Georgia State Poetry Society, 1983; Fulbright Grant to West Africa, 1987-88; Runner-up, Norma Farber First Book Award, 1991. Memberships: Associated Writing Programs; Modern Language Association; Session Chair for Regional Groups. Address: PO Box 290, Gautier, MS 39553, USA.

LEBRUN Claude Odile, b. 13 Aug 1929, France. Professor. m. Francois Lebrun, 7 Apr 1956, 2 s. Education: Lic de Lettres Modernes, 1953; Lic Libre d'Anglais, 1953; Diplome d'etudes Superieures de Lettres, 1954; Capes de Lettres Modernes, 1956. Publications: Invitation a Jean Sulivan, 1981; 1000 mots pour seussir (an lyci), 1987. Contributions to: Little Brown Bear. Address: Alle Cassandie, 41899 Couture Sur Loir, France.

LEBRUN HOLMES Sandra, b. 24 Apr 1924, Bulcoomatta Station, New South Wales, Australia. Writer; Film Maker; Researcher. m. Cecil William Holmes, 1956, 2 sons, 1 daughter. Education: Anthropology, Sydney University, 2 years. Publications: Yirawala Artist and Man, 1972; Yirawala Painter of the Dreaming, 1992. Contributions to: Milla Wah Milla, Sydney University, 1968; People Magazine; Life, 1968-70s; News; Reserve Bank Magazine; Others. Memberships: Australian Society of Authors; Film Directors Guild. Address: Box 439 PO, Potts Pt, New South Wales 2011, Australia.

LEDOUX Paul Martin, b. 4 Nov 1949, Halifax, Nova Scotia, Canada. Dramatist. m. Ferne Downey. Education: BA, Dalhousie University, Halifax; Postgraduate work, NSCAD, Halifax. Publications include: Love is Strange, 1985; Children of the Night, 1986; Fire, 1987; The Secret Garden, 1993; Also numerous teleplays & radio dramas. Honours: Best play, Quebec Drama Festival, 1975; Outstanding Drama, Chalmer Award, 1989; Dora Manor Moore Award, Best Canadian Drama, Toronto, 1990. Memberships: Chairman 1985-87, Playwrights Union of Canada; ACTRA; Dramatists Cooperative of Nova Scotia; SOCAN. Literary Agent: Katherine Martin. Address: 41 Cowan Avenue, Toronto, Ontario, M6K 2N1, Canada.

LEE Dennis Beynon, b. 31 Aug 1939, Toronto, Canada. Writer. m. (1) 1 son, 1 daughters, (2) Susan Perly, 1985. Education: Editor, House of Anansi Press, 1967-72; Consulting Editor, Macillan of Canada, 1972-78; Poetry Editor, McClelland and Stewart, 1981-84. Publications: Children's Poetry: Wiggle to the Laundromat, 1970; Alligator Pie, 1974; Nicholas Knock, 1974; Garbage Delight, 1977; Jelly Belly, 1983; Lizzy's Lion, 1984; The Ice Cream Store, 1991; Children's Tale: The Ordinary Bath, 1979; Adult Poetry: Kingdom of Absence, 1967; Civil Elegies, 1972; The Gods, 1979; The Difficulty of Living on Other Planets, 1988; Riffs, 1993; Adults Non-Fiction: Savage Fields, 1977. Contributions to: Magazines and journals. Honour: Governor General's Award for Poetry, 1972. Memberships: Writers' Union of Canada; PEN, Canada. Literary Agent: Sterling Lord Associates (Canada). Address: c/o Sterling Lord Associates (Canada), 10 St Mary Street No 510, Toronto, M4Y 1P9, Canada.

LEE Hamilton, b. 10 Oct 1921, Chowhsien, Shandong, China. Professor Emeritus (Education). m. Jean C Chang, 24 Aug 1945, 1 s, 3 d. Education: BS, National Peking Teachers University, 1948; MA, University of Minnesota, Minneapolis, USA, 1958; EdD, Wayne State University, Detroit, MI, 1964. Literary Appointmets: English Teacher, Taiwan High Schools, Taiwan, China, 1948-56; Research Associate, Wayne State University, Detroit, MI, USA, 1958-64; Visiting Professor of Chinese Literature, Seton Hall University, summer 1964; Assistant Professor, Moorhead State University, 1964-65; Associate Professor, University of Wisconsin, 1965-66; Professor, East Stroudsburg University, 1966-84; Visiting Scholar, Harvard University, summer 1965 and 1966; Visiting Fellow, Princeton University, 1976-78; Professor Emeritus, East Stroudsburg University, East Stroudsburg, PA, 1984. Publications: Readings In Instructional Technology, 1970; Reflection,

Chap Book, 1989; Revelation, Chap Book, 1991; Golden Voices, anthology, 1989; Works in numerous anthologies, 1974-. Contributions to: Education Tomorrow, 1974-76; World Future Society; Byline; Poetry Norwest; Today Poetry; Various small literary magazines, 1974-; Poets At Work. Honours: Numerous honourable mentions and awards in poetry contests, 1974-; Accomplishment Of Merit. Memberships: Poetry Society of America; Pennsylvania Poetry Society; Phi Delta Kappa; International Society of Poets Advisory Panel; Academy of American Poets; Former Member, numerous societies including: World Future Society; American Association Of University Professors; AACI. Address: 961 Long Woods Drive, Stroudsburg, PA 18360, USA.

LEE John, b. 1931, USA. Writer; Former Professor. Literary Appointments: Photographer, Fort Worth Star-Telegram, Fort Worth, TX, USA, 1952-57; Denver Post, Denver, CO, USA, 1958-60; Professor of Journalism, American University, Washington DC, 1965-67; University of Arizona, Tucson, 1967-71; New York University, 1971-74; California State University, Long Beach, 1975-76; Memphis State University, 1984-. Publications: Caught in The Act, 1968; Diplomatic Persuaders, 1968; Assignation in Algeria, 1971; The Ninth Man, 1976; The Thirteenth Hour, 1978; Lago, 1980; Stalag Texas, 1990. Literary Agent: Don Congdon Associates Inc. Address: c/o Don Congdon Associates Inc, 156 Fifth Avenue, Suite 625, New York, NY 10010, USA.

LEE Joyce Isabel, b. 19 June 1913, Murtoa, Australia. Pharmacist; Lecturer. m. Norman Edward, 18 Dec 1937, 2 sons. Education: Methodist Ladies' College; Registered Pharmacist, Victorian College of Pharmacy, Melbourne. Literary Appointments: Lecturer/Tutor (Poetry Writing) Victoria College of Advanced Education, Toorak Campus, 1981-. Publications: Sisters Poets 1, 1979, reprinted 1979, 1980; Abruptly from the Flatlands, 1984, reprinted 1984; Plain Dreaming, 1991. Contributions to: Meanjin; Poetry Australia; The Age; The Bulletin; Luna; Compass; Contempa; New Europe; Overland; Southerly; Premier Poets and various anthologies; New Oxford Book of Australian Verse, 1986; The Penguin Book of Australian Women Poets, 1986; Oxford Book of Love Poems, ed Jennifer Strauss, 1993; Walking the Dogs, 1994. Address: 13/205 Burke Road, Glen Iris, Victoria 3146, Australia.

LEE Kuei-shien, b. 19 June 1937, Taipei, Taiwan, China. Patent Agent; Chemical Engineer; Corporation President. m. Huei-uei Wang, 1965, 1 son, 1 daughter. Education: Chemical Engineering, Taipei Institute of Technology, 1958; German Literature, European Language Center of Educational Ministry, 1964; PhD, Chemical Engineering (Honoris Causa), Marquis Giuseppe Scicluna International University Foundation, 1985. Literary Appointments: Director, Li Poetry Society; Publisher, Inventors Journals; Examiner, Wu yong-fu Critique Prize; Director, Taiwan PEN. Publications: Essays include: Journey to Europe, 1971; Profile of the Souls, 1972; Essays on German Literature, 1973; On International Patent Practices, 1975; Critical Essays on Chinese Translation of English Poetry, 1976; Critical Essays: On Taiwanese Poems, 1987; Poetical Reaction, 1992; Poetical Witness, 1994; Poetry includes: Pagoda and Other Poems, 1963; The Loquat, 1964; Poems on Nankang, 1966; Naked Roses, 1976; Collected poems, 1985; Formation of Crystal, 1986; Transfusion, 1986; Eternal Territory, 1990; Praying, 1993; Image in the Evening, 1993; Anthologies include: Anthology of German Poems, 1970; Anthology of Black Orpheus, 1974; Year Book of Taiwanese Poems, 1987; Selected Poems of Li Poetry Society, 1992; Taiwan Literary Writings in 1993, 1994. Translations include: The Trial by Franz Kafka, 1969; Cat and Mouse by Gunter Grass, 1970; Rainer Maria Rilke by H E Holthusen, 1969; Duineser Elegien by R M Rilke, 1969; Die Sonnete an Orpheus by R M Rilke, 1969; Das Buch der Bilder, by R M Rilke, 1977; Selected Poems by Giosue Carducci, 1981; Selected Poems by Giogos Seferis, 1981; Selected Poems by Salvatore Quasimodo, 1981; Prussian Night by Alexander Solzhenitsyn, 1983. Address: Room 705, Asia Enterprise Center, No 142 Minchuan East Road, Sec 3, Taipei, Taiwan, China.

LEE Lance, b. 25 Aug 1942, NY, USA. Writer; Poet; Playwright. m. Jeanne Barbara Hutchings, 30 Aug 1962, 2 d. Education: Boston University; BA, Brandeis University, 1964; MFA, Yale School of Drama, 1967. Literary Appointments include: Lecturer, Bridgeport University, 1967-68; Instructor, Southern Connecticut State College, 1968; Assistant Professor, Senior Lecturer, University of Southern California, 1968-71; Lecturer, University of California, Los Angeles, 1971-73; Lecturer, Screenwriting, California State University, 1981-. Publications: Plays: Fox, Hounds and Huntress, 1973; Time's Up, 1979; Productions: Time's Up; Gambits; Fox, Hound and Huntress; Rasputin;

Textbook: The Understructure of Writing for Film and Television, 1988; Wrestling with The Angel (poetry), 1990. Contributions to: Numerous magazines and journals including: Glass Onion; The Journal; Poem; Lake Superior Review; Midwest Poetry Review; Cottonwood Review; Embers; Cross Currents; Los Angeles Times; California Writers Issue; Poetry Northwest; Poetry LA; Negative Capability. Honours: Fellowships: Arts of The Theatre Foundation, 1967; University of Southern California Research and Publication Grants, 1970-71; Rockefeller Foundation, 1971; NEA, 1976; Theatre Development Fund, 1976; Squaw Valley Community of Writers, 1982; Port Townsend (Centum), 1985; Theron Bamberger Award, Brandeis University. Memberships: Dramatists Guild; Authors League; American Academy of Poets; Poetry Society of America. Literary Agent: Samuel French, NY, USA. Address: 1127 Galloway Street, Pacific Palisades, CA 90272, USA.

LEE Laurie, b. 1914, United Kingdom. Author; Poet. Literary Appointments: Scriptwriter, Crown Film Unit, 1942-44; Publications Editor, Ministry of Information, 1944-46; Member, Green Park Film Unit, 1946-47; Caption Writer-in-Chief, Festival of Britain, 1950-51. Publications: The Dead Village, by Avigdor Dagan, translation, 1943; The Sun My Monument, 1944; Land at War, 1945; The Voyage of Magellan: A Dramatic Chronicle for Radio, 1946; The Bloom of Candles, 1947; Peasants' Priest (play), 1947; We Make a Film In Cyprus (with R Keene), 1947; New Poems (edited with C Hassall and Rex Warner), 1954; My Many-Coated Man, 1955; A Rose for Winter: Travels in Andalusia, 1956; Cider With Rosie (US edition as The Edge of Day), 1959; Poems, 1960; The Firstborn (essay on childhood), 1964; As I Walked Out One Midsummer Morning (autobiography), 1969; Pergamon Poets 10 (with Charles Causley), 1970; I Can't Stay Long, 1975; Innocence in The Mirror, 1978; Two Women, 1983; Selected Poems, 1983; A Moment of War, 1991. Address: c/o Andre Deutsch Limited, 105 Great Russell Street, London, WC1B 3LU, England.

LEE Li-Young, b. 1957, Jakarta, Indonesia. Publications: Rose; The City in Which I Love You; The Winged Seed. Honour: Lamont Poetry Selection, 1990.

LEE Robert E(dwin), b. 1918, USA. Dramatist; University Lecturer. Literary Appointments: Director, Radio Station WHK-WCLE, Cleveland, OH, 1937-38; Director, Young and Rubicam, NY and Hollywood, CA, 1938-42; Partner, Lawrence and Lee, 1942-; Vice-President, Lawrence and Lee Inc, NY and Los Angeles, CA, 1955-; Professor of Playwriting, College of Theatre Arts, Pasadena Playhouse, CA, 1962-63; Adjunct Professor, University of California, Los Angeles, 1966-; Co-Founder, American Playwrights Theatre. Publications: Television: The Revolutionary Industry, 1944; Shangri-La (with J Lawrence and James Hilton), 1956; With Jerome Lawrence: Inherit The Wind, 1955; Auntie Mame, 1956, musical, 1966; The Gang's All Here, 1959; Only in America, 1959; A Call on Kuprin, 1961; Sparks Fly Upward, 1967; The Incomparable Max, 1969; The Night Thoreau Spent in Jail, 1970; Jabberwock, 1972; The Crocodile Smile, 1972; First Monday in October, 1975; Sounding Brass, 1975; Whisper in The Mind (with Norman Cousins), 1990. Honour: Elected to Hall of Fame of American Theatre, 1990. Address: 15725 Royal Oak Road, Encino, CA 91436, USA.

LEE Tanith, b. 1947, United Kingdom. Freelance Writer of Science Fiction, Radio Plays, Children's Fiction. Publications: The Betrothed (short stories), 1968; The Dragon Hoard (juvenile), 1971; Princess Hynchatti and Some Other Surprises (juvenile), 1972; Animal Castle (juvenile), 1972; Companions on The Road (juvenile) (US as, Companions on The Road, and The Winter Players (1977), 1975; The Birthgrave, 1975; Don't Bite The Sun, 1976; The Storm Lord, 1976; The Winter Players (juvenile), 1976; East of Midnight (juvenile), 1977; Drinking Sapphire Wine (UK edition also includes, Don't Bite The Sun, 1979), 1977; Volkhavaar, 1977; Vazkor, Son of Vazkor (UK as, Shadowfire, 1979), 1978; Quest for The White Witch, 1978; Night's Master, 1978; The Castle of Dark (juvenile), 1978; Shon The Taken (juvenile), 1979; Death's Master, 1979; Electric Forest, 1979; Sabella: or, The Blood Stone, 1980; Kill The Dead, 1980; Day by Night, 1980; Delusion's Master, 1981; The Silver Metal Lover, 1982; Cyrion (short stories), 1982; Prince on a White Horse (juvenile), 1982; Sung in Shadow, 1983; Anackire, 1983; Red as Blood: or, Tales from The Sisters Grimmer, 1983; The Dragon Hoard, 1984; The Beautiful Biting Machine (short stories), 1984; Tamastara, or, The Indian Nights (short stories), 1984; Days of Grass, 1985; The Gorgon and Other Beastly Tales, 1985; Dreams of Dark and Light, 1986. Address: c/o Macmillan London Limited, 4 Little Essex Street, London, WC2R 3LF, England.

LEE Warner. See: **BATTIN B W.**

LEE Wayne C (Lee Sheldon), b. 1917, USA. Author. Publications: Prairie Vengeance, 1954; Broken Wheel Ranch, 1956; Slugging Backstop, 1957; His Brother's Guns, 1958; Killer's Range, 1958; Bat Masterson, 1960; Gun Brand, 1961; Blood on The Prairie, 1962; Thunder in The Backfield, 1962; Stranger in Stirrup, 1962; The Gun Tamer, 1963; Devil Wire, 1963; The Hostile Land, 1964; Gun in His Hand, 1964; Warpath West, 1965; Fast Gun, 1965; Brand of a Man, 1966; Mystery of Scorpion Creek, 1966; Trail of The Skulls, 1966; Showdown at Julesburg Station, 1967; Return to Gunpoint, 1967; Only The Brave, 1967; Doomed Planet (as Lee Sheldon), 1967; Sudden Guns, 1968; Trouble at Flying H, 1969; Stage to Lonesome Butte, 1969; Showdown at Sunrise, 1971; The Buffalo Hunters, 1972; Suicide Trail, 1972; Wind Over Rimfire, 1973; Son of a Gunman, 1973; Scotty Philip: The Man Who Saved The Buffalo, 1975; Law of The Prairie, 1975; Die Hard, 1975; Law of The Lawless, 1977; Skirmish at Fort Phil Kearney, 1977; Gun Country, 1978; Petticoat Wagon Train, 1978; The Violent Man, 1978; Ghost of a Gunfighter, 1980; McQuaid's Gun, 1980; Trails of The Smoky Hill (non-fiction), 1980; Shadow of The Gun, 1981; Guns at Genesis, 1981; Putnam's Ranch War, 1982; Barbed Wire War, 1983; The Violent Trail, 1984; White Butte Guns, 1984; War at Nugget Creek, 1985; Massacre Creek, 1985; The Waiting Gun, 1986; Hawks of Autumn, 1986; Wild Towns of Nebraska, 1988; Arikaree War Cry, 1992. Memberships: Western Writers of America, President, 1970-71; Nebraska Writers Guild, President, 1974-76. Address: PO Box 906 Imperial, Nebraska 69033, USA.

LEE William. See: **BURROUGHS William Steward.**

LEE William Rowland, b. Uxbridge, Middlesex, England. m. Zdene Pausarova, 9 July, Prague, 2 daughters. Education: Teacher's Diploma, University of London, 1934; Certificates in English Phonetics and French Phonetics, 1934, 35; PhD, Charles University, Prague, 1950; MA, Linguistics, University of London, 1954. Literary Appointments: Lecturer, Department of English, Charles University, Prague, 1946-50; Lecturer, English as a Foreign Language, University of London Institute of Education, 1952-57, 1959-62; Language Teaching Adviser, British Council, 1958, 59; Freelance Textbook Writer, Examiner and Lecturer, 1963-; Editor: English Language Teaching Journal, 1961-81; World Language English, 1982-84; English - a World Language, 1991-92. Publications: English Intonation: A New Approach, 1958; Teach Yourself Czech (with Z Lee), 1959; An English Intonation Reader, 1960; Spelling Irregularity and Reading Progress, 1960, 1972; Time for a Song with M Dodderidge, 1963; Simple Audio-Visual Aids to Foreign Language Teaching with H Coppen, 1964, 68; Language Teaching Games and Contests, 1979-86; The Dolphin English Course, 1970, 1973; A Study Dictionary of Social English, 1984; Cassell Elementary Dictionary of Techincal and Scientific English (with C V James), 1994. Contributions to: Magazines and professional publications. Honours: Honorary Fellow, Trinity College London, 1972; OBE, 1979; Medal of Honour, Poznan University, Poland. Memberships: Founder and Chairman (1967-84), The International Association of Teachers of English as a Foreign Language and member of other professional organizations. Address: 16 Alexandra Gardens, Hounslow, Middlesex, TW3 4HU, England.

LEECH Geoffrey Neil, b. 16 Jan 1936, Gloucester, England. University Professor. m. Frances Anne Berman, 29 Jul 1961, 1 s, 1 d. Education: BA English Language and Literature, 1959, MA, 1963, PhD, 1968, University College, London. Publications: English in Advertising, 1966; A Linguistic Guide to English Poetry, 1969; Towards a Semantic Description of English, 1969; Meaning and The English Verb, 1971, 2nd edition, 1987; A Grammar of Contemporary English (with R Quirk, S Greenbaum, J Svartvik), 1972; Semantics, 1974, 2nd edition, 1981; A Communicative Grammar of English (with J Svartvik), 1975; Explorations in Semantics and Pragmatics, 1980; Style in Fiction (with Michael H Short), 1981; English Grammar For Today (with R Hoogenraad, M Deuchar), 1982; Principles of Pragmatics, 1983; A Comprehensive Grammar of The English Language (with R Quirk, S Greenbaum, J Svartvik), 1985; The Computational Analysis of English (edited with R Gatside, G Sampson), 1987; An A-Z of English Grammar and Usage, 1989; Introducing English Grammar, 1992. Contributions to: A Review of English Literature; Lingua; New Society; Linguistics; Dutch Quarterly Review of Anglo-American Letters; TLS; Prose Studies; The Rising Generation; Transactions of The Philological Society. Honours: FilDr, University of Lund, 1987; FBA, 1987. Membership: Academia Europea. Literary Agent: The Peters, Fraser and Dunlop Group Limited, 503-4 The Chambers, Chelsea Harbour, London, SW10 0XF, England.

LEEDOM-ACKERMAN Joanne, b. 7 Feb 1947, Dallas, Texas, USA. Novelist. m. Peter Ackerman, 3 June 1972, 2 sons. Education: BA, Principia College, 1968; MA, Johns Hopkins University, 1969; MA, Brown University, 1974. Literary Appointment: Chair of International PEN's Writers in Prison Committee, 1994. Publications: No Marble Angels, 1985; The Dark Path to the River, 1988; Articles and poems in: What You Can Do: Practical Suggestions for Action on Some Major Problems in the Seventies, 1971; Bicentennial Collection of Texas Short Stories, 1974; Fiction and Poetry by Texas Women, 1975; Beyond Literacy, 1991; Edited, Women for All Seasons, 1989. Contributions to: Articles to: The Christian Science Monitor; The Los Angeles Times; The Houston Post. Address: 48 Phillimore Gardens, London W8 7QG, England.

LEES-MILNE James, b. 1908, United Kingdom. Author. Appointments: Private Secretary to Baron Lloyd, 1931-35; Staff Member, Reuters, 1935-36; Staff Member, National Trust, 1936-66. Publications: The National Trust (editor), 1945; The Age of Adam, 1947; National Trust (editor), 1945; The Age of Adam, 1947; National Trust Guide: Buildings, 1948; Tudor Renaissance, 1951; The Age of Inigo Jones, 1953; Roman Mornings, 1956; Baroque in Italy, 1959; Baroque in Spain and Portugal, 1960; Earls of Creation, 1962; Worcestershire: A Shell Guide, 1964; St Peter's 1967; English Country Houses: Baroque, 1970; Another Self, 1970; Heretics in Love, novel, 1973; Ancestral Voices, 1975; William Beckford, 1976; Prophesying Peace, 1977; Round the Clock, novel, 1978; Harold Nicolson, 2 vols 1980-81; The Country House, anthology, 1982; The Last Stuarts, 1983; Enigmatic Edwardian, 1986; Some Cotswold Country Houses, 1987; Venetian Evenings, 1988; The Fool of Love, 1987; Venetian Evenings, 1988; The Fool of Love, 1990; Bachelor Duke, 1991; People and Places, 1992; A Mingled Measure, 1994. Honours: FRSL; FSA. Address: Essex House, Badminton, Avon GL9 1DD, England.

LEESON Robert (Arthur), b. 31 Mar 1928, Barnton, Cheshire, England. Writer and Journalist. m. Gunvor Hagen, 25 May 1954, 1 son, 1 daughter. Education: Sir John Deane's Grammar School, Northwich, Cheshire, 1939-44; External Degree in English (Hons), London University, 1972. Literary Appointment: Literary Editor, Morning Star, London 1960-80. Publications: Third Class Genie (Childrens), 1975; Silver's Revenge (Childrens), 1978; It's My Life (Teen Fiction), 1980; Slambash Wangs of a Compo Gormer (Fantasy), 1987; Travelling Brothers (Six centuries history of travelling Craftsmen), 1979; Reading and Righting (Past, Present and Future of Fiction for the Young), 1985; Candy For King (Teen Fiction), 1983; Grange Hill Rules OK (School), 1980; Coming Home (Teen Fiction), 1991; Zarnia Experiment 1-6 (Science Fiction), 1993; Robin Hood, 1994. Contributions to: The Guardian, Times Education Supplement, Book for Your Children, Books for Keeps, School Librarian, Children's Literature in Education. Honour: Eleanor Farjeon Award for services to Children and Literature, 1985. Memberships: Writers' Guild of Great Britain (Chairman 1985-86); International Board on Books for Young People (British Section) Treasurer 1972-1991. Address: 18 McKenzie Road, Broxbourne, Hertfordshire EN10 7JH, England.

LEFEBURE Molly, b. United Kingdom. Author. Publications: Evidence for the Crown, 1955; Murder with a Difference, 1958; The Lake District, 1963; Scratch and Co, 1968; The Hunting of Wilberforce Pike, 1970; Cumberland Heritage, 1971; The Loona Balloons, 1974; Samuel Taylor Coleridge: A Bondage of Opium, 1974; Cumbrian Discovery, 1977; The Bondage of Love: A Life of Mrs Samuel Taylor Coleridge, 1986; The Illustrated Lake Poets; Blitz: A Novel of Love and War, 1988; The Coleridge Connection (Essays, ed with Richard Gravil), 1990; Thunder in the Sky (novel), 1991. Address: c/o Watson Little Ltd, 12 Egbert Street, London NW1 8LJ, England.

LEFF Leonard J, b. 23 Jan 1942, Houston, Texas, USA. Professor of English. m. Linda Ringer, 26 Jan 1969, 1 son. Education: BBA, University of Texas, Austin, 1963; MA, University of Houston, 1965; PhD, Northern Illinois University, 1971. Appointments: Instructor, English: McNeese State University, 1965-68; University of Illinois, Urbana-Champaign, 1971-72; Northern Illinois University, 1972-73; Assistant Professor, Associate Professor, Head of English, Bellevue College, 1973-79; Assistant Professor, 1979-82, Associate Professor 1983-91, Interim Head of English 1989-90, Professor 1991-, Oklahoma State University, Stillwater. Publications: Film Plots, vol I, 1983, vol II 1988; Hitchcock and Selznick: The Rich and Strange Collaboration of

Alfred Hitchcock and David O Selznick in Hollywood, 1987, paperback 1988, UK Edition 1988, UK paperback 1990, French translation 1990, Spanish translation 1992; The Dame in the Kimono: Hollywood, Censorship, and the Production Code from the 1920s to the 1960s (with Jerold Simmons), 1990. Literary Agent: Sobel Associates, New York City, New York, USA. Address: 3002 Loma Verde Ln, Stillwater, OK 74074, USA.

LEFFLAND Ella Julia, b. 25 Nov 1931, Martinez, California. Writer. Education: BA Fine Arts, San Jose State College, 1953. Publications: Mrs Munck, 1970; Love out of Season, 1974; Last Courtesies, 1979; Rumors of Peace, 1980; The Knight, Death of the Devil, 1990. Contributions to: New Yorker; Harper's; Atlantic Monthly; Mademoiselle; New York Magazine; New York Times. Honours: Gold Medal for Fiction, 1974, 1979; Silver Medal, 1991, Commonwealth Club of California; O Henry First Prize, 1977; Bay Area Book Reviewers Award for Fiction, 1990. Literary Agent: Lois Wallace. Address: Wallace Literary Agency, 177 East 70th Street, New York, NY 10021, USA.

LEGAT Michael Ronald, b. 24 Mar 1923, London, England. Writer. m. Rosetta Clark, 20 Aug 1949, 2 sons. Appointments: Editorial Director, Transworld Publishers Limited, 1956-73; Editorial Director, Transworld Publishers Limited, 1973-78. Publications: Dear Author..., 1972, revised 1989; Mario's Vineyard, 1980; The Silver Fountain, 1982; An Author's Guide to Publishing, 1983, revised 1991; Putting on a Play, 1984; The Shapiro Diamond, 1984; The Silk Maker, 1985; Writing for Pleasure and Profit, 1986, revised 1993; The Cast Iron Man, 1987; The Illustrated Dictionary of Western Literature, 1987; We Beheld His Glory, 1988; The Nuts and Bolts of Writing, 1989; How to Write Historical Novels, 1990; Plotting the Novel, 1992; Understanding Publishers' Contracts, 1992; Non-Fiction: A Writer's Guide, 1993. Contributions to: The Author; Writers' Monthly. Memberships: President, The Weald of Sussex Writers; Chairman, Writers' Holiday, Harlech; Society of Authors; Hon Sec, Society of Sussex Authors; President, Uckfield & District Writers Club. Literary Agent: Campbell Thomson and McLaughlin Limited. Address: Bookends, Lewes Road, Horsted Keynes, Haywards Heath, West Sussex RH17 7DP, England.

LEGERE Werner, b. 28 May 1912, Hohenstein-Ernstthal, Germany. Author. m. Ruth Corsa, 20 Oct 1942, 2 sons. Publications: Ich war in Timbuktu, 1955; Unter Korsaren Verschollen, 1955; Die Verschwoerung vom Rio Cayado, 1956; Schwester Florence, 1956; Der Ruf von Castiglione, 1960; Stern aus Jakob, 1963; Die Stiere von Assur, 1969; Der gefuerchtete Gaismair, 1976; In allen meinen Taten, 1982. Honours: Award for Art Prize: Adventure Books for Children and Young People, Board of Literature of the GDR, 1953; Art Prize, County Karl-Marx-Stadt, 1961; Artur Becker Medal, Silver, Free German Youth Organization, 1962; Johannes R Becher Medal, Silver, Kulturbund Association of the GDR, 1982; Culture Prize, County Karl-Marx-Stadt, 1982; Honorary Citizen, Hohenstein-Ernstthal, 1993. Memberships: Saxonian Writers' Union; Union of German Writers. Address: Lutherstrasse 20, Hohenstein-Ernstthal, D-09337, Germany.

LEGGATT Alexander Maxwell, b. 18 Aug 1940, Trafalgar Twp, Ontario, Canada. University Teacher. m. Margaret Anna Leggatt, 4 d. Education: BA, University of Toronto, 1962; MA, 1963, PhD, 1965, University of Birmingham. Literary Appointments: Associate Editor, Modern Drama, 1972-75; Editorial Board, English Studies in Canada, 1984-91. Publications include: Shakespeare's Comedy of Love, 1974; Shakespeare's Political Drama, 1988; Citizen Comedy in The Age of Shakespeare, 1973; Ben Jonson: His Vision and His Art, 1981; English Drama: Shakespeare to The Restoration, 1988; Harvester-Twayne New Critical Introductions to Shakespeare: King Lear, 1988; Shakespeare in Perfomance: King Lear, 1991; Jacobean Public Theatre, 1992. Contributions to: Many scholarly journals including: Shakespeare Quarterly; Shakespeare Studies; Shakespeare Survey; Essays in Criticism; Studies in English Literature; Modern Language Review. Honour: Guggenheim Fellowship, 1985-86. Memberships: Shakespeare Association of America, Trustee, 1986-89; International Shakespeare Association, Executive Committee, 1987-; International Association of University Professors of English; Association of Canadian University Teachers of English. Address: University College, University of Toronto, Toronto, Canada, M5S 1A1.

LEGUEY-FEILLEUX Jean-Robert, b. 28 Mar 1928, Marseilles, France. University Professor; Chairperson, Political Science Dept, St Louis University. m. Virginia Hartwell, 19 Sep 1953, 4 d. Education: Diplôme Supérieur, École Supérieure de Commerce, Marseilles, 1949; Diplôme Supérieur d'Enseignement Colonial, University d'Aix, 1949;

MA, University of FL, 1951; Certificate, English Life and Institutions, Cambridge, 1952; PhD, Georgetown University, 1965. Literary Appointments: Director of Research, Institute of World Polity, Georgetown University, 1960-66; National Panel of Judges for Fulbright Awards, 1973-75; Visiting Scholar, Harvard Law School, 1974-75. Publications: World Polity, Vol 2, 1960; The Law of Limited International Conflict, 1965; The Implications of Disarmament, 1977; Democracy in a High-Technology Society, 1988; The External Environment, 1991; Contributed to, Great Events from History: Human Rights, 1992. Contributions to: Peace Research Abstracts Journal (Canada); Respond; Prioritas; Bulletin of Peace Proposals (Norway); Chronicle of the UN Association. Honours: Fulbright Scholar, 1950; Distinguished Service, IIE, New York, 1976; Outstanding Educator, Nutshell Magazine, 1982; Pi Sigma Alpha; Pi Delta Phi. Memberships: Academic Council on the UN System; Gold Key Honor Society, Georgetown University; Political Science Honor Society; French Language Honor Society; Advisory Board, World News Report, St Louis. Address: 6139 Kingsbury Avenue, St Louis, MO 63112, USA.

LEGUM Colin, b. 3 Jan 1919, Kestell, South Africa. Journalist. m. 27 Jul 1960, 1 s, 3 d. Education: Secondary School, Kestell, South Africa. Literary Appointments include: Political Correspondent, Sunday Express, Johannesburg, 1936; Editor, The Forward, Johannesburg, 1939; Editor, Illustrated Bulletin, Johannesburg, 1942; Associate Editor, The Observer, London, 1949; Editor, Africa Contemporary Record; Co-Editor, Middle East Contemporary Survey, 1976; Editor, Third World Reports, 1982-. Publications include: Pan-Africanism; Congo Disaster; Must We Lose Africa; Attitude to Africa (with others); South Africa - Crisis for The West (co-author); The Battlefronts of Southern Africa, 1987. Contributions to: Journal of Contemporary African Affairs; New York Times; Washington Post; Christian Science Monitor; Jerusalem Post; London Review of Books. Memberships: Royal Institute of African Affairs; International Institute of Strategic Studies; African Publications Trust, Chairman; Africa Education Trust; Africa Studies Association of US; Diplomatic and Commonwealth Writers. Address: Wild Acre, Plaw Hatch, Near Sharpthorne, West Sussex, RH19 4JL, England.

LEHMANN David, b. 1948. Poet, Literary criticism. Publications: Some Nerve: Poems, 1973; Day One: Poems, 1979; The Perfect Murder: A Study in Detection, 1989; Operation Memory, 1990; Signs of the Times, 1991; The Line Forms Here, 1992; The Big Question, 1995. Honour: Fellow, American Academy & Institute of Arts & Letters, 1990.

LEHMANN Geoffrey, b. 1940, Australia. Tax Lawyer. m. 1981, 3 s, 2 d. Education: BA, LLM, University of Sydney. Appointment: Partner, Price Waterhouse. Publications: Ilex Tree (with Les A Murray), 1967; A Voyage of Lions, 1970; Conversation With a Rider, 1972; Spring Day in Autumn, 1974; Selected Poems, 1975; Ross' Poems, 1978; Nero's Poems, 1981; Children's Games, 1990; Spring Forest, 1992; Editor and co-editor of anthologies. Honour: Grace Levin Prize, 1967, 1981. Memberships: Literature Board of Australia Council, 1982-85. Literary Agent: Curtis Brown, Australia. Address: c/o Curtis Brown (Australia) Pty Limited, 27 Union Street, Paddington, NSW 2021, Australia.

LEIGH Meredith. See: KENYON Bruce Guy.

LEIGH Mike, b. 20 Feb 1943, Salford, Lancashire, England. Dramatist; Film and Theatre Director. m. Alison Steadman, 1973, 2 sons. Education: Royal Academy of Dramatic Arts; Camberwell School of Arts and Crafts; Central School of Art and Design; London Film School. Publications: Plays: The Box Play, 1965; My Parents Have Gone to Carlisle, The Last Crusade of the Five Little Nuns, 1966; Nenaa, 1967; Individual Fruit Pies, Down Here and Up There, Big Basil, 1968; Epilogue, Glum Victoria and the Lad with Specs, 1969; Bleak Moments, 1970; A Rancid Pong, 1971; Wholesome Glory, The Jaws of Death, Dick Whittington and His Cat, 1973; Babies Grow Old, The Silent Majority, 1974; Abigail's Party, 1977 (also TV play); Ecstasy, 1979; Goose-Pimples, 1981; Smelling A Rat, 1988; Greek Tragedy, 1989; It's A Great Big Shame! 1993; TV Films: A Mug's Game, Hard Labour, 1973; The Permissive Society, The Bath of the 2001 F A Cup, Final Goalie, Old Chums, Probation, A Light Snack, Afternoon, 1975; Nuts in May, Knock for Knock, 1976; The Kiss of Death, 1977; Who's Who, 1978; Grown Ups, 1980; Home Sweet Home, 1981; Meantime, 1983; Four Days in July, 1984; Feature Films: Bleak Moments, 1971; The Short & Curlies, 1987; High Hopes, 1988; Life is Sweet, 1990; Naked, 1993; Radio Play: Too Much of a Good Thing, 1979. Honours: Golden Leopard, Locarno Film Festival, Golden Hugo, Chicago Film

Festival, for Bleak Moments, 1972; George Devine Award, 1973; London 'Evening Standard' and 'Drama' London Critics' Choice best comedy awards, 1981, for Goose Pimples; MA (Hon), Salford University, 1991; OBE, 1993; Critics Prize, Venice Film Festival, 1988, for High Hopes; Best Director, Cannes Film Festival, 1993, for Naked. Literary Agent: The Peters Fraser and Dunlop Group Ltd. Address: The Peters Fraser and Dunlop Group Ltd, 503/4 The Chambers, Chelsea Harbour, London SW10 0XF, England.

LEIGH Richard Harris, b. 16 Aug 1943, NJ, USA. Writer. Education: BA Programme, Tufts University, 1961-65; MA Programme, University of Chicago, 1965-67; PhD Programme, State University of New York, Stony Brook, 1967-70. Literary Appointments: Special Collections Librarian, Simon Fraser University, Vancouver, 1970-72. Publications: The Holy Blood and The Holy Grail (with Michael Baigent and Henry Lincoln), 1982; The Messianic Legacy (with Michael Baigent and Henry Lincoln), 1986; The Temple and The Lodge (with Michael Baigent), 1989; The Dead Sea Scrolls Deception (with Michael Baigent), 1991; Various short pieces particularly, Madonna, in Random Review, 1982. Contributions to: Various journals and anthologies of short stories, some introductions to books by other people, particularly, essay on contemporary fiction as preface to Song of a Man Who Came Through, by Douglas Lockhart, 1978. Honour: Madonna selected among the best short stories of 1982, published in Random Review (hardback and paperback). Membership: Co-Founder of Pushkin Prize Programme in Ireland (with Seamus Heaney, Bernard McCabe, The Earl of Mount Charles, The Duchess of Abercorn). Literary Agent: Barbara Levy. Address: 21 Kelly Street, London, NW1 8PG, England.

LEIGH FERMOR Patrick (Michael), b. 1920, United Kingdom. Author. Publications: The Traveller's Tree, 1950; Julie de Carneilhan and Chance Acquaintances, by Colette, translation, 1951; A Time to Keep Silence, 1953; The Violins of Saint-Jacques, 1953; Mani, 1958; Roumeli, 1966; A Time of Gifts, 1977; Between the Woods and the Water, 1986; Three Letters from the Woods, 1991. Honours: DSO, OBE (Mil); DLitt; CLitt; Gold Medal of Honour of the Municipality of Athens. Literary Agent: Sheil Land Associates Ltd, 43 Doughty Street, London WC1N 2LF. Address: c/o Messrs John Murray Ltd, 50 Albemarle Street, London W1, England.

LEISY James Franklin (Frank Lynn), b. 1927, USA. Writer; Publisher; Company Director. Literary Appointments include: Founder, Chairman of Board, Chief Executive Officer, Wadsworth, 1956-85; Co-owner, Stephen Greene Press, 1978-85; Deputy Chairman, International Thomson Organisation, 1979-85; Chairman, International Thomson Books, 1980-85; Founder, Chairman of Board, Science Books International, 1981-83; Founder, Chairman of Board, Linguistics International, 1983-85; Founder, Franklin Beedle and Associates, 1985-; Director, Advisor, Mayfield Publishing Company, 1985-. Publications: Editor, Abingdon Song Kit, 1957; Editor, Let's All Sing, 1959; Songs For Swinging Housemothers (edited as Frank Lynn), 1961, 1963; Songs for Singing (edited as Frank Lynn), 1961; Editor, Songs for Pickin' and Singin', 1962; The Beer Bust Songbook (edited as Frank Lynn), 1963; Hootenanny Tonight, 1964; Folk Song Fest: Songs and Ideas for Performance Artistry, 1964; The Folk Song Abecedary, 1966; Editor, Alpha Kappa Psi Sings, 1967; The Good Times Songbook, 1974; Scrooge: The Christmas Musical, 1978; Alice: A Musical Play, 1980; Cuckoo Clock in a Music Box, 1980; Pinocchio: A Musical Play, 1981; Tiny Tim's Christmas Carol, 1981; The Pied Piper, 1982; The Nutcracker and Princess Pirlipat (as Julia Ericson), 1982; A Visit from St Nicholas, 1983; Pandora, 1984; Talkin' 'bout America, 1986; Mouse Country, 1987; The Dingalong Circus Holiday, 1987. Address: 183 Patricia Drive, Atherton, CA 94025, USA.

LELAND Christopher Towne, b. 17 Oct 1951. Writer; Professor. Education: BA English, Pomona College, Claremont, CA, 1973; MA Spanish, 1980, PhD Comparative Literature, University of California, San Diego, 1982. Literary Appointments: Professor of English, Wayne State University, 1990-. Publications: Mean Time, 1982; Fiction and The Argentine Reality, 1986; Mrs Randall, 1987; The Book of Marvels, 1990; The Last Happy Men: The Generation of 1922; The Professor of Aesthetics, 1994. Contributions to: Principal Translator, Open Door by Luise Valengnela, 1988. Honours: Finalist, PEN Hemingway Award, 1982; Fellow, Massachusetts Artists Foundation, 1985. Memberships: Poets and Writers; MLA. Literary Agent: M Marmur. Address: c/o Department of English, Wayne State University, Detroit, MI 48202, USA.

LELCHUK Alan, b. 15 Sept 1938, New York City, New York, USA. Writer. m. Barbara Kreiger, 7 Oct 1979, 2 sons. Education: BA, Brooklyn College, 1960; MA 1963, PhD English Literature 1965, Stanford University. Appointments: Brandeis University, 1966-81; Associate Editor, Modern Occasions, 1980-82; Amherst College, 1982-84; Dartmouth College, 1985-; Fulbright Writer-in-residence, Haifa University, Israel, 1986-87; Visiting Writer, City College of New York, autumn 1991; Editor, Publisher, Steerforth Press, South Royalton, Vermont, USA, 1993-. Publications: American Mischief, 1973; Miriam at Thirty-Four, 1974; Shrinking: The Beginning of My Own Ending, 1978; 8 Great Hebrew Short Novels (co-editor), in English translation, 1983; Miriam in Her Forties, 1985; On Home Ground, for young adults, 1987; Brooklyn Boy, 1989; Playing the Game, 1995. Contributions to: New York Times Book Review; Sewanee Review; The Atlantic; The New Republic; Dissent; New York Review of Books. Honours: Guggenheim Fellowship, 1976-77; Mishkenot Sha'Ananim Resident Fellow, 1976-77; Fulbright Award, 1986-87; Manuscript Collection, Mugar Memorial Library, Boston University. Memberships: PEN; Authors Guild. Literary Agent: Georges Borchardt Inc, 136 E 57th St, New York, NY 10022, USA. Address: RFD 2, Canaan, NH 03741, USA.

LELYVELD Joseph (Salem), b. 5 Apr 1937, Ohio, USA. Writer; Editor; Correspondent. Literary Appointments: Staff Member, New York Times, 1962; Correspondent in the Congo and South Afric, 1965-66, in London, England, 1966, in India and Pakistan, 1966-69, in Hong Kong, 1973-75, in South Africa, 1980-83; Staff Writer, New York Times Magazine, 1984-85; London Bureau Chief, 1985-86; Foreign Editor, 1987. Publications: Move Your Shadow: South Africa Black and White, 1985. Honours: Fulbright Fellowship to Burma, 1960; Page One Award, 1970; George Polk Memorial Award, 1972, 1984; John Smith Guggenheim Fellowship, 1984; Pulitzer Prize and Los Angeles Times Book Award, 1986.

LEM Stanislaw, b. 12 Sep 1921, Lvov, Russia. Author. m. Barbara Lesnik, 11 Aug 1953, 1 s. Education: Studied Medicine in Lvov, 1939-41, and Krakow, Poland, 1944-45. Literary Appointments: Lecturer, University of Krakow, part-time, 1973-. Publications: 40 books translated into 35 languages including: The Star Diaries, 1957, many later editions; Eden, 1959; Solaris, 1961; Memoirs Found in a Bathtub, 1961; The Invincible, 1964; The Cyberiad, 1965; His Master's Voice, 1968; Tales of Pirx the Pilot, 1968; A Perfect Vacuum, 1971; The Futurological Congress, 1971; The Chain of Chance, 1976; Fiasco, 1986. Contributions include: The New Yorker; Encounter; Penthouse; Omni. Honours include: Awards of Polish Ministry of Culture, 1965, 1973; Polish State Prize for Literature, 1976; Austrian State Award for European Literature, 1985; Prize of The Alfred Jurzykowski Foundation for Literature, 1987; Honorary PhD, University of Wroclaw. Membership: International Association of Poets, Playwrights, Editors, Essayists and Authors. Literary Agent: Franz Rottensteiner. Address: c/o Franz Rottensteiner, Marchettigasse 9 17, A 1060 Vienna, Austria.

LEMAIRE Michael (Desert Roving Reporter), b. 6 Aug 1936, Bordeaux, France. Writer. Education: BSCE, major Civil Engineering, 1957; Minors Literature and Journalism, 1958. Appointments: Proprietor, Lemaire Enterprises, Desert Hot Springs, CA, USA; Covering and publishing for many jazz festivals, worldwide. Publications: Love Me Or At Least Let Me Love You, 1988; A Romantic Interlude, 1990; Poems Published, 1990-91; Vindicated Episode at Salton Sea (novel), 1993; Tracks Through Time and Space (fantasy novel), 1993. Contributions to: San Diego Union; San Bernadino Bee; St Louis Post Dispatch; Kansas City Star; Washington Globe; London Times; Fresno Dixieland Society Jazz News Journal; St Louis Jazz on The River Publications; 1 Paris newspaper; 2 German newspapers, Frankfurt and Hamburg. Honours: Honorary Membership, International Writers and Artists Association; Rollex watch presented for coverages. Memberships: Writers Guild; National Writers Club; Jazz Journalists Association. Literary Agent: Suzanne Berwick Inc. Address: 6030 Shady Creek Road, Agoura, CA 92549, USA.

LEMANN Nancy Elise, b. 4 Feb 1956, New Orleans, USA. Writer. m. Mark Paul Clein, 5 Oct 1991. Education: BA, Brown University, 1978; Mfa, Columbia University, 1984. Publications: Lives of The Saints; The Ritz of The Bayou; Sportsmans Paradise. Contributions to: Chicago Tribune; Los Angeles Times; New Republic; New York Review of Books; New York Times; People; Washington Post. Memberships: PEN; Authors Guild. Address: 254 West 73rd Street, no 5 New York, NY 10023, USA.

LEMM Richard. Canadian. Poet. Publications: Prelude to the Bacchanal, 1991; A Difficult Faith, 1985. Honour: Canadian Authors Association Literary Award, 1991.

LEMMON David Hector, b. 4 Apr 1931, London, England.Writer. m. (Jean) Valerie Fletcher, 16 Aug 1958, 2 s. Education: Teachers Certificate, College of St Mark and John, 1953, BA Honours, English, 1968, London University; Associate, College of Preceptors, 1967; Final Certificate, English Speaking Board, 1967. Appointments include: Head of English: Torells Girls School, Thurrock, 1963-68; Nicholas Comprehensive School, Basildon, 1973-83; Examiner, A Level Theatre Studies, 1980-; Editor, TCCB's Official Tour Guide, Compiler, Test Match and Texaco Trophy programmes, 1984-89. Publications: Numerous books on cricket including: Benson and Hedges Cricket Year, annually, 1982-; Summer of Success, Great One Day Cricket Matches, Tich Freeman, 1982; Wisden Book of Cricket Quotations I, 1982, II, 1990; Johnny Won't Hit Today, The Book of One-Day Internationals, 1983; The Great Wicket-Keepers, A Walk to The Wicket (with Ted Dexter), Editor, Cricket Heroes, 1984; Ken McEwan, Percy Chapman, Cricket Reflections (with Ken Kelly), Cricket Mercenaries, 1985; The Great All-Rounder, 1987; The Official History of Essex CCC (with Mike Marshall), 1987, of Middlesex CCC, 1988, of Worcestershire CCC, 1989, of Surrey CCC, 1989; One-Day Cricket, The Crisis of Captaincy, 1988; Know Your Sport - Cricket (with Chris Cowdray), 1989; British Theatre Yearbook, 1989, 1990; Len Hutton, a Pictorial Biography, 1990; Cricket's Champion Counties, The Cricketing Greigs, 1991; Guinness Book of Test Cricket Captains, Benson and Hedges British Theatre Yearbook, 1992. Contributions include: Cricket World; The Guardian. Membership: Cricket Writers Club. Literary Agent: Malcolm Hamer, Headline Enterprises. Address: 26 Leigh Road, Leigh-on-Sea, Essex, SS9 1LD, England.

LEMON Lee Thomas, b. 9 Jan 1931, Kansas City, KS, USA. Professor. m. Maria Mullinaux, 5 May 1973, 3 s, 3 d. Education: BS, St Louis University, 1951; MA, Southern Illinois University, 1952; PhD, University of Illinois, 1961. Publications: Russian Formalists Critics, 1965; Partial Critics, 1965; Glossary of Literary Terms, 1971; Portraits of The Artist in Contemporary Fiction, 1985. Contributions to: Various articles on Modern Fiction, Literary Theory, Previews. Memberships: Associate Editor, Prairie Schooner. Address: 224 Andrews, WNL, Lincoln, NE 68588, USA.

LENGYEL Balazs, b. 21 Aug 1918, Budapest, Hungary. Writer. m. (1) Agnes Nemes Nagy, 1944, (2) Veronika Kerek. Education: Doctor of Law. Publications: Collections of essays: Green and Gold, 1988; Returning, 1990; Editor, Ujhold (New Moon), Literary year-book. Honours: Literary Award, Hungarian Writers' Union. Memberships: Presidium, Hungarian Writers' Union; Founding Member, Hungarian Academy of Arts, 1992. Address: 4 Apat Utca, Budapest 1033, Hungary.

LENT Blair (Ernest Small), b. 1930, USA. Children's Fiction Writer. Literary Appointments: Freelance Writer and Illustrator, 1963-. Publications: Pistachio, 1963; The Wave (with M Hodges), 1964; Baba Yaga (as Ernest Small), 1966; John Tabor's Ride, 1966; From King Boggen's Hall to Nothing-at-All, 1967; Why The Sun and The Moon Live in The Sky (with E Dayrell), 1968, as animated film, 1970; The Little Match Girl, by Hans Christian Andersen, 1968; Tikki Tikki Tembo (with A Mosel), 1968; The Angry Moon (with W Sleator), 1970; The Funny Little Woman (with A Mosel), 1972; Tales Told in India (with V Haviland), 1973; The Telephone (with K Chukovsky), 1977; I Stood Upon a Mountain (with A Fisher), 1979; Bayberry Bluff, 1987. Address: 10 Dana Street, Cambridge, MA 02138, USA.

LENTRICCHIA Frank, b. USA. Professor. Publications: The Gaiety of Language, 1968; Robert Frost: Modern Poetics & The Landscape of Self, 1975; Robert Frost: A Bibliography, 1976; After the New Criticism, 1980; Criticism & Social Change, 1983; Ariel & The Police, 1988; Critical Terms for Literary Study, 1990; New Essays on White Noise, 1991; Introducing Don DeLillo, 1991; The Edge of Night, 1994; The Edge of the Night: A Confession, 1994. Address: Department of English, Duke University, Durham, NC 27706-7706, USA.

LENZ Siegfried, b. 17 Mar 1926, Lyck, East Prussia, Germany. Novelist; Playwright. Education: University of Hamburg, 1945-48. Publications: Hawks were in the Air, 1951; Duel with Shadows, 1955; So Tender was Suleyken, 1955; The Man in the River, 1957; Jager des Spotts, 1958; The Lightship, 1960; Impressions of the Sea, 1962; The Survivor, 1963; Der Spielverderber, 1965; Begegnung mit Tieren, 1966;

Das Wrack, and Other Stories, 1967; The German Lesson, 1968; Collected Stories, 1970; An Exemplary Life, 1973; Einstein Crosses the Elbe at Hamburg, 1975; The Heritage, 1978; The Beginning of Something, 1981; The End of a War, 1984; Training Ground, 1985, 1991; The Selected Stories of Siegfried Lenz, 1989; The Rehearsal, 1990; Radio plays; Essays; Political texts. Honours include: Honorary Doctorate, University of Hamburg, 1976. Address: Preusserstrasse 4, 2000 Hamburg 52, Germany.

LEONARD Dick (Richard L), b. 12 Dec 1930, Ealing, Middlesex, England. Journalist; Former Member of Parliament. m. Irene Heidelberger, 29 Mar 1963, 1 son, 1 daughter. Education: MA, Essex University, 1969. Literary Appointments: Assistant Editor, The Economist, 1974-85; Brussels Correspondent, The Observer, 1989-; Various other editorial posts in magazines and broadcasting. Publications: Elections in Britain, 1968, 1991; The Backbencher and Parliament (co-author), 1972; Paying for Party Politics, 1975; The Socialist Agenda (co-author), 1981; World Atlas of Elections (co-author), 1986; The Economist Guide to the EU, 1988, 1992, 1994. Contributions to: Guardian; Financial Times; Sunday Times; New Society; Encounter; Leading newspapers, USA, Canada, Australia, New Zealand, Japan, India. Memberships: Fabian Society (Former Chairman); Reform Club. Address: 32 rue des Bégonias, 1170 Brussels, Belgium.

LEONARD Elmore, b. 11 Oct 1925, New Orleans, LA, USA. Novelist. m. Joan Shepard, 15 Sep 1979, 3 s, 2 d. Education: BA, University of Detroit, 1950. Publications include: 21 novels including: Hombre, 1961; City Primeval, 1980; Split Images, 1981; Cat Chaser, 1982; Stick, 1983; Labrava, 1983; Glitz, 1985; Bandits, 1986; Touch, 1987; Freaky Deaky, 1988; Killshot, 1989; Get Shorty, 1990; Maximum Bob, 1991; Rum Punch, 1992. Honours: Edgar Allen Poe Award, Mystery Writers of America, 1984; Michigan Foundation for The Arts Award for Literature, 1985; Edgar Allen Poe Award, Grand Master, 1992. Memberships: Writers Guild of America; PEN; Authors Guild; Western Writers of America; Mystery Writers of America. Address: c/o H N Swanson Literary Agent, 8523 Sunset, Los Angeles, CA 90069, USA.

LEONARD Hugh (John Keyes Byrne), b. 9 Nov 1926, Dublin, Ireland. Playwright. m. Paule Jacquet, 1955, 1 d. Publications: Stage Plays include: The Big Birthday, 1957; A Leap in The Dark, 1957; Madigan's Lock, 1958; A Walk on The Water, 1960; The Passion of Peter Ginty, 1961; Stephen D, 1962; The Poker Session, 1963; Dublin 1, 1963; The Saints Go Cycling In, 1965; Mick and Mick, 1966; The Quick and The Dead, 1967; The Au Pair Man, 1968; The Barracks, 1969; The Patrick Pearse Motel, 1971; Da, 1973; Thieves, 1973; Summer, 1974; Times of Wolves and Tigers, 1974; Irishmen, 1975; Time Was, 1976; A Life, 1977; Moving Days, 1981; The Mask of Moriarty, 1984; Writing for Television includes: Silent Song, 1967; Nicholas Nickleby, 1977; London Belongs to Me, 1977; The Last Campaign, 1978; The Ring and The Rose, 1978; Strumpet City, 1979; The Little World of Don Camillo, 1980; Kill, 1982; Good Behaviour, 1982; O'Neill, 1983; Beyond The Pale, 1984; The Irish RM, 1985; A Life, 1986; Troubles, 1987; Films: Herself Surprised, 1977; Da, 1984; Widows' Peak, 1984; Troubles, 1984; Autobiography: Home Before Night, 1979; Out After Dark, 1988. Honours: Honorary DHL (RI); Writers Guild Award, 1966; Tony Award; Critics Circle Award; Drama Desk Award; Outer Critics Award, 1978; Doctor of Literature, Trinity College, Dublin, 1988. Address: 6 Rossaun Pilot View, Dalkey, Co Dublin, Ireland.

LEONARD Tom, b. 22 Aug 1944, Glasgow, Scotland. Writer. m. Sonya Maria O'Brien, 24 Dec 1971, 2 sons. Education: MA, Glasgow University, 1976. Appointments: Writer-in-Residence, Renfrew District Libraries, 1986-88 and 1988-89; Writer-in-Residence, Glasgow University/Strathclyde University, 1991-92; Writer-in-Residence, Bell College of Technology, 1993-94. Publications: Intimate Voices (writing 1965-83), 1984; Radical Renfrew (editor), 1990; Situations Theoretical & Contemporary, 1986; Nora's Place, 1990; Places of the Mind: The Life and Work of James Thomson 'BV' Cafe, 1993; Reports From The Present: Selected Work 1982-94, 1995. Contributions to: Edinburgh Review. Honour: Joint Winner, Saltire Scottish Book of the Year Award, 1984. Literary Agent: 23 Hillhead Street, Glasgow G12, Scotland. Address: 56 Eldon Street, Glasgow G3 6NJ, Scotland.

LEONG GOR YUN. See: ELLISON Virginia Howell.

LEPAN Douglas Valentine, b. 25 May 1914, Toronto, Canada. Separated, 2 sons. Education: BA, University of Toronto, 1935; BA 1937, MA 1948, Oxford University. Appointments include: Counsellor and later Minister Counsellor, Canadian Embassey in Washington, 1951-55; Secretary and Director of Research, Royal Commission on Canada's Economic Prospects, 1955-58; Assistant Under Secretary of State for External Affairs, 1958-59; Professor of English Literature, Queens University, Kingston, 1959-64; Principal of University College, University of Toronto, 1964-70, Principal Emeritus, 1983-; University Professor, University of Toronto, 1970-79, University Professor Emeritus 1979-; Senior Fellow of Massey College, 1970-85; Senior Fellow Emeritus 1985-. Publications: The Wounded Prince and other poems, 1948; The Net and the Sword, 1953; Final Report on the Royal Commission on Canada's Economic Prospects, Ottawa 1957 chapters 1-7; The Deserter, 1964; Bright Glass of Memory, 1979; Something Still to Find, new poems, 1982; Weathering It complete poems 1948-87, 1987; Far Voyages poems, 1990. Honours: Guggenheim Fellowship 1948-49; Governor-General's Award for Poetry, 1953; Governor-General's Award for Fiction, 1964; Lorne Pierce Medal, Royal Society of Canada, 1976. Address: c/o Massey College, 4 Devonshire Place, Toronto, Ontario M5S 2E1, Canada.

LEPSCHY Anna Laura, b. 30 Nov 1933, Turin, Italy. University Professor. m. 20 Dec 1962. Education: BLitt, MA, Somerville College, Oxford, 1952-57. Publications: Viaggio in Terrasanta 1480, 1966; The Italian Language Today, 1977, 1991 (co-author); Tintoretto Observed, 1983; Narrativa e Teatro fra due Secoli, 1984. Contributions to: Italian Studies, Romance Studies, Studi Francesi, Studi sul Boccaccio, Studi Novecenteschi, Yearbook of the Pirandello Society, Modern Languages Notes, Lettere Italiane. Memberships: President, Pirandello Society, 1988-92; Chair, Society for Italian Studies, 1988-1995; Association for the Study of Modern Italy; Associazione Internazionale di Lingua e Letteratura Italiana. Address: Department of Italian, University College, Gower Street, London WC1E 6BT, England.

LERMAN Rhoda, b. 18 Jan 1936, New York, USA. Writer. m. Robert Lerman, 15 Sept 1957, 1 s, 2 d. Education: BA, Univesity of Miami, 1957. Literary Appointments: Visiting Professor of Creative Writing, SUNY, Buffalo, 1988, 1990; NEA Distinguished Professor of Creative Writing, Hartwick College, 1985; Chair of English Literature, SUNY, Buffalo, 1990. Publications: Call Me Ishtar, 1973, 1977; Girl That he Marries, 1976; Eleanor, A Novel, 1979; Book of the Night, 1984; God's Ear, 1989; Animal Acts, 1994. Literary Agent: Owen Laster. Address: William Morris Agency, 1350 Avenue of the Americas, New York, NY 10019, USA.

LERNER Laurence (David), b. 12 Dec 1925, Cape Town, South Africa. British Citizen. Professor; Poet. Education: MA, University of Cape Town, 1945; BA, Pembroke College, Cambridge. Appointments include: Kenan Professor, Vanderbilt University, Nashville, 1985-; Visiting Professor, Universities in USA, Europe. Publications include: Poems, 1955; Domestic Interior and Other Poems, 1959; The Directions of Memory: Poems, 1958-63; Selves, 1969; The Man I Killed, 1980; A.R.T.H.U.R & M.A.R.T.H.A: Or, The Loves of the Computers, 1980; Chapter and Verse: Bible Poems, 1984; Selected Poems, 1984; Rembrandt's Mirror, 1987; Play, The Experiment, 1980; Novels: The Englishmen, 1959; A Free Man, 1968; My Grandfather's Grandfather, 1985; Various works of Literary Criticism: Love & Marriage, 1979; The Frontiers of Literature, 1988. Honours include: Fellow, Royal Society of Literature, 1986. Address: 1-B Gundreda Road, Lewes, East Sussex, BN7 1PT, England.

LERNER Michael. Editor; Writer. 1 s. Education: BA, Columbia University, 1964; PhD, University of CA, 1972; PhD, Wright Institute. Publications: Socialism of Foods Antisemitism on the Left, 1992; Surplus Powerlessness, 1986; Jewish Renewal, 1994; The Politics of Meening, 1995; Blacks and Jews, 1995. Contributions to: NY Times; Wall Street Journal; Los Angeles Times; Time Magazine; Washington Post. Address: Tikkun Magazine, PO Box 1778, Cathedral Station, New York, NY 10025, USA.

LERNER Robert Earl, b. 8 Feb 1940, New York, USA. Historian. m. Erdmut Krumnack, 25 Oct 1963, 2 daughters. Education: BA, University of Chicago, 1960; MA 1962, PhD 1964, Princeton University. Publications: The Age of Adversity, 1968; The Heresy of the Free Spirit in the Later Middle Ages, 1972; One Thousand Years, co-author, 1974; The Powers of Prophecy, 1983; Western Civilizations, co-author, 12th edition, 1993. Contributions to: Numerous articles and reviews in professional journals. Honours: Fulbright Fellow, 1967; National Endowment for the Humanities Fellow, 1972; American Council of Learned Societies Fellow, 1979; Guggenheim Foundation Fellow, 1983; American Academy in Rome Fellow, 1983; Institute for Advanced Study, 1988; Historisches Kolleg Forschungspreis, 1992. Address: Dept of History, Northwestern University, Evanston, IL 60208, USA.

LESCHAK Peter M, b. 11 May 1951, Chisholm, MN, USA. Writer. m. Pamela Cope, May 1974. Education: Lumberjack, Roseburg, OR, USA, 1973; Printer, Baton Rouge, LA, USA, 1974; Water Plant Operator, Chisholm, 1975-79; Operator of Waste Water Plant, City of Hibbing, 1979-84; Writer, 1984-; Fire Chief of French, MN; Depot Outreach Artist, 1990-91. Publications: Letters from Side Lake, 1987; The Bear Guardian, 1990. Contributions to: Author of regular column in TWA Ambassador, 1985-86; Magazines; Editor of Twin Cities, 1984-86; Minnesota Monthly, 1984-. Honour: Minnesota Book Award, 1991. Memberships: Authors Guild; Minnesota Fire Chiefs Association. Address: Box 51, Side Lake, MN 55781, USA.

LESSING Doris May, b. 22 Oct 1919, Kermanshah, Persia. Writer. m. 1) Frank Charles Wisdom, 1939, div 1943, 1 son, 1 daughter, 2) Gottfried Anton Nicholas Lessing, 1945, div 1949, 1 son. Publications include: The Golden Notebook, 1962; The Children of Violence; Canopus in Argos: Archives, 1979; African Stories, 1964; The Grass Is Singing 1950; Briefing for a Descent into Hell, 1971; The Good Terrorist, 1985; Prisons We Choose To Live Inside, 1986; The Wind Blows Away Our Words - And Other Documents Relating to the Afghan Resistance, 1987; Opera Libretto for Philip Glass, The Making of the Representative for Planet 8, produced 1988; The Fifth Child, 1988; Doris Lessing Reader, 1990; London Observed (short stories), 1992; African Laughter: Four Visits to Zimbabwe, 1992. Literary Agent: Jonathon Clowes Ltd. Address: c/o Jonathon Clowes Ltd, Iron Bridge House, Bridge Approach, London NW1 8BD, England.

LESTER Andrew D, b. 8 Aug 1939, Coral Gables, Florida, USA. Professor of Pastoral Theology and Pastoral Counselling. m. Judith L Laesser, 8 Sept 1960, 1 son, 1 daughter. Education: BA, Mississippi College, Clinton, 1961; BD 1964, PhD 1968, Southern Baptist Theological Seminary, Louisville, Kentucky; Clinical Pastoral Education, Central State, Louisville General, Jewish and Children's Hospitals, Louisville, 1964-68; Clinical Training in Pastoral Counselling Service, Clarksville, Indiana, 1964-69; Diplomate, Association of Pastoral Counselors, 1979. Appointments: General Editor, Resources for Living series, 1989-90; Editor, series on Pastoral Counselling, 1992-, Westminster-John Knox Press. Publications include: Pastoral Care in Crucial Human Situations (editor with Wayne Oates), 1969; Sex Is More Than a Word, 1973; It Hurts So Bad, Lord!: The Christian Encounters Crisis, 1976; Coping with Your Anger: A Christian Guide, 1983; Pastoral Care with Children in Crisis, 1985; Spiritual Dimensions of Pastoral Care: Witness to the Ministry of Wayne E Oates (editor with Gerald L Borchert), 1985; Hope in Pastoral Care and Counselling, 1995. Address: Brite Divinity School, Texas Christian University, Fort Worth, TX 76129, USA.

LESTER Julius, b. 1939, USA. Professor of Judaic Studies; Writer; Musician; Singer. Appointments: Contributing Editor, SING OUT, New York, USA, 1964-69; Contributing Editor, Broadside of New York, 1964-70; Director, New Port Folk Festival, Rhode Island, 1966-68. Publications: The 12-String Guitar as Played by Leadbelly: An Instructional Manual (with Pete Seeger), 1965; To Praise Our Bridges: An Autobiography by Fanny Lou Hamer (edited with Mary Varela), 1967; Our Folk Tales: High John, The Conqueror, and Other Afro-American Tales (edited with Mary Varela), 1967; The Mud of Vietnam: Photographs and Poems, verse, 1967; Revolutionary Notes, 1969; Ain't No Ambulances for No Nigguhs Tonight, by Stanley Couch (editor), 1969; Look Out Whitey, Black Power's Gon' Get Your Mama, 1968; To Be a Slave, 1968; Black Folktales, 1969; Search for the New Land: History as Subjective Experience, 1969; The Seventh Son: The Thought and Writings of W E B Du Bois (editor), 2 vols, 1971; The Knee-High Man and Other Tales, 1972; Long Journey Home: Stories from Black History, 1972; Two Love Stories, 1972; Who I Am, 1974; All Is Well, autobiography, 1976; This Strange New Feeling, short stories, 1982; Do Lord Remember Me, 1984; The Tales of Uncle Remus: The Adventures of Brer Rabbit, 1987; More Tales of Uncle Remus: Further Adventures of Brer Rabbit, His Friends, Enemies and Others, 1988; How Many Spots Does a Leopard Have? and Other Tales, 1989; Further Tales of Uncle Remus: The Misadventure of Brer Rabbit, Brer Fox, Brer Wolf, The Dooding and Other Creatures, 1990; Falling Pieces of the Broken Sky, 1990; And All Our Wounds Forgiven, 1994. Address: 600 Station Road, Amherst, MA 01002, USA.

LETTE Kathy, b. 11 Nov 1958, Sydney, Australia. Writer. m. Geoffrey Robertson, 1 May 1990, 1 son, 1 daughter. Publications: Plays: Wet Dreams, 1985; Perfect Mismatch, 1985; Grommitts, 1986; Play, radio, I'm So Happy for You, I Really Am, 1991; Books: Puberty Blues, 1979; Hits and Ms, 1984; Girls' Night Out, 1988; The Llama Parlour, 1991; Foetal Attraction, 1993. Contributions to: Satirical columnist for the Sydney Morning Herald; The Bulletin; Cleo Magazine; Irregular contributor to the Guardian. Honours: Australian Literature Board Grant, 1982. Memberships: Judge and Organiser, The Hooker Prize, a yearly feminist spoof of The Booker Prize. Literary Agent: Mic Cheetan, Sheil Land and Associates. Address: c/o Sheil Land, 43 Doughty Street, London WC1N 2LF, England.

LEVANT Victor Avrom, b. 26 Nov 1947, Winnipeg, Manitoba, Canada. Professor; Film Consultant; Practising Gestalt Therapist. Education: BA Honours, Economics, Political Science, 1968, MA Political Science 1975, PhD Political Philosophy and International Relations 1981, McGill University; Institut des Sciences Politiques, Sorbonne, Paris, 1968-69. Appointments: Film Consultant: The World Challenge, TV series, 1984; Studio B, Office National du Film, 1984-86; Maximage Productions, 1987; Communications for The Making of an Etching: P Buckley Moss, 1988. Publications: How to Make a Killing: Canadian Military Involvement in the Indo-China War, 1972; How to Buy a Country: Monograph on Global Pentagon Contracts (co-editor), 1973; Capital and Labor: Partners? 1976; Capital et Travail, 1977; Quiet Complicity; Canada and the Vietnam War, 1987; The Neighborhood Gourmet, 1989; Le Gourmet du Quartier, 1989, 1990; Secrete Alliance: Le Canada dans las guerre du Vietnam, 1990. Address: 2243 Oxford, Montreal, H4A 2X7, Canada.

LEVENDOSKY Charles (Leonard), b. 4 July 1936. Journalist; Poet. Education: BS Physics 1958, BA Mathematics 1960, University of Oklahoma; MA Secondary Education, New York University, 1963. Appointments: HS Teacher, US Virgin Islands,1963-65; Tutor, Kyoto University, Japan, 1965-66; HS Tutor, New York, USA, 1966-67; Instructor of English, New York University, 1967-71; Visiting Poet (Poetryin the Schools), New York State, Georgia, New Jersey, 1971-72; Poet-in-Residence, Wyoming Council on the Arts, 1972-82; Editor for annual arts edition for the Casper Star-Tribune; Columnist for the Casper Star-Tribune, Wyoming, USA; Poet Laureate of Wyoming, 1988. Publications: Perimeters, 1970; Small Town America, 1974; Words and Fonts, 1975; Aspects of the Vertical, 1978; Distances, 1980; Wyoming Fragments, 1981; Nocturnes, 1982; Hands and Other Poems, 1986; Circle of Light, poetry, 1995. Contributions include: Numerous magazines and journals including: El Corno Emplumado; New York Quarterly; Thoreau Journal Quarterly; American Poetry Review; Poetry Now; Writers Forum; Northwest Review; Sun Dog; Sulphur River; Negative Capability; Poets on Blue Light Review; Dacotah Territory. Address: PO Box 3033, Casper, WY 82602, USA.

LEVENSON Christopher, b. 1934, United Kingdom. Educator; Poet; Translator. Appointments: Taught: International Quaker School, Eerde, Netherlands, 1957-58; University of Münster, Federal Republic of Germany, 1958-61; Rodway Technical High School, Mangotsfield, Gloucestershire, 1962-64; Member, English Department, Carleton University, Ottawa, Canada, 1968-; Editor, Arc, 1978-88. Publications: Poetry from Cambridge (editor), 1958; New Poets 1959 (with I Crichton Smith and K Gershon), 1959; Van Gogh, by Abraham M W J Hammacher, translation, 1961; The Golden Casket: Chinese Novels of Two Millennia, translation, 1965; The Leavetaking and Vanishing Point, by Peter Weiss, translation, 1966; Cairns, 1969; Stills, 1972; Into the Open, 1977; The Journey Back, 1978; No-Man's Land, 1980; Seeking Hearts Solace, translation, 1981; Light of the World, translation, 1982; Arriving at Night, 1986; The Return, 1986; Half Truths, 1991; Duplicities, New & Selected Poems, 1992. Honours include: Eric Gregory Award; Archibald Lampman Award. Address: Department of English, Carleton University, Ottawa, Ontario, K1S 5B6, Canada.

LEVER (Sir) Tresham Christopher Arthur Lindsay (3rd Baronet), b. 9 Jan 1932, London, England. Naturalist. m. Linda Weightman McDowell Goulden, 6 Nov 1975. Education: Eton College, 1945-49; Trinity College, Cambridge, BA 1954, MA 1957. Publications: Goldsmiths and Silversmiths of England, 1975; The Naturalized Animals of the British Isles, 1977; Naturalized Mammals of the World, 1985; Naturalized Birds of the World, 1987; The Mandarin Duck, 1990; They Dined on Eland: The Story of the Acclimatisation Societies, 1992; Naturalized Animals: The Ecology of Successfully Introduced Species, 1994; Contributor to several books on natural history. Memberships:

Fellow, Linnean Society of London. Address: Newell House, Winkfield, Berkshire SL4 4SE, England.

LEVERTOV Denise, b. 24 Oct 1923, Ilford, Essex, England. Professor; Writer. m. Mitchell Goodman, 1947, 1 son. Emigrated to US in 1948, naturalized in 1955. Education: Private education. Appointments: Teacher, YM-YMCA Poetry Center, New York, 1964; City College of New York, 1965 and Vassar, Poughkeepsie, New York, 1966-67; Visiting Lecturer, Drew University, Madison, New Jersey, 1965, University of California at Berkeley, 1969; Visiting Professor: Massachusetts Institute of Technology, Cambridge, 1969-70; University of Cincinnati, Ohio, Spring 1973; Professor, Tufts University, Medford, Massachusetts, 1973-79; Fannie Hurst Professor (Poet in Residence), Brandeis University, Waltham, Massachusetts, 1981-83; Professor, Stanford University, Stanford, California, 1981-; Poetry editor, The Nation, New York,1961-62 and Mother Jones, San Francisco 1976-78. Publications include: Verse: Life in the Forest, 1978; Collected Earlier Poems 1940-60, 1979; Candles in Babylon, 1982; Poems 1960-67, 1983; Oblique Prayers, 1984; Selected Poems, 1986; Poems 1968-72, 1987; Breathing the Water, 1987; A Door in the Hive, 1989; Evening Train (new poems), 1992; New and Selected Essays, 1992; Recordings, essays and edited works. Honours include: Honorary Scholar, Radcliffe Institute for Independent Study, Cambridge, Massachusetts, 1964-66; Longview Award, 1961; Guggenheim Fellowship, 1962; National Institute of Arts and Letters grant, 1966; Seven Honorary Doctorates; Recipient, NEA Senior Fellowship, 1991; Lannan Award, 1993/Honorary Doctorate, University of Santa Clara, 1993. Memberships: American Academy and Institute of Arts and Letters, 1980; Elmer Bobst Award, 1983; Corresponding Member, Academie Mallarme. Address: New Directions, 80 Eighth Avenue, New York, NY 10011, USA.

LEVEY Michael (Vincent) (Sir), b. 1927, United Kingdom. Writer; Former Director, National Gallery. Appointments: Slade Professor of Fine Art, Cambridge University, England, 1963-64; Slade Professor of Fine Art, Oxford, 1994-95; Assistant Keeper 1951-66, Deputy Keeper 1966-68, Keeper 1968-73, Director 1973-86, National Gallery, London, England. Publications: Painting in XVIIIth Century Venice, 1959, 2nd edition, 1980; 3rd edition, 1994; From Giotto to Cézanne, 1962; Dürer, 1964; Later Italian Pictures in the Collection of HM The Queen, 1964; Rococo to Revolution, 1966; Early Renaissance, 1967; The Life and Death of Mozart, 1971; Painting at Court, 1971; Art and Architecture of the 18th Century in France (with W W Kalnein), 1972; High Renaissance, 1974; The World of Ottoman Art, 1976; The Case of Walter Pater, 1978; Sir Thomas Lawrence, exhibition catalogue, 1979; The Painter Depicted, 1982; Tempting Fate, 1982; An Affair on the Appian Way, 1984; Tiepolo, 1986; Men at Work, 1988; The Soul of the Eye (anthology), 1990; Painting and Sculpture in France 1700-1789, 1992. Honours: Hawthornden Prize for Early Renaissance, 1968; Lieutenant of the Royal Victorian Order, 1965 - LVO; Banister Fletcher Prize for Tiepolo, 1986. Memberships: Fellow, British Academy - FBA; Fellow, Royal Society of Literature - FRSL. Address: 36 Little Lane, Louth, Lincolnshire LN11 9DU, England.

LEVI Peter (Chad Tigar), b. 1931, United Kingdom. Professor of Poetry; Author. Appointments: Fellow, St Catherine's College, Oxford, 1977-; Professor of Poetry, Oxford University, 1984-. Publications: Earthly Paradise, 1958; The Gravel Ponds: Poems, 1960; Beaumont: 1861-1961, 1961; Orpheus Head, 1962; Water, Rock and Sand, 1962; Selected Poems of Yevtushenko (translated with R Milber-Gulland), 1962; The Shearwaters, 1965; Fresh Water, Sea Water: Poems, 1965; Pancakes for the Queen of Babylon: Ten Poems for Nikos Gatsos, 1968; Ruined Abbeys, 1968; Life is a Platform, 1971; Death is a Pulpit, 1971; Guide to Greece, by Pausanias, translation, 2 vols, 1971; The Light Garden of the Angel King: Journeys in Afghanistan, 1972; Penguin Modern Poets 22 (with Adrian Mitchell and John Fuller), 1973; The English Bible from Wycliff to William Barnes (editor), 1974; Pope (editor), 1974; John Clare and Thomas Hardy, 1975; Collected Poems, 1976; The Psalms, translation, 1977; The Noise Made by Poems, 1977; Five Ages, 1978; The Head in the Soup, novel, 1979; The Hill of Kronos, 1980; Atlas of the Greek World, 1980; Private Ground, 1981; The Flutes of Autumn, 1983; The Echoing Green: Three Elegies, 1983; Grave Witness, novel, 1984; Shakespeare's Birthday, 1985; A History of Greek Literature, 1985; The Frontiers of Paradise: A Study of Monks and Monasteries, 1987; Goodbye to the Art of Poetry, 1989; Shadow and Bone, 1989; Shade Those Laurels (with Cyril Connolly), 1990; The Art of Poetry, Lectures, 1991; Life of Lord Tennyson, 1993. Memberships: Society of Jesus, 1948-77. Address: Prospect Cottage, Frampton on Severn, Gloucestershire, England.

LEVIN (Henry) Bernard, b. 19 Aug 1928. Journalist; Author. Education: BSc Economics, London School of Economics, University of London, England. Appointments: Writer, regular and occasional, many newspapers and magazines, UK and abroad including: The Times, London; Sunday Times; Observer; Manchester Guardian; Truth; Spectator; Daily Express; Daily Mail; Newsweek; International Herald Tribune; Writer, Broadcaster Radio and TV, 1952-. Publications: The Pendulum Years, 1971' Taking Sides, 1979; Conducted Tour, 1981; Speaking Up, 1982; Enthusiasms, 1983; The Way We Live Now, 1984; Hannibal's Footsteps, 1985; In These Times, 1986; To the End of the Rhine, 1987; All Things Considered, 1988; A Walk Up Fifth Avenue, 1989; Now Read On, 1990; If You Want My Opinion, 1992; A World Elsewhere, 1994. Honours: Numerous awards for journalism; Honorary Fellow, London School of Economics, 1977; CBE, 1990. Membership: Member, Order of Polonia Restituta (by Polish Government in Exile). Literary Agent: Michael Shaw, Curtis Brown Limited. Address: c/o The Times, 1 Pennington Street, London E1 9XN, England.

LEVIN Michael Graubart, b. 8 Aug 1958, New York City, New York, USA. Novelist. Education: BA, Amherst College, 1980; JD, Columbia University Law School, 1985. Appointments: Writers Programme, University of California, Los Angeles, 1990-; Visiting Professor of English, Stonehill College, 1993-94. Publications: Journey to Tradition, 1986; The Socratic Method, 1987; Settling the Score, 1989; Alive and Kicking, 1993; What Every Jew Needs To Know About, forthcoming. Contributions to: New York Times; Jerusalem Post. Honours: John Woodruff Simpson Fellowship, 1982, 1983. Memberships: Treasurer, Authors Guild Foundation Inc; PEN; Council Member, Authors Guild; Writers Guild of America East Inc. Literary Agents: Dan Green 1271 6th Ave, Rm 3309, New York, NY 10020, USA. Address: Box 181, Boston, MA 02101, USA.

LEVIN Torres (Tereska Torres), b. 3 Sept 1920, Paris, France. Writer. m. Meyer Levin, 25 Mar 1948, 3 sons, 1 daughter. Education: French Baccalaureat. Publications: Le Sable et l'ecume, 1945; Women's Barracks, 1951; Not Yet, 1952; The Dangerous Games, 1953; The Golden Cage, 1954; By Colette, 1955; The Only Reason, 1961; The Open Doors, 1968; The Converts, 1971; Les Annees Anglaises, 1980; Le Pays des Chuchotements, 1983; Les Poupees de Cendre, 1978; Les Maisons Hantees de Meyer Levin, 1990. Address: 65 Boulevard Arago, Studio 13, Paris 75013, France.

LEVINE Norman, b. 22 Oct 1923, Canada. m. 1) Margaret Emily Payne, 2 Jan 1952, dec 1978, 3 daughters, 2) Anne Sarginson, 10 Aug 1983. Education: BA 1948, MA 1949, McGill University, Montreal; Trinity College, Cambridge, England, 1945; King's College, London, 1949-50. Publications: Canada Made Me (travel), 1958; Short Stories: One Way Ticket, 1961; Thin Ice, 1979-80; Champagne Barn, 1984-85; I Don't Want to Know Anyone Too Well (stories), 1971; From A Seaside Town (novel), 1970; Something Happened Here (stories), 1991-92. Contributions to: Atlantic Monthly; Sunday Times; New Statesman; Spectator; Vogue; Harper's Bazaar; Encounter; Times Literary Supplement; Saturday Night. Literary Agent: Dr Ruth Liepman, Zurich, Switzerland. Address: c/o Liepman AG, Maienburgweg, CH-8044, Zurich.

LEVINE Paul. Publications: To Speak For the Dead, 1990; Night Vision, 1991; False Dawn, 1993; Mortal Sin, 1994; Slashback, 1995. Address: c/o Wm Morrow Publishing-Publicity Dept, 4th Floor 1350 Ave of the Americas, New York NY 10019, USA.

LEVINE Philip, b. 10 Jan 1928, MI, USA. Poet; Essayist; Professor. m. Frances Artley, 12 July 1954, 3 sons. Education: BA, 1950, MA, 1955, Wayne University; MFA, University of IA, 1957. Publications: Whatwork Is, 1991; New Selected Poems, 1991; A Walk with Tom Jefferson, 1988; The Bread Truth, 1994; The Simple Truth, 1994; They Feed the Lion, 1992. Contributions to: New Yorker; Atlantic; Harpers; Paris Review; Poetry; Hudson Review; Three Penny Review. Honour: National Book Award, 1980, 91. Address: 4549 N Van Ness Boulevard, Fresno, CA 93704, USA.

LEVINE Stuart (Esteban O'Brien Córdoba, Stephen O'Brien), b. 25 May 1932, New York, USA. College Professor; Editor. m. Susan Fleming Matthews, 6 June 1963, 2 sons, 1 daughter. Education: AB, Harvard University, 1954; MA 1956, PhD 1958, Brown University. Appointments: Founding Editor, American Studies, 1959-89; Exchange Professor, University of the West Indies, 1988; The Naples Chair (Fulbright Distinguished Lectureship), 1994-95; Professor Emeritus, University of Kansas, 1992-, (retired early to write fiction & perform

music). Publications: Materials for Technical Writing, 1963; The American Indian Today (with N O Lurie), 2nd edition 1970; Charles Caffin: The Story of American Painting, Editor, 1972; Edgar Poe: Seer and Craftsman, 1972; The Short Fiction of Edgar Allan Poe (with Susan Levine), 1976, 1989; The Monday-Wednesday-Friday Girl and Other Stories, 1994; Editor with Susan Levine, Eureka and Essays on Literature and Prosody, in The Collected Writing of Edgar Poe (ongoing). Address: 1644 University Drive, Lawrence, KS 66044, USA.

LEVINSON Harry, b. 16 Jan 1922, Port Jervis, New York, USA. Clinical Psychologist; Management Consultant. m. Roberta Freiman, 11 Jan 1946, div June 1972, 2 sons, 2 daughters. Education: BSEd 1943, MSEd 1947, Psychology, Emporia (Kansas) State University; PhD, Clinical Psychology, University of Kansas, 1952. Appointments: Editorial Advisory Board, Consultation, 1981-83; Editorial Review Board, Academy of Management Executive, 1986-89; Editorial Board, Family Business Review, 1987-; Panel of Editorial Advisors, Human Relations, 1990-. Publications include: Men, Management, and Mental Health, 1962; Organizational Diagnosis, 1972; The Great Jackass Fallacy, 1973; Executive Stress, 1975; Psychological Man, 1976; Emotional Health in the World of Work, 1980; Executive, 1981; Ready, Fire, Aim: Avoiding Management by Impulse, 1986; Designing and Managing Your Career (editor), 1989; Career Mastery, 1992. Contributions to: Numerous professional journals and magazines. Address: The Levinson Institute, 404 Wyman Street, Ste 400, Waltham, MA 02154, USA.

LEVINSON Leonard, (Nicholas Brady, Lee Chang, Glen Chase, Richard Hale Curtis, Gordon Davis, Clay Dawson, Nelson De Mille, Josh Edwards, Richard Gallagher, March Hastings, J Farragut Jones, Leonard Jordan, Philip Kirk, John Mackie, Robert Novak, Philip Rawls, Bruno Rossi, Jonathon Scofield, Jonathon Trask, Cynthia Wilkerson). b. 1935, New Bedford, Massachusetts, USA. m. (1) divorced, 1 d, (2) died. Education: Michigan State University. Publications include: over 70 titles including: (as Bruno Rossi) Worst Way To Die, 1974; Headcrusher, 1974; (as Nicholas Brady) Shark Fighter, 1975; (as Leonard Jordan) Operation Perfida, 1975; Without Mercy, 1981; (as Cynthia Wilkerson) Sweeter Than Candy, 1978; The Fast Life, 1979; (as Philip King) Hydra Conspiracy, 1979; (as Gordon Davis) The Battle of the Bulge, 1981; (as John Mackie) Hit the Beach, 1983; Nightmare Alley, 1985; (as Clay Dawson) Gold Town, 1989; (as J Farragut Jones) 40 Fathoms Down, 1990; (as Josh Edwards) Searcher, 1990; Warpath, 1991, (as Nelson De Mille)Rivers of Babylon; Cathedral; The Talbot Odyssey; Word of Honour; The Charm School; Gold Coast; The General's Daughter, 1993; Spencerville, 1994. Address: c/o Lowenstein Associates Inc Stel6, 121 W 27th Street, New York NY 10001, USA.

LEVINSON Riki Friedberg, b. Brooklyn, New York, USA. Author; Associate Publisher; Art Director. m. Morton Levinson, 7 Mar 1944, 1 daughter. Education: BA, Cooper Union School of Art & Sciences. Publications: Watch the Stars Come Out, 1985; I Go with My Family to Grandma's, 1986; DinnieAbbieSister-r-r! 1987; Touch! Touch! 1987; Our Home is the Sea, 1988; Honours: Watch the Stars Come Out, American Library Association Notable Book, 1985; Redbooks Top Ten Picture Books, 1985, I Go with My Family to Grandma's, Virginia Library Association's Jefferson Cup Honour Book, 1987; Georgia Book Award for DinnieAbbieSister-r-r-r! 1987. Memberships: Authors Guild, American Institute of Graphic Arts.

LEVIS Larry, b. 1946, USA. University Educator; Poet. Appointments: Instructor, California State University, Fresno, 1970; Lecturer, California State University, Los Angeles, 1970-72; Visiting Lecturer, University of Iowa, Iowa City, 1972; Assistant Professor, University of Missouri, Columbia, 1974-80; Associate Professor of English, University of Utah, Salt Lake City, 1980-. Publications: Wrecking Crew, 1972; The Rain's Witness, 1975; The Afterlife, 1977; The Dollmaker's Ghost, 1981; Winter Stars, 1985. Address: Department of English, University of Utah, Salt Lake City, UT 84112, USA.

LEVY Alan, b. 1932, USA. Journalist; Author; Editor. Appointments: Reporter, Courier-Journal, Louisville, Kentucky, 1953-60; Investigator, Carnegie Commission on Educational Television, 1966-67; Foreign Correspondent, 1967-, including Life Magazine and Good Housekeeping Magazine in Prague, Czechoslovakia, 1967-71; New York Sunday Times and International Herald Tribune in Vienna, Austria, 1971-91; Dramaturg, Vienna's English Theatre Ltd, 1977-82; Founding Editor in Chief, The Prague

Post, weekly English language newspaper, Prague, Czech Republic, 1991-. Publications: Draftee Confidential Guide (with B Krisher and J Cox), 1957, Revised Edition (with R Flaste), 1966; Operation Elvis, 1960; The Elizabeth Taylor Story, 1961; Wanted: Nazi Criminals at Large, 1962; Interpret Your Dreams, 1962, 2nd Edition, 1975; Kind-Hearted Tiger (with G Stuart), 1964; The Culture Vultures, 1968; God Bless You Real Good: My Crusade with Billy Graham, 1969; Rowboat to Prague, 1972; Good Men Still Live, 1974; The Bluebird of Happiness, 1976; Forever, Sophia, 1979, 2nd Edition, 1986; So Many Heroes, 1980, revised edition as So Many Heroes, 1980; The World of Ruth Draper, play, 1982; Just An Accident, libretto for requiem, 1983; Ezra Pound: The Voice of Silence, 1983; W H Auden: In the Autumn of the Age of Anxiety, 1983; Treasures of the Vatican Collections, 1983; Vladimir Nabokov: The Velvet Butterfly, 1984; Ezra Pound: A Jewish View, 1988; The Wiesenthal File, 1993. Contributions to: International Herald Tribune, Paris; ARTnews, New York City; New York Sunday Times; Reader's Digest; Travel & Leisure. Honours: New Republic Magazine's Younger Writer Award, Washington DC, 1957; Sigma Delta Chi, Regional Award for Best Enterprise Reporting in Coverage of Cuban Revolution, 1959; Bernard De Voto Fellowship in Prof Bread Loaf Writers Conference, Middlebury College, Vermont, USA, 1963; Best Article of 1978, Pacific Area Travel Association, San Francisco, 1978; Golden Johann Strauss Medal of City of Vienna for Services to Culture & Tourism, 1981, (with René Staar), Ernst Krenek Prize of City of Vienna for Best Work of New Music, Just an Accident?, 1986. Memberships: Authors Guild; Dramatists Guild; American PEN; Overseas Press Club of America; American Society of Journalists & Authors; Foreign Press Association of Vienna; Foreign Correspondents Association of Prague; Czech Union of Journalists. Literary Agent: Serafina Clarke, England. Address: c/o Serafina Clarke, Literary Agent, 96 Tunis Road, London W12 7EY, England.

LEVY Faye, b. 23 May 1951, Washington, District of Columbia, USA. Syndicated Columnist; Cooking Teacher. m. Yakir Levy, 28 Sept 1970. Education: BA, Sociology, Anthropology, Tel Aviv University, Israel, 1973; Grand Diplome, Ecole de Cuisine la Varenne, Paris, 1979. Appointments: Cookery Editor, La Varenne, Paris, France, 1977-81; Columnist, Bon Appetit Magazine, 1982-88; Columnist, At Magazine, Israel, 1988-; Syndicated Columnist, Los Angeles Times, USA, 1990-; Columnist, Jerusalem Post, 1990-. Publications: La Cuisine du Poisson, 1984; French Cooking Without Meat, in Hebrew, 1984; French Desserts, in Hebrew, 1985; Faye Levy's Chocolate Sensations, 1986; Fresh from France: Vegetable Creations, 1987; Fresh from France: Dinner Inspirations, 1989; Sensational Pasta, 1989; Fresh from France: Dessert Sensations, 1990; Faye Levy's International Jewish Cookbook, 1991; Faye Levy's International Chicken Cookbook, 1992; Faye Levy's International Vegetable Cookbook, 1993; Faye Levy's Favorite Recipes, in Hebrew, 1991. Literary Agent: Maureen Lasher. Address: 5116 Marmol Drive, Woodland Hills, CA 91364, USA.

LEWANDOWSKI Jan, b. 23 Feb 1933, Warsaw, Poland. Journalist; Writer. m. Iwona. Education: Warsaw University, 1951-54. Publications: Without the Song, 1965; The Stars of Small Orfelon, 1975; Do You Believe in UFO, M-mum? 1981; Everybody is Waiting for the Sentence, 1979; The Grenadier's Tomb, 1986. Contributions include: Kierunki; Prawo i zycie; Slowo Powszechne; Tygodniowy Magazyn Tim. Honours: Wlodziemierz Pietrzak Award, 1986; Awards, Union of Polish Journalists, 1974, 1976, 1978, 1980. Memberships: Union of Polish Writers; Union of Polish Journalists. Address: ul Prozna 12 m 17, 00-107 Warsaw, Poland.

LEWIN Michael Zinn, b. 21 July 1942, Cambridge, Massachusetts, USA. Writer. m. 1 son, 1 daughter. Education: AB, Harvard University, 1964; Churchill College, Cambridge, England. Appointments: High School Teacher, 1966-69; Freelance Writer, 1969-. Publications: How to Beat College Tests; Ask the Right Question; The Way We Die Now; The Enemies Within; Night Cover; The Silent Salesman; Missing Woman; Outside In; Hard Line; Out of Season (Out of Times in UK); Late Payments; And Baby Will Fall (Child Proof in UK); Called by A Panther, 1991; Underdog, 1993; Family Business, 1995; Various radio plays, stage plays and short stories. Honours: Edgar Nominations for Ask the Right Question, 1972 and The Reluctant Detective, 1985; Maltese Falcon Society Best Novel for Hard Line, 1987; Raymond Chandler Society of Germany, Best Novel, 1992 for Called By a Panther; Mystery Masters Award, 1994, for Magna cum Murder; Muncie Indiana. Memberships: Crime Writers Association; Mystery Writers of America; Private Eye Writers Association; Authors Guild; Co-editor, Crime Writers' Associations's Annual Anthology, 1992-. Literary Agent: Wallace Literary Agency (NY), A M Heath

(London). Address: 5 Welshmill Road, Frome, Somerset BA11 2LA, England.

LEWIS Anthony, b. 27 Mar 1927, New York City, USA. Newspaper Columnist; Legal Lecturer. m. (1) Linda Rannells, 8 July 1951, divorced 1982, 1 son, 2 daughters, (2) Margaret Hilary Marshall, 23 Sept 1984. Education: BA, Harvard University, 1948; HonDLitt, Adelphi University, 1964; Rutgers University, 1973; Williams College, 1978; Clark University, 1982; Hon LLD, Syracuse University, 1979; Colby College, 1983; Northeastern University, 1987. Appointments: Desk Editor, New York Times, 1948-52; Supreme Court Reporter, 1957-64; Chief, London Correspondent, 1964-72; Columnist, 1969-; Reporter, Washington Daily News, 1952-55; Lecturer, Law, Law School, Harvard University, 1975-90; James Madison Visiting Professor, Columbia University, 1983-. Publications: Gideon's Trumpet, 1964; Portrait of a Decade, 1964; Make No Law: The Sullivan Case and The First Amendment, 1991. Honours: Winner, Pulitzer Prize for National Correspondence, 1955, 1964. Address: New York Times, 2 Faneuil Hall Marketplace, Boston, MA 02109, USA.

LEWIS Bernard. Publications include: Turkey Today, 1940; Child Heroes of South Africa, 1940; The Arabs in History, 1950; The Emergence of Modern Turkey, 1961; The Middle East and the West, 1964; The Assassins: A Radical Sect in Islam, 1967; Race and Colour in Islam, 1971; Islam in History, 1973; The Jews of Islam, 1984; The Political Language of Islam, 1988; Islam and the West, 1993; The Shaping of the Modern Middle East, 1994; Cultures in Conflict: Christians, Muslims and Jews, 1994. Address: Dept of Near Eastern Studies, Princeton University, 110 Jone Hall, Princeton, NJ 08544, USA.

LEWIS Charles. See: DIXON Roger.

LEWIS David Levering, b. 1935. Little Rock, Arkansas, USA. Professor of History. m. (1) 3 children, (2) Ruth Ann Seward. Education: School of Law, University of Michigan; MA, Columbia University; PhD, London School of Economics. Publications: King: A Critical Biography, 1970; Prisoners of Honour: The Dreyfus Affair, 1974; When Harlem was in Vogue, 1981; The Race to Fashoda, 1988; W E B Dubois: Biography of a Race, 1868-1919, 1993; Harlem Renaissance Reader (editor), 1994. Honour: Pulitzer Prize, 1994. Address: Dept of History, Rutgers University, New Brunswick, NJ 08903, USA.

LEWIS Ernest Michael Roy (Roy Lewis), b. 6 Nov 1913, England. Author and Journalist. m. Christine May Tew, 1938, 2 daughters. Education: MA, University College Oxford: London School of Economics and University College London. Appointments: Editor and Washington Correspondent, The Economist, 1956-60; Editor, New Commonwealth, 1957-58; Leader Writer and Commonwealth Correspondent, The Times, 1961-81. Publications: The English Middle Class, 1949; Professional People, 1952; The British Business Man, 1961; The Evolution Man, 1960; Enoch Powell, 1979; Sierra Leone, 1954; The British in Africa, 1971; The Extraordinary Reign of King Ludd, 1990; A Force for the Future, 1976; A Walk with Mr Gladstone, 1991. Contributions to: Various newspapers, magazines and journals. Address: 2 Park House Gardens, Twickenham TW1 2DE, England.

LEWIS F(rances) R, b. 30 Apr 1939, USA. Writer. m. Howard D Lewis, 16 Apr 1961, 2 sons, 1 daughter. Education: BA, University of Albany, 1960. Appointments: Fiction Writing Instructor, 1989; Literary Manager, Public Radio Book Show, 1988; Writing Tutor, Johns Hopkins University, 1990. Publications: Short stories include: Cash on Delivery, 1991; How the World Grew Up, The Present, Husbands, 1992; Wanting, School Days, School Days, What You Eat, 1993; In Anthologies: Secrets, 1986; Gates to the City, 1986; Blue Moon 4, 1987; Next to the Last Straw, 1987; Gribiness, 1992; National Public Poets Playhouse: The Sound of Writing, 1992; The Book Club Book, 1993; Vital Signs, 1993; Each in Her Own Way, 1994. One-act Play: Fourth Floor Follies: A Literary Revue, 1989. Contributions to: Cream City Review; Salmon; San Jose Studies; Alasqa Quarterly Review; Kalliope; The William and Mary Review; The American Voice; Buffalo Spree; Blue Moon; Chariton Review; Albuquerque Journal; Alabama Literary Review; Ascent; Alaska Quarterly Review; Chariton Review; The American Voice; Cottonwood; Paragraph; Ararat; Capital Region Magazine; Jewish Currents; Rermafrost; Negative Capability; 13th Moon. Honours: Fellow, The Colony for the Arts; Fellow, The Millay Colony, 1991; PEN NEA Syndicated Fiction Project Awards, 1988, 1986; Finalist, Capricorn First Book Contest, The Writer's Voice, 1992;

Fellow, The MacDowell Colony for the Arts, 1993. Memberships: Poets & Writers Inc (listed writer); Hudson Valley Writers Guild (President, Secretary); International Women's Writing Guild; Associated Writing Programs; Address: PO Box 12093, Albany, NY 12212-2093, USA.

LEWIS Linda Joy, b. 20 June 1946, New York City, New York, USA. Writer. m. 31 Mar 1965, 1 son, 1 daughter. Education: BA, City College of New York, 1972; MEd, Florida Atlantic University, 1976. Publications: We Hate Everything But Boys, 1985; Is There Life After Boys, 1987; We Love Only Older Boys, 1988; 2 Young 2 Go 4 Boys, 1988; My Heart Belongs to That Boy, 1989; All for the Love of That Boy, 1989; Want to Trade 2 Brothers for a Cat, 1989; Dedicated to That Boy I Love, 1991; Preteen Means In Between, 1992. Membership: Authors Guild. Address: 2872 NE 26 Place, Ft Lauderdale, FL 33306, USA.

LEWIS Roy. See: LEWIS Ernest Michael Roy.

LEWIS Thomas Parker, b. 1936, USA. Children's Fiction Writer; Company President. Appointments: Coordinator, Institutional and Corporate Marketing Departments, Harper and Row, Publishers, Inc, New York City, 1964-82; President, Pro/Am Music Resouces, White Plains, New York, 1982-. Publications: Hills of Fire, 1971; The Dragon Kite, 1974; Clipper Ship, 1978; A Call for Mr Sniff, 1981; Mr Sniff's Motel Mystery, 1983; The Blue Rocket Fun Show, 1986. Address: 63 Prospect Street, White Plains, NY 10606, USA.

LEWIS-SMITH Anne Elizabeth, b. 14 Apr 1925, London, England. Writer; Poet. m. Peter Lewis-Smith, 17 May 1944, 1 son, 2 daughters. Appointments: Editor, 1st WRNS Magazine, Aerostat International Balloon and Airship, 1973-78; Editor, WWNT Bulletin, BAFM Newsletter, 1967-83; Assistant Editor, 1967-83; Editor, 1983-91, Envoi; Editor, British Association of Friends of Museums Yearbook, 1985-91; Publisher, Envoi Poets Publications, 1986-. Publications: Poetry: Seventh Bridge, 1963; The Beginning, 1964; Flesh and Flowers, 1967, 3 editions; Dandelion Flavour, 1971; Dinas Head, 1980; Places and Passions, 1986; In the Dawn, 1987. Contributions to: Poetry to over 40 magazines; Numerous articles to newspapers and magazines; Own Woman's page, 6 years; Feature to Cambridgeshire Life and Northamptonshire Life. Honours include: Tissadier Diploma, services to International Aviation; Debbie Warley Award, services to International Aviation; Dorothy Tutin Award, services to poetry. Membership: Fellow, PEN. Address: Pen Ffordd, Newport, Pembrokeshire, Dyfed SA42 0QT, Wales.

LEWISOHN Leonard C, b. 28 Aug 1953, New York, USA. Translator. m. Jane Ferril, 1973. Education: BA, International Relations, Pahlavi University, 1973-78; PhD, Persian Literature, University of London, 1983-88. Publications: Translations: Masters of the Path (A History of the Masters of the Nimatullahi Sufi Order), 1980; The Truths of Love: Sufi Poetry, 1982; Sufi Women, 1983, rprt 1990; Jesus in the Eyes of the Sufis, 1983; Spiritual Poverty in Sufism, 1984; Sufi Symbolism I (Parts of the Beloved's Body: Wine, Music, Mystical Audition, and Convival Gatherings, 1984; Books: The Legacy of Mediaeval Persian Sufism, editor, 1992; Persian Sufism from its Origins to Rumi, editor, 1993; A Critical Edition of the Divan of Maghribi, editor, 1993; Forthcoming: An Infidelity Beyond Faith: The Life, Works and Sufism of Mahmud Shabistari; The Occident of Mysteries: The Life, Literary School and Mystical Poetry of Muhammad Shirin Maghribi. Address: 41 Chepstow Place, London W2 4TS, England.

LEXAU Joan M (Joan L Nodset), b. American. Writer of Children's Fiction. Appointments: Editorial Secretary, Catholic Digest, St Paul, 1953-55; Advertising Production Manager, Glass Packer magazine, New York City, 1955-56; Reporter, Catholic News, New York City, 1956-57; Correspondent, Religious News Service, New York City, 1957; Children's Books Production Liaison, Harper and Row, Publishers, New York City, 1957-61. Publications: Olaf Reads, 1961; Cathy is Company, 1961; Millicent's Ghost, 1962; The Trouble with Terry, 1962; Olaf is Late, 1963; That's Good, That's Bad, 1963; Jose's Christmas Secret, 1963, revised edition as The Christmas Secret, 1973 (as Joan L Nodset), Who Took the Farmer's Hat? 1963; (as Joan L Nodset) Go Away, Dog, 1963; Banjie, 1964; Maria, 1964; (as Joan L Nodset) Where Do You Go When You Rung Away? 1964; (ed) Convent Life: Catholic Religious Orders for Women in North America, 1964; I Should Have Stayed in Bed! 1965; More Beautiful that Flowers, 1966; The Homework Caper, 1966; A Kite over Tenth Avenue, 1967; Finders Keepers, Losers Weepers, 1967; Every Day a Dragon, 1967; Three

Wishes for Abner, 1967; Striped Ice Cream! 1968; The Rooftop Mystery, 1968; A House So Big, 1968; Archimedes Takes a Bath, 1969; Crocodile and Hen, 1969; It All Began with a Drip, Drip, Drip...., 1970; Benjie on His Own, 1970; Me Day, 1971; A T for Tommy, 1971; That's Just Fine, and Who-o-o- Did It? 1971; (as Joan L Nodset) Come Here Cat, 1973; The Tail of the Mouse, 1974; I'll Tell on You, 1976; Beckie and the Bookworm, 1979; I Hate Red Rover, 1979; The Spider Makes a Web, 1979; Jack and the Beanstalk, 1980; The Poison Ivy Case, 1984; The Dog Food Caper, 1985; Don't Be My Valentine, 1985. Address: PO Box 270, Otisville, NY 10963, USA.

LEY Alice Chetwynd, b. 12 Oct 1913, Halifax, Yorkshire, England. Novelist. m. Kenneth James Ley, 3 Feb 1945, 2 sons. Education: Diploma in Sociology, London University. Literary Appointments: Tutor, Creative Writing, Harrow College of Further Education, 1962-84; Lecturer, Sociology & Social History, Harrow College of Further Education, 1968-71. Publications: 19 novels published in UK, USA, Germany, Holland, Scandinavia, Iceland, and Australia including: The Georgian Rake, 1960 (dramatised and broadcast on BBC Saturday Night Theatre, Radio, 1962 and 1966). Contributions to: Numerous journals. Honour: Gilchrist Award for Diploma in Sociology, 1962. Memberships: Romantic Novelists Association, Chairman 1970, Honorary Life Member 1987; Society of Women Writers & Journalists; Jane Austen Society. Address: 42 Cannonbury Avenue, Pinner, Middlesex HA5 1TS, England.

LEYTON Sophie, See: WALSH Sheila.

LEZENSKI Cezary Jerzy, b. 6 Jan 1930, Poznan, Poland. Journalist; Novelist. m. Antonina Czebatul, 1958, 1 son, 1 daughter. Education: Journalism, 1951; MA, Polish Philology, 1952, Jagiellonian University, Cracow. Appointments: Editor-in-Chief, Kurier Polski, 1969-81; Editor-in-Chief, Epoka Literacke, 1981-90; Editor-in-Chief, Poland Today, edited monthly in 7 languages in 104 countries 1991-1993. Publications: 21 books including: Powrot, novel, 1963; Zolnierskie Drogi, story, 1971; Pozostaly Tylko Slady Podkow, essay, 1978, 1984; Kwatera 139, biography, 1989; Kawaleria Polska XX Wieku, essay, 1991; 6 novels for young people. Contributions to: Nowe Ksiaski literary and science magazine, 1978-89. Honours: Polish Military Cross, 1944; Commander, Polonia Restitua, 1978; Order of Smile for young people's novels, 1979. Memberships: Society of Polish Writers; Vice-Chairman, Mazurek Dabrowski Society; Chancellor of Chapter of the Order of Smile (International); Board, Authors Agency, Poland; Polish Section; UNICEF. Literary Agent: Authors Agency, ul Danilowiczowsa, Warsaw, Poland. Address: ul Frascati 8/10A, 00-483 Warsaw, Poland.

LI Shizheng (Duo Duo), b. 28 Aug 195 1, Beijing, China. Writer. Publications: Looking out from Death, 1989; Statements, 1989; Der Mann im Käfig, 1990; Bang dat ik verloren raak, 1991; Een schrijftafel tussen de velden, 1991. Contributions to: Today magazine, regularly; Manhattan Review; American Poetry Review; Lettre, Germany; NRC newspaper, Netherlands. Honours: Poetry Award, Peking University, 1987. Membership: International PEN. Literary Agent: Jennifer Kavanagh, 44 Langham Street, London W1N 5RG, England. Address: Storkwinkel 12, 10711 Berlin, Germany.

LI Tien-yi, b. 14 Mar 1915, Juyzng, Honan, China. Professor. m. 14 Sept 1963, 1 son, 1 daughter. Education: BA, Nankai University, 1937; MA 1946, PhD 1950, Yale University. Appointments: Editor and Executive Secretary, Tsing Hua Journal of Chinese Studies, 1955-88; Director and Editor-in-Chief, Far Eastern Publications, Yale University, 1960-69. Publications: A Study of Thomas Hardy, 1937; Woodrow Wilson's China Policy 1913-1917, 1952; P'ai-an Ching-ch'i, editor, 2 vols, 1967; Chinese Fiction, a Bibliography of Books and Articles in Chinese and english, 1968; Chinese Historical Literature, 1970; Erh-k'o P'ai-an Ching-ch'i, editor, 2 vols 1980; Editor, Life and Letters. Contributions to: Tsing Hua Journal of Chinese Studies; Journal of Asian Studies; American Historical Review. Honours: Phi Tau Phi Honorary Society; Award from National Science Council, Taiwan; Award from Tunghai University, Taiwan. Memberships: American Oriental Society; Association for Asian Studies; American Historical Society; Board Member, American Chinese Language Teachers Association; Board Member and President, American Association for Chinese Studies; Director, Institute of Chinese Culture, The Chinese University of Hong Kong. Address: Department of East Asian Languages and Literatures, The Ohio State University, Columbus, OH 43210, USA.

LI Xueqin, b. 28 Mar 1933, Beijing, China. Professor. m. Xu Weiying, 20 Aug 1956, 2 sons. Education: Department of Philogophy, Tsinghua University, Beijing, 1952. Publications: On Geography of the Yin Dynasty, 1959; The Wonder of Chinese Bronzes, 1980; Eastern Zhou and Qin Civilizations, 1985; Essays on Comparative Archaeology, 1991; Origins of I-Ching, 1992; Selected works of Li Xueqin, 1989; Studies of Recently Discovered Bronzes, 1990. Memberships: Chairman, Association of the History of Pre-Qin Dynasties; Honorary Member, The American Oriental Society. Address: Institute of History, Chinese Academy of Social Sciences, 6 Ritan Lu, Beijing 100020, China.

LIBBY Ronald Theodore, b. 20 Nov 1941, Los Angeles, California, USA. Professor. m. Kathleen Christina Jacobson, 6 June 1982, 2 daughters. Education: BA Political Science, Washington State University, 1965; MA Political Science 1966, PhD Political Science 1975, University of Washington. Appointments: Book Reviewer, numerous professional journals and magazines including Comparative Politics, ORBIS, Journal of Modern African Studies, American Political Science Association, Social Science Quarterly. Publications: Toward an Africanized US Policy for Southern Africa, 1980; The Politics of Economic Power in Southern Africa, 1987; Hawke's Law: The Politics of Mining and Aboriginal Land Rights in Australia, 2nd Edition 1992; Protecting Markets: US Policy and the World Grain Trade, 1992. Contributions to: Listen to the Bishops, to Foreign Policy, 1983; Transnational Class Alliances in Zambia, to Comparative Politics, 1983; The United States and Jamaica: Playing the American Card to Latin American Perspectives, 1990; 11 more peer-reviewed articles to journals. Literary Agent: Oscar Collier, Collier Associates, 2000 Flat Run Road, Seaman, OH 45679, USA. Address: Department of Political Science, Southwest State University, Marshall, MN 56258, USA.

LICHTENBERG Jacqueline, b. 1942, American. Writer. Publications: House of Zeor, 1974, 3rd ed 1981; (with S Marshak and J Winston), Star Trek Lives! 1975; Unto Zeor, Forever, 1978, 1980; (with J Lorrah), First Channel, 1980, 1981; Channel's Destiny, 1982; Ren Sime, 1984; City of a Million Legends, 1985; Dushau, 1985; Farfetch, 1985; Outreach, 1986; (with Jean Lorrah), Zelerod's Doom, 1986; Those of My Blood, 1988.

LICKONA Thomas, b. 4 Apr 1943, Poughkeepsie, New York, USA. Professor of Psychology, Education; Counsellor. m. Judith Barker, 2 s. Education: BA; MA, Ohio University; PhD, State University of New York at Albany. Publications: Open Education: Increasing Alternatives for Teachers and Children, 1973; Foundations of Interpersonal Attraction, 1974; Moral Development and Behaviour, 1976; Raising Good Children: Helping Your Child Through the Stages of Moral Development, 1983; Education for Character: How Our Schools Can Teach Respect and Resposibility, 1991. Contributions include: Journal of Moral Education, Ethics in Education. Honours: Distinguished Achievement Award, American Association of Colleges of Teacher Education, 1973; Christopher Award, 1992. Memberships: Association of Moral Education; Ethics in Education. Address: Education Department, SUNY College at Cortland, Cortland, NY 13045-0900, USA.

LIDDELL (John) Robert, b. 1908, British. Writer of Novels/Short Stories, Literature, Travel, Translations. Appointments: Senior Assistant, Department of Western Manuscripts, Bodleian Library, Oxford, England, 1933-38; Lecturer, University of Helsingfors, Finland, 1939, and Farouk I University, Alexandria, 1941-46; Lecturer 1946-51 and Assistant Professor 1951-52, Fuad I University, Cairo; Head of English Department, Athens University, 1963-68. Publications: The Almond Tree, 1938; Kind Relations (in US as Take This Child), 1939; The Gantillons, 1940; Watering Place (stories), 1945; A Treatise on the Novel, 1947; The Last Enchantments, 1948; Unreal City, 1952; Some Principles of Fiction, 1953; Aegean Greece, 1954; The Novels of Ivy Compton-Burnett, 1955; Byzantium and Istanbul, 1956; The Morea, 1958; The Rivers of Babylon, 1959; (trans) Demetrios Sicilianos: Old and New Athens, 1960; The Novels of Jane Austen, 1963; Mainland Greece, 1965; An Object for a Walk, 1966; The Deep End, 1968; Stepsons, 1969; Abbé Tigrane: Ferdinand Fabre (trans), 1988; Cavafy: A Critical Biography, 1974; The Novels of George Eliot, 1977; Elizabeth and Ivy (memoir), 1986; The Aunts (novel), 1987; Twin Spirits (Emily and Anne Bronte), 1990. Honour: Hon DLitt, 1987. Address: c/o Barclays Bank, High Street, Oxford, England.

LIDDLE Peter (Hammond), b. 1934, British. Writer on History; Keeper of the Liddle Collection, University of Leeds. Appointments:

History Teacher, Havelock School, Sunderland, 1957; Head, History Department, Gateacre Comprehensive School, Liverpool, 1958-67; Lecturer, Notre Dame College of Education, 1967; Lecturer 1967-70, Senior Lecturer in History 1970-, Sunderland Polytechnic; Tutor, British Council, Lesotho and Chairman, Sunderland Industrial Archaeological Society, 1969; Fellow of the Royal Historial Society, 1982; Vice-President, British Audio-Visual Trust; Keeper of the Liddle Collection, University of Leeds, 1988. Publications: Men of Gallipoli, 1976; World War One: Personal Experience Material for Use in Schools, 1977; Testimony of War 1914-18, 1979; The Sailor's War 1914-18, 1985; Gallipoli: Pens, Pencils and Cameras at War, 1985; 1916: Aspects of Conflict, 1985 (ed and contributor) Home Fires and Foreign Fields, 1985; The Airman's War 1914-18, 1987; The Soldier's War 1914-18, 1988; Voices of War, 1988; The Battle of Somme, 1992; The Worst Ordeal: Britons at Home and Abroad 1914-18, 1994. Contributions to: Articles in: RUSI Journal; Army Quarterly; Rodina (Russian Journal); Journal of the Western Front Association; Founder and Editor, The Poppy & The Owl, Journal of the Friends of the Liddle Collection, The University of Leeds. TV Historical Consultancy: Voices of War, 1988; Henry Moore, Changing Step, 1994; The Battle of the Somme, Tyne Tees/Yorkshire TV; Oral History Cassette, Victoria Cross Holder Recollections, 1994. Memberships: Lecture Tours on Appointments Overseas: Canada 1990, Germany 1991, USA 1992, Canada 1992, Russia 1994. Address: Dipity House, 282 Pudsey Road, Leeds, LS13 4HK, England.

LIDE Mary Ruth (Harry Lorner), b. Cornwall, England. Writer. 3 sons, 1 daughter. Education: MA, History, Oxford University. Publications: The Bait (as Mary Lorner), 1961; Ann of Cambray, 1985; Gifts of the Queen, 1985; Hawks of Sedgemont, 1987; Diary of Isobelle, 1985; Hawks of Sedgemont, 1987; Diary of Isobelle, 1988; Tregaran, 1989; Command of the King, 1990; Robert of Normandy (as Mary Lorner), 1991; The Legacy, 1991; The Homecoming, 1992. Contributions to: Short stories; Poetry; Book reviews. Honours: Avery Hopwood Award for Poetry, 1955; Best Historical Novel for Ann of Cambray, 1984. Membership: Writers Guild, USA. Literary Agent: Goodman Associates, USA. Address: c/o Goodman Associates, 500 West End Avenue, New York, NY 10024, USA.

LIEBER Robert James, b. 29 Sept 1941, Chicago, Illinois, USA. Professor of Government. m. Nancy Lee Isaksen, 20 June 1964, 2 sons. Education: BA, High Honours, University of Wisconsin, 1963; PhD, Harvard University, 1968. Publications: British Politics and European Unity, 1970; Theory and World Politics, 1972; Oil and the Middle East War: Europe in the Energy Crisis, 1976; Eagle Entangled: US Foreign Policy in a Changing World (co-editor, co-author) 1979; The Oil Decade, 1983, 1986; Eagle Defiant, co-editor, co-author, 1983; Eagle Resurgent, co-editor, co-author, 1987; No Common Power, 1988,91,95; Eagle in a New World, co-editor, co-author, 1992. Contributions to: International Affairs; American Political Science Review; International Security; Foreign Policy; Politique Etrangere; Washington Quarterly; Washington Post; New York Times; Harpers. Address: Department of Government, Georgetown University, Washington, DC 20057, USA.

LIEBERMAN Herbert Henry, b. 22 Sept 1933, New Rochelle, New York, USA. Novelist; Playwright; Editor. m. Judith Barsky, 9 June 1963, 1 daughter. Education: AB, City College of New York, 1955; AM, Columbia University, 1957. Publications: The Adventures of Dolphin Green, 1967; Crawlspace, 1971; The Eighth Square, 1973; Brilliant Kids, 1975; City of the Dead, 1976; The Climate of Hell, 1978; Nightcall from a Distant Time Zone, 1982; Night Bloom, 1984; The Green Train, 1986; Shadow Dancers, 1989; Sandman Sleep, 1993. Honours: Charles Sergel, 1st Prize for Playwriting, University of Chicago, 1963; John Simon Guggenheim Fellow, Playwrighting, 1964; Grand Prix de Litterature Policiere, Paris, France, 1978. Memberships: Mystery Writers of America Inc; International Association of Crime Writers. Literary Agent: Georges Borchardt, New York, USA. Address: c/o Georges Borchardt, 136 East 57th Street, New York, NY 10022, USA.

LIEBERMAN Robert Howard, b. 4 Feb 1941, New York City, USA. m. Gunilla Anna Rosen, 2 sons. Education: Cornell University, 1958-59; BS, Electrical Engineering, Polytechnic Institute of Brooklyn, 1962; MS, Electrical Engineering/Biophysics, Cornell University, 1965. Publications: Baby, 1981; Paradise Rezoned, 1974; Goobersville Breakdown, 1979; Perfect People, 1986; Faces in a Famine, documentary film, 1984. Contributions to: Numerous articles and stories in US and Swedish Magazines. Honours: G K Hall Distinguished Fiction Series, 1980; CINE Golden Eagle for Faces in a

Famine, 1984. Membership: American Film Institute. Literary Agent: Jean Naggar Agency, 216 E 75th St, New York, NY 10021, USA. Address: 400 Nelson Road, Ithaca, NY 14850, USA.

LIEBERTHAL Kenneth Guy, b. 9 Sept 1943, Asheville, North Carolina, USA. Professor of Political Science. m. Jane Lindsay, 15 June 1968, 2 sons. Education: BA with distinction, Dartmouth College, 1965; MA, 1968, Certificate for East Asian Institute, 1968, PhD Political Science 1972, Columbia University. Appointments include: Instructor 1972, Assistant Professor 1972-75, Associate Professor 1976-82, Professor 1982-83, Political Science Department, Swarthmore College; Visiting Professor 1983, Professor 1983-, University of Michigan, Ann Arbor; Editorial Boards: China Economic Review; China Quarterly. Publications include: Policy Making in China: Leaders, Structures and Processes (with Michel Oksenberg), 1988; Research Guide to Central Party and Government Meetings in China 1949-86 (with Bruce Dixon), 1989; Co-editor, Contributor, Perspectives on Modern China: Four Anniversaries, 1991; Co-editor, Contributor, Bureaucracy, Politics and Policy Making in Post-Mao China, 1991; Governing China, 1995. Contributions to: Quarterly publication for Atlantic Council; Book reviews to American Political Science Review; China Economic Review; China Quarterly. Address: Center for Chinese Studies, 104 Lane Hall, 204 S State St, University of Michigan, Ann Arbor, MI 48109, USA.

LIEBMANN Irina, b. 23 July 1943, Moscow, USSR. Writer; Scripter; Reporter. 2 daughters. Education: MA, Sinology and Arts, Leipzig University. Publications: Berliner Mietshaus (Berlin Apartment House), 1983; Neun Berichte uber Ronald, der seine Grossmutter begraben wollte (Nine Reports on Ronald, Who Wanted to Bury His Grannie), radio play reprinted in Dialog, 1981; Henschelverlag: Sie Mussen jetzt gehen, Frau Muhsam (You'd Better Go Now, Frau Muhsam), radio play reprinted in Dialog; Hast du die Nacht genutzt? Story, reprinted in Neue Rundschau, Nr 4, 1987, and in Neue Deutsche Llte Ratur, Nr 2, 1988; Playwrights: Berliner Kindl, Schwerin, 1988. Contributions to: Wochenpost; Temperamente, Berlin 1975-80. Honours: 2nd Prize, Radio Drama Competitiono, 1979; Radio-drama Award for the GDR (Preis der Horer), 1980; 1st Prize, radio drama Competition, 1981; Award for the Benefit of Young Writers, 1984; Ernst-Willner Prize of the Editors, Klagenfurt, 1987. Memberships: Schriftstellerverband Verlag Halle/Saale. Address: Wolfshagener Str, DDR 1100 Berlin, Democratic Republic of Germany.

LIFTON Betty Jean, American. Writer of Children's fiction; Plays/Autobiography/Memoirs/Personal. Education: PhD (UMM Inst), 1992. Publications: Joji and the Dragon, 1957; Mogo the Mynah, 1958; Joji and the Fog, 1959; Kap the Kappa, 1960, play 1974; The Dwarf Pine Tree, 1963; Joji and the Amanojaku, 1965; The Cock and the Ghost Cat, 1965; The Rice-Cake Rabbit, 1966; The Many Lives of Chio and Goro, 1966; Taka-Chan and I: A Dog's Journey to Japan, 1967; Kap and the Wicked Monkey, 1968; The Secret Seller, 1968; The One-Legged Ghost, 1968; A Dog's Guide to Tokyo, 1969; Return to Hiroshima, 1970; The Silver Crane, 1971; The Mud Snail Son, 1971; Good Night, Orange Monster, 1972; (with Thomas C Fox) Children of Vietnam, 1972; (ed) Contemporary Children's Theater, 1974; Jaguar, My Twin, 1976; Lost and Found: The Adoption Experience, 1979; I'm Still Me, 1981; A Place Called Hiroshima, 1985; The King of Children, A Biography of Janusz Korczak, 1988; Tell Me a Real Adoption Story, 1991; The Adoptee's Journey (forthcoming). Address: 300 Central Park W, New York, NY 10024, USA.

LIFTON Robert Jay. Psychiatrist; Director, Center on Violence & Human Survival, John Jay College, New York City. Publications: The Nazi Doctors; Death in Life; The Protean Self: Human Resilience in an Age of Fragmentation, 1993. Address: c/o Basic Books, No 10 East 53rd Street, New York, NY 100022, USA.

LIGHTMAN Alan, b. 28 Nov 1948, TN, USA. Writer; Physicist. m. Jean Greenblatt, 28 Nov 1976, 2 d. Education: AB, Princeton University, 1970; PhD, CA Inst of Technology, 1974. Literary Appointments: Professor of Science & Writing, MA Institute of Technology, 1989. Publictions: Good Benito, 1995; Einsteins Dreams, 1993; Ancient Light, 1992; Origins: The Lives and Worlds of Modern Cosmologists, 1990; Great Ideas in Physics, 1992; A Modern Day Yankee in a Connecticut Court, 1986; Time Travel and Papa Joe's Pipe, 1984. Contributions to: Harpers; New Yorker; NY Review of Books; Granta. Honours: Association of Am Publishers Award, 1990; LL Winship Book Prize, 1993. Memberships: Am Association for the Advancement of Science; Am Physical Society. Literary Agent:

Gelfman Schneider Literary Agents. Address: Program in Writing and Humanistic Studies, MIT, Cambridge, MA, USA.

LILIAN Margaret. See: **CLARKE Brenda.**

LILIENTHAL Alfred M, b. 25 Dec 1913, New York City, USA. Author; Historian; Attorney; Lecturer. Education: BA, Cornell University, 1934; LLD, Columbia University School of Law, 1938; JD, 1969. Appointments: Editor, Middle East Perspective, 1968-85. Publications: What Price Israel? 1953; There Goes the Middle East, 1958; The Other Side of the Coin, 1965; The Zionist Connection I, 1978; The Zionist Connection II, 1982, Czech trans 1989, Japanese trans 1991, German trans 1994. Contributions to: Numerous journals including: Readers Digest; Mercury; Washington Reporter, Middle East Affairs. Honour: National Press Club Book Honours, 1982. Memberships: University Club; Cornell Club; National Press Club; Capital Hill Club. Address: 800 25 NW, Washington DC 210378, USA.

LILLINGTON Kenneth (James), b. 1916. British Writer of Novels/Short stories, Children's fiction, Plays/Screenplays, Literature; Lecturer in English Literature, Brooklands Technical College, Weybridge, Surrey, now retired. Publications: The Devil's Grandson, 1954; Soapy and the Pharoah's Curse, 1957; Conjuror's Alibi, 1960; The Secret Arrow, 1960; Blue Murder, 1960; A Man Called Hughes, 1962; My Proud Beauty, 1963; First (and Second) Book of Classroom Plays, 1967-68; Fourth (and Seventh) Windmill Book of One-Act Plays, 1967-72; Cantaloup Crescent, 1970; Olaf and the Ogre, 1972; (ed) Nine Lives, 1977; For Better for Worse, 1979; Young Map of Morning, 1979; What Beckoning Ghost, 1983; Selkie, 1985; Full Moon, 1986. Address: 90 Wodeland Avenue, Guildford, Surrey GU2 5LD, England.

LIM Shirley Geok-Lin, b. 27 Dec 1944, Malacca, Malaysia. Author. m. Dr Charles Bazerman, 27 Nov 1972, 1 son. Education: BA, 1st Class Honours 1967, MA, English & American Literature 1971, PhD 1973, Brandeis University, USA. Appointments include: Writer-in-residence, National University of Singapore, 1985. Publications: Crossing the Peninsula, 1980; Another Country, 1982; No Man's Grove, 1985; Modern Secrets, 1988; The Forbidden Stitch, 1989. Contributions include: Ariel; Asia; Asia Week; Commentary; Contact II; Journal of Ethnic Studies; Kunapipi; Meanjin; Pacific Quarterly Moana; Chelsea; Solidarity; Tengarra; Waves. Honours: Commonwealth Poetry Prize, 1980; 2nd Prize, Asia Week Short Story Competition, 1982; Summer Seminar Fellowship, National Endowment for the Humanities, 1978, 1987; Mellon Fellowships, 1983, 1987; Fulbright Award, Wien Aard, ISIAS Fellowship; American Book Award, 1990. Memberships include: Offices, Modern Language Association. Address: Stuart Lane, Katonah, NY 10536, USA.

LIMA Robert, b. 7 Nov 1935, Havana, Cuba. University Professor; Writer. m. Sally Murphy, 27 June 1964, 2 sons, 2 daughters. Education: BA, English & Philosophy 1957, MA Theatre & Drama 1961, Villanova University; PhD, Romance Literatures, New York University, 1968. Appointments: Professor of Spanish and Comparative Literature, 1965-; Poet-in-Residence, Pontificia Universidad Catolica del Peru, 1976-77; Writer-in-Residence, USIA, 1986. Publications: Criticism: The Theatre of Garcia Lorca, 1963; Ramon del Valle-Inclan, 1972; An Annotated Bibliography of Valle-Inclan, 1972; Dos Ensayos sobre Teatro Espanol de Los 20, 1984; The Lamp of Marvels by Valle-Inclan (translator), 1986; Valle-Inclan: The Theatre of His Life, 1988; Reader's Encyclopedia of American Literature (Editor of Revised edition), 1962; Barrenechea's Borges The Labyrinth Maker (Editor & Translator), 1965; Dark Prisms Occultism in Hispanic Drama, 1995; Poetry: Fathoms, 1981; The Olde Ground, 1985; Mayaland Poetry, 1992; Savage Acts: Four Plays by Valle-Inclan, 1993. Contributions to: Articles in USA and Hispania including: Revista de Estudios Hispanicos; Romanic Review; Saturday Review; Americas; Chicago Review; Washington Post; The Lima Times; The Philadelphia Inquirer; Modern Drama; The Chicagop Tribune; The Philadelphia Bulletin; The Christian Science Monitor; Over 300 poems published in journals, newspapers, books and anthologies in USA and abroad. Address: Pennsylvania State Universityi, N346 Burrowes Building, University Park, PA 16802, USA.

LIMBAUGH Rush, b. 1951, Cape Girardeau, Missouri. Radio Talent Show Host. Publications: The Way Things Ought to Be; See, I Told You So, 1993, Address: C/o Paramount Publishing Pocket Books, Attn Mngng Edtrl, 1230 Avenue of the Americas, New York, NY 10020, USA.

LIMBURG Peter R, b. 1929, American. Writer on Marine Science/Oceanography, Natural History. Appointments: Special Editor, Harper Encyclopaedia of Science, 1960-61; Senior Technology Editor, The New Book of Knowledge, 1961-66; Editor, School Department, Harcourt, Brace and World, publishers, 1966-69; Co-ordinating Editor, Collier's Encyclopaedia, 1969-70, all New York City President, Forum Writers for Young People, 1975-76, 1980-81. Publications: The First Book of Engines, 1969; The Story of Corn, 1971; What's in the Names of Fruit, 1972; What's in the Names of Antique Weapons, 1973; (with James B Sweeney), Vesselss for Underwater Exploration: A Pictorial History, 1973; Watch Out, It's Poison Ivy! 1973; What's in the Names of Flowers, 1974; (with James B Sweeney), 102 Questions and Answers about the Sea, 1975; What's in the Name of Birds, 1975; Chickens, Chickens, Chickens, 1975; What's in the Names of Stars and Constellations, 1976; Poisonous Plants, 1976; What's in the Names of Wild Animals, 1977; Oceanographic Institutions, 1979; The Story of Your Heart, 1979; Farming the Waters, 1980; Stories Behind Words, 1986. Memberships: American Society of Journalists and Authors (Chairman, Membership Committee, 1991-92); National Association of Science Writers. Address: RR 4, Banksville Road, Bedford, NY 10506, USA.

LIN David (Chi-Min), b. 4 Mar 1956, Hong Kong. Editor. m. Phoebe Chu, 19 Sept 1980, 1 son, 1 daughter. Education: Diploma, Secretarial Management, Hong Kong Baptist College, 1978; MSc, Journalism, Boston University, USA, 1985. Literary Appointments: Secretary, Managing Editor, Asia Lutheran News, Hong Kong, 1978-83; English Editor, Sampan Newspaper, Boston, USA, 1984-85; Interim English Editor, Lutheran World Information Weekly, Geneva, 1985; Editor, Asia Lutheran Press Services, Hong Kong, 1985-93. Publications: Asia Lutheran Press Services Biweekly News Dispatches, 1985-93; News Story for Religious News Service, New York, titled, Hong Kong Groups Quiz China Official on Treatment of Church Leaders, 1990; Asia Lutheran Quarterly Newsletter, 1991-93; Major works appeared in Chinese, English, German, French, Italian and Japanese. Contributions to: The Lutheran Magazine, Chicago, USA; Lutheran World Information, Geneva; Religious News Service, New York, USA; New Zealand Lutheran; Chinese Around The World Monthly, Hong Kong. Memberships: National Writers Club, Professional Member, USA, 1989-; East-West Literary Foundation, San Francisco, USA, Charter Member USA, 1992. Address: c/o World Association For Christian Communication, 357 Kennington Lane, London, SE11 5QY.

LINCOLN Bruce Kenneth, b. 5 Mar 1948, Philadelphia, USA. University Professor. m. Louise Gibson Hassett, 17 April 1971, 2 daughters. Education: BA (High Honours), Haverford College, 1970; PhD (Distinction), University of Chicago, 1976. Publications: Priests, Warriors and Cattle: A Study in the Ecology of Religions, 1981; Emerging from the Chrysalis: Studies in Rituals of Women's Initiation, 1981; Religion, Rebellion, Revolution, Editor, 1985; Myth Cosmos and Society, 1986; Discourse and the Construction of Society, 1989; Death, War and Sacrifice, 1991; Authority: Construction and Corrosion, 1994. Contributions to: Articles in Comparative Studies in Society and History; History of Religions; Journal of Indo-European Studies & other scholarly journals. Honours: American Council of Learned Societies Award for Best New Book in History of Religions for Priests, Warriors and Cattle, 1981; John Simon Guggenheim Memorial Fellowship, 1983-84; Discourse and the Construction of Society was selected as one of Outstanding Academic Books of 1989 by Choice. Address: University of Chicago Divinity School, Swift Hall, 1025 E 58th St, Chicago, IL 60637, USA.

LINCOLN Geoffrey. See: MORTIMER John Clifford.

LINCOLN W Bruce, Professor. Publications: In War's Dark Shadow: the Russians Before the Great War; Passage Through Armageddon: The Russians in War and Revolution; Red Victory: A History of the Russian Civil War; The Romanovs; Nikolai Miliutia; Nicholas I; Pter Semenov - Tian - Shanskii: the Life of A Russian Geographer. Contributions to: numerous scholarly journals. Address: Dept of History, Northern Illinois University, De Kalb, IL 60115 - 2893, USA.

LIND Levi Robert, b. 1906. American, Literature, Translations. University Distinguished Professor of Classics, University of Kansas, Lawrence, 1940-. Publications: Medieval Latin Studies: Their Nature and Possibilities, 1941; The Vita Sancti Malchi of Reginald of Canterbury, 1942; (trans) The Epitome of Andreas Vesalius, 1949; (trans) Lyric Poetry of the Italian Renaissance, 1954; (trans) Ten Greek Plays in Contemporary Translations, 1957; (trans) Latin Poetry in Verse Translation, 1957; (ed and trans) Ecclesiale by Alexander of Villa Dei, 1958; (trans) Berengario da Carpi, A Short Introduction to Anatomy, 1959; (trans) Vergil's Aeneid, 1963; (trans) Aldrovandi on Cickens: The Ornithology of Ulisse Aldrovandi (1600), 1963; Epitaph for Poets and Other Poems, 1966; (ed) Problemata Varia Anatomica: The University of Bologna MS 1165, 1968; Twentieth Century Italian Poetry: A Bilingual Anthology, 1974; (trans) Johann Wolfgang von Goethe, Roman Elegies and Venetian Epigrams, 1974; (trans) Studies in Pre-Vesalian Anatomy, 1974; (trans) Ovid, Tristia, 1974; (trans) Andre Chenier, Elegies Camille, 1978; (trans) Gabriele Zerbi Gerontocomia: On the Care of the Aged, and Maximianus, Elegies on Old Age and Love, 1988; An Epitaph Years After (poems), 1990; Berengario da Caspi, On Fracture of the Skull or Cranium (trans from Latin); Transactions of the American Philosophical Society Vol 80, Part 4, 1990; (ed) The Letters of Giovanni Garzoni, Bolognese Humanist and Physician (1419-1505), 1992. Contributions to: Articles in Classical and Modern Literature, 1980-. Address: 1714 Indiana Street, Lawrence, KS 66044, USA.

LIND William Sturgiss, b. 9 July 1947, Lakewood, Ohio, USA. Writer. Education: AB, Dartmouth College, 1969; MA, Princeton University, 1971. Appointments: Currently Associate Publisher, The New Electric Railway Journal. Publications: Maneuver Warfare Handbook, 1985; America Can Win: The Case for Military Reform (with Gary Hart), 1986; Cultural Conservation: Toward a New National Agenda (with William H Marshner), 1987; Cultural Conservation: Theory and Practice (editor with William H Marshner), 1991. Contributions to: Many articles to military journals including: Marine Corps Gazette; US Naval Institute Proceedings; Military Review; Parameters; General publications including: Washington Post; Harper's. Address: Free Congress Foundation, 717 2nd St NE, Washington, DC 20002, USA.

LINDBLOM Charles Edward, b. 21 Mar 1917, CA, USA. Professor. m. Rose K Winther, 4 June 1942, 2 sons, 1 daughter. Education: BA, Stanford University, 1937; PhD, Chicago University, 1945. Publications: Politics and Markets, 1977; Inquiry and Change, 1990; The Intelligence of Democracy, 1965; Politics, Economics & Welfare, 1953; Usable Knowledge, 1979; The Policy Making Process, 1968; Unions & Capitalism, 1949; Democracy & Market System, 1988. Honours: Various. Membership: American Pol Science Association. Address: 9 Cooper Road, North Haven, CT, USA.

LINDEY Christine, b. 26 Aug 1947. Art Historian. Education: BA Hons, History of European Art, Courtauld Institute, University of London, England. Publications: Superrealist Painting and Sculpture, 1980; 20th Century Painting: Bonnard to Rothko, 1981; Art in the Cold War, 1990. Address: c/o West Herts College, The Art School, Ridge Street, Watford, Herts WD2 5BY, England.

LINDGREN Gustav Torgny, b. 16 June 1938, Raggsjo, Sweden. m. Stina Andersson, 19 June 1959, 1 son, 2 daughters. Education: DPhil. Publications: Batseba, 1984; Ormens vag pa halleberget, 1983; Merabs skonhet, 1983; Legender, 1986; Ljuset, 1987; Skrammer dig minuten, 1981; Ovriga tragor, 1973; Karleksguden Fro, 1988; Brannvinsfursten, 1979; Till Sanningens lov, 1991. Honours: Prix Fomina, 1986; Guralid Prize, 1990. Memberships: Swedish Academy; PEN. Address: Trollenas, S-598 36 Vimmerby, Sweden.

LINDMAN-STRAFFORD Kerstin Margareta, b. 30 May 1939, Abo, Finland. Writer; Critic. 2 children. Education: BA, Hum Kand, 1961; MA, 1962. Appointments: Critic, UK Editor, Hufvudstadsbladet, Helsinki, 1964-; Cultural Presenter, OBS Kulturkvarten, Swedish Radio, 1975-. Publications: Sandhogen and Other Essays, 1974; Tancred Borenius, 1976; Landet med manga ansikten, 1979; English Writers in Literaturhandboken, 1984; Faeder och Dottrar, 1986; Moedrar och soener, 1990; Foeraendringen, 1994. Contributions to: Numerous journals and magazines. Honour: Finland's Swedish Literary Society Prize, 1976. Memberships: PEN; Finlands Svenska Litteraturforening. Address: 16 Church Path, Merton Park, London SW19 3HJ, England.

LINDSAY Hilarie Elizabeth, b. 18 Apr 1922, Sydney, Australia. Writer; Museum Curator; Company Director. m. Philip Singleton Lindsay, 19 Feb 1944, 1 son, 2 daughters. Education: Graduate William's Business College, 1938; BA (Deakin), 1985; Box 90 PO Leichhardt 2040 (NSW), 1992. Appointments: President, Terrey Hills Library, 1957-63, now patron. Publications: 101 Toys to Make, 1972;

So You Want to Be a Writer, 1977; You're On Your Own - Teenage Survival Kit, 1977; One for the Road, short stories, 1978; Midget Mouse Finds a House, 1978; Culinary Capers, 1978; The Short Story, 1979; Learn to Write, 1979; The Naked Gourmet, 1979; The Society of Women Writers Handbook, 1980; The Withered Tree, 1980; One Woman's World, 1980; Echoes of Henry Lawson, 1981; The Gravy Train, 1981; Mr Poppleberry and the Dog's Own Daily, 1983; Mr Poppleberry's Cuckoo Chook, 1983; Mr Poppleberry and the Milk Thieves, 1983; Murder at the Belle Vue, 1983; Mr Poppleberry's Birthday Pie, 1989; Midget Mouse Goes to Sea, 1989; Beyond the Black Stump of My Pencil, 1993; When I Was Ten, 1993 (with Len Fox); Sydney Life, 1994 (with P McGowan); Mrs Poppleberry's Cuckoo-Clock, 1995. Address: 19-25 Beeson Street, Leichhardt, NSW 2020, Australia.

LINDSAY (John) Maurice, b. 21 July 1918, Glasgow, Scotland. Editor; Poet. Education: Glasgow Academy and Royal Scottish academy of Music. Appointments include: Co Editor, Scottish Review, 1980-. Publications include: The Advancing Day, 1940; Predicament, 1942; No Crown for Laughter, 1943; The Enemies of Love: Poems, 1941-45, 1946; Selected Poems, 1947; At The Woods Edge, 1950; Ode for St Andrew's Night and Other Poems, 1951; The Exiled Heart: Poems, 1941-56, 1957; Snow Warning and Other Poems, 1962; On Later Day and Other Poems, 1964; The Business of Living, 1971; Comings and Goings, 1971; Selected Poems, 1942-72, 1973; The Run from Life: More Poems, 1942-72, 1975; Walking Without an Overcoat: Poems, 1972-76, 1977; Collected Poems, 1979; A Net to Catch the Wind and Other Poems, 1981; The French Mosquitoe's Woman and Other Diversions, 1985; Requiem for a Sexual Athlete and Other Poems and Diversions, 1988; The Scottish Dog (with Joyce Lindsay), 1989; Collected Poems, 1940-1990, 1991; On The Face Of It - Collected Poems Vol.2, 1993; The Theatre and Opera Lover's Quotation Book (with Joyce Lindsay), 1993; Plays: Fingal and Comala, 1953; The Abbot of Drimock and the Decision, Both to Music by Thea Musgrave, 1958, 1967; Guides to Scotland: Editions of Poetry. Honours: CBE, 1979; D Litt, University of Glasgow, 1982. Address: 7 Milton Hill, Milton, Dumbarton, Dumbartonshire GB2 2TS, Scotland.

LINDSEY Alton Anthony, b. 7 May 1907, Pittsburgh, Pennsylvania, USA. Ecologist; Writer; Explorer. m. Elizabeth Smith, 2 June 1939, 1 son, 1 daughter. Education: BS, Allegheny College, 1929; PhD, Cornell University, 1937. Appointments: 1947-, Purdue University, West Lafayette, Indiana, Assistant Professor; Full Professor; Emeritus Professor of Biology, 1973; Editor, Indiana Academy, 1963-65; Editor, Indiana Sesquicentennial Volume, 1965-67; Ford Foundation Grantee, researching and writing a book, 1967-69. Publications: Natural Features of Indiana, 1966; Natural Areas in Indiana and Their Preservation, 1969; Naturalists, Explorers and Pioneers, 1980; North American Wildlife, 1982; Naturalist on Watch, memoirs, 1983; The Bicentennial of John James Audubon, 1985. Contributions to: 72 technical articles to journals, 10 popular articles to quality magazines including: Presidential Farewell to Passenger Pigeons, to Natural History. Address: 191 Drury Lane, West Lafayette, IN 47906, USA.

LINE David. See: DAVIDSON Lionel.

LINETT Deena, b. 30 Aug 1938, Boston, Massachusetts, USA. College Professor. 2 sons, 1 daughter. Education includes: EdD, Rutgers University, 1982. Publications: On Common Ground, novel, 1983; The Translator's Wife, novel, 1986; Visit, 1990. Contributions to: Harvard Magazine; Sun Dog; South Coast Poetry Journal; Kalliope; Calliope; Taos Review; Phoebe; Mississipi Valley Review. Honours: Fellowships to Yaddo, 1981, 1985; Prizes for both novels; Visit chosen for PEN-Syndicated Fiction Project, 1990. Memberships: PEN; Modern Language Association; National Council of Teachers of English; Co-Director (with Martin White EdD), New Jersey (USA), Writing Project; Listed Writer, Poets and Writers. Address: English Department, Montclair State University, Upper Montclair, NJ 07043, USA.

LINGARD Joan Amelia, b. 8 Apr 1932, Edinburgh, Scotland. Author. 3 daughters. Education: Bloomfield Collegiate School, Belfast, 1943-48; General Teaching Diploma, Moray House Training College, Edinburgh. Appointments: Council Member, Member, Literary Committee, Scottish Arts Council, 1981-85; Edinburgh Book Festival Board, 1982-84; Chairman, Meet the Book Festival Committee, Edinburgh. Publications: Childrens Books: The Twelfth Day of July, 1970; Frying as Usual, 1971; Kevin & Sadie, Quintet, 1972-76; Across the Barricades, 1972; Into Exile, 1973; Maggie, Quartet, 1974-77; The Clearance, 1974; A Proper Place, 1975; The Resettling, 1975;

Hostages to Fortune, 1976; The Pilgrimage, 1976; The Reunion, 1977; The Gooseberry, 1978; The File on Fraulein Berg, 1980; Strangers in the House, 1981; The Winter Visitor, 1983; The Freedom Machine, 1986; The Guilty Party, 1987; Rags and Riches, 1988; Tug of War, 1989; Glad Rags, 1990; Between Two Worlds, 1991; Hands Off Our School! 1992; Night Fires, 1993; Novels: Liam's Daughter, 1963; The Prevailing Wind, 1964; The Tide Comes In, 1966; The Headmaster, 1967; A Sort of Freedom, 1968; The Lord on Our Side, 1970; The Second Flowering of Emily Mountjoy, 1979; Greenyards, 1981; Sisters by Rite, 1984; Reasonable Doubts, 1986; The Women's House, 1989; After Colette, 1993. Honours: Scottish Arts Council Bursary, 1967-68; Preis Der Leseratten ZDF, W Germany, 1986; Buxtehuder Bulle, W Germany, 1987. Memberships: Society of Authors in Scotland, Chairman 1982-86; Scottish PEN. Literary Agent: David Higham Associates Ltd, 5-8 Lower John St, Golden Square, London W1R 4HA, England.

LINGEMAN Richard, b. 2 Jan 1931, USA. Editor; Writer. m. Anthea Judy Lingeman, 3 Apr 1965, 1 daughter. Education: BA, Haverford College, Haverford, PA, USA. Appointments: Executive Editor, The Nation, 1978-; NY Times Book Review, 1969-78. Publications: Drugs from A to Z: A Dictionary, 1969; Don't You Know There's a War on? 1970; Small Town America, 1980; Theodore Dreiser: At the Gates of the City 1871-1907, 1986; Theodore Dreiser: An American Journey 1908-1945, 1990; Theodore Dreiser: An American Journey (paperback), 1993. Memberships: National Book Critics Circle; PEN American Center, Authors Guild. Address: The Nation, 72 Fifth Avenue, New York, NY 10011, USA.

LINK Arthur Stanley, b. 1920, American. History, Biography. George Henry Davis Professor of American History, Princeton University Emeritus. Appointments: Instructor in History 1945-48, Assistant Professor 1948-49, Member, Institute for Advanced Study 1949, 1954-55; Professor 1960-65; Edwards Professor of American History, 1965-76; Associate Professor of History, 1949-54 and Professor 1954-60, Northwestern University, Evanston, Illinois. Publications include: Wilson: The Road To the White House, 1947; Wilson: The New Freedom, 1956; Wilson: The Struggle for Normality, 1960; (with D S Muzzey) Our Country's History, 1964; Wilson: Confusions and Crises 1915-1916, 1964; Woodrow Wilson Pequena Biografia, 1964; Historia Moderna dos Estados Unidos, 3 vols, 1965; (ed) The Papers of Woodrow Wilson 1966-1993; (ed) The First Presbyterian Church of Princeton: Two Centuries of History, 1967; (ed with R W Patrick), Writing Southern History: Essays in Historiography in Honor of Fletcher M Green, 1967; Woodrow Wilson: A Profile, 1968; The Impact of World War I, 1969; (ed with W M Leary), The Diplomacy of World Power: The United States 1889-1920, 1970; (with S Coben), The Democratic Heritage: A History of the United States, 1971; Woodrow Wilson: Revolution, War and Peace, 1979; (co-author), The American People, 1981; 1987; (ed) Woodrow Wilson and a Revolutionary World 1982; Trans and ed, The Deliberations of Four by Paul Mantoux, 2 vols 1992; (ed) Brother Woodrow, A Memoir of Woodrow Wilson by Stockton Axson, 1993. Address: 5322 Bermuda Village, Advance, NC 27006, USA.

LINKLETTER Arthur Gordon, b. 1912, American. Writer on Human Relations, Social Commentary/Phenomena, Autobiography, Memoirs, Personal, Humour, Satire; Television Entertainer; Head, Linkletter Enterprises. Publications: People Are Funny, 1947; Kids Say the Darndest Things, 1957; (with A Gordon) Secret World of Kids, 1959; (with D Jennings) Confessions of a Happy Man, 1960; Kids Still Say the Darndest Things, 1961; Kids Sure Rite Funny, 1962; Oops! 1967; Wish I'd Said That, 1968; Linkletter Down Under, 1968; Drugs at My Doorstep, 1973; How to be a Super Salesman, 1973; Women Are My Favorite People, 1973; Yes, You Can! 1979; I Didn't Do It Alone, 1980; Hobo on the Way to Heaven, 1981; Public Speaking for Private People, 1981; Old Age is Not for Sissies, 1988. Address: 8484 Wilshire Bl Ste 205, Beverly Hills, CA 90211, USA.

LINNEY Romulus, b. 21 Sept 1930, PA, USA. Writer; Teacher. m. Margaret Andrews, 17 Sept 1967, 2 d. Education: BA, Oberlin College, 1953; MFA, Yale University, 1958; D Litt, Oberlin College, 1994. Literary Appointments: University of NC, 1963; Manhattan School of Music, 1961-70; University of PA, 1969-; Columbia University. Publications include: The Sorrows of Frederick, 1966; Child Byron, 1977; Holy Ghosts, 1977; Heathen Valley, 1962; *2*, 1993; Jesus Tales, 1980; Sand Mountain, 1986; Three Poets, 1989. Contributions to: About O'Neill; Eugene O'Neil Newsletter; Reviews & Short Stories to Journals & Newspapers. Honours: NEA Fellowship, 1974;

Rockefeller Fellowship, 1985; Award in Literature, 1984; Fellowship of Southern Writers. Memberships: Dramatists Guild; Corporation of Yaddo. Literary Agent: Peter Hagan. Address: 35 Claremont Avenue 9N, New York, NY 10027, USA.

LINSCOTT Gillian, b. 27 Sept 1944, Windsor, England. Journalist; Writer. m. Tony Geraghty, 18 June 1988. Education: Somerville College, Oxford, 1963-66; Honours Degree, English Language and Literature, Oxford University, 1966. Publications: A Healthy Body, 1984; Murder Makes Tracks, 1985; Knightfall, 1986; A Whiff of Sulphur, 1987; Unknown Hand, 1988; Murder, I Presume, 1990; Sister Beneath the Sheet, 1991; Hanging on the Wire, 1992; Stage Fright, 1993; Widow's Peck, 1994. Memberships: Society of Authors; Crime Writers Association; Mystery Writers of America. Literary Agent: Anthony Goff, David Higham Associates, London. Address: c/o David Higham Associates, 5-8 Lower John Street, Golden Square, London W1R 4HA, England.

LIPMAN Elinor, b. 16 Oct 1950, Massachusetts, USA. Fiction Writer. m. Robert M Austin, 29 July 1975, 1 son. Education: AB, Simmons College, Boston, 1972. Appointments: Managing Editor, The Massachusetts Teacher, monthly magazine, and MTA Today, monthly tabloid, 1975-81; Correspondent, Patriot Ledge, West Edition, 1973-74; Staff Writer, Promotion Department, WGBH-TV, Boston, 1973. Publications: Into Love and Out Again, stories, 1987; Then She Found Me, 1990, The Way Men Act, 1972, both novels; Isabel's Bed, forthcoming 1995. Contributions to: Short stories in: Yankee; Playgirl; Ascent; Ladies Home Journal; Cosmopolitan; Self; New England; Living; Redstart; Wigwag. Honours: Distinguished story citations in Best American Short Stories, 1984, 1985; Massachusetts Artists Foundation, Finalist in Playwriting, 1983. Memberships: The Author's Guild; PEN; Literary Agent: Elizabeth Grossman. Address: 67 Winterberry Lane, Northampton, MA 01060, USA.

LIPSEY David Lawrence, b. 21 Apr 1948. Editor. m. Margaret Robson, 1982, 1 daughter. Education: 1st Class Honours, PPE, Magdalen College, Oxford, England. Appointments: Research Assistant, General and Municipal Workers' Union, 1970-72; Political Adviser to Anthony Crosland, MP, 1972-77 (Dept of the Environment, 1974-76; FCO 1976-77; Prime Minister's Staff, 10 Downing Street, 1977-79; Journalist, 1979-80; Editor, 1986-, New Society; Political Staff, 1980-83, Economics Editor 1982-86, Sunday Times. Publications: Labour and Land, 1972; Editor, with Dick Leonard, The Socialist Agenda: Crosland's Legacy, 1981; Making Government Work, 1982. Memberships: Secretary, Streatham Labour Party, 1970-72; Chairman, Fabian Society, 1981-82; Fabin Executive, 1986-; Executive Committee, Charter for Jobs, 1984-86. Address: 44 Drakefield Road, London SW17 8RP, England.

LIPTZIN Sol, b. 1901, American. Writer on Cultural/Ethnic Topics, Literature, Biography. Appointments: Professor, City University, New York City, 1923-63 and American College, Jerusalem, 1968-74. Publications: Shelley in Germany, 1924; The Weavers in German Literature, 1926; Lyric Pioneers of Modern Germany, 1928; (ed) Heine, 1928; (ed) From Vovalis to Nietzsche, 1929; Arthur Schnitzler, 1932; Historical Survey of German Literature, 1936; Richard Beer-Hofmann, 1936; Germany's Stepchildren, 1945; (trans and ed) Peretz, 1946; Eliakum Zunser, 1950; English Legend of Henrich Heine, 1954; Generation of Decision, 1958; Flowering of Yiddish Literature, 1963; The Jew in American Literature, 1966; Maturing of Yiddish Literature, 1970; History of Yiddish Literature, 1972; (co-author) Einfuhrung in die jiddische Literatur, 1978; Biblical Themes in World Literature, 1985. Address: 21 Washington Street, Jerusalem, Israel.

LISTER Raymond George, b. 1919, British. Writer on Arts, Craft. Appointments: Managing Director and Editor, Golden Head Press, Cambridge, 1952-72; Senior Research Fellow, 1975-85, Fellow 1985-86, now Emeritus, Wolfson College, Cambridge, LittD (Cantab). Publications: The British Miniature, 1951; Silhouettes, 1953; Thomas Gosse, 1953; The Muscovite Peacock: A Study of the Art of Leon Bakst, 1954; Decorated Porcelains of Simon Lissim, 1955; Decorative Wrought Ironwork in Great Britain, 1957; The Loyal Blacksmith, 1957; Decorative Cast Ironwork in Great Britain, 1960; The Craftsman Engineer, 1960; Edward Calvert, 1962; Great Craftsmen, 1962; The Miniature Defined, 1963; Beulah to Byzantium, 1965; How to Identify Old Maps and Globes, 1965; Victorian Narrative Paintings, 1966; The Craftsman in Metal, 1966; Great Works of Craftmanship, 1967; William Blake, 1968; Samuel Palmer and His Etchings, 1969; Hammer and Hand: An Essay on the Ironwork of Cambridge, 1969; British Romantic

Art, 1973; Samuel Palmer, 1974; (ed) The Letters of Samuel Palmer, 2 vols, 1974; Infernal Methods: A Study of William Blake's Art Techniques, 1975; Apollo's Bird, 1975; For Love of Leda, 1977; Great Images of British Printmaking, 1978; Samuel Palmer: A Vision Recaptured, 1978; Samuel Palmer in Palmer Country, 1980; George Richmond, 1981; Bergomask, 1982; There Was a Star Danced, 1983; Prints and Printmaking, 1984; Samuel Palmer and The Ancients, 1984; The Paintings of Samuel Palmer, 1985; The Paintings of William Blake, 1986; Catalogue Raisonné of the Works of Samuel Palmer, 1988; British Romantic Painting, 1989; A M St Léon's Stenochoreography (translation), 1992; With My Own Wings (memoirs), 1994. Address: 9 Sylvester Road, Cambridge CB3 9AF, England.

LISTER Richard Percival, b. 23 Nov 1914, Nottingham, England. Author; Painter. m. Ione Mary Wynniatt-Husey, 24 June 1985. Education: BSc, Manchester University. Publications: Novels: The Way Backwards, 1950; The Oyster and the Torpedo, 1951; Rebecca Redfern, 1953; The Rhyme and the Reason, 1963; The Questing Beast, 1965; One Short Summer, 1974; Poems: The Idle Demon, 1958; The Albatross, 1986; Travel: A Journey in Lapland, 1965; Turkey Observed, 1967; Biography: The Secret History of Genghis Khan, 1969; Marco Polo's Travels, 1976; The Travels of Herodotus, 1979. Contributions to: Punch; New Yorker; Atlantic Monthly; others. Honour: FRSL, 1970. Membership: International Pen. Address: Flat H, 81 Ledbury Road, London W11 2AG, England.

LITOWINSKY Olga Jean, b. 9 Feb 1936, Newark, New Jersey, USA. Writer; Editor. Education: BS Hons History, Columbia University, 1965. Publications: The High Voyage, 1977, 1991; Writing and Publishing Books for Children in the 1990s, 1992; The New York Kids Book, 1978. Contributions to: Atlas; Publishers Weekly; The Writer; Writers' Digest; SCBW Bulletin. Honours: The Christopher Award, 1979. Memberships: Society of Children's Book Writers and Illustrations. Literary Agent: Curtis Brown Ltd, New York. Address: c/o Simon and Schuster, 15 Columbus Circle, NY 10023, USA.

LITTELL Robert, b. 1935, American. Writer of Mystery/Crime/Suspense. Formerly an editor with Newsweek magazine, based in Eastern Europe and the Soviet Union. Publications: (with Richard Z Cheznoff and Edward Klein), If Israel Lost the War (non-fiction), 1969; The Czech Black Book, 1969; The Defection of A J Lewinter, 1973; Sweet Reason, 1974; The October Circle, 1976; Mother Russia, 1978; The Debriefing, 1979; The Amateur, 1981; The Sisters, 1985; The Revolutionist; The Visiting Professor, 1994. Address: c/o Simon and Schuster, 1230 Sixth Avenue, New York, NY 10020, USA.

LITTLE Charles Eugene, b. 1 Mar 1931, Los Angeles, California, USA. Writer. m. Ila Dawson. Education: BA with distinction in Creative Writing, Wesleyan University, Connecticut, 1955. Appointments: Editorial Director, Open Space Action Magazine, 1968-69; Editor-in-Chief, American Land Forum, 1980-86; Books Editor, Wilderness Magazine, 1987-; Consulting Editor, Johns Hopkins University Press, 1989-. Publications: Challenge of the Land, 1969; Space for Survival (with J G Mitchell), 1971; A Town is Saved ... (with photos by M Mort), 1973; The American Cropland Crisis (with w Fletcher, 1980; Green Fields Forever, 1987; Louis Bromfield at Malabar (editor), 1988; Greenways for America, 1990; Hope for the Land, 1992; Discover America: The Smithsonian Book of the National Parks, 1995; The Dying of the Trees, 1995. Contributions to: Magazines and journals including: American Forests; Amicus Journal; Country Journal; Garden; Garden Design; Harrowsmith; Journal of Soil and Water Conservation; Smithsonian; Air and Space; Utney Reader; Wilderness; Many others. Literary Agent: Max Gartenberg, New York City, New York, USA. Address: 33 Calle del Norte, Placitas, NM 87043, USA.

LITTLE Geraldine Clinton, b. 20 Sept 1925, Portstewart, Ireland. Adjunct College Professor of English; Writer. m. Robert Knox Little, 26 Sept 1953, 3 sons. Education: BA, English, Goddard College, Plainfield, 1971; Master's in English, Trenton State College, 1976. Publications: Heloise & Abelard: A Verse Play, 1989; A Well-Tuned Harp, 1988; Hakugai: Poem from a Concentration Camp, 1983; Star-Mapped, 1989; Beyond the Boxwood Comb, 1988; Seasons in Space, 1983; Contrasts in Keening: Ireland, The Spinalonga Poems; Forthcoming: Women: In the Mask and Beyond; More Light Larger Vision: Out of Darkness. Contributions to: Shenandoah; The Literary Review; Massachusetts Review; Confrontation; Seneca Review. Honours: 5 from The Poetry Society of America; AWP Anniversary Award, 1986; Pablo Neruda Award, Nimrod, 1989; 3 grants from New

Jersey Council on the Arts. Memberships: Poetry Society of America, former Vice President; Haiku Society of America, President; PEN. Address: 519 Jacksonville Road, Mt Holly, NJ 08060, USA.

LITTLE Jean, b. 2 Jan 1932, Taiwan. Children's Writer. Education: BA, Victoria College, University of Toronto, Canada, 1955. Publications: Mine for Keeps, 1962; Home From Far, 1965; Spring Begins in March, 1966; When the Pie was Opened, 1968; Take Wing, 1968; One to Grow On, 1969; Look Through My Window, 1970; Kate, 1971; From Anna, 1972; Stand In the Wind, 1975; Listen for the Singing, 1977; Mama's Going to Buy You a Mockingbird, 1984; Lost and Found, 1985; Different Dragons, 1986; Hey, World, Here I Am, 1986; Little By Little, 1987; Stars Came Out Within, 1990; Jess was the Brave One, 1991; Revenge of the Small Small, 1992. Honours: Little, Brown Canadian Children's Book Award, 1961; Vicky Metcalf Award, 1974; Canada Council Children's Book Award, 1977; Canadian Library Association Children's Book of the Year Award, 1984; Ruth Schwartz Award, 1984; Boston Globe Horn Book Honor Book, 1988; Shortlisted for the 1988 Governor General's Children's Literature Award, 1989. Memberships: Writers' Union of Canada; CANSCAIP (Canadian Society for Children's Authors, Illustrators & Performers); Canadian Authors' Association; PEN; IBBY. Address: 198 Glasgow North, Guelph, Ontario, N1H 4X2, Canada.

LITTLEDALE Freya Lota, b. New York City, USA. Writer. 1 son. Appointments: Adjunct Professor, English Dept, Writing for Children and Adolescents, Fairfield University, 1984, 1986-92. Publications: The Magic Fish, 1967; King Fox and Other Old Tales, 1971; The Boy Who Cried Wolf, 1975; The Elves and the Shoemaker, 1975; Seven at One Blow, 1976 (revised under the title, The Brave Little Tailor, 1990); The Snow Child, 1978; Pinocchio, adaptation, 1979; I Was Thinking (poems), 1979; The Magic Plum Tree, 1981; The Wizard of Oz, adaptation, 1982; Fankenstein, adaptation, 1983; Sleeping Beauty, 1984; The Little Mermaid, adaptation, 1986; The Farmer in the Soup, 1987; The Twelve Dancing Princesses, 1988; Peter and the North Wind, 1988; King Midas and the Golden Touch, 1989; Rip Van Winkle, adaptation, 1991; Editor, various books including: A Treasure Chest of Poetry, 1964; Andersen's Fairy Tales, 1966; Thirteen Ghostly Tales, 1966; Ghosts and Spirits of Many Lands, 1970; Strange Tales from Many Lands, 1975; Plays includes: Stop That Pancake, 1975; The King and Queen Who Wouldn't Speak, 1975; The Giant's Garden, 1975; The Big Race, 1976. Contributions to: Various journals and magazines. Honours: One of the Children's Books of the Years, Child Study Association of America, Ghosts and Spirits of Many Lands, 1970; Children's Book Council/IRA Liaison Committee, 70 Favourite Paperbacks, 1986; International Reading Association Children's Choice Selection, The Magic Fish, 1987; IRA Children's Choice Selection, The Farmer in the Soup, 1988. Memberships: PEN; Authors Guild; Society of Children's Book Writers. Literary Agent: Curtis Brown. Address: c/o Curtis Brown Ltd, Ten Astor Place, New York, NY 10003, USA.

LITVINOFF Emanuel, b. 1915, British. Writer of Novels/Short Stories, Plays/Screenplays, Poetry; Director, Contemporary Jewish Library, London, 1958-88; Founder, Jews in Eastern Europe, journal, London. Publications: Conscripts: A Symphonic Declaration, 1941; The Untried Soldier, 1942; A Crown for Cain, 1948; The Lost Europeans, 1959; The Man Next Door, 1968; Journey Through a Small Planet, 1972; Notes for a Survivor, 1973; A Death Out of Season, 1974; (ed) Soviet Anti-Semitism: The Paris Trial, 1974; Blood on the Snow, 1975; The Face of Terror, 1978; (ed) The Penguin Book of Jewish Short Stories, 1979; Falls the Shadow, 1983. Address: c/o David Higham Associates, 5-8 Lower John Street, London W1R 4HA, England.

LIU Shaotang, b. 29 Feb 1936, Beijing, China. Writer. m. Zeng Caimei, 1 May 1955, 1 son, 2 daughters. Education: Beijing University, 1954-55. Appointments: Managing Director, Beijing Writers' Association, 1980; Director, Chinese Writers' Association, 1985; President, Beijing Learned Society of Writing, 1986; Vice President, Chinese Learned Society of Popular Literature, 1987; Essays in Narrow Study, 1992; I am Such a Man, 1993. Publications: The Sound of Oars on the Grand Canal, 1955; Catkin Willow Flats, 1980; The Flower Street, 1980; The Budding Lotus, 1981; The Suburbs of Beijing, 1984; Bean Shed, Melon Hut, Drizzle, 1985; This Year, 1986; Story-telling by Jing Liuting, 1987; Flowers Within Reach, 1987; Rural Weddings, 1988; Happiness and Sorrow Beside the River, 1990; Vigin Pond, 1991; A Solitary Village, 1991; The River at Sunset, 1992; Man and Ghost, 1993; Trilogy of Farmer Niu Bangs, 1993; Crossing the River, 1993; Two Lius Beside a River, 1994; Countrywoman Jing Chai, 1994; Officaldom, 1994; 11 novels, 28 novelettes, 60 short stories, 4

collections of prose, 9 collections of poems. Contributions to: Many influential literary magazines in China. Honours: Winner, China Novelettes, 1980; Winner, China Stories, 1980; Elected, Advanced Worker of Beijing, 1982; Awarded by the Beijing Government, for success in literary creation, 1985. Memberships: PEN, China Centre; Chinese Writers' Association. Address: Beijing Writers' Association, Beijing, China.

LIU Wu-chi (Hsiao Hsia), b. 1907. Chinese-American. Writer on History, Literature, Philosophy, Biography; Emeritus Professor. Appointments: Visiting Professor of Chinese Language and Literature, 1951-53 and Senior Editor and Associate Director of Research, Human Relations Area Files, 1955-60, Yale University, New Haven, Connecticut; Professor of Chinese and Director of Chinese Language and Area Center, University of Pittsburgh, Pennsylvania, 1960-61; Professor, 1961-76, Chairman, 1962-67, Emeritus Professor, 1976-, Department of East Asian Languages and Culture, Indiana University, Bloomington; Chairman of Board, Tsing Hua Journal of Chinese Studies, 1978-87; President, International Association for Nan-she, Studies, 1989-. Publications: (co-ed) Readings in Contemporary Chinese Literature, 5 vols, 1953-58, revised edition, 3 vols 1964-68; A Short History of Confucian Philosophy, 1955; Confucius: His Life and Time, 1955; (ed as Hsiao Hsia) China: Its People, Its Society, Its Culture, 1960; An Introduction to Chinese Literature, 1966; Su Man-shu, 1972; (co-ed and trans) Sunflower Splendor: Three Thousand Years of Chinese Poetry, 1975; (co-ed) K'uei Yeh Chi, 1976. Membership: Hon President, China Association of Nan-she and Liu Ya-tzu Studies. Address: 2140, Santa Cruz Avenue, Menlo Park, CA 94025, USA.

LIVAS Harriet (Haris) Parker, b. 1 Apr 1936, USA. Journalist; Author; Professor. m. John Livas, 18 June 1962, dec 1976, 3 sons, 3 daughters. Education: BS, Syracuse University, 1958; MLitt, University of Pittsburgh, 1960; PhD, Pacific Western University, 1990. Appointments: English Department, University of Maryland Overseas Faculty, 1966-78; Foreign Correspondent, 1978-82; Director of Feature Service Athens News Agency, Greece, 1982-88; Director, Hellenic Features International, Ministry of the National Economy, Greece, 1988-90; Humberside Council, UK, 1991; Beverley College, 1991-94; University of Hull, 1993-95. Publications: Contemporary Greek Artists, 1992. Contributions to: All articles for international distribution: Athens News Agency, 1982-88; Hellenic Features International, 1988-90. Address: 19 Thurlow Avenue, Beverley HU17 7QJ, England.

LIVELY Penelope Margaret, b. 17 Mar 1933, Cairo, Egypt. Writer. m. 27 June 1957, 1 son, 1 daughter. Education: Honours Degree, Modern History, Oxford University, England. Publications: (Fiction) The Road to Lichfield, 1977; Nothing Missing But the Samovar, and other Stories, 1978; Treasures of Time, 1979; Judgement Day, 1980; Next to Nature, Art, 1982; Perfect Happiness, 1983; Corruption and Other Stories, 1984; According to Mark, 1984; Pack of Cards: Stories, 1978-86; Moon Tiger, 1986, 1987; Passing On, 1989; City of the Mind, 1991; Cleopatra's Sister, 1993; (Non-fiction), The Presence of the Past: An Introduction to Landscape History, 1976; (Children's Books), Astercote, 1970; The Whispering Knights, 1971; The Driftway, 1972; Going Back, 1973; The Ghost of Thomas Kempe, 1974; A Stitch in Time, 1976; The Voyage of QV66, 1978; The Revenge of Samuel Stokes, 1981; The Stained Glass Window, 1976; Boy Without a Name, 1975; Fanny's Sister, 1976; Fanny and the Monsters, 1978; Fanny and the Battle of Potter's Piece, 1980; Uninvited Ghosts and Other Stories, 1984; Dragon Trouble, Debbie and the Little Devil, 1984; A House Inside Out, 1987; Passing On, 1989; City of the Mind, 1991. Contributions include: Numerous journals and magazines including: Quarto; Good Housekeeping; Vogue; Options; Over 21. Honours include: OBE, 1989; Treasures of Time, Arts Council National Book Award; Nothing Missing But the Samovar Southern Arts Literature Prize; Shortlisted for the Booker Prize: The Road to Lichfield, and According to Mark; Carnegie Medal, The Ghost of Thomas Kempe; A Stitch in Time, Whitbread Award; Moon Tiger, Booker Prize. Address: c/o Murray Pollinger, 222 Old Brompton Road, London SW5 0B2, England.

LIVERSAGE Toni, b. 31 Jan 1935, Hellerup, Denmark. Writer. m. 19 May 1962, 1 son, 1 daughter. Education: Magister artium in Slavonic Languages, Copenhagen University, Denmark, 1965. Publications: 10 books including: Women and History, 1972; Mary and the Revolution, 1974; Father and Daughters, 1977; From Gandhi to Greenham Common, 1987; The Great Goddess, 1990. Contributions to: Numerous articles about women's history, grass roots movements and other topics to magazines and journals. Honours: The Thit Jensen Award for Women's Literature, 1989. Membership: Danish Writers Union (International Committee Secretary). Address: Morlenesvej 26, 2840 Holte, Denmark.

LIVERSIDGE (Henry) Douglas, b. 12 Mar 1913, Swinton, Yorkshire, England. Journalist/Author. m. Cosmina Pistola, 25 Sept 1954, Holburn, London, England, 1 daughter. Publications include: White Horizon, 1951; The Last Continent, 1958; The Third Front, 1960; The Whale Killers, 1963; Saint Francis of Assisi, 1968; Peter the Great, 1968; Lenin, 1969; Joseph Stalin, 1969; Saint Ignatius of Loyola, 1970; The White World, 1972; Queen Elizabeth II, 1974; Prince Charles, 1975; Prince Phillip, 1976; Queen Elizabeth the Queen Mother, 1977; The Mountbattens, 1978. Contributions to: Numerous journals and newspapers. Address: 56 Love Lane, Pinner, Middlesex HA5 3EX, England.

LIVESAY Dorothy, b, 12 Oct 1909, Winnipeg, Manitoba, Canada. Teacher and Social Worker; Editor; Journalist; Broadcaster; University Professor. Education: BA, Modern Languages, University of Toronto, 1931; Diplome d'Etudes Superieures, Sorbonne, 1932; School of Social Work, University of Toronto, 1934; MEd, UBC, 1935. Publications include: The Unquiet Bed, 1968; Plainsongs, 1971; Collected Poems: The Two Seaons, 1972; Ice Age, 1975; Beginnings: A Winnipeg Childhood, 1976; Right Hand, Left Hand, 1977; The Woman I Am, 1978; The Raw Edges, 1981; The Phases of Love, 1983; Feeling the Worlds, 1985; The Self-Completing Tree: Selected Poems, 1986; The Husband: a Novella, 1990. Honours: Governor General's Award for Poetry, 1944, 1947; Lorne Pierce Medal, Royal Society of Canada, 1947; Queen's Canada Medal, 1977; Person's Case Award for the Status of Women, 1984; Order of Canada, 1987; Order of British Columbia, 1992. Memberships: Founder/editor of CVII; Founding Member, League of Canadian Poets, Amnesty International (Canada), and the Committee for an Independent Canada. Address: 647 Niagara Street, Victoria, British Columbia, V8V 1J1, Canada.

LIVINGS Henry, b. 20 Sept 1929, Prestwich, Lancashire, England. Writer of Short Stories, Plays/Screenplays, History. Education: Liverpool University, 1945-47. Publications: Stop it Whoever You Are, 1961; Nil Caborundum, 1963; Kelly's Eye and Other Plays, 1965; Eh? 1965; The Little Mrs Foster Show, 1967; Good Grief! 1968; Honour and Offer, 1969; The Ffinest Ffamily in the Land, 1970; Pongo Plays 1-6, 1971; The Jockey Drives Late Nights, 1972, 1976; Cinderella, 1976; Six More Pongo Plays, 1974; Jonah, 1975; That the Medals and the Baton Be Put in View: The Story of a Village Band 1875-1975, 1975; Pennine Tales, 1983; Flying Eggs and Things: More Pennine Tales, 1986; The Rough Side of the Boards, 1994; The Public, (translation, in Methuen Lorca Plays 3), 1994. Address: 49 Grains Road, Delph, Oldham OL3 5DS, England.

LIVINGSTON Myra Cohn, b. 17 Aug 1926, Omaha, Nebraska, USA. Writer. m. Richard Roland Livingston, 14 Apr 1952, dec 1990, 2 sons, 1 daughter. Education: BA, Sarah Lawrence College, 1948. Appointments: Poet-in-Residence, Beverly Hills Unified School District, 1966-84; Senior Instructor, University of California, Los Angeles, 1972-; Whispers and Other Poems,1958; The Malibu and Other Poems, 1972; No Way of Knowing: Dallas Poems, 1980; The Child as Poet: Myth of Reality, 1984; Climb into the Bell Tower, essays on poetry, 1990; 75 other books. Contributions to: The Horn Book; Top of the News; Childhood Education; Psychology Today; School Library Journal; The Reading Teacher; The Advocate; The New Advocate; Cricket Magazine; Many others. Literary Agent: Dorothy Markinko, McIntosh and Otis, 310 Madison Avenue, New York, NY 10017, USA. Address: 9308 Readcrest Drive, Beverly Hills, CA 90210, USA.

LIVINGSTONE Douglas (James), b. 5 May 1932, Kuala Lumpur, Malaya. South African Citizen. Poet. Education: Kearney College, Natal; University of Natal. Publications: The Skull in the Mud, 1960; Sjambok and Other Poems from Africa, 1964; Poems, 1968; Eyes Closed Against the Sun, 1970; The Sea My Winding Sheet and Other Poems, 1971; A Rosary of Bone, 1975-83; The Anvil's Undertone, 1978; Selected Poems, 1984; A Littoral Zone, 1991; Plays: A Rhino for the Boardroom, 1974; The Semblance of the Real, 1976. Honours include: D Litt, University of Natal, 1982; Rhodes University, 1990. Address: c/o Council of Scientific and Industrial Research, PO Box 17001, Congella, 4013 Natal, South Africa.

LLEWELLEN John. See: **JONES-EVANS Eric.**

LLEWELLYN Sam, b. 2 Aug 1948, Isles of Scilly. Author. m. Karen Wallace, 15 Feb 1975, 2 sons. Education: St Catherine's College, Oxford; BA (Hons), Oxford University. Appointments: Editor, Picador, 1973-76; Senior Editor, McClelland and Stewart, 1976-79; President, Publisher, Arch Books, 1982-; Captain, SY Hope, 1993-. Publications: Hell Bay, 1980; The Worst Journey in the Midlands, 1983; Dead Reckoning, 1987; Blood Orange, 1988; Death Roll, 1989; Pig in the Middle, 1989; Deadeye, 1990; Blood Knot, 1991; Riptide, 1992; Clawhammer, 1993; Maelstrom, 1994; The Rope School, 1994; The Magic Boathouse, 1994. Contributions to: Occasionally to: Country Living; The Telegraph; Esquire. Memberships: Society of Authors; Former Member, Crime Writers Association; The Academy. Literary Agent: Andrew Hewson, John Johnson, London, England. Address: c/o John Johnson, Clerkenwell House, Clerkenwell Green, London EC1, England.

LLOYD Geoffrey Ernest Richard, b. 25 Jan 1933. Professor. m. Janet Elizabeth Lloyd, 1956, 3 sons. Education: Charterhouse 1946-51; King's College, Cambridge, 1951-54, BA 1954, MA 1958, PhD 1958. Appointments: Fellow, King's College, Cambridge, 1957; Honorary Fellow, 1990; Cambridge University: Assistant Lecturer in Classics 1965-67, Lecturer in Classics 1967-74, Reader in Ancient Philosophy and Science 1974-83, Senior Tutor, King's College, Cambridge 1969-73; Bonsall Professor, Stanford University, 1981; Fellow, Japan Society for the Promotion of Science, 1981; Fellow, The British Academy, 1983-; Sather Professor, University of California at Berkeley, 1984; Visiting Professor, Peking University and Academy of Sciences, Beijing, 1987; A D Professor at Large, Cornell, 1990; Professor of Ancient Philosophy and Science, Cambridge University, 1983-, Master, Darwin College, Cambridge, 1989-; Chairman, East Asian History of Science Trust, 1992-. Publications include: Books include: Polarity and Analogy, 1966, translations in Spanish 1987, Italian 1992; Early Greek Science: Thales to Aristotle, 1970, translations: Spanish 1973, French 1974, Italian 1978, Japanese forthcoming; Greek Science After Aristotle, 1973, translations: Italian 1978, French 1990; Magic, Reason and Experience, 1979, translations: Italian 1978, French 1990; Science, Folklore and Ideology, 1983, translations: Italian 1987, Spanish forthcoming; Science and Morality in Greco-Roman Antiquity (Inaugural Lecture) 1985; The Revolutions of Wisdom, 1987, Italian forthcoming; Demystifying Mentalities, 1990 Italian 1991, French 1994 and Spanish forthcoming; Methods and Problems in Greek Science, 1991, translation Italian 1993, Rumanian, Portuguese and Greek forthcoming; Editor: Hippocratic Writings (introduction by GERL) 1978; Co-editor with G E L Owen, Aristotle On Mind and the Senses (Proceedings of the Seventh Symposium Aristotelicum) Cambridge Classical Studies, 1978. Contributions to: Numerous articles and books. Honour: Sarton Medal, 1987. Address: 2 Prospect Row, Cambridge CB1 1DU, England.

LLOYD John Nicol Fortune, b. 15 Apr 1946. Editor. m. 1) Judith Ferguson, 1974, div 1979, 2) Marcia Levy, 1983. Education: MA, Honours, Edinburgh University. Appointments: Editor, Time Out, 1972-73; Reporter, London Programme, 1974-76; Producer, Weekend World, 1976-77; Industrial Reporter, Labour Correspondent, Industrial and Labour Editor, Financial Times, 1977-86; Editor, New Statesman, 1986-87; Financial Times, 1987-. Publications: (with Ian Benson) The Politics of Industrial Change, 1982; (with Martin Adeney) The Miner's Strike: Loss Without Limit, 1986. Contributed to: Counterblasts, 1989. Honours: Journalist of the Year, Granada Awards, 1984; Specialist Writer of the Year, IPC Awards, 1985. Address: Flat 8, 14 Kutuzovsky Prospekt, Moscow, Russia.

LLOYD Kathleen Annie (Kathleen Conlon), b. 4 Jan 1943, Southport, England. Writer. m. Frank Lloyd, 3 Aug 1962, div, 1 son. Education: BA (Hons), King's College, Durham University. Publications: Apollo's Summer Look, 1968; Tomorrow's Fortune, 1971; My Father's House, 1972; A Twisted Skein, 1975; A Move in the Game, 1979; A Forgotten Season, 1980; Consequences, 1981; The Best of Friends, 1984; Face Values, 1985; Distant Relations, 1989; Unfinished Business, 1990. Contributions to: Atlantic Review; Cosmopolitan; Woman's Journal; Woman; Woman's Own. Memberships: Society of Authors. Literary Agent: Lavinia Trevor. Address: 26A Brighton Road, Birkdale, Southport PR8 4DD, England.

LLOYD Levannah. See: **PETERS Maureen.**

LLOYD Trevor Owen, b. 30 July 1934, London, England. University Teacher. Education: BA, Merton College, Oxford, 1956; MA, DPhil, Nuffield College, Oxford, 1959. Appointments: Lecturer 1959,

Professor 1973, Department of History, University of Toronto. Publications: Canada in World Affairs 1957-59, 1968; The General Election 1880, 1968; Suffragettes International, 1971; The Growth of Parliamentary Democracy in Britain, 1973; The British Empire 1558-1983, 1984; Empire, Welfare State, Europe: English History 1906-1992, 1993. Contributions to: Various journals. Honours: Guggenheim Fellowship, 1978-79. Memberships: William Morris Society; Victorian Studies Association of Ontario. Address: Department of History, University of Toronto, Toronto M5S 1A1, Canada.

LLOYD-JONES (Peter) Hugh (Jefferd) (Sir), b. 21 Sept 1922, St Peter Port, Jersey, Channel Islands. Classical Scholar. m. 1) Frances Hedley, 1953, div 1981, 2 sons, 1 daughter, 2) Mary R Lefkowitz, 1982. Education: Westminister School; Christ Church, Oxford; MA (Oxon), 1947. Publications: The Justice of Zeus, 1971, 2nd edition 1983; Blood for the Ghosts, 1982; Supplementum Hellenisticum (with P J Parsons), 1983; Sophoclis Fabulae (with N G Wilson), 1990; Sophoclea (with N G Wilson), 1990; Academic Papers (2 vols), 1990; Greek in a Cold Climate, 1991. Contributions to: Numerous. Honours: Honorary DHL, Chicago, 1970; Honorary PhD, Tel Aviv, 1984; Knight Bachelor, 1989. Memberships: Fellow, British Academy; Corresponding Fellow, Academy of Athens; American Academy of Arts and Sciences; American Philosophical Society; Rheinisch-Westfalische Akademie; Bagerische Akademie der Wissenschaften; Accademia di Lettere, Archeologia e Belle Arti, Naples. Address: 15 West Riding, Wellesley, MA 02181, USA.

LOADES David Michael, b. 19 Jan 1934. Academic. m. Judith Anne Atkins, 18 Apr 1987. Education: Perse School for Boys, Cambridge, England, 1945-53; Emmanuel College, Cambridge, 1955-61, BA 1958, MA, PhD 1961, LittD 1981. Appointments: Lecturer in Political Science, University of St Andrews, 1961-63; Lecturer in History, University of Durham, 1963-70; Senior Lecturer, 1970-77, Reader 1977-80, Professor of History, University College of North Wales, Bangor, 1980-. Publications include: Two Tudor Conspiracies, 1965; The Oxford Martyrs, 1970; The Reign of Mary Tudor, 1979; The Tudor Court, 1986; Mary Tudor, a life, 1989; The Tudor Navy, 1992; The Papers of George Wyatt (ed), 1968; The End of Strife (ed) 1984; Faith and Identity (ed), 1990. Contributions to: Journal of Ecclestical History and others. Memberships: Fellow, Royal Historical Society; Fellow, Society of Antiquaries of London. Address: Department of History, University College of North Wales, Bangor, Gwynedd LL57 2DG, Wales.

LOCHHEAD Douglas Grant, b. 25 Mar 1922, Guelph, Ontario, Canada. Writer. m. Jean St Clair Beckwith, 17 Sept 1949, 2 daughters. Education: BA, McGill University, 1943; MA, University of Toronto, 1947; BLS, McGill University, 1951. Appointments: Writer-in-Residence, Mount Allison University, 1987-90; President, Goose Lane Editions, 1989-. Publications: The Heart is Fire, 1959; It is All Around, 1960; Poet Talking, 1964; A & B & C &, poems, 1969; Millwood Road Poems, 1970; Prayers in a Field, 1974; The Full Furnace, 1976; High Marsh Road, 1980; Tiger in the Skull, selected poems, 1986; Dykelands, 1989; Upper Cape Poems, 1989; Black Festival, poems, 1992; Homage to Henry Alline & Other Poems, 1992. Contributions to: Canadian literary journals. Honours: Golden Dog Award, 1974; Fellow, Royal Society of Canada, 1976; DLitt, St Mary's University, 1987; LLD, Dalhousie University, 1987. Memberships: League of Canadian Poets, Vice Chairman 1968-72, Life Member; President, Bibliographical Society of Canada. Address: PO Box 1108, Sackville, New Brunswick, E0A 3CO, Canada.

LOCHHEAD Liz, b. 1947, British. Writer of Plays, Screenplays, Poetry; Art Teacher, Bishopsbriggs High School, Glasgow. Publications: Memo for Spring (poetry) 1972; Now and Then (screenplay), 1972; The Grimm Sisters (poetry), 1981; Blood and Ice (play), 1982; Dreaming Frankenstein, and Collected Poems, 1984; Silver Service (play), 1984; True Confessions and New Cliches, 1985. Address: c/o Salamander Press, 18 Anley Road, London W14 0BY, England.

LOCKE Elsie Violet, b. 17 Aug 1912, New Zealand. Writer. m. John Gibson Locke, 7 Nov 1941, 2 sons, 2 daughters. Education: BA, Auckland University, 1933; Hon DLitt, University of Canterbury, Christchurch, 1987. Publications: The Runaway Settlers, 1965; The End of the Harbour, 1968; The Boy with the Snowgrass Hair, 1976; Student at the Gates, 1981; The Kauri and the Willow, 1984; Journey under Warning, 1984; A Canoe in the Mist, 1984; Two Peoples One Land, 1988; Peace People, 1992. Contributions to: New Zealand

School Journal among others. Honours: Katherine Mansfield Award for Non-Fiction, essay, 1959; Honorary DLitt, University of Canterbury N2, 1987; Children's Literature Association of New Zealand award for distinguished services to children's literature, 1992. Memberships: Childrens Literature Association; Children's Book Foundation; NZ Society of Authors (incorporating PEN). Address: 392 Oxford Tce, Christchurch 1, New Zealand.

LOCKE Hubert Gaylord, b. 30 Apr 1934, Detroit, Michigan, USA. University Professor. 2 daughters. Education: BA, Latin and Greek, Wayne University, 1955; BD, New Testament Studies, University of Chicago, 1959; MA, Comparative Literature, University of Michigan, 1961. Literary Appointments: Associate Editor, Journal of Holocaust: Genocide Studies, 1989; Editorial Board, Studies in the Shoah, 1990. Publications: Detroit Riot of 1967; Care and Feeding of White Liberals, 1970; German Church Struggle and the Holocaust (with F Littell), 1974; Church Confronts and the Nazis, 1984; Exile in the Fatherland, 1986. Honours: Doctor of Divinity (hc), Payne Theological Seminary, 1967; Doctor of Humane Letters (hc), University of Akron, 1970; Doctor of Divinity (hc), Chicago Theological Seminary, 1971; Doctor of Humane Letters, University of Nebraska, 1992. Memberships: National Academy of Public Administration; Society for Values in Higher Education. Address: 7717 57th Avenue NE, Seattle, WA 98115, USA.

LOCKE Ralph P, b. 9 Mar 1949, Boston, Massachusetts, USA. Teacher; Musicologist; Author. Education: BA, cum laude Music, Harvard University, 1970; MA 1974, PhD 1980 in History & Theory of Music, University of Chicago. Literary Appointments: Music Critic, Boston After Dark and the Boston Phoenix, 1967-70; Co-Editor, Journal of Musicological Research; Senior Editor, Eastman Studies in Music. Publications: Music, Musicians, and the Saint-Simonians, 1986; Chapters in: Mendelssohn and Schumann, 1984; Music in Paris in the 1830s, 1987; Les Saint-Simoniens et L'Orient, 1989; Music and Society: The Early Romantic Era, 1991; Articles in: New Grove Dictionary of Music, 1980; New Harvard Dictionary of Music, 1986; Royal Opera (Covent Garden) Programme Book, 1991. Contributions to: 19th-Century Music; Cambridge Opera Journal; Journal of the American Musicological Society; Opera Quarterly; Opera News; Revue de Musicologie; Fontes artis musicae; Fenway Court. Honours: Music Library Association, Best Article, 1980; Galler Dissertation Prize, 1981; ASCAP - Deems Taylor Award, 1992; Grants from American Council of Learned Societies, National Endowment for the Humanities, Andrew Mellon Foundation. Memberships: Board of Directors, American Musicological Society; Board Member, Institute for Gounod Studies. Address: Department of Musicology, 26 Gibbs Street, Rochester, NY 14604-2599, USA.

LOCKE Robert Howard (Clayton Bess), b. 30 Dec 1944, Vallejo, California, USA. Librarian; Playwright; Author. Education: BA Speech Arts, California State University, Chico, 1965; MA Drama, San Francisco State University, 1967; MS Library Science, Simmons College, Boston, 1973. Publications: Written under the pen name Clayton Bess: Story for a Black Night, 1982; The Truth About the Moon, 1984; Big Man and the Burn-Out, 1985; Tracks, 1986; The Mayday Rampage, 1993; Plays: The Dolly; Play; Rose Jewel and Harmony; On Daddy's Birthday; Murder and Edna Redrum; Premiere. Honours: Best First Novel for Story for a Black Night, Commonwealth Club of California, 1982; Tracks, A Best Book for Young Adults, American Library Association. Address: c/o Lookout Press, PO Box 19131, Sacramento, CA 95819, USA.

LOCKERBIE D(onald) Bruce, b. 1935, American. Writer of Plays/Screenplays, Education, Literature, Theology/Religion. Scholar-in-Residence, Stony Brook School, New York, 1957-91; Visiting Consultant at American Schools in Asia and Africa, 1974; Visiting Lecturer/Consultant to American universities. Publications: Billy Sunday, 1965; Patriarchs and Prophets, 1969; Hawthorne, 1970; Melville, 1970; Twain, 1970; Major American Authors, 1970; (with L Westdahl), Success in Writing, 1970; Purposeful Writing, 1972; The Way They Should Go, 1972; The Liberating Word, 1974; The Cosmic Center: The Apostles' Creed, 1977; A Man under Orders: Lt Gen William K Harrison, 1979; Who Educates Your Child? 1980; The Timeless Moment, 1980; Asking Questions, 1980; Fatherlove, 1981; In Peril on the Sea, 1984; The Christian, The Arts and Truth, 1985; Thinking and Acting Like a Christian, 1989; Take Heart (with L Lockerbie), 1990; College: Getting In and Staying In (with D Fonseca), 1990. Address: PO Box 26, Stony Brook, NY 11790, USA.

LOCKLIN Gerald Ivan, b. 1941, American. Writer of novels/short stories, poetry. Professor of English, California State University - Long Beach, 1965-. Appointments: Instructor, California State University, Los Angeles, 1964-65. Publications: (with Ronald Koertge and Charles Stetler), Tarzan and Shane Meet the Toad (poetry); Poop and Other Poems, 1972; Son of Poop, 1973; Locked In (short stories), 1973; Toad's Europe, 1973; The Toad Poems, 1974; The Chase: A Novel, 1976; The Criminal Mentality (poems), 1976; The Four-Day Work Week and Other Stories, 1977; Toad's Sabbatical (poetry), 1978; Frisco Epic (poetry), 1978; Pronouncing Borges (poetry), 1978; The Cure: A Novel for Spreadreaders, 1979; A Weekend in Canada (short stories), 1979; Two Summer Sequences (poetry and prose), 1979; Two Weeks on Mr Stanford's Farm (poetry), 1980; The Last Toad (poetry), 1980; Two for the Seesaw and One for the Road (poetry), 1980; Scenes from Second Adolescence and Other Poems, 1981; By Land, Sea and Air (poetry), 1982; Why Turn a Perfectly Good Toad into a Prince? (poems and story), 1984; The Case of the Missing Blue Volkswagen (novella), 1985; Gringo and Other Poems, 1985; (with Ray Zepeda), We Love LA: The Olympic Boxing Poems, 1985; The Clubford Midget Shoots Pool (poems), 1986; The English Mini-Tour (poems), 1987; A Constituency of Dunces, 1988; Return to Ronnie Scott's, 1988; Toad Comes to Cleveland, 1988; On the Rack, 1988; Maybe the Confused Me with Ezra Pound, 1989; Lost and Found (poems), 1989; Toad on the Half-Shell, 1989; The Gold Rush, 1989; The Rochester Trip, 1990; The Conference, 1990. Address: English Department, California State University - Long Beach, Long Beach, CA 90840, USA.

LOCKRIDGE Ernest Hugh, b. 28 Nov 1938, USA. Novelist. m. Laurel Richardson, 12 Dec 1981, 2 sons, 3 daughters. Education: BA Indiana 1t, 1960; MA, Yale University, 1961; PhD, 1964. Appointments: Professor, Yale, 1963-71; Ohio State, 1971-; Visiting Writer, Eastern Kentucky University, 1977. Publications: Novels: Prince Elmo's Fire, 1974; Flying Elbows, 1975; Hartspring Blows His Mind, 1968; Criticism: 20th Century Studies of the Great Gatsby, 1968. Contributions to: Sewanee Review; Yale Review; The Ohio Journal; Journal of Literary Technique. Honours: Book of the month club selection, 1974; Distinguished Teaching Award, the Ohio State University, 1985. Membership: Phi Beta Kappa. Address: 143 W South St, Worthington, OH 43085, USA.

LODGE David John, b. 28 Jan 1935. Honorary Professor of Modern English Literature. m. Mary Frances Jacob, 1959, 2 sons, 1 daughter. Education: BA Honours, MA (London); PhD, Birmingham; National Service, RAC, 1955-57. Appointments: British Council, London, 1959-60; Assistant Lecturer 1960-62, Lecturer 1963-71, Senior Lecturer 1971-73, Reader English 1973-76, University of Birmingham; Harkness Commonwealth Fellow, 1964-65; Visiting Associate Professor, University of California, Berkeley, 1969; Henfield Writing Fellow, University of East Anglia, 1977. Publications: (Novels) The Picturegoers, 1960; Ginger, You're Barmy, 1962; The British Museum is Falling Down, 1965; Out of the Shelter, 1970, revised edition 1985; Changing Places, 1975; How Far Can You Go? 1980; Small World, 1984; Nice Work, 1988; Paradise News, 1991; (Criticism) Language of Fiction, 1966; The Novelist at the Crossroads, 1971; The Modes of Modern Writing, 1977; Working with Structuralism, 1981; Write On, 1986; After Bakhtin (essays), 1990; The Art of Fiction, 1992. Honours: Yorkshire Post Fiction Prize, 1975; Hawthornden Prize, 1976; Whitbread Book of the Year Award, 1980; Sunday Express Book of the Year Award, 1988. Address: Department of English, University of Birmingham B15 2TT, England.

LOEWE Michael Arthur Nathan, b. 2 Nov 1922, Oxford, England. University Lecturer (retired). Education: Magdalen College, Oxford, 1941; BA Hons (London) 1951, PhD 1962, University of London; MA (Cambridge) 1963. Publications: Records of Han Administration, 1967; Everyday Life in Early Imperial China, 1968, 2nd edition 1988; Crisis and Conflict in Han China, 1974; Ways to Paradise: The Chinese Quest for Immortality, 1979; Chinese Ideas of Life and Death, 1982; The Cambridge History of China, vol 1 1986; The Pride that was China, 1990; Early Chinese Texts, a Biographical Guide, 1993; Mythology and Monarchy in Han China, 1994. Contributions to: T'oung Pao; Bulletin of Museum of Far Eastern Antiquities; Asia Major; Bulletin of School of Oriental and African Studies. Membership: Fellow, Society of Antiquaries, 1972; Fellow, Clare Hall, 1963-90. Address: Willow House, Grantchester, Cambridge CB3 9NF, England.

LOGAN Ford. See: **NEWTON D(wight) B(ennett).**

LOGAN Jake. See: **RIFKIN Shepard.**

LOGAN Mark. See: **NICOLE Christopher Robin.**

LOGAN William, b, 1950. Publications: Moorhen, 1984; Difficulty: Poems, 1985; Sullen Weedy Lakes, 1988. Honour: Lavan Younger Poets Award, 1989.

LOGUE Christopher (Count Palmiro Vicarion), b. 1926, British. Plays/Screenplays, Poetry, Documentaries/Reportage, Translations. Contributor to Private Eye, London. Publications: Wand and Quadrant, 1953; Devil, Maggot, and Son, 1955; (trans) The Man Who Told His Love: Twenty Poems Based on Pablo Neruda's Los Cantoos d'Amores, 1958; The Trial of Cob and Leach: A News Play, 1959; Songs, 1959; Trials by Logue (Antigonne and Cob and Leach), 1960; Songs from the Lily-White Boys, 1960; Patrocleia, 1962; True Stories, 1966; Pax, 1967; The Girls, 1969; New Numbers, 1969; Twelve Cards, 1972; Savage Messiah (screenplay), 1972; True Stories from Private Eye, 1973; Puss-in-Boots Pop-up, 1976; Ratsmagic, 1976; The Crocodile, 1976; Abecedary, 1977; (ed) The Children's Book of Comic Verse, 1978; The Magic Circus (juvenile), 1979; Bumper Book of True Stories, 1980; Ode to Dodo: Poems, 1953-1978, 1981; War Music: An Account of Books 16-19 of the Iliad, 1981; Kings: An Account of Books 1-2 of the Iliad, 1992; (ed) London in Verse, 1982; (ed) Sweet and Sour: An Anthology of Comic Verse, 1983; (ed) The Oxford Books of Pseuds, 1983; (ed) The Children's Book of Children's Rhymes, 1987. Address: 41 Camberwell Grove, London SE5 8JA, England.

LOGUE John, b. 7 July 1933, Bay Minette, AL, USA. Writer. m. Helen Roberst, 15 Aug 1959, 3 sons. Education: BA, Auburn University, 1955. Appointments: Police Reporter, Montgomery Adviser, 1955; Reporter, United Press, 1957; Sportswriter, Atlanta Journal, 1957-67; Feature Writer, Southern Press Corporation, Birmingham, 1967-68; Managing Editor 1968-73, Creative Editor 1988-, Southern Living Magazine; Editor in Chief of Oxmoor House, 1973-. Publications: Follow the Leader, 1979; Replay: Murder, 1983; Flawless Execution, 1986; Boats Against the Current, 1987. Honours: Edgar Allen Poe Award nomination for Best First Novel from Mystery Writers of America, 1979. Memberships: PEN; Mystery Writers of America. Address: 2737 11th Avenue South, Birmingham, AL 35205, USA.

LOMAX Alan, b. 31 Jan 1915, Austin, TX, USA. Writer; Folklorist; Anthropologist. m. E Harold, 1937, 1 d. Education: Harvard College, 1932-33; BA, University of TX, 1936; Columbia University, 1939; Cantometrics, UCLA Media Division, 1981. Publications: Mister Jelly Roll, 1950; The Folksongs of North America, 1960; Hard Hitting Songs for Hard Hit People, 1967; Folksong Style and Culture, 1968; The Land Where the Blues Began, 1993. Contributions to: World of Music; Science. Honours: National Medal of Arts Award, 1986; National Book Critics Circle Award, 1993. Memberships: Am Anthropoligical Association; Fellow, American Folklore Society; American Association for Advancement of Science. Address: Association for Cultural Equity, 450 w 41st Str, 6th Floor, New York, NY 10036, USA.

LOMAX Marion, b. 20 Oct 1953, Newcastle-upon-Tyne, England. Poet; Lecturer. m. Michael Lomax, 29 Aug 1974. Education: BA (Hons), University of Kent, England, 1979; DPhil, University of York, England, 1983. Appointments: Creative Writing Fellow, University of Reading, 1987-88; Lecturer, Senior Lecturer in English, St Mary's College, Strawberry Hill, Middlesex, 1987-; Writer-in-Residence, Cheltenham Festival of Literature, Oct 1990. Publications: Stage Images and Traditions: Shakespeare to Ford, 1987; The Peepshow Girl, poems, 1989; Editor: Time Present and Past: Poets at the University of Kent 1965-1985, 1985; Four Plays of John Ford, in press. Contributions to: Over 60 poems to anthologies, magazines and journals including: Times Literary Supplement; London Magazine; Poetry Review; Writing Women; Reviews to: Times Literary Supplement; Poetry Wales; Modern Language Review. Honours: E C Gregory Award, Society of Authors, 1981; 1st Prize, Cheltenham Festival Poetry Competition, 1981; 3rd Place, Southern Arts Literature Award, 1992. Memberships: Poetry Society. Address: c/o Bloodaxe Books, England.

LOMBINO Salvatore A (Curt Cannon, Hunt Collins, Ezra Hannon, Evan Hunter, Richard Marsten, Ed McBain), b. 15 Oct 1916, New York, USA. Writer, Editor, Cooper Union and Hunter College. m. 1) Anita Melnick, 1949, 3 sons, 2) Mary Vann Finley, 1973, 1 step daughter. Publications: The Blackboard Jungle, 1954; Second Ending, 1956; Strangers When We Meet, 1958 (screenplay 1959); A Matter of Conviction, 1959; Mother and Daughters, 1961; The Birds (screenplay), 1962; Happy New Year Herbie, 1963; Buddwing, 1964; The Easter Man (play), 1964; The Paper Dragon, 1966; A Horse's

Head, 1967; Last Summer, 1968; Sons, 1969; The Conjurer (play), 1969; Nobody Knew They Were There, 1971; Every Little Crook and Nanny, 1972; The Easter Man, 1972; Come Winter, 1973; Streets of Gold, 1974; The Chisholms, 1976; Me and Mr Stenner, 1976; Love, Dad, 1981; 87th Precinct Mysteries, Far From the Sea, 1983; Lizzie, 1984; (under pseudonym Ed McBain): Cop Hater, 1956; The Mugger, 1956; The Pusher, 1956; The Con Man, 1957; Killer's Choice, 1957; Killer's Payoff, 1958; Lady Killer, 1958; Killer's Wedge, 1959; 'Til Death, 1959; King's Ransom, 1959; Give the Boys a Great Big Hand, 1960; The Heckler, 1960; See Them Die, 1960; Lady, Lady, I Did It, 1961; Like Love, 1962; The Empty Hours (three novelettes), 1962; Ten Plus One, 1963; Ax, 1964; He Who Hesitates, 1965; Doll, 1965; The Sentries, 1965; Eighty Million Eyes, 1966; Fuzz, 1968 (screenplay 1972); Shotgun, 1969; Jigsaw, 1970; Hail, Hail, The Gang's All Here, 1971; Sadie When She Died, 1972; Let's Hear It for the Deaf Man, 1972; Hail to the Chief, 1973; Bread, 1974; Where There's Smoke, 1975; Blood Relatives, 1975; So Long as You Both Shall Live, 1976; Long Time No See, 1977; Goldilocks, 1977; Calypso, 1979; Ghosts, 1980; Rumpelstiltskin, 1981; Heat, 1981; Ice, 1983; Beauty and the Beast, 1983; Jack and the Beanstalk, 1984; Lightening, 1984; Snow White and Rose Red, 1985; Eight Black Horses, 1985; Cinderella, 1986; Another Part of the City, 1986; Poison, 1987; Puss in Boots, 1987; Tricks, 1987; McBain's Ladies, 1988; The House That Jack Built, 1988; Lullaby, 1989; McBain's Ladies Too, 1989; Downtown, 1989; Vespers, 1990; Three Blind Mice, 1990. Address: c/o John Farquharson Ltd, 250 West 57th Street, New York, NY 10019, USA.

LOMER Harry. See: **LIDE Mary Ruth.**

LOMPERIS Timothy John, b. 6 Mar 1947, Guntur, A P, India. University Professor. m. Ana Maria Turner, 15 May 1976, 1 son, 1 daughter. Education: AB magna cum laude, Augustana College, Rock Island, Illinois, USA, 1969; MA, Johns Hopkins School of Advanced International Studies, Washington, District of Columbia, 1975; MA, Political Science, 1978, PhD, Political Science, 1981, Duke University, Durham; Olin Postdoctoral Fellow, Harvard University, 1985-86. Appointments: Assistant Professor, Political Science, Louisiana State University, Baton Rouge, 1980-83; Assistant Professor, Political Science, Duke University, Durham, North Carolina, 1983-; Fellow, Woodrow Wilson Center, Smithsonian Institution, 1988-89. Publications: The War Everyone Lost - And Won, 1984; The Hindu Influence on Greek Philosophy, 1984; Reading the Wind, 1987; From People's War to People's Rule: Insurgency, Intervention, and the Lessons of Vietnam. Contributions to: Vietnam: The Lesson of Legitimacy, to Conflict Quarterly, 1986; Giap's Dream, Westmoreland's Nightmare to Parameters, 1988. Honours: Bronze Star, 1973; Vietnamese Army Staff Medal, First Class, 1973; Helen Dwight Reid Award for Best Dissertation in International Relations, American Political Science Association, 1981; Finalist, Furniss Award for Best First Book in National Security, 1984. Membership: American Political Science Association. Address: Department of Political Science, Duke University, Durham, NC 27706, USA.

LONDON Herbert I, b. 1939, American. Writer on Education and Sociology; Professor of Social Studies, 1967-92, and Dean of the Gallatin Division, New York University, New York City (formerly Director of University Without Walls Programme); Presently, the John M Olin Professor of Humanities at New York University; Consultant, Hudson Institute, 1969-; Candidate for Governor of New York State, 1990; Candidate for Comptroller of New York State, 1994. Publications: (ed and contrib) Education in the Twenty-First Century, 1969; Non-White Immigration and the White Australia Policy, 1970; Fitting in: Crosswise at Generation Gap, 1974; (ed and contrib) Social Science Theory, Structure and Applications, 1975; The Overheated Decade, 1976; The Seventies: Counterfeit Decade, 1979; Myths That Rule America, 1981; Closing the Circle: A Cultural History of the Rock Revolution, 1984; Why Are They Lying to Our Children? 1984; Military Doctrine and the American Character, 1984; Armageddon in The Classroom, 1986; A Strategy For Victory Without War, 1989; The Broken Apple: Notes on New York In the 1980s, 1989; From The Empire State To The Vampire State; New York In A Downtown Transition, 1994. Address: 2, Washington Square Village, New York, NY 10012, USA.

LONDON Laura, See: **CURTIS Sharon.**

LONG Robert Emmet, b. 7 June 1934, New York, USA. Literary Critic; Freelance Writer. Education: BA 1956, PhD 1968, Columbia University; MA, Syracuse University, 1964. Appointments: Instructor,

English Dept, State University of New York, 1962-64; Assistant Professor, City University of New York, 1968-71. Publications: The Achieving of the Great Gatsby: F Scott Fitgerald 1920-25, 1979; The Great Succession: Henry James and the Legacy of Hawthorne, 1979; Henry James: The Early Novels, 1983; John O'Hara, 1983; Nathanael West, 1985; Barbara Pym, 1986; James Thurber, 1988; James Fenimore Cooper, 1990; The Films of Merchant Ivory, 1991; Ingmar Bergman: Film and Stage, 1994. Editor, 19 Reference Books including: American Education, 1985; Drugs and American Society, 1985; Vietnam, Ten Years After, 1986; Mexico, 1986; The Farm Crisis, 1987; The Problem of Waste Disposal, 1988; AIDS, 1989; The Welfare Debate, 1989; Energy and Conservation, 1989; Japan and the USA, 1990; Censorship, 1990; The Crisis in Health Care, 1991; The State of US Education, 1991; The Reunification of Germany, 1992; Immigration to the United States, 1992; Drugs in America, 1993; Banking Scandals: the S&L and BCCI, 1993; Religious Cults in America, 1994. Contributions to: Several hundred articles in magazines, journals and newspapers. Literary Agent: Harold Ober Associates, Inc, 425 Madison Avenue, New York, NY 10017, USA. Address: 254 South Third Street, Fulton, NY 13069, USA.

LONGLEY Michael, b. 27 July 1939, Belfast, Northern Ireland. Director; Poet. m. Edna Broderick, 1964, 1 s, 2 d. Education: BA, Trinity College, Dublin, 1963. Appointments include: Director, Arts Council of Northern Ireland, Belfast, 1970-. Publications: Ten Poems, 1965; Room to Rhyme, 1968; Secret Marriages: Nine Short Poems, 1968; Three Regional Voices, 1968; No Continuing City; Poems, 1963-68, 1969; Lares, 1972; An Exploded View: Poems, 1968-72; Fishing in the Sky, 1975; Penguin Modern Poets 26, 1975; Man Lying on a Wall, 1972-75; The Echo Gate, 1975-78, 1979; Selected Poems, 1963-80; Patchwork, 1981; Poems, 1963-83, 1985; Editor, Causeway: The Arts in Ulster, 1971; Selected Poems by Louis MacNeice, 1988. Honours include: Commonwealth Poetry Prize, 1985. Address: 32 Osborne Gardens, Malone, Belfast 9, Northern Ireland.

LONGMATE Norman Richard, b. 15 Dec 1925, Newbury, Berkshire, England. Freelance Writer. Education: BA, Modern History, 1950, MA 1952, Worcester College, Oxford. Appointments: Leader Writer, Evening Standard, 1952; Feature Writer, Daily Mirror, 1953-56; Administrative Officer, Electricity Council, 1957-63; Schools Radio Producer, 1963-65, Senior, subsequently Chief Assistant, BBC Secretariat 1965-83, BBC; Freelance Writer, 1983-. Publications: Editor, A Socialist Anthology, 1953; Oxford Triumphant, 1955; various detective stories, 1957-61; 3 career books for boys, 1961-64; King Cholera, 1966; The Waterdrinkers, 1968; Alive and Well, 1970; How We Lived Then, 1971; If Britain had Fallen, 1972; The Workhouse, 1974; The Real Dad's Army, 1974; The GI's, 1975; Milestones in Working Class History, 1975; Air Raid, 1976; When We Won the War, 1977; The Hungry Mills, 1978; The Doodlebugs, 1981; The Bombers, 1982; The Breadstealers, 1984; Hitler's Rockets, 1985; Defending the Island from Caeser to the Armada, 1989. Memberships: Vice-Chairman, North Surrey Area, Oxford Society; Society of Authors; Fortress Study Group; United Kingdom Fortification Club; Historical Association; Ramblers Association; Society of Sussex Downsmen; Prayer Book Society; Fellow, Royal Historical Society. Address: c/o Century Hutchison, 62-65 Chandos Place, London WC2 4NW, England.

LONGWORTH Philip, b. 1933, British/Canadian. Writer on History; Professor of History, McGill University, Montreal, 1984-. Publications: (trans) A Hero of Our Time, by Lermontov, 1962; The Art of Victory, 1965; The Unending Vigil, 1967, 1985; The Cossacks, 1969; The Three Empresses, 1971; The Rise and Fall of Venice, 1974; Alexis, Tsar of All the Russias, 1984; The Making of Eastern Europe, 1992. Contributions to: The Times Literary Supplement. Address: c/o Heath and Co, 79 St Martin's Lane, London WC2N 4AA, England.

LONGYEAR Barry (Brookes), b. 12 May 1942, Harrisburg, Pennsylvania, USA. Science Fiction; Freelance Writer 1977-. Appointments: Publisher, Sol III Publications, Philadelphia, 1968-72, and Farmington, Maine 1972-77. Publications include: City of Baraboo, 1980; Manifest Destiny (stories), 1980; Circus World (stories), 1980; Elephant Song, 1981; The Tomorrow Testament, 1983; It Came from Schenectady, 1984; Sea of Glass, 1986; Enemy Mine; Saint MaryBlue, 1988; Naked Came the Robot, 1988; The God Box, 1989; Infinity Hold, 1989; The Homecoming, 1989; Slag Like Me, 1994. Address: PO Box 100, Vienna Road Rt 41, New Shanon, ME 04955, USA.

LOOMIE Albert Joseph, b. 1922, American. History; Professor Emeritus of History, Fordham University, 1968-1993, (member of faculty 1958-); Member of the Jesuit Order, 1939-; Professor Emeritus, 1993-. Publications: (with C M Lewis), The Spanish Jesuit Mission in Virginia 1570-72, 1953; Toleration and Diplomacy: The Religious Issue in Anglo-Spanish Relations 1603-1605, 1963; The Spanish Elizabethans: The English Exiles at the Court of Philip II, 1964; Guy Fawkes in Spain, 1971; Spain and the Jacobean Catholics, vol I, 1973, vol II 1978; Ceremonies of Charles I: The Notebooks of John Finet 1628-41, 1987; English Polemics at the Spanish Court: Joseph Creswell's Letter to the Ambassador from England, The English and Spanish Texts of 1606, 1993. Address: Loyola-Faber Hall, Fordham University, New York, NY 10458-5198, USA.

LOPATE Phillip, b. 16 Nov 1943, Writer. m. Cheryl Cipriani, 31 Dec 1990. Education: BA, Columbia College, 1964; PhD, Union Institute, 1979. Appointments: Associate Professor: English, University of Houston, 1980-88, Creative Writing, Columbia University, 1988-91; Professor of English, Bennington College, 1992-; Professor of English, Hofstra University, at present. Publications: Bachelorhood, 1981; The Rug Merchant, 1987; Being With Children, 1975; Against Joie de Vivre, 1989; The Daily Round, 1976; Confessions of Summer, 1979; The Eyes Don't Always Want to Stay Open, 1972; The Art of the Personal Essay, 1994. Contributions to: Paris Review; Esquire; Vogue; New York Times; Film Comment; Journal of Contemporary Fiction; Harper's; Tikkun; Ploughshares. Literary Agent: Wendy Weil Agency. Address: c/o Wendy Weil Agency, 232 Madison Avenue, New York, NY 10016, USA.

LOPES Henri, b. 12 Sept 1937, Leopoldville, Belgian Congo. Writer (Novelist). m. Nirva Pasbeau, 13 May 1961, 1 son, 3 daughters. Education: Licence es Lettres, 1962, Diplome d'Etudes Superieures, History, 1963, University of Paris (Sorbonne). Publications: Tribaliques, 1971, English translations as Tribaliks, 1989; La Nouvelle Romance, 1976; Sans Tam-Tam, 1977; The Laughing Cry, 1988; Le Chercheur d'Afriques, 1990; Sur L'Autre Rive, 1992. Honours: Grand Prix de la Litterature d'Afrique Noire, 1972; Prix Jules Verne, 1990; Doctor Honoris Causa, University Paris-Val de Marne, France; Grand Prix de Littérature de Lafracophonie de L'Académie Française, 1993; Homme de Lettres 1993, 1994. Address: UNESCO, 7 Place de Fontenoy, 75352 Paris, France.

LOPEZ Barry Holstun, b. 6 Jan 1945, USA. m. Sandra Jean Landers, 10 June 1967. Education: BA cum laude, University of Notre Dame, 1966; MA, 1968; LDH Honorary, Whittier College, 1988. Publications: Arctic Dreams, 1986; Crossing Open Ground, 1988; Of Wolves and Men, 1978; Crow and Weasel, 1990; Winter Count, 1981; Desert Notes, 1976; Giving Birth to Thunder, 1978; River Notes, 1978; The Rediscovery of North American, 1991; Field Notes, 1994. Contributions to: Harper's; New York Times; North American Review; National Geographic. Honours: John Burroughs Medal, 1979; Christopher Medal, 1979, 1987; National Book Award, 1987; Award in Literature, American Academy, 1986; Guggenheim Fellowship, 1987; Lannan Foundation Award, 1990. Memberships: PEN American Center. Literary Agent: Peter Mason, Sterling Lord Literistic. Address: Peter Mason, Sterling Lord Literistic, 1 Madison Avenue, NY 10010, USA.

LORD Graham John, b. 16 Feb 1943, Mutare, Zimbabwe. Journalist. m. Jane Carruthers, 12 Sept 1962, 2 daughters. Education: BA Honours, Cambridge University, 1965. Literary Appointments: Literary Editor, Sunday Express, London, 1969-; Originator of Sunday Express Book of the Year Award, 1987, Judge 1987, 1988, 1989. Publications: Novels: Marshmallow Pie, 1970; A Roof Under Your Feet, 1973; The Spider and the Fly, 1974; God and All His Angels, 1976; The Nostradamus Horoscope, 1981; Time Out of Mind, 1986. Literary Agent: A M Heath, London. Address: Sunday Express, 245 Blackfriars Road, London SE1, England.

LORD Robert Needham, b. 18 July 1945, New Zealand. Playwright. Education: BA, Victoria University of Wellington; Diploma of Teaching, Wellington Teachers' College. Appointment: Burns Fellow, Otago University, 1987. Publications: Heroes and Butterflies, 1973; Well Hung, 1974; Bert and Maisy, 1987; The Travelling Squirrel, 1987; The Affair, 1987; Country Cops, 1988; China Wars, 1988; Glorious Ruins, 1990. Honours: Katherine Mansfield Young Writers Award, 1969; CAPS Grant, New York State, 1984; Burns Fellowship, 1987. Memberships: PEN; Dramatists Guild. Literary Agent: Gilbert Parker,

William Morris Agency, New York, USA. Address: Apartment 145, 250 West 85, New York, NY 10024, USA.

LORD Walter, b. 8 Oct 1917, Baltimore, Maryland, USA. Author. Education: BA, Princeton University, 1939; LLB, Yale University, 1946. Publications include: The Fremantle Diary, 1954; A Night to Remember, 1955, illustrated edition 1976; Day of Infamy, 1957; The Good Years, 1960; A Time to Stand, 1961; Peary to the Pole, 1963; The Past That Would Not Die, 1965; Incredible Victory, 1967; Dawn's Early Light, 1972; Lonely Vigil, 1977; Miracle of Dunkirk, 1982; The Night Lives On, 1986. Contributions include: Various magazines & journals including: American Heritage; Life; Look, Readers Digest. Address: 116 East 68th Street, New York, NY 10021, USA.

LORDE Audre. Poet. Publications; From A Land Where Other People Live, 1973; Black Unicorn, 1978; The Cancer Journals, 1980; Fami: A New Spelling of My Name, 1982; Chosen Poems Old and New, 1982; Sister Outsider, 1984; Our Dead Behind Us, 1986; Burst of Light, 1988; Undersong: Chosen Poems Old and New, 1992; The Marvellous Arithmetic of Distance, 1993. Contributions to: Nimrod; Callaloo. Address: c/o Charlotte Sheedy Literary Agency, 611 Broadway Suite 428, New York, NY 10012, USA.

LORENZ Sarah E,See:**WINSTON Sarah.**

LORRIMER Claire. See: **CLARK Patricia Denise.**

LOTT Bret, b. 8 Oct 1958, Los Angeles, CA, USA. Professor. m. Melanie Kai Swank, 28 June 1980, 2 sons. Education: BA, California State University, Long Beach, 1981; MFA, University of Massachusetts, Amherst, 1984. Appointments: Cook's Trainer, Big Yellow House Incorporated, Santa Barbara, 1977-79; Salesman, RC Cola, 1979-80; Reporter, Daily Commercial News, 1980-81, Los Angeles; Instructor in Remedial English, Ohio State University, Columbus, 1984-86; Assistant Professor of English, College of Charleston, 1986-. Publications: The Man Who Owned Vermont, 1987; A Stranger's House, 1988; A Dream of Old Leaves, 1989. Contributions to: Short stories represented in anthology, Twenty under Thirty, 1986; Fiction to periodicals including Missouri Review; Michigan Quarterly Review; Iowa Review; Yale Review; Yankee; Seattle Review; Redbook; Confrontation; Literary Reviews to periodicals, including New York Review of Books; Los Angeles Times; Michigan Quarterly Review. Memberships: Associated Writing Programs; Poets and Writers. Honours: Syndicated fiction Project Award from PEN/National Endowment for the Arts; Ohio Arts Council Fellowship in Literature, 1986; South Carolina Arts Commission Fellowship in Literature, 1987-88; South Carolina Syndicated Fiction Project Award, 1987. Address: Department of English, College of Charleston, Charleston, SC 29424, USA.

LOTTRIDGE Celia Barker. Canadian. Publications: Ticket to Curlew, 1992; The Name of the Tree, 1990; Ten Small Tales, 1994; The Wind Wagon, 1995. Honour: CLA Book of the Year for Children Award, 1993.

LOVAT Terence John, b. 29 Mar 1949, Sydney, New South Wales, Australia. University Professor of Education. m. Tracey Majella Dennis, 4 Jan 1986, 2 daughters. Education: BEd, 1982, MTh, 1983, MA (hons), 1984, PhD, 1988, Sydney University. Publications: Understanding Religion, 1987; What Is This Thing Called Religious Education?, 1989; Studies in Australian Society, 1989; Curriculum: Action on Reflection (with D Smith), 1990; Bioethics for Medical and Health Professionals (with K Mitchell), 1991; Teaching and Learning Religion, 1994; Editor: Sociology for Teachers, 1992; Studies in Religion, 1993. Contributions to: Over 30 including: British Journal of Religious Education; British Educational Research Journal; Journal of Education for Teaching; Action in Teacher Education. Memberships: Australian College of Education; European Association for Research on Learning and Instruction. Address: Department of Education, University of Newcastle, New South Wales 2308, Australia.

LOVE William F, b. 20 Dec 1932, Oklahoma City, Oklahoma, USA. Writer. m. Joyce Mary Athman, 30 May 1970, 2 daughters. Education: BA, St John's University, Minnesota, 1955; MBA, University of Chicago, 1972. Publications: The Chartreuse Clue, 1990; The Fundamental of Murder, 1991; Bloody Ten, 1992. Contributions to: The Enduring Legacy of Rex Stout, article, to Mostly Murder, 1991. Honours: Nominations (1 of top 5) for Macavity and Agatha Awards, for The Chartreuse Clue, 1991-. Memberships: Mystery Writers of America, Chairman of Committee to select winner of 1992 Edgar Award in category on Biographical-Critical Works; International Association of Crime Writers; Private Eye Writers of America; Authors Guild; Society of Midland Authors; PEN Midwest; Hinsdale Area United Way, Chairman 1991-93; Love Christian Clearing House; Theatre of Western Springs. Literary Agent: Arthur Pine Associates, 250 W 57th St, New York, NY 10019, USA. Address: 940 Cleveland, Hinsdale, IL 60521, USA.

LOVELL (Sir) (Alfred Charles) Bernard, b. 1913, British. Astronomy; Professor of Radio Astronomy and Director of Nuffield Radio Astronomy Laboratories at Jodrell Bank, University of Manchester, 1951-81. President, Royal Astronomical Society, 1969-71. Publications: Science and Civilization, 1939; World Power Resources and Social Development, 1945; (with J A Clegg), Radio Astronomy, 1952; Meteor Astronomy, 1954; (with R Hanbury Brown), The Exploration of Space by Radio, 1957; The Individual and the Universe, 1959; The Exploration of Outer Space, 1962; (with M Joyce Lovell), Discovering the Universe, 1963; Our Present Knowledge of the Universe, 1967; The Story of Jodrell Bank, 1968; Out of the Zenith: Jodrell Bank, 1957-70, 1973; The Origins and International Economics of Space Exploration, 1973; Man's Relation to the Universe, 1975; P M S Blackett: A Biographical Memoir, 1976; In the Center of Immensities, 1978; Emerging Cosmology, 1981; The Jodrell Bank Telescopes, 1985; (with F G Smith), Pathways to the Universe, 1988; Voice of the Universe, 1987; Astronomer by Chance, 1990; Echoes of War, 1991. Honours include: OBE, 1940; FRS 1995; Kt, 1961. Address: Jodrell Bank, Macclesfield, Cheshire, England.

LOVELL Mary Sybilla, b. 23 Oct 1941, Prestatyn, North Wales, UK. Writer. m. (2) Geoffrey A H Watts, 11 July 1991, 1 son, 2 step-sons, 2 step-daughters. Publications: Hunting Pageant, 1980; Cats as Pets, 1982; Boys Book of Boats, 1983; Straight on till Morning, 1987; The Splendid Outcast, 1988; The Sound of Wings, 1989; Cast No Shadow, 1991. Contributions to: Many technical articles on the subjects of accounting and software. Memberships: Society of Authors; MFHA, 1987-88; New Forest Hunt Club. Literary Agent: Robert Ducas, New York, USA. Address: Stroat House, Stroat, Gloucs NP6 7LR, England.

LOVELOCK Yann Rufus, b. 11 Feb 1939, Birmingham, England. Writer; Translator; Co-ordinator of Angulimala, Buddhist Prison Chaplaincy Organisation. m. Ann Riddell, 28 Sept 1961. Education: BA English Literature, St Edmund Hall, Oxford, 1963. Literary Appointments: Resident Writer in a number of schools also at Long Lartin Prison (1984) and other appointments for West Midlands Art Link. Publications: The Vegetable Book, 1972; The Line Forward, 1984; The Colour of the Weather, editor and translator, 1980; A Vanishing Emptiness, editor and part translator, 1989; A Townscape of Flanders, Versions of Grace (translation of Anton van Wilderode), 1990; Blue Cubes for a Catarrh and Songs of Impotence, poem, 1990; Some 25 other books of poems, experimental prose, anthologies and translations since 1960. Contributions to: Regular features in Dutch Crossing (London University); Poems in PN Review, Poetry Review, Ambit, Stand and others. Honour: Silver Medal, Haute Academie d'Art et de litterature de France, 1986. Memberships: Freundkreis Poesie Europe, Assistant Director. Address: 80 Doris Road, Birmingham, West Midlands B11 4NF, England.

LOVESEY Peter (Peter Lear), b. 10 Sept 1936, Whitton, Middlesex, England. Writer. m. Jacqueline Ruth Lewis, 30 May 1959, 1 son, 1 daughter. Education: BA Honours, English, University of Reading, England, 1958. Publications: The Kings of Distance, non-fiction sports, 1968; Wobble to Death, crime fiction, 1970; The Detective Wore Silk Drawers, 1971; Abracadaver, 1972; Mad Hatters Holiday, 1973; Invitation to a Dynamite Party, 1974; A Case of Spirits, 1975; Swing, Swing Together, 1976; Goldengirl as Peter Lear, 1977; Waxwork, 1978; Official Centenary History of the Amateur Athletic Association, 1979; Spider Girl, as Peter Lear, 1980; The False Inspector Dew, 1982; Keystone, 1983; Butchers, short stories, 1985; The Secret of Spandau, as Peter Lear, 1986; Rough Cider, 1986; Bertie and the Tinman, 1987; On the Edge, 1989; Bertie and the Seven Bodies, 1990; The Last Detective, 1991; Diamond Solitaire, 1992; Bertie and the Crime of Passion, 1993. Honours: Macmillan/Panther 1st Crime Novel Award, 1970; Crime Writers Association Silver Dagger, 1978; Gold Dagger, 1982; Grand Prix de Littérature Policière, 1985; Prix du Roman D'Aventures, 1987; Anthony Award, 1992. Memberships: Crime Writers Association, Chairman 1991-92; Detection Club; Society of Authors. Literary Agent: Vanessa Holt Associates Ltd. Address: 59 Crescent Road, Leigh-on-Sea, Essex SS9 2PF, England.

LOVETT Albert Winston, b. 16 Dec 1944, Abingdon, England. Academic. Education: BA 1965, PhD 1969, Cambridge, England. Publications: Philip II and Mateo Vazquez, 1977; Modern Europe 1453-1610, 1979; Early Habsburg Spain 1516 1598, 1986. Contributions to: Historical Journal (Cambridge); European History Quarterly; English Historical Review; Others. Memberships: Fellow, Royal Historical Society. Address: 26 Coney Hill Road, West Wickham, Kent BR4 9BX, England.

LOW Dorothy Mackie. See: LOW Lois.

LOW Lois, (Zoe Cass, Dorothy Mackie Low, Lois Paxton), b. 1916, British. Writer of Mystery/Crime/Suspense; Historical/Romance/Gothic fiction. Publications: Isle for a Stranger, 1962; Dear Liar, 1963; A Ripple on the Water, 1964; The Intruder, 1965; A House in the Country, 1968; (as Lois Paxton) The Man Who Died Twice, 1969; To Burgundy and Back, 1970; (as Lois Paxton), The Quiet Sound of Fear, 1971; (as Lois Paxton), Who Goes There? 1972; (as Zoe Cass), Island of the Seven Hills, 1974; (as Zoe Cass), The Silver Leopard, 1976; (as Zoe Cass), A Twist in the Silk, 1980; (as Lois Paxton), The Man in the Shadows, 1983. Memberships: Crime Writers Association; Society of Authors; Romantic Novelists Association, Chairman 1969-71. Literary Agent: A M Heath & Company Ltd, 79 St Martin's Lane, London WC2N 4AA. Address: 8 Belmont Mews, Abbey Hill, Kenilworth, Warwickshire CV8 1LU, England.

LOW Rachael, British. Appointments: Film, Researcher engaged in a history of British cinema: with British Film Institute, London, 1945-48, and Gulbenkian Research Fellow, Lucy Cavendish College, Cambridge, 1968-71; Fellow Commoner of Lucy Cavendish College, 1983. Publications: History of the British Film, 1896-1906, 1948; (with Roger Manvell), 1906-1914, 1949, 1914-1918, 1950, 1918-1929, 1971, 1929-39, 2 vols, 1979, 3rd vol, 1985. Address: c/o Allen & Unwin Ltd, 40 Museum Street, London WC1, England.

LOWDEN Desmond Scott, b. 27 Sept 1937, Winchester, Hants, England. m. 14 July 1962, 1 son, 1 daughter. Education: Pilgrims' School, Winchester; Marlborough College. Publications: Bandersnatch, 1969; The Boondocks, 1972; Bellman and True, 1975; Boudapesti 3, 1979; Sunspot, 1981; Cry Havoc, 1984; The Shadow Run, 1989; Chain, 1990. Honour: Crime Writers' Association Silver Dagger Award, 1989, for Shadow Run. Membership: Crime Writers' Association. Literary Agent: Deborah Rogers. Address: c/o Deborah Rogers, Rogers, Coleridge and White Ltd, 20 Powys Mews, London W11 1JN, England.

LOWE John Evelyn, b. 23 Apr 1928, London, England. Writer. m. (1) Susan Sanderson, 1956, 2 sons, 1 daughter, (2) Yuki Nomura, 1989, 1 daughter. Education: English Literature, New College, Oxford, 1950-52. Appointments: Associate Editor, Collins Crime Club, 1953-54; Editor, Faber Furniture Series, 1954-56; Deputy Story Editor, Pinewood Studios, 1956-57; Literary Editor, Kansai Time Out Magazine, 1985-89. Publications: Thomas Chippendale, 1955; Cream Coloured Earthenware, 1958; Japanese Crafts, 1983; Into Japan, 1985; Into China, 1986; Corsica - A Traveller's Guide, 1988; A Surrealist Life - Edward James, 1991; A Short Guide to the Kyoto Museum of Archaeology, 1991; Major contribution to the Encyclopaedica Britannica and the Oxford Junior Encyclopaedia. Contributions to: The American Scholar; Country Life; Listener; Connoisseur; Apollo; Others. Honours: Honorary Fellow, Royal College of Art. Memberships: Fellow, Society of Antiquaries; Fellow, Royal Society of Arts. Address: Paillole-Basse, 47360 Prayssas, France.

LOWE Robson, b. 7 Jan 1905, London, England. Editor; Author; Auctioneer. m. Winifred Marie Devine, 7 Mar 1928, 2 daughters. Education: Fulham Central School. Publications: Regent Catalogue of Empire Postage Stamps, 1933; The Encyclopaedia of Empire Postage Stamps (1 vol), 1935; Handstruck Postage Stamps of the Empire, 1937; The Birth of the Adhesive Postage Stamp, 1939; Masterpieces of Engraving on Postage Stamps, 1943; The Encyclopaedia of Empire Postage Stamps (7 vols) 1950-90; Sperati & His Work, 1956; The British Postage Stamp, 1968; Many monographs; Leeward Islands, 1990; The House of Stamps, Imitations, 1993. Contributions to: Edited the Philatelist 1935-74, 1982-; Contributed many articles to philatelic and postal history journals at home and abroad. Address: c/o The East India Club, 16 St James' Square, London SW1, England.

LOWE Stephen, b. 1 Dec 1947, Nottingham, England. Playwright. m. 1) Tina Barclay, 2) Tany Myers, 1 son, 1 daughter. Education: BA Hons, English and Drama, 1969; Postgraduate

Research, 1969-70. Appointments: Senior Tutor in Writing for Performance, Dartington College of Arts Performance, 1978-82; Resident Playwright, Riverside Studios, London, 1982-84; Senior Tutor, Birmingham University, 1987-88; Nottingham Trent University Advisory Board to Theatre Design Degree, 1987-. Publications: Stage Plays, Touched, 1981; Ragged Trousered Philanthropists, 1991; Moving Pictures and other Plays, 1985; Divine Gossip/Tibetan Inroads, 1988; Body and Soul in Peace Plays, vol I, 1985, vol 2, 1990; Cards, 1983. Contributions to: Englisch Amerikanische Studien, 1986; Debut on 2: A Guide to TV Writing, 1990; The Breath of Inspiration. Honours: George Devine Award for Playwriting, 1977. Memberships: Theatre Writers Union; Writers Guild; PEN. Literary Agent: S Stroud, Judy Daish Associates. Address: S Stroud, Judy Daish Associates, 83 Eastbourn Mews, London W2 6LQ, England.

LOWE-WATSON Dawn, b. 12 June 1929, London, England. Writer. m. David Lowe-Watson, 22 Oct 1951, sep, 3 sons. Education: Modern Arts Diploma, Queen's College, 1946. Appointments: Editorial Assistant, Weldons Publications, 1947; Editor, Markets and People, British Export Trade Research Organisation, 1950; Editorial Director, Perry Press Productions, 1951-54. Publications: The Good Morrow, 1980; Sound of Water, 1982; Black Piano, 1986; 12 radio plays, BBC Radio 4. Contributions to: As Dawn Valery, fiction to magazines; Features to many newspapers including Sunday Times. Honours: Authors Club 1st Novel Award for The Good Morrow, 1980; Elgin Prize for Sound of Water, 1983. Memberships: PEN; Society of Authors; Authors Club, Committee Member. Literary Agent: Rogers, Coleridge and White, England.

LOWELL Susan Deborah, b. 27 Oct 1950, Chihuahua, Mexico. Writer. m. William Ross Humphreys, 21 Mar 1975, 2 daughters. Education: BA 1972, MA 1974, Stanford University, USA, USA; MA, PhD, Princeton University., 1979. Appointments: University of Arizona, USA, 1974-76; University of Texas, Dallas, 1979-80; University of Arizona, 1989. Publications: Ganado Red: A Novella and Stories, 1988; I am Lavinia Cumming, 1993. Honours: Milkweed Editions National Fiction Prize, 1988; Mountain & Plains Booksellers Association 1994 Regional Book Award (Childrens category). Membership: Southern Arizona Society of Authors. Address: c/o Milkweed Editions, PO Box 3226, Minneapolis, MN 55403, USA.

LOWEN Alexander, b. 1910, American. Career: Writer on Human Relations, Psychiatry, Psychology, Sex; Psychiatrist in private practice since 1953; Associate Director, New England Heart Center; Executive Director, Institute for Bioenergetic Analysis, New York City. Publications: Physical Dynamics of Character Structure, 1958; Love and Orgasm, 1965; The Betrayal of the Body, 1967; Depression and the Body, 1973; Pleasure, 1975; Bioenergetics, 1975; (with Leslie Lowen) The Way to Vibrant Health, 1977; Fears of Life, 1980; Narcissism, 1983; Love, Sex and Your Heart, 1989; The Spirituality of the Body, 1990; Joy, the Surrender to the Body and to Life, 1993. Literary Agent: Raines and Raines, 71 Park Avenue, New York, NY 10016, USA. Address: Puddin Hill Road, New Canaan, Connecticut, USA.

LOWNIE Andrew James Hamilton, b. 11 Nov 1961, Kenya. Literary Agent. Education: Magdalene College, Cambridge, 1981-84; BA (Cantab); MA (Cantab); MSc, Edinburgh University, 1989. Appointments: Trustee, Iain Macleod Award, 1984; Hodder and Stoughton Publishers, 1984-85; Joined 1985, Director 1986-88, John Farquharson Literary Agents; Andrew Lownie Associates, 1988-; Denniston and Lownie, 1991-93; Parliamentary Candidate, Monklands West, 1992. Publications: North American Spies, 1992; Edinburgh Literary Guide, 1992; John Buchan, 1995 The Scottish Short Stories of John Buchan, 1995 Contributions to: Regularly to: Times; Spectator; Telegraph; Scotland on Sunday; Introductions to John Buchan's 'Huntingtower' & 'Courts of the Morning', 1994; Introductions to John Buchan reissues Alan Sutton, 1994. Honours: English Speaking Union Scholarship to Asheville School, North Carolina, USA, 1979-80; Fellow, Royal Geographical Society; Fellow, Royal Society of Arts. Address: 122 Bedford Court Mansions, Bedford Square, London WC1B 3AH, England.

LOWRY Lois, b. 20 Mar 1937, Honolulu, Hawaii. Writer. 2 s, 2 d. Education: Brown University, 1954-56; BA, University of Southern Maine, 1973. Publications include: The Giver, 1993; Number The Stars, 1989; Anastasia Krupnik, 1979; A Summer to Die, 1977. Honours: Newberry Medal, 1990, 94. Literary Agent: Claire Smith, Harold Ober

Associates inc, 425 Madison Avenue, NY 10017, USA. Address: c/o Agent.

LOXMITH John. See: BRUNNER John Kilian Houston.

LUARD Nicholas (James McVean), b. 1937, British. Writer of Mystery/Crime/Suspense, Environmental science/Ecology. Worked for NATO and in theatre and publishing. Publications: Mystery Novels: The Warm and Golden War, 1967; The Robespierre Serial, 1975; Travelling Horseman, 1975; The Orion Line, 1976; in US as Double Assignment, 1977; (as James McVean), Bloodspoor, 1977; The Dirty Area (in US as The Shadow Spy), 1979; (as James McVean), Seabird Nine, 1981; (as James McVean), Titan, 1984; Other: (with Dominick Elwes), Refer to Drawer, 1964; The Last Wilderness: A Journey Across the Great Kalahari Desert, 1981; The Wildlife Parks of Africa, 1985. Address: 227 South Lambeth Road, London SW8, England.

LUBINGER Eva, b. 3 Feb 1930, Steyr, Austria. Writer. m. Dr Walter Myss, 7 Oct 1952, 2 sons. Appointments: Wort und Welt, Innsbruck, Austria. Publications: Paradies mit Kleinen Fehlein, 1976; Gespenster in Sir Edward's Haus, 1978; Pflucke den Wind, lyric, 1982; Verlieb Dich nicht in Mark Aurell, 1985; Zeig mir Lamorna, 1985; Fleig mit Nach Samarkand, 1987. Contributions to: Prasent, weekly newspaper. Honours: Literature Prize for lyrics, Innsbruck, 1963; Literature Prize for Drama, Innsbruck, 1969. Membership: PEN, Austria. Literary Agent: Wort und Welt, Innsbruck. Address: Lindenbuhelweg 16, 6020 Innsbruck, Austria.

LUCARDO Max. Minister, Church of Christ; Author. m. Denalyn, 3 d. Publications: 11 books, adult & children's, including: The Applause of Heaven; Six Hours One Friday; On the Anvil, 1985; In The Eye of the Storm, 1991; He Still Moves Stones, 1993; When God Whispers Your Name, 1994. Address: Oak Hills Church of Christ, 8308 Fredericksburg Road, San Antonio, TX 78229, USA.

LUCAS Celia, b. 23 Oct 1938, Bristol, England. Writer. m. Ian Skidmore, 20 Oct 1971. Education: BA, Hons, Modern History, St Hilda's College, Oxford, 1961. Publications: Steel Town Cats, 1987; The Adventures of Marmaduke Purr Cat, 1990; Prisoners of Santo Tomas, 1975, paperback 1988; Anglesey Rambles (with husband), 1989 (under Skidmore); Glyndwr Country (with husband), 1988 (under Skidmore). Contributions to: Numerous journals and magazines. Honour: TIR NA N-OG Award for junior fiction with Welsh background, 1988. Membership: Welsh Academy (elected 1989). Address: Aberbraint, Llanfairpwll, Isle of Anglesey, Gwynedd LL61 6BP, Wales.

LUCAS John Randolph, b. 18 June 1929, London, England. Don. m. Helen Morar Portal, 17 June 1961, 2 sons, 2 daughters. Education: Scholar, Winchester, 1942-47; Scholar, Balliol, Oxford, 1947-51; 1st Class Mathematics Mods, 1948; 1st Class Lit Hum, 1951; BA, 1951; Harmsworth Senior Scholar, Merton College, Oxford, 1951-53; MA, 1954. Publications: Principles of Politics, 1966, 2nd edition 1985; The Concept of Probability, 1970; The Freedom of the Will, 1970; A Treatise on Time and Space, 1973; Democracy and Participation, 1976; Essays on Freedom and Grace, 1976; On Justice, 1980, 1989; Space, Time and Casuality, 1985; The Future, 1989; Spacetime and Electromagnetism, 1990; Responsibility, 1993. Honours: John Locke, 1952; FBA, 1988. Membership: President, British Society for the Philosophy of Science, 1991-93. Address: Merton College, Oxford OX1 4JD, England.

LUCAS Stephen E, b. 5 Oct 1946, White Plains, New York, USA. Professor. m. Patricia Vore, 14 June 1969, 2 sons. Education: BA, University of California, Santa Barbara, 1968; MA 1970, PhD 1973, Pennsylvania State University. Publications: Portents of Rebellion; Rhetoric and Revolution in Philadelphia 1765-1776, 1976; The Art of Public Speaking, 1983, 1986, 1989, 1992, 1995; Justifying America: The Declaration of Independence as a Rhetorical Document, 1989. Contributions to: The Schism in Rhetorical Scholarship, to Quarterly Journal of Speech, 1981; The Renaissance of American Public Address, to Quarterly Journal of Speech, 1988; The Stylistic Artistry of the Declaration of Independence, to Prologue, 1990; The Plakkaat van Verlatinge: A Neglected Model for the American Declaration of Independence, 1994. Honours: Golden Anniversary Book Award, Speech Communication Association, 1979. Memberships: Speech Communication Association; International Society for the History of Rhetoric; Society for Eighteenth-Century Studies; Organizations of American Historians. Address: Department of Communication Arts, University of Wisconsin, Madison, WI 57306, USA.

LUCIE-SMITH John Edward McKenzie (Peter Kershaw), b. 27 Feb 1933, Kingston, Jamaica, West Indies. Writer. Education: King's School, Canterbury; MA Hons, Modern History, Merton College, Oxford. Appointments: Settled in England in 1946; Education Officer, Royal Air Force, 1954-56; Advertising copywriter 1956-66; Freelance author, journalist and broadcaster 1966-; Consultant, curator or co-curator of a number of exhibitions of in Britain and the USA and author of exhibition catalogues. Publications include: Moments in Art since 1945 (entitled Late Modern in the US), 1969; A Concise History of French Painting, 1971; Symbolist Art, 1972; Eroticism in Western Art, 1972; Fantin-Latour, 1977; A Concise History of Furniture, 1979; A Cultural Calendar of Twentieth Century, 1979; Art in the Seventies, 1980; The Story of Craft, 1981; A History of Industrial Design, 1983; A Thames and Hudson Dictionary of Art Terms, 1984; Art of the 1930s, 1985; American Art Now, 1985; Lives of the Twentieth Century Artists, 1986; Sculpture Since 1945, 1987; Art of the Eighties, 1990; Art Deco Painting, 1990; Art and Civilization, 1992; The Faber Book of Art Anecdotes, 1992; Harry Holland, 1992; Wendy Taylor, 1992; Alexander, 1992; Other publications include four collections of his own verse, two standard anthologies (the Penguin Book of Elizabethan Verse and British Poetry Since 1945), a biography of Joan of Arc, a history of piracy and an autobiography. Membership: Fellow, Royal Literary Society. Address: c/o Rogers, Coleridge and White, 20 Powis Mews, London W11 1JN, England.

LUCKLESS John. See: **IRVING Clifford.**

LUCZAK Alojzy Andrzej, b. 12 June 1930, Poznan, Poland. Writer; Journalist. m. Wanda, 22 Dec 1954, 2 sons, 1 daughter. Education: Academy of Economyics, Poznan, 1956. Publications: Hungry, 1974; Against the Wind with Music, 1988; You Will Still be a Eagle for Me, 1976; Pro Sinfonika - The Life-art Among People, 1978; Music Itinerarium, 1979; Pro Sinfonica's Leading Ideas, 1980; Cinema Film: Go and Come Back with Poland, 1987. Contributions to: various journals and magazines. Honours: Prize, Polish Government (twice); Prize, Journal Polityka; Prize Children, Smile Order; Polish Literary Society; Polish Journalists Society; President, Great Polish Cultural Society; President, Pro Sinfonica. Address: ulica Nowowiejskiego 12 m 5, 61-731 Poznan, Poland.

LUDLUM Robert (Jonathon Ryder, Michael Shepherd), b. 25 May 1927, New York, United States of America. Author; Writer. m. Mary Ryducha, 31 Mar 1951, 2 sons, 1 daughter. Education: BA, Wesleyan University, 1951. Appointments include: Early Career devoted to the Theatre and Television as an Actor and Producer; Became Full-time Writer, 1975. Publications: The Scarlatti Inheritance, 1971; Trevayne (as Jonathon Ryder), 1973; The Cry of the Halidon (as Jonathon Ryde), 1974; The Road to Gandolfo (as Michael Shepherd), 1975; The Gemini Contenders, 1976; The Chancellor Manuscript, 1977; The Icarus Agenda, 1988. Honours: The Scarlatti Inheritance became bestseller and Book of the Month; The Icarus Agenda, New York Times Bestseller List, 1988.

LUEBKE Frederick Carl, b. 1927, American. Writer on History. Appointments: Charles Mach Distinguished Professor of History, Emeritus 1994, University of Nebraska, Lincoln, since 1987 (Professor, 1972-87, Associate Professor, 1968-72); Director, Center for Great Plains Studies, 1983-88; Editor, Great Plains Quarterly, 1980-84. Publications: Immigrants and Politics, 1969; (ed) Ethnic Voters and the Election of Lincoln, 1971; Bonds of Loyalty: German Americans and World War I, 1974; (ed) The Great Plains: Environment and Culture, 1979; (ed) Ethnicity on the Great Plains, 1980; (co-ed) Vision and Refuge: Essays on the Literature of the Great Plains, 1981; (co-ed) Mapping the North American Plains, 1987; Germans in Brazil: A Comparative History of Cultural Conflict During World War I, 1987; Germans in the New World: Essays in the History of Immigration, 1990; (ed) A Harmony of the Arts: The Nebraska State Capital, 1990; Nebraska: An Illustrated History, 1995. Address: 3117 Woodsdale Boulevard, Lincoln, NE 68502, USA.

LUELLEN Valentina. See: **POLLEY Judith Anne.**

LUHRMANN Tanya Marie, b. 24 Feb 1959, Ohio, USA. Associate Professor of Anthropology. Education: BA summa cum laude, Harvard University, 1981; MPhil, Social Anthropology 1982, PhD, Social Anthropology 1986, University of Cambridge. Appointments: Research Fellow, Christ's College, Cambridge, England, 1985-89; Dept of Anthropology, University of California at San Diego, USA, 1989-. Publications: Persuasions of the Witch's Craft, 1989.

Contributions to: Popol Vuh and Lacan, to Ethos, 1984; The Magic of Secrecy, to Ethos, 1989; Witchcraft, Morality and Magic in Contemporary England, to International Journal of Moral Social Studies; Others. Honours: Bowdoin Prize, 1981; National Science Foundation Graduate Fellow, 1982-85; Emanuel Miller Prize, 1983; Partingdon Prize, 1985; Stirling Prize, 1986; Fulbright Award, 1990. Memberships: American Anthropology Association; Society for Psychological Anthropology; Royal Anthropological Institute. Literary Agent: Jill Kneerim, Palmer and Dodge Agency. Address: UCSD-0101, La Jolla, CA 92093, USA.

LUKACS John, b. 1924, Budapest, Hungary. Publications include: A New History of the Cold War, 1966; Historial Consciousness, 1968; Decline and Rise of Europe, 1976; Philadelphia, Patricians and Phillistines, 1900-1950, 1981; Outgrowing Democracy: A History of the United States, 1984; Budapest 1900, 1988; Confessions of an Original Sinner, 1990; The End of the Twentieth Century At the End of The Modern Age, 1993; Destinations Past: Travelling Through History With John Lukacs, 1994. Contibutions to: National Review; Harpers; Bazaar. Address: c/o Ticknor & Fields Publicity, 10th Floor 215 Park Avenue South, New York, NY 10003, USA.

LUKAS J Anthony (Jay), b. 25 Apr 1933, New York, New York, USA. Journalist, (including foreign correspondent in the Congo and India); University Lecture in Public Communications; Radio Host. Appointments: Steering Committee, Reporter's Committee on Freedom of the Press; Exec Board, New York Committee for the Humanities; Senior Editor, Associate Editor, MORE Journalism Review, 1972-78. Publications include: The Barnyard Epithet & Other Obscenities: Notes on the Chicago Conspiracy Trial, 1970; Don't Shout - We Are Your Children, 1971; Nightmare: the Underside of the Nixon Years, 1975; Common Ground: A Turbulent Decade in the Lives of Three American Families, 1985. Contributions to: Esquire; Harpers; Saturday Review; New Republic; Readers Digest; Atlantic; Nation; MORE; American Scholar; Psychology Today. Honours: Pulitzer Prize (1968 Journalism, 1986 Book); George Polk Award, 1968; Mike Berger Award, 1968; Page One Award, 1968; American Book Award, 1985; National Book Critics Circle Award, 1985; Robert F Kennedy Award, 1986. Memberships: PEN (exec committee 1977-83); Committee on Public Justice. Address: 890 West End Avenue, New York, NY 10025, USA.

LUKAS Richard Conrad, b. 1937, American. Writer on History. Appointments: Research Consultant, US Air Force Historical Archives, 1957-58; Assistant Professor 1963-66, Associate Professor 1966-69, Professor 1969-83, University Professor of History 1983-89, Tennessee Technological University, Cookeville; Professor, Wright State University (Lake Campus), 1989-92; Adjunct Professor, University of South Florida, Fort Myers, 1993-. Publications: Eagles East: The Army Air Forces and the Soviet Union, 1941-45, 1970; (ed) From Metternich to The Beatles, 1973; The Strange Allies: The United States and Poland 1941-45, 1978; Bitter Legacy: Polish-American Relations in the Wake of World War II, 1982; Forgotten Holocaust: The Poles under German Occupation, 1986; Out of the Inferno: Poles Remember The Holocaust, 1989; Did The Children Cry?: Hitler's War Against Jewish and Polish Children, 1994. Honours: Doctor of Humane Letters (LHD), 1987; Polonia Restituta, 1988. Address: 1344 Rock Dove Court, D-104, Punta Gorda, FL 33950, USA.

LUKE Peter, b. 12 Aug 1919, England, Writer; Dramatist. m. June Tobin, 23 Nov 1963, 3 sons (1 dec), 4 daughters. Education: Eton, 1932-37; Byam Shaw School of Art, 1938; Atelier Andre Lhote, Paris, 1938-39. Appointments: Sub-editor, Reuters, 1946-47; Story Editor, ABC-TV, 1958-62; Editor, The Bookman, 1962-63; Editor, Tempo, 1963-64, ABC-TV; Drama Producer, BBC-TV, 1963-67; Director, Dublin Gate Theatre Co, 1977-80. Publications: The Play of Hadrian the Seventh, 1968; Sisyphus and Reilly, 1972; Telling Tales, short stories, 1981; The Other Side of the Hill, 1984; The Mad Pomegranate and the Praying Mantis, 1985; Yerma, translation, 1987; West End productions: Hadrian VII, 1968; Bloomsbury, 1974; Yerma (NT), 1987; Married Love, 1988; Editor: Enter Certain Players, Edwards-MacLiammoir, 1978; Paquito and the Wolf, for children, 1981. Contributions to: Envoy, Dublin; Cornhill; Pick of Today's Short Stories; Winter's Tales; Era, Ireland; New Irish Writing; Irish Times; Daily Telegraph; Independent on Sunday. Honours: MC 1944; Prix Italia, 1967; Nomination for Antoinette Perry Award, 1968-69; Nomination for Sony Award, 1990. Memberships: Writers' Guild of Great Britain; Society of Authors; International PEN. Literary Agent: Lemon, Unna and Durbridge Ltd, England. Address: c/o Lemon, Unna and Durbridge Ltd, 24 Pottery Lane, Holland Park, London W11 4LZ, England.

LUKE Thomas. See: **MASTERTON Graham**.

LUKER Nicholas John Lydgate, b. 26 Jan 1945, Leeds, England. University Senior Lecturer in Russian. 1 son. Education: Hertford College, Oxford, England, 1964-68; MA, French, Russian, Oxford; Lecteur d'Anglais, University of Grenoble, France, 1967; Postgraduate Scholar, Department of Slavonic Studies, 1968-70, PhD, 1971, University of Nottingham, England. Publications: Alexander Kuprin, 1978; Alexander Grin: The Seeker of Adventure, 1978; Alexander Grin: The Forgotten Visionary, 1980; An Anthology of Russian-Neorealism, 1982; Fifty Years on: Gorky and his Time, 1987; Alexander Grin: Selected Short Stories, 1987; From Furmanov to Sholokhov, 1988; In Defence of a Reputation, 1990; The Russian Short Story, 1900-1917, 1991. Contributions to: Numerous articles in various journals in field of Russian literature. Honours: Visiting Lecturer in Russian Victoria University of Wellington, New Zealand, 1976; Visiting Fellow, Department of Russian, University of Otago, Dunedin, New Zealand, 1991. Memberships: British Association of Slavists; Executive Committee, RLUSC for UK Universities. Address: Department of Slavonic Studies, University of Nottingham, Nottingham NG7 2RD, England.

LULUA Abdul-Wahid, b. 16 July 1931, Mowsil, Iraq. Professor of English Literature. m. Mariam Abdul-Bagi, 22 July 1962, 1 son, 1 daughter. Education: Licence-es-Lettres, English, Ecole Normale Superieure, University of Baghdad, 1952; EdM, English, Harvard University, USA, 1957; PhD, English, Western Reserve University, Cleveland, Ohio, 1962. Appointments: Lecturer, Assistant Professor, English Literature, Head, Department of European Languages, College of Education (formerly Ecole Normale Superieure), Baghdad, 1962-67; Assistant Professor, English Literature, University of Kuwait, 1967-70; Associate Professor, English Literature, Faculty of Arts, 1970-71, 1972-77; Visiting Scholar, Cambridge University, England, 1971-72; Freelance Translator, 1977; Associate Professor, English Literature, 1983, Professor, English Literature, 1983-89, Chairman, Department of English Language and Literature, 1983-84, Yarmouk University; Jordan; Professor, English Literature, United Arab Emirates University, 1989-. Publications: Critical Studies: In Search of Meaning, 1973, 2nd edition 1983; T S Eliot, The Waste Land; The Poet and the Poem, 1980, 2nd edition 1986; Blowing into Ashes, 1984, 2nd edition 1989; Aspect of the Moon, 1990; Arabic Poetry and the Rise of European Love Lyrics; English-Arabic translations: The Waters of Babylon and Sergeant Musgrave's Dance (John Arden), 1976; Timon of Athens (Shakespeare), 1977, 2nd edition 1984; Left-Handed Liberty and The Hero Rises Up (John Arden), 1978; William Blake (D G Gilham), 1982; The Critical Idion, 44 vols, 1969-82; Trends and Movements in Modern Arabic Poetry (Salma K Jayyusi); Cymbeline, Pericles (Shakespeare); Psychoanlytic Criticism (Elizabeth Wright); Arabic-English translations: Culture and Arts in Iraq, 1978; Revolution and Development in Iraq, 1980; Iraq: The Eternal Fire, 1981; The Long Days, novel, 1982; Battlefront Stories from Iraq, 1983; Modern Iraqi Poetry, 1987. Contributions to: Major Arabic magazines, Iraq and Middle East. Memberships: Modern Humanities Research Association, Cambridge; Association Internationale de Litterature Comparative. Literary Agent: Riad El-Rayyes Books, 56 Knightsbridge, London SW1X 7NJ, England.

LUNARI Luigi, b. 3 Jan 1934, Milan, Italy. Writer. m. Laura Pollaroli, 8 July 1961, 1 son, 1 daughter. Education: Degree in Law, University of Milan, 1956; Diploma in Common Law, City of London College, 1958; Composition & Orchestra Conducting, Academy Chigiana, Siena, 1978. Appointments: Director, Study Office of Piceolo Teatro, 1961-82; Professor, History of Dramatic Art, University of Modern Languages, 1984-. Publications: L'Old Vic di Londra, 1959; Laurence Oliver, 1959; Il movimento drammatico irlandese, 1960; Il teatro irlandese: storia e antologia, 1961; Henry Irving e il teatro inglese dell'800, 1962; Maria di Nazareth, 1986. Contributions to: Music & Drama Correspondent for the Daily Avanti, 1978-; Il giornale nuovo, 1991. Memberships: International Society of Authors; International Society of Dramatists; PEN Club. Address: 20047 Brugherid, Via Volturno 80, Milan, Italy.

LUND Gerald Niels, b. 12 Sept 1939, Fountain Green, Utah, USA. Educator. m. Lynn Stanard, 5 June 1963, 3 sons, 4 daughters. Education: BA Sociology 1965, MS Sociology 1969, Brigham Young University; Further graduate studies in New Testament at Pepperdine University, Los Angeles. Publications: The Alliance, 1983; Freedom Factor, 1987; One in Thine Hand, 1981; The Coming of the Lord, 1971; This is Your World, 1973; Leverage Point, 1986; Pillar of Light (vol 1 in A-part series called The Work and The Glory) Oct 1990; Like A Fire is Burning, vol 2 1991; Truth Will Prevail vol 3, 1992; They Gold To Refine, vol 4 1993; A Season of Joy, vol 5, 1994. Contributions to: Numerous articles in magazines and monographs on Biblical and religious themes. Honour: Outstanding Teacher, Continuing Education, Brigham Young University, 1985; Awarded Best Novel by Association of Mormon Letters, 1991, 1993. Address: 1157 E 1500 S, Bountiful, UT 84010, USA.

LUNN Janet Louise, b. 28 Dec 1928, Dallas, Texas, USA. Writer. m. Richard Lunn, 2 Mar 1950, 4 sons, 1 daughter. Education: Three Years at Queen's University, Kingston, Ontario; Writer-in-residence, Regina Public Library, Regina, Saskatchewan, 1982-83; Writer-in-residence, Kitchener Public Library, Kitchener, Ont, 1987; Writer-in-residence, Ottawa University, Ottawa, Ont, autumn 1993. Publications: The County, 1967; Double Spell, 1968; Larger Than Life, 1979; The Twelve Dancing Princesses, 1979; The Root Cellar, 1981; Shadow in Hawthorn Bay, 1986; Amos's Sweater, 1988; Duck Cakes for Sale, 1989; One Hundred Shining Candles, 1990; The Story of Canada, 1992; (Ed) Collection of Ghost Stories for Children, fall 1994. Contributions to: Magazine articles, book reviews, radio talk and interviews. Address: RR No 2 Hillier, Ontario, K0K 2J0, Canada.

LUO Bin Ji (Zhang Pujun), b. 17 Feb 1917, Jilin, China. Author/Novelist; Historian; Philologist. m. Zou Min Cai, 6 Oct 1949, 1 son, 1 daughter. Education: Completed Junior Middle School, 1933; Auditor, Peking University, 1934; Self-study, Peking Library, 1934-35. Appointments: Writer, 1936-; Propagandist, Shanghai, 1936; Minister, Chengxian County Propaganda Department, 1938; Chief Editor, magazines: Zhan Qi and Wen Xue Bao, 1939, 1941, North-East Culture, 1945. Publications: One Week and One Day, 1937; One Day of Shanghai, 1938; On the Border Line, 1939; Busy Summer, 1939; FEI YOU-WU, 1941; CHILDHOOD, 1944; An Unbending Man, 1944; Spring over Bei-Wang-Yuan and Other Stories, 1947; Blue River Tu-Men, 1947; May Lilac, play, 1947; Mother Wang, 1953; Old Wei Jun and Fang-fang, 1958; A Trading Post in the Mountains, 1963; Selected Short Stories, 1980; New Textual Research of Inscriptions on Bronze Objects, 1987; On Dragon, historical scientific paper (Japanese), 1987; Recollections of General Li Yan Lu, 1978; A Window for Looking at the Age, essayus, 1988; The Rear Area, short stories, 1990; Short Stories, 1990; The Ancient Society of China, 1990. Contributions to: Feng Huo; Literature; Lü Zhou; Ren Ming Ri Bao; Ren Ming Wen Xue; Writer, Centre Daily News, USA. Honours: October Literature Prize for A Brief Biography of Xiao Hong, 1984; Named Greqat Master of Short Story, The Muse of the Novel, The Father of Jin Wen. Memberships: Chinese Writers Association, Council Member 1979, Vice-Chair, Beijing Branch, 1963-88; Standing Council Committee Member, Chinese Literature and Art Association, 1979-; Standing Council Committee Member, Academy of Pacific History; Vice-Chair: Lao She Foundation, 1989-; Association of Literature and Art Shandong. Literary Agent: Zhang Xiao-xin. Address: The Beijing Branch of the Association of Chinese Writers, Liubukou, Beijing, China.

LUPOFF Richard Allen, b. 21 Feb 1935. Author. m. Patricia Enid Loring, 27 Aug 1958, 2 sons, 1 daughter. Education: BA, University of Miami, Florida, USA, 1956. Appointments: Editor, Canaveral Press, 1963-70; Contributing Editor, Crawdaddy Magazine, 1968-71; Contributing Editor Science Fiction Eye, 1988-90; Editor, Canyon Press, 1986-. Publications: Edgar Rice Burroughs: Master of Adventure, 1966; All in Colour for a Dime, 1971; Sword of the Demon, 1977; Space War Blues, 1978; Sun's End, 1984; Circumpolar!, 1984; Lovecrafts Book, 1985; The Forever City, 1987; The Comic Book Killer, 1988; The Classic Car Killer, 1992; The Bessie Blue Killer, 1994; The Sepia Siren Killer, 1994; many others. Contributions to: Ramparts; Los Angeles Times; Washington Post; San Francisco Chronicle; New York Times; Magazine of Fantasy and Science Fiction; many others. Honour: Hugo Award, 1963. Literary Agent: Henry Morrison, PO Box 235, Bedford Hills, NY 10507, USA. Address: 3208 Claremont Avenue, Berkeley, CA 94705, USA.

LURIE Alison, b. 3 Sept 1926, Chicago, Illinois, USA. Education: Radcliffe College, Cambridge, Mass, USA. Appointments: Frederic J Whiton Professor of American Literature, Cornell University; Editor, The Oxford Book of Modern Fairy Tales; Co-editor, The Garland Library of Children's Classics. Publications: Love and Friendship, 1962; The Nowhere City, 1965; Imaginary Friends, 1967; Real People, 1969; The War Between the Tates, 1974; V R Lang: Poems and Plays, 1975; Only Children, 1979; Clever Gretchen and other Forgotten Folktales, 1980; The Heavenly Zoo, 1980; The Language of Clothes, 1981; Fabulous Beast, 1981; Foreign Affairs, 1984; The Truth About Lorin Jones, 1988;

Don't Tell the Grownups: Subversive Children's Literature, 1990. Contributions to: Art and Antiques; Children's Literature; Harper's; House and Garden; Lear's; Ms; The New York Times Book Review; New York Woman; The Observer; Psychology Today; The Times Literary Supplement; Vanity Fair; Vogue. Honours: American Academy of Arts and Letters Award in Fiction, 1984; Radcliffe College Alumnae Award, 1987; Pulitzer Prize in Fiction, 1985; Prix Femina Etranger, 1989. Address: English Department, Cornell University, Ithaca, NY 14853, USA.

LURIE Morris, b. 30 Oct 1938, Melbourne, Australia. Writer. Education: Architecture studies, Royal Melbourne Institute of Technology, 1957-60, no degree. Appointments: Writer in Residence, Latrobe University, 1984; Holmesglen Tafe, 1992. Publications: Rappaport, 1966; The Twenty Seventh Annual African Hippopotamus Race, 1969; Flying Home, 1978; Outrageous Behaviour, 1984; Whole Life, 1987; Novels: Seven books for Grossmar 1983 and Madness 1991. Contributions to: Virginia Quarterly Review; The Times; Punch; Telegraph Magazine; The Age, National Times, Nation Review; The New Yorker; Stories broadcast on BBC, and plays on ABC. Honours: Bicentennial Banjo Award, 1988; State of Victoria Short Story Award, 1973; National Book Council Selection, 1980; Children's Book Council, 1983. Address: 2/3 Finchley Court, Hawthorn, Victoria 3122, Australia.

LUSTBADER Eric, b. 1946, American. Writer of novels, science fiction. Publications: The Sunset Warrior, 1976; Shallows at Night, 1977; Dai-San, 1978; Beneath an Opal Moon, 1978; The Ninja, 1980; Sirens, 1982; Black Heat, 1983; The Miko, 1984; Jian, 1985; Shan, 1986; French Kiss, 1989; Floating City, 1994. Address: c/o Henry Morrison Inc, Box 235, Bedford Hills, NY 10507, USA.

LUSTGARTEN Celia Sophie, b. 24 Oct 1941, New York City, New York, USA. Freelance Consultant; Writer. Publications: Short story in book, Shock Treatment, 1988. Contributions to: US publications: Shameless Hussy Review, 1978; Cow in the Road, 1986; Egad! 1986-87; Z Miscellanea, 1987; Bad Haircut, 1987; Ransom, 1988; For Poets Only, 1988; Famous Last Words, 1988; Perceptions, 1989, 1990, 1992; Stellanova, 1989; The Cacanadada Review, 1990; Grasslands Review, University of North Texas, 1990; The Key Move, 1981; Perceptions, 1993; Canadian publications: Room of One's Own, 1981; New Canadian Review, 1989; Chanticleer, 1989; Herspectives, 1990, 1991; New Zealand publications: Rhythm-and-Rhyme, 1985, 1986; UK publications: Spokes, 1985, 1986; T.O.P.S. 10 Poetry Magazine, 1985, 1986, 1987. Honours: First Prize, Short Story, Alternate Realities Society and Imaginative Fiction Society, Victoria, British Columbia, Canada, 1986. Membership: Poets & Writers, New York City, NY. Address: 317 Third Avenue, San Francisco, CA 94118, USA.

LUSTIG Arnost, b. 21 Dec 1926, Prague, Czechoslovakia. Came to US in 1970. Writer; Screenwriter; Educator. m. Vera Wieislitz, 24 July 1949, 1 son, 1 daughter. Education: MA, College of Political and Social Science, Prague, 1951, Ing 1954; Doctor of Hebrew Letters (hon), Spertus College, Judaica, 1986. Appointments include: Arab-Israeli Correspondent, Radio Prague, 1948-49; Correspondent, Czechoslovak Radio, 1950-68; Screenwriter, Barrandov Film Studios, Prague, 1960-68; Writer, Kibutz Hachotrim, Israel, 1968-69; Screenwriter, Jadran Film Studio, Zagreb, 1969-70; Visiting Lecturer, English 1971-72; Visiting Professor, English, Drake University, Des Moines, 1972-73; Professor, Literature and Film, American University, Washington, 1973-; Head, Czechoslovak film delegation, San Sebastian Film Festival, 1968. Publications include: Night and Hope, 1958; Diamonds of the Night, 1958; Street of Lost Brothers, 1959; Dita Saxova, 1962; My Acquaintance Vili Feld, 1962; A Prayer for Katarina Horovitzova, 1964; Nobody Will be Humiliated, 1964; Bitter Smells of Almonds, 1968; Darling, 1969; The Unloved (From the Diary of a Seventeen Year Old), 1986; Indecent Dreams, 1988; Films/Screenplays: Transport from Paradise, 1963; Diamonds of the Night, 1964; Dita Saxova, 1968; A Bit to Eat, 1960; The Triumph of Memory, 1989. Address: 4000 Tunlaw Road NW, Apt 825, Washington, DC 20007, USA.

LUTTWAK Edward (Nicolae), b. 1942, American. Writer on History, International Relations/Current Affairs, Politics/Government. Appointments: Associate, Center of Strategic and International Studies, Washington DC, 1978-87; Visiting Professor, Johns Hopkins University, Baltimore, 1974-78; Holder of Chair in Strategy, Center for Strategic and International Studies, Washington, DC; Director of Geo-Economics, Centre for Strategic and International Studies, 1991.

Publications: Coup D'Etat, 1968; Dictionary of Modern War, 1971; The Strategic Balance, 1972; The US-USSR Strategic Balance, 1974; The Political Uses of Sea Power, 1974; (co-author) The Israeli Army, 1975; The Grand Strategy of the Roman Empire, 1977; Strategy and Politics, 1980; The Grand Strategy of the Soviet Union, 1983; The Pentagon and the Art of War, 1985; Strategy and History: Collected Essays, 1985; (co-author) Yearbook of International Politics 1983-84, 1984, 1984-85, 1985; Strategy: The Logic of War and Peace, 1987; The Endangered American Dream, 1993. Contributions to: TLS; London Review of Books; Commentary New York Times; LA Times; Foreign Affairs. Address: CSIS, 1800 K Street NW, Washington, DC 20006, USA.

LUTYENS Mary (Esther Wyndham), b. 1908, British. Writer of Historical/Romance/Gothic publications, Biography. Publications: Forthcoming Marriages, 1933; Perchance to Dream, 1935; Rose and Thorn, 1936; Spider's Silk, 1938; Family Colouring, 1940; A Path of Gold, 1941; Together and Alone, 1942; So Near to Heaven, 1943; Julie and the Narrow Valley, 1944; And Now There Is You, 1953; Meeting in Venice, 1956; To Be Young, 1959; (ed) Lady Lytton's Court Diary, 1961; Effie in Venice, 1965; Millais and the Ruskins, 1967; (ed) Freedom from the Known by Krishnamurti, 1969; (ed) The Only Revolution by Krishnamurti, 1970; The Ruskins and the Grays, 1972; Cleo, 1973; Krishnamurti: The Years of Awakening, 1975; The Lyttons of India, 1979; Edwin Lutyens, 1980; Krishnamurti: The Years of Fulfilment, 1982; Krishnamurti: The Open Door, 1988; The Life and Death of Krishnamurti, 1989; Repv, 1991; Eight novels published by Mills & Boon. Contributions to: Apollo, TLS, Cornhill, Walpole Society Journal. Honours: FRSL. Literary Agent: Jane Turnbull, 13 Wendall Road, London W12 9RS. Address: 8 Elizabeth Close, Randolph Avenue, London W9 1BN, England.

LUTZ John Thomas, b. 11 Sept 1939, Dallas, Texas, USA. Writer. m. Barbara Jean Bradley, 15 Mar 1958, 1 son, 2 daughters. Education: Meramac Community College. Publications: The Truth of the Matter, 1971; Buyer Beware, 1976; Bonegrinder, 1977; Lazarus Man, 1979, 1980; Jericho Man, 1980, 1981; The Shadow Man, 1981, 1982; Exiled with Steven Greene, 1982; The Eye with Bill Pronzini, 1984; Nightlines, 1985; The Right to Sing the Blues, 1986; Tropical Heat, 1986; Ride the Lightning, 1987; Scorcher, 1987; Kiss, 1988; Shadowtown, 1988; Time Exposure, 1989; Flame, 1990; Diamond Eyes, 1990; SWF Seeks Same, 1990; Bloodfire, 1991; Hot, 1992; Dancing with the Dead, 1992; Spark, 1993; Shadows Everywhere, short stories, 1994; Torch, 1994; Thicker Than Blood, 1994. Contributions to: Ellery Queens Mystery Magazine; Hitchcocks Mystery Magazine; Mike Shayne Mystery Magazine; Executioner; Charlie Chan Mystery Magazine; Cavalier; Espionage; Works featured in numerous foreign publications, textbooks and anthologies; Several adaptations for radio mystery dramas. Honours: Scroll, Mystery Writers of America, 1981; Shamus Award, 1982; Shamus Nominee, 1983; Private Eye Writers of America; Peer Award Nominee, 1985; MWA Edgar Award, 1986; Shamus Award, 1988. Memberships: Board of Directors, Private Eye Writers of America; Midwest Chapter, Mystery Writers of America. Literary Agent: Dominick Abel, New York. Address: 880 Providence Avenue, Webster Groves, MO 63119, USA.

LUU Van Lang (Danh Khue), b. 5 Jan 1928, do luong, VN. Linguist. m. 10 Aug 1969, Bicho Thuoc (Giang), 2 sons. Edcucation: Beijing Institute of Russian Language, 1950-53; Doctoral Degree, Dissertation, 1964, printed 1968, Professor. Employment: Holder of the Chair of Foreign Language, Institute of Pedag. of Sciences, Hanoi University, 1955-56; Reader of Linguistics, HN University, 1957-61; Holder of the chair of Linguistics, Vinh College of Teacher Education, 1961-63; Vice-Director of Department of Terminology and Scientific Dictionaries, State Committee for Sciences, Member of the State Council for Science Terminology, 1964-68; Executive (Scientist of Institute of Linguistics, 1968-70; Head of the Section of Terminology, IL, 1971-78; Head of the Section of Grammer, IL, 1979-89; Member of Science Council, IL, 1968-94. Publications: Study on Russian morphology, 1956; On the declensio of Russian Words, 1957; On the problem of whether the language belongs to the superstructure 1957-58; An introduction to linguistic (co-author), 1961; On the use o foreign scientific terms, 1964, print, 1968; Russian-Vietnamese Linguistic Terms (Chief-redactor), 1969; A study of Vietnamese grammer from the viewpoint of nuclear stratus syntagm, 1968, 1970 Thoery of grammatology, 1971; Some contradictions in the conceptio of the word-group as the center of Vietnamese grammar, 1975; On th formation of scientific terms, 1977; Dictionary of Social Scientific term (Editor), 1979; The necessity of a distinction between morpheme (i lexicology) and syllabeme (in grammer) of Vietnamese language, 1980; To apply the theory of the typical sign with nuclear meaning to lexicography, 1978, 1981; The conception of Vietnamese word and phrase, 1981; Directly higher syntactic unit than work is syntaxeme, but not group word, 1983; Position of word and word building components in language system, 1984; The clause as a transitional unit between the syntaxeme and the sentence, 1985; On multi-strate nuclear grammar, 1985; The path to the establishment of the system of grammatical units, 1986; Problems of Vietnamese grammer (Editor-in-chief), 1988; About the principal of classification of the word classes in Vietnamese, 1988; The theory of typical sign with nuclear meaning in sematics and lexicography, 1989; The application of the theory of typical sign with nuclear meaning in explanatory dictionaries, 1991; On the viewpoint regarding functional grammar, 1992; The Problems on Grammar of Modern Vietnamese Language-Sentence Components, Editor-in-chief, 1994; My words (about 80) belong to the various domains, but most of them concentrate to present in detail on my nuclear multi-strats theory in gramma and my theory of typical sign with the nuclear meaning in semantics and lexicography (1978-81). Memberships: Member of Linguistics Society of Vietman.

LUXNER Mort(on Bennett), b. 2 June 1917, Newark, NJ, USA. Newspaper Editor. m. Trudie (Goldie) Wolfe, 2 Dec 1945, 1 s, 1 d. Education: Brooklyn College, NY; Washington & Lee Univ, Lexington VA; SMI, Waco, TX. Literary Appointments: Editor, The Stars and Stripes, Egyptian ed, 1944; Ed in Chief, The Craftsman, 1958; Ed, Western News, 1977; Ed, The Chronicle, 1979; Ed in Chief, The Broward News, 1983-. Publications: Birth of a Salesman. Contributions to: The Advertising Journal, 1980-92. Honours: Soldier Poet of World War II, 1943. Membership: Dir American Activities, IMPS, UK. Address: 1425 NW Terrace, Pompano Beach, FL 33063, USA.

LYALL Gavin Tudor, b. 9 May 1932, Birmingham, England. Author; Journalist. m. Katherine Whitehom, 4 Jan 1958, 2 sons. Education: MA, Pembroke College, Cambridge, 1956; MA 1986. Literary Appointments: Staff, Picture Post, 1956-57; Worked on BBC TV's Tonight programme 1958-1959; Staff, Sunday Times, 1959-63. Publications: The Wrong Side of the Sky, 1961; The Most Dangerous Game, 1964; Midnight Plus One, 1965; Shooting Script, 1966; Freedom's Battle Vol II, 1968; Venus with Pistol, 1969; Blame the Dead, 1972; Judas Country, 1975; Operation Warboard, 1976; The Secret Servant, 1980; The Conduct of Major Maxim, 1982; The Crocus List, 1985; Uncle Target, 1989; Spy's Honour, 1993. Contributions to: The Observer; Sunday Telegraph; Punch; London Illustrated News. Honours: Silver Dagger, Crime Writer's Association, 1964, 1965. Memberships: Crime Writers' Association (Chairman 1966-67); Detection Club; Society of Authors. Literary Agent: The Peters Fraser and Dunlop Group Ltd. Address: 14 Provost Road, London NW3 4ST, England.

LYKIARD Alexis, b. 1940, British. Writer of novels/short stories, poetry; translator. Creative Writing Tutor, Arvon Foundation, 1974-; Writer-in-Residence, Sutton Central Library (C Day Lewis Fellowship), 1976-77; Loughborough Art College (Arts Council of GB), 1982-83; Tavistock (Devon Libraries), 1983-85; HMP Channings Wood, 1988-89; HMP Haslar, 1992. Publications: Lobsters, 1961; Journey of the Alchemist, 1963; The Summer Ghosts, 1964; (ed) Wholly Communion, 1965; Zones, 1966; Paros Poems, 1967; A Sleeping Partner, 1967; Robe of Skin, 1969; Strange Alphabet, 1970; (trans), Lautréamont's Maldoror, 1970; (ed) Best Horror Stories of J Sheridan Le Fanu, 1970; Eight Lovesongs, 1972; The Stump, 1973; Greek Images, 1973; Lifelines, 1973; Instrument of Pleasure, 1974; (trans) The Piano Ship, 1974; (ed) The Horror Hom, by E F Benson, 1974; Last Throes, 1976; Milesian Fables, 1976; A Morden Tower Reading, 1976; (trans), Laure, by Emmanuelle Arsan, 1977; The Drive North, 1977; (ed) New Stories 2, 1977; (trans) Nea by Emmanuelle Arsan, 1978; (trans) Lautréamont Poésies, 1978; (ed) A Man with a Maid, 1982; Scrubbers, 1983; (ed) The Memoirs of Dolly Morton by Hugues Rebell, 1984; Cat Kin, 1985; Out of Exile, 1986; (trans) Secrets of Emmanuelle, by E Arsan, 1980; Vanna, by E Arsan, 1981; Oh Wicked Country! 1982; Nostradamus Countdown to Apocalypse by J-C de Fontbrune, 1983; Joy by Joy Laurey, 1983; Indiscreet Memoirs, by Alain Dorval, 1984; Nostradamus 2, by J-C de Fontbrune, 1984; Florian by Antoine S, 1986; Violette, by Marquise de Mannoury d'Ectot, 1986; The Exploits of a Young Don Juan, by Apollinaire/Irene by Aragon, 1986; (ed) Beat Dreams and Plymouth Sounds, 1987; (ed) Out of the Wood, 1989; (trans) Days and Nights, by Alfred Jarry, 1989; Safe Levels, 1990; (trans) Emmanuelle Exposed, by E Arsan, 1991; Living Jazz, 1991; Surrealist Games, by

André Breton, 1991; Beautiful is Enough, 1992. Address: c/o A M Heath and Co Ltd, 79 St Martin's Lane, London WC2N 4AA, England.

LYNCH Audry Louise, b. 18 July 1933, Cambridge, Massachusetts, USA. Guidance Counsellor; Community College English Instructor. m. Gregory Lynch, 8 Sept 1956, 1 son, 2 daughters. Education: BA, Harvard University, 1955; EdM, Boston University, 1968; EdD, University of San Francisco, 1983. Publications: With Steinbeck in the Sea of Cortez, 1991; Father Joe Young: A Priest and His People, 1993. Contributions to: Yankee Magazine; West Magazine; Parade Magazine; The Writer; The International Herald Tribune. Memberships: California Writers Club; The Writers Connection. Address: 20774 Meadow Oak Road, Saratoga, CA 95070, USA.

LYNCH Frances. See: **COMPTON D G.**

LYNCH John, b. 1927, British. Writer on History; Emeritus Professor. Appointments: Lecturer in History, University of Liverpool, 1954-61, Lecturer, Reader and Professor of Latin American History, University College, London, 1961-74; Professor of Latin American History and Director of Institute of Latin American Studies, University of London, 1974-87. Publications: Spanish Colonial Administration 1782-1810: The Intendant System in the Viceroyalty of the Río de la Plata, 1958; Spain Under the Habsburgs, 2 vols, 1964-69, 2nd rev ed 1981; (ed with R A Humphreys) The Origins of the Latin American Revolutions 1808-1826, 1965; The Spanish American Revolutions 1808-1826, 1973, 2nd rev ed 1986; Argentine Dictator: Juan Manuel de Rosas 1829-1852, 1981; (with others) The Cambridge History of Latin America, vol 3 1985, vol 4 1986; Bourbon Spain 1700-1808, 1989; Caudillos in Spanish America 1800-1850, 1992; Latin American Revolutions 1808-1826: Old and New World Origins, 1994. Honours: Order of Andrés Bello, Venezuela, 1979; Encomienda Isabel La Católica, Spain, 1988; Doctor, Honoris Causa, University of Seville, 1990; Membership: FRHistS. Address: 8 Templars Crescent, London N3 3QS, England.

LYNCH Timothy Jeremy Mahoney, b. 10 June 1952, San Francisco, California, USA. Lawyer; Classical Scholar; Author; Business Executive. Education: MS, JD, Civil Law, Taxation Law, Golden Gate University; MA, PhD, University of San Francisco, 1983; PhD, Classics, Divinity, Harvard University, 1988; JSD, Constitutional Law, Hastings Law Center, San Francisco; Postdoctoral research, Writing in Classics. Appointments: Chairman, Patristic, Biblical, Latin and Greek Literary Publications Group, Institute of Classical Studies; Chairman, Postdoctoral Research and Writing in Humanities Group, National Association of Scholars; Fellow, Harvard University Center for Hellenic Studies, June 1991, Apr 1993; Senior Research and Writing Fellow, Mediaeval Theological Philosophy manuscripts of St Gallen Monks, Medieval Academy of America. Publications include: History of Europe, 5 vols, 1987; Essays and papers on US-Soviet relations, Iran-British relations, 1988; Legal essays, 1990-94; Musical papers, 1994; History of Classical Tradition, 20 vols, 1995; Poems for children; Textbooks; Co-editor, co-author: Commentary on Classical Philology; Greek Hellenic Philosophy, Literary Translations and Commentary on Philodemus Project, 1995; 50 volumes on classical philology, literary styles and analysis of Old Testament Exegesis, history of mediaeval and modern moral and ecumenical theological institutes, other topics, 1966. Contributions to: Journals of Association of Trial Lawyers and Medieval Academy of America. Honours include: Member, International Platform Association; Eminent Scholar of the Year, National Association of Scholars, 1993. Memberships include: American Philological Association, President-Elect 1994-95; American Historical Association; Law Society of America. Literary Agent: National Endowment for the Humanities, Publications Office, Washington DC. Address: 540 Jones Street, Suite 201, San Francisco, CA 94102-2022, USA.

LYNDS Dennis (William Arden, Nick Carter, Michael Collins, John Crowe, Carl Dekker, Maxwell Grant, Mark Sadler), b. 15 Jan 1924, St Louis, Missouri, USA. Writer. m. (1) Doris Flood, 1949 (div 1956), (2) Sheila McErlean, 1961, div 1985, 2 daughters, (3) Gayle Hallenbeck Stone, 1986. Appointments include: Assistant Editor, Chemical Week, New York, 1951-52; Editorial Director, American Institute of Management, NY, 1952-54; Editor, Managing Editor, Chemical Engineering Progress, 1955-61; Editor (part-time), Chemical Equipment, Laboratory Equipment, NY, 1962-66; Instructor, Adult Education, Santa Barbara City College, California, 1966-68; Self-Employed Writer, 1961-. Publications include: Combat Soldier, 1962; Uptown Downtown, 1963; Why Girls Ride Sidesaddle, short stories, 1980; Freak, 1983; Minnesota Strip, 1987; Red Rosa, 1988; Castrato, 1989; Chasing Eights, 1990; The Irishman's Horse, 1991; Cassandra In Red, 1992; Crime, Punishment and Resurrection, 1992; Talking To The World, 1995; The Cadillac Cowboy, 1995. Literary Agent: Bleecker Street Associates, 88 Bleecker Street, Suite Suite 6P, New York, NY 10012, USA. Address: 12 St Anne Drive, Santa Barbara, California 93109, USA.

LYNN Frank. See: **LEISY James Franklin.**

LYNN Jonathon, b. 1943, British. Theatre and Film Director, Actor, Writer of Novels/Short Stories, Plays/Screenplays. Appointments: Artistic Director, Cambridge Theatre Company, 1976-81; Company Director of National Theatre, 1987. Publications: (with George Layton), Doctor in Charge, Doctor at Sea, Doctor on the Go (television series), 1971-74; (with George Layton), My Name is Harry Worth (television series), 1973; Pig of the Month (play), 1974; (with Barry Levinson), The Internecine Project (screenplay), 1974; (with George Layton), My Brother's Keeper (2 television series), 1975, 1976; A Proper Man (novel), 1976; (with Antony Jay), Yes Minister (television series), 1980-83, Yes Prime Minister, 1986, 1987; (hardback), The Complete Yes Minister, 1984; Yes Prime Minister, vols I and II, 1986, 1987; Clue (screenplay and direction), 1985; Nuns on the Run (screenplay and direction), 1990; My Cousin Vinny (director), 1992; The Distinguished Gentleman (director), 1992; Greed (director), 1993; Mayday (novel), 1993. Address: c/o Peters, Fraser and Dunlop Ltd, The Chambers, Chelsea Harbour, Lots Road, London SW10, England.

LYNTON Ann. See: **RAYNER Claire Berenice.**

LYON Bryce Dale, b. 22 Apr 1920, Bellevue, OH, USA. Professor. m. Mary Elizabeth Lewis, 3 June 1944, 1 son, 1 daughter. Education: AB, Baldwin-Wallace College, 1942; PhD, Cornell University, 1949. Appointments include: Assistant Professor of History, University of Colorado, Boulder, 1949-51; Assistant Professor of History, Harvard University, Cambridge, MA, 1951-56; Professor of History, University of California, Berkeley, 1959-65; Barnaby and Mary Critchfield Keeney Professor of History 1965-, Chairman of Department 1968-, Brown University, Providence. Publications include: Medieval Institutions: Selected Essays, 1954; A Constitutional and Legal History of Medieval England, 1960, 2nd edition 1980; A History of the World (with others), 1960; The High Middle Ages 1000-1300, 1964; Frankish Institutions Under Charlemagne (with M Lyon), 1968; A History of the Western World, 1969, 2nd edition 1974; The Origins of the Middle Ages: Pirenne's Challenge to Gibbon, 1972; Studies of West European and Medieval Institutions, 1978; The Wardrobe Book of William de Norwell: 12 July 1338 to 27 May 1340 (with H S Lucas and M Lyon), 1983; The Firth of Annales History: The Letters of Lucien Febvre and Marc Bloch to Henri Pirenne 1921-1935 (with Mary Lyon), 1991. Address: Department of History, Brown University, Brown Station, Providence, RI 02912, USA.

LYON Elinor. See: **WRIGHT Elinor.**

LYONS Arthur, b. 1946, American. Writer of Mystery/Crime/Suspense. Owner of gift shop and restaurant, Palm Springs, California, USA, 1967-. Publications: The Second Coming: Satanism in American (non-fiction), 1970, in UK as Satan Wants You: The Cult of Devil Worship, 1971; The Dead are Discreet, 1974; All God's Children, 1975; The Killing Floor, 1976; Dead Ringers, 1977; Castles Burning, 1980; Hard Trade, 1982; At the Hands of Another, 1983; Three with a Bullet, 1985; False Pretenses, 1993.

LYONS Elena. See: **FAIRBURN Eleanor M.**

LYONS Garry Fairfax, b. 5 July 1956, Kingston-upon-Thames, England. Writer. m. Ruth Caroline Willis, 6 Apr 1985, 1 son, 1 daughter. Education: BA, English Literature, University of York, 1978; MA, Drama & Theatre Arts, University of Leeds, 1982. Literary Appointments: Playwright in Residence, Major Road Theatre Company, 1983; Fellow in Theatre, University of Bradford, 1984-88. Major Productions: Echoes from the Valley, 1983; Mohicans, 1984; St Vitus' Boogie, 1985; Urban Jungle, 1985; The Green Violinist, 1986; Irish Night, 1987; Divided Kingdoms, 1989; The People Museum, 1989; Dream Kitchen, 1992; Frankie and Tommy, 1992; Wicked Yaar, 1994. Membership: Theatre Writers' Union. Literary Agent: Alan Brodie. Address: c/o International Creative Management, Oxford House, 76 Oxford Street, London W1N 0AX, England.

LYONS Mary E. Publications: Sorrow's Kitchen: The Life and Folklore of Zora Neal Hurston, 1990; Raw Head, Bloody Bones, 1991; Letters From a Slave Girl, 1992; Starting Home: The Story of Horace Pippin, 1993; Deep Blues, Bill Taylor, Self-Taught Artist, 1994. Honours: Golden Kite Award, Society of Children's Book Writers & Illustrators, 1993. Address: c/o MacMillan Publishing Publicity Dept, 20th Floor 866 Third Avenue, New York, NY 10022, USA.

LYONS Richard. Poet; Writer. Publications: Man & Tin Kettles, 1956; One Squeaking Straw: Eclogues, 1958; Poetry North: Five Poets of North Dakota (editor), 1970; Racer & Lame, 1975; Scanning the Land, 1980; Enough to Be a Woman, 1992. Contributions include: Kennebec; SD Review; ND Quarterly; Piedmont Literary Review. Honours: Lavan Younger Poets Award, American Academy of Poets, 1993. Address: 9 Deane street, Gardiner, Marine 04345, USA.

LYONS Thomas Tolman, b. 1934, American. Writer on Civil Liberties/Human Rights, History, Race Relations. Appointments: History Teacher, Mount Hermon School, 1958-63; History Teacher, Phillips Academy, Andover, Massachusetts, USA, 1963-. Publications: (ed) Presidential Power in the Era of the New Deal, 1964; (ed) Realism and Idealism in Wilson's Peace Program, 1965; (ed) Reconstruction and the Race Problem, 1968; Black Leadership in American History, 1970; The Supreme Court in Contemporary American Life, 1975; The Expansion of the Federal Union, 1978; After Hiroshima, 1979, 1985; The President: Teacher, Preacher, Salesman, 1984. Address: 38 Phillips Street, Andover, MA 01818, USA.

M

MABBETT Ian William, b. 27 Apr 1939. University Academic. m. Jacqueline Diana June Towns, 11 Dec 1971, 2 daughters. Education: Jesus College, Oxford, 1957-63; BA (Oxon), 1960, DPhil (Oxon), 1963, MA (Oxon), 1964. Publications: A Short History of India, 1968, 2nd edition, 1983; Modern China, The Mirage of Modernity, 1985; Kings and Emperors of Asia, 1985; Patterns of Kingship and Authority in Traditional Asia (editor), 1985; The Khmers (co-author), 1994. Contributions to: Hemisphere, Canberra; Asian Pacific Quarterly, Seoul; The Cambridge History of Southeast Asia, Cambridge. Honours: President, IXth World Sanskrit Conference, 1994. Memberships: Federation of Australian Writers; Australian Society of Authors. Address: c/o Department of History, Monash University, Clayton, Victoria 3168, Australia.

MABEY Richard Thomas, b. 20 Feb 1941, Berkhamsted, Hertfordshire, England, Writer; Broadcaster. Education: HA Hons, 1966, MA, 1971, St Cahterine's College, Oxford. Appointment: Senior Editor, Penguin Books, 1966-73. Publications: The Pop Process, 1969; Food for Free, 1972; Unofficial Countryside, 1973; Street Flowers, 1976; Plants with a Purpose, 1977; The Common Ground, 1980; The Flowering of Britain, 1980; In a Green Shade, 1983; Oak and Company, 1983; Frampton Flora, 1985; Gilbert White, 1986; The Flowering of Kew, 1988; Home Country, 1990; Whistling in the Dark, 1993. Contributions to: Times; Listener; Telegraph; Sunday Times; Observer; The Countryman; Nature; Modern Painters; The Independent. Honours: Information Book Award, Times Educational Supplement, 1977; Children's Book Award, New York Academy of Sciences, 1984; Whitbread Biography Award, 1986. Memberships: Guild of Food Writers; Botanical Society of British Isles, Council 1981-83; London Wildlife Trust, President 1982-92. Literary Agent: Richard Simon, London, England. Address: c/o Richard Simon.

MAC AVOY Roberta Ann, b. 1949, American. Publications: Tea with the Black Dragon, Damiano, 1983; Damiano's Lute, Raphael, 1984; The Book of Kells (co-author), 1985; Twisting the Rope, 1986; The Grey Horse, 1987; The Third Eagle, 1989; Lens of the World, 1990. Address: Underhill at Nelson Farm, 1669 Nelson Road, Scotts Valley, CA 95066, USA.

MACAULAY David. Publications: Cathedral, 1973; Castle, 1977; Great Moments in Architecture, 1978; Motel of the Mysteries, 1979; Unbuilding, 1980; Baaa, 1985; Why the Chicken Crossed the Road, 1985; The Way Things Work, 1988; Black & White, 1990; Ship, 1993; Short Cut, 1995. Honours: Caldecott Medal, 1991; Boston Globe/Horn Book Award, 1989.

MACAULEY Robie Mayhew, b. 3 May 1919. Editor; Writer. m. 19 July 1978, 1 son. Education: AB, Kenyon College, Gambier, Ohio, 1941; MA, University of Iowa, 1950; Postgraduate Study, University of London, England, 1965-66. Appointments: Editor, The Kenyon Review, 1958-66; Executive Editor, Houghton Mifflin Co, 1977-88. Publications: The Disguises of Love, novel, 1952; The End of Pity, stories, 1957; A Secret History of Time to Come, novel, 1978; Technique in Fiction, non-fiction, 1988; The Seven Basic Quarrels of Marriage, non-fiction, 1990. Contributions to: Esquire; Cosmopolitan; The Paris Review; Encounter; The Virginia Quarterly Review; New York Times Review of Books; Others. Honours: Rockefeller Foundation Grant, 1958-59; Guggenheim Foundation Grant, 1965-66; Honorary DLitt, Kenyon College, 1986. Membership: American PEN Center. Literary Agent: Kimberley Witherspoon, Witherspoon Associates, New York, USA. Address: c/o Witherspoon Associates, 157 W 57th St, Suite 700, New York, NY 10019, USA.

MACBETH George, b. 19 Jan 1932, Shotts, Lanarkshire, Scotland. Editor; Poet. Education: MA, New College Oxford, 1955. Appointments include: Editor, Poets Voice, 1958-65, New Comment, 1959-64, Poetry Now, 1965-76. Publications include: A Form of Words, 1954; The Broken Places, 1963; Penguin Modern Poets, 1964; A Doomsday Book: Poems and Poem Game, 1965; Missile Commander, 1965; The Screens, 1967; The Colour of Blood, 1967; The Night of Stones, 1968; A War Quartet, 1969; The Hiroshima Dream, 1970; The Burning Cone, 1970; A Prayer, Against Revenge, 1971; The Orlando Poems, 1971; A Farewell, 1972; Lusus: A Verse Lecture, 1972; A Litany, 1972; Shrapnel, 1973; The Vision, 1973; A Poet's Year, 1973;

In The Hours Waiting for the Blood to Come, 1975; Last Night, 1976; Buying a Heart, 1978; The Saddled Man, 1978; Poem for Breathing, 1979; Poem of Love & Death, 1980; The Long Darkness, 1983; The Cleaver Garden, 1986; Anatomy of a Divorce, 1981; Plays, The Doomsday Show, 1964; The Scene Machine, 1971; Novels, Stories for Children and Editions of Poetry. Honours include: Faber Memorial Award, 1964; Cholmondeley Award, 1977. Address: Moyne Park, Near Tuam, County Galway, Ireland.

MACCAIG Norman Alexander, b. 14 Nov 1914, Edinburgh, Scotland. Teacher; Lecturer. m. Isabel Munro, 6 Apr 1940, 1 son, 1 daughter. Education: MA, Hons, Classics, University of Edinburgh, 1928-32. Appointment: Writer-in-Residence, Edinburgh University, 1967-69. Publications: Collected Poems, 1985; Riding Lights, 1955; A Round of Applause, 1962; Tree of Strings, 1977; The Equal Skies, 1980; Voice-over, 1983; Measures, 1965; A Common Grace, 1960; Surroundings, 1966; A Man in My Position, 1969; The White Bird, 1973; The World's Room, 1974; A World of Difference, 1983; The Sinai Sort, 1957; Rings on a Tree, 1968; Collected Poems, 1985; Voice Over, 1988. Contributions to: The Listener; Sunday Observer; Spectator; New Statesman; Lines Review; Chapman; Agenda; Poetry Chicago. Honours: 8 Scottish Arts Council Awards, 1954-86; Society of Authors Awards, 1964 and 1967; Heineman Award, 1967; Cholmondely Award, 1975; OBE, 1979; DUniv (Stirling); ARSA, 1981; DLitt; FRSE, 1983; FRSL, 1965; Saltire Award, 1985; Queen's Gold Medal. Membership: Scottish Arts Club. Address: 11 Leamington Terrace, Edinburgh, Scotland.

MACCARTHY Fiona, b. 23 Jan 1940, London, England. Writer; Critic. m. David Mellor, 1966, 1 son, 1 daughter. Education: Oxford University, 1958-61; MA, English Language and Literature, Oxford. Appointments: Reviewer, The Times, 1981-91; Reviewer, The Observer, 1991-. Publications: The Simple Life: C R Ashbee in the Cotswolds, 1981; The Omega Workshops: Decorative Arts of Bloomsbury, 1984; Eric Gill, 1989; William Morris: A Life for our Time, 1994. Contributions to: Times Literary Supplement; New York Times Review of Books. Honours: Royal Society of Arts Bicentenary Medal, 1987; Honorary Fellowship, Royal College of Arts, 1989. Memberships: PEN Club. Literary Agent: Peters, Fraser and Dunlop, London, England. Address: The Round Building, Hathersage, Sheffield S30 1BA, England.

MACCOBY Michael, b. 5 Mar 1933, Mt Vernon, New York, USA. Consultant. m. Sandylee Weille, 19 Dec 1959, 1 son, 3 daughters. Education: BA 1954, PhD 1960, Harvard University; New College, Oxford, 1954-55; University of Chicago, 1955-56; Diploma, Mexican Institute of Psychoanalysis, 1964. Publications: The Gamesman, 1977; The Leader, 1981; Why Work, 1988; Social Character in a Mexican Village (with E Fromm), 1970; Sweden at the Edge, 1991; Social Change and Character in Mexico and the United States, 1970. Memberships: PEN; Signet Society; Cosmos; American Psychological Association; American Anthropological Association; National Academy of Public Administration. Address: 4825 Linnean Avenue NW, Washington, DC 20008, USA.

MACCREIGH James. See: **POHL Frederik.**

MACDONALD Alastair A, b. 24 Oct 1920, Aberlour, Scotland. Poet; University Professor Emeritus. Education: MA, Aberdeen University, 1948; BLitt, Christ Church, Oxford, 1953; PhD, Manchester Univeristy, 1956. Appointments: Senior Studentship in Arts (English), Manchester, 1953-55; Professor of English, Memorial University, Newfoundland, Canada, 1955-87; Professor Emeritus, 1992. Publications: Academic: Prose and verse in Fearful Joy, Papers from the Thomas Gray Bicentenary Conference, Ottawa, 1971, 1974; A Festschrift for Edgar Ronald Seary (co-editor, contributor), 1975; Introduction and Notes to reproduction in facsimile of Thomas Gray, An Elegy...The Eton Manuscript and First Edition 1751, 1976; Numerous essays, articles, book reviews; Books of Poetry: Between Something and Something, 1970; Shape Enduring Mind, 1974; A Different Lens, 1981; Towards the Mystery, 1985; A Figure on the Move, 1991; Selected and New Poems, in preparation; Collected Longer Poems, in preparation; Poetry in many anthologies, etc; Flavian's Fortune, novel, 1985. Contributions to: Aberdeen University Review; Dalhousie Review; Bulletin of Humanities Association of Canada; Review of English Studies; Queen's Quarterly, Canada; Studies in Scottish Literature; The University Review, USA. Honours: Prizes and Mentions for Poetry: Honourable Mention, Stroud Festival, 1967; Canadian Author and Bookman, prize for Best Poem in Vol 47, 1972; Prize, Best

Poem in New Voices in American Poetry, 1973, Vantage Press, New York, 1973; 1st Prize for Poetry, 1976, Honourable Mention, 1978, 2nd Prize, 1982, Newfoundland Government Arts & Letters Competition; Readings of own poetry: Many public readings, the most recent, by invitation for Habourfront Reading Series, Toronto, Canada, 1992. Memberships: Writers' Alliance of Newfoundland & Labrador; Scottish Poetry Library Association, Edinburgh; League of Canadian Poets. Address: Department of English, Arts & Administration Building, Memorial University, St John's, Newfoundland, A1C 5S7, Canada.

MACDONALD (Alexa Eleanor) Fiona, b. 25 Apr 1945, India. Writer. Publications: The Duke Who Had Too Many Giraffes; Little Bird I Have Heard. Contributions to: International Construction; Construction News; Underground Engineering. Memberships: PEN. Address: 41 Denne Place, London SW3 2NH, England.

MACDONALD Anne-Marie, b. 1958. Canadian. Dramatist. Publication: Goodnight Desdemona (Goodmorning Juliet), 1990. Honour: Canadian Authors Association Literary Award, 1991.

MACDONALD Elizabeth Anne, b. 15 May 1954, Great Yarmouth, Norfolk. Translator; Writer. m. Alastair Livingstone MacDonald, 4 June 1983, 1 daughter. Education: BA Hons, Cambridge, 1973-76; MA Hons, 1979; PhD Spanish, 1983; Institute of Linguists Diploma in Translation. Publications: Translation: Venus Unveiled, 1989; Japanese Paper. Contributions to: Medium Aevum; The Linguist. Honours: Newnham College Progress Prize, 1976, Scholarship 1976-77, Research Student 1977-79. Memberships: Winchester Writers' Circle' Society of Authors; Institute of Linguists. Address: 4 Burnett Close, Weeke, Winchester, Hampshire SO22 5JQ, England.

MACDONALD Jake M, b. 6 Apr 1949, Winnipeg, Manitoba, Canada. Writer. m. Carolyn MacKinnon, 18 June 1983, 1 daughter. Education: BA, University of Manitoba, 1971. Appointments: Writer, Fishing Guide in Northern Ontario, Summers 1969-; Freelance Writer. Publications: Novels: Indian River, 1981; Stonehouse; Radio Plays: Becoming, CBC Winnipeg, 1982; The Man from the Boy, CBC Winnipeg, 1983; Men who Say NO, CBC Winnipeg, 1984; The Highway is for Gamblers, CBC Winnipeg, 1985; The Longest Night of the Year, CBC 1986; Tax Dodge Lodge, Real Special Productions, 1986; Short Stories: The Bridge Out of Town (collection), 1986. Contributions to: Short stories in various anthologies; Articles contributed to periodicals. Memberships: Writers Union of Canada; Manitoba Writers Guild; Ducks Unlimited. Literary Agent: Sarah Parker and Associates, Toronto, Canada.

MACDONALD Malcolm. See: ROSS-MACDONALD Málcolm John.

MACDONALD (Margaret) Amy, b. 14 June 1951, Boston, Massachusetts, USA. Journalist. m. Thomas A Urquhart, 26 June 1976, 2 sons, 1 step-daughter. Education: University of Pennsylvania, PA, USA, 1969-73; BA, Centre de Formation et Perfectionement des Journalistes, 1982-83. Appointments: Stonecoast Writers Conference; Harvard University, Teacher. Publications: Little Beaver and the Echo; Rachel Fister's Blister; Let's Try, Let's Make a Noise, Let's Play, Let's Do It; A Very Young Housewife. Contributions to: Parents Magazine; Earthwatch Magazine; The Times; New Scientist; Guardian. Honours: Silver Stylus Award. Memberships: Society of Children's Book Writers. Address: 10 Winslow Road, Falmouth, ME 04105, USA.

MACDONALD Nancy Gardiner Bodman, b. 24 May 1910. m. Dwight MacDonald, 1934, div, 2 sons. Education: Vassar College, BA, 1932. Appointments: Institute of Persian Art & Archeology, 1932-33; Common Sensa Magazine, 1932-35; Partison Review, Business Manager, 1936-42; Political Magazine, 1943-47; Politics Packages Abroad, Director, 1945-50; International Rescue Committee, 1951-52; Spanish Refugee Aid, 1953-84. Publications: Are Hospitals Made for People? Homeage to the Spanish Exiles. Honours: Dama de la Order de la Liberacion de Espana; American Committee for Iberian Freedom; Spanish Civil War Historical Society; El Lazo de la Orden de Isabel La Catolica. Address: Spanish Refugee Aid, 386 Park Avenue South, New York, NY 10016, USA.

MACDONOGH Giles Malachy Maximilian, b. 6 Apr 1955, London, England. Author; Journalist. Education: Balliol College, Oxford, England, 1975-78; BA (Hons), Modern History, Oxford University, 1978; Ecole des Hautes Etudes Pratiques, France, 1980-83; MA (Oxon), 1992. Appointments: Freelance Journalist, 1983-; Editor, Made in

France, 1984; Columnist, Financial Times, 1989-; Contributor to various magazines and annual publicatins. Publications: A Palate in Revolution, Grimod de La Reynière and the Almanach des Gourmands, 1987; A Good German: Adam von Trott zu Solz, 1990; The Wine and Food of Austria, 1992; Brillat Savarin: The Judge and his Stomach, 1992; Syrah Grenache, Mourvèdre, 1992; Contributions in: Webster's Wine Guide, 1990-; Sainsbury's Pocket Wine Guide, 1992-; The Companion to Wine, 1992; Berghs Jahrbuuch der Gastronomie, 1992-; Le Guide BCBG, 1984. Contributions to: Financial Times (regularly); WINE; Decanter; Wine and Spirit; Food and Entertaining; Homes and Gardens; Opera Now. Honours: Shortlisted, Andre Simon Award, 1987; Glenfiddich Special Award, 1988. Memberships include: International PEN; Guild of Food Writers; Octagon of Wine Writers; The Academy. Literary Agent: Peter Robinson, Curtis Brown, London, England. Address: c/o Curtis Brown, 162 Regent Street, London W1, England.

MACDOUGALL Ruth Doan, b. 19 Mar 1939, Laconia, New Hampshire, USA. Writer. m. Donald K MacDougall, 9 Oct 1957. Education: Bennington College, 1957-59; BEd, Keene State College, 1961. Publications: The Lilting House, 1965; One Minus One, 1971; The Cost of Living, 1971; The Cheerleader, 1973; Wife and Mother, 1976; Aunt Pleasantine, 1978; The Flowers of the Forest, 1981; A Lovely Time Was Had By All, 1982; Snowy, 1993. Contributions to: Book Reviewer: The New York Times Book Review; Newsday; Others. Honours: Winner, PEN Syndicated Fiction Project, 1983, 1984, 1985. Memberships: National Writers Union. Address: RR1, Box 286, Center Sandwich, NH 03227, USA.

MACDOWELL Douglas Maurice, b. 1931, British. Appointments: Assistant Lecturer, Lecturer, Senior Lecturer, Reader in Greek and Latin, University of Manchester, England, 1958-71; Professor of Greek, University of Glasgow, Scotland, 1971-. Publications: Andokides: On the Mysteries (editor), 1962; Athenian Homicide Law, 1963; Aristophanes: Wasps (editor), 1971; The Law in Classical Athens, 1978; Spartan Law, 1986; Demosthenes: Against Meidias (editor), 1990. Honours: Fellow, Royal Society of Edinburgh, 1991; Fellow, British Academy, 1993. Address: University of Glasgow, Glasgow G12 8QQ, Scotland.

MACDOWELL John. See: PARKS T(imothy) Harold.

MACEACHERN Diane, b. 29 May 1952, Detroit, Michigan, USA. President, Vanguard Communications; Author. Education: BA, Literature, Science, Arts, 1974, MS, School of Natural Resources, 1977; University of Michigan. Publications: Save Our Planet: 750 Everyday Ways You Can Help Clean Up the Earth, 1990, translated into Chinese, Japanese, Italian. Contributions to: Frequently to: Family Circle; Good Housekeeping; Also articles to: Ladies Home Journal; Self; Lady's Circle; Bottom Line; National Wildlife; Syndicated column in Washington Post Writer's Group. Honours: William J Branstrom Freshman Prize, 1970; Honorary Alumni Award, 1990. Literary Agent: Ms Gail Ross. Address: 102 Tulip Avenue, Takoma Park, MD 20912, USA.

MACER-STORY Eugenia, b. 20 Jan 1945, Minneapolis, Minnesota, USA. Writer. m. Leon A Story, 1970, div 1975, 1 son. Education: BS, Speech, Northwestern University, 1965; MFA, Playwriting, Columbia University, New York City, 1968. Appointments: Fond du Lac Commonwealth Reporter, 1970; Polyarts, Boston, 1970-72; Joy of Movement, Boston, 1972-75; Magik Mirror, Salem, 1975-76; Magick Mirror Communications, Woodstock and New York City, 1977-. Publications include: Books: Congratulations: The UFO Reality, 1978; Angels of Time: Astrological Magic, 1981; Du Fu Man Chu Meets the Lonesome Cowboy: Sorcery and the UFO Experience, 1991, 2nd edition 1992; Articles: Espionage: Has Mind Control Supplanted the Cloak and Dagger, Pursuit, 1982; The Skyo UFO Sighting, Metascience, 1980; Plays: The Little Old Hermit of the Northwest Woods, 1972; Aphrodite - The Witch Play, 1979; Red Riding Hood's Revenge, 1980; The Observation Chamber, 1981; The UFO Show, 1981; The Sky Moth Project at Location 30, 1982; Six Way Time Play, 1983; Eternal Flowers of Ghost Mountain, 1985; Robin Hood's Nightgown, 1985; Cancelled & Interrupted Performances, 1986; All Souls Banquet, 1986; Poems with Percussion and Songs, 1986; Archaological Politics, 1986; Strange Inquiries, 1988; Divine Appliance, 1989; I Was Madelaine, 1989; The 13th Wife, 1989; The Zig Zag Wall, 1990; The Only Qualified Huntress, 1990; Wars with Pigeons, 1992; Battles with Dragons: Certain Tales of Political Yoga, 1993. Contributions to: Tri-Quarterly; Shadows; Woodstock Times; Omni; Frontiers of Science. Honour: Shubert Fellowship, 1968. Memberships:

Dramatists Guild; US Psychotronics Association. Address: Magick Mirror Communications, Box 741 - JAF Building, New York, NY 10116, USA.

MACFARLANE David, b. 1952. Canadian. Publications: The Danger Tree: memory, war, & the search for a family's past; Come From Away: memory, war, & the search for a family's past. Honour: Canadian Authors Association Literary Award, 1992.

MACGIBBON Jean, b. 1913, British. Appointment: Editorial Director, MacGibbon and Kee, Publishers, London, 1948-54. Publications: When the Weather's Changing, 1945; Peter's Private Army, 1960; Red Sail White Sail, 1961; Women of Islam by Assia Djebar (translator), 1961; The Red Sledge, 1962; Girls of Paris by Nicole de Buron (translator), 1962; Pam Plays Doubles, 1962; The View-Finder, 1963; A Special Providence, 1964; Sandy in Hollow Tree House, 1967; Liz, 1969; The Tall Ship, 1973; Hal, 1974; Jobs for the Girls, 1975; After the Raft Race, 1976; Three's Company, 1978; I Meant to Marry Him, 1985. Honours: Winner, 1st Other Award for Hal, 1974. Address: 8 Quay Street, Manningtree, Essex CO11 1AU, England.

MACGOWAN Christopher John, b. 6 Aug 1948, London, England. Educator. m. Catherine Levesque, 10 July 1988. Education: BA, Cambridge University (Kings College), 1976; MA 1979, PhD 1983, Princeton University, USA. Appointments: Research Assistant, The Writings of Henry D Thoreau, Princeton, 1981-83; Assistant Professor 1984-90, Associate Professor 1990-, College of William and Mary, Williamsburg, Virginia; Co-editor, Editor, various works of William Carlos Williams, 1984-92. Publications: William Carlos Williams' Early Poetry: The Visual Arts Background, 1984; The Collected Poems of William Carlos Williams, vol I, 1909-1939 (co-editor), 1986, vol II, 1939-62 (editor), 1988; William Carlos Williams' Paterson (editor), 1992. Contributions to: Several articles to William Carlos Williams' Review; John Witherspoon to Dictionary of Literary Biography, 1984; Editing William Carlos Williams: Paterson, 1991; Short articles on Harriet Monroe, Alfred Kreymborg and William Carlos Williams to Encyclopedia of American Writers. Honours: James Prize, King's College, Cambridge, England, 1976, 1977; Teaching Assistantship, Pennsylvania State University, 1976-77; Graduate Fellowship, Princeton University, 1977-81; Summer Grant, College of William and Mary, 1985, 1987, 1989; Summer Stipend, 1986, Fellowship 1990-91, National Endowment for the Humanities. Memberships: Modern Lanaguage Association; William Carlos Williams Society, President 1989-91. Address: Department of English, College of William and Mary, Williamsburg, VA 23187, USA.

MACGREGOR David Roy, b. 26 Aug 1925, London, England. Author. m. Patricia Margaret Aline Purcell-Gilpin, 26 Oct 1962, London. Education: BA 1948, MA 1950, Trinity College, Cambridge University; Hammersmith School of Building, 1954-55; Associate, Royal Institute of British Architects, 1957. Publications: The Tea Clippers, 1952, revised edition 1983; The China Bird, 1961; Fast Sailing Ships 1775-1875, 1973; Clipper Ships, 1977; Merchant Sailing Ships, 1775-1815, 1980; Merchant Sailing Ships 1815-1850, 1984; Merchant Sailing Ships 1858-1875, 1984. Contributions to: Mariner's Mirror; Journal of Nautical Archaeology. Honours: Gold Medal from Daily Express for Best Book of the Sea in 1973 for Fast Sailing Ships. Memberships: Fellow, Royal Historical Society, 1957; FSA, 1975; Council Member, Society of Nautical Research, 1959-63, 1965-69, 1974-77, 1980-85, Hon Vice-President, 1985; Ship's Committee, Maritime Trust, 1974. Address: 99 Lonsdale Road, London SW13 9DA, England.

MACGREGOR-HASTIE Roy Alasdhair Niall, b. 28 Mar 1929. Author; University Professor. m. Maria Grazia, 25 Dec 1977, 1 son. Education: New College, Royal Military Academy, Sandhurst, 1947-48; BA, University of Manchester; MFA, University of Iowa, USA; MEd, PhD, University of Hull. Appointments: Editor, The New Nation, 1955-56; Joint Editor, Miorita, 1977-; Editor, Prospice, 1967-77; Contributing Editor, numerous magazines and journals; Foreign Editor, Time and Tide, 1960-65; Japan Correspondent, 1989-. Publications: Books include: The Man from Nowhere, 1960; The Red Barbarians, 1961; Pope John XXIII, 1962; The Day of the Lion - A History of Eascism, 1964; Pope Paul VI, 1966; The Throne of Peter, 1967; Never to Be Taken Alive, 1985; Nell Gwyn, 1987; History of Western Civilisation, 1989; Getting it Right, 1990; Travel: The Compleat Migrant, 1962; Don't Send Me to Omsk, 1964; Signor Roy, 1967; Africa, 1968; Art History: Picasso, 1988; Poetry and Criticism: A Case for Poetry, 1960; Interim Statement, 1962; Eleven Elegies, 1969; Frames, 1972;

The Great Transition, 1975; Poems of Our Lord and Lady, 1976; Poeme, 1980; UNESCO Collection of rep works: Eminescu, The Last Romantic, 1972; Anthology of Contemporary Romanian Poetry (1969, 2 edn 1977, 3 edn 1982); Anthology of Bulgarian Poetry, 1978; Eminescu Centennial Commem Volume, 1989; Politics: The Mechanics of Power, 1966; Novel in translation, The Gypsy Tribe, 1974. Contributions to: Punch; Time and Tide; Twentieth Century; Spectator; New Statesman; Commonwealth Journal; Times Literary Daily Yoniuri; The Scotsman. Honours: Victoria Poetry Prize, 1986; UNESCO Author, 1989. Memberships: PEN; Society of Authors; British Association for Romanian Studies, Secretary 1966-77, President 1977-; International Association of Translators, President 1978-80; Asian History Association; Scottish Record Society. Literary Agent: Kurt Singer, Anahein, California, CA 72801, USA. Address: c/o Osaka Gakuin University, Kishibe, Suita, Osaka 564, Japan.

MACHUNG Anne, b. 30 Jan 1947, Long Beach, California, USA. Sociologist. m. Ron Rothbart, 27 Sept 1986. Education: BA summa cum laude, Seattle University, 1968; MA 1972, PhD 1983, University of Wisconsin. Publications: The Second Shift (with Arlie Hochschild), 1989. Contributions to: Talking Career, thinking job; Gender differences to work and family expectations of Berkeley seniors, to Feminist Studies, 1989. Honours: Distinguished Achievement for Bay Area Women Writers', National Women's Political Caucus, 1991. Memberships: American Sociological Association; National Women's Studies Association. Address: Institute for Study of Social Change, University of California-Berkeley, Berkeley, CA 94720, USA.

MACINTYRE Alasdair C. Philosopher. Publications: Marxism; An Interpretation, 1953; Difficulties in Christian Belief, 1960; A Short History of Ethics, 1967; The Religious Significance of Atheism, 1969; Against The Self-Images of the Age, 1971; After Virtue: A Study in Moral Theory, 1981; Is Patriotism a Virtue? 1984; Education and Values, 1987; Whose Justice? Whose Relationship? 1988; Three Rival Versions of Moral Enquiry, 1990; First Principles, Final Ends and Contemporary Philosophy, 1990. Address: Department of Philosophy, University of Notre Dame, 336 O'Shaughnessy, South Bend, IN 46556, USA.

MACINTYRE Stuart Forbes, b. 21 Apr 1947, Australia. Historian. m. 1) Margaret Geddes, 1971, 2) Martha Bruton, 1976, 2 daughters. Education: BA, University of Melbourne, 1968; MA, Monash University, 1971; PhD, Cambridge University, 1975. Appointments: Ernest Scott Professor, University of Melbourne, 1990-. Publications: A Proletarian Science; Little Moscows; Militant; Winners and Losers; Oxford History of Australia; A Colonial Liberalism. Honours: Blackwood Prize; Premiers Literary Award. Memberships: Academy of the Social Sciences in Australia; Council of the National Library of Australia. Address: History Department, University of Melbourne, Parkville, Victoria, Australia 3052.

MACK John E, b. 1931, New York, New York, USA. Professor Of Psychiatry, Cambridge Hospital, Massachussetts. Education: BA, Oberlin University, Harvard University Medical School. Nightmares and Human Conflict, 1970; A Prince of Our Disorder: The Life of T E Lawrence, 1976; Vivienne: The Life and Suicide of an Adolescent Girl, 1981; The Alchemy of Survival: One Woman's Journey, 1988; Abduction: Human Encounters With Aliens. Honour: Pulitzer Prize, 1977. Address: Dept of Psychiatry Cambridge Hospital, 1493 Cambridge Road, Cambridge, MA 02139, USA.

MACK William P, b. 6 Aug 1915, Hillsboro, Illinois, USA. US Navy Career Officer, 1935-75; Deputy Assisstant Secretary of Defense, 1968-71. m. Ruth McMillin, 11 Nov 1939, 1 s, 1 d. Education: BS, US Naval Academy; Naval War College; George Washington University. Publications: books, articles, editorials on nval subjectes, politics, history and fiction including: Naval Officers Guide, 1958; Naval Customs Traditions and Usage, 1978; Command at Sea, 1980; (novels) South to Java, 1988; Pursuit of the Sea Wolf, 1991; Checkfire, 1992; New Guinea, 1993; Straits of Messina, 1994. Honours: Alfred Theyer Mahan Award for Literary Excellence, Navy League, 1982. Address: 3607 Rundelac Road, Annapolis, MD 21403, USA.

MACKAY Claire Lorraine, b. 21 Dec 1930, Toronto, Ontario, Canada. Writer. m. Jackson F Mackay, 12 Sept 1952, 3 sons. Education: BA, Political Science, University of Toronto, 1952; Postgraduate study in Social Work; University of British Columbia, 1968-69; Certificate, rehabilitation counseling, University of Manitoba, 1971. Appointments include: Writer-in-residence, Metropolitan Toronto

Library, 1987. Publications: Mini-Bike Hero, 1974, 1978, 1984; Mini-Bike Racer, 1976, 1979, 1984; Mini-Bike Rescue, 1982; Exit Barney McGee, 1979; One Proud Summer, 1981; Minerva Program, 1984; Pay Cheques & Picket Lines, 1987; The Toronto Story, 1990; Touching All the Bases, 1994; Bats About Baseball, 1995. Contributions include: Articles, columns, short stories, verse, book reviews, in various newspapers & magazines. Address: 6 Frank Crescent, Toronto, Ontario, M6G 3K5, Canada.

MACKAY Eric Beattie, b. 31 Dec 1922. Editor. m. Moya Margaret Mayes Connolly, 1954, dec 1981, 3 sons, 1 daughter. Education: MA, Aberdeen University. Appointments: Aberdeen Bon-Accord, 1948; Elgin Courant, 1949; The Scotsman, 1950; Daily Telegraph, 1952; London Editor 1957, Deputy Editor 1961, Editor 1972-85, The Scotsman. Address: 5 Strathearn Place, Edinburgh EH9 2AL, Scotland.

MACKAY James Alexander, (Ian Angus, William Finlay, Bruce Garden, Peter Whittington), b. 21 Nov 1936, Inverness, Scotland. Author; Journalist. m. (1) Mary Patricia Jackson, 24 Sept 1960, diss. 1972, 1 son, 1 daughter, (2) Renate Finlay-Freundlich, 11 Dec 1992. Education: MA (Hons), History, 1958, DLitt, 1993, Glasgow University. Literary Appointments: Philatelic Columnist, The New Daily, 1962-67; Collecting Wisely in Financial Times, 1967-85; Editor-in-Chief, IPC Stamp Encyclopaedia, 1968-72; Antiques Advisory Editor, Ward Lock, 1972-79; Editor: The Burns Chronicle, 1977-; The Postal Annual, 1978-90; The Burnsian, 1986-89; Seaby Coin and Medal Bulletin, 1990-92; Consultant Editor, Antiques Today, 1992-. Publications: The Tapling Collection, 1964; Glass Paperweights, 1973, 1977, 1988; The Dictionary of Stamps in Colour, 1973; The Dictionary of Western Sculptors in Bronze, 1977; The Guinness Book of Stamps Facts and Feats, 1982, 1988; Complete Works of Robert Burns, 1986, 1990; Complete Letters of Burns, 1987; Burns A-Z: The Complete Word Finder, 1990; Burns: A Biography, 1992; 144 titles on philately, numismatics, applied and decorative arts, biography, Scottish literature, 1961-. Contributions to: Regular columns to: Stamps; Stamp Magazine; Gibbons Stamp Monthly; British Philatelic Bulletin; Stamp and Coin Mart; Coin News; Coin Monthly; Seaby Coin and Medal Bulletin; Coin Digest, Singapore; Studies in Scottish Literature, USA; Occasional contributions to many others worldwide. Honours: Silver Medal Amphile, Amsterdam, 1965; Vermeil Medal, Spellman Foundation, USA, 1982, 1987, 1990; Thomas Field Award for services to Irish Philatelic Literature, 1983; Saltire Book of the Year, 1993. Membership: The Burns Federation, Executive Council 1977-. Address: 5/75 Lancefield Quay, Glasgow G3 8HA, Scotland.

MACKAY Simon. See: NICOLE Christopher Robin.

MACKENZIE Andrew Carr, b. 30 May 1911, Oamaru, New Zealand. Journalist; Author. m. Kaarina Sisko Sihvonen, 1 Mar 1952, 1 son, 2 daughters. Education: Victoria University College, New Zealand, 1930-32. Literary appointment: London News Editor, Sheffield Morning Telegraph, England, 1963-76. Publications: The Unexplained, 1966; Frontiers of the Unknown, 1968; Apparitions and Ghosts, 1971; A Gallery of Ghosts (editor), 1972; Riddle of the Future, 1974; Dracula Country, 1977; Hauntings and Apparitions, 1982; Romanian Journey, 1983; A Concise History of Romania (editor), 1985; Archaeology in Romania, 1986; The Seen and the Unseen, 1987; A Journey into the Past of Transylvania, 1990. Contributions to: The Journal of the Society of Psychical Research. Membership: Society for Psychical Research, Vice-President 1989, Council Member 1970-91. Literary Agent: A M Heath, 79 St Martin's Lane, London WC2N 4AA, England. Address: 67 Woodland Drive, Hove, East Sussex BN3 6DF, England.

MACKENZIE David, b. 10 June 1927, Rochester, New York, USA. Professor of History. m. Patricia Williams, 8 Aug 1953, 3 sons. Education: AB, University of Rochester, 1951; MA & Certificate of Russian Institute, 1953; PhD, Columbia University, 1962. Appointments: US Merchant Marine Academy, 1953-58; Princeton University, 1959-61; Wells College, 1961-68; University of North Carolina, Greensboro, 1969-. Publications: The Serbs and Russian Pan-Slavism 1875-1878, 1967; The Lion of Tashkent: The Career of General M G Cherniaev, 1974; A History of Russia and the Soviet Union, 1977, 1982, 1987, 1993; Ilija Garasanin: The Balkan Bismarck, 1985; A History of the Soviet Union, 1986, 1991; Ilija Garasanin Drzavnik i Diplomata, 1987; Apis: The Congenial Conspirator, 1989; Imperial Dreams/Harsh Realities: Tsarist Russian Foreign Policy, 1815-1917, 1993; From Messianism to Collapse: Soviet Foreign Policy 1917-1991, 1994; Serbian edition of Apis, 1989; Japanese edition of

Apis, 1992; Chinese edition of A History of Russia, the Soviet Union and Beyond, 1994. Contributions to: The Journal of Modern History; Slavic Review; Canadian Slavic Studies; Russian Review; International History Review; East European Quarterly; Serbian Studies; Book Chapter: Russia's Balkan Policies under Alexander II 1855-1881, in Hugh Ragsdale, ed, Imperial Russian Foreign Policy, 1993. Address: 1000 Fairmont St, Greensboro, NC 27401, USA.

MACKENZIE Norman Hugh, b. 8 Mar 1915, Salisbury, Rhodesia. Educator; Writer. m. Rita Mavis Hofmann, 14 Aug 1948, 1 son, 1 daughter. Education: BA 1934, MA 1935, Diploma in Education 1936, Rhodes University, South Africa; PhD, University of London, England, 1940. Appointments include: Professor of English 1966-80, Emeritus Professor 1980-, Queen's University, Kingston, Ontario, Canada. Publications: South African Travel Literature in the 17th Century, 1955; The Outlook for English in Central Africa, 1960; Hopkins, 1968; A Reader's Guide to G M Hopkins, 1981; Editor: The Poems of Gerard Manley Hopkins (with W H Gardner), 1967, Revised edition 1970; Poems by Hopkins, 1974; The Early Poetic Manuscripts and Notebooks of Gerard Manley Hopkins in Facsimile, 1989; The Poetical Works of Gerard Manley Hopkins, 1990; The Later Poetic Manuscripts of Gerard Manley Hopkins in Facsimile, 1991; Various book chapters. Contributions to: International Review of Education; Bulletin of the Institute for Historical Research; Times Literary Supplement; Modern Language Quarterly; Queen's Quarterly; Others. Address: 416 Windward Place, Kingston, Ontario, K7M 4E4, Canada.

MACKENZIE Suzanne, b. 22 Mar 1950, Vancouver, Canada. University Professor. m. Alan Eric Nash, 29 May 1984. Education: BA Hons Simon Fraser University, BC, 1976; MA, University of Toronto, 1978; DPhil Geography, Sussex University, England. Publications: Visible Histories: Gender and Environment in a Post-War British City, 1989; Remaking Human Geography, 1989, co-editor; Gender Sensitive Theory and the Housing Needs of Mother led families, 1987, co-author. Contributions to: Cahiers de Geographie des Quebec, 1987, among others. Memberships: Canadian Association of Geographers; National Executive, 1988-90; Co-founder, CAG Women and Geography Studies Group; International Geographic Union, Executive Genere and Geography Working Group, 1989-. Address: Department of Geography, Carleton University, Ottawa, Ontario K1S 5B6, Canada.

MACKERRAS Colin Patrick, b. 26 Aug 1939, Sydney, Australia. Academic. m. Alyce Barbara Brazier, 29 June 1963, 2 sons, 3 daughters. Education: BA, Melbourne, 1961; BA Hons, Australia National University, 1962; MLitt, Cambridge, 1964; PhD, Australia National University, 1970. Publications: Western Images of China, 1989; The Rise of the Peking Opera 1770-1870, 1972; China: The Impact of Revolution, A Survey of Twentieth Century China, 1976; China Observed, 1967; The Chinese Theatre in Modern Times, 1975; Modern China, A Chronology from 1842 to the Present, 1982. Honour: Shared a Gold Citation of the Media Peace Prize awarded by the United Nations Association of Australia, 1981. Membership: Australian Writers' Guild. Address: Division of Asian and International Studies, Griffith University, Nathan, Qld 4111, Australia.

MACKESY Piers Gerald, b. 1924. British. Academic. Appointments: Harkness Fellow, Harvard University, USA, 1953-54; Fellow, 1954-87, Emeritus, 1988-, Pembroke College, Oxford, England; Visiting Fellow, Institute for Advanced Study, Princeton, New Jersey, USA, 1961-62; Visiting Professor, California Institute of Technology, 1966. Publications: The War in the Mediterranean 1803-1810, 1957; The War for America 1775-1783, 1964; Statesmen at War: The Strategy of Overthrow 1798-1799, 1974; The Coward of Minden: The Affair of Lord George Sackville, 1979; War without Victory: The Downfall of Pitt 1799-1802, 1984. Memberships: Council Member, National Army Museum, 1983-92; Council Member, Society for Army Historical Research, 1985-94; Fellow, British Academy, 1988. Address: Leochel Cushnie House, Leochel Cushnie, Alford, Aberdeenshire AB33 8LJ, Scotland.

MACKIE Alastair, b. 10 Aug 1925, Aberdeen, Scotland. English Teacher; Poet. Education: MA, University of Aberdeen, 1950. Appointments include: English Teacher, Waid Academy, Anstruther, 1959-. Publications: Soundings, 1966; To Duncan Glen, 1971; Clytach, 1972; At The Heich Kirk Yaird: A Hielant Sequence, 1974; Ingaitherins: Selected Poems, 1987; Editor, Four Gates of Lothian & Other Poems by Forbes Macgregor, 1979. Honours include: Scottish Arts Council Award, 1987. Address: 13 St Adrians Place, Anstruther, Fife, Scotland.

MACKIE John. See: **LEVINSON Leonard.**

MACKINNON Catherine. Professor of Law. Publications: Feminism Unmodified; Towards A Feminist Theory Of the State; Sexual Harrassment; Only Words,1993. Address: School of Law, University of Michigan, Ann Arbor, MI 48109-1189, USA.

MACKINNON Marianne H J, b. 4 June 1925, Berlin, Germany. Retired. 3 sons. Education: Translator Diploma, Hannover, 1946; Cambridge University Language Examination, English, 1949; State Registered Nurse, 1953; English Language and Literature, Strathclyde University, Scotland, 1983-85. Appointments: Author, Scottish Arts Council Register for Speakers in Schools and Public Schemes. Publications: Autobiographies: The Naked Years, 1987, paperback, 1989; The Alien Years, sequel, 1991; The Deluge, 1993. Honours: Constable Trophy, Scotland, 1982; Poetry and short story prizes, 1982-87; Research and Travel Award, Scottish Arts Council, 1989; Writer's Bursary, Scottish Arts Council, 1990. Memberships: PEN International; Society of Authors; The Royal Society of Literature. Literary Agent: A D Peters, London, England. Address: 54 Rosehill, Torrance, Glasgow G64 4HF, Scotland.

MACKSEY K(enneth) J(ohn), b. 1923. British. Writer; Military Historian. Appointments: Officer, Royal Tank Regiment, British Army, 1941-68, retiring with rank of Major, 1968; Deputy Editor, History of the Second World War, History of the First World War, Purnell, London, 1968-70. Publications: The Shadow of Vimy Ridge, To the Green Fields Beyond, 1965; Armoured Crusader: General Sir Percy Hobart, 1967; Africa Korps, Panzer Division, 1968; Crucible of Power: The Fight for Tunisia, 1969; Tank Force, Tank: A History of AFVs, 1970; Tank Warfare, Beda Fomm, 1971; The Guinness History of Land (Sea, Air) Warfare, 3 volumes, 1973-76; Battle, in US as Anatomy of a Battle, 1974; The Partisans of Europe in the Second World War, The Guinness Guide to Feminine Achievements, Guderian Panzer General, 1975; The Guinness Book of 1952 (1953, 1954), 3 volumes, 1977-79; Kesselring, 1978; Rommel's Campaigns and Battles, 1979; The Tanks, volume III of History of the Royal Tank Regiment, 1979; Invasion: The Germany Invasion of England, July 1940, 1980; The Tank Pioneers, 1981; History of the Royal Armoured Corps 1914-1975, 1983; Commando Strike, First Clash, 1985; Technology in War, 1986; Godwin's Saga, Military Errors of World War 2, 1987; Tank Versus Tank, 1988; For Want of a Nail, 1989; Penguin Encyclopedia of Modern Warfare, 1991; The Penguin Encyclopedia of Weapons and Military Technology, 1994. Literary Agent: Watson Little Ltd. Address: Whatley Mill, Beaminster, Dorset DT8 3EN, England.

MACKWORTH Cecily, b, Llantillio Pertholey, Gwent, Wales. Writer. m. Marquis de Chabannes la Palice, 1956, 1 daughter (by 1st husband). Publications: I Came Out of France, 1942; Francois Villon, A Study, 1947; A Mirror for French Poetry, 1942; The Mouth of the Sword, 1949; The Destiny of Isobella Eberhardt, 1952; Springs Green Shadow (novel), 1953; Guillaume Apollinaire and the Cubist Life, 1961; English Interludes, 1974; Ends of the World, Memoirs, 1987; Lucy's Nose (novel), 1992. Contributions to: Horizon; Life and Letters Today; Poetry Quarterly; Cornhill; Twentieth Century; Cultures for all Peoples (UNESCO); Critique; Les Lettres Nouvelles and several others. Honour: Darmstadt Award, 1965. Memberships: PEN (French); Association Internationale des Critiques Litteraires; Society of Authors, GB. Literary Agent: L Pollinger, 18 Madox Street, London, W1R 0EG. Address: 6 Rue des Countures-St-Gervais, Paris 75003, France.

MACKY Ahmad, b. 13 May 1943, Mauritius. Journalist; Chief Editor, The Student's World. m. Affroze Mudhawo, 8 Aug 1988, 1 daughter. Education: LSJ, London, 1968; BA, Honours, 1990. Publications: Six Strange Stories, 1975; Jaytoon, The Asian Woman, 1987; A monthly educational paper: The Student's World. Contributions to:Controversy; Star; The Guardian; BBC Wild Life; The Times.Memberships: National Union of Journalists, England; International Federation of Journalists. Address: Royal Road, Bel Air, Rivière Séche Flacq, Mauritius.

MACLAINE Allan H(ugh), b. 1924, American. Appointments: Instructor, Brown University, Providence, RI, 1947-50; Instructor, University of Massachusetts, Amherst, 1951-54; Assistant Professor 1954-56, Associate Professor 1956-62, Texas Christian University, Forth Worth; Professor of English 1962-, Dean of Division of University Extension 1967-71, University of Rhode Island, Kingston. Publications: The Student's Comprehensive Guide to the Canterbury Tales, 1964; Robert Fergusson, 1965; Allan Ramsay, 1985. Membership: President,

College English Association, 1965-66. Address: Department of English, University of Rhode Island, Kingston, RI 02881, USA.

MACLAVERTY Bernard, b. 14 Sept 1942, Belfast, Northern Ireland. Novelist. m. Madeline McGuckin, 1967, 1 s, 3, d. Education: BA, Queens University, Belfast, 1970. Publications: Bibliography: Secrets & Other Stories, 1977; Lamb (a novel), 1980; A Time to Dance & Other Stories, 1982; Cal (a novel), 1983; The Great Profundo & Other Stories, 1987; Walking the Dog & Other Stories, 1994; For Young Children: A Man in Search of a Pet, 1978; Andrew McAndrew, 1988, USA 1993; Radio Plays: My Dear Palestrina, 1980; Secrets, 1981; No Joke, 1983; The Break, 1988; Some Surrender, 1988; Lamb, 1992; Television Plays: My Dear Palestrina, 1980; Phonefun Limited, 1982; The Daily Woman, 1986; Sometime in August, 1989; Screenplays: Cal, 1984; Lamb, 1985; Drama Documentary: Hostages, 1992, USA 1993; Adaptation for TV: The Real Charlotte by Somerville & Ross, 1989. Honours include: Northern Ireland and Scottish Arts Councils Awards; Irish Sunday Independent Award, 1983; London Evening Standard Award for Screenplay, 1984; Award from Scottish Arts Council, 1988; Joint winner, Scottish Writer of the Year, 1988; Shortlisted for The Saltire Society Scottish Book of the Year, 1994. Address: 26 Roxburgh Street, Hillhead, Glsgow G12 9AP, Scotland.

MACLEAN Arthur. See: **TUBB E(dwin) C(harles).**

MACLEAN Fitzroy, Sir, b. 1911, British. Appointments: Former Conservative MP: Under Secretary of State for War, 1954-57. Publications: Eastern Approaches, 1949; Disputed Barricade, 1957; A Person from England, 1958; Back to Bokhara, 1959; Jugoslavia, 1969; A Concise History of Scotland, 1970; To the Back of Beyond, 1974; To Caucasus, 1976; Take Nine Spies, 1978; Holy Russia, 1979; Tito, 1980; The Isles of the Sea, 1985; Bonnie Prince Charlie, 1988; Portrait of the Soviet Union, 1988; All The Russias - The End of an Empire, 1992. Honours: Sir Fitzroy Maclean of Dunconnel Bt. KT CBE (CBE Military 1944), (Knight of the Thistle 1993). Address: Strachur House, Strachur, Argyll, PA27 8BX, Scotland.

MACLEOD Alison, b, 1920, British. Publications: Dear Augustine, 1958; The Heretics (in US as The Heretic), 1965; The Hireling (in UK as The Trusted Servant), 1968; City of Light (in UK as No Need of the Sun), 1969; The Muscovite, 1971; The Jesuit (in US as Prisoner of the Queen), 1972; The Portingale, 1976. Address: 63 Muswell Hill Place, London, N10 3RP, England.

MACLEOD Charlotte (Alisa Craig, Matilda Hughes), b. 1922, American. Appointment: Former Vice-President, NH Miller advertising agency, Boston (member of staff 1952-). Publications: As Charlotte MacLeod: Mystery of the White Knight, 1964; Next Door to Danger, 1965; The Fat Lady's Ghost, 1968; Mouse's Vineyard (juvenile), 1968; Ask Me No Questions, 1971; Brass Pounder (juvenile), 1971; Astrology for Sceptics (non-fiction), 1972; King Devil, 1978; Rest You Merry, 1978; The Family Vault, 1979; The Luck Runs Out, 1979; The Withdrawing Room, 1980; We Dare Not Go a Hunting, 1980; The Palace Guard, 1981; Wrack and Rune, 1982; Cirak's Daughter (juvenile), 1982; The Bilbao Looking Glass, 1983; Something the Cat Dragged In, 1983; Maid of Honour (juvenile), 1984; The Convival Codfish, 1984; The Curse of the Giant Hogweed, 1985; The Plain Old Man, 1985; Grab Bag, 1987; The Corpse in Oozak's Pond, 1987; The Recycled Citizen, 1988; The Silver Ghost, 1988; Vane Pursuit, 1989; The Gladstone Bag, 1990; As Matilda Hughes: The Food of Love, 1965; Headlines for Caroline, 1967; As Alisa Craig: A Pint of Murder, 1980; The Grub-and-Stakers Move a Mountain, 1981; Murder Goes Mumming, 1981; The Terrible Tide, 1983; The Grub and Stakers Quilt a Bee, 1985; The Grub-and-Stakers Pinch a Poke, 1988; Trouble in the Brasses, 1989; The Grub-and-Stakers Spin and Yarn, 1990; An Owl Too Many; Something in the Water. Address: c/o Jed Mattes, 175 W 73rd Street, New York, NY 10023, USA.

MACLEOD Robert. See: **KNOX William.**

MACMANUS Yvonne, b. 18 Mar 1931, Los Angeles, California, USA. Editor; Writer; Videoscripter. Education: Sundry courses at UCLA & USC, New York University and University of London, England. Publications: The Presence, 1982, 1987; You Can Write a Romance, 1983; Hugo (2 act play), 1990; Over 30 books published mostly pseudonymously; Corporate videoscripting. Contributions to: Training and Development Journal; Business Digest of Greater New Haven; Litchfield County Times. Honours: Honorary Daughter of Mark Twain.

Address: c/o Write On...!, Ste 1304, 4040 Mountain Creek Road, Chattanooga, TN 34715-6025, USA.

MACMULLEN Ramsay, b. 3 Mar 1928, NY, USA. Tchr. m. Margaret McNeil, 1 Aug 1992, 2 s, 2 d. Education: AB, 1950, AM, 1953, PhD, 1957, Harvard University. Publications include: Enemies of the Roman Order, 1969; Roman Social Relations, 1974; Paganism in the Roman Empire, 1981; Christianizing the Roman Empire, 1984; Corruption and the Decline of Rome, 1988. Contributions to: Selected Essays as Changes in the Roman Empire, 1990. The Eliza File; Documentary Editing, 1994. Honours: Porter Prize (College Art Assoc), 1964. Memberships: Association for Documentary Editing; Association of Ancient Historians; Friends of Ancient History; Society for the Promotion of Roman Studies. Address: 25 Temple Court, New Haven, CT 06511, USA.

MACNAB Roy Martin, B, 17 Sept 1923, Durban, South Africa. Retired Diplomat. m. Rachel Heron-Maxwell, 6 Dec 1947, 1 son, 1 daughter. Education: Hilton College, Natal, South Africa; MA, Jesus College, Oxford, England, 1955; DLitt et Phil, University of South Africa, 1981. Publications: The Man of Grass and other Poems, 1960; The French Colonel, 1975; Gold Their Touchstone, 1987; For Honour Alone, 1988; Co-editor Oxford Poetry, 1947; Poets in South Africa, 1958; Journey Into Yesterday, 1962; (editor) George Seferis South African Diary, 1990; The Cherbourg Circles, 1994. Contributions to: Times Literary Supplement; Spectator; Poetry Review; History To-day. Honour: Silver Medal, Royal Society of Arts, 1958. Address: c/o Travellers Club, London, SW1, England.

MACNEACAIL Aonghas, b, 7 June 1942, Uig, Isle of Skye, Scotland. Writer. m. Gerda Stevenson, 21 June 1980, 1 son. Literary Appointments: Writing Fellowships - The Gaelic College, Isle of Skye, 1977-79; An Comunn Gaidhealachm Oban, 1979-81; Ross-Cromarty District Council, 1988-90. Publications: Poetry Quintet, 1976; Imaginary Wounds, 1980; Sireadh Bradain Sicir/Seeking Wise Salmon, 1983; An Cathadh Mor/The Great Snowbattle, 1984; An Seachnadh/The Avoiding, 1986; Rocker and Water, 1990. Contributions to: Gairm (Gaelic) Cencrastus; Words; Acuarius; Cracked Locking Glass; Chapman Lines Review; Scottish Review; Edinburgh Review; Scotsman; West Highland Free Press; Akros Poetry, Australia; Pembroke Magazine, USA; International Poetry Review, USA; Tijdschrift Voor Poezie, Belgium; Honest Ulsterman, Ireland. Honours: Grampian TV Gaelic Poetry Award; Diamond of Jubilee Award, Scottish Association for the Speaking of Verse, 1985; An Comunn Gaidhealach Literary Award, 1985. Memberships: Council Member, Scottish Poetry Library Association, 1984-. Address: 1 Roseneath Terrace, Marchmont, Edinburgh EH9 1JS, Scotland.

MACNEIL Duncan. See: MCCUTCHAN Philip Donald.

MACSHANE Frank (Sutherland), b. 1927, American. Appointments: Assistant Professor of English, University of California, Berkeley, 1959-64; Associate Professor, Williams College, Williamstown, MA, 1964-67; Professor, Writing Division 1967-, Dean 1971-72, School of the Arts, Columbia University, NYC. Publications: The Visits of the Queen of Sheba by Miguel Serrano (trans), The Mysteries by Miguel Serrano (trans), 1960; Many Golden Ages, 1962; Impressions of Latin America (ed), The Serpent of Paradise by Miguel Serrano (trans), 1963; Critical Writings of Ford Madox Ford (ed), 1964; The American in Europe (ed), The Life and Work of Ford Madox Ford, 1965; C G Jung and Hermann Hesse: A Record of Two Friendships by Miguel Serrano (trans), 1966; The Ultimate Flower by Miguel Serrano (trans), 1969; El/Ella by Miguel Serrano (trans), Ford Madox Ford: The Critical Heritage (ed), 1972; Borges on Writing (ed with D Halpern and N T di Giovanni), 1973; The Life of Raymond Chandler, The Notebooks of Raymond Chandler, 1976; The Life of John O'Hara, Selected Letters of Raymond Chandler, 1981; The Collected Stories of John O'Hara (ed), Into Eternity: The Life of James Jones American Writer, 1985. Memberships: Director, Columbia Trans Center, NYC; Authors Guild. Address: c/o Aaron M Priest Literary Agency, 122 E 42nd Street, Suite 3902, New York, NY 10168, USA.

MACSWEENEY Barry, b. 1948, British. Writer. Appointments: Director Blacksuede Boot Press; Editor Harvest and the Blacksuede Boot, Barnet, Herts Former Freelance Journalist. Publications: Poems, 1965-68: The Boy from the Green Cabaret Tells of His Mother, 1969; The Last Bud, 1969; (with P Bland) Joint Effort, 1970; Flames on the Beach at Viareggio: Poems 1970; Our Mutual Scarlet Boulevard, 1970; Elegy for January: An Essay Commemorating the Bi-Centenary of

Chatterton's Death, 1970; The Official Biography of Jim Morrison, Rock Idol (poetry), 1971; Brother Wolf, 1972; 5 Odes, 1972; Dance Steps, 1972; Fog Eye, 1973; 6 Odes, 1973; Pelt Feather Log, 1975; Odes, 1979; Blackbird: Elegy for William Gordon Calvert, Being Book Two of Black Torch, 1980; Ranter, 1986.

MACTHOMAIS Ruaraidh. See: THOMSON Derick S.

MACVEAN Jean, b. Bradford, England. Writer. m. James Bernard Wright, 11 Oct 1952, 1 son, 1 daughter. Education: Sorbonne, Paris. Publications: The Intermediaries, novel; The Adjacent Kingdom (introduction, editing of Thomas Blackburn poems), 1980; Eros Reflected, poems, 1981; The Dolorous Death of King Arthur, 1992; The Price of an Eye, radio feature; Flight of the Swan, radio play; The Image of Freedom, play; Ideas of Love, poems. Contributions to: Another Look at Edith Sitwell, to Agenda and Contemporary Literary Criticism, USA; Thomas Blackburn, George MacKay Brown, to Temenos; The Poetry and Prose of Moelwyn Merchant, to Agenda; Poems to: Encounter; Yale Literary Magazine; Meridien; Agenda; The Tablet; Pen Anthology; Mandeville Press; Big Little Poems; Poetry London (Apple); Kathleen Raine - Living With Mystery, Agenda; (Co-editing) Kathleen raine - Special Issue, Agenda. Memberships: Fellow, International PEN Society; The Poetry Society. Address: 21 Peel Street, London, W8 7PA, England.

MACVEY John Wishart, b. 1923, British. Appointments: Research Chemist 1956-61, Company Technical Information Officer 1971-80, Nobel's Explosives Limited, Division of ICI; Plant Manager, 1961-62; Assistant Technical Information Officer, 1962-71. Publications: Speaking of Space (with C P Snow, B Lovell and P Moore), 1962; Alone in the Universe? 1963; Journey to Alpha Centauri, 1965; How We Will Reach the Stars, 1969; Whispers from Space, 1973; Interstellar Travel, Past, Present and Future, 1977; Space Weapons/Space War, 1979; Where Will We Go When the Sun Dies? 1980; Colonizing Other Worlds, 1984; Time Travel, 1987. Address: Mellendean, 15 Adair Avenue, Saltcoats, Ayrshire KA21 5QS, Scotland.

MADDISON Tyler. See: SMITH Moe Sherrard.

MADDOX Carl. See: TUBB E(dwin) C(harles).

MADELEY John, b. 14 July 1934, Salford, England. Writer; Broadcaster. m. Alison, 10 Mar 1962, 1 son, 1 daughter. Education: BA Hons Econ, 1972. Publications: When Aid is no Help, 1991; Trade and the Poor, 1992; Diego Garcia: Contrast to the Falklands, 1982; Human Rights Begin with Breakfast, 1981. Contributions to: Financial Times; The Observer; The Guardian; The Independent; International Agricultural Development (editor and publisher); Broadcasting: BBC and Deutsche Welle. Memberships: Society of International Development Journalists Group (Secretary). Address: 19 Woodford Close, Caversham, Reading, Berks RG4 7HN, England.

MADGETT Naomi Long, b. 5 July 1923, Norfolk, Virginia, USA. Poet; Publisher; Professor. m. Leonard P Andrews Snr. Education: BA, Virginia State College, 1945; MEd, English, Wayne State University; PhD, International Institute for Advanced Studies, 1980. Appointments: Staff Writer, The Michigan Chronicle; Service Representative, Michigan Bell Telephone Co; Teacher of English, Northwestern High School, Detroit, Michigan; Research Associate, Oakland University; Lecturer in English, University of Michigan, Ann Arbor; Associate Professor, Professor of English, now Emeritus Professor, Eastern Michigan University; Editor, Lotus Press, 1974-. Publications include: Songs to a Phantom Nightingale, 1941; One and the Many, 1956; Star By Star, 1965, 1970; Pink Ladies in the Afternoon, 1972; Exits and Entrances, 1978; A Student's Guide to Creative Writing, 1990; Phantom Nightingale: Juvenile, 1981. Contributions include: Numerous anthologies and journals including: Beyond the Blues, 1962; Afro-Amerikaanse Poezie, 1964; Ik Ben De Nieuwe Negar, 1965; Kaleidoscope, 1967; Ten, 1968; Black Voices, 1968; Black Poetry, 1969; Michigan Signatures, 1969; Black America, Yesterday and Today, 1969; Poems to Enjoy, 1970; Soulscript, 1970; Britain America, 1970; The Black Poets, 1971; New Black Voices, 1972; The Poetry of Black America, 1973; Love Has Many Faces, 1973; The Touch of a Poet, 1975; One Little Room, an Everywhere, 1975; The Freelance; Poet; English Journal; Ebony; Phylon; Negro Digest. Address: 16886 Inverness Ave, Detroit, MI 48221, USA.

MADSEN Richard Paul, b. 2 Apr 1941, California, USA. Sociologist. m. Judith Rosselli, 12 Jan 1974, 1 daughter. Education: BA, Maryknoll College, 1963; MTh, Maryknoll Seminary, 1968; MA, East Asian Studies, 1972, PhD, Sociology, 1977, Harvard University. Publications: Morality and Power in a Chinese Village, 1984; Chen Village (with Anita Chan and Jonathan Unger), 1984; Habits of the Heart (with Bellah, Sullivan, Swidler, Tipton), 1985; The Good Society (with Bellah, Sullivan, Swidler, Tipton), 1990. Honours: Wright Mills Award, for Morality and Power in a Chinese Village, 1985; For Habits of the Heart: Los Angeles Times Book Award, 1985; Jury nomination for Pulitzer Prize, 1986. Memberships: Association of Asian Studies, Governing Council for China and Inner Asia 1989-91; American Sociology Association. Address: Department of Sociology, University of California at San Diego, La Jolla, CA 92093, USA.

MADUBUIKE Ihechukwu Chiedozie, b. 9 Jluy 1944. Business Exective. m. 1980, 2 sons, 5 daughters. Education: BA, MA, PhD, Comparative Literature, SUNY at Buffalo, New York, 1973. Publications: A Handbook of African Names, 1976; Towards The Decolonisation of African Literature, 1980; The Sociology of the The Senegalese Novel, 1981; Ighota Abu Igbo (Understanding Igbo Poetry).Contributions to: Numerous articels and poems in national and international journals and magazines. Memberships: Newspapers Proprietors Association of Nigeria. Address: c/o PO Box 3538, Oweri, Imo State, Nigeria.

MAESTRO Giulio, b. 1942, American. Appointments: Assistant to Art Director, Design Organization Incorporated, 1965-66; Assistant Art Director, Warren A Kass Graphics Incorporated, 1966-69; Freelance Writer, Designer and Illustrator, 1969-. Publications: The Tortoise's Tug of War, 1971; The Remarkable Plant in Apartment 4, 1973; One More and One Less, 1974; Leopard is Sick, 1978; Leopald and the Noisy Monkeys, 1980; A Raft of Riddles, 1982; Riddle Romp, Just Enough Rosie, 1983; What's a Frank Frank? 1984; Razzle-Dazzle Riddles, 1985; What's Mite Might? 1986; Riddle Roundup, 1989; More Halloween Howls, 1992.

MAGEE Bryan, b. 12 Apr 1930, London, England. Writer. m. Ingrid Söderlund, 1954, (dec 1986), 1 daughter. Education: MA, Oxford, 1956; Yale University, 1955-56. Appointments: Theatre Critic, The Listener, 1966-67; Regular Columnist, The Times, 1974-76. Publications include: Go West Young Man, 1958; To Live in Danger, 1960; The New Radicalism, 1962; The Democratic Revolution, 1964; Towards 2000, 1965; One in Twenty, 1966; The Television Interviewer, 1966; Aspects of Wagner, 1968; Modem British Philosophy, 1971; Popper, 1973; Facing Death, 1977; Men of Ideas, 1978; The Philosophy of Schopenhauer, 1983; The Great Philosophers, 1987. Contributions to: numerous journals. Honours: Silver Medal, Royal Television Society, 1978. Memberships: President, Critics Circle; Society of Authors. Literary Agent: Peters, Fraser & Dunlop Group Limited,. Address: 12 Falkland House, Marloes Road, London, W8 5LF, England.

MAGEE Wes, b. 20 July 1939, Greenock, Scotland. Former Headteacher; Broadcaster; Full Time Author. m. Janet Elizabeth Parkhouse, 10 Aug 1967, 1 son, 1 daughter. Education: Teaching Certificate, 1967; Advanced Certificate in Education, 1972. Publications: Poetry: Urban Gorilla, 1972; No Man's Lane, 1978; A Dark Age, 1982; Flesh of Money, 1990; Other: Oliver the Daring Birdman, 1978; The Real Spirit of Christmas, 1979; All the Day Through, 1982; Dragon's Smoke, 1985; A Shooting Star, 1985; Story Starters, 1986; A Calandar of Poems, 1986; Don't Do That, 1987; A Christmas Stocking, 1987; Morning Break, 1989; The Witch's Brew, 1989; A Big Poetry Book, 1989; Read A Poem, Write A Poem, 1989; Madtail Miniwhale, 1989; Legend of The Ragged Boy, 1992; Scribblers of Scumbagg School, 1993. Contributions to: Journals and publications including poetry & reviews. Honours: New Poets Award, 1972; Poetry Book Society Recommendation, 1978; Cole Scholar (Florida, USA), 1985. Memberships: Poetry Society of Great Britian. Address: Santone House, Low Street, Sancton, York, YO4 3QX.

MAGNUSSON Magnus, b. 12 Oct 1929. Writer; Broadcaster. m. Mamie Baird, 1954, 1 son, 3 daughters (1 son dec). Education: MA, Jesus College, Oxford. Publications: Introducing Archaeology, 1972; Viking Expansion Westwards, 1973; The Clacken and the Slate, 1974; Hammer of the North, 1976, 2nd edition, Viking Hammer of the North, 1980; BC, The Archaeology of the Bible Lands, 1977; Landlord or Tenant? a View of Irish History, 1978; Iceland, 1979; Vikings! 1980; Magnus on the Move, 1980; Treasures of Scotland, 1981; Lindisfarne:

The Cradle Island, 1984; Iceland Saga, 1987; translations (all with Hermann Palsson): Njal's Saga, 1960; The Vinland Sagas, 1965; King Herald's Saga, 1966; Laxaela Saga, 1969; (all by Halldor Laxness): The Atom Station, 1961; Paradise Reclaimed, 1962; The Fish Can Sing, 1966; World Light, 1969; Christianity under Glacier, 1973; (by Samivel) Golden Iceland, 1967; Contributor: The Glorious Privilege, 1967; The Future of the Highlands, 1968; Strange Stories, Amazing Facts, 1975; Pass the Port, 1976; Book of Bricks, 1978; Chronicle, 1978; Discovery of Lost Worlds, 1979; Pass the Port Again, 1981; Second Book of Bricks, 1981; Introducted: Ancient China, 1974; The National Trust for Scotland Guide, 1976; Karluk, 1976; More Lives Than One? 1976; Atlas of World Geography, 1977; Face to Face with the Turin Shroud, 1978; Modem Bible Atlas, 1979; Living Legends, 1980; The Hammer and the Cross, 1980; Household Ghosts, 1981; Great Books for Today, 1981; The Voyage of Odin's Raven, 1982; Robert Burns: Bawdy Verse & Folksongs, 1982; Mastermind 4, 1982; Northern Voices, 1984; The Village, 1985; Secrets of the Bible Seas, 1985; Edited: Echoes in Stone, 1983; Readers Digest Book of Facts, 1985; Chambers Biographical Dictionary, 1990; The Nature of Scotland, 1991. Honours: Knight of the Order of the Falcon, Iceland, 1975; Knight Commander, 1986; Silver Jubilee Medal, 1977; Iceland Media Award, 1985; Hon KBE, 1989; Hon Fellow, Jesus College, Oxford, 1990; Honorary Degrees, and many other honours and awards. Memberships: Fellow, Society of Antiquaries of London, 1991; Fellow, Royal Scottish Geographical Society, 1991. Literary Agent: Deborah Rogers, Rogers, Coleridge & White, 20 Powis Mews, London W11 1JN, England. Address: Blairskaith House, Balmore-Torrance, Glasgow G64 4AX, Scotland.

MAGNUSSON Sigurdur A, b. 31 Mar 1928, Reykjavik, Iceland. Writer. Twice married, twice divorced, 2 sons, 3 daughters. Education: BA, New School for Social Research, New York, 1955. Appointments: Literary & Drama Critic, Morgunbladid, 1956-67; Editor in chief, Samvinnan, 1967-74; Member, International Writing Programme, University of Iowa, 1976, 1977; Member, West Berlin International Artists' Programme, 1979-80; Member, 11 Man 1986 Jury, Neustadt International Prize for Literature, Oklahoma; Member of Jury, Nordic Council's Prize for Literature, 1990-. Publications: In Icelandic. Poems: Scribbled in Sand, 1958; The Sea & the Rock, 1961; This is Your Life, 1974; In The Light of Next Day, 1978; Tropics - Selected Poems 1952-82, 1988. Essays: the Emperor's New Clothes, 1959; Sown to the Wind, 1967; In the Limelight, 1982. Novels: Night Visitors, 1961; Under a Dead Star, 1979; The Meshes of Tomorrow, 1981; Jacob Wrestling, 1983; The Tree of Knowledge, 1985; From the Snare of the Fowler, 1986. Short Stories: Trivialities, 1965. Play: Visiting, 1962. Biography: Bishop Sigurbjör - Life and Work, 1988. Travel Books on Greece, 1992 and India, 1953, 1962 (In Greek) Death of Balder and Other Poems, 1960; (In English) Northern Spinx - Iceland and the Icelanders from the Settlement to the Present, 1977, 2nd edition 1984; Iceland - Country and People, 1978, 1987; The Iceland Horse, 1978; The Postwar Poetry of Iceland, 1982; Icelandic Writing Today, 1982; Iceland Crucible - A Modern Artistic Renaissnace, 1985; The Icelanders 1990; Artistic, 1990; Magic of Greece, 1992. Contributions to: Numerous professional journals. Honours: Golden Cross of Phoenix, Greece, 1955; Cultural Council's Prize of Best Play, 1961; Cultural Prize for Best Novel, 1980. Memberships: Society of Icelandic Drama Critics, Chairman, 1963-71; Writers Union of Iceland, Chairman, 1971-78; Greek-Icelandic Cultural Society, Chairman, 1985-88; Amnesty International, Chairman 1988-89, 1993-95. Address: Barónsstig 49, 101 Reykjavik, Iceland.

MAGORIAN James, b. 24 Apr 1942, Palisade, Nebraska, USA. Writer; Poet; Author of children's stories. Education: BS, University of Nebraska, 1965; MS, Illinois State University, 1969; Graduate Studies, Oxford University 1972, Harvard University 1973. Publications: Author of 56 books including: The Garden of Epicus (poetry), 1971; Distances (poetry), 1972; School Daze (children's book), 1978; Safe Passage (poetry), 1977; The Edge of the Forest (poetry), 1980; Keeper of Fire (children's book), 1984; Ground-Hog Day (children's book), 1987; The Bad Eggs (children's book), 1989; The Invention of the Afternoon Nan (children's book), 1989. Contributions to: Western Poetry Quarterly; Poetry View; Nebraska Review; San Francisco Poetry Journal; Kansas Quarterly; The Louisville Review; Illinois Quarterly. Address: 1225 North 46th Street, Lincoln, NE 68503, USA.

MAGORIAN Michelle Jane, b. 6 Nov 1947, Southsea, Portsmouth, Hampshire, England. Writer; Actress. m. Peter Keith Venner, 18 Aug 1987, 1 son. Education: Diploma, Speech & Drama, Rose Bruford College of Speech and Drama, Kent, 1969; Ecole Internationale de Mime Marcel Marceau, Paris, France, 1969-70.

Publications: Novels: Goodnight Mister Tom, 1981, US edition 1982, also book and lyrics as musical; Back Home, 1984, 1985; A Little Love Song, 1991; Poetry: Waiting for My Shorts to Dry, 1989; Orange Paw Marks, 1991; In Deep Water, short story collection, 1992; Picture books; Short stories. Contributions to: Puffin Post. Honours: For Goodnight Mister Tom: Guardian Award for Children's Fiction, UK, 1981; Commended for Carnegie Medal, UK, 1981; Children's Award, International Reading Association, USA, 1982; Notable Children's Books of 1982, Best Book of Young Adults, 1982, YA Reviewers Choice, 1982, American Library Association; Western Australia Young Readers Book Award, 1983; Teachers Choice, NCTE, 1983; For Back Home: Best Books for Adults, American Library Association, 1984; Western Australia Young Readers Book Award, 1987; Goodnight Mister Tom (musical) winner, Buxon Opera House Quest for New Musicals. Memberships: Society of Authors, Children's Writers and Illustrators Committee; PEN; British Actors Equity. Literary Agent: Patricia White, Rogers, Coleridge and White. Address: 803 Harrow Road, Wembley, Middlesex HA0 2LP, England.

MAHAPATRA Jayanta, b. 22 Oct 1928, Cuttack, Orissa, India. Poet. m. Jyotsna Rani Das, 1951, 1 s. Education: MSc, Patna University, 1949. Appointments include: Visiting Writer, Universities, USA, Japan, Australia, UK, Germany, Mexico, Malaysia, Indonisia, Singapore; Poet in Residence, Rockefeller Foundation Cultural Centre, Italy, 1986. Publications include: Close the Sky, Ten by Ten, 1971; Svayamvara and Other Poems, 1971; A Rain of Rites, 1976; A Fathers Hours, 1976; Waiting, 1979; The False Start, 1980; Relationship, 1980; Life Signs, 1983; Dispossessed Nests, 1984, 1986; Selected Poems, 1987; Burden of Waves and Fruit, 1988; Temple, 1989; A Whiteness of Bone, 1992; Stories for Children and Translations. Honours include: National Academy of Letters Award, New Delhi, 1981; Rockefeller Foundation Award, 1986. Address: Tinkonia, Bagicha, Cuttack 753 001, Orissa, India.

MAHARIDGE Dale. Publications: Journey to Nowhere: The Saga of the New Underclass, 1985; And Their Children After Them, 1989; The Last Great American Hero, 1993. Honour: Pulitzer Prize, 1990. Address: c/o Pantheon Books Publicity Dept, 210 E 50th St 25th Floor, New York, NY 10022, USA.

MAHESHWARI Shriram, b. 27 Nov 1931, Kanpur. Teaching. m. Bimla, 30 May 1955, 3 sons, 2 daughters. Education: BA, 1951; MA Economics, 1953; MA Political Science, 1955, Agra University; MGA, Wharton School, University of Pensylvania, 1964; PhD, University of Delhi, 1965. Appointments: Professor of Political Science and Public Administration at Indian Institute of Public Administration, 1973-; Guest faculty at Jawaharla Nehur University, New Delhi, 1979-83; Director, The Centre for Political and Administrative Studies, 1991-; Visiting Professor, Dept of Political Studies, University of Guelph, Ont, Canada. Publications: Rural Development in India: A Public Policy Approach, 1986; The Higher Civil Service in Japan, 1986; The Higher Civil Service in France, 1991; Problems & Issues in Administrative Federalism, 1991; Administrative Reform in France, 1991; Indian Administration: An Historical Account, 1994. Contributions to: Various journals; The Philippines Journal of Public Administration; Indian Express; The Hindustan Times. Honours: Sardar Patel Prize for best work in Hindi, instituted by the Government of India, 1988. Memberships: President of Indian Public Administration Association, 1988-89; Indian Political Science Association. Address: 156 Golf Links, New Delhi 110003, India.

MAHFOUZ Naguib, b. 11 Dec 1911, Cairo, Egypt. Writer; Journalist; Civil Servant. m. 2 d. Education: Degree in Philosophy, University of Cairo, 1934. Appointments: Journalist, Ar-Risala; Minstry of Islamic Affairs, 1939; Department of Art; Head, State Cinema Organisation; Advisor to Minister of Culture; retired 1971. Publications: 16 collections of short stories including (in translation), The Time and the Place, 1991; 34 novels including (in translation), Midaq Alley, 1975; Mirrors, 1977; Miramar, 1978; Al-Karnak, 1979; Children of Gebelawi, (translated by Philip Stewart) 1981, new translation, 1995; The Thief and the Dogs, 1984; Wedding Song, 1984; The Beginning and the End, 1985; The Beggar, 1986; Respected Sir, 1986; The Search, 1987, Fountain and Tomb, 1988; (The Cairo Trilogy) Palace Walk, 1990, Palace of Desire, 1991, Sugar Street, 1992; The Journey of Ibn Fattouma, 1992; Adrift on the Nile, 1993; Al-Harafish, 1994; Arabian Nights and Days, 1995; (dates of translations' publication). Honours: Nobel Prize for Literature, 1988; Honorary Member, American Academy and Institute of Arts and Letters, 1992. Literary Agent: The

American Univesity in Cairo Press. Address: 113 Sharia Kasr El Aini, Cairo, Egypt.

MAHON Derek, b. 1914. British. Poet. Appointments: English Teacher, Belfast High School, Newtownabbey, Co Antrim, 1967-68; Lecturer in English, The Language Centre of Ireland, Dublin, Republic of Ireland; Poet-in-Residence: Emerson College, Boston, USA, 1976-77, New University of Ulster, Coleraine, Northern Ireland, 1977-79; Poetry Editor, New Statesman, London; Dream Critic: The Listener, London. Publications: Twelve Poems, 1965; Night-Crossing, 1968; Ecclesiastes, Beyond Howth Head, 1970; Modern Irish Poetry (editor), 1972; Lives, 1972; The Man Who Built His City in Snow, 1972; The Snow Party, 1975; Light Music, 1977; The Sea in Winter, Poems 1962-1978, 1979; Courtyards in Delft, 1981; The Chimeras by Nerval (translation), 1982; The Hunt by Night, 1982; A Kensington Notebook, 1984; Antarctica, 1985. Address: c/o Deborah Rogers Limited, 49 Belheim Crescent, London W11 2EF, England.

MAHONEY Rosemary, b. 28 Jan 1961, Boston, Massachusetts, USA. Writer. Education: BA, Harvard College, 1983; MA, Johns Hopkins University, 1985. Publications: The Early Arrival of Dreams; A Year in China; Whoredom in Kimmage; Irish Women Coming of Age, 1993. Honours: C E Horman Prize for Fiction, Harvard College, 1982; Henfield-Transatlantics Review Award for Fiction, 1985. Contributions to: Harper's Magazine Essay, 1994; The New York Times Op-Ed Page, What Are You? 1993; Mirabella Magazine Essay, 1993; Elle Magazine Essay, 1993; New York Times Book Review, Review of The Butcher Boy, 1993; New York Newsday Review, The Invisible Worm, 1993; The Washington Post Book World Review, Lipstick on the Host, 1993. Literary Agent: Wylie, Aitken and Stone, 250 West 57th St, New York, NY 10107, USA. Address: Houghton Mifflin Company, 215 Park Avenue South, New York, NY 10003, USA.

MAHY Margaret, b. 1936, New Zealand. Full-time Writer (Children's Fiction, Poetry, History). Appointments: Former Librarian, School Library Service, Christchurch; Writer-in-Residence: Canterbury University, 1984, College of Advanced Education, Western Australia, 1985. Publications: The Dragon of an Ordinary Family, 1969; Mrs Discombobulous, 1969; Pillycock's Shop, 1969; A Lion in the Meadow, 1969; The Procession, 1969; The Little Witch, 1970; Sailor Jack and the 20 Orphans, 1970; The Princess and the Clown, 1970; The Boy with Two Shadows, 1971; 17 Kings and 42 Elephants, verse, 1972; The First (Second, Third) Margaret Mahy Story Book: Stories and Poems, 3 vols, 1972-75; The Man Whose Mother Was a Pirate, 1972; The Railway Engine and the Hairy Brigands, 1973; Rooms for Rent, in UK as Rooms to Let, 1974; The Witch in the Cherry Tree, 1974; Clancy's Cabin, 1974; The Rare Spotted Birthday Party, 1974; Stepmother, 1974; The Bus under the Leaves, 1975; The Ultra-Violet Catastrophe! or, The Unexpected Walk with Great-Uncle Magnus Pringle, 1975; The Great Millionaire Kidnap, 1975; New Zealand: Yesterday and Today, 1975; Leaf Magic, 1975; The Boy Who Was Followed Home, 1975; The Wind Between the Stars, 1976; David's Witch Doctor, 1976; The Pirate Uncle, 1977; Nonstop Nonsense, 1977; The Great Piratical Rumbustification, 1979; Fearsome Robots and Frightened Uncles, 1980; Raging Robiots and Unruly Uncles, 1981; The Chewing-Gum Rescue, 1982; The Haunting, 1983; The Pirate's Mixed-Up Voyage, 1983; The Changeover, 1983; The Birthday Burglar and a Very Wicked Headmistress, 1984; The Catalogue of the Universe, 1985; Jam, 1985; The Tricksters, 1986; Aliens in the Family, 1986; The Downhill Crocodile Whizz and Other Stories, 1986; Memory, 1987; The Horrible Story and Others, 1987. Honours: Carnegie Medal, Esther Glen Medal, for The Haunting. Address: RD No 1, Lyttelton, New Zealand.

MAI Gottfried Erhard Willy, b. 11 May 1940, Finsterwalde, Germany. Theologian; Freelance Writer. m. Gunhild Flemming, 1 Sept 1962, 2 sons, 2 daughters. Education: Navigation Certificate, Nautical School, Bremen; Studied Theology and History, Universities of Bonn, Gottingen, Hamburg and Copenhagen; Dr Theol; Dr Phil. Publications include: The Protestant Church and the German Emigration to North America (1815-1914), 1972; Die niederdeutsche Reformbewegung, 1979; The German Federal Armed Forces 1815-1864, 1977, 1982; Geschichte der stadt Finsterwalde, 1979; Der Überfall des Tigers, 1982; Chronicle of the 4th Minesweeper Squadron Wilhelmshaven, 1985; Buddha, 1985; Napoleon - Temptation of Power, 1986; Zwischen Polor und Wonderkreis, 1987; Lenin - The Perverted Moral, 1987. Contributions to: Hospitium ecclesiae (Society for History), Bremen; Annual Books of Hermannsburg Mission Society; Annual Books of Gustav-Adolf-Werk, Kassel: Reader's Digest of World Mission, Erlangen; Annual Book of Lower Saxonian Church History, Blomberg;

German Solder Annual Book, Bonn; Others. Honours: Book Prize for History of AWMM, 1983. Address: Harlinger Weg 2, D 2948 Grafschaft, Germany.

MAIBAUM Matthew, b. 14 Aug 1946, Chicago, Illinois, USA. Consulting Social Scientist; Writer. Education: AB Honours, University of California, Berkeley, 1969; MPA, University of California, Los Angeles; PhD, California School of Professional Psychology, 1975; PhD, Political Sciences, Claremont Graduate School, 1980. Publications include: Sly Times, play, 1985; Wiggling in the Rain, play, 1987; The Lilac Bush, 1990; Monographs, articles and funded studies in ethnic studies, politics, intergroup relations. Contributions to: Various journals and books. Honours: Grant Aid Award, Society for the Psychological Study of Social Issues, 1972; Best Paper, California State Psychological Association, 1975; Other awards. Memberships: Authors Guild; Dramatists Guild; Pi Gamma Mu; Sigma Xi; Society of Authors, UK. Address: 15237 Sunset Blvd 24, Pacific Palisades, CA 90272, USA.

MAIDEN Jennifer, b. 7 Apr 1949, Penrith, NSW, Australia. Writer; Poet. m. David Toohey, 1984, 1 d. Education: BA, Macquarie University, NSW, 1974. Appointments include: Tutor, University of Western Sydney, 1991. Publications: Tactics, 1974; The Occupying Forces, 1975; The Problem of Evil, 1975; Birthstones, 1978; The Border Loss, 1979; For the Left Hand, 1981; The Trust, 1988; Selected Poems in Jennifer Maiden, 1990; The Winter Baby, 1990; Novels, The Terms, 1982; Play with Knives, 1990; Short Stories, Mortal Details, 1977. Honours include: Australia Council Grants or Fellowships. Address: PO Box 4, Penrith, NSW 2750, Australia.

MAIER Paul Luther, b. 1930, American. Appointments: Professor of Ancient History, Campus Chaplain to Lutheran students, Western Michigan University, Kalamazoo, 1958-. Publications: A Man Spoke, A World Listened: The Story of Walter A Maier, 1963; Pontius Pilate, 1968; First Christmas, 1971; First Easter, 1973; First Christians, 1976; The Best of Walter A Maier (ed), 1980; The Flames of Rome, 1981; Josephus - The Jewish War (associate ed), 1982; Josephus: The Essential Writings, 1988; In The Fullness of Time, 1991; A Skeleton in God's Closet, 1994; Josephus: The Essential Works, 1995. Address: Department of History, Western Michigan University, Kalamazoo, MI 49008, USA.

MAILER Norman Kingsley, b. 31 Jan 1923, Long Beach, USA. Writer. m. 1) Beatrice Silverman, 1944, div 1951, 1 daughter, 2) Adele Morales, 1954, div 1962, 2 daughters, 3) Lady Jeanne Campbell, 1962, div 1963, 1 daughter, 4) Beverly Rentz Bentley, 1963, div 1980, 2 sons, 1 daughter, 5) Carol Stevens, div, 1 daughter, 6) Norris Church, 1980, 1 son. Education: BS, Harvard University. Publications: The Naked and The Dead, 1948; Barbary Shore, 1951; The Deer Park, 1955 (dramatised 1967); Advertisements for Myself, 1959; Deaths for the Ladies (poems), 1962; The Presidential Papers, 1963; An American Dream, 1964; Cannibals and Christians, 1966; Why are We in Vietnam? (novel), 1967; The Armies of the Night, 1968; Miami and the Siege of Chicago, 1968; Moonshot, 1969; A Fire on the Moon, 1970; The Prisoner of Sex, 1971; Existential Errands, 1972; St George and the Godfather, 1972; Marilyn, 1973; The Faith of Graffiti, 1974; The Fight, 1975; Some Honourable Men, 1976; Genius and Lust - A Journey Through the Writings of Henry Miller, 1976; A Transit to Narcissus, 1978; The Executioner's Song, 1979; Of Women and Their Elegance, 1980; The Essential Mailer (Selections), 1982; Pieces and Pontifications, 1982; Ancient Evenings (novel), 1983; Tough Guys Don't Dance (novel), 1983; Haulot's Ghost, 1991. Contributions to: Numerous journals and magazines. Honours: National Book Award for Arts and Letters, 1969; Pulitzer Prize for Non-Fiction, 1969; 14th Annual Award for Outstanding Service to the Arts, McDowell Colony, 1973. Memberships: President, PEN, US Chapter, 1984-86; American Academy of Arts and Letters. Literary Agent: Wylie, Aitleen, Stone, 250 West 57th St, New York, NY 10119, USA. Address: c/o Rembar, 19th W 44th St, New York, NY 10036, USA.

MAINE David. See: **BARBET Pierre Claude Avice.**

MAIR Alexander Craig, b. 3 May 1948. Schoolteacher. m. Anne Olizar, 1 aug 1970, 2 sons, 1 daughter. Education: BA, Stirling University, 1971. Publications: A Time in Turkey, 1973; A Star for Seamen, 1978; The Lighthouse Boy, 1981; Britain at War 1914-19, 1982; Mercat Cross and Tolbooth, 1988; David Angus, 1989; Stirling, The Royal Burgh, 1990; The Incorporation of Glasgow Maltmen: A History, 1990. Memberships: Fellow, Scottish Society of Antiquaries;

Educational Institute of Scotland; Various local history groups. Address: 21 Keir Street, Bridge of Allan, Stirling, Scotland.

MAIRS Nancy Pedrick, b. 23 July 1943. Writer. m. George Anthony Mairs, 18 May 1963, 1 son, 1 daughter. Education: AB cum laude, Wheaton College, Massachusetts, 1964; MFA 1975, PhD 1984, University of Arizona. Publications: Instead It is Winter, 1977; In All the Rooms of the Yellow House, 1984; Plaintext, 1986; Remembering the Bone House, 1989; Carnal Acts, 1990; Ordinary Time, 1993; Voice Lessons, 1994. Contributions to: The American Voice; MSS; Tri Quarterly. Honours: Western States Book Award, 1984; Fellowship, National Endowment for the Arts, 1991. Memberships: The Authors Guild; Poets and Writers; National Women's Studies Association. Literary Agent: Barbara S Kouts. Address: 1527 East Mabel Street, Tucson, AZ 85719, USA.

MAJA-PEARCE Adewale, b. 3 June 1953, London, England. Researcher; Consultant; Writer. Education: BA, University of Wales, University College of Swansea, 1975; MA, School of Oriental and African Studies, 1986. Appointments: Researcher, Index on Censorship, London, 1986-; Consultant, Heinemann International, Oxford, 1986-. Publications: Christopher Okigbo: Collected Poems (editor), 1986; In My Father's Country: A Nigerian Journey, non-fiction, 1987; Loyalties, stories, 1987; How Many Miles to Babylon, non-fiction, 1990; The Heinemann Book of African Poetry in English (editor), 1990; Who's Afraid of Wole Soyinka? Essays on Censorship, 1991; A Mask Dancing: Nigerian Novelists of the Eighties, 1992. Contributions to: Various periodicals. Memberships: PEN; Society of Authors. Literary Agent: David Grossman Literary Agency, London, England. Address: 33 St George's Road, Hastings, East Sussex TN34 3NH, England.

MAJEWSKI Janusz, b. 5 Aug 1931, Lvov, Poland. Film Director; Scriptwriter. m. Zofia Nasierowska, 1960, 1 son, 1 daughter. Education: Cracow Polytechnic; State School of Drama and Film, Lodz, 1960. Appointments: Feature Film Set Designer, 1955-60; Short Film Director, 1961-67; Feature Film Director, 1967-; Professor, Higher State School of Film, TV and Drama, Lodz. Publications: Shorts: Rondeau, 1959; Fleischer's Album, 1963; Duel, 1964; Avatar, 1965; Feature films: The Lodger, 1966; Kokis, 1970; Jealousy and Medicine, 1973; Hotel Pacific, 1975; The Gorgonowa Case, 1977; Lesson of the Dead Language, 1979; The Epitaph for Barbara Radziwillowna, 1983; Daydream, 1985; Deserters, 1986; The Black Gorge, 1989; TV plays; TV series: Bona the Queen, 1982; Napoleon and Europe (Moscow episode), French production, 1989. Honours: Numerous awards and citations at national and international festivals; Several Polish awards including: Gold Cross of Merit, 1975; Knight's Cross, Order of Polonia Restituta, 1981. Memberships: Polish Film-makers Association, Secretary, General Board 1970-74, President 1983-; ZAIKS. Address: ul Forteczna 1a, 01-540 Warsaw, Poland.

MAKAREWICZ Roman, b. 13 Aug 1905, Cracow, Poland. Writer; Retired Senior Auditor. m. Irene Unverman, 19 Mar 1945, 2 sons. Education: Academy of Commerce, Poland, 1925; Diploma, Konsularakademie, Vienna, Austria, 1929; Postgraduate course, Hautes Etudes Internationales, Paris, France, 1929-30. Appointments include: Several poems in Gazeta Poranna and Gazeta Lwowska, Lwow, 1923-26; 1st public appearance, An Evening With The Authors, Municipal Casino, Lwow, 1923; Wrote, directed, "Hold on till Spring" show, Artillery Officers School, Wlodzimierz, 1930; Press Attache, Polish Consulate, Breslau and Correspondent, Polish Telegraph Agency, 1932-34; Co-Editor, Dzennik Zwiazkowy, Polish Daily, Chicago, Illinois, USA, 1946-48. Publications: Poems: Wiosna i Zima, 1972; Rapsody Kalifornijskie, 1983; Fraszki Frasujace, 1988; Postcards from Hawaii and Old Stories; Unpublished, registered drama: Gay Nineties on Broadway, Part 1, 1990, Part II, 1991. Contributions to: Dziennik Polski daily and Tydzien Polski weekly, London, 1970-80; New Horizon, New York, 1981-86. Honours: Participant, 9-hour document drama Struggles for Poland, WNET, 1986; Silver Poet Award, 1986; Golden Poet Award, 1987; World of Poetry, San Francisco; Certificate of Merit, Poetry in Paradise Association, Hawaii, 1987; Award of Merit, Iliad Press and National Authors Registry, 1991. Memberships: Past President, Los Angeles Municipal Accountants & Auditors Association; Commander, Polish Veterans in Exile, Southern California, 1966-67. Address: PO Box 575 Kilauen, Kauai, HI 96754, USA.

MAKARSKI Henryk, b. 17 Aug 1946, Biala, Podlaska, Poland. Writer. m. Maria Anna Koziolkiewicz, 24 Jul 1971, 1 s, 1 d. Education: MA, Polish Philology, Marie-Curie-Slowdoska University of Lublin,

1969. Appointments: Co-Editor of Youth Literary Columns, 1965-80. Publications: Drowning in the Hardened Soil, 1972; Desire, 1978; The Endless Staircase, 1980; The Easiest, The Hardest, 1984; On the Track of Great-Grandfather Walerian, 1983, 1987; Following the Purple Bird, 1986; The Gold Heart of the Emperor, 1989; 5 volumes of poetry; critical literary essays, short criminal sensation forms. Honours: Boleslaw Prus Literary; Award for Prose, 1984; Main Josef Czechowicz Award for Poetry, 1985; Over 25 Awards and Honours for prose, poetry and reportage. Membership: Polish Writers Association, Lublin Regional Board. Address: 20-850 Lublin, ul Radzynska 18 m 23, Poland.

MAKOWIECKI Andrzej, b. 5 Aug 1938, Warsaw, Poland. Writer; Reporter; Jazzman; Traveller. Education: State School of Music, Lodz, 1962; MA, Polish Philology, Lodz University, 1968. Literary Appointments: Editor, reporter, Odgiosy literary weekly, 1965-87; Correspondent, Polityka weekly, 1970-72; Reporter, Zwierciadlo, weekly, 1973-75. Publications include: Novels: Every Day Nearer to Heaven, 1972 (film 1983); The Catcher's Return, 1977, 1985; The Night of Saxophones, 1984; There Are No trains to Barcelona, 1987; The Quarter of the Sleeping Beauty, 1979; Napoleon's Rapier, 1986; also short stories. Contributions to: Polityka, Odglosy, Kultura; Tygodnik Kuturalny; Zycie Warszawy; Zwierciadlo. Honours: 1st Place, short story competition (sports subjects), Chief Committee for Physical Culture & Tourism, 1969; Various other literary awards & prizes. Memberships: Union of Polish Writers (ZLP); Association of Polish Journalists (ZDP); Association of Polish Authors (ZAIKS). Literary Agent: Dr Jacek Zaorski, Publishing House of Lodz, Lodz, ul. Pietrkowska 171. Address: 90-440 Lodz, ul. Pietrkowska 147 m. 1, Poland.

MALAND David, b. 1929. British. Headmaster. Appointments: Senior History Master, Stamford School, Lincolnshire, 1956-66; Headmaster, Cardiff High School, Glamorgan, Wales, 1966-69; Headmaster, Denstone College, Uttoxeter, 1969-78; High Manchester Grammar School, 1978-86. Publications: Europe in the Seventeenth Century, 1966; La Guerre de Trente Ans by G Pages (co-translator), 1970; Culture and Society in Seventeenth Century France, 1971; Europe in the Sixteenth Century, 1973; Europe at War 1600-1650, 1980. Address: Windrush, Underhill Lane, Westmeston, Nr Hassocks, East Sussex BN6 8XG, England.

MALGONKAR Manohar (Dattaray), b. 12 Jul 1913, Bombay, India. Education: BA, 1936, Bombay University. Appointments: Professional Big-Game Hunter, 1935-37; Cantonment Executive Officer, Government of India, 1937-42; Owner, Jagalbet Mining Syndiate, 1953-59; Self-employed farmer in Jagalbet, 1959-. Publications: Kanhoji Angray, Maratha Admiral: An Account of His Life and His Battles With the English, 1959; Distant Drum, 1960; Combat of Shadows, 1962; Puars of Dewas Senior, The Princes, 1963; A Bend in the Ganges, 1964; Spy in Amber, The Chatrapatis of Kolhapur, 1971; The Devil's Wind: Nana Saheb's Story, 1972; Bombay Beware, 1974; A Toast in Warm Wine, 1975; Rumble Tumble, 1976; Dead and Living Cities, Line of Mars, 1977; Shalimar (with K Shah), The Men Who Killed Ghandhi, 1978; Cue From the Inner Voice, The Garland Keepers, 1980; Inside Goa, Bandicoot Run, 1982; Princess, 1985. Address: PO Jagalbet, Londa, Belgaum District, India.

MALING Arthur (Gordon), b. 1923, American. Appointments: Reporter, The Journal, San Diego, CA, 1945-46; Executive, Maling Brothers Incorporated, Retail Shoe Chain, Chicago, 1946-72. Publications: Decoy, 1969; Go-Between, 1970; (in UK as Lambert's Son, 1972); Loophole, 1971; The Snowman, 1973; Dingdong, 1974; Bent Man, 1975; Ripoff, 1976; Schroeder's Game, When Last Seen (ed), 1977; Lucky Devil, Mystery Writers' Choice (ed), 1978; The Rheingold Route, The Koberg Link, 1979; From Thunder Bay, 1981; A Taste of Treason, 1983; Lover and Thief, 1988; Contributions to: The Christmas Bride, short story, 1991. Literary Agent: Harold Ober Associates. Address: 175 E Delaware Pl #6907, Chicago, IL 60611, USA.

MALINS Penelope, (Penelope Hobhouse), b. 20 Nov 1929, Northern Ireland. Writer; Designer. m. John Malins, 1 Nov 1965, 2 s, 1 d. Education: Cambridge Hons, Economics, 1951. Publications: The Country Gardener; Colour in Your Garden; Garden Style; Flower Gardens; Guide to the Gardens of Europe; The Smaller Garden; Painted Gardens; Private Gardens of England; Borders; Flower Gardens; Plants in Garden History; Garden Style. Contributions to: The Garden; Horticulture; Vogue; Antiques; Plants & Gardens. Literary

Agent: Felicity Bryan, Address: The Coach House, Bettiscombe, Bridport, Dorset, DT6 5NT, England.

MALLET-JONES Françoise, b. 6 July 1930, Antwerp, Belgium (French citizen). Novelist. Education: Bryn Mawr College, Pennsylvania, USA, and Sorbonne, Paris, 1947-49. Appointments include: Reader for Grasset publishers, from 1965. Publications: Into the Labyrinth, 1951, 1953; The Red Room, 1955; Cordelia and Other Stories, 1956, 1965; House of Lies, 1956; Cafe Celeste, 1958; The Favourite, 1961; Signs and Wonders, 1966; The Witches: Three Tales of Sorcery, 1968; The Underground Game, 1973; Allegra, 1976; Le Rire de Laura, 1985; La Tristesse du cerf-volant, 1988; Adriana Sposa, 1989; Divine, 1991; French version of Shelagh Delaney's play A Taste of Honey, 1960; Also: A Letter to Myself, 1964; The Paper House, 1970; Juliette Greco, 1975; Marie-Paule Belle, 1987. Honours include: Ordre National du Mérite, 1986. Address: c/o Flammarion et Cie, 26 rue Racine, 75278 Paris, France.

MALLINSON Jeremy John Crosby, b. 16 Mar 1937, Ilkley, Yorkshire, England. Zoological Director, Jersey Wildlife Preservation Trust. m. Odette Louise Guiton, 26 Oct 1963, 1 son, 1 daughter. Publications: Okavango Adventure, UK, 1973, USA, 1974; Earning Your Living With Animals, 1975; Modern Classic Animal Stories (editor), UK, 1977, in USA as Such Agreeable Friends, 1978; The Shadow of Extinction, 1978; The Facts About a Zoo, 1980; Travels in Search of Endangered Species, 1989. Contributions to: 135 articles in over 30 different journals and magazines. Honours: Chartered Biologist, 1990; Fellow, Institute of Biology, 1990. Memberships: Chairman, Editorial Board, International Zoo Yearbook; International Union of Zoo Directors; Honorary Director, Wildlife Preservation Trust International, Philadelphia, USA; Honorary Director, Wildlife Preservation Trust of Canada, Ontario; UK Trustee, The Dian Fossey Gorilla Fund; Species Survival Commission, International Union for the Conservation of Nature and Natural Resources. Literary Agent: Curtis Brown Ltd, London, England. Address: Jersey Wildlife Preservation Trust, Les Augres Manor, Trinity, Jersey, Channel Islands.

MALLON Maurus Edward, b. 10 July 1932, Greenock, Scotland. Teacher. Education: MA (Hons), Glasgow, 1956; BEd, Manitoba Univ, Canada, 1966. Publications: Basileus, 1971; The Opal, 1973; Pegaso, 1975; Way Of The Magus, 1978; Anogia, 1980; Bammer McPhie, 1984; Treasure Mountain, 1986; Postcards, 1991; Compenduism, 1993; Short Stories, from Ex Novo Mundo, 1990. Honours: Dave Smith Award, Best English Play, 1992. Memberships: National Writers Association USA; PEN. Literary Agents: NWA Agency. Address: Box 331, Deep River, Ontario, Canada KOJ 1PO.

MALONE Anne Patton. Publications: Women on the Texas Frontier: A Cross-Cultural Perspective, 1983; Sweet Chariot: Slave Family and Household Structure in Nineteenth Century Louisiana, 1994. Honours: Julia Cherry Sprull Prize, Southern Association of Women Historians; General L Kemper Williams Prize in Louisiana History. Address: PO Box 147, Marthaville, LA 71450-0147, USA.

MALONE Joseph Lawrence, b. 2 July 1937, New York City, USA. Professor. m. 31 Jan 1964, 2 sons. Education: AB, University of California, 1963; PhD, 1967. Appointments: Consultant, Contributing Editor, Member Advisory Board, The Academic American Encyclopedia, 1977-; Member Editorial Board, Hellas, 1990-. Publications: The Science of Linguistics in the Art of Translation; Tiberian Hebrew Phonology. Contributions to: Chicago Review; Yellow Silk; New York Times; Hellas; New Press; Reflect; Feasta; Webster Review; Paintbrush. Honours: Prize Story in the PEN Syndicated Fiction Project. Memberships: Linguistic Society of America; American Oriental Society; North American Conference on Afro Asiatic Linguistics. Address: 169 Prospect Street, Leonia, NJ 07605, USA.

MALOUF David, b. 20 Mar 1934, Brisbane, Australia. Education: BA, 1954, University of Queensland. Appointment: Junior Lecturer, English Department, Queensland University, 1955; Clerk, British Petroleum; Supply Teacher, London, 1959-1961; Teacher, Latin & English, Holland Park Comprehensive, 1962; Teacher, St Anselm's Grammer School, 1962-1968; Senior Tutor & Lecturer, English, University of Sydney, 1968-78. Publications: Novels: Johnno, 1975; An Imaginary Life, 1979 (USA 1978); Fly Away Peter, 1982; Child's Play with Eustace and the Prowler, 1982; Harland's Half Acre, 1984; The Great World, 1990; Remembering Babylon, 1993; Short Stories: Antipodes, 1985; Poetry: Interiors (in Four Poets, 1962); Bicycle and Other Poems, 1970; Neighbours in a Thicket, 1974; Poems 1976-77,

1977; First Things Last, 1981; Selected Poems, 1981; Selected Poems, 1982; Poems 1959-89, 1992; Play: Blood Relations, 1987; Opera Libretti: Voss, 1986; Mer de Glace; Baa Baa Black Sheep, 1993. Honours: Winner, NSW Premier's Award for Fiction; Winner: James Cook Award, 1975; Grace Leven Award, 1975; Gold Medal of the Australian Literature Society, 1975; Winner, Gold Medal of the Australian Literature Society, 1982; Victorian Premiers Award (Vance Palmer Prize) for Fiction, 1986; Commonwealth Writer's Prize, 1991; Miles Franklin Award, 1991; Prix Femina Etranger, 1991. Address: 53 Myrtle Street, Chippendale, NSW 2008, Australia.

MALPASS Eric Lawson, b. 14 Nov 1910, Derby, England. m. 3 Oct 1936, 1 s. Education: King Henry VIII School, Coventry, England. Publications: Morning's at Seven: At The Height of the Moon; Shakespeare Trilogy; Sweet Will; The Cleopatra Boy; A House of Women; 12 other novels. Contributions to: Argosy; BBC. Honours: Palma d'Oro Italian Award; Goldene Leinwand, Germany; Observer Short Stories Competition Award. Address: 3 Cedar Court, Rareridge Lane, Bishop's Waltham, Hants SO3 1DX, England.

MALZBERG Barry Norman (Mike Barry, Claudine Dumas, Mel Johnson, Lee W Mason; Francine de Natale, K M O'Donnell, Gerrold Watkins), b. 1939, USA. Freelance Writer (Mystery, Crime, Suspense, Historical, Romance, Gothic, Science Fiction, Fantasy). Appointments: Author, numerous novels for Midwood, Oracle, Soft Cover, Library and Traveler's Companion Series; Investigator, New York City Department of Welfare; Reimbursement Agent, New York State Department of Mental Hygiene; Editor, Scott Meredith Literary Agency, New York City; Editor, Amazing and Fantastic magazines, 1968; Managing Editor, Escapade, 1968. Publications include: Lady of a Thousand Sorrows (as Lee W Mason), 1977; Chorale, 1978; Shared Tomorrows: Collaboration in SF (edited with Bill Pronzini), 1979; The Who Who Loved the Midnight Lady, stories, 1980; The Arbor House Treasury of Horror and the Supernatural (co-editor), 1981; The Cross of Fire, 1982; The Remaking of Sigmund Freud, 1984; Uncollected Stars (co-editor), 1986; Editor with Martin Greenberg: Neglected Vision 1980; The Science Fiction of Mark Clifton, 1980; The Science Fiction of Kris Neville, 1984; 1986; Suspense as Mike Barry: Miami Marauder, 1974; Peruvian Nightmare, 1974; Detroit Massacre, 1975; Harlem Showdown, 1975; The Killing Run, 1975; Philadelphia Blow-Up, 1975; Phoenix Inferno, 1975; With Bill Pronzini: The Running of Beasts, 1976; Acts of Mercy, 1977; Night Screams, 1979; Prose Bowl, 1980. Address: Box 61, Teaneck, NJ 07666, USA.

MAMET David, b. 30 Nov 1947, Chicago, Illinois, USA. Dramatist. Publications: (plays) Sexual Perversity in Chicago; Speed-the-Plow; Oleanna; American Buffalo, 1976; Glengarry Glen Ross, 1983; (novel) The Village; (films/screenplays) House of Games; Things Change; Homicide; The Untouchables; The Verdict; Hoffa; (essays) Writing in Restaurants; Some Freaks; The Cabin; Warm and Cold; The Hero Pony. Honours: New York Drama Critics Circle Award, 1977; Pulitzer Prize, 1984. Address: c/o Howard Rosenstone/Wender, 3 E 48th St 4th Floor, New York, NY10017, USA.

MAMLEYEV Yuri, b. 11 Dec 1931, Moscow, Russia. Professor; Writer. m. Farida Mamleyev, 14 Apr 1973. Education: Forestry Institute, Moscow, 1955. Publications: The Sky Above Hell, 1980; Chatouny, 1986; La Dernier Comedie, 1900; Der Murder aus dem Nichts, 1992; Iznanka Gogena, 1982; Zivaja Smert, 1986; Shatuny, 1987; Ytopi Moyu Golovu, 1990; Golos iz Nichto, 1990; Vechnyi dom, 1991; Izbzannoe Moscow, 1993; Die Letzte Komödie, roman, Salzburg und Wien, 1994. Contributions to: Russian Literary Triquarterly; Apollon; Neue Russische Literatur; Russica New York; Kontinent; Voprosy filosofii, 1992, 1993, Moscow. Memberships: French PEN Centre. Address: 142 rue Legendre, 75017, Paris, France.

MANA Samira Al, b. 25 Dec 1935, Basra, Iraq. Librarian. m. Salah Niazi, Jul 1959, 2 d. Education: BA(Hon), University of Baghdad, 1958; Post Graduate Diploma in Librarianship, Ealing Technical College, 1976. Literary Appointments: Assistant Editor, Alightrab Al-Adabi, 1985-. Publications: The Forerunners and the Newcomers, 1972; The Song, 1976; A London Sequel, 1979; Only a Half, 1979; The Umbilical Cord, 1990. Contributions to: Alightrab Al-Adabi; Many short stories in Arabic magazines; translations in Dutch and English periodicals. Memberships: PEN Club. Address: 46 Tudor Drive, Kingston-Upon-Thames, Surrey, KT2 5PZ, UK.

MANCHEL Frank, b. 1 Jan 1935, USA. Writer; University Educator. Appointments: Professor of English, College of Arts and

Science, University of Vermont, Burlington; Film Reviewer and Critic-at-Large. Publications: Movies and How They Are Made, When Pictures Began to Move, The Lamancha Project, 1968; La Mancha Plus One, When Movies Began to Speak, 1969; Terrors of the Screen, La Mancha Plus Two, 1970; Cameras West, 1971; Yesterday's Clown: The Rise of Film Comedy, Film Study: A Resource Guide, 1973; An Album of Great Science Fiction Films, 1976; Women on the Hollywood Screen, 1977; The Talking Clowns, Gangsters on the Screen, 1978; The Box-Office Clowns, 1979; An Album of Great Sports Movies, 1980; An Album of Great Science Fiction Movies, 1982; An Album of Modern Horror Films, 1983; Film Study: An Analytical Biography, 4 vols, 1990. Address: Department of English, Old Mill, College of Arts and Science, University of Vermont, Burlington, VT 05405, USA.

MANDEL Leslie Ann, b. 29 Jul 1945. Writer; Businessowner. Education: BA, University of MN, 1967; Diploma, New York School Interior Design, 1969. Publications: 20 books icluding 2 novels. Contributions to: Vogue; Fortune; Campaign Electors Magazine. Memberships: Explorers Club; Coffee House; Business Executives for National Security. Literary Agent: Julian Bach. Address: 4 E 81, New York, NY 10028, USA.

MANDEL Oscar, b. 24 Aug 1926. Writer; Professor. Education: BA, 1947; MA, Columbia, 1948; PhD, OH State University, 1951. Publications: A Definition of Tragedy: The Theatre of Don Juan; Chi Po and The Sorcerer; The Gobble Up Stories; Seven Comedies by Marivaux; Five Comedies of Medieval France; Others inc. The Land of Upside Down; Ariadne and French Classical Tragedy; Sigismund, Prince of Poland; The Art of Alessandro Magnasco. Memberships: MLA; CAA. Address: Humanities and Social Science, CA Institute of Technology, Pasadena, CA 91125, USA.

MANES Christopher, b. 24 May 1957, Chicago, IL, USA. Author. 1 d. Education: BA, UCLA, 1979; MA, University of WI, 1981; JD, University of CA, 1992. Publications: Green Rage; Technology & Mountain Thinking; Radical Environmentalism; Place of the Wild, 1994; Post Modernism and Environmental Philosophy, 1994. Contributions to: Environmental Ethics; Orion Nature Quarterly; Penthouse; American Country; Wild Earth Journal; Lears; Amicus Journal; Encyclopedia of the Environment; English Language Notes; Humn Ecology Review; Wild Earth Journal. Memberships: Phi Beta Kappa; Writers Guild; CA State Bar. Literary Agent: Van der Leun. Address: 34542 Paseo Real, Cathedral City, CA 92234, USA.

MANFRED Frederick Feikema (Feike Feikema), b. 6 Jan 1912, Doon, Iowa, USA. Writer. div., 1 son, 2 daughters. Education: BA, Calvin College. Appointments: Writer-in-Residence, Macalaster College, St Paul, MN, 1949-51; University of South Dakota, 1968-82; Chair, Regional Heritage, Augustana College, Sioux Falls, Dakota, 1984. Publications: 25 books including: This is the Year, 1947; Lord Grizzly, 1954; Conquering Horse, 1959; Wanderlust Trilogy, 1962; King of Spades, 1966; Milk of Wolves, 1976; The Manly-Hearted Woman, 1976; Green Earth, 1977; Sons of Adam, 1980; Winter Count II, 1978; Prime Fathers, 1988; Selected Letters of Frederick Manfred, 1988. Contributions to: New Republic; Esquire; Minnesota History; American Scholar; The New Republic. Honours: Grant in Aid, American Academy of Arts and Letters, 1945; Honorary Life Membership, Western Literature Association, 1967; Iowa's Most Distinguished Contribution to Literature, 1980; Honorary DLitt, Augustana College; Honorary DHL, Morningside College; Honorary DHL, Buena Vista College. Memberships: Authors League; Society of Midland Writers; The Players. Address: Roundwind, RR3, Lucerne, MN 56156, USA.

MANGUEL Alberto (Adrian), b. 13 Mar 1948, Buenos Aires, Argentina. div, 1 s, 2 d. Education: Colegio Nacional de Buenos Airs, 1961-67; Universidad de Buenos Aires, 1967-68; London University, 1976. Appointments include: Theatre Critic, CBLT Morning, 1984-86; Head of Contemporary Reading Group, McGill Club, 1986-89; Contributing Editor, Saturday Night, 1988; Contributing Editor, Grand Street, 1991. Publications: The Oxford Book of Canadian Ghost Stories; Black Water; Dark Arrows; The Dictionary of Imaginary Places; News from a Foreign Country Came; Other Fires; The Gates of Paradise. Contributions to: Saturday Night; The WA Post; NY Times; The Village Voice; Rubicon; The Whig Standard. Honours: Juan Angel Fraboschi Gold Medal; Ricardo Monner Sans Gold Medal; McKitterick Prize, 1992; Canadian Authors Association Prize, 1992; Harbourfront Prize, 1992. Memberships: Writers Union of Canada; ACTRA; PEN Canada. Literary Agent: Lucinda Vardey Agency, Toronto, Ontario, M5A 2T6.

MANHEIM Werner, b. 17 Feb 1915, Poland. Pianist; Musicologist; Professor of Modern Foreign Languages. m. Eliane Housiaux, 18 Aug 1951. Education: BEd, University of Berlin, Germany; BMus, MMus, Cincinnati Conservatory of Music, USA; DFA, Chicago Musical College. Publications: Martin Buber, monograph, 1974; Sonette von der Vergänglichkeit, 1975; Klange der Nacht, 1977; Im Abendrot versunken, 1983; A Spark of Music, 1983; Wenn das Morgenrot aufblüht, 1985; Albert Conradi, monograph, 1985; Schatten über Blütentau, 1987; Noch fliessen die Tränen, 1987; An die Musik, 1988; Landschaft in Moll, 1988; In Nebel Gehüllt, 1989; Im Atem der Nacht, 1990; Geheimnisvoll das Licht, 1991; Herbstmusik, 1991; Timeless is a Silver Sparkle; Many translations and contributions in anthologies. Contributions to: Encounter; Poet; Poesie und Prosa; Lyrikmappe; Ocarina; Nachrichten aus den Staaten; UNIO; World Poetry; Gauke Jahrbuch; Anthology on World Brotherhood and Peace. Honours: Medal studiosis humanitatis, Poetenmunze zum Halben Bogen; Certificate of Merit, Adolf-Bartels-Gedachtais Ehrung; Distinguished Service. United Poets Laureate International, 1987; Golden Poets Awards, 1989, 1990, 1991. Memberships: International Circle of Authors; Plesse International; Board Member, German Senryu Center; Regensburg Autorenkreis; International Contributing Editor, Ocarina; International Poets Academy, 1987; German Haiku Society; World Poetry Society; American Association of Teachers of German. Address: 2906 Hazelwood Avenue, Fort Wayne, IN 46905, USA.

MANHIRE Bill, b. 1946, New Zealand. University Reader. Appointments: Editor, Amphedesma Press, Dunedin, 1971-75; Reader in English, Victoria University of Wellington. Publications: New Zealand Universities Arts Festival Yearbook (editor), 1969; Malady, 1970; The Elaboration, 1972; How to Take Off Your Clothes at the Picnic, 1977; New Zealand Listener Short Stories (editor), vol I, 1977, vol II, 1978; Dawn-Water, 1979; Zoetropes, 1981; Good Looks, 1982; Locating the Beloved and Other Stories, 1983; Zoetropes: Poems 1972-82; Some Other Country: New Zealand's Best Short Stories (edited with M McLeod), 1984; Maurice Gee, 1986. Address: Department of English, Victoria University of Wellington, Private Bag, Wellington, New Zealand.

MANKOWITZ Wolf, b. 7 Nov 1924, Bethnal Green, London, England. Writer; Theatrical Producer. m. Ann Margaret Seligmann, 1944, 4 sons. Education: MA, Downing College, Cambridge. Appointments: Extensive work in journalism, radio, TV, films and as Theatrical Producer; Expert in English Ceramics; Honorary Consul to Republic of Panama, in Dublin, 1971; Professor of Film and Dance, University of Mexico, 1982-89. Publications: Novels: Make Me an Offer, 1952; A Kid for Two Farthings, 1953; Laugh till You Cry, 1955; My Old Man's a Dustman, 1956; Cockatrice, 1963; The Biggest Pig in Barbados, 1965; Penguin Wolf Mankowitz, 1967; Raspberry Reich, 1978; Abracadabra!, 1980; The Devil in Texas, 1984; Gioconda, 1987; The Magic Cabinet of Professor Smucker, 1988; Exquisite Cadaver, 1989; A Night with Casanova, 1991; Short stories: The Mendelman Fire, 1958; The Blue Arabian Nights, 1972; The Day of the Women and the Night of the Men, 1975; Plays: The Bespoke Overcoat and Other Plays, 1955; Expresso Bongo, 1961; The Samson Riddle, 1972; Histories: The Portland Vase, 1953; Wedgwood, 1953; An Encyclopedia of English Pottery and Porcelain, 1957; Dickens of London (also TV script), 1976; Biography: The Extraordinary Mr Poe, 1978; Mazeppa, 1981. Honours: Venice Film Festival Award, 1955; Hollywood Oscar, 1955; British Film Academy Award, 1955, 1961; Critics Prize, Cork International Film Festival, 1972; Grand Prix, Cannes, 1973. Address: Bridge House, Ahakista, Co Cork, Republic of Ireland.

MANN Anthony Philip, b. 7 Aug 1942, North Allerton, Yorkshire, England. Writer; Theatre director. Education; BA, Hons, English and Drama, Manchester University, England, 1966; MA Design and Directing, Humboldt State University, California, USA, 1969. Literary Appointments: Trustee New Zealand Players, 1992; Advisory Board New Zealand Books, 1993. Publications: Eye of the Queen, 1982; Master of Paxwax, 1986; Fall of the Families, 1987; Pioneers, 1988; Wulfsyarn - A Mosaic, 1990; A Land Fit For Heroes, Vol 1, Into the Wild Wood, 1993, Vol 2, Stand Alone Stan, 1994; essay, I Believe, in volume of Essays by New Zealanders. Contributions to: Entry on New Zealand Science Fiction in Routledge Encyclopedia of Commonwealth Literature, 1994. Maurice Shadbolt - The Dramatist, 1994. Memberships: PEN, New Zealand; SFWA; British Society of Dowsers; NZADIE (New Zealand Association for Drama in Education). Literary Agent: Glenys Bean, Auckland, New Zealand. Address: 22 Bruce Avenue, Brooklyn, Wellington, New Zealand.

MANN Christopher Michael Zithulele, b. 6 Apr 1948, Port Elizabeth, South Africa. Director; Writer. m. Julia Georgina Skeen, 10 Dec 1980, 1 son, 1 daughter. Education: BA, Witwatersrand University, Johannesburg, 1969; MA, Oxford University, England, 1973; MA, London University, 1974. Publications: First Poems, 1977; A New Book of South African Verse (edited with Guy Butler), 1979; New Shades, 1982; Kites, 1990; Mann Alive, video and book presentation of aural poems, 1991. Contributions to: Numerous magazines and journals. Honours: Rhodes Scholar; Newdigate Prize for Poetry, Oxford; Olive Schreiner Prize for Poetry, South African Academy of English; Hon DLitt, University of Durban-Westville. Address: Box 444, Bothas Hill, Natal, South Africa.

MANN Jessica, British. Writer. Publications: A Charitable End, 1971; Mrs Knox's Profession, 1972; The Only Security, 1973; The Sticking Place, 1974; Captive Audience, 1975; The Eighth Deadly Sin, 1976; The Sting of Death, 1978; Funeral Sites, Deadlier Than the Male, 1981; No Man's Island, 1983; Grave Goods, 1984; A Kind of Healthy Grave, 1986; Death Beyond the Nile, 1988; Faith, Hope and Homicide, 1991; Telling Only Lies, 1992. Contributions to: Daily Telegraph; Sunday Telegraph; Various magazines and journals. Memberships: Detection Club; Society of Authors: PEN; Crime Writers Association. Literary Agent: Gregory & Radice, Riverside Studios, Crisp Road, London W6, England. Address: Lambessow, St Clement, Cornwall, England.

MANNERS Alexandra. See: **RUNDLE Anne.**

MANNING Paul, b. 22 Nov 1912, Pasadena, California, USA. Author. m. Louise Margaret Windels, 22 Mar 1947, 4 sons. Education: Alumnus, Occidental College, Los Angeles. Appointments: Editor, Time-Life, New York City, 1937-38; Editor, Everyweek, 1939; Chief European Correspondent in London, Newspaper Enterprise Association and Scripps Howard Newspaper Group, 1939-42; Joined Edward R Murrow as CBS News Commentator from London, England, 1942; Only journalist to witness and broadcast both German surrender ceremonies, Reims, France, and Japanese surrender aboard USS Missouri, Tokyo Bay. Publications: Mr England, Biography of Winston Churchill, 1941; Martin Bormann, Nazi in Exile, 1986; Hirohito: The War Years, 1986; The Silent War, KGB Against the West, 1987; Years of War, 1988. Contributions to: The New York Times; Reader's Digest; Saturday Evening Post; Articles to numerous journals including 8th Air Force News. Honours: Nominated for Pulitzer Prize, 1943, 1971, 1986; Special Citations, Secretary of War Robert Patterson and Secretary of Navy James Forrestal; Nominated for Congressional Medal for War Coverage, 1947. Membership: The Eighth Air Force Historical Society. Address: PO Box 3129, Jersey City, NJ 07302, USA.

MANNING Rosemary (Mary Voyle), b. 1911. British. Writer. Publications: Green Smoke, 1957; Dragon in Danger, 1959; Look Stranger, in US as The Shape of Innocence, 1960; Dragon's Quest, 1961; The Chinese Garden, 1962; Man on a Tower, 1965; Heraldry, Boney Was a Warrior, 1966; A Grain of Sand: Selections from Blake (editor), 1967; The Rocking Horse, 1970; Railways and Railwaymen, 1977; A Dragon in the Harbour, 1980; Down by the Riverside, 1983; A Time and a Time, 1986. Address: 20 Lyndhurst Gardens, London NW3 5NR, England.

MANO D Keith, b. 12 Feb 1942, NY, USA. Novelist; Screenwriter. m. Laurie Kennedy, 18 July 1980, 2 s. Education: BA, Columbia University; Clare College, Cambridge; Woodrow Wilson Fellow, Columbia. Appointments: Cont Editor, National Review, 1975-; Playboy, 1980; Book Editor, Esquire, 1979-80. Publications: Bishops Progress, 1968; Horn, 1969; War is Heaven, 1970; The Death & Life of Harry Goth, 1971; The Proselytizer, 1972; Take Five, 1982; The Bridge, 1973; Resistance, 1984; Topless, 1991. Contributions to: Regular Columnist, National Review Magazine; Playboy; Esquire; NY Times; People Magazine. Honours: MLA Award, 1968; Playboy Award, 1975; Literary Lion, 1987. Address: c/o National Review Magazine, 150 E 35th Street, NY 10016, USA.

MANOR Jason. See: **HALL Oakley Maxwell.**

MANSEL Philip Robert Rhys, b. 19 Oct 1951. Writer. Education: Eton College, 1964-69; Balliol Oxford, MA, 1974; University College, London, PhD, 1978. Publications: Louis XVIII; The Eagle in Splendor; Sultans in Splendor; The Court of France; e Charmeur de l'Europe: Charles Joseph de Ligne. Contributions to: History Today; Past & Present; Architectural Digest; Harpers and Queen; Spectator;

International Herald Tribune. Memberships: PEN; Society d' Histoire de la Restauraton Assciation. Literary Agent: Murray Pollinger. Address: 13 Prince of Wales Terrace, London W8 5PG, England.

MANSER Martin Hugh, b. 11 Jan 1952. Reference Book Editor. m. Yusandra Tun, 1979, 1 s, 1 d. Education: BA, Honours, University of York, 1974; MPhil, C.N.A.A., 1977. Publications: Concise Book of Bible Quotations, 1982; A Dictionary of Everyday Idioms, 1983; Listening to God, 1984; Pocket Thesaurus of English Words, 1984; Children's Dictionary, 1984; Macmillan Student's Dictionary, 1985; Penguin Wordmaster Dictionary, 1987; Guinness Book of Words, 1988; Dictionary of Eponyms, 1988: Visual Dictionary, Bloomsbury Good Word Guide, 1988; Printing and Publishing Terms, 1988; Marketing Terms, 1988; Bible Promises: Outlines For Christian Living, 1989; Oxford Learner's Pocket Dictionary, 2nd Edition, 1991; Guinness Book of Words, 1st Edition, 1988, 2nd Edition, 1991; Get To the Roots: A Dictionary of Words & Phrase Origins, 1992; The Lion Book of Bible Quotations, 1992; Oxford Learner's Pocket Dictionary with Illustrations, 1992; Guide to Better English, 1994; Editor, Chambers Compact Thesaurus, 1994; Editor, Bloomsbury Key to English Usage, 1994. Address: 102 Northern Road, Aylesbury, Bucks HP19 3QY, England.

MANSFIELD RICHARDSON Virginia D, b. 26 Apr 1955, Athens, OH, USA. Instructor of Journalism. m. Brian K Richardson, 31 Jul 1993. Education: BA, OH University, 1977; MA, George Mason University, 1993. Publications: Article in, The Best of Style Plus, 1984; Article in, Statistics: An Inferential Approach, 1984. Contributions to: The Washington Post; DVM, The Newsmagazine of Veterinary Medicine; City Magazine of Brussels. Honours: I D Wilson Award of 1987, for excellence in reporting veterinary issues; Sigma Delta Chi Journalism Honorary. Memberships: Association for Education in Journalism and Mass Communication. Address: 227 West Washington Street, # 12, Athens, OH 45701, USA.

MANTEL Hilary, b. 6 Jul 1952, Derbyshire, England. Author. m. Gerald McEwen, 23 Sept 1972. Education: London School Economics; Sheffield University; Bach Jurisprudence, 1973. Publications: Every Day is Mother's Day, 1985; Vacant Possession, 1986; Eight Months on Ghazzah Street, 1988; Fludd, 1989; A Place of Greater Safety, UK Edition 1992, US Edition 1993; A Change of Climate, 1994. Contributions to: Film column, Spectator, 1987-91; book reviews to range of papers. Honours: Shiva Naipaul Prize, 1987; Winifred Holtby Prize, 1990; Cheltenham Festival Prize, 1990; Southern Arts Literature Prize, 1990; Sunday Express Book of the Year Award, 1992. Memberships: Society of Authors Management Committee; Council of Royal Society of Literature; FRSL. Literary Agent: A M Heath, London. Address: c/o A M Heath & Co, 79 St Martin's Lane, London WC2, England.

MANWARING Randle (Gilbert), b. 3 May 1912, London, England. Poet; Author; Retired Company Director. m. Betty Rout, 9 Aug 1941, 3 s, 1 d. Education: Private Schools; MA, Keele, 1982; FSS; FPMI. Publications: Satires and Salvation, poetry, 1960; The Heart of This People, 1954; Christian Guide to Daily Work, 1963; Under the Magnolia Tree, poetry, 1965; In A Time of Unbelief, poetry, 1977; The Swifts of Maggiore, poetry, 1981; The Run of the Downs, 1984; Collected Poems, 1986; The Singing Church, 1990; Some Late Lark Singing, poetry, 1992. Contributions to: Anglo-Welsh Review; British Weekly; Poetry Review; Outposts; Envoi; This England; Country Life; The Field; SE Arts Review; John O'London's Weekly; Church of England Newspaper; The Lady; Pick; The Cricketer; Sussex Life; Limbo; Scrip; English; Oxford Magazine. Memberships: Downland Poets (Chairman 1981-83); Kent and Sussex Poetry Society; President of Society of Pension Consultants, 1968-70; Fellow of the Statistical Society; Society of Authors; Society of Sussex Authors; Fellow of the Statistical Society; Fellow of the Pensions Management Institute. Address: Marbles Barn, Newick, East Sussex, BN8 4LG, England.

MAPES Mary A. See: **ELLISON Virginia Howell**.

MAPLE Gordon Extra, b. 6 Aug 1932, Jersey, Channel Islands. Writer. m. Mabel Atkinson-Frayn, 29 Jan 1953, 1 son, 1 daughter. Publications: Plays: Limeade, 1963; Here's A Funny Thing, 1964; Dog, 1967; Elephant, 1968; Tortoise, 1974; Singo, 1975; Napoleon Has Feet, 1977; Pink Circle, 1984; Chateau Schloss, 1985; Popeye, Theatr Hafren, 1985; Keeping in Front, memoirs, 1986; Sour Grapes (with Miles Whittier), 1986; Yet Another Falklands Film, 1987. Honours: Evening Standard Awards, 1964, 1973; Oscar nomination, 1964; SWEAT Award for Sour Grapes, 1986. Memberships: BPM, Oxford

Yec; Fellow, Royal Society of Letters. Literary Agent: Fraser and Dunlop Ltd (scripts). Address: The Manor, Milton, nr Banbury, Oxfordshire, England.

MAPLES Evelyn Lucille Palmer, b. 7 Feb 1919, Ponce de Leon, MO, USA. Editor; Author. m. William Eugene Maples, 23 Dec 1938, 2 s, 1 d. Education: Southwest Missouri State University, 1936-38. Appointments: Proof Reader, Contributing Author, 1953, Copy Editor, Editor, 1963-81, Herald House. Publications: The Many Selves of Ann-Elizabeth, 1973; Norman Learns About the Sacraments, 1961; That Ye Love, 1971, 73; Endnotes, 1989; Contributions to: Various Journals; 3 Poems to Sisters in Christ, 1994. Honour: The Many Selves of Ann-Elizabeth, Winner, Midwestern Books Competition, 1983; Poetry Awards, 1984, 85. Memberships: American Association of Retired Persons; Scroll Club; MO Writers Guild. Address: 11336 Maples Road, Niangua, MO 65713, USA.

MARAS Karl. See: **BULMER Henry Kenneth**.

MARCEAU Felicien, b. 16 Sep 1913, Cortenberg, Belgium. Author; Playwright. Education: Plays: L'Oeuf, 1956; La Bonne Soupe, 1958; La Preuve par Quatre, 1964; Madame Princesse, 1965; La Babour, 1968; L'Homme en Question, 1973; A Nous de Jouer, 1979; novels: Bergere Legere, 1953; Les Elans du Coeur, 1955; Creezy, 1969; Le Corps de Mon Ennemi, 1975; Appelez-moi Mademoiselle, 1984; La Carriole du Pere Juniet, 1985; Les Passions Partagees, 1987; Un Oiseau Dans Le Ciel, 1989; La Terrasse de Lucrezia, 1993; Memoirs: Les Années Courtes, 1968; Une insolente Liberte ou Les Aventures de Casanova, 1983; Les Ingenus, 1992; Le Voyage de Noce de Figaro, 1994. Honours: Prix Pellman du Theatre, 1954; Prix Interallie, 1955; Prix Goncourt, 1969; Grand Prix Prince Pierre de Monaco, 1974; Grand Prix de Theatre, 1975; Prix Jean Gioano, 1993; Prix Jacques Audibuti, 1994. Memberships: Academie Francaise. Address: c/o Eds. Gallimard, 5 Rue Sebastien-Bottin, Paris 75007, France.

MARCH Jessica. See: AFRICANO Lillian.

MARCHANT Anyda (Sarah Aldridge). Founder and President, Naiad Press; Romantic Novelist. Publications: The Latecomer, 1974; All True Lovers, 1978; The Nesting Place, 1982; Madame Aurora, 1983; Misfortune's Friend, 1985; Magdelena, 1987; Keep To Me, Stranger, 1989; A Flight of Angels, 1992; Michaela, 1994. Address: The Naiad Press PO Box 10543, Talahassee, FL 32302, USA.

MARCHANT Catherine. See: **COOKSON Catherine (Ann)**.

MARCHBANKS Samuel,See:**DAVIES Robertson**.

MARCUS Jeffrey Scott, b. 4 Oct 1962, WI, USA. Novelist. Education: BA, University of Wisconsin Madison, 1980-84. Publications: The Art of Cartography, 1991; Forthcoming: The Captain's Fire. Contributions to: The New Yorker; Harper's; Antaeus; NY Times. Honour: Whiting Writers Award, 1992. Literary Agent: The Wallace Agency, 177 East 70th Street, NY 10021, USA. Address: 4735 N Woodruff Avenue, Milwaukee, WI 53211, USA.

MARCUS Joanna. See: **ANDREWS Lucilla Matthew**.

MARCUS Steven, b. 13 Dec 1928. University Professor; Literary Critic. m. Gertrud Lenzer, 20 Jan 1966, 1 son. Education: AB, 1948, PhD, 1961, Columbia University. Publications: Dickens: From Pickwick to Dombey, 1965; The Other Victorians, 1966; Engels, Manchester and the Working Class, 1974; Representations: Essays on Literature and Society, 1976; Doing Good (with David Rothman and others), 1978; Freud and the Culture of Psychoanalysis, 1984; Editor: The Life and Work of Sigmund Freud (with Lionel Trilling), 1960; The World of Modern Fiction, 2 volumes, 1968; The Continental Op, 1974. Contributions to: Partisan Review; Commentary; New York Review of Books; New Statesman; Times Literary Supplement; New York Times Book Review. Honours: ACIS Award, 1961; Guggenheim Fellowship, 1967-68; Honorary Visiting Professor, University of Leicester, England, 1968; Center for Advanced Study in the Behavioral Sciences, 1972-73; National Humanities Center, 1980-82; Fulbright Fellowship, 1982-84; DHL, Clark University, 1985. Memberships: American Academy of Arts and Sciences; Academy of Literary Studies; PEN. Literary Agent: Berenice Hoffman, New York City, USA. Address: Department of English and Comparative Literature, Columbia University, New York, NY 10027, USA.

MARFEY Anne, b. 19 Feb 1927, Copenhagen, Denmark. Writer; Adjunct Lecturer, Danish State University, Albany. m. Dr Peter Marfey, 6 Jan 1964, 1 son, 1 daughter. Education: Teachers' Certificate, Danish Teachers' College, Copenhagen, 1950; Postgraduate, Columbia University, 1961-62. Appointments: Freelance Writer, 1988-. Publications: Learning to Write, 1961; Vejen til hurtigere Laesning, 1962; Svante, 1965; Las Bedre, 1966; Amerikanere, 1967; Telefontraden, 1968; Skal Skal ikke, 1969; How Parents Can Help Their Child with Reading, 1976; Rose's Adventure, 1989; Moderne Dansk, 1989; The Duckboat, The Pump, The Pine Tree, 1994; The Chipmunk, 1994; In work: Sightsee New York's Roofs. Memberships: Danish Writers Guild; Dask Samvirke RepresentativeBoard Member, UN Albany. Address: 9 Tudor Road, Albany, NY 12203, USA.

MARGOSHES Dave, b. 8 July 1941, NJ, USA. Writer. m. Ilya Silbav, 29 Apr 1963. Education: BA, 1963, MFA, 1969, University of IA. Publications: Small Regrets, 1986; Walking At Brighton, 1988; Northwest Passage, 1990; Nine Lives, 1991. Contributions to: Many. Address: 2922 19th Avenue, Regina, Sask, S4T 1X5, Canada.

MARGULIES Donald. Dramatist. Education: State University of New York, Purchase. Publications: Sight Unseen, 1991; Luna Park; Gifted Childen; Resting Place; Found A Peanut; What's Wrong With This Picture?; Loman Family Picnic. Contributions to: 52nd Street Project. Honours: Obie Award, 1992. Memberships: New Dramatists; Dramatists Guild. Address: 320 W 88th Street, New York, NY 10024, USA.

MARINEAU Michele, b. 12 Aug 1955, Montreal, Canada. Writer; Translator. div. 1 son, 1 daughter. Education: BA, Traduction et Histoire de l'art, University of Montreal, 1988. Publications: Cassiopée ou L'été Polonais, 1988; L'été Des Baleines, 1989; L'Homme Du Cheshire, 1990; Pourquoi Pas Istambul?, 1991; La Route De Chlifa, 1992. Honours: Prix Du Gouverneur Général, 1988, 1993; Prix, Brive-Montreal, 1993; Prix, Alvine-Bélisle, 1993. Memberships: Union Des Ecrivaines Et Ecrivains, Quebec; Corporation Professionnelle Des Traducteurs Et Interprétes Agréés Du Quebec; Association Des Traducteurs Litteraires Du Canada; Communication-Jeunesse. Literary Agent: Editions Quebec/Amérique, 425 St Jean Baptiste, Montreal, Quebec, Canada. Address: 4405 rue de Brebeuf, Montreal, Quebec H2J 3K8, Canada.

MARK Jan(et Marjorie), b. 1943. British. Writer. Literary appointment: Arts Council Writer Fellow, Oxford Polytechnic, 1982-84. Publications: Thunder and Lightning, 1976; Under the Autumn Garden, 1977; The Ennead, 1978; Divide and Rule, 1979; The Short Voyage of the Albert Ross, Nothing to Be Afraid Of, 1980; Hairs in the Palm of the Hand, 1981; Aquarius, The Dead Letter Box, The Long Distance Poet, 1982; Handles, Feet, 1983; Childermas, 1984; At the Sign of the Dog and Rocket, Trouble Half-Way, 1985; Frankie's Hat, Out of the Oven, 1986; Zeno Was Here, 1987; Man in Motion, children's fiction, 1989.

MARKERT Joy, b. 8 May 1942, Tuttlingen, Germany. Author. Publications: Asyl, 1985; Malta, 1986; Film scripts: Harlis, 1973; Der letzte Schrei, 1975; Belcanto, 1977; Das andere Lacheln (with R van Ackeren), 1978; Ich fühle was, was du nicht fühlst, 1982; Theatre: Asyl, 1984; Erichs Tag, 1985; 30 radio plays, 1976-. Contributions to: German and Austrian radio stations; Various literary publications. Honours: German Film Prize, 1972; German Film Awards, 1977, 1980; Berlin Literary Awards, 1982, 1984. Memberships: German Authors Association; Berlin Film Makers. Address: Bredowstrasse 33, D-1000 Berlin, Germany.

MARKFIELD Wallace (Arthur), b. 1926, USA. Writer. Appointment: Film Critic, New Leader, New York City, 1954-55. Publications include: To an Early Grave, 1964; Teitelbaum's Window, 1970; You Could Live If They Let You, 1974; Multiple Orgasms, 1977; Radical Surgery, 1991. Address: c/o Alfred A Knopf Incorporated, 201 East 50th Street, New York, NY 10022, USA.

MARKHAM Edward Archibald, b. 1 Oct 1939, Montserrat, West Indies. British Citizen. Editor; Poet. Education: Universities, Wales, East Anglia, London. Appointments include: Lecturer, Abraham Moss Centre, Manchester, 1976-78; Writer in Residence, University of Ulster, Coleraine, 1988-91; Asst Editor, Ambit Magazine, London, 1980-; Editor, Artage, 1985-87; Sheffield Thursday, 1992-. Publications: Crossfire, 1972; Mad and Other Poems, 1973; Lambchops, 1976; Philpot in the City, 1976; Master Class, 1977; Love Poems, 1978; Games and Penalties, 1980; Love, Politics and Food, 1982; Family

Matters, 1984; Human Rites: Selected Poems, 1970-82; Lambchops in Papua New Guinea, 1985; Living in Disguise, 1986; Towards the End of the Century, 1989; Letter From Ulster & The Hugo Poems, 1993; Plays, The Masterpiece, 1964; The Private Life of the Public Man, 1970; Dropping Out is Violence, 1971; Short Stories, Something Unusual, 1981; Ten Stories, 1994; Hinterland (Ed), 1989; The Penguin Book of Caribbean Short Stories (Ed), 1995; Editor of Poetry & Short Stories. Honours include: C Day Lewis Fellowship, 1980-81. Address: c/o Bloodaxe Books Ltd, PO Box 1SN, Newcastle Upon Tyne, NE99 1SN, England.

MARKHAM Marion Margaret, b. 12 June 1929, Chicago, Illinois, USA. Writer. m. Robert Bailey Markham, 30 Dec 1955, 2 daughters. Education: BS, Northwestern University. Appointments: Contributing Editor, The Magazine Silver, 9 years. Publications: Escape from Velos, 1981; The Halloween Candy Mystery, 1982; The Christmas Present Mystery, 1984; The Thanksgiving Day Parade Mystery, 1986; The Birthday Party Mystery, 1989; The April Fools Day Mystery, 1991; The Valentine's Day Mystery, 1992; Strangler's Hand, for radio; Works in anthologies: The Handy Man; Hurricane Five. Contributions to: Short fiction to: 'Teen; Alfred Hitchcock's Mystery Magazine; London Mystery Magazine; Mike Shane Mystery Magazine; Buffalo Spree; Women's magazines, USA, UK, Australia; Over 200 articles to: Ford Times; Weight Watchers; Chicago Tribune; Others. Memberships: Board Member, Society of Midland Authors; Regional Vice-President, Mystery Writers of America; Authors Guild of America; Society of Children's Book Writers. Literary Agent: Alice Orr. Address: 2415 Newport Rd, Northbrook, IL 60062, USA.

MARKHAM Robert. See: **AMIS Kingsley (Sir).**

MARKO Katherine Dolores, b. 26 Nov 1913, Allentown, PA, USA. Writer. m. Alex Marko, 20 Oct 1945, 2 s, 1 d. Publications: Juvenile Books, The Sod Turners, 1970; God, When Will I Ever Belong, 1979; Whales, Giants of the Sea, 1980; How The Wind Blows, 1981; God, Why Did Dad Lose His Job, 1982; Away to Fundy Bay, 1985; Animals in Orbit, 1991; Hang Out the Flag, 1992. Contributions to: Children's Encyclopedia Britannica; Jack and Jill; Highlights for Children; Children's Playmate; Straight; Alive; The Friend; On the Line; Childlife; Christian Science Monitor; Young Catholic Messenger; Wow. Honours: Prizes for Short Stories, 1967; Child Study Association List, 1970; Honorable Mention, Manuscript at Conference, 1973. Memberships: Childrens Reading Round Table, Chicago; Society of Childrens Book Writers; Off Campus Writers Workshop. Address: 471 Franklin Boulevard, Elgin, IL 60120, USA.

MARKOWITZ Harry M (Max), b. 1927. Publications: Process Analysis in Metal-Working Industries, 1953; Portfolio Selection, 1959; Simscript: A Simulation Programming Language, 1963; Studies in Procss Analysis, 1963. Honours: Nobel Prize in Economics, 1990. Address: c/o Meredith Clarke Blackwell Publishers, 238 Main Street, Cambridge, MA 21242, USA.

MARKS Paula Mitchell, b. 29 Mar 1951, El Dorado, AK, USA. Professor; Writer. m. Alan Ned Marks, 2 Apr 1971, 1 d. Education: BA, St Edwards University, TX, 1978; MA, 1980, PhD, 1987, University of TX. Publications: And Die in the West, 1989; Turn Your Eyes Toward Texas, 1989; Precious Dust: The American Gold Rush Era 1848-1900, 1994. Contributions to: Am History Illustrated; Civil War Times; True West; Old West. Honours: T R Fehrenbach Texas History Award, 1990; Finalist, Western Writers of America, Non Fiction Book Award, 1990; Certificate of Commendation, 1990; Kate Broocks Bates Texas History Research Award, 1991. Memberships: Authors Guild; Western Writers of Am; Western History Association; TX State Historical Association. Address: St Edwards University, 3001 S Congress, Austin, TX 78704, USA.

MARKS Richard. See: **KRAUZER Steven M.**

MARKS Stanley, b. London, England. Writer. Education: Coursework (part) for Diploma of Journalism, Melbourne University, Australia. Appointments: Worked in Australia, UK, USA, Canada, for various Australian newspapers including Melbourne Herald and Sydney Daily Telegraph; British Commonwealth Press Union Exchange, Montreal Star and Toronto Telegram, Canada; New York Correspondent for Australian journals; Publicity Supervisor, Australian Broadcasting Commission; Public Relations Manager, Australian Tourist Commission. Publications: God Gave You One Face, 1964, paperback, 1966; Fifty Years of Achievement, on scouting in Victoria;

Animal Olympics, 1972; St Kilda Sketchbook, 1980; Welcome to Australia, 1981; Malvern Sketchbook, 1982; Out and About in Melbourne, 1988; Children Everywhere series, 1970s-80s: Ketut, Boy of Bali, republished in Danish, Hebrew, Braille; Graham Is An Aboriginal Boy; Rarua Lives In Papua New Guinea; Is She Fair Dinkum; Montague Mouse Who Sailed With Captain Cook And Discovered Australia (recorded). Contributions to: Features to newspapers and journals worldwide; Most Australian magazines and newspapers; MS Daily Cartoon Strip; New Zealand papers. Memberships: Australian Society of Authors; Fellowship of Australian Writers; Australian Travel Writers. Address: 348 Bambra Road, South Caulfield, Melbourne, Victoria 3162, Australia.

MARLATT Daphne Shirley, b. 11 July 1942, Melbourne, Victoria, Australia. Writer; Teacher. m. Gordon Alan Marlatt, 24 Aug 1963, div. 1970, 1 son. Education: BA, English, Creative Writing, University of British Columbia, Canada, 1968. Appointments: Writer-in-Residence, University of Manitoba, Canada, autumn 1982; Writer-in-Residence, McMaster University and Hamilton Poetry Centre, Jan 1985; Writer-in-Residence, University of Alberta, 1985-86; Writer-in-Residence, Mount Royal College, Calgary, May 1987; Poetry Instructor, Creative Writing Department, University of British Columbia, 1989-90; Writer-in-Residence, University of Western Ontario, 1993. Publications: What Matters: Writing, 1968-70, 1980; Frames of a Story, 1968; Vancouver Poems, 1972; Steveston, poetry, 1974; Our Lives, 1975; Zocalo, 1977; Net Work: Selected Writing, 1980; How Hug a Stone, 1983; Touch to My Tongue, 1984; Ana Historic, novel, 1988; Double Negative (with Betsy Warland), 1988; Ghost Works, 1993. Contributions to: Origin III; Imago; The Capilano Review; How(ever) I; Ellipse; Line; Co-editor, Tessera. Honours: MacMillan Award; Brissenden Award; Canada Council Grants. Memberships: West Coast Women and Words Society, Board Member 1982-83, 1986-87; PE N; Writers Union of Canada, 2nd Vice-Chair 1987-88; Federation of British Columbia Writers. Address: c/o 24 Byerson Avenue, Toronto, Ontario, Canada M5T 2P3.

MARLIN Brigid, b. 16 Jan 1936, Washington, District of Columbia, USA. Artist; Writer. div., 2 sons. Education: National College of Art, Dublin; Centre d'Art Sacré, Paris; Studio André L'Hôte, Paris; Beaux-Arts Académie, Montreal; Art Students League, New York; Atelier of Ernest Fuchs, Vienna. Publications: Author: From East to West, 1989; Paintings in the Mische Technique, 1990; Illustrator: King Oberon's Forest (Hilda von Stockem); Celebration of Love (Mary O'Hara); Bright Sun, Dark Sun (Nickolas Fisk); The Leap from the Chess-Board (Charles Sprague). Contributions to: Several to The Artists magazine; Article to: The Horn Book; The Lady; The Architect's Review. Honours: Special Children's Book Award, USA, 1958; 1st Prize, America Art Appreciation Award, 1987; 1st Prize, Visions of the Future, New English Library. Memberships: PEN Club; Authors Club; Free Painters Society; President, Inscape Group; Co-Chairman, WIAC. Address: 15 Pixies Hill Crescent, Hemel Hempstead, Herts HP1 2BU, England.

MARLOWE Hugh. See: **PATTERSON Harry.**

MARLOWE Joyce, b. 1929. British. Writer. Appointment: Professional Actress, 1950-65. Publications: The Man with the Glove, 1964; A Time to Die, 1966; Billy Goes to War, 1967; The House on the Cliffs, 1968; The Peterloo Massacre, 1969; The Tolpuddle Martyrs, 1971; Captain Boycott and the Irish, 1973; The Life and Times of George I, 1973; The Uncrowned Queen of Ireland, 1975; Mr and Mrs Gladstone, 1977; Kings and Queens of Britain, 1977; Kessie, 1985; Sarah, 1987. Address: 109 St Albans Road, Sandridge, St Albans AL4 9LH, England.

MARLOWE Stephen, b. 7 Aug 1928, New York City, USA. Novelist. m. (1) Leigh Lang, 1950, (2) Ann Humbert, 1964, 2 d. Education: AB, College of William and Mary in Virginia, 1949. Appointments: Writer in Residence, College of William and Mary, 1974-75, 1980-81. Publications: The Death and Life of Miguel de Cervantes, 1991; The Memoirs of Christopher Columbus, 1987; Translation, 1976; Colossus, 1972; The Shining, 1962; Nineteen Fifty-Six, 1981; The Valkyrie Encounter, 1978; The Summit, 1970; Come Over Red Rover, 1968; many works in genres of suspense and sci-fi. Honours: Prix Gutenberg du Livre, 1988. Literary Agent: Campbell Thompson and McLaughlin Ltd, 1 Kings Mews, London WC1N 2JA, England.

MARNY Dominique Antoinette Nicole, b. 21 Feb 1948, Neuilly, France. Novelist; Screenwriter; Journalist. m. Michel Marny, 5 Oct 1970, div., 1 daughter. Literary appointment: Director for J C Lattès, Mille et une femmes collection, 1993-. Publications: Crystal Palace, 1985; Les orages desirés, 1988; Les fous de lumière, 1991; Les desirs et les jours, 1993; Les courtisanes, 1994; Les belles de Cocteau, 1995. Contributions to: Madame Figaro; Vogue; Marie France. Honours: Prix Madame Europe, 1993. Membership: PEN Club. Address: 4 av de New York, 75016 Paris, France.

MARON Margaret, b. Greensboro, North Carolina, USA. m. Joseph J Maron, 20 Jun 1959, 1 s. Education: University of North Carolina. Publications; One Coffee With, 1981; Death of A Butterfly, 1984; Bloody Kin, 1985; Death in Blue Folders, 1985; Bootlegger's Daughter, 1992; Shooting at Loons, 1994. Contributions to: Redbook; McCall's; Alfred Hitchcock. Honours: Edgar Allen Poe, 1993; Memberships: Mystery Writers of America; North Carolina Writers Conference. Address: c/o Vicky Bijur Literary Agency, 333 West End Avenue, Suite 5B, New York, NY 10023, USA.

MAROWITZ Charles, b. 25 Jan 1934, NY, USA. Writer. m. Jane Elizabeth Allsop, 14 Dec 1982. Appointments include: Artistic Director, TX Stage Co; West Coast Correspondent, Theatre Week Magazine; Senior Editor, Matzoh Ball Gazette; Theatre Critic, LA Village View. Publications; The Method as Means, 1961; The Marowitz Hamlet, 1966; The Shrew, 1972; Artaud at Rodez, 1975; Confessions of a Counterfeit Critic, 1976; Marowitz Shakespeare, 1980; Act of Being, 1980; Sex Wars, 1983; Sherlocks Last Case, 1984; Prosperos Staff, 1986; Potboilers, 1986; Recycling Shakespeare, 1990; Burnt Bridges, 1991; Directing the Action, 1992; Cyrano de Berberai Translation, 1995. Contributions to: NY Times; Guardian; Sun Times; Plays & Players; Encore; New Stateman; Spectator; Village Voice; LA Times; Am Theatre Magazine; Theater Week Magazine. Honours: Order of Purple Sash, 1965; Whitbread Award, 1967; 1st Prize, Louis B Mayer Award, 1984. Memberships: Dramatists Guild; Writers Guild. Literary Agent: Gary Salt, c/o Paul Kohner Agency, CA, USA. Address: 3058 Sequit Drive, Malibu, CA 90265, USA.

MARQUEZ Gabriel Garcia, b. 6 Mar 1928, Aracataca, Columbia. Writer. m. Mercedes Barcha, 1958, 2 sons. Education: University of Bogota, 1946-51. Career: Journalist, Columbia and abroad, including several years in France; Originally Writer, short stories for magazines and newspapers; Social Activist; Recently forced to flee Columbia for alleged involvement with Colombian guerrillas; Homes in Paris and Mexico City. Publications: One Hundred Years of Solitude, 1970; The Autumn of the Patriarchs, 1976; Chronicle of a Death Foretold, 1982; Fragrance of Guava (with P Mendoza), 1983; Love in the Time of Cholera, fiction, 1988; Clandestine in Chile, non-fiction, 1989; The General in His Labyrinth, 1991. Honours: Nobel Prize for Literature, 1982; Love in the Time of Cholera on New York Times and Publishers Weekly bestseller lists, over 6 months, and won Los Angeles Times Book Prize for Fiction. Address: Agencia Literaria Carmen Balcelos, Diagonal 580, Barcelona, Spain.

MARQUIS Edward Frank. See: **MARQUIS Max**

MARQUIS Max, (Edward Frank Marquis), b. Ilford, Essex, England. Author. m. (1), 1 s, (2) Yvonne Cavenne, 1953. Appointments: News Writer and Reader, RDF French Radio, 1952; Sub Editor, Columnist; Continental Daily Mail, 1952, Evening News, London, 1955; Chief British Correspondent, L'Equipe, Paris, 1970. Publications: Sir Alf Ramsey: Anatomy of a Football Manager, 1970; The Caretakers, 1975; A Matter of Life, 1976; The Shadowed Heart, 1978; The Traitor Machine, 1980; Body guard to Charles, 1989; Vengeance, 1990; Deadly Doctors, 1992; Elimination, 1993; Undignified Death, 1994. Literary Agent: Rubert Crew Ltd. Address: C/o Rupert Crew Ltd, 1A Kings Mews, London WC1N 2JA, England.

MARR William W, b. 3 Sept 1936, China. Engineer. m. Jane J Liu, 22 Sept 1962, 2 s. Education: MS, Marquette University, 1963; PhD, University of WI, 1969. Appointments: Editing Advisor, Li Poetry Magazine, 1992; Editor, Chinese Poets, 1993. Publications: In The windy City, 1975; Selected Poems, 1983; White Horse, 1984; Selected Poems of Fei Ma, 1985; The Galloping Hoofs, 1986; Road, 1987; Selected Short Poem, 1991; Fly Spirit, 1992; Selected Poems, 1994. Contributions to: Li Poetry Magazine; Literary Taiwan; First Line; New Mainaland; Unitas Literary Magazine; Hong Kong Literature Monthly; Renmin Wenxue; Chinese Poets. Honours: Wu Cho Liu Poetry Award, 1982; Li Poetry Translation Award, 1982; Li Poetry Award, 1984.

Memberships: Li Poetry Society; First Line Poetry Society; Chinese Artists Association of North Am; President, IL State Poetry Society; The Am Society of Mechanical Engineers. Address: 737 Ridgeview Street, Downers Grove, IL 60516, USA.

MARRECO Anne. See: **ACLAND Alice.**

MARS JONES Adam, b. 26 Oct 1954, London. Education: BA, Cambridge University, 1976. Appointments: Film Critic, Reviewer, The Independent, London. Publications: Lantern Lectures and Other Stories, 1981; The Darker Proof: Stories from a Crisis (with Edmond White), 1987; Venus Envy, 1990; Monopolies of Loss, 1992; The Waters of Thirst; Editor, Mae West is Dead: Recent Lesbian and Gay Fiction. Honours: Maugham Award, 1982. Literary Agent: Peters, Fraser and Dunlop, 503-4 The Chambers, Chelsea Harbour, Lots Road, London SW10 0XF. Address: 3 Gray's Inn Square, London WC1R 5AH, England.

MARSDEN Peter Richard Valentine, b. 29 Apr 1940, Twickenham, Middlesex, England. Archaeologist. m. Frances Elizabeth Mager, 7 Apr 1979, 2 sons, 1 daughter. Education: Kilburn Polytechnic; Currently studying for higher degree, Oxford University. Publications: Londinium, 1971; The Wreck of the Amsterdam, 1974, UK, Dutch and US editions, revised edition, 1985; Roman London, 1980; The Marsden Family of Paythorne and Nelson, 1981; The Roman Forum Site in London, 1987; The Historic Shipwrecks of South-East England, 1987; Contributions to: Geographical Magazine; The Independent; The Times Literary Supplement; Illustrated London News; The Telegraph Colour Magazine; Various academic journals. Memberships: Fellow, Society of Antiquaries of London; Institute of Field Archaeologists. Address: 21 Meadow Lane, Lindfield, West Sussex RH16 2RJ, Sussex.

MARSHALL Gary, b. 13 Nov 1934, New York, New York, USA. Television, Stage, Film Producer, Director, Writer. m. 3 children. Education: BA, Northwestern University. Publications: (TV) Dick Van Dyke Show (contributor); The Odd Couple; Happy Days; Mork & Mindy; (screenplays) How Sweet It Is, 1968; The Grasshopper, 1970; Evil Roy Slade, 1971; (stage) Good News, 1978; The Roast, 1980; Wrong Turn At Lungfish, 1992. Address: c/o Jim Wyatt ICM, 8942 Wilshire Boulevard, Beverly Hills, CA 90211, USA.

MARSHALL Jack, b. 1937, USA. Publications: The Darkest Continent, 1967; Bearings, 1970; Floats, 1972; Bits of Thirst, 1974; Bits of Thirst and Other Poems and Translations, 1976; Arriving on the Playing Fields of Paradise, 1983; Arabian Nights, 1986. Address: 1056 Treat Avenue, San Francisco, CA 94110, USA.

MARSHALL James Vance. See: **PAYNE Donald Gordon.**

MARSHALL Joanne. See: **RUNDLE Anne.**

MARSHALL Rosalind Kay, b. Dysart, Scotland. Historian. Education: MA, Dip Ed, PhD, FRSL, FSA Scot, Edinburgh University, Scotland. Literary Appointments: Associate Editor of the Review of Scottish Culture, 1983-. Publications: The Days of Duchess Anne, 1973; Mary of Guise, 1977; Virgins and Viragos: A History of Women in Scotland, 1983; Queen of Scots, 1986; Bonnie Prince Charlie, 1988; Henrietta Maria, 1990; Elizabeth I, 1992; Mary I, 1993. Contributions to: various publications on social history. Honours: Hume Brown Senior Prize for PhD Thesis, also Jeremiah Dalziel Prize, 1970; Scottish Arts Council New Writing Award, 1973; Fellow of the Royal Society of Literature, 1974. Memberships: Member of Council, Scottish Record Society, 1993-; Scots Ancestry Research Society, 1988-; many historical societies. Address: Scottish National Portrait Gallery, Scotland.

MARSHALL Tom, b. 9 Apr 1938, Niagara Falls, Ontario, Canada. Professor of English. Education: BA, History, 1961, MA, English, 1965, Queen's University, Kingston, Ontario. Appointments: Professor of English, Queen's University, Kingston; Editor, Quarry, 1965-66, 1968-70; Poetry Editor, Canadian Forum, 1973-78. Publications: Books of poems: The Beast With Three Backs, 1965; The Silences of Fire, 1969; Magic Water, 1971; The Earth-Book, 1974; The White City, 1976; The Elements: Poems 1960-1975, 1980; Playing With Fire, 1984; Dance of the Particles, 1984; Ghost Safari, 1991; Criticism: The Psychic Mariner: A Reading of the Poems of D H Lawrence, 1970; Harsh and Lovely Land: the major Canadian poets and the making of a Canadian tradition, 1979; Multiple Exposures, Promised Lands, 1992; Fiction: Fourteen Stories High, 1971; Rosemary Goal, 1978; Glass

Houses, 1985; Adele at the End of the Day, 1987; Voices on the Brink, 1989; Changelings, 1991; Goddess Disclosing, 1992. Contributions to: Various journals. Memberships: Writers Union of Canada; League of Canadian Poets; PEN. Address: Department of English, Queen's University, Kingston, Ontario, Canada K7L 3N6.

MARSTEN Richard. See: **LOMBINO Salvatore A.**

MARTER Joan M, b. 13 Aug 1946, PA, USA. Professor. Education: AB, Temple University, 1968; MA, 1970, PhD, 1974, University of Delaware. Publications: Vanguard American Sculpture 1913-1939, 1979; Jose de Rivera, 1980; Design in America, 1983; Alexander Calder, 1991; Theodore Roszak Drawings, 1992. Contributions to: Archives of American Art Journal; Sculpture Magazine; Tema Celeste; Womens Studies Quarterly. Honours: Charles F Montgomery Prize, 1984; George Wittenborn Award, 1985; Diamond Achievement Award, 1993. Memberships: International Association of Art Critics; College Art Association of Am; Womens Caucus for Art. Address: Dept of Art History, Voorhees Hall, Rutgers University, New Brunswick, NJ 08903, USA.

MARTI René, b. 7 Nov 1926, Frauenfeld, Switzerland. Freelance Author and Journalist. m. Elizabeth Wahrenberger, 13 Oct 1955, 1 s, 2 d. Education: Commercial School, Lausanne; Cambridge Proficiency Class, Polytechnic School, London; Eidgenössisches Fähigkeiteugnis für kaufmännischen Abschluss (commercial qualification); Diploma, French and English; further study, Neuchâtel and Zurich; Literature-Science, Philosophy, Konstanz University, 12 terms. Publications: Das unauslöschliche Licht, 1954, French translation, La Lumiere qui ne s'eteint point, 1975; Die fünf unbekannten, lyric poetry, stories (main author), 1970; stories: Der unsichtbare Kreis, 1975; Stationen, 1986; poetry: Dorn des Herzens, 1967; Weg an Weg, 1979; Besuche dich in der Natur (with Lili Keller), 1983; Gedichte zum Verschenken (with Lili Keller), 1984; Die verbrannten Schreie, (9 set to music and recorded), 1989; Gib allem ein bisschen Zeit, 1993 (Renga with Brigitta Weiss); Lebensflamme - Vital Spark (in German and English, translated into English by Charly Stünzi), 1995. Contributions to: Over 140 anthologies; poems translated into English, French, Persian, Polish; book reviews; Teacher of French and English; Radio Collaborator; Poems set to music; Many Publications in newspapers and periodicals; Founder, New Press Agency (NPA), 1950. Address: Haus am Herterberg, Haldenstr 5, CH-8500, Frauenfeld, Switzerland.

MARTIN Alexander George, b. 8 Nov 1953, Baltimore, Maryland, USA. Writer. m. 28 July 1979, 2 sons. Education: Cambridge University, 1972-75; MA (Cantab), English; Diploma in Theatre, University College Cardiff, 1975-76. Publications: Boris the Tomato, 1984; Snow on the Stinker, 1988; the General Interruptor, 1989; Modern Poetry, 1990; Modern Short Stories, 1991. Honours: Betty Trask Award, 1988. Membership: Society of Authors. Literary Agent: David Higham Associates, London, England. Address: c/o D Higham Associates, 5-8 Lower John Street, London W1R 4HA, England.

MARTIN Chip. See: **MARTIN Stoddard H.**

MARTIN David Alfred, b. 30 Jun 1929, London, England. Professor. m. 30 Jun 1962, 3 s, 1 d. Education: Westminster College, Oxford, 1950-52, Teachers Diploma; London External Degree (BSc) 1959, PhD (London) 1964. Publications: Pacifism, 1966; A General Theory of Secularization, 1978; Dilemmas of Contemporary Religion, 1979; Cries for Cranmer and King James (editor), PN Review 13, 1979; The Breaking of the Image, 1980; Divinity in a Grain of Bread, 1989; Tongues of Fire, 1990. Contributor to: Regular contributor to The Times Supplements. Address: Cripplegate Cottage, 174 St John's Rd, Woking, Surrey, England.

MARTIN Desmond, b. 1 April 1916, Victoria, Australia. Grazier; Photographer (Retired). m. Cassie O'Dwyer 20 Oct 1951, 2 sons. Education: Assuption College, Kilmore, Victoria. Taff College Wodonga. Publications: Australia Astride; Many A Mile; A Century of Racing; A Tale of Twin Cities; Backing Up The Boys; The Tiniest Star; Pictorial History of Humeshire. Contributions to: The Horseman's Year; The Chronicle of The Horse; Over The Front; Hoofs and Horns, Herald/Weekly Times; Sporting Globe; Border Mail; Rag and Tube Journal of Australia Antique Aero Association. Memberships:Life Member, Murray Valley Hunt; Life Member Midland Hunt; Moonee Valley Racing Club; The Albury Club; Wodonga Pistol Club; Raeme Officers' Mess; Australian Antique Aircraft Association; Stockmans Hall of Fame. Address: 'Aherlo', 11 Elsa Court, Wodonga, NSW 3690, Australia.

MARTIN F(rancis) X(avier), b. 1922, Ireland. Appointments: Assisstant Lecturer 1959-62, Professor of Medieval History 1962-, University College, National University of Ireland, Dublin; Chairman, Council of Trustees, National Library of Ireland, 1977-. Publications: The Problem of Giles of Viterbo 1469-1532, 1960; Medieval Studies presented to Aubrey Gwynn (edited with J A Wyatt and J B Morrall), 1961; Friar Nugent: A Study of Francis Lavalin Nugent 1569-1635, 1962; The Irish Volunteers 1913-15, (editor), 1963; The Howth Gun-Running 1914: Recollections and Documents (editor), 1966; The Course of Irish History (editor with T W Moody), 1967, 1984; Leaders and Men of the Easter Rising, Dublin 1916 (editor), The Easter Rising, Myth, Fact and Mystery, 1967; The Scholar Revolutionary: Eoin MacNeil 1867-1945 and the Making of the New Ireland (editor with F J Byrne), 1973; A New History of Ireland (editor with T W Moody and J F Byrne), Volume: III 1974, VIII 1982, IX 1984, IV 1986, II 1987, V 1989; No Hero in the House: The Coming of the Normans to Ireland, 1977; The Conquest of Ireland by Giraldus Cambrensis (editor with A B Scott), 1978; Lambert Simnel: The Crowning of a King at Dublin, 24th May 1487, 1988; The Irish Augustinians in Rome: with Foreign Missions in 5 Continents - Europe (England and Scotland), India, Australia, North America, Africa (Nigeria and Kenya) 1656-1994, (edited with Clare O'Reilly, 8 contributors), 1994. Address: Department of Medieval History, University College Dublin, Dublin 4, Ireland.

MARTIN Fredric. See: **CHRISTOPHER Matthew F.**

MARTIN Laurence Woodward, b. 30 Jul 1928, United Kingdom. Professor. m. Betty Parnell, 19 Aug 1951, 1 s, 1 d. Education: Christ's College, Cambridge, 1945-48, BA, History, 1948, MA 1952; Yale University 1950-55, MA International Politics, 1951, PhD with Distinction, 1955. Publications: The Anglo-American Tradition in Foreign Affairs (with Arnold Wolfers), 1956; Peace Without Victory, 1958; The Sea in Modern Strategy, 1966; Arms and Strategy, 1973; Retreat From Empire (joint author) 1973; Strategic Thought in the Nuclear Age (editor/contributor), 1979; The Two-Edged Sword: Armed Force in the Modern World, 1982; Before the Day After, 1985; The Changing Face of Nuclear Warfare, 1987. Honours: Fellow, King's College, London, 1983-; Honorary Professor, University of Wales, 1985-; Honorary DCL, Newcastle, 1991. Memberships: International Institute of Strategic Studies; European Strategy Group. Address: The Royal Institute of International Affairs, 10 St James's Square, London SW1Y 4LE, England.

MARTIN (Roy) Peter, (James Melville), b. 5 Jan 1931, London, England. Author. 2 s. Education: BA Philosophy, 1953, MA, 1956, Birkbeck College, London University; Tubingen University, Germany, 1958-59. Appointments: Crime Fiction Reviewer, Hampstead and Highgate Express, 1983-; Occasional Reviewer, Times Literary Supplement. Publications: The Superintendent Otani mysteries, 13 in all; the Imperial way, 1986; A Tarnished Phoenix, 1990. Honours: MBE, 1970. Memberships: FRSA; Crime Writers Association; Mystery Writers of America; The Detection Club. Literary Agent: Curtis Brown, Haymarket House, London SW1Y 4SP, England.

MARTIN Philip (John Talbot), b. 28 Mar 1931, Melbourne, Australia. Poet; Teacher; Translator; Critic; Radio Broadcaster. Education: BA, University of Melbourne. Appointments include: English tutor, University of Melbourne, 1960-62; Lecturer, Australian National University, 1963; Lecturer, Senior Lecturer, English, Monash University, 1964-; Visiting Lecturer/Professor, University of Amsterdam 1967, Venice 1976, Carleton College, Northfield, Minnesota, USA 1983; Monash University, 1984-1988. Publications: Voice Unaccompanied, poems, 1970; Shakespeare's Sonnets: Self, Love & Art, criticism, 1972; A Bone Flute, poems, 1974; Lars Gustafsson: Selected poems (translation), 1982; A Flag for the Wind, poems, 1982; New & Selected Poems, 1988; Dictionary of Australian Poets (co-editor), 1980. Address: 25/9 Nicholson Street, Balmain 2041, Australia.

MARTIN Ralph Guy, b. 4 Mar 1920, Chicago, Illinois, USA. Writer. m. Marjorie Jean Pastel, 17 June 1944, 1 son, 2 daughters. Education: BJ, University of Missouri, 1941. Appointments: Reporter, Managing Editor, Box Elder News Journal, Brigham, Utah, 1940-41; Associate Editor: New Republic Magazine, 1945-48; Associate Editor, Newsweek Magazine, 1953-55; Executive Editor, House Beautiful, 1955-57; Publisher, President, Bandwagon Inc. Publications: Boy from Nebraska, 1946; The Best Is None Too Good, 1948; Ballots and

Bandwagons: Five Key Conventions since 1900, 1964; Skin Deep, 1964; The Bosses, 1964; President from Missouri, 1964; Wizard of Wall Street, 1965; World War II, Pearl Harbor to V-J Day, 1966; The GI War, 1967; A Man for All People, 1968; Jennie: The Life of Lady Randolph Churchill, The Romantic Years, 1969, Volume II, The Dramatic Years, 1971; Lincoln for the Performing Arts, 1971; The Woman He Loved: The Story of the Duke and Duchess of Windsor, 1974; Cissy: The Extraordinary Life of Eleanor Medell Patterson, 1979; A Hero for Our Times, An Intimate Study of the Kennedy Years, 1983; Charles and Diana, 1985; Golda Meir, The Romantic Luces, 1990; Co-author: Eleanor Roosevelt: Her Life in Pictures, 1958; The Human Side of FDR, 1960; Front Runner, Dark Horse, 1960; Money Money Money, 1960; Man of Destiny: Charles De Gaulle, 1961; Man of the Century: Winston Churchill, 1961; The Three Lives of Helen Keller, 1962; World War II: From D-Day to VE-Day, 1962. Contributions to: Numerous journals and magazines. Memberships: Authors League; Authors Guild; Century Association. Literary Agent: Sterling Lord. Address: 135 Harbor Road, Westport, CT 06880, USA.

MARTIN Reginald, b. 15 May 1956, Memphis, Tennessee, USA. Editor; Director of Professional Writing Programmes; Writer. Apppointments: Feature Editor, Reporter, News, Boston, Massachusetts, 1974-77; Instructor in English, Memphis State University, 1979-80; Research Fellow, Tulsa Center for the Study of Women's Literature, 1980-81; Editor, Continental Heritage Press, 1981; Instructor in English, Tulsa Junior College, Tulsa; Assistant Instructor in English, University of Tulsa, 1982-83; Assistant Professor, 1983-87, Associate Professor of Composition, 1988-, Memphis State University; Visiting Lecturer, Mary Washington College, 1984; Lecturer in Literary Criticism, University of Wisconsin, Eau Claire, 1988; Director of Professional Writing Programmes, 1987-. Publications: Ntozake Shange's First Novel: In the Beginning Was the Word, 1984; Ishmael Reed and the New Black Aesthetic Critics, 1988; An Annotated Bibliography of New Black Aesthetic Criticism, 1992. Contributions to: Stories, poems, articles and reviews to various anthologies and periodicals. Honours: Winner, Mark Allen Everell Poetry Contest, 1981; Winner in Fiction, 1982, Winner in Poetry, 1983, Friends of the Library Contest; Award in Service for Education, Alpha Kappa, 1984; Award for Best Novel, Deep South Writers Competition, 1987; Award for Best Critical Article, South Atlantic Modern Language Association, 1987; Award for Best Critical Article, College English Association, 1988. Memberships: Numerous professional associations. Address: PO Box 111306, Memphis, TN 38111, USA.

MARTIN Rhona (Madeline), b. 3 June 1922, London, England. Writer; Artist. m. (1) Peter Wilfrid Alcock, 9 May 1941, div., (2) Thomas Edward Neighbour, div., 2 daughters. Appointments: Former Fashion Artist, Freelance Theatrical Designer, Cinema Manager, Accounts Secretary and Office Manager; Served on Panel of SE Arts, Regional Arts Council, 1978-84; Full-time Writer, 1979-; Part-time Tutor, Creative Writing, University of Sussex, 1986-91. Publications: Gallows Wedding, 1978; Mango Walk, 1981; The Unicorn Summer, 1984; Goodbye Sally, 1987; Writing Historical Fiction, 1988. Contributions to: London Evening News; SE Arts Review; Cosmopolitan; Prima. Honours: Georgette Heyer Historical Novel Award, 1979. Memberships: Romantic Novelists Association; Society of Authors; Society of Women Writers and Journalists; PEN; Friends of the Arvon Foundation; Society of Limners. Literary Agent: Campbell, Thomson & McLaughlin, London, England. Address: 25 Henwood Crescent, Pembury, Kent TN2 4LJ, England.

MARTIN Robert Bernard (Robert Bernard), b. 11 Sept 1918, La Harpe, Illinois, USA. Writer. Education: AB, University of Iowa, 1943; AM, Harvard University, 1947; BLitt, Oxford University, England, 1950. Appointments: Professor of English, Princeton University, 1950-1975; Emeritus Professor, 1975; Citizens Professor of English, University of Hawaii, 1980-81, 1984-88, Emeritus Citizens Professor, 1988. Publications: The Dust of Combat: A Life of Charles Kingsley, 1959; Enter Rumour: Four Early Victorian Scandals, 1962; The Accents of Persuasion: Charlotte Bronte's Novels, 1966; The Triumph of Wit: Victorian Comic Theory, 1974; Tennyson: The Unquiet Heart, 1980; With Friends Possessed: A Life of Edward Fitzgerald, 1985; Gerard Manley Hopkins: A Very Private Life, 1991; 3 other critical books and 4 novels. Contributions to: Numerous magazines and journals. Honours: Fellow, Acls, 1966-67; Fellow, Guggenheim Foundation, 1971-72, 1983-84; Senior Fellow, NEH, 1976-77; Fellow, Rockefeller Research Center, 1979; Duff Cooper Award, Biography, 1981; James Tait Black Award, Biography, 1981; Christian Gauss Award, 1981; DLitt, Oxford, 1987; Fellow, National Humanities Center, 1988-89. Memberships: Fellow, Royal Society of Literature; Honorary Vice

President, Tennyson Society. Literary Agent: Curtis Brown. Address: 8 Walton Street, Oxford OX1 2HG, England.

MARTIN Ronald. See: **DELIUS Anthony.**

MARTIN Ruth. See: **RAYNER Claire Berenice.**

MARTIN Stoddard H (Chip Martin), b. 15 Dec 1948, Bryn Mawr, Pennsylvania, USA. Writer; Editor; Lecturer. m. Edin Harper Beard, 28 Sept 1974, separated. Education: BA, History, Stanford University, 1974; PhD, University College, London, England, 1978. Appointments: Co-Founder, Editor, Starhaven Books, La Jolla, California, 1979-; Co-Founder, Starhaven Productions, Brawley, 1983-; Guest Lecturer, California State University, 1984; Guest Lecturer, University of Gottingen, Germany, 1987; Lecturer, Harvard University, USA, 1987-. Publications include: Wagner to the Wasteland: A Study of the Relationship of Wagner to English Literature, 1982; California Writers: Jack London, John Steinbeck, The Tough Guys, 1983; Art, Messianism and Crime: A Study of Antinomianism in Modern Literature and Lives, 1986; Orthodox Heresy: The Rise of Magic in Religion and its Relation to Literature, 1988; Fiction, as Chip Martin: The Jew Hater, 1979; A Revolution of the Sun, 1982-86. Contributions to: Reviews; Times Literary Supplement; Numerous articles in professional and arts journals. Literary Agent: Jane Conway-Gordon, London W11 2SE, England. Address: 601 Franklin St, Cambridge, MA 02139, USA.

MARTIN Victoria Carolyn, b. 22 May 1945, Windsor, Berkshire, England. Writer. m. Tom Storey, 28 July 1969, 4 d. Education: Challow Court School, 1950-53; Silchester House School, Bucks, 1953-61; Winkfield Place, Berks, 1961-62; Byam Shaw School of Art, 1963-66. Publications: September Song, 1970; Windmill Years, 1975; Seeds of the Sun, 1980; Opposite House, 1984; Tigers of the Night, 1985; Obey the Moon, 1987. Contributions to: Woman; Woman's Own; Woman's Realm; Woman's Journal; Good Housekeeping; Woman's Weekly; Redbook; Honey, 1967-87. Literary Agent: Vanessa Holt. Address: Newells Farm House, Lower Beeding, Horsham, Sussex RH13 6LN, England.

MARTIN-JENKINS Christopher Dennis Alexander, b. 20 Jan 1945. Editor. m. Judith Oswald Hayman, 1971, 2 sons, 1 daughter. Education: BA, Modern History, MA, Fitzwilliam College, Cambridge. Appointments: Deputy Editor, 1967-70, Editor, 1981-87, Editorial Director, 1988-, The Cricketer; Sports Broadcaster, 1970-72, Cricket Correspondent, 1973-80, 1984-, BBC; Cricket Correspondent, Daily Telegraph, 1991-. Publications: Testing Time, 1974; Assault on the Ashes, 1975; MCC in India, 1977; The Jubilee Tests and the Packer Revolution, 1977; In Defence of the Ashes, 1979; Cricket Contest, 1980; The Complete Who's Who of Test Cricketers, 1980; The Wisden Book of County Cricket, 1981; Bedside Cricket, 1981; Sketches of a Season, 1981, 1989; Twenty Years On: Cricket's Years of Change, 1984; Cricket: A Way of Life, 1984; Cricketer Book of Cricket Eccentrics (editor), 1985; Seasons Past (editor), 1986; Quick Singles (joint editor), 1986; Grand Slam, 1987; Cricket Characters, 1987; Ball by Ball, 1990. Address: Daily Telegraph, Canada Square, Canary Wharf, London E14 9DT, England.

MARTINET Gilles, b. 8 Aug 1916, Paris, France. Journalist; Politician; Diplomat. m. Iole Buozzi, 1938, 2 daughters. Appointments: Editor in Chief, Agence France Presse, 1944-49, Observateur, 1950-61; Director, Observateur, 1960-64; Board of Directors, Nouvel Observateur, 1964-87; Matin 1973-81; Member European Parliament, 1979-81; Ambassador in Italy, 1981-85; Ambassadeur de France (dignity), 1984. Publications: Le Marxisme de notre temps, 1961; La conquete des pouvoirs, 1968; Les cinq communismes, 1971; Le systeme Pompidou, 1973; L'avenir depuis vingt ans, 1975; Les sept syndicalismes, 1977; Cassandre et les tueurs, 1986; Les Italiens, 1990; Le reveil du nationalisme francais, 1994. Address: 12 rue Las Cases, 75007 Paris, France.

MARTINI Teri, b. 1930, USA; Writer; Former Teacher. Appointments: Tenafly, New Jersey Board of Education. Publications: The Fisherman's Ring, True Book of Indians, 1954; Treasure of the Mohawk, True Book of Cowboys, 1956; Sandals on the Golden Highway, 1959; What a Frog Can Do, 1962; Mystery of the Hard Luck House, 1965; The Lucky Ghost Shirt, 1971; Patrick Henry, Patriot, 1972; Mystery of the Woman in the Mirror, 1973; John Marshall, 1974, Mystery Writers of Tunbridge Wells, 1975; The Dreamer Lost in Terror, 1976; To Love and Beyond, 1977; Dreams to Give, 1979; The Arundel Touch, 1980; Love's Lost Melody, 1986.

MARTINUS Eivor Ruth, b. 30 Apr 1943, Goteborg, Sweden. Writer; Translator. m. Derek Martinus, 27 Apr, 1963, 2 d. Education: Double Degree, English and Swedish Literature, Universities of Lund and Goteberg, 1981. Publications: Five original novels in Swedish; Strindberg Translations: Thunder in the Air, 1989; Chamber Plays, 1991, The Great Highway, 1990, three one act plays; other translations: My Life As A Dog; The Mysterious Barricades; A Matter of the Soul; Barrabas. Contributions to: Swedish Book Review; Swedish Books; Scandinavica. Memberships: Society of Authors; Swedish Writers Union; Swedish Playwrights Union; Swedish English Translators Association; SVEA-BRITT. Literary Agent: Tony Peake, Peake Associates, 14 Grafton Crescent, NW1 8SL, London, England. Address: 16 Grantham Road, London W4 2RS, England.

MARTONE Michael, b. 22 Aug 1955, Fort Wayne, IN, USA. Writer. m. Theresa Pappas, 3 Apr 1984. Education: AB, IN University, 1977; MA, Johns Hopkins University, 1979. Publications: Alive and Dead in Indiana, 1984; Safety Patrol, 1988; A Place of Sense, 1988; Fort Wayne is Seventh on Hitlers List, 1990; Townships, 1990; Fort Wayne is 7th on Hitlers List, 1993; Pensees: The Thoughts of Dan Quayle, 1994. Contributions to: Stories in, Antaeus; Ascent; Benzene; Shenandoah; Epoch; Iowa Review; Harpers; Northwest Review; Indiana Review; Denver Quarterly; Windless Orchard; Gargoyle; MI Review. Honours: National Endowment for the Arts Literary Fellowship, 1984; PEN Syndicated Fiction Award, 1988; Ingram Merrill Foundation Award, 1988; Pushcart Prize, 1989. Memberships: National Writers Union; PEN; Associated Writing Programs. Literary Agent: Sallie Gouverneur. Address: 348 Fellows Avenue, Syracuse, NY 13210, USA.

MARTY Martin E, b. 5 Feb 1928, West Point, Nebraska. Professor; Editor. m. (1) Elsa, dec, (2) Harriet Julia, 23 Aug 1982, 4 s, 1 d. Education: M Div, St Louis, 1952; STM, Lutheran School of Theology, 1954; PhD, University of Chicago, 1956. Appointments: Fairfax M Cone Distinguished Service Professor, University of Chicago, 1963; Senior Editor, Christian Century, Chicago, 1986; George B Caldwell Senior Scholar in Residence, Park Ridge Centre for the Study of Health, Faith & Ethics. Publications: Modern American Religion, The Irony of it All, 1986; Righteous Empire, 1972; Modern American Religion; The Noise of Conflict, 1919-1941; Fundamentlisms Observed, Fundamentalisms and Society, Fundamentalisms and the State, 1993. Contributions to: Various Magazines & Journals. Honours: Numerous Honours & Awards for Professional Services; 51 Honorary Degrees; National Book Award, 1972. Memberships: Am Academy of Religion; Am Society of Church History; Am Catholic Historical Association; Am Academy of Arts & Science; American Philosophical Society. Address: University of Chicago Divinty School, 1025 E 58th Street, Chicago, IL 60637, USA.

MARTZ Louis Lohr, b. 1913, USA. Appointments: Instructor, 1938-44, Assistant Professor, 1944-48, Associate Professor, 1948-54, Professor, 1954-57, Chairman of Dept, 1956-62, Douglas Tracy Smith Professor, 1957-71, Sterling Professor, 1971-, Yale University; Editorial Chairman, Yale Edition of the Works of Thomas More; Director, Beinecke Library, Yale, 1972-77; Acting Director, Yale Center for British Art, 1981. Publications include: The Later Career of Tobias Smollett, 1942; Pilgrim's Progress, 1949; The Poetry of Meditation, 1954; The Meditative poem, 1963; The Paradise within, 1964; The Poem of the Mind, 1966; The Wit of Love, 1969; Hero and Leander, 1972; Thomas More's Dialogue of Comfort, 1976; The Author in His Work, 1978; Poet of Exile (Milton) 1980; H D Collected Poems 1912-1944, 1983; H D Selected Poems, 1988; George Herbert and Henry Vaughan, 1986; Thomas More: The Search for the Inner Man, 1990; From Renaissance to Baroque Essays on Literature and Art, 1991; D H Lawrence, Quetzalcoatl, 1995; George Herbert, Selected Poems, 1994. Memberships: Am Academy of Arts & Science; British Academy of Arts & Science. Address: 994 Yale Station, New Haven, CT 06520, USA.

MARUTA Leszek, b. 8 Nov 1930, Torun, Poland. Writer; Journalist. (div), 1 s, 1 d. Education: Jagellonian University, 1949-52. Appointments: Staff, Gazeta Krakowska, Editor, 1969-71; Staff, Estrada Krakowska, Art Director, Scenarist, 1962-69; Director, WOK, Culture Centre of Tarnow, 1975-77; Staff, Lektura, literary monthly magazine, Editor, 1991-93. Publications: Almanach Mlodych, 1958; Stillife With Moustache, 1960; Haml-op Mopm C Ycamu, 1973; Silly Talk, 1975; Trumpet-call From The Crazy Tower, 1986; Heart Stew, 1989; In The Desert, In Wilderness and in Poland, 1992; The Cracow Joke - Is A Penny Worth, 1993; adaptions for radio TV and theatre. Contributions to: Numerous journals and magazines including: Zycie Literackie; Tak l Nie; Szpilki; Karuzela. Honours: Karuzela Literary Award, 1958Medal of Millenium, 1966; Award of the District Council of Cracow, 1972; Polish Radio Award, 1973; Award of the Governor of District Tarnow, 1976; Golden Cross of Merit, 1988; Golden Badge of the City of Cracow, 1988. Memberships: Polish Writers Union; Polish Journalistic Association, Secretary, Cracow Branch; Society of Authors; Society for the Humour of the Peoples; German Society for Military Music. Address: PL -123 Cracow (Kraków) ul, Krupnicza 22/12, Poland.

MARVIN Blanche, b. 17 Jan 1926, New York, New York, USA. Actress; Writer; Critic, Publisher, London Theatre Reviews; Director; Agent; Producer. m. Mark Marvin, 31 Oct 1950, 1 s, 1 d. Education: BA, Antioch College. Appointments: Secretary, PMA; Secretary, Royal Academy of Dancing; Editor and Artistic Director, Merri-Mimes. Publications: Sleeping Beauty, 1961, 1990; Scarface and Blue Water, 1971, 1990; Firebird, 1990; the Infanta, 1990; Pied Piper, 1990; 11 other plays; 4 plays for children, volume 1; 11 plays for children, volume 2. Contributions to: Dance Magazine; Theatre; New York City. Honours: Cue Magazine, Hall of Fame; Community Services, New York City; Children's Theatre Association Award; Emmy Award, TV film, Gertrude Stein & A Companion. Memberships: Writers Guild; Theatre Writers Union; PMA, Secretary; Equity; Screen Actors Guild; BAFTA; Royal Academy of Art. Literary Agent: Blanche Marvin. Address: 21a St John's Wood High Street, London NW8 7NG, England.

MARWICK Arthur, b. 1936, Britain. Appointments: Assistant Lecturer, University of Aberdeen, 1959-60; Lecturer, University of Edinburgh, 1960-69; Professor of History 1969-, Dean of Arts 1978-84, The Open University; Visiting Professor of History, State University of New York, Buffalo, 1966-67; Visiting Scholar, Hoover Institute, Visiting Professor, Stanford University, 1984-85; Directeur d'études invité, L'École des hautes études en sciences sociales, Paris, 1985; Visiting Professor, Rhodes College, Memphis, 1991; Visiting Professor, University of Perugia, 1991. Publications: The Explosion of British Society 1914-1962, 1963, 1971; Clifford Allen: The Open Conspiritor, 1964; The Deluge: British Society and the First World War, 1965, 1991; Britain in the Century of Total: War, Peace and Social Change 1900-1967, 1968; The Nature of History, 1970, 1981, 1989; War and Social Change in the Twentieth Century, 1974; The Home Front: The British and the Second World War, 1976; Women at War 1914-1918, 1977; Class: Image and Reality in Britain France and the USA Since 1930, 1980, 1990; Thames and Hudson Illustrated Dictionary of British History (ed), 1980; British Society Since 1945, 1982, 1990; Britain in Our Century: Images and Controversies, 1984; Class in the Twentieth Century (editor), 1986; Beauty in History: Society, Politics and Personal Appearance, c1500 to the Present, 1988; The Arts Literature and Society (editor), 1990; Culture in Britain Since 1945, 1991. Address: Flat 5, 67 Fittzjohn's Avenue, Hampstead, London NW3 6PE, England.

MARX Arthur, b. 1921, America. Film Writier; TV Writer; Director; Playwright. Publications: The Ordeal of Willie Brown, 1951; Life with Groucho, 1954; Not as a Crocodile, 1958; Son of Graucho, 1972; Everybody Loves Somebody Sometime, Especially Himself, 1974; Goldwyn, 1976; Red Skelton, 1979; The Nine Lives of Mickey Rooney, 1986; My Life with Groucho, 1988; The Impossible Years, 1965; Minnies Boys, 1970; My Daughters Rated X, 1975; Sugar and Spice, 1974; Groucho: A Life in Revue, 1986; The Ghost and Mrs Muir, 1987; Set to Kill, 1993; The Secret Life of Bob Hope, 1993. Contributions to: Los Angeles Magazine. Honour: Groucho: A Life in Revue, Nominated Laurence Oliver Award, 1957. Memberships: Dramatists Guild; Writers Guild of Am; International Association of Crime Writers; Authors Guild. Literary Agent: Scovil, Chichak & Galen, NY 10016, USA. Address: c/o Scovil, chichak & Galen, 381 Park Avenue South, New York, NY 10016, USA.

MASATSUGU Mitsuyuki, b. 25 Jan 1924, Taiwan. Writer. m. Kiyoko Takeda, 3 Nov 1951, 1 son, 1 daughter. Education: BS, Osaka University of Foreign Studies, Japan, 1945; Course in Industrial Management, Tokyo, 1952. Publications: How To Run A Successful Business, 1969; The Turning Point of Japanese Enterprises Overseas, 1972; The Modern Samurai Society, 1982; Zigzags To The Meiji Restoration - The Divine Puppet Dazzled the Blue-Eyed Imperialists, 1994. Contributions to: Occasionally to Japanese papers and magazines. Address: 3-35-16 Tomioka-nishi, Kanazawa-ku, Yokohama 236, Japan.

MASCHLER Thomas Michael (Mark Caine), b. 16 Aug 1933. Publisher. m. (1) Fay Coventry, 1970, 1 son, 2 daughters, (2) Regina Kulinicz , 1987. Appointments: Production Assistant, Andre Deutsch,

1955-56; Editor, MacGibbon and Kee, 1956-58; Fiction Editor, Penguin Books, 1958-60; Editorial Director, 1960-70, Chairman, 1970-, Publisher, Children's Books, 1991-, Jonathan Cape; Director, Random House, 1987-. Publications: Editor: Declarations, 1957; New English Dramatists Series, 1959-63. Address: 20 Vauxhall Bridge Road, London SW1V 2SA, England.

MASEFIELD Geoffrey (Bussell), b. 1911, Britain. Appointments: Agricultural Officer, Uganda, 1935-48; Lecturer in Tropical Agriculture 1948-76, Fellow, Wolfson College, Oxford University; Editor, Tropical Agriculture Journal, 1953-65. Publications: I Am Not Armed, 1938; This Springing Wilderness (with S Wood), 1942; The Uganda Farmer, 1948; Handbook of Tropical Agriculture, 1949; Short History of Agriculture in the British Colonies, 1950; Famine: Its Prevention and Relief, 1963; Food and Nutrition Procedures in Times of Disaster, 1967; The Oxford Book of Food Plants (with S G Harrison, M Wallis and B E Nicholson), 1969; Farming Systems of the World (with A N Duckham), 1970; History of the Colonial Agricultural Service, 1972. Honours: Doctor of Science, 1975. Address: Steepway, Adey's Lane, Wotton-under-Edge, Gloucestershire Gl2 7PS, England.

MASINI Eleonora Barbieri, b. 19 Nov 1928, Guatemala. Sociologist. m. Francesco Maria Masini, 31 Jan 1953, 3 s. Education: BA, 1948, Law Degree, 1952; Comparative Law Specialisation, 1953, Sociology Specialisation, 1969, Rome, Italy. Publications: Visions of Desirable Societies, 1983; Women - Households and Change (with Susan Stratige), 1991; Why Future Studies? 1992. Contributions to: Various articles to: Futures; Technological Forecasting and Social Change; Futurist. Memberships: Past Executive Council Chair, Past Secretary- General, Past President, World Futures Studies Federation; President for Europe, World Academy of Art and Science. Address: Via A Bertoloni 23, 00197 Rome, Italy.

MASLOW Jonathan Evan, b. 4 Aug 1948, Long Branch, New Jersey, USA. Writer. Education: BA with high honours, American Literature, Marlboro College, Vermont; MS, Columbia University Graduate School of Journalism. Publications include: The Owl Papers, 1983; Bird of Life, Bird of Death: A Political Ornithology of Central America, 1986; Sacred Horses: Memoirs of a Turkmen Cowboy, 1994; A Tramp in the Darien, film for BBC-WGBH-TV, 1990. Contributions to: Over 200 magazine articles to Atlantic Monthly, Saturday Review, GEO. Honours: George Varsell Award, American Academy of Arts and Letters, 1988; Guggenheim Fellow, 1989-90. Memberships: Authors Guild; National Writers Union. Literary Agent: The Robbins Office, New York City, USA. Address: Cutter's Way, Rd 3, Woodbine, NJ 08270, USA.

MASON Bobbie Ann, b. 1 May 1940, KY, US. Writer. m. Roger Rawlings, 12 Apr 1969. Education: BA, University KY, 1962; PhD, University of Connecticut. Publications: In Country, 1985; Shiloh, 1982; Feather Crowns, 1993; Love Life, 1989; Spence + Lila, 1988. Contributions to: The New Yorker. Honours: Hemingway Award for Best First Fiction, 1983. Memberships: Authors Guild; PEN. Literary Agent: Amanda Urban, ICM, 40 West 57 Str, New York, NY 10019, USA. Address: c/o Amanda Urban, ICM, 40 West 57th Str, NY 10019, USA.

MASON Francis K(enneth), b. 1928, Britain. Appointments: Editor, Flying Review International 1963-64; Managing Director, Profile Publications Limited, 1964-67; Managing Editor, Guiness Superlatives Limited, Enfield, middlesex, 1968-71; Managing Director, Alban Book Services Limited, Watton, Norfolk; Archivist and Researcher. Publications: Hawker Aircraft since 1920, 1961, 1972, 1990; Hawker Hurricane, 1962; Gloster Gladiator, North American Sabre (editor), 1963; The Hawker Hunter, 1965; The Hawker Sea Hawk, The Westland Lysander, 1966; The Hawker Siddley Kestrel, The Hawker Hunter Two-Seater, The Hawker Tempest, 1967; British Fighters of The Second World War, 1968; Air Facts and Feats, Battle Over Britain, 1969, 1972; British Gallantry Awards (editor), 1970; Know Britain, 1972; Know Aviation,1973; Ribbons and Medals (editor), 1974; A Dictionary of Military Biography, 1975, 1989; Famous Pilots and Their Planes, 1981; Lockheed Hercules, Phantom, 1984; War in the Air, 1985; Tornado, Luftwaffe Aircraft (with M Turner), 1986; The Hawker Typhoon and Tempest, 1987; The Avro Lancaster, 1989; The British Fighter Since 1912, 1992; The British Bomber Since 1914, 1994; a total of 87 hardback titles written. Contributions to: Radio and TV Commetaries, 1977-1991. Honour: International History Diploma (Paris), Aero Club of France, 1973. Membership: Founder Fellowship, Canadian Guild of

Authors, 1988; Fellow, The Royal Historical Society (London), 1969. Address: Beechwood, Watton, Thetford, Norfolk 1P25 6AB, England.

MASON Haydn Trevor, b. 1929, Britain. Appointments: Instructor in French, Princeton University, New Jersey, 1954-57; Lecturer 1964-65, Reader 1965-67, University of Reading: Professor of European Literature, University of East Anglia, Norwich, 1967-79; Editor, Studies on Voltaire and the Eighteenth Century, 1977-95; Professor of French Literature, University de Paris III, 1979-81; Professor of French, University of Bristol,1981-94, Emeritus Professor, 1994-; Scholar in Residence, University of Maryland, 1986; Chairman, Association of University Professors of French, 1981-82; President, Society for French Studies, 1982-84; British Society for Eighteenth Century Studies, 1984-86; Chairman, Board of Directors, Voltaire Foundation, University of Oxford, 1989-93; President, International Society for Eighteenth-Century Studies, 1991-95. Publications: Pierre Bayle and Voltaire, 1963; Marivaux: Les Fausses Confidences (editor), 1964; Leibniz-Arnauld Correspondence (translator and editor), 1967; Voltaire: Zadig and Other Stories (editor), 1971; Voltaire, 1974; Voltaire: A Life,1981; French Writers and Their Society 1715-1800, 1982; Cyrano de Bergerac: L'Autre Monde, 1984; Voltaire: Discours en vers sur l'homme (editor), 1991; Candide: Optimism Demolished, 1992. Honours: Officier dans L'Ordre des Palmes Academiques, 1985; Medaille D'Argent de la Ville de Paris, 1989. Address: Department of French, University of Bristol, Bristol BS8 1TE, England.

MASON Herbert (Molloy), b. 1927, USA. Publications: The Lafayette Escadrille, 1964; High Flew the Falcons, Famous Firsts in Exploration, 1965; The Texas Rangers, 1966; Bold Men, Far Horizons, The Commandos, 1967; The New Tigers, 1968; Duel for the Sky, 1969; The Great Pursuit, 1970; Death from the Sea, 1972; The Rise of the Luftwaffe, 1973; Missions of Texas, The Fantastic World of Ants, 1974; Secrets of the Supernatural, 1975; The United States Air Force, 1976; To Kill the Devil, 1979; The Luftwaffe, 1981; Hitler Must Die, 1985. Address: c/o John Hawkins and Associates, 71 West 23rd Street, New York, NY 10010, USA.

MASON Lee W. See: **MALZBERG Barry Norman.**

MASON Ronald Charles, b. 30 Jul 1912, Thames Ditton, England. Retired Staff Tutor, London University Extra Mural Department. m. Margaret Violet Coles, 8 Sept 1936, 2 s, 1 d. Education: BA, London University, 1947; Barrister at Law, Lincolns Inn, Called to the Bar, 1935. Publications include: The Spirit Above the Dust (Study of Herman Melville) 1951; Batsman's Paradise (cricket book) 1955; Jack Hobbs, 1960; Walter Hammond, 1962; Sing All A Green Willow (essays On cricket) 1967; Plum Warner's Last Season, 1970; Warwick Armstrong's Australians, 1971; Ashes in the Mouth, 1982; novels: Timbermills, 1938; The Gold Garland, 1939; Cold Pastoral, 1946; The House of the Living, 1947; songs: Songs From a Summer School, 1974 (with music by Geoffrey Bush); More Songs From a Summer School, 1980. Contributions to: Horizon; Penguin New Writing; Tribune; the Cricketer; Modern Reading; Notes and Queries. Memberships: MCC; Surrey County Cricket Club. Literary Agent: David Higham Associates Ltd. Address: 22 Rosehill Farm Meadow, Park Road, Banstead, Surrey SM7 3DE, England.

MASON Stanley, b. 16 Apr 1917, Blairmore, Alberta, Canada. Editor; Translator. m. Cloris Ielmini, 29 July 1944, 1 daughter. Education: MA, English Literature, Oriel College, Oxford. Appointments: Literary Editor, Graphis Magazine, 1963-83; Editor, Elements, Dow Chemical Europe House Organ, 1969-75. Publications: Modern English Structures (with Ronald Ridout), 4 volumes, 1968-72; A Necklace of Words, poetry, 1975; A Reef of Hours, poetry, 1983; Send Out the Dove, play, 1986; The Alps, verse translation of Albrecht von Haller's poem, 1987; The Everlasting Snow, poetry, 1993; Collected Poems, University of Salzburg, 1993; A German Treasury, translations, University of Salzburg, 1993. Contributions to: UK: Adelphi; Poetry Review; Envoi; Orbis; Doors; Pennine Platform; others; Canada: Canadian Forum; Dalhousie Review. Address: Im Zelgli 5, 8307 Effretikon, Switzerland.

MASSIE Allan, b. 1938, Singapore. Novelist. m. 3 children. Education: Trinity College, Cambridge. Publications: Change and Decay in All Around I See, 1978; The Las Peacock, 1980; The Death of Man, 1981; One Night in Winter, 1984; Augustus: The Memoirs of an Emperor, 1986; A Question of Loyalties, 1989; Tiberius, 1990; Muriel Spark, 1979; Ill Met by Gaslight: Five Edinburgh Murders, 1980; The Caesars, 1983; A Portrait of Scottish Rugby, 1984; Colette, 1986; 101

Great Scots, 1987; Byron's Travels, 1988; Glasgow: Portrait of a City, 1989; The Novel Today; A Critical Guide to the British Novel 1970-89, 1990. Honours: Niven Award, 1981; Scottish Arts Council Awards; Fellow, Royal Society of Literature. Address: c/o Hodder and Stoughton, 47 Bedford Square, London WC1B 3DP, England

MASSIE Robert K, b. 1929, Lexington, Kentucky, USA. Journalist; Professor of Journalism. m. Suzanne Rohrbach, 1 s, 2 d. Education: BA, Yale University; BA, Oxford University. Appointments: President, Author's Guild, 1987-91. Publications: Nicholas and Alexandra, 1967; Dreadnought; Journey, 1975; Peter The Great: His Life and Work, 1980; The Romanov Family Album, 1982. Honours: Christopher Award, 1976; American Library Citation, 1981; Pulitzer Prize, 1981. Memberships: Author's Guild; PEN; Authors League of America. Address: 60 West Clinton Avenue, Irvington, NY 10533, USA.

MASSON Jeffrey Moussaieff, b. 28 Mar 1941, Chicago, Illinois, USA (as Jeffrey Lloyd Masson). Former Professor of Sanskrit; Project Director, Sigmund Freud Archives, New York City, 1980-81; Co-Director, Freud Copyrights (1981-83). Publications: The Oceanic Feeling: The Origins of Religious Sentiment in Ancient India, 1980; The Assault on Truth: Freud's Suppression of the Seduction Theory, 1984; Complete Letters of Sigmund Freud to Wilhelm Fuess, 1887-1904 (editor and translator), 1985; A Dark Science: Women, Sexuality and Psychiatry in the Nineteenth Century (editor and translator), 1987; My Father's Guru: A Journey Through Spirituality and Disillusion, 1992. Contributions include: Atlantic Monthly; International Journal of Psycho-Analysis; New York Times; New York Review of Books. Address: c/o Elaine Markson Literary Agency, 44 Greenwich Avenue, New York, NY 10011, USA.

MAST Gerald, b. 1940, USA. Professor. Appointments: Instructor of English, New York University, 1964-65; Instructor of English, Oberlin College, Ohio, 1965-67; Assistant Professor, 1967-73, Associate Professor of Humanities, 1974-78, Richmond College, City University of New York; Professor, Department of English, College, Committee on General Studies in the Humanities, Committee on Art and Design, University of Chicago, Illinois, 1978-. Publications: A Short History of the Movies, 1971, 4th edition, 1986; The Comic Mind: Comedy and the Movies, 1973, 1979; Film Theory and Criticism: Introductory Readings (edited with Marshall Cohen), 1973, 3rd edition, 1985; Filmguide to Rules of the Game, 1974; The Movies in Our Midst: Readings in the Cultural History of Film America (editor), Howard Hawks Storyteller, 1982; Can't Help Singing: The American Musical on Stage and Screen, 1989. Address: c/o University of Chicago, 5811 S Ellis Avenue, Chicago, IL 60637, USA.

MASTERS Hilary Thomas, b. 2 Mar 1928, Kansas City, Missouri, USA. Novelist; Short Story Writer; Professor. div., 1 son, 2 daughters. Education: AB, Brown University, 1952. Appointments: Professor of English, Carnegie Mellon University; Member, Freedom to Write Committee, PEN, 1984. Publications: The Common Pasture, 1967; An American Marriage, 1969; Palace of Strangers, 1971; Last Stands: Notes from Memory, 1982; Hammertown Tales, 1986; The Harlem Valley Trio: Clemmons, 1985; Cooper, 1987; Strickland, 1990; Success, 1992. Contributions: Sports Illustrated; North American Review; Sewanee Review; The Georgia Review; New England Review; Kenyon Review. Memberships: PEN, New York Center; The Authors Guild. Literary Agent: Kit Ward, USA. Address: c/o Kit Ward, Box 515, North Scituate, MA 02060, USA.

MASTERTON Graham (Thomas Luke), b. 16 Jan 1946, Edinburgh, Scotland. Author. m. Wiescka Walach, 11 Nov 1975, 3 sons. Publications: The Manitou, 1975; Charnel House, 1976; Rich, 1977; Railroad, 1980; Solitaire, 1983; Maiden Voyage, 1984; Tengu, 1984; Lady of Fortune, 1985; Corroboree, 1985; Family Portrait, 1986; Night Warriors, 1987; Headlines, 1987; Silver, 1987; Death Trance, 1987. Contributions to: Article on technique, to The Writer, 1985; Article on horror writing, 1987; Twilight Zone, 1988. Honours: Special Award, Mystery Writers of America, 1977; Silver Medal, West Coast Review of Books, 1984. Membership: Literary Guild. Literary Agent: Wiescka Masterton. Address: c/o Sphere Books, 27 Wrights Lane, London W8 5TZ, England.

MASTROSIMONE William, b. 1947, USA. Writer. Publications: The Woolgatherer, 1981; Extremities, Shivaree, 1984; A Tantalizing, 1985; Nanawatai, 1986. Cat's-Paw, 1987. Address: c/o George Lane, William Morris Agency, 1350 Avenue of the Americas, New York, NY 10019, USA.

MATAS Carol, b. Winnipeg, Canada. Writer. m. Per Brask, 2 children. Education: London, Ontario, Canada; London, England. Publications include: Lisa, 1987; Jesper, 1989; Sworn Enemies, 1993; Daniel's Story, 1993; The Race, 1991; Of Two Minds (with Perry Nodelman), 1994; The Lost Locket, 1994; The Burning Time, 1994. Honours: Canadian Library Association Notable Book, for, Jesper 1989, The Race 1992; Geoffrey Bilson Award for Historical Fiction, for Lisa; New York Times Book Review Notable Book, for Lisa, 1990; International Reading Association Young Adults Choices, for Lisa's War, 1991; Governor General's Award, nominee, 1993. Address: c/o Writers Union of Canada, 24 Ryerson Avenue, Toronto, Ontario, M5T 2P3 Canada.

MATCHETT William Henry, b. 1923, USA. Appointments: Teaching Fellow, Harvard University, 1953-54; Instructor, 1954-56, Assistant Professor, 1956-60, Associate Professor, 1960-66, Professor, 1966-82, Professor Emeritus, 1983-, University of WA, Seattle; Modern Language Quarterly, 1963-82; Editorial Consultant, Poetry Northwest. Publications: Water Ouzel and Other Poems, 1955; Poetry From Statement to Meaning, The Phoenix and the Turtle; Shakespeare's Poem and Chester's Loues Martyr, 1965; The Life and Death of King John, 1966; Fireweed and Other Poems, 1980. Honours: Furioso Poetry Award, 1952; WA State Governors Award, 1982. Address: 1017 Minor Avenue, 702 Seattle, WA 98104, USA.

MATHERS Peter, b. 1931, Fulham, London. Novelist. Education: Sydney Technical College. Appointments: Researcher, Theatre Adviser, University of Pittsburgh, 1968. Publications: Trap, 1970; The Wort Papers, 1972; Story, A Change for the Better, 1984. Honours: Miles Franklin Award, 1967. Address: c/o Wav Publications, 499 The Parade, Magill, South Australia 5072, Australia.

MATHESON Rochard (Burton), b. 1926, USA. Writer. Career: Freelance Writer, especially of screenplays and TV plays including The Twilight Zone. Publications include: Someone Is Bleeding, 1953; Fury on Sunday, I Am Legend, Born of Man and Woman, 1954; Third from the Sun, 1955; The Shrinking Man, 1956; The Shores of Space, 1957; A Stir of Echoes, 1958; Ride the Nightmare, 1959; The Beardless Warriors, 1960; Shock!, 1961; Shock III, 1964; Shock IIII, 1966; Shock Waves, 1970; Hell House, 1971; Bid Time Return, 1975; What Dreams May Come, 1978; Shock 4, 1980; Earthbound, 1989; Collected Stories, 1989; By the Gun, 1994; Journal of the Gun Years. Address: PO Box 81, Woodland Hills, CA 91365, USA.

MATHIAS Roland Glyn, b. 4 Sept 1915, Talybont-on-Usk, Breconshire, Wales. Schoolmaster. m. Mary (Molly) Hawes, 4 Apr 1944, Chipping Norton, Oxfordshire, England, 1 son, 2 daughters. Education: BA, Modern History, 1936, BLitt (by thesis) 1939, MA 1944, Jesus College, University of Oxford, England; Doctor of Humane Letters (honoris causa), Georgetown University, Washington, USA, 1985. Literary Appointments: Editor, The Anglo-Welsh Review, 1961-76; Member, Welsh Arts Council, 1970-79; Chairman, Literature Committee, Welsh Arts Council, 1976-79; Visiting Professor, University of Alabama at Birmingham, 1971; Extra-Mural Lecturer, University College, Cardiff, 1970-77. Major Publications: Poems: Break in Harvest, 1946; The Roses of Tretower, 1952; The Flooded Valley, 1960; Absalom in the Tree, 1971; Snipe's Castle, 1979; Burning Brambles, selected poems, 1983; The Eleven Men of Eppynt, short stories, 1956; Whitsun Riot, Historical Research, 1963; Vernon Watkins, literary criticism, 1974; John Cowper Powys as Poet, literary criticism, 1979; A Ride Through the Wood, critical essays, 1985; Anglo-Welsh Literature - An Illustrated History, 1987. Contributions to: Very many periodicals and literary journals. Address: Deffrobani, 5 Maescelyn, Brecon, Powys LD3 7NL, Wales.

MATHIEU André (Andrew Matthew, Andrew Matthews), b. 10 Apr 1942, Beauce, Canada. Novelist. m. B Perron, 20 July 1963, 1 daughter. Education: BA, Laval University. Publications: Nathalie, 1982; La Sauvage, 1985; Aurore, 1990; Donald and Marion, 1990; Arnold's Treasure, 1994; 20 Others. Address: CP 55, Victoriaville, Qc, G6P 6S4, Canada.

MATHIS EDDY Darlene, b. 19 Mar 1937, IN, USA. Poet; Professor; Editor. m. Spencer Livingston Eddy, 23 May 1964, dec. Education: BA, Goshen College, 1959; MA, 1961, PhD, 1967, Rutgers University. Appointments: Poetry Editor, Forum, 1985-89; Poet in Residence, Ball State University, 1989-93. Publications: The Worlds of King Lear, 1968; Leaf Threads Wind Rhymes, 1985; Weathering, 1991. Contributions to: May Sarton: Woman and Poet, 1983; Contributor,

Florilegia, 1987; Am Literature; English Languages Notes; The Old Northwest. Honours: Woodrow Wilson National Fellow, 1959-62; Rutgers University Graduate Honours Fellowship & Dissertation Award, 1964-65, 1966; Numerous Research, Creative Arts Awards; Notable Woodrow Wilson Fellow, 1991. Memberships: Associated Writing Programs; American Association of University Professor; National Council of Teachers of English; American League of PEN Women. Address: Dept of English, RB 248, Ball State University, Muncie IN 47306, USA.

MATRAY James Irving, b. 6 Dec 1948, Evergreen Park, IL, USA. University Professor. m. Mary Karin Heine, 14 Aug 1971, 1 s, 1 d. Education: BA, Lake Forest College, 1970; MA, 1973, PhD, 1977, University of VA. Appointments: Glenville State College, 1976-77; CA State College, 1978-79; University of TX, 1979-80; New Mexico State University, 1980-; University of Southern CA, 1988-89. Publications: Trumans Plan for Victory, 1979; The Reluctant Crusade, 1941-50, 1985; Spoils of War, 1989; Historical Dictionary of the Korean War, 1991; Korea and the Cold War, 1993. Honours: Stuart L Bernath Article Award, 1980; Best Book Award, 1986; Best Reference Book Award, 1992. Memberships: Am Historical Association, Pacific Coast Branch; Society for Historian of America; Foreign Relations; Organization of Am Historians. Address: Box 3H Dept of History, New Mexico State University, Las Cruces, NM 88003, USA.

MATSON Clive, b. 13 Mar 1941, Los Angeles, California, USA. Poet; Playwright; Teacher. Education: Undergraduate work, University of Chicago, 1958-59; MFA, Poetry, School of the Arts, Columbia University. Publications: Mainline to the Heart, 1966; Space Age, 1969; Heroin, 1972; On the Inside, 1982; Equal in Desire, 1983; Hourglass, 1987; Breath of Inspiration, essay, 1987. Contributions to: Anthologies of poetry: 31 New American Poets, 1969; Loves, Etc, 1973; Take It to the Hoop, 1980; Hang Together, 1987; 8 others; Over 100 poetry journals including: Exquisite Corpse; Hanging Loose; Nine Items or Less; Yellow Silk; Jeopardy; Hawaii Review; Factor, Mexico City; Berkeley Poetry Review; Blue Unicorn; The Centennial Review; Dalmo'ma; Silver; Intrepid; The Floating Bear. Honours: Graduate Writing Fellowship, Columbia University, 1987-88. Memberships: Poets and Writers; Dramatists Guild; Theatre Bay Area; Bay Area Mineralogists. Literary Agent: Peter Beren, Berkeley, California, USA. Address: 472 44th Street, Oakland, CA 94609, USA.

MATSUMURA Takao, b. 7 Jan 1942, Yokohama, Japan. Professor of Economics. m. Rumiko Fukuoka, 20 May 1967, 1 son, 1 daughter. Education: BA, Economics, 1964, MA, Economics, 1966, Keio University; PhD, Social History, University of Warwick, England, 1976. Appointments: Associate Professor, 1972-81, Professor, 1982-, Department of Economics, Keio University; Visiting Fellow, Social History, Warwick University, 1987-88. Publications: The Labour Aristocracy Revisited: The Victorian Flint Glass Makers, 1850-1880, 1983. Contributions to: Journal of Historical Studies (in Japanese); Mita Economic Journal (in Japanese); Bulletin of the Society for the Study of Labour History. Honours: 7th Prize for Excellent Labour Publications, Japan Institute of Labour, 1984. Memberships: Japan Socio-Economic Society, Editorial Board; Japan Social Policy Society; Society for the Study of Labour History, International Board. Address: 7 chome 28-2, Okusawa, Setagaya-ku, Tokyo, Japan.

MATTHEW Andrew. See: MATHIEU André.

MATTHEW Christopher Charles Forrest, b. 8 May 1939, London, England. Writer; Broadcaster. m. Wendy Mary Mallinson, 19 Oct 1979, 2 sons, 1 daughter. Education: BA (Hons), Oxford; MA (Hons), St Peter's College, Oxford. Literary Appointment: Editor, Times Travel Guide, 1972-73. Publications: A Different World: Stories of Great Hotels, 1976; Diary of a Somebody, 1978; Loosely Engaged, 1980; The Long Haired Boy, 1980; The Crisp Report, 1981; Three Men in a Boat (annotated with Benny Green), 1982; The Junket Man, 1983; How to Survive Middle Age, 1983; Family Matters, 1987; The Simon Crisp Diaries, 1988; A Perfect Hero, 1991; The Amber Room, 1995; Radio Play: A Portrait of Richard Hillary; TV Scripts: The Good Guys, LWT, 1993; Radio Writer & Presenter: Fourth Column R4, 1990-93; Something to Declare, 1971-82; Points of Departure, 1980-82; Invaders, 1982-83; The Travelling Show (R4), 1984-85; Plain Tales from the Rhododendrons (R4), 1991; Cold Print (R4), 1992. Contributions to: Punch; Vogue; Daily Telegraph; Sunday Telegraph; High Life; World of Interiors; London Evening Standard; The Observer. Membership: Society of Authors. Address: c/o Andrew Lownie, 122

Bedford Court Mansions, Bedford Square, London WC1B 3AH, England.

MATTHEWS Andrew. See: **MATHIEU André.**

MATTHEWS Patricia Anne (P A Brisco, Patty Brisco, Laura Wylie), b. 1 July 1927, San Fernando, California, USA. Author. m. (1) Marvin Owen Brisco, 1946, div 1961, 2 sons, 2) Clayton Hartly Matthews, 1971. Education: California State University, Los Angeles. Appointments: Secretary, Administrator, California State University, 1959-77. Publications: Juveniles, mystery, romance, suspense, occult, Gothics, science fiction, including: Merry's Treasure, 1969; The Other People, 1970; The House of Candles, 1973; Mist of Evil, 1976, 1990; Love, Forever More, 1977; Raging Rapids, 1978; Love's Daring Dream, 1978; Love's Golden Destiny, 1979; Love's Many Faces, poetry, 1979; The Night Visitor, 1979, 1987; Love's Raging Tide, 1980; Love's Sweet Agony, 1980; Love's Bold Journey, 1980; Tides of Love, 1981; Embers of Dawn, 1982; Flames of Glory, 1983; Dancer of Dreams, 1984; Gambler in Love, 1985; Tame the Restless Heart, 1986; Destruction at Dawn, 1986; Twister, 1986; Enchanted, 1987; Thursday and the Lady, 1987; Mirrors, 1988; The Dreaming Tree, 1989; Sapphire, 1989; Oasis, 1989; The Death of Love, 1990; The Unquiet, 1991; Many others; With Clayton Matthews: Midnight Whispers, 1981; Empire, 1982; Midnight Lavender, 1985; The Scent of Fear, 1992; Taste of Evil, 1993; Vision of Death, 1993; The Sound of Murder, 1994. Contributions to: Short stories, poetry, articles, other writings, to magazines and anthologies include 2 recent stories to Magazine of Fantasy and Science Fiction. Honours: Porgie Award, West Coast Review of Books, Silver Medal, 1979, 1983, Bronze Medal, 1983; Romantic Times: Team Writing Award (with husband), 1983, Reviewers Choice Awards, Best Historical Gothics, 1986-87, Affaire de Coeur Silver Pen Readers Award, 1989. Memberships: RWA; MWA; Sisters in Crime; Novelists Ink. Literary Agent: Jay Garon. Address: c/o Jay Garon, 415 Central Park West, New York, NY 10025, USA.

MATTHEWS Peter John, b. 6 Jan 1945, Fareham, Hampshire, England. Freelance Author; Athletics Commentator, ITV. m. Diana Randall, 1969, 2 sons. Appointments: Director, Guinness Publishing 1981-84, 1989-: Sports Editor, Guinness Book of Records, 1982-91; Editor, Guinness Book of Records, 1991-. Publications: Guinness Book of Athletics Facts and Feats, 1982; International Athletics Annual, yearly from 1985; Track and Field Athletics - The Records (Guinness), 1986; Guinness Encyclopaedia of Sports Records and Results, from 1987; Cricket Firsts (with Robert Brooke), 1988; Guinness International Who's Who of Sport, 1993. Contributor to: Athletics publications. Address: 10 Madgeways Close, Great Amwell, Ware, Hertfordshire SG12 9RU, England.

MATTHEWS William, b. 11 Nov 1942, Cincinnati, Ohio, USA. Writer; Teacher. m. (1) Marie Harris, 4 May 1963, div. 1973, (2) Arlene Modica, 1984, (3) Patricia Smith, 1989, 2 sons. Education: BA, Yale University, 1965; MA, University of North Carolina, Chapel Hill, 1966. Appointments: Co-Editor, Co-Founder, Lillabulero Press and Magazine, 1966-74; Member, Editorial Board for Poetry, 1969-73, New Poets Editorial Board, 1988-90, Wesleyan University Press; Poetry Editor, Iowa Review, 1976-77; Teaching positions include: Bread Loaf Writers Conference, 1981-89, 1991, Brooklyn College, 1983-85, Columbia University, 1983-95, 1988, 1990-92; Professor, English: City College, New York University, 1985-, University of Michigan, 1987; Guest Poetry Editor, Indiana Review, 1987. Publications: Poetry books: Ruining the New Road, 1970; Sleek for the Long Flight, 1972; Sticks and Stones, 1975; Rising and Falling, 1979; Flood, 1982; A Happy Childhood, 1984, UK edition, 1985; Foreseeable Futures, 1987; A World Rich in Anniversaries (translations with Mary Feeney, from Jean Follain's prose poems), 1979; Curiosities, essays, 1989; Selected Poems and Translations 1969-1991, 1992. Contributions to: Atlantic Monthly; New Yorker; Ohio Review; Poetry; Others. Honours: National Endowment for the Arts Fellow, 1974, 1983; John Simon Guggenheim Fellow, 1980-81; Oscar Blumenthal Award, 1983; Ingram Merrill Fellow, 1984; Eunice Tietjens Memorial Prize, Poetry magazine, 1989; Residencies: Rockefeller Foundation Study and Conference Centre, Bellaggio, Italy, 1988; Harthomden Castle International Writers Retreat, Scotland, 1990. Memberships: PEN; Past Member, Past Chairman, Literature Panel, National Endowment for the Arts; Past President, Past Member, Board of Directors, Associated Writing Programs; Authors Guild; Past President, Poetry Society of America. Address: 523 W 121st Street, New York, NY 10027, USA.

MATTHIAS John Edward, b. 1941, USA. Appointments: Assistant Professor, 1967-71, Associate Professor, 1973-81, Professor, 1981, University of Notre Dame. Publications: Bucyrus, 1970; Contemporary British Poetry, 23 Modern British Poets, 1971; Hermans Poems, 1974; Turns, 1975; Crossing, Introducing David Jones, Contemporary Swedish Poetry, Five American Poets, 1979; Bathory and Iermontov, 1980; Rainmaker, 1983; Northern Summer, 1963-83, 1984; The Battle of Kosovo, 1987; David Jones, Man and Poet, 1989; Tva Dikter, 1989; A Gathering of Ways, 1991; Reading Old Friends, 1992. Address: Dept of English, University of Notre Dame, Notre Dame, IN 46556, USA.

MATTHIESSEN Peter, b. 22 May 1927, NY, USA. Writer. m. (1) Patricia Southgate, 8 Feb 1951, div, 1 son, 1 daughter, (2) Deborah Love, 16 May 1963, dec, 1 son, 1 daughter, (3) Maria Eckhart, 28 Nov 1980. Education: Sorbonne University, 1948-49; BA, Yale University, 1950. Appointments include: Writer, 1950-; Co Founder, 1951, Editor, 1951-, Paris Review. Publications include: Race Rock, 1954; Wildlife in America, 1959; The Cloud Forest, 1961; Under the Mountain Wall, 1962; At Play in the Fields of the Lord, 1965; Sal Si Puedes, 1970; The Tree Where Man Was Born, 1972; Seal Pool, 1975; Fartortuga, 1975; The Snow Leopard, 1978; Sand Rivers, 1981; In the Spirit of Crazy Horse, 1983; Indian Country, 1984; Killing Mister Watson, 1990; African Silences, 1991; Shadows of Africa, 1992. Honours: Various Awards and Honours including Atlantic Prize, 1950; Am Book Award, 1980; John Burroughs Medal; African Wildlife Leadership Foundation Award, 1982; Gold Medal for Distinction in Natural History, 1985. Memberships: Am Academy and Institute of Arts & Letters; (Advisor) NY Zoological Society. Address: PO Box 392, Bridge Lane, Sagaponack, NY 11962, USA.

MATTINGLEY Christobel Rosemary, 26 Oct 1931, Adelaide, South Australia. Writer. m. Cecil David Mattingley, 17 Dec 1953, 2 sons, 1 daughter. Education: BA, 1st Class Hons in German, 1951; Registration Certificate and Associate of the Library Association of Australia, 1971. Publications include: Windmill at Magpie Creek, 1971; The Great Ballagundi Damper Bake, 1975; Rummage, 1981; The Angel with the Mouth Organ, 1984; The Miracle Tree, 1985; Survival in Our Own Land: Aboriginal Experiences in South Australia since 1836, 1988; The Butcher, the Beagle and The Dog Catcher, 1990; Tucker's Mob, 1992; The Sack, 1993; No Gun for Asmir, 1993. Contributions to: Australian Library Journal; New Zealand Libraries; Landfall (NZ); Reading Time; Classroom; Magpies; Something About the Author Autobiography Series. Literary Agent: A P Watt, 20 John Street, London WC1N 2DR. Address: 3/6 Wynyard Grove, Wattle Park, South Australia 5066, Australia.

MATURA Thaddee, b. 24 Oct 1922, Poland. Monk. Education: Master in Theology; Master in Biblical Studies. Publications: Celibat et Communauté, 1967; La vie religieuse au tournant, 1971; Naissance d'un charisme, 1973; Le projet évangélique de François d'Assise, 1977; Le radicalisme évangélique, 1980; Ecrits de François d'Aroise, 1981; Suivre Jésus, 1983; Ecrits de Claire d'Assise, 1985; Une absence ardente, 1988; Dieu le Père très saint, 1990. Contributions to: About 150 items to various publications. Address: 84240 Grambois, France.

MAUMELA Titus Ntsieni, b. 25 Dec 1924, Sibasa, Venda, Southern Africa. Teacher. m. Rose Maumela, 27 June 1949, 2 sons, 1 daughter. Education: BA, University of South Africa, 1961. Publications: Novels: Elelwani, 1954; Mafangambiti, 1956 (English 1986) Vhavenda Vho-Matshivha, 1958; Vhuhosi Vhu tou Bebelwa, 1962; Zwa Mulovha Zwi a Fhela, 1963; Maela wa Vho-Mathavha, 1967; Musandiwa na Khotsi Vho-Liwalaga, 1968; Kanakana (youth), 1975; Ndi Vho-Muthukhuthukhu, 1977; Vho-Rammbebo, 1981; Tshiphiri Tsho Bvela Khagala, 1986; Talukanyani (youth), forthcoming; Dramas: Tshililo, 1957; A Hu Bebiwi Mbilu, 1975; Vhuhosi A Vhu Thetshelwi, 1975; Edzani, 1985; Tomolambilu, 1989; Short stories: Matakadzambilu, 1965; Zwiitavhathu, 1965; Maungedzo, 1972; Mihani Ya Shango, 1972; Mithetshelo, 1981; Mmbwa Ya La Inwe a i Noni, 1983; Nganea Pfufhi dza u takadza, 1989. Essay: Maanea A Pfadzaho, 1992; Folktales: Dzingaho na Dzithai dza Tshivenda, 1968; Salungano! Salungano! 1978; Language Manuals: Thikho ya Luvenda ya Forno 1, 1970; Thikho ya Luvenda ya Fomo II, na III, 1970; Luvenda Iwa Murole wa 5, 1975; Luvenda Iwa Fomo I, 1975; Luvenda Iwa Murole wa Fomo II, 1976; Luvenda Iwa Murole wa 8, 1978; Tshivenda tsho tambaho tsha, Murole wa 5 (with Prof T W Muloiwa and B H Maumela), 1986; Gondo la Tshivenda, Murole wa 5, 1987; Gondo la Tshivenda, Murole wa 6 (with M R Madiba), 1990; Gondo la Tshivenda, Murole wa 8 (with M R Madiba and F K Maselesele), 1992; Gondo la Tshivenda, Murole wa 9 (with M R Madiba), 1992; Gondo la Tshivenda, Murole wa 10 (with M R Madiba), 1992. Address: PO Box 2, Vhufuli, Venda, Southern Africa.

MAUPIN Armistead. Partner, Terry Anderson. Publications: Tales of the City; More Tales of the City; Further Tales of the City; Babycakes; Significant Others; Sure of You; Maybe the Man. Address: c/o Amanda Urban ICM, 40 W 57th Street, New York, NY 10019, USA.

MAVOR Elizabeth (Osborne), b. 17 Dec 1927, Glasgow, Scotland. Education: St Andrews, 1940-45; St Leonard's and St Anne's College, Oxford, England, 1947-50. Publications: Summer in the Greenhouse, 1959; The Temple of Flora, 1961; The Virgin Mistress: A Biography of the Duchess of Kingston (in US as The Virgin Mistress: A Study in Survival: The Life of the Duchess of Kingston), 1964; The Redoubt, 1967; The Ladies of Llangollen: A Study in Romantic Friendship, 1971; A Green Equinox, 1973; Life with the Ladies of Llangollen, 1984; The Grand Tour of William Beckford, 1986; The White Solitaire, 1988; The American Journals of Fanny Kemble, 1990; The Grand Tours of Katherine Wilmot, France 1801-3 and Russia 1805-7, 1992; The Captain's Wife, The South American Journals of Maria Graham 1821-23, 1993. Address: Curtis Brown Ltd, 28-29 Haymarket, London SW1Y 4SP, England.

MAXWELL Glyn Meurig, b. 7 Nov 1962, Welwyn Garden City, Hertfordshire, England. Writer. Education: Worcester College, Oxford, 1982-85; BA (Hons) 1st Class, English, Oxford, 1985; MA, Creative Writing, Boston University, USA, 1988. Publications: Tale of the Mayor's Son, poems, 1990; Out of the Rain, poems, 1992; Gnyss the Magnificent, verse-plays, 1993. Contributions to: Reviews to Independent; Times Literary Supplement; Vogue; Poetry Review; Verse; Poems to Times Literary Supplement; LRB; Sunday Times; Spectator; Independent; Atlantic Monthly; Partisan Review; Verse; The New Yorker. Honours: Poetry Book Society Choice, summer 1990; Shortlisted, John Llewellyn Rhys Memorial Prize, 1991; Poetry Book Society Recommendation, summer 1992; Eric Gregory Award, 1992; Somerset Maugham Travel Prize. Memberships: PEN; Poetry Society. Address: c/o Bloodaxe Books, PO Box 1SN, Newcastle-upon-Tyne NE99 1SN, England.

MAXWELL Gordon Stirling, b. 21 Mar 1938, Edinburgh, Scotland. Archaeologist. m. Kathleen Mary King, 29 July 1961, 2 daughters. Education: MA (Hons), St Andrews. Appointments: Curatorial Officer, Royal Commission for Ancient and Historical Monuments, Scotland, 1964-. Publications: The Impact of Aerial Reconnaissance on Archaeology (editor), 1983; Rome's Northwest Frontier, the Antonine Wall, 1983; The Romans in Scotland, 1989; A Battle Lost: Romans and Caledonians at Mons Graupius, 1990. Contributions to: Britannia; Proceedings of the Society of Antiquaries of Scotland; Glasgow Archaeological Journal. Memberships: Fellow, Royal Society of Arts; Fellow, Society of Antiquaries of London; Fellow, Society of Antiquaries of Scotland. Address: Micklegarth, 72a High Street, Aberdour, Fife KY3 0SW, Scotland.

MAXWELL Patricia Anne (Jennifer Blake, Maxine Patrick, Patricia Ponder, Elizabeth Trehearne), b. 9 Mar 1942, Louisiana, USA. Author. m. Jerry R Maxwell, 1 Aug 1957, 2 sons, 2 daughters. Appointments: Writer-in-Residence, University of Northeastern Louisiana. Publications: Over 40 novels including: Love's Wild Desire, 1977; Tender Betrayal, 1979; The Storm and the Splendor, 1979; Golden Fancy, 1980; Embrace and Conquer, 1981; Royal Seduction, 1983; Surrender in Moonlight, 1984; Midnight Waltz, 1985; Fierce Eden, 1985; Royal Passion, 1986; Prisoner of Desire, 1986; Louisiana Dawn, 1987; Southern Rapture, 1987; Perfume of Paradise, 1988; Love and Smoke, 1989; Spanish Serenade, 1990; Shameless, 1994. Honours: Historical Romance Author of the Year, 1985. Address: Route 1, Box 133, Quitman, LA 71268, USA.

MAXWELL William, b. Lincoln, Illinois, USA. Appointments: Former Fiction Editor, New Yorker; President, National Institute for Arts and Letters, 1969-72. Publications: novels, short stories, autobiographical memoirs, children's book, including: Bright Center of Heaven, 1934; The Folded Leaf, 1945; Time Will Darken It, 1948; The Chateau, 1961; The Old Man At the Railroad Crossing and Other Stories, 1966; Ancestors, 1971; Over By the River and Other Stories, 1977; So Long, See You Tomorrow, 1980; The Outermost Dream, 1989; Billy Dyer and Other Stories, 1992. Honours: Brandeis Creative Arts Medal; American Book Award; Howells Medal, American Academy

of Arts and Letters. Address: c/o The New Yorker, 25 West 43rd Street, New York, NY 10036, USA.

MAY Beatrice. See: **ASTLEY Thea.**

MAY Derwent James, b. 29 Apr 1930, Eastbourne, Sussex, England. Author; Journalist. m. Yolanta Izabella Sypniewska, 1 son, 1 daughter. Education: Lincoln College, Oxford, 1949-52; MA (Oxon). Appointments: Theatre and Film Critic, Continental Daily Mail, Paris, France, 1952-53; Lecturer in English, University of Indonesia, 1955-58; Senior Lecturer in English, Universities of Lodz and Warsaw, Poland, 1959-63; Chief Leader Writer, Times Literary Supplement, 1963-65; Literary Editor, The Listener, 1965-86; Literary and Arts Editor, Sunday Telegraph, 1986-90; Literary and Arts Editor, The European, 1990-91; European Arts Editor, The Times, 1992-. Publications: Novels: The Professionals, 1964; Dear Parson, 1969; The Laughter in Djakarta, 1973; A Revenger's Comedy, 1979; Non-fiction: Proust, 1983; The Times Nature Diary, 1983; Hannah Arendt, 1986; The New Times Nature Diary, 1993. Contributions to: Encounter; Hudson Review. Honours: Member, Booker Prize Jury, 1978; Hawthornden Prize Committee, 1987-. Membership: Beefsteak Club. Address: 201 Albany Street, London NW1, England.

MAY Gita, b. 16 Sept 1929, Brussels, Belgium. Professor of French. m. Irving May, 21 Dec 1847. Education: BA, Hunter College, New York, USA, 1953; MA, 1954, PhD, 1957, Columbia University. Appointments include: Professor of French, Columbia University, New York City, USA; Chair, Gottschalk Prize Committee, American Society for Eighteenth-Century Studies, 1979; Member, Executive Committee, Division on European Literary Relations, Modern Language Association of America, 1981-85; Department Chair, Columbia University, 1983-92; Elected to Academy of Literary Studies, 1986. Publications: Diderot et Baudelaire, critiques d'art, 1957; Diderot Studies III (edited with O Fellows), 1961; De Jean-Jacques Rousseau à Madame Roland: Essai sur la sensibilité préromantique et révolutionaire, 1964; Madame Roland and the Age of Revolution, 1970; Stendhal and the Age of Napoleon, 1977; Critical edition of Diderot's Essais sur la peinture, vol XIV for edition of complete works, 1984, paperback, 1984. Contributions to: Modern Language Association of America publications; French Review; Romanic Review; Stendhal Club; Many books including sections on Diderot and George Sand in European Writers. Honours: Hunter College Award, Outstanding Achievement, 1963; Guggenheim Fellow, 1964; Chevalier, Ordre des Palmes Académiques, 1968; Senior Fellow, National Endowment for the Humanities, 1971; Van Amringe Distinguished Book Award for Madame Roland and the Age of Revolution, Columbia University, 1971. Memberships: Modern Language Association of America, Executive Council 1980-83; American Society of Eighteenth Century Studies, President 1985-86; Past Member, Editorial Boards: Romanic Review; French Review; Eighteenth-Century Studies. Address: Department of French, Columbia University, 516 Philosophy Hall, New York, NY 10027, USA.

MAY Julian, b. 10 July 1931, Chicago, USA. Writer. m. Thaddeus e dikty, 1953, 2 s, 1 d. Publications: The Many Colored Land, 1981; The Golden Torc, 1982; The Nonborn King, 1983; The Adversary, 1984; Intervention, 1987; Black Trillium, 1990; Jack the Bodiless, 1991; 254 other books; Blood Trillium, 1992; Diamond Mask, 1994. Literary Agent: Scovil, Chichak, Galen, NY, USA. Address: Box 851 Mercer Island, WA 98040, USA.

MAY Naomi Young, b. 27 Mar 1934, Glasgow, Scotland. Novelist; Journalist; Painter. m. Nigel May, 3 Oct 1964, 2 sons, 1 daughter. Education: Slade School of Fine Art, London, England, 1953-56; Diploma, Fine Art, University of London. Publications: At Home, 1969, radio adaptation, 1987; The Adventurer, 1970; Troubles, 1976. Contributions to: Short stories to anthologies: New Writing and Writers; Rapunzel laas dein Haar herunter, in German translation; Also to magazines: Nova; London Review of Books; Encounter; PN Review; Woman's Realm; Articles mostly on positive aspects of life in Northern Ireland to: The Daily Telegraph; The Times; The Independent; The Observer; New Statesman and Society. Honours: History of Art Prize, Slade School of Fine Art. Membership: PEN. Address: 6 Lion Gate Gardens, Richmond, Surrey TW9 2DF, England.

MAY Robin (Robert) Stephen May, b. 26 Dec 1929, Deal, Kent, England. Writer. 2 sons, 1 daughter. Education: Bradfield College, 1943-48; Central School of Speech and Drama, 1950-53. Publications: Operamania, 1986; Theatremania, 1967; Wit of the Theatre, 1969;

Wolfe's Army, 1974; Who Was Shakespeare? 1974; The Gold Rushes, 1977; History of the American West, 1984; History of the Theatre, 1986; A Guide to the Opera, 1987. Contributions to: Miscellaneous magazines for young people. Membership: Society of Authors. Literary Agent: Rupert Crew Ltd, Kings Mews, London WC1, England. Address: 23 Malcolm Road, London SW19 4AS, England.

MAY Stephen James, (Julian Poole), b. 10 Sept 1946, Toronto, Canada. College Professor and Advisor; Educator; Novelist; Essayist; Historian; Critic. m. Caroline C May, 13 Oct 1972. Education: BA 1975, MA 1977, California State University, Los Angeles, USA; DLitt, International University, Bombay, India, 1992. Publications: Pilgrimage, 1987; Fire from the Skies, 1990; Footloose on the Santa Fe Trail, 1992; A Land Observed, 1993; Zane Grey: The Making of a Legend, 1993. Contributions to: Denver Post; Frontier Rocky Mountain News; Southwest Art; Artists of the Rockies; National Geographic. Memberships: Colorado Authors League; World Literary Academy. Literary Agent, Carl Brandt, New York City, USA. Address: 96 Hillside Terrace, Craig, CO 81625, USA.

MAYER Gerda, b. 9 June 1927, Carlsbad, Czechoslovakia. British Citizen. Poet. m. Adolf Mayer, 1949. Education: BA, Bedford College, London, 1963. Publications: Oddments, 1970; Gerda Mayer's Library Folder, 1972; Treble Poets 2, 1975; The Knockabourt Show, 1978; Monkey on the Analyst's Couch, 1980; The Candy Floss Tree, 1984; March Postman, 1985; A Heartache of Grass, 1988; Editor, Poet Tree Centaur: A Walthamstow Group Anthology, 1973. Address: 12 Margaret Ave, London E4 7NP, England.

MAYER Robert, b. 24 Feb 1939, Bronx, New York, USA. Writer. m. La Donna Cocilovo, 24 Feb 1989, 1 stepdaughter. Education: BA, City College of New York, 1959; MS, Journalism, Columbia University, 1960. Appointments: Reporter, Columnist, Newsday, 1961-71; Managing Editor, Santa Fe Reporter, 1988-90. Publications: Superfolks, 1977; The Execution, 1979; Midge and Decker, 1982; The Dreams of Ada, 1987; I, JFK, 1989; Sweet Salt, 1984; The Grace of Shortstops, 1984; The Search, 1986. Contributions to: Vanity Fair; New York Magazine; Travel and Leisure; Rocky Mountain Magazine; New Mexico Magazine; Santa Fe Reporter; Newsday. Honours: National Headliner Award, 1968; Mike Berger Award, 1969, 1971; Nominee, Edgar Allen Poe Award, 1988. Literary Agent: Philip Spitzer, New York, USA. Address: 135 Cedar Street, Santa Fe, NM 87501, USA.

MAYER Wolf, b. 23 June 1934, Stuttgart, Germany. Retired Senior Lecturer in Geology; now Visiting Scholar at the University of Canberra, 1994-. m. Veronica Mayer, 22 Aug 1959, 2 daughters. Education: BSc, University of New Zealand, 1962; MSc, University of Auckland, 1964; PhD, University of New England, 1972. Publications: Gemstone Identification, in Australian and New Zealand Gemstones, 1972; Gemstone Identification, in Australian Gemstones, 1974; Field Guide to Australian Rocks, Minerals and Gemstones, 1976, 3rd Edition, 1992; The Story of the Building Stones in the New Parliament House in Canberra, 1995. Contributions to: Numerous to professional journals on a variety of geological subjects. Memberships: Geological Society of Australia; History of Earth Science Society. Literary Agent: Curtis Brown, PO Box 19, Paddington, New South Wales 2021, Australia. Address: 22 Bennet St, Spence, ACT 2615, Australia.

MAYER-KOENIG Wolfgang, b. 28 Mar 1946, Vienna, Austria. Author; University Professor. Education: Extraordinary University Professor; Founder, Director, Austria University Cultural Centre; Dr.h.c.f.litt. Appointments: Editor, International Literature Magazine, LOG. Publications: Sichtbare Pavillons, 1968; Stichmarken, 1969; Vorlaeufige Versagung, 1985; Colloqui nella stanza, 1986; Chagrin non dechifre, 1986; In den armen unseres Waerters, 1979; Texte und Bilder, 1972; Karl Kraus als Kritiker, 1975; Robert Musils Moeglichkeitsstil, 1977; Sprache-Politik-Aggression, 1975; Schreibverantwortung, 1986; Ahatalom bonyolult angyala, 1988; A Complicated Angel, 1989; Colloquios Nelcuarto, 1990. Contributions to: Various journals including: Neue Wege-Wien; Literatur und Kritik-Wien; Meanjin Quarterly, Melbourne. Address: Hernalser Guertel 41, A 1170 Vienna, Austria.

MAYHAR Ardath, (John Killdeer, Frank Cannon), b. 20 Feb 1930, TX, USA. Writer; Teacher. m. Joe E Mayhar, 7 June 1958, 2 s. Publications include: How the Gods Wove in Kyrannon, 1979; Soul Singer of Tyrnos, 1981; Golden Dream: A Fuzzy Odyssey, 1982; Runes of the Lyre, 1982; Lords of the Triple Moons, 1983; Exile on Viahil, 1984; The World Ends in Hickory Hollow, 1985; The Saga of

Grittel Sundotha, 1985; Medicine Walk, 1985; Carrots and Miggle, 1986; Bloody Texas Trail, 1988; A Place of Silver Silence, 1987; Trail of the Seahawks, 1987; Feud at Sweet Water Creek, 1987; The Wall, Space & Time, 1987; Texas Gunsmoke, 1988; Monkey Station, 1989; Island in the Swamp, 1993; Blood Kin, 1993; Wilderness Rendezvous, 1992; Towers of the Earth, 1994; Far Horizons, 1994; Hunters of the Plains, 1995. Contributions to: The Twilight Zone Magazine; Isaac Asimovs Science Fiction Magazine; Espionage Magazine; Mike Shaynes Mystery Magazine; Mny Small & Literary Magazines. Honour: Balrog Award, 1985. Memberships: Science Fiction Writers of Am; Western Writers of Am. Literary Agent: Donald Maass. Address: PO Box 180, Chireno, TX 75937, USA.

MAYNARD Christopher, b. 1949, Canada. Editor; Publisher; Writer. Appointments: Editor, Macdonald Education, 1972-74; Editor, Intercontinental Book Productions, Maidenhead, Berkshire, England, 1976-77; Director, The Strip Limited, Maynard and How Publishing, London. Publications: Planet Earth, 1974; Prehistoric World, 1974; Great Men of Science (with Edward Holmes), 1975; The Amazing World of Dinosaurs, 1976; The Real Cowboy (co-author), 1976; The Amazing World of Money, 1977; Scimitar Paperbacks (editor), 1977-78; Economy Guide to Europe (co-author), 1978; New York (with Gail Rebuck), 1978; Indians and Palefaces (with Marianne Gray), 1978; The Razzmataz Gang, 1978; Father Christmas and His Friends, 1979; The First Great Kids Catalogue, 1987. Address: 78 Carlton Mansions, Randolph Avenue, London W9, England.

MAYNARD Fredelle Bruser, b. 9 July 1922, Foam Lake, Canada. Writer; Lecturer; TV Host. div., 2 daughters. Education: BA Honours, University of Manitoba, 1942; MA, University of Toronto, 1943; PhD, Harvard University, USA, 1947. Appointments: Radcliffe Institute Scholar, USA, 1967-69; Writer-in-Residence, University of Illinois, 1974. Publications: Raisins and Almonds, 1972; Guiding Your Child to a More Creative Life, 1973; The Child Care Crisis, 1985; The Tree of Life, 1988. Contributions to: Numerous journals in USA, Canada, England, Australia, South Africa. Honours: Governor General's Medal; Fellowship, Canadian Federation of University Women; Flavelle Fellowship, Harvard; Award for Excellence in Women's Journalism, University of Missouri; Senior Arts Award, Canada Council. Memberships: Phi Beta Kappa, 1947; Periodical Writers Association of Canada; Distinguished Affiliate, Ontario Association of Marriage and Family Therapy; Honorary Member, International Association for Promotion of Humanistic Studies in Gynaecology. Address: 25 Metcalfe Street, Toronto, Ontario, Canada M4X 1R5.

MAYNE Richard (John), b. 2 Apr 1926, London, England. Writer; Editor; Broadcaster. m. Jocelyn Mudie Ferguson, 2 daughters. Education: MA, PhD, Trinity College, Cambridge, 1947-53. Appointments: Rome Correspondent, New Statesman, 1953-54; Official of the European Community, Luxembourg and Brussels, 1956-1963; Personal Assistant to Jean Monnet, Paris, 1963-1966; Visiting Professor, University of Chicago, 1970; Director of the Federal Trust, London, 1971-73; Head of UK Offices of the European Commission, London, 1973-79; Film Critic, Sunday Telegraph, London, 1987-89; Film Critic, The European, 1990-; Paris Correspondent, 1963-73, Co-editor, 1985-90, Encounter. Publications: The Community of Europe, 1962; The Institutions of the European Community, 1968; The Recovery of Europe, 1970; The Europeans, 1972; Europe Tomorrow (ed), 1972; The New Atlantic Challenge (ed), 1975; The Memoirs of Jean Monnet (translation), 1978; Postwar: The Dawn of Today's Europe, 1983; Western Europe: A Handbook (ed), 1987; Federal Union: The Pioneers (with John Pinder), 1990; Europe: A History of its People (translation), 1990; History of Europe (translation), 1993; A History of Civilizations (translation), 1994. Contributions to: Numerous in UK, USA, France and Germany. Honour: Scott-Moncrief Prize for Translation from French, 1978. Memberships: Society of Authors; Royal Institute of International Affairs; Council Member, Federal Trust for Education & Research; Franco-British Council. Address: Albany Cottage, 24 Park Village East, Regent's Park, London NW1 7PZ, England.

MAYNE Seymour, b. 18 May 1944, Montreal, Canada. Poet; Editor; Translator. Education: BA, McGill University, 1965; MA, 1966; PhD, University of British Columbia, 1972. Appointments: Managing Editor, Very Stone House, 1966-69, Editor, Ingluvin Publications, 1970-73; Editor, Mosaic Press, 1974-82. Publications: Mouth, 1970; Name, 1975; Diaporas, 1977; The Impossible Promised Land, 1981; Vanguard of Dreams, 1984; Essential Words, 1985; Children of Abel,

1986; Simple Ceremony, 1990; Killing Time, 1992; Locust of Silence, 1993. Honours: Chester Macnaghten First Prize; J I Segal Prize; York Poetry Workshop Award; Am Literary Translators Association Poetry Award. Memberships: PEN; AM Klein Research & Publications Committee. Address: Dept of English, University of Ottawa, Ottawa, Ontario, Canada, KIN 6N5.

MAYNE William, b. 16 Mar 1928. Writer. Appointments: Lecturer, Creative Writing, Deakin University, Geelong, Australia, 1976, 1977. Publications: Published about 90 stories for children and young people, 1953-. Honours: Library Association's Carnegie Medal for Best Children's Book of the Year (1956), 1957; Guardian Award for Children's Fiction, 1993. Memberships: Fellow, Creative Writing, Rolle College, Exmouth, 1979-80. Address: c/o David Higham Associates, 5-8 Lower John Street, Golden Square, London W1R 4HA, England.

MAYOTTE Judith A (Moberly), b. 25 Jan 1937, Wichita, Kansas, USA. Author; Television Producer; Refugee Advocate; Adviser. m. Jack Parnell Mayotte, 10 June 1972 (dec. 9 Sept 1975). Education: BA, Mundelein College, Chicago; MA, PhD, Marquette University, Milwaukee, Wisconsin, 1976. Appointments: Special Adviser, US Department of State, Washington, District of Columbia; Producer, Writer, many TV programmes including Portrait of America series, WTBS (Turner Broadcasting). Publications: Disposable People: The Plight of Refugees, 1992. Contributions to: Journal of International Affairs, Columbia University, 1993; Numerous popular journals and newspapers; Maryknoll Magazine. Honours: Emmy, 1985; Mickey Leland Award, Refugee Voices, 1994; All University Alumni Merit Award for Professional Achievement, Marquette University, 1994; Honorary Doctor of Humanities, Seattle University, 1994; Annual Award, Refugees International, 1994. Memberships: Chairwoman, Women's Commission for Refugee Women and Children; Board of Directors, International Rescue Committee; Board of Directors, Refugees International; Senior Fellow, Refugee Policy Group; International Women's Media Foundation. Address: 1275 25th Street NW, Washington, DC 20037, USA.

MAYRÖCKER Friederike, b. 20 Dec 1924, Vienna, Austria. Writer; Poetess. Publications include: More than 50 books of poetry, children's books, novels, prose, radio plays, most recent being: Reise durch die Nacht, 1984; Das Herzzerreiszende der Dinge, 1985; Winterglück, 1986; Magische Blätter I, II, III, IV, 1983 and 1987; Stilleben, Das Besessene Alter; Veritas, 1993; Lection, 1994. Contributions include: Numerous articles in literary journals and magazines since 1946. Roswitha-von-Gandersheim-Preis, 1982; Anton-Wildgans-Preis, 1982; Grosser Österreichischer Staatspreis, 1982; Literaturpreis des Südwestfunk, 1985; Hauptpreis fur Literatur der Deutschen Industrie, 1989; Friedrich-Hölderlin Preis, 1993; Manuskripte, Preis, 1994. Memberships: Österreichischer Kunstsenat Wien; Kurie für Wissenschaft und Kunst; Akademie der Künste Berlin-West; Internationales Künstlergremium; Grazer Autorenversammlung; Deutsche Akademie für Sprache und Dichtung Darmstadt; Forum Stadtpark; Graz. Address: Zentagasse 16/40, A-1050 Wien, Austria.

MAYSON Marina. See: ROGERS Rosemary.

MAZER Norma Fox, b. 15 May 1931, NY, USA. m. Harry Mazer, 12 Feb 1950, 1 s, 3 d. Publications include: I Trissy, 1971; A Figure of Speech, 1973; Saturday, The Twelfth of October, 1975; Dear Bill, Remember me, 1976; The Solid Gold Kid, 1977; Up in Seth's Room, 1979; Mrs Fish, Ape and Me and the Dump Queen, 1980; Taking Terri Mueller, 1981; When We First Met, 1982; Summer Girls, Love Boys, and Other Stories, 1982; Someone To Love, 1983; Supergirl, 1984; Downtown, 1984; A My Name is Ami, 1986; Three Sisters, 1986; B My Name is Bunny, 1987; After the Rain, 1987; Silver, 1988; Heartbeat, 1989; Babyface, 1989; C, My Name is Cal, 1990; D, My Name is Danita, 1991; Bright Days, Stupid Nights, 1992; E My Name is Emily, 1991; Out of Control, 1993. Contributions to: English Journal; Alan Review; The Writer; Signal; Writing; Redbook; Playgirl; Voice; Ingeune. Literary Agent: Elaine Markson literary Agency, 44 Greenwich Avenue, NY 10011, USA. Address: Brown Gulf Road, Jamesville, NY 13078, USA.

MAZLISH Bruce, b. 15 Sept 1923, NY, USA. Historian. Education: BA, Columbia College, 1944; MA, 1946, PhD, 1955, Columbia University. Publications include: The Western Intellectual Tradition, 1960; In Search of Nixon, 1972; Kissinger: The European Mind in American Policy, 1972; The Revolutionary Ascetic, 1976; The

Meaning of Karl Marx, 1984; A New Science, 1989; The Leader, The Led and the Psyche, 1990; The Fourth Discontinuity, 1993; Conceptualizing Global History, 1993. Contributions to: Various Journals & Magazines. Honours: Fellow, Am Academy of Arts & Science, 1967; Clement Staff Essay Award, 1968; The Toynbee Prize, 1986-87. Address: 11 Lowell Street, Cambridge, MA, 02138, USA.

MAZUMDAR Maxim William, b. 27 Jan 1953, Bombay, India. Actor; Playwright. m. 16 Aug 1984. Education: BA, Loyola College, USA, 1972; DipEd, McGill University, Canada, 1973; MA, City University of New York, 1986. Appointments include: Head, Theatre Programme, Acadia University, 1985; Performance Studies, Memramcook School of Performing Arts, 1987; Artistic Director, Stephenville Festival, Stephenville, Newfoundland. Publications: Oscar Remembered, 1978; Rimbaud, 1979; Dance for Gods, 1980; Conversations with Diaghilev, Nijinsky, 1980; Invitation to the Dance, 1981; Tennessee and Me, 1983; Unholy Trinity, 1986; Journeys, 1987. Contributions to: Various journals and magazines. Honours: Nominee, ACTRA Award, 1976; Anik Award for CBC TV Script, The Fun of Being with Oscar, 1977; Winner, Canada Council Project Award, 1987. Memberships: Dramatists Guild, 1981; Playwrights Union of Canada, 1987; Canadian Actors Equity, Advisory Board, Atlantic Region. Address: c/o The Stephenville Festival, Box 282, Stephenville, Newfoundland, Canada A2N 2Z4.

MAZUR Bridget, b. 9 Jan 1958, Buffalo, New York, USA. Writer. m. Christopher Mazur, 1 Aug 1981, 1 son, 1 daughter. Education: BA, Medical Technology, State University of New York, 1980; MPH, University of California, 1981; MFA, Writing, Vermont College, 1990. Appointments: Instructor, Fiction and Non-Fiction Writing, Lebanon College, 1990-; Associate Editor, AIDS and Society: An International Research and Policy Bulletin. Publications: Our Lady of the Keyboard, 1989; The Problems and Pitfalls of Writing about Sex, 1989; A Woman's Place is Intuition, 1990; The Art of Baking, The Politics of Love, 1991; The Eye of the Needle, 1991; Atlas's Revenge, 1992. Honours: Fellowship, Vermont Council on the Arts, 1992. Membership: Poets and Writers. Address: PO Box 656, Norwich, VT 05055, USA.

MAZZARO Jerome Louis, b. 25 Nov 1934, Detroit, MI, USA. College Professor; Freelance Writer. Education: AB, Wayne State Univerity, 1954; MA, University of IA, 1956; PhD, Wayne State University, 1963. Appointments: Editor, Fresco, 1959-60, Modern Poetry Studies, 1970-78, Poetry Review, 1965-66; Contributing Editor, Salmagundi, 1967-, American Poetry Review, 1972-, Italian Americana, 1974-88. Publications include: Poetic Themes of Robert Lowell, 1965; Changing the Windows, 1966; Transformations in the Renaissance English Lyric, 1970; William Carlos Williams, 1973; Figure of Dante, 1981; Caves of Love, 1985; Rubbings, 1985; Juvenals Satires; Postmodern American Poetry. Contributions to: Numerous Journals. Honours: John Simon Guggenheim Memorial Fellowship, 1964-65; Hadley Fellowship, 1979-80. Memberships: Dante Society of America. Address: 147 Capen Building, Buffalo, NY 14226, USA.

MBURUMBA Kerina, b. 6 June 1932, Tsumeb, Namibia. Professor; Member of Parliament. m. Jane M Miller, 1957, 2 sons, 2 daughters. Education: BA, Lincoln University, Oxford, Pennsylvania, USA, 1957; Legal courses, American Extension School of Law, Chicago Correspondence School, 1953-57; Graduate courses, Graduate Faculty, New School for Social Research, 1957-59. Appointments include: Diplomatic Attaché of Republic of Liberia and Ethiopia, International Court of Justice, 1960-63; Adjunct Assistant Professor, School of Education, 1968-70, Associate Professor, Afro-American Studies, 1970-71, Associate Professor, Africana Studies Department, 1972-75, Brooklyn College, City University of New York, USA; Visiting Professor, Livingston College, Rutgers University, 1970-71; Director of Communications, Namibia Foundation, Namibia, 1976-78; Member, Constituent Assembly, Namibia; Member, National Assembly of Namibia, 1990-; Consultant; Lecturer. Publications include: Malcom X: The Apostle of Defiance, An African View (edited with H Newman), 1969; The Political History of Namibia 1884-1972, 1979; Namibia, The Making of a Nation. Contributions to: Ghanaian Times; The New African; Africa South; Egyptian Review. Honours: PhD (honoris causa), Political Science, Padjajaran University, Bandung, Indonesia, 1962. Address: PO Box 24861, Windhoek, Namibia, South West Africa.

MCADAM Douglas John, b. 31 Aug 1951, Pasadena, California, USA. Professor of Sociology. m. Tracy Lynn Stevens, 20 Feb 1988. Education: BA, Occidental College, Los Angeles, California, 1963; MA.

1977, PhD, 1979, State University of New York, Stony Brook. Publications: Politics of Privacy, 1980; Political Process and the Development of Black Insurgency 1930-1970, 1982; Freedom Summer, 1988. Contributions: Numerous articles to American Journal of Sociology and American Sociological Review. Honours: Finalist, Sorokin Annual Award for Best Book in Sociology, 1989. Membership: American Sociological Association. Address: Department of Sociology, University of Arizona, Tucson, AZ 85721, USA.

MCALLISTER Casey. See: **BATTIN B W.**

MCAULEY James J(ohn), b. 8 Jan 1936, Dublin, Ireland. Professor; Poet. m. Deirdre O'Sullivan, 1982. Education: University College Dublin; University of Arkansas, Fayetteville. Appointments include: Professor, Eastern Washington University, Cheney, 1978-; Editor, Dolmen Press, Dublin, 1960-66. Director, Eastern Washington University Press, 1993. Publication: Observations, 1960; A New Address, 1965; Draft Balance Sheet, 1970; Home and Away, 1974; After the Blizzard, 1975; The Exile's Recurring Nightmare, 1975; Recital, Poems, 1975-80, 1982; The Exile's Book of Hours, 1982; Coming and Going: New & Selected Poems, 1968-88, 1989; Play, The Revolution, 1966; Libretto Praise, 1981. Honours include: National Endowment for the Arts Grant, 1972; WA Governor's Award, 1976. Address: Eastern Washington University Press, MS#14, Eastern Washington University, Cheney, WA 99004-2431, USA.

MCBAIN Ed. See: **LOMBINO Salvatore A.**

MCBAIN Laurie (Lee), b. 1949, USA. Publications: Devil's Desire, 1975; Moonstruck Madness, 1977; Tears of Gold, 1979; Chance the Winds of Fortune, 1980; Dark Before the Rising Sun, 1982; Wild Bells to the Wild Sky, 1983; When the Splendor Falls, 1985. Address: c/o Harold Ober Associates, 425 Madison Avenue, New York, NY 10017, USA.

MCCAFFREY Anne (Inez), b. 1926, Irish. Appointments: Copywriter, Liberty Music Shops, 1948-50; Copywriter and Executive Secretary, Helen Rubinstein Incorporated, 1950-54. Publications: Restoree, 1967; Dragon-Flight, 1960; Decision at Doona, Alchemy and Academe (ed), 1969; Ship Who Sang, 1970; Dragonquest, The Mark of Merlin, Ring of Fear, 1971; To Ride Pegasus, Cooking Out of This World (ed), 1973; Kilternan Legacy, 1975; Dragonsong, 1976; Dragonsinger, Get Off the Unicorn, 1977; The White Dragon, Dinosaur Planet, 1978; Dragondrums, 1979; The Worlds of Anne McCaffrey, 1981; Crystal Singer, 1982; The Coelura, Moreta Dragonlady of Pern, 1983; Dinosaur Planet Survivors, Stitch in Snow, 1984; Killashandra,. 1985; Nerilka's Story, The Year of the Lucy, 1986; The Carradyne Touch, 1987; Dragons Dawn, 1988; Renegades of Pern, 1989; Sassinak (with Elizabeth Moon), 1990; The Death of Sleep (with Jody-Lynn Nye), 1990; The Rowan, 1990; Pegasus in Flight, 1990; All the Weyrs of Pern, 1992; Crystal Line, 1992; Powers That Be (with Elizabeth Ann Scarborough), 1994. Address: Dragonhold, Newcastle, Co Wicklow, Ireland.

McCALL Christina, Writer; Magazine Writer and Editor. Partner, Stephen Clarkson, 3 d. Appointments: Writer, Editor, Maclean's, Saturday Night. Education: English, University of Toronto. Publications: The Man From Oxbow, 1967; Grits: A Portrait of The Liberal Party, 1982; Trudeau and Our Times (with Stephen Clarkson), 2 vols, 1990, 1993; Trudeau, L'Homme, L'Utopie, L'Histoire, 1990. Honours: President's Medal, Best Magazine Article of the Year, 1970; Southam Fellowship, University of Toronto, 1977; National Magazine Award, gold medal, 1980; Canadian Author's Association Book of The Year, 1982; Governor General's Literary Award for Non-Fiction, 1990. Address: 44 Rosedale Road, Toronto, Ontario, M4W 2P6 Canada.

MCCALL Mabel Bunny, b. 6 Feb 1923, Bronx, New York, USA. Retired. m. T Ross, 31 Oct 1947 (dec. 1973). Publications: Poetry includes: Africa...Sings; The Rape of the Lady Called Harlem; She Walked to the Tune of a Different Drummer; Did I Pass You God?; Carnival Time; A Full Moon in the West Indies; Ode to a Rose of Darker Hue; Sweet Memories of Dixie Land; The Night My Spirit Took Flight; The Chosen One; My Trip to the Holy Land; In These Gardens of Granite, 1989; The Road Not Taken, 1990; Poems for All Seasons, collection of poems, 1991; Poetry in various anthologies including: Ode to a Cockroach, 1985; My Heart Speaks to Thee, 1985; The Heart of a Poet, 1985; The Art of Poetry, 1985; Dreams and Wishes, 1986; Sands of Time, 1986. Contributions to: Unification News; News World; Voice in the Wilderness; Many other journals and magazines. Honours:

Numerous including: Golden Poet Award, World of Poetry, 1985, 1986, 1987, 1988, 1989, 1990, 1991; Award of Merit Certificate, World of Poetry, 1990; 4th Place, Mug Poetry Contest, 1991; Guest Poet, Annual International Festival of Literary and Creative Arts, New York City, 1991. Memberships: World of Poetry; American Poetry Association; International Society of Poets. Address: 41-12 10th Street 4F, Long Island City, NY 11101, USA.

MCCARRY Charles, b. 1930, USA. Appointments: Editor, Lisbon Evening Journal, 1952-55; Reporter, Columnist, Vindicator, OH, 1955-56; Assistant to Secretary of Labor, 1955-58, Central Intelligence Agency, 1958-67; Freelance Journalist, Writer, 1967-83; Editor at Large, National Geographic, WA, 1983-90. Publications: Citizen Nader, 1972; The Miernik Dossier, 1973; The Tears of Autumn, 1975; The Secret Lovers, 1977; Double Eagle, 1979; The Better Angeles, 1979; The Great Southwest, 1981; The Last Supper, 1983; The Bride of the Wilderness, 1988; Second Sight, 1991; Shelleys Heart, 1985. Address: c/o William Morris Agency, 1350 Avenue of the Americas, NY 10019, USA.

MCCARTHY Cormac. Publications: The Orchard Keeper; Outer Dark; Child of God; Suttree; Blood Meridian; The Stonemason: A Play in Five Acts; All the Pretty Horses, 1991; The Crossing, 1994. Honours: National Book Critics Circle Awards, 1991; National Book Award, 1992. Address: 1510 North Brown, El Paso, TX 79902, USA.

MCCARTHY Gary W, b. 23 Jan 1943, California, USA. Western and Historical Novelist. m. Virginia Kurzwell, 14 June 1969, 1 son, 3 daughters. Education: BS, Agriculture, California State University; MS, Economics, University of Nevada. Appointments: Labour Economist, State of Nevada, Carson City, 1970-77; Economist, Copley International Corporation, La Jolla, California, 1977-79; Full-time Writer, 1979-. Publications: The Derby Man, 1976; Showdown at Snakegrass Junction, 1978; The First Sheriff, 1979; Mustang Fever, 1980; The Pony Express War, 1980; Winds of Gold, 1980; Silver Shot, 1981; Explosion at Donner Pass, 1981; The Legend of the Lone Ranger, 1981; North Chase, 1982; Rebel of Bodie, 1982; The Rail Warriors, 1983; Silver Winds, 1983; Wind River, 1984; Powder River, 1985; The Last Buffalo Hunt, 1985; Mando, 1986; The Mustangers, 1987; Transcontinental, 1987; Sodbuster, 1988. Literary Agent: Joseph Elder Agency. Address: 323 Matilija Street No 204, Ojai, CA 93023, USA.

MCCARTHY Rosemary P, b. 21 Oct 1928, Newark, New Jersey, USA. Public Health Nurse; Retiree, NYC Health Dept; Family Historian, Genealogist, Archivist; Artist; Lecturer. Education: BSN, St John's University, 1963; MEd, Columbia University Teachers College, 1973; Catholic University of American Institute of Adult Education, 1980-81; Long Island University, Southampton Campus, Summer, 1986. Publications include: The Family Tree of the Connors-Walsh Family of Kiltimagh, County Mayo, Eire & USA, with Branches in Great Britian & Throughout the World, 1979; Gradma, 1986; Editor, International Family Tree Newsletter, 1979-; International Family Directory, 1983-. Contributions to: O'Lochlainn's Journal of Irish Families; The Irish Genealogical Foundation. Memberships: Various nursing and public health organizations, civic & historical societies. Address: 814A Jefferson Street, Alexandria, VA 22314-4255, USA.

MCCARTHY William E(dward) J(ohn), b. 1925. British. College Fellow; Writer. Appointments: Research Fellow, Nuffield College, 1959-63; Staff Lecturer, Tutor, Industrial Relations, 1964-65, Fellow, Nuffield College and Centre for Management Studies, 1968-, Oxford University; Director of Research, Royal Commission on Trade and Unions and Employers Association, London, 1965-68; Senior Economic Adviser, Department of Employment, 1968-70; Special Adviser, European Economic Commission, 1974-75. Publications: The Future of the Unions, 1962; The Closed Shop in Britain, 1964; The Role of Shop Stewards in British Industrial Relations: A Survey of Existing Information and Research, 1966; Disputes Procedures in Britain (with Arthur Ivor Marsh); Employers' Associations: The Results of Two Studies (with V G Munns), 1967; The Role of Government in Industrial Relations, Shop Stewards and Workshop Relations: The Results of a Study, 1968; Industrial Relations in Britain: A Guide for Management and Unions (editor), 1969; The Reform of Collective Bargaining: A Series of Case Studies, 1971; Trade Unions, 1972, 1985; Coming to Terms with Trade Unions (with A J Collier), 1972; Management by Agreement (with N D Ellis), 1973; Wage Inflation and Wage Leadership (with J F O'Brien and V C Dowd), 1975; Making Whitley Work, 1977; Change in Trade Unions (co-author), 1981; Strikes in Post War Britain (with J W Durcun), 1985; Freedom at Work, 1985; The Future of

Industrial Democracy, 1988. Address: 4 William Orchard Close, Old Headington, Oxford, England.

MCCAULEY Martin, b. 1934, British. Appointments: Senior Lecturer in Soviet and East European Studies 1968-91; Senior Lecturer in Politics, 1991-; Chairman, Dept of Social Sciences, 1993-96, School of Slavonic and East European Studies, University of London, England. Publications: The Russian Revolution and the Soviet State 1917-1921 (ed with trans), 1975, 1980; Khruschchev and the Development of Soviet Agriculture: The Virgin Land Programme 1953-64, 1976; Communist Power in Europe 1944-1949 (ed and co-author), 1977, 1980; Marxism - Leninism in the German Democratic Republic: The Socialist Unity Party (SED), The Stalin File, 1979; The Soviet Union Since 1917, 1981; The Soviet Union, 1917-1991, 2nd edition 1993; Stalin and Stalinism, 2nd edition, 1995; The Origins of the Cold War, 2nd edition, 1995; The Soviet Union since Brezhnev (ed and contrib), 1983; The German Democratic Republic since 1945; Octobrists to Bolsheviks: Imperial Russia 1905-1917, 1984; Leadership and Succession in the Soviet Union, East Europe and China (ed and contrib), 1985; The Origins of the Modern Russian State 1855-81 (with Peter Waldron); The Soviet Union under Gorbachev (ed), 1987; Gorbachev and Perestroika (ed), 1990; Khrushchev, 1991; Directory of Russian MPs (ed), 1993; Longman Biographical Directory of Decision Makers in Russia and the Success States, 1994. Membership: Politics and Society Group; Economic and Social Research Council; East-West Initiative Group, 1991-93. Address: School of Slavonic and East European Studies, Senate House, Malet Street, London WC1E 7HU, England.

MCCGWIRE Michael Kane, b. 9 Dec 1924, Madras, India. m. Helen Jean Scott, 22 Nov 1952, 2 sons, 3 daughters. Education: RNC Dartmouth, 1938-42; University of Wales, BSc, 1967-70. Appointments: Officer, Royal Navy (Commander), 1942-67; Professor, Dalhousie University, 1971-79; Senior Fellow, The Brookings Institution, Washington, DC, 1979-90; Visiting Professor, Global Security Programme, Cambridge University, 1990-93. Publications: Author: Perestroika & Soviet National Security, 1991; Military Objectives & Soviet Foreign Policy, 1987; Editor: Soviet Naval Influence, 1977; Soviet Naval Policy, 1975; Soviet Naval Developments, 1973. Contributions to: Numerous. Honours: Order of the British Empire. Address: Hayes, Durlston, Swanage, Dorset, BH19 2JF, England.

MCCLANE Kenneth A, b. 19 Feb 1951, NY, USA. WEB Du Bois Professor. m. Rochelle Evette Woods, 22 Oct 1983, Education: AB, 1973, MA, 1974, MFA, 1976, Cornell University. Appointments: Visiting Professor, Colby College, 1975-76; Luce Visiting Professor, Williams College, 1983; Associate Professor, Cornell University, 1983-; Full Professor, Cornell University, 1989-93; WEB DuBois Professor, Cornell University; Martin Luther King Visiting Professor, Wayne State University. Publications include: Walls, 1985-90; Take Five, 1971-86; To Hear the River, 1981; Moons and Low Times, 1978; Out Beyond the Bay, 1975; Running Before the Wind, 1972. Contributions to: Antioch Review; Northwest Review; Community Review; Black Scholar. Honours: George Harmon Coxe Award, 1973; Corson Morrison Poetry Prize, 1973; Phi Beta Kappa, 1973; Lamont Poetry Prize Nominee, 1978. Memberships: Poets & Writers; Associated Writing Programme. Address: Dept of English, Rockefeller Hall, Cornell University, Ithaca, NY 14853, USA.

MCCLATCHY J D, b. 1945. Publications: Anne Sexton: the Artist & her Critics, (ed) 1978; Scenes from Another Life: Poems, 1981; Stars Principal: Poems, 1986; Kilim, 1987; Poets On Painters, (ed) 1988; White Paper on Contemporary Poetry, 1989; The Vintage Book of Contemporary American Poetry, (ed) 1990; The Rest of the Way: Poems, 1990. Honours: American Academy & Institute of Arts & Letters, 1991; Fellow, American Academy of Poets, 1991; Melville Cane Award, 1991.

MCCLINTOCK David, b. 4 July 1913, Newcastle upon Tyne, England. Writer. m. Elizabeth Anne Dawson, 6 July 1940, 2 sons, 2 daughters. Education: BA 1934, MA 1940, Trinity College, Cambridge. Publications include: Pocket Guide to Wild Flowers, with R S R Fitter, 1956; Supplement to Pocket Guide to Wild Flowers, 1957; Natural History of the Garden of Buckingham Palace, jointly, 1964; Companion to Flowers, 1966; Guide to the Naming of Plants, 1969, 2nd edition 1980; Wild Flowers of Guernsey, 1975; Supplement, 1987; Wild Flowers of the Channel Islands with J Bichard, 1975; Joshua Gosselin of Guernsey, 1976; The Heather Garden by H van de Laar, 1978, edited and rewritten; Guernsey's Earliest Flora, 1982. Contributions:

Over 900 to over 90 publications, in British Isles and abroad; 25 contributions to other books. Memberships include: Fellow, Linnean Society, Vice President, 1971-74, Editorial Secretary, 1974-78, Council, 1970-78; Botanical Society of the British Isles, President 1971-73; President, Kent Field Club, 1978-80; Royal Horticultural Society, Scientific Cttee, 1978-, Vice Chairman, 1983-93; President, Ray Society, 1980-83; Heather Society, President, 1990-. Address: Bracken Hill, Platt, Sevenoaks, Kent TN15 8JH, England.

MCCLOY Helen, b. 6 June 1904, New York, NY, USA. Foreign Correspondent; Writer. m. divorced, 1 daughter. Education: Sorbonne, Paris. Publications: Through A Glass Darkly, 1950; 2/3 of a Ghost, 1956; Before I Die, 1963; Mr Splitfoot, 1968; A Question of Time, 1971; Question of Time, 1971; Change of Heart, 1973; Sleepwalker, 1974; Minotaur Country, 1975; Changeling Conspiracy, 1976; Imposter, 1977; Smoking Mirror, 1979; Burn This, 1980. Honours: Edgar Allen Poe Awards, for mystery criticism, 1953, for Best Book, 1990.

MCCLURE Gillian Mary, b. 29 Oct 1948, Bradford, England. Author; Illustrator. m. 26 Sept 1971, 3 sons. Education: Horsham High School for Girls; BA, Combined Honours in French, English and History of Art, Bristol University; Teaching Diploma, Moray House. Literary Appointment: Represented UK at Eu Conference held in Turin on Children's Reading, 19th & 20th May 1994. Publications: What's the Time Rory Wolf? 1982; Prickly Pig, 1976; Cat Flap, 1990; What Happened to the Picnic? 1987; Fly Home McDoo, 1979; The Emperor's Singing Bird, 1974; Collaboration with Father Paul Coltman - Tog the Ribber, 1985; Witch Watch, 1989; Tinker Jim, 1992; The Christmas Donkey, 1993; The Illustrations for Norse Myths by Kevin Crossley Holland, 1993; Poems That Go Bump in the Night, 1994. Honours: Tog Ribber, Highly Commended: Smarties Award, 1985, and Highly Commended: Kate Greenaway Award, 1985; Shortlisted for the Smarties Award for Tinker Jim, 1992. Membership: CWIG Society of Authors, Committee Member 1989-; PLR Advisory Committee, 1992. Literary Agent: Curtis Brown. Address: 9 Trafalgar Street, Cambridge CB4 1ET, England.

MCCLURE James, b. 1939. British. Managing Director; Writer. Appointments: Photographer and Teacher, Natal, 1958-63; Journalist, Natal, Edinburgh, Oxford, 1963-69; Deputy Editor, Oxford Times Group, 1971-74; Managing Director, Sabensa Gakula Limited, Oxford, 1975-. Publications: The Steam Pig, 1971; The Caterpillar Cop, 1972; Four and Twenty Virgins, 1973; The Gooseberry Fool, 1974; Snake, 1975; Rogue Eagle, 1976; Killers, 1976; The Sunday Hangman, 1977; The Blood of an Englishman, 1980; Spike Island: Portrait of a British Police Division, 1980; The Artful Egg, 1984; Copworld, 1985. Address: 14 York Road, Headington, Oxford OX3 8NW, England.

MCCOLLEY Diane Laurene Kelsey, b. 9 Feb 1934, Riverside, California, USA. University Professor. m. Robert M McCrilley, 30 Aug 1958, 1 son, 5 daughters. Education: AB, University of California; PhD, University of Illinois. Publications: Miltons Eve; A Gust for Paradise; Others inc. Cambridge Companion of Milton; Medieval and Renaissance Texts and Studies. Contributions to: Milton Studies; Various Journals. Memberships: Milton Society of America; Modern Language Association; Renaissance Society of America. Address: Dept of English, Rutgers, The State University of New Jersey, Camden, NJ 08102, USA.

MCCOLLINS. See: PASZKOWSKI Kazimierz Jan.

MCCONICA James Kelsey, b. 1930, Canadian. Appointments: Instructor 1956-57, Assistant Professor of History 1957-62, University of Saskatchewan, 1976-, Pontifical Institute of Medieval Studies, Toronto; Visiting Fellow 1969-71, 1977, Research Fellow 1978-, All Souls College, Oxford; Associate Director, Center for Medieval Studies, 1973-76; President, University of St Michael's College, Toronto, 1984-; Research Fellow, All Souls College, Oxford, 1990-. Publications: English Humanists and Reformation Politics, 1965; The Correspondence of Erasmus 1515-1517 (ed), volumes III and IV of Collected Works of Erasmus, 1976, 1977; Thomas More: A Short Biography, 1977; The History of the University of Oxford: The Collegiate University, volume 3, 1986; Erasmus, 1991. Honours: Fellow, Royal Society of Canada, 1987; Foreign Member, Royal Belgian Academy. Memberships: American Society for Reformation Research; Renaissance Society of America; Royal Historical Society. Address: All Souls College, Oxford OX1 4AL, England.

MCCONKEY James Rodney, b. 2 Sept 1921, Educator; Writer. m. Gladys Jean Voorhees, 6 May 1944, 3 sons. Education: BA, Cleveland College, 1943; MA, Western Reserve University, 1946; PhD, University of IA, 1953. Appointments: Director, Morehead Writers Workshop, 1951-56; Director, Antioch Seminar, Writing & Publishing, 1957-59; Editorial Staff, Epoch Magazine, 1956-. Publications include: Court of Memory, 1983; The Tree House Confessions, 1979; Crossroads, 1968; The Novels of EM Forster, 1957; Night Stand, 1965; A Journey to Sahalin, 1971; Chekhov and Our Age, 1985; The Structure of Prose, 1963; Kentucky Writing, 1954; Rowan's Progress, 1992; Stories from My Life with the Other Animals, 1993. Contributions to: The New Yorker; Hudson Review; Shenandoah; Am Poetry Review; Yale Review; WA Post Book World. Honours: Saxton Literary Fellowship, 1962; National Endowment for the Arts Essay Award, 1968; Guggenheim Fellowship, 1969; Award in Literature, 1979. Literary Agent: Jane Gelfman, John Farquharson Limited. Address: 402 Aiken road, Trumansburg, NY 14886, USA.

MCCONNELL Will. See: **SNODGRASS W D.**

MCCORMICK John Owen, b. 20 Sept 1918, Thief River Falls, Minnesota, USA. Professor, Comparative Literature. m. Mairi MacInnes, 4 Feb 1954, 3 sons, 1 daughter. Education: BA 1941, MA 1947, University of Minnesota; PhD, Harvard University, 1951. Appointments: Senior Tutor and Teaching Assistant, Harvard University, Cambridge, MS, USA, 1946-51; Lecturer, Salzburg Seminar in American Studies, Austria, 1951-52; Professor of American Studies, Free University of Berlin, 1952-53, 1954-59; Professor of Comparative Literature, 1959-, now Emeritus, Rutgers University, New Brunswick, NJ. Publications: Catastrophe and Imagination, 1957; Versions of Censorship (with Mairi MacInnes), 1962; The Complete Aficionado, 1967; The Middle Distance: A Comparative History of American Imaginative Literature, 1919-1932, 1971; Fiction as Knowledge: The Modern Post-Romantic Novel, 1975; George Santayana: A Biography, 1987. Contributions to: Numerous magazines & journals. Honours: Guggenheim Fellow, 1964-65, 1968-81; Longview Award for Non-Fiction, 1960; Senior Fellow, NEH, 1983-84; American Academy and Institute of Arts and Letters Prize, 1988. Address: Hovingham Lodge, Hovingham, York YO6 4NA, England.

MCCORQUODALE Barbara Hamilton (Dame Barbara Cartland). Writer; Lecturer; Public Speaker. Publications: Over 521 books including: The Explosion of Love, 1980; A Heart is Stolen, 1980; The Power and the Prince, 1980; Free from Fear, 1980; A Song of Love, 1980; Love for Sale, 1980; Little White Doves of Love, 1980; The Perfection of Love, 1980; Lost Laughter, 1980; Punished with Love, 1980; Lucifer and the Angel, 1980; Ola and the Sea Wolf, 1980; The Pride and the Prodigal, 1980; The Goddess and the Gaiety Girl, 1980; Signpost to Love, 1980; Money, Magic and Marriage, 1980; Love in the Moon, 1980; Pride and the Poor Princess, 1980; The Waltz of Hearts, 1980; From Hell to Heaven, 1981; The Kiss of Life, 1981; Afraid, 1981; Dreams Do Come True, 1981; In the Arms of Love, 1981; For All Eternity, 1981; Pure and Untouched, 1981; Count the Stars, 1981; Kneel for Mercy, 1982; Call of the Highlands, 1982; A Miracle in Music, 1982; From Hate to Love, 1983; Lights, Laughter and a Lady, 1983; Diona and a Dalmatian, 1983; Moonlight on the Sphinx, 1984; Bride to a Brigand, 1984; Love Comes West, 1984; A Witch's Spell, 1984; White Lilac, 1984; Miracle for a Madonna, 1984; Royal Punishment, 1985; The Devilish Deception, 1985; Secrets of the Heart, 1985; A Caretaker of Love, 1985; The Devil Defeated, 1985; Love in the Ruins, 1989; The Duke's Dilemma, 1989; Beyond the Stars, 1990; Love Runs In, 1991; A Secret Passage to Love, 1992; A Train to Love, 1992; The Man of Her Dreams, 1993; Captured by Love, 1993; Love or Money, 1993; Danger to the Duke, 1993; The King without a Heart, 1993; A Battle of Love, 1993; Lovers in London, 1993. Honours include: Achiever of the Year Award, National Home Furnishing Association, 1981; Bishop Wright Air Industry Award, 1984; Gold Medal for Achievement, City of Paris, 1988; DBE, 1991. Address: Camfield Place, Hatfield, Hertfordshire, England.

MCCOURT James. Publications: Maurdrew Czgowdiwz, 1975; Kaye Wayfaring in "Avenged": four stories, 1984; Time Remaining, 1993. Contributions to: New Yorker; short stories in published anthologies. Address: c/o Vincent Virga 145 E 22nd St, New York, NY 10003, USA.

MCCRAW Thomas K, b. 1940, USA. Appointments: Newcomen Research Fellow, Harvard University, 1973-74; Assistant Professor, 1970-74; Associate Professor, University of TX, 1974-78; Visiting Associate Professor, 1976-78; Professor, 1978-, Straus Professor, 1989-, Harvard Business School, Boston; Editor, business History Review, 1994-. Publications: Morgan vs Lilienthal: The Feud Within the TVA, 1970; TVA and the Power Fight, 1933-39, 1971; Regulation in Perspective: Historical Essays, 1981; Prophets of Regulation, 1984; America vs Japan, 1986; The Essential Alfred Chandler, 1988. Contributions to: The American Scholar, 1985, 91, 92, 94. Honours: Recipient of Pulitzer Prize, 1985; Thomas Newcomen Book Award, 1985; William P Lyons Masters Essay Award, 1970. Memberships: MA Historical Society; Organisation of American Historians; AM Economic Association; Economic History Association; Business History Conference. Address: Harvard Business School, Soldiers Field, Boston, MA 02163, USA.

MCCREADY Jack. See: **POWELL Talmage.**

MCCRUMB Sharyn Elaine Atwood, b. 26 Feb 1948, Wilmington, North Carolina, USA. Writer. m. David McCrumb, 9 Jan 1982, 1 son, 2 daughters. Education: BA, University of North Carolina, 1970; MA, Virginia Tech, 1987. Publications: The Hangman's Beautiful Daughter; If Ever I Return Pretty Peggy O; Bimbos of the Death Sun; Missing Susan; Highland Laddie Gone; Sick of Shadows; Lovely in Her Bones; Paying the Piper; The Windsor Knot; Zombies of the Gene Pool; MacPherson's Lament. Contributions to: Ellery Queen; Crescent Review; Appalachian Heritage; Yorker; Mystery Scene. Honours: Notable Book, New York Times; Sherwood Anderson Short Story Contest; Best Appalachian Novel Award; Edgar Award; Macavity Award; Agatha Award. Memberships: Mystery Writers of America; Sisters in Crime; Appalachian Writers Association; Whimsey Foundation. Literary Agent: Dominick Abel. Address: Rowan Mountain Inc, PO Box 10111, Blacksburg, VA 24062, USA.

MCCULLAGH Sheila Kathleen, b. 3 Dec 1920, England. Writer. Education: Bedford Froebel College, 1939-42; MA, University of Leeds, 1949. Publications: Pirate Books, 1957-64; Tales and Adventures, 1961; Dragon Books, a series, 1963-70; One, Two, Three and Away, 1964-92; Tim Books, 1974-83; Into New Worlds, 1974; Buccaneers, 1980-84; Hummingbirds, 1976-92; Whizzbang Adventures, 1980; Where Wild Geese Fly, 1981; Puddle Lane, 1985-88; Penguins; Sea Animals; The Big Cats; Caterpillars and Butterflies; How Birds Live; Garden Birds; The Sea Shore, 1992. Honours: MBE, 1987. Membership: Society of Authors. Literary Agent: A P Watt. Address: 27 Royal Crescent, Bath, Avon BA1 2CT, England.

MCCULLOUGH Colleen, b. 1 June 1937, Wellington, New South Wales, Australia. Writer. Former Neurophysiologist. m. Ric Robinson, 1984. Education: Sydney University; Institute of Child Health, London University. Career: Neurophysiologist, 1967-77: Sydney; London and Birmingham, England; Yale University Medical School, New Haven, Connecticut, USA; Settled on Norfolk Island, Oceania, 1980. Publications: Tim (later filmed), 1974; The Thorn Birds (major bestseller, filmed as TV series), 1977; An Indecent Obsession (later filmed), 1981; Cooking with Colleen McCullough and Jean Easthope, 1982; A Creed for the Third Millennium, 1985; The Ladies of Missalonghi, 1987; The First Man in Rome, 1990; The Grass Crown, 1991; Fortune's Favorites, 1993. Honours: Doctor of Letters (honoris causa), Macquarie University, Sydney, 1993. Address: Out Yenna, Norfolk Island, Oceania (via Australia).

MCCULLOUGH David, b. 7 Jul 1933, Pittsburgh, Pennsylvania, USA. Writer. m. Rosalee Ingram Barnes, 18 Dec 1954, 3 s, 2 d. Education: BA, Yale University. Appointments: Advisory Board, Center for the Book, Library of Congress; Member, Harry S Truman Centennial Commission; Senior Contributary Editor, American Heritage; Contributary Editor, Parade. Publications: The Johnstown Flood, 1968; The Great Bridge, 1972; The Path Between the Seas: The Creation of the Panama Canal, 1870-1914, 1977; Mornings on Horseback, 1981; Truman, 1992; editor and contributor to numerous volumes on American History. Contributions include: Audubon; Architectural Forum; American Heritage; Geo; Smithsonian; New Republic; Psychology Today. Address: c/o Historical Sce of Western Pennsylvania - Attention Nina Devlp Dept, 4338 Bigelow Boulevard, Pittsburgh, PA 15213, USA.

MCCULLOUGH Kenneth Douglas, b. 18 July 1943, NY< USA. Writer; Teacher. 1 s. Education: BA, University of Delaware, 1966; MFA, University of IA, 1968. Publications: New and Selected Poems, 1993; Sycamore Oriole, 1991; Travelling Light, 1987; Elegy for Old Anna, 1983; Creosote, 1976; Migrations, 1973; The Easy Wreckage, 1971; New And Selected Poems, 1994. Contributions to: New Letters;

Confluence; Nimrod; Studia Mystica; The Devils Millhoppers; Crab Creek Review; Longhouse; The Devils Millhopper. Honours: Academy of Am Poets Award, 1969; National Endowment for the Arts Fellowship, 1974; Capricorn Book Award, 1985; Pablo Neruda Award, 1989. Memberships: Science Fiction Writers of America; Associated Writing Programmes; National Association of College Academic Advisers; Rocky Mountain Language Association; Rocky Mountain Modern Language Association.

MCCULLY Emily Arnold (Emily Arnold), b. 7 Jan 1939, Galesburg, Illinois, USA. Author; Illustrator. 2 sons. Education: BA, Brown University, 1961; MA, Columbia University, 1964. Publications: A Craving, novel, 1982; Picnic, 1985; Life Drawing, novel, 1986; Mirette on the High Wire, 1992; The Amazing Felix, 1993; Little Kit, or, the Industrious Flea Circus Girl, 1995; The Pirate Queen, 1995. Honours: O'Henry Award Collection, 1977; Caldecott Award, 1993. Memberships: PEN Society; Authors Guild. Literary Agent: Harriet Wasserman Literary Agency, New York City, USA. Address: c/o Harriet Wasserman, 137 E 36th Street, New York, NY 10026, USA.

MCCUNN Ruthanne Lum, b. 21 Feb 1946, San Francisco, CA, USA. Writer. m. Donald H McCunn, 15 June 1965. Education: BA, 1968. Publications: Illustrated History of the Chinese in America, 1979; Thousand Pieces of Gold, 1981; Pie Biter, 1983; Sole Survivor, 1985; Chinese American Portraits, 1988; Chinese Proverbs, 1991; Bibliography of Chinese and Chinese American Resource Materials; Directory of Language Resources; Wooden Fish Songs, 1995. Contributions to: Yihai. Honour: Before Columbus Foundation American Book Award, 1983. Memberships: Chinese Historical Society of Am; Asian Women Union; Am Civil Liberties Union; Chinese for Affirmative Action; Amnesty International. Literary Agent: Peter Ginsberg, Curtis Brown, San Francisco, USA. Address: 1007 Castro Street, San Francisco, CA 94114, USA.

MCCUTCHAN Philip Donald (Robert Conington Galway, Duncan MacNeil, T I G Wigg), b. 13 Oct 1920, Cambridge, England. Author. m. Elizabeth May Ryan, 30 June 1951, 1 son, 1 daughter. Publications include: More than 100 novels, 1957-, including series featuring Commander Shaw; Detective Chief Superintendent Simon Shard; Lieutenant St Vincent Halfhyde RN; Donald Cameron RNVR; Commodore John Mason Kemp, RNR; As Duncan MacNeil, series featuring Captain James Ogilvie of the 114th Highlanders, fighting Indian NW Frontier, 1890's, non-fiction: Tall Ships: The Golden Age of Sail, 1976; Great Yachts, 1979. Honour: Knight of Mark Twain, USA, 1978; Chairman, Crime Writers Association, 1965-66. Address: Myrtle Cottage, 107 Portland Road, Worthing, West Sussex BN11 1QA, England.

MCCUTCHEON Elsie Mary Jackson, b. 6 Apr 1937, Glasgow, Scotland. Author. m. James McCutcheon, 14 July 1962 (dec.), 1 daughter. Education: BA, Glasgow University, 1960; Jordanhill College of Education, 1961. Appointments: English Teacher, Glasgow, 1961-63; Publicity Officer, Norfolk Archaeological Rescue Group, 1976-78; Editor, Newsletter of Friends of the Suffolk Record Office, 1984-91. Publications: Summer of the Zeppelin; The Rat War; Smokescreen; Storm Bird; Twisted Truth. Contributions to: She; Good Housekeeping; Ideal Home; Scotland's Magazine; Scottish Field; Suffolk Fair; Eastern Daily Press. Honours: Runner-up, Guardian Award for Children's Fiction. Memberships: Bury St Edmunds Library Users Group; Writers Guild of Great Britain; Suffolk Local History Council; Suffolk Institute of Archaeology. Literary Agent: Vanessa Hamilton. Address: Wendover, Sharpers Lane, Horringer, Bury St Edmunds, Suffolk IP29 5PS, England.

MCCUTCHEON Hugh (Hugh Davie-Martin, Griselda Wilding), b. 1909. British. Author. Appointment: Town Clerk of Renfrew, Scotland, 1945-74. Publications: Alamein to Tunis, 1946; The Angel of Light, in US as Murder at the Angel, 1951; None Shall Sleep Tonight, 1954; Prey for the Nightingale, 1954; Cover Her Face, 1955; The Long Night Through, 1956; Comes the Blind Fury, 1957; To Dusty Death, 1960; Yet She Must Die, 1961; The Deadly One, 1962; Suddenly in Vienna, 1963; Treasure of the Sun, 1964; The Black Attendant, 1966; Killers Moon, in US as The Moon Was Full, 1967; The Scorpion's Nest, 1968; A Hot Wind from Hell, 1969; Brand for the Burning, 1970; Something Wicked, 1970; Red Sky at Night, 1972; Instrument of Vengeance, 1975; Night Watch, 1978; The Cargo of Death, 1980; As Hugh Davie-Martin: The Girl in My Grave, 1976; The Pearl of Oyster Island, 1977; Spaniard's Leap, 1979; Death's Bright Angel, 1982; As

Griselda Wilding: Promise of Delight, 1988; Beloved Wolf, 1991. Address: 19 Bentinck Drive, Troon, Ayrshire, Scotland.

MCDONALD Forrest, b. 7 Jan 1927, TX, USA. Historian. m. Ellen Shapiro, 1 Aug 1963, 3 s, 2 d. Education: BA, 1949, MA, 1949, PhD, 1955, University of TX. Publications include: Novus Ordo Seclorum, 1985; We the People: The Economic Origins of the Constitution, 1958; Alexander Hamilton: A Biography, 1979; Insull, 1962; E Pluribus Unum, 1965; The Presidency of George Washington, 1974; The Presidency of Thomas Jefferson, 1976; The Phaeton Ride, 1974; The American Presidency: An Intellectual History, 1994. Honours: Guggenheim Fellow, 1962-63; Fraunas Tavern Book Award, 1980; Am Revolution Round Table Book Award, 1986; 16th Jefferson Lecturer in the Humanities, 1987; Ingersoll Prize, 1990; Salvatori Book Award, 1994. Memberships: Philadelphia Society; Am Antiquarian Society. Address: PO Box 155, Coker, A: 35452, USA.

MCDONALD Gregory, b. 1937, USA. Full-time Writer. Appointments: Arts and Humanities Editor, Critic-at-Large, Boston Globe, 1966-73. Publications: Running Scared, 1964; Fletch series, 9 volumes, 1974-86; Flynn series, 3 volumes, 1977-85; Love among the Mashed Potatoes, 1978; Who Took Toby Rinaldi?, 1980; The Education of Gregory McDonald, 1985; Safekeeping, 1985; The Last Laugh (editor), 1986; A World Too Wide, 1987.

MCDONALD Ian (A.), b. 18 Apr 1933, St Augustine, Trinidad. Poet. m. Mary Angela Callender, 1948, 3 s. Education: Queens Royal College, Trinidad, Cambridge University, 1951-55. Appointments include: Director, Theatre Company of Guyana, Georgetown, 1981-; Chair, Demerara Publishers, 1988-. Publications: Selected Poems, 1983; Mercy Ward, 1988; Play, The Tramping Man, 1969; Novel, The Humming Bird Tree, 1969. Honours include: Fellow, Royal Society of Literature, 1970; Guyana National Award, 1987. Address: c/o Guyana Sugar Corporation, 22 Church Str, Georgetown, Guyana.

MCDONALD J O. See: HIBBERD Jean.

MCDONALD Robert Francis, b. 25 Oct 1943, Vancouver, British Columbia, Canada. Writer; Broadcaster. m. Catherine Donna Napier, 28 Aug 1965. Education: BA, 1964; Publications: Pillar and Tinderbox; The Problem of Cyprus; Greece in the 1990s; Greek Privatisation. Contributions to: The World Today; Economist Intelligence Unit Report on Greece and Cyprus. Membership: Commonwealth Journalists Association, London Management Committee. Address: 10 Chelwood Gardens, Richmond, Surrey TW9 4JQ, England.

MCDONALD Walter R(obert), b. 18 July 1934, Lubbock, Texas, USA. Professor of English. m. Carol Ham, 28 Aug 1959, 2 sons, 1 daughter. Education: BA, 1956, MA, 1957, Texas Technological College; PhD, University of Iowa, 1966. Appointments include: Faculties: US Air Force Academy, University of Colorado, Texas Tech University; Currently Paul W Horn Professor of English and Poet-in-Residence, Texas Tech University, Lubbock. Publications: Poetry: Caliban in Blue, 1976; One Thing Leads to Another, 1978; Anything, Anything, 1980; Working Against Time, 1981; Burning the Fence, 1981; Witching on Hardscrabble, 1985; Flying Dutchman, 1987; After the Noise of Saigon, 1988; Rafting the Brazos, 1988; Fiction: A Band of Brothers: Stories of Vietnam, 1989; Night Landings, 1989; The Digs in Escondido Canyon, 1991. Contributions to: Numerous journals and magazines including: Poetry; American Poetry Review; The Atlantic; The New York Review of Books; The Paris Review; The Nation; The Sewanee Review. Honours: Poetry Award, Texas Institute of Letters, 1976, 1985, 1987; George Elliston Poetry Prize, 1987; The Juniper Prize, 1988; Western Heritage Award for Poetry, National Cowboy Hall of Fame, 1990, 1992. Memberships: Past President, Texas Association of Creative Writing Teachers; PEN; Poetry Society of America; Associated Writing Programs; Councillor, The Texas Institute of Letters; Past President Conference of College Teachers of English of Texas. Address: Department of English, Texas Tech University, Lubbock, TX 79409, USA.

MCDOUGALL Bonnie Suzanne, b. 12 Mar 1941, Sydney, Australia. Professor. m. H Anders Hansson, 1980, 1 son. Education: BA, University of Sydney, 1965; MA, 1967; PhD, 1970. Publications: Introduction of Western Literary Theories into China; Mao Zedong's Talks at the Yanan Conference; Popular Chinese Literature and Performing Arts; The Yellow Earth: A Film by Chen Kaige; The August Sleepwalker; Old Snow; Brocade Valley. Contributions to: Journal of the Oriental Society of Australia; Modern Chinese Literature;

Renditions; Contemporary China; Stand; Grand Street; New Directions. Memberships: PEN; Edgar Wallace Society; British Association of Chinese Studies; Universities' China Committee in London; Amnesty International. Address: Dept of East Asian Studies, University of Edinburgh, 8 Buccleuch Place, Edinburgh EH8 9LW, Scotland.

MCDOUGALL Walter A(llan), b. 3 Dec 1946, Washington, District of Columbia, USA. Professor of History; Writer. m. Elizabeth Swoope, 8 Aug 1970, div. 1979. Education: BA cum laude, Amherst College, 1968; MA, 1971, PhD, 1974, University of Chicago. Appointments: Assistant Professor, 1975-83, Associate Professor, 1983-87, Professor of History, 1987-, University of California, Berkeley; Vestryman at St Peter's Episcopal Church. Publications include: France's Rhineland Diplomacy 1914-1924: The Last Bid for a Balance of Power in Europe, adaptation of PhD thesis, 1978; The Grenada Papers (edited with Paul Seabury), 1984; Social Sciences and Space Exploration: New Directions for University Instruction (contributor), 1984; ...the Heavens and the Earth: A Political History of the Space Age, 1985; Let the Sea Make a Noise, 1993. Contributions to: Numerous articles and reviews to periodicals. Honours include: Finalist, American Book Award for Non-Fiction, Association of American Publishers, 1985, Winner, Pulitzer Prize, History, Columbia University Graduate School of Journalism, 1986, both for ...the Heavens and the Earth; Visiting Scholar, Hoover Institution, 1986; Selected by Insight, America's Ten Best College Professors, 1987; Dexter Prize for Best Book, Society for the History of Technology, 1987. Memberships: American Church Union; Pumpkin Papers Irregulars; Delta Kappa Epsilon. Address: Department of History, University of California, Berkeley, CA 94720, USA.

MCDOWALL David Buchanan, b. 14 Apr 1945, London, England. Writer. m. 19 Apr 1975, 2 sons. Education: St Johns College, Oxford, MA. Publications: Palestine & Israel: The Uprising and Beyond; The Kurds: A Nation Denied; An Illustrated History of Britain; Britain in Close Up; Other inc. The Spanish Armada; The Kurds; Europe and the Arabs: Discord or Symbiosis?; Lebanon: A Conflict of Minorities; A Modern History of the Kurds, 1994; Scapegoat: The Palestinian Ordeal, 1994. Honours: The Other Award. Address: 31 Cambrian Road, Richmond, Surrey TW0 8JQ, England.

MCDOWELL Edwin S, b. 13 May 1935, Somers Point, NJ, USA. Journalist. m. Sathie Akimoto, 7 July 1973, 1 s, 2 d. Education: BS, Temple University, 1959. Publications: Novels, The Lost World, 1988; To Keep Our Honor Clean, 1980; Three Cheers and a Tiger, 1966. Memberships: Authors Guild. Address: c/o New York Times, 229 W 43rd Street, New York, NY 10036, USA.

MCDOWELL Michael (Nathan Aldyne, Axel Young), b. 1950, USA. Author. Publications: The Amulet, 1979; Cold Moon over Babylon, 1980; Gilded Needles, 1980; The Elementals, 1981; Katie, 1982; Cobalt, 1982; Wicked Stepmother, 1983; Blackwater, 6 vols, 1983; Slate, 1984; Toplin, 1985; Jack and Susan, 3 vols, 1985-87; With Dennis Schuetz: Vermilion (as Nathan Aldyne), 1980; Blood Rubies (as Axel Young), 1981. Address: c/o The Otte Company, 6 Goden Street, Belmont, MA 02178, USA.

MCELROY Colleen J, b. 30 Oct 1935, St Louis, MI, USA. Teacher; Writer, div, 1 s, 1 d. Education: BS, 1958, MS, 1963, KS State University; PhD, University of WA, 1973. Appointments: Professor, University of WA, 1973-; Editor, Dark Waters, 1973-79. Publications include: Queen of the Ebony Isles, 1984; Lie and Say You Love Mr, 1981; Winters Without Snow, 1979; Music From Home, 1976; Jesus and Fat Tuesday, 1987; Follow the Drinking Groud, 1987; The Halls of Montezuma, The New Voice, 1979; Driving Under the Cardboard Pines; What Madness Brought Me Here, 1990. Contributions to: 300 Poems and Short Stories in Various Journals. Address: Creative Writing Program GN30, Dept of English, University of WA, Seattle, WA 98195, USA.

MCELROY Joseph (Prince), b. 1930, USA. Author. Publications: A Smuggler's Bible, 1966; Hind's Kidnap, 1969; Ancient History, 1971; Lookout Cartridge, 1974; Plus, 1977; Ship Rock, 1980; Women and Men, 1987. Address: c/o Georges Borchardt, 136 E 57th Street, New york, NY 10022, USA.

MCELROYD Lee. See: KELTON Elmer Stephen.

MCEVEDY Colin (Peter), b. 1930. Writer. Publications: The Penguin Atlas of Medieval History, 1961; The Penguin Atlas of Ancient History, 1967; The Atlas World History, 3 vols (with Sarah McEvedy), 1970-73; The Penguin Atlas of Modern History, 1972; Atlas of World Population History (with Richard Jones), 1980; The Penguin Atlas of African History, 1980; The Penguin Atlas of Recent History (Europe since 1815), 1982; The Century World History FactFinder, 1984; Penguin Atlas of North American History, 1988; The New Penguin Atlas of Medieval History, 1992. Contributions to: The Bubonic Plague, Scientific American (vol 256 #2, 1988. Address: 7 Caithness Road, London W14, England.

MCEVOY Marjorie (Gillian Bond, Marjorie Harte), b. York City, England. Novelist. m. William Noel McEvoy, Cramlington, Northumberland, 1 son, 1 daughter. Publications: Doctors in Conflict, 1962; The Grenfell Legacy, 1967; Dusky Cactus, 1969; Echoes from the Past, 1968; Calabrian Summer, 1980; Sleeping Tiger, 1982; Star of Randevi, 1984; Temple Bells, 1985; Camelot Country, 1986; The Black Pearl, 1988. Contributions to: The Caravan; Modern Caravan; various newspapers and magazines. Membership: RNA. Address: 54 Miriam Avenue, Chesterfield, Derbyshire, England.

MCEWAN Ian Russell, b. 21 June 1948, Aldershot, Hampshire, England. Author. m. Penny Allen, 1982, 2 sons, 2 daughters. Education: BA, Honours, English Literature, University of Sussex; MA, University of East Anglia. Publications: Films: The Ploughman's Lunch, 1983; Last Day of Summer, 1984; Books: First Love, Last Rites, 1975; In Between the Sheets, 1978; The Cement Garden, 1978; The Imitation Game, 1981; The Comfort of Strangers, 1981; Or Shall We Die? (oratorio), 1982; The Innocent, 1989; Black Dogs, 1992; The Daydreamer, 1994. Address: c/o Jonathon Cape, 32 Bedford Square, London WC1B 3EL, England.

MCFARLANE James Walter, b. 1920. Writer. Publications: Translator, Knut Hamsun Pan, 1955; Ibsen and the Temper of Norwegian Literature, 1960; The Oxford Ibsen, 8 vols, 1960-77; Discussions of Ibsen, 1962; Thorkild Hansen: Arabia Felix, 1964; North West to Hudson Bay, 1970; Henrik Ibsen: A Critical Anthology, 1970; Modernism: European Literature 1890-1930, 1976; Knut Hamsun: Wayfarers, 1980; Slaves of Love and Other Norwegian Short Stories, 1982; Sigbjosn Obstfelder: A Priest's Diary, 1987; Ibsen and Meaning, 1988; Knut Hamsun, Letters 1879-1898, 1989; Cambridge Companion to Ibsen, 1994. Address: The Croft, Stody, Melton Constable, Norfolk NR24 2EE, England.

MCFEELY William. Publications: Grant: A Biography, 1981; Frederick Douglas,1991; Sapelo's People: A Long Walk into Freedom, 1994. Honours: Pulitzer Prize, 1982; Christopher Award, 1992. Address: Department of History, University of Georgia, Athens, GA 30609-4066, USA.

MCGAHERN John, b. 12 Nov 1934, Leitrim, Ireland. Author. m. Madeline Green, 1973. Education: University College, Dublin. Appointments: Research Fellow, University of Reading, 1968-71; O'Connor Professor, Colgate University, 1969, 1972, 1977, 1979, 1983, 1992; Visiting Fellow, Trinity College, 1988. Publications: The Barracks, 1963; The Dark, 1965; Nightlines, 1970; The Leavetaking, 1975; Getting Through, 1978; The Pornographer, 1979; High Ground, 1985; The Rockingham Shoot, BBC 2, 1987; Amongst Women, 1990; The Collected Stories, 1992. Address: c/o Faber & Faber, 3 Queen Square, London WC1N 3AU, England.

MCGARRITY Mark, (Bartholomew Gill), b. 1943, USA. Author; Freelance Writer. Publications include: Novels as Mark McGarrity, Little Augies Lament, 1973; A Passing Advantage, 1980; Neon Caesar, 1989; Mystery Novels as Bartholomew Gill, McGarr and the Politicans Wife, 1977; McGarr on the Cliffs of Moher, 1978; McGarr and the P M of Belgrave Square, 1983; The Death of a Joyce Scholar, 1989; The Death of Love, 1992; Death on a Cold Wild River, 1993. Contributions to: NJ Monthly; NJ Herald. Honours: Fellow, NJ Council of the Arts, 1981-82; 1st Place, NJ Press Association Critical Writing. Memberships: PEN. Literary Agent: Anita Diamant Agency, NY, USA. Address: 159 North Shore Road, Andover, NJ 07821, USA.

MCGARRY Jean, b. 18 June 1952, Providence, Rhode Island, USA. Writer; Teacher. Education: BA, Harvard University, 1970; MA, Johns Hopkins University, 1983. Appointment: Teacher, Johns Hopkins University. Publications: Airs of Providence, 1985; The Very Rich Hours, 1987; The Courage of Girls, 1992. Contributions to: Various US journals including: Antioch Review; Southern Review; Southwest Review; Sulfur; New Orleans Review. Honours: Short Fiction Prize,

Southern Review-Louisiana State University, 1985. Membership: Associated Writing Programs. Address: 100 West University Parkway, Baltimore, MD 21210, USA.

MCGINNISS Joe, b. 1942, USA. Writer. Appointment: Newspaper Reporter, 1964-68. Publications: The Selling of the President, 1968; The Dream Team, 1972; Heroes, 1976; Going to Extremes, 1980; Fatal Vision, 1983; Blind Faith, 1989. Address: c/o Morton L Janklow, 598 Madison Avenue, New York, NY 10022, USA.

MCGIVERN Maureen Daly. See: **DALY Maureen.**

MCGOUGH Roger, b. 9 Nov 1937, Liverpool, England. Poet. m. 20 Dec 1986, 3 sons, 1 daughter. Education: St Mary's College, Crosby; BA and Graduate Certificate of Education, Hull University. Literary Appointments: Fellow of Poetry, The University of Loughborough, 1973-75; Writer-in-Residence at West Australian College of Advanced Education, Perth, 1986. Publications include: The Mersey Sound (with Brian Patten and Adrian Henri), 1967; Strictly Private (editor), 1982; An Imaginary Menagerie, 1989; Blazing Fruit (selected poems 1967-87), 1990; Summer with Monika, reissued 1990; Pillow Talk, 1990; Melting in the Foreground, poems; The Lighthouse That Ran Away, 1991; You at the Back (selected poems 1967-87, volume 2), 1991; My Dad's Fire Eater, 1992; Defying Gravity, 1992; The Elements, 1993; Lucky, 1993; Stinkers Ahoy! 1994. Address: c/o The Peters, Fraser and Dunlop Group Ltd, 5th Floor, The Chambers, Chelsea Harbour, Lots Road, London SW10 0XF, England.

MCGOVERN Ann, b. 25 May 1930, New York City, New York, USA. Author. m. Martin L Scheiner, 6 June 1970, 3 sons, 1 daughter. Education: BA, University of New Mexico. Appointment: Publisher, The Privileged Traveler, 1986-90. Publications: Over 50 books including: If You Lived in Colonial Times, 1964; Too Much Noise, 1967; Stone Soup, 1968; The Secret Soldier, 1975; Sharks, 1976; Shark Lady, The Adventures of Eugenie Clark, 1978; Elephant Baby, 1982; Night Dive, 1984; Swimming with Sea Lions and Other Adventures in the Galapagos Islands, 1992. Contributions to: Signature; Saturday Review. Honours: Outstanding Science Book, National Science Teachers Association, 1976, 1979, 1984, 1993; Author of the Year, Scholastic Publishing Inc, 1978. Memberships: Explorers Club; PEN; Authors Guild; Society of Children's Book Writers; Society of Journalists and Authors. Literary Agent: Kirchoff Wohlberg Inc, New York, USA. Address: 30 E 62nd Street, New York, NY 10021, USA.

MCGRATH John (Peter), b. 1935. Playwright Director. Appointments: Over 40 plays performed; Director for Film and TV; Screenplays for TV and films. Publications: Events While Guarding the Bofors Gun, 1966; Adaptor: Bakke's Night of Fame, 1968; Random Happenings in the Hebrides: or, The Social Democrat and the Stormy Sea, 1970; Rules of the Game (translation with M Teitelbaum), 1970; The Fish in the Sea, 1973; The Cheviot, the Stag, and the Black, Black Oil, 1973; The Game's Bogey, 1974; Little Red Hen, 1975; Yobbo Nowt, 1975; Joe's Drum, 1979; Swings and Roundabouts, 1981; Blood Red Roses, 1981; A Good Night Out: Popular Theatre: Audience, Class and Form (non-fiction), 1981; The Bone Won't Break (non-fiction), 1990. Address: c/o Freeway Films, 67 George Street, Edinburgh EH, Scotland.

MCGRATH Morgan. See: **RAE Hugh Crauford.**

MCGRATH Patrick, b. 1950, London, England. Novelist. Education: BA, University of London. Appointments: Orderly, Ontario State Mental Hospital, Oakridge, 1971-; Teacher, Vancouver. Publications: The Grotesque, 1989; Spider, 1991; Stories, Blood and Water and Other Tales, 1989. Address: c/o Jane Gregory Agency, Riverside Studios, Crisp Road, London W6 9RL, England.

MCGRAW Eloise Jarvis, b. 9 Dec 1915, Writer. m. William Corbin McGraw, 29 Jan 1940, 1 s, 1 d. Education: BA, Principia College. Publications include: Moccasin Trail, 1952; Mara, Daughter of the Nile, 1953; The Golden Goblet, 1961; A Really Weird Summer, 1977; The Money Room, 1981; Sawdust in His Shoes, 1950; Techniques of Fiction Writing, 1959; Merry Go Round in Oz, 1963; Master Cornhill, 1973; Forbidden Fountain of Oz, 1980; Hideaway, 1983; The Seventeenth Swap, 1986; The Trouble with Jacob, 1988; Steady Stephanie, 1962; The Striped Ships, 1991; Tangled Webb, 1993. Contributions to: The Writer Magazine; Cricket Magazine. Literary Agent: Emilie Jacobson, Curtis Brown Limited, NY, USA. Address: 1970 Indian Trail, Lake Oswego, OR 97034, USA.

MCGREEVY Susan Brown, b. 28 Jan 1934, Chicago, Illinois, USA. Lecturer; Writer. m. Thomas J McGreevy, 16 June 1973, 3 children. Education: Mount Holyoke College, 1951-53; BA with honours, Roosevelt University, 1969; MA, Northwestern University, 1971. Appointments: Staff Consultant, Heart of America Indian Center, Kansas City, Missouri, 1973-75; Curator of North American Ethnology, Kansas City Museum of History and Science, 1975-77; Adjunct Professor, Ottawa University, Kansas City Campus, 1976-77; Director, 1978-82, Research Associate, 1983-, Member, Board of Trustees, 1987-, Wheelwright Museum of the American Indian, Santa Fe, New Mexico; Guest Lecturer, colleges and museums, 1978-; Member of Faculty, Northwestern University, Gallina, New Mexico, 1980-; Member, various Boards of Directors. Publications: Woven Holy People: Navajo Sandpainting Textiles (editor), 1983; Translating Tradition: Basketry Arts of the San Juan Paiutes (with Andrew Hunter Whiteford), catalogue, 1985; Guide to Microfilm Edition of the Washington N Matthews Papers (with Katherine Spencer Halpern), 1985. Contributions to: Various art journals. Honours: Grants from: National Historic Publications and Records Commission, 1980; National Endowment of the Humanities, 1981; National Endowment for the Arts, 1985. Memberships include: American Anthropological Association; American Association of Museums; American Ethnological Society. Address: Route 7, Box 129-E, Santa Fe, NM 87505, USA.

MCGREGOR Iona, b. 7 Feb 1929, Aldershot, England. Writer. Education: BA Hons, University of Bristol, England, 1950. Publications: Historical fiction for children: An Edinburgh Reel, 1968, 4th edition 1986; The Popinjay, 1969, 2nd edition 1979; The Burning Hill, 1970; The Tree of Liberty, 1972; The Snake and the Olive, 1974, 2nd edition 1978; Death Wore A Diadem, feminist crime novel, 1989; Non-fiction: Edinburgh and Eastern Lowlands, 1979; Wallace and Bruce, 1986; Importance of Being Earnest, Penguin Passnote, 1987; Huckleberry Finn, Penguin Passnote, 1988; Alice in Shadowtime, historical crime novel, 1992; Various radio scripts. Honour: Writer's Bursary, Scottish Arts Council, 1989. Membership: Scottish PEN. Address: 9 Saxe Coburg Street, Edinburgh EH3 5BN, Scotland.

MCGRORY Edward, b. 6 Nov 1921, Stevenston, Ayrshire, Scotland. Retired Sales Consultant. m. Mary McDonald, 20 Nov 1948, 1 son, 1 daughter. Education: BA, Open University, 1985. Publications: Selected Poems, 1984; Plain and Coloured, 1985; Pied Beauty, 1986; Orchids and Daisies, 1987; Light Reflections - Mirror Images (foreword by Iris Murdoch), 1988; Chosen Poems by Celebrities: Eddie McGrory's Poems, 1988; Masks and Faces (introduction by Duncan Glen), 1989; Illuminations, 1990; Letters from Flora (From My Correspondence with Dame Flora Robson DBE), 1991; Candles and Lasers (poetry), Lyrics for Musical Settings, 1992; My Brother Cain, novel, in progress. Memberships: Various literary societies. Address: 41 Sythrum Crescent, Glenrothes, Fife KY7 5DG, Scotland.

McGUANE Thomas, b. 11 Dec 1939, Wyandotte, Michigan, USA. Married, children. Education: BA, Michigan State University; MFA, Yale University. Appointments: Director, American Rivers; Director, Craighead Wildlife - Wilderness Institute, Montana. Publications: The Sporting Club; The Bushwacked Piano; Ninety-two in the Shade; Panama; Nobody's Angel; Something to be Desired; Keep the Change; To Skin a Cat; An Outside Chance; Nothing But the Skies, 1992. Honours: Richard and Hilda Rosenthal Award, American Academy and Institute of Arts and Letters; National Book Award, nominee. Address: c/o Farrar, Straus & Giroux, 19 Union Square West, New York, NY 10003, USA.

MCGUCKIAN Medbh, b. 1950, Ireland. Poet. Publications: Single Ladies: Sixteen Poems, 1980; Portrait of Joanna, 1980; Trio Poetry (with Damian Gorman and Douglas Marshall), 1981; The Flower Master, 1982; Venus and the Rain, 1984; On Ballycastle Beach, 1988; Marconi's Cottage, 1991. Address: c/o Peter Fallon, Gallery Press, Loughcrew, Oldcastle, Co Neath, Republic of Ireland.

MCILVANNEY William, b. 1936. Author; Poet. Publications: Remedy Is None, novel, 1966; A Gift from Nessus, novel, 1968; The Longships in Harbour, poetry, 1970; Landscapes and Figures, poetry, 1973; Docherty, novel, 1975; Laidlaw, mystery novel, 1977; The Papers of Tony Veitch, mystery novel, 1983; Weddings and After, poetry, 1984; The Big Man, novel, 1985; Glasgow 1956-1986, 1986; Walking Wounded, short stories, 1989. Address: c/o Vivienne Schuster, John Farquharson Limited, 162-168 Regent Street, London W1R 5TB, England.

MCINERNEY Jay, b. 1955, USA. Author. Appointments: Editor, Time Lif Publishers, Japan; Reader, Random House Publishers, NY; Fact Checker, New Yorker Magazine, 1980. Publictions: Bright Lights, Big City, 1984; Ransom, 1985; Story of My Life, 1988; Brightness Falls, 1992. Contributions to: Atlantic; Esquire; Granta; London Reviews of Books; New Yorker; NY Review of Books; The Observer; Paris Review; Vanity Fair. Literary Agent: Amanada Urban, ICM. Address: c/o ICM 40 W 57th Street, NT 10019, USA.

MCINERNY Ralph, b. 24 Feb 1929. Professor. m. 2 sons, 4 daughters. Education: BA, St Paul Seminary, St Paul, Minnesota, USA; MS, University of Minnesota, Minneapolis, 1953; PhL, Philosophy, 1953, PhD summa cum laude, 1954, Université Laval, Quebec, Canada. Appointments include: Editor, The New Scholasticism, 1975-89; Executive Director, Homeland Foundation, 1990-92; Publications: Novels: The Priest, 1973; The Gate of Heaven, 1975; Connolly's Life, 1983; The Noonday Devil, 1985; Frigor Mortis, 1989; Four on the Floor, 1989; The Search Committee, 1990; Sisterhood, 1991; Chambre Froide, 1991; Le Demon de Midi, 1992; Desert Sinner, 1992; Basket Case, 1992; Body and Soil, 1993; Philosophical books: Art and Prudence, 1988; First Glance at Thomas Aquinas, 1989; Beothius and Aquinas, 1990; Aquinas on Human Action, 1992. Honours: Honorary Doctor of Letters: St Benedict College, 1978, University of Steubenville, 1984; Fellow, Pontifical Roman Academy of St Thomas Aquinas, 1987; Sigma National Scholastic Honour Society, 1990; Thomas Aquinas Medal, University of Dallas, 1990; St Thomas Aquinas Medallion, Thomas Aquinas College, 1991; Thomas Aquinas Medal, American Catholic Philosophical Association, 1993; Board of Governors, Thomas Aquinas College, 1993. Memberships: Authors Guild; Mystery Writers of America; Metaphysical Society of America, President 1992-93; Fellowship of Catholic Scholars, President 1991-93. Address: 2158 Portage Avenue, South Bend, IN 46616, USA.

MCINNIS Don. See: **MCINNIS Harry Donald**.

MCINNIS Harry Donald, (Don McInnis), b. 18 Apr 1916, Worcester, Massachusetts, USA. Public Administrator; International Developer. m. Marjorie E Graber, 7 Aug 1948, 2 sons, 2 daughters. Education: AB, Clark University, 1938; Graduate studies: Clark University, 1938-39; American University, 1939-40; Johns Hopkins University, 1968-69. Career includes: Playwright, author of various successful stage productions. Publications: The Running Years, 1986; Cobwebs and Twigs, 1990; Will - Man from Stratford, play, 1992; New Work No Lines, play, 1994. Contributions to: Regularly to US personnel management journals, 1940's, 1950's. Honours: Special awards, US Government, Government of Guatemala, Republic of Korea. Memberships: Australian Writers Guild; US Dramatists Guild. Address: 22 Chauvel Circle, Chapman, ACT 2611, Australia.

MCINTIRE Carl Thomas, b. 4 Oct 1939, PA, USA. Professor. m. Rebekah Smick, 7 June 1980, 2 s, 2 d. Education: BA, Shelton College, 1961; MA, University of PA, 1962; MDiv, Faith Theol Seminary, 1966; PhD, University of PA, 1976. Publications: England Against the Papacy: God, History and Historians; History and Historical Understanding; Toynbee; Reappraisals; Herbert Butterfield: Writings on Christianity and History; Butterfield as Historian; The Legacy of Herman Dooyeweerd; Canadian Protestant and Catholic Mission; Christian Views of History. Contributions to: Many Articles and Reviews. Honours: 12 Fellowships & Research Grants. Memberships: Am Historical Association; Am Society of Church History; Canadian Church Historical Society. Address: Trinity College, University of Toronto, Toronto, Ontario, Canada M5S 1H8.

MCINTOSH Christopher (Angus), b. 1943. Writer (History). Appointments: Former Assistant Editor, Country Life Magazine; Illustrated London News. Publications: The Astrologers and Their Creed, 1969; Astrology, 1970; Eliphas Levi and the French Occult Revival, 1972; The Rosy Cross Unveiled, 1980; The Swan King, 1982; The Devil's Bookshelf, 1985. Address: 2 Abbey Road, Oxford OX2 0AE, England.

MCINTYRE Arthur (Milton), b. 31 Oct 1945, New South Wales, Australia. Artist; Writer. Education: Graduated, National Art School, Sydney, 1966; Postgraduate study, Sydney University, 1971-73. Career: Sydney Art Critic, The Australian, 1977-78; Sydney Art Critic, The Age, 1981-90. Publications: Australian Contemporary Drawing, 1988; Contemporary Australian Collage and Its Origins, 1990. Contributions to: Art Monthly, UK and Australia; Art and Australia; Island; Others. Honours: VAB Grant, Australia Council, 1987.

Memberships: National Gallery of Australia Association; NAVA; International Association of Art Critics. Address: 18 Malvern Ave, Croydon, New South Wales 2132, Australia.

MCKAY Don, b. Ontario, Canada. English Teacher; Creative Writer. Appointments: Editor, Brick Books, The Fiddlehead. Publications include: Lepender, 1978; Lightning Ball Bait, 1980; Birding or Desire, 1983; Sanding Down This Rocking Chair on a Windy Night, 1987; Night Field, 1991. Honours: Canadiann Author's Association Award, for poetry, 1983; National Magazine Award, for poetry, 1991; Governor General's Literary Award for Poetry, 1991. Address: Department of English, Univ of New Brunswick, Fredericton, New Brunswick, E3B 5A3, Canada.

MCKEAN John Maule Laurie, b. 7 Nov 1943, Glasgow, Scotland. Critic; Teacher; Designer. m. Polly Eupalinos, 1 son, 1 daughter. Education: BArch (Honours), University of Strathclyde, 1968; MA, Theory of Architecture, University of Essex, 1971. Appointments: Editor, The Architects' Journal, 1971-75; UK Correspondent, Architecture, 1975-80; Architecture Correspondent, City Limits, London, 1984. Publications: Essex University: A Case Study, 1971; The First Era of Modern Architecture of the Western World, 1980; Building Materials and Architectural Quality, 1982; Style Structure and Design, 1982; Masterpieces of Architectural Drawing, 1982; The Word Crystal, 1984; Suburban Prototype, 1986; Learning from Segal, 1987; Two Essays in Glasgow: Form Structure and Image of the City, 1987; The Royal Festival Hall, 1990. Contributions to: Spazio e Società; Architese, Switzerland; Building Design; Architects Journal; A A Files. Honours: Elected to CICA, 1990. Memberships: Royal Society of Arts; International Building Press, UK Branch, Committee Member 1974-76; Chartered Society of Designers; Royal Incorporation of Architects, Scotland; Design History Society; Construction History Society. Address: 34 Dukes Avenue, Muswell Hill, London N10, England.

MCKINLEY Hugh, b. 18 Feb 1924, Oxford, England. m. Deborah Waterfield, 15 Sept 1979. Appointments: Literary Editor, Athens Daily Post, 1966-77; European Editor, Poet, India, 1967-91; Editorial Panel, Bitterroot, USA, 1980-89. Publications: Poetry: Starmusic, 1976; Transformation of Faust, 1977; Poet in Transit, 1979; Exulting for the Light, 1983; Skylarking, 1994. Contributions to: Publications worldwide including: London Magazine; Orbis; Weyfarers; Pennine Platform; Candelabrum; Poetry Wales; Poet's Voice, UK; Hibernia; Kilkenny Magazine; Dublin Magazine, Ireland; Malahat Review, Canada; Bitterroot, The Smith Poetry International, USA; Laurel Leaves, Philippines; Poet India; Skylark, India; Suffolk Life; Poetry East; Nea Estia, S.H.Y (Greece); Al-Sharq (Israel); Forum (New Zealand); Ocarina (India). Honours: LittLD, International Academy of Leadership & President Marcos Medal, Philippines, 1967; DLitt, Free University of Asia, Karachi, India, 1973; Directorate, Academia Pax Mundi, Israel, 1978. Memberships: Suffolk Poetry Society; Life Member, Baha'i World Faith. Address: Roseholme, Curlew Green Kelsale, Suffolk, England.

MCKINNEY Jack, See: **DALEY Brian Charles**.

MCKISSACK Frederick (Lemuel), b. 1939. m. Patricia (L'Ann Carswell). Publications: with Patricia (L'Ann Carswell) McKissack: Abram, Abram Where Are We Going, 1984; Little Red Hen, 1985; Great African Americans Series, including Mary Church Tewell, 1991, Martin Luther King, Jr, 1991, Langston Hughes, 1992, Paul Robeson, 1992, Sojourner Truth, 1992; Long Hard Journey, 1989; African American Institute, 1994; Rebels Against Slavery, 1996. Honours: Jane Addams Childrens Book Award, 1990; Boston Globe/Horn Book Award, 1993.

MCKISSACK Patricia (L'Ann Carswell), b. 1944. m. Frederick (Lemuel). Publications: with Frederick (Lemuel) McKissack: Abram, Abram Where Are We Going, 1984; Little Red Hen, 1985; Great African Americans Series, including Mary Church Tewell, 1991, Martin Luther King, Jr, 1991, Langston Hughes, 1992, Paul Robeson, 1992, Sojourner Truth, 1992; Long Hard Journey, 1989; African American Inventors, 1994; Rebels Against Slavery, 1996. Honours: Jane Addams Childrens Book Award, 1990; Boston Globe/Horn Book Award, 1993.

MCKNIGHT Reginald, b. 26 Feb 1956, Germany. Writer; Professor. m. Michele Davis, 25 Aug 1985, 1 daughter. Education: AA, Liberal Arts and Science; BA; MA. Publications: Moustapha's Eclipse: I Get On the Bus; The Kind of Light That Shines on Texas. Contributions to: Prairie Schooner; Players; Kenyon Review; Massachusetts Review; New York Times Book Review. Honours: Bernice M Slote Award; Drue Heinz Prize; Special Citation, PEN

America; Henry Award; Award for Literary Excellence, Kenyon Review. Memberships: PEN America; African Literary Association. Literary Agent: Flannery, White and Store. Address: Department of English, BH228D, Carnegie Mellon University, Pittsburgh, PA 15213, USA.

MCKUEN Rod, b. 29 Apr 1933, Oakland, California, USA. Poet; Composer; Author; Performer; Columnist. Career: Many appearances, films, TV, concerts, nightclubs, and with symphony orchestras; Composer, modern classical music, film and TV scores; President, Stanyan and Discus Records, Tamarack and Stanyan Books, Rod McKuen Enterprises. Publications include: Poetry: And Autumn Came, 1954; Stanyan Street and Other Sorrows, 1966; Listen to the Warm, 1967; Lonesome Cities, 1968; Twelve Years of Christmas, 1968; In Someone's Shadow, 1969; A Man Alone, 1969; With Love, 1970; Caught in the Quiet, 1970; New Ballads, 1970; Fields of Wonder, 1971; The Carols of Christmas, 1971; And to Each Season, 1972; Pastorale, 1972; Grand Tour, 1972; Come to Me in Silence, 1973; Seasons in the Sun, 1974; America, an Affirmation, 1974; 1974; Moment to Moment, 1974; Beyond the Boardwalk, 1975; The Rod McKuen Omnibus, 1975; Celebrations of the Heart, 1975; Alone, 1975; The Sea Around Me, 1977; Hand in Hand, 1977; Coming Close to the Earth, 1978; We Touch the Sky, 1979; Love's Been Good to Me, 1979; Looking for a Friend, 1980; The Power Bright and Shining, 1980; Rod McKuen's Book of Days, 1981; The Beautiful Stranger, 1981; Too Many Midnights, 1981; The Works of Rod McKuen: Vol I, Poetry 1950-1982, 1982; Watch for the Wind..., 1982; Rod McKuen-1984 Book of Days, 1983; The Sound of Solitude, 1983; Suspension Bridge, 1984; Another Beautiful Day, 1984, vol 2, 1985; Valentines, 1986; Prose: Finding My Father: One Man's Search for Identity, 1976; An Outstretched Hand, 1980. Honours: 41 Gold and Platinum Records; Grand Prix du Disque, Paris, 4 times; Nominee, Pulitzer Prize, 1973; Grammy, Best Spoken Word Album, Lonesome Cities, 1969; Entertainer of the Year, 1975; Man of the Year Award, University of Detroit, 1978; Nominee, Academy Awards; Others. Memberships: Numerous professional and civic organisations. Address: PO Box G, Beverly Hills, CA 92013, USA.

MCLANATHAN Richard, b. 12 Mar 1916, Methuen, USA. Author; Art Historian. m. Jane Fuller, 3 Jan 1942, Education: AB, 1938, PhD, 1951, Harvard University. Appointments: Visiting Professor, Number of US & European Universities; Museum Curator, Director, Trustee. Publications include: Images of the Universe, 1966; The Pageant of Medieval Art & Life, 1966; The American Tradition in the Arts, 1968; The Brandywine Heritage, 1971; Art in America, 1973; East Building, A Profile, Ntional Gallery of Art, 1978; The Art of Marguerite Stix, 1977; World Art in American Museums, 1983; Gilbert Stuart, 1986; Michelangelo, 1993. Contributions to: Numerous Journal and Mgazines. Honours include: Society of Gellows, Harvard university, 1943; Prix de Rome, 1948; Distinguished Service Award USIA, 1959; Rockefeller Senior Felloe, 1975; US National Commission for UNESCO, 1976-79. Memberships: Am Association of Museums; NY State Council on the Arts. Literary Agent: Lucy Kroll Agency. Address: The Stone School House, Phippsburg, ME 04562, USA.

MCLAREN Colin Andrew, b. 14 Dec 1940, Middlesex, England. Manuscript Librarian. m. Jan Foale, 25 Mar 1964, 1 son, 1 daughter. Education: BA, MPhil, Dip Arch Administration, University of London. Publications: Rattus Rex, 1978; Crows in a Winter Landscape, 1979; Mother of the Free, 1980; A Twister over the Thames, 1981; The Warriors under the Stone, 1983. Contributions to: Writes, broadcasts and adapts regularly for BBC Radio 3 and 4. Honours: Winner, Society of Authors Award for Best Adaptation, for Munchhausen, 1986. Memberships: Society of Authors; Crime Writers Association. Literary Agent: A P Watt Ltd. Address: c/o The Library, University of Aberdeen, Aberdeen, Scotland.

MCLAREN John David, b. 7 Nov 1932, Melbourne, Australia. Professor; Academic. Education: BA (Hons), BEd, PhD, Melbourne University; MA, Monash University. Appointments: Associate Editor, Overland, 1968-; Editor, Australian Book Review, 1978-86; Editor, Overland, 1993-. Publications: Our Troubled Schools, Melbourne, 1968; A Nation Apart, Melbourne, 1983 (editor); Australian Literature, an historical introduction, Melbourne, 1989; Xavier Herbert's Capricornia and Poor Fellow My Country, Melbourne, 1981; Towards a New Australia, Melbourne (editor), 1972; The New Pacific Literatures: culture and environment in the European Pacific, 1993. Address: Humanities Department, Victoria University of Technology, PO Box 14428, MMC, Melbourne Vic 3000, Australia.

MCLEAN Allen Campbell, b. 1922. Author. Publications: The Hill of the Red Fox, 1955; The Islander (in United States of America as The Gates of Eden), 1962; The Glass House, 1969; The Year of the Stranger, 1971; The Highlands and Islands of Scotland, 1976; Ribbon of the Fire, 1985; A Sound of Trumpets, 1985. Address: Anerley Cottage, 16 Kingsmills Road, Inverness, IV2 3JS, Scotland.

MCLEAN Antonia Maxwell, b. 1 Aug 1919, Retired. m. Ruari McLean, 24 Jan 1945, 2 sons, 1 daughter. Education: MA, Downs School, Seaford, Sussex; Somerville College, Oxford. Publications: Humanism and the Rise of Science in Tudor England; Benjamin Fawcett, Victorian Colour Printer. Contributions to: Sunday Mail Supplement. Address: Carsaig, Pennyghael, Isle of Mull PA70 6HD, Scotland.

MCLEISH Kenneth, b. 10 Oct 1940, Glasgow, Scotland. Author; Translator. m. Valerie Elizabeth Heath, 30 May 1967, 2 sons. Education: BA, BMus, MA, Worcester College, Oxford, 1963. Publications: The Theatre of Aristophanes, 1980; Penguin Companion to 20th Century Arts, 1985; Listener's Guide to Classical Music, 1986; Shakespeare's People, 1986; The Good Reading Guide, 1988; Guide to Human Thought (ed), 1993; Read a Book a Week, 1992; Crucial Classics (with Valerie McLeish), 1994; Forthcoming: Guide to Shakespeare's Plays, Guide to the Myths and Legends of the World, Key Thinkers (ed); over 50 children's books including: The Oxford First Companion to Music, 1979; Children of the Gods (Myths & Legends of Ancient Greece), 1984; Myths and Folktales of Britain and Ireland, 1986; Stories from the Bible, 1988; Translator: Aeschylus, Euripides, Ibsen, Feydeau, Labiche, Sophocles, Aristophanes. Contributions to: Reviewer, General Books, Sunday Times, Independent on Sunday. Literary Agent: A P Watt & Co. Address: c/o A P Watt, 20 John Street, London WC1N 2DR, England.

MCLELLAN David Thorburn, b. 10 Feb 1940, Hertford, England. University Teacher. m. Annie Brassart, 1 July 1967, 2 daughters. Education: MA 1962, DPhil 1968, St John's College, Oxford, England. Publications: Simone Weil: Utopian Pessimist, 1989; Karl Marx: His Life and Thought, 1974; Marxism and Religion, 1987; Ideology, 1986; Marxism After Marx, 1980; Engels, 1977; The Young Hegelians and Karl Marx, 1969; Unto Caesar: The Political Importance of Christianity, 1993. Literary Agent: The Peters, Fraser & Dunlop Group Ltd. Address: Eliot College, University of Kent, Canterbury CT2 7NS, England.

MCLERRAN Alice, b. 24 June 1933, West Point, NY, USA. Writer. m. Larry Dean McLerran, 8 May 1976, 2 s, 1 d. Education: BA, 1965, PhD, 1969, University of CA; MS, 1973, MPH, 1974, Harvard School of Public Health. Publications: The Mountain that Loved a Bird, 1985; Secrets, 1990; Rexaboxen, 1991; 1 Want to go Home, 1992; Dreamsong, 1992; Hugs, 1993; Kisses, 1993; The Ghost Dance, 1995. Honours: Southwest Book Award, 1991. Memberships: The Authors Guild; Society of Childrens Book Writers & Illustrators. Address: 2524 Colfax Avenue South, Minneapolis, MN 55405, USA.

MCMAHON Barrie, b. 2 Jun 1939, Perth, Australia. Education Public Servant. m. Jan Murphy, 7 May 1960, 2 s. Education: Teachers Certificate; Teachers Higher Certificate; BA; MA; Graduate Diploma Design Education and Film. Publications: all with Robyn Quin) Exploring Images, 1984; Real Images, 1986; Stories & Stereotypes, 1987; Meet the Media, 1988; Australian Images, 1990; Understanding Soaps, 1993. Contributions to: Australian Journal of Education; Canadian Journal of Education Communication; Education Para la Reception, Mexico; Tijdschrift voor Theaterwetenschap, Germany. Honours: Curtin University, School of English Prize. Memberships: Australian Teachers of Media. Address: PO Box 8064 Perth Business Centre, Pier Street, Perth 6849, Western Australia.

MCMANUS James, b. 22 Mar 1951, NY, USA. Poet; Novelist. m. Jennifer Arra, 9 July 1992, 1 son, 1 daughter. Appointments: Professor, The School of Art Institute, Chicago, 1981. Publications: Great America; Girl with Electric Guitar; Ghost Waves; Chin Music; Curtains; Out of the Blue; Antonio Salazar is Dead; Going to the Sun, 1995. Contributions to: Paris Review; Atlantic Monthly; Parnassus; NY Times; Am Poetry Review; Honest Ulsterman; Tri Quarterly; Harvard Magazine; The Best Am Poetry. Honour: Fellow, Guggenheim Foundation, 1994-95. Memberships: PEN; AWP. Literary Agent: Bob Cornfield. Address: SAIC, 37 S Wabash, Chicago, IL 60603, USA.

MCMASTER Juliet Sylvia, b. 2 Aug 1937, Kenya University Professor. m. Rowland McMaster, 10 May 1968, 1 s, 1 d. Education:

BA, 1959, MA, 1962, St Annes College, Oxford; MA, 1963, PhD, 1965, University of Alberta. Appointments: Assistant professor, 1965-70, Associate Professor, 1970-76, Professor, 1976-86, University Professor, 1986-, University of Alberta. Publications include: Thackeray: The Major Novels, 1971; Jane Austen's Achievement, 1976; Trollope's Palliser Novels, 1978; Jane Austen on Love, 1978; The Novel from Sterne to James, 1981; Dickens the Designer, 1987; The Beautifull Cassandra, 1993. Contributions to: 19th-Century Fiction; Victorian Studies; Modern Language Quarterly; English Studies in Canada. Honours: Canada Council Post; Doctoral Fellowship, 1969-70; Guggenheim Fellow, 1976-77; McCalla Professorship, 1982-83; University of Alberta Research Prize, 1986; Killam Research Fellowship, 1987-88; Molson Prize Winner; 1994. Memberships: Jane Austen Society of North Am; Association of Canadian University Teachers of English. Address: Dept of English, University of Alberta, Edmonton Alta, Canada T6G 2E5.

MCMILLAN James (Coriolanus), b. 30 Oct 1925. Journalist. m. Doreen Smith, 7 Apr 1953, 3 sons, 1 daughter. Education: MA (Economics), Glasgow University, Scotland. Publications: The Glass Lie, 1964; American Take-Over, 1967; Anatomy of Scotland, 1969; The Honours Game, 1970; Roots of Corruption, 1971; British Genius (with Peter Grosvenor), 1972; The Way We Were 1900-1950 (trilogy), 1977-80; Five Men at Nuremberg, 1984; The Dunlop Story, 1989; From Finchley to The World-Margaret Thatcher, 1990. Literary Agent: Curtis Brown, London. Address: Thurleston, Fairmile Park Road, Cobham, Surrey KT11 2PL, England.

MCMILLAN Terry, b. 18 Oct 1951, MI, USA. Writer. 1 s. Education: BA, University of CA; MFA, Columbia University. Literary Appointments: Guest Columnist, New York Times Hers Column; Reviewed Books for New York Times Book Review, The Atlanta Constitution, Philadelphia Inquirer; Visiting Professor, University of Wyoming; Associate Professor, University of AZ; Visiting Professor, Stanford University. Publications include: Mama, 1987; Disappearing Acts, 1989; Breaking Ice, 1990; Waiting to Exhale, 1992; A Day Late and a Dollar Short, 1995. Honours: Natl Book Award; National Endowment for the Arts Fellowship; NY Foundation for the Arts Fellowship; Doubleday Columbia University Literary Fellowship. Address: Free At Last, PO Box 2408, Danville, CA 94526, USA.

MCMILLEN Neil Raymond, b. 1939, American. Appointments: Assistant Professor of History, Ball State University, Muncie, IN 1967-69; Assistant Professor, 1969-70, Associate Professor, 1970-78, Professor of History, 1978-, University of Southern Mississippi, Hattiesburg. Publications: The Citizens' Council: Organized Resistance to the Second Reconstruction, 1971; Thomas Jefferson: Philosopher of Freedom, 1973; A Synopsis of American History (with C Sellers and H May), 1984, 7th edition 1992; Dark Journey: Black Mississippians in the Age of Jim Crow, 1989. Honour: Bancroft Prize, 1990. Address: Department of History, University of Southern Mississippi, Hattiesburg, MS 39401, USA.

MCMONIGAL Valwyn Christina, b. 6 June 1938, Sydney, New South Wales, Australia. Home Economics Teacher (retired). m. Geoffrey G McMonigal, 28 Sept 1957, 2 sons, 2 daughter. Education: School Leaving Certificate, 1954. Publications: Cookbooks: Popular Potato, 1989; Pumpkin and Other Squash, 1994; Australia Wide Cookbook (with panavisions by Ken Duncan), 1994. Contributions: Short stories in: ITA; Gippsland Literary Magazine; Sailing. Honours: Short Story Awards, Fellowship of Australian Writers, 1983, 1985. Memberships: Australian Society of Authors; Patron, Girl Guide Association; Vice-President, Wine and Food Appreciation Society. Address: 23 Grevillea Crs, Berkeley Vale, New South Wales 2261, Australia.

MCMULLEN Mary, b. 1920, American. Publications: Stranglehold, 1951, in UK as Death of Miss X, 1952; The Doom Campaign, 1974; A Country Kind of Death, The Pimlico Plot, 1975; Funny, Jonas, You Don't Look Dead, 1976; A Dangerous Funeral, Death By Request, 1977; Prudence Be Damed,The Man with Fifty Complaints,1978; Welcome to the Grave, But Nellie Was So Nice, 1979; My Cousin Death, Something of the Night, 1980; The Other Shoe, 1981; Better Off Dead, Until Death Do Us Part, 1982; A Grave Without Flowers, 1983; The Gift Horse, 1985; The Bad-News Man, 1986. Address: c/o Doubleday and Company Incorporated, 245 Park Avenue, New York, NY 10017, USA.

MCMURTRY Larry (Jeff), b. 3 June 1936, Wichita Falls, Texas, USA. m. Josephine Ballard, 15 July 1959, (div) 1 son. Education: BA, North Texas State College, MA, Rice University, Houston, Texas, Stanford University. Career: Instructor and Professor of English and Creative Writing, 1961-71; Writer. Publications: Horseman Pass By (in UK as Hud), 1961; Leaving Cheyenee, 1963; The Last Picture Show, 1966, screenplay with Peter Bogdanovitch, 1971; In a Narrow Grave, 1968; Moving On, 1970; All My Firends Are Going to be Strangers, 1972; It's Always We Rambled, 1974; Terms of Endearment, 1975; Somebody's Darling, 1978; Cadillac Jack, 1982; The Desert Rose, 1983; Lonesome Dove, 1985; Texasville, 1987; Anything For Billy, 1989; (with Diana Ossana) Pretty Boy Floyd, 1994; Buffalo Girls, 1990; The Evening Star, 1992; Flim Flam: Essays on Hollywood, 1988; Streets of Laredo, 1993. Honours include: Pulitzer Prize, 1986; Jesse H Jones Award, Texas Institute of Letters, 1962; Academy of Motion Picture Arts and Sciences Award (Oscar), 1972. Membership: Texas Institute of Letters. Address: c/o Simon and Schulster, 1230 Sixth Avenue, New York, NY 10020, USA.

MCNALLY Terrebnce, b. 3 Nov 1939, St Petersburg, Florida, USA. Appointments: Stage Manager, Actors Studio, NYC, 1961; Tutor, 1961-62; Film Critic, The Seventh Art, 1963-65; Assistant Editor, Columbia College Today, 1965-66. Publications: Apple Pie, Sweet Eros Next and Other Plays, 1969; Three Plays: Cuba Si!, Bringing It All Back Home, Last Gasps, 1970; Where Has Tommy Flowers Gone? 1972; Bad Habits: Ravenswood and Dunelawn, 1974; The Ritz and Other Plays,1976; The Rink, 1985; And Things That Go Bump In the Night, 1990; Until Your Heart Stops, 1993; Frankie and Jonny in the Clair De Lune, 1990; Lips Together, Teeth Apart, 1992. Honours include: Stanley Award, 1962; Obic Awaerd for Bad Habits; American Academy of Arts and Letters Citation; National Institute of Arts and Letters Citation. Address: 218 West 10th Street, New York, NY 10014, USA.

MCNAMARA Eugene Joseph, b. 18 Mar 1930, Oak Park, Illinois, USA. Professor; Editor; Poet; Writer. m. Margaret Lindstrom, 19 July 1952, Chicago, Illinois, USA. 4 s, 1 d. Education: BA, MA, DePaul University, PhD, Northwestern University, 1964. Literary Appointments: Editor, Mainline, 1967-72; Editor, University of Windsor Review, 1965-; Editor, Sesame Press, 1973-80. Professor of English, University of Windsor. Major Publications: Poems: For the Mean Time, 1965; Outerings, 1970; Dillinger Poems, 1970; Love Scenes, 1971; Passages, 1972; Screens, 1977; Forcing the Field, 1980; Call it a Day, 1984; Short Stories: Salt, 1977; Search for Sarah Grace, 1978; Spectral Evidence, 1985; The Moving Light, 1986. Contributions to: Queens Quarterly; Saturday Night; Chicago; Quarry; Denver Quarterly; and others (several hundred poems). Address: 166 Randolph Place, Windsor, Ontario, N9B 2T3, Canada.

MCNEIL Florence Ann, b. 8 May 1940, Vancouver, British Columbia, Canada. Writer. m. David McNeal, 3 Jan 1973. Education: BA, 1960, MA, 1965, University of British Columbia, Vancouver. Publications include: Miss P and Me, 1982; All Kinds of Magic, 1984; Catrionas Island, 1989; Emily, 1975; A Balancing Act, 1979; Ghost Towns, 1975; Barkerville, 1984; The Overlanders, 1982; Rim of the Park, 1972; Breathing Each Others Air, 1994. Contributions to: Many Magazines, Journals and Anthologies. Honours: Thea Koetner Award, 1963; The MacMillan Prize, 1963; National Magazine Award for Poetry, 1980; BC Book Awards, 1989; Our Choice Toronto Childrens Book Centre, 1985; Many Canada Council Grants. Memberships: League of Canadian Poets; Canadian Writers Union; Canadian Society for Childrens Authors, Illustrators and Performers; British Columbia Writers Federation. Address: 20 Georgia Wynd, Delta, British Columbia, Canada V4M 1A5

MCNEILL Anthony, b. 17 Dec 1941, St Andrew, Jamaica. Lecturer; Poet. m. Olive Samuel, 1970. Education: MA, Johns Hopkins University, 1971. Appointments include: Lecturer, Excelsior Community College, 1982-83. Publications: Hello Ungod, 1971; Reel From The Life Movie, 1975; Credences at the Altar of Cloud, 1979; Co Editor, The Caribbean Poem: Anm Anthology of 50 Caribbean Voices, 1979. Honours include: Jamaica Festival Prize, 1966, 1971. Address: c/o L Wint, Camperdown, Linstead PO, Jamaica, West Indies.

MCNEISH James, b. 1931, New Zealander. Appointment: Writer-in-Residence, Berlin Kunstler-program, 1983. Publications: Tavern in the Town, 1957; Fire Under the Ashes, 1965; Mackenzie, 1970; The Mackenzie Affair, 1972; Larks in a Paradise (co-author), 1974; The Glass Zoo, 1976; As for the Godwits, 1977; Art of the Pacific (with Brian Brake), 1980; Belonging: Conversations in Israel, 1980; Joy,

1982; Walking on My Feet, 1983; The Man from Nowhere: A Berlin Diary, 1985; Lovelock, 1986; Penelope's Island, 1990; The Man from Nowhere & Other Prose, 1991; My Name is Paradiso, 1995. Literary Agent: James Hale, London, England. Address: c/o James Hale, 47 Peckham Rye, London SE15 3NX, England.

MCNULTY Faith, b. 1918, American. Appointments: Staff Writer, The New Yorker Magazine, 1953-. Publications: Arty the Smarty, Wholly Cats (with E Keiffer), When a Boy Wakes Up in the Morning, 1962; When a Boy Goes to Bed at Night, 1963; The Whooping Crane, 1966; Must They Die? 1971; Prairie Dog Summer, 1972; The Great Whales, Woodchuck, 1974; Whales, 1975; Mouse and Tim, 1978; How to Dig a Hole to the Other Side of the World, 1979; The Burning Bed, The Wildlife Stories of Faith McNultry, 1980; Hurricane, 1983; The Lady and the Spider, 1986. Address: c/o The New Yorker, 25 West 43rd Street, New York, NY 10036, USA.

MCPHEE David Ross, b. 6 Apr 1930, Lansing, Michigan, USA. Bookseller (retired). m. Ute Bartholemy, 31 Oct 1963, 1 son, 1 daughter. Education: Barker College, 1946. Career: Manager: Henry Lawson's Australiana Bookshop; Swains Book Department; Antiquarian Department, Angus & Robertson. Publications: Some Common Snakes and Lizards of Australia, 1959, 1963; Observer's Book of Snakes and Lizards of Australia, 1979. Contributions to: Wildlife, Bulletin. Membership: Scientific Member, Royal Zoological Society of New South Wales. Address: 64 Catherine St, St Ives, New South Wales 2075, Australia.

MCPHEE John, b. Princeton, New Jersey, USA. Education: Princeton High School; Deerfield Academy; Princeton University; Cambridge University. Appointments: Staff Writer, New Yorker; Teacher, Princeton University. Publications include: A Sense of Where You Are; The Headmaster; A Roomful of Hovings; Oranges; Levels of the Game; The Crofter and the Laird; The Deltoid Pumpkin Seed; Pieces of the Frame; The Survival of the Bark Canoe; Encounters with the Archdruid; The Curve of Binding Energy; The John McPhee Reader; Coming into the Country, 1977; Giving Good Weight, 1979; In Suspect Terrain, 1982; Rising from the Plains, 1986; Heirs of General Practice, 1986; The Control of Nature, 1989; Looking for a Ship, 1990. Honours: Nominated for National Books Award; Award from Am Academy and Institute of Arts & Letters, 1977. Membership: Geological Society of Am; Am Academy of Arts & Letters. Address: 475 Drakes Corner Road, Princeton, NJ 08540, USA>

MCPHERSON James Allen, b. 16 Sept 1943, GA, USA. Writer; Teacher, 1 d. Education: BA, Morris Brown College, 1965; LLB, Harvard Law School, 1968; MFA, University of IA, 1971. Appointments include: University of CA, 1969-70; Morgan State University, 1974-75; University of VA, 1976-81; University of IA, 1981-. Publications include: Hue & Cry, 1969; Railroad, 1976; elbow Room, 1977; A World Unsuspected, 1987; Crabcakes, 1996. Contributions to: Atlantic Monthly; Atlantic; Esquire; NY Times; Readers Digest; Chicago Tribune; Playboy; Yale Review; Ploughshares; IA Review. Honours: Atlantic First Award, 1968; Atlantic Grant, 1969; Award Literature National Academy of Arts & Letters, 1970; Guggenheim Fellowship, 1973; Pulitzer Prize, 1978; McArthur Award, 1981; Award for Excelence in Teaching, 1991; University of IA Green Eyeshades Award, 1994. Memberships: Authors League. Literary Agent: Carl Brandt. Address: c/o Carl Brandt, 1501 Broadway, New York, NY 10036, USA.

MCPHERSON James Munro, b. 11 Oct 1936, Valley City, USA. m. Patricia Rasche, 28 Dec 1957, 1 d. Education: BA, Gustavus Aldophus College, 1958; PhD, Johns Hopkins University, 1963. Appointments: Instructor, 1962-65, Assistant Professor, 1965-66, Associate Professor, 1966-72, Professor, 1972-82, Edwards Professor, 1982-91, George Henry Davis Professor, 1991-, Princeton University; Commonwealth Fund Lecturer, University College, London, 1982. Publications: Battle Cry of Freedom, 1988; The Abolitionist Legacy, 1975; Ordeal by Fire, 1982; Abraham Lincoln and the Second American Revolution, 1991; Images of the Civil War, 1992; Gettysburg, 1993; What The Fought For, 1861-1865, 1994. Contributions to: Altantic Monthly; NT Review; New Republic; Am Historical Review; Journal of Am History; Southern Historical Review; New England Quarterly. Honours: Anisfield Wolf Award, 1965; Pulitzer Prize, 1989; Michael Award, 1989; DHL Gustavus Adolphus College, 1990; DHL Lehigh University, 1991, Gettysburg College, 1991, Muhlenberg College, 1994. Memberships: Am Historical Association; Society of Am Historians;

Southern Historical Association; Am Philosophical Society. Address: 15 Randall Road, Princeton, NJ 08540, USA.

MCPHERSON Sandra, b. 2 Aug 1943, San Jose, CA, USA. Writer; Teacher. m. (1) Henry Carlile, 24 July 1966, div, 1 daughter; (2) Walter Pavlich, 3 Jan 1995. Education: BA, San Jose State, 1965; University of WA, 1965-66. Publications: Elegies for the Hot Season, 1970, 1982; Radiation, 1973; The Year of Our Birth, 1978; Sensing, 1980; Patron Happiness, 1983; Pheasant Flower, 1985; Streamers, 1988; The God of Indeterminacy, 1993. Contributions to: American Poetry Review; Field; Grand Street; Yale Review; New Republic; New Yorker; Many Others. Honours: Ingram Merrill Foundation Grant, 1972, 1984; NEA Grant, 1974, 80, 85; Guggenheim Foundation Fellowship, 1976; National Book Award Nominee, 1979; Oregon Arts Commission Fellowship, 1984; American Academy & Institute of Arts and Letters Award in Literature, 1987. Address: c/o English Dept, University of CA, Davis, CA 95616, USA.

MCQUEEN Cilla, b. 22 Jan 1949, Birmingham England. Teacher; Artist; Poet. m. Ralph Hotere, 1974, 1 d. Education: MA, Dunedin University, Otago, 1970. Publications: Homing in, 1982; Anti Gravity, 1984; Wild Sweets, 1986; Benzina, 1988; Berlin Diary, 1990; Crikey, 1994; Play, Harlequin and Colombine, 1987; Radio Play, Spacy Calcutta's Travelling Truth Show, 1986. Honours include: Robert Burns Fellowship, 1985 and 1986; Goethe Institute Scholarship, 1988; New Zealand Book Award for Poetry, 1983, 1989, 1991. Address: PO Box 69, Portobello, Dunedin, New Zealand.

MCQUOWN Norman Anthony, b. 30 Jan 1914, IL, USA. Techer. m. 7 Nov 1942, 2 d. Education: AB, 1935, AM, 1936, University of IL, PhD, Yale University. Appointments: University of IL, 1935-36; Escuela Nacional de Antropologia, 1939-42; Hunter College of the City of NY, 1945-46; University of Chicago, 1946-. Publications include: Language, Culture and Education, 1982; El Microanalisis de Entevistas, 1983; Spoken Turkish, 1946; Konusulan Ingilizce, 1954; El Tzeltal Hablado, 1957; Handbook of Middle American Indians, 1967. Contributions to: International Journal of Am Linguistics; Am Anthropologist; Revista Mexicana de Antropologia; Estudios de Cultura Maya. Honours: Diploma, Sociedad Mexicana de Antropologia, 1981; Certificate of Merit, 1983; Alexander von Humboldt Stiftungspreis, 1988. Memberships: Linguistic Society of Am; Am Anthropological Assn; Address: 1126 East 59th Str, Chicago, IL 60637, USA.

MCRAE Hamish Malcolm Donald, b. 20 Oct 1943, Barnstaple, Devon, England. Journalist. m. Frances Annes Cairncross, 10 Sept 1971, 2 daughters. Education: Fettes College, Edinburgh 1957-62; Trinity College, Dublin, 1962-66, Honours Degree Economics & Political Science. Literary Appointments: Editor, Euromoney, 1972; Financial Editor, The Guardian, 1975; Editor, Business and City, The Independent, 1989; Associate Editor, The Independent, 1991. Publications: Capital City - London as a Financial Centre (with Frances Cairncross), 1973, 5th edition 1991; The Second Great Crash (with Frances Cairncross), 1975; Japan's role in the emerging global securities market, 1985; The World in 2020, 1994. Contributions to: Numerous magazines and journals. Honours: Financial Journalist of the Year, Wincott Foundation, 1979; Special Merit Award, Amex Bank Review Essays, 1987. Address: 6 Canonbury Lane, London N1 2AP, England.

MCTRUSTRY Christlfor (Chris) John, b. 29 Oct 1960, Wellington, New South Wales, Australia. Screenwriter; Novelist. m. Patricia Rose Dravine, 1 Nov 1986, 1 son, 1 daughter. Education: Bachelor of Creative Arts, 1989, Master of Creative Arts, 1990, University of Wollongong. Publications: Television: Neighbours, 1989, 1990, 1991, 1992, 1993; A Country Practice, 1991; Home and Away, 1992, 1993; Radio: Alien Evangelist, 4x30 minute comedy series, 1992; Novel: The Cat Burglar, 1995. Memberships: Australian Writers Guild; Australian National Playwrights Centre; Australian Society of Authors. Literary Agent: Shauna Crawley, Crawley Management, Glebe, Sydney, New South Wales, Australia. Address: 22 Stanleigh Crescent, West Wollongong, New South Wales 2500, Australia.

MCVEAN James. See: LUARD Nicholas.

MCWHIRTER George, b. 26 Sept 1939, Belfast, Northern Ireland. Writer; Translator; Professor. m. Angela Mairead Cold, 26 Dec 1963, 1 s, 1 d. Education: BA, Queen Univerity; MA, University of British Columbia. Appointments: Co-Editor in-Chief, 1977, Advisory Editor, 1978-89, Prism International Magzine; Professor, University of

British Columbia, 1982-. Publications include: Catalan Poems, 1971; Bodyworks, 1974; Queen of the Sea, 1976; Gods Eye, 1981; Coming to Grips with Lucy, 1982; The Island Man, 1980; Fire Before Dark, 1983; Paula Lake, 1984; Cage, 1987; The Listeners, 1991; A Bad Day to be Winning, 1992; A Staircase for All Souls, 1993; Shadow Light, 1995; Musical Dogs, 1995. Contributions to: Numerous Magazines & Journals. Honours: McMillan Prize, 1969; Commonwealth Poetry Prize, 1972; F R Scott Prize, 1988; Ethel Wilson Fiction Prize, 1988. Memberships: League of Canadian Poets; Writers Union of Canada; PEN; Literary Translators Association of Canada. Address: 4637 West 13th Avenue, Vancouver BC, Canada V6R 2V6.

MCWHIRTER Norris Dewar, b. 12 Aug 1925, London, England. Author; Editor; Broadcaster. m. (1) Carole Eckert, 28 Dec 1957 (dec 1987), 1 son, 1 daughter, (2) Tessa Mary Pocock, 26 Mar 1991. Education: BA 1947, MA 1948, Trinity College, Oxford, England. Appointments: Athletics Correspondent, Observer, 1951-67, Star 1951-60; Editor, Athletics World, 1952-56; Founder Editor, Guinness Book of Records, 1955. Publications: Get To Your Marks, 1951; Guinness Book of Records, 1955-86 (30 languages); Dunlop Book of Facts, 1964-73; Guinness Book of Answers, 1976-; Ross, Story of a Shared Life, 1976; Guinness Book of Essential Facts, 1979. Contributions to: Encyclopedia Brittanica; Whitakers Almanack. Honour: CBE, 1980. Memberships: Royal Institution. Address: c/o Guinness Publishing Co, 33 London Road, Enfield, Middlesex EN2 6DJ, England.

MCWILLIAM Candia Frances Juliet, b. 1 July 1955, Edinburgh, Scotland. Writer. m. (1) Earl of Portsmouth, 10 Feb 1981, (2) F E Dinshaw, 27 Sept 1986, 2 sons, 1 daughter. Education: Sherborne School for Girls, 1968-73; Girton College, Cambridge, England, BA, 1973-76. Publications: A Case of Knives, 1988; A Little Stranger, 1989; Debatable Land, 1994. Honours: Betty Trask Prize; Scottish Arts Council Prize; Guardian Fiction Prize. Memberships: Society of Authors; PEN; Fellow of the Royal Society of Literature. Literary Agent: Janklow & Nesbit. Address: c/o Bloomsbury Publishing, 2 Soho Square, London W1V 5DE, England.

MCWILLIAMS Peter, b. 1950. Publisher; Writer. Come Live With Me and Be My Life, 1967; Surviving the Loss of a Love, 1971; The Personal Computer Book; Portraits, 1992; Life 101 Series (with John Rozer), including: You Can't Afford the Luxury of a Negative Thought; Life 101; Do It! Lets Get Off Our Butts; Weather 101. Ain't Nobody's Business If You Do; Life 102. Contributions to: Playboy. Address: Prelude Press, 8159 Santa Monica Boulevard, Los Angeles, CA 9046, USA.

MEAD Matthew, b. 1924, British. Appointments: Editor, Satis Magazine, Edinburgh, 1960-62. Publications: A Poem in Nine Parts, 1960; Identities, 1964; Kleinigkeiten, 1966; Identities and Other Poems, 1967; the Administration of Things, Penguin Modern Poets 16 (with Harry Guest and J Beeching), 1970 In the Eyes of the People, 1973; Minusland, 1977; The Midday Muse, 1979; A Roman in Cologne, 1986. Address: c/o Anvil Press, 69 King George Street, London, SE10 8PX, England.

MEADES Jonathon Turner, b. 21 Jan 1947, Salisbury, Wiltshire, England. Journalist; Writer; Broadcaster. m. (1) Sally Browne, (2) Frances Bentley, 3 daughters. Education: Kings College, Taunton, 1960-64; Royal Academy of Dramatic Art, 1967-69. Publications: Filthy English; Peter Knows What Dick Likes; Pompey. TV: The Victorian Horse, Abroad in Britain, Further Abroad, Jerry Building. Contributions to: The Times; Sunday Times; The Observer; The Independent. Memberships: Water Rats; Pro Celeb Golfers. Literary Agent: Aitken, Stone and Wylie. Address: c/o Jonathon Cape, Vauxhall Bridge Road, London SW1, England.

MEASHAM Donald Charles, b. 19 Jan 1932. Retired Teacher, Higher Education. m. Joan Doreen Barry, 15 Dec 1954, 1 son, 1 daughter. Education: BA (Hons), Birmingham University, 1953; MPhil, Nottingham University, 1971. Appointments: Member (Deputy Chairman) Literature Panel, East Midlands Arts, 1980-84; Founding Editor 1983, Business Manager and Continuing Co-editor 1988-, Staple Magazine. Publications: Leaving, 1965; Fourteen, 1965; English Now & Then, 1965; Larger Than Life, 1967; Quattordicenni, 1967; The Personal Element, 1967; Lawrence & The Real England, 1985; Ruskin: The Last Chapter, 1989. Contributions to: Tribune; TLS; Teacher; Renaissance and Modern Studies; Other People's Clerihews, edited G

Ewart. Address: Tor Cottage, 81 Cavendish Road, Matlock, Derbyshire DE4 3HD, England.

MEDOFF Mark, b. 18 Mar 1940. Playwright. m. Stephanie Thome, 3 d. Education: BA, University of Miami; MA, Stanford University, DHL, Gallaudet College. Appointments: Dramatist in Residence, New Mexico State University, Las Cruses, New Mexico; Liteature and Theatre Panel, National Endowment for the Arts. Publications: Plays: When You Comin' Back, Red Ryder, 1973-74; The Wager; Children of a Lesser God, 1979; The Majestic Kid, 1981; Revised Edition, 1989; The Hands Of Its Enemy, 1984; The Heart Outright, 1986; Big Mary, 1989; Stumps, 1989; The Hero Trilogy (When You Comin' Back, Red Ryder, The Heart Outright, The Majestic Kid), 1989; Stephanie Hero, 1990; Kringle's Window, 1991; Others: Film Scripts: Good Guys Wear Black, 1977; When You Comin' Back, Red Ryder, 1978; Off Beat, 1985; Apology, 1986; Children of a Lesser God, 1987; Clara's Heart, 1988; City of Joy, 1992. Contributions to: The Washington Post; Los Angeles Times; Journal of Teachers of English, Dramatics Magazine; Reader's Digest; New York Times Magazine; Albuquerque Journal Impact; Esquire. Honours include: For When You Comin' Back, Red Ryder, OBIE Award, Drama Desk Award, New York Outer Critics Award, Best Plays, 1973-74; Westhafer Award for Excellence in Creative Activity, New Mexico State University, 1974; Guggenheim Fellowship in Playwriting, 1974-75; Best Plays for The Wager, 1974-75; Outstanding Play Script for Firekeeper, Texas Review of Books, 1978; Governor's Award for Excellence in the Arts, State of New Mexico, 1980; For Children of a Lesser God: Antoinette Perry Award for Best Play, Drama Desk Award, New York Outer Critics Circle Award, 1979-80; Best Plays, 1980-81; Los Angeles Drama-Logue Critics Award, Best Play, Society of West End Theatre, 1981; Distinguished Alumnus, University of Miami, 1987; John Conley Scholar, American Academy of Otolaryngology-Head and Neck Surgery, 1987; California Media Access Award for film script of Children of a Lesser God. Memberships: Writers Guild of America; Actors Equity Association; Screen Actors Guild. Literary Agent: Gilbert Parker, William Morris Agency. Address: Box 3585, Las Cruces, NM 88003, USA.

MEDVEDEV Roy (Alexandrovich), b. 1925, Russian. Appointments: School Teacher, Sverdlovsk region, 1952-54; School Director, Leningrad region; Deputy Editor-in-Chief, Prosveshchenie Publishing House, 1957-60; Head of Department of Vocational Education, Research Institute of Education, Moscow, Russia, 1961-71; Deputy of the Supreme Soviet of the USSR 1989-91. Publications: Let History Judge, Questions of Madness (with Zhores A Medvedev), 1971; On Socialist Democracy, 1975; Khrushchev: The Years in Power (with Zhores A Medvedev), Political Essays, 1976; Problems in the Literary Biography of Mikhail Sholokov, 1977; Samizdat Register (ed), 2 volumes, 1977-80; The October Revolution, On Stalin and Stalinism, 1979; On Soviet Dissent, Nikolai Bukharin: The Last Years, 1980; Leninism and Western Socialism, 1981; All Stalin's Men, 1983; China and the Superpowers, 1986; Let History Judge, 1989; Time of Change (with G Chiesa), 1990; Brezhnev: A Political Biography, 1991. Contributions to: Over 300 professional and general articles. Literary Agent: Dr Zhores A Medvedev, 4 Osborn Gardens, Mill Hill, London NW7 1DY, England. Address: Abonement Post Box 258, Moscow A-475, 125475, Russia.

MEDVEDEV Zhores (Alexandrovich), b. Russia, 1925, British. Appointments: Seniro Research Fellow, MRC National Institute for Medical Research Division of Genetics, London, 1993-; Associate Ed, Experimental Gerontolotyg; Senior Research Scientists K Timiraisev Academy of Agricultural Sciences, Moscow, 1951-62; Head of Laboratory of Molecular Radiobiololgy, Research Institute of Medical Radiology, Obninsk, Kaluga Reion, USSR, 1963-69; Senior Research Scientist, Laboratory of Proteins, Research Institute of Biochemistry and Physiology of Farm Animals, Borovsk, Kaluga Region, USSR, 1970-72. Publications: Protein Biosynthesis, 1966; The Rise and Fall of T D Lysenko, 1969; Molecular-Genetic Mechanisms of Development, 1979; (with Roy A Medvedev), Questions of Madness, 1971; Medvedev Papers, 1971; Ten Years After Ivan Denisovich; (with Roy A Medvedev) Khrushchev: The Years in Power, 1976; Soviety Science, 1978; Nuclear Disaster in the Urals, 1979; Andropov, 1983; Gorbachev, 1986; Soviet Agriculture, 1987.

MEDVIE Victor Cornelius, (C Monk), b. 6 June 1905, Budapest, Hungary. Consultant Physician. m. Sheila Mary Wiggins, (dec 1989), 9 May 1946, 1 s, 2 d. Education: Prince Eszterhazy Symnasium, Vienna, 1916-24; MD, University of Vienna, 1930; MRCS LRCP, St

Bartholomews Hospital London, 1941; MRCP, 1943, FRCP, 1965. Publications include: The Mental and Physical Effects of Pain, 1949; The Royal Hospital of St Bartholomews 1923-1973, (joint editor), 1974; A History of Endocrinology, 1982; reprinted 1984, 2nd edition 1993. Contributions to: About 80 papers for Medical Scientific Journals, 1931-92. Honours: CBE, 1965; Chevalier de l'ordre National du Merite, 1981; Buckston Browne Prize, Harveian Society of London, 1948; Golden MD, Diploma of the University of Vienna, 1991. Memberships: London PEN, 1946; Harveian Society, President, 1970; Osler Club of London, President, 1983; Section of History of Medicine (Royal Society of Medicine), President 1986-87; The Garrick Club, 1972-. Address: 38 Westmoreland Terrace, London, SW1V 3HL. England.

MEEK Jay, b. 23 Aug 1937, Grand Rapids, MI, USA. Professor; Writer. m. Martha George, 29 Aug 1966, 1 d. Education: BA, University of MI; MA, Syracuse University. Appointments: Guest Member, Writing Faculty, Sarah Lawrence College, 1980-82; Associate Professor, MIT, 1982-83; Writer in Residence, Memphis State University, 1984; Professor, University of North Dakota. Publications: The Week the Dirigible Came, 1976; Drawing on the Walls, 1980; Earthly Purpose, 1984; Stations, 1989; After the Storm, 1992; Windows, 1994. Contributions to: Poetry; Paris Review; Yale Review; VA Quarterly Review; Numerous Other. Honours: Award NEA, 1972-73; Award John Simon Guggenheim Memorial Foundation, 1985; Bush Artist Fellowship, 1989. Memberships: Poetry Editor, North Dakota Quarterly. Address: University of North Dakota, University Station 7209, Grand Forks, ND 58202, USA.

MEGGED Aharon, b. 10 Aug 1920, Wloclawek, Poland. Writer. m. Eda Zoritte, 11 May 1944, 2 sons. Appointments: Editor, MASSA, 1953-55; Literary Editor, Lamerchav Daily, 1955-68; Cultural Attaché, Israel Embassy, London, England, 1968-71; Columnist, Davar Daily, 1971-85. Publications: Hedva and I, 1953; Fortunes of a Fool, 1960; Living on the Dead, 1965; The Short Life, 1971; Asahel, 1978; Heinz, His Son and the Evil Spirit, 1979; Journey in the Month of Av, 1980; The Flying Camel and the Golden Hump, 1982; Foiglmann, 1987; The Turbulent Zone (essays), 1985; The Writing Desk (literary essays), 1988; The Selvino Children (documentary), 1984; Anat's Day of Illumination, 1992; Longing for Olga, 1994; Plays: Hedva and I, 1955; Hannah Senesh, 1963; Genesis, 1965; The High Season, 1968. Contributions to: Atlantic Monthly; Encounter; Midstream; The Listener; Moment; Present-Tense; Partisan Review; Ariel. Address: 26 Rupin Street, Tel Aviv 63457, Israel.

MEHROTRA Arvind Krishna, b. 16 Apr 1947, Lahore, Pakistan. Lecturer; Poet. Education: MA, University of Bombay, 1968. Appointments include: Lecturer, University of Hyderbad, 1977-78; Founder, Ezra Fakir Press, Bombay, 1966. Publications: Bharatmata: A Prayer, 1966; Woodcuts on Paper, 1967; Poems, Poemes, Poemas, 1971; Nine Enclosures, 1976; Distance in Statute Miles, 1982; Middle Earth, 1984; Editor, Twenty Indian Poems, 1990; Twelve Modern Indian Poets, 1991. Honours include: Homi Bhabha Fellowship, 1981. Address: Dept of English Studies, University of Allahabad, Allahabad 211002, Uttar Pradesh, India.

MEHTA Ved (Parkash), b. 21 Mar 1934, Lahore, India. Writer. m. Linn Fenimore Cooper Cary, 1983, 2 d. Education: Arkansas School for the Blind, BA, Pomona College, 1956; BA, Hons, Modern History, Oxford University, England, 1959; MA, 1962; M, Harvard University, 1961. Appointments: Staff Writer, The New Yorker, 1961-; Visiting Scholar, Case Western Reserve, 1974; Writer and Commentator of Television Documentary Film Chachaji, My Poor Relation, PBS, 1978, BBC, 1980; Beatty Lecturer, McGill University, 1979; Visiting Professor of Literature, Bard College, 1985, 1986; Noble Foundation Visiting Professor of Art and Cultural History, Sarah Lawrence College, 1988; Visiting Fellow of Literature, Balliol College, Oxford, 1988-89; Visiting Professor of English, New York University, 1990-93; Lecturer in History, 1990, 1991, 1992; Lecturer in English, 1991-91; Associate Fellow 1988-; Residential Fellow, 1990-93, Berkeley College, Arnold Bernhard Visiting Professor of English and History, Williams College; Randolph Distinguished Professor, Vassar College. Publications: Fact to Face, 1957; Walking to Indian Streets, 1960, revised edition, 1971; Fly and the Fly-Bottle, 1963, 2nd edition 1983, introduction by Jasper Griffin; The New Theologian, 1966; Delinquent Chacha, 1967; Portrait of India, 1970, 2nd edition, 1993; John is Easy to Please, 1971; Mahatma Gandhi and his Apostles, 1977, reissued 1993; The New India, 1978; Photographs of Chachaji, 1980; A Family Affair: India Under Three Prime Ministers, 1982; Three Stories of the Raj, 1986; Rajiv Gandhi's Legacys, in progress. Continents of Exile,

(autobiographical series); Daddyji, 1972; Mamaji, 1979; Vedi, 1982; The Ledge Between the Stream, 1984; Sound-Shadows of the New World, 1986; The Stolen Light, 1989; Up At Oxford, 1993. Honours: Phi Beta Kappa, 1955; Hazen Fellow, 1956-59; Harvard Prize Fellow, 1959-60; Guggenheim Fellow, 1971-72, 1977-78; Ford Foundation Travel and Study Grantee, 1971-76; Public Policy Grantee, 1979-82; Member Council on Foreign Relations, 1979-; Member Usage Panel, American Heritage Dictionary, 1982; MacArthur Prize Fellow, 1982-87; Fellow, New York Institute for the Humanities, 1988-92; Association of Indians in America Award, 1978; Distinguished Service Award, Asian/Pacific American Library Association, 1986; New York City Mayor's Liberty Medal, 1986; Centenary Barrows Award, Pomona College, 1987; Honorary D.Litt, Pomona, 1972, Bard 1982; Williams, 1986; Honorary D.Univ Stirling (Scotland) 1988. Literary Agent: Anthony Sheil, Georges Borchardt. Address: c/o The New Yorker, 20 West 43rd Street, New York, NY 10036, USA.

MEIDINGER Ingeborg Lucie, b. 16 Mar 1923, Berlin. Writer. Education: Studies of History & German Literature; DPhil. Publications include: 50 works of novels, poetry, stories, radio plays, essays & critiques including: Welterlebnis in deutscher Gegenwartsdichtung, 1956; Der Mond von Gestern (novel), 1963; Ordentliche Leute (stories), 1976; Zukunfts-chronik (poetry), 1978 and others. Contributions to: ORF, Vienna; Die Presse, Vienna; Zeitwende; Die Welt; Nurnberger Zeitung and others. Honours include: Hans Sachs Drama Prize, 1976; Max Dauthendey Plaque, 1979; International Molle Literary Prize, Sweden, 1979 and others. Memberships: PEN; European Authors Association Die Kogge (Chairman 1967-1988). Address: Schobertweg 1 a, D-91056 Erlangen, Germany.

MEINKE Peter, b. 29 Dec 1932, Brooklyn, New York, USA. Writer; Teacher. m. Jeanne Clark, 14 Dec 1957, 2 s, 2 d. Education: AB, Hamilton College, 1955; MA, University of Michigan, 1961; PhD, University of Minnesota, 1965. Appointments: Director, Writing Workshop, Eckerd College, St Petersburg, Florida, 1966-93 (retired); Fulbright Senior Lecturer, University of Warsaw, Poland, 1978-79; Jenny Moore Writer-in-Residence, Washington DC, 1981-82; James Thurber Writer-in-Residence, Columbus, Ohio, 1987; McGee Writer-in-Residence, Davisdon College, North Carolina, 1989; Writer-in-Residence, University of Hawaii. Publications: The Piano Tuner, 1986; Night Watch on the Chesapeake, 1987; Trying to Surprise God, 1981; The Night Train and the Golden Bird, 1977; Far from Home 1988; Underneath the Lantern, 1987; The Rat Poems, 1978; Liquid Paper: New and selected Poems, 1981. Contributions to: Poems and stories in The Atlantic, The New Yorker, Poetry, Yankee, Grand Street, The Virginian Quarterly. Honours: NEA Creative Writing Fellowships, 1974, 1989; Gustav Davidson Award, PSA, 1976; Lucille Medwick Award, PSA, 1984; Emily Dickinson Award, PSA, 1992; Emily Clark Balch Award for Short Fiction, 1982; Flannery O'Connor Award for Short Fiction, 1986; Robert A Staub, Outstanding Teacher Award, Eckead College, 1990. Memberships: PSA; PEN. Address: 147 Wildwood Lane SE, St Petersburg, FL 33705, USA.

MEJIA GONZALEZ Eduardo, b. 13 Oct 1948, Editor. m. Lourdes Eguiluz, 9 Aug 1973, 1 s, 1 d. Appointments: Journalist, Novedades, 1973-85; Contenido, 1990-; Editor, Universidad Veracruzana, 1980-84; Fondo de Cultura Economica, 1985-90; Dragon, 990-. Publications: Leave Me Space; For Example, You; A Wave Smash on the Rock; Matrimonial Promise. Contributions to: Revista de la Universidad de Mexico; La Palabra y el Hombre; Sabado; Siemprol; Nexos. Address: Thiers 213-5, 11590 Mexico, DF Mexico.

MELCHETT Sonia. See: SINCLAIR Sonia Elizabeth.

MELCHIOR Ib J, b. 1917, Copenhagen, Denmark, Author; Playwright; Freelance Writer. Appointments include: Actor, State Manager, Director, English Players, 1937-39; Stage Manager, Radio City Music Hall, Center Theatre, 1941-42; Television Writer, Actor, Director, NY City, 1947-50; Associate Producer, G L Enterprises, 1952-53; Writer, Director, 12 Feature Films, 60 Documentary Films, 1959-76. Publications include: Rosmersholm, 1946; Hedda Gabler, 1947; Order of Battle, 1972; Sleeper Agent, 1975; The Haigerloch Project, 1977; The Watchdogs of Abaddon, 1979; The Marcus Device, 1980; Hour of Vengeance, 1982; Eva, 1984; V-3, 1985; Code Name: Grand Guignol, 1987; Steps and Stairways, 1989; Quest, 1990; Hitlers Werewolves, 1991; Case By Case, 1993. Honours: Golden Scroll, 1976; Hamlet Award, 1982; Outstanding American-Scandinavian, 1995. Memberships: Authors Guild; Writers Guild of AM; Directors Guild of

Am; Manuscript Society. Address: 8228 Marmont Lane, Los Angeles, CA 90069, USA.

MELDRUM James. See: **KYLE Duncan.**

MELEAGROU Evie, b. 28 May 1930, Nicosia, Cyprus. Author. m. Dr John Meleagrou, MD, 26 Nov 1952, 1 s, 2 d. Education: Pancyprian Gymnasium, Nicosia; High School Diploma, Ecole Saint Joseph, Nicosia; Dimplme de la Literature Francaise, Athenaeum Institute, Athens; Philosophical Studies, University of London, BA. Classics. Literary Appointments: Producer Literary Programmes, CBC, 1952-55; Editor, Cyprus Chronicles, 1960-72; Secretary, Cyprus Chronicles Cultural Centre, 1960-74; Cyprus Representative, World Writers Conference, 1965. Publications: Solomons Family, 1957; Anonymous City, 1963; Eastern Mediterranean, 1969; Conversations with Che, 1970; Penultimate Era, 1981; Persona is the unknown Cypriot Woman (literary Essays and poetry), 1993; The Virgin Plunge in the Ocean Depths (short stories and novelles), 1993; Cyprus Chronaca (historical essay), 1974-1992; Translations. Honours: Severian Literary Prize, 1945; 1st Pancyprian Prize Short Story Competition, 1952; Pancyprian Novella Competition, 1957; Cyprus National Novel Award, 1970, 1982; Panhellenic National Novel Award, 1982. Memberships: Cyprus Chronicles Cultural Centre, General Secretary; Cyprus Cultural Association of Women, General Secretary; The First Cypriot Writers Association, Secretary 1961-70; Association of Greek Writers, Athens; Cyprus State Literary Awards Committee, 1969-79; Agent: Dodoni Publishing House, 3 Asklipios Street, Athens, 10679, Greece. Address: 22 Messolongi Street, Nicosia, Cyprus.

MELLEN Joan, b. 1941, United States of America. Writer. Publications: A Film Guide to the Battle of Algiers, 1973; Marilyn Monroe, 1973; Women and Their Sexuality in the New Film, 1973; Voices from the Japanese Cinema, 1975; The Waves at Genji's Door: Japan Through Its Cinema, 1976; Big Bad Wolves: Masculinity in the American Film, 1978; The World of Luis Bunuel, 1978; Natural Tendencies, 1981; Priviledge: The Enigma of Sacha Bruce, 1983; Bob Knight: His Own Man, 1988. Address: PO Box 359, 25 Elm Ridge Road, Pennington, NJ 08534, USA.

MELLERS Wilfrid Howard, b. 26 Apr 1914. University Teacher. 3 daughters. Education: Leamington College, 1933; BA, 1936; MA, 1938, Cambridge University; DMus, Birmingham University. Appointments: University Teacher, 1945-81. Publications: Man and His Music, 1957, revised edition, 1987; Francois Couperin and the French Classical Tradition, 1950, revised 1987; Bach and the Dance of God, 1980; Beethoven and the Voice of God, 1984; Music in a New Found Land, 1987; Vaughan Williams and the Vision of Albion, 1989; The Music of Percy Grainger, 1992; Francis Poulenc, 1993. Contributions to: Various journals and encyclopaedias. Honours: OBE, 1982; DPhil (City University), 1980; Honorary Member of the Sonneck Society (for services to American music). Address: Oliver Sheldon House, 17 Aldwark, York Y01 2BX, England.

MELLING John Kennedy, b. 11 Jan 1927, Westcliff-on-Sea, Essex, England. Chartered Accountant; Lecturer; Broadcaster. Education: Thirsk School, 1932-38; Westcliff High School for Boys, 1938-42. Literary Appointments: Editor, Chivers Black Dagger Series of Crime Classics, 1986-91; Dramatic Critic, The Stage, 1957-90; Editor, The Liveryman Magazine, 1970-75. Publications: Discovering London's Guilds & Liveries, 5 editions, 1973-95; Murder Done To Death, 1995; Discovering Lost Theatres, 1969; Discovering Theatre Ephemera, 1973; Southend Playhouses from 1793, 1969; Plays: George..From Caroline, 1971; The Toast Is..series, 1979-83; Editor, Crime Writers' Handbook of Practical Information, 1989; Play: Murder at St Dunstans', 1982. Contributions to: The Times; Sunday Times; The Poisoned Pen; The Accountant; The Stage; Fur Weekly News; Essex Countryside; Evening Echo; Art & Antiques Weekly; Food & Cookery; Essex Police Magazine. Honours: Knight Grand Cross; Order of St Michael; Fellow, Royal Society of Arts, Crime Writers' Association, committee, 1985-88. Memberships: Mystery Writers of America; British Academy of Film & TV Arts; Fellow, Institute of Taxation; Fellow, Faculty of Building; Member Cookery & Food Association. Address: 85 Chalkwell Avenue, Westcliff-on-Sea, Essex, SS0 8NL, England.

MELLOW James R, 28 Feb 1926, MA, USA. Writer; Biographer; Art Critic. Education: BS, Northwestern University, 1950. Appointments: STaff, 1955-61, Editor in Chief, 1961-65, Arts Magazine; Art Critic, NY International, 1965-69; Art Critic, New Leader, 1969-72; Art Critic, NY Times, 1969-74. Publications: Charmed Circle, 1974; Nathaniel

Hawthorne in His Times, 1980; Invented Lives, 1984; The Best in Arts, 1962; New York, The Art World, 1964; Hemingway: A Life Without Consequences, 1993. Contributions include: NY Times; WA Post; Chicago Tribune; Chicago Sun Times; Saturday REview; Gourmet; Horizon. Honours: National Book Award, 1983. Memberships: National Book Critics Circle; Authors Guild. Literary Agent: Georges Borchardt Inc, NY, USA. Address: PO Box 297, Clinton, CT 06413, USA.

MELLY (Alan) George (Heywood), b. 1926. Writer; Jazz Singer. Appointments: Jazz Singer, Mick Mulligan's Band, 1949-61; Writer, Flook Strip Cartoon, 1956-71; Pop Music Critic, 1965-67; TV Critic, 1967-71, Film Critic, 1971-73, Observer Newspaper, London; Compere, George, Granada TV Show, 1974. Publications: 1 Flook, 1962; Owning Up, 1965; Revolt into Style, 1970; Flook by Trog, 1970; Rum, Bum and Concertina, 1977; Media Mob (with B Fantoni), 1980; Great Lovers, 1981; Tribe of One, 1981; Mellymobile, 1982; Swans Reflecting Elephants, 1982; Scouse Mouse, 1984; It's All Writ Out For You, The Life and Works of Scottie Wilson, 1986; Paris and the Surealists, with Michael Woods, 1991. Address: 33 St Lawrence Terrace, London W10 5SR, England.

MELNIKOFF Pamela Rita, b. London, England. Journalist; Author. m. Edward Harris, 29 Mar 1970. Education: North London Collegiate School. Appointments: Reporter, Feature Writer, The Jewish Chronicle, 1960-70; Film Critic, The Jewish Chronicle, 1970-. Publications: The Star and the Sword; Plots and Players; Prisoner in Time; Others inc, The Ransomed Menorah; Works Performed: Cantata Heritage (Librettist), World Premiere in London, June 1993. Contributions to: The Jewish Quarterly; Poetry Review. Honours: Golden Pen Award; Poetry Societys Greenwood Prize. Memberships: PEN; Society of Authors; Guild of Jewish Journalists; Critics Circle. Address: 25 Furnival Street, London EC4A 1JT, England.

MELODY A, b. Cumberland, MD, USA. Author, Scientist. Education: BS, Mathematics, 1971; MA, Mathematics, 1972. Publications: Love Is In The Earth - A Kaleidoscope Of Crystals, 1991; Love Is In The Earth - Laying On Of Stones, 1992; Love Is In The Earth - Mineralogical Pictorial, 1994. Address: 3440 Youngfield Street, Suite 353, Wheatridge, CO 80033, USA.

MELOSH Barbara. Publications: The Physician's Hand, 1982; American Nurses in Fiction (editor), 1984; Engendering Culture: Manhood and Womanhood in New England, 1991; Gender and American History Since 1890 (editor), 1993. Address: 604 A Street NE, Washington, DC 20002, USA.

MELTON David, b. 1934, United States of America. Children's Writer; Poet. Publications: Todd (autobiographical), 1968; I'll Show You the Morning Sun (poem), 1971; Judy: A Remembrance (biography/poetry), 1971; When Children Need Help, 1972; This Man, Jesus, (childrens book) 1972; Burn the Schools, Save the Children, 1975; Children of Dreams, Children of Hope (with Raymundo Veras), 1975; A Boy Called Hopeless (childrens novel), 1976; How to help Your Preschooler Learn More, Faster and Better, 1976; And God Created...(poems), 1976; Theodore, 1978; The Survival Kit for Parents and Teenagers, 1979; The One and Only Autobiography of Ralph Miller, 1979; Harry S Truman, 1980; Promises to Keep, 1984; Written and Illustrated by..., 1985. Address: 7422 Rosewood Circle, Prairie Village, KSD 66208, USA.

MELVILLE Anne. See: **POTTER Margaret.**

MELVILLE James. See: **MARTIN (Roy) Peter.**

MELVILLE Jennie. See: **BUTLER Gwendoline (Williams).**

memphis slim. See: **SULLIVAN Larry Michael.**

MENASHE Samuel, b. 16 Sept 1925, NY, USA. Education: BA, Queens College; University of Paris. Publications: The Many Names Beloved, 1961; No Jerusalem But This, 1971; Fringe of Fire, 1973; To Open, 1974; Collected Poems, 1986. Contributions to: Poems in the Times Literary Supplement; Temonos; Poetry Nation Review; Poetry Durham; Proteus. Honour: Longview Foundation Award, 1957. Membership: PEN. Address: 75 Thompson Street, New York, NY 10012, USA.

MENDES Bob. See: **MENDES David.**

MENDES David (Bob Mendes), b. 15 May 1928, Antwerp, Belgium. Accountant. Education: Graduate in Accountancy, 1953. Publications: Day of Shame, 1988; The Chunnel Syndrome, 1989; The Fourth Sura, 1990; The Fraud Hunters, 1991; Vengeance, 1992; Races/Riots, 1993; Link, 1994. Contributions to: VIT Magazine; Sodipa. Honours: The Golden Halter, 1993; Dutch Award for the Best Thriller 1993, for Vengeance. Memberships: Flemish Writers Guild; PEN Club. Literary: Dan Wright, Ann Wright Literary Agency, 136 East 56 Street, NY 10022, USA. Address: Wezelsebaan 191, B 2900 Schoten, Belgium.

MENENDEZ Albert J, b. 1942, United States of America. Writer. Publications: The Bitter Harvest: Church and State in Northern Ireland, 974; Church-State Relations: An Annotated Bibliography, 1975; The Sherlock Holmes Quiz Book, 1975; The American Political Quiz Book, 1976; Religion at the Polls, 1977; Classics of Religious Liberty, 1978; John F Kennedy: Catholic and Humanist, 1974; The Dream Lives On, 1982; Christmas in the White House, 1983; Religious Conflict in America, 1985; School Prayer and Other Religious Issues in American Education, 19785; The Subject is Mudrder, 1985; The Road to Rome, 1986; Religion and the US Presidency, 1986; The Catholic Novel, 1987. Address: 8120 Fenton Street, Silver Spring, MD 20910, USA.

MERCHANT Carolyn b. 12 Jul 1936, Rochester, New York, USA. University Professor. Education: AB, Vasser College; MA, PhD, University of Wisconsin. Publications: The Death Of Nature: Women, Ecology and the Scientific Revolution, 1980; Ecological Revolutions: Nature, Gender, and Science in New England, 1993. Contributions to: academic journals including: Isis; British Journal For the History of Science; Environment. Memberships: American Society for Environmental History; American Council of Learned Societies (Fellow, 1978); British Society for thr History of Science; Society for the History of Technology; Center for the Advanced Study in the Behavioural Sciences (Fellow, 1978). Address: College of Natural Resources, University of California at Berkeley, Berkeley, CA 94720-0001, USA.

MERCHANT William Moelwyn, (Rev. Prof), b. 5 June 1913, Writer; Sculptor. m. Maria Eluned Hughes, 1938, 1 s, 1 d. Education: Exhibitioner, University College, Cardiff, BA, 1st Class Honours, English, 1933; 2nd Class 1st Div, History, 1934; MA, 1950; DLitt, 1960. Publication: Wordsworth's Guide to the Lakes, 1952, USA, 1953; Reynard Library Wordsworth, 1955, USA, 1955; Shakespeare and the Artist, 1959; Creed and Drama,1965; Editor, Merchant of Venice, 1967; Editor, Marlowe's Edward the Second, 1967; Comedy, 1972; Tree of Life (Libretto, music by Alun Hoddinott), 1972; Breaking the Code (poems), 1975; Editor, Essays and Studies, 1977; No Dark Glass, (poems), 1979; R S Thomas: a critical evaluation, 1979; Confrontation of Angels (poems), 1986; Jeshua (novel), 1986; Five from the Heights (novel), 1989; A Bundle of Papyrus (novel), 1989; Fragments of a Life (Autobiography), 1990; Inherit the land (short stories), 1992; Triple Heritage (novel), 1992. Contributions include: The Times Literary Supplement; Warburg Journal; Shakespeare Survey; Shakespeare Quarterly; Shakespeare Jahrbich; Encyclopedia Britannica. Honours: FRSL, 1976; Founder, Llanddewi Brefi Arts Festival, 1975; Honorary Fellow, University College of Wales, 1975; Hon, HLD, Wittenberg University, Ohio, 1973; Welsh Arts Council Literary Award, 1991. Address: 32A Willes road, Leamington Spa, Warwickshire, England.

MEREDITH Christopher, b. 15 Dec 1954, Tredegar, Wales. Writer; Senior Lecturer, University of Glamorgan. m. V Smythe, 1 Aug 1981, 2 sons. Education: BA (Joint Honours), Philosophy and English, University College Wales, Aberystwyth, 1976. Publications: Poems: This, 1984; Snaring Heaven, 1990; Novels: Shifts, 1988; Griffri, 1991. Contributions to: Literary magazines in Wales, England and USA. Honours: Eric Gregory Award, 1984; Welsh Arts Council Young Writer's Prize, 1985; Welsh Arts Council Fiction Prize, 1989; Griffri shortlisted for Book of the Year Award, 1992. Membership: Yr Academi Gymreig (English language Section). Address: c/o Seren Books, Andmar House, Tondu Road, Bridgend, Mid Glamorgan, Wales.

MEREDITH Donald Clynton, b. 12 Apr 1938, Inglewood, CA, USA. Writer. m. Jo Ann, 15 Oct 1962. Education: AA, Orange Coast College, 1959; Long Beach State College, 1959-60; San Francisco State College, 1961-62. Publications: Morning Line, 1980; Home Movies, 1982. Contributions to: Image Magazine; The TX Review; The Short Story Review; Kingfisher; Folio; Slipstream; Poets and Writers; Modern Maturity Magazine; Executive Magazine. Honours: National Endowment for the Arts Grant, 1982, 88; Pushcart Prize, 1983-84; Best Story Award, 1990. Memberships: Poets and Writers; National Writers

Union. Address: 708 Gravenstein Hwy North, #124, Sebastopol, CA 95472, USA.

MEREDITH William. Poet. Publications: Love Letters From an Impossible Land, 1944; Ships and Other Figures, 1948; The Open Sea, 1958; Shelley: Selected Poems, 1962; Alcools: Poems 1898-1913 by Guillaume Apollinaire (translator), 1964; Wreck of the Thresher, 1964; Earth Wife, 1970; Hazard, the Painter, 1975; The Cheer, 1980; Poets of Bulgaria (editor), 1986; Partial Accounts, 1987; Poems are Hard to Read, 1991. Honours: Pulitzer Prize, 1988. Address: 6300 Bradley Avenue, Bethseda, MD 20817, USA.

MERRILL Christopher, b. 24 Feb 1957, MA, USA. Writer. m. 4 June 1983. Education: BA, Middlebury College, 1975-79; MA, University of WA, 1979-82. Appointments: Ingram Merrill Fellow, 1991. Publications: Workbook; Fevers & Tides; The Forgotten Language; From the Faraway Nearby; The Grass of Another Country; Outcroppings; Watch Fire, 1994. Contributions to: The Paris Review; Poetry East; Poetry Wales; Poetry Northwest; Mississippi Review; Praire Schooner; New VA Review; Sierra Magazine; Northern Lights; Seneca Review. Honours: Sherman Brown Neff Fellow; Columbia: A Magazine of Poetry & Prose Editors Award; Ingram Merrill Award; Praire Schooners Readers Choice; John Ciardi Fellow. Memberships: Elizabeth Grassman, Sterling Lord Literistic, NY 10010, USA. Address: 2214 SE 59th Avenue, Portland, OR 97215, USA.

MERRILL (Josephine) Judith Grossman, (Cyril Judd), b. 1923, Canada. Writer. Appointments include: Freelance Writer and Lecturer, 1949-; Research assistant, Ghostwriter, 1943-47; Editor, Bantam Books, New York City, 1947-49; Director, Milford Science Fiction Writers Conference, 1956-61; Writing Reacher, Adult Education programme, Port Jervis, New York, 1963-64; Book Editor, Fantasy and Science Fiction, 1965-69; Radio Documentaries for Canadian Broadcasting Corporation, 1971-75; Video Documentaries and Commentories for TV Ontario, 1978-81; Writer-in-Residence, Centennial College (Toronto), 1983; Toronto Public Libraries, 1987; Brampton Public Libraries, 1989. Publications: Shadow on the Hearth, 1950; Shot in the Dark, 1950; Beyond the Human Ken, 1952; As Cyril Judd: Gunner Cade, 1952; Outpost Mars, 1952; Sin in Space, 1956; Beyond the Barriers of Space and Time, 1954; Human? 1954; Galaxy of Ghouls, 1955; Off the Beaten Orbit, 1959; S-F: The Year's Greatest Science Fiction and Fantasy 1-6, continued as The Year's Best S-F, 7th-11th Annual, 12 vols, 1956-68, as SF '57-'59, 3 vols (in United Kingdom as Annual SF and the Best of Sci-Fi, 5 vols 1965-70); The Tomorrow People, 1960; Out of Bounds, (short stories), 1960; SF: The Best of the Best, 1967; Daughters of Earth (short stories), 1968; England Swings SF, 1968 (in United Kingdom abridged edition as The Space-Time Journal), 1972; Survival Ship and Other Stories, 1973; The Best of Judith Merrill (short stories), 1976; Tesseracts: Canadian S-F, 1985; Daughters of Earth and Other Stories, 1985. Address: 40 St George Street, Toronto, Ontario, Canada, M5S 2E4.

MERSSERLI Douglas John, b. 30 May 1947, Waterloo, Iowa, USA. Publisher; Poet; Fiction Writer. Education: BA, University of Wisconsin; MA, 1974, PhD, 1979, University of Maryland. Appointments: Assistant Professor, Literature, Temple University, 1979-85; Director, Contemporary Arts Education Project Inc, 1982-; Publisher, Sun & Moon Press, 1976-. Publications: Djuna Barnes: A Bibliography, 1976; Dinner on the Lawn, 1979; Some Distance, 1982; River to Rivet: A Poetic Manifesto, 1984; Language, Poetries, Editor, 1987; Maxims from My Mother's Milk/Hymns to Him: A Dialogue, 1988; Contemporary American Fiction, Editor, 1983; Silence All Round Marked: An Historical Play in Hysteria Writ, 1992; Along Without: A Film for Poetry, 1992. Contributions to: Roof; Mississippi Review; Paris Review; Boundry 2; Art Quarterly; Los Angeles Times. Memberships: Modem Language Association. Address: c/o Sun & Moon Press, PO Box 481170, Los Angeles, CA 90048, USA.

MERTZ Barbara Louise Gross, (Barbara Michaels, Elizabeth Peters), b. 29 Sept 1927, Canton, IL, USA. Writer. div, 1 s, 1 d. Education: PhD, University of Chicago, 1952. Publications include: Temples, Tombs & Hieroglyphs, 1964, 78, 90; Red Land, Black Land: The World of Ancient Egyptians, 1966, 89, 90; Sons of the Wolf, 1967; The Dark on the Other Side, 1970; Greygallows, 1972; The Crying Child, 1973; Wait For What Wil Com, 1978; Street of the Five Moons, 1978; Summer of the Dragon, 1979; The Love Talker, 1980; The Curse of the Pharaohs, 1981; The Copenhagen Connection, 1982; Silhouette in Scarlet, 1982; Die for Love, 1984; The Mummy Case, 1985; Lion in the Valley, 1986; Trojan Gold, 1987; Deeds of the Disturber, 1988;

Naked Once More, 1989; The Last Camel Died at Noon, 1991; Vanish with the Rose, 1991; Houses of Stone, 1993; The Snake, The Crocodile and the Dog, 1992; Night Trainto Memphis, 1994. Contributions to: The Writer; WA Post; BAltimore Sun; Encyclopaedia Britannica; Americana World Book. Honour: Doctor of Humane Letters, Hood College, 1992. Memberships: Authors Guild; Myustery Writers of Am. Literary Agent: Dominick Abel. Address: c/o Dominick Abel, 498 West End Avenue, New York, NY 10024, USA.

MESERVE Walter Joseph, b. 1923, USA. Playwright; Writer. Publications include: The Complete Plays of W D Howells, 1960; Outline History of American Drama, 1965; Discussions of Modern American Drama, 1966; American Satiric Comedies, 1969; Robert E Sherwood, 1970; Modern Drama from Communist China, 1970; Studies in Death of a Salesman, 1972; Modern Literature from China, 1974; An Emerging Enterainment: The Drama of the American People to 1828, 1977; The Revels History of Drama in English VIII: American Drama, 1977; Cry Woolf, 1982; Heralds of Promise: The Drama of the American People During the Age of Jackson 1829-1849, 1986; Whos Where in the American Theatre, 1990; A Chronological Outline of World Theatre, 1992; An Outline History of American Drama, 1994. Honours: Fellowship, National Endowment for the Humanities, 1973, 78, 83; Fellowship, Guggenheim Foundation, 1984. Address: PO Box 174, Brooklin, Maine 04616, USA.

MESSENT Peter Browning, b. 24 Oct 1946, Wimbledon, England. University Lecturer. m. Brenda, 10 July 1972, div, 1 son, 1 daughter. m Carin, 9 July 1994. Education: BA Hons, American Studies, Manchester University, Manchester, England, 1969; MA, 1972; PhD, Nottingham, 1991. Appointments: Temporary Lecturer in American Literature, Manchester University, 1972-73; Lecturer in American Studies, Nottingham University, Nottingham, England, 1973-; Senior Lecturer in American and Canadian Studies, Nottingham University, 1994, Reader in Modern American Literature, Nottingham, 1995. Publications: Ernest Hemingway, 1992; New Readings of the American Novel, 1990; Henry James: Selected Tales, 1992 (editor); Twentieth Century Views: Literature of the Occult, 1981 (editor). Contributions to: Books and journals and magazines including Journal of American Studies, Essays in American Humor; Essays in Arts and Sciences. Memberships: Hemingway Society; British Association for American Studies; Mark Twain Circle. Address: Department of American and Canadian Studies, University of Nottingham, Nottingham NG7 2RD, England.

MESSER Thomas M, b. 1920, USA. Writer. Appointments: Teaching Assignments, Harvard University, 1960, Bernard College, 1965, Art Museum Curatorships 1971, Weslyan University, 1966, Vienna Hochschule Fur Angewandte Kunst, 1984, Frankfurt Goethe University, 1991-93. Publications: The Emergent Decade: Latin American Painters and Painting in the 1960's; Edvard Munch, 1973; Pablo picasso, 1974; Sixty Works: The Peggy Guggenheim Collection, 1982; Acquisitions Priorities, 1983; Edward Munch, 1986; Jean Dubuffet, 1990; Antoni Tapiea/Eduardo Chikida, 1993; Nicola de Stach, 1994. Memberships include: International Council of Museums; National Endowment for the Arts; Kandinsky Society; Curatorships: La Caixa Foundation, Barcelona; Schien Kunsthalle, Frankfurt. Address: 303 E 57th Street, New York, NY 10022, USA.

MESTAS Jean-Paul, b. 15 Nov 1925, Paris, France. Engineer; Poet; Critic; Essayist; Lecturer; Translator; Consultant. m. Christaine Schoubrenner, 23 Dec 1977, 2 s, 1 d. Education: Graduated, Institute of Political Studies, Paris, 1947; LLB, 1947; BA, 1947. Publications: Soliels noirs, 1965; Part de Vivre, 1968; Resurgences, 1969; Romance Limousine, 1970; Chateau de Paille, 1971; Plaise aux souvenire, 1972; L'Aventue des choses, 1973; Le retour d'Ulysse, 1974; Traduire la Memoire, 1975; Pays Nuptial, 1977; Memoire d'Exil, 1978; Cette idee qui ne vivra pas, 1979; En ce royaume d'ombre et d'eau, 1982; Entre deux temps, 1983; En Ecoutnat vieillir les lapes, 1983; Ismene, 1984; Entre les colonns du vent, 1984; Dans la longue authomne du coeur, 1985; L'ancre et le cyclone, 1987; La terre est pleine de hailons, 1988; Entre les violons du silence, 1988; Chant pour Chris, 989; La Lumiere arriva des mains, 1990; Roses de Sable, 1990. Works in anthologies, monographs, essays, including: Rencontre avec Manes Sperber, 1979; En prenant ainsi conscience du Monde...Ilaire Voronca, 1979; Sur les portes et aux fronts des hommes: Alberto E Mazzocchi, 1981; Comme une vie Qui marche: Mara Guimaraes, 1981; Present de Voronca, 198; Dans sa harpe d'oiseuz lilas: Henry Rougier, 1984; Privire Asupra Poeziei Romance de Azi: Revista de Istoriei si teorie literara 1, 1985, 2, 1986; Seigneur, que ne m'as-tu fait pierre: Ion Caraion, 1986; Dans

ce pays comme au debut du monde: Audrey Bernard et Jeanne Maillet, 1986; Nichita Stanescu ou les epines de la gloire, 1988. Contributions to: Numerous magazines and journals in some 50 countries. Honours: Excellence in Poetry, Int Poet, NY, 1982; Premio della Cultura Carlo Alianello, Palermo, 1991. Memberships: Associate, Emeritus Academician: International Academy of Madras; Academy of Human Sciences, Brazil; Accademia Internazionale, Naples; Life Member, International Writers and Artists, New York. Address: 65 Avenue du Parc d Proce, 44 100 Nantes, France.

MESTERHAZI Marton, b. 7 July 1941, Budapest, Hungary. Radio Drama Script Editor. m. Agnes Pécsvari, 7 July 1962, 1 son, 1 daughter. Education: MA, Hungarian English and French, Budapest, 1964; PhD, English Literature, 1987. Publications: The World of Sean O'Casey, 1983; Sean O'Casey in Hungary, 1926-1986, 1993; Translations: The Selected Essays of Arnold J Toynbee, 1971; Ian McEwan: The Comfort of Strangers, 1984; Brian Friel: The Communication Cord, 1990. Contributions to: Nagyvilag, (literary monthly). Honours: Outstanding Programmes Prizes, Hungarian Radio. Memberships: Hungarian Irish Cultural Society; Chamber of Hungarian Radio Programme Makers. Literary Agent: Artisjus, Hungarian Copywright Office. Address: Hungarian Radio, Drama H-1800, Budapest, Hungary.

METCALF John Wesley, b. 12 Nov 1938, Carlisle, England. Writer. m. Myrna Teitelbaum, 3 s, 2 d. Education: BA, Bristol University, 1960. Appointments: Writer in Residence, University of New Brunswick, 1972-73, Loyola of Montreal, 1976, University of Ottawa, 1977, Concordia University, 1980-81, University of Bologna, 1985. Publications: The Lady Who Sold Furniture, 1970; The Teeth of My Father, 1975; Girl in Gingham, 1978; Kicking Against the Pricks, 1982; Adult Entertainment, 1986; Some 25 Texts and Anthologies Edited; How Stories Mean, 1993; Shooting The Stars, 1993; Freedom from Culture, 1994. Contributions to: Many Publications in Canada & USA. Honours: Canada Council Arts Award, 1968, 69, 71, 74, 76, 78, 80, 83, 85. Literary Agent: Denise Bukowski, The Bukowski Agency, 125B Dupont Street, Toronto, Ontario, Canada. Address: 128 Lewis Str, Ottawa Ontario, Canada K2P 0S7.

METCALF Paul, b. 7 Nov 1917, MA, USA. Writer. m. Nancy Harman Blackford, 30 May 1942, 2 d. Education: Taft School, Watertown, CT, 1936. Appointments: Writer in Residence, University of KS; Writers Conference, Lecturer, Teacher, University of IN; Visiting Professor, University of CA; Writer in Residence, The Centrum Foundation; Writer in Residence, State University of NY. Publications: Genoa; Apalache; Waters of Potowmack; Where Do You Put The Horse?; Headlands. Contributions to: Innumerable. Honours: The Morton Dauwen Zabel Award; American Academy and Institute of Arts and Letters. Address: RFD 1, Box 60, Chester, MA 01011, USA.

METLITZKI Dorothee, b. 27 July 1914, Koenigsberg, Germany. Professor Emeritus. 1 daughter. Education: BA (Hons), 1936, MA, 1938, University College, School of Oriental Studies, University of London; PhD, Yale University, 1957. Appointments: Instructor, Hebrew University, Jerusalem, 1939-44; Instructor, British Council, British Institute, Cairo, Egypt, 1945-47; Lecturer, Associate Professor, University of California, Berkeley, USA, 1957-65; Senior Lecturer, Professor, 1965-85, Professor Emeritus, 1985-, Yale University, New Haven, Connecticut. Publications: Essential Poetry (co-author), 1942; Melville's 'Orienda', 1961, Reprinted, 1971; The Matter of Araby in Medieval England, 1977. Contributions to: On the Origin of Fedallah in Moby-Dick, in American Literature, 1955; The Pearl-Poet as Bazalel, in Medieval Studies, 1964-64. Honours: Fellowship, American Council of Learned Studies, 1963-64. Membership: Former President, Oriental Club, Yale University. Address: 305 Crown Street, Room 226, Yale University, New Haven, CT 06517, USA.

METZ Jerred, b. 5 May 1943, Lakewood, New Jersey, USA. Writer; Social Service Administrator. m. Sarah Barker, 14 May 1978, 1 s, 1 d. Education: BA, 1965, MA, 1967, University of Rhode Island; PhD, University of Minnesota, 1972. Appointments: Poetry Editor, Webster Review, 1973-. Publications: Halley's Coment, 1910: Fire in the Sky, 1985; Drinking the Dipper Dry: Nine Plain-Spoken Lives, 1980; Angels in the House, 1979; Three Legs Up, Cold as Stone, Six Legs Down, Blood and Bone, 1977; The Temperate Voluptary, 1976; Speak Like Rain, 1975. Contributions to: Numerous peoms and short stories in magazines and journals. Literary Agent: Mary Yost. Address: 56200 Jackson Street, Pittsburgh, PA 15206, USA.

METZGER Deena, b. 17 Sept 1936, Brooklyn, NY, USA. Writer; Poet; Playwright; Essayist; Teacher; Lecturer; Healer; Counselor. m. (1)H Reed Metzger, 26 Oct 1957, (2)Michael Ortiz Hill, 20 Dec 1987, 2 s. Education: BA, Brooklyn College; MA, University of CA; PhD, International College, Los Angeles. Appointments: Faculty Member, CA Institute of the Arts, 1970-75; Professor, Los Angeles Valley College, 1966-69, 1973-74, 1975-79; Founded, Director, Writing Program of Feminist Studio Workshop and Womens Building, 1973-77; Teaching Writing Privately, 1976-. Publications: Dark Milk, 1978; The Book of Hags, 1978; The Axis Mundi, 1981; Dreams Against the State; The Woman Who Slept with Men to Take the War Out of Them and Tree; What Dinah Thought, 1989; Looking for the Faces of God, 1989; A Sabbath Among the Ruins, 1992; Writing For Your Life: A Guide to Companion to the Inner Worlds, 1992. Literary Agent: Muriel Nellis. Address: PO Box 186, Topanga, CA 90290, USA.

MEWSHAW Michael, b. 1943, USA. Author. Publications: Man in Motion, 1970; Walking Slow, 1972; The Toll, 1974; Earthly Bred, 1976; Intro 9, 1978; Land Without Shadow, 1979; Life for Deth, 1980; short Circuit, 1983; Year of the Gun, 1984; Blackballed, 1986; Money to Burn, 1987; Playing Away, 1988; True Crime, 1991; Ladies of the Court, 1993. Contributions to: NY Times; WA Post. Memberships: PEN; TX Institute of Letters. Address: c/o Owen Laster, William Morris Agency, 1350 Sixth Avenue, New York, NY 10019, USA.

MEYER Ben F, b. 5 Nov 1927, Chicago, USA. Professor. m. Denise Oppliger, 27 Mar 1969. Education: BA, 1952; MA, 1953; PHI, 1952; SSL, 1961; STD, Gregorian University (summa cum laude), 1965. Publications: The Man for Others, 1970; The Church in Three Tenses, 1971; Spanish Translation, El Hombre Para Los Demas, 1973; The Aims of Jesus, 1979; The Early Christians, 1986; TV Script, Christianity, 1974; Critical Realism and the New Testament, 1989; Lonergan's Hermeneutics (co-edited with S E McEvenue), 1989; Christus Faber, The Master Builder and the House of God, 1992; One Loaf, One Cup, 1993; Five Speeches that Changed the World, 1994; Reality and Illusion in New Testament Scholarship, 1995. Contributions to: Editorial Consultant; Method; Boston; Ex Auditu; Princeton; Articles in Various Journals. Memberships: Canadian Society of Biblical Studies; Studiorum Novi Testament Societas. Address: Dept of religious Studies, McMaster University, Hamilton, Ontario, Canada L8S 4K1.

MEYER E Y, b. 11 Oct 1946, Liestal, Switzerland. Novelist; Essayist; Dramatist. m. Florica Malureanu. Publications: Ein Reisender in Sachen Umsturz, 1972; In Trubschachen, 1973; Eine entfernte Aehnlichkeit, 1975; Die Ruckfahrt, 1977; Die Halfte der Erfahrung, 1980; Playdoyer, 1982; Sundaymorning, 1984; Das System des Doktor Maillard oder Die Welt der Maschinen, 1994. Contributions to: Numerous periodicals. Honours: Literature Prize of the Province of Basel, 1976; Gerhart Hauptmann-Prize, 1983; Prize of the Swiss Schiller-Foundation, 1984; Welti-Prize for the Drama, 1985. Memberships: Swiss Writers Association; Swiss-German PEN Centre. Address: Brunnen-Gut, CH 3027 Berne, Switzerland.

MEYER June. See: **JORDAN June.**

MEYER Lynn. See: **SLAVITT David Rytman.**

MEYER Michael, b. 11 June 1921, London, England. Freelance Writer. 1 daughter. Education: MA, Christ Church, Oxford. Appointments: Lecturer in English Literature at Uppsala University, Sweden, 1947-50's; Visiting Professor of Drama at Dartmouth College, 1978; University of Colorado, 1986; Colorado College, 1988; Hofstra University, 1989; UCLA, 1991. Publications: (Editor with Sidney Keyes and Contributor), Eight Oxford Poets, 1941; Editor, Collected Poems of Sidney Keyes, 1945; Editor, The Minos of Crete, by Sidney Keyes, 1948; The End of the Corridor (novel), 1951; The Ortolan (play), 1967; Henrik Ibsen: The Making of a Dramatist, 1967; Henrik Ibsen: The Farewell to Poetry, 1971; Henrik Ibsen: The Top of a Cold Mountain, 1971; Lunatic and Lover (play), 1981; Editor, Summer Days, 1981; Ibsen on File, 1985; Strindberg, a Biography, 1985; File on Strindberg, 1986; Not Prince Hamlet (memoirs), (USA Words Through a Windowpane), 1989; The Odd Women (play), 1993; Numerous translations including all the major plays of Ibsen (1960-86) and of Strindberg (1964-91). Honours: Gold Medal of the Swedish Academy, 1964; Whitbread Biography Prize, 1971; FRSL, 1971; Knight Commander of the Order of the Polar Star (Swedish), 1977; Royal Norwegian Order of Merit, 1995. Literary Agent: David Higham

Associates Ltd. Address: 4 Montagu Square, London W1H 1RA, England.

MEYER Nicholas, b. 1945, United States of America. Author. Publications: Target Practice, 1974; The Seven Percent Solution, 1974; The West End Horror, 1976; Black Orchid (with Barry J Kaplan), 1978; Confessions of a Homing Pigeon, 1981; The Canary Trainer, 1993. Address: c/o Bloom and Dekom, 9255 Sunset Boulevard, Los Angeles, CA 90069, USA.

MEYER Paul J, b. USA. Corporate President. m. Jane Gurley Meyer, 3 sons, 2 daughters. Appointments: Insurance Sales, 1948-57; Sales Executive, Word Inc, Waco, Texas, 1958-59; Founder, President, SMI Inc, Leadership Management Inc, 1960-. Publications: Building Financial Success; Dynamics of Creative Selling; Dynamics of Personal Goal Setting; Dynamics of Personal Motivation; Dynamics of Personal Time Control; Dynamics of Success Attitudes; Dynamics of Successful Communication; Dynamics of Successful Management; Effective Communication; Effective Management Development; Effective Motivational Management; Effective Personal Leadership; Effective Personal Productivity; Effective Selling Strategies; Effective Supervisory Management; Effective Time Management; Making of a Champion; Personal Success Planner; Sales Manager's Motivation Program. Contributions to: Over 200 journals and magazines. Honours include: Honorary Doctorate of Aviation Education, Embry-Riddle Aeronautical University, 1971; Honorary Doctorate of Humane Letters, Fort Lauderdale University, 1971; Honorary Doctorate of Letters, East Texas Baptist University, 1989; The Barnabas Award, 1990; Golden Key National Honor Society, 1992; Baylor University Alumnus Honoris Causa Award, 1992. Memberships past and present include: Life Member, Baylor University Alumni Association; Gamma Beta Phi; American Management Association; American Franchise Association; Waco Chamber of Commerce; National Speakers Association. Hobbies: Cycling; Flying; Golf; Mountain hiking; Scuba diving; Skiing; Tennis (Texas-ranked player). Address: 2524 N Valley Mills Drive, Waco, TX 76710, USA.

MEYERS Jeffrey, b. 1939, USA. Writer. Publications include: Fiction and the Colonial Experience, 1973; The Wounded Spirit: A Study of Seven Pillars of Wisdom, 1973; T E Lawrence: A Bibliography, 1975; A Reader's Guide to George Orwell, 1975; George Orwell: The Critical Heritage, 1975; Painting and the Novel, 1975; A Fever at the Core, 1976; George Orwell: An Annotated Bibliography of Criticism, 1977; Married to Genius, 1977; Homosexuality and Literature, 1890-1930, 1977; Katherine Mansfield: A Biography, 1978; The Enemy: A Biography of Wyndham Lewis, 1980; Wyndham Lewis: A Revolution, 1980; D H Lawrence and the Experience of Italy, 1982; Hemingway: The Critical Heritage, 1982; D H Lawrence and the Experience of Italy, 1982; Disease and the Novel, 1860-1960, 1984; Hemingway: A Biography, 1985; D H Lawrence and Tradition, 1985; The Craft of Literary Biography, 1985; The Legacy of D H Lawrence, 1987; Manic Power: Robert Lowell and His Circle, 1987; Robert Lowell: Interviews and Memoirs, 1988; The Biographer's Art, 1989; The Spirit of Biography, 1989; T E Lawrence: Soldier, Writer, Legend, 1989; Graham Greene: A Revaluation, 1989; D H Lawrence: A Biography, 1990; Joseph Conrad: A Biography, 1991; Edgar Allan Poe: His Life and Legacy, 1992; Scott Fitzgerald: A Biography, 1994; Edmund Wilson: A Biography, 1995. Membership: Royal Society of Literature. Literary Agent: Sandy Dijkstra Agency. Address: 84 Stratford Road, Kensington, CA 94707, USA.

MEYLAKH Michael, b. 20 Dec 1944, Tashkent. Translator; Journalist; Literary Critic; Poet. m. Rita Ilukhin, 24 Dec 1989. Education: University of Leningrad, 1967; Institute of Linguistics, Academy of Sciences, 1967-70. Appointments: La Pensée Russe, Correspondent, 1988-. Publications: V Nabokov, (translations); The Language of the Troubadours; Daniel Harms Collected Works; Alexander Vvedensky Complete Works; Anna Akhmatova Poems; The Lives of the Troubadours, 1994; The OBERIU Poets, 1994. Contributions to: La Pensée Russe; Financial Times; Appolo; Times Literary Supplement; Continent. Honours: Political Prisoner in Russia, 1983-87. Memberships: PEN; Association Internationale d'Etudes Occiaties; Union of Russian Authors, 1993; Union of Russian Journalists, 1993. Address: Bolchoy 21-v, Komarovo, St Petersburg, Russia 189643.

MEYNELL Hugo Anthony, b. 23 Mar 1936, England. m. 24 Feb 1969, 1 Adopted s, 3 d. Education: Eton College, 1949-54; Cambridge University, 1959. Appointments: Lecturer, University of Leeds, 1961-81;

Visiting Professor, Emory University, 1978; Professor, Religious Studies, University of Calgary, 1981. Publications: Introduction to the Philosophy of Bernard Lonergan; The Intelligible Universe; Freud, Mare & Morals; The Art of Handel's Operas; The Nature of Aesthetic Value; Others inc. God and the World. Contributions to: The New Scholastic; Heythrop Journal; New Blackfriars. Memberships: Canadian Society for Religious Studies; Canadian Philosophical Association; Royal Society of Canada. Address: Dept of Religious Studies, University of Calgary, Calgary, Alberta, Canada T2N 1N4.

MEZEY Katalin, b. 30 May 1943, Budapest, Hungary. General Secretary of Hungarian Writers Trade Union. m. Janos Olah, 1 Mar 1971, 2 sons, 1 daughter. Education: Zurich University, Philology, German Literature, 1964; Philology, Hungarian Literature and Adult Education, Eotvos University in Budapest. Appointments: Poet (or Writer), Journalist and Translator, 1970-; Secretary, 1987, General Secretary 1992, Trade Union of Hungarian Writers, Founder and Editor of Publishers, Szephalom Konyvmuhely, 1989-. Publications: Books: Waiting for the Bus, 1970; Materials Study, 1977; Green Jungle, 1978; Csutka-Jutka's Teles, 1981; Live Film, 1984; Again and Again, 1985; Holes in the Classbook, 1987; Letters to the Native Country, 1989; Paul Whowas in Nopossible-Land, 1987; Continental Writer, 1991; The Two Princes, Who Are the Same, 1994. Address: Pesthidegkut 2 pf 5, Budapest 1286, Hungary.

MFAUME Rogers, b. 20 June 1946, Tanga, Tanzania. Lawyer; Journalist; Author. Educations: Lenigrand Univ, 1988; Kharkov University; MA, Tashkent University. Appointments: Legal Advisor, 1989; Author, 1990. Publications: Kiswahili For All, Part 1, 1990; Kiswahili For All, Part 2, 1992; Juvenile Delinquency, 1994; Lecturer, Aarhus Center for Kiswahili Language, Denmark. Contributions to: Chief Editor, Afro-New Magazine. Memberships: Dansk Forfatter Forening, 1991; The Danish Writer's Union; Ledernes Hovedorganisation, Denmark; Executives Organization, Denmark. Literary Agent: Tandan. Address: PO Box 2641, Aarhus, DK-8200, Denmark.

MIALL Robert. See: **BURKE John Frederick.**

MIANOWSKA Aleksandra Jadwiga, b. 16 July 1912, Rusocice, Poland. Voluntary Nurse; Literary Chief; Lecturer; Actress; Actress; Stage Director; Author. m. Walery Bigay Mianowski, 27 June 1936 (dec). Educcation: School of Political Sciences, 1936; Polish and Classical Philology, 1937; Doctor of Law, 1947; Diploma of Stage Director, 1960; DrPhil, 1968. Appointments: Voluntary Nurse, hospitals for Polish prisoners-of-war; With Voluntary Audience, Cracow and towns in Southern Poland, 1956-81. Publications: Underground Print: Polish Society in the novels of Eliza Orzeszkowa, 1944; Robinson Cruzoe, adaptation of 2 volumes, 1945; Stories for a Little Brother; Sutkovski of Stephan Zerömski on the Polish Stages, 1975; Theatre. Contributions to: Odra; Przekroj; The Literary Life; Newspaper of Polish Underground; Polish Daily. Honours: Just Among the Peoples, Yad-Vashem, 1980. Membership: Society of Authors. Address: Karmelicka 9/3, 31-133 Cracow, Poland.

MICHAEL John,See:**CRICHTON Michael.**

MICHAEL Judith (pseudonym of husband and wife, Judith Barnard and Michael Fain). Publications: Deceptions; Possessions; Private Affairs; A Ruling Passion; Inheritance; Sleeping Beauty; Pot of Gold, 1993; A Tangled Web, 1994. Address: c/o Ann Patty, Editor-in-Chief, Crown Books, 201 East 50th Street, New York, NY 10022, USA.

MICHAELIS Bo Tao, b. 19 July 1948, Copenhagen, Denmark. Teacher; Critic; Author. m. Annette Gertrud Begtorp, 9 Oct 1976, 1 s, 1 d. Education: Studied Sorbonne, Paris, 1969-70; Univesity of Copenhagen. Appointments: Critic, Berlingkse Tidende, 1984-89; Reader, Gyldendal, 1985-; Chairman, palle Rosenkrantz, 1989-; Film Critic, Teacher, Danish Filmschool, 1989-. Publications: Portrait of the Private Eye as a petit Bourgeois; An Analysis of the Philip Marlowe Novels by Raymond Chandler; Lyst of Labyrint. Contributions to: Levende Billeder; Kosmorama; Dansk Noter; Essays on inc, Jorgen Gustava Brandt; Paul Auster; John Le Carre. Memberships: The Danish Writers Union; The Academy of Danish Crime Literatre; Union of Grammar School Teachers. Address: Standboulevarden 7, 4th 200 Copenhagen O, Denmark.

MICHAELS Anne, b. 1958. Canadian. Poet. Publications: The Weight of Oranges, 1985; Miner's Pond, 1992. Honour: Canadian Authors Association Literary Award, 1992.

MICHAELS Barbara. See: **MERTZ Barbara Louise Gross.**

MICHAELS Dale. See: **RIFKIN Shepard.**

MICHAELS Fern. Novelist; Animal Rights Activists. Married; 5 children. Publications: over 20 novels, including: Texas Sunrise; Texas Rich; Texas Heart; Texas Fury; For All Their Lives; To Have and to Hold; All She Can Be; Vixen in Velvet; Captive Embraces; Captive Innocence; Sin of Omission; Sins of the Flesh; Seasons of Her Life, 1994; Desperate Measures, 1994; Serendipity, 1994. Address: c/o Carol Fass Ballantine Publishing, 201 E 50th Street, New York, NY 10022, USA.

MICHAELS Kristin,See:**WILLIAMS Jeanne.**

MICHAELS Steve. See: **AVALLONE Michael Angelo.**

MICHAELS Wendy Faye, b. 25 May 1943, Melbourne, Victoria, Australia. Consultant. 3 sons. Education: BA; MA, Graduate Diploma, Educational Studies; ATCL; ASDA; MACE, PhD in progress. Publications: Played upon a Stage; When the Hurly Burly is Done; Up and Away; Inside Drama; Played upon Shakespeare's Stage; The Playwright At Work; A Deed without a Name; A Madman Shakes a Dead Geranium. Contributions to: Jeda; EQ; The Nadie Journal; The Australian. Membership: Australian Society of Authors. Address: 2 Marooba Road, Northbridge, New South Wales 2063, Australia.

MICHENER James Albert, b. 3 Feb 1907, NY, USA. Writer. m. (1) Patti Koon, 1935, div, (2) Vange Nord, 1948, div, (3) Mari Yoriko Sabusawa, 1955. Education: Swarthmore College; Colorado State College of Education; OH State University; Universities of PA, VA; Harvard and St Andrews. Appointments: Teacher, 2929-36; Professor, CO State College of Education, 1936-41; Associate Editor, Macmillan Co, 1941-46; US Naval Reserve, 1944-46. Publications include: Unit in the Social Studies, 1940; Tales of the South Pacific, 1947; The Fires of Spring, 1949; Return to Paradise, 1951; The Bridges at Toko ri, 1953; Floating World, 1955; The Bridge at Andau, 1957; Selected Writing, 1957; The Hokusai Sketchbook, 1958; Japanese Prints, 1959; Report of the Country Chairman, 1961; The Source, 1965; The Qulity of Life, 1970; kent State, 1971; The Drifters, 1971; Centennial, 1974; Sports in Am, 1976; Poland, 1983; Legacy, 1987; The World in My Home, 1992; Writers Handbook, 1992; My Lost Mexico, 1992; Creatures of the Kingdom, 1993; Literary Reflections, 1993; Recessional, 1994. Honours: Pulitzer Prize, 1947; Einstein Award, 1957; Medal of Freedom, 1977; Gold Medal Spanish Institute, 1980. Memberships: President Kennedys Food for peace Programme; NASA. Address: TX Center for Writers, University of TX, Austin, TX 78713, USA.

MICHIE Jonathan, b. 25 Mar 1957, London, England. Economist. m. Carolyn Downs, 5 Nov 1988, 1 son. Education: Balliol College, Oxford University, 1976-79; Queen Mary College, London University, 1979-80; Balliol College, Oxford University, 1980-85. Publications: The Economic Legacy; Wages in the Business Cycle; Beyond the Casino Economy; The Economics of Restructuring and Intervention; Unemployment in Europe, 1994; Managing the Global Economy, 1995. Memberships: Cambridge Journal of Economics. Address: Robinson College, Cambridge CB3 9AN, England.

MIDDLETON Christopher, b. 10 June 1926, Truro, Cornwall, England. University Teacher. Education: BA, 1951, DPhil, 1954, University of Oxford. Publications: Torse 3, 1962; Nonsequences, 1965; Our Flowers & Nice Bones, 1969; The Lonely Suppers of W V Balloon, 1975; Carminalenia, 1980; Serpentine, 1985; Two Horse Wagon Going By, 1986; Selected Writings, 1989; The Balcony Tree, 1992; The Pursuit of the Kingisher Essays, 1983. Honours: Sir Geoffrey Faber Memorial Prize, 1963; Guggenheim Poetry Fellowship, 1974-75; Schlegel Tieck Translation Prize, 1985. Address: Germanic Languages, EPS 3 154 University of TX, Austin, TX 78712, USA.

MIDDLETON Osman Edward, b. 25 Mar 1925, Christchurch, New Zealand. Writer; Author. m. 1949 (div), 1 son, 1 daughter. Education: Auckland University College, 1946, 1948; University of Paris, France, 1955-56. Appointments include: Robert Burns Fellow, University of Otago, 1970-71; Visiting Lecturer, University of Canterbury, 1971, also universities of Zurich, Frankfurt, Giessen, Kiel,

Erlangen, Regensburg, Turin, Bologna, Pisa, Venice, Rome, 1983; Writer in Residence, Michael Karolyi Memorial Foundation, Vence, France, 1983. Publications: The Stone & Other Stories, 1959; A Walk on the Beach, 1964; The Loners, 1972; Selected Stories, 1976; Confessions of an Ocelot, 1979; 10 Stories, 1953; From the River to the Tide, juvenile, 1962. Contributions to: Anthologies worldwide; Numerous magazines & journals. Honours: Achievement award, 1959, Scholarship in Letters, 1965, NZ Literary Fund; Hubert Church Prose Award, 1964; NZ Government Bursary winner, study in France, 1955-56; Joint Winner, NZ Prose Fiction Award, 1976; Member PEN, 1959-80; Committee, NZ Association of the Blind & Partially Blind, 1970-1995. Address: 20 Clifford Street, Dalmore, Dunedin, New Zealand.

MIDDLETON Roger, b. 19 May 1955, England. Education: BA, First Class Honours, Victoria University of Manchester, 1976; PhD, Cambridge University, 1981. Appointments; Lecturer in Economic History, University of Durham, Durham, England, 1979-87; Senior Lecturer in Economic History, University of Bristol, Bristol, England, 1987-. Publications: Towards the Managed Economy, 1985. Contributions to: Economic, History and Computing journals. Honours: T S Ashton Prize from Economic History Society, 1980 for best paper of the year by a young scholar in the Society's journal, Economic History Review. Memberships: Royal Economic Society, Economic History Society; Conference of Socialist Economists; Association of History and Computing; Institute of Fiscal Studies; Software Review; Economic History Review. Address: Department of Economic and Social History, University of Bristol, Bristol, BS1 1TB, England.

MIDDLETON Stanley, b. 1 Aug 1919, Bulwell, Nottingham, England. Writer. m. Margaret Shirley Charnley (nee Welch), 21 Dec 1951, 2 daughters. Education: BA London, 1940; MEd, 1952, MA (Hon), 1975, Nottingham. Publications: Holiday, 1974; Harris's Requiem, 1960; Entry into Jerusalem, 1983; Valley of Decision, 1990; Changes and Chances, 1990; Two Brothers, 1978; In a Strange Land, 1979; Blind Understanding, 1982; Recovery, 1988; Vacant Places, 1990; A Place to Stand, 1992; Married Past Redemption, 1993; Catalysts, 1994; Toward the Sea, 1995. Contributions to: Critical Quarterly; Fiction Magazine; Cambridge Review. Honours: Booker Prize, 1974. Memberships: Fellow of PEN. Literary Agent: Hutchinson. Address: 42 Caledon Road, Sherwood, Nottingham, England.

MIDWOOD Barton A, b. 10 Mar 1938, Brooklyn, NY, USA. Writer. m. Laura Melim, 10 Oct 1988, 3 s, 2 d. Education: BA, University of Miami, 1959. Appointments: Fiction Reviewer, Esquire Magaine, 1970-72. Publications: Bodkin; Phantoms; The Nativity; Bennett's Angel. Contributions to: Esquire; Atlantic; Paris Review; Dutton Review; Transatlantic Review; Columbia Magazine. Honours: Robert Frost Prize; NEA; Aga Khan Prize; Guggenheim. Membership: PEN. Address: 64 Meadow Street, Garden City, NY 11530, USA.

MIESEL Sandra Louise, b. 25 Nov 1941, New Orleans, Los Angeles, USA. Freelance Writer. m. John Louis Miesel, 20 June 1964, 1 s, 2 d. Education: BS, College of St Francis, 1962; MS, University of IL, 1965; MA, Univ of IL, 1966; abd, Indiana University, 1989. Publications: Shaman; Dreamrider; Against Times Arrow; A Separate Star; Heads to the Storm. Contributions to: Amazing; National Catholic Register; Catholic Twin Circle; Catholic Heritage; Our Sunday Visitor. Memberships: Lambda Iota Tau; Delta Epsilon Sigma; Phi Alpha Theta. Address: 8744 N Pennsylvania Street, Indianapolis, IN 46240, USA.

MIGHTON John, b. 1957. Canadian. Dramatist. Publications: Scientific Americans, 1990; Possible Worlds & A Short History of the Night, 1991. Honour: Governor General's Award, 1992.

MIKHAIL Edward H, b. 1928, Canadian. Appointments: Lecturer, Assistant Professor, University of Cairo, 1949-66; Associate Professor of English, 1966-72, Professor of English Literature, 1972-. University of Lethbridge. Publications: The Social and Cultural Setting of the 1890's, 1969; John Galsworthy the Dramatist, 1971; Comedy and Tragedy: A Bibliography of Criticsm, Sean O'Casey: A Bibliography of Criticism, A Bibliography of Modern Irish Drama 1899-1970, 1972; Dissertations on Anglo-Irish Drama, 1973; The Sting and the Twinkle: Conversations with Sean O'Casey (co-ed), 1974; J M Synge: A Bibliography of Criticis, 1975; Contemporary British Drama, 1950-1976: An Annotated Critical Bibliography, 1976; W B Yeats: Interviews and Recollections, J M Synge: Interviews and Recollections, English Drama, 1900-1950. Lady Gregory: Interviews and Recollections, 1977; Oscar Wilde: An Annotated Bibliography of Criticism, 1978; A Research

Guide to Modern Irish Dramatists, Oscar Wilde: Interviews and Recollections, The Art of Brendan Behan, 1979; Brendan Behan: An Annotated Bibliography of Criticism, 1980; An Annotated Bibliography of Modern Anglo-Irish Drama, Criticism, Brendan Behan: Interviews and Recllections, 1982; Sean O'Casey ahd His Critics, 1985. The Abbey Theatre, 1987. Address: 6 Coachwood Point West, Lethbridge, Alberta, Canada, T1J 4B3.

MIKHALKOV Sergey Vladimirovich, b. 13 Mar 1913, Moscow, Russia. Poet; Playwright; Childrens Writer. Education: Literary Institute, Moscow. Publications: Uncle Steve, 1936; Collected Works, 2 volumes; Film Script: Frontline Friends, 1941; Plays: After Mark Twain, 1938; Red Neckerchief; Selected Works, 1947; I Want to Go Home, 1949; Lobsters, 1952; Zaika-Zasnaika, 1955; Basni Mikhalkova, 1957; Sombrero, 1958; A Monument to Oneself, 1958; Campers, 1959; Collected Works, 4 volumes, 1964; Green Grasshopper, 1964; We Are Together, My Friend and I, 1967; In the Museum of Lenin, 1968; Fables, 1970; Disobedience Day, 1971; The Funny Bone (articles), 1971; Collected Works, 3 volumes 1970-71; Selected Works, 1973; Bibliographical Index, 1975. Honours: 4 Orders of Lenin; Hero of Socialist Labour, 1973; Red Banner; Red Banner of Labour; Red Star; Lenin Prize, 1970; 4 State Prizes; Merited Worker of Arts of RSFSR. Memberships: Academy of Pedagogical Sciences; Commission for Youth Affairs. Address: USSR Union of Writers ulitsa Vorovskogo 52, Moscow, USSR.

MIKKOLA Marja-Leena (Pirinen), b. 18 Mar 1939, Salo, Finland. Writer. Education: Candidate of Philosophy, Helsinki University, 1963. Publications: Naisia, 1962; Raskas Puuvilla, 1971; Laakarin Rouva, 1972; Anni Manninen, 1977; Maailman Virrassa, 1981; Jalkeen Kello Kymmenen, 1984; Translations of Poetry: Sylvia Plath: Sanantuojat, 1987; Dylan Thomas: Rakkaus on Viimeinen Valo, 1990; Anna Ahmatova: Runoja, 1992. Contributions to: Pamasso; Kultuurivihkot. Honours: Eino Leino Award, 1968; State Prize for Literature, 1971, 1972, 1977, 1984. Membership: Finnish Writers Union. Literary Agent: Otava, Helsinki. Address: Kalervonk 12 c 16, 00610 Helsinki, Finland.

MIKLOWITZ Gloria D, b. 18 May 1927, NY, USA. Writer. m. Julius Miklowitz, 28 Aug 1948, 2 s. Education: Hunter College of NY, 1944-45; BA, University of MI, 1948; NY University, 1948. Appointments: Instructor, Pasadena City College, 1970-80. Publications include: Did You Here What Happened to Andrea; Close to the Edge; The War Between the Classes; Anything to Win; The Emerson High Vigilantes; Suddenly Super Rich; Standing Tall, Looking Good; Desperate Pursuit; The Killing Boy; Past Forgiving. Contributions to: Numerous Journals, Magazines & Newspapers. Honours: 3 Novels Made TV Specials for Children; Western Australia Young Book Award, 1984; Bucks Herald for Teens Publishers Award, 1990; Wyoming Soaring Eagle Award, 1993. Memberships: PEN; Society of Childrens Book Writers; SC Council of Literature for Children and Young People. Literary Agent: Curtis Brown, NY, USA. Address: 5255 Vista Miguel Drive, La Canada, CA 91011, USA.

MILBURN Robert Leslie Pollington, b. 28 July 1907. Clerk in Holy Orders. m. Margery Kathleen Mary Harvie, 15 April 1944, 1 son, dec, 1 daughter. Education: Oundle, 1921-26; Sidney Sussex College, Cambridge; Worcester College, Oxford, 1934-57; Dean of Worcester, 1957-68; Master of the Temple, 1968-80. Publications: Early Christian Interpretation of History; early Christian Art & Architecture; Saints and their Emblems in English Churches. Contributions include: Many articles. Membership: Society of Antiquaries. Address: 5 St Barnabas, Newland Malvern, Worcs WR13 5AX, England.

MILES Betty, b. 1928, American. Publications: A House for Everyone, 1958; The Cooking Book, What Is the World? 1959; Having a Friend, A Day of Summer, 1960; Mr Turtle's Mystery, 1961; A Day of Winter, 1962; The Feast on Sullivan Street, 1963; The Bank Street Readers (assoc ed), 1965; A Day of Autumn, 1967; Joe Finds a Way, 1969; A Day of Spring, 1970; Just Think! 1971; Save the Earth! The Real Me, 1974; Just the Beginning, 1975; All It Takes Is Practise, 1976; Looking On, 1977; The Trouble with Thirteen, 1979; Maudie and Me and the Dirty Book, 1980; The Secret Life of the Underwear Champ, 1981; I Would If I Could, 1982; Sink or Swim, 1986; Save the Earth An Action Handbook for Kids, 1991. Address: 94 Sparkill Avenue, Tappan, NY 10983, USA.

MILES John. See: BICKHAM Jack Miles.

MILIONIS Christoforos, b. 4 Nov 1932, Greece. Writer. m. Tatiana Tsaliki, 28 Dec 1969, 1 daughter. Education: Diploma, Classical Greek Literature. Appointments: Conferences: University of Milano, 1991; Union Santore Santarosa, Torino, 1991; University of Triesta, 1991; University of Köln, 1988; Congress: University of Trieste, 1990. Publications: Short Stories: Chiristis Anelkystiros, 1993; Kalamas ke Acherontas, 1985; The Shirt of Centaur, 1982; The Short Stories of Trial, 1978; Novels: Silvestros, 1987; Dytiki Sinikia, 1980; Acrokeraunia, 1976. Contributions to: Endochora, Dokimasia; I Lexi; To Dentro; Anti; Grammata ke Technes; Kathimerini; Ta Nea. Honour: 1st State Award of Short Stories, 1986. Memberships: Society of Greek Writers; Union of Greek Philologists. Literary Agent: Editions Kedros, G Gennadiou Str 3, Athens 106 78, Greece. Address: 1, Agathiou Str, Athens 114 72, Greece.

MILKOMANE George Alexis Milkomanovich, (George Bankoff, George Borodin, George Braddin, Peter Conway, Alex Redwood, George Sava), b. 15 Oct 1903. Author; Consulting Surgeon. m. Jannette Hollingdale, 1939, 2 s. 2 d. Publications: (Autobiography, Medical) The Healing Knife, 1937; Beauty from the Surgeon's Knife, 1938; A Surgeon's Destiny, 1939; Donkey's Serenade, 1940; Twice the Clock Round, 1941; A Ring at the Door, 1941; Surgeon's Symphony, 1944; The Come by Appointment, 1946; The Knife Heals Again, 1948; The Way of a Surgeon, 1949; Strange Cases, 1950; A Doctor's Odyssey, 1951; Patients' Progress, 1952; A Surgeon Remembers, 1953; Surgeon Under Capricorn, 1954; The Lure of Surgery, 1955; A Surgeon at Large, 1957; Surgery and Crime, 1957; All this and Surgery Too, 1958; Surgery Holds the Door, 1960; A Surgeon in Rome, 1961; A Surgeon in California, 1962; Appointments in Rome, 1963; A Surgeon in New Zealand, 1964; A Surgeon in Cyprus, 1965; A Surgeon in Australia, 1966; Sex, Surgery, People, 1967; The Gates of Heaven are Narrow, 1968; Bitter Sweet Surgery, 1969; One Russian's Story, 1970; A Stranger in Harley Street, 1970; A Surgeon and his Knife, 1978; Living with your Psoriasis (essays), 1978; (Politica and Historical Books): Rasputin Speaks, 1941; Valley of Forgotten Peole, 1942; The Chetniks, 1943; School for War, 1943; They Stayed in London, 1943; Russia Triumphant, 1944; A Tale of Ten Cities, 1944; War Without Guns, 1944; Caught by Revolution, 1952; (Novels): Land Fit for Heroes, 1945; Link of Two Hearts, 1945; Gissy, 1946; Call it Life, 1946; Boy in Samarkand, 1950; Flight from the Palace, 1953; Pursuit in the Desert, 1955; The Emperor Story, 1959; Punishment Deferred, 1966;. Man Without Label, 1967; Alias Dr Hotzman, 1968; City of Cain, 1969; The Imperfect Surgeon, 1969; Nothing Sacred, 1970; Of Guilt Possessed, 1970; A Skeleton for My Mate, 1971; The Beloved Nemesis, 1971; On the Wings of Angels, 1972; The Sins of Andrea, 1972; Tell Your Grief Softy, 1972; Cocaine for Breakfast, 1973; Return from the Valley, 1973; Sheilah of Buckleigh Manor, 1974; Every Sweet Hath Its Sour, 1974; The Way of the Healing Knife, 1976; Mary Mary Quite Contrary, 1977; Crusader's Clinic, 1977; Pretty Polly, 1977; No Man is Perfect, 1978; A Stranger in his Skull, 1979; Secret Surgeon, 1979; Crimson Eclipse, 1980; Innocence on Trial, 1981; The Price of Prejudice, 1982; The Killer Microbes, 1982; Betrayal In Style, 1983; Double Identity, 1984; A Smile Through Tears, 1985; Bill of Indictment, 986; Rose By Any Other Name, 1987; The Roses Bloom Again, 1988; numerous novels as Geoge Broodin. Address: c/o A P Watt Ltd, 20 John Street, London, WC1N 2DR. England.

MILLAR Margaret (Ellis), b. 5 Feb 1915, Kitchener, Ontario, Canada. Writer. m. Kenneth Millar (Ross Macdonald), 1938, (dec 1983), 1 d. (dec). Education: Kitchener-Waterloo Collegiate, 1929-33; University of Toronto, 1933-36. Appointments: Screenwriter, Warner Brothers, Hollywood, 1945-46; Freelance Writer. Publications include: Crime Publications include: The Listening Walls, 1959; A Stranger in My Grave, 1960; How Like and Angel, 1962; The Fiend, 1964; Beyond This Point Are Monsters, 1971; Ask For Me Tomorrow, 1977; The Murder of Miranda, 1980; Mermaid, 1982; Banshee, 1983; Spider Webs, 1986, 1987; Novels: Experiment in Springtime, 1947; It's All in the Family, 1948; The Cannibal Heart, 1949, 1950; Wives and Lovers, 1954; Autobiography: The Birds and Beasts Were There, 1968; various short stories. Honours: Mystey Writers of America Edgar Allan Poe Award, 1956; Grand Master Award, 1982; Los Angeles Times Woman of the Year Award, 1965. Memberships: President, Mystery Writers of America, 1957-58. Literary Agent: Harold Ober Associates. Address: Harold Aber Associates, 425 Madison Avenue, New York, NY 10017, USA.

MILLAR Ronald (Graeme) (Sir), b. 1919, British. Appointment: Deputy Chairman, Theatre Royal, Haymarket, London, 1977-. Publications: Plays: Frieda, 1947; Waiting for Gillian, 1955; The Bride

and the Bachelor, 1958; A Ticklish Business, 1959; The More the Merrier, The Bride Comes Back, 1960; The Affair, 1962; The Affair, The New Men, The Masters; Three Plays Based on the Novels and with a Preface by C P Snow, 1964; Robert and Elizabeth, Number 10, 1967; They Don't Grow on Trees, 1969; Abelard and Heloise, 1970; The Case in Question, 1975; A Coat of Varnish, 1982; A View from the Wings (autobiography), 1993. Honour: Kt, 1980. Address: 7 Sheffield Terrace, London W8 7NG, England.

MILLARD Hamilton. See: KIRK-GREENE Anthony.

MILLER Arthur, b. 17 Oct 1915, New York, USA. Playwright. m. (1)Mary Grace Slattery, 1940 (div 1956), 1 s, 1 d, (2)Marily Monroe, 1956 (div 1951), (3)Ingeborg Morath, 1962. 1 d. Education: University of Michigan. Publications: The Man Who Had All the Luck, 1943; Situation Normal, 1944; Focus, 1945; All My Sons, 1947; Death of a Salesman, 1949; The Crucible, 1953; A View from the Bridge, 1955; A Memory of Two Mondays, 1955; Collected Plays, 1958; The Misfits (screenplay), 1959; After the Fall, 1964; Incident at Vichy, 1964; I Don't Need You Any More, (short stories), 1967; The Price (play) 1968; In Russia (with Inge Morath) 1969; Chinese Encounters (with Inge Morath) 1972; The Creation of the World and Other Business (play), 1972; Up From Paradise (musical), 1974; The American Clock, 1980; Playing for Time (play), 1981; Elegy for a Lady (play), 1983; Some Kind of Love Story (play) 1983; Salesman in Beijing (journal) 1984; The Archbishop's Ceiling, 1986; Danger, Memory! (two one-acts), 1987; Timebends (autobiography), 1987. Honours: Theatre Guild National Award, 1938; New York Drama Critics Circle Award, 1947, 1949; Pulitzer Prize for rama, 1949; Antoinette Perry Award, 1953; American Acadey of Arts and Letters Gold Medal for Drama, 1959; Anglo-American Award, 1966; Cretive Arts Award Brandeis University, 1970; Kennedy Centre Award, 1984; Hon D.Litt, Unviersity of East Anglia, 1984. Membership: President, International PEN, 1965-69. Address: c/o ICM, 40 W 57th Street, New York, NY 10019, USA.

MILLER Donald George, b. 30 Oct 1909, USA. Clergyman. Professor. m. Eleanor Chambers, 21 July 1937, 2 s, 1 d. Education: AB, Greenville College, 1930; STB, 1933; STM, 1934; MA, 1934; PhD, 1935, New York University; LLD, Waynesburg College, 1963; LittD, WA & Jefferson College, 1965. Appointments: Co Editor, Interpretation, 1947-62; Associate Editor, Laymans Bible Commentary, 1957-65; Editorial Board, Ex Auditu, 1985-. Publications include: Nature and Mission of the Church, 1957; Fire in thy Mouth, 1954; The Way to Biblical Preaching, 1957; The Gospel According to Luke, 1959; The Authority of the Bible, 1972; The Scent of Eternity: On A Life of Harris Elliott Kirk of Baltimore, 1989; This rock: A Commentary on 1 Peter, 1993. Contributions to: Over 35 Journals. Memberships: Society of Biblical Literature. Address: 401 Russell Avenue, Apt 405, Gaithersburg, MD 20877, USA.

MILLER Douglas Taylor, b. 27 May 1937, Professor. Author. m. Susanne Elin Nielson, 22 May 1982, 1 s, 1 d. Education: BA, Colby College, 1958; MA, Columbia University, 1959; PhD, MI State University, 1965. Publications: Jacksonian Aristocracy, Class and Democracy in New York, 1830-1860, 1967; The Birth of Modern America, 1820-1850, 1970; Then Was The Future, 1973; The Fifties, 1977; Visions of America, 1988; Frederick Douglass and the Fight for Freedom, 1988; Henry David Thoreau, 1991; On Our Own, Americans, in the Sixties, 1995; The Nature of Jacksonian American, 1972. Contributions to: Am Quarterly; Educational Theory; NY History; Journal of Popular Culture; Americana; Tijdschrift Voor De Studie Van Nord America. Literary Agent: Virginia Barber, NY, USA. Address: Dept of History, MI State University,East Lansing, MI 48824, USA.

MILLER Frederick Walter Gascoyne, b. 1904, New Zealand. Appointments: Former Journalist, Otago Daily Times, Dunedin: The Press, Christchurch: Southland Daily News: and Southland Times: (Journalist from 1922). Publications: Gold in the River, 1946; Golden Days of Lake County, 1949, 5th edition 1973; Beyond the Blue Mountains, 1954, 1978; West to the Fiords, 1954, 1976; Waikaia: The Golden Century, 1966; Ink on My Fingers, 1967; The Story of the Kingston Flyer, 1976; King of Counties: A History of the Southland County: Hokonui: The School and the People, 1982; Murihiku - The Tail, an epic poem dealing lightly with the history of Southland for the 1990 commemoration. Honours: OBE; OSM, 1995. Memberships: Life Member, NZ Journalists Union; Invercargill Lions Club. Address: 191 Princes Street, Invercargill, New Zealand.

MILLER Hugh, b. 1937, British. Appointments: Editorial Assistant, Scottish ITV, Glasgow, 1958-60; Technical and Photographic Assistant to a Forensic Pathologist, University of Glasgow, 1960-62; Manager 1963-64, Co-Owner 1965-70, Unique Studios, London; Editor, Bulletin 1967-69, General 1968-71. Publications: A Pocketful of Miracles, 1969; Secrets of Gambling, 1970; Professional Presentations, 1971; The Open City, Levels, Drop Out, Short Circuit, Koran's Legacy, 1973; Kingpin, Double Deal, Feedback, 1974; Ambulance, 1975; The Dissector, A Soft Breeze from Hell, 1976; The Saviour, 1977; The Rejuvenators, Terminal 3, 1978; Olympic Bronze, Head of State, 1979; District Nurse, 1984; Honour a Physician, 1985; Eastenders, Teen Eastenders, 1986; Snow on the Wind, 1987; Silent Witnesses, 1988; The Paradise Club, 1989; An Echo of Justice, 1990; Home Grown, 1990; Home Ground, 1990; An Echo of Justice, 1991; Skin Deep 1992; Scotland Yard (co-author), 1993; Unquiet Minds, 1994. Literary Agent: Peters, Fraser & Dunlop Ltd. Address: The Chambers, Chelsea Harbour, London SW10 0XF, England.

MILLER Jim (James), b. 1947. Publications: Jim Miller Sings, 1975; History and Human Existence: From Marx to Merleau - Poetry, 1979; Rousseau: A Dreamer of Democracy, 1984; Democracy in the Streets, 1987; The Passion of Michel Foucault, 1993. Address: c/o Paramount Publishing, Simpan & Schuster Attn Mngl Edtel, 1230 Avenue of the Americas, New York, NY 10020, USA.

MILLER Jim Wayne, b. 21 Oct 1936, North CA, USA. Professor; Writer. m. Mary Ellen Yates, 17 Aug 1958, 2 s, 1 d. Education: AB, Berea College, 1958; PhD, Vanderbilt University, 1965. Appointments: Invited Reader, 50th Anniversary Meeting, South Atlantic Modem Language Association, 1978; Folger Shakespeare Library, WA, 1981; Writer in Residence, The Centre College of KY, 1984; East TN Stte University, 1985. Publications include: The Mountains Have Come Closer, 1980; Dialogue with a Dead Man, 1974, 1978, 1990; Brier, His Book, 1988; Vein of Words, 1984; Nostalgia for 70, 1986; Newfound, 1989; I Have a Place, 1981; The Figure of Fulfillment, 1975; His First Best Country, 1987; The Examined Life, 1989; His First, Best Country, 1993. Contributions to: The Writer; Appalchian Journal; Appalachian Heritage; Modem Philology; The Louisville Magazine; Southern Folklore. Honours: Alice Lloyd Memorial Award, 1967; Western KY Award, 1976; Thomas Wolfe Literary Award, 1980; Zoe Kinkaid Brockman Memorial Award; Denny C. Plattner Appalachian Heritage Award, 1994. Memberships: KY Poetry Society; Appalachian Studies Conference. Address: IWFAC 258, Western KY University, Bowling Green, KY 42101, USA.

MILLER Jonathan (Wolfe), b. 1934, British. Appointments: Co-author and appeared in Beyond the Fringe, London and NYC, 1961-64; Editor of Monitor (BBC TV documentary series), 1965; Research Fellow in the History of Medicine, University College, 1970-73; Associate Director, National Theatre, 1973-75; Produced The Body in Question, (BBC series) 1978; Executive Producer, BBC Shakespeare Series,1979-80; Research Fellow in Neuropsychology, University of Sussex, Brighton. Publications: McLuhan, 1971; Freud: The Man, His World, His Influence (ed), 1972; The Body in Question,1978; Darwin for Beginners,1982; Subsequent Performances, 1986; Editor, The Don Giovanni Book: Myths of Seduction and Betrayal, 1990. Honour: CBE, 1983. Address: c/o IMG Artists (Europe), Media House, 3 Burlington Lane, London, W4 2TH, England.

MILLER Karl (Fergus Connor), b. 1931, British. Appointments: Assistant Principal, HM Treasury, 1956-57; Producer, BBC Television, 1957-58; Literary Editor, The Spectator, 1958-61 and the New Statesman, 1961-67; Editor, The Listener, 1967-73; Lord Northcliffe Professor of Modern English Literature, University College, London, 1974-92; Editor, London Review of Books, 1979-89, co-editor, 1989-92. Publications: Poetry from Cambridge 1952-54 (ed), 1955; Writing in England Today: The Last Fifteen Years (ed), 1968; Memoirs of a Modern Scotland (ed), A Listener Anthology August 1967 - June 1970 (ed), 1970; A Second Listener Anthology (ed), 1973; Cockburn's Millennium, 1975; Robert Burns (ed), 1981; Doubles: Studies in Literary History, 1985; Authors, 1989; Rebecca's Vest, 1993. Honour: James Tait Black Award for Cockburn's Millennium; A Scottish Arts Council Book Award for Rebecca's Vest. Membership: Fellow, Royal Society of Literature. Address: 26 Limerston Street, London SW10, England.

MILLER Kerby A, b. 30 Dec 1944, Phoenix, AZ, USA. Professor. m. Patricia Mulholland, June 1979, 2 s, 1 d. Education: BA, Pomona College, CA, 1966; MA, University of CA, 1967; PhD, 1976. Appointments: Assistant Professor, University of MI, 1978-84;

Associate Professor, 1984-89, Professor, 1989. Publications: Emigrants and Exiles. Contributions to: Irish Historical Studies; Journals of American Ethnic History; Journal of Urban History; various book-length collections. Honours: Merle Curti Award; Theodore Saloutos Award; Pulitzer Prize finalist. Memberships: American Historical Association; Organization of American Historians; Irish Historical Society; Immigration History Society; Irish Social & Economic History Society. Address: History Dept, 101 Read Hall, University of Missouri, Columbia, MO 65211, USA.

MILLER Lily Poritz, b. 7 June 1938, South Africa. Editor; Writer. m. Stephen Harris Miller, 6 Aug 1966. Education: The Fay School; The Am Academy of Dramatic Arts; The New School for Social Research. Appointments: Editor, Collier Macmillan and McGraw Hill; Teacher, City University of NY; Senior Editor, McClelland and Stewart Limited; Lily Poritz Miller Editorial Services. Publications: The Proud One, 1974; My Star of Hope, 1962; New Voices, 1963. Honour: Samuel French Award, 1974. Memberships: PEN International; Dramatists Guild of Authors League of Am; Playwrights Union of Canada. Address: PO Box 505, Station Q, Toronto, Ontario, Canada M4T 2M5.

MILLER Marc William, b. 29 Aug 1947, Annapolis, Maryland, USA. Writer. m. Darlene File, 24 Sep 1981, 1 s, 1 d. Education: BS, Sociology, University of Illinois, 1969. Appointments: Staff, Grenadier Magazine, 1977-79; Journal of the Travellers' Aid Society, 1979085; Staff, Challenge Magazine, 1986-92; Contributing Editor, Fire & Movement Magazine, 1977-84. Publications: Traveller, 1977; Imperium, 1977; 2300 AD, 1986; Mega Traveller, 1988; Mega Traveller II, Quest for the Ancients, 1991; Spellbound, 1992; 8 science fiction simulation games; 8 historical simulation games; 4 role-playing games, 3 computer games, Triplanetary, 1973; Chaco, 1974; Coral Sea, 1974; Their Finest Hour, 1976; The Russo-Japanese War, 1976; Battle for Midway, 1976; Mayday, 1978; Belter, 1979; Asteroid, 1980; Twighlight's Peak, 1980; Verdun, 1980; 1942! 1981; Safari Ship, 1984; Translations: Various editions in German, French, Spanish, Portuguese, Swedish, Italian and Japanese. Contributions to: Journal of Travellers' Aid Society; Moves; The Travellers' Digest; Fire & Movement; other professional journals. Honours: Charles Roberts Award, 1978, 1979, 1980, 1981; H G Wells Award, 1979, 1980; Game Designers Guild Select Award, 1978, 1980, 1981; Games 100, 1981, 1982, 1983, 1984, 1991; Elected to Adventure Gaming Hall of Fame, 1982. Memberships: Science Fiction Writers of America; Game Deisigners' Guild, President, 1979-81; Acadmey of Adventure Gaming Arts and Sciences; United States Army Air Defense Artillery, 1969-89, Captian, 1975-89; The Children's Foundation, Board of Directors; City of Bloomington Human Relations Commission; Rotary; Scabbard and Blade. Address: PO Box 193, Normal, IL 61761, USA.

MILLER Margaret J. See: DALE Margaret Jessy.

MILLER Merton H. Publications: The Theory of Finance (with Eugene F Fama), 1972; Macroeconomics: A Neoclassical Introduction, 1974; Financial Innovations and Market Volatility. Honours: Nobel Prize Economics, 1990. Address: Graduate School of Business, University of Chicago 1101 E 58th Street, Chicago, IL 60637-1511, USA.

MILLER Olga Eunice, b. 27 Mar 1920, Maryborough, Queensland, Australia. Aboriginal Historian; Consultant; Artist. separated, 3 sons, 2 daughters. Education: Junior Public Examination Status, Maryborough Girls Grammar Schools, 1935. Publications: Legends of Moonie Jarl (co-author), 1964; Fraser Island Legends, 1993, New Edition, 1994; TV programmes: Legends of Our Land, 1965; Across Australia, 1988; Radio programmes: This Was Our Town, 1965; Fraser Island Legends, 1983. Contributions to: Facts about Artefacts, 1965, First 200 Years, 1983, Maryborough Chronicle. Honours: Advance Australia Foundation Award, 1992. Address: 4/227 Ellena St, Maryborough, Queensland 4650, Australia.

MILLER Seumas Roderick Macdonald, b. 11 Mar 1953, Edinburgh, Scotland, England. University Professor. Education: BA, Australia National University, 1976; MA, Oxford University, England, 1978; Higher Diploma in Journalism, Rhodes University, 1984; Diploma in Education, State College of Victoria, Australia, 1979; Doctorate in Philosophy, Universityof Melbourne, Australia, 1985. Publications: Re-thinking Theory, 1992. Contributions to: Numerous articles in internationally distributed professional philosophy journals and other academic journals. Address: University of Melbourne, Parkville, Vic 3052, Australia.

MILLER Sue, b. 1943. Publications: The Good Mother, 1986; Inventing the Abbotts and Other Stories, 1987; Family Pictures: A Novel, 1990; For Love, 1993. Address: c/o Harper Collins Attn Athr MI Dept, 7th Floor 10 E 53rd Street, New York, NY 10022, USA.

MILLER Vassar (Morrison), b. 1924, American. Appointments: Instructor in Creative Writing, St John's School, Houston, 1975-76. Publications: Adam's Footprint, 1956; Wage War on Silence: A Book of Poems, 1960; My Bones Being Water: Poems, 1963; Onions and Roses, 1968; If I Could Sleep Deeply Enough, 1974; Small Change, Approaching Nada, 1977; Selected and New Poems, 1982; Struggling to Swim on Concrete, 1984; Despite This Flesh (ed), 1985; If I Had Wheels or Love: Collected Poems, 1991. Address: 1615 Vassar Street, Houston, TX 77006, USA.

MILLER Walter M(ichael), b. 1922, American. Appointments: Engineer; Freelance Writer, mainly of SF Short Stories and Novellas. Publications: A Canticle for Leibowitz, 1960; Conditionally Human, 1962; The View from the Stars, 1964; The Best of Walter M Miller Jr, 1980; The Darfstellar and Other Stories, 1982; The Science Fiction Stories of Walter M Miller Jr, 1984; Beyond Armegeddon (co-ed), 1985.

MILLETT Kate (Katherine Murray), b. 1934, USA. Leader in Feminist Movement. Publications: Sexual Politics, 1970; Flying, 1974; The Prostitution Papers, 1976; Sita, 1977; The Basement, 1980; Going to Iran, 1982; The Loony Bin Trip, 1990; The Politics of Cruelty, 1994. Address: c/o Georges Borchardt Incorp, 136 East 57th Street, New York, NY 10022, USA.

MILLHAUSER Steven, b. 3 Aug 1943, NY, USA. Novelist; Writer. m. Cathy Allis, 16 June 1986, 1 son, 1 daughter. Education: BA, Columbia College, 1965; Brown University, 1968-71. Publications: Edwin Mullhouse: the Life and Death of an American Writer, 1972; Portrait of a Romantic, 1976; In the Penny Arcade, 1986; From the Realm of Morpheus, 1986; The Barnum Museum, 1990; Little Kingdoms, 1993. Honours: Prix Medicis Etranger, 1975; Award in Literature, 1987. Literary Agent: Amanda Urban, CIM. Address: Saratoga Springs, NY, USA.

MILLHISER Marlys, b. 27 May 1938, IA, USA. Author. m. David Millhiser, 25 June 1960, 1 s, 1 d. Education: BA, University of IA, 1960; MA, University of Colorado, 1963. Publications: Michaels Wife, 1972, 73; Nella Waits, 1974, 75; Willing Hostage, 1976, 77; The Mirror, 1978, 79; Nightmare County, 1981, 82; The Threshold, 1984, 85; Murder at Moot point, 1992; Death of the Office Witch, 1993, 95; Murder in a Hot Flash, 1995. Contributions to: Column for Mystery Scene Magazine; Malice Domestic; Ellery Queen Mystery Magazine. Honours: Top Hand Award, 1975, 85. Memberships: Authors Guild; Mystery Writers of Am; Sisters in Crime; Western Writers of Am; Colorado Authors League. Literary Agent: Deborah Schneider, Gelfman Schneider. Address: 1843 Orchard Avenue, Boulder, CO 80304, USA.

MILLIEX Tatiana Gritsi, b. 20 Oct 1920, Athens, Greece. Writer. m. Roger Milliex, 1 June 1939, 1 son, 1 daughter. Education: Diploma, French Institute in Athens, 1938. Publications: Imeroloyio, 1951; 3 editions; Allazoume? 1958, French translation, 1985, 3 editions; Kai Idou Ippos Chloros, 1963, 6 editions; Anadromes, 1983, 2 editions; Apo Tin Alli Oxhtitou Chronou, 1988, French translation, Paris, 1992, 3 editions; H Tripoli Tou Pontou, 1977, 4 editions; Se Proto Prosopo, 1958, 5 editions; Onirika, 1991; To Aloni Tis Ekatis, 1993 (short stories), 1993. Contributions to: Variety of Greek and Cypriot magazines and journals. Honours: State Prize for short story, 1951, 1985, Novel, 1964 and 1974; Prize of Athens Academy, 1973; Prize Nikiphoros Vrettakos, 1995. Memberships: Greek Writers Society. Literary Agent: Castaniotis, odos Zalongou, 16078, Athens, Greece. Address: 20 Odos Metsovou, BP 26180 Exarchin, Athens, Greece.

MILLIGAN Spike. See: MILLIGAN Terence Alan.

MILLIGAN Terence Alan (Spike Milligan), b. 1918, Irish. Writer of Plays/Screenplays, Poetry, Humour/Satire. Radio and TV Personality: The Goon Show, BBC Radio; Show Called Fred, ITV; World of Beachcomber, Q5-Q10, BBC-2 Television; Curry and Chips, BBC; Oh in Colour, BBC; A Milligan for All Seasons, BBC. Publications: (with J Antrobus) The Bed Sitting Room (play); Oblommov (play); Son of Oblommov (play); Silly Verse for Kids, 1959; A Dustbin of Milligan, 1961; Puckoon, 1963; The Little Pot Boiler, 1963; A Book of Bits, 1965; The Bedside Milligan, 1968; Milliganimals, 1968; The Bald Twit Lion, 1970; Milligan's Ark, 1971; Adolf Hitler: My Part in

His Downfall, 1971; The Goon Show Scripts, 1972; Small Dreams of a Scorpion, 1972; Rommel? Gunner Who? 1973; Badjelly the Witch, 1973; More Goon Show Scripts, 1974; Spike Milligan's Transport of Delights, 1974; Dip the Puppy, 1974; The Great McGonagal Scrapbook, 1975; (with Jack Hobbs) The Milligan Book of Records, Games, Cartoons and Commercials, 1975; Monty: His Part in My Vistory, 1976; Mussolini: His Part in My Downfall, 1978; A Book of Goblins, 1978; Open Heart University (verse), 1979; Indefinite Articles and Slunthorpe, 1981; The 101 Best and Only Limericks of Spike Milligan, 1982; The Goon Cartoons, 1982; Sir Nobonk and the Terrible Dragon, 1982; The Melting Pot, 1983; More Goon Cartoons, 1983; There's A Lot About, 1983; Further Transports of Delight, 1985; Floored Masterpieces and Worse Verse, 1985; Where Have All the Bullets Gone, 1985; Goodbye Soldier, 1986; The Mirror Running, 1987; Startling Verse for All the Family, 1987; The Looney, 1987; William McGonall Meets George Gershwin, 1988; It Ends with Magic..., 1990; Peacework, 1991; Condensed Animals, 1991; Dear Robert, Dear Spike, 1991; Depression and How to Survive It (with Anthony Clare), 1993; Hidden Words, 1993; The Bible - Old Testament According to Spike Milligan, 1993; Lady Chatterley's Lover According to Spike Milligan, 1994; Wuthering Heights According to Spike Milligan 1994. Honours: TV Writer of the Year Award, 1956; Writing and Appearing Awarded Golden Rose and Special Comedy Award, Montreux, 1972; CBE, 1992; Lifetime Achievement Award, British Comedy Awards, 1994. Address: Spike Milligan Productions, 9 Orme Court, London W2, England.

MILLINGTON Barry (John), b. 1 Nov 1951, Essex, England. Music Journalist. Education: BA, Cambridge University, England, 1974. Publications: Wagner; Selected Letters of Richard Wagner; Wagner Compendium; Wagner in Performance; Wagner's Ring of the Nibelung: A Companion, 1993; Reviews Editor, BBC Music Magazine. Contributions to: Times; Opera. Membership: Critics Circle. Address: 50 Denman Drive South, London NW11 6RH, England.

MILLS Claudia, b. 21 Aug 1954, NY, USA. Writer. m. Richard W Wahl, 19 Oct 1985, 2 s. Education: BA, Wellesley College, 1976; MA, Princeton University, 1979; PhD, 1991. Publications include: Luisas American Dream, 1981; At The Back of the Woods, 1982; The Secret Carousel, 1983; All the Living, 1983; Boardwalk with Hotel, 1985; The One and Only Cynthia Jane Thornton, 1986; Melanie Magpie, 1987; Cally's Enterprise, 1988; Dynamite Dinah, 1990; Hannah on her Way, 1991; Dinah in Love, 1993; Phoebe's Parade, 1994; The Secret Life of Bethany Barrett, 1994. Memberships: Authors Guild; WA Children's Book Guild; Society of Children's Book Writers. Address: 2575 Briarwood Drive, Boulder, CO 80303, USA.

MILLS Derek Henry, b. 19 Mar 1928, Bristol, England. University Fellow; Consultant. m. Florence Cameron, 26 May 1956, 1 son, 1 daughter. Education: BSc, honours, University of London, 1949-53; MSc, University of London, 1957; PhD, University of London, 1963; FIFM; FLS. Literary Appointments: Editor, Fisheries Management, 1974-84; John Buchan Journal, 1979-83; Co-editor, Aquaculture & Fisheries Management, 1985-93; Co-editor, Fisheries Management & Ecology, 1994-. Publications: Salmon and Trout: A Resource, its Ecology, Conservation and Management, 1971; Introduction to Freshwater Ecology, 1972; Scotland's King of Fish, 1980; The Salmon Rivers of Scotland, 1981, 1992; The Fishing Here Is Great!, 1985; The Ecology and Management of Atlantic Salmon, 1989; Freshwater Ecology: Principles and Applications, 1990. Contributions to: Numerous, including: Blackwood Magazine; The Field; The Fly Fishers'Journal; The John Buchan Journal; Salmon and Trout Magazine; Fisheries Research. Memberships: John Buchan Society; Trollope Society; Society of Authors; PEN; Fellow, Institute of Fisheries Management; Fellow, Linnean Society of London; Atlantic Salmon Trust; Fly Fishers' Club. Address: Valerna, Aldie Crescent, Darnick, Melrose, TD6 9AY, Scotland.

MILLS Ralph Joseph, b. 16 Dec 1931, University Professor. m. 25 Nov 1959, 1 s, 2 d. Education: BA, Lake Forest College, 1954; MA, 1956, PhD, 1963, Northwestern University. Appointments: Teacher, Northwestern University, 1957-59; University of Chicago, 1959-65; University of IL, 1965-. Publications: Criticism: Theodore Reothke, 1963; Contemporary American Poetry, 1965; Edith Sitwell, 1966; Kathleen Raine, 1967; Selected Letters of Theodore Roethke, 1968; Each Branch, 1976-85, 1986; Living with Distance, 1979; March Light, 1983; A While, 1989; A Window in Air, 1993; Nine Poems, 1993. Contributions to: Accent; Boundary 2; NY Times Book Review; Poetry; New Letters; Kayak; Tar River Review; The Nation; New England

Review; Mississippi Valley Review. Honours: English Speaking Union Fellowship, 1956-57; Poetry Prize, 1979; Carl Sandburg Prize, 1983-84. Address: 1451 North Astor Street, Chicago, IL 60610, USA.

MILLWARD Eric, b. 12 Mar 1935, Longnor, Staffordshire, England. Poet. m. Rosemary Wood, 1975. Education: Buxton College, Derbyshire, 1946-54. Publications: A Child in the Park, 1969; Dead Letters, 1978; Appropriate Noises, 1987. Honours include: Arts Council Writers Award, 1979. Address: 2 Victoria Row, Knypersley, Stoke on Trent, Staffordshire ST8 7PU, England.

MILNE Christopher Robin, b. 21 Aug 1920, London, England. Author. m. Lesley Elizabeth De Selincourt, 25 July 1948, 1 daughter. Education: BA, Honours, Trinity College, Cambridge, England. Appointments: Bookseller, 1951-76; Writer, 1976-. Publications: The Enchanted Places, 1974; The Path Through the Trees, 1979; The Hollow on the Hill, 1982; The Windfall, 1985; The Open Garden, 1988. Membership: Fellow, Royal Society of Arts. Address: Glebe House, Manor Way, Totnes, Devon, England.

MILNE W(illiam) Gordon, b. 1921, American. Appointments: Joined faculty, 1951, Professor of English, 1964-, Chairman, Department of English, 1964-75, Chairman of American Studies, 1976-, Lake Forest College, IL. Publications: George William Curtis and the Genteel Tradition, 1956; The American Political Novel, 1966; The Sense of Society: A History of the American Novel of Manners, 1977; Stephen Crane at Brede: An Anglo-American Literary Circle of the 1890's, 1980; Ports of Call: A Study of the American Nautical Novel, 1986. Address: Box 273, Rye Beach, NH 0387, USA.

MILOSZ Czeslaw, b. 30 June 1911, Lithuania, naturalised US Citizen, 1970. Poet; Author; Professor. Education: University of Wilno, Mjuris, 1934. Publications: Poemat o czasie zastyglym, 1933; Trzy zimy, 1936; Ocalenie, 1945; Zniewolony umysl, 1953; Zdobycie wladzy, 1953; Dolina Issy, 1955; Traktat poetycki, 1957; Rodzinna Europa, 1958; Postwar Polish Poetry, 1965; Widzenia nad Zatoka San Francisco, 1969; The History of Polish Literature, 1970; Prywatnes obowiazki,1972; Selected Poems, 1973; Ziemia Ulro, 1977; Emperor of the Earth, 1977; Bells in Winter, 1978; Hymn o perle, 1982; Visions from San Francsco Bay, 1983; The Witness of Poetry, 1983; Separtate Notebooks, 1984; The Land of Ulro, 1985; Nieobjeta Ziema, 1986; Unattainable Earth, 1987; Kroniki, 1987; Collected Poems, 1988; Provinces, 1991. Honours: Prix Litteratire Europeen, 1953; Neustadt International Prize for Literature, 1978; Nobel Prize in Literature, 1980; National Medal of Arts, 1989. Memberships: American Academy and Institute of Arts and Letters. Address: Dept of Slavic Languages and Liteatures, 5416 Dwinelle Hall, University of California, Berkeley, CA 94720, USA.

MILWARD Alan Steele, b. 19 Jan 1935, Stoke-on-Trent, England. University Teacher. Education: BA 1956, PhD 1960, London University, England. Publications include: The German Economy at War, 1965; The New Order and the French Economy, 1970; The Economic and Social Effects of the Two World Wars on Britain, 1971, 1984; The Fascist Economy in Norway, 1972; War, Economy and Society 1939-1945, 1979; The Reconstruction of Western Europe 1945-1951, 1984; The European Rescue of the Nation-State, 1992. Contributions to: History and Economics Journals, Times Literary Supplement, London Review of Books. Honours: Honorary MA, Manchester University, England, 1976; FBA 1987; Fellow, Royal Norwegian Academy of Letters, 1994. Memberships: Economic History Society; Economic History Association; German History Society; University Association for Contemporary European Studies (former President); British Academy. Address: Department of Economic History, London School of Economics, Houghton Street, London WC2A 2AE, England.

MINARIK Else H(olmelund), b. 1920, American (born Danish). Publications: Little Bear, 1957; No Fighting, No Biting!, 1958; Father Bear Comes Home, 1959; Cat and Dog, Little Bear's Friends, 1960; Little Bear's Visit, 1961; Little Giant Girl and the Elf Boy, 1963; The Winds That Come from Far Away and Other Poems, 1964; A Kiss for Little Bear, My Grandpa Is a Pirate, by Jan Loof (trans), 1968; What If!, 1987; It's Spring!, 1989; Percy and The Five Houses, 1989; The Little Girl and the Dragon, 1991; Am I Beautiful? 1992. Memberships: PEN Club, Authors Guild. Address: c/o Green Willow Books, 1350 Avenue of the Americas, New York, NY 10016, USA.

MINARIK John Paul, b. 6 Nov 1947, McKeesport, PA, USA. Engineer; Poet. Education: BS, Carnegie Mellon University, 1970; BA, University of PA, 1978. Appointments include: Editor, Academy of Prison Arts, 1973-. Publications: A Book, 1974, 77; Patterns in the Dusk, 1977; Past the Unknown, Remebered Gate, 1980; Kicking Their Hells with Freedom, 1980; Light from Another Country, 1984. Contributions include: Bulletin, Poetry Society of America; New Orleans Review; Prison Writing Review; Journal of Popular Culture; Small Pond; Interstate; Backspace; Gravide; Joint Conference; Nitty Gritty. Honour: Honorable Mention, International PEN, 1976-77. Address: PO Box 99901, Pittsburgh, PA 15233, USA.

MINATOYA Lydia, b. 8 Nov 1950, NY, USA. Writer. 1 son. Education: BA, Lawrence University, 1972; MA, George Washington University, 1976; PhD, University of MD, 1981. Publication: Talking to High Monks in the Snow, 1992. Honours: PEN Jerard Fund Award, 1991; American Library Association Notable Book, 1992; NY Public Lib Notable Book, 1992; Pacific Nova West Booksellers Award, 1993; Govenors Writers Award. Literary Agent: Ellen Levene Agency. Address: Harper Collins, 10 E 53rd Street, New York, NY 10022 5299, USA.

MINEAR Richard H, b. 31 Dec 1938, IL, USA. Historian. m. Edith Christian, 1962. 2 s. Education: BA, Yale University, 1960; MA, 1962, PhD, 1968, Harvard University. Appointments: Assistant Professor, OH State University, 1967-70; Associate Professor, University of MA, 1970; Professor, 1975-. Publications: Hiroshima: Three Witnesses, 1990; Requiem for Battleship Yamato, 1985; Japanese Tradition and Western Law, 1970; Victors' Justice, 1971; Through Japanese Eyes, 1974; Black Eggs, 1994. Contributions to: Numerous Magazines & Journals. Memberships: Association for Asian Studies. Address: History Dept, University of MA, Amherst, MA 01003, USA.

MINER Earl Roy, b. 21 Feb 1927, WI, USA. Professor. m. Virginia Lane, 15 July 1950, 1 s, 1 d. Education: BA, 1949, MA, 1955, PhD, University of MN. Publications include: The Japanese Tradition in British and American Literature, 1958; Japanese Court Poetry, 1961; Drydens Poetry, 1967; Comparative Poetics, 1992. Contributions to: Proffesional Journals. Honours: Fulbright Lectureships, 1960-61, 1966-67, 1985; Am Council of Learned Societies, 1963; Guggenheim Fellow, 1977-78; Yamagato Banto Prize, 1988; Koizumi Yakumo Prize, 1991; Howard T Behrman Prize, 1993; Order of the Rising Sun with Gold Rays and Neck Ribbon, Japanese Govt, 1994. Memberships: Am Society for 18th Century Studies; Milton Society of America; Renaissance Society of Am; Association for Asian Studies; Am & International Comparative Literature Associations. Address: 22 McCosh, Princeton University, Princeton, NJ 08544, USA.

MINGAY Gordon Edmund, b. 20 June 1923, Long Eaton, Derbyshire, England. Emeritus Professor. m. Mavis Tippen, 20 Jan 1945. Education: BA, 1st Class, 1952, PhD 1958, University of Nottingham, England. Appointment: Editor, The Agricultural History Review, 1972-84. Publications: English Landed Society in the Eighteenth Century, 1963; The Agricultural Revolution 1750-1880 (with J D Chambers), 1966; Britain and America: A Study of Economic Change 1850-1939 (with P S Bagwell), 1970; The Gentry, 1976; Rural Life in Victorian England, 1976; The Victorian Countryside, 1981; Enclosure and the Small Farmer in the Age of the Industrial Revolution, 1968; Arthur Young and his Times, 1975; The Transformation of Britain 1830-1939, 1985; The Agrarian History of England and Wales, Volume VI (edited), 1989; A Social History of the English Countryside, 1990; Land and Society in England 1750-1980, 1994. Contributions to: The Economic History Review; The Agriculture History Review; Agricultural History. Honour: FRHS, 1968. Memberships: Head, British Agricultural History Society, Editor 1972-84, President 1987-89; Economic History Society. Address: Mill Field House, Selling Court, Selling, Faversham, Kent ME13 9RJ, England.

MINOGUE Valerie Pearson, b. 26 Apr 1931, Llanelli, South Wales. Research Professor. m. Kenneth Robert Minogue, 16 June 1954, 1 son, 1 daughter. Education: BA, Girton College, Cambridge, England, 1952; MLitt, 1956. Appointments: Assistant Lecturer, University College, Cardiff, Wales, 1952-53; Contributor, Cambridge Italian Dictionary, 1956-61; Lecturer, Queen Mary College, London, England, 1962-81; Professor, University of Wales, Swansea, 1981-88; Research Professor, 1988-. Publications: Nathalie Sarraute: The War of the Words; Proust: Du Coté de chez Swann; Zola: L'Assommoir; Romance Studies. Contributions to: Quadrant; The Literary Review; Modern Language Review; French Studies; Romance Studies; Forum for Modern Language Studies. Memberships: Association of University Professors of French; Modern Humanities Research Association; Society for French Studies; Romance Studies Institute. Address: 92 Eaton Crescent, Swansea, West Glamorgan SA1 4QP, Wales.

MINOT Susan Anderson, b. 7 Dec 1956, Boston, MA, USA. Writer. m. Davis McHenry, 30 Apr 1988, div. Education: BA, Brown University, 1978; MFA, Columbia University, 1983. Publications: Monkeys, 1986; Lost & Other Stories, 1989; Folly, 1992. Contributions to: The New Yorker; Grand Street; The Paris Review; Mademoiselle; Harper's; GQ; New England Monthly; Conde Nasts Traveler; Esquire; NY Times Magazine; Atlantic Monthly. Honour: Priz Femina Etranger, 1987. Literary Agent: Georges Borchardt.

MINTER David Lee, b. 1935, USA. Appointments: Universitatslektor, University of Hamburg, 1965-66; Lecturer, Yale University, CT, 1966-67; Assistant Professor, 1967-69, Associate Professor, 1969074, Professor, 1974-80, Rice University, Houston; professor, Dean of Emory College, Vice President for Arts & Sciences, Emory Universiy, 1981-90; Professor, Rice University, 1991-. Publications include: The Interpreted Design as a Structural Principle in American Prose, 1969; William Faulkner: His Life & Work, 1980; The Harper American Literature, 1986; The Norton Critical Edition of The Sound and the Fury, 1987; A Cultural History of The American Novel: Henry James to William Faulkner, 1994. Address: Dept of English, Rice University, PO Box 1892, Houston, TX 77251, USA.

MIRABELLI Eugene, Jr, b. 1931, United States of America. Author. Publications: The Burning Air, 1959; The Way In, 1968; No Resting Place, 1972; The World at Noon, 1993. Address: 29 Bennett Terrace, Delmar, NY 12054, USA.

MIRZA Mohd Z Ahan Azurdah, b. 17 Mar 1945, India. Teacher. m. Haleema Begum, 3 Oct 1963, 2 s, 1 d. Education: MA, Urdu, 1970; B.Ed, 1971, PhD, 1977. Publications: Mirza Salamet Ali Debeer, 1981, 1985; Ghubar Kalwan, 1984; Essay, 1983; Thorns & Thistles, 1986; Sheereen Ke Khatoot, 1974; Ghubari Khayal, 1973; Fibori Hing Ribrir, 1980, 1981; Ratan Nath Sarshar, 1987; Kante, 1975. Contributions to: Indian Literature; Enquiry; many other professional journals. Honours: WP, 1981, 1985, AP, 1981, WB, 1981, Urdu Academy; National Acadmy of Letter, 1984. Memberships include: General Secretary, Brazni Iqbal Kind; Vice President, Kaharrin Cultural League; Chairman, Haghmin Council of Historical and Cultural Research. Address: Hasanabad Rainawari, Srinagar, Kashmir, India 190003.

MISTRY Rohinton, b. 1952, Bombay, India. Emigrated to Toronto, Canada, 1975. m. Freny Elavia. Education: BSc, University of Bombay; BA, University of Toronto. Appointments: Worked in banking for 10 years; Part-time student, English and Philosophy, University of Toronto. Publications: Short stories published in major Canadian Literary Journals and Anthologies; Tales from Firozsha Baag, 1987; The Faber Book of Contemporary Canadian Short Stories, 1990; Condolence Visit; Such A Long Journey, 1991. Honours: Smith/Books in Canada First Novel Award; Hart House Prize for Fiction, 1983, 1984; Shortlisted, Booker Prize, 1991; Winner, Commonwealth Writer's Prize, 1992. Address: c/o Linda Vardley Agency, 297 Seaton Street, Toronto, Ontario, M5A 2T6 Canada.

MITCHELL Adrian, b. 24 Oct 1932, London, England. Writer. Education: Christ Church, Oxford. Appointments: Granada Fellow, University of Lancaster, 1968-69; Fellow, Centre for the Humanities, Wesleyan University, 1972; Resident Writer, Sherman Theatre, Cardiff, 1974-75; Visiting Writer, Billericay Comprehensive School, 1978-80; Judith Wilson Fellow, Cambridge University, 1980-81; Resident Writer, Unicorn Theatre for Children, 1982-83. Publications: Tyger, 1971; Man Friday, 7:84, 1973; For Beauty Douglas; On the Beach at Cambridge, 1984; Nothingmas Day, 1984; The Pied Piper, 1986; Adaptation, various works including: Peer Gynt, 1980; Novels: Strawbery Drums, 1989; TV plays. Contributions include: Oxford Mail; London Magazine, Times Literary Supplement; Observer; New Yorker; Peace News Tribune; New Statesman; Sunday Times; Daily Mail; Evening Standard; Sanity. Memberships: Theatre Writers Union. Agent: The Peter Fraser & Dunlop Group Ltd. Address: c/o The Peter Fraser and Dunlop Group Ltd, 5th Floor, The Chambers, Chelsea Harbour, Lots Road, London, SW10 0XF, England.

MITCHELL David John, b. 24 Jan 1924, London, England. Freelance Writer. m. 1955, 1 son. Education: Bradfield College, Berkshire; Trinity College, Oxford, 1944-47; MA (Hons), Modern History. Appointments: Staff Writer, Picture Post, 1947-52. Publications: Women on the Warpath, 1966, as Monstrous Regiment, USA; The Fighting Pankhursts, 1967; 1919 Red Mirage, 1970, translated as L'Annata Rossa dell'Europa, Italy, 1972; Pirates, 1976; Queen Christabel, 1977; The Jesuits: A History, 1980; The Spanish Civil War, 1982; Travellers in Spain, 1990, translated as Viajeros por España. Contributions to: Articles and reviews to: Times; Times Literary Supplement; New Statesman; New Society; Guardian; Daily Telegraph; London Magazine; History Today. Honours: US Literary Guild Alternate Choice for Pirates, 1976; UK Historical Guild Selection for Pirates, 1976. Memberships: Society of Authors. Address: 20 Mountacre Close, Sydenham Hill, London SE26 6SX, England.

MITCHELL (Sibyl) Elyne Keith, b. 30 Dec 1913, Melbourne, Australia. Author; Grazier. m. Thomas Walter Mitchell, 4 Nov 1935, deceased. 2 sons (1 dec), 2 daughters. Publications: Australia's Alps, 1942; Speak to the Earth, 1945; Soil & Civilization, 1946; Flow River, Blow Wind, 1953; Silver Brumby Series (for children), 1958-77; Kingfisher Feather (children), 1962; Winged Skis (children), 1964; Light Horse to Damascus, 1971; Light Horse, the Story of Australia's Mounted Troops, 1978; Colt from Snowy River, series, 1979-81; The Snowy Mountains, 1980; Chauvel Country, 1983; Discoverers of the Snowy Mountains, 1985; A Vision of the Snowy Mountains, 1988; Towong Hill, Fifty Years on an Upper Murray Cattle Station, 1989; Silver Brumby, Silver Dingo, 1993; Silver Brumby, film, 1993. Contributions to: Quadrant; Poetry Australia; The Canberra Times; The Age; The Australian. Honours: Children's Book Week Award; Silver Brumby, Highly Commended, Winged Skis and Silver Brumby's Daughter, Commended; Order of Australia Medal, 1990; Honoray Doctor of Letters, Charles Sturt University, 1993. Memberships: Australian Society of Authors. Literary Agent: Curtis Brown Ltd. Address: Towong Hill, Corryong, Victoria 3707, Australia.

MITCHELL Geoffrey Duncan, b. British. Appointments: Senior Research Worker, University of Liverpool, England, 1950-52; Lecturer in Sociology, University of Birmingham, England, 1952-54; Lecturer and Senior Lecturer 1954-67, Professor 1967-86, Emeritus Professor of Sociology and Research Fellow, Institute of Population Studies, University of Exeter, England. Publications: Neighbourhood and Community (with T Lupton, M W Hodges and C S Smith), 1954; Sociology: The Study of Social Systems, 1959, 1972; A Dictionary of Sociology (ed and contributor), A Hundred Years of Sociology, 1968; A New Dictionary of Sociology (ed and contributor), 1979; The Artificial Family (with R Snowden), 1981; Artificial Reproduction (with R and E Snowden), 1983. Contributions to: New Scientist; Journal of Medical Ethics; Sociological Review. Honours: MBE, 1946; OBE, 1984. Address: 26 West Avenue, Exeter, Devon, England.

MITCHELL Jerome, b. 7 Oct 1935, TN, USA. University Lecturer. Education: BA, Emory University, 1957; MA, 1959, PhD, 1965, Duke University. Appointments: Assistant Professor, University of IL, 1965-67; Associate Professor, 1967-72, Professor, 1972-, University of Georgia; Fulbright Guest Professor, University of Bonn, 1972-73; Visiting exchange Professor, University of Erlangen, 1975; Richard Merton Guest Professor, University of Regensburg, 1978-79. Publications: Thomas Hoccleve: A Study in Early 15th Century English Poetic, 1968; The Walter Scott Operas, 1977; Scott, Chaucer and Medieval Romance, 1987; Hoccleve's Works: The Minor Poems, 1970; Chaucer, The Love Poet, 1973; Old and Middle English Literature, 1994. Contributions to: Various Scholarly Journals. Memberships: South Atlantic Modern Language Association; Gesellschaft für Englische Romantik; Edinburgh Sir Walter Scott Club. Address: English Dept, University of Georgia, Athens, GA 30602, USA.

MITCHELL (Charles) Julian, b. 1 May 1935, Epping, Essex, England. Author. Education: BA 1958, Wadham College, Oxford. Appointments: Midshipman, Royal Naval Volunteer Reserve, 1953-55. Publications: Imaginary Toys, 1961; A Disturbing Influence, 1962; As Far as You Can Go, 1963; The White Father, 1964; A Heritage and Its History (adapter play), 1965; A Family and a Fortune (adaptation) play, 1966; A Circle of Friends, 1966; The Undiscovered Country, 1968; Jennie Lady Randolph Churchill: A Portrait with Letters (with Peregrine Churchill), 1974; Half-Life, play, 1977; Another Country, play, 1982, film 1984; Francis, play, 1983; After Aida, play, 1985; Falling Over England, play, 1994; August (adaptation of Uncle Vanya), play 1994, film 1995. Contributions to: Welsh History Review, The Monmouthshire Antiquary. Literary Agent: The Peters, Fraser & Dunlop Group. Address: 47 Draycott Place, London SW3 3DB, England.

MITCHELL Juliet, b. 1940, New Zealand. Part-time Psycho-Analyst; Freelance Writer; Broadcaster and Lecturer. Appointments: Lecturer in English, University of Leeds, England, 1962-63; Lecturer in English, University of Reading, 1965-70; Luce Lecturer, Yale University, 1984-85; A D White Professor-at-Large, Cornell University, 1994-2000. Publications include: Women: The Longest Revolution, 1966; Woman's Estate, 1972; Psycho-Analysis and Feminism, 1974; Rights and Wrongs of Women (co-editor), 1977; Feminine Sexuality (co-editor), 1982; Women: The Longest Revolution, 1983; What is Feminism (co-editor), 1986; The Selected Writings of Melanie Klein, 1986; Before I was I (co-editor), 1991. Literary Agent: Deborah Rogers. Address: 275 Lonsdale Road, London SW13 9QB, England.

MITCHELL K L. See: **LAMB Elizabeth Searle.**

MITCHELL Margaretta Meyer Kuhlthau, b. 27 May 1935, Brooklyn, NY, USA. Photographer. m. 23 May 1959, 3 d. Education: BA, Smith College, 1957; MA, University of CA, 1985. Appointments include: University of CA Ext Program, 1976-78; City College, 1980; Civic Arts, 1980-84; Carleton College, Visiting Professor, 1988; Teacher, Academy of Art, San Francisco, 1990-94. Publications include: Recollections: Ten Women of Photography, 1979; To a Cabin, 1973; Gift of Place, 1969; Introduction to After Ninety by Imogen Cunningham, 1977; Dance for Life, 1985; Flowers, 1991. Contributions to: Ramparts; Vermont Life; Camera Art. Honour: Phi Beta Kappa, 1957. Memberships: American Society of Media Photographers. Address: 280 Hillcrest Road, Berkeley, CA 94705, USA.

MITCHELL Michael Robin, b. 10 Apr 1941, Rochdale, Lancashire. University Lecturer. m. Jane Speakmen, 3 Jan 1970, 3 s. Education: MA, 1960-64; B.Litt, 1966-68, Lincoln College, Oxford. Publications: Translator: Gyorgy Sebestyen: The Works of Solitude, 1991; Gustav Meyrink: The Angel of the West Window, 1991; Meryrink: The Green Face, 1992; Herbert Rosendorfer: The Architect of Ruins, 1992; The Dedalus Book of Austrian Fantasy (Editor and translator), 1992. Peter Hacks: Theatre for a Socialist Society, 1991, (author); Harrap's German Grammar, 1989 (co-author). Address: 4 Mount Hope, Bridge of Allan, Stirling, Scotland.

MITCHELL Roger, b. 8 Feb 1935, Boston, MA, USA. Poet; Teacher, 2 d. Education: AB, Harvard College, 1957; MA, University of Colorado, 1961; PhD, Manchester University, 1963. Appointments: Editor, The MN Review, 1973-81; Director, IN University Writers Conference, 1975-85; director, Creative Writing Program, IN University, 1978-. Publications: Letters from Siberia, 1971; Moving, 1976; A Clear Space on a Cold Day, 1986; Adirondack, 1988; Clear Pond, 1991. Contributions to: Poetry; Poetry Northwest; Triquarterly; Ploughshares; New Republic; Times Literary Supplement; Poetry East; MA Review. Honours: Abby M Copps Award, 1971; Midland Poetry Award, 1972; Borestone Mountain Award, 1973; PEN Award, 1977; Arvon Foundation Award, 1985, 1987; NEA Creative Writing Fellowship, 1986; Chester H Jones Award, 1987. Membership: Associated Writing Programs. Address: 1010 E First Street, Bloomington, IN 47401, USA.

MITCHELL William John Thomas, b. 24 Mar 1942, CA, USA. College Professor; Editor. m. Janice Misurell, 11 Aug 1968, 1 s, 1 d. Education: BA, MI State University, 1963; MA, PhD, 1968, Johns Hopkins University. Appointment: Editor, Critical Inquiry, 1979-. Publications include: Blake's Composite Art, 1977; The Language of Images, 1980; The Politics of Interpretation, 1983; Iconology, 1986; Picture Theory, 1994; Landscape and Power, 1993; Art and the Public Sphere, 1993. Contributions to: Times Literary Supplement; London Review of Books; Partisan Review; Salmagundi; AfterImage; New Literary History; Representations. Honours: American Philosophical Society Essay Prize, 1968; National Endowment for the Humanities Fellowship, 1978, 1986; Guggenheim Fellow, 1983. Memberships: Modern Language Association; PEN; Academy of Literary Studies. Address: English Dept, University of Chicago, 1050 E 59th Street, Chicago, IL 60637, USA.

MITCHELL W(illiam) O(rmond), b. 13 Mar 1914, Weyburn, Saskatchewan, Canada. Novelist. Education: Universities of Manitoba, Alberta, 1942. Appointments: Director, Banff School of Fine Arts, Alberta, 1975-86; Writer in Residence, University of Calgary, 1968-71, University of Windsor, Ontario, 1979-87. Publications: Who Has Seen the Wind, 1947; The Kite, 1962; The Vanishing Point, 1973; How I Spent My Summer Holidays, 1981; Since Daisy Creek, 1985; Ladybug Ladybug, 1988; Roses Are Difficult Here, 1990; Jake and the Kid, 1961; According to Jake and the Kid: A Collection of New Stories, 1989; Plays include Wild Rose, 1967; The White Christmas of an Archie Nicotine, 1971; Back to Beulah, 1976; The Kite, 1981; For Those in Peril on the Sea, 1982; Screeplays, Radio Plays and TV Plays. Honours include: Canadian Authors Association Award, 1983; D Litt University of Ottawa, 1972; Officer, Order of Canada, 1972. Address: c/o McClelland & Stewart Inc, 481 University Avenue, Suite 900, Toronto, Ontario M5G 2E9, Canada.

MITCHELL HAYES Minnie M, b. 30 Nov 1948, USA. Fiction Writer. m. James E Hayes, 2 s. Education: BAS, University of IL; MFA, Vermont College, 1991; Fellow, Ragdale Artist Colony, IL, 1992. Appointments: Freelance Journalist; PR Work; Political Speech Writing; Teacher, Columbia college, il. Contributions to: Redbook Magazine; Gallery Magazine; North Am Review; Hawaii Review; Writers Digest; Tomorrow Magazine; Whetstone. Honours include: Screenwriting Fellowships; 1 of 25 Distinguished Stories of 1989; Katherine Anne Porter Prize, 1994. Memberships: Poets & Writers; The Wednesday Writers; PEN Midwest; Off Campus Writers Workshop. Literary Agent: Philip G Spitzer. Address: 431 Sheridan Road, Kenilworth, IL 60043, USA.

MITCHISON Naomi, b. 1 Nov 1989, Edinburgh, Scotland. Novelist. m. Gilbert Richard Mitchison, 1916, 3 sons, 2 daughters. Publications: The Conquered, 1923; When the Bough Breaks, 1924; Cloud Cuckoo Land, 1925; Black Sparta, 1928; Anna Comnena, 1928; Nix-Nought-Nothing, 1928; Barbarian Stories, 1929; The Corn King and the Spring Queen, 1931; The Delicate Fire, 1932; We Have Been Warned, 1935; The Fourth Pig, 1936; Socrates (with R H S Crossman), 1937; Moral Basis of Politics, 1938; The Kingdom of Heaven, 1939; As It Was in the Beginning (with L E Gielgud), 1939; The Blood of the Martyrs, 1939; Re-Educating Scotland, 1945; The Bull Calves, 1947; Men and Herring (with D Macintosh), 1949; The Big House, 1950; Lobsters on the Agenda, 1952; Travel Light, 1952; Swan's Road, 1954; Graeme and the Dragon, 1954; Land the Ravens Found, 1955; To the Chapel Perilous, 1955; Little Boxes, 1956; Behold Your King, The Far Harbour, 1957; Other People's Worlds, Five Men and a Swan, 1958; Judy and Lakshmi, 1959; Rib of the Green Umbrella, 1960; The Young Alexander, 1960; Karensgaard, 1961; Memoirs of a Spacewoman, 1962; The Fairy Who Couldn't Tell a Lie, 1963; When We Became Men, 1964; Return to the Fairy Hill, 1966; Friends and Enemies, 1966; African Heroes, 1968; The Family at Ditlabeng, 1969; The Africans: A History, 1970; Sun and Moon, 1970; Cleopatra's People, 1972; A Danish Teapot, 1973; A Life for Africa, 1973; Sunrise Tomorrow, 1973; Small Talk (autobiography), 1973; All Change Here, (autobiography), 1975; Solution Three, 1975; Snakel 1976; The Two Magicians, 1979; The Cleansing of the Knife and Other Poems, 1979; You May Well Ask: A Memoir 1920-40, 1979; Images of Africa, 1980; The Vegetable War, 1980; Mucking Around, (autobiography) 1981; What Do You Think Yourself? 1982; Not by Bread Alone, 1983; Among You Taking Notes, 1985; Early in Orcadia, 1987; A Girl Must Live, 1990; Sea-Green Ribbons, 1991; The Oathtakers, 1991. Honours: CBE, 1985; Member, Bakgatla Tribe SE Botswana; Hon DLitt, Strathclyde, 1983, Stirling, Dundee; Open University, 1994. Address: Carradale House, Carradale, Campbeltown, Scotland.

MITCHISON Rosalind Mary, b. 11 Apr 1919, Manchester, England. m. 21 June 1947, 1 son, 3 daughters. Education: Oxford University, 1938-42; MA, 1945. Publications: A History of Scotland, 2nd edition, 1982; Life in Scotland, 1978; Lordship to Patronage: Scotland 1603-1749, 1989; Sexuality and Social Control: Scotland 1660-1780 (co-author Leah Leneman), 1989; Coping with Destitution: Poor Relief in Western Europe. Honour: Hon DLitt, 1992. Memberships: Fellow, Royal Historical Society; The Scottish History Society, President, 1981-84; Fellow, Royal Society of Edinburgh. Address: Great Yew, Ormiston, East Lothian EH35 5NJ, Scotland.

MITEHAM Hank. See: **NEWTON D(wight) B(ennett).**

MITFORD Jessica, b. 11 Sep 1917. Writer. m. (1) Esmond Marcus David Romilly, (dec 1941), 2 daughters, (2) Robert Edward Treuhaft, 1 son. Literary Appointments: Distinguished Professor, San Jose State University, California, 1973-74; Instructor Yale University, 1976. Publications: Hons and Rebels (autobiography), 1960; The American Way of Death, 1963; The Trial of Dr Spock, 1970; The American Prison Business, 1973; A Fine Old Conflict, 1977; The Making of a Muckraker (essays), 1979; Faces of Philip: A Memoir of Philip Toynbee, 1984; Grace Had an English Heart, The Story of Grace Darling, Heroine and Victorian Superstar, 1988; The American Way of

Birth, 1992. Contributions to: Numerous, including: Harpers; Atlantic Monthly; McCall's. Honours: Guggenheim Fellowship, 1972. Memberships: Authors Guild; National Writers Union. Address: 6411 Regent Street, Oakland, CA 94618, USA.

MITSON Eileen Nora, b. 22 Sept 1930, Langley, Essex, England. Housewife; Author. m. Arthur Samuel Miston, 22 Sept 1951, 2 daughters (1 dec). Education: Cambridge Technical College and School of Art, 1946-47. Publications: Beyond the Shadows, 1968; The Inside Room, 1973; Reaching for God, 1978; Creativity (co-author), 1985; Amazon Adventure, 1969; A Kind of Freedom, 1976; Author of 2 other adult and 2 children's novels. Contributions to: Regular Columnist for Christian Woman Magazine (now Woman Alive), 1982-1994. Address: 39 Oaklands, Hamilton Road, Reading, Berkshire RG1 5RN, England.

MO Timothy, b. 1950, Hong Kong. Novelist. Education: Mill Hill School, London; St John's College, Oxford. Appointments: Journalist, Boxing News, New Statesman, Times Educational Supplement. Publications: The Monkey King, 1980; Sour Sweet, 1982; An Insular Possession, 1986; The Redundancy of Courage, 1991. Honours: Geoffrey Faber Memorial Prize, 1978; Hawthornden Prize, 1982. Address: c/o Chatto and Windus, 20 Vauxhall Bridge Road, London SW1V 2SA, England.

MOAT John, b. 1936, United Kingdom. Author; Poet. Publications: 6d per Annum, 1966; Heorot, novel, 1968; A Standard of Verse, 1969; Thunder of Grass, 1970; The Tugen and the Toot, novel, 1973; The Ballad of the Leat, 1974; Bartonwood, Juvenile, 1978; Fiesta and the Fox Reviews and His Prophecy, 1979; The Way to Write (with John Fairfax), 1981; Skeleton Key, 1982; Mai's Wedding, novel, 1983; Welcombe Overtunes, 1987; The Missing Moon, 1988; Firewater and the Miraculous Mandarin, 1990; Practice, 1994. Address: Crenham Mill, Hartland, N Devon EX39 6HN, England.

MODIANO Patrick Jean, b. 30 July 1945. Novelist. m. Dominique Zehrfuss, 1970, 2 daughters. Publications: La place de l'etoile, 1968; La ronde de nuit, 1969; Les boulevards de ceinture, 1972; Lacombe Lucien (screenplay), 1973; La polka (play), 1974; Villa triste (novel), 1975; Interrogatoire d'Emmanuel Berl, 1976; Livret de famille (novel), 1977; Rue des boutiques obscures, 1978; Une Jeunesse, 1981; Memory Lane, 1981; De si Braves Garcons (novel), 1982; Poupee blonde, 1983; Quartier perdu, 1985; Dimanches d'Aout, 1986; Une aventure de Choura, 1986; Remise de Peine, 1987; Vestiaire de l'enfance, 1989; Voyage de Noces, 1990; Fleurs de Ruine, 1991; Un Cirque Passe, 1992. Honours: Prix Roger Nimier, 1968; Prix Goncourt, 1978; Chevalier des Arts et des Lettres. Address: c/o Editions Gallimard, 5 rue Sebastien Bottin, 75007 Paris, France.

MOFFAT Gwen, b. 3 July 1924, Brighton, Sussex, England. Author. m. Gordon Moffat, 1948, 1 daughter. Publications: Space Below My Feet, 1961; The Corpse Road, 1974; The Buckskin Girl, 1982; The Storm Seekers, 1989; The Stone Hawk, 1989; Rage, 1990; Lady with a Cool Eye, 1973; Deviant Death, 1973; Miss Pink at the Edge of the World, 1975; Over the Sea to Death, 1976; A Short Time to Live, 1976; Persons Unknown, 1978; Die like a Dog, 1982; Last Chance Country, 1983; Grizzly Tail, 1984; Hard Option, 1975; Two Star Red, 1964; On My Home Ground, 1968; Survival Count, 1972; Hard Road West, 1981; Snare, 1987; The Raptor Zone, 1990; Pit Bull, 1991; Veronica's Sisters, 1992; The Outside Edge, 1993; Cue the Battered Wife, 1994. Contributions to: Guardian; Sunday Times; Sunday Telegraph; Sunday Express; Glasgow Herald; Scotsman; Argosy; Good Housekeeping; Homes and Gardens; She; The Lady. Memberships: The Society of Authors; The Crime Writers Association; Mystery Writers of America. Literary Agent: Gregory and Radice, London. Address: c/o Gregory and Radice, Riverside Studios, Crisp Road, Hammersmith, London W6 9RL, England.

MOFFEIT Tony A, b. Claremore, Oklahoma, USA. Poet; Librarian. Education: MLS, University of Oaklahoma; BS, Psychology, Oaklahoma State University, 1964. Appointments: Director, Pueblo Poetry Project, 1980-; Poet in Residence, University of Southern Colorado, 1987-95. Publications: Pueblo Blues, 1986; Dancing With The Ghosts of the Dead, 1986; Black Cat Bone, 1986; The Spider Who Walked Underground, 1985; Hank Williams Blues, 1985; Coyote Blues, 1985; Shooting Chant, 1984; Outlaw Blues, 1983; La Nortenita, 1983; Luminous Animal, 1989; Boogie Alley, 1989; Poetry Is Dangerous, the Poet is an Outlaw, 1995; Contributions to: Numerous journals and magazines. Honours: Jack Kerouac Award for Pueblo Blues, 1986;

National Endowment for the Arts Fellowship in Poetry, 1992. Membership: American Library Association. Address: 1501 E 7th, Pueblo, CO 81001, USA.

MOFFETT Judith, b. 1942, USA. Author; Poet; University Lecturer. Appointments: Assistant Professor, Behrend College, Pennsylvania State University, Erie, 1971-75; Visiting Lecturer, Programme in Creative Writing, University of Iowa, Iowa City, 1977-78; Visiting Lecturer, 1978-79, Assistant Professor of English, 1979-86; Adjunct Assistant Professor, 1986-1989; Associate, 1989-1993; Adjunct Professor, 1993-1994, University of Pennsylvania, Philadelphia. Publications: Keeping Time, verse, 1976; Gentleman, Single, Refined, and Selected Poems 1937-59, by Hjalmar Gullberg, translation, 1979; Whinny Moor Crossing, verse, 1984; James Merill: An Introduction to the Poetry, criticism, 1984; Penterra, science fiction, 1987; The Ragged World, science fiction, 1991; Two That Came True, science fiction, 1991; Time, Like an Ever-Rolling Stream, science fiction, 1992; Homestead Year: Back to the Land in the Suburbs (non fiction), 1995. Literary Agent: Martha Millard. Address: 951 S Laird Ave, Salt Lake City, UT 84105, USA.

MOHAMED N P, b. 1 July 1929, Calicut, India. Author. m. 27 Nov 1954, 4 s, 3 d. Education: Intermediate, Madras University. Appointments: Assistant Editor, Kerala Kaumundi, 1987. Publications: Thopplyum Thattavum 1952; Maram, 1959; Hiranya Kashipu, 1976; Abudabi-Dubai, 978; Ennapadem, 1981; Avar Nalupaer, 1987. Contributions to: Various literary journals, peridocials. Honours: Madras Government Award, Short Stories, 1959; Kerala Sahitya Academy Award, 1969, 1981. Memberships: Kerala Sahitya Academy, Executive Committee; Central Academy of Letters, Advisory Member in Malayasian. Address: Suthalam, Calicut-Pin 6730007, Kerala, India.

MOHLER James Aylward, b. 22 Jul 1923, Ohio, USA. Professor; Writer; Clergyman. Education: LittB, Xavier University, 1946; PhL, 1949; STL, 1956, Jesuit School of Theology, Loyola University; MSIR, Loyola University, 1959; PhD, University of Ottowa, 1964; STD, University of St Paul, 1966. Publications include: Speaking of God (co-author), 1967; Man Needs God, 1967; The Beginning of Eternal Life, 1968; Dimension of Faith, 1969; Cosmos, Man, God, Messiah, 1973; The School of Jesus, 1973; Dimension of Love, 1975; Sexual Sublimation and the Sacred, 1978; The Sacrament of Suffering, 1979; Dimensions of Prayer, 1981; Love Marriage and the Family, 1982; Paradise, Gardens of the Gods, 1985; Late Have I Loved You, 1991; A Speechless Child is The Word of God, 1993. Contributions to: Numerous articles in books and magazines. Memberships: Association of Asian Studies; American Academy of Religion; Catholic Theological Society. Literary Agent: Bill Holub. Address: Rodman Hall, John Carroll University, Cleveland, OH 44118, USA.

MOHR Steffen, b. 24 July 1942, Leipzig, Germany. Author. 3 s, 4 d. Education: Diplomas of Theatre, University of Leipzig and Institute of Literature, Leipzig. Publications: At the Beginning of this Travel, 1975; Andy, Set the Fashion, 1975; A Day Full of Music, 1976; Interrogation Without Order, 1979; Remarkable Causes of Captain Merks, 1980; Flowers from the Heaven-meadow, 1982; Today I'll Kill 10 past 12, 1980; Moritz and the Golden Princess, 1986; Don't Look too Closely, 1989 co-author with Professor Bostzky of West Berlin (the first book written by an author of the GDR and an author of the FDR); The Corpse in the Baobad, 1992; Films: Women With and Without (TV film) 1985; Five Minutes to Six (TV film) 1989-90; Radio-drama: Wriggling, 1990; Youth and the dog of the Lord, 1992. Memberships: SYNDIKAT, Union of Crime Writers of Federal Republic of Germany; AIEP; Free Society of Literature (founder and 2nd Chairman). Address: Liechtensteinstr 35, Leipzig, Germany.

MOHRT Michel, b. 28 Apr 1914, Morlaix, France. Writer; Editor. m. Francoise Jarrier, 1955, 1 s. Education: Law School, Rennes. Appointments: Lawyer, Marseilles Bar until 1942; Professor, Yale University, 1947-52; Editor, Head of English Translations, Les Editions Gallimard, 1952-. Publications: Novels: Le repit: Mn royaume pour un cheval,1949; Les nomades; Le seviteur fidele; La prison maritime, 1961; La campagne d'Italie, 1965; L'ours des Adirondacks, 1969; Deux Americaines a Paris, 1974; Les moyens du bord, 1975; La guerre civile, 1986; Le Telesiege, 1989; Essays: Motherland, homme libre, 1943; Le nouveus Roman American, 1956; Lair du large,1969; Vers l'Ouest, 1988; Benjamin on Lettes sur l'Incorestauce, 1989. Plays: Une jeu d'enfer, 1970 (narration); La maison du pere, 1979; Vers l'Ouest, 1988; Benjammin on Liettes sur l'Inconstances, 1989; Le Telesieze, 1989; U Soiz, a loudres, 1991; Ou Liqude et ou s'en Va, 1992. Honours:

Chevalier Legion d'honneur, Croix de guerre; Grand Prix du roman de l'Academie Francaise for La Prison Maritme, 1962; Grand Prix de la Criique Litteraire, 1970; Grand prix du Litteraure de l'Academie Francaise, 1983. Memberships: Academic Francaise, 1985; Garrick Club. Address: Editions Gallimard, 5 rue Sebastien-Bottin, Paris 75007, France.

MOJATABAI Ann Grace, b. 8 Jun 1937, New York City, USA. Author; Educator. m. Fathollah Motabai, 27 April 1960, div 1966, 1 son, 1 daughter. Education: BA, Philosophy, Antioch College, 1958; MA, Philosohy, Columbia University, 1968; MS in LS, Columbia University, 1970. Appointments: Lecturer in Philosophy, Hunter College, 1966-68; Lecturer in English, Harvard University, 1978-83; Writer in Residence, University of Tulsa, 1983-. Publications: Mundome, 1974; The 400 Eels of Sigmund Freud, 1976; A Stopping Place, 1979; Autumn, 1982; Blessed Assurance, 1986; Ordinary Time, 1989; Called Out, 1994. Contributions to: The New York Times Book Review; The New Republic; Philosophy Today; The Philosophical Journal. Honours: Radcliffe Institute Fellow, 1976-78; Guggenheim Fellow, 1981-82; Richard and Hinda Rosenthal Award, American Academy and Institute of Arts and Letters, 1983; Academy Award in Literature, The American Academy of Arts and Letters, 1993. Memberships: The Mark Twain Society; PEN; Texas Institute of Letters; Phi Beta Kappa. Literary Agent: Georges Borchardt. Address: 2102 S Hughes, Amarillo, TX 79109, USA.

MOLDON Peter Leonard, b. 31 Mar 1937, London, England. Writer; Freelance Designer. Education: Hampton Grammar School, 1948-55; Regent Street Polytechnic, 1958-59. Publications: Your Book of Ballet (illustrated & designed by author), 1974, revised edition 1980; Nureyev (designed by author), 1976; The Joy of Knowledge Encyclopaedia (ballet articles), 1976. Contributions to: The Dancing Times. Honours: Your Book of Ballet, selected as one of the Children's Books of the Year, National Book League, 1974, shown at Frankfurt Book Fair by British Council, 1974. Address: 11 Oxlip Road, Witham, Essex CM8 2XY, England.

MOLE John Douglas, b. 12 Oct 1941, Taunton, Somerset, England. Teacher; Writer. m. Mary Norman, 22 Aug 1968, 2 sons. Education: MA, Magdalene College, Cambridge, England, 1961-64. Publications include: In & Out of the Apple, 1984; Homing, 1987; Boo To A Goose (for children), 1987; The Mad Parrot's Countdown, 1990; The Conjuror's Rabbit, 1992; Depending on the Light, 1993; Selected Poems, 1995; Passing Judgements: Poetry in the Eighties (critical essays), 1989. Contributions to: Encounter; TLS; TES; Spectator. Honours: Eric Gregory Award Winner, 1970; Signal Award, for the year's outstanding contribution to children's poetry, 1988; Cholmondeley Award, 1994. Memberships: Society of Authors. Address: 11 Hill Street, St Albans, Hertfordshire AL3 4QS, England.

MOLLENKOTT Virginia Ramey, b. 1932, USA. Professor of English. Appointments: Faculty Member, Shelton College, 1955-63; Faculty Member, Nyack College, 1963-67; Assistant Editor, Seventeenth Century News, 1964-73; Professor of English, William Paterson College of New Jersey, 1967-. Publications: Adamant and Stone Chips: A Christian Humanist Approach to Knowledge, 1967; In Search of Balance, 1969; Adam Among the Television Trees: An Anthology of Verse by Contemporary Christian Poets (editor), 1971; Women, Men and the Bible, 1977, revised, 1988; Is the Homosexual My Neighbour (with Letha Scanzoni), 1978, updated & expanded, 1994; Speech, Silence, Action, 1980; Views From the Intersection (with Catherine Barry), 1983; The Divine Feminine: Biblical Imagery of God as a Female, 1983; Godding: Human Responsibility and the Bible, 1987; Women of Faith in Dialogue (editor), 1987; Sensuous Spirituality: Out from Fundamentalism, 1992. Memberships: Modern Language Association; Milton Society of America; Evangelical & Ecumenical Women's Caucus. Address: 11 Yearling Trail, Hewitt, NJ 07421, USA.

MOLLOY Michael John, b. 22 Dec 1940. Editor. m. Sandra June Foley, 1964, 3 d. Appointments: Sunday Pictorial, 1956; Daily Sketch, 1960; Daily Mirror, 1962-85; Editor, Daily Mirror, 1969; Assistant Editor, Daily Mirror, 1970; Deputy Editor, 1975; Editor, Daily Mirror, 1975-85; Director, Mirror Group Newspapers, 1976-; Editor-in-Chief, Mirror Group, 1985-; Editor, Sunday Mirror, 1986-. Publications: The Black Dwarf, 1985; The Kid from Riga, 1986; The Harlot of Jericho, 1988; The Century. Address: 62 Culmington Road, London, W13, England.

MOMADAY Navarre Scott, b. 27 Feb 1934, Lawton, Oklahoma, USA. Writer; Painter; Professor. m. Regina Heitzer, 21 July 1978, 4 d.

Education: BA, University of New Mexico, 1958; MA, 1960, PhD, 1963, Stanford University. Appointments: Visiting Professor, Columbia University, Princeton, 1979; Writer-in-Residence, Southeastern University, 1985; Aspen Writers Conference, 1986. Publications: House Made of Dawn, 1968; The Way to Rainy Mountain, 1969; The Names, 1976; The Gourd Dancer, 1976; The Ancient Child, 1989; Enchanted Circle, 1993; In the Presence of the Sun, 1992; (with Linda Hozan) The Native Americans, 1993. Honours: Pulitzer Prize, Fiction, 1969; Premio Mondello, Italy, 1979; Honorary Degrees, various universities. Membership: PEN. Literary Agent: Julian Bach Agency. New York. Address: c/o Julian Bach Literary Agency, New York, USA.

MOMI Balbir Singh, b. 20 Nov 1935, Armagarh, India. Teacher; Education Officer; Writer; Translator. m. Baldev Kaur, 28 Oct 1954, 4 daughters. Education: Honours, 1953, MA, 1970, in Punjabi, Honours in Persian, 1974, PhD, 1977. Panjab University, Chandigarh (Candidate); OT, Education Department, PB University, 1957. Appointments: School Teacher, 1954-71; Research and Evaluation Officer, Editor of Pankrian, 1971-73; Subject Officer, 1976-79, Public Relations Officer, Subject Expert, 1979-82, PB School Education Board, retired 1993, Chandigarh. Lecturer, Research Assistant, GND University, Amritsar, 1974-76; Literary Editor, Perdesi Punjab, Toronto, Canada, 1982-85. Publications include: short sory collections: Masale Wala Gohora, 1959; Je Main Mar Jawan, 1965; Sheeshe Da Samunder, 1968; Phul Khire Har, 1973; Sar Da Boojha, 1973; novels: Jeeha Jee, 1964; Peela Gulab, 1975; Ek Phul Mera Vi, 1986; dramas: Laudha Vela and Noukrian Hi Nukrian, 1960-64; translations into Punjabi: Tobha Tek Singh; Nangian Awazan; Sat Gawache Lok; Jai Kantan Ki Kahanian. Contributions include: Amar kahanian; Panj Darya; Preet Lari; Kavita; Lok Sahit; Pritam; Punjabi Sahit; Khoj Dapan; Jan Sahit; Punjabi Duniya; Arsee; Ajit; Punjabi Tribune; Sardal; M4.Navat Sahit; Indo Canadian Times; Punjabi Tribune: The Sikh Press; Canasia; Daily Punjabi; Bitter Almond (short story), Ajit and Simawan, 1994. Honours: Promotion of Culture Award, Punjab, 1968; Literary Awards: Kala Kendar Amritsar, 1975; Guru Nanek Dev University, Amritsar, 1989; Sahit Sameekhia Board, Jalandhar, 1989; CIPSA Award, Toronto Canada, 1990; Baltimore, Punjabi Society Award, 1993; honoured by Kamzoj Vichar Manch, PB, India, 1993; Honoured by International Cultural Forum, Chandigarh, India, 1994. Memberships: General Secretary, Panch Kala Feroxohur, 1950-70; Punjabi Sahit Sabha, Chandigarh, 1971-82; President, International Perdesi Punjab Sahit Sabha, Toronto, 1982-90; Senior Vice President, International Cultural Forum, India & Canada, 1993-. Literary Agent: Dr K S Third, Punjabi University, PB, India. Address: 17 Donaldson Drive, Brampton, Ontario, Canada L6Y 3H1.

MOMMSEN Katharina Zimmer, b. 18 Sep 1925, Berlin, Germany. Professor of Literature. m. Momme H Mommsen, 23 Dec 1948. Education: Abitur, Berlin, 1943; DPhil, Tubingen, 1956; Dr.Phil.Habil, Berlin, 1962. Appointments: Researcher, German Academy of Sciences, Berlin, 1949-61; Docent, Professor, Free University of Berlin, 1962-70; Professor, German Literature, Carleton University, Ottawa. 1970-74, Stanford University, USA, 1974-. Publications: Goethe und 1001 Nacht, 1960; Goethe und Diez, 1961; Goethe und der Islam, 1964; Natur und Fabelreich in Faust II, 1968; Schillers Anthologie, 1973; Kleists Kampf mit Goethe, 1974; Gesellschaftkritik bei Fontane und Thomas Mann, 1974; Herders Journal Meiner Reise, 1976; Hofsmannsthal und Fontane, 1978; Who is Goethe?, 1983; Goethe - Warum?, 1984; Goethes Marchen, 1984; Goethe und die arabische Welt, 1988. Contributions to: numerous journals and magazines. Honours: Guggenheim, 1976; Alexander von Humboldt Forschungspreis, 1980; Bundesverdienskreuz 1 Klasse, 1985; Endowed Chair as Albert Guerard Professor of Literature, Stanford University. Memberships: various professional organisations. Address: Stanford University, Dept of German Studies, Stanford, CA 94305, USA.

MONACO James Frederick, b. 15 Nov 1942, New York, USA. Writer; Publisher. m. Susan R Schenker, 24 Oct 1976, 2 sons, 1 daughter. Education: BA, Muhlenberg College, 1963; MA, Columbia University, 1964. Publications: How to Read a Film, 1977, 1981, 1995; American Film Now, 1979, 1984; Connoisseurs Guide to the Movies, 1985; The New Wave, 1976; Media Culture, 1977; Celebrity, 1977; The International Encyclopedia of Film, 1991; The Movie Guide, 1992; Cinemania: Interactive Movie Guide, 1992. Contributions to: Numerous professional journals including: New York Times; Village Voice; American Film; Christian Science Monitor; many other publications. Memberships: Authors Guild; Writers Guild. Literary Agent: Virginia Barber. Address: UNET Inc, 31 E 12 St, New York, NY 10003, USA.

MONAGAN John Stephen, b. 23 Dec 1911, Waterbury, Connecticut, USA. Attorney at Law. m. Rosemary Brady, 23 May 1949, 2 sons, 3 daughters. Education: AB, Dartmouth College, 1933; JD, Harvard Law School, 1937. Publications: Horace Priest of the Poor; The Grand Pajandrun Mellow Years of Justice Holmes. Contributions to: NY Times Magazine; NY Times Book Review; Washington Post Book World; Washington Times; NY State Bar Journal; American Bar Association Journal; Boston Globe Magazine; US Supreme Court Historical Society Journal; Hartford Courant. Memberships: Cosmos Club; American Conn and DC Bar Associations; President, Association Former Members of Congress; Member of Congress, 1959-73. Address: 3043 West Lane Keys, NW, Washington, DC 20007-3057, USA.

MONCURE Jane Belk, b. 16 Dec 1926, Orlando, Florida, USA. Teacher; Author: Consultant. m. James Ashby Moncure, 14 Jun 1952, 1 son. Education: BS Degree, Virginia Commonwealth University, 1952; Masters Degree, Columbia University, 1954. Appointments: Instructor, Early Childhood Ed, University of Richmond, Virginia, 1972-73; Burlington Day School, Burlington, North Carolina, 1974-78. Publications: First Steps to Reading - Sound Box Books/The Child's World (24 books) 1970's; Magic Castle Books/ The Child's World (27), 1980's; First Steps to Math, (10 books), 1980's; Word Bird, (27 books), 1980's & 90's; Discovery World, (15 books) 1990's. Honours: Outstanding Service to Young Children, 1979; C S Lewis Gold Medal Award, Best Children's Book of the Year, 1984. Address: Cove Cottage, Seven Lakes Box 3336, West End, NC 27376, USA.

MONETTE Madeleine, b. 3 Oct 1951, Montreal, Canada. Author. m. William R Leggio, 27 Dec 1979. Education: MA, Literature, University of Quebec. Publications: Le Double Suspect, 1980; Petites Violences, 1982; Fuites et Poursuites, 1982; Plages, 1986; L'Aventure, la Mesaventure, 1987; Amades et melon, 1991; Nouvelles de Montreal, 1992; Contributions to: Quebec francais; Possibles, Arcade; Le Devoir; Trois; Moebius; Ecrits du Canada-Francais; Nuit Blanche; Le Sabord (Canada) Sud; Europe (France); Beaconand Romance Language Annual (USA). Honours: Robert-Cliche Award, Quebec City International Book Fair, 1980; Grants, Canadian Council of Arts, 1981, 1984, 1991, 1993. Memberships: Quebec Writers Union. Address: 2 Charlton Street, 11K, New York, NY 10014, USA.

MONEY David Charles, b. 5 Oct 1918, Oxford, England. Schoolmaster. m. Madge Matthews, 30 Nov 1945, 1 son. Education: Honours Degree, Chemistry, 1940, Honours Degree, Geography, 1947, St John's College, Oxford University. Publications: Human Geography, 1954; Climate, Soils and Vegetation, 1965; The Earth's Surface, 1970; Patterns of Settlement, 1972; Environmental Systems, series, 1978-82; Foundations of Geography, 1987; Climate and Environmental Systems, 1988; China - The Land and the People, 1984, revised 1989; China Today, 1987; Australia Today, 1988; Environmental Issues - The Global Consequences, 1994. Honours: Honorary Member, for Services to Education, The Geographical Association. Memberships: Fellow, The Royal Geographical Society; The Farmer's Club. Address: 52 Park Avenue, Bedford MK40 2NE, England.

MONEY Keith, b. 1934, Auckland, New Zealand. Author; Artist; Photographer. Publications include: Salute the Horse, 1960; The Horseman in Our Midst, 1963; The Equestrian World, 1963; The Art of the Royal Ballet, 1964, 1967; The Art of Margot Fonteyn, 1965, 1975; The Royal Ballet Today, 1968; Fonteyn: The Making of a Legend, 1973; John Curry, 1978; Anna Pavlova: Her Life & Art, 1982; The Bedside Book of Old Fashioned Roses, 1985; Some Other Sea: The Life of Rupert Brooke, 1988-89; Fonteyn and Nureyev: The Great Years, 1994; Margot, assoluta, 1993; Collaborations: Pat Smythe, Peter Beales. Contributions to: Numerous journals & magazines; also screenplays, anthologies. Address: Carbrooke Hall Farm, Thetford, Norfolk, England.

MONGRAIN Serg, b. 15 Jan 1948, Trois Rivieres, Quebec, Canada. Educations: Mathematical Université du Quebec a Trois Rivieres, 1972. Publications: L'Oeil du l'idée, 1988, 1991; Le calcul des heures, 1993; As Photographer: Lis: écris, 1981; L'image titre, 1981; Agrestes, 1988; Many exhibition catalogues in art. Contributions to: Numerous contributions of magazines and poetry review. Memberships: Union des écrivains du Quebec. Address: 994 rue Sainte Cecile, Trois Rivieres, Quebec G9A 1L3, Canada.

MONK C. See: MEDVE Victor Cornelius.

MONOD Jean, b. 19 Oct 1941, Paris, France. Writer; Ethrologist; Film Maker. m. (1)Marie Laure Chaude, 1962, (2)Kagumi Onodera, 1989, 3 s, 2 d. Education: University Paris, 1974. Appointments: Lecturer, 1970; Editor in Chief, Aiou, 1987; Editorial Board, Ethnies, 1989; Editorial Board, Dock(k)s, 1991. Publications: Les Barjots; Un Riche Cannibale; Wora, La Deesse Cachee; Luniere d Ailleirs; Raid; Le Foetus Astra; others inc L'eau Du Premier Soir. Contributions to: Le Monde; Canal; Liberation; Les Temps Modernes; Journal de la Societe des Americanistes; L'Autre Journal. Honours: Prix Georges Sadoul; Prix Louis Marinde L'Academie des Sciences; d'Ortre-Mer. Address: L'Espinassounel, 48330 Saint Etienne Valle Francaise, france.

MONSARRAT Ann Whitelaw, b. 8 Apr 1937, Walsall, England. Writer. m. Nicholas Monsarrat, 22 Dec 1961. Publications: An Uneasy Victorian: Thackeray the Man, 1980; And the Bride Wore ... The Story of the White Wedding, 1973. Contributions to: Journalist, West Kent Mercury, 1954-58; Daily Mail, London, 1958-61; Tatler, 1993-94; UNESCO Courier, 1994; Assistant Editor, Stationery Trade Review, 1961. Literary Agent: Campbell Thomson and McLaughlin, London, England. Address: San Lawrenz, Gozo, Malta.

MONTAG Tom b. 1947, USA. Poet; Editor, Publisher. Appointments: Formerly Researcher, Centre for Venture Management; Editor, Publisher, Monday Morning Press, Milwaukee, 1971-; Editor, Publisher, Margins Books, 1974-. Publications: Wooden Nickel, 1972; Twelve Poems, 1972; Measurers, 1972; To leave This Place, 1972; Making Hay, 1973; The Urban Ecosystem: A Holistic Approcah (edited with F Stearns), 1974; Making Hay and Other Poems, 1975; Ninety Notes Toward Partial Images and Lover Prints, 1976; Concerns: Essays and Reviews: 1977; Letters Home, 1978: The Essential Ben Zen, 1992. Address: c/o Sparrow Press, 193 Waldron Street, West Lafayette, IN 47906, USA.

MONTAGU OF BEAULIEU Edward John Barrington Douglas-Scott-Montagu, (Lord), b. 1926, United Kingdom. Author; Founder/Trustee, National Motor Musuem, Beaulieu. Appointments: Founder, Publisher, Veteran and Vintage Magazine, 1956-79. Publications: The Motoring Montagus, 1959; Lost Causes of Motoring, 1960; Jaguar: A Biography, 1961, 1962, 1967, 1981, 1982, 1986, 1990; The Gordon Bennett Races, 1963; Rolls of Rolls Royce, 1966; The Gilt and Gingerbread, 1967; Lost Causes of Motoring in Europe, vol I, 1969, vol II 1971; More Equal Than Others, 1970; History of the Steam Car (with A Bird), 1971; The Horseless Carriage, 1975; Early Days on the Road, 1976; Behind the Wheel, 1977; Royalty on the Road, 1980; Home, James, 1982; The British Motorist, 1987; English Heritage, 1987. Address: Palace House, Beaulieu, Brockenhurst, Hants SO42 7ZN, England.

MONTAGU Robert, b. 25 Nov 1949. Writer; Businessman. m. Marzia Brigante Colonna, 23 May 1970, 2 s, 2 d. Education: Eton College, 1962-66; Diploma in Communications Studies, Polytechnic of Central London, 1973. Honours: Shortlisted for Faber Prize, 1988. Literary Agent: Jane Conway-Gordon, 1 Old Compton Street, London, W1, England. Address: The Old Manor, Evershot, Dorest, England.

MONTAGUE John (Patrick), b. 1929. Ireland. Author; Educator. Appointments: Worked for State Tourist Board, Dublin, 1956-61; Currently Lecturer in Poetry, University College, Cork. Publications: Forms of Exile, 1958; The Old People, 1960; Poisoned Lands and Other Poems, 1961; The Dolmen Miscellany of Irish Writing (editor) 962; Death of a Chieftain and Other Stories, 1964; All Legendary Obstacles, 1966; Patriotic Suite, 1966; A Tribute ot Austin Clarke on His Seventieth Birthday, 9th May 1966 (edited with Liam Miller), 1966; Home Again, 1967; A Chosen Light, 1967; The Rough Field, 1972; Hymn to the New Omagh Road, 1968; The Bread God: A Lecture, with illustrations in Verse, 1968; A New Siege, 1969; The Planter and the Gael (with J Hewitt), 1970; Tides, 1970; Small Secrets, 1972; The Rough Field, play, 1972; A Fair House, translation from Irish, 1973; The Cave of Night, 1974; O'Riada's Farewell,1974; The Faber Book of Irish Verse (editor), 19734; A Slow Dance, 1975; The Great Cloak, 1978; Selected Poems, 1982; The Dead Kingdom, 1984; Mount Eagle, 1989. Address: Department of English, University College, Cork, Republic of Ireland.

MONTE Bryan Robert, b. 3 Nov 1957, Cleveland, Ohio, USA. Writer. Editor. Education: BA, English Literature, University of California, Berkeley, 1983; MA, Graduate Writing Programme, Brown University, 1986. Appointments: California Poet in the Schools, 1983-84; University Fellow, Brown University, 1984-86; Writing

Specialist, Massachusetts Public Schools, 1986-87; Assistant Bibliographer, John Carter Brown Library, 1986. Publcations: No Apologies, Editor, 1983-; The Mirror of the Medusa, poetry, 1987; Neurotika, poetry, 1988. Contributions to: James White Review; Bay Windows; Addvocate. Honours: Youth and Creative Arts Award Winner, The Saints Herald, 1976-78; Joan Lee Yang Memorial Poetry Prize Winner, University of California, 1982; many other honours and awards. Literary Agent: Jayne Walker. Address: 1835 Ednamary Way, No E, Mountain View, CA 94040, USA.

MONTELEONE Thomas Francis, b. 14 Apr 1946, Baltimore, Maryland, USA. Writer. m. Elizabeth, 2 sons, 1 daughter. Education: BS, Psychology, 1964, MA, English Literature, 1973, University of Maryland. Publications: The Time Swept City, 1977; The Secret Sea, 1979; Night Things, 1980; Dark Stars and Other Illuminations, 1981; Guardian, 1981; Night Train, 1984; Lyrica, 1987; The Magnificent Gallery, 1987; Crooked House, 1988; Fantasma, 1989; Borderlands, 1990; Borderlands 2, 1991; Borderlands 3, 1992; The Blood of the Lamb, 1992; Borderlands 4, 1993; The Blood of the Lamb, 1993. Contributions to: National & International Science Fiction; Dark Fantasy; Suspense; Cemetary Dance; anthologies. Honours: Finalist, John W Campbel Award, 1973; Nebula Award, best short story, 1976, 1977; Winner, Gabriel Award, best television drama, 1984; Bronze Award, International Film & TV Festival, New York, (best drama), 1984; Bram Stoker Award for Superior Achievement - novel, The Blood of the Lamb, 1993. Memberships: Secretary, 1976-79, Science Fiction Writers of America; Vice President, 1987-88, Horror Writers of America. Literary Agent: Howard Morhaim, 175 Fifth Avenue, New York, NY 10010, USA.

MONTGOMERY David, b. 6 Nov 1948, Bangor, Northern Ireland. Journalist. m. Heidi Kingstone, 6 May 1989. Education: BA, Politics & History, Queen's University, Belfast, 1967-70. Appointments: Sub-editor, Daily and Sunday Mirror, Manchester, 1973-76; Back Bench Executive, Daily and Sunday Mirror, London, 1976-80; Chief Sub-editor, The Sun, 1980-82; Assistant Editor, Sunday People, 1982-84; Assistant Editor, News of the World, 1984-85; Editor, News of the World, 1985-87; Director, Sky Television plc, 1986-90; Editor, Today, Managing Director, London Live Television Ltd, 1991; Director, Caledonian Newspaper Publishing Ltd, owner of George Outram, 1992; Chief Executive, Mirror Group Newspapers, 1992. Honours: Design Award, Best Colour & Outstanding Contribution to Newspaper Design, 1988; Media Week Consumer Press, 1989; The British Environment & Media Awards, 1989. Address: 13 Warrington Crescent, London W9, England.

MONTGOMERY Marion, b. 16 Apr 1925. Teacher: Writer. m. Dorothy Carlisle, 20 Jan 1952, 1 son, 4 daughters. Education: AB, 1950, MA, 1953, University of Georgia; Creative Writing Workshop, University of Iowa, 1956-58. Appointments: Associate Editor, Modern Age; Managing Editor, Western Review, 1957-58; Assistant Director, University of Georgia Press, 1950-52. Publications: Dry Lightening (poems), 1960; The Wandering of Desire, 1962; Darell, 1964; Stones From the Rubble, 1965; The Gull and Other Georgia Scenes, 1969; T S Eliot: An Essay on the American Magus, 1970; Fugitive, 1974; The Reflective Journey Towards Order, 1974; Eliot's Reflective Journey to the Garden, 1979; The Prophetic Poet and the Popular Spirit, 3 vols, 1981. 1983, 1984; Possum and Other Receipts for the Recovery of Southern Being, 1987; Liberal Arts and Community, 1990; Virtue and Modern Shadows of Turning, 1990; The Men I Have Chosen For Fathers: Literary and Philosophical Passages, 1990. Contributions to: over 200 essays, 300 poems, 30 stories in periodicals. Honours: Best American Short Stories, 1971; Eugene Saxton Memorial Award, 1960; Earhart Foundation Fellowship, 1973-74. Membership: Philadelphia Society. Address: Box 115, Crawford, GA 30630, USA.

MONTI Nicolas, b. 8 Jan 1956, Milan, Italy. Architect; Writer. Education: Liceo Gonzaga, Milan, 1974; Paris VI University, 1976; Polytechnic School of Architecture, Milan, 1984. Publications: Mediterranean Houses; Cunha Moraes, Viagens en Angola; Italian Modern: A Design Heritage; Africa Then; Emilio Sommariva; Luca Comerio, Fotografo e Cineasta; Design Ethno, 1994. Contributions to: AI; Area; Camera Mainichi; Corto Maltese; Domina; Domus; Geodes; Il Giornale dell'Ingegnere; Lagola; La Mia Casa; Modo; PM; Personal Time; Progresso Fotografico; Zoom; Blue Rosso; Aperture. Honours: Study Tour of Japan, Essay Contest. Memberships: Ordine degli Architetti; Collegio degli Ingegneri; Società degli Architetti. Literary Agent: Melanie Jackson AGency, 250 West 57th Street, New York City, New York, USA. Address: Via Borghetto 5, 20122 Milan, Italy.

MONTPETIT Charles, b. 3 Jan 1958, Montreal, Canada. Novelist; Scriptwriter; Cartoonist. Education: BA, Communications, Concordia University, 1979. Publications: Moi Ou La Planète, 1973; Une Conquête De Plus, 1981; Temps Perdu, 1984; Temps Mort, 1989; La Première Fois, 1991; Copie Carbone, 1993. Contributions to: Numerous Magazines and Journals. Honours: Actuelle-Jeunesse Prize, 1973; Three Radio-Canada Scriptwriting Competitions, 1978, 1979, 1991; Governor General Award, 1989; White Raven, 1992; Signet d'Or, 1993. Memberships: Communication Jeunesse; Canadian Society of Children's Authors, Illustrators and Performers; Canadian Children's Book Centre; SF Canada; Union Des Écrivaines Et Écrivains du Québec. Address: 4282C Fullum Street, Montreal H2H 2J5, Canada.

MOONEY Bel, b. 8 Oct 1946, Liverpool, England. Writer; Boradcaster. m. Jonathan Dimbleby, 23 Feb 1968, 1 s, 1 d. Education: BA, Honours, 1st Class, University College, London, 1968. Publications: The Year of the Child, 1979; Liza's Yellow Boat, 1980; The Windsurf Boy, 1983; Diffenences of Opinion, 1984; I Don't Want to! 1985; The Anderson Question, 1985; Father Kismass and Mother Claws, 1985; The Stove Haunting, 1986; The Fourth of July, 1988; From This Day Forward, 1989; A Flower of Jet, 1990; But You Promised! 1990; Why Not? 1990; I Know! 1991; Perspectives for Living Conversations on Bereavement and Love, 1992; Lost Footsteps, 1993; Contributions include: All major British Newspapers and Magazines (Freelance), 1970-87; Columnist, Daily Mirror, 1979-80; Sunday Times, 1982-983; Book Reviews; Interviews. Literary Agent: David Higham Associates. Address: c/o David Higham Associates, 5-8 Lower John Street, London, W1R 3PE, England.

MOONMAN Eric, b. 29 Apr 1929, Liverpool, England. Professor of Health Management; Director of Research. m. Jane Moonman, 10 Sept 1962, div. 1991, 2 sons, 1 daughter. Appointments include: Professor of Health Management, Chair, Essex Radio PLC, City University, 1990-; Consultant, International Red Cross (Africa), 1992-. Education: Diploma, Society Sciences, Liverpool University, 1955; MSc, Management Science, Manchester University, 1966. Publications: The Manager and the Organization, 1961; Communications in an Expanding Organization, 1970; The Reluctant Partnership, 1971; The Alternative Government, 1984; The Violent Society, 1987. Contributions to: Times; New York Times; Observer. Honours: OBE. Memberships: Fellow, Institute of Management; Fellow, Royal Society of Arts. Address: 1 Beacon Hill, London N7 9LY, England.

MOORCOCK Michael (John) (Desmond Read, Edward P Bradbury), b. 18 Dec 1939, Mitcham, Surrey, England. Writer (Novels, Short Stories, Science Fiction, Fantasy). Literary appointments: Editor: Tarzan Adventures, 1956-58, Sexton Blake Library, 1959-61, New Worlds, London, 1964-79. Publications include: The Stealer of Souls and other Stories (with James Cawthorn), 1961; Caribbean Crisis, 1962; The Fireclown, 1965, as The Winds of Limbo, 1969; The Sundered World, 1965, as The Blood Red Game, 1970; Stormbringer, 1965; Michael Kane series: Warriors of Mars, 1965, as The City of the Beast, 1970; The Distant Suns (with Philip James), 1975; The Quest for Tanelorn, 1975; The Adventures of Una Persson and Catherine Cornelius in the Twentieth Century, 1976; The End of All Songs, 1976; Moorcock's Book of Martyrs, 1976; The Lives and Times of Jerry Cornelius, 1976; Legends from the End of Time, 1976; The Sailor on the Seas of Fate, 1976; The Transformation of Miss Mavis Ming, 1977, as Messiah at the End of Time, 1978; The Weird of the White Wolf, 1977; The Bane of the Black Sword, 1977; Sojan, for children, 1977; Condition of Muzak, 1977; Glorianna, 1978; Dying for Tomorrow, 1978; The Golden Barge, 1979; My Experiences in the Third World War, 1980; The Russian Intelligence, 1980; The Great Rock'n'Roll Swindle, 1980; Byzantium Endures, 1981; The Entropy Tanga, 1981; The Warhound and the World's Pain, 1981; The Brothel in Rosenstrasse, 1982; The Dancers at the End of Time, omnibus, 1983; The Retreat from Liberty, 1983; The Language of Carthage, 1984; The Opium General and Other Stories, 1984; The Chronicles of Castle Brass, 1985; Letters from Hollywood, 1986; The City in the Autumn Stars, 1986; The Dragon in the Sword, 1986; Death is No Obstacle, 1992; Editor: The Best of New Worlds, 1965; England Invaded, 1977; New Worlds: An Anthology, 1983. Address: c/o Anthony Sheil Associates, 43 Doughty Street, London WC1N 2LF, England.

MOORE Barbara, b. 1934, USA. Writer. Appointments: Reporter, Fort Worth Star-Telegram, Fort Worth, Texas, 1955-57; Denver Post, Denver, Colorado, 1958-60; San Antonio Light, San Antonio, Texas, 1963-65. Publications: Hard on the Road, 1974; The Fever Called

Living, 1976; Something on the Wind, 1978; The Doberman Wore Black, 1983; The Wolf Whispered Death, 1986. Literary Agent: Harold Matson Co Inc, USA. Address: c/o Harold Matson Co Inc, 276 Fifth Avenue, New York, NY 10001, USA.

MOORE Brian, b. 25 Aug 1921, Belfast, Northern Ireland. Author. m. Jean Denney, Oct 1967, 1 son. Education: Saint Malachy's College, Belfast. Publications: The Lonely Passion of Judith Hearne, 1955; The Feast of Lupercal, 1957; The Luck of Ginger Coffey, 1960; An Answer from Limbo, 1962; The Emperor of Ice-Cream, 1965; I am Mary Dunne, 1968; Fergus, 1970; The Revolution Script, 1971; Catholics, 1972; The Great Victorian Collection, 1975; The Doctor's Wife, 1976; The Mangan Inheritance, 1979; The Temptation of Eileen Hughes, 1981; Cold Heaven, 1983; Black Robe, 1985; The Color of Blood, 1987; Lies of Silence, 1990; No Other Life, 1993. Honours: Que, Literary Prize, 1958; US National Arts and Letters Award, 1961; Fiction Award, Governor General of Canada, 1961; 75 W H Smith Award, 1973; Heinemann Award, Royal Society of Literature, 1986; Sunday Express Book of the Year Award, 1987; Guggenheim Fellow, 1959; Canadian Council Senior Fellow, 1962, 1976; Scottish Arts Council International Fellow, 1983; Hon D.Litt, The Queen's University of Belfast, 1989; Hon D.Litt, The National University of Ireland, University College, Dublin, 1991. Address: 33958 Pacific Coast Highway, Malibu, CA 90265, USA.

MOORE Charles Hilary, b. 31 Oct 1956. Editor. m. Caroline Mary Baxer, 1981. 1 son, 1 daughter. Education: BA, Trinity College, Cambridge. Appointments: Joined Editorial Staff, 1979, Leader Writer, 1981-83, Deputy Editor, 1990-92, The Daily Telegraph; Assistant Editor, Political Columnist, 1983-84, Editor, 1984-90, Fortnightly Columnist, 1990-, The Spectator; Weekly Columnist, The Daily Express, 1987-; Editor, The Sunday Telegraph, 1992-. Publications: Violent Universe, 1969; The Mind of Man, 1970; The Restless Earth, 1972; The Life Game, 1973; The Weather Machine, 1974; The Human Conspiracy, 1976; The Key to the Universe, 1977; Spaceships of the Mind, 1978; Einstein's Universe, 1979; Nuclear Nightmares, 1979; The Comet is Coming!, 1980; Timescales, 1983; The English Channel, 1986; Scientific Europe, 1990; Spaceship Earth, 1991; Giotto to the Comets, 1992; Out of this World, 1995. Membership: Beefsteak Club. Address: 16 Thornhill Square, London N1 1BQ, England.

MOORE Christopher Hugh, b. 9 June 1950, England. Historian; Writer. m. Louise Brophy, 7 May 1977. Education: BA, Honours, University of British Columbia, 1971; MA, University of Ottawa, 1977. Publications: Louisbourg Portraits, 1982; The Loyalists, 1984; Co-author, The Illustrated History of Canada, 1987; and many Radio Documentaries, School Texts, Educational Software Programmes, Historical Guidebooks on Canadian History. Contributions to: Numerous scholarly journals and magazines. Honours: Governor General's Literary Award, 1982; Secretary of State's Prize for Excellence in Canadian Studies, 1985; Canadian Historical Association Award of Merit, 1984. Memberships: Writers Union of Canada; Canadian Historical Association; Ontario Historical Society; Heritage Canada Foundation. Address: 620 Runnymede Road, Toronto, Ontario, M6S 3A2, Canada.

MOORE Eric. See: BRUTON Eric.

MOORE John Evelyn (Captain), b. 1 Nov 1921, Sant'Ilario, Italy. Editor; Author; Retired Naval Officer. m. (1) Joan Pardoe, 1945, 1 son, 2 daughters, (2) Barbara Kerry. Appointments include: Editor, Jane's Fighting Ships, 1972-87; Editor, Jane's Naval Review, 1982-87. Publications: Jane's Major Warships, 1973; The Soviet Navy Today, 1975; Submarine Development, 1976; Soviet War Machine (jointly), 1976; Encyclopaedia of World's Warships (jointly), 1978; World War 3 (jointly), 1978; Seapower and Politics, 1979; Warships of the Royal Navy, 1979; Warships of the Soviet Navy, 1981; Submarine Warfare: Today and Tomorrow (jointly), 1986. Membership: Fellow, Royal Geographical Society. Address: Elrmhurst, Rickney, Hailsham, Sussex BN27 1SF, England.

MOORE Patrick Alfred Caldwell, b. 4 Mar 1923, Pinner, Middlesex, England. Astronomer; Author. Appointments: BBC TV Series, The Sky at Night 1957-; Radio Braodcasts; Editor, Year Book of Astronomy, 1962-; Director, Armagh Planetarium, 1965-68; Composer, Perseus and Andromeda (opera), 1975; Theseus, 1982. Publications: Numerous, including Guide to the Moon, 1976; Atlas of the Universe, 1980; History of Astronomy, 1983; Guinness Book of Astronomy (revised edition), 1983; The Story of the Earth (with Peter Cattermole), 1985; Halley's Comet (with Heather Couper), 1985;

Patrick Moore's Ammchair Astronomy, 1985; Stargazing, 1985; Exploring the Night Sky with Binoculars, 1986; the A-Z of Astronomy, 1986; Astronomny for the Under Tens, 1987; Stargazing, 1988; Men of the Stars, 1988; The Planet Neptune, 1989; Mission to the Planets, 1990; A Passion for Astronomy, 1991; The Earth for Under Tens, 1992; Fireside Astronomy, 1992. Honours: Goodacre Medal, British Astronomical Association, 1968; Jackson Gwilt Gold Medal, Royal Astronomical Society, 1977; Klumpke Medal, Astronomical Society of the Pacific, 1979; Hon D.Sc, Lancaster, 1974; OBE, 1969; CBE, 1988; Minor Planet No 2602 named "Moore" in his honour. Memberships: Past President, British Astronomical Association. Address: Farthings, 39 West Street, Selsey, West Sussex, England.

MOORE Peter Dale, b. 20 June 1942, Nantyglo, Wales. University Lecturer. m. Eunice P Jervis, 18 Dec 1966, 2 daughters. Education: BSc, 1963, PhD, 1966, University of Wales. Publications: Peatlands; Biography; Pollen Analysis; Atlas of Living World; Encylopedia of Animal Ecology; Mitchell Beazeley Guide to Wild Flowers; European Mires; Methods in Plant Ecology. Contributions to: New Scientist; Nature; Plants Today; Journal of Ecology. Memberships: British Ecological Society; Cambridge Philosophic Society; Botanical Society of British Isles. Address: Division of Life Sciences, Kings College, Campden Hill Road, London W8 7AH, England.

MOORE Ruth Nulton, b. 19 June 1923, Easton, Pennsylvania, USA. Writer. m. Carl Leland Moore, 15 June 1946, 2 s. Education: BA, Bucknell University; MA, Columbia University. Publications: Frisky the Playful Pony, 1966; Hiding the Bell, 1968; Peace Treatry, 1977; Ghost Bird Myster, 1977; Mystery of the Lost Treasure, 1978; Tomas and the Talking Birds, 1979; Wilderness Journey, 1979; Mystery at Indian Rocks, 1981; The Sorrel Horse, 1982; Danger in the Pines, 1983; In Search of Liberty, 1983; Mystery of the Missing Stallions, 1984; Mystery of the Secret Code, 1985; The Christmas Surprise, 1989; Distant Thunder, 1991; Mystery at Captain's Cove, 1992; Mystery at the Spanish Castle, 1990. Contributions to: Jack and Jill; Children's Activities. Honours: C S Lewis Honor Book Medal, 1983; Religion in Media Silver Angel Award, 1984. Memberships: Children's Authors and Illustrators of Philadelphia. Literary Agent: McIntosh and Otis, Address: 3033 Center Street, Bethlehem, PA 18017, USA.

MOORE Sally, b. 12 Feb 1936, Buffalo, New York, USA. Writer; Photographer. m. Richard E Moore, 10 Dec 1960, 1 son, 2 daughters. Education: Mount Holyoke College, MA, South Hadley; Sarah Williston Scholar. Publications:Country Roads of Pennsylvania, 1993. Contributions to: Travel Articles: US Air Magazine, Delta Sky Magazine, Snow Country, New York Times. Memberships: Society of American Travel Writers; American Association of Journalists & Authors. Address: 1226 Blossom Terrace, Boiling Springs, PA 17007, USA.

MOORE Susanna, b. 9 Dec 1948, Bryn Mawr, Pennsylvania, USA. Film Industry; Writer. Married, 1 d. Publications: The Whiteness of Bones; Sleeping Beauties; My Old Sweetheart, 1982. Honours: PEN/ Ernest Hemingway Citation; Sue Kaufman Prize from American Academy and Institute of Arts and Letters, 1983; American Book Award, nominee, 1983. Address: c/o Amanda Urban ICM, 40 West 57th Street, New York, NY 10019, USA.

MOOREHEAD Caroline, b. 1944, United Kingdon. Writer; Journalist. Appointments: Reporter, Time Magazine, Rome, Italy, 1968-69; Feature Writer, Telegraph Magazine, London, 1969-70; Features Editor, Times Educational Supplement, 1970-73; Feature Writer, The Times Newspaper, London, 1973-88; Human Rights Columnist Indepdent, 1988-. Publications: Myths and Legends of Britain (editor and translator), 1968; Fortune's Hostages, 1980; Sidney Bernstein: A Biography, 1983; Freya Stark: A Biography, 1985; Troublesome People, 1988; Betrayal Children in Today's World, 1989; Bertrand Rundei: A Life, 1992. Address: 36 Fitzroy Road, London, NW1, England.

MOORHOUSE Frank, b. 21 Dec 1938, Nowra, Queensland, Australia. Education: University of Queensland; WEA. Appointments: President, Australian Society of Authors, 1979-82; Chairman, Copyright Council of Australia, 1985. Publications: Futility and Other Animals, 1969; The Americans, Baby, 1972; The Electrical Experience, 1974; Conference-Ville, 1976; Tales of Mystery and Romance, 1977; Everlasting Secret Family and Other Secrets, 1980; Days of Wine and Rage, 1980; Room Service, 1986; Forty-Seventeen, 1988; Lateshows, 1990. Contributions to: Bulletin. Honours: Henry Lawson Short Story

Prize, 1970; National Award for Fiction, 1975; Winner, Awgie Award, Best Script, for Conference-Ville; Gold Medal for Literature, Australian Literary, 1989. Memberships: Australian Royal Automobile Club, Sydney; Crouchos Club, London; Member, Order of Australia. Literary Agent: Rosemary Creswell, Australia. Address: c/o Rosemary Cresswell, Private Bag 5, PO Balmain, New South Wales 2041, Australia.

MOORHOUSE Geoffrey, b. 29 Nov 1931, Bolton, Lancashire, England. Author. m. Marilyn Isobel Edwards, 2 s, 1 d, previous marriage. Publications: The Other England, 1963; Against All Reason, 1969; Calcutta, 1971; The Missionaries, 1973; The Fearful Void, 1974; The Diplomats, 1977; The Boat & The Town, 1979; The Best Loved Game, 1979; Lord's 1983; Indian Britannica, 1983; To the Frontier, 1984; Apples in the Snow, 1990; Hell's Foundation: a town, it's myth and Gallipolis, 1992. Contributions to: The Guardian; The Times; Observer; London Magazine; Books and Bookmen. Honours: Fellow, Royal Geographical Society, 1972; Fellow, Royal Society of Liteature, 1982; Cricket Society Literary Award, 1979; Thomas Cook Literary Award, 1984. Literary Agent: A P Watt Ltd, London. Address: Park House, Gayle, Near Hawes, N Yorks, DL8 3RT, England.

MORAES Dominic, b. 19 July 1938. Writer; Poet. Education: Jesus College, Oxford. Appointments: Consultant, UN Fund for Population Activities, 1973-, (on loan to India), Managing Editor, the Asia Magazine, Hong Kong, 1972-. Publication include: A Beginning, 1957; Gone Away, 1960; My Son's Father (autobiography), 1968; The Tempest Within, 1972-73; The People Time Forgot, 1972; A Matter of People, 1974; Voices for Life (essays), 1975; Mrs Gandhi, 1980; Bombay, 1980; Ragasthan: Splendour in the Wilderness, 1988; books of poems and travel books on India. Honours: Hawthornden Prize for A Beginning, 1957. Address: c/o 521 Fifth Avenue, New Yrok, NY 10017, USA.

MORAN John Charles, b. 4 Oct 1942, Nashville, Tennessee, USA. Editor; Foundation Director, Researcher; Librarian. Education: BA, 1967, MLS, 1968, George Peabody, Nashville, Tennessee. Appointments: Director, F Marion Crawford Memorial Society, Nashville, Tennessee, 1975-; Editor, The Romantist, 1977-; Editor, The Worthies Library, 1980-. Publications: An F Marion Crawford Companion, 1981; Seeking Refuge in Torre San Nicola, 1980; In Memoriam: Gabriel Garcia Moreno 1875-1975, 1975; Editor, Francesca Da Rimini (1902), 1980; Bibliography of Marketing of Fruits and Vegetables in Honduras, 1975-85, 1985; Editor, The Satanist, (1912) Forthcoming; Last Days and Death of Dr & Gen William Walker, forthcoming; Editor, Anne Crawford von Rabe's, A Shadow on a Wave, 1981, 1994. Contributions to: Numerous professional journals and magazines. Honours: Special Guest, Il Magnifico Crawford Conference on Francis Marion Crawford, Sant' Agnello Di Sorrento, 1988. Membership: Director, F Marion Crawford Memorial Society, 1975-. Address: F Marion Crawford Society, Sarascinesca House, 3610 Meadowbrook Ave, Nashville, TN 37205, USA.

MORAY WILLIAMS Ursula, b. 19 Apr 1911, Petersfield, Hampshire, England. Writer of Children's Books. m. Conrad Southey John, 28 Sept 1935, 4 sons. Education: Winchester Art College. Publications: Approximately 70 titles, 1931-, including: Jean-Pierre; Adventures of the Little Wooden Horse; Gobbolino the Witch's Cat; Further Adventures of Gobbolino and the Little Wooden Horse; Nine Lives of Island Mackenzie; The Noble Hawks; Bogwoppit; Jeffy the Burglar's Cat; Good Little Christmas Tree; Cruise of the Happy-Go-Gay; Bellabelinda and the No-Good Angel; The Moonball. Contributions to: Cricket USA; Puffin Post; The EGG; Storyteller 1, 2, Christmas numbers; Various Australian magazines. Membership: West of England Writers Guild. Literary Agent: Curtis Brown, London, England. Address: Court Farm House, Beckford, near Tewkesbury, Gloucestershire, England.

MORENCY Pierre, b. 8 May 1942, Quebec, Canada. Writer. Education: BA, College de Levis, 1963; Licence es Lettres, Universite Laval, Quebec, Canada, 1966. Appointments: freelance Writer at Radio Canada, 1967- 91. Publications: Lumière des Oiseaux, 1992; L'Oeil Americain, 1989; The Eye is an Eagle, 1992; A Season for Birds, selected poems, 1990; Quand nous serons, 1988; Effets Personnels, 1986; Les Passeuses, 1976; Glimmer on the Mountain, 1992; Les Paroles Qui Marchent Dans La Nuit, 1994. Honours: Prix Alain Grandbois, 1987; Prix Quebec-Paris, 1988; Prix Ludger Duvernay, 1991; Prix France Quebec, 1992. Memberships: Union Des Ecrivains

Quebecois; PEN Club: Ordre Des Arts et Des Lettres de France, (chevalier). Address: 155 Avenue Laurier, Quebec, Canada, G1R 2K8.

MORENO Armando, 19 Dec 1932, Porto, Portugal. University Professor and Medical Doctor. m. Maria Guinot Moreno, 3 Oct 1987. Education: Licentiate in Medicine, 1960; Doctor of Medicine, 1972; Aggregation in Medicine, 1984; Licentiate in Literature, 1986. Literary Appointments: 1st Congresso Luso-Brasilerio de Literaturea, Porto, 1984; Oration Sapientia, Universidad Tecnica de Lisboa, Lisbon; 1st Congresso Internacional de Lingua Portuguesa, Lisbon, 1989; Ciclo de Conferencias O Corpo Morfologica, Porto, 1990. Publications include: Historias Quase Clinicas (short stories) 3 vols, 1982, 1984, 1988; A Chamada (short stories), 1982; As Carreiras (Romance), 1982; O Bojador (Romance) 1982; Biologia fdo Conto (literary Study about short story) 1987; Cais do Sodre (short Stoies), 1988. Also Medical Books (6 vols), poetry, plays. Contributions to: Magazines, including Noticias Medicas, Geofarma, Espaco Medico, Intercidades, and journals, such as O Diario, Journal de Letras, Letras e Letras. Honours: Theatre Play Award, Fialho de Almeida, 1982; Literary Award, Abel Salazar, 1986; Great Award to Romance, Cidade de Amadora, 1990. Memberships: Associacao Portuguesa de Escritories; Sociedade Portugeusa de Escritores Medocos; Sociedade de Ciencias Medicas de Lisboa; Sociedade Portuguesa de Anatomia. Address: Rua Almirante Matos Moreira 7, 2775 Carcavelos, Portugal.

MORETON John. See: **COHEN Morton Norton**.

MORGAN Claire,See:HIGHSMITH (Mary) Patricia.

MORGAN David Henry, b. 28 Sept 1928, Invercargill, New Zealand. Consultant; Trainer; Technical Writer. m. Patricia Margaret Taylor, 30 Dec 1961, 2 sons, 1 daughter. Education: MA, University of New Zealand, 1961. Publications: Thinking and Writing, 1966; Effective Business Letters, 1970; Working with Words, 1989; Resource Packages and Distance Education Packages on Writing and Communication. Contributions to: Articles to professional journals. Memberships: Australian Society for Technical Communication; Institution of Scientific & Technical Communicators; Association for Teachers of Technical Writing; Council for Programs in Technical and Scientific Communication. Address: PO Box 687, Civic Square ACT 2608, Australia.

MORGAN Edmund Sears, b. 17 Jan 1916, MN, USA. Historian. m. (1)Helen Mayer, 7 June 1939, (2)Marie Caskey, 22 June 1983, 2 daughters. Education: AB, 1937, PhD, 1942, Harvard University. Literary Appointments: Brown University, 1946-55; Yale University, 1955-. Publications: The Puritan Family, 1944; The Stamp Act Crisis, 1953; The Gentle Puritan, 1962; American Slavery American Freedom, 1975; Inventing the People; The Birth of the Republic, 1956; The Puritan Dilemma, 1958. Contributions to: Various. Memberships: American Philosophical Soceity; British Academy, American Academy of Arts & Science. Address: Dept of History, Yale University, New Haven, CT 06520, USA.

MORGAN Edwin (George), b. 1920, Scotland. Writer; Poet; Emeritus Professor. Appointments: Assistant Lecturer, Lecturer, Senior Lecturer, 1947-71, Reader, 1971-75, Titular Professor, English, 1975-80, University of Glasgow; Visiting Professor. University of Strathclyde, 1987-90; University College of Wales, Aberystwyth, 1990-. Publications: The Vision of Cathkin Braes, 1952; The Cape of Good Hope, 1955; Starryveldt, 1965; Scotch Mist, 1965; Sealwear, 1966; Emergent Poems, 1967; The Second Life, 1968; Gnomes, 1968; Proverbfolder, 1969; Penguin Modern Poets 15 (with others), 1969; The Horseman's Word: A Sequence of Concrete Poems, 1970; Twelve Songs, 1970; The Dolphin's Song, 1971; Instamatic Poems, 1972; Glasgow Sonnets, 1972; From Glasgow to Saturn, 1973; The Whittrick: A Poem in Eight Dialogues, 1973; Essays, 1974; East European Poets, 1976; Hugh MacDiarmid, 1976; The New Divan, 1977; Colour Poems, 1978; Star Gate: Science Fiction Poems, 1979; Poems of Thirty Years, 1982; Grafts/Takes, 1983; 4 Glasgow Subway Poems, 1983; Sonnets from Scotland, 1984; Selected Poems, 1985; From the Video Box, 1986; Newspoems, 1987; Themes on a Variation, 1988; Tales from Limerick Zoo, 1988; Collected Poems, 1990; Nothing Not Giving Messages, 1990; Crossing the Border: Essays on Scottish Literature, 1990; Hold Hands Among the Atoms, 1991; Evening Will Come They Will Sew the Blue Sail, 1991; Sweeping Out the Dark, 1994; Translations: Beowulf, 1952; Poems from Eugenio Montale, 1959; Sovpoems..., 1961; Sandor Weores and Ferenc Juhasz: Selected Poems (co-translator), 1970; Wi the Haill Voice: Poems by

Mayakovsky, 1972; Fifty Renascence Love-Poems, 1975; Rites of Passage: Selected Translations, 1976; Platen: Selected Poems, 1978; Rostand's Cyrano de Bergerac, 1992; Editor: Collins Albatross Book of Longer Poems: English and American Poetry from the 14th Century to the Present Day, 1963; Scottish Poetry One to Six (co-editor), 1966-72; New English Dramatists 14, 1970; Scottish Satirical Verse, 1980. Address: 19 Whittingehame Court, Glasgow G12 0BG, Scotland.

MORGAN Michaela, b. 7 Apr 1951, Manchester, England. Writer; Teacher. m. Colin Holden, 1 son. Education: BA, University of Warwick, 1973; PGCE, University of Leicester, 1975. Literary appointments: Writer in Residence, HM Prisons, Ashwell and Stocken, Leicester, 1992. Publications: The Monster is Coming; The Edward Stories; Dinostory; The Helpful Betty Stories;. Harraps Junior and Longmans Project. Contributions to: Poetry anthologies for children. Honours: Included, Children's Book of the Year; Children's Choice, International Reading Association and United Kingdom Reading Association award. Memberships: Society of Authors; NAWE. Literary Agent: Rosemary Sandberg, Bowerdean Street, London SW6, England. Address: 9 Main Street, Bisbrooke, Oakham, Rutland, Leics LE15 9EP, England.

MORGAN Mihangel. See: MORGAN-FINCH Mihangel Ioan.

MORGAN (Colin) Pete(r), b. 7 June 1939, Leigh, Lancashire, England. Poet. Education: Normanton School, Buxton, 1950-57. Appointments include: Creative Writing for Northern Arts, Loughborough University, 1975-77. Publications: A Big Hat or Waht, 1968; Loss of Two Anchors, 1970; Poems for Shortie, 1973; The Grey Mare Being the Better Steed, 1973; I See You on My Arm, 1975; Ring Song, 1977; The Poets Deaths, 1977; Alpha Beta, 1979; The Spring Collection, 1979; One Greek Alphabet, 1980; Reporting Back, 1983; A Winter Visitor, 1984; The Pete Morgan Poetry Pack, 1984; Plays, Still the Same Old Harry, 1972; All The Voices Going Away, 1979; Television Documentaries. Honours include: Arts Council of Great Britain Award, 1973. Address: c/o Fordon Fraser Publications, Eastcotts Road, bedford MK4Z 0JX, England.

MORGAN Robin. Editor-in-Chief; MS Magazine. Publications: (non-fiction) The Demon Lover; Anatomy of Freedom; Going Too Far; The New Woman (editor); Sisterhood is Powerful (editor); Sisterhood is Global (editor); (poetry) Monster; Lady of the Beasts; Death Benefits; Depth Perception; Upstairs in the Garden; Dry Your Smile (fiction). c/o MS Magazine, 230 Park Avenue, New York, NY 10169, USA.

MORGAN-FINCH Mihangel Ioan (Mihangel Morgan), b. 7 Dec 1959, Aberdare, Wales, England. University Lecturer. Education: BA, University of Wales, 1990; PhD Candidate, University of Wales. Publications: Beth Yw Rhif Ffôn Duw, 1991; Diflaniad Fy Fi, 1988; HenLwybr A Storiau Eraill, 1992; Saith Pechod Marwol, 1993; Dirgel Ddyn, 1993; Te Gyda'r Frenhines, 1994. Contributions to: Stories, Poems, Articles, Interviews in the following Welsh Journals: Barn; Barddas; Taliesin; Tu Chwith; Poetry Wales. Honours: Prose Medal, Eisteddfod, 1993; BBC Wales Arts Awards, Runner Up, 1993; Welsh Arts Council, Book of the Year Short List, 1993-94. Memberships: Gorsedd Beirdd; Ynys Prydain. Address: Porth Ceri, Talybont, Aberystwyth, Dyfed, Wales.

MORIARITY J. See: KELLY Tim.

MORIER Henri, b. 23 May 1910, Geneva, Switzerland. Emeritus Professor; Writer. Education: Licence ès lettres, with distinction, Modern Romance Languages, 1933, Doctorat ès lettres, 1944, dissertation, 1956, University of Geneva. Appointments: High School Teacher of Literature, 1945-47; Extraordinary Professor, History of the French Language, 1952, Ordinary Professor, 1956, Director, Centre of Poetics and Experimental Phonetics, 1962, Emeritus Professor, 1980, University of Geneva. Publications: La Technique de L'Examen, 1941; Poèmes nocturnes, 1944; Aubades, 1947; Le Rythme du Vers libre symboliste, 3 volumes, 1943-44, re-edition, 1975; La Psychologie des Styles, 1959, 1985; Dictionnaire de Poétique et de Rhétorique, 1961, 4th Edition, 1989. Address: Les Caryatides, 7 rue du Bief, 74100 Ambilly, France.

MORITZ Albert F(rank), b. 1947. Canadian. m. Theresa. Publications: Signs & Certainties, 1979; Music & Exile, 1980; Black Orchid, 1981; Leacock: A Biography, 1985; Oxford Illustrated Literary Guide to Canada, 1987; The Pocket Canada, 1987; Song of Fear, 1992. Honour: Fellow, American Academy & Institute of Arts & Letters, 1991.

MORLAND Dick. See: HILL Reginald (Charles).

MORLEY Don, b. 28 Jan 1937, Derbyshire, England. Photographer; Journalist. m. Josephine Mary Munro, 17 Sept 1961, 2 sons. Education: National Certificates, Electrical Engineering, Photography. Appointments: Former Picture Editor, The Guardian; Former Chief Photographer, Sports World Magazine, British Olympic Association; Chief Photographer, Moto Course. Founder Member/Director All Sport Photographic Ltd, 1975. Publications: Action Photography, 1975; Motorcycling, 1977; Everyone's Book of Photography, 1977; Everyone's Book of Motorcycling, 1981; The Story of the Motorcycle, 1983; Motorbikes, 1983; Classic British Trial Bikes, 1984; Classic British Moto Cross Machines, 1985; The Classic British Two Stroke Trials Bikes, 1987; The Spanish Trials Bikes, 1987; Trials: A Riders Guide, 1990; BSA (History in Colour), 1990; Triumph (History in Colour), 1990; Norton (History in Colour), 1990; BMW (History in Colour), 1993. Contributions to: Magazines and journals worldwide. Honours: Winner, 17 national and international photography awards. Memberships: Founder, Honorary Life Member, Chairman, 5 years, Professional Sports Photographers Association; Guild of Motoring Writers; Sports Writers Association of Great Britain. Address: 132 Carlton Road, Reigate, Surrey RH2 0JF, England.

MORLEY Patricia Marlow, b. 25 May 1929, Toronto, Canada. Writer; Educator. m. Lawrence W Morley, (div), 3 sons, 1 daughter. Education: BA Hon, English Language and Literature, University of Toronto, 1951; MA, English, Carleton University, 1967; PhD, English Literature, University of Ottawa, 1970. Appointments: Assistant Professor, 1972-75; Associate Professor, 1975-80; Professor of English and Canadian Studies, 1980-89; Fellow, 1979-89, Lifetime Honorary Fellow, 1989-, Simone de Beauvoir Institute, Concordia University. Publications include: The Mystery of Unity: Theme and Technique in the Novels of Patrick White, 1972; The Immoral Moralists: Hugh Maclennan and Leonard Cohen, 1972; Robertson Davies: Profiles in Canadian Drama, 1977; The Comedians: Hugh Hood and Rudy Wiebe, 1977; Morley Callaghan, 1978; Kuralek: A Biography, 1986, 1988. Margaret Laurence, The Long Journey Home, 1991; As Though Life Mattered,: Leo Kennedy's Story, 1994. Contributions to: Reviews, articles to professional and mainstream journals. Honours: Award for non-fiction, 1987; Ottawa-Carleton Literary Award, 1988; D S Litt (Doctor of Sacred Letters), Thorneloe College, Laurentian U, 1992. Memberships: The Writer's Union of Canada. Address: Box 137, Manotick, Ontario, Canada K4M 1A2.

MORLEY Sheridan Robert, b. 5 Dec 1941, Ascot, Berkshire, England. Journalist; Biographer; Broadcaster. m. Margaret Gudejko, 18 July 1965, div. 1990, 1 son, 2 daughters. Education: MA (Hons), Merton College, Oxford, 1964. Appointments: Arts Editor, Punch, 1974-88; Drama Critic, International Herald Tribune, 1975-; Drama Critic, Spectator, 1992-; Film Critic, Sunday Express, 1992-94. Publications: A Talent to Amuse, 1st biography of Noel Coward, 1969; The Other Side of the Moon, 1st biography of David Niven, 1979; Odd Man Out, 1st biography of James Mason, 1984; Gladys Cooper; Gertrude Lawrence; Oscar Wilde; Tales From The Hollywood Raj; Elizabeth Taylor; Marlene Dietrich; Katherine Hepburn; Review Copies; Our Theatres in the 80's; Spread A Little Happiness, 1986; Shooting Stars: Our Theatres in the Eighties, 1990; Methuen Book of Theatrical Short Stories, 1992; Robert My Father, 1993; Audrey Hepburn, 1993; Methuen Book of Movie Stories, 1994. Contributions to: The Times; Punch; Herald Tribune; Spectator; Sunday Times; Playbill, USA; Variety, USA; The Australian. Honours: BP Arts Journalist of the Year, 1990. Memberships: Critics Circle; Garrick Club. Literary Agent: Curtis Brown, 28 Haymarket London, SW1 45P. Address: 5 Admiral Square, Chelsea Harbour, London SW10 0UU, England.

MORNER (Carl) Magnus (Birgersson), b. 31 Mar 1924, Mellosa, Sweden. University Professor. m. Aare Ruth Puhk, 2 Dec 1947, 2 sons, 1 daughter. Education: University studies, 1946-54, PhD, 1954, Stockholm. Publications include: The Political and Economic Activities of the Jesuits in the Plata Region; Race Mixture in the History of Latin America; La Corona Española y los Foráneos en los Pueblos de Indios de America; Historia Social Latinoamericana; The Andean Past; Local Communities and Actors in Latin America's Past, 1994. Contributions to: Numerous magazines and journals. Honours: Loubat Prize; 2 Doctor honoris causa degrees; President, 48th International Congress of Americanists. Memberships: Regia Societatis Scientiarum et Litterarum Gothoburgensis; Association of European Latin Americanist Historians. Address: Äppelstigen 5, S-647 00 Mariefred, Sweden.

MORPURGO Jack Eric, b. 26 Apr 1918, London, England. Author; Literary Agent; University Professor. m. Catherine Noel Kippe Cammaerts, 16 July 1947 (dec 1993), 3 sons, 1 daughter. Education: Christ's Hospital, England; University of New Brunswick, Canada; BA, College of William and Mary, USA, 1938; Durham University, England, 1939; Institute of Historical Research, 1946. Appointments: Editor, Penguin Books, 1945-69; Editor, Penguin Parade, 1949-50; General Editor, Penguin History of England and Penguin History of the World, 1949-69; Assistant Director, Nuffield Foundation, 1951-54; Director General, National Book League, 1954-69; Professor of American and Canadian Studies, University of Geneva, Switzerland, 1968-70; Professor of American Literature, University of Leeds, England, 1969-83. Publications: American Excursion, 1949; Leigh Hunt: Autobiography (editor), 1949; Charles Lamb and Elia, 1949; History of the United States (co-author), 2 volumes, 1955, 1959, 1971, 1976; The Road to Athens, 1963; Barnes Wallis: A Biography, 1972; Their Majesties: Royall Colledge, 1976; Allen Lane: King Penguin, 1979; Christ's Hospital (with G A T Allan), 1986; Master of None: An Autobiography, 1990; Christ's Hospital: An Introductory History, 1990; Charles Lamb and Elia, 1993; Editions of Trelawny, Keats, Cobbett, Fenimore Cooper, Lewis Carroll, Marlowe and others. Contributions to: Times Literary Supplement; Daily Telegraph; Yorkshire Post; Quadrant, Australia; Mayfair, Canada. Honours: 4 honorary doctorates, USA institutions; Special Literary Award, Yorkshire Post, 1980. Memberships: Army and Navy Club; Pilgrims. Literary Agent: Sexton Agency and Press Limited. Address: Managing Director: P & M Youngman Carter Ltd., 12 Laurence Mews, Askew Road, London W12 9AT, England.

MORRELL David. Writer; former Professor of Literature. Publications: (fiction) First Blood, 1972; Testament, 1975; The Totem, 1979; Blood Oath, 1982; The 100-year Christmas, 1983; Brotherhood of the Rose, 1984; Rambo, 1985; Fraternity of the Stone, 1985; League of Night and Stone, 1985; Rambo III, 1988; The Covenant of the Frame, 1990; Assumed Identity, 1993; Desperate Measures, 1994. (Non-fiction) John Barth: An Introduction, 1976; Fireflies, 1988. Address: c/o Henry Morrison Inc, PO Box 235, Bedford Hills, NY 10507, USA.

MORRIS Colin, b. Liverpool, England. Writer; Producer; Director; Actor; Interviewer (BBC TV, ITV). Publications: Stage play productions: Desert Rats, 1945; Italian Love Story, 1945; Reluctant Heroes, 1950; Television plays: The Unloved, 1954; Who Me, 1959; Jacks and Knaves, 1960; Women in Crisis, 1963; The Newcomers, 1965; King of the River, 1967; Walk with Destiny, 1974; Television serials: Reluctant Bandit, 1966; The Dragon's Opponent, 1973; Television series: The Carnforth Practice, 1974; Heart to Heart; Turning Point; My Way; Women of Today; My Life; My Marriage; My Family, 1986; Numerous dramatised documentaries, 1954-74. Contributions to: Evening Standard; Sunday Mirror. Honours: Atlantic Award in Literature, 1946; 4 Best Script Awards, 1955, 1956, 1958, 1961. Address: 75 Hilway, London N6, England.

MORRIS Desmond John, b. 24 Jan 1928, Purton, Wiltshire, England. Zoologist. m. Ramona Baulch, 30 July 1952, 1 son. Education: BSc. Birmingham University, 1951; DPhil, Oxford University, 1954. Publications include: The Biology of Art, 1962; The Naked Ape, 1967; The Human Zoo, 1969; Manwatching, 1977; Catwatching, 1986; Dogwatching, 1986; The Animal Contract, 1990; Animal-Watching, 1990; Babywatching, 1991; Christmas Watching, 1992; The World of Animals, 1993; The Human Animal, 1994; The World Guide to Gestures, 1994. Contributions to: Many journals and magazines. Membership: Scientific Fellow, Zoological Society of London. Address: c/o Jonathan Cape, Random Century House, 20 Vauxhall Bridge Road, London, SW1V 2SA, England.

MORRIS Janet Ellen, b. 25 May 1946, Boston, Massachusetts, USA. Writer. m. 31 Oct 1970. Publications include: Silistra Quartet, 1976-78, 1983-84; Dream Dance Trilogy, 1980-83; Heroes in Hell, series (10 vols), 1984-88; Beyond Sanctuary, (3 vols), 1985-86; Warlord, 1986; I the Sun, 1984; The Little Helliad, 1986; Outpassage, 1987; City at the Edge of Time, 1988; Tempus Vabound, 1989, Target, with David Drake, 1989; Kill Ratio, 1987; Warrior's Edge, 1990; Threshold, 1991; Trust Territory, 1992; American Warrior, 1992; The Stalk, 1994. Contributions to: 50 short stories in publications including: The Yacht; Argos: New Destinies. Honours: Hellva Award for Best Novel, for 40 Minute Wars, 1985. Memberships: Science Fiction Writers of America; Mystery Writers of America; BMI (Broadcast Music Inc); New York Academy of Science; National Intelligence Study Center; Association of Old Crows. Literary Agent: Perry Knowlton, Curtis Brown Ltd. Address: c/o Curtis Brown Ltd, 10 Astor Place, New York, NY 10003, USA.

MORRIS Julian,See:**WEST Morris.**

MORRIS Katherine Emily, b. 9 Apr 1913, New South Wales, Australia. Teacher (retired). m. Vincent Darcy Morris, 17 Jan 1942, 1 son, 1 daughter. Education: Sydney Teachers College, 1931, 1932, 1933. Publications: Down by the River (with E Laird), 1967; The Frog, 1968; The Platypus, 1974; Mudeye - The Story of a Dragonfly, 1978; The Wonderful Caterpillar, 1978; Polly and Taddy - The Story of Two Frogs, 1978; Buzzy - The Honey Bee, 1978; Slim and Flash - The Garden Lizards, 1980; Pep, Joe and Ana - The Ants' Story, 1980; Tip the Long-necked Tortoise, 1983; Ringo the Ringtail Possum, 1983; The Fairy Penguins, 1983; How the Sun was Made, 1984; Why Rabbit's Nose Twitches, 1984; Collin's Children's Annual: Little Friend Tortoise, 1984. Address: 39 Hawkesbury Rd, Springwood, New South Wales 2777, Australia.

MORRIS Mary, b. 14 May 1947, Chicago, Illinois, USA. Writer. m. Larry O'Connor, 20 Aug 1989, 1 daughter. Education: BA, Tufts College, 1969; MA, Columbia University, 1973; MPhil, 1977. Appointments: Princeton University, 1980-87, 1991-94; New York University, 1988-94; Sarah Lawrence College, 1994. Publications: A Mother's Love, Nothing to Declare: Memoirs of a Woman Travelling Alone; The Waiting Room; Vanishing Animals & Other Stories; The Bus of Dreams; Wall to Wall; Crossroads. Contributions to: The Paris Review: The New York Times; Triquarterly; New Woman; Vogue; McCalls; Ontario Review; Agni Review. Honours: National Endowment for the Arts; Rome Prize; Guggenheim; Creative Public Service Award; Friends of American Writers Award; Princeton University Fellowship. Memberships: American PEN; Authors Guild; Friends of the American Academy, Rome. Literary Agent: Amanda Urban, ICM. Address: c/o Amanda, ICM 40 W, 57th Street, New York, NY 10019, USA.

MORRIS Mervyn, b. 1937, Kingston, Jamaica. Lecturer; Poet. Education: University of West Indies, Kingston; St Edmund Hall, Oxford. Appointments include: Senior Lecturer, University of West Indies, 1970; Reader, West Indian Literature. Publications: The Pond, 1973; On Holy Week, 1976; Shadowboxing, 1979; Editions of West Indian Poetry, including Seven Jamaican Poets, 1971; Jamaica Women: An Anthology of Poems, 1980; Focus, 1983; An Anthology of Contemporary Jamaican Writing; The Faber Book of Contemporary Caribbean Short Stories, 1990. Honours include: Institute of Jamaica Musgrave Medal, 1976. Address: Dept of English, University of West Indies, Mona, Kingston 7, Jamaica.

MORRIS Sara. See: **BURKE John Frederick.**

MORRIS Vera. See: **KELLY Tim.**

MORRISON Anthony (Tony) James, b. 5 July 1936, England. Television Producer; Writer. Appointments: Partner, South American Pictures; Director, Nonesuch Expeditions Ltd. Publications: Steps to a Fortune (co-author), 1967; Animal Migration, 1973; Land Above the Clouds, 1974; The Andes, 1976; Pathways to the Gods, 1978; Lizzie: A Victorian Lady's Amazon Adventure (co-editor), 1985; The Mystery of the Nasca Lines, 1987; Margaret Mee, In Search of Flowers of the Amazon (editor), 1988; QOSQO, Navel of The World, 1995. Membership: Chairman, Finance Committee, Margaret Mee Amazon Trust. Address: 48 Station Road, Woodbridge, Suffolk IP12 4AT, England.

MORRISON Bill, b. 22 Jan 1940, Ballymoney, Northern Ireland. Playwright; Theatre Director. div., 1 son, 1 daughter. Education: LLB (Honours), Queen's University, Belfast, 1962. Appointments: Resident Playwright, Victoria Theatre, Stoke-on-Trent, England, 1968-71; Resident Playwright, Everyman Theatre, Liverpool, 1976-79; Associate Director, 1981-83, Artistic Director, 1983-85, Liverpool Playhouse. Publications: Stage plays: Flying Blind, 1979; Scrap, 1982; Be Bop A Lula, 1988; A Love Song for Ulster, 1993, 1994; Radio and stage plays: Sam Slade Is Missing, 1971; The Love of Lady Margaret, 1972; Ellen Cassidy, 1978; The Emperor of Ice Cream, 1977; Blues in a Flat, 1989; The Little Sister, 1990; Radio plays: The Great Gun-Running Episode, 1973; Simpson and Son, 1977; Maguire, 1978; The Spring of Memory, 1981; Affair, 1991; Three Steps to Heaven, 1992; Waiting for Lefty, 1994; TV plays: Shergar, 1986; A Safe House, 1990; Force of Duty, 1992. Honours: Best Programme, Pye Radio Awards, for The Spring of Memory, 1981. Membership: Director, Lagan Pictures Ltd. Literary Agent: Alan Brodie, London, England. Address: c/o Alan Brodie, International Creative Management Ltd, 76 Oxford Street, London W1N 0AN, England.

MORRISON (Philip) Blake, b. 8 Oct 1950, Burnley, Lancashire. Literary Editor; Poet. m. Katherine Ann Drake, 1976, 2 s, 1 d. Education: BA, University of Nottingham, 1972; PhD, University College London, 1978. Appointments include: Literary Editor, The Observer, 1987-89; Literary Editor, Independent on Sunday, 1990-. Publications include: Dark Glasses, 1984-89; The Ballad of the Yorkshire Ripper and Other Poems, 1987; The Movement: English Poetry and Fiction of the 1950's, 1980; Seamus Heaney, 1982; The Yellow House, 1987; Co Editor, The Penguin Book of Contemporary British Poetry, 1982; And when did you last see your father? 1994. Honours include: Somerset Maugham Award, 1984; Dylan Thomas Prize, 1985; Fellow, Royal Society of Literature, 1988; J R Ackerley Prize, 1994. Address: c/o the Independent on Sunday, 40 City Road, London EC1Y 2DB, England.

MORRISON Dorothy Jean Allison, b. 17 Feb 1933, Glasgow, Scotland. Author; Lecturer. m. James F T Morrison, 12 Apr 1955, 1 son, 1 daughter. Education: MA (Honours), Glasgow University. Appointments: Principal Teacher of History, Montrose Academy, 1968-73; Lecturer in History, Dundee College of Education, 1973-83; Advisor to Scottish History series, History at Hand series, Scotland's War series, Scottish TV. Publications: Old Age, 1972; Young People, 1973; Health and Hospitals, 1973; The Civilian War (with M Cuthbert), 1975; Travelling in China, 1977; The Romans in Britain, 1978, 2nd Edition, 1980; Billy Leaves Home, 1979; Story of Scotland (with J Halliday), I, 1979, 1980, II, 1982; The Great War, 1914-18, 1981; Historical Sources for Schools, I Agriculture, 1982; History Around You, 1983; People of Scotland, I, 1983, II, 1985; Ancient Greeks (with John Morrison), 1984; Handbook on Money Management, 1985; Modern China, 1987; The Rise of Modern China, 1988; Montrose Old Church - A history, 1991; Scotland's War, 1992; A Sense of History - Castles, 1994. Address: Craigview House, Usan, Montrose, Tayside DD10 9SD, Scotland.

MORRISON Joan, b. 20 Dec 1922, Hinsdale, Illinois, USA. Writer. m. Robert Thornton Morrison, 19 Jun 1943, 2 sons, 1 daughter. Education: BA, University of Chicago, 1944. Publications: American Mosaic: From Camelot to Kent State. Contributions include: New York Times; McCalls; Mademoiselle. Honours: Ambassador Award; New York Times Notable Book of the Year. Memberships: Authors Guild; National Society of Arts & Letters; Oral History Association; American Studies Association. Literary Agent: John Ware, 392 Central Park West, New York, NY 10025.

MORRISON Sally, b. 29 June 1946, Sydney, New South Wales, Australia. Writer. 1 son. Education: BSc (Hons), Australian National University, 1970. Publications: Who's Taking You to the Dance, novel, 1979; I Am a Boat, short stories, 1989; Mad Meg, novel, 1994. Contributions to: The Bulletin; Australian Literary Supplement; Overland; Quadrant; Island; Sydney Morning Herald; Age Monthly Review. Honours: Project Assistance Grants, Victorian Ministry of the Arts, 1988, 1993, 1994; Writer's Grants, Australia Council Literary Board, 1990, 1991, 1992. Memberships: Fellowship of Australian Writers; Australian Society of Authors; Victorian Writers Centre. Literary Agent: Margaret Connolly. Address: c/o Margaret Connolly and Associates, PO Box 48, Paddington, NSW 2021, Australia.

MORRISON Toni, b. 18 Feb 1931, Lorraine, Ohio, USA. Publications: The Bluest Eye; Sula, 1974; Song of Solomon, 1977; Tar Baby, 1981; Beloved, 1987; Jazz, 1992; Playing in the Dark: Witness and the Literary Imagination; Honours: National Book Critics Circle Award, 1978; Pulitzer Prize, 1988; Nobel Prize for Literature, 1993. Address: c/o Janklow & Nesbit, 598 Madison Avenue, New York, NY 10022, USA.

MORRISON Wilbur Howard, b. 21 Jun 1915, Plattsburgh, New York, USA. Freelance Writer. Education: Plattsburgh State Normal School, 1922-30; Plattsburgh High School, 1930-34. Publications: Hellbirds, the Story of the B-29s in Combat, 1960; The Incredible 305th; The Can Do Bombers of WWII, 1962; Wings Over the Seven Seas: US Naval Aviation's Fight For Suirvival, 1974; Point of No Return: The Story of The Twentieth Air Force, 1979; Fortress Without a Roof: The Allied Bombing of the Third Reich, 1982; Above and Beyond, 1941-45, 1983; Baja Adventure Guide, 1990; The Elephant and the Tiger: The

Full Story of the Vietnam War, 1990; Donald W Douglas: A Heart With Wings, 1991; Twentieth Century American Wars, 1993; The Adventure Guide to the Adirondacks and Catskills, 1995; Papers, Manuscripts, Memorabilia, housed in American Heritage Center, University of Wyoming, PO Box 3924, Laramie, Wyoming 82071-3924, available for qualified researchers. Membership: Dramatists Guild. Address: 2036 E Alvarado Street, Fallbrook, CA 92028, USA.

MORRISS Frank, b. 28 Mar 1923, Pasadena, California, USA. Writer; Teacher. m. Mary Rita Moynihan, 11 Feb 1950, 1 son, 3 daughters. Education: BS, Regis College, Denver, Colorado, 1943; LLD, Georgetown University School of Law, Washington DC, 1948; Doctor of Letters, Register College of Journalism, Denver Colorado, 1953. Appointments: News Editor, Denver Catholic Register, 1960; Associate Editor, Vermont Catholic Tribune, 1961; News Editor, National Register, 1963; Founding Editor, Twin Circle, 1967; Contributing Editor, Wanderer, St Paul, Minnesota, 1968-. Publications: The Divine Epic, 1973; The Catholic as Citizen, 1976; Abortion (co-author), 1979; Saints for the Small, (children's book) 1965; Alfred of Wessex, (children's book), 1959; Submarine Pioneer, (children's book), 1961; The Conservative Imperative, 1970; The Adventures of Broken Hand (children's book), 1957; Boy of Philadelphia (children's book), 1955; The Forgotten Revelation: A Christmas Celebration, (editor and contributor), 1985; A Neglected Glory, 1976; A Little Life of Our Lord, 1993. Contributions to: The Wanderer, columns, fiction, poetry; The World of Poetry, anthology of prizewinners. Honours: George Washington Award for newspaper writing on two occasions; Honorable Mention, World of Poetry. Membership: The Fellowship of Catholic Scholars (USA). Address: 3505 Owens Street, Wheat Ridge, CO 80033, USA.

MORROW Ann Patricia (Kenny), b. Dublin, Republic of Ireland. Journalist. m. (2) G W K Fenn Smith, 19 May 1984, 2 stepsons, 1 stepdaughter. Education: University College, Dublin. Appointments: Fleet Street: Daily Express, IPC Magazines, Daily Telegraph. Publications: The Queen; The Queen Mother; Highness; Picnic in a Foreign Land; Princess. Contributions to: The Times; The Daily Telegraph. Membership: PEN. Literary Agent: Michael Shaw, Curtis Brown. Address: c/o Curtis Brown, 4th Floor - Haymarket House, 28-29 Haymarket, London, SW1 4SP, England.

MORT Graham Robert, b. 11 Aug 1955, Middleton, England. Poet. m. Maggie Mort, 12 Feb 1979, 3 sons. Education: BA, Liverpool University, 1977; St Martin's College, Lancaster, 1980. Appointments: Creative Writing Course Leader, Open College of the Arts, 1989-. Publications: A Country on Fire; Into The Ashes; A Halifax Cider Jar; Sky Burial; Snow from the North; Starting To Write; The Experience of Poetry, Storylines. Contributions to: Numerous literary magazines and journals. Honours: 1st Prize, Cheltenham Poetry Competition, 1979, 1982; Duncan Lawrie Prize, Arvon Poetry Competition, 1982, 1992, 1994; Major Eric Gregory Award, 1985; Authors Foundation Award, 1994. Memberships: Society of Authors; National Association of Writers in Education. Address: The Beeches, Riverside, Clapham, Lancaster LA2 8DT, England.

MORTIMER John Clifford (Geoffrey Lincoln), b. 21 Apr 1923, London, England. Barrister; Playwright; Novelist. m. (1) Penelope Ruth Fletcher, 1 son, 1 daughter, (2) Penelope Gallop, 2 daughters. Education: Brasenose College, Oxford. Appointments: Called to the Bar, 1948; QC, 1966; Master of the Bench, Inner Temple, 1975; Publications include: Charade, 1947; Rumming Park, 1948; Answer Yes or No, 1950; Like Men Betrayed, 1953; Three Winters, 1956; Will Shakespeare, 1977; Rumpole of the Bailey, 1978; The Trials of Rumpole, 1979; Rumpole's Return, 1981; Clinging to the Wreckage, autobiography, 1982; In character, 1983; Rumpole and the Golden Thread, 1983; Rumpole's Last Case, 1986; Paradise Postponed, 1986; Character Parts, interviews, 1986; Summers Lease, 1988; Rumpole and the Age of Miracles, 1988; Titmuss Regained, 1989; Rumpole à la Carte, 1990; Rumpole on Trial, 1992; Dunster, novel, play, 1992; Plays: The Dock Brief and Other Plays, 1959; The Wrong Side of the Park, 1960; Two Stars for Comfort, 1962; The Judge, 1967; Come As You Are, 1970; The Bells of Hell; Villians, 1992; Film scripts: John and Mary, 1970; Edwin, 1984; TV series: Rumpole of the Bailey, 6 series; Brideshead Revisited, 1981; Unity Mitford, 1981; The Ebony Tower, 1984; Paradise Postponed, 1986; Summer Lease, 1989. Contributions to: Various periodicals. Honours include: Italia Prize, Short Play, 1958; British Academy Writers Award, 1979; Writer of the Year, BAFTA, 1980; Book of the Year, Yorkshire Post, 1982; Susquehanna University, 1985; CBE, 1986; Hon LLD: Exeter, 1986, St Andrew, 1987;

Hon DLitt, Nottingham. Memberships: Chairman, Royal Society of Literature, 1989-; Chairman, Royal Court Theatre, 1990-; President, Howard League for Penal Reform, 1991-. Address: c/o The Peter Fraser and Dunlop Group Ltd, 5th Floor, The Chambers, Chelsea Harbour, Lofs Road, London SW10, England.

MORTIMER Penelope (Ruth) (Penelope Dimont, Ann Temple), b. 19 Sept 1918, Rhyl, Flint, Wales. Author. Education: University College, London. Appointments: Film Critic, The Observer, London, 1967-70. Publications: Johanna (as Penelope Dimont), 1947; A Villa in Summer, 1954; The Bright Prison, 1956; With Love and Lizards (with John Mortimer), travel, 1957; Daddy's Gone A-Hunting, US Edition as Cave of Ice, 1958; Saturday Lunch with the Brownings, 1960; The Pumpkin Eater, 1962; My Friend Says It's Bullet-Proof, 1967; The Home, 1971; Long Distance, 1974; About Time: An Aspect of Autobiography, 1979; The Handyman, 1983; Queen Elizabeth: A Life of the Queen Mother, 1986; Portrait of a Marriage, screenplay, 1990; About Time Too, autobiography, 1993. Honours: Whitbread Prize, 1979; Literary Agent: Anthony Sheil, 43 Doughty Street, London WC1N 2LF, England. Address: 19 St Gabriel's Road, London NW2 4DS, England.

MORTIMER-DUNN Gloria Dawn Cecilia, b. 22 July 1928, Sydney, New South Wales, Australia. Designer; Teacher. m. Bernard Mortimer-Dunn, 24 Dec 1954. Education: Honours Diploma in Art (Design and Craft), Art Department, East Sydney Technical College (now Sydney Institute of Technology, East Sydney Campus, Design and Crafts). Publications: Pattern Design, 1960; Fashion Making, 1964; Fashion Design, 1972, UK Edition as ABC of Fashion; Pattern Design for Children, 1995. Address: 15 Roberts Street, Rose Bay, New South Wales 2029, Australia.

MORTON Frederic, b. 5 Oct 1924, Vienna, Austria. Author. m. Marcia Colman, 28 Mar 1957, 1 daughter. Education: BS, College of City of NY, 1947; MA, New School for Social Research, NY. Publications include: The Rothschilds, 1962; A Nervous Splendor, 1978; Thunder at Twilight, 1991; The Forever Street, 1987. Contributions to: NY Times; Esquire; Playboy; Atlantic Monthly; Harpers Magazine; NY Magazine; Hudson Review; Nation Magazine. Honours: National Book Award, Twice Nominated. Memberships: PE Club; Authors Guild. Literary Agent: Lantz Harris Lit Agency, 888 Seventh Avenue, NY, USA.

MORTON G L. See: **FRYER Jonathan.**

MORTON Harry Edwin Clive, (Pindar Pete), b. 24 Mar 1931, Gordonvale, Queensland, Australia. Sugar Cane Grower. m. Desma Baird, 18 Jan 1958, 1 son, 2 daughters. Education: Cairns High School; Townsville Grammar School. Publications: The Cane Cutters (with G Burrows), 1986; Smoko the Farm Dog, 1989; By Strong Arms, 1995. Contributions to: Australian, UK and Canadian magazines; Australian, Italian and US anthologies; Short stories and features, Australian Cane Grower, 1960-. Honours: Fellowship of Australian Writers Regional History, 1986; Vaccari Historical Trust, 1987. Address: PO Box 166, Gordonvale, North Queensland 4865, Australia.

MORTON Henry (Harry) Albert, b. 20 July 1925, Gladstone, Manitoba, Canada. Writer. Associate Professor of History (retired). Education: BA, BEd, University of Manitoba; MA, University of Cambridge, England; PhD, University of Otago, New Zealand. Publications: And Now New Zealand, 1969; The Wind Commands, 1975; Which Way New Zealand, 1975; Why Not Together?, 1978; The Whale's Wake, 1982; The Farthest Corner, 1988. Honours: Sir James Wattie Award, Book of the Year, for The Wind Commands, 1976. Memberships: Blenheim Club; PEN New Zealand. Address: 55B Brooklyn Drive, Blenheim, Marlborough, New Zealand.

MOSBY Aline, b. 27 July 1922, Missoula, Montana, USA. Journalist. Education: BA, University of Montana School of Journalism, 1943; Postgraduate studies, Columbia University, New York City, 1965. Appointments: Journalist, Time magazine, 1943; Journalist, Foreign Correspondent, United Press International, 1943-85; Freelance Writer, Paris, France, 1985-; Lecturer, Keedick Agency; Guest Instructor, University of Montana. Publications: The View from Number 13 People's Street. Address: 1 Rue Maître Albert, Paris 75005, France.

MOSES Elbert Raymond Jr, b. 31 Mar 1908, New Concord, Ohio, USA. Professor Emeritus. m. (1) Mary M Sterrett, 21 Sept 1933, (dec 1984), 1 son, (2) Caroline M Chambers, 19 June 1985. Education:

AB, University of Pittsburgh; MSc, PhD, University of Michigan. Publications: A Guide to Effective Speaking, 1956, 1957; Phonetics: History & Interpretation, 1964; Three Attributes of God, 1983; Adventure in Reasoning, 1988; Beating the Odds, 1992; The Range, Great Poems of Our Time, 1993; Where Is Virtue, 1993; Reflections Within, 1993. Contributions to: American Speech & Hearing Magazine; Journal of American Speech; Speech Monographs; Veterans Voices. Honours include: Paul Harris Fellow, Rotary, 1971; Certificate, Humanitarian Services, Nicaraguan Government, 1974; Phi Delta Kappa Service Key, 1978; Certificate, Services to Education, 1981; Life Patron, American Biographical Institute, 1985; Grand Ambassador of Achievement, HE, American Biographical Institute, 1985; Life Fellow, World Literary Academy, 1987. Memberships: Lifetime, International Society of Poets, 1993. Address: 2001 Rocky Dells Drive, Prescott, AZ 86303-5685, USA.

MOSKOWITZ Bette Ann. Publications: Leaving Barney, 1988. Contributions include: Appearances. Address: The Jonathon Dolger Agency, 49 East 96th Street, New York, NY 10128, USA.

MOSKOWITZ Faye Stollman, b. 31 Jul 1930, Detroit, Michigan, USA. English Professor; Writer. m. Jack Moskowitz, 29 Aug 1948, 2 sons, 2 daughters. Education: BA, George Washington University, 1970; MA, 1979; PhD (abd), 1974. Publications: A Leak in the Heart; Whoever Finds This; I Love You; And the Bridge is Love; Her Face in the Mirror. Jewish Women Write about Mothers and Daughters, (editor), 1994. Contributions to: the New York Times; Washington Post; Chronicle of Higher Education; Womans Day; Feminist Studies; Calyx; Christian Science Monitor; Wigwag Magazine. Honours: Michael Karolyi Foundation: Breadloaf Scholar; EdPress Merit Award; Pen Syndicated Fiction Award; Literary Friends of DC Library. Memberships: Jenny McKean Moore Fund for Writers. Literary Agent: Russell & Volkenning. Address: 3306 Highland Place, NW Washington, DC 20008, USA.

MOSLEY Jonathan Philip, b. 8 June 1947, Grimsby, England. University Professor. m. Shu Ching Huang, 11 Aug 1988. Education: Leeds University, BA, 1968; University of East Anglia, MA, 1970; PhD, 1976. Publications: Ingmar Bergman: The Cinema as Mistress; Bruges-La-Morte; Tea Masters, Tea Houses. Contributions to: Numerous articles & Reviews. Memberships: British, American & International Comparative Literature Associations; International Council of Francophone Studies; Society for Cinema Studies. Address: Pennsylvania State University, Worthington Scranton Campus, 120 Ridge View Drive, Dunmore, PA 18512, USA.

MOSLEY Nicholas (Lord Ravensdale), b. 25 June 1923, London, England. Author. Education: Balliol College, Oxford, 1946-47. Publications: Spaces of the Dark, 1951; The Rainbearers, 1955; Corruption, 1957; African Switchback, 1958; The Life of Raymond Raynes, 1961; Meeting Place, 1962; Accident, 1965; Experience and Religion: A Lay Essay in Theology, 1965; Assassins, 1966; Impossible Object, 1968, screenplay, 1975; Natalie, Natalia, 1971; The Assassination of Trotsky, 1972, screenplay, 1973; Julian Grenfell: His Life and the Times of His Death 1888-1915, 1976; Catastrophe Practice, 1979; Imago Bird, 1980; Serpent, 1981; Rules of the Game: Sir Oswald and Lady Cynthia Mosley 1896-33, 1982; Beyond the Pale: Sir Oswald Mosley and Family 1933-1980, 1983; Judith, 1986; Hopeful Monsters, 1990; Efforts at Truth, 1994. Honours: Whitbread Prize. Address: 2 Gloucester Crescent, London NW1 7DS, England.

MOSLEY Walter, b. 1952, Los Angeles, California, USA. m. Joy Kellman. Education: Goddard College, BA, Johnson State University; City College, New York. Appointments: PEN (Executive Board); National Book Awards (Board Of Directors). Publications: Devil in a Blue Dress, 1990; A Red Death, 1991; White Butterfly, 1992; Black Betty, 1994; R L's Dream, 1995; (in progress) The Little Yellow Dog; The Bad Boy Bobby Brown. Honours: Edgar Award, Nominee; Golden Dagger Award, nominee, (twice). Address: c/o Paramount Publishing Pocket Books, Attn Mngng Edtrl, 1230 Avenue of the Americas, New York, NY 10020, USA.

MOSS Norman Bernard, b. 30 Sept 1928, London, England. Journalist. m. Hilary Sesta, 21 July 1963, 2 sons. Education: Hamilton College, New York City, 1946-47. Appointments: Staff Journalist with newspapers, news agencies and radio networks. Publications: Men Who Play God - The Story of the Hydrogen Bomb, 1968; A British-American Dictionary, 1972, Revised Editions, 1978, 1982, 1990, 1994; The Pleasures of Deception, 1976; The Politics of Uranium,

1982; Klaus Fuchs: The Man Who Stole the Atom Bomb, 1987; The Politics of Global Warming, 1992. Honours: Magazine Writer of the Year, Periodical Publishers Association, 1982. Memberships: International Institute of Strategic Studies; Society of Authors. Literary Agent: Michael Shaw, Curtis Brown Group. Address: 21 Rylett Crescent, London W12 9RP, England.

MOTION Andrew Peter, b. 26 Oct 1952, London, England. Writer. m. Jan Dalley, 9 June 1985, 2 sons, 1 daughter. Education: BA (1st Class Honours), MLitt, University College, Oxford, 1970-76. Literary appointments: Editor, Poetry Review, 1980-82; Editorial Director, Chatto and Windus, 1982-89. Publications: Dangerous Play, Selected Poems, 1979-84; The Lamberts, biography, 1986; Natural Causes, poems, 1987; The Pale Companion, novel, 1989; Love in a Life, poems, 1991; Famous for the Creatures, novel, 1991; Philip Larkin: A Writer's Life, biography, 1993; The Price of Everything, poems, 1994. Contributions to: Regularly to: Times Literary Supplement; The Observer; LRB. Honours: ARVON/Observer Prize; John Llewelyn Rhys Prize; Dylan Thomas Prize; Somerset Maugham Award; Whitbread Prize for Biography. Membership: Fellow, Royal Society of Literature. Literary Agent: Pat Kavanagh, The Peters, Frazer and Dunlop Group Ltd. Address: c/o Faber and Faber, 3 Queen Square, London WC1 3AU, England.

MOTT Michael, (Charles Alston), b. 8 Dec 1930, London, England. Writer. m. (1) Margaret Ann Watt, 6 May 1961 (dec 1990), 2 daughters, (2) Emma Lou Powers, 16 Nov 1992. Education: Diploma Central School of Arts & Crafts, London; Intermediate Law Degree, Law Society, London; BA, History of Art, Courtauld & Warburg Institutes, London; Honorary Doctor of Letters, St Mary's College, Notre Dame, 1983. Literary Appointments: Editor, Air Freight, 1954-59; Assistant Editor, Adam International Review, 1956-66; Editor, Books on Fine Arts, Thames and Hudson, 1961-64; Assistant Editor, The Geographical Magazine, 1964-66; Poetry Editor, The Kenyon Review, 1966-70; 25 years teaching experience including positions as Visiting Professor and Writer-in-Resident at Kenyon College, 1966-70; SUNY, Buffalo, 1968; Concordia University, Montreal, Canada, 1970 and 1974; Emory University, 1970-77; The College of William and Mary, 1978-79, 1985-86; Professor of English, Bowling Green State University, 1980-92; Retired Professor Emeritus, 1992. Publications include: novels: The Notebooks of Susan Berry, 1962; Master Entrick, 1964; Helmet and Wasps, 1964; The Blind Cross, 1968; poetry: Absence of Unicorns, Presence of Lions, 1977; Counting the Grasses, 1980; Corday, 1986; Piero de Cosimo: The World of Infinite Possibility, 1990; Taino, 1992; biography: The Seven Mountains of Thomas Merton, 1984. Contributions to: Encounter; Poetry Chicago; The Sunday Times (London); The Kenyon Review; Southern Review; Iowa Review; Pearl (Denmark). Honours: Governor's Award in Fine Arts, State of Georgia, 1974; Guggenheim Fellowship, 1979-80; Runner-up, Pulitzer Prize in Biography, 1984; The Christopher Award, 1984; Ohioana Book Award, 1985; Olscamp Research Award, 1985; Nancy Dasher Book Award, 1985; Phi Beta Kappa, Alpha Chapter, 1994. Memberships: Arts Club: Fellow Royal Geographical Society, 1953-; Academy of American Poets; Amnesty International; British Lichen Society; Geographical Club. Literary Agent: The Peter Frazer and Dunlop Group Ltd, London. Address: 122 The Colony, Williamsburg, VA 23185, USA.

MOTTRAM Eric, b. 1920, England. Professor; Poet. Education: Cambridge University. Appointments include: Professor, Kings College, University of London, 1983; Other University Appointments in USA, India, Europe. Publications include: Inside the Whale, 1970; The He Expression, 1973; Local Movement, 1973; Two Elegies, 1974; Against Tyranny, 1975; 1922 Earth Raids and Other Poems, 1973-75, 1976; Homage to Braque, 1976; Spring Ford, 1977; Tunis, 1977; Elegy 15: Neruda, 1978; Precipe of Fishes, 1979; 1980 Mediate; Elegies, 1981; A Book of Herne, 1975-81; Interrogation Rooms: Poems, 1980-81; Address, 1983; Three Letters, 1984; The Legal Poems, 1984; Selected Poems, 1989; Peace Projects and Brief Novels, 1989; Studies and Editions of American Literature. Address: Dept of English, Kings College, University of London, The Strand, London WC2R 2LS, England.

MOULD Daphne Desire Charlotte Pochin, b. 15 Nov 1920, Salisbury, England. Author. Education: BSc 1st Class Honours, Geology, 1943, PhD, Geology, 1946, University of Edinburgh. Publications include: The Celtic Saints, 1956; The Irish Saints, critical biographies, 1963; The Aran Islands, 1972; Ireland from the Air, 1972; Irish Monasteries, 1976; Captain Roberts of the Sirius, 1988; Discovering Cork, 1991. Contributions to: Numerous and various;

Broadcaster on Radio Telefis Eireann. Honours: LLD, National University of Ireland, 1993. Membership: Aircraft Owners and Pilots Association. Address: Aherla House, Aherla, Co Cork, Republic of Ireland.

MOUNT William Robert Ferdinand, b. 2 July 1939, London, England. Novelist; Journalist; Editor. m. Julia Lucas, 20 July 1968, 2 sons, 1 daughter. Education: BA, Christ Church, Oxford, 1961. Literary appointments: Political Correspondent, 1977-82, Literary Editor, 1984-85, Spectator; Head of Prime Minister's Policy Unit, 1982-84; Columnist, Daily Telegraph, 1985-90; Editor, Times Literary Supplement, 1991-. Publications: Very Like a Whale, 1967; The Theatre of Politics, 1972; The Man Who Rode Ampersand, 1975; The Clique, 1978; The Subversive Family, 1982; The Selkirk Strip, 1987; Of Love and Asthma, 1991; The British Constitution Now, 1992; Umbrella, 1994. Contributions to: Spectator; Encounter; National Interest; Politique Internationale. Honours: Hawthornden Prize for Of Love and Asthma, 1992. Address: 17 Ripplevale Grove, London N1, England.

MOUNTFIELD David. See: **GRANT Neil David Mountfield**.

MOUNTJOY Roberta Jean. See: **SOHL Gerald A.**

MOUNTZOURES Harry Louis, b. 9 Jul 1934, Fishers Island, NY, USA. Writer. m. Mary Ann Cawley, 8 Oct 1964, 1 son. Education: BA, Wesleyan University, 1956. Publications: The Empire of Things; The Bridge. Contributions to: The New Yorker; the Atlantic; Redbook; McCalls. Honours: Atlantic First Prize. Memberships: PEN International. Address: 29 Old Black Point Road, Niantic, CT 06357, USA.

MOURE Erin, b. Calgary, Alberta, Canada. Poet. Education: University of Calgary, UBC. Publications include: Wanted Alive, 1985; Domestic Fuel, 1985; Furious, 1988; WSW (West South West), 1989; Sheepish Beauty, Civilian Love, 1992; The Green Word, 1992. Honours: Pat Lowther Award for Domestic Fuel; Governor General's Award for Poetry, for Furious, 1988. Address: c/o The Writtien Union of Canada, 24 Ryerson Avenue, Toronto, Ontario, M5T 2P3, Canada.

MOWAT David, b. 16 Mar 1943, Cairo, Egypt. British Citizen. Playwright. Education: BA, New College, Oxford, 1964. Appointments include: Director of Playwriting Workshop, Actors Centre London, 1984-. Publications: Jens, 1965; Pearl, 1966; Anna Luse, 1968; Dracula, 1969; Purity, 1969; The Normal Woman, and Tyypi, 1970; Adrift, 1970; The Others, 1970; Most Recent Least Recent, 1970; Inuit, 1970; Liquid, 1971; The Diabolist, 1971; John, 1971; Amalfi, After Webster, 1972; Phoenic and Turtle, 1972; Morituri, 1972; My Relationship with Jayne, 1973; Come, 1973; Main Sequence, 1974; The Collected Works, 1974; The Memory Man, 1974; The Love Maker, 1974; X to C, 1975; Kim, 1977; Winter, 1978; The Guise, 1979; Hiroshima Nights, 1981; The Midnight Sun, 1983; Carmen, 1984; The Almas, 1989; Radio Plays. Honours include: Arts Council Bursaries. Address: 7 Mount Street, Oxford OX2 6DH, England.

MOXHAM Gwenyth Constance, b. 3 Sept 1943, Adelaide, South Australia, Australia. Teacher. m. Kenneth Ewing Moxham. 14 May 1966, 1 son, 1 daughter. Education: Associate in Arts and Education, 1965, BA, 1966, University of Adelaide; Diploma of Teaching, Adelaide Teachers College, 1966; TO; MACE. Publication: They Built South Australia' Engineers, Technicians, Manufacturers, Contractors and their Work (with D A Cumming), 1986. Contributions to: Australian Dictionary of Biography, 1995. Honours: Publication assisted by Jubilee 150 Board of South Australia, 1986. Memberships: Australian Reading Association, Secretary, Adelaide Branch 1986-88; Australian College of Education. Address: 6 Barr Smith Drive, Urrbrae, South Australia 5064, Australia.

MOYES Gertrude Patricia, b. 19 Jan 1923, Bray, Ireland. Author. m. (1) John Moyes, 29 Mar 1952, (2) John Haszard, 13 Oct 1962. Publications: Time Remembered, translation, 1958; Henry Tibbett mysteries, 1959-89: Dead Men Don't Ski; The Sunken Sailor; Death On the Agenda; Murder A La Mode; Johnny Underground; Murder Fantastical; Death and the Dutch Uncle; Many Deadly Returns; Season of Snows and Sins; The Curious Affair of the Third Dog; Black Widower; The Coconut Killings; Who Is Simon Warwick?; Angel Death; A 6-Letter Word for Death; Night Ferry to Death; Black Girl, White Girl, 1989; Twice in a Blue Moon, 1993; How To Talk To Your Cat; Helter Skelter. Contributions to: Ellery Queen Mystery Magazine. Honours; Edgar Special Scroll, Mystery Writers of America, for Many Deadly

Returns, circa 1963. Memberships: Crime Writers Association; Mystery Writers of America; Detection Club; Authors Guild. Literary Agents: Curtis Brown Ltd, London, England; The Karpfinger Agency, New York, USA. Address: Po Box 1, Virgin Gorda, British Virgin Islands.

MOYNIHAN Daniel Patrick, b. 1927, USA. United States Senator; Author. Publications: Beyond the Melting Pot (with Nathan Glazer), 1963; Defenses of Freedom: The Public Papers of Arthur J Goldberg (editor), 1966; Equal Educational Opportunity (co-author), 1969; Maximum Feasible Misunderstanding: Community Action in the War on Poverty, 1969; On Understanding Poverty: Perspectives From the Social Sciences (editor), 1969; Toward a National Urban Poverty (editor), 1970; The Politics of a Guaranteed Income, 1973; Coping, 1973; Ethnicity: Theory and Experience (edited with Nathan Glazer), 1975; A Dangerous Place (with S A Weaver), 1978; Counting Our Blessings: Reflections on the Future of America, 1980; Loyalties, 1984; Family and Nation, 1986; Came the Revolution: Argument in Reagan Era, 1988; On the Law of Nations, 1990; Pandaemonium: Ethnicity in International Politics, 1993. Address: United States Senate, Washington, DC 20510, USA.

MOYNIHAN John Dominic, b. 31 July 1932, London, England. Journalist; Author. 1 son, 2 daughters. Education: Chelsea School of Art. Literary appointments: Bromley Mercury, 1953-54; Evening Standard, 1954-63; Daily Express, 1963-64; The Sun, 1964-65; Assistant Literary Editor, Sports Correspondent, 1989-; freelance, The Sunday Telegraph; The Sunday Times; The Independent on Sunday; The Daily Express. Publications: The Soccer Syndrome, 1966, 1987; Not All a Ball, autobiography, 1970; Park Football, 1970; Football Fever, 1974; Soccer, 1974; The Chelsea Story, 1982; The West Ham Story, 1984; Soccer Focus, 1989; Kevin Keegan: Black and White, 1993. Contributions to: Sunday Telegraph Magazine; New Statesman; Spectator; Harper's and Queen; The Observer; The Melbourne Age Sunday Supplement, Australia; The Radio Times; Now Magazine; Serve and Volley; Evening Standard; Daily Express; The Sunday Times; Country Life; Catholic Herald; Badminton, Tennis World; The European; World Soccer. Memberships: Society of Authors; Sports Writers Association; Football Writers Association; Lawn Tennis Writers Association; Chelsea Arts Club; Scribes. Literary Agent: Scott Ferris Associates, London, England. Address: 102 Ifield Road, London SW10, England.

MPHAHLELE Es'kia. See: **MPHAHLELE Ezekiel.**

MPHAHLELE Ezekiel (Es'kia Mphahlele), b. 17 Dec 1919, Pretoria, South Africa. Author; Professor of African Literature. Education includes: MA, University of South Africa, Pretoria, 1956. Appointments: Teacher of English and Afrikaans, Orlando High School, Johannesburg, 1942-52; Fiction Editor, Drum magazine, Johannesburg, 1955-57; Lecturer in English Literature, University of Ibadan, Nigeria, 1957-61; Director of African Programmes, International Association for Cultural Freedom, Paris, France, 1961-63; Director, Chem-chemi Creative Centre, Nairobi, Kenya, 1963-65; Lecturer: University College, Nairobi, 1965-66; University of Denver, Colorado, USA, 1966-74; University of Pennsylvania, Philadelphia, 1974-77; Professor of African Literature, University of the Witwatersrand, Johannesburg, South Africa, 1979-. Publications: Man Must Live and Other Stories, 1947; Down Second Avenue, autobiography, 1959; The Living Dead and Other Stories, 1961; The African Image, essays, 1962, 2nd Edition, 1974; Modern African Stories (edited with E Komey), 1964; African Writing Today (editor), 1967; In Corner B and Other Stories, 1967; The Wanderers, novel, 1971; Voices in the Whirlwind and Other Essays, 1972; Chirundu, novel, 1979; The Unbroken Song, 1981; Bury Me at the Marketplace, 1984; Father Come Home, 1984; Afrika My Music: An Autobiography 1957-1983, 1986. Address: African Studies Institute, University of the Witwatersrand, Johannesburg 2001, South Africa.

MUAMBA Muepu, b. 23 Nov 1946, Tshilundu, Zaire. Journalist; Writer. Education: Institut St Ferdinand, Jemappes, Belgium. Literary appointments: Literary Director, Editions Les Presses Africaines, Kinshasa, Zaire; Literary Critic, Salongo and Elima. Publications include: Ventre Creux, short stories; Suppliqué; Anthologie d'une jeune littérature (selected by Oliver Dubuis); Afrika in eigener Sache (with Jochen Klicker and Klaus Paysan), essays on Africa, 1980; Poems in various anthologies; Devoir d'ingérence, nouvelles et poèmes, 1988; Ma Terre d'O, poems, in press. Contributions to: Salongo; Elima; Culture et Authenticité, Kinshasa; Beto, Dusseldorf. Literary Agent: Dr phil Maria Kohlert-Németh, Germany. Address: c/o Dr phil M Kohlert-Neméth, Schaumainkai 99, 6000 Frankfurt am Main 70,

Germany.

MUGGESON Margaret Elizabeth (Margaret Dickinson, Everatt Jackson), b. 30 Apr 1942, Gainsborough, Lincolnshire, England. Partner in Retail Store. m. Dennis Muggeson, 19 Sept 1964, 2 daughters. Education: Lincoln College of Technology, 1960-61. Publications: Pride of the Courtneys, 1968; Brackenbeck, 1969; Portrait of Jonathan, 1970; The Road to Hell (as Everatt Jackson), 1975; Abbeyford Trilogy, 1981; Lifeboat!, 1983; Beloved Enemy (as Margaret Dickinson), 1984; Plough the Furrow, 1994. Membership: The Romantic Novelists Association. Literary Agent: Darley Anderson, Darley Anderson Books, Estelle House, 11 Eustace Road, London SW6 1JB, England. Address: 17 Seacroft Drive, Skegness, Lincolnshire PE 25 3AP, England.

MÜHRINGER Doris Agathe Annemarie, b. 18 Sept 1920, Graz, Austria. Writer; Poet. Publications include: Gedichte I, 1957; Das Marchen von den Sandmannlein, children's picture book, 1961; Gedichte II, 1969; Staub offnet das Auge: Gedichte III, 1976; Tag, mein Jahr (with H Valencak), 1983; Vogel, die ohne Schlaf sind: Gedichte IV, 1984; Tanzen unter d Netz, short prose, 1985; Das hatten die Ratten vom Schatten: Ein Lachbuch, 1989, 2nd edition, 1992; Reisen wir (Ausgewählte Gedichte aus vier Jahrzehnten), 1995. Contributions to: Numerous literary magazines in 9 countries. Honours: Georg Trakl Prize, 1954; Award of Achievement, Vienna, 1961; Lyrics Prize of Steiermark, 1973; Austrian State Scholarship, 1976; Award of Achievement, Board of Austrian Literar-Mechana, 1984; Großer Literaturpreis des Landes Steiermark, 1985. Memberships: PEN; Association of Austrian Writers; Poium; Kogge. Address: Goldeggasse 1, A-1040 Vienna, Austria.

MUIR Kenneth (Arthur) (Mark Finney), b. 1907, England. Emeritus Professor. Appointments: King Alfred Professor of English Literature, 1951-74, Emeritus Professor, 1974-, University of Liverpool; Editor, Shakespeare Survey, 1965-79. Publications: Elizabethan Lyrics, 1953; John Milton, 1955; Shakespeare's Sources, 1957; Shakespeare and the Tragic Pattern, 1959; Shakespeare as a Collaborator, 1960; Last Periods, 1961; Life and Letters of Sir Thomas Wyatt, 1963; Introduction to English Literature, 1967; New Companion to Shakespeare Studies (with S Schoenbaum), 1971; Shakespeare's Tragic Sequence, 1972; Shakespeare the Professional, 1973; The Singularity of Shakespeare, 1977; The Sources of Shakespeare's Plays, 1977; Shakespeare's Comic Sequence, 1979; Shakespeare, Contrasts and Controversies, 1985; King Lear, 1986; Antony and Cleopatra, 1987; Editor: Collected Poems of Sir Thomas Wyatt, 1949; Macbeth, 1951; King Lear, 1952; The Pelican Book of English Prose, 1, 1956; The Life and Death of Jack Straw (edited with F P Wilson), 1957; John Keats, 1958; Unpublished Poems of Sir Thomas Wyatt and his circle, 1961; Richard II, 1963; Othello, 1968; Collected Poems of Sir Thomas Wyatt (edited with Patricia Thomson), 1969; Shakespeare's Plays in Quatro (edited with Michael Allen), 1982; Three Plays of Thomas Middleton, 1975; Troilus and Cressida by Shakespeare, 1982; Interpretations of Shakespeare, 1985; Translations: Five Plays of Jean Racine, 1960; Four Comedies of Calderon, 1980; Three Comedies of Calderon (translated with Ann L Mackenzie), 1985; Calderon's The Schism in England (with Mackenzie), 1990; Calderon's Jealousy the Worst Monster (with Mackenzie), 1995. Honours: Honorary Doctorate: Rouen, 1967; Dijon, 1976; Fellow, British Academy, 1970; 3 collections of essays in his honour, 1974, 1980, 1987; Chairman, 1974-86, Vice President, 1986, International Shakespeare Association; Fellow, Royal Society of Literature, 1978; President, English Association, 1987. Address: 6 Chetwynd Road, Oxton, Birkenhead, Merseyside L43 2JJ, England.

MUIR Richard, b. 18 June 1943, Yorkshire, England. Author; Photographer. Education: 1st class honours, Geography, 1967, PhD, 1970, Aberdeen University, Scotland. Literary appointment: Editor, National Trust Regional Histories and Countryside Commission National Park Series. Publications: Modern Political Geography, 1975; Geography, Politics and Behaviour (with R Paddison); The English Village; Shell Guide to Reading the Landscape; Lost Villages of Britain; History from the Air; National Trust Guide to Prehistoric and Roman Britian (with Humphrey Welfare); Visions of the Past (with C Taylor); East Anglian Landscapes (with J Ravensdale); Shell Countryside Book (with E Duffey); Reading the Celtic Landscape; National Trust Guide to Dark Age and Medieval Britain; Landscape and Nature Photography; National Trust Book of Rivers (with N Muir); Hedgerows: Their History and Wildlife (with N Muir), 1987; Old Yorkshire, 1987; The Countryside Encyclopaedia, 1988; Fields (with Nina Muir), 1989; Portraits of the

Past, 1989; Barleycorn, fiction, 1989; The Dales of Yorkshire, 1991; The Villages of England, 1992; The Coastlines of Britain, 1993. Contributions to: Geographical Magazine; Sunday Times Magazine; Observer Magazine; Various academic articles. Honours: Yorkshire Arts Literary Prize, 1982-83. Honours: Waterfall Close, Station Road, Birstwith, Harrogate, Yorkshire, England.

MUKHERJEE Bharati, b. 27 July 1940, Calcutta, India; Canadian Citizen, 1972. Associate Professor; Author. m. Clarke Blaise, 19 Sept 1963, 2 sons. Education: BA, University of Calcutta, 1959; MA University of Baroda; MA PhD University of Iowa. Appointments: Associate Professor, McGill University, Montreal, Canada, 1966-. Publications: Tiger's Daughter, 1972; Wife, 1975; Kautilya's Concept of Diplomacy, 1976; Days and Nights in Calcutta (with Clark Blaise), 1977; The Middleman, 1989. Honours: National Book Critics Circle Award, 1988. Address: Department of English, McGill University, Montreal, Quebec, Canada.

MULDOON Paul, b. 1951, Armagh, Ireland. Radio Producer; Poet. Education: Queen's University, Belfast. Appointments: Radio Producer, BBC Northern Ireland; Lecturer, Princeton University, USA; Various teaching posts at Universities of Princeton, Berkeley and Amhurst, USA, 1987-. Publications: Knowing My Place, 1971; Poetry Introduction 2, 1972; New Weather, 1973, new edition, 1994; Spirit of Dawn, 1975; Mules, 1977; Names and Addresses, 1978; Why Brownlee Left, 1980; Immram, 1980; Quoof, 1983; Faber Poetry Cassette with Ted Hughes, 1983; The Wishbone, 1984; Selected Poems of Paul Muldoon, 1986; Faber Book of Contemporary Irish Poetry (editor), 1986; Meeting the British, 1987; Madoc: A Mystery, 1990; Shining Brow (an opera libretto), 1993; The Annals of Chile, 1994. Address: Faber and Faber, 3 Queen Square, London WC1N 3AU, England.

MULFORD Wendy, b. 1941, England. Lecturer; Poet. m. John James. Education: BA, MA, Cambridge University; M Phil, University of London. Appointments include: Senior Lecturer, Thames Polytechnic, London, 1968-82. Publications: Bravo to Girls and Heroes, 1977; No Fee: A Line or Two for Free, 1979; Reactions to Sunsets, 1980; The Light Sleepers: Poems, 1980; Some Poems, 1968-78, 1982; River Whose Eyes, 1982; The ABC of Writing and Other Poems, 1985; Late Spring Next Year, 1979-85; Lusus Naturae, 1990; This Narrow Place: Sylvia Townsend Warner, Valentine Ackland: Life, Letters and Politics, 1930-51, 1988; Editor, the Virago Book of Love Poetry, 1990. Address: c/o Curtis Brown Limited, 162-68 Regent Str, London W1R 5TB, England.

MULISCH Harry, b. 29 July 1927, Haarlem, Netherlands. Novelist; Poet; Playwright. Education: Haarlem Lyceum. Appointments include: Director of De Bezige Bij Publishers. Publications: Between Hammer and Anvil, 1952; Blackmailing Life, 1953; The Diamond, 1954; The Horses' Leap and the Salt Sea, 1955; The Miracle, 1956; The Black Life, 1956; The Decorated Man, 1957; The Stone Bridal Bed, 1959; The Narrator, 1970; What Happened to Sergeant Massuro, 1972; The Limit, 1975; Two Women 1975, 1981; Collected Stories 1947-77; Symmetry and Other Stories, 1982; The Assault, 1982, 1985; The Decorated Man, 1984; The Room, 1984; Last Call, 1985, 1989; The Pupil, 1987; The Elements, 1988; Incident: Variations on the Theme, 1989; The Discovery of Heaven, 1992; Plays: Oidipous, Oidipous, 1972; Visiting Time, 1974; The People and Paternal Love, 1975; Axel, 1977; Verse: Words, Words, Words, 1973; The Birds: Three Ballads, 1974; Light in the Eyes, 1975; Kinsfolk, 1975; Language is an Egg, 1976; What Poetry Is, 1981; Opus Gran, 1982; Egyptian, 1983; The Poems 1974-83, 1987; Also: Oedipus as Freud, 1988; The Picture and the Clock, 1989; The Pillars of Hercules, 1990. Honours include: Knight, Order of Orange Nassau, 1977. Address: Van Miereveldstraat 1, 1071 DW Amsterdam, Netherlands.

MULLER Heiner, b. 9 Jan 1929, Eppendorf, Saxony, Germany. Playwright. Appointments include: Staff member, Berliner Volksbühne, from 1976. Publications include: Ten Days Which Shook the World (after John Reed), 1957; The Correction, 1959; Herakles 5, 1966; Oedipus Tyrann (after Hölderlin), 1967; Philoktet, 1968 As; You Like It (after Shakespeare), 1968; Drachenoper (after Dessau), 1969; Macbeth (after Shakespeare), 1972; Zement, 1973; Traktor, 1974; Mauser (after Sholokhov), 1975; Germania Tod in Berlin, 1978; The Life of Grundling, 1979; Die Hamletmaschine, 1979; Der Bau, 1980; The Mission: or, Memory of a Revolution, 1980; Quartett (after Laclos), 1981; Heartpiece, 1983; Bildbeschreibung, 1985; The Civil Wars (with Robert Wilson), 1985; Anatomie Titus Fall of Rome, 1985; Quai West, 1986;

Revolutionsstücke, 1988; Stücke: Texte über Deutschland, 1957-79, 1989; Also: Explosions of a Memory and Other Writings, 1989; The Battle: Plays, Prose, Poems, 1989. Honours include: Lessing Prize, 1975. Address: c/o Reclam-Verlag, Nonnenstrasse 38, 7031 Leipzig, Germany.

MULLIN Chris John, b. 12 Dec 1947, Chelmsford, England. Member of Parliament. m. Nguyen Thi Ngoc, 14 Apr 1987, 1 daughter. Publications: Error of Judgement; The Truth About The Birmingham Bombings; A Very British Coup; The Last Man Out of Saigon; The Year of the Fire Monkey. Honours: BAFTA Awards; US Emmy, Best Drama. Literary Agent: Pat Kavanagh, Peters, Frazer and Dunlop. Address: The House of Commons, London SW1, England.

MULVIHILL Maureen Esther, b. 2 Oct 1944, Detroit, Michigan, USA. Writer; Scholar; Teacher. m. Daniel R Harris, Composer-Musician, 18 Jun 1983. Education: BPhil, Monteith College, 1966, MA, English Literature, 1968, Wayne State University, Detroit, Michigan; PhD, University of Wisconsin-Madison, 1983; Post-Doctoral, Yale Centre for British Art, Yale University, 1986; Columbia University Rare Book School, 1986. Appointments: Writer, State of Wisconsin - Office of the Governor, Office of the Mayor, 1975-82; Corporate Communications Director, Gruntal & Co, Inc, Wall Street, New York City, 1983-85; Communications Consultant, New York City, 1985-; Visiting Scholar and Lecturer in Universities of: New York, Princeton, Utah State, McMaster (Canada), Detroit, also Brooklyn Museum, Georgian Court College (New Jersey), Metropolitan State College (Colorado), Marymount Manhatten College, Fordham Univ at Lincoln Ctr, (New York). Publications include: Poems by Ephelia, 1992, 1993; essays in Restoration, 1987; Scriblerian, 1989; Curtain Calls, 1991; Studies in 18th-C Culture, 1992; Diet of British & American Writers, 1985; British Women Writers, 1989; Encyclopedia of Continental Women Writers, 1991; forthcoming: Medieval Women Writers, British Publishers to 1830; works-in- progress: Stewardess of Culture: Stuart Women Writers & Patronesses. Honours include: Frances Hutner Award (Princeton Research Forum, New Jersey); Fellow, National Endowment for the Humanities; Undergrad & grad scholarships. Memberships: Princeton Research Forum; Institute for Research in History, NYC; Modern Language Association; American Society for 18th-C Studies; Society for Textual Scholarship; Bibliographical Society of America. Address: 45 Plaza St W, Park Slope, Brooklyn, NY 11217, USA.

MUMME Ivan Albert, b. 10 Apr 1928, Adelaide, South Australia. Writer; Publisher. m. Margaret Hastings Davidson, 17 Jan 1953, 1 s, 2 d. Education: BSc, Adelaide University, 1948; BSc (Honours), Adelaide University, 1949; M ENG Sc, University Of New South Wales, 1967; PhD, Macquarie University, 1990. Publications: The Emerald, 1982; Gold Fossicking In Australia, 1984; World Of Sapphires, 1988. Contributions to: SA Chronicle; Roysoc; NSW & SA Qld Mining Journal; Gemmology Association; Australian Lapidary Magazine; Gem And Treasure Hunter; The Earth Exchange; Lapidary Club NSW; Australia Amateur Mineralogist Memberships: Vice President, The Earth Exchange Museum Society, Sydney; Former Chairman, Board of Studies And Examination; The Gemmological Association of Australia. Address: 46 Turriell Pt Road, Port Hacking, NSW 2229, Australia.

MUNDSTOCK Karl, b. 26 Mar 1915, Berlin, Germany. Writer. m. 10 July 1943, 1 son, 1 daughter. Education: Studied Machine Engineering. Publications include: Helle Nächte, novel, 1962; Aliund die Bande vom Lanseplatz, children's book, 1955; Gespenster Edes Tod und Auferstehung, children's book, 1956; Tod an der Grenze, short stories, 1961; Meine 1000 Jahre Jugend, autobiography, 1980; Zeit der Zauberin, 1985. Honours: Medal for Anti-Facism, 1958; Order for Merit (Silver), 1974; FDGB Prize for Literature, 1982; Goethe Prize of Berlin, 1984; GDR National Prize, 2nd Class, 1985. Memberships: Deutscher Schriftsteller-Verband; Deutsches PEN-Zentrum-Ost. Literary Agent: Mitteldeutscher Verlag, Halle/Saale. Address: Wolfshagener Str 75, 13187 Berlin-Pankow, Germany.

MUNONYE John (Okechukwu), b. 22 Apr 1929, Akokwa, Nigeria. Novelist. m. Regina Nwokeji, 1957, 1 d, 1 s. Education: Cert Ed, University of London, 1953. Appointments: Chief Inspector of Education, East Central State, 1973-76, Imo State, 1976-77. Publications: The Only Son, 1966; Obi, 1969; Oil Man of Obange, 1971; A Wreath for Maidens, 1973; A Dancer of Fortune, 1974; Bridge to a Wedding, 1978; Short Stories, Silent Child, 1973; Pack Pack Pack, 1977; Man of Wealth, 1981; On A Sunday Morning, 1982; Rogues,

1985. Honours: Member, Order of the Niger, 1980. Address: PO Box 436 Orlu, Imo State, Nigeria.

MUNRO Alice, b. 10 July 1931, Wingham, Ontario, Canada. Novelist; Story Writer. Education: University of Western Ontario, 1949-51. Appointments: Artist in Residence, University of Western Ontario, 1974-75; University of British Columbia, Vancouver, 1980. Publications: Novel, Lives of Girls and Women, 1971; Stories: Dance of the Happy Shades, 1973; Something I've Been Meaning to Tell You: 13 Stories, 1974; Personal Fictions, 1977; Who Do You Think You Are, 1979; The Moons of Jupiter, 1982; The Progress of Love, 1986; Friends of My Youth, 1990; Play, How I Met My Husband, 1974. Honours: Governor General Award; Canada Australia Literary Prize, 1978; D Litt, University of Western Ontario, 1976. Address: c/o Writers Union of Canada, 24 Ryerson Street, Toronto, Ontario M5T 2PW, England.

MUNRO David Mackenzie, b. 28 May 1950. Freelance Geographical Reference Editor. m. Wendy Jane Nimmo, 22 Nov 1985. Education: BSc, 1973, PhD, 1983, University of Edinburgh. Appointment: Editor, Chambers World Gazetteer, 1984-. Publications: Chambers World Gazetteer (editor), 1988; Ecology and Environment in Belize (editor), 1989; A World Record of Major Conflict Areas (with Alan J Day), 1990; The Hutchinson Guide to the World (associate editor), 1990; Contributor: Longman's Encyclopedia; Hutchinson's Encyclopedia; Oxford Encyclopaedic English Dictionary. Contributions to: Geographical Magazine. Address: Department of Geography, University of Edinburgh, Drummond Street, Edinburgh EH8 9XP, Scotland.

MUNRO John Murchison, b. 29 Aug 1932, Wallasey, Cheshire, England. University Administrator. m. Hertha Ingrid Bertha Lipp, 12 Aug 1956, 2 sons, 2 daughters. Education: BA, English Literature, University of Durham, 1955; PhD, English Literature, Washington University, St Louis, USA, 1960. Appointments: Part-time Instructor of English, Washington University, St Louis, Missouri, USA, 1956-60; Instructor, University of North Carolina, 1960-63; Assistant Professor, University of Toronto, Canada, 1963-65; Professor, American University of Beirut, Lebanon, 1965-87; Director, Outreach Services, Professor of Mass Communications, 1987-, Associate Dean for External Affiars, 1990-, American University in Cairo, Egypt. Publications: English Poetry in Transition, 1968; Arthur Symons, 1969; The Decadent Poets of the 1890's, 1970; Selected Poems of Theo Marzials, 1974; James Elroy Flecker, 1976; A Mutual Concern: The Story of the American University of Beirut, 1977; Cyprus: between Venus and Mars (with Z Khuri), 1984; Selected Letters of Arthur Symons (with Karl Beckson), 1988; Theatre of the Absurd: Lebanon, 1982-88, 1989; Middle East Times (senior editor). Contributions to: Various scholarly articles in literary journals; Journalism on Middle Eastern subjects. Honours: Fulbright Research Award, University of California, Los Angeles, summer 1987. Address: American University in Cairo, 113 Kasr el Aini Street, Cairo, Egypt.

MUNRO Rona, b. 7 Sept 1959, Aberdeen, Scotland. Playwright. Education: MA, Edinburgh University, 1980. Appointments include: Dramatist in Residence, Paines Plough Theatre Company, London, 1985-86. Publications: Fugue, 1983; Piper's Cave, 1985; Saturday at the Commodore, 1989; Bold Girls, 1990; Your Turn to Clear the Stair, 1992; Plays for Stage, Radio, TV and Film. Honours include: Evening Standard Award, 1991. Address: Casarotto Ramsay Ltd, National House, 60-66 Wardour Street, london W1V 3HP, England.

MUNRO Ronald Eadie. See: **GLEN Duncan Munro.**

MUNSCH Robert N, b. 11 Jun 1945, Pittsburgh, Pennsylvania, USA. Writer. m. Ann D Metta, 20 Jan 1973, 1 son, 2 daughters. Education: BA, History, Fordham University, 1969; MA, Anthropology, Boston University, 1971; MEd, Child Studies, Tuft's University, 1973. Appointments: Day care Teacher, Boston and Coos Bay, 1972-75; Lecturer, Department of Family Studies, University of Guelph, 1975-80, Assistant Professor, 1980-84; Full time writer, 1984-. Publications: 26 books including: The Paper Bag Princess, 1980; Love You Forever, 1986. Honours: Canadian Bookseller's Association Author of the Year, 1991. Memberships: Writer's Union of Canada; Canadian Association of Children's Authors, Illustrators and Performers; Canadian Author's Association; Contact: Writer's Union of Canada. Address: c/o Writers Union of Canada, 24 Ryerson Ave, Toronto, Ontario, Canada, M5T 2P3.

MURATA Kiyoaki, b. 19 Nov 1922, Ono, Hyogo, Japan. Educator; Author. m. (1) Minako Iesaka, 1960, div. 1981, 2 sons, 1 daughter, (2) Kayoko Matsukura, 1987. Education includes: MA, University of Chicago, USA. Appointments: Editorial Writer, 1957-66, Managing Editor, 1971-76, Executive Editor, 1976-77, Managing Director, 1976-83, Editor-in-Chief, 1977-83, The Japan Times; Director, Japan Graphic Inc, 1977-82; Professor, International Communications, Yachiyo International University, 1988. Publications: Japan's New Buddhism - An Objective Account of Soka Gakkai, 1969; Japan - The State of the Nation, 1979; Kokuren Nikki-Suppon Wan no Kaiso (UN Diary - Recollections of Turtle Bay), 1985; An Enemy Among Friends, 1991. Honours: Honorary LLD, Carleton College; Vaughn Prize, Japan Newspaper Editors and Publishers Association. Address: 19-12 Hiroo 2 chome, Shibuya-ku, Tokyo 150, Japan.

MURDOCH Iris (Jean) (Dame), b. 15 July 1919, Dublin, Ireland. Writer; Philsopher. m. John O Bayley. Education: Somerville College, Oxford. Publications: Sartre: Romantic Rationalist, 1953; Under the Net, 1954; The Flight from the Enchanter, 1955; The Sandcastle, 1957; The Bell, 1958; A Severed Head, 1961, play, 1963; An Unofficial Rose, 1962; The Unicorn, 1963; The Italian Girl, 1964, play, 1967; The Red and the Green, 1964; The Time of the Angels, 1966; The Nice and the Good, 1968; Bruno's Dream, 1969; A Fairly Honourable Defeat, 1970; The Sovereignty of Good, 1970; The Servants and the Snow, play, 1970; An Accidental Man, 1971; The Three Arrows, play, 1972; The Black Prince, 1973; The Sacred and Profane Love Machine, 1974; A Word Child, 1975; Henry and Cato, 1976; The Sea, the Sea, 1978; The Fire and the Sun, 1978; Nuns and Soldiers, 1980; Art and Eros, play, 1980; The Philosopher's Pupil, 1983; The Good Apprentice, 1985; Acastos, Platonic Dialogues, 1986; The Book of the Brotherhood, 1987; The Message to the Planet, 1989; Metaphysics as a Guide to Morals, 1992. Honours include: Honorary DLitt, Universities of Sheffield, Belfast, East Anglia (Norwich), Caen, London; Fellow, 1948-63, Honorary Fellow, 1963, St Anne's College, Oxford; James Tait Black Prize for Fiction, 1974, Whitbread Literary Award for Fiction, 1974; Booker Prize for Fiction, 1978; Gifford Lecture, University of Edinburgh, 1982; DBE, 1987. Memberships: Various professional organisations. Address: c/o Ed Victor Ltd, 162 Wardour Street, London W1V 4AT, England.

MURNANE Gerald, b. 1939, Melbourne, Victoria, Australia. Novelist. m. 3 s. Education: BA, University of Melbourne, 1969. Appointments: Lecturer, Victoria College, Melbourne; Senior Lectuer, Deakin University, Melbourne. Publications: Tamarisk Row, 1974; A Lifetime on Clouds, 1976; The Plains, 1982; Landscape with Landscape, 1985; Inland, 1988; Velvet Waters, Stories, 1990. Address: 2 Falcon Street, Macleod, VA 3085, Australia.

MURPHEY Rhoads, b. 13 Aug 1919, Philadelphia, Pennsylvania, USA. Professor, History and Asian Studies. m. Eleanor Albertson, 12 Jan 1952, 2 sons, 2 daughters. Education: AB, 1941, AM, 1942, History, Harvard University: AM, China, 1948, PhD, Eastern History & Geography, 1950, ibid. Publications include: Shanghai: Key to Modern China, 1953; Introduction to Geography, 1969, 4th edition 1978; Scope of Geography, 1969, 4th edition, 1987; Mozartian Historian, 1976; Outsiders (award), 1977; Fading of the Maoist Vision: The Chinese, 1986; also: A New China Policy, 1965; Approaches to Modern Chinese History, 1967; Treaty Ports, 1975; The Human Adventure, 1990; 50 Years of China to Me, 1994; A History of Asia, 1995; Civilisations of the World, 1995. Contributions to: Various Professional Journals. Honour: Best Book of Year, 1978. Memberships include: Board of Directors, 1959-, President, 1986-, Editor, Monographs, Association of Asian Studies. Address: Department of History, University of Michigan, Ann Arbor, Michigan 48109, USA.

MURPHY C L. See: **MURPHY Lawrence Agustus.**

MURPHY Clive, b. 28 Nov 1935, Liverpool, England. Writer. Education: BA, LLB, Trinity College, Dublin, 1958; Incorporated Law Society of Ireland, 1958. Publications: Freedom for Mr Mildew and Nigel Someone; Summer Overtures, 1976; Oral history: The Good Deeds of a Good Woman; Born to Sing; Four Acres and a Donkey; Love, Dears!; A Funny Old Quist; Oiky; At The Dog in Dulwich; A Stranger in Gloucester; Dodo, 1993; Endsleigh, 1994. Contributions to: Over 21; PEN Broadsheet; Cara; Books and Bookmen; Panurge. Honours: Adam International Review 1st Novel Award. Memberships: PEN; Society of Authors; Associate, Royal Society of Literature. Address: 132 Brick Lane, London E1 6RU, England.

MURPHY Jim, b. 25 Sep 1947, Newark, New Jersey, USA. Children's Book Editor. m. Elaine Kelso, 12 Dec 1970. Education: BA, Rutgers University; Radcliffe College. Publications: Weird and Wacky Inventions, 1978; Rat's Christmas Party, 1979; Harold Thinks Big, 1980; Death Run, 1982; Two Hundred Years of Bicycles, 1983; The Indy 500, 1983; Trackers, 1984; Baseball's All-Time Stars, 1984; Guess Again: More Weird and Wacky Inventions, 1985; The Long Road to Gettysburg, 1992. Contributions to: Cricket. Honours: Golden Kite Award Society of Children's Book Writers and Illustrators, 1993. Address: 138 Wildwood Avenue, Upper Montclair, NJ 07043, USA.

MURPHY Joseph Edward, b. 13 Mar 1930, Minneapolis, Minnesota, USA. Writer. m. Diana E Kuske, 4 Jul 1958, 2 sons. Education: BA, Princeton University, 1952; University of Minnesota. Publications: South of the Pole by Ski; The Random Character in Interest Rates; Stock Market Probability; With Interest: Adventure Beyond the Clouds. Contributions to: Princeton Alumni journals; American Alpine journals; Journal of Quantitative Financial Analysis. Honour: 2nd Prize, Friends of American Writers. Memberships: American Alpine Club; Chartered Financial Analysts. Literary Agent: Vicki Lansky, Minneapolis. Address: 2116 W Lake Isles, Minneapolis, MN 55405, USA.

MURPHY Lawrence Agustus, (Steven C Lawrence, C L Murphy), b. 1924, USA. Educator: Author. Education: PhD. Appointments: English Teacher, Department Chairman, South Junior High School, Brockton, Massachussets, 1951-87; President, Treasurer, Steven C Lawrence Productions, Brockton; Instructor in Creative Writing, Stonehill College, North Easton, Massachussets, 1967. Publications: The Naked Range, 1956; Saddle Justice, 1957; Brand of a Texan, 1958; The Iron Marshal, 1960; Night of the Gunmen, 1960; Gun Fury, 1961; With Blood in their Eyes, 1961; Slattery and Bullet Welcome for Slattery, 1961; Slattery, published as The Lynchers, 1975; Walk a Narrow Trail and A Noose for Slattery, 1962; Longhorns North and Slattery's Gun Says No, 1962; A Texan Comes Riding, 1966; Buffalo Grass (with Charlotte Murphy jointly as C L Murphy), 1966; That Man From Texas, 1972; Edge of the Land, 1974; Six-Gun Junction, 1974; North to Montana, 1975; Slattery Stands Alone, 1976; A Northern Sage,: The Account of the North Atlantic-Murmansk, Russia Convoys, 1976; Trial for Tennihan, 1976; Day of the Commancheros, 1977; Gun Blast, 1977; Slattery Stands Alone, 1979; Through Which We Serve, 1985; The Green Concord Stagecoach, 1988. Memberships: Navy League of the United States; United States Navy League; The Battle of Normandy Foundation; United States Navy Memorial Foundation; Christian Coalition; The American Air Museum in Britain; Massachussetts Maritime Academy Alumni Association; Boston University Alumni Association; Liberty Ship - John W Brown Memorial; Merchant Marine Veterans of World War II; US Navy Veterans of World War II. Address: 30 Mercedes Road, Brockton, MA 02401, USA.

MURPHY Walter Francis, b. 21 Nov 1929, Charleston, South Carolina, USA. McCormick Professor of Jurisprudence, Princeton University. m. Mary Therese Dolan, 28 Jun 1952, 2 daughters. Education: AB Magna cum Laude, University of Notre Dame, 1950; AM, George Washington University, 1954; PhD, University of Chicago, 1957. Publications include: Upon This Rock, fiction, 1987; The Vicar of Christ, fiction, 1979; Elements of Judicial Strategy, 1964; American Democracy, several editions 1963-83; Courts, Judges & Politics, editions 1961-95; The Roman Enigma, fiction, 1981; Congress & the Court, 1962; Comparative Constitutional Law, 1977; American Constitutional Interpretation, 2nd ed 1995; Wiretapping on Trial, 1965. Contributions to: Numerous legal academic & professional journals. Honours: Chicago Foundation for Literature, 1980; Guggenheim Fellowship, 1973; Fulbright Award, 1980. Memberships: Fellow, American Academy of Arts & Sciences; Various Offices, American Political Science Associaton, Law & Society Association. Literary Agent: Robert Lantz, Lantz Office, 888 7th Avenue, NYC. Address: Department of Politics, Princeton University, Princeton, NJ 08544, USA.

MURPHY Albert, b. 12 May 1916, Nokomis, Alabama, USA. Writer. m. 31 May 1941, 1 daughter. Education: BS, Tuskegee University, 1939; MA, New York University, 1948. Publications: The Omni-Americans, 1970; South to a Very Old Place, 1971; The Hero and the Blues, 1973; Train Whistle Guitar, 1974; Stomping the Blues, 1976; Good Morning Blues, 1985; The Spyglass Tree, novel, 1991. Honours: Lillian Smith Award for Fiction for Train Whistle Guitar; Deems Taylor Award for Music Criticism for Stomping the Blues, American Society of Composers, Authors and Publishers, 1977;

Honorary DLitt, Colgate, 1975; The Lincoln Center Alumni Emeirto Award, 1991. Memberships: American PEN; Authors Guild. Literary Agents: Wylie, Aitken and Stone. Address: 45 West 132nd Street, New York, NY 10037, USA.

MURRAY Beatrice. See: **POSNER Richard.**

MURRAY Frances. See: **BOOTH Rosemary Sutherland.**

MURRAY John. See: **WRIGHT David.**

MURRAY Les, b. 1938, Australia. Poet. Appointments: Scientific and Technical Translator, Australian National University, Canberra, Australian Capital Territory, 1973-80; Co-Editor, Poetry Australia, 1973-80; Poetry Reader, Angus and Robertson Publishers, 1976-91; Literary Editor, Quadrant, 1990-; Honorary Vice-President, Poetry Society of Great Britain, 1993. Publications: The Ilex Tree (with Geoffrey Lehmann), 1965; The Weatherboard Cathedral, 1969; Poems Against Economics, 1972; Lunch and Counter Lunch, 1974; Selected Poems: The Vernacular Republic, 1976, 2nd Edition, 1983; Ethnic Radio, 1978; The Peasant Mandarin, prose, 1978; The Boys Who Stole the Funeral, 1980; The Vernacular Republic: Poems 1961-1981, 1982; Equanimities, 1982; The People's Otherworld, 1983; Persistence in Folly, 1984; The Australian Year (with Peter Solness), 1986; The Daylight Moon, 1986; Dog Fox Field, 1991; Collected Poems, Australia, 1991, USA and UK, 1992; Blocks and Tackles, prose, 1991; The Paperbark Tree: Selected Prose, UK, 1992; Translations from the Natural World, verse, 1992; Editor: New Oxford Book of Australian Verse, 1986; Collins Dove Anthology of Australian, Religious Verse, 1986; Fivefathers: Five Australian Poets of the Pre-Academic Era, 1994. Honours: Officer, Order of Australia, 1989. Literary Agent: Margaret Connolly and Associates, New South Wales, Australia. Address: c/o Margaret Connolly and Associates, 37 Ormonde Street, Paddington, New South Wales 2021, Australia.

MURRAY Rona, b. 10 Feb 1924, London, England. Lecturer; Poet. m. Walter Dexter, 1972. Education: MA, University of British Columbia, Vancouver, 1965; PhD, University of Kent, Canterbury, 1972. Appointments include: Lecturer, University of Victoria, 1977-82. Publications: The Enchanted Adder, 1965; The Power of the Dog and Other Poems, 1968; Ootischenie, 1974; Selected Poems, 1974; An Autumn Journal, 1980; Journey, 1981; Adam and Eve in Middle Age, 1984; Journey Back to Peshawar: Memoir/Travel; Plays, Blue Ducks' Feather and Eagledown, 1958; One, Two, Three, Alary, 1970; Creatures, 1980; Short Stories, The Indigo Dress and Other Stories, 1986; Co Edutor, The Art of Earth: An Anthology, 1979. Honours include: Canada Council Grants; Pat Lowther Award, 1982. Address: 3825 Duke Road, RR4 Victoria, British Columbia, V9B 5T8, Canada.

MURRAY Terry (Kate Fournis, Chris Yarrow), b. 8 Jul 1954, Chicago, IL, USA. Medical Journalist. Education: BJ, Carleton University, Canada, 1976. Literary Appointments: Senior Staff Writer, The Medical Post, 1982; Consultant, Global Programme on Aids, World Health Organization, 1987. Contributions to: The Medical Post; Australian Doctor; Spotlight. Honours: Special Award For Unusual Excellence, Association for Education in Journalism, 1977; Kenneth R Wilson Memorial Award, Canadian Business Press. Memberships: Canadian Association Of Journalists; Periodical Writers Association of Canada. Address: 205-105 Raglan Avenue, Toronto, Ontario, Canada, M6C 1A7.

MURRAY Virginia R, b. 8 Nov 1914, Virginia, USA. Secondary English Teacher, Retired. m. Herbert H Murray, 27 Feb 1943, 1 son, 1 daughter. Education: BA, Randolph-Macon Woman's College, (Phi Beta Kappa), 1936; Graduate Work: English, University of Virginia, 1938-40, Physics and Law, George Washington University, 1946. Appointments: Newspaper Advisor, Editor, Literary Magazine, Randolph School, Huntsville, 1965-72. Publications include: Poems, published in various journals and anthologies; Poetry programmes. Honours include: Edwin Morkham Poetry Society Awards, San Jose, CA, USA, 1959, 1960; Many awards in Alabama State Poetry Society and the Alabama Conclave Annual Contests, 1983-93; Poet, Author Contest Award, 1983.Memberships: Alabama State Poetry Society; Alabama Writers Conclave; Huntsville Branch National League of American Pen Women; Past President, Alabama State Association NLAPW; Alpha Delta Kappa; Poets and Writers; Academy of American Poets; American Association of University Women; Huntsville Literary Association. Address: 8905 Strong Drive SE, Huntsville, AL 35802, USA.

MURRELL John, b. 15 Oct 1945, USA. Canadian Citizen. Playwright. Education: BA, University of Calgary. Appointments include: Head, Theatre Section, Canada Council, 1988. Publications: Metamorphosis, 1970; Haydn's Head, 1973; Power in the Blood, 1975; Arena, 1975; Teaser, 1975; A Great Noise, A Great Light, 1976; Memoir, 1977; Uncle Vanya, After Chekhov, 1978; Mandragola, After Machiavelli, 1978; Bajazet, After Racine, 1979; The Seagull, After Chekhov, 1980; Farther West, 1982; New World, 1985; October, 1988; Democracy, 1991. Address: c/o Talonbooks, 201-1019 East Cordova, Vancouver, British Columbia V6A 1MB, Canada.

MURTI Kotikalapudi Venkata Suryanarayana, b. 31 May 1929, Parlakemidi, India. Retired Professor of English; Teacher; Research Guide; Researcher; Creative Writer; Journalist; Linguist. Education includes: MA, English Language and Literature, 1963, PhD, English, 1972; Andhra University; Certificate in Linguistics, Central Institute of English and Foreign Languages, Hyderabad, 1969. Publications: Books of poetry in English: Allegory of Eternity, 1975; Triple Light, 1975; Sparks of the Absolute, 1976; Spectrum, 1976; Symphony of Discords, 1977; Araku, 1982; Youth and Science, 1994; Other works: Waves of Illumination, 1978; Iham to Param, 1979; Lilahela, 1981; The Sword and the Sickle: A Study of Mulk Raj Anand's Novels, 1981; Kohinoor in the Crown: Critical Studies in Indian English Literature, 1987; Old Myth and New Myth: Letters from MRA to KVS, 1991; Pranavam tho Pranayam, poetry in Telugu, 1994. Address: 43-21-9A Venkatarazu Nagar, Visakhapatnam 530 016, (AP), India.

MUSGRAVE Susan, b. 12 Mar 1951, Vancouver Island, British Columbia, Canada. Poet; Novelist; Columnist; Reviewer; Non-fiction Writer. m. Stephen Reid, 1986, 2 daughters. Publications: Poetry include: Songs of the Sea-Witch, 1970; Entrance of the Celebrant, 1972; Grave-Dirt and Selected Strawberries, 1973; A Man to Marry, a Man to Bury, 1979; Cocktails at the Mausoleum, 1992; Forcing the Narcissus, 1994; Non-Fiction include: Great Musgrave, 1989; Musgrave Landing: Musgrave, 1990; Leonardo, 1990; The Embalmer's Art, 1991; Musings on the Writing Life, 1994. Contributions to: Canadian Literature in the Seventies; Gangsters, Ghosts & Dragonflies; New Oxford Book of Canadian Verse; Antologia de la Poesia anglocanadiense contemporanea; The New Canadian Poets; The Norton Introduction to Poetry; The Norton Anthology of Modern Poetry; The Great Big Book of Canadian Humour. Address: 10301 West Saanich Road, PO Box 2421, Sidney, British Columbia, V8L 3Y3, Canada.

MUSGROVE Frank, b. 1922, England. Professor Emeritus. Appointments include: Professor Emeritus of Education, University of Manchester. Publications: The Migratory Elite, 1963; Youth and the Social Order, 1964; The Family, Education and Society, 1966; Society and the Teacher's Role (with P H Taylor), 1969; Patterns of Power and Authority in English Education, 1971; Ecstasy and Holiness, 1974; Margins of the Mind, 1977; School and the Social Order, 1979; Education and Anthropology, 1982; The North of England: A History from Roman Times to the Present, 1990. Contributions to: Articles to African Studies, 1952; Africa, 1952, 1953; History, 1955; Economic History Review, 1959, 1961; Sociological Review, 1959, 1961, 1963, 1967, 1975; British Journal of Sociology, 1961, 1976, 1981; Paedagogica Historica, 1962; British Journal of Social and Clinical Psychology, 1962; Others. Honours: Fellow, Royal Anthropological Institute, 1952; Fellow, Royal Society of Arts, 1970; The Chancellor's Lectures, University of Wellington, New Zealand, 1970; Doctor of Letters, Open University, 1982. Address: DIB SCAR, The Cedar Grove, Beverley, East Yorkshire HU17 7EP, England.

MUSKE Carol Anne (Carol Muske Dukes), b. 17 Dec 1946, St Paul, Minnesota, USA. Professor; Writer. m. David Dukes, 31 Jan 1983, 1 stepson, 1 daughter. Education: BA, Creighton University, 1967; MA, State University of California, San Francisco. Literary Appointments: Assistant Editor, Antaeus Magazine; Founder, Art W/O Walls; President, Poetry Society of America West. Publications: Dear Digby, 1989, paperback, 1990; Red Trousseau, poetry, 1993; Saving St Germ, novel, paperback, 1995; Applause; Wyndmere; Skylight; Camouflage. Contributions to: New Yorker; New York Times; Los Angeles Times; Poetry; American Poetry Review; Others. Honours: Castagnola Award, 1979; Guggenheim Fellow, 1981; National Endowment for the Arts Fellow, 1984; Ingram Merrill Award, 1988. Memberships: PEN; Poetry Society of America; Authors Guild. Literary Agent: Charles Verrill, Darhansoff & Verrill, Park Avenue, New York City, New York, USA. Address: c/o Department of English, University of Southern California, University Park, Los Angeles, CA 90089, USA.

MUSSER Joe, b. 1936, USA. Writer; Company President. Appointments: Director, Creative Services, 1966-73, President, 1963-, Four Most Productions Inc, Wheaton, Illinois. Publications: The Centurian, radio play, 1963; Dawn at Checkpoint Alpha, radio play, 1966; Behold a Pale Horse, 1970; Doctor in a Strange Land (co-author), 1968; Road to Spain, screenplay, 1971; The Rapture, screenplay, 1972; Joni (with Joni Eareckson) 1976; Josh, 1981; The Coming World Earthquake, 1982; A Skeptic's Quest, 1984. Address: c/o Tynedale House, 351 Executive Drive, Wheaton, IL 68187, USA.

MUSSEY Viginia T H. See: **ELLISON Virginia Howell.**

MUSTO Barry (Robert Simon), b. 1930, England. Novelist; Short Story Writer. Appointments: Public Relations Consultant. Publications: The Lawrence Barclay File, 1969; Storm Centre, 1970; The Sunless Land (as Robert Simon), 1974; The Fatal Flaw, 1974; Code Name, Bastille; No Way Out; The Weighted Scales; The Lebanese Partner, 1984. Membership: Crime Writers Association. Address: Thistles, Little Addington, Kettering, Northants, England.

MYERS Jack Elliot, b. 29 Nov 1941, Lynn, Massachusetts, USA. Professor of English. m. Thea Temple, 25 Sep 1993, 3 sons, 1 daughter. Education: BA, University of Massachussetts, 1970; MFA, University of Iowa, 1972. Literary Appointments: Poetry Editor of Cimarron Review, 1989; Distinguished Writer-in-Residence, Witchita State University, 1992, University of Idaho, 1993. Publications: Black Sun Abraxas, 1970; Will It Burn, 1974; The Family War, 1977; I'm Amazed That You're Still Singing, 1981; A Trout in the Milk, 1982; New American Poets of the '80's, 1984; The Longman Dictionary & Handbook of Poetry, 1985; As Long As You're Happy, 1986; New American Poets of the '90's, 1991; A Profile of 20th Century American Poetry, 1992; Blindsided, 1993. Contributions include: Esquire; American Poetry Review; Antaeus; Poetry; A Magazine of Verse; Iowa Review; Minnesota Review; Virginia Quarterly Review; Georgia Missouri and Southern Poetry Reviews; Ploughshares; South-West Review; Fiction International; The Nation. Honours: Texas Institute of Letters Poetry Award, 1978, 1993; Elliston Book Award, 1978; National Endowment for the Arts Fellowship 1982, 1986; Texas Institute Award in Poetry, 1993. Memberships: Vice-President, Associated Writing Programs; 1991-94; PEN; Texas Association of Creative Writing Teachers. Address: Dept of English, Southern Methodist University, Dallas, TX 75275, USA.

N

NABOKOV Dmitri, b. 10 May 1934, Berlin, Germany. Operatic Bass; Writer; Translator. Education: AB cum laude, Harvard University; Longy School of Music, 1955-57. Career includes: Has sung leading bass operatic roles and performed in concert in major theatres in many countries of North and South America and Europe. Publications: Translations including numerous works of Vladimir Nabokov, 1957-; Translator, editor, commentator: The Man from the USSR and Other Plays (Vladimir Nabokov), 1984; The Enchanter (Vladimir Nabokov), 1986; The Selected Letters of Vladimir Nabokov, 1940-1977, 1989. Contributions to: Articles and essays to various collections and periodicals. Honours: Cum Laude Society; Served with AUS, 1957-59; Winner, International Opera Contests: Reggio Emilia, 1960, Parma, 1966; Participant, award-winning recording of Madrigals by Gesualdo, 1963. Memberships: Offshore Powerboat Racing Association; American Powerboat Racing Association; American Alpine Club; Ferrari Club, Switzerland; Chevalier du Tastevin. Literary Agent:, Smith and Skolnik, New York, USA. Address: Chemin de la Caudraz, CH-1820 Montreux, Switzerland.

NADICH Judah, b. 13 May 1912, Baltimore, Maryland, USA. Rabbi. m. Martha Hadassah Ribaloe, 26 Jan 1947, 3 daughters. Education: AB, College of New York, 1928-32; Jewish Theological Seminary of America, 1932-36; MA, Columbia University, 1935-36; Rabbi, Doctor of Hebrew Literature, 1953, Doctor of Divinity (honoris Causa), 1966. Publications: Eisenhower and the Jews, 1953; Translator of The Flowering of Modern Hebrew Literature by Menachem Ribalow, 1957; Editor, Al Halakhah Ve-Aggadah, by Louis Ginzberg, 1960; Jewish Legends of the Second Commonwealth, 1983; Legends of the Rabbis, 1994; Yom Kippur, a brochure for Armed Forces of USA; Articles on Eisenhower and Jews in the Military in Encyclopeadia Judaica and Jewish-American History and Culture, an Encyclopeadia. Contributions to: Articles published in The Reconstructionist; Hadoar; Jewish Book Annual; Essays in Jewish Booklore; Congress Weekly; Conservative Judaism; Shma; The Jewish Frontier; Journal of Jewish Social Studies. Memberships: President, The Jewish Book Council of America, 1970-72; President, The Rabbinical Assembly, 1972-74. Address: Park Avenue Synagogue, 50E 87th Street, New York, NY 10028, USA.

NADOLNY Sten, b. 29 July 1942, Zehdenick/Havel, Germany. Author. Education: Abitur, 1961; Dr phil, Modern History, 1977. Publications: Netzkarte, 1981; Die Entdeckung der Langsamkeit, 1983; Selim oder die Gabe der Rede, 1990; Das Erzählen und die guten Absidhten, 1990. Honours: Ingeborg Bachmann Prize, 1980; Hans Fallada Prize, 1985; Vallombrosa Prize, Florence, 1986. Memberships: PEN; Bayerishe Akademie der Schönen Künste. Literary Agent: R Piper & Co Verlag, Germany. Address: c/o R Piper & Co Verlag, Georgenstrasse 4, D 8000 Munich 40, Germany.

NAGARAJA RAO C K (Rajanna, Haritas, Haida), b. 12 June 1915, Chellakere, India. Author; Journalist. m. Rajamani Nagarajo Rao, 18 May 1934, 2 sons, 6 daughters. Education: Intermediate Engineering Exam, Mysore University, 1933; Hindi Preaveshika Exam, 1937. Publications: Wild Jasmine, 1937; Mushrooms, 1942; Shoodramuni, 1943; Dayadadavanala, 1944; Sangama, 1944; Place and Date of Mahakavi Lakshmeesha, 1969; Pattamahadevi Shantaladevi, 1978; Sankole Basava, 1979; Sampanna Samaja, 1979; Savilladavaru, 1982; Kuranganayani, 1983; Ekalavya, 1988; Veeranganga Vishnuvardhana, 1992. Contributions to: Illustrated Indian Weekly; Mirror; Quarterly Journal of Mythic Society; PEN; Vani; Prabhata; Prakasha; Janapragati?; Subodha; Vakchitra; Prajamata; Prajavani. Honours: Award for Research and Criticism, 1969-70, Best Creative Literature of the Year, 1978, Karnataka State Sahitya Akademi; Moorthidevi Sahitya Puraskar of Bharatiya Jnanpith, 1983. Memberships: Kannada Sahitya Parishat; Karnataka Lekhakar Sangha; PEN All India Centre; Mythic Society; Authors Guild of India. Address: 7/61/2 Mandaara, 1 Main Road, Padmanabhanagar, Bangalore 560 070, India.

NAGATSUKA Ryuji, b. 20 Apr 1924, City of Nagoya, Japan. Professor. m. 20 July 1949. Education: Graduated, Section of French Literature, University of Tokyo, 1948. Appointments: Professor, Nihon University, 1968-. Publications: Napoleon tel qu'il était, 1969; J'étais un kamikaze, 1972; George Sand, sa vie et ses oeuvres, 1977; Napoleon,

2 volumes, 1986; Talleyrand, 1990. Contributions to: The Yomiuri Shimbun. Honours: Prix Pierre Mille, 1972; Prix Senghor, 1973. Membership: Association Internationale des Critiques Littéraires, Paris. Address: 7-6-37 Oizumigakuen-cho, Nerima-ku, Tokyo, Japan.

NAGEL Paul C, b. 1926. USA. Writer on History & Biography. Appointments: Professor of History, 1964-69, Dean, College of Arts and Sciences, 1965-69, University of Kentucky, Lexington; Professor of History, 1969-78, Vice-President for Academic Affairs, 1970-74, University of Missouri, Columbia; Professor of History and Head of Department, University of Georgia, Athens, 1978-81; Director Virginia Historical Society, 1981-85; Distinguished Lee Scholar, R F Lee Memorial Foundation, 1986-; Contributing Editor, American Heritage Magazine, 1983-; Visiting Scholar, Duke University, 1991-92; Visiting Scholar, University of Minnesota, 1992-; Visiting Scholar, Carleton College 1992-. Publications: One Nation Indivisible: The Union in American Thought 1776-1861, 1964; This Sacred Trust: American Nationality 1798-1898, 1971; Missouri: A History, 1977; Descent From Glory: Four Generations of the John Adams Family, 1983; Extraordinary Lives: The Art and Craft of American Biography (co-author), 1986; The Adams Women, 1987; The Lees of Virginia, Seven Generations of an American Family, 1990; Massachussetts and the New Nation (co-author), 1992. Honour: Virginia Cultural Laureate, 1988-. Memberships: Fellow, Pilgrim Society; Fellow, Society of American Historians; President, Southern Historical Association; Massachussetts Historical Society, (Corresponding Member). Address: 12800 Marion Lane West, Apt 502, Minnetonka, MN 55305, USA.

NAGY Paul, b. 23 Aug 1934, Hungary. Writer. div. Education: Bachelor's degree, Hungary, 1953; Diploma, French Language and Literature, Sorbonne, Paris, 1962. Appointments: Co-Founder, Atelier Hongrois, 1962; Co-Founder, p'ART video-review, 1987. Publications: Books: Les faineants de Hampstead, 1969; Sadisfaction IS, 1977; Journal in-time, 1984; Points de Repères "Postmodernes": Lyotard, Habermas, Derrida, 1993; Journal in-time II, 1994; Projections-performances, 1978-; Visual multimedia works, 1980-. Contributions to: Change; Change International; Rampike; Lotta poetica; Others. Membership: Union des Ecrivains Français. Address: 141 Ave Jean Jaures, 92120 Montrouge, France.

NAHAL Chamal, b. 2 Aug 1927, Sialkot, India (now Pakistan). Writer (Novels, Short Stories, Literature, Philosophy). Appointments: Member, Department of English, Delhi University, 1963-; Columnist, Talking About Books, The Indian Express newspaper, 1966-73; Associate Professor of English, Long Island University, New York, USA, 1968-70. Publications: The Weird Dances, short stories, 1965; A Conversation with J Kristnamurti, 1965; D H Lawrence: An Eastern View, 1970; Drugs and the Other Self (editor), 1971; The Narrative Pattern in Ernest Hemingway's Fiction, 1971; The New Literatures in English, 1985; The Bhagavad-Gita: A New Rendering, 1987; Novels: My True Faces, 1973; Azadi, 1975; Into Another Dawn, 1977; The English Queens, 1979; The Crown and the Loincloth, 1982; Sunrise in Fiji, 1988; The Salt of Life, 1990. Address: 2/1 Kalkaji Extension, New Delhi 110019, India.

NAIFEH Steven, b. 19 Jun 1952, Tehran, Iran. Art Lecturer; Public Relations Consultant. Education: AB, Princeton University; MA, JD, Harvard University. Publications: Culture Making: Money, Success, and the New York Art World, 1976; Moving Up in Style, 1980; Gene Davis, 1981; From Primitive to Modern: One Hundred Years of Nizenzu Art, c. 1982 ; The Arts Book, c. 1982; What Every Client Needs to Know About Using A Lawyer, 1982; Pillars of Wisdom: New Buildings for the World of Islam, c. 1983; Why Can't Men Open Up? 1984; The Best Lawyers in America: Directory of Experts, 1990; Jackson Pollack: An American Saga, 1990; The Best Doctors in America, 1992; Final Justice, 1993. Honours: Pulitzer Prize, 1991. Address: 129 First Avenue SW, Aiken, SC 29801, USA.

NAIMAN Anatoly G, b. 23 Apr 1936, Leningrad, Russia. Poet; Writer. m. Galina Narinskaia, 1969, 1 son, 1 daughter. Education: Degree in Organic Chemistry, Leningrad Technological Institute, 1958; Postgraduate Diploma in Screenwriting, Moscow, Russia, 1964. Appointments: Visiting Professor in Russian and Poetry, Bryn Mawr College, USA, 1991; Visiting Fellow, All Souls College, Oxford, UK, 1991-92. Publications: Remembering Anna Akhmatova, 1989; The Poems of Anatoly Naiman, 1989; The Statue of A Commander and other Stories, 1992; Translations into Russian include: Songs of Troubadours, 1979; Flemanca, 1983, 1984; Floire et Blanceflor, 1985; Le Roman de Renard, 1986; Le Roman de Sept Sages, 1989; The

Poems of Giacomo Leopardi, 1967, 1989. Contributions to: The New Worlds; October; The Star; Literaturnaia Gazeta; Russkaia Mysl; L'Espresso; TLS. Honours: Lativian Union of Writers Translators Prize. Memberships: Leningrad Four (group of Poets), 1960-66; Writers Committee, Leningrad, 1965-70, Moscow 1970-; PEN Club, France, 1989-. Literary Agent: Andrew Nurnberg Associates, London. Address: Dmitrovskoye Schosse 29 fl 56, Moscow, Russia.

NAIPAUL Vidiadhar Surajprasad, b. 17 Aug 1932, Trinidad. Writer. m. Patricia Hale, 1955. Education: BA, Honours, English, University College, Oxford, 1954. Publications: The Mystic Masseur, 1957; The Suffrage of Elvira, 1958; Miguel Street, 1959; A House for Mr Biswas, 1961; The Middle Passage, 1962; Mr Stone and the Knights Companion, 1963; An Area of Darkness, 1965; The Mimic Men, 1967; A Flag on the Island, 1967; The Loss of Eldorado, 1969; In a Free State, 1971; India: A Wounded Civilization, 1977; A Bend in the River, 1979; The Return of Eva Perion, 1980; Among the Believers, 1981; Finding the Centre, 1984; The Enigma of Arrival, 1987; A Turn in the South, 1989. Contributions to: Various journals and magazines. Honours: Recipient, numerous honours and awards including: Rhys Memorial Prize, 1958; W H Smith Literary Award, 1968; Booker Prize, 1971; Bennet Award, 1980; Jerusalem Prize, 1983; Ingersoll Prize, 1986; DLitt, Cambridge University, 1983. Memberships: Fellow, Royal Society of Literature; Society of Authors. Literary Agent: Gillon Aitken. Address: c/o Aitken & Stone, 29 Fernshaw Road, London SW10 0TG, England.

NAKAYAMA Kiyoshi, b. 30 Mar 1935, Professor of English, 1 son, 1 daughter. Education: BA, French, Tenri University, Nara, 1955; MA, English Literature, Kansai University, Osaka, 1962. Publications: Selected Essays of John Steinbeck, 1981; Tanoshi Mokuyobi, 1984; Uncollected Stories of John Steinbeck, 1986; John Steinbeck's Writings: The California Years, 1989; John Steinbeck: Asian Perspectives, 1992; Steinbeck in Japan: A Bibliography, 1992; Of Mice and Men: A Play in Three Acts (co-editor), 1993. Contributions to: Kansai University English Literature Society Bulletin; San Jose Studies; Essays on Collecting John Steinbeck's Books; Steinbeck Quarterly; Monterey Life. Honours: The Richard W and Dorothy Burkhardt Award, 1992. Memberships: John Steinbeck Society of Japan, Executive Director; International John Steinbeck Society, Executive Board; The Japan American Literature Society, Executive Board 1994-. Address: 594 Takabatake Honyakushi-cho, Nara-shi, Nara 630, Japan.

NAKAYAMA Shigeru, b. 22 June 1928, Japan. Professor. m. Motoko Watanabe, 8 July 1962, 1 son, 1 daughter. Education: BA, Tokyo University, 1951; PhD, Harvard University, 1959. Publications: History of Japanese Astronomy, 1969; Chinese Science, 1973; Science and Society in Modern Japan, 1974; Characteristics of Scientific Development in Japan, 1977; Academic and Scientific Traditions, 1984; Science, Technology and Society in Postwar Japan, 1991. Memberships: International Council for Science Policy Studies; Vice President, Académie Internationale d'Histoire des Sciences; President, International Society of the History of East Asian Science, Technology and Medicine. Address: 3-7-11 Chuo, Nakano, Tokyo, Japan.

NANDA Bal Ram, b. Rawalpindi, India (now Pakistan). Historian; Writer. m. Janak Khosla, 24 May 1946, 2 sons. Education includes: MA, History, 1st class, University of Punjab. Lahore, 1939. Appointment: Director, Nehru Memorial Museum and Library, New Delhi, 1965-79. Publications: Mahatma Gandhi, A Biography, 1958; The Nehrus, Motilal and Jawaharlal, 1962; Gandhi, A Pictorial Biography, 1972; Gokhale, The Indian Moderates and the British Raj, 1977; Jawaharlal Nehru, A Pictorial Biography, 1980; Gandhi and His Critics, 1986; Gandhi, Pan-Islamism, Imperialisn and Nationalism in India, 1989; In Gandhi's Footsteps: Life and Times of Jamnalal Bajaj, 1990; Editor: Socialism in India, 1972; Indian Foreign Policy: The Nehru Years, 1975; Science and Technology in India, 1977; Essays in Modern Indian History, 1980. Contributions to: Numerous newspapers, magazines and journals. Honours: Rockefeller Fellowship, 1964; National Fellowship, Indian Council of Social Science Research, New Delhi, 1979; Dadabhai Naoroji Memorial Prize, 1981; Padma Bhushan, 1988. Memberships: Institute for Defence Studies and Analyses, New Delhi; Authors Guild of India; Indian International Centre. Address: S-174 Panchshila Park, New Delhi 110017, India.

NANSE. See: **KUO Nancy.**

NAPIER William (Bill) McDonald, b. 29 June 1940, Perth, Scotland. Astronomer. m. Nancy Miller Baillie, 7 July 1965, 1 son, 1

daughter. Education: BSc, 1963; PhD, 1966. Publications: The Cosmic Serpent, 1982; The Cosmic Winter, 1990; The Origin of Comets, 1990. Contributions to: Occasionally to: New Scientist; Astronomy Today. Honours: Joint recipient, Arthur Beer Memorial Prize, 1986-87. Membership: Fellow, Royal Astronomical Society. Address: Royal Observatory, Blackford Hill, Edinburgh EH9 3HJ, Scotland.

NARANG Gopi Chand, b. 1 Jan 1931, Dukki, Baluchistan, India. Professor. m. Manorama Narang, 9 Dec 1973, 2 sons. Education: Honours, 1st in 1st Class, Urdu, 1948, Honours, 1st in 1st Class, Persian 1958, Punjab University; MA, 1st in 1st Class, Urdu, 1954, PhD, 1958, Diploma in Linguistics, 1st Division, 1961, University of Delhi; Postdoctoral courses in Acoustic Phonetics and Transformational Grammar, Indiana University, USA, 1964. Appointments: Currently Professor of Urdu Language and Literature, Delhi University. Publications include: Karkhandari Dialect of Delhi Urdu, 1961; Puranon Ki Kahaniyan, 1976; Anthology of Modern Urdu Poetry, 1981; Urdu Afsana, Riwayat aur Masail, 1982; Safar Ashna, 1982; Usloobiyat-e-Mir, 1985; Saniha-e-Karbala bataur Sheri Istiara, 1987; Amir Khusrau ka Hindavi Kalaam, 1988; Adabi Tanqeed aur Usloobiyat, 1989; Rajinder Singh Bedi, anthology, 1990; Urdu Language and Literature: Critical Perspectives, 1991; Sakhtiyat, Pas-Sakhtiyat, Mashriqi Sheriyat, 1993. Address: D-252 Sarvodaya Enclave, New Delhi 110017, India.

NARAYAN Rasipuram Krishnaswamy, b. 10 Oct 1906, Madras, India. Novelist. Education: Maharajas College, Mysore, 1930. Appointments: Owner, Indian Thought Publications, Mysore. Publications include: Swami and Friends: A Novel of Malgudi, 1935; The Bachelor of Arts, 1937; The Dark Room, 1939; The English Teacher, 1945; The Financial Expert, 1952; The Guide, 1958; The Man Eater of Malgudi, 1962; The Vendor of Sweets, 1967; The Painter of Signs, 1976; Talkative Man, 1986; The World of Nagaraj; Stories: Malgudi Days, 1943; Cyclone and Other Stories, 1944; An Astrologers Day and Other Stories, 1947; Lawley Road, 1956; A Horse and Two Goats, 1970; Essays, Travel Writing and Memoirs. Honours: English Speaking Union Award, 1975; D Litt University of Delhi; Fellow, Royal Society of Literature, 1980. Address: 15 Vivekananda Road, Yadavagiri, Mysore 2, India.

NARDON Anita Lucia, b. 2 Apr 1931, Belgium. Multi-Lingual Secretary; Art Critic. div., 3 sons. Appointments: Staff, Peau de Serpent. 1962-78; Le Drapeau Rouge, 1980-91; IDEART, 1989; Montrer, 1991. Publications: Poetry: 18 Booklets; La Chanson d'Isis; Novel: L'Obj a Teret et la Chute; Tale: Contes pour Yannick; Art Books: more than 10 artist's monographies; 50 Artistes de Belgique, Vol IV, V. Contributions: Various monthly art magazines. Honours: Médaille d'argent Arthur Rimbaud; Prix Ville de Toulon, France; Prix Silarus Francia; Médaille de Bronze, Poésiades de Paris. Memberships: PEN; Association of French Speaking Belgian Writers; Association International des Critiques d'Art. Address: Rue Jourdan 57, 1060 Brussels, Belgium.

NARULA Surinder Singh, b. 8 Nov 1917, Amritsar, India. Teacher. m. Pritama, 10 Apr 1950, 3 daughters. Education: MA, English, 1942. Appointments: Former Principal & Head, Post Graduate Department of English and American Literatures, Government College, Ludhiana. Publications: 13 novels, 6 collections of short stories, 8 books of literary criticism, 3 collections of poetry and 12 books on socio cultural subjects including: Peo Puttar, 1946; Sil Alune, 1963; History of Panjabi Literature, 1958; Gatha, epic poem, 1985; Gali Gwand, 1971; Nili Bar; Rang Mahal. Contributions to: Numerous professional journals. Honours: Rattingon Gold Medalist, 1938; J S Hailey Prizeman, 1938; Panjab Government Shiromani Sahityakar; Panjab Arts Council Award; Sahitya Shri Award, Bhartiya Bhasha Sangam; Rotary International Award; Panjabi Sahitya Akademi Silver Jubilee Robe of Honour; Vishav Panjabi Sammelan Gold Medal; many other honours and awards. Memberships: various professional organisations. Address: 684 Gurdevnagar, Civil Lines, Ludhiana 141001, India.

NASH Gary B, b. 1933, American. Writer on History; Professor of History, University of California at Los Angeles, USA, 1966-. Appointments: Assistant Professor of History, Princeton University, New Jersey, 1964-66; Associate Director, National Center for History in the Schools, 1988-. Publications: Quakers and Politics: Pennsylvania 1618-1726, 1968; Class and Society in Early America, 1970; (ed with Richard Weiss), The Great Fear: Race in the Mind of America, 1970; Red, White and Black: The Peoples of Early America, 1974, 1982-91; The Urban Crucible: Social Change, Political Consciousness and the

Origins of the American Revolution, 1979; (ed with David Sweet), Struggle and Survival in Colonial American, 1980; (co-ed), The Private Side of American History, 2 vols, 1983-87; (with J R Jeffrey), The American People, 2 vols, 1985-89; Retracing the Past, 2 vols, 1985-89I; Race, Class and Politics, 1986; Forging Freedom: The Formation of Philadelphia's Black Community, 1720-1840, 1988; Race and Revolution, 1991. Address: 16174 Alcima Avenue, Pacific Palisades, CA 90272, USA.

NASH Gerald David, b. 16 Jul 1928, Berlin, Germany. University Professor. m. 19 Aug 1967, 1 d. Education: BA, New York University, 1950; MA, Columbia University, 1952; PhD, University of California, 1957; Appointments: Stanford University, 1957-58, 1959-60; Northern Illinois University, 1959-60; Harvard University, 1960-61; University of New Mexico, 1961-. Publications: State Government & Economic Development, 1964; US Oil Policy, 1968; The Great Transition, 1971; The American West in 20th Century, 1973; The Great Depression and World War II, 1979; American West Transformed, World War II, 1985; Issues in American Economic History, 1964; F D Roosevelt, 1967; Urban West, 1979; Half Century of Social Security, 1988; Perspectives on 20th Century West, 1988; World War II and the West: Reshaping the Economy, 1990; Creating the West: Historical interpretations, 1890-1990, 1991; A P Giannini and the Bank of America, 1992. Contributions to: 40 Articles in professional journals. Honours: Phi Beta Kappa, 1950; Newberry Fellow, 1955; Huntington Library Fellow, 1979; NEH Fellow, 1981. Memberships: Phi Alpha Theta, Historian, 1974-84; Editor, The Historian, 1974-84; Organisation of American Historians; Western History Association. Address: Dept of History, University of New Mexico, Albuqueque, NM 87131, USA.

NASH Padder. See: **SEWART Alan.**

NASSAUER Rudolf, b. 1924, British. Writer of Novels/Short Stories, Poetry. Publications: Poems 1947; The Holigan, 1959; The Cuckoo, 1962; The Examination, 1973; The Unveiling, 1975; The Agents of Love, 1976; Midlife Feasts, 1977; Reparations, 1981; Kramer's Goats, 1986. Address: 51, St James' Gardens, London W11, England.

NASSENBAUM Stephen, Historian. Publications: The Great Awakening of Yale College, 1972; The Salem Witchcraft Papers (editor), 1977; Sex, Diet and Debility in Jacksonian America, 1988; Salem Village Witchcraft: A Documentary Record (editor), 1993. Address: Department of History, University of Massachussetts at . Amherst, Amherst, MA 01003-0128, USA.

NATALE Francine de. See: **MALZBERG Barry Norman.**

NATHAN David, b. 9 Dec 1926, Manchester, England. Journalist. m. Norma Ellis, 31 Mar 1957, 2 sons. Appointments: Copy Boy, Copy Taker, News Chronicle, Manchester, 1942-44, 1947; Reporter, St Helen's Reporter, 1947-49; Reporter, Feature Writer, Theatre Critic, London Editor, Nottingham Guardian, 1949-52; Daily Mail, 1952-54; Associated Press, 1954-55; Reporter, Feature Writer, Theatre Critic, Daily Herald/Sun, 1955-69; Theatre Critic, 1970-, Deputy Editor, 1978-91, Jewish Chronicle. Publications: Hancock (with Freddie Hancock), 1969; A Good Human Story, television play, 1978; The Freeloader, novel 1970; The Laughtermakers, 1971; Radio Plays: The Belman of London, 1982; The Bohemians, 1983; Glenda Jackson, a critical profile, 1984; John Hurt, An Actor's Progress, 1986; The Story So Far, novel 1986; Shaw and Politics (contributor). Contributions to: The Times Saturday Review; Daily Telegraph; Sunday Telegraph; Independent; Harper's and Queens; TV Times; Observer Colour Magazine. Honours: Highly Commended, Writer's Award, Royal Television Society, 1978. Membership: Critics Circle, President 1986-88, Trustee. Literary Agent: Harvey Unna and Stephen Durbridge Limited. Address: 16 Augustus Close, Brentford Dock, Brentford, Middlesex, England.

NATHAN Edward Leonard, b. 8 Nov 1924, Los Angeles, California, USA. Teacher; Poet. m. Carol G Nash, 27 June 1949, 1 son, 2 daughters. Publications: Western Reaches, 1958; Glad and Sorry Seasons, 1963; The Day the Perfect Speakers Left, 1969; Returning Your Call, 1975; Dear Blood, 1980; Holding Patterns, 1982; Carrying On: New & Selected Poems, 1985; Translations include: First Person, Second Person by Agyeya, 1971; The Transport of Love, 1976; Grace and Mercy in Her Wild Hair, 1982; Songs of Something Else, 1982; Happy as a Dog's Tail, 1986; On the Skin (translation with C Milosz of poetry of Aleksander Wat), 1989. Contributions to: Salmagundi; New

Yorker; New Republic; Kenyon Review. Honours: Guggenheim Fellowship, 1976-77; Nominee, National Book Award, 1975; National Institute of Arts and Letters Award for Creative Literature, 1971; Ameican Institute of Indian Studies Fellowship, 1965-66; Creative Arts Fellowship, UCB, 1973-74. Address: 40 Beverly Road, Kensington, CA 94707, USA.

NATHAN Robert S, b. 13 Aug 1948. Education: BA cum laude, Amherst College, 1970. Appointments: Producer, NBC Television Series, Law and Order; Writer and Co-writer; Writer, television film, In the Deep Woods, 1992. Publications: The White Tiger, 1988; Rising Higher, 1981; Amusement Park, 1977; In the Deep Woods, 1989; The Legend, 1986; The Religion, 1982. Contributions to: All Things Considered; The New Republic; New York; Harper's; The New York Times Book Review. Honours: Notable Book of the Year, New York Times; Book of the Month Club Selection. Address: c/o Adam Berkowitz, William Morris Agency, New York, USA.

NATUSCH Sheila Ellen, b. 14 Feb 1926, New Zealand, Writer; Illustrator. m. Gilbert G Natusch, 28 Nov 1950. Education: MA, Otago University, 1948. Publications: Animals of New Zealand, 1967; Brother Wohlers, 1969, 2nd edition 1992; New Zealand Mosses, 1970; Wild Fare for Wilderness Foragers, 1970; Native Plants, revised edition, 1976; Hell and High Water, 2nd edition, 1992; The Cruise of the Acheron, 1978; On the Edge of the Bush, 1978; Wellington, 1981; A Bunch of Wild Orchids, 3rd edition, 1983; A Pocketful of Pebbles, 1983; Southward Ho, 1985; William Swainson of Fern Grove, 1987; Roy Traill of Stewart Island, 1991; An Island Called Home, 1992. Contributions to: Marine News; New Zealand Gardener; NZ Fisherman. Honours: Hubert Church Award for Brother Wohlers, PEN New Zealand, 1969. Address: 46 Owhiro Bay Parade, Wellington 6002, New Zealand.

NAU Henry Richard, b. 10 Dec 1941, USA. Associate Dean; Professor of Political Science and International Affairs. m. Marion M Nau, 1 daughter. Education: BS, Economics, Politics, Science, Massachusetts Institute of Technology, 1963; MA with distinction, International Relations, 1967, PhD, International Relations, 1972, School of Advanced International Relations, Johns Hopkins University. Publications: National Politics and International Technology: Nuclear Reactor Development in Western Europe, 1974; Technology Transfer and US Foreign Policy, 1976; Domestic Trade Policies and the Uruguay Round (editor, contributor), 1989; The Myth of America's Decline: Leading the World Economy into the 1990s, 1990; 18 book chapters; Monographs. Contributions to: Perspective; Orbis; International Organization; Columbia Journal of World Business; Journal of International Affairs; Policy Studies Journal; The Washington Quarterly; World Affairs; Geopolitics of Energy; Economic Impact; Foreign Policy; Western Political Quarterly; The National Interest; International Economy; Dokumentation; National Review; CEO International Strategies. Honours: Dean's List, Massachusetts Institute of Technology; Proctor and Gamble Fellowship, Massachusetts Institute of Technology, 1958-63; NDEA Title IV Fellowship, 1965-68; Ford Foundation Foreign Area Fellowship Grant, 1968-70; Phi Beta Kappa, 1973; National Science Foundation Grant, 1974-75; International Affairs Fellowship, Council of Foreign Relations, 1975-76; Superior Honor Award, Department of State, 1977; Fellowship, Woodrow Wilson International Center for Scholars, 1987; Fellowship, Smith-Richardson Foundation, 1987. Memberships: North-South Roundtable on Trade, Society for International Development, Islamabad; Board of Editors and Executive Committee, International Organization 1977-81. Address: 7409 River Falls Drive, Potomac, MD 20854, USA.

NAUMOFF Lawrence Jay, b. 23 Jul 1946, Charlotte, North Carolina, USA.Author. (div) 1 s. Education: BA, University of North Carolina, Chapel Hill, 1969. Publications: The Night of the Weeping Women, 1988; Rootie Kazootie, 1990; Taller Women, 1992; Silk Hope, NC, 1994. Contributions to: Various literary magazines, short stories. Honours: Thomas Wolfe Memorial Award,1969; National Endowment for the Arts Grant, 1970; $30,000 Whiting Foundation Writers Award, 1990. Membership: PEN. Literary agent: Barbara Lowenstein (USA); Adam Stein (UK). Address: PO Box 901, Carrboro, NC 27510, USA.

NAVASKY Victor S, b. 5 July 1932, NY, USA. Editor; Writer. m. Anne Dandy Strongin, 27 Mar 1966, 1 son, 2 daughters. Education: AB, Swarthmore College, 1954; JD, Yale Law School, 1959. Publications: Kennedy Justice, 1971; Naming Names, 1980. Contributions to: The Nation; Many Magazines & Journals. Honour: American Book Award, 1981. Memberships: American PEN; Authors Guild; Committee to

Protect Journalists. Literary Agent: Lynn Nesbit. Address: 33 West 67th Street, New York, NY 10023, USA.

NAVON Robert, b. 18 May 1954, New York City, New York, USA. Editor; Philosopher. Education: BA, Lehman College, City University of New York, 1975; MS, State University of New York, Geneseo, 1978; MA studies, New School, 1982-86; PhD candidate, University of New Mexico, 1991-. Publications: Patterns of the Universe, 1977; Autumn Songs: Poems, 1983; The Pythagorean Writings, 1986; Healing of Man and Woman, 1989; Harmony of the Spheres, 1991; Cosmic Patterns, volume 1, 1993; Great Works of Philosophy, 7 vols (editor). Honours: New York State Regents Scholar, 1971; Phi Beta Kappa, 1975; Intern, Platform Association, 1980. Memberships: Society of Ancient Greek Philosophy; American Philosophical Association. Address: PO Box 81702, Albuquerque, NM 87198, USA.

NAVRATIL Jan, b. 13 May 1935, Slovakia. Writer. m. Libusa Nigrovicova, 5 Sept 1959, 1 son, 1 daughter. Education: Pedagogic Facultyat University, 1959. Publications: Lampas maleho plavcika, 1980, 1983, 1989; Gulata Kocka, 1985, 1987; Kto vidi na dno, 1981; Len srdce prvej velkosti, 1970, 1984; Pramienok, 1983, 1989; Plachetnica Nonsens, 1967; Diskoteka L, 1983; Z hliny a rosy, 1981; Riekanky, 1988; Belasy majak, 1985; Kral s gitarou, 1988; Ciarky na dlani, 1989; Tri cervene klobuciky, 1973; Rozpravka o duhovej lodi, 1984. Honours: Janusz Korczak Award, 1981; Frano Kral Award, 1980; Union of Slovak Writers Award, 1981, 1985; Mlade leta Award, 1966, 1970, 1990; Maxim Gorki Diploma, 1987; HCh Anderson Diploma, 1982. Memberships: ssa OOUnion of Slovak Writers; Friends of Children's Books Club. Literary Agent: Agencef Litteraire Slovaque, Partizanska ul c 21, 815 30 Bratislava, Slovakia. Address: Obezna Street 13, 926 01 Sered, Slovakia, Slovaki.

NAYAK Harogadde Manappa, b. 5 Feb 1931, Hosamane, India. Teacher. m. Yashodharamma, 11 May 1955, 1 son, 1 daughter. Education: BA, Honours, University of Mysore, 1955; MA, Calcutta University, 1959; PhD, Indiana, USA, 1964. Appointments: Editor, Prabuddha Karnataka, 1967-84; Adviser, Grantha Loka, 1976-. Publications: Namma Maneya Deepa, 1956; Revindranath Tagiore, 1960; Kannada - Literary and Colloquial, 1967; Sulangi, 1975; Sangati, 1987; Janapada Swarupa, 1971; more than 60 books. Contributions to: Indian PEN; Kannada Prabha; Prajamata; Prajavani; Inchara; Prabuddha Karnataka; Sudha; Taranga. Honours: Calcutta University Gold Medal, 1959; Mysore University Jubilee Award, 1978; Karnataka State Award, 1982; Karnataka Sahitya Akademy Award, 1985; Presided over 57th All India Kannada Literary Conference, 1985. Memberships: Indian National Academy of Letters, Executive Committee; National Book Trust, India, Trustee; Indian PEN; Kannada Sahitya Parisht; Karnataka Janapada Parisht, President. Address: Godhuli, Jayalakshmi Puram, Mysore 570-021, Karnataka, India.

NAYLOR Gloria, b. 1950, American. Novelist. Appointments: Missionary for the Jehovah's Witnesses, New York, North Carolina and Florida, 1968-75; Telephone Operator, New York City Hotels, 1975-81; Writer-in-Residence, Commington Community of the Arts, Massachusetts, 1983; Visiting Professor, George Washington University, Washington DC, 1983-84; Visiting Writer, New York University, 1986; Columnist, New York Times, 1986. Publications: The Women of Brewster Place: A Novel in Seven Stories, 1982; Linden Hills, 1985. Address: c/o Ticknor and Field, 52 Vanderbilt Avenue, New York, NY 10017, USA.

NAYLOR Phyllis Reynolds. Publications: Over 60 books for adults and children including: The Galloping Goat, 1965; Knee-Deep in Ice Cream and Other Stories, 1967; How To Find Your Wonderful Someone: How to Keep Him, 1971; To Walk the Sky Path, 1973; Getting Along In Your Family, 1976; How I Came To Be A Writer, 1978; All Because I'm Older, 1981; Old Sadie and the Christmas Bear, 1984; Unexpected Pleasures, 1986; Alice in Rapture, Sort Of, 1989; The Craft of Writing, 1989; Send No Blessings, 1990; Shiloh, 1991; All But Alice, 1992; The Fear Place, 1994. Honours: Newberry Medal, American Library Association, 1992. Address: 9910 Holmhurst Road, Bethseda, MD 20817, USA.

NEAL Ernest Gordon, b. 20 May 1911, Boxmoor, Hertfordshire, England. Retired School Teacher; Biologist. m. Helen Elizabeth Thomson, 30 Apr 1937, 3 sons. Education: BSc, MSc, PhD, London University and Extension, 1931-35. Publications: Exploring Nature with a Camera, 1946; The Badger, 1948; Woodland Ecology, 1953; Topsy

and Turvy My Two Otters, 1961; Uganda Quest, 1971; Biology for Today (with K R C Neal), 1974; Badgers, 1977; Badgers in Closeup, 1984; Natural History of Badgers, 1986; On Safari in East Africa, A Background Guise, 1991; The Badger Man, Memoirs of a Biologist, 1994. Contributions to: Country Life; The Field; Illustrated London News; Times; Wildlife Magazine; Sunday Times; Countryman; Countryside Magazine; Mammal Review. Honours: Fellow, Institute of Biology, 1965; Stamford Raffles Award, Zoological Society of London, 1965; MBE, 1976. Memberships: Society of Authors; Chairman, President, Mammal Society; British Ecological Society; Chairman, Vice-President, Somerset Wildlife Trust. Address: 42 Park Avenue, Bedford MK40 2NF, England.

NEEDLE Jan, b. 1943, England. Writer for Children and Adults. Publications: Albeson and the Germans, 1977; My Mate Shofiq, 1978; A Fine Boy for Killing, 1979; The Size Spies, 1979; Rottenteeth, 1980; The Bee Rustlers, 1980; A Sense of Shame, 1980; Wild Wood, 1981; Losers Weepers, 1981; Another Fine Mess, 1981; Brecht (with Peter Thomson), 1981; Piggy in the Middle, 1982; Going Out, 1983; A Game of Soldiers, TV serial, 1983, book, 1985; A Pitiful Place, 1984; Great Days at Grange Hill, 1984; Tucker's Luck, 1984; Behind the Bike Sheds, 1985; Tucker in Control, 1985, TV Series, 1985; Wagstaffe, The Wind-Up Boy, 1987; Soft Soap, TV play, 1987, TV series, 1988; Truckers, TV series, 1987; Uncle in the Attic, 1987; Skeleton at School, 1987; In the Doghouse, 1988; The Sleeping Party, 1988; Mad Scramble, 1989; As Seen on TV, 1989; The Thief, TV series, 1989; The Thief, novel, 1990; The bully, novel, 1992; The Bill, TV series, 1992. Literary Agents: For drama: Rochelle Stevens and Co, London, England; For novels: David Higham Associates, 5-8 Lower John Street, London W1R 4HA, England. Address: c/o Rochell Stevens and Co, 2 Terretts Place, Upper Street, London N1 1QZ, England.

NEELY Mark Edward, Jr, b. 10 Nov 1944, Amarillo, Texas, USA. Director, Louis A Warren Library; University Professor. m. Sylvia Eakes, 15 Jun 1966. Education: BA, PhD, Yale University. Appointments: Member of Advisory Board, Indiana Historical Bureau; Editorial Advisory Committee, Indiana Magazine of History; Member of Editorial Board, Ulysses S Grant Association; Editor, Lincoln Lore. Publications: Abraham Lincoln Encyclopaedia, 1981; The Lincoln Image: Abraham Lincoln and the Popular Print, 1984; Insanity File: The Case of Mary Todd Lincoln, 1986; The Confederate Image: Prints of the Lost Cause, 1987; The Fate of Liberty: Abraham Lincoln and Civil Liberties, 1991; The Last Best Hope of Earth: Abraham Lincoln and the Promise of America, 1993. Honours: Pulitzer Prize, 1992. Memberships: Abraham Lincoln Association (Board of Directors, 1981-); Society of Indiana Archivists (President 1980-81); Indiana Association of Historians (President 1987-88). Address: Dept of History, St Louis University, 221 North Grand Avenue, St Louis, MO 63103, USA.

NEHAMAS Alexander, b. 22 Mar 1946, Athens, Greece. University Professor. m. Susan Glimcher, 22 Jun 1983, 1 s. Education: BA, Swarthmore College, Usa, 1967; PhD, Princeton University, 1971. Publications: Nietsche: Life as literature, 1985; Plato's Symposium, 1989; Aristotle's Rhetoric: Philosophical Essays, 1994; Plato's Phaedrus, 1995. Contributions to: Various including: Cavafy's World of Art, Sartre's Freud Scenario; Grand Street. Honours: Fellow, National Endowment for the Humanities, USA, 1977-78; Guggenheim Fellow, 1984-85; Phi Beta Kappa, Romanwell Professor, 1991; Sather Professor of Classical Literature, University of California, Berkeley, 1993; DPhil (Hon), University of Athens. Memberships: American Philosophical Association, Excutive Committee, 1989-92; American Society for Aesthetics; Modern Language Association; Modern Greek Studies Association; American Academy of Arts and Sciences. Address: Department of Philosophy, Princeton University, Princeton, NJ 08544, USA.

NELSON Marguerite. See: FLOREN Lee.

NELSON Mildred (Pearson), b. 28 Mar 1915, Arkansas, USA. Writer. m. Arthur Lee Nelson, 7 Jul 1935, 1 s, 1 d. Education: BA, English Literature, University of Arkansas, 1936. Publications: Taste of Power, 1964; The Dark Stone, 1972; The Island, 1973. Contributions to: Fiction and Poetry to many journals and magazines including: Crosscurrents; McCalls; Georgia Review; Christian Science Monitor; Colorado Quarterly; Light Year Anthology, '86. Honours: PEN Syndicated Fiction award, 1984; World Order of Narrative Poets Award, 1985; Poetry Arts Project Award, 1989. Memberships: Authors Guild & League of America; PEN; Poets and Writers, Literary Agent: Jay

Garon, New York, USA. Address: 1508 Circa del Lago B-307, Lake San Marcos, CA 92069, USA.

NELSON Richard, b. 1950, American. Writer of Plays/Screenplays. Appointments: Literary Manager, BAM Theatre Co, Brooklyn, 1979-81; Associate Director, Goodman Theatre, Chicago, 1980-83; Dramaturg, Guthrie Theatre, Minneapolis, 1981-82. Publications: The Vienna Notes (in Word Plays I), 1980; Il Campiello (adaptation), 1981; An American Comedy and Other Plays, 1984; Between East and West (in New Plays USA 3), 1986; Principia Scriptoriae, 1986; (ed), Strictly Dishonorable and Other Lost American Plays, 1986; Rip Van Winkle, 1986; Jungle Coup (in Plays from Playwrights Horizons), 1987; Accidental Death of an Anarchist (adaptations), 1987. Address: 32 South Street, Rhinebeck, NY 12572, USA.

NELSON-HUMPHRIES Tessa, b. Yorkshire, England. Professor of English Literature; Lecturer; Writer. m. (1) Kenneth Nelson-Brown, 1 Jun 1957, (dec 1962), (2) Cecil H Unthank, 26 Sep 1963, (dec 1979). Education: BA, MA, University of North Carolina; PhD, Liverpool University, UK. Contributions to: Michigan Quarterly Review; Southern Folklore Quarterly; Dalesman; Let's Live; Cats Magazine; Bulletin, Society of Childen's Book Writers; Child Life; Vegetarian Times; Bulletin, Society of Women Writers and Journalists; The Lookout; Joycean Literary Arts Guild Magazine; Alive; British Vegetarian; Blue Unicorn; Candles and Lamps; Envoi (UK) Hardback anthology, 1990; Outposts; poetry in Z-Miscellaneous, 1987-88; Childrens Digest; New Mexico Vegetarian Journal; Bulletin Cavaliers of The West; Mesilla Valley Writers Journal. Honours: Short story Prize, Society of Women Writers, UK, 1975; Julia Cairns Trophy, poetry (UK), 1978; Mellon Award, writing and travel in China, 1981; James Still Fellowship in Humanities, University of Kentucky, for biography of L E Landon, 1983; also, Danforth, Fulbright, AAUW Awards; Article Prize, 1985, Fiction Prize 1987, SWWJ; Poetry Prizes, (Julia Cairns Competition), 1988, 1989; Mellon Awards, a travel study, Spain, 1988, 1989. Memberships: Society of Children's Book Writers, USA; Society of Women Writers & Journalists, UK; New Mexico Education Association; Association Poets & Writers, USA; MENSA. Address: 3228 Jupiter Rd, 4 Hills, Las Cruces, MN 88012-7742, USA.

NEMEROV Howard, b. 29 Feb 1920, New York City, USA. English Teacher. m. Margaret Russell, 26 Jan 1944, 3 sons. Education: AB, Harvard College, 1941. Appointments include: Faculties, Hamilton College 1946-48, Bennington 1948-66, Brandeis University 1966-69, Washington University, Missouri 1969-, (Edward Mallinckrodt Distinguished University Professor, English, 1976-); Consultant in Poetry, Library of Congress, 1963-64; Poet Laureate of the United States, 1988-. Publications include: Collected Poems of HN, 1977; Journal of the Fictive Life, 1965; The Homecoming Game, novel, 1958; Sentences, poems, 1980; Inside the Orion, poems, 1984; New & Selected Essays, 1985; Total, 26 books, poetry, fiction, criticism, memoirs; Most recent: The Oak in the Acorn: On Remembrance of Things Past & On Teaching Proust, Who Will Never Learn, 1987; War Stories: Poems About Long Ago & Now, 1987; Trying Conclusions, 1991. Contributions to: Numerous magazines & journals. Honours include: National Book Award, Pulitzer Prize, 1978; Bollingen Prize, poetry, 1980; Aiken/Taylor Award, poetry, 1987; National Medal of Arts, poetry, 1987. Memberships: American Academy of Arts & Letters; American Academy of Arts & Sciences; Chancellor, Academy of American Poets. Address: Department of English, Washington University, St Louis, Missouri 63130, USA.

NESTOR Elena, b. 13 Aug 1951, Romania. French Teacher; Journalist. Education: Diploma in Philology, Bucharest University, 1967-72; Diploma, Paris, 1987-90; Studies, Philosophy, History of Religions, France, 1987-91; Master, Comparing Literature, France, 1990. Literary Appointments: Eugene ionesco, 1986; Emil Cioran, 1986; Zaharia Stancu; Eugen Jebeleanu; Marin Sorescu; Augustin Buzura. Publications: The Soul of Fire, 1973; Rainy Weathers, stories, 1976; One Day, One Man, One Act, 1978; Leisure Romance, 1979. Contributions to: Romania Literature; Romania Libera; Scinteia Tineretului; Ramuri; Orizont; Vatra; Astra; Luceafarul Tribuna. Memberships: Writers Union, Denmark; Writers Union, Romania; Romania-American Academy, USA; Scoala Ardelesna Foundation, Romania. Address: Strandgade 6, 1401 Copenhagen, Denmark.

NEUBERGER Julia Babette Sarah, b. 27 Feb 1950, London, England. Rabbi; Author; Broadcaster. m. Anthony John Neuberger, 17 Sept 1973, 1 son, 1 daughter. Education: Newnham College,

Cambridge, 1969-73; BA, Assyriology, Hebrew, Cambridge, MA, USA, 1975; Rabbanic Ordination, Leo Baeck College, 1977. Publications: Jadaism, for children, 1986; Caring for Dying People of Different Faiths, 1987; Days of Decision, 4 vols (editor), 1987; Whatever's Happening to Women? 1991; A Necessary End (editor with John White), 1991; Ethics and Healthcare: Research Ethics Committees in the UK, 1992; The Things that Matter (ed), an anthology of Women's Spiritual Poetry, 1993. Contributions to: Jewish Chronicle; Journal of STD and AIDS; Vogue; Cosmopolitan; Others; Reviews to: Sunday Times; Telegraph; Sunday Express; Mail on Sunday; Evening Standard. Membership: Fellow, Royal Society of Arts. Literary Agent: Carol Smith. Address: 36 Orlando Road, London SW4 0LF, England.

NEUGEBOREN Jay, b. 30 May 1938, New York, USA. Writer. Education: BA, Columbia University, 1959; MA, Indiana University, 1963. Appointments: Visiting Writer, Stanford University, 1966-67; Writer in Residence, University of Massachusetts, 1971-. Publications: The Stolen Jew, 1981; Before My Life Began, 1985; Big Man, 1966; Sams Legacy, 1974; POLI, 1989; Corky's Brother, 1969. Contributions to: The Atlantic: The American Scholar; Tri Quarterly; Sport, and others. Honours: Transatlantic Review Novella Award, 1967; National Endowment for Arts Fellow, 1974, 1989; Guggenheim Fellow, 1978; Present Tense Award, Best Novel, 1981; Wallant Memorial Prize, Best novel, 1985; PEN Syndicated Fiction Prize, 1982-88. Memberships: Authors Guild; PEN. Literary Agent: Richard Parks, New York City, USA. Address: 35 Harrison Avenue, Northampton, MA 01060, USA.

NEUMEYER Peter F, b. 4 Aug 1929. Professor; Writer. m. Helen Wight Snell, 28 Dec 1952, 3 s. Education: BA, 1951, MA, 1955, PhD, 1963, University of California, Berkeley. Appointments: Assistant Professor, Harvard University, 1963-69; Associate Professor, SUNY (Stony Brook), 1969-75; Professor Chairman, Department of English, West Virginia University, 1975-78; Professor, San Diego State University, 1978-. Publications: Kafkas, The Castle, 1969; Donald and the ..., 1969; Donald Has a Difficulty, 1970; The Faithful Fish, 1971; Elements of Fiction (coeditor), 1974; Homage to John Clare, 1980; Image and Makes (coeditor), 1984; The Phantom of the Opera (adapted), 1988; The Annotated Charlotte's Web, 1994; The Annotated Charlotte's Web, 1994. Contribution to: The Creation of Charlottes Web from Drafts to Book, Horn Book, Oct and Dec 1982; Franz Kafka, Sugar Baron, Modern Fiction Studies, Spring 1971. Address: 7968 Windsor Drive, La Mesa, CA 91941, USA.

NEUSTADT Richard E, b. 1919, USA. Writer on Politics and Government. Appointments: Associate Dean of Kennedy School of Government, 1965-75, Director Institutes of Politics, 1966-71, Lucius Littauer Professor, 1975-86, Douglas Dillon Professor of Government, 1987-89, Emeritus, 1989-, Harvard University, Cambridge, Massachusetts; Economist, Office of Price Administration, Washington DC, 1942; US Navy, 1942-46, Staff Member, Bureau of the Budget 1946-50; Member, White House Staff 1950-53; Professor of Government, Columbia University, New York City, 1954-65; Special Consultant, Sub-Committee on National Policy Machinary, US Senate, Washington DC, 1959-61; Member, Advisory Board, Commission on Money and Credit, 1960-61; Special Consultant to President Kennedy, 1961-63; Bureau of the Budget, 1961-70; Department of State, 1963 and to President Johnson, 1964-66; Council on Foreign Relations, 1963; Associate Member, Nuffield College, Oxford, 1964-67, 1990-93; Visiting Professor, University of Essex, 1994-95. Publications: Presidential Power, 1960, 1990; Alliance Politics, 1970; The Swine Flu Affair (with Harvey Fineberg), 1978, republished as The Epidemic That Never Was, 1982; Thinking in Time (with E R May), 1986. Memberships: International Institute of Strategic Studies, 1968. Address: Harvard, 79 JFK St, Cambridge, MA 02138, USA.

NEUSTATTER Angela Lindsay, b. 24 Sept 1943, Buckinghamshire, England. Journalist. Author. 2 sons. Education: Regent Street Polytechnic, London; Diploma in Journalism. Publications: Hyenas in Petticoats - A Look at 20 Years of Feminism, 1989; Twiggy - Health and Beauty, 1985; Mixed Feelings, 1986; Getting the Right Job; Working for Yourself. Contributions to: Guardian; The Times; Observer; Sunday Telegraph; Daily Telegraph. Honours: Mixed Feelings selected for Feminist Top Twenty List, 1986 and winner of the Institute for the Study of Drug Dependency award, 1994. Literary Agent: Jane Bradish-Ellames, Curtis Brown. Address: 32 Highbury Place, London N5, England.

NEVES Augusto. See: CARDOSO PIRES Joao.

NEVILLE Robert Cummings, b. 1 May 1939, St Louis, Missouri, USA. Philosophy and religion educator. m. Elizabeth Egan, 3 daughters. Education: BA, 1960; MA, 1962; PhD, 1963, Yale University; Ordained Elder, United Methodist Church, 1966. Publications: God the Creator, 1968; The Cosmology of Freedom, 1974; Operating on the Mind, (ed with Gaylin & Meister), 1975; Soldier Sage Saint, 1978; Creativity and God, 1980; Reconstruction of Thinking, 1981; The Tao and the Diamon, 1982; the Puritan Smile, 1987; New Essays in Metaphysics (editor), 1987; The Recovery of the Measure, 1989; A Theology Primer, 1991; Behind the Masks of God, 1991; The Highroad around Modernism, 1992; Eternity and Time's Flow, 1993; Normative Cultures, 1995; The Truth of the Broken Symbols, 1995. Contributions to: Articles to professional journals. Memberships: American Academy of Religion, Board of Directors, 1982-; Chairman, Research and scholarship Committee, 1990-92; Long-range Planning Committee, 1985-92; Vice-President, President Elect, President, 1990-92, Executive Committee, 1990-92, Missouri East Annual Conference, United Methodist Church; American Theological Society (Exec Comm 1980-83); American Philosophical Association; (Exec Comm 1983-85); Metaphysical Society of America, President, 1988. Address: Boston University School of Theology, 745 Commonwealth Avenue, Boston, MA 02215, USA.

NEVINS Francis M(ichael) Jr, b. 1943, USA. Writer of Mystery, Crime, Suspense Literature. Appointments: Assisstant Professor, 1971-75, Associate Professor,1975-78, Professor, 1978-, St Louis University School of Law; Admitted to the New Jersey Bar, 1967; Assistant to the Editor in Chief, Clark Boardman Co, law publishers, New York City, 1967; Served in US Army, 1968-69; Staff Attorney, Middlesex County Legal Services Corp, New Brunswick, New Jersey, 1970-71. Publications: novels: Publish and Perish, 1975; Corrupt and Ensnare, 1978; The 120 - Hour Clock, 1986; The Ninety Million Dollar Mouse, 1987. Non-fiction: Detectionary (with 4 co-authors), 1971; Royal Bloodline: Elley Queen, Author and Detective, 1974; Missouri Probate: Intestacy, Wills and Basic Administration, 1983; The Films of Hopalong Cassidy, 1988; Cornell Woolrich: First You Dream , Then You Die, 1988; Bar-20: The Life of Clarence E Mulford, Creator of Hopalong Cassidy, 1993; fiction edited or co-edited: Nightwebs, 1971; The Good Old Stuff, 1983; Exeunt Murderers, 1983; Buffet for Unwelcome Guests, 1983; More Good Old Stuff, 1985; Carnival of Crime, 1985; Hitchcock in Prime Time, 1985; The Best of Ellery Queen, 1985; Leopold's Way, 1985; The Adventures of Henry Turnbuckle, 1987; Better Mousetraps, 1988; Mr President- Private Eye, 1988; Death on Television, 1989; Little Boxes of Bewilderment, 1989; The Night My Friend, 1991; non-fiction edited or co-edited: The Mystery Writer's Art, 1970; Mutiplying Villainies, 1973. Honours: Edgar Award from Mystery Writers of America for Royal Bloodline: Ellery Queen Author and Detective, 1975; Edgar Award from Mystery Writers of America for Cornell Woolrich: First You Dream, Then You Die, 1988. Address: 7045 Cornell, University City, MO 63130, USA.

NEVZGLIADOVA Elena Vsevolodovna (Elena Ushakova), b. 2 June 1939, Leningrad, Russia; Poet; Literary Critic. m. Aleksandr Semyonovich Kushner, 1 son. Education: Graduate, 1962, PhD, 1974, Philological Faculty, Leningrad University. Publications: Nochnoe Solntse, (A Night Sun), 1991. Contributions to: Neva; Znamya; Syntaxis; Raduga; Zvezda; Novii Mir; Almanakh Petropol. Memberships: Writers' Union. Address: Kaluzhskii per 9 apt 48, St Petersburg 193015, Russia.

NEW Anthony Sherwood Brooks, b. 14 Aug 1924, London, England. Architect. m. Elizabeth Pegge, 11 Apr 1970, 1 son, 1 daughter. Education: Northern Polytechnic School of Architecture, 1941-43, 1947-51. Publications: Observer's Book of Postage Stamps, 1967; Observer's Book of Cathedrals, 1972; A Guide to the Cathedrals of Britain, 1980; A Guide to the Abbeys of England and Wales, 1985; New Observer's Book of Stamp Collecting, 1986; A Guide to the Abbeys of Scotland, 1988. Memberships: Fellow, Society of Antiquaries; Fellow, Royal Institute of British Architects; Institution of Structural Engineers. Address: 26 Somerset Road, New Barnet, Herts EN5 1RN, England.

NEWBY (Percy) Howard, b. 25 June 1918, Crowborough, Sussex, England. Author. m. 12 July 1945, 2 daughters. Education: St Paul's College, Cheltenham. Publications: A Journey to the Interior, 1945; The Picnic at Sakkara, 1955; Something to Answer For, 1968; Kith, 1977; Feelings Have Changed, 1981; Leaning in the Wind, 1986; Coming in with the Tide, 1991; Something About Women, 1995; 12 other novels; 3 historical studies; 2 works of literary criticism; 2

children's books. Honours: Atlantic Award, 1946; Somerset Maugham Prize, 1948; Yorkshire Post Fiction Award, 1968; Booker Prize, 1969; CBE, 1972. Membership: Society of Authors. Literary Agent: David Higham Associates. Address: Garsington House, Garsington, Oxford OX44 9AB, England.

NEWCOMER James William, b. 14 Mar 1912, Gibsonburg, Ohio, USA. College Professor; Vice Chancellor Emeritus. m. 17 Aug 1946, 1 s, 2 d. Education: PhB, Kenyon College; MA, University of Michigan; PhD, University of Iowa. Publications: Criticism: Maria Edgeworth the Novelist, 1967; Maria Edgeworth, 1973; Lady Morgan the Novelist, 1990; poetry: The Merton Barn Poems, 1979; The Resonance of Grace, 1984; The Grand Duchy of Luxembourg (history), 1984; The Nationhood of Luxembourg (essays), 1994; Luxembourg (essays), 1995. Contributions to: College English; Nineteenth Century Fiction; Criticism; Books at Iowa; Arlington Quarterly; Descant; Sands. Honours: Phi Beta Kappa; Officer in Order of Merit and Honorary Member, L'Institut Grand-Ducal, Duchy of Luxembourg. Address: 1100 Elizabeth Boulevard, Fort Worth, TX 76110, USA.

NEWLANDS Willy (William Newlands of Lauriston), b. 5 Nov 1934, Perth, Scotland. Travel Writer. m. (1) 1 son, 2 daughters, (2) Dorothy Straton Walker, 1985. Career includes: Scripwriter, Presenter, TV travel series, Grampian/STV, 1993-94. Contributions to: Articles on travel and wildlife to Daily Telegraph, The Observer, Mail on Sunday, The Guardian, The Times, Daily Express, The Field. Honours: Churchill Fellow, 1968; Travel Writer of the Year, 1983-84, 1987-88. Address: Lauriston Castle, by Montrose, Angus DD10 0DJ, Scotland.

NEWMAN Andrea, b. 7 Feb 1938, Dover, England. Writer (div). Education: BA, Honours, English, 1960, MA, 1972, London University. Publications: A Share of the World, 1964; Mirage, 1965; The Cage, 1966; Three Into Two Won't Go, 1967; Alexa, 1968; A Bouquet of Barbed Wire, 1969; Another Bouquet, 1977; An Evil Streak, 1977; Mackenzie, 1980; A Sense of Guilt, 1988; Triangles, 1990; A Gift of Poison, 1991. Contributions to: Woman; Woman's Own; Woman's Realm; Marie-Claire; GQ; Living; TV Scripts for Bouquet of Barbed Wire; Another Bouquet; Mackenzie; A Sense of Guilt. Memberships: PEN; Writers' Guild. Literary Agent: A P Watt. Address: A P Watt, 20 John Street, London WC1N 2DR, England.

NEWMAN Aubrey N, b. 1927, British. Writer on History, Biography; Professor in History, University of Leicester, England. Appointments: Research Fellow, Bedford College, University of London, 1954-55; President, Jewish Historical Society of England, 1977-79. Publications: The Parliamentary Diary of Sir Edward Knatchbull 1722-1730, 1963; The Stanhopes of Chevening: A Family Biography, 1969; (compiler with Helen Miller); A Bibliography of English History, 1485-1760; The United Synagogue 1870-1970, 1977; The Jewish East End 1940-1939, 1981; The Board of Deputin, 1760-1985, a brief survey, 1987; The World Turned Inside Out, new views on George II, 1988. Address: Department of History, University of Leicester, Leicester, England.

NEWMAN G F, b. 22 May 1945, England. Writer. Publications: Sir, You Bastard, 1970; You Nice Bastard, 1972; You Flash Bastard, 1974; The Govnor, 1977; The Nation's Health, 1982; Law and Order, 1977, 1983; The List, 1984; The Men with Guns, 1985; Set a Thief, 1986; The Testing Ground, 1987; Operation Bad Apple, play; An Honourable Trade, play. Literary Agent: Elaine Steel. Address: Wessington Court, Woolhope, Hereford HR1 4QN, England.

NEWMAN John Kevin, b. 17 Aug 1928, Bradford, Yorkshire, England. Classics Educator. m. Frances M Stickney, 8 Sept 1970, 1 s, 2 d. Education: BA, Lit Humaniores, 1950, BA, Russian, 1952, MA, 1953, Oxford University; PhD, Bristol University, 1967. Appointments: Classics Master, St Francis Xavier College, Liverpool, 1952-54; Classics Master, Downside School, Somerset, 1955-69; Faculty, 1969-, Professor Classics, 1980-, University of Illinois, Urbana, USA; Editor, Illinois Classical Studies, 1982-87. Publications: Augustus and the New Poetry, 1967; The Concept of Vates in Augustan Poetry, 1967; Latin Compositions, 1976; Golden Violence, 1976; Dislocated: An American Carnival, 1977; Pindar's Art, 1984; The Classical Epic Tradition, 1986; Roman Catullus, 1990; Lelio Gudiccioni, Latin Poems, 1992. Honours: Silver Medals, Vatican, Rome, 1960, 1962, 1965. Membership: Senior Common Room, Corpus Christi College Oxford, 1985-86. Address: 703 W Delaware Ave, Urbana, IL 61801, USA.

NEWMAN (Jerry Coleman) Joseph, b. 17 Feb 1935, Montreal, Quebec, Canada. Novelist. Education: George Williams & Tomoto Universities, 1959. Appointments: Assistant Professor, 1972-77, Associate Professor, 1977-, University of British Columbia, Vancouver. Publications: We Always Take Care of Our Own, 1965; A Russian Novel, 1973; Stories: New Canadian Writing, 1969; A Time to Heal, 1971; Your Green Coast, 1973; That Old David Copperfield Kind of Crap, 1973; The Best Lay I Ever Had, 1974; Fallin in Love Again, 1974; The Game of Limping, 1975; The Last Beginning, The Last, The Last, 1975; Radio & TV Plays. Honours: Canada Bursary and Grants. Address: Dept of Creative Writing, University of British Columbia, Vancouver, British Columbia V6T 1W5, Canada.

NEWMAN Leslea, b. 5 Nov 1955, Brooklyn, New York, USA. Writer; Teacher of Women's Writing Workshops. Education: BS, Education, University of Vermont, USA, 1977; Certificate in Poetics, Naropa Institute, 1980. Appointment: Massachusetts Artists Fellowship in Poetry, 1989. Publications: A Letter to Harvey Milk, 1988; Good Enough to Eat, 1986; Love Me Like You Mean It, 1987; Heather Has Two Mommies, 1989; Bubbe Meisehs by Shayneh Maidelehs, 1989; Secrets, 1990. Contributions to: Sojourner, Heresies, Dark Horse, Siniste Wisdom, Telephone, Common Lives, Lilith, New Age Magazine. Honour: 2nd Place Finalist, Raymond Carver Short Story Competition, 1987. Memberships: Authors Guild and Authors League of America; Poets and Writers Inc. Address: PO Box 815, Northampton, MA 01061, USA.

NEWMAN Margaret. See: **POTTER Margaret.**

NEWMAN Peter Charles, b. 19 May 1929, Vienna. Author; Journalist. Education: MA, Economics, University of Toronto and McGill. Appointments: Assistant Editor, The Financial Post, 1951-55; Ottawa Editor, Maclean's Magazine, 1955-64; Ottawa Editor, Toronto Daily Star, 1964-69; Editor-in-Chief, Toronto Daily Star, 1969-71; Editor-in-Chief, Maclean's Magazine, 1971-82; Director, Maclean Hunter Limited, 1972-83; Weekly interview show, Global Television Network, 1981-87; Senior Contributing Editor, Macleans. Publications: Flame of Power, 1959; The Distemper of our Times, 1968; The Canadian Establishment, 1975; The Establishment Man, 1982; Company of Adventurers, 1985; Caesers of the Wilderness, 1987; Empire of the Bay, 1989. Honours: Companion Order of Canada, National Newspaper Award, Feature Writing, 1966; President's Medal, University of Western Ontario, 1974; Quill Award as Journalist of Year, 1977; Knight-Commander in the Order of St Lazarus, 1983; National Business Writing Achievement Award, 1986; The Bob Edwards Award, 1989. Address: 2594 Panorama Drive, Deep Cove, North Vancouver, British Columbia, V7G 1V5, Canada.

NEWTON David Edward, b. 18 June 1933, Grand Rapids, Michigan, USA. University Educator; Science Writer. Education: AS, Grand Rapids Junior College, 1953; BS with high distinction, Chemistry, 1955, MA, Education, 1961, University of Michigan; DEd, Science Education, Harvard University, 1971; Various short courses, Cornell University, Oregon State University, Atlanta University, Hampshire College. Publications: Many books including: Chemistry Problems, 1962, 3rd edition 1984; Understanding Venereal Disease, 1973, 2nd edition 1978; Math in Everyday Life, 1975, 2nd edition 1991; Scott Foresman Biology (with Irwin Slesnick, A LaVon Blazar, Alan McCormack, Fred Rasmussen), 1980, 2nd edition 1985; Science and Social Issues, 1983, 3rd edition 1992; Biology Updated, 1984, 2nd edition 1987; Chemistry Updated, 1985, 2nd edition 1989; An Introduction to Molecular Biology, 1986; Science Ethics, 1987; Particle Accelerators, 1989; Taking a Stand Against Environmental Pollution, 1990; Land Use, 1991; James Watson and Francis Crick: A Search for DNA and Beyond, 1992; Contributions to books: Numerous teaching aids. Contributions to: The Bulletin of the National Association of Secondary School Principals; School Science and Mathematics; The High School Journal; Journal of Homosexuality; Appraisal; Several others. Honours: Sloane Scholarship, University of Michigan, 1958; Star '60 Award, National Science Teachers Association; William Payne Scholar, Horace Rackham Graduate School, University of Michigan, 1961-62; Shell Merit Fellow, 1964; Outstanding Young Science Educator of the Year, AETS, 1968. Memberships: Phi Beta Kappa; Phi Kappa Phi; Phi Lambda Upsilon; Delta Pi Alpha; National Science Teachers Association; Association for the Education of Teachers in Science; American Association for the Advancement of Science; National Association of Science Writers, Reviewer, Reviewer, Children's Science Book Review Committee. Address: Instructional Horizons Inc, 297 Addison Street, San Francisco, CA 94131, USA.

NEWTON D(wight) B(ennett), b. 1916, American. Writer of Westerns/Adventure. Appointments: Freelance writer since 1946; Story consultant and staff writer for TV series Wagon Train, 1957, Death Valley Days, 1958 and Tales of Wells Fargo. Publications: Shotgun Guard, 1950, in UK as Stagecoach Guard, 1951; Six-Gun Gamble, 1951; Guns along the Wickiup, 1953; Rainbow Rider, 1954, in US paperback as Triple Trouble, 1978; Syndicate Gun, 1972; Massacre Valley, 1973; Range Tramp, 1975; Bounty on Bannister, 1975; Broken Spur, 1977; as Dwight Bennett: Stormy Range, 1951, in UK (as D B Newton) Range Feud, 1953; Lost Wolf River, 1954; Border Graze, 1952; Top Hand, 1955; The Avenger, 1956; Cherokee Outlet, 1961; The Oregon Rifles, 1962; Rebel Trail, 1963; The Big Land, 1972; The Guns of Ellsworth, 1973; Hangman's Knot, 1975; The Cheyenne Encounter, 1976; West of Railhead, 1977; The Texans, 1979; Disaster Creek, 1981; as Clement Hardin: Hillbent for a Hangrope, 1954; Cross Me in Gunsmoke, 1957; The Lurking Gun, 1961; The Badge Shooters, 1962; Outcast at Ute Bend, 1965; The Ruthless Breed, 1966; The Paxman Feud, 1967; The Oxbow Deed, 1967; Ambush Reckoning, 1968; Sheriff of Sentinel, 1969; Colt Wages, 1970; Stage Line to Rincon, 1971; as Dan Temple: Outlaw River, 1955; The Man from Idaho, 1956; Bullet Lease, 1957; The Love Goddess, 1962; Gun and Star, 1964; as Hank Mitchum: Station 1: Dodge City, 1982; Station 2: Laredo, 1982; Station 3: Tombstone, 1983 ; Station 6: Santa Fe, 1983; Station 11: Deadwood, 1984; Station 13: Carson City, 1984; Station 20: Leadville, 1985; Station 26: Tulsa, 1986. Memberships: Founding Member 1953, Secretary/Treasurer 1953-58, 1967-71, Western Writers of America. Literary Agent: Golden West Literary Agency, Oregon, USA. Address: 11 N W Kansas Avenue, Bend, OR 97701, USA.

NEWTON Suzanne, b. 1936, USA. Writer of children's fiction. Appointments: Consultant in Creative Writing in North Carolina's public schools, 1972; Freelance writer, Writer in Residence, Meredith College, Raleigh, North Carolina. Publications: Purro and the Prattleberries, 1971; c/o Arnold's corners, 1974; What are You Up To, William Thomas, 1977; Reubella and Old Focus Home, 1978; MV Sexton Speaking, 1981; I Will Call it Geogie's Blues, 1983; An End to Perfect, 1984; A Place Between, 1986; Where are You When I Need You? 1991. Address: 841 - A Barringer Drive, Raleigh, NC 27606, USA.

NEY James W, b. 28 Jul 1932, Nakura, Kenya. Educator. m. J Marie Allen, 12 Jun 1954, 2 s. Education: AB, 1955; AM, Wheaton College, IL, 1957; EdD, University Of Michigan. Publications include: Linguistics, Language Learning And Composition In The Grades, 1975; Semantic Structures For The Syntax Of Complements And Auxiliaries In English, 1981; Transformational Grammar, 1988; American College Life In English Communication, 1991; American English In A Situational Context, 1991; GRE Time Saver, 1992; GMAT Time Saver, 1993. Contributions include: Written Communication, Volume 3, 1986; The Modern Language Journal, 1990; Lenguas Modernas, 1992. Memberships: Teachers of English to Speakers of Other Languages; Linguistic Society of America; Canadian Linguistic Association. Address: English Department, Arizona State University, Tempe, AZ 85287-0302, USA.

NEYREY Jerome H, b. 5 Jan 1940, New Orleans, Louisiana, USA. Professor. Education: BA, 1963; MA, 1964; MDiv, 1970; MTh, 1972; PhD, 1977; STL, 1987. Appointments: Weston School of Theology, 1977-92; University of Notre Dame, Notre Dame, Indiana, 1992-. Publications: The Passion According to Luke, 1983; Christ is Community, 1983; An Ideology of Revolt, 1988; Calling Jesus Names, 1988; The Resurrection Stories, 1988; Paul, In Other Words, 1990; The Social World of Luke - Acts, 1991. Contributions to: Articles regularly to: Catholic Biblical Quarterly; Journal of Biblical Literature; Biblica; Novum Testamentum; New Testament Studies. Honours: Bannan Fellowship, Santa Clara University, 1984-85; Young Scholars Grant, 1984; ATS Grant, 1989; Visiting Professor, Pontifical Biblical Institute, Rome, 1989; Lilly Foundation, 1989; Plowshares, 1990. Memberships: Catholic Biblical Association; Society of Biblical Literature, New England Region President 1990; Executive Secretary, Context Group. Address: Department of Theology, University of Notre Dame, Notre Dame, IN 46556, USA.

NEZZLE. See: **SAUNDERS Nezzle Methelda.**

NGUGI J(ames) T, (Wa Thiongio Ngugi), b. 5 Jan 1938, Kamiriithu, Kenya. Literary and Political Journalist; Author. Education: University College, Kampala; Leeds University, Yorkshire. Literary appointment: Former Editor, Penpoint magazine, Kampala, Uganda. Publications: As J T Ngugi or Ngugi Wa Thiong'o: The Black Hermit, play, 1962; This Time Tomorrow, play, 1964; Weep not, Child, 1964; The River Between, 1965; A Grain of Wheat, 1967; Homecoming: Essays on African and Caribbean Literature, Culture and Politics, 1972; Secret Lives, 1974; Petals of Blood, 1977; The Trial of Dedan Kimathi (with M G Mugo), 1977; Writers in Politics, 1980; Devil on the Cross, 1981; Detained: A Writer's Prison Diary, 1981; Education for a National Culture, 1981; I Will Marry When I Want, play, 1982; Barrel of a Pen: Resistance to Repression in Neo-Colonial Kenya, 1983. Contributions to: Sunday Nation, Nairobi. Address: c/o William Heinemann Ltd, 10 Upper Grosvenor Street, London W1X 9PA, England.

NGUGI Wa Thiongio. See: NGUGI J(ames) T.

NGUYEN Ngoc Huy, b. 2 Nov 1924, Cholon, Vietnam, immigrated to the USA, 1975. Research Associate; Writer. m. Thu Thi Duong, 1952 (dec 1974), 1 son, 1 daughter. Education: Graduate of Institute of Political Studies, 1958, Licence en Droit 1959, DES en Science Politique, 1960, Doctorate en Science Politique, 1963, University Paris. Appointments include: Member of central executive committee of Vietnam's Dai Viet Nationalist Party 1945-64; Founder and General Secretary of Vietnam's Neo Dai Viet Party, 1964-75; Research Associate, Harvard Law School, Harvard University, Cambridge, Massachusetts, 1976-. Publications: Hon Viet (Vietnamese Soul), poems, 1950, 2nd edition (Paris) 1984, 3rd edition (San Jose, California) 1985; Dan toc sinhton (The Doctrine of the Nation's Survival) 2 vols Dai Viet Party, 1964; De tai Nguoi uu tu trong chanh tri Trung Quoc co thoi (Elite Notions in Traditional Chinese Political Thought), 1969; Lich su cac hoc thuyet chanh tri (A History of Political Theories), 2 vols, 1970-71; (Translator from Chinese into Vietnamese) Han Fei, Han Phi Tu (Master Han Fei) 2 vols, Lua Thieng, 1974; (with Stephen B Young), Understanding Vietnam, 1982; A New Strategy to Defend the Free World Against Communist Expansion, 1985; Pour une strategie de defense du monde libre contre l'expansion communiste (A New Strategy to Defend the Free World Against Communist Expansion), 1985; Cac an so chanh tri trong tieu thuyet vo hiep Kim Dung (The Hidden Political Thoughts in Jin Yung's Martial-Arts Fiction Novels), 1986; (with Ta Van Tai and Tran Van Liem), The Le Code: Law in Traditional Vietnam: A Comparative Sino-Vietnamese Legal Study With Historical-Juridicial Analysis and Annotations, 1987; (with Stephen B Young), Viture and Law: Human Rights in Traditional China and Vietnam, 1988. Contributions to: Poems and periodicals. Address: 72-74 Shirley Avenue, Revere, MA 02151, USA.

NI CHUILLEANAIN Eilean, b. 28 Nov 1942. Lecturer. m. Macdara Woods, 27 June 1978, 1 son. Education: BA 1962, MA 1964, University College, Cork; BLitt, Lady Margaret Hall, Oxford, 1969. Appointments: Lecturer in Mediaeval and Renaissance English, Trinity College, Dublin, 1966-; Professor of American History & Institutions, Oxford University, 1969-78. Publications: Acts and Monuments, 1972; Site of Ambush, 1975; Cork, 1977; The Second Voyage, 1977, 1986; The Rose-Geranium, 1981; Irish Women: Image and Achievement (editor), 1985; The Magdalene Sermon, 1989. Contributions to: An Editor of Cyphers Literary Magazine; Articles in Journal of Ecclesiastical History; Poems in many magazines. Honours: Irish Times Poetry Prize, 1966; Patrick Kavanagh Pize, 1972. Address: 2 Quarry Hollow, Headington, Oxford OX3 8JR, England.

NICHOL B(arrie) P(hillip), b. 1944, Canadian. Novels/Short Stories, Poetry. Appointment: Co-editor, Gronk Magazine, Toronto. Publications include: Cycles Etc, 1965; Scraptures 2-4, 10-11, 5 vols, 1965-67; (with D Aylward), Strange Grey Town, 1960; Tonto or, 1966; Calendar, 1966; A Little Pome for Yur Fingertips, 1966; Fodder, Fodder, 1966; Portrait of David, 1966; A Vision of the U of T Stacks, 1966; Langwedge, 1966; Alaphbit, 1966; Stan's Ikon, 1966; The Birth of O, 1966, followed by later titles including: The Teaching of Arress Kinken, 1982; Three Drafts, 1982; Ruins of C, 1983; Song for Saint Ein, 1983; New H Blues, 1983; Haiku (for David A), 1983; Hologram 4, 1983; Wall, 1983; Possibilities of the Poem, 1984; To the End of the Block (for children), 1984; Theory 1-4, 1984; Zygal, 1985; The Martyrology Book 6, 1987.

NICHOLLS Christine Stephanie, b. 23 Jan 1943, Bury, Lancashire, England. Editor. m. Anthony James Nicholls, 12 Mar 1966, 1 son, 2 daughters. Education: BA, 1964, MA, 1968, Lady Margaret Hall, Oxford; DPhil, St Antony's College, Oxford, 1968. Appointments: Henry Charles Chapman Research Fellow, Institute of Commonwealth Studies, London University, 1968-69; Freelance Writer, BBC, 1970-74; Research Assistant, 1975-76; Joint Editor, 1977-89, Editor, 1989-, Dictionary of National Biography Supplements. Publications: The

Swahili Coast, 1971; Cataract (with P Awdry), 1985; Dictionary of National Biography 1961-70 (joint editor), 1981, 1971-80 (joint editor), 1986, 1981-85 (joint editor), 1990, Missing Persons (editor), 1990. Address: 27 Davenant Road, Oxford OX2 8BU, England.

NICHOLS Grace, b. 18 Feb 1950, Guyana. Journalist; Teacher; Poet. Education: University of Guyana, Georgetown. Appointments include: Freelance Journalist, Guyana, 1977. Publications: I Is a Long Memories Woman, 1983; The Fat Black Womans Poems, 1984; Come on Into My Tropical Garden, 1988; Lazy Thoughts of a Lazy Woman, 1989; Novel, Whole of a Morning Sky, 1989; Editor, Black Poetry, 1988; Stories for Children: Trust You Wriggly, 1980; Leslyn in London, 1984; The Discovery, 1986. Honours include: British Arts Council Bursay, 1988. Address: c/o Anthea Morton Saner, Curtis Brown Ltd, 162-68 Regent Str, London W1R 5TB, England.

NICHOLS John, b. 1940, Berkeley, California, USA. Freelance Writer; Photographer. 1 s, 1 d. Education: Hamilton College, New York. Publications: The Sterile Cuckoo, 1965; The Wizard of Loneliness, 1966; The Milagro Beanfield War, 1974; The Magic Journey, 1978; A Ghost in the Music, 1979; If Mountains Die, 1979; The Nirvana Blues, 1981; The Last Beautiful Days of Autumn, 1982; On the Mesa, 1986; American Blood, 1987; A Fragile Beauty, 1987; The Sky's the Limit, 1990; An Elegy for September, 1992; Keep It Simple, 1993; Conjugal Bliss, 1994; The Holiness of Water, 1995. Address: Box 1165, Taos, NM 87571, USA.

NICHOLS Pamela Amber McCurdy, b. 25 June 1956, Columbus, Ohio, USA. Nurse. m. Jerry Lee Nichols, 26 June 1974, 1 s, 1 d. Education: Nursing degree WVNCC, Wheeling WVA, 1994. Literary appointments: Teacher of Poetry, Monroe County School, 1980. Publications: After the Battle, 1979; Touch the Sun, 1982; Lampslight, 1986; Oh Beloved, My Beloved (Part 1), 1987; For My Persecuted Brethren, 1988; Wedding Song, 1989. Contributions to: International Marriage Encounter Magazine; Northern Lights Literary Magazine WVNCC. Honours: Award of Merit, 1986, 1987, 1988. Memberships: National Society of Published Poets. Address: 46430 Buckio Road, Woodsfield, OH 43793, USA.

NICHOLS Peter Richard, b. 31 July 1927. Playwright. m. Thelma Reed, 1960, 1 son, 3 daughters (1 dec). Appointments: Actor, 1950-55; Teacher, Primary and Secondary Schools, 1958-60; Arts Council Drama Panel, 1973-75; Playwright in Residence, Guthrie Theater, Minneapolis, Minnesota, USA, 1976. Publications: TV plays: Walk on the Grass, 1959; Promenade, 1960; Ben Spray, 1961; The Reception, 1961; The Big Boys, 1961; Continuity Man, 1963; Ben Again, 1963; The Heart of the Country, 1963; The Hooded Terror, 1963; When the Wind Blows, 1964, later adapted for radio; The Brick Umbrella, 1968; Daddy Kiss It Better, 1968; The Gorge, 1968; Hearts and Flowers, 1971; The Common, 1973; Films: Catch Us If You Can, 1965; Georgy Girl, 1967; Joe Egg, 1971; The National Health, 1973; Privates on Parade, 1983; Stage plays: A Day in the Death of Joe Egg, 1967; The National Health, 1969; Forget-me-not Lane, 1971; Chez Nous, 1973; The Freeway, 1974; Privates on Parade, 1977; Born in the Gardens, 1979, televised, 1986; Passion Play, 1980, Poppy, musical, 1982; A Piece of My Mind, 1986; Feeling You're Behind, autobiography, 1984. Honours: Standard Best Play Award, Joe Egg, 1967, National Health, 1969, Passion Play, 1983; Evening Standard Best Comedy, Society of West End Theatre Best Comedy, Ivor Novello Best Musical Awards, Privates On Parade, 1977; Society of West End Theatre Best Musical, Poppy, 1982; Fellow, Royal Society of Literature, 1983; Tony Award, 1985. Literary Agent: Rochelle Stevens, 2 Terrett's Place, London N1 8PS, England. Address: 22 Belsize Park Gardens, London NW3 4LH, England.

NICHOLS (Joanne) Ruth, b. 4 Mar 1948, Toronto, Canada. Novelist; Theologian. m. W N Houston, 21 Sept 1974. Education: BA Hons, University of British Columbia, 1967; MA Religious Studies 1972, PhD Theology 1977, McMaster University. Publications: A Walk Out of the World, 1969; The Marrow of the World, 1972; Song of the Pearl, 1976; The Left-Handed Spirit, 1978; What Dangers Deep: A Story of Philip Sidney, 1992; Ceremony of Innocence, 1969; The Burning of the Rose, 1989. Honours: Award, Shankar's International Literary Contest for Children, 1965, 1963; Gold Medal, Canadian Association of Children's Librarians, 1972; Woodrow Wilson Fellow, 1968; Fellow of The Canada Council 1971-72; Research Fellow of The Canada Council, 1978. Address: 276 Laird Drive, Toronto, MY6 3XY, Canada.

NICHOLSON Christina. See: NICOLE Christopher Robin.

NICHOLSON Geoffrey Joseph, b. 4 Mar 1953, Sheffield, England. Writer. m. Tessa Robinson, 31 Jan 1984, div 1989. Education: Gonville and Caius College, Cambridge, 1972-75; MA, English, Cambridge; MA, Drama, University of Essex, Colchester, 1978. Publications: Street Sleeper, 1987; The Knot Garden, 1989; What We Did On Our Holidays, 1990; Hunters and Gatherers, 1991; Big Noises, 1991; The Food Chain, 1992; Day Trips to the Desert, 1992; The Errol Flynn Novel, 1993; Still Life with Volkswagens, 1994. Contributions to: Regularly, Ambit magazine. Honours: Shortlisted, Yorkshire 1st Work Award, 1987. Literary Agent: A P Watt, London, England. Address: 23 Sutherland Avenue, London W9 2HE, England.

NICHOLSON Margaret Bede (Margaret Yorke), b. 1924. Author. Appointments: Assistant Librarian, St Hilda's College, Oxford, 1959-60; Library Assistant, Christ Church, Oxford, 1963-65; Chairman, Crime Writers Association, 1979-80. Publications: Summer Flight, 1957; Pray Love Remember, 1958; Christopher, 1959; Deceiving Mirror, 1960; The China Doll, 1961; Once a Stranger, 1962; The Birthday, 1963; Full Circle, 1965; No Fury, 1967; The Apricot Bed, 1968; The Limbo Ladies, 1969; Dead in the Morning, 1970; Silent Witness, 1972; Grave Matters, 1973; No Medals for the Major, 1974; Mortal Remains, 1974; The Small Hours of the Morning, 1975; Cast for Death, 1976; The Cost of Silence, 1977; The Point of Murder, 1978; Death on Account, 1979; The Scent of Fear, 1980; The Hand of Death, 1981; Devil's Work, 1982; Find Me a Villain, 1983; The Smooth Face of Evil, 1984; Intimate Kill, 1985; Safely to the Grave, 1986; Evidence to Destroy, 1987; Speak for the Dead, 1988; Crime in Question, 1989; Admit to Murder, 1990; A Small Deceit, 1991; Criminal Damage, 1992; Dangerous to Know, 1993; Almost the Truth, 1994; Pieces of Justice, 1994. Address: c/o Curtis Brown, 162-168 Regent Street, London, W1R 5TB, England.

NICHOLSON Robin. See:NICOLE Christopher Robin.

NICK Dagmar, b. 30 May 1926, Breslau, Germany. Writer. Education: Psychology and Graphology studies, Munich, 1947-50. Publications: Poetry: Martyrer, 1947; Das Buch Holofernes, 1955; In den Ellipsen des Mondes, 1959; Zeugnis und Zeichen, 1969; Fluchtlinien, 1978; Gezählte Tage, 1986; Im Stillstanmd der Stunden, 1991; Prose: Einladung nach Israel, 1963; Rhodos, 1967; Israel gestern und heute, 1968; Sizilien, 1976; Götterinseln der Ägäis, 1981; Medea, ein Monolog, 1988; Lilith, eine Metamorphose, 1992. Contributions to: Zeit; Frankfurter Allgemeine Zeitung; Akzente; Merian; Westermanns Monatshefte; Horen; Chicago Review; International Poetry Review; Chariton Review. Honours: Liliencron Prize, Hamburg, 1948; Eichendorff Prize, 1966; Honorary Award, Gryphius Prize, 1970; Roswitha Medal, 1977; Kulturpreis Schlesien des Landes Niedersachsen, 1986; Gryphius Prize, 1993. Memberships: PEN Club; Association of German Writers. Address: Kuglmüllerstrasse 22, D 80638 Munich, Germany.

NICOL Abioseh (Davidson Sylvester Hector Willoughby Nicol), b. 1924, Sierra Leone. Author; Honorary Fellow, Christ's College, Cambridge; Former Diplomat. Publications: Alienation: An Essay, 1960; Africa: A Subjective View, 1964; The Truly Married Woman and Other Stories, 1965; Two African Tales, 1965; Africanus Horton: The Dawn of Nationalism in Modern Africa, US Edition Black Nationalism in Africa, 1867, 1969; New and Modern Roles for Commonwealth and Empire, 1976; The United Nations and Decision Making, 1978; Nigeria and the Future of Africa, 1980; Paths to Peace, 1981; The United Nations Security Council, 1981; Creative Women, 1982. Memberships: President, World Federation of United Nations Associations, 1983-87. Address: Christ's College, Cambridge CB2 3BU, England.

NICOL Davidson Sylvester Hector Willoughby. See: NICOL Abioseh.

NICOL Dominik, b. 25 Sept 1930, North Oltenia, Rumania. Writer; Photographer. Education: Baccalaureat Diploma, Rm Valcea Lyceum, 1949; Diploma in Technology and Chemistry of Antibiotics, Bucharest, 1954. Publications: Self encounter, 1979; Vacuum (colocviu de abis), 1979; Ten Oneiric sketches, 1980; Rendez-Vous sau Intalnire cu mine insumi, 1987; Vacuum-Void (bilingual edition), play, 1988; Pe portativul vietii - journal literar - 1992. Contributions to: Micro- Magazin, New York; Tricolorul magazine, Ontario; Stindardul magazine, Munich; Saptamana Muncheneza magazine, Munich; Meridiane magazine, New York; Lupta magazine, Providence, Rhode Island. Address: PO Box 411, Times Square Sta, New York, NY 10108, USA.

NICOL Donald MacGillivray, b. 1923, England. Historian; Retired Professor. Appointments include: Koraes Professor of Modern Greek and Byzantine History, Language and Literature, King's College, University of London; Retired, 1988. Publications: The Despostate of Epiros, 1957; Meteora: The Rock Monasteries of Thessaly, 1963, 2nd Edition, 1975; The Byzantine Family of Kantakouzenos 1100-1460, 1968; The Last Centuries of Byzantium 1261-1453, 1972, 2nd Edition, 1993; Byzantium: Its Ecclesiastical History and Relations with the Western World, 1972; Church and Society in the Last Centuries of Byzantium, 1979; The End of the Byzantine Empire, 1979; The Despotate of Epiros 1267-1479: A Contribution to the History of Greece in the Middle Ages, 1984; Studies in Late Byzantine History and Prosopography, 1986; Byzantium and Venice, 1988; Joannes Gennados - The Man, 1990; A Biographical Dictionary of the Byzantine Empire, 1991; The Immortal Emperor, 1992. Address: 16 Courtyards, Little Shelford, Cambridge CB2 5ER, England.

NICOLE Christopher. See: NICOLE Christopher Robin.

NICOLE Christopher Robin (Daniel Adams, Leslie Arlen, Robin Cade, Peter Grange, Nicholas Grant, Caroline Gray, Mark Logan, Simon Mackay, Christina Nicholson, Robin Nicholson, Christopher Nicole, Alan Savage, Alison York, Andrew York), b. 7 Dec 1930, Georgetown, Guyana. Novelist. m. Diana Bachmann, 8 May 1982, 4 sons, 3 daughters. Education: Harrison College, Barbados; Queen's College, Guyana; Fellow, Canadian Bankers Association. Publications: As Christopher Nicole: Ratoon, 1962; Caribee Series, 1974-78; Byron, 1979; The Haggard Series, 1980-82; The China Series, 1984-86; The Japan Series, 1984-86; Black Majesty, 2 volumes, 1984-85; The Old Glory series, 1986-88; Ship with No Name, 1987; The High Country, 1988; The Regiment, 1988; The Pearl of the Orient, 1988; As Andrew York: The Eliminator Series (9 Spy Thrillers), 1966-75); The Operation Series, 1969-71; Where the Cavern Ends, 1971; The Tallant Series, 1977-78; Dark Passage, 1976; The Combination, 1984; As Peter Grange: King Creole, 1966; The Devil's Emissary, 1968; As Robin Cade: The Fear Dealers, 1974; As Mark Logan: The Tricolour Series, 1976-78; As Christina Nicholson: The Power and the Passion, 1977; The Savage Sands, 1978; The Queen of Paris, 1983; As Alison York: The Fire and the Rape, 1979; The Scented Sword, 1980; As Robin Nicholson: The Friday Spy, 1981; As Leslie Arlen: The Borodin Series, 1980-85; As Daniel Adams: The Brazilian Series, 1982-83; As Simon Mackay: The Anderson Series, 1984-85; As Caroline Gray: First Class, 1984; Hotel de Luxe, 1985; White Rani, 1986; Victoria's Walk, 1986; The Third Life, 1988; Shadow of Death, 1989; Blue Water, Black Depths, 1990; The Daughter, 1992; Golden Girl, 1992; Spares, 1993; Spawn of the Devil, 1993; As Christopher Nicole: The Happy Valley, 1989; The Triumph, 1989; The Command, 1989; Dragon'd Blood, 1989; Dark Sun, 1990; Sword of Fortune, 1990; Sword of Empire, 1990; Days of Wine & Roses, 1991; The Titans, 1992; Resumption, 1992; The Last Battle, 1993; Bloody Sunrise, in progress; Bloody Sunset, in progress; As Alan Savage: Ottoman, 1990; Mughal, 1991; The Eight Banners, 1992; Queen of Night, 1993; The Last Bannerman, 1993; Queen of Lions, in progress; As Nicholas Grant: Khan, 1993; Total of 114 Books - 107 novels, 4 juveniles, 1 history, 1 sporting history and 1 technical; Also several books written jointly with wife, Diana Bachmann. Contributions to: Numerous journals and magazines. Memberships: Society of Authors; Literary Guild of America; Mark Twain Society. Literary Agent: David Higham Associates Ltd, 5-8 Lower John Street, Golden Square, London W1R 4HA, England. Address: Curtis Brown & John Farquharson Ltd, 162-168 Regent Street, London W1R 5TB, England.

NICOLSON Nigel, b. 19 Jan 1917. Author; Director. m. Philippa Janet, 1953 (div 1970), 1 son, 2 daughters. Education: Balliol College, Oxford. Publications include: The Grenadier Guards, 1939-45, 1949 (official history); People and Parliament, 1958; Lord of the Isles, 1960; Great Houses of Britain, 1965, revised edition 1978; Editor, Harold Nicholson: Diaries and Letters, 3 volumes, 1966-68; Great Houses, 1968; Alex (F M Alexander of Tunis), 1973; Portrait of a Marriage, 1973; Editor, Letters of Virginia Woolf, 1975-80 (6 volumes); The Himalayas, 1975; Mary Curzon, 1977; Napoleon: 1812, 1985; The World of Jane Austin, 1991; Vita and Herald: The Letters of Vita Sackville-West and Harold Nicolson, 1910-1962, 1992. Honours: Whitbread Award; MBE, 1945; FSA; FRSL. Address: Sissinghurst Castle, Kent, England.

NIEDZIELSKI Henryk Zygmunt, b. 30 Mar 1931, France. Educator. m. 26 July 1977, 3 s, 1 d. Education: BA, 1959, MA, 1963, PhD, 1964, Romance Philology, University of Connecticut, USA.

Appointments: Editor in Chief, Language & Literature in Hawaii, 1967-72; Correspondent, France Amerique, 1969-72; Editorial Board, Conradiana, 1971-76; Editorial Board, Science et Francophonie, 1985-91. Publications: Le Roman de Helcanus, 1966; The Silent Language of France, 1975; Studies on the Seven Sages of Rome, 1978; Jean Misrahi Memorial Volume, 1977; 6 language teaching books; The Silent Language of Poland, 1989; Polish Body Language (film). Contributions to: La Democratie au foyer La Tribune des l'enfance, 1970; articles in various professional journals; Journal of American Translators Association. Honours: Distinguished Fellow, University of Auckland, New Zealand, Foundation, 1989; Silver Cross of Merit of the Polish People's Republic, 1989. Memberships: Medieval Academy of America; International Arthurian Society; American Association of Teachers of French, President, Hawaii, 1981-83; Hawaii Association of Translators, Founding President, 1982; International Association of Teachers of English As a Foreign Language; Founding Director, Chopin Society of Hawaii, 1990. Address: 2425 W Orange Avenue, Anaheim, CA 92804, USA.

NIELSEN Helen Berniece (Kris Giles), b. 1918, USA. Author. Publications: The Kind Man, 1951; Gold Coast Nocturne, 1951, UK Edition, Murder by Proxy, 1952, US Paperback, Dead on the Level, 1954; Obit Delayed, 1952; Detour, 1953, US Paperback, Detour to Death, 1955; The Woman on the Roof, 1954; Stranger in the Dark, 1955; The Crime is Murder, 1956; Borrow the Night, 1957, US Paperback, Seven Days Before Dying, 1958; The Fifth Caller, 1959; False Witness, 1959; Sing Me a Murder, 1960; Woman Missing and Other Stories, 1961; Verdict Suspended, 1964; After Midnight, 1966; A Killer in the Street, 1967; Darkest Hour, 1969; Shot on Location, 1971; The Severed Key, 1973; The Brink of Murder, 1976; Line of Fire, 1987.

NIEMANN Linda Grant, b. 22 Sep 1946, Pasadena, California, USA. Railroad Brakeman. Education: BA, University of California, Santa Cruz, 1968; PhD, University of California, Berkeley, 1975. Publications: Boomer: Railroad Memoirs, 1990. Honours: Non-Fiction Award, Bay Area Book Reviewers Association, 1991. Memberships: PEN West; National Writers Union. Address: PO Box 7409, Santa Cruz, CA 95061, USA.

NIEMINEN Kai Tapani, b. 11 May 1950, Helsinki, Finland. Poet; Translator. m. 1991, 1 daughter. Publications: Joki vie ajatukseni, 1971; Syntymästä, 1973; Kiireettä, 1977; Tie jota oli kuljettava, 1979; Vain mies, 1981; Elämän vuoteessa, 1982; Oudommin kuin unessa, 1983; En minä tiedä, 1985; Milloin missäkin hahmossa, 1987; Keinuva maa, 1989; Fuuga/Fugue (English translation by Hebert Lomas), 1992; Translations from Japanese include: Joutilaan mietteitä, 1978; Kapea tie pohjoiseen, 1981; Harhojen maja, 1984; Kokoro, 1985; Rakasta sinä vain, 1986; Genjin tarina, volume 4, 1990; Makiokan sisarukset, 1991; Kwaidan, 1991. Contributions to: Numerous translations of Japanese poetry, essays on Japanese literature and culture, to various publications. Honours: National Literary Awards for Translations, Ministry of Education, 1978, 1982, 1991; National Literary Awards for Poems, 1986, 1990. Memberships: Finnish Authors Society; Finnish PEN, President 1991-94; Eino Leinon Seura. Literary Agent: Tammi Publishers. Address: Baggböle 99 A, 07740 Gammelby, Finland.

NIGG Joseph Eugene, b. 27 Oct 1938, Davenport, Iowa, USA. Editor; Writer. m. (1) Gayle Madsen, 20 Aug 1960, div 1979, 2 s, (2) Esther Muzzillo, 27 Oct 1989. Education: BA, Kent State University, 1960; MFA, Writers Workshop, University of Iowa, 1963; PhD, University of Denver, 1975. Appointments: Assisstant Editor, Essays in Literature, 1974-75; Associate Editor, Liniger's Real Estate, 1979-85; Fiction Editor, Wayland Press, 1985-92. Publications: The Book of Gryphons, 1982; A Guide to the Imaginary Birds of the World, 1984; Winegold, 1985; The Strength of Lions and the Flight of Eagles, 1982; The Great Balloon Festival, 1989; Wonder Beasts, 1995. Contributions to: various journals and magazines. Honours: Non-fiction Book of the Year, 1983, 1985, Colorado Authors League; Mary Chase Author of the Year, Rocky Mountain Writers Guild, 1984; Non-fiction Book of the Year, 1989, Colorado Authors League. Memberships: Colorado Authors League, Publicity Chairman, Membership Chairman; Rocky Mountain Writers Guild, Board of Directors. Address: 1114 Clayton St, Denver, CO 80206, USA.

NILE Dorothea. See: AVALLONE Michael Angelo.

NIMS John Frederick, b. 20 Nov 1913, Chicago, USA. Professor; Editor of Poetry. m. Bonnie Larkin, 1 s, 1 d. Education: AB, 1937, MA, 1939, University of Notre Dame; PhD, University of Chicago,

1945. Appointments: Professor, numerous Universities including: University of Notre Dame, University of Florence, University of Madrid, University of Illinois, Harvard University, Williams College; Editor, Poetry Chicago, 1978-84. Publications: The Iron Pastoral, 1947; A Fountain in Kentucky, 1950; The Poems of St John of the Cross, translation, 1958, 3rd edition, 1979; Knowledge of the Evening, 1960; Of Flesh and Bone, 1967; Sappho to Valery: Poems in Translation, 1971, 3rd edition, 1992; Western Wind: an introduction to Poetry, 1974; The Harper Anthology of Poetry, 1981; The Kiss: A Jambalaya, poems 1982; Selected Poems, 1982; A Local Habitation: essays on Poetry, 1985; The Six-Cornered Snowflake, 1991; Zany in Denim, 1993. Contributions to: Numerous magazines, journals and reviews including: Poetry; Hudson Review; Atlantic; Harpers; Times Literary Supplement; Saturday Review. Honours include: National Institute of Arts and Letters Award, 1967; Creative Arts Poetry Award, Brandeis University, 1972; Fellowship, Academy of American Poets, 1982; Guggenheim Fellowship, 1986-87; Aiken-Taylor Award, 1991; Melville Cane Award, 1992; Hardison Poetry Prize, 1993. Address: 3920 Lake Shore Drive, Chicago, IL 60613, USA.

NIOSI Jorge Eduardo, b. 8 Dec 1945, Buenos Aires, Argentina. University Professor. m. Graciela Ducatenzeiler, 25 Nov 1971, 2 daughters. Education: Licence, Sociology, National University of Buenos Aires, 1967; Advanced Degree, Economics, IEDES, Paris, 1970; Doctorate, Sociology, Ecole Pratique, Paris, 1973. Publications: Technology and National Competitiveness, 1991; Les entrepeneurs dans la politique argentine, 1976; The Economy of Canada, 1978; Canadian Capitalism, 1981; Firmes Multinationales et autonomie nationale, 1983; Canadian Multinationals, 1985; La montee de l'ingenierie canadienne, 1990, 1990. Editor: New Technology Poilcy and Social Innovation in the Firm, 1994. Contributions to: Nearly 30 Magazines and journals including: Recherches sociographiques; Sociologie et societe; Tiers Monde; World Development; Technovation; Revue francaise d'economie. Honours: John Porter Award, Canadian Sociology and Anthropology Association, 1983; Fellow, Statistics Canada, 1989-92. Memberships: International Sociological Association; Canadian Sociology and Anthropology Association; International Management of Technology Association; Royal Society of Canada. Address: CREDIT, UQAM, Box 8888, Station Centre Ville, Montreal, Quebec, Canada H3C 3P8.

NISBET Jim, b. 20 Jan 1947. Writer, Publications: Poems for a Lady, 1978; Gnachos for Bishop Berkeley, 1980; The Gourmet, novel, 1980; Morpho (with Alaistair Johnston), 1982; The Visitor, 1984; Lethal Injection, novel, 1987; Death Puppet, novel, 1989; Laminating the Conic Frustum, 1991; Small Apt, 1992; Sous le Signe de la Razoir, 1994; Ulysses' Dog, 1993. Literary Agent: William Morris Agency, New York, USA. Address: c/o Mr Matthew Bialer, William Morris Agency, 1350 Avenue of the Americas, New York, NY 10019, USA.

NISH Ian Hill, b. 3 June 1926, Edinburgh, Scotland. Professor (retired). m. Rona Margaret Speirs, 29 Dec 1965, 2 daughters. Education: University of Edinburgh, 1943-51; University of London, 1951-56. Appointments: University of Sydney, New South Wales, Australia, 1957-62; London School of Economics and Political Science, England, 1962-91. Publications: Anglo-Japanese Alliance, 1966; The Story of Japan, 1968; Alliance in Decline, 1972; Japanese Foreign Policy, 1978; Anglo-Japanese Alienation 1919-52, 1982; Origins of Russo-Japanese War, 1986; Contemporary European Writing on Japan, 1988; Japan's Struggle with Internationalism, 1931-33, 1993. Honours: CBE, 1990; Order of the Rising Sun, Japan, 1991. Memberships: European Association of Japanese Studies, President 1985-88; British Association of Japanese Studies, President 1986. Address: Oakdene, 33 Charlwood Drive, Oxshott, Surrey KT22 0HB, England.

NITYANANDA Datta, b. 1934, India. Producer and Film Director. Eduction: BA, Commerce, Calcutta University, 1954; Diploma in Fine Arts, Calcutta, India. Career: Chief Assistant Director to Satyajit Ray (Oscar Winner 1992), in several films including: World of Apu (Apur Samaar-a Trilogy, award winning); Three Daughters; Tin Kanya (Rabindranath Tagore's) award winning, 1956-68; Associate Director to Hrishikesh Mukherjee, a reputed Film Director, 1971-1978 including work on award winning films: Alhiman; Namak Haram; Independent Producer and Director, 1965-87, produced adn directed two award winning films in Bengali - Sesh Prahar, and Baksa Badal, Green Revolution (for Government of India), You Are The Creator of Your Destiny, (Swami Vivekananda's Message to Youths) - award winning. Other Honours include: Award for Short Story Writer, The Whistle, published in Bengali Monthly Journal; Parichay, Award Winner for a Dance Drama, written, directed and choreographed, entitled Shilpir Navajanma, (New Birth of an Artist), award winner as the Best New Film Director for Sesh Prahar, 1962; Award Winner, for Best Script Writer, and Best Comedy Film Production, Baksha Badal, 1966. Address: 818 Webster St, Hayward, CA 94544, USA.

NIVEN Alastair Neil Robertson, b. 25 Feb 1944, Edinburgh, Scotland. Arts Council of England, Director of Literature. m. Helen Margaret Trow, 22 Aug 1970, 1 son, 1 daughter. Education: BA, 1966, MA, 1968, University of Cambridge; MA, University of Ghana, 1968; PhD, University of Leeds, 1972. Appointments: Lecturer, English: University of Ghana, 1968-69; University of Leeds, England, 1969-70; Lecturer, English Studies, University of Stirling, Scotland, 1970-78; Visiting Professor, Aarhus University, Denmark, 1975-76; Honorary Lecturer, University of London, 1979-84; Editor, Journal of Commonwealth Literature, 1979-92; Chapman Fellow, Institute of Commonwealth Studies, 1984-85; Visiting Fellow, Australian Studies Centre, London, 1985; Director of Literature, Arts Council of Great Britain, 1987-94, Arts Council of England, 1994-. Publications: D H Lawrence: The Novels, 1978; The Yoke of Pity: The Fictional Writings of Mulk Raj Anand, 1978; The Commonwealth of Universities (with Hugh W springer), 1987; Truth into Fiction or Raja Rao's The Serpent and the Rope, 1988; Editor: The Commonwealth Writer Overseas, 1976; Under Another Sky, 1987; Study guides on William Golding, R K Narayan, Elechi Amadi. Contributions to: Articles or book chapters to The Times; Ariel; The Literary Criterion; Commonwealth Essais et Etudes. Honours: Commonwealth Scholar, 1966-68; Laurence Olivier Awards Panel, 1989-91; Judge, Booker Prize, 1994. Memberships: Greater London Arts Association Literature Advisory Panel, Chairman 1980-84; Association for Commonwealth Literature and Language Studies, Secretary 1986-89; UK Council for Overseas Student Affairs, Executive Committee Chairman 1987-92; Commonwealth Trust. Address: Eden House, 28 Weathercock Lane, Woburn Sands, Buckinghamshire MK17 8NY, England.

NIVEN Larry (Laurence Van Cott), b. 30 Apr 1938, Los Angeles, California, USA. m. Marilyn Joyce Wisowaty, 6 Sept 1969. Education: California Institute of Technology, 1956-58; BA, Mathematics, Washburn University, Kansas, 1962. Publications: Neutron Star, 1966; Ringworld, 1970; Inconstant Moon, 1971; The Hole Man, 1974; The Borderland of Sol, 1975; Protector, 1974; N-Space; Playgrounds, 1991; Achilles' Choice (co-author); Football, with Jerry Pournelle, 1985; The Gripping Hand, with Jerry Pournelle, 1993; Dream Park, with Steven Barnes, 1981; The California Voodoo Game. Articles, speeches, TV scripts, contributions to books, magazines and comics. Honours: Honorary Doctor of Letters, Washburn University, 1984; Science Fiction Achievement Awards, 1966, 1970, 1971, 1974, 1975; Nebula Best Novel, 1970; Australian Best International Science Fiction, 1972, 1974; Inkpot Award, San Diego Comic Convention, 1979. Literary Agent: Eleanor Wood, Spectrum Literary Agency, 111 8th Vanalden Avenue, Tarzana, CA 91356, USA.

NIXON Richard (Milhous), b. 1913, USA. Former Lawyer; Former US Senator; Former US President; Former President of the United States; Author. Publications: Six Crises, 1962; Memoirs, 1978; The Real War, 1980; Leaders, 1982; Real Peace: A Strategy for the West, 1983; No More Vietnams, 1985; Victory Without War, 1988; In the Arenal: A Memoir of Victory, Defeat and Renewal, 1990; Seize the Moment: America's Challenge in a one Superpower World, 1992. Address; 577 Chestnut Ridge Road, Woodcliff Lake, NJ 07675, USA.

NJEMOGA-KOLAR Ana, b. 5 July 1951, Padina, Yugoslavia. Writer. m. Samo Kolar, 5 Apr 1980. Education: Faculty of Philosophy, Novi Sad University; Qualified Secondary School Teacher of Slovak Language and Literature. Appointments: Junior Journalist, Radio Novi Sad, 1976-81; Senior Journalist, Editor, TV Novi Sad, 1981-82; Co-Founder, Editorial Board Member, IGROPIS magazine (on children's theatre), 1990; Currently freelance. Creative works: Children's radio and magazine short stories include: Olivera; The New Theatre Lovers; At May Table; Children's radio plays include: The Invented Case; Love, translated into 4 languages; Adults' radio dramas include: An Unsuccessful Experiment, translated into 4 languages; Departure of Mr Tom, The Tent at the Edge of the Fair, Slovakia Radio Bratislava, 1993; TV and theatre children's plays include: Love, performed 1988; A Quiet Small Daydream Creature, performed 1990. Honours: 2nd Prize, Yugoslav Competition for Best Children's Play, Radio Sarajevo, 1988; 2nd and 3rd Prizes, Competition for Best Children's Radio Story, Radio Novi Sad, 1988-89; 2nd Prize,

Competition for Best Children's Story, Pioneers magazine, 1990; 1st Prizes, Republic Competition for Best Children's Story, 1990, for Children's Theatre Play, 1990; 1st Prize, Competition for Best Theatre Play for Adults, New Life literary magazine, 1991. Membership: Vojvodina Journalists Association. Address: PO Box 11, 07 801 Secovce, Slovakia.

NJERI Itabari Lord, b. Brooklyn, NY, USA. Journalist; Author. Education: BS, Boston University; MS, Columbia University Graduate School of Journalism. Publications: Every Goodbye Ain't Gone, 1989; The Last Plantation, 1993; Sushi & Girls: the Challenge of Diversity, 1993. Contributions to: Essence; Emerge; Harpers. Honours: South Carolina Associated Press Award, 1980; Lincoln University UNITY Media Award, 1982; Penney, University of Missouri Journalism Prize, 1983; Los Angeles Press Club Award, 1989; National Association of Black Journalists Award, 1990; American Book Award, 1990.

NKOSI Lewis, b. 1936, South Africa. Novelist; Playwright; Essayist. Appointments: Staff Member: Ilange Lase Natal (Zulu newspaper), Durban, South Africa, 1955-56; Drum magazine and Golden City Post, Johannesburg, 1956-60; South African Information Bulletin magazine, Paris, France, 1962-68; Radio Producer, BBC Transcription Centre, London, England, 1962-64; Literary Editor, New African magazine, London, 1965-68. Publications: The Rhythm of Violence, 1964; Home and Exile, essays, 1965; The Transplanted Heart: Essays on South Africa, 1975; Tasks and Masks: Themes and Styles of African Literature, 1981; Mating Birds, novel, 1986. Address: Flat 4, Burgess Park Mansions, Fortune Green Road, London NW6, England.

NOAKES Vivien, b. 16 Feb 1937, England. Writer. m. Michael Noakes, 9 July 1960, 2 sons, 1 daughter. Education: BA 1st Class Honours, English, Senior Scholar, Somerville College, Oxford University. Publications: Edward Lear: The Life of a Wanderer, 1968, revised, 1979, revised, 1985; Edward Lear 1812-1888, The Catalogue of the Royal Academy Exhibition, 1985; The Selected Letters of Edward Lear, 1988; The Painter Edward Lear, 1991. Contributions to: The Times; The Times Literary Supplement; Daily Telegraph; New Scientist; Punch; Harvard Magazine; Tennyson Research Bulletin. Literary Agent: Watson, Little Limited. Address: 146 Hamilton Terrace, London NW8 9UX, England.

NOBLE Jayne. See: DOWNES Mary Raby.

NOBLE John Appelbe, b. 1914, Australian. Travel, Exploration and Adventure. Appointments: Ship's Captain, Union Steamship Co, New Zealand, 1951-58; Ship's Pilot, Port Phillip Sea Pilots, Williamstown, Victoria, 1959-79; Editor, Journal of the Co of Master Mariners of Australia, Harbour Press, Sydney, 1966-71; Melbourne Branch Master, Co of Master Mariners of Australia, 1974-75. Publications: Australian Lighthouse, 1967; Hazards of the Sea, 1970; Port Phillip: Pilots and Defence, 1973, 1978; Port Phillip Panorama, 1975; The Golden Age of Sail, 1985.

NODSET Joan L. See: LEXAU Joan M.

NOEL. See: ADAMS Douglas.

NOEL Arthur. See: RAVEN Simon.

NOEL Lise, b. 19 Apr 1944, Montreal, Quebec, Canada. Writer; Professor; Columnist. Education: DENS Education, 1972, BA, 1965, Licence in Letters, 1970, MA, History 1975, PhD, History, 1982, all at The University of Montreal; 1 year study, The University of Aix-en-Provence, France. Publications: Intolerance, The Parameters of Oppression, 1994. Contributions to: Critère; Liberté; Possibles (Literary and, or Cultural Magazines); Service Social (Scholarly); Le Devoir. Honours: Hachette-Larousse, 1967; Governor General's Award, Non Fiction, 1989. Memberships: Editorial Boards of: Liberté, 1982-87; Critère, 1983-85. Address: 2608 Chemin Cote Sainte Catherine, Montreal, Quebec H3T 1B4, Canada.

NOEL-HULME Ivor, b. 1927, United Kingdom. Author; Archaeological Researcher. Appointments: Archaeological Director, Colonial Williamsburg Foundation, Williamsburg, Virginia, USA, 1957-; Research Associate, Smithsonian Institution, 1959-; Vice-President, Society for Post-Medieval Archaeology, UK, 1967-76; Council Member, Institute of Early American History and Culture, 1974-76; Board Member, Jamestown Yorktown Foundation, 1987-. Publications:

Archaeology in Britain, 1953; Tortoises, Terrapins and Turtles (co-author), 1954; Treasure in the Thames, 1956; Great Moments in Archaeology, 1957; Here Lies Virginia, 1963; 1775: Another Part of the Field, 1966; Historical Archaeology, 1969; Artifacts of Colonial America, 1970; All the Best Rubbish, 1974; Early English Delftware from London and Virginia, 1976; Martin's Hundred, 1982. Address: PO Box 1711, Williamsburg, VA 23187, USA.

NOF Shimon Y, b. 22 Mar 1946, Haifa, Israel. Professor of Industrial Engineering. m. Nava C Vardinon, 1972, 2 d. Education: BSc, 1969, MSc, 1972, Industrial Engineering and Management, Techion, Haifa, Israel; PhD, Industrial and Operations Engineering, University of Michigan, Ann-Arbor, USA, 1976. Appointments: Deputy Editor, Computor and Knowledge Engineering, 1984-; Special Issue Editor, Material Flow, 1984-85; Consulting Editor, Encyclopedia of Robotics, 1984-88; Editorial Board: Handbook of IE, 1989-92, International Journal of Production Planning and Control, 1991-; Advisory Board, International Journal of Informatics; Editorial Board: International Journal of Industrial Engineering, 1993-, Computers and Knowledge Engineering, 1984-93, Computing & Emerging Methodologies/IIE Transactions, 1993-. Publications: Handbook of Industrial Robotics, 1985; International Encyclopedia of Robotics and Automation, 1988; Robotics and Material Flow, 1986; Co-editor: Concise Encyclopedia of Robotics and Automation, 1990; Advanced Information Technology for Industrial Material Flow Systems, 1989; Information and Collaboration Models of Integration (editor). Contributions to: Journals and Proceedings articles on computor applications in manufacturing and industrial robotics. Honours: Fulbright Grant, 1972; The Silent Hoist Doctoral Award, 1975; American Association of Publishers Awards of Excellence, 1975, 1988; Fellow, Institute of Industrial Engineers; Association of Computing Machinary; Institue of Management Science; Japan Industrial Management Association; Society of Manufacturing Engineers; International Federation of Production Research. Address: 1287 Grissom Hall, Purdue University, W Lafayette, IN 47907, USA,

NOLAN Patrick, b. 2 Jan 1933, Bronx, New York, USA. Teacher. 3 s. Education: MA, University of Detroit; PhD, English Literature, Bryn Mawr College. Appointments include: Instructor, University of Detroit; Professor, Villanova University. Publications include: Films: Hourglass Moment, 1969; Jericho Mile, 1978; plays: Chameleons, 1981; Midnight Rainbows, 1991. Contributions: Origin of Fear in the Emperor Jones, in O'Neill Newsletter, 1980; Jungian View of Desire Under the Elms, ibid, 1981. Honours: Emmy Award, Academy of TV Arts & Sciences, 1979; Citation, Teaching Excellence, Philadelphia Magazine, 1980. Membership: Writes Guild of America, West; Dramatists Guild. Literary Agent: Richard Barber, 544 82nd Street, New York, NY 10028, USA. Address: English Department, Villanova University, Villanova, PA 19085, USA.

NOLAN William F(rancis) (Frank Anmar, Mike Cahill, F E Edwards, Michael Phillips), b. 1928, American. Writer of novels/short stories, mystery/crime/suspense, science fiction/fantasy, poetry, film, literature, sports, biography. Publications: Over 600 appearances in 255 publications Worldwide, 200 anthology appearances and 40 scripts for films and television; (ed) Ray Bradbury Review, 1952; (ed with C Beaumont), Omnibus of Speed of Speed, 1958; (with J Fitch) Adventure on Wheels, 1959; Barney Oldfield, 1961; Phil Hill: Yankee Champion, 1962; Impact 20 (stories), 1963; (ed with C Beaumont), When Engines Roar, 1964; Men of Thunder, 1964; John Huston: King Rebel, 1965; (ed) Man Against Tomorrow, 1965; (ed), The Pseudo-People, 1965; Sinners and Supermen, 1965; (ghost ed), Il Meglio della Fantascienza, 1967; (with G C Johnson), Logan's Run, 1967; (ed), 3 to the Highest Power, 1968; Death is for Losers, 1968; The White Cad Cross-UP, 1969; (ed), A Wilderness of Stars, 1969; Dashiell Hammett: A Casebook, 1969; (ed), A Sea of Space, 1970; (ed), The Future is Now, 1970; (ed), The Human Equation, 1971; (ghost ed), The Edge of Forever, 1971; Space for Hire, 1971; Steve McQueen: Star on Wheels, 1972; Carnival of Speed, 1973; Alien Horizons (stories), 1974; Hemingway: Last Days of the Lion, 1974; The Ray Bradbury Companion, 1975; Wonderworlds (stories), 1977; Logan's World, 1977; Logan's Search, 1980; (ed with M Greenberg), Science Fiction Origins, 1980; (ed), Max Brand's Best Western Stories, 3 vols, 1981-87; Hammett: A Life at the Edge, 1983; McQueen, 1984; Things Beyond Midnight (stories), 1984; Look Out for Space, 1985; The Black Mask Boys, 1985; The Work of Charles Beaumont (bibliography), 1986; Dark Encounters (poems), 1986; (ed), Max Brand: Western Giant, 1986; Logan: A Trilogy, 1986; (with Boden Clarke), The Work of William F Nolan (bibliography), 1988; (as Terence Duncan), Rio Renegades, 1989; (ed with M Greenberg), Urban Honnons, 1990; How to Write

Horror Fiction, 1990; Blood Sky, 1991; Helltracks, 1991; (ed with M Greenberg), The Bradbury Chronicles, 1991; 3 Fon Space, 1992; Helle on Wheels, 1992; Saturday's Shadow, 1992; Six in Darkness (stories), 1993; (ed), Max Brand's Detective Stories, 1993; Night Shapes (stories), 1993. Address: Loni Perkins Associates Literary Agency, 301 W 53rd St, New York, NY 10019, USA.

NONHEBEL Clare, b. 7 Nov 1953, London, England. m. Robin Nonhebel, 30 Aug 1975. Education: BA (Honours), French Studies, University of Warwick. Appointments: Freelance Feature Writer, 1980-84. Publications: Cold Showers, 1985; The Partisan, 1986; Story in Winter's Tales anthology, 1987; Incentives, 1988; Child's Play, 1991. Contributions to: Annabel; Various other women's magazines; Mind Your Own Business; Other business journals; Occasional items for newspapers. Honours: Joint Winner, Betty Trask Award, 1984. Literary Agent: Curtis Brown. Address: c/o Curtis Brown, Haymarket House, 28/29 Haymarket, London, SW1Y 4SP.

NOON Ed. See: **AVALLONE Michael Angelo.**

NOONE Edwina. See: **AVALLONE Michael Angelo.**

NORDBRANDT Henrik, b. 21 Mar 1945, Copenhagen, Denmark. Writer. Education: Turkish & Arabic Studies. Publications: Digte, 1966; Miniaturer, 1967; Syvsoverne, 1969; Omgivelser, 1972; Opbrud ogankomstr, 1974; Ode til blaeksprutten, 1976; Guds hus, 1977; Selected Poems, 1978; Amenia, 1982; Violinbyggernes by, 1985; Glas, 1986; Istid, 1987. Contributions to: various journals and magazines. Honours: 12 Literary Awards including big prize of Danish Academy, Danish Critic's Prize for Best Book of the Year & Life Grant of Honour, Danish State. Address: Gyldendal, Klareboderne 3, Copenhagen 1001 K, Denmark.

NORDLAND Rodney Lee, b. 17 July 1949, USA. Journalist. Education: BA, Pennsylvania State University. Appointments: Foreign Correspondent, Asia, Philadelphia Inquirer, 1972-83; Bureau Chief, Newsweek Magazine, 1984-85; Correspondent-at-Large, Newsweek Magazine, 1986-. Publications: Names and Numbers: A Journalist's Guide, 1978; The Watergate File, 1984. Contributions to: numerous newspapers and magazines in USA, France, Germany. Honours: Pulitzer Prize, Local Reporting, 1978; Thomas L Stokes Award, 1978; Edward J Meeman Award, 1978; Pulitzer Prize, 1st Finalist, Foreign Reporting, 1982; George Polk Special Award, Foreign Correspondent, 1982. Memberships: Board of Governors, Pen & Pencil Club; Society of Professional Journalists; Investigative Reporters & Editors; Overseas Press Club. Literary Agent: Betty Martin, New York. Address: 496 La Guardia Pl, No 450, New York, NY 10012, USA.

NORLING Bernard, b. 23 Feb 1924, Hunters, Washington, USA. Retired University Professor. m. Mary Pupo, 30 Jan 1948. Education: BA, Gonzaga University, 1940-42, 1946-48; Military, Bard College, 1943-44; Military, Hamilton College, 1944; Military, Washington and Lee College, 1945; MA 1949, PhD 1955, Notre Dame University. Appointments: Instructor, 1952-55, Assistant Professor 1955-61, Associate Professor 1961-71, Professor 1971-86, History Department, University of Notre Dame. Publications: Towards a Better Understanding of History, 1960; Timeless Problems in History, 1970; Understanding History Through the American Experience, 1976; Return to Freedom, 1983; Behind Japanese Lines, 1986; The Nazi Impact On a German Village, 1993. Contributions to: Numerous articles magazines and journals. Honour: Best Teacher of Freshman, University of Notre Dame, 1968. Memberships: Indiana Association of Historians; Michiana Historians, President 1993. Address: 504 E Pokagon, South Bend, IN 46617, USA.

NORMAN Barry Leslie, b. 21 Aug 1933, London, England. Writer; Broadcaster. m. Diana Narracott, 1957, 2 daughters. Appointments: Entertainments Editor, Daily Mail, London, 1969-71; Weekly Columnist, The Guardian, 1971-80; Writer & Presenter, BBC 1 Film, 1973-81, 1983-88, The Hollywood Greats, 1977-79, 1984, The British Greats 1980, Omnibus, 1982, Film Greats, 1985; Talking Pictures, 1988; Radio 4 Today 1974-76, Going Places 1977-81, Breakaway 1979-80. Publications: Novels: The Matter of Mandrake, 1967; The Hounds of Sparta, 1968; End Product, 1975; A Series of Defeats, 1977; To Nick a Good Body, 1978; Have a Nice Day, 1981; Sticky Wicket, 1984; Non-fiction: Tales of the Redundance Kid, 1975; The Hollywood Greats, 1979; The Movie Greats, 1981; Talking Pictures, 1987; 100 Best Films of the Century, 1992; Thriller: The Birddog Tape, 1992. Honours: BAFTA Richard Dimbleby Award, 1981.

Address: c/o Curtis Brown, 162-168 Regent Street, London W1R 5TA, England.

NORMAN Geraldine (Geraldine Keen, Florence Place), b. 13 May 1940, Wales. Journalist. m. Frank Norman, July 1971. Education: MA (Honours), Mathematics, St Anne's College, Oxford University; University of California, USA. Publications: The Sale of Works of Art (as Geraldine Keen), 1971; 19th Century Painters and Paintings: A Dictionary, 1977; The Fake's Progress (co-author), 1977; The Tom Keating Catalogue (editor), 1977; Mrs Harper's Niece (as Florence Place), 1982; Biedermeier Painting, 1987; Top Collectors of the World (co-author), 1993. Contributions to: The Independent, regular reports. Honours: News Reporter of the Year, 1976. Literary Agent: Gillon Aitken. Address: 5 Seaford Court, 220 Great Portland Street, London W1, England.

NORMAN Hilary, b. London, England. Writer. Education: Queen's College, London. Appointments: Director, Henry Norman textile manufacturing and retail firm, London, 1971-79; Production Assistant, Capital Radio, London, 1980-82; Production Assistant, British Broadcasting Corporation, 1982-85; Writer, 1985-. Publications: Novels: In Love and Friendship, 1986, 1987; Château Ella, 1988; Shattered Stars, 1991; Fascination, 1992; Spellbound, 1993; Laura, 1994. Contributions to: Stories to Woman's Own. Literary Agents: John Hawkins Associates, 71 West 23rd Street, New York, NY 10010, USA; A M Heath and Company, London, England. Address: c/o A M Heath Co Ltd, 79 St Martins Lane, London WC2N 4AA, England.

NORMAN John, b. 20 Jul 1912, Syracuse, New York, USA. Professor Emeritus. m. Mary Lynott, 28 Dec 1948, Pittsburgh, Pennsylvania, 4 d. Education: BA, 1935, MA, 1938, Syracuse University; PhD, Clark University, 1942. Publications include: Edward Gibbon Wakefield: A Political Reappraisal, 1963; Labor and Politics in Libya and Arab Africa, 1965; Poems in Periodicals and anthologies: Our World's Most Treasured Poems, 1991; Arcadia Poetry Anthology, 1992; A Question of Balance, National Library of Poetry, 1992. Contributions to: Funk and Wagnall's Encyclopedia Yearbook; Encyclopedia Yearbook; Encyclopedia Americana; Industrial and Labor Relations Review; Far Eastern Historical Review. Honours: Prizes for Poetry by World Poetry, 1991. Address: 94 Cooper Road, John's Pond, Ridgefield, CT 06877, USA.

NORMAN Marsha, b. 1947, USA. Novelist; Dramatist. Appointments: Teacher, Brown School, Louisville, and Book Reviewer, Louisville Times, mid 1970s; Resident Writer, Actors Theatre, Louisville, 1977-80. Publications: Plays: Getting Out, 1977; Third and Oak: The Laundromat, The Pool Hall, 2 vols, 1980-85; Night, Mother, 1983; The Holdup, 1987; Novel: The Fortune Teller, 1987; Traveler in the Dark, 1988; Four Plays: Sarah and Abraham; Musical Book & Lyrics - The Secret Garden, 1991. Literary Agent: The Tantleff Agency, Jack Tantleff, 375 Greenwich Suite, 700, New York, NY 10019, USA. Address: c/o Samuel Liff, William Morris Agency, 1350 Avenue of the Americas, New York, NY 10019, USA.

NORRIE Philip Anthony, b. 5 Feb 1953, Sydney, New South Wales, Australia. Medical Practitioner. m. Belinda Jill Vivian, 6 June 1974, 2 sons. Education: MB, BS, University of New South Wales, 1977; Certificate, Family Planning Association, 1980; MSc, University of Sydney, 1993; MSocSc honours degree in progress, Charles Sturt University. Literary appointments: Wine Writer, Australian Medical Business Review, 1994; Winews, 1994. Publications: Vineyards of Sydney, Cradle of Australian Wine Industry, 1990; Lindeman - Australia's Classic Winemaker, 1993; Penfold - Time Honoured, 1994; Australia's Wine Doctors, 1994; Leo Buring - Australia's Wine Authority, 1994. Contributions to: Australasian Journal of Psychopharmacology; Australian Doctor; Australian Medical Observer; Journal of Medical Biography; The Australian. Memberships: Australian Medical Association; Australian National Trust; Royal Australian Historical Society; Australian Society of the History of Medicine; New South Wales Society of the History of Medicine; Founder, President, Australian Medical Friends of Wine Society. Address: 22 Ralston Rd, Palm Beach, New South Wales 2108, Australia.

NORRIS Ken, b. 3 Apr 1951, Bronx, NY, USA. Associate Professor; Poet. m. Susan Hamlett, 1987. Education: PhD, McGill University, Montreal, 1980. Appointments include: Associate Professor, Canadian Literature, University of ME. Publications: Report on the Second half of the Twentieth Century, 1977-88; The Perfect Accident, 1978; The Book of Fall, 1979; Autokinesis, 1980; Sonnets and Other

Dead Forms, 1980; To Sleep, To Love, 1982; Eight Odes, 1982; Whirlwinds, 1983; The better Part of Heaven: Pacific Writings, 1984; One Night, 1985; In The spirit of the Times, 1986; Islands, 1986; In The House of No, 1991; Editions of Canadian Poetry. Honours include: Canada Council Arts Grant, 1982. Address: Dept of English, University of Maine, 304 Neville Hall, Orno, ME 04469, USA.

NORRIS Leslie, b. 21 May 1921, Glamorgan, Wales. Professor: Poet. m. Catherine Mary Morgan, 1948. Education: M Phil, University of Southampton, 1958. Appointments include: Humanities Professor, Brigham Young University. Publications include: Tongue of Beauty, 1941; Poems, 1946; The Ballard of Billy Rose, 1963; The Loud Winter, 1967; Finding Golf, 1967; Ranssoms, 1970; His Last Autumn, 1972; Moutains, Polecats, Pheasants and Other Hegies, 1973; At The Publishers, 1976; Revenna Bridge, 1977; Islands off Maine, 1977; Merlin and the Snakes Egg, 1978; Hyperion, 1979; Water Voices, 1980; Walking the White Fields, 1967-80; A Tree Sequence, 1984; Selected Poems, 1986; Sequences, 1988; Norris's Ark, 1988; A Sea in the Desert, 1989; Short Stories, Sliding, 1976; The Gift from Cardigan, 1988; Glyn Jones, 1973. Honours include: Welsh Arts Council Awards; Katherine Mansfield Award, 1981. Address: 849 South Carterville Road, Orem, UT 84058, USA.

NORSE Harold George, b. 6 July 1916, New York City, USA. Author. Education: BA, Brooklyn College, 1938; MA, New York University, 1951. Appointments: Instructor in English, Cooper Union College, New York, 1949-52, Lion School of English, Rome, 1956-57, United States Information Service School, Naples, 1958-59; Instructor in Creative Writing, San Jose State University, California, 1973-75; Currently freelance writer. Publications: Best Hotel (novel), 1975 (Germany), 1983 (USA), 1985 (Italy, Switzerland); Karma Circuit (poetry), 1967 (London), 1974 (USA); Carnivorous Saint (poetry), 1977; Hotel Nirvana (poetry), 1974; Love Poems (poetry), 1986; Memoirs of a Bastard Angel (autobiography), 1989, 1990 (UK), 1991 (France); Mysteries of Magritte (poetry), 1984; The Roman Sonnets of Giuseppe Gioacchino Belli (translations), 1960, 1974. Contributions to: Antaeus; City Lights Review; Kayak; Kenyon Review; Poetry Flash; The Advocate; Exquisite Corpse; Semiotexte; Commentary; Harpers & Queen; Transatlantic Review; Christopher Street; Isis (Oxford); Paris Review; Saturday; Sewanee Review. Honours: National Endowment for the Arts, Poetry Fellowship 1974; R H de Young Museum Grant, 1974. Membership: PEN. Literary Agent: Writers House. Address: Box 263, 537 Jones Street, San Francisco, CA 94102, USA.

NORTH Andrew. See: NORTON Alice Mary.

NORTH Elizabeth (Stewart), b. 1932, United Kingdom. Author; Teacher of Creative Writing. Appointments: Writer-in-Residence, Bretton Hall College of Higher Education, 1984-85. Publications: Make Thee an Ark, radio play, 1969; Wife Swopping, radio play, 1969; The Least and Vilest Things, novel, 1971; Pelican Rising, novel, 1975; Enough Blue Sky, novel, 1977; Everything in the Garden, novel, 1978; Florence Avenue, novel, 1970; Dames, novel, 1981; Ancient Enemies, novel, 1982; The Real Tess, radio feature, 1984; Jude the Obscure, adaptation for radio, 1985. Address: 8 Huby Park, Huby, Leeds, England.

NORTON Alice Mary, (Andrew North, André Norton), b.1912, USA. Writer of science fiction/ fantasy, children's fiction. Former Librarian, Children's Department, Cleveland Public Library. Publications include: Outside, 1975; White Jade Fox, 1975; Merlin's Mirror, 1975; No Light Without Stars, 1975; Knave of Dreams, 1975; Perilous Dreams, 1976; Wraiths of Time, 1976; Red Hart Magic, 1976; Velvet Shadows, 1977; Opal-eyed Fan, 1977; Trey of Swords (short stories), 1977; Quag Keep, 1978; Yurth Burdon, 1978; Zarathor's Bane, 1979; Snow Shadow, 1979; Iron Butterflies, 1980; Voorlooper, 1980; Lore of Witchworld, (short stories), 1980; Gryphon in Glory, 1981; Forerunner, 1981; Star Ka'ats and Winged Warriors (with Dorothy Madlee), 1981; Moon Called, 1982; Wheel of Stars, 1983; Ware Hawk, 1983; Stand and Deliver, 1984; House of Shadows (with Phyllis Miller), 1984; Gryphon's Eyrie, 1984; Werewrath, 1984; Flight in Yiktov, 1986; Gate of a Cat, 1987; Serpent's Tooth, 1988; as Collections: Moon Mirror, 1988; Grand Master's Choice, 1989; Wizard's World, 1989; Dare to Go Hunting, 1990; Black Trillium (with Bradley & May), 1990; Jekyll Legacy (with Bloch), 1990; Storms of Victory, (with Griffin), 1991; Elevebane (with Lackey), 1991; Anthologies ed: Magic in Iftker I, 1986, Magic in Iftker II, 1987, Tales of Witch World I, 1987, Tales of Witch World II, 1988, Four from Witch World, 1989, Cat Fantastic, 1989; Tales of Witch World III, 1990; Cat Fantastic, 1991; Elvenbane, 1991;

Mark of Cat, 1992; Flight of Vengeance, 1992; Golden Trillium, 1993; On Wings Of Magic, 1993; Empire of Eagle, 1993; Brother to Shadows, 1993; Hands of Lyr, 1994; Firehand, 1994. Literary Agent: Russell Galen. Address: 1600 Spruce Avenue, Winter Park, FL 32789, USA.

NORTON André. See: **NORTON Alice Mary.**

NORTON Augustus Richard, b. 2 Sept 1946, New York, USA. Professor; Army Officer (Colonel). m. Deanna J Lampros, 27 Dec 1969, 1 son. Education: BA, magna cum laude 1974, MA, Political Science 1974, University of Miami; PhD, Political Science, University of Chicago, 1984. Publications: Amal and the Shia: Struggle for the Soul of Lebanon, 1987; International Terrorism, 1980; Studies in Nuclear Terrorism, 1979; NATO, 1985; Touring Nam: The Vietnam War Reader, 1985; The International Relations of the Palestine Liberation Organization, 1989; UN Peacekeepers: Soldiers with a Difference, 1990; Political Tides in the Arab World, 1992. Contributions to: Numerous magazines including Survival & Foreign Policy; Current History; New Outlook; New Leader; Middle East Journal. Address: Department of Social Science, USMA, West Point, NY 10996, USA.

NORWICH John Julius, b. 15 Sept 1929. Writer; Broadcaster. m. (1) Anne Clifford, 5 Aug 1952, 1 son, 1 daughter, (2) Mollie Philipps, 14 June 1989. Education: University of Strasbourg, 1947; New College, Oxford, 1949-52. Publications: Mount Athos, 1966; Sahara, 1968; The Normans in the South, 1967; The Kingdom in the Sun, 1970; A History of Venice, 1977, 1981; Christmas Crackers 1970-79, 1980; Glyndebourne, 1985; The Architecture of Southern England, 1985; A Taste for Travel, 1985; Byzantium: The Early Centuries, 1988; More Christmas Crackers 1980-89, 1990; Venice: A Traveller's Companion, 1990 (editor); The Oxford Illustrated Encyclopaedia of the Arts, 1990; Byzantium, the Apogee, 1991. Contributions to: Numerous magazines and journals. Honours: Commander, Royal Victorian Order; Commendatore, Ordine al Merito della Repubblica Italiana. Memberships: Fellow, Royal Society of Literature; Fellow, Royal Geographical Society; Beefsteak. Literary Agent: Felicity Bryan, 2A North Parade, Oxford, England. Address: 24 Blomfield Road, London W9 1AD, England.

NORWOOD Warren, b. 1945, USA. Science Fiction Writer. Appointments: Assistant Manager, University Bookstore, University of Texas, Arlington, 1973-76; Manager, Century Bookstore, Ft Worth, Texas, 1976-77; Publisher's Representative in Fort Worth, 1978-83; Taught Creative Writing, Tarrant County Junior College, 1983. Publications: The Windhover Tapes, comprising An Image of Voices, 1983; Flexing the Warp, 1983; Fize of the Gabriel Ratchets, 1983, and A Planet of Flowers, 1984; The Seren Cenacles (with Ralph Mylius), 1983; Double Spiral War, comprising Midway Between, 1984, Polar Fleet, 1985, and Final Command, 1986.

NOSKOWICZ-BIERON Helena, b. 5 July 1931, Sobolow, Poland. Journalist. m. Wladystaw Bieron, 27 Dec 1956, 2 sons. Education: BA, Journalism, Jangiellonian University, Cracow, 1964; MA Journalism, University of Warsaw, 1964. Appointments: Reporter for the Polish Radio in Cracow, 1953-63; Columnist for Echo Krakowa, daily, 1964-81; Editor, Underground Press, 1981-89; Columnist, Gazeta Krakowska and Dziennik Polski, 1989-. Publications: Ciagle czekaja z obiadem, 1978; Kto Ukradl Zloty Fon, 1991. Contributions to: Zycie Literackie weekly; St Uzba Zdrowia monthly; Polityka, weekly; Architektura i Biznes; Solidarnosc matopolska. Honours: Book of the Year about Cracow, 1978; Association of Polish Journalists prizes and awards. Memberships: Association of Polish Journalists, Secretary, Cracow Chapter, 1981-82. Address: ul Batorego 19/16, 31-135 Krakow, Poland.

NOSSITER Bernard Daniel, b, 10 Apr 1926. Journalist. m. Jacqueline Robinson, 1950, 4 sons. Education: BA, Dartmouth College; MA, Harvard University. Appointments: National Economics Correspondent, 1955-62, European Economics Correspondent, 1964-67, South Asia Correspondent, 1967-68, National Bureau Reporter, 1968-71, London Correspondent, Washington Post; UN Bureau Chief, New York Times, 1979-83. Publications: The Mythmakers, 1964; Soft State, 1970; Britain: A Future that Works, 1978; The Global Struggle for More, 1987. Contributions to: American Economics Review; Harvard Business Review; Annals American Academy Political Science. Memberships: Nieman Fellow, Harvard, 1962-63; Reform Club, Council of Foreign Relations. Address: 6 Montagu Place, London W1H 1RF, England.

NOTLEY Alice, b. 8 Nov 1945, Bisbee, Arizona, USA. Poet. m. Douglas Oliver, 10 Feb 1988, 2 sons (Ted Berrigan). Education: BA Barnard College, 1967; MFA, The Writers' Workshop, University of Iowa, 1970. Publications: Alice Ordered Me to Be Made, 1976; When I Was Alive, 1980; How Spring Comes, 1981; Waltzing Matilda, 1981; Margaret and Dusty, 1985; At Night the States, 1988; Beginning with a Stain; Homer's Art, 1991; The Scarlet Cabinet (with Douglas Oliver), 1992. Contributions to: Co-editor of Scarlet & frequent contributor. Honours: NEA Award, 1979; The Poetry Center Book Award, 1982; GE Foundation Award, 1984; NYFA Fellowship, 1991. Address: 61 rue Lepic, 75018, France.

NOVAK Maximillian Erwin, b. 26 Mar 1930, New York City, USA. University Professor. m. Estelle Gershgoren, 21 Aug 1966, 2 sons, 1 daughter. Education: Phd, University of California, 1958; DPhil, St John's University, Oxford, 1961. Appointments: Assistant Professor, University of Michigan, 1958-62; Assistant Professor, Professor, University of California, Los Angeles, 1962-. Publications: Economics and The Fiction of Daniel Defoe, 1962; Defoe and The Nature of Man, 1963; Congreve, 1970; Realism Myth and History in The Fiction of Daniel Defoe, 1983; Eighteenth Century English Literature, 1983; Editor, The Wild Man Within, 1970; English Literature in The Age of Disguise, 1977; California Dryden Volumes X and X111, 1971, 1984. Contributions to : Essays in Criticism; PMLA; JEGP; MP; PQ; SEL; Kenyon Review; SP; Studies in The Literary Imagination; MLR; TSLL. Address: Deparment of English, University of California, Los Angeles, CA 90095-1530, USA.

NOVAK Michael, b. 1933, PA, USA. Professor. m. Karen Laub, 1 s, 2 d. Education: AB, Stonehill College, 1956; BT, Gregorian University, Rome, 1958; Theological studies at Catholic University; MA, History and Philosophy of Religion, Harvard University, 1966. Appointments include: Teaching Fellow, Harvard University, 1961-63; Tenured Chair, University Professor and Ledden-Watson Distinguished Professor of Religion, Syracuse University, 1976; Resident Scholar, American Enterprise Institute, 1978-, currently holds George Frederick Jewett Chair in Religion and Public Policy and is Director of Social and Political Studies at The Institute, Washington DC; W Harold and Martha Welch Chair as Professor of American Studies at The University of Notre Dame for autumn semesters of 1987 and 1988; Headed US Delegation to the Experts' Meeting on Human Contacts at The Conference on Security and Cooperation in Europe (continuation of the Helsinki Accord negotiations), March 1986; W Harold and Martha Welch chair, Professor of American Studies, University of Notre Dame, 1987, 1988. Publications include: Wrote text of New Consensus on Family and Welfare, 1987; This Hemisphere of Liberty, 1990; Choosing Presidents, 1992; The Catholic Ethic and The Spirit of Capitalism, 1994; Works of fiction include: The Tiber Was Silver, 1961; Naked I Leave, 1970; Free Persons and The Common Good, 1989. Contributions include: Author and Editor of numerous monographs and over 200 articles; many articles, essays and columns in journals; Editor-in-chief, Crisis, 1993-; Writings ha ve appeared in every major Western language and in Bengali, korean and Japanese. Address: American Enterprise Institute, 1150 17th Street NW, Washington DC, 20036, USA.

NOVAK Robert. See: **LEVINSON Leonard.**

NOVE Alec, b. 1915, United Kingdom. Emeritus Professor of Economics, University of Glasgow, Scotland. Publications: The Soviet Economy, 1961; Was Stalin Really Necessary, 1964; The Soviet Middle East (with J A Newth), 1967; An Economic History of the USSR, 1969, 3rd edition 1993; Socialist Economics (edited with D M Nuti), 1972; Efficiency Criteria for Nationalised Industries, 1973; Stalinism and After, 1975; The Soviet Economic System, 1977; Political Economy and Soviet Socialism, 1979; The Economics of Feasible Socialism, 1983; Socialism, Economics and Development, 1986; Studies in Economics and Russia, 1990; Glasnost in Action, 1990; The Stalin Phenomenon (editor), 1993. Address: Hamilton Drive, Glasgow G12 8DP, Scotland.

NOWRA Louis, b. 1950, Melbourne, Victoria, Australia. Playwright. Education: La Trobe University, Victoria. Appointments include: Co-Artistic Director, Lighthouse Company, Sydney, 1983. Publications include: Albert Names Edward, 1975; Inner Voices, 1977; Visions, 1978; Inside the Island, 1980; The Precious Woman, 1980; The Song Room, 1981; Lulu, after Wedekind, 1981; Royal Show, 1982; The Prince of Homburg, After Kleist, 1982; The Golden Age, 1985; Whitsunday Opera Libretto, 1988; Byzantine Flowers, 1989; Summer of the Aliens, 1989; Cosi, 1992; Radiance, 1993; Crow, 1994; Radio & TV Plays; Novels, The Misery of Beauty, 1976; Palu, 1987. Honours include: Australian Literature Board Fellowships. Address: Hilary Linstead & Associated, Suite 302, Easts Tower, 9-13 Bronte Road, Bondi Junction, NSW 2022, Australia.

NOYES Stanley Tinning, b. 7 Apr 1924, San Francisco, CA, USA. Teacher; Writer. m. Nancy Black, 12 Mar 1949, 2 s, 1 d. Education: BA, English, 1950, MA, English, 1951, University of California, Berkeley. Literary Appointments: Literary Arts Coordinator, New Mexico Arts Division, 1972-86. Publications: No Flowers For a Clown, novel, 1961; Shadowbox, novel, 1970; Faces and Spirits, poems, 1974; Beyond The Mountains Beyond The Mountains, poems, 1979; The Commander of Dead Leaves, poems, 1984; Los Comanches: The Horse People, 1751-1845, history, 1993. Contributions to: San Francisco Review; New Mexico Quarterly; Sumac; The Cold Mountain Review; San Marcos Review; Puerto del Sol; The Greenfield Review; High Plains Literary Review; Floating Island; others. Honours: MacDowell Fellow, 1967. Membership: PEN American Center. Literary Agent: Maria Theresa Caen, 2901 Scott Street, San Francisco, CA 94123, USA. Address: 634 East Garcia, Santa Fe, NM 87501, USA.

NOZICK Robert, b. 16 Nov 1938, NY, USA. Professor; Writer. m. Gjertrud Schnackenberg, 5 Oct 1987, 1 s, 1 d. Education: AB, Columbia College, 1959; PhD, Princeton University, 1963. Literary Appointments: Assistant Professor, Princeton University, 1964-65; Assistant Professor, Harvard University, 1965-67; Associate Professor, Rockefeller University, 1967-69; Professor, Harvard University, 1969-; Arthur Kingsley Professor of Philosophy, Harvard University, 1985-. Publications: Anarchy State & Utopia, 1974; Philosophical Explanations, 1981; The Examined Life, 1989; The Nature of Rationality, 1993. Honours: National Book Award, 1975; Ralph Waldo Emerson Award, 1982. Memberships: PEN; Am Academy of Arts & Science; Am Philosophical Association. Literary Agent: Georges Borchardt. Address: Emerson Hall, Harvard University, Cambridge, MA 02138, USA.

NUDELSTEJER Sergio, b. 24 Feb 1924, Warsaw, Poland. Writer; Journalist. m. Tosia Malamud. Education: National University of Mexico. Publications: Theodor Herzl, Prophet of Our Times, 1961; The Rebellion Of Silence, 1971; Albert Einstein: A Man in His Time, 1980; Franz Kafka: Concience of An Era, 1983; Borges: Getting Near to His Literary Work, 1987; Rosario Castellanos: The Voice, The Word, The Memory, Anthology, 1984; Elais Canetti: The Language of Passion, 1990; Spies of God-Authors of End of Century, 1992 and Stefan Zweig: The Concience of Man, 1992. Contributions to: Writer, daily newspaper Excelsior; Writer, Revista de Revistas, Plural and Coloquio published in Argentina Magazines; Editor, Tribuna Israelita. Address: Heraclito 331, Appartment 601, Polanco, Mexico 11560, Mexico D F.

NUGENT Neill, b. 22 Mar 1947, Newcastle-on-Tyne, England. Professor. m. Maureen Nugent, 12 Sept 1969, 2 daughters. Education: BA, Politics, Social Administration, University of Newcastle, 1969; MA, Government, University of Kent, 1970; London School of Economics, 1970-71. Publications: The British Right (with R King); Respectable Rebels (with R King); The Left in France (with D Lowe); The Government and Politics of the European Union, 1994; The European Business Environment (with R O'Donnell), 1994; The European Union: Annual Review of Activities, 1993 and 1994. Contributions to: numerous articles on aspects of British and European politics to academic and professional journals. Memberships: Political Studies Association; University Association for Contemporary European Studies; European Community Studies Association, USA. Address: Department of Politics and philosophy, Manchester Metropolitan University, Chatham/Undercroft Building, Manchester M15 6BR, England.

NULAND Sherwyn B. Physician; Professor. m. children. Appointments: Physician; Professor of Surgery & History of Medicine, Yale University; Literary Editor, Connecticut Medicine; Chairman, Board of Managers, Journal of the History of Medicine & Allied Sciences. Publications: Doctors: the Biography of Medicine; How We Die: Reflections on Life's Final Chapter; Face of Mercy; Medicine: the Art of Healing/Origins of Anaesthesia. Contributions to: New Yorker; New Republic; Discover. Honours: National Book Award, 1994.

NUNIS Doyce B(lackman), b. 1924. American. Professor of History; Writer. Appointments: Associate Professor 1965-68, Professor of History 1968-, Emeritus 1989, University of Southern California, Los Angeles; Editor, Southern California Quarterly, 1962-; President, Board of Trustees, Mission Santa Barbara Archive, 1971-; Historian, El Pueblo de Los Angeles State Historic Park, 1971-80. Publications include: Andrew Sublette, Rocky Mountain Prince, 1960; (ed), The Golden Frontier, 1962; (ed), Josiah Belden, 1841 California Overland Pioner, 1962; (ed), Letters of a Young Miner, 1964; (ed), California Diary of Farm Dean Atherton, 1964; (ed), Journey of James A Bull, 1967; (trans with L Jay Oliva), A California Medical Journey, by Pierre Garnier, MD, 1967; Trials of Issac Graham, 1968; Past is Prologue: Centennial Profile of Pacific Mutual Life Insurance Co, 1968; (ed), Hudson's Bay Company's First Fur Brigade to Sacramento Valley: Alexander McLeod's 1829 Hunt, 1968; (ed), Sketches of a Journey on the Two Oceans, by Abbe Henri-J-A Alric, 1971; (ed), San Francisco Vigilance Committee of 1856: Three Views, 1971; (ed), The Drawing of Ignacio Tirsch, SJ, 1972; (ed), Los Angeles and Its Environs in the Twentieth Century: A Bibliography of a Metropolis, 1973; A History of American Political Thought, 2 vols, 1975; The Mexican War in Baja, California, 1977; (ed), A Frontier Doctor, by Henry F Hoyt, 1979; (ed), Angeles from the Days of the Pueblo, 1981; (ed), The Letters of Jacob Baegart, 1749-1761: Jesuit Missionary in Baja California, 1982; (ed), Transit of Venus: The First Planned Scientific Expedition in Baja California, 1982; Men, Medicine and Water: The Building of the Los Angeles Aqueduct 1908-1913, 1982; (ed), Frontier Fighter by George W Coe, 1984; (ed), Southern California Historical Anthology, 1984; (ed), The Life of Tom Horn, 1987; (co-ed), A Guide to the History of California, 1988. Memberships: Sheriff, Los Angeles Corral of Westerners, 1973; President, Zamorano Club, 1975-76; Atheneaum, London. Address: Department of History, University of Southern California, Los Angeles, CA 90089, USA.

NUNN Frederick McKinley, b. 1937, United States of American. Writer (History, Politics/Government). Appointments include: Editorial Advisory Board, Military Affairs, 1973-78; Board of Editors, Latin American Research Review, 1984-85. Publications: Chilean Politics, 1920-31; The Honorable Mission of the Armed Forces, 1970; The Military in Chilean History: Essays on Civil-Military Relations, 1810-1973, 1976; Yesterdays Soldiers: European Military Professionalism in South America 1890-1940, 1983; The Time of the Generals: Latin American Professional Militarism in World Perspective, 1992. Address: Department of History, Portland State University, PO Box 751, Portland, OR 92707, USA.

NUTTALL Jeffrey, b. 8 July 1933, Clitheroe, Lancashire, England. Artist. div., 5 sons, 1 daughter. Education: Intermediate Examination, Arts and Crafts, Hereford School of Art, 1951; NDD, Painting (Special Level), Bath Academy of Art, Corsham, 1953; ATD, Institute of Education, London University, 1954. Appointments: Sergeant Instructor, Royal Army Education Corps, 1954-56; Art Master, Secondary Modern Schools, Leominster, 1956-59, East Finchley, London, 1956-63, Barnet, 1963-67; English Master, Greenacre Secondary Modern, Great Yarmouth, 1967-68; Lecturer, Foundation Course, Bradford College of Art, 1968-70; Senior Lecturer, Fine Art, Leeds Polytechnic, 1970-81; Head, Fine Art Department, Liverpool Polytechnic, 1981-84; Part-time teaching, 1984-; Occasional broadcasts, London Weekend TV, Granada TV, Yorkshire TV, BBC Radio; Exhibited paintings in numerous exhibitions. Publications include: Verse: Objects, 1973; Sun Barbs, 1974; Grape Notes/Apple Music, 1979; Scenes and Dubs, 1987; Mad with Music, 1987; Fiction: The Gold Hole, 1968; Snipe's Spinster, 1973; The Patriarchs, 1975; Anatomy of My Father's Corpse, 1976; What Happened to Jackson, 1977; Muscle, 1980; Teeth, 1994; Non-fiction: King Twist, A Portrait of Frank Randle, 1978; Performance Art, Vol I: Memoirs, 1979, Vol II: Scripts, 1979; Knuckleduster Funnies, 4 issues (contributor, edited with Robert Banks), comic book, 1986; The Pleasures of Necessity, 1989; The Bald Soprano, 1989; Graphics: Come Back Sweet Prince, 1965; Oscar Christ and the Immaculate Conception, 1970; The Fox's Lair, 1972. Contributions to: Poetry criticism, Guardian, 1979-82; Criticism and comment, numerous journals; Columnist, Observer Review. Honours: No 3 Winner, Teeth, Novel in a Day Competition, Groucho Club, 1994. Address: 71 White Hart Lane, Barnes, London SW13 0PP, England.

NUWER Henry (Hank) Joseph, b. 19 Aug 1946, Buffalo, NY, USA. Author. m. (1) Alice Cemiglia, 28 Dec 1968, (div 1980), (2) Jenine Howard, 9 Apr 1982, 2 s. Education: BS, State University College of New York, Buffalo, 1968; MA, New Mexico Highlands University, 1970;

PhD equivalency, Ball State University, 1988. Literary Appointments: Assistant Professor of English, Clemson University, 1982-83; Associate Professor of Journalism, Ball State University, 1985-89; Senior Writer, Rodale Press Book Division, Emmaus, PA, 1990-91; Historian, Cedar Crest College, 1991-93; Editor, Arts Indiana Magazine, 1993-. Publications include: Non-fiction: Strategies of The Great Baseball Managers, 1988; Recruiting in Sports, 1989; Steroids, 1990; Sports Scandals, 1994; Broken Pledges: The Deadly Rite of Hazing, 1990; How To Write Like an Expert, 1995; Come Out, Come Out Wherever You Are, (with Carole Shaw) 1982; Fiction: The Bounty Hunter series, (with William Boyles) 4 volumes, 1980-82; Non-fiction works in progress: Biography of Jesse Owens; History of Cedar Crest College. Address: Arts Indiana, 47 S Pennsylvania, Suite 701, Indianapolis, IN 46204, USA.

NYE Joseph S(amuel) Jr, b. 1937, New Jersey, USA. University Professor. m. Molly Harding, 3 sons. Education: BA summa cum laude, Princeton University, 1958; Degree in Philosophy, Politics, Economics, Oxford University, England; PhD, Political Science, Harvard University, 1964. Appointments: Instructor, 1964-66, Assistant Professor 1966-69, Associate Professor 1969-71, Professor of International Security 1971-, Director, Center for Science and International Affiars, 1985-90, Director Center for International Affairs, 1990-, Harvard University, Cambridge, Massachusetts; Deputy to Under-Secretary of State for Security Assistance, Science and Technology, 1977-79; Editorial Board, Foreign Policy and International Security magazines. Publications: Pan-Africanism and East African Integration, 1965; International Regionalism (editor), 1968; Peace in Parts: Integration and Conflict in Regional Organization, 1971; Conflict Management by International Organizations, 1972; Transnational Relations and World Politics (author, edited with R O Keohane), 1972; Power and Independence, 1977; Energy and Security (edited with David Deese), 1980; Living with Nuclear Weapons, 1983; The Making of America's Soviet Policy, 1984; Global Dilemmas (edited with Samuel P Huntingdon), 1985; Hawks, Doves, and Owls (co-author), 1985; Nuclear Ethics, 1986; Fateful Visions (co-editor), 1988; Bound to Lead: The Changing Nature of American Power, 1990; Understanding International Conflicts, 1993. Contributions to: Professional and scholarly journals; New York Times; Washington Post; Los Angeles Times; Boston Globe; Christian Science Monitor; Atlantic Monthly; New Republic. Honours: Rhodes Scholar, Oxford; Distinguished Honor Award, Department of State, 1979. Memberships: Fellow, American Academy of Arts and Sciences; Senior Fellow, Aspen Institute; International Institute for Strategic Studies; Advisory Committee, Institute for International Economics; Director, United Nation Association. Address: Center for International Affairs, Harvard University, 1737 Cambridge Street, Cambridge, MA 02138, USA.

NYE Nelson (Clem Colt, Drake C Denver), b. 28 Sept 1907, Chicago, USA. Writer. m. 1) 1 daughter, 2) Ruth Hilton, 1937. Education: Studied art and engineering. Publications: Pistols for Hire, 1941; Not Grass Alone, 1961; Maverick Marshal, 1958; Riders by Night, 1950; Horse Thieves, 1987; Mule Man, 1988; Wild Horse Shorty, 1944; The Parson of Gunbarrel Basin, 1955; Wide Loop, 1952; Gunfight at the OK Corral; Trail of Lost Skulls, 1967. Contributions to: Ford Times; The Speed Horse; Quarter Horse Journal; Western Horseman; Thoroughbred Record; Blood Horse. Honours: Spur Award for Best Western Critic, 1954; Spur Award for Best Western Novel, 1959; Editorial Award, Quarter Racing Owners of America, 1972. Memberships: Western Writers of America Incorporated, Co-Founder, twice President, twice Judge, Director; Judge, Best Western category, 1989. Address: 2290 W Ironwood Ridge Drive, Tucson, AZ 85745, USA.

NYE Robert, b. 1939. Poet; Novelist; Literary Critic. Literary appointments: Poetry Editor, The Scotsman, 1967-; Poetry Critic, The Times, London, 1971-. Publications: Juvenilia, 1, poems, 1961, 2, poems, 1963; Taliesin, juvenile, 1966; March Has Horse's Ears, juvenile, 1966; Doubtfire, novel, 1967; Beowulf, 1968; Tales I Told My Mother, 1969; Sawney Bean (with Bill Watson), 1969; Sisters, 1969; Darker Ends, poems, 1969; Wishing Gold, 1970; Fugue, screenplay, 1971; Poor Pumpkin, 1971; A Choice of Sir Walter Raleigh's Verse, 1972; The Mathematical Princess and Other Stories, 1972; Cricket, 1972; A Choice of Swinburne's Verse; The Faber Book of Sonnets, 1976; Penthesilia, 1976; Falstaff, novel, 1976; The English Sermon 1750-1850, 1976; Divisions on a Ground, poems, 1976; Out of the World and Back Again, juvenile, 1977; Merlin, novel, 1978; The Bird of the Golden Land, 1980; Faust, novel, 1980; Harry Pay the Pirate, juvenile, 1981; The Voyage of the Destiny, novel, 1982; The Facts of

Life and Other Fictions, 1983; Three Tales, for children, 1983; PEN New Poetry 1 (editor), 1986; William Barnes, selected poems (editor), 1988; The Memoirs of Lord Byron, novel, 1989; A Collection of Poems 1955-1988, 1989; The Life and Death of My Lord Gilles de Rais, novel, 1990; First Awakenings: The Early Poems of Laura Riding (edited with Elizabeth Friedmann and Alan J Clark), 1992; Mrs Shakespeare, novel, 1993; A Selection of the Poems of Laura Riding (editor), 1994; 14 Poems, 1994; Spine Chilling Tales, juvenile, 1995; Henry James and other poems, 1995; Collected Poems, 1995. Honours: Gregory Award, for Poetry, 1963; The Guardian Fiction Prize, 1976; Hawthornden Prize, 1977; Travel Scholarship, Society of Authors, 1991. Membership: Fellow, Royal Society of Literature, 1976. Literary Agent: Sheil Land Associates Ltd, England. Address: c/o Sheil Land Associates Ltd, 43 Doughty Street, London WC1N 2LF, England.

NYE Simon Beresford, b. 29 July 1958, Burgess Hill, Sussex, England. Writer. Education: BA, French, German, Bedford College, London University, 1980; Diploma, Technical Translation, Polytechnic of Central London, 1985. Publications: Men Behaving Badly, 1989, 1992, as situation comedy, 2 series, Thames TV, 1992, BBC, 1994; First Awakenings: The Early Poems of Laura Riding (edited with Wideboy, 1991, as comedy drama series Frank Stubbs Promotes, Carlton TV, Series I, 1993, Series 2, 1994; Translator: The Vienna Opera, 1985; Braque, 1986; Matisse: Graphic Works, 1987. Contributions to: Sunday Times. Honours: Winner, Best ITV Sitcom, for Men Behaving Badly, ITV Comedy Awards, 1993. Literary Agent: Rod Hall, A P Watt Ltd, London, England. Address: 5 Nassington Road, London, NW3 2TX, England.

O

O'BALANCE Edgar, b. 1918. Freelance Writer; Journalist. Publications: The Arab-Israeli War, 1956; The Sinai Campaign, 1956, 1959; The Story of the French Foreign Legion, 1961; The Red Army of China, 1962; The Indo-China War 1945-1954, 1964; The Red Army of Russia, 1964; The Greek Civil War 1948-1960, 1966; The Algerian Insurrection 1954-1962, 1967; The Third Arab-Israeli War 1967, 1972; The Kurdish Revolt 1961-1970, 1973; Arab Guerilla Power, 1974; The Electronic War in the Middle East 1968-1970, 1974; The Wars in Vietnam 1954-1972, 1975; The Secret War in the Sudan 1955-1972, 1977; No Victor, No Vanquished, 1978; The Language of Violence, 1979; Terror in Ireland, 1979; The Bloodstained Cedars of Lebanon, 1980; The Tracks of the Bear, 1982; The Gulf War, 1988; The Cyanide War, 1989; Terrorism in the 1980s, 1989; Wars in Afghanistan: 1839-1990, 1991; The Second Gulf War; The Civil War in Yugoslavia; Civil War in Bosnia: 1992, 1994. Membership: Former Chairman, Military Commentators Circle. Address: Wakebridge Cottage, Wakebridge, Matlock, Derbyshire, England.

O'BRIAN Geoffrey, b. 4 May 1948, New York, New York, USA. Freelance Writer; Translator. m. Kaalii Francis, 18 March 1977. Education: Yale University; BA, State University of New York at Stony Brook; Nichibei Kaiwa Gaku-in, Tokyo, Japan. Appointments: Co-editor, Pony Tail, 1968-70, Montemora, 1975-76; Editor, Frogpond, 1981; Executive Editor, Library of America. Publications: poems in anthologies including: Open Poetry, 1973; Active Anthology, 1974; selected Poetry of Vincente Huidobro, 1981; Hard Boiled America: The Lurid Years of Paperbacks, 1981; Dream Time: Chapters from the Sixties, 1988; The Book of Maps, 1989; The Reader's Catalog (ed). Contributions to: Stony Brook; Chicago Review; Soho News; Village Voice; Res Gestae; Airplane; Wind Chimes; Dyslexia; New Observations. Address: c/o W W Norton Co, 500 Fifth Avenue, New York, NY 10110; USA.

O'BRIEN Conor Cruise (Donat O'Donnell), b. 1917, Ireland. Writer (History, Politics/Government). Education includes: PhD. Appointments include: Member, Irish Delegation to United Nations, New York City, 1956-60; Labour Member of Dail Eirann (Irish Parliament) for Dublin North East, 1969-77; Minister of Posts and Telegraphs, 1973-77; Pro-Chancellor, Dublin University, 1973-; Consultant Editor, The Observer newspaper, London, 1981-. Publications: Maria Cross, 1952; Parnell and His Party, 1957; The Shaping of Modem Ireland, 1959; To Katanga and Back, 1962; Conflicting Concepts for the U.N., 1964I Writers and Politics, 1965; The United Nations: Sacred Drama, 1967; Murderous Angels, play, 1968; Power and Consciousness, 1969; Albert Camus, 1969; Edmund Burke: Reflections on the Revolution in France, 1969; Conor Cruise O'Brien Introduces Ireland, 1969; The Suspecting Glance (with M Cruise O'Brien), 1970; A Concise History of Ireland, 1971; States of Ireland, 1972; King Herod Advises, play, 1973; Neighbours, 1980; The Siege: The Saga of Israel and Zionism, 1986; Passion and Cunning and Godland, 1988; Reflections on Religion and Nationalism, 1988; The Great Melody: A Thematic Biography and Commented Anthology of Edmund Burke, 1992, Paperback Edition, 1993. Contributions to: Contributing editor, The Atlantic Monthly Bulletin. Literary Agent: Lady Greene, Greene and Heaton Ltd, 37a Goldhawk Road, London W12 8QQ, England. Address: Whitewater, Howth Summit, Dublin, Republic of Ireland.

O'BRIEN Edna, b. 15 Dec 1936, Tuamgraney, County Clare, Republic of Ireland. Author. m. 1954, div. 1964, 2 sons. Education: Pharmaceutical College of Ireland. Publications: The Country Girls, 1960, film, 1983; The Lonely Girl, 1962; Girls in Their Married Bliss, 1963; August is a Wicked Month, 1964; Casualties of Peace, 1966; The Love Object, 1968; A Pagan Place, 1970, play, 1971; Night, 1972; A Scandalous Woman, short stories, 1974; Mother Ireland, 1976; Johnny I Hardly Knew You, novel, 1977; Arabian Days, 1977; Mrs Reinhardt and Other Stories, 1978; The Wicked Lady, screenplay, 1981; Virginia, play, 1981; The Dazzle, children's book; Returning: A Collection of New Tales, 1982; A Christmas Treat, 1982; Home Sweet Home, play, 1984; Stories of Joan of Arc, film, 1984; A Fanatic Heart, Selected Stories, 1985; Flesh and Blood, play, 1987; Madame Bovary, play, 1987; Vanishing Ireland, 1987; Tales for the Telling, children's book; The High Road, fiction, 1989; Lantern Slides, short stories, 1990; Time and Tide, 1992. Honours: Yorkshire Post Novel Award, 1971; Kingsley Amis

Award. Address: c/o Douglas Rae Management, 28 Charing Cross Road, London WC2 0DB, England.

O'BRIEN Stephen. See: LEVINE Stuart.

O'BRIEN Tim. b. 1946, Austin, MN, USA. Education: BA, Macalester College. Publications: If I Die in a Combat Zone, Box Me Up & Ship Me Home, 1973; Nothern Lights, 1975; Going After Cacciato: a novel, 1978; The Nuclear Age, 1985. Honours: Fellow, American Academy & Institute of Arts & Letters, 1982; O Henry Memorial Award, 1976; National Book Award, 1979; Vietnam Veterans of America Award, 1987; Heartland Prize, Chicago Tribune, 1990.

O'BRIEN CORDOBA Esteban. See: LEVINE Stuart.

O'CASEY Brenda. See. HAYCRAFT Anna (Margaret).

O'CONNELL Richard (James), b. 25 Oct 1928, New York City, USA. Poet; Educator. Education: BS, Temple University, 1956; MA, Johns Hopkins University, 1957. Publications: Brazilian Happenings, 1966; Terrane, 1967; Epigrams From Martial, 1976; Hudson's Fourth Voyage, 1978; Irish Monastic Poems, 1984; Temple Poems, 1985; Hanging Tough, 1986; Battle Poems, 1987; Selected Epigrams, 1990; New Epigrams from Martial, 1991; The Caliban Poems, 1992; RetroWorlds, 1993; Simulations, 1993; Voyages, 1995. Contributions to: New Yorker; Paris Review; Atlantic Monthly; National Review; Quarterly Review of Literature; Littack; Acumen; Texas Quarterly and others. Honours: Fulbright Lecturer, University of Brazil,1960; Fulbright Lecturer, University of Navarre, Pamplona, Spain, 1962-63; Contemporary Poetry Prize, 1972; Yaddo Foundation Writing Residency, 1974, 1975. Memberships: American PEN Club; Modern Language Association. Address: 1150 Hillsboro Mile, #815, Hillsboro Beach, FL 33062, USA.

O'CONNOR Patrick, b. 8 Sept 1949, London, England. Writer; Editor. Appointments: Deputy Editor, Harpers and Queen, 1981-86; Contributing Editor, F M R, 1986; Editor-in-Chief, Publications, Metropolitan Opera Guild, 1987-89; Consulting Editor, The New Grove Dictionary of Opera, 1989-91. Publications: Josephine Baker (with B Hammond), 1988; Toulouse-Lautrec: The Nightlife of Paris, 1991; The Amazing Blonde Woman, 1991. Contributions to: The Times Literary Supplement; Literary Review; Daily Telegraph; Gramophone; Opera; House and Garden; Music and Letters; The Independent. Memberships: National Union of Journalists; PEN. Literary Agent: Deborah Rodgers, London, England. Address: c/o Rodgers, Coleridge and White, 20 Powis Mews, London W11 1JN, England.

O'CONNOR Robert Patrick. See: PATRICK Robert.

O'DANIEL Janet (Lillian Janet), b. United States of America. Author. Publications: Touchstone (novel with L Ressler), 1947; City Beyond Devil's Gate (with L Ressler), 1950; O Genesee, 1958; The Cliff Hangers, 1961; Garrett's Crossing (children), 1969; A Part for Addie (children), 1974; As Evelyn Claire: Storm Remembered, 1984; No More Heartache, 1986; Prescription for Love, 1987; As Amanda Clark: Flower of the Sea, 1985. Address: 211 Birchwood Avenue, Upper Nyack, NY 10960, USA.

O'DONNELL Donat. See: O'BRIEN Conor Cruise.

O'DONNELL K M. See: MALZBERG Barry Norman.

O'DONNELL Kevin Jr, b. 1950, United States of America. Author. Appointments: Assistant Lecturer in English, Hong Kong Baptist College, 1972-73; American English Language Institute, Taipei, 1973-74; Managing Editor, 1979-81, Publisher 1983, Empire, New Haven, Connecticut. Publications: Bander Snatch, 1979; Mayflies, 1979; Caverns, 1981; Reefs, 1981; War of Omission, 1982; Lava, 1982; ORA:CLE, 1984; The Electronic Money Book (non-fication with the Haven Group), 1984; Cliffs, 1986.

O'DONNELL M R. See: ROSS-MACDONALD Malcolm John.

O'DONNELL Michael, b. 20 Oct 1928. Author; Broadcaster. m. Catherine Dorrington Ward, 1953, 1 son, 2 daughters. Education: MBBChir, St Thomas' Hospital Medical School, London, England. Appointments: Editor, Cambridge Writing, 1948; Scriptwriter, BBC Radio, 1949-52; General Medical Practitioner, 1954-64; Editor, World Medicine, 1966-82; Scientific Adviser: O Lucky Man, 1972; Inside

Medicine, 1974; Don't Ask Me, 1977; Don't Just Sit There, 1979-80; Where There's Life, 1981-83. Publications: (TV Plays): Suggestion of Sabotage, 1963; Dangerous Reunion, 1964; Resolution, 1964; (TV Documentaries): You'll Never Believe It, 1962; Cross Your Heart and Hope to Live, 1975; The Presidential Race, 1976; From Europe to the Coast, 1976; Chasing the Dragon, 1979; Second Opinion, 1980; Judgement on Las Vegas, 1981; Is Your Brain Really Necessary, 1982; Plague of Hearts, 1983; Medical Express, 1984; Can You Avoid Cancer, 1984; O'Donnell Investigates...Booze, 1985; O'Donnell Investigates....food, 1985; O'Donnell Investigates...the food business, 1986; Health, Wealth and Happiness, 1989; What is This Thing Called Health, 1990; Radio: Serious Professional Misconduct, 1992. Contributor to: Stop the Week (BBC), 1976-; Chairman, My Word (BBC), 1983; (Books), Cambridge Anthology, 1952; The Europe We Want, 1971; My Medical School, 1978; The Devil's Prison, 1982; Doctor! Doctor! an Insider's Guide to the Games Doctors Play, 1986; The Long Walk Home, 1988; Dr Michael O'Donnell's Executive Health Guide, 1988. Contributions to: Punch; New Scientist; Vogue; The Times; Sunday Times; Daily Telegraph; Daily Mail; The Listener. Literary Agent: A P Watt. Address: Handon Cottage, Markwick Lane, Loxhill, Godalming, Surrey GU8 4BD, England.

O'DONNELL Peter (Madeleine Brent), b. 1920. Author. Appointments: Writer of Strip Cartoons: Garth, 1953-66; Tug Transom, 1954-66; Romeo Brown, 1956-62; Modesty Blaise, 1963-. Publications: Modesty Blaise, 1965; Sabre-Tooth, 1966; I, Lucifer, 1967; A Taste for Death, 1969; The Impossible Virgin, 1971; Pieces of Modesty, short stories, 1972; The Silver Mistress, 1973; Murder Most Logical, play, 1974; Last Day in Limbo, 1976; Dragon's Claw, 1978; The Xanadu Talisman, 1981; The Night of Morningstar, 1982; Dead Man's Handle, 1985; As Madeleine Brent: Tregaron's Daughter, 1971; Moonraker's Bride, 1973; Kirkby's Changeling, 1975; Merlin's Keep, 1977; The Capricorn Stone, 1979; The Long Masquerade, 1981; A Heritage of Shadows, 1983; Stormswift, 1984; Golden Urchin, 1986. Address: 49 Sussex Square, Brighton BN2 1GE, England.

O'DONOVAN Joan Mary, b. 31 Dec 1914, Mansfield, England. Retired. Appointment: Former General Advisor for Education, Oxfordshire, retired 1977. Publications: Dangerous Worlds, 1958; The Visited, 1959; Shadows on the Wall, 1960; The Middle Tree, 1961; The Niceties of Life, 1964; She, Alas, 1965; Little Brown Jesus, 1970; Argument with an East Wind, 1986. Contributions to: Times Educational Supplement; The Guardian; Punch; Vogue; Harper's and Queen. Memberships: Society of Authors; International PEN. Address: 14 Rue du Four, 24600 Ribérac, France.

O'DRISCOLL Dennis, b. 1 Jan 1954, Thurles, County Tipperary, Ireland. Editor: Poet. m. Julie O'Callaghan, 1985. Education: University College Dublin, 1972-75. Appointments include: Literary Organiser, Dublin Arts Festival, 1977-79; Editor, Poetry Ireland Review, 1986-87. Publications: Kist, 1982; Hidden Extras, 1987; Co Editor, The First Ten Years: Dublin Arts Festival Poetry, 1979. Honours include: Irish Arts Council Bursary. Address: Ketu, Breffni Gate, Church Road, Dalkey, County Dublin, Ireland.

O'FAOLAIN Julia, b. 6 June 1932, London, England. Writer. m. Lauro Rene Martines, 14 Dec 1957, 1 son. Education: BA 1952, MA 1953, University College, Dublin; Scholarship, Italian Government for Study at Rome University, 1952-53; Travelling Studentship, National University of Ireland, 1953-55. Publications: No Country for Young Men, 1980; Women in the Wall, 1975; The Obedient Wife, 1982; The Irish Signorina, 1984; Daughters of Passion, 1982; Man in the Cellar, 1974; We Might See Sights! and Other Stories, 1968; Godded and Codded, 1970; Editor, Not in God's Image: Women in History from the Greeks to the Victorians, with Lauro Martines, 1973; Novel, The Judas Cloth, 1992. Contributions to: numerous magazines & newspapers. Membership: Society of Authors. Literary Agent: Deborah Rogers Ltd, Literary Agency, 20 Powis Mews, London W11 1JN, England.

O'FARRELL Patrick James, b. 17 Sept 1933, Greymouth, New Zealand. Professor of History. m. Deirdre Genevieve MacShane, 29 Dec 1956, 3 sons, 2 daughters. Education includes: MA, New Zealand, 1956; PhD, Australian National University, 1961. Appointments include: Professor, School of History, University of New South Wales, Australia. Publications: The Catholic Church in Australia, A Short History, 1968; Documents in Australian Catholic History, 2 volumes, 1969; Harry Holland, Militant Socialist, 1969; Ireland's English Question, 1971; England and Ireland since 1800, 1975; Letters from Irish Australia, 1984; The Catholic Church and Community. An Australian History,

1985; The Irish in Australia, 1986; Vanished Kingdoms Irish in Australia and New Zealand, 1990; Through Irish Eyes, Australian and New Zealand Images of the Irish, 1788-1948, 1994. Contributions to: Historical, literary and religious journals. Honours: New South Wales Premier's Literary Award, 1987. Memberships: Australian Society of Authors; Fellow, Australian Academy of the Humanities. Address: School of History, University of New South Wales, Sydney 2052, New South Wales, Australia.

O'FLAHERTY Patrick Augustine, b. 6 Oct 1939, Long Beach, Newfoundland, Canada. Professor; Writer. 3 s. Education: BA (Hons); MA; PhD. Publications: The Rock Observed, 1979; Part of The Main: An Illustrated History of Newfoundland and Labrador (with Peter Neary), 1983; Summer of The Greater Yellowlegs, 1987; Priest of God, 1989; A Small Place in The Sun, 1989; By Great Waters (with Peter Neary); Come Near at Your Peril: A Visitor's Guide to The Island of Newfoundland, 1992 (revised 1994); Benny's Island, 1994. Contributions to: Weekend Magazine; Saturday Night; Canadian Forum; Queen's Quarterly; Globe and Mail; Ottawa Citizen; others. Membership: The Writers Union of Canada. Address: Box 2676 St Johns, Newfoundland, Canada, A1C 6K1.

O'GRADY Desmond James Bernard, b. 27 Aug 1935, Limerick City, Ireland. Poet. 1 son, 2 daughters, 2 step-sons. Education: MA, 1964; PhD, 1982, Harvard University, USA. Publications include: Chords and Orchestrations, 1956; Reilly, 1961; Separazioni, 1965; The Dying Gaul, 1968; Separations, 1973; Sing Me Creation, 1977; Alexandrian Notebook, 1989; The Seven Arab Odes, 1990; Ten Modern Arab Poets, 1991. Contributions to: Batteghe Oscure; The Transatlantic Review; The Atlantic Monthly; Poetry Ireland; Translation, and others. Memberships: The Irish Aosdana; Irish Academy of Letters; Amnesty International. Address: Kinsele, Co Cork, Ireland.

O'GRADY Tom, b. 26 Aug 1943. Teacher; Poet; Vintner. Education: BA, University of Baltimore, 1966; MA, Johns Hopkins University, 1967; Advanced Studies of English and American Literature, University of Delaware, 1972-74. Literary Appointments: Lecturer in English, Johns Hopkins University, 1966-67; Catonsville College, 1969-71; University of Delaware, 1972-74; Hampden-Sydney College, 1974-76; Adjunct Professor, English, Poet in Residence, Hampden-Sydney College, 1976-. Publications include: Establishing a Vineyard, (sonnet sequence) 1977; Photographs, 1980; The Farmville Elegies, 1981; Co-founder, Editor, The Hampden-Sydney Poetry Review; Translation of, Jaroslav Siefert (1984 Nobel Laureate in Literature); The Casting of Bells; Mozart in Prague; Eight Days; In The Room of The Just Born, (a collection of poems) 1989; Editor, The Hampden-Sydney Poetry Anthology, 1990; Carvings of The Moon, A Cycle of Poems, 1991; Shaking The Tree: A Book of Works and Days, 1993. Contributions to: Newsletters; Dryad; Enoch; Scene; Pyx; Nimrod; New Laurel Review. Address: P O Box 126, Hampden-Sydney, VA 23943, USA.

O'HEHIR Diana, b. 23 May 1922, USA. Writer; Professor of English. (div) 2 s. Education: MA, Aesthetics of Literature, 1957; PhD, Humanities, 1970, Johns Hopkins University, Baltimore. Publications: Novels, I Wish This War Were Over, 1984; The Bride Who Ran Away, 1988; Poetry, Summoned, 1976; The Power to Change Geography, 1979; Home Free, 1988. Honours: Devins Award for Poetry, 1974; Helen Bullis Poetry Award, 1977; Di Castagnola Award for Poetry, 1981; Runner-up, Pulitzer Prize in Fiction, 1984; Guggenheim Award in Fiction, 1984; NEH Award in Fiction, 1984. Memberships: Poetry Society of America; Modern Language Association; Authors Guild; Poets and Writers. Literary Agent: Ellen Levine. Address: English Department, Mills College, Oakland, CA 94613, USA.

O'LEARY Liam, b. 25 Sept 1910, Youghal, County Cork, Eire. Film Historian. Education: University College, Dublin. Appointments: Editorial Staff, Ireland Today, 1936-37. Publications: Invitation to the Film, 1945; The Silent Cinema, 1965; Rex Ingram, Master of the Silent Cinema, 1980; International Dictionary of Films and Filmmakers, 1985; Cinema Ireland: A History, in progress. Contributions to: Ireland Today, Film Critic; Irish Times; Films and Filming; Kosmorama; The Leader; Irish Press; Envoy; The Bell; film scripts, 1948; gaelic translations of Shakespeare Masterlinck, 1946. Honours: Medal for services in film section, Brussells International Film Fair, 1958; Medal for contribution to Irish Film Industry, National Film Studios of Ireland. Address: The Garden Flat, 2 Otranto Place, Sandycove, Co Dublin, Ireland.

O'MALLEY Mary, b. 19 Mar 1941, Bushey, Hertfordshire, England. Playwright. Appointments include: Resident writer, Royal Court Theatre, 1977. Publications: Superscum, 1972; A 'Nevolent Society, 1974; Oh If Ever a Man Suffered, 1975; Once a Catholic, 1977; Look out, Here Comes Trouble, 1978; Talk of the Devil, 1986; TV Plays; A Consideration of Silk, 1990. Honours include: Evening Standard Award, 1978. Address: c/o Salmon Publishing, The Bridge Mills, Galway, Ireland.

O'MORRISON Kevin, b. St Louis, MO, USA. Playwright; Novelist; Lyricist; Director; Actor. m. Linda Soma, 30 Apr 1966. Education: Private tutoring to BA equivalent in European Philosophy. Appointments include: Television: The Watergate Coverup Trial, 1975; Concealed Enemies, 1986; Lonesome Dove, 1988; Law and Order, 1990,1991; Actor, Film: Funny Farm, 1987; Sleepless in Seattle, 1992; Adjunct Professor, Theatre, University of Missouri, 1976; Director, The Morgan Yard, 1976; Actor, Film, Lightening Jack, 1993-94; Play, Songs In a Strange Land, 1993. Publications include: Television Plays: And Not a Word More, 1960; A Sign for Autumn, 1962; Radio Play: Ladyhouse Blues, (Adaptation of Stage Play) 1981; Stage Plays: The Mutilators, 1988; Songs in a Strange Land, 1989; 50 monologues for Men and Women, 1989; Ladyhouse Blues, The Morgan Yard, A Party For Lovers, The Long War; The Nightgatherers, (on hold); Screenplays: The Cosmic Connection, 1992; Ladyhouse Blues, 1992; Novels: The Deadfile, 1992; Murder In Mind, (novel in progress); Lyrics for Songs: The Dark Wind of Missouri; I Need Someone, 1992. Honours: Creative Artists Public Service Playwright Fellowship, 1975; NEA Playwright Fellowship, 1981. Agent: Samuel Liff, William Morris Agency, 1325 Avenue of Americas, NYC 10019, USA.

O'NEILL Michael Stephen Charles, b. 2 Sept 1953, Aldershot, England. Reader in English. m. Rosemary Ann McKendrick, 1977, 1 son, 1 daughter. Education: Exeter College, Oxford, 1972-75; BA (Hons), Class I, English, 1975; MA (Oxon), 1981; DPhil (Oxon), 1981. Appointments: Co-Founder, Editor, Poetry Durham, 1982-94; Former Lecturer, now Reader in English, 1993-, University of Durham. Publications: The Human Mind's Imaginings: Conflict and Achievement in Shelley's Poetry, 1989; Percy Bysshe Shelley: A Literary Life, 1989; The Stripped Bed, poems, 1990; Auden, MacNeice, Spender: The Thirties Poetry (with Gareth Reeves), 1992; Shelley Special Issue, Durham University Journal, 1993; Editor: Shelley, critical reader, 1993; The 'Defence of Poetry' Fair Copies, 1994. Honours: Eric Gregory Award, 1983; Cholmondeley Award, 1990. Address: Department of English, University of Durham, Durham DH1 3JT, England.

O'NEILL Patrick Geoffrey, b. 1924. Writer. Publications: A Guide to No 1953; Early No Drama,1958; An Introduction to Written Japanese, 1966; Japanese Kana Workbook, 1967; A Programmed Introduction to Literary Style Japanese, 1968; Japanese Names, 1972; Essential Kanji: 2000 Japanese Characters, 1973; Tradition and Modern Japan (ed), 1982; A Reader of Handwritten Japanese, 1984; Japan on Stage (tr), 1990. Address: School of Oriental and African Studies, University of London, Thornaugh Street, London WC1E 7HP, England.

O'NEILL Paul, b. 26 Oct 1928, St John's Newfoundland, Canada. Author. Education: National Academy of Theatre Arts, NY, USA. Publications: Spindrift & Morning Light, 1968; The Oldest City, 1975; Seaport Legacy, 1976; Legends of a Lost Tribe, 1976; A Sound of Seagulls, 1984; Upon this Rock, 1984; Also: The City in Your Pocket, 1974; The Seat Imperial, 1983; Breakers, 1982; Radio and stage plays; TV and film scripts. Contributions to: Numerous magazines and journals, poetry publications, newspapers, and reviews. Honours include: Regional History Prize, Canadian Historical Association; Literary Heritage Award, Newfoundland Historical Society; Robert Weaver Award, National Radio Producers Association of Canada, 1986; Honorary Doctor of Laws, Memorial University of Newfoundland, 1988; Order of Canada, 1990; Newfoundland and Labrador Arts Hall of Honour, 1991; Canada Commemorative Medal, 1992. Memberships: Former VP, Canadian Authors Association; Former President, Newfoundland Writers Guild; Executive, Atlantic Region Representative, Writers Union of Canada; Canadian Radio Producers Association; Chairman, Newfoundland and Labrador Arts Council, 1988-89. Address: 115 Rennies Mill Road, St John's, Newfoundland, A18 2P2, Canada.

O'ROURKE Andrew Patrick, b. 26 Oct 1933, Plainfield, New Jersey, USA. County Executive, Westchester County, New York. Separated, 1988, 1 son, 2 daughters. Education: BA, Fordham College,

1954; JD, Fordham Law School, 1962; LLM, New York University Graduate Law School, 1965. Publications: Red Banner Mutiny, 1986; Hawkwood, 1989. Contributions to: Bar journals and digests; The Proceedings of the Naval Institute; Journal of Ancient and Medieval Studies. Honours: Honorary DHL, Mercy College, 1984; Honorary LLD, Manhattanville College, 1986; Honorary JD, Pace University, 1988. Literary Agent: Jane Dystel, Acton and Dystel Inc, 928 Broadway, New York City, NY 10010, USA. Address: 148 Martine Avenue, White Plains, NY 10601, USA.

O'SULLIVAN Vincent (Gerard), b. 28 Sept 1937, Auckland, New Zealand. Editor; Poet. Education: MA, University of Auckland, 1959; B Litt, Lincoln College, Oxford, 1962. Appointments include: Former Visiting Fellow, Yale University, New Haven; Writer in Residence, VA University. Publications include: Our Burning Time, 1965; Revenants, 1969; Bearings, 1973; From the Indian Funeral, 1976; Brother Jonathan, Brother Kafka, 1980; The Rose Ballroom and Other Poems, 1982; The Butcher Papers, 1982; The Pilate Tapes, 1986; Plays, Shuriken, 1985; Jones and Jones, 1989; Novel, Miracle: A Romance, 1976; The Boy, The Bridge, The River, 1978; Dandy Edison for Lunch and Other Stories, 1981; New Zealand Poetry in the Sixties, 1973; Katherine Mansfield's New Zealand, 1974; Editions of New Zealand Literature. Honours include: New Zealand Book Award, 1981. Address: c/o John McIndoe Limited, 51 Crawford Street, PO Box 694, Dunedin, New Zealand.

O'TOOLE James, b. 15 Apr 1945, San Francisco, CA, USA. Business Educator; Writer. m. Marilyn Louise Burrill, 17 Jun 1967, 2 children. Education: BA, Magna Cum Laude, University of Southern California, 1966; DPhil, Oxford University, 1970. Appointments include: Professor of Management, 1980-; University Associate's Chair of Management, 1982-; Director of Twenty Year Forecast Project for Center for Futures Research, 1973-81; Co-ordinator of general field investigations for President's Commission on Campus Unrest, 1970, University of Southern California, Los Angeles; Director of Aspen Institute Project on Education, Work and The Quality of Life, 1973-74; Executive Director of Town Hall of California Study of Los Angeles Public Pension Plans, 1978-79; Host of Why in The World, (Television) 1981, 1983; Speaker for US Information Agency in Italy and West Germany, 1976; Executive Director, The Leadership Institute, 1991; Senior Fellow, Aspen Institute, 1994. Publications include: Work, Learning and The American Future, 1977; (with others) Tenure, 1979; Making America Work, 1981; Editor, Working: Changes and Choices, 1981; Vangard Management: Redesigning The Corporate Future, 1985; The Executive's Compass: Business and The Good Society, 1993. Address: 19912 Pacific Coast Highway, Malibu, CA 90265, USA.

OAKES John Bertram, b. 23 Apr 1913, Elkins Park, PA, USA. Journalist. m. Margery C Hartman, 1945, 1 s, 3 d. Education: Princeton University; Queen's College, Oxford; AM; ILD. Appointments: Reporter, Trenton Times, 1936-37; Political Reporter, Washington Post, 1937-41; served US Army, 1941-46; Editor, Review of The Week, Sunday New York Times, 1946-49; Editorial Board, 1949-61; Editorial Page Editor, 1961-76; Senior Editor, 1977-78; Contributing Columnist, 1977-90. Publications: The Edge of Freedom, 1961. Contributions to : Essays Today, 1955; Foundations of Freedom, 1958; Tomorrow's American, 1977; On The Vineyard, 1980; The March to War, 1991; Cast a Cold Eye, 1991. Address: 1120 Fifth Avenue, New York, NY 10128, USA.

OAKES Philip, b. 1928, England. Author. Literary Appointments: Scriptwriter, Granada TV and BBC, London, 1958-62; Film Critic, The Sunday Telegraph, London, 1963-65; Assistant Editor, Sunday Times Magazine, 1965-67; Arts Columnist, Sunday Times, London, 1969-80. Publications: Unlucky Jonah: Twenty Poems, 1954; The Punch and Judy Man (with Tony Hancock), screenplay, 1962; Exactly What We Want, novel, 1962; In the Affirmative, 1968; The God Botherers, US Edition as Miracles: Genuine Cases Contact Box 340, novel, 1969; Experiment at Proto, novel, 1973; Tony Hancock: A Biography, 1975; The Entertainers (editor), 1975; A Cast of Thousands, novel, 1976; The Film Addict's Archive, 1977; From Middle England, memoirs, 1980; Dwellers All in Time and Space, memoirs, 1982; Selected Poems, 1982; At the Jazz Band Ball: A Memory of the 1950's, 1983; Shopping for Women, novel, 1994. Address: Fairfax Cottage, North Owersby, Lincolnshire LN8 3PX, England.

OAKLEY Ann, b. 1944, England; Sociologist; Director of Research Unit; Professor of Sociology. Publications: Sex, Gender and Society, 1972; Housewife, 1974; The Sociology of Housework, 1974; The Rights and Wrongs of Women (edited with J Mitchell), 1976;

Becoming a Mother, 1979; Women Confined, 1980; Subject Women, 1981; Miscarriage (with A McPherson and H Roberts), 1984; Taking It Like a Woman, 1984; The Captured Womb, 1984; What is Feminism (edited with J Mitchell), 1986; Telling the Truth about Jerusalem, 1986; The Men's Room, 1989; Matilda's Mistake, 1990; The Secret Lives of Eleanor Jenkinson, 1992; Social Support and Motherhood, 1992; Scenes Originating in the Garden of Eden, 1993; Essays on Women, Medicine and Health, 1993; Young People, Health & Family Life, (with J Brannen, K Dodd & P Storey); The Politics of the Welfare State (edited with S Williams), 1994. Literary Agent: Tessa Sayle Agency, London, England. Address: c/o Tessa Sayle Agency, 11 Jubilee Place, London SW3, England.

OAKLEY Graham, b. 1929, United Kingdom. Children's Fiction Writer. Appointments: Scenic Artist, theatres and Royal Opera House, 2 years; Designer, BBC TV, 1962-77. Publications: The Church Mouse, 1972; The Church Cat Abroad, 1973; The Church Mice series, 1974-; Magical Changes, 1979; Hetty and Harriet, 1981; Henry's Quest, 1986. Address: c/o Macmillan Children's Books, 4 Little Essex Street, London WC2R 3LF, England.

OANDASAN William Cortes, b. 17 Jan 1947, Santa Rosa, California, USA. Poet; Educator. m. 28 Oct 1973, 2 daughters. Education: BA, 1974; MA, 1981; MFA, 1984; Instructor Credential, 1989. Appointments: Editor, A Publications, 1976-; Senior Editor, American Indian Culture and Research Journal, University of California, Los Angeles, 1981-86; Instructor, English Department, University of Orleans, Louisiana State University, 1988-90. Publications: Moving Inland, 1983; Round Valley Songs, 1984; Summer Night, 1989; The Way to Rainy Mountain: Internal and External Structures, in Approaches to Teaching World Literature, 1988; Poetry in Harper's Anthology of 20th Century Native American Poetry, 1988. Contributions to: Colorado Review; Southern California Anthology; California Courier; American Indian Culture and Research Journal. Honours: Publishing Grant, National Endowment for the Arts, 1977; American Book Award, 1985; Summer Scholr Award for Writers, 1989; Research Council Grant, 1989. Memberships: Associated Writers Program; Executive Director, A Writers Circle; Modern Language Association; Society for the Study of Multi-Ethnic Literatures; Association for the Study of American Indian Literatures; National Association on Ethnic Studies; Philological Society of the Pacific Coast. Literary Agent: Florence Feiler. Address: 3832 West Avenue 43, No 13, Los Angeles, CA 90041, USA.

OATES Joyce Carol, b. 16 Jun 1938, Lockport, New York, USA. Professor. Publications: 24 novels and collections of stories, poetry, plays, including: Black Water; Because it is Bitter and Because it is My Heart; Solstice; Mysteries of Winterthurm; Bellefleur; Childworld; Do With Me What You Will; Expensive People; A Garden of Earthly Delights; With Shuddering Fall; Foxfire; Haunted: Tales of the Grotesque, 1994; What I Lived For, 1994. Honours: National Book Award, nominee; National Book Critics Circle Award, nominee; Pulitzer Prize, nominee; Rhea Award for the Short Story, 1990. Address: 9 Honeybrook Drive, Princeton, NJ 08540, USA.

OATES Stephen B(aery), b. 1936, USA. Writer (History). Publications: Confederate West of The River, 1961; Rip Ford's Texas, 1963; The Republic of Texas, 1968; Visions of Glory: Texans on The Southwestern Frontier, 1970; To Purge This Land With Blood: A Biography of John Brown, 1970; Portrait of America: From The Cliff Dwellers to The End of Reconstruction, 1973; Portrait of America: From Reconstruction to The Present, 1973; The Fires of Jubilee: Nat Turner's Fierce Rebellion, 1975; With Malice Toward None: The Life of Abraham Lincoln, 1977; Our Fiery Trial: Abraham Lincoln, John Brown and The Civil War Era, 1979; Let The Trumpet Sound: The Life of Martin Luther King, Jr, 1982; Abraham Lincoln, The Man Behind the Myths, 1984; Biography as High Adventure, 1986; William Faulkner, The Man and The Artist, 1987; A Woman of Valor: Clara Barton and The Civil War, 1994. Contributions to : New York Times; American Heritage; The New Republic; The Nation; Timeline. Honours: Christopher Award, 1977,1982; Robert F Kennedy Memorial Book Award, 1983; Nevins-Freeman Award for Life-time Achievement, 1993. Memberships: Society of American Historians; The American Antiquarian Society; Gerard McCauley Agency. Address: 10 Bride Path, Amherst, MA 01002, USA

OBARSKI Marek, b. 2 July 1947, Poznan, Poland. Novelist; Poet; Critic; Translator. m. Aleksandra Zaworska, 27 Mar 1982, 2 sons, 1 daughter. Appointments: Director, The Flowering Grass Theatre,

1974-79; Director, Literary Department, Nurt literary magazine, 1985-90; Critic, Art for Child magazine, 1989-90; Editor, 1991-93, currently Translator, The Publishing House Rebis; Editor, Europe literary quarterly, 1992-94. Publications: The Sunken Pipes, 1969; The Countries of Wolves, 1971; The Lighting of Flight, 1978; The Body of Cloud, 1983; The Dancing Stoat, 1985; The Flower of Embryo, 1987; The Straw Giant, 1987; The Forest Altar, 1989; The Meat and Infinity, 1994; The Face of Demon, forthcoming. Contributions to: Various journals and literary magazines. Honours: Medal of Young Art, 1984; Stanislaw Pietak Award, 1985; Nomination, Natalia Gall Award, Switzerland, 1988. Memberships: The Ecologic Association of Creators; Union of Polish Letters, 1979-83; Union des Gens de Lettres Polonaises. Address: O WI Lokietka 13 F m 58, 61-616 Poznan, Poland.

OBSTFELD Raymond (Pike Bishop, Jason Frost, Don Pendleton, Carl Stevens), b. 22 Jan 1952, Williamsport, Pennsylvania, USA. Writer; Teacher. Education: BA, Johnston College, University of Redlands, 1972; MA, University of California, Davis, 1976. Appointments: Lecturer, Assistant Professor, 1976-, English, Orange Coast College. Publications: (Novels), The Whipping Boy, 1988; Brainchild, 1987; Redtooth, 1987; Masked Dog, 1986; The Remington Factor, 1985; Dead Bolt, 1982; Dead Heat, 1981; Dead-End Option, 1980; The Golden Fleece, 1979; (as Jason Frost): Invasion USA, 1985; Warlord No 5: Terminal Island, 1985; Warlord No 4: Prisonland, 1985; Warlord No 3: Badlands, 1984; Warlord No 2: Cutthroat, 1984; Warload, 1983; (as Don Pendleton): The Fire Eaters, 1986; Savannah Swingsaw, 1985; Flesh Wounds, 1983; Bloodsport, 1982; (as Pike Bishop), Judgement at Poisoned Well, 1983; Diamondback, 1983; (as Carl Stevens): Ride of the Razorback, 1984; The Centaur Conspiracy, 1983; Poetry Book, The Cat with Half a Face, 1978; poetry in various anthologies; Plays; Screenplays. Contributions to: numerous journals and magazines. Honour: Nominee, Edgar Allen Poe Award for Dead Heat, 1981. Memberships: Mystery Writers of America. Address: 190 Greenmoor, Irvine, CA 92714, USA.

ODA Beth Brown, b. 7 Mar 1953, Cleveland, Ohio, USA. Writer. m. 2 sons, 1 daughter. Education: AB, Bryn Mawr College; MFA, Goddard College; EdD Temple University; PhD, University of Pennsylvania. Appointments include: Professor of English, Nassau State College, New York City, 1982. Publications: Poetry: Lightyears, 1973-1976, 1982; Blue Cyclone, 1982; Kaze, 1985; Satin Tunnels, 1988; Boca Raton, 1986; Riccardo, 1986; Also: Book of Hours, translation of Rainer Maria Rilke; Modern German Poetry, translation; Sun Stone, translation of Octavio Paz. Contributions to: Pennsylvania Review; Philadelphia Inquirer; Callaloo; Journal of Black Studies. Honours: CBS Writing fellowships, 1981-82; Publication Fellowship, Pennsylvania Council on the Arts; Goddard College Scholarship, 1977; Bread Loaf Writers Conference Scholarship, 1977. Memberships: Poetry Society of America; Academy of American Poets: Poets & Writers. Literary Agent: Riccardo Muti, conductor, Philadelphia Orchestra. Address: 4238 Chestnut Street No 4, Philadelphia, PA 19104, USA.

ODAGA Asenath (Bole), b. 1938, Kenyan, Writer of Novels/Short Stories, Children's fiction, Plays/Screenplays, Mythology/Folklore; Freelance Writer 1982-. Appointments: Tutor, Church Missionary Society Teacher Training College, Ngiya, 1957-58; Teacher, Butere Girls School, 1959-60; Headmistress, Nyakach Girls School 1961-63; Assistant Secretary, Kenya Dairy Board, Nairobi, 1965-67; Secretary, Kenya Library Services, Nairobi, 1968; Advertising Assistant, East African Standard Newspaper and Kerr Downey and Selby Safaris, both Nairobi, 1969-70; Assistant Director, Curriculum Development Programme, Christian Churches Educational Association, Nairobi, 1974-75; Research Fellow, Institute of African Studies, University of Nairobi, 1976-81. Publications include: Kip Goes to the City (children's fiction), 1977; Poko Nyar Mugumba (Poko Mugumba's Daughter, children's folktale), 1978; (ed with David Kirui and David Crippen), God, Myself and Others (pastoral handbook), 1976; Thu Tinda: Stories from Kenya (folktales), 1980; The Two Friends (folktales), 1981; Miaha (in Luo: The Bride, play), 1981; Simbi Nyaima (The Sunken Village, play), 1982; Oral Literature: A School Certificate Course (school text book non-fiction), 1982; Ange ok Tel (Regret Never Comes First, children's fiction), 1982; Kenyan Folk Tales, 1982; Sigendini gi Timbe Luo Moko (Stories and Some Customs of the Luo), 1982; A Reed on the Roof, Block Ten, With Other Stories, fiction, 1982; Mouth and Pen: Literature for Children and Young People in Kenya, Research on Childrens Lit in Kenya, 1983; My Home (reader), 1983; The Shade Changes (fiction), 1984; Yesterday's Today: The Story of

Oral Literature, 1984; The Storm (fiction), 1986; Nyamgondho the Son of Ombare and Other Luo Stories, 1986; Between the Years (fiction), 1987; A Bridge in Time (fiction), 1987; Munde and his Friends (children's fiction), 1987; Munde goes to the Market (children's fiction), 1987; The Rag Ball (children fiction), 1987; The Silver Cup (children fiction), 1988; The Storm (adolescent's fiction), 1988; Rianan (fiction), 1990; A Night on A Tree (fiction), 1991; Luo Sayings, 1992. Address: PO Box 1743 Kisumu, Kenya, Africa.

ODELL Peter Randon, b. 1930. Writer (Earth Sciences, Economics, Geography); Professor. Publications: An Economic Geography of Oil, 1963; Oil: The New Commanding Height, 1966; Natural Gas in Western Europe: A Case Study in the Economic Geography of Energy Resources, 1969; Oil and World Power: A Geographical Interpretation, 1970, 8th Edition, 1986; Economics and Societies in Latin America: A Geographical Interpretation (with D A Preston), 1973, 1978; Energy Needs and Resources, 1974, 1978; The North Sea Oil Province (with K E Rosing), 1975; The West European Energy Economy: The Case for Self-Sufficiency, 1976; Optimal Developments of North Sea Oilfields (with K E Rosing), 1976; The Pressures of Oil: A Strategy for Economic Revival (with L Valenilla), 1978; British Offshore Oil Policy: A Radical Alternative, 1980; The Future of Oil (with K E Rosing), 1980, 1983; Energie: Geen Probleem? (with J A van Reyn), 1981; The International Oil Industry: An Inter-disciplinary Perspective (with J Rees), 1986; Global and Regional Energy Supplies: Recent Fiction and Fallacies Revisited, 1991. Address: 7 Constitution Hill, Ipswich IP1 3RG, England.

ODELL Robin Ian, b. 19 Dec 1935, Totton, Hampshire, England. Editor. m. Joan Bartholomew, 19 Sept 1959. Publications: Jack the Ripper in Fact and Fiction, 1965; Exhumation of a Murder, 1975; Jack the Ripper: Summing-up and Verdict (with Colin Wilson), 1987; With J H H Gaute: The Murderers' Who's Who, 1979; Lady Killers, 1980; Murder Whatdunit, 1982; Murder Whereabouts, 1986; With Christopher Berry-Dee: Dad Help Me Please, 1990; A Question of Evidence, 1992; Lady Killer, 1992; The Long Drop, 1993. Contributions to: Crimes and Punishment; The Criminologist. Honours: FCC Watts Memorial Prize, 1957; International Humanist and Ethical Union, 1960; Edgar Award, Mystery Writers of America, 1980. Memberships: Paternosters; Our Society (Crimes Club); Crime Writers Association. Literary Agent: Curtis Brown. Address: 11 Red House Drive, Sonning Common, Reading RG4 9NT, England.

ODGERS Darrel Allan, b. 7 Mar 1957, Smithton, Australia. Secretary; Manager; Writer. m. Sally P Farrell, 26 May 1979, 1 s, 1 d. Education: School's Board Certificate. Publications: Timedetector, forthcoming 1995. Memberships: Aust Soc Authors. Address: PO Box 87, Latrobe, Tasmania 7307, Australia.

ODGERS Sally Farrell, (Tegan James), b. 26 Nov 1957, Latrobe, Tasmania, Australia. Freelance Writer and Lecturer. m. Darrel Allan Odgers, 26 May 1979, 1 son, 1 daughter. Publications include: Dreadful David, 1984; Five Easy Lessons, 1989; Kayak, 1991; Shadowdancers, 1994; Anna's Own, forthcoming; Tasmania, A Guide; Drummond; Timedetector (with D Odgers). Contributions to: Lucky; Organic Growing; Australian Women's Weekly; Good House Keeping; The Australian Author; Writer's News. Honours: Journalism Award, Circular Head Festival, 1993. Memberships: Australian Society of Authors; Society of Women Writers. Address: PO Box 87, Latrobe, Tasmania 7307, Australia.

OFFEN Yehuda, b. 4 Apr 1922, Altona, Germany. Writer. m. Tova Arbisser, 28 Mar 1946, 1 daughter. Education: BA, London University, England, 1975; MA, Comparative Literature, Hebrew University, Jerusalem, Israel, 1978. Publications: Poems: L'Lo L'An, 1961; Har Vakhol, 1963; Lo Agadat Khoref, 1969; Nofim P'nima, 1979; B'Magal Sagur, short stories, 1979; N'Vilat Vered, 1983; Shirim Bir'hov Ayaif, 1984; P'Gishot Me'ever Lazman, 1986; Massekhet Av, 1986; Stoning on the Cross Road, short stories, 1988; Who Once Begot a Star, 1990; Silly Soil, 1992; Back to Germany, 1994. Contributions to: Most magazines, literary journals and publications in Israel; Various publications in USA, Poland, Germany, Italy, India; Some songs recorded. Honours: ACUM Prize for Literature, 1961, 1979, 1984; Talpir Prize for Literature, 1979; Efrat Prize for Poetry, 1989. Memberships: Hebrew Writers Association, Israel; International Academy of Poets, USA; PEN Centre, Israel; ACUM (Société des Auteurs, Compositeurs et Editeurs en Israel); National Federation of Israeli Journalists; International Federation of Journalists, Brussels. Address: 8 Gazit Street, Tel-Aviv 69417, Israel.

OFFUTT Andrew J(efferson) V), b. 1934, Louisville, Kentucky, USA. Author. m. Mary Joe McCabe, 19 Oct 1957, 2 sons, 2 daughters. Education: BA, PhD, University of Louisville. Publications: Author of over 100 works including: Evil is Live Spelled Backwards, 1970; The Great 24 Hour Thing, 1971; The Castle Keeps, 1972; Messenger of Zhuvastou, 1973; Ardor on Aros, 1973; The Galactiv Rejects (juvenile), 1973; Operation: Super Ms, 1974; Sword of the Gael, 1975; The Genetic Bomb (with D Bruce Berry), 1975; Chieftain of Andor, 1976 (in United Kingdom as Clansman of Andor), 1978); The Undying Wizard, 1976; Demon in the Mirror (with Richard K Lyon), 1977; Sign on the Moonbow, 1977; The Mists of Doom, 1977; My Lord Barbarian, 1977; Swords Against Darkness 1-5, 5 vols, 1977-79; Conan and the Sorcerer, 1978; The Sword of Skelos, 1979; The Iron Lords, 1979; Shadows out of Hell, 1979; King Dragon, 1980; When Death Birds Fly (with Keith Taylor), 1980; The Tower of Death (with Keith Taylor), 1980; The Eyes of Sarsis (with Richard K Lyon), 1980; Conan the Mercenary, 1980; Web of the Spider (with Richard K Lyon), 1981; The Tower of Death (with Keith Taylor), 1982; The Lady of the Snowmist, 1983; The Shadow of the Sorcery, 1993. Honour: 1st Prize in Words of If, short story contest. Membership: Science Fiction Writers of America. Address: Funny Farm, Haldeman, KY 40329, USA.

OGAWA Masaru, b. 1915, Los Angeles, USA. Journalist. m. Ayame Fukuhara, 1942, 1 son, 2 daughters. Education: University of California, Los Angeles; Tokyo Imperial, and Columbia Universities. Appointments: Domei News Agency, 1941-46; Kyodo News Service, 1946-48; The Japan Times, 1948-; Chief, Political Section, 1949; Assistant Managing Editor, 1950, chief Editor, 1952, Managing Editor, 1958-64, Director, 1959-, Executive Editor, 1964-68, Senior Editor, 1968-71, Chief Editorial writer 1969-71, Editor 1971-77, Adviser 1977-, weekly columnist; Chairman, Asia-Pacific Magazine, Manila, 1981-. Honours: Hon DLitt, Lewis and Clark College, Portland, Oregon; Phi Beta Kappa, 1937 UCLA; Vaughn-Uyeda (Journalism) Prize, 1967. Memberships: Life Member, Foreign Correspondents Club of Japan, 1973-; Executive Director, American Japan Society, 1981-; Tokyo Club, 1986-. Address: 14-banchi, 4 chome, Mejiro, Toshima-ku, Tokyo, Japan.

OGBURN Charlton, b. 15 Mar 1911, Atlanta, USA. Writer. m. (1) Mary C Aldis, 6 Jun 1945 (div 1951), 1 s, (2) Vera Weidman, 24 Feb 1951, 2 d. Education: SB, cum laude, Harvard, 1932; Graduate, National War College, 1952. Publications: The White Falcon, 1955; The Bridge, 1957; Big Caesar, 1958; The Marauders, 1959; US Army, 1960; The Gold of The River Sea, 1965; The Winter Beach, 1966; The Forging of Our Continent, 1968; The Continent in Our Hands, 1971; Winespring Mountain, 1973; The Southern Appalachians: A Wilderness Quest, 1975; The Adventure of Birds, 1976; Railroads: The Great American Adventure (National Geographical Society), 1977; The Mysterious William Shakespeare: The Myth and The Reality, 1984 (second edition, 1992). Contributions to: Magazines and Journals. Address: 403 Hancock Street, Beaufort, SC 29902, USA.

OGILVY George. See: **AYERST David.**

OGLETREE Thomas Warren, b. 1933, United States of America. Writer (Philosophy, Theology/Religion). Publications: Christian Faith and History: A Critical Comparison of Ernst Troelsch and Karl Barth, 1965; The Death of God Controversy, 1966; Openings for Marxist-Christian Dialogue, 1968; From Hope to Liberation: Toward a New Marxist-Christian Dialogue (with H Apthekerand S Bliss), 1974; Lifeboat Ethics: The Moral Dilemmas of World Hunger (with George Lucas Jr), 1976; The Use of the Bible in Christian Ethics, 1983; Hospitality to the Stranger: Dimensions of Moral Understanding, 1985. Address: Office of the Dean, Drew University, Theological School, Madison, NJ 07940, USA.

OGUNYEMI Wale, b. 1939, Ogbajo, Oyo State, Nigeria. Playwright. Education: Studied in Nigeria. Appointments include: Senior Artist, Institute of African Studies, University of Ibadan. Publications: Business Headache, 1966; The Scheme, 1967; Be Mighty Be Mine, 1968; Eshu Elegbara, 1968; Aare Akogun, After Macbech, 1968; Obaluaye, Musical, 1968; Ijake War, 1970; Kiriji, 1971; The Vow, 1972; The Divorce, 1975; Langbodo, 1977; Eniyan, After Everyman, 1982; The Sign of the Rainbow; TV and Radio Pays. Honours include: Nigerian Writers Guild Award, 1982. Address: c/o Institute of African Studies, University of Ibadan, Ibadan, Nigeria.

OJALA Ossi Arne Atos, b. 22 Mar 1933, Savonlinna, Finland. Amateur Theatre Director; Teacher; Copywriter. Education: BA,

University of Helsinki. Publications include: Novels: Saarella Tapahtuu (The Island), 1963; Valkoinen Vaara (White Danger), 1966; Kahvila Sinuhe (Sinuhe Cafe), 1967; Toisenlainen Rakkaustarina (Different Love Story), 1981; Ja Aika Pysahtyi (Time Stopped), 1985; Ennen Hiljaisuutta Mina Huudan (Before Stillness I Will Cry Out), 1985; Suolintu (The Crane), 1966; Also over 30 broadcast plays, including Haapaveden Kannel, 1986. Contributions to: Theater; Ita-Hame; Kaleva; Kainuun Sanomat; Opistolehti. Honours: Otava Prize, 1964; 1st Prize, novel competition, 1966; Best Finnish novel for young people, 1967. Memberships: Suomen Kirjailijaliitto; Suomen Noytelmakirkjailijaliitto; Salpausselan Kirjailijat; Pirkkalaiskirjailijat. Literary Agents: WSOY, Helsinki; Kustannusoy Pohjoinen, Oulu. Address: Keskustie 39, 19600 Hartola, Finland.

OKAI John, b. 1942, Ghana. Lecturer; Poet. Education: MA, Gorky Literary Institute, Moscow, 1967; M Phil, University of London. Appointments include: Lecturer; Author, University of Ghana. Publications: Flowerfall, 1969; The Oath of fontomfrom and Other Poems, 1971; Lorgorligi Logarithms and Other Poems, 1974. Honours include: Royal Society of Arts Fellowship, 1968. Address: Dept of Modern Languages, University of Ghana, PO Box 25, Legon, Ghana.

OKARA Gabriel, b. 21 Apr 1921, Bumodi, Ijaw District, Rivers State, Western Nigeria. Publishing Director; Poet. Education: Government College Umuahia. Appointments include: Director, Rivers State Publishing House, Port Harcourt, 1972-. Publications: Poetry from Africa, 1968; The Fisherman's Invocation, 1978; Novel, The Voice, 1964. Honours include: Commonwealth Poetry Prize, 1979. Address: PO Box 219, Port Harcourt, Nigeria.

OKON Zbigniew Waldemar, b. 21 July 1945, Chelm, Poland. Teacher. m. Halina Pioro Maciejewska, 6 Oct 1969, 2 sons, 1 daughters. Education: Marie Curie-Sklodowska University, Lublin. Publications: Outlooks and Reflections, 1968; The Soldiers of the Chalk Hills, 1970; Impatience of the Tree, 1979; Intimidation By Twilight, 1986; Calling Up the Darkness, 1987. Contributions to: Poetry in various journals and magazines. Honours: 1st Prize Winner, Poetry Competitions, 1964, 1966, 1968, 1974; The Czechowicz Literary Prize, 1987. Memberships: Stowarzyszenie Ziemi Chelmskiej; Chairman, Pryzmaty, 1983; Union of Polish Literary Men. Address: Ul Kolejowa 86/19, 22-100 Chelm, Poland.

OKRI Ben, b. 1959, Minna, Nigeria. Novelist; Poet; Short Story Writer. Education: University of Essex, Colchester. Appointments: Broadcaster, Network Africa, BBC World Service, 1984-85; Poetry Editor, West Africa, 1981-87; Fellow Commoner in Creative Arts, Trinity College, Cambridge; Writer and Reviewer, New Statesman, Observer, Guardian, The Times, London, New York Times and many International newspapers, journals and magazines. Publications: Flowers and Shadows, 1980; The Landscapes Within, 1982; The Famished Road, 1991; Songs of Enchantment, 1993; Short Stories: Incidents at the Shrine, 1986; Stars of the Curfew, 1988; Poetry: An African Elegy. Honours: Booker Prize Winner, 1991; Paris Review for Fiction; Premio Letterario Internazionale Chianti Ruffino-Antico Fattore, 1993; Premio Grinzane Cavour Prize, 1994. Address: c/o Jonathan Cape Ltd, 20 Vauxhall Bridge Road, London SW1V 2SA, England.

OLDKNOW Antony, b. 15 Aug 1939, Peterborough, England. Poet; Literary Translator; Professor. Education: BA, Leeds, 1961; Postgraduate Diploma, Phoenetics, Edinburgh, 1962; PhD, University of North Dakota, USA, 1983. Appointments include: Editor, Publisher, Scopcraeft Press Inc, 1966-; Travelling Writer, The Great Plains Book Bus, 1979-81; Writer-in- Residence, Wisconsin Arts Board, 1980-83; Poetry Staff, Cottonwood, 1984-87; Professor of Literature, Eastern New Mexico University, 1987-; Associate Editor, Blackwater Quarterly, 1993. Publications: Lost Allegory, 1967; Tomcats and Tigertails, 1968; The Road of The Lord, 1969; Consolation for Beggars, 1978; Anthem for Rusty Saw and Blue Sky, 1975; Miniature Clouds, 1982; Ten Small Songs, 1985; Clara d'Ellébeuse, (translated novel) 1992; The Villages and Other Poems, (translated book) 1993. Contributions to : Numerous Journals, Magazines and Reviews; Poems in American Poetry Review, 1992 and Men of Our Time, 1993. Address: Department of Languages and Literature, Eastern New Mexico University, Portales, NM 88130, USA.

OLDS Sharon, b. 1942, San Francisco, California, USA. Poet. Education: Stanford University; Columaz University. Publications: Satan Says, 1980; The Dead and the Living, 1984; The Gold Cell, 1987; The Father, 1993. Contributions include: American Poetry Review; Bastard Review; Gettysburg Review; Iron; Paris Review; Salmongurdi; Threepenny Rview. Honours: San Francisco Poetry Center Award, 1981; Lamont Poetry Selection, 1983; National Book Center Circle Award, 1984. Address: c/o Knopf Publishers, 201 E 50th Street, 20th Floor Reception, New York, NY 10022, USA.

OLDSEY Bernard, b. 18 Feb 1923, Wilkes-Barre, PA, USA. Professor, Editor; Writer. m. Ann Marie Re, 21 Sep 1946, 1 s, 1 d. Education: BA, 1948, MA, 1949, PhD, 1955, Pennsylvania State University. Appointments: Instructor to Associate Professor, English, Pennsylvania State University, 1951-69; Senior Fulbright Professor, American Literature, Universidad de Zaragoza, Spain, 1964-65; Professor, English, West Chester University, 1969-; Editor, College Literature, 1974-; University Professor, University of Innsbruck, Austria, 1985. Publications: From Fact To Judgement, 1957; The Art of William Golding, 1967; The Spanish Season, novel, 1970; Hemingway's Hidden Craft, 1979; Ernest Hemingway: Papers of A Writer, 1981; British Novelists, 1930-1960, 1983; Critical Essays on George Orwell, 1985. Address: 1003, Woodview Lane, West Chester, PA 19380, USA.

OLIVER (Symmes) Chad(wick), b. 1928, United States of America. Author. Publications: Shadows in the Sun, 1954; Mists of Dawn (juvenile fiction), 1952; Another Kind (short stories), 1955; The Winds of Time, 1957; Unearthly Neighbors, 1960; Ecology and Cultural Continuity as Contributing Factors in the Social Organization of the Plains Indians, 1962; The Wolf is My Brother (western novel), 1967; The Shores of Another Sea, 1971; The Edge of Forever edited by William F Nolan (short stories), 1971; Giants in the Dust, 1976; Cultural Anthropology: The Discovery of Humanity, 1980; Broken Eagle, Winner Western Heritage Award for Best Novel of 1989. Address: 301 Eanes Road, Austin, TX 78746, USA.

OLIVER Douglas Dunlop, b. 14 Sept 1937, Southampton, England. Poet; Novelist; Prosodist. m. (1) Janet Hughes, July 1962, (2) Alice Notley, Feb 1988, 2 stepsons, 2 daughters. Education: BA, Literature, 1975, MA, Applied Linguistics, 1982, University of Essex. Appointments: Journalist, newspapers in England, Agence France-Presse, Paris, 1959-72; University Lecturer, Literature, English, various, 1975-; Editorial Board, Franco-British Studies; Co-Editor, Scarlet magazine. Publications: Oppo Hectic, 1969; The Harmless Building, 1973; In the Cave of Succession, 1974; The Diagram Poems, 1979; The Infant and the Pearl, 1985; Kind, 1987; Poetry and Narrative in Performance, 1989; Three Variations on the Theme of Harm, 1990; Penniless Politics, 1991; The Scarlet Cabinet (with Alice Notley), 1992. Contributions to: Anthologies including: A Various Art, 1987; The New British Poetry 1968-1988, 1988; Numerous poems, articles, fiction, to magazines and journals. Honours: Eastern Arts Grant, 1977; South-East Arts Grant for publication of Kind, 1987; Fund for Poetry Grants, 1990, 1991. Literary Agent: John Parker, MBA Associates, 45 Fitzroy Street, London W1P 5HR, England. Address: c/o British Institute in Paris, 11 Rue de Constantine, 75007 Paris, France.

OLIVER Mary, b. 1935. Poet. Publications: House of Light; Dream Work; American Primitive; Twelve Moons; The River Styx, Ohio and Other Poems; No Voyage and Other Poems; Sleeping in the Forest; The Night Traveler; New and Selected Poems, 1991; A Poetry Handbook, 1994; White Pine, 1994. Contributions incl: Poetry, Virginia Quarterly Review, Cream City Review, Country Journal, Harvard Magazine, Paris Review, Kenyon Review, Wilderness. Honours: National Book Award, 1992; Pulitzer Prize. Address: c/o Molly Malone Cook Agency Box 338, Provincetown, MA 02657, USA.

OLIVER Paul H, b. 25 May 1927, Nottingham, England. Author; Lecturer in Architecture and Popular Music. m. Valerie Grace Coxon, 19 Aug 1950. Education: Drawing Exam Distinction, 1945; Painting Exam, National Diploma in Design, 1947; Art Teachers' Diploma, 1948; Diploma in Humanities, History of Art, Distinction, 1955, University of London, England. Appointments: Editor, Architectural Association Journal, 1961-63; Reviewer for Arts Review, 1965-70; Member, Cambridge University Press Popular Music Editorial Board, 1980-. Publications: Bessie Smith, 1959; Blues Fell This Morning, 1960; Conversation with the Blues, 1965; Screening the Blues, 1968; The Story of the Blues, 1969; Shelter and Society (ed), 1970; Savannah Syncopators: African Retentions in the Blues, 1970; Shelter in Africa, 1971; Shelter, Sign and Symbol, 1975; Dunroamin' The Suburban Semi and Its Enemies (with Ian Davis and Ian Bentley), 1981; Songsters and Saints: Vocal Traditions on Race Records, 1984; Blues Off the Record: Thirty Years of Blues Commentary, 1984; Dwellings: The House Across the World, 1987; Blues Fell This Morning (1960, revised edition

1990; Black Music in Britain (ed), 1990; Blackwell's Guide to Blues Records (ed), 1989; Architecture - An Invitation (with Richard Hayward), 1990. Contributions to: Articles and reviews published in: RIBA Journal; Architects Journal; Architectural Association Journal and Quarterly; Arts Review; Architectural Review; Third World Planning Review; Habitat International Building Design; Building: Architectural Design; Hi-Fi News and Record Review; Journal of Musicology; Popular Music Yearbook; Black Music Research; Musical Traditions; Jazz Review; Blues Unlimited; MELUS. Honours: Prix d'Etrangers, Paris for Le Monde du Blues, French translation of Blues Fell This Morning, 1962; Prix du Disque, Paris, for The Story of the Blues, 1962; Honorary Fellow, AmCAS University of Exeter, 1986; Honorary Fellow, Oxford Polytechnic, 1988; Sony Radio Award Best Special Music Programme, 1988. Memberships: Fellow, Royal Anthropological Institute; Architectural Association; International Association for the Study of Popular Music; Standing Committee, and Honorary Fellow, Centre for American and Commonwealth Arts & Studies, University of Exeter, Society of Architectural Historians (USA), Vernacular Architecture Forum (USA). Address: Wootton-by-Woodstock, Oxon, England.

OLIVER Reginald Rene St John, b. 7 July 1952, London, England. Actor; Dramatist. Education: BA Hons, University College, Oxford, 1975. Literary Appointments: Literary Consultant to Drama Panel, Arts Council of Great Britain, 1983-86; Director of Publications, Seeds Ltd, 1986-. Publications: Zuleika, 1975; Interruption to the Dance, 1977; You Might as Well Live, 1978; The Shewstone, 1981; Passing Over, 1982; Absolution, 1984; Back Payments, 1985; Rochester (A Dramatic Biography), 1986; A Portrait of Two Artists, 1986; Imaginary Lines, 1987. Contributions to: Numerous magazines and journals. Honours: Time Out Award Best Fringe Play; International Theatre Award, 1985. Memberships: Honorary President, Dramatist's Club; British Actors Equity; Theatre Writers Union. Literary Agent: Margaret Ramsay (Ltd). Address: The Bothy, Wormington Grange, Broadway, Worcs, England.

OLIVER Roland Anthony, b. 1923. Writer (Area Studies, History). Publications: The Missionary Factor in East Africa, 1952; Sir Harry Johnston and the Scramble for Africa, 1957; The Dawn of African History, 1958; A History of East Africa (with G Mathew), 1961; A Short History of Africa (with J D Fage), 1961; The Middle Age of African History, 1966; Africa Since 1800 (with A Atmore), 1967; Papers in African Prehistory (with J D Fage), 1970; Africa in the Iron Age (with B M Fagan), 1975; Cambridge History of Africa, 8 vols, 1975-86; The African Middle Ages 1400-1800 (with A Atmore), 1980; The African Experience, 1991. Address: Frilsham Woodhouse, Newbury, Berkshire, RG16 9XB, England.

OLIVIER Richard, b. 9 Aug 1945, Etterbeek, Belgium. Playwright; Film Producer. m. Monique Licht, 16 Sept 1967, 1 son. Education: Institut des Arts et Diffusion. Publications: Amin Dada, 1er Empereur de Belgique, 1980; Adaptation of Gulliver for children's television; Films include: Leurs Trucs en Plumes; Le Charme de l'Ambiguité; Strip School; Black Paris; Marvin Gaye Transit Ostende; La Chanson Rebelle; Le Buteur Fantastique; Les Fous du Roi; Chants de Femmes; Chants d'Amour, Chants d'Amore; Wilchar, les larmes noires; Marchienne de vie; Musical comedy: King Singer; Big Dady Dada; L'Irrésistible Ascension de John Travol'rat; Theatre: Un Amour de Vitrine, 1987. Contributions to: Le Soir Illustré; Pourquoi Pas?; Moustique; Time-Life Books; A la recherche du cinéma perdu. Honours: Prix RTBF, La Louvière, 1969; Prix Ondas, Spain, 1974; Label of Quality Prize, CNC, 1977, 1981, 1983; Prix du Jury, Festival Automoto, Paris, 1980; Prize, Belgian Authors and Writers (SABAM), 1982, 1984; Prix BNP, Rennes, France, 1984. Membership: Director, Audiovisual Committee, SABAM. Address: 24 avenue de Messidor, 1180 Brussels, France.

OLLARD Richard, b. 1923. Writer (History, Biography). Literary appointments include: Editor, Williams Collins and Sons, London, 1960-83. Publications: Historical Essays 1600-1750 (edited with H E Bell), 1963; The Escape of Charles II, 1967; Man of War: Sir Robert Holmes and the Restoration Navy, 1969; Pepys, 1974, new illustrated edition, 1991; The War Without an Enemy: A History of the English Civil Wars, 1976; The Image of the King: Charles I and Charles II, 1979; An English Education: A Perspective of Eton, 1982; For Veronica Wedgwood These Studies on 17th Century History (edited with Pamela Tudor Craig), 1986; Clarendon and His Friends, 1987; Fisher and Cunningham: a study in the personalities of the Churchill era, 1991; Cromwell's Earl: A Life of Edward Mountagu, 1st Earl of Sandwich,

1994. Honours: Fellow, Royal Society of Literature, 1970; Fellow, Society of Antiquaries, 1984. Address: c/o Curtis Brown Limited, 162-168 Regent Street, London W1, England.

OLMSTEAD Andrea Louise, b. 5 Sep 1948, Dayton, OH, USA. Musicologist. m. Larry Thomas Bell, 2 Jan 1982. Education: BM, Hartt College of Music, 1972; MA, New York University, 1974. Appointments: Faculty, The Juilliard School, 1972-80; The Boston Conservatory, 1981-. Publications: Roger Sessions and His Music, 1985; Conversations With Roger Sessions, 1987; The New Grove 20th Century American Masters, 1987; The Correspondence of Roger Sessions, 1992. Contributions to: Journal of The Arnold Schoenberg Institute; American Music; Musical Quarterly; Tempo; Musical America; Perspectives of New Music; MLA Notes. Honours: Two NEH Grants; Outstanding Academic Book, Choice, 1986. Memberships: Sonneck Society; Pi Kappa Lambda. Address: 73 Hemenway Street, Apt 501, Boston, MA 02115, USA.

OLNEY Ross R(obert), b. 1929. American, Writer of Children's non-fiction, Recreation/Leisure/Hobbies, Sports-Physical education/Keeping fit, Biography. Appointments: Writing Instructor, UCLA, USC, UCSB and several Community Colleges. Publications include: (with P Olney), Quick and Easy Magic Fun, 1974; Light Motorcycle Repair, 1975; Motorcycling, 1975; Photographing Actions Sports, 1976; Simple Appliance Repair, 1976; Superstars of Auto-Racing, 1976; Gymnastics, 1976; Hand Gliding, 1976; How to Understand Soccer, 1976; Auto Racing's Young Lions, 1977; (with Chan Bush), Better Skateboarding for Boys and Girls, 1977; (with Mary Ann Duganne), How to Make Your Car Run Better, 1977; This Game Called Hockey, 1978; The Young Runner, 1978; A J Foyt, 1978; Illustrated Auto Racing Dictionary for Young People, 1978; Janet Guthrie, 1978; Modern Auto-Racing Superstars, 1978; Modern Racing Cars, 1978; (with Chan Bush), Roller Skating, 1979; Tricky Discs, 1979; How to Understand Auto Racing, 1979; (with Pat Olney), Magic, 1979; Out to Launch: Model Rockets, 1979; Modern Motorcycle Superstars, 1980; Auto Racing Micro Style, 1980; (with Chan Bush), Better Kite Flying for Boys and Girls, 1980; The Amazing Yo-Yo, 1980; Model Airplanes, R/C Style, 1970; The Young Bicyclist, 1980; Listen to Your Car, 1981; Farm Giants, 1982; Modern Speed Record Superstas, 1982; Windsurfing, 1982; Winners, 1982; Construction Giants, 1983; (with Pat Olney), How to Have More of It, 1983; (with Pat Olney), How Long? 1984; The Farm Combine, 1984; Super-Champions of Auto Racing, 1984; Ocean-Going Giants, 1985; Car of the Future, 1986; The Shell Auto Car Guide, 1986; (with Ross D Olney), The Amazing Transistor, 1986. Contributions to: Reader's Digest, all editions, Westways and others. Memberships: Board of Directors, Greater Los Angeles Press Club, Immediate Past President, American Auto Racing Writers and Broadcasters. Literary Agent: Gloria R Mosesson. Address: GRM Associates, 290 West End Avenue, New York, NY 10023, USA.

OLSEN Lance, b. 14 Oct 1956, USA. Writer; Critic; Teacher. m. Andrea Hirsch, 3 Jan 1981. Education: BA Hons, University of Wisconsin, 1978; MFA, University of Iowa, 1980; MA, 1982, PhD, 1985, University of Virginia. Literary Appointments: Director of Creative Writing Program, University of Idaho, 1994. Publications: Ellipse of Uncertainty, 1987; Circus of The Mind in Motion, 1990; Live From Earth, 1991; William Gibson, 1992; My Dates With Franz, 1993; Natural Selections, (poems with Jeff Worley) 1993; Scherzi, I Believe, 1994; Tonguing The Zeitgeist, 1994; Lolita, 1995; short stories, poems, essays, reviews in journals and magazines. Contributions to: Hudson Review; Fiction International; Iowa Review; VLS; Mississippi Review; Mondo 2000; Alaska Quarterly; New Stories from The South; Shenandoah; College English. Address: Bear Creek Cabin, 1490 Ailor Road, Deary, ID 83823, USA.

OLSEN Theodore Victor (Joshua Stark, Christopher Storm, Cass Willoughby), b. 25 Apr 1932, Rhinelander, Wisconsin, USA. Freelance Writer. m. Beverly Butler, 25 Sept 1976, Sun Prairie. Education: BSc English, University of Wisconsin, 1955. Publications: 49 books including: Haven of the Hunted, 1956; The Rhinelander Story, 1957; The Man from Nowhere, 1959; McGivern, 1960; High Lawless, 1960; Gunswift, 1960; Ramrod Rider, 1960; Brand of the Star, 1961; Brothers of the Sword, 1962; Savage Sierra, 1962; The Young Duke, 1963; Break the Young Land, 1964; The Sex Rebels, 1964; A Man Called Brazos, 1964; Canyon of the Gun, 1965; Campus Motel, 1965; The Stalking Moon, 1965; The Hard Men, 1966; Autumn Passion, 1966; Bitter Grass, 1967; The Lockhart Breed, 1967; Blizzard Pass, 1968; Arrow in the Sun, 1969; Keno, 1970; A Man Named Yuma, 1971; Eye of the Wolf, 1971; There Was a Season, 1973; Mission to the West,

1973; Run to the Mountain, 1974; Track the Man Down, 1975; Day of the Buzzard, 1976; Westward They Rode, 1976; Bonner's Stallion, 1977; Rattlesnake, 1979; Roots of the North, 1979; Allegories for one Man's Moods, 1979; Our First Hundred Years, 1981; Blood of the Breed, 1982; Birth of a City, 1983; Red is the River, 1983; Lazlo's Strike, 1983; Lonesome Gun, 1985; Blood Rage, 1987; A Killer is Waiting, 1988; Under the Gun, 1989; The Burning Sky, 1991; The Golden Chance, 1992. Contributions to: 20 short stories in Ranch Romances, 1956-57. Honour: Award of Merit, State Historical Society of Wisconsin, 1983; WWA Spur Award for Best Western Paperback Novel, 1992. Membership: Western Writers of America. Literary Agent: Jon Tuska, Golden West Literary Agency, 2327 S E Salmon St, Portland, OR 97214. Address: PO Box 856, Rhinelander, WI 54501, USA.

OLSON David John, b. 18 May 1941, Brantford, ND, USA. Professor; Chairman; Political Science. m. Sandra Jean Crabb, 11 Jun 1966, 1 d. Education: BA, Concordia College, 1963; MA, 1966, PhD, 1971, University of Wisconsin. Publications: Black Politics, 1971; Theft of The City, 1974; To Keep The Republic, 1975; Commission Politics, 1976; Governing The United States, 1977. Contributions to: Journal of Politics; Transactions; American Political Science Review. Honours: Rockefeller Fellow, 1964; Vilas Fellow, 1966; Brookings Predoctoral Fellow, 1968; Frederick Bachman Lieber Distinguished Teaching Award, 1973; Harry Bridges Endowed Chair in Labor Studies, 1992; Distinguished Labor History Professor, Labor Archives and Research Center, San Francisco State University, 1994. Memberships: Western Political Science Association, Vice President, 1984, President, 1985; American Political Science Association; Midwest Political Science Association; Southern Political Science Association. Address: 6512 E Green Lake Way North, Seattle, WA 98103, USA.

OLSON Toby, b. 17 Aug 1937, Berwyn, IL, USA. Poet; Novelist. m. Miriam Meltzer, 27 Nov 1966. Education: BA, Occidental College, CA, 1965; MA, Long Island University, 1968. Appointments include: Faculty, New School for Social Research, New York City, 1968-73; Assistant Professor, Long Island University, 1968-74; Professor of English, Temple University, 1975-. Publications: Life of Jesus, 1976; Seaview, 1982; We Are The Fire, 1984; Woman Who Escaped From Shame, 1986; Utah, 1987; Dorit in Lesbos, 1990; At Sea, 1993; Unfinished Building, 1993. Contributions include: Numerous magazines including: American Book Review; Inside Outer Space; American Experience; Radical Reader; Nation; Ohio Review; Minnesota Review; New York Quarterly; New York Times; Choice; Sun; Caterpillar; American Poetry Review; Boundary 2; Conjunctions; Sun and Moon. Literary Agent: Ellen Levine. Address: 329 South Juniper Street, Philadelphia, PA 19107, USA.

OLSON Walter Karl, b. 20 Aug 1954, Detroit, MI, USA. Writer; Editor. Education: BA, Yale University, 1975. Publications: New Directions in Liability Law, (editor) 1988; The Litigation Explosion, 1991. Literary Agent: Writers' Representatives Inc, 25 W 19th Street, New York, NY10011-4202, USA. Address: Manhattan Institute, 52 Vanderbilt Avenue, New York, NY 10017, USA.

OLUDHE-MACGOYE Marjorie Phyllis, b. 21 Oct 1928, Southampton, England. Bookseller. m. D G W Oludhe-Macgoye, 4 June 1960, dec'd 1990, 3 sons, 1 daughter. Education: BA, English, 1948, MA, 1953, London University. Publications: Growing Up at Lina School, (juvenile), 1971, 2nd Edition, 1988; Murder in Majengo, (novel), 1972; Song of Nyarloka and Other Poems, 1977; Coming to Birth, (novel), 1986; The Story of Kenya, (history), 1986; The Present Moment, (novel), 1987; Street Life, (novella), 1988; Victoria and Murder in Majengo, 1993; Homing In, (novel), 1994. Contributions to: London Magazine; Literary Review; Ghala; Zuka; Alfajiri; Most anthologies of East African poetry; Heinemann Book of African Poetry in English. Honours: BBC Arts in Africa Poetry Award (3), 1982; Sinclair Prize for Fiction, 1986. Address: PO Box 70344, Nairobi, Kenya.

OMAN Julia Trevelyan, b. 11 July 1930, Kensington, England. Designer. m. Roy Strong (Sir), 10 Sept 1971. Education: Royal College of Art, London. Appointments include: Designer, BBC Television, 1955-57; Art Director: The Charge of the Light Brigade, 1967; Laughter in the Dark, 1968; Designer: Brief Lives, 1967, 40 Years On, 1968; Enigma Variations, 1968; Production Designer: Julius Caesar, 1969; The Merchant of Venice, 1970; Eugene Onegin, 1971; The Straw Dogs, 1971; Othello, 1971; Samuel Pepys, 1971; Getting On, 1971; Othello, 1972; Un Ballo in Maschera, 1973; La Boheme, 1974; The Importance of Being Ernest, 1976; Diefledermaus, 1977; Hayfever, 1980; Otello,

1983; The Consul, 1985; Mr and Mrs Nobody, 1986; A Man for All Seasons, 1987; The Best of Friends, 1988. Publications: Street Children; Elizabeth R; Mary Queen of Scots; The English Year. Contributions to: Architectural Review; Vogue; Honours include: DES; RCA, 1954; RDI, 1977; Fellow, Chartered Society of Designers; CBE, 1986; Hon D Litt, Bristol, 1986. Designer of the Year Award - Award for ACE Cable TV Excellence; Literary Agent: Felicity Bryan. Address: Oman Productions Limited, The Laskett, Much Birch, Hereford HR2 8HZ, England.

OMOLEYE Mike, b. 26 Jan 1940, Oyo Ekiti, Ondo State, Nigeria. Journalist; Publisher. m. M A Omoleye, 1970, 4 sons, 3 daughters. Education: Diploma in Journalism. Appointments: Freelance Journalist, 1960-63; Reporter, Morning Post and Sunday Post, 1964-69; Special Roving Features Writer, 1969-71, News Editor, 1972-73, Assistant Editor, 1974-76, Daily Sketch and Sunday Sketch; Managing Director, Omoleye Publishing Company Limited, 1976-; Publisher, Sunday Glory, 1986-. Publications: You Can Control Your Destiny, 1974; Fascinating Folktales, 1976; Great Tales of the Yorubas, 1977; Mystery World Under the Sea, 1979; Awo As I Know Him, 1982; The Book of Life, 1982; Self Spiritual Healing, 1982; Issues at Stake, 1983; Make the Psalms Perform Wonders for You, 1990; Awo Speaks of Revolution, 1991. Contributions to: Numerous articles to Nigerian newspapers; Former columnist, Sunday Post, Daily Sketch, Sunday Sketch, Sunday Tribune. Address: GPO 1265, Ibadan, Oyo State, Nigeria.

OMURA Jimmie Matsumoto, b. 27 Nov 1912, Winslow, Washington, USA. Journalist; Editor; Publisher. m. Haruko Motoishi, 8 Mar 1951, 2 sons. Education: Graduated, Broadway High School, Seattle, 1932; Home Courses, Landscape Construction. Appointments: Editor, Junior High Newspaper, 1928-29; Journalism Delegate to State of Washington Student Leaders Conference, 1931; Editor, New Japanese American News, Los Angeles, California, 1933-34; Editor, New World Daily News, San Francisco, 1934-35; Editor, New World Sun, San Francisco, 1935-36; Publisher, Current Life Magazine, San Francisco, 1940-42; Selected among All-Time Nisei Essayist, 1941 Special Edition, Japanese American News, San Francisco; Editor & Public Relations, The Rocky Shimpo, Denver, Colorado, 1944, 1947. Publications: The Passing Show Column, Japanese American News, 1939-40; Nisei America: Know the Facts, Rocky Nippon, 1943; The Passing Parade, The Colorado Times, 1942; Plain Speaking, The Hokube Mainichi, 1984-88; Editorials, Current Life Magazine, 1940-42; Testimony Against Eviction, Tolan Congressional Committe, San Francisco Hearings, 1942; Wartime Editorials Advocating Restoration of Civil Liberties as Prelude to Military Service, Rocky Shimpo, 1944; Debunking JACL Fallacies, The Rafu Shimpo, 1989; Japanese American Journalism in World War II, Frontieers of Asian American Studies, 1989. Contributions to: The Formation of Nisei Perspectives, UCLA's Amerasia Journal, 1983 a requested commentary and two book reviews, 1984 (requested) and volunteered California Daily News; Great Northern Daily; Colorado Times; Rocky Nippon; Hokubei Mainichi; Asian Week; Hawaii Herald; New York Daily News; Nichibei; Rikka Magazine, Canada. Honours: Tolan Testimony included in Americans Betrayed, Morton Grodzin, 1949, as Introductory Feature in Japanese Section, To Serve the Devil, Paul Jacobs and Saul Landau, 1971, Chapter aphorism in Years of Infamy, Michi Weglyn, 1976; Over 400 editorials used for UCLA classroom studies, 1945; Historical book Dedication & Tolan Statement Epigraph in Keeper of Concentration Camps, Richard Drinnon, 1986; Symbol of Wartime Resistance, Smithsonian Institution Bi-Centennial Exhibit, For a More Perfect Union: Japanese Americans & The US Constitution, 1987; 1st and only recipient, Lifetime Achievement Award, Asian American Journalists Association, 1989. Memberships: Vice President, Associated Landscape Contractors of America; President, Landscape Contractors of Colorado, 2 terms; Nursery Advisory Committee, Colorado Department of Agriculture, 7 terms; Life Member, World Parliament of Chivalry, Sydney, Australia, 1990; Maison Internationale des Intellectuels, The Academie MIDI, Paris, France, 1992; Liberty Lobby, Charter Member, US Committee for Battle of Normandy Museum; National Trust for Historic Preservation; Smithsonion Associates; Public Citizen; People For the American Way; HALT; The Statue of Liberty/Ellis Island Centennial Foundation. Address: 1455 South Irving Street, Denver, CO 80219, USA.

ONDAATJE Michael, b. 12 Sept 1943, Colombo, Ceylon. Playwright; Poet; Novelist; Film Maker. m. Linda Spalding, 2 sons. Education: BA, University of Toronto, Canada, 1965; MA Queen's University. Publications: The Dainty Monsters, 1967; The Collected

Works of Billy the Kid, 1970, 1989, as play, 1973; Leonard Cohen, 1970; The Broken Ark, 1971; Rat Jelly, 1973; Elimination Dance, 1978; Coming Through Slaughter, novel, 1979; Rat Jelly and Other Poems, 1979; There's a Trick with a Knife That I'm Learning to do, 1979; The Long Poem Anthology, 1979; Running in the Family, 1983; Secular Love, poems, 1985; In the Skin of a Lion, novel, 1986; The Cinnamon Peeler, poetry, 1989; The English Patient, 1992. Honours: Canadian Author's Association Award, Poetry, 1980; Joint Winner Booker Prize, 1992; Governor's General Literary Award, 1992. Address: Department of English, Glendon College, York University, 2275 Bayview Avenue, Toronto, Ontario, Canada.

ONEAL Elizabeth, b. 1934, United States of America. Children's Fiction and Non Fiction Writer. Publications: War Work, 1970; The Improbable Adventures of Marvelous O'Hara Soapstone, 1971; The Language of Goldfish, 1980; A Formal Feeling, 1982; In Summer Light, 1985; Grandma Moses, Painter of Rural American, 1986. Address: 501 Onondaga Street, Ann Arbor, MI 48104, USA.

ONG Walter Jackson, b. 30 Nov 1912, Kansas City, MO, USA. Priest, Society of Jesus; University Professor. Education: BA, Rockhurst College, 1933; PhL, 1940, MA, 1941, STL, 1948, St Louis University; PhD, Harvard University, 1955; Various Honorary Doctorates. Appointments include: Professor, 1959-, Professor of Humanities in Psychiatry, 1970-, University Professor of Humanities, 1981-, Emeritus Professor, 1984-, St Louis University; Visiting Professor at various universities: Lincoln Lecturer, 1974, Zaire, Cameroun, Nigeria, Senegal; Wolfson College Lecturer, Oxford University, 1985; Lecturer, Finland, Austria, 1968; Israel, Egypt, 1969; USIA Lecturer, Sweden, Tunisia, Morocco, 1975; Korea, Japan, 1980. Publications include: Rhetoric, Romance and Technology, 1971; Interfaces of The Word, 1977; Fighting For Life: Contest, Sexuality and Consciousness, 1981; Orality and Literacy, 1982; Hopkins, The Self and God, 1986; Faith and Contexts, 2 Volumes, 1992. Contributions to: Over 300 articles across the USA, Europe and other continents. Address: St Louis University, St Louis, MO 63103, USA.

ONYEAMA Charles Dillibe Ejiofor, b. 6 Jan 1951, Enugu, Nigeria. Publisher; Author; Journalist. m. Ethel Ekwueme, 15 Dec 1984, 4 sons. Education: Premier School of Journalism, Fleet Street, London, England. Appointments: Member, Anambra Book Fair Planning Committee, 1987-90; Member, Board of Directors, Star Printing and Publishing Company Limited, 1992-94; Managing Director, Delta Publications (Nigeria) Limited. Publications: Nigger at Eton, 1972; John Bull's Nigger, 1974; Sex Is A Nigger's Game, 1975; The Book of Black Man's Humour, 1975; I'm The Greatest, 1975; Juju, 1976; Secret Society, 1977; Revenge of the Medicine Man, 1978; The Return, 1978; Night Demon, 1979; Female Target, 1980; The Rules of the Game, 1980; The Story of an African God, 1982; Modern Messiah, 1983; Godfathers of Voodoo, 1985; African Legend, 1985; Correct English, 1986; Notes of a So-Called Afro-Saxon, 1988. Contributions to: Books and Bookmen; The Spectator; The Times; Daily Express; Sunday Express; Drum; West Africa; Roots; The Guardian; Evening News. Memberships: President, Delta Book Club; Councillor, 5-man Caretaker Committee, Udi Local Government Council, Enugu State, 1994-. Literary Agent: Elspeth Cochrane Agency, London, England. Address: 8B Byron Onyeama Close, New Haven, PO Box 1171, Enugu, Enugu State, Nigeria.

OPIE Iona, b. 1923. Writer. Publications: A Dictionary of Superstitions (with Moira Tatem), 1989; The People in the Playground, 1993; With Peter Opie: The Oxford Dictionary of Nursery Rhymes, 1951; The Oxford Nursery Rhyme Book, 1955; The Lore and Language of Schoolchildren, 1929; Puffin Book of Nursery Rhymes, 1963; A Family Book of Nursery Rhymes, 1964; Children's Games in Street and Playground, 1969; The Oxford Book of Children's Verse, 1973; Three Centuries of Nursery Rhymes and Poetry for Children, 1973; The Classic Fairy Tales, 1974; A Nursery Companion, 1980; The Oxford Book of Narrative Verse, 1983; The Singing Game, 1985; Babies: an unsentimental anthology, 1990; I Saw Esau, 2nd Edition. Honours: Honorary MA (Oxon), 1962; Honorary MA, Open University, 1987; Honorary DLitt, Southampton, 1987; Honorary DLitt, Nottingham, 1991. Address: Westerfield House, West Liss, Hampshire GU33 6JQ, England.

OPITZ May, (May Ayim), b. 3 May 1960, Hamburg, Germany. Poet; Educator; Speech Therapist. Education: Adult Education, MA, 1986; Speech Therapist Diploma, 1990. Appointments: Vaterland-Mutterprache, Berlin, 1991; CELAFI, Toronto, 1992; Black

Bookfair, London, 1993; Zesde Internationale MEP-festival, Utrecht, Netherlands, Panafst Ghana, 1994. Publications: Showing our Colors, 1992; Entfernte Verbindungen, 1993; Daughters of Africa, 1992; Schwarze Frauen der Welt, 1994. Contributions to: Conditions 14, Baltimore, 1987; The Black Scholar, Vol 19, Oakland, 1988; Beiträge zur feministischen Wissenschaft 30/31 Köln, 1991; MS, Vol III, Nr 6, New York, 1993. Memberships: Co-founder, Literatue frauen, 1989; Deutscher Schriftstellerverband; Co-founder, Initiative of Black Germans, 1986. Literary Agent: Orlanda Frauenverlag, Grobgörschenstr 40, 10827 Berlin, Germany. Address: Hohenstaufenstr 63, 10781 Berlin, Germany.

OPPENHEIMER Joel (Lester), b. 1930, United States of America. Playwright; Poet. Publications: The Dancer, 1952; The Dutiful Son, 1957; The Great American Desert (play), 1961; The Love Bit and Other Poems, 1962; Miss Right (play), 1962; Like a Hill (play), 1963; A Treatise, 1966; Sirventes on a Sad Occurrence, 1967; In Time: Poems 1962-1968, 1969; On Occasion, 1973; The Wrong Season (on baseball), 1973; The Woman Poems, 1975; Pan's Eyes (short fiction), 1975; Names, Dates and Places, 1978; Just Friends/Friends and Lovers, 1978; Marilyn Lives! 1981; At Fifty, 1982; Poetry: The Ecology of the Soul, 1983; New Spaces, 1985; Why Not, 1987. Address: PO Box 281, Henniker, NH 03242, USA.

ORFALEA Gregory Michael, b. 9 Aug 1949, Los Angeles, California, USA. Writer; Editor. m. Eileen Rogers, 4 Aug 1984, 3 sons. Education: AB with honours, English, Georgetown University; MFA, Creative Writing, University of Alaska. Appointments: Reporter, Northern Virginia Sun, 1971-72; Professor, Santa Barbara City College, Santa Barbara, California,1974-76; Editor, Political Focus, 1979-81; Editor, Small Business Administration, 1985-91; Editor, Resolution Trust Corporation, 1991-. Publications: Before the Flames, 1988; The Capital of Solitude, 1988; Grape Leaves, 1988; Imagining America: Stories of the Promised Land, 1991. Contributions to: Triquarterly; Enoch: The Christian Science Monitor; The Washington Post. Honours: California Arts Council Award, 1976; American Middle East Peace Research Award, 1983; District of Columbia Commission on the Arts and Humanities, 1991. Membership: American PEN. Literary Agent: Thomas Wallace, The Wallace Group, New York City, New York, USA. Address: 6001 34th Pl NW, Washington, DC 20015, USA.

ORGEL Doris (Doris Adelberg),b. 15 Feb 1929, Vienna, Austria. Writer. m. Shelley Orgel, 25 June 1949, 2 sons, 1 daughter. Education: BA, Barnard College, 1960. Appointments: Senior Staff Writer,Editor, The Publications and Media Group of The Bank Sheer College of Education, 1961-. Publications: Sarah's Room, 1963; The Devil in Vienna, 1978; My War with Mrs Galloway, 1985; Whiskers Once and Always, 1986; Midnight Soup and a Witch's Hat, 1987; Starring Becky Suslow, 1989; Nobodies And Somebodies, 1991; Next Time I Will, 1993; The Mouse Who Wanted To Marry, 1993; Ariadue, Awake, 1994; Some 30 others - retellings, translations, light verse and original stories for children; Novels for young adults: Risking Love, 1985; Crack in the Heart, 1989. Contributions to: Several stories to Cricket magazine. Literary Agent: Writers House, USA. Address: c/o Writers House, 21 West 26th Street, New York, NY 10010, USA.

ORIOL Jacques (Jacques F G Vandievoet), b. 1 Oct 1923, Brussels, Belgium. Geography Teacher (retired); Poet; Essayist; Critic. 1 son. Education: Agregation, secondary school teaching, 1951. Publications: Travel writing, poetry, essays; Titles include: Les Belges au Kenya pour l'éclipse du siècle, series of 5 newspaper articles, 1973, book edited 1991; Quarantaine, 1983; Dédicaces, 1984; Midi, déjà Minuit, 1985; Nous ferons se lever une clarté très haute, 1985; L'Un, Le Multiple et le Tout, 1985; Voyage, 1986; Co-author with Années Quatre-Vingts group: L'an prochain a Valparaiso, 1986; Etat critique, 1987; Bruxelles a venir, 1987; Icare selon les écrivains grecs et latins (in Phréatique, Paris), 1988; Icare ou l'éternelle jeunesse (id), 1988; Poète aujourd'hui, comment dire? 1989; Douze chants pour renouer les liens d'amour en floréal, 1989; Demi-deuil, 1990; Contre la réforme de l'orthographe (collective work), 1990; Un un mot comme en cent (ana), 1992; Dilecta, 1993. Contributions to: Reviews to various literary journals. Honours: 1st Prize, Classical Poetry, Rosati, Arras, 1985; Cup, Nord Pas-de-Calais Regional Council, 1985; Francois Villon Prize, National Association of French Writers, 1986; Silver Medal, High School of French Contemporary Culture, 1987; 1st Prize, Classical Poetry, Ecole de la Loire, Blois, 1989. Memberships include: Belgian Section, PEN Club; Association of Belgian Authors; Executive, Union of Walloon Writers and Artists; Sociedad de Escritores de Chile; Leader, Années Quatre-Vingts Group; Association pour la au suavegarde et l'expansion de la langue française; Collaborator in Belgium of the parisian review, Vericuetos. Address: 210 avenue Moliere, boite 10, B-1060 Brussels, Belgium.

ORLEDGE Robert Francis Nicholas, b. 5 Jan 1948, Bath, Avon, England. Professor of Music. Education: Associate, Royal College of Organists, 1964; Clare College, Cambridge; BA (Hons), Music, 1968, MA, 1972, PhD, 1973, Cambridge University. Publications: Gabriel Fauré, 1979, Revised Edition, 1983; Debussy and the Theatre, 1982; Charles Koechlin (1867-1950): His Life and Works, 1989; Satie the Composer, 1990. Contributions to: Articles and reviews to: Music and Letters; Musical Quarterly; Musical Times; Music Review; Current Musicology; Journal of the Royal Musical Association. Memberships: Royal Musical Association; Centre de Documentation Claude Debussy; Association des Amis de Charles Koechlin; Fondation Erik Satie. Address: Windermere House, Windermere Terrace, Liverpool L8 3SB, England.

ORLOVA Alexandra, b. 22 Feb 1911, Russia. Musicologist. m. (1) Georgi Orlov, 1935, dec 1940, 2 sons, (2) Mikhail Glukh, 23 Apr 1963, dec 1973. Education: Leningrad Institute of Art History, 1928-30; Extra-mural studies, Leningrad University, 1930-33. Appointments: Freelance Writer, 1950-. Publications: Glinka: Literary Legacy, vol I, 1952, vol II, 1953; Glinka in the memory of contemporaries, 1955; Rimsky-Korsakov, Chronicle of his life and works (in Russian), 4 vols, 1969-71; Glinka in Petersburg, 1971; Musorgsky in Petersburg, 1974; Mikhail Glukh. Essay on his life and works, 1977; Musorgsky: Days and Works. Biography in documents, 1983; Glinka's Life in Music. Biography in documents, 1988; Tchaikovsky: A self-portrait, 1990; Musorgsky Remembered, 1991. Contributions to: Numerous contributions to collections, newspapers and magazines, USSR, USA, France, Germany. Memberships: Former Member, Union of Soviet Composers. Address: 97 Van Wagenen Ave, Apt 1D, Jersey City, NJ 07306, USA.

ORLOWSKI Wladyslaw, b. 27 June 1922, Warsaw, Poland. Writer. m. Halina Radzikowska, 4 Nov 1954, 2 sons. Education: MA, University of Lodz, 1947; PhD, Institute of Art, Polish Academy of Sciences, Warsaw, 1970. Publications: Other's Love, Other's Suffering, 1976; The Splinters, 1987; Call from the Empty Space, 1982; The Sunrise of the Passed Day, 1988; From the Book to the Screen, 1961; The Justice in Kyoto, play, 1961. Contributions to: 400 articles to numerous journals and magazines. Honours: Literary Prize: Minister of Defence, 1965, City of Lodz, 1987. Memberships: Society of Polish Writers, President, Lodz Branch, 1984-. Address: ul Brzezna 18 m 5, 90-303 Lodz, Poland.

ORMEROD Roger, Author. Publications: Time to Kill, 1974; The Silence of the Night, 1974; Full Fury, 1975; A Spoonful of Luger, 1975; Sealed with a Loving Kill, 1976; The Colour of Fear, 1976; A Glimpse of Death, 1976; Too Late for the Funeral, 1977; The Murder Come to Mind, 1977; A Dip into Murder, 1978; The Weight of Evidence, 1978; The Bright Face of Danger, 1979; The Amnesia Trap, 1979; Cart Before the Hearse, 1979; More Dead than Alive, 1980; Double Take, 1980; One Breathless Hour, 1981; Face Value, 1983; Seeing Red, 1984; The Hanging Doll Murder, 1984; Dead Ringer, 1985; Still Life with Pistol, 1986; A Death to Remember, 1986; An Alibi Too Soon, 1987; The Second Jeopardy, 1978; An Open Window, 1988; By Death Possessed, 1988; Guilt on the Lily, 1989; Death of an Innocent, 1989; No Sign of Life, 1990; Hung in the Blance, 1990; Farewell Gesture, 1990. Address: c/o Constable, 10 Orange Street, London WC2H 7EG, England.

ORMSBY Frank, b. 30 Oct 1947, Enniskillen County, Fermanagh, Northern Ireland. Schoolmaster. Education: BA, English, 1970, MA, 1971, Queen's University, Belfast, Northern Ireland. Appointment: Editor, The Honest Ulsterman, 1969-89. Publications: A Store of Candles, 1977, 1986; A Northern Spring, 1986; Poets from the North of Ireland, editor, 1979, new edition 1990; Northern Windows: An Anthology of Ulster Autobiography, Editor, 1987; The Long Embrace: Twentieth Century Irish Love Poems, editor, 1987; Thine in Storm and Calm: An Amanda McKittrick Ros Reader, Editor, 1988. Address: 36 Strathmore Park North, Belfast BT15 5HR, Northern Ireland.

ORNSTEIN Robert E, b. 17 Feb 1942, New York, New York, USA. Assisstant Professor of Medical Psychology; President, Langley Porter Institute. Education: BA, Queens College, City of New York; PhD, Stanford University. Publications: On the Experience of Time, 1968; On The Psychology of Meditation, 1971; Psychology of

Consciousness, 1974; The Healing Brain (co-author), 1987; New World, New mind: Moving Towards Conscious Evolution (co-author), 1989; The Roots of the Self, 1993. Contributions to: Psychonomic Science; Psychophysiology; Psychology Today. Honours: Creative Talent Award, American Institute for Research, 1968; UNESCO Award, Best Contribution to Psychology, 1972; Media Award, American Psychological Foundation, 1973. Memberships: International Society for the Study of Time; Institute for the Study of Human Consciousness; Biofeedback Society. Address: Langley Porter Institute, 401 Parnassus, San Francisco, CA 94143, USA.

ORSZAG-LAND Thomas, b. 12 Jan 1938, Budapest, Hungary. Writer. Publications: Berlin Proposal, 1990; Free Women, 1991; Translations: Bluebeard's Castle, 1988; Splendid Stags, 1992; 33 Poems by Radnoti, 1992; Poems by Nezei, 1995. Contributions to: Nature; Contemporary Review; Spectator; New York Times; Observer; Guardian; Financial Times; Times Higher Education Supplement; Others. Memberships: Fellow, International PEN; Foreign Press Association; Royal Institute of International Affairs; Society of Authors. Address: PO Box 1213, London N6 5HZ, England.

ORTEGA Julio, b. 29 Sept 1942, Peru. Writer; Professor. m. Claudia J Elliott, 21 Mar 1986. Education: Doctoral of Literature, Catholic University, Lima, Peru. Appointments: Professor, University of Texas, Austin, 1978-86, Brandeis University 1987-; Correspondent, Diario 16, Madrid, Republica, Lima, Unomasuno, Mexico. Publications: Poetics of Change, 1984; Adios Ayachucho, 1986; Latin America in its Literature, 1980; La Contemplacion y la fiesta, 1969; Figuracion de la persona, 1971; The Land in the Day, 1978; Rituales, 1976; Ceremonias, 1974; Acto subersivo, 1984; Mediodia, 1970; Relato de la Utopia, 1973; Teoria poetica de Vallejo, 1986; La Lima del 900, 1986; Antologia de la poesia hispanoamericana, 1987. Contributions to: London Magazine; TriQuarterly; L'Arc; Sulfur; New Orleans Review; Syntaxis; Vuelta; Mundo Nuevo. Honours: Guggenheim Fellowship, 1974; Director, NEH, 1981, 1987; Premio Cope for Short Story, Lima, 1981; National Prize, Theatre, Peru, 1968, 1971. Memberships: President, Peruvian Association of Culture; Archives de la Litterature Latinoamericaine, Paris; Latin American Studies Association. Literary Agent: Carmen Balcells, Barcelona. Address: Romance and Comp Lit, Brandeis University, Waltham, MA 02254, USA.

ORTIZ Simon J, b. 1941, United States of America. Author; Poet. Appointments include: Editor, Quetzeal Chinle, Arizona, 1970-73; Consultant Editor, Pueblo of Acoma Press, 1982-. Publications: Naked in the Wind, 1970; Going for the Rain, 1976; A Good Journey, 1977; The People Shall Continue, 1977; Howbah Indians (short stories), 1978; Song, Poetry, Language, 1978; Fightback, 1980; From Sand Creek, 1981; A Poem is a Journey, 1981; Blue and Red (for children), 1982; The Importance of Childhood, 1982; Fightin': New and Collected Stories, 1983; Woven Stone, 1992. Address: 308 Sesame SW, Albuquerque, NM 87105, USA.

OSBORN Betty Olive, b. 15 July 1934, Melbourne, Victoria, Australia. Writer; Historian. m. Bruce Jamieson Osborn, 23 Apr 1962, 1 son, 3 daughters. Education: BA, University of Melbourne, 1959. Career: Journalist, Argus, 1952-57; Book Editor, Melbourne University Press, 1958-62. Publications: History of Holy Trinity Bacchus Marsh, 1971; The Bacchus Story, 1973; Pieces of Glass, play, 1977; Maryborough, A Social History 1854-1904 (with Trenear DuBourg), 1985; Maryborough: Against the Odds 1905-1961, 1995. Contributions to: Argus Weekend Magazine; Age Literary Supplement; Wimmera-Mallee Country Bulletin. Honours: Montague Grover Prize, 1955. Memberships: Fellowship of Australian Writers (Victoria) Inc; Graduate Union, Melbourne University; Committee Member, Midlands Historical Society; Life Member, Bacchus Marsh and District Historical Society. Address: 18 Douglass St, Maryborough, Victoria 3465, Australia.

OSBORNE Charles Thomas, b. 24 Nov 1927, Brisbane, Australia. Author; Critic; Musicologist. Education: Brisbane High School, 1941-44; Griffith University, 1994. Literary Appointments: Assistant Editor, The London Magazine, 1958-66; Literature Director, Arts Council of Great Britain, 1966-86; Chief Theatre Critic, London Daily Telegraph, 1987-92. Publications: The Complete Operas of Verdi, 1969; W H Auden: The Life of a Poet, 1980; Letter to W H Auden and other Poems, 1984; Giving It Away, 1986; The Bel Canto Operas, 1994; Volumes on Mozart, Wagner, Puccini & Strauss. Contributions to: Times Literary Supplement; Encounter; Spectator; Encyclopedia dell Speltacolo; Annual Register, Harvard Advocate. Honours: Gold Medal,

1993. Memberships: PEN; Royal Society of Literature; Critics' Circle. Literary Agent: Aitken & Stone, 29 Fernshaw Road, London SW10 0TG, England. Address: 125 St George's Road, London SE1 6HY, England. 192.

OSBORNE John, (James), b. 1929. Writer; Playwright. Appointments: Co-Director, Woodfall Films, 1958-; Director, Oscar, Lowenstein Plays Limited, London, 1960-; Council, English Stage Company, 1960-. Publications: Look Back in Anger, 1956; The Entertainer, 1958, screenplay 1960; Epitaph for George Dillon (with A Creighton), 1957; The World of Paul Slickey, 1959; A Subject for Scandal and Concern, 1961; Luther, 1961; Plays for England: The Blood of the Bambers, Under Plain Cover, 1963; Tom Jones (screenplay), 1964; Innadmissible Evidence, 1965; (adaptor) A Bond Honoured, 1966; A Patriot for Me, 1966; Time Present and The Hotel in Amsterdam, 1968; The Right Prospective: A Play for Television, 1969; Very Like a Whale, 1970; West of Suez, 1971; (adaptor) Hedda Gabler, 1972; The Gifts of Friendship, 1972; A Sense of Detachment, 1972; A Place Calling Itself Rome, 1973; Four Plays, 1973; (adaptor) The Picture of Dorian Gray, 1973; The End of Me Old Cigar, 1975; Watch It Come Down, 1975; You're Not Watching Me, Mummy, and Try a Little Tenderness, 1978; A Better Class of Person (autobiography), 1981; Too Young to Fight, Too Old to Forget, 1985; A Better Class of Person and God Rot Tunbridge Wells, 1985; The Father (adapt & trans), 1989; Déjavu (play), 1991; Almost a Gentleman (autobiography), 1991. Contributions to: Various newspapers and journals. Address: The Hurst, Clunton, Craven Arms, Shropshire, England.

OSBORNE Maggie (Margaret Ellen), b. 10 June 1941, Hollywood, California, USA. Author; Novelist. m. George M Osborne II, 27 Apr 1972, 1 son. Publications: Partners (with Carolyn Bransford), 1989; As Margaret St George: Castles and Fairy Tales, 1986; Dear Santa, 1989; Winter Magic, 1986; The Heart Club, 1987; Where There's Smoke, 1987; Heart's Desire, 1988; Jigsaw, 1990; American Pie, 1990; Lady Reluctant, 1991; Chase The Heart, 1987; Alexa, 1980; Salem's Daughter, 1981; Portrait in Passion, 1981; Yankee Princess, 1982; Rage to Love, 1983; Flight of Fancy, 1984, As Maggie Osborne: Emerald Rain, 1991; Happy New Year Darling, 1992; Murder by The Book, 1992; Cache Poor, 1993; The Pirate and His Lady, 1992; A Wish and A Kiss, 1993; The Accidental Princess, 1994; The Drop.in Bride, 1994; The Wives of Bowie Stone, 1994. Literary Agent: Meg Ruley, Jane Rotrosen Agency, 318 E 51st St, New York City, NY 10022. Address: Box E, Dillon, CO 80435, USA.

OSBORNE Mary Pope, b. 20 May 1949, Fort Sill, Oklahoma, USA. Writer. m. Will Osborne, 16 May 1976. Education: BA, University of North Carolina. Publications: Run, Run, As Fast As You Can, 1982; Love Always, Blue, 1983; Best Wishes, Joe Brady, 1984; Mo to the Rescue, 1985; Last One Home, 1986; Beauty and the Beast, 1987; Christopher Columbus, Admiral of the Ocean Sea, 1987; Pandora's Box, 1987; Jason and the Argonauts, 1988; The Deadly Power of Medusa (with Will Osborne), 1988; Favorite Greek Myths, 1989; A Visit to Sleep's House, 1989; Mo and His Friends, 1989; American Tall Tales, 1990; Moonhorse, 1991; Spider Kane Series, 1992; Magic Treehouse Series, 1993; Mermaid Tales, 1993; Molly and the Prince, 1994; Haunted Waters, 1994. Address: Brandt & Brandt Agency, 1501 Broadway 2310, New York, NY 10036, USA.

OSBOURNE Ivor Livingstone, b. 6 Nov 1951, Jamaica. Author; Publisher. Partner, Charline Mertens, 2 daughters. Publications: Novels: The Mercenary, 1976; The Mango Season, 1979, 1987; Prodigal, 1987; The Rasta Cookbook, Optima, 1990; The Exotic Cookbook of Optima, 1990. Contributions to: Various journals and magazines. Literary Agent: Peter Bryant Writers, 3 Kidderpire Gardens, Hampstead, London, England. Address: 27c Chippenham Road, Maida Vale, London W9 2AH, England.

OSERS Ewald, b. 13 May 1917, Prague, Czechoslovakia. Translator; Author. m. Mary Harman, 3 June 1942, 1 son, 1 daughter. Education: Prague University; BA (Hons), University of London. Appointments: Chairman, Translators Association, 1971; 1980-81; Chairman, Translators Guild, 1975-79; Vice-Chairman, Institute of Linguists, 1975-80; Vice-President, International Federation of Translators, 1977-81, 1984-87; Editorial Director, Babel, 1979-87; Member, International Book Committee, 1981-87. Publications: Poetry: Wish You Were Here, 1976; Arrive Where We Started, 1995; Volume of own poetry translated into Czech, 1986; Translator, over 110 books including 31 volumes of poetry; English translation of Jaroslav Seifert,

Czech Nobel Prize Winner. Contributions to: Over 30 magazines, UK, USA, Canada, Australia, India, Germany, Poland, Yugoslavia, Bulgaria. Address: 33 Reades Lane, Sonning Common, Reading, Berkshire RG4 9LL, England.

OSOFISAN Femi, b. 16 June 1946, Nigeria. Playwright. Education; BA, 1969, PhD, 1974, University of Ibadan. Appointments include: Professor, University of Ibadan; Visiting Professor, American Universities. Publications include: You Have Lost Your Fine Face, 1969; Red is the Freedom Road, 1974; A Restless Run of Locusts, 1975; The Chattering and the Song, 1974; Once upon Four Robbers, 1978; Farewell to a Cannibal Rage, 1978; Birthdays Are Not for Dying, 1981; The Oriki of a Grasshopper, 1981; No More the Wasted Breed, 1982; Midnight Hotel, 1982; Aringindin and the Nightwatchman, 1989; Another Raft, 1989; Yungba Yungba and the Dance Contest; TV Plays; Novels, Kolera Kolej, 1975; Cordelia, 1990; Verse, Minted Coins, 1986. Honours include: Fulbright Fellowships, 1986. Address: Dept of Theatre Arts, University of Ibadan, Ibadan, Nigeria.

OSTRIKER Alicia, b. 11 Nov 1937, New York City, USA. m. 1 Dec 1958, 1 son, 2 daughters. Education: BA, Brandeis University, 1959; PhD, University of Wisconsin, 1964. Appointments: Faculty, English Department, Rutgers University, 1965-. Publications: Poetry: The Mother/Child Papers, 1980; A Woman Under the Surface, 1982; The Imaginary Lover, 1986; Green Age, 1989; Criticism: Vision & Verse in William Blake; Writing Like a Woman; Stealing the Language: Emergence of Women's Poetry in America; Criticism: Feminist Revision and the Bible, 1993; Essays: The Nakedness of the Fathers: Biblical Visions and Revisions, 1994. Contributions to: The Atlantic; Paris Review; Antzeus; New York Times Book Review; Nation; Partisan Review; Hudson Review; Poetry; American Poetry Review; Iowa Review; New Yorker. Honours: Poetry Fellowship, National Endowment for the Arts, 1977; Guggenheim Fellowship, 1984-85; William Carlos Williams Award, Poetry Society of America, 1986. Memberships: PEN; Poetry Society of America; Modern Language Association. Literary Agent: Ellen Levine. Address: 33 Philip Drive, Princeton, NJ 08540, USA.

OSTROM Hans Ansgar, b. 29 Jan 1954, USA. Writer; Teacher. m. Jacqueline Bacon, 18 July 1983, 1 son. Education: BA, 1975, PhD, English, 1982, University of California, Davis. Appointments: Contributing Reviewer, Choice, 1987-; Columnist, Morning News Tribune, Tacoma, Washington, 1990-. Publications: The Living Language, 1984; Lives and Moments, 1991; Three to Get Ready, 1991; The Coast Starlight, 1992; Water's Night (with Wendy Bishop), 1992; Colors of a Different Horse, 1993; Langston Hughes: The Short Fiction, 1993. Contributions to: Reviews, poems, stories to: Ploughshares; San Francisco Chronicle; Poetry Northwest; Webster Review; San Francisco Review of Books. Honours: Harvest Prize in Poetry, 1978; Redbook Prize in Fiction, 1985. Memberships: National Book Critics Circle; Modern Language Association; Mystery Writers of America. Address: English Department, University of Puget Sound, Tacoma, WA 98416, USA.

OTTEN Charlotte F, b. 1 Mar 1926, Chicago, Illinois, USA. Professor of English. m. Robert T Otten, 21 Dec 1948, 2 sons. Education: AB, 1949; MA, 1969; PhD, 1971. Publications: Environ: D With Eternity, 1985; A Lycanthropy Reader, 1986; The Voice of the Narrator in Children's Literature, 1989; English Women's Voices, 1991; The Virago Book of Birth Poetry, 1993; Bantam Book of Birth Poetry, 1995. Contributions to: Amherst Review; Anglican Theological Review; Commonweale South Florida Poetry Review; South Coast Poetry Review; Manhattan Poetry Review; Descant; Kentucky Poetry Review; The Macguffin; Interim; Southern Humanities Review; Whiskey Island Magazine; Shakespeare Quarterly; Milton Studies; N&Q; English Literary Renaissance; Huntington Library Quarterly; English Studies; Chaucer Review; Signal; Concerning Poetry. Address: English Department, Calvin College, Grand Rapids, MI 49546, USA.

OTTO-RIEKE Gerd, b. 3 Mar 1950, Schlagsdorf. Journalist. Education: Diplom-Volkswirt, Hamburg University, 1977. Appointments: Chairman, Junge Presse Schleswig-Holstein, 1968-73; Vice Chairman, Deutsche Jugendpresse, 1969-73; Staff, Interpress and F Reinecke Verlag, Hamburg, 1977-81; Editor in Chief, Deutscher Verkehrsverlag, Hamburg, 1981-85; Editor in Chief, Jaeger Verlag Industriemagazin, Munich, 1988-. Publications: Der Formaltaeten-Wegweiser, 1982; Der Grosse Hobby und Erlebnis-Urlaubsfuehrer, 1986; Landgangfuehrer fuer Schiffsbesatzungen, 1986. Contributions to: various articles in professional journals. Memberships: Hamburger Journalisten-Verband;

Luftfahrt Presse Club. Address: Wrangelstrasse 28, D 2000 Hamburg 20, Germany.

OUELLETTE (Marie Léonne) Francine, b. 11 Mar 1947, Montreal, Canada. 1 daughter. Education: Fine Arts Diploma in Sculpture, 1968; Pilot Licence, 1973. Publications: Au Nom Du Père Et Du Fils, 1984; Le Sorcier, 1985; Sire Gaby Du Lac, 1989; Les Ailes Du Destin, 1992; Le Grand Blanc, 1993. Honours: France-Québec, Jean Hamelin, 1986; Prix, Du Grand Public, 1993. Memberships: Union des écrivains Québécois UNEQ. Literary Agent: Michel Ouellette. Address: CP 30, 1044 ch Presquîle, Lac Des Iles, Québec J0W 1J0, Canada.

OUSMANE Sembene, b. 1 Jan 1923, Ziguinchor, Casamance Region, Senegal. Writer; Film-maker. Education: Studied Film Production under Marc Donski, USSR. Appointments: Plumber; Bricklayer; Apprentice Mechanic; Founder, Editor, 1st Wolof Language Monthly, Kaddu. Publications: Novels: Le docker noir, 1956; O Pays mon beau peuple, 1957; Les bouts de bois de Dieu, 1960; Voltaïque, 1962; L'harmattan, 1964; Vehi-Ciosane suivi du mandat, 1966; Xala, 1974; Fat ndiay Diop, 1976; Dernier de l'empire, 1979. Honours: 1st Prize for Novelists, World Festival of Negro Arts, Dakar, 1966; Grand Prix pour les lettres, President of Republic of Senegal, 1993; Numerous international awards. Memberships: Association des Ecrivain du Sénégal; Societé des Gens de Lettres, France; Société Africaine de Culture; Corresponding Member, German Academy of Letters; President, International PEN Club, Senegal Section. Address: PO Box 8087, Yoff, Dakar, Senegal.

OVERY Paul (Vivian), b. 1940. Writer. Appointments: Art Critic, The Listener, London, 1966-68; Art Critic, The Financial Times, London, 1968-70; Chief Art Critic, The Times, London, 1973-78; Literary Editor, New Society, London, 1970-71. Publications: Edouard Manet, 1967; De Stijl, 1969; Kandinsky: The Language of the Eye, 1969; Paul Neagu: A Generative Context, 1981; The Rietveld Schroder House (co-author), 1988; De Stijl, 1991; The Complete Rietveld Furniture (with Peter Vöge), 1993; A Recognition of Restrictions, essay, 1994. Contributions to: Lions and Unicorns: The Britishness of Postwar British Sculpture; Art in America, 1991; Carpentering the Classic; A Very Peculiar Practice; The Furniture of Gerrit Rietveld, Journal of Design History, 1991; Equipment for Utopia, Art Journal, 1994. Memberships: Society of Authors; National Union of Journalists. Literary Agent: John Johnson. Address: 92 South Hill Park, London NW3 2SN, England.

OVESEN Ellis, b. 18 July 1923, Writer; Artist; Composer. m. 27 Aug 1949, 2 sons. Education: MA, cum laude, University of Wisconsin, 1948; California Teachers Credential, San Jose State University, 1962; Extra classes in poetry writing. Appointments: Teacher of English, University of Wisconsin, 1946-48; Writer, Advertising Department, Du Pont Mag, Delaware, 1948-49; Publicity Chairman, AAUW, Eastern Seaboard, 1949-53; Teacher of English, San Jose State U, 1962-63; Teaching Poetry, 1963-90. Publications: Gloried Grass, 1970; Haloed Paths, 1973; To Those Who Love, 1974; The Last Hour: Lives Touch, 1975; A Time for Singing, 1977; A Book of Praises, 1977; The Green Madonna, 1984; The Keeper of the Word, 1985; The Wing Brush, 1986; The Year of the Snake, 1989; The Flowers of God, 1985, 1990; Beloved I, 1980, II 1990; The Year of the Horse, 1990; A Time for Singing: Another Man's Mocassins; Memories of South Dakota. Contributions to: Poet India; Los Altos Town Crier; Paisley Moon; Fresh Hot Bread; Samvedana; The Plowman. Honours: National Honour Society, 1941; Los Altos Hills Poet, 1976-90; Honorary Doctorate, World Academy of Arts and Culture, 1986; Dame of Merit, Knights of Malta, 1988; World Poet, 1989; Golden Poet Award, 1988, 1989, 1991; Research Fellow, 1992. Memberships include: National Writers Club; California Writers Club; Poetry Society of America; California State Poetry Society, President; Penisula Poets, Founder and President; NLAPW; Womens Museum of Art, Charter Member, Washington DC; San Francisco Poetry Society' South Dakota Music Composers. Address: Box 482, Los Altos, CA 94023, USA.

OVSTEDAL Barbara Kathleen, b. England. Writer. m. Inge Ovstedal, 1945, 1 son, 1 daughter. Education: West Sussex College of Art. Publications: The Warwyck Trilogy, 1979-80; This Shining Land, 1985; The Silver Touch, 1987; To Dance With Kings, 1988; The Golden Tulip, 1991; The Venetian Mask, 1992; The Sugar Pavilion, 1993; The Fortuny Gown, 1995. Contributions to: Good Housekeeping; Country Life; Woman; Woman's Own; Woman's Weekly; Others. Memberships: Society of Authors; Romantic Novelists Association. Literary Agent:

Laurence Pollinger Ltd, London, England. Address: c/o Laurence Pollinger Ltd, 18 Maddox Street, London W1R 0EU, England.

OWEN Alun (Davies), b. 24 Nov 1925. Writer. m. Mary O'Keefe, 1942, 2 sons. Publications include: Everyday Except Christmas, 1957; I'm All Right Jack, 1959; The Servant, 1963; (Television), Glas y Dorlan, BBC Wales; Author, Stage Productions: The Rough and Ready Lot, 1959; Progress to the Park, 1959; Progress to the Park, 1959; The Rose Affair, 1966; A Little Winter Love, 1963; Maggie May, 1964; The Game, 1965; The Goose, 1967; Shelter, 1971; There'll Be Some Changes Made, 1969; Norma, 1969; We Who Are About To, 1969; The Male of the Species, 1974; (Screen), The Criminal, 1960; A Hard Day's Night, 1964; Caribbean Idyll, 1970; (Radio), Two Sons, 1957; It Looks Like Rain, 1959; Earwig, series, 1984; (Television), No Trams to Lime Street, 1959; After the Funeral, 1960; Lena, Oh My Lena, 1960; The Ruffians, 1960; The Ways of Love, 1961; Dare to be a Daniel, 1962; The Hard Knock, You Can't Wind'em All, 1962; The Strain, Let's Imagine Series, The Stag, A Local Boy, 1963; The Other Fella; The Making of Jericho, 1966; The Wake, 1967; The Web, 1972; Ronnie Barker Show (3 scripts); Buttons, Flight, 1973; Lucky Norma, 1974; Left, 1975; Forget Me Not, 6 plays, 1976; The Look, 1978; The Runner, 1980; Sealink, 1980; Cafe Society, 1982; Colleagues, 1982; Tiger, 1984; Lovers of the Lake, 1984; Widowers, 1985. Membership: Chelsea Arts Club. Literary Agent: Blake Friedmann, London. Address: c/o Julian Friedmann, Blake Friedman Literary Agency, 37-41 Gower Street, London WC1E 6HH, England.

OWEN Charles, b. 14 Nov 1915, England. Author; Management Consultant; Royal Navy Officer (retired). m. Felicity, 14 Feb 1950, 1 son, 1 daughter. Education: Royal Navy Colleges, Dartmouth & Greenwich, England. Publications: Independent Traveller, 1966; Britons Abroad, 1968; The Opaque Society, 1970; No More Heroes, 1975; The Grand Days of Travel, 1979; Just Across The Channel, 1983. Contributions to: Various magazines & journals. Honours: Distinguished Service Cross, 1943. Memberships: Society of Authors; Writers Guild of Great Britain; PEN; West Country Writers Association. Address: Flat 31, 15 Portman Square, London W1H 9HD, England.

OWEN Douglas David Roy, b. 17 Nov 1922, Norton, Suffolk, England. University Professor (retired). m. Berit Mariann Person, 31 July 1954, 2 sons. Education: University College, Nottingham, 1942-43; St Catharine's College, Cambridge; BA, 1948, MA, 1953, PhD, 1955, Cambridge; Sorbonne and Collège de France, Paris, 1950-51. Appointments include: Founder, General Editor, Forum for Modern Language Studies, 1965-. Publications: The Evolution of the Grail Legend, 1968; The Vision of Hell, 1970; The Song of Roland, translation, 1972, new expanded edition, 1990; The Legend of Roland: a Pageant of the Middle Ages, 1973; Noble Lovers, 1975; Chrétien de Troyes: Arthurian Romances, translation, 1987; Guillaume le Clerc: Fergus of Galloway, translation, 1989; A Chat Round The Old Course (by DDRO), 1990; Eleanor of Aquitaine: Queen and Legend, 1993; The Romance of Reynard the Fox, 1994; Edited with R C Johnston: Fabliaux, 1957; Two Old French Gauvain Romances, 1972. Contributions to: Over 30 Festschrift papers and articles to British and foreign journals; Many reviews including several for The Times Literary Supplement; 3 broadcast talks. Memberships: International Arthurian Society; Société Rencesvals; International Courtly Literature Society. Address: 7 West Acres, St Andrews, Fife KY16 9UD, Scotland.

OWEN Eileen, b. 27 Feb 1949, Concord, New Hampshire, USA. Editor; Writer. m. John D Owen, 19 June 1971, Chichester, New Hampshire. Education: BA, Spanish, University of New Hampshire, 1971; BA, English, 1979; MA, Creative Writing, 1981, University of Washington. Publication: Facing the Weather Side, 1985. Contributions to: Poetry Northwest; Dark Horse; Tar River Review of Poetry; Passages North; Sojourner; Welter; The Seattle Review; Mississippi Mud; Hollow Springs Review; Signpost; Back Door Travel; Arts and Artists; and other publications. Honours: Artist-in-Residence, Ucross Foundation, Wyoming, 1984 and 1988; Poems selected King County Arts Commission, 1983; Poems selected in competition Seattle Arts Commission, 1983 and 1987; Honorable Mention, Washington Poets Association, 1981. Address: 18508 90th Avenue W, Edmonds, WA 98020, USA.

OWEN Warwick (Jack Burgoyne), b. 1916, New Zealand. Writer. Appointments: Assistant Lecturer, Lecturer, Senior Lecturer in English, University College of North Wales, 1946-65; Professor, Emeritus Professor of English, McMaster University, 1965-. Publications: Wordsworth's Preface to Lyrical Ballads, 1957;

Wordsworth and Coleridge Lyrical Ballads 1798, 1967, 1969; Wordsworth as Critic, 1969, 1971; Prose Works of William Wordsworth, 3 vols (with J W Smyser), 1974; Wordsworth's Literary Criticism, 1974; William Wordsworth: The Fourteen-Book Prelude, 1985. Address: Department of English, McMaster University, Hamilton, Ontario L8S 4L9, Canada.

OWUSU Martin, b. 11 July 1943, Agona, Kwaman, Ghana. Playwright. Education: PhD, Brandeis University, MA, 1979. Appointments include: Senior Lecturer, University of Ghana, Legon, 1987. Publications include: The Story Ananse Told, 1967; The Mightier Sword, 1967; The Adventures of Sasa and Esi, Sasa and the King of the Forest, 1968; The Adventures of Sasa and Ensi, Sasa and the Witch of the Forest, 1968; Anane, 1968; Python: The Legend of Aku Sika, 1989; The Pot of Okro Soup and A Bird Called Go Back for the Answer. Honours include: Awards for Acting and for TV. Address: School of Performing Arts, University of Ghana, PO Box 25, Legon, Near Accr, Ghana.

OXLEY William, b. 1939. Poet; Philosopher; Translator; Actor; Traveller; Freelance Writer. Publications: The Dark Structures, 1967; New Workings, 1969; Passages from Time: Poems from a Life, 1971; The Icon Poems, 1972; Sixteen Days in Autumn, travel, 1972; Opera Vetera, 1973; Mirrors of the Sea, 1973; Eve Free, 1974; Mundane Shell, 1975; Superficies, 1976; The Exile, 1979; The Notebook of Hephaestus and Other Poems, 1981; Poems of a Black Orpheus, 1981; The Synopthegms of a Prophet, 1981; The Idea and Its Imminence, 1982; Of Human Consciousness, 1982; The Cauldron of Inspiration, 1983; A Map of Time, 1984; The Triviad and Other Satires, 1984; The Inner Tapestry, 1985; Vitalism and Celebration, 1987; The Mansands Trilogy, 1988; Mad Tom on Tower Hill, 1988; The Patient Reconstruction of Paradise, 1991; Forest Sequence, 1991; In the Drift of Words, 1992; The Playboy, 1992; Cardboard Troy, 1993; The Hallsands Tragedy, 1993; Collected Longer Poems, 1994. Address: 6 The Mount, Furzeham, Brixham, South Devon TQ5 8QY, England.

OZ Amos, b. 4 May 1939, Jerusalem, Israel. Author. M. Nily Zuckerman, 5 Apr 1960, 1 son, 2 daughters. Education: BA cum laude, Hebrew Literature, Philosophy, Hebrew University, Jerusalem, 1965. Appointments: Teacher, Literature, Philosophy, Hulda High School and Givat Brenner Regional High School, 1963-86; Visiting Fellow, St Cross College, Oxford, England, 1969-70; Writer in Residence, Hebrew University, Jerusalem, 1975, 1990; Visiting Professor, University of California, Berkeley, USA, 1980; Writer in Residence, Professor of Literature, The Colorado College, Colorado Springs, 1984-85; Writer in Residence, Visiting Professor of Literature, Boston University, Massachusetts, 1987; Full Professor of Hebrew Literature, Ben Gurion University, Beer Sheva, Israel, 1987-; The Slopes of Lebanon. Publications: 13 books (novels, short stories, essays), 1965-90, including: My Michael, 1982; Black Box, 1987; To Know a Woman, 1989; Fima, 1991; The Silence of Heaven, 1993; Don't Pronounce It Night, 1994. Address: c/o Deborah Owen Ltd, 78 Narrow Street, London E14, England.

OZICK Cynthia, b. 17 Apr 1928, New York City, USA. Author. m. Bernard Hallote, 7 Sept 1952, 1 daughter. Education: BA, cum laude, English, New York University, 1949; MA, Ohio State University, 1950; LHD (Hon), Yeshiva University, 1984; Hebrew Union College, 1984; Williams College, 1986, Hunter College 1987; Jewish Theological Seminary America, 1988; Adelphi University, 1988; SUNY, 1989; Brandeis University, 1990. Publications: Trust, 1966; The Pagan Rabbi and Other Stories, 1971; Bloodshed and Three Novellas, 1976; Levitation: Five Fictions, 1982; Art and Ardor: Essays, 1983; The Cannibal Galaxy, 1983; The Messiah of Stockholm, 1987; Metaphor and Memory: Essays, 1989; The Shawl, 1989; The Pagan Rabbi & Other Stories, 1991. Contributions to: Poetry, criticism, reviews, translations, essays and fiction in numerous periodicals and anthologies. Honours: Phi Beta Kappa Orator, Harvard University, 1985; Mildred and Harold Strauss Living Award, American Academy of Arts and Letters, 1983; Rea Award for short story, 1986; Guggenheim Fellow, 1982. Memberships: PEN; Authors League; American Academy of Arts and Sciences; American Academy and Institute of Arts and Letters; Phi Beta Kappa. Address: c/o Raines & Raines, 71 Park Avenue, New York, NY 10016, USA.

P

PAANANEN Eloise Engle, b. 12 Apr 1923. Writer. m. 1) P R Engle, 1 son, 1 daughter, 2) Lauri A Paananen, 26 Oct 1973. Education: Bachelor Degree, Foreign Affairs, George Washington University, Washington D C. Publications: 29 books on military history, culture, travel, nutrition and foods and hundreds of articles and stories for magazines and newspapers; The Winter War - The 1939-40 the Russo-Finnish Conflict, reissued in America as The Soviet Attack on Finland; Man in Flight, 1979; America's Maritime Heritage: The Military, 1993. Memberships: Society of Women Geographers, American Society of Journalists and Authors. Honours: Outstanding Books for Children; CINDY Award for film, More than Shelter; Best Book Awards for The Winter War, American's Maritime Heritage, Man in Flight. Address: 6348 Crosswoods Drive, Falls Church, VA 22044, USA.

PACKARD Vance, b. 22 May 1914, Granville Summit, USA. Author; Teacher. m. Virginia Mathews, 1938, 2 sons, 1 daughter. Education: AB, MS, Pennsylvania State University; Columbia University. Appointments: Reporter, Boston Record, 1937-38; Writer, Editor, Associated Press Feature Service, 1938-42; Editor, Staff Writer, American Magazine, 1942-56; Staff Writer, Collier's Magazine, 1956. Publications: The Hidden Persuaders, 1957; The Status Seekers, 1959; The Waste Makers, 1960; The Pyramid Climbers, 1962; The Naked Society, 1964; The Sexual Wilderness, 1968; A National of Strangers, 1972; Our Endangered Children, 1983; The People Shapers, 1989; The Ultra Rich, 1989. Honours: Distinguished Alumni Awards, Pennsylvania State University, Columbia University. Memberships: Board, National Book Committee; Authors Guild; President, Society of Magazine Writers, 1961; American Academy of Political and Social Sciences; American Sociology Association. Address: 87 Mill Road, New Canaan, CT 06840, USA.

PACNER Karel, b. 29 Mar 1936, Janovice-n-Uhl, Czechoslovakia. Science Journalist. m. 1971-73. Education: Dipl Ing (Master's degree), Economics, Economics University, Prague, 1959. Appointments: Mlada fronta (now Mlada fronta Dnes) daily newspaper, 1959-. Publications: In Czech: On both sides of Space, 1968; ... and the giant leap for mankind (Apollo 11), 1971, 1972; We are Searching Extra-Terrestrial Civilisation, 1976; Columbuses of Space, 1976; Soyuz is Calling Apollo, 1976; The Constructor-in-Chief, 1977; Nine Space Days, 1978; Message of Space Worlds, 1978; The Trip on Mars; Towns in Space, 1986; The Humanized of Galaxy, 1987; Discovered secrets of UFO, 1991. Contributions to: Several Czech magazines especially Letectvi a kosmonautika. Honours: Literary awards for several books from publishing houses. Memberships: Community of Writers in Czech Republic; Czechoslovak Society of Arts and Sciences in USA, Czechoslovak Branch. Address: K Vidouli 216, 15500 Prague 4, Czech Republic.

PADEL Ruth, b. 8 May 1946, London, England. Writer. m. Myles Burnyent, 15 Aug 1984, 1 daughter. Education: Greats, Lady Margaret Hall, Oxford; BA, 1969; MA, 1975; PhD, 1976. Publications: Alibi, poems, 1985; Summer Snow, poems, 1990; In and Out of the Mind: Greek Images of the Tragic Self, 1992; Angel, book of poems, 1993; Whom Gods Destroy: Elements of Greek and Tragic Madness, book on history of ideas, 1995 Collections on: Women in Antiquity; The Anthropology of the Self; Essays on George Steiner. Contributions to: Essays to Bête Noire; Encounter; Gender and History; Articles on ancient and modern Greek poetry to Classical Quarterly; Proceedings of Cambridge Philogical Society; Poems and reviews to Times Literary Supplement, 1975-94; Poems to The Times; The Sunday Times; London Review of Books; Acumen; Oxford Magazine; Critical Quarterly; The Observer; New Statesmen; Poetry Nation Review; Kenyon Review; Poetry; Poetry Review; Cambridge Review; Bête Noire; Poetry Ireland Review; New Yorker; Harvard Review; Various anthologies including Virago Book of Women's Love Poetry. Honours: Prize-winning Poems, National Poetry Competition, 1985, 1992, 1994; Royal Literary Fund Grant, 1991; Wingate Fellowship, 1992; Poetry Book Society Recommendation for Angel, 1993. Memberships: Royal Zoological Society; Hellenic Society; PEN; Society of Authors. Address: 5a Thurlow Road, London NW3 5PJ, England.

PADFIELD Peter Lawrence Notton, b. 3 Apr 1932, Calcutta, India. Author. m. Dorothy Jean Yarwood, 23 Apr 1960, 1 son, 2 daughters. Publications: The Titanic and the Californian, 1965; An Agony of Collisions, 1966; Aim Straight: A Biography of Admiral Sir Peter Scott, 1966; Broke and the Shannon: A Biography of Admiral Sir Philip Broke, 1968; The Battleship Era, 1972; Guns at Sea: A History of Naval Gunnery, 1973; The Great Naval Race: Anglo-German Naval Rivalry 1900-1914, 1974; Nelson's War, 1978; Tide of Empires: Decisive Naval Campaigns in the Rise of the West, Volume I 1481-1654, 1979, Volume II 1654-1763, 1982; Rule Britannia: The Victorian and Edwardian Navy, 1981; Beneath the Houseflag of the P & O, 1982; Dönitz, The Last Führer, 1984; Armada, 1988; Himmler, Reichsführer - SS, 1990; Hess: Flight for the Führer, 1991, revised, updated edition, 1993; War beneath the Sea: Submarine Conflict 1939-1945, 1995; Novels: The Lion's Claw, 1978; The Unquiet Gods, 1980; Gold Chains of Empire, 1982; Salt and Steel, 1986. Address: Westmoreland Cottage, Woodbridge, Suffolk, England.

PADHY Pravat Kumar, b. 27 Dec 1954, India. Geologist. m. Namita Padhy, 6 Mar 1983, 2 daughters. Education: MSc, Applied Geology, 1979; MTech, Mineral Exploration, 1980; PhD, Applied Geology. Career include: Wrote 4-line poem at age 13; Currently Senior Geologist, ONGC, Baroda, Gujarat. Publications: Silence of the Seas, 1992; Anthologised in: RJES Intercontinental Poetry, 1979; Modern Trends in Indo-Anglian Poetry, 1982; Prevalent Aspects of Indian-English Poetry, 1983-84; Premier Poets, 1986; Anti-war, Vol II, 1988; East-West Voices, 1988; Contemporary Indian English Poetry, 1988; Snows to the Seas, 1989; Contemporary Indian English Love Poetry, 1990; World Poetry, 1991; World Poetry, 1992. Contributions to: Hesperus Review; Writer's Life Line; Skylark; Poetry; Poesie; Poetry Time; Commonwealth Quarterly; Canopy; Creative Forum; Poet Crit; Kavita India; Literary Horizon; By Word; Creative Art and Poetry; Others. Honours: Certificate of Honour for poem I Wish Every Day, Writer's Life Line, Canada, 1986. Address: 166 HIG Complex, Chandrasekharpur, Sailashri Vihar, Bhubaneshwar, Orissa, India.

PADMANABHAN Neela, b. 26 Apr 1938, Thiruvanantha Puram. Deputy Chief Engineer. m. U Krishnammal, 3 July 1963, 1 son, 3 daughters. Education: SSLC, 1953; Kekala University, Intermediate, 1956; BSC, 1959, BSc (Engg), 1963; FIE, Institute of Engineers, Calcutta, 1991. Publications: Thalaimurakal; Pallikondapuram; Uravukal; Therodum Veedhi; Paavam Seyyathavargal; Samuka Chintaanai; Moondravathu Naal. Contributions to: Ezhutthu; Ilakkiavattam Nadai; Caravan; Mirror; Indian Literature; Indian Writing Today; Kumudam. Honours: Rajah Sir Annamalai Chettiar Award; Tamil Annai Prize; Tamil Development Council of Tamil Nadu Government. Memberships: Authors Guild of India; PEN; Poetry Society of India; Centre of Indian Writers. Address: 39 1870 Kuriyathi Road, Manacaudpo, Thiruvanantha Purah 695009, India.

PADOVANO Anthony Thomas, b. USA. Professor. Education: BA magna cum laude, Seton Hall University, South Orange, New Jersey, 1956; STB magna cum laude, 1958, STL magna cum laude, 1960, STD magna cum laude, 1962, Pontifical Gregorian University, Rome; PhL magna cum laude, St Thomas Pontifical International University, Rome, 1962; MA, American Literature, New York University, 1971; PhD, Fordham University, New York, 1980. Appointments: Professor of Systematic Theology, Darlington School of Theology, Mahwah, New Jersey, 1962-74; Professor of American Literature, Ramapo College of New Jersey, Mahwah, 1971-. Publications: The Cross of Christ, the Measure of the World, 1962; The Estranged God, 1966, Paperback, 1967, Spanish Edition, 1968; Who is Christ, 1967, Chinese Edition, 1969, Spanish Edition, 1972; Belief in Human Life, 1969; American Culture and the Quest for Christ, 1970, Paperback, 1971; Dawn Without Darkness, 1971, German Edition, 1984; Free to be Faithfull, 1972; Eden and Easter, 1974; A Case for Worship, 1975; Presence and Structure, 1975; America: Its People, Its Promise, 1975; Trilogy, 1982; The Human Journey: Thomas Merton, Symbol of a Century, 1982, Paperback, 1984; Contemplation and Compassion, 1984; Winter Rain, play, 1985; His Name is John, play, 1986; Christmas to Calvary, 1987; Love and Destiny, 1987; A Celebration of Life, 1987; Summer Lightening, play, 1988; Conscience and Conflict, 1989; The Church Today: Belonging and Believing, 1990; Reform and Renewal, 1991; Scripture in the Streets, 1992; A Retreat with Thomas Merton, 1995. Contributions to: Ave Maria; The Catholic World; Preaching; National Catholic Reporter; St Anthony Messenger; New Catholic World; The Beacon; Creation. Address: 9 Millstone Drive, Morris Plains, NJ 07950, USA.

PAGE Eleanor. See: COERR Eleanor Beatrice.

PAGE Emma. See: TIRBUTT Honoris.

PAGE Geoff, b. 7 July 1940, Grafton, New South Wales, Australia. Teacher; Writer. m. Carolyn Mau, 4 Jan 1972, 1 son. Education: BA (Hons); DipEd. Literary appointments: Writer-in-Residence: Australian Defence Force Academy, Curtin University, Wollongong University and Edith Cowan University. Publications: The Question, in Two Poets, 1971; Smalltown Memorials, 1975; Collecting the Weather, 1978; Cassandra Paddocks, 1980; Clairvoyant in Autumn, 1983; Shadows from Wire: Poems and Photographs of Australians in the Great War (editor), 1983; Benton's Conviction, novel, 1985; Century of Clouds: Selected Poems of Guillaume Apollinaire (translator with Wendy Coutts), 1985; Collected Lives, 1986; Smiling in English, Smoking in French, 1987; Footwork, 1988; Winter Vision, novel, 1989; Invisible Histories, stories and poems, 1990; Selected Poems, 1991; Gravel Corners, 1992; On the Move (editor), 1992; Human Interest, 1994. Honours: Literature Board Grants, Australia Council, 1974, 1983, 1987, 1989, 1992. Memberships: Australian Society of Authors; Australian Teachers Union. Address: 8 Morehead Street, Curtin, ACT 2605, Australia.

PAGE Katherine Hall, b. 9 July 1947, New Jersey, USA. Writer. m. Alan Hein, 5 Dec 1975, 1 son. Education: AB, Wellesley College, 1969; EdM, Tufts University, 1974; EdD, Harvard Univrsity, 1985. Publications: Faith Fairchild mystery series: The Body in the Belfry, 1990, 1991; The Body in the Bouillon, 1991, 1992; The Body in the Kelp, 1991, 1992; The Body in the Vestibule, 1992, 1993. Honours: Agatha for Best First Domestic Mystey, Malice Domestic, 1991. Memberships: Mystery Readers International; Mystery Writers of America; The Authors Guild; Sisters in Crime; The American Crime Writers League; Society of Children's Bookwriters and Illustrators. Literary Agent: Faith Hamlin, Greenburger Associates Inc, New York, NY, USA. Address: c/o St Martin's Press, 175 Fifth Avenue, New York, NY 10010, USA.

PAGE Louise, b. 7 Mar 1955, London. Playwright. Education: BA, University of Birmingham, 1976. Appointments include: Resident Playwright, Royal Court Theatre, 1982-83. Publications: Want Ad, 1977; Glasshouse, 1977; Tissue, 1978; Lucy, 1979; Hearing, 1979; Flaws, 1980; House Wives, 1981; Salonika, 1982; Real Estate, 1984; Golden Girls, 1984; Beauty and the Beast, 1985; Diplomatic Wives, 1989; Adam Wasxa Gardener, 1991; Like to Live, 1992; Hawks and Doves, 1992; Radio & TV Plays. Honours include; George Devine Award, 1982. Address: 6J Oxford & Cambridge Mansions, Old Marylebone Road, London NW1 5EC, England.

PAGE Norman, b. 8 May 1930, University Teacher. Author. m. Jean Hampton, 29 Mar 1958, 3 sons, 1 daughter. Education: BA 1951, MA 1955 Emmanuel College, Cambridge; PhD University of Leeds, 1968. Publications include: The Language of Jane Austen, 1972; Speech in the English Novel, 1973, 2nd edition 1988; Thomas Hardy, 1977; A E Housman: A Critical Biography, 1983; A Kipling Companion, 1984; E M Forster, 1988; Tennyson: An Illustrated Life, 1992. Contributions to: London Review of Books; Modern Language Review; Notes and Queries; Etudes Anglaises; Bulletin of the New York Public Library. Honours: Guggenheim Foundation Fellowship, 1979; Fellow, Royal Society of Canada, 1982; University of Alberta Research Prize, 1983. Memberships: Thomas Hardy Society, Vice-President, Editor of Thomas Hardy Journal; Newstead Abbey Byron Society; Tennyson Society, Chairman, Publications Board. Address: 23 Braunston Road, Oakham, Rutland LE15 6LD, England.

PAGE Patricia Kathleen, b. 23 Nov 1916, Dorset, England. Writer; Painter. m. Arthur Irwin, 16 Dec 1950, 1 stepson, 2 stepdaughters. Publications: Novel: The Sun and the Moon, 1944; Poetry: As Ten as Twenty, 1940; The Metal and the Flower, 1954; Cry Araratl-Poems New and Selected, 1967; The Sun and the Moon and Other Fictions, 1973; Poems Selected and New, 1974; Editor, To Say the Least, 1979; Evening Dance of the Grey Flies (poems and a short story), 1981; The Travelling Musicians, text, 1984; The Glass Air, poetry, essays and drawings, 1985; Brazilian Journal, prose, 1988; I-Sphinx, A Poem of Two Voices; A Flask of Sea Water, fairy story, 1989; The Glass Air, Poems Selected and New, 1991; The Travelling Musicians, children's book, 1991; The Goat that Flew, fairy story, 1993; Hologram, 1994. Address: 3260 Exeter Road, Victoria BC, V8R 6H6, Canada.

PAGE Robin, b. 1943. Writer. Publications: Down with the Poor, 1971; The Benefits Racket, 1972; Down Among the Dossers, 1973; The Decline of an English Village, 1974; The Hunter and the Hunted, 1977; Weather Forecasting: The Country Way, 1977; Cures and Remedies:

The Country, 1978; Weeds: The Country Way, 1979; Animal Cures: The Country Way, 1979; The Journal of a Country Parish, 1980; Journeys into Britain, 1982; The Country Way of Love, 1983; The Wildlife of the Royal Estates, 1984; Count One to Ten, 1986; The Fox's Tale, 1986; The Duchy of Cornwall, 1987; The Fox and the Orchid, 1987. Address: Bird's Farm, Barton, Cambridgeshire, England.

PAGLIA Camille, b. 2 Apr 1947, NY, USA. Writer; Professor. Education: BA, State University of NY, 1968; M Phil, 1971, PhD, 1974, Yale University. Publications: Sexual Personae: Art and Decadence from Nefertiti to Emily Dickinson, 1990; Sex, Art, & American Culture, 1992; Vamps & Tramps: New Essays, 1994. Literary Agent: Janklow & Nesbit, NY, USA. Address: Dept of Humanities, University of the Arts, 320 S Broad Street, Philadelphia, PA 19102, USA.

PAINE Lauran Bosworth, b. 25 Feb 1916, Duluth, Minnesota, USA. Author. m. Mona Margarette Lewellyn, 26 June 1982, 1 son, 4 daughters. Education: Pacific Military Academy, 1930-32; St Alban's Episcopal School, 1932-34. Publications: Numerous psuedonyms; Over 600 westerns include: Geronimo, 1950; Decade of Deceit, 1955, ad Dakota Death-Trap, 1986; Outpost, 1963; The Border Guns, 1965, as Arizona Drifter, 1966; Avenger's Trail, 1967; Rainey Valley, 1971; The Blue Hills, 1975; Mule-Train, 1978; The Loner, 1978; Deuce, 1979; The Trail Drive, 1983; The Sand Painting, 1987; The Bushwhacker, 1989; The Sheridan Stage, 1989; The Bandoleros, 1990; Alamo Jefferson, 1990; The Left-Hand Gun, 1991; Strangers in Buckhorn, 1991; The Undertaker (The Legend of El Cajonero), 1991; The Sqaw Men, 1992; Devil's Canyon, 1992; Over 75 mysteries include: Case of the Hollow Men, 1958; Murder Now Pay Later, 1969; The Killer's Conscience, 1971; The Ivory Penguin, 1974; The Underground Men, 1975; Over 100 romances; Non-fiction includes: Northwest Conquest (Conquest of the Great Northwest), 1959; The General Custer Story, 1960; Tom Hom: Man of the West, UK Edition, 1962, US Edition, 1963; Viet-Nam, 1965; Bolivar the Liberator, 1970; The Hierarchy of Hell, 1972; Gentleman Jonny: The Life of General John Burgoyne, 1973; Saladin: A Man for All Ages, 1974; Witches in Fact and Fantasy, 1972; The CIA at Work, 1977; The Technology of Espionage, 1978; D-Day, 1981; America and Americans, 1984; The Abwehr (German Military Intelligence in World War Two) 1984. Literary Agent: Jon Tuska, 2327 Salmon Street, Portland, OR 97214, USA. Address: 9413 North Hiway 3, Fort Jones, CA 96032, USA.

PAJOR John Joseph, b. 5 Feb 1948, South Bend, Indiana, USA. Poet. m. Cass Pajor, 18 Nov 1989, 3 sons, 1 daughter. Education: Graduate Welder and Medical Assistant,Vocational College; College credits, University. Appointments include: Readings and poetry concerts, radio, drama, Italy, USA, Canada, over 30 years. Literary Appointments: Juror, Seattle METRO Poetry Bus Project, 1994. Publications: Dies Faustus, Revised Edition, 1976; In Transit, 1978; A Collection Of 2, 1979; Auditions, 1979; Traveler, 1979; Works: On Tour; African Violets, 1989; Challenger, 1990; Sacred Fire, 1990; Chiaroscuro, 1991; Wilderness - land of the raining moon, 1991; The ErpslchOrd I & II, registered 1992 & 93, unpublished; SLAMdunk, 1993; Of A Brave Boy's Journeying, 1994; AXIS/Falcon Rising, 1994. Contributions to: Numerous small contributions to various publications, over last 30 years. Honours: Literary Honorarium, National Poetry Awards, USA, 1978. Address: 848-51st Street, Port Townsend, WA 98368, USA.

PALEY Grace, b. 11 Dec 1922, New York, New York, USA. m. Robert Nicholls, 2 children. Publications: The Little Disturbances of Man, 1956; Leaning Forward; 365 Reasons Not to Have Another War; Long Walks and Intimate Talks; Enormous Changes at the Last Minute, 1974; Later the Same Day, 1985. Address: 126 W 11th Street #21, New York, NY 10011, USA.

PALIN Michael Edward, b. 5 May 1943. Freelance Writer and Actor. m. Helen M Gibbins, 1966, 2 sons, 1 daughter. Education: BA, Brasenose College, Oxford. Appointments: Actor, Writer: Monty Python's Flying Circus, BBC TV, 1969-74; Ripping Yarns, BBC TV 1976-80; Writer, East of Ipswich, BBC TV, 1986; Films: Actor and Joint Author: And Now for Something Completely Different, 1970; Monty Python and the Holy Grail, 1974; Monty Python's Life of Brian, 1978; Time Bandits, 1980; Monty Python's The Meaning of Life, 1982; Actor, Writer, Co-Producer, The Missionary, 1982; Around the World in 80 Days, BBC, 1989; Actor: Jabberwocky, 1976; A Private Function, 1984; Brazil, 1985; A Fish Called Wanda, 1988; Contributor, Great Railway Journeys of the World, BBC TV, 1980; Actor, Co-Writer, American Friends (film), 1991; Actor, GBH (TV Channel 4), 1991. Publications:

Monty Python's Big Red Book, 1970; Monty Python's Brand New Book, 1973; Dr Fegg's Encyclopaedia of All World Knowledge, 1984; Limericks, 1985; For Children: Small Harry and the Toothache Pills, 1981; The Mirrorstone, 1986; The Cyril Stories, 1986; Around the World in 80 Days, 1989; Pole to Pole, 1992. Honours: Writers Guild, Best Screenplay Award for American Friends, 1991. Address: 68a Delancey Street, London NW1 7RY, England.

PALMER Alan Warwick, b. 28 Sept 1926, Ilford, Essex. Retired Schoolmaster. m. Veronica Mary Cordell, 1 Sept 1951. Education: Bancroft's School, Woodford Green, Essex, MA 1950, MLitt 1954, Oriel College, Oxford. Publications: Alexander I, Tsar of War and Peace, 1974; The East End, 1989; Bernadotte: Napolean's Marshal, Sweden's King, 1990; The Chancelleies of Europe, 1982; Crowned Cousins: The Anglo-German Royal Connection, 1986; Penguin Dictionary of Twentieth Century History, 4th edition, 1990; The Decline and Fall of the Ottoman Empire, 1992. Contributions to: History Today; The Times etc. Memberships: Fellow of the Royal Society of Literature, 1979; International PEN, 1989. Literary Agent: Campbell, Thomson and McLaughlin Ltd. Address: 4 Farm End, Woodstock, Oxford OX20 1XN, England.

PALMER Diana. See: KYLE Susan Eloise Spaeth.

PALMER Frank Robert, b. 1922. Writer. Publications: Morphology of the Tigre Noun, 1962; Linguistic Study of the English Verb, 1965; Selected Papers of J R Firth 1951-1958, 1968; Prosodic Analysis, 1970; Grammar, 1971, 1984; The English Verb, 1974, 1987; Semantics, 1976, 1981; Modality and the English Modals, 1979, 1990; Mood and Modality, 1986; Grammatical Roles and Relations, 1994. Contributions to: Over 50 learned journals. Memberships: Linguistic Society of America; Vice-President, Philological Society; Academia Europaea; Fellow, British Academy. Address: Whitethorns, Roundabout Lane, Winnersh, Wokingham, Berkshire RG11 5AD, England.

PALMER John, b. 13 May 1943, Sydney, Nova Scotia, Canada. Playwright; Director. Education: BA, English, Careton University, Ottawa, Canada, 1965. Appointments: Dramaturge, Associate, Factory Theatre Lab, Toronto, Canada, 1970-73; Co-Founder, Co-Artistic Director, Literary Manager, Toronto Free Theatre, 1972-76; Resident Playwright, Canadian Rep Theatre, Toronto, 1983-87; Course Director, Final Year Playwrighting, York University, Toronto, 1991-93; Resident Playwright, National Theatre School of Canada, 1993-94. Publications: 2 Plays: The End, and A Day at the Beach, 1991; Before the Guns, Memories for my Brother, Part I, Dangerous Traditions: Four Passe-Muraille Plays, 1992; Henrik Ibsen On the Necessity of Producing Norwegian Drama, 1992-93; Selected Plays. Contributions to: Theatre Byline, Woodstock Sentinel Review, 1968; The Man Behind the News, short story, to Canadian Forum, 1973; Henrik Ibsen to: Canadian Theatre Review and This Magazine, 1977. Address: 32 Monteith St, Toronto, Ontario, M4Y 1K7, Canada.

PALMER Peter John, b. 20 Sept 1932, Melbourne, Victoria, Australia. Teacher. m. Elizabeth Fischer, 22 Dec 1955, 1 son, 1 daughter. Education: BA, 1953, BEd, 1966, University of Melbourne. Publications: The Past and Us, 1957; The Twentieth Century, 1964; Earth and Man, 1980; Man on the Land, 1981; Man and Machines, 1983; Macmillan Australian Atlas (Executive Editor), 1983, 3rd Edition, 1990, 4th Edition, 1993. Challenge, 1985; Geography 10 (author, illustrator), 1992; Editor, contributor, illustrator: Confrontation, 1971; Interaction, 1974; Expansion, 1975; Survival, 1976; Three Worlds, 1978. Address: 34 Ardgower Court, Lower Templestowe, Victoria 3107, Australia.

PALMER Tony, b. 29 Aug 1941, London, England. Film Director; Author. Publications: Born Under A Bad Sign; Trials of Oz; Electric Revolution; Biography of Liberace; All You Need Is Love; Charles II; Julian Bream, A Life on the Road; Menuhin, A Family Portrait. Contributions to: Observer; Sunday Times; New York Times; Spectator; Punch; Daily Mail; Life Magazine. Honours: Italia Prize, twice; Gold Medal, New York Film and TV Festival, 6 times; Fellini Prize; Critics Prize, Sao Paulo; Special Jury Prize, San Francisco. Membership: Garrick Club. Address: Nanjizal, St Levan, Cornwall, England.

PALOMINO JIMENEZ Angel, b. 2 Aug 1929, Toledo, Spain. Novelist; Journalist; Television Writer. Education: Linguistics, Science and Chemistry studies, Central University, Madrid; Technician in Management. Publications: Numerous works of poetry, short stories, essays and novels including: El Cesar de Papel, 1957; Zamora y

Gomora, 1968; Torremolinos Gran Hotel, 1971; Memorias de un Intelectual Antifranquista, 1972; Un Jaguar y una Rubia, 1972; Madrid Costa Fleming, 1973; Todo Incluido, 1975; Divorcio para une Virgen Rota, 1977; La Luna Se Llama Perez, 1978; Plan Marshall para 50 Minutos, 1978; Las Otras Violaciones, 1979; Adiós a los Vaqueros, 1984; Este muerto no soy yo, 1989; Caudillo, 1992; De carne y sexo, 1993. Contributions to: Estafeta Literaria; ABC; Semana. Honours: Numerous literary prizes including: International Prize, Press Club, 1966; Miguel de Cervantes National Literary Prize, 1971; Finalist, Planeta Prize, 1977. Memberships: Royal Academy of Fine Arts and Historical Sciences; National Academy of Gastronomy; Spanish Association of Book Writers; International Federation of Tourism Writers; International Association of Literary Critics. Literary Agent: Editorial Planeta, Barcelona, Spain. Address: Conde de Penalver 17, 28006 Madrid, Spain.

PALSSON Einar, b. 10 Nov 1925, Reykjavik, Iceland. Headmaster. m. Birgitte Laxal, 24 Dec 1948, 2 sons, 1 daughter. Education: Cand phil, University of Iceland, 1946; Certificate of Merit, Royal Academy of Dramatic Art, London, 1948; BA, Danish and English Literature, University of Iceland, 1957. Appointments: Chairman, Reykjavik City Theatre (Leikfélag Reykjaviku), 1950-53; Play Producer, Reykjavik City Theatre, National Theatre and Icelandic State Radio, 1952-63. Publications: Spekin og Sparifotin, essays, 1963; The Roots of Icelandic Culture, 10 vols: 1. The Background of Njals Saga, 1969; 2. Religion and the Settlement of Iceland, 1970; 3. Time and Ekprosis, 1972; 4. Stone Cross, 1976; 5. The Ominous Beat, 1978; 6. The Celtic Heritage, 1981; 7. The Dome of Heaven, 1985; Egils Saga and the Two Wolves, 1990; 10. The Ancient Althing at Thingvellir, 1991; Icelandic in Easy Stages, textbook I, 1975; II, 1977. Contributions to: Numerous to Icel Morgunbladid; Lesbok; Special prints: monographs and lectures. Honours: Prize for 1-act play Trillan, Icelandic Cultural Council, 1962. Memberships: Rithofundasamband Islands; The Nordic Society, Director 1966-69; The Reykjavik City Theatre. Address: Solvallagata 28, 101 Reykjavik, Iceland.

PAMA Cornelis, b. 5 Nov 1916, Rotterdam, Netherlands. Editor; Author. m. Heather Myfanwy Woltman, 1 Mar 1977, 1 son, 2 daughters. Education: Dutch Publishing Diploma. Appointments: Manager, Bailliere, Tindall & Cox Ltd, London, 1948-55; General Manager, W & G Foyle, Cape Town, South Africa, 1955-67; Honorary Editor: Arma, 1955-, Familia, 1965-; Director, A A Balkema Publishers, Cape Town, 1967-72; Editor, Tafelberg Publishers, Cape Town, 1972-80; Editor-in-Chief, Nederlandse Post, Cape Town, 1980-. Publications include: Lions and Virgins, 1964; Genealogies of Old South African Families, 3 volumes, 2nd Edition, 1966; The South African Library 1810-1968, 1968; The Heraldry of South African Families, 1970; Vintage Cape Town, 1973; Bowler's Cape Town, 1975; Regency Cape Town, 1978; Handboek der Heraldiek, 5th Edition, 1987; 21 other books on genealogy and heraldry. Contributions to: Historical, genealogical and heraldic journals. Honours include: Extraordinary Gold Medal, South African Academy of Arts and Sciences, 1966; J Bracken Lee Award, Salt Lake City; Gold Medal Pro Merito Genealogicae, Deutsche Zentralstelle für Familiengeschichte, Germany, 1976; Distinguished Fellow, American College of Heraldry; Distinguished Fellow, New Zealand Heraldry Society. Memberships: PEN South African Centre; South African Academy of Arts and Sciences; Afrikaanse Skrywerskring. Address: PO Box 4839, Cape Town 8000, South Africa.

PAMPEL Maria, b. 4 Apr 1913, Muhlheim, Rhur, Germany. Author. m. Adolf Pampel, 1 June 1936, 1 daughter. Education: Business Training; Correspondence Course, English; Organist's Examination; International Famous Writers School. Publications: Die Tur Steht offen, 1965, 1976; Heilige mitkleinen Fehlern, 1977; Land der dunklen Walder, 1977; Wer in der Liebe bleibt, 1978; Ein Streiter vor dem Herrn, 1979; Das Freuen lernen, 1979, recorded on tape, 1983; 7 small volumes, series, Die Feierabendstende; Various little books: Die Kleinen Freuden des Alltags, 1986; Calendars, children's devotions book. Honours: Diploma of Merit, Universityie delle Arti, Italy, 1982; Albert Einstein Academy Bronze Medal, peace proposition, Universal Intelligence Data Bank of America, 1986; Honorary Doctorate, International University Foundation, USA, 1986. Address: Lortzingstrasse 9, Bad Sachsa, 3423, Federal Republic of Germany.

PANICHAS George Andrew, b. 21 May 1930, Springfield, Massachusetts, USA. Educator; Literary Critic; Scholar. Education: BA, American International College, 1951; MA, Trinity College, Hartford, Connecticut, 1952; PhD, Nottingham University, UK, 1962. Appointments include: Instructor, Assistant/Associate Professor,

Professor of English, University of Maryland, 1962-. Editor, Modern Age, quarterly review; Advisory editor, Continuity, history journal. Publications include: Adventure in Consciousness: The Meaning of D H Lawrence's Religious Quest, 1964; Epicurus, 1967; The Reverent Discipline: Essays in Literary Criticism & Culture, 1974; The Burden of Vision: Dostoevsky's Spiritual Art, 1977, 1985; The Courage of Judgement: Essays in Literary Criticism, Culture & Society, 1983; Co-author: Renaissance & Modern Essays (presented to Vivian de Sola Pinto, 70th birthday), 1966; Editor: numerous books including: Politics of 20th Century Novelists; Modern Age: The First 25 Years. Contributions to: Articles, translations, reviews, essays, to books, anthologies, journals, USA & Europe. Honours include: Fellow, Royal Society of Arts, UK, 1971-; Grant, Earhart Foundation, 1982. Memberships include: Awards committee, Richard M Weaver Fellowship, 1983-; Jury panel, Ingersoll Prizes, 1986-; Academic Board, National Humanities Institute, 1985-. Address: Department of English, University of Maryland, College Park, MD 20742, USA.

PANIKER Ayyappa, b. 12 Sept 1930, Kavalam, India. Professor. m. Sreeparvathy Paniker, 6 Dec 1961, 2 daughters. Education: BA Honours, Travancore, 1951; MA, Kerala, 1959; CTE, Hyderabad, 1966; AM, PhD, Indiana, USA, 1971. Appointments: Founder Editor, Kerala Kavita, 1965; General Editor, Kerala Writers in English; Editor, World Classics Retold in Malayalam; Editor, Indian Journal of English Studies; Director, Workshop in Literary Translation, 1987; Chief Editor, Medieval Indian Literature. Publications: Ayyappa Panikerude Kritikal 1, 1974, 1981; Ayyappa Panikerude Lekhanangal, 1982; Ezhukavitalum Patanagalam, 1984; Ayyappa Panikerude Kritikal II, 1984; Cuban Poems, translation, 1984; Granth Sahib, translation, 1986; Mayakovski's Poems, 1987; Dialogues, 1988; Vallathol: A Centenary Perspective; Ayyappa Panikerude Kritikal III 1981-89, 1989; Pattu Kavitakal Patanagalum, 1989; Thakazhi Sivasankara Pillai, 1989; Gotrayanam, 1989; Indian Literature in English, A Perspective of Malayalain Literature, 1990; Spotlight on Comparative Indian Literature, 1992; Avatarikakal, 1993. Address: 111 Gandhinagar, Trivandrum 695014, India.

PANIKER Salvador, b. 1 Mar 1927, Barcelona, Spain. Publisher; Writer. Education: Lic Philos; Doctor of Industrial Engineering. Publications: Conversaciones en Cataluna, 1966; Los Signos y las Cosas, 1968; Conversaciones en Madrid, 1969; La Dificultad de Ser Español, 1979; Aproximacion al Origen, 1982; Primer Testamento, 1985; Ensayos retroprogresivos, 1987; Segunda Memoria, 1988; Lectura de los Griegos, 1992. Contributions to: La Vanguardia; El País; Revista de Occidente. Honours: International Press Prize, 1969. Address: Numancia 117-121, Barcelona 08029, Spain.

PAPADIMITRAKOPOULOS Elias, b. 23 Aug 1930, Pyrgos, Ilias, Greece. Physician. m. Niobe Kataki, 30 Dec 1957. Education: Thessaliniki's University Mdical School, 1949-55; Military Medical School, 1949-55. Appointments: Co Editor, Skapti Ili, 1965-66; O Chartis, 1983-87; Yiati, 1985-. Publications: Toothpaste with Chlorophyll; Maritime Hot Baths; The General Archivist. Contributions to: Tram; To Dendro; Anti; Yiati; I Lexi; O Chartis; To Tetarto. Memberships: Society of Greek Writers. Address: 23 Lazaradon Street, 11363 Athens, Greece.

PAPAGEORGIOU Kostas G, b. 4 July 1945, Athens, Greece. Author; Producer, Greek Radio. Education: Law Diploma, 1968; Literature, Philology, University of Athens, 1969-72. Appointments: Editor, Grammata ke Technes, 1982-; Member, Commission for Literary Awards, Ministry of Culture, 1982-84; Member, Commission for Authors' Pensions, 1991-. Publications: Piimata, 1966; Sillogi, 1970; Epi pigin Kathise, 1972; Ichnographia, poetry, 1975; To Giotopato, prose, 1977; To Ikogeniako dendro, poetry, 1978; To skotomeno ema, 1982; Kato ston ipno, poetry, 1986; I genia tou 70, 1989; Rammemo Stoma, poetry, 1990. Contributions to: Anti; Diavazo; Lexi; Dendro; Tram; Tomes; Chronico. Membership: Eteria sigrafeon (Greek Authors Union). Literary Agent: Kedros Publishing House, Athens, Greece. Address: Kerasountos 8, 11528 Athens, Greece.

PAPAKOU-LAGOU Avgi, b. 1923, Greece. Schoolteacher; Writer. m. 23 Dec 1948, 2 sons. Education: Diploma of Schoolteacher, 1946. Appointment: Agricultural News, 1978-82. Publications: (In Greek), The Fairy Child and Other Fairy Tales, 3rd edition; A Summer Different from the Others; The Festival Stories; The Little Maestro; Father's Secret, 1980; A Sunbeam Tells a Tale; In the Chestnut Grove; The Wonderful Sunbeams; Like a Fairy Tale I, II, III, IV; The Animals Warning, 1983; The Little Boatbuilder, Toto and his Kite, 1981; The

Superior Truth: Once Upon a Time in a Marvellous City; Biographies: Modern Persons and Literary Works (in co-operation); Joyful Return, 1988; Editor: Andronikos a' Komnlnos (Historical), 1988; What and Where: The Heroic Mouse: Don't Cry My Little Girl; The Golden Pomegranate, 1974; The Golden Apple, 1976; The Brave Ringworm, 1984; Christmas - New Year, Happy Holidays, 1986; Happy Return, 1987. Contributions to: Agricultural News; Act of Roumeli; Studies; Student; Farm Youth; Hunting News; Attican; Intellectual Problems; Essays. Honours: 1st Prize, Literary Company, 1978; 1st Prize, Circle of Children's Books, 1979; Award, Circle of Children's Books, 1979. Memberships: Circle of Children's Book Writers, 1975; Society of Greek Writers; Greek Committee, 1983, UNICEF, 1981-. Address: Vasiliadou 9, GR 11141, Athens, Greece.

PAPALEO Joseph, b. 13 Jan 1926. Professor of Literature and Writing; Fiction Writer. m. 4 sons. Education: BA, Sarah Lawrence College, 1949; Diploma di Profitto, University of Florence, Italy, 1951; MA, Columbia University, 1952. Appointments: Teacher, Fieldston Prep School, 1952-60; Professor, Literature Writing, Sarah Lawrence, 1960-68, 1969-92; Guest Professor, Laboratorio de Cibernetica, Naples, Italy, 1968-69. Publications: All the Comforts, novel, 1968, paperback, 1969; Out of Place, novel, 1971; Picasso at Ninety One, 1988; The Bronx Book of the Dea, short stories; My Life Story (Sicilian Zen Version), short stories in 3 anthologies: Delphinium Blossoms, From The Margin, Imagining America, 1991, 1992. Contributions to: Short stories and poems to: Harper's; New Yorker; Penthouse; Commentary (many); Patterson Literary Review; Rolling Coulter; Attenzione; Accent Review (Oberlin University); Remington Review; The Dial; Swank; Grove Press Review; Sarah Lawrence Journal; Many others. Honours: Guggenheim Fellowship, 1974; Ramapo College Poetry Prize, 1986. Memberships: Authors Guild; Italian American Writers Association; American Association of University Professors. Address: 60 Puritan Avenue, Yonkers, NY 10710, USA.

PAPAS William, b. 1927, South Africa. Author. Appointments: Formerly Cartoonist, The Guardian, The Sunday Times Newspapers, Punch Magazine; Book Illustrator, Painter, Print Maker. Publications: The Press, 1964; The Story of Mr Nero, 1965; The Church, 1965; Parliament, 1966; Freddy the Fell-Engine, 1966; The Law, 1967; Tasso, 1967; No Mules, 1967; Taresh, the Tea Planter, 1968; A Letter from India, 1968; A Letter from Israel, 1968; Theodore, or, The Mouse Who Wanted to Fly, 1969; Elias the Fisherman, 1970; The Monk and the Goat, 1971; The Long-Haired Donkey, 1972; The Most Beautiful Child, .1973; The Zoo, 1974; People of Old Jerusalem, 1980; Papas' America, 1986; Papas Portland, 1994. Membership: Savage Club, London. Address: 422 NW 8th Avenue, Portland, OR 97209, USA.

PAPASTRATU Danae, b. 20 Mar 1936, Patras, Greece. Author; Journalist. Education: Diploma, Law, Athens University, 1959; Greek-American Institute, 1965; Université de Paris-Sorbonne, 1969. Appointments: Protevoussa Journal; News of Municipalitis; Collector Magazine; Nautical Greece. Publications: Travels with the Polar Book, 1978; A vol d'oiseau, 1979; We Will See in Philippi, 1981; Without Periphrasis, Poetry Collection, 1981; An Essay about Poetry, 1983; A Study about Women in General; Editor, Director, Perigramma, 1985-; Runnings Through Time and Space; Diadromes sto Horo and Hrono, travel book, 1989; Anichnetsis, essays, 1992. Contributions to: Many articles to professional journals including: Thessaliki Estia; Davlos; Meteora; Vue Touristique, Brussels; Nautiki Ellas; Perigramma; Nautiki Ellas; Tourist Life; Research Society and Economist; Touristiki Zoi; Cameiros; 2 TV conferences. Literary Agent: Koridis, Editor, Mariomihali str 49, Athens 10680, Greece. Address: Bouboulinas 1a, Hilioupolis 16345, Athens, Greece.

PAPAZOGLOU Orania, b. 13 July 1951, Bethel, Connecticut, USA. Writer. m. William L DeAndrea, 1 Jan 1984, 2 sons. Education: AB, Vassar College, 1973; AM, University of Connecticut, 1975; Doctoral Study at Michigan State University, 1975-80. Career: Assistant to the Editor, 1980-81, Executive Editor 1981-83, Greek Accent (magazine); Full-time writer, 1983-. Publications: Sweet, Savage Death (novel), 1984; Wicked Loving Murder (novel), 1985; Death's Savage Passion (novel), 1986; Sancify (novel), 1986; Rich, Radiant Slaughter, 1988. Contributions to: Columnist for Mystery Scene; Contributor to magazines, including Working Woman, Mother and Intro. Literary Agent: Meredith Bernstein, New York. Address: c/o Meredith Bernstein, 470 West End Avenue, New York, NY 10024, USA.

PAPIER Tadeusz Zenon, b. 9 July 1914. Writer. m. Helena Grochowska, 15 July 1944, 2 daughters. Education: University of

Warsaw, 1936-39; University of Lodz, 1946-50. Appointments: Editor, Orka na ugorze,1938; Teacher, 1939-44; Editor, Wies, 1945-49; Editor, Lodz Teatrainia, 1949; Editor, Wytwomia Filmow Fabularnych, 1950-55; Editor, Osnowa, 1966-67; Editor in Chief, Socio-political Department, Wydawnictwo, Lodz, 1968-74. Publications: Powtorna smierc Boryny, 1965; Narodziny Gerty, 1968; Ciche jeziora, 1976; Cienie na piaskowej jorze, 1976; Wiktoria i general, 1980; Moje Lipce, 1986; Rodzina Szafrancow, 1988; Magdalena w nocy, 1971; Anita, 1979; Szum jodly w miescie, 1984; Author of short stories and reports. Contributions to: numerous journals and magazines. Honours: Literary Award, Lodz Region, 1965; Literary Award, Lodz, 1983. Memberships: Country Department, Polish Writers' Society; Society of Authors. Address: Al Kosciuszki 98 m 14, 90-442 Lodz, Poland.

PAPINEAU David Calder, b. 30 Sept 1947, Como, Italy. Philosopher. m. Rose Wild, 6 July 1986, 1 daughter. Education: BSc (Hons), University of Natal, 1967; BA (Hons), Cambridge University, 1970; PhD, Cambridge. Appointments include: Editor, British Journal for the Philosophy of Science, 1993-. Publications: For Science in the Social Sciences, 1978; Theory and Meaning, 1979; Reality and Representation, 1987; Philosophical Naturalism, 1993. Honours: Professor, King's College, London, 1990-; President, British Society for the Philosophy of Science, 1993-95. Address: Department of Philosophy, King's College, London WC2R 2LS, England.

PARGETER Edith, (Ellis Peters), b. 1913. Writer (Mystery, Crime, Suspense, Historical); Translator. Education: BEM, 1994; MA Birmingham 1994. Publications include: The Hounds of Sunset, 1976; Afterglow and Nightfall, 1977; The Marriage of Meggotta, 1979; As Ellis Peters: Never Pick Up Hitch Hikers!, 1976; A Morbid Taste for Bones, 1977; Rainbow's End, 1978; One Corpse Too Many, 1979; Monk's-Hood, 1980; Saint Peter's Fair, 1981; The Leper of Saint Giles, 1981; The Virgin in the Ice, 1982; The Sanctuary Sparrow, 1983; The Devil's Novice, 1983; Dead Man's Ransom, 1984; The Pilgrim of Hate, 1984; An Excellent Mystery, 1985; The Raven in the Foregate, 1986; The Rose Rent, 1986; The Hermit of Eyton Forest, 1987; The Confession of Brother Haluin, 1988; The Heretic's Apprentice, 1989; The Potter's Field, 1989; The Summer of the Danes, 1991; The Holy Thief, 1992; Brother Cadfael's Penance, 1994; Translations include: Legends of Old Bohemia, by Alois Jirasek, 1963; May, by Karel Hynek Macha, 1965; The End of the Old Times, by Vladislav Vancura, 1965; A Close Watch on the Trains, by Bohumil Hrabal, 1968; Report on My Husband, by Josef Slanska, 1969; A Ship Named Hope, by Ivan Klima, 1970; Mozart in Prague, by Jaroslav Seifert, 1970. Honours: Cartier Diamond Dagger Award, Crime Writers Association, 1993; OBE, New Year's Honours, 1994. Memberships: The Welsh Academy, 1990; Society of Authors; Crime Writers Association; Mystery Writers of America. Literary Agent: Deborah Owen Ltd, 78 Narrow Street, London E14 8BP, England. Address: Troya, 3 Lee Dingle, Madeley, Telford, Shropshire TF7 5TW, England.

PARINI Jay, b. 2 Apr 1948, Pittston, Pennsylvania, USA. Poet; Novelist; Literary Critic; Professor. m. Devon Stacey Jersild, 21 Jun 1981. Education: AB, Lafayette College; B Phil, PhD, University of St Andrew. Appointments: Editor, North Star poetry series; Member, Vermont Council on the Humanities and Social Sciences, 1975-; Member, Vermont Council of the Arts, 1980-82; Editorial Committee, Juniper Prize for Poetry, University of Massachussetts Press, 1984-. Publications: (poems) Singing in Time, 1972; Anthracite Country, 1982; Town Life, 1988; (novels) The Love Run, 1980; The Patch Boys, 1988; The Last Station, 1990; Theodore Roeyuke: An American Romantic, 1979; A Vermont Christmas, 1988; The Columbia History of American Poetry (editor), 1993; (work in progress) Biography of John Steinbeck, 1995; editor of several poetry anthologies. Address: Rr 1 Box 195, Middlebury, VT 05753, USA.

PARIS Bernard Jay, b. 19 Aug 1931, Baltimore, Maryland, USA. University Professor. m. Shirley Helen Freedman, 1 Apr 1949, 1 son. Education: AB, 1952, PhD, 1959, Johns Hopkins University. Appointments: Instructor, Lehigh University, 1956-60, Assistant Professor, 1960-64, Associate Professor, 1964-67; Professor, 1967-81, Michigan State University; Professor, English, University of Florida, 1981-; Director, Institute for Psychological Study of the Arts, 1985-92; Director, International Karen Horney Society, 1991-. Publications: Experiments in Life, George Eliot's Quest for Values, 1965; A Psychological Approach to Fiction: Studies in Thackeray, Stendhal, George Eliot, Dosteovsky and Conrad; Character and Conflict in Jane Austen's Novels, 1978; Psychoanalyst's Search for Self-Understanding, 1994; Editor, Third Force Psychology and the

Study of Literature, 1986; Shakespeare's Personality (co-ed), 1989; Bargains with Fate: Psychological Crises and Conflicts in Shakespeare and His Plays, 1991; Character as a Subversive Force in Shakespeare: The History and The Roman Plays, 1991; Karen Horney: A Psychoanalyst's Search for Self-Understanding, 1994. Contributions to: Numerous essays in scholarly and literary journals. Honours: Phi Beta Kappa, 1952; Fellow, NEH, 1969; Fellow, John Simon Guggenheim Foundation, 1974. Memberships: Modern Language Association of America; Honorary Member, Association for the Advancement of Psychoanalysis; Scientific Associate, American Academy of Psychoanalysis. Address: Department of English, University of Florida, Gainesville, FL 32611, USA.

PARIS I Mark, b. 28 Feb 1950, Baltimore, Maryland, USA. Translator. Life Partner: John L Gibbons. Education: Baltimore Polytechnic Institute, 1963-67; BA, Johns Hopkins University, 1971; MA, Columbia University, 1973; MPhil, 1994. Appointments: Reid Hall, Columbia University extension, Paris, France, Instructor, 1974; Barnard College, New York City, Instructor in French, 1975-80; Freelance Translator, 1976-. Publications: Louis Grodecki, Gothic Architecture, 1977; Raymond Cogniat, Georges Braque, 1980; Maurice Sérullaz, Velázquez, 1981; José Alcina Franch, Pre-Columbian Art, 1983; Danielle and Vadime Elisseeff, The Art of Japan, 1985; Jacques-Yves Cousteau and Yves Paccalet, Jacques Cousteau-Whales, 1988; Kostas Papaioannou, The Art of Greece, 1989; Alain Erlande-Brandenburg, Gothic Art, 1989; Françoise Cachin, Gauguin: The Quest for Paradise, 1992; Robert Delort, The Life and Lore of the Elephant, 1992; Alain Gheerbrant, The Amazon: Past, Present and Future, 1992; Jean-Guy Michard, The Reign of the Dinosaurs, 1992; Jean-Pierre Maury, Newton: The Father of Modern Astronomy, 1992; Henri Loyrette, Degas: The Man and His Art, 1993; Trinh Xuan Thuan, The Birth of the Universe: The Big Bang and After, 1993; Yvette Gayrard-Valy, Fossils: Evidence of Vanished Worlds, 1994; France Borel, The splendor of Ethnic Jewelry, 1994; Xavier Girard, Matisse: The Wonder of Color, 1994; Bertrand Jestaz, Renaissance Art, forthcoming. Honours: Maryland Senatorial Scholar, 1967-71; Woodrow Wilson Fellow, 1971; National Defense Education Act Fellow, 1971-74; President's Fellow, Columbia University, 1975-76; F J E Woodbridge Distinguished Fellow, Columbia University, 1975-76. Memberships: Phi Beta Kappa. Address: 160 West End Avenue, New York, NY 10023, USA.

PARISI Joseph Anthony, b. 18 Nov 1944, Duluth, Minnesota, USA. Editor; Writer; Consultant. Education: BA Honours, College of St Thomas, 1966; MA, University of Chicago, 1967; PhD Honours, ibid, 1973. Appointments include: Associate Editor, 1976-83, Acting Editor, 1983-85, Editor, 1985-, Poetry Magazine. Publications include: Editor, The Poetry Anthology 1912-77, 1978; Marianne Moore: The Art of a Modernist, 1989; Writer, Producer, "Poets in Person", 14 part audio series, broadcast over NPR, 1991; Author: Voices & Visions Reader's Guide, 1987; Author: Poets in Person Reader's Guide, 1992. Contributions to: Articles, Reviews to: Yale Review; Georgia Review; Shenandoah; Modern Philology; TriQuarterly; Booklist; Poetry; Mandarin Oriental; Chicago Tribune Book World; Chicago Sun-Times Book Week; Sewanee Review. Honours: Fellowship, University of Chicago, 1966-69; Alvin M Bentley Scholarship; Delta Epsilon Sigma. Memberships: Society of Midland Authors; Modern Language Association. Address: c/o Poetry, 60 West Walton Street, Chicago, IL 60610, USA.

PARK (Rosina) Ruth (Lucia), b. Australia. Author; Playwright. Publications: The Uninvited Guest (play), 1948; The Harp in the South, 1948; Poor Man's Orange (in United States of America as 12 and a Half Plymouth Street), 1949; The Witch's Thorn, 1951; A Power of Roses, 1953; Pink Flannel, 1955; The Drums Go Bang (autobiographical with D'Arcy Niland), 1956; One-a-Pecker, Two-a-Pecker (in United States of America as The Frost and the Fire), 1961; The Good Looking Women, 1961; The Ship's Cat, 1961 (in United States of America as Serpent's Delight, 1962); Uncle Matt's Mountain, 1962; The Road to Christmas, 1962; The Road Under the Sea, 1962; The Hole in the Hill (in USA as The Secret of the Maori Cave), 1964; The Muddle-Headed Wombat series, 11 vols, 1962-76; Shaky Island, 1962; Airlift for Grandee, 1964; Ring for the Sorcerer, 1967; The Sixpenny Island (in United States of America as Ten-Cent Island), 1968; Nuki and the Sea Serpent, 1969; The Companion Guide to Sydney, 1973; Callie's Castle, 1974; The Gigantic Balloon, 1975; Swords and Crowns and Rings, 1977; Come Danger, Come Darkness, 1978; Playing Beatie Bow, 1980; When the Wind Changed, 1980; The Big Brass Key, 1983; The Syndey We Love, 1983; Missus, 1985; My Sister Sif, 1986; The Tasmania We

Love, 1987; Callie's Family: James, 1991; A Fence Around the Cuckoo, 1992; Fishing in the Styx, 1993. Address: c/o Curtis Brown Pty Limited, PO Box 19, Paddington, NSW 2021, Australia.

PARKER Franklin, b. 2 June 1921, New York, USA. Writer; Educationalist. m. Betty June Parker, 1950. Education: BA, Berea College, 1949; MS, University of Illinois, 1950; EdD, Peabody College of Vanderbilt University, 1956. Publications include: African Development and Education in Southern Rhodesia, 1960, reprinted, 1974; Government Policy and International Education, 1965; Church and State in Education, 1966; Strategies for Curriculum Change: Cases from 13 Nations, 1968; International Education: Understandings and Misunderstandings, 1969; George Peabody, A Biography, 1971, hardback and paperback reprint with new material, 1995;American Dissertations on Foreign Education: Abstracts of Doctoral Dissertations (20 vols), 1971-90; What We Can Learn From the Schools of China?, 1977; Education in Puerto Rico and of Puerto Ricans in the USA, Vol. 1, 1978, Vol. 2, 1984; British Schools and Ours, 1979; Women's Education (2 vols), 1979, 1981; US Higher Education: Guide to Information Sources, 1980; Education in the People's Republic of China, Past and Present: Annotated Bibliography, 1986; Education in England and Wales: An Annotated Bibliography, 1991. Contributions to: Over 500 articles and book reviews in magazines and journals. Honours include: Distinguished Alumnus Award, Peabody College of Vanderbilt University, 1970; Claude Worthington Benedum Professor of Education, Emeritus, West Virginia University, 1968-86; Distinguished Alumnus Award, Berea College, Berea, KY, 1989. Address: PO Box 100, Pleasant Hill, TN 38578, USA.

PARKER Gordon, b. 1940. Author; Playwright. Appointment: Book Reviewer, BBC Radio and ITV. Publications: The Darkness of the Morning, 1975; Lightning in May, 1976; The Pool, 1978; Action of the Tiger, 1981; Radio plays: The Seance, 1978; God Protect the Lonely Widow, 1982. Address: 14 Thornhill Close, Seaton Delaval, Northumberland, England.

PARKER Jean. See: **SHARAT Chandra G S.**

PARKER Robert B(rown), b. 1932, United States of America. Author. Appointments include: Technical Writer, Group Leader, Raytheon Company,1957-59; Copywriter, Editor, Prudential Insurance Company, Boston, 1959-62; Partner, Parker Farman Company, Advertising Agency, Boston, 1960-62. Publications: Fiction: The Godwulf Manuscript, 1973; God save the Child, 1974; Mortal Stakes, 1975; Promised Land, 1976; The Judas Goat, 1978; Wilderness, 1979; Looking for Rachel Wallace, 1980; Early Autumn, 1981; A Savage Place, 1981; Surrogate, 1982; Ceremony, 1982; The Widening Gyre, 1983; Love and Glory, 1983; Valediction, 1984; A Catskill Eagle, 1985; Taming a Sea Horse, 1986; Pale Kings and Princes, 1987; Crimson Joy, 1988; Playmates, 1989; Poodle Springs (completion of unfinished novel by R Chandler), 1989; Stardust, 1990; Perchance to Dream, 1991; Pastime, 1991; Double Deuce, 1992; Other: The Personal Response to Literature, 1971; Order and Diversity, 1973; Sports Illustrated Training with Weights, 1974; Three Weeks in Spring (with Joan H Parker), 1978; Playmates (USA); All Our Yesterdays, 1994; Walking Shadow, 1994; Paper Dolls. Address: Helen Brann Agency, 94 Curtis Road, Bridgewater, CT 06752, USA.

PARKES Joyce Evelyne, (J E Dubois), b. 30 June 1930, Serang, West Java, Indonesia. Writer; Archivist. 1 son, 2 daughters. Education: Archivist's course, 1 year, 1948-49, Java. Publications: The Land of Sand And Stone, 1977; Silver and Gold, 1977; Changes, 1977; Publisher: The Light of the World (Geoffrey Thurley), 1979; Green Rose (Tadeusz Rozewicz, translated by Geoffrey Thurley), 1982. Contributions to: Canberra Times; Artlook; Weekend Australian; Fling!; POETRY Australia; Overland; Westerly; Fremantle Arts Review; Prints; Wordhord; Celebrations; Breakaway; Labor Voice; Kalla Yeedip Arts; Overseas; Sepia, UK; Mother Tongues, Canada; Road of Poems and Borders, Finland; Pen International, UK; Social Images, Stet, A Spin of Golden Wattle, Austarlian Writer, The Western Review. Memberships: Newsletter Editor, Former Executive Committee Member, Fellowship of Australian Writers; W B Yeats Society; PEN, Former Board Member, Perth Centre, Archivist, Past President; KSP Foundation. Address: No 16 John Str, Darlington, Western Australia 6070, Australia.

PARKES Roger Graham, b. 15 Oct 1933, Chingford, Essex, England. Novelist; Scriptwriter. m. Tessa Isabella McLean, 5 Feb 1964, 1 son, 1 daughter. Education: National Diploma of Agriculture; Member, Royal Agricultural College. Literary appointments: Staff Writer, Farming Express and Scottish Daily Express, 1959-63; Editor, Farming Express, 1963; Staff Script Editor, Drama, British Broadcasting Corporation Television, London 1964-70. Publications: Death Mask, 1970; Line of Fire, 1971; The Guardians, 1973; The Dark Number, 1973; The Fourth Monkey, 1978; Alice Ray Mortons Cookham, 1981; Them and Us, 1985; Riot, 1986; Y-E-S, 1986; An Abuse of Justice, 1988; Troublemakers, 1990; Gamelord, 1991; The Wages of Sin, 1992. Contributions to: Daily Express; Sunday Express. Honours: Grand Prix de Littérature, for The Dark Number, Paris, France, 1974; Runner-up, Prix Jeunesse, for television play Secrets, Munich, Germany. Memberships: Writers Guild of Great Britain; Magistrates Association. Literary Agents: Watson Little Ltd, London England; The Sharland Organisation, London, England. Address: Cartlands Cottage, Kings Lane, Cookham Dean, Berkshire SL6 9AY, England.

PARKIN Molly, b. 1932. Author. Appointments: Former Fashion Editor, Nova Magazine, Harper's Bazaar Magazine, The Sunday Times Newspaper, London. Publications: Love All, 1974; Uptight, 1975; Full Up, 1976; Write Up, 1977; Switchback, 1978; Good Golly, Ms Molly, 1978; Fast and Loose, 1979; Molly Parkin's Purple Passages, 1979; Up and Coming, 1980; Bite of the Apple, 1981; Love Bites, 1982; Breast Stroke, 1983; Cock-a-Hoop, 1985. Address: c/o St Martin's Press, 175 fifth Avenue, New York, NY 10010, USA.

PARKINSON Michael, b. 28 Mar 1935, Yorkshire, England. TV Presenter; Writer. m. Mary Heneghan, 3 sons. Appointments: Began career as Journalist with local paper, then worked on The Guardian, Daily Express, Sunday Times, Punch, The Listener; joined Granada TV as interviewer/reporter, 1965; Executive Producer and Presenter, London Weekend TV, 1968; Presenter, Cinema, 1969-70, Tea Break, Where in the World, 1971; hosted own chat show "Parkinson" (BBC), 1972-82, "Parkinson One to One" Yorkshire TV, 1987-; Presenter, Give Us a Clue, 1984-, All Star Secrets, 1985; Desert Island Discs, 1986-88; Parky, 1989; LBC Radio, 1990; Help Squad, 1991; Daily Telegraph, 1991-. Publications: Football Daft, 1968; Cricket Mad, 1969; Sporting Fever, 1974; George Best: An Intimate Biography, 1975; A-Z of Soccer (joint author), 1975; Bats in the Pavilion, 1977; The Woofits, 1980; Parkinson's Lore, 1981; The Best of Parkinson, 1982. Address: c/o Michael Parkinson Enterprises Ltd, IMG, 23 Eyot Gardens, London W6 9TR, England.

PARKS Suzan-Lori, b. 1964. Dramatist; Instructor in Playwriting. Education: Mt Holybrooke College;; Drama Studios, London, UK. Publications: (plays) Imperceptible Mutabilities in the Third Kingdom, 1989; Betting on the Dust Commander, 1990; Death of the Last Black Man in the Whole World, 1990; Devotees of the Garden of Love, 1992; (video) Poetry Spots; Alive From Off Center; (radio) Locomotove; The Third Kingdom; Pickling; (film) Anemone Me. Honours: Obie, 1990; Whiting Writer's Award, 1992; numerous grants and fellowships. Address: c/o Kelly Rosenheim Whiting Writers Awards, Mrs Giles Whiting Foundation, 30 Rockerfeller Plaza Room 3530, New York, NY 10112, USA.

PARKS T(imothy) Harold, (John MacDowell), b. 19 Dec 1954, Manchester, England. Educator; Translator; Author. Publications: Tongues of Flame, 1985; Loving Roger, 1986; Home Thoughts, 1987; Family Planning, 1989; Cara Massimina (as John MacDowell), 1990; Goodness, 1991; Italian Neighbours, 1992; Shear, 1993; Short stories: Keeping Distance, 1988; The Room, 1992; Translations: La Cosa, short stories, 1985; Notturno indiano, novel, 1988; L'uomo che guarda, novel, 1989; Viaggio a Romas, 1989; Il filo dell'orrizonto, novel, 1989; La donna di Porto Pim, I volatili del Beato Angelico, short story collections, 1991; C'un punto della terra, 1991; I beati anni del castigo, novel, 1991; Le nozze di Cadmo e Armonia, 1993; La strada di San Giovanni, stories, 1993. Contributions to: Numerous articles, reviews and talks for BBC Radio 3. Honours: Somerset Maugham, 1986; Betty Trash 1st Prize, 1986; Llewellyn Rhys, 1986; Winner, Joh Floria Prize for Best Translation from Italian. Membership: Authors Society. Literary Agent: Curtis Brown. Address: Via delle Primule 6, Montorio, 37033 Verona, Italy.

PARLAKIAN Nishan, b. 11 July 1925, New York City, New York, USA. Professor of Drama; Playwright. m. Florence B Mechtel, 1 son, 1 daughter. Education: BA, Syracuse University, 1948; MA, 1950, MA, 1952, PhD, 1967, Columbia University. Appointments: Editorial Board, Ararat, 1970-; Editorial Board, MELUS, 1977-80; Editor, Pirandello Society Newsletter, Editor, Armenian Church Magazine; Associate Editor, Pirandello Society Annual. Publications: Original plays: The Last Mohigian, 1959; Plagiarized, 1962; What Does Greta Garbo Mean to

You?, 1973; Grandma, Pray for Me, 1988; Translated plays: For the Sake of Honor, 1976; Evil Spirit, 1980; The Bride, 1987; Be Nice I'm Dead, 1990. Contributions to: Armenian Literature Between East and West, to Review of National Literature, 1984. Honours: Prizewinner, Stanley Awards, 1961; International Arts Award for Playwriting, Columbus Countdown, 1992. Memberships: Modern Language Association; Vice President, Pirandello Society of America. Literary Agent: Ann Elmo. Address: 415 W 115th Street, New York City, NY 10025, USA.

PARMELEE David Freeland, b. 20 June 1924, Oshkosh, Wisconsin, USA. Research Curator; Former Professor. m. Jean Marie Peterson, 4 Dec 1943, 1 daughter. Education: BA, Lawrence University, Appleton, Wisconsin, 1950; MSc, University of Michigan, Ann Arbor, 1952; PhD, University of Oklahoma, Norman, 1957. Career includes: Professor, University of Minnesota, 1970-92; Research Curator of Ornithology, University of Nevada, Las Vegas, 1992-. Publications: The Birds of West-Central Ellesmere Island and Adjacent Areas, 1960; The Birds of Southeastern Victoria Island and Adjacent Small Islands, 1967; Bird Island In Antarctic Waters, 1980; Antarctic Birds, 1992. Contributions to: Arctic; Antarctic Journal US; Auk; Beaver; Bird-Banding; Condor; Ibis; The Living Bird; Loon; Wilson Bulletin. Honours: Antarctic Place Name 'Parmelee Massif' at 70°58' S, 62°10'W, Geographic Names Division, Defense Mapping Agency, Topographic Center, Washington DC, 1977; Native Son Award, Michigan Rotary International, 1982. Memberships: Past President, Organization of Biological Field Stations; British Ornithological Society; Cooper's Ornithological Society; Wilson Ornithological Society; Fellow, Explorers Club. Literary Agent: University of Minnesota Press. Address: Marjorie Barrick Museum of Natural History, 4505 Maryland Parkway, Box 454012, Las Vegas, NV 89154-4012, USA.

PARMET Herbert Samuel, b. 28 Sept 1929, New York City, USA. Historian; Author. m. 12 Sept 1948, 1 daughter. Education: BA, State University of New York at Oswego; MA, Queens College, The City University of New York. Publications: Richard Nixon and His America, 1990; JFK: The Presidency of John F Kennedy, 1983; Jack: The Struggles of John F Kennedy, 1980; Eisenhower and the American Crusades, 1972; The Democrats: The Years after FDR, 1976; Never Again: A President Runs for a Third Term, 1968; Aaron Burr: Portrait of an Ambitious Man, 1967. Contributions to: American Historical Review; Journal of American History; Journal of Southern History. Memberships: The Authors Guild; The Authors League. Literary Agent: Timothy Seldes, Russell & Volkening. Address: Marsten Lane, Hillsdale, NY12529, USA.

PARQUE Richard, b. 8 Oct 1935, Los Angeles, California, USA. Writer; Teacher. m. Vo Thi Lan, 1 May 1975, 3 sons. Education: BA, 1958, MA, 1961, California State University, Los Angeles; California State Teaching Credential, 1961; Postgraduates studies, University of Redlands. Publications: Sweet Vietnam, 1984; Hellbound, 1986; Firefight, 1987; Flight of the Phantom, 1988; A Distant Thunder, 1989. Contributions to: Numerous articles to magazines, many poems to poetry journals; commentary for newspapers. Honours: Bay Area Poets Award, 1989; Vietnam novels have been placed in the Colorado State University Vietnam War Collection. Memberships: Authors Guild; Academy of American Poets. Address: PO Box 327, Verdugo City, CA 91046, USA.

PARRINDER John Patrick, b. 11 Oct 1944, Wadebridge, Cornwall, England. Literary Critic. 2 daughters. Education: Christ's College, 1962-65, Darwin College, 1965-67, Cambridge; MA, PhD, Cambridge University. Appointments: Fellow, King's College, Cambridge, 1967-74; Lecturer in English, 1974-80, Reader, 1980-86, Professor, 1986-, University of Reading. Publications: H G Wells, 1970; Authors and Authority, 1977, 2nd enlarged edition, 1991; Science Fiction: Its Criticism and Teaching, 1980; James Joyce, 1984; The Failure of Theory, 1987; Editor: H G Wells: The Critical Heritage, 1972; Science Fiction: A Critical Guide, 1979. Contributions to: London Review of Books; Many academic journals. Honours: President's Award, World Science Fiction, 1987. Memberships: Vice-President, H G Wells Society; Science Fiction Foundation. Address: Department of English, University of Reading, PO Box 218, Reading, Berkshire RG6 2AA, England.

PARTLETT Launa (Launa Gillis), b. 19 May 1918, Miles, Queensland, Australia. Retired Editress; Freelance Writer of Articles. m. Charles Henry Partlett, 19 June 1943 (dec.), 1 son, 1 daughter. Education: Art Classes; Writing courses. Literary Appointments: Social

Editress, St George Call Newspaper, starting 1960; Freelance articles for The Leader Newspaper. Publications: Guluguba Pioneers - Stories from Queensland Rural Community, 1986; John Jones and Family: Rocky River Gold (co-author), 1987; Contributor: Wendy Lowenstein's Weevils in the Flour, 1978; Les Philpott's The Bundeena Book, 1979; Demented Bliss, poetry anthology, 1989-90; The Tin Wash Dish, poetry anthology, 1989. Contributions to: Walkabout; Bundeena Newsletter; Argus, Melbourne; Antique Collector; Woman's Day; New Idea; Numerous newspapers. Honours: Newshound Certificate, Leader Newspaper, 1984. Memberships: Book Society, Australia; Miles Historical Society; Former Member: Art Society of New South Wales; Bankstown Art Society. Address: 3/11 Parry Avenue, Narwee, New South Wales 2209, Australia.

PARTNOY Alicia, b. 7 Feb 1955, Bahia Blanca, Argentina. Literature Professor; Translator; Human Rights Lecturer. m. Antonio Leiva, 2 daughters. Education: Certificate of Translation, English/Spanish, American University, USA, 1986; MA, Latin American Literature, The Catholic University, USA, 1991. Appointments: Lecturer on Latine American Literature, The Maryland Institute - College of Arts, Baltimore, USA, 1992; Acquisitions Editor, Latin American Series, Cleis Press, San Francisco, USA, 1989-. Publications: The Little School: Tales of Disappearance and Survival in Argentina, 1986 (USA), 1987 (UK); Ed: You Can't Drown the Fire: Latin American Women Writing in Exile, 1988 (USA), 1989 (UK); Revenge of the Apple - Venganza de la Manzana, 1992. Honours: Writer's Choice, Pushcart Foundation, juror Tobias Wolff, Sept 1986; Writer's Choice, Pushcart Foundation, juror Bobbie Ann Mason, Oct 1986. Membership: Board of Directors, Amnesty International, USA, 1992. Address: PO Box 21425, Washington, DC 20009, USA.

PARTRIDGE Derek, b. 24 Oct 1945, London, England. Professor of Computer Science. m. 27 Aug 1971, 2 daughters. Education: BSc, Chemistry, University College, London, 1968; PhD, Computer Science, Imperial College, London, 1972. Appointments: Editor, Computational Science, book series, Ablex Publishing Corporation, Norwood, NJ, USA. Publications: Artificial Intelligence: Applications in the Future of Software Engineering, 1965; A New Guide to AI, 1991; Engineering AI Software, 1992. Contributions to: More than 100 articles to professional magazines and journals. Memberships: American Association for Artificial Intelligence; Society for Artificial Intelligence and Simulation of Behaviour. Address: Department of Computer Science, University of Exeter, Exeter EX4 4PT, England.

PARTRIDGE Frances Catherine, b. 15 Mar 1900, London, England. Writer. m. Ralph Partridge, 2 Mar 1933, 1 son. Education BA (Hons), English, Moral Sciences, Newnham College, Cambridge, 1921. Appointments: Worked at antiquarian bookshop, 1922-28; Edited The Greville Memoirs (with Ralph Partridge), 1928-38; Translator, 20 books from French and Spanish. Publications: A Pacifist's War, 1978; Memories, 1981; Julia, 1983; Everything to Lose, 1985; Friends in Focus, 1987; The Pasque Flower, 1990; Hanging On, 1990; Other People, 1993. Contributions to: Many book reviews and obituaries to various publications. Memberships: Fellow, Linnean Society; International PEN. Literary Agent: Gill Coleridge, 20 Powis Mews, London W11 1JN, England. Address: 15 West Halkin Street, London SW1X 8JL, England.

PASCALIS Stratis, b. 4 Mar 1958, Athens, Greece. Poet; Translator. m. Sophie Phocas, 28 Feb 1982, 2 daughters. Education: Graduated, Political Sciences, University of Athens, 1983. Publications: Poetry: Anactoria, 1977; Excavation, 1984; Hermaphrodite's Night, 1989; Sour Cherry Trees in the Darkness, 1991; Translations: 49 Scholia on the poems of Odysseus Elytis, by Jeffrey Carson, 1983; Phaedra, by Racine, 1990; The Horla and other stories of madness and terror, by Guy de Maupassant, 1992. Contributions to: Poems, translations essays, articles to Greek magazines: Efthini; Lexi; To Dendra; Spira; Chartis; To Vima, newspaper. Honours: Maris P Ralli Prize for 1st Book of a Young Poet, 1977. Membership: Society of Greek Writers. Address: Diamandidou 36, Palio Psychiko, Athens 15452, Greece.

PASCHEN Elise Maria, b. 4 Jan 1959, Chicago, Illinois, USA. Arts Administrator. Education: BA with honours, Harvard University, 1982; MPhil, 1984, DPhil, 1988, Oxford University, England. Appointments: Executive Director, Poetry Society of America. Publications: Houses: Coasts, 1985. Contributions to: Poems to: Poetry Magazine; Poetry Review, England; Oxford Magazine; Poetry Ireland Review; Oxford Poetry; The Harvard Advocate. Honours: Lloyd McKim

Garrison Medal for poetry, Harvard, 1982; Joan Grey Untermyer Poetry Prize, Harvard/Radcliffe, 1982; Richard Selig Prize for poetry, Magdalen College, Oxford, 1984. Memberships: Harvard Club; National Arts Club; Former Member: Signet Literary Society, Harvard; John Florio Society, Magdalen College; Oxford University Poetry Society. Address: Poetry Society of America, 15 Gramercy Park, New York, NY 10003, USA.

PASKANDI Géza, b. 18 May 1933, Szatmarhegy-Ville Satumare, Rumania. Writer. m. Anna-Maria Sebök, 24 Apr 1970, 1 daughter. Education: University Bolyai-Kolozsvar-Cluj, 1953-57. Appointments: Journalist, Szatmarnemeti, Bucharest, Kolozsvar, 1949-54; Editor, Editions Kriterion, Kolozsvar, 1970-73; Review Kortars, Budapest, Hungary. Publications: Tales, Radio Plays, Screenplays, 1970-90; Drama, 1970, 1975, 1987; Poetry, 1972, 1979, 1989; Essays, 1984; Novels, 1988, 1989; Works have appeared in 8 other languages; 40 dramas performed in Hungary, 7 in other countries. Contributions to: Magazines: Kortars; Helikon; Tiszataj; Nagyvilag; Eletunk; Hitel; Kelet-Nyugat; Irodalmi Szemle; Journals: Magyar Nemzet; Uj Magyarorszag. Honours: Award, Rumanian Writers Assocation, 1970; Jozsef Attila Award, Hungary, 1977; Award for Hungarian Art, 1991; Medallion, 1956; Kossuth Award, Hungary, 1992. Memberships: PEN Club; Hungarian Writers Association; Moricz Zsigmond Literary Society; Hungarian Academy of Arts. Address: Nagyszalonta utca 50, 1112 Budapest, Hungary.

PASSMORE Jacki, b. 2 July 1947, Queensland, Australia. Food Writer; Cookbook Author. 1 daughter. Career: Food Writer: Queensland Newpapers, Sunday Mail, Courier Mail, 1993. Publications: Asia The Beautiful Cookbook, 1987; The Encylopedia of Asian Food and Cooking, 1990; The Complete Spanish Cookbook, 1992; Festival Foods of Thailand, 1992; The Noodle Shop Cookbook, 1994; 15 others. Memberships: Queensland Wine Writers Club; International Association of Culinary Professionals, USA. Literary Agent: Judith Weber, Sobel Weber Associates Inc, 146 East 19th St, New York, NY 10003, USA. Address: 50 Turin St, West End, Brisbane, Queensland 4101, Australia.

PASTERNAK Bogdan, b. 30 July 1932, Poland. Journalist. (div), 1 son, 2 daughters. Education: Magister, University of Lodz, Poland, 1965. Appointments: Contributing Editor, Przemianv; Editor in Chief, Gossip, 1981-; Head, House of Creative People, Kielce, 1984-. Publications: Poetry: Wicker Words, 1965; The Cage, 1973; Returns, 1975; The Simplest Dimension, 1980; The Secret Message, 1985; Novel, Black Angel, in print. Contributions to: Tygodnik Kulturalny (Cultural Weekly); Zycie Literackie (Literary Life); Radar; Okolice (Surroundings). Honours: Transformations Awards, 1981; President of Kielce Award, Outstanding Achievements in Literature, 1983. Membership: Polish Writers' Association. Address: Checinska St 11/95, 25-020 Kielce, Poland.

PASZKOT Jan. See: PASZKOWSKI Kazimierz Jan.

PASZKOWSKI Kazimierz Jan (Rideamus, Jan Paszkot, McCollins, Vapuru), b. 19 Sept 1895, Lvov, Poland. Writer; Publicist; Publisher. m. 1925-69, 2 daughters. Education: Military College, Vienna, 1915; High School of Political Science, Warsaw, 1925; Privat Akademie für Buchwesen und Litteraturwissenschaft, Meyers Institut, Leipzig, 1926-28. Appointments: Charter Member, Polish Writers Association, 1918; Director, Ignis publishing company, Warsaw, 1924; Served to Colonel, Polish Army. Publications: Grzech utajony, novel, 1923; Milosc na Wschodzie, story, 1923; Madrosci Wschodu, poems, 1923; Przygody Wicka i Wacka, comics, 1924; RAF kontra Luftwaffe, story, 1947; Swiat basni i legend, story, 1947; Translations: Mysli, by R Tagore; Odrodzenie, by R Tagore. Contributions to: Verses to the press. Membership: Polish Writers Association. Address: ul Kasprzaka 40 m 24, Lodz, Poland.

PATCHETT Ann. Education: BA, Sarah Lawrence College. Publications: The Patron Saint of Liars, 1992; Taft, 1994. Honours: American Library Association Notable Books Council Selection, 1992. Address: c/o Carol Fass Ivy Publishing, 201 East 50th Street, New York, NY 10022, USA.

PATEL Gieve, b. 18 Aug 1940, Bombay, India. Poet; Painter. m. Toni Diniz, 1969, 1 d. Eduction: St Xaviers College, Bombay; Grant Medical College, Bombay. Publictions: Poems, 1966; How Do You Withstand, Body, 1976; Mirrored, Mirroring, 1990; Plays, Princes, 1971; Savaska, 1982; Mister Behram, 1987. Honours include: Woodrow

Wilson Fellowship, 1984. Address: 5E Malabar Apartments, Nepean Road, Bombay 400 036, India.

PATERAKIS Yolanda, b. 27 Oct 1934, Greece. Author. m. Andreas Paterakis, 14 Sept 1963, 1 son, 1 daughter. Education: Greek Literary Certificate, 1954; University of Cambridge, 1958. Appointments: Member, Circle of the Greek Children's Book, 1976-; General Secretary, National Society of Greek Authors, 1976-. Publications: Grandma's Lace Cap, 1976; My Brother, My Little Man, 1977; Moonmen Come to Earth, 1977; Three Stories and a Truth, 1978; A Trick That Becomes True, 1978; The Lady of the Aegean Sea, 1978; The Ship Comes from Psaza, 1978; The Lionhearted, 6 volumes, 1979; The Secret of the Blessed Island, 1979; A Pearl Swims on the Sea, 1979; An Adventure in the Big Forest, 1981; Glory and Sacrifice, 1981; Under the Sun of Cephalonia, 1982; A Child That Conquers the Victory, 1984; Tales of the Greek Islands, 1990; The Last Ally, 1990; The Secret of the Whelk, 1991, 2nd Edition, 1993; Under the Shadow of the Stone Column, novel, 1994. Address: 17 Kritonis Str, 11634 Athens, Greece.

PATERSON Aileen (Francis), b. 30 Nov 1934, Burntisland, Fife, Scotland, England. Author; Illustrator of Children's Books. m. Hamish Paterson, 5 Apr 1963, 2 sons, 4 daughters. Education: DA, Edinburgh, 1955; Moray House Teaching Qualification, 1961. Publications: Maisie Comes to Morningside, 1984; Maisie Goes to School, 1988; Maisie In The Rainforest, 1992; Maisie and the Puffer, 1992; Maisie Goes To Hollywood, 1994; The Pigs of Puddledub; Maisie Digs Up The Past; What Maisie Did Next. Contributions to: Scotsman; Scotland on Sunday; Scotland's Languages Magazine; The Insider. Memberships: Committee, Society of Authors in Scotland. Literary Agent: Gina Pollinger. Address: 8 Carlyle Place, Edinburgh EH7 5SR, Scotland, England.

PATERSON Alistair (Ian Hughes), b. 1929. Full-time Poet and Writer; Formerly Lt Cdr, RNZN; Dean of general studies NZ Police; Education Officer with NZ Dept of Education. Publications: Caves in the Hills (selected poems), 1965; Birds Flying, 1973; Cities and Strangers, 1976; The Toledo Room: a poem for voices, 1978; 15 Contemporary New Zealand Poets (editor), 1980; Qu'appelle, 1982; The New Poetry, 1982; Incantations for Warriors, 1982; Oedipus Rex, 1986; Short Stories from New Zealand (editor), 1988; Climate and Mate (Journals of NZ literature), (editor), 1972-82. Honours: Fulbright Fellow, 1977; The Auckland University's John Cowie Reid Award for Longer Poems, 1982. Memberships: Chairman, Auckland Branch PEN (Int), 1982-86; Member, NZ PEN (Int), National Council, 1982-87. Address: PO Box 9612, Newmarket, Auckland, New Zealand.

PATERSON Katherine (Womeldorf), b. 31 Oct 1932, Qing Jiang, China. Public School Teacher; Writer. m. John Barstow Paterson, 2 sons, 2 adopted daughters. Education: AB, King College; MA, Presbyterian School of Christian Education; MRS, Kobe University School of Japanese Language, Union Theological Seminary. Publications: Sign of the Chrysanthemum, 1973; The Great Gilly Hopkins, 1978; Jacob Have I Loved, 1980; Consider the Lilies: Plants of The Bible, 1986; Park's Quest, 1988; The Spying Heart, 1989; Tale of the Mandarin Ducks, 1990; The King's Equal, 1992; Flip-Flop Girl, 1994; Angel & the Donkey, 1996. Honours: American Library Association Awards, 1974, 1976, 1977, 1978; Newbery Medals, 1978, 1981; National Book Award, 1979; Christopher Award, 1979; Parents Choice Award, 1983; Laura Ingalls Wilder Award, 1986; Regina Medal Award, Catholic Library Association, 1988; Boston Globe/Horn Book Award, 1991;

PATERSON Neil, b. 31 Dec 1915, Greenock, Scotland. Author. m. 6 July 1939, 1 son, 2 daughters. Education: MA, Edinburgh University, 1936. Appointments: Variously Member, Chairman of Production, Director and Consultant, Films of Scotland, 1954-79; Director, Grampian Television, 1960-86; Chairman, Literature Committee, Scottish Arts Council, 1967-76; Member, Arts Council Great Britain, 1973-76; Governor, British Film Institute, 1958-60; Governor, National Film School, 1970-80; Governor, Pitlochry Theatre, 1966-76. Publications: The China Run; Behold Thy Daughter; And Delilah; Man on the Tightrope; The Kidnappers; Stories & Screenplays. Honours: Atlantic Award in Literature, 1946; American Film Academy Award (Oscar), 1959. Address: St Ronans, Crieff, Perthshire, Scotland.

PATHAK Jayant Himatlal, b. 20 Oct 1920, India. Retired Professor. m. 7 Feb 1945, 1 son, 1 daughter. Education: BA, 1943; MA, 1945; PhD, 1960. Appointments: Professor, Gujarati, 1953-80; Director,

C G Vidyabhavan Institute of Learning and Research, 1963-75. Publications: Modern Trends in Gujarati Poetry, 1963; Vananchal, 1967; Bhavayitree, 1974; Anunaya, poems, 1978; Mrugaya, poems, 1983; Kimapidravyam, 1987; Taru Raga, 1987; Shuli Upar Sej, 1988; Be Akshar Anandna, poetry. Contributions to: Sanskriti; Kavita; Kavyalok; Akhand Anand. Honours: Kumar Medal, 1957; Narmad Gold Medal, 1976; Ranjitram Gold Medal, 1976; Akademie Award, 1978; Dhanji Kanji Gold Medal, 1987. Memberships: Narmad Sahitya Sabha, Surat, President, Past Vice-President; Board of Studies, Board of Publications, South Gujarat University; President, Gujarati Sahitya Parishad, Ahmedabad, Sectional President 1974, President 1989-91; Gujarat Sahitya Akademie, Gandhinagar. Address: 23 Kadambpalli, Nanpura, Surat 395001, India.

PATILIS Yannis, b. 21 Feb 1947, Athens, Greece. Poet, Teacher of Literature. m. Elsa Liaropoulou, 2 sons. Education: Degree, Law School, University of Athens, 1971; Degree, Department of Byzantine & Neo-Hellenic Studies, School of Philosophy, University of Athens, 1977. Publications: Poetry: The Little Guy and the Beast, 1970; But Now Be Carefull, 1973; In Favour of Fruition, 1977; Tokens, 1980; Non-Smoker in the Land of Smokers, poems, 1970-80 (above volumes collected, 1982); Warm Midday, 1984; The Scribe's Mirror, 1989; Trips in the Same City, poems, 1970-90 (above volumes collected), 1993; 1983-85 co-founder and co-editor of poetry and music journal, Nesus (Island) and of the critical journal Kritike Kai Keimena (Critique and Texts); 1986- editor and publisher of Planodion, a journal of literature and the politics of culture. Many poems translated into various languages, notably English, French, German, Italian, Russian, Hungarian and Serbo-Croatin. Memberships: Society of Greek Writers. Address: 23 G Mistriotou Street, 112 55 Athens, Greece.

PATON WALSH Jill, b. 1937, United Kingdom. Children's Fiction Writer. Publications: Hengest's Tale, 1966; The Dolphin Crossing, 1967; Fireweed, 1969; Wordhoard (with Kevin Crossley-Holland), 1969; Goldengrove, 1972; Farewell Great King, for adults, 1972; Toolmaker, 1973; The Dawnstone, 1973; The Emperor's Winding Sheet, 1974; The Huffler, 1975; The Island Sunrise: Prehistoric Culture in the British Isles, 1975; Unleaving, 1976; Children of the Fox: Crossing to Salamis, 1977; The Walls of Athens, 1978; Persian Gold, 1978; A Chance Child, 1978; The Green Book, 1981; Babylon, 1982; A Parcell of Patterns, 1983; Lost and Found, 1984; Gaffer Samson's Luck, 1985; Lapsing, 1985. Address: 72 Water Lane, Histon, Cambridge CB4 4LR, England.

PATRICK John. See: AVALLONE Michael Angelo.

PATRICK John, b. 17 May 1905, Louisville, USA. Dramatist. Education: Harvard and Columbia Universities. Appointments: Radio Writer, 1932-35; Film Writer, Hollywood, 1936-37; Freelance Dramatist, London and New York, 1940-. Publications: Plays: The Willow and I, 1942; The Hasty Heart, 1945; The Story of Mary Surratt, 1947; The Curious Savage, 1950; Lo and Behold, 1951; The Teahouse of the August Moon, 1953; Good as Gold,1957; Everybody Loves Opal, 1962; It's Been Wonderful, 1965; Everybody's Girl, 1966; Scandal Point, 1967; Love is a Time of Day, 1969; Macbeth Did It, 1971; The Dancing Mice, 1971; Lovely Ladies, Kind Gentlemen (Musical), 1971; The Small Miracle (TV), 1972; Anybody Out There? 1972; The Enigma, 1974; Opal's Husband, 1975; Divorce Anyone? 1976; Suicide, Anyone? 1976; Love Nest for Three, Sex on the Sixth Floor, 1977; Girls of the Garden Club; A Barrel Full of Pennies, 1960; Opal is a Diamond, 1972; The Savage Dilemma, 1972; Noah's Animals, 1973; Opal's Baby, 1974; People! 1976; Opals Million Dollar Duck, 1979; The Magenta Moth, 1983; The Reluctant Rogue, 1984; Cheating Cheaters, 1985; The Gay Deceiver, 1988; Sense and Nonsense (verse), 1989; The Doctor Will See You Now, 1991; Films: Enchantment, 1948; The President's Lady, 1952; Three Coins in the Fountain, 1954; Mister Roberts, 1954; A Man Splendoured Thing, 1955; High Society, 1956; Les Girls, 1957; Some Came Running, 1958; The World of Suzie Wong, 1960; Gigot, 1961; Main Attraction, 1963; Shoes of the Fisherman, 1968. Honours: Pulitzer Prize, 1954; Drama Critics Circle Award Tony Award and Donelson Foreign Correspondent Award, 1957; Hon DFA, 1972; Doctor Humane Letter, Camrus College; William Inge Award for Lifetime Achievement in the Theater, 1986. Address: Fortuna Mill Estate, Box 2386, St Thomas, US Virgin Islands 00801, USA.

PATRICK Maxine. See: Patricia Anne.

PATRICK Robert (Robert Patrick O'Connor), b. 1937, USA. Dramatist. Appointments: Feature Editor, Astrology Magazine, 1971-72. Publications: Robert Patrick's Cheap Theatricks, 1972; Play-by-Play:

A Spectacle of Ourselves, 1972; Kennedy's Children, 1973; My Cup-Runneth Over, 1978; Mutual Benefit Life, 1978; One Man, One Woman: Six One Act Plays, 1978; Mercy Drop and Other Plays, 1980; Untold Decades: Seven Comedies of Gay Romance, 1989.

PATRICK Susan. See: CLARK Patricia Denise.

PATRICK William. See: HAINING Peter Alexander.

PATRIDES C(onstantinos) A(postolos), b. 1930, USA. Professor of English. Appointments: Lecturer to Associate Professor, University of California, Berkeley, 1957-64; Lecturer to Professor, University of York, 1964-78; G B Harrison Professor of English, University of Michigan, Ann Arbor, 1978-. Publications: Milton's Lycidas: The Tradition and the Poem (editor), 1961; Milton and the Christian Tradition, 1966; Milton's Epic Poetry (editor), 1967; Approaches to Paradise Lost (editor), 1968; The Cambridge Platonists (editor), 1969; Sir Walter Raleigh's The History of the World (editor), 1971; The Poetry of John Milton (general editor), 1972; The Grand Design of God: The Literary Form of the Christian View of History, 1972; John Milton: Selected Prose (editor), 1974; The English Poems of George Herbert (editor), 1974; Aspects of Time (editor), 1976; Sir Thomas Browne: The Major Works (editor), 1977; Approaches to Marvell (editor), 1978; The Age of Milton (co-editor), 1980; Approaches to Sir Thomas Browne (editor), 1982; Premises and Motifs in Renaissance Thought and Literature, 1982; George Herbert: The Critical Heritage (editor), 1983; The Apocalypse in English Renaissance Thought and Literature (co-editor), 1984; The Complete English Poems of John Donne (editor), 1985; An Annotated Critical Biography of Milton, 1987. Address: Department of English, University of Michigan, Ann Arbor, MI 48109, USA.

PATTEN Brian, b. 7 Feb 1946, Liverpool, England. Poet. Publications: Little Johnny's Confession, 1967; Notes to the Hurrying Man, 1969; The Irrelevent Song, 1975; Mr Moon's Last Case, 1975; Vanishing Trick, 1976; Gossip, 1979; Love Poems, 1980; Gargling with Jelly, 1985; Storm Damage, 1989; Grave Thawing Frozen Frogs, 1990; Grinning Jack, 1990; The Puffin Book of 20th Century Children's Verse (editor), 1991. Contributor to: TLS; Sunday Times; Independent; Guardian; Sunday Telegraph. Literary Agent: Rogers Coleridge and White.

PATTERSON Henry (Harry), (Martin Fallon, James Graham, Jack Higgins, Hugh Marlowe), b. 27 July 1929. Novelist. m. (1) Amy Margaret Hewitt, 1958, div. 1984, 1 son, 3 daughters, (2) Denise Lesley Anne Palmer, 1985. Education: BSc Honours, External, London School of Economics.; FRSA. Appointments: NCO, The Blues, 1947-50, 1950-58. Publications include: As Jack Higgins: Prayer for the Dying, 1973, filmed, 1985; The Eagle Has Landed, 1975, filmed, 1976; Storm Warning, 1976; Day of Judgement, 1978; Solo, 1980; Luciano's Luck, 1981; Touch the Devil, 1982; Exocet, 1983; Confessional, 1985, filmed, 1985; Night of the Fox, 1986, filmed, 1990; Season in Hell, 1989; Coldharbour, 1990; The Eagle Has Flown, 1991; As Harry Patterson: The Valhalla Exchange, 1978; To Catch a King, 1979, filmed, 1983; Dillinger, 1983; Many others under pseudonyms, including: The Violent Enemy, filmed, 1969; The Wrath of God, filmed, 1972; Some books translated into 42 languages. Address: c/o Ed Victor, 162 Wardour Street, London W1V 3AT, England.

PATTERSON James, b. 1947. Publications: The Thomas Berryman Number, 1976; The Season of the Machete, 1977; The Jericho Commandment, 1979; Virgin, 1980; Black Market, 1986; The Midnight Club, 1989; The Day America Told the Truth, 1991; Along Came the Spider, 1993; The Second American Revolution, 1994; Kiss the Girls, 1995. Address: c/o Anna Crespo 9th Flr Warner Brks, 1271 Avenue of the Americas, New York, NY 10020, USA.

PATTERSON Michael Wyndham (formerly Michael Wyndham Richards), b. 7 Sept 1939, London, England. University Professor. m. 1) Ellinor von Einsiedel, (2) Diana (Dixi) Patterson, 3 sons, 5 daughters. Education: BA, Mediaeval and Modern Languages, 1962, DPhil, 1968, Oxford. Publications: German Theatre Today, 1976; The Revolution in German Theatre 1900-1933, 1981; Peter Srein, 1981; Georg Büchner: Collected Works (editor), 1987; The First German Theatre, 1990. Address: Department of Visual and Performing Arts, De Montfort University, Leicester GB-LE4 9BH, England.

PATTERSON Orlando, Professor; Author. Education: BSc, Economics, University College of the West Indies-London University

(External), 1962; PhD, Sociology, London School of Economics, 1965. Appointments include: Professor, Sociology, 1971-, John Cowles Professor of Sociology, 1993, Harvard University, Cambridge, Massachusetts, USA; Associate Editor, American Sociological Review, 1989-92. Publications: Fiction: The Children of Sisyphus, UK, 1964, US, 1965, Dutch edition, 1980; An Absence of Ruins, 1967; Die the Long Day, US, 1972, paperback, 1973, UK, 1974; Non-fiction: The Sociology of Slavery: Jamaica, 1655-1838, 1967, 1969; Ethnic Chauvinism: The Reactionary Impulse, 1977; Slavery and Social Death: A Comparative Study, 1982; Freedom: vol 1, Freedom in the Making of Western Culture, 1991, Spanish edition, 1994, vol 2, A World of Freedom: Freedom, 1995. Contributions to: British Journal of Sociology; New Left Review; New Left Review; Times Literary Supplement; Social and Economic Studies; Public Scholar; Social Research; Change; Latin American Research Review; Harvard Educational Review; American Scholar; Annual Review of Sociology; Journal of Basic Writing; Journal of Family History; Reviews in American History; Slavery and Abolition; Dissent; Salmagundi; Several books. Honours: Best Novel in English, Dakar Festival of Negro Arts, 1965; AM, 1971, Walter Channing Cabot Faculty Prize, 1983, Harvard; Co-winner, Ralph Bunche Award, Best Scholarly Work on Pluralism, American Political Science Association, 1983; Distinguished Contribution to Scholarship, American Sociological Association, 1983; National Book Award, Non-Fiction, 1991; DHL, Trinity College, Connecticut, 1992; UCLA Medal, 1992. Memberships: Fellow, American Academy of Arts and Sciences; American Sociological Association. Address: Department of Sociology, William James Hall, Room 520, Harvard University, Cambridge, MA 02138, USA.

PATTISON Robert, b. 28 Oct 1945, Orange, New Jersey, USA. Teacher. Education: AB, Yale University; MA, University of Sussex, 1968; PhD, Columbia University, 1974; Languages: Greek, Latin, French. Appointments: Adjunct Lecturer, Richmond College, CUNY, 1974; Adjunct Instructor, Queensborough Community College, CUNY, 1974-75; Instructor, English, St Vincent's College, St John,s University, New York, 1975-77; Professor of English, Southampton College, Long Island University, Southampton, New York, 1978-. Publications: The Child Figure in English Literature, 1978; Tennyson and Tradition, 1980; On Literacy, 1982; The Triumph of Vulgarity, 1987; The Great Dissent: John Henry Newman and the Liberal Hersey, 1991. Contributions to: The Nation; ADE Bulletin; University of Toronto Quarterly; Mosaic; The New York Times; Dickens Studies Newsletter; Various edited volumes. Honours: Long Island University Trustees Award for Scholarship, 1979 and 1985; Rockefeller Foundation Fellowship, 1980-81; Guggenheim Fellowship, 1988-87. Address: PO Box 2106, Southampton, NY 11969, USA.

PAUL Barbara Jeanne, b. 5 June 1931, Maysville, Kentucky, USA. Writer. (div), 1 son. Education: AB, Bowling Green State University, 1955; MA, University of Redlands, 1957; PhD, University of Pittsburgh, 1969. Appointments: Mellon Fellow, University of Pittsburgh, 1967-69. Publications: An Exercise for Madmen, 1978; The Fourth Wall, 1979; Pillars of Salt, 1979; Bibblings, 1979; First Gravedigger, 1980; Under the Canopy, 1980; Your Eyelids Are Growing Heavy, 1981; Liars and Tyrants and People Who Turn Blue, 1982; A Cadenza for Caruso, 1984; The Renewable Virgin, 1984; Prima Donna at Large, 1985; Kill Fee, 1985; But He Was Already Dead When I Got There, 1986; A Chorus of Detectives, 1987; The Three-Minute Universe, 1988; He Huffed and He Puffed, 1989; Good King Sauerkraut, 1989; In-Laws and Out Laws, 1990; You Have The Right To Remain Silent, 1992; The Apostrophe Thief, 1993. Contributions to: various magazines & journals. Memberships: American Crime Writers League; Science Fiction and Fantasy Writers of America; Sisters in Crime; Mystery Writers of America; President, GEnie Chapter of SinC. Literary Agent: Joshua Bilmes, Scott Meredith Agency. Address: c/o Scott Meredith Literary Agency, 845 Third Avenue, New York, NY 10022, USA.

PAUL Jeremy, b. 29 July 1939, Bexhill, Sussex, England. Writer. m. Patricia Garwood, 26 Nov 1960, 4 daughters. Education: King's, Canterbury & St Edmund Hall, Oxford. Creative works: Numerous TV plays, series and adaptations, 1960-, including: Upstairs, Downstairs, 1971-75; Country Matters, 1972; The Duchess of Duke Street, 1976; Danger, UXB, 1977; A Walk in the Forest, 1980; The Flipside of Dominick Hide (with Alan Gibson), 1980; Sorrell and Son, 1983; The Adventures, Return and Memoirs of Sherlock Holmes, 1984-94; Lovejoy, 1991-94; Theatre includes: David Going Out, 1971; Manoeuvres, 1971; Visitors (with Carey Harrison), 1980; The Secret of Sherlock Holmes, 1988; The Watcher, 1989; Scraps (with Leslie

Stewart and Keith Strachan), musical; The Lady or the Tiger (with Michael Richmond and Nola York), 1976; Countess Dracula, film, 1970. Memberships: MCC; Writers Guild of Great Britain; Director, Parachute Productions. Address: c/o William Morris Agency, 31-32 Soho Square, London W1V 5DG, England.

PAULIN Tom, b. 1949, United Kingdom. Author. Publications: Thomas Hardy: The Poetry of Perception, 1975; Theoretical Locations, 1975; A State of Justice, 1977; Personal Column, 1978; The Strange Museum, 1980; The Book of Juniper, 1981; Liberty Tree, 1983; Ireland and the English Crisis, 1985; The Riot Act, play, 1985; The Faber Book of Political Verse (editor), 1986; Hard Lines 3 (co-editor), 1987. Address: Faber and Faber Ltd, 3 Queen Street, London WC1N 3AU, England.

PAULSON Ronald (Howard), b. 1930, USA. Professor of English. Appointments: Instructor, 1958-59, Assistant Professor, 1959-62, Associate Professor, 1962-63, University of Illinois; Professor of English, Rice University, Houston, Texas, 1963-67; Professor of English, Johns Hopkins University, Baltimore, Maryland, 1967-75, 1984-; Professor of English, Yale University, New Haven, Connecticut, 1975-84. Publications: Theme and Structure in Swift's Tale of a Tub, 1960; Fielding: The Critical Heritage (edited with T Lockward), 1962; Fielding: 20th Century Views (editor), 1962; Hogarth's Graphic Works, 1965; The Fictions of Satire, 1967; Satire and the Novel, 1967; Hogarth: His Life, Art and Times; Rowlandson: A New Interpretation, 1970; Emblem and Expression in English Art of the 18th Century 1795; Satire: Modern Essays in Criticism (editor), 1975; The Age of Hogarth, 1975; Popular and Polite Art in the Age of Hogarth and Fielding, 1979; Literary Landscape: Turner and Constable, 1982; Book and Painting; Shakespeare, Milton and the Bible, 1982; Representations of Revolution, 1983; Breaking and Remaking, 1989; Hogarth's Graphic Works (rev ed), 1989; Figure and Abstraction in Contemporary Painting, 1990; Hogarth, I: The Modern Moral Subject, 1991; Hogarth, II: High Art and Low, 1992; Hogarth, III: Art and Politics, 1993. Address: Johns Hopkins University, Baltimore, MD 21218, USA.

PAUWELS Rony (Claude Van De Berge), b. 30 Apr 1945, Assenede, Belgium. Docent of Declamation. m. Drongen Pauwells, 30 Jan 1973. Education: Koninklijk Conservatorium, Gent. Appointments: Docent Declamation, Academy of Arts, Ecklo; Universities of Brussels, Gent, Louvain-La-Neuve; University of Bonn, Germany, 1989. Publications: De koude wind du over het zand waeut, 1977; Het bewegen van her hoge gras op de top van de hevvel, 1981; Hiiumaa, 1987; Attu, 1988; Aztlan, 1990; Poetry: De zang van de maskers, 1988; De Mens in der ster, 1991; Het Silhouet, 1993. Contributions to: Journals: De Standaard; Literary magazines: Diogenes; Letters; Randschrift; DW and B; Bzulletin; Poeziekrant. Honours: 1st Prize, Declamation, Koninklijk Conservatorium, 1966; Scriptores Christianie, 1973; Dirk Martens Prize for Prose, 1975; E Bayie Prize, 1976; A De Pesseroy Poetry Prize, 1982; Inter-Provincial Prize, Flanders, 1983. Membership: VVF (Flemish Writers). Address: Oude Molenstraat 2, 9960 Assenede, Belgium.

PAVEY Don (Jack Adair), b. 1922, England. Former Senior Lecturer. Appointments: Formerly Senior Lecturer, Art and Design, Kingston Polytechnic; Editor, Athene, Journal of Society for Education Through Art, 1972-80. Publications: Methuen Handbook of Colour and Colour Dictionary (editor), 1963, 1967, 1978; Art-Based Games, 1979; Genius, 1980; Colour, 1981; The Artist's Colourmen's Story, 1985. Contributions to Journal of the Royal College of Art; Athene; Inscape; Colour Group Journal; Journal of Academic Gaming and Simulation in Education and Training; Times Educational Supplement. Honours: Freedom of the City of London (Guild of Painter Stainers), 1987. Memberships: Council Member, Society for Education Through Art, 1972-83; Founder, Chairman, Junior Arts and Science Centres, 1970-80; Life Fellow, Royal Society of Arts; Design Research Society; Colour Group, Great Britain; Founder, Trustee, National Art Education Archives, Bertton Hall, Wakefield, 1985-86. Address: 30 Wayside, Sheen, London SW14 7LN, England.

PAVLOVICH. See: AKSENOV Vasilii.

PAXTON Lois. See: LOW Lois.

PAYNE Donald Gordon (Ian Cameron, Donald Gordon, James Vance Marshall), b. 3 Jan 1924, London, England. Author. m. Barbara Back, 20 Aug 1947, 4 sons, 1 daughter. Education: MA, History, Oxford. Publications include: Walkabout, 1959; A River Ran

Out of Eden, 1963; The Island at the Top of the World, 1970; To the Farthest Ends of the Earth, History of the Royal Geographical Society, 1980; Mountains of the Gods, 1984; Lost Paradise: The Exploration of the Pacific, 1987; Many other books. Contributions to: Reader's Digest; National Geographic. Literary Agent: John Johnson. Address: Pippacre, Westcott Heath, Dorking RH4 3JZ, Surrey, England.

PAYNE Laurence, b. 1919, United Kingdom. Author; Actor. Appointments: Numerous stage, film, television and radio roles; Drama Teacher: Royal College of Music, London; St Catherine's School, Guildford, Surrey. Publications: The Nose of My Face, 1962, US Paperback Edition The First Body, 1964; Too Small for His Shoes, 1962; Deep and Crisp and Even, 1964; Birds in the Belfry, 1966; Spy for Sale, 1969; Even My Foot's Asleep, 1971; Take the Money and Run, 1982; Malice in Camera, 1983; Vienna Blood, 1984; Dead for a Ducat, 1985; Late Knight, US Edition Knight Fall, 1987. Address: c/o Hodder and Stoughton, 47 Bedford Square, London WC1B 3DP, England.

PAYNE Peggy, b. 8 Jan 1949, Wilmington, North Carolina, USA. Writer. m. Dr Bob Dick, 8 Dec 1983. Education: AB, English, Duke University. Publications: Revelation, 1988; Co-author, The Healing Power of Doing Good, 1992. Contributions to: Cosmopolitan; Ms; Family Circle; Travel & Leisure; New York Times; Washington Post; McCall's. Honours: Annual Fiction Award, given by Crucible, 1978; NEH Fellowship, 1979. Memberships: Society of American Travel Writers; American Society of Journalists and Authors. Address: 512 St Mary's Street, Raleigh, NC 27605, USA.

PAZ Octavio, b. 31 Mar 1914, Mexico City. Poet; Philosopher; Essayist; Critic; Director; Revista Vuelta. m. Marie José Tramini, 1 daughter. Education: National University of Mexico; Guggenheim Fellowship, USA, 1944. Appointments: Secretary, Mexican Embassy, Paris, 1946; New Delhi, 1952; Chargé d'Affaires ad interim, Japan, 1952; Posted Minister Secretariat for External Affairs, Mexico, 1953-58; Extraordinary and Plenipentiary Minister to Mexican Embassy, Paris, 1959-62; Ambassador to India, 1962-68; Simon Bolivar Professor of Latin American Studies, Cambridge, 1970; Visiting Professor of Spanish American Literature, University of Texas, Austin and Pittsburgh University, 1969-70; Charles Eliot Norton Professor of Poetry, Harvard University, 1971-72; Editor, Plural Mexico City, 1971-75. Publications include: Poetry: Hombre, 1937; Libertad bajo Palabra, 1949; Aguila o Sol? 1951 (trans: Eagle or Sun? 1970); Semillas para un Himno, 1956; Piedra de Sol, 1957 (trans: Sun Stone, 1960); La Estacion Violenta, 1958; Discos Visuales, 1968; Ladera Este, 1969; La Centena, 1969; Topoemas, 1971; Renga, 1971; New Poetry of Mexico (Anthol), 1972; Pasado en Claro, 1975; Vuelta, 1976; Poemas 1935-1975, 1979; Arbol adentro, 1987; in English: Early Poems (1935-57), 1963; Configurations, 1971; A Draft of Shadows and Other Poems, 1979; Airborn/Hijos del Aire, 1981; Selected Poems, 1984; Collected Poems (1957-87), 1987; Prose: el Laberinto de la soledad, 1950; El Arco y la Lira, 1956; Las Peras del Olmo, 1957; Postdata, 1970; El Mono Gramatico, 1971. Honours: Prizes include: Internat Poetry Grand Prix, 1963; National Prize for Literature, Mexico, 1977; Golden Eagle, Nice, 1978; Ollin Yoliztli, Mexico, 1980; Cervantes, Spain, 1982; Neustact International Prize for Literature, USA, 1982; T S Eliot Prize, Ingersoll Foundation, USA, 1987; Novel Prize for Literature, 1990. Address: c/o Revista Vuelta, Presidente Canonza 210, Coyascan, Mexico 4000 DF, Mexico.

PEARCE Ann Philippa, b. Great Shelford, Cambridgeshire, England. Freelance Writer of Childrens Books. m. Martin James Christie, 9 May 1963, 1 daughter. Education: MA, Cambridge University. Appointments: Script Writer, Producer, School Broadcasting, Radio, 1945-58; Children's Editor, Andre Deutsch Limited, 1960-67. Publications: Minnow on the Say, 1954; Tom's Midnight Garden 1958; Mrs Cockle's Cat, 1961; A Dog So Small, 1962; (with Sir Brian Fairfax-Lucy), The Children of the House, 1968, reissued as The Children of Charlecote, 1989; The Squirrel Wife, 1971; What the Neighbours Did and Other Stories, 1972; The Shadow Cage and other Stories of the Supernatural, 1977; The Battle of Bubble and Squeak, 1978; The Elm Street Lot, 1979; The Way to Sattin Shore, 1983; Lion at School and Other Stories, 1985; Who's Afraid? and other Strange Stories, 1986; Emily's Own Elephant, 1987; The Toothball, 1987; Freddy, 1988; Old Belle's Summer Holiday, 1989; Here Comes Ted, 1992. Contributions to: Times Literary Supplement; The Guardian; Children's Book Reviewer, 1960-75. Honours: Carnegie Medal, for Tom's Midnight Garden, 1959; New York Herald Tribune Spring Festival Prize, for A Dog So Small; Whitbread Prize for Battle of Bubble

and Squeak, 1979. Membership: Society of Authors. Address: c/o Viking-Kestrel Books, 27 Wright's Lane, London W8 5TZ, England.

PEARCE Brian Leonard (Joseph Redman), b. 8 May 1915, Weymouth, Dorset, England. Translator. m. 1) Lilla Fox, 1950, 1 son, 2 daughters, 2) Fanny Greenspan, 1954, 3) Margaret Mills, 1966. Education: University College, London, 1934-37; BA Honours (Upper IInd), History, London, 1937. Appointments: Honorary Visiting Fellow: Aberdeen University; Glasgow University; School of Slavonic and East European Studies; University of London, 1992. Publications: How Haig Saved Lenin, 1987; Translations: The New Economics (E Preobrazhensky), 1965; Islam and Capitalism (M Rodinson), 1974; The Communist Movement, Part 1 (F Claudin), 1975; How the Revolution Armed (L D Trotsky), 1979-81; The Thinking Reed (Boris Kagarlitsky), 1988; Bread and Circuses (Paul Veyne), 1990; Others. Contributions to: Sbornik and its successor Revolutionary Russia. Honours: Scott-Moncrieff Prize, 1975, 1979, 1990. Membership: Translators Association. Address: 42 Victoria Road, New Barnet, Herts EN4 9PF, England.

PEARCE Brian Louis, b. 4 June 1933, West London, England. Poet; Novelist; Lecturer; Former College Librarian. m. Margaret Wood, 2 Aug 1969, 1 daughter. Education: University College, London; MA; Fellow, Library Association; Fellow, Royal Society of Arts. Appointments: Examiner in English Literature, Library Association, 1964-70; Member, Writers in Schools Scheme, Greater London Arts, 1984-; Tutor in Creative Writing, Richmond-upon-Thames College; Occasional Lecturer, National Portrait Gallery, London, 1990-. Publications: Fiction: Victoria Hammersmith, novel, 1988; London Clay, stories, 1991; The Bust of Minerva, 1992; A Man in his Room, 1992; Battersea Pete, 1994; The Servant of his Country, 1994; A Man in his Room, 1992; The Servant of his Country, 1994; Poetry: Selected Poems 1951-73, 1978; The Vision of Piers Librarian, 1981; Office Hours, 1983; Browne Study, 1984; Dutch Comfort, poetry, prose, translations, 1985; Gwen John Talking, 1985; Palgrave: Selected Poems (editor), 1985; Thomas Twining of Twickenham, 1988; Jack o'Lent, 1991; Leaving the Corner: Selected Poems 1973-1985, 1992; Criticism: The Fashioned Reed: the poets of Twickenham from 1500, 1992; Thames Listener: poems 1949-89, 1993; Plays: The Eagle and the Swan, 1966; Shrine Rites, 1990; Criticism: The Fashion Reed: the poets of Twickenham from 1500, 1992; Other Thomas Twining of Twickenham, 1988; The Palgraves to John Murray; letters edited, 1995. Contributions to: New Poems, PEN, 1976, 1977; New Poetry, Arts Council anthologies, 1977, 1980, 1983; Emotional Geology: The Writings of Brian Louis Pearce, 1993. Honours: 5th-6th Place, 1-Act Verse Play Competition, Poetry Society, 1964; 1st Prize, Christian Poetry Competition, 1989. Memberships: Browning Society; Palgrave Society; PEN; Poetry Society; Chairman, Richmond Poetry Group, 1974-84. Address: 72 Heathfield South, Twickenham, Middlesex TW2 7SS, England.

PEARCE Mary Emily, b. 7 Dec 1932, London, England. Writer. Publications: Apple Tree Lean Down, 1973; Jack Mercybright, 1974; The Sorrowing Wind, 1975; Cast a Long Shadow, 1977; The Land Endures, 1978; Seedtime and Harvest, 1980; Polsinney Harbour, 1983; The Two Farms, 1985; The Old House at Railes, 1993. Memberships: Society of Authors; National Book League. Address: Owls End, Shuthonger, Tewkesbury, Gloucestershire, England.

PEARSALL Derek Albert, b. 28 Aug 1931, Birmingham, England. Professor of English. m. Rosemary Elvidge, 30 Aug 1952, 2 sons, 3 daughters. Education: BA, 1951, MA, 1952, University of Birmingham. Appointments: Assistant Lecturer, Lecturer, King's College, University of London, 1959-65; Lecturer, Senior Lecturer, Reader, 1965-76, Professor, 1976-87, University of York; Visiting Professor, 1985-, Gurney Professor of English, 1987-, Harvard University, Cambridge, Massachusetts, USA. Publications: John Lydgate, 1970; Landscapes and Seasons of the Medieval World (with Elizabeth Salter), 1973; Old English and Middle English Poetry, 1977; Langland's Piers Plowman: An Edition of the C-Text, 1978; The Canterbury Tales: A Critical Study, 1985; The Life of Geoffrey Chaucer: A Critical Biography, 1992. Memberships: Council Member, Early English Text Society; Fellow, Medieval Academy of America, 1988-90; New Chaucer Society, President 1988-90; Fellow, American Academy of Arts and Sciences. Address: Harvard University, Department of English, Warren House, Cambridge, MA 02138, USA.

PEARSALL Ronald, b. 1927, England. Author. Publications: Is That My Hook in Your Ear?, 1966; Worm in the Bud, 1969; The

Table-Rappers, 1972; The Possessed, 1972; The Exorcism, 1972; Diary of Vicar Veitch, 1972; A Day at the Big Top, 1973; The Wizard and Elidog, 1973; Victorian Sheet Music Covers, 1973; Victorian Popular Music, 1973; Edwardian Life and Leisure, 1973; Collecting Mechanical Antiques, 1973; Collecting Scientific Instruments, 1974; Inside the Antique Trade (with Graham Webb), 1974; Edwardian Popular Music, 1975; Night's Black Angels, 1975; Collapse of Stout Party, 1975; Popular Music of the 1920s, 1976; Public Purity Private Shame, 1976; The Alchemists, 1976; The Belvedere, 1976; Conan Doyle, 1977, 1989; Antique Hunter's Handbook, 1978; Tides of War, 1978; Thomas en Olihond, 1979; The Iron Sleep, 1979; Making and Managing an Antique Shop, 1979, Revised Edition, 1986; Tell Me Pretty Maiden, 1981; Practical Painting, 1983, 1990 (4 volumes), 1993; Joy of Antiques, 1988, paperback, 1992; The Murder in Euston Square, 1989; Antique Furniture for Pleasure and Profit, 1990; Lifesaving, 1991; Painting Abstract Pictures, 1991; Encyclopedia of Everyday Antiques, 1992; Antique Furniture Almanac, 1992. Address: Sherwell, St Teath, Bodmin, Cornwall PL30 3JB, England.

PEARSE Lesley Margaret, b. 24 Feb 1945, Rochester, Kent, England. Novelist. m. Nigel Pearse, 4 Mar 1976, 3 daughters. Education: Northbrook School Lee, London. Publications: Georgia, 1992; Tara, 1993. Contributions to: Numerous short stories: Womans Home; Womans My Weekly; Winners, owned by Littlewoods Pools. Memberships: Romantic Writers Association. Literary Agent: Darley Anderson, Estelle House, 11 Eustace Road, Fulham, SW6 1JB, London. Address: 1 Clyde Terrace, Knowle, Bristol, BS4 3DQ, England.

PEARSON Ridley, b. 13 Mar 1953, Glen Cove, New York, USA. Author. Education: Kansas University, 1972; Brown University, 1974. Publications: Never Look Back, 1985; Blood of the Albatross, 1986; The Seizing of Yankee Green Mall, 1987; Undercurrents, 1988; Probable Cause, 1990; Hard Fall, 1992; The Angel Maker, 1993; No Witnesses, 1994. Honours: Raymond Chandler Fulbright Fellow, 1990-91. Memberships: Writers Guild of America; Mystery Writers of America; The Authors Guild Inc; International Crime Writers Association. Literary Agent: Al Zuckerman. Address: PO Box 670, Hailey, ID 83333, USA.

PEARSON William Harrison (Bill), b. 18 Jan 1922, Greymouth, New Zealand. Writer; Retired University Teacher. Education: Greymouth Technical High School, 1934-38; MA, Canterbury University College, Christchurch, 1948; PhD, King's College, University of London, England, 1952. Publications: Coal Flat, 1963, 5th Edition, 1985; Henry Lawson Among Maoris, 1968; Fretful Sleepers and Other Essays, 1974; Rifled Sanctuaries, 1984; Six Stories, 1991. Honours: Co-Recipient, Landfall Readers Award, 1960; New Zealand Book Award for Non-Fiction, 1975. Address: 49 Lawrence Street, Herne Bay, Auckland, New Zealand.

PECK Michael Scott, b. 22 May 1936, New York, New York, USA. Psychiatrist; Management Consultant. m. Lily Ho, 27 Dec 1959, 1 s, 2 d. Education: Middlebury College; AB, Harvard University; MD, Case Western Reserve University. Appointments: Founder, Foundation for Community Encouragement; Practising Psychiatrist with Government (incl Office of US Surgeon General) and private practice. Publications: A Different Drum: A Bed By The Window; The Friendly Snowflake; A World Waiting To Be Born; Meditations From the Road; The Road Less Travelled: A New Psychology of Love, Traditional Values and Spiritual Growth, 1978; People Of The Lie: The Hope For Healing Human Evil, 1983; What Return Can I Make? The Dimensions of Christian Experience, 1985; Further Along the Road Less Travelled, 1993. Address: Bliss road, New Preston, CT 06777, USA.

PECK Richard, b. 5 Apr 1934, Decatur, Illinois, USA. Writer. Education: BA, DePauw University, 1956; MA, Southern Illinois University, 1959. Publications: The Ghost Belonged to Me, 1975; Are You in the House Alone?, 1976; Amanda/Miranda, 1980; This Family of Women, 1983; Remembering the Good Times, 1985; Prinbers Ashley, 1987; Don't Look and It Won't Hurt, 1972; Secrets of the Shopping Mall, 1979; New York Time, 1981; Close Enough To Touch, 1981; Blossom Culp and the Sleep of Death, 1986; Princess Ashley, 1987; Those Summer Girls I Never Met, 1988; Unfinished Portrait of Jessica, 1991. Contributions to: New York Times; School Library Journal. Honours: Edgar A Poe Award, American Society of Mystery Writers, 1977; Citations for 3 Young Adult Novels, American Library Associations Best of the Best Listing; American Library Association Margaret Edwards Young Adult Author Award, 1990. Memberships:

Authors Guild; Authors League. Literary Agent: Sheldon Fogelman, New York. Address: 155 E 72nd St, New York, NY 10021, USA.

PECK Robert Newton, b. USA. Author. Publications: A Day No Pigs Would Die, 1972; Millie's Boy, 1973; Path of Hunters: Animal Struggle in a Meadow, 1973; Soup, 1974; Soup for Me, 1975; Wild Cat, 1975; Bee Tree and Other Stuff, verse, 1975; Fawn, 1975; I Am the King of Kazoo, 1976; Rabbits and Redcoats, 1976; Hamilton, 1976; Hang for Treason, 1976; King of Kazoo (music and lyrics), play, 1976; Last Sunday, 1977; Trig, 1977; Patooie, 1977; The King's Iron, 1977; Soup for President, 1978; Eagle Fur, 1978; Trig Sees Red, 1978; Basket Case, 1979; Hub, 1979; Mr Little, 1979; Clunie, 1979; Soup's Drum, 1980; Secrets of Successful Fiction, 1980; Trig Goes Ape, 1980; Soup of Wheels, 1981; Justice Lion, 1981; Trig or Treat, 1982; Banjo, 1982; Soup in the Saddle, 1983; Soup's Goat, 1984; Spanish Hoof, 1985; Soup on Ice, 1985; Jo Silver, 1985; Soup on fire, 1987; My Vermont, 1987; Hallapoosa, 1988; Arly, 1989; Soup's Hoop, 1990; Higbee's Halloween, 1990; Little Soup's Hayride, 1991; Little Soup's Birthday, 1991; Arly II, 1991; Soup in Love, 1994; Soup Ahoy, 1994; A Part of the Sky, 1994; Soup 1776, 1995. Honours: Mark Twain Award, Missouri, 1981. Address: 500 Sweetwater Club Circle, Longwood, FL 32779, USA.

PECKHAM Morse, b. 1914, USA. Distinguished Professor Emeritus of English and Comparative Literature. Appointments: Instructor 1946-47, Assistant Professor 1948-49, Rutgers University, New Brunswick, New Jersey; Assistant Professor, 1949-52, Associate Professor 1952-61, Director, Institute for Humanistic Education for Business Executives, 1953-54; Director, University Press, 1953-55; Professor, 1961-67, University of Pennsylvania, Philadelphia; Distinguished Professor of English and Comparative Literature, 1967-80, Distinguished Professor Emeritus, 1980-, University of South Carolina, Columbia. Publications: On the Origin of Species: A Variorum Text, by Charles Darwin (editor), 1959; Humanistic Education for Business Executives: An Essay in General Education, 1960; Word, Meaning, Poem: An Anthology of Poetry (edited with Seymour Chapman), 1961; Beyond the Tragic Vision: The Quest for Identity in the Nineteenth Century, 1962; Man's Rage for Chaos: Biology, Behaviour and the Arts, 1965; Romanticism: The Culture of the Nineteenth Century (editor), 1965; Paracelsus, by Robert Browning (editor), 1969; Art and Pornography: An Experiment in Explanation, 1969; The Triumph of Romanticism; Speculation on Some Heroes of a Culture Crisis, 1970; Pippa Passes, by Robert Browning (editor), 1971; Luria, by Robert Browning (editor), 1973; Romanticism and Behaviour: Collected Essays II, 1976; Sordello, by Robert Browning (editor), 1977; Explanation and Power: The Control of Human Behavior, 1979; Romanticism and Ideology, 1985; The Birth of Romanticism, 1986. Address: 6478 Bridgewood Road, Columbia, SC 29206, USA.

PEDERSEN Ellen Miriam Kamp, b. 16 Feb 1948, Copenhagen, Denmark. Writer; Translator. Education: MA English & Phonetics, 1972-76; Danish Degree; Literary Appointments: Summer Course on Science Fiction, Danish Adult Education Centre, 1989. Publications: Slaver of New York, 1989; Black Robe, Danish translation, 1992; Denny Alice, 1993; Numerous translations and articles; Book and taped interviews for Radio. Contributions to: Mind & Behavior; Studies in the Humanities; Danish Newspapers, Journals and Magazines. Honours: Danish Award, for theory and criticism, 1980. Memberships: SFRA; Bylaws Committee; Officer, Danish Translators Association; Danish Writers Guild. Address: Jerichausgade 49.2, 1777 Kobenhavn V, Denmark

PEET Bill, b. 1915, USA. Children's Fiction Writer. Appointments: Formerly Artist and Screenwriter for Walt Disney Productions. Publications: Hubert's Hair-Raising Adventure, 1959; Huge Harold, 1961; Smokey, 1962; The Pinkish Purplish Bluish Egg, 1963; Ella, 1964; Randy's Dandy Lions, 1964; Kermit the Hermit, 1965; Chester the Worldly Pig, 1965; Capyboppy, 1966; Farewell to Shady Glade, 1966; Jennifer and Josephine, 1967; Buford the Little Big-Horn, 1967; Fly Homer Fly, 1969; The Whingdingdilly, 1970; The Wump World, 1970; How Droofus the Dragon Lost His Head, 1971; The Caboose Who Got Losse, 1971; Countdown to Christmas, 1972; The Ant and the Elephant, 1972; The Spooky Tail of Preewit Peacock, 1973; Merle the High Flying Squirrel, 1974; The Gnats of Knotty Pine, 1975; Big Bad Bruce, 1976; Eli, 1978; Cowardly Clyde, 1979; Encore for Eleanor, 1981; The Luckiest One of All, 1982; No Such Things, 1983; Pamela Camel, 1984; The Kweeks of Kookatumdee, 1985; Zella Zack and Zodiak, 1986; Jethro and Joel Were a Troll, 1987; Bill Peet - An

Autobiography, 1989; Cock-A-Doodle Dudley, 1990. Address: Houghton Mifflin Ci, 1 Beacon Street, Boston, MA 02107, USA.

PEIRCE Neal R, b. 1932, USA. Writer; Editor. Appointments: Political Editor, Congressional Quarterly, 1960-69; Fellow, Woodrow Wilson Center for Scholars, 1971-74; Co-Founder, Contributing Editor, The National Journal, Washington, District of Columbia, 1969-; Syndicated Columnist, Washington Post Writers Group. Publications: The People's President, 1968, 2nd edition, 1981; The Megastates of America, 1972; The Pacific States of America, 1972; The Great Plains States of America, 1973; The Deep South States of America, 1974; The Border South States, 1975; The New England States, 1976; The Mid-Atlantic States of America, 1977; The Great Lakes States of America, 1980; the Book of America, 1983; Corrective Capitalism, 1987; Enterprising Communities, 1989; Citisates, 1993; Breakthroughs: Recreativity The American City, 1994. Address: 610 G Street SW, Washington, DC 20024, USA.

PELIKAN Jaroslav, b. 17 Dec 1923, OH, USA. m. Sylvia Buric, 9 June 1946. Education: MA, Yale University, 1961; DD, Concordia College, MN, 1960; Litt D, Wittenberg University, 1960; Hum D, Providence College, 1966; LLD, Keuka College, 1967; LHD, Vaplaraiso University, 1966; DTheol, University of Hamburg, 1971; ThD, St Olaf College, 1972; STD, Dickinson College, 1986; Dr Sc Hist, Comenius University, 1992. Publictions include: From Luther to Kierkegaard, 1950; Luther the Expositor, 1959; Development of Doctrine, 1969; Scholarship and Its Survival, 1983; The Excellent Empire, 1987; Eternal Feminines, 1990; Christianity and Classical Culture, 1993. Honours include: Abingdon Award, 1959; Religious Book Award, 1974; Achievement Award, 1980; Award for Excellence, 1989; Literary Lions Award, 1992; Newberry Library Umanita Award, 1990; Joseph A Sittler Medal, 1993. Address: Dept of History, Yale University, PO Box 208324, New Haven, CT 06520 8324, USA.

PELUFFO Luisa, b. 20 Aug 1941, Buenos Aires, Argentina. Writer. m. Pablo Masilorens, 24 Apr 1971, 2 sons. Education: Drawing Teacher's degree, National Fine Arts School, 1959; Stage Direction, National Drama School, 1975. Appointments: Staff: Panorama Magazine, Buenos Aires, 1969-70; Channel 7 TV, Buenos Aires, 1970-71; La Nacion newspaper, 1971-76. Publications include: Materia Viva, poems, 1976; Conspiraciones, short stories, 1982, 1989; Materia de Revelaciones, poems, 1983; Todo Eso Oyes, novel, 1989; La Otra Orilla, poems, 1990; La Doble Vida, 1993. Address: Palacios 465, (8400) Bariloche, Provincia de Rio Negro, Argentina.

PEMBERTON Margaret, b. 10 Apr 1943, Bradford, England. Writer. m., 1 son, 4 daughters. Appointments; Chairman, Romantic Novelists Association. Publications include: Harlot, 1981; Lion of Languedoc, 1981; The Flower Garden, 1982; Silver Shadows, Golden Dreams, 1985; Never Leave Me, 1986; Multitude of Sins, 1988; White Christmas in Saigon, 1990; An Embarrassment of Riches, 1992; Zadruga, 1993; Moonflower Madness, 1993; Tapestry of Fear, 1994; Numerous other novels including: Forever, Pioneer Girl; African Enchantment; Guilty Secret; Vengeance in the Sun. Memberships: Crime Writers Association; Romantic Novelists Association; PEN; Society of Authors. Literary Agent: Carol Smith. Address: 13 Manor Lane, London SE13 5QW, England.

PENA MUNOZ Margarita, b. 21 Aug 1937, Mexico. Writer; Scholar. m. B Lima, 6 Nov 1971, 1 sons. Education: BD, Hispanic Literature, 1963; MD, Hispanic Literature, 1965, University of Mexico; PhD, El Colegio de Mexico, 1968. Appointments: Researcher, Literary Researching Centre, 1969-75, Professor 1975-87, University of Mexico. Publications: Flores de varia poesia, 1980, 1987; America's Discovery and Conquest, An Anthology of Chronicles, 1982; To Pass Over in Silence, 1983; Mofarandel, 1986; Living Again, 1980. Contributions to: various journals and magazines. Memberships: International Hispanists Association; PEN; International Institute of Latin-American Literature; Latin-American Linguistics Association, University of Mexico. Address: Cerrada del Convento 45, Casa 2, Tlalpan, Mexico DF 14420, Mexico.

PENDLETON Don. See: **OBSTFELD Raymond.**

PENDLETON Don. See: **GARSIDE Jack Clifford.**

PENN John. See: **TROTMAN Jack.**

PENNANT-REA Rupert Lascelles, b. 23 Jan 1948, Zimbabwe. Economist. m. Helen Jay, 2 sons, 1 daughter, 2 stepdaughters.

Education: BA, Economics, Trinity College, Dublin, 1970; MA, University of Manchester, 1972. Appointments: Economics Correspondent, 1977, Economics Editor, 1981; Editor, 1986-93, The Economist; Deputy Governor, Bank of England, London, 1993-. Publications: Gold Foil, 1978; Co-author: Who Runs the Economy?, 1979; The Pocket Economist, 1983; The Economist Economics, 1986. Honours: Winner, Wincott Prize for Financial Journalism, 1984. Memberships: Reform Club; MCC; Harare. Literary Agent: Curtis Brown. Address: Bank of England, Threadneedle Street, London EC2R 8AH, England.

PEPPE Rodney Darrell, b. 24 June 1934, Eastbourne, East Sussex, England. Author; Artist. m. Tatjana Tekkel, 16 July 1960, 2 sons. Education: Eastbourne School of Art, 1951-53, 1955-57; London County Council Central School of Art, 1957-59; NDD, Illustration (special subject) and Central School Diploma. Publications include: The Alphabet Book, 1968; The House That Jack Built, 1970; Odd One Out, 1974; Henry series, 1975-84; The Mice Who Lived in a Shoe, 1981; The Kettleship Pirates, 1983; The Mice and the Clockwork Bus, 1986; Huxley Pig series, 1989; The Mice and the Travel Machine, 1993. Contributions to: Making First Books, to Books for Your Children, autumn 1978; Something about the Author Autobiography Series, volume 10. Membership: Society of Authors. Address: Barnwood House, Whiteway, Stroud, Gloucestershire GL6 7ER, England.

PERERA Victor Haim, b. 12 Apr 1934, Guatemala. Writer. m. Padma Hejmadi, 8 Aug 1960 (div 1974). Education: BA, Brooklyn College, 1956; MA, University of Michigan, 1958. Appointments: Editorial Staff, The New Yorker, 1963-66; Reporter, The New York Times Magazine, 1971-75; Contributing Editor, Present Tense, 1974-89; Editorial Board, Tikkun, 1990-. Publications: The Conversion, 1970; The Loch-Ness Monster Watchers, 1974; The Last Lords of Palenque (with Robert D Bruce), 1982; Rites: A Guatemalan Boyhood, 1986; Testimony: Death of A Guatemalan Village, by Victor Montejo (trans from Spanish), 1987; Unfinished Conquest: The Guatemalan Tragedy, 1993; The Cross and The Pear Tree: A Sephardic Journey, 1995. Contributions to: New Yorker; Atlantic Monthly; The Nation; The New York Review; Partisan Review. Honours: Avery Hopwood Major Award in the Essay, 1962; National Endowment of the Arts Writing Award, 1980; PEN Fiction, (Short Story) Award, 1984; Present Tense/Joel Cavior Award in Biography, 1987; Lila Wallace, Reader's Digest Writing Award, 1992-94. Memberships: PEN American Centre. Literary Agent: Gloria Loomis, Watkins-Loomis Agency. Address: c/o Watkins-Loomis Agency, 133 East 35th Street, New York, NY 10016, USA.

PERI ROSSI Chistina, b. 12 Nov 1941, Montevideo, Uruguay. Writer. Education: Professor of Comparative Literature, 1963. Appointments: Professor of Literature, Montevideo, 1963-72; Professor of Comparative Literature and Latin American Literature, Universidad Autonoma de Barcelona, Spain, 1983. Publications: La Nave de los locos, novel; Solitano de amor, novel; Babel barbara, poetry; El museo de los esfuerzos inutiles, short stories; La rebelion de los ninos, short stories; Europa despues de la Uwia, poetry; Una pasion prohibida, short stories; La tarde del dinosaurio, short stories. Contributions to: Marcha, Uruguay; In Spain: Quimera; El Viejo Topo; El Pais; La Vanguardia; Efe. Honours: ARCA Prize, narrative, Uruguay, 1968; 1st Prize, MARCHA, novel, Uruguay, 1969; In Spain: Inventarios Provisionales de Poesia, poetry, 1974; Civdad de Palma, poetry, 1975; Benito Perez Galdos Prize, narrative, 1979; Cibtat de Barcelona Award, poetry, 1991; Award for babel barbara in English, Quarterly Review of Literature Poetry Series, Princeton, USA, 1992. Membership: Asociacion Colegial de Escritores de Espana. Literary Agent: International Editors, Barcelona, Spain. Address: Travessera de les Corts No 171 4o 1a, 08028, Barcelona, Spain.

PERKINS George Burton, b. 16 Aug 1930, USA. University Professor. m. Barbara Miller, 9 May 1964, 3 d. Education: AB, Tufts College, 1953; MA, Duke University, 1954; PhD, Cornell University, 1960. Appointments: Teaching Assisstant, Cornell University, 1957-60; Assisstant Professor, Farleigh Dickinson University, 1963-66; Lecturer, American Literature, Edinburgh University, 1966-67; Professor, Eastern Michigan University, 1967-; General Editor, Journal of Narrative Technique, 1970-92. Publications: Writing Clear prose, 1964; The Theory of the American Novel, 1970; Realistic American Short Fiction, 1972; American Poetic Theory, 1972; The American Tradition in Literature (with Bradley, Beatty, Long), 4th 5th 6th 7th editions, 1974, 82, 85, 90; The Practical Imagination (with Frye, Baker), 1985; Contemporary American Literature (with B Perkins), 1991;

Kaleidoscope (with B Perkins), 1993. Contributions to: Essays and reviews in Nineteeth-Century Fiction; Journal of American Folklore; The Dickensian; New England Quarterly; others. Honours: Duke University Fellow 1953-54; Cornell University Fellow, 1954-55; Phi Kappa Phi, 1956; Distinguished Faculty Award, Eastern Michigan University, 1978; Fellow, Institute for Advanced Studies in the Humanities, Edinburgh University, 1981; Senior Fulbright Scholar, University of Newcastle, Australia, 1989. Memberships: various professional organisations. Address: 1316 King George Bulevard, Ann Arbor, MI 48108, USA.

PERKINS Michael, b. 11 Nov 1942, Lansing, Michigan, USA. Writer; Arts Programme Director. m. Renie (Shoemaker) McCune, 20 June 1960, 1 son, 2 daughters. Education: Ohio University, Athens, 1963; New School for Social Research, 1962; City College New York, 1966. Appointments: Editor, Tompkins Square Press, 1966-68; Editor, Croton Press Ltd, 1969-72; Editor, Ulster Arts Magazine, 1978-79; Senior Editor, Masquerade Books, New York City, 1992-; Programme Director, Woodstock Guild, 1987-. Publications: Evil Companions, 1968 and 1992; Down Here, 1969; The Secret Record, 1977 and 1992; The Persistence of Desire, 1977; The Good Parts, 1994; Gift of Choice, 1993. Contributions to: Acumen England, 1993; Mother Jones; The Nation; Village Voice; Choice; Eleven. Honours: Panelist, New York Foundation for the Arts. Memberships: Authors Guild; National Book Critics Circle. Literary Agent. John Brockman. Address: 750 Ohayo Mt Road, Glenford, NY 12433, USA.

PERRETT Bryan, b. 9 July 1934, Liverpool, England. Author; Military Historian. m. Anne Catherine Trench, 13 Aug 1966. Education: Liverpool College. Appointment: Defence Correspondent to Liverpool Echo, during Falklands War and Gulf War. Publications include: A History of Blitzkrieg, 1983; The Czar's British Squadron (with A Lord), 1981; Knights of the Black Cross - Hitler's Panzerwaffe and its Leaders, 1986; Desert Warfare, 1988; Encyclopaedia of the Second World War (with Ian Hogg), 1989; Canopy of War, 1990; Liverpool: A City at War, 1990; Last Stand - Famous Battles Against The Odds, 1991; The Battle Book - Crucial Conflicts in History from 1469 BC to the Present, 1992; At All Costs - Stories of Impossible Victories, 1993; Seize and Hold - Master Strokes of the Battlefield, 1994; Iron Fist - Crucial Armoured Engagements, 1995. Contributions to: War Monthly; Military History; World War Investigator; War in Peace (partwork); The Elite (partwork). Memberships: Rotary Club of Ormskirk; Royal United Services Institute. Literary Agent: Watson Little Ltd, London, England; McIntosh and Otis, New York, USA. Address: 7 Maple Avenue, Burscough, Nr Ormskirk, Lancashire L40 5SL, England.

PERRIAM Wendy Angela, b. 23 Feb 1940, London, England. Author. m. (1) 22 Aug 1964, 1 daughter, (2) John Alan Perriam, 29 July 1974. Education: St Anne's College, Oxford, 1958-61; BA (Hons), History, 1961, MA, 1972, Oxford; London School of Economics, 1963-64. Publications: Novels: Absinthe for Elevenses, 1980; Cuckoo, 1981; After Purple, 1982; Born of Woman, 1983; The Stillness of The Dancing, 1985; Sin City, 1987; Devils, for a Change, 1989; Fifty-Minute Hour, 1990; Bird Inside, 1992; Michael, Michael, 1993; Breaking and Entering, 1994. Contributions to: Stories and articles to magazines and newspapers including: She; Cosmopolitan; Penthouse; Esquire; Sunday Times; Evening Standard; Daily Mail; Poems and short stories to Arts Council Anthology and South East Arts Anthologies: Seven Deadly Sins, 1985; The Literary Companion to Sex, 1992; Best Short Stories, 1992. Memberships: PEN; Society of Authors; British Actors Equity Association. Literary Agent: Curtis Brown, London, England. Address: c/o Curtis Brown, 4th Floor, Haymarket House, 28/29 HAymarket, London SW1Y 4SP, England.

PERRIE Walter, b. 5 June 1949, Scotland. Poet; Critic. Education: MA Honours, Mental Philosophy, University of Edinburgh, 1975; MPhil, University of Stirling, 1989. Appointments: Scotland/Canada Exchange Fellow, 1984-85; Co-Editor, Margin, 1986-91. Publications: Metaphysics and Poetry (with Hugh MacDiarmid), 1974; Poem on a Winter Night, 1976; Lamentation for the Children, 1977; By Moon and Sun, 1980; Out of Conflict, 1982; Concerning the Dragon, 1984; Roads That Move: A Journey through Eastern Europe, 1991. Contributions to: Chapman; Lines Review; New Edinburgh Review; Numerous others. Honours: Writer's Bursary, Scottish Arts Council, 1976, 1983, 1994; Book Award, Scottish Arts Council, 1976, 1983; Gregory Award for Poetry, 1978; Merrill-Ingram Foundation Award, New York, 1986; Writing Fellow, University of Stirling, 1991. Memberships: PEN, Scotland; Society of Authors. Address: 10 Croft Place, Dunning, Perthshire PH2 0SB, Scotland.

PERRY George Cox, b. 7 Jan 1935, London, England. Writer. m. 1 Jul 1976, 1 s. Education: BA, 1957, MA, 1961, Trinity College, Cambridge. Publications: The Films of Alfred Hitchcock, 1965; A Competitive Cinema, co-author, 1966; Penguin Book of Comics, 1967, 1971; The Great British Picture Show, 1974, 1985; Rule Britannia - The Victorian World, 1974; Hitchcock, 1975; Movies From the Mansion, 1976; Forever Ealing, 1981; Diana- A Celebration, 1982; Life of Python, 1984; Rupert: A Bear's Life, 1985; Bluebell, 1986; The Complete Phantom of the Opera, 1987. Contributions to: The Times; Sunday Times; Radio Times; Los Angeles Times; Illustrated London News, Film Critic, 1982-. Literary Agent: Deborah Rogers Ltd, London, England. Address: 7 Roehampton Lane, London SW15 5LS, England.

PERRY Ritchie (John Allen), b. 1942, England. Teacher; Author. Publications: The Fall Guy, 1972; Nowhere Man, US Edition as A Hard Man to Kill, 1973; Ticket to Ride, 1973; Holiday with a Vengeance, 1974; Your Money and Your Wife, 1975; One Good Death Deserves Another, 1976; Dead End, 1977; Brazil: The Land and Its People, 1977; Copacabana Stud (as John Allen), 1977; Dutch Courage, 1978; Bishop's Pawn, 1979; Up Tight (as John Allen), 1979; Grand Slam, 1980; Fool's Mate, 1981; Foul Up, 1982; MacAllister, 1984; Kolwezi, 1985; Presumed Dead, 1988; Comeback, 1991; Children's books: George H Ghastly, 1982; George H Ghastly to the Rescue, 1982; George H Ghastly and the Little Horror, 1985; Fenella Fang, 1986; Fenella Fang and the Great Escape, 1987; Fenella Fang and the Wicked Witch, 1989; The Creepy Tale, 1989; Fenalla Fang and the Time Machine, 1991; The Runton Werewolf, 1994. Literary Agent: Peters, Fraser and Dunlop. Address: The Linhay, Water Lane, West Runton, Norfolk NR27 9QP, England.

PERUTZ Kathrin, b. 1939, USA. Author; Executive. Appointments: Executive Director, Contacct Program Inc. Publications: The Garden, 1962; A House on the Sound, 1964; The Ghosts, 1966; Mother is a Country: A Popular Fantasy, 1968; Beyond the Looking Glass: America's Beauty Culture, 1970; Marriage is Hell: The Marriage Fallacy, 1972; Reigning Passions, 1978; Writing for Love and Money, 1991. Also as Johanna Kingsley: Scents, 1985; Faces, 1987. Memberships: PEN; Authors Guild. Literary Agent: Elaine Markson. Address: 16 Avalon Riad, Great Neck, NY 10021, USA.

PESETSKY Bette, b. 16 Nov 1932, Milwaukee, Wisconsin, USA. Writer. m. Irwin Pesetsky, 25 Feb 1956, 1 son. Education: BA, Washington University, 1954; MFA, University of Iowa, 1959. Publications: Stories Up to A Point, 1982; Author from a Savage People, 1983; Midnight Sweets, 1988; Digs, 1988; Confessions of a Bad Girl, 1989; Late Night Muse, 1991; Cast a Spell, 1993. Contributions to: The New Yorker; Vanity Fair; Ms; Vogue; Paris Review; Ontario Review; Stand. Honours: Creative Writing Fellowship, National Endowment for the Arts, 1979-80; Creative Writing Public Service Award, New York Council for the Arts, 1980-81. Memberships: PEN. Literary Agent: Goodman Associates, USA. Address: Hilltop Park, Dobbs Ferry, NY 10522, USA.

PESSEN Edward, b. 31 Dec 1920, New York, USA. Historian; Author. m. Adele Barlin, 25 Nov 1940, Brooklyn, New York, 2 s, 3 d. Education: BA 1947, MA 1948, PhD 1954, Columbia University, New York, USA. Literary Appointments: City College of New York, 1948-54; Fisk University, Nashville, Tennessee, 1954-56; Staten Island Community College, 1956-70; Baruch College and Graduate School & University Centre, City University of New York, 1970-. Major Publications: Most Uncommon Jacksonians, 1967; Jacksonian America: Society, Personality & Politics, 1969, revised edition, 1978; Riches, Class & Power before the Civil War, 1973; Three Centuries of Social Mobility in America, 1974; The Log Cabin Myth: Social Backgrounds of the Presidents, 1984; Riches, Class and Power (new ed), 1989. Contributions to: Journal of American History; American Historical Review. Honours: National Book Award Finalist, 1974; Guggenheim Foundation Fellowship, 1977; Rockefeller Foundation Fellow, 1978; Fulbright Lecturer, Moscow State University, USSR, 1985. Memberships: President, Society of Historians of the Early American Republic, 1985-86; American Historical Association; American Antiquarian Society; Organisation of American Historians; Southern Historical Association. Address: City University of New York, 17 Lexington Avenue, New York, NY 10010, USA.

PETE Pindar. See: MORTON Harry Edwin Clive

PETECKI Bohdan Antoni, b. 5 Jul 1931, Krakow, Poland. Writer. m. Janina Rogowska, 19 Jul 1966, 1 d. Education: MA, Oriental

Studies, Jagiellonian University, Cracow. Journalist, Polish Radio Station, Katowice, 1958-68; Sub-Editor, TV Broadcasting Station, Katowice, 1968-72; 1st Sub Editor, Polish Radio Broadcasting Station, 1972-75; Sub Editor, Weekly Magazine, Panorama, 1978-. Publications: 1001 Swiatow, 1983; X-A Uwolnij gwiadzy, 1977, 1981; Strefy zerowe, 1972; Tylko cisza, 1974; Bal na pieciu ksiezycach, 1981; Pierszy Ziemianin, 1983; Youth Novels: Sola z nieba polnocnego, 1977; Wiatr od Slonca, 1980; Krolowa komoscu, 1979; Science Fiction Novels: Operocja wieczuosc, 1975; Rubin przerywa milczeniel, 1976; Contributions to: various journals and magazines, Honours: Diploma of Honour, National Publishers Iskry, Warsaw, 1977; Novel of the Year, Magzine Fantastyka, 1984. Memberships: Polish Writer's Association, Vice President, Katowice, 1985-. Address: ul Baltycka 51A, 40-778 Katowice, Poland.

PETERFREUND Stuart Samuel, b. 30 June 1945, Brooklyn, New York, USA. English Professor. m. 12 Sept 1981. Education: AB, Cornell University, 1966; MFA, University of California, Irvine, 1968; PhD, University of Washington, 1974. Appointments include: University of Arkansas, 1975-78, Assistant Professor, 1978-82, Associate Professor 1982-91, Full Professor, 1991-, Chair, 1991-, Northeastern University. Publications: The Hanged Knife & Other Poems, 1970; Harder Than Rain, poems, 1977; Interstatements, poems, 1986; Literature and Science: Theory and Practice, 1990. Contributions to: Poetry in various journals including: Cimarron; Cincinnati Poetry Review; Epoch; Poetry Northwest; Shenandoah; and others. Articles, English Romantic Literature, various scholarly journals. Address: Department of English 406 HO, Northeastern University, 306 Huntington Avenue, Boston, MA 02115, USA.

PETERKIEWICZ Jerzy, b. 29 Sept 1916, Fabianki, Poland. Novelist; Poet. Education: University of Warsaw; MA, University of St Andrews, Scotland, 1944; PhD, King's College, London, England, 1947. Publications: Prowincja, 1936; Wiersze i poematy, 1938; Pogrzeb Europy, 1946; The Knotted Cord, 1953; Loot and Loyalty, 1955; Polish Prose and Verse, 1956; Antologia liryki angielskiej, 1958; Future to Let, 1958; Isolation, 1959; Five Centuries of Polish Poetry (with Burns Singer), 1960, enlarged edition, 1970; The Quick and the Dead, 1961; That Angel Burning at My Left Side, 1963; Poematy Londynskie, 1965; Inner Circle, 1966; Green Flows the Bile, 1969; The Other Side of Silence (The Poet at the Limits of Language), 1970; The Third Adam, 1975; Easter Vigil and Other Poems, by Karol Wojtyla (Pope John Paul II) (editor, translator), 1979; Kula magiczna, Poems 1934-52, 1980; Collected Poems, by Karol Wojtyla (Pope John Paul II) (editor, translator), 1982; Poezje wybrane, Selected Poems, 1986; Literatura polska w perspektywie europejskiej, essays translated from English, 1986; Modlitwy intelektu, poems, 1988; Messianic Prophecy, 1991; In the Scales of Fate, an autobiography, 1993; The Place Within: The Poetry of Pope John Paul II, (editor & translator) 1994. Essays; Poems; Radio plays, BBC 3. Contributions to: Numerous periodicals. Literary Agent: John Johnson Ltd, 45-47 Clerkenwell Green, London EC1R 0HT, England. Address: 7 Lyndhurst Terrace, London NW3 5QA, England.

PETERS Catherine Lisette, b. 30 Sept 1930, London, England. Lecturer; Writer. m. (1) John Glyn Barton, 14 Jan 1952, 3 sons, (2) Anthony Storr, 9 Oct 1970. Education: BA 1st Class Honours, 1980, MA, 1984, Oxford University. Appointments: Editor, Jonathan Cape, 1960-74; Lecturer in English, Somerville College, Oxford, 1981-92. Publications: Thackeray's Universe, 1987; The King of Inventors: A Life of Wilkie Collins, 1991. Contributions to: Dickens Studies Annual; Victorian Periodicals Review; Editions of Armadale and Hide and Seek by Wilkie Collins (World's Classics), Vanity Fair by W M Thackeray and The Moonstone by Wilkie Collins (Everyman Books); The Art of Literary Biography. Memberships: Wilkie Collins Society; Society of Authors; Fellow, Royal Society of Literature; International PEN. Literary Agent: Michael Sissons, Peters, Fraser and Dunlop. Address: 45 Chalfont Road, Oxford OX2 6TJ, England.

PETERS Elizabeth. See: MERTZ Barbara Louise Gross.

PETERS Ellis. See: PARGETER Edith.

PETERS Lance, b. 8 May 1934, Auckland, New Zealand. Author; Screenwriter. m. Laura Chiang, 25 Feb 1981, 2 sons. 2 daughters. Appointments: London Representative, Seymour Theatre Centre, 1973-74; Feature Writer, TV Times London Correspondent, 1974-76. Publications: Carry On Emmannuelle, 1978; The Dirty Half Mile, 1981; Cut-Throat Alley, 1982; Enemy Territory, 1988; God's Executioner,

1988; The Civilian War Zone, 1989; The Red Collar Gang, 1989; The Dirty Half Mile (Again), 1989; Gross Misconduct, 1993; Savior in the Grave, 1994; Extensive TV writing: comedy, documentary and drama; 5 feature film screenplays; Assault with a Deadly Weapon, stage play. Contributions to: Numerous popular magazines. Memberships: Honorary Life Member, Australian Writers Guild, President 1970-72; Australian Society of Authors; Writers Guild of Great Britain; British Academy of Film and Television Arts. Literary Agents: Gelfman and Schneider, 250 W 5th Street, New York, NY 10107, USA; Catherine Hanen, Attorney, 2049 Century Park East, Suite 3100, Century City, CA 90067, USA (personal manager). Address: 291 Fitzwilliam Road, Vaucluse, Sydney, New South Wales 2030, Australia.

PETERS Margaret McCullough, b. 13 May 1933, USA. Writer; Professor. 1 s, 1 d. Education: BA, 1961, MA, 1965, PhD, 1969, University of Wisconsin-Madison. Appointments: Kathe Tappe Vernon Professor of Biography, Dartmouth College, 1978; Professor Emerita, University of Wisconsin; Reviewer, New York Times Book Review. Publications: Charlotte Brontë, Style in the Novel, 1973; Unquiet Soul: A Biography of Charlotte Brontë, 1975; Bernard Shaw and the Actresses, 1980; Mrs Pat: The Life of Mrs Patrick Campbell, 1984; The House of Barrymore, 1990; As Lonely As God, in the Genius of Shaw; Editor, Bernard Shaw's Mrs Warren's Profession, Facsimile edition. Contributions to: Biography; Language and Style; The Annual of Bernard Shaw Studies; The Southwest Review: The British Studies Monitor; Harvard magazine; Brontë Society Transactions. Honours: Best Prose Award, Friends of American Writers, 1975; Banta Award, 1980, 1984; George Freedley Memorail Award for Best Drama Book, 1980, 1984; English Speaking Union Ambassador Award, 1990; American Council of Learned Societies Fellow; Guggenheim Fellow; Wisconsin Institute for the Humanities Fellow; Rockefeller Fellow. Memberships: Bernard Shaw Society; Brontë Society; Tennessee Williams Society; Authors Guild. Literary Agent: 511 College Street, Lake Mills, WI 53551, USA.

PETERS Mark. See: TAYLOR Peter Mark.

PETERS Maureen (Veronica Black, Catherine Darby, Belinda Grey, Levannah Lloyd, Judith Rothman, Sharon Whitby), b. 1935, British. Writer of mystery/crime/suspense/historical romance/Gothic/biography. Publications include: (as Sharon Whitby) No Song at Morningside, 1981; (as Belinda Grey), Glen of Frost, 1981; (as Levannah Lloyd), A Maid Called Wanton, 1981, Mail Order Bride, 1981, Cauldron of Desire, 1981, Dark Surrender, 1981; (as Veronica Black), The Dragon and the Rose, 1982; Red Queen, White Queen, 1982; Imperial Harlot, 1983; My Lady Troubadour, 1983; Alianor, 1983; Lackland's Bride, 1983; (as Veronica Black) Bond Wife, 1983; (as Sharon Whitby), Childen of the Rainbow, 1983; (as Catherine Derby) A Circle of Rowan, 1983; A Song For Marguerite, 1984; My Philippa, 1984; (as Veronica Black) Hoodman Blind, 1984; (as Catherine Darby) The Rowan Maid, 1984, Song of the Rowan, 1984, Sangreal, 1984; Fair Maid of Kent, 1985; Isabella, The Sea Wolf, 1985; the Vinegar Seed, 1985; (as Catherine Darby) Sabre, 1985, Sabre's Child, 1985, House of Sabre, 1986, Heart of Falme, 1986; The Vinegar Blossom, 1986; (as Catherine Darby) A Breed of Sabres, 1987, Morning of a Sabre, 1987; The Luck Bride, 1987; The Vinegar Tree, 1987. Address: c/o Hale, 45-47 Clerkenwell Green, London EC1R OHT, England.

PETERS Natasha. See: CLEAVER Anastasia.

PETERS Richard. See: HAINING Peter Alexander.

PETERS Richard Stanley, b. 31 Oct 1919, Missouri, India. Emeritus Professor. m. Margaret Lee Duncan, 16 July 1943, 1 son, 2 daughters. Education: Queen's College, Oxford; Birkbeck College, London; BA (Oxon); BA, London; PhD, London, 1949. Appointments: Part-time Lecturer, 1946-49, Full-time Lecturer, 1949-58, Reader in Philosophy, 1958-62, Birkbeck College, University of London; Visiting Professor, Harvard University, USA, 1961; Professor, Philosophy of Education, 1962, Emeritus Professor, 1982-, Institute of Education, London; Part-time Lectureships, Bedford College, London, and London School of Economics, 1966; Visiting Fellow, Australian National University, Canberra, 1969. Publications: Ethics and Education, 1945; Hobbes, 1956; Social Principles of the Democratic State (co-author), 1958; Authority, Responsibility and Education, 1960; Logic of Education (co-author), 1970; Reason and Compassion, 1973; Psychology and Ethical Development, 1974; Essays on Educators, 1981; Moral Education and Moral Development, 1981; Editor, International Library of the Philosophy of Education. Address: Flat 3, 16 Shepherd's Hill, Highgate, London N6 5AQ, England.

PETERS Robert Louis, b. 20 Oct 1924, Wisconsin, USA. Poet; Critic; Actor; Professor of Literature. 3 sons, 1 daughter. Education: BA, 1948; MA, 1949; PhD, MacDowell and Yaddo Colonies. Publications: The Crowns of Apollo: Swinburne's Principles of Literature and Art, 1965; Songs for a Son, 1967, (poems); The Gift to be Simple, 1975, (poems); The Great American Poetry Bake-Off: First, Second, Third & Fourth Series, 1979, 1985, 1987 & 1990; What Dillinger Meant To Me, 1984; Hawker, 1984; The Peters Black and Blue Guide to Current Literary Periodicals, 1983, 1985, 1987; Kane, 1985; Shaker Light, 1987; Hawker, 1989; Goodnight Paul, 1992; Snapshots For A Serial Killer, 1992; Poems: Selected & New, 1992; Zapped: Two Novellas, 1993; Love Poems For Robert Mitchum, 1993. Contributor to: American Book Review; Poetry Now; Contact 11; Pearl; Western Humanities Review; Where The Bee Sucks: Workers, Drones & Queens of Contemporary Poetry, 1994; numerous others. Honours: Guggenheim Fellow, 1966-67; NEA Fellowship, 1974; Alice Faye de Castagnola Prize, 1984; Larry P Fine Award for Criticism, 1985; Jack Kerouac Award for Poetry. Memberships: PEN; Authors Guild. Address: Dept of English, University of California, Irvine, CA 92717, USA.

PETERS Thomas J. Founder and Chief, the Tom Peters Group; Management Consultant; Author; Lecturer. Publications: In Search of Excellence: Lessons From America's Best Run Companies, 1982; A Passion For Excellence; Thriving on Chaos; Liberation Management; The Tom Peters Seminars: Crazy Times Call For Crazy Organsations, 1994. Address: The Tom Peters Group, 555 Hamilton Avenue, Palo Alto, CA 94301, USA.

PETERSEN Peter James, b. 23 Oct 1941, Santa Rosa, California, USA. Writer; Teacher. m. Marian Braun, 6 July 1964, 2 daughters. Education: AB, Stanford University; MA, San Francisco State University; PhD, University of New Mexico. Appointments: English Instructor, Shasta College. Publications: Would You Settle for Improbable, 1981; Nobody Else Can Walk It for You, 1982; The Boll Weevil Express, 1983; Here's to the Sophomores, 1984; Corky & the Brothers Cool, 1985; Going for the Big One, 1986; Good-bye to Good O'Charlie, 1987; The Freshman Detective Blues, 1987; I Hate Camping, 1991; Liars, 1992; The Sub, 1993; I Want Answers and a Parachute, 1993; Some Days, Other Days, 1994. Honours: Fellow, NEH, 1976-77. Memberships: Society of Children's Book Writers. Literary Agent: Ruth Cohen, PO Box 7626, Menlo Park, CA 94025, USA. Address: 1243 Pueblo Court, Redding, CA 96001, USA.

PETERSON Donald Macandrew, b. 23 Jun 1956. Lecturer in Cognitive Science. Education: MA, Philosophy and Psychology, Edinburgh University, 1978; PhD, Philosophy, University College London, 1985, MSc, Dlc, in Foundations of Advanced Information Technology, Imperial College, London, 1986. Publication: Wittgenstein's Early Philosophy - Three Sides of the Mirror, 1990. Contributions to: a number of professional journals and magazines. Membership: Society of Artificial Intelligence and the Simulation of Behaviour. Address: Department of Computor Science, University of Birmingham, Birmingham B15 2TT, England.

PETERSON Robert, b. 2 June 1924, Denver, Colorado, USA. 1 daughter. Education: BA, University of California, Berkeley, 1947; MA, San Francisco State College, 1956. Appointments: Writer-in-Residence, Reed College, Protland, Oregon, 1969-71. Publications: Home for the Night, 1962; The Binnacle, 1967; Wondering Where You Are, 1969; Lone Rider, 1976; Under Sealed Orders, 1976; Leaving Taos, 1981; The Only Piano Player in La Paz, 1985; Waiting for Garbo: 44 Ghazals, 1987. Honours: Grant in Poetry, National Endowment for the Arts, 1967; Amy Lowell Travelling Fellowship, 1972-73; National Poetry Series, Leaving Taos, 1981. Memberships: Authors Guild; PEN. Address: PO Box 417, Fairfax, CA 94978, USA.

PETERZEN (Anna Karin) Elisabet, b. 15 Apr 1938, Stockholm, Sweden. Author, 1 d. Education: London School of Foreign Trade, 1960; Stockholm University, 1980-83. Appointment: Women's Committee, Swedish Union of Authorss, 1985-88. Publications: Marmor och Ebenholts, 1964; Njutning, 1967; Trygghet, 1968; Aktenskaps Brott, 1969; Den konstgjorda mannen, 1973; En mans liv (Mustafa Said), 1974; Roman, 1976; Ljusnatten, 1981; Lura Livet, 1981; Sista Sticket, 1983; Mamsell Caroline, 1986; Djursager, 1987; Nubiens Hjarta, 1989. Honours: 1st Prize, Best 2rd World Novel, Mustafa Said, 1976; 1st Prize, Best Book Club Novel, Mamsell Caroline, 1986.

Membership: Swedish Union of Authors, 1970-. Address: Osmo, Sweden.

PETOCZ Andras, b. 27 Aug 1959, Budapest, Hungary. Writer; Poet. 2 d. Education:Graduated, Faculty of Arts, Lorand Eotvos Univeristy, Budapest, 1986. Appointments: Chief Editor, literary Periodical Jelenlet (Presence) 1981-83; an editor of literary periodical Magyar Muhely (Hungarian Workshop) 1989-91; Editor and publisher of Medium Art, an underground literary periodical during the communist regime, 1983-89; Leader of the Medium-Art Studio, a centre of experimental art. Publications: Letter Pyramid (Betupiranis) 1984, poems; Attempts at an Autobiography (Oneletrajzi kiserletrek), 1984; Non-figurative, 1989 poems and visual poems; Ivisible presence (Lathatlan jelenlet) 1990, poems; Scale with no Meaning (A jelentes nelkuli hangsor) poems 1988; Dignity of Existence-in-Gesture (A jelben-letezes meltosaga) essay, 1990; Wake up, Gergely Csutoras! (Csutoras Gergely ebresztese) poems for children, 1991; The Typed Fear (Az irogepelt felelem) poems, 1992; Writer and director of two video films: Dialogue (Parbeszed) 1989 and Approaches to a Thing-Found (Kozeltesek egy talalt targyhoz) 1990. Contributions to: DOC/K/S France; Rampike, Canada; Magyar Muhely, Budapest; Holmi, Budapest; New Hungarian Quarterly, Budapest. Honours: Lajos Kassak, 1987; Robert Graves Prize for best Hungarian poem of the Year, 1990; Prize for best book by Szepirodalmi Publishers, 1989. Memberships: Hungarian Writers Association; Art Association of the Hungarian Republic; Hungarian Workshop Committee; Member of Advisory Board of Writer's Committee in Tokaj; Young Artists Club, Budapest. Address: Studio of Medium-Art, Donati u 6, H-1015 Budapest, Hungary.

PETRINGENARU Adrian, b. 19 Oct 1933, Bucharest, Romania. Film Director; Author. m. Liliana Lazar, 1970, 1 d. Education: PhD, University of Paris, 1981. Appointments: Art Critic, Romanian Weekly Magazine, Contemporanul, 1963-70. Publications: Image and Symbol in the World of Brancusi, 1983; films: The Prodigal Father, 1974; Pyre and Flame, 1979; The Woman From the Great Bear, 1982; The Hidden Castle, 1987; documentary films: Steps to Brancusi, 1966; 6000 Years, 1967; animated films: Brezaia, 1968; In John's Forest, 1970; Byzance After Byzance, 1972; Long Way, 1976; The Principle of the field, 1979; Art Expertise, 1980; Competition, 1981; The Final, 1982; Perpetual Reborn, 1986. Contributions to: various magazines, journals and newspapers. Honours: Golden Prize, Film Festival Santarem, 1975, 1980; Silver Prize, Film Festival, Mamaia, 1970; Honour Diplomas, Film Festivals, London, 1970, Salonica, 1977, Leipzig, 1979, 1984, Lucca, 1984, 1986; National Romanian Prizes for Films, 1977, 1981. Memberships: ASIFA, CIDALC; Romanian Film-makers Institution. Address: Str Ciucea 5, Bloc L 19, Apt 33, Bucharest, CP 7210, Romania.

PETROSKI Catherine, b. 7 Sep 1939, St Louis, Missouri, USA. Writer. m. Henry Petroski, 15 July 1966, 1 s, 1 d. Education: BA, MacMurray College, 1961; MA, University of Illinois, 1962. Appointments: National Endowment for the Arts Writing Fellowship, 1978-79; Alan Collins Fellow, Bread Loaf, 1982; National Endowment for the Arts Fellow, 1983-84. Publications: Gravity and Other Stories, 1981; Beautiful My Manr in the Wind, 1983; The Summer That Lasted Forever, 1984. Contributions to: Short fiction in Virginia Quarterly Review, Mississippi Review, Southern Humanities Review, North American Review, Prairie Schooner and others; reviews of fiction and non- fiction to Chicago Tribune and others. Honours: Berlin Prize, 1960; Texas Institute of Letters Prize, 1976; PEN Syndicated Fiction Prizes, 1983, 84, 85, 88. O Henry Award, 1989; AAUW North Carolina Literary and Historical Association Book Prize; 1984 Honorary DLitt conferred by MacMurray College. Memberships: The Author's Guild; The Author's League of America; National Book Critics Circle. Literary Agent: Georges Borchard, 136 East 57th Street, New York, NY 10022, USA. Address: 2528 Wrightwood Avenue, Durham, NC 27705, USA.

PETROSKI Henry, b. 6 Feb 1942, NY, USA. Engineer; Writer. m. Catherine Ann Groom, 15 July 1966, 1 s, 1 d. Education: BME, Manhattan College, 1963; MS, 1964, PhD, 1968, University of IL. Publications: To Engineer is Human, 1985; The Pencil, 1990; The Evolution of Useful Things, 1992; Design Paradigms, 1994; Beyond Engineering, 1986. Honours: IL Arts Council Award, 1976. Memberships: ASCE; ASME. Address: School of Engineering, Duke University, Durham, NC 27708, USA.

PETROVITS Loty, b. 12 Aug 1937, Athens, Greece. Author. m. Andreas Andrutsopoulos, 23 July 1966, 1 son, 1 daughter. Education:

University of Michigan; Istituto Italiano di Cultura in Atene, 1960. Literary appointments: Editorial Correspondent, Phaedrus, 1980-88; Associate Editor, Bookbird, 1982-; Co-Editor, Diadromes, 1986-. Publications: O Mikros Adelfos, 1976, Japanese translation, 1988; Tris Fores Ki Enan Kero, 1977; Gia Tin Alli Patrida, 1978; Sto Tsimentenio Dasos, 1981; Zetete Mikros, 1982; Spiti Gia Pente, 1987, Japanese translation, 1990; Istories pou kanenas den xerei, 1984; Istories me tous dodeca mines, 4 volumes, 1988; Lathos Kyrie Noygerl, 1989; 13 more books for children and 4 for adults; Translations from English into Greek include: Blowfish Live in the Sea, by Paula Fox, 1979; The Camelthorn Papers, by Ann Thwaite, 1987. Contributions to: Phaedrus; Bookbird; Diadromes; Efthini; Diavazo; Kypriaki Martyria; Helidonia; Gia Hara. Address: 129 Aristotelous Street, GR 11251 Athens, Greece.

PETTIFER Julian, b. 21 July 1935. Freelance Writer; Broadcaster. Education: St John's College, Cambridge. Appointments: TV Reporter, Writer, Presenter: Southern TV, 1958-62; Tonight, 1962-64, 24 Hours, 1964-69, Panorama, 1969-75, BBC; Presenter, Cuba - 25 Years of Revolution, series, 1984, Host, Busman's Holiday, 1985-86, ITV; Numerous TV documentaries including: Vietnam War Without End, 1970; The World About Us, 1976; The Spirit of 76, 1976; Diamonds in the Sky, 1979; Nature Watch, 5 series, 1981-90; Automania, 1984; The Living Isles, 1986; Africawatch, 1989; Missionaries, 1990; BBC Assignment, 1993-94; BBC Correspondent, 1994-95. Publications: Co-author: Diamonds in the Sky: a social history of air travel, 1979; Nature Watch, 1981; Automania, 1984; The Nature Watchers, 1985; Missionaries, 1990; Nature Watch, 1994. Honours: Reporter of the Year Award, Guild of Television Directors and Producers, 1968; Vice-President, Royal Society for Nature Conservation, 1992-; Trustee, Royal Botanic Gardens, Kew, 1993-; President, Royal Society for the Protection of Birds, 1994. Address: c/o Curtis Brown, 28/29 Haymarket, London SW1Y 4SP, England.

PEYREFITTE (Pierre) Roger, b. 17 Aug 1907, Castres (Tarn), France. Author. Education: BA, Ecole des Sciences Politiques, Paris. Publications: Les amitiés particulières, 1944-45; Mademoiselle de Murville, 1946; Le prince des neiges, 1947; L'oracle, 1948; Les amours singulières, 1949; La Mort d'une mère, 1950; Les ambassades, 1951; Du Vesuve a l'Etna, 1952; Les clés de St Pierre, 1955; Jeunes Proies, 1956; Chevaliers de Malte, 1957; L'exile de Capri, 1959; Le Spectateur nocturne, 1960; Les fils de la lumière, 1961; La nature du prince, 1963; Les Juifs, 1965; Notre Amour, 1967; Les Americains, 1968; Des Francais, 1970; La Coloquinte, 1971; Manouche, 1972; La muse garçonnière, 1973; Tableaux de chasse ou la vie extraordinaire de Femand Legros, 1976; Propos secrets, 1977; La Jeunesses d'Alexandre, 1977; L'enfant de coeur, 1978; Roy, 1979; Les conquêtes d'Alexandre, 1979; Propos Secrets II, 1980; Alexandre Le Grand, 1981; L'illustre écrivain, 1982; La soutane rouge, 1983; Henry de Montherlant-Roger Peyrefitte correspondence, 1983; Voltaire, sa Jeunesse et son Temps, 1985; L'Innominato, nouveaux propos secrets, 1989; Reflexion sur De Gaulle, 1992. Honours: Prix Theophaste Renaudot. Address: 9 avenue du Marechal Manoury, 75016, Paris, France.

PEYTON K(athleen) W(endy), (Kathleen Herald), b. 2 Aug 1929. Writer. m. Michael Peyton, 1950, 2 daughters. Education: ATD, Manchester School of Art. Publications: As Kathleen Herald: Sabre, the Horse from the Sea, 1947, USA, 1963; The Mandrake, 1949; Crab the Roan, 1953; As K M Peyton: North to Adventure, 1959, USA, 1965; Stormcock Meets Trouble, 1961; The Hard Way Home, 1962; Windfall, 1963, USA as Sea Fever, 1963; Brownsea Silver, 1964; The Maplin Bird, 1964, USA, 1965; The Plan for Birdsmarsh, 1965, USA, 1966; Thunder in the Sky, 1966, USA, 1967; Flambards Trilogy, 1969-71; The Beethoven Medal, 1971, USA, 1972; The Pattern of Roses, 1972, USA, 1973; Pennington's Heir, 1973, USA, 1974; The Team, 1975; The Right-Hand Man, 1977; Prove Yourself a Hero, 1977, USA, 1978; A Midsummer Night's Death, 1978, USA, 1979; Marion's Angels, 1979, USA, 1979; Flambards Divided, 1981; Dear Fred, 1981; Going Home, 1983, USA, 1983; The Last Ditch, 1984, USA as Free Rein, 1983; Froggett's Revenge, 1985; The Sound of Distant Cheering, 1986; Downhill All The Way, 1988; Darkling, 1989; Skylark, 1989; No Roses Round The Door, 1990; Poor Badger, 1991, USA, 1991; Late to Smile, 1992; The Boy Who Wasn't There, 1992, USA, 1992; The Wild Boy and Queen Moon, 1993; Snowfall, 1994. Honours: New York Herald Tribune Award, 1965; Carnegie Medal, 1969; Guardian Award, 1970. Address: Rookery Cottage, North Farnbridge, Chelmsford, Essex CM3 6LP, England.

PEYTON Richard. See: HAINING Peter Alexander.

PFANNER (Anne) Louise, b. 6 Mar 1955, Sydney, New South Wales, Australia. Illustrator; Writer. m. (1) Glenn Woodley, 24 Dec 1976, (2) Tim Maddox, 12 Jan 1987, 4 sons. Education: Diploma, Graphic Design, 1977; BA, Visual Communication, 1986. Career includes: Regular exhibits of illustrations. Publications: Louise Builds a Boat, 1986; Louise Builds a House, 1987; Illustrator: Your Book of Magic Secrets (R Deutch), 1991. Contributions to: Illustrations to various magazines; Regular illustrations to Sydney's Child; Illustrations to Favourite Stories from Playschool, 1991; Wrote and illustrated story, El Nido, for Playschool. Membership: Society of Book Illustrators, Sydney. Literary Agent: Barbara Mobbs, PO 126, Edgecliffe, New South Wales 2027, Australia. Address: 4 Catalpa Avenue, Avalon, New South Wales 2107, Australia

PFEFFER Susan Beth, 1948, USA. Children's Fiction Writer. Publications: Just Morgan, 1970; Better Than All Right, 1972; Rainbows and Fireworks, 1973; The Beauty Queen, 1974; Whatever Words You Want To Hear, 1974; Marly The Kid, 1975; Kid Power, 1977; Starring Peter and Leigh, 1979; Awful Eveline, 1979; Just Between Us, 1980; About David, 1980; What Do You Want When Your Mouth Won't Open, 1981; A Matter of Principle, 1982; Courage, Dana, 1983; Fantasy Summer, 1984; Paperdolls, 1984; On The Move, 1985; Starting With Melodie, 1985; Make Me a Star, series, 6 Vols, 1986; The Friendship, 1986; Getting Even, 1986; HardTimes High, 1986; Address: 14 S Railroad Avenue, Middletown, NJ 10940, USA.

PHELAN Mary Kay, b. 1914, USA. Children's Author. Publications: The White House, 1962; The Circus, 1963; Mother's Day, 1965; Mr Lincoln Speaks at Gettysburg, 1866; The Fourth of July, 1966; Election Day, 1967; Four days at Philadelphia, 1967; Midnight Alarm: the Story of Paul Revere's Ride, 1968; Probing the Unknown: The Story of Dr Florence Sabin, 1969; The Great Chicago Fire, 1971; Martha Berry, 1971; Mr Lincoln's Inaugural Journey, 1972; The Story of the Boston Tea Party, 1973; The Burning of Washington 1914, 1975; The Story of the Boston Massacre, 1976; Waterway West: The Story of the Erie Canal, 1977; The Story of the Louisiana Purchase, 1979; The Story of the United States Constitution, 1987.

PHELPS Gilbert Henry, b. 23 Jan 1915. Writer. m. (1) 1 s, 1d, (2) Kay Batchelor, 23 Oct 1972, 3 ss. Education: BA, 1st Class Honours, Fitzwilliam, Cambridge, 1934-37; Research and Teaching, St John's College, Cambridge, 1937-39; MA, 1941. Appointments: Lecturer and Tutor, Cambridge University Board of Extra-Mural Studies, 1937-39; Senior Producer, BBC Third Programme, 1950-55; Editor, Latin-American Series, 1972-77; Broadcaster and BBC Script Writer; Introductions for Folio Society. Publications include: novels: The Dry Stone, 1953; The Heart in the Desert, 1954; A Man in His Prime, 1955; The Centenarians, 1958; The Love Before the First, 1960; The Winter People, 1963; Tenants of the House, 1971; The Old Believer, 1973; The Low Roads, 1975; non-fiction: The Russian Novel in English Fiction, 1956; The Last Horizon: Travels in Brazil, 1964; A Survey of English Literature, 1965; The Byronic Byron, 1971; The Tragedy of Paraguay, 1975; Squire Waterton, 1976; An Introduction to Fifty British Novels 1600-1900, 1979; From Myth to Modernism: A Short Guide to the World Novel, 1988; Post-War Literature and Drama, 1988. Contributions to: The Pelican Guide to English Literature, 1987; The Cambridge Journal;Slavonic Review; World Review; New Statesman; Times Literary Supplement. Memberships: Fellow, Royal Society of Literature; Society of Authors, Panel of Judges for various literary awards; Southern Arts, Chairman, Literature Panel, 1976-79; PEN; Fellow, Royal Commonwealth Society. Address: The Cottage, School Road, Finstock, Oxford OX7 3DJ, England.

PHILANDERSON Flavian Titus, (John Stimulus, Flavian P Stimulus, Johnny Goad), b. 3 Mar 1933, Penang, British Malaya. High School Teacher; Freelance Journalist; Writer. m. Martha Bernadette Pillai, 29 Dec 1956, 2 sons, 2 daughters. Education: Overseas School Certificate A, University of Cambridge, 1951; Teacher Training, Ministry of Education, British Administration, Malaya; Fiction Writing, Premier School of Journalism, Fleet Street, London. Publications: A Course in Primary English (co-author), set texts for ESL students, 1969; Sun Never Sets; Zigzags; Optics of Being; Window in the Sky, novel, 1982; Diary of a Sydney Girl, 1992; All Flesh Is Grass, 1995. Contributions to: Various, 1953-84, 1989-91, including: Straits Echo and Times of Malaya; Her World; Wm Own. Memberships: Australian Society of Authors; Royal Australian Historical Society; History Teachers Association; Fellowship of Australian Writers; Independent Teachers Association; National Geographical Association. Address: 32 Hillcrest Avenue, Winston Hills, Sydney, New South Wales 2153, Australia.

PHILLIPS Caryl, b. 13 Mar 1958, St Kitts, West Indies. British Citizen. Playwright; Novelist. Education: BA, Oxford University, 1979. Appointments include: Visiting Writer, Amherst College, MA, 1990. Publications: Strange Fruit, 1980; Where There is Darkness, 1982; The Shelter, 1983; The Wasted Years, 1984; Playing Away, Screenplay, 1987; Novelist: The Final Passage, 1985; A State of Independence, 1986; Cambridge, 1991; Higher Ground, 1989; Crossing the River, 1993; The European Tribe, non-fiction, 1987; Radio & TV Plays. Honours: Martin Luther King Memorial Prize, 1987; Guggenheim Fellow, 1992; James Tait Black Memorial Prize, 1993; Lannan Foundation Fiction Award, 1994. Address: c/o Haymarket House, 28/29 Haymarket, London SW1Y 4SP, England.

PHILLIPS Edward O, b. 26 Nov 1931, Montreal, Canada. Teacher; Writer. Education: BA, McGill University, 1953; LL.L, University of Montreal, 1956; AMT, Harvard University, 1957; MA, Boston University, 1962. Publications: Sunday's Child, 1981; Where Theres A Will, 1984; Buried on Sunday, 1986; Hope Springs Eternal, 1988; Sunday Best, 1990; The Landlady's Niece, 1992. Contributions to: Short stories to various Canadian journals. Honours: Arthur Ellis Award, 1986. Memberships: Canadian Writers Union; Union des ecrivains quebecois; PEN. Literary Agent: Lucinda Vardy Agency, Toronto, Canada. Address: 425 Wood Avenue, Westmount, Quebec, H3Y 3J3, Canada.

PHILLIPS Jayna Anne, b. 1952, USA. Writer. Appointments: Has taught: Humboldt State University, Arcata, California; Boston University, Massachusetts; Williams College, Williamstown, Massachusetts. Publications: Sweethearts, short stories, 1976; Counting, short stories, 1978; Black Tickets, short stories, 1979; How Mickey Made it, short stories, 1981; Fast Lanes, short stories, 1984; Machine Dreams, novel, 1984; Shelter, 1994. Literary Agent: Lynn Nesbit, ICM, USA. Address: c/o Lynn Nesbit, ICM, 40 West 57th Street, New York, NY 10019, USA.

PHILLIPS Michael. See: **NOLAN William F(rancis)**.

PHILLIPS Shelley, b. 18 Mar 1934, Melbourne, Victoria, Australia. Psychological Consultant; Writer. 2 daughters. Education: BA (Hons), English, History, University of Melbourne; BA, Psychology, University of Western Australia; PhD, Sydney University, 1972; Visiting Scientist, Programme Associate, Tavistock Clinic, London, 1975-76, 1978-79, 1982-83. Publications: Young Australian. The Attitudes of Our Children, 1979; Relations With Children. The Psychology of Human Development in a Changing World, 1986; Beyond the Myths. Mother Daughter Relations in Psychology, History, Literature and Everyday Life, 1991; Contributing author: Advances in Child Development, 1981; The Sociogenesis of Language and Human Conduct, 1982; Chapters in many books about psychological development and relationships. Contributions to: International and professional journals including: Oxford Review of Education; Paedagogica Historica; Psychologia; Journal of Psychology; Child Study Journal; Selected Papers Unit for Child Studies, University of New South Wales; Sensibilities; Australian and New Zealand Journal of Sociology; Inventory of Marriage and Family Literature. Honours include: Prox Accesit Arts Convocation Prize, University of Western Australia, 1959; Honorary academic appointments: University of Birmingham, England, 1975, Georgia State University, USA, 1975, University of Alberta, Canada, 1976; London University Institute of Education, 1979, Institute of Early Childhood Studies, Melbourne, 1982; University College, London, 1983; Research grants. Memberships: Australian Society of Authors; Committee Member, Society of Women Writers; Jane Austen Society; National Trust; Australian Psychological Society; Board of Educational and Developmental Psychologists; Alumni of Universities of Melbourne, Sydney and New South Wales. Address: Sydney, New South Wales, Australia.

PHILLIPSON (Charles) Michael, b. 16 June 1940, Gatley, Cheshire, England. Freelance Painter; Writer. m. Julia Hauxwell, 1 Sept 1971, 1 son, 2 daughters. Education: BA, 1961, MA, 1964, Nottingham University. Publications: Making Fuller Use of Survey Data, 1968; Sociological Aspects of Crime and Delinquency, 1971; New Directions in Sociological Theory (co-author), 1972; Understanding Crime and Delinquency, 1974; Problems of Reflexivity and Dialectics in Sociological Inquiry (co-author), 1975; Painting, Language and Modernity, 1985; In Modernity's Wake, 1989. Contributions to: Reviews to sociology journals; Articles and reviews to Artscribe International, 1986-88. Address: Derlwyn, Glandwr, Hebron, Whitland, Dyfed SA34 0YD, Wales.

PHILP Peter, b. 10 Nov 1920, Cardiff, Wales. Writer. m. 25 Sept 1940, 2 sons. Publications: Beyond Tomorrow, 1947; The Castle of Deception, 1952; Love and Lunacy, 1955; Antiques Today, 1960; Antique Furniture for the Smaller Home, 1962; Furniture of the World, 1974. Contributions to: The Times; Antique Dealer and Collectors Guide; Antique Collecting; Antique Furniture Expert (with Gillian Walkling), 1991. Honours: Arts Council Award, 1951; C H Foyle Award, 1951. Membership: Society of Authors. Address: 77 Kimberley Road, Cardiff CF2 5DP, Wales.

PHIPPS Christine, b. 5 Dec 1945, Bristol, England. University Lecturer; Counsellor. div. Education: BA 1st Class Honours, Hull University, 1968; MLitt, St Hugh's College, Oxford University, 1971; Advanced Diploma in Linguistics, Lancaster University, 1986; Advanced Diploma in Counselling, Wigan College of Technology, 1989. Publication: Buckingham: Public and Private Man (George Villiers 1628-1687), 1985. Contributions to: Notes and Queries Journal, Oxford University. Address: 21 Hurstway, Fulwood, Preston, Lancashire PR2 4TT, England.

PHIPSON Joan. See: **FITZHARDINGE Joan Margaret**.

PICANO Felice, b. 22 Feb 1944, New York City, USA. Author. Education: BA cum laude, Queens College, City of New York University, 1960. Publications: Smart As The Devil, 1975; Eyes, 1976; Deformity Lover and Other Poems, 1977; The Lure, 1979; Late in the Season, 1980; An Asian Minor, 1981; Slashed to Ribbons in Defense of Love and Other Stories, 1982; House of Cards, 1984; Ambidextrous, 1985; Men Who Loved Me, 1989; To the Seventh Power, 1989; The New Joy of Gay Sex, 1992; Dryland's End, 1995; Like People In History, 1995. Contributions to: Men on Men; The Violet Quill Reader; Numerous magazines and journals. Honours: Finalist, Ernest Hemingway Award; PEN Syndicated Short Fiction Award; Chapbook Award, Poetry Society of America. Memberships: PEN Club; Writers Guild of America; Authors Guild; Publishing Triangle. Literary Agent: Malaga Baldi. Address: 95 Horatio Street 423, New York City, NY 10014, USA.

PICARD Barbara Leonie, b. 4 Dec 1917, Richmond, Surrey, England. Author. Publications: Ransom for a Knight, 1956; Lost John, 1962; One is One, 1965; The Young Pretenders, 1966; Twice Seven Tales, 1968; Three Ancient Kings, 1972; Tales of Ancient Persia, 1972; The Iliad and Odyssey of Homer, 1986; French Legends, Tales and Fairy Stories, 1992; German Hero-sagas and Folk-tales, 1993; Tales of the Norse Gods, 1994; Selected Fairy Tales, 1994. Address: Oxford University Press, Walton Street, Oxford, England.

PICARD Robert George, b. 5 July 1951, Pasadena, California, USA. Professor; Author. m. Elizabeth Carpelan, 15 Sept 1979, 2 daughters and 1 son. Education: BA, Loma Kinda University, 1974; MA, California State University, Fullerton, 1980; PhD, University of Missouri, 1983. Appointments: Editor, Journal of Media Economics, 1988-; Associate Editor, Political Communication and Persuasion, 1989-91. Publications: Media Economics: Concepts and Issues, 1989; Press Concentration and Monopoly, 1988; The Ravens of Odin: The Press in the Nordic Nations, 1988; The Press and the Decline of Democracy, 1985; In The Camera's Eye: News Coverage of Terrorist Events, 1991; Media Portrayals of terrorism: Functions and Meaning of News Coverage, 1993; The Cable Networks Handbook, 1993; Joint Operating Agreements: The Newspaper Preservation Act and its Application, 1993. Address: 2806 Gertrude Street, Riverside, CA 92506, USA.

PICK Frederick Michael, b. Jun 1949, Leicestershire, England. Antique Dealer; Designer/Director; Author; Lecturer. Education: MA, History & Law, Gonville & Caius College, Cambridge. Publications: The English Room, 1985; The National Trust Pocket Guide to Furniture, 1985; The English Country Room, 1988; Biography of the Late Sir Norman Hartnell KCVO, in progress. Contributions to: Antique Collector; Apollo; Art and Auction (USA); Antique and New Art; Connoisseur; Harpers and Queen; Journal of the Thirties Society; the Times; Vogue (Germany). Honour: 1969 Exhibitioner in History, Gonville and Caius, Cambridge. Memberships: Society of Authors; Founder Committee Member, The Twentieth Century Society; The Royal Society for Asian Affairs; The British Antique Dealer Association; Committee and Council Member The Lansdowne Club. Address: 114 Mount Street, London W1Y 5RA, England.

PICKARD Tom, b. 7 Jan 1946, Newcastle-on-Tyne, England. Writer/Director (Freelance). m. Joanna Voit, 22 Jul 1978, 2 s, 1 d.

Publications: Guttersnipe - City Lights, novella, 1971; Hero Dust, poetry, 1979; Jarrow March, oral history, 1982; Custom and Exile, poetry, 1985; We Make Ships, oral history, 1989; Tell Them in Gdansk, TV documentary (director), 1989; Word of Mouth, international poetry series (director and series editor). Honours: Arts Council Writer-in-Residence at Warwick University, 1979-80. Memberships: General Council, ACTT. Literary Agent: Judy Daish Associates, England. Address: c/o Judy Daish Assocates, 83 Eastbourne Mews, London W2 6LQ, England.

PICKERING Edward Davies, Sir, b. 4 May 1912. Journalist. Appointments: Chief Sub Editor, Daily Mail, 1939; RA 1940-44; Staff, Supreme HQ Allied Expeditionay Force, 1944-45; Managing Editor, Daily Mail, 1947-49, Daily Express 1951-57; Editor, Daily Express, 1957-62; Director, Beaverbrook Newspapers, 1956-63; Managing Director, Beaverbrook Publications, 1962-63; Editorial Director & Director, The Daily Mirror Newspapers Ltd, 1964-68; Editorial Director, International Publishing Corporation, Chairman IPC, Newspaper Division, Chair, Daily Mirror Newspapers Ltd, 1968-70; Chairman, IPC Magazines Ltd, 1970-74; Chairman, Mirror Group Newspapers Ltd, 1974-77; Director, Reed Publishing Holdings, 1977-81, Times Newspapers Holdings, 1981-, William Collins, 1981-. Honours: HonDLitt, City University, London, 1986. Memberships: Vice President, Periodical Publishers Association, 1971-. Address: Chatley House, Norton St Philip, Somerset, England.

PICKERING Howard Charles, b. 14 April 1943, Brisbane, Australia. Teacher. m. Lorraine Pickering (Purdy), 13 Dec 1965, 1 son, 1 daughter. Education: Advanced Trade. Publications: Senior Graphics, 1988; Junior Graphics, 1989; Introducing Graphics, 1990. Memberships: Industrial Technology and Design Teachers Association of Queensland; President, Secretary, Treasurer, Editor, Institute of Technology Education NSW; Queensland Society for Information Technology. Address: 11 Kiriwina Street, Fig Tree Pocket, Queensland 4069, Australia.

PICTON Bernard. See: KNIGHT Bernard.

PIECHOCKI Stanisław Ryszard, b. 8 Feb 1955, Olsztyn, Poland. Lawyer. m. Elzbieta Piechocki, 29 Oct 1979, 1 daughter. Education: MSc, Department of Law, University of Torun, 1978. Publications: Na krancu drogi (On the End of Way), story, 1975; Przedostatni przystanek (The Last But One Stop), novel, 1980; Tekturowe czolgi (The Cardboard Tanks), novel, 1983; Przyladek burz (Cape of Storm), novel, 1989; Czysciec zwany Kortau (Purgatory called Kortau), report, 1993; Przysposobienie dziecka (Adoption of Child), science material, 1993; Dzieje olsztynskich ulic (History of Streets in Olsztyn), tales, 1994. Contributions to: Local magazines and journals, Olsztyn; Historical publications relating to former East Prussia. Honours: Ignacy Krasicki Memorial Medal for Best First Novel, 1980; Award, Minister of Culture and Art, 1984. Memberships: Polish Writers Association; President, Revisory Commission, Olsztyn; Polish Lawyers Association; Society of the Friends of Warmia and Masuriás Literature, Member of Authorities. Address: ul Iwaszkiewicza 16 m 28, 10-089 Olsztyn, Poland.

PIELMEIER John, b. 3 Feb 1949, Altoona, Pennsylvania, USA. Dramatist; Actor. m. Irene O'Brian, 9 Oct 1982. Education: BA, Catholic University of America; MFA, Pennsylvania State University. Publications: Agnes of God, 1983; Haunted Lives (A Witches Brew, A Ghost Story, A Gothic Tale), 1984. Honours include: Christopher Award, 1984; Humanitas Award, 1984. Memberships: Writers Guild of America; Dramatists Guild; American Federation of Television and Radio Artists; Actors Equity Association. Literary Agent: Artists Agency, USA. Address: C/o Artists Agency, 230 West 55th Street, New York, NY 10019, USA.

PIERACCINI Giovanni, b. 25 Nov 1918, Viareggio, Italy. Journalist; Politician. m. Vera Verdiani. Education: University of Pisa. Appointments: Organiser, Young Socialist Federation; Editorial Staff, La Nazione del Popolo, 1944-46; Joint Editor, Nuovo Corriere, 1946-48; Editor, Avanti, 1959-63. Memberships: President, Commercial Industry, Commerce and Tourism; Minister for Scientific and Technological Affairs; President, Socialist Group in Senate; President, Assitalia Insurance Co, SEC; ISLE, SIAC (from 1979; Minister Public Affairs (1963/64); Minister Budget Affairs (1965/68); Minister Merchant Navy (1973/74); Member of Parliament in six legislatures (Deputy and Senator); Managemnet of the Italian Socialist Party; Board of Directors of STET and UNIORIAS; Board of Management of ANIA.

PIERARD Richard V, b. 1934, USA. Professor of History. Appointments: Member, Indiana Governor's Advisory Commission on Libraries and Information Services, 1980-81. Publications: Protest and Politics: Christianity and Contemporary Affairs (edited with R G Clouse and R D Linder), 1968; The Unequal Yoke: Evangelical Christianity and Political Conservatism, 1970; The Cross and the Flag (edited with R G Clouse and R D Linder), 1972; Politics: A Case for Christian Action (with R D Linder), 1973; Twilight of the Saints (with R D Linder), 1978; Streams of Civilization, vol II (with R G Clouse), 1980; Bibliography on the Religious Right in America, 1986; Civil Religion and the Presidency (with R D Linder) 1988; Two Kingdoms: The Church and Culture Through the Ages (with R G Clouse and E M Yarnauchi) 1993. Address: Department of History, Indiana State University, Terre Haute, IN 47809, USA.

PIERCE Meredith Ann, b. 5 Jul 1958, Seattle, Washington, USA. Novelist. Education: AA Liberal Arts, 1976, BA English, 1978, MA English, 1980, University of Florida. Publications: The Darkangel, 1982; A Gathering of Gargoyles, 1984; The Woman Who Loved Reindeer, 1985; Birth of the Firebringer, 1985; Where the Wild Geese Go, 1988; Rampion (novella), in Four From the Witch World, 1989, Andre Norton (ed); The Pearl of the Soul of the World (vol III of the Darkangel Trilogy), 1990. Contributions to: Scholastic Magazine; Mythlore XXXi; The Horn Book; The Alan Review; The New Advocate. Honours: National First Prize, Scholastic Creative Writing Awards Contest, Scholastic Magazine, 1973; Graduate Teaching Assisstant Award, Univerity of Florida, English Department, 1979-80; The Darkangel; International Reading Association's Children's Book Award, Listed on American Language Association's Best Books for Young Adults Roster; ALA Best of the Best Books List, Chosen for New York Times Notable Children's Book List; Appeared on Parents' Choice Award Book Roster, 1982; Jane Tinkham Broughton Fellow in Writing for Children, Bread Loaf Writers' Conference, 1984; A Gathering of Gargoyles: ALA Best Books For Young Adults semifinalist, 1985; The Woman Who Loved Reindeer: Parents: Choice Book Award for Literature, 1985, AIA Best Book for Young Adults, 1985, New York Public Library's Books for the Teenage Participant, 1986; The Darkangel: Califomia Young Reader Medal, 1986; Where The Wild Geese Go: Florida Department of State's Division of Cutural Affairs Individual Artist Fellowship Special Award for Children's Literature, 1987. Memberships: Phi Beta Kappa; Secretary-Treasurer Children's Literature Association's annual convention, 1982; The Author's Guild Inc; Science Fiction Writers of America. Address: 703 NW 19th Street, Gainsville, FL 32603, USA.

PIERCY Margo, b. 31 Mar 1936, Detroit, Michigan, USA. Poet and Writer. Publications include: (poetry) Gone to Soldiers; Breaking Camp; Hard Loving; To Be Of Use; The Moon Is Always Female; Available Light, 1988; He, She and It, 1991; Mars and Her Children, 1992; The Longings of Women, 1994; (non-fiction) Going Down Fast; Women on the Edge of Time; Braided Lives; (play) The Last White Class. Address: Box 1473, Welfleet, MA 02667, USA.

PIERRE José, b. 24 Nov 1927, Bénesse-Maremne, France. Writer. m. Nicole Pierre, 5 Sept 1953. Education includes: Docteur ès-Lettres, Sorbonne, Paris, 1979. Career includes: Director of Research, Centre National de la Recherche Scientifique. Publications: Qu'est-ce que Thérèse? -C'est les marronniers en fleurs, novel, 1974; Gauguin aux Marquises, novel, 1982; L'Univers Surréaliste, history of art, 1983; André Breton et la peinture, 1987; L'Univers Symboliste, history of art and literature, 1991; Plays: Magdeleine LeClerc, le dernier amour du Marquis de Sade, 1993. Contributions to: La Quinziane Littéraire, 1969-76. Memberships: Société des Gens de Lettres; Association Internationale des Critiques d'Art, Section France. Address: 2 rue Cournot, 75015 Paris, France.

PIKE Charles R. See: BULMER Henry Kenneth.

PIKE Charles R. See: HARKNETT Terry.

PILCHER Rosamunde, (Jane Fraser), b. 1924. Writer (Romance, Plays, Screenplays). m. Graham Pilcher, 4 children. Appointments: During World War II: Worked for Foreign Office in Bedfordshire; Served with Women's Royal Naval Service, Portsmouth, England and Trincomalee, Sri Lanka, with East Indies Fleet. Publications: A Secret to Tell (as Rosamunde Pilcher); April, 1957; On My Own, 1965; Sleeping Tiger, 1967; Another View, 1969; The End of the Summer, 1971; Snow in April, 1972; The Empty House, 1973; The Day of the Storm, 1975; Under Gemini, 1977; Wild Mountain Thyme, 1978; The Carousel, 1981; Voices in Summer, 1984; The Blue

Bedroom and Other Stories, 1985; The Shell Seekers, 1988; September, 1989; Flowers in the Rain, 1991; Plays with C C Gairdner: The Piper of Order; The Dashing White Sergeant, 1955; The Tulip Major, 1959. Contributions to: Woman and Home; Good Housekeeping. Address: Over Pilmore, Invergowrie, by Dundee, Scotland.

PILGRIM Anne. See: **ALLAN Mabel Esther.**

PILGRIM Constance Maud Eva, b. 3 Dec 1911, London, England. Writer. m. (1) Paul Smither, 29 Dec 1934 (dec 2 Sep 1943), 1 s, 1 d,(2) Richard Pilgrim, 10 Sep 1957 (dec 5 Jun 1979). Education: Textile Design, Eastbourne School of Art; English Literature Course, Oxford. Publications: Dear Jane, Biographical research, Jane Austen, 1971, re-print, 1991; This is Illyria, lady, life/rambles & friends of Jane Austen, 1991; also: You Precious Winners All, study of the Winter's Tale completed and left in MSS by Reverend Richard Pilgrim (1979) seen through press by C Pilgrim, published 1983. Contributions to: Persuasions, 1988 (journal of JASNA, Jane Austen Society of North America); varoious journals and magazines. Memberships: The Society of Authors: West Country Writers Association: The Jane Austen Society, Bath & Bristol. Address: 24 Withington Court, Abingdon, Oxfordshire, OX14 3QB, England.

PILKINGTON Roger Windle, b. 17 Jan 1915, St Helens, England. Author. m. (1) Miriam Jaboor, 27 July 1937, (2) Ingrid Geijer, 11 Oct 1972. Education: Magdalene College, Cambridge, 1933-37; MA (Cantab); PhD. Publications: 20 volumes in Small Boat series, including: Small Boat Down the Years, 1988; Small Boat in the Midi, 1989; Scientific philosophy and Christianity, notably: World Without End, 1960; Heavens Alive, 1962; Children's books including: The Ormering Tide, 1974; I Sailed on the Mayflower, 1990; One Foot in France, 1992; View from the Shore, 1995. Contributions to: Sunday Telegraph; Guardian. Honours: Chevalier, Compagnons du Minervois. Membership: Master, Glass Sellers Company, 1968. Address: Les Cactus, Moutouliers 34 310, France.

PILLING Christopher (Robert), b. 20 Apr 1936, Birmingham, England. Writer; Teacher. m. Sylvia Hill, 6 Aug 1960, 1 son, 2 daughters. Education: BA Hons, University of Leeds, 1957; Diplôme d'Etudes Françaises, Université de Poitiers, 1955; Certificate of Education, Loughborough College, 1959. Appointments: Assistant d'Anglais, Ecole Normale d'Institeurs, Moulins, Allier, France, 1957-58; Teacher, French, Physical Education: Wirral Grammar School, Cheshire, England, 1959-61; King Edward's Grammar School for Boys, Camp Hill, Birmingham, 1961-62; Teacher, French, Housemaster, Ackworth School, Yorkshire, 1962-73; Head, Modem Languages, Housemaster, Knottingley High School, West Yorkshire, 1973-78; Head, French, Teacher, German, Latin, Keswick School, Cumbria, 1980-88; Reviewer, Times Literary Supplement, 1973-74. Publications: Snakes and Girls, 1970; In All The Spaces On All The Lines, 1971; Foreign Bodies, 1992; Cross Your Legs and Wish, 1994; Various broadsheets; Books containing poems include: Oxford Book of Christmas Poems; The Oxford Book of Verse in English Translation; PEN Anthologies; Peterloo Anthologies; Four Poetry and Audience Poets, 1971; Adam's Dream, 1981; Northern Poetry 2, The New Lake Poets, 1991; Poetry Book Society Anthology, 1992; The Forward Book of Poetry, 1994. Contributions to: New Welsh Review; Observer; Times Literary Supplement; London Magazine; New Statesman; Critical Quarterly; Encounter; Ambit; Arts Council New Poetry; Spectator; Lettres d' Europe; The Independent; Poetry Review; Pennine Platform. Address: 25 High Hill, Keswick, Cumbria CA12 5NY, England.

PILON Jean-Guy, b. 12 Nov 1930, St Polycarpe, Québec, Canada. Writer; Radio Producer & Broadcaster. Education: Law Graduate, University of Montreal, 1954. Appointments include: Founder 1959, Director 1959-79, Review, Liberte; Head, Cultural Broadcast Service, 1970-85; Producer, Radio Canada. Publications include: Poetry: La Fiancee du Matin, 1953; Les Cloitres de l'Ete, 1955; L'Homme et le Jour, 1957; La Mouette et le Large, 1960; Recours au Pays, 1961; Pour Saluer une Ville, 1963; Comme eau retenue, 1969, revised 1985; Saisons pour la Continuelle, 1969; Silences pour une Souveraine, 1972. Articles: tourism, literature, writers, poets. Contributions to: La Presse, Le Devoir, 1960-80; Frequent service to various national juries including Prix David & international juries including Prix Gilson, Prix Canada-Belgique. Honours include: Québec Poetry Prize, Prix David, 1956; Louise Labe Prize, 1969; France-Canada Prize, 1969; Van Larberghe Prize, Paris, 1969; Govemor-General of Canada Prize, 1970; Athanase David Prize, 1984; Officer, Order of Canada, 1987. Memberships: President, Intemational

Québec Writers Union; Royal Society of Canada; President de l'Academie des lettes du Québec, depuis, 1982; Officer de l'Ordre des Atrts et des lettres (France), 1993. Address: 5724 Cote Saint-Antoine, Montréal, Québec, H4A 1R9, Canada.

PINCHER (Henry) Chapman, b. 29 Mar 1914, Ambala, India. Freelance Writer; Novelist; Business Consultant. m. (1) 1 daughter, 1 son. (2) Constance Wolstenholme, 1965. Education: BSc Honours, Botany, Zoology, 1935. Appointments: Staff, Liverpool Institute, 1936-40; Royal Armoured Corps, 1940; Defence Science and Medical Editor, Daily Express, 1946-73; Assistant Editor, Daily Express, Chief Defence Correspondent, Beaverbrook Newspapers, 1972-79. Publications: Breeding of Farm Animals, 1946; A Study of Fishes, 1947; Into the Atomic Age, 1947; Spotlight on Animals, 1950; Evolution, 1959; It's Fun Finding Out (with Bernard Wicksteed), 1950; Sleep and How to Get More of It, 1954; Sex in Our Time, 1973; Inside Story, 1978; Their Trade is Treachery, 1981; Too Secret Too Long, 1984; The Secret Offensive, 1985; Traitors - the Labyrinth of Treason, 1987; A Web of Deception, 1987; The Truth about Dirty Tricks, 1991; One Dog and Her Man, 1991; Pastoral Symphony, 1993; A Box of Chocolates, 1993; Novels: Not with a Bang, 1965; The Giantkiller, 1967; The Penthouse Comspirators, 1970; The Skeleton at the Villa Wolkonsky, 1975; The Eye of the Tornado, 1976; The Four Horses, 1978; Dirty Tricks, 1980; The Private World of St John Terrapin, 1982; Contamination, 1989. Honours: Granada Award, Journalist of the Year, 1964; Reporter of the Decade, 1966; Honorary DLitt, Newcastle-upon-Tyne, 1979. Address: The Church House, 16 Church Street, Kintbury, Near Hungerford, Berkshire RG15 0TR, England.

PINGET Robert, b. 19 Jul 1919, Geneva, Switzerland. Writer. Education: Univwersity of Geneva. Appointments: Former Barrister, later Painter; Teacher, French in England; literary career, 1951-. Publications: Fantoine et Agapa, 1951; Mahu et la Materiau, 1952; Le renard et la Loussoule, 1955; Graal Filibuste, 1956; Baga, 1958; Le Fiston, 1959; Lettre morte (play), 1959; La manivelle (play), 1960; Clope au dossier, 1961; Architruc (play), 1961; L'hypothese (play), 1961; L'inquisitore, 1962; Quelqu'un, 1965; Autour de Mortin (dialogue), 1965; Le libera, 1968; La passacaille, 1969; Fable, 1971 Identite, Abel et Bela (play), 1971; Paralchimie, 1973; Cette voix, 1975; L'Apocryphe, 1980; Monsieur Songe, 1982; Le harnais, 1984. Honours: Prix des Critiques, 1963; prix Femina, 1965. Address: c/o Editions de Minuit, 7 rue Bernard-Palissey, 75006, Paris, France.

PINNER David John, b. 6 Oct 1940. Writer. m. Catherine, 23 Oct 1965, 1 s, 1 d. Education: Royal Academy of Dramatic Art, 1959-60. Publications: stage plays: Dickon, 1965; Fanghom, 1966; The Drums of Snow, 1969; the Potsdam Quartet, 1973; An Evening with The GLC, 1974; The Last Englishman, 1975; Lucifer's Fair, 1979; Screwball, 1985; The Teddy Bears' Picnic, 1988; TV plays: Juliet and Romeo, 1975; 2 Crown Courts, 1978; The Potsdam Quartet, 1980; The Sea Horse; novels: Ritual, 1967, 1968; With My Body, 1968; Corgi, 1969; There'll Always Be an England, 1984. Address: Barnes, London, England.

PINNEY Lucy Catherine, b. 25 July 1952, London, England. Author; Journalist. m. Charles Pinney, 14 June 1975, 2 sons, 1 daughter. Education: BA Honours, English, Education, York University, 1973. Publications: The Pink Stallion, 1988; Tender Moth, 1994; Short story in The Best of the Fiction Magazine Anthology, 1986. Contributions to: The Sunday Times; The Observer; The Daily Mail; The Telegraph; Company; Cosmopolitan; Country Living; Country Homes and Interiors; She magazine. Honours: Runner-up, Betty Trask Prize, 1987. Membership: West Country Authors Association. Literary Agent: Lisa Eveleigh, A P Watt Ltd. Address: Egremont Farm, Payhembury, Honiton, Devon EX14 0JA, England.

PINNOCK Winsome, b. 1961, London. Playwright. Education: BA, Goldsmiths College, London, 1982; MA, Birkbeck Coll, London. Appointments include: Playwright in Residence, Royal Court Theatre, London, 1991; Playwright in Residence, Tricycle Theatre, Kilburn, 1990; Playwright in Residence, Clean Break Theatre Company, 1994. Publications: The Wind of Change, 1987; Leave Taking, 1988; Picture Palace, 1988; A Rock in Water, 1989; A Hero's Welcome, 1989; Talking in Tongues, 1991; TV Plays, Episodes in South of the Border and Chalkface Series; Screenplay, Bitter Harvest. Honours include: Thames TV Award, 1991; George Devine Awd, 1991. Address: c/o Lemon, Unna and Durbridge, 24 Pottery Lane, Holland Park, London W11 4LZ, England.

PINSDORF Marion Katheryn,b. 22 June 1932, Teaneck, New Jersey, USA. Corporate Officer; Journalist; Professor. div. Education: BA cum laude, Drew University, Madison, New Jersey, 1954; MA, 1967, PhD, 1976, Brazilian Economic History, Graduate School of Arts and Sciences, New York University. Appointments: Business include: Vice President, Corporate Communications, Textron Inc, 1977-80, Ina Corporation, 1980-82; Member of the Board of Directors, AMFAC Inc, 1982-88; Vice President, 1971-77, Senior Consultants Programme and Senior Consultant, Hill and Knowlton, Inc, 1988-90; Academic Appointments include: Adjunct Assistant Professor, Brazilian Studies, Brown University, Providence, Rhode Island, 1979-; Senior Fellow in Communications, Graduate School of Business, 1988-, Fordham University. Publications: Books: Communicating When Your Company is Under Seige: Surviving Public Crises, 1987, 2nd ed. underway; German-Speaking Entrepreneurs: Builders of Business in Brazil South, 1990. Numerous articles, reviews and academic presentations. Contributions to: Public Relations Journal; Drew Magazine; PR Quarterly; Executive Challenge; Business Journalism Review; Executive Communications; Risk Management, FOCUS and a numer of others. Memberships include: Board of Directors, The Americas Society, 1990-; The Arthur Page Society; The Northeast Brazilianists; Authors Guild, 1992-. Address: 114 Leonia Avenue, Leonia, NJ 07605, USA.

PINTER Harold, b. 10 Oct 1930. Actor; Playwright. m. Lady Antonia Fraser. Publications: Plays: The Room, 1957; The Birthday Party, 1957; The Dumb Waiter, 1957; The Hothouse, 1958; A Slight Ache, 1958; A Night Out, 1959; The Caretaker, 1959; Night School, 1960; The Dwarfs, 1960; The Collection, 1961; The Lover, 1962; Tea Party, 1964; The Homecoming, 1964; The Basement, 1966; Landscape, 1967; Silence, 1968; Old Times, 1970; Monologue, 1972; No Man's Land, 1974; Betrayal, 1978; Family Voices, 1980; A Kind of Alaska, 1982; Victoria Station, 1982; One for the Road, 1984; Mountain Language, 1988; The New World Order, 1991; Party Time, 1991; Moonlight, 1993; Screenplays: The Caretaker, 1962; The Servant, 1962; The Pumpkin Eater, 1963; The Quiller Memorandum, 1965; Accident, 1966; The Birthday Party, 1967; The Go-Between, 1969; The Homecoming, 1969; Langrishe Go Down, 1970; A la Recherche de Temps Perdu, 1972; The Last Tycoon, 1974; The French Lieutenant's Woman, 1980; Betrayal, 1981; Victory, 1982; The Turtle Diary, 1984; The Harmdmaid's Tale, 1987; The Heat of the Day, 1988; Reunion, 1989; The Trial, 1989; The Comfort of Strangers, 1989. Honours include: Honorary degrees, Reading, 1970, Birmingham, 1971, Glasgow and East Anglia, 1974, Stirling, 1979, Brown, USA, 1982, Hull, 1986; Evening Standard Drama Award, 1960; Best British Screenplay, Screenwriters Guild, 1963; Italia Prize, 1963; Best Screen Writing of Year, New York Film Critics, 1964; British Film Academy Award, 1964; Whitbread Award, 1967; Writers Guild Prize, Best Screenplay Award, 1971; Donatello Prize and Ennio Flaiano Award, Italy, 1982; Elmer H Bobst Award, New York University; Many more. Memberships: Fellow, Royal Society of Literature; Honorary Member, American Academy and Institute of Arts and Letters. Address: c/o Judy Daish Associates Ltd, 83 Eastbourne Mews, London W2 6LQ, England.

PIONTEK Heinz, b. 15 Nov 1925, Kreuzburg, Silesia, Germany. Writer. m. Gisela Dallman, 1951. Education: Theologisch-Philosophische Hochschule, Dillengen. Publications: poems: Die Furt, 1952; Die Rauchfahne, 1953; John Keats: Poems, 1960; Mit einer Kranichfeder, 1962; Klartext, 1966; Fruh im September, 1982; Helldunkel, 1987; stories: Vor Augen, 1955; Kastanien aus dem Feuer, 1963; Winterage-Sommernachte, 1977; novels: Die mittleren Jahre, 1967; Dichterleben, 1976; Juttas Neffe, 1979; Windrichtungen (journey reports), 1963; Liebeserklarungen (essays), 1969; Leid und Zeit und Ewigkeit, Anthology, 1987. Honours: Tukan Preis, 1971; Literatur preis des Kulturreises im BDI, 1974; Georg-Buchner Presi, 1976; Werner-Egk Preis, 1981; Obserschlesischer Kulturpreis, 1984; Bundeverdienstkreux, 1st class, 1985. Addrss: Dulfer Strasse 97, 8000 Munchen 50, Germany.

PIRIE David Tarbat, b. 4 Dec 1946, Dundee, Scotland. Writer. m. Judith Harris, 21 June 1983, 1 son, 1 daughter. Education: University of York; University of London. Appointments: Tutor; Film Critic, Editor, Time Out Magazine, 1980-84. Publications: Heritage of Horror, 1974; Mystery Story, 1980; Anatomy of the Movies, 1981. Films: Rainy Day Women, 1984; Wild Things, 1988; Black Easter, 1993; Wildest Dreams, 1995. TV: Never Come Back, BBC serial, 1989; Ashenden, BBC serial, 1990; Natural Lies, TV serial, 1991. Contributions to: Various journals. Honours: Drama Prize for Rainy Day Women, New York Festival, 1985; Best Network Series Prize for Never Come Back, Chicago Film

Festival, 1990. Membership: Screenwriters Studio, Dartington Hall, 1990. Literary Agent: Stephen Durbridge, London, England. Address: c/o Lemon Unna and Durbridge, 24 Pottery Lane, London W11, England.

PIRSIG Robert Maynard, b. 6 Sept 1928, MN, USA. Author. m. Wendy Kimball, 28 Dec 1978, 1 son, 1 daughter. Education: BA, 1950, MA, 1958, University of MN. Publication: Zen and the Art of Motorcycle Maintenance, 1974; Lila, 1991. Literary Agent: Janklow & Nesbit, NY, USA. Address: c/o Bantam Books, 1540 Broadway, New York, NY 10036, USA.

PISERCHIA Doris (Elaine), b. 1928, USA. Author. Publications: Mister Justice, 1973; Star Rider, 1974; A Billion Days of Earth, 1976; Earthchild, 1977; Spaceling, 1978; The Spinner, 1980. Address: c/o DAW Books, New American Library, PO Box 120, Bergenfield, NJ 07621, USA.

PISKOR Stanilaw, b. 13 Aug 1944, Poland. Writer; Art Historian. m. 29 Sep 1969, 1 s, 1 d. Education: Degree in History of Art, Adam Mickiewicz University, Poznan, 1969; Doctor, Philology, Silesian University, Katowice, Poland, 1985. Publications: Confessions, 1975; Dispute Over Poetry, 1977; The Moveable Country, 1980; The Polish Identity, 1988; On the Bridge Of Europe, 1992; plays: The Glass Pane, 1976; The Overflow, 1979; The Slaughter House, 1980. Contributions to: Editor in Chief, a literary-artistic magazine, Studio, 1981-93; articles in Nowy Wyraz; Tworzosc; Pismo; Odra; Poezja; Pogaldy. Honours: Private Artistic Award - Julian Przybos, Medal for vanguard creation and promotion; Award of W Rzymowski, Warzawa, 1988; Award of Literary Foundation, Warsawa, 1988; Literary Award of Solidarity, Katowice, 1993. Memberships: Association of Polish Writers, 1980; Association of Art Historians in Poland. Literary Agent: ZAIKS, Warsaw, ul Hipoteczna 2. Address: Ul Jaworznicka 38, 32-520 Jaworzno, Poland.

PISTORIUS Vladimir, b. 10 Jan 1951, Ostrava, Czechoslovakia. Editor. m. Jitka Pistoriusova, 17 Apr 1976, 1 s. Education: Graduated, Faculty of Mathematics and Physics, Charles University, Prague, 1974, majoring in Cosmology. Appointments: Directed KE-78, one of Czech samizdat book editions, 1978-89; Editor-in-Chief, Mlada fronta Publishers, 1990-. Publications: A prece, KE 78, Praha, 1978; Jak se chyta slunce, Albatros, Praha, 1981; Filkovi na kalhoty, KE 78, Praha, 1984; Stamouci literatura, SPN, Praha, 1991. Contributions to: Kriticky sbornik; Literani noviny; Lidove noviny. Membership: Czech Writer's Society. Address: Skalecka 17, 170 00 Praha 7, Czechoslovakia.

PITCHER George, b. 1925, USA. Emeritus Professor of Philosophy. Publications: Truth (editor), 1964; The Philosophy of Wittgenstein, 1964; Wittgenstein: A Collection of Critical Essays (editor), 1966; Ryle (edited with O P Wood), 1970; A Theory of Perception, 1971; Berkeley, 1977; A Life of Grace, 1987. Address: 18 College Road West, Princeton, NJ 08540, USA.

PITCHER Harvey John, b. 26 Aug 1936, London, England. Writer. Education: BA, 1st Class Honours, Russian, Oxford University. Publications: Understanding the Russians, 1964; The Chekhov Play: A Nw Interpretation, 1973, 1985; When Miss Emmie was in Russia, 1974, 1984; Chekov's Leading Lady, 1979; Chekhov: The Early Stories, 1883-1888 (with Patrick Miles), 1982, 1994; The Smiths of Moscow, 1984; Lily: An Anglo-Russian Romance, 1987; In Russian translation: Myur i Meriliz: Shotlandtsy v Rossii (Muir and Mirrielees: Scots in Russia), 1993. Contributions to: The Times Literary Supplement. Address: 37 Bernard Road, Cromer, Norfolk NR27 9AW, England.

PITT Barrie William Edward, b. 7 Jul 1918, Galway, Ireland. Historian. m. (1) Phyllis Kate Edwards, 1943, 1 s (dec), (2)Sonia Deidre Hoskins, 1953, diss, 1971, (3) Frances Mary Moore, 1983. Appointments: Historical Consultant to BBC series, The Great War, 1963; Editor, Purnell's History of the Second World War, 1964; Editor-in-Chief, Ballantine's Illustrated History of World War 2, US Book Series, 1967; Editor, Purnell's History of the First World War, 1969; Editor-in-Chief, Ballantine's Illustrated History of the Violent Century, 1971; Editor, British History Illustrated, 1974-78. Publications: The Edge of Battle, 1958; Zeebrugge, St George's Day, 1918, 1958; Coronel and Falkland, 1960; 1918 The Last Act, 1962; The Battle of the Atlantic, 1977; The Crucible of War: Year of Alamein, 1942, 1982; Special Boat Squadron, 1983. Contributions to: Encyclopaedia Britannica, The Sunday Times. Address: 10 Wellington Road, Taunton, Somerset, TA1 4EG, England.

PITT David Charles, b. 15 Aug 1938. Social Anthropologist; Ecologist; Sociologist. m. Carol Haigh, 13 Feb 1959, 3 s, 4 d. Education: BA, University of New Zealand, 1959-61; BLitt, MLitt, DPhil, Balliol College, Oxford University, England, 1962-66. Appointments: Professor, School of Social Sciences, University of Waitkato, New Zealand, 1972-80; Consultant, United Nations and World Health Organisation, Geneva, 1980-. Publications: Tradition and Economic Progress - OUP, 1970; Social Dynamics of Development - Pergamon, 1976. Honours: Vernadsky Medal, USSR Academy of Sciences, 1989. Memberships: Fellow, Royal Anthropological Institute; Commission Chairman, International Union of Anthropolgical and Ethnological Sciences. Address: 1265 La Cure, Switzerland.

PITT David George, b. 12 Dec 1921, Musgravetown, Newfoundland, Canada. Author; University Professor (retired). m. Marion Woolfrey, 5 Jun 1946, 1 s, 1 d. Education: BA (Hons) English, Mt Allison University, 1946; MA, 1948, PhD, 1960, University of Toronto. Appointment: Professor of English Literature, Memorial University of Newfoundland, 1949-83. Publications: Elements of Literacy, 1964; Windows of Agates, 1966; Critcal Views on Canadian Writers: E J Pratt, 1969; Toward the First Spike: The Evolution of a Poet, 1982; Goodly Heritage, 1984; EJ Pratt: the Truant Years, 1987; Tales From the Outer Fringe, 1990. Honours: Medal for Biography, University of British Columbia, 1984; Artist of the Year, Newfoundland Arts Council, 1988; Honorary LLD, Mt Allison University, 1989. Memberships: Association of Canadian University Teachers of English; Humanities Association of Canada. Address: 7 Chestnut Place, St John's, Newfoundland, Canada A1B 2T1.

PITT-KETHLEY Fiona, b. 21 Nov 1954, Edgware, Middlesex, England. Writer; Poet. Education: BA Hons, Fine Art, Chelsea School of Art, 1976. Publications: Sky Ray Lolly, 1986, reissue, 1990; Private Parts, 1987 reissue, 1991; Journeys to The Underworld, 1988, peperback, 1989; The Perfect Man, 1989, London, privately printed, 1984, Rome, 1985; The Tower of Glass, 1985; Gesta, 1986; The Misfortunes of Nigel, 1991; The Literary Companion to Sex, 1992, paperback, 1993; The Pan Principle, 1994. Contributions to: Numerous magazines and newspapers including: The Independent; The Guardian; The Times. Memberships: Society of Sussex Authors; Chelsea Arts Club; Film Artistes Association. Literary Agent: Giles Gordon, Sheil Land Associates. Address: c/o Giles Gordon, Sheil Land Associates, 43 Doughty Street, London.

PITTER Ruth, b. 7 Nov 1897, Ilford, Essex, England. Poet. Education: Cobom School for Girls, East London. Publications: First Poems, 1920; First and Second Poems, 1921-25, 1927; Persephone in Hades, 1931; A Mad Lady's Garland, 1934; A Trophy of Arms, 1926-35; The Spirit Watches, 1939; The Rude Potato, 1941; The Bridge, 1939-44; Pitter in Cats, 1947; Urania, 1949; The Ermine, 1942-52; Still by Choice, 1966; Poems, 1926-66, 1968; End of Drought, 1975; A Heaven to Find, 1987; Collected Poems, 1990. Honours include: Compnion of Literature, Royal Society of Literature, 1974; CBE, 1979. Address: The Hawthoms, 71 Chilton Road, Long Crendon, Aylesbury, Buckinghamshire.

PITTOCK Murray George Hornby, b. 5 Jan 1962, Nantwich, England. Academic. m. Anne Grace Thomton Martin, 15 Apr 1989, 2 daughters. Education: MA, 1st Class, English Language and Literature, Glasgow University, 1983; Snell Exhibitioner, Balliol College, Oxford, 1983-86; DPhil, Oxford, 1986; British Academy Postdoctoral Research Fellow, University of Aberdeen, 1988-89. Appointments: Daily Express schools work, 1982-83; Lecturer, Pembroke College, Oxford, 1986-87; Editorial Assistant, Waverley Novels Project, 1987-88; Junior Research Fellow, Linacre College, Oxford, 1988-; Lecturer, University of Edinburgh, 1989-. Publications: Lionel Johnson: Selected Letters (editor), 1988; The Invention of Scotland, 1991; Clio's Clavers, 1992; Spectrum of Decadence, 1993. Contributions to: Over 50 articles to journals including: Victorian Poetry; Scottish Literary Journal; Irish University Review; Nineteenth-Century Fiction; British Journal for Eighteenth-Century Studies; Press, radio and TV appearances, UK, USA. Honours: Winner, 1 of 10 1st Prizes, National Children's Writing Contest, 1973; Sir James Robetson Prize for Literature, 1976; Buchanan Prize, 1979; Bradley Medal, 1983; English-Speaking Union Scholar, 1984; BP Humanities Research Prize, Royal Society of Edinburgh, 1992. Memberships: Council, Association for Scottish Literary Studies; Fellow, Royal Historical Soc. Address: Department of English Literature, David Hume Tower, George Square, Edinburgh EH8 9JX, Scotland, England.

PIVOT Bernard, b. 5 May 1935, Lyons, France. Journalist. m. Monique Dupuis, 1959, 2 d. Education: Centre de Formation des Journalistes. Appointments: Staff, Figaro Litteraire, then Literary Editor, Figaro, 1958-74; Chronique pour sourire on Europe 1, 1970-73; Columnist, le Point, 1974-77; producer, presenter, Ouvrez les guillemets, 1973-74, Apostophes, Channel 2, 1975-; Editor, Lire, 1975-. Publications: L'Amour en vogue (novel), 1959; La vie oh la! la!, 1966; Les critiques litteraires, 1968; Beaujolaises, 1978; Le Football en vert, 1980. Honours: Grand Prix de la Critique l'Academie Francaise, 1983. Address: 7 Avenue Niel, 75017, France.

PLACE Florence. See: **NORMAN Geraldine.**

PLAGEMANN Bentz, b.1913, USA. Author. Appointments: Bookstores, Cleveland, Chicago, Detroit, New York, 1932-42; Instructor, Journalism, New York University, 1946-47. Publications: William Walter, 1941; All For the Best, 1946; Into The Labyrinth, 1948 (in USA paperback as Downfall, 1952, 2nd US paperback edited as the Sin Underneath, 1956; My Place to Stand (autobiography), 1949; This is Gogle, or The Education of a Father (in UK as My Son Goggle), 1955; The Steel Cocoon, 1958; Half the Fun, 1961; Father to the Man, 1964; The Best is Yet to Be, 1966; The Heart of Silence, 1967; A World of Difference, 1969; This Happy Place: Living the Good Life in America (reminiscences), 1970; How to Write a Story (juvenile), 1971; The Boxwood Maze (gothic novel), 1972; Wolfe's Cloister (gothic novel), 1974. Address: c/o Harold Matson Company, 276 Fifth Avenue, New York, NY 10001, USA.

PLAIN Belva, b. 1918, USA. Author. Publications: Evergreen, 1978; Random Winds, 1980; Eden Burning, 1982; Crescent City, 1984; The Golden Cup, 1986; Blessings, 1989.

PLANO Jack Charles, b. 1921, USA. Writer. Appointments include: Editor, New Issues Press, Western Michigan University, Kalamazoo. Publications: The United Nations and the India-Pakistan Dispute, 1966; The American Political Dictionary (with M Greenberg), 1962, 9th edition, 1993; Forging World Order (with R E Riggs), 1967, 1971; The International Relations Dictionary (with R Olton), 1969, 4th edition, 1988; Dictionary of Political Analysis (with R E Riggs), 1973, revised edition with R E Riggs and H S Robin, 1982; Political Science Dictionary (with M Greenberg, R Olton and R E Riggs), 1973; International Approaches to the Problems of Marine Pollution; The Latin American Political Dictionary (with Ernest E Rossi), 1980, 2nd edition, 1993; The Public Administration Dictionary (with R Chandler), 1982, 1988; The United Nations (with R E Riggs), 1987, 2nd edition, 1993. Address: Department of Political Science, Western Michigan University, Kalamazoo, MI 49008, USA.

PLANT Richard (Stefan Brockhoff), b. 22 Aug 1910. Education: PhD, University of Basel, Switzerland, 1936. Publications: Die Kaste mit dem Grossen S, 1935; Taschenbuch des Films, 1938; The Dragon in the Forest, 1950-51; Lizzie Borden (opera text), 1966; The Pink Triangle, 1986, 1991; Detective novels under Stefan Brockoff 1936-38, reissued 1950. Contributions to: The New Yorker; The Saturday Review; the New York Times. Honours: Best Non-Fiction Book for the Pink Triangle, 1991; Best Non-Fiction Book, Lambda Report. Membership: American PEN. Address: 23 Perry Street, apt 4, New York, NY 10014, USA.

PLANTE David (Robert), b. 1940, USA. Author. Publications: Argo, or the Voyage of a Balloon, by A Embiricos (translation with N Stangos), 1967; The Ghost of Henry James, 1970; Slides, 1971; Realtives, 1972; The Darkness of the Body, 1974; Figures in the Bright Air, 1976; The Family, 1978; The Country, 1980; The Woods, 1982; Difficult Women, 1983; The Foreigner, 1984; The Catholic, 1985; The Native, 1987; Address: c/o Deborah Rogers Agency, 44 Blenheim Crescent, London, W11 2EF, England.

PLANTEY Alain, b. 19 July 1924, Mulhouse, France. Author; Councellor of State; Diplomat; Chairman of The International Court of Arbitration, International Chamber of Commerce; Member of The French Academie des Sciences Morales et Politiques. m. Christiane Wioland, 4 d. Education: University of Bordeaux; LLD, University of Paris, 1949; Diploma, National School of Public Administration, Paris, 1949. Publications include: Traite Pratique de La Fonction Publique, 1955, 3rd edition 1971; Prospective de L'Etat Paris, 1974; La Fonction Internationale Paris, 1977; La Negociation Internationale, 1980, 1994; De La Politiqu Entre Les Etats, 1987, 1992; International Civil Service, 1981; La Funcion Publica Internacional y Europea, 1982; Tratado de

Derecho Diplomatics, 1991; La Fonction Publique, Garté Général, 1992. Contributions to: Various journals and magazines including: Le Monde. Honours: Award, Academy of Moral and Political Sciences, 1979; Award, Academy Française, 1982; Commander, Legion d'Honneur, Palmes Academiques. Memberships: Various professional organisations. Address: 6 Avenue Sully Prudhomme, Paris 75007, France.

PLATE Andrea, (Andrea Darvi), b. 29 July 1952, Los Angeles, USA. Teacher; Writer. m. Thomas Plate, 22 Sept 1979, 1 daughter. Education: MA, Jounalism, USC; BA, English, University of California, Berkeley. Appointments: Assistant Professor, Communications Department, Fordham University, 1988-90; Senior Lecturer, Journalism, University of Southern California, 1990-92; Senior Lecturer, Journalism, Santa Monica College, 1993-; English Teacher, Oakwood School, 1994-. Publications: Secret Police, 1981. Contributions to: Freelance Pieces for LA Times, New York Times, New York Newsday, Chicago Tribune, TV Guide. Address: 812 16th Street #2, Santa Monica, CA 90403, USA.

PLATER Alan Frederick, b. 15 Apr 1935. Freelance Writer. m. (1) Shirley Johnson, 1958 (div 1985), 2 s, 1 d, (2) Shirley Rubinstein, 1986, 3 ss. Publications: theatre: A Smashing Day (also televised); Coal the Coalhouse Door; And a Little Love Besides; Swallows on the Water; Trinity Tales; The Fosdyke Saga; Fosdyke Two; On Your Way, Riley! Skyhooks: A Foot on the Earth; Prez: Rent Party, 1989; Sweet Sorrow, 1990; Going Home, 1990; I Thought I Heard A Rustling, 1991; films: The Virgin and the Gypsy; It Shouldn't Happen to a Vet; Priest of Love; TV plays: So Long Charlie; See the Pretty Lights; To See How Far It Is (trilogy); Land of Green Ginger; Willow Cabins; The Party of the First Part; The Blacktoft Diaries; Thank You, Mrs Clinkscales; A day in Summer, 1989; Misterioso, 1991; biographies: The Crystal Spirit; Pride of Our Alley; Edward Lear - at the Edge of the Sand; Coming Through; TV series and serials: Z Cars; Softly, Softly; Shoulder to Shoulder; Trinity Tales; The Good Companions; The Consultant; The Biederbecke Connection, 1989; Fortunes of War, 1987; A Very British Coup, 1988; Maigret, 1992; radio: The Journal of Vasilije Bogdaovic; books: The Biederbecke Affair, 1985; The Biederbecke Tapes, 1986; Misterioso, 1987; The Biederbecke Connection, 1992; plays and shorter pieces in anthologies. Contributions to: Punch; The Guardian; The Listener. Honours: Writer's Guild Radio Award, 1972; Sony Radio Award, 1983; Honorary Fellow, Humberside College of Further Education, 1983; Hon DLitt, Hull, 1985; RTS Writer's Award, 1984-85; Broadcasting Press Guild, Best Drama Series, 1987 and 1988; BAFTA, Best Drama Series, 1988; BAFTA, The Writer's Award, 1988; Royal Telvision Society, Best Drama Series, A Very British Coup, 1988; A Very British Coup also won: The International Emmy (USA), The Golden Fleece of Georgia (USSR), Best Series and Grand Prix of the Banff Television Festival (Canada). Memberships: President, Writer's Guild of Great Britain, 1991; FRSL, 1985; FRSA, 1991. Literary Agent: Alexandra Cann. Address: c/o 68e Redcliffe Gardens, London SW10 9HE, England.

PLATT Charles, b. 1944. Author; Poet; Freelance Writer. Appointments: Formerly Worked for Clive Bingley Publishers, London; Designer, Productions Assisstant, New Worlds Magazine, London. Publications: The Garbage World, 1967; The City Dwellers, 1970; Highway Sandwiches (poetry), 1970; The Gas (poetry), 1970; Planet of the Voles, 1971; New Worlds 6 (edited with Michael Moorcock), 1973 (in USA as New Worlds 5, 1974); New Worlds 7 (edited with Hilary Bailey), 1974 (in US as New Worlds 6, 1975); Sweet Evil, 1977; Dream Makers: The Uncommon People Who Write Science Fiction, 1980. Address: c/o Gollancz, 14 Henrietta Street, London WC2E 8QJ, England.

PLAYER Corrie Lynne (Oborn), b. 14 Oct 1942, Ogden, Utah, USA. Journalist; Technical Writer; Teacher. m. Gary Farnsworth Player, 5 s, 3 d. Education: AA, English, Speech, Weber College; BA, English, Creative Writing, 1964, MA, Education, 1965, Stanford University. Publications: Anchorage Altogether, non-fiction, 1972, revised edition, 1977. Contributions to: Baby Talk, 1986; Parents Magazine, 1986; McCall's, 1987; American Baby, 1988; Woman's Day, 1988; Ladies Home Journal, 1989; Family Circle, 1992; I'd Rather Raise an Elephant, column, Daily Spectrum, 1990-. Honours: Non-Fiction Book, Oklahoma Writers Federation, 1986, 1988; Article, League of Utah Writers, 1991; Inspirational Article, National Writers Club, 1991. Memberships: Founder, 1st President, San Luis Obispo Nightwriters, 1988-89; Founder, 1st President, Cedar City Nightwriters; Oklahoma Writers Federation; League of Utah Writers; National Writers Club; National Foster Parents Association; Former Member, American Society of University Professors. Address: 429 West 400th South, Cedar City, UT 84720, USA.

PLAYER Trezevant,See:**YEATMAN Ted P.**

PLEIJEL Agneta, b. 26 Feb 1940, Stockholm, Sweden. Author. m. Maciej Zaremba, 27 Nov 1982, 1 d. Education: MA, 1970. Appointments: Norstedts Publishing Co, Stockholm. Publications: Kollontay, play, 1979; Angels, Dwarfs, poetry volume, 1981; The Hill on the Black Side of the Moon, film, 1983; Eyes of a Dream, poetry volume, 1984; He Who Observeth the Wind, novel, 1987; Dog Star, novel, 1989. Contributions to: Several, mostly in Sweden/Scandinavia. Memberships: President, Swedish PEN Club. Address: Tantogatan 45, 117 42 Stockholm, Sweden.

PLIMPTON George Ames, b. 18 Mar 1927, New York, New York, USA. Writer; Editor; Actor. m. Freddy Medora Espy, 1 s, 1 d. Education: AB, Harvard University; BA, MA, Kings College, Cambridge University. Appointments: Editor-in-Chief, Paris Review, 1853-; Contributing Editor, Sports Illustrated; Director, American Literature Anthology Program, 1967-; Advisor, John F Kennedy Oral History Project. Publications include: interviews, literature, TV scripts, sports writings, including: Writers at Work: The Paris Interviews (editor), issued periodically since 1957; Out of My League, 1961; Paper Lion (football anecdotes), 1966; Pierre's Book: The Game of Court Tennis, 1971; One More July: A Football Dialogue with Bill Curvy, 1977; The Curious Case of Sidd Finch, 1987; Fireworks: A History and a Celebration, 1984; Open Net, 1985; Poets at Work, 1989; Women Writers at Work, 1989; Paris Review Anthology (editor), 1990; The Writer's Chapbook (editor), 1990. Address: Paris Review, 541 E 72nd Street, Suite 1-C, New York, NY 10021, USA.

PLINGE Walter. See: **THURGOOD Nevil.**

PLOWDEN Alison, b. 18 Dec 1931, Simla, India. Writer. Publications: Elizabethan Quartet: The Young Elizabeth, 1971; Danger to Elizabeth, 1973; Marriage with My Kingdom, 1977; Elizabeth Regina, 1980; The House of Tudor, 1976; Elizabethan England, 1982; The Young Victoria; Jane Grey and The House of Suffolk; 2 Queens in One Isle; Caroline and Charlotte; Lords of The Land; The Elizabethan Secret Service; The Stuart Princesses, in preparation; Dramatised documentaries for BBC, Radio and TV; Radio plays. Honours: Writers Guild of Great Britain Award; Best British Educational TV Script for Mistress of Hardwick, BBC1, 1972. Literary Agent: John Johnson, England. Address: c/o John Johnson Authors Agents, Clerkenwell House, 45-47 Clerkenwell Green, London, EC1R 0HT, England.

PLUCKROSE Henry Arthur (Richard Cobbett), B. 1931, British. Writer of children's fiction, Education Head, Teacher, Prior Weston School, London, 1968-, Editor, Let's Go series. Appointments: Teacher of elementary school-aged children in Inner London, 1954-68. Publications: Let's Make Pictures, 1965; Creative Arts and Crafts; A Handbook for Teachers in Primary Schools, 1966; Intorducing Crayon Techniques, 1967; Lets Work Large: A Handbook of Art Techniques for Teachers in Primary Schools, 1967; Introducing Acrylic Painting, 1968; (compiler) The Art and Craft Book, 1969; (editor with Farnk Peacock) A Dickens Anthology, 1970; Creative Themes, 1970; (editor) A Book of Crafts, 1971; Art and Craft Today, 1971; (editor) Let's Use the Locality, 1971; (editor) Let's Paint, 1971; (editor) Let's Print, 1971; (editor) Let's Make a Picture, 1971; (editor) Let's Make A Puppet, 1971; Art, 1972; Churches, 1975; Castles, 1975; Open School, Open Society, 1975; Houses, 1976; Monastries, 1976; Seen in Britain, 1978; (with Peter Wilby) The Condition of English Schooling, 1979; Saxon and Norman England, 1979; Medieval England, 1979; Children in Their Primary Schools, 1980; Victorian Britain, 1981; 20th Century Britain, 1981; Tudor Britain, 1981; Stuart Britain, 1981; Ancient Greeks, 1981; Arctic Lands, 1982; Hearing, 1985; Smelling, 1985; Tasting, 1985; Touching, 1985; Seeing, 1985; Growing, 1986; Shape, 1986; Floating and Sinking, 1986; Moving, 1987; Counting, 1987. Address: 3 Butts Lane, Danbury, Essex, England.

PLUHAR Zdenek, b. 16 May 1913, Brno, Czechoslovakia. Writer; Author. m. Marie Janir, 6 Dec 1979, 1 d. Education: Diploma Jugenieur, 1937. Publications: V sest vecer v Astorii 1982; Opustis-li mne, 1957; At hodi kamenem, 1962; Minutu ticha za me lasky, 1969 Konecna stanice, 1971; Jeden stribny, 1974; Opona bes poblesku, 1985; Krize rostou k Pacifiku, 1974; Mraky tahnou nad Savojskem, 1949; Bronzova spirala, 1953; Modre udoli, 1954 and numerous other novels.

Contributions to: Literalrm mesicmk; Kmen and numerous others. Honour: National Artist, State Prize. Membership: Srak Cescosloveurlch spisorarelu. Address: Narvdru 37, Praha 1, Czechoslovakia.

PLUMB John Harold (Sir), b. 20 Aug 1911, Leicester, England. Historian; Professor of Modern English History at University of Cambridge. Education: University College, Leicester, Christ's College, Cambridge; BA, PhD, LittD. Literary Appointments: Editor, History of Human Society, 1959-; European Advisory Editor, Horizon, 1959-; Historical Advisor, Penguin Books. Publications include: England in The Eighteenth Century, 1950, 1953; Sir Robert Walpole, volume 1, 1956, volume II, 1960, both reprinted, 1972; The First Four Georges, 1956; The Renaissance, 1961; Crisis in The Humanities, 1964; The Growth of Political Stability in England 1675-1725, 1967; Death of The Past, 1969; In The Light of History, 1972; The Commercialisation of Leisure, 1974; Royal Heritage, the book of the BBC television series, advisor and co-author with Huw Wheldon, 1977; New Light on The Tyrant, George III, 1978; The Making of an Historian, 1988; The American Scene, 1988. Honours include: Knight; Several Honorary Degrees. Memberships include: Fellow, British Academy; Fellow, Royal Historical Society; Fellow, Society of Antiquaries; Fellow, Royal Society of Literature; Honorary Foreign Member, American Academy of Arts and Sciences. Address: Christ's College, Cambridge, CB2 3BU, England.

PLUMME Don E. See: **KATZ Bobbi.**

PLUNKETT James, b. 21 May 1920, Dublin, Ireland. Novelist. Education: Dublin College of Music. Appointments: Senior Producer, Radio Telefis Eireann, 1974-85. Publications include: Strumpet City, 1969; The Gems She Wore: A Book of Irish Places, 1972; Farewell Companions, 1977; The Circus Animals 1990; Short Stories: The Trusting and the Maimed, Other Irish Stories, 1959; Collected Short Stories, 1977; Plays, Homecoming 1954; Big Jim, 1954; The Risen People, 1958; Radio Plays; TV Plays and Programmes; Boy on the Back Wall and Other Essays, 1987. Honours: Yorkshire Poet Award, 1969; President, Irish Academy of Letters, 1980-82. Literary Agent: Peter Fraser and Dunlop Group, 503-4 the Chambers, Chelsea Harbour, Lots Road, London SW10 0XF. Address: 29 Parnell Road, Bray, County Wicklow, Ireland.

POAGUE Leland Allen, b. 15 Dec 1948, San Francisco, USA. English Professor. m. Susan Eileen Jensen, 24 Aug 1969, 2 d. Education: BA, English, San Jose State College, 1970; PhD, English, University of Oregon, 1973. Appointments: Instructor, 1973-74, Assisstant Professor 1974-78, SUNY, Geneseo; Visiting Assisstant Professor, University of Rochester, 1977; Assisstant Professor 1978-81; Associate Professor 1981-86; Professor 1986-, Iowa State University. Publications: A Hitchcock Reader (edited with Marshall Deutelbaum), 1986; Howard Hawks, 1982; Billy Wilder and Leo McCarey, 1980; The Cinema of Earnest Lubitsch; The Hollywood Films, 1978; The Cinema of Frank Capra: An Approach to Film Comedy, 1975; The Possibility of Film Criticism (with William Cadbury), 1989; All I Can See is the Flags, 1988; Cavell and the Fantasy of Criticism, 1987. Contributions to: Various journals. Address: English Department, Iowa State University, Ames, IA 50011, USA.

POCOCK Tom (Guy Allcot), b. 18 Aug 1925, London, England. Author; Journalist. m. Penelope Casson, 26 Apr 1969, 2 d. Publications: Nelson and His World, 1968; Chelsea Reach, 1970; Fighting General, 1973; Remember Nelson, 1977; The Young Nelson in The Americas, 1980; 1945: The Dawn Came Up Like Thunder, 1983; East and West of Suez, 1986; Horatio Nelson, 1987; Alan Moorehead, 1990; The Essential Venice, 1990; Sailor King, 1991; Rider Haggard and The Lost Empire, 1993; Norfolk, 1995. Contributions to: numerous newspapers and magazines. Literary Agent: Andrew Lounie. Address: 22 Lawrence Street, London, SW3 5NF, London.

PODOPULU Soula, b. 16 Aug 1935, Greece. Schoolmistress. m. 26 Dec 1963, 2 s. Education: Pedagogic Academy Arsakiou Psihiku of Athens, 1955. Publications: Small Stories, 1977; Difficult Years, 1979; The Forty Sifters, 1983; With The Sea-Gulls, 1986; Myrtle or Mirsini, 1985; Konstadi's and the Pigeon, 1987; Uneasy Days, 1981; The Consent of Silence, 1986. Contributions to: Instructivestep; Kycladiko Light; New Thoughts; New Fireside; Open School; Free Spirit; The Modern Woman; Fire Grand. Honours: Literary Award, Pedagogic Academia, 1955; Prize, Lyceum of Greek Women, 1982; Prize, Delphian Amphichtionen, 1982; Award, Feminine Company, 1982;

Award, Delphian Amphictionion, 1984; Award, Literary Men of Prefecture Karolicha, 1985; Prize, Hellenic Organisation of Tourism, 1986. Memberships: Company of Greek Authors; Circle of Hellenic Childrens Book Authors; Union of Greek Scientist Women. Address: Ragavi 98, Athens 114-75, Greece.

POGREBIN Lett Cottin, b. 9 Jun 1939, New York City, USA. Author. m. Bertrand Pogrebin, 1963, 1 s, 2 d. Education: BA, cum laude, Brandeis University, 1959. Appointments: Editor MS magazine, 1971-; Contributor to various anthologies, 1974-. Publications: Free to be... A Family, editor, 1987; Among Friends, 1986; Family Politics, 1983; Growing Up Free, 1980; Getting Yours, 1975; How to Make It in a Man's World, 1970; Stories for Free Childrn, editor, 1982. Contributions to: Columnist Ms, 1988-, Newsday, 1986-; New York Times, 1983; Ladies Home Journal, 1097-81; Moment Magazine; TV Guide; McGill Journal of Education; Boardroom Reports. Honours include: Poynter Fellow, Yale University, National Honorary Life Member, Pioneer Women, 1984; Matrix Award, 1981; Emmy Award, 1974; Clarion Award, Women in Communication, etc. Memberships: Founding Member, National Women's Political Caucus; Women's Forum; National Commission for Women's Equality of the American Jewish Congress; UJA Federation Task Force on Women; New York Network; Board of Directors; Action for Children's Television; Author's Guild; Child Care Action Campaign; Women's Action Alliance; Jewish Fund for Justice; International Centre for Peace in the Middle East; Board of Trustees; Public Education Association. Address: c/o Ms Magazine, 1 Times Square, New York, NY 10036, USA.

POHL Frederik (James MacCreigh), b. 1919, American. Writer of novels/short stories, science fiction/fantasy. Member of the Council, Author's Guild, 1976-. Appointments: Book Editor and Associate Circulation Manager, Popular Science Publishing Co, New York City, 1946-49; Literary Agent, New York City, 1949-53; Editor, Galaxy Publishing Co, New York City, 1960-69; Executive Editor, Ace Books, New York City, 1971-72; Science Fiction Editor, Bantam Books, New York City, 1973-79. Publications include: The Space Merchants, 1953; Gladiator-at-Law, 1954; Search the Sky, 1956; Wolfbane, 1957 (all novels in collaboration with C M Kornbane); Slave Ship, 1957; Drunkard's Walk, 1960 (solo novels); Other Short Novels, 1962; (with C M Kornbluth) The Wonder Effect, 1962; A Plague of Pythons, 1963, revised edition as Demon in the Skull, 1984; The Abominable Earthman, 1963; (ed) The Seventh GalaxyReader, 1964; (with Jack Williamson) The Reefs of Space, 1964; (with Jack Williamson) Starchild, 1965; (ed) Star Fourteen, 1966; (ed) The If Reader of Science Fiction, 1966; The Frederik Pohl Omnibus, 1966; Digits and Dastards, 1968; The Age of Pussyfoot, 1969; (with Jack Williamson) Rogue Star, 1969; Day Million (short stories) 1970; (ed) Nightmare Age, 1970; Practical Politics, 1972, 1971; (ed with C Pohl) Science Fiction: The Great Years, 1974; Man Plus, 1977; Gateway, 1978; Jem, 1979; Beyond the Blue Event Horizon, 1980; The Cool War, 1981; Syzygy, 1982; Starburst, 1982; (with Jack Williamson) Rendezvous, 1984; The years of the City, 1984; Black Star Rising, 1985; The Coming of the Quantum Cats, 1986; The annals of the Heechee, 1987; Chernobyl, 1987; Narabedla, 1988; The Day the Martians Came, 1988; Homegoing, 1989; The World at the End of Times, 1990; The Gateway Trip, 1990; Outnumbering the Dead, 1990; Mining the Oort, 1991; (with Jack Williamson) The Singers of Time, 1991; Stopping at Slowyear, 1992; The Voices of Heaven, 1994. Memberships: President, Science Fiction Writers of America, 1974-76; President, World SF, 1980-82. Address: c/o World, 855 S Harvard Drive, Palatine, IL 60067, USA.

POIDEVIN Leslie Oswyn Sheridan, b. 28 Jan 1914, Cremorne, New South Wales, Australia. Medical Doctor (Gynaecologist and Obstetrician). m. Rosemarie Slaney Poole, 18 Sept 1946, 2 daughters. Education: Faculty of Medicine, Sydney University, 1932-37; MBBS, 1938; MRCOG, 1951, FRCOG (London), 1961; MD, 1961, MS, 1965, University of Adelaide. Appointments: Head of Department of Obstetrics, University of Adelaide, 1952-58. Publications: Caesarean Section Scars, 1965; Samurais and Circumcision, 1985; Goodbye Doctor, 1986; Doctor Goes Farming, 1987; The Lucky Doctor, 1988; Doctor in Heaven, 1989; Come In Doctor, 1990; And The Winner Is..., 1992. Contributions to: The Lancet, British Medical Journal, Journal of Obstetrics and Gynaecology of British Empire, Medical Journal of Australia, 1951-83. Address: 9 St Albans Drive, Burnside, South Australia 5066, Australia.

POIRIER Louis, (Julien Grace), b. 27 July 1910, St Florent le Vieil, Maine et Loire, France. Education: Ecole des Science, Politiques, 1933; Ecole Normale Superieure, 1934. Appointments: Professor,

Numerous Public Schools in France; Assistant to Faculty, Caen University, 1935-47; Professor, Lycee Claude Bernard, Paris, 1947-70; Guest Professor, University of Wisconsin, USA, 1970; Writer, 1939-. Publications include: Un Beau Teribeux, 1945; Liberto Grande, 1946; Un Balcon un Feret, 1961; Lettrines, 1967; La Presqu'ile, 1974; Les Eaux Etroites, 1976; En Lisant, en Ecrivant, 1981; La Forme d'une Ville, 1985; Cavrets du Guard Chemin, 1992. Honours: Prix Goncourt, 1951. Address: 61 Rue de Grenelle, 75007 Paris, France.

POIRIER Richard, b. 9 Sep 1925, Gloucester, Massachusetts, USA. Literary Critic. Education: University of Paris, France, 1946; BA, Amherst College, USA, 1949; MA, Yale University, 1950; Fulbright Scholar, Cambridge University, England, 1952; PhD, Harvard University, 1960. Appointments: Williams College, 1950-52; Harvard University, 1955-62; Rutgers University, 1962-; Editor, Partisan Review, 1963-71; Vice-President, Founder, Library of America, 1980-; Editor, Raritan Quarterly, 1980-. Publications: Comic Sense of Henry James, 1960; A World Elsewhere, 1966; The Performing Self, 1971; Norman Mailer, 1976; Robert Frost: The Work of Knowing, 1977; The Renewal of Literature, 1987; Poetry and Pragmatism, 1992; In Defense of Reading, co-editor, 1962. Contributions to: Daedalus; New Republic; Partisan review; New York Review; London Review of Books; various others. Honours: Phi Beta Kappa, 1949; Fulbright Fellow, 1952; Bolingen Fellow, 1963; Guggenheim Fellow, 1967; NEH Fellow, 1972; HHD Amherst College, 1978; Award, American Academy of Arts & Letters, 1980; Literary Lions of NY, 1992. Memberships: Poets, Playwrights, Editors, Essayists and Novelists; American Academy of Arts and Sciences; Century Club. Address: 104 West 70th Street 9B, New York, NY 10023, USA.

POL Lotte Constance, van de, b. 11 May 1949, Enschede, Netherlands. Historian. m. Egmond Elbers, 15 Mar 1985, 2 daughters. Education: MA History and English 1977, University of Amsterdam. Appointments: Teacher of History, Hervormd Lyceum, Amsterdam 1977-78; Rijks Pedagogische Academie (Teacher Training College), Amersfoort 1977-81; Research Fellow, Department of History, Erasmus University, Rotterdam 1982-88. Publications: Books: Daar was laatst een meisje loos Nederlandse vrouwen als matrozen en soldaten. Een historisch onderzoek, co-author, 1981; F L Kersteman, De Bredasche Heldinne, co-author, 1988; The tradition of female transvestism in early modern Europe, co-author, 1989; Vrouwen in mannenkleren. De geschiedenis van een tegendraadse traditie. Europa 1500-1800, co-author, 1989, 2nd ed 1991; Frauen in Männerkleidern. Weibliche Transvestiten und ihre Geschichte, co-author, 1990; Forthcoming: Het Amsterdams Hoerdom. Prostitutie en prostituées in Amsterdam 1650-1750, 1995; Several articles in professional journals including: Republican heroines: cross-dressing women in the French Revolutionary armies, co-author, 1989; In volumes: Women and political culture in the Dutch Revolutions 1780-1800, co-author, 1990; The Lure of the Big City, Female Migration to Amsterdam; An International Debate on Women in Seventeenth Century and Italy, 1994. Address: Jan van Scorelstraat 127, 3583 CM Utrecht, The Netherlands.

POLAND Dorothy Elizabeth Hayward (Alison Farely, Jane Hammond), b. 1937. Author. Publications: as Alison Farely: The Shadows of Evil, 1963; Plunder Island, 1964; High Treason, 1966; Throne of Wrath, 1967; Crown of Spledour, 1968; The Lion and the Wolf, 1969; Last Roar of the Lion, 1969; Leopard From Anjou, 1970; King Wolf, 1974; Kingdom under Tyranny, 1974; Last Howl of the Wolf, 1975; The Cardinal's Neices,1976; The Tempestuous Countess, 1976; Archduchess Arrogance, 1980; Scheming Spanish Wueen, 1981; Spain for Mariana, 1982; as Jane Hammond: The Hell Raisers of Wycombe, 1970; Fire and the Sword, 1971; The Golden Courtesan, 1975; Shadow of the Headsman, 1975; The Doomtower, 1975; Witch of the White House, 1976; Gunpowder Treason, 1976; The Red Queen, 1976; The Queen's Assassin, 1977; The Silver Madonna, 1977; Conspirator's Moonlight, 1977; Woman of Vengeance, 1977; The Admiral's Lady, 1978; The Secret of Petherick, 1982; The Massingham Topaz, 1983; Beware the King's Enchantress, 1983; Moon in Aries, 1984; Eagle's Talon, 1984; Death in the New Forest, 1984. Address: Horizons, 95 Dock View Road, Barry, Glamorgan, Wales.

POLE J(ack) R(ichon), b. 14 Mar 1922, Historian. m. Marilyn Mitchell, 31 May 1952 (diss 1988), 1 s, 2 d. Education: BA, Oxon, 1949; MA, 1979; PhD, Princeton, 1953; MA, Cantab, 1963. Publications: Political Representation in England and The Origins of The American Republic, 1966, 1971; Foundations of American Independence, 1972; The Pursuit of Equality in American History, 1978; Paths to The

American Past, 1979; The Gift of Government, 1983; Colonial British America, co-editor, 1983; The American Constitution, for and against, editor, 1987; The Blackwell Encyclopedia of The American Revolution, co-editor, 1991; The Pursuit of Equality in American History, revised 2nd edition, 1993. Contributions to: Numerous articles in British and American historical journals, also in the Spectator, The New York Times, TLS, London Review of Books. Honours: New Jersey Scholar, Princeton, 1953; Charles Randall Award, Southern Historical Association, USA, 1959. Memberships: FBA; FR Hist S; MCC. Address: 20 Divinity Road, Oxford, OX4 1LJ, England.

POLENBERG Richard, b. 1937, USA. Writer (History). Publications: Reorganising Roosevelt's Government 1936-1939, 1966; America at War: The Home Front 1941-1945, 1968; War and Society: The United States 1941-1945, 1972; Radicalism and Reform in the New Deal, 1972; The American Century: A History of the United States since the 1890's (with Walter LeFeber and Nancy Woloch), 1975, 4th edition, 1991; One Nation Divisible: Class, Race and Ethnicity in the United States since 1938, 1980; Fighting Faiths: The Abrams Case, The Supreme Court and Free Speech, 1987. Address: Department of History, McGraw Hall, Cornell University, Ithaca, NY 14853, USA.

POLIAKOFF Stephen, b. 1953, UK. Dramatist. Publications: Lay-By (co-author), 1972; Hitting Town and City Sugar, 1976; Strawberry Fields, 1977; Shout Across the River, 1979; American Days, 1979; The Summer Party, 1980; Favourite Nights and Caught on a Train, 1982; Banners and Soft Targets, 1984; Breaking the Silence, 1984; Coming in to Land, 1987; Plays One, 1989. Literary Agent: Margaret Ramsey Ltd, England. Address: c/o 33 Devonia Road, London N1 8JQ, England.

POLING-KEMPES Lesley Ann, b. 9 Mar 1954, Batavia, New York, USA. Writer. m. James Kempes, 31 May 1976, 1 s, 1 d. Education: Bachelor of University Studies cum laude, University of New Mexico, 1976. Publications: Harvey Girls: Women Who Opened The West, 1989. Contributions to: short fiction to: Puerta del Sol; Writer's Forum 16; Best of the West 3; Higher Elevations; Articles to New Mexico Magazine. Honours: Zia Award for Excellence, New Mexico Press Women, 1991. Literary Agent: Sydelle Kramer-Frances Goldin Agency. Address: PO BOx 36, Abiquiu, NM 87510, USA.

POLLAND Madelaine Angela (Frances Adrian), b. 1918, United Kingdom. Novelist; Short Story Writer; Children's Fiction Writer. Appointments: Assistant Librarian, Hertfordshire, 1939-42; 1945-46. Publications include: The White Twilight, 1962; Chuiraquimba and The Black Robes, 1962; City of The Golden House, 1963; The Queen's Blessing, 1963; Flame over Tara, 1964; Thicker Than Water, 1964; Mission to Cathay, 1965; Queen Without Crown, 1965; Deirdre, 1967; The Little Spot of Bother (US edition, Minutes of a Murder), 1967; To Tell My People, 1968; Stranger in The Hills, 1968; Random Army (US edition, Shattered Summer), 1969; To Kill a King, 1970; Alhambra, 1970; A Family Affair, 1971; Package to Spain, 1971; Daughter to Poseidon (US edition, Daughter of The Sea, 1972; Prince of The Double Axe, 1976; Double Shadow (as Francis Adrian), 1977; Sabrina, 1979; All Their Kingdoms, 1981; The Heart Speaks Many Ways, 1982; No Price Too High, 1984; As It Was In The Beginning, 1987; Rich Man's Flowers, 1990; The Pomegranate House, 1992. Literary Agent: A P Watt Limited, 20 John Street, London, WC1N 2DR. Address: Edificio Hercules 634, Avenida Gamonal, Arroyo de La Miel, Malaga, Spain.

POLLARD Jane (Dana James), b. 22 Nov 1944, Goole, Yorkshire, England. Author. m. (3) Michael Pollard, 2 June 1992, 2 s, 1 d. Publications: Historical Romances: Harlyn Tremayne, 1984; The Consul's Daughter, 1986; Contemporary Romance: Doctor in The Andes, 1984; Desert Flower, 1986; Doctor in New Guinea, 1986; Rough Waters, 1986; The Marati Legacy, 1986; The Eagle and The Sun, 1986; Heart of Glass, 1987; Tarik's Mountain, 1988; Snowfire, 1988; Pool of Dreaming, 1988; Dark Moon Rising, 1989; Love's Ransom, 1989; A Tempting Shore, 1992; Bay of Rainbows, 1993. Contributions to: Falmouth Packet; West Briton; Western Morning News; Woman's Way; Radio Cornwall; BFBS Gibraltar, GIB TV. Memberships: Executive, Royal Cornwall Polytechnic Society; Romantic Novelists Association; Society of Authors. Literary Agent: Dorothy Lumley, Dorian Literary Agency, Upper Thornehill, 27 Church Street, St Marychurch, Torquay, Devon, TQ1 4QY. Address: 32 Cogos Park, Comfort Road, Mylor, Falmouth, Cornwall, TR11 5SE, England.

POLLARD John (Richard Thornhill), b. 1914, United Kingdom. Retired Senior Lecturer in Classics. Publications: Journey to The Styx, 1955; Adventure Begins in Kenya, 1957; Africa for Adventure, 1961; African Zoo Man, 1963; Wolves and Werewolves, 1964, 2nd edition, 1991; Helen of Troy, 1965; Seers, Shrines and Sirens, 1965; The Long Safari, 1967; Virgil: The Aeneid Appreciation (with C Day Lewis), 1969; Birds in Greek Life and Myth, 1977; Divination and Oracles: Greece, Civilization of The Ancient Mediterranean, 1986; A Country to Composer, 1994. Address: The Yard, Red Wharf Bay, Anglesey, LL75 8RX, Wales.

POLLEY Judith Anne (Valentina Luellen, Judith Stewart, Helen Kent), b. 15 Sep 1938, London, England. Author. m. Roy Edward Polley, 28 Mar 1959, 1 s. Education: High School, Belgravia and Maida Vale, London. Publications include: About 50 Romance novels including: To Touch The Stars, 1980; Beloved Enemy, 1980; Don't Run From Love, 1981; Moonshadow, 1981; Prince of Deception, 1981; Beloved Adversary, 1981; Shadow of The Eagle, 1982; Silver Salamander, 1982; The Wind of Change, 1982; The Measure of Love, 1983; The Peaceful Homecoming, 1983; The Valley of Tears, 1984; Moonflower, 1984; Elusive Flame of Love, 1984; Mistress of Tanglewood, 1984; Black Ravenswood, 1985; The Lord of Darkness, 1985; Devil of Talland, 1985; Passionate Pirate, 1986; Where the Heart Leads, 1986; Love The Avenger, 1986; The Devil's Touch, 1987; My Lady Melisande, 1987; Dark Star, 1988; Love and Pride (Book 1), 1988; The Web of Love (Book 2), 1989; Winter Embers, Summer Fire, 1991; To Please a Lady, 1992; One Love, 1993; Hostage of Love, 1994; many foreign editions and translations. Contributions to: Woman's Weekly Library; Woman's Realm; Woman's Weekly Fiction series; The Museum of Peace and Solidarity, Samarkand, Uzbekistan. Membership: Founding Member, English Romantic Novelists Association. Address: Calcada, 8150 Sao Braz de Alportel, Algarve, Portugal.

POLLITT Katha. Poet: Essayist; Feminist. Publications: Antarctic Traveller: Poems, 1982; Reasonable Creatures: Essays on Women and Feminism, 1994. Contributions to: Nation. Honours: Whiting Writers Award, 1992. Address: 317 W 93rd Street, New York, NY 10025, USA.

POLLOCK John Charles, b. 1923, London, England. Clergyman; Writer. Education: MA, Trinity College, Cambridge; Ridley Hall, Cambridge. Publications include: Moody Without Sankey, 1963; The Keswick Story, 1964; The Christians from Siberia, 1964; Billy Graham, 1966, revised edition, 1969; The Apostle, 1969; A Foreign Devil in China, USA, 1971, UK, 1972, revised edition USA, 1988; George Whitefield and The Great Awakening, USA, 1972, UK, 1973; Wilberforce, USA, 1978; UK, 1977; Billy Graham Evangelist to The World, 1979; The Siberian Seven, USA, 1980, UK, 1979; Amazing Grace: John Newton's Story, 1981; The Master: A Life of Jesus, USA, 1985, UK, 1984; Billy Graham: Highlights of The Story, 1984, USA, 1985 (as To All The Nations); The Cambridge Seven, revised centenary edition, 1985; Shaftesbury: The Poor Man's Earl, 1985; A Fistful of Heroes: Great Reformers and Evangelists, 1988; John Wesley, 1989; On Fire for God: Great Missionary Pioneers, 1990; Fear No Foe: A Brother's Story, 1992; Gordon: The Man Behind The Legend, 1993. Contributions to: Churchman; Church of England Newspaper; Christianity Today; Sunday Telegraph. Membership: English Speaking Union. Address: Rose Ash House, South Molton, Devon, EX36 4RB, England.

POLOMÉ Edgar Charles, b. 31 Jul 1920. Centennial Professr of Liberal Arts, University of TX. m. Sharon Looper Rankin, 8 Feb 1991, 1 s, 1 d. Education: BA, University of Brussels, 1941; MA, Catholic University of Louvain, 1943; PhD, University of Brussels, 1949.Publications: Swahili Language Handbook, 1967; Language in Tanzania, 1980; The Indo-Europeans in the fourth and third millenia, 1982; Essays on Germanic Religion, 1989; Guide to Language Change, 1990; Language Society & Paleoculture, 1992. Contributions to: Many articles and reviews on Indo-european and African language studies. Honours: First Prize, Society for Language and Culture, Umeaa, Sweden, 1991. Memberships: Fellow, American Anthropological Association; Linguistic Society of America; Linguistic Society of India; African Studies Association; Association for Indian Studies; American Institute of Indian Studies; American Oriental Society, President SW branch, 1980-83, 1986-89; Modern Language Association; Société de Linguistique de Paris; Indogermanische Gesellschaft; Societas Linguistica Europaea; Dravidian Linguistic

Association; ACTUAL, President 1975-77; SALA. Address: 2701 Rock Terrace Dr, Austin, TX 78704, USA.

POLONSKY Anthony, b. 1940, British. Appointments: Lecturer in East European History, University of Glasgow, 1968-70; Lecturer in International History, London School of Economics, 1970-, London University 1981-; Secretary, Association of Contemporary Historians, London, 1975-. Publications: Politics in Independent Poland, 1972; The Little Dictator, 1975; The Great Powers and the Polish Question, 1976; The Beginnings of Communist Rule in Poland (with B Druckier), 1978; The History of Poland since 1863 (co-author), 1981. Address: 27 Dartmouth Park Road, London NW5, England.

POLUNIN Nicholas, b. Checkendon, Oxford, England. m. Helen Eugenie Campbell, 3 Jan 1948, 2 s, 1 d. Education: Open Scholar, Christ Church, 1928-32; BA 1st Class Honours, Botany with special subject in Ecology, Oxford University; MA, DPhil, DSc, Oxon; MS, Yale University (Henry Fellow), 1933-34; Research Associate, 1936-37; Foreign Research Associate, 1937-; Fellow, 1950-54, Harvard University. Appointments include: Professor of Botany, University of Ife, Ibadan, Nigeria, 1962-66; Founding Dean, Faculty of Science, Planned Campus for Ile-Ife; Guest Professor, University of Geneva, 1959-61, 1975-76; Founder, Editor, Biological Conservation, 1967-74; Environmental Conservation, 1974-; President, Foundation for Environmental Conservation, 1975-; and of The World Council for The Biosphere, 1984-; Originator of Biosphere Day (21 Sep, first in 1991). Publications include: More than 600 research and other scientific papers, editorials, reviews and books; Editor, The Environmental Future, 1972; Growth Without Ecodisasters?, 1980; Ecosystem Theory and Application, 1986; Maintainance of The Biosphere (with Sir John Burnett), 1989; Surviving with The Biosphere (with Sir John Burnett), 1993; Editor of about 30 volumes (including new editions) of Plant Science Monographs and World Crops Books, 1954-72; Convener and General editor, Environmental Monographs and Symposia, 1979-; Chairman of Board, Cambridge Studies in Environmental Policy, 1984-; Co-editor, Environmental Challenges I, from Stockholm to Rio and Beyond, 1993, Book II: Population and Global Security, 1994. Honours: Recipient, various honours and awards including: International Sasakawa Environment Prize, 1987. Address: Environmental Conservation, 7 Chemin Taverney, 1218 Grand-Saconnex, Geneva, Switzerland.

POLYAKOV Vasiliy Ivanovich, b. 10 Dec 1913, Kursk, USSR. Retired 1985. Agricultural Journalist; Politician. Education: Agricultural Technical School Voronezh; Institute of Journalism, Leningrad. Appointments: Agronomist, 1933-38; CPSU, 1939-; Head of Department Executive Secretary Editorial Board, Sotsialisticheskoe Zemidelie, 1938-41; Pravda, 1946-60, later Editor, Agricultura Department, and Member, Editorial Board; Editor, Rural Life, 1960-62; Head Agriculture, Central Committtee of CPSU, 1962; Chairman, USSR Bureau of Agriculture, 1962-64; Secretary, Central Committee, CPSU, 1962-64; Deputy Chief Editor, Ekonomicheskaya Gazeta, 1964-; Deputy to USSR Supreme Soviet until 1970. Honours: Orders of Lenin, Red Banner of Labour, Patriotic War 1st and 2nd Classes, Red Star.

PONDER Patricia. See: **MAXWELL Patricia Anne.**

POOLE Josephine. See: **HELYAR Jane Penelope Josephine.**

POOLE Julian. See: **MAY Stephen James.**

POPE Dudley Bernard Egerton, b. 29 Dec 1925, Kent, England. Author. m. Kathleen Patricia Hall, 17 Mar 1954, 1 d. Education: Ashford Grammer School. Publications: The Ramage Series (18 volumes), the York series (5 volumes), The Battle of the River Plate, 1956; 73 North, 1958; England Expects, 1959; At 12 Mr Byng Was Shot, 1962; The Black Ship, 1963; fiction: Ramage Series includes: Ramage's Trial, 1984; Ramage's Challenge, 1985; Ramage and the Dido, 1989. Honours: Book Society Choice (1) Ramage; Book Society Alternative Choice (2) Ramage and the Drumbeat, Ramage and the Freebooters; Book Club Associates' Choice (1) Buccaneer; World Book Club Choice (1) Decoy. Address: C/o Campbell Thomson and McLaughlin, 31 Newington Green, London N16 9PU, England.

POPE Pamela Mary Alison, b. 26 Apr 1931, Lowestoft, Suffolk, England. Novelist. m. Ronald Pope, 3 Apr 1954, 2 d. Education: Newland High School, Hull. Publications: The Magnolia Seige, 1982; The Candleberry Tree, 1982; Eden's Law, 1983; The Wind in The East,

1989; The Rich Pass By, 1990; Neither Angels Nor Demons, 1992; A Collar of Jewels, 1994. Contributions to: Good Housekeeping; Woman; Woman's Realm; Vanity Fair; True; Loving; Hampshire Magazine; Hampshire Life; London Evening News. Memberships: Romantic Novelists Association; Society of Authors; Society of Women Writers and Journalists. Address: 1 Rhiners Close, Sway, Lymington, Hampshire, SO41 6BZ.

POPE Ray, b. 1924, British. Appointment: Geography Teacher, Chippenham High School for Girls, 1966-. Publications: Strosa Light, 1965; Nut Case, 1966; Salvage from Strosa, 1967; The Drum, Desperate Breakaway, 1969; One's Pool, 1969; The Model-Railway Men series, 3 volumes, 1970-78; Is It Always Like This? 1970; Telford series, 5 volumes, 1970-79; Hayseed and Company, 1972. Address: The Vatican, 49 High Street, Marshfield, Chippenham, Wiltshire, England.

POPESCU Christine, (Christine Pulleln-Thompson), b. 30 Oct 1930, London, England. Author. m. Julian Poescu, 6 Oct 1954, 2 s, 2 d. Literary Appointment: Speaker, Eastern Arts, 1984. Publications: 95 books for children including Phantom Horse series, 1956; Pony Patrol series 1970's; Black Pony Inn series; Father Unknown, 1980; A Home for Jessie series, 1986; Stay at Home Ben, Careless Ben, 1987, 88; The Road Through the Hills, 1988; Across the Frontier, 1990; The Long Search, 1991; I Want That Pony, 1993; Collection: Horse and Pony Stories. Contributions to: Riding magazines. Memberships: PEN; Society of Authors; Eastern Arts; The Book Trust; Chairman Mellis Parish Council. Literary Agent: Jennifer Luithlen Agency. Address: The Old Parsonage. Mellis, Eye, Suffolk, IP23 8EE, England.

POPHAM Hugh, b. 1920, British. Writer; Author. Publications: Against the Lightning, 1944; The Journey and the Dream, 1945; To the Unborn-Greetings, 1946; Beyond the Eagle's Rage, 1951; Sea Flight, 1954; Cape of Storms, 1957; Monsters and Marlinspikes (in US as the Fabulous Flight of the Pegasus), 1958; The Sea Beggars, 1961; The Shores of Violence, 1963; The House at Cane Garden, 1965; The Somerset Light Infantry, 1968; Gentlemen Peasants, 1968; Into Wind, 1969; The Dorset Regiment, 1970; A Thirst for The Sea, 1979; F.A.N.Y. The Story of the Women's Transport Service, 1985.

PORAD Francine Joy, b. 3 Sept 1929, Seattle, Washington, USA. Poet; Painter. m. Bernard L Porad, 12 June 1949, 3 sons, 3 daughters. Education: BFA, University of Washington, 1976. Appointments: Editor: Brussels Sprout, Haiku Journal, 1988-. Publications: Pen and Inklings, 1986; Connections, 1986; After Autumn Rain, 1987; Blues on the Run, 1988; Free of Clouds, 1989; Without Haste, 1990; Round Renga Round, 1990; A Mural of Leaves, 1991; Hundreds of Wishes, 1991; Joy is My Middle Name, 1993; The Patchwork Quilt, 1993. Contributions to: Leading Haiku journals in the USA, Canada, Japan, England and Romania (total of 49 poetry publications). Honours: Cicada Chapbook Award, 1990; San Francisco International Haiku Honorable Mention, 1991; International Tanka Awards (3) 1991; Juror, International Haiku, Senryu & Tanka Competition, 1992; International Tanka Awards, 1992, 1993; 1st Prize, Poetry Society of Japan International Tanka Competition, 1993; Haiku Society of America Merit Book Award, 1994; Juror, New Zealand International Poetry Competition, 1995. Memberships: Haiku Society of America, President, 1993-95; Association of International Renku; Treasurer, National League of American Pen Women. Address: 6944-SE 33rd, Mercer Island, WA 98040, USA.

PORKERT Manfred Bruno, b. 16 Aug 1933, Decin, Czechoslovakia. University Professor of Chinese Studies and Chinese Medicine, div, 1 d. Education: PhD, Universite de Paris (Sorbonne) 1957; Dr phil habil, Chinese Medicine, Munich University, 1969. Appointments: Editor, Translator, Kindlers Literatur-Lexicon, 1959-62; Executive Editor-in-Chief: International Normative Dictionary of Chinese Medicine, China Academy, Peking, 1989-. Publications: The Theoretical Foundations of Chinese Medicine, 1974; Essentials of Chinese Diagnostics, 1976, 1983; Klinische Chinesische Pharmakologie, 1978; Klassische chinesische Rezeptur, 1984; (with C H Hempen) Systematische Akupunktur, 1985; Booklength literary translation of Chinese "Pingyozhuan: Der Aufstand der Zauberer, 1987; Some 400 professional articles, 200 translations. Memberships: International Chinese Medicine Society (SMS), Founding President 1978-85, Honorary President 1985-. Address: Institut fur Ostasienkunde der Universitat Munchen, Kaulbachstrasse 51a, Munchen 22, Germany.

PORRINO Stefania, b. 1 Apr 1957, Rome, Italy. Dramatist; Professor. Education: Laurea in Lettere, University La Sapienza, Rome, 1980; Diploma di Pianoforte, Conservatorio Di Musica, S Cecilia, Rome, 1987. Publications: Lilli, 1987; Il Rond Del Caffe Ristoro, 1992; Maria Antonietta, 1992; Plays: Invenzione A Tre Voci, 1983; Lilli, 1984; Michelangelo: L'Amico Del Tempo Bruno, 1985; Dostoevskij, 1987. Contributions to: The Monthly Theatre Review, Ridotto. Memberships: Sindacato Nazionale Autori Drammatici; Comitato Esecutivo. Address: Via Flaminia 334, 00196 Roma, Italy.

PORTAL Ellis. See: **POWE Bruce Allen**.

PORTER Bern(ard Harden), b. 14 Feb 1911, Porter Settlement, Maine, USA. Writer. Education: BS, Colby College, 1932; ScM, Brown University, 1933; DSc (Hon), Institute of Advanced Thinking, 1969. Publications: Author, 86 books including: Dieresis, 1976; The Wastemaker, 1980; I've Left, 1982; The Book of Do's, 1984; Here Comes Everybody's Don't Book, 1984; Sweet End, 1984; Last Acts, 1985; Dear Me, 1985; Gee-Whizzels, 1986; H L Mencken: A Bibliography, 1987; First Publications of F Scott Fitgerald, 1987; Sounds That Arouse, 1992. Contributions to: various magazines, 1932-89. Honours: Carnegie Authors Award, 1976; PEN Award, 1976; NEA, 1981. Memberships: Fellow, Society of Programmed Instruction, 1970-; Member, Maine Writers & Publishers Alliance, 1980-. Address: 22 Salmond Way, Belfast, ME 04915, USA.

PORTER Bernard (John), b. 1941, British. Appointments: Fellow, Corpus Christie College, Cambridge, 1966-68; Lecturer, 1968-78, Senior Lecturer in History, 1978-, University of Hull; Reader in History, 1986-92; Professor of Modern History, University of Newcastle, 1992-. Publications: Critics of Empire: British Radical Attitudes to Colonialism in Africa 1896-1914, 1968; The Refugee Question in Mid-Victorian Politics, 1979; Britain, Europe and The World 1850-1982: Delusions of Grandeur, 1983, 1987; The Lion's Share: A Short History of British Imperialism 1850-1982, 1984; The Origins of The Vigilant State: The London Metropolitan Police Special Branch Before The First World War, 1987; Plots and Parania: A History of Political Espionage in Britain 1790-1988, 1989; Britannia's Burden: The Political Development of Britain 1857-1990, 1994. Address: Department of History, The University, Newcastle on Tyne, NE1 7RU, England.

PORTER Brian (Ernest), b. 1928, British. Appointments: Lecturer in Political Science, University of Khartoum, 1963-65; Lecturer 1965-71, Senior Lecturer in International Politics 1971-85; University College, Aberystwyth; Acting Vice-Counsel, Muscat, 1967; Honorary Lecturer in International Relations, University of Kent, Canterbury, 1984-. Publications: Britain and the Rise of Communist China, 1967; The Aberystwyth Papers: International Politics 1919-1969 (editor), 1972; The Reason of States (joint author), 1982; Home Fires and Foreign Fields: British Social and Military Experience in the First World War (joint author), 1985; The Condition of States (joint author), 1991; (co-edited) MartinWright's Intrenational Theory, 1991. Address: Rutherford College, University of Kent, Canterbury, Kent.

PORTER Burton F, b. 22 June 1936. University Professor; Author; Academic Dean; m. 31 Dec 1981, 1 son, 1 daughter, 1 stepdaughter. Education: BA cum laude, University of Maryland, 1959; PhD, St Andrews, Postgraduate, Oxford University, England, 1962. Appointments: Associate Professor, Russell Sage College, 1971-87; Full Professor and Department Head, Drexel University, 1987-91; Dean of Arts and Sciences, Western New England College, 1991-. Publications: Deity and Morality, 1968; Philosophy: A Literary and Conceptual Approach, 1974, 2nd Edition, 1980, 3rd Edition, 1995; Personal Philosophy, 1976; The Good Life, 1980, 2nd edition, 1994; Reasons for Living, 1988; Religion and Reason, 1992. Contributions to: Excerpt from The Moebius Strip, in Boulevard, 1990. Memberships: American Philosophical Association; Modern Language Association. Address: 30 Fearing Street, Amherst, MA 01002, USA.

PORTER Catherine Marjorie, b. 27 Jun 1947, Oxford, England. Writer; Translator. 1 s, 1 d. Education: BA, Hons, Russian, Czech, School of Slavonic Studies, University of London, 1970. Publications: Fathers and Daughters, 1976; Alexandra Kollontai: A Biography, 1980; Blood and Laughter: Images of the 1905 Revolution, 1983; Moscow in World War 2, 1987; Women in Revolutionary Russia, 1987; Larissa Reisner: A Biography, 1988; Translations: Sofia Tolstoya's Diary, 1985; Love of Worker Bees, 1977; A Great Love, 1981; Ship of Widows, 1985; Arise and Walk, 1990; The Best of Ogonoyok, 1990; Little Vera, 1990. Contributions to: articles and book reviews to: Independent;

Guardian; New Statesman and Society; Independent on Sunday. Honours: People's Publishing Prize for translation of Ship of Widows, 1986; Shortlisted, Independent Foreign Fiction Award for Wagibin's Arise and Walk, 1990; numerous drama translations. Membership: Society of Authors. Literary Agent: AnnMcDermid, Curtis Brown.

PORTER Joshua Roy, b. 1921, British. Appointments: Fellow, Chaplain and Tutor, Oriel College, Oxford and University Lecturer in Theology, Oxford University, 1949-62; Canon and Prebendary of Wightring, Chichester Cathedral and Theological Lecturer, 1965-; Dean, Faculty of the Arts 1968-71, Department Head and Professor of Theology 1972-86, University of Exeter. Publications: Eight Oxford Poets (with J Heath-Stubbs and S Keyes), 1941; Poetry from Oxford in War-Time (with W Bell) World in the Heart, 1944; Promise and Fulfilment (with F F Bruce), Moses and Monarchy, 1963; The Extended Family in the Old Testament, 1967; A Source Book of the Bible for Teachers (with R C Walton), Proclamation and Presence (edited with J I Durham), 1970; The Non-Juring Bishops, 1973; The Journey to the Other World (with H R E Davidson),1975; The Book of Leviticus, 1976; Animals in Folklore (edited with W D M Russell), The Monarchy, the Crown and the Church, 1978; Tradition and Interpretation (with G W Anderson), 1979; A Basic Introduction to the Old Testament (with R C Walton), Folklore Studies in the Twentieth Century (co-editor), 1980; Divination and Oracles (with M Loewe and C Blacker), The Folklore of Ghosts (with H R E Davidson), 1981; Israel's Prophetic Tradition (co-author), 1982; Tracts for Our Times (co-author), 1983; The Hero in Traditional Folklore (with C Blacker), 1984; Arabia and the Gulf: From Traditional Society to Modern States (with I Netton), 1986; (contributor to) The Seer in Celtic & Other Traditions, 1989; Schöpfung und Befreiung, 1989; Synodical Government in the Church of England, 1990; Christianity & Conservatism, 1990; Oil of Gladness, 1993; Boundaries and Thresholds (H R E Davidson), 1993. Membership: Wiccamical Canon & Prebendary of Exceit, Chichester Cathedral, 1988-. Address: 36 Theberton Street, Barnsbury, London N1 OQX, England.

PORTER Michael E, b. 1947. Professor; Management Consultant. Publications: Interbrand Choice, 1976; Competitive Strategy, 1980; Competitive Advantage, 1985; Competition in Global Industries, 1986; The Competitive Advantage of Nations, 1990. Contributions to: Harvard Review; Wall Street Journal. Honours: McKinsey Foundation Award for The Best Harvard Review Article, 1973. Address: Harvard Business School, Aldrich Hall 200 Soldiers Field Rd, Boston, MA 02163, USA.

PORTER Peter Neville Frederick, b. 16 Feb 1929, Brisbane, Australia. Freelance Writer; Poet. m. Jannice Henry, 1961 (dec 1974), 2 d. Appointments: Journalist, Brisbane, to 1951; in England: Clerk, Bookseller, Advertising Writer, then became full-time Poet, Journalist, Reviewer and Broadcaster, 1968. Publications: Once Bitten, Twice Bitten, 1961; Penguin Modern Poets No 2, 1962; Poems, Ancient and Modern, 1967; A Porter Folio, 1969; The Last of England, 1970; Preaching to the Converted, 1972; Translator, After Martial,1972; (with Arthur Boyd) Jonah, 1973, The Lady and the Unicorn, 1975; Living in a Calm Country, 1975; Joint Editor, New Poetry 1, 1975; The Cost of Seriousness, 1978; English Subtitles, 1981; Collected Poems, 1983; Fast Forward, 1984; (with Arthur Boyd) Narcissus, 1985; Possible Worlds, 1989; The Chain of Babel, 1992. Honour: Duff Cooper Prize, 1983. Address: 42 Cleveland Square, London W2, England.

PORTIS Charles McColl, b. 28 Dec 1933, El Dorado, Arkansas, USA. Writer. Education: BA, University of Arkansas, 1958. Publications: Novels: Norwood, 1966; True Grit, 1968; The Dog of the South, 1979; Masters of Atlantis, 1985; Gringos, 1991. Literary Agent: Janklow and Nesbit Associates, 598 Madison Avenue, New York, USA. Address: 7417 Kingwood, Little Rock, AR 72207, USA.

PORTOCALA Radu, b. 27 Mar 1951, Bucharest, Romania. Writer; Journalist. m. Delphine Beaugonin, 21 Dec 1987, 2 daughters. Education: Master of International Relations, Paris, 1986; BA, Romanian, Paris, 1986. Publications: Autopsie Du Coup D'Etat Roumain, 1990; Câlâtorie in Cusca Hidrelor, 1994; La Chute Dans L'Enthousiasme, in print; Several volumes of poetry in Romanian. Contributions to: Le Point; Est & Ouest; Cuvintul, Bucharest; Voice of America; Radio France Internationale. Address: 7 Rue Du Docteur Roux, 75015 Paris, France.

PORTWAY Christopher, b. 30 Oct 1923, Halstead, Essex, England. Travel Journalist; Author; Novelist; Travel Editor. m.

Jaroslava Krupickova, 4 Apr 1957, 1 s, 1 d. Publications: Journey to Dana, 1955; The Pregnant Unicorn, 1969; All Exits Barred, 1971; Corner Seat, 1972; Lost Vengeance, 1973; Double Circuit, 1974; The Tirana Assignment, 1974; The Anarchy Pedlars, 1976; The Great Railway Adventure, 1983; Journey Along the Spine of The Andes, 1984; The Great Travelling Adventure, 1985; Czechmate, 1987; Indian Odessy, 1993; A Kenyan Adventure, 1993. Contributions to: Times; Daily Telegraph; Times Educational Supplement; Guardian; Country Life; The Lady; Railway Magazine; In-Flight Magazines; Various holiday and travel magazines. Honours: TD; FRGS; Winston Churchill Fellow, 1993. Address: 22 Tower Road, Brighton, BN2 2GF, England.

POSEJPAL Matej. See: VANICEK Zdenek.

POSNER Gerald, b. 20 May 1954, CA, USA. Attorney; Writer. m. Trisha D Levene, Apr 1984. Education: BA, University of CA, 1972-75; JD, Hastings College of Law, 1975-78. Publications: Mengele: The Complete Story, 1986; Warlords of Crime, 1988; Bio-Assassins, 1989; Hitler's Children, 1991; Case Closed, 1993. Contributions to: NY Times; New Yorker; Chicago Tribune; US News & World Report. Honour: Pulitzer Finalist, 1993. Memberships: National Writers Union; Authors Guild; PEN. Literary Agent: William Morris Agency. Address: 515 Madison Avenue, Suite 905, New York, NY 10022, USA.

POSNER Richard, (Jonathon Craig, Iris Foster, Beatrice Murray, Paul Todd, Dick Wine), b. 1944, American. Appointments: English Teacher, Sachem High School, Ronkonkoma, NY; Instructor of Composition, Queenborough Community College, Bayside. Publications: The Dark Sonata (as B Murray), 1971; The Moorwwod Legacy (as I Foster), The New York Crime Book (as J Craig), Deadly Sea Deadly sand (as I Foster), the Sabbath Quest (as I Foster), The Crimson Moon (as I Foster), Allegro with Passion (as D Wine), The Mafia Man,the Seven-Ups, 1973; The Trigger Man, Welcome Sinner, 1974; Blood All Over (as P Todd), The Image and the Flesh, Lucas Tanner: A Question of Guilt, Lucas Tanner: A Matter of Love, Lucas Tanner: For Her to Decide, 1975; The Lovers, 1978; Impassioned, 1980; Infidelities, 1982; Tycoon, 1983; Jade Moon, The Goldshield (with Marie Castoire), 1984; Bright Desires, 1985.

POSTER Mark, b. 1941, American. Appointments: Professor of History, University of California at Irvine, 1978-; Member, Editorial Board, The 18th Century: A Journal of Interpretation. Publications: The Utopian Thought of Restif de la Bretonne, Harmonian Man: Selected Writings of Charles Fourier (editor), 1971; Existential Marxism in Postwar France, 1976; Critical Theory of the Family, 1978; Satre's Marxism, 1979; Foucalt, Marxism and History, 1984; Baudrillard: Selected Writings (edited and introduced by Mark Poster), 1988; Critical Theory and Poststructuralism, 1989; The Mode of Information, 1990; Postsuburban California: The Social Transformation of Orange County Since 1945, (edited, Rob Kling, Spencer Olin and Mark Poster), 1991. Address: History Department, University of California at Irvine, Irvine, CA 92717, USA.

POSTMA Johannes, b. 14 Jan 1935. University Professor. Education: BA, Graceland College, 1962; MA, University of Kansas, 1964; PhD, Michigan State University, 1970. Appointments: Instructor, Western Michigan University, 1964-68; Assisstant Professor to full Professor, Mankato State University, 1969-; Visiting Professor, Leiden Rijksunversiteit, 1986-87. Publication: The Dutch in the Atlantic Slave Trade, 1600-1815, 1990. Memberships: American Historical Association; Social Science History Association; Royal Institute of Linguistics and Anthropology. Address: 50 Woodview Drive, Mankato, MN 56001, USA.

POSTMAN Neil. Writer; Professor of Media Ecology. Publications:the Disappearence of Childhood; Technopoly; Television and the Teaching of English, 1961; The Uses of Language, 1965; Language and Reality, 1966; Teaching as a Subversive Activity (with Charles Weingartner), 1969; The Soft Revolution: A Student Handbook for Turning Schools Around, (with Charles Weingartner), 1971; Teaching as a Conserving Activity, 1979. Contributions include: Atlantic; Nation. Address: Dept of Communications, Arts & Sciences, NY University, New York, NY 10003-6607, USA.

POTOK Chaim, b. 17 Feb 1929, NY, USA. Writer. m. Adena Sara Mosevitsky, 8 June 1958, 1 s, 2 d. Education: BA, Yeshiva University, 1950; MHL, Rabbinic Ordination, Jewish Theological Seminary, 1954; PhD, University of PA, 1965. Publications: The Chosen, 1967; The Promise, 1969; My Name is Asher Lev, 1972; In the Beginning, 1975;

The Book of Lights, 1981; Wanderings, 1978; Davitas Harp, 1985; The Gift of Asher Lev, 1990; I am the Clay, 1992. Contributions to; The New York Times Sunday Book Review; Esquire; Commentary; Triquarterly; Moment. Honours: Wallant Prize, 1967; Athenaeum Award, 1970; National Jewish Book Award, 1991. Memberships: PEN; Drama Guild; Writers Guild. Literary Agent: Owen Laster, William Morris Agency. Address: 20 Berwick Road, Merion, PA 19066, USA.

POTTER Beverley Ann, b. 3 Mar 1944, Summit, New Jersey, USA. Psychologist; Publisher; Business Executive. Education: BA, 1966, MS, 1968, San Francisco State University; PhD, Stanford University, 1974. Publications: Chlorella: The Amazing Alchemist; Turning Around: Keys to Motivation and Productivity, 1980, 81, 85, 89; Beating Job Burnout: How to Transform Work Pressure into Productivity, 1980, 81, 85; The Way of the Ronin: Riding the Waves of Change at Work, 1985, 86, 89; Preventing Job Burnout: A Work Book, 1987; Drug Testing at Work: A Guide for Employers and Employees, 90; The Pathfinder's Craft: Tools for Personal Leadership, 1993; Brain Boosters: Foods & Drinks That Make You Smarter, 1993. Contributions to: Numerous contributions to journals and magazines. Memberships: North California Booksellers Association: Bay Area Organisation Development Network - formerly National Speakers Association. Address: PO Box 1035, Berkeley, CA 94701, USA.

POTTER Jeremy, b. 25 Apr 1922, London, England. Writer; Publisher. m. 11 Feb 1950, 1 s, 1 d. Education: MA, Queen's College, Oxford. Publications: Good King Richard?, 1983; Pretenders, 1986; Independent Television in Britain, volume 3: Politics and Control 1968-80, 1989 and volume 4: Companies and Programmes 1968-80, 1990; Tennis and Oxford, 1994; Novels: Hazard Chase, 1964; Death in Office, 1965; Foul Play, 1967; The Dance of Death, 1968; A Trail of Blood, 1970; Going West, 1972; Disgrace and Favour, 1975; Death in The Forest, 1977; The Primrose Hill Murder, 1992; The Mystery of the Campden Wonder, 1995. Address: The Old Pottery, Larkins Lane, Headington, Oxford, OX3 9DW, England.

POTTER Margaret (Anne Betteridge, Anne Melville, Margaret Newman), b. 21 Jun 1926, Harrow, Middlesex, England. Author. m. Jeremy Potter, 11 Feb 1950, 1 s, 1 d. Education: Major Scholar, Modern History, St Hugh's College, Oxford; MA, Oxon; Book Production course, London School of Printing. Literary Appointments: Editor, Children's Missionary Magazine, 5 years. Publications include: As Margaret Newman: The Boys Who Disappeared; Trouble on Sunday; The Motorway Mob; Tilly and The Princess; Unto the Fourth Generation; Lochandar; As Anne Betteridge: A Portuguese Affair; A Little Bit of Luck; Shooting Star; Love in A Rainy Country; The Girl Outside; Journey From a Foreign Land; The Sacrifice; A Time of Their Lives, short stories; The Temp; A Place for Everyone; The Tiger and The Goat; As Anne Melville: The Lorimer Line; The House of Hardie; Grace Hardie; The Hardie Inheritance; The Dangerfield Diaries; The Tantivy Trust; A Clean Break; The Russian Tiara; Standing Alone; Snapshots, short stories. Contributions to: Fiction Reviews; Travel articles; Short stories in magazines. Memberships: Adviser, Citizens Advice Bureau, 8 years; Grant Allocation Committee, King Edward VII Fund, 5 years. Address: c/o Peters Fraser and Dunlop, 5th Floor, The Chambers, Chelsea Harbour, Lots Road, London, SW10 0XF, England.

POULIN Gabrielle, b. 21 June 1929, St Prosper, Quebec, Canada. Writer. Education: MA, University Montreal; Lic Letters; Dip Higher Studies; DLitt, University Sherbroke. Appointments: Writer in Residence, Ottawa Public Library, 1988. Publications: Les Miroirs d'un poète: image et reflets de Paul Eluard, 1969; Cogne la caboche, 1979; L'Age de l'interrogation, 1937-52, 1980; Les Mensonges d'Isabelle, (novel), 1983; All the Way Home, originally published as Cogne la caboche, translated by Jane Pentland, 1984; La Couronne d'oubli, (novel), 1990; Petites Fugues pour une saison seche (poetry) 1991; Le Livre de däraison (novel), 1994. Contributions to: Voix et images; Lettres québécoises; Relations. Honours: Prize, Swiss Embassy 1967; Grant, Arts Council of Canada on 11 occasions, 1968-83, 1985; Press Lit Prize, 1979;Champlain Lit Prize, 1979; Ottawa Carleton Lit Prize, 1993; Alliance françoise Lit Prize, 1984; Salon du Livre de Toronto Lit Prize, 1994. Memberships: Union Quebecois Writers; Sociätä des äcrivains canadiens de l'Outaouais. Literary Agent: René Dionne, Lettres Francaises, University of Ottawa. Address: 1997 Avenue Quincy, Ottawa, Ontario, K1J 6B4, Canada.

POULSEN Morten, (Morti Vizki), b. 18 Jan 1963, Copenhagen, Denmark. Author. Education: Japanese, University of Copenhagen. Publications: Himmelstormere, 1986; Begge Ben, 1990; Det Sidste Rum, 1993; Vingens Kniv, 1993. Honours: Klaus Rifbderg Award, 1986; Nordic Radio Prize, 1989; Laureate of State, 1990; Marguerite Viby Award, 1994. Memberships: Editor of "The Blue Gate". Literary Agent: Gyldendal. Address: Sankt Jorgens Alle 7, 1669 Kobenhavn V, DK, Denmark.

POUPLIER Erik, b. 16 Jun 1926, Svendborg, Denmark. Writer. m. Annalise Hansen, 28 Sep 1947, 1 d. Education: Trained as journalist. Publications: In Danish: Lend Me Your Wife, 1957; My Castle in Ardèche, 1968; The Gentle Revolt, 1970; The Discreet Servant of The Death, 1972; The Adhesive Pursuer, 1973; Murder, Mafia and Pastis'er, 1974; My Castle in Provence, 1979; The Old Man in Provence, 1980; The Clumsy Kidnappers, 1981; The World of Annesisse, 1982; The Galic Cock, 1984; My Own Provence, 1984; The Cuisine of Provence, 1985; Panic in Provence, 1986; All Year Round in Provence, 1987; Machiavelli, 1987; The Anaconda-Coup in Provence, 1988; Long Live the Grandparents, 1988; Barbaroux and the Flood, 1989; Always Around the Next Corner (memoirs), 1990; Pearls of Provence, 1991; Barbaroux and The Nuns, 1992; Merry-Go-Round, 1993; The 4 Seasons of Provence, 1995. Contributions to: Jyllands Posten, Denmark. Memberships: Danish Author's Society; Société d'Ecrivains de Nice et de Cannes; Danish Press Association. Address: Les Charmettes, Chemin de Plateau, 83550 Vidauban, France.

POURNELLE Jerry Eugene, (Wade Curtis), b. 1933, USA. Freelance Writer, Lecturer and Consultant. Publications: Red Heroin (as Wade Curtis), 1969; The Strategy of Technology: Winning the Decisive War (with Stefan Possony), 1970; Red Dragon (as Wade Curtis), 1971; A Spaceship for the King, 1973; Escape From the Planet of the Apes, novelization of screenplay, 1973; The Mote in God's Eye (with Larry Niven), 1974; 20/20 Vision (editor), 1974; Birth of Fire, 1976; Inferno (with Larry Niven), 1976; West of Honor, 1976; High Justice, short stories, 1977; The Mercenary, 1977; Lucifer's Hammer, (with Larry Niven), 1977; Exiles to Glory, 1978; Black Holes (editor), 1979; A Step Further Out, non-fiction, 1980; Janisseries, 1980; Oath of Fealty (with Larry Niven), 1981; Clan and Crown (with Roland Green), 1982; There Will Be War (co-editor), 1983; Mutual Assured Survival (with Dean Ing), 1984; Men of War (co-editor), 1984; Blood and Iron (co-editor), 1984; Day of the Tyrant (co-editor), Footfall (with Larry Niven), 1985; Warriors (co-editor), 1986; Imperial Stars: The Stars at War, Republic and Empire (co-editor), 2 vols, 1986-87; Guns of Darkness (co-editor), 1987; Storms of Victory (with Roland Green), 1987; Legacy of Hereot (with Larry Niven), 1987; Prince of Mercenaries, 1989; The Gripping Hand (with Larry Niven), 1993. Contributions to: non-fiction articles to Galaxy magazine, 1974-78; Consulting Editor and Columnist, Byte magazine. Memberships: Fellow, Operations Research Society of America; Fellow, American Association for the Advancement of Science; President, Science Fiction Writers of America, 1974. Address: 121901 1/2 Ventura Blvd, Box 372, Studio City, CA 91604, CA, USA.

POWE Bruce Allen (Ellis Portal),b. 1925, Canada. Appointments: Special Assistant, Minister of Mines and Technical Surveys, 1951-57; Editorial Assistant, Imperial Oil Limited, 1957-60; Executive Director, Ontario Liberal Association, 1960-63; Vice President, Public Relations, Baker Advertising Limited, 1964-66; Vice President of Public Affiars, Canadian Life and Health Insurance Association, Toronto, 1966-90. Publications: Expresso '67, 1966; Killing Ground: The Canadian Civil War (as E Portal), 1968, under own name, 1972; The Last Days of the American Empire, 1974; The Aberhart Summer, 1983; The Ice Eaters, 1987. Address: 158 Ridley Boulevard, Toronto, Ontario M5M 3M1, Canada.

POWE Bruce William,b. 23 Mar 1955, Ottawa, Ontario, Canada. Author; Teacher. m. Robin Leslie Mackenzie, 7 Sept 1991, 1 son, 1 daughter. Education: BA, Special Honours, York University, Toronto; MA, University of Toronto. Publications: A Climate Charged, 1984; The Solitary Outlaw, 1987; Noise of Time, text for Glenn Gould Profile, 1989; A Tremendous Canada of Light, 1993; Outage: A Journey into the Electric City, 1995. Contributions to: The Globe and Mail; The Toronto Star; The Antigonish Review; The Bennington Review; Exile; Modem Drama. Honours: York University Book Award, 1977; Special MA Scholarship to University of Toronto, 1979; Explorations Grant, Canada Council, 1980; Maclean-Hunter Fellowship, 1989; Ontario Arts Council Awards, 1990, 1991, 1992, 1994. Literary Agent: Dean Cooke, Livingston Cooke-Curtis Brown, Canada. Address: 18 Berkinshaw Crescent, Toronto, Ontario M3B 2T2, Canada.

POWELL Anthony (Dymoke), b. 21 Dec 1905, London, England. Writer. m. Lady Violet Pakenham, 1934, 2 s. Education: Balliol College, Oxford. Literary Appointments: With Duckworth Publishers, 1926-35; Literary Editor, Punch, 1953-59; Trustee, National Portrait Gallery, 1962-76. Publications include: The Soldier's Art, 1966; The Military Philosophers, 1968; The Garden God and The Rest I'll Whistle: The Text of Two Plays, Books Do Furnish a Room, 1971; Temporary Kings, 1973; Hearing Secret Harmonies, 1975; Infants of The Spring, 1976; Messengers of Day, 1978; Faces in My Time, 1980; The Strangers All Are Gone, 1982; O, How The Wheel Becomes It!, 1983; To Keep The Ball Rolling (abridged memoirs), 1983; The Fisher King, 1986; Miscellaneous Verdicts (criticism), 1990; Under Review (criticism), 1992. Honours: CBE, 1956; CH, 1988; Orders of White Lion (Czechoslovakia), Leopold II (Belgium), Oaken Crown and Croix de Guerre (Luxembourg); James Tait Black Prize; Hon DLitt: Sussex, Leicester, Kent, Oxford, Bristol; Honorary Fellow, Balliol College, Oxford, 1974; W H Smith Award, 1974; The Hudson Review Bennett Award, 1984; Ingersoll Foundation; Hon DLitt, Wales, 1992. Address: The Chantry, Near Frome, Somerset, BA11 3LJ, England.

POWELL (Elizabeth) Dilys, TV Film Critic; Film Critic. m. (1) Humfry Payne, 1926 (dec 1936), (2) Leonard Russell, 1943 (dec 1974). Education: Somerville College, Oxford. Appointments: Editorial Staff, Sunday Times, 1928-31, 1936-41; Film Critic, 1939-76, TV Film Critic, 1976-, The Sunday Times, Film Critic, Punch, 1979-1992. Publications: Descent From Parnassus, 1934; Remember Greece, 1941; The Traveller's Journey is Done, 1943; Coco, 1952; An Affair of the Heart, 1957; The Villa Ariadne, 1973; The Golden Screen (Collected Reviews), 1989; The Dilys Powell Film Reader (Collected Reviews), 1991. Honour: CBE, 1974; Hon Fellow, Somerville College, 1992. Memberships: Board of Governors, British Film Institute, 1948-52, Fellow, 1986; Independent Television Authority, 1954-57; Cinematograph Films Council, 1965-69; President, Classical Association, 1966-67; Honorary Member, ACTT. Address: 14 Albion Street, Hyde Park, London W2 2AS, England.

POWELL (John) Enoch, b. 1912, British. Poetry; Classics; History; Politics/Government; Translations. Appointments: Conservative Member of Parliament for Wolverhampton South-West, 1950-74; Ulster Unionist Member of Parliament (UK) for South Down, Northern Ireland, 1974-87. Publications: The Rendel Harris Papyri, 1936; First Poems, 1937; A Lexicon to Herodotus, 1938; The History of Herodotus, 1939; Casting Off and Other Poems, 1939; Herodotus, Book VIII, 1939; Llyfr Blegywryd, 1942; Thucydidis Historia, 1942; Herodotus (translation), 1949; One Nation (with others), 1950; Dancer's End and The Wedding Gift, 1951; The Social Services: Needs and Means, 1952; Change Is Our Ally (with others), 1954; Biography of A Nation (with A Maude), 1955; Saving in A Free Society, 1960; Great Parliamentary Occasions, 1960; A Nation Not Afraid, 1965; A New Look at Medicine and Politics, 1966; The House of Lords in The Middle Ages (with K Wallis), 1968; Freedom and Reality, 1969; Income Tax at 4/3 in The Pound, 1970; The Common Market: The Case Against, 1971; Still To Decide, 1972; No Easy Answers, 1973; Wrestling With The Angel, 1977; Joseph Chamberlain, 1977; A Nation or No Nation, 1978; Collected Poems, 1990; Enoch Powell on 1992, 1992; Evolution of the Gospel, 1994. Address: 33 South Eaton Place, London, SW1W 9EN, England.

POWELL Geoffrey Stewart (Tom Angus), b. 25 Dec 1914, Scarborough, Yorkshire, England. Soldier; Writer. m. Felicity Wadsworth, 15 Jul 1944, 1 son, 1 daughter. Education: Scarborough College, 1923-31; Army Staff College, 1945-46; United States Command and General Staff College, 1950-51; Joint Services Staff College, 1953-54; BA, Open University, 1981. Publications: The Green Howards, 1968; The Kandyan Wars, 1973; Men at Amhem, 1978, (1st edited under the pseudonym Tom Angus); Suez: The Double War (with Roy Fullick), 1979; The Book of Campden, 1982; The Devil's Birthday: The Bridges to Amhem, 1984; Plumer: The Soldier's General, 1990; The Green Howards: 300 Years of Service, 1992; Buller: A Scapegoat: A Life of General Sir Redvers Buller, VC, 1994. Contributions to: Numerous to journals and magazines. Honours: Fellow, Royal Historical Society, 1989. Literary Agent: A M Heath and Company. Address: c/o Army and Navy Club, Pall Mall, London, SW1, England.

POWELL Neil, b. 11 Feb 1948, London, England. Writer; Editor. Education: BA, 2:1 English and American Literature, 1966-69, MPhil, English Literature, 1969-71, University of Warwick. Publications: At The Edge (poems), 1977; Carpenters of Light (criticism), 1979; A Season of Calm Weather (poems), 1982; Selected Poems of Fulke Greville

(edited), 1990; True Colours: New and Selected Poems, 1991; Unreal City (novel), 1992; The Stones on Thorpeness Beach (poems), 1994. Contributions to: Critical Quarterly; Encounter; Gay Times; The Guardian; The Listener; London Magazine; New Statesman; PN Review; Poetry Review; Times Literary Supplement. Honours: Gregory Award, Society of Authors, 1969; Authors' Foundation Award, 1992. Memberships: Greenpeace; Poetry Society; Society of Authors. Literary Agent: A P Watt. Address: c/o Carcanet Press Limited, 402-406 Corn Exchange Buildings, Manchester, M4 3BQ, England.

POWELL Padgett, b. 25 Apr 1952, Gainesville, Florida, USA. Professor of Creative Writing. m. Sidney Wade, 22 May 1984, 2 daughters. Education: BA, College of Charleston 1975; MA, University of Houston, 1982. Appointments: Freight Handler, Household Mover and Orthodontic Technician in Southern United States, including Jacksonville, Florida, Florence, South Carolina and Charleston, South Carolina, 1968-75; Day Labourer, Houston, Texas, 1975; Roofer in Texas, 1975-82; Writer, 1983-; Professor of Creative Writing, University of Florida, Gainesville, 1984-. Publications: Edisto (novel), 1984; A Woman Named Drown (novel), 1987; Contributor, Alex Harris (ed) A World Unsuspected: Portraits of Southeren Childhood, 1987; Typical (stories), 1991. Contributions to: Stories to periodicals, including Esquire, The New Yorker and Grand Street. Honours: Edisto named one of the year's five best books, 1984 by Time; American Book Award nominee for first fiction, 1984 and Whiting Foundation Writers' Award 1986, both for Edisto; American Academy and Institute of Arts and Letters Rome Fellowship in Literature 1987. Memberships: PEN; Authors Guild; Writers Guild of America, East. Literary Agent: Cynthia Cannell, Janklow & Nesbit, 598 Madison Avenue, NY 10022, USA. Address: Department of English, University of Florida, Gainesville, FL 32611, USA.

POWELL Talmage, b. 1920, USA. Author. Publications: novels: The Girl From the Big Pine, 1961; The Cage, 1969; Mission Impossible - The Priceless Particle, 1969; The Thing in B-3, 1969; Mission: Impossible - The Money Explosion, 1979; Dark Over Arcadia (as Anne Talmage), 1971; Mystery novels: The Killer is Mine, 1959; The Smasher, 1959; The Girl's Number Doesn't Answer, 1960; Man-Killer, 1960; The Girl Who Killed Things, 1960; What a Madman Behind Me, 1962; Start Screaming Murder, 1962; The Raper (as Jack MaCready), 1962; Murder with a Past (as Ellery Queen), 1963; Beware the Young Stranger (as Ellery Queen), 1965; Corpus Delectable, 1965; Where is Bianca (as Ellery Queen), 1966; Who Spies, Who Kills (as Ellery Queen), 1966, other: Cellar Team, juvenile, 1972. Contributions to: anthologies: numerous including: Bad Girls, 1958; The Saint Mystery Library, 1959; Best Detective Stories of the Year, 1961; The Fireside Treasury of Modern Hunour, 1963; Mink is for a Minx, 1964; Alfred Hitchcock's Death Mate, 1973 and many more. More recent works include: Alfred Hitchcock's A Choice of Evils, 1983; Alfred Hitchcock's Grave Suspicans, 1984; Alfred Hitchcock's Crime Watch, 1984; Alfred Hitchcock's A Brief Darkness, 1987; 14 Vicious Valentines, 1988; Dixie Ghosts, 1988; More Wild Westerns, 1989; A Treasury of American Mysteries, 1989; Curses! 1989; Lighthouse Horrors, 1990; Back From the Dead, 1990; Loaded for Bear, 1990. A volume of short stories, written for Hitchcock, 25 Twisted Tales of Revenge and Intrigue, 1989; 25 TV/ Motion pictures, stories and/or screenplays; translations in 11 languages. Address: 33 Caledonia Road, Kenilworth, Asheville, NC 28803, USA.

POWELL Violet, b. 1912, British. Publications: Five out of Six, 1960; A Substantial Ghost, 1967; The Irish Cousins, 1970; A Compton-Burnett Compendium, 1973; Within the Family Circle, 1976; Maragaret, Countess of Jersey, 1978; Flora Annie Steel, Novelist of India, 1981; The Constant Novelist, 1983; The Album of Anthony Powell's Dance to the Music of Time (editor), 1987; The Life of A Provincial Lady: A Study of E M Delderfield and Her Works, 1988; A Jane Austen Compendium, 1993. Address: The Chantry, Nr Frome, Somerset, BA11 3LJ, England.

POWELL-SMITH Vincent, (Francis Elphinstone, Justiciar, Santa Maria), b. 28 May 1939, Westerham, Kent, England. Advocatem, m. (1) 2 d, (2) Martha Marilyn Du Barry, 4 Apr 1989. Education: University of Birmingham: International Faculty of Comparative Law, Luxembourg; Inns of Court School of Law, London; Gray's Inn; LLB, Honours: LLM; DLitt; Dip Com; DSL. Appointments: Professor of Construction Law, Universiti Teknologi Malaysia, 1990-; Joint Editor, Construction Law Reports, 1984-;Consultant Editor, Emden's Building Contracts and Practice, 1980; Series Editor, Architectural Press Library of Building Control. Publications: The Building Regulations Explained,

8th edition, 1990; Building Contract Claims, 2nd edition, 1988; Horse and Stable Management, 1984; The JCT Standard Building Contract, 2nd edition, 1990; Building Contract Dictionary, 2nd edition, 1990; Horse Business Management, 1989; Law of Boundaries and Fences; You and the Law, 1986; Author of over 60 books. Contributions to: Legal Correspondent, Contract Journal, 1974-; Legal Correspondent, Surveyor, 1980-; Architect's Journal; Law Society's Gazette; Financial Times; Daily Telegraph; The Field; New Law Journal. Honours: Liveryman, Worshipful Company of Paviors; Freeman of the city of London; Knight of Honour, Royal Yugoslavian Order of St John; Kt Commander, Order of Polonia Restituta. Memberships: Fellow, Chartered Institute of Arbitrators; Fellow, British Academy of Experts. Address: Apartado 127, 8126 Quarteira Codex, Portugal.

POWER Edward, b. 16 Jun 1951, Mooncoin, Co Kilkenny, Ireland. Writer; Historian. Education: Mooncoin BNS; Mooncoin Vocational · and Technical School. Appointments: Worked for photographic firm in London; Literature Officer, Waterford Arts Centre, 1986-87; Publisher and Editor, Riverine literary magazine; Press Correspondent, Kilkenny People newspaper; Local historian. Publications: Poetry and short stories included in: The Second Blackstaff Book of Short Stories, 1991, The Kilkenny Anthology, The Cloverdale Anthology of Irish poets, 1992. Contributions to: New Irish Writing (Irish Press & Sunday Tribune); Poetry Ireland Review; Cyphers; Cloverdale Anthology; Kilkenny Magazine; Passages 4; The Salmon; Criterion. Honours: Winner, Waterford Literary Competition for Short Fiction, 1981; Shortlisted for Hennessey Award, 1987; Story, entitled Faith Healer, won first place in competition organised by Kilkenny County Council & the Book Centre & Radio Kilkenny, 1991; shortlisted for US based Cloverdale Literary Prize for Irish Poetry, 1992. Address: Chapel Street, Mooncoin, Co Kilkenny, Ireland.

POWERS J(ames) F(arl), b. 1917, USA. Academic; Author. Appointments: Faculty Member: Marquette University, Milwaukee, 1949-51; University of Michigan, Ann Arbor, 1956-57; Smith College, Northampton, Massachusetts, 1965-66; St John's University, Collegville, Minnesota, 1976-. Publications: Prince of Darkness and Other Stories, 1947; The Presence of Grace, short stories, 1956; Morte d'Urban, novel, 1962; Look How the Fish Live, 1975. Address: c/o Alfred Knopf Inc, 201 East 50th Street, New York, NY 10022, USA.

POWERS M L. See: TUBB E(dwin) C(harles).

POWERS Robert M, b. 9 Nov 1942, Levington, Kentucky, USA. Author. m. 1 Sept 1961, 1 daughter. Education: BA, University of Arizona, 1969; University of Edinburgh, Scotland, 1968; MA, University of Western New Mexico. Appointments: Aerospace Editor, Revisa Aerea, 1980; Contributing Editor, Final Frontier, 1987; Professor of Creative Writing, Pirna College, Tucson, 1986-. Publications: Planetary Encounters, 1978, 1980; Shuttle, 1979; The Coattails of God, 1981; Mars, 1986; Other Worlds Than Ours, 1983; Viking Mission to Mars, with others, 1975; In The Belly of The Bomb (pending). Contributions: Over 200 magazine articles, 1970-. Honours: Best Book on Science, Library Journal, for Shuttle, 1980; Best Space Book, Av. Space Writers International, 1979, 1980, 1982. Memberships: Authors League and Guild; Fellow, Royal Astronomical Society, England; Aviation Space Writers Association International; Royal Astronomical Society of Canada; Société Astronomique de France. Literary Agent: Maggie Nouch, London, England. Address: Valencia Mountain Observatory, HCR-1, Box 470, Tucson, AZ 85736, USA.

POWNALL David, b. 19 May 1938, Liverpool, England. Author. Education: BA, 1960, University of Keele. Appointments: Resident Writer: Century Theatre Touring Group, 1970-72; Duke's Theatre, Lancaster, 1972-75; Paines Plough Theatre, Coventry, 1975-80. Publications: Verse: An Eagle Each (with J Hill), 1972; Another Country, 1978; Fiction: The Raining Tree War, 1974; African Horse, 1975; My Organic Uncle and Other Stories, 1976; God Perkins, 1977; Light on A Honeycomb, 1978; Beloved Latitudes, 1981; Plays: The Dream of Chief Crazy Horse, 1975; Music to Murder By, 1978; Motocar and Richard III, Part Two, 1979; An Audience Called Edouard, 1979; Beef (in Best Radio Plays of 1981), 1982; Master Class, 1983; Ploughboy Monday (in Best Radio Plays of 1985), 1986; Other: Between Ribble and Lune: Scenes from the North-West, 1980; The Bunch From Bananas (for children), 1980. Address: 136 Cranley Gardens, London, N10 3AH, England.

POYER Joe, b. 30 Nov 1939, Battle Creek, Michigan, USA. Author. m. Bonnie Prichard, Oct 1987. Education: BA,

Communications, Michigan State University, 1961. Appointments include: Field Editor, International Combat Arms, Journal of Defence Technology; Freelance Specialist, high technology military affairs & weaponry; Novelist, Owner and Publisher, North Cape Publications; Editor, Safe & Secure Living; Editor, International Military Review. Novels: North Cape, 1968; Balkan Assignment, 1971; Chinese Agenda, 1972; Shooting of the Green, 1973; Devoted Friends, 1982; Time of War, 2 vols, 1983, 1985. Also: The Contract; Vengeance 10; Tunnel War; Day of Reckoning; Publications: The 54-70 Springfield, 1991; US Winchester Trench and Riot Guns, 1993; Pocket Guide, 45-70 Springfield, 1994. Contributions to: Journals as listed, aslo international Defence Images. Literary Agent: Diane Cleaver, 55 5th Avenue, New York City. Address: PO Box 1027, Tustin, CA 92681, USA.

POYNDER Edward. See: GRIGG John.

PRABHASHANKAR T G (Premi), b. 7 May 1942, Tumkur, India. Professor of Hindi, Bangalore University. m. Anu Prabha, 16 Mar 1969, 1 s, 1 d. Education: MA Hindi, Mysore University, 1965; PhD, Karnatak University, Dharwar, 1977. Appointments: Editor, Basava Marg, half yearly Hindi Magazine, Bangalore. Publications: Kavyabala, poetry in Hindi, 1975; Kannada Aur Hindi Sahitya Ka Tulanatmak Adyayan, 1977; Adhunik Hindi Kavita Par Gandhivad Ka Prabhav, PhD thesis, 1981; Basava Darshan, essay, translation, 1983; Shresta Jeevania, biographies, 1984; Talash, poetry in Hindi, 1988; Kanasugala Kannadi, poetry in Kannada. Contributions to: Hindi Poems and articles to leading Hindi magazines: Kadambini; Aaj Kal; Samakaleen Bharatia Sahitya; Bhasha. Honours: Karnatak State Monetary Award for translation of Basava Darshan, 1983; Souhardh Samman Cash Award, Uttar Pradesh Government, 1990. Memberships: Vice-President, Poets International, Bangalore; Convenor, Authors Guild of India, Bangalore Chapter. Address: Prabhu Priya 391, VI Main 111 Block 111 Stage, Basavaeswar Nagar, Bangalore 5600079, India.

PRABHOT Kaur, b. 6 Jul 1927, Langarial, India. Poet; Politician. m. Brigadier Narenderpal Singh, 1948, 2 d. Education: Punjab University. Publications: 35 books including: Poems: Supne Sadhran, 1949; Do Rang, 1951; Pankheru, 1956; Iala (in Persian), 1958; Bankapasi, 1958; Pabbi, 1962; Khali, 1967; Waddershi Sheesha, 1972; Madhiantar, 1974; Chandra Yug, 1978; Dreams Die Young, 1979; Him Hans, 1982; Samrup, 1982; ishq Shara Ki Nata, 1983; short stories: Kinke, 1952; Aman de Na, 1965; Zindgi de Kujh Pal, 1982. Honours: Most Distinguished Order of Poetry, World Poetry Society, 1974; Woman of the Year, UPLI, Philippines, 1975; Sewa Sifta Award, 1980; NIF Cultural Award, 1982; Josh Kenya Award, 1982; Delhi State Award, 1983; Poet Laureat, Punjab Government. Memberships: Legislative Council, Punjab 1966-; Sahitya Akademi. Address: D-203 Defence Colony, New Delhi 110024, India.

PRALL Stuart Edward, b. 2 June 1929, Saginaw, Michigan, USA. Professor of History; Author. m. Naomi Shafer, 20 Jan 1958, 1 son, 1 daughter. Education: BA, Michigan State University, 1951; MA, University of Rhode Island, 1953; University of Manchester, England, 1953-54; PhD, Columbia University, 1960. Appointments: Queens College & Graduate School, University Center, City University of New York, 1955-58, 1960-; Newark State College, New Jersey, 1958-60; Executive Officer, PhD Program in History, Graduate School, CUNY, 1988-94. Publications: The Agitation for Law Reform during the Puritan Revolution, 1640-1660, 1966; The Puritan Revolution: A Documentary History, 1968, 1969, 1973; The Bloodless Revolution: England, 1688, 1972, 1974, 1985; A History of England, 1984, 1991; Church and State in Tudor and Stuart England, 1993. Contributions to: The Development of Equity in Tudor England, to American Journal of Legal History. Honours: Fulbright Scholar, University of Manchester, 1953-54; Fellow, Royal Historical Society, 1978. Memberships: American Historical Association; North American Conference on British Studies. Address: 1479 Court Place, Hewiett, NY 11557, USA.

PRANDOTA Miroslaw, b. 4 Nov 1938, Cserk, Poland. Journalist. m. Ewa Umiecka, 30 Mar 1987, 2 s. Education: Polish Philology, 1963; Psychology, 1970, both Catholic Universities of Lublin. Appointments: Psychiatric Hospital, Gnezio, 1970; The Cultural Weekly, Warssaw. Publications: The Last Fight of Gladiators, 1982; Dance of Life, 1983; The Catch Those Days, 1977; The Four Minors and One Major, 1979; Queers, 1985; Waiting For The Wind, 1985; Hazardsman and Magicians, The Image of the Public Man, 1986; On the Black, 1987. Contributions to: Renaissance. Honours: Literary Award, President of the Union of Polish Writers, 1977; Ministry of Culture Prize, 1987.

Membership: Union of Polish Writers. Address: Karolkowa 66/74 m. 46, 01-193, Warsaw, Poland.

PRANTERA Amanda, b. 23 Apr 1942, England. Author. Publications: Strange Loop, 1984; The Cabalist, 1985; Conversations with Lord Byron on Perversion, 163 Years After His Lordship's Death, 1987; The Side of The Moon, 1991; Pronto-Zoe, 1992; The Young Italians, 1993. Literary Agent: Jane Conway Gordon, London. Address: Jane Conway Gordon, 1 Old Compton Street, London, W1V 5PH, England.

PRASAD Madhusudan, b. 3 Jan 1950, Allahabad, India. Reader in English, University of Allahabad, India. m. Kiran Srivastava, 29 May 1971, 4 d. Education: BA 1967, MA English, 1969, DPhil 1974, University of Allahabad. Appointments: Associate Editor, Orbit, 1983-, Gaya, Bihar, India. Publications: D H Lawrence: A Study of His Novels, 1980; Anita Desai: The Novelist, 1981; In The Dark, stories, 1982; editor, Indian-English Novelists: An Anthology of Critical Essays, 1982; editor, Contemporary Indian-English Stories, 1983, 1984, 1988; editor, Perspectives of Kamala Markanddaya, 1984; editor, The Poetry of Jayanta Mahapatra: A Critical Study, 1986; editor, Living Indian-English Poets: An Anthology of Critical Essays, 1989. Contributions to: Numerous research papers published in journals, magazines and books, including: World Literature Today (USA); Journal of South Asian Literature (USA); World Literature Written in English (Canada); Indian Literature; Thought; The Literary Half-Yearly (Mysore). Address: 134-112 Kothaparcha off G T Road, Allahabad 211 003, India.

PRATCHETT Terry, b. 1948, England. Author. m. 1 d. Appointments: Worked as a Journalist, now full-time Writer. Publications: The Colour of Magic, 1983; Wyrd Sisters, 1989; Truckers, 1990; Small Gods, 1991; Reaper Man, 1991; Lord and Ladies, 1992; Witches Abroad, 1992; The Light Fantastic: Equal Rites; Mort; Sorcery; Strata; The Dark Side of the Sun. Address: c/o Corgi.

PRATHER Richard, (David Knight, Douglas Ring) b. 1921, USA. Author. Publications: Case of the Vanishing Beauty, 1950; Bodies in Bedlam, 1951; Everybody Has a Gun, 1951; Find This Woman, 1951; Way of a Wanton, 1952; Darling It's Death, 1952; Lie Down Killer, 1952; Dagger of Flesh, 1952; Pattern for Murder (as David Knight), 1952; The Peddler (as Douglas Ring), 1952; Too Many Crooks, 1953; Always Leave 'em Dying, 1954; Pattern for Panic, 1954; Strip for Murder, 1955; The Wailing Frail, 1956; Dragnet: Case No 561 (as David Knight), 1956; Have Gat, Will Travel, collection, 1957; Three's a Shroud, collection, 1957; Slab Happy, 1958; Take A Murder, Darling, 1958; Over Her Dear Body, 1959; Double in Trouble (with Stephen Marlowe, 1959; Dance With the Dead, 1960; The Comfortable Coffin (editor), anthology, 1960; Shell Scott's Seven Slaughters, collection, 1961; Dig That Crazy Grave, 1961; Kill the Clown, 1962; The Cockeyed Corpse, 1964; Dead Heat, 1964; The Trojan Hearse, 1964; Kill Him Twice, 1965; Dead Man's Walk, 1965; The Meandering Corpse, 1965; The Khubla Knan Caper, 1966; Gat Heat, 1967; The Cheim Manuscript, 1969; The Shell Scott Sampler, 1969; Kill Me Tomorrow, 1969; Shell Scott's Murder Mix, 1970; Dead-Bang, 1971; The Sweet Ride, 1972; The Sure Thing. Memberships: Former Director, Mystery Writers of America.

PRATT John Clark, b. 19 Aug 1932, St Albans, VT, USA. Writer; Educator. m. (2) Doreen Goodman, 28 June 1968, 1 son, 5 daughters. Education: BA, University of California, 1954; MA, Columbia University, New York, 1960; PhD, Princeton University, 1965. Appointments: Instructor, English, 1960-65; Assistant Professor, 1965-69, Associate Professor, 1969-73, Professor, 1973-75, USAF Academy; Professor, Colorado State University, 1975-; President, Pratt Publishing Company, 1989-. Publications: The Meaning of Modern Poetry, 1962; John Steinbeck, 1970; One Flew Over the Cuckoo's Nest (editor), 1973, Revised Editions, 1995; Co-Editor, Middlemarch Notebooks, 1978; Vietnam Voices, 1984; The Laotian Fragments, 1985; Co-Author, Reading The Wind: The Literature of the Vietnam War, 1986; Writing from Scratch: The Essay, 1987; The Quiet American (editor), 1995. Contributions to: Vietnam War Literature; Vietnam-Perkasie; Fourteen Landing Zones; Unaccustomed Mercy. Honours: Fulbright Lecturer, University of Lisbon, Portugal, 1974-75; Fulbright Lecturer, Leningrad State University, USSR, 1980; Honours Professor, Colorado State University, 1989. Address: Department of English, Colorado State University, Ft Collins, CO 80523, USA.

PRATT Minnie Jo. Publications: The Sound of One Foot, 1981; We Say We Love Each Other, 1985; Crime Against Nature, 1988;

Rebellion: Essays, 1980-1991, 1991; S/he, 1995. Honours: Lamont Poetry Selection, 1989.

PRAWER Siegbert Salomon, b. 15 Feb 1925, Cologne, Germany. Author; Artist; Educator. Literary Appointments include: Taylor Professor of German, Oxfod Univ, 1969-85; Honorary Fellow, Queen's College, Oxford; Dean of Degrees, Queen's College, Oxford, 1974-92; Professor of German, Westfield College, London University, 1964-69; Co-editor, Oxford German Studies, 1971-75; Anglica Germanica, 1973-79. Publications: German Lyric Poetry, 1952; Mörike und seine Leser, 1960; Heine's Buch der Lieder: A Critical Study, 1960; Heine, The Tragic Satirist, 1962; editor, The Penguin Book of Lieder, 1964; The Uncanny in Literature (lecture), 1965; co-editor, Essays in German Language, Culture and Society, 1969; editor, The Romantic Period in Germany, 1970; Heine's Shakespeare (lecture), 1970; editor, Seventeen Modern German Poets, 1971; Comparative Literary Studies, 1973; Karl Marx and World Literature, 1976; Caligari's Children, the film as Tale of Terror, 1980; Heine's Jewish Comedy, 1983; Frankenstein's Island: England and the English in The Writings of Heinrich Heine, 1986; Israel at Vanity Fair, Jews and Judaism of The Writings of W M Thackeray, 1992. Honours: Fellow, British Academy; Corresponding Fellow, German Academy of Language and Literature; Honorary Fellow (Honorary Director, 1965-68), London University Institute of Germanic Studies; Honorary Member of Modern Language Association of America; President, Honorary Fellow, British Comparative Literature Association, (President 1984-86); Holder of two Goethe Medals in Gold; Gundolf Prize, German Academy of Language and Literature; Honorary Doctorates from the Universities of Birmingham, England and Cologne, Germany. Address: Queen's College, Oxford, England.

PREBBLE John (Edward Curtis), b. 1915, United Kingdom. Author. Publications: Where the Sea Breaks, 1944; The Edge of Darkness (USA as The Edge of The Night), 1948; Age Without Pity, 1950; The Mather Story, 1954; The Brute Streets, 1954; The High Girders (USA as Disaster at Dundee), 1956; My Great-Aunt Appearing Day, 1958, reissued with additions as Spanish Stirrup, 1973; Mongaso (with John A Jordan) (USA as Elephants and Ivory), 1959; The Buffalo Soldiers, 1959; Culloden, 1961; The Highland Clearances, 1963; Glencoe, 1966; The Darien Disaster, 1968; The Lion in The North, 1971; Mutiny, 1975; John Prebble's Scotland, 1984; The King's Jaunt: George IV in Edinburgh, 1988; Landscapes and Memories, 1993. Honours: McVitie Award, Scottish Writer of The Year, 1993. Memberships: Fellow, Royal Society of Literature; Society of Authors; International PEN; Writer's Guild. Literary Agent: Curtis Brown. Address: 905 Nelson House, Dolphin Square, London, SW1V 3PA, England.

PRELUTSKY Jack, b. 1940, USA. Full-time Writer. Publications: The Bad Bear, translation, 1967; A Gopher in the Gardens and Other Animal Poems, 1967; No End of Nonsense, translation, 1968; Lazy Blackbird and Other Verses, 1969; Three Saxon Nobles and Other Verses, 1969; The Terrible Tiger, verse, 1969; Toucans Two and Other Poems, 1971; Circus, verse, 1974; The Pack Rat's Day and other Poems, 1974; Nightmares: Poems to Trouble Your Sleep, 1976; It's Halloween (Christmas Thanksgiving, Valentine's Day), verse, 4 vols, 1977-83; The Snopp on the Sidewalk and Other Poems, 1977; The Mean Old Mean Hyena, verse, 1978; The Queen of Eene, verse, 1978; The Headless Horseman Rides Tonight: More Poems to Trouble Your Sleep, 1980; Rainy Day Saturday, verse, 1980; Rolling Harvey Down the Hill, verse, 1980; The Sheriff of Rottenshot, verse, 1982; Kermits Garden of Verses, 1982; The Baby Uggs are hatching, verse, 1982; The Random House Book of Poetry for Children, 1983; It's Snowing, It's Snowing, 1984; What I Did Last Summer, 1984; New Kid on the Block, 1984; My Parents Think I'm Sleeping, 1985; Ride a Pink Pelican, 1986. Address: c/o Greenwillow Books, 105 Madison Avenue, New York, NY 10016, USA.

PRESCOTT J(ohn) R(obert) V(ictor), b. 1931, Australia. Professor of Geography, University of Melbourne. Publications: The Geography of Frontiers and Boundaries, 1965, revised edition as Frontiers and Boundaries, 1978; The Geography of State Policies, 1968; The Evolution of Nigeria's International and Regional Boundaries 1861-1971, 1971; Political Geography, 1972; The Political Geography of The Oceans, 1975; The Map of Mainland Asia by Treaty, 1975; Our Fragmented World: An Introduction to Political Geography (with W G East), 1975; The Frontiers of Asia and Southwest Asia (with H J Collier and D F Prescott), 1976; The Last of Lands: Antartica (with J Lovering), 1979; Austrlai's Continental Shelf (with other), 1979; Maritime Jurisdiction in Southeast Asia, 1981; Australia's Maritime Boundaries,

1985; The Maritime Political Boundaries of The World, 1985; Political Frontiers and Boundaries, 1987; Aboriginal Frontiers and Boundaries in Australia (with S Davis), 1992. Address: Department of Geography, University of Melbourne, Parkville, Victoria 3052, Australia.

PRESS John Bryant, b. 11 Jan 1920, Norwich, England. Retired Officer of The British Council. m. Janet Crompton, 20 Dec 1947, 1 s, 1 d. Education: Corpus Christi College, Cambridge, England. Publications include: The Fire and The Fountain, 1955; The Chequer'd Shade, 1958; A Map of Modern English Verse, 1969; The Lengthening Shadows, 1971; John Betjeman, 1974; Poets of World War II, 1984; A Girl with Beehive Hair, 1986. Contributions to: Encounter; Southern Review; Art International. Honours: Royal Society of Literature Heinemann Award, 1959; 1st Prize, Cheltenham Poetry Festival, 1959. Memberships: Fellow of Royal Society of Literature, 1959; Member of Council, 1960-88. Address: 5 South Parade, Frome, Somerset, BA11 1EJ, England.

PRESS Lloyd Douglas Jr (Skip Press), b. 26 Jul 1950, Commerce, Texas, USA. Writer. m. Debra Ann Hartsog, 30 Jul 1989, 1 s, 1 d. Education: Honours Programme, East Texas State University, Commerce. Publications: A Woman's Guide to Firearms, 1986; Cliffhanger,1992; The Devil's Forest Fire, 1993; Knucklehead, 1993; A Rave of Snakes, 1993; The Ormportance of Mark Twain, 1993. Contributions to: Boy's Life; Disney Adventures; Reader's Digest; Writer's Digest; many others. Honours: Siver Medal, New York International Film Festival, 1987. Memberships: Dramatist's Guild; Poets and Writers; Independent Writers of Southern California, Vice-President 1990-91; Poets, Essayists and Novelists. Address: 2132 Palos Verdes Drive West 6, Palos Verdes Estates, CA 90274, USA.

PRESS Skip. See: PRESS Lloyd Douglas Jr.

PRESTON Ivy Alice Kinross, b. 11 Nov 1913. Writer. m. Percival Edward James Preston, 14 Oct 1937, 2 s, 2 d. Publications: The Silver Stream (autobiography), 1958; Hospital on the Hill, 1967; Voyage of Destiny, 1974; The House Above the Bay, 1976; Fair Accuser, 1985; Stranger From the Sea, 1987; 40 romance novels, reprinted in 9 languages and 130 editions. Contributions to: short stories, articles, radio talks, to most New Zealand publications including the Listener. Holme Station Arts Festival, 1990. Memberships: President Secretary, South Canterbury Writers Guild; New Zealand Women Writers Society; Life Member, South Island Writers Association. Romance Writers of America; Romantic Novelists Association, London. Literary Agent: Robert Hale Ltd, London England. Address: 95 Church Street, Timaru, Southe Canterbury, New Zealand.

PRESTON Peter John, b. 23 May 1938. Editor. m. Jean Mary Burrell, 1962, 2 s, 2 d. Education: MA English Literature, St John's College, Oxford. Literary Appointments: Editorial Trainee, Liverpool Daily Post, 1960-63; Political Reporter, 1963-64; Education Correspondent, 1965-66; Diary Editor, 1966-68; Features Editor, 1968-72; Production Editor, 1972-75, The Guardian; British Executive Chairman and European Vice-Chairman, IPI, 1988-94. Honour: Hon DLitt, Loughborough, 1982. Address: The Guardian, 119 Farringdon Road, London, EC1R 3ER, England.

PRESTON Richard McCann, b. 5 Aug 1954. m. 11 May 1985. Education: BA summa cum laude, Pomona College, 1977; PhD, English and American Literature, Princeton University, 1983. Appointments: Lecturer in English, Princeton University, 1983; Visiting Fellow, Princeton University Council of the Humanities, 1994-95; Regular contributor to The New Yorker Magazine, 1986-. Publications: First Light, 1987; American Steel, 1991; The Hot Zone, 1994. Contributions to: "The Mountains of Pi", The New Yorker, 1992; New York TimesLos Angeles Times; National Geographic Traveler; Mercury; Blair & Ketchum's Country Journal. Honours: American Institute of Physics Science Writing Award, 1988; Asteroid 3686 named 'Preston', 1989; AAAS, Westinghouse Award, 1992; MIT McDermott Award, 1993. Memberships: The Authors Guild. Literary Agent: Lynn Nesbit. Address: c/o Lynn Nesbit, Janklow & Nesbit Associates, 598 Madison Avenue, New York, NY 10022, USA.

PREUSS Paul F, b. 7 Mar 1942, Albany, Georgia, USA. Writer. m. (1) Marsha May Pettit, 1963, 1 daughter, (2) Karen Reiser, 1973, (3) Debra Turner, 1993. Education: BA cum laude, Yale University, 1966. Publications: The Gates of Heaven, 1980; Re-entry, 1981; Broken Symmetries, 1983; Human Error, 1985; Starfire, 1988;Volumes of the Venus Prime Series, with Arthur C Clark, 1987-91; Short Stories in The

Planets, 1985, The Microverse, 1989; The Ultimate Dinosaur, 1992; Core, 1993. Contributions to: Science Writer, principally for Science 80 - Science 85 and Discover; Numerous book reviews, currently for The Washington Post. Memberships: Northern California Science Writers Association; National Book Critics' Circle; Bay Area Book Reviewers' Association. Literary Agent: Jean V Naggar, New York. Address: PO Box 590773, San Francisco, CA 94159, USA.

PREVOTS Naima Wallenrod, b. 27 May 1935, Brooklyn, New York, USA. Professor, The American University, Washington DC. m. Martin Wallen, 26 Aug 1979, 1 son, 1 daughter. Education: BA, Brooklyn College, 1955; MS, University of Wisconsin, 1960; Attended Juilliard School, 1957-58; PhD, University of Southern California. Publications: A Vision for Music, 1984; Sound Waves, 1985; Dancing in the Sun - Hollywood Choreographers, 1987; American Pageantry: A Movement for Art and Democracy, 1990. Contributions to: Dance Magazine; Dance Research Journal; Dance Chronicle; California Historical Society. Honours: Phi Beta Kappa; Fulbright Fellowship; National Endowment for the Humanities Fellowship; University-wide Award for Research and Professional Contribution. Memberships: ssa OOBoard Member, Dance History Scholars; Board Member, Fulbright Association. Address: 5219 Mass Avenue, Bethesda, MA 20816, USA.

PRICE A(lice) Lindsay, b. 21 Oct 1927, Augusta, GA, USA. Writer; Artist; Publisher. Education: BA, Oklahoma State University, 1949; MA, University Of Tulsa, 1970; Scholar In Residence, Voices And Visions, 1990 and 1992. Publications: Faces Of The Waterworld, 1976; Our Dismembered Shadow, 1982; Swans Of The World In Nature, History, Myth And Art, 1994. Contributions include: Enwright House; Rhino; Commonweal; Gryphon; Phoenix; Nimrod; Greenfield Review; Suncatcher. Honours: Fist Award, Nimrod, 1970; Pegasus Award, 1981; Church And The Artist, 1990; Arts And Humanities Literary Award, 1992. Memberships: Poets And Writers. Address: 3113 So, Florence Avenue, Tulsa, OK 74015, USA.

PRICE (Alan) Anthony, b. 16 Aug 1928. Author; Journalist; Editor. m. (Yvonne) Ann Stone, 1953, 2 s, 1 d. Education: Exhibitor, MA, Merton College, Oxford. Literary Appointment: Editor, The Oxford Times, 1972-88. Publications: The Labyrinth Makers, 1970; The Alamut Ambush, 1971; Colonel Butler's Wolf, 1972; October Men, 1973; Other Paths to Glory, 1974; Our Man in Camelot, 1975; War Game, 1976; The '44 Vintage, 1978; Tomorrow's Ghost, 1979; The Hour of The Donkey, 1980; Soldier No More, 1981; The Old Vengeful, 1982; Gunner Kelly, 1983; Sion Crossing, 1984; Here Be Monsters, 1985; For The Good of The State, 1986; A New Kind of War, 1987; A Prospect of Vengeance, 1988; The Memory Trap, 1989; The Eyes of The Fleet, 1990. Honours: CWA Silver Dagger, 1970; CWA Gold Dagger, 1974; Swedish Academy of Detection Prize, 1978. Literary Agent: A P Watt. Address: Wayside Cottage, Horton cum Studley, Oxford, OX33 1AW, England.

PRICE Glanville, b. 16 Jun 1928, Rhaeadr, Wales. University Professor. m. Christine Winifred Thurston, 18 Aug 1954, 3 s, 1 d. Education: University of Wales, Bangor, 1946-50; University of Paris, 1950-53; BA, Wales, 1949; MA, Wales, 1952; Docteur de l'Université de Paris, 1956. Appointments: Professor of French, University of Stirling, 1967-72, University of Wales, Aberystwyth, 1972-92; Research Professor, University of Wales, 1992-; Joint Editor, The Year's Work in Modern Language Studies, 1972-92. Publications: The Present Position of Minority Languages in Western Europe, 1969; The French Language, Present and Past, 1971; editor, William, Count of Orange: Four Old French Epics, 1975; Romance Linguistics and the Romance Languages (with Kathryn F Bach), 1977; The Languages of Britain, 1984; Ireland and the Celtic Connection, 1987; An Introduction to French Pronunciation, 1991; A Comprehensive French Grammar, 1992; The Celtic Connection, editor, 1992. Contributions include: numerous to various journals including: Romance Philology; Studia Neophilologica; Archivum Linguisticum; Modern Language Review; Orbis; Bulletin of the Board of Celtic Studies; Seventeenth-Century French Studies; Cercetari de Linguistica; Semasia. Memberships: Modern Humanities Research Association (Chairman 1979-90); Philological Society; Society for French Studies. Address: Department of European Languages, University of Wales, Aberystwyth, Dyfed, Wales, SY23 3DY.

PRICE Jennifer, See: HOOVER Helen Mary.

PRICE (Edward) Reynolds, b. 1933, USA. Professor of English; Writer. Appointments: Editor, The Archive, Durham, North Carolina,

1954-55; Faculty Member, 1958-, James B Duke Professor of English, 1977-, Duke University, Lexington, Virginia, 1964-. Publications: A Long and a Happy Life, 1962; The Names and Faces of Heroes, short stories, 1963; A Generous Man, 1966; Love and Work, 1968; Late Warning: Four Poems, 1968; Permanent Errors, short stories, 1970; Things Themselves, essays, 1972; Presence and Absence: Version from the Bible, 1973; The Surface of the Earth, 1975; Early Dark, play, 1977; A Palpable God, 1978; The Source of Light, 1981; Vital Provisions, 1982; Mustian, 1983; Private Contentment, 1984; Kate Vaiden, 1985; Clear Pictures: First Lover First guides, 1989; Good Hearts; The Tongues of Angels; Blue Calhoun, 1992; A Full and Happy Life, 1993; A Whole New Life, 1994. Honours include: National Book Critics Circle Award, 1986. Address: 4813 Duke Station, Durham, NC 27706, USA.

PRICE Richard. Author; Screenwriter. Publications: Bloodbrothers, 1976; Ladies Man, 1978; The Breaks, 1984; Clockers, 1992. Address: c/o Janklow & Nesbit, 598 Madison Avenue, New York, NY 10022, USA.

PRICE Roger (David), b. 1944, United Kingdom. Historian; Professor of European History. Literary Appointments: Professor of Modern History, University of Wales, Aberystwyth, 1994-. Publications: The French Second Republic: A Social History, 1972; The Economic Modernization of France, 1975; Revolution and Reaction: 1848 and The Second French Republic (editor and contributor), 1975; 1848 in France, 1975; An Ecomomic History of Modern France, 1981; The Modernization of Rural France: Communications Networks and Agricultural Market Structures in 19th Century France, 1983; A Social History of 19th Century France, 1987; The Revolutions of 1848, 1989; A Concise History of France, 1993. Honours: DLitt, University of East Anglia, 1985. Membership: Fellow, Royal Historical Society, 1983. Address: Department of History and Welsh History, University of Wales, Aberystwyth, Dyfed, Wales, SY23 3DY.

PRICE Stanley, b. 12 Aug 1931, London, England. Writer. m. Judy Fenton, 5 Jul 1957, 1 s. Education: MA, University of Cambridge, England. Publications: novels: Crusading for Kronk, 1960; A World of Difference, 1961; Just for the Record, 1962; The Biggest Picture, 1964; stage plays: Horizontal Hold, 1967; The Starving Rich, 1972; The Two of Me, 1975; Moving, 1980; Why Me? 1985; screenplays: Arabesque, 1968; Gold, 1974; Shout at the Devil, 1975; TV plays: All Things Being Equal, 1970; Exit Laughing, 1971; Minder, 1980; The Kindness of Mrs Radcliffe, 1981; Moving, 1985; Star Quality, series, 1986; The Bretts, 1990, Close Realtions, 1986-87. Contributions to: The Observer; Sunday Telegraph; New York Times; Los Angeles Times; Punch; Plays and Players; New Statesman; The Independent; Town. Memberships: Writer's Guild; Dramatists Club. Literary Agent: Douglas Rae, England. Address: Douglas Rae, 28 Charing Cross Road, London WC2, England.

PRICE Susan, b. 1955, UK. Children's Fiction Writer. Publications: Devil's Piper, 1973; Twopence a Tub, 1975; Sticks and Stones, 1976; Home from Home, 1977; Christopher Uptake, 1981; The Carpenter, stories, 1981; In A Nutshell, 1983; From Where I Stand, 1984; Ghosts at Large, 1984; Odin's Monster, 1986; The Ghost Drum, 1987; The Bone Dog, 1989; Forbidden Doors, 1990. Honours The Other Award, 1975; The Carnegie Medal, 1987. Membership: The Society of Authors. Literary Agent: A M Heath & Co Ltd, 79 St Martins Lane, London. Address: c/o Faber & Faber Ltd, 3 Queen Square, London WC 1N 3AU, England.

PRICE Victor, b. 10 Apr 1930, Newcastle, Co Down, Northern Ireland. Education: BA Hons, Modern Languages (French and German), Queen's University, Belfast, 1947-51. Appointments: With the BBC, 1956-90, ending as Head of German Language Service. Publications: Novels: The Death Of Achilles, 1963; The Other Kingdom, 1964; Caliban's Wooing, 1966; The Plays Of Georg Buchner, 1971; Two Parts Water (poems), 1980. Contributions to: Financial Times; The Scotsman; BBC World Service; Deutschland Funk; Channel Four. Address: 22 Oxford Gardens, London, W4 3BW.

PRIEST Christopher (McKenzie), b. 1943, United Kingdom. Freelance Writer. Publications: Indoctrinaire, 1970; Fugue for a Darkening Island, US Edition Darkening Island, 1972; Inverted World, 1974; Your Book of Film-Making, 1974; Real-Time World, 1974; The Space Machine, 1976; A Dream of Wessex, US Edition, The Perfect Lover, 1977; Anticipations (editor), 1978; An Infinite Summer, 1979; Stars of Albion (co-editor), 1979; The Affirmation, 1981; The Glamour,

1984; The Quiet Woman, 1990. Literary Agent: Maggie Noach. Address: c/o Bloomsbury Publishing Ltd, 2 Soho Square, London, W1V 5DE, England.

PRIESTLAND Gerald Francis, b. 26 Feb 1927, Berkhamstead, England. Author; Broadcaster. m. Helen Sylvia Rhodes, 14 May 1949, 2 s, 2 d. Education: Scholar, Charterhouse School 1940-45, New College Oxford 1945-48; BA Honours (Oxon), PPE, 1948. Literary Appointments: BBC correspondent; Foreign Affairs 1954-69, Religious affairs 1976-82. Publications: Priestland's Progress, 1981; The Case Against God, 1984; Something Understood, autobiography, 1986; The Future of Violence, 1974; The Dilemmas of Journalism, 1979; Frying Tonight, 1970; America the Changing Nation, 1968; Yours Faithfully, 2 volumes, 1979, 1981; Gerald Priestland at Large, 1983; Priestley Right and Wrong, 1983; West of Hayle River, 1980. Contributions include: numerous articles on religious , ethical & social issues in UK newspapers and magazines, including: Listener; Times; Sunday Telegraph; Observer; International Christian Digest. Honours: Honorary Fellow, Manchester Polytechnic, 1978; Honorary Master, Open University, 1985; Sandford St Martin Prize, religious broadcasting, 1981. Membership: West Country Writers. Literary Agent: MBA, 45 Fitzroy Street, London, W1P 5HR. Address: 4 Temple Fortune Lane, London NW11 7UD, England.

PRIESTLEY Brian, b. 10 Jul 1946, Manchester, England. Writer; Musician. Education: BA (Hon) French; Diploma of Education, Leeds University. Publications: Mingus, A Critical Biography, 1982; Charlie Parker, 1984; John Coltrane, 1987; Jazz - The Essential Companion (with Ian Carr and Digby Fairweather), 1987; Jazz on Record, A History, 1988; Jazz Piano (volumes 1-6), 1983-90. Contributions to: Reviws and articles. Address: Flat 3, $3 Ponder Street, London N7 8UD, England.

PRIETO Mariana Beeching, b. 1912, USA. Children's Writer; Teacher. Appointments: Teacher of Creative Writing, Dade County Schools Adult Division, Miami, Florida, 1956-; Teacher of Creative Writing, University of Miami, 1960-62; Coordinator, Miami Writers Club. Publications: Spanish and How, 1944; Pattern for Beauty, 1945; His Cuban Wife, novel, 1954; The Wise Rooster, 1962; El Gallo and Itzo, 1964; A Kite for Carlos, 1965; Tomato Boy, 1966; Johnny Lost, 1969; When the Monkeys Wore Sombreros, 1969; Play It In Spanish (editor), 1973; The Birdman of Papantla, 1973; Fun Jewelry, 1973; Hickless Cocktails and Harmless Highballs, 1980; Poem, Miami Herald, 1993; Poem, Coral Gables Journal, 1992. Contributions to: Travel articles to International Travel News, 1982. Honours: Coral Gables Journal First Prize, 1992. Memberships: Miami Writers Group; Miami Pioneers; Friends of The Everglades. Address: 2499 SW 34th Avenue, Miami, FL 33145, USA.

PRINCE Alison, b. 26 Mar 1931, Kent, England. Writer. m. Goronwy Siriol Parry, 26 Dec 1957, 2 sons, 1 daughter. Education: Beckenham Grammar School; Slade School Diploma, London University; Art Teacher's Diploma, Goldsmith's College. Appointment: Fellow in Creative Writing, Jordanhill College, Glasgow, 1988-90. Publications: The Doubting Kind (young adults), 1974; How's Business (children's book), 1985; The Ghost Within (supernatural stories), 1987; The Blue Moon Day, (childrens), 1989; The Necessary Goat (essays on creativity), 1992. Other publications: A Haunting Refrain; Haunted Children; A Job for Merv; Goodbye Summer; Nick's October; The Sinister Airfield; The Type One Robot; Kenneth Grahame: An Innocent in the Wild Wood, (biography), 1994. Contributions to: New Statesman; The Scotsman; The Herald; Scottish Child; various educational journals. Honour: Runner-up for Smarties Prize, 1986. Memberships: Scottish PEN; Society of Authors. Address: Burnfoot, Whiting Bay, Isle of Arran, KA27 8QL, Scotland.

PRINCE F(rank) T(empleton), b. 1912, United Kingdom. Former Professor of English; Author; Poet. Appointments. Professor of English, University of Southampton, 1957-74; Professor of English, University of the West Indies, Jamaica, 1975-78; Fannie Hurst Professor, Brandeis University, Waltham, Massachusetts, USA, 1978-80. Publications: Poems, 1938; Soldiers Bathing and Other Poems, 1954; The Italian Element in Milton's Verse, 1954; The Stolen Heart, 1957; Samson Agonistes, by Milton (editor), 1957; The Poems, by Shakespeare (editor), 1960; Sir Thomas Wyatt, by Sergio Baldi, translation, 1961; Paradise Lost, books I and II, by Milton (editor), 1962; The Doors of Stone: Poems, 1938-62, 1963; William Shakespeare: The Poems, 1963; Comus and Other Poems by Milton (editor), 1968; Memoirs in Oxford, 1970; Penguin Modern Poets 20 (with John

Heath-Stubbs and Stephen Spender), 1971; Drypoints of the Hasidim, 1975; Afterword on Rupert Brooke, 1977; Collected Poems, 1979; The Yuan Chen Variations, 1981; Later on, 1983; Walks in Rome, 1987; Collected Poems, 1993. Address: 32 Brookvale Road, Southampton, Hants, SO17 1QR, England.

PRINGLE-JONES Jennifer Suzanne, b. 26 May 1946, Tasmania, Australia. Journalist. m. 21 Jul 1967, 1 s, 2 d. Education: Dux of School, St Michael's Collegiate School, 1962. Appointments: Staff, Mercury Newspaper, 1962-67; Journalist, ABC Radio/TV 1967-71, TAS/TV 1978-86, Commonwealth Scientific & Industrial Research Organisation, 1986-. Publications: Discovering Tasmania, 1981; Explore Tasmania, First Edition, 1983; Tasmania is a Garden, 1985; Explore Tasmania, Second Edition, 1989; Tasmania the Beautiful Island, 1989. Contributions to: Fodor's Travel Guides; Herald and Weekly Times Publications; Ansett Transport Industries publications; Vogue Australia; The Design Series; Australian Country Style; Contrasts Australia Logies 1981, 1983; numerous scriptng awards; National Tourism Award; TV News Reporters Award. Membership: Australian Journalists Association; Australian Day Council; Queen Elizabeth II Silver Jubilee Trust for Yung Australians; Advisory Board, St John's Hospital. Address: 29 Amanda Crescent, Sandy Bay, Tasmania 7005, Australia.

PRIOR Allan, b. 1922, United Kingdom. Author. Publications: A Flame in the Air, 1951; The Joy Ride, 1952; The One-Eyed Monster, 1958; One Away, 1961; The Interrogators, 1965; The Operators, 1966; The Loving Cup, 1968; The Contract, 1970; Paradiso, 1972; Affair, 1976; Never Been Kissed in the Same Place Twice, 1978; Theatre, 1981; A Cast of Stars, 1983; The Big March, 1983; Her Majesty's Hit Man, 1986; Fuhrer - the Novel, 1991; The Old Man and Me, 1994. Address: Summerhill, Waverley Road, St Albans, Herts, England.

PRITCHARD Margaret (Marged) Jones, b. 29 Aug 1919, Tregaron, Dyfed, Wales, England. Modern Languages Teacher; Lecturer for Welsh Learners. m. Robert Gwilym Pritchard, 5 Apr 1949, 1 son. Education: Honours Degree in French, 1940; First Class Teaching Diploma, Bangor, 1941. Literary Appointments: Literary Adjudicator, Welsh Arts Council, 1991. Publications: Cregyn Ar y Traeth, 1974; Gwylanod yn y Mynydd, 1975; Clymau and Disgwyl, 1976; Mid Mudan Mo'r Môr, 1976; Enfys y Bore, 1980; Nhw Oedd Yno, 1986; Adar Brith. Contributions to: Taliesin; Traethodydd; Barn; y Genhinen; y Faner. Honours: Welsh Arts Council Prize, 1975. Memberships: Welsh Academy, Adjudicator of Prose, 1993. Literary Agent: Gomer Press, Dyfed. Address: Glaslyn, Minffordd, Penrhyndeudraeth, Gwynedd LL48 6HL, Wales.

PRITCHARD R(obert) John, b. 30 Nov 1945, Los Angeles, USA. Freelance Writer and Broadcaster. m. (1) Sonia Magbanna Zaide, 15 Aug 1969, div 1984, 1 son, 1 daughter, (2) Lady Elayne Antonia Lodge, 20 Dec 1989. Education: AB, University of California, 1967; MA, 1968, PhD, 1980, London School of Economics, England. Appointments: Managing Editor, Millennium: Journal of International Studies, 1974-78; Research Assistant in History, 1973-81; Consultant Editor/Compiler, Tokyo War Trial Project, The London School of Economics, 1981-87; Director/Company Secretary, Integrated Dictionary Systems Ltd, 1988-90; Lecturer in History, University of Kent, 1990-93; Fellow in War Studies, Kings College, London, 1990-93; Simon Senior Research Fellow in History, University of Manchester, 1993-94; Director, Historical Enterprises, 1993-. Publications include: Reichstag Fire & Ashes of Democracy, 1972; Tokyo War Crimes Trial Complete Transcripts, Proceedings of International Military Tribunal for Far East (with S M Zaide), 22 volumes, 1981; Tokyo War Crimes Trial, Index and Guide (with S M Zaide), 5 volumes, 1981-87; co-author, General History of the Philippines, volume 1, American Half Century 1898-1946, 1984; Far Eastern Influences on British Strategy Towards the Great Powers 1937-39, 1987; Overview of the Historical Importance of the Tokyo War Trial, 1987; co-author, Total War: Causes & Courses of 2nd World War, 1989; co-author, The Japanese Army's Secret of Secrets, 1989; Japan and the 2nd World War (with Lady Toshiko Marks), 1989; ed. The British War Crimes Trials in the Far East, 1946-48, (21 volumes), forthcoming for 1995; co-author, From Pearl Harbour to Hiroshima, 1993; The Misconduct of War and the Rule of Law, forthcoming. Literary Agent: Sheila Watson, Watson, Little Ltd., 12 Egbert Street, London, NW1 8LJ. Address: 11 Charlotte Square, Margate, Kent, CT9 1LR, England.

PRITCHARD William H, b. 12 Nov 1932, Binghamton, New York, USA. Professor. m. 24 Aug 1957, 3 sons. Education: BA, Amherst

College, 1953; MA, PhD, Harvard University, 1960. Appointments: Teaching, Amherst College, 1958-. Publications: Randall Jarrell, A Literary Life, 1990; Frost: A Literary Life Reconsidered, 1984, 2nd edition, 1993; Lives of the Modern Poets, 1980; Seeing Through Everything, English Writers 1918-1940, 1977; Wyndham Lewis, 1968; Playing It By Ear: Literary Essays and Reviews, 1994. Honours: Fellowships from Guggenheim; National Endowment for the Humanities; American Council of Learned Societies; Henry Clay Folger, Professor of English, Amherst College. Memberships: Advisory Editor, the Hudson Review; Assoxiation of Literary Scholars and Critics. Literary Agent: Watkins-Loomis Agency. Address: 62 Orchard Street, Amherst, MA 01002, USA.

PRITCHETT Victor Sawdon (Sir), b. 16 Dec 1900, Ipswich, Suffolk, England. Author; Critic. m. Dorothy Rudge Roberts, 1936, 1 son, 1 daughter. Appointments: Lectured in 4 Universities in USA; Resident Writer, Smith College, 1967, 1970-72; Clark Lectures Cambridge, 1969. Publications: Marching Spain; Clare Drummer; The Spanish Virgin; Shirley Sanz; Nothing Like Leather; Dead Man Leading; You Make Your Own Life; In My Good Books; It May Never Happen; Why Do I Write? (with Elizabeth Bowen & Graham Greene); The Living Novel; Mr Beluncle; Books in General; The Spanish Temper; Collected Short Stories; When My Girl Comes Home; London Perceived; The Key to My Heart; Foreign Faces; New York Proclaimed; The Living Novel and Later Appreciations; Dublin; A Cab at the Door (autobiography), 1968; Blind Love (short stories); George Meredith and English Comedy, 1970; Midnight Oil, (autobiography volume II), 1971; Balzac, 1973; The Camberwell Beauty (stories), 1974; Turgenev, 1977; The Gentle Barbarian, 1977; Selected Stories, 1978; The Myth Makers (essays), 1979; On the Edge of the Cliff (stories), 1979; The Tale Bearers, 1980; Oxford Book of Short Stories, Editor, 1981; Collected Stories, 1982; The Turn of the Years, 1982; more Collected Stories, 1983; A Man of Letters; Chekhoo, 1988; (stories), A Careless Widow, 1989; At Home & Abroad, 1990; Lasting Impression, 1990; The Complete Essays, 1991. Honours: Hon D.Lit., Leeds, 1972, Columbia University, New York, Sussex University, 1978, Harvard, 1985; PEN Biography Award for Balzac, 1974; CH, 1993; Knighted, 1975; CBE, 1968; CLIT (Royal Society of Literature), 1988. Memberships: President, Society of Authors, 1977-. Address: 12 Regent's Park Terrace, London, NW1, England.

PROCASSION Michael, b. 1946, USA. Playwright. Publications: The Shadow Box, 1977; Black Angel, 1984; The Lady and the Clarinet, 1985; Ice; Breaking Up; The Bonfire of the Vanities. Honours: Pulitzer Prize and Antoinette Perry 'Tony' Award for the Shadow Box. Literary Agent: Dramatists Play Service, USA. Address: c/o Dramatists Play Service, 440 Park Avenue South, New York, NY 10016, USA.

PROCHNOW Herbert Victor, b. Wilton, Wisconsin, USA. Various positions with The First National Bank of Chicago between 1933 and 1969, President, 1961-69; Secretary to Federal Advisory Council, Federal Reserve System. m. Laura Virginia Stinson (dec 1977), 1 s. Education: BA, Ma, University of Wisconsin; PhD, Northwestern University. Appointments: Financial Columnist, Chicago Tribune, 1968-70. Publications include: Practical Bank Credit, 1939; The Public Speaker's Treasure Chest, 1986; The Changing World of Banking, 1974; The Toastmaster's Treasure Chest, 1988; Inspirational Thoughts on the Ten Commandments, 1970; The Federal Reserve System, 1960; The Eurodollar, 1970; Dilemmas Facing the Nation, 1979; Bank Credit, 1981; Editor and co-author of over 80 books. Honours: Order of Vesa, Sweden; Commanders Cross of the Order of Merit, Federal Republic of Germany; Business Statesmanship Award, Harvard Business School Association; Ayres Leadership Award, Reutgers University; Silver Plaque Highest Award, National Conference of Christians and Jews; Hon LLD, University of Wisconsin and Northwestern University; Hon Lett D, Millikin University; LLD Ripon College, Lake Forest University; DHL, Thiel College. Memberships include: Beta Gamma Sigma. Address: 1st National Bank Plaza, Chicago, IL 60670, USA.

PROSE Francine, b. 1 Apr 1947, Brooklyn, New York, USA. University Professor. m. Howard Michaels, 24 Sep 1976, 2 children. Education: BA, Radcliffe College; MA, Harvard University. Publications: The Peaceable Kingdom; Primitive People; Bizpot Dreams; Women and Children First; Judah the Pious, 1973; Stories From Our Living Past, 1974; The Glorious One, 1974; Marie Laveau, 1977; Animal Magnetism, 1978; Household Saints, 1981; Hungry Hearts, 1983. Contributions to: Mademoiselle; Atlantic; Village Voice; Commentary. Honours: Jewish Book Council Award; Edgar Lewis

Wallant Memorial Award, 1984. Memberships: PEN; Associated Writing Programs. Address: c/o George Borchardt Inc, 136 East 57th Street, New York, NY 10022, USA.

PROSSER Harold Lee, b. 31 Dec 1944, Springfield, Missouri, USA. Author; Composer; Interfaith Minister. div 1988, 2 daughters; re-married Debra Cunningham Phipps, 6 Dec, 1994. Education: AA, Santa Monica College, 1968; BS, 1974, MSED, 1982, Southwest Missouri State University. Publications: Dandelion Seeds: 18 Stories, 1974; Goodbye Lon Chaney Jr, Goodbye, 1977; Desert Woman Visions: 100 Poems, 1987; Jack Bimbo's Touring Circus Poems, 1988; Charles Beaumont (biography), 1994; Contributed several essays to book, Reader's Guide to 20th Century Science Fiction (ed M P Fletcher), 1989; Over 900 publications since 1963; Numerous musical compositions for publication. Contributions to: Antaeus; Doppleganger; Imagine; Dialogue; Moon; Night Music; Singing Guns Journal; Social Education; Fantasy; Several Essays to book, New Encyclopeadia of Science Fiction (ed James Gunn). Honours: Manuscripts permanently housed and stored at the following universities under title: The H L Prosser Collection: 1. Golden Library, Eastern New Mexico University at Portales, New Mexico; 2. Archival Heritage Centre, University of Wyoming at Laramie, Wyoming; 3. Donnelly Library, New Mexico Highlands University at Las Vegas, New Mexico. Memberships: Composer Member of ASCAP; Vedanta Society; ordained Interfaith Minister, 1994 from New Mexico Theological Seminary. Address: 1313 South Jefferson Avenue, Springfield, MO 65807-1605, USA.

PROUX F Annie, b. 1935. Publications: Postcards, 1992; Shipping News, 1993; Heart Soup and Other Stories. Honours: PEN/Faulkner Award, 1993; National Book Award, 1993; Pulitzer Prize, 1994; Irish Times International Fiction Prize, 1994. Address: Durgan Hill Road, Vershire, VT 05079, USA.

PRUITT William O, b. 1 Sept 1922, Easton. University Professor. m. Erna Nauert, 5 Feb 1951, 1 son, 1 daughter. Education: BSc, University of Maryland, 1947; MA, University of Michigan, 1948; PhD, University of Michigan, 1952. Publications: Wild Harmony; Boreal Ecology; Author of 65 Scientific Papers: Author of 40 Popular Articles. Honours: Fellow, Artic Institute of North America; Fellow, The Explorers Club; Seton Medal, Manitoba Naturalists Society; Northern Science Award and Centenary Medal, Government of Canada; Stefansson Award, University of Manitoba; DSc (Hon) University of Alaska, 1993. Memberships: American Society of Mammalogists, Arctic Institute; Sigma Xi. Address: Department of Zoology, The University of Manitoba, Winnipeg, Manitoba, Canada, R3T 2N2.

PRUTKOV Kozma. See: **SNODGRASS W D.**

PRVULOVICH Zika Rad, (Dr Peters), b. 4 Dec 1920, Vlahovo, Serbia, Yugoslavia. Retired University Senior Lecturer. m. Janet Mary Atkins, 11 Aug 1959, 1 son, 1 daughter. Education: BA (Mod), Trinity College, Dublin, 1951; BA (Oxon), 1952; DPhil (Oxon), 1956; MA (Oxon), 1957. Publications: Njegoseva Teorija Saznauja i Sistem, 1981; Prince-Bishop Hjegosh's Religious Philosophy, 1984; Serbia between the Swastika and the Red Star, 1986; Tajna Boga i Tajna Sveta, Pt 1 of a Trilogy, 1991; The Ray of the Microcosm, translation of Prince-Bishop Njegosh's poem Luca Mikrokozma (bilingual edition with critical commentary and Introduction in English), 1992. Contributions to: Many contributions to various literary, political, religious and philosophical journals and magazines. Honours: The Wray Prize in Philosophy, Dublin University, 1951. Memberships: Honorary Librarian, Dublin University Philosophical Society; PEN, English Section; Honorary Member, Serbian Writers Club; Society of Serbian Writers and Artist, England; Philosophy of Education Society of Great Britain; Oriel Society; University of Birmingham Common Room. Address: 26 Wheeler's Lane, King's Heath, Birmingham, B13 0SA, England.

PRYBLA Jan, b. 21 Oct 1927, Poland. Professor of Economics. m. Jacqueline Meyer, 1958, 1 s, 1 d. Education: BComm, 1949; MES, 1950, PhD, 1953, National University of Ireland; Diploma in Higher European Studies, University of Strasbourg, France, 1952. Appointments: Currently Professor of Economics, Pennsylvania State University, University Park, USA. Publications: The Political Economy of Communist China, 1970; The Chinese Economy: Problems and Policies, 1978, 1981; Issues in Socialist Economic Modernization, 1980; Market and Pplan Under Socialism: The Bird in the Cage, 1987; Reforms in China and Other Socialist Economies, 1990; China and the Crisis of Marxism-Leninism (co-author), 1990; Editor, Comparative

Economic Sytstems, 1969. Contributions to: Current History; Asian Survey; Problems of Communism; Slavic Review; Comparative Economic Studies; Review of World Economy; Social Research; The Annals; Pacific Affairs. Memberships: President, Conference on European Problems; Board of Directors, American Association for Chinese Studies; Association for Comparative Economic Studies. Address: 523 Kern Building, University Park, PA 16802, USA.

PRYCE-JONES David, b. 15 Feb 1936, Vienna, Austria. m. 29 July 1959, 1 son, 2 daughters. Education: BA, MA, Magdalen College, Oxford, 1956-59. Appointments: Literary Editor: Time & Tide, 1961; Spectator, 1964. Publications: Owls & Satyrs, 1961; The Sands of Summer, 1963; Next Generation, 1964; Quondam, 1965; The Stranger's View, 1967; The Hungarian Revolution, 1969; Running Away, 1969; The Face of Defeat, 1971; The England Commune, 1973; Unity Mitford, 1976; Vienna, 1978; Shirley's Guild, 1981; Paris in the Third Reich, 1983; Cyril Connolly, 1984; The Afternoon Sun, 1986; The Closed Circle, 1989; Inheritance, 1992; You Can't Be Too Careful, 1993; The War That Never Was, 1995. Contributions to: numberous journals and magazines. Honour: Wingate Prize, 1986. Memberships: Royal Society of Literature. Literary Agent: The Peters Fraser and Dunlop Group Ltd. Address: Lower Pentwyn, Gwenddwr, Powys, LD2 3LQ, Wales.

PRYNNE J H, b. 24 June 1936, England. Publications include: Kitchen Poems, 1968; Day light Songs, 1968; The White Stones, 1969; Brass, 1971; Into The Day, 1972; Wound Response, 1974; High Pink on Chrome, 1975; News of Warring Clans, 1977; Down where changed, 1979; Poems, 1982; The Oval Window, 1983; Bands Around the Throat, 1987; Word Order, 1989; Not-You, 1993; Her Weasles Wild Returning, 1994. Address: Gonville & Caius College, Cambridge, CB2 1TA, England.

PRYOR Adel, See: **WASSERFALL Adel.**

PRYOR Bonnie Helen, b. 22 Dec 1942, Los Angeles, California, USA. Author. m. Robert E Pryor, 2 sons, 4 daughters. Publications: Grandpa Bear, 1985; Rats, Spiders and Love, 1986; Amanda and April, 1986; Grandpa Bear's Christmas, 1986; Mr Z and the Time Clock, 1986; Vinegar Pancakes and Vanishing Cream, 1987; House on Maple Street, 1987; Mr Munday and Rustlers, 1988; Seth of Lion People, 1989; Plumtree War, 1989; Porcupine Mouse, 1989; Perfect Percy, 1989; Mr Munday and Space Creatures, 1989; Merry Christmas Amanda and April, 1990; 24 Hour Lipstick Mystery, 1990; Greenbrook Farm, 1991; Jumping Jenny, 1992; Beaver Boys, 1992; Lottie's Dream, 1992; Poison Ivy and Eyebrow Wigs, 1993; Horses in the Garage, 1993; Birthday Blizzard, 1993; Marvelous Marvin and the Werewolf Mystery, 1994. Contributions to: Women's Circle, 1983; Woman's World, 1984; Writers, 1989. Honours: Irma Simonton Black Award from Bank Street College, 1989 for Procupine Mouse; Children's Choice, 1986, for Mr Z and the Time Clock; Outstanding Book List, National Society of Science Teachers and National Society of Social Studies, 1987 for House on Maple Street; National Society of Science Teachers Award for Seth of Lion People, 1990. Memberships: Society of Children's Book Writers. Address: 19600 Baker Road, Gambier, OH 43022, USA.

PRZYBYSZ Janusz Anastazy, b. 31 May 1926, Poznan, Poland. Journalist; Writer. m. Danuta Maria Magolewska, 10 Sept 1951, 1 daughter. Education: Poznan University, 1950. Publications: The Note-book of one Untermensch, 1972; The Dog Which in Sopot Get Out, 1980; A Short Fragment of a Family Story, 1981; Eintopfkommando, 1986; The Long Lesson of Gymnastics, 1990; Stories: Family Secrets, 1972; Thirteenth on Friday, 1975; In the Almonds and Icings Smell, 1978; Short Satirical Works: The Adventures of Gentlemen, 1962; My Good Unknown, 1966; Our Beloved Little World, 1968; Dreadful Lovely is this World, 1973. Contributions to: Kaktus, 1957-61; Tydzien, 1973-81; Wprost, 1982; Karuzela, 1966-90; Gazeta Poznanska, 1966-. Honours: Reymont Literary Prize, 1987; City of Poznan Prize for Cultural Activity and Arts, 1988. Memberships: Polish Writers Association, 1972-90, Vice-Chairman Poznan Association, 1978-81; Association of Authors and Composers; Polish Journalists Association. Address: ul. Galileusza 6A, m 6, 60-159 Poznan, Poland.

PRZYMANOWSKI Janusz, b. 20 Jan 1922, Warsaw, Poland. Author; Journalist. m. Aleksandra Nowinska, 2 Jun 1984, 1 d. Education: University of Warsaw, 1964. Publications: Four from the Tank Corps and the Dog (novel TV film 21 x 1 hour, translated into 18

languages) 1963; 101 Nights on the Front; Studzianki, 1964; novels: Summoned; Dogged; Tired; Wire Entanglement (1.5 hour film); Turnout; Who Speaks Yes? (TV film, 7 x 15 mins); Nest of Bricks; Tricks of Jonaton Kost: Who I Am? Memory; Over 200 songs. Honours: Literary Prize, Ministry of National Defence, 1959, 1961, 1966, 1967, 1987; Literary Prize, Prime Minister, 1977; Literary Prize, Minister of Culture and Art, 1967. Membership: Union of Polish Authors. Address: ul Deuga, 30/34 m. 00-238 Warsawa, Poland.

PRZYPKOWSKI Andrzej Jozef, b. 9 Jul 1930, Poland. Writer. m. Halina Sienska, 17 Mar 1980, 1 d. Education: University of Warsaw, 1952. Publications: Gdzies we Francji, 1966; Gdy Wrocisz do Montpellier, 1969; Na ma jutra w Saint-Nazaire, 1971; Taniec marihuany, 1977; Palm City, 1978; Victoria, 1980; 18 novels, 1 travel book, including latest novel Miraz, 1987. Contributions to: Nlke; Argumenty. Honour: Order of Polonia Restituta, 1980. Memberships: Union of Polish Writers; National Council of Culture. Literary Agent: Authors Agency Ltd, Warsaw. Address: Graniczna 62, 05-540 Zalesie Gorne, Poland.

PUGH Dan(iel Lovelock), b. 11 Mar 1924, England. Engineer's Buyer (retired); Poet. M. Doris Irene Wheatcroft, 22 Sep 1951, 1 s, 4 d. Education: Evening and Correspondence Courses in Trades Unionism and Local Government, 1944-46; Old Testament, New Testament, Art of Teaching, Preaching, Child Psychology, 1951-55; Work Study, 1974. Contributions to: Poetry and creative articles to various publications, mainly UK, also South Africa, New Zealand, USA. Honours: Poem in top 5% Rhyme Revival Competition, 1981, published in 1982 Anthology; Haiku in Top 100 (of 5200), BHA-JA: Contest, 1991; Sonnet recommended, Age Concern Competition, 1991; Winner, Hrafnhon Magazine International Literary Competition, 1991; Mirrors, Tanka Award Poet, (USA), 1992. Memberships: Christian Writers Forum; Fellowship of Christian Writers. Literary Agent: Gerald England, New Hope International (overseas placements). Address: 8 Wyvern Terrace, Melton Mowbray, Leicestershire, LE13 1AD, England.

PUGLISI Angela Aurora, b. 28 Jan 1949, Messina, Italy. Professorial University Lecturer, Georgetown University, Washington DC. Education: BA cum laude, Dunbarton College, USA, 1972; MFA, Painting, 1974, MA, Art History, MA, Language and Literatures, 1977, PhD, Comparative Literature, 1974-83, Education Consultant-US Government 1983-; Catholic University of America; Georgetown University DC, 1986-. Publications: Towards Excellence in Education through Liberal Arts, 1984; Homage, 1985; Nature's Canvas, 1985; Sonnet, 1985; Primavera, 1986; Sand Dunes, 1986; Sun's Journey, 1986; Jet d'Eau, 1986; Ocean Waves, 1986; Prelude, 1987; Ethics in Journalism, 1989; Woodland Revisited, 1988. Artistic Publications 1989-90. Contributions to: Catholic Academy of Sciences, 1989-. Honours include: Certificate in Recognition of Outstanding Service to Education and Education Reform. Memberships: Chairperson, Admissions Committee, Catholic Academy of Sciences, USA, 1990-; Founding Member, Italian Cultural Center Casa Italiana; Corcoran College of Art Association; Charter Member N Museum of Women in the Arts; Board of Directors, SEE. Address: 2843 Cedar Lane, Vienna, VA 22180, USA.

PUJUN Zhang. See: LUO Bin Ji.

PULLEIN-THOMPSON Christine. See: POPESCU Christine.

PULSFORD Petronella, b. 4 Feb 1946, Leeds, Yorkshire, England. Actress; Writer; Director. Education: BA, Hons, English, St Hilda's College, Oxford. Publication: Lee's Ghost, novel, 1990. Honour: Constable Trophy for Fiction, 1989. Memberships: Society of Authors; Equity. Address: 8 Thomas Street West, Savile Park, Halifax, West Yorks, HX1 3HF, England.

PUNNOOSE Kunnuparambil P, b. 26 Mar 1942, Kottayam, India. Editor. m. Santhamma, 9 Jan 1967, 1 s, 2 d. Education: College Graduate, 1962. Literary Appointments: Managing Editor, Concept Publishing Company, 1974-75; Managing Editor, Asian Literary Market Review, 1975-; Director, Darsan Books (P) Limited, 1983-; General Convener, Kottayam International Book Fair, 1984-. Publications: Directory of American University Presses, 1979; American Book Trade in India, 1981; Bookdealers in India and The Orient, 1992; Studying in India, 1994. Contributions to: Over 100 articles on the art and craft of writing and the business of book and magazine publishing. Honours: Kottayam International Book Fair Award, 1989, 1994. Memberships: Authors Guild of India; Kerala Book Society; Afro-Asian Book Council,

New Delhi. Literary Agent: Jaffe Publishing Management Service. Address: Kunnuparambil Buildings, Kurichy, Kottayam 686549, India.

PURCELL Sally (Anne Jane), b. 1 Dec 1944, England. Poet. Education: MA, Lady Margaret Hall, Oxford, 1970. Publications: The Devil's Dancing Hour, 1968; The Holly Queen, 1972; Provençal Poems, 1969; Ed, George Peele, 1972; Dark of Day, 1977; By The Clear Fountain, 1980; Guenevere and the Looking Glass, 1984; Lake & Labyrinth, 1985; Four Poems, 1985; Co Author, Heraldic Symbols, 1986; Through Lent with Blessed Ramon Lull, 1994; Co Editor, The Happy Unicorns, 1971; Editor, The Poems of Charles of Orleans, 1973; The Early Italian Poets, 1981; Monarchs and the Muse, 1972; Translations: Dante, De Vulgari Eloquentia, 1979; Gaspara Stampa, 1985; Nikos Gatsos, Amorgós, 1986. Honours include: Arts Council Award, 1971. Address: c/o Anvil Press Poetry, 69 King George Street, London, SE10 8PX.

PURDUE Arthur William, b. 29 Jan 1941. University Lecturer. m. 29 Aug 1979, 1 d. Education: BA Hons, History, King's College, London, 1962; Diploma of Education, King's College, Durham University, 1963; Master of Letters, University of Newcastle-upon-Tyne, 1974. Publications: The Civilization of The Crowd (with J M Golby), 1984; The Making of The Modern Christmas (with J M Golby), 1986; The Monarchy and The British People (with J M Golby), 1988. Contributions to: Salisbury Review; Times Higher Education Supplement; New Society; Country Life; Northern History; International Review of Social History. Memberships: Trollope Society; Fellow, Royal Historical Society. Address: The Old Rectory, Allendale, Hexham, Northumberland, NE47 9DA, England.

PURDY A F (Fred Wellington), b. 30 Dec 1918, Wooler, Ontario, Canada. Poet. Education: Trenton Collegiate Institute, Ontario. Appointments include: Poet in Residence, Universities of Manitoba & Western Ontario, 1975-78. Publications include: The Crafte So Long to Lerne, 1959; Poems for all the Annettes, 1962; The Old Woman and the May Flowers, 1962; The Blur in Between, 1960-61; Wild Grape Wine, 1968; Love in a Burning Building, 1970; Selected Poems, 1972; Hiroshima Poems, 1972; Sex and Death, 1973; Sundance at Dusk, 1976; The Poems of Al Purdy, 1976; A Handful of Earth, 1977; No Second Spring, 1977; Moths in the Iron Curtain, 1977; Being Alive, 1958-78; The Stone Bird, 1981; Bursting into Song, 1982; Collected Poems, 1986; Two, Al Purdy, 1990; A Woman on the Shore, 1989; Novel, A Splinter in the Heart, 1990; Editions of Modern Canadian Poets. Honours include: Governor Generals Award, 1987; Order of Canada, 1987. Address: Rural Route 1, Ameliasburgh, Ontario KOK 1AO, Canada.

PURDY Carol Ann, b. 5 Jan 1943, Long Beach, California, USA. Writer; Social Worker. m. John Purdy, 8 June 1963, 1 son, 2 daughters. Education: BA, California State University, Long Beach, 1964; MSW, California State University, Sacramento, 1990. Publications: Iva Dunnit And The Big Wind, 1985; Least of All, 1987; The Kid Power Program, Groups for High Risk Children, 1989; Mrs Merriwether's Musical Cat, 1994. Memberships: Society of Children's Book Writers; National Association of Social Workers. Literary Agent: Faith Hamlin, Stanford J Greenburger Literary Agency. Address: 25310 68th Avenue, Los Molinos, CA 96055, USA.

PURDY James, b. 23 July, Ohio, USA. Writer. Publications: 63 Dream Place, 1957; Malcolm, 1959; The Nephew, 1960; Eustace Chisholm and the Works, 1967; Jeremy's Version (novel), 1970; The House of the Solitary Maggot, 1974; In a Shallow Grave, 1976; Narrow Rooms, 1978; On Glory's Course, 1983; Out With The Stars, (novel), 1983; In the Hollow of His Hand, 1986; The Candles of Your Eyes, 1987; Garments The Living Wear, (novel) 1989; Souvenirs, 1989 (play); Introduction Essay: Weymouth Sands, 1984, Collected Poems, 1989; Ruth Elder, (full length play), 1990; In The Night of Time & Four Other Plays, (full length plays), 1992. Contributions to: Conjunctions Magazine; The Village Voice; The Antioch Review; Esquire, Life Magazine. Honours: Guggenheim, 1958, 1962; Ford Fellowship, 1960; The Morton Dauwen Zabel Award in Fiction, The American Academy of Arts & Letters, New York, 1993. Literary Agent: Curtis Brown Ltd, 10 Astor Place, New York. Address: 236 Henry Street, Brooklyn, NY 1201, USA.

PURNELL Kathryn Isabell, b. Vancouver, British Columbia, Canada. Writer; Editor; Tutor. m. William Ernst Purnell, 2 daughters. Education: Melbourne University, Australia. Career: Editor, Society of Women Writers, Australia, 1980-91; Writer in Comunity, City of

Melbourne, East Melbourne Library, Victoria, 1993. Publications: Larpent - The History of a Ship and a District, 1989; Books of poetry: Pandora, 1979; Safari, 1979; Trillium, 1981; Otway Country, 1984; Fairy Trees, 1990; A Harpsicord of Water, 1994; Essays on poetry: Magic Perhaps; The Perpetual Evaluation; Editor, poetry anthologies: Spin of Pink Health, 1980; Spin of Gold Wattle, 1982; Editor, prose anthologies, 1984-89: Journeys; Arrivals; Remember; Series Editor, Gold Wattle Poets Nos 1-32, 1983-92; The Beautiful Hill, 1993. Contributions to: Luna magazine, 1975-91; Literary magazines, education magazines, book reviews, Australia and overseas. Honours: Prose Award, 1967; Poetry Awards, 1972, 1973, 1975, 1976, 1979. Memberships: Past State President, Past Federal President, Society of Women Writers, Australia; Past Vice-President, International PEN; Victorian Writers Centre; Past Chair, Human Rights Committee, United Nations Association, Victoria, Australia; Retired National Board, Young Women's Christian Association. Address: East Melbourne, Victoria, Australia.

PURSER Philip John, b. 28 Aug 1925, Letchworth, England. Journalist; Author. m. Ann Elizabeth Goodman, 18 May 1957, 1 s, 2 d. Education: MA, St Andrews University, 1950. Literary Appointments: Staff, Daily Mail, 1951-57; Television Critic, Sunday Telegraph, 1961-87. Publications: Peregrination 22, 1962; Four Days to The Fireworks, 1964; The Twentymen, 1967; Night of Glass, 1968; The Holy Father's Navy, 1971; The Last Great Tram Race, 1974; Where is He Now?, 1978; A Small Explosion, 1979; The One and Only Phyllis Dixey, 1978; Halliwell's Television Companion (with Leslie Halliwell), 1982, 1986; Shooting The Hero, 1990; Poeted: The Final Quest of Edward James, 1991; Done Viewing, 1992. Contributions to: Numerous magazines and journals. Memberships: Writers Guild of Great Britain; British Academy of Film and Television Arts; The Academy Club. Literary Agent: David Highams Associates. Address: 10 The Green, Blakesley, Towcester, Northamptonshire, NN12 8RD, England.

PURVES Libby (Elizabeth Mary), b. 2 Feb 1950, London, England. Journalist/Broadcaster. m. PaulHeiney, 2 Feb 1980, 1 s, 1 d. Education: BA 1st class honours, Oxford, 1971. Appointments: Presenter/Writer, BBC, 1975-; Editor, Tatler, 1983. Publications: Adventures Under Sail (editor), 1962; Britain at Play, 1982; The Sailing Weekend Book, 1984; How Not to Be a Perfect Mother, 1987; The English and Their Horses, 1988; One Summer's Grace, 1989; How Not to Raise a Perfect Child, 1991. Contributions to: Regularly to the Times and Sunday Express; many magazines, Britain and Australia. Honours: Best Book of the Sea, 1984. Literary Agent: A P Watt, 20 John Street, London WC1, England. Address: Vale Farm, Middleton, Saxmundham, Suffolk 1P17 3LT, England.

PUZO Mario, b. 15 Oct 1920, New York, New York, USA. The Dark Arena, 1955; The Fortunate Pilgrim, 1965; Runaway Summer of Davie Shaw, 1966; The Godfather, 1969; The Godfather Papers and Other Confessions, 1972; Inside Las Vegas, 1977; Fools Die, 1978; The Sicilian, 1984; The Fourth K, 1990. Address: c/o Wm Targ Putnam Publishing, 200 Madison Avenue, New York, NY 10016, USA.

PYBUS Rodney, b. 5 June 1938, Newcastle Upon Tyne, Northumberland. Lecturer: Poet. m. Ella Johnson, 1961, 2 s. Education: MA, Gonville & Caius College, Cambridge, 1965. Appointments include: Lecturer, Macquarie University, Sydney, 1976-79; Literature Officer, Northern Arts, Cumbria, 1979-81. Publications: In Memoriam Milena, 1973; Bridging Loans and Other Poems, 1976; At The Stone Junction, 1978; The Loveless Letters, 1981; Wall, 1981; Talitha Cumi, 1983; Cicadas in Their Summers, 1965-85, 1988; Flying Blues, 1994; Co Editor, Adams Dream, 1981. Honours include: Arts Council Fellowships. Address: 21 Plough Lane, Sudbury, Suffolk CO10 6AU, England.

PYNCHON Thomas, b. 8 May 1937, Glen Cove, Long Island, New York, USA. Writer. m. Melanie Jackson. Education: BA, Cornell University, 1958. Appointments include: Boeing Aircraft, Seattle, Washington. Publications: V (novel), 1963; The Crying of Lot 49 (novel), 1966; Gravity's Rainbow (novel), 1973; Been Down So Long It Looks Like Up To Me, 1983; Slow Leaner, 1984; several short stories including: Mortality and Mercy in Vienna, 1976; Lowlands, 1978. Contributions to: Short stories and essays to periodicals including New York Times Magazine, New York Times Book Review, Cornell Writer, Holiday, Cornell Alumni News, Saturday Evening Post, Kenyon Review. Honours: William Faulkner Novel Award from National Institute of Arts and Letters for the Crying of Lot 49, 1967; National Book Award for Gravity's Rainbow, 1974.

Q

QAZI Moin, b. 4 Apr 1956, Nagpur, India. Bank Executive and Author. m. Nahid Qazi, 30 Dec 1984, 2 sons. Education: LLB, 1983; MA, 1989; PhD, 1993. Publication: A Wakeful Heart (collection of poems) 1990 published by Writers' Workshop, Calcutta; The Real Face, 1991; The Elegant Costumes of the Deccan, The Mission of Muhammad. Contributions to: About 1000 articles and 150 poems to Indian and foreign publications including The Times of India; The Statesman; Indian Express; The Economic Times; Financial Express; The Hindustan Times; Business Standard; The Hindu; Mainstream; Third World Features (Malaysia); SIDA Rapport (Sweden); Depth News (Philippines); Poetry International; Asiaweek (Hongkong); First Time Symphony; New Hope International and Irish Poetry Review, UK; Prophetic Voices, USA; Resurgence, Australia; The Observer; The Telegraph; Christian Science Monitor. Address: Samiullah Khan Marg, Sadar, Nagpur 440001, India.

QUANDT William B, b. California, USA. Middle East Specialist, Brookings Institution; University Professor. m. Helena Gibson, 1 d. Resolution and Political Leadership, 1969; The Comparative Study of Political Ethics, 1970; Algerian Military Development, 1972; The Politics of Palestinian Nationalism, 1973; Decade of Delusions, 1977; Saudi Arabia in the 1980's, 1981; Camp David: Peacemaking in Politics, 1986; The Middle East: Ten Years After Camp David, 1988; The United States and Egypt, 1990; Peace Process: American Diplomacy and the Arab-Israeli Conflict Since 1967, 1994. Address: 2238 44th Street N W, Washington, DC 20007, USA.

QUARRY Nick. See: **ALBERT Marvin H.**

QUARTUS Appleton. See: **CREGAN David.**

QUEEN Ellery. See: **POWELL Talmage.**

QUICK Barbara, b. 28 May 1954, Los Angeles, California, USA. Writer. m. John Quick, 1 Aug 1988. Education: BA, Hons, Literature, University of California, Santa Cruz. Publications: Northern Edge (novel) 1990, revised edition, 1995. Contributions to: New York Times Book Review. Honours: Northern Edge was selected as one of 26 books for B Dalton's Discover; Great New Writer series, 1990; 2nd place, Ina Coolbrith Poetry Prize, 1977. Literary Agent: Elizabeth Wales, Levant & Wales. Address: c/o Elizabeth Wales, 108 Hayes Street, Seattle, WA 98109, USA.

QUIJADA Rodrigo, b. 23 Nov 1942, Punta Arenas, Chile. Lawyer. m. Broughton Maria Isabel, 6 May 1979, 1 d. Education: Lawyer, Chile University, 1971; Criminology Researcher, 1970; Sexologist and Marriage Counsellor, 1970. Appointments: Public Relations Manager, Orbe Publishers, 1966-69; Executive Editor, Hera Magazine, 1967-69; Creative Director, Multivision Audiovisual, 1976-; Literature Coordinator, Fonatur, Mexico Latinamerican Section Editor, Le Monde Diplomatique Mexico. Publications: Graduacion, 1970; Tiempo de Aranas 1967; Bajo un Silencio, 1963; Techo Circular, 1973; Manual de Educacion Sexual, 1972; Elementos de Derecho Penal, 1975; short stories, essays. Contributions to: numerous journals and magazines. Honours: Zig-Zag Publishers Prize, 1966; Municipal Prize, 1967. Memberships: PEN; Chilean Association of Writers; Mexican Association of Writers; Chilean Association of Sexology; Cultural Multivision Institute. Address: Matias Romero 227, Mexico 12, CP 03100, Mexico.

QUILLER Andrew. See: **BULMER Henry Kenneth.**

QUIN Robyn, b. 10 Jun 1954, Perth, Australia. Academic. m. Rod Quin. Education: Teachers Certificate; BA; MA; Graduate Diploma, Film and TV. Publications: (All with Barrie McMahon) Exploring Images, 1984; Real Images, 1986; Stories and Stereotypes, 1987; Meet the Media, 1989; Australian Images, 1990; Understanding Soaps, 1993. Contributions to: Australian Journal of Education; Canadian Journal of Educational Communication; Education Para la Reception, Mexico; Tijdschrift voor Theaterwetensschap, Germany. Honours: Cuitin University School of English Prize. Memberships: Australian Teachers of Media, WA. Address: PO Box 8064, Perth Business Centre, Pier Street, Perth 6849, Western Australia.

QUINNEY Richard, b. 16 May 1934. University Professor. Education: Bs, Caroll College, 1956; MA, Nortwestern University, 1957; PhD, University of Wisconsin, 1962. Appointments: Instrutor, Department of Sociology and Anthropology, St Lawrence University, 1960-62; Assisstant Professor, Department of Sociology, University of Kentucky, 1962-65; Associate Professor, 1965-70, Professor 1970-73, Department of Sociology, New York University; Research and writing leaves, Department of Sociology, University of North Carolina at Chapel Hill, Sabbatical fron New York University 1971-74; Visiting Professor 1975-78, Adjunct Professor1980-83, Department of Sociology, Brown University; Distinguished Visiting Professor 1978-79, Adjunct Professor, 1980-83, Department of Sociology, Boston College; Professor, Department of Sociology, Northen Illinois University, 1983-. Publications: Many Books including: Criminology: Analysis and Critique of Crime in America, 1975, 1979; Class, State and Crime: On The Theory and Practice of Criminal Justice, 1977, 1980; ed. Capitalist Society: Readings for a Critical Sociology, 1979; Providence: The Reconstruction of Social and Moral Order, 1980; Marxism and Law, co-editor Piers Beirne, 1982; Social Existence: Metaphysics, Marxism and the Social Sciences, 1982; Criminology as Peacemaking, co-editor Harold E Pepinsky, 1991; Journey to a Far Place: Autobiographical Reflections, 1991. Contributions to: Numerous articles contributed to professional journals including: Social Problems; Southwestern Social Science Quarterly; Journal of Criminal Law, Criminology and Police Science; Journal of Research in Crime and Deliquency; Sociometry; American Behavioural Scientist; British Journal of Criminolgy. Honours: Edwin Sutherland Award, for contributions to criminological theory, American Society of Criminology, 1984; Delegate, Crime Prevention and Criminal Justice Delegation to the People's Republic of China, sponsored by the Eisenhower Foundation and Northern Illinois University, 1985; Fulbright Award, Lectureship at University College, Galway, Ireland, 1986; President's Award, Western Society of Criminology, 1992. Address: Department of Sociology, Northern Illinois University, Dekalb, IL 60115, USA.

QUINOT Raymond G A, b. 12 Feb 1920, Brussels, Belgium. Hr Director; Writer. m. Suzanne Cambron, 3 Sept 1952. Appointments: Hr Secretary, International PEN Club, French Speaking Centre Belgium; Administrator: Association of Belgian Writers, Royal Association of Walloon Writers, Foundation Charles Plisnier, International Biennal of Poetry of Liege. Publications: 50 books (essays and poetry) including: The Adventures of Jaune and Jaunette; Charles de Ligne, Walloon and European Prince; Thoughts of a Gentleman; My Cities; The Nice October; Solo for a Reader; Langston Hughes or the Black Star; Present. Contributions to: Numerous, magazines, journals and anthologies throughout the world. Honours: Jury Member, Prize of the Ministry of the French Community in Belgium; Laureate of Prizes Max Rose, Interfrance, Davaine (Academie Francaise, Paris), Ville de Bruxelles, Rime d'Or; Bouvier-Parvillez, Royal Academy, Brussels. Address: 76 (bte 7) Avenue du Onze Novembre, 1040 Brussels, Belgium.

QUINTAVALLE Uberto Paolo, b. 1 Nov 1926, Milan, Italy. Writer. m. Josephine Hawke, 1970, 5 s. Education: D Litt, University of Milan, 1949; Playwriting, Yale Drama School, 1950. Publications: La festa, 1953; Segnati a dito, 1956; Capitale Mancata, 1959; Tutti compromessi, 1961; Rito Romano, rito ambrosiano, 1964; Carolinda, 1974; Il Dio riciclato, 1989; La Corriere della sera; Il gionale. Memberships: PEN Club, Secretary General of the Italian Division. Address: Via Mangili 2, 20121 Milan, Italy.

QUIRK Randolph (Lord), b. 12 July 1920, Isle of Man, England. Academic; Past President, The British Academy. Education: BA 1947, MA 1949, PhD 1951, DLitt 1961, University College, London; Yale University, USA. Publications: The Use of English, 1968; Elicitation Experiments in English, 1970; Grammar of Contemporary English, 1972; University Grammar of English, 1974; The Linguist & the English Language, 1974; Style & Communication in the English Language, 1982; Comprehensive Grammar of the English Language, 1985; Words at Work, 1987; A Student's Grammar of the English Language, 1990; English in Use, 1990; An Introduction to Standard English, 1993; Grammatical and Lexical Variance in English, 1995. Honours: CBE, 1976; KT, 1985; Life Peerage, 1994; Honorary Doctorates: Paris & over 20 other Universities. Address: University College London, Gowen Street, London WC1E 6BT, England.

QUIROGA Elena, Writer. Publications: Viento del Norte, 1951; La Sangre, 1952; Algo Pasa en la Calle, 1954; La Enferma, 1954; La Careta, 1955; Placida la Joven, 1956; la Ultima Corrida, 1958; Tristura,

1960; Escribo tu Nombre, 1965. Honours: Nadal Prize, 1950; Critics Prize, 1960; Escribo tu Nombre chosen to represent Spain in Romulo Gallegos Literary Competition, 1965. Address: Real Academia de la Historia, Leon 21, Madrid 14, Spain.

R

RABAN Jonathon. Publications include: the Technique of Modern Fiction, 1968; The Society of the Poem, 1971; Soft City, 1974; Arabia A Journey Through the Labyrinth, 1979; Old Glory: An American Voyage, 1981; Foreign Land: a Novel, 1986; Coasting, 1987; For Love and Money: A Writing Life, 1989; God, Man and Mrs Thatcher, 1989; Hunting Mr Heartbreak, 1991. Contributions to: New York Review of Books. Address: 3030 Humes Place west, Seattle, WA 98119, USA.

RABE Berniece, b. 11 Jan 1928. Author. m. 30 July 1946. 3 sons, 1 daughter. Education: BSEd, National College; Graduate work in Psychology and Administration, Northern Illinois and Roosevelt Universities; Master's degree, Columbia College, Chicago. Appointments include: Writing Instructor, Columbia College, Chicago, 2 years; Consultant, Missouri Council of the Arts. Publications: Rass, 1973; Naomi, 1975; The Girl Who Had No Name, 1977; The Orphans, 1978; Who's Afraid, 1980; Margaret's Moves, 1987; A Smooth Move, 1987; Rehearsal for the Bigtime, 1988; Where's Chimpy, 1988; Tall Enough To Own The World, 1988; Magic Comes In It's Time, 1993; The Legend of the First Candy Cares, 1994; Picture books: The Balancing Girl, 1982; Can They See Me; Two Peas in a Pod; 2 film scripts. Contributions to: Short stories and articles. Honours include: 3rd Place, Mark Twain Award, 1973; Honor Book, 1975, Golden Kite Award, 1977, National Society of Children's Book Writers Award, 1975; Midland Author's Award, 1978; Notable Book of the Year, American Library Association, 1982; National Children's Choice Award, 1987. Memberships include: Board of Directors, Society of Midland Authors; Board of Directors, Off Campus Writers; Board of Directors, Fox Valley Writers. Address: 724 Denton, Texas, TX 76205, USA.

RABE David, b. 10 Mar 1940, Duburque, Iowa, USA. Playwright; Feature writer; Consultant. m. (1) Elizabeth Pan, 1969, 1 s, (2) Jill Clayburgh, March 1979. Education: BA, Lores College; MA, Villanova University. Publications: Plays, including: The Coming; Sticks and Bones, 1971; The Orphan, 1973; In The Boom Boom Room, 1973; Streamers, 1975. Honours: Associated Press Award, 1970; Obie Award, 1971; Drama Desk Award, 1971; Drama Guild Award, 1971; Elizabeth Hull- Kate Warriner Award, 1971; Outer Circle Award, 1971; Antoinette Perry Award, 1971-72; National Institute and American Academy Award in Literature, 1976; New York Drama Critics Circle Award, 1976. Address: c/o Grove Atlantic Inc, 841 Broadway, New York, NY 10003-4793, USA.

RACHLIN Nahid, b. 6 June 1944, Abadan, Iran. Writer; Instructor. m. Howard Rachlin, 1 daughter. Education: BA, Psychology, Lindenwood College, St Charles, Missouri, USA; 24 credits in Creative Writing, Columbia University. Appointments: New York University, School of Continuing Education, 1978-90; Marymount Manhattan College, 1986-87; Hofstra University, 1988-90; Yale University, 1989-90; Hunter College, 1990; Barnard College, 1991-. Publications: Foreigner, W W Norton, 1978; John Murray, 1978; Married to a Stranger, 1983, reissued in paperback, City Lights; Veils, 1992. Contributions to: Redbook; Shenandoah; Crosscurrents; Fiction; Prism International; Ararat; Confrontation; Minnesota Review; Four Quarters; Columbia Magazine; New Laurel Review; Blueline; New Letters; Mississippi Mud; City Lights Journal; Pleiades; North Atlantic Review; Chanteh. Honours: Doubleday-Columbia Fellowship; Stegner Fellowship, Stanford; National Endowment for the Arts Grant; Bennet Certificate Award; PEN Syndicated Fiction Project. Memberships: PEN. Address: Apt PHC, 501E, 87th Street, New York, NY 10128, USA.

RADDALL Thomas Head, b. 13 Nov 1903, Hythe, Kent, England. Novelist. Education: Halifax Academy. Appointments: Full Time Writer, 1938-. Publications include: Saga of the Rover, 1931; His Majestys Yankees, 1942; Roger Sudden, 1944; Prides Fancy, 1946; Son of the Hawk, 1950; Tidefall, 1954; The Wings of Night, 1956; The Governor's Lady, 1961; Short Story Collections, Pied Piper of Dipper Creek and Other Tales, 1939; Tambour and Other Tales, 1945; A Muster of Arms and Other Stories, 1954; At the Tide's Turn and Other Stories, 1959; The Dreamers, 1986; Uncollected Short Stories and Histories of Nova Scotia and Its People. Honours: D Litt, St Mary's University, Halifax, 1969; Officer, Order of Canada, 1970. Address: 44 Park Street, Liverpool, Nova Scotia BOT 1JO, Canada.

RADLEY Sheila. See: **ROBINSON Sheila Mary.**

RADTKE Gunter, b. 23 Apr 1925, Berlin, Germany. Author. Education: Trainee Journalist. Publications: Davon Kommst du Nicht Los, 1971; Die Dunne Haut Der Luftballons, 1975; Der Krug Auf Dem Weg Zum Wasser, 1977; Gluck aus Mangel an Beweisen, 1978; Suchen Wer Wir Sind, 1980; Gedanken zum Selbermachen, 1987; Wolkenlandschaften, 1988; Nicht so ernst wie es ist, 1990; Notizen zur greifbaren Nähe, 1993. Contributions to: Numerous literary magazines, newspapers and broadcasting stations. Honours: German Short Story Prize, 1971; George Mackensen Prize, 1973; The First Roman Literature Prize, 1975; Literature Prize Markische Culture Conference, 1979; Prize from Europ Writers Corporation DIE KOGGE, 19933. Memberships: Die Kogge; Association of German Writers; NGL Hamburg and Berlin; PEN. Literary Agent: Deutsche Verlags-Anstalt. Address: Postfach 86, Keitum/Sylt, Germany.

RAE Hugh Crauford (James Albany, Robert Crawford, R B Houston, Morgan McGrath, Stuart Stern, Jessica Sterling), b. 22 Nov 1935, Glasgow, Scotland. Novelist. m. Elizabeth Dunn, 3 Sep 1960, 1 d. Appointments: Scottish Arts Council, 1975-80. Publications include: Skinner, 1965; Night Pillow, 1966; A Few Small Bones, 1968; The Saturday Epic, 1970; Harkfast, 1976; Sullivan, 1978; Haunting at Waverley Falls, 1980; Privileged Strangers, 1982; As Jessica Stirling: The Spoiled Earth, 1974; The Hiring Fair, 1976; The Dark Pasture, 1978; The Deep Well at Noon, 1980; The Blue Evening Gone, 1982; The Gates at Midnight, 1983; Treasures on Earth, 1985; Creature Comforts, 1986; Hearts of Gold, 1987; as James Albany: Warrior Caste, Mailed Fist, Deacon's Dagger, 1982; Close Combat, Matching Fire, 1983; Last Bastion, Borneo Story, 1984. Membership: Scottish Association Of Writers. Address: Drumore Farm Cottage, Balfron Station, Stirlingshire, Scotland.

RAE John Malcolm, b. 20 Mar 1931, London, England. Director, The Portman Group. Education: MA, Sidney Sussex College, Cambridge University, 1955; PhD, King's College, London University. Publications: The Custard Boys, 1960; Conscience and Politics, 1970; The Golden Crucifix, 1974; The Treasure of Westminster Abbey, 1975; Christmas is Coming, 1976; Return to the Winter Place, 1979; The Third Twin: A Ghost Story, 1980; The Public School Revolution, 1981; Letters from School, 1987; Too Little, Too Late? 1989; Delusions of Grandeur, 1993. Contributions to: Encounter; Times Literary Supplement; Times Educational Supplement; The Times; Sunday Telegraph. Honour: Recipient, United Nations Award for Film Script, Reach for Glory, 1962. Literary Agent: The Peters Fraser Dunlop Group Ltd. Address: 101 Millbank Court, 24 John Islip St, London SW1P 4LG, England.

RAELIN Joseph A, b. 10 Apr 1948, Cambridge, Massachusetts, USA. Professor of Management. m. Abby P Dolin, 4 Aug 1974, 2 sons. Education: Diplome, University of Paris, Sorbonne, 1969; BA, 1970, EdM, 1971, Tufts University; PhD, State University of New York, Buffalo, 1977. Appointments: The Wallace E Carroll School of Management, Boston College, Massachusetts, 1976-, currently Professor of Management. Publications: Building A Career: The Effect of Initial Job Experiences and Related Attitudes on Later Employment, 1980; The Salaried Professional: How to Make the Most of Your Career, 1984; The Clash of Cultures: Managers Managing Professionals, 1986, paperback, 1991. Contributions to: Co-Editor, Management Learning; Some 50 articles in professional journals, proceedings and magazines. Memberships: Academy of Management (US). Address: The Wallace E Carroll School of Management, Boston College, Chestnut Hill, MA 02167, USA.

RAFFEL Burton Nathan, b. 27 Apr 1928, NY, USA. Writer; Translator; Editor; Teacher; Lawyer. m. Elizabeth Clare Wilson, 16 Apr 1974, 3 s, 3 d. Education: BA, Brooklyn College, 1948; MA, Ohio State University, 1949; JD, Yale University, 1958. Literary Appointments include: Editor, Foundation News, 1960-63; Denver Quarterly, 1976-77. Publications include: Beowulf (translation), 1963; Four Humours (poems), 1979; How To Read A Poem, 1984; Signet Book of American Stories (anthology), 1985; After Such Ignorance (novel), 1986; Chretien de Troyes, Yvain (translation), 1987; Rabelais, Gargantua and Portaguel (translation), 1990; Complete Poetry and Prose of Chairil Anwar (translation), 1993; Cervantes, Don Quijote (translation), 1994; Various other books of criticism, history. Contributions to: Hudson Review; Saturday Review of Literature; Asian Wall Street Journal; Arion; Tri-Quarterly; Atlantic Monthly; Literary Review; Times Literary Supplement; Yale Review; Books Abroad; Science Digest; Thought; London Magazine; East-West Review. Honour: Frances Steloff Prize, fiction, 1978. Address: Raffel, 203 Mannering Avenue S, Lafayette, LA 70508, USA.

RAGON Michel, b. 24 June 1924, Marseille, France. Author. m. Francoise Antoine, 28 Dec 1968. Education: Docteur es Lettres. Publications: Droles de Metiers (novel), 1953; L'Accent de ma mere (novel), 1980; Les Mouchoirs rouges de Cholet (novel), 1982; Histoire mondiale de l'architecture et de l'urbanisme modernes, 3 vols, 19781-78; Histoire de la litterature proletarienne, 1974; 25 ans d'art vivant, 1986; 12 other novels; 15 monographs about painters and architects. Numerous works conveyning modern art and architecture. Honours: Member, Royal Academy of Denmark; Member, Academy of Brittany; Laureate, Academie Francaise; Grande Medaille d'Argent and Grande Medaille de Vermeil, Academie d'Architecture. Memberships: Societe des Gens de Lettres; International Association of Art Critics. Address: 4 rue du Faubourg Poissonniere, 75010 Paris, France.

RAIJADA Rajendrasinh, b. 1 July 1943, Sondarda, India. Headmast, High School, Keshod. m. Gulabkumari Raijada, 21 Feb 1969, 2 sons, 1 daughter. Education: BEd, Gujarati, 1973, MA, Gujarati, 1975, Saurashtra University, Rajkot; PhD, Mysticism in Modern Gujarati Poetry, Sardar Patel University, Vallabhvidyanagar, 1979. Appointments: Central Committee Member, Gujarati Sahitya Parishad, Amdavad, 1975-77; Language Expert, Gujarat State Text Book Board, Gandhinagar, 1975-82; Resource Person, National Education Policy, 1986; Adviser, Gujarat Sahitya Academy, Gandhinagar, 1991. Publications: Radha Madhav, translation from Hindi), 1970; Farva avyo chhun, poetry, 1976; Gulmahor ni niche, short stories, 1977; Rahasyavad, essays, 1980; Hun, Kali chhokari ape Suraj, poetry, 1982; Darsdhan ane Itishas, collection of articles, 1983; Sant Parampara Vimarsh, criticism, 1989; Tantra Sadhana, Maha Panth Ane Anya Lekho, collection of articles, 1993. Address: Sondarda, via Kevadra 362227, Gujarat, India.

RAILSBACK Brian Evan, b. 24 Sep 1959, Glendale, CA, USA. Assistant Professor of English. m. Sandra Lea Railsback, 6 Aug 1983, 2 s, 1 d. Education: AA, 1981; BA Journalism, 1982; MA English, 1985; PhD English, 1990. Literary Appointments: John Cady Fellow, Ohio University, 1989; Assistant Professor, English, Western Carolina University, NC, 1990-. Contributions to: Scholarly articles to: San Jose Studies; Steinbeck Quarterly; Short story to Tamaqua; Reviews to various Magazines and journals. Memberships: American Writing Programs; Modern Language Association; International Steinbeck Society. Address: PO Box 1001, Cullowhee, NC 28723, USA.

RAINE Craig Anthony, b. 3 Dec 1944, Shildon, England. Writer. m. Ann Pasternak Slater, 27 Apr 1972, 3 s, 1 d. Education: Honours Degree, English Language and Literature, Oxford, 1966; BPhil, English Studies, Oxford, 1968. Literary Appointments: Reviews Editor, The New Review, 1977-79; Editor, Quarto, 1979-80; Poetry Editor, New Statesman, 1981; Poetry Editor, Faber, 1981-91. Publications include: A Martian Sends a Postcard Home, 1979; The Onion Memory, 1978; Rich, 1984; The Electrification of The Soviet Union, 1987; 1953, 1990; Haydn and The Valve Trumpet, 1990. Contributions to: Observer; Sunday Times; Independent on Sunday; New Statesman; Listener; Encounter; London Review of Books; TLS; Literary Review; Grand Street; New Yorker. Honours: Southern Arts Literature Award, 1980; Cholmondeley Award, 1983; Fellow, New College, Oxford, 1991-. Memberships: PEN; Royal Society of Literature. Address: New College, Oxford.

RAINE Kathleen Jessie, b. 1908. Poet; Scholar. m. Charles Madge (div), 1 s, 1 d. Education: Girton College, Cambridge. Publications: Stone and Flower, 1943; Living in Time, 1946; The Pythoness, 1949; The Year One, 1952; Collected Poems, 1956; Blake and Tradition (Andrew Mellon Lectures, WA), 1962; The Hollow Hill (poems), 1965; Defending Ancient Springs (criticism), 1967; William Blake, 1970; The Lost Country (verse), 1971; On a Deserted Shore (verse), 1973; Yeats, The Tarot and The Golden Dawn (criticism), 1973; Faces of Day and Night, 1973; Farewell Happy Fields (autobiography), 1973; Death in Life and Life in Death (on Yeats), 1974; The Land Unknown (autobiography), 1975; The Oval Portrait (verse), 1977; The Lion's Mouth (autobiography), 1977; David Jones and The Actually Loved and Known (criticism), 1978; L'Imagination Creatice de William Blake, French translation of verse, Isis errant, 1978; Sur un rivage desert, 1978; From Blake to a Vision (criticism), 1979; Le Premier Jour, 1980; Spanish translation, En una desierta orilla, 1980; Co-Editor, Temenos, 1981-; Collected Poems, 1981; The Human Face of God, 1982; The Inner Journey of The Poet and Other Papers

(criticism), 1982; Yeats the Initiate, 1986; La bueul du Lion, 1987; The Preserve (verse), 1988; Selected Poems, 1988; Le Royaume Invisible, 1991. Honours: Honorary Doctorates from universities of: Leciester, 1974; Durham, 1979; Caen, France, 1987; Prix de Heilleur Liore Etranger, 1978; W H Smith and Son Award, 1972. Address: 47 Paultons Square, London, SW3, England.

RAJA P, b. 7 Oct 1952, Pondicherry, India. Lecturer in English. m. Periyanayaki, 6 May 1976, 2 sons, 1 daughter. Education: BA, English, 1973; MA, English Language & Literature, 1975; PhD, Indian Writing in English, 1992. Appointments: Regular contributor to about 15 journals in India; Literary Editor to Pondicherry Today (fortnightly); One among the 8 member committee to translate the works of the Tamil Poet Bharathidasan into English - appointed by Government of Pondicherry. Publications: From Zero to Infinity (poems), 1987; Folktales of Pondicherry, 1987; A Concise History of Pondicherry, 1987; Tales of Mulla Nasruddin, 1989; The Blood and Other Stories, 1991; M P Pandit: A Peep Into His Past, 1993; Many Worlds of Manoj Das, 1993; The Best Woman in My Life and Other Stories, 1994; Sudden Tales the Folks Told, 1995; Translations from Tamil: The Stupid Guru and his Foolish Disciples, 1981, The Sun and the Stars, 1982. Address: 74 Poincare Street, Olandai-Keerapalayam, Pondicherry 605004, India.

RAJANNA. See: NAGARAJA RAO C K.

RAJIC Negovan, b. 24 June 1923, Belgrade, Yugoslavia. Writer. m. Mirjana Knezevic, 28 Mar 1970, 1 son, 1 daughter. Education: Attended University of Belgrade, 1945-46; Diplome d'etudes techniques superieures, 1962, Diploma in Electrical Engineering, 1968, Conservatoire des Arts et Metiers, Paris. Appointments: Fought with Resistance during World War II, escaped Yugoslavia 1946, arrived Paris, 1947, resumed studies in Engineering; Research Engineer, Physical Laboratory, Ecole Polytechnique de Paris, 1956-63; Researcher in Electronics, France, 1963-69; Came to Canada, 1969 becoming Professor of Mathematics, Cegep Trois Rivieres to 1987. Publications: Les Hommes-Taupes, 1978; English translation The Master of Srappado, 1984; Sept roses pour une boulangere, 1987, English translation, Seven Roses for a Baker, 1988; Service penitentiaire, 1988, English translation The Shady Business, 1989; Numerous articles and short stories. Honours: Prix Esso du Cercle du Livre de France, 1978; Prix Air Canada best short story, 1980; Prix Slobodan Yovanovitch Association des ecrivains et artistes serves en exile, 1984; Prix litteraire de Trois-Rivieres, 1988. Memberships: PEN International; Association of Writers of Quebec; Honorary Member, Association of Serbian Writers, Belgrade. Address: 300 Dunant, Trois-Rivieres, Quebec, G8Y 2W9, Canada.

RAJU Chethput, b. 28 Jan 1916, Vellore, North Arcot District, Tamil Nadu, India. Retired Commercial Executive and Manager. m. Eashwari Raju, 14 Nov 1947, 2 sons. Education: BA English (Special), 1957. Publications: This Modern Age and Other Poems, poems in English, 1954; No Exit, poems in English, 1970. Contributions to: Poetry Review, London; Poetry Nippon, Japan; The National Library of Poetry, USA; Purpose, USA; Others. Honours: Prizewinner, All India Poetry Contest, 1991, 1992. Memberships: PEN India; Associate, Chartered Insurance Institute; LCC, London. Adddress: 3 Ganga Vihar, 318 Bhalchandra Road, Matunga, CR, Bombay 400 019, India.

RAMA RAO Vadapalli Vijaya Bhaskara, b. 1 Jan 1938, Srikakulam District, A P, India. Educator. m. Ramani Rama Rao, 15 Apr 1959, 1 son, 3 daughters. Education: BA, Economics, 1957; BA, English, 1958; MA, English, 1961; Diploma in Teaching English, 1966; Diploma in French, 1979; PhD, 1980. Publications: In English: Poosapati Ananda Gajapati Raju, biography, 1985; Tapaswi, novel, 1989; Graham Greene's Comic Vision, criticism, 1990; Into That Heaven of Freedom, novel, 1991; Warm Days Will Never Cease, forthcoming; Translation, Trapped, novel, from English to Telugu, 1991; 6 novels in Telugu: Sparasarekhalu, 1977; Neetikireetalu, 1977; Maguvalu - Manasulu, 1980; Gaalipadagalu - Deepakalikalu, 1981; Tapaswi, 1985; Avagaahana, forthcoming; The Joy of the Divine, 1994; The Drunken Boat, 1994; Malapalli, English translation, 1994; Novel, forthcoming 1995; Unnava, Sahitya Akademi monograph, 1994; Major novels, books published. Contributions to: 15 literary reviews in English and about 125 short fiction in Telugu to magazines and journals; About 400 English and about 20 Telugu feature and newspaper articles. Address: 19-5-13 Kanukurti st, Vizianagaram 535 002, India.

RAMA RAU Santha (Rama Rau Wattles), b. 24 Jan 1923, Madras, India. Freelance Writer. m. (1) Faubion Bowers, 24 Oct 1951, divorced 1966, 1 son, (2) Gurdon W Wattles, 1970. Education: BA, Honours, Wellesley College, USA, 1945. Publications: Home to India, 1945; East of Home, 1950; This India, 1953; Remember the House, 1955; View to the South-East, 1957; My Russian Journey, 1959; A Passage to India, 1962 (dramatisation of E M Forster's Novel); Gifts of Passage, 1962; The Cooking of India, 1970; The Adventuress, 1970; A Princess Remembers, 1976; An Inheritance, 1977. Contributions to: numerous journals and magazines. Honours: Honorary Degrees: Bates College, 1960, Roosevelt University, 1962, Brandeis University, 1962, Russell Sage College, 1965; Awards: Mlle Mag Merit Award, 1965; Association of Indians in America, 1977. Literary Agent: William Morris Agency. Address: c/o William Morris Agency, 1350 6th Avenue, New York, NY 10019, USA.

RAMAMURTI Krishnamurthy Sitaraman (Madhuram Ramamurti), b. 4 Nov 1930, Madras, India. Professor of English; Dean. m. Rajesnari Ramamurti, 4 Jul 1958, 2 d. Education: BSc Physics, 1950, MA English Language and Literature, 1954, University of Madras; MA, English Literature, Muslim University, Aligarh, 1963; Diploma, Teaching of English, Central Institute of English, Hyderabad; PhD, Madurai University, 1975. Literary Appointments: Lecturer, English, St Aloysius College, Mangalore, 1954-65; Professor, Head, Department of English, Sri Palaniasndowar Arts College, Palmi, 1965-76; Lecturer, 1976-78, Reader, 1978-84, Professor, 1984-91, Dean, College Development Council, 1991-, Bharathidasan University, Tiruchirapalli. Publications: Editor, The Spanish Tragedy (Thomas Kyd), 1978; Vazhithunai (novel), 1980; Perspectives on Modern English Prose, 1985; Rise of The Indian Novel, in English, 1986; Variety in Short Stories, 1988. Contributions to: About 12 short novels and short stories in Tamil to leading journals; about 12 feature articles to leading newspapers including: The Hindu; Indian Express; about 70 research papers to standard literary journals; about 20 book reviews and review articles. Honour: Prize for novel, 1980. Memberships: Indian Association of English Teachers; Comparative Literature Association of India; Executive Committee, Indian Association of Canadian Studies. Address: Bharatidasan University, Tiruchirapalli 620024, India.

RAMAMURTI Madhuram. See: RAMAMURTI Krishnamurthy Sitaraman.

RAMANUJAN Attipat Krishnaswami, b. 16 Mar 1929, Mysore, Karnataka, India. Professor: Poet. m. Molly Daniels, 1962, 1 s, 1 d. Education: MA, University of Mysore, 1950; PhD, Indiana University, 1963. Appointments include: William E Colvin Professor, University of Chicago, 1983-; Visiting Professor, Universities of WI, CA, MI, 1965-73. Publications: The striders, 1966; No Lotus in the Naval, 1969; Relations, 1972; Selected Poems, 1976; And Other Poems, 1977; Second Sight, 1986; Novel, Mattobbana Atmacaritre, 1978; Proverbs, 1955; The Literatures of India, 1975; Translations of Indian Poetry. Honours include: National Endowment for the Arts Grants; Americn Academy. Address: Foster Hall, University of Chicago, 1130 East 59th Str, Chicago, IL 60637, USA.

RAMDIN Ronald Andrew, b. 20 Jun 1942, Marabella, Trinidad. Historian; Writer; Lecturer. m. Irma de Freitas, 20 Dec 1969, 1 s. Education: Diploma in Speech and Drama, New Era Academy of Drama and Music, 1963; Diploma in Industrial Relations and Trade Union Studies, University of Middlesex, 1977; BSc Economics, London School of Ecnomics and Political Science, 1982. Publications: From Chattel Slave to Wage Earner, 1982; Introductory Text: The Black Triangle, 1984; The Making of The Black Working Class in Britain, 1987; Paul Robeson: The Man and His Mission, 1987; World in View: West Indies, 1990; Arising From Bondage: A History of East Indians in The Caribbean 1838-1991, forthcoming. Contributions to: Anglo-British Review; City Limits; Dragon's Teeth; Race Today; Caribbean Times; West Indian Digest; History Workshop Journal. Honours: Scarlet Ibis Medal, Gold Award, Trinidad and Tobago High Commission, London, 1990; Hansib, Caribbean Times, Community Award, Britain, 1990. Address: The British Library, Humanities and Social Science Section, Great Russell Street, London, WC1B 3DG, England.

RAMIREZ-DE-ARELLANO Diana, b. 3 June 1919, New York City, USA. Professor Emeritus; Poet; Writer. Education: BA, University of Puerto Rico, 1941; MA TC, University of Columbia, 1946; Licentiate Degree and Title, University of Madrid, 1959; Doctorate Degree and Title, 1952 and 1961. Appointments: Poetry Chair, City College, City University of New York, 1970-; President and Director of Publications,

Ateneo de New York. Publications include: Los Ramirez de Arellano de Lope de Vega, literary editor, 1954; Camminos de la Creación Poética en Pedro Salinas, literary critcism, 1957; Angeles de Ceniza (poetry) 1958; Privilegio (poetry), 1959; Poesiá Contemporánea en Lengua Española, 1961; Tree at Vespers (bilingual) (poetry), ed 1987; Un Vuelo Casi Humano (poetry); Albatros Sobre el Alma (poetry); Poesia Diacunista de Taller, CUNY; Memorias del Ateneo PR de NY 1961-67; Adelfazar (Elegiá) 1994. Contributions to: Numerous journals in Puerto Rico and Spain. Honours: First Prize in Literature, Institute of Literature, Puerto Rico, 1958; Prize for Literary Criticism, Institute of Literature, Puerto Rico, 1961; Order of Merit, Republic of Ecuador, 1971; International Prize for Poetry, Ministry of Education and Arts, Bolivia, 1964; Professor Emeritus, City University of New York, 1984. Memberships include: Hispanic Society of America; American Association of Spanish and Portuguese (Professor Emeritus); President, Josefina Romo Arregui Memorial Foundation; PEN Club International, Puerto Rican Chapter; Royal Academy of Doctors of Madrid, USA Representative. Address: 23 Harbor Circle, Centerport, NY 11721, USA.

RAMKE Bin, b. 19 Feb 1947, Pt Neches, TX, USA. Teacher; Editor; Poet. m. 31 May 1967, 1 s. Education: BA, Louisiana State University, 1970; MA, University of New Orleans, 1971; PhD, Ohio University, 1975. Literary Appointments: Professor of English, Columbus College, Georgia, 1976-85; Professor of English, University of Denver, 1985-; Editor, Contemporary Poetry Series, University of Georgia Press, 1984-; Poetry Editor, The Denver Quarterly, 1985-. Publications: The Difference Beteewn Night And Day, 1978; White Monkeys, 1981; The Language Student, 1987; The Erotic Light of Gardens, 1989. Contributions to: Poetry; New Yorker; Paris Review; Essays and reviews in Georgia Law Review; Denver Quarterly. Honours: Yale Younger Poets Award, 1977; Texas Institute of Arts and Letters Award, poetry, 1978. Memberships: PEN, American Centre; Associated Writing Programmes. Address: Department of English, University of Denver, Denver, CO 80208, USA.

RAMNEFALK (Sylvia) Marie Louise, b. 21 Mar 1941, Stockholm, Sweden. Education: FK 1964, FL 1968, FD 1974, Stockholm University. Appointments: Script Supervisor, TV-Theatre, 1967-68; University Teacher, Stockholm University, 1960s; Umea University, 1970s; School for Librarians, Boras, 1970s, 1980s; Karlstad University, 1986-87; Literary critic, several papers and magazines. Publications: Nagon har jag sett, poems, 1979; Author of 6 other poetry books including: Adam i Paradiset, 1984; Tre larodiktare, Studier i Harry Martinsons, Gunnar Ekelofs och Karl Vennbergs lyrik, 1974; Opera librettos: Love Love Love, 1973; Nagon har jag sett, 1987. Contributions to: Numerous newspapers and magazines including: Aftonbladet; Var Losen. Honours: Recipient of several Scholarships. Memberships: Statens Kulturrad, 1981-89; Forfattarforlaget, Executive Board, 1977-82, President 1982-84; Sveriges Forfattarforbund, Executive Board, 1979-83; Forfattarnas Fotokopieringsfond, President 1985-87; Swedish PEN. Address: Vastra Valhallavagen 25A, S-182 Djursholm, Sweden.

RAMPERSAD Arnold, b. 13 Nov 1941, Trinidad, West Indies. University Professor. m. 1985, 1 child. Education: BA, MA, Bowling Green State University; MA, PhD, Harvard University. Publications: Melville's Israel Potter: A Pilgramage and Progress, 1969; The Art and Imagination of W E B Dubois, 1976; Life of Langston Hughes, Vol I 1902-1941: I Too Sing America, 1986, Vol II 1941-1967: I Dream A World, 1988; Slavery and The Literary Imagination (co-editor), 1989; Days of Grace: A Memoir (with Arthur Ashe), 1993. Honours: Ansfield Wolf Book Award in Race Relations, Cleveland Foundation, 1987; Clarence L Hotte Prize, Phelps Stoke Fund, 1988; Pulitzer Prize Finalist, 1989; American Book Award, 1990. Address: Department of English, Princeton University, Princeton, NJ 08544, USA.

RAMSAY Jay. See: RAMSAY-BROWN John Andrew.

RAMSAY-BROWN John Andrew (Jay Ramsay), b. 20 Apr 1958, Guildford, Surrey, England. Poet; Writer; Translator; Administrator; Editor; Teacher. Education: Charterhouse School; BA Honours, English Language and Literature, Pembroke College, Oxford, 1980; Foundation Year diploma in Psychosynthesis, London Institute, 1987. Literary Appointments: Co-founder and administrator of Angels of Fire 1983-88: 4 major film festivals in London, of poetry and related media (music, dance, video), appearing on ITV South of Watford and BBC2 Open Space, 2 documentaries, 1985; Project Director of Chrysalis - The Poet In You, founded 1990, including its two-part course by post, for students in Britain and abroad, editing one-to-one sessions, retreats, and the workshop, The Sacred Space of The Word. Publications: Psychic Poetry - a manifesto, 1985; Co-editor, Angels of Fire (anthology of radical poetry in the 80's), 1986; The White Poem (with photographs by Carole Bruce), 1988; Editor, Transformation - The Poetry of Spiritual Consciousness, 1988; The Great Return, books 1 to 5, published in 2 volumes, 1988; Raw Spiritual - Selected Poems, 1986; Trwyn Meditations, 1987; Transmissions, 1989; Strange Days, 1990; Journey to Eden (with Jenny Davis), 1991; For Now (with Geoffrey Godbert), 1991; The Rain, The Rain, 1992; St Patrick's Breastplate, 1992; Tao Te Ching, a new translation, 1993. Contributions to: Poetry Review; Literary Review; City Limits; Acumen; Resurgence; Jungle, Paris; Apart, Germany; Island, Athens; Forum (the journal of Psychosynthesis. Memberships: Poetry Society; Psychosynthesis Education and Trust, London. Address: c/o The Diamond Press, 5 Berners Mansions, 34-36, Berners Street, London, W1P 3DA, England.

RAND Peter, b. 23 Feb 1942, San Francisco, CA, USA. Writer. m. Bliss Inui, 19 Dec 1976, 1 s. Education: MA, Johns Hopkins University, 1975. Literary Appointments: Fiction Editor, Antaeus, 1970-72; Editor, Washington Monthly, 1973-74; Teaching Fellow, Johns Hopkins University, 1975; Lecturer-in-English, Columbia University, NY, 1976-91. Publications: Firestorm, 1969; The Time of The Emergency, 1977; The Private Rich, 1984; Gold From Heaven, 1988. Contributions include: New York Times; Washington Post; Penthouse; Washington Monthly; Antaeus. Honour: CAPS, 1977. Memberships: PEN; Authors Guild; Poets and Writers; East Asian Institute, Columbia University; Research Associate, Fairbank Center, Harvard University. Literary Agent: Wendy Weil. Address: 24 Winslow Road, Belmont, MA 02178, USA.

RANDALL Clay. See: ADAMS Clifton.

RANDALL Michael Bennett, b. 12 Aug 1919. Appointments: Assistant Editor, Sunday Chronicle, 1952-53; Editor, Sunday Graphic, 1953; Assistant Editor, Daily Mirror, 1953-56; Assistant Editor, News Chronicle, 1956-57; Assistant Editor, Daily Mail, 1957-61; Deputy Editor 1961-63, Editor 1963-66; Managing Editor, News, Sunday Times, 1967-72, Senior Managing Editor, 1972-78. Publication: The Funny Side of the Street, 1988. Honours: Hannen Swaffer Award, Journalist of 1965-66. Address: 39 St Anne's Crescent, Lewes, East Sussex BN7 1SB, England.

RANDALL Rona, b. Birkenhead, Cheshire, England. Free-lance Journalist; Short Story Writer; Novelist; Non-Fiction Writer. m. 1 son. Literary Appointments: Editorial Dept, UK Magazine, Woman's Journal, 4 years. Publications: 56 published novels including: Dragonmede, 1974; The Watchman's Stone, 1976; The Eagle at the Gate, 1978; The Mating Dance, 1979; The Ladies of Hanover Square, 1981; Curtain Call, 1982; The Drayton Trilogy: The Drayton Legacy, 1985; The Potter's Niece, 1987; The Rival Potters, 1990. Non-fiction: Jordan & the Holy Land, 1968; The Model Wife, 19th Century Style, 1989; Writing Popular Fiction, 1992. Literary Agent: Curtis Brown Ltd. Address: Conifers, Pembury Road, Tunbridge Wells, Kent TN2 4ND, England.

RANSLEY Peter, b. Leeds, England. Writer. m. Cynthia Harris, 14 Dec 1974, 1 son, 1 daughter. Plays include: Numerous TV plays including, Plays for Today, Minor Complications, Kate the Good Neighbour; Series, Bread or Blood, BBC, 1982, The Price (Channel 4), 1985; Series, Underbelly, BBC, 1991, Seaforth, BBC 1994; Film The Hawk, 1992; Books: The Price, based on the series, The Hawk, 1988; Bright Hair about the Bone, 1989; Theatre: Runaway, Royal Court, 1974; Ellen & Disabled, Hampstead Theatre Club, 1972. Honours: Gold Medal, Kate, 1st Commonwealth TV Film Festival, 1980; Award, Royal Television Society's Writer's, Minor Complications, 1981. Agent: Norman North, The Peters Fraser Dunlop Group Ltd. Address: The Chambers, Chelsea Harbour, Lots Road, London SW10, England.

RANSOM Bill, b. 6 June 1945, USA. Writer. 1 daughter. Education: BA, University of Washington. Appointments: NDEA Title IV Fellow, American Minority Literature, University of Nevada, Reno, 1971-72; Poetry in the Schools, Master Poet, NEA, 1974-77. Publications: Novels: The Jesus Incident, 1979; The Lazarus Effect, 1983; The Ascension Factor, 1988; Jaguar, 1990; Viravax, 1993; Burn, 1995; Poetry: Finding True North, 1974; The Single Man Looks at Winter, 1983; Last Call, 1984; Waving Arms at the Blind, 1975; Last Rites, 1979; Semaphore, 1993; Learning the Ropes, (poetry, essays and short fiction), 1995. Contributions to: Numerous journals and magazines. Honours: NEA Discovery Award, 1977. Memberships:

Poetry Society of America; Poets Essayists & Novelists; InternationalAssociation of Machinists and Aerospace Workers; Science Fiction, Fantasy Writers of America; Poet's Writers inc. Literary Agent: Ralph Vicinanza, New York. Address: Southern Utah University, Box 9473, Cedar City, UT 84720, USA.

RAO Raja, b. 5 Nov 1908, Hassan, Mysore, India. Novelist. Education: BA, University of Madras, 1929; Sorbonne, Paris, 1930-33. Appointments: Professor, University of Texas, Austin, 1965. Publications: Kanthapura, 1938; The Serpent and the Rope, 1960; The Cat & Shakespeare: A Tale of India, 1965; Comrade Kirilov, 1976; The Chessmaster and his Moves, 1988; Story Collections: The Cow of the Barricades and Other Stories, 1947; The Policeman and the Rose, 1978; On the Ganga Ghat, 1989; Alien Poems and Other Stories, 1983; The Chess Master and his Moves, 1978. Honours: Neustaft International Prize, 1988. Address: Dept of Philosophy, University of TX, Austin, TX 78712, USA.

RAPHAEL Adam Eliot Geoffrey, b. 22 Apr 1938, London, England. Journalist. m. Caroline Rayner Ellis, 15 May 1970, 1 s, 1 d. Education: BA Honours, History, Oxford University. Literary Appointments: London, 1965-68, Foreign Correspondent in WA, USA, 1969-73, The Guardian; Political Correspondent, 1976-82, Political Editor, 1982-87, The Observer; Presenter, BBC Newsnight, 1987-88; Assistant Editor, The Observer, 1988-. Publication: My Learned Friend (non-fiction), 1989. Honours: Journalist of The Year, Granada Awards, 1973; Journalist of The Year, IPC Awards, 1973. Address: 50 Addison Avenue, London, W11 4QP, England.

RAPHAEL Frederic Michael, b. 14 Aug 1931, Chicago, USA. Writer. m. 17 Jan 1955, 2 sons, 1 daughter. Education: St John's College, Cambridge, England. Publications: Obbligato, 1956; The Earlsdon Way, 1958; The Limits of Love, 1960; The Trouble With England, The Graduate Wife, 1962; Lindmann, 1963; Darling, 1965; Orchestra and Beginners, 1967; Two for the Road (film script with preface), 1968; Like Men Betrayed, 1970; Who Were You With Last Night? 1971; April, June and November, 1972; Richard's Things, 1973; California Time, 1975; The Glittering Prizes, 1976; Somerset Maugham (biography), 1977; Sleeps Six (short stories), 1979; Cracks in the Ice: Views and Reviews, 1979; Oxbridge Blues (short stories), 1980; Byron (biography), 1982; Heaven and Earth, 1985; Think of England I, 1990; A Double Life, 1993; Of Gods and Men (Greek mythology revisited) 1993; The Latin Lover, short stories, 1994; Translations (with Kenneth McLeish) The Poems of Catullus, 1978; The Plays of Aeschylus (with introduction, two volumes), 1991. Contributions include: Sunday Times (London); Times Literary Supplement; The Spectator. Honours: Lippincott Prize, 1961; Writers' Guild, 1965, 1966; USA Academy Award, 1966; British Academy Award, 1966; Royal TV Society Award, 1976; ACE (US Cable TV) Award, 1985, 1991. Membership: Fellow, Royal Society of Literature. Literary Agent: Deborah Rogers, Rogers, Coleridge and White, 20 Powis Mews, London W11 1JN, England.

RASKY Harry, b. 9 May 1928, Canada. Writer; Director; Producer; Commentator. m. Ruth Arlene Werkhoven, 21 Mar 1965, 1 son, 1 daughter. Education: BA, 1949, LLD, 1982, University of Toronto. Publications: Nobody Swings on Sunday, 1980; Tennessee Williams - A portrait in Laughter and Lamentation; Teresa Stratas; 40 feature-length documentaries including: Tennessee Williams' South, 1972; Homage to Chagall - The Colours of Love, 1975; The War against the Indians, 1992. Contributions to: The Nation; Saturday Night; Financial Post; Directors Guild of America News. Honours: Canadian Radio Award,1951; Nominations, Writers Guild of America Award, 1972, 1978, 1980; 10 Awards, Writers Guild of Canada. Memberships: Writers Guild of Canada; Writers Guild of America; Writers Union of Canada; Directors Guild of America; Academy of Motion Pictures Arts and Sciences, Hollywood; Academy of TV Arts and Sciences, New York; Academy of Canadian Cinema, Toronto. Literary Agent: Lucinda Vardy Agency. Address: CBC, Box 500, Terminal A, Toronto, Ontario, Canada.

RASS Rebecca Rivka, b. 9 Dec 1936, Israel. Writer; Journalist; College Professor. 1 d. Education: Tel-Aviv University, 1958-60; Ba, Empire State College, NY, 1977; MFA, Brooklyn College, NY, 1979. Literary Appointments: New York Cultural Correspondent, Yediodth Ahronoth, Tel-Aviv, Israel, 1965-; New York Art Critic, Zero Magazine, Amsterdam, 1978-80. Publications: From A-Z, prose-poetry, 1969, 1984; From Moscow to Jerusalem, 1976; The Fairy Tales of My Mind (novel), 1978, Spanish edition, 1986; The Mountain, 1982, Hebrew edition, 1988; Word War I and Word War II, 1984. Contributions to:

Algemeen Handelsbladt, Amsterdam; Aftenposten, Norway; Rotterdam Courant; Vrij Nederland; San Francisco Chronicle. Honours: Grants, PEN American Center, 1976, 1977; CAPS Award for Fiction, 1981; Yaddo Grant, 1982. Memberships: New York Press Club; PEN; Poets and Writers. Address: 54 West 16th Street, New York, NY 10011, USA.

RATHER Dan, b. 1931. Broadcaster; Journalist. m. Jean Goebel, 1 s, 1 d. Education: University of Houston; South Texas School of Law. Literary Appointments: Writer, Sports Commentator with KSAM-TV; Teacher, Journalism, Houston Chronicle; with CBS; with radio station KTRH, Houston, 4 years; News and Current Affairs Director, CBS Houston TV affiliate KHOU-TV late 1950's; joined CBS News, 1962; Chief, London Bureau, 1965-66; worked in Viet-Nam, White House, 1966; Anchorman CBS Reports, 1974-75; Co-anchorman, 60 Minutes, CBS TV, 1975-81; Anchorman, Dan Rather Reporting CBS Radio Network, 1977-; Co-Editor, Show Who's Who, CBS TV, 1977; Anchorman, Managing Editor, CBS Evening News with Dan Rather, 1981-. Publications: The Palace Guard (with Gary Gates), 1974; The Camera Never Blinks (with Mickey Herskowitz), 1977; I Remember, 1991; Who's Here, 1994. Address: CBS News, 524 West 57th Street, New York, NY 10019, USA.

RATNER Rochelle, b. 2 Dec 1948, Atlantic City, USA. Poet; Novelist; Critic. Literary Appointments: Poetry Columnist, Soho Weekly News, 1976-82; Executive Editor, American Book Review, 1978-; Small Press Columnist, Library Journal, 1985. Publications: A Birthday of Waters, 1971; False trees, 1973; Pirate's Song, 1976; The Tightrope Walker, 1977; Quarry, 1978; Combing The Waves, 1979; Sea Air in a Grave Ground Hog Turns Toward, 1980; Hide and Seek, 1980; Practicing to Be a Woman: New and Selected Poems, 1982; Trying to Understand What it Means to be a Feminist, 1984; Bobby's Girl, 1986. Contributions to: New York Times; Hanging Loose; Shenandoah; Antaeus; Salmagundi. Memberships: PEN; National Book Critics Circle; Poetry Society of America. Address: 314 East 78th Street, New York, NY 10021, USA.

RAUBENHEIMER George H (George Harding), b. 26 Jun 1923, Pretoria, South Africa. Ceramics Manufacturer; Writer. m. Shirley Hall, 26 Apr 1958, 2 s, 2 d. Education: Matriculation, 1940. Publications: North of Bushman's Rock, 1965; Dragon's Gap, 1967; The Gun Merchants, 1969; The Skytrap, 1972; Crossfire, 1980; Screenplay: Mr Kingstreets War (co-writer), 1970; Television scripts: Taskforce, 1981; Tilly, 1985; currently working on television scripts for SATV. Memberships: South African Military History Association; South African Air Force Association. Address: 19 Lystanwold, Saxonwold 2196, Johannesburg, South Africa.

RAVEN Simon (Arthur Noel), b. 28 Dec 1927, London, England. Author. m. Susan Mandeville Kilner, 1951, divorced, 1 son. Education: Charterhouse, King's College, Cambridge, England, 1948-52, Honours Degree in Classics. Literary Appointment: Fellow, Royal Society of Literature, 1993. Publications: Alms for Oblivion, 10 volumes, 1964-76; Shadows on the Grass, memoirs, 1982; The First Born of Egypt, 7 vols, 1984-92; In the Image of God; Bird of Ill Omen, 1989; Is There Anybody There? Said The Traveller, memories of a private nuisance, 1991; TV: The Pallisers, in 26 Episodes; Edward & Mrs Simpson, 7 episodes; In the Image of God; The Blackheath Poisonings: 3 Part TV Serial based on Julian Symonds novel of that name, 1993. Contributions to: The Observer; The Listener; The Spectator. Membership: PEN; Royal Society of Literature. Literary Agent: Curtis Brown. Address: c/o Curtis Brown, 162 Regent Street, London W1R 51B, England.

RAVVIN Norman, b. 26 Aug 1963, Calgary, Alberta, Canada. Novelist; University Instructor. Education: BA (Hons), 1986, MA, English, 1988, University of British Columbia; PhD, University of Toronto, 1994. Publications: Café des Westens, novel, 1991. Contributions to: Stories: My Father and the Sky, to West Coast Review, 1986; Family Architecture, to Western Living; A Jew's House (short story), to Parchment: Contemporary Canadian Jewish Writing, 1993; Articles: Strange Presences on the Family Tree: The Prague Orgy to English Studies in Canada, 1991; An Irruption of the Archaic: Poe and the Grotesque to Mosaic, 1992. Honours: Alberta Culture and Multiculturalism New Fiction Award, 1990; PhD Fellowship, Social Sciences and Humanities Research Council of Canada. Memberships: Writers Guild of Alberta; Association of Canadian College and University Teachers of English; Modern Language Society of America. Address: c/o Red Deer College Press, 56 Ave and 32nd St, Box 5005, Red Deer, Alberta, T4N 5H5, Canada.

RAWLS John, b. 21 Feb 1921, Baltimore, Maryland, USA. University Professor of Philosophy, Princeton University, Cornell University, Massachussetts Istitute of Technology, Harvard University. Appointments: Co-Editor, Philosophical Review, 1956-59. Publications: A Theory of Justice, 1971; Political Liberalism, 1993. Address: 9 Winthrop Road, Lexington, MA 02173, USA.

RAWLS Philip. See: **LEVINSON Leonard.**

RAWORTH Thomas Moore, b. 19 Jul 1938, London, England. Writer. m. Valarie Murphy, 4 s, 1 d. Education: MA, University of Essex, 1967-70. Literary Appointments: Poet-in-Residence, Literature Department, University of Essex, England, 1969-70; Poet-in-Residence, Northeastern Illinois University, Chicago, USA, 1973-74; Poet-in-Residence, King's College, Cambridge, England, 1977-78; London and Cambridge Correspondent, Rolling Stock, Boulder, USA; Editor, designer and publisher, Infolio, 1986. Publications: The Relation Ship, 1967, USA, 1969; The Big Green Day, 1968; A Serial Biography, 1969, USA, 1977; Lion Lion, 1970; Moving, 1971; Act, 1973; Ace, 1974, USA, 1977; Common Sense, 1976; Logbook, 1977; Nicht Wahr, Rosie?, 1979; Writing, 1982; Tottering State, Selected Poems, 1963-83, 1988, USA, 1984; Lazy Left Hand, 1986; Visible Shivers, 1987; Eternal Sections, 1991. Contributions to: Numerous magazines and journals in UK, USA, France, Italy, Spain, Romania, Hungary, Germany. Honours: Alice Hunt Barlett Prize, 1969; Cholmondeley Award, 1971. Membership: PEN. Address: 3 St Philip's Road, Cambridge, CB1 3AQ, England.

RAWSON Claude Julien, b. 8 Feb 1935, Shanghai, China. George M Bodman Professor of English, Yale University. m. Judith Ann Hammond, 14 July 1959, 3 sons, 2 daughters. Education: Magdalen College, Oxford, England, 1952-57; BA, 1955; MA, BLitt, 1959. Appointments: Editor, Modern Language Review, and Yearbook of English Studies, 1974-88; General Editor, Unwin Critical Library, 1975-; Executive Editor, Cambridge History of Literary Criticism, 1983-; General Editor, Blackwell Critical Biographies, 1986-; Chairman and General Editor, Yale Editions of the Private Papers of James Boswell, 1990-. Publications: Henry Fielding, 1968; Focus Swift, 1971; Henry Fielding and the Augustan Ideal under Stress, 1972, 1991; Gulliver and the Gentle Reader, 1973, 1991; Fielding: A Critical Anthology, 1973; The Character of Swift's Satire, 1983; English Satire and the Satiric Tradition, 1984; Order from Confusion Sprung: Studies in 18th Century Literature, 1985, 1994; Thomas Parnell's Collected Poems (edited with F P Lock), 1989; Satire and Sentiment 1660-1800, 1994; Editor: Jonathan Swift: A Collection of Critical Essays, 1995. Literary Agent: The Peters Fraser and Dunlop Group Ltd. Address: 50 Malthouse Lane, Kenilworth, Warwickshire CV8 1AD, England.

RAY David Eugene, b. 20 May 1932, Oklahoma, USA. Writer; Professor of English. m. Suzanne Judy Morrish, 21 Feb 1970, 1 son, 3 daughters. Education: BA, 1952; MA, 1957, University of Chicago. Appointments: Instructor in English, Wright Junior College, 1957-58; Northern Illinois University, 1958-60; also Associate Editor, Epoch, Cornell University, 1960-64; Assistant Professor, Reed College, 1964-66; Lecturer in Writers Workshop, University of Iowa, 1969-70; Visiting Associate Professor, Bowling Green State University, 1970-71; Professor of English, University of Missouri, 1971-; Editor, News Letters, 1971-85; Visiting Professor, Syracuse University, 1978-79; University of Rajasthan, India, 1981-82; Exchange Professor, University of Otago, New Zealand, 1987; Visiting Fellow, University of Western Australia, 1991; Professor Emeritus, 1995-. Publications include: X-Rays, 1965; Dragging the Main, 1968; Gathering Firewood, 1974; The Tramp's Cup, 1978; The Farm in Calabria and Other Poems, 1979; The Touched Life, 1982; On Wednesday I Cleaned Out My Wallet, 1985; Sam's Book, 1987; The Maharani's New Wall, 1989; Not Far From The River, 1990; Wool Highways, 1993; Kangaroo Paws, 1994. Contributions to: numerous journals and newspapers, including New York Times; The Paris Review; Harpers; Ontario Review; Poetry; The London Magazine; The Saturday Review, and many others. Honours include: New Republic Magazine, Young Writers Award, 1958; Kansas City Star Poetry Award, 1974; Associated Writing Programs Poetry Contest, Winner, 1982, 1983; PEN Syndicated Fiction Awards, 1982-86; Amelia Magazine, Poem Prize, 1987; Maurice English Award for Poetry, 1988; Poetry Society of America's Emily Dickinson Award, 1988; H G Roberts Foundation Awards in Poetry and Creative Essay, 1993; Poetry Society of America's Wm Carlos Williams Award for Wool Highways, 1994. Memberships: PEN; Poetry Society of America; Phi Kappa Phi Honorary Society; Friends Association for Higher Education. Address: 2033 E 10th Street, Tucson, AZ 85719, USA.

RAY Robert Henry, b. 29 Apr 1940, San Saba, Texas, USA. Professor of English. m. Lynette Elizabeth Dittmar, 1 Sept 1962, 2 daughters. Education: BA, 1963, PhD, 1967, University of Texas at Austin. Appointments: Assistant Professor of English, 1967-75, Associate Professor of English, 1975-85, Professor of English, 1985-, Baylor University. Publications: The Herbert Allusion Book, 1986; Approaches to Teaching Shakespeare's King Lear, 1986; A John Donne Companion, 1990. Contributions to: Recent Studies in Herbert in English Literary Renaissance, 1988; Herbert's Words in Donne's Mouth, Modern Philology, 1987; Marvell's To His Coy Mistress, and Sandys's Translation of Ovid's Metamorphoses, The Review of English Studies, 1993. Honours: Phi Beta Kappa, 1962. Memberships: Modern Language Association of America; John Donne Society. Address: Department of English, PO Box 97406, Baylor University, Waco, TX 76798, USA.

RAY Robert J, b. 15 May 1935, Amarillo, TX, USA. m. (1) Ann Allen (div), (2) Margot M Waaie, Jul 1983. Education: BA 1957, MA 1959, PhD 1962, University of Texas, Austin. Literary Appointments: Instructor, 1963-65, Assistant Professor, 1965-68, Associate Professor, 1968-75, Professor, 1976, Beloit College, Beloit, WI; Certified Tennis Instructor, San Diego, CA, 1976-81; Freelance Writer, 1981-; Partner of Owning The Store, 1983-88; Writing Teacher: Valley College, 1984-88; University of California, Irvine, 1985-88; Adjunct Professor, Chapman College, 1988-. Publications: The Art of Reading: A Handbook on Writing (with Ann Ray), 1968; The Heart of The Game (novel), 1975; Cage of Mirrors (novel), 1980; Small Business: An Entrepreneur's Plan (with L A Eckert and J D Ryan), 1985; Bloody Murdock (novel), 1987; Murdock for Hire (novel), 1987; The Hitman Cometh (novel), 1988; Dial M for Murder (novel), 1988; Murdock in Xanadu (novel), 1989. Membership: Mystery Writers of America, Fictionaries. Literary Agent: Ben Kamsler, H N Swanson Inc. Address: c/o Ben Kamsler, H N Swanson Inc, 8523 Sunset Boulevard, Los Angeles, CA 90069, USA.

RAYMOND Derek, See: COOK Robert William Arthur.

RAYMOND Diana Joan, b. 25 Apr 1916, London, England. Novelist. m. Ernest Raymond, 20 Aug 1940, 1 son. Publications: Incident on a Summer Day, 1974; Emma Pride, 1981; House of the Dolphin, 1985; The Dark Journey, 1978; The Dancers All Are Gone, 1983; Horseman Pass By, 1977; 22 novels including: Strangers' Gallery, 1958; Guest of Honour, 1960; The Climb, 1962; The Small Rain, 1954; The Best of the Day, 1972; Lily's Daughter, 1988; Roundabout, 1995. Honours: Book Society Choice, The Small Rain, 1954. Membership: Society of Authors. Literary Agent: A P Watt Ltd. Address: 22 The Pryors, East Heath Road, London NW3 1BS, England.

RAYMOND Mary. See: KEEGAN Mary Constance.

RAYMOND Patrick Ernest, b. 25 Sep 1924, Cuckfield, Sussex, England. Royal Air Force, retired. m. Lola Pilpel, 27 May 1950, 1 s. Education: Art School, Cape Town, South Africa. Appointments: RAF, rising to Group Captain, 1942-77. Publications: A City of Scarlet and Gold, 1963; The Lordly Ones, 1965; The Sea Garden, 1970; The Last Soldier, 1974; A Matter of Assassination, 1977; The White War, 1978; The Grand Admiral, 1980; Daniel and Esther, 1989. Literary Agent: A P Watt Limited. Address: 24 Chilton Road, Chesham, Buckinghamshire, HP5 2AU, England.

RAYNER Claire Berenice (Sheila Brandon, Ann Lynton, Ruth Martin), b. 22 Jan 1931, London, England. Writer; Broadcaster. m. Desmond Rayner, 23 June 1957, 2 sons, 1 daughter. Education: State Registered Nurse (Gold Medal), Royal Northern Hospital, London, 1954; Midwifery, Guy's Hospital. Appointments include: 'Agony Aunt' for Petticoat, The Sun, Sunday Mirror, Today; Medical Correspondent for Womans Own; Woman; various other journals. Regular radio series, TV appearances: consumer affairs, family advice, personal problems, Kitchen Garden (with Keith Fordyce). Publications: Over 90 books: broad range of medical subjects, fiction. Medical titles include: Your Baby, 1965; Essentials of Out-Patient Nursing, 1967; 101 Key Facts of Practical Baby Care, 1967; Home Nursing & Family Health, 1967; Parents Guide to Sex Education, 1968; Childcare made Simple, 1973; Safe Sex, 1987; The Don't Spoil Your Body Book, 1989; Fiction Titles: 7 romantic novels (as Sheila Brandon); 12 volume saga, medical/theatrical fiction, The Performers, 1973-86; 6 volume saga, The Poppy Chronicles, 1987-92; Various other novels including, Clinical Judgements, 1989; Postscripts, 1991. Contributions to: Papers & magazines as above; professional journals including: The Lancet,

Medical World, Nursing Times, Nursing Mirror. Honours: Freeman, City of London, 1981; Award, Medical Journalists Association, 1987; Hon Fellow, University of N London, 1988; Best Specialist Consumer Columnist Award, 1988. Memberships include: Fellow, Royal Society of Medicine; Fellow, Royal Society of Arts; Society of Authors. Literary Agent: Desmond Rayner, Holly Wood House, Roxborough Avenue, Harrow-on-the-Hill, Middlesex HA1 3BU, England.

RAYNER Mary Yoma, b. 30 Dec 1933, Mandalay, Burma. Author. m. (1) Eric Rayner, 6 Aug 1960, 2 sons, 1 daughter, (2) Adrian Hawksley, 9 Mar 1985. Education: Honours Degree, English, University of St Andrews, Scotland. Publications: Witch-Finder, 1975; Mr & Mrs Pig's Evening Out, 1976; Garth Pig & The Icecream Lady, 1977; The Rain Cloud, 1980; Mrs Pig's Bulk Buy, 1981; Crocodarling, 1985; Mrs Pig Gets Cross, 1986; Reilly, 1987; Oh Paul! 1988; Rug, 1989; Marathon and Steve (USA), 1989; Bathtime for Garth Pig, 1989; Open Wide, 1990; The Echoing Green, 1992; Garth Pig Steals the Show, 1993; One by One, Ten Pink Piglets, 1994. Memberships: Society of Authors; Member of Advisory Committee, Public Lending Right, 1989-93. Literary Agent: Laura Cecil. Address: c/o Pan Macmillan Ltd, Cavaye Place, London SW10 9PG, England.

RAYSON Hannie, b. 31 Mar 1957, Brighton, Melbourne, Australia. Playwright. Education: BA, University of Melbourne, 1977; Dip Ed in Dramatic Arts, Victoria College of Arts, 1980. Appointments include: Writer in Residence, various institutions. Publications: Please Return to Sender, 1980; Mary, 1981; Leave it Till Monday, 1984; Room to Move, 1985; Hotel Sorrento, 1990; TV Play, SLOTH, 1992; Falling From Grace, 1994. Honours include: Australian Writers Guild Award, 1986 and 1991. Address: Hilary Linstead & Associates, Suite 302, Easts Tower, 9-13 Bronte Road, Bondi Junction, NSW 2022, Australia.

RAZ Joseph, b. 21 Mar 1939, Israel. Professor of the Philosophy of Law, Oxford University. Education: Magister Juris, Hebrew University, Jerusalem, 1963; DPhil, Oxford University, 1967. Publications: The Concept of a Legal System, 1970, 1980; The Authority of Law, 1979; Practical Reason and Norms, 1975, 2nd ed 1990; The Morality of Freedom, 1986; Ethics in the Public Domain, 1994. Contributions to: Articles contributed to numerous magazines and journals. Honours: W J M Mackenzie Book Prize of the Political Studies Association of the UK, 1987; The Elaine and David Spitz Book Prize of the Conference for the Study of Political Thought, New York, both prizes for the book The Morality of Freedom. Membership: Fellow, British Academy, 1987-; Honorary Foreign Member, American Academy of Arts & Sciences, 1992; Honorary Doctor, Katolieke University, Brussel, 1993. Address: Balliol College, Oxford OX1 3BJ, England.

READ Anthony, b. 21 Apr 1935, Staffordshire, England. Writer. m. Rosemary E Kirby, 29 Mar 1958, Great Barr, West Midlands, 2 daughters. Education: Central School of Speech & Drama, London, 1952-54. Publications: The Theatre, 1964; Operation Lucy, with David Fisher, London & USA, 1980; Colonel Z, with David Fisher, London 1984, USA 1985; The Deadly Embrace, with David Fisher, London & USA, 1988; Kristallnacht, with David Fisher, London & USA, 1989; Conspirator, with Ray Bearse, USA & London, 1991; The Fall of Berlin, with David Fisher, London 1992, USA 1993; Berlin: The Biography of a City, with David Fisher, London & USA, 1994; Over 100 television films, plays, serials. Honours: Pye Colour TV Award, 1983; Wingate Literary Prize, 1989. Memberships: Trustee, Chairman 1981-82, Writers Guild of Great Britain. Literary Agent: Books, Murray Pollinger; TV & Film, Stephen Durbridge, Lemon, Unna & Durbridge Ltd. Address: 7 Cedar Chase, Taplow, Buckinghamshire, England.

READ Desmond. See: MOORCOCK Michael (John).

READ Elfreida, b. 2 Oct 1920, Vladivostok, Russia. Writer. m. George Read, 1 s, 1 d. Education: Cambridge Entrance Standard, Shanghai Public School for Girls. Publications: The Message of The Mask; Brothers by Choice; Days of Wonder, Autobiography: Part 1, A Time of Cicadas, Part II, Guns and Magnolias, Part III, Congee and Peanut Butter; Growing Up In China; Fresh Lettuce and New Faces; The Dragon and The Jadestone; The Enchanted Egg; The Spell of Chuchuchan; The Magic of Light; Magic for Granny; Kirsten and The Villains; Race Against The Dark; No One Need Ever Know. Contributions to: Poetry to various literary magazines. Honours: Canadian Centennial Contest for Children's Stories; Poetry in British Columbia; Playwriting Contest, UN International Co-op Year, Junior Literary Guild, NY; CBC Literary Contest. Membership: Writers Union.

Address: 2686 W King Edward Avenue, Vancouver, British Columbia, Canada, V6L 1T6.

READ Miss. See: **SAINT Dora Jessie.**

READ Piers Paul, b. 7 Mar 1941, Beaconsfield, England. Writer. m. Emily Albertine Boothby, 29 July 1967, 2 sons, 2 daughters. Education: MA, St John's College, Cambridge, England. Publications: Game in Heaven with Tussy Marx, 1966; The Junkers, 1968; Monk Dawson, 1969; The Upstart, 1973; A Married Man, 1979; The Free Frenchman, 1986; The Professor's Daughter, 1975; Polonaise, 1976; The Villa Golitsyn, 1981; A Season in the West, 1988; On the Third Day, 1990; Non-Fiction: Alive, 1974; The Train Robbers, 1978; Quo Vadis? the subversion of the Catholic Church, 1991; Ablaze, 1993. Contributions to: The Spectator, The Tablet. Honours: FRSL; Sir Geoffrey Faber Memorial Prize, 1968; Hawthornden Prize, 1969; Somerset Maugham Award, 1969; Thomas More Award, 1976; James Tait Black Memorial Prize, 1988. Memberships: Society of Authors, Council Member. Literary Agent: Aitken and Stone. Address: 50 Portland Road, London W11 4LG, England.

READE Hamish. See: **GRAY Simon John Halliday.**

READING Peter, b. 27 Jul 1946, Liverpool, England. Poet. m. Diana Gilbert, 5 Oct 1968, 1 d. Education: BA, Liverpool College of Art, 1967. Appointments: Teacher, large comprehensive school in Liverpool; Lecturer, Department of Art History, Liverpool College of Art, 1968-70; Various jobs in Animal Feed Mill, Shropshire; Fellowship, Sunderland Polytechnic, 1981-83. Publications: Water and Waste, 1970; For The Municipality's Elderly, 1974; The Prison Cell and Barrel Mystery, 1976; Nothing for Anyone, 1977; Fiction, 1979; Tom O'Bedlam's Beauties, 1981; Diplopic, 1983; 5 x 5 x 5 x 5 x 5, 1983; C, 1984; Ukulele Music, 1985; Stet, 1986; Essential Reading, 1986; Final Demands, 1988; Perduta Gente, 1989; Shitheads, 1989; Evagatory, 1992; 3 in 1, 1992; Last Poems, in progress. Honours: Cholmondeley Award for Poetry, 1978; First Dylan Thomas Award, 1983 for Diplopic; Whitbread Award, Poetry Category, 1986; Lannan Foundation, USA, Literary Fellowship Award, 1990; Elected Fellow of The Royal Society of Literature, 1988.

READSHAW Grahame George Cochrane, b. 23 Feb 1933, Toowoomba, Queensland, Australia. Medical Practitioner. m. Laurel Gray, 27 Oct 1956, 2 sons, 2 daughters. Education: MB, BS, 1955; Diploma of Ophthalmology, 1964; Fellow, Royal Australian College of Ophthalmology, 1978. Publications: Looking Up, Looking Back at Old Brisbane (with R Wood), 1987; Keep It Simple System for Watercolour Painting, 1992. Contributions to: Medical Journal of Australia; Australian Journal of Ophthalmology; Australian Artist Magazine. Honours: Grumbacher Gold Medallion for Painting, 1983. Memberships: Royal Queensland Art Society; Watercolour Society of Queensland; Australian Medical Association; Royal Australian College of Ophthalmologists; Aviation Medical Society of Australia and New Zealand. Address: 44 Victoria Avenue, Chelmer, Queensland 4068, Australia.

REAKES Janet Elizabeth, b. 26 Jan 1952, Bristol, England. Genealogist. Education: Diploma Of Family History Studies; Accredited Genealogist (GSU). Publications: How To Trace Your Convict Ancestors, 1986; A To Z of Genealogy - A Handbook, 1987, 1991, 1993; How To Trace Your Family Tree And Not Get Stuck On A Branch, 1987; How To Trace Your English Ancestors, 1987; How To Trace Your Irish Ancestors, reprinted 1993; How To Write The Family Story, 1993. Contributions to: Columnist, Sunday Mail, Queensland, Australia; Former Columnist, Sunday Sun; Telegraph; Mirror; New Idea; Womens Weekly; Herald; Sun. Memberships: Australian Authors. Address: PO Box 937, Hervey Bay, Queensland, Australia.

REANEY James (Crerar), b. 1 Sept 1926, South Easthope, Ontario, Canada. Poet; Playwright. Education: MA, University College, Ontario, 1949; PhD, 1958. Appointments include: Profesor, Middlesex College, University of Western Ontario, -. Publications include: Verse; The Red Heart, 1949; A Suit of Nettles, 1958; Twelve Letters to a Small Town, 1962; The Dance of Death at London, 1963; Selected Shorter and Longer Poems, 1975-76; Imprecations: The Art of Swearing, 1984; Plays, Night Blooming Cereus, 1959; The Killdeer, 1960; One Man Masque, 1960; The Sun and the Moon, 1965; Listen to the Wind, 1966; The Canada Tree, 1967; Genesis, 1968; Masque, 1972; The Donnellys: A Trilogy, 1973-75; Baldoon, 1976; King Whistle, 1979; Antler River, 1980; Gyroscope, 1981; The Shivaree, Opera

Libretto for John Beckwith, 1982; I, The Parade, 1982; The Canadian Brothers, 1983; Lewis Carroll's Alice Through the Looking-Glass adapted for the stage, premiered at Stratford Festival, 1994. Honours include: D Litt, Carleton University, 1975; Officer, Order of Canada, 1975. Address: Dept of English, University of Western Ontario, London, Intario N6A 3K7, Canada.

RECHEIS Kathe, b. 11 Mar 1928, Engelhartszell, Austria. Freelance Writer of Children's and Young People's Literature. Publications: Geh heim und vergiss Alles, 1964; Fallensteller am Bibersee, 1972; London 13 Juli, 1974; Der weite Weg des Nataiyu, 1978; Wo die Wolfe glucklich sind, 1980; Der Weisse Wolf, 1982; Weisst du dass die Baume reden, 1983; Lena - Unser Dorf und der Krieg, 1987; Tomasita, 1989; Wolfsaga, 1994; others. Honours: Austrian State Prize for Childrens and Young Peoples Literature, 1961, 1963, 1964, 1967, 1971, 1972, 1975, 1976, 1979, 1980, 1984, 1987, 1992; YBBY Certificate of Honour for Der weite Weg des Nataiyu and for Der Weisse Wolf and Lena-Unser Dorf und der Krieg; Österreichischer Würdigungspreis für Kinder-und Jugendliteratur 1986 für das Gesamtwerk. Memberships: Austrian Writers Association; PEN Club. Address: Rembrandtstrasse 1/28, A 1020 Vienna, Austria.

RECKFORD Barry, b. 1930, Jamaica. Playwright. Education: Oxford University, 1952. Appointments include: Honorary Dramatist, Tricycle Theatre, Kilburn, Publications: Adella, 1954; Flesh to a Tiger, 1958; You in Your Small Corner, 1960; Skyvers, 1963; Don't Gas the Blacks, 1969; A Liberated Woman, 1970; Give the Gaffers Time to Love You, 1973; X, 1974; Streetwise, 1982; White Witch, 1985; Radio play: Malcolm X, 1973; Television plays: In the Beautiful Caribbean, 1972, and Club Havana, 1975; Also: Does Fidel Eat More Than Your Father: Cuban Opinion, 1971. Address: c/o Tricycle Theatre, 269 Kilburn High Road, London NW6 7JR, England.

REDDIN Keith. Dramatist, Publications: Life and Limb, 1985; Desperadoes/Throwing Sweets/Keyhole Lover: Three Plays, 1986; Life During Wartime, 1991; The Innocent's Crusade, 1993. Honours: Whiting Writer's Award, 1992. Address: c/o Kelly Rosenheim, Mrs Giles Whiting Foundation, 30 Rockerfeller Plaza Room 3500, New York, NY 10112, USA.

REDDY T Vasudeva, b. 21 Dec 1943, Mittapalem, India. Lecturer in English. m. 5 Nov 1970, 2 s, 1 d. Education: BSc, 1963; MA English, 1966; PhD English, 1985; PGDTE, 1983. Literary Appointment: Lecturer in English, 1966-. Publications: When Grief Rains (poems), 1982; The Vultures (novel), 1983; The Broken Rhythms (poems), 1987; Jane Austen, 1987; Jane Austen: Matrix of Matrimony, 1987; The Fleeting Bubbles (poems), 1989. Contributions to: Poems, critical articles and reviews to various journals and magazines. Honours: Award of International Eminent Poet, 1987; Honorary DLitt, World Academy of Arts and Culture, CA, 1988; State Award for Best Teacher, 1991, University College Teachers, Andhra Pradesh, India. Memberships: International Poets Academy, Madras; World Poetry Society, CA; American Biographical Institute, USA; Research Board of Advisors, ABI, USA; Government College Teachers Association, Andhra Pradesh, India. Address: Narasingapuram Post, Via Chandragiri, Pin 517 102, A P, India.

REDGROVE Peter William, b. 2 Jan 1932. Poet; Analytical Psychologist. m. Penelope Shuttle, 2 sons, 1 daughter, 1 daughter by previous marriage. Publications: Poetry: The Collector, 1960; The Nature of Cold Weather, 1961; At the White Monument, 1963; The Force, 1966; Penguin Modern Poets, 11, 1968; Work in Progress, 1969; Dr Faust's Sea Spiral Spirit, 1972; Three Pieces for Voices, 1972; The Hermaphrodite Album (with Penelope Shuttle), 1973; Sons of My Skin: Selected Poems, 1975; From Every Chink of the Art, 1977; Ten Poems, 1977; The Weddings at Nether Powers, 1979; The Apple-Broadcast, 1981; The Working of Water, 1984; The Man Named East, 1985; The Mudlark Poems and Grand Buveur, 1986; In the Hall of Saurians, 1987; The Moon Disposes: Poems 1954-87, 1989; The First Earthquake, 1989; Dressed as for a Tarot Pack, 1990; Under the Reservoir, 1992; The Laborators, 1993; The Cyclopean Mistress, 1993; Abyssophone, 1995; (Novels): In the Country of the Skin, 1973; The Terrors of Dr Treviles (with Penelope Shuttle), 1974; The Glass Cottage, 1976; The Sleep of the Great Hypnotist, 1979; The God of Glass, 1979; The Beekeepers, 1980; The Facilitators, 1982; Tales from Grimm, 1989; My Father's Trapdoors, 1994; (Plays): Miss Carstairs Dressed for Blooding, 1976; (Radio) In the Country of the Skin, 1973; The Holy Sinner, 1975; Dance of the Putrefact, 1975; The God of Glass, 1977; Martyr of the Hives, 1982; Florent and the Tuxedo

Millions, 1982; The Sin-Doctor, 1983; Dracula in White, 1984; The Scientists of the Strange, 1984; Time for the Cat-Scene, 1985; Trelamia, 1986; Six Tales from Grimm, 1987; (Television) The Sermon, 1963; Jack Be Nimble, 1980; (Non-fiction): The Wise Wound (with Penelope Shuttle), 1978, 1986; The Black Goddess and the Sixth Sense, 1987. Honours include: Imperial Tobacco Award, 1978; Giles Cooper Award, 1981; Prix Italia, 1983. Literary Agent: David Higham Associates. Address: c/o David Higham Associates, 5-8 Lower John Street, Golden Square, London W1R 4HA, England.

REDMAN Joseph. See: **PEARCE Brian Leonard.**

REDWOOD Alec. See: **MILKOMANE George Alexis Milkomanovich.**

REED Eliot. See: **AMBLER Eric.**

REED Ismael, b. 22 Feb 1938, Chattanooga, Tennessee, USA. Poet; Essayist. Publications include: The Free-Lance Pallbearer, 1967; Yellow Back Radio Broke-Down, 1969; Conjure: Selected Poems, 1963-1970, 1972; Chattanooga: Poems, 1973; The Last Days of Louisiana Red, 1974; Flight to Canada, 1976; Shrovetide in Old New Orleans, 1978; The Terrible Twos, 1982; Reckless Eyeballing, 1986; Writin' is Fightin', 1988; New and Collected Poems, 1988; The Terrible Threes, 1989, Japanese by Spring, 1993; Airing Dirty Laundry, 1994. Address: Dept of English, University of California at Berkeley, Berkley, CA 94720-0001, USA.

REED Jane Barbara, b. England. Journalist. Appointments: Editor, Woman's Own, 1969-79; Publisher, IPC Magazines, 1979-81; Editor, Woman, 1981-83; Managing Director, Holbom Publishing, 1983-85; Managing Editor, Today, 1987-89; Director, Corporation Affairs, News International, 1989-. Publications: Girl About Town, 1965; Kitchen Sink or Swim, Co-author, 1982. Contributions to: Woman's Own; Times; Sunday Times; Guardian; Today. Memberships: Vice-Chairman, Media Society; Member, Executive Council, The Literacy Trust. Address: 1 Virginia Street, London E1 9XY, England.

REED Jeremy, b. 1951, Jersey, Channel Islands. Poet. Education: BA, University of essex, Colchester. Publications include: Target, 1972; Vicissitudes, 1974; Diseased Near Deceased, 1975; Emerald Cat, 1975; Ruby Onocentaur, 1975; Blue Talaria, 1976; Count Bluebeard, 1976; Jacks In His Corset, 1978; Saints and Psychotics: Poems 1973-74; Walk on Through, 1980; Bleecker Street, 1980; No Refuge Here, 1981; A Long Shot to Heaven, 1982; A Man Afraid, 1982; By The Fisheries, 1984; Elegy for Senta, 1985; Skies, 1985; Border Pass, 1986; Selected Poems, 1987; Engaging Form, 1988; The Escaped Image, 1988; Nineties, 1990; Dicing for Pearls, 1990; Novels, The Lipstick Boys, 1984; Blue Rock, 1987; Madness: The Price of Poetry, 1990. Honours include: Somerset Maugham Award, 1985. Address: c/o Jonathan Cape Limited, 20 Vauxhall Bridge Road, London SW1V 2SA, England

REED John (Reginald), b. 30 May 1909, Aldershot, Hants, England. Retired Schoolmaster; Music Critic. m. Edith Marion Hampton, 30 Oct 1936, 2 sons, 2 daughters. Education: County High School, Aldershot, 1920-27; London University, 1927-30, 1934-35, Diploma of Education, 1930, BA Hons, English Language and Literature, 1935. Appointment: Guardian, Music Critic, 1974-81. Publications: Schubert: The Final Years, 1972; Schubert (Great Composers Series), 1978; The Schubert Song Companion, 1985; Schubert (Master Musicians Series), 1986. Contributions to: Music Times, Listener, Music and Letters and many others. Honour: Duckles Award for best reference book on a musical topic published in 1985, by Music Library Association of America, March 1987; Honorary Member, International Franz Schubert Institute of Vienna, 1989. Membership: Schubert Institute (United Kingdom), Chairman 1991-94. Address: 130 Fog Lane, Didsbury, Manchester M20 0SW, England.

REED Michael Arthur, b. 25 Apr 1930, Aylesbury, Bucks, England. University Professor. m. Gwynneth Vaughan, 1 Oct 1955, 1 son. Education: BA 1954, MA 1958, University of Birmingham; LLB, University of London, 1966; PhD, University of Leicester, 1973. Publications: The Buckinghamshire Landscape, 1979; The Georgian Triumph, 1983; The Age of Exuberance, 1986; The Landscape of Britain, 1990; Editions of Ipswich Probate Inventories and of Buckinghamshire Probate Inventories; A History of Buckinghamshire, 1993. Contributions to: Articles in The Agricultural History Review; Records of Bucks; other journals. Memberships: Fellow, Royal

Historical Society, 1985; Fellow, Society of Antiquaries of London, 1985. Address: Department of Information and Library Studies, Loughborough University, Loughborough, Leicestershire, England.

REEDER Carolyn, b. 16 Nov 1937, WA, USA. Writer; Teacher. m. Jack Reeder, 15 Aug 1959, 1 s, 1 d. Education: BA 1959, MEd 1971, The American University. Publications: Historical fiction for children: Shades of Grey, 1989; Grandpa's Mountain, 1991; Moonshiner's Son, 1993; adult fiction, co-authored with Jack Reeder: Shenandoah Heritage, 1978; Shenandoah Vestiges, 1980; Shenandoah Secrets, 1991. Honours: Scott O'Dell Award for Historical Fiction, 1989; Child Study Association Award, 1989; Jefferson Cup Award, 1990; ALA Notable Book for 1989; an Honour Book for the Jane Addam's Children's Book Award, 1989; Notable Trade Book in the Language Arts, 1989; An International Reading Association Young Adult Choice for 1991. Address: 7314 University Avenue, Glen Echo, MD 20812, USA.

REEDER Hubert, b. 17 Mar 1948, Plainfield, NJ, USA. Writer. Education: BS degree, 1989. Publications: Gates Found I, 1977; Gates Found II, 1982; third book, in progress. Honours: Awards of Merit, World of Poetry, 1984, 1985, 1987, 1988; Editor's Choice Award, National Library of Poetry, twice in 1989; Poet of Merit Award, American Poetry Society. Memberships: World of Poetry; American Poetry Society. Address: PO Box 128, East Orange, NJ 07019, USA.

REEDY George Edward, b. 5 Aug 1917, East Chicago, IN, USA. College Professor. m. Lilian Greenwald, 22 Mar 1948 (dec), 2 s. Education: BA, University of Chicago, 1938. Publications: Who Will Do Our Fighting For Us?, 1969; Twilight of The Presidency, 1970, revised edition as Johnson to Reagan, 1987; The Presidency in Flux, 1973; Lyndon B Johnson, A Memoir, 1982; The US Senate, Paralysis or Search for Consensus, 1986. Contributions to: Articles, political topics in New York Times; Washington Post; World Book Encyclopaedia Yearbook; Annals, American Academy of Political and Social Science. Honours: Annual Political Book Award, Washington Monthly, 1970; Knight of Golden Quill, Milwaukee Press Club, 1986. Memberships: American Academy of Political and Social Science; American Political Science Association; American Committee on Irish Studies. Literary Agent: Mike Hamilburg. Address: 2535 North Stowell Avenue, no 1, Milwaukee, WI 53211, USA.

REEMAN Douglas Edward (Alexander Kent), b. 15 Oct 1924, Thames Ditton, Surrey, England. Author. m. Kimberley June Jordan, 5 Oct 1985. Publications: A Prayer for the Ship, 1958; High Water, 1959; Send a Gunboat, 1960; Dive in the Sun, 1961; The Hostile Shore, 1962; The Last Raider, 1963; With Blood and Iron, 1964; HMS Saracen, 1965; Path of the Storm, 1966; The Deep Silence, 1967; The Pride and the Anguish, 1968; To Risks Unknown, 1969; The Greatest Enemy, 1970; Against the Sea, 1971; Rendezvous - South Atlantic, 1972; Go In and Sink! 1973; The Destroyers, 1974; Winged Escort, 1975; Surface with Daring, 1976; Strike from the Sea, 1978; A Ship Must Die, 1979; Torpedo Run, 1981; Badge of Glory, 1982; The First to Land, 1984; D-Day: A Personal Reminiscence, 1984; The Volunteers, 1985; The Iron Pirate, 1986; In Danger's Hour, 1988; The White Guns, 1989; Killing Ground, 1990; The Horizon, 1993; Sunset, 1994; The Douglas Reeman Omnibus, 1994. As Alexander Kent: To Glory We Steer, 1968; Form Line of Battle, 1969; Enemy in Sight! 1970; The Flag Captain, 1971; Sloop of War, 1972; Command a King's Ship, 1974; Signal - Close Action! 1974; Richard Bolitho - Midshipman, 1975; Passage to Mutiny, 1976; In Gallant Company, 1977; Midshipman Bolitho and the 'Avenger', 1978; Captain Richard Bolitho, RN, 1978; The Inshore Squadron, 1978; Stand Into Danger, 1980; A Tradition of Victory, 1981; Success to the Brave, 1983; Colours Aloft! 1986; Honour This Day, 1987; With All Despatch, 1988; The Only Victor, 1990; The Bolitho Omnibus, 1991; Beyond the Reef, 1992; The Darkening Sea, 1993; For My Country's Freedom, 1995. Contributions to: Various journals and magazines. Address: Peters, Fraser & Dunlop, The Chambers, Chelsea Harbour, London SW10 0XF, England.

REES Barbara Elizabeth, b. 9 Jan 1934, Worcester, England. Writer. m. Larry Herman, 1 Sept 1967, div 1978, 1 daughter. Education: BA Honours, English Language and Literature, University of Oxford; MA. Appointments: Arts Council of Great Britain Creative Writer in Residence, North London Polytechnic, 1976-78. Publications: Try Another Country, 3 short novels, 1969; Diminishing Circles, UK 1970, USA 1971, Netherlands 1972; Prophet of the Wind, USA 1973, UK 1975, 1976; George and Anna, 1976; The Victorian Lady, 1977; Harriet Dark, UK and USA 1978, USA 1980. Contributions to: Good

Housekeeping; Melbourne Herald; Annabella; Det Nye; Woman's Own. Honour: Arts Council Award, 1974. Address: 102 Savernake Road, London NW3 2JR, England.

REES Brian, b. 20 Aug 1929, Strathfield, Sydney, Australia. Parliamentary Researcher; Writer. m. (1) Julia Birley (dec), 17 Dec 1959, (2) Juliet Akehurst, 3 Jan 1987, 2 s, 3 d. Education: First Class Historical Tripos, Parts I and II, Trinity College, Cambridge. Appointments: Assistant Master, Eton College, 1952-65; Headmaster, Merchant Taylor's School, 1965-73; Headmaster, Charterhouse, 1973-81; Headmaster, Rugby School, 1981-84. Publications: A Musical Peacemaker (Biography of Sir Edward German), 1987; Editor, History and Idealism, 1990; Stowe: Story of a Public School, 1993. Address: 52 Spring Lane, Flore, Northamptonshire, NN7 4LS, England.

REES-MOGG William (Baron), b. 14 Jul 1928, Bristol, England. Journalist. m. Gillian Shakespeare Morris, 1962, 2 s, 3 d. Education: Balliol College, Oxford. Literary Appointments: Financial Times, 1952-60, Chief Leader Writer, 1955-60, Assistant Editor, 1957-60; City Editor, Sunday Times, 1960-61, Political and Economic Editor, 1961-63, Deputy Editor, 1964-67; Editor, The Times, 1967-81; Director, The Times Limited, 1968-81; Vice-Chairman, BBC, 1981-86; Chairman, Arts Council, 1982-89; Chairman, Broadcasting Standards Council, 1988-. Publications: The Reigning Error: The Crisis of World Inflation, 1974; An Humbler Heaven, 1977; How to Buy Rare Books, 1985; Blood in The Streets, 1988; The Great Reckoning, 1991; Picnics on Vesurius, 1992. Honours: Hon LLD, Bath; Kt, 1981. Memberships: President, Oxford Union, 1951; International Committee, Pontifical Council for Culture; President, The Trollope Society. Address: 17 Pall Mall, London, SW1, England.

REEVE F(ranklin) D(oller), b. 18 Sep 1928, Philadelphia, PA, USA. Writer. Education: PhD, Columbia University, 1958. Literary Appointments: Professor of Letters, Wesleyan University, 1970-; Visiting Lecturer, English, Yale University, 1972-86; Visiting Professor, Columbia University, 1992. Publications include: The Russian Novel, 1966; In The Silent Stones, 1968; The Red Machines, 1968; Just Over The Border, 1969; The Brother, 1971; The Blue Cat, 1972; White Colors, 1973; Nightway, 1987; The White Monk, 1989; Concrete Music, 1989; Editor, Poetry Review, 1982-84; Translations, Russian Literature including two-volume Anthology of Russian Plays, 1961-63; The Russian Novel, 1966; An Arrow in The Wall, 1987; The Garden, 1990; The Trouble With Reason, 1993. Contributions to: Poems, essays, stories in American Poetry Review; New England Review; Yale Review; Sewanee Review; Manhattan Poetry Review; Confrontation; New Yorker; Kansas Quarterly; North American Review; Kenyon Review; Gettysburg Review; Poetry: A Magazine of Verse; New York Times Book Review. Honours: Literature Award, American Academy - National Institute of Arts and Letters, 1970; PEN, Syndicated Fiction Award, 1985, 1986. Memberships: PEN, American Centre; Poetry Society of America, Vice-President, 1982-84; Board of Directors, Poets House. Literary Agent: Robert Lewis. Address: Mount Holly, UT 05758, USA.

REGAN Dian Curtis, b. 17 May 1950, Colorado Springs, CO, USA. Children's Book Author. m. John Regan, 25 Aug 1979. Education: BS Honours, Education, University of Colorado, Boulder, 1980. Literary Appointments: Speaker, numerous writers' conferences, USA. Publications: I've Got Your Number, 1986; The Perfect Age, 1987; Game of Survival, 1989; The Kissing Contest, 1990; Jilly's Ghost, 1990; Liver Cookies, 1991; The Class With The Summer Birthdays, 1991; The Curse of The Trouble Dolls, 1992; My Zombie Valentine, 1993; Princess, 1993; Cripple Creek Ghost Mine, 1993; Thirteen Days of Halloween, 1993. Contributions to: Assignments for Writer's Digest; Column, Byline Magazine, 5 years; Fiction, non-fiction, poetry to various children's publications. Honours: Children's Choice Award, 1987; Pick of The List, American Library Association, 1989; Oklahoma Cherubim Award, 1990, 1991, 1992. Memberships: Authors Guild; Society of Children's Book Writers; Oklahoma Writers Federation. Literary Agent: Curtis Brown Limited, New York, USA.

REGINALD Robert, b. 11 Feb 1948, Fukuoka, Japan. Professor; Librarian; Publisher; Author. m. Mary Alice Wickizer, 15 Oct 1976, 1 stepson, 1 stepdaughter. Education: AB Honours, Gonzaga University, 1969; MS, University of Southern California, 1970. Literary Appointments: Associate Editor, Forgotton Fantasy, 1970-71; Editor, Newcastle Publishing Company, 1971-; Publisher, Borgo Press, 1975-; Editor, LTF Newsletter, 1987; Six Reprint Series. Publications include: Cumulative Paperback Index, 1973; Phantasmagoria, 1976; Science Fiction and Fantasy Literature, 1979; The Holy Grail Revealed, 1982; Candle For Poland, 1982; Lords Temporal and Lords Spiritual, 1985; Futurevisions, 1985; The Work of William F Nolan, 1988; The Work of Ian Watson, 1989; Reference Guide to Science Fiction, Fantasy and Horror, 1990. Contributions to: 107 articles and reviews. Honours: Title II Fellowship, University of Southern California, 1969-70; Nomination as Finalist for Hugo Award, 1980; Choice Magazine, Book of The Year, 1980; Winner $2500 Meritorious Performance and Professional Promise Award, California State University, 1987. Memberships include: American Association of University Professors; Blue Earth County Historical Society; Horror Writers of America; International Association for The Fantastic in Arts; Science Fiction Writers of America. Address: Box 2845, San Bernardino, CA 92406, USA.

REGISTER Cheri. See: **REGISTER Cheryl**.

REGISTER Cheryl (Cheri Register), b. 30 Apr 1945, Albert Lea, MN, USA. Writer; Freelance Teacher. m. 1966-85, 2 d. Education: BA Honours, 1967, MA Honours, 1968, PhD Honours, 1973, University of Chicago. Appointments: Co-founder, organizer and workshop leader, Emma Willard Task Force on Education, MN, 1970-73; Co-ordinator of Women's Center, University of Idaho, Moscow, 1973-74; Assistant Professor of Women's Studies and Scandinavian Languages and Literatures, University of Minnesota - Twin Cities, Minneapolis, 1974-80; Writer and Freelance Teacher, 1980-. Publications: As Cheri Register: Sexism in Education (co-author), 1971; Kvinnokamp och litteratur i USA och Sverige (Women's Liberation and Literature in The United States and Sweden), 1977; Editor and contributor, A Telling Presence: Westminster Presbyterian Church 1857-1982, 1982; Mothers, Saviours, Peacemakers: Swedish Women Writers in The Twentieth Century, 1983; Living With Chronic Illness: Days of Patience and Passion, 1987; Are Those Kids Yours?, American Families With Children Adopted from Other Countries, 1990. Contributions to: Various edited volumes and to magazines. Honour: Jerome Foundation Travel and Study Grant, 1991. Address: 4226 Washburn Avenue S, Minneapolis, MN 55410, USA.

REICH Ali. See: **KATZ Bobbi**.

REICH Robert. Married, 2 s. Education: BA, Dartmouth College; LLB, Yale University; Oxford University. Appointments: US Secretary Of Labor, 1994-; Director, Policy Planning for Federal Trade Commission, Carter Administration; Assisstant to Solicitor General, Ford Administration. Publications: The Resurgent Liberal; Tales of a New America; New Deals: The Chrysler Revival and the American System; The Next American Frontier; Minding America's Business; The Work Of Nations. Contributions to: New Republic; The American Prospect (Chairman of the Editorial Board); Harvard Business Review; The Atlantic. Address: Dept of Law, 200 Constitution Avenue, N W Suite S2018, Washington, DC 20210, USA.

REID Alastair, b. 22 Mar 1926, Whithorn, Wigtonshire, Scotland. Writer; Translator; Poet. Education: MA, University of St Andrews, Scotland, 1949. Appointments include: Visiting Lecturer at Universities in the UK and USA; Staff Writer, Correspondent, New Yorker, 1959-. Publications: To Lighten my House, 1953; Oddments, Inklings, Omens Moments, 1959; Corgi Modern Poets in Forcus 3, 1971; Weathering: Poems and Translations, 1978; Passwords: Places, Poems, Preoccupations, 1963; Mother Goose in Spanish, 1967; Whereabouts: Notes on Being a Foreigner, 1987; An Alastair Reid Reader, 1995; Stories for Children and Translations from Spanish of Pablo Neruda, Jorge Luis Borges and other America writers. Honours include: Scottish Arts Council Award, 1979. Address: c/o New Yorker, 20 West 43rd Str, NY 10036, USA.

REID Christine, b. 12 Mar 1942, Belfast, Northern Ireland. Playwright. Education: Queens University, Belfast, 1982-83. Appointments include: Writer-in-residence at the Young Vic Theatre, London, 1988-89. Publications: Did You Hear The One About The Irishman?, 1982; Tea in a China Cup, 1983; Joyriders, 1986; The Last of a Dyin' Race, 1986; My Name, Shall I Tell You My Name?, 1987; The Belle of Belfast City, 1989; Les Miserables, after Hugo, 1992 (Plays produced in New York, London, Belfast and Nottingham). Honours include: George Devine Award, 1986. Address: c/o Alan Brodie Representation, 91 Regent Street, London W1R 7TB, England.

REID Christopher, b. 13 May 1949, Hong Kong. Poet; Freelance Journalist. m. Lucinda Gane, 7 Jul 1979. Education: Exeter College, 1968-71, graduated 1971. Literary Appointments: Part-time librarian,

Ashmolean Classics Library; Actor; Filing-clerk; Flyman, Victoria Palace Theatre; nanny and tutor; Freelance journalist; Poet. Publications: Books: Arcadia, Oxford 1979; Pea Soup, Oxford and NY, 1982; Katerina Brac, London, 1985. Honours include: Prudence Farmer Award, with Craig Raine, 1978, 1980; Eric Gregory Award, Society of Authors for typescript of Arcadia, 1978; Somerset Maughan Award for Arcadia, 1980; Hawthornden Prize for Arcadia, 1981.

REID Michaela Ann (Lady), b. 14 Dec 1933. Author. m. Alexander James Reid, 15 Oct 1955, 1 son, 3 daughters. Education: Law Tripos, Part 1, Girton College, Cambridge University. Publications: Ask Sir James; Sir James Reid, Personal Physician to Queen Victoria and Physician-in-Ordinary to Three Monarchs, 1987, 1989, 1990. Address: Lanton Tower, Jedburgh, Roxburghshire, Scotland.

REID Philip. See: **INGRAMS Richard Reid.**

REID Victor Stafford, b. 1 May 1913, Kingston, Jamaica, West Indies. Journalist; Novelist; Biographer. m. Monica Victoria Jacobs, 10 Aug 1935, 2 s, 2 d. Literary Appointments: Newspaper and Magazine Editor, Jamaica. Publications: Novels: New Day; The Leopard; The Jamaicans; Sixty-Five; The Young Warriors; Mount Ephraim; Nanny Town; Biographies: The Horses of The Morning; About Norman Manley, National Hero of Jamaica; various novels and short stories in USA and Europe; numerous translations. Honours: Canada Council Fellow, 1959-60, 1960-61; Guggenheim Fellow, 1961-62; Mexican Escritores, 1962; Musgrave Gold Medal for Literature; Norman Manley Award for Excellence; The Order of Jamaica. Membership: Chairman, Historic Foundation Research Centre; Past Chairman, Jamaica National Trust Commission; Jamaica Library Association. Address: Box 129, Kingston 10, Jamaica, West Indies.

REIF Stefan Clive, b. 21 Jan 1944, Edinburgh, Scotland. Academic. m. Shulamit Stekel, 19 Sept 1967, 1 son, 1 daughter. Education: BA Hons 1964, PhD 1969, University of London; MA, University of Cambridge, England, 1976. Appointments: Editor, Cambridge University Library's Genizah Series published by Cambridge University Press, 1978-. Publications: Shabbethai Sofer and his Prayer-book, 1979; Interpreting the Hebrew Bible, 1981; Published Material from the Cambridge Genizah Collections, 1988; Genizah Research after Ninety Years, 1992; Judaism and Hebrew Prayer, 1993. Contributions to: Over 180 articles in Hebrew and Jewish studies. Address: Taylor-Schechter Genizah Research Unit, Cambridge University Library, West Road, Cambridge CB3 9DR, England.

REIG June, b. 1 Jun 1933, NY, USA. Author; Television Writer and Director; Illustrator. m. Robert Maxwell, 26 Nov 1969. Education: BA summa cum lauda, State University of New York, Albany, 1954; MA Dramatic Arts, New York University, 1962. Publications: The Heart of Christmas NBC Special, 1965; Stuart Little, NBC TV, 1965; An Afternoon at Tanglewood, NBC TV Special, 1966; Bill Cosby and As I See It, NBC TV Special, 1969; A Day With Bill Cosby, NBC TV Special, 1971; Tut, The Boy King, NBC TV, 1977; Diary of The Boy-King Tutankh-Amen, 1978. Contributions to: Scholastic Magazine; Jack and Jill; American Harp Journal; New York Times Drama Section. Honours: Peabody, 1966; Prix Jeunesse, 1966; Emmy nominee, 1966, 1976; American Library Association, 1967; Brotherhood Award, NCCJ, 1968; The Christopher, 1970; Ohio State, 1970; ACT Achievement, 1970. Memberships: Writers Guild of America; Directors Guild of America; National Academy of Television Arts and Sciences. Address: Bunny Chord Productions Inc, 119 West 57th Street, Suite 1106, New York, NY 10019, USA.

REIN Evgeny Borisovich, b. 29 Dec 1935, St Petersburg, Russia. Writer. m. Nadejda Rein, 21 Jan 1989, 1 s. Education: Graduated, Mechanical Engineer, Leningrad Technological Institute, 1959. Publications: Books of poems: The Names of Bridges, 1984; Shore Line, 1989; The Darkness of Mirrors, 1989; Irretrievable Day, 1991; Counter-Clockwise, 1992. Contributions to: Over 100 contributions to Russian, European and US magazines. Honours: Smena Magazine Award, 1970; Tallinn Magazine Award, 1982. Memberships: Russia Writers Union; Russian PEN Centre. Address: ulitza Kuusinena 7, apt 164, 123308 Moscow, Russia.

REISEL Vladimir, b. 19 Jan 1919, Brodzany, Slovakia. Editor. m. Margita Rihova, 16 Aug 1945, 1 son, 1 daughter. Education: Philosophical Faculties, Prague & Bratislava Universities, 1937-42. Literary Appointments: Deputy Editor, Slovensky Spisovatel publishing house, 1960-72; Editor, Slovenske Pohlady, monthly review, 1972-87.

Publications: Vidim vsetky dni a noci, 1939; Neskutocne mesto, 1943; Zrkadlo a za zrkadlom, 1945; More bez odlivu, 1960; Oci a brezy, 1972; Rozlucky, 1980; Zena a muz, 1983; Trpké planky, 1988; Poezia Laca Novomeskeho, critical essays, 1946. Contributions to: Numerous daily papers, literary & critical journals. Honours: State Prize, Slovak Socialist Republic, 1973; Artist of Merit, 1974. Membership: Committee, Union of Slovak Writers. Literary Agent: Lita, Bratislava. Address: Sutazna 19, 821 08 Bratislava, Slovakia.

REITER David Philip, b. 30 Jan 1947, Cleveland, OH, USA. Publisher; Writer. m. Cherie Lorraine Reiter, 26 Apr 1992. Education: BA, Independent Study, University of Oregon; MA, American Literature, University of Alberta, Canada; PhD, Creative Writing, University of Denver, 1982. Literary Appointments: Lecturer, Cariboo University College, Canada, 1975-84; Lecturer, University of British Columbia, 1984; Lecturer, British Columbia Institute of Technology, 1984; Lecturer, University of Canberra, Australia, 1986-90. Publications: The Snow in Us, 1989; Changing House, 1991; The Cave After Saltwater Tide, in press. Contributions to: Widely in Australian, Canadian, US and UK journals. Honours: Queensland Premier's Poetry Award, 1989; Imago-QUT Short Story Competition, 1990. Literary Agent: Debbie Golvan, Melbourne, Victoria, Australia. Address: 15 Gavan Street, Ashgrove, Queensland 4060, Australia.

REKAI Catherine Kati, b. 20 Oct 1921. Writer; Journalist; Broadcaster. m. John Rekai, 15 Aug 1941, 2 d. Education: Budapest, Hungary. Publications: The Adventures of Micky, Taggy, Puppo and Cica, and How They Discover, series of travel books for children on major cities and countries of the world, 16 titles. Contributions to: Columnist, Magyar Elet (Hungarian Life); Spark Magazine, performing arts in Canadian magazine; Broadcaster, cultural events Chin-Radio International. Honours: Award for contribution to Canadian Unity, 1979; Knighthood of St Ladislaus, 1980; Prix Saint-Exupery-Valeur Jeunesse, 1988; Rakoczi Foundation Award, 1991. Memberships: Chair External Committee, Writers Union of Canada; Vice-President, Ethnic Journalists and Writers Club; Board of Directors, Secretary, Canadian Scene; Board of Directors, Smile Theatre Company; Director, Performing Arts Magazine. Address: 623-21 Dale Avenue, Toronto, Canada, M4W 1K3.

REMEC Miha, b. 10 Aug 1928, Pluj, Yugoslavia. Journalist. m. Mira Iskra, 1 Jul 1970, 3 s. Literary Appointments: Editorial Staff, Daily Newspaper, Delo, 1953-. Publications: Novels: Solstice, 1969; Recognition, 1980; Iksion, 1981; Mana, 1985; The Big Carriage, 1986; Two Short Novels: The Hunter and The Unchaste Daughter, 1987; Dramas: The Dead Kurent, 1959; The Happy Dragons, 1963; Workshop of Clouds, 1966; The Plastionic Plague, 1982; Fairytales From The Dragon's Castle; Votlina, The Cave (novel), 1978; 20 short stories, poems. Contributions to: Articles in numerous professional magazines and journals. Honours: Literary Award for Drama, 1950, 1976; SFera Award, for novel, 1981; SFera Award, for short story, 1987. Memberships: Slovene Writers Association; World Science Fiction Organization; SFera Science Fiction Club. Literary Agent: Ziga Leskovsek, Ljubljana, Yugoslavia. Address: Pod lipami 58, Ljubljana 61000, Yugoslavia.

REMNICK David, b. 1959. Journalist; Former Foreign Correspondent in Moscow, Russia. married, 2 s. Education: Princeton University. Publications: Lenin's Tomb: The Last Days of the Soviet Empire, 1993. Contributions to: New Yorker; Washington Washington Post; New York Review of Books. Honours: Pulitzer Prize, 1994; Helen Bernstein Award, New York Public Library, 1994. Address: c/o Random House 201 E 50th Street, 12th Floor Reception, New York, NY 10022, USA.

REMY Pierre-Jean (Jean-Pierre Angremy), b. 21 Mar 1937. Diplomat; Author. m. Odile Cail, 1963 (div 1979), 1 s, 1 d. Appointments: Served in Hong Kong, 1963; Second Secretary, Peking, 1964, London, 1966; First Secretary, London, 1968; Counsellor, Ministry of Foreign Affairs, 1971; Director, Programme Co-ordinator, ORTF, 1972; Cultural Counsellor, French Embassy, London, 1975-79; French Ministry of Culture, 1979-81; Consul General de France, Florence, 1985-87. Publications: Et Gulliver mourut de sommeil, 1961; Midi ou l'attentat, 1962; Gauguins a gogo, 1971; La sac du palais d'ete, 1971; urbanisme, 1972; une mort sale, 1973; La vie d'Adrian Putney, 1973; Ava, La mort de Floria Tosca, memoires secrets pour servir a l'histoire de ce siecle, 1974; Rever la vie, 1975; La figure dans la pierre, 1976; Chine: Un itineraire, 1977; Les Enfans du parc, 1977; Si j'etais romancier, 1977; Callas, une vie, 1978; Les nouvelles aventures du

Chevalier de la Barre, 1978; orient Express, 1979; Cordelia ou l'Angleterre, 1979; Don Giovanni, 1979; Pandora, 1980; Slaue pour moir le monde, 1980; Un voyage d'hiver, 1981; Don Juan, 1982; Le dernier ete, 1983; Maa Hari, 1983; La vie d'un hero, 1985; une ville immortelle, 1986; Des Chatevoux Allamagne, 1987; Toscanes, 1989. Honours: Chevalier, Legion d'Honneur; Chevalier, Ordre national du Merite; Commander, des Arts et des Lettres. Address: Consulat de France, 2 Piazza Ognissanti, 50123 Florence, Italy.

RENAS Y. See: **ELBERG Yehuda.**

RENAUD (Ernest) Hamilton Jacques, b. 10 Nov 1943, Montreal, Canada. Author; Conceptor; Writer; Teacher; Translator; Speaker. 2 sons, 1 daughter. Appointments: Critic and Researcher, Radio Canada, 1965-67; Reporter, Metro-Express, Montreal, 1966; Critic, Le Devoir, Montreal, 1975-78; Teacher, hatha-yoga, Montreal, 1975-76; Teacher, Creative Writing Workshop, Quebec University, Montreal, 1980-89; Researcher, Senator Jacques Hebert, Senate of Canada, 1990. Publications: 18 titles, some of which are under pen-names including short stories, novels, poetry, short and long essays; Electrodes, Poetry, 1962; Le Cassé, stories, 1964; Clandestines, Novel, 1980; L'espace du Diable, Stories, 1989; Les Cycles du Scorpion, poetry, 1989; La Constellation Du Bouc Emissaire, a study in proto-totalitarianism in Quebec and Canada, 1993; Translations in English of: Le Casse: Flat Broke and Beat, by Gerald Robitaille, 1967; Broke City, by David Homel, 1984. Contributions to: Nouvelles Literaires; La Presse; The Montreal Gazette; The Ottawa Citizen; Perspectives; Forces; Moebius; Parti Pris; Breves; Sexus; Nyx; L'Analyste; Liberte. Memberships: Spokesman and Speaker for Equality Party and Political Adviser and Researcher to Equality Party's Leader and Elected Member of Quebec National Assembly, Robert Libman, 1989. Address: 205 Ivy Crescent 3, Ottawa, Ontario, K1M 1X9, Canada.

RENDELL Ruth (Barbara Vine), b. 17 Feb 1930, London, England. Crime. Novelist. m. Donald Rendell, 1950, div, remarried 1977, 1 son. Education: Loughton High School, Essex, England. Publications include: From Doon with Death, 1964; To Fear a Painted Devil, 1965; Vanity Dies Hard, 1966; A New Lease of Life, 1967; Wolf to the Slaughter, 1967 (televised 1987); The Secret House of Death, 1968; The Best Man to Die, 1969; A Guilty Thing Surprised, 1970; One Across Two Down, 1971; No More Dying Then, 1971; Murder Being Once Done, 1972; Some Lie and Some Die, 1973; The Face of Trespass, 1974 (televised, An Affair in Mind, 1988); Shake Hands for Ever, 1975; The Fallen Curtain (short stories), 1976; A Sleeping Life, 1978; Make Death Love Me, 1979; Means of Evil (short stories), 1979; The Lake of Darkness, 1980 (televised, Dead Lucky, 1988); Put on by Cunning, 1981; Master of the Moor, 1982; The Fever Tree (short stories), 1982; The Speaker of Mandarin, 1983; The Killing Doll, 1984; The Tree of Hands, 1984 (film 1989); An Unkindness of Ravens, 1985; The New Girl Friend (short stories), 1985; Live Flesh, 1986; A Dark-Adapted Eye (as Barbara Vine), 1987; Heartstones, 1987; Talking to Strange Men, 1987; A Fatal Inversion (as Barbara Vine), 1987 (televised 1992); (ed) A Warning to the Curious - The Ghost Stories of M R James, 1987; Collected Short Stories, 1987; The House of Stairs (as Barbara Vine), 1988; The Veiled One, 1988 (televised 1989); The Bridesmaid, 1989; Ruth Rendell's Suffolk, 1989; (with Colin Ward) Undermining the Central Line, 1989; Going Wrong, 1990; Gallowglass (as Barbara Vine), 1990 (televised 1993); The Copper Peacock, 1991; King Solomon's Carpet, 1991; Kissing the Gunner's Daughter, 1992. Honour: Arts Council National Book Award for Genre Fiction, 1981; Crime Writers Association, Cartier Diamond Dagger Award, 1991. Address: Nussteads, Polstead, Suffolk CO6 5DN, England.

RENIER Elizabeth. See: **BAKER Betty (Lou).**

RENO Dawn Elaine, b. 15 Apr 1953, Waltham, Massachusetts, USA. Writer. m. Robert G Reno, 25 Feb 1978, 1 daughter, 1 stepdaughter, 3 stepsons. Education: AA cum laude, Liberal Arts, Bunker Hill, Community College, Boston, Massachusetts, 1976; BA summa cum laude, Liberal Studies, Johnson State College, Johnson, Vermont, 1990. Appointments: Assistant Editor, Vermont Woman, 1988-91; Reporter, New England County Antiques, 1979-86; Columnist, Daytona Beach News Journal, 1992-93. Publications: Collecting Black Americana, 1986; American Indian Collectibles, 1989; American Country Collectibles, 1991; Jenny Moves, 1984; Jenny's First Friend, 1984; All That Glitters, 1992; Collecting Advertising, 1993. Contributions to: Journals including: The Writer; Black Ethnic Collectibles; Better Homes and Gardens; Tours and Resorts; New England Get Aways; Dolls; Antique Trader Weekly; Green Mountains

Review; Burlington Free Press. Honours: Semi-finalist, Writers' Digest Contest, non-fiction, 1986; Fiction Award, Johnson State College, 1990; Fellowship at Virginia Centre for the Creative Arts, 1990; Fellowship at Vermont Studio Colony, 1993. Memberships: League of Vermont Writers; Society of Children's Book Writers; National Writers Union. Address: 3280 Shingler Terrace, Deltona, FL 32738, USA.

REPLANSKY Naomi, b. 23 May 1918. Poet. Education: BA, University of California, Los Angeles, USA, 1956. Appointments: Poet in Residence, Pitzer College, Claremont, California, 1981. Publications: Ring Song, 1952; Twenty-One Poems, Old and New, 1988; The Dangerous World, New and Selected Poems, 1994. Contributions to: Ploughshares; Missouri Review; The Nation; Feminist Studies. Honours: Nominated for National Book Award, 1952. Memberships: PEN American Center; Poetry Society of America. Address: 711 Amsterdam Avenue, New York, NY 10025, USA.

RESTAK Richard Martin, b. 4 Feb 1942, Wilmington, Delaware, USA. Physician; Author. m. Carolyn Serbent, 18 Oct 1968, 3 daughters. Education: MD, Georgetown Medical School, 1966; Trained in Neurology and Psychiatry. Appointments: Consultant, Encyclopedia of Bioethics, 1978; Special Contributing Editor, Science Digest, 1981-85; Editorial Board, Integrative Psychiatry: An International Journal for the Synthesis of Medicine and Psychiatry, 1986. Publications: Premeditated Man: Bioethics and the Control of Future Human Life, 1975; The Brain: The Last Frontier: Explorations of the Human Mind and Our Future, 1979; The Self Seekers, 1982; The Brain, 1984; The Infant Mind, 1986; The Mind, 1988; The Brain Has A Mind of It's Own, 1991; Receptors, 1994; Modular Brain, 1994, Works in anthologies. Contributions to: Saturday Review; Psychology Today; Science Digest; The Wilson Quarterly; Semiotica; Vogue; Publisher's Weekly; Newsday; Washington Post; Los Angeles Times; Washington Post Outlook; Washington Post Education Review; New York Times Book Review; Washington Times; New York Tomes; Washington Post Book World; The Sciences; Psychology Today; Zygon Journal of Religion and Science. Honours: Summer Fellowship, National Endowment for the Humanities, 1976; Claude Bernard Science Journalism Award, National Society for Medical Research, 1976; Distinguished Alumni Award, Gettysburg College, 1985. Memberships: American Academy of Neurology; American Academy of Psychiatry and the Law; American Psychiatric Association; Behavioral Neurology Society; New York Academy of Sciences; Royal Society of Medicine, London, 1984; Semiotic Society of America, 1985; International Neuropsychological Society; National Book Critics Circle; International Brotherhood of Magicians; Philosophical Society of Washington; Georgetown Clinical Society, 1974-84, President 1983-84; International Platform Association. Literary Agent: Sterling Lord, One Madison Ave, New York, USA. Address: 1800 R Street NW, Suite C-3, Washington DC 20009, USA.

REUSS-IANNI Elizabeth, b. 9 Jan 1944, New Orleans, LA, USA. Anthropologist. m. Francis A J Ianni, 28 May 1971. Education: BS, Political Science, Northwestern University, 1964; MA, Anthropology, New York University, 1970. Publications: A Family Business: Kinship and Social Control in Organized Crime (with F A J Ianni), 1972; The Crime Society (with F A J Ianni), 1979; Street Cops vs Management Cops: The Two Cultures of Policing, 1983. Contributions to: Organized Crime in Encyclopaedia of Crime and Punishment, 1985. Memberships: American Anthropological Association; Society of Applied Anthropology; International Association on Organized Crime. Address: Villa L'Aquila, Clover Road, Newfoundland, NJ 07435, USA.

REUTHER David Louis, b. 2 Nov 1946, Detroit, Michigan, USA. Children's Book Publisher and Author. m. Margaret Alexander Miller, 21 July 1973, 1 son, 1 daughter. Education: BA, Honours, University of Michigan, Ann Arbor, 1968. Publications: Adult: The Hidden Game of Baseball, (co-author) 1984; Total Baseball, 1989; Total Baseball (rev) 1991; The Whole Baseball catalog, 1990; Co-Editor, The Armchair Angler, 1986; The Armchair Book of Baseball, 1985; The Armchair Mountaineer, 1984; The Armchair Traveler, 1989; The Armchair Aviator, 1983; The Armchair Quarterback, 1982; Children: Fun To Go, 1982; Save-the-Animals Activity Book, 1982. Contributions to: The Horn Book, 1984. Memberships: American Library Association; Society of Children's Book Writers; Authors Guild; Children's Book Council, Board of Directors, 1985-88 and 1991-94, Treasurer, 1986, Chairman, 1993, Chairman, Book Week Committee, 1987; American Booksellers Association CBC Joint Committee, 1990-93. Address: 271 Central Park West, New York, NY 10024, USA.

REYES Carlos, b. 2 June 1935, Marshfield, USA. Poet; Teacher. m. (1) Barbara Ann Hollingsworth, 13 Sept 1958, (div 1973), 1 son, 3 daughters, (2) Karen Ann Stoner, 21 May 1979 (div 1992), (3) Elizabeth Atly, 27 Dec 1993. Education: BA, University of Oregon, 1961; MA, ABD, University of Arizona, 1965. Appointments: Governor's Advisory Committee on the Arts, Oregon, 1973; Poet to the City of Portland, 1978; Poet in Residence, in various public schools in Oregon and Washington; Editor, Hubbub, 1982-90. Publications: The Shingle Weaver's Journal, 1980; The Prisoner, 1973; At Doolin Quay, 1982; Nightmarks, 1990; A Suitcase Full of Crows; poems, 1995. Contributions to: various journals and magazines. Honours: Oregon Arts Commission Individual Artist Fellowship, 1982; Yaddo Fellowship, 1984. Memberships: Board, Portland Poetry Festival Inc, 1974-84; PEN, Northwest; Co-Chair, PEN Northwest, 1992-93. Address: 3222 NE Schuyler, Portland, OR 97212, USA.

REYNOLDS Graham, b. 10 Jan 1914, Highgate, London, England. Writer; Art Historian. Education: BA Honours, Queens College, Cambridge University. Publications: Nicholas Hilliard and Isaac Oliver, 1947, 1971; English Portrait Miniatures, 1952, revised edition 1988; Painters of the Victorian Scene, 1953; Catalogue of the Constable Collection, Victoria and Albert Museum,1960, revised 1973; Constable, The Natural Painter, 1965; Victorian Painting, 1966, revised 1987; Turner, 1969; Concise History of Watercolour Painting, 1972; Catalogue of Portrait Miniatures, Wallace Collection, 1980; The Later Paintings and Drawings of John Constable, 2 volumes 1984; English Watercolours, 1988; The Earlier Paintings of John Constable, 2 volumes, 1995; Catalogue of Portrait Minatures, Metropolitan Museum of Art, New York, 1995. Contributions to: Times Literary Supplement; Burlington Magazine; Apollo; New Departures; Palindromes and Anagrams, anthology; A W Bergerson, editor 1973. Honours: Mitchell Prize for The Later Paintings and Drawings of John Constable, 1984; OBE, 1984; FBA, 1993. Membership: Honorary Keeper of Minatures, Fitzwilliam Museum, Cambridge, 1994. Literary Agent: A M Heath & Company Limited. Address: The Old Manse, Bradfield St George, Bury St Edmunds, Suffolk IP30 0AZ, England.

REYNOLDS Keith (Kev) Ronald, b. 7 Dec 1943, Ingatestone, Essex, England. Author; Photojournalist; Lecturer. m. Linda Sylvia Dodsworth, 23 Sept 1967, 2 daughters. Publications: Walks and Climbs in the Pyrenees, 1978, 1983; Mountains of the Pyrenees, 1982; The Weald Way and Vanguard Way, 1987; Walks in The Engadine, 1988; The Valais, 1988; Walking in Kent, 1988; Classic Walks in the Pyrenees, 1989; Classic Walks in Southern England, 1989; The Jura, 1989; South Downs Way, 1989; Eye on the Hurricane, 1989; The Mountains of Europe, 1990; Visitors Guide to Kent, 1990; The Cotswold Way, 1990; Alpine Pass Route, 1990; Classic Walks in the Alps, 1991; Chamonix to Zermatt, 1991; The Bernese Alps, 1992; Walking in Ticino, 1992; Central Switzerland, 1993; Annapurna, A Trekker's Guide, 1993. Contributions to: The Great Outdoors; Climber and Hill Walker; Environment Now; Trail Walker; Country Walking; High. Memberships: Outdoor Writers' Guild. Address: Freshfields, Crockham Hill, Edenbridge, Kent TN8 6RT, England.

REYNOLDS Kimberley Kay Griffith, b. 8 Jan 1955, Columbus, OH, USA. Lecturer in English. m. Peter Lloyd Reynolds, 9 Oct 1976, 1 s, 1 d. Education: BA summa cum laude, C W Post College, Long Island, NY, 1975; BA 1984, MA 1985, PhD 1988, University of Sussex. Publications: Girls Only? Gender and Popular Children's Fiction, 1880-1910; An Illustrated Dictionary of Art Terms. Contributions to: Assorted articles and chapters in academic journals; Books on The Box; The BBC Chronicles of Narnia for Critical Survey, Volume 3 No 3, 1991. Address: 10 Dorset Road, Lewes, East Sussex, BN7 1TH, England.

REYNOLDS Sydney, b. 22 Jan 1939, Richmond, Surrey, England. Journalist. m. Jennifer Knapp, 26 Jan 1963, 4 s. Literary Appointments: Night Editor, Associate Iliffe Press, 1962-65; Sub-Editor, Daily Telegraph, 1965-84; Art Editor, Sunday Telegraph, 1984-86. Contributions to: The Artist; Daily Telegraph; The Lady; Scottish Field; American in Britain; Majesty; Music and Musicians; Art and Antiques; Universe; Woodworker; Melbourne Herald and Sun; Drum; Ulster Tatler; almost every County magazine in Britain; Sunday Times of Ceylon; Camera Weekly; Private Eye; UK Press Gazette; The Times, Malta; Dog World; Feathered World; Morning Advertiser; The Guardian; The Stage and Television Today; What's On In London; History Today; Manchester Evening News; Cats; Western Mail; Baptist Times; PR Week; New Statesman and Society; Evening Argus, Brighton; Decanter; Grocer; Amateur Gardening; Our Dogs; Farmers Weekly;

Artists and Illustrators Magazine; Horse and Hound. Address: 113 Bridgewater Road, Berkhamstead, Hertfordshire, England.

REYNOLDS Vernon, b. 14 Dec 1935, Berlin, Germany. University Teacher. m. Frances Glover, 5 Nov 1960, 1 son, 1 daughter. Education: BA, PhD, London University; MA, Oxford University. Publications: Budongo: A Forest and its Chimpanzees, 1965; The Apes, 1967; The Biology of Human Action, 1976, 2nd edition 1980; The Biology of Religion (with R Tanner), 1983; Primate Behaviour: Information, Social Knowledge and the Evolution of Culture (with D Quiatt), 1993. Memberships: Fellow, Royal Anthropological Institute; Chairman, Biosocial Society; Primate Society of Great Britain; Society for the Study of Human Biology. Address: Institute of Biological Anthropology, Oxford University, 58 Banbury Road, Oxford OX2 6QS, England.

RHODAS Virginia, b. Rhodes, Greece. Freelance Journalist; Writer. Education: Journalism, Human and Public Relations, Eastern and Western Philosophy, Argentina and Europe. Literary Appointments: Journalist, newspaper corrector, secretary, several magazines and journals; Director, International Poetry Letter. Publications include: There Will Come a Day...and Other Poems, 1968; Brother Century XXI; Open Letter to Humanity; Listen to Me, Humanity, 1985; From The Greek Nucleous... To Your Heart; 6 Theatre Plays; short stories, essays, children's stories; Work translated into Greek, various other languages. Contributions to: Numerous magazines and journals, worldwide. Honours: Awards: Orthodox Church, Argentina (poetry, essay), 1968; World Poetry Society, 1975; Academy of Arts and Culture, 1981; Honorary Doctorate, World University, USA, 1984; Prix Goddes Athenea, International Society of Greek Writers. Memberships: YWCA; Christian Committee for World Prayer; Argentine Writers Society; Latin American Regent; World Poetry International Society (WPIS); International Society of Greek Writers, Athens, Greece. Literary Agents: WPIS, Gerigramme, Greece; Literary Horizon, India. Address: Rivadavia 2284, PB J 1034 Buenos Aires, Argentina.

RHODES Anthony, b. 24 Sep 1916, Plymouth, Devon, England. Writer. m. Rosaleen Forbes, 9 Apr 1956. Education: Royal Military Academy, Woolwich; MA, Trinity College, University of Cambridge, England; Licence et Lettres, University of Geneva, Switzerland. Publications include: Sword of Bone, 1942; The Uniform, 1949; A Sabine Journey, 1952; A Ball in Venice, 1953; The General's Summer House, 1954; The Dalmation Coast, 1955; Where The Turk Trod, 1956; The Poet as Superman: A Life of Gabriele D'Annunzio, 1959; Rise and Fall of Louis Renault, 1966; The Prophet's Carpet, 1969; Princes of The Grape, 1970; Art Treasures of Eastern Europe, 1971; The Vatican in The Age of The Dictator, 1922-45, 1973; Propaganda in The Second World War, 1976; The Vatican in The Age of The Liberal Democracies, 1983; The Vatican in The Age of The Cold War, 1992; 15 book-length translations from French, Italian and German. Contributions include: Encounter; Sunday Telegraph. Honour: Cavaliere Commendatore del'Ordine di San Gregorio Magno (Papal Title). Memberships: Society of Authors; PEN; Bucks Club; Beefsteak Club. Literary Agent: Anthony Sheil. Address: 46 Fitzjames Avenue, London, W14, England.

RHODES Philip, b. 2 May 1922, Sheffield, England. Medical Practitioner; Professor, Postgraduate Medical Education; Retired 1987. m. Elizabeth Worley, 26 Oct 1946, 3 sons, 2 daughters. Education: Clare College, Cambridge University, England, 1940-43; St Thomas' Hospital, London, England, 1943-46, MA (Cantab) 1946; MB Chir (Cantab) 1946; FRCS (Eng) 1953; FRCOG 1964; FRACMA 1976; FFOM 1990; FRSA 1990. Publications include: Fluid Balance in Obstetrics, 1960; Introduction to Gynaecology & Obstetrics, 1967; Woman: A Biological Study, 1969; Reproductive Physiology, 1969; The Value of Medicine, 1976; Dr John Leake's Hospital, 1978; Letters to a Young Doctor, 1983; Outline History of Medicine, 1985; Associate Editor, The Oxford Companion to Medicine, 1986; Wakerley, A Village in Northamptonshire, 1994. Contributions to: Lancet; British Medical Journal; British Journal of Obstetrics & Gynaecology; Practitioner. Honours include: Annual Prize, Bronte Society, 1972. Memberships: Medical Committee, Society of Authors; British Medical Association. Address: 1 Wakerley Court, Wakerley, Oakham, Leicester LE15 8PA, England.

RHODES Richard, b. 4 July 1937, Kansas City, Kansas, USA. Writer. Education: BA cum laude, Yale University, 1959. Appointments: Writer Trainee, Newsweek, 1959; Assistant to Policy Adviser, Radio Free Europe, New York, 1960; English Instructor, Westminster College, 1960-61; Book Editing Manager, Hallmark Cards Inc, 1962-70;

Contributing Editor, Harper's, 1970-74; Freelance Writer, 1974-. Publications: Non-fiction: The Inland Ground, 1970; The Ozarks, 1974; Looking for America, 1979; The Making of the Atomic Bomb, 1988; A Hole in the World, 1990; Making Love, 1992; Dark Sun, 1995; How to Write, 1995; Fiction: The Ungodly, 1973; Holy Secrets, 1978; The Last Safari, 1980; Sons of Earth, 1981. Contributions to: Numerous journals and magazines including: Playboy; Redbook; Harper's Audience; Esquire; American Heritage; Quest. Honours: National Book Award in Non-fiction, National Book Critics Circle Award in Non-fiction, 1987; Pulitzer Prize in Non-fiction, 1988. Memberships: Authors Guild. Literary Agent: Morton L Janklow. Address: c/o Morton L Janklow Associates, 598 Madison Avenue, New York, NK 10022, USA.

RHONE Trevor Dave, b. 24 Mar 1940, Kingston, Jamaica, West Indies. Playwright; Director; Screenwriter. m. Camella King, 5 Mar 1974, 2 s, 1 d. Education: Diploma Speech and Drama, Rose Bruford College of Speech and Drama, 1963. Literary Appointments: Resident playwright, Barn Theatre, Kingston, 1968-75. Publications: Old Time Story, 1981; Two Can Play, 1984. Honours: Silver Musgrave Medal, Institute of Jamaica, 1972; Commander of The Order of Distinction, National Honour, Jamaica, 1980; Gold Musgrave Medal, 1988; Academy Award, Film Canada, 1989. Literary Agents: Yvonne Brewster, 32 Buckley Road, London, NW6 7LU, England; I C M,New York, USA. Address: 1 Haining Mews, Kingston 5, Jamaica, West Indies.

RICARD Charles, b. 9 Jan 1922, Gap, France. Author. m. J Balmens, 28 Jul 1951. Education: Professeur de Lettres. Publications: Novels: Le puits, 1967; La derniere des revolutions, 1968; A propos d'un piano casse, 1977; Le Pot-a-Chien, 1979; Alerte rouge aux cites soleils, 1985; Le mercredi des Cendres, 1986; Le Chemin des Oiseaux, 1991; Rédé, 1992; Les Mysteres du Villaret, 1993; Books of Poetry: si j'avais su, 1960; Je Voudrais, 1963; Les ombres du chemin, 1964. Contributions to: Various magazines and journals. Honours: Several major prizes including: Gold Medal, International Competition of Clubs of Cote d'Azur; Gold Medal, International Competition, Lutece, 1976; Prix Diamant, 1985; Prix du Vimeu, 1986. Memberships: Academy of The French Provinces; Associate, Society of French Poets; Associate, Gens de Lettres de France. Address: 20 rue du Super-Gap, 05000 Gap, France.

RICCHIUTI Paul B(urton), b. 4 July 1925, Redford Township, Michigan, USA. Writer. Education: Andrews University, 1949-52; Loma Linda University, 1953. Appointments: Layout and Design Artist, Pacific Press Publishing Association, 1955-. Publications: For Children: I Found a Feather, 1967; Whose House is It?, 1967; Up in the Air, 1967; When You Open Your Bible, 1967; Jeff, 1973; Amy, 1975; Five Little Girls, 1975; Let's Play Make Believe, 1975; My Very Best Friend, 1975; Elijah Jeremiah Phillip's Great Journey, 1975; Yankee Dan, 1976; General Lee, 1978; Mandy, 1978; Mike, 1978; Jimmy and the Great Balloon, 1978; Charlie Horse, 1992; Mrs White's Secret Sock, 1992; Ellen (adult biography of Ellen G White), 1977; End of the World Man and Other Stories, 1989; Rocky and Me, 1989; New Dog in Town, 1991. Contributions to: Work represented in anthologies, including: The Family Album, 1975, 1976; Articles, stories and poems to magazines including: Signs of the Times; Our Little Friend; Primary Treasurer; These Times; Adventist Review, and to newspapers. Address: 5702 E Powerline, Nampa, ID 83687, USA.

RICE Anne, b. 14 Oct 1941, New Orleans, Louisiana, USA. m. Stan. 1 son. Address: c/o Jackson & Nesbit, 598 Madison Avenue, New York, NY 10022, USA.

RICH Adrienne, b. 1929 Baltimore, Maryland, USA. Education: BA, Radcliffe College. Appointments: Professor. Contributions to: Yale Review. Honours: Fellowship of American Academy of Poets, 1992; Los Angeles Times Book Award, 1992; National Book Award, 1973; Bess Hokin Prize, 1963; Tietjens Memorial Prize, 1968; Shelley Memorial Award, 1971; Fund of Human Dignity Award, 1981; Brandis University Creative Arts Medal, 1987; Ruth Lilly Prize, 1986; National Poetry Association Award for Distinguished Service, 1989; Commonwealth Award, 1991; Leonsie Marshall Nation Prize, 1992; Frost Silver Medal, 1992. Address: Dept of English, Stanford University, Building 40, Stanford, CA 94305-2087, USA.

RICH Frank Hart, b. 2 Jun 1949, WA, USA. Journalist. m. Gail Winston, 1976, 2 s. Education: Harvard College. Literary Appointments: Film Critic, Senior Editor, New Times Magazine, 1973-75; Film Critic, New York Post, 1975-77; Film and Television Critic, Time Magazine,

1977-80; Chief Drama Critic, New York Times, 1980-. Address: New York Times, 229 West 43rd Street, New York, NY, 10036, USA.

RICHÉ Pierre, b. 4 Oct 1921, Paris, France. Professor Emeritus, University of Paris X. m. Suzanne Grenier, 20 Dec 1953. Education: Agregé, History, 1948; Docteur es lettres, 1962. Publications: Education et Culture dans l'Occident Barbare, 1962, translated into Italian, English, Japanese; Ecoles et Enseignement dans le Haut Moyen Age, 1970; La Vie Quotidienne dans l'Empire Carolingien, 1973, translated into English, Polish, German, Japanese; Dhuoda Manuel pour Mon Fils (editor, translator), 1975; Les Carolingiens une Famille Qui fit l'Europe, 1983, translated into German, Italian, English; Gerbert d'Aurillac Pape de l'an Mil, 1987, translated into Italian, Spanish; Petite Vie de Saint Bernard, 1989, translated into Italian, Portuguese, Corean; Japanese L'Europe Barbare de 476 a 774, 1989. Contributions to: Le Moyen Age; Revue d'Histoire de l'Eglise de France; Notre Histoire; Histoire de l'Education; Others. Honours: Officier des Palmes Academiques; Prix Gobert, 1963; Prix de Courcel, 1969, 1988; Prix George Goyau, 1974. Memberships: Résident Member, Societé Nationale des Antiquaires de France; Board Member, Societé d'Histoire de France; President d'honneur Centre International de Recherche et de Documentation sur le monachisme Celtique; Membre de la Section d'Histoire Medievale et de Philologie du Comité des Travaux Historiques et Scientifiques. Address: 99 Rue Bobillot, Paris 75013, France.

RICHARD Mark, b. 1955, Louisiana, USA. Education: BA, Washington & Lee University. Publications: Ice at the Bottom of the World, 1989; Fishboy, 1993. Contributions to: Esquire; Harpers; New Yorker; Grand Street; Shanandoah; Best American Short Stories. Honours: Pushcart Prize; Ernest Hemmingway Foundation Award, 1990.

RICHARDS Alun, b. 27 Oct 1929, Pontypridd, Wales. Author. m. Helen Howden, 8 Jul 1956, 3 s, 1 d. Education: Diploma, Social Science and Education, University of Wales. Literary Appointment: Editor, Penguin Book of Welsh Short Stories and Penguin Book of Sea Stories, volumes 1-11. Publications: The Elephant You Gave Me, 1963; The Home Patch, 1966; A Woman of Experience, 1969; Home to An Empty House, 1974; Ennal's Point, 1979; Dai Country, 1979; The Former Miss Merthyr Tydfil and Other Stories, 1980; Barque Whisper, 1982; Autobiography, Days of Absence, 1987. Contributions to: Guardian; Planet; Western Mail. Honours: Arts Council Prize for Collected Short Stories, 1974; Royal National Lifeboat Institution Public Relations Award, 1983; Japan Foundation Fellowship, 1984. Memberships: Writer Guild of Great Britain. Literary Agent: Harvey Unna and Stephen Durbridge Limited. Address: 326 Mumbles Road, Swansea, SA3 5AA, Wales.

RICHARDS David Adams, b. 1950, Newcastle, New Brunswick, Canada. Education: St Thomas University, New Brunswick, Canada. Publications: The Coming of Winter, 1974; Blood Ties, 1976; Dancers at Night, 1978; Lives of Short Duration, 1981; Road to the Stilt House, 1985; Nights Below Station Street, 1988; Evening Snow Will Bring Such Peace, 1990; For Those Who Hunt the Wounded Down, 1993. Honours: Norman Epstein Prize; Selected for "45 Below", 1986; Governor General's Award, 1988; Maclean's Award; Canada Authors Association Literary Award, 1991; Canada-Australian Literary Award, 1992.

RICHARDS Denis George, b. 10 Sept 1910, London, England. Writer. m. Barbara Smethurst, 6 Jan 1940, 4 d. Education: Trinity Hall, Cambridge, 1928-31; 1st Class Hons BA, 1931; MA, 1935. Publications: An Illustrated History of Modern Europe, 1938; An Illustrated History of Modern Britain, 1951; Royal Air Force, 1939-45 (3 volumes with H St G Saunders), 1953, 1954; Offspring of The Vic: A History of Morley College, 1958; Britain Under The Tudors and Stuarts, 1958; The Battle of Britain: The Jubilee History (with Richard Hough), 1989; The Few and The Many, 1990; Others mostly in collaboration; The Hardest Victory: RAF Bomber Command in The Second World War, 1994. Contributions to: Books and Bookmen; Daily Telegraph Supplement; Financial Times. Honours: C P Robertson Memorial Trophy, 1956; OBE, 1990. Memberships include: PEN, Honorary Treasurer, English Centre in 1960's; Arts Club; Society of Authors; Garrick Club. Address: 16, Broadlands Road, London, N6 4AN, England.

RICHARDS Hubert John, b. 25 Dec 1921, Weilderstadt, Germany. Lecturer; Writer. m. 22 Dec 1975, 1 s, 1 d. Education: STL (Licence in Theology), Gregorian University, Rome, Italy; LSS (Licence in Scripture), Biblical Institute, Rome. Publications: The First Christmas: What Really Happened?, 1973, USA 1986; The Miracles of Jesus: What Really Happened?, 1975, USA 1986; The First Easter: What Really Happened?, 1977, USA 1986; Death and After: What Will Really Happen?, 1979, USA 1986; What Happens When You Pray?, 1980; Pilgrim To The Holy Land, 1985; Various books for children, 1986-; Focus on The Bible, 1990; The Gospel According To St Paul, 1990; God's Diary, 1991, USA 1991; Pilgrim To Rome, 1993. Contributions to: Regular articles and reviews in various publications. Membership: Chairman, Norfolk Theological Society. Address: 59 Park Lane, Norwich, Norfolk, NR2 3EF, England.

RICHARDS James, Sir (Jim Cladpole), b. 13 Aug 1907, London, England. Editor; Journalist; Writer; Historian. Education: Diploma, Architectural Association, School of Architecture, London, 1929; Associate, Royal Institute of British Architects, 1930. Publications: High Street, 1938; Introduction to Modern Architecture, 1940; The Castles on The Ground, 1946; The Functional Tradition, 1958; Editor, The Anti-Rationalists, 1973; Editor, Who's Who in Architecture, 1977; Eight Hundred Years of Finnish Architecture, 1978; Memoirs of An Unjust Fella, 1980; Goa, 1981; National Trust Book of English Architecture, 1981; National Trust Book of Bridges. Contributions to: Architectural Review; Architects Journal; Times; Times Literary Supplement; Listener; New Statesman; Country Life; Editor, Architectural Review, 1937-71; Architectural Correspondent, The Times, 1947-71; Editor, European Heritage, 1974-75. Honours include: CBE, 1959; Bicentenary Medal, Royal Society of Arts, 1971; Knight, 1972; Honorary Fellow, American Institute of Architects, 1984; Commander, Order of The White Rose of Finland, 1985. Literary Agent: Curtis Brown Limited. Address: 29 Fawcett Street, London, SW10, England.

RICHARDS Ronald Charles William (Allen Saddler), b. 15 Apr 1923, London, England. Writer; Journalist. Publications: Novels: The Great Brain Robbery, 1965; Gilt Edge, 1966; Talking Turkey, 1968; Betty, 1974; Children's Books: The King and Queen series; Mr Wizz; Jerry and The Monsters; Jerry and The Inventions; The Relay Race; Smudger's Seaside Spectacular; Smudger's Saturday Special; Sam's Swop Shop; 24 radio plays for BBC: TV Barnet (with Doris Richards); The Concert Party (documentary); I Should Say So (radio series); Stage: Them; All Basic Comforts; Kindly Leave The Stage; King and Queen Show (for children); Better Dead; Champagne and Kippers. Contributions to: As Drama Critic: The Guardian; The Stage; Plays and Players; Plays International; Entertainment; Feature writer to: The Guardian; Sunday Times Magazine; The Observer Magazine; Time Out; The Daily Telegraph; Daily Express; Nova; Western Morning News; Columnist for: The Western Morning News; Sunday Independent. Memberships: Writers Guild, Chairman, Westcountry Branch, 1974-87; Drama Panel, SW Arts; Editor Western Front/Westward Look (BBC Radio 3); Tutor, Arvon, Beaford, Exeter and Devon Arts Centre. Literary Agent: Jane Conway-Gordon. Address: 5 St Johns Hall, Station Road, Totnes, TQ9 5HW, Devon, England.

RICHARDS Sean. See: **HAINING Peter Alexander.**

RICHARDSON Boyce. Canadian. Publications: Future of Canadian Cities, 1972; James Bay: the Plot to the North Woods, 1972; Strangers Devour the Land, 1975; A Time to Change: Canada's Place in a World in Crisis, 1990; People of Terra Nullius: Betrayal & Rebirth in Aboriginal Canada, 1993. Honour: Canadian Author's Association Literary Award, 1994.

RICHARDSON Joanna, b. London, England. Biographer. Education: The Downs School, Seaford, Sussex; MA, St Anne's College, Oxford. Literary Appointments: FRSL, 1959; Member of Council, Royal Society of Literature, 1961-86. Publications include: The Pre-Eminent Victorian: A Study of Tennyson, 1962; The Everlasting Spell: A Study of Keats and His Friends, 1963; Editor, Essays by Divers Hands (transactions Royal Society of Literature), 1963; Introduction to Victor Hugo: Choses Vues (The Oxford Library of French Classics), 1964; Edward Lear, 1965; George iV: A Portrait, 1966; Creevey and Greville, 1967; Princess Mathilde, 1969; Verlaine, 1971; Enid Starkie, 1973; Translator, Verlaine, poems, 1974; Translator, Baudelaire, poems, 1975; Victor Hugo, 1976; Zola, 1978; Keats and His Circle: An Album of Portraits, 1980; Paris Under Siege, 1982; Colette, 1983; The Brownings, 1986; Judith Gautier, 1987; Portrait of A Bonaparte, 1987; Baudelaire, 1994. Address: c/o Curtis Brown Ltd, Haymarket House, 28-29 Haymarket, London, England.

RICHARDSON Ruth, b. London, England. Historian. Education: BA Hons, English Literature, 1977; MA, History, 1978; DPhil, History, 1985. Literary Appointments: Research Fellow, Institute of Historical Research, University of London; Wellcome Research Fellow, Department of Anatomy, University College, London. Publications: Death, Dissection and The Destitute, 1988, paperback, 1989; chapter in Conference Proceedings volume: La Compañia de La Vida, La Muerte, el Entierro y La Resurrección: el Entierro Metropolitano en el Reino Unido, 1600-1990, 1993; The Builder Illustrations Index, 1843-83 (co-author with Robert Thorne, foreward by HRH Prince Charles), 850 pages, 1994; Contributions to books includes: Why Was Death So Big in Victorian Britain?, 1989; Contributions to Journals include: Notorious Abominations, architecture and the public health in The Builder 1843-1883, 1992; Victorian Periodicals: Architecture (with Robert Thorne), 1994. Contributions include: Inspector General James Barry MD: Putting The Woman in Her Place, to British Medical Journal, 1989; Somnambulism, Vampirism and Suicide: The Life of Dr John Polidori, to Proceedings of The Royal College of Physicians, Edinburgh, 1991. Honours: Leverhulme Research Fellowship, 1992-92; Monkton Copeman Medal, Society of Apothecaries, London, 1993; Fellow, Royal Historical Society. Memberships: Society of Authors; Folklore Society; Trustee, Museum of Soho. Address: Institute of Historical Research, University of London, WC1E 7HU, England.

RICHESON Cena Golder, b. 11 Apr 1941, Oregon, USA. Author; Instructor; Public Speaker. m. Jerry Richeson, 3 Jun 1961, 2 s. Education: BA, California State University. Literary Appointments: Staff, Anderson Press, 1974-77; Instructor: Shasta College, 1974-76; Liberty High School Adult Education, 1985-86. Publications: Love Is Where You Find It; For Love's Sake; Go For Broke, Honorable Decision. Contributions to: Numerous magazines and journals. Honours: Poet of The Year, J Mark Press, 1974; Non-fiction Writing Award, Writer's Digest Annual Contest, 1976; Non-fiction article, 3rd place, Williamette Writers Annual Convention, 1976. Memberships: California Writers Club; Western Writers of America; Society of Children's Book Writers; Zane Grey's West Society. Address: PO Box 268, Knightsen, CA 94548, USA.

RICHIE Donald, b. 17 Apr 1924, Ohio, USA. Writer; Critic. Divorced. Education: Bachelor's Degree, Columbia University, NY, USA, 1953; Presidential Citation, New York University. Literary Appointments: Film Critic: Stars and Stripes, 1947-49; Variety, 1961-65; Japan Times, 1954-69; Literary Critic: Newsweek, 1973-76; Japan Times, 1973-. Publications: The Japanese Film: Art and Industry (with J Anderson) 1959; The Films of Akira Kurasawa, 1965; Ozu, 1974; Japanese Cinema: An Introduction, 1990; The Inland Sea, 1971; Different People: Pictures of Some Japanese, 1987; Tokyo Nights, 1988; Companions of The Holiday, 1968; Zen Inklings, 1982; A Taste of Japan, 1984; A Lateral View, 1987; The Honourable Visitors, 1994. Address: 304 Shato Nezu, Yanaka 1 1-18 Taito Ku, Tokyo 110, Japan.

RICHLER Mordecai, b. 27 Jan 1931, Montreal, Canada. Writer. m. Florence Wood, 1960, 3 s, 2 d. Education: Sir George Williams University; Canada Council Junior Arts Fellowship, 1959, 1960; Fellowship, Creative Writing, Guggenheim Foundation, New York, 1961; Canada Council, Senior Arts Fellowship, 1967. Literary Appointments: Writer in Residence, Sir George Williams University, 1968-69; Visiting Professor, Carleton University, Ottawa, 1972-74; Editorial Board, Book of The Month Club, New York, 1976. Publications: Novels: The Acrobats, 1954; Son of A Smaller Hero, 1955; A Choice of Enemies, 1957; The Apprenticeship of Duddy Kravitz, 1959; The Incomparable Atuk, 1963; Cocksure, 1968; St Urbain's Horseman, 1971; Images of Spain, 1978; Joshua Then and Now, 1980; Solomon Grusky Was Here, 1989; Broadsides, 1991; Stories: The Street, 1972; Film Scripts: No Love For Johnny; Life at The Top; The Apprenticeship of Duddy Kravitz; TV Plays: The Trouble with Benny; Essays: Hunting Tigers Under Glass, 1969; Shovelling Trouble, 1973; Home Sweet Home, 1984; Editor, Canadian Writing Today, 1970; For Children: Jacob Two-Two Meets the Hooded Fang, 1975; The Best of Modern Humour, editor, 1983; Solomon Guksky War Hero, 1989. Honours: Canadian Governor Generals Award for Fiction, 1969; Golden Bear, Berlin Film Festival, 1974. Address: Apartment 80C, 1321 Sherbrooke Street West, Montreal, Quebec H3G 1J4, Canada.

RICHTER Anne, b. 25 Jun 1939, Brussels, Belgium. Writer; Teacher of French. Widow, 1 d. Education: Licence of Philosophy and Letters, Free University of Brussels, 1963. Publications: Short stories: La Fourmi a Fait le Coup, 1954, English translation New York, 1956,

London, 1957; Les Locataires, 1967; La Grande Pitié de la Famille Zintram, 1986; Essays: Georges Simenon et l'Homme Désintégré, 1964; Milosz, 1965; Le Fantastique Féminin, Un Art Sauvage, 1984; Simenon Malgré Lui, 1993; Anthologies: L'Allemagne Fantastique, 1973; Les Contes Fantastiques de Guy de Maupassant, 1974; Le Fantastique Féminin, 1977; Histoires de Doubles et de Miroirs, 1981; Roger Bodart: La Route du Sel, 1993. Contributions to: Literary reviews in Le Magazine Littéraire, La Revue Générale. Honours: Prizes of Belgian Academy of French Literature and Language. Memberships: Committee member, PEN International; Asrobiation of Belgian Authors; International Association of Literary Critics. Address: 93 Boulevard Louis Schmidt, bte 13, 1040 Brussels, Belgium.

RICHTER Hans Peter, b. 28 Apr 1925, Cologne, Germany. m. Elfriede Feldmann, 20 May 1952, 1 s, 3 d. Education: Universitites of Cologne, Bonn, Mainz, Tubingen; Prof Dr rer pol. Publications include: Karussell und Luftbailon (Uncle and His Merry-Go-Round), 1958; Das Pferd Max (Hengist The Horse), 1959; Damals war es Friedrich (Friedrich), 1961, 40th edition, 1993, translated into 15 languages, over 4 million copies sold; Wir waren dabei (I Was There), 1962; Saint Just, 1975; Die Zeit der jungen Soldaten (The Time of The Young Soldiers), 1980; Wissenschaft von der Wissenschaft, 1981; Translations: Montaigne, 1989; F Mein Vater, 1992. Contributions to: Numerous magazines, journals, radio and television. Honours: Jugendbuchpreis, 1961; Auswahilliste, 1962; Cite Internationale des Arts, Paris, 1965-66; Mildred Batchelder Book Award, 1971; Best Book, Japanese Library Association. Address: 58 Franz-Werfel Strasse, D 6500 Mainz 1, Germany.

RICHTER Harvena, b. 13 Mar 1919, Reading, PA, USA. Writer. Education: BA, UNM, 1938; MA, NYU, 1955; PhD, NYU, 1966. Literary Appointments: Lecturer, NYU, 1955-66; Lecturer, UNM, 1969-89. Publications: The Human Shore, 1959; Virginia Woolf: the Inward Voyage; 1970; Writing To Survive: the Private Notebooks of Conrad Richter, 1988; The Yaddo Elegies and other poems, 1995. Contributions to: The New Yorker; Atlantic; New Letters; Chelsea; South Dakota Review; Christian Science Monitor. Honours: AAUW Fellowship; residence grants at Yaddo, MacDowell, VCCA, Wurlitzer Foundation; Ragdale Foundation. Memberships: Authors Guild of the Authors League; AAUW; Kappa Kappa Gamma. Literary Agent: John Hawkins, Assoc. Address: 1932 Candelaria Road NW, Albuqueque, NM 87107, USA.

RICHTER Milan, b. 25 Jul 1948, Bratislava, Czechoslovakia. Writer; Translator; Diplomat. m. Adreinna Matejovova, 1 Oct 1980, 1 s, 2 d. Education: German and English Linguistics and Literature, Faculty of Philosophy, Comenius University, Bratislava, 1967-72; PhD, 1985. Appointments include: Head of The Slovak Embassy in Oslo, Norway, 1993; Part Time Editor, Dotyky Literary Magazine, 1988-89; Fulbright Research Scholar, University of California, LA, USA, 1990; Part Time Editor, Revue Svetovej Literatury, 1991. Publications include: Poetry in Slovak: The Secure Place, 1987; Roots in The Air, 1992; In German: Wurzeln in der Luft, selected poems, 1992; Translations into Slovak language: Selected poems by E Dickinson, E Hemingway, J W Goethe, Urfast, E Lindegrn, A Lundkvist, P Neruda, E Jandl, E Cardenal. Contributions to: London Magazine; Paris Review; Massachusetts Review; Literary Review; City Lights Review; Literary Olympians, 1992; Jacaranda Review; Akzente, Sprache im Technischen Zeitalter, Germany; Manuskripte, Podium, Wespennest, Austria; Anthologies in Denmark and Sweden. Prairie Schooner, Oxford Magazine. Address: Sidlisko 714, CS 900 42 Dunajska Luzna, Slovakia.

RICKEL Annette U, Professor of Psychology; Licenced Psychologist. Education: BA< Michigan State University, 1963; MA, 1965, PhD, 1972, University of Michigan. Publications : Co-editor with Gerrard M and Iscoe I, Social and Psychological Problems of Women: Prevention and Crisis Intervention, 1984; Preventing Maladjustment from Infancy Through Adolescence (with Allen L), 1987; Teenage Pregnancy and Parenting, 1989. Contributions to: Articles in various journals including: The International Review of Education; Journal of Community Psychology; Journal of Abnormal Child Psychology; Clinical Social Work Journal; International Journal of Women's Studies; Personnel Psychology. Honours: Fellow, American Psychological Association, President APA Division 27 - Community Psychology, 1984-85, Secretary-Treasurer APA Division 27, 1979-82; Fellow, American Council on Education, 1990-91. Memberships: Society For Research in Child and Adolescent Psychopathology; International Association of Applied Psychologists; American Association for Higher Education; American Educations Research Association; Psi Chi; Sigma

Xi. Address: Wayne State University, Department of Psychology, 71 West Warren, Detroit, MI 48202, USA.

RICKS Christopher B, b. England. Appointments: University Professor. Address: Dept of English, Boston University, 236 Bay State Road, Boston, MA 02215, USA.

RIDEAMUS. See: PASZKOWSKI Kazimierz Jan.

RIDGWAY Judith Anne, b. 10 Nov 1939, Stalybridge, England. Writer. Education: BA Class II, Division 1, Keele University, 1962. Publications include: Home Cooking For Money, 1983; Booklets: Making the Most of Rice, 1983; Making the Most of Pasta, 1983; Making the Most of Potatoes, 1983; Making the Most of Bread, 1983; Making the Most of Eggs, 1983; Making the Most of Cheese, 1983; The Little Lemon Book, 1983; Barbecues, 1983; Cooking Round the World, 1983; Cooking with German Food, 1983; The Little Bean Book, 1983; Frying Tonight, 1984; Running Your Own Wine Bar, 1984; Sprouting Beans and Seeds, 1984; Man in the Kitchen, 1984; The Little Rice Book, 1984; Successful Media Relations, 1984; Running Your Own Catering Company, 1984; Festive Occasions, 1986; The Vegetable Year, 1985; Nuts and Cereals, 1985; Cooking Without Gluten, 1986; Vegetarian Wok Cookery, 1986; Wining and Dining At Home, 1985; Cheese and Cheese Cookery, 1986; 101 Ways With Chicken Pieces, 1987; The Wine Lovers Record Book, 1988; Pocket Book of Oils, Vinegars and Seasoning, 1989; The Little Red Wine Book, 1989; The Vitamin and Mineral Diet Cookbook, 1990; Catering for a Wedding, 1991; Vegetarian Delights. 1992; Quick After Work Pasta Cookbook, 1993; Best Wine Buys in The High Street, 1991, 1992, 1993; 1994, 1995; Food For Sport, 1994; Quick After Work Vegetarian Cookbook, 1994; The Noodle Cookbook, 1994; The Catering Management Handbook, 1994. Memberships: Society of Authors; Guild of Food Writers; Circle of Wine Writers. Literary Agent: Clarissa Rushdie, A P Watt Ltd. Address: 124 Queens Court, Queensway, London, W2 4QS, England.

RIDLER Anne (Barbara), b. 30 Jul 1912. Author. m. Vivian Ridler, 1938, 2 s, 2 d. Education: King's College, London. Publications include: Poetry: Selected Poems (New York), 1961; Some Time After, 1972; (Contributor) Ten Oxford Poets, 1978; New and Selected Poems, 1988; Collected Poems, 1994; Plays: The Jesse Tree (libretto), 1972; The King of The Golden River (libretto), 1975; The Lambton Worm (libretto), 1978; A Measure of English Poetry (criticism), 1991; The Trial of Thomas Cranmer; Translations: Così fan Tutte, 1986; Gluck's Orpheus, 1988; Don Giovanni, 1990; Figaro, 1991; Coronation of Poppea, 1992; Operas of Monteverdi (contributor), 1992; Tancredi, 1993; Biography: A Victorian Family Postbag, 1988; Editor, Shakespeare Criticism, 1919-35, 1935-60, 1963; A Little Book of Modern Verse, 1941; Best Ghost Stories, 1945; Supplement to Faber Book of Modern Verse, 1951; The Image of the City and Other Essays by Charles Williams, 1958; Poems of James Thomson, 1963; Thomas Traherne, 1966; (with Christopher Bradby) Best Stories of Church and Clergy, 1966; Selected Poems of George Darley, 1979; Poems of William Austin, 1983. Address: 14 Stanley Road, Oxford, OX4 1QZ, England.

RIDLEY Jasper Godwin, b. 25 May 1920, West Hoathly, Sussex, England. Author. m. Vera Pollakova, 1 Oct 1949, 2 s, 1 d. Education: Sorbonne Paris University, 1937; Magdalen College, Oxford University, 1938-39; Certificate of Honour, Council of Legal Education, 1945. Publications: Nicholas Ridley, 1957; Thomas Cranmer, 1962; John Knox, 1968; Lord Palmerston, 1970; Mary Tudor, 1973; Garibaldi, 1974; The Roundheads, 1976; Napolean III and Eugenie, 1979; The History of England, 1981; The Statesman and The Fanatic, 1982; Henry VIII, 1984; Elizabeth I, 1987; The Tudor Age, 1988; The Love Letters of Henry VIII, 1988; Maximillian and Juárez, 1992; Tito, 1994. Contributions to: The Prime Ministers, 1975; Garibaldi Generale Della Liberta, 1984; Childhood in Sussex, 1988; English Heritage Journal, 1989. Honours: James Tait Black Memorial Prize, 1970. Memberships: Vice-President, English PEN; Fellow, Royal Society of Literature; Life President, Tunbridge Wells Writers Circle; Sussex Authors; Court of Assistants, Worshipful Company of Carpenters (Master 1988, 1990). Literary Agent: Curtis Brown (London and New York). Address: 6 Oakdale Road, Tunbridge Wells, Kent, TN4 8DS, England.

RIDOUT Ronald, b. 23 Jul 1916, Farnham, Surrey, England. Author. m. 10 Feb 1940, 1 s, 2 d. Education: BA Honours, Oxon. Publications: 509 titles, 1st English Today, 1948; most recent: Ronald Ridout's Children's Dictionary, 1983; Now I Can Write, 1984; Now I Can

Spell, 1984; Ronald Ridout's English A-Z, 1985; Getting on With Spelling, 1986; The Methuen Activity Picture Dictionary, 1987. Membership: Society of Authors, 1st Chairman, Educational Writers Section. Literary Agent: A P Watt and Company. Address: St Lucia, West Indies.

RIDPATH Ian, b. 1 May 1947, Ilford, Essex, England. Writer; Broadcaster. Publications: Over 30 books on astronomy and space, including: Worlds Beyond, 1975; Encyclopedia of Astronomy and Space, Editor, 1976; Messages From The Stars, 1978; Stars and Planets, 1978; Young Astronomer's Handbook, 1981; Hamlyn Encyclopedia of Space, 1981; Life Off Earth, 1983; Collins Guide to Stars and Planets, 1984; Gem Guide to The Night Sky, 1985; Secrets of The Sky, 1985; A Comet Called Halley, 1985; Longman Illustrated Dictionary of Astronomy and Astronautics, 1987; Monthly Sky Guide, 1987; Star Tales, 1989; Norton's Star Atlas (editor), 1989; Book of The Universe, 1991; Atlas of Stars and Planets, 1992. Address: 48 Otho Court, Brentford Dock, Brentford, Middlesex, TW8 8PY, England.

RIES Hans, b. 22 Dec 1941, Gilching, Germany. Research Scientist. m. Gitta Maikl, 24 May 1968, 1 son. Literary Appointments: Wilhelm Busch Museum, Hannover, 1980-; Vice President, International Youth Library, Munich, 1992-. Publications: Wilhelm Buschals Zeichner nach der Natur, 1982; Zwischen Hausse und Baisse, Börse und Geld in der Karikatur, 1987; Illustration und Illustratoren 1871-1914, 1992; Co-operator, Allgemeines Künstlerlexikon, 1985-. Contributions to: Börsenblatt für den Deutschen Buchhandel, Aus dem Antiquariat. Address: Römerstr 93, D 82205 Gilching, Germany.

RIFBJERG Klaus Thorvald, b. 15 Dec 1931, Copenhagen, Denmark. Author. m. Inge Merete Gerner, 28 May 1955, 1 s, 2 d. Education: Princeton University, 1950-51; University of Copenhagen, 1951-56. Literary Appointments: Library Critic, Information, 1955-57, Politiken, 1959-; Editor, Vindrosen, 1959-64; Literary Director, Gyldendal Publishers, 1985-92. Publications include: Anna (Jeg) Anna, 1970; Marts, 1970, 1970; Leif den Lykkelige JR, 1971; Til Spanien, 1971; Lena Jorgensen, Klintevej 4, 2650, Hvidovre, 1971; Brevet til Gerda, 1972; RR, 1972; Spinatfuglene, 1973; Dilettanterne, 1973; Du skal ikke vaere ked af det Amalia, 1974; En Hugorm i solen, 1974; Vejen ad Hvilken, 1975; Tak for turen, 1975; Kiks, 1976; Tango, 1978; Dobbeltgoenger, 1978; Drengene, 1978; Joker, 1979; Voksdugshjertet, 1979; Det sorte hul, 1980; Short stories: Og Andre Historier, 1964; Rejsende, 1969; Den Syende Jomfru, 1972; Sommer, 1974; Non-fiction: I medgang Og Modgang, 1970; Plays: Gris Pa Gaflen, 1962; Hva' Skal Vi Lave, 1963; Udviklinger, 1965; Hvad en Mand Har brug For, 1966; Voks, 1968; Ar, 1970; Narrene, 1971; Svaret Blaeser i Vinden, 1971; Det Korte af det lange, 1976; Twist, 1976; Et bortvendt ansigt, 1977; Deres majestaet!, 1977; Poems: Livsfrisen, 1979. Honours: Danish Dramatists, 1966; Danish Academy Award, 1966; Golden Laurels, 1967; Grand Prize, Danish Academy of Arts and Letters, 1968; Soren Gyldendal Award, 1969; Nordic Council Award, 1971; Grant of Honour, Danish Writers Guild, 1973; PH Prize, 1979; Holberg Medal, 1984; H C Andersen Prize, 1987. Membership: Danish Academy of Arts and Letters, 1967; Professor of Staics, 1986; Doctor H C Luna University, 1992. Address: Kristianiagade 22, DK 2100, Copenhagen, Denmark.

RIFKIN Shepard (Jake Logan, Dale Michaels), b. 14 Sep 1918, New York City, USA. Writer; Out-of-Print Book Dealer. Education: City College of New York, 1936-38. Publications: Desire Island, 1960; What Ship? Where Bound?, 1961; Ladyfingers, 1969; The Murderer Vine, 1970; McQuaid, 1974; The Snow Rattlers, 1977; McQuaid in August, 1979; Historical Westerns include: Texas, Blood Red, 1956; The Warring Breed, 1962; King Fisher's Road. Contributions to: Story Magazine, 1947; Atlantic First, 1961. Membership: Authors League. Literary Agent: Knox Burger, 39 1-2 Washington Square South, New York, NY 10012, USA. Address: 105 Charles Street, New York, NY 10014, USA.

RIGHTMIRE G Philip, b. 15 Sept 1942, Boston, Massachusetts, USA. Professor of Anthropology. m. Berit Johansson, 20 Aug 1966, 1 son, 1 daughter. Education: BA, Harvard University, 1964; MS, 1966, PhD, 1969, University of Wisconsin. Appointments: Assistant Professor, Associate Professor, Professor, State University of New York, Binghamton. Publications: The Evolution of Homo Erectus, 1990. Contributions to: Articles in Science; Nature; American Journal of Physical Anthropology; Journal of Human Evolution; Paleobiology; Evolutionary Anthropology and other journals and in encyclopaedias'.

Memberships: American Association for the Advancement of Science; Sigma Xi. Address: 4004 Fuller Hollow Road, Vestal, NY 13850, USA.

RIGONI Orlando Joseph, b. 1917, USA. Author. Publications: Twisted Trails; Ambuscade; Pikabo Stage; House of Haddon; Headstone for a Trailboss; As Carolyn Bell: House of Clay; Sixgun Song; Showdown at Skeleton Flat; Massacre Ranch; A Nickle's Worth of Lead; The Guns of Folly; A Close Shave at Pozo; Bullet Breed; Hunger Range; Drover Man; As Leslie Ames: The Hungry Sea; The Hidden Chapel; The Phantom Bride; Wind Over The Citadel; The Big Brand; Muskeg Marshal; King's Castle; Castle on The Island; The Angry Wind; Brand of The Bow; Bride of Donnebrook; Hill of Ashes; As James Wesley: Texas Justice; Showdown at Mesa Bend; Maverick Marshal; Brand X; Four Graves to Jericho; Showdown at The MB Ranch; Diamond Range; Trail to Boothill; Bitteroot Showdown, 1985. Address: 2900 Dogwood Avenue, Morro Bay, CA 93442, USA.

RILEY James Andrew, b. 25 July 1939, Sullivan County, Tennessee, USA. Author; Feature Writer. m. Dorothy Elizabeth Taylor, 14 Oct 1960, 2 sons. Education: BS, 1961, MA, 1966, East Tennessee State University; EdS, Nova University, 1982. Publications: The All-Time All-Stars of Black Baseball, 1983; Dandy, Day, and the Devil, 1987; The Hundred Years of Chet Hoff, 1991; Biographical Encyclopedia of the Negro Baseball Leagues, 1994; Contributor to: Insiders Baseball, 1983; Biographical Dictionary of American Sports: Baseball, 1987, 1989-1992 Supplement, 1991; The Baseball Encyclopedia, Negro League Section (editor), 1990; The Ballplayers, 1990; Baseball Chronology, 1991. Contributions to: Baseball Research Journal, 1981, 1982, 1985, 1991; Oldtyme Baseball News (feature writer), 1989, 1990, 1991, 1992, 1993; All-Star Game: Official Major League Baseball Program, 1993, 1994; The Diamond: Official Chronicle of Major League Baseball, 1993, 1994; Athlon Baseball, 1994. Honours: Society for American Baseball Research-MacMillan Research Award, 1990; MacMillan-Society for American Baseball Research Research Award, 1994. Membership: Society for American Baseball Research. Address: PO Box 560968, Rockledge, FL 32956-0968, USA.

RILEY Samuel Gayle III, b. 8 Oct 1939, Raleigh, North Carolina, USA. University Professor. m. Mary Elaine Weisner, 14 May 1966, div 1986, 1 son, 1 daughter. Education: AB, Davidson College, 1961; MBA, 1962, PhD, Mass Communication Research, 1970, University of North Carolina, Chapel Hill. Appointments: Assistant Professor, Journalism, Temple University, 1970-74; Associate Professor, Journalism, Georgia Southern University, 1971-81; Professor, Communication Studies, Virginia Polytechnic Institute and State University, 1981-. Publications: Magazines of the American South, 1986; Index to Southern Periodicals, 1986; American Magazine Journalists (Dictionary of Literary Biography), 4 vols, 1988, 1989, 1990, 1994; Index to City and Regional Magazines of the United States, 1989; Regional Interest Magazines of the United States, 1991; GR8 PL8S, 1991; Corporate Magazines of the United States, 1992; Consumer Magazines of the British Isles, 1993; The Best of the Rest, 1993. Contributions to: Articles to scholarly journals including: American Journalism; Journalism Quarterly; American Periodicals; Mass Communications Review; Journalism History; Hundreds of articles to US newspapers and magazines; Over 700 reference book entries. Memberships: Association for Education in Journalism and Mass Communications; Research Society of American Periodicals; American Journalism Historians Association. Address: 1865 Mountainside Drive, Blacksburg, VA 24060, USA.

RINALDI Nicholas Michael, b. 2 Apr 1934, Brooklyn, NY, USA. Writer; College Professor. m. Jacqueline Tellier, 29 Aug 1959, 3 s, 1 d. Education: AB Classics, Shrub Oak, 1957; MA 1960, PhD 1963, English Literature, Fordham. Literary Appointments: Instructor, Assistant Professor, St John's University, 1960-65; Lecturer, City University of New York, 1966; Associate Professor, Columbia University, Summer 1966; Professor, University of Connecticut, Summer, 1972; Assistant Professor, Professor, Fairfield University, 1966-. Publications: The Resurrection of The Snails, 1977; We Have Lost Our Fathers, 1982; The Luftwaffe in Chaos, 1985; Bridge Fall Down (novel), 1985. Contributions to: Yale Review; New American Review; Prairie Schooner; Carolina Quarterly. Honours: Joseph P Slomovich Memorial Award for Poetry, 1979; All Nations Poetry Award, 1981, 1983; AWP Award Series Publication, We Have Lost Our Fathers, 1982; New York Poetry Forum Award, 1983; Eve of St Agnes Poetry Award, 1984; Charles Angoff Literary Award, 1984. Memberships: Associated Writing Programme; Poetry Society of

America. Literary Agent: International Creative Management. Address: 190 Brookview Avenue, Fairfield, CT 96432, USA.

RING David. See: **PRATHER Richard.**

RINGGOLD Faith, b. 10 Aug 1930, NY, USA. Painter; Sculptor; Performance Artist Writer; Teacher. 2 children. Education: BS, MA, City College of NY. Literary Appointments: Professor, University of CA. Publications: Who's Afraid of Aunt Jemima, 1983; Tar Beach, 1991; The Woman On A Bridge Series, 1988; Aunt Harriets Underground Railroad In The Sky, 1992; Dinner At Aunt Connies House; The Dinner Quilt. Honours include: Caldecott Honor; Coretta Scott King Award; National Endowment for the Arts Award, 1978, 1989; La Napoule Foundation Award, 1990; John Simon Guggenheim Memorial Foundation Fellowship, 1987; Creative Artists Public Service Award, 1971; In Many Private & Public Art Collections.

RIO-SUKAN Isabel del, b. 8 Sep 1954, Madrid, Spain. Translator; Writer; Language Consultant. m. Huseyin B Sukan, 31 Jul 1981, 2 d. Education: MA, Information Sciences, Madrid Central University, 1977; Incorporated Linguist, Institute of Linguists, London, 1985. Literary Appointments: Broadcaster, Arts and Literary Programmes; Editor, BBC Spanish Section, London, 1978-82; UN Supernumerary Translator, 1988-. Publications: BBC Get By in Spanish, 1992; Ciudad del Interior (poetry), 1993; Translations: The Secret Garden, by F H Burnett, 1990; Into Cuba, by P Marshall, 1991. Memberships: Society of Authors, London; The Translators Association, London; Institute of Linguists; ITI; AITC; APETI; Equity. Address: 3 Meadow Place, Edensor Road, London, W4 2SY, England.

RIOS Juan, b. 28 Sep 1914, Barranco, Lima, Peru. Poet; Dramatist; Journalist; Critic. m. Rosa Saco, 16 Sep 1946, 1 d. Publications: Cancion de Siempre, 1941; Malstrom, 1941; La Pintura Contempranea en el Peru, 1946; Teatro (1), 1961; Ayar Manko, 1963; Primera Antologia Poetica, 1981. Honours: National Prize, Playwriting, 1946, 1950, 1952, 1954, 1960; National Poetry Prize, 1948, 1953. Memberships: Writers' Fellowship, UNESCO, Europe and Egypt, 1960-61; Academia Peruana de la lengua Correspondiente a la Espanola. Address: Bajada de Banos 109, Barranco, Lima 04, Peru.

RIPLEY Alexandra, b. 8 January 1934, Charleston, South Carolina, USA. m. 2 children. Education: AB, Vassar College. Address: c/o William Morris Agency, 1350 Avenue of The Americans, New York, NY 10019, USA.

RIPLEY Michael David (Mike Ripley), b. 29 Sep 1952, Huddersfield, England. Chief Press Officer, The Brewers Society. m. Alyson Jane White, 8 Jul 1978, 2 d. Education: BA Honours, Economic History, University of East Anglia. Literary Appointments: Crime Fiction Critic, The Sunday Telegraph, 1989-91; Crime Critic, The Daily Telegraph, 1991-. Publications: Just Another Angel, 1988; Angel Touch, 1989; Angel Hunt, 1990; Angels in Arms, 1991; Short stories: The Body of The Beer, 1989; Smeltdown, 1990; Gold Sword, 1990. Contributions to: The 'Britcrit' Column in Mystery Scene, USA. Honours: Scholarship to public school; Runner-up, Punch Magazine Awards for Funniest Crime Novel, 1988; Last Laugh Award, Crimw Writers Association, 1989, 1991; The Angel Literary Award for Fiction, 1990. Memberships: Crime Writers Association; Sisters in Crime, USA; The Dorothy L Sayers Society. Literary Agent: David Higham Associates. Address: c/o David Higham Associates, 5-8 Lower John Street, London, W1R 4HA, England.

RIPLEY Mike. See: **RIPLEY Michael David.**

RIPPON Angela, b. 12 Oct 1944, Plymouth, England. Television and Radio Presenter; Writer. m. Christopher Dare, 1967. Education: Grammar School, Plymouth, England. Appointments include: Editor, Presenter, Producer, Westward Television, 1969-73; News Reporter, National News, 1973-76; Newsreader, Nine O'Clock News, 1976-81; Interview with HRH The Prince of Wales and Lady Diana Spencer on the eve of their wedding and presented live coverage of the wedding day, BBC, Jul 1981; TV-am, 1982; Arts and Entertainment Officer, WNEV Television Channel 7, Boston, MA, USA, 1984-85; Autumn 1989, began weekly series entitled The Health Show, which launched BBC Radio 5; September 1990: Anchorwoman for LBC's 3-hour daily breakfast programme, The Angela Rippon Morning Report, rescheduled as Angela Rippon's Drive Time Show in February 1992. Publications: Riding, 1980; Mark Phillips - The Man and His Horses, 1982; Angela Rippon's West Country, 1982; Victoria Plum, 1983; In

The Country, 1980; Badminton - A Celebration, 1987; Many recordings. Honours: Radio and Television Industries Award for Newsreader of The Year, 1976, 1977, 1978; Television Personality of The Year, 1977; Sony Award for The Health Show, 1990. Memberships: International Club for Women in Television, Vice-President, 1979-; Chairman, English National Ballet Association; Board Member, American College, London. Address: c/o International Management Group, Media House, 3 Burlington Lane, Chiswick, London, W4 2TH, England.

RITCHIE Elisavietta Artamonoff, b. 29 June 1932, Kansas City, Missouri, USA. Writer; Poet; Translator; Teacher; Editor; Photographer. m. (1) Lyell Hale Ritchie, 2 sons, 1 daughter, (2) Clyde Henri Farnsworth, 22 June 1991. Education: Degré Supèrieur, Mention Très Bien, Sorbonne, Paris, 1951; Cornell University, 1951-53; BA, University of California, Berkeley, 1954; MA, French Literature, minor Russian Studies, American University, 1976; Advanced Russian courses, Georgetown University. Appointments: US Information Agency Visiting Poet, Brazil, 1972; Far East 1977; Yugoslavia, Bulgaria, 1979; Founder, Director, The Wineberry Press, 1983-; President, Washington Writers Publishing House, 1986-89; Leader, Creative Writing Workshops. Publications: Timbot, 1970; Tightening The Circle Over Eel Country, 1974; A Sheath of Dreams And Other Games, 1976; Moving To Larger Quarters, 1977; Raking The Snow, 1982; The Problem With Eden, 1985; Flying Time: Stories and Half-Stories, 1992; A Wound-Up Cat and Other Bedtime Stories, 1993; Elegy for the Other Woman, 1995; The Arc of the Storm, 1995; Works in numerous anthologies. Contributions to: Fiction, poetry, articles, reviews, translations, photographs: New York Times; Washington Post; Christian Science Monitor; Paris Herald Tribune; Miami Herald; Poetry; American Scholar; Ascent; Washingtonian; National Geographic; New Letters; Epoch; The Poetry Review; Many others, USA, abroad. Honours: New Writer's Award for Best 1st Book of Poetry, Great Lakes Colleges Association, 1975-76; Graduate Teaching Fellowship, American University; Fellow, Virginia Center for the Creative Arts; 4 times PEN Syndicated Fiction Winner; 4 Individual Artist Grants, DC Commission for the Arts. Memberships: Writer's Center; Washington Independent Writers; PEN; Committee for Poetry in the Greater Washington Area; Amnesty International; Poetry Society of America; Poets and Writers; Environmental organisations. Literary Agent: Nina Graybill, Ronald Goldfarb and Associates, 918 Sixteenth St NW 400, Washington DC 20006, USA. Address: 3207 Macomb Street NW, Washington DC 20008, USA.

RITTER Erika, b. 1948, Saskatchewan, Canada. Playwright. Education: BA, McGill University, Montreal, 1968; MA, University of Toronto, 1970. Appointments include: Dramatist in Residence, Stratford Festival, Ontario, 1985. Publications: A Visitor from Charleston, 1975; The Splits, 1978; Winter, 1671, 1979; The Automatic Pilot, 1980; The Passing Scene, 1982; Murder at McQueen, 1986; Urban Scrawl, 1984; Ritter in Residence, 1987; Essays and Sketches. Honours include: ACTRA Award, 1982. Address: c/o Shain Jaffe, Great North Artists, 350 Dupont Street, Toronto, Ontario M5R 1V9, Canada.

RITTERBAND Olly, b. 28 Dec 1923, Miercurea-Niraj, Rumania. Artist; Author. m. Daniel Ritterband, 25 Dec 1949, 2 daughters. Education: Royal Danish Academy of Fine Arts; Ecole Nationale Superieure Des Beaux-Arts, Paris; Accademia Del Mosaico, Ravenna, Italy; Photographer, Josef Porjes, Transylvania; Teacher, Royal Danish Academy of Fine Arts, Copenhagen. Publications: I Will Not Die, 1982; Will To Survive, 1990; Lecture, The Holocaust. Contributions to: Articles about the Holocaust. Honours: Diplomas, Lodge of Denmark, 1979. Memberships: The Danish Authors Association; President, Friends of Mosaics Art; Committee Member, Gentofte Society of Culture; Committee Member, Society of Jewish History. Address: Niels Andersensvej 65, Hellerup, DK-2900, Denmark.

RITVO Harriet, b. 19 Sept 1946, Cambridge, Massachusetts, USA. Historian. Education: AB, 1968, PhD, 1975, Harvard University. Appointments: Currently, Professor of History and Writing, Massachusetts Institute of Technology. Publications: The Animal Estate: The English and Other Creatures in the Victorian Age; The Macropolitics of 19th-Century Literature (co-editor with Jonathan Arac). Contributions to: Numerous essays and reviews on 18th and 19th-Century cultural history, and on the relationship between humans and other animals. Honours: Whiting Writers' Award, 1990. Memberships: PEN American Center; National Book Critics Circle, (US); American Historical Association; History of Science Society; Society for the History of Natural History. Address: E51 230 Massachusetts Institute of Technology, Cambridge, MA 02139, USA.

RIVA Maria Elizabeth, b. 13 Dec 1924, Berlin, Germany. US Citizen. Author; Former Actress. m. William Riva, 4 July 1947, 4 sons. Publication: Marlene Dietrich by Her Daughter, 1992. Contributions to: Various. Honours: Various acting awards, 1946-55. Literary Agent: International Transactions Inc. Address: 133 RR2, Wassaic, NY 12592, USA.

RIVARD Ken J, b. 30 June 1947, Montreal, Canada. Special Education Teacher. m. Micheline Rivard, 19 Sept 1972, 2 daughters. Education: BEd, University of Montreal, 1970; MEd, McGill University, 1974. Publications: Poetry books: Kiss Me Down To Size, 1983; Frankie's Desires, 1987; Chapbooks: Losing His Thirst, poetry, 1985; Working Stiffs, short fiction, 1990; Short, Short Fiction: If She Could Take All These Men, 1995. Contributions to: Short fiction and poetry to: Alberta Diamond Jubilee Anthology, 1979; Lyrical Voices, USA, 1979; Alberta Poetry Yearbook; Alive; Antigonish Review; Border Crossings; Canadian Forum; Cross-Canada Writers Quarterly; Dalhousie Review; Didsbury Booster; Going for Coffee - An Anthology of Contemporary North American Working Poems, 1981; Glass Canyons, 1985; Matrix; New Quarterly; Open Windows Anthology, 1988; Poems N'Things; Poetry Canada; Poetry Toronto; Paririe Journal of Canadian Literature; Prism International; Queen's Quarterly; Sans Crit; Small Press Lynx, 1991; Transition; Vortex; Wascana Review; Waves; Whetstone; Various other magazines and anthologies. Memberships: Writers Guild of Alberta; League of Canadian Poets. Literary Agent: Joanne Kellock. Address: 120 Whiteview Place NE, Calgary, Alberta, T1Y 1R6, Canada.

RIVERO Andres, b. 18 Jul 1936. Writer. m. Pilar Eloisa, 19 May 1959, 3 s. Education: Doctor of Literature. Publications: Enterrado Vivi, 1961; Cuentos Pam Entender, 1978; Recuerdos, 1979; Sorpresivemente, 1981; Somos Como Somos, 1982. Contributions to: Several publications throughout Latin America and The United States of America. Honours: Kiwanis, 1965; Club Leonistico Cubano, 1978; Cruzada Educativa, 1985; ACCA, Miami, 1990. Memberships: Poets and Writers, NY. Address: PO Box 650909, Miami, FL 33265, USA.

RIVERS Joan, b. 1935, Brooklyn, New York, USA. American Comedienne; Actress; Recording Artist; Columnist; Playwright; Screenwriter; Author. Publications: Contemporary Theatre, Film, and Television Volume I, 1984; Current Biography, 1970; Having a Baby Can Be a Scream, 1974; The Life and Hard Times of Heidi Abromowitz: A Totally Unauthorized Biography, 1984; Enter Talking, 1986; Still Talking, 1991; Creator, TV Series, Husband and Wives, 1976; Author, Screenplay, The Girl Most Likely To. Contributions to: Detroit Free Press; New York Times Book Review; People; Time; Columnist, Chicago Tribune, 1973-76. Address: c/o Richard Grant & Associates, 8484 Wilshire Boulevard, Suite 500, Beverly Hills, CA 90211, USA.

RIVERS Jose,Dramatist. Honours: Whiting Writers Award, 1992. Address: c/o Kelly Rosenheim, Mrs Giles Whiting Foundation, 30 Rockefeller Plaza. Rm 3500, NY 10112, USA.

RIVET Albert Lionel Frederick, b. 30 Nov 1915, Streatham, London, England. Emeritus Professor of Roman Provincial Studies. m. Audrey Catherine Webb, 8 Apr 1947, 1 s, 1 d. Education: BA Classics, 1938, MA Classics, 1946, Oriel College, Oxford. Literary Appointments include: Army, 1940-46 (Ciphers 1941-46 ending as Major, Chief Cipher Officer EA Command); Bookseller, 1946-51; Assistant Archaeology Officer Ordnance Survey, 1951-64; Lecturer 1964, Reader 1967, Professor 1974, retired 1981, but Research Professor, 1988-90, Classics Department, University of Keele. Publications: Town and Country in Roman Britain, 1958, 2nd edition, 1964; The Iron Age in Northern Britain (editor and bibliography), 1966; The Roman Villa in Britain (editor and chapter), 1969; The Place-Names of Roman Britain (with C Smith), 1979; Gallia Narbonensis, 1988. Contributions to: Various journals including: Antiquaries Journal; Antiquity; Archaeologia Cantiana; Archaeological Journal; Archaeological News Letter. Memberships include: The British Academy, Elected FBA 1981, British Member, Sub-Committee of Tabula Imperii Romani, 1970-81, Deputy Chairman, 1979-81, Chairman, 1981-87; Royal Commission on The Historical Monuments of England, Commissioner, 1979-85, Chairman of National Monuments Records Committee, 1981-85; Society for The Promotion of Roman Studies, Member, 1964-, President, 1977-80, Vice-President, 1976-; Society of Antiquaries of London FSA, 1953-. Address: 7 Springpool, Keele, Staffordshire, ST5 5BN, England.

RIVKIN J F, b. 1951, USA. Publications: Silverglass, 1986; Web of Wind, 1987; Witch of Rhostshyl, 1989; Mistress of Ambiguities, 1991;

The Dreamstone, 1991. Membership: Science Fiction and Fantasy Writers of America. Address: 1430 Massachusetts Avenue, Suite 306, Cambridge, MA 02138, USA.

RIVOYRE Christine Berthe Claude Denis de, b. 29 Nov 1921. Journalist; Author. Education: University of Syracuse, USA. Literary Appointments: Journalist, Le Monde, 1950-55; Literary Director, Marie-Claire, 1955-65; Member, haut Comite de la Langue Francaise, Conseil Superieur des Lettres, Prix Medicis Jury. Publications: L'alouette au miroir, 1956; La mandarine, 1957; La tete en fleurs, 1960; La glace a l'ananas, 1962; Les sultans, 1964; Le petit matin, 1968; Le seigneur des chevaux (with A Kalda), 1969; Fleur d'agonie, 1970; Boy, 1973; Le voyage a l'envers, 1977; Belle alliance, 1982; Reine-Mere, 1985. Honours include: Chevalier, Legion d'honneur; Chevalier, des Arts et des Lettres Prix Paul Morand, 1984. Address: Dichats Ha, Onesse Laharie, 40110, Morceux, France.

RIZKALLA John Ramsay, b. 2 Nov 1935, Manchester, England. Writer. Education: Baccalaureat Francais, 1st and 2nd part, 1952-53; BA Hons, Manchester University, 1958. Publications: The Jericho Garden, 1988; Contributor of short stories to: Winter's Tales 28, ed A Mclean, 1982; A Christmas Feast, ed J Hale, 1983; BBC Radio 3, 1984; Signals, ed A Ross, 1991. Contributions to: London Magazine; Panurge; Literary Review; New Review; Encounter; 2 Plus 2; Argo; Short Story International (USA); Blackwood Magazine; Weirdbook (USA). Memberships: Society of Authors. Address: c/o Murray Polinger, 222 Old Brompton Road, London, SW5 0BZ, England.

RIZVI Sajid, b. 2 Feb 1949, Lucknow, India. Writer; Publisher. m. Shirley Joseph, 31 Jul 1975, 1 s. Education: BA, University of Karachi, 1969; Diploma in Advanced Journalism, Thomson Centre of Journalism, Cardiff, 1974. Appointments: Apprentice Proofreader, appointed in 1964, age 15, becoming City Editor in 1970, Morning News, English Language Daily, Karachi; Executive Editor, Tehran Journal, Tehran, 1976; Chief Correspondent, United Press International (UPI), Tehran, 1977-80; UPI Chief Correspondent, Ankara, 1980; UPI Middle East Correspondent, London, 1981-84; Diplomatic Editor, Compass News Features, Luxembourg, 1984-87; Independent Correspondent, 1987-; founded The Centre for Near East, Afro-Asia Research (NEAR), 1987. Publications: Numerous articles on current affairs and the arts in various publications; work syndicated throughout the world since joining UPI in 1977. Address: Centre for Near East Asia and Africa Research, 172 Castlenau, London, SW13 9DH, England.

RIZZUTO Sharida, b. New Orleans, LA, USA. Writer; Publisher. Education: BA History, University of New Orleans, 1992. Contributions to: The Collinsport Record; The Collinwood Journal; The Vampire Journal; Nightshade; Horizons West; The Haunted Journal; Baker Street Gazette; The Salem Journal; Mixed Bag; Pen & Ink; Jack The Ripper Gazette; News From The Abyss & Abyss Forum; Vampire Nights; Horizons Beyond; Movie Memories; Hollywood Nostalgia. Memberships: National Writers Club; Horror Writers Of America; Mystery Writers Of America; Small Genre Association. Literary Agents: Elaine Wolfe. Address: PO Box 517, Metairie, LA 70004-0517, USA.

ROBB Graham Macdonald, b. 2 Jun 1958, England. Writer. m. Margaret Robb, 2 May 1986. Education: BA 1st Class Honours, 1981; PGCE, Goldsmiths College, London, 1982; PhD, Vanderbilt University, Nashville, TN, USA, 1986. Publications: Le Corsaire - Satan en Silhouette, 1985; Baudelaire Lecteur de Balzac, 1988; Scenes de La Vie de Boheme (editor), 1988; Baudelaire, translation 1989; La Poésie de Baudelaire et La Poésie Française, 1993; Balzac, 1994. Contributions to: Times Literary Supplement; Revue d'Histoire Litteraire de La France; French Studies. Honours: Postdoctoral Research Fellow; British Academy Fellowship, 1987-90. Memberships: Society of Authors; Societe d'Histoire Litteraire de La France. Literary Agent: Gill Cloeridge, Rogers, Coleridge and White. Address: 139 Hollow Way, Oxford, OX4 2NE, England.

ROBBE-GRILLET Alain, b. 18 Aug 1922, Brest, France. Writer; Film-Maker; Agronomist. m. Catherine Rstakian, 1957. Publications: Novels: Les Gommes, 1953; Le Voyeur, 1955; La Jalousie, 1957; Dans le Labyrinthe, 1959; La Maison de Rendez-vous, 1965; Projet pour une Revolution a New York, 1970; Topologie d'une Cite Fantome, 1976; La Belle Captive, 1977; Un Regicide, 1978; Souvenirs du Triangle d'Or, 1978; Djinn, 1981; Le Miroir qui Revient, 1984; Angélique ou l'Enchantment, 1987; Les Derniers Jours de Corinthe, 1994; Short stories: Instantanes, 1962; Essay: Pour un Nouveau Roman, 1964; Films, L'Annee Derniere a Marienbad, 1961; Films Directed:

L'Immortelle, 1963; Trans-Europ-Express, 1967; L'Homme qui Ment, 1968; L'Eden et Apres, 1970; Glissements Progressifs du Plaisir, 1974; Le Jeu Avec le Feu, 1975; La Belle Captive, 1983. Honours: Chevalier, Legion d'Honneur; Officier, Ordre National du Merite; Prix Louis Delluc, 1963. Memberships: Various professional organisations. Address: 18 Boulevard Maillot, 92200 Neuilly-sur-Seine, France.

ROBBINS Harold, b. 1916, USA. Author. m. Grace, 1 d. Publications: Never Love a Stranger, 1948; The Dream Merchants, 1949; A Stone for Danny Fisher, 1952; Never Leave Me, 1953; 79 Park Avenue, 1955; Stiletto, 1960; The Carpetbaggers, 1961; Where Love Has Gone, 1962; The Adventurers, 1966; The Inheritors, 1969; The Betsy, 1971; The Pirate, 1974; The Lonely Lady, 1976; Dreams Die First, 1977; Memoires of Another Day, 1979; Goodbye Janette, 1981; Spellbinder, 1982; Descent from Xanadu, 1984; The Storyteller, 1985; The Pirhanas, 1991. Address: c/o New English Library, 47 Bedford Square, London, WC1B 3DP, England.

ROBBINS Kenneth Randall, b. 7 Jan 1944, Georgia, USA. Professor. m. Dorothy Dodge, 14 May 1988, 1 s, 1 d. Education: AA, Young Harris College, 1964; BSEd, Georgia Southern University, 1966; MFA, University of Georgia, 1969; PhD, Southern Illinois University-Carbondale, 1982. Literary Appointments: Literary Manager, Barter Theatre, Abingdon, VA, 1979; Presenter, Black Hills Writers Conference, 1986-90; Programme Development, Aspen Writers Conference, 1987; Convener, Breadloaf Writers Conference, 1981-82; currently Editor, Wayne S Knutson Dakota Playwriting Series. Publications: The Dallas File (play), 1982; Buttermilk Bottoms (novel), 1987. Contributions to: Calling The Cows, story, ND Quarterly; Dynamite Hill, play, NPR and BBC-Radio 3; The House Across the Street, story, St Andrews Review; Out of Irony, essay, Southern Quarterly; Concerning The Altered Text, essay, Theatre Topics. Honours: Toni Morrison Prize for Fiction, 1986; Associated Writing Programmes Novel Award, 1986; Festival of Southern Theatre Award, 1987, 1990. Memberships: Dramatists Guild; Playwright's Centre, Minneapolis; The Loft, Minneapolis; American College Theatre Festival, PAC Chair, Region V; Association of Theatre in Higher Education; Society for Humanities and Technology; Southeastern Theatre Conference. Address: 118 Willow, Vermillion, SD 57069, USA.

ROBBINS Thomas Eugene,b. 1936, Blowing Rock, North Carolina. m. Terrie (divorced), 1 son. Education: Washington & Lee University; Richmond Professional Institute; University of Washington. Appointments: Copy Editor; Writer. Address: c/o Bantam Publishers Attn Author, Mail Dept-1540 Broadway, NY 10036, USA.

ROBERSON John Royster, b. 7 Mar 1930, Roanoke, Virginia, USA. Editor; Writer. m. Charlene Grace Hale, 17 Sept 1966, 1 son, 1 daughter. Education: BA, 1950, MA, 1953, University of Virginia; Certificates of French Studies, 1st and 2nd Degrees, University of Grenoble, France, 1952; Diploma in Mandarin Chinese, US Army Language School, Monterey, California, 1956. Appointments: From Assistant to Senior Editor, Holiday, 1959-70; Copywriter, N W Ayer Advertising, 1971-76; From Associate to Senior Staff Editor, Reader's Digest Condensed Books, 1976-. Publications: China from Manchu to Mao 1699-1976, 1980; Japan from Shogun to Sony 1543-1984, 1985; Transforming Russia 1692-1991, 1992. Contributions to: Atlantic; Holiday; Reader's Digest; Studies in Bibliography; Virginia Magazine of History and Biography. Honours: Raven Society, University of Virginia, 1950; Rotary International Fellowship, University of Grenoble, 1951-52. Memberships: International House of Japan; US China People's Friendship Society; Director of Publications, Science Education Center, Fairfield County, Connecticut. Address: 16 Hassake Road, Old Greenwich, CT 06870, USA.

ROBERT Adrian. See: **JOHNSTON Norma.**

ROBERTS Andrew, b. 13 Jan 1963, London, England. Author. Education: MA 1st Class Honours, Modern History, Gonville and Caius College, Cambridge, 1985. Publications: The Holy Fox: A Biography of Lord Halifax; Eminent Churchillians, 1994. Contributions to: Sunday Telegraph; Spectator; Literary Review; American Spectator. Memberships: Beefsteak Club; University Pitt Club, Cambridge; Brooks. Address: 14 Cadogan Gardens, London, SW3 2RS, England.

ROBERTS Brian, b. 1930, England. Writer. Appointments: Teacher of English and History, 1955-65. Publications: Ladies In The Veld, 1965; Cecil Rhodes and The Princess, 1969; Churchills in Africa, 1970; The Diamond Magnates, 1972; The Zulu Kings, 1974; Kimberley:

Turbulent City, 1976; The Mad Bad Line: The Family of Lord Alfred Douglas, 1981; Randolph: A Study of Churchill's Son, 1984; Cecil Rhodes: Flawed Colossus, 1987; Those Bloody Women: Three Heroines of The Boer War, 1991. Literary Agent: Andrew Lownie, 122 Bedford Court Mansions, Bedford Square, London, WC1B 3AH, England. Address: North Knoll Cottage, 15 Bridge Street, Frome BA11 1BB, England.

ROBERTS Eirlys Rhiwen Cadwaladr, b. 3 Jan 1911, United Kingdom. Journalist. m. John Cullen, 1941. Education: BA Honours, Classics, Girton College, Cambridge. Literary Appointments: Editor, Which? magazine, 1958-73; Head of Research and Editorial Division, Consumers' Association. Publication: Consumers, 1966. Contributions to: Various journals and magazines. Honours: OBE, 1971; CBE, 1977. Membership: Royal Society of Arts. Address: 8 Lloyd Square, London, WC1X 9BA, England.

ROBERTS Gildas Owen, b. 5 Dec 1932, Johannesburg, South Africa. University Professor. m. Patricia Margaret Howe, 10 June 1963, 2 sons, 2 daughters. Education: Graduated, Selborne College, 1948; BA, Law, 1951, MA, 1953, BEd, 1955, STC, 1975, University of Cape Town; PhD, Ohio State University, 1966. Publications: Joseph of Exeter: The Iliad of Dares Phrygius, 1970; Seven Studies in English, 1971; Angels of God (novel), 1974; Chemical Eric (novel), 1974; Lotus Man (novel), 1983; Beowulf (verse translation), 1984; Gander Snatch (novel), 1991. Contributions to: Poems and short stories in Tickle Ace (literary magazine) and others.

ROBERTS I M. See: **ROBERTS Irene.**

ROBERTS Irene, (Roberta Carr, Elizabeth Harle, I M Roberts, Ivor Roberts, Iris Rowland, Irene Shaw), b. 1925, United Kingdom. Writer. Appointments: Woman's Page Editor, South Hams Review, 1977-79; Tutor, Creative Writing, Kingsbridge Community College, 1978-. Publications include: Shadows on the Moon, 1968; Thunder Heights, 1969; Surgeon in Tibet, 1970; Birds Without Bars, 1970; The Shrine of Fire, 1970; Sister at Sea, 1971; Gull Haven, 1971; Moon Over the Temple, 1972; The Golden Pagoda, 1972; Desert Nurse, 1976; Nurse in Nepal, 1976; Stars Above Raffael, 1977; Hawks Burton, 1979; Syphony of Bells, 1980; Nurse Moonlight, 1980; Weave Me A Moonbeam, 1982; Jasmine for a Nurse, 1982; Sister on Leave, 1982; Nurse in the Wilderness, 1983; Moonpearl, 1986; Sea Jade, 1987; Kingdom of the Sun, 1987; Song of the Nile, 1987; juveniles: Holiday's for Hanbury, 1964; Laughing is for Fun, 1964; as Ivor Roberts: Jump into Hell, 1960; Trial by Water, 1961; Green Hell, 1961; as Iris Rowland: Blue Feathers, 1967; Moon Over Moncrieff, 1969; Star Drift, 1970; Rainbow River, 1970; The Wild Summer, 1970; Orange Blossom for Tara, 1971; Blossoms in the Snow, 1971; Sister Julia, 1972; Golden Bubbles, 1976; Hunter's Dawn, 1977; Golden Triangle, 1978; Forgotten Dreams, 1978; Temptation, 1983; Theresa, 1985; as Roberta Carr: Sea Maiden, 1965; Fire Dragon, 1967; Golden Interlude, 1970; as Elizabeth Harle: Golden Rain, 1964; Gay Rowan, 1965; Sandy, 1967; Spray of Red Roses, 1971; The Silver Summer, 1971; The Burning Flame, 1979; Come to Me Darling, 1983; as Irene Shaw: Moonstone Manor, 1968, (Murder Mansion 1976, USA); The Olive Branch, 1968; as I M Roberts: The Throne of the Pharoahs, 1974; Hatsheput, Queeen of the Nile, 1976; Hour of the Tiger, 1985; Jezebel Street, 1994; Sparrows Can't Sing, 1995. Literary Agent: Judith Murdoch, 19 Chalcot Square, London NW1 8YA. Address: Alpha House, Higher Town, Marlborough, Kingsbridge, South Devon TQ7 3RL, England.

ROBERTS Ivor. See: **ROBERTS Irene.**

ROBERTS John Morris, b. 14 Apr 1928. Warden, Merton College, Oxford, 1985-1994; Hon Fellow, 1981-84, 1994-; m. Judith Cecilia Mary Armitage, 1964, 1 s, 2 d. Education: Scholar; Hon Fellow, Keble College, Oxford, 1981. Appointments include: Senior Proctor, Oxford University, 1967-68; Vice-Chancellor and Professor, Southampton University, 1979-85; Member, Institute of Advanced Study, Princeton, 1960-61; Visiting Professor, University of South Carolina, 1961; Secretary of Harmsworth Trust, 1962-68; Member, Council, European University Institute, 1980-88; USA/UK Education Commission (Fulbright), 1981-87; Governor of BBC, 1988-93; Board Member, British Council, 1992. Publications: French Revolution Documents 1, 1966; Europe 1880-1945, 1967, 1990; The Mythology of The Secret Societies, 1972; The Paris Commune from The Right, 1973; Revolution and Improvement: The Western World 1775-1847, 1976; History of The World, 1976, revised edition 1993; The French Revolution, 1978; The Triumph of The West, 1985; (General Editor)

Purnell's History of The 20th Century; Shorter Illustrated History of The World, 1994. Contributions to: Articles and reviews to learned journals; Editor, English Historical Review, 1967-77; Presenter, TV series, The Triumph of The West, 1985. Honours: Hon D Litt, Southampton University, 1987; Cavalier of The Order of Merit of The Italian Republic, 1989. Memberships: General Committee, Royal Literary Fund, 1975-; Trustee, National Portrait Gallery, 1984-; President, Council, Taunton School, 1978-88; Board Member, Royal Literary Fund. Literary Agent: A D Peters. Address: Merton College, Oxford, OX1 4JD, England.

ROBERTS Keith John Kingston (Alistair Bevan), b. 1935, United Kingdom. Author; Freelance Graphic Designer and Advertising Copywriter. Literary Appointments: Assistant Editor, Science Fantasy, 1965-66; Assistant Editor, 1965-66, Managing Editor, 1966, Science Fiction Impulse. Publications: The Furies, 1966; Pavane, 1968; The Inner Wheel, 1970; Anita, 1970; The Boat of Fate, 1971; Machines and Men, 1973; The Chalk Giants, 1974; The Grain Kings, 1975; Ladies from Hell, 1979; Molly Zero, 1980; Kiteworld, 1985; Kaeti and Company, 1986; The Lordly Ones, 1986. Address: 23 New Street, Henley-on-Thames, Oxon, RG9 2BP, England.

ROBERTS Kevin, b. 1940, Australia. Author. Appointment: Instructor, Malaspina University College. Publications: Cariboo Fishing Notes (poetry), 1973; Five Poems, 1974; West Country (poetry), 1975; Deepline (poetry), 1978; S'Ney'mos (poetry), 1980; Heritage (poetry), 1981; Stonefish (poetry), 1982; Flash Harry and The Daughters of Divine Light (fiction), 1982; Black Apples (play), 1983; Nanoose Bay Suite (poetry), 1984; Picking the Morning Colour (fiction), 1985; Tears in a Glass Eye (novel), 1989; Red Centre Journal (art and poetry show), 1985. Address: Box 55, Lantzville, British Columbia, Canada, V0R 2H0.

ROBERTS Michele, English-French Poet, Playwright and Novelist. Career: Frequent reviewer, broadcaster; Tutor of Creative Writing; Has taken several Arvon Foundation Courses. Publications: A Piece of the Night, (novel), 1978; Tales I Tell My Mother, (stories), 1978; The Wild Girl, (novel), 1984; The Book of Mrs Noah, (novel), 1986; The Mirror of the Mother, (poetry), 1986; More Tales I Tell My Mother, (story), 1988; The Journey Woman, (play), 1988; The Seven Deadly Sins, (stories), 1989; The Seven Cardinal Virtues, (stories), 1990; In the Red Kitchen, (novel), 1990; Psyche and the Hurricane, (poetry), 1991; God, (stories), 1992; The Heavenly Twins, (screenplay), 1992; Daughters of the House, (novel), 1993; During Mother's Absence, 1993; Also published in a number of anthologies and co-authorships. Honours: Winner, 35th Annual W H Smith Literary Award, 1993.

ROBERTS Nora, b. 10 Oct 1950. Writer. m. 6 Jul 1985, 2 s. Education: Graduated, High School, 1968. Publications: Irish Thoroughbred, 1981; This Magic Moment, 1983; The MacGregors, 1985; Hot Ice, 1987; Sacred Sins, 1987; Brazen Virtue, 1988; The O'Harleys, 1988; Sweet Revenge, 1989; Public Secrets, 1990; The Calhoun Women, 1991; Genuine Lies, 1991; Carnal Innocence, 1992; Honest Illusions, 1992; Divine Evil, 1992; Private Scandals, 1993; Hidden Riches, 1994. Honours: Romance Writers of America (RWA), Golden Medallion, 1982, 1983, 1984, 1986; RWA Hall of Fame, 1986; RWA Rita Award, 1990; Waldenbooks Award, 1986, 1987, 1989, 1990, 1991; B Dalton Award, 1990, 1991. Memberships: Romance Writers of America; Mystery Writers of America; Novelists Inc; Crime Writers; Sisters-in-Crime. Address: c/o Writers House, 21 West 26th Street, New York, NY 10010, USA.

ROBERTS Selyf, b. 20 May 1912, Corwen, Gwynedd, Wales. Retired Bank Officer. m. 28 Aug 1945, 1 d. Publications: Translations into Welsh: Alice in Wonderland (abridged) 1951, (full translation), 1982; Through the Looking Glass, 1984; essays: Deg o'r Diwedd, 1958; Mesur Byr, 1977; Hel Meddliau, 1982; Dr R P Howells (imaginary biography), 1974; Tocyn Dwyffordd, 1984; novels: Cysgod yw Arian, 1959; Helynt ar Hoelion, 1960; A Eilw ar Ddfnder, 1962; Wythnos o Hydref, 1965; Ymweled ag Anwiredd, 1975; Lach o'r Cadwynau, 1977; Tebyg Nid Oes, 1981; Teulu Meima Lloyd, 1986; Gorwel Agos, 1989; Arts Council Award Winning Novel; Cyfrinach Mai, 1993. Contributions to: Essays and Short Stories to: Y Llenor; yr Eugrawn; Taliesin; Genhinen; various anthologies. Honours: Honorary Member, Gorsedd of Bards; Winner of Prose Medal, National Eisteddfod of Wales , Pwlheli, 1955. Memberships: Yr Adaemi Gymreig: Chairman, Undeb Awduron Cymru (union of Welsh Authors) 1975-86. Address: Hafod Las, Trefonen Road, Oswestry, Shropshire SY11 2TW, England.

ROBERTS Willo Davis, b. 29 May 1928, Grand Rapids, Michigan, USA. Freelance Writer. m. David Roberts, 20 May 1949, 2 sons, 2 daughters. Publications: 88 books including: Murder at Grand Bay, 1955; The Girl Who Wasn't There, 1957; Nurse Kay's Conquest, 1966; The Tarot Spell, 1970; King's Pawn, 1971; White Jade, 1975, Paperback Edition, 1976; 8 volumes in The Black Pearl Series, 1978-80, The Search for Willie, 1980; A Long Time To Hate, 1982; Keating's Landing, 1984; The Annalise Experiment, 1985; To Share A Dream, 1986; Madawaska, 1988; Books for children and young adults: The View from the Cherry Tree, 1975; Don't Hurt Laurie, 1977; The Girl with the Silver Eyes, 1980; The Pet Sitting Peril, 1983; Eddie and the Fairy God Puppy, 1984; Baby Sitting Is A Dangerous Job, 1985; The Magic Book, 1986; Sugar Isn't Everything, 1987; Megan's Island, 1988; Nightmare, 1989; Scared Stiff, 1991; Dark Secrets, 1991; Jo and the Bandit; What Are We Going To Do About David; Caught; The Absolutely True Story of My Trip To Yellowstone With The Terrible Rupes. Honours: Young Hoosier Award, Evansville Book Award, Georgia Children's Book Award, Young Readers of Western Australia Award, 1977; Mark Twain Award, 1980; Mark Twain Award, Young Hoosier Award, South Carolina Children's Book Award, Nevada Young Reader's Award, 1985; Pacific Northwest Writers Achievement Award, 1986; Edgar Allen Poe Award, 1988; The Florida Sunshine State Award, 1994; California Young Reader Medal; 1984, 1994. Memberships: Mystery Writers of America, Founder, Northwest Seattle Chapter, Past Regional Vice President; Society of Children's Book Writers; Seattle Freelances; Pacific Northwest Writers Conference. Literary Agent: Emilie Jacobson, Curtis Brown Ltd, New York, USA. Address: 12020 Engebretson Road, Granite Falls, WA 98252, USA.

ROBERTSON Barbara Anne, b. 1931, Canada. Biographer. Publications: The Wind Has Wings (compiled with M A Downie), 1968, Enlarged Edition, The New Wind Has Wings, 1984; Wilfrid Laurier: The Great Conciliator, 1971; The Well-Filled Cupboard (with M A Downie), 1987; Doctor-Dwarf and other poems for Children, (ed with M A Downie), 1990; new edition, Sir Wilfrid Laurier: The Great Conciliator, 1991. Address: 52 Florence Street, Kingston, Ontario, K7M 1Y6, Canada.

ROBERTSON Charles, b. 22 Oct 1940, Glasgow, Scotland. Parish Minister; Chaplain to Her Majesty the Queen in Scotland, (Clergyman). m. 30 July 1965, 1 son, 2 daughters. Education: MA, Edinburgh University, 1964. Publications: Editor, contributor: Common Order; Saint Margaret Queen of Scotland and her Chapel; Singing the Faith; Worshipping Together; Hymns for a Day; Songs of God's People. Contributions to: Record of Church Service Society; Scottish Journal of Theology (reviewer). Memberships: Chairman, Joint Liturgical Group; Secretary, Panel on Worship. Address: Manse of Canongate, Edinburgh EH8 8BR, Scotland.

ROBERTSON Denise, b. 9 Jun 1933, Sunderland, England. Writer; Broadcaster. m. (1) Alexander Robertson, 19 Mar 1960, (2) John Tomlin, 3 Nov 1973, 5 s. Publications: Year of Winter, 1986; Land of Lost Content, 1987; Blue Remembered Hills, 1987; Second Wife, 1988; None to Make You Cry, 1989; Remember The Moment, 1990. Contributions to: Numerous. Honour: Constable Fiction Trophy, 1985. Literary Agent: Carol Smith, 25 Hornton Court, East Kensington High Street, London, W8 7RT, England. Address: 9 Springfield Crescent, Seaham, County Durham, England.

ROBERTSON James, b. 18 Jul 1930, Danville, VA, USA. Professor of History. m. Elizabeth Green, 1 Jun 1952, 2 s, 1 d. Education: BA, Randolph-Macon College, 1954; MA 1955, PhD 1959, Emory University; LittD, Randolph-Macon College, 1980. Literary Appointments: Associate Professor of History, University of Montana, 1965-67; Professor, Head, History Department, 1967-75, C P Miles Professor of History, 1976-, Virginia Polytechnic Institute and State University. Publications: The Stonewall Brigade, 1963; Civil War Books: The Civil War Letters of General Robert McAllister, 1965; A Critical Bibliography, 1965-67; Recollections of a Maryland Confederate Soldier, 1975; Four Years in The Stonewall Brigade, 1978; The 4th Virginia Infantry, 1980; Civil War Sites in Virginia: A Tour-Guide, 1982; The 18th Virginia Infantry, 1983; Tentinting Tonight: The Soldiers' View, 1984; General A P Hill, 1987; Soldiers Blue and Gray, 1988. Contributions to: More than 150 articles in historical journals and history magazines. Honours include: Freeman-Nevins Award, 1981; Bruce Catton Award, 1983; William E Wine Award for Teaching Excellence, 1983; A P Andrews Memorial Award, 1985; James Robertson Award of Achievement, 1985; Jefferson Davis Medal, United Daughters of The Confederacy. Memberships: Board of Trustees,

Virginia Historical Society; Organization of American Historians; Southern Historical Association; Confederate Memorial Society. Address: Department of History, Virginia Polytechnic Institute and State University, Blacksburg, VA 24061-0117, USA.

ROBINETTE Joseph Allen, b. 8 Feb 1939, Rockwood, TN, USA. College Professor; Playwright. m. Helen M Scitz, 27 Aug 1965, 4 s, 1 d. Education: BA, Carson-Newman College, 1960; MA 1966, PhD 1972, Southern Illinois University. Publications: The Fabulous Fable Factory, 1975; Once Upon a Shoe (play), 1979; Legend of The Sun Child (musical), 1982; Charlotte's Web (dramatization), 1983; Charlotte's Web (musical with Charles Strouse), 1989; Anne of Green Gables (dramatization), 1989; The Lion, The Witch and The Wardrobe (dramatization), 1989; The Trial of Goldilocks (operetta), 1990; Dorothy Meets Alice (musical), 1991. Contributions to: Children's Theatre News; Opera For Youth News. Honours: Charlotte Chorpennlag Cup, National Children's Playwriting Award, 1976. Memberships: American Society of Composers, Authors and Publishers; American Association for Theatre in Education; Opera for Youth; ASSITEJ. Address: Department of Speech and Theatre, Rowan State College, Glassboro, NJ 08028, USA.

ROBINS Patricia. See: **CLARK Patricia Denise.**

ROBINSON David Julien, b. 6 Aug 1930. Film Critic. Education: BA Hons, Kings College, Cambridge. Appointments: Associate Editor, Sight and Sound, Editor, Monthly Film Bulltin, 1956-58; Programme Director, NFT, 1959; Film Critic, Financial Times, 1959-74; Editor, Contrast, 1962-63; Film Critic, The Times, 1974-93. Publications: Hollywood in the Twenties, 1969; Buster Keaton, 1969; The Great Funnies, 1972; World Cinema, 1973, 2nd edition, 1980 (US edition The History of World Cinema, 1974, 1980); Chaplin: The Mirror of Opinion, 1983; Chaplin: His Life and Art, 1985; Editor, Translator, Luis Bunuel (J F Aranda); Editor, Translator, Cinema in Revolution (anthology); Music of the Shadows, 1990; Masterpieces of Animation, 1991; Richard Attenborough, 1992; Georges Méliès, 1993; Lantern Images: Iconography of the Magic Lantern, 1993. Contributions to: The Times; The Guardian; The Australian; Sight and Sound. Honours: Roger Machin Prize, 1985; Commise Prize, 1987-88; Diego Fabbri Prize, 1989; Fellini Prize, 1991. Literary Agent: Curtis Brown Ltd. Address: 96-100 New Cavendish Street, London W1M 7FA, England.

ROBINSON Ian, b, 1 Jul 1934, Manchester, England. Writer. m. Adelheid Armbrüster, 21 Dec 1959, 1 s, 1 d. Education: MA, Oriel College, Oxford, 1955-58. Appointments: Editor, Oasis Magazine, 1969-; Publisher, Oasis Books, 1970-; Deputy Chairman, The Poetry Society of Great Britain, 1977-78. Publications: Poetry: Accidents, 1974: Three, 1978; Short Stories, 1979; Maida Vale Elegies, 1983; Journal, 1987; Fiction: P4.Obsequies, 1979; Fugitive Aromas, 1979; Blown footage, 1980; Dissolving Views, 1986; Graphic Book: The Glacier in the Cupboard, 1995. Contributions to: Prism International, Vancouver; The Canadian Fiction Magazine; London Magazine; Prospice; Blue Cage; Poesie Europe, Germany; Osiris, USA; 200 others. Memberships: Association of Little Presses; Society of Fulham Artists. Address: 12 Stevenage Road, London SW6 6ES, England.

ROBINSON Jancis Mary, b, 22 Apr 1950. Wine Writer; Broadcaster. m. Nicholas Laurence Lander, 1981, 1 s, 2 d. Education: MA, St Anne's College, Oxford, 1971. Appointments: Editor, Wine & Spirit, 1976-80; Founder, Editor, Drinker's Digest (now Which? Wine Monthly), 1977-82; Editor, Which Wine Guide, 1980-82; Sunday Times Wine Correspondent, 1987-88; Evening Standard Wine Correspondent, 1987-88; Regular Contributor to Financial Times, 1989-, ed, 1994; Freelance Journalist, on wine food and people, 1980-; Freelance TV & Radio Broadcaster, 1983-; Writer, Presenter, The Wine Programme, 1983, 1985, 1987; 'Jancis Robinson Meets...', 1988; Matters of Taste, 1989; The Vintner's Tale,1992; Wine Judging and Lecturing, 1983. Publications: The Wine Book, 1979, revised edition, 1983; The Great Wine Book, 1981; Masterglass, 1983, revised edition, 1987; How to Choose and Enjoy Wine, 1984; Vines Grapes and Wines, 1986; Food and Wine Adventures, 1987; The Demon Drink, 1988; Vintage Timecharts, 1989; The Oxford Companion to Wine. Honours: Glenfiddich Trophy, 1983; Master of Wine, 1984; Andre Simon Memorial Prize, Wine Guild Award, Cliquot Book of the Year, 1986. Membership: Master of Wine, 1984. Literary Agent: Caradoc king, A O4.P Watt Agency. Address: c/o A P Watt, 20 John Street, London, WC1N 2DR, England.

ROBINSON Jeffrey, b.19 Oct 1945, New York, NY, USA. Author. m. Aline Benayoun, 27 Mar 1985, 1 s, 1 d. Education: BS, Temple University, Philadelphia, Pennsylvania. Publications: Bette Davis, Her Stage and Film Career, 1983; Teamwork, 1984; The Risk Takers, 1985; Pietrov and Other Games (fiction), 1985; Minus Millionaires, 1986; The Ginger Jar (fiction), 1986; Yamani - The Inside Story, 1988; Rainier and Grace, 1989; The Risk Takers - Five Years On, 1990; The End of the American Century, 1992; The Laundrymen, 1994; Bardot - Two Lives, 1994; The Margin of the Bulls (fiction), 1995. Contributions to: More than 700 articles and short stories published in major magazines and journals worldwide. Honours: Overseas Press Club, 1984; Benedictine - After Dinner Speaker of the Year, 1990. Membership: PEN. Literary Agent: Mildred Marmur Associates Ltd., Suite 127, 2005 Palmer Ave, Larchmont, NY 10538, USA. Address: c/o Mildred Marmur.

ROBINSON Kim Stanley, b. 1952, USA. Author. Literary Appointments: Visiting Lecturer: University of California, Davis, 1982-84, 1985; University of Califomia, San Diego, 1982, 1985. Publications: The Novels of Philip K Dick, 1984; The Wild Shore, 1984; Icehenge, 1985; The Memory of Whiteness, 1985; The Planet on The Table, 1986; The Gold Coast (fiction), 1989; Green Mars, Red Mars, 1994. Address: 17811 Romelle Avenue, Santa Ana, CA 92705, USA.

ROBINSON Robert Henry, b. 17 Dec 1927, Liverpool, England. Writer; Broadcaster. m. Josephine Mary Richard, 1958. 1 s, 2 d. Education: Raynes Park Grammar School; MA, Exeter College, Oxford. Publications: Landscape With Dead Dons, 1956; Inside Robert Robinson, 1965; The Conspiracy, 1968; The Dog Chairman, 1982; Everyman Book of Light Verse, editor), 1984; Bad Dreams, 1989; Prescriptions of a Pox Doctor's Clerk, 1991; TV & Radio Programmes: Call My Bluff; Stop the Week; Brain of Britain; Robinson Country; Ad Lib. Contributions to: Times; Listener; Sunday Times. Address: 16 Cheyne Row, London, SW3, England.

ROBINSON Roland (Edward), b. 1912, British. Appointments: Member, Kirsova Ballet, 1944-47; Ballet Critic, 1956-66, Book Reviewer, Sydney Morning Herald; Editor, Poetry Magazine, Sydney; President, Poetry Society of Australia. Publications: Beyond The Grass-Tree Spears (verse), 1944; Language of The Sand, 1948; Legend and Dreaming: Legends of The Dream-Time of The Australian Aborigines, 1952; Tumult of The Swans, 1953; The Feathered Serpent: The Mythological Genesis and Recreative Ritual of The Aboriginal Tribes of The Northern Territory of Australia, 1956; Black-Feller, White-Feller, 1958; Deep Well, 1962; The Man Who Sold His Dreaming, 1965; Aborigine Myths and Legends, 1966; Grendel, 1967; Editor, The Australian Aborigine in Colour, Wandjina: Children of The Dreamtime: Aboriginal Myths and Legends, 1968; Selected Poems, 1971; The Drift of Things 1914-1952, 1973; The Shift of Sands 1952-62, 1976; A Letter to Joan, 1978; Selected Poems, 1984; Selected Poems, 1989; The Nearest The White Man Gets, 1989. Address: 10 Old Main Street, Belmont North, New South Wales 2280, Australia.

ROBINSON Shella Mary (Shella Radley, Hester Rowan), b. 18 Nov 1928, Cogenhoe, Northamptonshire, England. Writer. Education: BA, University of London. Publications: Death and The Maiden, 1978; The Chief Inspector's Daughter, 1981; A Talent for Destruction, 1982; Blood on The Happy Highway, 1983; Fate Worse Than Death, 1985. Literary Agent: Curtis Brown. Address: c/o Curtis Brown, 162-168 Regent Street, London, W1R 5TB, England.

ROBINSON Spider, b. 1948, American. Literary Appointments: Realty Editor, Long Island Commercial Review, Syosset, NY, 1972-73; Freelance Writer, 1973-; Book Reviewer, Galaxy Magazine, 1975-77. Publications: Telempath, 1976; Callahan's Crossing Saloon, 1977; Stardance (with Jeanne Robinson), 1979; Antinomy, 1980; Time Travelers Strictly Cash, 1981; Mindkiller, 1982; Melancholy Elephants, 1984; Night of Power, 1985; Callahan's Secre, 1986; Time Pressure, Callahan and Company, 1987; Lady Slings The Booze Off The Wall at Callahan's, 1994.

ROCHARD Henri. See: **CHARLIER Roger Henri.**

ROCHE Billy (William Michael), b. 11 Jan 1949, Wexford, Ireland. Playwright. Education: Christian Brothers Secondary School, 1966. Appointments include: Singer with The Roach Band, 1975-80; Playwright-in-residence at The Bush Theatre, London, 1988. Publications: A Handful of Stars, 1987 (in London, 1988); Amphibians, 1987; Poor Beast in the Rain, 1989; Belfry, 1991; The Cavalcaders,

1993-94 (plays produced in Wexford, Dublin and London); Novel: Tumbling Down, 1986. Honours include: London Theatre Fringe Award, 1992; Time Out Award, 1992. Address: c/o Leah Schmidt, Curtis Brown Group, 162-68 Regent Street, London W1R 5TB, England.

ROCHE George Charles III, b. 16 May 1935, Denver, CO, USA. College President. m. June Bernard, 2 s, 2 d. Education: BS, Regis College, CO, 1956; MA 1961, PhD 1965, University of Colorado. Publications: The Bewildered Society, 1972; Going Home, 1986; A World Without Heroes: A Modern Tragedy, 1987; A Reason for Living, 1989; One by One, 1990. Contributions to: Columns in several newspapers; Human Events - The American Spectator. Honour: Freedom Leadership Award, Freedoms Foundation, 1972. Memberships: Mont Pelerin Society; The Philadelphia Society; American Association of Presidents of Independent Colleges and Universities. Address: Hillsdale College, Hillsdale, MI 49242, USA.

ROCHE Paul, b. 1928, British. Literary Appointments: Instructor, Smith College, Northampton, MA, 1957-59; Poet-in-Residence, California Institute of The Arts, Valencia, 1972-74. Publications: The Rat and The Convent Dove and Other Tales and Fables, 1952; O Pale Galilean, 1954; The Oedipus Plays of Sophocles (translation), 1958; The Rank Obstinacy of Things: A Selection of Poems, Vessel of Dishonour, 1962; The Orestes Plays of Aeschylus, 1963; Prometheus Bound, by Aeschylus (translation), 1964; 22 November 1963 (The Catherisis of Anguish), 1965; Ode to The Dissolution of Morality, All Things Considered: Poems (in USA as All Things Considered and Other Poems), The Love-Songs of Sappho (translation), 1966; To Tell The Truth: Poems, Te Deum for J Alfred Prufrock, Oedipus The King, 1967; 3 Plays of Plautus (translation), 1968; Philoctetes lines 676-729 by Sophocles (translation), Lament for Erica: A Poem, 1971; Three Plays of Euripides: Alcestis Medea The Bachhae (translation), Enigma Variations and..., The Kiss, 1974; New Tales from Aesop for Reading Aloud, With Duncan Grant in Southern Turkey, 1982.

ROCKWELL John (Sargent), b. 16 Sep 1940, WA, USA. Education: BA, Harvard University, 1962; Graduate Study, University of Munich, 1962-63; MA 1964, PhD 1972, University of California. Appointments: Music Critic and Writer. Worked in radio and on television on opera programmes and various freelance jobs for stations such as, WHRB-Radio, Cambridge, MA, KPFA-Radio, Berkeley, CA and KPED-TV, San Francisco, CA, 1965-69; West Coast Correspondent, Opera News, NY, 1968-72; Music and Dance Critic, Tribune, Oakland, CA, 1969; Assistant Music and Dance Critic, Los Angeles Times, Los Angeles, CA, 1970-72; Freelance Music Critic, 1972-74, Staff Music Critic, 1974-, New York Times, NY; Lecturer in cultural history at Princeton University, 1977-79; Lecturer in Music at Brooklyn College of The City University of New York, 1980. Publications: Contributor, Jim Miller (editor) The Rolling Stone Illustrated History of Rock and Roll, 1976; Robert Wilson: A Theater of Images (with Robert Stearns), 1980; All American Music: Composition in The Late Twentieth Century, 1983; Sinatra: An American Classic, 1984; Contributor, editorial adviser, Stanley Sadie and H Wiley Hitchcock, editors, New Grove Dictionary of American Music, 1986. Contributions to: Other volumes and to periodicals. Honours: German academic Exchange Fellowship, 1962-63; Woodrow Wilson Fellowship, 1963-64; All American Music: Composition in The Late Twentieth Century, nominated for 1983 National Book Critics Circle Award. Memberships: Music Critics Association, Treasurer, 1977-81; Phi Beta Kappa. Literary Agent: Robert Cornfield, 145 West 79th Street, New York, NY 10024, USA. Address: New York Times, 229 West 43rd Street, New York, NY 10036, USA.

RODDY Lee, b. 22 Aug 1921, Marion County, IL, USA. Author; Lecturer. m. Cicely Price, 17 Oct 1947, 1 s, 1 d. Education: Graduated, Oakdale High School, Oakdale, CA, 1940; AA, Los Angeles City College, CA, 1945. Publications: The Life and Times of Grizzly Adams (ghosted), 1977, became an NBC-TV prime time television series; The Lincoln Conspiracy (ghosted), 1977, made the New York Times best-seller list, and was also a motion picture; Jesus, 1979, became a film, now available in 200 languages worldwide; Ghost Dog of Stoney Ridge, 1985; Dooger, Grass hopper Hound, 1985; The City Bear's Adventures, 1985; The Hair-Pulling Bear Dog, 1985; Secret of The Shark Pit, 1988; Secret of The Sunken Sub, 1990; The Overland Escape, 1989; The Desperate Search, 1989; Danger on Thunder Mountain, 1990; Secret of The Howling Cave, 1990; The Flaming Trap, 1990; Mystery of The Phantom Gold, 1991; The Gold Train Bandits, 1992; Giants on The Hill, in progress; Ladd Family Adventures, in progress. Honours: 29 of Lee Roddy's nearly 60 books, all published

since 1974, have been best-sellers, award winners, book club selections, made into movies or television programmes; Recognised as one of 15 distinguished alumni in the 100 year history of Oakdale High School, 1992. Memberships: Authors League; Authors Guild of America; National Society of Children's Book Writers; Northern California Chapter, Society of Children's Book Writers. Literary Agent: S Rickley Christian, President of Alive Communications, Colorado Springs, CO, USA. Address: PO Box 700, Penn Valley, CA 95946, USA.

RODEFER Stephen (Jean Calais), b. 20 Nov 1940, Bellaire, OH, USA. Writer; Lecturer. 3 s. Education: BA, Amherst College, 1959-63; MA, State University of New York, Buffalo, 1963-67; MA, San Francisco State University, 1980-81. Literary Appointments: Teaching Fellow, 1963-66, Instructor, 1966-67, State University of New York, Buffalo; Assistant Professor, Co-Director of Writing Programme, University of New Mexico, 1967-71; Editor, Duende Press, Placitas, NM, 1972-75; Language Arts Specialist, Berkeley Unified School District, CA, 1976-81; Lecturer, San Francisco State University, CA, 1981-85; Curator, Archive for New Poetry, 1985-87, Lecturer in Poetry, 1985-89, University of California, San Diego; Lecturer, University of California, Berkeley, 1990-. Publications: The Knife, 1965; Villon (as Jean Calais), 1976; One or Two Love Poems From The White World, 1976; The Bell Clerk's Tears Keep Flowing, 1978; Plane Debris, 1981; Four Lectures, 1982; Oriflamme Day (co-author Benjamin Friedlander), 1984; Safety (translations of Sappho and The Greek Anthology), 1985; Emergency Measures, 1987. Contributions to: Sulfur; Conjunctions; Temblor; Oblek; Writing; This; Sur. Honours: Faculty Fellowship for Poetry, Research Foundation, State University of New York, Buffalo, 1967; Co-winner, Annual Book Award for Four Lectures, American Poetry Centre, San Francisco, 1983; Public Arts Council Grant, 1987; Fund for Poetry Award, NY, 1988. Memberships: American Literary Translators Association; American Association of University Professors; Poets Theatre. Address: 6434 Raymond Street, Oakland, CA 94611, USA.

RODGERS Carolyn M, American. Appointments: Former Midwest Editor, Black Dialogue, New York City; Editor, Founder, Poetry Newsletter, Rare Form, 1st issue winter 1994-95. Publications: Paper Soul, 1968; Two Love Raps, Songs of a Blackbird, Now Ain't That Love, 1969; For H W Fuller, 1970; Long Rap/Commonly Known as a Poetic Essay, 1971; How I Got Ovah: New and Selected Poems, 1975; The Heart as Ever Green, 1978; Translation, 1980; Eden and Other Poems, 1983; A Little Lower Than 'the Angels, 1984; Morning Glory, 1989; We're Only Human, 1994. Contributions to: The Black Scholar; Nation; Caprice; Essence; Ebony; Nommo. Honours: Society of Midland Authors Award; National Endowment of The Arts Award; National Book Award Nominee. Address: 12750 South Sangamon, Chicago, IL 60643, USA.

RODGERS Daniel Tracy, b. 29 Sept 1942, Darby, Pennsylvania, USA. Professor of History. m. Irene Wylie Rodgers, Dec 1971, 2 sons. Education: AB-BSc in Engineering, Brown University, 1965; PhD History, Yale University, 1973. Publications: The Work Ethic in Industrial America 1850-1920, 1978; Contested Truths: Keywords in American Politics since Independence, 1987. Contributions include: Reviews in American History; Journal of American History. Honours: Frederick Jackson Turner Award of the Organization of American Historians, 1978. Address: Department of History, Princeton University, Princeton, NJ 08544, USA.

RODRIGUES Santan Rosario, b. 23 Sep 1948, Goa. Public Relations Expert. m. Patricia Rodriguez, 23 Sep 1983. Education: MA, English Literature, Bombay university, India. Appointments: Fouder, Editor, Kavi India Poetry quarterly, 1976-83; Poetry Editor, imprint, 1877-78; Poetry Editor, Gomanta Times, 1989-90. Publications: I Exist, 1976; 3 Poets, 1978; The Householder Yogi, 1982; Poems in: New Poetry by Indian Men; Indian English Poetry since 1950; Goan Literature. Contributions to: Illustrated Weekly of India; Journal of Indian Writing in English; Times of India; Gentleman; Debonair. Honours: Travel Grant, Sahiya Akademi, 1976-77. Memberships: India PEN; The Asiatic Society; Bombay English Association; Vice President, Association of Business Communicators of India. Address: 7 Gautam Apts, 45-624 Kastur Park, Shimpoli Road, Borivali (W) Bombay 400092, India.

RODRIGUEZ Judith, b. 13 Feb 1936, Perth, Western Australia. Lecturer; Poet. m. Thomas Shapcott, 1982. Education: University of Queensland; MA, Girton College, Cambridge, 1965; Certificate

Education, University of London, 1968. Appointments include: Lecturer, Colleges & Universities in London, West Indies, Australia; Lecturer, Victoria College, 1989-92; Senior Lecturer, Deakin University, 1993-. Publications: Nu-Plastik Fanfare Red and Other Poems, 1973; Water Life, 1976; Shadow on Glass, 1978; Arapede, 1979; Mudcrab at Gambaros, 1980; Witch Heart, 1982; Floridian Poems, 1986; New & Selected Poems, 1988; The Cold, 1992; Poor Johanna (play, written with Robyn Archer, produced Adelaide 1994; published in Heroines 1991); Lindy (Libretto, commissioned by Australian Opera), 1994; Editor, Mrs Noah and the Minoan Queen, 1983; Co Editor, Poems from the Australians 20th Anniversary Competition, 1985; Editor, Collected Poems of Jennifer Rankin, 1990. Honours include: AM (Member, Order of Australia), 1994; Australian Council Fellowships. Address: PO Box 231, Mont Albert, Vic 3127, Australia.

RODWAY Anne. See: **BRENNAN Patricia Winifred.**

ROECKER William Alan, b. 17 Jan 1942, Madison, Wisconsin, USA. Writer. m. Debbie Sue Huntsman, 31 Dec 1985. Education: BS, 1966, MFA, 1967, University of Oregon. Appointments: Assistant Editor, Northwest Review, 1967; Instructor, Associate Professor, English, University of Arizona, 1968-74; Editor, Windsport Magazine, 1981-82; Saltwater Editor, Today's Fishermen, 1985; Associate Editor, South Coast Sportfishing, 1987; Senior Editor, South Coast Sportfishing, 1988; Senior Managing Editor, California Angler Magazine, 1992; Saltwater Editor, Fishing & Hunting News, 1993. Publications: Willamette, poems, 1970; Stories that Count, 1971; You Know Me, poems, 1972; Closer to the Country, poems, 1976; Standup Fishing: Saltwater Methods, Tackle & Techniques, 1990. Contributions to: Numerous journals & magazines. Honours include: Haycox Award, 1966; Neubergr Award, 1967; Runner Up, Yale Younger Poets, 1971; NEA Award, 1973; Gray Prize, Hang Gliding Journalism, 1984. Memberships: Outdoor Writers Association of America; Outdoor Writers Association of California. Address: PO Box 586071, Oceanside, CA 92058, USA.

ROEHRS Herma Erika, b. 11 Apr 1922, Bethany, Tanunda, South Australia, Australia. Retired Secondary School Principal. Education: BA, 1945, DipEd, 1953, Adelaide University. Publications: Loose Leaves: Reminiscences of a Pioneer North Queensland Missionary 1988, (Translated German works of W G F Poland). Contribution to: Lutheran Almanac: Yearbook of the United Evangelical Lutheran Church in Australia, 1964. Literary Agent: Openbook Publishers, Box 1368, GPO Adelaide, South Australia 5001, Australia. Address: 11 Wellington St, Glandore, South Australia 5037, Australia.

ROGERS Floyd. See: **SPENCE William John Duncan.**

ROGERS Ingrid, b. 3 May 1951, Rinteln, Germany. Pastor; Teacher; Writer. m. H Kendall Rogers, 9 Jun 1972, 1 s, 1 d. Education: DUEL, Sorbonne Nouvelle, Paris, France, 1971; Oxford University, England, 1972-73; Staatsexamen, 1974, PhD 1976, Philipps University, Marburg; Doctor of Ministry Degree, Bethany Theological Seminary, 1988. Publications: Tennessee Williams: A Moralist's Answer to The Perils of Life, 1976; Peace Be Unto You, 1983; Swords into Plowshares, 1983; In Search of Refuge, 1984; Glimpses of Clima, 1989. Honours: Christopher Book Award, 1985; Angel Award of Excellence, 1985, for In Search of Refuge; Fellowships from The Evangelische Studienwerk Villigst, 1971-74, 1974-76. Address: Manchester College, Box 64, N Manchester, IN 46962, USA.

ROGERS Jane Rosalind, b. 21 Jul 1952, London, England. Novelist. 1 s, 1 d. Education: BA Hons, English Literature, New Hall, Cambridge, 1974; Post-graduate Certificate of Education; Leicester University, 1976. Literary Appointments: Writer-in Residence, Northern College, Barnsley, South Yorkshire, 1985-86; Writer-in Residence, Sheffield Polytechnic, 1987088; Judith E Wilson Fellow, Cambridge, 1991. Publications: Separate Tracks, 1983, 1984; Her Living Image, 1984, 1986; The Ice is Singing, 1987; Mr Wroe's Virgins, 1991; Promised Lands, 1995; Screenplay: Dawn and the Candidate, 1989; BBC Serial of Mr Wroe's Virgins, 1993. Contributions to: Various Magazines. Honours: North West Arts Writers Bursary, 1985; Somerset Maughn Award for Her Living image, 1985; Samuel Beckett Award, 1990, for Dawn and the Candidate, Fellow of the Royal Society of Literature, 1994. Memberships: Society of Authors. Literary Agent: Pat Kavanagh, The Peter Faser & Dunlop Group Ltd. Address: c/o Pat Kavanagh, The Peter Fraser & Dunlop Group Ltd, 5th Floor, The Chambers, Chelsea Harbour, Lots Road, London SW10 OXF, Engalnd.

ROGERS Linda, b. 10 Oct 1944, Port Alice, Canada. Poet; Teacher. m. Ken Rogers, 11 Jun 1966, 3 s. Education: MA, English Literature, University of British Columbia. Literary Appointments: University of British Columbia, 1970-71; Writers Workshops, National Poets Festival, 1983-84; Creative Writing Design, University of Victoria, 1986-. Publications: Queens of The Next Hot Stars, 1981; I Like to Make a Mess, 1985; I Think I am Ugly, 1985; Witness, 1985; Setting the Hook, 1986; Singing Rib, 1987; Worm Sandwich, 1989; Woman at Mile O, 1990; Children's Magic Flute, 1990; Anthology of BC Poets in French, 1990. Contributions to: Editor, Poetry Canada Review; Canadian Literature; Malahat Review; Vancouver Sun; Monday Magazine. Honours: Pat Lowther, runner-up, 1982; Cross Canada Writers Poetry Prize, 1986; Seattle Arts Council Poetry Prize, 1987; BC Writers Poetry Prize, 1988; Aya Press Poetry Prize, 1989. Memberships: League of Canadian Poets; Writers Union of Canada; PEN; Director, Pacific Opera Association; Vice-President, Federation of BC Writers. Address: 228 Douglas Street, Victoria, British Columbia, Canada.

ROGERS Michael Alan, b. 29 Nov 1950, Santa Monica, California, USA. Novelist; Journalist. Education: BA, Creative Writing, Stanford University, 1972. Appointments: Associate Editor, Rolling Stone, 1972-76; Editor-at-Large, Outside, 1976-78; Visiting Lecturer in Fiction, University of California, 1981-82; Senior Writer, Newsweek, 1983-. Publications: Mindfogger, 1973; Do Not Worry about the Bear, 1978; Biohazard, 1979; Silicon Valley, 1983; Forbidden Sequence, 1989. Contributions to: Esquire; Rolling Stone; Newsweek; Playboy; Look; Outside; Many others. Honours: Distinguished Science Writing Award, American Association for the Advancement of Science, 1974; Computer Press Association, 1987; Software Publishers Association, 1991. Memberships: Authors Guild. Literary Agent: Gail Hochman, Brandt and Brandt, New York, USA. Address: c/o Newsweek, 388 Market St, Suite 1650, San Francisco, CA 94111, USA.

ROGERS Pat, b. 1938, British. Literary Appointments: Fellow, Sidney Sussex College, Cambridge, 1964-69; Lecturer, King's College, University of London, 1969-73; Professor of English, University College of North Wales, Bangor, 1973-76, University of Bristol, 1977-86; DeBartolo Professor, Liberal Arts, University of South Florida, Tampa, 1986-. Publications: Editor, A Tour Through Great Britain, by Daniel Defoe, 1971; Grub Street: Studies on a Sub-culture, 1972, revised edition as Hacks and Dunces, 1980; Defoe: Editor, The Critical Heritage, 1972; The Augustan Vision: An Introduction to Pope, 1976; Editor, The Eighteenth Century, 1978; Henry Fielding: A Biography, Robinson Crusoe, 1979; Editor, Swift: Complete Poems, Literature and Popular Culture in the Eighteenth Century, 1983; Eighteenth-Century Encounters, 1985; Editor, The Oxford Illustrated History of English Literature, 1987; The Economy of Arts in The 18th Century, 1989; An Outline of English Literature, 1992; Essays on Pope, 1993; Johnson and Boswell in Scotland, 1993. Address: Department of English, University of South Florida, Tampa, FL 33620, USA.

ROGERS Rosemary (Marina Mayson), b. 7 Dec 1932, Sri Lanka. Writer. m. (1) Summa Navaratnam, 16 Jan 1953 (div), 2 s, 2 d, (2) Leroy Rogers, 1957 (div 1964), (3) Christopher M Kadison, 1984. Education: BA, English, 1952. Publications: Sweet Savage Love, 1974; Wildest Heart, 1974; Dark Fires, 1975; Wicked Loving Lies, 1976; The Crowd Pleasers, 1978; The Insiders, 1979; Lost Love, Last Love, 1980; Love Play, 1981; Surrender to Love, 1982; The Wanton, 1984; Bound by Desire, 1988. Contributions to: Star Magazine; Good Housekeeping. Memberships: Writers Guild of America; Authors Guild. Literary Agent: Morton Janklow and Associates Inc. Address: 300 East 56th Street, Apt 27J, New York, NY 10022, USA.

ROGERS Samuel Shepard (Sam Shepard), b. 5th Nov 1943, Fort Sheridan, IL, USA. Actor. (1) O-Lan Johnson, 9 Nov 1969 (div), 1 s, (2) now domestic partner, Jessica Lange, 1 s, 1 d. Education: Mount Antonio Junior College. Publications: Five Plays: Chicago; Icarus's Mother; Red Cross; Fourteen Hundred Thousand; Melodrama Play, 1967; La Turista, 1968; Operation Sidewinder, 1970; The Unseen Hand and Other Plays, Mad Dog Blues and Other Plays, 1971; Hawk Moon, 1973; The Tooth of Crime and Geography of a Horse Dreamer, 1974; Action and The Unseen Hand, 1975; Angel City and Other Plays, 1976; Rolling Thunder Logbook, 1977; Buried Child and Other Plays, 1979, in UK as Buried Child and Seduced and Suicide in B Flat, 1980; Four One-Act-Plays, 1980; True West, Seven Plays, 1981; Motel Chronicles, 1982; Fool for Love and Other Plays, Paris Texas, 1984; A Lie of The Mind, 1985; Curse of The Starving Class, 1990; Seduced, 1990; States of Shock, 1992; Simpatico, 1994. Honours include: Obie Awards, 1966,

1967, 1968, 1973, 1975, 1977, 1979, 1984; National Institute and American Academy Award for Literature, 1974; Pulitzer Prize, 1979; New York Drama Critics Circle Award, 1986. Membership: American Academy and Institute of Arts and Letters. Address: c/o Loris Berman, Little Theatre Building, 240 West 44th Street, New York, NY 10036, USA.

ROGGEMAN William Maurits, b. 9 Jul 1935, Brussels, Belgium. Journalist. m. 8 Jan 1975, 1 son, 1 daughter. Education: Economic Sciences, University of Ghent. Publications: Poetry; Rhapsody in Blue, 1958; Baudelaire Verliefd, 1964; Memoires, 1985; Een Leegte die Verdwijnt, 1985; Al Wie Omkijkt is Gezien, 1988; De Uitvinding van de Tederheid, 1994; novels: De Centauren, 1963; De Verbeelding, 1966; De belegering van een Luchtkasteel, 1990; essays: Cesare Pavese, 1961; Beroepsgeheim, 1975. Contributions to: De Vlaamse Gids; Nieuw Vlaams Tijdschrift; Avenue; De Gids. Honours: Dirk Martensprize, 1963; Louis Paul Boon Prize, 1974; Prize, City of Brussels, 1975. Memberships: Vereniging van Vlaamse Letterkundigen; Secretary, Flemish PEN Centre. Address: Luchtlaan 4, 1700 Dilbeek, Belgium.

ROHEN Edward, (Bruton Connors), b. 10 Feb 1931, Dowlais, South Wales. Writer. m. Elizabeth Mary Jarrett, 4 Apr 1961, 1 d. Education: ATD, Cardiff College of Art, 1952. Appointments: served with UN in Korea, 1952-54; Permanently Commissioned Contributor, Twentieth Century Magazine, 1966-68. Publications: Nightpriest, 1965; Poems/Poemas, 1976; A Hundred and One Seppuku for Maria, 1987; Sonnets for Maria Marriage, 1988; Sonnets Second Sequence for Maria, 1989; Bruised Concourse, 1973; Scorpio Broadside 15, 1975. Contributions to: Poetry anthologies; Poetry Wales; Anglo Welsh Review; Tribune; Irish Press; Mabon; Argot and Edge; Little Word Machine; Second Aeon; Carcanet; Poetry Nippon; Riverside Quarterly; Littack; Wormwood Review. Memberships: The Welsh Academy; Ex Member, Poets Society of Japan; Academician of Centro Cultural Literario e Artistico de o Jornal de Felgeiras, Portugal; Korean War Veterans Club and Society. Address: 57 Kinfauns Road, Goodmayes, Ilford, Essex IG3 9QH, England.

ROHRBACH Peter Thomas (James Cody), b. 27 Feb 1926, New York City, USA. Writer. m. Sheila Sheehan, 21 Sept 1970, 1 daughter. Education: BA, MA, Catholic University of America. Publications: 17 books including: Conversation with Christ, 1981; Stagecoach East, 1983; American Issue, 1985; The Largest Event: World War II, 1993; National Issue, 1994. Contributions to: Time-Life; Washington Star; America; Aviation News; PAMA News; AIA Journal; Various encyclopaedias. Memberships: Authors Guild of America; Poets, Playwrights, Editors, Essayists & Novelists; Washington Independent Writers. Address: 9609 Barkston Court, MD 20850, USA.

ROLAND Alex, b. 7 Apr 1944, Providence, Rhode Island, USA. Historian. m. 31 June 1979, 3 sons. Education: BS, US Naval Academy, 1966; MA, University of Hawaii, 1970; PhD, Duke University, 1974. Publications: Model Research: The National Advisory Committee for Aeronautics, 1985; Men in Arms: A History of Warfare and its Interrelationships with Western Society, 1991; Underwater Warfare in the Age of Sail, 1978; Men in Arms: A History of Warfare and its Interrelationships with Western Society (5th ed), 1991. Memberships: Society of Military History; Society for the History of Technology; History of Science Society. Address: Department of History, Duke University, Durham, NC 27708, USA.

ROLICKI Janusz Andrzej, b. 22 Oct 1938, Wilno, Poland. Journalist; Writer. m. Ewa Stasko, 11 Jul 1976, 1 d. Education: MA, Warsaw University, 1962. Literary Appointments: Staff, Polityka, 1961-67; Staff, Kultura, 1967-74. Publications: Bralem lapowki, 1966; Z syciem pod pache, 1968; Przodem do przodu, 1972; Kockana mamo wyroh mi alibi, 1976; Nie tylko bralem, 1978; Dygnitarz, 1982; adaptations for films and television. Contributions to: Numerous magazines and journals. Honours: Boleslaw Prus Award, 1977; Drozdze Award, 1978. Membership: Union of Polish Writers. Address: Warszawa Dzika 6m 74, 00-172, Warsaw, Poland.

ROLLS Eric Charles, b. 25 Apr 1923, Grenfell, New South Wales, Austalia. Author; Farmer. m. (1) Joan Stephenson, 27 Feb 1954, (dec 1985) 2 s, 1 d, (2) Elaine van Kempen, 1988. Publications: Sheaf Tosser, 1967; They All Ran Wild, 1969; Running Wild, 1973; The River, 1974; The Green Mosaic, 1977; Miss Strawberry Verses, 1978; A Million Wild Acres, 1981; Celebration of the Senses, 1984; Doorways: A Year of the Cumberdeen Diaries, 1989; Selected Poetry,

1990; Sojurners: Flowers and the Wide Sea, 1992; From Forest to Sea, 1993. Contributions to: The Bulletin; Overland; National Times; The Age; Sydney Morning Herald; various others. Honours include: David Myer Trust Award for Poetry, 1968; Captain Cook Bicentennial Award for Non-Fiction, 1970; John Franklin Award for Children's Book, 1974; Braille Book of the Year, 1975; The Age Book of the Year, 1981; Talking Book of the Year, 1982; Fellow, Australian Academy of the Humanities, 1985; Australian Creative Fellow, 1991; Member of the Order of Australia, 1991. Memberships: Australian Society of Authors: National Book Council. Literary Agent: Anthony A Williams. Address: Anthony A Williams Management Pty Ltd, First Floor, 50 Oxford Street, Paddington, NSW 2021, Australia.

ROLOFF Michael, b. 19 Dec 1937, Berlin, Germany, US Citizen 1952-. Playwright. Education: BA, Haverford College, USA, 1958; MA, Stanford University, 1960. Literary Appointments include: Editor, Farrar, Straus and Giroux, NY, 1966-70; Staff, Lantz-Donadio Literary Agency, 1970-72; Senior Editor, Continuum Books, 1972-75; Publicity Manager, Urizen Books, 1975-81. Publications: Screenplays: Feelings, 1982; Darlings and Monsters, 1983; Graduation Party, 1984; Plays: Wolves of Wyoming, 1985; Palombe Blue, 1985; Schizzohawk, 1986; Poetry: Headshots, 1984; It Won't Grow Back, 1985; Fiction: Darlings and Monsters Quartet, 4 titles, 1986-; numerous translations from German. Memberships: Executive Committee, 1977-81, PEN. Literary Agent: Rosica Colin Limited. Address: Box 6754, Malibu, California 90264, USA.

ROMAINE-DAVIS Ada, b. 7 June 1929, Cumberland, MAryland, USA. Nurse Educator; Medical Historian. m. John F Davis, 1 Aug 1953, 2 sons, 1 daughter. Education: Diploma, Kings County Hospital School of Nursing, Brooklyn, New York; BS, MS, PhD, University of Maryland, Baltimore and College Park; MD, College Park; Post-doctoral Studies, History of Science & Technology/Medicine, University of Maryland; Certified Adult Nurse Practitioner, American Nurses Certification Center. Appointments: Associate Professor, Johns Hopkins University School of Nursing, Baltimore. Publications: John Gibbon and His Heart-Lung Machine, 1992; Home Health Care: An Annotated Bibliography, 1992; Home Health Care: Brief Bibliography, 1994; Editor, Encyclopedia of Home Care for the Elderly, 1995. Contributions to: American Journal of Nursing; Health Care Trends & Transitions; Nurse Practitioner; Journal of the Academy of Nurse Practitioners. Honours: Honorable Mention, American Medical Writers Association, 1993. Memberships: American Historical Association; Society for the History of Medicine; National Organization of Nurse Practitioner Faculties; American Academy of Nurse Practitioners; Sigma Theta Tau. Address: 6400 Wilmett Road, Bethesda, MD 20817, USA. 6. 30.

ROMBOTIS Anastasios, (Tasos Korfis), b. 12 Oct 1929, Corfu, Greece. Vice-Admiral (retired). m. Helen Moniakis, 5 Feb 1959, 1 son, 1 daughter. Education: Various professional schools and academies, Hellenic War Navy, Greece and in USA; NATO Defence College, Rome, 1971-72. Appointments: Director, Prosperos book publishers, 1973-; Director, Anacyclisis literary magazine, 1985-90. Publications: Poetry: Diary 1, 1963; Diary 2, 1964; Diary 3, 1968; Diarios, 1971; Handiwork, 1977; Poems, collection, 1983; Pafsilipa, 1987; 153 Graffiti, 1992; Prose: Journey without Polar Star, 1953; A Desert House, 1973, 1978; Knowledge of the Father, 1984; Essays: The Poet Romos Filyras, 1974, 1992; The Poet Nikos Kavadias, 1978, 1991; Glances at the Poets 1920-1940, 1978; Deposits in short terms, 1982; The Poet Napoleon Lapathiotis, 1985; Glances at the literature 1920-1940, 1991; Translations: Lustra (Ezra Pound), 1977; Poems (William Carlos Williams), 1979, 1989; Poems (Ezra Pound), 1981, 1987; Coexistences, 1982; The Writer Stratis Doukas 1895-1936, biography, 1988. Contributions to: Frequently to Diagenios, 1958-80; Numerous poems, prose pieces, essays to notable magazines, Athens and other cities. Honours: 1st Efstathiou Award for Journey without Pole Star, The Cyprian Petters, 1952; 1st Award for The poet Nikos Kavadias, Ministry of Shipping, 1973; 2nd State Prose Award for Knowledge of the Fathers, 1984. Memberships: Society of Writers. Address: Alkiviadou 9, 10439 Athens, Greece.

ROME Anthony. See: **ALBERT Marvin H.**

ROME Tony. See: **ALBERT Marvin H.**

ROMER Stephen Charles Mark, b. 20 Aug 1957, Bishops Stortford, Hertfordshire, England. University Lecturer. m. Bridget Strevens, 17 Jul 1982, 1 s. Education: Radley College, 1970-74; Trinity Hall, Cambridge, English Tripos: Double First, 1975-78; Harvard

University, 1978-79; British Institute, Paris, 1980-81; PhD Cantab, May 1985. Publications: The Growing Dark, 1981; Firebird 3, 1985; Idols, 1986; Plato's Ladder, 1992. Contributions to: TLS; PN Review; Cambridge Quarterly; Poetry Review; New Statesman; Poetry Book Society Anthology, 1986, 1992; Stand, Oxford Poetry. Honour: Gregory Award for Poetry, 1985. Address: 6 rue de Verneuil, 75007 Paris, France.

ROMERIL John, b. 26 Oct 1945, Melbourne, Victoria, Australia. Playwright. Education: BA, Monash University, Clayton, 1970. Appointments include: Writer in residence with various Australian groups and at the National University, Singapore, 1974-87. Publications: A Nameless Concern, 1968; The Litchen Table, 1968; The Man from Chicago, 1969; In a Place Like Somewhere Else, 1969; Chicago Chicago, 1970; Marvellous Melbourne, 1970; Dr Karl's Kure, 1970; Whatever Happened to Realism, 1971; Rearguard Action, 1971; Hackett Gets Ahead, 1972; Bastardy, 1972; Waltzing Matilda, 1974; The Floating World, 1974; The Golden Holden Show, 1975; The Accidental Poke, 1977; Mickey's Moomba, 1979; Centenary Dance, 1984; The Kelly Dance, 1984; Definitely Not the Last, 1985; Koori Radio, 1987; Top End, and History of Australia (co-author), 1989; Lost Weekend, 1989; Black Cargo, 1991; The Reading Boy, 1991; Working Out, 1991; Television plays. Honours include: Victorian Government Drama Fellowship, 1988. Address: Almost Managing, PO Box 1034, Carlton, Victoria 3053, Australia.

ROMEU Jorge Luis (Beltran de Quiros), b. 10 Dec 1945, Havana, Cuba. Educator; Writer. m. Zoila Barreiro, 25 July 1970, 3 sons. Education: Diplomas: Language, 1964, Literature, 1966, Teaching, 1970, Alliance Francaise de La Havane; Licenciado en Matematicas, University of Havana, 1973; MS, 1981, MPh, 1987, PhD, 1990, Syracuse University, USA. Appointments: Editor, Club Las Palmas Newsletter; Member, Collaborators Group, El Vecino, Rochester, New York; Member, Collaborators Group, AIC Newsletter, Miami, Florida; Monthly Column, Syracuse Post Standard; Radio Commentator, WAER-FM, Syracuse University Public Radio Station; Associate Professor of Statistics, State University of New York, Cortland. Publications: Los Unos, Los Otros y El Seibo, 1971; La Otra Cara de la Moneda, 1984; Thinking of Cuba, collection of 28 published Oped pieces on Castro's dictatorship and Latin American problems, 1992. Contributions to: Over 20 technical articles to statistics and engineering journals, USA, UK, Spain, Cuba; Over 100 articles, 1988-, to Herald-American; El Nuevo Herald; The Post Standard; The Press; Cortland Standard; El Vecino; Diario Montanes; Correo Gallego. Address: PO Box 6134, Syracuse, NY 13217, USA.

ROMTVEDT David William, b. 7 Jun 1950, Oregon, USA. Writer. m. Margo Brown, 30 May 1987. Education: BA, Reed College, 1972. Literary Appointment: State Literature Consultant, WY, 1987. Publications: Free and Compulsory for All, 1984; Moon, 1984; Letters from Mexico, 1987; Black Beauty and Kiev The Ukraine, 1987; Crossing The River, Poets of The Western US, 1987; How Many Horses, 1988; A Flower Whose Name I Do Not Know, 1992; Crossing Wyoming, 1992. Contributions to: Paris Review; Canadian Forum; American Poetry Review; Poets and Writers Magazine. Honours: NEA Residency Award, 1979; NEA Fellowship, Poetry, 1987; Pushcart Prize, 1991; National Poetry Series Award, 1991. Address: 457 N Main, Buffalo, WY 82834, USA.

ROMVARY Susan, b. 20 Aug 1925, Miskolc, Hungary. Bookkeeper; Controller. m. John Romvary, 22 Nov 1947, 1 son. Education: Pazmany Peter University, Budapest, Hungary, 1947-49; Thomas More Institute, Montreal, 1973; Concordia University, 1975. Publications: Zsuzsa not Zsazsa - Balance with a smile, 1992. Contributions to: Anthologies: New Canadian Review, 1987-89, Mozaik, 1993; Articles in Literary Journals: London, Montreal, Toronto, New York. Honours: 1st Prize, Canadian Authors Association, 1987, 1988; 1st Prize, Hungarian Literary Association, 1988. Memberships: Vice President, Canadian Authors Association; Vice President, Hungarian Authors Association. Editor: Mrs Judith Isherwood. Address: 4000 De Maisonneuve West, Westmount, Quebec, H3Z 1J9, Canada.

RONAY Egon, b. Pozsony, Hungary. Publisher; Journalist. m. Barbara Greenslade, 1967, 1 s, (2 d by previous marriage). Education: LLD, University of Budapest; Academy of Commerce, Budapest. Appointments: Trained in kitchens of family firm and abroad; managed 5 restaurants in family firm; emigrated from Hungary, 1946; General Manager 3 London restaurants, opened The Marquee 1952-55; columnist, food, wine, eating-out and tourism, Daily Telegraph, Sunday Telegraph, 1954-60; weekly column, The Evening News, 1968-74; Food Columnist, The Sunday Times 1986-91. Publications: Egon Ronay's Guide to Hotels and Restaurants, annually 1956-, Egon Ronay's Just a Bite, annually 1979-85, Egon Ronay's Pub Guide, annually 1980-85, Egon Ronay's Guide to 500 Good Restaurants in Europe's main Cities, annually, 1983-85, sold out the Guides in 1987; The Unforgettable Dishes of My Life, 1989; various other tourist guides to Britain, to ski resorts in Europe, to Scandinavian Hotels and Restaurants, and to eating places in Greece. Memberships: Academie des Gastronomes, France, 1979; Founder, President, The British Academy of Gastronomes, 1983-; Founding Vice President, International Academy of Gastronomy, 1987-. Address: 37 Walton Street, London SW3 2HT, England.

RONDINI Adele, b. 30 Jan 1921, Italy. Headmaster, Secondary School, retired. m. 1 Dec 1951, 2 s. Education: Degree in Arts; Postgraduate Qualifications in Arts and French. Appointments: Various positions, 1965-. Publications: Fosombron Sparita, 1969; Fosombron Spareta, 1970; Le Journal De Jean Pierre; Rimpianto a Due Voci, 1972; Editor, La tombola Di Papa (Latino), 1983. Contributions to: Various magazines and journals. Honours: Picchio d'Argento delle Monde, Rome, for Poetry, 1970; Accademia Tiberina, Roma Caripodoglio, for Poetry, 1968; 1st Prize, Poetry, G Pascoli, 1979. Memberships: President, AMES, 1981-; President, Fondaz Artistica Monassi, 1981-; President, Le Rondini Cultural Club, 1987-; Vice President, Le Migliori Mondo, Rome; Public Relations, CIAS, Rome. Address: Via Mondragone u/12, 00179 Rome, Italy.

ROOK William Alan, b. 31 Oct 1909, Ruddington, Nottinghamshire. Poet. Education: BA, 1939, Oxford University. Publications: Songs from a Cherry Tree, 1938; Soldiers, this Solitude, 1942; These Are My Comrades, 1943; We Who Are Fortunate, 1945; Literary Criticism, Not as a Refuge, 1948; Diary of an English Vineyard, 1972. Honours include: Royal Society of Literature; OBE, 1980. Address: Stragglethorpe Hall, Lincoln, LN5 0QZ, England.

ROOKE Daphne Marie, b. 6 Mar 1914, Boksburg, South Africa. Novelist. m. 1 Jun 1937, 1 d. Publications: novels: A Grove of Fever Trees, 1950, reprint 1989; Mittee, 1951, reprint 1987; Ratoons, 1953; reprint 1990; Wizards County, 1957; Beti, 1959; A Lover for Estelle, 1961; The Greyling; Diamond Jo; Boy on the Mountain; Margaretha De La Porte; juvenile books: A Horse of His Own; Double Ex. Contributions to: John Bull; Woman (Sydney). Honours: 1st prize, APB Novel Competition, 1946. Address: 54 Regatta Court, Oyster Row, Cambridge CB5 8NS, England.

ROOKE Leon, b. 11 Sep 1934, NC, USA. Author. Literary Appointments: Writer-in-Residence: University of North Carolina, 1965-66; University of Victoria, 1972-73; University of Southwest Minnesota, 1974-75; Visiting Professor, University of Victoria, 1980-81; Writer-in-Residence, University of Toronto, 1984-85; University of Western Ontario, 1990-91; Short-term Residencies: University of Winnipeg; University of Lethbridge; University of Toronto. Publications: Novels: Last One Home Sleeps in The Yellow Bed, 1968; Vault, 1974; The Broad Back of The Angel, 1977; The Love Parlour, 1977; Fat Woman, 1980; The Magician in Love, 1980; Death Suite, 1982; The Birth Control King of The Upper Volta, 1983; Shakespeare's Dog, 1983; Sing Me No Love Songs I'll Say You No Prayers, 1984; A Bolt of White Cloth, 1984; How I Saved The Province, 1990; The Happiness of Others, 1991; A Good Baby, 1991; Who Do You Love?, 1992; Stage Plays: A Good Baby, 1991; The Coming, 1991; 4 others. Contributions to: About 300 short stories in leading North American journals. Honours: Canada and Australia Literary Prize, 1981; Best Paperback Novel of The Year, for Fat Woman, 1981; Governor General's Award, for Shakespeare's Dog, 1984; Numerous short story prizes and awards; North Carolina Award for Literature, 1990. Memberships: PEN; Writers' Union of Canada. Literary Agent: Liz Darhansoff. Address: 209 Main Street, Eden Mills, Ontario, Canada, N0B 1P0.

ROOM Adrian Richard West, b. 27 Sept 1933, Melksham, England. Writer. Education: Honours Degree, Russian, University of Oxford, England, 1957; Diploma, Education, University of Oxford, 1958. Publications include: Place-Names of the World, 1974; Great Britain: A Background Studies English-Russian Dictionary(Russian Language), 1978; Room's Dictionary of Confusables, 1979; Place-Name Changes since 1900, 1980; Naming Names, 1981; Room's Dictionary of Distinguishables, 1981; Dictionary of Trade Name Origins, 1982; Room's Classical Dictionary, 1983; Dictionary of Cryptic Crossword Clues, 1983; A Concise Dictionary of Modern Place-Names in Great

Britain and Ireland, 1983; Guide to British Place-Names, 1985; Dictionary of Changes in Meaning, 1986; Dictionary of Coin Names, 1988; Guinness Book of Numbers, 1989; Dictionary of Dedications, 1990; A Name for Your Baby, 1992; The Street Names of England, 1992; Brewer's Dictionary of Names, 1992; Corporate Eponymy, 1992; Place-Name Changes 1900-91, 1993; The Naming of Animals, 1993; Hutchinson Pocket Dictionary of First Names, 1994; Hutchinson Pocket Dictionary of Confusible Words, 1994; African Place-Names, 1994; Cassell Dictionary of Proper Names, 1994; A Dictionary of Irish Place-Names, 1994. Memberships: Royal Geographical Society; Society of Authors; English Place-Name Society; American Name Society; Translators Association; Association for Language Learning; Britain-Russia Centre. Address: 12 High Street, St Martin's, Stamford, Lincolnshire PE9 2LF, England.

ROONEY Lucy, b. 13 Jul 1926, Liverpool, England. Former Lecturer; Religious sister of Notre Dame de Namur. Education: Teaching Certificate, Universities of Manchester and Liverpool; City and Guilds Advanced Handloom Weaver, 1965. Publications: Co-author: Mary, Queen of peace, 1984; Medjugorje Unfolds, 1986; Medjugorje Journal, 1987; Medjugorje Retreat, 1989; The Contemplative Way of prayer, 1986; Lord Jesus Teach Me To Pray, 1988; Our Lady Comes to Scotttsdale, 1992; Return to God: The Scottsdale Message, 1993; Medjugorje Unfolds in Peace and in War, 1994. Contributions to: Religious Journals. Address: 52 Warriner Gardens, London SW11 4DU, England.

ROOSE-EVANS James Humprey, b. 11 Nov 1927. Theatre Director; Author. Education: MA, Oxon; Ordained non-stipendiary priest in Anglican Church, 1981. Appointments: Founder, Hampstead Theatre, 1959, West End productions include: Under Milk Wood, An Ideal Husband, Cider With Rosie, Private Lives, Spitting Image, 84 Charing Cross Road, The Best Of Friends, Temptation. Founder, Artistic Director, The Bleddfa Trust, Centre for Caring and the Arts in the Welsh Marches; Distinguished Visiting Fellow, Ohio State University; Gian Carlo Menotti Artist-in-Residence, Charleston College, South Carolina. Publications include: Inner Journey Outer Journey (The Inner Stage, in USA); Darling Ma: The Letters of Joyce Grenfell (editor), 1988; The Time of My Life: War Memoirs of Joyce Grenfell (editor), 1989; 84 Charing Cross Road (play adapted from a book by Helene Hanff); seven children's books, a saga, The Adventures of Odd and Elsewhere; London Theatre; Directing a Play; A Pride of Players, 1993; play: Re:JOYCE! for Maureen Lipman; Directed revival of Venus Observed, by Christopher Fry, Chichester Festival, 1992; Passages of the Soul, 1994; Cider With Rosie, by Laurie Lee, adaptation for the stage. Contributions to: Reviews for: Financial Times; Hampstead and Highgate Express; The Tablet; Catholic Herald; Weekly column, Something Extra, in Woman; documentaries for BBC; Featured on TV and radio. Honours: Nomination, Best Director, 1981, by Society of West End Theatre Managers, for production of 84 Charing Cross Road; Best Director and Best Play, New York, for 84, Charing Cross Road. Memberships: The Garrick Club; The Dramatists Club. Literary Agent: Sheil Land Associates, Address: 43 Doughty Street, London, WC1N 2LF. Theatre Agent: Jeremy Conway, Conway Van Gelder, 18-21 Jeremt Street, London, SW1Y 6HP, England

ROOT William Pitt, b. 28 Dec 1941, Austin, Minnesota, USA. Poet; Professor. m. Pamela Uschuk, 6 Nov 1988, 1 daughter. Education: BA, University of Washington, 1964; MFA, University of North Carolina, Greensboro, 1966; Stegman Fellow, Stanford University, 1967-68. Appointments: Assistant Professor, Michigan State University, 1967-68; Visiting Writer-in-Residence: University of Southwest Louisiana, 1976, Amherst College, 1971, University of Montana, 1978, 1980, 1982-85, Wichita State University 1976, Pacific Lutheran University 1990, Professor, Hunter College, 1986-. Publications: Selected Odes of Pablo Neruda, 1994; Faultdancing, 1986; Invisible Guests, 1984; Reasons for Going It On Foot, 1981; In the World's Common Grasses, 1981; Striking the Dark Air for Music, 1973; The Storm and Other Poems, 1969;A Journey South, 1977; Trace Elements from a Recurring Kingdom, 1994. Contributions to: The Atlantic; Nation; Harpers; Poetry; New Yorker; APR; Poetry East; Triquarterly; Commonwealth. Honours: Academy of American Poets Prize, 1967; Borestone Mt Best Poems of the Year, 1974; Stanley Kumitz Poetry Award, 1981; Guy Owen Poetry Award, 1984; Pushcart Awards, 1977, 1980, 1985; Grants from Rockefeller 1969-70, Guggenheim 1970-71, NEA 1973-74, US/UK Exchange Artist, 1978-79. Address: English Department, Hunter College, 695 Park Avenue, New York City, NY 10021, USA.

ROPER David, b. 30 Nov 1954, Hessle, Yorkshire, England. Critic. Education: MA, AKC, King's College, London. Appointments: Editor, Square One, 1978; Editor, Gambit, 1978-85; Editor, Platform, 1981-82; Drama editor, Event, 1981-82; Theatre Critic, Daily Express, 1982-87; Editor, Plays and Players, 1983-84; Arts Correspondent, BBC 1987-90; Channel 4 TV, 1990-93; Director, Heavy Entertainment Limited, 1993-. Publications: The Pineapple Dance Book, 1983; Bart! (the biography of Lionel Bart), 1994. Contributions to: Tatler; Event; Time Out; Sunday Telegraph; Daily Express; Sunday Express; Daily Mail; Harpers & Queen. Literary Agent: David Higham Associates, London. Address: PO Box 5055, London W12 OZX, England.

ROSCA Ninotchka, b. Philippines. Writer. Education: AB, Comparative Literature, University of The Philippines; Graduate Studies in Khmer Civilization. Publications: Novels: State of War, 1988; Twice Blessed, 1992; Short Stories: Bitter Country, 1972; Monsoon Collection, 1982. Honours: New York Foundation for The Arts, Fiction Fellowship, 1986; NYFA, Fiction Fellowship, 1991. Memberships: Board of Directors, PEN International, Women's Committee, and PEN American Center. Literary Agent: Sterling Lord Literistic. Address: c/o Sterling Lord Literistic, 1 Madison Avenue, NY 10010, USA.

ROSE Andrew Wyness, b. 11 Feb 1944, Headingley, Leeds, Engalnd. Barrister. Eduction: Trinity College, Cambridge, 1963-67; MA; LLM; Called to Bar, Grays Inn, London, 1968. Appointments: Barrister, 1968-88. publications: Stinie: Murder on the Common, 1985; Scandal at the Savoy, 1991. Honours: Shortlisted, Golden Dagger Award for Non-fiction, Crime Writers Association. Address: Brock House, 26 The Street, Sutton Waldron, Blandford Forum, Dorset, DT11 8N2, England.

ROSE Daniel Asa, b. 20 Nov 1949, New York City, USA. Writer. m. (1) Laura Love, 30 Nov 1974, div. 2 sons, (2) Shelley Roth, 5 Sept 1993. Education: AB, English, Honours, Brown University, 1971. Appointments: Travel Columnist, Esquire; Travel Editor, Dimension. Publications: Flipping for it, 1987; Small Family with Rooster, 1988; Various Screenplays, poems, stories, reviews and literary essays. Contributions to: Esquire; New York Times; LA Times; Partisan Review; The New Yorker; Vanity Fair; Conde Nast Traveller; North American Review; Southern Review. Honours: PEN Literary Award, 1987, 1988; O Henry Prize, 1980. Address: 138 Bay State Road, Renoboth, MA 02769, USA.

ROSE Joel Steven, b. 1 Mar 1948, Los Angeles, CA, USA. Writer. m. Catherine Texier, 2 d. Education: BA, Hobart College, 1970; MFA, Columbia University. Publications: Kill The Poor (novel), 1988; Co-editor, Between C and D, 1988; Co-editor, Love is Strange, 1993. Contributions to: New York Times; New York Newsday; Bomb; New Observations; Confrontation; Between C and D; Autremont. Honours: NEA Award, Fiction Writing, 1986; New York State Council on The Arts, 1986-87. Memberships: Poets and Writers; Co-ordinating Council of Literary Magazines; Writers Guild of America. Literary Agent: Michael Carlisle, William Morris Agency. Address: 255 East 7th Street, New York, NY 10009, USA.

ROSE Kenneth Vivian, b. 15 Nov 1924. Writer. Education: Repton School; Scholar, MA, New College, Oxford. Appointments: Assisstant Master, Eton College, 1948; Editorial Staff, Daily Telegraph, 1952-60; Founder, Writer, Albany Column, Sunday Telegraph, 1961-. Publications: Superior Person: A Portrait of Curzon and his Circle in Late Victorian England, 1969; The Later Cecils, 1975; William Harvey: a Monograph, 1978; King George V, 1983; Kings Queens and Courtiers: Intimate Portraits of the Royal House of Windsor, 1985; Harold Nicolson (in Founders & Followers: Literary Lectures on the London Library, 1992). Contributions to: Dictionary of National Biography. Honours: Fellow of the Royal Society of Literature, 1976; Wolfson Award for History, 1983; Whitbread Award for Biography, 1983; Yorkshire Post Biography of the Year Award, 1984. Address: 38 Brunswick Gardens, London W8 4 AL, England.

ROSE Mark, b. 4 Aug 1939, NY, USA. Prof. 1 son. Education: AB, Princeton University, 1961; B Litt, Merton College, 1963; PhD, Harvard University, 1967. Literary Appointments: Yale University, 1967-74; University of IL, 1974-77; University of CA, 1977-. Publications: Authors & Owners: The Invention of Copyright, 1993; Shakespearian Design, 1972; Alien Encounters: Anatomy of Science Fiction, 1981; Heroic Love, 1968; Spenser's Art, 1975. Contributions to: New Republic; The NY Times Book Review; Many Scholarly Journals. Honours: National Book Critics Circle Award nomination, 1993; Eaton Prize, 1983. Memberships: Modern Language Association of America;

Shakespeare Society of Am. Address: 1135 Oriole Rod, Montecite, CA 93108, USA.

ROSE Mitchell, b. 22 Nov 1951, PA, USA. Literary Agent; Editor. Education: BA, Bard College, 1974; MFA, Goddard College, 1980. Literary Appointments: Freelance Writer, 1975-80; Editor and Managing Editor for trade magazines, 1980-83; Editor, New American Library, 1983-86; Literary Agent and Editor, 1986-. Publications: The Victorian Fairy Tale Book, 1988; The Wizard of Oz: The Official Pictorial History, 1989; Gone With The Wind: The Definitive Illustrated History, 1989; The Film Encyclopaedia, 1990; Dr Derning, 1990; At Dawn We Slept, 1991; Harper Dictionary of American Government and Politics, 1992; Lawrence of Arabia, 1992; Judy Garland, 1992; Healing Through Nutrition, 1993; Kennedy As President, 1993. Contributions to: Boston Phoenix. Membership: Authors Guild. Address: The Mitchell S Rose Literary Agency, 688 Avenue of The Americas, New York, NY 10010, USA.

ROSE Richard, b. 9 Apr 1933, St Louis, Missouri, USA. Professor of Public Policy, and Director, Centre for Study of Public Policy, University of Strathclyde, Glasgow. m. Rosemary J Kenny, 14 Apr 1956, 2 s, 1 d. Education: BA distinction, Johns Hopkins University, USA; DPhil, Oxford University, England, 1960. Appointments include: Editor, Journal of Public Policy, 1985-. Publications include: Politics in England, 1964, 5th edition 1989; Governing Without Consensus: an Irish Perspective, 1971; Electoral Behaviour, 1974; International Almanac of Electoral History, with T T Mackie, 1972, 1982, 1991; Problem of Party Government, 1974; Managing Presidential Objectives, 1976; Can Government Go Bankrupt? with B G Peters, 1978; Do Parties Make a Difference? 1980, 1984; Presidents & Prime Ministers, co-editor, 1980; Understanding the United Kingdom, 1982; Understanding Big Government, 1984; Nationwide Competition for Votes, 1984; Public Employment in Western Nations, 1985; Voters Begin to Choose, with d McAllister, 1986; Ministers & Ministries, 1987; Taxation by Political Inertia, 1987; The Post-Modern President, 1988, 1991; Ordinary People in Public Policy, 1989; The Loyalty of Voters, with d McAllister, 1990; Lesson Drawing in Public Policy, 1993; Inheritance in Public Policy, 1994; What is Europe?, 1995. Contributions to: Times; Telegraph; New Society; Economist; Various TV Stations. Honours: Guggenheim Fellowship, 1974; Fellow, Woodrow Wilson International Centre, Washington DC, USA, 1974; Japan Foundation Fellow, 1984; Fellow, British Academy, 1992; Honorary Foreign Member, Finnish Academy of Arts & Sciences; American Academy of Arts & Sciences. Address: CSPP, University of Strathclyde, Glasgow G1 1XH, Scotland.

ROSEN Michael Wayne (Landgrave of Hesse), b. 7 May 1946, Harrow, England. Writer; Performer. m. 30 Nov 1987, 3 s, 2 stepdaughters. Education: Middlesex Hospital Medical School, 1964-65; Wadham College, Oxford, 1965-69; National Film School, 1973-76. Literary Appointments: Writer-in-Residence: Vauxhall Manor Comprehensive School, 1976-77; London Borough of Brent, 1983-84; John Scurr Primary School, 1984-87, 1988-90; Western Australia College of Advanced Education, 1987. Publications: Mind Your Own Business, 1974; Quick Let's Get Out Of Here, 1983; Don't Put The Mustard In The Custard, 1984; The Kingfisher Book of Poetry, 1984; The Hypnotiser, 1988; We're Going on a Bear Hunt, 1989; You Can't Catch Me; Nasty; You're Thinking About Doughnuts; The Class 2 Monster; The Wicked Tricks of Till Owlyglass; Spollyolly Diddly Tiddlyitis. Contributions to: New Statesman; The Guardian; Times Educational Supplement; Jewish Socialist. Honours: Signal Poetry Award, 1982; The Other Award, 1984; Smarties Award, 1989. Membership: Equity. Literary Agent: The Peters Fraser and Dunlop Group Limited. Address: c/o The Peters Fraser and Dunlop Group Limited, 5th Floor, The Chambers, Chelsea Harbour, Lots Road, London, SW10 0XF, England.

ROSEN Norma, b. New York City, New York, USA. Writer. m. Robert S Rosen, 1960, 1 son, 1 daughter. Education: BA, Mt Holyoke College, 1946; MA, Columbia University, 1953. Appointments: Teacher, Creative Writing, New School, New York, 1965-69;; University of Pennsylvania, 1969; Harvard University, 1971; Yale University, 1984; New York University, 1987-. Publications: Fiction: Joy to Levine!, 1962; Green, 1967; Touching Evil, 1969; At the Center, 1982; John and Anzia: An American Romance, 1989; Accidents of Influence: Writing as a Woman and a Jew in America, essays, 1992; Contributed essays to anthologies Out of the Garden, 1994 and Reading Ruth, 1994. Contributions to: Many. Honours: Saxton, 1960; CAPS, 1976; Bunting,

1971-73. Memberships: PEN; Authors Guild; Phi Beta Kappa. Literary Agent: 133 East 35th Street, New York, NY 10016, USA.

ROSENBERG Bruce Alan, b. 27 July 1934, New York City, USA. Teacher; Writer. m. Ann Harleman, 20 June 1981, 3 sons. Education: BA, Hofstra University, 1955; MA, Pennsylvania State University, 1960; PhD, Ohio State University, 1965. Publications: The Art of the American Folk Preacher, 1970; Custer and the Epic of Defeat, 1975; The Code of the West, 1982; The Spy Story, 1987; Ian Fleming, 1989; Can These Bones Live?, 1988. Contributions to: Over 60 professional journals. Honours: James Russell Lowell Prize, 1970; Chicago Folklore Prize, 1970, 1975. Memberships: Folklore Fellows International. Address: 55 Summit Avenue, Providence, RI 02906, USA.

ROSENBERG Liz, b. 3 Feb 1957, Glen Cove, NY, USA. Associate Professor of English. m. (1) John Gardner, 14 Feb 1982, (2) David Bosnick, 8 Dec 1985, 1 s. Education: BA, Bennington College; MA, Johns Hopkins University. Appointment: Amanuensis for Ved Mehta, The New York, 1977. Publications: Poetry: The Fire Music, 1986; Children of Pardin, 1993; Children's Books: Adelaide and The Night Train, 1989; Window, Mirror Man, 1990; The Scrap Doll, 1991; Monster Mama, 1993. Contributions include: The New York Times; The New Yorker; The Nation; Southern Review; Poetry. Honours: Atlantic 1st Award, 1976; Pennsylvania Council of The Arts Award, 1982; National Kelloggs Fellowship, 1982-85; Agnes Starrett Poetry Prize, 1985. Memberships: Association of Writers and Poets; Poets and Writers. Address: c/o English Department, State University of New York, Binghamton, NY 13902, USA.

ROSENBERG Nancy Taylor. m. Jerry. Career: Law Enforcement in Texas, New Mexico, California. Address: c/o Dytton Publicity, 375 Hudson Street, New York, NY 10014, USA.

ROSENBERG Peter Michael, b. 11 Jul 1958, London England. Freelance Writer. Education: BSc Class 2 (ii), Applied Sciences with Social Sciences, University of Sussex, 1979. Publications: Novels: The Usurper (co-author), 1988; Kissing Through a Pane of Glass, 1993; Touched By a God or Something, 1994; Because It Makes My Heart Beat Faster, 1995. Contributions to: Wanna Come Back to My place, comic fiction, to Jennings Magazine, 1987; Travel articles, book reviews, 1987-91, to: Literary Review; The Adventurer; Girl About Town; Midweek; LAW Magazine; Nine to Five; TNT Magazine; Trailfinders; New Zealand News; Poetry to PEN New Poetry II; The Insufferable Being of Lightness, New York Diary, Sharon's Secret, On Reflection, The Black Envelope, to Radio LBC, 1986-87. Honours: 2nd Prize, Betty Trask Award, 1992. Literary Agent: Christopher Little, 49 Queen Victoria Street, London EC4N 4SA, England. Address: 430 St Ann's Road, London N15 3JJ, England.

ROSENBLATT Joseph, b. 26 Dec 1933, Toronto, Canada. Writer. m. Faye Smith, 13 Oct 1969, 1 son. Education: George Brown College. Literary Appointments: Writer in Residence, University of Western Ontario, 1980; University of Victoria, 1981; Saskatoon Library, 1985; University of Rome, 1987. Publications: Top Soil, 1976; The Sleeping Lady, 1980; Brides of The Stream, 1983; Poetry Hotel, 1985; Escape From The Glue Factory, 1985; Bumble Bee Dythyramb, 1970; Kissing Goldfish of Siam, 1989; Beds and Consenting Dreamers, 1994. Contributions to: Tamarack Review; Canadian Forum; The Nation; Exile; Prism Internationa; Ariel Review of International; English Literature. Honours: Governor Generals, 1976; B C Book, 1986. Memberships: Writers Union of Canada; League of Canadian Poets. Address: 221 Elizabeth Avenue, Qualicum Beach, BC V9K 1G8, Canada.

ROSENBLUM Martinjack, b. 19 Aug 1946, Appleton, Wisconsin, USA. Official Harley-Davidson Motorcycle Company Archivist; Admissions Specialist. m. Maureen Rice, 6 Sept 1970, 2 d. Education: BS, English, 1969; MA, English, 1971; PhD, Modern American Poetry, 1980, Univesity of Wisconsin. Career: Guest Lecturer, University of East Anglia, Norwich, England, 1975; Poetry Contest Judge, University of Wisconsin, Oshkosh, 1979; Poet-in-Residence, Wisconsin Review, University of Wisconsin, Oshkosh, 1987. Publications: Home, 1971; On, 1972; The Werewolf Sequence, 1974; Brite Shade, 1984; Conjunction, 1987; Scattered on: Omens and Curses, 2nd edition, 1987; Stone Fog, 1987; Burning Oak, 1987; Georgaphics, 1987; Music Lingo, 1987; Backlit Frontier, 1987; Harley-Davidson Poems, 1988; The Holy Ranger: Harley-Davidsion Poems, 1989; Ameican Outlaw Visionary, 1989; I Am The Holy Ranger, A Collection of Poems and Songs on Cassette, 1989; The Holy Ranger's Free Hand, an album of songs on CD and Cassette, 1990; Harley-Davidson Inc, 1903-1993, 1994. Address: 2521 East Stratford Court, Shorewood, WI 53211, USA.

ROSENFELD Albert Hyman, b. 31 May 1920, Philadelphia, USA. Science Writer. m. 24 Aug 1948, 1 s, 1 d. Education: BA, History and Social Science, New Mexico State University. Literary Appointments include: Associate Editor, 1956-58, Senior Science Editor, 1958-60, Life; Managing Editor, Family Health, 1969-71; Senior Science Editor, Saturday Review, 1973-80; Contributing Editor, Geo, 1979-81, Science Digest, 1980-82. Publications include: The Quintessence of Irving Langmui, 1962; The Second Genesis: The Coming Control of Life, 1969; Prolongevity, 1976; Editor, Mind and Supermind, 1977; Editor, Science, Invention and Social Change, 1978; Responsible Parenthood (with G W Kliman), 1980; Prolongevity II, 1985. Contributions to: Life; Time; Fortune; Sports Illustrated; McCall's Redbook; Harper's; Readers Digest; Think; Saturday Review; Better Homes and Gardens; Physicians World; Horizon; Geo; Prime Time; Science Digest. Honours include: Aviation Space Writers Award, 1964; Westinghouse Writing Award AAAS, 1966; Lasker Award, 1967; Claude Bernard Science Journalism Award, 1974; National Magazine Award, 1975; James P Grady Medal, American Chemical Society, 1981; Honorary DLett, New Mexico State University. Memberships: 3 times President, Council for The Advancement of Science Writing; National Association of Science Writers; Authors Guild. Address: 25 Davenport Avenue, New Rochelle, NY 10805, USA.

ROSENGARTEN Theodore,b. 17 Dec 1944, Brooklyn, New York, USA. m. 1974, 1 son. Education: AB, Amherst College; PhD, Harvard University. Appointments: Writer; Mechanic. Honours: National Book Award, 1974. Address: PO Box 8, McClellanville, SC 29458, USA.

ROSENSTAND Peder Tuxen, b. 2 Nov 1935, Copenhagen, Denmark. Poet; Artist; Painter; Professor. m. Anni Rosenstand, 1960, 3 sons, 1 daughter. Education: Royal Danish Academy of Art; University of Copenhagen, Denmark. Publications: Osteklokken, 1974; Blik, 1988; Dramatic Works for Danish, Swedish and Norway TV; Painting Exhibitions Held in: Germany, England, New York, USA, Sweden, Denmark, Italy, 1962-94. Contributions to: Essays, Articles to Pinqvinen. Memberships: University of Stockholm; Authors Society, Copenhagen, Denmark. Address: Gl Mollerup, 4673 Rodvig Stevns, Tlf 53707030, Denmark.

ROSENTHAL Barbara Ann, b. 17 Aug 1948, Bronx, New York, USA. Writer; Artist. 2 daughters. Education: BFA, Carnegie-Mellon University, 1970; MFA, Queens College, 1975. Career: Editor-in-Cheif, Patterns, 1967-70; Editor, Parsons College Faculty Affairs Committee Newsletter, 1986-88; Adjuct Lecturer, English, The College of Staten Island (CUNY), New York City. Publications include: Clues to Myself, 1982; Sensations, 1984; Old Address Book, 1985; Homo Futurus, 1986; Children's Shoes, 1993; Poetry and short story antholgies: In The West of Ireland, 1992; Call It Courage: Women Transcending Violence, 1993. Contributions to: Numerous professional journals and lit-art magazines including: Feelings, 1990-91; Poetry Motel, 1993; Spit, 1990, 1993; Parting Gifts, 1993; Poetry and Short Anthologies: Cradle and All, 1990; Contributions to: MacGuffin Reader, 1994; Bohemian Chronicle, 1993. Honours: Recipient, various honours and awards; Listed Writer, Poets and Writers Directory. Address: 727 Avenue of the Americas, New York, NY 10010, USA.

ROSENTHAL Jack Morris, b. 8 Sep 1931. Writer. m. Maureen Lipman, 1973, 1s, 1 d. Education: BA, English Literature & Language, Sheffield University. Appointments: Television: Writer of over 250 productions including:That Was the Week That Was, 1963; 150 episodes of Coronation Street, 1961-69; The Evacuees, 1975; Bar Mitzvah Boy, 1976; Ready When You Are, Mr McGill, 1976; Spend, Spend, Spend, 1977; The Knowledge, 1979; P'tang Yang Kipperbang, 1982; Mrs Capper's Birthday, 1985; London's Burning, 1986; Fools on the Hill, 1986; Day to Remember, 1986; And a Nightingale Sang, 1989; Bye Bye Baby, 1992; Wide-eyed and Legless, 1994; stage: 5 plays including: Smash!, 1981; films: 6 feature films including: Lucky Star, 1980; Yentl (co-written with Barbra Streisand), 1983; The Chain, 1985; The Wedding Gift, 1994. Publications: Contributions to: The Television Dramatist, 1973; Anthology, First Love, 1984; numerous TV plays and series. Honours: BAFTA Writer's Award, 1976; RTS Writer's Award, 1976; CBE for Services to Drama, 1994; Royal Television Society Hall of Fame, 1993; MA (Hon), University of Salford, 1994. Literary Agent: William Morris Agency, Address: William Morris Agency, 31, Soho Square, London W1, England.

ROSS Alan, b. 6 May 1922, Calcutta, India. Author; Publisher; Journalist. m. Jennifer Fry, 1949, div 1985, 1 son. Education: St John's College, Oxford. Appointments include: Royal Navy, 1942-45; Staff, The Observer, 1950-71, toured Australia as Correspondent, 1964-65; West Indies 1960-68; Editor, London Magazine, 1961-; Managing Director, London Magazine Editions (Publishers), 1965-. Publications: The Derelict Day, 1947; Time Was Away, 1948; The Forties, 1950; The Gulf of Pleasure, 1951; The Bandit on the Billiard Table, 1954; Something of the Sea, 1954; Australia 55, 1956, 2nd edition 1983; Abroad, Editor, 1957; Cape Summer and the Australians in England, 1957, 2nd edition 1986; To Whom It May Concern, 1958; The Onion Man, 1959; Through the Caribbean, 1960; The Cricketer's Companion, Editor, 1960; Danger on Glass Island, 1960; African Negatives, 1962; Australia, 63, 1963; West Indies at Lord's, 1963, 2nd edition 1986; North from Sicily, 1965; Poems 1942-1967, 1968; Tropical Ice, 1972; The Taj Express, 1973; Editor, London Magazine Stories 1-11, 1964-80; Editor, Living in London, 1974; Open Sea, 1975; Editor, Selected Poems of Lawrence Durrell, 1977; Death Valley and Other Poems, 1980; Editor, The Turf, 1982; Colours of War, 1983; Ranji, 1983; Editor, Living Out of London, 1984; Blindfold Games, 1986; The Emissary, 1986; Coastwise Lights, 1988. Honours: Atlantic Award for Literature, Rockefeller Foundation, 1946; FRSL, 1971; CBE, 1982. Address: 4 Elm Park Lane, London SW3, England.

ROSS Angus. See: **GIGGAL Kenneth.**

ROSS Catherine. See: **BEATY Betty Smith.**

ROSS Gary Earl, b. 12 Aug 1951, Buffalo, NY, USA. Writing Educator. m. 23 Dec 1970, 2 s, 1 d. Education: BA, English, 1973, MA, Humanities, 1975, University at Buffalo. Literary Appointments: Writing Educator, State University of New York Educational Opportunity Center at Buffalo, 1977-. Publications: Editor, Guiding The Adult Learner, 1979; Editor, Developmental Perspectives, 1981; Practical Considerations for Computer-Assisted Writing Instruction for Disadvantaged Learners, 1990; Teaching Creative Writing, 1990; Strategies for Addressing Technophobia in Adult Learners, 1991. Contributions to: Short stories to: Pure Light; Arts in Buffalo; Best for Men; EdVantage; Word Worth Anthology of Fiction; Starsong; Slipstream; A Poetry Mag; Live Writers!; Ohio Renaissance Review; Innisfree; Starsong; Gas; BLFO Journal; Artvoice; Buffalo News; Buffalo Magazine; ELF; Poetry to: A Poetry Mag; American Poetry Anthology; Hearts on Fire; Pure Light; Homunulus; Non-fiction to: EdVantage; Development Perspectives; Spectrum; Colloquy; Newsletter; Buffalo News. Honours: Hearts on Fire Award, American Poetry Association, 1983; LIFT Program Fiction Fellowship, 1989; Just Buffalo Fiction Writer-in-Residence, 1987, 1992. Memberships: Just Buffalo Literary Organization; Niagara-Erie Writers, Board Chair, 1987-89; United University Professions; International Society for Exploration of Teaching Alternatives. Address: SUNY EOC at Buffalo, 465 Washington Street, Buffalo, NY 14203, USA.

ROSS Helaine, See **DANIELS Dorothy.**

ROSS James, See: **WELCH Colin.**

ROSS John Munder, b. 20 June 1945, New York City, USA. Psychoanalyst. m. 1 s. Education: BA magna cum laude, Harvard College, 1967; MA, 1973, PhD, 1974, Clinical psychology, New York University, Certificate in Psychoanalysis, NYU Medical Centre, 1984; Training and Supervisory Analysis, Columbia, Psycholanalyst Centre, Clinical Progress, Cornell University Medical Centre. Publications: Tales of Love, Sex and Danger, 1986; The Male Paradox, 1992; The Oedipus Papers, 1988; Father and Chld, 1982; New Concepts in Psychoanalytic Psychotherapy; What Men Want, 1993. Contributions to: New York Times; Express Magazine; Journal of American Psychoanalytic Association; The Washington Post; The American Journal of Psychiatry; American Psychological Association Monitor; Mademoiselle Magazine, among others. Literary Agent: Suzanne Gluck, ICM 40 West 57th St, NYC 10019, USA. Address: 243 West End Ave, Suite 101, New York, NY 10023, USA.

ROSS Jonathon. See: **ROSSITER John.**

ROSS Leonard Q. See: **ROSTEN Leo C.**

ROSS Malcolm. See: **ROSS-MACDONALD Malcolm John.**

ROSS (James) Sinclair, b. 22 Jan 1908, Shellbrook, Saskatchewan, Canada. Novelist. Appointments: Staff Member, Union Bank of Canada, 1924-68; Resident, Vancouver, 1981. Publications: As For Me and My House, 1941; The Well, 1958; Whir of Gold, 1970; Sawbones Memorial, 1974; The Lamp at Noon and Other Stories, 1968; The Race and Other Stories. Address: c/o Writers Union of Canada, 24 Ryerson Avenue, Toronto, Ontario, M5T 2P3, Canada.

ROSS-MACDONALD Malcolm John (Malcolm Macdonald, Malcolm Ross, M R O'Donnell), b. 1932, Chipping, Sodbury, Gloucestershire, England. Freelance Writer; Editor; Designer. m. Ingrid Giehr, 2 daughters. Appointments include: Lektor, Folk University, Sweden, 1959-61; Executive Editor, Aldus Books, 1962-65; Visiting Lecturer, Hornsey College of Art, 1965-69. Publications: The Big Waves, 1962; Executive Editor, Macdonald Illustrated Encyclopaedia, 10 volumes, 1962-65; Co-author, designer, Spare Part Surgery, 1968; Machines in Medicine, 1969; The Human Heart, 1970; Also numerous other titles under pen-names including: World Wildlife Guide, 1971; Beyond the Horizon, 1971; Every Living Thing, 1973; World from Rough Stones, 1974; Origin of Johnny, 1975; Life in the Future, 1976; The Rich Are With You Always, 1976; Sons of Fortune, 1978; Abigail, 1979; Goldeneye, 1981; The Dukes, 1982; Tessa'd'Arblay, 1983; In Love & War, 1984; Mistress of Pallas, 1986; Silver Highways, 1987; The Sky with Diamonds, 1988; A Notorious Woman, 1989; His Father's Son, 1989; An Innocent Woman, 1989; Hell Hath No Fury, 1990; A Woman Alone, 1990; The Captain's Wives, 1991; A Woman Scorned, 1991; A Woman Possessed, 1992; All Desires Known, 1993; To the End of Her Days, 1993; Dancing on Snowflakes, 1994; For I Have Sinned, 1994; Kernow & Daughter, 1994; Crissy's Family, 1995. Contributions to: Sunday Times; New Scientist; Science Journal; Month; Jefferson Encyclopaedia. Membership: Authors Guild; Society of Authors. Address: c/o David Higham Ltd, 5-8 Lower John Street, London W1R 4HA, England.

ROSSER J(ill) Allyn, b. 1957. Publication: Bright Moves, 1990. Honours: Lavan Younger Poets Award, 1991; Morse Poetry Prize, 1990.

ROSSI Bruno. See: LEVINSON Leonard.

ROSSI Maria Francesca, (Francesca Duranti), b. 2 Jan 1935, Genoa, Italy. Writer. m. (1) Enrico Magnani, 1956, (2) Massimo Duranti, 1970, 1 s, 1 d. Education: Laurea in Giurisprudenza, University of Pisa. Publications: La bambina, 1976; Piazza, Mia Bella Piazza, 1978; The House on Moonlake, 1984; Happy Ending, 1987; Effetti Personalia, 1988; Ultima Stesura, 1991. Contributions to: Il Secoloxx; Il Giornale; Il Messaggero. Honours: Martina Franca Citta Di Milano, Bagutta, 1984; Basilicata Hemingway Campiello, 1988; Prix Lectrices d'Elle, Castiglioncello, 1991. Address: Villa Rossi, Gattaiola, Lucca, Italy.

ROSSITER John. See: CROZIER Brian Rossiter.

ROSSITER John (Jonathon Ross), b. 1916, British. Appointments: Detective Chief Superintendent, Wiltshire Constabulary, 1939-69; Columnist, Wiltshire Courier, Swindon, 1963-64. Publications: The Blood Running Cold (as J Ross), Diminished by Death (as J Ross), 1968; Dead at First Hand (as J Ross), The Deadest Thing You Ever Saw (as J Ross), 1969; The Murder Makers, The Deadly Green, 1970; The Victims (as J Rossiter), 1971; A Rope for General Dietz, Here Lies Nancy Frail (as J Rossiter), 1972; The Manipulators, 1973; The Burning of Billy Toober (as J Rossiter), The Villains, 1974; The Golden Virgin (in US as The Deadly Gold), (as J Rossiter), 1975; I Know What It's Like to Die (as J Rossiter), 1976; The Man Who Came Back, 1978; A Rattling of Old Bones (as J Rossiter), 1979; Dark Flight, Dark Blue and Dangerous (as J Rossiter), 1981; Death's Head (as J Ross), 1982; Dead Eye (as J Ross), 1983; Dropped Dead (as J Ross), 1984; Burial Deferred (as J Rossiter), 1985; Fate Accomplished (as J Ross), 1987; Sudden Departures (as J Ross), 1988; A Time for Dying (as J Ross), 1989; Daphne Dead and Done for (as J Ross), 1990; Murder be Hanged (as J Ross), 1992; The Body of a Woman (as J Ross), 1994. Contributions to: Police Review. Membership: Crime Writers Association, Soho, London. Address: 3 Leighton Home Farm Court, Wellhead Lane, Westbury, Wilts BA13 3PT, England.

ROSSNER Judith, b. 1935, American. Publications: To the Precipice, 1966; Nine Months in the Life of an Old Maid, 1969; Any Minute I Can Split, 1972; Looking for Mr Goodbar, 1975; Attachements, 1977; Emmeline, 1980; August, 1983; His Little Women, 1990; Olivia or The Weight of the Past, 1994. Contributions to: Stories and essays to magazines and journals. Memberships: Authors Guild; PEN. Address: c/o Wendy Weil Agency, 232 Madison Ave, New York, NY 10016, USA.

ROSTEN Leo C (Leonard Q Ross), b. 11 Apr 1908. Author; Social Scientist. m. (1) Priscilla Ann Mead, 1935 (dec), 1 s, 2 d, (2) Gertrude Zimmerman, 1960. Education: PhD, University of Chicago; London School of Economics, Honorary Fellow, 1975. Publications include: The Movie Makers, 1941; The Dark Corner, 1945; Editor, Guide to The Religions of America, 1957; The Return of Hyman Kaplan, 1959; Captain Newman, MD, 1961; The Story Behind The Painting, 1961; The Many Worlds of Leo Rosten; The Leo Rosten Bedside Book, 1965; A Most Private Intrigue, 1967; The Joys of Yiddish, 1968; A Trumpet for Reason, 1970; People I Have Loved, Known or Admired, 1970; Rome Wasn't Burned in a Day, 1971; Leo Rosten's Treasury of Jewish Quotations, 1973; Dear "Herm", 1974; Editor, The Look Book, 1975; The 3.10 to Anywhere, 1976; O Kaplan! My Kaplan!, 1976; The Power of Positive Nonsense, 1977; Passions and Prejudices, 1978; Editor, Infinite Riches: Gems from a Lifetime of Reading, 1979; Silky!, 1979; King Silky!, 1980; Hooray for Yiddish!, 1983; Leo Rosten's Giant Book of Laughter, 1985; The Joys of Yinglish, 1989; Leo Rosten's Carnival of Wit, 1984. Contributions to: Learned journals. Honours: Grants, Rockefeller Foundation and Carnegie Corporation, 1938-40; Distinguished Alumnus Award, University of Chicago, 1970; Honorary DHL, University of Rochester, 1973, Hebrew Union Theological College, 1980; many other honours and awards. Memberships: Various professional organisations. Address: 36 Sutton Place South, New York, NY 10022, USA.

ROSTON Murray, b. 1928, British/Israeli. Appointments: Professor of English Literature, Bar-Ilan University, Ramat Gan, Israel (joined faculty 1956). Publications: Prophet and Poet: The Bible ad the Growth of Romanticism, 1965; Biblical Drama in England from the Middle Ages to the Present Day, 1968; The Soul of Wit: A Study of John Donne, 1974; Milton and the Baroque, 1980; Sixteenth-Century English Literature, 1982; Renaissance Perspectives in Literature and the Visual Arts, 1987; Changing Perspectives in Literature and the Visual Arts (1650-1820), 1990; Victorian Contexts in Literature and the Visual Arts, 1995. Address: 51 Katznelson Street, Kiryat Ono, Israel.

ROSZKOWSKI Janusz, b. 11 Mar 1928, Lapy, Poland. Journalist. m. Natalia Roszkowska, 1960, 1 son. Education: Academy of Political Sciences, Warsaw. Appointments: Journalist, Polish Press Agency, Warsaw, 1953-, Reporter 1953-61, Deputy Editor in Chief, Home Section, 1967-68, Editor in Chief, Home Section 1968-71, Deputy Editor in Chief, 1969-71, Editor in Chief (acting), 1971-72, Editor in Chief, 1972-86. Publications: Literary Critic, regular contributions to weekly Kultura, 1967-76. Honours: Boleslaw Prus Award, 1st Class, 1973; Juliusz Fuczik Hon Medal of International Journalist Association; Order of Banner of Labour, 2nd Class; Cross Order of Polonia Restituta. Memberships: Polish Workers Party, 1947-48; PZPR, 1948-90; Free Journalist, 1991; Association of Poland's Journalists; Polish Journalists Association, Vice-President of PJA; President, Polish Committee for Radio and TV, 1986-89; Polish Ambassador, Copenhagen, 1989-91. Address: ul Ladowa 1/3m, 14, 00-759 Warsaw, Poland.

ROTBLAT Joseph, b. 1908, British. Literary Appointments: Professor, 1950-76, Emeritus, Medical College of St Batholomew's Hospital, University of London; President, Pugwash Conferences on Science and World Affairs, 1988-; Editor, Physics in Medicine and Biology, 1960-73. Publications include: Radioactivity and Radioactive Substances (with Sir James Chadwick), 1961; Science and World Affairs, 1962; The Uses and Effects of Nuclear Energy (co-author), 1964; Editor, Aspects of Medical Physics, 1966; Pugwash: The First Ten Years, 1967; Scientists in The Quest for Peace: A History of The Pugwash Conferences, 1972; Nuclear Reactors: To Breed or Not to Breed, 1977; Nuclear Energy and Nuclear Weapon Proliferation, 1979; Nuclear Radiation in Warfare, 1981; Scientists, The Arms Race and Disarmament, 1982; The Arms Race at a Time of Decision, 1984; Nuclear Strategy and World Security, 1985; World Peace and The Developing Countries, 1986; Strategic Defence and The Future of The Arms Race, 1987; Co-existence, Co-operation and Common Security, 1988; Verification of Arms Reductions, 1989; Global Problems and Common Security, 1989; Nuclear Proliferation: Technical and Economic Aspects, 1990; Global Security Through Co-Operation, 1990; Towards A Secure World in The 21st Century, 1991; Striving for Peace, Security and Development in The World, 1992; A Nuclear-Weapon-Free World: Desirable? Feasible?, 1993. Honours:

CBE, 1965; Albert Einstein Peace Prize, 1992. Address: 8 Asmara Road, London, NW2 3ST, England.

ROTH Andrew, b. 23 Apr 1919. Political Correspondent. m. Mathilda Anna Friederich, 1949 (div 1984), 1 s, 1 d. Education: BSS, City College of New York; MA, Columbia University; Harvard University. Literary Appointments: Reader, City College, 1939; Research Associate, Institute of Pacific Relations, 1940; Editorial Writer, The Nation, 1945-46; Foreign Correspondent, Toronto Star Weekly, 1946-50; London Correspondent, France Observateur, Sekai, Singapore Standard, 1950-60; Political Correspondent, Manchester Evening News, 1972-84; Political Correspondent, New Statesman, 1984-; Director, Parliamentary Profiles, 1955-. Publications: Japan Strikes South, 1941; French Interests and Policies in The Far East, 1942; Dilemma in Japan, 1945; The Business Background of MPs, 1959, 7th edition, 1980; The MPs Chart, 1967, 5th edition, 1979, 6th edition, 1987; Enoch Powell: Tory Tribune, 1970; Can Parliament Decide..., 1971; Heath and The Heathmen, 1972; Lord on The Board, 1972; The Prime Ministers, volume II (Heath Chapter), 1975; Sir Harold Wilson: Yorkshire Walter Mitty, 1977; Parliamentary Profiles, volumes I-IV, 1984-85, 2nd edition, 1988-90; New MPs of '92, 1992; Mr Nice Guy and His Chums, 1993. Address: 34 Somali Road, London, NW2 3RL, England.

ROTH Lane, b. 10 Apr 1943, New York City, USA. University Professor. Eduction: BA, Sociology and Psychology, New York University, 1964; MA, 1974, PhD, 1976, Mass Communication, Florida State University. Publications: Film Semiotics, Metz an Leone's Trilogy, 1983; The Power of Imagination: Archetypal Images in science Fiction Films. Contributions to: Research articles in refereed scholarly journals of the humanities, philosophy, English, communiction and cinema; Chapter in scholarly book on film. Honours: National German Honors, 1964. Memberships: International Association for the Fantastic in the Arts; World Communication Association. Address: Communication 10050, Lamar University, Beaumont, TX 77710, USA.

ROTH Philip, b. 19 Mar 1933, Newark, NJ, USA. Writer. Education: MA, Bucknell and Chicago Universities. Publications: Goodbye Columbus, 1959; Novels: Letting Go, 1962; When She Was Good, 1967; Portnoy's Complaint, 1969; Our Gang, 1971; The Breast, 1972; The Great American Novel, 1973; My Life as a Man, 1974; Reading Myself and Others (essays), 1975; The Professor of Desire, 1977; The Ghost Writer, 1979; A Philip Roth Reader, 1980; Zuckerman Unbound, 1981; The Anatomy Lesson, 1983; The Prague Orgy, 1985; The Counterlife, 1986; The Facts, 1988; Deception, 1990; Patrimony, 1991; The Conversion of The Jews, 1992; Goodbye Columbus and 5 Short Stories, 1993. Honours: Guggenheim Fellowship, 1959-60; Rockefeller Grant, 1965; Ford Foundation Grant, 1966. Membership: National Institute of Arts and Letters. Address: Wylie, Aitken and Stone, 250 West 57th Street, New York, NY 10107, USA.

ROTHENBERG Jerome Dennis, b. 11 Dec 1931, New York City, USA. Poet. m. Diane Brodatz, 25 Dec 1952, 1 s. Education: BA, City College, City University of New York, 1952; MA, University of Michigan, 1953. Career: Professor, English and Comparative Literature, State University of New York at Binghamton, 1986-88; Professor, Visual Arts and Literature, University of California at San Diego, 1988-. Publications include: New Young German Poets, 1959; White Sun Black Sun, 1960; Sightings 1-1X, 1964; The Gorky Poems, 1966; Between 1967; Poems 1964-67, 1968; Technicians of the Sacred, 1968; Poems for the Game of Silence, 1971; Shaking the Pumpkin, 1972; America a Prophecy, 1973; Revolution of the Word, 1974; Poland/1931, 1974; A Big Jewish Book, 1977; A Seneca Journal 1978; Vienna Blood, 1980; Pre-Faces, 1981; Symposium of the Whole, 1983; That Dada Strain, 1983; New Selected Poems, 1986; Khurbn and Other Poems, 1989; Exiled in the Word, 1989; Further Sightings and Conversations, 1989; The Lorca Variations, 1993; Gematria, 1994. Address: c/o New Directions, 80 Eighth Avenue, New York, NY 10012, USA.

ROTHENSTEIN John Knewstub Maurice, Sir, b. 11 Jul 1901. Director of The Tate, 1938-64 and other Art Galleries; University Professor. Education: MA, Oxford University, 1927; PhD, University College, London, 1931. Publications include: An Introduction to English Painting, 1934; Augustus John, 1944; Modern English Painters, 3 volumes, 1952-74; Turner, 1960; Sickert, 1961; Paul Nash, 1961; Summers Lease, 1965; Brave Day, Hideous Night, 1966; Francis Bacon (autobiography in 3 volumes), 1967; Time's Thievish Progress, 1970; Edward Burra, 1972; Stanley Spencer, The Man, 1979; Modern English Painters, updated edition, 1984; John Nash, 1983; Stanley Spencer, 1989. Honours include: Knight, 1952; CBE, 1948; Knight Commander, Order Aztec Eagle, Mexico, 1953; Honorary Fellow, Worcester College, Oxford, 1953; Fellow, University College, London, 1976-; Knight Commander, Order St Gregory The Great, 1977. Memberships include: Athenaum Club. Address: Beauforest House, Newington, Dorchester-on-Thames, Oxford, OX9 8AG, England.

ROTHMAN Judith, See: **PETERS Maureen.**

ROTIMI Ola, b. 13 Apr 1938, Sapele, Nigeria. Playwright. Education: BFA, Boston University, 1963; MFA, Yale University, 1966. Appointments include: Head of the Department of Creative Arts at the University of Port Harcourt, from 1982. Publications: Our Husband Has Gone Mad Again, 1966; The Gods Are Not To Blame, 1968; Kurunmi: An Historical Tragedy, 1969; Holding Talks, 1970; Ovonramwen Nogbaisi, 1971; Imitation into Madness, 1973; Grip Am, 1973; Akassi Youmi, 1977; If: A Tragedy of the Ruled, 1979; Hopes of the Living - Dead, 1985; Has directed his own plays in Ife-Ife and Port Harcourt. Honours include: Oxford University Press Prize, 1970. Address: Department of Creative Arts, University of Port Harcourt, PMB 5323, Port Harcourt, Rivers State, Nigeria.

ROUDINESCO Elisabeth, b. 10 Sept 1944, Paris, France. Writer; Historian. Education: State Doctor of Letters, History and Human Science, University of Paris; Chargee de Conférence a l'Ecole des Hautes Etudes en Sciences, Paris. Publications: Historie ole la Psychahalyse en France 1885-1985, 2 volumes, 1982-1986, 1990; Madness and Revolution, 1991-92; Jacques Lacan Esquisse d'une vié Histoire ol'un Systéme de Pensee, 1993; Seven Other Books. Contributions to: Chronicle, Liberation, Literary Supplement. Memberships: Du Comité de la Maison des Ecrivains, Paris; Vice President, Sociéte International d'historie de la Psychiatrie et de la Psycharialyse, Paris. Literary Agents: Claude Durand, Olivier Bétourné, c/o Librairue Arthéme Fayard. Address: 89 ave Denfert-Rochereau, 75014 Paris, France.

ROUDYBUSH Alexandra, b. 14 Mar 1911, Hyres, France. Novelist. m. Franklin Roudybush, Dean of Roudybush Foreign Service School, France. Education: London School of Economics, 1929. Literary Appointments: Journalist, London Evening Standard, Correspondent at Washington, 1930; Time Magazine, 1931; Assistant to Drew Pierson, 1933; French News Agency, 1933; National Academy of Science, WA, 1934; News and Special Events of CBS Broadcasting Company, 1935; White House Correspondent, MBC Radio, 1940-48. Publications: Before The Ball Was Over, 1965; Death of a Moral Person, 1967; Capital Crime, 1969; House of The Cat, 1970; A Sybarite Death, 1972; Suddenly in Paris, 1975; The Female of The Species, 1977; Bloodties, 1981; In preparation - Beyond Gehenna, a story about Armenia; Elspeth and The Cooking Fairy. Memberships: Crime Writers of USA; Crime Writers of UK. Address: Sauveterre de Rouerque, 12800 Aveyron, France.

ROUNDTREE Owen. See: **KRAUZER Steven M.**

ROUSSEAU George, b. 1941, American. Literary Appointments: Osgood Fellow, English Literature, Princeton University, NJ, 1965-66; Instructor in English Literature, Harvard University, Cambridge, MA, 1966-68; Professor of Eighteenth-Century Studies, University of California, Los Angeles (joined faculty, 1968). Publications: Editor, This Long Disease My Life: Alexander Pope and The Sciences (with Marjorie Hope Nicholson), 1968; John Hill's Hypochondriasis, 1969; The Augustan Milieu: Essays Presented to Louis A Landa (edited with Eric Rothstein), 1970; Tobias Smollett: Bicentennial Essays Presented to Lewis M Knapp (co-editor), 1971; Editor, Organic Form: The Life of an Idea; English Poetic Satire: Wyatt to Byron (edited with Neil Rudenstine), 1972; Goldsmith: The Critical Heritage, 1974; The Renaissance Man in the 18th Century, 1978; The Ferment of Knowledge: Studies in The Historiography of Eighteenth Century Science (edited with Roy Porter), 1980; The Letters and Papers of Sir John Hill, Tobias Smollett: Essays of Two Decades, 1982; Editor, Literature and Science, 1985; Sexual Underworlds of The Enlightenment (co-editor), 1987; Exoticism and The Enlightenment (co-editor), 1988; The Languages of Psyche, 1990; Enlightenment Crossings, 1991; Perilous Enlightenment, 1991; Enlightenment Borders, 1991; Hysteria Beyond Freud, 1993. Honour: The Clifford Prize, 1987. Membership: Many international societies in Literature, Cultural History and Medicine. Address: 2424 Castilian Drive, Outpost Estates, Los Angeles, CA 90068, USA.

ROVNER Arkady, b. 28 Jan 1940, Odessa, Russia. Writer; Publisher; Teacher. m. Victoria Andreyeva, 5 Aug 1969, 1 s. Education: MA, Philosophy, Philosophy Department, 1965, Moscow University, Russia; Graduate Programme, Department of German and English, 1965-67, Moscow Pedagogical Institute, Russia; Graduate Programme, Department of Foreign Studies, American University, WA, USA, 1974-75; Doctoral Studies, Department of Religion, Columbia University, 1976-87. Literary Appointments: Publisher, Gnosis Press, 1978-; Instructor, Faculty Member, New York University, 1981-85; Instructor, The New School, NY, 1981-. Publications include: Gostii iz oblastii, 1975, 1991; Kalalatsy, 1980, 1990; Khod korolyom, 1989; Etagy Gadesa, 1992; The noumenal agent; The Step Towards Gnosis; The Russian Idea; In Search of Miraculous; Principles and Applications; V F Ern; A Hermit From The Mountain Arumachala; Krishnamurti; The Third Literature (with Victoria Andreyeva). Contributions to: Communication; Writers Introduce Writers; Short Story International; City; Central Park; Another Chicago Review; Spring; Appalachian Quarterly; Science and Religion. Honours: Cammington Community of The Arts, USA, 1983; Mme Karolyi Foundation, Vance, France, 1984. Membership: American PEN Center; The Union of Russian Writers. Address: PO Box 42, Prince Street Station, New York, NY 10012, USA.

ROWAN Deidre, See: **WILLIAMS Jeanne.**

ROWAN Hester. See: **ROBINSON Sheila Mary.**

ROWBOTHAM David Harold, b. 27 Aug 1924, Toowoomba, Queensland, Australia. Author; Journalist. m. Ethel Jessie Matthews, 14 Jan 1952, 2 d. Education: BA< University of Queensland, 1965; MA (QUAL), 1969. Literary Appointments include: Australian Delegate, World Congress of Poets, 1981; Cultural Visitor, USA, Library of Congress, 1988; Commonwealth Literary Fund Lecturer in Australian Literature, 1956, 1961, 1964; National Book Reviewing Panel, Australian Broadcasting Commission, 1954-63; Literary Editor, Brisbane Courier-Mail, 1980-87. Publications: Ploughman and Poet (poems), 1954; Town and City (stories), 1956; Inland (poems), 1958; The Man in The Jungle (novel), 1964; All The Room (poems), 1964; Bungalow and Hurricane (poems), 1967; The Makers of The Ark (poems), 1970; The Pen of Feathers (poems), 1971; Mighty Like a Harp (poems), 1974; Selected Poems, 1975; Maydays (poems), 1980; New and Selected Poems, now in preparation for Penguin Books. Contributions to: Numerous magazines and journals. Honours include: Pacific Star, World War II, 1945; Emeritus Fellow of Australian Literature, Australia Council, 1989; Second Prize for Poetry, NSW Captain Cook Bi-Centenary Celebrations Literary Competition, 1970; Grace Leven Prize, 1964; Third Prize for Poetry, Sydney Morning Herald Competition (jointly), 1949; Henry Lawson Prize for Poetry, University of Sydney, 1949; Ford Memorial Medal for Poetry, University of Queensland, 1948; Order of Australia, Queen's Birthday Honours, 1991. Memberships include: Australian Journalists Association; International Federation of Journalists; President, State Branch, Fellowship of Australian Writers, 1982. Address: 28 Percival Terrace, Holland Park, Brisbane, Queensland 4121, Australia.

ROWE Brian, See: **CRESSWELL Helen.**

ROWE Peter G, Appointments: Dean, Graduate School of Design, Harvard University. Address: Graduate School of Design, Harvard University, Cambridge, MA 02138-3800, USA.

ROWETT Helen Graham Quiller, b. 30 Dec 1915, London, England. Retired Lecturer. Education: Girton College, Cambridge, 1935-39; BA, Natural Science, 1938; Part II, Zoology, 1939; MA, 1942. Publications: Guides to Dissection Parts 1-5, 1950-53, translations into Sinhalese, Spanish, Malaysian; The Rat as a Small Mammal, 1960, 3rd edition, 1974; Guide to Dissection, 1962, revised edition 1970; Histology and Embryology, 1962; Basic Anatomy and Physiology, 1959, 3rd edition full revised 1988; Two Moorsway Guide, 1976, 4th edition, fully revised, 1993; Roundabout Family Rambling, 1995. Honours: Grisedale Research Scholarship, Manchester, 1939-40. Memberships: Society of Authors; Committee Member, West Country Writers; Institute of Biology; Fellow, Royal Society of Arts. Address: 3 Manor Park, Dousland, Yelverton, Devon PL20 6LX, England.

ROWINSKI Alexander, b. 9 Mar 1931, Poland. Author. m. Hanna Gis, 13 Sep 1975, 1 s, 1 d. Education: BA, Philosophical and Social Sciences, Warsaw University, 1953. Literary Appointments: Staff, Dziennik Zachodni, 1954-57, Prawo i Zycie, 1959-70, Kultura, 1972-78;

Editor in Chief, Przeglad Tygodniowy, 1982-83. Publications: Anioly Warszawy, 1970, 3rd edition, 1974; Wstapcie do klasztoru, 1966, 2nd edition, 1970; Rozkoszny Pantoffelland, 1974; Wlepszym towarzystwie, 1975; Tamci zolnierze, 1979, 2nd edition, 1988; Swiat sie konczy, 1972; Spadek po synach slonca, 1987. Contributions to: Numerous magazines and journals. Honours: Julian Brun's Award, 1960; Polish Journalists Association's Award, 1966; Award, Zycie Literackie, 1969; Ksawery pruszynski's Award, 1975. Memberships: ZAIKS; Polish Authors Association, Presidium Member. Literary Agent: Agencja Autorska, Warsaw. Address: ul Jazgarzewska 10, 00-730 Warsaw, Poland.

ROWLAND Iris. See: **ROBERTS Irene.**

ROWLAND J(ohn) R(ussell), b. 10 Feb 1925, Armidale, New South Wales, Australia. Diplomat; Poet. Education: BA, University of Sydney, 1945. Appointments include: Australian Ambassador to France, 1978-82; Visiting Fellow at the Australian National University, 1982-83. Publications: The Feast of Ancestors, 1965; Snow, 1971; Time and Places: Poems of Locality, 1975; The Clock Inside, 1979; Sixty, 1989; Granite Country, 1994; Translator, The Sculptor of Candles, 1985. Honours include: Officer, Order of Australia, 1981. Address: 15 Grey Street, Deakin, ACT 2600, Australia.

ROWLAND Peter Kenneth, b. 1938, British. Appointments: Administration Officer, London Waste Regulation Authority. Publications: The Last Liberal Governments: The Promised Land 1905-1910, 1968; The Last Liberal Governments: Unfinished Business 1911-1914, 1971; Lloyd George, 1975; Macaulay's History of England in the 18th Century (ed), 1980; Macaulay's History of England from 1485 to 1685 (ed), 1985; Autobiography of Charles Dickens (ed), 1988; The Disappearance of Edwin Drood, 1991. Address: 18 Corbett Road, London E11 2LD, England.

ROWLAND Robin F, b. 17 Jun 1950, Tanga, Tanzania. Writer. Education: Lawrence Park Collegiate, Toronto, Canada; BA, Anthropology, York University, Toronto, 1973; Bachelor of Journalism, Carleton University, Ottawa, 1975. Literary Appointments: Reporter, Sudbury Star, Sudbury, Ontario, Canada, 1975-76; Editor, CBC National Radio News, Toronto, 1977-80; Writer, Editor, CBC Teletext, Toronto, 1982-85; Freelance Writer, CTV National News, Toronto, 1988-. Publications: King of The Mob, Rocco Perri and The Women Who Ran His Rackets, 1987; Undercover: Cases of The RCMP's Most Secret Operative (with James Dubro), 1991; Radio Plays: A Truthful Witness, 1985; King of The Bootleggers, 1986; Hot Coffee, 1988. Membership: Science Fiction and Fantasy Writers of America. Address: Eridani Productions, Suite 1005, 268 Poplar Plains Road, Toronto, Ontario, Canada, M4V 2P2.

ROWLAND-ENTWISTLE (Arthur), Theodore (Henry), b. 30 July 1925, Clayton-le-Moors, Lancashire, England. Writer. Education: BA (Hons), Open University. Publications: Famous Composers (with J Cooke), 1974; Animal Worlds, with J Cooke, 1975; Famous Explorers, with J Cooke, 1975; Facts and Records Book of Animals, 1975; Famous Kings and Emperors, with J Cooke, 1977; The World You Never See: Insect Life, 1976; Our Earth, 1977; The Restless Earth, 1977; Exploring Animal Homes, 1978; Seashore Life (as T E Henry), 1983; Fishes (as James Hall-Clarke), 1983; Fact Book of British History, with J Cooke, 1984; Heraldy, 1984; Houses, 1985; World of Speed, 1985; Confucius, 1986; Stamps, 1986; Nebuchadnezzar, 1986; Rivers and Lakes, 1986; Focus on Rubber, 1986; Great British Architects, 1986; Great British Inventors, 1986; Great British Kings and Queens, 1986; Great British Reformers, 1986; Focus on Coal, 1987; The Royal Marines, 1987; The Secret Service, 1987; The Special Air Service, 1987; Jungles and Rainforests, 1987; Three-Dimensional Atlas of the World, 1988; Flags, 1988; Guns, 1988; Focus on Silk, 1989; Weather and Climate, 1991. Contributions to: Various encyclopaedias and periodicals. Memberships: FRGS; FZS. Literary Agent: Rupert Crew Ltd. Address: West Dene, Stonstile Lane, Hastings, Sussex TN35 4PE, England.

ROWSE A(lfred) L(eslie), b. 4 Dec 1903, St Austell, Cornwall, England. Writer; Poet; Professor Emeritus. Education: MA, Christ Church, Oxford, 1929. Appointments include: Fellow of All Souls College, Oxford, 1925-74; Research Associate at the Huntington Library, San Merino, California, USA, 1962-69. Publications include: Poems of a Decade, 1941; Poems Chiefly Cornish, 1944; Poems Partly American, 1959; The Road to Oxford, 1978; A Life: Collected Poems, 1981; Transatlantic: Later Poems, 1989; Tudor Cornwall: Portrait of a

Society, 1941; A Cornish Childhood, 1942; The England of Elizabeth, 1950; The Cornish in America, 1969; The Churchills: The Story of a Family, 1956-58; The Elizabethans and America; William Shakespeare: A Biography, 1963; Christopher Marlowe: A Biography, 1964; Shakespeare's Southampton, 1965; The Elizabethan Renaissance, 1971-72; Shakespeare the Man, 1973; Oxford in the History of the Nation, 1975; Matthew Arnold, Poet and Prophet, 1976; Homosexuals in History, 1977; Simon Forman: Sex and Society in Shakespeare's Age, 1994; The Byrons and Trevanions, 1978; A Man of the Thirties, 1979; Memories of Men and Women, 1980; Shakespeare's Globe: His Intellectual and Moral Outlook, 1981; Eminent Elizabethans, 1983; Shakespeare's Self-Portrait, 1984; Froude the Historian, 1987; The Poet Auden, 1987; Discovering Shakespeare, 1989; Editions of Shakespeare. Honours include: Fellow, Royal Society of Literature; Benson Medal. Address: Trenarren House, St Austell, Cornwall, PL26 6BH, England.

ROYCE Kenneth. See: **GANDLEY Kenneth Royce.**

ROYSTER Charles, b. 27 Nov 1944, Nashville, Tennessee, USA. Education: AB, MA, PhD, University of California, Berkeley. Appointments: Professor of History. Contributions to: William & Mary Quarterly. Honours: Bancroft Prize, 1992; John D Rockefeller III Book Award, 1979. Address: Dept of History, Louisiana State University, Baton Rouge, LA 70803-3601, USA.

ROZHDESTVENSKY Robert Ivanovich, b. 20 Jun 1932, Kosikha Village, Russia. Author; Poet. Publications include: Poetry: Flags of Spring, 1955; To My Contemporary, 1962; Radius of Action, 1965; Vera's Son, 1966; The Dedication, 1970; Requiem, 1970; In All Earnestness, 1970; The Artist Aleksandra Bill, 1970; The Heart's Radar, 1971; The Return: Verse of Several Years, 1972; The Line, 1973; In The Twenty Years, 1973; Before The Holiday: Verse and Poems, 1974; Selected Works, 1974; Two Hundred and Ten Steps, 1978; The Voice of The Town, 1979; The Seventies, 1979; This is The Time, 1980; verse translated into many languages. Honours: Order of Red Banner; Order of Lenin; State Prize, 1979; several medals. Address: USSR Union of Writers, Ulitsa Vorovskogo 52, Moscow, Russia.

RU Zhi-juan, b. 13 Sep 1925, Shanghai, China. Teacher; Editor; Author. m. Wang Xiao Ping, 9 Sep 1950, 1 s, 2 d. Literary Appointments: Vice-Chairman, Chinese Writers Association, Shanghai Branch; Vice Chief Editor, Shanghai Literature. Publications: Short Stories: Lily Flower, 1958; Tall White Poplar, 1959; Quite Maternity Hospital, 1967; The Story Which has Been Montaged It Wrong, 1978; A Path on the Prairie, 1980; Novels: She Comes From That Path, 1983; Flower Cherisher Has Gone, 1982; Plays: No 800 Locomotive Starts Off, 1951; The Soldier Without Gun, 1954; Film: If You Say You Need, 1959; Essays: Talking About My Creative Experience, 1984; Mother and Daughter Toured in America Together, 1986. Honour: National Best Short Story Prize, 1978. Membership: Chinese Writers' Association. Address: 675 Ju Lu Road, Shanghai, China.

RUAS Charles Edward, b. 14 Nov 1938, Tientsin, China. Author. m. Agneta Danielsson, 10 June 1967, div 1976, 1 sons. Education: BA 1960, MA 1963, PhD 1970, Princeton University; The Sorbonne University of Paris, 1964. Publications: Conversations with American Writers, 1986; Entering the Dream: Lewis Carol, 1994; Trans: Michel Foucault, Death & the Labyrinth: The Life and Works of Raymond Roussel, 1989; Pierre Assouline: An Artful Life: D H Kahnweiler, 1990; Contributions to: The New York Times; The Village Voice; The Soho News; The Paris Review. Honours: Best of the year, New York Times Book Review; Fulbright Lecturer, 1992; Danforth Fellow, NEA, NYSCA. Memberships: Pen International; Writers Room. Literary Agent: Irene Skolnick, Curtis Brown Association.

RUBENS Bernice Ruth, b. 26 July 1928, Cardiff, Wales. Author. m. Rudi Nassauer, 1947, 2 daughters. Education: BA, University of Wales. Appointments: Author, Director, documentary films on Third World subjects. Publications: Novels: Set on Edge, 1960; Madame Sontsatzka, 1962; Mate in Three, 1964; The Elected Member, 1968; Sunday Best, 1970; Go Tell the Lemming, 1972; I Sent a Letter to My Love, 1974; Ponsonby Post, 1976; A Five-year Sentence, 1978; Spring Sonata, 1979; Birds of Passage, 1980; Brothers, 1982; Mr Wakefield's Crusade, 1985; Our Father, 1987; Kingdom Come; A Solitary Grie, 1991; Mother Russia, 1992; Autobiopsy, 1993. Honours: Booker Prize, 1970; American Blue Ribbon (documentary film), 1972; Hon DLitt, University of Wales. Membership: Fellow, University College, Cardiff.

Literary Agent: Mark Lucas, Peters, Fraser & Dunlop. Address: 16a Belsize Park Gardens, London NW3 4LD, England.

RUBIN Larry Jerome, b. 14 Feb 1930, Bayonne, New Jersey, USA. Professor of English, Georgia Institute of Technology. Education: BA, 1951; MA, 1952; PhD, 1956, Emory University. Literary Appointments: Smith-Mundt Fellow, University of Krakow, Poland, 1961-62; Fulbright Lecturer, University of Bergen, Norway, 1966-67; Free University of West Berlin, 1969-70; University of Innsbruck, Austria, 1971-72. Publications include: 3 books of poetry: The World's Old Way, 1963; Lanced in Light, 1967; All My Mirrors Lie, 1975; Poems in 55 Anthologies including: A Geography of Poets, 1979; The Norton Introdution to Poetry, 3rd Edition, 1986. Contributions to: Poetry to various literary journals including: New Yorker; Poetry; Saturday Review; Yale Review; The Nation; Esquire; Transatlantic Review; London Magazine; American Scholar; Harper's Magazine; Virginia Quarterly Review; Quarterly Review of Literature; Encounter; Sewanee Review; Antioch Review; New York Quarterly; New Letters; Massachusetts Review; University of Windsor Review. Address: Box 15014, Druid Hills Branch, Atlanta, GA 30333, USA.

RUBIN Rivka Leah Jacobs, b. 22 Feb 1952, Philadelphia, PA, USA. Writer. m. Gerald E Rubin, 25 Nov 1981, 1 s. Education: BA, History, 1981, MA, Sociology, 1982, Marshall University. Publications: Experimentum Crucis, 1981; The Boy From The Moon, 1985; The Milk of Paradise, 1985; Morning on Venus, 1985. Honours: Honourable Mention for Poetry, Poetry Manuscript, West Virginia Writers Inc, 1983; Honourable Mention, Writers of The Future Contest, 1985. Memberships: Science Fiction Writers of America; West Virginia Sociological Association. Address: 1285 26th Street, Huntington, WV 25705, USA.

RUBINSTEIN Gillian Margaret, b. 29 Aug 1942, Berkhamsted, England. Author. m. Philip Rubinstein, 1973, 1 son, 2 daughters. Education: BA, MA, Modern Languages, Oxford University, 1961-64; Postgraduate Certificate of Education, University of London, 1972. Publications: Space Demons, 1986; Beyond the Labyrinth, 1988; Answers to Brut, 1988; Melanie and the Night Animal, 1988; Skymaze, 1989; Flashback, 1990; At Ardilla, 1991; Dog In, Cat Out, 1991; Squawk and Screech, 1991; Galax-Arena, 1992; Keep Me Company, 1992; Mr Plunkett's Pool, 1992; The Giant's Tooth, 1993; Foxspell, 1994. Honours: Honour Book, Australian Children's Book Council, 1987, 1989; Senior Fellowship, Australia Council, 1988, 1989-92; National Children's Book Award, 1988, 1990; New South Wales Premier's Award, 1988; Book of the Year, CBA, 1989. Memberships: Australian Society of Authors. Literary Agent; Australian Literary Management, Middle Park, Australia. Address: c/o Australian Literary Management, 2a Armstrong St, Middle Park, Victoria 3206, Australia.

RUBINSTEIN Hilary Harold, b. 24 Apr 1926, London. Literary Agent and Writer. m. Helge Kitzinger, 6 Aug 1955, 3 sons, 1 daughter. Education: Cheltenham College; MA, Merton College, Oxford. Appointments: Director, Victor Gollancz Ltd, 1953-63; Deputy Editor, The Observer Magazine, 1964-65; Managing Director, A P Watt, 1965-92; Managing Director, Hilary Rubinstein Books, 1992-. Publications: The Complete Insomniac (Cape 1974, Coronet 1976) published in the USA as Insomniacs of World Goodnight; Good Hotel Guide, founded and published annually since 1978, published in the USA as Europe's Wonderful Hotels and Inns; Editor: Hotels and Inns, 1984. Contributions to: Times; Guardian; Observer; New Statesman; Telegraph Magazine; Conde Nast Traveler. Memberships: Literature Panel 1973-79, Literature Financial Committee, 1975-77, Arts Council; Council Institute of Contemporary Arts, 1976-92; Trustee, Open College of the Arts, 1987-; Society of Authors. Address: 61 Clarendon Road, London W11 4JE, England.

RUDKIN James David, b. 29 June 1936, London, England. Dramatist. m. Alexandra Margaret Thompson, 3 May 1967, 2 s, 2 d. Education: MA, St Catherine's, Oxford, 1957-61. Appointment: Judith E Wilson Fellow, University of Cambridge, 1984. Publications: Afore Night Come (stage play), 1964; Ashes (stage play), 1974; Cries From Casement as His Bones are Brought to Dublin (radio play), 1974; Penda's Fen (TV Film), 1975; Hippolytus (translation from Euripides), 1980; The Sons of Light (stage play), 1981; The Triumph of Death (stage play), 1981; Peer Gynt (translation from Ibsen), 1983; The Saxon Shore (stage play), 1986; Rosmersholm (translation from Ibsen), 1990; When We Dead Waken (translation from Ibsen), 1990. Contributions to: Drama; Tempo; Encounter. Honours: Evening Standard Most Promising Dramatist Award, 1962; John Whiting Drama

Award, 1974; New York OBIE (Ashes), 1977; New York Film Festival Gold Medal (Testimony), 1987, screenplay award; Sony Silver (The Lovesong of Alfred J Hitchcock), 1994, radio drama award. Membership: Hellenic Society; PEN. Literary Agent: Casarotto Ramsay Limited. Address: c/o Casarotto Ramsay Limited, National House, 60-66 Wardour Street, London, W1V 3HP, England.

RUDMAN Mark, b. 11 Dec 1948, New York City, USA. Writer; Teacher; Editor. m. Madelaine Bates, 28 Dec 1977, 1 s. Education: BA, New School for Social Research, 19071; Columbia University School of the Arts, 1974. Career: Editor-in-Chief, Pequod, 1983-. Publications: The Nowhere Steps, 1990; Diverse Voices, 1993; By Contraries, 1987; Robert Lowell, 1983; My Sister-Life, 1982, revised, 1992; Memories of Love: Selected Poems of Bohdan Boychuk, 1989; Rider, 1994; Realm of Unknowing: Meditations on Art & Suicide, 1995; Square of Angels, 1976. Address: 817 West End Avenue, New York City, NY 10025, USA.

RUDOLF Anthony, b. 6 Sept 1942, London, England. Editor; Poet. Education: BA, Trinity College, Cambridge, 1964. Appointments include: Co-founder and Editor, Menard Press, London, 1969; Advisory Editor, Modern Poetry in Translation, 1973-83, and Jewish Quarterly, 1975-82. Publications: The Manifold Circle, 1971; The Same River Twice, 1976; After the Dream: Poems 1964-79, 1980; From Poetry to Politics: The Menard Press 1969-84; Translations of French and Russian literature. Address: 8 The Oaks, Woodside Avenue, London N12 8AR, England.

RUDOLPH Lee, b. 28 Mar 1948. Mathematician. Education: BA, Princeton University, 1969; PhD, MIT, 1974. Literary Appointments: Assistant Copy Editor, Standard-Times, New Bedford, 1987. Publications: Curses and Songs and Poems, 1974; The Country Changes, 1978; Anthologies in: Contemporary Poetry, 1974; Tygers of Wrath, 1981; Contemporary New England Poetry, 1987. Contributions to: Kayak; Quarterly Review of Literature; Toy Son; Counter-Measures; 17 research articles in Mathematical Journals and Proceedings of Symposia, 1976-88; The New Yorker. Honours: Bain-Swiggett Memorial Award, Krull Memorial Academy of American Poets, 1966-69; Book of The Month Club, College English Association, Writing Fellowship, 1969-70. Memberships: Past Treasurer, Alice James Poetry Co-operative; National Writers Union. Address: PO Box 251, Adamsville, RI 02801, USA.

RUDOMIN Esther. See: **HAUTZIG Esther.**

RUELL Patrick. See: **HILL Reginald (Charles).**

RUELLAND Jacques G, b. 14 Aug 1948, Spa, Belgium. Professor, History of Sciences, Philosophy of Sciences. m. Krystyna Brylska-Ruelland, 17 Nov 1977, 1 daughter. Education: BA Philosophy, 1975; MA Philosophy, 1983; MA History, 1985; PhD History of Sciences, 1994. Literary Appointments: Société des écrivains canadiens, Montreal, 1992; Société des écrivains canadiens, Quebec, 1993; Société des écrivains canadiens, Chicoutimi, 1994. Publications: Pierre du Calvet 1735-1786, 1986; Valentin Jautard 1736-1787, 1989; Orwell et 1984: trois approches, 1988; De l'épistémologie à la politique, 1991; Histoire de la guerre sainte, 1993; La Moisson littéraire, 1993. Contributions to: Les Arts, Nouméa, New-Caledonia; Philosopher, Montreal; Philosophiques, Montreal; Archives de philosophie, Paris. Honours: Honourary Member, Fondation Aérovision, Quebec. Memberships: President, Musée des arts graphiques, Quebec, 1986-; President, Société des arts et des lettres, Brossard, 1993-; General President, Société des écrivains canadiens, 1993-. Address: 360 rue de Venise, Brossard, Quebec J4W 1W7, Canada.

RUFFIN Paul, b. 14 May 1941, Millport, AL, USA. Professor of English. m. Sharon Krebs, 16 Jun 1973, 1 s, 1 d. Education: BA 1964, MA 1968, Mississippi State University; PhD, University of Southern Mississippi. Literary Appointments: Editor, The Texas Review, 1976-. Publications: The Man Who Would Be God and Other Stories; What I Like About The South; Southern Fiction for The Nineties; Lighting The Furnace Pilot; Our Women; The Storm Cellar; Co-author, Contemporary New England Poetry; A Sampler; Contemporary Southern Short Fiction: A Sampler; To Come Up Grinning; A Tribute to George Garrett. Contributions to: American Way; Southern Review; Ploughshares; Alaska Quarterly Review; Michigan Quarterly Review. Memberships: Texas Institute of Letters; South Central Modern Language Association; Conference of College Teachers of English;

Texas Association of Creative Writing Teachers. Address: 2014 Avenue N 1-2, Huntsville, TX 77340, USA.

RUGANDA John, b. 1941, Uganda. Playwright. Education: BA, Makerere University, Kampala. Appointments include: Senior Fellow in Creative Writing at Makerere University, from 1973; Founder-member of the Nairobi Travelling Theatre, Kenya. Publications: The Burdens, 1972; Black Mamba, 1972; Covenant of Death, 1973; The Floods, 1979; Music Without Tears, 1981; Echoes of Silence, 1985; Plays produced in Kampala and Nairobi. Address: c/o Heinemann Kenya, PO Box 45314, Nairobi, Kenya.

RUIZ Benardo, b. 6 Oct 1953, Mexico DF. Author; Critic. m. Virginia Abrin Batule, 18 Nov 1978, 2 sons. Education: BA, Spanish and Latin American Literature, Universdidad Nacional Autonoma de Mexico. Career: Editor, Universidad Autonoma Metropolitana, 1979; Production Manager, Premia Editora, 1982; Staff, Tiempo de Mexico, 1982; Casa del Teiempo, 1983-84; Editor, Ministry of Labour, 1985-88; Advisor, National Council of Culture and Art; Advisor, Presidence of the Republic, 1990-91; Director, INBA, Centro Nacional De Informacion y Promocion De La Literatura, 1992. Publications include: Viene la Muerte (short stories), 1976; La otra orilla (short stories) 1980; Olvidar tu nombre (novel) 1982; Vals sin fin (short stories), 1982 revised 1986; El Tuyo, el mismo (poetry), 1986; Los caminos del hotel (fiction) 1991; Juego De Cartas (poetry), 1992. Contributions to: Excelsior, Revista de la Universidad, Casa del Tiempo, Plural, Revista de Bellas Artes; PC Semanal; Tierro Adentro; Nexos, Personal Computing. Honours: Literature Scholarship, Instituto Nacional de Ballas Artes, 1973; Honorary Mention: National Essay Award Jose Revueltas, 1978. Memberships: Asociacion de Escritores de Mexico; Sociedad General de Escritores de Mexico; Asociacion de Criticos de Mexico. Address: Arizona 94-6, Col Napoles, CP 03810, Mexico DF.

RULE Jane, b. 28 Mar 1931, Plainfield, NJ, USA. Literary. Education: Mills College, California. Appointments: Teacher of English, Concord Academy, MA, 1954-56; Assistant Director of International House, 1958-59; Intermittent Lecturer in English, 1959-70; Visiting Lecturer in Creative Writing, University of British Columbia, Vancouver, 1972-73. Publications: The Desert of The Heart, 1964; This Is Not You, 1970; Against The Season, 1971; Lesbian Images, 1975; Themes For Diverse Instruments, 1975; The Young in One Another's Arms, 1977; Contract With the World, 1980; Outlander, 1981; Inland Passage, A Hot-Eyed Moderate, 1985; Memory Board, 1987; After The Fire, 1989. Honours: Canadian Author's Association, Best Novel of the Year, 1978, Best Story of the Year, 1978; US Gay Academic Union Literature Award, 1978; Canadian Institute for the Blind, 1991. Address: The Fork, Rte 1, S19 C 17, Galiano, BC Canada, V0N 1P0.

RUMENS Carol Ann, b. 10 Dec 1944, Forest Hill, London, England. Writer. m. 23 Jul 1966, 2 d. Education: BA Honours, University of London, 1966. Appointment: Fellow, Royal Society of Literature, 1984. Publications: Unplayed Music, 1981; Star Whisper, 1983; Direct Dialling, 1985; Selected Poems, 1987; Plato Park (novel), 1987; From Bekin to Heaven (poetry), 1989. Contributions to: Times Literary Supplement; Observer; Punch; Question; Literary Review; Poetry Review. Honour: Alice Hunt Bartlett Award (jointly), 1981; Cholmondeley Award, 1984; Prudence Farmer Award, 1983. Memberships: International PEN; Society of Authors; Society for Cultural Relations with Russia. Literary Agent: The Peters, Fraser and Dunlop Group Limited. Address: c/o Chatto and Windus, 30 Bedford Square, London, WC1, England.

RUNDLE Anne (Marianne Lamont, Alexandra Manners, Joanne Marshall, Jeanne Sanders), British. Publications: The Moon Marriage, 1967; Swordlight, 1968; Cuckoo at Candlemass (as J Marshall), 1968; Cat on a Broomstick (as J Marshall), The Dreaming Tower (as J Marshall), Dragonscale, 1969; Rakehell, Tamlane, Dark Changeling (as M Lamont), Green Glass Moon (as M Lamont), Flower of Silence (as J Marshall), 1970; Babylon Was Dust (as J Marshall), Bitter Bride Bed (as M Lamont), 1971; Lost Lotus, Amberwood, 1972; Wildboar Wood (as J Marshall), The Trelised Walk, Sea-Song, The Stone Maiden (as A Manners), 1973; Candles in The Wood (as A Manners), Heron Brook, Spindrift (as J Sanders), Follow a Shadow (as J Marshall), Valley of Tall Chimneys (as J Marshall), 1974; The Singing Swans (as A Manners), 1975; Judith Lammeter, 1976; Sable Hunter (in US paperback as Cardigan Square) (as A Manners), Nine Moons Wasted (as M Lamont), 1977; Grey Ghyll, The Peacock Bed (as J Marshall), Wildford's Daughter (as A Manners), 1978 (in UK as The White Moths, 1979); Horns of The Moon (as M Lamont), 1979; Echoing

Yesterday (as A Manners), 1981; Trilogy, Karran Kinrade (as A Manners), 1982; A Serpent's Tooth (as M Lamont), 1983; Trilogy, The Red Bird (as A Manners), Trilogy, The Gaming House (as A Manners), 1984; Moonbranches, 1986. Address: Cloy Cottage, Knowe Road, Brodick, Isle of Arran, Scotland.

RUNHAM. See: **ACKROYD Peter.**

RUSAN Otila Valeria. See: **BLANDIANA Ana.**

RUSH Norman, b. 24 Oct 1933, San Francisco, California, USA. Writer. m. Elsa, 10 July 1955, 1 s, 1 d. Education: BA, Swarthmore College, 1956. Career: Part-time writer and self-employed dealer in antiquarian books, 1958-73; Instructor in English and history and Co-Director of College A, Rockland Community College, Suffern, New York, 1973-78; Co-Director, US Peace Corps, Botswana, Africa, 1978-83; Full-time writer, 1983-. Publications: Whites: Stories, 1986; Mating (novel), 1991. Contributions to: Short stories in anthologies, including Best American Short Stories, periodicals. Membership: PEN American Center; American Economic Association. Literary Agent: Wylie, Aitken and Stone Inc, New York. Address: 10 High Tor Road, New City, NY 10956, USA.

RUSHDIE (Ahmed) Salman, b. 19 Jun 1947, Bombay, India. Writer. m. (1) Clarissa Luard, 1976 (diss 1987), 1 s, (2) Marianne Wiggins, 1988. Education: MA, King's College, Cambridge. Literary Appointments: Actor, Fringe Theatre, London, 1968-69; Advertising Copywriter, 1969-73; Part-time Copywriter, 1976-80. Publications: Grimus, 1975; Midnight's Children, 1981; Shame, 1983; The Jaguar Smile: A Nicaraguan Journey, 1987; The Satanic Verses, 1988; Haroun and The Sea of Stories, 1990; Imaginary Homelands (essays), 1991; The Wizard of Oz, 1992; Television films: The Painter and The Pest, 1985; The Riddle of Midnight, 1988. Contributions to: New York Times; The Guardian; Granta; New Yorker. Honours: Booker McConnell Prize for Fiction, 1981; Arts Council Literature Bursary, 1981; English Speaking Union Literary Award, 1981; James Tait Black Memorial Book Prize, 1981; Prix du Meilleur Livre Etranger, 1984; Nominated for Whitbread Prize, 1988; Booker Prize, 1993. Memberships: PEN; Production Board, British Film Institute; Advisory Board, Institute of Contemporary Arts; Fellow, Royal Society of Literature; Executive, Camden Committee for Community Relations, 1975-82. Address: c/o Aitken and Stone Limited, 29 Fernshaw Road, London, SW10 0TG, England.

RUSHTON William (George), b. 1937, British. Literary Appointments: Founder Editor, 1961 and Contributor, Private Eye Magazine, London; Numerous appearances on the stage, in film and as broadcaster. Publications: William Rushton's Dirty Book, 1964; How To Play Football: The Art of Dirty Play, 1968; The Day of The Grocer, 1971; The Geranium of Flut, 1975; Superpig, 1976; Pigsticking: A Joy of Life, 1977; The Reluctant Euro, 1980; The Fifth Amendment, 1981; W G Grace's Last Case, 1984; Adam and Eve, 1985; Don't Open That Trapdoor, The Alternative Gardener, 1986; Marylebone Versus the Rest of The World, 1987; Spy Thatcher, editor, 1987; Every Cat in The Book, 1993. Membership: The Academy Club. Literary Agent: Roger Hancock Limited, 4 Water Lane, London, NW1 8NZ, England. Address: Wallgrave Road, London, SW5, England.

RUSSELL James. See: **HARKNETT Terry.**

RUSSELL John, b. 1919, British. Appointments: Honorary Attache, Tate Gallery, 1940-41; served in the Ministry of Information, 1941-43, The Naval Intelligence Division, Admiralty, London, 1943-46; Regular Contributor, 1945-49, Art Critic, 1949-74, The Sunday Times; Art Critic, 1974-; Chief Art Critic, 1982-, The New York Times. Publications: Shakespeare's Country, 1942; British Portrait Painters, 1945; Switzerland, Logan Pearsall Smith, 1950; Erich Kleiber, 1956; Paris, 1960, 1983; Seurat, Private View (with Bryan Robertson and Lord Snowdon), 1965; Max Ernst, 1967; Henry Moore, 1968; Ben Nicholson, Pop Art Redefined (with Suzi Gablik), 1969; The World of Matisse, 1970; Francis Bacon, Edouard Vuillard, 1971; The Meanings of Modern Art, 1981, new and enlarged edition, 1990; Reading Russell, 1989. Address: 166 East 61st Street, New York, NY 10021, USA.

RUSSELL John Leonard, b. 22 Jun 1906, Wye, Kent, England. Catholic Priest; Lecturer in Philosophy (retired). Education: Christ's College, Cambridge, 1925-29, 1931-35; MA, 1932; PhD, 1935. Publications: Science and Metaphysics, 1958; Theology of Evolution (with E Nemesszeghy) 1972. Contributions to: Annals of Science;

British Journal for The History of Science; Heythrop Journal; Journal for The History of Astronomy; Month; Nature. Memberships: British Society for The History of Science; British Society of The Philosophy of Science. Address: 114 Mount Street, London, W1Y 6AH, England.

RUSSELL Martin James, b. 25 Sep 1934, Bromley, Kent, England. Writer. Publications: No Through Road, 1965; The Client, 1975; Mr T, 1977; Death Fuse, 1980; Backlash, 1981; The Search for Sara, 1983; A Domestic Affair, 1984; The Darker Side of Death, 1985; Prime Target, 1985; Dead Heat, 1986; The Second Time is Easy, 1987; House Arrest, 1988; Dummy Run, 1989; Mystery Lady, 1992. Memberships: Crime Writers' Association; Detection Club. Literary Agent: Curtis Brown. Address: 15 Breckonmead, Wanstead Road, Bromley, Kent, BR1 3BW, England.

RUSSELL Nicholas, b. 9 Oct 1938, Teddington, Middlesex, England. University Professor; Journalism Teacher. m. Sharon Elizabeth Plows, 20 Jun 1964, 2s. Education: BA English Honours, McGill University, 1966; MA English Honours, University of London, 1966; PhD Journalism, University of Wales, 1994. Publications: Morals and the Media, 1994; Monographs, Trials & Tribulations, 1986; The Quarrymen of History, 1987. Contributions to: Many Magazines and Journals. Memberships: Commonwealth Association if Journalists; Commonwealth Association of Journalism Educators; Association for Education in Journalism. Address: School of Journalism, University of Regina, Regina, S4S OA2, Canada.

RUSSELL Ray, b. 4 Sept 1924, Chicago, Illinois, USA. Author; Editor. m. Ada Beth Stevens, 5 Sept 1950, 1 s, 1 d. Education: Chicago Conservatory; Goodman Theatre School of Drama (division of Art Institute, Chcago). Publications: Sardonicus, 1961; The Case Against Satan, 1962; The Little Lexicon of Love, 1966; Unholy Trinity, 1967; The Colony, 1969; Sagittarius, 1971; Prince of Darkness,1971; Incubus, 1976; Holy Horatio, 1976; Princess Pamela, 1979; The Book of Hell, 1980; The Devil's Mirror, 1980; The Bishop's Daughter, 1981; Haunted Castles, 1985; The Night Sound (poetry) 1987; Dirty Money, 1988; Absolute Power, 1992; Stories in 100 anthologies and textbooks. Contributions to: The Paris Review; Verbatim; Theology Today; Ellery Queen; Fantasy and Science Fiction Magazine; Playboy (Associate Editor 1954-55, Executive Editor, 1955-60, Contributing Editor, 1968-74); Editor, The Permanent Playboy (anthology) 19569, 40 other anthologies 1960-74; Film screenplays for Warner Brothers, Universal, Columbia, MGM, Twentieth Century Fox, American International. Honours: Sri Chinmoy Poetry Award, 1977; World Fantasy Lifetime Achievement Award, 1991; Bram Stoker Award, 1993. Literary Agent: H N Swanson Inc, Los Angeles. Address: c/o H N Swanson Inc, 8523 Sunset Boulevard, Los Angeles, CA 890069, USA.

RUSSELL Roy, b. Blackpool, Lancashire, England. Author; Dramatist. Publications include: Television plays and series: No Hiding Place; Fothgale; The Saint; The Troubleshooters; A Man of Our Times; Champion House; Sexton Blake; Dixon of Dock Green; Doomwatch; Crime of Passion; Crown Court; A Family at War; The Onedin Line; Intimate Strangers; A House in Regent Street (4 plays); Tales of The Unexpected; The Woodcutter Operation; Last Video and Testament; The Irish RM; Henry's Leg; BBC Playhouse Children's TV Dramas and Radio Plays; Documentary Films: The Lonely Sea and The Sky; Prince Bernhard, Pilot Royal; Prince Charles, Pilot Royal; Stage Plays include: The Eleventh Commandment; Books include: A Family at War; Towards Victory. Contributions to: Various magazines and journals. Honours; Laurel Award for Distinguished Services to Writers; Writers Guild of Great Britain. Memberships: Writers Guild of Great Britain; Society of Authors. Literary Agent: Lemon Unna and Durbridge Limited. Address: c/o Lemmon Unna and Durbridge Limited, 24 Pottery Lane, Holland Park, London, W11 4LZ, England.

RUSSELL Sharman Apt, b. 23 July 1954, California, USA. Teacher; Writer. m. Peter Russell, 24 Jan 1981, 1 s, 1 d. Education: BS, Conservation and Natural Resources, UC Berkeley; MFA, English and Creative Writing, University of Montana. Publications: Songs of the Fluteplayer, 1991; Kill the Cowboy: A Battle of Mythology in the West, 1993; The Humpbacked Fluteplayer, 1993; Frederick Douglas, 1987; Built to Last, 1986 (co-author). Contributions to: Countryside; Harrowsmith; The Massachusetts Review; The North American Review; The Missouri Review; The New York Times; New Women; The Threepenny Review. Literary Agent: Felicia Eth (adult); Martha Casselman (children's). Address: Rt 15 Box 2560, Mimbres, NM 898049, USA.

RUSSELL William Martin (Willy), b. 23 Aug 1947. Author. m. Ann Seagroatt, 1969, 1 s, 2 d. Education: Certificate of Education, St Katherine's College of Education, Liverpool. Appointments: Ladies Hairdresser, 1963-69; Teacher, 1973-74; Fellow, Creative Writing, Manchester Polytechnic, 1977-78. Publications include: Theatre: Blind Scouse, 1971-72; When The Reds (adaptation), 1972; John, Paul, George, Ringo and Bert (musical), 1974; Breezeblock Park, 1975; One For The Road, 1976; Stags and Hens, 1978; Educating Rita, 1979; Blood Brothers (musical), 1983; Our Day Out (musical), 1983; Television Plays: King of The Castle, 1972; Death of a Young Young Man, 1972; Break In (for schools), 1974; Our Day Out, 1976; Lies (for schools), 1977; Daughter of Albion, 1978; Boy With Transistor Radio (for schools), 1979; One Summer (series), 1980; Radio Play: I Read The News Today (for schools), 1979; Screenplays: Band on The Run, 1979; Educating Rita, 1981; Shirley Valentine (stage play), 1986. Honours: Honorary MA, Open University; Honorary Director, Liverpool Playhouse. Address: c/o Margaret Ramsay Limited, 14A Goodwin's Court, St Martin's Lane, London, WC2, England.

RUSSO Albert, b. 26 Feb 1943, Kamina, Zaire. Writer. 1 s, 1 d. Education: Abschluss Diplom, Heidelberg; BSc, General Business Administration, New York University, USA. Appointment: Member of Jury of The Prix de l'Europe (with Ionesco), 1982-. Publications: Incandescences, 1970; Eclats de malachite, 1971; La Pointe du diable, 1973; Mosaïque New Yorkaise, 1975; Your Son Léopold, Princes and Gods and Triality, excerpts of which have appeared in reviews in North America, UK, India and Africa; Albert Russo Anthology, 1987; Mixed Blood (novel), 1990; Le Cap des illusions (novel), 1991; Futureyes/Dans la nuit bleu fauve (poetry in English and in French), 1992; Kaleidoscope (poetry collection), 1993; Éclipse sur le Lac Tanganyika (novel), 1994 Stories broadcast by the BBC World Service. Contributions to: Numerous professional journals. Honours: Various awards and honours including: Willie Lee Martin Short Story Award, USA, 1987. Memberships: PEN; Authors Guild of America; Writers and Poets; Association of French Speaking Writers. Address: BP 640, 75826 Paris Cedex 17, France.

RUTSALA Vern, b. 5 Feb 1934, McCall, Idaho, USA. Writer; Teacher. m. Joan Colby, 6 May 1957, 2 s, 1 d. Education: BA, Reed College, 1956; MFA, University of Iowa, 1960. Publications include: The Window, 1964; Small Songs, 1969; The Harmful State, 1971; Laments, 1975; The Journey Begins, 1976; Paragraphs, 1978; The New Life, 1978; Walking Home from the Icehouse, 1981; Backtracking, 1985; The Mystery of Lost Shoes, 1985; Ruined Cities, 1987; Selected Poems, 1991; Little-Known Sports, 1994. Contributions to: The New Yorker; Esquire; Poetry; Hudson Review; Harpers; The Atlantic; American Poetry Review; Paris Review. Honours: NEA Fellowship, 1974, 1979; Northwest Poetry Prize, 1976; Guggenheim Fellowship,1982; Carolyn Kizer Poetry Prize, 1988; Master, Fellowship, Oregon Arts Commission, 1990; Hazel Hall Award, 1992; Juniper Prize, 1993; Duncan Lawrie Prize Arvon Foundation, 1994. Memberships: PEN, Poetry Society of America; AWP. Address: 2404 NE 24th Avenue, Portland, OR 97212, USA.

RUTTER Michael Llewellyn, b. 15 Aug 1933, Brummanna, Lebanon. Professor; Child Psychiatry, University of London; Honorary Director, Medical Research Council, Child Psychiatry Unit; Director, Research Centre in Social, Genetic and Developmental Psychiatry. m. Marjorie Heys, 27 Dec 1958, 1 s, 2 d. Education: MB ChB, University of Birmingham Medical School, 1950-55; Academic DPM, University of London, 1961; MD, University of Birmingham, 1963; Fellow, Royal College of Psychiatrists, London, 1971; Fellow, Royal College of Physicians, London, 1972; FRS, 1987. Publications include: Child and Adolescent Psychiatry: Modern Approaches (co-editor), 3rd edition, 1994; Depression in Young People: Development and Clinical Perspectives (co-editor), 1986; Language Development and Disorders (co-editor), 1987; Treatment of Autistic Children (co-author), 1987; Parenting Breakdown: The Making and Breaking of Intergenerational Links (co-author), 1988; Assessment and Diagnosis in Child Psychopathology, 1988; Straight and Devious Pathways From Childhood to Adulthood, 1990; Biological Risk Factors for Psychosocial Disorders, 1991; Developing Minds: Challenge and Continuity Across The Lifespan, 1993. Contributions to: Numerous professional and medical/psychiatric journals. Honours include: Honorary Doctorate, University of Leiden, 1985; Founding Member, Academia Europaea, 1988; Foreign Honorary Member, American Academy of Arts and Sciences, 1989; Honorary Doctorate, Catholic University, Louvain, 1990; Honorary Doctor of Science, University of Chicago, 1991; Honorary Doctor of Science, University of Minnesota, 1993; Honorary

Doctor of Science, University of Birmingham, 1990; Honorary Doctor of Medicine, University of Edinburgh, 1990; Foreign Associate Member, US National Academy of Education, 1990; Honorary Doctorate, University of Gent, 1994. Address: MRC Child Psychiatry Unit, Institute of Psychiatry, De Crespigny Park, Denmark Hill, London, SE5 8AF, England.

RUYSLINCK Ward. See: **DE BELSER Raymond.**

RUZICKA Penelope Susan (Penny Kane), b. 23 Jan 1945, Kenya. Consultant. m. Ladislav Ruzicka, 21 Mar 1984. Education: MSc, Economics, University of Wales, 1986. Publications: Womens Health; From Womb to Tomb, 1991; The Which? Guide to Birth Control, 1983; The Second Billion: Population and Family Planning in China, 1987; Famine in China, 1959-61, 1988; Choice Not Chance, 1978; Editor, China's One Child Family, 1985; Differential Mortality, 1989; Tradition, Development and The Individual, 1986; Asking Demographic Questions, 1985; Victorian Families in Fact and Fiction, 1994. Memberships: International Union for The Scientific Study of Population; Vice-President, Family Planning, Australia. Literary Agent: Bruce Hunter, David Higham Associates. Address: The Old School, Majors Creek Near Braidwood, NSW 2622, Australia.

RYAN John Gerald Christopher, b. 4 Mar 1921, Edinburgh, Scotland. Artist; Writer. m. Priscilla Ann Blomfield, 3 Jan 1950, 1 s, 2 d. Education: Ampleforth College, York, 1930-40; Regent Street Polytechnic Art School, 1946-47. Appointments: Cartoonist; Catholic Herald 1965-. Publications: 14 children's picture books, Captain Pugwash, 1956-86; Tiger Pig; 12 Noah's Ark Stories; 2 Dodo books; Mabel and The Tower of Babel, 1990; Adventures of Sir Cumference, 1990; Jonah, a Whale of a Tale, 1994; Soldier Sam and Trooper Ted, 1994. Contributions to: Eagle and Girl Magazines; Harris Tweed Extra Special Agent, 1950-60. Membership: Society of Authors. Literary Agent: Jane Gregory. Address: Gungarden Cottage, Rye, East Sussex, TN31 7HH, England.

RYBICKA Zofia, b. 28 Nov 1920, Klony, Poland. Writer; Critic; Translator. m. Waldemar Jerzy Rybicki, 2 Jan 1955, div 1958. Education: Secondary School for Kindergarten Teachers, 1934-37; ITT Lyceum, 1945-46; Secondary School Certificate, 1946, Gdansk-Wrzeszcz; Graduated, Diplomatic Consular Faculty, Academy of Political Science, Warsaw, 1950; Diploma, Organ, High Music School, Gdansk-Wrzeszcz, 1952; MPh, Polish Philology and Literature Faculty, Warsaw University, 1953. Appointments include: Soldier-Club Manager, Poznan, 1938-39; Typist, Lublin, 1940-44; Gestapo prisoner, 1942; Polish Army, 1944-45; Proof Reader, Press House, Gdansk, 1947-50; Grammar School Teacher, Lyceum for Kindergarten Teachers, Gdansk-Wreszcz, 1952-55; Editor, Ministry of National Defence Publishing House, Warsaw, 1955-75; Head, German and Scandinavian Department, Polish Publishing House, PIW, Warsaw, 1975-81. Publications include: 48 short prose pieces translated from German into Polish including: Bodo Uhse: Mexikanische Erzahlungen, 1960; Erika Runge: Bottroper Protokolle, 1973; Adelbert von Chamisso: Peter Schlemihls wundersame Geschichte, 1979; Hermann Hesse: Der Lateinschüler, 1979; Conrad F Meyer: Die Hochzeit des Mönchs, 1979; Heinrich Mann: Das Herz, 1979; Friedrich Durrenmatt: Die Panne, 1979; Adolf Muschg: short stories in U szczytuszczescia, 1981; Robert Musil: Vereinigungen, 1982; Others: Essays, speeches, treatises of Max Horkheimer, Theodor W Adorno, Heinrich Mann, Klaus Mann, Thomas Mann, in Woberc faszyzmu; 15 novels including: Dieter Noll: Die Abenteuer des Werner Holt, Roman einer Jugend, 1964; Roman einer Heimkehr, 1966; Christa Wolf: Der geteilte Himmel, 1966; Kurt David: Der Schwarze Wolf, 1966; Tenggeri, Sohn des Schwarzen Wolfs, 1968; Die Uberlebende, 1975; Gerold Späth: Commedia, 1986; Others: Nicolaus v Below; Als Hitlers Adjutant, memoirs, 1990. Contributions to: Articles, essays, reviews to various publications. Honours: Silver Cross of Merit, 1975; Knight's Cross, Polonia Restituta, 1979; Medal of Victory and Freedom, 1945, 1984; Other military orders. Memberships include: Polish Writers Union; ZAIKS; Stowarzyszenie Tlumacy Polskich; Polish Association of Editors. Address: ul Ks J Popieluszki 17b m 68, 01 595 Warsaw, Poland.

RYCE-MENUHIN Joel, b. 11 Jun 1933, USA. Analytical Psychologist; Former International Concert Pianist. m. Yaltah Menuhin, 11 Jun 1960. Education: BMus, 1953; BSc Honours, 1976; MPhil, 1982. Publications: The Self in Early Childhood, 1988; Jungian Sandplay - The Wonderful Therapy, 1992; Jung and The Monotheisms, 1993. Contributions to: Clinical Papers in Journal of Analytical Psychology; Harvest; Chiron; Free Association Journal; British Journal of Projective

Psychology; Guild of Pastoral Psychology. Memberships: IAAP, PEN; Former Chairman, G C Jung Analytical Psychol Club and Guild of Pastorial Psychology, London; Founding Director, British and Irish Sandplay Society. Address: 85 Canfield Gardens, London, NW6 3EA, England.

RYDELL Forbes. See: **FORBES DeLoris Stanton.**

RYDER Jonathon. See: **LUDLUM Robert.**

RYDER Susan Margaret (Baroness Ryder of Warsaw, Sue Ryder), b. 3 Jul 1923, Leeds, England. Social Worker; Founder of Sue Ryder Foundation; Doctor of Essex University, 1993. m. Lord Cheshire of Woodhall, 5 Apr 1959, dec, 1 s, 1 d. Education: School Certificate. Publications: And The Morrow is Theirs, 1st autobiography; Child of My Love, 2nd autobiography, 1986; Remembrance, annual magazine of Sue Ryder Foundation. Honours: Order of The British Empire, 1957; Order of Polonia Restituta, 1965; Medal of Yugoslav Flag with Gold Wreath and Diploma, 1971; Companion, Order of St Michael and St George, 1976; Golden Order of Merit, Poland, 1976; Created Baroness Ryder of Warsaw in Poland and of Cavendish in Suffolk, England, 1978; Order of Smile, Poland, 1980; Commander's Cross of the Order of Polonia Restituta and Order of Merit, Poland, 1992; Honorary LLD, Liverpool, 1973, Exeter, 1980, London, 1981, Leeds, 1984, Kent, 1986, Cambridge, 1989; Honorary DLitt, Reading, 1982. Memberships: Special Operations Executive Club; Trustee, The Leonard Cheshire Foundation; Co-Founder, The Ryder Cheshire Foundation; Trustee, The World War Memorial Fund for Disaster Relief. Address: Sue Ryder Home, Cavendish, Sudbury, Suffolk, CO10 8AY, England.

RYERSON Stanley B, b. 1911. Historian; Comedian. Address: Dept of History, University of Quebec, PO Box 8888, Station Centreville, Montreal, Quebec Hc3 3P8, Canada.

RYLANT Cynthia,b. 6 June 1954, Hopewell, Virginia, USA. m. (divorced), 1 son. Education: BA, Morris Harvey College; MA, Marshall University; MLS, Kent State University. Appointments: Writer; Children's Librarian; Lecturer in English. Honours: Child Study Association of America Best Book, 1985; Citations from American Library Association, New York Times; Newbery Award, 1993; Boston Globe Honorary Book Award, 1991; English Speaking Union Book-Across-the-Sea Ambassador of Honour Award, 1984; National Council for Social Studies, Best Book, 1985. Address: c/o Dell Publishing Attn Author, Mail Dept 1540 Broadway, New York, NY 10036, USA.

RYZMAN Leonard, b. Melbourne, Victoria, Australia. Professional Speaker; Author. Education: BEc, BA, DipEd, Monash University; Graduate Diploma in Human Relations Education, Melbourne University. Publications: Leonardo Da Vinci 1452-1519: The Concise Biography, 1983; Murder on the Management Express, 1985; Make Your Own Rainbow, 1990; All You Need Is Life, 1994; All Things Must Pass But Here Comes The Sun, play. Contributions to: Columnist and contributor to numerous magazines including: Flight Deck; Australian Wellbeing. Membership: National Speakers Association of Australia. Literary Agent: Curtis Brown (Australia), Paddington, New South Wales, Australia. Address: c/- Curtis Brown (Aust), PO Box 19, Paddington, New South Wales, Australia.

S

S Elizabeth Von. See: FREEMAN Gillian.

SACHS Marilyn, b. 18 Dec 1927, USA. Writer. m. Morris Sachs, 26 Jan 1947, 1 s, 1 d. Education: BA. Hunter College, New York, MS, Library Science, Columbia University New York. Publications include: Fiction: Amy Moves In, 1964; Veronica Ganz, 1968; The Bears' House, 1971; The Truth About Mary Rose, 1973; A Pocket Full of Seeds, 1973; Dorrie's Book, 1975; A Summer's Lease, 1979; Class Pictures, 1980; Call Me Ruth, 1982; Fourteen, 1983; The Fat Girl, 1984; Underdog, 1985; Baby Sister, 1986; Almost Fifteen, 1987; Fran Ellen's House, 1987; Just Like a Friend, 1989; At The Sound of the Beep, 1990; (co-editor) Big Book for Peace, 1990; Circles, 1991; What My Sister Remembered, 1992; Thirteen, Going on Seven, 1993. Address: 733 31st Ave, San Francisco, CA 94121, USA.

SACHS Murray, b. 10 Apr 1924, Toronto, Canada. Literary Scholar; Teacher. m. Miriam Blank, 14 Sept 1961, 1 s, 1 d. Eduction: BA Modern Languges, University of Toronto, 1946; MA, French, 1947, PhD, French, 1953, Columbia University, New York, USA. Career includes: Assistant Professor of Romanic Languages, Williams College, 1954-60; Professor of French and Comparative Literature, Brandeis University, 1960-; Massachusetts, USA and others. Publications: The Career of Alphonse Daudet, 1965; The French Short Story in the 19th Century, 1969; Anatole France: The Short Stories, 1974; The Legacy of Flaubert in L'Hénaurme Siècle, 1984; Kamouraska in Women Writers of Quebec, 1985. Contributions to: Pmla; Symposium; Nineteenth-Century French Studies, Modern Language Review; L'Esprit Crèateur; Raison D'Etre: Foreign Languages and the Liberal Arts Today, in Managing The Foreign Language Department: A Chairperson's Primer, 1993, and others. Address: Dept of Romance and Comparative Literature, Shiffman Humanities Center, Brandeis University, Waltham, MA 02254, USA.

SACKS Oliver, b. London, England. Education: London, Oxford, California, New York. Appointments: Professor of Clinical Neurology, Albert Einstein College of Medicine, New York, USA. Address: Clinical Neurology, Albert Einstein College of Medicine, 1300 Morris Park, Bronx, NY 10461-1924, USA.

SADDLEMYER (Eleanor) Ann, b. 28 Nov 1932, Prince Albert, Saskatchewan, Canada. Critic; Theatre Historian; Educator. Education: BA, 1953, Honours, English Diploma 1955, University of Saskatchewan; MA, Queen's University, 1956; PhD, Bedford College, University of London, England, 1961. Career: University of Victoria, Victoria, British Columbia, 1960-71; Victoria College, University of Toronto, 1971-; Director, Graduate Centre for Study of Drama, University of Toronto, 1972-77, 1985-86; Berg Chair, New York University, USA, 1975; Master, Massey College, University of Toronto, 1988-95; Board of Directors, Colin Smythe Publishers. Publications: The World of W B Yeats, 1965; In Defence of Lady Gregory, Playwright, 1966; J M Synge Plays Books I and II, 1968; Lady Gregory Plays, 4 volumes, 1971; Theatre Business, 1982; The Collected Letters of J M Synge, 2 volumes, 1983-84; Synge and Modern Comedy, 1968; Letters to Molly: J M Synge to Maire O'Neill, 1971; Lady Gregory Fifty Years After, 1987; Early Stages, Essays on the Theatre in Ontario, 1800-1914, 1990. Address: 100 Lakeshore Road East, # 803, Oakville, Ontario, Canada L6J 6M9.

SADDLER Allen. See: RICHARDS Ronald Charles William.

SADGROVE Sidney Henry (Lee Torrance), b. 1920, British. Appointments: Artist, Teacher and Writer, 1949-. Publications: You've Got To Do Something, 1967; A Touch of The Rabbits, The Suitability Factor, 1968; Stanislaus and The Princess, 1969; A Few Crumbs, 1971; Stanislaus and The Frog, Paradis Enow, 1972; Stanislaus and The Witch, 1973; The Link, 1975; The Bag, Half Sick of Shadows, Bleep, All in The Mind, 1977; Icary Dicary Doc, Angel, 1978; Filling, 1979; First Night, Only on Friday, 1980; Hoodunnit, 1984; Pawn en Prise, 1985; Just For Comfort, 1986; Tiger, 1987; State of Play, 1988; Warren, 1989; Dear Mrs Cornfett, 1990. Memberships: Writers Guild of Great Britain. Address: Pimp Barn, Withyham, Hartfield, Sussex, TN7 4BB, England.

SADIE Stanley (John), b. 1930, British. Literary Appointments: Professor, Trinity College of Music, 1957-65; Music Critic, The Times, 1964-81; Editor, The Musical Times, London, 1967-87; Editor, The New Grove Dictionary of Music and Musicians, 1970-. Publications: Handel, 1962; The Pan Book of Opera (in USA as The Opera Guide) (with A Jacobs), 1964, 3rd edition, 1984; Mozart, 1965; Beethoven, 1967; Handel, 1968; Handel Concertos, 1973; New Grove Dictionary of Music and Musicians, editor, 20 volumes, 1980; Mozart, 1982; New Grove Dictionary of Musical Instruments, editor, 3 volumes, 1984; The Cambridge Music Guide (in USA as Stanley Sadie's Music Guide), Mozart Symphonies, The New Grove Dictionary of American Music (co-edited with H Wiley Hitchcock), 4 volumes, 1986; The Brief Music Guide, 1987; The Grove Concise Dictionary of Music (editor), 1988; History of Opera (editor), 1989; Performance Practice (co-edited with Howard M Brown), 2 volumes, 1989; Man and Music (general editor), 8 volumes, 1989-93; The New Grove Dictionary of Opera (editor), 4 volumes, 1992. Address: 12 Lyndhurst Road, London, NW3 5NL, England.

SADLER Mark. See: LYNDS Dennis.

SAEE John Islamudin, b. 12 Sept 1959, Panjsher, Afghanistan, now Australian Citizen. Lecturer in Management of Consumer Science. Education: Certificate, German Language and Literature, Hamburg University, Germany; BA, Social Sciences, Flinders University, South Australia, 1980; MCom, University of New South Wales, 1983; PhD, International Management, University of Technology, New South Wales, in progress. Publications: AMP Management Requirements Definition Study (co-author), 1986; Sales Unit Management System User's Reference Manual, 1986; User's Acceptance Testing Specifications, 1986-87. Contributions: Consumerism: its implications for marketing in the 1990s, 1991; New Marketing Methods Point to a Future of Seafood, 1991; Realising Employees Creative Potentialities: A Matter of Managerial Psychology, 1992; Strategic Marketing Responses to Female Business Travellers: A Matter of Contemporary Marketing Management, 1992; Culture, Multiculturalism and Racism: An Australian Perspective, 1993; Intercultural Communication Competence within Australian Organisations, 1994; Australian Small Enterprise Management Challenges, Problems and Opportunities: The Strategic Entrepreneurial Educational Responses and Solutions; Others in various publications including: Journal of Home Economics of Australia; The Commercial Horticulture; Food Manufacturing News; Journal of Australian Institute of Management; Journal of Manufacturers News; Journal of Professional Building Surveyors. Memberships: Australian Institute of Management; Professional Member, Australian and New Zealand Academy of Management; International Communication Association. Address: Thorpe, Melbourne, Victoria, Australia.

SAFIRE William, b. 1929, American. Career: Reporter, New York Herald-Tribune Syndicate, 1949-51; Correspondent, WNBC-WNBT, Europe an the Middle East, 1951; Radio-TV producer, WMBC, NYC, 1954-55; Vice-President, Tex McCrary Incorporated, 1955-60; President, Safire Public Relations, 1960-68; Special Assistant to President Nixon, 1969-73; Columnist, New York Times, WA 1973-. Publications: The Relations Explosion, 1963; Plunging into Politics, 1964; Safire's Political Dictionary, 1968 1st edition 1972, 2nd edition 1978, 3rd edition; Before the Fall, 1975; Full Disclosure, 1977; Safire's Washington, On Language, 1980; What's the Good Word?, Good Advice (with Leonard Safir), 1982; I Stand Corrected, 1984; Take My Word For It, 1986; You Could Look It Up, 1988; Language Maven Strikes Again, 1990; Leadership (with Leonard Safir), 1990; Fumblerules, 1990; The First Dissident, 1992; Lend Me Your Ears, 1992; Good Advice on Writing (with Leonard Safir), 1992; Quoth The Maven, 1993; Safire's New Political Dictionary, 1993; In Love with Norma Loquendi, 1994. Address: New York Times, 1627 Eye Street NW, Washington, DC 20006, USA.

SAGAN Carl, b. 1934, Brooklyn, New York, USA. m. (1) divorced, 3 children; (2) Ann Druyan, 2 children. Education: BA, PhD, Astrophysics, University of Chicago. Appointments: Consultant to NASA; University Professor at Stanford University (Genetics); Harvard University (Astronomy); Cornell University (Space Science). Honours: Pultzer Prize, 1978; Joseph Priestly Award; NASA Medals for Exceptional Scientific Achievement; Distinguished Public Service. Address: Dept of Astronomy, Cornell University, 426 Space Science Building, Ithaca, NY 14853-0001, USA.

SAGAN Françoise, b. 21 June 1935, Carjac, France. Novelist; Playwright. Education: Sorbonne, Paris. Publications: Bonjour Tristesse, 1954; A Certain Smile, 1956; Those Without Shadows, 1957; Aimez-vous Brahms, 1959; Wonderful Clouds, 1961; La Chamade, 1965; The Heart-Keeper, 1968; A Few Hours of Sunlight, 1969, 1971; Scars on the Soul, 1972; Lost Profile, 1974; Silken Eyes, 1976; The Unmade Bed, 1977; Le Chien Couchant, 1980, 1985; Incidental Music, 1981; The Painted Lady, 1981; The Still Storm, 1983; Engagements of the Heart, 1985, 1988; La Maison de Raquel Vega, 1985; Painting in Blood, 1987; The Leash, 1989; Les Faux-fuyants, 1991; Plays: Castle in Sweden, 1960; Les Violons parfois, 1962; Landru (screenplay for Claude Chabrol), 1963; Bonheur, impair et passe, 1964; The Dizzy Horse, 1966; Un piano dans l'herbe, 1970; Le Sang doré des Borgia (screenplay), 1977; Il fait beau jour et nuit, 1978; Opposite Extremes, 1987; Also: Mirror of Venus, 1965; Réponses 1954-74, autobiographical conversations, 1974; Brigitte Bardot, 1975; Dear Sarah Bernhardt, 1987; La Sentinelle de Paris, 1988; The Eiffel Tower, 1989; Editor, Sand & Musset: lettres d'amour, 1985.

SAGGS Henry William Frederick, b. 2 Dec 1920, Weeley, Essex, England. Professor of Semitic Languages. m. Joan Butterworth, 21 Sep 1946, 4 d. Education: King's College, London, 1939-42, 1946-48; School of Oriental and African Studies, London, 1949-52; BD, 1942, MTh, 1948; MA, 1950; PhD, 1953. Literary Appointments: Lecturer, then Reader in Akkadian, School of Oriental and African Studies, London, 1953-66; Professor of Semitic Languages, University College Cardiff, University of Wales, 1966-83. Publications: The Greatness That Was Babylon, 1962, revised 1987; Everyday Life in Babylon and Assyria, 1965, 1987; The Encounter With The Divine in Mesopotamia and Israel, 1978; The Might That Was Assyria, 1984, 1990; Civilization Before Greece and Rome, 1989; Abridged edition of H A Layard, Nineveh and Its Remains, 1970. Contributions to: Iraq; Sumer; Journal of Cuneiform Studies; Journal of Theological Studies; Archiv fuer Oreintforschung; Revue d'Assyriologie; Journal of Semitic Studies; Bibliotheca Orientalis. Memberships: Society of Authors; Society of Antiquaries; British School of Archaeology in Iraq, Council Member; Savage Club; Royal Asiatic Society. Address: Eastwood, Bull Lane, Long Melford, Suffolk, CO10 9EA, England.

SAHAY Akhowri Chittaranjan, b. 2 Jan 1925, Muzaffarpur, India. Poet; Writer. m. Akhowri Priyamvada, 17 Jun 1945, 3 s, 1 d. Education: BA, Honours Distinction, 1945, MA English, 1947, Patna University; MDEH, National University of Electro Homeopathy, Kanpur, 1964; PhD Englaish, Stanton University, NY, 1985. Appointments include: Lecturer, Integrated Department of English, L S College, Muzaffarpur, Bihar, 1968-74; Associate Professor, English, Postgraduate Language Block, Bihar University, Muzaffarpur, 1974-85; Chief Editor, Kavita India Quarterly Poetry Journal, 1987-. Publications: Hindi Poetry: Van Yoothi, 1939; Van Shephali, 1941; Van Geet, 1942; Ajab Desh, 1945; Hindi short stories for children: Dick Aur Ostrich, 1946; Motilal Tota, 1948; Rani Sahiba, 1964; English Poetry Books: Roots and Branches, 1979; Emerald Foliage, 1981; Pink Blossoms, 1983; Golden Pollens, 1985; English Prose: The Rubaiyat and Other Essays, 1980; My Interest in Occultism, 1982; Works in numerous anthologies. Contributions include: Numerous journals, India and abroad including: Byword; Creative Forum; Canopy; Kavita India; Literary Endeavour; Poetry Time; Prophetic Voices; Poetry Review; Skylark; The Commonwealth Quarterly; Poets International; The Plowman; The Quest. Honours: Various prizes, medals, certificates of merit, literary excellence, during school and college. Memberships: The Poetry Society, India, UK; PEN All-India Centre; International Writers Association; Writers Club, Madras; World Poetry Society; United Writers Association, Madras. Address: Kavita India House, South East Chaturbhujasthan, Muzaffarpur, Bihar 842001, India.

SAHGAL Nayantara, b. 10 May 1927, India. Writer. m. (1) 2 Jan 1949, div, 1 s, 2 d, (2) 17 Sep 1979. Education: BA History, Wellesley College, MA, USA, 1947. Literary Appointments include: Advisory Panel for English, Satitya Akademi, 1972-75; Research Scholar, Radcliffe Institute, Cambridge, MA, 1976; Writer-in-Residence, Southern Methodist University, Dallas, TX, 1973, 1977; Member, Indian Delegation to The UN, 1978; Fellow, Woodrow Wilson International Center for Scholars, Washington DC, 1981-82; Fellow, National Humanities Center, NC, 1983-84; Member, Jury for Commonwealth Writers Prize, 1990, 1991. Publications: Fiction: A Time to Be Happy, 1958; This Time of Morning, 1965; Storm in Chandigarh, 1969; The Day in Shadow, 1972; A Situation in New Delhi, 1977; Rich Like Us, 1985; Plans for Departure, 1986; Mistaken Identity, 1988; Non-fiction: Prison and Chocolate Cake, 1954; From Fear Set Free, 1962; The

Freedom Movement in India, 1970; Indira Gandhi: Her Road to Power, 1982; Relationship: Extracts from a Correspondence (with E N Mangat Rai), 1994. Contributions to: Articles and short stories, India and abroad including: London Magazine; Vogue; The Far Eastern Economic Review; The New Republic; Cosmopolitan; Dallas Times-Herald; The Times; Christian Science Monitor. Honours: Sinclair Prize for Fiction, UK, for Rich Like Us, 1985; Sahitya Akademi Award for Rich Like Us, 1986; Commonwealth Writers Prize, Eurasia, for Plans for Departure, 1987; Elected Foreign Honorary Member, American Academy of Arts and Sciences, 1990; Book Society Recommendation for A Time To Be Happy. Memberships: Vice-President, People's Union for Civil Liberties, India, twice. Literary Agent: Bill Hamilton, A M Heath and Company, 79 St Martin's Lane, London, WC2N 4AA, England. Address: 181 B Rajpur Road, Dehra Dun 248009, UP, India.

SAID Edward, b. Beirut, Lebanon. Appointments: Professor of English Literature; Activist for Palestinian Self-determination. Honours: National Aorke Critics Circle Award, Nominee. Address: Dept of English, Columbia University, 2960 Columbia University, NY 1027-6902, USA.

SAIL Lawrence Richard, b. 29 Oct 1942, London, England. Poet; Writer. m. (1) Teresa Luke, 1966, div 1981, 1 s, 1 d, (2) Helen Bird, 1994. Education: Honours Degree in Modern Languages, St John's College, Oxford, 1961-64. Literary Appointments: Editor, South West Review, 1981-85; Chairman, The Arvon Foundation, 1990-94; Programme Director, Cheltenham Festival of Literature, 1991. Publications: Opposite Views, 1974; The Drowned River, 1978; The Kingdom of Atlas, 1980; Devotions, 1987; Aquamarine, 1988; Editor, First and Always, 1988; Out of Land: New and Selected Poems, 1992; Building into Air, 1995. Contributions to: Poetry Review; PN Review; Stand. Honours: Hawthornden Fellowship, 1992; Arts Council Writers' Bursary, 1993. Memberships: Senior Common Room, St John's College, Oxford; Advisory Board, British Centre for Literary Translation; Management Committee, Peterloo Poets; The Society of Authors. Address: Richmond Villa, 7 Wonford Road, Exeter, Devon, EX2 4LF, England.

SAINSBURY Maurice Joseph, b. 18 Nov 1927, Sydney, New South Wales, Australia. Consultant Psychiatrist. m. Erna June Hoadley, 22 Aug 1953, 1 son, 2 daughters. Education: MB, BS, Sydney, 1952; DPM, Royal College of Physicians and Surgeons, 1960; MRANZCP, 1963; FRANZCP, 1971; MRCPsych, 1971; FRCPsych, 1975; MHP, University of New South Wales, 1980. Publications: Key to Psychiatry, 1st edition, 1973, 3rd edition, 1980; Sainsbury's Key to Psychiatry (with L G Lambeth), 4th edition, 1988. Contributions to: Variety of articles to medical journals. Honours: Reserve Force Decoration, 1985; Member, Order of Australia (AM), 1987; Consultant Psychiatrist to Australian Army, 1976-86. Memberships: Past President, Royal Australian and New Zealand College of Psychiatrists; President, After Care Association of New South Wales; Part-time Member, Guardianship Board, New South Wales; Part-time Member, Mental Health Review Tribunal, New South Wales; Consultant Psychiatrist to Chelmsford Royal Commission, 1988-90. Address: 3 Bimbil Place, Killara, New South Wales 2071, Australia.

SAINT Dora Jessie, (Miss Read), b. 1913, United Kingdom. Novelist; Short Story and Children's Fiction Writer. Publications: Village School, 1955; Village Diary, 1957; Storm in The Village, 1958; Hobby Horse Cottage, 1958; Thrush Green, 1959; Fresh From The Country, 1960; Winter in Thrush Green, 1961; Miss Clare Remembers, 1962; The Market Square, 1966; The Howards of Caxley, 1967; Country Cooking, 1969; News from Thrush Green, 1970; Tyler's Row, 1972; Christmas Mouse, 1973; Battles at Thrush Green, 1975; No Holly for Miss Quinn, 1976; Village Affairs, 1977; Return to Thrush Green, 1978; The White Robin, 1979; Village Centenary, 1980; Gossip From Thrush Green, 1981; A Fortunate Grandchild, 1982; Affairs at Thrush Green, 1983; Summer at Fairacre, 1984; At Home in Thrush Green, 1985; Time Remembered, 1986; The School at Thrush Green, 1987; The World at Thrush Green, 1988; Mrs Pringle, 1989; Friends at Thrush Green, 1990; Changes at Fairacre, 1991; Celebrations at Thrush Green, 1992; Farewell to Fairacre, 1993; Tales From A Village School, 1994. Membership: Society of Authors. Address: Strouds, Shefford Woodlands, Newbury, Berkshire, RG16 7AJ, England.

SAINT-DENIS Janou, b. 6 May 1930, Montreal, Canada. Actress; Poet. m. 30 Oct 1952, deceased, 25 Apr 1956, 1 son, 1 daughter. Education: Diploma-es Lettres et Sciences, Couvent d'Hochelaga, Montreal, 1946; Diploma, Conservatoire Lassalle (theatre), 1950;

Diploma, Université du Théatre des Nations, Paris, France, 1962. Literary Appointments: Established Poetry Readings in Montreal, 1959, Paris, 1961-71; Started Poetry Shows, 1975, named "Place aux Poetes"; For the last 20 years, Poet and a Moderator; Founded, Les Productions du Soudain (Poetry Company). Publications: Mots a dire, Mauxa dire, 1972; Claude Gauvreau, le Cygne, 1977; Place aux Poetes, 1977; Les Carnets de l'Audace, 1981; La Roue du Feu Secret, 1985; Hold-Up Mental, 1988; Memoire Innee, 1990. Contributions to: Moebius; Les Cahiers de la femme; Atelier Littéraire de la Mauricie; Revue de l'Université d'Ottawa; Sorcieres; Femme Plurielle, Xceteras, Cahier des Arts Visuels; Arcade; Le Sabord. Honours: Membre d'Honneur de l'U.N.E.Q; U. Memberships: Union des Ecrivaines et Ecrivans du Quebec; Société des Ecrivains Canadiens, Montreal Section; Société Littéraire de Laval; Union des Artistes; CAPAC. Address: 4445 Rue St Dominique, Montreal, Quebec, H2W 2B4, Canada.

SAKAMOTO Yoshikazu, b. 16 Sep 1927, USA. Professor. m. Kikuko Ono, 2 Jun 1956, 2 d. Education: Faculty of Law, University of Tokyo, 1951. Publications: Editor, Strategic Doctrines and Their Alternatives, 1987; Co-editor, Democratizing Japan: The Allied Occupation of Japan, 1987; The Political Analysis of Disarmament, 1988; Militarization and Regional Conflict, 1988; International Politics in Global Perspective, 1990; Editor and Contributor, Global Transformation, 1994. Honours: Fulbright Grant; Rockerfeller and Eisenhower Fellowships; The Mainichi Press National Book Award, 1976. Memberships: Secretary General, International Peace Research Association, 1979-83; Jury, UNESCO Prize for Peace Education, 1984-89; American and Japanese Political Science Associations; Japanese Association of American Studies; International Peace Research Association. Address: 8-29-19 Shakujii-machi, Nermaku, Tokyo 177, Japan.

SALE Kirkpatrick, b. 1937, American. Career: Board Member, PEN American Centre, 1976-; Exploratory Project for Conditions of Peace, 1984-90; Learning Alliance, 1985-; Secretary, 1980-86, Co-director, 1986-, E F Schumacher Society; Contributing Editor, Nation, NYC, 1986-. Publications: SDS, 1973; Power Shift, 1975; Human Scale, 1980; Dwellers in the Land: The Bioregional Vision, 1985; The Conquest of Paradise: Christopher Columbus and the Columbian Legacy, 1990.; The Green Revolution: The American Environmental Movement 1962-1992, 1993; Rebels Against the Future: The Luddites and Their War on the Industrial Revolution, 1995. Address: 113 West 11th Street, New York, NY 10011, USA.

SALE Medora, b. Canada. Address: c/o Maxwell Macmilan Canada, Attn Merrill Matthews Pblcty, 1200 Eglinton Avenue East Suite 200, Don Mills, Ontario M3C 3N1, Canada.

SALINGER Jerome David, b. 1919, American. Publications: The Catcher in the Rye, 1951; Nine Stories (in UK as For Esme - With Love and Squalor and Other Stories), 1953; Franny and Zooey, 1961; Raise High the Roof Beam, Carpenters, and Seymour: An Introduction, 1963. Address: c/o Harold Ober Associates, 425 Madison Avenue, New York, NY 10017, USA.

SALISBURY Frank B(oyer), b. 1926, American. Career: Assistant Professor of Botany, Pomona College, Claremont, CA, 1954-55; Assistant Professor of Plant Physiology, 1955-61, Professor, 1961-66, Colorado State University, Fort Collins; Natioanl Science Foundation Postdoctoral Fellow, Tubingen, West Germany, Insbruck, Austria, 1962-63; Professor of Plant Physiology, 1966-; Head of Plant Science Department, 1966-70; Professor of Botany, 1968-, Utah State University, Logan; Technical Representative in Plant Physiology, US Atomic Energy Commission, 1973-74; Guest Professor, University of Innsbruck, Austria, 1983; Guest Professor, Lady Davis Fellow, Hebrew University of Jerusalem 1983; Editor, Americas and Pacific Countries, Journal of Plant Physiology. Publications: The Flowering Process, 1963; Vascular Plants: Form and Function (with R V Parke), 1964, 1970; Truth by Reason and by Revelation, 1965; Plant Physiology, (with C Ross), 1969, 3rd edition, 1986, 4th edition, 1991; The Biology of Flowering, 1971; Botany (with W A Jensen), 1972, 1984; The Utah UFO Display: A Biologist's Report, 1974; The Creation, 1976; Biology (co-author), 1977. Contributions: over 200 journal and magazine articles. Memberships: Various advisory boards for US National Aeronautics and Space Agency (NASA); American Society of Plant Physiologists, Ed Board, 1967-1992; Botanical Society of America; American Society for Gravitational and Space Biology, Founder's Award, 1994; American Institute of Biological Sciences, Ed Board,

1972-1978; Fellow, AAAS; Utah Academy of Arts and Sciences; Sigma Xi; Phi Kappa Phi; The Planetary Society; Ecological Society of America. Address: Plants, Soils and Biometeorology Department, Utah State University, Logan, UT 84322-4820, USA.

SALISBURY John. See: CAUTE David.

SALISBURY Robert H(olt), b. 1930, American. Career: Joined faculty, 1955, Chairman, Department of Political Science, 1966-73, Chairman, Centre for the Study of Public Affairs, 1974-75; Professor, Washington University, St Louis; Guggenheim Fellowship, 1990; Rockefeller Study Centre (Bellagio) Visiting Scholar, 1990. Publications: Functions and Policies of American Geovemement (co-author), 1958, 3rd edition, 1967; American Government: Readings and Problems (with Eliot, Chambers and Prewitt), 1959, 1965; Democracy in the Mid-Twentieth Century (ed with Chambers), 1960; as Democracy Today, 1962; State Politics and the Public Schools (with Masters and Eliot), 1964; Interest Group Politics in America, 1970; Governing America: Public Choice and Political Action, 1973; Citizen Participation in the Public Schools, 1980; Interest and Institutions, Substance and Structure in American Politics, 1992; The Hollow Core, (with Heinz, Laumann and Nelson), 1993. Memberships: Chairman, Department of Political Sciences, Washington University, 1986-92. Address: 337 Westgate, St Louis, MO 63130, USA.

SALKEY (Felix) Andrew (Alexander), b. 30 Jan 1928, Colon, Panama. Education: BA Hons, University of London, 1955. Appointments: Regular outside Contributor, Interviewer and Scriptwriter, BBC External Services (Radio), London, 1952-76; English Teacher in a London Comprehensive School, 1957-59; Professor of Writing, Hampshire College, Amherst, MA, 1976-. Publications include: Drought, The Shark Hunters, 1966; Riot, Caribbean Prose, 1967; The Late Emancipation of Jerry Stover, 1968; The Adventures of Catullus Kelly, Jonah Simpson, 1969; Havana Journal, Breaklight: Caribbean Poetry (editor), 1971; Georgetown Journal, Caribbean Essays (editor), 1972; Breaklight: An Anthology of Caribbean Poetry (in USA as Breaklight: The Poetry of The Caribbean) (editor), 1972; Anancy's Score, Caribbean Essays (editor), Jamaica, 1973; Caribbean Folk Tales and Legends (editor), 1975; Come Home, Malcolm Heartland, 1976; Writing in Cuba Since The Revolution (editor), 1977; In The Hills Where Her Dreams Live, 1979; The River That Disappeared, Danny Jones, Away, 1980; Anancy, Traveller, 1992; Brother Anancy and Other Stories, 1993; In the Border Country and other stories. Address: Flat 8, Windsor Court, Moscow Road, Queensway, London, W2, England.

SALOM Philip, b. 8 Aug 1950, Bunbury, Western Australia, Australia. Lecturer; Poet. Education: BA, Curtin University, Perth, 1976; Dip Ed, 1981. Appointments: Lecturer, Murdoch University, 1994-; Tutor and Lecturer, Curtin University, 1982-93; Writer-in-residence: Singapore National University, 1989; B R Whiting Library/Studio, Rome, 1992. Publications: The Silent Piano, 1980; The Projectionist: Sequence, 1983; Sky Poems, 1987; Barbecue of the Primitives, 1989; Playback, 1991; Tremors, 1992; Feeding the Ghost, 1993; Drama/Play, Always Then and Now, 1993. Honours include: Commonwealth Poetry Prize, 1981, 87; Western Australian Premier's Prize (fiction) 1992; Australia/New Zealand Literary Exchange Award, 1992; Australia Council Fellowships. Address: 795 Mills Road, Glen Forest, Western Australia, 6071, Australia.

SALTER Charles A, b. 12 Oct 1947, Fort Worth, Texas, USA. Research Psychologist, Army Officer. m. 13 May 1972, 1 s, 2 d. Education: BS magna cum laude, Tulane University, 1969; MA, University of Pennsylvania, 1970, PhD, 1973; MS, 1987, SD, 1989, Harvard University School of Public Health. Career: Editor, Alternative Careers for Academics Bulletin, 1978; Syndicated Columnist, Suburban Features, 1983-85; Editor, The Professional Chef's Guide to Kitchen Management, 1985; Knight's Foodservice Dictionary, 1987; Foodservice Standards in Resorts, 1987; On the Frontlines, 1988; Getting it Off, Keeping it off, 1988; Literacy and the Library, 1991; Psychology for Living, 1977; Looking Good Eating Right, 1991; The Vegetarian Teen, 1991; Food Risks and Controversies, 1993; The Nutrition-Fitness Link, 1993. Literary Agent: Ruth Wreschner, 10 West 74th St, NY 10023, USA. Address: MCMR-PLC Fort Detrick, MD 21702-5012, USA.

SALTER James, b. 10 June 1925, USA. Writer. m. Ann Altemus, 5 June 1951 (divorced 1976), 2 s, 3 d. Publications: The Hunters, 1957; The Arm of Flesh, 1960-; A Sport and a Pastime, 1967; Light Years,

1976; Sold Faces, 1980; Dusk and Other Stories, 1989. Contributions to: The Paris Review; Antaeus; Grand Street; Vogue; Esquire, and others. Honours: Grant, American Academy of Arts and Letters, 1982; PEN-Faulkner Award, 1989. Memberships: PEN USA. Literary Agent: Peter Matson, Sterling Lord Literistic, One Madison Avenue, New York, NY 10010, USA. Address: Box 765, Bridgehampton, NY 11932, USA.

SALTER Mary Jo, b. 15 Aug 1954, Grand Rapids, MI, USA. Poet. Education: BA, Harvard University; MA, New Hall, Cambridge University. Publications: Henry Purcell in Japan, 1985; Unfinished Painting, 1987; The Moon Come Home, 1989; Sunday Skaters, 1994. Honours: Discovery Prize, Nation Magazine; Lamont Poetry Selection, 1988.

SALTMAN Judith, b. 11 May 1947, Vancouver, Canada. Associate Professor of Children's Literature and Librarianship; Writer. m. Bill Barringer, 1 d. Education: MA, Simmons College, 1982. Career: Children's Librarian, Toronto Public Library, Toronto, Canada, 1970-72; Children's Librarian, West Vancouver Memorial Library, West Vancouver, British Columbia, 1973-79; Children's Librarian, Vancouver Public Library, 1980-83; Assistant Professor, 1983-88, Associate Professor of Children's Literature and Librarianship, 1988-, University of British Columbia, Vancouver. Member, Interanational Board on books for Young People. Publications: (ed) Riverside Anthology of Children's Literature, 6th edition, 1985; Goldie and the Sea (juvenile), 1987; Modern Canadian Children's Books, 1987; The New Republic of Childhood, 1990. Address: School of Library, Archival and Information Studies, University of British Columbia, 831-1956 Main Mall, Vancouver, British Columbia, Canada, V6T 1Z1.

SALTZMAN Arthur Michael, b. 10 Aug 1953, Chicago, Illinois, USA. Professor. m. Marla Jane Marantz, 26 July 1980, 1 d. Education: University of Illinois, AB, 1971; AM, 1976; PhD, 1979. Career: Teaching Fellow, University of Illinois, 1975-80; Assistant Professor, Missouri Southern State College, 1981-86; Associate Professor, 1986-92; Professor, 1992-. Publications: The Fiction of William Gass: The Consolation of Language, 1986; Understanding Raymond Carver, 1988; Designs of Darkness in Contemporary American Fiction, 1990; The Novel in the Balance, 1993. Contributions to: Articles in Contemporary Literature; Review of Contemporary Fiction; Literary Review; Denver Quarterly; Chicago Review; Studies in Contemporary Satire; Journal of Modern Literature; Critique; and others. Honours: List of Excellent Teachers; Bresee Graduate Fiction Award; Phi Beta Kappa; NEH Summer Stipend; Outstanding Teachers Award. Memberships: Modern Language Association; PEN. Address: 2301 West 29th Street, Joplin, MO 64804, USA.

SAMBROOK Arthur James, b. 5 Sep 1931, England. University Teacher. m. Patience Ann Crawford, 25 Mar 1961, 4 s. Education: BA, 1955, MA, 1959, Worcester College, Oxford; PhD, University of Nottingham, 1957. Publications include: A Poet Hidden: the Life of R W Dixon, 1962; The Scribleriad, etc, editor, 1967; William Cobbett, 1973; James Thomson, The Seasons, editor, 1981; The Eighteenth Century: The Intellectual and Cultural Context of English Literature 1700-1789, 1986, 2nd edition, 1993; Liberty, The Castle of Indolence and Other Poems, 1986; English Pastoral Poetry, 1983; James Thomson 1700-1748, A Life: Biographical Critical, 1992; William Cowper, The Task and Other Poems, editor, 1994; Biographical articles on various English writers in numerous reference books; over 100 articles and reviews in Church Quarterly Review; 18th Century Life; 18th Century Studies; English; English Language Notes; Garden History; Journal of English and German Philology; Library; Modern Language Review; Times Literary Supplement; English Miscellany; English Studies; Notes and Queries; The Scriblerian; Review of English Studies. Contributions to: The Rossettis and Contemporary Poets in The Sphere History of Literature, 1970, 2nd edition, 1987; Pope and The Visual Arts, in Alexander Pope, 1972; Augustan Poetry, in Encyclopaedia of Literature and Criticism, 1990; Thomson Abroad: Traversing Realism Unknown, in All Before Them; The Rights of Man, in Eighteenth-Century Studies, 1992. Address: Department of English, Southampton University, Southampton, Hampshire, England.

SAMPSON Anthony Terrell Seward, b. 3 Aug 1926, Durham, England. Writer. m. 31 May 1965, 1 son, 1 daughter. Education: Christ Church, Oxford University, 1947-50. Appointments: Editor, Drum Magazine, South Africa, 1951-55; Staff, Observer, 1955-66; Editorial Advisor, Brandt Commission, 1978-80; Columnist, Newsweek International, 1977-; Chairman, Society of Authors, 1992-94. Publications: Drum, 1956; Anatomy of Britain, 1962; New Europeans,

1968; The Sovereign State of ITT, 1973; The Seven Sisters, 1975; The Arms Bazaar, 1977; The Money Lenders, 1981; Black and Gold, 1987; The Midas Touch, 1989; The Essential Anatomy of Britain: New Patterns of Power in The Nineties, 1992; Company Man: The Rise and Fall of Corporation Life, 1995. Contributions to: Numerous journals including: Newsweek; New York Times; Times; Observer. Honour: Prix International De La Presse, Nice, 1976. Literary Agent: The Peters Fraser and Dunlop Group Limited, London. Address: 27 Ladbroke Grove, London, W11, England.

SAMPSON Geoffrey (Richard), b. 1944, British. Language Engineering Consultant. Appointments: Fellow, Queens, College, Oxford, 1969-72; Lecturer, London School of Economics, 1972-74; Lecturer, 1974-76, Reader, 1976-84, University of Lancaster; Professor of Linguistics, University of Leeds, 1985-90; Director, Centre for Advanced Software Applications, University of Sussex, 1991-. Publications: The Form of Language, 1975; Liberty and Language, 1979; Making Sense, School of Linguistics, 1980; An End to Allegiance, 1984; Writing Systems, 1985; The Computational Analysis of English (with Garside and Leech), 1987; English For The Computer, 1995. Membership: MBCS. Address: School of Cognitive and Computing Sciences, University of Sussex, Falmer, Brighton, BN1 9QH, England.

SAMPSON Ronald Victor, b. 12 Nov 1918, St Helen's, Lancashire, England. m. 9 Jan 1943, 2 d. Education: Keble College, Oxford, 1936-39, 1946-47, 1948-51; Nuffield College, Oxford, 1950-51; MA, 1947; DPhil, 1951. Publications: Progress in The Age of Reason, 1957; Equality and Power, 1965, USA edition as The Psychology of Power, Brazilian edition as Psicanalize do Poder, Mexican edition as Igualdad y Poder; Tolstoy: The Discovery of Peace, 1973, USA edition as The Discovery of Peace; Chapter on Limits of Religious Thought, in 1959 - Entering an Age of Crisis, 1959. Contributions to: The Nation, New York; Resurgence; Peace News; The Pacifist; Academic journals; Pamphlets and translations, Housmans and Peace Pledge Union. Membership: English PEN. Address: Beechcroft, Hinton Charterhouse, Bath, Avon, England.

SAMS Eric, b. 3 May 1926, London, England. Civil Servant (retired). m. Enid Tidmarsh, 30 Jun 1952, 2 s. Education: Corpus Christi, Cambridge, 1947-50; BA 1st Class Honours, 1950; PhD, 1972. Publications: The Songs of Hugo Wolf, 1961, 1983, 1992; The Songs of Robert Schumann, 1969, 1975, 1993; Brahms Songs, 1971, in French 1989; Shakespeare's Edmund Ironside, 1985, 1986; The Real Shakespeare, 1995. Contributions to: Times Literary Supplement; Notes and Queries; Connotations. Honours: Leverhulme Grant, 1984; Honorary Patron, Songmakers Almanac, 1980-; Honorary Member, Guildhall School of Music and Drama, 1983-. Address: 32 Arundel Avenue, Sanderstead, Surrey, CR2 8BB, England.

SAMUELS Warren Joseph, b. 1933, American. Career: Assistant Professor of Economics, University of Missouri, 1957-58; Georgia State College, Atlanta, 1958-59; Assistant Professor of Economics, 1959-62, Associate Professor, 1962-68, University of Miami, FL; Professor of Economics, 1968-, Director of Graduate programs, Placement Officer, Department of Economics 1969-73, Michigan State University, East Lansing; President Elect 1971-71, President, 1972-73, Economics Society of Michigan; Editor, Journal of Economic Issues, 1971-81. Publications: The Classical Theory of Economic Policy, 1966; A Critique of Administrative Regulation of Public Utilities (ed with H M Trebing) 1972; Pareto on Policy, 1974; The Economy as a System of Power, (ed) 2 volumes, 1979; Taxing and Spending Policy (co-ed); The Methodology of Economic Thought (ed), 1980; Research in the History of Economic Thought and Methodology (ed) volume 1, 1983. Memberships: Editorial Board, History of Political Economy, 1969-89; Public Utilities Taxation Committee, National Tax Association, 1971-73; Member of Executive Committee 1972-73, President 1981-82, History of Economics Society; President, Association for Social Economics, 1988. Address: 4397 Cherrywood Drive, Okemos, MI 48864, USA.

SANBORN Margaret, b. 1915, American. Publications: Robert E Lee, a Portrait: 1807-1861, 1966; Robert E Lee, The Complete Man, 1861-1870, 1967; The American: River of El Dorado, 1974; The Grand Tetons, 1981; Yosemite: Its Discovery, Its Wonders and Its People, 1981; Mark Twain: The Bachelor Years (biography), 1990; Robert E Lee, a Portrait; revised; 2 vols in one vols 1995. Address: 527 Northern Avenue, Mill Valley, CA 94941, USA.

SANDEN Einar, b. 8 Sept 1932, Tallinn, Estonia. Writer; Historian. m. Dr Elizabeth Gorell, 6 Sept 1994. Education: MA 1983, PhD, 1984, USA. Appointments: Managing Director, Owner, Boreas Publishing House, 1975; Councillor, Estonian Government in Exile, 1975-1990. Publications: KGB Calling Eve, 1978; The Painter From Naissaar, 1985; Ur Eldinum Til Islands, 1988; An Estonian Saga, 1995. Contributions to: Editor of various Estonian periodicals. Honours: Distinguished Freedom Writer Poet of 1968, UPLI, Manila, The Philippines; Cultural Award, Fraternity Sakala, Toronto, 1984. Memberships: PEN Centre for Writers in Exile, 1954-80; Royal Society of Literature, London, 1960; Association of Estonian Writers Abroad, 1970; English PEN, 1976; Estonian National Council, 1959; Association for The Advancement of Baltic Studies, USA, 1980; Estonian Academic Association of War History, Tallinn, 1988. Address: Boreas House, 63 Ninian Road, Cardiff, CF2 5EL, England.

SANDERS Jeanne. See: **RUNDLE Anne.**

SANDERS Scott Russell, b. 26 Oct 1945, TN, USA. Writer; Teacher. m. Ruth Ann McClure, 27 Aug 1967, 1 son, 1 daughter. Education: BA, Brown University, 1967; PhD, Cambridge University, 1971. Literary Appointments: Cambridge Review, 1969-71; Minnesota Review, 1976-80; North American Review, 1982-; Orion, 1992-. Publications: Staying Put, 1993; Secrets of the Universe, 1991; The Invisible Company, 1989; The Paradise of Bombs, 1987; Bad Man Ballad, 1986; In Limestone Country, 1985; Fetching the Dead, 1984; Wilderness Plots, 1983. Contributions to: Harpers; Omni; Georgia Review; North American Review; Orion; OH Review; Notre Dame Magazine; Gettysburg Review. Honours: Associated Writing Programs Award; Kenyon Review Award; Guggenheim Fellowship. Address: 1113 East Wylie Street, Bloomington, IN 47401, USA.

SANDERSON John Michael, b. 23 Jan 1939, Glasgow, Scotland. University Reader. Education: MA, 1963, PhD, 1966, Queens' College, Cambridge, 1957-63. Appointments: General Editor of McMillan Economic History Society Studies in Economic and Social History Series, 1992-; Council of Economic History Society, 1994. Publications: The Universities and British Industry, 1850-1970, 1972; The Universities in The 19th Century, 1975; Education Economic Change and Society in England, 1780-1870, 1983, second edition, 1992, Japanese edition, 1993; From Irving to Olivier, A Social History of The Acting Profession in England, 1880-1983, 1984; Educational Opportunity and Social Change in England, 1900-1980s, 1987; The Missing Stratum, Technical School Education in England, 1900-1990s, 1994. Contributions to: Economic History Review; Journal of Contemporary History; Contemporary Record; Business History; Northern History; Past and Present. Membership: Economic History Society. Address: School of Economic and Social Studies, University of East Anglia, Norwich, Norfolk, England.

SANDERSON Stewart F(orson), b. 1924, British. Appointments: Secretary Archivist, 1952-58, Senior Research Fellow, Editor of Scottish Studies, 1957-60, University of Edinburgh; Joint Secretary, Section H, British Association for The Advancement of Science, 1957-63; Lecturer in Folk Life Studies and Director of The Folk Life Survey, 1960-64; Director of The Institute of Dialect and Folk Life Studies, 1964-83; Chairman of The School of English, 1980-, University of Leeds; President, Folklore Society, 1971-73; member of The Council, Society of Folk Life Studies, 1974-79, 1981-; Governor, British Institute of Recorded Sound, 1979-. Publications: Hemingway, 1961, 1970; The City of Edinburgh (with others), 1963; Studies in Folk Life (with others), 1969; The Secret Common-Wealth and A Short Treatise of Charms and Spells (editor), 1976; To Illustrate the Monuments (with others), 1976; The Linguistic Atlas of England (editor)(with H Orton and J Widdowson), 1978; Ernest Hemingway: For Whom The Bell Tolls, 1980. Address: England.

SANDFORD Jeremy. Playwright; Author; Journalist; Musician; Performer. m. (1) Nell Dunn, 1956, 3 s, (2) Philippa Finnis, 1987. Education: Eton; Oxford. Appointments: Director, Hatfield Court New Age Conference Centre; Editor, Romano Drom (Gypsy Newspaper), 1970-73. Publications: Synthetic Fun, 1967; Cathy Come Home, 1967; Whelks and Chromium, 1968; Edna The Inebriate Woman, 1971; Down and Out in Britain, 1971; In Search of the Magic Mushroom, 1972; Gypsies, 1973; Tomorrow's People, 1974; Prostitutes, 1975; Smiling David, 1975; Figures and Landscapes: The Art Of Lettice Sandford, 1991; Hey Days in Hay, 1992. Contributor to: The Guardian; Sunday Times; Observer. Honours: Italia Prize, 1967; Writers Guild, Best Television Play, 1967, 1971; BECTU (then ACTT) Best Television Play,

1967. Memberships: Writers Guild; BECTU, Hereford Traveller Support Group. Address: Hatfield Court, Near Leominster, HR6 0SD, England.

SANDOZ G Ellis, b. 1931, USA. Writer. Publications: Political Apocalypse: A Study of Dostoevsky's Grand Inquisitor, 1971; Conceived in Liberty, 1978; A Tide of Discontent: The 1980 Elections and Their Meaning, 1981; The Voegelinian Revolution: A Biographcal Introduction, 1981; Eric Voegelin's Thought: A Critical Appraisal, 1982; Election '84; Landslide Without a Mandate? 1985; Autobiographical Reflections, 1989; A Government of Laws: Political Theory, Religion and the American Founding, 1990; Eric Voegelin's Published Essays, 1966-1985, 1990. Political Sermons of the American Founding 1730-1805, 1991; Eric Voegelin's Significance for the Modern Mind, 1991; The Roots of Liberty: Magna Carta, Ancient Constitution and The Anglo-American Tradition of Rule of Law, 1993. Address: Department of Political Science, Louisiana State University, Baton Rouge, LA 70803, USA.

SANDS Martin. See: **BURKE John Frederick.**

SANDY Stephen, b. 2 Aug 1934, Minneapolis, MN, USA. Education: BA, Yale, 1955; MA, Harvard, PhD, Harvard, 1963. Career: McGee Professor of Writing, Davidson College, 1994. Publications: Stresses in the Peaceable Kingdom, HM Co, 1967; Roofs, Houghton Mifflin, 1971; Riding to Greylock, Alfred A Knopf, 1983; To A Mantis, 1987; Man in the Open Air, 1988; The Epoch, 1990; Thanksgiving Over the Water, 1992; A Cloak for Hercules, verse translation, forthcoming. Contributions to: Agenda; American Poetry Review; The Atlantic; Harvard Magazine; Michigan Quarterly Review; Iowa Review; The New Yorker; The Paris Review; Salmagundi; Southwest Review and others. Memberships: Poetry Society of America. Honours: Ingram Merrill Foundation Fellowship, 1985; Vermont Council on the Arts Fellowship, 1988; National Endowmwnet for the Arts Fellowship, 1988. Address: Box 524, North Bennington, VT 05257, USA.

SANDYS Elspeth Somerville, b. 18 Mar 1940, Timaru, New Zealand. Writer. 1 son, 1 daughter. Education: MA, Auckland, New Zealand; LTCL (Music); FTCL (Speech, Drama). Publications: Catch a Falling Star, 1978; The Broken Tree, 1981; Love and War, 1982; Finding Out, 1991; Best Friends', a collection of short stories, 1993. Contributions to: Various Magazines including: Landfall, New Zealand; PEN, England; Folio Society, England; Writer numerous radio plays, BBC. Memberships: Writers Guild. Literary Agent: Diana Tyler, MBA Literary Agents Ltd. Address: c/o MBA Literary Agents Ltd, 45 Fitzroy Street, London, W1P 5HR, England.

SANJIAN Avedis K, b. 1921, USA. Writer (History, Literature, Medieval Peleography). Publications: The Armenian Communities in Syria Under Ottoman Dominion, 1965; Colophons of Armenian Manuscripts 1301-1480: A Source For Middle Eastern History, 1969; A Catalogue of Medieval Armenian Manuscripts in the United States, 1976; (with Andreas Tietze), Eremia Chelebi Komurjian's Armeno-Turkish Poems, The Jewish Bride, 1981; David Anhaght: the Invincible Philosopher, 1986; (with Thomas F Mathews) Armenian Gospel Iconography: The Tradition of the Glajor Gospel, 1991. Memberships: American Oriental Society; Middle East Studies Association; Society for Armenian Studies; Society for the Study of Caucasia. Address: 545 Muskingum Place, Pacific Palisades, CA 90272, USA.

SANTA MARIA. See: **POWELL-SMITH Vincent.**

SANTINI Rosemarie, b. New York City, USA. Writer. Education: Hunter College. Career: Senior Editor, True Story Magazine. Publcations: Ask Me What I Want; Beansprouts; All My Children, 3 vols; Abracadabra; Forty-One Grove Street; The Sex Doctors; The Secret Fire, 1978-82; A Swell Style of Murder, 1986; The Discenchanted Diva, 1988; Blood Sisters, 1990; Private Lies, 1991. Contributions to: Short stories regularly to Women's World; Non-fiction to: Ladies Home Journal; Playboy Magazine; Working Woman; Regulary to Daily New Sunday Magazine; Penthouse Forum; Essence Magazine; Playbill Magazine; Weekend Magazine; Antholgies: The Dream Book; Kerouac and Friends; Side By Side; Varieties of the American Experience, 1993. Memberships: PEN; Mystery Writers of America; Authors Guild; Poets and Writers; Poetry Society of American; Society of American Journalists and Authors; Dramatists Guild; National Academy of TV Arts and Sciences; International Assocaition of Crime Writers; Sisters in Crime; Novelists Inc; Board of

Directors, Mystery Writers of America. Address: c/o Pratt University, 295 Lafayette Street, New York, NY 10012, USA.

SANTOS Helen. See: **GRIFFITHS Helen.**

SAPERSTEIN David, b. Brooklyn, New York, USA. Novelist; Screenwriter; Film Director. m. Ellen-Mae Bernard, 1 son, 1 daughter. Education: Chemical Engineering and Chemistry, CCNY; Film Institute, CCNY. Career: Assistant Professor, Film, New York University Graduate Film and TV School, 1992-93. Publications: Cocoon, 1985; Fatal Reunion, 1987; Metamorphosis: The Cocoon Story Continues, 1988; Red Devil, 1989; and 19 screenplays. Honours: Writers Guild of America, Best Story for Screen Nomination, 1985. Memberships: Writers Guild of America; Directors Guild of America. Literary Agent: Susan Schulman; Motion Picture Agent: Joel Gottler-Renaissance/Swanson. Address: c/o Ebbets Field Productions, PO Box 42, Wykagyl Station, New Rochelle, NY 10804, USA.

SAPP (Eva) Jo (Barnhill), b. 4 Feb 1944, San Antonio, TX, USA. Writer; Editor. m. David Paul Sapp, 1 s, 1 d. Education: BA Hons English Creative Writing, 1976, MA 1982, PhD coursework completed, 1985, University of Missouri. Literary Appointments: Editorial Assistant, 1978-80, Senior Fiction Advisor, 1980-81, Associate Editor: Special Projects, 1981-92, Fiction, 1986-88, Missouri Review; Editorial Consultant, Cultural Plan of Action, 1987-. Publications: Co-editor, The Best of The Missouri Review: Fiction 1978-90; Missouri Review Online: 1986-88. Contributions to: Intro 15 and 16; Norton Anthology, 1994; Washington Review; Kansas Quarterly; North American Review; Flash Fiction, 1992. Honours: Honorable mention, Deep South, 1981; McKinney Prize, 1984; Editor's Book Awards Nominee, 1988; Missouri Arts Council Grant, 1988; Elmer Holmes Bobst Award Nominee, 1992. Memberships: Poets and Writers; Associated Writing Programmes; Columbia Commission on The Arts, Secretary, 1986-87, Vice-Chair, 1987-88, Chair, 1988-. Address: Missouri Review, 1507 Hillcrest Hall, University of Missouri, Columbia, MO 65211, USA.

SARAC Roger. See: **CARAS Roger Andrew.**

SARANTI Galatia, b. 8 Nov 1920, Greece. Writer. m. Stavros Patsouris, 26 Dec 1948, 2 sons. Education: Law Faculty, University of Athens, 1947. Publications: Novels: Lilacs, 1949; The Book of Johannes and Maria, 1952; Return, 1953; Our Old House, 1959; The Limits, 1966; Cracks, 1979; The Waters of Euripoe, 1989; Short stories: Bright Colours, 1962; Remember Vilna, 1972. Contributions to: Nea Hestia; Helliniki Ahmiozptia; Epoches; Diabazo. Honours: Kostas Ouranis Prize, 1953; State Prize, 1957, 1974; Academy of Athens Literature Prize, 1979. Memberships: National Society of Greek Writers; PEN Club. Literary Agents: Hestia, Solonos 60, Athens 10672, Greece. Address: Kallidromidy 87-89, 10683 Athens, Greece.

SARGENT Lyman Tower, b. 9 Feb 1940, Rehoboth, Massachusetts, USA. Professor of Political Science. m. (1) Patricia McGinnis, 27 Dec 1961 (divorced), 1 s. (2)Mary T Weiler, 14 Aug 1985 (divorced). Education: BA, International Relations, Macalester College, 1961; MA, American Studies, 1962; PhD, Political Science, 1965, Univerity of Minnesota. Career: University of Wyoming, 1964-65; University of Missouri-St Louis, 1965-; University of Exeter, 1978-79, 1983-84; London School of Economcs, 1985-85; Editor, Utopian Studies, 1988-; Co-editor, Syracuse University Press, Series on Utopianism and Communitarism, 1988-. Publications: Contemproary Political Ideologies: A Comparative Analysis, 1969, 1972, 1975, 1978, 1981, 1984, 1987, 1990, 1993; New Left Thought: An Introducton, 1972; British and American Utopian Literature 1516-1975: An Annotated Bibligraphy, 1979; British and American Utopian Literature, 1516-1985; An Annotated, Chronological Bibliography, 1988; Contemporary Political Ideologies: A Reader, 1990; Techniques of Political Analysis: An Introduction 1970; Editor: IVR NORTHAM IV Consent: Concept, Capacity, Conditions, Constraints, 1979. Address: Department of Political Science, Univerity of Missouri- St Louis, 8001 Natural Bridge Road, St Louis, MO 63121, USA.

SARGESSON Jenny. See: **DAWSON Jennifer.**

SARKAR Anil Kumar, b. 1 Aug 1912, India. Professor Emeritus. m. Aruna Sarkar, 1 Nov 1941 (dec) 1 s, 3 d. Education: MA 1st Class, 1935, PhD, 1946, D.Litt, 1960, Patna University. Career: Professor, Rajendra College, 1940-44; Senior Lecturer, University of Ceylon, Colombo and Peredeniya, 1944-64; Visiting Professor, University of New Mexico, Albuquerque, USA, 1964-65; Full Professor of Philosophy

and West-East Philosophy, 1965-82, California State University, Hayward, USA; Research Director, Professor of Asian Studies, 1968, now Professor Emeritus, California Institute of Integral Studies, San Francisco, 1980-. Publications: An Outline of Whitehead's Philosophy, 1940; Changing Phases of Buddhist Thought, 1st and 2nd editions,1968-75, 3rd edition, 1983; Whitehead's Four Principles From West-East Perspectives, 1974; Dynamic Facets of Indian Thought, vol 1, 1980, vol 2-4, 1987-88; Experience in Change and Prospect Pathways from War to Peace, 1989; Sri Aurobindo's Vision of the Super Mind - Its Indian and Non-Indian Interpreters, 1989; Buddhism and Whitehead's Process - Philosopy, 1990; Zero - Its Role and Prospects in Indian Thought and its Impact on Post-Einsteinian Astrophysics, 1992; The Mysteries of Vajrayana Buddhism: From Atisha to Dalai Lama, 1993; Whitehead's Four Principles From West-East Perspectives (enlarged 2nd edition) 1994; Triadic Avenues of India's Cultural Prospects - Philosophy, Physics and Politics, 1994. Contributions to: Indian, American and other journals. Address: 818 Webster Street, Hayward, CA 94544, USA.

SARNA Jonathan D, b. 10 Jan 1955. Joseph H & Belle R Braun Professor of American Jewish History, Brandie University. m. Ruth Langer, 8 June 1986, 1 s, 1 d. Education: BHL Honours, Hebrew College, Boston, USA, 1974; BA Summa cum laude, Highest Honours in Judaic Studies and History, 1975, MA, Judaic Studies, 1975, Brandeis Univerity; MA, Yale University, 1976; MPhil, History, Yale University, 1978; PhD, History, Yale Univerity, 1979. Career: Abstracter-Consultant, ABC-CLIO, 1980-94; Editor, North Aerican Judaism section, Religious Studies Review, 1984-94; Publication Committee, Jewish Publication Society, 1985-; Editorial Committee, Queen City Heritage, 1985-; Editrorial Board: American Jewish History, 1988-, Religion and American Culture, 1989-; Associate Editor, American National Biography. Publications include: Jews in New Haven (editor), 1978; Mordecai Manuel Noah: Jacksonian Politician and American Jewish Communal Leader, 1979; Jacksonian Jew: The Two Worlds of Mordecai Noah, 1981; People Walk on Their Heads: Moses Weinberger's Jews and Judaism in New York (Translator, editor), 1982; Jews and the Founding of the Republic (co-editor), 1985; The American Jewish Experience: A Reader, 1986; American Synagogue History: A Bibliography and State-of-the-Field Survey (with Alexandra S Korros), 1988; American Jews and Chuch-State Relations: The Search for Equal Footing, pamphlet, 1989; JPS: The Americanization of Jewish Culture (A History of the Jewish Publication Society 1888-1988),1989; The Jews of Cincinnati (with Nancy H Klein), 1989; Ethnic Diversity and Civic Identity: Patters of Conflict and Cohesion in Cinncinnati Since 1820, 1992; Yuhude Artsot Ha-Berit, 1992; A Double Bond: The Constitutional Documents of American Jewry; Relgion and State in American Jewish History; Observing America's Jews: Selected Writing of Marsall Skalre; Masterworks of Modern Jewish Writing (general editor), 10 vols; American Jewish Life (editor with Moses Rischin), 5 vols; Contributions to Articles and reviews to American, Jewish History; Jerusalem Post; The Principal; Canadian Jewish Historical Society Journal; Library Journal; Juidaica Book News. Address: Department of NEJS, Brandeis University, Waltham, MA 02254, USA.

SARNA Nahum Mattathias, b. 27 Mar 1923, London, England. Emeritus Professor, Biblical Studies. m. Helen Horowitz, 23 Mar 1947, 2 sons. Education: BA, 1944; MA, 1946, University of London; PhD, Dropsie College, Philadelphia, USA, 1955. Career: Univesity College, London, 1946-49; Gratz College, Philadelphia, USA, 1951-57; Jewish Theological Seminary, New York, 1957-65; Faculty, 1965-, Dora Golding Professor of Biblical Studies, 1967-, Professor Emeritus, 1985-, Brandeis University, Editor, Editorial Boards, Various scholarly journals; General Editor, Jewish Publications Society Torah Commentary; Editor, Proceedings of the American Academy for Jewish Research; Visiting Professor, Columbia University, 1964-65, 1992; Yale University, 1992-94; Distinguished Professor Florida Atlantic University, 1995-. Publications include: Understanding Genesis, 1966; Exploring Exodus, 1985; Commentary on Genesis, 1989; Commentary on Exodus, 1991; Songs of the Heart: An Introduction to the Book of Psalms, 1993. Contributions to: Journal of Biblical Literature; Journal of Near Eastern Studies; Journal of Americal Oriental Society; Harvard Theological Review; Biblical Archaeologist; Biblical Archaeology Review; various scholarly journals. Honours: Award, Jewish Book Council, 1967; Senior Fellow, American Council of Learned Societies, 1971-72; Fellow, American Academy for Jewish Research, 1974-; Council, World Union of Jewish Studies, 1981-; Fellow, Institute for Advanced Studies, Hebrew University, 1982-83; Honorary Doctorate, Gratz College, 1984; Jewish Institute of Religion, 1987; Honorary

Doctorate, 1991. Memberships include: Past president, Association for Jewish Studies; American Academy for Jewish Research; American Oriental Society; Israel Exploration Society; Palestine Exploration Society; World Union of Jewish Studies; Board of Advisors of the Dead Sea Scrolls Foundation. Address: 7886 Chula Vista Crescent, Boca Raton, FL 33433, USA.

SAROYAN Aram, b. 25 Sept 1943, New York City, USA. Writer. m. Gailyn McClanahan, 9 Oct 1968, 1 s, 2 d. Education: University of Chicago, Illinois; New York and Columbia Universitie. Publications: Aram Saroyan, 1968; Pages, 1969; Words and Photographs, 1970; The Street: An Autobiographical Novel, 1974; Genisis Angels: The Saga of Lew Welch and the Beat Generation, 1979; Last Rites: The Death of William Saroyan, 1982; William Saroyan, 1983; Trio: Portrait of an Intimate Friendship, 1985; The Romantic, 1988; Friends in the World: The Education of a Writer, 1992; Rancho Mirage: An American Tragedy of Manners, Madness and Murder, 1993. Contibutions to: New York Times Book Reivew; Los Angeles Times Book Review; Nation Village Voice; Mother Jones; Paris Review. Honors: Poetry Award, NEA, 1967, 1968. Memberships: President, PEN Center USA West, 1992-93. Address: 732 Blue Oak Avenue, Thousand Oaks, CA 91320, USA.

SARTORI Eva Maria, b. Subotica, Yugoslavia. Author. Publications: Pierre, Mon Amour, 1967; Wie Eine Palme im Wind, 1968; Oh, Diese Erbschaft, 1969; Die Rheinhagens, 1980; Spuren, Die Kein Wind Verweht, 1981; Damals in Dahlem, 1982; Königin Luise, 1983; Der Sünder und Die Heilige, 1984; Streite Nicht Mit Dem Wind, 1985; Venedig Sehen und Sterben, 1986; Das Geheimnis Der Roten Rose, 1987; Das Schicksal Stellte Die Weiche, 1987; Ein Herz Sucht eine Heimat, 1989; Bittere Vergangenheit, 1989; Aller Reichtum Dieser Welt, 1989; Warten Auf Die Liebe, 1990; Und Dennoch Liebe Ich Dich, 1991; Wir Wissen Weder Tag Noch Stunde, 1991; Der Kaktuskavalier, 1993; Die Dombergs, 1994. Contributions to: Neue Welt; 7 Tage; Frau Aktuell; Die Aktuelle; Frau Mit Herz; Das Neue Blatt; TV Hören und Sehen; Romanwoche. Honours: Doctoral Membership, Literature, World University. Memberships: Freier Deutscher Autorenverband; Fellow, International Biographical Association. Literary Agent: Grit Peters. Address: Kirchenstrasse 32, DG 84533 Stammham, Germany.

SATTERTHWAIT Walter, b. 23 Mar 1946, USA. Writer. 1 d. Education: Reed College, 1969-72. Publications: Cocain Blues, 1980; The Aegean Affair, 1981; Wall of Glass, 1987; Miss Lizzie, 1989; At Ease With The Dead, 1990; Wilde West, 1991; A Flower In The Desert, 1992; The Hanged Man, 1993 (UK Title: The Death Card, 1994). Contributions to: Alfred Hitchcock's Mystery Magazine; Santa Fe Reporter. Memberships: Mystery Writers of America; Private Eye Writers of America. Literary Agent: Dominick Abel. Address: PO Box 5452, Clearwater, Florida 34618, USA.

SAUNDERS Ann Loreille (Ann Cox-Johnson), b. 23 May 1930, London, England. Historian. m. Bruce Kemp Saunders, 4 Jun 1960, 1 s, 1 d. Education: Plumptre Scholar, Queen's College, London, 1946-48; BA Hons, University College, London, 1951; PhD, Leicester University,1965. Literary Appointments include: Archivist, Marylebone Public Library, London, 1956-63; Honorary Editor, Costume Society, 1967-; Honorary Editor, London Topographical Society, 1975-. Publications include: London, City and Westminster, (Arthur Mee re-written) 1975; Art and Architecture of London, 1984, Paperback, 1988, 1992; John Bacon, R A, 1740-1799, (as Ann Cox-Johnson); St Martin-in-The-Fields, short history and guide, 1989; The Royal Exchange, 1991; 2 solid catalogues. Contributions to: Articles and reviews to Burlington Magazine, Geographic Magazine, London Journal. Honours: Prize for Best Specialist Guide Book of The Year, British Tourist Board, 1984; Fellow of University College, London, 1992. Memberships: Fellow, Society of Antiquaries; Costume Society; London Topographical Society. Address: 3 Meadway Gate, London, NW11 7LA, England.

SAUNDERS James, b. 8 Jan 1925, London, England. Playwright. m. Audrey Cross, 1951, 1 s, 2 d. Publications: Plays: Moonshine, 1958; Alas, Poor Fred, The Ark, 1959; Committal, Barnstable, Return to A City, 1960; A Slight Accident, 1961; Double Double, 1962; Next Time I'll Sing To You, The Pedagogue, Who Was Hilary Maconochie?, 1963; A Scent of Flowers, Neighbours, 1964; Triangle, Opus, 1965; A Man's Best Friend, The Borage Pigeon Affair, 1969; After Liverpool, 1970; Games, Savoury Meringue, 1971; Hans Kohlhaas, 1972; Bye Bye Blues, 1973; The Island, 1975; Bodies, 1977; Birdsong, 1979; Fall, 1981; Emperor Waltz, 1983; Scandella, 1985; Making It Better, 1992; Retreat, 1995. Television: Watch Me I'm a Bird, 1964; Bloomers,

(series) 1979;TV adaptations of works by D H Lawrence, Henry James, H E Bates and R F Delderfield; Screenplays: Sailor's Return; The Captain's Doll. Honours: Arts Council of GB Drama Bursary, 1960; Evening Standard Drama Award,1963; Writer's Guild TV Adaptation Award, 1966; Arts Council Major Bursary, 1984; BBC Radio Play Award, 1986; Moliére Award (Paris), 1990. Address: c/o Casarotto Ramsay Ltd, 60-66 Wardour Street, London, W1V 3HP, England.

SAUNDERS Nezzle Methelda (Nezzle), b. 26 May 1940, Smithville, Jamaica, West Indies. Cook; Performance Writer. m. 27 Jul 1960, 3 s, 4 d. Education: Diploma (Office Practice), South Nottingham College of Further Education, 1976; City And Guilds Certificate (Community Care), 1989. Literary Appointments: Schools And Community Centres (Radio Programmes), 1986-1994; Channel 4 (TV Programme), 1988. Publications: Divine Inspiration, 1986 And 1989; Insight, 1987; Children's And Student's Anthology, 1988. Contributions: The Voice; East Midlands Foreward; Jamaica Gleaner; Evening Post (local). Honours: Bursary Award (Research In Creative Writing), Nottinghamshire County Council Leisure Services. Memberships: Committee, Chronicle Of Minority Arts; Partnership, Arts Development Group, 1987-; Lecturer, Afro-Caribbean Family And Friends, 1990-93. Address: 48 Finsbury Avenue, Sneinton Dale, Nottingham, NG2 4LL, England.

SAUVAIN Philip Arthur, b. 1933. Freelance Writer. Appointments include: Senior Lecturer in Geography, James Graham College, Leeds, 1963-68; Head of Environmental Studies Department, Charlotte Mason College of Education, Ambleside, 1968-74. Publications include: Environment Books: Looking Around Town and Country, 1975; A First Look at Winds (Dinosaurs, Discoveries, Ice and Snow) 5 volumes, 1975-78; Imagining The Past: First Series (6 books) 1976, Second Series (6 books) 1979; Looking Back, 1977; Macmillan Local Studies Lit, 1979; Looking Around Cards, 1979; Certificate Mapwork, 1980; The British Isles, 1980; Story of Britain Series (4 books) 1980; Science Discussion Pictures, 1981; Britain's Living Heritage, 1982; History of Britain (4 books) 1982; Theatre, 1983; Macmillan Junior Geography (4 books) 1983; Hulton New Geographies (5 books) 1983; History Map Books (2 books) 1983, 1985; Hulton New Histories (5 books) 1984, 1985; France and The French, 1985; European and World History, 1815-1919, 1985; Modern World History, 1919 Onwards, 1985; How History Began, 1985; Castles and Crusaders, 1986; What to Look For (4 books) 1986; British Economic and Social History, 2 volumes, 1987; Exploring Energy (4 books) 1987; GCSE History Companion series (3 books) 1988; How We Build (3 books) 1989; The World of Work (3 books) 1989; Skills for Geography, 1989; Skills for Standard Grade History, 1990; Exploring the Past: Old World, 1991; Changing World, 1992; Expanding World, 1993; The Way It Works (3 books) 1991; History Detectives (3 books) 1992,1993; Great Battles and Sieges (4 books) 1992,1993; Breakthrough: Communications, 1992; The Era of The Second World War, 1993; Robert Scott in the Antarctic, 1993; Target Geography (8 books) 1994. Address: 70 Finborough Road, Stowmarket, Suffolk, IP14 1PU, England.

SAVA George. See: **MILKOMANE George Alexis Milkomanovich.**

SAVAGE Alan. See: **NICOLE Christopher Robin.**

SAVAGE Thomas (Tom), b. 14 July 1948, New York City, USA. Poet, Critic. Education: BA, English, Brooklyn College, City University of New York, 1969; Master's Degree, Columbia University School of Library Service, 1980. Career: Teaching Assistant, Naropa Institute School of Poetics, 1975; Teacher, Words, Music, Words for Poets and Composers, St Mark's Poetry Project, 1983-85; Editor, Roof Magazine, 1976-78; Editor, Gandhabba Magazine, 1981-93. Publications: Poetry Books: Personalities, 1978; Slow Waltz on the Glass Harmonica, 1980; Filling Spaces, 1980; Housing Preservation and Development, 1988; Political Conditions/Physical States, 1994; Processed Words. Contributions to: Downtown; Cover; The World; City Magazines; Transfer; The Poetry Project Newsletter; Mudfish; Appearances. Honours: PEN Grant, 1978; Grant from Co-ordinating Council of Literary Magazines for Gandhabba, 1981-82. Memberships: CCLM. Address: 622 E 11th St 14, New York, NY 10009, USA.

SAVITT Sam, b. Wilkies-Barre, PA, USA. Author; Artist. m. Bette Orkin, 28 Mar 1946, 1 s, 1 d. Career: Dean of the School, American Academy of Equine Art. Publications include: Midnight, 1957; Rodeo, 1963; Vicki and the Black Horse, 1964; Sam Savitts True Horse

Stories, 1970; Vicki and the Brown Mare, 1976; The Dingle Ridge Fox and Other Stories, 1978; Wild Horse Running, 1973; One Horse, One Hundred Miles, One Day, 1981; A Horse to Remember, 1986; Step a Bit, 1956; There Was A Horse, 1961; Around The World With Horses, 1962; A Day At The LBJ Ranch, 1965; America's Horses, 1966; Equestrian Olympic Sketchbook, 1968; Draw Horses with Sam Savitt, 1981. Contributions to: Equus Magazine; Western Horseman Magazine. Honours: Boys Clubs of America Book Award, 1957; Library Guild, 1973. Memberships: Authors Guild; American Academy of Equine Art; Society of Animal Artists; Society of Illustrators. Address: Box 302, North Salem, NY 10560, USA.

SAVOY Douglas Eugene (Gene), b. 11 May 1927, Bellingham, Washington, USA. Bishop; Writer; Educator; Explorer. m. Sylvia Ontaneda, 7 July 1971, 2 sons, 1 daughter. Publications include: Antisuyo: The Search for the Lost Cities of the High Amazon, 1970; The Child Christ, 1973; The Decoded New Testament, 1974; On the Trail of the Feathered Serpent, 1974; The Prophecies of Jamil, 7 volumes, 1976-83; The Essaei Document: Secrets of an Eternal Race, 1978; The Lost Gospel of Jesus: Hidden Teachings of Christ, 1978; The Secret Sayings of Jamil: The Image & The World, 7 volumes, 1976-87; 39 texts, 400 audio tapes: Lectures on Religious Systems and Theology, 3 documentary videos. Articles on Peruvian Culture, Philosophy, Religion. Contributions to: Various publications. Memberships include: Authors Guild; Explorers Club, NYC; Geographical Society, Lima, Peru; Andean Explorers Foundation & Ocean Sailing Club. Literary Agent: Ted Chichak, Galen Literary Agency, 381 Park Ave S, Suite 1020, New York, NY 10016. Address: 2025 LaFond Drive, Reno, NV 89509, USA.

SAWYER Robert J, b. Canada. Education: Bachelor of Applied Arts, Radio and Television, Ryerson Polytechnical Institute, Toronto, Canada. Appointments: Book Reviewer for The Globe and Mail, Quill & Quire, Canadian Book Review Annual; Writer and Narrator for CBC Radio's Ideas Series. Publications: Author of Five Science-Fiction Novels, Several Short Stories, and over 200 magazine articles, including: Golden Fleece, 1990; Far-Seer, 1992; Fossil Hunter, 1993;End of an Era, 1994. Memberships: Writers' Guild of Canada; Crime Writers of Canada; Mystery Writers of America; Board Director, Science Fiction and Fantasy Writers of America. Honours: CompuServe HOMer Award, for best first science-fiction novel; Best Science-Fiction Novel, The Magazine of Fantasy & Science Fiction, 1990; Aurora Award, Honouring Excellence in Science-Fiction, five-time nominee. Address: 617-7601 Bathurst Street, Thornhill, Ontario L4J 4H5, Canada.

SAWYER Roger Martyn, b. 15 Dec 1931, Stroud, England. Author. m. Diana Margaret Harte, 30 Aug 1952, 2 s. Education: Wycliffe College, BA Hons, Diploma in Education, T G James Prize for Education, University of Wales, 1952-58; PhD History, Southampton University, 1979. Publications: Casement: The Flawed Hero, 1984; Slavery in The Twentieth Century, 1986; Children Enslaved, 1988; The Island From Within (editor), 1990; 'We Are But Women': Women in Ireland's History, 1993. Contributions to: Immigrants and Minorities; South. Honour: Airey Neave Award, 1985. Memberships: Anti-Slavery International (council member); Society of Authors, Bembridge Sailing Club; Retired member, Incorporated Association of Preparatory Schools. Address: Ducie House, Darts Lane, Bembridge, Isle of Wight, PO35 5YH, England.

SAY Allen. Honours: Caldecolt Medal, 1994; Boston Globe/Horn Book Award, 1994. Address: c/o Houghton Mifflin Childrens Books, Publicity Dept, 222 Berkeley Street, Boston, MA 02115, USA.

SAYER Ian Keith Terence, b. 30 Oct 1945, Norwich, Norfolk, England. Company Director; Author. 2 sons, 3 daughters. Education: Sunbury Grammar School, 1957-62. Publications: Nazi Gold, The Story of the World's Greatest Robbery, 1984; America's Secret Army, The Untold Story of the Counter Intelligence Corps, 1989; Hitler's Last General, The Case Against Wilhelm Mohnke, 1989. Contributions to: Columnist, Freight News Express, 1984-89. Address: c/o FRX International Ltd, FRX House, Staines Road, Hounslow, Middlesex, TW3 3LF, England.

SAYLOR John Galen, b. 1902, USA. Writer. Publications: Factors Associated with Participation in Cooperative Programs of Curriculum Planning, 1941; Secondary Education: Basic Principles and Practices (with W M Alexander), 1950; Curriculum Planning for Better Teaching in Secondary Education: Basic Principls and Practices (with W M Alexander), 1959; Curriculum Planning for Modern Schools (with W M Alexander), 1966; The High School: Today and Tomorrow (with W M Alexander), 1971; Planning Curriculum for Schools (with W M Alexander), (2nd edition with W M Alexander and Aruthur J Lewis, 1981), 1974; Antecedent Developments in the Movement to Competacy-based programs of Teachers Education, 1976; Who Planned The Curriculum: A Curriculum Plans Reservoir Model, with Historical Examples, 1982; A History of the Department of Secondary Education, Univesity of Nebraska, Lincoln, 1871-1980, 1982; A Saylor Lineage, 1983; A Smith Lineage, 1985; The Gilchrist Lineage, 1987. Address: 3001 S 51st Street, No 377, Lincoln, NB 68505, USA.

SAYLOR Steven, b. England. Address: c/o St Martin's Press Attn Author, Mail Dept 175 Fifth Avenue, New York, NY 10010, USA.

SCAGLIONE Aldo, b. 10 Jan 1925, Torino, Italy. University Professor. m. Jeanne M Daman (dec 1986), 28 June 1952. Education: DLitt, Univesity of Torino, Italy, 1948. Career includes: University of California, Berkeley, 1952-68; University of North Carolina, 1968-87; Professor and Chairman, Department of Italian, New York University, 1987. Publications include: Nature and Love in the Late Middle Ages, 1963; Ars Grammatica, 1970; The Classical Theory of Composition, 1972; The Theory of German Word Order, 1981; The Liberal Arts and the Jesuit College System, 1986; Knights at Court, 1991. Contributions to: Various scholarly journals. Memberships: Medieval Academy of America; Boccaccio Association of America, President, 1980-83; American Association for Italian Studies, Honorary President,1989. Honours: Knighted to the Order of Merit of the Republic of Italy; Fulbright Scholar, 1951; Guggenheim Fellow, 1958; Newberry Fellow, 1964; Fellow University of Wisconsin Institute for the Humanities, 1981; W R Kenan Professor, UNC - Chapel Hill, 1969-87; E M Remarque Professor of Literature, NYU, 1991-. Address: 3 Reading Ave, Frechtown, NJ 08825, USA.

SCAGNETTI Jack, b. 24 Dec 1924, Piney Fork, Ohio, USA. Literary; Talent Agent; Author. m. Doris Woolford, 19 July 1951, 1 s, 1 d. Education: Graduate, Detroit Southwestem High School. Publictions: Life and Loves of Gable; Laurel and Hardy Scrapbook; Intimate Life of Rudolph Valentino; Movie Stars in Bathtubs. Cars of the Stars; Bee Pollen; Nature's Miracle Health Food; Bicycle Motorcross; Famous Custom and Show Cars; The Joy of Walking Co-author; Gold for Begniners; Racquetball Made Easy; Racquetball for Women. Contributions to: Motor Trent; Popular Hot Rodding; Golf Magazine; Golf Digest; Golf Tips Magazine. Memberships: Writers Guild of America; Academy of Televison Arts and Sciences. Address: 5118 Vineland Ave, # 102, Hollywood, CA 910601, USA.

SCALAPINO Robert Anthony, b. 1919, USA. Writer. Career: Robson Research Professor of Government; Editor, Asian Survey Journal, 1962-. Publications: Decomcracy and the Party Movement in Pre-War Japan, 1953; Parties and Politics in Contemporary Japan (withJ Masumi), 1962; North Korea Today, 1964; The Japanese Communist Movement 1920-1966, 1968; Communism in Korea, 2 vols (with Chong-Sik Lee), 1972; Elites in the People's Republic of China, 1972; American-Japanese Relations in a Changing Era, 1972; Asia and the Major Powers, 1972; Asia and the Road Ahead, 1975; The Foreign Policy of Modern Japan, 1977; The Early Japanese Labour Movement, 1984; Modern China and Its Revolutionary Process, vol 1 (with G T Yu), 1985; Major Powers Relations in Northeast Asia, 1987; The Politics of Development - Perspectives on Twentieth Century Asia, 1989; The Last Leninists: The Uncertain Future of Asia's Communist States, 1992. Address: Institute of East Asian Studies, University of California, Berkeley, CA 94720, USA.

SCAMMELL William, b. 2 Jan 1939, Hythe, Hampshire, England. Poet; Critic. Education: BA, University of Bristol, 1967. Appointments include: Lecturer in English at the University of Newcastle, 1975-1991; Chairman of the Northem Arts Literature Panel, 1982-85. Publications: Yes and No, 1979; A Second Life, 1982; Time Past, 1982; Jouissance, 1985; Eldorado, 1987; Keith Douglas: A Study, 1988; Bleeding Heart Yard, 1992; The Game: tennis poems, 1992; Five Easy Pieces, 1993; Barnacle Bill, 1994; Editor: Between Comets: for Norman Nicholson at 70, 1984; This Green Earth: Nature Poetry 1400-1980, 1992; The Poetry Book Society Anthology 3, 1992; The New Lake Poets, 1991; Winter Pollen: Occasional Prose of Ted Hughes, 1994. Honours include: British Arts Council award, 1985; Northem Arts Writers award, 1988, 1991, 1994. Address: Centre for Continuing Education, The University, Newcastle upon Tyne NE1 7RU, England.

SCANNELL Vernon, b. 23 Jan 1922, Spilsby, England. Author. m. 4 Oct 1954, 3 s, 2 d. Appointments: Writer in Residence, Berinsfield, Oxon, 1975-76; Visiting Poet, Shrewsbury School, 1973-75; Poet in Residence, King's School, Canterbury, 1979. Publications: New and Collected Poems, 1980; The Tiger and The Rose, Autobiography, 1971; Ring of Truth, Novel, 1983; Argument of Kings, Autobiography, 1987; Funeral Games, (poetry) 1987; Winterlude, (poetry) 1983; The Fight, (novel) 1952; The Wound and The Scar, (novel) 1953; The Face of The Enemy, (novel) 1960; The Dividing Night, 1962; The Big Time, (novel) 1967; Soldiering On, (poetry) 1989; A Time For Fires, (poetry) 1991; Drums of Morning, Growing Up in The 30's, (autobiography) 1992. Collected Poems 1950-1993, 1994. Contributions to: The Listener; The Observer; Sunday Times; Encounter; London Magazine; TLS; American Scholar; Yale Literary Magazine. Honours: Heinmann Award for Literature, 1960; Cholmondoley Poetry Prize, 1974. Memberships: Fellow, Royal Society of Literature, 1961. Address: 51 North Street, Otley, West Yorkshire, LS21 1AH, England.

SCARBOROUGH William Kauffman, b. 17 Jan 1933, Baltimore, Maryland, USA. University Professor; Historian. m. Patricia Estelle Carruthers, 16 Jan 1954, 1 s, 1 d. Education: AB, 1954, PhD, 1962, University of North Carolina; MA, Cornell University, 1957. Publications: The Overseer: Plantation management in the Old South, 1966; Reprinted, 1984; The Diary of Edmund Ruffin, 3 vols, 1972-89; Heartland of the Cotton Kingdom, in A History of Mississippi, 1973; Slavery -The White Man's Burden, in Perspecitves and Irony in American Slavery, 1976; Science on the Plantation, in Science and Medicine in the Old South, 1989. Contributions to: Agricultural History, 1964; Civil War Times Illustrated, 1976; Virginia Magazine of History and Biography, 1989. Honours: Phi Beta Kappa, 1953; President, Mississippi Historical Society, 1979-80; Jules and Frances Landry Award for The Diary of Edmund Ruffin, Vols I-III, Louisiana State University Press, 1989. Memberships: Organization of American Historians; Southern Historical Association; Agricultural History Society; Mississippi Historical Society; St George Tucker Society; South Carolina Historical Society. Address: Department of History, University of Soutern Mississippi, Southern Station, Box 5047, Hattiesburg, MS 39406, USA.

SCARF Maggie (Margaret), b. 13 May 1932, Philadelphia, Pennsylvania, USA. Writer. m. Herbert Eli Scarf, 28 June 1953, 3 daughters. Education: BA, South Connecticut State University, 1989. Appointments: Contributing Editor, The New Republic, 1975-; Writer-in-Residence, Johnathan Edwards College, Yale University, New Haven, Connecticut, 1992-. Publications: Body, Mind, Behavior, 1976; Unfinished Business, 1980; Intimate Partners, 1987. Contributions to: (1) The New York Times Magazine; Psychology Today; Atlantic Monthly; New Republic; Self; Cosmopolitan; Family Therapy Networker. Honours: Ford Foundation Fellow, 1973-74; Nieman Fellow, Harvard, 1975-76; Fellow, Center for Advanced Study, Stanford, 1977-78, 1985-86; Alica Patterson Fellow, 1978-79; Garantee The Smith Richardson foundation Inc., 1991, 1992, 1993, 1994; Connecticut U. award Outstanding Contribution, 1987; Connecticut Psychological Society, Certificate of Appreciation, 1988. Memberships: PEN; Elizabethan Club, Yale University; Connecticut Society of Psychoanalytic Psychologists; Member, Advisory Board, American Psychiatric Prize. Literary Agent: Janklow and Nesbit. Address: Jonathan Edwards College, Yale University, 68 High Street, New Haven, CT 06517, USA.

SCARFE Norman, b. 1 May 1923, Felixstowe, England. Education: MA Hons, History, Oxford, 1949. Literary Appointments: Chairman of Centre of East Anglia Studies, University of East Anglia; Founder, Honorary General Editor, Suffolk Records Society, 1958-92. Publications: Suffolk, 1960, 1988; Essex, 1968,1982; Cambridgeshire, 1983; The Suffolk Landscape, 1972, 1987; Suffolk in The Middle Ages, 1986; Assault Division, 1947; A Frenchman's Year in Suffolk, (1784), 1988; Innocent Espionage - The La Rochefoucauld Brother's Tour of England in 1785, 1995. Contributions to: Proceedings, Suffolk Institute of Archaeology; Aldeburgh Festival Annual Programme Book; Country Life; The Book Collector; The Dictionary of National Biography. Honours: Hon D Litt, University of East Anglia, 1989; MBE, 1994. Memberships: International PEN; Founder Chairman, Suffolk Book League, 1982; Fellow, Society of Antiquaries. Literary Agent: John Welch, Milton House, Milton, Cambridge, CB4 6AD, England. Address: The Garden Cottage, 3 Burkitt Road, Woodbridge, Suffolk, IP12 4JJ, England.

SCARFE Wendy Elizabeth, b. 1933, Australia. Author; Poet. Publications: Shadow and Flowers (poetry), 1974, 1984; The Lotus Throne (novel), 1976; Neither Here Nor There (novel), 1984; Laura My Alter Ego (novel), 1988; The Day They Shot Edward (novel), 1991; With Allan John Scarfe: A Mouthful of Petals, 1967; Tiger on a Rein, 1969; People of India, 1972; The Black Australians, 1974; Victims or Bludgers? Case Studies in Poverty in Australia, 1974; J P, His Biography, 1975; Victims or Bludgers? A Poverty Inquiry for Schools, 1981; Labor's Titan: The Story of Percy Brookfield 1878-1921, 1983; All That Grief (with Allan Scarfe), 1994. In progress: The Sculptor (novel) and No Taste For Carnage (biography with Allan Scarfe). Honours: with Allan Scarfe, Australia Council Literature Board Special Purpose Writers Grant, 1980, 1988. Memberships: Fellowship of Australian Writers. Address: 8 Bostock Street, Warrnambool, Victoria 3280, Australia.

SCHALLER George B, b. 26 May 1933, Berlin, Germany. m. Kay Morgan, 26 August 1957, 2 sons. Education: BS Zoology, BA, Anthropology, University of Alaska; MS, PhD, University of Wisconsin. Appointments: Professor; Researcher. Contributions to: zoological journals and popular periodicals; Wildlife Conservation; National Geographic; International Wildlife; Life. Honours: National Book Award, 1973. Address: The Wildlife Conservation Society, Bronx Park, NY 10460, USA.

SCHAU Jens Michael, b. 25 May 1948, Ronne, Bornholm. Writer; Psychologist; Screen Writer; Playwright. Education: Bachelor in History, University of Copenhagen, 1974; PhD, Psychology, University of Copenhagen, 1978. Publications: I Familiens Skod, 1982; Byen og Oen, 1983; Himlen begynder ved Jorden, 1984; Far, Mor og Born, 1988; En lille Prins, 1994; TV Films: Boksning; Naeste Sommer måske, 1988; Radioplay: Sonner, 1984. Contributions to: Magazines and Journals. Honours: Statens Kunstfond, 1983, 84, 85. Literary Agent, Claus Clausen, Tiderne Skifter, Pilestraede 51,5, 1001 Kobenhavn K. Address: Tiderne Skifter & Gyldendal Publisher, Klarebodeme 3,1115 Kobenhavn K, Denmark.

SCHEFFER Victor B(lanchard), b. 1906, USA. Writer. Publications: The Year of the Whale, 1969; The Year of the Seal, 1970; The Seeing Eye, 1971; A Voice for Wildlife, 1974; A Natural History of Marine Mammals, 1976; Adventures of a Zoologist, 1980; The Amazing Sea Otter, 1981; Spires of Form, 1983; The Shaping of Environmentalism in America, 1991. Address: 1750 152d Ave NE, Sivler Glen # C-214, Bellevue, WA 98007, USA.

SCHEIBER Harry N, b. 1935, USA. Writer; Professor of Law, Past Chair of Jurisprudence and Social Policy, University of California, Berkeley. Career: Co-Editor, History of American Economy Series, Johnson Reprint; Member of Editorial Boards, Publius: Journal of Federalism, Review's in American History; Founding Director, Berkeley Seminar on Federalism, 1986-; Academic Director, National Endowment of the Humanities Institute on Constitutionalism, University of California, Berkeley, 1987-90; Co-ordinator for Marine Affairs, California Sea Grant College Program; Academic Chair for History and Civics, National Assessment of Educational Progress, 1986-88; The Stefan Reisenfeld Professor of Law and History, University of California, Berkeley Associate Dean, 1990-93; Chair, University of California, Berkeley, Faculty Senate, 1994-95. Publications: The Wilson Administration and Civil Liberties, 1960; United States Economic History, 1964; Co-author, American: Purpose and Power, 1965; The Condition of American Federalism 1966; Co-author and Editor, The Frontier in American Development, 1969; The Old Northwest, 1969; Ohio Canal Era, 1820-1861, 1969, 2nd edition, 1987; Black Labor in American History, 1972; Agriculture in the Development of the Far West, 1975; Co-author, Legal Culture and the Legal Profession, 1995; Co-author, American Economic History, 1976; Co-editor, American Law and the Constitutional Order, 1978, 1990; Editor, Perspectives on Federalism, 1987; Co-editor and contributing author, Power Divided, 1989; Editor, Federalism of the Jucicial Mind, 1993. Honours: Guggenheim Fellow, 1967, 1989; Fellow, Centre for Advanced Study in Behavioural Science,1966, 1971; Distinguished Fulbright Lecturer (Australia), 1984; Fellow, National Endowment for the Humanites, 1986; Fellow, University of California Humanities Research Institute, 1989. Address: School of Law, University of California, Berkeley, CA 94708, USA.

SCHELL Orville Hickok, b. 20 May 1940, New York City, New York, USA. Writer. 1 s. Education: BA magna cum laude, Harvard College; MA, PhD (ABD), University of California, Berkeley.

Publications: Mandate of Heaven, 1994; Discos and Democracy; China in the Throes of Reform; To Get Rich is Glorious - China in the 1980's; Watch Out for the Foreign Guests: China Confronts the West; Modern Meat. Contributions to: Granta, New Yorker; Atlantic Monthly; New York Times Magazine; Rolling Stone. Honours: Alice Patterson Fellowship, 1981; MacDowell Colony Fellow, 1984, 1987; John Simon Guggenehim Fellow, 1989-90. Memberships: PEN; Authors Guild. Literary Agent: Amanda Urban, ICM. Address: 40 W 57th St, New York, NY 10019, USA.

SCHELLENBERG James Arthur, b. 7 June 1932, Vinland, Kansas, USA. Social Scientist. m. 28 Dec 1974, 3 s, 1 d. Education: AB, Baker University, 1954; MA, 1955, PhD, 1959, University of Kansas. Publications: An Introduction to Social Psychology, 1970; Revised Edition, 1974; Masters of Social Psychology, 1978, with subsequent Swedish, Spanish, Japanese and Malay Editions; The Science of Conflict, 1982; Conflict Between Communities, 1987; Primitive Games, 1990; An Invitation to Social Psychology, 1993; Exploring Social Behaviour, 1993. Address: 124 Madison Blvd, Terre Haute, IN 47803, USA.

SCHELLING Thomas Crombie, b. 14 Apr 1921, Oakland, California, USA. Professor. m. Corinne Saposs, 13 Sept 1947, 4 s. Education: BA, Unversity of California, Berkeley, 1944; PhD, Economics, Harvard Universty, 1951. Publcations: National Income Behaviour, 1951; International Economics, 1958; Strategy of Conflict, 1960; Arms and Influence 1967; Micromotives and Macrobehaviour, 1978; Choice and Consequence, 1984; Contributions to: Numerous journals, magazines and newspapers. Honours: Frank E Seidmen Distinguished Award in Political Economy, 1977; Distinguished Fellow, American Economic Association, 1986; National Academy of Sciences award for Behavioural Research Relevant to the Prevenion of Nuclear War, 1993. Memberships: American Economic Association, President 1991; National Academy of Sciences; American Academy of Arts and Sciences. Address: Department of Economics, University of Maryland, College Park, MD 20742, USA.

SCHEPISI Frederic Alan, b. 26 Dec 1939, Melbourne, Australia. Film Writer; Producer; Director. m. (1) Joan Mary Ford, (2) Rhonda Elizabeth Finlayson, 1973, 3 s, 4 d, (3) Mary Rubin, 1984. Appointments: TV Production Manager, Patron Advisory Service, Melbourne, 1961-64; Victorian Manager, Cinesound Productions, Melbourne, 1964-66; Managing Director, The Film House, Melbourne, 1964-66; Governing Chairman, 1979-. Publications: Films: The Devil's Playground, 1975; The Chant of Jimmie Blacksmith, 1978; Barbarosa, 1981; Iceman, 1983; Plenty, 1984-85; Roxanne, 1986; Evil Angels, 1987; Russia House, 1989; Mr Baseball, 1991; Six Degrees of Separahon, 1993; IQ, 1994. Honours: Australian Film Awards, Best Film, The Devil's Playground, 1975; Australian Film Awards, Best Film, Best Achievement in Direction, Best Screenplay adapted from another source and the AFI Members Prize Special Award, for Evil Angels, 1989. Address: 159 Eastern Road, South Melbourne, Victoria, Australia 3205.

SCHEVILL James (Erwin), b. 1920, USA. Author; Poet; Playwright. Publications: Tensions (poetry), 1947; The American Fantasies (poery), 1951; Sherwood Anderson: His Life and Work, 1951; High Sinners, Low Angels, 1953; The Right to Greet (poetry) 1956); The Roaring Market and the Silent Tomb (biolgraphy), 1956; Edited Six Historians, by Ferdinand Schevill, 1986; Selected Poems 1945-59,1959; Voices of Mass and Capital A, 1962; Private Dooms and Public Destinations: Poems 1945-62, 1962; The Master, 1963; The Stalingrad Elegies (poetry), 1964; The Black President, 1965; Release (poetry), 1968; Violence and Glory: Poems 1962-1968, 1969; Lovecraft's Follies (play), 1971; Breakout! In Search of New Thearical Environments, 1972; The Buddhist Car and Other Characters (poetry), 1973; Pursuing Elegy, 1974; Cathedral of Ice, 1975; The Arena of Ants (novel) 1977; The Mayan Poems, 1978; Fire of Eyes: A Guatemalan Seuqence, 1979; Edison's Dream, 1982; The American Fantasies: Collected Poems 1945-82, 1983; The Invisible Volcano (poem), 1985; Oppenheimer's Chair (play), 1985; Collected Short Plays, 1986; Ambiguous Dancers of Fame: Collected Poems 1945-86, 1987; Bem Porter: A Personal Biogrphy, 1992; Five Plays, 1993; Winter Channels (poems), 1994. Honours: Literary Award, American Academy and Institute of Arts and Letters, New York, 1991. Literary Agent: Helen Merill, 435 W 23St, Suite 1A, New York, NY 10011, USA. Address: 1309 Oxford Street, Berkeley, CA 94709, USA.

SCHEVING Hans, b. 27 June 1958, Copenhagen, Denmark. Architect. Education: Architect, Royal Academy of Fine Arts, School of Architecture, Copenhagen, 1984. Publications: Rom, A Guide to Rome, 1988; London, A Guide to London, 1993. Contributions to: Danish Architects Journal, Arkitekten; Danish Weekly Journal, Weekend Avisen. Memberships: Danish Architects Association. Address: Rojenvaengets Hoveovej 29, DK 2100, Copenhagen, Denmark.

SCHLAFLY Phyliss Stewart, b. 15 Aug 1924, St Louis, USA. Author; Lawyer. m. Fred Schlafly, 20 Oct 1949, 4 s, 2 d. Educaion: BA, Washington University, 1944; MA, Harvard University, 1945; LLD, Niagara University, 1976; JD, Washington University Law School, 1978. Career: Syndicated Columnst, Copley News Service, 1976-. Publications: A Choice No an Echo, 1964; The Gravedigges, 1964; Strike from Space, 1965; Safe Not Sorry, 1967; The Betrayers, 1968; Mindszentry the Man, 1972; Kissinger on the Couch, 1975; Ambush a Vladivostok, 1976; The Power of the Positive Woman, 1977; Author of First Reader, 1994; Editor, Child Abuse in the Classroom, 1984; Pronography's Victims, 1987; Equal Pay for Unequal Work, 1984; Who Will Rock the Cradle! 1989; Contributions to: The Phyllis Schlafly Report (monthly newsletter, 1967 - to date); Numerous journals and magazines; Broadcaster, Commentator. Honours: Commission on the Bicentennial of the US Constitution, 1985-91; DAR, various office including Chairman, National Defence 1977-80, 1983-; American, Illlinois Bar Assocations; Phi Beta Kappa, Pi Sigma Alpha; 10 Honour Awards, Freedoms Foundation; Named Woman of Achievement in Public Affairs; One of Ten Most Admired Women in World Good Housekeeping Poll, 1977, and many others. Address: 68 Danforth Road, Alton, IL 62002, USA.

SCHLESINGER Arthur Jr, b. 15 Oct 1917. Columbus, Ohio, USA. Writer; Educator. m. (1) Marian Cannon, 1940, div 1970, 2 s, 2 d, (2) Alexandra Emmet, 1971, 1 s. Education: Harvard Univesity; Peterhouse, Cambridge, England. Publications: Orestes A Brownson: A Pilgrim's Progress, 1939; The Age of Jackson, 1945; The Vital Center (English title The Politics of Freedom), 1949; The General and the President (with R H Revere), 1951; The Age of Roosevelt: Volume 1, The Risis of the Old Order, 1957, Volume II, The Coming of the New Deal, 1958, Volume III, The Politics of Upheaval, 1960; Kennedy or Nixon, 1960; The Politics of Hope, 1963; Paths of American Thought (editor with Morton White), 1963; A Thousand Days: John F Kennedy in the White House, 1965; The Bitter Heritage: Vietnam and American Democracy, 1941-66, 1967; The Crisis of Confidence, 1969; History of American Presidential Elections (editor with F L Israel), 1971; The Imperial Presidency, 1973; Rober Kennedy and His Times, 1978; Cycles of American History, 1986; The Disuniting of America, 1992. Contributions to: Various magazines and newspapers. Honours include: Honorary D.Litt, University of Oxford, 1987; and honorary degrees from many other universities and colleges; Pulitzer Prize for History, 1946, for Biography, 1966. Address: City University of New York, 33 West 42nd Street, New York, NY 10036, USA.

SCHMIDMAN Jo Ann, b. 18 Apr 1948, Omaha, Nebraska, USA. Theatre Director; Playwright. Education includes: BFA, Boston University, 1970. Appointments include: Producing Artistic Director, Omaha Magic Theatre, 1968-; Artist-in-Schools, performing arts and poetry, Nebraska Arts Council, Nebraska Curriculum Frameworks in the visual performing Arts, Team Member, 1994. Publications include: Plays, This Sleep Among Women, 1974; Running Gag, 1980; in High Energy Musicals from the Omaha Magic Theatre; Astro Bride, 1985; Velveeta Meltdown, 1985; Co-editor (with M Terry and S Kimberlain) Right Brain, Vaction Photos, new plays and production photogrpahs from The Omaha Magic Theatre, 1972-92; Plays produced (unpublished) include: This Sleep Among Women, 1978; Change Yer Image, 1981; Aliens Under Glass, 1982; Watch Where We Walk, 1983; X-Rayed-Late: E-Motion in Action, with M Terry, 1984; Walking Through Walls, with Megan Terry, 1987; Sea of Forms, with M Terry, 1987; Body Leaks, 1990; Sound Fields, with M Terry and Kimberlain, 1992; Belches on Couches, with B Terry and S Kimberlain, 1993. Address: 2309 Hanscom Boulevard, Omaha, Nebraska, NE 68105, USA.

SCHMIDT-NIELSEN Knut, b. 24 Sept 1915, Norway. Scientist; Writer. Education: Dr Phil, Copenhagen, 1946; Dr Med, honoris causa, Lund, Sweden, 1983. Literary Appointments: Editor and Editorial Boards of numerous Scientific Journals. Publcations: Animal Physiology, 1975, 4th edition, 1990; Scaling: Why is Animal Size So Important, 1984; How Animals work, 1972; Desert Animals, 1964. Contributions to: more than 200. Honours: Honorary Dr Philosophy,

Univerity of Troudheim, Norway,1993. Memberships: Royal Society, London; National Academy of Sciences, USA; Academe des Sciences, Paris. Address: Department of Zoology, Duke University, Durham, NC 27706, USA.

SCHMITT Peter, b. 1958. Publications: Country Airport, 1989; Hazard Duty, 1995. Honours: Lavan Younger Poets Award, 1991.

SCHMOOKERL Andrew Bard, b. 19 Apr 1946, Long Branch, New Jersey, USA. Writer; Speaker; Consultant. m. 28 Sept 1986, 2 s, 1 d. Education: BA summa cum lade, Harvard College, 1967; PhD, Thelogical Union and University of California, 1977. Publications: The Parable of the Tribes, The Problem of Power in Social Evolution, 1984, second edition, 1995; Out of Weakness: Healing the Wounds that Drive us to War, 1988; Sowing and Reapings: The Cycling of Good and Evil in the Human System, 1989; The Illusion of Choice: How the Market Economy Shapes Our Destiny, 1992; Fools Gold: The Fate of Values in a World of Goods, 1993; Living Posthumously: Confronting the Loss of Vital Powers (unpublished). Address: 86 Sunset Ridge Road, Broadway, VA 22815, USA.

SCHNAPPER Dominique Aron, b. 9 Nov 1934. Director of Studies. m. Antoine Schnapper, 28 Nov 1958, 1 s, 2 d. Education: IEP, 1957; Doctorate, Sorbonne, 1967; Doctorat d'Etat, 1979. Appointments: Director of Studies, Ecole des Hautes Etudes en Sciences Sociales, Paris. Publications: L'Italie Rouge et Noire, 1971; Juifs et Israelites, 1980; L'épreuve du Chomage, 1981; La France de L'Intégration, 1991; L'Europe des Immigrés, 1992; La Communauté des Citoyens, 1994. Memberships: Societe Francaise de Sociologie; Societe Francaise de Sciences Politiques; Society of Friends of Raymond Aron. Address: 75 Bd St Michel, 75005 Paris, France.

SCHNEEBAUM Tobias, b. 25 Mar 1922. Writer; Lecturer. Education: BA, City College of New York, 1942; MA, Cultural Anthropology, Goddard College,1977. Publications: Keep the River on Your Right, 1969; Wild Man, 1979; Life with the Asmat, 1981; Asmat Images, 1985; Where the Spirits Dwell, 1988; Embodied Spirts, 1990. Contributions to: Pacific Arts (about 10 articles); 4 articles in The New York Native; The Asmat, in Louisiana Revy, Copenhagen, 1991. Honours: Fulbright Fellowship, 1955; CAPS Grant, 1974; JDR 3rd Fund Grant, 1975, 1978; Ingram Merrill Foundation, 1982, 1989; Ludwig Vogelstein Foundation, 1985. Memberships: PEN; Explorers Club. Literary Agent: Don Congdon, Don Congdon Assocaites Inc. Address: 463 West Street 410A, New York, NY 10014, USA.

SCHOEMPERLEN Diane Mavis, b. 9 July 1954, Thunder Bay, Ontario, Canda. Writer; Teacher. 1 s. Education: BA, English, Lakehead University, Ontario, 1976. Career: Teacher: Kingston School of Writing, Queens University, Ontario, 1986-93; St Lawrence College, Kingston, 1987-; University of Toronto Summer Writers' Workshop, 1992; Editor, Corning Attractions, Oberton Press, 1994-. Publications: Double Exposures, 1984; Frogs and other Stories, 1986; Hockey Night in Canada, 1987; The Man of My Dreams, 1990; Hockey Night in Canada and other Stories, 1991; In The Language of Love, 1994. Contributions include: 87 and 90 Best Canadian Stories; Macmillan Anthology 1 & 3; Oxford Canadain Short Stories. Honours: WGA Award for Short Fiction, 1987; Silver National Magazine Award, 1989; The Man of my Dreams shortlisted for Governor General's Award and Trillium Award. Memberships: Writer's Union of Canada. Literary Agent: Bella Pomer, Toronto, Ontario. Address: 32 Dunlop Street, Kingston, Ontario, Canada, K7L 1L2.

SCHOENEWOLF Gerald Frederick, b. 23 Sept 1941, Fredericksburg, Texas, USA. Psychoanalyst; Writer. m. (1) Carol Slater, 1964-1969. 1 daughter, (2) Theresa Lamb, 1979-84. Education: BA, Goddard College, Plainfield, Vermont; MA, California State University, Dominguez Hills, PhD, The Union Institute, Cincinnati, Ohio. Publications: 101 Common Therapeutic Blinders (with R Robertiello), 1987; 101 Therapeutic Successes, 1989; Sexual Animosity between Men and Women, 1989; Turning Points in Analytic Therapy: The Classic Cases, 1990; Turning Points in Analytic Therapy: From Winnicott to Kernberg, 1990; The Art of Hating, 1991; Jennifer and Her Selves, 1991; Counterresistance, 1993; Erotic Games: Bringing Intimacy Back into Relationships, 1995. Contributions to: Numerous papers and short stories to various publications. Memberships: American Psychological Association; National Association for the Advancement of Psychoanalysis. Literary Agent: Don Congdon. Address: R.R.I, Box 304F, Bushkill, PA 18324, USA.

SCHOFIELD Caroline (Carey), b. 29 Dec 1953, Surrey, England. Writer. m. Laurence King, 14 Jun 1985. Education: BA Cantab, 1976. Publications: Mesrine, 1980; Jagger, 1984; Russia At War, 1987; Inside The Soviet Army, 1991; The Russian Elite: Inside Spetsnaz and The Airborne Forces, 1993. Contributions to: Various publications.' Memberships: International Institute of Strategic Studies; Royal United Services Institute. Address: 6 St Martins Road, London, SW9, England.

SCHOFIELD Michael, b. 1919. Sociologist; Writer. Publications: The Sexual Behaviour of Young People, 1965; The Sociological Aspects of Homosexuality, 1965; Society and The Young School Leaver, 1967; Drugs and Civil Liberties, 1968; Social Research, 1969; Co-author, Behind The Drug Scene, 1970; The Strange Case of Pot, 1971; Co-author, The Rights of Children, 1972; The Sexual Behaviour of Young Adults, 1973; Promiscuity, 1976; The Sexual Containment Act, 1978. Address: 28 Lyndhurst Gardens, London, NW3 5NW, England.

SCHOFIELD Paul. See: **TUBB E(dwin) C(harles).**

SCHOFIELD William Greenough, b. 13 June 1909, Providence, Rhode Island, USA. Author. m. 21 Nov 1934, 2 sons, 1 daughter. Appointments: Feature Writer, Providence Journal, 1936-40; Chief Editorial Writer, Columnist, Foreign Correspondent, Boston Traveler, 1940-67; Manager, Editorial Services, Raytheon Co., 1967-70; Director, Public Information Consultant, Public Affairs, Publications Editor, Boston University, 1970-79. Publications: Ashes in the Wilderness, 1942; The Cat in the Convoy, 1946; Payoff in Black, 1947; The Deer Cry, 1948; Seek for a Hero, 1956; Sidewalk Statesman, 1959; Destroyers - 60 Years, 1962; Treason Trail, 1964; Eastward the Convoys, 1966; Freedom by the Bay, 1974; Frogmen - First Battles, 1987; others. Contributions to: Readers Digest; Catholic Digest; Redbook; Skipper; Information; Boston Sunday Herald. Honour: Achievement Award, US Dept. of Interior, 1976. Address: 16 Hunnewell Circle, Newton, MA 02158, USA.

SCHOLEY Arthur (Edward), b. 1932. Children's Writer; Playwright. Publications: The Song of Caedmon, (with Donald Swann) 1971; Christmas Plays and Ideas for Worship, 1973; The Discontented Dervishes, 1977; Sallinka and The Golden Bird, 1978; Twelve Tales For a Christmas Night, 1978; Wacky and His Fuddlejig, (with Donald Swann) 1978; Singalive, (with Donald Swann) 1978; Herod and The Rooster, (with Ronald Chamberlain) 1979; The Dickens Christmas Carol Show, 1979; Baboushka, (with Donald Swann) 1979; Candletree, (with Donald Swann) 1981; Five Plays for Christmas, 1981; Four Plays About People, 1983; Martin The Cobbler, 1983; The Hosanna Kids, 1985; Make a Model Christmas Crib, 1988; Who'll Be Brother Donkey?, 1990; Brendan Ahoy!, (with Donald Swann) 1994. Address: 1 Cranbourne Road, London, N10 2BT, England.

SCHOULTZ Solveig von, b. 5 Aug 1907, Borga, Finland. Author. m. Erik Bergman, 7 Jul 1961. Education: Teacher's Qualification; PhD, honouris causa, 1986. Publications: Poetry: Eko av ett rop, 1946; Natet, 1956; Sank ditt ljus, 1963; De fyra flojtspelarna, 1975; Bortom traden hors havet, 1980; En enda minut, 1981; Vattenhjulet, 1986; Alla träd vantar faglar, 1988; Ett sätt att räkna tiden, 1989; Samtal med en fjäril, 1994; Short Novels: Ingenting ovanligt, 1948; Narmare nagon, 1951; Den blomstertid, 1958; Aven dina kameler, 1965; Rymdbruden, 1970; Somliga momar, 1976; Kolteckning, ofullbordad, 1983; Ingen dag forgaves, 1984; Nästa dag, 1991; Längs vattenbrynet, 1992; Samtal med en fjäril, 1994; Plays for TV and Radio. Address: Berggatan 22C, Helsinki 10, Finland.

SCHRAG Peter, b. 1931, United States of America. Writer (Education, Politics). Appointments: Reporter, El Paso Herald Post, Texas, 1953-55; Assistant Secretary, Amheret College, Massachusetts, 1956-66; Associate Education Editor, 1966-68, Executive Editor, 1968-73; Saturday Review, New York City; Editor, Change, New York City, 1969-70; Editor, Editorial page Sacramento Bee, 1978-; Lecturer, University of Massachusetts, 1970-72; University of California, Berkeley, 1990-. Publications: Voices in the Classroom, 1965; Village School Downtown, 1967; Out of Place in America, 1970; The Decline of the WASP (in United Kingdom as The Vanishing American), 1972; The End of the American Future, 1973; Test of Loyalty, 1974; The Myths of the Hyeractive Child (with Diane Divoky), 1975; Mind Control, 1978. Address: Sacramento Bee, 21st and Q Streets, Sacramento, CA 95816, USA.

SCHRAMM David Normah, b. 25 Oct 1945, St Louis, Missouri, USA. Louis Block Professor in the Physical Sciences. m. Judith Jane Gibson, 20 June 1986, 2 sons. Education: SB Physics, Mass. Institute of Technology, 1967; PhD Physics, California Institute of Technology, 1971. Appointments: Editorial Commission, Ann, Rev. of Nucl. Science, 1976-80; Associate Editor, American Journal of Physics, 1978-81; Editor, Theoretical Astrophysics Series, University of Chicago Press, 1981-; Columnist, Outside Magazine, 1979-; Astrophysics Editor, Physics Reports, 1981-; Correspondent, Comments on Nuclear and Particle Physics, 1984-; Associate Editor, Particle World, 1990-. Publications: Co-author: From Quarks to the Cosmos: Tools of Discovery, 1989; The Shadows of Creation: Dark matter and the Structure of the Universe, 1991. Honours: Richtmyer Memorial Award Lecturer, American Association of Physics Teachers, 1984; Alexander von Humboldt Award, 1986; Einstein medal, Eotovos University, Hungary, 1989; Lilienfeld Award, American Physical Society, 1993; University of Chicago Graduate Teaching Award, 1994; Aspen Center for Physics, Chair, 1992-95; British North American Committee, Chair Information Technology Working Group, 1993-; American Academy of Art and Sciences, Fellow, 1994-. Memberships: National Academy of Sciences, Chair Astrophysics Panel, 1989-92; American Physics Society, Fellow, 1975-; American Astronomical Society, Executive Commission, 1977-78; Secretary, Treasurer, 1979-82; The Meteoritical Society, Fellow, 1981-; International Astronomical Union, 1973-. Literary Agent: John Brockman Associates Inc. Address: University of Chicago, 5640 South Ellis Avenue, AAC 140, Chicago, IL 60637, USA.

SCHRAMM Werner, b. 28 Apr 1926, Germany. Author; Painter. Education: Teacher Training Institute; Langemarck Studies (wounded during World War II). Publications include: Das antike Drama 'Die Bacchantinnen' in der Neugestaltung durch H Wolfgang Philipp, 1980; Hugo Wolfgang Philipps Tragikomödie 'Der Clown Gottes', 1983; Moderner deutscher Roman, 1983; Stefan Zweig: Bildnis eines genialen Charakters, 1984. Honours include: Lifetime Deputy Governor, 1989; World Decoration of Excelle nce, 1989; Medal of Honour, 1990; International Order of Merit, 1990; LPIBA, 1990; IOM, 1990; HE, 1991; FABI, 1991; Cultural Doctorate in Literature, 1991; Research Advisor of The Year, 1991; Professional of The Year, 1991; Grand Ambassador of Achievement, 1991; Silver Shield of Valor, 1992; Doctor of Arts, Albert Einstein International Academy Foundation, 1993; Man of The Year, 1993; Pictoral Testimonial of Achievement and Distinction, 1993. Memberships: American Biographical Institute Research Association's Board of Governors, 1989; Fellowship of The International Biographical Association, 1989; ABI Research Board of Governors, 1989; IBC Advisory Council, 1990; International Order of Merit, 1990; Lifetime Achievement Academy, 1991; ABI Research Board of Advisors, 1991; Men's Inner Circle of Achievement, 1993. Address: Eckenerweg 8, D 25524 Itzehoe, Germany.

SCHREINER Samuel Agnew, Jr, b. 6 June 1921, Mt Lebanon, Pennsylvania, USA. Author. m. Doris Moon, 22 Sept 1945, 2 daughters. Education: AB, Princeton University, USA, 1942; Summa Cum Laude. Publications: Thine Is The Glory, 1975; The Condensed World of the Reader's Digest, 1977; Pleasant Places, 1977; Angelica, 1978; The Possessors and the Possessed, 1980; The Van Alens, 1981; A Place Called Princeton, 1984; The Trials of Mrs Lincoln, 1987; Cycles, 1990; Mayday! Mayday!, 1990, Contributions to: Reader's Digest; Woman's Day; McCalls, Redbook, Parade. Literary Agent: Harold Ober Associates. Address: 111 Old Kings Highway South, Darien, Ct 06820, USA.

SCHUCHMAN Joan. See: **FEINBERG Joan Miriam**.

SCHULBERG Budd, b. Los Angeles, California, USA. Education: BA, Dartmouth College. Honours: Oscar; Antoinette Perry Award. Address: c/o Russell & Volkening Agency, 50 West 29th Street, NEw York, NY 10001, USA.

SCHULLER Gunther, b. 22 Nov 1925, USA. Writer (music). Appointments: Publisher, Editor, Margun Music Inc, Newton Centre, MA, USA; Producer, G M Recordings Inc, Newton Centre, MA, USA. Publications: Horn Technique, 1962; Early Jazz: Its Roots and Musical Development, 1968; Musings, 1985; The Swing Era, 1988. Memberships: American Academy of Arts and Letters, 1977; President, New England Conservatory of Music, Boston, 1967-77. Address: 167 Dudley Road, Newton Centre, MA 02159, USA.

SCHULTZ John, b. 28 July 1932, Columbia, Missouri, USA. Writer; Teacher. m. Anne Gillian Bray, 10 Dec 1962 (div), Nov 1975; (2)

Betty E Schiflett, 9 May 1992, 1 son, 1 daughter. Appointments: Head, Master of Fine Arts in Creative Writing, Columbia College, Chicago, 1990-; Head, Master in Teaching Writing, 1983-, and Chair, Fiction Writing Department, Columbia College, Chicago, 1967-. Publications: The Tongues of Men, 1969; Custom, 3x3 and 4xY, 1962-67; No One Was Killed, 1969; Motion Will be Denied, 1972; Writing From Start to Finish, 1982, 1990; The Chicago Conspiracy Trial, 1993. Contributions to: The Georgia Review. Honours: Editor, F Magazine; Originator and developer of the Story Workshop Method. Memberships: MLA; AWP; NCTE: CCCC. Literary Agent: Jeff Herman. Address: 3636 N, Janssen, Chicago, IL 60613, USA.

SCHULZ Max Frederick, b. 1923, United States of America. Writer. Appointments: Professor of English, 1963-, Chairman, 1968-80, University of Southern California, Los Angeles; Associate Editor, Critique Magazine, 1971-85; Curator, USC Fisher Gallery, 1993-. Publications: The Poetic Voices of Coleridge, 1963, revised edition, 1965; Essays in American and English Literature, Presented to Bruce Robert McElderry Jr., 1967; Radical Sophistication: Studies in Contemporary Jewish-American Novelists, 1969; Bruce Jay Friedman, 1973; Black Humor Fiction of the Sixties: A Pluralistic Definition of Man and His World, 1973; Paradise Preserced: Recreations of Eden in 18th and 19th Century England, 1985; the Muses of John Barth: Tradition and Metafiction from Lost in the Funhouse to the Tidewater Tales, 1990. Address: Fisher Gallery, University of Southern California, Los Angeles, CA 90089, USA.

SCHUNCKE Michael, b. 8 May 1929, Dresden Blasewitz, Germany. Special Teacher; Author; Consultant. m. Dorothea Czibulinski-Dressler, 22 Dec 1956, 2 d. Education: Theory of Music, 1945-49; Advertising, Academy of Mannheim, 1953-54; Seminars in writing, advertising, marketing. Appointments: Vice Chairman, Poetical Ludwig-Finckh-Freundeskreis Gaienhofen, 1989-93. Publications: Wanderer Zwischen 2 Welten, 1975; Sprecht die Sprache der Adressaten, 1982; Schlüsselworte erfolgreicher Anzeigen, 2 Auft, 1986; Praktische Werbehilfe, 1987; Atmosphäre eines Jugend in Baden-Baden; Many articles for advertising and music history; Sammelbände der Robert-Schumann-Ges Zwickau, 1961-66; Catalogue for Exhibition, Ludwig Schuncke and Musikerfamilie Schuncke, 1984. Contributions to: Ein unbek Mendelssohn-Bild v J P Lyser/ Max F Schneider Basel, 1958; Werbeforschung und praxis, 1985,1991; Histories of Corporates; Newsletter of the Rachmaninoff Society, 1992; Aufsatze in Muttersprache; Das System der Text-CI, 1991; Schuncke - Archives for Music, Literature, History, (special themes). Honours: Goldene Hans Buchholz Medaille, 1974; Awards in Community. Memberships: Gesellschaft fur Deutsche Sprache; Poetical Ludwig-Finckh-Freundeskreis Gaienhofen; Robert Schumann Gesellschaft; Mendelssohn Gesellschaft. Address: Lichtental, Heschmattweg 11, D 76534 Baden Baden, Germany.

SCHWANDT Stephen (William), b. 5 Apr 1947, Chippewa Falls, Wisconsin, USA. Educator. m. Karen Sambo, 13 June 1970, 2 sons. Education: BA, Valparaiso University, 1969; BS, St Cloud State University, 1972; MA, University of Minnesota - Twin Cities, 1972. Appointments: Teacher of Composition and American Literature, Irondale High School, New Brighton, Minnesota, 1974-; Instructor at Concordia College, St Paul, Minnesota, 1975-80 and Normandale Community College, 1983-. Publications: The Last Goodie, 1985; A Risky Game, 1986; Holding Steady, 1988; Guilt Trip, 1990; Funnybone, 1992. Contributions to: Various newspapers. Memberships: National Education Association; Authors Guild; Book Critics Circle; National Council for Teachers of English; The Loft. Literary Agent: Marilyn Marlow, Curtis Brown Ltd, New York. Address: Marilyn Marlow, Curtis Brown Ltd, 10 Astor Place, New York, NY 10003, USA.

SCHWARTZ Eli, b. 1921, United States of America. Writer. Publications: Co-Author, Study of the Probable Effects of a Move Toward Land Value Taxation in the City of Bethlehem, 1958; Corporation Finance, 1962; Editor and Co-Author with J.R. Aronson, Management Policies in Local Government Finance, 1987; Trouble in Eden: A Comparison of the British and Swedish Economicies, 1980; Theory and Application of the Interest Rate, 1993. Address: Rauch Bus Center, 37, Lehigh University, Bethlehem, PA 18015, USA.

SCHWARTZ Elliott S, b. 19 jan 1936, Brooklyn, New York, USA. Composer; Professor. m. Dorothy Feldman, 26 June 1960, 1 son, 1 daughter. Education: AB, Columbia College, 1957; MA, EdDrn, Columbia University, 1962; Composition study with Otto Luening, Jack Beeson and Paul Creston. Piano study with Alton Jones, Thomas

Richner. Appointments: University of Masachusetts, 1960-64; Bowdoin College, 1964-91; Visiting Professor, The Ohio State University, 1985-86, spring term, 1989, 90, 91; Visiting fellowships and extended residencies at the University of California, San Diego (Center for Music Experiment), University of California, Santa Barbara (College of Creative Studies), Trinity College of Music, London, Cambrdige University (Robinson College). Publications: Electronic Music: A Listener's Guide, 1973, revised 1985; The Symphonies of Ralph Vaughan Williams, 1965; Contemporary Composers on Contemporary Music, 1967; Music: A Listener's Guide, 1982; Music Since 1945, 1993. Contributions to: Many essays, reviews for The Musical Quarterly, Musical America, Perspectives of New Music, Music and Musicians, NOTES, Music Educators Journal, Nutida Musik, Contact. Honours: Gaudeamus Prize (Netherlands) 1970; Maine State Award in the Arts and Humanities, 1970; National Endowment for the Arts Composition Grants 1975-83; Rockefeller Foundation Bellagio Residency, 1980 and 1989. Memberships: President, College Music Society; Former Vice President, American Society of University Composers. Address: 10 Highview Road, PO Box 451, South Freeport, ME 04078, USA.

SCHWARTZ John Burnham, b. 8 May 1965, New York, USA. Writer. Education: BA, East Asian Studies, Harvard University, 1987. Publications: Bicycle Days, novel, 1989. Contributions to: New York Times Book Review, New York Times. Honours: Lyndhurst Prize, 1991. Memberships: Authors Guild; The Poet's Theatre, Cambridge, MA. Literary Agent: Amanda Urban, International Creative Management. Address: c/o Amanda Urban, International Creative Management, 40 West 57th, New York, NY 10019, USA.

SCHWARTZ Lynne Sharon, b. 1939, United States of America. Author; Full Time Writer. Publications: Rough Strife (novel), 1980; Balancing Acts (novel), 1981; Disturbances in the Field (novel), 1983; Acquainted with the Night (stories), 1984; We Are talking about Homes (stories), 1985; The Melting Pot and Other Subversive Stories, 1987; Leaving Brooklyn, 1989; A Lynne Sharon Schwartz Reader: Selected Prose and Poetry, 1992; The Fatigue Artist, 1995. Honours: National Endownment for the Arts Fellowship, 1984; Guggenheim Fellowship, 1985; New York State Foundation for the Arts Fellowship, 1986. Memberships: PEN American Centre; Authors Guild; National Book Critics Circle; National Writers Union. Literary Agent: Liz Darhansoff. Address: c/o Darhansoff & Verrill, 1220 Park Ave, New York, NY 10128, USA.

SCHWARTZ Ros, b. 24 Oct 1952, London, England. Translator. Partner, Andrew Cowen, 1 son, 1 daughter. Education: Licence-ès-Lettres, Universite de Paris VIII, 1978. Publications: Translations: I Didn't Say Goodbye (Claudine Vegh), 1984; The Blue Bicycle (Régine Deforges), 1985; Black Docker (Ousmane Sembéne), 1987; Desperate Spring (Fettouma Touati), 1987; The Net (Ilie Nastase), 1987; Cuisine Extraordinaire, 1988; Return to Beirut (Andrée Chedid), 1989; Women in Evidence (Sébastien Japrisot), 1990; Dining with Proust (Anne Borel), 1992; The Dragon Book (Ciruelo), 1992. Memberships: Translators Association, Chairwoman, 1991-92; Society of Authors; Institute of Translation and Interpreting; Women in Publishing. Address: 34 Uplands Road, London, N8 9NL, England.

SCHWARTZ Sheila, b. 15 Mar 1936, New York, USA. Professor; Author; Lecturer. div, 1 son, 1 daughter, (1 dec). Education: BA, Adelphi University; MA Teachers College, Columbia; EdD, New York University. Publications: How People Lived in Ancient Greece and Rome, 1967; How People Lived in Mexico, 1969; Teaching the Humanities, 1970; Earth in Transit, 1977; Like Mother, Like Me, 1978; Growing Up Guilty, 1978; Teaching Adolescent Literature, 1979; The Solid Gold Circle, 1980; One Day You'll Go, 1981; Jealousy, 1982; The Hollywood Writer's Wars, 1982; Bigger is Better, 1987; Sorority, 1987; The Most Popular Girl, 1987. Contributions to: Writing In America, 1989. Honours: Excellence in Letters, New York State, 1979; Excellence in Teaching, New York State, 1979; Annual award of Adolescent Literature Association for Contribution to the Field, 1981; Fulbright Fellow, University College, Cork, Republic of Ireland. Literary Agent: Harvey Klinger. Address: State University College, New Paltz, HY 12561, USA.

SCHWARTZ Stephan Andrew, b. 10 Jan 1942, Cincinnati, Ohio, USA. Writer; Researcher; Businessman. m. (1) 1 daughter, (2) Hayden Oliver Gates, 1 step-daughter. Education: Humanities, University of Virgina. Appointments: Editor, Subtle Energies. Publications include: The Secret Vaults of Time, 1978; The Alexandria Project, 1983; Television Writing: Project Deep Quest; The Alexandria Project; Small

World; Master of the House; Conversations at the Smithsonian; Psychic Detectives; Report from the Unknown. Contributions to: Stories from Omni, 1984; Psychic Detectives, 1985; The Millennium Agenda: Visions of a Multi-racial America; Within Your Lifetime; Washington Post; Omni; Harpers; The Washingtonian; Venture Inward. Memberships: Senior Fellow, Philosophical Research Society; Fellow Royal Geographical Society; Explorer's Club of New York; Past President and founding member, Society for the Anthropology of Conciousness; Society for Historic Archaeology; Society of Underwater Archaeology; Associate, Parapsychology Association; Board International Society for Subtle Energies and Energy Medicine; Board, California USSR Trade Association Director, World Children's (Organ) Transplant Fund. Literary Agent: ICM. Address: 4470-107 Sunset Blvd, No 339, Los Angeles, CA 90027, USA.

SCHWARZ Daniel Roger, b. 12 May 1941, Rockville Centre, New York, USA. Professor of English. 2 sons. Education: BA, Union College, 1963; MA, 1965, Phd, 1968, Brown University. Appointments: Assistant, Associate and Full Professor, Cornell University, 1968-; Distinguished Visiting Cooper Professor, University of Arkansas at Little Rock, 1988; Citizen's Chair in Literature, University of Hawaii, 1992-93. Publications: Narrative and Representation in the Poetry of Wallace Stevens, 1993; The Case for a Humanistic Poetics, 1991; Reading Joyce's Heritage, 1987; The Humanistic Heratage: Critical Theories of the English Novel from James to Hillis Miller, 1986; Conrad: The Later Fiction, 1983; Disraeli's Fiction, 1979; The Transformation of the English Novel, 1890-1930, 1989; Conrad: Almayer's Folly to Under Western Eyes, 1980. Contributions to: Modern Fiction Studies; 19th Century Fiction; JEGP; James Joyce Quarterly; Studies in the Novel; Sewanee Review; Diacritics, Novel; University of Toronto Quarterly. Honours: Nine NEH Summer Seminars for College and High School Teachers, 1984-1993; American Philosophical Society Grant, 1981. Memberships: International Association of University Professors of English. Address: 304 Rockefeller Hall, Department of English, Cornell University, Ithaca, New York, 14853, USA.

SCHWERIN Doris Belle, b. 24 June 1922, Peabody, Massachusetts, USA. Author; Composer. m. Jules V Schwerin, 2 Mar 1946, 1 son. Education: Boston University; New England Conservatory of Music; Diploma, Julliard School of Music, 1943; Student of George Antheil and Stefan Wolpe. Publications: Diary of a Pigeon Watcher, 1976; Leanna, novel in 6 movements, 1978; The Tomorrow Book, children's book, 1984; Rainbow Walkers, UK Edition as The Missing Years; The Tree That Cried, children's book, 1988; Cat and I, memoir, 1990. Contributions to: MS Magazine. Honours: Charles Sergal National Play Award, University of Chicago, 1971. Memberships: PEN; Assocation of American Composers, Authors and Publishers; Authors Guild; Authors League. Address: 317 West 83rd Street, New York, NY 10024, USA.

SCHWERNER Armand, b. 1927, Antwerp, Belgium. Writer; Poet; Translator; Musician. Education: Cornell University, USA; University of Geneva, Switzerland; BA, French, French Literature, MA, English, Comparative Literature, Graduate study, Department of Anthropology, Columbia University, USA. Appointments: Professor, Department of English, Speech and World Literature, College of Staten Island, New York, USA. Publications: The Lightfall, 1963; The Domesday Dictionary (with D Kaplan), 1963; (if personal), 1968; The Tablets I-VIII, 1968; Seaweed, 1969; The Tablets I-XZ, 1971; The Bacchae Sonnets, 1974; The Tablets I-XVIII, audiotape, 1974; Redspell, from the American Indian, 1975; Tablets XVI, XVII, XVIII and other poems, 1975; Bacchae Sonnets, 1977; the work, the joy and the triumph of the will, 1978; Philoctetes, translation from Sophocles, stereo cassette, 1978; Sound of the River Naranjana and the Tablets I-XXIV, 1983; Tablets I-XXVI, 1989; Works including translations, in numerous anthologies. Honours: Faculty Research Fellowship, State University of New York, summers 1970, 1972; Faculty Research Fellowship, City University of New York, summer 1971; Creative Writing Fellowship, National Endowment for the Arts, 1973, 1979, 1987; Creative Writing Fellowship, Creative Artists Public Service Programme, 1973, 1975; National Endowment for the Humanities Summer Seminar, Princeton University, 1978, Fordham University, New York, 1981, Columbia University, Paris, France, 1985; Creative Incentive Fellowship, Professional Staff Congress-City University of New York, 1986, 1992; Grant for Poetry, Greater New York Arts Development Fund, 1987, ; Grant for Contribution to Contemporary Poetry, 1991. Memberships: Poets Advisory Board: Poets House, 1989-, New York; PEN, America; NCTE; MLA; National Council of the Teachers of English, 1989-; Modern Languages Association, 1992-; Board of Tibetan Museum, Staten Island, 1995-;

National Book Critics' Circle, 1995-. Address: 20 Bay Street Landing B-3C, Staten Island, NY 10301, USA.

SCIARRILLO Carmen Francisca Maria Vivern, b. 8 Jul 1919. Author; Piano Teacher. Publications: La Educacion Musical En La Escuela Primaria, 1964; Cuentos Musicales Escenificados, 1965; Marcha Para Mi Escuela, La Escarapela, 1967; Cinco Canciones Para Jardin de Infantes, 1969; Canciones Para Mi Escuela, 1970; Cancionero Didactico Escolar, 1970; Comedias Musicales Escolares, 1972; La Educacion Musical En La Escuela Primaria, 1979. Honours: Ten Confs. by LRA Radio Nacional; Narrator and Coordinator, Firsts Musical Educational Congress at The Medical University, 1970. Literary Agent: Rogelio Sciarrillo. Address: Ignacio Fermin Rodriguez 2427, Capital Federal CP 1406, Buenos Aires, Argentina.

SCOBIE Stephen, b. Canada. Honours: Govenor General's Award for Poetry, 1980. Address: 4728 Parkside Crescent, Victoria, British Columbia, V8N 2C3, Canada.

SCOFIELD Jonathan. See: **LEVINSON Leonard.**

SCOTT Anna Heather, b. Sydney, New South Wales, Australia. Writer, Editor. 1 son, 2 daughters. Education: Diploma of Nursing (Registered Nurse), Royal Prince Alfred Hospital, Sydney, New South Wales, 1956. Career: Writer, Editor, Sydney magazines, 1978-90, including: Australian Home Journal, Better Homes and Gardens, Cosmopolitan, Harpers Bazaar, Vogue Australia, Vogue Living, Vogue Entertaining, Australian Design Series; Tutor, The Writing School, Sydney, 1987-89. Publication: Triumph over Arthritis, 1991. Contributions to: Numerous publications. Memberships: Australian Society of Authors; Society of Editors, New South Wales; Australian Journalists Association. Address: c/- Cosmosis Editorial, 69 Cove Blvd, North Arm Cove, New South Wales 2324, Australia.

SCOTT Arthur Finley, b. 30 Nov 1907, Kronstad, Orange Free State, South Africa. Teacher; Author. m. (1) Margaret Ida Scott, Jun 1935, (deceased), (2) Margaret Clare Scott, Jan 1954, (deceased), 2 d. Education: Emmanual College, Cambridge, England, BA, 1930, MA, 1934, Cambridge University; Graduate Study, Education, Oxford University, 1930. Appointments include: Senior Lecturer, English, Borough Road College of Education, London, 1952-73; University Teacher, London University, 1968-73; Reader of English educational publications, MacMillan, Harrap, Heineman, Cambridge University Press; Director, Scott and Finley Limited. Publications: Over 130 books including: Meaning and Style, 1938; New Reading, 10 books, 1956-60; Parrish Poetry Books, 4 books, 1958-59; The Craft of Prose, 1963; Current Literary Terms: Dictionary of Their Origin and Use, 1965; New Horizons (with N K Aggarwala), 10 books, 1968-71; The Stuart Age, 1974; Who's Who in Chaucer, 1974; The Roman Age, 1977; The Saxon Age, 1979; Early Hanoverian Age, 1980; America Grows, 1982; What Fire Kindles Genius, 1982; What Makes a Prose Genius, 1983. Honours: Exhibition, Arthur Finley Scott Collection of Books held at University of Southern Mississippi, 1968, 1969; Life Fellow, International Biographical Association. Memberships: Royal Society of Literature; Society of Authors; Life Member, National Book League; Past Chairman, Kettering Three Arts Society. Address: 59 Syon Park Gardens, Isleworth, Middlesex, TW7 5NE, England.

SCOTT Dennis, b. 1939, Jamaica. Drama Principal; Poet. m. Joy Scott. Education: Jamaica College, University of the West Indies at Kingston. Appointments include: Principal of the School of Drama at Kingston, Jamaica. Publications: Journeys and Ceremonies. 1969; Uncle Time, 1973; Dreadwalk: Poems 1970-78, 1982; Plays: Terminus, 1966, and An Echo in the Bone, 1985. Honours include: Commonwealth Poetry Prize, 1974. Address: School of Drama, 1 Arthur Wint Drive, Kingston, Jamaica.

SCOTT Donald Fletcher, b. 29 Nov 1930, Norfolk, England. Medical Consultant (retired). m. Adrienne Mary Moffett, 2 Sept 1967 (dec 1992), m. Dr Mary Paterson, 5 Jan 1994, 1 s, 1 d. Education: MB, ChB, Edinburgh University, Scotland, 1951-57; DPM, London University, 1965; FRCP, Royal College of Physicians, London, 1979. Publications: About Epilepsy, 1969; Fire and Fire Raisers, 1974; Understanding EEG, 1976; Coping With Suicide, 1989; Beating Job Burnout, 1989; The History of Epileptic Therapy, 1992. Contributions to: Over 100 articles mainly to medical/psychological journals. Memberships: Electro-Encephalogram Society, former Meeting Secretary; Association of British Neurologists; Association of British Clinical Neurophysiology; British Society of Clinical Neurophysiology;

Association of British Neurologists. Address: 25 Park Gate, Blackheath, London, SE3 9XF, England.

SCOTT Gail, b. Ottawa, Canada. Writer. 1 daughter. Appointments: Writer in Residence, University of Alberta, 1994-95; Writer in Residence, Concordia University, Montreal, 1991-92; Writing Instructor, 1981-90; Journalist, Montreal Gazette, The Globe and Mail, Toronto, 1970-79. Publications: Heroine, 1987; Spaces like Stairs, 1989; Spare Parts, 1982; La Theorie, un Dimanche, 1988; Serious Hysterics (anthology), 1992; Resurgences (anthology), 1992; Main Brides, 1994. Contributions to: Critical journals, Spirale and Tessera, (Founding Editor); Massachusetts Review, 1990; West Coast Line, 1991; However, 1992; American Voice, 1993; Books in Canada, 1994; Poetics Journal, 1994. Honours: Quebec Society for the Promotion of English Language Literature - shortlisted for Heroine, 1987, Main Brides, 1994. Memberships: Writer's Union of Canada; L'Union Des Ecrivains Quebecois. Literary Agent: French Language, Fré délique Porrettic, Paris. Address: c/o Coach House Press, 50 Prince Arthur Avenue, Ste. 107, M5R 1B5.

SCOTT John A, b. 23 Apr 1948, Littlehampton, Sussex, England. Lecturer; Poet. Education: Monash University, Victoria, Australia. Appointments include: Lecturer in Writing at Wollongong University, New South Wales, from 1989. Publications: The Barbarous Sideshow, 1975; From the Flooded City, 1981; Smoking, 1983; The Quarrel with Ourselves; And Confession, 1984; St Clair: Three Narratives, 1986; Singles: Shorter Works, 1981-86, 1989; Translation, 1990; Novel: Blair, 1988; The Book of Rats, 1981; Radio scripts. Honours include: Victorian Premier's Prize, 1986. Address: c/o Pan/Picador (Australia) Ltd, PO Box 124, Chippendale, New South Wales 2008, Australia.

SCOTT John Peter, b. 8 Apr 1949, London, England. University Teacher. m. Jill Wheatley, 4 Sep 1971, 1 s, 1 d. Education: Kingston College of Technology, 1968-71; BSc, (Soc), London, 1971; London School of Economics, 1971-72; PhD, Strathclyde, 1976. Appointments: Lecturer in Sociology, Strathclyde University, Scotland, 1972-76; Lecturer 1976-87, Reader 1987-91, Professor 1991-94, in Sociology, University of Leicester; Professor of Sociology, Essex University, 1994-; Editor, Network Newsletter, British Sociological Association, 1985-89; Editor, Sociology Review (formerly Social Studies Review, 1986-. Publications: Corporations, Classes and Capitalism, 1979, 2nd edition, 1985; The Upper Classes, 1982; The Anatomy of Scottish Capital (with M Hughes), 1982; Directors of Industry (with C Griff), 1984; Networks of Corporate Power (joint editor) 1985; Capitalist Property and Financial Power, 1986; A Matter of Record, 1990; The Sociology of Elites (3 Vols, editor), 1990; Who Rules Britain, 1991; Social Network Analysis, 1992; Power (3 vols, editor), 1994; Poverty and Wealth, 1994. Contributions to: Numerous articles for professional journals and magazines. Membership: Chairperson, 1992-93, General Secretary, British Sociological Association. Address: Department of Sociology, University of Essex, Colchester, CO4 3SQ, England.

SCOTT Jonathan Henry, b. 22 Jan 1958, Auckland, New Zealand. Historian. Education: BA, 1980, BA Hons, 1981, Victoria University of Wellington, New Zealand; PhD, Cambridge, 1986. Publications: Algernon Sidney and the English Republic, 1623-1677, 1988; Algernon Sidney and the Restoration Crisis, 1677-83, 1991. Contributions to: Historical Journal, 1988; The Politics of Religion in Restoration England, 1990; Contributor of Poetry to literary Journals, 1984-86. Contributions to: Revolution and Restoration: England in the 1650s, 1992; History of Political Thought, vol XIII, no 4, winter, 1992; Political Discourse in Early Modern Britain, 1993. Address: Downing College, Cambridge CB2 1DQ, England.

SCOTT Nathan A, Jr, b. 1925, American, Writer on Literature, Philosophy, Theology/Religion. William R Kenan, Professor Emeritus of Religious Studies and Professor Emeritus of English, University of Virgina, Charlottesville, 1976-. Advisory Editor, Literature and Theology, Religion and Literature, Callaloo and Religion and Intellectual Life. Appointments: Associate Professor of Humanities, Howard University, Washington DC, 1948-55; Shailer Mathews Professor of Theology and Literature and Co-Editor, The Journal of Religion, University of Chicago, 1955-76; Fellow, School of Letters, Indiana University, Bloomington, 1965-72. Publications include: (ed) The Climate of Faith in Modern Literature, 1964; Samuel Beckett, 1965; (ed) Four Ways of Modern Poetry, 1965; (ed) Man in the Modern Theatre, 1965; The Broken Center: Studies in the Theological Horizon of Modern Literature, 1966; Ernest Hemingway, 1966; (ed) The Modern Vision of Death, 1967; (ed) Adversity and Grace: Studies in Recent American

Literature, 1968; Craters of the Spirit: Studies in the Modern Novel, 1968; Negative Capability: Studies in the New Literature and the Religious Situation, 1969; The Unquiet Vision: Mirrors of Man in Existentialism, 1969; Nathanael West, 1971; The Wild Prayer of Longing: Poetry and the Sacred, 1971; Three American Moralists: Mailer, Bellow, Trilling, 1973; (ed) The Legacy of Reinhold Niebuhr, 1975; The Poetry of Civic Virtue: Eliot, Malraux, Auden, 1976; Mirrors of Men in Existentialism, 1978; The Poetics of Belief: Studies in Coleridge, Arnold, Pater, Santayana, Stevens and Heidegger, 1985; Visions of Presence in Modern American Poetry, 1993; Reading George Steiner, 1994. Address: 1419 Hilltop Road, Charlottesville, Virgina 22903, USA.

SCOTT Paul Henderson, b. 7 Nov 1920, Edinburgh, Scotland. Essayist; Historian; Critic; Former Diplomat. Education: Royal High School, Edinburgh; MA, MLitt, Edinburgh University. Publications: 1707: The Union of Scotland and England, 1979; Walter Scott and Scotland, 1981; John Galt, 1985; Towards Independence: Essays on Scotland, 1991; Andrew Fletcher and the Treaty of Union, 1992; Edited: Scotland: A Concise Cultural History, 1993; Defoe in Edinburgh, 1994. Contributions to: Articles and reviews in: The Scotsman; The Herald; The Economist; Books in Scotland and many others. Honours: Andrew Fletcher Prize, 1993. Memberships: President, Scottish Centre, International PEN; Vice Chairman, Saltire Society; Convener, Advisory Council for the Arts in Scotland; Association for Scottish Literary Studies. Address: 33 Drumsheugh Gardens, Edinburgh, EH3 7RN, Scotland.

SCOTT Rosie, b. 22 Mar 1948, New Zealand. Writer. m. 28 Nov 1987, 2 d. Education: MA Hons, English, 1968; Graduate Diploma, Drama, 1984. Appointments: Member, Queensland Literary Board, Committee member Australian Society of Authors, 1991-92. Publications: Flesh and Blood, poetry, 1984; Queen of Love, stories, 1989; novels: Glory Days, 1988; Nights With Grace, 1990; Feral City, 1992; Lives on Fire, 1993; Movie Dreams, 1995. Contributions to: Literary essays, poems, stories to: Rolling Stone; Metro; Island; Austalian Book Review; 24 Hours; Australian Author. Honours: Sunday Times Bruce Mason Award for play, Say Thank You For the Lady, 1986; Glory Days, shortlisted, National Book Award, 1988; Feral City, shortlisted, Australian National Book Awards; Australian Writers Fellowship, Category A, 1992; Shortlisted for Australian-Canada Literary Award, 1993. Memberships: PEN New Zealand; Australian Society of Authors; Greenpeace; ACF. Literary Agent: Margaret Connelly, Paddington, Australia. Address: 21 Darghan St, Glebe, NSW 2037, Australia.

SCOTT Roy Vernon, b. 1927, United States of America. Writer. Publications: The Agrarian Movement in Illinois 1880-1896, 1962; The Reluctant Farmer: The Rise of Agricultural Extension to 1914, 1970; The Public Career of Cully A. Cobb: A Study in Agricultural Leadership (with J.G. Shoalmire), 1973; Southern Agriculture Since the Civil War (with George L. Robinson Jr.), 1979; Railroad Development Programs in the Twentieth Century, 1985; The Great Northern Railway: A History (with R. W. Hidy and others), 1988; Eugene Beverly Ferris and Agricultural Science in the Lower South, 1991; Wall-Hart: A History of Sam Walton's Retail Phenomenon (with Sandra S Vance), 1994. Address: Department of History, Mississippi State University, Mississippi State, MI 39762, USA.

SCOTT Sally Elisabeth, b. 30 May 1948, London, England. Writer; Illustrator. Education: BA, Hons, Philosophy and English Literature, York University, 1970. Publications: The Magic Horse, 1985, The Three Wonderful Beggars, 1987, The Elf-King's Bride, 1981, all self-illustrated; Illustrator, Tales and Legends of India. Memberships: Society of Authors. Literary Agent: Bruce Hunter, David Higham Associates Ltd, 5-8 Lower John Street, Golden Square, London, W1R 4HA, England.

SCOTT Tom, b. 1918. Poet; Childrens Writer. Appointment: Former Editor, Scottish Literature Series, Pergamon Press, Oxford. Publications: Seeven Poems o Maister Francis Vilton, 1953; An Ode til New Jerusalem, 1956; The Ship and Ither Poems, 1963; A Possible Solution to the Scottish Question, 1963; Dunbar: A Critical Exposition of the Poems, 1966; The Oxford Book of Scottish Verse (with J McQueen), 1966; Late Medieval Scots Poetry: A Selection from the Makars and their Heirs Down to 1610, 1967; At the Shrine o the Unkent Sodger: A Poem for Recitation, 1968; Tales of Robert the Bruce, 1969; The Penguin Book of Scottish Verse, 1970; Brand the Builder, 1975; The Tree, 1977; Tales of Sir William Wallace, 1981; The Dirty

Business, 1986; Collected Shorter Poems, 1993. Address: Duddington Park, Edinburgh 15, Scotland.

SCOTT William (Bill) Neville, b. 1923, Australia. Author. Publications: Focus on Judith Wright, 1967; Some People (short stories), 1968; Brother and Brother (verse), 1972; The Continual Singing: An Anthology of World Poetry, 1973; Portrait of Brisbane, 1976; The Complete Book of Australian Folklore, 1976; Bushranger Ballads, 1976; My Uncle and Other People (short stories), 1977; Boori (children's fiction), 1978; Tough In The Old Days (autobiography), 1979; Ned Kelly After a Century of Acrimony (with John Meredith), 1980; The Second Penguin Australian Songbook, 1980; Darkness Under The Hills (children's fiction), 1980; Reading 360 series (The Blooming Queensland Side, On The Shores of Botany Bay, The Golden West, Bound For South Australia, Upon Van Diemen's Land, The Victorian Bunyip), 6 volumes, 1981; Australian Bushrangers, 1983; Reading 360 series, 6 volumes, 1983; Penguin Book of Australian Humorous Verse, 1984; Shadows Among the Leaves (children's fiction), 1984; The Long and The Short and The Tall (folklore), 1985; Following the Gold (poems for children), 1989; Many Kinds of Magic (short stories), 1990; Hey Rain (cassette, songs and poems) 1992; The Currency Lad (fiction) 1994; Songbird In Your Pocket (cassette, songs and poems) 1994; Pelicans And Chihuahuas (folklore), 1995; The Banshee, The Bollocky and The Boiler (short stories), 1995. Honours: Medal of The Order of Australia for work as a folklorist, 1992. Address: 157 Pratten Street, Warwick, Queensland 4370, Australia.

SCOTT TANNER Amoret, b. 27 Mar 1930, Vancouver, British Columbia, Canada. Social Historian. m. Ralph Tanner, 24 Aug 1985. Publications: Hedgerow Harvest, 1979; Parrots, 1982; With Christopher Scott: Collecting Bygones, 1964; Tobacco and the Collector, 1966; Dummy Board Figures, 1966; Discovering Smoking Antiques, 1970, 1981; Discovering Stately Homes, 1973, 1981, 1989; Staffordshire Figures (Shire Album), 1986, 1993. Contributions to: The Saturday Book; Country Life; Antique Collector; Antiquarian Book Monthly. Memberships: Founder Member, Member of Council, Ephemera Society. Address: The Footprint, Padworth Common, Reading, RG7 4QG, England.

SCOTT-STOKES Natascha (Norton), b. 11 Apr 1962, Munich, Germany. Travel Writer. m. Benoit Le Blanc, 27 Feb 1992. Education: BA Hons Humanities, Middlesex Polytechnic; MA Latin American Studies, University of London. Appointments: Associate Editor, Writer's Newsletter, 1989-90. Publications: An Amazon and A Donkey, 1991; Co-author: Germany, the Rough Guide, 1989; The Cadogan Guide to Central America, 1992; The Amber Trail, 1993. Contributions to: The Lima Times; Writers Newsletter. Memberships: Writers Guild of Great Britain; PEN English Centre; Fellow, Royal Geographical Society. Address: 55 Leconfield Road, London N5 2RZ, England.

SCOVELL E(dith) J(oy), b. 1907, Sheffield, Yorkshire, England. m. Charles Elton, 1937. Education: BA, Somerville College, Oxford, 1930. Publications: Shadows of Chrysanthemums and Other Poems, 1944; The Midsummer Meadow and Other Poems, 1946; The River Steamer and Other Poems, 1956; The Space Between, 1982; Ten Poems, 1984; Listening to Collared Doves, 1986; Collected Poems, 1988; Selected Poems, 1991. Honours include: Cholmondeley Award, 1989. Address: 51 Diamond Court, Oxford, OX2 TAA, England.

SCRUTON Roger V, b. 27 Feb 1944, Bulingthorpe, England. Professor of Philosophy, Boston University. Education: BA, Philosophy, 1965, PhD 1972, Jesus College, Cambridge. Literary Appoinyments: Editor, Salisbury Review, 1982-. Publications: The Meaning of Conservatism, 1980; The Aesthetics of Architecture, 1979; A Dictionary of Political Thought, 1982; Fortnight's Anger, 1981; The Aesthetic Understanding, 1983; Sexual Desire, 1986; Art and Imagination, 1974; Politics of Culture, 1981; Short History of Modern Philosophy, 1981; Thinkers of the New Left, 1986; A Land Held Hostage, 1987; Untimely Tracts, 1987; The Philosopher on Dove Beach, 1990; Francesca, 1991; A Dove Descending and Other Poems, 1991; Conservative Texts, an Anthology, 1992; Xanthippic Dialogues, 1993; Modern Philosophy, 1994. Contributions to: Times; Times Literary Supplement; Spectator; Guardian; Field; Salisbury Review; Encounter. Literary Agent: Curtis Brown.

SCULLY Vincent Joseph, b. 1920. Appointments: Professor of History of Art, Yale University and University of Miami, Florida; Architecture. Address: Dept of Art History, Yale University, PO Box 2009, Yale Station, New Haven, CT 06520-2009, USA.

SCUPHAM John Peter, b. 24 Feb 1933. Writer. m. Carola Nance Braunholtz, 10 Aug 1957, 3 s, 1 d. Education: The Perse School, Cambridge; Hons Degree in English, Emmanuel College, Cambridge. Literary Appointment: Proprietor and Founder of the Mandeville Press. Publications include: Prehistories, 1975; The Hinterland, 1977; Summer Palaces, 1980; Winter Quarters, 1983; Out Late, 1986; The Air Show, 1988; Selected Poems, 1991. Membership: Fellow, Royal Society of Literature. Address: Old Hall, Norwich Road, South Burlingham, Norwich, Norfolk NR13 4EY, England.

SEAGER Ralph William, b. 3 Nov 1911, Geneva, New York, USA. Writer. m. Ruth M Lovejoy, 1932, 3 sons. Education: Graduated from Penn Yan Academy, 1928; Studied basic and advance verse, University of California at Berkeley, 1950-51; Studied with Pulitzer Poet Robert Peter Tristram Coffin at University of New Hampshire Writers' Conference, 1954 and John Holmes, Harvard Phi Beta Kapa Poet, 1956; Litt D, Keuka College, 1970; Professor Emeritus, 1977. Apppointments: Assistant Professor of English, Keuka College, teaching a creative course in Verseand and Writing since 1960; Served with United States Navy in the South Pacific campaigns during World War II; Judge for Arizona Poetry Society, 1992-1994. Publications include: Books of Verse: Songs from a Willow Whistle, 1956; Beyond the Green Gate, 1958; Christmas Chimes in Rhyme, 1962; Cup, Flagon and Fountains, 1965; A Choice of Dreams, 1970; Wheatfields and Vineyards, 1975; The Manager Mouse and Other Christmas Poems, 1977; Hiding in Plain Sight, 1982; The Love Tree, 1985; The First Quartet (with 3 other poets), 1988; Books in prose: The Sound of an Echo, 1963; Little Yates and the United States, 1976; The First Baptist Church - One Hundred Fifty Years (co-author), 1980; One-Room Schoolhouse - anthology, 1993. Contributions to: Poems in publications including The Saturday Evening Post; New York Times; Ladies' Home Journal; Director or instructor of numerous poetry workshops; IDEALS; Time of Singing; On Silver Wings and others. Address: 311 Keuka Street, Penn Yan, NY 14527-1153, USA.

SEAGRAVE Sterling, b. 15 Apr 1937, USA. Writer. m. (1) Wendy Law-Yone, 1967, (2) Peggy Sawyer, 1982, 1 s, 1 d. Education: In India, USA, Latin America. Publications: Yellow Rain, 1981; Soldiers of Fortune, 1981; The Soong Dynasty, 1985; The Marcos Dynasty, 1988; Dragon Lady, 1992. Contributions to: Atlantic: Far Eastern Economic Review; Esquire; Time; Smithsonian. Membership: Authors Guild. Literary Agents: Robert Gottlieb (New York), Sappho Clissett (UK), William Morris Agency. Address: c/o William Morris Agency, 31 Soho Sq, London W1V 5DG, England.

SEAL Basil. See: **BARNES Julian Patrick**.

SEALEY Leonard George William, b. 7 May 1923, London, England. Educational Author, Consultant. m. (1) Joan Hearn, Mar 1944 (dec), (2) Nancy Verre, August 1972, 5 sons. Education: Teachers Certificate, Peterborough College, England; DipED, MEd, University of Leicester. Publications: The Creative Use of Mathematics, 1961; Communication and Learning (co-author), 1962; Exploring Language, 1968; Basic Skills in Learning, 1970; Introducing Mathematics, 1970; The Lively Readers, 1973; Our World Encyclopedia (Editor), 1974; Open Education, 1977; Children's Writing, 1979. Memberships: Fellow of the Royal Society of Arts; Phi Delta Kappa (Harvard Chapter Honorary). Address: 136 Sandwich Road, Plymouth, MA 02360, USA.

SEALTS Merton M, Jr, b. 8 Dec 1915, United States of America. Writer. Publications: Melville as Lecturer, 1957; Billy Budd, Sailor by Herman Melville (with H Hayford), 1962; The Journals and Miscellaneous Notebooks of Ralph Waldo Emerson 1835-1838, vol V, 1965; Melville's Reading, 1966, 1988; Emerson's Nature: Origin, Growth, Meaning (with A.R. Ferguson), 1969, 1979; The Journals and Miscellaneous Notebooks of Ralph Waldo Emerson 1847-1848, vol X, 1973; The Early Lives of Melville: Nineteenth Century Biographical Sketches and Their Authors, 1974; Pursuing Melville, 1940-1980: Chapters and Essays, 1982; Emerson on the Scholar, 1992. Honours: Jay B. Hubbell Medal for achievement in American Literature, awarded by the American Literature Section, Modern Language Association, 1992; Annual award for the best article appearing in ESQ: A Journal of the American Renaissance, named for me by the editors, 1992: The Merton M. Sealts, Jr. Prize. Address: 6209 Mineral Point Road, Apt. 1106/08, Madison, WI 53705-4537, USA.

SEARLE Ronald, (William Fordham), b. 1920. Publications: Forty Drawings, 1946; Le Nouveau Ballet Anglais, 1947; Hurrah for St Trinian's, 1948; The Female Approach, 1949; Back to The Slaughterhouse, 1951; Souls in Torment, 1953; Rake's Progress, 1955; Merry England, 1956; Which Way Did He Go, 1961; Searle in the Sixties, 1965; From Frozen North to Filthy Lucre, 1964; Pardong M'sieur, 1965; Searle' Cats, 1969; Hommage à Toulouse Lautrec, 1969; Secret Sketchbook, 1970; The Addict, 1971; More Cats, 1975; Drawings From Gilbert and Sullivan, 1975; The Zoodiac, 1977; Ronald Searle, 1978; The King of Beasts, 1980; The Big Fat Cat Book, 1982; Winespeak, 1983; Ronald Searle in Perspective, 1984; Ronald Searle's Golden Oldies, 1985; To the Kwai - and Back, 1986; Something in the Cellar, 1986. Ah Yes I Remember it Well: Paris 1961-1975, 1987; The Non-Sexist Dictionary, 1988; Slightly Foxed - but still desirable, 1989; The Curse of St Trinian's, 1993; Marquis de Sade meets Goody Two Shoes, 1994. Address: c/o Tessa Sayle, 11 Jubilee Place, London, SW3 3TE, England.

SEDGWICK Eva Kossofsky, Contributions to: Numerous Academic and Professional Journals, Including: Raritan; Delta; Critical Inquiry. Address: Dept of English, Duke University, Durham, NC 27706-7706, USA.

SEDGWICK Fred, b. 20 Jan 1945, Dublin, Ireland. Lecturer in Education; Poet. Education: St Luke's College, Exeter; MA, University of East Anglia at Norwich, 1984. Appointments include: Head of Downing Primary School, Suffolk; Education Lecturer. Publications: Really in the Dark, 1980; From Another Part of the Island, 1981; A Garland for William Cowper, 1984; The Living Daylights, 1986; Falernian, 1987; Lighting Up Time: On Children's Writing, 1990; Editor, This Way That Way: A Collection of Poems for Schools, 1989. Address: 1 Mornington Avenue, Ipswich, Suffolk IP1 4LA, England.

SEDLEY Kate. See: **CLARKE Brenda**.

SEE Carolyn (Monica Highland), b. 13 Jan 1934, California, USA. Writer. m. (1) Richard See, 18 Feb 1954, (2) Tom Sturak, 30 Apr 1960, 2 daughters. Education: PhD, University of California, Los Angeles (UCLA), 1953. Appointments include: Professor of English, UCLA. Publications include: The Rest is Done with Mirrors, 1970; Blue Money, 1974; Mothers, Daughters, 1977; Rhine Maidens, 1980; Golden Days, 1985; When Knaves Meet, 1988; The Mirrored Hall in the Hollywood Dance Hall, 1991; Dreaming: Hard Luck and Good Times in America, 1995. As Monica Highland: Lotus Land, 1983; 1-10 Shanghai Road, 1985; Greetings From Southern California, 1987; Precious Cargo, 1990; Two Schools of Thought (with John Espey), 1991. Contributions to: Esquire; McCalls; Atlantic; Sports Illustrated; California Magazine; Contributing editor, book reviews, Los Angeles Times; Contributing book Reviewer, Washington Post. Honours: Samuel Goldwyn Award, 1963; Sidney Hillman Award, 1969; Grant, National Endowment for the Arts, 1974; Bread and Roses Award, National Womens Political Caucus, 1988; Vesta Award, 1989; Guggenheim Fellowship in Fiction, 1989; Lila Wallace Grant, 1993. Memberships: President, PEN Centre USA West, 1993-94. Literary Agent: Anne Sibbold at Janklow Nisbet. Address: PO Box 107, Topanga, Ca 90290, USA.

SEED Cecile Eugenie, (Jenny Seed), b. 18 May 1930, Cape Town, South Africa. Author. m. Edward (Ted) Robert Seed, 31 Oct 1953, 3 s, 1 d. Publications: The Great Thirst, 1985; The Great Elephant, 1985; Place Among the Stones, 1987; Hurry, Hurry, Sibusiso, 1988; The Broken Spear, 1989; The Prince of the Bay, 1989; The Big Pumpkin, 1990; Old Grandfather Mantis, 1992; The Hungry People, 1993; A Time to Scatter Stones, 1993. Honours: MER Award for Place Among the Stones, 1987; Runner-up, Noma Award, for Ntombi's Song. Address: 10 Pioneer Crescent, Northdene, Natal 4093, South Africa.

SEED Jenny. See: **SEED Cecile Eugenie**.

SEGAL L, b. 8 Mar 1928, Vienna, Austria. Writer. m. David I. Segal, 3 Nov 1960 (dec), 1 son, 1 daughter. Education: BA, English, Bedford College, University of London, England, 1948. Appointments: Professor, Writing Division, School of Arts, Columbia University, Princeton University, Sarah Lawrence College, Bennington College, USA; Professor of English, University of Illinois, Chicago, Illinois; The Ohio State University. Publications: Novels: Other People's Houses, 1964; Lucinella, 1976; Her First American, 1985; Children's books: Tell Me a Mitzi, 1977; The Story of Mrs Brubeck and How She Looked for Trouble and Where She Found Him, 1981; The Story of Mrs Lovewright and Purrless Her Cat, 1985; Translations: Gallows Songs (with W D Snodgrass), 1968; The Juniper Tree and Other Tales from Grimm, 1973; The Book of Adam to Moses; The Story of King Soul and King

David. Contributions to: Short stories and articles to: New York Times Book Review; Partisan Review; New Republic; The New Yorker; Others. Honours: Guggenheim Fellow, 1965-66; Grantee, Council of Arts and Humanities, 1968-69; Grantee, Artists Public Service, 1970-71; Grantee, CAPS, 1975; Grantee, National Endowment for the Arts, 1982; Grantee, National Endowment for the Humanities, 1983; Academy of Arts and Letters Award, 1986. Address: 280 Riverside Drive, New York, NY 10025, USA.

SEGAL Stanley Solomon, b. 9 Nov 1919, London, England. Educator. m. Tamar Shuster, 29 Apr 1945, 1 s, 1 d. Education: Certificate in Education, Goldsmiths College, University of London, 1950; Diploma in Education of Handicapped Pupils, Istitute of Education, London, 1954; Masters Degree in Education, University of Leicester, School of Education, 1970; Appointed Professor of Special Education, Bulmershe College of Higher Education, 1981. Literary Appointments: Honorary Editor, Forward Trends in the Treatment of the Backward Child, 1954-74; Honorary Editor, British Journal of Special Education, 1974-93. Publications: No Child is Ineducable, 1967, 1974; Teaching Backward Pupils, 1963; Eleven-Plus Rejects? 1961; Backward Pupils in the USSR, 1965; From Care to Education, 1970; Society and Mental Handicap, 1984; The Space Age Readers, 1963; The Working World Series, 1965; The Creative Arts in the Development of People With Mental Handicaps, 1990. Contributions to: Times Educational Supplement; Teachers World; The Teacher; Parents Voice; Mental Health. Honour: OBE for Services to the Education of Handicapped Children. Memberships: Life President, National Council for Special Education; Magistrates Association; Association of Professions for the Mentally Handicapped (former Chairman); Life Member, National Association for Special Educational Needs, 1994-; Founder-Chairman, International Information Centre on Special Needs Education. Address: 11 Ravensdale Avenue, Finchley, London N12 9HP, England.

SEGHERS Greta Irene Pieter, b. 11 Feb 1942, Beveren, Waas, Belgium. writer; History Teacher. m. Ludo de Cock, 12 Jul 1966, 1 s, 1 d. Education: Secondary Teacher Training, Dutch, History. Appointments: Member, Editorial staff, Dietsche Warande en Belfort, 1984; Member, Literary Commission, East Flanders, 1991. Publications: Het blauwe meisje, stories, 1980; Wat ge leest en schrijft, dat zijt ge zelf, essay, 1985; Het eigenzinnige leven van Angèle Manteau, biography, 1992; Novels: Afkeer van Faulkner, 1977; Omrent de man die wederkwam, 1978; Ontregeling en Misverstand, 1983; De zijpaden van het paradijs, 1988; Hoe moordend is mijn school, 1990; Een Dunne Wand, stories, 1994. Contributions to: short stories to: De Brakke Hond; De Vlaatse Gids/ NVT; Het Laaste Nieuws; Dietsche Warande en Belfort; Kreatief; interviews to: Knack; Intermediair; and others. Honours: Best Debut prize, 1977; Yang Prize, 1977; Prize, 1983, Honorable Mention, 1985, Province of East Flanders. Membership: Dietsche Warande en Belfort. Address: Tuinlaan 14, 9120, Vrasene, Belgium.

SEIDMAN Hugh, b. 1 Aug 1940, USA. Poet. Education: Massachusetts Institute of Technology, 1957; BS, cum laude, Polytechnic Institute of Brooklyn, 1961; MS, University of Minnesota, 1964; MFA, with Distinction, Columbia University, 1969. Appointments include: Teacher of poetry for workshops, lectures and courses including: Visiting Poet, Writer's Voice, New York City, 1988; Faculty Member, New School for Social Research, 1976-. Publications: People Live, They Have Lives, 1992; Throne/Falcon/Eye, 1982; Blood Lord, 1974; Collecting Evidence, 1970. Honours: New York Foundation for the Arts, Poetry Fellowship, 1990; National Endowment for the Arts, Creative Writing Fellowship, 1972, 1985; Writers Digest, Poetry Prize, 1982; Resident Fellow, Yaddo, 1972, 1976, 1988; Resident Fellow, MacDowell Colony, 1974, 1975, 1989; Poetry Grant, Creative Artists Public Service Programme, 1971; Discovery Grant, National Endowment for the Arts, 1970; Yale Series of Younger Poets Prize, for Collecting Evidence, 1969. Memberships include: American PEN; Poetry Society of America; Authors Guild; Authors League; Board Member, Millay Colony for the Arts, 1975-79; Maryland Arts Council, Panelist, 1978; Massachusetts Council on the Arts, Panelist, 1977; Reviewer, New York Tines Book Review, 1975-85. Address: 463 West Street, New York, NY 10014, USA

SEIFMAN Eli, b. 4 Aug 1936, New York, USA. Distinguished Service Professor of Social Sciences. Education: BA, 1957, MS, 1959, Queens College, City University of New York; PhD, New York University, 1965. Publications: History of New York State Colonization Society, 1966; Social Studies: Structure, Models & Strategies, 1969;

Teacher's Handbook, 1971; Towards a New World Outlook, 1976; Education & Socialization Modernization, 1987; Contributions to: Asian Affairs; Asian Thought & Society; American Journal of Chinese Medicine; History of Education Quarterely; Social Education; Pennsylvania History; Teaching History; Liberian Studies Journal. Honours: Phi Beta Kappa, 1956; Phi Alpha Theta, 1956; Kappa Delta Pie, 1963; Book Award, Phi Lamda Theta, 1973. Memberships: American Historical Association; Royal Society for Asian Affairs; National Council for Social Studies; Historical Association. Address: Social Sciences Interdisciplinary Programme, State University of New York, NY 11794, USA.

SELBOURNE David, b. 1937. Writer; Playwright. Publications: The Play of William Cooper and Edmund Dew-Nevett, 1968; The Two-Backed Beast, 1969; Dorabella, 1970; Samson and Alison Mary fagan , 1971; The Damned, 1971; Class Play, 1973; Brook's Dream: The Politics of Theatre, 1974; What's Acting? And Think of a Story Quickly! 1977; An Eye To India, 1977; An Eye to China, 1978; Through the Indian Looking Glass, 1982; The Making of A Midsummer Night's Dream, 1983; Against Socialist Illusion: A Radical Argument, 1985; In Theory and In Practice: Essays on the Politics of Jayaprakash Narayan, 1986; Left Behind: Journeys into British Politics, 1987; A Doctor's Life: The Diaries of Hugh Selbourne MD 1960-63, 1989; Death of the Dark Hero: Eastern Europe 1987-90, 1990; The Spirit of the Age, 1993; Not an Englishman: Conversations With Lord Goodman, 1993; The Principle of Duty, 1994. Honour: Member, Academy of Savignano, Italy, 1994. Address: c/o Ed Victor, 162 Wardour Street, London W1, England.

SELBY Stephen, b. 5 Jun 1952, Darley Dale, Derbyshire, England. Playwright. m. Ann Spence, 6 Mar 1982, 1 d. Education: Social Science & Philosophy. Appointments: Writer, Director, Producer, Noc On Theatre, 1987-; Writer, Director, Producer, Hurdles of Time Theatre, 1991-. Publications: Better Looking Corpse; Contentious Work; Archie Pearson the One legged Shoemaker; Eviction; Cuts: Nottingham by the Sea; Hurdles of Time; Erewash Giants, 1993. Memberships: Theatre Writers Union. Literary Agent: Hurdles of Time. Address: 53 Percival Road, Sherwood, Nottingham NG5 2FA, England.

SELLMAN Roger Raymond, b. 24 Sept 1915, London, England. Schoolmaster; Lecturer; Devon County Inspector of Schools (retired). m. Minnie Coutts, 10 Aug 1938. Education: MA, Dip Ed Oxford University; PhD, Exeter University. Publications: Methuen's Outline Series: Castles and Fortresses, 1954; The Crusades, 1955; Roman Britain, 1956; English Churches, 1956; The Vikings, 1957; Elizabethan Seamen, 1957; Prehistoric Britain, 1958; Civil War and Commonwealth, 1958; The Anglo Saxons, 1959; Ancient Egypt, 1960; Norman England, 1960; Medieval English Warfare, 1960; The First World War, 1961; The Second World War, 1964; Garibaldi and the Unification of Italy, 1973; Bismarck and the Unification of Germany, 1973; The Prairies, 1974; Historical Atlases and Textbooks: Outline Atlas of Eastern History, 1954; Outline Atlas of World History, 1970; Modern World History, 1972; Students Atlas of Modern History, 1973; Modern British Economic and Social History, 1973; Historical Atlas for First Examinations, 1973; Modern European history, 1974; Local History: Illustrations of Dorset History, 1960; Illustrations of Devon History, 1962; Devon Village Schools in the Nineteenth Century, 1968; Aspects of Devon History, 1985. Contributions to: The Victorian Countryside, 1981; The Devon Historian ; Devon and Cornwall Notes and Queries. Address: Pound Down Corner, Whitestone, Exeter EX4 2HP, England.

SELTZER Joanne, b. 21 Nov 1929, Detroit, Michigan, USA. Poet; Writer. m. Stanley Seltzer, 10 Feb 1951, 1 son, 3 daughters. Education: BA, Univesity of Michigan; MA, College of Saint Rose. Publications: Adirondack Lake Poems, 1985; Suburban Landscape, 1988; Inside Invisible Walls, 1989. Contributions to: Blueline; Waterways; The Village Voice; Small Press Review; Minnesota Review; Studia Mystica; Glens Falls Review; Poetry Now; Primavera; Earth's Daughters; The Greenfield Review; Calliope. Honours: Winner, Fifth Annual All Nations Contest, 1978; Honourable Mention, Robert Browning Award, World Order of Narrative Poets, 1984; 1st Prize Tie, 2nd Place Tie, 2 Honourable Mentions, World Order of Narrative Poets Contest, 1986; Residency, Ragdale Foundation, 1988; World Order of Narrative Poets: 2 second place ties, 2 third place ties and 4 Honourable Mentions, 1988; Mishkenot Sha'Ananim (Jerusalem), 1989; Residency, Act I Creativity Center, 1990; New York State S.O.S. Grant, 1991. Memberships: The Poetry Society of America; Associated Writing Programs; International Womens's Writing Guild; American

Literary Translators Association. Address: 2481 McGovern Drive, Schenectady, New York 12309, USA.

SELVON Samuel Dickson, b. 20 May 1923, Trinidad. Canadian Citizen. Education: Naparima College, Trinidad, 1935-39. Appointments: Civil Servant, Trinidad High Commission, London, 1950-53; Full Time Writer, 1954. Publications: A Brighter Sun, 1952; An Island is a World, 1955; The Lonely Londers, 1956; Turn Again Tiger, 1958; I Hear Thunder, 1963; The Housing Lark, 1964; The Plains of Caroni, 1970; Those Who Eat the Cascadura, 1972; Moses Ascending, 1975; Moses Migrating, 1983; Eldorado West One, 1988; Story Collection, Ways of Sunlight, 1959; Radio Plays, Foreday Morning, Selected Prose, 1946-86, 1989. Honours: Guggenheim Fellowship, 1954; Trinidad Government Scholarship, 1962; D Litt, University of Warwick, 1989. Address: 4031 Charleswood Drive, NW Calgary, Alberta T2L 2EI, Canada.

SELZER Richard. m. Janet. Appointments: Former Professor of Surgery at Yale Medical School; Professor of Writing, Yale University; Writer of Essays and Short Stories. Contributions to: Vanity Fair; Harpess; Esquire. Honours: National Magazine Award; Pushcart Prize; American Medical Writers Award. Address: 6 St Ronan Terrace, New Haven, CT 06511, USA.

SEMMLER Clement William, b. 23 Dec 1914, Eastern Well, S.A. Broadcaster; Writer. m. (div) 1 son, 1 daughter. m. Catherine Helena Wilson, 20 Dec 1974, 1 d. Education: MA, Adelaide University, 1938; D Litt, University of New England, Armidale, 1968; Fellow, College of Fine Arts, University of NSW. Publications: The Banjo of the Bush, 1966; The ABC-Aunt Sally and the Sacred Cow, 1981; Twentieth Century Australian Literary Criticism (editor), 1967; Douglas Stewart, (critical study), 1974; The War Diaries of Kenneth Slessor, 1985; The War Dispatches of Kenneth Slessor, 1987; For the Uncanny Man, (essays), 1963; Literary Australia, (editor) 1965; Kenneth Slessor, 1966; The Art of Brian James, 1972; Barcroft Boake, 1965; A Frank Hardy Swag (editor), 1982; The War Diaries of Kenneth Slessor, 1985; The War Dispatches of Kenneth Slessor, 1987; Pictures on the Margin (memoirs), 1991; AB 'Banjo' Paterson: Bush Ballads, Poems, Stories and Journalism (editor). Contributions to: The Bulletin; Quadrant; Book Reviewer, The Australian; the Courier Mail. Honours: OBE, 1972; AM, 1988. Membership: Consulting Editor, Poetry Australia. Address: the Croft, St Clair Street, Bowral, NSW Australia 2576.

SEN Amarta Kumar, b. Bengal, India. m. (1) Deb Sen, (divorced) 2 children, (2) Eva (deceased) 2 children; (3) Martha Nussbaum (divorced). Contributions to: Numerous Professional Journals, Conference Proceedings and Volumes of Essays. Address: Dept of Philosophy, Harvard University, Emerson Hall, Cambridge, MA 02138-6598, USA.

SENGUPTA Preety, b. 17 May 1944, Ahmedabad, India. 'Traveller by Religion'. Writer; Poet. m. Chandan Sengupta, 21 June 1975. Education: Masters in English Literature. Appointments: Teacher English Literature, India 1968; Secretary of Tagore Society, New York, 1973-80. Publications: Poorva; Dikdigant; Khandit Aakash; Sooraj Sange Dakskin Panthe; Ghar Thi Door na Ghar; Antim Kshitijo; Dhaval Aalok, Dhaval Andhar; O Juliet; Joy of Travelling Alone; 'White Days, White Nights', 1993. Contributions to: Kumar; Nireekshak; Kavita; Kavilok; Janmabhoomi Pravasi; Gujarat Mitra; Pen India; Skylark; Indian Express; Hinduism Today, a monthly. Honours: Highest Literary Award in Gujarat; Six awards for various literary works; Vishwa-Gurjari Award, 1994. Memberships: Poetry Society of America; Pen of India. Address: 15 Stewart Place, White Plains, New York, 10603, USA.

SEPAMLA (Sydney) Sipho, b. 1932, Johannesburg, South Africa. Editor; Poet. Education: Studied as teacher. Appointments include: Editor, New Classic and S'ketsh magazines. Publications: Hurry Up To It, 1975; The Blues Is You In Me, 1976; The Soweto I Love, 1977; The Root Is One, 1979; Children of the Earth, 1983; Selected Poems, 1984; Novels: A Ride on the Whirlwind, 1981, and Third Generation, 1986. Address: c/o Skotaville Publishers, PO Box 32483, Braamfontein 2017, South Africa.

SEQUIERA Isaac J F, b. 5 Jan 1930, Hyderabad, India. University Professor. Education: BA, 1955; MA, 1958; PhD, 1970, Utah. Publications: The Theme of Initiation in Modern American Fiction, 1975; A Manifesto for Humour, 1985; Popular Culture: East and West, 1991; Studies in American Literature, 1991; Viewpoints USA, 1992.

Contributions to: Research journals in USA, Korea and India. Honours: Seaton Scholar, 1947; Fulbright Smith-Mundt, 1966; American Council of Learned Societies Fellow, 1979; UGC Council Lecturer, 1983, Professor Emeritus, 1991. Memberships: Modern Language Association, USA; Indian Association of American Studies; American Studies Association, USA; President: Poetry Society, 1975-80, Dramatic Circle, 1980-, Hyderabad. Address: Senior Academic Fellow, American Studies Research Centre, ASRC Hyderabad 500007, AP India.

SEROTE Mongane Wally, b. 8 May 1944, Johannesburg, South Africa. Cultural Attaché; Poet. Education: MFA, Columbia University, New York, 1979. Appointments include: Cultural Attaché for the ANC's Department of Arts and Culture, South Africa. Publications: Yakhal'imkomo, 1972; Tsetlo, 1974; No Baby Must Weep, 1975; Behold Mama, Flowers, 1978; The Night Keeps Winking, 1982; Selected Poems, 1982; A Tough Tale, 1987; Novel: To Every Birth Its Blood, 1981. Honours include: Fulbright Scholarship. Address: 28 Penton Road, PO Box 38, London N1 9PR, England.

SERVADIO Gaia Cecilia, b. 13 Sep 1938, Paduoa, Italy. Writer; Journalist. 2 s, 1 d. Education: St Martin's School of Art, London, England; National Diploma Graphic Art. Appointments: Associazone Italiana Lecturer, 1970; Manchester Museum Lecturer, 1982; Consultant Editor, Editore Italy, 1987; Director of Debates and Literary Talks, Accademia Italiana, 1988-89. Publications: Melinda, 1968; Don Juan/Salome, 1969; il Metodo, 1970; Mafioso, 1972; A Siberian Encounter, 1973; Luchino Visconti, a Biography, 1985; A Profile of a Mafia Boss: Insider Outsider, 1986; To a Different World: La donna nel Rinascimento; Il Lamento di Arianna, 1987; Una infanzia diversa, 1988; La Storia di R, 1990; La Vallata, 1991; Incontri, essays, 1993; The Real Traviata, 1994; La mia umbria, (editor), 1994. Contributions to: Arts Correspondent: Il Corriere della Sera. Honour: Cavaliere Ufficiale della Republica Italiana, 1980. Memberships: Society of Authors: Foreign Press Association, Vice President 1974-79; London Symphony Orchestra, Executive Committeee, 1980-87; Mahler Festival, 1982-83. Literary Agent: Artellus, 30 Donet House, Gloucester Place, London NW1 5AD, England. Address: 31 Bloomfield terrace, London SW1 W8PQ, England.

SERVICE Alastair Stanley Douglas, b. 8 May 1933. m. (1) Louisa Anne Hemming, 28 Feb 1959, div 1983, 1 s 1 d; (2) Zandria Madeleine Pauncefort, 21 Feb 1992. Education: Modern History, Queen's College, Oxford, 1953-55. Publications: Edwardian Architecture, 1977; Architects of London: 1066 to Today, 1979; Anglo-Saxon and Norman Buildings - A Guide, 1981; The Megaliths of Europe - A Guide, 1979; Lost Worlds, 1980; Edwardian Interiors, 1981; London 1900, 1978; A Birth Control Plan For Britain, 1972; Victorian/Edwardian Hampstead, 1990; Edwardian Architecture and its Origins, 1975; Standing Stones of Europe: The Great Neolithic Monuments, 1993. Contributions to: The Guardian; Architectural Review; New Statesman; Architects Journal; The Oldie. Memberships: Society of Architectural Historians of GB; The Victorian Society; Family Planning Association, National Chairman, 1975-80; Health Education Authority , Vice-Chairman, 1978-89; Wessex Region Health Authority, Chairman, 1993-; Wiltshire & Bath Health Commission, Chairman, 1992- 94. Address: Swan House, Avebury, Nr Marlborough, Wilts, SN8 1RA, England.

SETH Vikram, b. 20 June 1952, Calcutta, India. Poet; Novelist. Education: BA, 1975, MA, 1978, Corpus Christi College, Oxford; MA, Stanford University California, 1979; PhD, Economics, Stanford University, USA. Appointments include: Senior Editor, Stanford University Press, 1985-86; Several years in China, Research at the University of Nanking. Publications: Mappings (poetry), 1982; From Heaven Lake: Travels Through Sianking and Tibet (non-fiction), 1983; The Humble Administrator's Garden (poetry), 1985; All You Who Sleep Tonight (poetry translation); The Golden Gate (verse novel); 1986; A Suitable Boy, 1994; in progress: Arion and the Dolphin, (opera). Honours include: Guggenheim Fellowships; Commonwealth Poetry Prize, 1986; Winner, Thomas Cook Travel Book Award, 1983; Winner, Commonwealth Poetry Prize; Winner, 36th Annual W H Smith Literary Award, 1994. Address: c/o Anthony Sheil Associates, 42 Doughty Street, London WC1N 2LF, England.

SETTLE Mar y Lee. Honours: Literature Award, American Academy & Institute of Arts and Letters, 1994. Address: 544 Pembroke Avenue, Norfolk, VA, USA.

SEWART Alan, (Padder Nash), b. 26 Aug 1928, Bolton Lancashire, England. Writer. m. Dorothy Teresa Humphreys, 13 Oct 1962, 2 s, 1 d. Education: LLB, University of London. Publications include: Tough Tontine, 1978; A Ribbon for My Repute, 1978; The Salome Syndrome, 1979; The Women of Morning, 1980; In That Rich Earth. 1981; Smoker's Cough, 1982; Death Game - Five Players, 1982; If I Should Die, 1983; Dead Man Drifting, 1984; The Educating of Quinton Quinn, 1984. Non-fiction: Murder in Lancashire, 1988; Leisure Guides, Lancashire (with Dorothy Sewart), 1989. As Alan Sewart Well: Mr Crumblestone's Eden, 1980; Where Lionel Lies, 1984; Candice is Dead, 1984; As Padder Nash: Grass, 1983; Coup de Grass, 1983; Wayward Seeds of Grass, 1983; Grass and Supergrass, 1984: others in press. Contributions to: Police Review. Membership: Crime Writers Association. Address: 7 Knott Lane, Easingwold, York YO6 3LX, England.

SEWELL Elizabeth, b. 9 Mar 1919, Coonoor, India. Writer; Lecturer. Education: Cambridge University, BA, 1942, MA, 1945, PhD, 1949. Publications: The Orphic Voice; The Field of Nonsense; Paul Valéry: The Mind in the Mirror; An Idea; The Structure of Poetry; The Dividing of Time; The Singular Hope; Now Bless Thyself. Contributions to: USA, Canada, England, France, Austria, Netherlands. Honours: Honorary Degree, Various American Colleges & Universities; National Award; Zoe Kincaid Brockman Award. Memberships: PEN; Lewis Carroll Society of North America; North Carolina Writers Network. Literary Agent: Harold Ober Associates Inc, New York. Address: 854 West Bessemer Avenue, Greensboro, NC 27408, USA.

SEWELL Stephen, b. 1953, Sydney, New South Wales, Australia. Playwright. Education: BS, University of Sydney, 1975. Publications: The Father We Loved on a Beach by the Sea, 1976; Traitors, 1979; Welcome the Wright World, 1983; The Blind Giant is Dancing, 1983; Burn Victim (with others), 1983; Dreams in an Empty City, 1986; Hate, 1988; Miranda, 1989; Sisters, 1991; King Golgrutha, 1991; In the City of Grand-Daughters, 1993; Dust, 1993 (plays produced in Sydney, Adelaide, Brisbane, Melbourne and London). Honours include: New South Wales Premier's Award, 1985. Address: Hilary Linstead and Associates, Suite 302, Easts Towers, 9-13 Bronte Road, Bondi Junction, New South Wales 2022, Australia.

SEYERSTED Per, b. 18 May 1921, Oslo, Norway. University Professor. Education: MA, Harvard, USA, 1959; DPhil, Oslo, 1969. Appointments: Chair, American Literature, University of Oslo, 1973-1991; Member, Editorial Committee, Norway-America Association Yearbook, 1980-; Associate Editor, Studies in American Fiction, 1985-. Publications: Gilgamesj, 1967, 1979, 1988; Kate Chopin: A Critical Biography, 1969, 1980, 1990; The Complete Works of Kate Chopin (editor), 1969, 1981, 1993; A Kate Chopin Miscellany (editor), 1979; Leslie Marmon Silko, 1980; Scando-Americana: Papers on Scandinavian Emigration to the United States (editor), 1980; Dakky Kiaer (editor), 1980; From Norwegian Romantic to American Realist: Studies in the Life And Writings of Hjalmar Hjorth Boyesen, 1984; The Arctic: Canada and the Nordic Countries (editor), 1991. Contributions to: Some 40 articles to 25 journals, including, The Indian in Knickerbocker's New Amsterdam, in The Indian Historian, 1974. Honours: Fellow, American Council of Learned Societies, 1964-66; Fellow, Norwegian Research Council for Science and Letters, 1966-69. Memberships: Norsk faglitteraer forfatterforening; Modern Language Association; Elected Member, Norwegian Academy for Science and Letters, Chairman, Literature Section; Nordic Association for American Studies, President 1973-79; Nordic Association for Canadian Studies, Vice President, 1984-93. Address: Department of British and American Studies, University of Oslo, PB 1003 Blindern, 0315 Oslo, Norway.

SEYMOUR Alan, b. 6 June 1927, Perth, Western Australia, Australia. Playwright. Education: Perth Modern School. Appointments include: Former Actor, Theatre Critic and Journalist. Publications: Swamp Creatures, 1958; The One Day of the Year, 1960; The Gaiety of Nations, 1965; A Break in the Music, 1966; The Pope and the Pill, 1968; Oh Grave, Thy Victory, 1973; Structures, 1973; The Wind from the Plain, 1974; The Float, 1980 (plays produced in Australia, Adelaide, London, Glasgow, Europe and Japan); Radio and Television plays; Novels: The One Day of the Year, 1967, and The Coming Self-Destruction of the United States, 1969. Honours include: Australia Council for the Arts Grant. Address: 74 Upland Road, London SE22 0DB, England.

SHAABAN Bouthaina, b. 1 Apr 1953, Syria. University Professor. m. Khalil Jawad, 2 Sept 1981, 2 daughters. Education: BA,

English Literature, Damascus University, Syria, 1975; MA, English Literature, Warwick University, England, 1978; PhD, English Literature, Warwick University, England, 1982. Appointments: Lecturer, Constantine University, Algeria, 1982-84; Damascus University, Syria, 1985-90; Fullbright Professor,Duke University, USA, 1990-91; Associate Professor, Damascus University, Syria, 1991-. Publications: Both Right and Left-Handed Arab Women Talk About Their Lives, London, 1988, USA, 1991; Poetry and Politics; Shelly and the Chartist Movement, (Arabic), Dartalas, Damascus, 1993. Contributions to: Executive Editor, Foreign Literature Quarterly, Arab Writers Union; Keats-Shelly Journal; Al MawKif Al Adabi; Al Nashir al-Arabi. Honours: Fulbright, Duke University, 1990-91; Rockefeller, Rice University, 1992-93. Memberships: International PEN; Keats-Shelley Society; FIT, Arab Writers Union. Address: Arab Writers Union, Damascus, PO Box 3230, Syria.

SHADBOLT Maurice (Francis Richard), b. 4 June 1932, Auckland, New Zealand. Novelist. m. Bridget Armstrong, 1978. Education: University of Auckland. Appointments: Journalist, New Zealand, 1952-54; Documentry Screenwriter, Director, New Zealand Film Unit, 1954-57; Full Time Writer, 1957-. Publications: Among the Cinders, 1965; This Summer's Dolphin, 1969; An Ear of the Dragon, 1971; Danger Zone, 1975; The Lovelock Version, 1980; Season of the Jew, 1986; Monday's Warrior, 1990; Story Collections: The New Zealander: A Sequence of Stories, 1959; Summer Fires and Winter Country, 1963; The Presence of Music: Three Novellas; Figures in Light: Selected Stories; Play, Once on Chunk Bair, 1982; Guides and Histories of New Zealand. Honours: James Wattie Award, 1973, 1991; New Zealand Book Award, 1981; CBE, 1989. Address: Box 60028 Titirangi, Auckland 7, New Zealand.

SHAFFER Anthony (Joshua), b. 15 May 1926, Liverpool, England. Playwright. m. Diane Cilento, 1985. Education: Graduated Trinity College, Cambridge, 1950. Appointments include: Former Barrister and Journalist. Publications: The Savage Parade, 1963, revived 1987; Sleuth, 1970; Murderer, 1970; Widow's Weeds, 1977; Whodunnit, 1977; Screenplays for Mr Forbush and the Penguins, 1971; Frenzy, 1972; Sleuth, 1973; The Wicker Man, 1974; Masada, 1974; Death on the Nile, 1978; Absolution, 1979; Evil under the Sun, 1982; Appointment with Death, 1988; Sommersby, 1994; Novels: How Doth the Little Crocodile (with Peter Shaffer), 1952; Withered Murder (with Peter Shaffer), 1955; The Wicker Man, 1978; Absolution, 1979. Honours include: Tony Award, 1971; Six Edgars (Edgar Allan Poe Awards, given by the Mystery Writers of America); Grande Prix Filmes Fantastique Paris. Address: c/o Peters, Fraser and Dunlop Group, 503-504 The Chambers, Chelsea Harbour, Lots Road, London SW10 0XF, England.

SHAFFER Peter Levin, b. 15 May 1926, Liverpool, England. Playwright. Education: BA, Trinity College, Cambridge, 1947-50. Appointments: With Acquisition Department, New York Public Library, 1951-54; Boose & Hawkes, Music Publishers, 1954-55; Literary critic, Truth, 1956-57; Music Critic, Time and Tide, 1961-62. Publications: Plays: Five Finger Exercise, 1958; The Private Ear and the Public Eye, 1962; The Royal Hunt of the Sun, 1964; Black Comedy, 1965; White Lies, 1967; Shrivings, 1970; Equus, 1973; Amadeus, 1979; the Collected Plays of Peter Shaffer, 1982; Yonadab, 1985; Lettice and Lovage, 1987; Whom Do I Have the Honour of Addressing? radio play, 1990; The Gift of the Gorgon, 1992. Honours: Standard Drama Award, 1958, 1979; Antoinette Perry Award, 1975, 1981; New York Drama Critics Award, 1960, 1975; Academy Award (Oscar), 1984; CBE, 1987; Hambourg Shakespeare Prize, 1987; William Inge Award for Distinguished Contribution to American Theatre, 1992. Literary Agent: Rachel Daniels. Address: London Management, 2-4 Noel Street, London W1V 3RB, England.

SHAH Idries, b. 16 June 1924. Author. Appointments: Director, Institute for Cultural Research, 1966; Advisor, Harcourt Brace Jovanovitch Publishers, USA, 1975-79. Publications include: Oriental Magic, 1956; Destination Mecca, 1957; The Sufis, 1964; Exploits of the Incomparable Mulls Nasrudin, 1966; Tales of the Dervishes, 1967; Caravan of Dreams, 1968; The Book of the Book, 1969; The Dermis Probe, 1970; Ten Texts, 1971; the Magic Monastery, 1972; Subleties of the Inimitable Mull Nasrudin, 1973; The Elephant in the Dark, 1974; Neglected Aspects of Sufi Study, 1977; the Hundred Tales of Wisdom, 1978; World Tales, 1979; Letters and Lectures, 1981; Seeker After Truth, 1982; Kara Kush, 1986; Darkest England, 1987; The Natives Are Restless, 1988; The Commanding Self, 1994. Honours: 5 First Prizes, UNESCO World Book Year, 1972; Gold Medal, Distinguished Services to Poetry, 1973; Award for Outstanding Contributions to Human Thought, USA, 1975; Governor, Royal Hospital, 1980-. Memberships: Fellow, Institute of Directors, 1970; Fellow, Royal Society of the Arts, 1972; Member, The Athenaeum, 1973; Society of Authors; PEN; London Authors Club. Literary Agent: A P Watt Ltd; Jonathon Clowes Ltd. Address: PO Box 457, London NW2 4BR, England.

SHAH Tahir, b. 16 Nov 1966, London, England. Author. Education: BA, International Relations, US International University. Publications: Monographs: The Development and Collapse of Gond Society; Secret Societies of Serra Leone; Moriscos and the Demise of the Arab Empire in Spain; Private International Law; The Conflict of Law; Macumba; African-based Religions in South America; The Ainu; First People of Japan; The Kafirs of Kafiristan; The Celtic Druids; Journey Through Namibia, 1994; Spectrum Guide to Jordan, 1994. Contributions to: International Press; articles on travel, Middle Eastern society and culture, human thought. Memberships: Institute for Cultural Research, London; Institute for the Study of Human Knowledge, San Francisco; Association of Crypto-Zoology, Arizona; Wig & Pen Club, London. Address: PO Box 2227, London NW2 3BP, England.

SHAHEEN Jack G, b. 21 Sept 1935, Pittsburgh, Pennsylvania, USA. Professor; Journalist. m. Bernice Marie, 22 Jan 1966, 1 son, 1 daughter. Education: BFA, Carnegie Institute of Technology, 1957; MA, Pennsylvania State University 1964; PhD, University of Missouri, 1967. Appointments: Consultant, CBS News, 1993; Arts Critic, WSIE Radio, 1970-85. Publications: The TV Arab, 1984; Nuclear War Films, 1978. Contributions to: The Wall Street Journal, Newsweek; The Washington Post; The Los Angeles Time; Journal of Popular Film and Television; Journal of Popular Culture; The Television Quarterly. Honours: Outstanding Book of the Year, Choice Magazine, 1984; Scholar-Diplomat, Department of State, 1978; Fulbright Scholar, 1974, 1981. Literary Agent: James C G Conniff, Megadot. Address: 1526 Weber Lane, Edwardsville, IL, 62025, USA.

SHANE John. See: **DURST Paul.**

SHAPCOTT Thomas W(illiam), b. 21 Mar 1935, Ipswich, Queensland, Australia. Poet; Playwright. m. Judith Rodriquez, 1982. Education: BA, University of Queensland, Brisbane, 1968. Appointments include: Director, Austrlia Council Literature Board, 1983-90. Publications include: Time on Fire, 1961; Twelve Bagatellers, 1962; The Mankind Thing, 1964; A Taste of Salt Water, 1967; Inwards to the Sun, 1969; Begin with Walking, 1972; Shabbytown Calendar, 1975; Seventh Avenue Poems, 1976; Selected Poems, 1979; Turning Full Circle, 1979; Welcome, 1983; Travel Dice, 1987; Play, The Seven Deadly Sins, 1970; Novels, The Birthday Gift, 1982; White Stag of Exile, 1984; Hotel Bellevue, 1986; The Search for Galina, 1989; Editor of Australian Poetry; Poetry as a Creative Learning Process, 1978. Honours include: D Litt, Macquarie University, 1989; Office, Order of Australia, 1989. Address: 62 Cremome Road, Cremorne, NSW 2060, Australia.

SHAPIRO Harvey, b. 27 Jan 1924, Chicago, Illinois, USA. Poet; Journalist. m. Edna Kaufman, 23 July 1953, 2 sons. Education: BA, Yale University, 1947; MA, Columbia University, 1949. Publications: Poetry: The Eye, 1953; Mountain Fire, Thornbush, 1961; Battle Report, 1966; This World, 1971; Lauds & Nightsounds, 1978; The Light Holds, 1984; National Cold Storage Company: New Selected poems, 1988; A Day's Portion, 1994. Address: 43 Pierrepont Street, Brooklyn, NY 11201, USA.

SHARAT Chandra G S, (Jean Parker), b. 3 May 1938, India. Professor of English and Creative Writing. m. Jane Ronnermann, 1966, 1 son, 2 daughters. Education: AB, LLB, University of Mysore, India; MS, SUNY, NY; LLM, University of Toronto, Canada; MFA, University of Iowa, USA. Appointments: Editor: Kamadhenu, 1970-75; South Asian Review, 1989-; Consultant, Centre for Research in New Literature in English, Flinders University, Australia. Publications: Bharata natyam Dancer, 1968; April in Nanjangud, 1971; Once or Twice, 1974; The Ghost of Meaning, 1978; Heirloom, 1982; Family of Mirrors, 1993; Immigrants of Loss, 1993. Contributions to: London Magazine; Strand; Encounter; Outposts; New Welsh Review; New York Quarterly; Poetry Australia; Paris Review; New Criterion, International Quarterly. Honours: NEH Fellow, 1981; Florida State Poetry Award, 1980; Distinguished Visiting Professor, Poetry/Fiction, Purdue University, 1985, University of Hawaii. 1987. Memberships: Modern Language Association; Associated Writing Programme; South Asian Language Association. Address: Department of English, University of

Missouri, Kansas City, MO 64110, USA. Residence: 9916, Juniper, Overland Park, Kansas 66207, USA.

SHARMA Sita Sharan, b. 26 Mar 1931, Samhu, Begusarai, India. Sarvodaya Worker. m. Sharada, 26 Feb 1970, 1 s. Education: Studied under Bhoodan Movement Leader Acharya Vinoba Bhave. Publications: Acharya Sri Tulasi Jaise Maine samajha; Ram Kathaki Parmapara Main Agni Pariksha; Bihar Ki Jhanki; Trilochan Kavita; Shakti Pooja; Perak Kathaye; Manas Marmonk; Karnatka Ki Jhanki. Contributions to: Hindi articles in many weeklies and souvenirs. Honours: Lai Bahadur Sastrys Award: Anuvrat Pravartak Award. memberships include: Authors Guild of India; Poet International Organisation; Daxina Bhareth Hindi Prachara sabha; Bharativa Sanskriti Vidya Pitj; State Sarvodaya Mandala. Address: 19 Vallabha Niketa, Kumara Park East, Bangalore 560001, India.

SHARMA Vera, b. 10 Feb 1926, Bombay, India. writer; Housewife. M. 10 Mar 1949, 1 daughter. Publications: Random Thoughts; The Unrepentent and Other Stories; The Early Bird & Other One Act Plays; The Hermaphrodite & Other Indian Poems; The Blind Musician; Naina & Other Indian Stories; The Chameleon and Six Other Radio Plays; An Unusual Indian Girlhood, 1994. Contributions to: Illustrated Weekly of India; PEN Journal; Debonair; MAFIL; Kunnapipi. Honours: Prizes, National Newspaper Competitions; Free Press Journal; Bharat Jyoti; Deccan Herald. Memberships: PEN Bombay; Asiatic Society of Bombay. Address: 106, 6th Road, Tilaknagar, Goregaon W, Bombay, India.

SHARP Ronald Alan, b. 19 Oct 1945, Cleveland, Ohio, USA. Professor of English. m. Inese Brutans, 22 June 1968. 2 sons. Education: BA, Kalamazoo College, 1967; MA, University of Michigan, 1968; PhD, Univeristy of Virginia, 1974. Appointments include: John Crowe Ransom Professor of English, Kenyon College, 1985-; Founding Co-editor, Kenyon Review, 1978-82. Publications: Keats, Skepticism and the Religion of Beauty, 1979; Friendship and Literature: Spirit and Form, 1986; The Norton Book of Friendship, 1991; Reading George Steiner, 1994; Three Short Plays of Federico Garcia Lorca, 1979. Contributions to: New Literary History, American Literature, Modern Philology, Kenyon Review, Keats-Shelly Journal. Honours: Fellow: English Speaking Union, National Humanities Center, National Endowment for Humanities, American Council of Learned Societies; Director, Keats Bicentennial Conference at Harvard University. Memberships: Modern Language Association of America; Keats-Shelly Association of America; Wordsworth-Coleridge Assocation; North American Society for the Study of Romanticism; Ohio College English Group. Literary Agent; Timothy Seldes at Russell & Volkening. Address: Department of English, Kenyon College, Gambier, OH 43022, USA.

SHARPE Thomas (Tom) Ridley, b. 30 Mar 1928, London, England. Author. m. Nancy Anne Looper, 6 Aug 1969. 3 d. Education: Lancing College, 1942-46; Pembroke College, Cambridge, 1948-52. Publications: Riotous Assembly, 1971; Indecnt Exposure, 1973; Porterhouse Blue, 1974; Blott on the Landscape, 1975; Wilt, 1976; The Great Pursuit, 1977; The Throwback, 1978; The Wilt Alternative, 1979; Ancestral Vices, 1980; Vintage Stuff, 1982; Wilt on High, 1984. Contributions to: Numerous magazines and journals. Honours: Laureat Le Grand Prix De L'Humour Noir, Paris, 1986; Le Legion de l'Humour, Aphia, Paris, 1986. Membership: The Society of Authors. Literary Agent: Richard Scott Simon. Address: 38 Tunwells Lane, Great Shelford, Cambridge CB2 5LT, England.

SHAVELSON Melville, b. 1 April 1917, New York City, USA. Writer; Director. m. Lucille T Myers, 2 Nov 1938, 1 son, 1 daughter. Education: AB, Cornell University, 1937. Appointments: Writer, Bob Hope Pepsodent Show, NBC Radio, 1934-43. Publications: Screenplays Including: The Princess and the Pirate, 1944; Wonder Man, 1944; Room for One More, 1951; I'll See You in My Dreams, 1952; Writer, Director: The Seven Little Foys, 1954; Beau James, 1956; Houseboat, 1957; The Five Pennies, 1958; It Started in Naples, 1959; On the Double, 1960; Yours, Mine and Ours, 1968; The War Between Men and Women, 1972; The Legend of Valentino, 1975; Deceptions, 1985; Writer, Director, Producer: The Pigeon That Took Rome, 1962; A New Kind of Love, 1963; Cast a Giant Shadow, 1966; Mixed Company, 1974; The Great Houdinis, 1976; Ike, 1979; Author, Broadway Musical: Jimmy, 1969; Books: How to Make a Jewish Movie, 1970; Lualda, 1975; The Great Houdinis, 1976; The Eleventh Commandment, 1977; Ike, 1979; Don't Shoot It's Only Me, 1990. Honours include: President, Writers Guild of America, West, 1969-71,

1979-81, 1985-87; Academy Award Screenplay Nominations, 1955, 1958; Screenwriters Guild Award, 1959; Christopher Award, 1959; Screenwriters Award Nominations, 1952, 1958, 1959, 1962, 1968, 1972, 1975; Screen Writers Award, Best Written American Musical, 1959; Award of Merit, United Jewish Appeal, 1966; Writers Guild Laurel Award; Writers Guild Valentine Davies Award. Address: 11947 Sunshine Terrace, Studio City, CA 91604, USA.

SHAW Brian. See: **TUBB E(dwin) C(harles).**

SHAW Bynum (Gillette), b. 10 July 1923, Alamance County, North Carolina, USA. Professor of Journalism. m. (1) Louise N Brantley (dec), 30 Aug 1948, (2) Emily P Crandall (dec), 19 June 1982, (3) Charlotte E Reeder, 26 Nov 1986, 2 daughters. Education: BA, Wake Forest College, 1951. Pubications: The Sound of Small Hammers, 1962; The Nazi Hunter, 1968; Divided We Stand, The Baptists in American Life, 1974; Days of Power, Nights of Fear, 1980; W W Holden: A Political Biography (with Edgar E Folk), 1982; The History of Wake Forest College, Vol IV, 1988; Oh, Promised Landl, 1992. Contributions to: Esquire; New Republic; Moneysworth; New York Times; The Baltimore Sun. Honours: Sir Walter Raleigh Award in Fiction, 1969. Memberships: North Carolina Writers Conference, Chairman, 1972. Address: 2700 Speas Road, Winston-Salem, NC 27106, USA.

SHAW Irene. See: **ROBERTS Irene.**

SHEARER Jill, b. 14 Apr 1936, Melbourne, Victoria, Australia. Playwright. Appointments include: Secretary in Brisbane, 1966-79. Publications: The Trouble with Gillian, 1974; The Foreman, 1976; The Boat, 1977; The Kite, 1977; Nocturne, 1977; Catherine, 1978; Stephen, 1980; Release Lavinia Stannard, 1980; A Woman Like That, 1986; Shimada, 1987; Comrade, 1987; The Family, 1994; (plays produced in Brisbane, Melbourne and New York). Honours include: Australia Council Grant, 1987; Arts Queensland Fellowship, 1993. Address: c/o Playlab Press, PO Box 185, Ashgrove, Brisbane 4060, Queensland, Australia.

SHEEHAN Neil. m. Susan Sheehan. Appointments: Journalist, (obtained the Pentapon Papers, 1971, leading to Pulitzer Prize for New York Times). Honours: National Book Award, 1988; Pulitzer Prize, 1988. Address: c/o The New Yorker, 25 W 43rd Street, New York, NY 10036, USA.

SHEEHY Gail, b. 27 November 1937, Mamaroneck, New York, USA. m. (1) Albert Sheehy, 20 August 1960, (divorced), 1 daughter, (2) Clay Felker, 1985, 1 adopted daughter. Education: BS, University of Vermont; Columbia University. Appointments: Journalist; Editor; Writer. Contributions to: Cosmopolitan; McCall's; Glamour; Good Housekeeping; Paris Match. Memberships: Authors' Guild; Authors' League of America; PEN American Center (advisory Board); Common Cause; National Organization for Women; Newswoman's Club of New York. Honours: Front Page Award, Newswoman's Club of America, 1964, 1973; National Magazine Award, 1972; Anisfield-Wolf Book Award, 1986. Address: c/o Wm Morrow Publishing Pblcty Dt, 4th Floor, 1350 Ave of The Americas, NY 10019, USA.

SHELBOURNE Cecily. See: **EBEL Suzanne.**

SHELBY Graham. Writer. Publications: The Knights of Dark Renown, 1969; The Kings of Vain Intent, 1970; The Villains of the Piece, 1972; The Devil is Loose, 1973; The Wolf at the Door, 1975; The Cannaways, 1978; The Cannaway Concern, 1980; The Edge of the Blade, 1986; Demand the World, 1990. Literary Agent: A P Watt Ltd, 20 John Street, London WC1N 2DR, England.

SHELDON John. See: **BLOCH Robert.**

SHELDON Lee. See: **LEE Wayne C.**

SHELDON Roy. See: **TUBB E(dwin) C(harles).**

SHELTON Mark Logan, b. 19 May 1958, Chicago, Illinois, USA. Writer. m. Eve Shelnutt, 29 May 1982. Education: AB, Western Michigan University, 1980; MFA, University of Pittsburgh, 1982. Publications: Working in a Very Small Place, 1989, 1990, 1991; The Next Great Thing: The Sun, The Stirling Engine and The Drive to Change The World, 1994. Contributions to: Ohio, Pittsburgh, Milwaukee Journals, Columbus Dispatch, Library Journal. Honours: Best Sports

Stories, Sport News; A Dozen Sigma Delta Chi Awards. Memberships: Judge, Ohioana Library Association Book Awards, 1990-. Literary Agent: Tim Seldes, Russell and Volkening, 50W 29th St, NY 10001, USA. Address: 25 Andover Street, Worcester, MA 01606, USA.

SHELTON Richard, b. 1933. Poet. Address: English Department, University of Arizona, Ticson, AZ 85721, USA.

SHEPARD Sam. See: **ROGERS Samuel Shepard.**

SHEPHERD Michael. See: **LUDLUM Robert.**

SHEPHERD Robert James, b. 14 Feb 1949, Solihull, Warwickshire, England. Author; Journalist; TV Producer; Director. Education: Tudor Grange GS, Solihull, 1960-67; University of Kent, BA, MA, 1968-72. Appointments: Leader and Features Writer, Investors Chronicle, 1983; Editorial Team, Producer, A Week in Politics, 1983-88; Parliamentary Lobby Correspondent, 1984-87; Producer: documentaries, Democracy in Danger, All the Presidency Men, 1992; What Has Become of Us, 1994. Publications: Public Opinion and European Integration, 1975; A Class Divided, 1988; Ireland's Fate, 1990; The Power Brokers, 1991; Iain Macleod, 1994. Contributions to: Political Quarterly; New Statesman; Investors Chronicle; Marxism Today; Guardian; The Times; The Irish Independent; The Sunday Press; Ireland of the Welcomes. Honour: Prix Stendhal (television), 1993. Memberships: Society of Authors; International PEN; National Union of Journalists; BECTU. Literary Agent: Michael Shaw, Curtis Brown, 162-8 Regent Street, London, W1R 5TB, England.

SHEPPARD David (Rt Rev), b. 6 Mar 1929, Reigate, Surrey, England. Bishop. m. Grace Isaac, 19 June 1957, 1 d. Education: MA, Trinity Hall, Cambridge. Publications: Parson's Pitch, 1964; Built as a City, 1974; Bias to the Poor, 1983; Better Together (with Archbishop Derek Worlock), 1988; with Christ in the Wilderness (with Archbishop Derek Worlock), 1990; With Hope in Our Hearts (with Archbishop Derek Worlock), 1994; Contributions to: Woman's Own columnist, 1957-74; Occaisonal contributor to various other publications, Honours: Honorary LLD, Liverpool University, 1981; Honorary DTech, Liverpool Polytechnic, 1987; Hon DD, Cambridge University; Freeman of the City of Liverpool. Memberships: Chairman Church of England Board for Social Resposibility, 1991. Address: Bishop's Lodge, Woolton Park, Liverpool L25 6DT, England.

SHER Steven Jay, b. 28 Sep 1949, USA. Writer. m. Nancy Green, 11 Mar 1978, 1 s, 1 d. Education: BA, CCNY, 1970; MA, University of Iowa, 1972; MFA, Brooklyn College, 1978. Appointments: Director, Creative Writing, Spalding University, 1979-81; Oregon State University, 1981-86; University of North Carolina, Wilmington, 1986-89; Visiting Writer, Willamette University, 1993; Western Oregon State College, 1991-95. Publications: Nickelodeon, 1978; Persnickety, 1979; Caught in The Revolving Door, 1980; Trolley Lives, 1985; Man With A Thousand Eyes and Other Stories, 1989; Traveler's Advisory, 1994; Northwest Variety: Personal Essays by 14 Regional Authors, (co-editor) 1987. Contributions to: The Anthology of Magazine Verse and Yearbook of American Poetry, 1980, 1981, 1986-87; Blood to Remember: American Poets on The Holocaust, 1991; On The Threshold of A Dream, 1992. Honours: All Nations Poetry Contest, 1977; Weymouth Centre Residency, 1988; North Carolina Writers Network, Writers and Readers Series Competition, 1989; Oregon Book Awards Finalist (poetry), 1994. Memberships: Academy of American Poets; AWP; Poetry Society of America; Poets and Writers; President, Willamette Literary Guild. Address: 3930 NW Witham Hill Dr C 26, Corvallis, OR 97330, USA.

SHERATON Mimi, b. 10 Feb 1926, Brooklyn, NY, USA. Food Critic. m. (1) William Sheraton, 20 Aug 1945, (div 1954), (2) Richard Falcone, 30 Jul 1955, 1 s. Education: BS, New York University, 1947. Appointments include: Managing Editor of Supplemental Division, House Beautiful, New York City, 1954-56; Freelance Writer, 1956-69; Food Critic, New York Magazine, 1967-75; Food Critic, New York Times, 1975-83; Food Critic, Time, New York City, 1984; Food Editor, Condé Nast Traveler, 1987-91; Contributing Editor, New Woman, 1994-, Harper's Bazaar, 1993-1995; Publisher of newsletter, Mimi Sheraton's Taste, 1987-1990. Publications: Visions of Sugar Plums, 1968; From My Mother's Kitchen, 1979 & 1991; Mimi Sheraton's New York Times Guide to New Restaurants, 1983; (with Alan King) Is Salami and Eggs Better Than Sex?, 1985; Mimi Sheraton's Favorite New York Restaurants, 1986, 1989; The Seducer's Cookbook, 1962; City Portraits, 1963; The German Cookbook, 1965; The Whole World

Loves Chicken Soup, 1995. Contributions to: Magazines including: Town and Country; Vogue; Vanity Fair. Honours: Penney Missouri Award from School of Journalism at University of Missouri, Columbia, 1974; Front Page Award, Newswomen's Club of New York, 1977. Literary Agent: Owen Laster, William Morris Agency, 1350 Avenue of The Americas, New York, NY 10019, USA.

SHERMAN Eileen Bluestone, b. 15 May 1951, Atlantic City, USA. Author; Playwright; Lyricist; Instructor; Lecturer. m. Neal Jonathan Sherman, 10 Jun 1973, 1 s, 1 d. Education: BA, Theatre Arts, English, Finch College, NY, 1973; MA, Theatre Arts, State University of New York, Albany, 1976. Publications: The Odd Potato, 1984; Monday in Odessa, 1986; Independence Avenue, 1990; Musical plays produced: Me, Myself and I; The Odd Potato; Rotten Apples; The Sabbath Pedlar; Independence Avenue; Rockwell, 1992; Dramatic play produced: Monday In Odessa; Scriptwiter: The Magic Door, Television series, 1987-1990. Honours: Outstanding Social Studies Trade Book, Monday In Odessa, 1986; Children's Book Council; National Jewish Book Award, Childrens Literature, 1986; Emmy Award, Best Children's Special, Nothing is Simple, (co-writer), 1988; Emmy Award, Best Children's Special, The Odd Potato, 1989; The Teacher's Choice Award, Independence Avenue, 1991. Memberships: Authors Guild Inc; Society of Childrens Book Writers; National League of American Pen Women; The Dramatists Guild. Address: 10720 Horton, Overland Park, KS 66211, USA.

SHERRIN Edward George (Ned), b. 18 Feb 1931, Lowham, Somerset, England. Director; Producer; Presenter; Writer. Education: MA, Oxford University; Barrister-at-Law. Publications: Cindy-Ella (with Caryl Brahms), 1962; Rappel (with C B), 1964; Benbow Was His Name (with C B), 1967; Ooh La La (with C B), 1973; After You Mr Feydeau (with C B), 1975; A Small Thing Like an Earthquake, 1983; Song by Song (with C B), 1984; Cutting Edge, 1984; 1956 and All That (with Neil Shand) 1984; The Metropolitan Mikado (with Alistair Beaton) 1985; Too Dirty for the Windmill (with C B), 1986; Loose Ends, 1990; Theatrical Anecdotes, 1991; Ned Sherrin in his Anecdotage, 1993. Literary Agent: Rivers Scott. Address: c/o Scott-Ferris, 15 Gledhooa Gardens, PO Box 317, London, SW5 0AY, England.

SHERRY (Michael) Norman, b. 6 July 1935, Tirana, Albania. Writer; Professor of Literature. Education: BA, English Literature, University of Durham, England; PhD, University of Singapore, 1963. Career: Lecturer in English Literature, University of Singapore, 1961-66; Lecturer, Senior Lecturer, University of Liverpool, England, 1966-70; Professor of English, University of Lancaster, 1970-82; Fellow, Humanities Research Center, North Carolina, USA, 1982; Mitchell Distinguished Professor of Literature, Trinity University, San Antonio, Texas, 1983-. Publications: Conrad's Eastern World, 1966; Jane Austen, 1966; Charlotte and Emily Brontë, 1969; Conrad's Western World, 1971; Conrad and His World, 1972; Conrad: The Critical Heritage, 1973; Conrad in Conference, 1976; The Life of Graham Greene, Vol 1 1904-39, 1989, Vol 2 1939-55, 1994; Editor: An Outpost of Progress and Heart of Darkness, 1973; Lord Jim, 1974; Nostromo, 1974; The Secret Agent, 1974; The Nigger of Narcissus, Typhoon, Falk and Other Stories, 1975; Joseph Conrad: a commemoration, 1976. Contributions to: The Academic American Encyclopedia; Guardian; Daily Telegraph; Oxford Magazine; Modern Language Review; Review of English Studies; Notes and Queries; BBC; Times Literary Supplement; Observer. Honours: Fellow, Royal Society of Literature, 1986; Edgar Allan Poe Award, 1989; Guggenheim Fellowship, 1989-90. Memberships: Savile. Literary Agent: Graham Carleton Greene. Address: Trinity University, 715 Stadium Dr, San Antonio, TX 78212, USA.

SHERWIN Byron Lee, b. 18 Feb 1946, NY, USA. m. 24 Dec 1972, 1 s. Education: BS, Columbia University, 1966; MA, New York University, 1969; BHL, MHL, Rabbinic Ordination Jewish Theological Seminary of America, 1966, 1970; PhD, University of Chicago, 1978. Publications: Mystical Theology and Social Dissent. 1982; In Partnership With God, 1990; No Religion is An Island, 1991; Toward a Jewish Theology, 1992; Judaism, 1978; Encountering The Holocaust, 1979; Abraham Joshua Heschel, 1979; Golem Legend, 1985; How To Be A Jew: Ethical Teachings of Judaism, 1992. Contributions to: More than 100 articles and monographs in English, Hebrew and Polish journals. Memberships: Founding President, Midwest Jewish Studies Association. Honour: Man of Reconciliation, Polish Council of Christians and Jews, 1992. Address: 618 S Michigan Avenue, Chicago, IL 60605, USA.

SHIELDS Carol A, b. 2 Jun 1935, USA. Writer; Teacher. m. Donald Shields, 20 Jul 1957, 1 s, 4 d. Education: BA, Hanover College, 1957; MA, University of Ottawa, 1975. Publications: The Republic of Love; Swann; Various Miracles; The Orange Fish; Small Ceremonies; The Box Garden; Happenstance; A Fairly Conventional Woman; Others; Intersect; Comins to Canada; Departures and Arrivals; Thirteen Hands; The Stone Diaries, 1993. Honours: Canadian Authors Award; Arthur Ellis Award; Marion Engel Award; Nominee, Booker Prize, 1993; Governor General's Award, 1993; Manitoba Book of The Year, 1994. Memberships: The Writers Union of Canada; PEN. Literary Agent: Bella Pomer. Address: 701-237 Wellington Crescent, Winnipeg Man, Canada, R3M 0A1.

SHIPLER David K, b. 1942. m. Debby Shipler, 2 sons, 1 daughter. Appointments: Journalist, New York Times; Foreign Correspondent, Saigon, Moscow, Jerusalem. Contributions to: New Yorker; New York Times. Honours: Pulitzer Prize, 1987; George Polle Award, 1982; Overseas Press Club Award. Address: c/o Ramdom House, 201 E 50th Street, 12th Floor Reception, NY 10022, USA.

SHIPMAN David, b. 4 Nov 1932, Norwich, England. Writer. Education: Merton College, Oxford. Publications include: Great Movie Stars: Golden Years, 1970, revised, updated, 1979, 1989; Great Movies Stars: International Years, 1972, revised, updated, 1980, 1989; Brando, monograph, 1974, full-length biography retitled Marlon Brando, 1989; Story of Cinema, 2 volumes, UK 1982, 1984, 1 volume US 1984; Good Film & Video Guide, 1984, revised and expanded, 1986; Pictorial History of Science Fiction Films, 1985; Caught in the Act: Sex & Eroticism in the Cinema, 1985; Movie Talk: Who Said What About Whom in the Movies, 1989; The Great Movie Stars: The Independent Years, 1991; Judy Garland, 1992; Cinema: The First Hundred Years, 1993; Contributions to: Films & Filming; Radio Times; Independent; Contemporary Review. Membership: British Film Institute, Consultant, 1989. Literary Agent: Frances Kelly. Address: c/o The Frances Kelly Agency, 111 Clifton-Upon-Thames, Surrey KY2 6PL, England.

SHOR Ira Neil, b. 2 Jun 1945. Professor of English. Education: BA, 1966, MA, 1968, University of Michigan; PhD, 1971, University of Wisconsin. Publications: Culture Wars: School and Society in The Conservative Restoration, 1969-91, 1992; A Pedagogy for Liberation, 1986; Freire for The Classroom, 1987; Critical Teaching and Everyday Life, 1987; Empowering Education, 1992. Contributions to: Harvard Education Review, College English, Journal of Education. Honours: Fellowships, 1966, 1982, 1983; Chancellor's Scholar, City University of NY, 1985. Address: English Doctoral Programme, City University of New York, 33 West 42nd Street, New York, NY 10036, USA.

SHORT Brian Michael, b. 27 Feb 1944, Canterbury, Kent, England. University Senior Lecturer. m. (1) 2 s, (2) Valerie, 17 Dec 1979, 1 s. Education: North Western Polytechnic, 1963-73. Publications: The South East From AD100; The English Rural Community. Contributions to: Many, including: Agricultural History Review; Journal of Peasant Studies; Sussex Archaeological Collections. Honour: Fellow, Royal Society of Arts. Memberships: Institute of British Geographers; Agricultural History Society; Sussex Archaeological Society. Address: CCS, Arts B, University of Sussex, Falmer, Brighton, BN1 9QN, England.

SHRAPNEL Norman, b. 5 Oct 1912, Grimsby, England. Journalist; Critic. Publications: A View of the Thames, 1977; The Performers; Politics as Theatre, 1978; The Seventies; Britain's Inward March, 1980. Contributions to: The Guardian; Times Literary Supplement; National Geographical Society Publications. Honours: Recipient, Pol Writer of the Year, 1969. Address: 27A Shooters Hill Rd, Blackheath, London SE3, England.

SHREEVE James Marion, b. 26 Feb 1951, Ohio, USA. Writer. m. Christine Kuethe, 8 Jun 1985, 1 daughter, 1 stepson, 1 stepdaughter. Education: BA, Brown University, 1973; MFA, University of Iowa, 1979. Publications: The Sex Token, 1976; Nature: The Other Earthlings, 1987; Lucy's Child, (co-author) 1989. Contributions to: Discover; MD; Science, Science Illustrated. Literary Agent: Victoria Pryor, Arcadia Ltd. Address: 10549 St Paul Street, Kensington, MD 20895, USA.

SHRIMSLEY Bernard, b. 1931, United Kingdom. Newspaper Editor. m. Norma Jessie Alexandra Porter, 1952, 1 d. Appointments: Assisstant Editor, Daily Mirror, London, 1964-68; Editor, Liverpool Daily Post, 1968-69; Deputy Editor, 1969-72, Editor, 1972-75, The Sun,

London; Editor, The News of the World, London, 1975-80; Editor-designate/Editor, The Mail on Sunday, London, 1980-82; Assoiate Editor, Daily Express, London, 1983-; British Press Awards judge, 1989-95; Vice Chairman, British Press Council, 1989-90. Publications: The Candidates, 1968; Lion Rampant, 1984. Membership: Society of Authors. Literary Agent: John Farquharson Ltd, England. Address: Daily Express: Ludgate House, 245 Blackfriars Road, London SE1 9UX, England.

SHUBIN Seymour, b. 14 Sep 1921, Philadelphia, USA. Author. m. Gloria Amet, 27 Aug 1957, 1 s, 1 d. Education: BA, Temple University. Appointments: Managing Editor: Official Detective Stories Magazine; Psychiatric Reporter. Publications: Anyone's My Name, 1953; Manta, 1958; Wellville, USA, 1961; The Captain, 1982; Holy Secrets, 1984; Voices, 1985; Never Quite Dead, 1989; Remember Me Always, 1994. Contributions to: Saturday Evening Post; Reader's Digest; Redbook; Family Circle; Story; Ellery Queen's Mystery Magazine; Emergency Medicine; Official Detective Stories Magazine; Perspective in Biology and Medicine. Honours: Edgar Allan Poe, Special Award; Special Citation for Fiction, Athenaeum of Philadelphia; Certificate of Honor, Temple University. Memberships: American Society of Authors and Journalists; Authors Guild; Mystery Writers of America; PEN, American Center. Address: 122 Harrogate Road, Wynnewood, PA 19096, USA.

SHUKMAN Harold, b. 23 Mar 1931. University Teacher of Modern Russian History. m. (1) Ann King Farlow 1956, (div 1970), 2 s, 1 d, (2)Barbara King Farlow. Education: BA Hons, Nottingham, 1956; DPhil, 1961; MA, 1961, Oxford. Publications: Lenin and the Russian Revolution, 1977; Blackwells Encyclopedia of the Russian Revolution, 1988; Andrei Gromyko Memories, (editor and translator), 1989; Children of the Arbat, (translator), 1988; Heavy Sand, (translator), 1981; Triumph and Tragedy: Stalin (editor & translator), 1991, Stalin's Generals (editor); Lenin: His Life and Legacy (editor & translator). Contributions to: Commentary; TLS; THES; Independent; Times; English Historical Review; Economist; Soviet (East European) Jewish affairs. Memberships: Authors Society; Translators Association; Royal Historical Society, Fellow. Address: St Antony's College, Oxford OX2 6JF, England.

SHUMSKY Zena. See: COLLIER Zena.

SHUPE Anson (David Jr), b. 21 Jan 1948, Buffalo, NY, USA. Sociology Professor. m. Janet Ann Klickua, 27 Jun 1970, 1 s, 1 d. Education: BA, College of Wooster, Ohio, 1970; MA, 1972, PhD, 1975, Indiana University. Publications: Moonies in America, 1979; The New Vigilantes, 1980; Strange Gods, 1981; The Family Secret, 1983; The Mormon Corporate Empire, 1985; The Darker Side of Virtue, 1991; Co-editor, The Politics of Religion and Social Change; Secularization and Fundamentalism Reconsidered; The Violent Couple, 1994. Contributions to: The Wall Street Journal; GEO; The Christian Century; Religious Broadcasting; Fort Worth Star Telegram; Dallas Morning News; Fort Wayne Journal; Gazette. Memberships: American Sociological Association; Association for The Sociology of Religion; Society for The Scientific Study of Religion; Religious Research Association. Literary Agent: Jeffrey H Herman, The Jeff Herman Agency, 500 Greenwich Street, Suite 5016, NY 10013, USA. Address: Sociology and Anthropology Department, Indiana Purdue University, Fort Wayne, IN 46805, USA.

SHUSTERMAN Richard Mark, b. 3 Dec 1949. Philosopher. m. Rivka Nahmani, 16 Aug 1970, 2 s, 1 d. Education: BA, Hebrew University, 1971; MA, 1973, PhD, 1979, St Johns College, Oxford University. Publications: Pragmatist Aesthetics; The Interpretive Turn; Analytic Aesthetics; T S Eliot and The Philosophy of Criticism; The Object of Literary Criticism; L'Art à L'état Vif, 1992; Kunst Leben, 1994. Contributions to: British Journal of Aesthetic; New Literary History; Poetics Today; Philosophical Quarterly; Critique; Journal of Aesthetics; Political Theory. Honours: NEH Fellowship. Memberships: American Philosophical Association; British Society of Aesthetics; American Society for Aesthetics. Address: 1810 Hemlock Circle, Abington, PA 19001, USA.

SHUTTLE Penelope Diane, b. 12 May 1947, Staines, Middlesex, England. Writer. m. Peter Redgrove, 16 Sept 1980, 1 d. Publications: Novels: An Excusable Vengeance, 1967; All the Usual Hours of Sleeping, 1969; Wailing Monkey Embracing A Tree, 1974; Rainsplitter in the Zodiac Garden, 1976; The Mirror of the Giant, 1979; The Terrors of Dr Treviles (with Peter Redgrove), 1974; The Glass Cottage, 1976;

poetry: The Orchard Upstairs, 1980; The Child-Stealer, 1983; The Lion From Rio, 1986; Adventures With My Horse, 1988; The Hermaphrodite Album (with Peter Redgrove), 1973; Taxing the Rain, 1992; psychology and sociology: The Wise Wound: Menstruation and Everywoman (with Peter Redgrove) 1978, updated 1986, 1989, 1990, reissued 1994; Alchemy For Women (with Peter Redgrove): sequel to the Wisewound; Rider 1995. Numerous pamphlet collections, broadsheets, radio dramas, recordings, readings and television features. Contributions to: Times Literary Supplement; Encounter; Outposts; The Aylesford Review; The Poetry Review; Pequod; Poetry Book Society Xmas Supplements, 1978, 1980, 1981; Poetry Australia; Poetry Southwest; Poetry Chicago; The Literary Review; The Manhatten Review; Stand; Poetry Book Society Anthology 1987/88. Honours: Joint 3rd prize, Radio Times Drama Bursaries Competition, 1974; 3 Arts Council Awards, 1969, 1972, 1985; Greenwood Poetry Prize, 1972; E C Gregory Award, 1974. Address: c/o David Higham Ass Ltd, 5-8 Lower John Street, London W1R 4HA, England.

SIATOPOULOS Dimitrios, b. 1 Apr 1917, Athens, Greece. Attorney-at-Law; Journalist; Writer. m. 27 Dec 1947, 1 son, 1 daughter. Education: Law degree, Athens University, 1944; Science of Political Economics degree, Athens University. Career: Regular speaker at universities, literature clubs, conferences, 1950-. Publications: 35 books including: Melody of Wings, 1954; Theatre in Greece during the Revolution of 1821, 1971; Biography of Painter El Greco, 1978; Iliades of Omeros, translation from ancient original language to modern Greek, 1991; Biography of Greek Poets Kavafis and Palamas, 1993. Contributions to: Numerous Greek magazines and newspapers including main dailies, 1945-. Honours: National Prize for Young Writers, 1954; 1st Prize, Academy of Athens, 1971; 1st National Prize for Literature, 1978. Memberships: President, Greek Section, International Association of Literature Critics; Numerous Literature Committes. Address: 20 Omirou Str, 106 72 Athens, Greece.

SIDDONS Anne Rivers, b. 9 Jan 1936, GA, USA. Novelist. m. Heyward L Siddons, 11 June 1966, 4 s. Education: BA, Auburn University, 1958. Publications include: John Chancellor Makes Me Cry, 1975; Heartbreak Hotel, 1976; The House Next Door, 1978; Homeplace, 1986; Peachtree Road, 1988; King's Oak, 1990; Outer Banks, 1991; Colony, 1992; Hill Towns, 1993; Downtown, 1994. Contributions to: Articles & Essays in Various Am Magazines. Honours: GA Author of the Year, 1988; Honor Doctor of Letters, 1992. Memberships: Authors Guild; International Womans Forum; Woodward Academy. Literary Agent: Virginia Barber Literary Agency, 101 5th Avenue, New York, NY 10003, USA. Address: 3767 Vermont Road NE, Atlanta, GA 30319-1208, USA.

SIDWHA Napsi, b. Karachi, Pakistan. m. 3 children. Education: Kinnaird College for Women, Lahore, Pakistan. Appointments: Former Professor; Writer; Social Worker among Asian Women. Honours: Sitara-i-Imtiaz, Pakistan, 1991; Liberater Prize, Germany. Address: 17119 Beaver Spring Drive, Houston, TX 77090, USA.

SIEPMANN Mary Aline, (Mary Wesley), b. 24 June 1912. Writer. m. (1) 2nd Baron Swinfen, 1937 (diss 1945), 2 s, (2) Eric Siepmann, 1952 (d 1970), 1 s. Education: LSE. Publications: Speaking Terms (for children), 1968; The Sixth Seal (for children), 1968; Haphazard House (for children), 1983; Jumping the Queue, 1983; The Camomile Lawn, 1984; Hamessing Peacocks, 1985; The Vacillations of Poppy Carew, 1986; Not That Sort of Girl, 1987; Second Fiddle, 1988; A Sensible Life, 1990; A Dubious Legacy, 1992; An Imaginative Experience, 1994. Honours: Hon Degree, Open University; Hon Degree, Exeter University; Hon Fellow, London School of Economics; CBE, 1995. Membership: PEN. Literary Agent: Rachel Calher, Tessa Sayle Agency, 11 Jubilee Place, London SW3 3TE. Address: c/o Transworld Publishers Ltd, London W5 5SA, England.

SIGAL Clancy, b. 6 Sept 1926, Chicago, USA. Education: BA, 1950, University of California, Los Angeles. Publications: Weekend in Diplock, 1960; Going Away, A Report, A Memoir, 1963; Zone of the Interior, 1976. Address: c/o Jonathon Cape, 30 Bedford Square, London WC1B 3EL, England.

SIGGINS Maggie, b. Toronto, Ontario, Canada. Appointments: Former Magazine Writer; Political Columnist; Television Producer; Journalism Professor; Writer. Publications: Basset: A Biography, 1979; Brian and the Boys: A Story of Gang Rape, 1984; A Canadian Tragedy: JoAnn and Colin Thatcher, 1985; Revenge of the Land, 1991. Honours: Southam Fellowship, 1974-75; Max Bell Chair in Journalism, 1983-84;

Arthur Ellis Award, Crime Writers of Canada,1986; Governor General's Award for Non-Fiction, for "Revenge of the Land", 1992. Address: 2831 Retailack Street, Regina, Saskatchewan, S4S 1S8, Canada.

SILKIN Jon, b. 2 Dec 1930, London, England. Poet; Critic; Editor. m. Loma Tracy, 3 s (1 dec), 1 d. Education: Degree in English, 1962. Literary Appointments: Journalist, 1947; Visiting Poet, University of Iowa, 1968, 1991; Distinguished Writer-in-Residence, The American University, 1989; University of Tsukuba, 1991-; Publications include: The Peaceable Kingdom, 1954, 1975; The Two Freedoms, 1958; The Re-ordering of the Stones, 1961; Nature with Man, 1965; Poems New and Selected, 1966; Amana Grass, 1971; Out of Battle: Criticism of Poets of World War I, 1972, 1987; Poetry of the Committed Individual: anthology of poetry from Stand, 1973; The Principle of Water, 1974; The Little Time-Keeper, 1976; Editor, The Penguin Book of First World War Poetry, 1979; The Psalms With Their Spoils, 1980; Selected Poems, 1980, enlarged edition, 1988; Gurney, a play in verse, 1985; Editor, The War Poems of Wilfred Owen, 1985, 1990; Editor with Jon Glover, the Penguin Book of First World War Prose, 1989; The Ship's Pasture (Poems), 1986; The First Twenty-four Years, Contemporary Authors Biography Series, Volume 5, 1987; Natan Zach, Against Parting, translation, 1967; The Lens- Breakers, 1992; Selected Poems, 1994; The War Poems of Wilfred Owen (editor), 1994. Honours: Geoffrey Faber Memorial Prize for Nature with Man, 1966; Awarded Gregory Fellowship in Poetry, University of Leeds, 1958; Visiting Poet, Mishkenot Sha'ananim, Jerusalem, 1980; Bingham Poet, University of Louisville, USA, 1981; Elliston Poet, University of Cinncinnati, 1983; Visiting Poet, yearly festival, University of Notre Dame, 1985; Fellow, Royal Society of Literature; Visiting Poet, Writer's Conference, University of North Alabama, 1987. Memberships: Royal Society of Literature, Literary Fellow, Dumfries & Galloway Arts Association. Literary Agent: Laurence Pollinger. Address: 13 Queens Terrace, Newcastle upon Tyne NE2 2PJ, England.

SILLIMAN Ron, b. 8 May 1946, WA, USA. Writer. m. Krishna Evans, 4 June 1986, 2 sons. Education: Merritt College, 1965-66, 1969; San Fransisco State University, 1966-69; University of CA, 1970-71. Literary Appointments: Lectures, SF State University, 1981; Visiting Lecturer, UC San Diego, 1982; Writer in Residence, New College, 1982; Poet in Residence, CA Institute of Integral Studies, 1984-90. Publications: Ketjak, 1978; Tjanting, 1981; In The American Tree, 1986; The New Sentence, 1987; What, 1988; Toner; Demo to Ink; Leningrad; The Age of Huts. Honours: NEA Fellowship, 1979; Poetry Center Book Award, 1985. Memberships: National Writers Union; Modern Language Association. Address: 1819 Curtis Street, Berkeley, CA 94207 1617, USA.

SILLITOE Alan, b. 4 Mar 1928, Nottingham, England. Author. Publications: Saturday Night and Sunday Morning, 1958; The Loneliness of the Long Distance Runner, 1959; The General, 1960; Key to the Door, 1961; The Ragman's Daughter, 1963; Roads to Volgagrad, 1964; A Falling Out of Love, Poems, 1964; The Death of William Posters, 1965; A Tree on Fire, 1967; The City Adventures of Marmalade Jim, (for children) 1967; Love in the Environs of Voronezh (poems), 1968; Guzman, Go Home, 1968; All Citizens are Soldiers, (play, with Ruth Fainlight,) 1969; A Start in Life, 1970; Travels in Hihilon, 1971; Raw material, 1972; Men, Women and Children, 1973; The Flame of Life, 1974; Mountains and Caverns, Selected Essays, 1975; The Widower's Son, 1976; Big John and the Stars (for children), 1977; Three Plays, 1978; Snow on the Side of Lucifer, 1979; The Storyteller, 1979; Marmalade Jim at the Farm (for children), 1980; The Second Chance, 1981; Her Victory, 1982; The Saxon Shore Way, with Fay Godwin, 1983; The Lost Flying Boat, 1983; Sun Before Departure, poems, 1984; Down From the Hill, 1984; Marmalade, Jim and the Fox (for children), 1985; Life Goes On, 1985; Tides and Stone Walls, poems, 1986; Nottinghamshire, with D Sillitoe, 1987; Out of the Whirlpool, 1987; The Open Door, 1988; Last Loves, 1990; Leonard's War, 1991. Address: c/o The Savage Club, 9 Fitzmaurice Place, London SW1, England.

SILLS Leslie Elka, b. 26 Jan 1948, Brooklyn, NY, USA. Artist; Author; Lecturer. m. Robert J Oresick, 9 Jul 1978, 1 s. Education: BA, Psychology, Boston University, 1969; MA, School of The Museum of Fine Arts, Boston, 1970-73. Publications: Inspirations: Pilgrims and Pioneers: New England Women in The Arts, 1987; Stories About Women Artists, 1989; Visions: Stories About Women Artists, 1993. Contributions to: School Arts Magazine; Sojourner. Honours: Notable Book Award, American Library Association, 1989, 1994; Booklist: Editor's Choice - Best Books of 1989 and 1993; Best 10 Books for

Children, Parenting Magazine, 1989; Recommended List, Biographies for Children, 1991; New York City Public Library Recommended List, 1989, 1993; Pick of The Lists - American Bookseller, 1989, 1993; School Library Journal, Best Books, 1993. Memberships: New England Authors and Illustrators of Children's Books; National Women's Caucus for Art, Boston, Co-Chair, 1984-85. Literary Agent: Marie Brown, Marie Brown Associates, New York City, NY, USA. Address: 38 St Paul Street, Brookline, MA 02146, USA.

SILLS-DOCHERTY Jonathon John (John Docherty), b. 7 Jan 1941, Bowden, Cheshire, England. Humorous Writer; Lyricist; Poet. Education: Fielden Park College, West Didsbury, Manchester, 1977; Poetry Workshop, 1981, Extramural Department, 1986-87, University of Manchester. Appointments include: Editor, Guardian Society, 1974; Reporter, Dun & Bradstreet, 1975; Proof Reader, sub-editor, biography compiler, Odd Fellow Magazine. Publications include: A Walk Around the City & Other Groans, 1969, revised 1973; Words on Paper, 1977; from Bottoms to Tops & Back Again, 1977, limited edition, 1987; Ballads of Ecstasy & Perspicacity, 1987; Ballads of North West John (plus cassette tape), 1987; tribute ballads to Nigel Mansell and Eddie 'The Eagle' Edwards, and other lyrics. Contributions to: News/Views House Journal, Mappin & Webb; Sunday Times; Sunday Telegraph; Manchester Evening News; Stretford & Urmston Journal; Daily Mail; Star; Artful Reporter; What's On in Hulme; Dun & Bradstreet Report Magazine; Radio Manchester; Letters to, dancer on: The Hitman & Her, and Juice, Granada TV, Manchester. Honours: North West Arts Poetry Award, 1978; Double prizewinner, Tribute for St George's Day, Granada TV, 1978; Various Other prizes, awards, including most prolific letter writer to Manchester Evening News. Memberships include: Turner Society; Court School of Dancing; Independent Order of Odd Fellows; Friend, North West Arts, Manchester City Art Gallery; Authors North; Subscriber, Manchester Academy of Fine Arts. Address: 5 Farm Avenue, Stretford, Manchester M32 9TW, England.

SILMAN Roberta, b. 29 Dec 1934, NY, USA. Writer. m. Robert Silman, 14 Jun 1956. Education: BA, English Literature, Cornell University, 1956; MFA, Writing, Sarah Lawrence College, 1975. Publications: Somebody Else's Child, 1976; Blood Relations, 1977; Boundaries, 1979, UK 1980; The Dream Dredger, 1986; Beginning The World Again, 1990. Contributions to: Numerous magazines in USA and UK including: Atlantic Monthly; New Yorker; McCall's; Redbook; Family Circle; Hadassah. Honours: Child Study Association Award, Best Children's Book, 1976; Honourable Mention, Hemingway Award, 1978; Janet Kafka Prize, 1978, 1980; Guggenheim Fellowship, 1979; NEA, Fellowship, 1983; National Magazine Award, Fiction, 1984; PEN Syndicated Fiction Project Award, 1983, 1984. Memberships: PEN; Authors Guild; Poets and Writers; Phi Beta Kappa. Literary Agent: Philippa Brophy, Sterling Lord Literistic. Address: 18 Larchmont Street, Ardsley, NY 10502, USA.

SILVER Eric, b. 1935. Honours: Christopher Award, 1993. Address: c/o Grove Atlantic Inc, 841 Broadway, NY 10003-4793, USA.

SILVER Richard. See: BULMER Henry Kenneth.

SILVERMAN Kenneth, b. 5 February 1936, New York, USA. University Professor. m. Sharon Medjuck, 8 September 1957 (divorced), 1 son, 1 daughter. Education: BA, MA, PhD, Columbia University. Appointments: Institute of Early American History & Culture, Executive Council; Early American Literature, Editorial Board, 1971-73, 1977-80; William & Mary Quarterly, Editorial Board, 1985-. Memberships: Modern Language Association of America; PEN; American Antiquarian Society; Society of American Historians. Address: Dept of English, New York University, 19 University Place, NY 10003, USA.

SILVERMAN-WEINREICH Beatrice. See:WEINREICH Beatrice.

SILVIS Randall Glenn, b. 15 Jul 1950, Rimersburg, PA, USA. Novelist; Playwright. m. Rita Lynne McCanna, 25 Sep 1982, 2 s. Education: BS, Clarion University, 1973; MEd, Indiana University, 1976. Literary Appointments: James Thurber Writer In Residence, Thurber House, Columbus, 1989; Mercyhurst College, PA, 1989-90; Ohio State University, 1991,1992. Publications: The Luckiest Man In The World; Excelsior; An Occasional Hell; Under The Rainbow; Driven To Acts Of Kindness. Contributions to: Prism International; Manoa; Destination Discovery; Pittsburgh Magazine. Honours: National Endowment For The Arts Fellowship; Drue Heinz Literature Prize; National Playwright Showcase Award; Fulbright Senior Scholar

Research Grant; James Thurber Writer In Residence. Address: PO Box 297, St Petersburg, PA 16054, USA.

SIMIC Charles, b. 1938, Belgrade, Yugoslavia. Education: New York University. Appointments: Professor, University of New Hampshire. Honours: Pulitzer Prize, 1990; Edgar Allen Poe Award; PEN Translation Prize; Awards from American Academy of Arts & Letters, Poetry Society of America. Address: Box 192, Strafford,NH 03884, USA.

SIMIONESCU Mircea Horia, b. 23 Jan 1928, Tirgoviste, Romania. Writer. m. Teodora Dinca, 26 Feb 1953, 2 d. Education: BA, Literature, Bucharest University, 1964. Publications: The Well Tempered Ingenious Man, 4 volumes, 1969, 1970, 1980, 1983; After 1900, About Noon, 1974; Ganymede's Kidnapping, 1975; Endless Dangers, 1978; Advice For the Dauphin, 1979; Ulysse and the Shadow, 1982; The Banquet, 1982; The Cutaway, 1984; Sale By Auction, 1985; Three Looking Glasses, 1987; The Siege of the Common Place, 1988; The Angel with the Apron, 1992. Contributions to: various magazines and journals, Radio & TV programmes in Romania; PEN Club. Honours: Prize, for prose, Writers Union of Romania, 1974. Memberships: Writers Union of Romania; Journalists Union of Romania. Address: 3 Belgrad Str, Bucharest, CD 71248, Romania.

SIMKIN Tom, b. 11 Nov 1933, Auburn, NY, USA. Geologist. m. Sharon Russell, 3 Jul 1965, 1 s, 1 d. Education: BS, Swarthmore College, 1955; MSE, 1960, PhD, 1965, Princeton University. Publications: Volcanoes Of The World, 1981, (second edition) 1994; Krakatau 1883; The Volcanic Eruption And Its Effects, 1983; Global Volcanism, 1975-85, 1989; Volcano Letter, 1987; Paricutin: The Volcano Born In A Mexican Cornfield, 1993. Contributions to: Various scientific journals. Honours: Choice Outstanding Academic Book Award, 1984. Memberships: Editor, International Association Of Volcanology; Catalog And Active Volcanoes; President, 1990, Geological Society Of Washington; Secretary For Americas, 1970-90, Charles Darwin Foundation For Galapagos Isles; 1972-, American Geophysical Union. Address: Smithsonian Institution, National Museum Of National History MS119, Washington, DC 20560, USA.

SIMMERMAN Jim, b. 5 Mar 1952, Denver, CO, USA. English Professor; Poet. Education: BS, Education, University of Missouri, 1973; MA, English, University of Missouri, 1976; MFA, Creative Writing, University of Iowa 1980. Literary Appointments include: Member, Literary Panel, 1984, 1986; Literary Grants Panel, 1987; Arizona Commision On The Arts; Editorial Board, Pushcart Prize Series, 1985-. Publications: Home, 1983; Bad Weather, 1987; Once Out of Nature, 1989; Yoyo, 1994; Moon Go Away, I Don't Love You No More, 1994; Numerous Poems. Contributions to: Literary journals and anthologies (poetry) including: Antaeus; Bread Loaf Anthology of Contemporary American Poetry; Anthology of Magazine Verse; Missouri Review; Western Humanities Review. Honours: Poetry Fellowships, 1983, 1987 Arizona Commission On The Arts; Creative Writing Fellowship Grant, National Endowment For The Arts, 1984; Poetry Fellowship, Fine Arts Work Centre, 1984; Pushcart Writers Choice Selection, 1984; Pushcart Prize, 1985. Memberships: Associated Writing Programs; Board of Directors (1992-95) and Secretary (1994-95), Associated Writing Programs. Address: c/o English Department, Box 6032, Northern Arizona University, Flagstaff, AZ 86011, USA.

SIMMONS Michael, b. 17 Oct 1935, England. Journalist. m. Angela Thomson, 20 Apr 1963, 2 s. Education: BA, Hons, Manchester, 1960. Appointments: Political correspondent, Glasgow Herald, 1964-67; East Europe Correspondent, Financial Times, 1968-72; Third World Editor, 1978-81, East Europe Editor, 1983-89, diplomatic correspondent, 1980-92, Community Affairs, 1993, Guardian. Publications: Berlin: Dispossessed City, 1988; The Unloved Country: Portrait of East Germany, 1989; Reluctant President: A Political Life of Vaclav Havel, 1991; Voices from the South, 1983, (co-editor). Contributions to: Various magazines newspapers and journals. Memberships: Society of Authors; Trinity Cricket Club. Literary Agent: Tessa Sayle, London SW3 3TE, England. Address: The Guardian, London, EC1 3ER, England.

SIMMS Suzanne. See: GUNTUM Suzanne Simmons.

SIMON Barney, b. 13 Apr 1933, Johannesburg, South Africa. Playwright. Education: Studied in Johannesburg. Appointments include: Co-founder and Director, The Market Theatre, Johannesburg, 1978. Publications: Phiri, 1972; Hey Listen, 1973; People, and People Too,

1973; Joburg Sis, 1974; Storytime, 1975; Medea, after Grillparzer, 1978; Cincinatti, 1979; Call me Woman, 1980; Cold Stone Jug, 1980; Marico Moonshine and Manpower, 1981; Woza Albert, 1981; Black Dogonj Mayama, 1984; Born in the RSA, 1985; Outers, 1985; Written by Hand, 1987; Score Me with Ages, 1989; Eden and Other Places, 1989; Inyanga- About Women in Africa, 1989; Singing the Times, 1992 (all plays created in collaboration with participants); Television plays. Honours include: Edinburgh Festival Fringe Awards, 1982, 1987; Los Angeles Critics Award, 1982; Rockefeller Grants. Address: c/o The Market Theatre, PO Box 8656, Johannesburg 2000, South Africa.

SIMON Claude, b. 10 Oct 1913, Madagascar. Writer. Education: College Stanislas, Paris. Publications: Le tricheur, 1945; La corde raide, 1947; Gulliver, 1952; Le sacre de printemps, 1954; Le vent, 1957; L'herbe, 1958; La route des Flandres, 1960; Le palace, 1962; Histoire, 1967; La bataille de Pharsale, 1969; Orion aveugle, 1970; Les corps conducteurs, 1971; Tryptyque, 1973; Lecon de choses, 1975; Les Georgiques, 1981; Le chevelure de Bérénice, 1984; Discours de Stockholm, 1986; L'invitation, 1987; L'acacia, 1989; The Georgies, 1989. Honours: Prix de l'Express for La Route des Flandres, 1960; Prix Medicis for Histoire, 1967; Doctor (honoris causa), University of Bologna, 1989; Grand Croix Ordre National du Mérite, 1990. Address: Editions de Minuit, 7 rue Bernard-Palissey, 75006 Paris, France.

SIMON Herbert Alexander, b. 1956. Honours: Nobel Prize in Economics, 1978. Address: Dept of Psychology, Carnegie Mellon University, Pittsburgh, PA 15213, USA.

SIMON Robert. See: MUSTO Barry.

SIMON Sheldon Weiss, b. 31 Jan 1937, USA. Professor Of International Politics. m. Charlann Scheid, 23 Apr 1962, 1 s. Education: BA, University Of Minnesota, 1958; MA, Princeton University, 1960; PhD, University Of Minnesota, 1964. Appointments include: Director, Center For Asian Studies, ASU, 1980-88; Visiting Professor, University Of British Columbia, 1972-73, 1979-80; Visiting Professor, Carleton University, 1976; Visiting Professor, Montrey Institute Of International Studies, 1991; Visiting Professor, American Graduate School Of International Management, 1991-92. Publications: East Asian Security In The Post-Cold War Era,1993; The Future Of Asian-Pacific Security Collaboration, 1988; The Ajean States And Regional Security, 1982; The Military And Security In The Third World, 1976; War And Politics In Cambodia, 1974; Asian Neutralism And US Policy, 1975; The Broken Triangle; Peking, Djakarta And The PKI, 1969. Research papers in Asian Survey, Pacific Affairs, Problems Of Communism, Third World Quarterly, Journal Of International Affairs, Journal Of Northeast Asian Studies, Australian Outlook, New Zealand International Review, Indochina Issues; The Australian Journal of International Affairs; The Pacific Review. Address: Department of Political Science, Arizona State University, Tempe, AZ 85287-2601, USA.

SIMON Werner, b. 5 Jun 1914, Bremen, Germany. Psychiatrist. m. Elizabeth Strawn, 24 Apr 1939. Education: Medical School, University Of Frankfurt, Germany, 1932-36; MD Degree, University Of Bern, Switzerland,1937. Appointments: Chief Of Psychiatry, Veterans Administration Medical Center, Minneapolis, 1948-71; Consultant, Hennepin County Medical Center, Minneapolis, 1971-; Emeritus Professor Of Psychiatry, University Of Minnesota Medical School. Publications include: Differential Treatment And Prognosis In Schizophrenia, 1959; Suicide Among Physicians, 1989; The Veterans Administration Center Develops in Minnesota Psychiatry Evolves-Bernstein, 1989; Chapters in several books, over 55 papers in professional journals. Memberships: Minnesota Psychiatric Society, President 1967-69; American Psychiatric Association, Life Fellow; American College Of Physicians, Fellow; International Association For Suicide Prevention; Minnesota Society Of Neurological Sciences. Address: 8915 River Ridge Road, Minneapolis, MN 55425, USA.

SIMONS Beverley, b. 31 Mar 1938, Flin Flon, Manitoba, Canada. Playwright. Education: McGill University; BA, University of British Columbia at Vancouver, 1959. Publications: Twisted Roots, 1956; The Birth, 1957; A Play, 1957; The Elephant and the Jewish Question, 1968; Crabdance, 1969; Green Lawn Rest Home, 1973; Preparing, 1973; Prologue, Triangle and the Crusader, 1976; If I Turn Around Quick, 1976; Leela Means to Play; Television Play, The Canary, 1968. Honours include: Canada Council grant and award.

SIMPSON Alan, b. 27 Nov 1929. Author; Scrptwriter. m. Kathleen Phillips, 1958, (dec 1978). Publications: Author, scriptwriter (with Ray

Galton), 1951-; TV: Hancock's Half Hour, 1954-61; Comedy Playhouse, 1962-63; Steptoe and Son, 1962-74 (translated into Dutch, Scandinavian and USA); Galton-Simpson Comedy, 1969; Clochemerle, 1971; Casanova '74, 1974; Dawson's Weekly, 1975; The Galton and Simpson Playhouse, 1976-77; The Lost Steptoes, 1994; Films: The Rebel, 1960; The Bargee, 1961; The Wrong Arm of the Law, 1963; The Spy With the Cold Nose, 1966; Loot, 1969; Steptoe and Son, 1971; Den Siste Fleksnes, 1974; Skraphandlarne, 1975; Theatre: Way Out in Picadilly, 1966; The Wind in the Sassafras Trees, 1968; Albert och Herbert, 1981; Fleksnes, 1983; Mordet pa Skolgatan 15, 1984; Books: Hancock, 1961; Steptoe and Son, 1963; The Reunion and Other Plays, 1966; Hancock Scripts, 1974; The Best of Hancock, 1986. Honours: Scriptwriters of the Year, Guild of TV Producers and Directors, 1959; Best Comedy TV Series, Steptoe and Son, 1962, 1962, 1963, 1964, 1965, Screenwriters Guild; John Logie Baird Award, 1964; Best Comedy series, Dutch TV, 1966; Best Comedy Screenplay, Scriptwriters Guild, 1972. Address: c/o Tessa Le Bars Management, 54 Birchwood Road, Petts Wood, Kent BR5 1NZ, England.

SIMPSON Dorothy (née Preece), b. 1933, United Kingdom. Author. Appointments: Teacher of English and French: Dartford Grammer School for Girls, Kent, 1955-59; Erith Grammer School, Kent, 1959-61; Teacher of English, Seacre School, Maidstone, Kent, 1961-62. Publications: Harbinger of Fear, 1977; The Night She Died, 1981; Six Feet Under, 1982; Puppet for a Corpse, 1983; Close Her Eyes, 1984; Last Seen Alive, 1985; Dead on Arrival, 1986; Element of Doubt, 1987; Suspicious Death, 1988; Dead by Morning, 1989; Doomed to Die, 1991; Wake the Dead, 1992; No Laughing Matter, 1993. Honour: Siver Dagger Award for Last Seen Alive, 1985. Literary Agent: Curtis Brown, England. Address: c/o Peter Robinson, Curtis Brown, 4th Floor, Haymarket House, 28/29 Haymarket, London SW1Y 4SP, England.

SIMPSON Elizabeth Robson, b. 16 Oct 1910, Sydney, New South Wales, Australia. Zoologist; Painter; Writer. m. Alfred Moxon Simpson, 3 Aug 1938, 1 son. Education: BSc, 1931, 1st Class Honours, 1933, MSc, 1935, University of Adelaide, South Australia. Publications: The Hahndorf Walkers and the Beaumont Connection, 1983; The Clelands of Beaumont, 1986; Beaumont House, the Land and its People, 1993. Contributions: 10 papers on larval trematodes, in Transactions of Royal Society of South Australia. Honours: John Bagot Scholarship and Medal, University of Adelaide, 1929; Fellow, Royal South Australian Society of Arts; Award, Genealogical Society of South Australia, 1987. Memberships include: Queen Adelaide Club; Lyceum Club of South Australia Inc; Tatlers; Fellow, Royal Society of South Australia, 1938-46. Literary Agent: Ms Carol Cheshire. Address: Beaumont Press, 2nd Floor, 135 Waymouth St, Adelaide, South Australia 5000, Australia.

SIMPSON John Cody Fidler, b. 9 Aug 1944, Cleveleys, England. Television Journalist. m. Diane Jean Petteys, 14 Aug 1965, (separated), 2 d. Education: MA, Magdalene College, Cambridge, 1963-66. Literary Appointments: Editor, Granta, 1965; Trainee, sub-editor, producer, reporter, BBC Radio News, 1966-72; BBC correspondent, Dublin 1972, Brussels 1975, Johannesburg 1977; Political editor, 1980; Diplomatic editor, BBC TV & Radio, 1988-; Contributing Editor, The Spectator, 1990-. Publications: The Best of Granta, 1967; Moscow Requiem, novel, 1981; A Fine & Private Place, novel, 1983; The Disappeared, 1985; Behind Iranian Lines, 1988; Despatches from the Barricades, 1990; From the House of War: Baghdad and the Gulf, 1991; The Darkness Crumbles: the Death of Communism, 1992; In the Forests of the Night: Encounters with Terrorists, Drugs-Runners and the Opressors in Peru, 1993. Contributions to: Articles, reviews: The Listener, Harper's; Granta; The Spectator. Honour: CBE, 1991. Membership: Athenaeum; Chelsea Arts Club. Literary Agent: Jacintha Alexander Associates. Address: c/o BBC Television News, Television Centre, Wood Lane, London W12, England.

SIMPSON Louis Aston Marantz, b. 27 Mar 1923, Jamaica, West Indies. Writer; Teacher. m. (1) Jeanne Rogers, 1949, (div 1954) 1 s, (2) Dorothy Roochvarg, 1955, (div 1979) 1 s, (3) Miriam Bachner (née Butensky), 1985. Education: Columbia University, NY. Appointments: Editor, Bobbs-Merrill Publishing Company, NY, 1950-55; Instructor, Assistant Professor, Columbia University, 1955-59; Professor, University Of California, Berkeley, 1959-67; Professor, State University Of New York, Stony Brook, 1967-93. Publications: Poetry: The Arrivistes: Poems 1940-49, 1949; Good News Of Death And Other Poems, 1955; The New Poets Of England And America, Editor, 1957;

A Dream Of Governors, 1959; At The End Of The Open Road, 1963; Selected Poems, 1965; Adventures Of The Letter I, 1971; Searching For The Ox, 1976; Caviare At The Funeral, 1980; People Live Here: Selected Poems, 1949-83; The Best Hour Of The Night, 1983; Collected Poems, 1988; In The Room We Share, 1990. Prose: James Hogg: A Critical Study, 1962; Riverside Drive, 1962; An Introduction To Poetry, Editor, 1967; North Of Jamaica, 1971; Three On The Tower: The Lives And Works Of Ezra Pound, T S Eliot and William Carlos Williams, 1975; A Revolution In Taste, 1978; A Company Of Poets, 1981; The Character Of The Poet, 1986; Selected Prose, 1989; Ships Going into the Blue, 1994; The King My Father's Wreck, 1995 . Address: 186 Old Field Road, Setauket, NY 11733, USA.

SIMPSON Matt(hew William), b. 13 May 1936, Lancs, England. Lecturer: Writer. m. Monika Ingrid Weydert, 13 Dec 1962, 1 s, 1 d. Education: Cambridge University, 1955-58; Liverpool University, 1958-59. Appointments: Literature Panel of Merseyside Arts Association, 1970-75; Chairman, Executors of the Widows Project, 1980-; Poet-in-Residence, Tasmanian Poetry Festival, 1994. Publications: An Elegy for the Galosherman, 1990; Making Arrangements, 1982; The Pig's Thermal Underwear, 1992, 1993; To Tasmania with Mrs Meredith, 1994; Catching Up with History, 1995. Contributions to: Major UK journals and magazines; reviews, criticisms, poetry for children, in a number of anthologies. Memberships: Poetry Society of Great Britain. Address: 29 Boundary Drive, Liverpool L25 0QB, England.

SIMPSON N(orman) F(rederick), b. 1919, United Kingdom. Author. Appointments: Teacher, City of Westminster College, London, and Extramural Lecturer, 1946-62; Literary Manager, Royal Court Theatre, London, 1976-78, Publications: The Hole, 1958; One Way Pendulum, 1960; The Form, 1961; The Hole and Other Plays and Sketches, 1964; The Cresta Run, 1966; Some Tall Tinkles: Television Plays, 1968; Was He Anyone, 1973; Harry Bleachbaker, novel, 1974, US Edition Man Overboard, 1976; Inner Voices, 1983. Address: c/o Mrs Holder, Hillview, Lower Inkpen, Berkshire, RG15 ODX, England.

SIMPSON Ronald Albert, b. 1 Feb 1929, Melbourne, Victoria, Australia. m. Pamela Bowles, 27 Aug 1955, 1 s, 1 d. Education: Trained Primary Teachers' Certificate, 1951; Associate Diploma in Fine Art, Royal Melbourne Institute of Technology, 1966. Appointments: Teacher, Junior and Secondary Schools, Australia and England, 1951-68; Lecturer, Senior Lecturer, The Chisholm Institute of Technology, Melbourne, Victoria, 1968-87. Publications: The Walk Along The Beach, 1960; This Real Pompeii, 1964; After the Assassination, 1968; Diver, 1972; Poems from Murrumbeena, 1976; The Forbidden City, 1979; Editor, Poems From the Age, 1979; Selected Poems, 1981; Words For A Journey, 1986; Dancing Table, 1992; Poetry Editor, The Age. Honours: The Australia Council for Travel, 1977, Category A Fellowship to write poetry, 1987; FAW Christopher Brennan Award, 1992. Membership: Australian Society of Authors. Address: 29 Omama Road, Murrumbeena, Melbourne, Victoria 3163, Australia.

SIMS George Frederick Robert, b. 3 Aug 1923, Hammersmith, London, England. Rare Book Dealer; Author. m. Beryl Simcock, 2 s, 1 d. Education: Lower School of John Lyon, Harrow, 1934-40. Publications: The Terrible Door, 1964; Sleep No More, 1966; The Last Best Friend, 1967; The Sand Dollar, 1969; Deadhand, 1971; Hunters Point, 1973; The End of the Web, 1976; Rex Mundi, 1978; Who Is Cato? 1981; the Keys of Death, 1982; Coat of Arms, 1984; The Rare Book Game, 1988; Last of the Rare Book Game, 1990; The Despain Papers, 1992. Contributions to: Black Mask; Saturday Book; London Magazine; American Book Collector; Book Collector; Antiquarian Book Monthly Review. Memberships: Crime writers Association: the Detection Club. Address: Peacocks, Hurst, Reading, Berkshire RG10 0DR, England.

SINCLAIR Andrew Annandale, b. 21 Jan 1935, Oxford, England. Writer; Historian. m. Sonia Melchett, 25 July 1984, 2 s. Education: Major Scholar, BA, PhD, Trinity College, Cambridge, 1955-59; Harkness Fellow, Harvard University, 1955-59; ACLS Fellow, Stanford University, 1964-65. Appointments: Founding Fellow, Churchill College, 1961-63; Lecturer, University College, London, 1966-68; Publisher, Lorrimer Publishing, 1968-89. Publications: The Breaking of Bumbo, 1959; My Friend Judas, 1959; Prohibition: The Era of Excess, 1961; Gog, 1967; Magog, 1972; Jack: A Biography of Jack London, 1977; The Other Victoria, 1981; King Ludd, 1988; War Like A Wasp, 1989; The War Decade: An Anthology of the 1940's, 1989; The Need

To Give, 1990; The Far Corners of the Earth, 1991; The Naked Savage, 1991; The Strength of the Hills, 1991; The Sword and the Grail, 1992; Francis Bacon: His Life and Violent Times, 1993; In Love and Anger, 1994. Contributions to: The Sunday Times; The Times; The New York Times; Atlantic Monthly. Honours: Somerset Maughn Prize, 1967; Venice Film Festival Award, 1971. Memberships: Fellow, Society of American Historians, 1970; Fellow, Royal Literary Society, 1968. Literary Agent: Aitken & Stone. Address: 16 Tite Street, London SW3 4HZ, England.

SINCLAIR Iain, b. 11 June 1943, Cardiff, Wales. Poet; Novelist. m. Mary Hadman, 1967. Education: Trinity College, Dublin; Courtauld Institute, London. Publications: Back Garden Poems, 1970; Muscats Würm, 1972; The Birth Rug, 1973; Lud Heat, 1975; Brown Clouds, 1977; The Penances, 1977; Suicide Bridge, 1979; Fluxions, 1983; Fresh Eggs and Scalp Metal, 1983; Autistic Poses, 1985; Significant Wreckage, 1988; Selected Poems, 1970-87; Plays, An Explanation, 1963; Cords, 1964; Novels, White Chappell, Scarlet Tracings, 1987; Downriver, 1991; Radon Daughters, 1994. Address: 28 Albion Drive, London E8 4ET, England.

SINCLAIR James. See: **STAPLES Reginald Thomas.**

SINCLAIR Olga Ellen, (Ellen Clare, Olga Daniels), b. 23 Jan 1923, Norfolk, England. Writer. m. Stanley George Sinclair, 1 Apr 1945, 3 s. Publications: Gypsies, 1967; Hearts By the Tower, 1968; Bitter Sweet Summer, 1970; Dancing in Britain, 1970; Children's Games, 1972; Toys, 1974; My Dear Fugitive, 1976; Never Fall in Love, 1977; Master of Melthorpe, 1979; Gypsy Girl, 1981; Ripening Vine, 1981; (as Olga Daniels) The Gretna Bride, 1985; When Wherries Sailed By, 1987; (as Olga Daniels) Lord of Leet Castle, 1984; The Bride From Faraway, 1987; The Untamed Bride, 1988; Gretna Green; A Romantic History, 1989; (as Olga Daniels) The Arrogant Cavalier, 1991. Memberships: Society of Authors; Romantic Novelists Association; Society of Women and Journalists; President, Norwich Writer's Circle. Address: Dove House Farm, Potter Heigham, Norfolk NR29 5LJ, England.

SINCLAIR Sonia Elizabeth, (Sonia Graham, Sonia Melchett), b. 6 Sep 1928, Nainital, India. Writer. m. (1) Julian Mond, Lord Melchett (dec Jun 1973), 1 s, 2 d, (2) Andrew Sinclair, 1984. Education: Royal School, Bath; Queen's Secretarial College, Windsor, England. Appointments: Writer, Member of Board of Directors, English Stage Company and The Royal National Theatre. Publications: (as Sonia Graham) Tell Me Honestly (nonfiction), 1964; (as Sonia Melchett) Someone is Missing, (nonfiction), 1987; (as Sonia Melchett) Passionate Quests - Five Contemporary Women Travellers., 1989. Contributions To: Periodicals including: Vogue; Harper's & Queen; Tatler; Portraits; Marie-Claire. Address: 16 Tite Street, London SW3 4HZ, England.

SINGER Adam. See: **KARP David.**

SINGER June Flaum, b. 17 Jan 1932, Jersey City, NJ, USA. Writer. m. Joseph Singer, 7 Sep 1950, 1 s, 3 d. Education: Ohio State University, Columbus, 1948-50. Publications: The Bluffer's Guide To Interior Decorating, 1972; The Bluffer's Guide To Antiques, (American editor), 1972; The Debutantes, 1981; Star Dreams, 1982; The Movie Set, 1984; The Markoff Women, 1986; The President's Women, 1988; Sex In The Afternoon, 1990; Till The End Of Time, 1991; Brilliant Divorces, 1992. Memberships: The Southern California Society of Women Writers; PEN West; Authors Guild. Literary Agent: Roslyn Targ. Address: 780 Stone Canyon Road, Bel-Air, CA 90077, USA.

SINGER Kurt Deutsch, b. 10 Aug 1911, Vienna, Austria. News Commentator; Author; Publisher. m. (1) Hilda Tradelius, 23 Dec 1932, 1 s, 1 d, (2) Jane Sherrod, 9 Apr 1955 (dec 1985), (3) Katherine Han, 8 Apr 1989. Education: University Of Zurich, Switzerland, 1930; Labor College, Stockholm, Sweden, 1936; PhD, Div College of Metaphysics, Indianapolis, 1951. Appointments: Founder, Ossietzky Committee; Founder, Niemöller Committee; Co-founder, Pro-Allied Newspaper Trots Allt; Editor, 1940, News Background; University Lecturer, 1945-49; Editor, 1958-59; President, 1953-, Singer Media Corporation; Director, 1987-, Oceanic Press Service, San Clemente, CA. Publications include: Tales Of The Macabre, 1971; Ghouls And Ghosts, 1972; Satanic Omnibus, 1973; Gothic Horror Omnibus, 1974; Dictionary Of Household Hints And Help, 1974; They Are Possessed, 1976; True Adventures Into The Unknown, 1980; I Spied - And Survived, 1980; First Target Book Of Horror, (two editions) 1984, (two editions) 1985; Solve A Crime, 1994. Contributions To: Magazines and

Journals including: Readers Digest, Saturday Evening Post, Folket in Bild, Sweden Style, Hong Kong. Honours: Instrumental in Awarding Nobel Peace Prize, 1936 to Carl Von Ossietzky. Memberships: UN Speakers Research; UN Children's Emergency Fund; Menninger Foundation; National Geographic Society; Smithsonian Association; Vice President, International Platform Association; President, United School Assemblies. Literary Agent: Oceanic Press, San Clemente, CA 92673, USA. Address: c/o Singer Media Corporation, Seaview Business Park, 1030 Calle Cordillera Unit 106, San Clemente, CA 92673, USA.

SINGER Marilyn, b. New York City, USA. Writer. m. Steven Aronson, 31 Jul 1971. Education: BA, Queens College,1969; MA, NY University, 1979. Publications: It Can't Hurt Forever; Tarantulas On The Brain; The Course Of True Love Never Did Run Smooth; Ghost Host; Turtle In July; Several Kinds Of Silence; Horsemaster; Sky Words, 1994; The Painted Fan, 1994; Family Reunion, 1994; Please, Don't Squeeze Your Boa, Noah!, 1995. Contributions to: Yes; Encore; Corduroy; The Archer. Honours: Childrens Choice Award; Parents Choice Award; American Library Association Best Book Award; Maud Hart Lovelace Award; NCTE Award; The New York Times Best Illustrated Children's Books of 1989. Memberships: Authors Guild; PEN American Centre; Society Of Childrens Book Writers and Illustrators. Literary Agent: Marilyn Malin, Foreign Rights Only. Address: 42 Berkeley Place, Brooklyn, NY 11217, USA.

SINGER Sarah Beth, b. 4 Jul 1915, USA. Poet. m. 23 Nov 1938, 1 s, 1 d. Education: BA, 1934; Graduate Courses, 1960-64. Literary Appointments: Consulting Editor, Poet Lore, 1976-81; Publicity Chairman For State of Washington by The National League of American Penwomen, 1992. Publications: After The Beginning, 1975; Of Love and Shoes, 1987; The Gathering, 1992; Anthology of poems, Filtered Images, 1992. New York Times; Poet Lore; Yankee; McCall's: The Lyric; Voices; Christian Science Monitor; Judaism; The Round Table; The Shakespeare Newsletter; Poetry Column of The Journal of The American Medical Association. Address: 2360 43rd Avenue East, Seattle, WA 98112, USA.

SINGH Charu Steel, b. 15 May 1955, UP, India. Teacher. m. Maya, 6 June 1987, 1 son. Education: BA, 1974; MA, 1976; PhD, 1978. Appointments: MBS College Gangapur, 1977-79; Lecturer, Kashi Vidyapith University, 1979-91; Reader, 1991-. Publications: The Chariot of Fire; Auguries of Evocation; Contemporary Literary Theory; Literary Theory: Possibilities and Limits; Four Collections of poems; Confederate Gestures; Self- Reflexive Materiality; Concentric Imagination. Contributions to: The Literary Criterion; Journal of Literary Criticism; Modern Language Review; Years Work in English Studies. Honours: British Council Fellowship; Prestigious University Grants; Fellowship Indian Institute of Advanced Study Shimla. Memberships: Journal of Indian Writing in English; American Studies Research Centre; Indian PEN. Address: 36 Brahmanand Nagar, Ext 1, Durga Kund, Varanasi 221005, India.

SINGH Khushwant, b. 2 Feb 1915, Hadali, India. Novelist. Education: BA, Government College, Lahore, 1934; LLB, Kings College, London, 1938. Appointments: Lawyer, High Court, Lahore, 1939-47; Visiting Lecturer, Oxford, Rochester, Princeton, Swarthmore & Hawaii Universities, 1965-67; Member, Indian Parliament, 1980-. Publications: Train to Pakistan, 1956; I Shall Not Hear the Nightingale, 1959; Story Collections, The Mark of Vishnu and Other Stories, 1950; The Voice of God and Other Stories, 1957; A Bride for the Sahib and Other Stories, 1967; Black Jasmine, 1971; The Collected Stories, 1989; Writing on Sikh History and Translations; Selected Writings: Delhi: A Novel; Sex, Scotch & Scholarship; Not a Nice Man To Know. Honours: Punjab Government Robe of Honour, 1970; Mohan Singh Award, Padma Bushan, Indian, 1974. Address: 49E Sujan Singh Park, New Delhi, 110 003 India.

SINGH Ram Krishna, b. 31 Dec 1950, Varanasi, India. Teacher. m. Durga, 1 Mar 1978, 1 son, 1 daughter. Education: BA, University of Gorakhpur, 1970; MA Banaras Hindu University, 1972; PhD English, Kashi Vidyapith, 1981. Appointments: Guest Editor, Language Forum, New Delhi, 1986; Board of Advisors, Canopy, 1986-; Co-editor, Creative Forum, 1987-; General Editor, Creative Forum New Poets' Series, 1992-: Advisory Council, Poecrit, 1991-, International Journal of Translation, 1992-, Editorial Associate, Indian Book Chronicle, 1992-, Associate Editor, Young Poet, 1994-. Appointments: Professor and Head, Dept of HSS, Indian School of Mines. Publications: Savitri: A Spiritual Epic, 1984; My Silence, 1985; Using Contemporary English

Idioms, 1985-86; Sound and Silence, edited, 1986; Indian English Writing, 1981-85, edited, 1987; Using English in Science and Technology, 1988; Memories Unmemoried, 1988; Practising English in Science and Technology, 1990; Flight of Phoenix, 1990; Music Must Sound, 1990; Recent Indian English Poets: Expressions and Beliefs, edited 1992; I Do Not Question, 1994; Krishna Srinivas: The Poet of Inner Aspiration, 1984; My Silence and Other Selected Poems, 1995; General English Practice, 1995. Contributions to: Indian Journal of English Studies; Littcrit; The Literary Endeavour; Language Forum; Journal of Indian Writing in English; Commonwealth Quarterly; Poet; Indian Literature; Skylark; Fantasy; Prophetic Voices; Noreal; Triveni; CER*BER*US; Puck and Pluck; Forum; Creative Inspiration; International Poetry; Kanora; BAFA Newsletter; Poiesis; World Poetry; Canopy; Poetry; Kaiser-e-Hind; Poetcrit; Manxa; Creative Forum; Young Poets; Kavita India; Quill; Unilit; Haritham; Thirteen Poetry Magazine; The Call Beyond. Honours: Hon DLitt, World Academy of Arts and Culture, 1984; Certificate of Excellences, International Writers and Artists Association, 1987, 1988; International Eminent Poet and Fellowship of International Poets Academy, Madras, 1987; Michael Madhusudan Award of Michael Madhusudan Academy, Calcutta, 1994. Memberships include: International Writers and Artists Association; World Poetry Society Intercontinent; International Poets Academy, Madras; PEN, Bombay; International Association of Teachers of English as a Foreign Language, UK; Honorary Secretary, Dhanbad Chapter of SID, Rome. Address: Type VI-4 Indian School of Mines, Dhanbad 826004, India.

SIONIL JOSE Francisco, b. 3 Dec 1924, Rosales, Pangasinan, Philippines. Novelist. m. Tersita G Jovellanos. Appointments: Publisher, Editor, Solidarity Magazine, 1966-; Manager, Solidaridad Galleries, Manila, 1967-. Publications: The Pretenders, 1962; Tree, 1978; My Brother, My Executioner, 1979; Mass, 1982; Po-on, 1985; Ermita, 1988; Spiderman, 1991; Story Collections, The Pretenders and Other Stories, 1962; The God Stealer and Other Stories, 1968; Waywaya and Other Short Stories for the Philippines, 1980; Two Filipino Women, 1982; Platinum and Other Stories, 1983; Olvidon and Other Stories, 1988. Honours: National Press Club Awards; British Council Grant, 1967; Rockefeller Foundation Bellagio Award, 1979; Ramon Magsaysay Memorial Award for Literature, 1980; International House of Japan Fellowship, 1983. Address: Solidaidad Publishing House, 531 Padre Faura, Ermita PO Box 3959, Manila, Philippines.

SIPHERD Ray, b. 27 Aug 1935, PA, USA. Novelist; TV Writer; Editor. m. Anne Marie Foran, 4 Oct 1986. Education: BA, Yale University, 1957. Publications: The Christmas Store, 1993; The Courtship of Peggy McCoy, 1990; Down on the Farm with Grover, 1980; When Is My Birthday, 1988; The White Kite, 1972; Big Birds Animal Alphabet, 1987; The Counts Poem, 1989; Ernie & Berts Telephone Call, 1978; Sherlock Hemlock & The Outer Space Creatures, 1981. Honours: TV Emmy Awards, 1969, 74, 85. Memberships: Writers Guild of America; American Society of Composers Authors & Publishers. Literary Agent: Michael V Carlisle, William Morris Agency, 1350 Avenue of the Americas, NY, USA. Address: PO Box 366, Newtown, CT 06470, USA.

SIROF Harriet Toby, b. 18 Oct 1930, New York City, USA. Writer; Teacher. m. 18 Jun 1949, 1 s, 1 d. Education: BA, New School for Social Research, 1962. Publications: A New-Fashioned Love Story, 1977; The IF Machine, 1978; The Junior Encyclopedia of Israel, 1980; Save The Dam!, 1981; That Certain Smile, 1981; The Real World, 1985; Anything You Can Do, 1986; Because She's My Friend, 1993; The Road Back: Living With A Physical Disability, 1993. Contributions to: Colorado Review; Descent; Inlet; Maine Review; North American Review; New Orleans Review; Sam Houston Review; San Jose Studies; Woman; Voices of Brooklyn. Honours: Junior Literary Guild Selection of The Real World, 1985. Memberships: Authors Guild; Society of Children's Book Writers. Address: Harriet Sirof, 792 East 21 Street, Brooklyn, NY 11210, USA.

SISLER Harry Hall, b. 13 Mar 1917. Chemist; Educator; Dean Emeritus. m. Helen E Shaver, 29 Jun 1940, 2 s, 2 d, Hannelore L Wass, 13 Apr 1978. Education: BSc, Honours, Ohio State University, 1936; MSc, Chemistry, 1937; PhD, 1939, University Of Illinois. Appointments: Board Of Publication, Journal of Chemical Education, 1956-58; Editor, Reinhold Publication Corporation, 1958-78; Assistant to Editor, Death Studies, 1978-; Consulting Editor, Dowden, Hutchinson and Ross, 1971-78. Publications include: Chemistry in Non-Aqueous Solvents, 1961; Electronic Structure, Properties and The Periodic Law, 1963; The Chloramination Reaction, 1977; Chemistry- A Systematic

Approach, 1980; Starlight, (poems) 1976; Of Outer and Inner Space, (poems) 1980; Earth, Air, Fire and Water, (poems) 1989; numerous others. Contributions to: Over 200 articles in major scientific and scholarly journals. Address: 6014 NW 54th Way, Gainesville, FL 32606-3244, USA.

SISSON Charles Hubert, b. 22 Apr 1914, Bristol, England. Retired Civil Servant. m. Nora Gilbertson, 19 Aug 1937, 2 daughters. Education: BA, 1st Class Honours, University of Bristol, 1931-34; Postgraduate studies, Berlin and Paris, 1934-36. Publications: The Spirit of British Administration, 1959; Christopher Homm, 1965; Art and Action, 1965; Essays, 1967; David Hume, 1976; The Avoidance of Literature, 1978; The Divine Comedy of Dante, 1980; Collected Poems, 1984; On the Lookout (autobiography), 1989; An Asiatic Romance, 1953; In the Trojan Ditch, 1974; Anglican Essays, 1983; In Two Minds: Guesses at Other Writers, 1990; Jeremy Taylor: Selected Writings, 1990; English Perspectives: Essays on Liberty and Government, 1992; Is There a Church of England? 1993; What and Who (poems), 1994; Verse translations of Catullus, Lucretius, Virgil, Du Bellay, Racine. Contributions to: Agenda; London Magazine; London Review of Books; New Criterion, New York; New York Times Review of Books; PN Review; Spectator; Times Literary Supplement. Honours: FRSL, 1975; Honorary DLitt, Bristol, 1980; C.H. (Companion of Honour), 1993. Literary Agent: Laurence Pollinger Limited. Address: Moorfield Cottage, The Hill, Langport, Somerset TA10 9PU, England.

SISSON Rosemary Anne, b. 13 Oct 1923, London, England. Writer. Education: BA, Honours, UCL; Mlit, Newnham College, Cambridge University. Appointments: Junior Lecturer, University of Wisconsin, 1949-50; Lecturer, University College, London, 1950-53; Lecturer, University of Birmingham, 1953-54; Dramatic Critic, Stratford-upon-Avon Herald, 1954-57. Publications: The Bretts, 1987; Beneath the Visiting Moon, 1986; Bury Love Deep, 1985; The Manions of America, 1981; The Queen and the Welshman, 1979; The Stratford Story, 1975; The Exciseman, 1972; The Killer of Horseman's Flats, 1973; Escape from the Dark, 1976; The Queen and the Welshman, 1979; The Manions of America, 1982; Bury Love Deep, 1985; Beneath the Visiting Moon, 1986; The Bretts, 1987; The Young Indiana Jones Chronicles, 1993-. Contributions to: Numerous magazines and journals. Honours: Writers Guild of Great Britain, Laurel Award for services to Writers. Memberships: Co-chair, The Writers Guild of Great Britain; Writers Guild of America; BAFTA; Dramatists' Club; Academy Club. Literary Agent: Andrew Mann Limited. Address: 167 New King's Road, Parson's Green, London SW6, England.

SIZER John, b. 14 Sept 1938, Grimsby, England. University Professor. m. 1965, 3 sons. Education: BA, Nottingham University, 1961-64; DLitt, Loughborough University of Technology, 1989; FCMA; FBIM; FRSA. Publications: An Insight into Management Accounting, 1969, 1979 and 1989; Perspectives in Management Accounting, 1981; A Casebook of British Management Accounting Vol I and II, 1984 and 1985; Institutional Responses to Financial Reductions in University Sector, DES 1987. Contributions to: Numerous articles in Accounting, Management and Higher Education journals. Honour: CBE, 1989. Membership: Fellow, Chartered Institute of Management Accountants. Address: Scottish Higher Education Funding Council, Donaldson House, 97 Haymarket Terrace, Edinburgh EH12 5HD, Scotland.

SKALDASPILLIR Sigfriur. See: BROXON Mildred Downey.

SKARSAUNE Oskar, b. 2 July 1946, Trondheim, Norway. Professor. m. Karin, 4 Aug 1973, 2 sons, 1 daughter. Education: Norwegian Lutheran School of Theology, Olso, Norway, 1972; Doctor of Theology, University of Oslo, 1982. Appointments: Co Editor, Luthersk Kirketidende, 1985-. Publications: The Proof from Prophecy, Incarnation, Myth or Fact; Da Skriften Ble Apnet; Fra Jerusalem Til Rom Og B. Contributions to: Several articles. Address: PO Box 27, Bekkelaget, 0137 Oslo, Norway.

SKELTON Geoffrey David, b. 11 May 1916, Springs, South Africa. Writer; Translator. m. Gertrude Klebac, 4 Sept 1947, 2 sons. Education: Plymouth College, City of London School, 1927-34. Appointments: BBC, England, 1956-67. Publications: Wagner at Bayreuth, 1965, 1976; Wieland Wagner, 1971; Paul Hindemith, 1975; Richard and Cosima Wagner, 1982; Wagner in Thought and Practice, essays, 1991; Cosima Wagner's Dairies: An Abridgement, 1994; Translations from German: The Marat-Sade, play by Peter Weiss (with Adrian Mitchell), 1964; Cosima Wagner's Diaries, 1978, 1980; Works by Max Frisch, Freidrich Heer, Günter Herburger, Robert Lucas;

Training Ground, novel by Siegfried Lenz, 1991. Honours: American PEN Prize for Translation (with Adrian Mitchell) for Marat-Sade, 1967; Schlegel-Tieck Translation Prize for Frieda Lawrence by Robert Lucas, 1973, for Training Ground, 1992; Yorkshire Post Music Award for Paul Hindemith, 1975. Memberships: Radiowriters Association, Executive Committee 1969-72; Translators Association, Executive Committee 1972-74, 1979-81, Chairman 1974. Literary Agent: David Higham Associates. Address: 49 Downside, Shoreham, West Sussex BN43 6HF, England.

SKOCPOL Theda, b. Detroit, Michigan, USA. m. 1 son. Appointments: Professor, Harvard University. Contributions to: 10 books and numerous articles; Numerous Academic Journals. Honours: Ralph Waldo Emerson Prize, Phi Beta Kappa, 1995; J David Greenstone Award and Woodrow Wilson Foundation Award, American Political Science Association, 1993; Allan Sharlin Memorial Award, Social Science History Association, 1993; Political Sociology Section Book Award, American Sociological Association, 1993. Address: Dept of Government, Harvard University, William James Hall, Cambridge, MA 02138-3800, USA.

SKRZYNECKI Peter, b. 6 Apr 1945, Imhert, Germany. Australian Citizen. Lecturer; Poet. m. Kate Magrath, 1 son, 2 daughters. Education: University of Sydney. Appointments include: Lecturer, University of Western Sydney, 1987. Publications: There, Behind the Lids, 1970; Headwaters, 1972; Immigrant Chronicle, 1975; The Aviary: Poems, 1975-77; The Polish Immigrant, 1982; Night Swim, 1989; Novel, The Beloved Mountain, 1988; Josephs Coat: An Anthology of Multicultural Writing, 1985; Short Story, The Wild Dogs, 1987. Honours include: Captain Cook Bicentenary Award, 1970. Address: 6 Sybil Street, Eastwood, NSW 2122, Australia.

SKVORECKY Josef, b. 27 Sept 1924, Nachod, Czechoslovakia (Canadian citizen). Novelist. Education: PhD, Charles University, Prague, 1951. Appointments include: Professor of English, University of Toronto, Canada, 1975-90. Publications: The Views in the February Night, 1948, 1989; The Cowards, 1958, 1970; Murder for Luck, 1962; The Menorah, 1964; The Life of High Society, 1965; The Bass Saxophone, 1967; A Babylonian Story, 1967; The End of the Nylon Age, 1967; Miss Silver's Past, 1969; The Bitter World: Selected Stories 1946-67; The Tank Battalion, 1969; The Miracle Game, 1972, 1991; Sins for Father Knox, 1973, 1990; The Swell Season, 1975; The Engineer of Human Souls, 1977, 1985; Dvorák Society, 1985; A Bride from Texas, 1992; Play: God in Your House, 1980; Screenplays, television plays; Essays; Translations of Henry James, Hemingway, Faulkner, Sinclair Lewis and American crime writers. Honours include: Honorary Citizen, City of Prague, 1990. Address: 487 Sackville Street, Toronto, Ontario, Canada M4X 1T6.

SLADE Jack. See: GERMANO Peter B.

SLADE Peter, b. 7 Nov 1912, Fleet, Hampshire, England. Actor; Director; Drama Advisor; Drama Therapist. m. 25 Nov 1939, 2 daughters. Education: Public School, Lancing, 1926-30; Central School of Speech and Drama, 1st Class Certificate in Acting, 1933-34. Publications: Child Drama, 1954; Introduction to Child Drama, 1958; Experience of Spontaneity, 1968; Natural Dance, 1977; Contribution to Drama in Therapy, Vol 1, New York, 1981; in progress: Child Play (its importance for personal development); Education pamphlets published by the Educational Drama Association. Contributions to: Athene Arts; Guild of Pastoral Psychology; Educational Drama Association. Honour: The Queen's Silver Jubilee Medal, 1977. Memberships: Director, 1948-77, President 1977-, Educational Drama Association; Patron Institute of Dramatherapy. Address: Swingletrees, Park Crescent, Stow on the Wold, Cheltenham, Gloucestershire GL54 1DT, England.

SLATER Ian David, b. 1 Dec 1941, Queensland, Australia. Author; Lecturer; Editor. m. Marian Ella Wray Johnston, 18 Dec 1968, 1 s, 1 d. Education: BA, University of British Columbia, 1972; MA, 1972; PhD, 1977. Appointments: Visiting Lecturer, University of Ljubljana, 1984; Writer in Residence, Simon, Fraser University, 1986; Writer in Residence, Sechelt and Festival of The Arts, 1988. Publications: Orwell - The Road To Airstrip One; Firespill; Sea Gold; Air Glow Red; World War III series; Deep Chill; Storm. Honours: Royal Institute Scholarship; Mark Eastman United Nations Award. Memberships: Authors Guild Of America; UBC Faculty Club. Literary Agent: Henry Dunow. Address: 4074 West 17th Avenue, Vancouver BC, Canada, V6S 1A6.

SLATTA Richard Wayne, b. 22 Oct 1947, North Dakota, USA. Professor of History. m. Maxine P Atkinson, 15 Jun 1983, 1 s. Education: BA cum laude, Pacific Lutheran University, 1969; MA Portland State University, 1974; PhD History, University of Texas at Austin, 1980. Publications: Gauchos and The Vanishing Frontier, 1992; Cowboys of The Americas, 1994; The Cowboy Encyclopedia, 1994. Contributions to: The Futurist, 1987; Family Computing, 1986; Criminal Justice History: An International Review, 1990; Social Science Computer Review. Honours: Western Heritage Award for Nonfiction, National Cowboy Hall of Fame, 1991; Hubert Herring Book Prize, 1984. Memberships: American Historical Association; Conference on Latin American History; Western History Association. Address: History Department, North Carolina State University, Raleigh NC 27695, USA.

SLAVITT David Rytman (Henry Sutton, David Benjamin, Henry Lazarus, Lynn Meyer), b. 1935, USA. Novelist; Poet; Film Editor; Book Reviewer; Poetry Critic; Lecturer. Education: BA, Magna Cum Laude, Yale University, 1956; MA, Honors, Columbia University, 1957. Literary Appointments: Associate Editor, Newsweek Magazine, 1958-65; Associate Professor of English, Temple University, 1978-80; Lecturer in English, Columbia University, 1985-86; Lecturer in English, University of Pennsylvania, 1989-; Poetry Critic, The New England Review and Seven Arts; Book Reviewer for various journals. Publications include: Writer for Newsweek, 1958-65; Screenplays; Performance Pieces; Translations; Poetry: Equinox, 1989; Eight Longer Poems, 1990; Crossroads, 1994; The Gift, 1995; Non-Fiction: Physicians Observed, 1987; Virgil, 1991; Fiction: Turkish Delights, 1993; The Cliff, 1994; Pseudonymous Novels: The Idol, (David Benjamin) 1979; The Proposal, (Henry Sutton) 1980; numerous others. Literary Agent: William Morris Agency, USA. Address: c/o William Morris Agency, 1350 Avenue of The Americas, New York, NY 10019, USA.

SLIDE Anthony Clifford, b. 7 Nov 1944, Birmingham, England. Film Historian; Archivist. Appointments: Editor, Filmmakers, 1982-. Publications include: The American Film Industry; A Historical Dictionary, 1986; Early American Cinema, 1970; Early Women Directors, 1977; The Big V: A History Of The Vitagraph Company, 1987; The Vaudevillians, 1981; Silent Portraits, 1990; book review column, Classic Images, 1989-; Nitrate Won't Wait: A History of Film Preservation in The United States, 1992; Before Video: A History of The Non-Theatrical Film, 1992; Gay And Lesbian Characters and Themes in Mystery Novels, 1993; The Encyclopedia of Vaudeville, 1994. Honours: The American Film Industry: A Historical Dictionary, named Outstanding Reference of The Year, American Library Association; Honorary Doctor of Letters, Bowling Green University, 1990. Address: 4118 Rhodes Avenue, Studio City, CA 91604, USA.

SLOAN Carolyn, b. 15 Apr 1937, London. England. Freelance Journalist; Children's Author. m. David Hollis, 15 May 1961, 2 s. Education: Harrogate College; Tutorial Schools in Newcastle, Guildford. Appointments: Editorial Secretary, Features Assistant, Queen Magazine, 1956-60; Press Officer, Yvonne Arnaud Theatre, 1976-80. Publications include: The Sea Child, 1987; Helen Keller, 1984; Don't Go Near The Water, 1988; The Penguin and the Vacuum Cleaner, 1974; Skewer's Garden, 1983; The Friendly Robot, 1986; T-Boys Weekend, 1988; Working Dogs, 1991; Working Elephants, 1991; Working Horses, 1992; Gracie, 1994. Contributions to: Features Contributed to Daily Telegraph, Sunday Telegraph, Radio Times. Memembership: Society of Authors. Literary Agent: Murray Pollinger. Address: 7 Dapdune Road, Guildford, Surrey, GU1 4NY, England.

SLOMAN Anne, b. 24 Apr 1944, London, England. Journalist. m. Martyn Sloman, 22 Apr 1972, 2 sons. Education: BA, Honours, Politics, Philosophy and Economics, St Hilda's College, Oxford University, 1963-66. Appointments: Radio Producer 1967-72, TV Producer 1972-73, Senior Producer, Radio, Current Affairs, Executive Producer, General Election and US Presidential Results Coverage, 1973-81, Assistant Editor, Today Programme, 1981-82, Editor, Special Current Affairs, 1983-, BBC; Editor, Special Current Affairs 1983-94; Deputy Head of Weekly Programmes (TV & Radio) BBC, News & Current Affairs, 1994-. Publications: Co-author: British Political Facts 1900-79, 1980; No Minister, 1982; But Chancellor, 1983; With Respect Ambassador, 1985; The Thatcher Phenomenon, 1986. Honours: Award, Outstanding Programme Contribution, Broadcasting Guild of Journalists; Broadcasting Press Guild Radio Award, Outstanding Programme: The Thatcher Phenomenon, 1985; Outstanding Contribution: My Country Right or Wrong, 1988. Address: 29 Church Crescent, London N10, England.

SLOTKIN Richard, b. 1942. Honours: National Book Award, Nominee. Address: Dept of English, Weslyan University, Middletown, CT 06459-0260, USA.

SMALL Ernest. See: **LENT Blair.**

SMALL Michael Ronald, b. 3 Jan 1943, Croydon, Surrey, England. Teacher; Short Story Writer; Poet; Textbook Writer. Education: BA, London University; BEd, La Trobe University, Australia; MA, University of Windsor, Canada. Publications: Her Natural Life and Other Stories, 1988; Film: A Resource Book for Studying Film as Text (with Brian Keyte), 1994. Contributions to: Numerous to journals and magazines including: Harvard Review; University of Windsor Review; Westerly. Memberships: Victorian Fellowship of Australian Writers, former Committee Member. Address: 71 Strabane Avenue, Box Hill North, Victoria 3129, USA.

SMALLEY Stephen Stewart, b. 11 May 1931, London, England. Clerk in Holy Orders. m. Susan Jane Paterson, 13 July 1974. Education: BA 1955, MA 1958, PhD 1979, Jesus College, Cambridge; BD 1957, Eden Theological Seminary, USA; Deacon 1958, Priest 1959, Ridley Hall, Cambridge. Appointments: Assistant Curate, St Paul's, Portman Square, London, 1958-60; Chaplain, Peterhouse, Cambridge, 1960-63, Acting Dean 1962-63, Lecturer and Senior Lecturer, University of Ibadan, Nigeria, 1963-69; Lecturer and Senior Lecturer, University of Manchester, 1970-77, also Warden of St Anselm Hall, 1972-77; Canon Residentiary and Precentor of Coventry Cathedral, 1977-86, Vice-Provost 1986; Dean, Chester Cathedral, 1987-. Publications: John: Evangelist and Interpreter, 1978; 1,2,3 John, 1984; The Spirit's Power, 1972; Thunder and Love: John's Revelation and John's Community, 1994; (Ed) Christ and Spirit in the New Testament, 1973. Contributions to: Numerous articles and reviews in learned journals, including Journal of Theological Studies, New Testament Studies, Journal of Biblical Literature, Expository Times, Novum Testamentum. Honours: Foundation and Lady Kay Scholar, Jesus College, Cambridge, 1948, 1955; Select Preacher, University of Cambridge, 1963-64; Manson Memorial Lecturer, University of Manchester, 1986; Member, Archbishops' Doctrine Commission of the Church of England, 1981-86. Memberships: Studiorum Novi Testamenti Societas; Chester City Club. Address: The Deanery, 7 Abbey Street, Chester CH1 2JF, England.

SMARANDACHE Florentin, b. 10 Dec 1954, Balcesti, Vilcea, Romania. Mathematician; Writer. Education: MA, Faculty of Mathematics and Computer Science, University of Craiova. Publications: Books written in Romanian: Formule Pentru Spirit (Formulas for The Spirit), 1981; Culegere de Exercitii Poetice (Collection of Poetical Exercises), Editor El Kitab, 1982; Legi de Compozitie Interna. Poeme Cu...Probleme! (Laws of Internal Composition. Poems With...Problems!) Editor El Kitab, 1982; Sentimente Fabricate in Laborator (Feelings Made in Laboratory)(poems) Editor El Kitab, 1984; Strain de Cauza (Out in Left Field)(sketch), 1990; America: Paradisul Diavolului, 1992; Books in French: Le Sens du Non-Sens (The Sense of Non-sense), 1983,1984; Anti-Chambres, Anti-Poesies, Bizarreries (Ante-Rooms, Ante-Poems, Wiersnesses) Editor Claude Le Roy, 1989; Books in English: Nonpoems, 1990; Circles of Light, Dark Snow, 1992; Philosophia Paradoxae, 1995; FUGIT, 1995; Intâmplàri cu Pàcalà, 1994; Anthologies: Ora Planetei (Planet Time), 1980; Clair de Signes (Clear Signs), 1989; Cristal (Crystal), 1990; Anthology of The Paradoxist Literary Movement, 1993. Contributions to: Literary Magazines in Romania, France, England, United States of America, Japan. Memberships: US Mathematical Association; Romania Mathematical Association; Reviewer to Zentralblatt fur Mathematik, West Germany. Address: PO Box 42561, Phoenix, AZ 85080, USA.

SMEDS Dave, b. 23 Feb 1955, Reedley, CA, USA. Author. m. Connie Willeford, 26 Jun 1982, 1 s, 1 d. Education: BA English, Psychology, Sonoma State University. Publications: The Sorcery Within, 1985; The Schemes of Dragons, 1989; Piper in The Night, forthcoming. Contributions to: Isaac Asimov's Science Fiction Magazine; Lui; Mayfair; The Magazine of Fantasy and Science Fiction; Inside Karate; Anthologies include: Dragons of Light, 1980; Far Frontiers, Volume 6, 1986; In The Field of Fire, 1987; Full Spectrum 4 1993, Sword and Sorceress 4, 1987. Memberships: Science Fiction Writers of America; Author's Guild. Address: 164 Jack London Drive, Santa Rosa, CA 95409, USA.

SMEED John William, b. 21 Feb 1926, London, England. Emeritus Professor in German. m. Gay Jones, 24 Mar 1952. Education: BA, MA, PhD, University of Wales. Publications: Jean Paul's Dreams, 1966; Faust in Literature, 1975; The Theophrastan Character, 1985; German Song and its Poetry, 1987; Don Juan. Variations on a Theme, 1990; Famous Poets, neglected Composers, Songs to Lyrics by Goethe, Heine, Mörike and others, 1992. Contributions to: Literary Periodicals in England, Germany and USA. Honours: University of Wales Fellowship, 1953; Leverhulme Research Fellowship, 1983. Address: 53 Claypath, Durham DH1 1QS, England.

SMELSER Neil Joseph, b. 22 Jul 1930, MO, USA. University Professor of Sociology. m. (1) Helen Margolis, 10 Jun 1954, (div 1965), (2) Sharin Hubbert, 20 Oct 1967, 2 s, 2 d. Education: BA 1952, PhD 1958, Harvard University; BA 1954, MA 1959, Oxford University; Graduate, San Francisco Psychoanalytic Institute, 1971. Appointments: Director, Center for Advanced Study in The Behavioral Sciences, Stanford, CA. Publications: Economy and Society, 1956; Social Change in The Industrial Revolution, 1959; Theory of Collective Behaviour, 1962; The Sociology of Economic Life, 1962, 1973; Sociology, 1981, 1984, 1987. 1991; Handbook of Sociology, editor, 1988; Social Paralysis and Social Change, 1991. Contributions to: American Behavioural Scientist; American Sociologist. Address: Center for Advanced Study in The Behavioral Sciences, 202 Junipero Serra Boulevard, Stanford, CA 94305, USA.

SMIRNOV Igor Pavlovich, b. 19 May 1941, Leningrad, Russia. Professor of Russian Literature. m. Johanna Renate Luise Elisabeth Döring-Smirnov, 16 July 1979. Education: MA, Leningrad State University, 1963; Dr Phil Sci, Institute of Russian Literature, Leningrad, 1967. Appointments: Editorial Board, Elementa, Journal of Slavic Studies and Comparative Cultural Semiotics, Los Angeles, 1992; New Literary Review, Moscow, 1992. Publications: Meaning in Art and the Evolution of Poetic Systems, 1977; The Emergence of the Inter-text, 1985; Towards a Theory of Literature, 1987; Being and Creating, 1990; An Old Russian Culture, Russian National Specifically and the Logic of History, 1991; Psychohistory of Russian Literature from Romanticism Till Now, 1995. Contributions to: Russian Literature; Wiener Slawistischer Almanach. Address: Guerickestr 35, 80 805 München, Germany.

SMITH A C H, b. 31 Oct 1935, Kew, England. Writer. Education: MA, Cambridge University. Literary Appointments: Literary Associate, Royal Shakespeare Co, 1964-1974; Senior Research Associate, University of Birmingham, 1965-69; Fellowship in Drama, University of Bristol, 1976-79; Visiting Professor, Emory University, Atlanta, USA, 1986; Director, Cheltenham Festival of Literature, 1978-79; Chairman, Playwrights Company, 1979-83; Visiting Professor, University of Texas, USA, 1990-91, 1994. Publications: The Crowd, 1965; Zero Summer, 1971; Orghast at Persepolis, 1972; Paper Voices, 1975; Treatment, 1976; The Jericho Gun, 1977, Edward and Mrs Simpson, 1978; Extra Cover, 1981; The Dark Crystal, 1982; Wagner, 1983; Sebastian the Navigator, 1985; Lady Jane, 1985; Labyrinth, 1986. Contributions to: New Society; Transatlantic Review; Listener; Times; Telegraph Magazine; Sunday Times; Observer; Guardian; BBC and ITV. Honours: Writing Awards, Arts Council, 1970-71, 1974-75, 1980, Memberships: Writers Guild of Great Britain; Literary Advisory Panel, Southwest Arts, 1972-75. Literary Agent: Aitken and Stone. Address: 21 West Shrubbery, Bristol, BS6 6TA, England.

SMITH Barbara Herrnstein, b. 6 Aug 1932, NY, USA. Educator. m. R J Herrnstein, 28 May 1951, (div 1961), T H Smith, 21 Feb 1964, (div 1974), 2 d. Education: BA 1954, MA 1955, PhD, English and American Literature, 1965, Brandeis University. Appointments: Faculty, Literature and Language, Bennington College, 1961-73; Communications, English and Communications, Comparative Literature and Literary Theory, University of Pennsylvania, 1973-87; Professor of Comparative Literature and English, Duke University, 1987-; Northrop Frye Chair in Lit Theory, University of Toronto, 1990. Publications: Poetic Closure: A Study of How Poems End, 1968; On The Margins of Discourse: The Relation of Literature to Language, 1978; Contingencies of Value; Alternative Perspectives for Critical Theory, 1988; The Politics of Liberal Education, co-editor, 1991. Contributions to: Critical Inquiry; South Atlantic Quarterly; University of Toronto; Cardozo Law Review; Annals of Scholarship; Common Knowledge. Address: 325 Allen Building, Box 90015, Duke University, Durham, NC 27706, USA.

SMITH Bernard William, b. 3 Oct 1916, Sydney, New South Wales, Australia. Art Historian and Critic. m. Kate Beatrice Hartley Challis, 16 May 1941, 1 son, 1 daughter. Education: BA, Sydney University, 1952; Warburg Institute, London, England, 1948-50; PhD, Australian National University, 1956. Appointments: Category A Literary Fellowship, Australia Council, 1990-91. Publications: Place, Taste and Tradition, 1945; European Vision and the South Pacific, 1960; Australian Painting, 1962; The Architectural Character of Glebe, Sydney (with K Smith), 1973; Documents on Art and Taste in Australia, 1975; The Boy Adeodatus, 1984; The Art of Captain Cook's Voyages (with R Joppien), 3 vols, 1985-87; The Death of the Artist as Hero, 1988; The Critic as Advocate, 1989; Imagining the Pacific, 1992; Noel Counitian, 1993. Contributions to: Journal of the Warbury and Courtauld Institutes, Modern Painters (London); Meanjin, Scripsi, Australian Society. Honours: Co-Recipient, Ernest Scott Prize for History, Melbourne, 1962; Henry Lawson Prize for Poetry, 1964; Honorary LittD, University of Melbourne, 1976; Aistralian National Book Council Prize, The Nettie Palmer Prize for Non-Fiction, and the Talking Book Award, all for the Boys Adeodatus, 1984. Memberships: Australian Society of Authors; Australian Academy of the Humanities, President 1977-80; Australian Humanities Research Council, 1956-69, Secretary 1962-65; Fellow, Society of Antiquaries; UNESCO Committee for Letters, Australia, 1963-69. Address: 168 Nicholson Street, Fitzroy, Victoria 3065, Australia.

SMITH Bradley F, b. 5 Oct 1931, Seattle, USA. Writer; Teacher. m. 31 Dec 1983, 2 daughters. Education: BA 1957; MA, 1960, University of California, Berkeley. Publications: Reaching Judgement at Nuremberg, 1977; The Shadow Warriors, 1983; Himmler Geheimreden, 1974; Operation Sunrise, (with Elena Agarossi), 1979; The War's Long Shadow, 1986; Adolf Hitler, his Family, Childhood, and Youth, 1967; The Road to Nuremberg, 1981; The American Road to Nuremberg, 1981; The Ultra-Magic Deals and the Special Relationship, 1940-46, 1992-93 (Presido US & Airline UK). Contributions to: Encounter; Los Angeles Times; The Independent; The Washington Post; The American Historical Review; Vierteljahrshefte fur Zeitgeschichte. Honours: Shortlisted for Los Angeles Times Book of theYear, 1981; Observer Book of the Year, 1977. Memberships: Phi Beta Kappa; Authors Guild. Address: 104 Regents Park Road, London, NW1 8UG, England.

SMITH Bryan. See: **KNOTT William Cecil.**

SMITH (Clarice) Holly, b. 12 July 1931, Sydney, New South Wales, Australia. Editor; Writer; Creative Writing Tutor. Education: Teachers Certificate, New South Wales Department of Education, 1954; International Correspondence School courses, Short Story, Radio Playwriting, TV Scriptwriting, Public Relations, 1960-94; Certificate, Advertising Copywriting, 1988; Diploma, Journalism, 1989. Career: Own business, Proofreading and Editing Services, 1988-; Planned, wrote, conducted 2 series of radio interviews, Meet the Authors (14 interviews), 1990, 1993; Tutor, The Writing School, June 1991-. Publications: The Metric Primer, 1973; Gleb and the Golden Ball, 1994. Contributions: Various articles in magazines and newspapers including: Outdoors and Fishing, Ski Australia, Avalon News, Children's book reviews, Australian (NSW Teachers Federation newspaper). Honours: Best Newsletter Award as Editor of Pens, New South Wales Fellowship of Australian Writers Inc regionals, 1993. Fellowship of Australian Writers, Ex-Editor of Newsletter, Society of Editors, Manly Warrington Media Co-op, Former Member, Australian Society of Authors, New South Wales (Australia) Teachers Federation, Actors Equity. Address: 6 Park Avenue, Avalon Beach, New South Wales 2107, Australia.

SMITH Delia. Cookery Writer and Broadcaster. m. Michael Wynn Jones. Appointments: Several BBC TV Series; Cookery Writer, Evening Standard, later the Standard, 1972-85; Columnist, Radio Times. Publications: How to Cheat at Cooking, 1971; Country Fare, 1973; Recipes from Country Inns and Restaurants, 1973; Family Fare, book 1, 1973; book 2, 1974; Evening Standard Cook Book, 1974; Country Recipes from "Look East", 1975; More Country Recipes from "Look East", 1976; Frugal Food, 1976; Book of Cakes, 1977; Recipes from "Look East", 1977; Food for Our Times, 1978; Cookery Course, part 1, 1978, part 2, 1979, part 3, 1981; The Complete Cookery Course, 1982; A Feast for Lent, 1983; A Feast for Advent, 1983; One is Fun, 1985; Editor, Food Aid Cookery Book, 1986; A Journey into God, 1988; Delia Smith's Christmas, 1990; Delia Smith's Summer Collection, 1993. Contributions to: Consultant Food Editor, Sainsbury's The Magazine. Honours: 1994 Special Award from the Andre Simon Memorial Fund;

OBE, 1995. Literary Agent: Deborah Owen Ltd, 78 Narrow Street, London, E14 8BP. Address: c/o Deborah Owen Ltd, 78 Narrow Street, London, E14 8BP.

SMITH Dudley (Sir), b. 14 Nov 1926, Cambridge, England. Member of Parliament, Deputy Lieutenant, Warwickshire. m. (1) diss, 1 son, 2 daughters, (2) Catherine Amos, 1976. Appointments: Various provincial and national newspapers as journalist and senior executive, 1943-66; Assistant News Editor, Sunday Express, 1953-59; Divisional Director, Beecham Group, 1966-70; Member of Parliament. Publications include: Harold Wilson: A Critical Biography, 1964; They Also Served, 1945; Author of several WEU Assembly Reforms on Defence. Honours: Kt, 1983; D.L., 1989. Memberships: Secretary General European Democratic Group, Council of Europe, 1985-; Chairman, United and Cecil Club, 1975-80; President, Western European Assembly. 1993-. Address: Church Farm, Weston under Wetherley, Nr. Leamington Spa, Warwickshire, England.

SMITH Emma, b. 21 Aug 1923, Newquay, Cornwall, England. Writer. m. Richard Llewellyn Stewart-Jones (dec 1957), 31 Jan 1951, 1 son, 1 daughter. Publications: Maiden's Trip, 1948; The Far Cry, 1949; Emily, 1959; Out of Hand, 1963; Emily's Voyage, 1966; No Way of Telling, 1972; The Opportunity of a Lifetime, 1978. Contributions to: Various magazines. Honours: Atlantic Award, short stories, 1948; John Llewellyn Rhys Memorial Prize, 1948; James Tait Black Memorial Prize, 1949. Literary Agent: Curtis Brown. Address: c/o Curtis Brown, 162-168 Regent Street, London, W1R 5TB, England.

SMITH Genevieve Douglas, b. 14 Aug 1923, McKees Rocks, Pennsylvania, USA. Educator; Education Administration; Writer. m. William Reeves Smith, 6 Jan 1946, 1 daughter. Education: Westminster College, Pennsylvania, BBA, 1945; University of Tennessee, MS, 1971: Ed.D, 1973. Publications: Techniques and Activities for Teaching Business Skills - Featuring the Mini-Company, 1977; Genevieve Smith's Deluxe Handbook for the Executive Secretary, 1979; I'd Rather Be The Boss!, 1992. Contributions to: Simplified Grading for Multiple-Subject Classes, Journal Business Education, 1971; Office Education in The Round, Journal Business Education, 1972; The Mini-Company, Journal Business Education, 1973; Directing A Prevocational Workshop, American Vocational Journal, 1974; Using Management Information Systems for Planning, Catalyst for Change 1976; Mini-Company, Journal Business Education, 1973; The Camel Hopscotch Magazine; A New Way To Fly, Teen Quest, 1989. Memberships: Tennessee Writers' Alliance; Knoxville Writers' Guild; International Women's Writing Guild; Society Childrens Book Writers; Pi Lambda Theta; Phi Delta Kappa; National Business Education Association; American Education Research Association. Address: 1205 Snowdon Drive, Knoxville, TN 37912 USA.

SMITH Gregory Blake, b. 24 Jul 1951, Torrington, CT, USA. Novelist; College Professor. 1 s. Education: AB, Bowdoin College, 1975; MA, Boston Universit, 1981; MFA, University of Iowa, 1983. Publications: The Devil in The Dooryard, 1986; The Divine Comedy of John Venner, 1992. Honours: Stegner Fellowship, Stanford University, 1985; National Endowment for The Arts Fellow, 1988. Literary Agent: Paula Diamond. Address: Department of English, Carleton College, Northfield, MN 55057, USA.

SMITH Iain Crichton, b. 1 Jan 1928, Glasgow, Scotland, Writer, m. 16 July 1977, 2 stepsons. Education: MA Honours, English, Aberdeen University, 1949; D.Litt, Aberdeen University, 1988. Publications inclued: Thistles and Roses (poems), 1961; The Law and the Grace (poems), 1965; Consider the Lilies (novel), 1968; The Last Summer (novel), 1969; The Black and the Red (short stories), 1973; On the Island (short stories), 1974; The Hermit and Other Stories, 1977; Selected Poems, 1982; A Life (poems), 1985; The Village and Other Poems, 1989; Collected Poems, 1992; Bibliography of Iain Crichton Smith by Grant Wilson, 1988; Mirror and Marble - The Poetry of Iain Crichton Smith by Carol Gow, 1992; Critical Essays on Iain Crichton Smith, 1992. Contributions to: Spectator; The Literary Review; Times Literary Supplement; BBC; Encounter; Poetry Review; New Statesman. Honours: 8 Scottish Arts Council Awards; LLD, Dundee University; DLitt, Glasgow University; OBE; FRLS; P.E.N. Award, 1970; Commonwealth Poetry Prize, 1986; Saltire Award for Scottish Book of the Year awarded to Collected Poems, 1992. Address: Tigh Na Fuaran, Taynuilt, Argyll, Scotland.

SMITH Julie, b. 1944. Publications: Death Turns a Trick, 1982; Huckleberry Fiend, 1987; New Orleans Mourning, 1990; Axeman's

Jazz, 1991; Jazz Funeral, 1993; New Orleans Beat, 1994; House of Blues, 1995. Honour: Edgar Allen Poe Award, 1991.

SMITH Ken(neth Roger), b. 14 Apr 1944. Writer; Professor. m. 14 Jul 1992, 3 s, 1 d. Education: BA, University of Arizona, 1976; MFA, 1980. Literary Appointments: Fiction Editor, The Poetry Miscellany, 1986-. Publications: Decoys and Other Stories; Angels and Others. Contributions to: The Atlantic; Sonora Review; Triquarterly; Crazyhorse. Honours: Arizona Commission on The Arts Fellowship; PEN Fiction Award; John Gardner Fellowship; Kentucky Arts Council Fellowship. Membership: Associated Writing Program. Literary Agent: Ms Jean V Naggar. Address: Rt 10 Box 1006, Ringgold, GA 30736, USA.

SMITH Lee, b. 1944. Writer. Address: 44 Cedar Street, Chapel Hill, NC 27514, USA.

SMITH Lew. See: **FLOREN Lee.**

SMITH Moe Sherrard, (Tyler Maddison), b. 22 June 1939, Leeds, England. Author; Journalist; Adjudicator; Literary Agent. m. Thomas Maddison Smith, 14 Mar 1962. Literary Appointments: Freelance Author, 1960-; Editor, Driving Mirror Magazine, 1975-84; Principal, Writing Tutorial, 1975-; Scribe Magazine, 1975-78; Pocklington Post, 1988-90; Managing Editor. Publications: Write A Successful Novel; The Essential Guide to Novel Writing (PCW/PC disc); Cold Blast of Winter; Rubbings; Wholly Love; Yorkshire Air Museum Guide Book. Contributions to: Numerous. Honours: Numerous Competitions. Memberships: Various Writers Groups and Committees; Magistrates Association; Member of Society of Women Writers and Journalists. Literary Agent: Sherrard Smith Associates. Address: c/o Sherrard Smith Associates, Garthend House, Millington, York YO4 2TX, England.

SMITH Page, b. 1917, USA. Professor Emeritus; Writer. Appointments: Fellow, Institute of Early American History and Culture, 1951-53; Assistant to Professor, University of California, 1953-64; Provost, 1964-70, Professor, 1970-73, Professor Emeritus of Historical Studies, 1973, Cowell College, University of California, Santa Cruz. Publications: James Wilson, Founding Father, 1956; John Adams, 1962; The Historian and History,1964; As A City Upon A Hill: The Town In American History, 1966; Daughters of The Promised Land: Women in American History, 1970; Jefferson, 1976; A New Age Now Begins: A People's History of The American Revolution, 1976; The Chicken Book (co-author), 1976; A Letter From My Father, 1976; The Religious Origins Of The American Revolution (editor), 1976; The Constitution: A Documentary and Narrative History, 1978; The Shaping of America, 1980; The Nation Comes Of Age, 1981; Trial By Fire: The Civil War and Reconstruction, 1982; The Rise of Industrial America, Vol 6, People's History of US, 1984; America Enters The World, 1985, vols 111, 1V, V, V1 and V11 of A People's History of The United States; Dissenting Opinions, 1984; Redeeming The Time, vol V111, People's History of The United States, 1987; Killing The Spirit: Higher Education in The United States, 1990; Rediscovery Christianity: A History of Modern Demcolacey and The Christian Ethic, 1994. Address: 235 Pine Flat Road, Santa Cruz, CA 95060, USA.

SMITH Patrick D, b. 8 Oct 1927, Mendenhall, MS, USA. Writer; Lecturer. m. Iris Doty, 1 Aug 1948, 1 s, 1 d. Education: BA, University of Mississippi, 1947; MA, 1959. Appointments: Director, Public Relations, Hinds Community College, 1959-62; Director, Public Information, University of Mississippi, 1962-66; Director, College Relations, Brevard Community College, 1966-88. Publications: A Land Remembered; Allapattah; Angel City; Forever Island; The River Is Home; The Beginning. Contributions to: More than 1000. Honours: Tebeay Prize; Outstanding Author Award; Outstanding Florida Author Award; Best Writer Award; Toastmasters International Communication Achievement Award; Environmental Writers Award; Medal of Honor. Memberships: Space Coast Writers Guild; Authors Guild; Poets and Writers. Address: 1370 Island Drive, Merritt Island, FL 32952, USA.

SMITH Peter Charles Horstead, b. 1940, United Kingdom. Author. Appointments: Editor, Photo Precision Ltd, printers and publishers, 1972-75. Publicatons: Destroyer Leader, 1968; Task Force 57, 1969, 2nd Edition, 1994; Pedestal, 1970; 2nd Edition, 1987, 3rd Edition, 1994; Stuka at War, 1970, 2nd Edition, 1980; Hard Lying, 1971; British Battle Cruisers, 1972; War in the Aegean (with Edwin Walker), 1974; Heritage of the Sea, 1974; Battle of the Malta Striking Forces (with Edwin Walker), 1974; Destroyer Action (editor and contributor),

1974; R A F Squadron Badges, 1974; The Story of the Torpedo Bomber, 1974; The Haunted Sea (editor), 1974; Per Mare Per Terram: A History of the Royal Marines, 1974; Arctic Victory, 1975, 2nd Edition, 1994; The Battle of Midway, 1976; Fighting Flotilla, 1976; Undesirable Properties (editor and contributor), 1977; The Great Ships Pass. 1977; Hit First, Hit Hard, 1979; The Phantom Coach (editor and contributor), 1979; Action Imminent, 1980; Haunted Shores (editor and contributor), 1980; Impact: The Dive Bomber Pilots Speak, 1981; Cruisers in Action (with J R Dominy), 1981; Dive Bomber, 1982; Rendezvous Skerki Bank, fiction, 1982; Hold the Narrow Sea. 1984; Uninvited Guests, 1984; H M S Wild Swan, 1985; Into the Assault, 1985; Vengeance, 1986; Jungle Dive Bombers at War, 1987; Victoria's Victories, 1987; Dive Bombers in Action, 1988; The Royal Marines A Pictorial History (with Derek Oakley), 1988; Battleship Royal Sovereign, 1988; Stuka Squadron, 1990; Close Air Support, 1990. Contributions to: Cambridgeshire Life; Warship International (USA); Mariners Mirror; The Army Quarterly; Navy International; War Monthly, Fly Past; World War Investigator; Images of War; World War II (USA); Military History (USA); In Flight (USA); Defense Update (USA). Honour: Royal Marines Historical Society Award for 1987/88. Memberships: The Society of Authors, London; The Royal Marines Historical Society, Eastney; The American Aviation Historical Society. Address: Foxden, 12 Brooklands Road, Riseley, Bedford, MK44 1EE, England.

SMITH Ralph Bernard, b. 9 May 1939, Bingley, England. University Professor. Education: Burnley Grammer School, Lancashire 1950-56; BA 1959, Phd 1963, University of Leeds. Appointments: Lecturer, then Reader in the History of South East Asia, School of Oriental and African Studies, University of London, 1962-88; Professor of the International History of Asia, School of Oriental and African Studies, University of London, 1989-. Publications: Land and Politics in the England of Henry VIII, 1970; Vietnam and the West, 1968, 1971; An International History of the Vietnam War: Vol I, 1983, Vol II, 1985, Vol III, 1991. Contributions to: Articles in learned journals (Fields of History, Asian Studies); Book reviews in various periodicals. Address: School of Oriental and African Studies, Russell Square, London, WC1, England.

SMITH Robert Edward, b. 10 Mar 1943, Holyoke, MA, USA. Professor. m. Pauletta Verett, 28 Jul 1968. Education: BA, Harding University, 1964; MFA, University of Oregon, 1966; PhD, University of Missouri, Columbia, 1969. Publications: Principles of Human Communication; The Gift Horses Mouth; Janice, Bobby and Sarah; Cyrano of The Hill Country. Contributions to : Karamu; Descant; Four Quarters; Tales; Texas Review. Honours: Writer in Residence, Amerika Haus. Memberships: Texas Creative Writing Association; Speech Communication Association; Central States Communication Association. Literary Agent: Nat Sobel and Associates. Address: 520 Terry Lane, West Lafayette, IN 47906, USA.

SMITH Sarah W R, b. 9 Dec 1947, Boston, MA, USA. Writer. m. Frederick S Perry, 26 Aug 1979, 1 s, 1 d. Education: BA, Radcliffe College, 1968; University of London, 1968-69; PhD, Harvard University, 1975. Appointments: Assistant Professor, Northeastern University, 1975-76; Assistant Professor, Tufts University, 1976-82. Publications: The Vanished Child; King of Space; Samuel Richardson; Future Boston (co- author);Honours: Fulbright; Harvard Graduate Prize Fellow; Bowdoin Prize; Mellon Fellow. Memberships: Science Fiction Writers of America; Signet Society; Boston Computer Society; Mystery Writers of America; Sisters in Crime. Literary Agent: Jane Otte, The Otte Company. Address: 32 Bowker Street, Brookline, MA 02146, USA.

SMITH Terry Lamson, b. 10 Nov 1937, Sydney, Australia. Journalist; Author. m. Sybilla Smith, 24 Feb 1970, 2 sons. Education: Shore School, Sydney. Publications: The Complete Book of Australian Golf, 1975-78-88; Australian Golf, The First 100 Years, 1982; The Champions - Australia's Sporting Greats, 1990; Bedside Book of Cricket Centuries, 1991; I Love Youse All- The Jeff Fenech Story, 1993; Path to Victory: Wallaby Rugby Power in the 80s, 1987; Aussie Golf Trivia, 1985; More Aussie Golf Trivia, 1988. Contributions to: Australian Golf & Rugby Correspondent, London Daily Telegraph; Rugby & Boxing Writer, Sydney Daily Telegraph Mirror. Memberships: Elanora Country Club. Address: 6 Shannon Avenue, Killarney Heights, Sydney 2087, Australia.

SMITH Vivian (Brian), b. 3 June 1933, Hobart, Tasmania. Lecturer; Poet. m. Sybille Gottwald, 1960, 1 son, 2 daughters. Education: PhD, University of Sydney, 1971. Appointments include: Reader, University of Sydney, 1982; Literary Editor, Quadrant

Magazine, Sydney, 1975-90. Publications: The Other Meaning, 1956; An Island South, 1967; Familiar Places, 1978; Tide Country, 1982; Selected Poems, 1985; The Poetry of Robert Lowell, 1975; Tasmania and Australian Poetry, 1984; Editor of Volumes of Australian Poetry. Honours include: NSW Premiers Prize, 1983. Address: 19 McLeod Street, Mosman, NSW 2099, Australia.

SMITH Wilbur Addison, b. 9 Jan 1933, Zambia, Author. 2 sons, 1 daughter. Education: BCom, Rhodes University, 1953. Publications include: The Courtney novels, 6 volumes 1964-87; When the Lion Feeds; The Sound of Thunder; A Sparrow Falls; The Burning Shore; Power of the Sword; Rage, The Ballantyne novels, 4 volumes 1980-84; A Falcon Flies; Men of Men; The Angels Weep; The Leopard Hunts in Darkness. Also: The Dark of the Sun, 1965; Shout at the Devil, 1968; Gold Mine, 1970; Diamond Hunters, 1971; The Sunbird, 1972; Eagle in the Sky, 1974; The Eye of the Tiger, 1975; Cry Wolf, 1976; Hungry as the Sea, 1978; Wild Justice, 1979; A Time to Die; Golden Fox, 1990; Elephant Song, 1991; River God, 1993; The Seventh Scroll, 1995. 25 books total. Contributions to: Numerous journals & magazines. Literary Agent: Charles Pick. Address: c/o Charles Pick, Flat 3, 3 Bryanston Place, London, W1H 7FN, England.

SMITH Z Z. See: **WESTHEIMER David.**

SMITHYMAN Kendrick, b. 9 Oct 1922. m. (1) Mary Stanley Smithyman, (dec 1980), 3 sons, (2) Margaret Ann Edgcumbe, 1981. Education: Seddon Memorial Technical College, Auckland; Auckland Teachers College, Auckland University College. Appointments: Visiting Fellow, Commonwealth Literature, University of Leeds, England, 1969. Publications: Seven Sonnets, 1946; The Blind Mountain, 1951; The Gay Trapeze, 1955; The Night Shift: Poems on Aspects of Love (co-author), 1957; Inheritance, 1962; Flying to Palmerston, 1968; Earthquake Weather, 1974, The Seal in the Dolphin Pool, 1974; Dwarf with a Billiard Cue, 1978; Stories about Wooden Keyboards, 1985; Are You Going to the Pictures?, 1987; Selected Poems, 1989; Auto/Biographies, 1992. Editor: Novels by William Satchell, 1971, 1985; Short stories by Greville Texidor, 1987. Contributions to: Academic Journals; Anthologies including: A Book of New Zealand Verse, 1951; An Anthology of New Zealand Verse, 1966; Poems of Today, 1967; Poetry New Zealand, 1971-; Fifteen Contemporary New Zealand Poets, 1980; Oxford Book of Contemporary New Zealand Poetry, 1982; Penguin Book of New Zealand Verse, 1985; Penguin Book of Contemporary Verse, 1989. Honour: D Litt, University of Auckland, 1986. Address: 66 Alton Avenue, Northcote, Auckland, New Zealand.

SMITTEN Richard, b. 22 Apr 1940. 1 d. Education: BA, University of Western Ontario. Appointments: Marketing Manager, Vick Chemical Company; Executive Vice President, MTS International. Publications: Twice Killed; The Man Who Made It Snow; The Godmother; Legal Tender; The Bank Of Death; Capital Crimes; Death Stream; Kathy: A Case of Nymphomania; Several film projects. Address: 3675 Skyline Drive, Jensen Beach, FL 34957, USA.

SMUCKER Barbara C, b. 1 Sep 1915, Newton, KS, USA. Writer; Librarian. m. 21 Jan 1939, 2 s, 1 d. Education: BS, Kansas State University, 1936. Publications: Henry's Red Sea, 1955; Cherokee Run, 1957; Wigwam in The City, 1966; Runaway To Freedom, 1979; Days of Terror, 1979; Amish Adventure, 1983; Incredible Jumbo, 1990; Garth and The Mermaid, 1992. Contributions to: Autobiography, To Something About The Author, 1991; Writers on Writing; A Guide to Writing and Illustrating Children's Books; Canadian Children's Literature; Books translated into many languages; Teresita Sagia. Address: 20 Pinebrook Drive, Bluffton, OH 45817, USA.

SMYTH Dacre, b. 5 May 1923, London, England. Former Naval Officer. m. Jennifer Haggard, 11 Jan 1952, 1 son, 4 daughters. Education: RAN College, 1940. Publications: The Bridges of the Yarra, 1979; The Lighthouses of Victoria, 1980; Historic Ships of Australia, 1982; Old Riverboats of the Murray, 1982; Views of Victoria, 1984; The Bridges of Kananook Creek, 1986; Waterfalls of Victoria, 1988; Gallipoli Pilgrimage, 1990; Immigrant Ships to Australia, 1992; Pictures in My Life, 1994. Honours: Runner-up, Griffin Press Literary Award, 1990. Memberships: Fellowship of Australian Writers; Victoria Artists Society; Australian Guild of Realist Artists. Address: 22 Douglas Street, Toorak, Vic 3142, Australia.

SMYTHE Colin Peter, b. 2 Mar 1942, Maidenhead, Berkshire, England. Publisher; Literary Agent. Education: Bradfield College,

Berkshire, 1955-59; Trinity College, Dublin University, 1959-63; BA, 1963; MA, 1966. Publications: Some small volumes of poetry, 1978-79; A Guide to Coole Park: Home of Lady Gregory, 1973, revised 1983; Editor, Lady Gregory, Our Irish Theatre, 1973; Editor, Lady Gregory, Poets and Dreamers, 1974; Editor, Lady Gregory, Seventy Years 1852-1922, 1974; Editor, Robert Gregory 1881-1918, 1981; Editor with Ann Saddlemyer, Lady Gregory Fifty Years After, 1986; General Editor: The Coole Edition of Lady Gregory's Writings, 1970-; General Editor, with Henry Summerfield: The Collected Works of G W Russell - AE, 1978-; General Editor: Irish Literary Studies series. Honours: Officer, Most Venerable Order of St John; Knight Commander of Grace, Benemerenti Medals in Silver and Gold, Sacred & Military Constantinian Order of St George; Knight, Order of Polonia Restituta, and Gold Cross of Merit; Grand Cross of Merit of the "Causa Monarquica"; Benemerenti Medal in Bronze of Vatican Council II. Memberships: Honorary Member, Mark Twain Society; International Association for the Study of Anglo-Irish Literature; British Association for Irish Studies; Canadian Association for Irish Studies; American Conference for Irish Studies; Fellow, Royal Society of Arts, London; Editorial Board of Yeats Annual; Visiting Professor, University of Ulster; Honorary Research Associate, Athenaenm Club; Royal Holloway and Bedford College, University of London; Academic Advisor, Publisher, Princess Grace Irish Library, Monaco. Address: PO Box 6, Gerrards Cross, Bucks SL9 8XA, England.

SNEYD Lola, Poet, Short Story Writer; Journalist. Publications: The Asphalt Octopus, 1983; The Concrete Giraffe, 1984; Ringette is Fun, 1985; Nature's Big Top, 1987; Classy Cats, 1991. Memberships: Canadian Authors' Association; Canadian Society of Children's Authors, Illustrators & Performers; League of Canadian Poets. Honours: Canadian Children's Book Centre Our Choice; Lynn Harrington Award, Canadian Authors' Association, 1983. Address: 7 Wheeler Avenue, Toronto, Ontario, M4L 3V3, Canada.

SNODGRASS W D, (S S Gardons, Will McConnell, Kozma Prutkov), b. 5 Jan 1926, USA. Poet; Professor. m. (4) Kathleen Brown, 20 Jun 1985, 1 s. 1 d, previous marriages. Education: BA, 1949, MA, 1951, MFA, 1953, State University of Iowa. Appointments include; English Departments: Cornell, Rochester, Wayne State, Syracuse Universities, 1955-77; Distinguished Visiting Professor, Old Dominion University, 1978-79; Distinguished Professor of Creative Writing and Contemporary Poetry, University of Delaware, 1979-94. Publications include: Poems: Heart's Needle, 1959; After Experience, 1967; Remains, (as S S Gardens) 1970, (as W D Snodgrass) 1985; The Fuehrer Bunker, cycle of poems in progress, 1977; If Birds Build With Your Hair, 1979; D D Byrde Calling Jennie Wrenne, 1984; A Colored Poem, 1986; The House The Poet Built, 1986; A Locked House, 1986; The Kinder Capers, 1986; Selected Poems, 1957-87, 1987; W D's Midnight Carnival, 1988; The Death of Cock Robin, 1989; Each In His Season, 1993; The Fuhrer Bunker: The Complete Cycle, 1995. Also critical essays, translations of songs. Honours include: Numerous awards and grants including: National Institute of Arts and Letters, 1960; Pulitzer Prize, 1960; Guinness Poetry Award, UK, 1961; Guggenheim Fellowship, 1972-73; Centennial Medal, Government of Romania, 1977. Memberships: Poetry Society of America; International PEN. Address: R D I, Box 51, Erieville, NY 13061, USA.

SNOWMAN Daniel, b. 4 Nov 1938. BBC Producer. m. Janet Linda Levison, 1 son, 1 daughter. Education: BA (Double First Class) History, Cambridge. 1961; MA, Government, Cornell University, New York, USA. 1963. Appointments: Lecturer in History and American Studies, University of Sussex, 1963-67; BBC Producer 1967-; currently Chief Producer, BBC Radio Features and Arts; Visiting Professor of History, California State University, 1972-73. Publications: America Since 1920; 1968; Eleanor Roosevelt, 1970; Kissing Cousins (British and American Culture) 1977; If I Had Been.... Ten Historical Fantasies, 1979; The Amadeus Quartet, 1981; The World of Placido Domingo, 1985; Beyond the Tunnel of History, 1990; Pole Positions: The Polar Regions and the Future of Planet, 1993; Plácido Domingo's Tales From The Opera, 1994. Contributions to: Numerous chapters in books and articles and reviews. Memberships: Regular singer with London Philharmonic Choir 1967-, former Chairman. Literary Agent: Dinah Wiener, 27 Arlington Road, London, NW1 7ER. Address: 47 Wood Lane, Highgate, London, N6 5UD, England.

SNYDAL James Matthew, b. 6 May, Williston, ND, USA. Writer. m. Kathryn Church, 25 Jul 1970. Education: BA, University of Washington, Seattle, 1971. Publications: Numerous poems including: City Life Along the Home Front, 1942, in Poem The Nukes, 1983, in

Alternatives: An American Poetry Anthology, 1988, in The New Poet's Anthology, 1987; Empire of Light, On May 4 1985, The Fifteenth Anniversary of My Antiwar Demonstration Arrest, February 5 1989, On Bainbridge Island in American Poetry Confronts The 1990s; Book reviews in Small Press Review and many others; Poems in New York Quarterly, Albany Review and others. Contributions to: Inscape; Big Moon; Permafrost; Pacific; Poetry Seattle; Vegetable Box; Yakima; Maniac; Poetry Now; Snowy Egret; Matrix; Fine Madness. Address: 11034 Old Creosote Hill Road, Bainbridge Island, WA 98110, USA.

SNYDER Dianne. Publications: Boy of the Three-Year Nap, 1987; George & the Dragon Word, 1991. Honours: Boston Globe/Horn Book Award, 1988.

SNYDER Francis Gregory, b. 26 June 1942, Madison, Wisconsin, USA. Law Professor. m. Sian Miles, 20 Aug 1967, 1 son. Education: BA, Yale, 1964; Fulbright Scholar, Institut d'Etudes Politiques de Paris 1964-65; JD, Harvard Law School, 1968; Certificat de Droit et Economie des Pays d'Afrique, 1969; Doctorat de Spécialité, 1973, Université de Paris I; US Attorney, MA, 1968. Publications: European Community Law, 2 vols, 1993; New Directions in European Community Law, 1990; Law of the Common Agricultural Policy, 1985; International Law of Development, (co-editor), 1987; The Political Economy, (co-editor), 1987; Capitalism and Legal Change, 1981; One=Party Government in Mali, 1965; Labour, Law and Crime, (co-editor), 1987; Policing and Prosecution in Britain 1750-1850, (co-editor), 1989; Law and Population in Senegal, 1977. Contributions to: Over 50 articles and 100 reviews to various journals. Honours include: Officier dans l'Ordre des Palmes Academiques, 1988; Research Associate International Development Research Center, 1978. Memberships include: Law and Society Association. Address: Department of Law, European University Institue, Badia Fiesolana I-50016, San Domenico di Fiesole (Fi), Italy.

SNYDER Gary, b. 1930, San Francisco, California. Appointments: Professor of English, University of California, Davis, 1985-. Contributions to: Yale Review; Grand Street. Honours: Pulitzer Prize, 1975. Address: Dept of English, University of California, Davis, CA 95616, USA.

SNYDER Zilpha Keatley, b. 11 May 1927, CA, USA. Writer. m. 18 Jun 1950, 2 s, 1 d. Education: BA, Whittier College, 1948. Publications: Season of Ponies, 1964; The Velvet Room, 1965; Black and Blue Magic, 1966; The Egypt Game, 1967; The Changeling, 1970; The Headless Cupid, 1971; The Witches of Worm, 1972; The Princess and The Giants, 1973; The Truth About Stone Hollow, 1974; The Famous Stanley Kidnapping Case, 1979; Blair's Nightmare, 1984; The Changing Maze, 1985; And Condors Danced, 1987; Squeak Saves The Day And Other Tooley Tales, 1988; Janie's Private Eyes, 1989; Libby on Wednesday, 1990; Song of The Gargoyle, 1991; Fool's Gold, 1993; Cat Running, 1994; numerous others. Address: 52 Miller Avenue, Mill Valley, CA 94941, USA.

SOCOLOFSKY Homer Edward, b. 20 May 1922, Tampa, KS, USA. Emeritus Professor of History. m. Helen Margot Wright, 23 Nov 1946, 4 s, 2 d. Education: BS, 1944, MS, 1947, Kansas State University; PhD, University of Missouri, 1954. Literary Appointments: History Editor, Kansas Quarterly, 1969-92; Book Review Editor, Journal of The West, 1978-92. Publications: Arthur Capper, Publisher, Politician, Philanthropist, 1962; Historical Atlas of Kansas (with Huber Self), 1972, 1989; Landlord William Scully, 1979; The Presidency of Benjamin Harrison (with Allan Spetter), 1987; Governors of Kansas, 1990; Kansas History: An Annotated Bibliography (with Virgil Dean), 1992. Contributions to: Over 40 articles in journals and anthologies. Address: Department of History, Kansas State University, Manhattan, KS 66506, USA.

SOFOLA Zulu, b. 22 June 1935, Issele-Uku, Nigeria. Playwright. Education: PhD, University of Ibadan, 1977. Appointments include: Head of Department at the University of Ilorin, Kwara State, Nigeria, from 1989. Publications include: The Disturbed Peace of Christmas, 1969; Wedlock of the Gods, 1971; The Operators, 1973; King Emene, 1975; Old Wines are Tasty, 1975; The Sweet Trap, 1975; The Wizard of Law, 1976; The Deer and the Hunter's Pearl, 1976; Memories in the Moonlight, 1977; Song of a Maiden, 1977; Queen Umu-Ako of Oligbo, 1989; Eclipse and the Fantasia, 1990; Lost Dreams, 1991; The Showers, 1991; The Love of the Life; Has produced her own plays in the United States and Nigeria. Honours include: Fulbright Fellowship,

1988. Address: Department of the Performing Arts, University of Ilorin, Ilorin, Kwara State, Nigeria.

SOHAIL Khalid, b. 9 July 1952, Pakistan. Psychiatrist. Education: MBBS, Pakistan, 1974; FRCP(C), Canada, 1982. Publications: Discovering New Highways in Life, psychotherapy, 1991; From One Culture To Another, essays, 1992; Literary Encounters, interviews, 1992; Pages of my Heart, poems, 1993; A Broken Man, stories, 1993; Collections of poems, stories, essays and translations of World Literature. Contributions to: American Poetry Anthology, 1987, 1989; Global Safari, Canada, 1994; Afkar & Rujhanat, Pakistan; Shair, Saughat, India; Frank, France. Honours: Honourary Cultural Doctorate in Literature, World University, USA, 1993; Rahul Award, Calcutta, India, 1994. Memberships: Writers Union of Canada; Fellow, Royal College of Physicians & Surgeons, Canada. Address: PH6 100 White Oaks Court, Whitby, Ontario, L1P 1B7, Canada.

SOHL Gerald A, (Nathan Butler, Roberta Jean Mountjoy, Jerry Sohl, Sean Mei Sullivan), b. 13 Dec 1913, Los Angeles, CA, USA. Author; Screenwriter. m. Jean Gordon, 28 Oct 1943, 1 s, 2 d. Publications: As Jerry Sohl: The Haploids, 1952; The Altered Ego, 1954; The Time Dissolver, 1957; The Odious Ones, 1959; Night Slaves, 1963; The Spun Sugar Hole, 1971; Underhanded Chess, 1973; Underhanded Bridge, 1975; I, Aleppo, 1976; Death Sleep, 1983; Various other novels as Roberta Jean Mountjoy, Nathan Butler, Sean Mei Sullivan; Staff Writer, Television Programmes including: Star Trek; Alfred Hitchcock Presents; The New Breed; Episodes; various other programmes; Filmscripts including: 12 Hours To Kill; Die, Monster, Die; Night Slaves. Contributions to: Playboy; Galaxy; If; Magazine of Fantasy and Science Fiction; Science Fiction Adventures; Imagination; Space; Infinity; Various anthologies. Memberships: Charter member, Science Fiction Writers of America; Writers Guild of America (West); Authors Guild; Authors League. Address: 3020 Ash Court, Thousand Oaks, CA 91360, USA.

SOHL Jerry. See: SOHL Gerald A.

SOHOLM Ejgil, b. 19 Apr 1936, Nykobing Mors, Denmark. Librarian; Author; Translator; Freelance Journalist. m. Kirsten Kynne Frandsen, 28 Apr 1961, 2 sons, 1 daughter. Education: MA, Aarhus Universitet, 1963; Sr Librarian, State & University Library, Aarthus, 1968-; Lecturer in Danish Literature, Aarhus University, 1968-73. Literary Appointments: Editor, DF-Revy, 1978-82. Publications: Roman om en forbrydelse, 1976; Fra frihedskamp til lighedsdrom, 1979; Storm P for Ping, 1986; Ordkvartet Århus, 1990; Angli gjorde det, 1992; Translation of a considerable number of children's books. Contributions to: Bibliotek 70, 1981-; Information, 1983-. Memberships: The Danish Writers Union. Address: PO Box 1302, DK-8210 Århus V, Denmark.

SOLINGER Rickie. Honours: New York Times Citation, 1992. Address: 1017 Maxwell Avenue, Boulder, CO 80302, USA.

SOLOW Robert M. Contributions to: Numerous Professional Journals. Honours: Nobel Prize in Economics, 1987. Address: Dept of Economics, Massachusetts Institute of Technology, 77 Massachusetts Avenue, Cambridge, MA 02139-4307, USA.

SOMERS Suzanne. See: DANIELS Dorothy.

SOMERSET FRY Peter George Robin Plantagenet, b. 3 Jan 1931, England. Author; Journalist. m. (2) Daphne Diana Elizabeth Caroline Yorke, 1958 (dec 1961), (3) Hon Mrs Leri Butler, 1961 (div. 1973), (4) Pamela Fiona Ileene Whitcombe, 1974. Education: Lancing College; St Thomas's Hospital Medical School, London; St Catherine's College, Oxford. Appointments include: Editorial staffs: Atomics & Nuclear Energy 1957-58, Tatler & Bystander 1958; Information Officer, Ministry of Public Buildings & Works, 1967-70; Head of Information at COSIRA, 1970-74; Editor of Books, HM Stationery Office, 1975-80; General editor, Macmillan History in Pictures series, 1977-1980. Publications include: Mysteries of History, 1957; The Cankered Rose, 1959; Rulers of Britain, 1967, 3rd edition, 1973; They Made History, 1971, 1973; The World of Antiques, 1970, 4th edition 1972; Antique Furniture, 1971, 1972; Children's History of the World, 1972, 11th edition, 1987; Zebra Book of Famous Men, 1972: Zebra Book of Famous Women, 1972; Collecting Inexpensive Antiques, 1973, 5th edition, 1980; British Medieval Castles, 1974; Great Caesar, 1974; 1000 Great Lives, 1975, 9th edition, 1987; 2000 years of British Life, 1976; Chequers: The Country Home of Britain's Prime Minsters, official history, 1977; 3,000 Questions & Answers, 1977, 12th edition, 1984;

Boudicca, 1978; The David & Charles Book of Castles, 1980; Beautiful Britain, 1981; Great Cathedrals, 1982; The History of Scotland (with Fiona Somerset Fry), 1982, 1985 and 1992; Rebellion Against Rome, 1982; Roman Britain; History & Sites, 1984; 3,000 More Questions & Answers, 1984; Junior Illustrated Dictionary, 1987; A History of Ireland (with Fiona Somerset Fry), 1988, 1991; Castles of the British Isles, 1990; The Tower of London, 1990; Kings & Queens of England and Scotland, 1990, 1991, 1992, 1993 twice; Handbook of Antique Furniture, 1992; Dorling Kindersley History of the World, 1994 . Memberships include: Council, East Anglian Writers 1977-82; Senior member Wolfson College, Cambridge since 1980; Co-founder, Congress of Independent Archaeologists, 1985; Eastern Region Manager, Charities Aid Foundation, 1987-1991; Antique Furniture Consultant, Christchurch Mansion, Ipswich Museum since 1987. Address: Wood Cottage, Wattisfield, Bury St Edmunds, Suffolk, IP22 1NE, England.

SOMLYO György, b. 28 Nov 1920, Balatonboglar, Hungary. Writer; Magazine Director. div, 1 son. Education: Budapest, University, 1945-46; Sorbonne, Paris, France, 1947-48. Appointments: Director, Literary section, Radio Budapest, 1954-55; Secretary, International Poetry Meeting, days of Poetry in Budapest, 1966, 1970; Director, magazine Arion, 1966. Publications: Airon's Canto; Stone Cercles, collected poems 1-2, 1978; Phyloctetes's Blessing, essay, 1980; Shadow Plan, novel, 1977; The Rampe, novel, 1984; The Trip, French Poetry from Baudelaire To..., translation, 1984; Parisiens, 1987; Beyond Myself, Selected Poems, 1988; Palimpsest, poems, 1990; Talisman, 101 Sonnets, 1990; Two-steps in Paris, novel, 1990; Cities, essays, 1991; No Secret, poems, 1992; Milán Füst, biographical essey, 1993; An Indisputable Place, essays in poetry, 1994; The Foath Chamber, poems, 1994, 1001 Sonnets from the World Literature, (editor), 1991. Literary Agent: Artisjus. Address: Irinyi ju. 39, Budapest H-1111, Hungary.

SONENBERG Maya, b. 24 Feb 1960, New York City, USA. Writer; Professor. Education: MA Graduate Writing Programme, Brown University, 1984; BA, Wesleyan University, 1982. Literary Appointments: English Department Instructor, Sonoma State University, 1986; Lecturer, Chabot College, 1989-90; Assistant Professor, Oregon State University, 1990-93; Assistant Professor, University of Washington, 1993-. Publications: Cartographies, 1989. Contributions to: The Writer; Grand Street; Chelsea; The Cream City Review; Columbia; Gargoyle. Honours: McDowell Colony Fellow, 1987; Drue Heinz Literature Prize, 1989; Centre For The Humanities Faculty Fellow, Oregon State University, 1992-93. Memberships: Associate Writing Programmes; Modern Language Association. Address: English Department, GN-30, University of Washington, Seattle, WA 98195, USA.

SONTAG Susan, b. 16 Jan 1933, New York, USA. Writer; Film & Play Director. m. Philip Rieff, 1950 (div), 1 son. Education: University of California, Berkeley; BA, University of Chicago; MA English, MA Philosophy, Harvard University; St Anne's College; Oxford University. Publications include: The Benefactor, 1963; Against Interpretation, 1966; Death Kit, 1967; Styles of Radical Will, 1969; On Photography, 1977; Illness as Metaphor, 1978; I, etcetera, 1978; Under the Sign of Saturn, 1980; A Sontag Reader, 1982; AIDS and Its Metaphors, 1989; The Way We Live Now, a story with six coloured etchings by Howard Hodgkin, 1991; The Volcano Lover, 1992; Alice in Bed, 1993. Contributions to: Essays and stories included in The New York Review of Books; The Times Literary Supplement; Art in America; The Threepenny Review; Granta. Memberships: PEN America Center, President, 1987-89; The American Academy of Arts and Letters, 1979. Honours: Fellowships: Rockefeller Foundation, 1965 & 74, Guggenheim Foundation, 1966 & 75; National Book Critics Circle Award for On Photography, 1978; Officier de l'Ordre des Arts et des Lettres, 1984; Malaparte Prize, Italy, 1992; John D and Catherine T MacArthur Foundation Fellowship, 1990-95; Honorary Doctorates: Columbia University and Harvard University, 1993; Montblanc de la Culture's Cultural Achievement Award, 1994. Address: c/o Wylie, Aitken & Stone, 250 West 57th Street, Suite 2114, New York, NY 10107, USA.

SORENSEN Knud, b. 10 Mar 1928, Hjorring, Denmark. Writer. m. Anne Marie Dybor Jorgensen, 4 July 1950, 2 sons. Education: Graduate Royal Vet and Agricultural University of Copenhagen, 1952. Publications: Revolutionen i Toving, 1972; Bondeslutspil, 1980; St St Blicher Digterog Samfordsborger, 1984; Historier fra engang, 1989; Naboskab, 1991; Sandemoses ryg, 1992; Den Rode Kaffekande.

Smaborgerlige digte, 1965; Slutsdelen, 1977; Beretninger fra en dansk udkant, 1978; Historie om Martin, 1979; Hvad skal vi med solnedgangen (digte), 1977; Marginaljord (noveller), 1987; Danmark mellem land og by, 1988; Historier fra engang, 1989; Op over den lave jord. In bog om Hohan Skjoldborg og hans tid, 1990; Naboskab, 1991; Sandemoses ryg, 1992; Rundt omkring, 1993; Samhorighed, 1994; Hvor bor Kulturen, 1994. Contributions to: Hvedekorn; Chancen; Kritik; Fredag; Aktuelt; Jyllands-Posten; Fyens Stiftstidende; Arhus Stiftstidende. Address: Skjelholmvehj 2, DK 7900 Nykobing Mors, Denmark.

SORENSEN Villy, b. 13 Jan 1929, Frederiksberg, Denmark. Writer. Education: Philosophical And Philological Studies in Copenhagen, Freiburg, Germany. Publications: Strange Stories; Harmless Tales; Tutelary Tales; Seneca, the Humanist at the Court of Nero; Another Metamorphosis; Four Biblical Tales; The Downfall of the Gods. Honours: Prize of the Danish Academy; Henrik Steffens Preis; The Nordic Prize of the Swedish Academy. Memberships: The Danish Academy. Address: Skovvej 6, DK 2930 Klampenborg, Denmark.

SORESTAD Glen Allan, b. 21 May 1937, Vancouver, Canada. Writer. m. Sonia Diane Talpash, 17 Sep 1960, 3 s, 1 d. Education: University of Saskatchewan, 1963; MEd, 1976. Publications: Prairie Pub Poems; Ancestral Dances; Jan Lake Poems; Air Canada Owls; West Into Night. Contributions to: Numerous. Honours: Hilroy Fellowship; Founder Award. Memberships: The Saskatchewan Writers Guild; League of Canadian Poets; Writers Union of Canada; International PEN. Address: 668 East Place, Saskatchewan, Sask, Canada S7J 2Z5.

SOSKIN V H. See: **ELLISON Virginia Howell.**

SOSUKE Shibasaki. See: **CIVASAQUI Jose.**

SOTO Gary, b. Sacramento, California, USA. Poet; Essayist. Honours: American Book Award, 1985; Bess Hoskin Prize; Discovery - The Nation Prize; Academy of American Poets Award. Address: 43 The Crescent, Berkeley, CA 94708, USA.

SOULE Gardner, b. 16 Dec 1913, Paris, Texas, USA. Author. m. (1) Janie Lee McDowell, 20 Sept 1940, dec, (2) Mary Muir Dowhing, 23 Apr 1994. Education: BA, Rice University, 1933; BSc, 1935, MSc, 1936, Columbia University. Appointments: Associated Press, 1936-41; US Naval Reserve, 1942-45; Managing Editor, Better Homes & Gardens, 1945-50. Publications: Tomorrow's World of Science, 1963; The Maybe Monsters, 1963; UFO's and IFO's, 1967; Trail of the Abominable Snowman, 1965; The Ocean Adventure, 1966; The Mystery Monsters, 1965; Wide Ocean, 1970; British Edition, 1974; Men Who Dared the Sea, 1976; German Edition, 1978; The Long Trail, How Cowboys and Longhorns Opened the West, 1976; Mystery Monsters of the Deep, 1981; Mystery Creatures of the Jungle, 1982; Antarctica, 1985; Christopher Columbus, 1989; Books translated into Spanish, Japanese, Thai, three languages in India. Contributions to: Popular Science Monthly; United Features; London Express Syndicate; Boy's Life; Illustrated London News. Honours: Navy League Commendation, 1956. Memberships: Sigma Delta Chi; Columbia University Club. Address: Apt 53, 517 West 113th Street, New York, NY 10025, USA.

SOULE Maris Anne, b. 19 Jun 1939, Oakland, CA, USA. Writer; Teacher. m. William L Soule, 11 May 1968, 1 s, 1 d. Education: BA, University of California, Davis, 1961; Secondary Teaching Credential, University of California, Berkeley. Publications include: First Impressions, 1983; No Room for Love, 1984; Lost and Found, 1985; Sounds Like Love, 1986; A Winning Combination, 1987; The Best of Everything, 1988; The law of Nature, 1988; Storybook Hero, 1989; Jared's Lady, 1991; No Promises Made, 1994; Stop The Wedding!, 1994. Memberships: Romance Writers of America Inc; Mid-Michigan Chapter, RWA Inc, Chapter Adviser; Novelists Inc. Literary Agent: Denise Marcil Literary Agency, New York, USA. Address: RRI Box 173B, Fulton, MI 49052, USA.

SOURITZ Elizabeth, b. 25 Feb 1923, Berlin, Germany. Ballet Historian. m. Vladimir Varkovitsky, 4 Sept 1948, dec 1974, 1 daughter. Education: Graduate, State Institute of Theatre Art, 1949; Candidate in Arts Degree, Institute of Research in Arts, Moscow, 1976. Publications: Soviet Choreographers in the 1920s, 1979, 1990. Contributions to: Soviet ballet; Ballet Review; Dance Research Journal; World Ballet and Dance; La Danza Italiana; Studies in Dance History, Dance Chronicle; Encyclopedias: Pipers Enzyclopädie des Musik Theaters; International

Encylopedia of Ballet (St James Press). Honours: The de la Torre Bueno Prize, Dance Perspectives Foundation, USA, 1991. Memberships: Union of Theatre Workers of the USSR; Association Européenne des Historiens de la danse. Address: Victorenco Street 2/1 Apt 79, Moscow 125167, Russia.

SOUSTER Raymond (John Holmes, Raymond Holmes), b. 1921, Canada. Author; Banker (retired). Publications include: On Target (as John Holmes), 1972; 100 Poems of 19th Century Canada (edited with D Lochhead), 1974; Change Up, 1974; Sights and Sounds (edited with R Woollatt), 1974; These Loved, These Hated Lands (edited with R Woollatt), 1974; Double Header, 1975; Rain Check, 1975; Extra Innings, 1977; Vapour and Blue; The Poetry of W W Campbell (editor), 1978; Hanging In: New Poems, 1979; Comfort of The Fields: The Best-Known Poems of Archibald Lampman (editor), 1979; Collected Poems, 7 volumes, 1980-88; Going the Distance: New Poems, 1979-82, 1983; Powassan's Drum: Selected Poems of Duncan Campbell Scott (edited with Douglas Lochhead), 1983; Queen City, Toronto in Poems and Pictures (with Bill Brooks), 1984; Jubilee of Death: The Raid on Dieppe, 1984; Windflower: The Selected Poems of Bliss Carman (edited with Douglas Lochhead), 1986; It Takes All Kinds: New Poems, 1986; The Eyes of Love, 1987; Asking For More, 1988; Collected Poems of Raymond Souster, Volume 6, 1988; Running Out The Clock, 1991; Collected Poems of Raymond Souster, Volume 7, 1992; Riding The Long Black Horse, 1993; Old Bank Notes, 1993. Address: 39 Baby Point Road, Toronto, Ontario, Canada, M6S 2G2.

SOUTHALL Ivan Francis, b. 8 June 1921, Melbourne, Australia. Writer. m. (1) Joy Blackburn, 8 Sept 1945 (div.), 1 son, 3 daughters, (2) Susan Westerlund Stanton, 11 Nov 1976. Appointments include: Whitall Poetry & Literature Lecturer, Library of Congress, USA, 1973; May Hill Arbuthnot Honour Lecturer, University of Washington, USA, 1974; Writer-in-residence, Macquarie University, Sydney, 1979. Publications include: Softly Tread the Brave, 1960; Hills End, 1962; Ash Road, 1965; To the Wild Sky, 1967; Let the Balloon Go, 1968; Josh, 1971. Also: They Shall Not Pass Unseen, 1956; Bread & Honey, 1970; Head in the Clouds, 1972; Matt & Jo, 1973; What About Tomorrow, 1977; City Out of Sight, 1984; Christmas in the Tree, 1985; Rachel, 1986; Blackbird, 1988. Address: PO Box 25, Healesville, Victoria 3777, Australia.

SOUTHAM B(rian) C(harles), b. 1931, United Kingdom. Publisher. Appointments: Lecturer in English Literature, University of London, 1961-63; Currently Publisher, The Athlone Press, London. Publications: Volume the Second (editor), 1963; Jane Austen's Literary Manuscripts, 1964; Selected Poems of Lord Tennyson (editor), 1964; Jane Austen: The Critical Heritage (editor), 2 vols, 1966, 87; Critical Essays on Jane Austen (editor), 1968; Minor Works of Jane Austen (edited with R W Chapman), 1969; A Student's Guide to the Selected Works of T S Eliot, 1969, 6th edition 1994; Tennyson, 1971; Jane Austen (editor), 1975; Jane Austen: Northanger Abbey and Persuasion (editor), 1976; Jane Austen: Sense and Sensibility, Pride and Prejudice, and Mansfield Park (editor), casebooks, 3 vols, 1976; T S Eliot (editor), 1981. Membership: Chairman, Jane Austen Society. Address: 3 West Heath Drive, London, NW11 7QG, England.

SOUTHERN Terry (Maxwell Kenton), b. 1 May 1924, USA. Author. Publications: Candy Kisses (with D Burnett), screenplay, 1955; Flash and Filigree, 1958; Candy (as Maxwell Kenton with Mason Hoffenberg), 1958, under real names, 1964; The Magic Christian, 1959, screenplay, 1971; Writers in Revolt (co-editor), 1963; Dr Strangelove (with S Kubrick), screenplay, 1964; The Loved One (with Christopher Isherwood), screenplay, 1965; The Journal of the Loved Ones: The Production Log of a Motion Picture, 1965; The Cincinnati Kid (with Ring Lardner Jr), screenplay, 1966; Barbarella, screenplay, 1967; Red-Dirt Marijuana and Other Tales, short stories, 1967; Easy Rider, screenplay, 1968; End of the Road, screenplay, 1969; Blue Movie, 1970; The Rolling Stones on Tour, 1978. Address: R F D, East Canaan, CT 06024, USA

SOWANDE Bode, b. 2 May 1948, Kaduna, Nigeria. Playwright. Education: Universities of Ife, Dakar and Sheffield; MA, 1974; PhD, 1977. Appointments include: Senior Lecturer at the Department of Theatre Arts, University of Ibadan, 1977-90. Publications: The Night Before, 1972; Lamps in the Night, 1973; Bar Beach Prelude, 1976; A Sanctus for Women, 1976; Afamoko - the Workhorse, 1978; Farewell to Babylon, 1978; Kalakuta Cross Currents, 1979; The Master and the Frauds, 1979; Barabas and the Master Jesus, 1980; Flamingo, 1982; Circus of Freedom Square, 1985; Tornadoes Full of Dreams, 1989;

Arede Owo, after L'Avare by Molière, 1990; Mammy-Water's Wedding, 1991; Ajantala-Pinocchio, 1992; Radio and Television plays; Novels: Our Man the President, 1981; Without a Home, 1982; The Missing Bridesmaid, 1988. Honours include: Chevalier De L'Ordre Des Arts Et Des Lettres (France), 1991; Patron of the Arts Award (Pan African Writers Association), 1993; Association of Nigerian Authors Drama Awards. Address: c/o Odu Themes Meridian, 33 Oyo Road, Orita, PO Box 14369, Post Office UI, Ibadan, Nigeria.

SOYINKA Wole, b. 13 July 1934, Abeokuta, Nigeria. Poet; Playwright. Education: University College Ibadan, University of Leeds, 1957. Appointments include: Professor, Head of Department, University of Ife, Nigeria, 1975-85; Visiting Professor, Univerisities in USA & Nigeria. Publications include: Verse, Idanre and Other Poems, 1967; Poems from Prison, 1969; A Shuttle in the Crypt, 1972; Mandelas Earth and Other Poems, 1988; Plays, The Swamp Dwellers, 1958; The Lion and the Jewel, 1959; The Invention, 1959; A Dance of the Forests, 1960; The Trials of Brother Jero, 1960; The Strong Breed, 1964; Kongis Harvest, 1964; Before the Blackout, 1965; The Road, 1965; Madmen and Specialists, 1970; The Jero Plays, 1973; The Bacchae, 1973; Death and the Kings Horseman, 1976; Golden Accord, 1980; Requiem for a Futurologist, 1983; A Play of Giants, 1984; Radio & Television Plays, Editor, Poems of Black Africa, 1975. Honours include: D Litt, University of Leeds, 1973, University of Lagos, 1989; Commander, Federal Republic of Nigeria, 1986. Address: PO Box 935, Abeokuta, Nigeria.

SPACHE George Daniel, b. 22 Feb 1909, New York, USA. Psychologist; Reading Specialist. m. Evelyn B Schoonover, 28 Oct 1968, 1 s, 4 d. Education: BS, 1933; MA, 1934; PhD, 1937, School of Education, New York University. Publications include: Good Books for Poor Readers, 1954; Resources in Teaching Reading, 1955; Faster Reading for Business, 1958; Toward Better Reading, 1963; Good Reading for Poor Readers, 10th edition, 1978; Reading in The Elementary School, 5th edition, 1985; Art of Efficient Reading, 4th edition, 1988; Vision and School Success (with Lillian B Hinds and Lois B Bing), 1990; various case studies, papers and articles in professional journals. Address: 4042 Wilshire Circle E, Sanasota, FL 34238, USA.

SPACKS Patricia Meyer, b. 1929, USA. Professor of English. Appointments: Instructor in English, Indiana University, Bloomington, 1954-56; Instructor in Humanities, University of Florida, 1958-59; Instructor, 1959-61, Assistant Professor, 1961-63, Associate Professor, 1965-68, Professor of English, 1968-79, Wellesley College, MA; Professor of English, 1979-89, Chairman, Department of English, 1985-88, Yale University, New Haven, CT; Edgar F Shannon Professor of English, University of Virginia, 1989-; Chairman, Department of English, 1991-. Publications: The Varied God, 1959; The Insistence of Horror, 1962; 18th Century Poetry (editor), 1964; John Gay, 1965; Poetry of Vision, 1967; Late Augustan Prose (editor), 1971; An Argument of Images, 1971; Late Augustan Poetry (editor), 1973; The Female Imagination, 1975; Imagining a Self, 1976; Contemporary Women Novelists, 1977; The Adolescent Idea, 1981; Gossip, 1985; Desire and Truth, 1990; Boredom: The Literary History of A State of Mind, 1995. Honour: American Academy of Arts and Sciences, 1994. Memberships: A SECS, Modern Language Association, 2nd Vice-President, 1992, 1st Vice-President, 1993, President, 1994. Address: Department of English, University of Virginia, Charlottesville, VA 22903, USA.

SPALDING Linda, b. Canada. m. Michael Ondastje. Address: c/o Michael Ondastje, Gledon College, 2275 Bayview Avenue, Toronto, Ontario M4N 3M6, Canada.

SPARK David Brian, b. 5 Oct 1930, Darlington, England. Journalist. m. 20 Sept 1958, 1 son, 1 daughter. Education: MA Modern Languages, Trinity Hall, Cambridge, 1948-51. Literary Appointments: Assistant Editor, The Northern Echo, 1965-66; Leadwriter, Westminster Press, 1967-86; Editor, National Press Agency, 1972-82; Assistant London Editor, Westminster Press, 1982-86; Editor Commonwealth Journalists Association Newsletter, 1986-. Publications: Practical Newspaper Reporting, 1966, 1993; Who to Ask about Developing Countries, 1992. Contributions to: Financial Times; The Independent. Memberships: Commonwealth Journalists Association; Association of British Science Writers. Address: 47 Seagry Road, Wanstead, London, E11 2NH, England.

SPARK Muriel Sarah, Dame, b. 1 Feb 1918, Edinburgh, Scotland. Writer. m. S O Spark, 1937, marriage dissolved, 1 son.

Education: James Gillespies's School for Girls; Heriot Watt College, Edinburgh. Appointments: Political Intelligence Department, British Foreign Office, World War II; General Secretary, Poetry Society, Editor, Poetry Review, London, 1947-49. Publications include: The Comforters, 1957; Robinson, 1958; Memento Mori, 1959; The Bachelors, 1960; The Ballard of Peckham Rye, 1960; The Prime of Miss Jean Brodie, 1961 (adapted to stage 1966, 1994, filmed 1969, and BBC TV 1978); The Girls of Slender Means, 1963; The Mandelbaum Gate, 1965; The Driver's Seat, 1970; The Abbess of Crewe, 1974; The Takeover, 1976; Territorial Rights, 1979; Loitering With Intent, 1981; The Only Problem, 1984; The Stories of Muriel Spark, 1987; A Far Cry From Kensington, 1989: Symposium, 1990; Autobiography: Curriculum Vitae, 1992; The Essence of the Brontës, 1993; The French Window and The Small Telephone (for children), 1993; Omnibus I, 1993; Omnibus II, 1994. Honours: Hon D.Litt, University of Strathclyde, Glasgow, 1971; OBE; Hon D.Litt, University of Edinburgh, 1989; C.Litt, 1991; Honorary Member, American Academy, 1978; Awards: The Observer Story Prize, 1951; Italia Prize for Radio Drama, 1962; James Tait Black Memorial Prize, 1966; Prize du Meilleur Recueil de Nouvelles Etrangères Foundation FNAC, 1987; Scottish Book of the Year, The Saltire Society and the Royal Bank of Scotland, 1987; Ingersoll Foundation; T S Eliot Award, 1992. Address: c/o David Higham Associates Ltd, 5-8 Lower John Street, Golden Square, London, W1R 4HA, England.

SPARSHOTT Francis Edward, b. 19 May 1926, Chatham, England. University Teacher; Author. m. Kathleen Elizabeth Vaughan, 7 Feb 1953, 1 d. Education: King's School, Rochester; Corpus Christi College, Oxford, 1943-44, 1947-50; BA, MA, 1950. Publications: An Enquiry into Goodness, 1958; The Structure of Aesthetics, 1963; A Divided Voice, poems, 1965; The Concept of Criticism, 1967; A Cardboard Garage, poems, 1968; Looking for Philosophy, 1972; The Naming of The Beasts, poems, 1979; The Rainy Hills, poems, 1979; The Theory of The Arts, 1982; The Hanging Gardens of Etobicoke, poems, 1983; Storms and Screens, poems, 1987; Off The Ground, 1988; Sculling to Byzantium, poems, 1989; Taking Life Seriously, 1994; Views From The Zucchini Gazebo, poems, 1994; A Measured Pace, poems, 1995. Contributions to: numerous. Honour: 1st Prize for Poetry, CBC Literary Competition, 1981. Memberships: League of Canadian Poets, President 1977-79; PEN International, Canadian Centre; Canadian Philosophical Association, President, 1975-76; American Society for Aesthetics, President 1981-82. Address: 50 Crescentwood Road, Scarborough, Ontario, Canada, M1N 1E4.

SPECTOR Ronald H, b. 1943. Professor of History. Address: Dept of History, George Washington University, 2029 G Street NW, WA 20006-4211, USA.

SPELLMAN Cathy Cash, b. New Jersey, USA. Novelist; Journalist. 3 daughters. Education: Vassar College. Publications: Notes to My Daughters; So Many Partings; An Excess of Love; Paint the Wind; Bless the Child. Contributions to: Vogue; Town and Country; Mademoiselle; Harper's Bazaar; Cosmopolitan; Omni. Memberships: Writers Guild; Vassar Club; The Fashion Group. Literary Agent: Robert Gottlieb; William Morris.

SPENCE Alan, b. 5 Dec 1947, Glasgow, Scotland. Novelist; Playwright. Education: Glasgow University, 1966-69, 1973-74. Appointments: Writer in Residence, Glasgow University, 1975-77, Traverse Theatre, Edinburgh, 1982, Edinburgh University, 1990. Publications: Novel, The Magic Flute, 1990; Short Story Collection, Its Colours They are Fine, 1977; Plays, Sailmaker, 1982; Space Invaders, 1983; Changed Days, 1991; Verse, Plop, 15 Haiku, 1970; Glasgow Zen, 1981. Address: 21 Waverley Park, Edinburgh, EH8 8ER, Scotland.

SPENCE Bill. See: SPENCE William John Duncan.

SPENCE Jonathan, b. 1936, England. Professor of History. m. Helen Mexander. Education: BA, MA, Cambridge University; PhD, Yale University. Contributions to: New York Reviewer of Books. Honours: Los Angeles Times Book Award; MacArthur Fellowship. Address: Dept of History, Yale University, PO Box 1504a, Yale Station, New Haven, CT 06520-7425, USA.

SPENCE William John Duncan (Jessica Blair, Jim Bowden, Kirk Ford, Floyd Rogers, Bill Spence), b. 20 Apr 1923, Middlesborough, England. Author. m. Joan Mary Rhoda Ludley, 8 Sep 1944, 1 s, 3 d. Education: St Mary's Teachers Training College,

1940-42. Publications: Harpooned, 1981; Romantic Rydale, (with Joan Spence) 1977, 1987; The Medieval Monasteries of Yorkshire, (with Joan Spence) 1981; 36 Westerns, (by Jim Bowden, Floyd Rogers, Kirk Floyd); 3 War Novels; 1 Romance; Stories from Yorkshire Monasteries, (with Joan Spence) 1992; 2 Historical Sagas, (by Jessica Blair) 1993; AA Leisure Guide North York Moors, (co-author); The Red Shawl, 1994; A Distant Harbour, (by Jessica Blair). Contributions to: Yorkshire Gazette and Herald; Writing manuals for The Writing School. Memberships: Society of Authors; Whitby Literary and Philosophical Society; Hakluyt Society. Address: Post Office, Ampleforth College, York, YO6 4EZ, England.

SPENCER Colin, b. 17 Jul 1933, London, England. Writer; Novelist; Playwright. m. Gillian Chapman, 2 Oct 1959, 1 s. Education: Selhurst Grammar School; Brighton Art School. Publications include: Novels: Panic; How The Greeks Kidnapped Mrs Nixon; Asylum; The Victims of Love; Non-Fiction: Reports From Behind with Chris Barlas; Which of Us Two?; The Heretic's Feast - A History of Vegeterianism; Plays: Spitting Image; The Trial of St George; The Sphinx Mother; Why Mrs Neustadter Always Loses; Keep It In The Family; Flossie (Television); Cookery Books: Colin Spencer's Vegetarian/Wholefood Cookbook; Al Fresco; Feast for Health; Mediterranean Vegetarian Cooking; The Romantic Vegetarian; The Adventurous Vegetarian; Vegetable Pleasures; Faber Book of Food, an anthology, (Co-editor). Address: Two Heath Cottages, Tunstall, Woodbridge, Suffolk, IP12 2HQ, England.

SPENCER Elizabeth, b. Carrollton, MS, USA. Fiction Writer. m. John Arthur Rusher, 29 Sep 1956. Education: AB, cum laude, Belhaven College; MA, Vanderbilt University. Appointments include: Writer-in-Residence, Adjunct Professor, 1977-86, Concordia University, Montreal; Visiting Professor, University of North Carolina at Chapel Hill, 1986-92. Publications: Fire in The Morning, 1948; This Crooked Way, 1952; The Voice at The Back Door, 1956; The Light in The Piazza, 1960; No Place for an Angel, 1967; Ship Island and Other Stories, 1968; The Snare, 1972; The Stories of Elizabeth Spencer, 1981; The Salt Line, 1984; Jack Of Diamonds, 1988; For Lease or Sale, drama, 1989; The Night Travellers, 1991. Contributions to: The New Yorker; The Atlantic; Southern Review; Kenyon Review. Literary Agent: Eugene Winick, McIntosh & Otis, 310 Madison Avenue, New York, NY 10017, USA. Address: 402, Longleaf Drive, Chapel Hill, NC 27514, USA.

SPENCER LaVyrle, b. 17 August 1943, Brownsville, Minnesota, USA. m. David F Spencer, 10 February 1962, 2 daughters. Honours: Historical Romance of the Year Award, Romance Writers of America, 1982, 1983, 1984. Address: c/o Putnam Publishing, 200 Madison Avenue, NY 10016, USA.

SPIEGELMAN Art. Cartoonist. m. Françoise Mouly, 1 son, 1 daughter. Appointments: Contributing Editor, cover artist for The New Yorker, 1992-; Co-Founder, Editor of "Raw". Publications: The Wild Party, 1994. Contributions to: New York Times; Playboy. Honours: Pulitzer Prize (x2), for MAUS, A Survivor's Tale; National Book Critics Award, Nominee. Address: c/o Pantheon Books Pblcty Dept, 201 E 50th Street, 25th Floor, NY 10022, USA.

SPIERENBURG Pieter Cornelis, b. 2 June 1948, Haarlem, Netherlands. Historian. Education: Dissertation, University of Amsterdam, 1978. Publications: The Spectacle of Suffering; The Broken Spell; The Prison Experience. Contributions to: Social Science History; Journal of Social History. Memberships: Secretary, International Association for The History of Crime and Criminal Justice. Address: Erasmus University, Department of History, PO Box 1738, 3000 Dr Rotterdam, Netherlands.

SPINELLI Eileen, Poet; Children's Book Writer. Contributions to: A Room of One's Own; Muse; Footwork. Address: 331 Melville Road, Phoenixville, PA 19460, USA.

SPINELLI Jerry, b. 1941. Publications: Maniac Magee, 1989; Space Station 7th Grade, 1982; Picklemania, 1993; Who Put That Hair in My Toothpaste, 1984; Night of the Whale, 1985; Jason & Marcelline, 1986; School Daze, 1991; Tooter Pepperday, 1995. Honours: Boston Globe/Horn Award, 1990; Newbery Medal, 1991.

SPRIGEL Olivier. See: BARBET Pierre Claude Avice.

SPRIGGE Timothy Lauro Squire, b. 14 Jan 1932, London, England. University Professor. m. Giglia Gordon, 4 Apr 1959, 1 s, 2 d. Education: BA, 1955; MA; PhD, 1961, Cantab. Literary Appointments: Editorial Board, Journal of Applied Philosophy; Journal et Idealistic Studies; The Journal of Speculative Philosophy; Studia Spinozana. Publications: The Correspondence of Jeremy Benthan, 1968; Facts, Words and Beliefs, 1970; Santayana: An Examination of His Philosophy, 1974; The Vindication of Absolute Idealism, 1983; Theories of Existence, 1984; The Rational Foundation of Ethics, 1987; James and Bradley: American Truth and British Reality, 1993. Contributions to: Various professional journals, including: Mind; Philosophy; Inquiry; Journal of Applied Philosophy; Utilitas. Honour: Fellow, The Royal Society of Edinburgh. Memberships: Mind Association; Scots Philosophical Club. Address: David Hume Tower, University of Edinburgh, George Square, Edinburgh, EH8 9JX, Scotland.

SPRING Michael, b. 14 Oct 1941, New York City, USA. Editor; Writer. (div), 2 s. Education: BA, Haverford College, Haverford, PA, 1964; MA, English Literature, Columbia University, 1970. Publications: Great Weekend Escape Book, 3rd edition, 1987, 4th edition, 1990; Great European Itineraries, 1987, 3rd edition, 1994; American Way of Working (editor), 1980; A Student's Guide to Julius Caesar, 1984; Editor, 50 volumes, Barron's Book Notes series, 1984; Vice President and Editorial Director, Fodor's Travel Publications, 140 titles; Contributing Editor, Conde Nast's Traveler magazine. Contributions include: Travel and Leisure; Signature; Modern Bride; Travel expert, CNN TV Travel Show, 1992-. Honours: Distinguished Achievement Award in Educational Journalism, Educational Press Association of America, 1987. Address: c/o Random House, 201 East 50th Street, New York, NY 10022, USA.

SPRINGER Nancy, b. 5 Jul 1948, New Jersey, USA. Novelist. m. Joel H Springer, 13 Sep 1969, 1 s, 1 d. Education: BA, English Literature, Gettysburg College, 1970. Appointments: Personal Development Plan Instructor, University of Pittsburg, 1983-85; Leisure Learning Instructor, York College, PA, 1986-91; Education Instructor, Franklin and Marshall College, 1988-. Publications include: The Black Beast, 1982; The Sable Moon, 1981; The Golden Swan, 1983; Wings of Flame, 1985; Chains of Gold, 1986; A Horse to Love (juvenile), 1987; Madbond, 1987; Chance and Other Gestures of The Hand of Fate, 1987; The Hex Witch of Seldom, 1988; Not on A White Horse (juvenile), 1988; Apocalypse, 1989; They're All Named Wildfire (juvenile), 1989; Red Wizard (juvenile), 1990; Colt (juvenile), 1991; The Friendship Song (juvenile), 1992; The Great Pony Hassle (juvenile), 1993; Stardark Songs (poetry), 1993; Larque on The Wing, 1994; The Boy on A Black Horse (juvenile), 1994; Metal Angel, 1994; Music of Their Hooves (poetry, juvenile), 1994. Contributions to: Magazines and journals. Honours include: Distinguished Alumna, Gettysburg College, 1987; Nominee, Hugo Award, 1987; Nominee, World Fantasy Award, 1987; International Reading Association Children's Choice, 1988; Joan Fassler Memorial Book Award, 1992; International Reading Association Young Adult's Choice, 1993. Memberships: Society of Children's Book Writers; Central Pennsylvania Writers' Organization; Board Member, Children's Literature Council of Pennsylvania; Board Member, Pennwriters, President, 1992-93; Novelists Inc; Society of Children's Book Writers. Literary Agent: Jean V Naggar. Address: c/o Virginia Kidd Agency, Box 278, 538 E Harford Street, Milford, PA 18337, USA.

SPRINKLE Patricia Houck, b. 13 Nov 1943, West Virginia, USA. Writer. m. Robert William Sprinkle, 12 Sep 1970, 2 s. Education: AB Vassar College, 1965. Appointments: Managing Editor, United Pub Co, Atlanta, 1967-68; Director of PR, Kendall College, 1970; Staff Writer, Presbyterian Church, 1968-70, 1971-73. Publications: Hunger: Understanding the Crisis Through Games, 1980; Murder at Markham, 1988; Murder in The Charleston Manner, 1990; Murder on Peachtree Street, 1991; Somebody's Dead in Snellville, 1992; Death of A Dunwoody Matron, 1993; Women Who Do Too Much: Stress and The Myth of The Superwoman, 1992; Do I Have To? What To Do About Children Who Do Too Little Around The House, 1993; In God's Image: Meditations For The New Mother, 1988; Housewarmings: For Those Who Make a House a Home, 1992; A Gift From God, 1994; A Mystery Bred in Buckhead, 1994. Contributions include: Guideposts; Presbyterian Survey; Parents of Teenagers; MWA Annual. Memberships: Penwomen; Sisters in Crime; Mystery Writers of America. Literary Agent: Dominick Abel. Address: 15086 SW 113 Street, Miami, FL 33196, USA.

SPURLING John Antony, b. 17 Jul 1936, Kisumu, Kenya. Writer. m. Hilary Spurling, 4 Apr 1961, 2 s, 1 d. Education: BA, St

John's College, Oxford, 1960. Literary Appointments: Henfield Writing Fellow, University of East Anglia, 1973. Publications: Plays: MacRune's Guevara, 1969; In The Heart of The British Museum, 1972; Shades of Heathcliff, 1975; The British Empire, Part One, 1982; The Ragged End (novel), 1989; Beckett The Playwright (with John Fletcher), 1972, third edition 1985; Grahame Greene, 1983. Contributions to: Art critic of The New Statesman, 1976-88; Freelance contributor at various times to The Spectator, The Times, The Sunday Times, The Observer, The Independent, Modern Painters, TLS, The Guardian, The Daily Telegraph. Literary Agent: Patricia MacNaughton, MLR, 200 Fulham Road, London, SW10 9PN. Address: C/O Patricia MacNaughton, MLR, 200 Fulham Road, London, SW10 9PN, England.

SRIVASTAVA Ramesh Kumar, b. 2 Jan 1940, Banpur. India. m. Usha Rani Srivastava, 27 Jun 1959, 2 s. Education: BA, 1957; MA, 1961; PhD, 1972. Literary Appointments: Editor, The Summit, 1970-72; Associate Editor, 1976-88; Editor, 1988-93, The Punjab Journal of English Studies. Publications: Love and Animality: Stories, 1984; Cooperative Colony: Stories, 1985; Neema, (novel) 1986; Six Indian Novelists in English, 1987; Games They Play and Other Stories, 1989; Critical Studies in English and American Literature, 1993; Under The Lamp: Stories, 1993. Contributions to: Art of Living; The Sunday Tribune; Indian Book Chronicle; Indian Express; Games They Play and Other Stories; Punjab Journal of English Studies; Indian Journal of English Studies; Bharat Protiva; Gueta Journal of English Studies; Encyclopaedia of Indian Literature; University News. Honours: Fulbright Fellowship, 1969; Senior Fulbright Grant, 1984. Memberships: Authors Guild of India; Indian PEN; Modern Language Association. Address: B 16 Gurunanak Dev University, Amritsar 143005, India.

SSUJEN. See: KUO Nancy.

ST AUBYN Giles R (The Hon), b. 11 Mar 1925, London, England. Writer. Education: Wellington College; MA, Trinity College, Oxford University. Publications: Lord Macaulay, 1952; A Victorian Eminence, 1957; The Art of Argument, 1957; The Royal George, 1963; A World to Win, 1968; Infamous Victorians, 1971; Edward V11, Prince and King, 1979; The Year of Three Kings 1483, 1983; Queen Victoria: A Portrait, 1991. Honour: LVO. Memberships: Fellow, Royal Society of Literature; Society of Authors. Address: Apartment 2, Saumarez Park Manor, Route de Saumarez, Câtel, Guernsey, Guernsey, Channel Islands, GY5 7TH.

ST CLAIR Elizabeth. See: COHEN Susan.

ST CLAIR Margaret, b. 17 Feb 1911, Kansas, USA. Writer. m. Eric St Clair, 25 May 1932. Education: MA Greek, University of California, 1934. Publications: Agent of The Unknown, 1956; The Green Queen, 1956; The Games of Neith, 1960; Sign of the Labrys, 1963; Message From The Eocene, 1964; The Worlds of Futurity, 1964; The Dolphins of Altair, 1967; The Shadow People, 1969; The Dancers of Noyo, 1973; Change The Sky and Other Stories, 1974; The Best of Margaret St Clair, 1985; The Lack of Teddy Bears (autobiography), 1989. Contributions to: More than 100 pieces of short fiction published in various journals and magazines. Memberships: Former member, Authors League of America; Science Fiction Writers of America. Literary Agent: Julie Fallowfield, McIntosh and Otis, New York City. Address: 684 Benicia Drive 44, Santa Rosa, CA 95409, USA.

ST CLAIR William, b. 7 Dec 1937, London, England. Author; Formerly Under-Secretary, Her Majesty's Treasury. 2 d. Education: St Johns College, Oxford, 1956-60. Appointments: Fellow, All Souls College, Oxford, 1992; Visiting Fellow, 1981-82; Fellow, Huntington Library, 1985. Publications: Lord Elgin and The Marbles, 1967, revised 1983; That Greece Might Still Be Free, 1972; Trelawny, 1978; The Godwins and The Shelleys: The Biography of A Family, 1989; Policy Evaluation, A Guide for Managers, 1988; Executive Agencies, A Guide to Setting Targets and Judging Performance, 1992; Consultant to OECD, 1992-;. Honours: Heinemann Prize, Royal Society of Literature, 1973; Time Life Prize and Macmillan Silver Pen for Non-fiction, 1990. Memberships: International President, Byron Society; Fellow, British Academy; Fellow, Royal Society of Literature. Literary Agent: Deborah Rogers. Address: 52 Eaton Place, London, SW1, England.

ST DAWN Agnes Grace Galasso, b. 24 Apr 1921, Paterson, NJ, USA. Poet; Speaker. 1s. Education: PhD, National Academy of Management, China; The World Academy of Arts and Culture. Literary Appointments: National Adviser, American Biographical Research Institute. Publications: The Gift of Peace; God Gave Me His Peace;

Trust God - Love God; Creator Yahweh Is His Name; Is We Want God To Come; Mystery Of the Holy Spirit. Honours: Poet Laureate of Spiritual Revelation; American Poet of Bi-Centennial Distinction; Dame of High Grace of the Knights of Malta, LF; World Decoration of Excellence, ABI; ABI Gold Commemorative Medal of Honour; World Poet Resource Center Award; Golden Poet Award; Silver Shield of Valour, 1991-2; National Library of Poetry, Editors Choice Award; Woman of the Year, ABI, 1990; Woman of the Year, IBC, 1992; Hon Doctorate, Humane Letters, China; Hon Doctorate, Divinity, Universal Orthodox College. Memberships: Life Fellow, American Biographical Research Institute; International Life Fellow, PLatform Association; Life Fellow, IBC; United Poets Laureate International. Address: 340 Elliot Place, Paramus, NJ 07652, USA.

ST JOHN David. See: **HUNT Everette Howard.**

ST JOHN Lucia. See: **DIORIO Mary Ann Lucia.**

ST JOHN Nicole. See: **JOHNSTON Norma.**

STACEY Tom, b. 11 Jan 1930, Bletchingley, England. Author. Education: Oxford University. Publications: the Hostile Sun,1953; The Brothers M, 1960; Summons to Ruwenzori, 1964; Today's World, 1968; The Living and The Dying, 1975; The Pandemonium, 1979; The Worm in The Rose, 1985; Deadline, 1988; Bodies and Souls, 1989; Decline, 1991. Contributions to: Numerous Journals. Honours: John Llewellyn Rhys Memorial Prize, 1954; Granada Award, 1961; Fellow, Royal Society of Literature, 1977. Literary Agent: Jacintha Alexander. Address: 128 Kensington Church Street, London, W8, England.

STACK George Joseph, b. New York, NY, USA. Professor of Philosophy. 1 s, 1 d. Education: BA Social Science, Pace University, NY, 1960; MA Philosophy, 1962, PhD Philosophy, 1964, Pennsylvania State University, State College. Publications: Kierkegaard's Existential Ethics, 1977, Japan, 1985, UK, 1992; Berkeley's Analysis of Perception, Mouton and Co, 1970, Humanities Press, 1972, Peter Lang, 1992; On Kierkegaard: Philosophical Fragments, Fini Lokkes Vorlag, Copenhagen, 1976, Humanities Press, 1976; Sartre's Philosophy of Social Existence, 1978; Lange and Nietzsche, 1983; Nietzsche and Emerson, 1992; Nietzsche: Man, Knowledge, Will to Power, 1994. Contributions to: Over 312 articles and reviews published in professional journals. Memberships: American Philosophical Association; Society for The Advancement of American Philosophy; North American Nietzsche Society. Address: Department of Philosophy, 139 FOB, SUNY Brockport, Brockport, NY 14420, USA.

STADTLER Beatrice, b. 26 Jun 1921, Cleveland, OH, USA. Educator; Writer. m. Oscar Stadtler, 31 Jan 1945, 1 s, 2 d. Education: Diploma, Sunday School Teachers, 1957; Bachelor, Judaic Studies, 1971; MSc, Religious Education, 1983; Master of Jewish Studies, 1988. Appointments: Weekly column, Cleveland Jewish News for Youth, 1962; Weekly column, Boston Jewish Advocate, 1975. Publications include: The Holocaust: A History of Courage and Resistance, 1975; Significant Lives, 1976; Rescue From The Sky, translated into Hebrew, 1978; Chapters In: The Holocaust, 1976, and Genocide; A Search for Conscience; Chapter: Anthology on Armed Jewish Resistance during The Holocaust, 1939-45; Chapter, The Second Jewish Catalog, Heranca Judaica; A History of Israel Through Her Postage Stamps, 1993; Chapters in: Holocaust Literature: A Handbook of Critical Historical and Literary Writings: Jewish Women in The Holocaust Resistance; Juvenile and Youth books about The Holocaust. Address: 24355 Tunbridge Lane, Beachwood, OH 44122, USA.

STAINES David, b. 8 Aug 1946, Toronto, Ontario, Canada. Educator; Writer. Education: BA, University of Toronto, 1967; AM, 1968, PhD, 1973, Harvard University. Literary Appointments: Assistant Professor of English, Harvard University, 1973-78; Honorary Research Fellow, University College, London, 1977-78; Associate Professor, 1978-85, Professor of English, 1985-, University of Ottawa; Five College Professor of Canadian Studies, Smith College, 1982-84. Publications: Editor: The Canadian Imagination: Dimensions of a Literary Culture, 1977; Stephen Leacock: A Reappraisal, 1986; The Forty-Ninth and Other Parallels: Contemporary Canadian Perspectives, 1986; Author: Tennyson's Camelot: The Idylls of The King and Its Medieval Sources, 1982; Translator: The Complete Romances of Chretien de Troyes, 1990. Contributions to: Studies in Philology; Modern Language Review; Speculum; many others. Address: Department of English, University of Ottawa, Ottawa, Ontario, Canada, K1N 6N5.

STAINES Trevor. See: **BRUNNER John Kilian Houston.**

STALLWORTHY Jon, b. 18 Jan 1935, London, England. Poet. m. Gillian Waldock, 25 Jun 1960, 3 children. Education: Dragon School, Oxford, 1940-48; Rugby School, Warwickshire, 1948-53; Served as Lieutenant in Oxfordshire and Buckinghamshire Light Infantry, seconded to the Royal West African Frontier Force; Served fifteen months in Nigeria, 1954-55; BA, 1958, B Litt, 1961, Magdalen College, Oxford. Literary Appointments include: Visiting Fellow, All Souls College Oxford, 1971-72; John Wendell Anderson Professor of English Literature, Cornell University, Ithaca, NY, USA, 1977-86; Reader in English Literature, Oxford University, 1988-92; Professor of English Literature, Oxford University, 1992-. Publications include: A Dinner of Herbs, 1970; Hand in Hand, London, 1974, New York, 1974; The Apple Barrel: Selected Poems 1955-63, 1974; Wilfred Owen: A Biography, London, 1974, New York, 1975; Poets of The First World War, 1974; A Familiar Tree, London, 1978, New York, 1978; The Anzac Sonata: New and Selected Poems, London, 1986, New York, 1987; Louis MacNeice (biography), London, 1995, New York, 1995; Other works include: Boris Pasternak, Selected Poems, translated by Stallworthy and France, 1982; The Complete Poems and Fragments of Wilfred Owen (editor), 1983; The Oxford Book of War Poetry (editor), 1984; The Poems of Wilfred Owen (editor), 1985; First Lines: poems written in youth from Herbert to Heaney, 1987; Henry Reed: collected poems, 1991. Memberships: FRSL; FBA. Address: Wolfson College, Oxford, OX2 6UD, England.

STAMPER Alex. See: **KENT Arthur (William Charles).**

STAMPP Kenneth M, b. 1912, Milwaukee, Wisconsin, USA. Professor of History. m. 2 children. Education: PhD, University of Wisconsin. Contributions to: American Historical Review; Mississippi Valley Historical Review; Journal of Negro History; North Carolina Historical Review; Journal of Southern History. Address: Dept of History, University of California, 3229 Dwinelle Hall, Berkeley, CA 94720, USA.

STANBROUGH Harvey Ernest, b. 19 Nov 1952, Alamogordo, New Mexico, USA. Poet; College Instructor; US Marine (retired). m. Mona Griffith, 23 June 1984, 3 sons, 2 daughters. Education: AA, Liberal Arts, 1993; BA and MA, English, in progress, Publications: Melancholy and Madness, chapbook, 1993; If I Could Write a Poem on the Sea, in The Best of Feelings anthology, 1993; Taps, in The Best of Feelings, 1994; A Poet's Wish, in the Road Less Travelled anthology and poetry textbook, 1994; Excerpt from Courage Defined, in Poets Market, 1995. Contributions to: Numerous to: Feelings; The Formalist; Tucumcari Literary Review; Many other small press publications. Honours: Awards in contests. Membership: President, Alpha Mu Pi Chapter, Phi Theta Kappa. Address: 810 South Michigan, Roswell, NM 88201, USA.

STANFIELD Anne. See: **COFFMAN Virginia.**

STANFILL Dorothy McMahen, b. 22 Dec 1911, Stanton, TN, USA. Freelance Writer, retired. m. Charles Tillman Stanfill, 21 Jun 1941, dec, 1 s. Education: BA, 1962. Appointments: Fiction Editor, Old Hickory Review, 1969. Publications: Kaiharine and The Quarter Mile Drag; Goodbye Ocie May. Contributions to: Numerous including: Texas Review; Mississippi Review; Delta Scene; Southern Review; South and West; New Writers, Pen Women Magazine. Honours: 2 First places, Deep South Writers Conference; Numerous State and National Prizes. Memberships: ASPW; Jackson Writers Group. Literary Agent: Diane Cleaver, Nat Sohel. Address: 1585 Hollywood Drive, Apt B 10, Jackson, TN 38305, USA.

STANGL Jean, b. 14 May 1928, MO, USA. Author; Teacher. m. Herbert Stangl, 14 Aug 1946, 3 sons. Education: Master Early Childhood, 1977; BA Human Development, 1975; Community College, Adult Education Credential. Publications: Paper Stories; Crystals and Crystal Gardens; Tools of Science; H20 Science; Story Sparklers. Contributions to: Numerous. Honours: International Reading Association; Literacy Award; Honorary Life Member Parent/Teacher Association. Memberships: Ventura County Reading Association; Society of Children's Book Writers and Illustrators; National Association for The Education of Young Children; Beatrix Potter Society. 1658 Calle La Cumbre, Camarillo, CA 93010, USA.

STANLEY Bennett. See: **HOUGH Stanley Bennett.**

STANTON Vance. See: AVALLONE Michael Angelo.

STAPLES Reginald Thomas (Robin Brewster, James Sinclair, Robert Tyler Stevens), b. 26 Nov 1911, London, England. Company Director. m. Florence Anne Hume, 12 Jun 1937, 1 s. Education: West Square Grammar School, 1923-28. Publications include: The Summer Day Is Done; Appointments in Sarajevo; The Fields of Yesterday; Shadows in The Afternoon; Warrior Queen; Down Lambeth Way; Flight From Bucharest; Women of Cordova; The Professional Gentleman; The Hostage. Memberships: Society of Authors; The Brevet Flying Club. Literary Agent: Sheila Watson, Watson Little Ltd. Address: Wenvoe, Dome Hill, Caterham, Surrey, CR3 6EB, England.

STARER Robert, b. 8 Jan 1924, Vienna, Austria. Composer. m. Johanna Herz, 27 Mar 1942, 1 s. Education: State Academy Vienna, 1937-38; Jerusalem Conservatoire, 1938-43; Juilliard School, 1947-49. Publications: Rhythmic Training; Continuo a Life of Music. Contributions to: New Yorker; Musical America; New York Times; London Times. Honours: Guggenheim Fellowship, 1957, 1964; American Academy Institute of Arts and Letters. Memberships: ASCAP; American Academy of Arts and Letters, 1994. Literary Agent: John Hawkins. Address: PO Box 946, Woodstock, NY 12498, USA.

STARK Joshua. See: OLSEN Theodore Victor.

STARK ADAM Pegie, b. 4 July 1949, South Bend IN. Designer; Artist; Teacher. m. Dr G Stuart Adam, 23 Feb 1994. Education: BFA, IN, 1975; MA, School of Journalism, IN, 1981; PhD in Mass Communications, 1984. Publications: Author & Designer; Eyes on the News, 1990; Color & Design, 1995; Designer: Contemporary Newspaper Design, 2nd edition, 1992. Contributions to: IFRA journal, Germany; Society of Newspaper Design journal. Honours: Society of Newspaper Design, 17 awards, 1987-88; First place, "Eyes on the News", FL Design Competition, 1991. Memberships: Society of Newspaper Design; Association for the Education of Journalism and Mass Communication. Address: 5232 Beach Drive SE, St Petersburg, FL 33705, USA.

STARNES John Kennett, b. 5 Feb 1918, Montreal, Canada. Retired Diplomat. m. Helen Gordon Robinson, 10 May 1941, 2 s. Education: Institute Sillig, Switzerland, 1935-36; University of Munich, Germany, 1936; BA, Bishops University, 1939. Appointments: Counsellor, Canadian Embassy, Bonn, 1953-56; Head of Defence Liaison, Ottawa, 1958-62; Ambassador to Federal Republic of Germany, 1962-66; Ambassador United Arab Republic and The Sudan, 1966-67; Assistant Undersecretary, State for External Affairs, 1967-70; Director General, RCMP Security Service, 1970-73; Member Council, International Institute for Strategic Studies, 1977-85. Publications: Deep Sleepers, 1981; Scarab, 1982; Orions Belt, 1983; The Cornish Hug, 1985; Film and TV rights to first three books sold 1983; Latonya (novel), 1994. Contributions to: Numerous Newspapers, journals and periodicals. Honours: Centennial Medal; DCL; Commemorative Medal for 125th Anniversary of The Confederation of Canada, 1992; Doctor of Civil Law (Honoris Causa), Bishop's University, 1975. Memberships: International Institute of Strategic Studies; Canadian Institute of International Affairs; Director, The Canadian Writers Foundation. Address: Apt 9 100 Rideau Terrace, Ottawa, Ontario, Canada, K1M 0Z2.

STAROBINSKI Jean, b. 17 Nov 1920, Geneva, Switzerland. Writer. m. Jacqueline Sirman, 15 Aug 1954, 3 s. Education: PhD, Geneva, 1958; MD, Lausanne, 1960. Publications: Jean Jacques Rousseau: La Transparence et L'Obstacle, 1957; La Relation Critique, 1970; 1789: Les Emblemes de La Raison; Montaigne en Mouvement, 1983; Le Remede dans Le Mal, 1989; Largesse, 1994. Contributions to: Le Monde; Magazine Litteraire; TLS; New York Book Review; Hudson Review; La Repubblica; Leggere; NZZ; FAZ. Honours: Cheval. Legion D'Honneur, 1980; AAAS; British Academy; Prix Europeen de L'Essai, 1983; Balzan Prize, 1984; Prix de Monaco, 1988; Goethe Prize, 1994. Memberships: President, Recontres Intern. Address: Universite de Geneva, CH 1211, Geneva, Switzerland.

STARR Paul. Professor; Writer; Founder and Editor of 'The American Prospect. m. Sandra Starr, 4 children. Honours: Pulitzer Prize, 1984; Bancroft Prize, 1984; James Hamilton Award, American College of Health Care Executives; C Wright Award, Society for the Study of Social Problems. Address: Dept of Sociology, Princeton University Green Hall, Princeton, NJ 08544-1010, USA.

STAVE Bruce M(artin), b. 17 May 1937, New York City, USA. Historian. m. Sondra T Astor, 16 Jun 1961, 1 s. Education: AB, Columbia College, 1959; MA, Columbia University, 1961; PhD, University of Pittsburgh, 1966. Appointments: Professor, 1975; Director, Center for Oral History, 1981-; Chairman, Department of History, 1985-94, University of Connecticut. Publications include: The New Deal & The Last Hurrah, author, 1970; The Discontented Society, co-editor, 1972; Socialism and The Cities, contributing editor, 1975; The Making of Urban History, 1977; Modern Industrial Cities, 1981; Talking About Connecticut, 1985, 1990; Mills and Meadows: A Pictorial History of Northeast Connecticut, co-author, 1991; From The Old Country: An Oral History of European Migration to America, co-author, 1994. Contributions to: Journal of Urban History; Americana Magazine; International Journal of Oral History. Honours include: Fulbright Professorships, India, 1968-69, Australia, New Zealand, Philippines, 1977, China, 1984; NEH Fellow, 1974. Memberships include: American Historical Association; Organization of American Historians; Immigration History Society; President, New England Historical Association, 1994-1995. Address: 200 Broad Way, Coventry, CT 06238, USA.

STEAD C(hristian) K(arlson), b. 17 Oct 1932, Auckland, New Zealand. Author; University Educator. Education: BA, Auckland University, 1954. Appointments: Lecturer in Literature, University of New England, New South Wales, Australia, 1956-57; Faculty Member, 1960-86, Professor of English, 1969-86, Auckland University, New Zealand; Chairman, New Zealand Literary Fund, 1973-75. Publications: Whether the Will Is Free: Poems 1954-62, 1964; The New Poetic: Yeats to Eliot, 1964; Smith's Dream, novel, 1971; Crossing the Bar, 1972; Quesada: Poems 1972-74, 1975; Walking Westward, 1978; Five for the Symbol, short stories, 1981; In the Glass Case: Essays on New Zealand Literature, 1981; Geographies, 1982; Poems of a Decade, 1983; Paris, 1984; All Visitors Ashore, novel, 1984; Pound, Yeats, Eliot, and the Modernist Movement, 1986; The Death of the Body, novel, 1986; Editor: New Zealand Short Stories: Second Series, 1966; Measure for Measure: A Casebook, 1971; Selected Letters and Journals of Katherine Mansfield, 1973; Collected Stories of Maurice Duggan, 1981. Address: 37 Tohunga CRescent, Parnell, Auckland 1, New Zealand.

STEADMAN Mark Sidney, b. 2 Jul 1930, Statesboro, GA, USA. College Professor. m. Joan Marie Anderson, 29 Mar 1952, 3 sons. Education: BA, Emory University, 1951; MA, Florida State University, 1956; PhD, 1963. Appointments: Writer in Residence, Clemson University, 1980. Publications: McAfee County; A Lion's Share; Angel Child; Bang Up Season. Contributions to: Southern Review; South Carolina Review; Kennesaw Review; Nova. Honours: Winthrop Fiction Award; NEA Creative Writing Fellowship. Memberships: South Carolina Writers Workshop; South Atlantic Modern Language Association. Literary Agent: Lois Wallace. Address: 450 Pin Du Lac Drive, Central, SC 29630, USA.

STEARNS Peter, b. 3 Mar 1936, London, England. m. Carol 26 Mar 1978, 1 son, 3 daughters. Education: AB, 1957, AM, 1959, PhD, 1963, Harvard University. Literary Appointments: Dean, College of Humanities & Social Science, Carnegie Mellon University. Publications include: European Society in Upheaval, 1967; The Impact of the Industrial Revolution, 1972; Old Age in Europen Society, 1977; The Other Side of Western Civilization, 1984; Be A Man, Males in Modern Society, 1990; American Cool, 1994. Contributions to: Numerous inc. Journal of Social History; Forum Press; Business History Review; Network News Exchange; American Historical Review; Perspectives. Honours: Phi Beta Kappa; Social Science Research Council Fellowship; American Philosophical Society Grant; Guggenheim Fellowship; Koren Prize; Newcomen Special Award; Elliott Dunlap Smith Teaching Award. Memberships: American Historical Association; International Society for Research. Address: Carnegie Mellon University, Pittsburgh, PA 15213, USA.

STEBEL Sidney Leo, (Leo Bergson, Steve Toron), b. 28 June 1923, Iowa, USA. Writer. m. Jan Mary Dingler, 10 Sept 1954, 1 daughter. Education: BA English Literature, University of Southern California, 1949. Appointments: Adjunct Professor, Masters of Professional Writing, USC, 1991. Publications: The Collaborator, 1968; The Vorovich Affair, 1975; The Shoe Leather Treatment, 1983; Spring Thaw, 1989; The Boss's Wife, 1992; The Widowmaster, 1967; Main Street, 1971. Contributions to: West Magazine; Air Mail; Botteghe Obscure; Story Magazine; Connoiseur's World 90 Cal. Anthology; Architectural Digest; Calendar; LA Times; Sunday Book Review;

Southern California Anthology, 1994. Honours: International Secretary, PEN Centre, USA West. Memberships: Writers Guild of America West; Author's Guild; Australian Writers Guild. Literary Agent: Don Congdon, New York City. Address: 1963 Mandeville Canyon Road, Los Angeles, CA 90049, USA.

STEEL Ronald, b. 25 Mar 1931, USA. Writer; Professor. Education: BA, Northwestern University, 1953; MA, Harvard University, 1955. Publications: The End Of Alliance: America and The Future of Europe, 1964; Pax Americana, 1967; Imperialists and Other Heroes, 1971; Walter Lippmann and The American Century, 1980; Temptations of a Superpower, 1995. Contributions to: New York Review of Books; New Republic. Honours: Sidney Hillman Prize, 1967; National Book Critics Award, 1980; Bancroft Prize, 1980; American Book Award, 1981; Los Angeles Times Book Prize, 1980; Washington Monthly Book Prize, 1981. Memberships: Council on Foreign Relations; Society of American Historians; American Historical Association. Literary Agent: Morton Janklow, New York. Address: School of International Relations, University of Southern California, Los Angeles, CA 90089, USA.

STEELE Shelby. Professor. Honours: National Book Critics Circle Award, 1990. Address: Dept of English, San Jose University, 1 Washington Square, San Jose, CA 95192-0090, USA.

STEFFLER John Earl, b. 13 Nov 1947, Toronto, Canada. Writer; Professor. m. Shawn O'Hagan, 30 May 1970, 1 s, 1 d. Education: MA, University of Guelph, 1974; BA, University of Toronto, 1971. Publications: An Explanation of Yellow; The Grey Islands; The Wreckage of Play; The Afterlife of George Cartwright; Flights of Magic. Contributions to: Malahat Review; Canadian Literature; Event; Poetry Canada; Queens Quarterly; Descant; Orbis; Fiddlehead. Honours: Norma Epstein Prize; Canada Council Award; Ontario Arts Council Award; Thomas Raddall Atlantic Fiction Award, 1993; Smith Books/Books in Canada First Novel Award, 1993; Newfoundland Arts Council Artist of The Year Award, 1993. Memberships: League of Canadian Poets; PEN; Writers Alliance of Newfoundland and Labrador. Literary Agent: Susan Schulman, 454 West 44th Street, New York, NY 10036, USA. Address: Department of English, Sir Wilfred Grenfell College, Memorial University of Newfoundland, Corner Brook, NF, Canada, A2H 6P9.

STEIN Clarissa Ingeborg (Sara Cristiens), b. 3 Sept 1948, Munich, Germany. Editor; Poet. m. Herbert Stein, 26 May 1981, 1 daughter. Education: Diplom Finanzwirt- (FH), Beamtenfachhochschule, Herrsching, Bavaria, 1975. Literary Appointments: Editor, Papyrus Publishing, 1991-. Publications: New Melodies Neue Melodien, 1992; Notes from My Land, poems, 1993. Membership: Toyota Landcruiser Club, Australia. Address: 16 Grand View Crescent, Upper Ferntree Gully, Victoria 3156, Australia.

STEIN Peter Gonville, b. 29 May 1926, Liverpool, England. Professor of Law. m. Anne M Howard, 16 Aug 1978, 3 daughters from previous marriage. Education: BA, 1949, LLB, 1950, Gonville and Caius College, Cambridge; University of Pavia, 1951-52; Admitted as Solicitor, 1951. Appointments: Regius Professor of Civil Law at The University of Cambridge, 1968-93; Professor of Jurisprudence, University of Aberdeen, 1956-68. Publications: Regulae Iuris: From Juristic Rules to Legal Maxims, 1966; Legal Values in Western Society (with J Shand), 1974, Italy, 1981; Legal Evolution: The Story of An Idea, 1980, Japan, 1989; Legal Institutions: The Development of Dispute Settlement, 1984, Italy, 1987; The Character and Influence of The Roman Civil Law, historical essays, 1988; The Teaching of Roman Law in Twelth Century England (with F de Zulueta), 1990. Honours: Fellow, British Academy, 1974; Hon Dr Iuris, Gottingen University, 1980; Foreign Fellow, Italian National Academy (Lincei), 1987; Belgian National Academy, 1991; Hon Dott. Giur. Ferrara University, 1991; QC (Hon), 1993. Memberships: Vice-President, Selden Society, 1984-87; President, Society of Public Teachers of Law, 1980-81. Address: Queens College, Cambridge, CB3 9ET, England.

STEINBACH Meredith Lynn, b. 18 Mar 1949, Ames, Iowa, USA. Novelist; Professor. m. Charles Ossian Hartman, 5 May 1979, div 1991, 1 s. Education: BGS, 1973, MFA, 1976, University of Iowa. Literary Appointments: Teaching Fellow, University of Iowa, 1975-76; Writer in Residence, Antioch College, 1976-77; Lecturer, Fiction, Northwestern University, 1977-79; Visiting Assistant Professor, University of Washington, 1979-82; Bunting Fellow, Radcliffe-Harvard, 1982-83; Assistant Professor, Brown University, 1983-; Associate Professor, Brown University. Publications: Novels: Zara, 1982; Here

Lies The Water, 1990; The Birth of The World As We Know It (forthcoming). Short stories: Reliable Light, 1990. Contributions to: Tri-Quarterly Magazine; Antaeus; Massachusetts Review; Antioch Review; South West Review; Black Warrior Review. Honours: Pushcart Prize, Best of The Small Presses, 1977; Fellow NEA, 1978; Bunting Fellow, Bunting Summer Fellow, Mary Ingraham Bunting Institute, Radcliffe College, Harvard, 1982-83; Rhode Island Artists Fellowship, 1986-87; O Henry Award, 1990. Memberships: PEN; Associated Writing Programme. Address: 2 Rue de Versailles, 34150 Montpeyroux, France.

STEINER-ISENMANN Robert, b. 19 May 1955, Basel, Switzerland. Writer. 1 daughter. Education: Theology, Zurich University. Publications: Gaetano Donizetti Sein Leben und seine Opern, 1982; Espoirs-hopfnungen, revue, 1988, 1993; Windspeil der Leidenschaft, poems, 1994. Contributions to: Poems in many Anthologies, Magazines and Journals. Memberships: Association Suisse des Ecoivains; Association Valaisanne des Écrivains; PEN Club des Écrivains, section Suisse Allemande. Address: Café de la Rosablanche, 1996 Basse-Nendaz/VS, Switzerland.

STEINHARDT Nancy R Shatzman, b. 14 Jul 1954, St Louis, MO, USA. Art Historian. m. Paul Joseph Steinhardt, 1 Jul 1979, 3 sons, 1 daughter. Education: AB, Washington University, 1974; AM, 1975, PhD, 1981, Harvard. Publications: Chinese Imperial City Planning, 1990; Chinese Traditional Architecture, 1984. Contributions to: More than 20 scholarly articles and 10 reviews. Memberships: College Art Association; Association for Asian Studies; Society of Architectural Historians. Address: Department of Asian and Middle Eastern Studies, University of Pennsylvania, Philadelphia, PA 19104-6305, USA.

STENDAL Grant Vincent, b. 8 Dec 1955, Rochdale, England. Writer. Education: BA, Flinders University of South Australia, 1982; BA (Honours), University of Tasmania, 1985; PhD candidate, University of Adelaide, 1994-. Publications: At Work: Australian Experiences, 1984; Job Representatives Handbook, Revised Edition, 1989. Contributions to: The National Times; Journal of Industrial Relations; Asia Pacific Human Resource Management; Nuovo Paese; Australasian Farming; Training and Development in Australia; AITD Training and Development Newsletter; Quarterly Training News; Industrial Relations Society of South Australia Newsletter; Industrial Relations Society News Bulletin; Flinders Journal of History and Politics; Togartus; The New Voice; Linkage; Public Service Review (South Australia); Red Tape; Labour Studies Briefing; Jane Sheet; Inmate; Short and Curly; Postscripts; Empire Times; On Dit. Honours: International Travel Grant, Australian Industrial Relations Society, 1994. Memberships: Australian Industrial Relations Society. Address: Department of Politics, University of Adelaide, Adelaide, South Australia 5005, Australia.

STEPHAN John Jason, b. 8 Mar 1941, Chicago, Illinois, USA. Professor; Historian. m. 22 June 1963. Education: BA 1963, MA 1964, Harvard University; PhD, University of London, England, 1969. Appointments: Far Eastern Editor, Harvard Review, 1962; Visiting Fellow, St Antony's College, Oxford, 1977; Editorial Board, University of Hawaii Press, 1980-92; Visiting Professor of History, Stanford University, 1986; Research Fellow, Kennan Institute of Advanced Russian Studies, 1987; Editor, Encyclopedia of Siberia, 1988-. Publications: Sakhalin: A History, 1971; The Kuril Islands: Russo-Japanese Frontier in the Pacific, 1974; The Russian Fascists, 1978; Hawaii Under the Rising Sun, 1984; Soviet-American Horizons in the Pacific, with V.P. Chichkanov, 1986; The Russian Far East: A History, 1994. Contributions to: Washington Post; Modern Asian Studies; American Historical Review; Pacific Affairs; Pacific Community; Journal for Asian Studies; New York Times; Siberica; Pacifica; Australian Slavic and E European Studies. Honours: Fulbright Fellowship, 1967-68; Japan Culture Translation Prize, 1973; Japan Foundation Fellowship, 1977; Sanwa Distinguished Scholar, Fletcher School of Law & Diplomacy, Tufts University, 1989; Distinguished Invited Speaker, Canadian Historical Association, 1990. Memberships: Authors Guild; PEN; International House of Japan, Life Member; American Association for the Advancement of Slavic Studies, Life Member; American Historical Association; Canadian Historical Association. Literary Agent: John Hawkins & Associates, New York, USA. Address: Dept of History, University of Hawaii, 2530 Dole St, Honolulu, HI 96822, USA.

STEPHENS Michael Gregory, b. 4 Mar 1946. Writer. 1 daughter. Education: City College of New York,BA, MA, 1976; Yale University, MFA, 1979. Appointments: Columbia University, Lecturer, 1977-91;

Fordham University, Assistant Professor, 1979-85; Princeton University, Lecturer, 1987-91; New York University, Lecturer, 1989-91. Publications: Seasons at Coole; Lost in Seoul; Shipping Out; Jigs and Reels; Circles End; After Asia, poetry, 1993; The Brooklyn Book of the Dead, novel, 1994; Green Dreams: Essays under the Influence of the Irish, essays/creative non-fiction, 1994. Contributions to: Ohio Review; Poet Lore; Poetry New York; Ontario Review; Paris Review; Fiction; Fiction International; Peguod; NY Times; Washington Post; Rolling Stone; Village Voice; Baltimore Sun; International Herald Tribune. Honours: Associated Writing Programs Award in Creative Non-Fiction, for Green Dreams, 1993. Memberships: PEN. Address: c/o Spuyten Duyvil Press, Box 1852, New York, NY 100025, USA.

STEPHENS Reed. See: **DONALDSON Stephen Reeder.**

STEPHENSON Hugh, b. 18 Jul 1938, England. Writer; Journalist; Teacher. m. (1) Auriol Stevens, 1962, 2 s, 1 d, (2) Diana Eden, 1990. Education: MA, New College, Oxford; University of California, Berkeley, USA. Appointments include: HM Diplomatic Service, 1964-69; Staff, The Times, 1968; Editor, The Times Business News, 1972-81; Editor, New Statesman, 1982-86; Professor of Journalism, City University, 1986-. Publications: The Coming Clash, 1972; Mrs Thatcher's First Year, 1980; Claret and Chips, 1982. Honour: President, Oxford Union, 1962. Memberships include: Committee to Review Functioning of Financial Institutions, 1977-80. Address: Z/L Department of Journalism, City University, Northampton Square, London, EC1, England.

STERLING Jessica. See: **RAE Hugh Crauford.**

STERLING Maria Sandra. See: **FLOREN Lee.**

STERN Gerald, b. 22 Feb 1925, Pittsburgh, PA, USA. m. (divorced), 1 son, 1 daughter. Education: BA, University of Pittsburgh; MA, Columbia University. Publications: Lucky Life; The Red Coal; Paradise Poems; Lovesick; Leaving Another Kingdom: Selected Poems; Bread Without Sugar; Selected Essays (ff). Honours: Lamont Poetry Selection, 1977; Governor's Award for Excellence in the Arts, State of Pennsylvania, 1980; Ben Holkin Award, Poetry, 1980; Bernard F Connor's Award, Paris Review, 1981; American Poetry Review Award, 1982; Melville Cane Award, 1982; Jerome J Shestack Poetry Prize, American Poetry Review, 1984; Fellow, American Academy of Poets, 1993.

STERN Howard. Radio Talk Show Host. m. Alison Stern. Address: c/o Paramount Publishing Simoon & Schuster Attn Managing Editorial, 1230 Ave of The Americas, NY 10020, USA.

STERN Richard G, b. 25 Feb 1928, New York City, USA. Writer; Professor. m. (1) Gay Clark, (2) Alane Rollings, 3 sons, 1 daughter. Education: BA, University of North Carolina; MA, Harvard University; PhD, University of Iowa. Publications: Golk, 1960, reissued, 1987; In Any Case, 1962, reissued, 1981; Stitch, 1965, reissued, 1986; Other Men's Daughter, 1973; A Father's Words, 1986; Noble RoT Stories, 1949-89; Europe or Up & Down with Baggish and Schreiber, 1961; One Person and Another, 1993; Shares and Other Fictions, 1992; The Position of the Buoy, 1986; Sistermony, 1995. Contributions to: Numerous journals and magazines, worldwide. Honours: Longwood, 1954; American Academy Arts & Letters, 1968; Friends of Literature, 1968; Sandburg, 1979; Award of Merit for the Novel, 1985. Address: 1050 E 59th St, Chicago, IL 60637, USA.

STERN Richard Martin, b. 17 Mar 1915, Fresno, California, USA.Writer. m. Dorothy Helen Atherton, 20 Dec 1937, 1 daughter (adopted). Education: Harvard College, 1933-36. Appointments Include: Editorial Board, The Writer, 1976-. Publications: Bright Road to Fear, 1958; Search for Tabatha Carr, 1960; These Unlucky Deeds, 1960; High Hazard, 1962; Cry Havoc, 1963; Right Hand Opposite, 1963; I Hide, We Seek, 1964; The Kessler Legacy, 1967; Brood of Eagles, 1969; Merry Go Round, 1969; Manuscript For Murder, 1970; Murder in the Walls, 1971; Stanfield Harvest, 1972; Death in the Snow, 1973; The Tower, 1973; Power, 1974; The Will, 1976; Snowbound Six, 1977; Flood,1979; The Big Bridge, 1982; Wildfire, 1985; Tsunami, 1988; Tangled Murders, 1989; You Don't Need An Enemy, 1989; Missing Man, 1990; Interloper, 1990. Contributions to: Short stories, serials to national magazines, 1942-68, including: Saturday Evening Post; Colliers; Good Housekeeping; Cosmopolitan; McCalls; Redbook American Liberty. Honour: Edgar Award, Mystery Writers of America, 1958. Memberships: Past President, Mystery Writers of America; Crim Writers Association, UK; Authors Guild, USA. Literary Agent: Brandt &

Brandt, 1501 Broadway, NY 10036, USA. Address: Route 9 Box 55, Santa Fe, NM 87505, USA.

STERN Steve, b. 21 Dec 1947, TN, USA. Writer; Teacher. Education: BA, Thodes College; MFA, University of Arkansas. Literary Appointments: Visiting Lecturer, University of WI, 1987; Associate Professor, Skidmore College, 1994. Publications include: Lazar Malkin Enters Heaven, 1986; Harry Kaplan's Adventures Underground, 1991; Plague of Dreamers, 1994; The Moon and Ruben Shein, 1984; Isaac and the Undertaker's Daughter, 1983; Mickey and the Golem, 1986; Hershel and the Beast, 1987. Contributions to: Epoch; Tikkun; The Quarterly; Nimrod; Gureka Review; Alaska Quarterly; Jewish Forward. Honours: O Henry Prize, 1981; Edward Lewis Wallant Award, 1988; Pushcart Writers Choice Award, 1984. Literary Agent: Liz Darhansoff. Address: Dept of English, Skidmore College, Saratoga Springs, NY 12866, USA.

STERN Stuart. See: **RAE Hugh Crauford.**

STERNBERG Robert J, b. 8 Dec 1949, Newark, New Jersey, USA. Psychology Educator. m. Alejandra Campos, 11 Aug 1991, 1 son, 1 daughter. Education: BA summa cum laude, Yale University, 1972; PhD, Stanford University, 1975. Literary Appointments: Associate Editor, Intelligence, 1977-82; Associate Editor, Child Development, 1981-84; Consulting Editor, Memory & Cognition, 1979-81; Journal of Educational Psychology, 1979-81; American Journal of Psychology, 1979-81 and 1989-; Human Intelligence International Newsletter, 1979-89; Roeper Review, 1984-90; Journal of Experimental Psychology: General, 1985-88; Cognitive Development, 1986-90; Developmental Review, 1986-90; Psychological Review, 1989-90; Journal of Personality and Social Psychology, 1989; Editor, Psychological Bulletin, 1991-. Publications: Beyond IQ: A Triarchic Theory of Human Intelligence, 1985; Intelligence Applied: Understanding Your Intellectual Skills, 1986; Practical Intelligence: Nature and Origins of Competence in the Everyday World (edited with Richard K Wagner), 1986; The Triangle of Love, 1987; The Triarchic Mind, 1988; The Nature of Creativity (editor), 1988; Metaphors of Mind: Conceptions of the Nature of Intelligence, 1990. Contributions to: Phi Delta Kappan, 1990; Educational Leadership, 1990; Journal of Reading, 1991; Human Development, 1991. Honours Include: Distinguished Scientific Award for an Early Career Contribution to Psychology of the APA, 1981; Boyd R McCandless Young Scientist Award, APA (Div 7), 1982; Fellow, American Psychological Association, 1983; Distinguished Scholar Award, National Association for Gifted Children, 1985; Research Review Award, American Educational Research Association (co-recipient), 1986; Outstanding Book Award, American Educational Research Association, 1987; Mensa Education and Research Foundation (MERF) Award for Excellence, 1989; Doctor Honoris Causa, Complutense Universidad, Madrid, Spain. Memberships Include: President, Divisions 1 & 15, American Psychological Association; Fellow, American Psychological Association; Fellow, American Psychological Society; American Association for the Advancement of Science; American Educational Research Association; Society for Research in Child Development. Address: Department of Psychology, Yale University, Box 208205, New Haven, CT 06520, USA.

STERNLICHT Sanford, b. 20 Sept 1931, New York, USA. University Professor. m. Dorothy Hilkert, 6 June 1956 (dec 1977), 2 sons. Education: BS, State University of New York at Oswego, 1953; MA, Colgate University, 1955; PhD, Syracuse University, 1962. Publications: Gulls Way, 1961; Love in Pompeii, 1967; McKinley's Bulldog, 1977; USF Constellation: Yankee Race Horses, 1981; John Webster's Imagery and the Western Canon, 1972; TheBlack Devil of the Bayous, 1971; John Masefield, 1977; C S Forester, 1981; Padraic Colum, 1985; R F Delderfield, 1988; Johnn Galsworthy, 1987; Stevie Smith, 1991; Stephen Spender, 1992; Siegfried Sassoon, 1993. Contributions to: 300 articles, poems, stories in US, UK, Canadian and Belgian publications. Honour: Poetry Society of America Fellow, 1965. Memberships: PEN America; Modern Language Association; Shakespeare Association of America. Address: 126 Dorset Road, Syracuse, NY 13210, USA.

STEVENS Carl. See: **OBSTFELD Raymond.**

STEVENS Graeme Roy, b. 17 Jul 1932, Lower Hutt, New Zealand. Palaeontologist. m. Diane Louise Morton Ollivier, 20 Oct 1962, 2 s, 1 d. Education: BSc, 1954, MSc 1st Class, 1956, University of New Zealand; PhD, University of Cambridge, England, 1960;

Fellowship, Royal Society of New Zealand, 1976. Appointments: UNESCO Sub Commission for The Natural Sciences, 1976; Advisory Committee on Adult Education, 1979; Book Resources Panel, National Library of New Zealand, 1981. Publications: Rugged Landscape, 1974; Geology of The Tararuas, 1975; New Zealand Adrift, 1980; Lands in Collision, 1985; Geology of New Zealand, 1978; Prehistoric New Zealand, 1988; The Great New Zealand Fossil Book, 1990; On Shaky Ground, 1991; 151 scientific papers. Contributions to: various professional journals. Honours: Hamilton Prize, Royal Society of New Zealand, 1959; McKay Hammer Geological Society of New Zealand, 1956; Wattie Book of The Year Award (non-fiction), 1974, 1980; Doctor of Science, Victoria University of Wellington, 1989. Memberships: Royal Society of New Zealand, Home Secretary; Geological Society of New Zealand, Publisher. Address: 19A Wairere Road, Belmont, Lower Hutt, New Zealand.

STEVENS John. See: TUBB E(dwin) C(harles).

STEVENS Lynsey. See: HOWARD Lynette Desley.

STEVENS Peter, b. 17 Nov 1927, Manchester, England. Canadian Citizen. Professor; Poet. Education: BA, Nottingham University; MA, McMaster University, 1963; PhD, University of Saskatchewan, 1968. Appointments include: Professor, University of Windsor, 1973. Publications: Plain Geometry, 1968; Nothing But Spoons, 1969; A Few Myths, 1971; Breadcrusts and Glass, 1972; Family Feelings and Other Poems, 1974; Momentary Stay, 1974; The Bogman Pavese Tactics, 1977; An All That Jazz, 1980; Coming Back, 1981; Revenge of the Mistresses, 1981; Out of the Willow Trees, 1986; Editor of Literary Volumes. Honours include: Canada Council Award, 1969. Address: Dept of English, University of Windsor, Windsor, Ontario N9B 3P4, Canada.

STEVENS Robert Tyler. See: STAPLES Reginald Thomas.

STEVENS William Christopher. See: ALLEN Stephen Valentine.

STEVENSON David, b. 30 Apr 1942. University Professor. m. Wendy McLeod, 2 s. Education: BA, Dublin, 1966; PhD, 1970, D Litt, 1989, Glasgow. Literary Appointment: Editor, Northern Scotland, 1980-90. Publications include: The Scottish Revolution, 1973; Revolution and Counter-Revolution in Scotland, 1977; Alastair MacColla and The Highland Problem, 1980; Scottish Covenanters and Irish Confederates, 1981; The Origins of Freemasonry, 1988; The First Freemasons, 1988. Contributions to: many historical journals. Memberships: Scottish History Society, Honorary Secretary, 1976-84; Fellow, Royal Society of Edinburgh, Royal Historical Society, Society of Antiquaries of Scotland. Address: St John's House, University of St Andrews, St Andrews, KY16 9QW, Scotland.

STEVENSON John, (Mark Denning), b. 8 May 1926, London, England. Freelance Novelist; Columnist. m. Alison, 1951, div. Appointments: Fiction Editor, 1981-82; Book Review Columnist, Mystery News, 1982-90; Instructor of Crime and Suspense and Advanced Novel Writing, Writer's Digest Schools, 1989-. Publications: Writing Commerical Fiction, 1983; Ransom, 1989; Den of Inequity, 1983; Merchant of Menace, 1980; Beyond the Prize, 1978; Die Fast, Die Happy, 1976; Shades of Gray, 1976; 20 novels of suspense, mystery and adventure under a variety of pseudonyms; 2 non-fiction books; numerous short stories. Contributions to: Numerous journals and magazines. Honours: 4th Prize, Crime Writers International Congress, Stockholm, 1981; Awarded Life Membership in MWA in recognition of his contributions to the field of Mystery, 1993. Memberships: Regional Vice President, Mystery Writers of America, 1984, 1985. Address: 2005 Ivar Ave, No 3, Los Angeles, CA 90068, USA.

STEWART Bruce Robert, b. 4 Sep 1927, Auckland, New Zealand. Writer. m. Ellen Noonan, 16 Oct 1950, 3 s, 3 d. Education: BA, Auckland. Publications include: A Disorderly Girl, 1980; The Turning Tide, 1980; The Hot and Copper Sky, 1982; The Hallelujah Boy, (play); Shadow of a Pale Horse, (play); Television plays: The Devil, Makes Sunday, Jungle, Juice, The Sin Shifter, Old Man March is Dead, A Laugh at The Dark Question, The Daedalus Equations; Radio plays: Stars in My Hair, Hector's Fixed Idea, Me and My Shadow, 1988; The Dog That Went to War, (Television mini series) 1989; Speak Low, 1993, (stage play and radio). Contributions to: Film Criticism, The Month, 1970-80; Reviews and Criticisms in publications

including: The New Statesman, Times Literary Supplement; The Tablet. Honours: Edgar Allen Poe Award, USA, 1963; Charles Henry Foyle Award, UK, 1968. Memberships: Writers Guild of Great Britain; Writers Guild of Australia; British Film Institute; Co-Chairman, WGGB, 1978-80. Literary Agent: Harvey Unna. Address: c/o Harvey Unna, 24 Pottery Lane, Holland Park, London, W11, England.

STEWART David. See: HIGHAM Robin.

STEWART Judith. See: POLLEY Judith Anne.

STEWART Leslie, b. 23 May 1949, Benghazi, Libya. Scriptwriter; Director; Author; Lyricist. 2 sons. Education: St Edward's College, Malta. Publications: Two of Us, novel, 1989; Three Minute Heroes, play, 1985; Good Neighbours, play, 1987; Wide Games, play, 1987; TV Films & Plays: Three Minute Heroes, 1982; Wide Games, 1984; The Amazing Miss Stella Estelle, 1984; Good Neighbours, 1984; Space Station: Milton Keynes, 1985; The Little Match Girl, 1986; Janna, Where Are You?, 1987; Boogie Outlaws, TV serial, 1987; Q.P.R. Askey Is Dead, 1989; Two of Us, 1988; That Green Stuff, 1990; Radio: The Key To My Father's House, 1992; Canada Park, 1994; Stage: Shoot-Up At Elbow Creek, musical, 1976; The Little Match Girl, musical, 1977; Directed: The Soldier, stage, 1983; The Little Match Girl, stage, 1983; Shoot-Up at Elbow Creek, stage, 1985; Space Station: Milton Keynes, with Colin Rogers, TV Film, 1985; Lola, Terry, She's Not There, with Colin Rogers, TV shorts, 1985; A Game Of Soldiers, stage, 1987; That Green Stuff, TV Film, 1990; A Foot In The Door, TV Film, 1992; Filigree, TV Documentary, 1993. Honours: EMMY nomination, 1987; Ivor Novello Award, 1988. Memberships: Writer's Guild of Great Britain; British Academy of Film & Television Arts; Associate Member, The Performing Rights Society. Literary Agent: Jane Annakin, William Morris Agency (UK) Ltd, Address: York Villa, Station Road, Haddenham, Cambridgeshire CB6 3XD, England

STEWART Mary Florence Elinor (Lady), b. 17 Sep 1916, Sunderland, England. Writer. m. Frederick Henry Stewart, 24 Sep 1945. Education: BA, 1938; DipEd, 1939; MA, 1941, Durham University. Publications: Madam, Will You Talk?, 1954; Thunder On The Right, 1957; My Brother Michael, 1959; The Moonspinners, 1962; The Crystal Cave, 1970; The Little Broomstick, 1971; Touch Not The Cat, 1976; A Walk in Wolf Wood, 1970; Thornyhold, 1988; Frost on The Window and Other Poems, 1990; Stormy Petrel, 1991. Contributions to: Many articles to various magazines. Honours: Frederick Niven Prize; Scottish Arts Council Award; Honorary Fellow, Newnham College, Cambridge. Memberships: PEN; New Club. Address: 79 Morningside Park, Edinburgh, EH10 5EZ, Scotland.

STIBBE Mark W G, b. 16 Sept 1960, London, England. Clerk in Holy Orders. m. Alison Heather Stibbe, 30 July 1983, 2 sons, 1 daughter. Education: BA/MA, Cambridge University, 1982; PhD, Nottingham University, 1989. Publications: John as Storyteller, 1992; The Gospel of John as Literature, 1993; John: A New Biblical Commentary, 1993; A Kingdom of Priests, 1994; John's Gospel, 1994. Contributions to: Numerous articles to Renewal; Anglicans for Renewal; Various New Testament journals; Journal of Pentecostal Theology. Literary Agent: Edward England. Address: St Mark's Vicarage, 19 Graven Close, Grenoside, Sheffield S30 3QT, England.

STICKLAND Caroline Amanda, b. 10 Oct 1955, Germany. Writer. m. William Stickland, 3 Aug 1974, 1 d. Education: BA Hons, English and American Literature, University of East Anglia, 1977. Publications: The Standing Hills, 1986; A House of Clay, 1988; The Darkness of Corn, 1990. Honours: Betty Trask Award, 1985. Memberships: Society of Authors; Mrs Gaskell Society; Jane Austen Society. Address: 81 Crock Lane, Bothenhampton, Bridport, Dorset, DT6 4DQ, England.

STILES Martha Bennett, b. 30 Mar 1933. Writer. m. Martin Stiles, 18 Sept 1954, 1 son. Education: BS, University of Michigan, 1954. Publications: Darkness Over the Land, 1966; Sarah the Dragon Lady, 1986; Kate of Still Waters, 1990; The Star in the Forest, 1977; The Strange House at Nowburyport, 1963. Contributions to: Winter Love Story; Tri Quarterly; Wolfe County Tri Quarterly; The Harvesters; New Orleans Review; The Pastoral Life; Virginia Quarterly. Honours Include: Society of Children's Bookwriters Grant, 1988; Al Smith Fellowship, Kentucky Arts Council, 1992. Memberships: Paris Arts Club; King Library Associates. Literary Agent: Jean Naggar. Address: 861 Hurne Bedford Road, Paris, KY 40361, USA.

STILLINGER Jack, b. 1931, USA. Professor of English. Appointments: Assistant Professor, 1958-61, Associate Professor, 1961-64, Professor of English, 1964-, University of Illinois, Urbana-Champaign. Publications: The Early Draft of John Stuart Mill's Autobiography (editor), 1961; Anthony Munday's Zelauto (editor), 1963; William Wordsworth: Selected Poems and Prefaces (editor), 1965; The Letters of Charles Armitage Brown (editor), 1966; Twentieth Century Interpretations of Keat's Odes (editor), 1968; John Stuart Mill: Autobiography (editor), 1969; John Stuart Mill: Autobiography and Other Writings (editor), 1969; The Hoodwinking of Madeline and Other Essays on Keat's Poems, 1971; The Texts of Keat's Poems, 1974; The Poems of John Keats, 1978; Mill's Autobiography and Literary Essays (editor), 1981; Keat's Complete Poems, 1982; John Keats: Poetry Manuscripts at Harvard, 1990; Multiple Authorship and the Myth of Solitary Genius, 1991; Coleridge and Textual Instability: The Multiple Versions of the Major Poems, 1994. Honours: Fellow, American Academy of Arts and Sciences, 1993. Address: English Building, University of Illinois, 608 S Wright St, Urbana, IL 61801, USA.

STIMULUS Flavian P. See: **PHILANDERSON Flavian Titus.**

STIMULUS John. See: **PHILANDERSON Flavian Titus.**

STINE R L. Children's Book Author. Address: c/o Scholastic Attn Publicity Dept, 555 Broadway, NY 10021, USA.

STIVENS Dal(las George), b. 1911, Australia. Author. Literary Appointments: Australian Department of Information, 1944-50; Press Officer, Australia House, London, England, 1949-50; Foundation President, 1963-64; Vice-President, 1964-66, President, 1967-73, Australian Society of Authors; Chairman, Literary Committee, Captain Cook Bicentenary Celebrations, 1969-70; Member, New South Wales Advisory Committee, ABC, 1971-73. Publications: The Tramp and Other Stories, 1936; The Courtship of Uncle Henry: Short Stories, 1946; The Gambling Ghost and Other Stories, 1946; Jimmy Brockett: Portrait of a Notable Australian, 1951; Ironbark Bill, 1955; The Wide Arch, 1958; Coast to Coast: Australian Stories, 1957-58 (editor), 1959; A Guide to Book Contracts (with B Jefferis), 1967; Three Persons Make A Tiger, 1968; A Horse of Air, 1970; The Incredible Egg: A Billion Year Journey, 1974; The Unicorn and Other Tales, 1976; The Bushranger, 1979; The Demon Bowler and Other Cricket Stories, 1979. Address: 5 Middle Harbour Road, Lindfield 2070, New South Wales, Australia.

STOKER Alan. See: **EVANS Alan.**

STOLOFF Carolyn, b. 14 Jan 1927. Poet; Painter; Teacher. Education: Distinction Literature and Fine Arts, Dalton School; University of Illinois; BS Painting, columbia School of General Studies; Art Studies, Xavier Gonzalez, Eric Isenburger, Hans Hofmann; Poetry Study, Workshops with Stanley Kunitz. Appointments: Teaching: Manhattanville College, 1955-74; Painting and Drawing, 1957-74; Chairman of Art History and Studio Art, 1960-65; Seminar in Creative Writing, Poetry, 1969-74; Discussion Group, Women's House of Detention, 1971-72; English and Creative Writing, Baird House, 1973; Visiting Writer, Stephen's College, 1975, Hamilton College, 1985, Summer Writers Workshop, University of Rochester, 1985; Poets in Public Service, 1989-90. Publications: Stepping Out, 1971; Dying to Survive, 1973; In the Red Meadow, 1973; Lighter-than-Night Verse, 1977; Swiftly Now, 1982; A Spool of Blue, New and Selected Poems, 1983; You Came To Meet Someone Else, 1993. Contributions to: Numerous magazines and anthologies including: The New Yorker, Chelsea, Caliban, Partisan Review, Poetry Northwest, New Yorker Book of Poems, Alcatraz, New Directions 53, Rising Tides. Honours Include: MacDowell Colony Residence Grants, 1961, 1962, 1970, 1976; Helene Wurlitzer Foundation, New Mexico, 1972, 1973, 1974; National Council on the Arts Award for achievement, 1968; Theodore Roethke Award from Poetry Northwest, 1967; First Prize for Poetry, The Miscellany, 1972. Address: 24 West 8th Street, New York, NY 10011, USA.

STONE Gerald Charles, b. 22 Aug 1932, Surbiton, Surrey, England. University Lecturer. m. Vera Fedorovna Konnova, 10 Apr 1974, 2 s, 2 d. Education: BA, London University, School of Slavonic and East European Studies, 1964, 1969; PhD, London University, 1969. Publications: The Smallest Slavonic Nation: The Sorbs of Lusatia, 1972; The Russian Language Since The Revolution (with Bernard Comrie), 1978; An Introduction to Polish, 1980, 2nd edition, 1992; The Formation of The Slavonic Literary Languages, (edited with Dean Worth), 1985; Oxford Slavonic Papers (editor since 1982).

Honours: FBA, 1992. Memberships: The Philological Society, Member of Council, 1981-86; The Society for Slovene Studies. Address: 6 Lathbury Road, Oxford, OX2 7AU, England.

STONE Joan Elizabeth, b. 22 Oct 1930, Port Angeles, Washington, USA. Professor of English. 4 sons, 1 daughter. Education: BA 1970, MA 1974, PhD 1976, University of Washington. Appointments: Poet in Residence, The Colorado College, 1979-; Associate Professor of English, University of Washington, 1975; Visiting Professor of Poetry, University of Montano, 1974. Publications: A Letter to Myself to Water, 1981; Our Lady of the Harbor, 1986; The Swimmer and Other Poems, 1975; Alba, 1976. Contributions to: Yale Review; Poetry Northwest; Seattle Review; New American and Canadian Poetry; Kansas Quarterly; The Southern Poetry Review; Texas Quarterly; Beloit Poetry Journal. Honours: Borestone Mountain Awards, Best Poems, 1973, 1974; Academy of American Poets Award, University of Washington, 1969, 1970, 1972. Address: 312 E Yampa Street, Colorado Springs, CO 80903, USA.

STONE Lawrence, b. England. Contributions to: New York Reviewer of Books; Professional Journals in USA and England. Address: Dept of History, Princeton Unviersity, Dickinson Hall, Princeton, NJ 08544-1017, USA.

STOPPARD Miriam, b. 12 May 1937. Writer; Broadcaster. m. Tom Stoppard, 1972 (diss 1992), 2 s, 2 stepsons. Education: Royal Free Hospital School of Medicine, University of London; King's College Medical School, University of Durham, Newcastle-Upon-Tyne; MB, BS, Durham, 1961; MD Newcastle, 1966. Appointments include: Senior House Officer in Medicine, 1962-63, Royal Victoria Infirmary, King's College Hospital, Newcastle-Upon-Tyne; Research Fellow, Department of Chemical Pathology, 1963-65, Registrar in Dermatology, 1965-66; Senior Registrar in Dermatology, 1966-68, University of Bristol; MRCP, 1964; TV Series: Where There's Life, 1981-; Baby and Co, 1984-; Woman to Woman, 1985-; Miriam Stoppard's Health and Beauty Show, 1988-. Publications: Miriam Stoppard's Book of Baby Care, 1977; My Medical School (contributor), 1978; Miriam Stoppard's Book of Health Care, 1979; The Face and Body Book, 1980; Everywoman's Lifeguide, 1982; Your Baby, 1982; Fifty Plus Lifeguide, 1982; Your Growing Child, 1983; Baby Care Book, 1983; Pregnancy and Birth Book, 1984; Baby and Child Medical Handbook, 1986; Everygirl's Lifeguide, 1987; Feeding Your Family, 1987; Miriam Stoppard's Health and Beauty Book, 1988; Every Woman's Medical Handbook, 1988; Lose 7lbs in 7 Days, 1990; Test Your Child, 1991; The Magic of Sex, 1991; Conception, Pregnancy and Birth, 1993; The Menopause, 1994. Contributions to: Over 40 medical journals. Honours: State Scholarship, 1955; Medical Research Scholarship, 1963-65. Memberships: Dermatology and Endocrinology Sections, Royal Society of Medicine; Heberden Society; British Association of Rheumatology and Rehabilitation. Address: Iver Grove, Iver, Buckinghamshire, England.

STOPPARD Tom, b. (as Thomas Straussler) 3 Jul 1937, Zlin, Czechoslovakia (now British citizen). Writer. m. (1) Jose Ingle, 1965 (div 1972), 2 s, (2) Dr Miriam Moore-Robinson, 1972, 2 s. Education: Grammar School, Yorkshire, England. Appointments include: Journalist, Bristol, 1954-60; Freelance journalist, London, 1960-64. Publications include: On The Razzle, 1981; The Real Thing, 1982; Rough Crossing, 1984; Dalliance (adaptation, Schnitzler's Liebelei), 1986; Hapgood (Aldwych Theatre), 1988; The Love for Three Oranges (English Libretto for Prokofiev's opera) Glyndebourne, 1983; Largo Desolato (adaptation of Vaclev Havel), 1987; Tango (adaptation Mrowzek) RSC, 1966; The House of Bernard Alba (Greenwich), 1973; Film scripts: Empire of The Sun, 1987; Russia House, 1989; Largo Desolato by Vaclav Havel (trans), 1987; Hapgood, 1988; Billy Bathgate, 1990; Resencrantz and Guildenstem Are Dead (also directed), 1990; Stage: Arcadia, Royal National Theatre, 1993. Radio Plays include: In The Native State, 1991. Also screenplays, television plays, novels, short stories. Honours include: Honorary degrees, various universities; John Whiting Award, Arts Council, 1967; New York Drama Critics Award, best play, 1968; Antonette Perry Tony Award, 1968, 1976, 1984; Evening Standard Awards, 1967, 1972, 1978, 1982, 1993; Italia Prize, radio drama, 1968; Shakespeare Prize, 1979. Memberships include: Committee of the Free World, 1981-. Address: c/o The Peters Fraser and Dunlop Group Ltd, 503/4 The Chambers, Chelsea Harbour, Lots Road, London, SW10 0XF, England.

STORM Christopher. See: **OLSEN Theodore Victor.**

STORR (Charles) Anthony, b. 18 May 1920, Bentley, England. Psychiatrist; Author. m. (1) Catherine Cole, 6 Feb 1942, 3 d, (2) Catherine Barton, 9 Oct 1970. Education: Winchester College; MB BChir, Cantab, 1944, MA Cantab, 1946, Christ's College, Cambridge; Westminster Hospital FRCP (London), 1975; FRCP Psych, 1972. Publications: The Integrity of The Personality, 1960; Sexual Deviation, 1964; Human Aggression, 1968; Human Destructiveness, 1972; The Dynamics of Creation, 1972; Jung, 1973; The Art of Psychotherapy, 1979; The Essential Jung,1983; Solitude: A Return to the Self, 1988; Churchill's Black Dog and Other Phenomena of the Human Mind (USA, Churchill's Black Dog, Kafka's Mice and Other Phenomena of The Human Mind), 1989; Freud, 1989; Music and The Mind, 1992. Contributions to: Reviews for New York Times, Washington Post, The Independent, The Spectator, Times Literary Supplement. Honours: Fellow, Royal Society of Literature, 1990; Honorary Fellow, Royal College of Psychiatrists, 1993. Memberships: Fellow, Green College, Oxford, 1979, Emeritus, 1984. Literary Agent: The Peters Fraser and Dunlop Group Ltd. Address: 45 Chalfont Road, Oxford, OX2 6TJ, England.

STORR Catherine (Lady Balogh), b. 1913, United Kingdom. Novelist; Short Story Writer; Children's Fiction Writer; Former Psychiatrist. Appointment: Assistant Editor, Penguin Books, London, 1966-70. Publications: Clever Polly Series, 4 volumes, 1952-80; Stories for Jano, 1952; Marianne Dreams, 1958; Marianne and Mark, 1959; Robin, 1962; Flax Into Gold, libretto, 1964; Lucy, 1964; The Catchpole Story, 1965; Rufus, 1969; Puss and The Cat, 1969; Thursday, 1971; Kate and The Island, 1972; Black God, White God, 1972; Children's Literature (editor), 1973; The Chinese Egg, 1975; The Painter and The Fish, 1975; Unnatural Fathers, 1976; The Story of The Terrible Scar, 1976; Tales from The Psychiatrist's Couch, short stories, 1977; Winter's End, 1978; Vicky, 1981; The Bugbear, 1981; February Yowler, 1982; The Castle Boy, 1983; Two's Company, 1984; Cold Marble, short stories, 1985; Daljit and The Unqualified Wizard, 1989; The Spy Before Yesterday, 1990; We Didn't Think of Ostriches, 1990; Babybug, 1992; Finn's Animal, 1992; The Mirror Image Ghost, 1994. Honours: Prize from Friends of The Earth for The Boy and The Swan, 1985. Membership: Royal Society of Medicine. Literary Agent: Pat Kavanagh, Peters Fraser and Dunlop, 5th Floor The Chambers, Chelsea Harbour, London, SW10 0XF, England. Address: Flat 5, 12 Frognal Gardens, London, NW3, England.

STOTT Mike, b. 2 Jan 1944, Rochdale, Lancashire, England. Playwright. Education: Manchester University. Appointments include: Resident Writer at the Hampstead Theatre Club, 1975. Publications: Mata Hari, 1965; Erogenous Zone, 1969; Funny Peculiar, 1973; Lenz, after Buchner, 1974; Plays for People Who Don't Move Much, 1974; Midnight, 1974; Other People, 1974; Lorenzaccio, after De Musset, 1976; Followed by Oysters, 1976; Soldiers Talking Cleanly, 1978; The Boston Strangler, 1978; Grandad, 1978; Strangers, 1979; Ducking Out, 1982; Dead Men, 1982; Penine Pleasures, 1984; The Fling, 1984; The Fancy Man, 1988; Radio and Television plays. Address: c/o Michael Imison Playwrights, 28 Almeida Street, London N1 1TD, England.

STOW (Julian) Randolph, b. 28 Nov 1935, Geraldton, Western Australia. Education: Universities of Western Australia & Sydney, 1956. Appointments: Lecturer, English University of Leeds, Yorkshire, 1961-62, University of Western Australia, 1962-64; Harkness Fellow, USA, 1964-66; Resident in England, 1966. Publications: A Haunted Land, 1956; The Bystander, 1957; To The Islands, 1958; Tourmaline, 1963; The Merry Go Round in the Sea, 1965; Midnite (for children), 1967; Visitants, 1979; The Girl Green as Elderflower, 1980; The Suburbs of Hell, 1984; Librettos to Music by Peter Maxwell Davies: Eight Songs for a Mad King, 1969; Miss Donnithornes Maggot, 1974; Verse Collections: Act One, 1957; Outrider: Poems, 1956-62; A Counterfeit Silence: Selected Poems, 1969; Randolph Stow (omnibus volume, ed A J Hassall), 1990. Honours: Miles Franklin Award, 1958; Britannica-Australia Award, 1966; Grace Levew Prize, 1969; Arts Council of Great Britain Bursary, 1969; Commonwealth Literary Fund Grant, 1974; Patrick White Award, 1979. Address: c/o Richard Scott Simon, Anthony Sheil Associates, 43 Doughty Street, London WC1N 2LF, England.

STRAND Mark, b. 1934, Summerside, Prince Edward Island, Canada. Poet; Writer. m. 1 son, 1 daughter. Appointments: Professor of English, John Hopkins University, Baltimore, MD, USA. Contributions to: New Yorker; Grand Street. Memberships: Academy of American Poets; American Academy of Arts & Letters. Honours: Bollingen Prize, 1993; MacArthur Fellowship, 1987; Poet Laureate of United States, 1990-91. Address: c/o Harry Ford Alfred A Knopf, 201 E 50th Street, New York, NY 10022, USA.

STRANDBERG Keith William, b. 21 Aug 1957, Toledo, Ohio, USA. Professional Writer. m. Carol Anne Hartman, 25 Sept 1982, 2 sons. Education: Ba, Chinese Language & Literature, 1979; BA, Physical Education, 1979. Publications: No Retreat, No Surrender, (feature film), 1986; Raging Thunder, 1987, (feature film); Stir Fry Cooking, 1985; Blood Brothers (film), 1989; The King of the Kickboxers (film), 1990; American Shaolin (film), 1991; Self Defense Choices for Women (video), 1992; Action Film Making Master Class (book), 1993; American Dragons (feature film), 1994; The Hate Stops Here (feature film), 1994. Contributions to: Berlitz; The Doctor's Press; Philadelphia Magazine; Online Access; Econ; Law Enforcement Technology; Corrections Forum; Soap; Karate/Judo Journal; Top Fighter; Impact; Karate International; Travel & Leisure; Rider; D & B Reports; Far East Traveler; BabyTalk; The China Business Review; American Motor Cyclist; Black Belt; Child Life; Motorworld. Honours: International Martial Arts Hall of Fame, 1993; Writer of the Year, 1994; World Martial Arts Hall of Fame, 1994. Memberships: National Writer's Club; National Martial Arts Advisory Board. Literary Agent: Shirley Strick, Los Angeles. Address: 3634 Peregrine Circle, PA 17554, USA.

STRANGER Joyce. See: WILSON Joyce Muriel.

STRATTON Thomas. See: DE WEESE Thomas Eugene.

STRAUB Peter Francis, b. 2 Mar 1943, Milwaukee, Wisconsin, USA. Novelist. m. 27 Aug 1966. Education: BA, University of Wisconsin, 1965; MA,Columbia University, 1966. Publications: Open Air (poetry), 1972; Marriage, 1973; Julia, 1975; If You Could See Me New, 1977; Ghost Story, 1979; Shadowland, 1980; Floating Dragon, 1983; The Talisman (with Stephen King), 1984; Koko, 1988; Mystery, 1989; Houses Without Doors, 1990. Contributions to: Reviews to TLS; New Statesman; Washington Post. Honours: British Fantasy Award, Auguest Derleth Award for Floating Dragon, 1983; World Fantasy Award, Best Novel for Koto, 1988; World Fantasy Award, Best Novell for The Ghost Village, 1993. Memberships: MWA; HWA; Authors League; Authors Guild; PEN. Literary Agent: Robert J Schuster. Address: 53 W 85th Street, New York, NY 10024, USA.

STRAUBING Harold Elk, b. 19 Feb 1918, New York, USA. Writer. m. Helen Mozlin, 13 Mar 1943, 1 daughter. Education: BA, Long Island University, 1940. Appointments: Artist and Writer, Fleischer Studios, Miami, Florida, 1940-42; US Army, wrote animated cartoon series, Snafu, 1942-45; Goodman Publications, Comic Books Editor, 1945-47; Comics Editor of the Newspaper and its Syndicate, New York Herald Tribune, New York, 1947-51; Comics Editor, Associated Press News-Features, 1951-52; Editor, Lev Gleason Publications, 1952-54; Magazine Editor, Crestwood Publishing Company, New York, 1954-61; Executive Editor, General Manager, American Art Enterprises Inc, North Hollywood, California, 1961-75; Executive Editor, Chatsworth Enterprises Inc, Chatsworth, California, 1975-82; Writer, 1982-; Producer and Director of Radio Dramas, Chairman of Board of Directors of Oceanside Community Theatre, Oceanside, New York. Publications: Little Girl with Red Nails (3-act play) readings of script given in New York in 1961; Target Number One (novel), 1983; Civil War - Eyewitness Reports, 1985, reprinted as The Fateful Lightning, 1987; The Last Magnificent War, 1988 to be issued as an oral reading by Books on Tape, Autumn 1990; Bandages, Bullets and Beans, to be published, Autumn 1990; A Touch of War, 1991; In Hospital and Camp, 1993; Hey! Look at Me! I'm Talkin, 1994; Forthcoming: Motion Pictures Finds It's Voice; Devil Clan. Honour: Fletcher Pratt Award for nomination from Civil War Round Table of New York, 1985 for Civil War: Eyewitness Reports. Memberships: Writers Guild of America West; Mystery Writers of America. Address: 5336 Corteen Place 1, North Hollywood, CA 91607, USA.

STRAUS Dennis David, (Ascher/Straus), b. New York, USA. Writer. Education: MA, Columbia University. Publications: Letter to an Unknown Woman; The Planet; The Menaced Assassin. Contributions to: ChicagoReview; Paris Review; Epoch; Top Stories; Chelsea; Exile; Calyx; Zone; Controntation; Central Park; New American Writing; Top Top Stories (anthology_; Is Years in Exile (anthology); The Living Underground (anthology). Honours: Panache Experimental Fiction Prize; Pushcart Prize; Caps Fellowship. Address: PO Box 176, Rockaway Park, NY 11694, USA.

STRAUS/ASCHER. See: **ASCHER Sheila & STRAUS Dennis David.**

STRAUSS Jennifer, b. 30 Jan 1933, Heywood, VA, Australia. Lecturer; Poet. m. Wermer Strauss, 1958, 3 sons. Education: BA, University of Melbourne, 1954; University of Glasgow, 1957-58; PhD, Monash University, 1992. Appointments include: Senior Lecturer, 1971, Associate Professor, 1992-, Monash University, Melbourne. Publications: Children and other Strangers, 1975; Winter Driving, 1981; Labour Ward, 1988; Co Editor, Middle English Verse: An Anthology, 1985; Boundary Conditions: The Poetry of Gwen Harwood, 1992; The Oxford Book of Australian Love Poems (ed), 1993. Memberships include: Literature Committee for the Victorian Ministry for the Arts, 1983-85; Premiers Literary awards Committee. Address: 2-12 Tollingtom Avenue, East Malvern, VA 3145, Australia.

STRAUSSLER Thomas. See: **STOPPARD Tom.**

STRAWSON Galen John, b. 5 Feb 1952, Oxford, England. Philosopher. m. Jose Said, 20 Jul 1974, diss, 1994, 1 s, 2 d. Education: BA Philosophy, 1973, MA, 1977, Cambridge; BPhil, 1977, DPhil, 1983, Oxford. Appointments: Assistant Editor, 1978-87, Consultant, 1987-, Times Literary Supplement, London. Publications: Freedom and Belief, 1986; The Secret Connection, 1989; Mental Reality, 1994. Contributions to: TLS; Sunday Times; Observer; London Review of Books; Independent on Sunday; Mind; American Philosophical Quarterly; Inquiry; Analysis, Philosophical Studies. Honours: R A Nicholson Prize for Islamic Studies, Cambridge, 1971; T H Green Prize for Moral Philosophy, Oxford, 1983; Fellow, Jesus College, Oxford. Membership: Mind Association. Address: Jesus College, Oxford, OX1 3DW, England.

STREET Pamela, b. 3 Mar 1921, Wilton, Wiltshire, England. Writer. (div) 1 d. Education: The Godolphin School, Salisbury, 1930-38; Salisbury and South Wiltshire College of Further Education, 1967-69. Publications: My Father, A G Street, 1969, reprinted 3 times, Second edition, 1984; Portrait of Wiltshire, 1971, 1980; The Illustrated Portrait of Wiltshire, 1986, paperback edition, 1994; Arthur Bryant - Portrait of a Historian, 1979; Light of Evening, 1981; The Stepsisters, 1982; Morning Glory, 1982; Portrait of Rose, 1986; Personal Relations, 1987; The Mill-Race Quartet, 1988; The Timeless Moment, 1988; Mr Brown and Prudence (radio story), 1988; The Beneficiaries, 1989; Doubtful Company, 1990; Guilty Parties, 1991; Late Harvest, 1991; The Colonel's Son, 1992; Hindsight, 1993; Keeping it Dark, 1994. Contributions to: The Field; Punch; The Farmer's Weekly; The Sunday Times; The Lady. Address: Flat 5, 47 South Street, London, W1Y 5PD, England.

STRESHINSKY Shirley, b. 7 Oct 1934, Alton, Illinois, USA. Writer. m. Ted Streshinsky, 16 June 1966, 1 son, 1 daughter. Education: BA, University of Illinois. Publications: And I Alone Survived, 1978; Hers The Kingdom, 1981; A Time Between, 1984; Gift of the Golden Mountain, 1988; The Shores of Paradise, (novel), 1991; Audubon: Life and Art in The American Wilderness, (bio), 1993. Contributions to: Over 100 articles in journals and magazines including: Redbook; Ms; Glamour; Ladies Home Journal; McCalls. Honours: Best Human Interest Article, Society Magazine Writers Association, 1968; Educational Press Award, 1968. Membership: Authors Guild. Literary Agent: Claire Smith, Harold Ober Associates, New York, USA. Address: PO Box 674, Berkeley, CA 94701, USA.

STROM Robert Duane, b. 21 Jan 1935, Chicago, Illinois, USA. Professor. m. Shirley Kaye Mills, Apr 1962, 2 sons. Education: BS, Macalester College, 1958; MA, University of Minnesota, 1959; PhD, University of Michigan, 1962. Publications: Teaching in the Slum School, 1965; Psychology for the Classroom, 1969; Teachers and the Learning Process, 1971;Education for Affective Achievement (with E P Torrance), 1973; Values and Human Development, 1973; Learning Processes, 1976; Parent and Child Development, 1978; Growing Through Play: Parents and Children, 1981; Educational Psychology, 1982; Human Development and Learning, 1989; Becoming A Better Grandparent, 1991; Grandparent Education, 1991; Achieving Grandparent Potential, 1992. Contributions to: Over 200 articles to journals of education, psychology, educational research, aging and human development, child development, creativity and exceptional children. Honours: NATO Scholar, University of Ankara, Turkey, 1967; Fulbright Scholar, Canberra, Australia, 1975; Fulbright Scholar, University of Stockholm, Sweden, 1985; Research Fellow, Japan Society for the Promotion of Science, 1995. Memberships: American

Psychological Association. Address: Arizona State University, Tempe, AZ 85287, USA.

STRONG Eithne, b. 28 Feb 1923, W.Limerick, Ireland. Writer. m. Rupert Strong, 1943, 2 s, 7 d. Education: BA, H Dip Ed, Trinity College, Dublin. Publications: Sarah, in Passing; Flesh - The Greatest Sin, (revised edition 1993); Songs of Living; Degrees of Kindred; Patterns; Cirt Oibre; Fuil agus Fallai; My Darling Neighbour; Aoife faoi Ghlas (poetry in Irish), 1990; An Sagart Pinc (poetry in Irish), 1990; Let Live (poetry in English), 1990; Spatial Nosing (poetry in English), 1993; The Love Riddle (novel), 1993; works included in many anthologies. Contributions to: numerous journals and magazines. Memberships: Several professional bodies including: Poetry Ireland; PEN; Irish writers' Union. Address: 17 Eaton Square, Monkstown, Co Dublin, Ireland.

STRONG Jonathan, b. 13 Aug 1944, Evanston, Illinois, USA. Novelist; Teacher. Education: BA, Harvard University, 1969. Publications: Secret Words, 1992; Elsewhere, 1985; Ourselves, 1971; Tike, 1969; Companion Pieces, 1993; An Untold Tale (novel), 1993; Forthcoming: Offspring (novel). Contributions to: Partisan Review; Triquarterly; Shenandoah;Esquire; Transatlantic Review. Honours: Rosenthal Award, 1970; O Henry Story Award, 1967, 1970; National Endwoment for the Arts Award, 1986. Memberships: New England Gilbert and Sullivan Society; Sir Arthur Sullivan Society. Address: English Department, Tufts University, Medford, MA 02155, USA.

STRONG Pat. See: **HOUGH Richard Alexander.**

STRONG Roy (Colin) (Sir), b. 1935, United Kingdom. Author. Appointments: Assistant Keeper, 1959-67, Director, Keeper, Secretary, 1967-73, National Portrait Gallery, London; Museum Director, Victoria and Albert Museum, 1974-87. Publications include: The Cult of Elizabeth: Elizabethan Portraiture and Pageantry, 1977; And When Did You Last See Your Father?, The Victorian Painter and British History, 1978; The Renaissance Garden in England, 1979; Britannia Triumphans: Inigo Jones, Rubens and Whitehall Palace, 1980; The English Miniature (co-author), 1981; Designing for The Dancer (contrib), 1981; The English Year (with J T Oman), 1982; The New Pelican Guide to English Literature (co-author), 1982; The English Renaissance Miniature, 1983; Artists of The Tudor Court Catalogue (with J Murrell), 1983; Art and Power, 1984; Glyndebourne: A Celebration (co-author), 1984; Strong Points, 1985; Henry, Prince of Wales and England's Lost Renaissance, 1986; Creating Small Gardens, 1986; Gloriana: Portraits of Queen Elizabeth I, 1987; A Small Garden Designer's Handbook, 1987; Cecil Beaton, The Royal Portraits, 1988; Creating Small Formal Gardens, 1989; Sidney's Achievements (contrib), 1990; England and the Continental Renaissance (co-author), 1990; Lost Treasures of Britain, 1990; The Garden Trellis, 1991; Small Period Gardens, 1992; Royal Gardens, 1992; A Celebration of Gardens, 1991. Contribution to: The Art of The Emblem, 1993; A Countrylife, 1994; William Larkin, 1994; Successful Small Gardens, 1994. Literary Agent: Felicity Bryan. Address: The Laskett, Much Birch, Hereford, HR2 8HZ, England.

STRUTTON Bill, b. 23 Feb 1918, Moonta, South Australia. Writer. m. Virginia Bolt, 18 Apr 1970, 1 s, 2 d. Education: South Australian Country Studentship, Kadina Memorial High School, 1932; Adelaide, 1933-35. Appointments: Feature Writer, Australian Consolidated Press, 1945-58. Publications: A Jury of Angels, 1957; The Secret Invaders (with Michael Pearson), 1959; Island of Terrible Friends, 1961; Dr Who and The Zarbi, 1965; The Carpaccio Caper, 1973; Many screenplays for popular TV series, Britain, USA and Australia, 1958-75. Memberships: Crimewriters Association; Writers Guild of Great Britain; Honorary Life Member, The Critics Circle, Great Britain. Literary Agent: David Higham Associates, Lower John Street, London, England. Address: Federico Martin Carreras 2, 17200 Palafrugell, Gerona, Spain.

STUART Sidney. See: **AVALLONE Michael Angelo.**

STUBBS Jean, b. 23 Oct 1926, Denton, Lancashire, England. Author. m.(1) Peter Stubbs, 1 May 1948, 1 s, 1 d, (2) Roy Oliver, 5 Aug,1980. Education: Manchester School of Art, 1944-47; Diploma, Lorebum Secretarial College, Manchester, 1947. Appointments: Reviewer, Books and Bookmen, 1965-76; Copywriter, Henry Melland, 1964-66; Writer-in-Residence for Avon, 1984. Publications: The Rose Grower, 1962; The Travellers, 1963; Hanrahan's Colony, 1964; The Straw Crown, 1966; My Grand Enemy, 1967; The Passing Star, 1970;

The Case of Kitty Ogilvie, 1970; An Unknown Welshman, 1972; Dear Laura, 1973; The Painted Face, 1974; The Golden Crucible, 1976; Kit's Hill,1979; The Ironmaster, 1981; The Vivian Inheritance, 1982; The Northern Correspondent, 1984; 100 Years Around the Lizard, 1985; Great Houses of Cornwall,1987; A Lasting Spring, 1987; Like We Used To Be, 1989; Summer Secrets, 1990; Kelly Park, 1992; Charades, 1994. Contributions to: Numerous stories in various women's magazines also to Winter's Tales, Writer's Crimes, Ghost Books, Penguin Modern Stories. Honours: Tom Gallon Trust Award for short story writing, 1964; Daughter of Mark Twain, 1973. Memberships: PEN; Society of Women Writers and Journalists; Detection Club; Lancashire Writers Association; West Country Writers. Literary Agent: Jennifer Kavanagh, 39 Camden Park Road, London, NW1 9AX, England. Address: Trewin, Nancegollan, Helston, Cornwall, TR13 0AJ, England.

STUEWE Paul William, b. 5 Oct 1943, Rochester, New York, USA. Editor; Writer. m. Denna Groetzinger, 30 Aug 1976, 1 son, 2 daughters. Education: BA, Columbia University, 1965; MA, University of Toronto, 1993. Appointments: Contributing Editor, Quill & Quire, 1979-90; Editor, Books in Canada, 1990-. Publications: Dont Deal Five Deuces; The Storms Below; Hugh Garners Life And Works; Clearing the Ground. Contributions to: Too Numerous. Honours: Shortlisted, City of Toronto Book Award. Memberships: Canadian Society of Magazine Editors. Address: 149 Essex Street, Toronto, M6G 1T6, Canada.

STYLES Frank Showell (Glyn Carr), b. 14 Mar 1908, England. Author. m. Kathleen Jane Humphreys, 1954, 1 s, 2 d. Appointments include: Royal Navy, 1939-46 (retired as Commander); Professional author, 1946-76; Led 2 private Arctic expeditions, 1952-53; Himalayan expedition, 1954. Publications include: A Tent on Top, 1971; Vincey Joe at Quiberon, 1971; Admiral of England, 1973; A Sword for Mr Fitton, 1975; Mr Fitton's Commission, 1977; The Baltic Convoy, 1979; A Kiss for Captain Hardy, 1979; Centurion Comes Home, 1980; The Quarterdeck Ladder, 1982; Seven-Gun Broadside, 1982; The Malta Frigate, 1983; Mutiny in The Caribbean, 1984; The Lee Shore, 1985; Gun-Brig Captain, 1987; HMS Cracker, 1988; Nelson's Midshipman, 1990; A Ship for Mr Fitton, 1991; The Independent Cruise, 1992; Mr Fitton's Prize, 1993; Mr Fitton and The Black Legion, 1994; Other works include: First on The Summits, 1970; First up Everest, 1970; The Forbidden Frontiers: A Survey of India from 1765-1949, 1970; Welsh Walks and Legends, 1972; Snowdon Range, 1973; The Mountains of North Wales, 1973; Glyder Range, 1974; Backpacking: A Comprehensive Guide, 1976; Backpacking in The Alps and Pyrenees, 1976; Backpacking in Wales, 1977; Welsh Walks and Legends: South Wales, 1977; As Glyn Carr: Death on Milestone Buttress, 1951; Murder on the Matterhorn, 1951; The Youth Hostel Murders, 1952; The Corpse in the Crevasse, 1952; Deth Under Snowden, 1953; A Corpse at Camp Two, 1955; Murder of an Owl, 1956; The Ice-Axe Murders, 1958; Swing Away, Climber, 1959; Holiday With Murder, 1961; Death Finds A Foothold, 1962; Lewker in Norway, 1963; Death of a Weirdy, 1965; Lewkwer in Tirol, 1967; Fat Man's Agony, 1969. Honour: Fellow, Royal Geographic Society, 1954. Address: Trwyn Cae Iago, Borth y Gest, Porthmadog, Gwynedd, LL49 9TW, Wales.

STYRON William (Clark) Jr, b. 11 June 1925, Newport News, Virginia, USA. Writer. m. Rose Burgunder, 4 May 1953, 1 son, 3 daughters. Education: LLD, Davidson College, 1942-43; AB, LLD, Duke University, 1943-47. Publications: Lie Down in Darkness, 1951; The Long March, 1953; Set This House on Fire, 1960; The Confessions of Nat Turner, 1967; Sophie's Choice, 1979; This Quiet Dust, 1982; Darkness Visible, 1990; A Tidewater Morning, 1993. Contributions to: Articles, essays and reviews to numerous journals. Honours: Pulitzer Prize, 1968; American Book Award, 1980; Prix Mondial Cino del Duca, 1985; Commandeur Ordre des Arts et des lettres, 1985; Edward MacDowell Medal, 1988; Decorated Commandeur Legion d'Honneur, France, 1988; Elmer Holmes Bobst Award for fiction, 1989; Howells Medal, 1970; National Medal of Arts, 1993; National Arts Club Gold Medal, 1995. Memberships: Honorary Member, Academie Goncourt, France; American Academy of Arts and Letters. Literary Agent: Don Congdon, 156 Fifth Avenue, New York, NY 10010, USA. Address: 12 Rucum Road, Roxbury, CT 06783, USA.

SUBRAMAN Velinda (Mary Bumgarer). Education: BA, Regents College, New York, 1987; MA, California State University, 1990. Appointments: Poetry Editor, Gypsy Magazine and Vergin Press, 1983-. Publications: Poetry Books: Skin Divers (co-author Lyn Lifshin), 1988; Halloween, 1989;Fighting Woman, 1986; Heather and Mace, 1985; The Jesuit Poems, 1989; Numberg Poems, 1983; Eye of the Beast, 1986; Snow Summits, 1988; In the Sun He Dreams His

Playmate, 1987; Body Parts, 1987; Work in Anthologies: A New Geography of Poets, 1992; Mondo Barbie, 1993; We Speak for Peace, 1993; The World of 2:nes, 1992. Contributions to: Atom Mind; Catalyst; Borderlands; Dog River Review; Owen Wister Review; Poppourri; Human Quest; Silent Skies; Social Justice; The Baltimore Sun; Puerto del Sol; Genre; Open; Rio Grande Review; Slipstream; Amelia; Bogg; Samisdat; Gargoyle; Second Coming; The Plough. Honours: Guest Speaker, California State University, Long Beach, 1994. Address: PO Box 370322, El Paso, TX 79937, USA.

SUDAMA Bhikkhoo. See: **GOKANI Pushkar Haridas.**

SUGERMAN Danny, b. 1954, Los Angeles, USA. Writer. Education: University of California, Los Angeles. Appointments: Office Boy, Junior Assistant, Doors' West Hollywood. Publications: No One Here Gets Out Alive, 1980; The Doors Illustrated History; Wonderland Avenue; Appetite For Destruction; Consultant, Oliver Stone's new film on The Doors. Contributions to: Numerous Magazines and Journals. Honours: No 1 Slot, Bestseller Lists, various Books. Address: Far Arden Inc, c/o Laura Lizer & Assoc, 12711 Ventura Blvd Site 440, Studio City, CA 91604, USA.

SUGIMOTO Yoshio, b. 7 Dec 1939, Japan. University Professor. m. Machiko Satow, 19 Jun 1966, 1 s, 2 d. Education: Political Science, Kyoto University, 1964; PhD Sociology, University of Pittsburgh, 1973. Publications: Popular Disturbance in Postwar Japan, 1981; Images of Japanese Society, 1986; Democracy in Contemporary Japan, 1986; The Japanese Trajectory, 1988; Constructs for Understanding Japan, 1989; The MFP Debate, 1990. Honours: Japan Intercultural Publications Award, 1987. Memberships: Fellow, Australian Academy of The Humanities. Address: School of Sociology and Anthropology, La Trobe University, Bundoora, Melbourne, Victoria 3083, Australia.

SUHRAWARDY (Rizvi) Nilofar, b. 25 Feb 1963, Allahbad, India. Writer; Journalist. Education: BA, University of Delhi, 1984; MA, JNU, 1986; MPhil, JNU, 1989; MA, School of Journalism and Mass Communication, UW-Madison, USA, 1992. Appointments include: Times of India. Contributions to: Wisconsin State Journal; Austin-American Statesman; The Badger Herald, USA; Impact International, England; Arab News, Saudi Arabia; Indian publications include, Mainstream; The Times of India; Hindustan Times; The Sunday Mail; The Indian Post; Free Press Journal; National Herald; The Evening News; Women's Era; presently working in the Times of India. Address: 375 B Pocket II, Mayur Vihar. Ph I, Delhi-91, India.

SUKNASKI Andrew, b. 30 July 1942, Wood Mountain, Saskatchewan, Canada. Editor; Poet. Education includes: University of British Columbia, Vancouver, 1967-68. Appointments include: Editor of Three Legged Coyote, Wood Mountain, 1982-. Publications: This Shadow of Eden, 1970; Circles, 1970; Rose Wayn in the East, 1972; Old Mill, 1972; The Zen Pilgrimage, 1972; Four Parts Sand: Concrete Poems, 1972; Wood Mountain Poems, 1973; Suicide Notes, Booke One, 1973; These Fragments I've Gathered for Ezra, 1973; Leaving, 1974; Blind Mans House, 1975; Leaving Wood Mountain, 1975; Octomi, 1976; Almighty Voice, 1977; Moses Beauchamp, 1978; The Ghosts Call You Poor, 1978; Two For Father, 1978; In The Name of Narid: New Poems, 1981; Montage for an Interstellar Cry, 1982; The Land They Gave Away: Selected and New Poems, 1982; Silk Trail, 1985. Honours include: Canada Council Grants. Address: c/o Thistledown Press, 668 East Place, Saskatoon, Sasketchewan S7J 2Z5, Canada.

SULLIVAN Larry Michael (memphis slim), b. 30 Jul 1948, Millington Naval Base, TN, USA. Civil Servant; Writer; Poet. m. (1) Mary Jo Hulme, 22 Mar 1968, div 1971, (2) Kathryn Sue Curry, 1 Jul 1984, 1 son, 2 step-daughters. Education: BS Education, 1970, MS, 1976, University of TN, Knoxville. Literary Appointments: Foreign Correspondent, Knoxville Libra, 1971; National/International News Editor, Great Speckled Bird, 1976. Publications: Free Venice Beachhead, 1981-89; Snatsu Tu (Spanish poetry). Creative works: Art work shown at Venice Art Festivals, 1992-93, Fourth Dimension Gallery, Venice, 1992-93. Honours: Pi Lambda Theta, 1975; Alpha Xi Chapter. Memberships: President, Venice Town Council, 1989-90; President, Venice-Ocean Park Food Co-op, 1989-92; President, Venice City Hood Committee, 1989-91. Address: PO Box 1132, Venice, CA 90294, USA.

SULLIVAN Sean Mei. See: **SOHL Gerald A.**

SULLIVAN Thomas William, b. 20 Nov 1940, Highland Park, Michigan, USA. Author; Teacher. 1 son, 1 daughter. Education: BA, 1964. Publications: Diapason, 1978; The Phases of Harry Moon, 1988; Born Burning, 1989; Drummers on Glass, 1991; Approx 50 short stories published. Contributions to: Over 30 articles in magazines including: Omni; Best of Omni; Twilight Zone; Michigan Magazine. Honours: Pushcart Nomination, 1985; Cash Awards, Hemingway Days Festival Literary Contest, 1985; DADA Literary Contest, 1985, 1987; Nebula Award Nomination, 1987; Pulitzer Prize Nomination, 1989. Memberships: SFWA; MENSA; Literary Guild; Society of the Black Bull; Arcadia Mixture. Literary Agent: Bill Thompson, The Literary Group. Address: 17376 Catalpa, Lathrup Village, MI 48076-3549, USA.

SULLIVAN Walter Seager, b. 12 Jan 1918, New York, USA. Journalist; Author. m. Mary E Barrett, 1950, 1 son, 2 daughters. Education: Yale University. Appointments Include: New York Times, 1940-; (US Navy 1940-46). Positions as: Foreign Correspondent, Far East, 1948-50; United Nations, 1950-52; Germany & Berlin, 1952-56; US Antarctic Expeditions, 1946-47, 1954-55, 1956-57, 1976, 1991; Science News Editor, 1960-63; Science Editor, 1964-87. Governor, Artic Institute of North America, 1959-66; Councillor, American Geographical Society, 1959-81. Publications Include: Quest for a Continent, 1957; White Land of Adventure, 1957; Assault on the Unknown, 1961; We Are Not Alone, 1964; Continents in Motion, 1974; Black Holes: The Edge of Space, The End of Time, 1979; Landprints, 1984; We Are Not Alone, 1993 (hard cover), 1994 (paperback). Honours Include: Public Welfare Medal, National Academy of Sciences, Public Service Award, National Science Foundation, John Wesley Powell Award, US Geological Survey Fellow, Westinghouse Award, 1963, 1968, 1972, American Association for the Advancement of Science; Honorary Degrees in various universities; International Non-Fiction Book Prize, Frankfurt, 1965; American Institute Physics/US Steel Foundation Award, Physics & Astronomy, 1969; Science-in-Society Journalism Award, National Association of Science Writers, 1976. Memberships: American Academy of Arts & Sciences. Literary Agent: Oscard Associated, New York, USA. Address: New York Times, Times Square, NY 10036, USA.

SULLOWAY Frank Jones, b. 2 Feb 1947, Concord, New Hampshire, USA. Historian of Science. Education: AB summa cum laude, 1969, AM, History of Science, 1971, PhD, 1978, Harvard University. Publications: Freud, Biologist of the Mind, 1979; Darwin and his Finches, 1982; Freud and Biology: The Hidden Legacy, 1982; Darwin's Conversion, 1982; Darwin and the Galapagos, 1984; Darwin's Early Intellectual Development, 1985; Reassessing Freud's Case Histories, 1991. Honours: Pfizer Award, History of Science Society, 1980; MacArthur Foundation Fellowship, 1984-89. Memberships: Fellow, American Association for the Advancement of Science; Electorate Nominating Committee, Section on the History and Philosophy of Science, 1988-91, 1994-97; History of Science Society, Finance and Development Committees. Address: Massachusetts Institute of Technology, Programme in Science, Technology & Society, Bldg E51-128, Cambirdge, MA 02139, USA.

SUMMERFOREST Ivy B. See: **KIRKUP James.**

SUMMERS Anthony (Bruce), b. 21 Dec 1942, UK. Author; Journalist. m. (4) 27 Jun 1992, 3 sons. Education: BA, Modern Languages, New College Oxford, 1964. Appointments: Researcher, World In Action Programme, Granada TV, 1963; Newsreader, Writer, Swiss Broadcasting Corporation 1964-65; Scriptwriter, BBC-TV News, 1965; BBC-TV Current Affairs Programmes, 1965-73, rising to Senior Film Producer. Publications: The File On the Tsar (with Tom Mangold), 1976; Conspiracy (Who Killed President Kennedy?), 1980; Goddess: The Secret Lives of Marilyn Monroe, 1985; Honeytrap: The Secret Worlds of Stephen Ward (with Stephen Dorril), 1987; Official and Confidential, The Secret Life of J Edgar Hoover, 1993. Contributions to: Sunday Times; Observer; Independent. Honour: Golden Dagger, Crime Writers Association, for best Non-Fiction, 1980; Memberships: PEN; Authors Guild; NVJ; BECTV. Literary Agent: Sterling Lord Literistic Inc, (New York City). Address: One Madison Avenue, New York City, NY 10010, USA.

SUNDERLAND Eric, b. 18 Mar 1930, Ammanford, Dyfed, Wales. Vice Chancellor, University College, Bangor. m. 19 Oct 1957, 2 d. Education: BA Class 1, Geography with Anthropology, University of Wales; MA Anthropology (by thesis), University of Wales; PhD Anthropology (by thesis), University College, London. Publications: Elements of Human and Social Geography; some anthropological

perspectives, 1973; Genetic Variation in Britain (co-editor), 1973; The Operation of Intelligence: biological pre-conditions for the operation of intelligence (co-editor), 1980; Genetic and Population Studies in Wales (co-editor), 1986. Contributions to: Approx 90 papers to journals; Approx 50 book reviews. Address: Bryn, Ffriddoedd Road, Bangor, Gwynedd, LL57 2EH, Wales.

SUTHERLAND Efua, b. 27 June 1924, Cape Coast, Ghana. Playwright. Education: BA, Homerton College, Cambridge. Appointments include: Founding Director of Ghana Drama Studio, University of Ghana Writer's Workshop, and Kusum Agoromba children's theatre group. Publications: Foriwa, 1962; Edufa, after Alcestis by Euripides, 1962; Anansegoro: You Swore an Oath, 1964; Vulture, Vulture: Two Rhythm Plays, 1968; Ananse and the Dwarf Brigade, 1971; The Marriage of Anansea: A Storytelling Drama, 1971; Versions and adaptations of plays and stories by Chekhov and Lewis Carroll; Also Playtime in Africa, children's verse, 1960; The Original Bob: The Story of Bob Johnson, 1970; The Voice in the Forest: A Tale from Ghana, 1983. Address: Institute of African Studies, University of Ghana, PO Box 25, Legon, Ghana.

SUTHERLAND Margaret, b. 16 Sep 1941, Auckland, New Zealand. Author. Married, 2 s, 1 d. Education: Registered Nurse. Appointments: Literary Fellow, Auckland University, 1981; Scholarship in Letters, New Zealand Government, 1984; Australia Council Writers Fellowship, Category B, 1992, Category A, 1995. Publications: The Fledgling, 1974; The Love Contract, 1976; Getting Through, 1977, (USA, Dark Places, Deep Regions, 1980); The Fringe of Heaven, 1984; The City Far From Home, 1992; Children's Books: Hello I'm Karen, 1974. Contributions to: Literary and Popular New Zealand Magazines and Journals. Honours: Katherine Mansfield Short Story Award; Scholarship in Letters, New Zealand, 1981. Memberships: Federation of Australian Writers; Australian Society of Authors. Address: 10 Council Street, Speers Point, NSW 2284, Australia.

SUTHERLAND SMITH Beverley Margaret, b. 1 July 1935, Australia. Writer. (div) 2 s, 2 d. Publications include: A Taste For All Seasons, 1975, revised 1991; A Taste of Class, 1980; A Taste In Time, 1981; Chocolates and Petit Fours, 1987; Gourmet Gifts, 1985; Delicious Desserts, 1989; Oriental Cookbook, 1990; Simple Cuisine, 1992; Vegetables, 1994. Contributions to: Gourmet Magazine; Epicurean Magazine; The Age; Golden Wings; German Geographical Magazine; Herald and Weekly Times. Memberships: International Association of Culinary Professionals; Ladies Wine and Food Society of Melbourne; Chaine des Rotisseurs; Wine Press Club; Amities Gastronomiques Internationales. Literary Agent: Curtis Brown (Australia and USA). Address: 29 Regent Street, Mount Waverley, Melbourne, Victoria 3149, Australia.

SÜTO András, b. 17 Jun 1927, Pusztakamarás, Transylvania, Romania (Hungarian origin). Witer; Journalist. m. Eva Szabo, 1949, 2 children. Appointments include: Journalist, Vilagossag Daily Newspaper, Kolozsvár; Contributor, later editor-in-chief, Falvak Népe, 1949-54; Deputy chief editor, Igaz Szo literary monthly, Marosvásárhely, Tirgu Mures, 1955- 57; Chief editor, Uj Elet, pictorial, Marosvásárhely, 1957-89; Vice President, Writers Federation, Socialist Republic of Romania, 1973-81. Publications include: Emberek indulnak, short stories, 1953; Félrejaro Salamon, short novel, 1956; Anyam könnyu álmot iger, novel, 1970; Rigó és apostol, essays, travelogue, 1970; Engedjétek hozzam jönni a szavakat, novel, 1977; Az Idö Markában, essays, 1984; Sárkány alszik veled, interviews, 1991; Szemet széért, journalism, diary, 1993; Heródes napjai, diary, 1994; Dramatic works: Tékozló szerelem, play, 1963; Pompás Gedeon, play, 1968; Egy lócsiszár virágvasarnápja, 1975; Csillag a máglyán, 1975; Cain and Abel, 1978; A szuzai menyagzö, 1981; Advent a Hargitán, 1987; Az Alomkommandó; Szemet szóért, diary notes, 1993; Az ugató madár, play, 1993; Herodes napjai, diary notes, 1994; Vadpávamenyegzó, story book, 1994; Books translated into Romanian, German, Russian, Bulgarian, Slovak, Ukranian; Plays performed, Budapest, Bucharest, Cluj, Novi-Sad, Zagreb, Bratislva, New York. Honours: State Prize, Literature, Romania, 1953, 1954; Herder Prize, Vienna, Austria, 1979; Kossuth Prize, 1992. Address: Tirgu Mures, Marosvasarhely, Str Marasti Nr 36, Romania.

SUTTON Henry. See: **SLAVITT David Rytman.**

SUTTON Keith Ashley, b. 27 Jan 1944, Moorabbin, Victoria, Australia. Editor; Writer. div., 1 son. Education: BA, Australian National University, Canberra, 1972; Associate Diploma in Professional Writing,

Canberra College of Advanced Education (now University of Canberra), 1974. Career: Editor, Publications, Department of Foreign Affairs, Canberra, 1977-85; Editor to Australian Auditor-General, Canberra, 1985-88. Publications: How to Stuff Up a Small Business (with Gavin Byrne and Neville O'Neill), 1990; Blueprint for the Casino Industry: Federal Hotels and Wrest Point, 1992; Australia's Coins and Notes, 1993. Memberships: Australian Society of Authors; Canberra Society of Editors; National Press Club. Address: 38A Northgate Gardens, Forbes St, Turner, ACT 2601, Australia.

SUTTON Shaun Alfred Graham, b. 14 Oct 1919, England. Stage and Television Director; Producer; Writer. m. Barbara Leslie, 1948, 1 s, 3 d. Education: Latymer Upper School; Embassy School of Acting, London. Appointments include: Stage Manager, London Theatres, 1938-40; Royal Navy, 1940-46; Director, Buxton Repertory Theatre, Embassy Theatre, 1947-51; Director, On Monday Next, Comedy Theatre, 1949; Entered BBC TV service, 1952, produced and wrote many children's TV plays and serials; Directed television series including Z Cars. Softly Softly, Sherlock Holmes, Kipling, Detective; Head, BBC Drama Serials Department, 1966-68; Head of BBC TV Drama Group, 1969-81; Producer, Skakespeare series, 1981-84; Theatre Night series, 1984-89; Produced: Merlin of The Crystal Cave, Re-Joyce, 1991-92. Publications: A Christmas Carol (stage adaptation), 1949; Queen's Champion, children's novel, 1961; The Largest Theatre in The World, 1982. Honours: OBE, 1979; Fellow, Royal TV Society; Director, Prime Time Television. Memberships: BAFTA. Address: 15 Corringham Court, Corringham Road, London, NW11 7BY, England.

SWAIM Alice Mackenzie, b. 5 June 1911, Craigdam, Scotland. Writer; Consultant; Contest Judge. m. William Thomas Swaim, 27 Dec 1932, 2 daughters. Education: BA, Wilson College, 1932. Appointments: Newspaper Columnist, Cornucopia, Tejas, Carlisle, Pennsylvania Evening Sentinel, 1953-70; National Contest Judge, 1954-85; Newspaper Columnist, Touchstone, New Hampshire, 1970-85; Poetry Therapy Consultant, 1971-75; Public Relations Director, 2nd World Congress of Poets; Writer, Concordia Greeting Card Company, 1981-82. Publications: Let The Deep Song Rise, 1952; Up To The Stars, 1954; Sunshine in a Thimble, 1958; Crickets are Crying Autumn, 1960; The Gentle Dragon, 1962; Pennsylvania Profile, 1966; Scented Honeysuckle Days, 1966; Here On The Threshhold, 1966; Beneath a Dancing Star (Italy), 1968; Beyond My Catnip Garden, 1970; And Miles to go, 1981; Unicorn and Thistle, 1981; Children in Summer, 1983; As Wrens Sing Madringals, 1987; Horizon - Makers, 1991; Beneath a Dancing Star, 1991; A Time of Promise, 1993. Contributions to: Poet; Lyric; Nostalgia; Opus; Poetic Page; Mediphors; Iliad (HM); Cader Co; Creative Arts; Harp Strings; Voices International; Arcadia; Apropos. Honours Include: Over 800 Awards and Citations, including: Medals from Philippines, Italy and USA; American Heritage Award, JFK Library of Minorities, 1974; 1st Prize, Writer's Digest Contest, 1988; 1st Prize, Poet, 1993; Spring Poet Laureate, Verses, 1994; 3rd Prize, CFCP, 1994; Woman of the Year Award, American Biographical Institute, 1994; 3 Commemorative Awards, World Who's Who of Women, 1994; Presidents Award for Literary Excellence, Iliad Press, 1994. Memberships: Poetry Society of America; Academy of American Poets; National Federation of State Poetry Societies; Marketing Editor, Poetry Society of New Hampshire; Poetry Society of Pennsylvania, Kentucky and California. Address: 322 North Second Street, Apt 1606, Harrisburg, PA 17101, USA.

SWAN Gladys, b. 15 Oct 1934, New York City, USA. Writer. m. 9 Sept 1955, 2 daughters. Education: BA, Western New Mexico University, 1954; MA, Claremont Graduate School. Appointments: Distinguished Visiting Writer in Residence, University of Texas, El Paso, 1984-85; Visiting Professor, Ohio University, 1986-87; Associate Professor, University of Missouri, 1987-. Publications: On the Edge of the Desert (short stories), 1979; Carnival for the Gods (novel), 1986; Of Memory and Desire (short stories), 1989; Do You Believe in Cabeza de Vaca?, 1991; Ghost Dance: A Play of Voices, 1992. Contributions to: 37 Short Stories to various magazines including: Sweanee Review; Virginia Quarterly Review; Writer Forum; Ohio Review; Mid-American Review; Kenyon Review; Manoa; Shenandoah; Southwest Review; Passport. Honours: Fulbright Fellowship, Writer-in-Residence, Yugoslavia, 1988; Honorary Doctorate of Humane Letters, Western North Mexico University, 1992. Memberships: Authors Guild; Associated Writing Programmes; PEN American Center. Literary Agent: Jonathan Dolger Agency. Address: 2601 Lynwood Dr, Columbia, MO 65203, USA.

SWAN Robert Arthur, b. 2 Oct 1917, Broken Hill, Australia. Retired Civil Servant. m. Marie Kathleen McClelland, 14 Oct 1949, dec'd 1984, 1 d. Education: BA, University Of Melbourne, 1950. Publications: Argonauts Returned And Other Poems, 1946; Australia In The Antarctic: Interest, Activity And Endeavour, 1961; To Botany Bay: If Policy Warrants The Measure, 1973; 12 Collections of Poems, 1982- 1994. Contributions: Royal Historical Society Of Victoria; Royal Australian Historical Society; Australia Defence 2000; Australia And World Affairs; Australian Dictionary Of Biography; British National Biography. Membership: Fellow, Royal Geographical Society, London; United Services Institute, Sydney; Commando Association, Australia; Z Special Unit Association, Australia. Address: 64 Beach Drive, Woonona, NSW 2517, Australia.

SWAN Susan, b. 9 June 1945, Ontario, Canada. Novelist. m. Barry Haywood, 25 Mar 1969, 1 daughter. Education: BA, McGill University. Literary Appointments: Professor, York University. Publications: The Biggest Modern Woman of the World; The Wives of Bath; The Last of the Golden Girls; Unfit for Paradise. Honours: Guardian Fiction Finalist, 1993; Ontario Trillum Finalist, 1993; Governor General Finalist, 1983; Best First Novel Finalist, 1993. Literary Agent: Kim Witherspoon Associates, NY, USA. Address: 151 Robert Street, Toronto, M5S 2K6, Ontario, Canada.

SWANN Lois, b. 17 Nov 1944, NY, USA. Author; Reader; Calliope's Chamber; Teacher. m. (1) T G Swann, 15 Aug 1964, 1 son, 1 daughter, div 1979, (2) Kenneth E Arndt, 3 Sep 1988. Education: BA, Marquette University, 1966. Publications: The Mists Of Manittoo, 1976; Torn Covenants, 1981; Edited and Overwrote: John Milton: The True Wayfaring Christian, 1986. Contributions to: House Beautiful's; Home Decorating; Cincinnati Entertainment. Honours: Ohioana Library Association Award For First Novelists, 1976; Papers archived in Twentieth Century Collection, Boston University. Address: 22 Sagamore Road, Bronxville, NY 10708, USA.

SWANSON Judith Ann, b. 4 Nov 1957, Los Angeles, California, USA. University Professor. m. David R Mayhew, 20 Nov 1987. Education: BA, Colorado College, 1979; MSc, with distinction, London School of Economics & Political Science, 1980; PhD, University of Chicago, 1987. Publications: Book: The Public and the Private in Aristotle's Political Philosophy, 1992; Articles: The Political Philosophy of Aeschylus's Prometheus Bound; Justice as Seen by Prometheus, Zeus and Co, Interpretation 22, 1994; Aristotle on Liberality: Its Relation to Justice and its Public and Private Practice, 1994. Contributions to: Several Book Reviews in, The American Political Science Review; Presidential Studies Quarterly. Honours: National Honor Society, 1975; Graduated 3rd in high school class of 142, 1975; Honors at Entrance, Colorado College, 1975; Alpha Lambda Delta, National Honor Society, 1975-76; Dean's List, Colorado College, 1975-76, 1976-77, 1977-78; Pi Gamma Mu, 1978; Edith Bramhall Award for Academic Excellence, Colorado College, 1979; Phi Beta Kappa, 1979; Earhart Foundation Fellowship, University of Chicago, 1980-84; Josephine de Karman Fellowship, 1983-84; National Endowment for the Humanities Fellowship for University Teachers, 1990-91; Boston University Faculty Seed Research Grant, 1990. Memberships: American Political Science Association; Conference for the Study of Political Thought; International Association for Greek Philosophy; Society for Greek Political Thought; The Claremont Institute Society for the Study of Political Philosophy & Statesmanship; American Philosophical Association. Address: Department of Political Science, Boston University, 232 Bay State Road, Boston, MA 02215, USA. 6.

SWANTON Ernest William, b. 11 Feb 1907, London, England. Author. m. Ann Marion Carbutt, 11 Feb 1958. Education: Cranleigh School, 1921-24. Appointments: Evening Standard Staff, 1927-39; Daily Telegraph Staff, 1946-75; Editorial Director, The Cricketer, 1965-89, President 1990-. Publications: History of Cricket, 1938-1962 (with H S Altham), 1962; Barclays World of Cricket, 1st edition, 1966, 2nd edition, 1980, 3rd edition, 1986; As I Said at The Time, 1983; Essential E W Swanton, 1990. Contributions to: The Cricketer. Honours: OBE, 1965; Appointed Life Vice-President, MCC; CBE, 1994. Literary Agent: Curtis Brown, John Farquharson. Address: Delf House, Sandwich, Kent, CT13 9HB, England.

SWARD Robert Stuart, b. 23 June 1933, Chicago, Illinois, USA. University Professor; Writer. 2 sons, 3 daughters. Education: BA honours, University of Illinois, 1956; MA, University of Iowa, 1958; Postgraduate Work, University of Bristol, England, 1960-61; Middlebury College, Vermont, USA, 1959-60. Appointments: Poet-in-Residence,

Cornell University, 1962-64; Poet-in-Residence, University of Victoria, British Columbia, Canada, 1969-73; Visiting Writer, University of California-Extension, Santa Cruze, 1986-; Writer-in-Residence, Aspen Writers Conference, 1968; Writer-in Residnece, Foothill Writers Conference, summer, 1988-; Canada Council Fellowship; Exploration Grant; Writer, Writing Programme, Language Arts Department, Cabrillo College, 1989-; Poet-in-Residence, University of California, Santa Cruz, 1987-. Publications Include: Uncle Dog and Other Poems, 1962; Kissing the Dancer and Other Poems, 1964; Thousand-Year-Old Fiancee, 1965; Horbortom Stringbottom, 1970; Hannah's Cartoon, 1970; Quroum/Noah, 1970; Half a Life's History: Poems New and Selected, 1983; Poet Santa Cruz, 1985; Five Iowa Poems and One Iowa Print, 1975; Honey Bear on Lasqueti Island, 1978; The Three Roberts, (co-authors Robert Zend and Robert Priest), 1985; Four Incarnations, New & Selected Poems, 1957-91; Family (co-authors Prof David Swanger, Prof Tilly Shaw, Prof Charles Atkinson), 1994. Contributions to: The New Yorker; Poetry, Chicago; Transatlantic Review; The Paris Review; Tri-Quarterly; Chicago Review; New York Times; Antioch Review; Poetry Northwest; The Nation. Honours: Fulbright Fellowship, 1960-61; Guggenheim Fellowship, 1965-66; D H Lawrence Fellowship, 1966; McDowell Colony Fellowship, 1959-80s; Montalvo Literary Arts Award, Biennial Poetry Competition; Djerassi Foundation Residency, 1990; Harbourfront, International Poetry Festival, Toronto, 1993. Memberships: Writers Union of Canada, Newsletter Committee Chairman; League of Canadian Poets; National Writers Union, USA. Address: PO Box 7062, Santa Cruz, CA 95061, USA.

SWARTZ Jon David, b. 28 Dec 1934, Houston, Texas, USA. Psychologist; Professor; University Administrator. m. Carol Joseph Hampton, 20 Oct 1966, 2 sons, 1 daughter. Education: BA 1956, MA 1961, PhD 1969, Senior Postdoctoral Fellowship in Community Psychology and Community Mental Health, Counseling-Psychological Services Center and Hogg Foundation for Mental Health, 1973-74, University of Texas, Austin. Publications: Inkblot Perception and Personality (with W H Holtzman), 1961; Mental Retardation (with C C Cleland), 1969; Administrative Issues in Institutionsfor the Mentally Retarded, 1972; Multihandicapped Mentally Retarded, 1973; Personality Development in Two Cultures (with W H Holtzman), 1975; Profound Mental Retardation (with C C Cleland), 1976; The Profoundly Mentally Retarded (editor), 1978; Exceptionalities Through the Lifespan (with C C Cleland), 1982; Holtzman Inkblot Technique, 1956-82, 4th edition, 1983; Jesse Daniel Ames: An Exhibition at Southwestern University, 1986; HIT: An Annotated Bibliography (Supplement), 1988; Clara Harmon Lewis Collection, 1989; Handbook of Old-Time Radio: A Comprehensive Guide to Golden Age Radio Listening and Collecting, 1993; Other separate works. Contributions to: Over 350 articles and reviews in over 100 journals and magazines. Honours Include: Psi Chi, 1959; US Office of Education Fellow, 1964-66; Franklin Gilliam Prize, 1965; Mu Alpha Nu, 1965; Phi Kappa Phi, 1967; Sigma Xi, 1968; Spencer Fellow, National Academy of Education, 1972-74; Postdoctoral Fellow, 1973-74; Delta Tau Kappa, 1976; Phi Delta Kappa, 1980; Faculty Fellowship Award, 1981. Memberships: San Gabriel Writers League; Fellow, American Association for the Advancement of Science; Fellow, American Psychological Society; Fellow, Society for Personality Assessment; American Library Association; Southwestern Psychological Association; American Academy on Mental Retardation; Board Member, Western Research Conference on Mental Retardation; Bell County Psychological Association, 1991-. Address: 1401 East 18th Street, Georgetown, TX 78626, USA.

SWEARER Donald Keeney, b. 2 Aug 1934, Wichita, Kansas, USA. College Professor of Religion. m. 17 June 1964, 1 son, 1 daughter. Education: AB cum laude, 1956, MA 1965, PhD 1967, Princeton University, New Jersey. Publications: Buddhism in Transition, 1970; Secrets of the Lotus, 1971; Wat Haripunjaya: The Royal Temple of the Buddha's Relic, 1976; Dialogue, the Key to Understanding Other Religions, 1977; Buddhism, 1977; Buddhism and Society in Southeast Asia, 1981; For the Sake of the World. The Spirit of Buddhist and Christian Monasticism, 1989; Me-and-Mine, Selected Essays of Bhikkhu Buddhadasa, 1989; Ethics, Wealth and Salvation, 1989. Contributions to: Journal of the American Academy of Religion; Journal of Ecumenical Studies; Journal of Religious Ethics; Philosophy East and West; Journal of the Siam Society; Religious Studies Review. Honours: Phi Beta Kappa, 1956; Kent Fellow, 1964-65; Asian Religions Fellowship, Society for Religion in Higher Education, 1967-68; Senior Fellowship, National Endowment for the Humanities, 1972-73; Humanities Fellowship, Rockefeller Foundation, 1985-86; Senior

Research Fellowship, Fulbright (CIES), 1989-90; Charles and Harriet Cox McDowell Professor of Religion, 1992-; Fulbright-Hays Fellowship, 1994; Guggenheim Fellow, 1994. Memberships: American Academy of Religion, Vice-President, Mid-Atlantic Region, 1971-72; Association for Asian Studies, Board of Directors, SE Asia Council, 1977-80; American Society for the Study of Religion; Society for Buddhist-Christian Studies. Address: 109 Columbia Avenue, Swarthmore, PA 19081, USA.

SWEDE George, b. 20 Nov 1940, Riga, Latvia. Writer; Professor. m. Anita Krumins, 23 July 1974, 2 sons. Education: BA, University of British Columbia, 1964; MA, Dalhousie University, 1965. Appointments: Director, Poetry and Things, 1969-71; Poetry Editor, Poetry Toronto, 1980-81; Reviews and Poetry Editor, Writers' Quarterly, 1982-88; Judge, Japan Air Lines Haiku Contest, 1987 and 1990; Poetry Editor, Writers' Magazine, 1988-90; Judge, Haiku Society of American Henderson Award, 1989; Mirrors, International Tanka Awards, 1991. Publications Include: Poetry: Tell-Tale Feathers, 1978; Endless Jigsaw, 1978; Canadian Haiku Anthology (editor), 1979; Wingbeats, 1979; A Snowman, Headless, 1979; As Far As The Sea Can Eye, 1979; This Morning's Mockingbird, 1980; Eye To Eye With A Frog, 1981; All Of Her Shadows, 1982; Tick Bird, 1983; Frozen Breaths, 1983; I Throw Stones At The Mountain, 1988; Flaking Paint, 1983; Night Tides, 1984; Bifids, 1984; Time is Flies, 1984; The Space Between (with LeRoy Gorman & Eric Amann), 1986; High Wire Spider, 1986; Multiple Personality, 1987; Where Even The Factories Have Lawns (with John Curry), 1988; Leaping Lizard, 1988; Holes in my Cage, 1989; The Universe Is One Poem (editor), 1990; I Want To Lasso Time, 1991; Leaving My Loneliness, 1992; There Will Always Be A Sky (editor), 1993. Essays: The Modern English Haiku, 1981. Fiction: Moonlit Gold Dust, 1979; Quillby, The Porcupine Who Lost His Quills (with Anita Krumins), 1980; Missing Heirloom, 1980; Seaside Burglaries, 1981; Downhill Theft, 1982; Undertow, 1982; Dudley and the Birdman, 1985; Dudley and the Christmas Thief, 1986. Prose: Creativity: A New Psychology, 1993. Contributions to: Poetry, short stories and articles in over 125 different magazines around the world. Honours: Haiku Society of America Book Award, 1980; High/Coo Press Chapbook Competition Winner, 1982; Museum of Haiku Literature Award, 1983, 1985, 1993; Canadian Children's Book Centre Our Choice Award, 1984, 1985, 1987, 1991, 1992; First Prize, Haiku In English, Mainichi Daily News, 1993. Memberships: League of Canadian Poets; The Writers Union of Canada; PEN; Haiku Canada, co-founder 1977; Haiku Society of America; Canadian Society for Authors, Illustrators and Performers; Canadian Authors Association. Address: Box 279, Station P, Toronto, M5S 2S8, Canada.

SWEENEY Matthew, b. 6 Oct 1952, County Donegal, Ireland. Poet. m. Rosemary Barber, 1979. Education: University College Dublin, 1970-782; BA, Polytechnic of North London, 1978. Appointments include: Writer in Residence, Farnham College, Surrey, 1984-85; Publicist and Events Assistant for the Poetry Society, 1988-90. Publications: Without Shores, 1978; A Dream of Maps, 1981; A Round House, 1983; The Lame Waltzer, 1985; Blue Shoes, 1989; for Children, The Chinese Dressing Gown, 1987. Honours include: Cholmondeley Award, 1987. Address: 11 Dombey Street, London WC1N 3PB, England.

SWETZ Frank Joseph, b. 7 July 1937, New York City, USA. University Professor. Education: BA, Marist College, 1962; MA, Fordham University, 1963; DED, Columbia University, 1971; Dip (Supervision), 1969. Publications: Mathematics Education in China, 1974; Was Pythagoras Chinese?, 1977; Socialist Mathematics Education, 1979; Capitalism and Arithmetic, 1987; The Sea Island Mathematical Manual, 1992; From Five Fingers to Infinity, 1994; Mathematical Modelling in School Curriculum, 1991. Contributions to: Mathematics Teacher; American Mathematical Monthly; Historia Mathematics; Journal of Developing Areas; Science Teacher; USA Today; Physics Teacher; Educational Studies in Mathematics; Curriculum Review. Honours: Edpress Awards, 1971, 1984; Fulbright Asean Research Fellowship, 1985; Outstanding Research Awards Penn State University, 1986, 1989. Memberships: National Council of Teachers of Mathematics; PA Council Teachers of Mathematics; International Study Group on History of Pedagogy of Mathematics. Address: 616 Sandra Avenue, Harrisburg, PA 17109, USA.

SWIFT Graham Colin, b. 4 May 1949, London, England. Author. Education: Queens' College, Cambridge, 1967-70; MA, York University, 1970-73. Publications: The Sweet Shop Owner, 1980; Shuttlecock, 1981; Learning to Swim and Other Stories, 1982; Waterland, 1983; The

Magic Wheel (edited with David Profumo), 1986; Out Of This World, 1988; Ever After, 1992. Honours: Nominated for Booker Prize, 1983; Geoffrey Faber Memorial Prize, 1983; Guardian Fiction Award, 1983; Royal Society of Literature Winifred Holtby Award, 1983; Premio Grinzane Cavour, Italy, 1987; Prix du Meilleur Livre Étranger, France, 1994. Literary Agent: A P Watt Ltd. Address: 20 John Street, London, WC1N 2DR, England.

SWIFT Robert. See: **KELLY Tim.**

SWINBURNE Richard Granville, b. 26 Dec 1934, Smethwick, Staffordshire, England. Professor. m. Monica Holmstrom, 1960, (separated 1985) 2 d. Education: BA, 1957; B Phil, 1959; Dp Theol, 1960; MA, 1961, University of Oxford. Publications: Space and Time, 1968, 2nd edition, 1981; The Coherence of Theism, 1977, revised 1993; The Existence of God, 1979, revised 1991; Faith and Reason, 1981; The Concept of Miracle, 1971; An Introduction to Confirmation Theory, 1973; Personal Identity (with S Shoemaker), 1984; The Evolution of The Soul, 1986; Responsibility and Atonement, 1989; Revelation, 1992; The Christian God, 1994. Contributions to: Many philosophical journals. Honour: FBA, 1992. Address: Oriel College, Oxford, OX1 4EW, England.

SWINDELLS Robert, b. 1939, Bradford, England. Appointments: RAF; Shop Assistant; Clerk; Printer; Engineer; Teacher, 1969-1977; Full-Time Writer. Publications: The Ice Palace; A Serpent's Tooth; Follow a Shadow; Daz for Zoe; You Can't Say I'm Crazy; The Go-Ahead Gang; When Darkness Comes, 1973; Brother In The Land, 1986; Time Line, 1995; Stone Cold, 1995. Honours: Children's Rights Workshop Other Award, 1984 for Brother in the Land; Children's Book Award for Brother in the Land and Room 13, 1980; Carnegie Award, 1994 for Stone Cold.

SZABO Istvan, b. 18 Feb 1938, Hungary. Film Director; Scenario Author. m. Vera Gyurey. Education: Budapest Academy of Theatre & Film Arts. Appointments include: Leading member, Hungarian Film Studios; Tutor, College of Theatre & Film Arts, Budapest; Numerous productions, films, plays, documentaries, television. Honours include: Bela Balazs Prize, 1967; Kossuth Prize; Grand Prix, Oberhausen, 1971, 1977; Grand Prix, Locarno, 1973; Silver Bear of Berlin, Academy Award nomination, 1981; Academy Award, David di Donatello Prize (Italy); Italian Critics' Prize; UK Critics' Prize, 1982; BAFTA Award, 1986; Akademy Award Nomination, 1985, 1988; Silver Bear of Berlin, 1992; European Script Writer of the Year, 1992. Memberships: Academy of Motion Pictur Arts & Sciences; Akademie der Kunste, Berlin. Address: I.S.L. - film, 1149 Budapest, Róua-uta, 174 Hungary.

SZABO Magda, b. 5 Oct 1917, Hungary. Author. m. Tibor Szobotka, 1948. Education: Graduated as Teacher, 1940; Dr phil, Classical Philology. Career: Teacher, secondary schools, 1940-44, 1950-59; Started literary career as poet, has since written novels, plays, radio dramas, essays, film scripts; Works translated into 31 languages including English, French, German, Italian, Russian, Polish, Swedish. Publications: Neszek (Noises), poems; Okut (Old Well), autobiography; The sadness of Demigods, essays, 1992; Children's novels: Szigetkek (Blue Island); Tunder Lala (Lala the Fairy); Abigel (Abigail); Novels: Az oz (The Fawn); Fresko (Fresco); Disznotor (Night of Pig Killing); Pilatus (Pilate); A Danaida (The Danaid); Mozes 1.22 (Genesis 1.22); Katalin utca (Kathleen Street); A szemlelok (The Onlookers); Regimodi tortenet (Old-fashioned Story); Az ajso (The Door); The moment, 1991; Plays: Az a Szep Fenyes Nap (The Bright Beautiful Day); A Merani Fiu (The Boy of Merano); A Csata (The Battle), 1982; Bela Kiraly (King Bela); A Macskak Szerdaha (The Wednesday of the Cats), 1985. Honours: Jozsef Attila Prize, 1959, 1972; Kossuth Prize, 1978; Getz Corporation Prize, 1992. Memberships: Academy of Sciences of Europe; Hungarian Szechenyi Academy of Arts. Literary Agent: Artisjus, Budapest, Hungary. Address: Julia-utca 3, H-1026 Budapest II, Hungary.

SZASZ Imre, b. 19 Mar 1927, Budapest, Hungary. Writer; Translator. m. Elizabeth Windsor, 23 Sept 1965, 2 daughters. Education: Degree in English and Hungarian Literature, Budapest University, 1950. Appointments: Publishing House Editor, 1949-68; Literary Editor, Cultural Weekly, Budapest, 1968-90; General Secretary, Hungarian PEN Centre, 1989-94. Publications: Come at Nine, 1969; Dry Martini, 1973; One Went Hunting, 1985; Menesi Street, 1986; This is the way the world ends, 1986; Self-portrait with background, 1986; I'll go when you dismiss me, 1991. Contributions to: Magazines and journals. Honours: Jozef Attila Award, 1954, 1989;

Book of the Year, 1989. Memberships: Hungarian Writers Union; Hungarian PEN Centre; Hungarian Journalists Union. Address: Szeher ut 82, Budapest 1021, Hungary.

SZIRTES George Nicholas, b. 29 Nov 1948, Budapest, Hungary. Poet. m. Clarissa Upchurch, 11 July 1970, 1 son, 1 daughter. Education: BA (1st class Honours), Fine Art, Leeds College of Art, England. Publications: The Slant Door, 1979; November and May, 1981; The Kissing Place, 1982; Short Wave, 1984; The Photographer in Winter, 1986; Selected Poems, Hungary, 1987; Metro, 1988; Bridge Passages, 1991; Blind Field, 1994; Translations from Hungarian: Imre Madach's Tragedy of Man, 1987; Dezsö Kosztolányi's Anna Édes, 1992; Ottó Orbán's The Blood of the Walsungs, 1993; Zsuzsa Rakovszky's New Life, 1994. Contributions to: Numerous journals and magazines. Honours: Faber Memorial Prize, 1980; Arts Council Bursary, 1984; British Council Fellowship, 1985; Cholmondeley Award, 1987; Dery Prize for Translation, 1991; Decorated, Hungarian Republic, 1991; Shortlisted, Whitbread Poetry Prize, 1992. Memberships: Fellow, Royal Society of Literature; PEN. Address: 20 Old Park Road, Hitchin, Hertfordshire SG5 2JR, England.

SZUCS Andrew Eric, b. 25 Apr 1946, Cleveland, OH, USA. Writer; Publisher. m. Laura Jean Nyhan, 4 Jun 1971, 2 s. Education: BA, Communications University of Dayton, 1968; Diploma Electronic Technology, Cleveland Institute of Electronics, 1972; MBA, Wright State University, 1984. Contributions to: Leading Edge Magazine; Other publications since 1970. Honours: Aviation/Space Writers Assoc Midwest Journalism Award, 1986. Memberships: National Press Club, Wash DC; Aviation/Space Writers Association. Address: 1135 Mint Springs Drive, Fairborn, OH 45324-5728, USA.

T

TA Tai Van, b. 16 Apr 1938, Vietnam. Legal Scholar and Attorney. m. Lien-Nhu Tran, 26 Oct 1967, 1 son, 3 daughters. Education: LLB, Saigon University Law School, 1960; MA, PhD, Government and Foreign Affairs University of Virginia, 1964-65; LLM, Harvard Law School, 1985-. Publications: The Vietnamese Tradition of Human Rights, 1988; Co-author: Investment Law and Practice in Vietnam, 1990; The Le Code: Law in Traditional Vietnam, 1987; The Laws of Southeast Asia, 1986; Law and the State in Traditional East Asia, 1986. Contributions to: American Journal of Comparative Law; Journal of Asian History; Asian Thought and Society; UNHCR Refugee Abstracts; Vietnam Forum. Honours: Fulbright, 1960; US Agency for International Development, 1962; Asia Foundation, 1971; Ford Foundation, 1975, 1978. Memberships: Massachusetts Bar Association; Association of Asian Studies; American Political Science Association; Vietnam Council on Foreign Relations. Address: Harvard Law School, Pound Hall 423, Cambridge, MA 02138, USA.

TABORI George, b. 24 May 1941, Budapest, Hungary (British citizen). Playwright. Education: Zrinyl Gymnasium, Hungary. Appointments include: Formerly, Artistic Director of the Berkshire Theater Festival at Stockridge, Massachusetts, USA. Publications: Flight into Egypt, 1952; The Emperor's Clothes, 1953; Miss Julie, version of Strinberg, 1958; Brouhaha, 1958; Brecht on Brecht, 1962; The Resistible Rise of Arturo Ui, after Brecht, 1963; Andora, after Max Frisch, 1963; The Niggerlovers, 1967; The Cannibals, 1968; Mother Courage, after Brecht, 1970; Clowns, 1972; Talk Show, 1976; Changes, 1976; Mein Kampf: A Farce, 1989; Weisman and Copperface, 1991 (plays premiered in New York, London, Washington, Edinburgh and Munich); Screenplays; Novels: Beneath the Stone the Scorpion, 1945; Companions of the Left Hand, 1948; Original Sin, 1947; The Caravan Passes, 1951; The Journey: A Confession, 1958; The Good One, 1960. Address: c/o Suhrkamp Verlag, Lindenstrasse 29-35, Postfact 4229, 6000 Frankfurt am Main, Germany.

TABORSKI Boleslaw, b. 7 May 1927, Torun, Poland. Writer; Translator; Broadcaster. m. Halina Junghertz, 20 Jun 1959, 1 d. Education: BA, MA, Bristol University. Appointments: Producer, BBC World Service (Polish Section), 1959-89; Editor, Arts in Action (BBC WS), 1985-93; Visiting Professor, Grad Center, CUNY, New York, 1982. Publications include: poetry: Times of Passing, 1957 Grains of Night, 1958; Crossing the Border, 1962; Lesson Continuing, 1967; Voice of Silence, 1969; Selected Poems, 1973; Web of Words, 1977; For the Witnesses, 1978; Observer of Shadows, 1979; Love, 1980; A Stranger's Present, 1983; Art, 1985; The Stillness of Grass, 1986; Life and Death, 1988; Politics, 1990; Shakespeare, 1990; Goodnight Nonsense, 1991; criticism: New Elizabethan Theatre, 1967; Polish Plays In English Translations, 1968; Byron and the Theatre, 1972; The Inner Plays of Karol Wojtyla, 1989; co-author: Crowell's Handbook of Contemporary Drama, 1971; Polish Plays in Translation, 1983; Numerous translations into English and Polish. Contributions include: Gambit; Stand; Theatre Research; Theatre Quarterly; Miesiecznik Literacki, Tulanr Drama Review; Polish Review; Dialog; Kultura; Wiez; Teatr. Honours: Polish Writers Association Abroad Award, 1954; Jurzykowski Foundation Award, New York, 1968; Merit for Polish Culture Badge and Diploma, Warsaw, 1970; Koscielski Foundation Award, Geneva, 1977; SI Witkiewicz ITI Award, Warsaw, 1988; ZAIKS Translation Award, Warsaw, 1990. Memberships: Honorary Committee Leon Shiller Foundation, 1987-; Association of Authors, ZAIKS, 1985-; Council Gallery in the Provinces Foundation, Lublin, 1990-; Association of Polish Writers, Warsaw, 1991-; Council The Pro Europa Foundation, Warsaw, 1994-; World Association of Polish Home Army (AK), Ex-Servicemen, Warsaw, 1992-. Address: 66 Esmond Road, Bedford Park, London W4 1JF, England.

TACEY Elisabeth Irene, b. 24 Nov 1960, Chichester, Sussex, England. Science Journalist. Education: BS, 1982, PhD, 1986, King's College, London. Publications: PhD Thesis on Antifouling Paints for Ships, Detailed Treatise on Paint used to Release Barnacles. Contributions to: Financial Times; The Times; The Guardian; The Independent; South China Morning Post; Many More. Memberships: Fringe Club; a Hong Kong Arts Club; National Union of Journalists; Convocation of University of London. Address: 111 Ramsden Road, South Clapham, London SW12, England.

TADEUSZ Rozewicz, b. 9 Oct 1921, Radomsko, Poland. Poet; Playwright. m. Wiestawa Koztowska, 1949. Education: University of Cracow. Publications include: Face of Anxiety; Conversation with the Prince; The Green Rose; The Card Index; The Witnesses; White Marriage; The Trap. Contributions to: Various Journals. Honours: State Prize, 1955, 56; Literary Prize, City of Cracrow, 1959; Prize of Minister of Culture and Art, 1962; State Prize, 1st Class, 1966; Prize, Minister of Foreign Affairs, 1974, 1987; Austrian National Prize, European Literature, 1982; German Literary Award, 1994. Memberships: Bavarian Academy of Fine Arts. Address: Authors Agency, ul Hispoteozna 2, Warsaw.

TADEUSZ T. See: **WITTLIN Thaddeus.**

TAGLIABUE John, b. 1 July 1923, Cantu, Italy. College Teacher. m. Grace Ten Eyck, 11 Sept 1946, 2 daughters. Education: BA 1944, MA 1945, and advanced Graduate Work, 1947-48, Columbia, New York City. Literary Appointments: Professor, English Department, Bates College, Maine; Fulbright Lecturer, University of Indonesia, 1993. Publications: The Great Day, 1984; The Doorless Door, 1970; The Buddha Uproar, 1970; A Japanese Journal, 1966; Poems, 1959. Contributions to: More than 1500 poems published in magazines including: The Atlantic Monthly; Chelsea; Centennial Review; Carolina Quarterly; Chicago Review; Epoch; Greenfield Review; Hudson Review; Harpers; Kayak; Kenyon Review; Literature East and West; Massachusetts Review; New York Quarterly; The Nation; Northeast; Poetry (Chicago); Poetry Northwest. Honours: Bellagio Writing Grant; Karolyi Foundation Writing Grant; Fulbright Lecturer, 1950-52, University of Pisa; 1958-60, Tokyo University; 1984, Fudan University, China. Memberships: PEN; Academy of American Poets; Main Writers and Publ. Alliance; Poetry Society of America. Address: 12 Abbott Street, Lewiston, ME 04240, USA.

TAIT Arch, b. 6 June 1943, Glasgow, Scotland. Translator; University Lecturer. Education: Trinity Hall, Cambridge, MA, 1966, PhD, 1971. Appointments: Lecturer, University of East Anglia, 1970; Lecturer, University of Birmingham, 1983; Editor, Gals: New Russian Writing, 1991. Publications: Lunacharsky, The Poet Commissar, 1984; Translated: The Russian Style, 1991; Is Comrade Bulgakov Dead, 1993. Memberships: Translators Association; Society of Authors; British Association for Slavonic & East European Studies. Address: Dept of Russian Literature, University of Birmingham, Birmingham, B15 2TT, England.

TAKAMURA Hiromasa, b. 4 Apr 1943, Japan. Professor. m. Eiko Numata, 15 Oct 1972, 1 d. Education: MA, Kansai University, 1968. Appointments: Professor. Onatani Womens University, 1984-. Publications: Steinbeck and Drama, 1990; Canadian Folktales, 1991; A Study Guide to Steinbeck's The Long Valley, 1992; Steinbeck and River, 1992; Steinbeck and His Dramatic World, 1992. Memberships: The Steinbeck Quarterly; International John Steinbeck Society; John Steinbeck Society of Japan. Address: 10-22 Yamatecho, Tondabayashi, Osaka 584, Japan.

TALBOT Michael, b. 4 Jan 1943, Luton, Bedfordshire, England. Professor. m. Shirley Mashiane, 26 Sept 1970, 1 s, 1 d. Education: ARCM, Royal College of Music, 1960-61; BA, 1964; BMus, 1965; PhD, 1969, Clare College, Cambridge. Publications: Vivaldi, 1978; Antonio Vivaldi: A Guide to Research, 1988; Tomaso Albinoni: The Venetian Composer and his World, 1990; Benedetto Vinaccesi: A Musician in Brescia and Venice in the Age of Corelli, 1994. Contributions to: Music and Letters; Journal of Royal Musical Association; Rivista Italiana di Musicologia; Informazioni e Studi Vivaldiani; Honours: Cavaliere del, Ordine el Merite Della Repubblica Italiana. Fellow, British Academy. Address: 36 Montclair Drive, Liverpool L18 0HA, England.

TALBOT Norman Clare, b. 14 Sept 1936, Gislingham, Suffolk, England. University Professor; Poet; Fiction Writer; Editor; Literary Consultant. m. 17 Aug 1960, 1 s, 2 d. Education: BA, Durham University, Hatfield College, 1956-59; PhD, Leeds University, 1959-62. Appointments: Lecturer, 1962, Senior Lecturer, 1968, Associate Professor, 1973-, Newcastle University College, University of NSW. Publications include: The Major Poems of John Keats, 1967; Son of a Female University, 1972; The Fishing Boy, 1975; Find the Lady, 1978; A Glossary of Poetic Terms, 1980; Where Two Rivers Meet, 1981; The Kelly, Haiku, 1985; Another Site to be Mined: New South Wales Anthology, 1986; Wearing the Heterocom: An Anthology of Narrative Poetry, 1989. Contributions to: Numerous Magazines including, Poetry Australia; Makar; Southern Review; Northern Perspective; Southerly;

The Australian; The Age; The Sydney Morning Herald; Aspect. Honours: E C Gregory Memorial Award, 1965; ACLS Fellowship, 1967-68; Visiting Professorship, Universities of East Anglia, 1975-76; aarhus, 1976; Eugene, 1983; Leicester, 1984; Oxford, 1987-88. Memberships: William Morris Society; Australian Victorian Studies Association; Australian Universities Language & Literature Association; Federation of Australian Universities Staffs Association. Literary Agent: Richard Deutch, Pymble, NSW. Address: PO Box 170, New Lambton 2305, Australia.

TALLENT Elizabeth, b. 8 Aug 1954, WA, USA. Writer; Professor. m. Barry Smoots, 28 Sept 1975, 1 s. Education: BA, IL State University. Publications: Honey, 1993; Time with Children, 1987; Museum Pieces, 1985; In Constant Flight, 1983; Married Men & Magic Tricks, 1982. Contributions to: New Yorker; Paris Review. Honours: Bay Area Book Reviewers Association Fiction Award; National Endowment of the Arts Fellowship, 1992. Memberships: Poets & Writers. Literary Agent: Andrew Wylie. Address: English Dept, University of CA, Davis 95616, USA

TALMAGE Anne. See: **POWELL Talmage.**

TAN Amy, b. 1952, Oakland, California, USA. m. Contributions to: Atlantic; San Francisco Focus; Seventeen. Address: c/o Putnam Publishing, 200 Madison Avenue, NY 10016, USA.

TANG Victor, b. 12 Apr 1942, China. Business Executive, IBM. m. Wendy Chu, 3 June 1968, 1 son, 2 daughters. Education: BSEE, Purdue University, USA, 1963; MS, Mathematical Physics, 1965; Advanced Research and Studies, Pennsylvania State University, 1967-69; MBA, Columbia University, 1983. Publications: Digital Private Branch Exchanges (PBX), Chapter 6, 1989; The Silverlake Project, 1992;Competitive Marketing, Part I and II (with Philip Kotler), 1993. Contributions to: Methodology and Declarative Language for Displays, 1975; Traffic Management in VTAM-NCP Network, 1977; Flat Panel Displays, 1984; ISDN - New Vistas in Information Processing, 1987; ISDN - Strategic Analysis, 1989; AS-400 New Product Launch Process, 1992; Organizational Implications of EIS, 1992. Memberships: Eta Kappa Nu, Electrical Engineering Honour Society; Pi Mu Epsilon, Mathematics Honour Society; Beta Gamma Sigma, Business Honour Society; Sigma Pi Sigma, Physics Honour Society. Address: 55 Deerfield Lane South, Pleasantville, NY 10570, USA.

TANNER Tony, b. 1935, England. Appointments: Fellow, Kings College, Cambridge, 1964-; Reader in Faculty of English, Cambridge University, 1984-; Professor, 1989-. Publications include: The Reign of Wonder, 1965; Mansfield Park, 1966; Henry James Modern Judgements, 1968; City of Words 1950-1970, 1971; Adultery in the Novel: Contact and Transgression, 1980; Jane Austen, 1986; Venice Desired, 1992. Address: Kings College, Cambridge, Englnd.

TANSKA Natalie, (Jana Dankova), b. 30 Dec 1929, Praha, Czech. Writer. m. Jan Valek, 20 Oct 1960. Education: Academy of Performing Arts, 1954. Appointments: Theatre Critic, Cultural Life, 1956-63; Script Writer, Film Studios, Koliba, 1965-68. Publications: The Duel; An English Lesson; Fluff and Muff; The Postscripts; Wont You Get Lost in a Crowd; Shop No 004; Men Women Dictionary. Contributions to: Cultural Life; Mlada Fronta; Mona. Honours: Frano Kral Award; Award for Best Radio Play; Publishers Award for Best Book; Three Roses Award; London Writers Competition, Runner Up, 1991. Membership: PEN. Address: Vikova 7 Praha 4, Post Code 140 00, Czech.

TAPPLY William G, b. 16 July 1940, MA, USA. Writer. 1 s, 2 d. Education: BA, Amherst College, 1962; MA, Harvard University, 1963. Publications include: The Dutch Blue Error, 1984; The Vulgar Boatman, 1987; Dead Winter, 1989; Client Privilege, 1990; The Snake Eater, 1993; Sportsman's Legacy, 1993; The Seventh Enemy, 1995. Contributions to: Worcester Magazine; Field & Stream Magazine. Honour: Scribner Crime Novel Award, 1984. Membership: Mystery Writers of Am. Literary Agent: Jed Mattes. Address: 187 Great Road C#1, Acton, MA 01720, USA.

TARRANT John. See: **EGLETON Clive Frederick William.**

TART Indrek, (Julius Ürt), b. 2 May 1946, Tallinn, Estonia. Physicist; Poet; Literary Critic. m. Aili Arelaid Tart, 7 Feb 1980, 1 s, 1 d. Education: Tallinn 4thSecondary School; Tartu University. Appointments: Institute of Cybernetics, 1969-80; Institute of Chemical

Physics & Biophysics, Estonian Academy of Sciences, 1980-92; Tallinn Pedagogical University, 1992-; Estonian National Commission for UNESCO, Director of Information, 1992-93; Chairman, Young Writers Tallinn Branch, Estonian Writers Union, 1978-83. Publications include: Haljendav Ruumala, 1981; Väike Luuletaja ja Teised, 1993; in Koik Siin Maailmas: Estonian Haikus Anthology, 1980; in Eesti Luule Aastaraamat, 1986, 87, 88, 89, 90; Translations into Estonian; Poems of William Carlos Williams, Adrienne Rich, Norman Dubie, Raymond Carver, Charles Tomlinson, R S Thomas, Iain Crichton Smith. Contributions to: Looming; Keel ja Kirjandus; Noorus. Honour: Honorary Fellow, Writing, University of Iowa. Membership: Estonian Writers Union. Address: Kurni 17-1, Tallinn, EE0016, Estonia.

TARTT Donna, b. Greenwood, Mississippi, USA. Education: University of Mississippi; Bennington College. Address: c/o Knopf Publishers, 201 E 50th St 20th Floor Reception, NY 10022, USA.

TARUSKIN Richard,Critic. Address: Dept of Music, University of California, Berkeley, CA 94720-0001, USA.

TATE James, b. 1943, Kansas City, Missouri, USA. Poet. Appointments: Professor, Massachusetts, Amherst. Publications include: Worshipful Company of Fletchers, 1994. Contributions to: American Poetry Review; Poetry; Massachusetts Review. Honours: Pulitzer Prize, 1992; William Carlos Williams Award, 1992; National Book Award, 1994; Yale Series of Younger Poets Award, 1967. Address: 16 Jones Road, Amherst, MA 01002, USA.

TAVIRA Luis de, b. 1 Sept 1948, Mexico. Playwriter; Theatre Director. 3 sons. Education: Licentiate, Literature & Dramatic Arts, UNAM, 1972; Master of Philosophy, Instituto Libre de Filosofia, Mexico, 1976. Appointments: Director, Centro Universitario de Teatro, UNAM, 1978-82; Director, Centro de Experimentacion Teatral, INBA, Mexico, 1985-90; Director, Casa del Teatro, AC Mexico, 1990-. Publications: Poetry: Coloquio con la Soledad, 1972; La Tarde y el rio, 1978; Tarde Perpetua, 1992; Dramas: La Sombra del Caudillo, 1982; Teoria y Praxis del Teatro Mexico, 1982; Lances de amor, 1984; La Pasion de Pentesilea, 1988; Zozobra, 1990; La Septima Morada, 1991; Novedad de la Patria, play, 1984. Contributions to: Weekly column Proscenio, to La Jornada Semanal, Sunday edition of journal, La Jornada; Process review. Honours: Best Play, AMCT, Mexico, 1985; Best Mise en scene, Festival of Theater of Americans, Montreal, 1985; Best Director, ATP, California, USA, 1987; Premio Ollantay, EICIT, Madrid, 1989; Best Director, APT, 1993. Memberships: International Association of Critics and Theatrologists. Address: Offico 59, Prados de Coyoacan, Mexico DF, Mexico CF 04810, USA.

TAYLOR Andrew John Robert, b. 14 Oct 1951, Writer. m. Caroline Jane Silverwood, 8 Sept 1979, 1 s, 1 d. Publications include:Waiting for the End of the World, 1984; Our Fathers Lies, 1985; Freelance Death, 1987; The Second Midnight, 1987; Blacklist, 1988; Toyshop, 1990; Childrens Books, Hairline Cracks, 1988; The Private Nose, 1989; Double Exposure, 1990; Blood Relation, 1990; The Sleeping Policeman, 1992; The Barred Window, 1993; Odd Man Out, 1993; Negative Image, 1992; The Invader, 1994; An Air That Kills, 1994; Double Exposure; Private Nose; Snapshots. Honours: Winner of 1982 John Creasey Award; Shortlisted for an Edgar; Shortlisted for 1985 Gold Dagger. Memberships: Society of Authors; Crime Writers Association. Literary Agent: Richard Scott Simon. Address: c/o Richard Scott Simon Limited, 43 Doughty Street, London WC1N 2LF, England.

TALYOR Andrew McDonald, b. 19 Mar 1940, Warrnambool, Australia. Professor. m. Beate Josephi, 1981, 1 s, 1 d. Eduction: MA, Melbourne University, 1971. Appointments: Member, Literature Board of Australia Council, 1978-81; Chair, Writers Week of Adelaide Festival of Arts, 1980, 1982; Member, South Australian Arts Finance Advisory Committee, 1988-91. Publications include: Miracles of Disbelief, 1985; Reading Australian Poetry, 1987; Selected Poems, 1960-85, 1988; Folds in the Map, 1991. Contributions to: Australia, USA, Britain, Europe, India. Honours: AM, 1990. Memberships: Australian Society of Authors; PEN International; Australian Society of Authors; Association for the Study of Australian Literature. Address: English Dept, Edith Cowan University, Mount Lawley, Western Australia 6050.

TAYLOR Beverly White,b. 30 Mar 1947, Mississippi, USA. University Professor. Education: BAE, University of Mississippi, 1969; MA 1970, PhD 1977, Duke University. Appointments: Assistant Professor of English, 1977-84, Associate Professor 1984-92, Professor 1992-, University of North Carolina at Chapel Hill. Publications: The

Return of King Arthur, 1983; Arthurian Legend and Literature, 1984; Francis Thompson, 1987; The Cast of Consciousness, 1987; Gender and Discourse in Victorian Literature and Art, 1992. Contributions to: Periodicals and Encyclopaedias on 19th century and Arthurian literature. Memberships: Victorians Institute, President 1989-90, VP 1987-88, Secretary 1985-86; Tennyson Society; Browning Institute; Modern Language Association; International Arthurian Society. Address: Department of English, University of North Carolina, Chapel Hill, NC 27599, USA.

TAYLOR Drew (Hayden), b. 1962. Canadian. Dramatist. Publications: Bootlegger Blues, 1991; Someday: a Play, 1993. Honours: Canadian Author's Association Literary Awards, 1992.

TAYLOR H Baldwin. See: **WAUGH Hillary Baldwin.**

TAYLOR John Laverck, b. 25 May 1937, England. College Principal; Bramley Professor. m. Jennifer Margaret Green, 21 Sept 1981, 1 s, 2 d. Education: DipArch, Leeds, 1960; MSc, Urban Design, Columbia, 1963; PhD, Sheffield, 1969. Appointments: Editor, Salzburgh Journal of Urban Planning & Development, 1970-76. Publications include: Simulationa in the Classroom, 1974; Learning and the Simulation Game, 1978; Guide on Simulationa dn Gaming for Environmental Education, 1984; Planning for Urban Growth, 1972; Instructional Simulation Systems in Higher Education, 198; Feedback on Instructional Simulations Systems, 1992. Contributions to: Over 80 Articles and Papers in Various Journals. Honours: Fulbright Fellow, 1962-64; Salzbury Fellow, 1965-66; Nuffield School Science Fellow, 1968-74; Various Visiting Professorships; OBE, 1990; BT Visiting Fellow, 1993-94; HEI Professional Fellow, UNECIA, 1993. Memberships: Conference of College Principals; Freeman of the City of London; Higher Education International The Rual Buildings Preservation Trust. Address: Tapton Hall Barn, Balmoak Lane, Chesterfield, Derbyshire S41 0TH.

TAYLOR John Vernon, b. 11 Sept 1914, Cambridge, England. Retired Bishop. m. Peggy Wright, 5 Oct 1940, Oxford, 1 s, 2 d. Education: MA, Trinity College, Cambridge University; MA, St Catherines Oxford University; D Ed, London University Institute of Education. Publications include: Christianity and Politics in Africa, 1955; The Growth of the Church in Buganda, 1958; The Primal Vision, 1963; The Go between Goti, 1972; Enough is Enough, 1975; Weep Not For Me, 1985; A Matter of Life and Death, 1986; A Christmas Sequence and Other Poems, 1989; Kingdom Come, 1989; The Christlike God, 1992. Honours: Honorary Doctor of Divinity, 1962; Collins Religious Book Prize, 1974; Honorary Fellow, New Coll & Magdalen College, Oxford, 1986, Trinity College, Cambridge, 1987; Honorary Doctor of Literature, 1991. Address: 65 Aston Street, Oxford, OX4 1EW, Englnd.

TAYLOR John William Ransom Dr, OBE, b. 8 June 1922, England. Author; Editor. m. Doris Alice Haddrick, 1946, 1 s, 1 d. Appointments include: Editor, Contributing Editor, Correspondent, Various Journals, Emeritus, Aircraft, Aviation; Editor in Chief, James All the Worlds Aircraft, 1959-. Publications include: Spitfire, 1946; Civil Aircraft Markings, 1950-78; military Aircraft Recognition, 1953-79; Science in the Atomic Age, 1956; Janes All the Worlds Aircraft, 1956-; Russian Aircraft, 1957; US Military Aircrft, 1959; Pictorial History of Royal Air Force, 1968-70, 1980; Aircraft Aircraft, 1967; Rockets & Missiles, 1971; Civil Aircraft of the World, 1970-79; British Civil Aircraft Register, 1971; History of Aviation, 1973, 1978; Janes Aircrat Pocket Books, 1973; Helicopters of the World, 1976-79; Aircraft, Strategy and Operations of the Soviet Air Force, 1986; CFS Birthplace of Air Power, 1987; Soviet Wings, 1991. Honours include: FRAeS; FRHistS; AFAIAA; Honorary DEng; Freeman of City of London, 1987; C P Robertson Memorial Trophy, 1959; Order of Merit, 1981; Paul Tissandier Diploma, 1990; Lauren D Lyman Award, 1990. Address: 36 Alexandra Drive, Surbiton, Surrey KT5 9AF, England.

TAYLOR Judy, (Julia Marie Hough), b. 12 Aug 1932, Wales. Writer. m. Richard Hough, 1980. Appointments include: The Bodley Head Publishers, 1951-; Director, Bodley Head Limited, 1967-84; Chatto, Bodley Head & Jonathan Cape Limited, 1973-80; Chatto, Bodley Head & Jonathan Cape Australia Pty Limited, 1977-80; Consultant to Penguin, Beatrix Potter, 1981-87. Publications include: Sophie & Jack, 1982; My First Year: A Beatrix Potter Baby Book, 1982; Sophie & Jack in the Snow, 1984; Dudley & The Monster, 1986; Dudley Goes Flying, 1986; Dudley in a Jam, 1986; Dudley & The Strawberry Shake, 1986; That Naughty Rabbit Beatrix Potter and Peter Rabbit, 1987; Beatrix Potter 1866-1943; Beatrix Potters Letters A Selection,

1989; SO I SHall Tell You a Story, 1993. Contributions to: Numerous Professional Journals. Honour: MBE, 1971. Memberships include: Publishers Association Council; Book Development Association; Unicef International Art Committee; UK Unicef Greetings Card Committee; Beatrix Potter Society; FRSA. Address: 31 Meadowbank, Primrose Hill Road, London NW3 1AY, England.

TAYLOR Laurie Aylma, b. 3 Sept 1939, Tappan, New York, USA. Writer. m. Allen Sparer, 17 July 1971, 2 daughters. Education: BA, Ohio Wesleyan University, 1960. Publications: Footnote to Murder; Only Half a Hoax; Deadly Objectives; Shed Light on Death; The Blossom of Erda; Changing the Past; Love of Money; Poetic Justice; A Murder Waiting to Happen; Cats Paw. Contributions to: Anthologies: Best of Fantasy, 1994; Xanadu, 1994; Several others. Honours: Minnesota Voices Project; Lois Phillips Hudson Prize. Memberships: Poets & Writers; Mystery Writers of America; Science Fiction and Fantasy Writers of America. Literary Agent: Frances Collin. Address: 4000 York Avenue South, Minneapolis, MN 55410, USA.

TAYLOR Mildred D, b. Jackson, MS, USA. Publications: Roll of Thunder, Hear My Cry, 1976; Let the Circle Be Unbroken, 1981; The Gold Cadillac, 1987; The Friendship, 1987; The Road to Memphis, 1990. Honours: Boston Globe/Horn Book Award, 1988; Council on International Books for Children, 1973; Newbery Medal, 1977; Buxtehuder Bulle Award, 1985; Coretta Scott King Award, 1982, 1988; Christopher Award, 1988.

TAYLOR Peter Mark, (Mark Peters), b. 5 Dec 1936, Huddersfield, England. Full-time Author. m. Rosemary Hughes Grey, 21 July 1958, 1 son. Education: Grammar school, Huddersfield College. Career: Managing Director, Arrow Books (London), 1966-70; Managing Director, Hutchinson Australia, 1970-74; Managing Director, Methuen Australia, 1974-76. Publications: More than 20 books including: An End to Silence - The Building of the Overland Telegraph Line, 1980; Australia - The First Twelve Years, 1982; Pastoral Properties of Australia, 1984; An Australian Country Life, 1986; Station Life in Australia, 1988; An Atlas of Australian History, 1990. Contributions to: Sydney Morning Herald; The Australian; This Australia. Membership: Union Club, Sydney. Address: 36 Sundance Way, Runaway Bay, Queensland 4216, Australia.

TAYLOR Renée (Gertrude), b. 19 July 1929, Napier, New Zealand. Playwright. Education: BA, University of Auckland, 1979. Appointments: Member of women's writers collective groups, 1979-84; Director and actress with the Napier Repertory Players. Publications: Secrets: Two One-Woman Plays, 1982; Breaking Out, 1982; Setting the Table, 1982; What Did You Do in the War, Mummy?, 1982; Asking For It, 1983; Dancing, 1984; Wednesday to Come, 1984; Groundwork, 1985; Pass It On, 1986; Born to Clean, 1987; Jeannie Once, 1990; Touch of the Sun, 1991; Missionary Position, 1991; The Glass Box, 1992; Tiggy Tiggy Touchwood, 1992; Novel: Willy Nilly, 1990; Daisy and Lily, 1993; Does This Make Sense To You? 1995; Television plays and short stories. Honours include: Queen Elizabeth II Arts Council grant and award. Address: c/o Playmarket, PO Box 9767, Wellington, New Zealand.

TAYLOR Theodore Langhans, b. 23 June 1921, Statesville, North Carolina, USA. Writer. m. (1) Gwen Goodwin, 25 Oct 1946, 2 sons, 1 daughter, (2) Flora Gray, 18 Apr 1982. Publications: The Magnificent Mitscher, 1954; Fire on the Beaches, 1957; The Cay, 1968; The Children's War, 1971; The Maldonado Miracle, 1973; Teetoncey, 1974; Jule, 1979; The Trouble with Tuck, 1981; Battle of the Midway Island, 1982; HMS Hood vs Bismarck, 1983; Battle in the English Channel, 1984; Sweet Friday Island, 1984; The Cats of Shambala, 1985; Walking Up A Rainbow, 1986; The Stalker, 1987; The Hostage, 1988; Sniper, Monocolo, 1989; Tuck Triumphant, 1990; The Weirdo, 1991; Maria, 1992; To Kill a Leopard, 1993; Timothy of The Clay, 1993. Contributions to: Saturday Evening Post; McCall's; Ladies Home Journal; Saturday Review of Literature; Argosy. Honours: Lewis Carroll Shelf Award; Jane Addams Peace & Freedom Foundation Award; Western Writers of America Award; George G Stone Center Award; Edgar Allan Poe Award; International Association of School Librarians Award. Literary Agent: Gloria Loomis, Watkins-Loomis, New York City, USA. Address: 1856 Catalina Street, Laguna Beach, CA 92651, USA.

TEALE Ruth. See: **FRAPPELL Ruth Meredith.**

TEBBEL John, b. 16 Nov 1912, Boynce City, USA. Writer; Retired Professor. m. 29 Apr 1939, 1 daughter. Education: BA 1935,

LittD, Hon, 1948,Central Michigan University; MS, Columbia University. Publications: The Life and Good Times of William Randolph Hearst, 1952; George Horace Lorimer and the Saturday Evening Posts, 1952; History of Book Publishing in the United States, Volumes I, IV, 1972-81; The Media in America, 1974; The Press and the Presidency, 1985; Between Covers, 1987; The Magazine in America, 1991; Turning The World Upside Down, 1993; Over 40 others. Contributions to: Over 500 articles in national magazines and professional journals. Honours: Graduate, School of Journalism, Columbia University, 50th Anniversary Awards, 1963; Alumni Award, 1975; Publishing Hall of Fame, 1985. Memberships: Society of Professional Journalists; Authors Guild. Literary Agent: William B Goodman. Address: 4033 The Forest At Duke, 2701 Pickett Road, Durham, NC 27705, USA.

TELFER Barbara Jane, b. 13 Aug 1945, Wellington, New Zealand. Author. m. Maxwell Bryant Telfer, 14 Mar 1970, 2 daughters. Education: New Zealand School Dental Nurse Certificate, 1965. Publications: The Great New Zealand Puzzle Book, 1987; The Great International Puzzle Book, 1988; The Great Crafty Ideas Book, 1988; A Book of Australian Puzzles, 1988; The Great Number Puzzle Book, 1990; Summertime Puzzles, 1992; Astro Puzzles, 1992; World of Puzzles, 1992; Mystery Word Puzzles (3), 1993; The Windsor Street Mystery, 1993; The Great Christmas Activity Book, 1993; The Great Junior Puzzle Book, 1994; The Second Great Number Puzzle Book, 1994; The Zoo Mystery, 1994. Contributions: Craft pages in: Jabberwocky Magazine; Kiwikids. Address: 9 Regent Street, Rotorua, New Zealand.

TELFER Tracie. See: **CHAPLIN Jenny.**

TEMKO Allan Bernard,b. 4 Feb 1924. Writer; Teacher. m. Elizabeth Ostroff, 1 July 1950, 1 son, 1 daughter. Education: AB, Columbia, 1947; University of California, Berkeley, 1949-51; Sorbonne, 1948-49, 1951-52. Appointments: Architecture Critic, San Francisco Chronicle, 1961-; Art Editor, 1979-82. Publications: Notre Dame of Paris; Eero Saarinen; No Way to Build A Ballpark. Contributions to: The New Yorker; Harpers; Horizon; New York Times; Washington Post. Honours Include: Gold Medal; Commonwealth Club of California; Journalism Award; Silver Spur Award; Manufactures Hanover Art World Award; Critics Award; Professional Achievement Award; Pulitzer Prize; Fellowships & Grants. Literary Agent: Fifi Oscard, New York City. Address: c/o San Francisco Chronicle, 901 Mission Street, San Francisco, CA 94103, USA.

TEMPLE Ann. See: **MORTIMER Penelope (Ruth).**

TEMPLE Dan. See: **NEWTON D(wight) B(ennett).**

TEMPLE Frances. Publications: A Taste of Salt: A Story of Modern Haiti, 1992; Grab Hands & Run, 1993; The Ramsey Scallop, 1994; Tiger Soup, 1994; Tonight, by Sea, 1995. Honours: Jane Addams Childrens Book Award, 1993.

TEMPLE Nigel Hal Longdale, b. 21 Jan 1926, England. Painter; Architectural and Garden Historian; Photographer; Lecturer. m. Judith Tattersill, 1 son, 1 daughter. Education: National Diploma in Design, 1951; Art Teacher's Diploma, Sheffield, 1953; MLitt, Architecture, Bristol, 1978; PhD, Keele, 1985. Publications include: Farnham Inheritance, 1956, 1965; Farnham Buildings and People, 1963, 1973; Looking at Things, 1968; Seen and Not Heard, 1970; John Nash and the Village Picturesque, 1979; Blaise Hamlet (a brief guide), 1986; George Repton's Pavilion Notebook: a catalogue raisonné, 1993. Contributions to: Country Life; Journal of Garden History; Architectural Review; Garden History; Georgian Group Journal; Others. Honours: Fellow, National Society for Art Education, 1964; Companion, Guild of St George. Memberships: Royal West of England Academy; Council Member, Garden History Society. Photographic Agents: Robert Harding, Garden Picture Library. Address: 4 Wendover Gardens, Christchurch Road, Cheltenham, Gloucestershire GL50 2PA, England.

TEMPLE Paul. See: **DURBRIDGE Francis Henry.**

TEMPLE (Robert) Philip, b. 20 Mar 1939, Yorkshire, England. Author. m. Daphne Evelyn Keen, 12 June 1965, div., 1 son, 1 daughter. Appointments: Katherine Mansfield Memorial Fellowship, Menton, France, 1979; Robert Burns Fellowship, University of Otago, Dunedin, New Zealand, 1980; Berliner Kunstlerprogramm Fellowship, West Berlin, 1987. Publications: The World at Their Feet, 1969; Ways to the Wilderness, 1977; Beak of the Moon, 1981; Sam, 1984; New Zealand

Explorers, 1985; Kakapo, 1988; Making Your Vote Count, 1992; Temple's Guide to the New Zealand Parliament, 1994; Dark of the Moon, 1993; The Explorer Stations; Moa; Legend of the Kea; Walking Track Guide Series; Author, 5 photographic books and 3 other non-fiction books. Contributions to: Associate Editor, Landfall, 1972-75. Honours: Wattie Award, 1970; New Zealand Literary Fund Grants and Bursaries, 1972, 1976, 1986, 1987, 1991, 1992. Memberships: PEN, New Zealand Centre, 1970-; PEN Representative, New Zealand Authors Advisory Committee, 1986-88, 1993-; New Zealand Writers Guild, 1981-; New Zealand Alpine Club, 1960-86, Editor, New Zealand Alpine Journal, 1968-70, 1973. Literary Agent: John Johnson Limited, London, England. Address: 147a Tomahawk Road, Dunedin, New Zealand.

TEMPLETON Fiona, b. 23 Dec 1951,Scotland. Writer; Director; Performer. Education: MA Hons, French/Spanish, Edinburgh University, 1973; Auditrice Libre, Aix-en-Provence University, 1971-72; MA Poetics, New York University, 1985. Publications: London, 1984 (poem); Elements of Performance Art (theory & textbook), 1976; Performance pieces produced include: Thought/Death, 1980; Cupid and Psyche, 1981; There Was Absent Achilles, 1982; The Seven Deadly Jealousies, 1982; Under Paper Spells, 1982; Experiments in the Destruction of Time, 1983; Five Hard Pieces including The New Three Act Piece, 1983; Out of the Mouths, 1984; A/Version, 1985; You - The City (play), produced 1988, published 1990; Delirum of Interpretations, 1991. Contributions to: Boundary 2; Pessimistic Labor 2; Poetics Journal 5; JAA 6; ABC No Rio; Appearances; Sun & Moon 11; Wallpaper 5/6; Musics 9; Partisan Review 2; Poetry Project Newsletter 3/91; Big Allis 1, 5; Blatant Artifice 2/3; Raddle Moon 12, Conjuctions 20; The Art of Practice (anthology); Writing from the Other Side (anthology); Writing 28. Honours: Foundation for Contemporary Performance Arts Grant, 1987; New York State Council on the Arts Individual Artists' Project Grant, 1988; National Endowment for the Arts Interarts Grant, 1987-88; Art Matters Award, 1988; New York Foundation for the Arts Fellowship, Interarts, 1985, 1989; Jerome Fund for Performance Art Award, 1984; PEN Writers Grant, 1985; National Endowment for the Arts Visual Arts (New Genres) Fellowship, 1983; Abendzeitung (Munich) Stern Des Jahres Award for Theatre, 1991. Membership: New Dramatists. Address: c/o Downtown Arts, 280 Broadway Room 412, New York, NY 10007, USA.

TENE Benjamin, b. 10 Dec 1914, Warsaw, Poland. Writer. m. Sarah Tene, 1937, 1 son, 1 daughter. Appointment: Editor, Michmar L'iladim. Publications: Mehora, 1939; Massa Begalil, 1941; Beheret hadwai, 1945; Tmolim Al Hasaf, 1947; Ktsir Hapele, for children, 1957; Hazamir, 1963; Shirim Upoemot, 1967; Translation: Poems and Ballads by Itzik Manger; Mismor Lehag, for children, 1973; Prose books: In the Shade of the Chestnut Tree, 1973; Schoolboys Before the Storm, 1976; The Story of Mor, 1977; City of My Youth, 1979; A Friend in Need, 1981; The Third Courtyard, 1982. Honours: Alfred Jurzykowski Foundation Award, 1970; Zew Award, 1974, 1981; Lamdan Award, 1980; Itzik Manger Award, 1987. Membership: Association of Hebrew Writers in Israel. Address: Kami 8, Ramat Aviv, 69025 Tel-Aviv, Israel.

TENNANT Emma Christina (Catherine Aydy), b. 20 Oct 1937, London, England. Author. 1 son, 2 daughters. Publications: The Colour of Rain, 1963; The Crack, 1973; The Last of the Country House Murders, 1975; Hotel De Dream, 1976; The Bad Sister, 1978; Wild Nights, 1979; Woman Beware Woman, 1983; Black Marina, 1984; The Adventures of Robina, 1986; The House of Hospitalities, 1987; A Wedding of Cousins, 1988; The Bad Sister, 1989; Sisters and Strangers, 1990; Faustine, 1991; The ABC of Writing, 1992; Tess, 1993; Pemberley, 1993; An Unequal Marriage, 1994. Contributions to: London Review of Books. Membership: Fellow, Royal Society of Literature. Literary Agent: Curtis Brown, London, England. Address: c/o Curtis Brown and Associates, 162-168 Regent Street, London W1R 5TB, England.

TERDIMAN Richard, Professor of Literature & History, University of California, Santa Cruz. Education: BA, Amherst College; PhD, Yale University. Address: Dept of General Literature, University of California, 1156 High Street, Santa Cruz, CA 95064, USA.

TEREHATA Jun. See: **KIRKUP James.**

TERKEL Louis,b. 16 May 1912, New York, USA. Writer. m. Ida Goldberg, 2 July 1939, 1 son. Education: PhB, JD, University of Chicago. Appointments: Civil Servant; Stage Actor; Cimema Manager; Radio & TV Broadcaster; Writer. Honours: Pulitzer Prize, 1985; Ohio

State University Award, 1959; UNESCO Prix Italia Award, 1962. Address: 850 West Castlewood Terrace, Chicago, IL 60640, USA.

TERLECKI Tymon Tadeusz Julian, b. 10 Aug 1905, Poland. Writer; Professor Emeritus. m. (1) Antonia Kopczynskam 1946, dec. 1983, (2) Nina Taylor, 1987. Education includes: PhD, King John Casimir University, 1932. Appointments: Co-Editor, Zycie Sztuki, 1932-35, 1938-39; Editor: Teatr, 1936-39; Scena Polska, 1936-38; Wiedza o Teatrze, 1938-39; Co-Founder, Editor, Polska Walczaca, 1939-49; Editorial Adviser, Polish Review, New York. Publications: Rodowód poetycki Ryszarda Berwinskiego, 1937; Krytyka Personalistyczna, 1957; Egzystencjalizm chrzescijanski, 1958; Pani Helena, 1962; Stanislaw Wyspianski, 1983; Rzeczy teatralne, 1984; Szukanie Rownowagi, 1985; Londyn-Paryz, 1987. Contributions to: Kultura, Paris; Wiadomósci; Many Polish periodicals. Honours: Theatrical Book of the Year, 1985; Stanislaw Vincenz Prize, 1985; Radziszewski Prize, Catholic University of Lublin, 1990; Honorary Doctorate, University of Wroclaw, 1990. Memberships: Polish Hist-Lit Society of Paris, 1950; Co-founder, Union of Polish Writers Abroad, Chairman 1955-59, 1965-66; Co-Founder, Association of Polish Writers; Polish Society of Arts and Sciences Abroad, 1952-; Polish Institute of Arts and Sciences of America. Address: 325 Woodstock Road, Oxford OX2 7NX, England.

TERLECKI Wladyslaw Lech, b. 18 May 1933, Czestochowa, Poland. Writer. m. Lucyna Basaj, 1955, 1 son, 1 daughter. Education: University of Wroclaw. Appointments: Staff: Wspolczesnosc, 1958-65; Drama Section, Polish Radio, 1965-70. Publications: Cobble Stones, 1956; Fire, 1962; The Conspiracy, 1966; High Season, 1966; The Wormwood Star, 1968; Two Heads of a Bird, 1970; Pilgrims, 1972; Return from Tzarskoe Selo, 1973; Black Romance, 1974; Rest After the Race, 1975; Tea with the Man Who is Not Here, 1976; The Forest Grows, 1977; Cien Karla, Cien Olbrzyma, 1983; Lament, 1983; Pismak, 1984, 1988; Zwierzeta Zostaly Oplacone, 1987; Kill the Tzar, 1992; Numerous film scripts and theatre plays. Honours: Koscielski Prize, Switzerland, 1973; ODRA Award, 1978; Literatura Award, 1981; Drama Award, Teatr Polski, 1987. Memberships: PEN; Polish Film-Makers Union; Association of Polish Writers. Address: ul Mazurska 1, 05-806 Komorow, Poland.

TERRILL Ross, b. Melbourne, Australia. Education: Wesley College, 1956; BA, University of Melbourne, 1962; PhD, Harvard University, 1970. Professional Appointments: Australian Army, 1957-58; Tutor, University of Melbourne, 1962-63; Staff Secretary, Australian Student Christian Movement, 1962, 1964-65; Teaching Fellow, Harvard, 1968-70; Lecturer, Harvard, 1970-74; Research Associate, East Asian Studies, Harvard, 1970-; Contributing Editor, Atlantic Monthly, 1970-84; Research Fellow, Asia Society, 1978-79; Associate Professor, 1974-78; Author, 1979-. Publications include: China In Our Time, 1992; The Australians, 1987; The White Boned Demon, 1984 and 1992; Mao: A Biography, 1980 and 1993; Flowers on an Iron Tree, Five Cities of China, 1975; 800,000,000: The Real China, 1972. Contributions to: Foreign Affairs; Image; Boston Globe Magazine; World Monitor; Los Angeles Times Magazine; National Geographic; The New Republic; Atlantic Monthly; Worldview; L'Actualite. Honours: National Magazine Award, 1972; George Polk Memorial Award, 1972; Sumner Prize, 1970; Frank Knox Memorial Fellowship, 1965. Literary Agent: Barbara Lowenstein.

TERRY William. See: HARKNETT Terry.

TESH Ruby Nifong, b. 5 Oct 1917, Winston-Salem, NC, USA, Teacher of Organ & Piano, Choir Director, Poet. m. Luther E Tesh, 27 Sep 1936, 2 s. Education: Winston-Salem Public School. Publications: Fleeting Inspiration, 1988; Random Thoughts, 1992. Contributions to: World of Poetry; American Anthology of Southern Poetry; The Mountain Laurel; The Carroll News; Sparrowgrass Poetry Forum; New Voices in American Poetry. Honours: Honorary Charter Membership for Outstanding Achievement in Poetry, International Society of Poets. Address 2409 Friedberg Church Rd, Winston-Salem, NC 27127, USA.

THAYER Geraldine, See: DANIELS Dorothy.

THELLE Notto Reidar, b. 19 Mar 1941, Hong Kong. Professor of Theology. m. Mona Irene Ramstad, 2 sons, 3 daughters. Education: Candidate of Theology, 1965, degree in Practical Theology, 1966, DTheol, 1982, Oslo University. Appointments: Missionary in Japan, 1969-85; Associate Director, The Centre for the Study of Japanese Religions, Kyoto. Publications: Buddhism and Christianity in Japan:

From Conflict to dialogue, 1854-1899, 1987; Norwegian books: Who Can Stop the Wind?, 1991; The Human and the Mystery, 1992; I Seek Your Face, 1993. Contributions to: Japanese Religions; Japan Christian Quarterly; Cross Currents; Inter-religio; Update; Japan Missionary Bulletin; International Bulletin of Mission Studies; Current Dialogue; A number of Norwegian journals. Address: Nordengveien 29, 0755 Oslo 7, Norway.

THELWELL Norman, b. 3 May 1923, Berkenhead, Cheshire, England. Artist; Writer; Cartoonist. m. 11 Apr 1949, 1 son, 1 daughter. Education: NDA, ADT, Liverpool College of Art, 1947-50. Appointments: Art Teacher, Wolverhampton College of Art, 1950-57. Publications: Angels on Horseback, 1957; Thelwell Country, 1959; A Place of Your Own, 1960; Thelwell in Orbit, 1961; A Leg at Each Corner, 1962; The Penguin Thelwell, 1963; Top Dog, 1964; Thelwell's Riding Academy, 1965; Drawing Ponies, 1966; Up the Garden Path, 1967; The Compleat Tangler, 1967; The Thelwell Book of Leisure, 1968; This Desirable Plot, 1970; The Effluent Society, 1971; Penelope, 1972; Three Sheets in the Wind, 1973; Belt Up, 1975; Thelwell Goes West, 1976; Thelwell's Brat Race, 1978; A Plank Bridge by a Pool, 1979; Thelwell's Gymkhana, 1980; Pony Calvalcade, 1981; A Mill Stone Round My Neck, 1982; Some Damn Fool's Signed the Rubens Again, 1983; Magnificat, 1984; Thelwell's Sporting Prints, 1985; Wrestling with a Pencil, 1986; Play It As It Lies, 1987; Penelope Rides Again, 1988; The Cat's Pyjamas, 1992. Contributions to: Punch, 1952-77; Cartoonist for News Chronicle, 1956-60, Sunday Dispatch, 1960-62, Sunday Express, 1962-72; Numerous other journals and magazines. Literary Agent: Momentum Licensing Ltd, London, England. Address: Herons Mead, Timsbury, Romsey, Hampshire SO51 0NE, England.

THEROUX Paul Edward, b. 10 Apr 1941, MA, USA. Writer. m. Anne Castle, 1967, 2 s. Education: BA, University of MA. Appointments include: Lecturer, Various Universities. Publications include: Novels, Waldo, 1967; Fong & The Indians, 1968; Murder in Mount Holly, 1969; Girls at Play, 1969; Sinning with Annie, 1972; Saint Jack, 1973; The Family Arsenal, 1976; The Consuls File, 1979; The Mosquito Coast, 1981; The London Embassy, 1982; Doctor Slaughter, 1984; Doctor de Marr, 1990; The Old Patagonian Express, 1979; The Kingdon by the Sea, 1983; The Imperial Way, 1985; Riding the Iron Rooser, 1988; The Traveling World, 1990; Happy Isles of Oceania, 1992. Honours: Honorary Degrees, USA; Whitbread Award, 1978; James Tait Black Award, 1982; Yorkshire Post Best Novel, 1982; Thomas Cook Travel Book Prize, 1989; Honorary DLitt, 1985. Address: c/o Hamish Hamilton Limited, 27 Wrights Lane, London W8 5TZ, England.

THIELE Colin Milton, b. 16 Nov 1920, Eudunda, South Australia, Australia. Author. m. Rhonda Gladys Gill, 17 Mar 1945, 2 daughters. Education: BA, DipEd, DipT, University of Adelaide. Publications: 90 books including: The Sun on the Stubble; Storm Boy; Blue Fin; The Fire in the Stone; Seashores and Shadows. Contributions to: Meanjin; The Australian; The Australian Author; The Sydney Morning Herald; The Adelaide Advertiser. Honours: Companion, Order of Australia; Grace Levin Poetry Prize; Austrian State Prize; Australian Children's Book of the Year Award; Netherlands Silver Pencil Award. Memberships: Australian Society of Authors; Australian College of Education. Address: Endeavour Lane, King Scrub, via Dayboro, Queensland 4521, Australia.

THIRY August, b. 24 Apr 1948, Grazen, Belgium. Professor. m. Simonne Rutten, 28 July 1972, 2 daughters. Education: MA, Germanic Languages, 1972; Slavonic Languages, Russian, 1975. Appointments: Editor, Cultural Magazine, 1976-82; Reviewer, Russian Literature, 1990-. Publications: Het Paustovski Syndroom; Onder Assistenten; Russische Literatuur in de zoste Eeuw; Montagne Russe. Contributions to: Jeugd en Cultuur; Kreatief; Argus; Dietsche Warande; Nieuw Wereldttydschrift; Slavica Gandensia. Honours: De Brakke Hond Story Award; Guido Gezelle Novel Award. Literary Agent: Lionel Deflo. Address: Dorenstraat 196, 3020 Herent, Belgium.

THISTLETHWAITE Frank, b. 24 July 1915, Emeritus Professor. m. Jane Hosford, 1940, 2 sons (1 dec), 3 daughters. Education: Exhibitioner and Scholar, St John's College, Cambridge; BA 1st class honours, History, English Literature, 1938; Commonwealth Fund Fellow, University of Minnesota, 1938-40; MA (Cantab), 1941. Appointments include: Editor, The Cambridge Review, 1937; British Press Service, New York, USA, 1940-41; Various university teaching positions; Founding Chancellor, 1961-80, Emeritus Professor, 1980-, University of East Anglia, Norwich, England; Visiting Scholar, various

American universities. Publications: The Great Experiment: An Introduction to the History of the American People, 1955; The Anglo-American Connection in the Early Nineteenth Century, 1958; Dorset Pilgrims, 1989; Chapters in New Cambridge Modern History, New Universities in the Modern World. Contributions to: Historical journals. Honours: Honorary LHD, Colorado, 1972; Honorary Fellow, RIBA, St John's College, Cambridge, 1974; CBE, 1979; Honorary DCL, East Anglia, 1980; Honorary Professor of History, University of Mauritius, 1981. Memberships include: Founding Chairman, British Association of American Studies; Fellow, Royal Historical Society. Address: 15 Park Parade, Cambridge CB5 8AL, England.

THOM James Alexander, b. 28 May 1933, Gosport, Indiana, USA. Novelist. m. Dark Rain, 20 May 1990. Education: AB, Butler University, Indianapolis, Ind, 1961. Appointments: Reporter & Columnist, The Indianapolis Star, 1961-67; Lecturer in Journalism, Indiana University, 1978-80. Publications Include: Spectator Sport, 1978; Long Knife, 1979; Follow the River, 1982; From Sea to Shinging Sea, 1984; Staying Out of Hell, 1985; Panther in the Sky, 1989; The Children of First Man, 1994. Contributions to: National Geographic; Readers Digest; Washington Post Book World and others. Memberships: Authors Guild; Western Writers of America. Literary Agent: Mitch Douglas, International Creative Management, New York. Address: 10061 West Stogsdill Road, Bloomington, IN 47404, USA.

THOMANECK Jurgen Karl Albert, b. 12 June 1941, Stettin, Germany. University Professor. m. Guinevere Ronald, 3 Aug 1964, 2 daughters. Education: Universities of Kiel, Tübingen, Aberdeen; Aberdeen College of Education. Publications: Deutsches Abiturienten Lexikon, 1974; Fremdsprachenunterricht und Soziolinguistik, 1981; Police and Public Order in Europe, 1985; The German Democratic Republic, 1989; Plenzdorf's Die Neuen Leiden des Jungen W, 1991. Contributions to: Learned journals. Membership: Fellow, Royal Society of Arts. Address: 17 Elm Place, Aberdeen AB2 3SN, Scotland.

THOMAS David Arthur, b. 6 Feb 1925, Wanstead, England. Retired Marketing Executive. m. Joyce Irene Petty, 3 Apr 1948, 1 daughter. Education: Northampton Polytechnic, 1948-53. Publications: With Ensigns Flying, 1958; Submarine Victory, 1961; Battle of the Java Sea, 1968; Crete 1941: The Battle at Sea, in US Nazi Victory, 1972; Japan's War at Sea, 1978; Royal Admirals, 1982; Compton Mackenzie: A Bibliography, 1986; Companion to the Royal Navy, 1988; Illustrated Armada Handbook, 1988; The Atlantic Star, 1990; Christopher Columbus, Master of the Atlantic, 1991. Membership: Fellow, Royal Society of Arts. Address: Cedar Lodge, Church Lane, Sheering, Bishop's Stortford, Hertfordshire, England.

THOMAS Donald Michael, b. 27 Jan 1935, Redruth, Cornwall, England. Poet; Novelist. 2 sons, 1 daughter. Education: BA 1st Class Honours, English, MA, New College, Oxford. Appointments include: Schoolteacher, 1959-63; Lecturer, Hereford College of Education, 1964-78. Publications: Poetry: Penguin Modern Poets 11, 1968; Two Voices, 1968; Logan Stone, 1971; Love and Other Deaths, 1975; The Honeymoon Voyage, 1978; Dreaming in Bronze, 1981; Selected Poems, 1983; Puberty Tree, 1992; Novels: The Flute Player, 1979; Birthstone, 1980; The White Hotel, 1981; Ararat, 1983; Swallow, 1984; Sphinx, 1986; Summit, 1987; Pictures at an Exhibition, 1993; Eating Pavlova, 1994; Translations: Requiem, and Poem Without a Hero (Akhmatova), 1976; Way of All the Earth (Akhmatova), 1979; Bronze Horseman (Pushkin), 1982; Fiction: Lying Together, 1990; Flying into Love, 1992. Address: The Coach House, Rashleigh Vale, Tregolis Road, Truro TR1 1TJ, England.

THOMAS Elizabeth Marshall, b. 13 Sept 1931, Boston, Massachusetts, USA. m. 14 Jan 1956, 1 son, 1 daughter. Education: AB, Radcliffe, 1954. Publications: The Harmless People, 1959; Warrior Herdsmen, 1966; Reindeer Moon, 1987; The Animal Wife, 1990; The Old Way, 1990; The Hill People, 1953; The Hidden Life of Dogs, 1993; The Tribe of Tiger: Cats and Their Culture, 1994. Contributions to: Behavioural Ecology and Sociobiology; Studying War; Anthropological Perspectives. Honours: Doctorate of Letters (Hon), Franklin Pierce College, 1992; Radcliffe Alumni Recognition Award, 1989; PEN Hemingway Citation, 1988; Brandeis Creative Arts Award, 1968. Memberships: PEN; Authors Guild; Authors League; Society of Women Geographers. Literary Agent: John Taylor Williams at Palmer & Dodge. Address: 80 East Mountain Road, Peterborough, NH 03458, USA.

THOMAS Franklin Richard,b. 1 Aug 1940, Indiana, USA. Professor. m. Sharon Kay Myers, 2 June 1962, 1 son, 1 daughter.

Education: AB, MA, Purdue University; PhD, Indiana University, 1970. Appointments: Purdue University, 1969-70; Professor, Michigan State University, 1971-; Research Associate, Indiana University, 1978-79. Publications: Poetry: Fat Grass, 1970; Frog Praises Night, 1980; Alive With You This Day, 1980; The Landlocked Heart: Poems from Indiana, 1980; Heart Climbing stairs, 1986; Corolla, Stamen & Style, 1986; The Whole Mystery of the Bregn, 1989;Scholarship: The Literary Admirers of Alfred Stieglitz, 1983; Americans in Denmark, 1989; Novel: Prism: The Journal of John Fish, 1992. Contributions to: Numerous journals and magazines. Honours: Several including: MacDowell Colony Fellowship; Fulbright Teaching Awards to Denmark, 1974-75, 1985-86; Michigan Council for the Arts Award for Poetry, 1990. Address: Dept of American Thought & Language, Michigan State Unviersity, E Langsing, MI 48824, USA.

THOMAS Lee. See: FLOREN Lee.

THOMAS Victoria. See: DE WEESE Thomas Eugene.

THOMPSON Diana Pullein. See: FARR Diana.

THOMPSON Ernest Victor, b. 14 July 1931, London, England. Author. m. Celia Carole Burton, 11 Sept 1972, 2 sons. Publications: Chase the Wind, 1977; Harvest of the Sun, 1978; The Music Makers, 1979; Ben Restallick, 1980; The Dream Traders, 1981; Singing Spears, 1982; The Restless Sea, 1983; Cry Once Alone, 1984; Polrudden, 1985; The Stricken Land, 1986; Becky, 1988; God's Highlander, 1988; Lottie Trago, 1989; Cassie, 1990; Wychwood, 1991; Blue Dress Girl, 1992; Mistress of Polrudden, 1993; The Tolpuddle Woman, 1994; Various books on Cornish and West Country subjects. Contributions to: Approximately 200 short stories to magazines. Honours: Best Historical Novel, 1976. Memberships: Society of Authors; Vice-President, West Country Writers Club; Patron, Cornwall Drama Association; Vice-Patron, Mevagissey Male Choir; Royal Society of Literature. Address: Parc Franton, Pentewan, St Austell, Cornwall, England.

THOMPSON Jean Louise, b. 1 Jan 1950, Chicago, Illinois, USA. Writer. Education: MFA, Bowling Green State University, 1973; BA, University of Illinois, 1971. Appointments: Graduate Assistant, Bowling Green State University, 1971-73; Professor, University of Illinois, 1973-; Warren Wilson College, 1988; Distinguished Visiting Writer, Wichita State University, 1991; San Francisco State University, 1992. Publications: The Woman Driver; Little Face and Other Stories; My Wisdom; The Gasoline Wars. Contributions to: Numerous, including: The New Yorker; Indiana Review; Carolina Quarterly; Epoch; Mademoiselle; Southwest Review; Descant; Fiction International; Best American Short Stories. Honours: Reader, Associated Writing Programs Novel Contest; Guggenheim Fellow; McGinnis Memorial Award; National Endowment for the Arts Fellowship; Canarad Fellow. Literary Agent: David Black. Address: 203 Smith Road, Urbana, IL 61801, USA.

THOMPSON Judith, b. 20 Sept 1954, Montreal, Canada. Playwright. Education: BA, Kingston University, Ontario, 1976; National Theatre School at Montreal, 1976-79. Publications: The Crackwalker, 1980; White Biting Dog, 1984; Pink, 1986; Tornado, 1987; I am Yours, 1987; The Other Side of the Dark, 1989; Lion in the Streets, 1990; Hedda Gabler, after Ibsen, 1991 (has produced her plays in London, New York and Toronto); Radio and television plays. Honours include: Governor-General's Awards. Address: c/o Great North Artists, 350 Dupont Street, Toronto, Ontario, Canada M5R 1V9.

THOMPSON Lloyd Arthur, b. 1932. Publications: Africa in Classical Antiquity, (ed) 1969; Rome & Race, 1987; Romans & Blacks, 1989; Culture & Civilization, (ed) 1991. Honours: American Book Award, 1990.

THOMPSON Tom (Eduarde Batarde), b. 21 Oct 1953, Parkes, New South Wales, Australia. Publisher; Writer. m. Elizabeth Butel, 20 Nov 1984, 1 daughter. Education: BA, Macquarie University. Career: Publisher, Australian Bicentennial Authority, 1984-; Publisher, Literature, Angus & Robertson. Publications: Island Hotel Dreams, 1977; Neon Line, 1978; From Here, 1978; The View from Tinsel Town, 1985; Growing Up in the Sixties, 1986. Contributions to: Sydney Morning Herald; Australian; Australian Book Review; Age; National Times. Membership: Australian Society of Authors. Address: PO Box 157, Kings Cross, New South Wales 2011, Australia.

THOMSON Derick S, (Ruaraidh MacThòmais), b. 5 Aug 1921, Stornoway, Scotland. University Professor, retired. m. Carol Galbraith, 1952, 5 sons, 1 daughter. Education: MA, University of Aberdeen, 1947; BA, University of Cambridge, 1948. Literary Appointments: Editor of Gaelic Quarterly, Gairm, 1952-. Publications: An Introduction to Gaelic Poetry, 1974, 1990; Creachadh Na Clàrsaich, Plundering the Harp, 1982; The Companion to Gaelic Scotland, 1983, 1994; European Poetry in Gaelic, 1990. Contributions to: Lines Review; Chapman; Stand; Orbis. Honours: Ossian Prize, 1974; FRSE, 1977; FBA, 1992. Memberships: President, Scottish Gaelic Texts Society; Glasgow Arts Club. Address: 263 Fenwick Road, Giffnock, Glasgow G46 6JX, Scotland.

THOMSON Edward. See: **TUBB E(dwin) C(harles).**

THOMSON Elizabeth (Liz) Mary, b. 12 Sept 1957, London, England. Writer; Editor. Education: BA Honours, Music, University of Liverpool, 1979. Appointments: Staff Writer, Publishing News, Books; Numerous radio appearances, BBC and IBA. Publications: Conclusions on the Wall: New Essays on Bob Dylan, 1980; Folk Songs and Dances of England/Folk Songs and Dances of Scotland (arranger), 1982; With David Gutman: The Lennon Companion, 1987; The Dylan Companion, 1991; The Bowie Companion, 1993. Contributions to: Woman's Journal; Melody Maker; Books and Bookmen; The Listener; The Times; The Standard; The Bulletin, Australia. Memberships: Society of Authors; National Union of Journalists; International Association for the Study of Popular Music; Charter 88; Greenpeace. Address: 24 Grosvenor Park Road, Walthamstow, London E17 9PG, England.

THOMSON June Valerie, b. 24 June 1930, Sandgate, Kent, England. Writer. div., 2 sons. Education: BA (Hons), English, Bedford College, University of London. Publicatins include: Not One of Us, 1972; A Question of Identity, 1978; Deadly Relations, 1979; Shadow of a Doubt, 1981; To Make a Killing, 1982; A Dying Fall, 1985; No Flowers by Request, 1987; Rosemary for Remembrance, 1988; The Spoils of Time, 1989; Past Reckoning, 1990. Contributions to: Several short stories to various magazines. Honours: Prix du Roman d'Aventures, France, 1983. Memberships: Crime Writers Association; Detection Club. Literary Agent: Michael Shaw, Curtis Brown and Associates, 162-168 Regent Street, London W1R 5TB, England. Address: 177 Verulam Road, St Albans, Hertfordshire AL3 4DW, England.

THORBURN James Alexander,b. 24 Aug 1923, Martins Ferry, Ohio, USA. Professor of English (retired). m. (1) Lois McElroy, 3 July 1954, 1 son, 1 daughter, (2) June Yingling, 18 Apr 1981. Education: BA 1949, MA 1951, Ohio State University; PhD, Linguistics, Louisiana State University, 1977. Appointments Include: Head, English, Sheridan Rural Agricultural School, Michigan; Instructor, English, University of Missouri, Monmouth College, Illinois, Texas Western College; Instructor, English, In Charge, English, University of Missouri, St Louis; Instructor, English, Louisiana State University, 1961-70; Professor, English & Linguistics, Southeastern Louisiana University, 1970-89. Contributions to: Book Review Editor, Experiment; Editor, Valedictory Issue of Innisfree; Articles in numerous periodicals & anthologies including: National Poetry Anthology; Spring Anthology; Ardentia Verba; Iaudamus Te; Poetry Dial Anthology; Prairie Poet; Poetry Digest; Writers Digest; Cardinal Poetry Quarterly; Poet Lore; Translator, several old Portuguese & old Provencal lyrics into modern English verse, Beowulf into modern English verse. Honours: La Sociedad Nacional Hispanica, Sigma Delta Pi; Phi Mu Alpha Sinfonia; The Honor Society of Phi Kappa Phi; Professor Emeritus of English & Linguistics, Louisiana Board of Trustees for State Colleges & Universities & Southeastern Louisiana University, 1989. Memberships: Numerous professional organizations including: Avalon World Arts Academy; Life Member, Modern Language Association; Linguistic Association of the South and Southwest; Southern Conference on Linguistics; American Dialect Society; Conference on Christianity and Literature. Address: 739 Southeastern Louisiana University, Hammond, LA 70402, USA.

THORNE Nicola. See: **ELLERBECK Rosemary Anne L'Estrange.**

THORNHILL Richard. See: **POLLARD John.**

THORNTON Caroline Rouse, b. 29 Oct 1937, Parramatta, New South Wales, Australia. Freelance Writer; Teacher. m. 1 Sept 1970. Education: FTCL, 1962; BA, 1970, MEd, 1982, University of Western Australia. Publications: Rouse Hill House and the Rouses, 1988;

Ebenezer, material for libretto, 1990. Memberships: President, Graduate Dramatic Society; Past President, University of Western Australia Choral Society; Royal Australian Historical Society. Address: 18 Doonan Rd, Nedlands, Western Australia 6009, Australia.

THORPE David Richard, b. 12 Mar 1943. Schoolmaster; Political Biographer. Education: BA (Hons), 1965, MA, 1969, Selwyn College, Cambridge. Literary appointment: Appointed Official Biographer of Lord Home of the Hirsel, 1990. Publications: The Uncrowned Prime Ministers: A Study of Sir Austen Chamberlain, Lord Curzon and Lord Butler, 1980; Selwyn Lloyd, 1989. Contributions to: Th Blackwell Biographical Dictionary of British Political Life in the 20th Century, 1990. Memberships: Johnson Club; United Oxford and Cambridge University Club. Literary Agent: Graham C Greene, CBE (Ed Victor). Address: Brooke Hall, Charterhouse, Godalming, Surrey GU7 2DS, England.

THORPE Dobbin. See: **DISCH Thomas Michael.**

THORSTENSEN Alana. See: **DI SCIASCIO Eve Francesca.**

THRING Meredith Wooldridge, b. 17 Dec 1915, Melbourne, Victoria, Australia. Professor of Engineering. m. 14 Dec 1940, 2 sons, 1 daughter. Education: BA 1st Class Honours, Physics, Trinity College, Cambridge, 1937; ScD, Cambridge, 1964. Publications: Man, Machines and Tomorrow, 1973; Machines: Master or Slaves of Man?, 1973; How to Invent, 1977; The Engineer's Conscience, 1980, reprinted, 1992; Robots and Telechirs, 1983. Contributions to: More than 150 scientific and technical articles to journals. Memberships: Fellow, Fellowship of Engineering; Fellow, Institution of Electrical Engineers; Fellow, Institution of Mechanical Engineers; Fellow, Institute of Physics; Fellow, Institution of Chemical Engineers; Senior Fellow, Institute of Energy, President 1962-63. Address: Bell Farm, Brundish, Suffolk IP13 8BL, England.

THUBRON Colin Gerald Dryden, b. 14 June 1939, London, England. Writer. Appointments: Editorial Staff, Hutchinson and Company Limited, London, 1959-62; Freelance Filmmaker, British Broadcasting Corporation Television, London, 1963-64; Editorial Staff, Macmillan Company, New York City, USA, 1964-65. Publications: Mirror To Damascus, 1967; The Hills of Adonis: A Quest in Lebanon, 1968; Jerusalem, 1969; Journey Into Cyprus, 1975; The God In The Mountain, novel, 1977; Emperor, novel, 1978; The Venetians, 1980; The Ancient Mariners, 1981; The Royal Opera House Covent Garden, 1982; Among The Russians, 1983; A Cruel Madness, 1984; Behind The Wall: A Journey Through China, 1987; Falling, 1989; Turning Back The Sun, 1991. Contributions to: Times; Times Literary Supplement; Independent; Sunday Times; Sunday Telegraph; New York Times; Granta, Honours: Fellow, Royal Society of Literature, 1969; Silver Pen Award, 1985; Thomas Cook Award, 1988; Hawthornden Prize, 1989. Memberships include: PEN. Literary Agent: Gillow Aitken and Stone. Address: Garden Cottage, 27 St Ann's Villas, London W11 4RT, England.

THUERY Jacques Henri André, b. 27 Nov 1951, Rodez, France. Engineer. m. Beatriz L López, 25 Aug 1983, 1 s, 1 d. Education: Electronics Engineering, Enseeiht, Toulouse, France. Publications: Les Micro-Ondes Et Leurs Effets Sur La Matière, 1983; Microwaves: Industrial Scientific And Medical Applications, 1992. Memberships: Société Des Lettres, Sciences Et Arts De L'Aveyron; IEEE; SEE; ISF. Address: 3866 Corina Court, Palo Alto, CA 94303-4508, USA.

THURGOOD Nevil, (Walter Plinge), b. 29 Dec 1919, Stansted Mountfitcher, Essex. Self Employed Actor, Director, Writer. m. Eva Mary Hopper, 23 Aug 1941, 4 sons. Education: Technical College Certificate, 1936. Publications: The Furtive Fortunes of Fickle Fate and Sir Jaspers Revenge, 1984; Good Evening Ladies & Gentlemen, 1988; Sleeping Beauty, unpublished; Thurgood, A family history, private publication. Memberships: Life Member, Actors Equity; Australian Writers Guild; British Music Hall Society. Address: The Croft, 329 Mount Macedon Road, Mount Macedon, Vic 3441, Australia.

THURSTON Jarvis,See:**VAN DUYN Mona.**

TIBBER Robert. See: **FRIEDMAN Eve Rosemary.**

TIBBER Rosemary. See: **FRIEDMAN Eve Rosemary.**

TICKLE Phyllis A, b. 12 Mar 1934, Johnson City, Tennessee, USA. Writer. m. Dr Samuel M Tickle, 17 June 1955, 3 sons, 4 daughters. Education: BA, East Tennessee State University; MA, Furman University. Appointments: Poet-in-Residence, Memphis Brooks Museum, 1977-85; Director, St Lukes Press, 1975-89; Director, Trade Publishing Group, The Wimmer Companies, 1989; Director Emeritus, 1992-; Religion Editor, Publishers Weekly, 1992-. Publications: The Story of Two Johns, 1976; American Genesis, 1976; On Beyong Koch, 1981; The City Essays, 1983; Selections, 1984; What the Heart Already Knows, 1985; Final Sanity, 1987; Ordinary Time, 1988; The Tickle Papers, 1989. Contributions to: The Episcopalian; The Tennessee Churchman; The Dixie Flyer; The Feminist Digest; 365 Meditations For Women, 1989; Disciplines, 1989. Honours: Individual Artists Fellowship in Literature, 1983. Memberships: Vice President, President, Tennessee Literary Arts Association; Chair, Publishers Association of the South. Literary Agent: Mary Jane Ross. Address: 3522 Lucy Road South, Lucy Community, Millington, TN 38053, USA.

TIEDE Tom, b. 24 Feb 1937, USA. Journalist; Author. Education: BA, Washington State University, 1959. Appointments: Instructor, Lecturer in Field, 1965-; Currently, Senior Editor, National Correspondent, Newspaper Enterprise Association, the Scripps-Howard Syndicate; Publisher, "The News", Georgia. Publications: Your Men at War, 1966; Coward, 1968; Calley: Soldier or Killer?, 1970; Welcome to Washington, Mr Witherspoon, 1982; The Great Whale Rescue, 1986; American Tapestry, 1990; The Man Who Discovered Pluto, 1991. Honours: Ernie Pyle Memorial Award for War Reporting; National headlines Award for Feature Writing; Freedom's Foundation Award; George Washington Medal. Address: Mill Run Bourne, Box 1919, Richmond Hill, GA 31324, USA.

TIGAR Chad. See: **LEVI Peter.**

TIGHE Carl, b. 26 Apr 1950, Birmingham, England. Writer. Education: BA Hons, English, 1973, MA, 1974, University College, Swansea; PDESL, Leeds University, 1979. Appointments: Script Reader, BBC Wales Radio and TV, 1985-87. Publications: Little Jack Horner, 1985; Baku!, 1986; Gdansk: National Identity in the Polish-German Borderlands, 1990; Rejoice! And Other Stories, 1992; Anthology contributions to: The Best Short Stories of 1989; Minerva Book of Short Stories: Poetry Street 2; Telling Stories, vol 3, BBC, 1994; Best Short Stories of 1994. Contributions to: Planet; Ambit; 20/20; Literary Review; Margin; Poetry Wales; The Works; Passport; Literature and History; Monthly Review; Journal of European Studies; Metropolitan. Honours: Welsh Arts Council Literary Bursary, 1983; All London Drama Prize, 1987; British Council Travel Bursary, 1990; Rejoice! And Other Stories shortlisted for Irish Times First Fiction Prize, 1993. Memberships: PEN; Writers Guild; Welsh Union of Writers; Welsh Academy. Address: 36 Oak Road, Withington, Manchester M20 9DA, England.

TILLMAN Barrett, b. 24 Dec 1948, Pendleton, Oregon, USA. Author. Education: Oregon State University, 1967-68; BS, Journalism, University of Oregon, 1971. Appointments: Editorial Committee, American Aviation Historical Society, 1971-77; Founder, Publisher, Champlin Museums Press, 1982-87; Managing Editor, The Hook Magazine, 1986-89. Publications: Warriors, 1990; On Yankee Station, 1987; the Dauntless Dive Bomber of WWII, 1976; Hellcat: The F6F in WWII, 1979; Corsair: The F4U in WWII and Korea, 1979; Avenger at War, 1979; Pushing the Envelope: The Career of Fighter Ace & Test Pilot Marion Carl, 1994. Contributions to: Naval Institute Proceedings, Naval History, The Hook, Soldier of Fortune, USAF Fighter Weapons Review, Wings, Airpower, Air Progress, American Aviation Historical Society Journal. Honours: Outstanding Contributor's Award, AAHS Journal, 1976; USAF Historical Foundation Writing Award, 1981; North American Society of Oceanic History, 1987; Captain Emile Louis Bonnot Award from the Naval Order of the United States, for lifetime achievement in naval writing, 1994; Admiral Arthur W Radford Award for Naval History and Literature, 1994. Memberships: Founder, Conference of Historic Aviation Writers; Life Member, US Naval Institute; Tailhook Association; Association of Naval Aviation. Literary Agent: Robert Gottlieb, William Morris Agency, New York. Address: Box 567, Athena, OR 97813, USA.

TILLY Charles,Historian; Professor. Contributions to: Professional Journals. Address: Centre for Studies of Social Change, New School for Scl Rsc, 64 University Place, New York, NY 10003-4520, USA.

TINDALL Gillian Elizabeth, b. 4 May 1938, London, England. Novelist; Biographer; Historian. m. Richard G Landown, 1 son. Education: BA 1st Class, MA, University of Oxford. Publications: Novels: No Name in the Street, 1959; The Water and the Sound, 1961; The Edge of the Paper, 1963; The Youngest, 1967; Someone Else, 1969, 1975; Fly Away Home, 1971; The Traveller and His Child, 1975; The Intruder, 1979; Looking Forward, 1983; To the City, 1987; Give Them All My Love, 1989; Spirit Weddings, 1992; Short stories: Dances of Death, 1973; The China Egg and Other Stories, 1981; Biography: The Born Exile on George Gissing, 1974; Non-fiction: A Handbook on Witchcraft, 1965; The Fields Beneath, 1977; City of Gold: The Biography of Bombay, 1981, 1992; Rosamund Lehmann, an Appreciation, 1985. Contributions to: Encounter: The Observer; Guardian; New Statesman; Evening Standard, 1973-; The Times, 1983-; The Independent, 1987-. Honours: Somerset Maugham Award for Fly Away Home, 1972. Memberships: Fellow, Royal Society of Literature; PEN. Address: c/o Curtis Brown Limited, 162-168 Regent Street, London W1, England.

TINNISWOOD Peter, b. 21 Dec 1936, Liverpool, England. FormerJournalist. Publications include: A Touch of Daniel, 1969; Mog, 1970; I Dodn't Know You Cared, 1973; Except You're A Bird, 1974; Tale froma Long Room, 1981-82; The Brigadier Down Under, 1983; The Brigadier in Season, 1984; Call it a Canary, 1985; The Village Fete; The Brigadier and Uncle Mort; Radio & TV Plays. Honours: Best First Novel of Year, 1969; Book of Month Choice, 1969; Winfred Holiby Award, 1974; Sony Award for Radio, 1987; Giles Cooper Award, 1987; Writers Guild Comedy Award, 1991. Memberships: Royal Society of Literature. Literary Agent: Jonathan Clowes Agency. Address: c/o Jonathan Clowes Agency, Ironbride Bridge House, bridge Approach, London NW1 8BD, England.

TIPTON David John, b. 28 Apr 1934, Birmingham, England. Author. m. twice, div., 2 sons, 3 daughters. Education: Saltley College, Birmingham, 1957-59; Essex University, 1976-77. Appointments: Editor, Rivelin Press, 1974-84; Editor, Redbeck Press, 1984-. Publications: Poetry: Peru, The New Poetry, translations, 1970, 1977; Millstone Grit, 1972; Nomads and Settlers, 1980; Wars of the Roses, 1984; Green and Purple, 1993; The South American Poems, 1994; Biography, fiction: Atahualpa, 1976; Freak Summer, 1984. Contributions to: Ambit; London Magazine; Stand; Poetry Review; Poetry, Chicago; Evergreen Review; Twentieth Century; Tribune; Outposts. Address: 24 Aireville Road, Frizinghall, Bradford BD9 4HH, Yorkshire, England.

TIRBUTT Honoris (Emma Page), Author. Publications: In Loving Memory, 1970; Family and Friends, 1972; A Fortnight by the Sea, 1973, US edition as Add a Pinch of Cyanide; Element of Chance, 1975; Missing Chance, 1980; Every Second Thursday, 1981; Last Walk Home, 1982; Cold Light of Day, 1983; Scent of Death, 1985; Final Moments, 1987; A Violent End, 1988; Deadlock, 1991; Mortal Remains, 1992; In the Event of My Death, 1994. Address: c/o The Crime Club, Harper Collins Publishers, 77-85 Fulham Palace Road, London W6 8JB, England.

TIRION Wil, b. 19 Feb 1943, Breda, Netherlands. Uranographer; Graphic Artist. m. Cokkie van Blitterswijk, 23 Dec 1975, 1 son, 1 daughter. Education: High School, 1959; Famous Artists Schools, 1968; Self-taught, Uranography. Publications include: Sky Atlas 2000.0, 1981; Bright Star Atlas 2000.0, 1989; Cambridge Star Atlas 2000.0, 1991, French (Canadian) Edition, 1993; Co-author: Collins Guide to Stars and Planets, 1984, 2nd Edition, 1993, US Edition, 1985, Spanish Edition, 1986, Italian Edition, 1986, German Edition, 1987; Uranometria 2000.0, Vol I, 1987, Vol II, 1988; Monthly Sky Guide, 1987, Dutch Edition, 1988, Spanish Edition, 1989, Italian Edition, 1989, Danish Edition, 1990, 2nd Danish Edition, 1994; Binocular Astronomy, 1992; The Southern Sky Guide, 1993; Star charts, maps, drawings, in other books. Contributions to: Maps to: Zenit; Sterrengids; Sternfuehrer; Aarde en Hemel; Astronomy; Sky and Space (Southem Astronomy). Honours: Dr J van der Bilt Prize, Netherlands, 1987. Memberships: NVWS (Dutch Organisation of Amateur Astronomers); British Astronomical Association. Address: Wisselspoor 221, 2908 AD Capelle A/D IJsell, Netherlands.

TLALI Miriam (Masoli), b. 1940, Sophiatown, Johannesburg, Novelist. Education: University of the Witwatersrand, Johannesburg. Publications: Miriam at the Metropolitan, 1975; Amandla, 1980; Stories, Mihloti, 1984; Footprints in the Quag, Stories and Dialogues from

Soweto, 1989. Address: c/o Pandora Press, 77-85 Fulham Palace Road, London W6 8JB, England.

TOCH Henry, b. 15 Aug 1923. Tax Consultant. m. Margaret Schwarz, 3 Apr 1958. Education: Bachelor of Commerce, 2nd Class Honours (Upper Division), London School of Economics and Political Science, University of London, 1950. Appointments: Formerly Monthly Columnist, Law for Business. Publications: How to Pay Less Income Tax, 1958, 4 editions, re-issued, 1986; Tax Savings for Businessmen, 1960, 3 editions; Income Tax, handbook, 1966, 14 editions; Economics for Professional Studies, 1974, 3 editions; How to Survive Inflation, 1977; How to Pass Examinations in Taxation, 1979; Cases in Income Tax, 1981; Essentials of British Constitution and Government, 1983; Taxation Made Simple, 1985, 2 editions. Contributions to: Cooperative News, over 15 years; Journal of Business Law. Memberships: The Financial Intermediaries Manager and Brokers Regulatory Association. Address: Candida, 49 Hawkshead Lane, North Mymms, Hatfield, Herts AL9 7TD, England.

TODD Paul. See: POSNER Richard.

TOFFLER Alvin,b. 4 Oct 1928, New York City, USA. Author. m. Adelaide Elizabeth (Heidi) Farrell Toffler, 29 Apr 1950, 1 daughter. Education: BA, New York University. Literary Appointment: Associate Editor, Fortune Magazine, 1959-61. Publications: (Mostly in collaboration with Heidi Farrell Toffler): Future Shock, 1970; The Third Wave, 1980; Previews & Premises, 1983; The Adaptive Corporation, 1984; Powershift, 1990; War and Anti-War, 1993; The Culture Consumers, 1964; Editor: Learning for Tomorrow, 1973; The Futurists, 1972. Contributions to: New York Times Magazine; Annals, American Academy of Political & Social Science; Observer, UK; Sunday Times, UK; Christian Science Monitor; Nouvelle Observateur; Nouvelle Economiste; Washington Post; Wall Street Journal; Readers Digest; Technology & Culture; Playboy; Horizon; Nation; New Republic. Honours: Prix de Meilleur Livre Etranger, 1971; McKinsey Foundation Book Award, 1970; Author of Year, American Society of Journalists & Authors; 6 Honorary Degrees; Officer de l'Ordre des Arts et Sciences; Fellow, American Association for the Advancement of Science; Centennial Award, Institute of Electrical & Electronics Engineers; Medal, President of Italy. Memberships Include: Authors League; American Society of Journalists & Authors; World Future Studies Federation; International Institute for Strategic Studies; Former Trustee, Antioch University. Literary Agent: Curtis Brown Ltd. Address: c/o Curtis Brown Ltd, 10 Astor Place, New York, NY 10003, USA.

TOFFLER Heidi, b. 1 Aug 1929, New York City, USA. Author. m. Alyin Toffler, 29 Apr 1950, 1 daughter. Education: BA, Long Island University. Publications: (Mostly in collaboration with Alvin Toffler): Future Shock, 1970; War and Anti-War, 1993; The Third Wave, 1980; Previews & Premises, 1983; The Adaptive Corporation, 1984; Powershift, 1990; The Culture Consumers, 1964; Editor, Learning for Tomorrow, 1973; The Futurists, 1972. Contributions to: New York Times Magazine; Annals, American Acadamy of Political & Social Science; Observer, UK; Sunday Times, UK; Christian Science Monitor; Nouvelle Observateur; Nouvelle Economiste; Washington Post; Wall Street Journal; Readers Digest; Technology & Culture; Playboy; Horizon; Nation; New Republic. Honours: 2 Honorary Doctorates; Medal, President of Italy. Literary Agent: Curtis Brown Ltd. Address: c/o Curtis Brown Ltd, 10 Astor Place, New York, NY 10003, USA.

TOLGYESSY Juraj, b. 27 Jan 1931, Dun Streda, Slovakia. Professor. m. Eva Cicha, 8 Aug 1967, 1 son, 2 daughters. Education: Slovak Technical University, 1953; PHD, Chemicotechnological University, 1959; DSc, Lomonosov State University, 1968; Slovak Technical University, 1972. Appointments: Founder, Editor, Journal of Radioanalytical and Nuclear Chemistry, 1967-. Publications: Radiometric Titrations; Isotope Dilution Analysis; Nuclear Analytical Chemistry; Emanation Thermal Analysis; Radionuclide X-Ray Fluorescence Analysis of Environmental Samples; Others include chamistry and biology of water, air and soil. Honours: Prize, Slovak Academy of Sciences; Award, Hungarian Academy of Sciences. Address: Radlinskeho 9, 812 37 Bratislava, Slovakia.

TOMALIN Claire, b. 1933, London. Author. m. (1) Nicholas Tomalin, dec, 1973, (2) Michael Frayn, 5 children. Appointments: Worked in publishing and journalism for over thirty years; Literary Editor, the New Statesman and Sunday Times until 1986. Publications: Books: The Life and Death of Mary Wollstonecraft; Shelley and His World, Katherine Mansfield: A Secret Life; The Invisible Woman: The

Story of Nelly Ternan and Charles Dickens; Mrs Jordan's Profession: The Story of an Great Actress and Future King; The Winter Wife (play). Honours: Winner, Whitbread Literary First Book Prize, 1974; Shortlisted for the NCR Award; Recipient of James Tait Black Memorial Prize; Hawthorden Prize.

TOMASZEWSKA Marta, b. 10 Apr 1933, Warsaw, Poland. Author. Education: MA, University of Warsaw, 1956. Appointments: Reporter, Swiat Mlodych, 1950-52; Editor, Cultural Section, Walka Mlodych, 1956-58, Motywy, 1961-67; Author, 1967-. Publications: Zorro Put On Your Glases, 1974; Tapatiki, Cycle Volumes I-IV, 1974-84; The Wig, 1974; Night After the Day of Love, 1977; Serpent in Paradise, 1978; The Tapatiki's Expedition, musical play, 1982; The Giant in the Pirates Cavern, or Mystery of Fourthwall, 1986; The Travel to Om Land, 1979; The Queen of Invisible Riders, 1988; Tetratys, 1991; If You Go With Me, 1993; Some 30 other novels. Contributions to: Fantasy; Fantastyka; Fantazia; Usmiech Numeru; Claudia. Honours: Polish Prime Minister's Award, 1981; Eagle's Pen, Young Readers Award, 1986; Cross, Order of Polonia Restituta, 1986; XII Premio Europeo di Litteratura Giuvanile-Lista d'Oneren Arrativa, for The Queen of Invisible Riders, 1988; Ibby Awards Certificate of Honour for Writing, for The Giant in the Pirates Cavern, or Mystery of Fourthwall, 1988. Memberships: ZAIKS, 1967; Polish Writers Union, 1969; Association of Polish Writers (Stowarzyszenie Pisarzy Polskich), 1994. Address: Natolinska 3 m 64, Warsaw 00-562, Poland.

TOMLINSON Catherine Twaddle Dimond, b. 1 Mar 1917, Ipswich, Queensland, Australia. Home Economics Teacher; Author. m. (1) D J Linton, Jan 1944 (killed in action, 1945), (2) H F B Tomlinson, Dec 1950, 1 son, 1 daughter. Education: 3-year Trained Teacher, Queensland Education Department, 1934-36; Diploma, Domestic Science, Department of Public Instruction of Queensland, Technical Branch, 1942; BA, University of Queensland, St Lucia, Brisbane, 1987. Publications: Recipes with a Difference, 1962; Competitive Cookery, 1972; Successful Cookery, 1983. Contributions to: Journal of Home Economics Association, Australia; Queensland Home Economics Association Magazine; Home Economics Education 1881-1981; A Centenary History of Home Economics 1881-1981 (J E Logan); History of South Brisbane College of Technical and Further Education, Boolarong (B McKeering), 1988. Memberships: Australian Society of Authors; Alumni Association of the University of Queensland Inc; Standing Committee, Women's College, University of Queensland; Life Member, Ipswich (Queensland) Girls' Grammar School Old Girls' Association. Address: 12 Wiseman Street, Kenmore, Queensland 4069, Australia.

TOMLINSON Charles, b. 8 Jan 1927, Stoke-on-Trent, England. Emeritus Professor. Education: BA, Queens' College, Cambridge; MA, London. Publications: Poems: The Necklace, 1955, 1966; Seeing is Believing, 1958; Versions from Tyutchev (with H Gifford), 1960; A Peopled Landscape, 1963; Castilian Ilexes (with H Gifford), 1963; American Scenes, 1966; The Way of a World, 1969; Poems (with A Clarke, T Connor), 1964; Poems (with A Brownjohn, M Hamburger), 1969; The Poem as Initiation, 1968; Renga (with O Paz), 1971, 1972, 1979, 1983; Words and Images, 1972; Written on Water, 1972; The Way In, 1974; Selected Poems, 1951-74, 1978; The Shaft, 1978; Air Born/Hijos del Aire (with O Paz), 1979; The Flood, 1981; Translations, 1983; Notes from New York, 1984; Eden, 1985; Collected Poems, 1985, enlarged, 1987; The Return, 1987; Annunciations, 1989; Selected Poems, 1989; Poems, The Door in the Wall, 1992; Selected Poems of Attilio Bertolucci, translation, introduction, 1993; Prose: In Black and White, 1976; Some Americans: A Literary Memoir, 1981; Poetry and Metamorphosis (The Clark Lectures), 1983; Editor, The Oxford Book of Verse in English Translation, 1980; George Oppen: Selected Poems, 1990; Eros Englished, erotic poems from the Greek and Latin, 1991; Essays on Marianne Moore and William Carlos Williams, Poetry of Williams and Octavio Paz. Honours: Fellow, Royal Society of Literature; D H Lawrence Fellowship, University of New Mexico, 1963; National Translation Centre Award, University of Texas, 1968; Cheltenham Poetry Prize, 1976; Honorary Fellow: Queens' College, Cambridge, 1976, Royal Holloway and Bedford New College, London, 1990; Arts Council Travelling Exhibition, 1978-81; Cholmondeley Award, Poetry, 1979; Honorary DLitt: Keele and Colgate, 1981, New Mexico, 1986; Honorary Professor, Keele, 1989; Cittadella European Poetry Prize, 1991; Emeritus Professor, 1992; Bennett Award, Poetry, New York, 1993. Address: Ozleworth, Glos GL12 7QB, England.

TOMLINSON Gerald, b. 24 Jan 1933, Elmira, New York, USA. Writer; Editor; Publisher. m. (Mary) Alexis Usakowski, 19 Aug 1966, 2 sons. Education: BA, Marietta College, Marietta, Ohio, 1955; Columbia Law School, New York City, 1959-60. Appointments: Associate Editor, Business and Professional Books, Prentice Hall, 1960-63; Associate Editor, School Department, Harcourt Brace Jovanovich, 1963-66; Senior Editor, English Department, Holt, Rinehart and Winston, 1966-69; Executive Editor, K-12 English, Silver Burdett and Ginn, 1969-82; Publisher, Home Run Press, 1985-. Publications: On a Field of Black, novel, 1980; School Administrator's Complete Letter Book, 1984; Baseball Research Handbook, 1987; Speaker's Treasury of Sports Anecdotes, Stories and Humor, 1990; Encyclopedia of Religious Quotations, 1991; The New Jersey Book of Lists (co-author), 1992; Murdered in Jersey, 1994. Contributions to: 24 mystery short stories in: Ellery Queen's Mystery Magazine; Alfred Hitchcock's Mystery Magazine; Mike Shayne Mystery Magazine; Mystery Monthly; 10 articles to: The National Pastime; Baseball Research Journal; other Sports magazines. Honours: Best Detective Stories of the Year, E.P. Dutton, 1976; Mystery Writers of America Annual Anthologies, 5 appearances, 1977-87. Memberships: Authors Guild; Mystery Writers of America; Society for American Baseball Research. Address: 19 Harbor Drive, Lake Hopatcong, NJ 07849, USA.

TOMLINSON Mary Teresa, b. 15 Aug 1935, England. Journalist; Public Relations/Lecturer; Specialist in European Community Affairs and Tourism. m. Noel Tomlinson, 15 Aug 1959, 1 son, 1 daughter. Education: English, Accountancy and Economics Diploma; School of Economics, 1952-54; School of Drama and Music; School of Art, 1955-56. Appointments: Partner, Ays Press and Public Relations. Publications include: Around the World in Cookery and Cakes, 1980; Wool on the Back (with Peter Taylor), 1987. Contributions to: Lady; Nursery World; Devon Life; RAF News; Cotswold Life; Sunday Times; Times; Debretts' Best of Britain, 1990; Hollis Europe. Honours: Nominee, Woman of Europe Award, 1990; Member, Club of Rhodes, UK, 1991-. Memberships: Society of Women Writers and Journalists; Institute of Journalists; Officer, Chartered Institute of Journalists. Address: Mayfield Cottage, 51 Ebrington, nr Campden, Glos GL55 6NQ, England.

TOONA Elin-Kai,b. 12 July 1937, Tallinn, Estonia. Freelance Writer. m. Donald Frederick Gottschalk, 9 Oct 1967, 1 son. Publications: Puuingel, 1965; Lotukata, 1968; Sipelgas Sinise Kausi All, 1973; In Search of Coffee Mountains, US Edition, 1977, UK Edition, 1979; Lady Cavaliers, 1977; Pictures, and DP Camp Child, poetry in Visions, 1988; Kalevikula Vimne Tutar (Estonian novel published in Sweden), 1988; Kolm Valget Tuvi (novel published in Lund, Sweden), 1992; Reprints: Estonia, Sipelgas Sinise Kausi All, 1991; Kalevikula Viimne Tutar, 1992; Lotukata; Kolm Valgettuvi. Contributions to: Estonia; Regular column for The Coastal Illustrated, St Simons Island, Georgia, 1974-75; Coastal Quarterly, Georgia; Indian River Life, Florida, Lady's Circle, New York; Talent Magazine, International Platform Association; St Petersburg Times, Florida; New Writers Magazette, Florida; Storyteller Magazine; Eesti Haal, London; Vaba Eesti Sona, New York; Tulimuld, Sweden; Mana, Canada/USA; Triinu; Scripts/Contributions to Radio Liberty, Voice of America. Honours: 1st Prize for Young Estonian Writers in England, 1952; Certificate of Merit for short story The Old Farm, Storyteller Magazine, London, 1962; 1st Prize for Short Story Competition 13, Writer's Review, London, 1966; The H Visnapuu Literary Award for Estonians for novel Puuingel, World Association of Estonians, 1966; Ennu Literary Prize for juvenile novel Lotukata, Estonians, USA, 1968; Certificate of Commendation for The Square, Golden Windmill Radio Drama Contest, Radio Nederland Wereldomroep, 1971; 1st Prize for Photo Turks in a Field, National Examiner Contest, 1983; 1st Prize, Florida State Award for Non-Fiction and 2nd Prize, Florida State Award for Photo Journalism, National League of American Pen Women, 1985; Honourable Mention for short stories Sand Prints and When Butterflies Pass Over, Short Story Contest, National League of American Women, 1988; Lauri Literary Prize for Estonian Novel, Kolm Valget Tuvi, 1993. Memberships: International PEN, Estonian Branch; All Estonian Literary Associations Worldwide; Fellow, International Biographical Association; National League of American Pen Women; International Platform Association. Address: 27554 US 19N, 37 Clearwater, FL 34621, USA.

TOPOLSKI Daniel, b. 4 June 1945, London, England. Writer; Broadcaster. Partner, Susan Gilbert, 2 daughters. Education: BA Geography, Diploma Social Anthropology, MA Geography, New College, Oxford, 1964-68. Publications: Muzungu: One Man's Africa, 1976; Travels with my Father: South America, 1983; Boat Race: The

Oxford Revival, 1985; True Blue: The Oxford Mutiny, 1988; Henley: The Regatta, 1989. Contributions to: Telegraph; Times; 'You' Magazine; Hello; Radio Times; Tatler; Vogue; Life; Madamoiselle; Daily Mail; Observer; Evening Standard; BBC. Honours: True Blue, Sports Book of the Year, 1990; Radio Travel Program of the Year, 1994. Memberships: Churchill Fellow; Fellow of RGS; Henley Steward; Leander Club; London RC. Literary Agent: Peter's Fraser & Dunlop, c/o Mark Lucas, 503/4 The Chambers, Chelsea Harbour, London, SW10 OXF. Address: 69 Randolph Avenue, London W 9 1DW, England. 192.

TOREKULOVICH. See: **AITMAYOV Chingiz.**

TORON Steve. See: **STEBEL Sidney Leo.**

TORRANCE Lee. See: **SADGROVE Sidney Henry.**

TORRANCE Thomas Forsyth, b. 30 Aug 1913, Chengdu, China. Minister of Religion; Professor of Theology. m. Margaret Edith Spear, 2 Oct 1946, 2 sons, 1 daughter. Education: MA, 1934; BR, 1937; DrTheol, 1946; DLitt, 1971; FRS (Edinburgh), 1979; FBA (London), 1982. Appointments: Founder, Editor, Scottish Journal of Theology, 1948-88. Publications: The Doctrine of Grace, 1949; Calvin's Doctrine of Man, 1949; Kingdom and Church, 1956; Conflict and Agreement in the Church, 2 vols, 1959-60; Theology in Reconstruction, 1965; Theological Science, 1969; God and Rationality, 1971; Theology in Reconciliation, 1975; Space, Time and Resurrection, 1976; Space, Time and Incarnation, 1979; The Ground and Grammar of Theology, 1980; Christian Theology and Scientific Culture, 1980; Divine and Contingent Order, 1981; Reality and Scientific Theology, 1984; The Humanity of John Calvin, 1987; The Trinitarian Faith, 1988; The Christian Frame of Mind, Reason, Order and Openness in Theology and Natural Science, 1989; Karl Barth, Biblical and Evangelical Theological Theologian, 1990; Senso del divino e scienza mnoderna, 1992; Theological Dialogue between Orthodox and Reformed Churches (editor), 1993; Royal Priesthood, 1993; Divine Meaning. Studies in Patristic Hermeneutics, 1994; Trinitarian Perspectives. Toward Doctrinal Agreement, 1994. Contributions to: Numerous. Honours: DD, Montreal, 1950; DrTheol, Geneva and Paris, 1959; DD, St Andrews, 1960; DrTeol, Oslo, 1961; DSc, Heriott-Watt University, Edinburgh, 1983; DrTheol, Debrecen, Hungary; Moderator, General Assembly, Church of Scotland, 1976-77. Memberships: British Academy; International Academy of Religious Sciences, President 1972-81; International Academy of the Philosophy of Sciences; Center of Theological Inquiry, Princeton, USA; Royal Society of Edinburgh, Committee Member 1985. Address: 37 Braid Farm Road, Edinburgh EH10 6LE, Scotland.

TORRES Tereska. See: **LEVIN Torres.**

TOTH Susan Allen,Address: 4820 Penn Avenue South, Minneapolis, MN 55409, USA.

TOURNOER Michel Edouard, b. 19 Dec 1924, Paris, France. Author. Literary appointment: Editions Gallimard, Paris. Publications: Friday or The Other Island, 1969; The Erl King (The Ogre), 1972; Gemini, 1981; The Four Wise Men, 1982; The Fetishist, 1984; Gilles et Jeanne, 1987; The Golden Droplet, 1987. Honours: Grand Prix du Roman, Académie Française, 1967; Prix Goncourt, 1970. Memberships: Académie Goncourt, France; Akademie der Kunste, Berlin, Germany. Address: 78460 Choisel, Chevreuse, France.

TOWNSEND John Rowe, b. 10 May 1922. Author. m. Vera Lancaster, 3 July 1948 (dec. 1973), 1 son, 2 daughters. Education: MA, Cambridge University. Publications: Gumble's Yard, 1961; The Intruder, 1969; Noah's Castle, 1974; The Islanders, 1981; The Invaders, 1992; Written for Children, history of children's literature, 5th edition, 1990. Honours: Silver Pen Award, International PEN, 1970; Horn Book Award, Boston Globe, 1970; Edgar Award, Mystery Writers of America, 1970; Christopher Award, 1981. Memberships: Society of Authors, former Member of Management Committee and Chairman, Children's Writers Group. Address: 72 Water Lane, Histon, Cambridge CB4 4LR, England.

TOWNSEND Peter Wooldridge, b. 22 Nov 1914, Rangoon, Burma. Author. m. Marie Luce Jamagne, 21 Dec 1959, 1 s, 2 d. Education: Haileybury; Royal Air Force College, 1933-35; Royal Air Force Staff College, 1942-43. Publications include: Earth my Friend, 1960; Duel of Eagles, 1970; The Last Emperor, 1975; Time and Chance, 1978; The Smallest Pawns in the Game, 1979-80; The Girl in the White Ship, 1982; The Postman of Nagasaki, 1984; Nostalgia Britannica, 1994; Duel in the Dark, 1986. Contributions to: Daily Telegraph; Daily Mail; Daily Express; Sunday Express; Evening Standard; Paris Match; Journal du Dimanche; Le Figaro; Le Figaro Litteraire; Madame Figaro; Le Temps Retrouve. Membership: European Academy of Science, Arts & Letters. Address: La Mare aux Oiseaux, 78610 St Leger en Yvelines, France.

TOWNSEND Sue, b, 4 Feb 1946, Leicester, England. Author. Publications: The Secret Diary of Adrian Mole Aged Thirteen and Three-Quarters, 1982; The Growing Pain of Adrian Mole, 1984; The Diaries of Adrian Mole, combined volume issued in USA, 1986; Bazaar and Rummage, Groping for Words, Womberang: Three Plays, 1984; True Confessions of Adrian Albert Mole; Mr Bevan's Dream, 1989; Ten Tiny Fingers, Nine Tiny Toes, play, 1989; Adrian Mole from Minor to Major, 1991; The Queen and I, 1992; Adrian Mole - The Wilderness Years, 1993. Contributions to: London Times; New Statesman; Observer; Sainsburys Magazine, Le Temps. Memberships: Writers Guild; PEN. Literary Agent: Sheil Land Associates Ltd. Address: c/o Giles Gorden Agency, 43 Doughty Street, London, England.

TOWNSEND Thomas (Tom) L, b. 1 Jan 1944, Illinios, USA. Novelist. m. Janet L Simpson, 17 Apr 1965. Education: Arkansas Military Academy. Publications: Texas Treasure Coast, 1978; Where the Pirates Are, 1985; Trader Wooly, 1987; Trader Wooly and the Terrorists, 1988; Queen of the Wind, 1989; Trader Wooly and the Ghost in the Colonel's Jeep, 1991; The Holligans, 1991; Battle of Galveston, 1990; Bubba's Truck, 1992; The Ghost Flyers, 1993; A Fair Wind to Glory, 1994. Honours: Friend of American Writers Award, 1986; Texas Blue Bonnet Master List, 1986; Silver Award, Best Children's Video, Houston International Film Festival, 1986. Address: PO Box 905, Kemah, TX 77565, USA.

TOYNBEE Polly, b. 27 Dec 1946, England. Journalist; Writer. m. Peter Jenkins, 1970, 1 son, 2 daughters, 1 stepdaughter. Education: St Anne's College, Oxford. Literary appointments: Reporter, The Observer, 1968-71; Editor, Washington Monthly, USA, 1972-73; Feature Writer, Observer, 1974-76; Columnist, The Guardian, 1977-88; Social Affairs Editor, BBC, 1988-. Publications: Leftovers, 1966; A Working Life, 1970, 1972; Hospital, 1977, 1979; The Way We Live Now, 1981; Lost Children, 1985. Honours: Catherine Pakenham Award for Journalism, 1975; British Press Awards, 1977, 1982. Address: BBC TV, TV Centre, Wood Lane, London W12, England.

TRACEY Hugh. See: EVANS Stuart.

TRACHITENBERG Paul, b. 1948. Poet. Address: 9431 Krepp Drive, Huntington Beach, CA 92646, USA.

TRANBARGER Ossie Elmo, b. 6 Apr 1914, MO, USA. Docent, Independence Museum. m. Jack Tranbarger, 1 s. Education: College Honours, Creative Writing, Journalism, Lit & Mass Communications. Publications: Private Encounters; Wont of the Pen; Museum Ghosts. Contributions to: KS Quarterly; Little Balkans Review; numerous magazines. Honours: IWW in Poetry; DHL, University of Asia. Memberships: NLAPW, former KS State President; Midwest Fed Chapperal Poets, former KS State Regent; KS Authors, former President 3rd District; World Poetry Society; UPLI; Ozark Writers & Artists Guild; Int Poets Shrine; Int Clover Poetry Association. Address: 619 West Main St, Independence, KS 67301, USA.

TRANTER Nigel Godwin (Nye Tregold), b. 23 Nov 1909, Glasgow, Scotland. Author; Novelist. m. May Jean Campbell Grieve, 11 July 1933, 1 son (dec.), 1 daughter. Appointments: Accountant, Inspector, family insurance company, Edinburgh, 1929-39; Full-time Writer, Lecturer, Broadcaster, 1946-; Chairman, National Forth Road Bridge Committee, 1953-57; President, 1962-66, now Honorary President, PEN Scottish Centre; Chairman, Society of Authors, 1966-72; Vice-President, Scottish Teachers of History Association, 1990. Publications: Historical, romantic, Gothic, Western, adventure and children's fiction; Western novels as Nye Tredgold; Non-fiction; Numerous titles include: The Fortified House in Scotland, 5 vols, 1962-86; Robert the Bruce, trilogy: The Steps to the Empty Throne, 1969, The Path of the Hero King, 1970, The Price of the King's Peace, 1971; The Queen's Scotland, 4 vols, non-fiction, 1971-77; Portrait of the Border Country, non-fiction, 1972; The Wisest Fool, 1974; The Wallace, 1975; Stewart Trilogy: Lords of Misrule, 1976, A Folly of Princes, 1977, The Captive Crown, 1977; Macbeth the King, 1978; Margaret the Queen, 1979; Portrait of the Lothians, non-fiction, 1979; David the

Prince, 1980; True Thomas, 1981; Nigel Tranter's Scotland: A Very Personal View, 1981; The Patriot, 1982; Lord of the Isles, 1983; Unicorn Rampant, 1984; The Riven Realm, 1984; James, By the Grace of God, 1985; Rough Wooing, 1986; Columba: The Story of Scotland, non-fiction, 5 vols, 1987; Cache Down, 1987; Flowers of Chivalry, 1988; Mail Royal, 1989; Warden of the Queen's March, 1989; Crusader, 1991; Kenneth, 1990; Footbridge to Enchantment, 1992; Children of the Mist, 1992; Druid Sacrifice, 1993; Tapestry of the Boar; Price of a Princess. Honours: Honorary DLitt, Strathclyde; Honorary MA, Edinburgh; OBE, 1983; Scot of the Year, 1991; Honorary President, Saltire Society. Address: Quarry House, Aberlady, East Lothian EH32 0QB, Scotland.

TRAPIDO Barbara (Louise), b. 5 Nov 1941, Cape Town, South Africa. Writer. m. Stanley Trapido, 29 Apr 1963, 1 son, 1 daughter. Education: BA Hons, English; Postgraduate Certificate, London. Publications: Brother of the More Famous Jack, 1982; Noah's Ark, 1985; Temples of Delight, 1990; Juggling, novel, 1994. Contributions to: Spectator; Sunday Telegraph; Sunday Times. Honours: Whitbread, 1982; Shortlisted for Sunday Express Book of the Year Award, 1990. Literary Agent: Felicity Bryan, Oxford, England. Address: c/o Felicity Bryan, 2a North Parade, Oxford OX2 6PE, England.

TRASK Jonathan. See: LEVINSON Leonard.

TRAVIS Millicent Elizabeth. See: LANE M Travis.

TREANOR Oliver, b. 1 May 1949, Warrenpoint, Northern Ireland. Catholic Priest. Education: Queen's University, Belfast; BA (Hons); PGCE; Dip Phil; STB, 1977, STL, 1979, STD, 1984, Pont Universita Gregoriana, Rome. Publication: Mother of the Redeemer, Mother of the Redeemed, 1988. Contributions to: Observatore Romano, Vatican City; Priests and People, Durham, England; Theology Digest, USA; Religious Life Review, Dublin. Address: St Malachy's College, Belfast BT15 2AE, Northern Ireland.

TREASE (Robert) Geoffrey, b. 11 Aug 1909, Nottingham, England. Author. m. Marian Granger Boyer, 11 Aug 1933, 1 daughter. Education: Open Scholar in Classics, Queen's College, Oxford, 1928-29. Publications: 105 books including: Bows Against the Barons, 1934; Cue for Treason, 1940; Tales Out of School, 1948; No Boats on Bannermere, 1949; A Whiff of Burnt Boats: An Early Autobiography, 1971; Laughter at the Door: A Continental Autobiography, 1974; Tomorrow is a Stranger, 1987; The Arpino Assignment, 1988; A Flight of Angels, 1988; Shadow Under the Sea, 1990; Calabrian Quest, 1990; Aunt Augusta's Elephant, 1991; Song for a Tattered Flag, 1992; Fire on the Wind, 1993; Bring Out the Banners, 1994. Contributions to: Daily Telegraph; Times Literary Supplement; Times Educational Supplement; The Author. Honours: New Play Prize for After the Tempest, Welwyn Theatre Festival, 1938; New York Herald Tribune Award for This Is Your Century, Book Festival, 1966; Fellow, Royal Society of Literature, 1979. Memberships: Society of Authors, Chairman 1972-73, Council Member 1973-; PEN. Literary Agent: Murray Pollinger, London, England. Address: c/o Murray Pollinger, 222 Old Brompton Road, London SW5 0BZ, England.

TREAT Lawrence, b. 21 Dec 1903, New York City, USA. Writer. m. 7 May 1943. Education: AB, Dartmouth College, 1924; LLb, Columbia Law School, 1927. Publications: V as in Victim, 1945; Big Shot, 1951; Venus Unarmed, 1961; P as in Police, 1970; Lady Drop Dead, 1960; H as in Haunted, 1946; 20 other books; Originator of Pictorial Crime Puzzles: Bringing Sherlock Home, 1935; rime and Puzzlement, 1981; Crime and Puzzlement 2, 1982; Crime and Puzzlement 3, 1988; You're the Detective, 1983; Cluedo Armchair Detective, 1983; Crime and Puzzlement, My Cousin Phoebe, 1991; Crime and Puzzlement on Martha's Vineyard, 1993. Contributions to: Numerous journals including: Ellery Queen's Mystery Magazine; Hitchcock Mystery Magazine; The Saint; Redbook. Honours: Edgar Allan Poe Award, 1965, 1979; Short Story Award, International Crime Writers Convention, 1981; Special Edgar Allan Poe Award, TV Alfred Hitchcock Hour. Memberships: Mystery Writers of America, Past President, Director, Treasurer, Founder; Boston Authors Club. Literary Agent: Vicky Bijur. Address: c/o Vicky Bijur, 333 West End Avenue, New York, NY 10023, USA.

TREBORLANG Robert, b. 19 Dec 1943, Jerusalem, Israel. Writer; Poet. m. Moi Moi Cumines, 6 May 1971. Education: BA, Language, University of Sydney, 1968. Publications include: How to Survive in Australia, 1985; How to be Normal in Australia, 1987; How to Make it Big in Australia, 1989; She Vomits Like A Lady, 1991; Staying Sane in Australia, 1991; Men, Women and Other Necessities, 1992; How to Mate in Australia, 1993; The Little Book of Aussie Wisdom, 1994; A Hop through Australia's History, 1993; The Little Book of Aussie Insults, 1994. Contributions to: 24 Hours; The Australian; The Australian Jewish Times. Honours: Literature Grant, Australia, 1976. Memberships: Australian Journalist Association, Section of Media; Entertainment and Arts Alliance. Address: PO Box 997, Potts Point, New South Wales 2011, Australia.

TREGLOWN Jeremy Dickinson, b. 24 May 1946, Anglesey, North Wales. Biographer; Editor; Critic. m. (1) Rona Bower, 1970, div. 1982, 1 son, 2 daughters, (2) Holly Urquhart Eley, 1984. Education: BLitt, MA (Oxon); PhD, London. Appointments: Lecturer in English, Lincoln College, Oxford, 1974-77; University College, London, 1977-80; Assistant Editor, 1980-82, Editor, 1982-90, Times Literary Supplement; Chairman of Judges, Booker Prize, 1991; Ferris Professor of Journalism, Princeton University, USA, 1992; Professor of English, University of Warwick, England, 1993-. Publications: Letters of John Wilmot, Earl of Rochester (editor), 1980; Spirit of Wit: Reassessments of Rochester (editor), 1982; Introduction, R L Stevenson, In the South Seas, 1986; Selection, and Introduction, The Lantern Bearers: Essays by Robert Louis Stevenson, 1987; Introductions to reprints of complete novels of Henry Green, 1991-; Roald Dahl: A biography, 1994. Contributions to: Numerous magazines and journals. Membership: Council, Royal Society of Literature. Literary Agent: Rogers, Coleridge and White. Address: Gardens Cottage, Ditchley Park, Enstone, Nr Chipping Norton, Oxon OX7 4EP, England.

TREGOLD Nye. See: **TRANTER Nigel Godwin.**

TREHEARNE Elizabeth. See: **MAXWELL Patricia Anne.**

TRELFORD Donald Gilchrist, b. 9 Nov 1937, Coventry, England. Journalist; Broadcaster. m. (1) Janice Ingram, 1963, 2 sons, 1 daughter, (2) Katherine Louise Mark, 1963, 1 daughter. Education: MA, Selwyn College, Cambridge. Appointments: Pilot Officer, RAF, 1956-58; Staff, newspapers in Coventry and Sheffield, 1961-63; Editor, Times of Malawi and Correspondent in Africa, The Times, Observer, BBC, 1963-66; Deputy News Editor, 1966, Assistant Managing Editor, 1968, Deputy Editor, 1969-75, Director, Editor, 1976-93, Observer; Professor of Journalism Studies, Sheffield University, 1993-. Publications: Siege; County; Champions; Sunday Best; Snookered, 1985; Child or Change (with Gary Kasparov), 1988; Len Hutton Remembered, 1992. Contributions to: The Queen Observed, 1986; Saturday's Boys, 1990. Honours: Editor, Newspaper of the Year, Granada TV Press Awards, 1982; Commended, International Editor of the Year, 1984; Honorary DLitt, Sheffield University, 1990. Memberships: British Executive Committee, International Press Institute, 1976-; Fellow, Royal Society of Arts, 1988-. Literary Agent: Michael Sissons, Peters Fraser and Dunlop, 503/4 Chelsea Harbour, London SW10 0XF, England.

TREMBLAY Gail Elizabeth,b. 15 Dec 1945, Buffalo, New York, USA. Poet; Artist; Faculty Member, The Evergreen State College. Education, BA, Drama, University of New Hampshire, 1967; MFA, Creative Writing, University of Oregon, 1969. Publications: Night Gives Woman the Word, 1979; Talking to the Grandfathers, 1980; Indian Singing in 20th Century America, 1990. Contributions to: Wooster Review; Denver Quarterly; Calyx; Northwest Review; Maize. Honour: Alfred E Richards Poetry Prize, 1967. Memberships: Board Member, Woman's Caucus for Art; Vice-President of the Board, Indian Youth of America; Native American Writers Circle of the Americas. Address: Seminar 3127, The Evergreen State College, Olympia, WA 98505, USA.

TREMLETT George William, b. 5 Sept 1939, England. Author; Journalist; Bookseller. m. Jane Mitchell, 1971, 3 sons. Publications: 17 biographies of Rock Musicians, published in many different countries, 1974-77; Living Cities, 1979; Caitlin (with Mrs Caitlin Thomas), 1986; Clubmen, 1987; Homeless, Story of St Mungo's, 1989; Little Legs (with Roy Smith), 1989; Rock Gold, 1990; Dylan Thomas: In The Mercy of His Means, 1991; Gadaffi: The Desert Mystic, 1993; David Bowie, 1994. Honours: OBE, for community and local government work. Memberships include: Advisory Panel, BBC Community Programme Unit, 1985-. Literary Agents: A M Heath & Co Ltd, London, England; Tony Secunda, San Francisco, USA. Address: Corran House, Laugharne, Carmarthen, Dyfed SA33 4SJ, Wales.

TRENHAILE John Stevens, b. 1949. British. Publications: Kyril, 1981; A View from the Square, 1983; Nocturne for the General, 1985; The Mahjong Spies, 1986; The Gates of Exquisite View, 1987; The Scroll of Benevolence, 1988; Kyrsalis, 1989; Acts of Betrayal, 1990; Blood Rules, 1991; The Tiger of Desire, 1992; A Means to Evil, 1993. Address: c/o Blake Friedman, Literary Agents, 37-41 Gower Street, London WC1E 6HH, England.

TRENTON Gail. See: **GRANT Neil David Mountfield.**

TRESILLIAN Richard. See: **ELLIS Royston.**

TREVELYAN (Walter) Raleigh, b. 6 July 1923, Port Blair, Andaman Islands. Author. Literary appointments: Publisher, 1948-88, with Collins, Hutchinson, Michael Joseph (Editorial Director, 13 years), Hamish Hamilton, Jonathan Cape, Bloomsbury. Publications: The Fortress, 1956; A Hermit Disclosed, 1960; The Big Tomato, 1966; Princes Under the Volcano, 1972; The Shadow of Vesuvius, 1976; A Pre-Raphaelite Circle, 1978; Rome '44, 1982; Shades of the Alhambra, 1984; The Golden Oriole, 1987; La Storia dei Whitaker, 1989; Grand Dukes and Diamonds, 1991; A Clear Premonition, 1994; Italian Short Stories: Penguin Parallel Texts (editor), 1965. Contributions to: National Trust publications; Apollo; Connoisseur; Harpers Queen; John Ryland's Bulletin; Reviews in most leading daily and Sunday papers. Honours: John Florio Prize for translation from Italian, The Outlaws by Luigi Meneghello. Memberships: Committee Member, Fellow, PEN; Fellow, Royal Society of Literature; Brooks's; Groucho Club; Chairman, Anglo-Italian Society for Protection of Animals. Literary Agent: A M Heath, 79 St Martin's Lane, London WC2N 4AA, England. Addresses: 18 Hertford Street, London W1Y 7DB, England; St Cadix, St Veep, Lostwithiel, Cornwall PL22 0PB, England.

TREVOR Meriol, b. 15 Apr 1919, London, England. Author. Education: BA, St Hugh's College, Oxford, 1942. Publications: Newman: The Pillar of the Cloud, Newman: Light in Winter, 2 volumes, 1962; Pope John, 1967; The Arnolds, 1973; The City and the World, 1970; The Golden Palaces, 1985; James II: The Shadow of a Crown, 1988; 16 historical novels, 1956-; 2 biographical books; 12 books for older children, 1949-66. Contributions to: Reviewer for Times Literary Supplement, 1960s, 1970s. Honours: James Tait Black Memorial Prize, 1962; Elected Fellow, Royal Society of Literature, 1967. Address: 41 Fitzroy House, Pulteney Street, Bath BA2 4DW, England.

TREVOR William. See: **COX William Trevor.**

TRICKETT (Mabel) Rachel, b. 20 Dec 1923, Lathom, Lancashire, England. Novelist. Education: MA, Lady Margaret Hall, Oxford, 1947. Appointments: Principal, St Hughe's College, Oxford, 1973-91. Publications: The Return Home, 1952; The Course of Love, 1954; Point of Honour, 1958; A Changing Place, 1962; The Elders, 1966; The Visit to Timon, 1970; Plays, Antigone (1954) and Silas Marner (1960), music by John Joubert; The Honest Muse: A Study in Augustan Verse, 1967; Browning's Lyricism, 1971; Tennyson's Craft, 1981. Honours: Rhys Memorial Prize, 1953; Honorary Fellow, Lady Margaret Hall, 1978. Address: Flat 4, 18 Norham Gardens, Oxford OX2 6QB, England.

TRIER MORCH Dea, b. 9 Dec 1941, Copenhagen, Denmark. Writer; Graphic Artist. m. Troels Trier, 1 son, 2 daughters. Education: Graduated, The Royal Academy of Fine Arts, Copenhagen, 1964; Postgraduate studies, Academies of Fine Arts, Warsaw, Cracow, Belgrade, Leningrad, Prague, 1964-67. Appointments: Chairman, Danish Writers Associtin, 1990-91. Publications: Sorgmunter socialisme, 1968; Polen, 1970; Vinterbom, 1976, translated into 22 languages; En Trekant, 1977; Ind i verden, 1977; Kastaniealleen, 1978; Den Indre By, 1980; Aftenstjernen, 1982; Morgengaven, 1984; Da jeg opdagede Amerika, 1986; Skibet i flasken, 1988; Barnet uden navn, 1990; Pengene og livet, 1990; Landskab i to etager, 1992; Graphic works, mainly illustrations of own novels, exhibited in 22 countries in Europe, USA, Latin America, Asia. Honours: Elected Danish Author of the Year, 1977; Awarded Government Stipend for Life, 1985, for Work, 1994; The Hvass Foundation, 1985; Peter Sabroe Children's Prize, 1987; Tagea Brandt Travel Fellowship, 1988. Contributions to: Vindrosen; Clarté; Dagens Nyheter; ALEF magazine on Jewish culture; Ugeskrift for læger; Information; Others. Memberships: PEN Club, Denmark; Union of Danish Graphic Artists; The Danish Fiction Writers Association. Literary Agent: Gyldendal Publishing, Copenhagen, Denmark. Address: Jens Juels Gade 7, 2100 Copenhagen, Denmark.

TRIGGER Bruce Graham, b. 18 June 1937, Cambridge, Ontario, Canada. Professor of Anthropology. m. Barbara Marian Welch, 7 Dec 1968, 2 daughters. Education: BA, University of Toronto, 1959; PhD, Yale University, 1964. Appointments: *Assistant Professor,* Northwestern University, 1963-64; Assistant Professor, 1964-67, Associate Professor, 1967-69, Professor, 1969-, McGill University. Publications: History and Settlement in Lower Nubia, 1965; The Huron: Farmers of the North, 1969, revised, 1990; The Children of Aataentsic, 1976, revised 1987; Time and Traditions, 1978; Vol ed Handbook of North American Indians, Vol 15, Northeast 1978; Natives and Newcomers, 1985; The History of Archaeological Thought, 1989; Early Civilizations: Ancient Egypt in Context, 1992; Late Nubian Settlement at Arminna West, 1967; Beyond History, 1968; Cartier's Hochelaga and the Dawson Site, 1972; Nubia Under the Pharaohs, 1976; Gordon Childe, 1980. Contributions to: Antiquity; American Antiquity; World Archaeology; Man. Editor, Native and Northern Series, McGill-Queen's University Press. Honours: Canadian Silver Jubilee Medal, 1977; Cornplanter Medal, 1979; Innis-Gerin Medal, Royal Society of Canada, 1985; DSc, University of New Brunswick, 1987; John Porter Prize, 1988; DLitt, University of Waterloo, 1990; Prix du Québec, 1991; Honorary Member, Prehistoric Society, England, 1991; Honorary Fellow, Society of Antiquaries of Scotland, 1993. Memberships: Various professional organizations. Address: Department of Anthropology, McGill University, 855 Sherbrooke Street West, Montreal, Quebec, H3A 2T7, Canada.

TRIPP Miles Barton (John Michael Brett, Michael Brett), b. 5 May 1923, Ganwick Corner, England. Writer. Publications include: Kilo Forty, 1963; The Eighth Passenger, 1969; A Man Without Friends, 1970; High Heels, 1987; The Frightened Wife, 1987; The Cords of Vanity, 1989; Video Vengeance, 1990; The Dimensions of Deceit, 1993. Memberships: Society of Authors; Crime Writers Association, Chairman 1968-69; Detection Club. Literary Agent: The Peters Fraser and Dunlop Group Ltd, London, England. Address: The Peters Fraser and Dunlop Group Ltd, 5th Floor, The Chambers, Chelsea Harbour, Lots Road, London SW10 0XF, England.

TRISTRAM Uvedale Francis Barrington, b. 20 Mar 1915. Journalist. m. Elizabeth Frances Eden-Pearson, 8 Sept 1939, 1 daughter. Appointments: Morning Post; Assistant Editor, Aeropilot; Managing Editor, Hulton Publications, 1960-61; Editorial Manager, Longacre Press, 1961-62; Director of Information and Broadcasting, Basutoland, 1962-67; Director of Information, UK Freedom from Hunger Campaign, 1967-73; Founder Editor, World Hunger. Publications: Adventure in Oil, 1958; John Fisher; Basutoland, 1961. Contributions to: Sunday Telegraph; Time and Tide; Tablet; Universe; Catholic Herald; Commercial Times. Honours: Rics Award, Best Property Column in Weekly Paper, 1988, 1991; ISVA Provincial Property of the Year, 1990. Memberships: Guild of Catholic Writers, Master of the Keys 1987-91, Deputy Master 1991-; Institute of Journalists. Address: 19 Mallards' Reach, Weybridge, Surrey KT13 9HQ, England.

TROLLOPE Joanna (Caroline Harvey), b. 9 Dec 1943. Writer. m. (1) David Roger William Potter, 1966, 2 daughters, (2) Ian Bayley Curteis, 1985, 2 Stepsons. Education: MA, St Hugh's College, Oxford, 1972. Appointments: Information and Research Department, Foreign Office, 1965-67; Teaching posts at Farnham Girl's Grammar School, Adult education, English for Foreigners and Daneshill School, 1967-79. Publications: Eliza Stanhope, 1978; Parson Harding's Daughter, 1979; Leaves from the Valley, 1980; The City of Gems, 1981; The Steps of the Sun, 1983; Britannia's Daughters: a study of women in the British Empire, 1983; The Taverners' Place, 1986; The Choir, 1988; A Village Affair, 1989; A Passionate Man, 1990; The Rector's Wife, 1991; The Men and the Girls, 1992; A Spanish Lover, 1993; The Country Habit: an anthology, 1993; as Caroline Harvey: Legacy of Love, 1992; A Second Legacy, 1993; Forthcoming: The Best of Friends, 1995; Contributions to newspapers and magazines. Hobbies: Reading; Conversation; Very long baths. Address: c/o Peters, Fraser & Dunlop, Fifth Floor, The Chambers, Chelsea Harbour, SW10 0XF, England.

TRONSKI Bronisław, b. 24 Sept 1921, Wilno, Poland. Journalist; Writer. m. Janina Zajacowna, 3 July 1980, 1 son, 1 daughter. Education: Academy of Political Sciences, 1946-48; MA, Law, Jagiellonian University, Cracow, 1949. Appointments: Staff: Socjalistyczna Agencja Prasowa, 1946-48, Agencja Robotnicza, 1948-64, Polska Agencja Prasowa, 1964; Foreign Correspondent, Far East, 1959-60, Balkan Countries, 1972-76, Algieria and Tunisia, 1980-82; Special Correspondent, European countries. Publications: Tedy przeszła Smierc, 1957; Na Dachu Swiata, 1961; Stonce Nad

Stara Planina, 1979; W Cieniu Nadziei, 1980; Trucja Bez Tajemnic, 1981; Algierskie Osobliwosci, 1984; Test Pan Wolny, 1987; Tanczacy prezydent, 1988; Mozaika sródziemnomorska, 1988; Smak ziemi obiecanej, 1990; Stambul, 1992; I w Ostrej swiecisz Bramie, sladami mlodego Adama Mickiewicza, 1993; Translations of dramas. Contributions to: Numerous journals and magazines. Honours: Award, President of Polish Parliament; Award, Parliament Reporters Club, 1965, 1966; Award, Publishing Company Epoka, 1979; Golden Pen Award, Bulgarian Journalists Association; Award, Polonia Club, Polish Journalists Association, 1985; Award, Weekly Kultura, 1988; Award, Counsel Fund of Literature, 1988; Award, International Publishers Club, 1990; Many others. Memberships: Polish Writers Association; Polish Journalists Association; Authors and Composers Association; Vice-President, Union of Warsaw Insurgents, 1991-. Address: Rakowiecka Street 33, App 30, 02-519 Warsaw, Poland.

TROTMAN Jack (John Penn), Canadian. Writer. Appointments: Officer, British Army Intelligence Corps, 1940-46; Foreign Office, 1946-48; Joint Intelligence Bureau, Ottawa, Canada, 1949-65; Canadian Department of National Defence, 1965-73; NATO International Staff, Paris, France, 1973-77; President, National Trust for Jersey, Channel Islands, 1984-87, 1990-92. Publications: Notice of Death, US as An Ad for Murder, 1982; Deceitful Death, US as Stag-Dinner Death, 1983; A Will to Kill, 1983; Mortal Term, 1984; A Deadly Sickness, 1985; Unto the Grave, 1986, Barren Revenge, 1986; Accident Prone, 1987; Outrageous Exposures, 1988; A Feast of Death, 1989; A Killing to Hide, 1990; A Knife Ill-Used, 1991; Death's Long Shadow, 1991; A Legacy of Death, 1992; A Haven of Danger, 1993; Widow's End, 1993; The Guilty Party, 1994. Address: c/o Murray Pollinger, 222 Old Brompton Road, London SW5 0BZ, England.

TROW George W S, b. 28 Sept 1943, Greenwich, Connecticut, USA. Education: AB, Harvard University, 1965. Appointments: Staff Writer, New Yorker, New York City, 1966-. Publications: Prairie Avenue (three-act play) first produced Off-Broadway at the South Street Theatre, April 1979; The Tennis Game (three-act play) first produced Off-Broadway at the Theatre of the Open Eye, Feb 1978; Dramatists Play Service, 1979; Elizabeth Dead (one-act play) first produced in New York City at the Cubiculo Theatre, Nov 1980; Bullies (collection of stories) Little, Brown, 1980; Within the Context of No Context (nonfiction essays, contains Within the Context of No Context and Within That Context, One Style), Boston, 1981; The City in the Mist (novel) Little Brown, 1984; "Needs" in The Best American Essays, 1992, Ticknor & Fields New York, 1992. Contributions to: Periodicals, including New Yorker and Harper's. Honours: Jean Stein Award from the American Academy and Institute of Arts and Letters, 1986, for essays, Within the Context of No Context and The Harvard Black Rock Forest and for novel, The City in the Mist; Fellow, John Simon Guggenheim Foundation, 1994-95. Literary Agent: Andrew Wylie, Wylie & Aitken, 250 W 57th Street, NY 10107, USA. Address: c/o New Yorker, 20 West 43rd Street, New York, NY 10036, USA.

TRUCK Robert-Paul (Count), b. 3 May 1917, Calais, France. Writer (Poet and Historian). m. Jeanne Brogniart, 24 July 1942, 1 daughter. Education: Baccalaureat, 1935; French Naval School, 1938; Naval Officer, 1939. Literary Appointments: Poet, 1938; Art Critic, 1940; Lecturer, 1948; Literary Critic, 1966; Historian, 1975. Publications: Heures folles, poems, 1938; Au bord de la nuit, poems, 1948; Intersignes, poems, 1953; Medecins de la honte (with Betty Truck), 1975; Mengele, l'ange de la mort (with Betty Truck), 1976; Vertiges, poems, 1989; 1492-1992 (Foreword of Les Poetes et l'Amerique), 1991; Bois des Iles, poems, 1992; Marche des Rois, poem, 1994; Cicatrices, poems, 1994; Poems in anthologies: Les Poetes de la Vie, Les Poetes de la Mer, Poeti Francesi d'Oggi, Carterie Poetique, 1984, Flammes Vives, L'Encyclopedie Poetique, Les Grandes Anthologies, Parnassus of World Poets. Contributions to: Les Cahiers du Nord; Maintenant; Quo Vadis, Points et Contrepoints; Elysees-Jonchere; Nostra; Historia; Life; L'Eco del Popolo; Washington Post, Annuaire National des Lettres. Honours: Master of the Intellectual Elite, Milan, Italy, 1953; Diploma of Honour, Relations Latines, Milan, 1954; Selection Diploma, Academic Institute of Paris, 1981; Diploma of Honour, La Gloire International Prize, Rome, Italy, 1982; Certificate of Merit, Men of Achievement, 1982; Diploma di Benemerenza, 1983, Targa d'Onore, 1983; Gold Palms, 1984, Leonardo da Vinci International Academy, Rome, Doctor of Literature (Honoris Causa), The Marquis Giuseppe Scicluna (1855-1907) International University Foundation, Delaware, USA, 1987; Commemorative Medal of Honor, American Biographical Institute, 1987; Medal for Peace, Albert Einstein International Academy Foundation, Missouri, USA, 1989; Shield of

Valor, American Biograhcial Institute, 1992; Cross of Merit with Collar Ribbon, Albert Einstein International Academy Foundation, USA, 1992. Memberships: Fellow, International Academy of Poets, Cambridge, England; Fellow, World Literary Academy, Cambridge; Titular Member, Leonardo da Vinci International Academy; Academic Institute of Paris; Society of French Poets. Address: Varouna, 49 Rue de Lhomel, 62600 Berck-Plage, France.

TRUMAN Jill, b. 12 June 1934, Enfield, Middlesex, England. Teacher; Writer. m. Tony Truman, 31 Mar 1956 (dec. 1975), 1 son, 3 daughters. Education: BA, English Literaturem, 1955; Postgraduate Certificate in Drama, 1979. Publications: Letter to My Husband, book, 1988; The Web, theatre, 1991; Radio plays for BBC Radio 4 and 5: Letter to My Husband, 1986; Gone Out-Back Soon, 1988; Travels in West Africa, 1990; Flit, 1992; For Lizzie, radio play for Celebration Radio, 1994; Commissions: Kings of the Night, musical for Southmead Music Project, 1993; Cholne, The Puppet Van, 1994. Contributions to: Letter to My Husband serialised in magazines, UK, USA, Australia, Belgium. Honours: Special Commendation for Women's Radio Group for facilitating Nine Lives, New London Playwrights Festival, 1992. Membership: Writers Guild of Great Britain. Literary Agent: June Hall. Address: 34 Wellington Park Road, Clifton, Bristol BS8 2UW, England.

TSALOUMAS Dimitris, b. 13 Oct 1921, Leros, Greece. Teacher; Poet. m. Isle Wulff, 1958, 2 sons, 2 daughters. Appointments include: Teacher, Victorian Schools, 1958-82; Writer in Residence, Oxford University, 1989; Writer in Residence, Melbourne University, Queensland University, La Trobe University. Publications: Resurrection, 1967; Triptych for a Second Coming, 1974; Observations for a Hypochondriac, 1974; The House with the Eucalyptus, 1975; The Sick Barber and Other Characters, 1979; The Book of Epigrams, 1981; The Observatory: Selected Poems, 1983; Falcon Drinking: The English Poems, 1988; Portrait of a Dog, 1991; The Barge, 1993. Editor, Translator of Poetry. Honours include: Australia Council Grant and Fellowship; National Book Council Award, 1983; Wesley M Wright Prize for Poetry, 1994; Patrick White Award, 1994. Address: 72 Glenhuntly Road, Elwood, VA 3184, Australia.

TSUYUKI Shig eru. See: KIRKUP James.

TUBB E(dwin) C(harles) (Chuck Adams, Jud Cary, J F Clarkson, James S Farrow, James R Fenner, Charles S Graham, Charles Grey, Volsted Gridban, Alan Guthrie, George Holt, Gill Hunt, E F Jackson, Gregory Kern, King Lang, Mike Lantry, P Lawrence, Chet Lawson, Arthur MacLean, Carl Maddox, M L Powers, Paul Schofield, Brian Shaw, Roy Sheldon, John Stevens, Edward Thomson, Douglas West, Eric Wilding), b. 15 Oct 1919, London, England. Writer. Literary appointment: Editor, Authentic Science Fiction magazine, London, 1956-57. Publications include: Over 100 under various pseudonyms; Science fiction/fantasy: Saturn Patrol, 1951; Argentis, 1952; Planetoid Disposals Ltd, 1953; The Living World, 1954; Alien Dust, 1955; The Space-Born, 1956; Touch of Evil, 1959; Moon Base, 1964; Ten From Tomorrow, short stories, 1966; Death Is A Dream. 1967; COD Mars, 1968; STAR Flight, 1969; The Jester at Scar, 1970; Lallia, 1971; Century of the Manikin, 1972; Mayenne, 1973; Veruchia, 1973; Zenya, 1974; Atilus the Slave, 1975; Jack of Swords, 1976; Haven of Darkness, 1977; Incident on Ath, 1978; Stellar Assignment, 1979; The Luck Machine, 1980; Suspense and Western novels: The Fighting Fury, 1955; Scourge of the South, 1956; Wagon Trail, 1957; Target Death, 1961; Too Tough To Handle, 1962; Airborne Commando, 1963; The Quillian Sector, 1978; Web of Sand, 1979; Iduna's Universe, 1979; The Terra Data, 1980; World of Promise, 1980; Nectar of Heaven, 1981; The Terridae, 1981; The Coming Event, 1982; Earth is Heaven, 1982; Melome, 1983; Stardeath, 1983; Angado, 1984; Symbol of Terra, 1984; The Temple of Truth, 1985. Contributions to: 230 stories to magazines and journals. Literary Agent: Carnell Literary Agency. Address: 67 Houston Road, London SE23 2RL, England.

TUCKER Eva Marie, b. 18 Apr 1929, Berlin, Germany. Writer. m. 11 Mar 1950 (widowed 1987), 3 daughters. Education: BA Honours, German, English, University of London. Appointments: C Day Lewis Writing Fellow, Vauxhall Manor School, London, 1978-79; Hawthornden Writing Fellowship, 1991. Publications: Contact, novel, 1966; Drowning, novel, 1969; Radetzkymarch by Joseph Roth, translation, 1974; Contributions to: BBC Radio 3 and 4; Encounter; London Magazine; Woman's Journal; Vogue; Harpers; Spectator; Listener; PEN International. Memberships: English PEN; Turner Society. Address: 63B Belsize Park Gardens, London NW3 4JN, England.

TUCKER Helen, b. 1926, American. Appointments: Reporter, Times-News, Burlington, 1946-47, Times-News, Twin Falls, 1948-49, Statesman, Boise, 1950-51, Raleigh Times, 1955-57; Continuity Writer, Radio KDYL, Salt Lake City, Utah, 1952-53; Continuity Supervisor, Radio WPTF, Raleigh, 1953-55; Editorial Assistant, Columbia University Press, 1959-60; Director of Publicity and Publications, North Carolina Museum of Art, Raleigh, 1967-70. Publications: The Sound of Summer Voices, 1969; The Guilt of August Fielding, 1972; No Need of Glory, 1973; The Virgin of Lontano, 1974; A Strange and Ill-Starred Marriage, 1978; A Reason for Rivalry, 1979; A Mistress to the Regent, An Infamous Attachement, The Halverton Scandal, 1980; A Wedding Day Deception, 1981; The Double Dealers, Season of Dishonor, 1982; Ardent Vows, 1983; Bound by Honor, 1984; The Lady's Fancy, 1991; Bold Impostor, 1991. Honours: First Woman to receive the Distinguished Alumni Award, Wake Forest University, 1971; Franklin County Artist of the Year Award, 1992. Address: 2930 Hostetler Street, Raleigh, NC 27609, USA.

TUCKER Martin, b. 8 Feb 1928, Philadelphia, Pennsylvania, USA. Author; Professor of English. Education: BA, New York University, 1949; MA, University of Arizona, 1954; PhD, New York University, 1963. Literary Appointments: Editor, Confrontation magazine, 1970-; Executive Board, PEN American Center, 1973-; Governing Board, Poetry Society of America, 1984-88. Publications: Joseph Conrad, 1976; Africa in Modern Literature, 1967; Homes of Locks and Mysteries, 1982 (poems); Sam Shepard, 1992; Literary Exile in the United States, 1991; Ed: The Critical Temper, Vols I-V 1970-89; Ed: Modern British Literature, Vols I-IV 1967-76. Contributions to: New York Times Book Review; The Nation; The New Republic; The Saturday Review; Research in African Literature; Northern Centinel; Abiko (Japan); North Atlantic Review; African Publishing Book Record; The Literary Review. Honours: NEA/Co-ordinating Council and Literary Magazine Award for Editorial Distinction on Confrontation, 1976, 1984; English-Speaking Union Award, 1982. Memberships: PEN; Poetry Society of America; Authors Guild; National Book Critics Circle; African Literature Association; Modern Language Association; African Studies Association; Phi Beta Kappa. Address: 90 A Dosoris Lane, Glen Cove, NY 11542, USA.

TUCKMAN Bruce W, b. 24 Nov 1938, New York, USA. College Professor. m. Darby Godwin, 26 July 1980, 1 son, 1 daughter. Education: BS, Psychology, Rensselaer Polytechnic Institute, 1960; MA, Psychology, 1962, PhD, Psychology, 1963, Princeton University. Appointments: Research Associate, Princeton University, 1963; Adjunct Professor, University College, University of Maryland, 1963-65; Research Psychologist, Naval Medical Research Institute, Bethesda, Maryland, 1963-65; Associate Professor of Education, 1965-70, Professor of Education,1970-78, Rutgers University; Director of Research, Graduate School of Education, Rutgers University, 1975-78; Dean, School of Education, Baruch College of The City University of New York, 1978-82; Senior Research Fellow, Center for Advanced Study in Education, City University of New York, 1982-83; Dean, 1983-85, Professor, 1985-, College of Education, The Florida State University. Consulting Editor, Journal of Experimental Education, 1987-93; Executive Editor, 1993-; Contributing Editor and Columnist, Educational Technology Magazine, 1981-. Publications: Conducting Educational Research, 1972, 1978, 1988; Evaluating Instructional Programs, 1979, 1985; Testing for Teachers, 1975, 1988; Effective College Management, 1987; Analyzing and Designing Educational Research, 1985; Preparing to Teach the Disadvantaged, 1969; Long Road to Boston (novel) 1988; Educational Psychology, 1992; Conducting Educational Research, 1994 (4th ed). Contributions to: Executive Editor, Journal of Experimental Education, 1993-; Runner's World; Phi Delta Kappan; Journal of Educational Psychology; American Education Research Journal; Journal of Educational Research. Honours: National Institute of Mental Health Fellowship, 1961-63; New Jersey Association of English Teachers Author's Award, 1969; Phi Delta Kappa Research Award, 1973; Outstanding Teaching Award, 1993; Florida State University Teaching Award, 1993. Memberships: Fellow, American Psychological Association; American Educational Research Association; Gulf Winds Track Club. Address: Department of Educational Research, B 197 Florida State University, Tallahassee, FL 32306, USA.

TUDOR Andrew Frank, b. 19 Nov 1942, Edinburgh, Scotland. University Lecturer. Education: BA, Sociology, 1965. Publications: Theories of Film, 1973; Image and Influence, 1974; Beyond Empiricism, 1982; Monsters and Mad Scientists, 1989. Contributions to: Film Critic for New Society, 1975-82. Address: Department of Sociology, University of York, Heslington, York YO1 5DD, England.

TUDOR-CRAIG Pamela Wynn (Wedgewood), b. 26 June 1928, London, England. Art Historian. m. (1) Algernon James Riccarton Tudor-Craig, 27 July 1956 (dec. 1969), 1 daughter, (2) Sir John Wedgwood, 1 May 1982 (dec. 1989). Education: 1st Class Honours degree, 1949, PhD, 1952, Courtauld Institute, University of London. Appointments: Taught at numerous American colleges with houses in England, currently Grinell, London and American Heritage Association. Publications: Richard III, 1973; Secret Life of Paintings (co-author), 1986; Bells Guide to Westminster Abbey (co-author), 1986; Age of Chivalry, Royal Academy (contributor), 1987; Exeter Cathedral, 1991; Anglo-Saxon Wall Paintings, 1991; Television: The Secret Life of Paintings, own series, 1986. Contributions to: Arts page, Church Times, 1988-; Harlaxton Medieval Studies, 3 issues; Anglo-Saxon England; British Archaeological Journal; Royal Archaeological Journal; Others. Honours: Honorary Doctor of Humanities, William Jewell College, 1983. Memberships: Fellow, Society of Antiquaries, 1958-, Council Member 1989-92; Committees for the Care of Churches and Cathedrals; Cathedrals Advisory Commission, 1975-90; Paintings Committee; Fabric Committees for Westminster Abbey, Peterborough Cathedral, Southwell Cathedral; Cultural Affairs Committee, English-Speaking Union. Address: Home Farm, Leighton Bromswold, Nr Huntingdon PE18 0SL, England.

TUFTY Barbara Jean, b. 28 Dec 1923, Iowa City, Iowa, USA. Conservation Writer and Editor. m. Harold G Tufty, 29 Dec 1948, 2 sons, 1 daughter. Education: Ba, Botany, Duke University; Postgraduate classes, New School for Social Research, New York City, 1946; Sorbonne, Paris, France, 1948; University of Colorado, 1949, 1950, 1951. Appointments: Editor, Union Carbide and Carbon Corporation, 1945-47;Writer, University of Coloradop, Extension Center, 1949-51; Editor, Freelance Writer, Tufty Associates; Science Writer, Science Service, 1948-72; Science Writer, National Academy of Sciences, 1970-72; Editor, National Science Foundation, 1972-84; Conservation Writer and Editor, Audubon Naturalist Society, 1986-. Publications: 1001 Questions Answered About Natural Land Disasters, 1969, paperback, 1978; 1001 Questions Answered About Storms, 1970, paperback, 1986; Cells, Units of Life, 1973; Crafts in the Ivory Coast, translation, French to English, 1963; Wildflowers of the Washington-Baltimore Area, co-author, 1995. Contributions to: Books: Science Year Encyclopedia, 1970; Women in Science, 1979; Book of Biology, 1985; Magazines: The Atlantic Naturalist; Mosaic Magazine; Science News Letter; Bombay Natural History Society Journal; Coal Age; Iron Age. Honours: Chi Delta Phi, 1945; Honorary Life Member (1st Woman), Bombay Natural History Society, 1960; Thomas Stokes Honourable Mention Writing Award, 1972; Catherine O'Brien Honourable Mention Writing Award, 1972; Writing Fellowships at Ossabaw Island Institute, Library of Congress. Memberships Include: Washington Independent Writers; National Association of Science Writers; The Nature Conservancy; American Association for the Advancement of Science; New York Academy of Sciences; Washington Environmental Writers Association; Environmental Writers Association. Address: 3812 Livingston Street NW, Washington, DC 20015, USA.

TUGENDHAT Julia. See: **DOBSON Julia Lissant.**

TULLY William Mark, b. 24 Aug 1935, Calcutta, India. Journalist. m. Margaret Tully, 13 Aug 1960, 2 sons, 2 daughters. Education: Trinity Hall, Cambridge, 1956-59. Publications: Amritsar; Mrs Gandhi's Last Battle; Raj to Rajiv; No Full Stops in India. Honours: OBE; Dimbleby Award, British Academy of Film and Television Arts; Broadcasting Press Guild; Padmashri. Literary Agent: Gill Coleridge. Address: 1 Nizamuddin East, New Delhi 110013, India.

TUOHY John Francis (Frank), b. 2 May 1925, Uckfield, Sussex, England. Writer. Education: MA Honours, King's College, Cambridge, 1946. Publications: The Animal Game, 1957; The Warm Nights of January, 1960; The Ice Saints, 1964; Portugal, 1970; W B Yeats, 1976; Collected Stories, 1984. Contributions to: Numerous magazines and journals. Honours: Katherine Mansfield Prize, 1960; James Tait Black Memorial Prize, 1964; Geoffrey Faber Memorial Prize, 1964; William Heinemann Award, 1978. Memberships: PEN; Society of Authors. Literary Agent: The Peters Fraser and Dunlop Group Ltd, London, England. Address: Shatwell Cottage, Yarlington, Nr Wincanton, Somerset BA9 8DL, England.

TURBILL Janice Betina, b. 13 Mar 1944, Sydney, Australia. University Lecturer. Education: BA, Macquarie University, 1979; MED, Sydney University, 1985; PhD, Wollongong University, 1994. Publications: No Better Way To Teach Writing, 1982; Now We Want To Write, 1983; Towards a Reading Writing Classroom, (with Andrea Butler) 1984; Coping with Chaos, (with B Cambourne), 1987; Responsive Evaluation, (with B Cambourne), 1994; contributed to other books in USA and Australia and to Frameworks: Staff Development Program in Literacy & Learning. Memberships: Society of Authors of Australia; Fellow, Australian College of Education. Address Faculty of Education University of Wollongong, NSW, Australia 2522.

TURK Frances Mary, b. 14 Apr 1915, Huntingdon, England. Novelist. Publications: Numerous books including: Paddy O'Shea, 1937; The Precious Hours, 1938; Paradise Street, 1939; Lovable Clown, 1941; Angel Hill, 1942; The Five Grey Geese, 1944; Salutation, 1949; The Small House at Ickley, 1951; The Gentle Flowers, 1952; The Dark Wood, 1954; The Glory and the Dream, 1955; Dinny Lightfoot, 1956; No Through Road, 1957; The White Swan, 1958; The Secret Places, 1961; The Guarded Heart, 1964; Legacy of Love, 1967; Fair Recompense, 1969; Goddess of Threads, 1975; A Visit to Marchmont, 1977; Candle Corner, 1986. Contributions to: The Writer; Woman's Way; Land Girl; Home and Country; Cambridgeshire Life; Beds and Northants Life; Sunday Companion; Peterborough Evening Telegraph; Many other journals. Memberships: Romantic Novelists Association; Many other professional organisations. Address: Hillrise, Brampton Road, Buckden, Huntingdon PE18 9UH, England.

TURNBULL Gael Lundin, b. 7 Apr 1928, Edinburgh, Scotland. Writer; Former Medical Practitioner. m. (1) Jonnie May Draper, 1952, 3 d. (2) Pamela Jill Iles, 1983. Education: BA, Cambridge University, 1948; MD, University of PA, 1951. Publications: A Trampoline, 1968; Scantlings, 1970; A Gathering of Poems, 1950-80, 1983; A Year and a Day, 1985; A Winter Journey, 1987; While Breath Persist, 1992; Numerous Collections Since 1954. Contributions to: Numerous Journals and Magazines. Honour: Alice Hunt Bartlett Award, 1969. Address: 12 Strathearn Place, Edinburgh, EH9 2AL, Scotland.

TURNER Alberta Tucker,b. 22 October 1919, New York City, USA. Poet; Professor. m. 9 Apr 1943, 1 son, 1 daughter. Education: BA, Hunter College, 1940; MA, Wellesley College, 1941; PhD, Ohio State University, 1946. Appointments: Director, Cleveland State University Poetry Centre, 1964-90; Editor, Field: Contemporary Poetry & Poetics, 1969-; Professor, English, Cleveland State University, 1978-90; Emeritas Professor, 1990-. Publications: 50 Contemporary Poets: The Creative Process, 1977; 45 Contemporary Poems: The Creative Process, 1985; To Make a Poem, 1982; Poets Teaching, 1980; A Belfry of Knees, 1983; Lid and Spoon, 1977; Learning to Count, 1974; Responses to Poetry, 1990; Beginning With And: New Selected Poems, 1994. Contributions Include: Stand; Poetry; Prairie Schooner; Missouri Review; Atlantic Monthly; Poetry Now. Honours: Ohio Arts Council Grant for Poetry, 1980; Cleveland Artists Prize for Literature, 1985; Ohioana Award for Poetry, 1986; Governor's Award for the Arts in Education, 1988. Memberships: PEN; Milton Society of America. Address: 482 Caskey Court, Oberlin, OH 44074, USA.

TURNER Brian (Lindsay), b. 1944, Dunedin, New Zealand. Editor; Poet. Education: Otago Boys High School, 1957-61. Appointments include: Managing Editor, John McIndoe Ltd, Dunedin, 1975-86. Publications: Ladders of Rain, 1978; Ancestors, 1981; Listening to the River, 1983; Bones, 1985; All That Blue Can Be, 1989; Beyond, 1992; New Zealand High Country: Four Seasons, 1983; The Guide to Trout Fishing in Otago, 1994. Honours include: Robert Burns Fellowship, 1984; New Zealand Book Award for Poetry, 1993; Scholarship in Letters, 1994. Address: 2 Upper Junction Road, Sawyers Bay, Dunedin, New Zealand.

TURNER Frederick, b. 19 Nov 1943, East Haddon, Northamptonshire, England. Professor of Humanities; Writer. m. Mei Lin Chang, 25 June 1966, 2 sons. Education: Christ Church, Oxford University, 1962-67; BA 1965, MA 1967, BLitt 1967, English Language and Literature, Oxford. Appointments: Assistant Professor of English, University of California, Santa Barbara, USA, 1967-72; Associate Professor of English, Kenyon College, 1972-85; Editor, Kenyon Review, 1978-83; Visiting Professor of English, University of Exeter, England, 1984-85; Founders Professor of Arts and Humanities, University of Texas at Dallas, Richardson, USA, 1985-. Publications: Shakespeare and the Nature of Time, 1971; Between Two Lives, 1972; The Return, 1979; The New World, 1985; The Garden, 1985; Natural

Classicism, 1986; Genesis: an Epic Poem, 1988; Rebirth of Value, 1991; Tempest, Flute and Oz, 1991; April Wind, 1991; Beauty, 1991; Foamy Sky: the Major Poems of Miklos Radnoti (translation with Zsuzanna Ozsvath), 1992; The Culture of Hope, 1995. Contributions to: Essays in Harper's; Poetry; New Literary History; Poems in Poetry; Southern Review; Poetry Nation Review. Translations in New Hungarian Quarterly; Partisan Review. Honours: Ohioana Prize for Editorial Excellence, 1980; Djerassi Foundation Grant and Residency, 1981; Levinson Poetry Prize, 1983; Missouri Review Essay Prize, 1986; PEN Golden Pen Award, 1992. Memberships: PEN; Modern Language Association. Address: 2668 Aster Drive, Richardson, TX 75082, USA.

TURNER George (Reginald), b. 8 Oct 1916, Melbourne, Australia. Appointments: Employment Officer, Commonwealth Employment Service, Melbourne, 1945-49, Wangaratta, VA, 1949-50; Textile Technician, Bruck Mill, Wangaratta, 1951-64; Senior Employement Officer, Volkswagen Limited, 1964-67 . Publications include: Young Man of Talent, 1959; A Stranger and Afraid, 1961; A Waste of Shame, 1965; The Lame Dog Man, 1967; Beloved Son, Transit of Cassidy, 1978; Vaneglory, 1982; Yesterdays Men, 1983; The Sea and Summer, 1987; A Pursuit of Mircles, 1990; The Destiny Makes, 1993. Honours: Miles Franklin Award, 1962; Arthur C Clarke Award, 1987. Membership: Australian Society of Authors. Literary Agent: Cherry Weiner, 28 Kipling Way, NJ, USA. Address: 4/296 Inkerman Street, East St Kilda, VA 3183, Australia.

TURNER George William, b. 26 Oct 1921, Dannevirke, New Zealand. University Teacher (retired). m. Beryl Horrobin, 18 Apr 1940, 2 sons. Education: BA (NZ), 1944; MA (NZ), 1948; Diploma, New Zealand Library School, 1948; Diploma in English Linguistic Studies, University College, London, England, 1964. Appointments: Tutor and Lecturer, University of Canterbury, New Zealand, 1955-64; Reader, University of Adelaide, 1965-86. Publications: The English Language in Australia and New Zealand, 1966, 2nd edition 1972; Good Australian English (editor), 1972; Stylistics, 1973; Australian Pocket Oxford Dictionary, 2nd edition (editor) 1984; Australian Concise Oxford Dictionary (editor), 1986; The Australian Oxford Paperback Dictionary (co-editor with Beryl Turner), 1989. Contributions to: The Verses in Gunnlaugs saga Ormstungu in the Journal of English and Germanic Phiology, 1977; The Language of Literature in Beitrage zur Phonetik und Linguistik, 1986; English in Australia in The Cambridge History of the English Language, 1994. Honours: Fellow, Australian Academy of the Humanities, 1974; Festschrift: Lexicographical and linguistic studies, edited by T L and Jill Burton, D S Brewer, 1988. Address: 3 Marola Avenue, Rostrevor, SA 5073, Australia.

TURNER Len. See: **FLOREN Lee.**

TURNER Mary. See: **LAMBOT Isobel Mary.**

TURNER Philip William (Stephen Chance), b. 3 Dec 1925, Rossland, British Columbia, Canada. Writer; Dramatist. m. Margaret Diana Samson, 23 Sept 1950, 2 sons, 1 daughter. Education: BA/MA, English Lanaguage & Literature, Oxford University, 1946. Publications: The Bible Story, 1968; The Grange at High Force, 1965; Septimus & the Danedyke Mystery, 1973; The Candlemass Treasure, 1988; Plays: Christ in the Concrete City, 1956, 1965; How Many Miles to Bethlehem? 1987. Honour: Carnegie Medal, 1965. Literary Agent: Watson Little, London, England. Address: St Francis, 181 West Malvern Road, Malvern, Worcs, England.

TURNILL Reginald, b. 12 May 1915, Dover, England. Writer; Broadcaster. m. 10 Sept 1938, 2 s. Education: Fleet Street Reporter. Appointments: Reporter, Industrial Correspondent, Press Association, London, 1930-56; Industrial Correspondent, 1956-58; Aerospace & Defence Correspondent, 1958-75, British Broadcasting Corporation. Publications include: The Language of Space, 1970; Observer's Book of Manned Spaceflight, 1972, 75, 78; Observer's Unmanned Spaceflight, 1974; Observer's Spaceflight Directory, 1978; Space Age, 1980; Jane's Spaceflight Directory, 1984, 86, 87, 88; Space Technology International, 1989, 90, 91, 92; World Aerospace Development, 1993; Celebrating Concorde, 1994. Contributions to: Zodiac; Executive Travel; Aerospace; Aviation Week; Space Technology. Memberships: British Interplanetary Society; Royal Aeronautical Society. Address: Somerville Lodge, Hillside, Sandgate, Kent CT20 3DB, England.

TUSIANI Joseph,b. 14 Jan 1924, San Marco in Lamis, Foggia, Italy. University Professor. Education: DLit, University of Naples, Italy

and College of Mount St Vincent, USA. Publications Include: The Complete Poems of Michelangelo, 1960; Envoy from Heaven, 1965; Tasso's Jerusalem Delivered, 1970; Gente Mia and Other Poems, 1978; Rosa Rosarum, poems in Latin, 1984; In Exilio Rerum, in Latin, 1985; Autobiography: La Parola Difficile, 1988; La Parola Nuova, 1991; La Parola Antica, 1992; Confinia Lucis et UmbZae, poems in Latin, 1990; Il Ritozno, 1992; Annemale Parlante, poems in the Apulian dialect, 1994; Dante's Lyric Poems, 1992. Contributions to: Numerous journals including: New York Times; New Yorker; Catholic World; Sign; Spirit; Classical Outlook; La parola. Honours: Greenwood Prize, Poetry Society of England, 1956; Alice Fay di Castagnoia Award, Poetry Society of America, 1969; Spirit Gold Medal, Catholic Poetry Society of America. Memberships: Past Vice President, Poetry Society of America; Past Director, Catholic Poetry Society of America. Address: 2140 Tomlinson Avenue, Bronx, NY 10461, USA.

TUTOLA Amos, b. June 1920, Abeokuta, Western Nigeria. Novelist. Education: Anglican Central School, Abeokuta. Appointments: Visiting Research Fellow, University of Ife, 1979. Publications: The Palm Wine Drinkard, His Dead Palm Wine Tapester in the Dead's Town, 1952; My Life in the Bush of Ghosts, 1954; Simbi and the Styr of the Dark Jungle, 1955; Ajaiyi and His Inherited Poverty, 1967; The Witch Herbalist of the Remote Town, 1981; The Wild Hunter in the Bush of the Ghosts, 1982; Pauper Brawler and Slanderer, 1987; T Yoruba Folktales, 1986; The Village Witchdoctor and Other Stories, 1990; Co Editor, Winds of Change: Modern Stories from Black Africa, 1977. Address: PO Box 2251, Ibadan, Nigeria.

TUTTLE Lisa, b. 16 Sept 1952, Houston, TX, USA. Writer. Education: BA, Syracuse University, 1973. Publications include: Windhaven, 1981; Familiar Spirit, 1983; Catwitch, 1983; Children's Literary Houses, 1984; Encyclopedia of Feminism, 1986; A Spaceship Built of Stone & Other Stories, 1987; Heroines: Women Inspired by Women, 1988; Lost Futures, 1992; Memories of the Body, 1992. Contributions to: TV Critic; Austin Am Statesman; City Limits; Time Out; Fiction Magazine. Honour: John W Campbell Award, 1974. Literary Agent: Caradoc King, A P Watt Limited. Address: c/o A P Watt Limited, 20 John Street, London WC1N 2DL, England.

TUTTLE William McCullough, b. 7 Oct 1937. Professor of History. m. Linda L Stumpp, 12 Dec 1959 (divorced), 2 sons, 1 daughter. Education: BA, Denison University, 1959; MA, University of Wisconsin, 1964; PhD, University of Wisconsin, 1967. Appointments: Assistant Professor, 1967-70, Associate Professor, 1970-75, University of Kansas; Senior Fellow in Southern and Negro History, Johns Hopkins University, 1969-70; Research Fellow, Harvard University, 1972-73; Professor of History, University of Kansas, 1975-; Visiting Professor, USC, 1980; Intra-University Professor, University of Kansas, 1982-83; Associate Fellow, Stanford Humanities Center, 1983-84; Research Associate, University of California, Berkeley, 1986-88. Publications: Race Riot: Chicago in the Red Sumer of 1919, 1970; W E B DuBois, 1973; Co-author, Plain Folk, 1982; Co-author,A People & a Nation, 1982, 1986, 1990, 1994; Daddy's Gone to War: The Second World War in the Lives of America's Children, 1993. Contributions to: Journal of American History, American Studies, Labor History, Technology and Culture and other journals. Honours: National Endowment for the Humanities, Younger Humanist Fellowship, 1972-73; Award of Merit, American Association for State and Local History, 1972; Guggenheim Fellowship, 1975-76; Evans Grant 1975-76; Beveridge Grant, 1982; Fellowship for Independent Study and Research, 1983-84; National Endowment for the Humanities, Projects Research Grant, 1986-89; Hall Humanities Research Fellow, 1990. Memberships: Society of American Historians; American Historical Association; Organization of American Historians (Nominating Board 1979-81). Address: 21 Winona Avenue, Lawrence, KS 66046, USA.

TWICHELL Chase, b. 1950. Publications: Northern Spy: Poems, 1981; The Odds, 1986; Perdido, 1991; The Practice of Poetry, 1992. Honours: Fellow, American Academy & Institute of Arts & Letters, 1994.

TWINING William Lawrence, b. 22 Sept 1934, Kampala. Professor. m. Penelope Elizabeth wall Morris, 31 Aug 1957, 1 s, 1 d. Education: BA, 1955, MA, 1960, DCL, 1990, Brasenose College, Oxford; JD, 1958, University of Chicago; LLD, 1980, University of Victoria. Appointments: Editor, Law in Context Series, 1965-; Editor, Jurists Series, 1979-. Publications include: Karl Llewellyn and the Realist Movement, 1973, 1985; Law Publishing and Legal Information, 1981; How to Do Things With Rules, 1991; Theories and Evidence,

Bentham and Wigmore, 1985; Learning Lawyers Skills, 1989; Rethinking Evidence, 1990; Analysis of Evidence, 1991; Evidence and Proof, 1992. Contributions to: Numerois Journals. Honour: LLD, University of Victoria. Memberships: Society of Public Teachers of Law; Commonwealth Legal Education Association; UK Association for Legal and Social Philosophy. Address: Faculty of Laws, University College, Ednsleigh Gardens, London WC1H 0EG, England.

TWUM Michael Kyei, b. 30 Apr 1954, Writer; Poet. m. Maureen Twum, 22 Aug 1986, 1 s. Education: Modern School of Commerce, Ghana, 1974; University of Bonn, West Germany, 1981. Appointments: Lifetime Deputy Governor, ABIRA, USA, 1987. Publications include: Golden Poems from Africa, 1982; Beyond Expectations, 1983; Great Adventures of an African, 1983. Contributions to: Several Magazines and Newspapers. Honours: Silver Medal, 1985, Gold Medal, 1987, ABI, USA; Certificates, IBC, England. Memberships: National Association of Writers; World Institute ot Achievement; IBC; PEN International. Literary Agent: Vantage Press, NY, USA. Address: 78 Acacia Road, Mitcham, Surrey, CR4 1ST, England.

TYLER Anne, b. 1941, American. Publications: If Morning Ever Comes, 1964; The Tin Can Tree, 1965; A Slipping Down Life, 1970; The Clock Winder, 1972; Celestial Navigation, 1974; Searching for Caleb, 1976; Earthly Possessions, 1977; Morgan's Passing, 1980; Dinner at the Homesick Restaurant, 1982; The Best American Short Stories, 1983 (ed with Shannon Ravenel), 1983; The Accidental Tourist, 1985; Breathing Lessons, 1988; Saint Maybe, 1991; Tumble Tower (juvenile), 1993; Ladder of Years, 1995. Honours: National Book Critics Circle Award for Fiction, 1985; Pulitzer Prize for Fiction, 1989. Memberships: American Academy of Arts and Letters; American Academy of Arts and Sciences. Literary Agent: Timothy Seldes, Russell & Volkening Inc. Address: 222 Tunbridge Road, Baltimore, MD 21212, USA.

TYLER W T. See: HAMRICK Samuel J, Jr.

TYSON Remer Hoyt, b. 2 July 1934, Statesboro, Georgia, USA. Journalist. m. Virginia Curtin Knight, 18 Feb 1984, 1 son, 1 daughter. Education: Georgia Teacher College, 1952-54; University of Georgia, 1954-56; Art degree, Harvard University, Nieman Fellow 1967-68; Harvard Business School, 1981. Publication: They Love a Man in the Country, 1988. Memberships: Foreign Correspondents Association of Southern Africa; East Africa Foreign Correspondents Association. Address: 3 Woking Drive, Northwood, Mt Pleasant, Harare, Zimbabwe.

U

UDICK Robert Alan, b. 27 Nov 1957, Bellevue, NE, USA. Professor Of Political Science And Communication. Education: BA (History), Louisiana State, 1980; MA (Political Science), 1983; PhD (Social Sciences), Syracuse University, 1994. Contributions to: Mass Comm Review, The Hutchins Paradox; C Wright Mills And Francis, A Letter From History, spring 1994; Socialist Review, Fukuyama, winter 1993. Memberships: National Board Of Directors, Educators For Social Responsibility. Address: 2320 Magazine, Apt C, N O, LA 70130, USA.

UHNAK Dorothy, b. 1933. Appointments: Detective, NYC Transit Police Department, 1953-67. Publications: Policewoman, 1964; The Bait, 1968; The Witness, 1969; The Ledger, 1970; Law and Order, 1973; The Investigation, 1977; False Witness, 1981; Victims, 1985; The Ryer Avenue Story, 1993. Contributions to: The Writer, magazine; TV Guide, weekly magazine; Book Reviewer; New York Times; Washington Post. Honours: Edgar (Mystery Writers of America), 1969; Legrande Prix de la Litterateur Policiere, 1971. Memberships: PEN; Writers Guild of America. Literary Agent: Alice Martell, Martell Agency, 555 5th Avenue, NY 10017, USA. Address: c/o Simon and Schuster Inc, 1230 Sixth Avenue, NY 10020, USA.

ULAM Adam Bruno, b. 8 April 1922, Lwow, Poland. Professor and Director, Russian Research Center, Harvard University. 2 sons. Education: AB, Brown University, 1943; PhD, Harvard University, 1947. Publications: Stalin: The Man and His Era (revised edition 1989); Expansion and Co-existence, 1968; The Bolsheviks, 1965; The Kirov Affair (novel) 1988; The Unfinished Revolution, 1960; A History of Soviet Russia, 1980. Contributions to: Los Angeles Times, New York Times, the international press; Magazines such as Commentary, The New Republic. Honour: Honorary LLD, Brown University. Memberships: American Philosophical Society; American Academy of Arts and Sciences. Literary Agent: Julian Bach. Address: Russian Research Center, Harvard University, 1737 Cambridge Street, Cambridge, MA 02138, USA.

ULRICH Betty Garton, b. 28 Oct 1919, Indianapolis, Indiana, USA. Writer. m. Reverend Louis E Ulrich, 5 Jan 1946, 3 sons, 2 daughters. Education: BS, Education. Publications: Away We Go, 1970; Every Day With God, 1972, re-issued in paperback, 1980, translated into 4 foreign languages; Rooted in the Sky: A Faith To Cope With Cancer, 1989. Contributor to: Co-Founder, Contributing Editor to Writers' Journal; Articles, short stories, poems in over 30 publications including Christian Herald; Eternity; Scope; The Lutheran; Reader's Digest; Redbook; Guideposts, Lighthouse. Memberships: Wisconsin Regional Writers Association; Indianhead Writers Association; Wisconsin Council for Writers. Literary Agent: Steven Griffith. Address: PO Box 265, Stone Lake, WI 54876, USA.

ULRICH Laurel Thatcher, b. 11 July 1938, ID, USA. m. Gael Dennis Ulrich, 22 Sept 1958, 3 sons, 2 daughters. Education: B, University of Utah, 1960; MA, Simmons College, 1971; PhD, University of New Hampshire, 1980. Literary Appointments: Assistant Professor, Humanities Program, 1980-84, History, 1985-88, Associate Professor, History, 1988-92, Professor, 1992-, University of New Hampshire. Publications: A Midwifes Tale, 1990; Good Wives, 1991. Contributions to: Several inc. Journal of Mormon History; Dress; William & Mary Quarterly; Families and Children; Foodways in the Northest. Honours include:Pulitzer Prize, 1991; Bancroft Prize, 1991; John S Dunning Prise, 1990; New England Historical Association Award, 1991; Charles Frankel Award, 1993; Guggenheim Fellowship, 1991-92; Gary Lindberg Award, 1991. Memberships: American Historical Association. Address History Dept, Horton Social Science Ctr, University of New Hampshire, Durham, NH 03824, USA.

UNDERHILL Charles. See: HILL Reginald (Charles).

UNDERWOOD Michael. See: EVELYN John Michael.

UNGER Barbara, b. 2 Oct 1932, New York City, USA. College Professor. m. (1) 2 daughters, (2) Theodore Sakano, 31 July 1986. Education: BA, MA, City College of New York. Appointments: Professor, Rockland Community College, Suffern, 1969-. Publications: Dying for Uncle Ray; Blue Depression Glass; Learning to Foxtrot; Inside the Wind; Basement; The Man Who Burned Money.

Contributions to: Massachusetts Review; The Nation Beloit Poetry Journal; Midstream; Kansas Quarterly; Carolina Quarterly; Southern Humanities Review. Honours: NEH Fellow; National Poetry Award; Goodman Award; Judah Magnes Award; Roberts Writing Award; John Williams Narrative Poetry Award. Memberships: AWP; PSA. Address: 101 Parkside Drive, Suffern, NY 10901, USA.

UNGER J Marshall, Professor of Japanese. Education: AB 1969, AM 1971, University of Chicago, Far Eastern Languages and Civilsations; MA 1973, PhD 1975, Yale University, Linguistics. Publications: The Fifth Generation Fallacy: Why Japan is Betting Its Future on Artificial Intelligence, 1987; Sixteen chapters and essays in anthologies including: Language Engineering versus Machine Engineering: A Linguist's view of the Character Input Problem, 1989; Japanese and That Other Altaic Languages?, 1990; Summary Report of the Altaic Panel, 1990; Kanji to arufabetto no yomikaki noryoku, 1990; 21 articles in professional journals; Eight book reviews including: The Phonology of Eight-Century Japanese, 1981; A History of Writing Japan, 1991. Honours: 8 major postdoctoral grants including support from the Control Data Corporation 1980-82, the Japan Foundation 1985 and the National Museum of Ethnology, Suita, Osaka, Japan, 1991. Memberships: Chair, Curriculum Framework Taskforce; Educational Testing Service Committee of Examiners. Address: Department of Hebrew and East Asian Languages and Literatures, University of Maryland, College Park, MD 20742, USA.

URE Jean Ann, b. 1 Jan 1943, Caterham, Surrey, England. Writer. m. Leonard Gregory, 12 Aug 1967. Eduction: Webber Douglas Academy of Dramatic Art, 1965-66. Publications: See You Thursday, 1981; A Proper Little Norryeff, 1982; If It Werent for Sebastian, 1982; Hi There, Supermouse, 1983; The You Two, 1984; One Green Leaf, 1987; Play Nimrod for Him, 1990; Plague 99, 1989. Honour: Lanc Book Award, 1989. Membership: Society of Authors. Literary Agent: Maggie Noach, 21 Redan Street, London. Address: 88 Soutbridge Road, Croydon, CR0 1AF, England.

URQUHART Jane, b. 21 June 1949, Canada. Writer. m. (1) Paul Brian Keele, 6 Jan 1969, (2) Tony Urquhart, 5 May 1976, 1 daughter. Education: BA, University Guelph, Canada. Appointments: Writer in Residence: University of Ottawa, Ottawa, Canada, 1990; Memorial University, St John's, Newfoundland, 1992. Publications: The Whirlpool, 1986; Storm Glass, 1987; Changing Heaven, 1990; False Shuffles, 1982; The Little Flowers of Madam de Montespan, 1984; Away (novel), 1993. Contributions to: Brick Magazine; The Globe and Mail Book Pages; Quill and Quire; Malahat Review. Honours: Short listed for Seal First Novel Award, Le Prix de Meilleur Livre Etranger, France, 1992; The Trillium Award, Canada, 1993. Memberships: Writer's Union of Canada; PEN International. Literary Agent: Ellen Levine Literary Agency, New York. Address: c/o Writers Union of Canada, 24 Ryerson Avenue, Toronto, Ontario, M5T 2P3, Canada.

URSELL Geoffrey Barry, b. 14 Mar 1943, Moose Jaw, Saskatchewan, Canada. Writer; Editor. m. Barbara Davies, 8 July 1967. Education: BA, University of Manitoba, 1965; MA, 1966; PhD, University of London, 1973. Appointments: Writer in Residence, Saskatoon Public Library, 1984-85; Winnipeg Public Library, 1989-90; Editor, Grain, 1990. Publications: Way Out West; The Look Out Tower; Perdue; Trap Lines; Saskatoon Pie; The Running of the Deer. Contributions to: This Magazine; Saturday Night; Canadian Forum; Quarry; Border Crossings; Canadian Fiction Magazine; NeWest Review; Western People. Honours: Clifford E Lee National Playwriting Award; Special Commendation in Commonwealth Poetry Prize; Books in Canada First Novel Award. Memberships: PEN; Writers Union of Canada; Playwright's Union of Canada; Saskatchewan Writers Guild; Sk Playwrights Centre. Address: c/o Coteau Books, 401-2206 Dewdney Avenue, Regina, Saskatchewan, S4R 1H3, Canada.

USHAKOVA Elena. See: NEVZGLIADOVA Elena Vsevolodovna.

USHERWOOD Elizabeth Ada, b. 10 July 1923, Author. m. Stephen Dean Usherwood, 24 Oct 1970. Publications: Visit Some London Catholic Churches, 1982; The Counter Armada - 1596, 1983; We Die for the Old Religion, 1987; Women First, 1989; A Saint in the Family, 1992. Contributions to: The Universe; Catholic Herald; Other Papers & Periodicals. Address: 24 St Marys Grove, London N1 2NT, England.

V

VACHSS Andrew Henry, b. 19 Oct 1942, New York City, USA. Attorney at Law, Consultant, Writer. Education: BA, Case Western Reserve University, 1965; JD, magna cum laude, New England School of Law, 1975. Appointments Include: Director, Libra Inc, Massachusetts, 1971; Deputy Director, Medfield-Norfolk Prison Project, Massachusetts, 1971-72; Director, Intensive Treatment Unit (ANDROS II) Massachusetts, 1972-73; Project Director, Department of Youth Services, Massachusetts, 1972-73; Planner Analyst, Crime Control Co-ordinator's Office, New York, 1974-75; Director, Advocacy Associates, New York and New Jersey, 1973-75; Director, Juvenile Justice Planning Project, New York City, 1975-85; Adjunct Professor, College of New Resources, New York City, 1980-81; Attorney, Private Practice, New York City,1976-; Numerous consultancy appointments. Publications: Non-fiction: The Life-Style Violent Juvenile: The Secure Treatment Approach, 1979; The Child Abuse-Delinquency Connection - A Lawyer's View, 1989; Novels: Flood, DIF,1986; Pocketbooks, 1986; Strega, 1987, NAL, 1988; Blue Belle, 1988, NAL 1990; Hard Candy, 1989, NAL 1990; Blossom, 1990, Ivy, 1991; Sacrifice, 1991, Ivy 1992; Shella, 1993; Down in The Zero, 1994; Born Bad - The Collected Short Stories, 1994. Contributions to: Numerous articles and short stories contributed to magazines and anthologies; Emotional Abuse: The Hidden Wound, 1994. Honours: The Grand Prix de Litterature Policiere, 1988 for Strega; The Falcon Award, 1988, Maltese Falcon Society of Japan for Strega; The Deutschen Krimi Preis 1989 for Flood. Membership: PEN American Centre; National Association of Counsel for Children; American Society of Criminology; American Professional Society on the Abuse of Children. Address: 299 Broadway, Suite 1803, New York City, NY 10007, USA.

VAGGE Ornello, (Lionello Grifo), b. 10 Aug 1934, Rome Italy. Author; Journalist; Novelist; Poet; Writer. Widower. Education: Doctor of Political & Social Sciences, 1958. Publications: La Mia Poesia - My Poetry - Mi Poesia, 1989; Sottovoce Parole in Cerca di Musica, 1980; Sottovoce, Poesia come Musica, and Sempre Sottovoce, Poesia come Vita, 1992; Potgtosem, 1991; My Poetry, 1993; Handbook for Aspiring Businessmen, 1978; Philosophical Repertory 1970-1989; A Character and Other Short Stories; Hommage to Woman, 1994. Contributions to: Numerous contributions to journals and magazines in Europe. Honours: Commenda Della Republica Italiana, Rome, 1973; Communeauté Européenne Des Journalistes Prize, Malta, 1972; Genti e Paesi Prize, La Spezia, 1990. Memberships: Life Member, Dante Alighieri Society, Rome; International Society of Poets, Maryland, USA; Ordine Nationale Giornalisti Italiani; Roman Press Association; Italian Society of Authors & Publishers; International Federation of Dog Breeders. Address: Apartado Correos 32, E-30380 La Manga Del Mar Menor, Spain.

VALDAR Colin Gordon, b. 18 Dec 1918, England. Journalist; Consultant Editor. m. (1) Evelyn Margaret Barriff, 1940, div, 2 s, (2) Jill Davis. Appointments include: Freelance Journalist, 1936-39; Successively Production Editor, Features Editor, Assistant Editor, Sunday Pictorial, 1942-46; Features Editor, 1946-51, Assistant Editor, 1951-53, Daily Express; Editor, Sunday Pictorial, 1953-59; Editor, Daily Sketch, 1959-62; Director, Sunday Pictorial Newspaper, 1957-59; Director, Daily Sketch & Daily Graphic, 1959-62; Chairman, Bouverie Publishing Company, 1964-83; Founder, UK Press Gazette, 1965. Address: 2A Ratcliffe Wharf, 18-22 Narrow Street, London E14 8DQ, England.

VALENCAK Hannelore, b. 23 Jan 1929, Donawitz, Austria. Writer. m. 2) Viktor Mayer, 28 Apr 1962, 1 son. Education: PhD, Physics, University of Graz, Styria, Austria. Publications: Novels: Die Hohlen Noahs, 1961; Ein Fremder Garten, 1964, 1970; Zuflucht hinter der Zeit, 1967, 1977; Vohof der Wirklichkeit, 1972; Das magische Tagebuch, 1981; various short stories, poetry & books for young people. Contributions to: Neue Deutsche Hefte; Literatur und Kritik; Dimension, USA; Others. Honours: National Advancement Award, 1957; Peter Rosegger Prize, Styrian Regional Government, 1966; Austrian Children's Book Prize, 1977; Amade Prize, Monaco, 1978; various other awards. Memberships: Austrian PEN Club; Austrian Writers Union; Styrian Writers Union; Podium. Address: Schwarzspanierstrasse 15/2/8, A-1090 Vienna, Austria.

VALENTINE Alec. See: **ISAACS Alan**.

VALERIO Anthony, b. 13 May 1940, USA. Author. 1 son, 2 daughters. Education: BA, Columbia College, 1962. Appointments: Book Editor, Major Publishing Houses, 1966-72; Instructor of Writing, 1986-88. Publications: Bart: A Life of A Bartlett Gianmathi; Valentino and the Great Italians; The Mediterranean Runs Through Brooklyn. Contributions to: Paris Review; Philadelphia Magazine; Patterson Review; Anthologies; Dream Streets; Columbus Review. Memberships: PEN. Address: 106 Charles Street, 14 New York, NY 10014, USA.

VALERY Anne. See: **FIRTH Anne Catherine**.

VALGARDSON William Dempsey, b. 7 May 1939, Winnipeg, Canada. Writer; Professor. div. 1 son, 1 daughter. Education: BA, United College, 1961; BEd, University of Manitoba, 1966; MFA, University of Iowa, 1969. Appointments: Associate Professor, 1970-74; Professor, University of Victoria, 1974-. Publications: Bloodflowers; God Is Not A Fish Inspector; Gentle Sinners, What Can't Be Changed, Should'nt be Mourned; The Girl with the Botticelli Face; Red Dust; The Carpenter of Dreams; In The Gutting Shed. Contributions to: The Saturday Evening Post; Readers Digest; TV Guide; The Globe and Mail; The Time Colonist; EnRoute. Honours: Presidents Medal; First Prize CBC Annual Literary Competition; First Novel Award; CAA Silver Medal; The Ethel Wilson Literary Prize, 1992. Memberships: CACLALS; ACTRA; The Writers Union of Canada; PWAC. Literary Agent: Denise Bukowski. Address: 1908 Waterloo Road, Victoria, BC, V8P 1J3, Canada.

VALLBONA (Rothe) de Rima Gretchen, b. 15 Mar 1931, San José, Costa Rica. Professor; Author. m. Carlos Vallbona, 26 Dec 1956, 1 son, 3 daughters. Education: BA, BS, Colegio Superior de Senoritas, San José, 1948; MA, University of Costa Rica, 1962; DML, Middlebury College, 1981. Appointments: Professor, Hispanic Literature, Liceo J.J. Vargas Calvo, Costa Rica, 1955-56, University of St Thomas, Houston, 1964-; Member, Editorial Board: Letras Femeninas, 1975-, Alba de America, 1981-, Foro Literario, 1979-89; Co-Director, Foro, 1984-89;Contributing Editor, The America's Review, 1989-. Publications: Noche en vela, 1968; Polvo del camino, 1971; Yolanda Oreamuno, 1972; la obra en prosa de Eunice Odio, 1981; Mujeres y agonias, 1982; Las sombras que perseguimos, 1983; La Salamandra rosada, 1979; Cosecha de pecadores, 1988; El aréngel del perdòn, 1990; Mundo demonio y mujer, 1991; Los infiernos de la mujer y algo mas, 1992; Vida i sucesos de la Morja Alférez, 1992; Flowering Inferno - Tales of Sinking Hearts, 1993. Contributions to: Articles, poems & short stories in Spanish, French, English and Portuguese in various professional journals and magazines. Honours: Aquileo J Echeverria Costa Rican Novel Prize, 1968; Agripina Montes del Valle Novel Prize, Colombia, 1978; Jorge Luis Borges Short Story Prize, Argentina, 1977; Literary Award, Southwest Conference of Latin American Studies, 1982; Ancora Literary Award, Costa Rica, 1984; El Lazo de Dama de la Orden del Mérito Civil, condecorated by His Royal Majesty D Juan King Carlos I of Spain, 1988; Cullen Foundation Professor of Spanish, 1989. Memberships: Comunidad de Escritores Latinoamericanos de Costa Rica; Associacion de Literatura Femenina Hispanica; National Writers Association; Cultural Secretary, Instituto Literario y Cultural Hispanico; and others. Agent: Dr Nick Kanellos, Arte Publico Pres. Address: University of St Thomas, 3800 Montrose Blvd, Houston, TX 77006, USA.

VALTINOS Thanassis, b. 16 Dec 1932, Arcadia, Greece. Writer; Screenplay Writer. 1 daughter. Education: Cinematography Studies, Athens, 1950-53. Publications: The Book of the Days of Andreas Kordopatis, 1972; The Descent of the Nine, 1978; Three Greek One-Act Plays, a novel, 1978; Deep Blue Almost Black, 1985; Data on the Decade of the Sixties, 1989; Woodcock Feathers, 1992; You Will Find My Bones in the Rain, 1992; Saint Orthocosta. Contributions to: I Lexi, Greece; To Thendro, Greece; Akzente, Germany; Le Monde, France; To Tram, Greece; Shenandoah, USA; Meanjin, Australia. Honours: Screen Play Prize, Cannes Film Festival, 1984; Greek State Prize for Literature, 1989. Memberships: President, Greek Society of Writers; International Theatre Institute; Greek Society of Playwrights; The European Academy of Science and Arts (Academia Scientiarum et Artium Europaea). Address: Astydamantos 66-68, Athens 11634, Greece.

VAN COTT Laurence. See: **NIVEN Larry**.

VAN DE BERGE Claude. See: **PAUWELS Rony**.

VAN DE LAAR Waltherus Antonius Bernardinus (Victor Vroomkoning), b. 6 Oct 1938, Boxtel, Netherlands. Teacher; Poet. m. Inge Gorris, 22 Jan 1968, 1 son, 1 daughter. Education: Master's degree, Dutch Linguistics and Literature, 1978. Appointments: Contact publishing house, Amsterdam, 1966-67; Teacher, Interstudie teacher's training college, Arnhem, 1977-83; Co-Writer, Kritisch Literatur Lexicon reference book for literature, 1981-. Publications: De einders tegemoet, 1983; De laatste dingen, 1983; Circuit des souvenirs, 1984; Klein museum, 1987; Groesbeek Tijdrit, 1989; Echo van een echo, 1990; Oud zeer, 1993. Contributions to: Avenue; Bzzlletin; Tirade; De Tweede Ronde; Maatstaf; Preludium; Parmentier; Dietsche Warande and Belfort; Yang; Kreatief; Poeziekrant; Nieuw Wereldtijdschrift. Honours: Pablo Neruda Prize, 1983. Memberships: Lira; Former Member, Literair Cafe Nijmegen. Address: Aldenhof 70-17, 6537 DZ Nijmegen, Netherlands.

VAN DER VAT Dan, b. 28 Oct 1939, Alkmaar, The Netherlands. Author & Journalist. m. Christine Mary Ellis, 1962, 2 daughters. Education: BA, honours, Classics, University of Durham, England, 1960. Appointments: The Journal, Newcastle Upon Tyne, 1960; Daily Mail, 1963; The Sunday Times, 1965; The Times, 1967, including ten years as foreign correspondent; The Guardian, 1982-88; Chief Foreign Leader-Writer; Full-time author, 1989-. Publications: The Grand Scuttle, 1982; The Last Corsair, 1983; Gentlemen of War, 1984; The Ship That Changed the World, 1985; The Atlantic Campaign, 1939-45, 1988; The Pacific Campaing, 1941-45, 1991; Freedom was Never Like This: A Winter's Journey in East Germany, 1991; Stealth at Sea - History of the Submarine, 1994. Contributions to: Newspapers, magazines, radio and TV. Honours: Best First Work Award, Yorkshire Post, 1982; Best Book of the Sea Award, King George's Fund for Sailors, 1983. Memberships: Society of Authors; London Library. Literary Agent: Michael Shaw, Curtis Brown, 162 Regent Street, London W1R 5TA. Address: c/o Curtis Brown, 162 Regent Street, London W1R 5TA, England.

VAN DER WEE Herman, b. 10 July 1928, Lier. Professor of Social & Economic History. m. Monique Verbreyt, 27 Feb 1954, 1 son, 1 daughter. Education: BA Philosophy, 1949, LLD 1950, Licentiaat Political and Social Sciences (MA status), 1951, Doctor in Historical Sciences, 1963, KU Leuven, Belgium; Graduate Studies, Sorbonne, Paris, France and London School of Economics, England. Publications: Prix et salaires, Manuel Méthodologique, 1956; The Growth of the Antwerp Market and the European Economy (14th-16th centuries), 3 vol, 1963; La Banque Nationale de Belgique et la politique monétaire entre les deux guerres, 1975; Prosperity and Upheaval, The World Economy, 1945-1980, 1986, several translations; Histoire economique mondiale, 1945-1990, 1990; Banking in Europe (Middle Ages-Early Modern and Modern Times), 1992. Contributions to: Annales (Economies, Sociétés, Civilisations); Vierteljahrschrift fur Sozial- und Wirtschaftsgeschichte; The Business History Review; The Economic History Review; Journal of European Economic History; Bijdragen tot de Geschiedenis. Honours: De Sassart Prize for national History (1961-1967) of the Royal Academy of Belgium, 1968; Fulbright-Hayes Award, 1975, 1981; Quinquennial Solvay Prize for Social Sciences (1976-1980), National Foundation of Scientific Research, Belgium, 1981; Amsterdam Prize, Historical Sciences, Royal Academy of the Netherlands, 1992; Dr hon causa, Catholic University of Brussels, 1994; Knighted (Baron), 1994. Memberships: Foundation Member, Academia Europeae (Cambridge, England), 1986, Member of Council, 1987-90; Chairman, Advisory Council, West European Programme, Wilson International Centre for Scholars, Washington DC, 1986-92; President, Advisory Council, Leuven Institute for Central and East European Studies, 1990-94; President of Board of Trustees, Leuven University Press, 1990-94; President, International Economic History Association, 1986-90; Honorary President, 1990-, Royal Academy of Belgium, Class of Arts, 1972-; Corresponding Fellow,British Academy & Royal Academy of the Netherlands; Honorary Foreign Member, American Academy of Sciences, 1993-; Scientific Committee, Exec, Instituto Internationale di Storia Economica Francesco Datini, 1986-; External Member, Research Council, European University Institute of Florence. Address: De Hettinghe, B-9170, St Pauwels, Belgium.

VAN DUYN Mona, (Jarvis Thurston), b. 1921, Waterloo, Iowa, USA. Poet. Appointments: University Professor; Founder (1947), Editor, (to 1970), "Perspective, a Quarterly of Literature". Memberships: National Institute of Arts and Letters; American Academy of Poets. Honours: Pulitzer Prize, 1991; Bollingen Prize, 1971; Poet Laureate of the United States, 1992-93; National Book Award, 1971; Ruth Lilly Prize, 1989. Address: 7505 Teasdale Avenue, St Louis, MO 63130, USA.

VAN OVER Raymond, b. 29 June 1934, Inwood, Long Island, New York, USA. Writer. Appointments: Editor, Garret/Helix Press, 1962-65; International Journal of Parapsychology, 1965-68; Film, Story Editor, 20th Centry Fox, Columbia Pics, 1968-72; Book Reviewer, Book of the Month Club, 1970-71; Staff Writer, Governor Nelson Rockefeller's Commission to Preserve the Adirondacks, 1972-73; Instructor, Hofstra University, New York, 1973-76; Instructor, New York University, 1973-76. Publications Include: Explorer of the Mind, 1967; I Ching, 1971; A Treasury of Chinese Literature, 1972; Psychology and Extrasensory Perception, 1972; Unfinished Man, 1972; The Chinese Mystics, 1973; Taoist Tales, 1973; The Psychology of Freedom, 1974; Eastern Mysticism, 2 vols, 1977; Total Meditation, 1973; Sun Songs, 1980; Smearing the Ghost's Face with Ink, 1983; Monsters You Never Heard Of, 1983; Screenwriter, documentaries, 1973-; Khomeini, A Biography, 1985; The Twelfth Child, 1990; Whisper, 1991; In A Father's Rage, 1991. Contributions to: Various journals and magazines. Memberships: Author's Guild; United Nations, NGO, Global Education Motivators; Voting Member American Society for Psychical Research. Literary Agent: Paul Mahon, 1735 Connecticut Avenue NW, Washington, DC 20015, USA. Address: 2905 Rittenhouse Street NW, Washington, DC 20015, USA.

VAN VEGHEL L(awrence) A, b. 28 July 1947. Writer; Compressor Engineering Tech. Education: Milwaukee Institute of Technology, 1969. Appointments: Midwest Outdoors, 1975, Fishing & Hunting Editor and Wisconsin Editor; Badger Sportsman, 1975, Contributing Writer; Secretary and Media Director, 1989, Wisconsin Council of Sport Fishing Organizations. Publications: 153 Technical Manuals on Industrial Refrigeration Units and Compressors, 1975-85. Contributions to: Over 1000, Including: Above the Bridge; Outdoor Beacon; Midwest Outdoors; Badger Sportsman; Walleye Magazine; Outdoors Unlimited; Wisconsin Outdoor News; Metro Parent; Washington Island Observer; Milwaukee Journal; Woods & Waters; Authorship; Writers Digest. Honours: Raconteurs Inc, Member of the Year, 1991; Honorary Citizen of Boys Town. Memberships: Outdoor Writers Association of America; Association of Great Lakes Outdoor Writers; Wisconsin Regional Writers Association; Wisconsin Outdoor Communicators Association, Director; Writers Ink, Vice President; Raconteurs Inc, Director and Historian; National Writers Club; Wisconsin Fishing Club, Secretary and Media Director; Wisconsin Humane Society; Animal Protection Institute; Wisconsin Waterfowl Association; Bass Anglers Sportsman Society; North American Fishing Club; American Life League; Wisconsin Council of Sport Fishing Organizations, Secretary & Media Director; Coalition On The Advancement of Sportfishing and Tourism; Rogers Street Fishing Village; Wildlife Forever; National Fresh Water Fishing Hall of Fame. Address: 5557 So Disch Avenue, Cudahy, WI 53110, USA.

VANCE William L, b. 19 April 1934. Educator; Writer. Education: AB 1956, Oberlin College, Ohio; MA English Language and Literature, 1957, PhD English Language and Literature, 1962, University of Michigan, Ann Arbor. Appointments: Boston University, Assistant Professor of English, 1962-67, Associate Professor of English, 1967-73, Professor of English, 1973-. Publications: America's Rome, vol 1: Classical Rome, 1989; America's Rome, vol 2: Catholic and Contemporary Rome, 1989; American Literature, 2 vols, co-editor, 1970; The Faber Book of America, co-editor, 1992; Immaginari a confronto, co-editor, 1993. Contributions to: Numerous contributions to scholarly journals and to exhibition catalogues. Honours: Senior Writing Prize, Oberlin, 1956; Ralph Waldo Emerson (Phi Beta Kappa) Prize, 1990; Association of American Publishing Prize, 1989; John Simon Guggenheim Fellowship, 1990-91; National Book Critic's Circle Award Nomination, 1990; LLD (Hon) University of South Dakota, 1992. Membership: American Literature Section of Modern Language Association of America. Address: 255 Beacon Street, Boston, MA 02116,USA.

VANDERHAAR Gerard A, b. 15 Aug 1931, Louisville, Kentucky, USA. Professor. m. Janice Marie Searles, 22 Dec 1969. Education: BA 1954, Providence College; STD 1965, University of St Thomas, Rome. Appointments: Taught on faculties of St John's University, New York 1964-65, Providence College 1965-68, Wesleyan University 1968-69, Christian Brothers University 1971-. Publications: A New Vision and a New Will for Memphis, 1974; Christians and Nonviolence in the Nuclear Age, 1982; Enemies and How to Love Them, 1985; Way of Peace: A Guide to Nonviolence, Co-Editor, 1987; The Philippines: Agony and Hope, Co-Author, 1989; Active Nonviolence: A Way of Personal Peace, 1990; Why Good People Do Bad Things, 1994; Booklets: Nonviolence, Theory and Practice, 1980; Nonviolence in Christian Tradition, 1983.

Contributions to: Articles in Encyclopaedia of World Biography; Fellowship; Cross Currents; The Wesleyan Public Affairs Review; Pax Christi; The Encyclopaedic Dictionary of Religion; Pro Mundi Vita; and others. Honours: Outstanding Educators of America, 1971; Distinguished Service Award, United Nations Association, 1981; Catholic Press Association Book Award for Spirituality, 1991; Tennessee Higher Education Commission Award for Community Service, 19994. Memberships: American Academy of Religion; American Association of University Professors; Pax Christi; National Conference of Christians and Jews; Fellowship of Reconciliation; War Registers League. Address: Christian Brothers University, 650 East Parkway South, Memphis, TN 38104, USA.

VANDIEVOET Jacques F G. See: **ORIOL Jacques.**

VANE Brett. See: **KENT Arthur (William Charles).**

VANICEK Zdenek, (Alois Bocek, Matej Posejpal), b. 24 June 1947, Chlumec, Czechoslovakia. Professor of International Relations; Freelance Journalist; Writer; Poet. 1 son, 1 daughter. Education: BA, College of Economics, Prague, 1972; MA, LLD, Charles University of Law, 1979; PhD, Diplomatic Academy, Prague, 1981. Publications: The Theory and the Practice of British Neo-Conservatism, 1988; Under The Range of Mountains of Five Fingers, in preparation; On The Edge Of Rain, a selection of poems, 1988-92, 1994; To The Ends Of The Earth, 1992; Amidst The Ruins Of Memories, 1990. Contributions to: Lidé a Zeme, principal correspondent, Czech geographical monthly; Various Czech daily newspapers and magazines; Poems published in US and England Literary Magazines. Honours: Honorary Member, 56 Group Wales, England, 1986; Honorary Silver Medal, Czechoslovak Society for International Relations, Prague, 1986; Bronze Medal for the Preparation of the World Postage Stamp Exhibition, Prague, 1988; Honorary Member, American-Czechoslovak Society, USA, 1990; Commemorative Medal, Greek Olympic Committee, 1990; Official Pontifical Medal, 1990; The International Man for the Year, England, 1993; The Twentieth Century Award for Achievement, England, 1993; Numerous other awards and honours. Memberships: National Geographic Society, USA; The Poetry Society, England; Corresponding Member, British Art Medal Society, England; Society for Cultural & University Links with Wales & Scotland; Czechoslovak-British Society; Union of Creative Arts. Literary Agent: Art Van, Prague, Czech Republic. Address: Vladislavova 8, 110 00 Prague 1, Czech Republic.

VANSITTART Peter, b. 27 Aug 1920, Bedford, England. Education: Worcester College, Oxford. Publications: I Am the World, 1942; Enemies, 1947; The Overseer, 1949; Broken Canes, 1950; A Verdict of Treason, 1952; A Little Madness, 1953; The Game and the Ground, 1956; Orders of Chivalry, 1958; The Tournament, 1959; A Sort of Forgetting, 1960; Carolina, 1961; Sources of Unrest, 1962; The Friends of God, 1963; The Siege, The Lost Lands, 1964; The Dark Tower, 1965; The Shadow Land, 1967; The Story Teller, 1968; Green Knights Black Angels, Pastimes of a Red Summer, 1969; Landlord, 1970; Vladivostok: Figures in Laughter, 1972; Marlborough House School, Worlds and Underworlds, 1974; Quintet, 1976; Lancelot, Flakes of History, 1978; Harry, the Death of Robin Hood, 1980; Voices from the Great War, 1981; Three Six Seven, 1982; Voices 1870-1914, John Masefield's Letters from the Front, 1984; Aspects of Feeling, Paths from a White Horse, The Ancient Mariner and the Old Sailor, 1985; Happy & Glorious, 1987; Parsifal, 1988; Voices of the Revolution, 1989; The Wall, 1990; A Choice of Murder, 1992; London, 1992; In the Fifties, 1991; A Safe Conduct, 1995. Memberships: F R S L. Literary Agent: Anthony Sheil. Address: 9 Upper Park Road, Hampstead, London NW3, England.

VAPURU. See: **PASZKOWSKI Kazimierz Jan.**

VARVERIS Yannis, b. 25 Nov 1955. Writer. m. 6 Oct 1982, 1 son. Education: University of Athens; Sorbonne III, Paris. Publications: In Imagination and Reason; The Leak; Invalids of War; Death Extends; Bottoms Piano; Mr Fog, poetry, 1993; Translations: The Girl from Samos, 1993. Contributions to: Numerous. Memberships: Society of Writers; Greek Union of Theatrical Critics; Grece ITI. Address: 51 Omirou Str, 10672 Athens, Greece.

VAS DIAS Robert, b. 19 Jan 1931, London, England. Writer. m. div, 1 . Education: BA, Grinnell College; Columbia University. Appointments: Director, Aspen Writers Workshop, Aspen, 1964-67; Poet in Residence, Thomas Jefferson College, MI, 1971-74; Editor,

Publisher, Permanent Press, 1972-; General Secretary, Poetry Society, Director, National Poetry Centre, London, 1975-78; Joint Editor, Ninth Decade, 1983-; Contributing Editor, High Plains Literary Review; Adviser, Contemporary Poets. Publications include: Inside Outer Space, 1970; Speech Acts and Happenings, 1972; Making Faces, 1975; Poems Begining, The World, 1979. Contributions to: Chelsea; Choice; Encounter; Maps; Mulch; The Nation; The New Yorker; Partisan Review; Poetry Review; Stony Brook; Sumac; American Book Review; Margin; Oasis. Honours: CAPS Fellowship, NY State Council on Arts, 1975; C Day Lewis Fellowship in Poetry, 1980. Address: 5B Compton Avenue, Canonbury, London N1 2XD, England.

VASILIU Emanuel, b. 7 Sept 1929, Chisinau, Moldova. Professor. m. Maria Laura Stoka, 1 Aug 1952. Education: Bucharest University. Appointments: Lecturer, 1956, Associate Professor, 1968, Full Professor, 1970, Bucharest University; Researcher, 1951-53, Scientific Secretary, 1956-60, Institute of Liguistics of Romanian Academy; Researcher, Centre for Phonetic and Dialectal Researches, 1960-65; Dean, Bucharest University, 1990-92; Director, Institute of Phonetics and Dialectology, Romanian Academy, 1990-. Publications include: Romanian Phonology, 1965; Outline of a Semantic Theory of Kernel Sentences, 1972; Meaning, Analyticity, Knowledge, 1984; Introduction to Text Theory, 1990; Introduction to Language Theory, 1992. Contributions to: Studies and Papers Published in Romanian and Foreign Journals. Honours: State Award, 1953; B P Hasdeu Award, 1960. Memberships include:Societas Linguistica Europaea; International Pragmatic Association; Romanian Society of Romance Linguistics; Romanian Society of Linguistics; International Association of Phonetic Sciences. Address: Intrarea Lucaci 3, 784111 Bucharest, Romania.

VASSANJI Moyez G, b. Nairobi, Kenya. Full-time Writer. Education: BS, Massachusetts Institute of Technology; PhD, University of Pennsylvania. Appointments: Lecturer, Researcher, University of Toronto; Writer-in-Residence, International Writing Program, University of Iowa, 1989. Publications: Uhuru Street, 1992; No New Land, 1991; The Gunny Sack, 1989; The Book of Secrets, 1994. Honours: Commonwealth Regional Prize, best first novel, 1990; Griller Prize, best work of fiction, 1994; F G Bressani Literary Prize, 1994; Harbourfront Literary Award, 1994. Address: 39 Woburn Avenue, Toronto, Ontario, M5M 1K5, Canada.

VEGE Nageswara Rao, b. 18 Jan 1932, Peda, India. Physician; Surgeon. Education: BA, Andhra University; MD, Parma University. Publications include: Poetry, Life and Love, 1965; The Light of Asoka, 1970; Peace and Love, 1981; Pace e Vita, 1963; Santi Priya, 166; Pace e Amore, 1981; Templi Trascurati, 1983; The Best of Vege, 1992; 100 Opionions of Great Men on Life, 1992. Contributions to: International Herald Tribune; Indian Express; Paris France; Epoca; Espresso; Various English & Italian Newspapers. Honours include:Gold Medal Plaque; Poet of the Year; Diploma of Award; Guiseppe Ungaretti Award, 1982; Grand Prix Mediterranee, 1982; Schiller Award, 1985; Greenwood Poetry Forum Award, 1985; La Ballata Award, 1991; Viareggio Award, 1992. Memberships: International PEN; World Doctors Writers Association; Italian Writers Association; Swiss Writers Association; Scrittori della Svizzera Italiana; World Culture Organization. Address: Via Monte Ceneri 20, 6516 Gerra Piano TI, Switzerland.

VEGH Claudine, b. 24 Dec 1934, Paris, France. Psychiatrist. m. Marcel Vegh, 8 July 1956, 1 son, 1 daughter. Education: Doctor of Medicine, 1962; Doctor of Psychiatry, 1976. Publications: I Didn't Say Goodbye, 1980. Honours: Wizo's Award, 1981. Memberships: Apostrophes, Paris, 1980. Literary Agent: Gallimard. Address: 4 Rue de la Renaissance, Paris 75008, France.

VENDLER Helen (Hennessy), b. 1933, American. Appointments: Instructor, Cornell University, Ithaca, New York, 1960-63; Lecturer, Swarthmore College and Haverford College, Pennsylvania, 1963-64; Assistant Professor, Smith College, Northampton, 1964-66, Associate Professor 1966-68, Professor 1968-85, Boston University; Kenan Professor of English, Harvard University, Cambridge, 1985-; Porter University Professor, 1990-. Publications: Yeats's Vision and the Later Plays, 1963; On Extended Wings: Wallace Stevens' Longer Poems, 1969; The Poetry of George Herbert, 1975; Part of Nature, Part of Us: Modern American Poets, 1981; The Odes of John Keats, 1983; Wallace Stevens: Words Chosen Out of Desire, 1984; The Harvard Book of Contemporary American Poetry (ed), 1986; The Music of What Happens, 1988; Soul Says, 1995; The Given and the Made, 1995; The

Breaking of Style, 1995. Honours: ACLS, Guggenheim, Wilson and NEH Fellowships. Memberships: MLA, President, 1980; American Academy of Arts and Sciences, Vice President 1992-; American Philosophical Society; American Academy of Arts and Letters, Norwegian Academy of Arts and Sciences. Address: Department of English, Harvard University, 8 Prescott Street, Cambridge, MA 02138, USA.

VENN George Andrew Fyfe, b. 10 Dec 1943, Tacoma, WA, USA. Professor; Writer; Editor; Poet; Critic. m. Elizabeth Cheney, 1s, 1d. Education: BA, College of ID, 1967; MFA, Creative Writing, University of MT, 1970; also attended Central University, Quito, Ecuador; University of Salamanca, Spain; City Literary Institute, London. Literary Appointments: Writer-on-Tour, Western States Arts Foundation, 1977; Foreign Expert, Changsha Railway University, Hunan, China, 1981-82; General Editor, Oregon Literature Series, 1989-94; Writer-in-Residence, Eastern OR State College. Publications: Sunday Afternoon: Grande Ronde, 1975; Off The Main Road, 1978; Marking The Magic Circle, 1988; Oregon Literature Series, 1992-94; many poems, essays, stories. Contributions to: Oregon Humanities; Writer's Northwest Handbook; NW Review; Northwest Reprint Series; Poetry Northwest; Willow Springs; Clearwater Journal; Oregon East; Portland Review. Honours: Pushcart Prize, 1980; Oregon Book Award, 1988; Stewart Holbrook Award, 1994. Memberships: Executive Board, OR Council of Teachers of English; Editorial Board, Northwest Folklore. Address: Dept of English, Eastern OR State College, La Grande, OR 97850, USA.

VENTURI Robert, b. 25 June 1925, PA, USA. Architect. m. Denise Scott Brown, 23 Aug 1967, 1 son. Education: AB, Princeton University, 1947; MFA, American Academy in Rome, 1950. Publications: Complexity and Contradiction in Architecture, 1966; Learning From Las Vegas, 1972; A View from The Campidoglio: Elected Essays, 1953-84, 1984. Contributions to: Numerous, RSA Journal. Honours: AIA Medal, 1978; Pritzker Archiecture Prize, 1991. Memberships: American Institute of Architects; American Academy in Rome; Academia Nazionale di San Luca; American Academy of Arts & Science; American Academy of Arts & Letters; RIAS. Address: Venturi, Scott Brown & Associates, 4236 Main Street, Philadephia, PA 19127, USA.

VERDUIN John Richard Jr, b, 6 July 1931, Muskegon, Michigan, USA. University Professor. m. Janet M Falk, 26 Jan 1963, 1 son, 1 daughter. Education: BS, Science, University of Albuquerque, 1954; MA, Education Administration, 1959, PhD, Curriculum, 1962, Michigan State University. Publications: Cooperative Curriculum Improvement, 1967; Conceptual Models in Teacher Education, 1967; Adults Teaching Adults, 1977; The Adult Educator, 1979; Curriculum Building for Adult Learning, 1980; The Lifelong Learning Experience, 1986; Adults and Their Leisure, 1984; Handbook for Differential Education for the Gifted, 1986; Differentielle Erziehung Besonders Begabter, 1989; Distance Education: The Foundation of Effective Practice, 1991; Uzaktan Egitim: Etkin Uygulama Esaslari, 1994. Contributions to: Lifelong Learning; Leisure Quarterly; Gifted Education Press Newsletter; Dialogue on Aging; Science Education; NAPCAE Exchange; Illinios Career Education Journal. Memberships: American Association for Supervision and Curriculum Development; IACEA; Phi Delta Kappa. Address: 107 North Lake Lane, Carbondale, IL 62901, USA.

VERMA Daya Nand, b. 12 Dec 1930, Multan City. Author; Palmist. m. 28 Jan 1951, 1 d. Publications include:Yaun Vyavhar Anusheelan; Zindabad Murdabad; Kam Bhav Ki Nayee Vyakhya; Palmistry Ke Goorh Rahsya; Mansik Saphalta; Hum Sab Aur Voh; Dhyn Toga; Palmistry Ke Anubhoot Praypg. Contributions to: Gyanodya; Hamara Mun; Prakashit Man; All The Sec rets of Palmistry, 1992; Palmistry: How to Master It, 1994. Honours: Literary Award; Honoured Vishva Yoga Conference. Memberships: Authors Guild of India; Film Writers Association; Bhartiya Lekhak Sangathan; PEN; AKhil Bhartiya Hindi Prakahak Sangh; Creater Kailash Residents Association; All Indian Hindi Publishers Association; Afro Asian Book Council. Address: W21 Greater Kailash 1, New Delhi 110048, India.

VERMEIREN Koen, b. 18 Dec 1953, Antwerp, Belgium. Education: Study Germanic Philogy, 1978; Doctor of Literature & Philosophy, 1984. Appointments: Teacher, Writers Academy of Antwerp. Publications: Hermans and Wittgenstein; De Vrolijke Eenzaamheid; Schaduwen; Dood Spoor; De Droomexpres; De Kus Van Selena; Herr Ludwig; De Gek op De Heuvel. Contributions to:

Numerous. Honours: ANV Visser Neerlandia Award; August Beernaert Award. Address: Visbeekbaan 32, 2275 Wechelderzande, Belgium.

VERMES Geza, b. 22 June 1924, Mako, Hungary. Professor Emeritus. m. Pamela Curle, 12 May 1958, dec. Education: Universities of Budapest & Louvain, 1945-52; DTheol; MA; DLitt; Honorary DD; Honorary DLitt. Appointments: Editor, Journal of Jewish Studies, 1971; Director, Forum for Qumran Research, Oxford Centre for Hebrew Studies, 1991-94. Publications include: Scripture and Tradition in Judaism, 1961, 1973; The Dead Sea Scrolls in English, 1962, 75, 87; Jesus the Jew, 1973, 81, 94; Postbiblical Jewish Studies, 1975; Jesus and the World of Judaism, 1982; The Religion of Jesus the Jew, 1993; The History of the Jewish People in the Age of Jesus Christ by E Schuerer, 3 vols, 1973-87. Contributions to: Journal of Jewish Studies; Journal of Semitic Studies; Jewish Chronicle; The Times; TLS; NY Review of Books. Memberships: British Academy; British Association for Jewish Studies; European Association for Jewish Studies. Address: West Wood Cottage, Foxcombe Lane, Boars Hill, Oxford OX1 5DH, England.

VERNON Annette Robyn. See: CORKHILL Annette Robyn.

VESTER Frederic, b. 23 Nov 1925, Germany. Biochemist. m. Anne Pillong, 2 Feb 1950, 1 s, 2 d. Education: Paris University; Hamburg University. Publications include: Denken, Lernen, Vergessen, 1978; Neuland des Denkens, 1984; Unsere Welt ein Vernetztes System, 1983; Phaemomen Stress, 1978; Januskopf Landwirtschaft, 1986; Krebs Fehlgesteuertes Leben, 1977; Wasser Leben, 1987; Ausfahrt Zukunft, 1991. Contributions to: About 200 Articles in Professional Journals. Honours: Adolf Grimme Prize, 1974; German Environment Protection Medal, 1975; Deutscher Umwelthilfe Authors Prize, 1979; Emmy und Karl Kaus Preis, 1982; Philip Morris Research Prize, 1984; Essen City Prize for Journalism, 1984; Bayerische Umweltmedaille, 1992. Memberships: FBS; ASIM; GEK; DEG; Club of Rome, 1993. Address: Studiengruppe fur Biologie, und Unwelt Gmbh, Nussbaumstr 14, 80336 Munich, Germany

VICARION Palmiro (Count). See: LOGUE Christopher.

VICKERS Hugo, b. 12 Nov 1951, Writer. Education: Eton; Strasbourg University. Appointments: Director, Burkes Peerage, 1974-79; Editor, Cocktails and Laughter, 1983-; Lecturer, England, Italy, Ireland, Australia; Broadcaster, TV and Radio, 1973-; Writes Obituaries. Publications include: Gladys, Duchess of Marlborough, UK, 1979, USA, 1980; We Want the Queen, 1977; Debretts Book of the Royal Wedding, 1981; Cecil Beaton: The Authorised Biography, 1985; Vivien Leigh, 1988, 89; Cecil Beaton, 1993; Loving Garbo, 1994; Royal Orders, 1994. Contributions to: Burkes Guide to the Royal Family; Burkes Royal Families of the World; Burkes Guide to the British Monarchy; Book Reviewer for the Times; Reviews & Occasional Articles. Memberships include: Lay Steward of St Georges Chapel; Commemorative Collectors Society; Royal Society of Literature; Historic Houses Association. Hobbies: Travelling; Diarist; Photographer; Collecting Press Cuttings of the Royal Family. Literary Agent: Gillon Aitken, Aitken & Stone, 29 Fernshaw Road, London. Address: 62 Lexham Gardens, London W8 5JA, England.

VICKY. See: BHARGAVA Vishal.

VIDAL Gore, (Edgar Box), b. 3 Oct 1925, West Point, New York, USA. Writer. Education: Graduate, Phillips Exeter Academy, 1943. Publications: (novels) Williwaw, 1946; In a Yellow Wood, 1947; The City and the Pillar, 1948; The Season of Comfort, 1949; A Serch for the King, 1950; Dark Green, Bright Red, 1950; The Judgment of Paris, 1952; Messiah, 1954; Julian, 1964; Washington DC, 1967; Myra Breckinridge, 1968; Two Sisters, 1970; Burr, 1973; Myron, 1974; Kalki, 1978; Creation, 1981; Duluth, 1983; Lincoln, 1984; Empire, 1987; A Thirsty Evil, 1956; (play) Visit to a Small Planet, 1957; (TV and Broadway productions) The Best Man, 1960; Romulus, 1966; Weekend, 1968; An Evening with Richard Nixon, 1972; Gore Vidal's Lincoln, 1988; (essays) Rocking the Boat, 1962; Reflections upon a Sinking Ship, 1969; Homage to Daniel Shays, 1973; Matters of Fact and of Fiction, 1977; The Second American Revolution, 1982; Armageddon?, 1987 (London); United States: Essays 1952-1992, 1993; (films) The Catered Affair, 1956; The Left-Handed Gun, 1958; The Best Man, 1964; (teleplays) The Death of Billy the Kid, 1958; Dress Gray, 1986. Honours: National Book Award, 1993. Address: c/o Random House, 201 East 50th Street, New York, NY 10022, USA.

VIDOR Miklos Janos, (Nicholas John), b. 22 May 1923, Budapest, Hungary. Writer. m. 22 Aug 1972. Education: Doctor of German & Hungarian Literature and Aesthetics, 1947. Appointments: Freelance Writer; Chairman, Youth Dept, Hungarian Writers Union, 1991; Vice President, Hungarian PEN CLub, 1994. Publications include: On The Border, 1947; Empty Season, 1966; Meeting, 1986; Strangers, 1958; Pawn on the Chessnord, 1968; Hurt People, 1973; Challenge, 1975; Just One Day More, 1981; The Death and Resurrection of the Back, 1991; Short Stories inc, Cadet with Mandoline, 1981; Archi 5 Vpelgo, 1993; 5 Vols of Lyrics. Contributions to: Nagyvilag; Liget; Magyar Nemzet. Honours: Jozsef Attila Prize, 1955; Officers Cross of the Hungarian Republic, 1993. Memberships: Hungarian Art Foundation; Union of Hungarian Writers; PEN. Literary Agent: Artisjus, 1051 Budapest. Address: 17 Puskin u, H 1088 Budapest, Hungary.

VIERROS Tuure Johannes, b. 20 Dec 1927, Kankaanpaa, Finland. Senior Teacher. m. Enni Luodetlahti, 22 June 1954, 2 s, 1 d. Education: University of Helsinki, 1952. Publications include: Loukkauskivet, 1959; Laivurinsolmu, 1961; Harjahirsi, 1963; Lahella Kuolon Rantaa, 1967; Harhaoppinen, 1971; Komeett, 1972; The Kankaanpaa Quarter, 1976; Valhetta Kaikki Totuus, 1979; Ei Saavu Satamaan, 1981; Samum, 1983; Julmat Jumalat, 1990; Various Textbooks, Approx 30 Vols. Contributions to: Various Journals and Magazines. Honours: R SVR, 1986; Nortamo Prize of Satakunnan Kirjallinen Kerho, 1966; Literary Prize of Pori Town, 1960, 62; Honor Prize of Uusi Kirjakerho, 1982; First Prize, Literary Game of Kalevala Festival Year, 1985; Literary Prize of Suomen Maakuntakirjailijat, 1992. Memberships: Finnish Society of Authors; PEN; Authors in Helsinki. Literary Agent: Kirjayhtyma. Address: Untuvaisentie 7 G 94, 00820 Helsinki, Finland.

VILLA GILBERT Mariana Soledad Magdalena, b. 21 Feb 1937, Croydon, England. Writer. Education: Various Schools including Newbury High School, Berkshire. Publications: Mrs Galbraith's Air, 1963; My Love All Dressed in White, 1964; Mrs Cantello, 1968; A Jingle Jangle Song, 1968; The Others, 1970; Manuela A Modern Myth, 1973; The Sun in Horus, 1986. Address: 28 St Martins Road, Canterbury, Kent CT1 1QW, England.

VINCENT John James, b. 29 Dec 1929, Sunderland, England. Methodist Minister. m. Grace Johnston Stafford, 4 Dec 1958, 2 s, 1 d. Education: BD, Richmond College, London University, 1954; STM, Drew University, 1955; DeTheol, Basel University, 1960; Ordained, Methodist Church, 1956. Appointments: Director, Urban Theology Unit, 1969-; Editor, New City Journal, 1971-; Adjunct Professor, New York Theological Seminary, 1979-87; Honorary Lecturer, Sheffield University, 1990-. Publications include: Christ and Methodism, 1964; Here I Stand, 1967; Secular Christ, 1968; The Race Race, 1970; The Jesus Thing, 1973; Stirrings, Essays Christian and Radical, 1975; Alternative Church, 1976; Disciple and Lord, 1976; Starting all over Again, 1981; Into the City, 1982; OK Lets Be Methodists, 1984; Radical Jesus, 1986; Mark at Work, 1986; Britain in the 90's, 1989; Liberation Theology fron the Inner City, 1992; A Petition of Distress from the Cities, 1993; A British Liberation Theology. Memberships: Studiorum Novi Testamenti Societas; Alliance of Radical Methodists; Methodist Church of Great Britain, 1989-90. Address: 178 Abbeyfield Road, Sheffield, S4 7AY, England.

VINE Barbara. See: RENDELL Ruth.

VINGE Vernor Steffen, b. 2 Oct 1944, Waukesha, Wisconsin, USA. Writer; Teacher. Education: PhD, Mathematics, University of California, San Diego. Publications: True Names; Marooned in RealTime; Peace War; Threats and Other Promises; Witling; Tatja Grimm's World. Literary Agent: Sharon Jarvis & Co, Toad Hall Inc, RR2 Box 16B, Laceyville, PA 18623, USA. Address: Department of Mathematical Sciences, San Diego State University, San Diego, CA 92182, USA.

VIRTUE Noel, b. 1947, New Zealand. Novelist. Appointments: Zookeeper during the 1970s. Publications: The Redemption of Elsdon Bird, 1987; Then Upon the Evil Season, 1988; In the Country of Salvation, 1990; Always the Islands of Memory, 1991; Among the Animals: A Zookeeper's Story, 1988. Address: c/o Hutchinson, 20 Vauxhall Bridge Road, London SW1V 2SA, England.

VISWANATHAN Subrahmanyam, b. 23 Oct 1933, Sholavandan, Tamil Nadu, India. Professor. m. Nirmala Nilakantan, 26 June 1960, 1

d. Education: BA, 1953, MA, 1958, University of Madras; PhD, 1977, Sri Venkateswara University. Appointments: Lecturer, Sri Venkateswara University, 1959-77; Reader, 1977-82, Professor, 1982-, University of Hyderabad. Publications: The Shakespeare Play as Poem, 1980; On Shakespeares Dramaturgy, 1992; Shakespear in India, 1987; Critical Essays, 1982. Contributions to: Learned Journals and Collections of Essays and Papers, About 50. Honour: The Indian UGC National Lecturer in English Literature, 1986-87. Address: A14 Staff Quarters, University of Hyderabad, Hyderabad 500134, India.

VITIELLO Justin, b. 14 Feb 1941, New York, USA. Professor of Italian. Education: BA, Brown University 1963; PhD, University of Michigan, 1970. Appointments: Assistant Professor of Comparative Literature, University of Michigan, 1970-73; Assistant, Associate then Full Professor of Italian, Temple University, 1974-. Publications: Il carro del pesce di Vanzetti, 1989; Vanzetti's Fish Cart, 1991; Sicily Within, 1992; Confessions of a Joe Rock, 1992; Subway Home, 1994. Contributions to: Many in the area of Medieval and Renaissance Italian, Sicilian & Spanish Poetry. Address: Clivo Delle Mura Vaticane, 23-00136 Rome, Italy.

VITZ Robert Carl, b. 26 Dec 1938, Minneapolis, USA. Professor. m. Margaret Markel, 13 June 1964, 2 sons, 1 daughter. Education: DePauw University, BA, 1960; Miami University, MA, 1967; University of North Carolina, PhD, 1971. Appointments: Purdue University, Assistant Professor, 1971-72; Northern Kentucky University, Professor, 1972-. Publications: The Queen and the Arts; Painters of Reform. Contributions to: Queen City Heritage; New York History; The Old Northwest; Filson Club Quarterly. Honour: Post Corbett Award. Memberships: The Literary Club; Organization of American Historians; Cincinnati Historical Society. Address: 43E Vernon Ln, Ft Thomas, KY 41075, USA.

VIVIAN Daisy. See: KENYON Bruce Guy.

VIZINCZEY Stephen, b. 12 May 1933, Kaloz, Hungary. Writer. m. Sept 1963, 3 d. Education: University of Budapest, 1949-50; Academy of Theatre Arts, Budapest, 1951-56. Appointments: Editor, Exchange Magazine, 1960-61; Producer, Canadian Broadcasting Corporation, 1962-65. Publications: In Praise of Older Women, 1965; The Rules of Chaos, 1969; An Innocent Millionaire, 1983; Truth and Lies in Literature, 1986; The Man with the Magic Touch, 1994. Contributions to: Currently; Observer; ABC. Memberships: PEN. Address: 70 Coleherne Court, Old Brompton Road, London SW5 0EF, England.

VIZKI Morti. See: POULSEN Morten.

VLAD Alexandru, b. 31 July 1950, Romania. Author. m. Maria Vlad, 4 Mar 1985, 2 s. Education: BA, Cluj Napoca University. Appointment: Assistant Editor, Vatra, 1990-. Publications: The Giffins Wing, 1981; The Way to the South Pole, 1985; In The Cold of the Summer, 1985; Joseph Conrd, The Duel, 1989; W H Hudson Green Mansions, 1992; Atena, Atena, 1994; Reinventing Politics, 1994. Contributions to: Steaua; Vatra; Amfiteatru; Astra; Trubuna; New Glass; 22; Romania Literara. Memberships: Union of Writers; N Steinhardt Memorial Foundation. Address: Str Lugoslaviei Nr 72 Bl, B4 Ap23 3400 Cluj Napoc, Romania.

VOGASSARIS Angelo-Eftihios (Felix), b. 6 May 1935, Piraeus, Greece. Educator; Writer. div. Education: Degree in Philosophy & Greek Literature, University of Athens; Diploma, Germanistics, Munich German Academy; Diploma, English, French. Appointments: Editor, Writer, Common Market News, Ionian and Popular Bank of Greece, to 1977; Ex-Director, Experimental Evening High School; High School Teacher, Greek Literature; Pedagogy Advisor. Publications: A Man, A Life, A Death, Costas Cariotakis, 1968, 2nd edition, 1969; The Poet Andrea Calvos, 1968; Andrea Calvos, Poet of Virtue, Patriotism and Liberty, essay, 1970; Dionyssios Solomos and Liberty, essay, 1972; Windspeed Eight to Ten Beaufort, novel, 1974; Nicolas Kavvadias (Marabu): The Poet of the seaways, 1979; The Ghost of Che Guevara, 2 novels, 1982; Paul Nor (Nicolas Nicolaides) The satirical, the lyrical, the theatrical, the antifascist), essay, 1985; Harry's Night Encounter in Aphrodite Street, novel, 1988-89; Forthcoming: In the Land of Portugal; The Monkey's Love, contemporary tragedy; The Star, tragi-comedy; Fury and Disgust of Citizen 'A' tragi-comedy; Poetry: Languor; Silence, Better Silence (in memory of the 40 years anniversary of the Spanish writer Federico Garcia Lorca), 1977; Memory of Bobby Sands Who Died in the Maze Prison, 1984; The Fury and Loneliness Monologue of a Citizen 'A' 1992; Radio plays include: George Gershwin's Life; Al Johnson's Life; Cole Porter's Life; Voyage to Tilsit; The Death of a Salesman, radio version; Madness on Mountains. Contributions to: Prose to newspapers and magazines. Memberships: Association of Greek Writers; President, Piraeus Literary & Arts Society; Represented Greek Writers in Poetry & Literature, International Meetings, most European Countries, USA, USSR. Address: 1-3 Aristotelous str, GR 18535 Piraeus, Greece.

VOGEL Paula Anne, b. 16 November 1951, Washington DC, USA. Dramatist. Education: BA, Catholic University of America. Appointments: Instructor, Consultant of Playwriting and Theatre Arts. Memberships: Dramatists Guild. Honours: Obie Award, 1992; Heerbes-McCalmon Playwriting Award, 1975, 1976; American College Theatre Festival Award, 1977; American National Theatre and Academy-West Award, 1978. Address: Dept of English, Brown University, Box 1852, Providence, RI 02912, USA.

VOIGT Ellen Bryant, b. 9 May 1943, Danville, Virginia, USA. Poet; Teacher. m. Francis G W Voigt, 5 Sept 1965, 1 son, 1 daughter. Education: BA, Converse College, Spartanburg, South Carolina, 1964; MFA, University of Iowa, Iowa City, Iowa, 1966. Appointments: Faculty Member: Iowa Wesleyan College, 1966-69, Goddard College 1969-79, Massachusetts Institute of Technology, 1979-82, Warren Wilson College, 1981-; Participant: Indiana, Tucson, Napa Valley, Catskills and Breadloaf Writers Conferences. Publications: Two Trees, 1992; The Lotus Flowers, 1987; The Forces of Plenty, 1983; Claiming Kin, 1976. Contributions to: New Yorker; Atlantic; American Poetry Review; Antioch Review; Partisan Review; Pequod; Ploughshares; Georgia Review; Ohio Review; Poetry; New Republic. Honours: Fellowship, National Endowment for the Arts, 1975; Fellowship, Guggenheim Foundation, 1978; Haines Award for Poetry, Fellowship of Southern Writers, 1993; Doctor of Literature, Converse College, 1989; Emily Clark Balch Award, 1987. Address: Box 16, Marshfield, VT 05658, USA.

VOLLMAN William T, b. 1959. Computer Programmer; Writer. Education: Deep Springs College. Honours: Whiting Writers Award. Address: c/o Kelly Rosenheim Whiting Writers Awards-Mrs Giles Whiting, 30 Rockefeller Plaza, Room 3500, NY 10112, USA.

VON MOLLER Ilona Katrina, b. 8 April 1941, Budapest, Hungary. Teacher; Musician; Wife-Mother. m. Erich Baron von Moller-Harteneck, 6 April 1968, 1 son, 2 daughter. Education: MusB, Adelaide, 1962; BA Melbourne, 1966; L.Mus.A, 1962; TSTC, Melbourne, 1966. Publications: Strings and Things. Memberships: Soroptomist Soc; ISME; Concert Master Maroondah Symphony Orch. Address: Moller House, 37 Craig Road, Donvale, Victoria 3111, Australia.

VON TROTTA Margarethe, b. 21 Feb 1942, Berlin, German. Screen Writer, Director. m. (1)1 s, (2)Volker Schloendorff. Appointments: Screenwriter, Director; Actress, 1960's. Publications include: Schwestern; Oder, Die Balance des Gluecks; Fischer Taschenbuch Verlag, 1979; Die Bleierne Zeit, 1981; Heller Wahn, 1983; Rosa Luxemburg, 1986; F Greno, 1986; Other Screenplays. Honours: Golden Lion from Venice Film Festival, 1981. Memberships: Akademie der Kunste; European Film Academy. Address: c/o German Film & TV Academy, Pommernallee 1, 1 Berlin 19, Germany.

VONARBURG Elisabeth, b. 1947, France. Education: PhD, Creative Writing. Appointments: Literature Teacher at various Universities in Quebec; Singer; Songwriter; Literary Editor of "Solaris", 1979-90. Publications: The Silent City, 1986; Comment écrire des histoires, 1986; Histoires de la Princess et du Dragon, 1991; Ailleurs et du Fapon, 1992. Honours: Casper Awards, best science fiction short story in French, 1987, 1990, 1991; Best Science Fiction Book, 1991, 1992; Grand Prix de la Science-Fiction Francaise, Prix Rosny Ainé, and Prix Boréal, 1981. Address: 266 Belleau, Chicoutini, Quebec, G7H 2Y8, Canada.

VONNEGUT Kurt, b. 11 Nov 1922, USA. Author. m. Jane Marie Cox, 1 Sept 1945, div, 1 s, 2 d. adopted 3 nephews, (2)Jill Krementz, 1979. Education: Cornell University; University of Chicago, 1945-47. Publictions include: Player Piano, 1951; Siren of Titan, 1959; Welcome to the Monkey House, 1968; Slaughterhouse Five, 1969; Deadeye Dick, 1982; Galapagos, 1985; Bluebeard, 1987; Hocus Pocus, 1990; Fates Worse than Deth, 1991. Contributions to: Various Journals and

Magazines. Membership: National Institute Arts & Letters. Address: c/o Donald C Farber, 99 Park Avenue, NY 10016, USA.

VOTH Alden H, b. 4 May 1926, Goessel, Kansas, USA. University Professor. m. 18 Aug 1956, 1 son, 1 daughter. Education: BA Economics 1950, Bethel College; MS Economics 1953, Iowa State University; PhD International Relations 1959, University of Chicago. Appointments: Upland College, Upland, California, 1960-63; San Jose State University, 1963-91; American University in Cairo (2 year leave-of-absence from San Jose State University) 1965-67. Publications: Moscow Abandons Israel for the Arabs, 1980; The Kissinger Legacy: American Middle East Policy, 1984. Contributions to: Vietnam: Studying a Major Controversy, Journal of Conflict Resolution, 1967; Portugal in Africa: Angola and Mozambique, Contemporary Review, 1968; The Moral Dimension of International Relations, Rocky Mountain Social Science Journal, 1972. Honours: Wall Street Journal Award, 1950; Excellence in Teaching Award, American University in Cairo, 1967; Most Influential Professor Award, SJSU, 1987, 1989 & 1991; Research Grant for the Study of African Politics, AUC, 1966; Fellow, National Council on US-Arab Relations, 3-week guest of the Iraqi and UAE governments, 1990. Memberships: Pomona Valley American Association for the United Nations, Member of the Board of Trustees 1961-63; International Studies Association; American Political Science Association; Western Political Science Association. Address: 1385 Kimberly Drive, San Jose, CA 95118, USA.

VOYLE Mary. See: **MANNING Rosemary.**

VROOMKONING Victor. See: **VAN DE LAAR Waltherus Antonius Bernardinus.**

VUONG Lynette Dyer, b. 20 June 1938, Owosso, Michigan, USA. Author-Lecturer. m. Ti Quang Vuong, 9 Jan 1962, 2 sons, 2 daughters. Education: University of Wisconsin, Milwaukee, 1958-61; Graduated, Registered Nurse, Milwaukee County Hospital School of Nursing, 1959, University of Houston, 1992-. Publications: The Brocaded Slipper and Other Vietnamese Tales, 1982; A Friend for Carlita, 1989; The Golden Carp and Other Tales from Vietnam, 1993; Sky Legends of Vietnam, 1993. Contributions to: Highlights For Children; Guide; Trails; Reflection; Face-To-Face; Venture; Discoveries; Straight; In Touch; Davis Nursing Survey; Hi-Call; Teens Today; Romance Writers Report; Contact; Family and Friends; Partners; Bread for Children; Between Times. Honours: Texas Bluebonnet Award List Title (The Brocaded Slipper), 1984; Georgia Children's Book Award Nominee, The Brocaded Slipper, 1985; Romance Writers of America Golden Heart Award, 1st Place in Mainstream Division, The Shadow of The Sickle, unpublished manuscript; Catholic Library Association's Ann Martin Book Award, 1991. Memberships: Associated Authors of Children's Literature, Houston (past President); Romance Writers of America; Society of Children's Book Writers; Golden Key National Honor Society; Classical Association of Houston. Address: 1521 Morning Dove Drive, Humble, TX 77396, USA.

W

WADDELL Evelyn Margaret (Lyn Cook), b. 4 May 1918, Weston, Ontario, Canada. Children's Librarian. m. Robert John Waddell, 19 Sept 1949, 1 son, 1 daughter. Education: BA English Language & Literature, BLS, University of Toronto. Publications: All as Lyn Cook: The Bells on Finland Street, 1950, 1991; The Little Magic Fiddler, 1951; Rebel on the Trail, 1953; Jady and the General, 1955; Pegeen and the Pilgrim, 1957; The Road to Kip's Cove, 1961; Samantha's Secret Room, 1963, 1991; The Brownie Handbook for Canada, 1965; The Secret of Willow Castle, 1966; The Magical Miss Mittens, 1970; Toys from the Sky, 1972; Jolly Jean-Pierre, 1973; If I Were All These, 1974; A Treasure for Tony, 1980; The Magic Pony, 1981; Sea Dreams, 1981; The Hiding Place (historical novel for young people), 1990; A Canadian ABC (poetry with art by Thoreau MacDonald), 1990. Honours: Honorary Member, Academy of Canadian Writers, Vicky Metcalf Award, 1978. Memberships: Writers Union of Canada; Canadian Society of Children's Authors, Illustrators and Performers. Address: 72 Cedarbrae Blvd, Scarborough, Ontario, M1J 2K5, Canada.

WADDINGTON FEATHER John Joseph, b. 10 July 1933, Keighley, Yorkshire, England. Anglican Priest; Publisher. m. Sheila Mary Booker, 23 July 1960, 3 d. Education: BA, Leeds University. Appointment: Co Editor, Orbis, 1971-80. Publications: Yorkshire Dialect, 1969; Garlic Lane, 1970; Easy Street, 1971; One Mans Road, 1979; Quills Adventures in the Great Beyond, 1980; Tall Tales from Yukon, 1983; Khartoum Trilogy, 1985; Quills Adventures in Wasteland, 1986; Quills Adventures in Grozzieland, 1988; Six Christian Monologues, 1990; Shropshire Volumne in Poets England Series, 1994. Contributions to: Various Journals and Magazines. Honours: Bronte Society Prize, 1963; Cyril Hodges Poetry Award, 1976. Memberships: Yorkshire Dialect Society; Bronte Society; Royal Society of Arts. Address: Fair View, Old Coppice, Lyth Bank, Shrewsbury, Shropshire, SY3 0BW, England.

WADE David, b. 1929, England. Appointments: Radio Critic, The Listener, 1965-67, The Times, 1967-89. Publications: Trying to Connect You; The Cooker; The Guthrie Process; The Gold Spinners; Three Blows in Anger; The Ogden File; The Carpet Maker of Samarkand; The Nightingale; Summer of 39; The Facts of Life; A Rather Nasty Crack; On Detachment; The Tree of Strife; Power of Attorney; Alexander. Address: Willow Cottage, Stockland Green Road, Southborough, Kent TN3 0TL, England.

WAELTI-WALTERS Jennifer Rose, b. Wolverhampton, England. Professor of French and Women's Studies. Education: BA Hons, 1964, PhD, 1968, University of London: Licence-ès-Lettres, Université de Lille, France, 1965. Publications: Alchimie et littérature (Butor), 1975; J M G Le Clézio, 1977; Michel Butor, a view of his World and a Panorama of his Work, 1977; Icare ou l'évasion impossible (J M G Le Clézio), 1981; Fairytales and the Female Imagination, 1982; Jeanne Hyvrard (with M Verthuy), 1989; Feminist Novelists of the Belle Epoque, 1991; Michel Butor, 1992; Feminisms of The Belle Epoque (with S Hause), 1994. Contributions to: Numerous magazines and journals. Honours: APFUCC Prize, Best Book of Literary Critism in French, 1989. Memberships: Canadian Research Institute for the Advancement of Women; Canadian Women's Studies Association; Association des Professeurs de Français des Universités et Collèges Canadiens. Address: Women's Studies, University of Victoria, Victoria BC, V8W 3P4, Canada.

WAGNER-MARTIN Linda C, b. 1936, American. Appointments: Former Teacher, Wayne State University, Detroit; Bowling Green State University, Ohio; Michigan State University, East Lansing; Hanes Professor of English and Comparative Literature, University of North Carolina, Chapel Hill; Editor, The Centennial Review. Publications: The Poems of William Carlos Williams, 1964; Denise Levertov, Intaglios, 1967; The Prose of William Carlos Williams, 1970; Phyllis McGinley, 1971; William Faulkner: Four Decades of Criticism (ed), 1973; T S Eliot (ed), Ernest Hemingway: Five Decades of Criticism (ed), 1974; Hemingway and Faulkner: Inventors/Masters, 1975; Introducing Poems (with C David Mead), 1976; Ernest Hemingway: A Reference Guide, Robert Frost: The Critical Heritage, Speaking Straight Ahead: Interviews with William Carlos Williams, 1977; William Carlos Williams: A Reference Guide, 1978; Dos Passos: Artist as American, Joyce

Carol Oates: Critical Essays (ed), 1979; American Modern, 1980; Songs for Isadora, 1981; Ellen Glasgow: Beyond Convention, 1982; Sylvia Plath: Critical Essays, 1984; The Sun Also Rises (ed), Ernest Hemingway: Six Decades of Criticism (ed), 1987; Sylvia Plath, A Biography 1987; Sylvia Plath: The Critical Heritage (ed), 1988; Anne Sexton: Critical Essays (ed), The Modern American Novel, 1914-1945, 1989; Co-ed of The Heath Anthology of American Literature (1989, 1994); Wharton's The House of Mirth: A Novel of Admonition, 1990; Denise Levertov: Critical Essays (ed), 1990; Plath's The Bell Jar, 1991; Telling Women's Lives: The New Biography, 1994; Co-ed of The Oxford Comparion to Women's Writing in the United States, 1995; Favoured Strangers: Gertrude Stein and Her Family, 1995; New Essays on Go Down Moses, 1995; Co-ed of The Oxford Book of Women's Writing in the United States, (anthology) 1995. Address: Department of English, University of North Carolina, Chapel Hill, NC 27514, USA.

WAINWRIGHT Geoffrey, b. 16 July 1939, Yorkshire, England. Theologian (Professor of Systematic Theology); Minister, Methodist Church. m. Margaret Wiles, 20 Apr 1965, 1 son, 2 daughters. Education: BA, 1960, MA, 1964, BD, 1972, DD, 1987, Cambridge University; Dr Theol, Geneva University, 1969. Appointments: Editor, Studia Liturgica, 1974-87; Co-Editor, Dictionary of the Ecumenical Movement, World Council of Churches, Geneva, Switzerland, 1991. Publications: Christian Initiation, 1969; Eucharist & Eschatology, 1971, 1981; The Study of Liturgy (co-editor), 1978, 1992; Doxology, 1980; The Ecumenical Moment, 1983; The Study of Spirituality (co-editor), 1986; On Wesley and Calvin, 1987; Keeping the Faith - Essays to Mark the Centenary of Lux Mundi (editor), 1989. Contributions to: Numerous articles to dictionaries, encyclopedias and theological journals. Honours: Numerous named lectureships throughout the world. Memberships: Societas Liturgica, President 1983-85; Chairman, International Dialogue between World Methodist Council and Roman Catholic Church; Faith and Order Commission, World Council of Churches, 1976-91; Secretary, American Theological Society. Address: The Divinity School, Duke University, Durham, NC 27708, USA.

WAINWRIGHT Jeffrey, b. 19 Feb 1944, Stoke On Trent, England. Poet; Critic. m. 2 children. Education: BA, 1965, MA, 1967, University of Leeds. Appointments: Lecturer, University of Wales, 1967-72; Visiting Lecturer, Lond Island University, 1970-71; Senior Lecturer, Manchester Polytechnic, 1972-. Publications include: The Important Man, 1970; Hearts Desire, 1978; Selected Poems, 1985; Michael Schmidt and peter Jones, British Poetry Since 1970, 1980; Blacke Morrison and Andrew. Motion, The Penguim Book of Ontemporary British Poetry, 1982; Peter Robinson, Geoffrey Hill, 1985; The Red Headed Pupil, 1994; Le Cid, 1994. Contributions to: Various Periodicals including Stand; Agenda; PN Review; Poetry Review. Address: 11 Hesketh Avenue, Didsbuty, Manchester, M20 8QN, England.

WAITE Peter Busby, b. 12 July 1922, Toronto, Ontario, Canada. Professor of History. m. Masha Maria Gropuzzo, 22 Aug 1958. Education: BA (Hons), 1948, MA, 1950, University of British Columbia, PhD, University of Toronto, 1954. Publications: The Life and Times of Confederation, 1864-1867, 1962; Canada 1874-1896, 1971; John A Macdonald, his life and world, 1975; The Man from Halifax: Sir John Thompson, Prime Minister, 1985; Lord of Point Grey: Larry MacKenzie of UBC, 1987; Between Three Oceans: Challenges of a Continental Destiny, 1840-1900, Chapter IV, Illustrated History of Canada, 1988; The Loner: The Personal Life and Ideas of R B Bennett 1870-1947, 1992; The Lives of Dalhousie University: Volume I, Lord Dalhousie's College, 1818-1925, 1994. Contributions to: Some 55 articles to numerous magazines and journals. Honours: Fellow, Royal Society of Canada, 1972; Runner-up, Governor-General's Gold Medal Prize, 1985; Lieutenant-Governor's Medal for Lord of Point Grey, British Columbia, 1987; LL.D Dalhousie, 1991; D.Litt, University of New Brunswick, 1991; Memorial University of Newfoundland, 1991; Carleton University, 1993; Officer of the Order of Canada, 1993. Memberships: President, Canadian Historical Association, 1968-69; Chairman, Humanities Research Council, 1968-70; Chairman, Aid to Publications Committee, Social Science Federation, 1987-89. Address: 960 Ritchie Drive, Halifax, Nova Scotia, B3H 3P5, Canada.

WAKEMAN (Frederic) Evans, b. 12 Dec 1937, Kansas City, USA. Professor. div, 2 sons, 1 daughter. Education: BA, Harvard College, 1959; MA, 1962, PhD, 1965, University of California, Berkeley. Appointments: Editorial Advisor, Modem Asian Studies, 1980-81; Editorial Advisory Board, American Historical Review, 1981; President,

Social Science Research Council, 1986-89; President, American Historical Association, 1992; Haas Professor of Asian Studies, Berkeley, 1989-; Director, Institute of East Asian Studies, Berkeley. Publications: Strangers at the Gate: Social Disorder in South China, 1839-1861, 1966; Nothing Concealed: Essays in Honor of Liu Yu-Yun, 1970; Co-Editor, Conflict & Control in Late Imperial China, 1975; History and Will, 1976; The Great Enterprise: The Manchu Reconstruction of Imperial Order in Seventeenth Century China, 1985, 2 volumes; Co-Editor, Shanghai Sojourners, 1992. Contributions to: American Historical Review; New York Review of Books; The China Quarterly; Journal of Asian Studies. Honours: History and Will, nominated for National Book Award, 1974; The Great Enterprise, Winner, Levenson Prize, 1986; The Great Enterprise, Winner, Lilienthal Award. Memberships: American Historical Association; Association for Asian Studies; American Academy of Arts and Sciences. Address: Institute of East Asian Studies, University of California, Berkeley, CA 94720, USA.

WAKEMAN John, b. 29 Sept 1928, London, England. Editor; Writer. m. Hilary Paulett, 15 Mar 1957, 4 s, 1 d. Education: Associate, British Library Association, 1950; BA, University of East Anglia, 1989; MA, 1990. Publications include: A Room for Doubt, 1985; Wilson Library Bulletin, 1959-61; World Authors, 1950-70, 1975, 1970-75, 1980; Worl Film Directors, 1987, 88; The Rialto, 1985; The Bech Hut, 1987. Contributions to: Poems; Essays, Reviews in, Ambit; Encounter; London Magazine; New Statesman; NY Times; NY Times Book REview; Observer; Poetry; Times; Times Literary Supplement; Punch. Honours: World Film Directors Selected by Library Journal as 1 of Best Refence Books of 1988; 1 of Outstanding Academic Books of 1989; Eastern Arts Travel Bursary, 1991; Hawthornden Fellowship, 1992. Literay Agent: Michael Shaw, Curtis Brown, London W1R 5TB. Address: 32 Grosvenor Road, Norwich, Norfolk, NR2 2PZ.

WALCOTT Derek (Alton), b. 23 Jan 1930, Castries, St Lucia, West Indies. Poet; Playwright. m. Norline Metivier, 1982. Education: BA, University College of the West Indies at Mona, Jamaica, 1953. Appointments include: Visiting Professor at Boston and other American universities, from 1981. Publications include: 25 Poems, 1948; Poems 1951; In a Green Night: Poems 1948-60, 1962; Selected Poems, 1964; The Castaway and Other Poems, 1965; The Gulf and Other Poems, 1969; Another Life, 1973; Sea Grapes, 1976; The Star-Apple Kingdom, 1980; Selected Poetry, 1981; The Fortunate Traveller, 1981; Midsummer, 1984; Collected Poems 1948-84, 1986; The Arkansas Testament, 1988; Omeros, 1989; Plays: Harry Dernier, 1952; The Sea at Dauphin, 1954; The Charlatan, 1954; Ti-Jean and His Brothers, 1957; Batai, carnival show, 1964; Dream on Monkey Mountain, 1967; Franklin: A Tale of the Islands, 1969; The Joker of Seville, 1974; O Babylon, 1976; Remembrance, 1977; Pantomime, 1978; The Isle is Full of Noises, 1982; Beef, no Chicken, 1989. Honours include: Fellow, Royal Society of Literature, 1966; OBE, 1972; Queen's Gold Medal for Poetry, 1988; Nobel Prize for Literature, 1992. Address: 165 Duke of Edinburgh Avenue, Diego Martin, Trinidad.

WALDENFELS Hans, b. 20 Oct 1931, Essen, Ruhr. University Professor. Education: Lic Phil, 1956; Lic Theol, 1964; Dr Theol, 1968; Dr Theol Habil, 1976; Ordained Roman Catholic Priest, 1963. Publications include: Faszination des Buddhismus, 1982; Kontextuelle Fundamentalheologie, 1988; An der Grenze des Denkbaren, 1988; Lexikon der Religionen, 1989; Begegnung der Religionen, 1990. Memberships: Internationales Institut fur Missionswissenschaftliche Forschungen; International Association for Mission Studies; Deutsche Vereinigung fur Religionsgeschichte; Deutsche Gesellschaft fur Missioswissenschaft; Rotary Club. Address: Grenzweg 2, D 4000 Dusseldorf 31, Germany.

WALDROP Rosmarie, b. 24 Aug 1935, Kitzingen/Main, Germany. Writer; Translator; Editor. m. 21 Jan 1959. Education: Undergraduate studies, Universities of Wurzburg, Freiburg and Aix-Marseille; MA, 1960, PhD, 1966, University of Michigan, USA. Appointments: Editor, Publisher, Burning Deck Press, USA, 1963-; Wesleyan University, 1964-70; SMU, 1977; Brown University, 1977-78, 1983, 1990-91; Tufts University, 1978-81. Publications: The Road is Everywhere or Stop This Body, 1978; Streets Enough to Welcome Snow, poems, 1986; The Reproduction of Profiles, poems, 1987; The Hanky of Pippin's Daughter, novel; A Form/of Taking/It All, novella, 1990; The Book of Questions by Edmond Jabes (translator), 7 vols bound as 4, 1976-84; Lawn of Excluded Middle, poems, 1993. Contributions to: Conjunctions; Sulfur; Oblek; Denver Quarterly; Temblor. Honours: Major Hopwood Award in Poetry, 1963; Howard

Fellowship, 1974-75; Columbia Translation Center Award, 1978; NEA Arts Award, 1988; Award from the Fund for Poetry, 1990; DAAD Fellowship, 1993; Harold Morton Landon Translation Award, 1994. Memberships: PEN. Address: 71 Elmgrove Avenue, Providence, RI 02906, USA.

WALES Robert, b. 12 July 1933, Greenock, Scotland. Writer. m. (1)Joan Marie Austin, 1947, 2 s, 3 d, (2)Susan Clare Richardson, 1970, 1 s. Publications: The Cell, 1971; Harry, 1985; The Navigator, 1989; Films, TV & Theatre Plays; TV Series, Short Stories. Memberships: Society of Authors; Writers Guild. Literary Agent: Peters Fraser & Dunlop, The Chambers, Chelsea Harbour, London. Address: 2 Thorne Street, Barnes, London SW13 0PR, England.

WALKER Alexander, b. 22 Mar 1930, Portadown, Northern Ireland. Journalist; Film Critic. Education: BA, Queens University, Belfast; College d'Europe, BElgium; University of MI, USA. Appointments include: Lecturer, University of MI, 1952-54; Features Edutor, Birmingham Gazette, UK, 1954-56; Leader Writer, Film Critic, Evening Standard, 1960-; Columnist, Vogue Magazine, 1974-86; Frequent Broadcaster; Author, TV Series; Author, Co Producer, TV Programmes. Publications include: The Celluloid Sacrifice: Aspects of Sex in the Movies, 1966; Stardom: The Hollywood Phenomenon, 1970; Rudolph Valentino, 1976; Garbo, 1980; Peter Sellers: Authorised Biography, 1981; Joan Crawford, 1983; Dietrich, 1984; National Heros: British Cinema Industry in the 70's * 80's, 1985; Its Only a Movie, Ingrid, 1988; Elizabeth: The Life of Elizabeth Taylor, 1990; Zinnemann, 1991; Fatal Charm: The Life of Rex Harrison, 1992; Audrey: Her Real Story, 1994. Contributions to: Encounter; Various Other British & Foreign Publications. Honours: Critic of the Year, 1970, 1974; British Press Awards; Chevalier de l'Ordre des Arts et des Letters, 1981; Award of Golden Eagle. Memberships: British Screen Advisory Council; British Film Institute. Address: 1 Marlborough, 38-40 Maida Vale, London W9 1RW, England.

WALKER Andrew Norman, b. 19 May 1926, Looe, Cornwall, England. Retired BBC Journalist. m. Avril Anne Elizabeth Dooley, 20 June 1956, 2 s, 2 d. Publications: The Modern Commonwealth, 1975; The Commonwealth: A New Look, 1978; A Skyful of Freedom, 1992. Contributions to: Occasional Articles in Janes Defence Weekly; Commonwealth Magazine. Membership: Commonwealth Journalists Association. Address: 9 Chartwell Court, Brighton, East Sussex BN1 2EW, England.

WALKER David Maxwell, b. 9 April 1920, Glasgow, Scotland. University Professor, Retired. m. Margaret Knox, 1 Sept 1954. Education: MA, 1946, LLB, 1948, LLD, 1985, Glasgow University; PhD, 1952, LLD, 1960, Edinburgh University; LLB, 1957, LLD, 1968, London University. Publications include: The Oxford Companion to Law, 1980; Principles of Scottish Private Law, 4 vols, 1988; Law of Delict in Scotland, 1981; Law of Contracts in Scotland, 1994; The Scottish Jurists, 1985; Law of Prescription and Minitation in Scotland, 1990; Stairs Institutions of the Law of Scotland, 1981; Legal History of Scotland, 3 vols; The Scottish Legal System, 1993. Contributions to: Numerous, Mostly to Juridical Review and Scots Law Times. Honours: Honorary LLD, 1974; Fellow, British Academy, 1976; Fellow, Royal Society of Edinburgh, 1980; CBE, 1986. Memberships: Faculty of Advocates; Society of the Middle Temple; Stair Society; Scottish History Society; Society of Antiquaries of Scotland. Address: 1 Beaumont Gate, Glasgow, G12 9EE.

WALKER Geoffrey De Quincey, b. 27 Oct 1940, Waratah, NSW, Australia. Professor of Law. m. Patricia Mary Kehoe, 7 Dec 1990. Education: LLB, 1962; LLM, 1963; SJD, 1966. Publictns: Australian Monopoly Law, 1967; Initiative and Referendum: The People's Law, 1987; The Rule of Law: Foundation of Constitutional Democracy, 1988. Contributions to: Over 60 Articles. Honour: Gowen Fellow, University of PA, 1966. Address: T C Beirne School of Law, University of Queensland, Qld 4072, Australia.

WALKER George F(rederick), b. 23 Aug 1947, Toronto, Ontario, Canada. Playwright. Education: Graduated Riverdale Collegiate, Toronto, 1965. Appointments include: Resident Playwright, New York Shakespeare Festival, 1981. Publications: The Prince of Naples, 1971; Ambush at Tether's End, 1971; Sacktown Rag, 1972; Baghdad Saloon, 1973; Beyond Mozambique, 1974; Ramona and the White Slaves, 1976; Gossip, 1977; Zastrozzi, The Master of Discipline, 1977; Filthy Rich, 1979; Rumours of our Death (musical), 1980; Theatre of the Film Noir, 1981; Science and Madness, 1982; The Art of War: An Adventure,

1983; Criminals in Love, 1984; Better Living, 1986; Beautiful City, 1987; Nothing Sacred, after Turgenev, 1988; Love and Anger, 1990; Radio and television plays. Honours include: Canada Council Grants. Address: c/o Great North Artists, 350 Dupont Street, toronto, Ontario, Canada M5V 1V9.

WALKER Harry. See: **WAUGH Hillary Baldwin.**

WALKER Lou Ann, b. 9 Dec 1952, Hartford City, Indiana, USA. Writer. m. Speed Vogel, 8 Sept 1986, 1 daughter. Education: Attended Ball State University, 1971-73; Degree in French Language and Literature, University of Besancon, 1975; BA, Harvard University, 1976. Appointments: Reporter, Indianapolis News, 1976; Assistant to Executive Editor, New York (magazine) New York, 1976-77; Assistant to Executive Editor, Cosmopolitan, New York City, 1979-80; Associate Editor, Diversion (magazine) New York City, 1980-81; Editor, Direct (magazine) New York City, 1981-82; Sign Language Interpretor for New York Society for the Deaf; Consultant on special project for handicapped people for Museum of Modern Art, 1980-85; Consultant to Broadway's Theater Development Fund and sign language advisor on many Broadway shows, 1984-; Contributing Editor, New York Woman, 1990-92. Publications: Amy: The Story of a Deaf Child, photographs by Michael Abramson, 1985; A Loss for Words: The Story of Deafness in a Family (autobiography) 1986; Hand, Heart and Mind, 1994; Roy Lichtenstein: The Artist at Work, 1994. Contributions to: The New York Times Book Review; The Chicago Sun-Times (Book Reviews); Esquire; The New York Times Magazine; New York Woman; Life. Honours: Rockefeller Foundation Humanities Fellowship, 1982-83; Christopher Award for A Loss for Words, 1987; National Endowment for the Arts Creative Writing Grant, 1988. Membership: Authors Guild. Literary Agent: Liz Darhansoff. Address: c/o Darhansoff & Verrill, 13th Floor, 1220 Park Avenue, New York, NY 10128, USA.

WALKER Ted, b. 28 Nov 1934, Writer. m. (1)Lorna Ruth Benfeld, 11 Aug 1956, dec, 2 s, 2 d. (2)Audrey Joan Hicks, 8 July 1988. Education: St Johns College, Cambridge. Appointments: Chairman of Judges Panel, Cholmondeley Award for Poetry, 1974-90. Publications include: Fox ion a Barn Door, 1965; The Solitaries, 1967; The Night Bathers, 1970; Burning the Ivy, 1978; The High Path, 1982; You've Never Heard Me Sing, 1985; In Spain, 1987; Hands at a Live Fire, 1987; The Last of England, 1992. Contributions to: The New Yorker; The New Statesman; The Times literary Supplement; The Listener; The Atlantic Monthly; The London Magazine; The Observer; Encounter; The Poetry Review; Sunday Telegraph. Honours: The Eric Gregory Award, 1964; The Cholmondeley Award, 1966; The Alice Hunt Bartlett Award, 1969; The Society of Authors Travel Bursary, 1978; The Ackerley Award, 1982. Memberships: Royal Society of Literature. Literary Agent: David Higham Associates Limited, London. Address: Argyll House, The Square, Eastergate, Chichester, West Sussex PO20 6UP, England.

WALKER Wilbert Lee, b. 22 July 1925, Durham, NC, USA. Retired Public Administrator. m. Grace Clayborne, 15 June 1951, 1 son. Education: BA Morgan State University, 1950; MSW, SocialWork, Howard University, Washington DC, 1954. Publications: The Deputy's Dilemma, 1987; Servants of All, 1982; Stalemate at Panmunjon, 1980; The Pride of our Hearts, 1978; We are Men, 1972. Honours: Trinity Presbyterian Church Literary Award, 1978; Alpha Phi Alpha Literary Award, 1979. Memberships include: Mid Atlantic Writers Association; Committee of Small Magazines, Editors and Publishers; National Association of Social Workers, life member; Delta Lambda Chapter, Alpha Phi Alpha Fraternity, Past President. Address: PO Box 18625, Baltimore, MD 21216, USA.

WALL Ethan. See: **HOLMES Bryan John.**

WALL Geoffrey. See: **CHADWICK Geoffrey.**

WALL Mervyn, b. 23 Aug 1908, Dublin, Ireland. Retired Chief Executive, Irish Arts Council. m. Fanny Freehan, 25 Apr 1950, 1 s, 3 d. Education: BA, National University of Ireland, 1928. Appointments: Civil Servant, 1934-48; Programme Officer, Radio Eireann, 1948-57; Irish Arts Council, Chief Executive, 1957-75; Book Reviewer, Radio Critic, Radio Broadcaster. Publications include: The Unfortunte Fursey, 1946; The Return of Fursey, 1948; No Trophies Raise, 1956; Forty Foot Gentlemen Only, 1962; A Flutter of Wings, 1974; The Garden of Echoes, 1988; Plays. Contributions to: Journals in Ireland, Britain & USA. Honours: Best European Novel of Year, 1952. Memberships: Irish Academy of Letters; Irish Writers Union. Address: 16 Castlepark Road, Sandycove, Dun Laoghaire, Co Dublin, Ireland.

WALLACE Betty Frances, b. 28 June 1926, Gastonia, North Carolina, USA. Retired Teacher/Educator; Librarian. m. William Andrew Wallace Jr, 4 Sept 1948, 1 son, 2 daughters. Education: BFA Degree, Painting, University of Georgia, 1948; Postgraduate Study, Georgia State University, 1967-69, 1972-73; Tift College, 1976; Elementary Certification, Art Certification, Georgia State University, 1976; Teacher of Gifted Certification, West Georgia College, 1981. Publications: Through a Time Sieve, 1984; With Wings Afire, 1990; Poems include: The Bayeaux Tapestry, 1980; House of the Muses, 1980; The Lo Moth, 1983; Retreat without Maximilian, 1983; Ballade for the Lady, 1984; Posture of Sleep, 1988. Contributions to: New York Herald Tribune; American Mentor; Hampton News; Anthologies, Georgia State Poetry Society; American Poetry Anthology; New Worlds Unlimited. Honours include: New York Poetry Forum, Villanelle, 1983; Daniel Whitehead Hicky National Awards, 1983, 1988; Author of Year in Poetry, 1985; Free Verse, Nevada State Poetry Society, 1987; Yearbook Dedication, HAWKS, 1986; Teacher of Year, 1987; Blue Ribbon Award, Southern Poetry Association, 1989. Memberships include: Georgia State Poetry Society, Charter Member; Southern Poetry Association; American Association of University Women; National Geographics Association. Address: 30 Woodlawn Avenue, Hampton, GA 30228, USA.

WALLACE Ian Robert, b. 31 Mar 1950, Ontario, Canada. Author; Illustrator. Education: Ontario College of Art, 1969-73, 1973-74. Publications: Julie News, 1974; The Sandwich, co-author, 1975; The Christmas Tree House, 1976; Chin Chiang and the Dragon's Dance, 1984; Very Last First Time, 1985, Illustrator; The Sparrow's Song, 1986; Morgan the Magnificent, 1987; Architect of the Moon, 1988; Illustrator, 1988; The Name of the Tree, Illustrator; Mr Kneebone's New Digs, 1991, Author/Illustrator; The Year of Fire, 1992, Illustrator; The Mummer's Song, 1993, Illustrator; Hansel & Gretel, 1994, Illustrator. Contributions to: The New Advocate; Quill & Quire. Honours: Runner Up, City of Toronto Book Awards, 1976; IODE Book Award, 1985; Canadian Library Association's Amelia Francis Howard-Gibbon Award, 1985; Ibby Honour Book, 1986; ALA Notable Book, 1986; White Raven Book, Bologna Children's Book Fair, 1987; Mr Christie's Award, 1990; Elizabeth Mrazik-Cleaver Award, 1990; Hans Christian Anderson Award Nominee (Illustration), 1992. Memberships: Writers Union; The Authors Guild. Address: 184 Major Street, Toronto, Ontario, M5S 2L3, Canada.

WALLACE Ronald William, b. 18 Feb 1945, Cedar Rapids, Iowa, USA. Poet; Professor of English. m. Margaret Elizabeth McCreight, 3 Aug 1968, 2 daughters. Education: BA, College of Wooster, 1967; MA, 1968, PhD, 1971, University of Michigan. Appointments: Director of Creative Writing, University of Wisconsin, Madison, 1975-; Series Editor, Brittingham Prize in Poetry, 1985-; Director, Wisconsin Institute for Creative Writing, 1986-. Publications: Henry James and the Comic Form, 1975; Installing the Bees, 1977; Cucumbers, 1977; The Last Laugh, 1979; The Facts of Life, 1979; Plums, Stones, Kisses and Hooks, 1981; Tunes for Bears to Dance to, 1983; God Be With The Clown, 1984; The Owl in the Kitchen, 1985; People and Dog in the Sun, 1987; Vital Signs, 1989; The Makings of Happiness, 1991; Time's Fancy, 1994. Contributions to: The New Yorker; The Atlantic; The Nation; Poetry; Southern Review; Poetry Northwest; Others. Honours: Hopwood Award for Poetry, 1970; Council for Wisconsin Writers Awards, 1978, 1979, 1984, 1985, 1986, 1988; Helen Bullis Prize in Poetry, 1985; Robert E Gard Award for Excellence in Poetry, 1990; Posner Poetry Prize, 1992; Gerald A Bartell Award in the Arts, 1994. Memberships: Poets and Writers; Associated Writing Programs. Address: Department of English, University of Wisconsin, Madison, WI 53706, USA.

WALLACE-CRABBE Chris(topher Keith), b. 6 May 1934, Richmond, Victoria, Australia. Professor of English; Poet. m. Sophie Feil, 1 son, 1 daughter. Education: BA, 1956, MA, 1964, University of Melbourne. Appointments include: Reader in English, 1976, Professor of English, 1988, University of Melbourne. Publications: No Glass Houses, 1956; The Music of Division, 1959; Eight Metropolitan Poems, 1962; In Light and Darkness, 1964; The Rebel General, 1967; Where the Wind Came, 1971; Selected Poems 1955-72; Act in the Noon, 1974; The Shapes of Gallipoli, 1975; The Foundations of Joy, 1976; The Emotions are not Skilled Workers, 1979; The Amorous Cannibal and Other Poems, 1985; I'm Deadly Serious, 1988; Novel: Splinters, 1981; Melbourne or the Bush: Essays on Australian Literature and Society, 1973; Editor, volumes of Australian poetry. Honours: Dublin Prize, 1986.

WALLER Jane Ashton, b. 19 May 1944, Bucks, England. Writer; Cermist. m. Michael Vaughan Rees, 11 June 1982. Education: Oxford Art College, 1962-63; Sir John Cas Colleg, 1966-69; MA, Royal College of Art, 1982; BA, Hornsey Art College, 1985. Publications include: A Stitch in Time, 1972; Some Things for the Children, 1974; Some Dinosaur Poems for Children, 1975; A Mans Book, 1977; Some Bedtime Tales for Children, 1978; Happy Day Stories for Children, 1980; The Thirties Family Knitting Book, 1981; Below thg Green Pond, 1982; The Mans Knitting Book, 1984; Women in Wrtime, 1987; Women in Uniform, 1989; Handbuilt Ceramics, 1990; Saving the Dinosaurs, 1994. Contributions to: Ceramic Review. Honour: The Herbert Read Literary Award, 1981. Literary Agent: Mike Shaw, Curtis Brown. Address: 22 Roupell Street, Waterloo, London, SE1 8SP, England.

WALLER John Stanier, (Sir), b. 27 July 1917, England. Author; Poet; Journalist. m. Anne Eileen Mileham, 1974. Education: BA, 1939, Worcester College, Oxford; QU Dip Ed, 1940. Appointments include: Founder, Editor, Kingdom Come, Quarterly, 1939-41; Features Editor, British Ministry of Information, Middle East, 1943-45; Chief Press Officer, British Embassy, Baghdad, 1945; News & Features Editor, MIME, 1945-46; Dramatic Critic, Cairo Weekly, The Sphinx, 1943-46; Lecturer, Tutor, Carlisle & Gregson Limited, 1953-54; Information Officer, Overseas Press Service Division, 1940-42; Director, Literature Limited, 1940-42; Richard Congreve Limited, 1948-50. Publications include: The Confessions of Peter Pan, 1941; Fortunate Hamlet, 1941; Spring Legend, 1942; The Merry Ghosts, 1946; Crusade, 1946; The Kiss of Stars, 1948; Collected Poems of Keith Douglas, 1951, 66; Shaggy Dog, 1953; Goldenhair & The Two Black Hawks, 1971; Return to Oasis, 1980. Contributions to: Numerous Anthologies, Periodicals, UK & Abroad. Honours: Greenwood Award, 1947; Keats Prize, 1974; Royal Society of Literature, Fellow, 1948. Memberships include: Salamander Society of Poets. Address: Winchcombe, 37A Madeira Road, Ventnor, Isle of White, PO38 1TQ, England.

WALLER Robert James. Professor of Management; Writer; Photographer; Bar Musician. Contributions to: Des Moines Register. Address: PO Box 219, Cedazr Falls, IA 50613, USA.

WALLINGTON Vivienne Elizabeth, (Elizabeth Duke), b. 8 Feb 1937, Adelaide, South Australia. Former Librarian; Writer. m. John Wallington, 18 Apr 1959, 1 son, 1 daughter. Education: Matriculated, Girton G.S. Adelaide, 1954; Library Registration, Prelim + 6 Subjects, 1954-59. Publications: Somewhere, 1982; Butterfingers, 1986; Names are Fun, 1990; Outback Legacy, 1993; Shattered Wedding, 1994. Contributions to: Travel Articles, Melbourne Sun, Newcastle Herald, West Australian, Adelaide Advertiser; Feature Article, Prime Time. Memberships: ASA; FAW; Society of Women Writers; Romance Writers of America; Romance Writers of Australia; ALIA. Address: 38 Fuller Street, Mitcham, Vic 3132, Australia.

WALLS Ian Gascoigne, b. 28 Apr 1922, Glasgow, Scotland. Horticulturist. m. Eleanor McIntosh McCaig, 11 Aug 1947, 2 d. Education:West of Scotland Agricultural College, 1949. Appointments: Gardening Writer, Glasgow Herald. Publications include: Gardening Month by Month, 1962; Creating Your Garden, 1967; Complete Book of the Greenhouse, 1973, 79, 83, 88, 93; Tomato Growing Today, 1972, 77; A-Z of Garden Pests and Problems, 1979; Modem Greenhouse Methods, 1984; Profit from Growing Vegtables, Fruits and Flowers, 1988; Simple Tomato Growing, 1988; Simple Vegtable Growing, 1988; Growing Tomatoes, 1989; Making Your Garden Pay: Low Cost Gardening, 1992; Hydroponics, UK Reissue; Bowling Green Care and Maintenance. Contributions to: The Grower; The Greenock Telegraph. Memberships: Glasgow Wheelers CC; Milngavie Horticultural Society. Literary Agent: Robert Crewe Limited, Kings News, London, England. Address: 17 Douglaston Avenue, Milngavie, Glasgow, G62 6AP, Scotland.

WALSER Martin, b. 24 Mar 1927, Wasserburg, Germany. Writer. Education: Theological Philosophical College, Regensburg; PhD, University of Tubingen. Publications include: Ehen in Philippsburg, 1957; Halbzeit, 1960; Das Einhorn, 1966; Der Sturz, 1973; Jenseits de Liebe, 1976; Ein Fliehendespferd, 1978; Das Schwanenhaus, 1980; Brief on Lord Liszt, 1982; Messmers Gedanken, 1985; Die Vej Teidigung Derkindheit, 1991; Ohne einander, 1993. Honours: Grip 47 Proze, 1955; Hermann Hesse Prize, 1957; Gerhart Hauptmann, 1962; Schiller Prize, 1965; Georg Buechner Prize, 1981; Order pour le Merite fur Wissensdaften und Kinste, 1993; Officer de l'ordre des Arts et des Lettres, 1994. Memberships: German Academy for Language and

Literature; Association German Writers; PEN; Academy of Arts, Berlin. Address: 777 Uberlingen Nussdorf, Zum Hecht 36, Germany.

WALSH Sheila, (Sophie Leyton), b. 1928, Writer. Publications include: The GOlden Songbird, 1975; The Sergeant Majors Daughter, 1977; A Fine Silk Purse, 1978; The Incomparable Miss Brady, 1980; The Rose Domino, 1981; A Highly Respectable Marriage, 1983; The Runaway Bridge, 1984; Cousins of a Kind, 1985; The Inccorigible Rake, 1985; An Insubstantial Pageant, 1986; Bath Intrigue, 1986; Lady Aurelias Bequest, 1987; Minervas Marquis, 1988; The Nabob, 1989-90; A Woman of Little Importance, 1991; Until Tomorrow, 1993; Remember Me, 1994; A Perfect Bride, 1994. Honours: Best Romantic Novel of Year, 1983. Memberships: Romantic Novelists Association; Soroptimist International of Southport. Literary Agent: Irvine, 11 Upland Park Road, Oxford, England. Address: 35 Coudray Road, Southport, Merseyside PR9 9NL, England.

WALSHE Aubrey Peter, b. 12 Jan 1934, Johannesburg, South Africa. Professor, Political Science. m. Catherine Ann Pettifer, 26 Jan 1957, 1 son, 3 daughters. Education: BA, Hons Oxford 1956, Wadham College; DPhil Oxford 1968, St Antonys College. Appointments: Lecturer, University of Lesotho 1959-62; Professor, University of Notre Dame, Indiana, USA, 1967-. Publications: The Rise of African Nationalism in South Africa, 1971; Black Nationalism in South Africa, 1974; Church versus State in South Africa, 1983; Southern Africa, Cambridge History of Africa, vol 7, ch 11, 1986. Contributions to: Journal of Modem African Studies; Journal of Church and State; Cross Currents; The Review of Politics; New York Times; Journal of African History; Transafrica Forum; Christianity and Crisis; and others. Literary Agent: Christopher Hurst, London. Address: Department of Government, University of Notre Dame, Notre Dame, IN 46556, USA.

WALTER John Christopher, b. 1933. Publications: The Harlem Fox: J Raymond Jones & Tammamy, 1989; Transforming the Curriculum, 1991. Honour: American Book Award, 1990.

WALTER Richard, b. 11 July 1944, New York, USA. Writer; Educator. m. Patricia Sandgrund, 18 June 1967, 1 son, 1 daughter. Education: BA History 1965, Harpur College, State University of New York; MS Communications 1966, Newhouse School of Public Communications, Syracuse University; Postgraduate Study, Department of Cinema, University of Southem California, 1967-70. Appointments: Professor and Screenwriting Chairman, Department of Film and Television, University of California, Los Angeles, 1977-. Publications: Barry and the Persuasions, 1976; The Whole Picture, 1995; Screenwriting: The Art, Craft and Business of Film and Television Writing, 1988; Screenplays: Group Marriage; Return of Zorro; Dynamite Lady; Mrs Charlie; Split; Young Love; Marked Man; Jackie Whitefish. Contributions to: Asian Wall Street Journal; Los Angeles Times; Los Angeles Herald Examiner. Memberships: Writers Guild of America; PEN Centre West; University Film and Video Association. Literary Agent: Henry Dunow at Harold Ober Associates, NYC. Address: Department of Film and Television, University of California, Los Angeles, CA 90024, USA.

WALVIN James, b. 2 Jan 1942, Manchester, England. Historian; Professor. m. Jennifer, 2 s. Education: BA, Keele University, 1964; MA, McMaster University, 1970. Publications include: Black-White, The Negro and ENglish Society, 1973; The Peoples Game, Social History of Football, 1975; Victorian Values, 1987; Slavery and the Slave Trade, 1983; England, Slaves and Freedom, 1986; Black Ivory, A History of British Slavery, 1993. Honour: Martin Luther King Memorial Prize, 1974. Membership: Royal Historical Society. Literary Agent: The Peters, Fraser and Dunlop Group Limited. Address: Dept of History, University of York, Heslington, York YO1 5DD, England.

WALWICZ Ania, b. 19 May 1951, Swidnica, Poland (Australian citizen). Artist; Poet. Education: Dip Ed, University of Melbourne, 1984. Appointments include: Writer-in-residence, Deakin and Murdoch Universities, 1987-88. Publications: Writing, 1982; Boat, 1989; Plays: Girlboytalk, 1986; Dissecting Mice, 1989; Elegant, 1990. Honours include: Australian Council Literature Board grants; Fellowship, 1990. Address: 9 Cremorne Street, Fitzroy, Victoria 3065, Australia.

WALZER Michael. Political Philosopher; Professor. m. Judith Walzer. Contributions to: Dissent; New Republic. Address: Institute for Advanced Study, Olden Lane, Princeton, NJ 08540, USA.

WAMBAUGH Joseph, b. 22 Jan 1937, PA, USA. Author. m. 26 Nov 1955, 1 son, 1 daughter. Education: BA; MA, California State University, Los Angeles. Publications: The New Centurions, 1971; The Blue Knight, 1972; The Onion Field, 1973; The Choirboys, 1975; The Glitter Dome, 1981; The Delta Star, 1983; Lines and Shadows, 1984; The Secrets of Harry Bright, 1985; Echoes in the Darkness, 1987; The Blooding, 1989; The Golden Orange, 1990; Fugitive Nights, 1992; Finnegan's Week, 1993. Address: c/o Wm Morrow & Co, 105 Madison Avenue, New York, NY 10016, USA.

WANDOR Michelene Dinah, b. 20 Apr 1940, London. Writer. m. Edward Victor, 1963, div, 2 s. Education: BA, Newnham College; MA, University of Essex; LTCL, DipTCL, Trinity College of Music. Appointments: Poetry Editor, Time Out, 1971-82. Publications include: Carry on Understudies, 1981; Routledge, 1986; Look Back in Gender, 1987; Gardens of Eden, 1990; Five Plays, 1984; Guests in the Body, 1987. Contributions to: Regular Reviewer for the Listener; The Sunday Times. Honour: International Emmy for the Film, Belle of Amherst, 1987. Membership: Writers Guild. Address: 71 Belsize Lane, London NW3 5AU, England.

WARD John Hood, b. 16 Dec 1915, Newcastle Upon Tyne, England. Former Senior Principal, Civil Service. m. Glayds Hilda Thorogood, 27 July 1940, Great Crosby, 1 s, 2 d. Education: Royal Grammar School. Publications include: A Late Harvest, 1982; The Dark Sea, 1983; A Kind of Likeness, 1985; A Song At Twlight, 1989; Grandfather Best and The Protestant Work Ethic, 1991; Tales of Love and Hate, 1993; The Brilliance of Light, 1994. Contributions to: Over 100 Short Stories, 200 Poems, Various Commercial & Literary Magazines, Commercial Radio & BBC Radio. Honours: Imperial Service Order, 1977; City of Westminister Arts Council Poetry Prize, 1977; Wharfedale Music Festival Open Poetry Prize, 1978; Society of Civil Service Authors Jubilee Open Compeition, 1987; H E Bates Short Story Prize, 1988; High Peak Community Writers Open Poetry Competition, 1988, 89; Open Short Story Competition, 1988; West Sussex Writers Club Open Short Story Competition First Prize, 1991. Membership: Society of Civil Service Authors. Address: 42 Seal Road, Bramhall, Stockport, Cheshire SK7 2JS, England.

WARD Philip, b. 10 Feb 1938, Harrow, England. Chartered Librarian; Professional Writer. m. 4 Apr 1964, 2 d. Education: University for Foreigners, Perugia; Coimbra University. Appointments: Honorary Editor, The Private Library, 1958.64; Coordinator, Library Services, Tripoli, Libya, 1963-71; Director, National Library Services, 1973-74. Publications include: The Oxford Companion to Spanish Literature, 1978; Lost Songs, 1981; A Dictionary of Common Fallacies, 1978-80; A Lifetimes Reading, 1983; Japanese Captitals, 1985; Travels in Oman, 1987; Wright Magic, 1990; Bulgaria, 1990; Sofia Portrait of a City, 1989. Honours: Fellow, Royal Geographical Society; Royal Society of Arts; Guinness Poetry Award, 1959; 1st Prize, International Travel Writers Competition, 1990. Membership: Private Libraries Association. Address: c/o Oxford University Press, Walton St, Oxford OX2 6DP, England.

WARD Ronald Bentley, b. 6 Oct 1928, Sydney, New South Wales, Australia. University Lecturer. m. Brenda Madden, 7 Jan 1955, 1 son, 1 daughter. Education: Trades Certificate, 1948; Diploma, Sydney Technical College, 1955; BEng, University of New South Wales, 1961; MBA, Macquarie University, 1975; PhD, 1994. Appointments: Currently Lecturer, School of Mechanical Engineering, University of Technology, Sydney. Publications: The Engineering of Management, 1987; The Engineering of Communication, 1988, revised edition, 1989; A Plant for Appropriate Technology, 1991; Procedures of student conferences on engineering communication (edited with H McGregor), 1989, 1990; Procedures of student conference on topics in management (editor), 1990. Contributions to: Various conference proceedings and symposia, Australia and overseas. Memberships: Institution of Engineers, Australia; Australian Institute of Management. Literary Agent: C Weiner, NJ, USA. Address: 13 Landscape Avenue, Forestville, NSW 2087, Australia.

WARDLE (John) Irving, b. 20 July 1929, England. Drama Critic. m. (1) Joan Notkin, 1958, div, (2) Fay Crowder, 1963, div, 2 s, (3) Elizabeth Grist, 1975, 1 s, 1 d. Education: BA, Wadham College, Oxford; ARCM, Royal College of Music. Appointments: Sub Editor, Times Educational Supplement, 1956; Deputy Theatre Critic, Observer, 1960; Editor, Gambit, 1973-75; Drama Critic, The Times, 1963-; Theatre Critic, The Independent on Sunday, 1989. Publications: The Theatres of George Devine, 1978; The Houseboy, 1974; Theatre

Criticism, 1992. Address: 51 Richmond Road, New Barnet, Herts, England.

WARE Wallace. See: **KARP David.**

WARMINGTON William Allan, b. 1922, Retired Lecturer. m. Chairman Wind, 1951, 2 s. Education: BA, University of Bristol. Publications: A West African Trade Union; (joint author) Organizationl Behaviour and Performance; Studies in Industrialization; Plantation and Village in the Cameroons. Contributions to: Journal of Management Studies; Personnel Review; Others. Address: Westington Corner, Chipping Campden, Gloucestershire, England.

WARNER Francis, (Robert Le Plastrier), b. 21 Oct 1937, Yorkshire, England. Poet; Dramatist; Vice Master of St Peters College. m. (1)Mary Hall, 1958, div, 2 d. (2)Penelope Anne Davis, 1983, 1 s, 1 d. Education: Christs Hospital, London College of Music; BA, MA, ST Catharines College, Cambridge. Appointments include: Fellow, Tutor, St Peters College, Oxford, University Lecturer, CUF, 1965-; Vice Master, St Peters College, 1987; Pro Senior Proctor, University of Oxford, 1989-90. Publications include: Poetry, Perennia, 1962; Early Poems, 1964; Lucca Quartet, 1975; Morning Vespers, 1980; Spring Harvest, 1981; Collected Poems, 1960-84, 1985; Plays, Maquetes, 1972; Requiem, 1972; Killing Time, 1976; Meeting Ends, 1974; Moving Reflections, 1983; Virgil and Caesar, 1992; Various Other Publications. Contributions to: Various Anthologies, Journals. Honour: Messing International Award, 1972. Address: St Peters College, Oxford, OX1 2DL, England.

WARNER Val, b. 15 Jan 1946, Middlesex, England. Writer. Education: BA, 1968, Somerville College, Oxford. Appointments: Freelance Copy Editor, 1972-77. Publications include: Under the Penthouse, 1973; Before Lunch, 1986; Translation, The Centenary Corbiere, 1975; Editor, Collected Poems & Prose of Charlotte Mew, 1981, 82; These Yellow Photos, 1971. Contributions to: Poems; Encounter; Tribune; The Scotsman; Critical Quarterly; Poetry Review; Ambit; Poetry Wales; Lines Review; RN Review; Antaeus; Cencrastus; Other poetry; Outposts; Pequod; Green River Review; Verse; Gairfish; The Honest Ulsterman; New Writing Scotland. Honours: Gregory Award for Poetry, 1975; Writer in Residence, University College of Swansea, 1979-81. Membership: PEN. Address: Carcanet Press Limited, 208-212 Corn Exchange Buildings, Manchester M4 3BQ, England.

WARREN Rosanna. Poet; Translator. Contributions to: Atlantic Monthly; Boulevard; Chelsea. Honours: Lamont Poetry Section, 1993; Lavan Younger Poets Award, 1992. Address: 11 Robinwood, Needham, MA 02192, USA.

WARTOFSKY Victor, b. 15 June 1931, New York, USA. Writer. m. Tamar Chachik, 1957, 1 son, 2 daughters. Education: BA, Journalism. Publications: Mr Double and Other Stories; Meeting the Pieman; Year of the Yahoo; The Passage; Prescription for Justice; Terminal Justice; Screenplays: Death be my Destiny; The Hellbox; Feathers. Contributions to: USIA America; Fifty Plus; Macabre; Quartet; True. Address: 8507 Wild Olive Drive, Potomac, MD 20854, USA.

WASSERFALL Adel, (Adel Pryor), b. 2 Dec 1918, Haugesund, Norway. Writer; Housewife. m. Education: Cape Technical College, South Africa. Publications include: Novels, Tangled Paths, 1959; Clouded Glass, 1961; Hidden Fire, 1962; Out of the Night, 1963; Hearts in Conflict, 1965; Forgotten Yesterday, 1966; Valley of Desire, 1967; Sound of the Sea, 1968; Free of a Dream, 1969; German Edition, 1973; A Norwegian Romance, 1976; All Is Not Gold, 1979; Flame of Jealousy. Honours: English Composition Prize, 1934; Sir William Thorne Award, 1937; Short Story Contest Award, 1946. Address: 8 Iona Street, Milnerton 7441, Cape South Africa.

WATERMAN Andrew, b. 28 May 1940, London, England. Senior Lecturer; Poet. Education: BA, University of Leicester, 1966; Worcester College, Oxford, 1966-68. Appointments: Senior Lecturer, University of Ulster at Coleraine. Publications: Last Fruit, 1974; Living Room, 1974; From the Other Country, 1977; Over the Wall, 1980; Out for the Elements, 1981; Selected Poems, 1986; In the Planetarium, 1990; Editor, The Poetry of Chess, 1981; Hamburger Heaven, 1995. Honours include: Cholmondeley Award, 1977. Address: 15 Hazelbank Road, Coleraine, County Londonderry, Northern Ireland.

WATERS John Frederick, b. 27 Oct 1930, Somerville, Massachusetts, USA. Professional Writer. Education: BS, University of Massachusetts. Publications Include: Marine Animal Collectors (Grades 7 and Up), 1969; The Crab From Yesterday, Grades 2-5, 1970; The Sea Farmers, 1970; What Does An Oceanorapher Do, 1970; Saltmarshes and Shifting Dunes, 1970; Turtles, 1971; Neighborhood Puddle, 1971; Some Mammals Live in the Sea, 1972; Green Turtle: Mysteries, 1972; The Royal Potwasher, 1972; Seal Harbour, 1973; Hungry Sharks, 1973; Giant Sea Creatures, 1973; The Mysterious Eel, 1973; Camels: Ships of the Desert, 1974; Carnivorous Plants, 1974; Exploring New England Shores, 1974; The Continental Shelves, 1975; Creatures of Darkness, 1975; Victory Chimes, 1976; Maritime Careers, 1977; Fishing, 1978; Summer Seals, 1978; The Hatchlings, 1979; Crime Labs, 1979; A Jellyfish is Not a Fish, 1979; Flood, 1991; Watching Wales, 1991; The Raindrop Houmey, 1991; Deep Sea Vents, Grades 5 Up, 1994. Contributions to: Cape Cod; Compass. Honours: Junior Literary Book Choice (twice); Outstanding Science books for Children Awards (6 times). Memberships include: Past President, Southeastern Massachusetts Creative Writers Club; Organizer, Cape Cod Writers; 12 O'Clock Scholars; Society of Children's Book Writers. Address: Box 735, Chatham, MA 02633, USA.

WATERTON Betty Marie, b. 31 Aug 1923, Oshawa, Ontario, Canada. Writer, Children's Books. m. Claude Waterton, 7 Apr 1942, 1 son, 2 daughters. Publications: A Salmon for Simon, 1978; Pettranetta, 1980; Mustard, 1983; The White Moose, 1984; Quincy Rumpel, 1984; Orff, 27 Dragons (and a Snarkel !), 1984; The Dog Who Stopped the War, (adaptation and translation), 1985; Starring Quincy Rumpel, 1986; Quincy Rumpel, PI, 1988; Morris Rumpel and the Wings of Icasus, 1989; Plain Noodles, 1989; Quincy Rumpel and the Sasquatch of Phantom Cove, 1990; Quincy Rumpel and the Woolly Chaps, 1992; Quincy Rumpel and the Mystifying Experience, 1994. Honours: A Salmon for Simon, Co-winner, Canada Council Award for Children's Literature, 1978. Memberships: Canadian Society of Children's Authors, Illustrators and Performers; The Federation of BC Writers. Address: 10135 Tsaykum Road, RR1, Sidney BC, V8L 3R9, Canada.

WATKINS Floyd C, b. 19 Apr 1920, Cherokee County, Georgia, USA. Professor; Author; Farmer. m. Anna E Braziel, 14 June 1942, 1 son, 2 daughters. Education: BS, Georgia Southern, 1946; AM, Emory University, 1947; PhD, Vanderbilt University, 1952. Appointments: Instructor, Emory University, 1949, Professor 1961; Candler Professor, American Literature, 1980; Candler Professor Emeritus, 1988; Visiting Professor, Southeastern University, Oklahoma, summers 1961, 1970; Visiting Professor, Texas A & M University, 1980. Publications: Co-Editor, The Literature of the South, 1952; Thomas Wolfe's Characters, 1957; Co-author, Old Times in the Faulkner Country, 1961; The Flesh and the Word, 1971; In Time and Place, 1977; Then and Now: The Personal Past in the Poetry of Robert Penn Warren, 1982; Co-author, Some Poems and Some Talk About Poetry, 1985. Address: 519 Druand Drive NE, Atlanta,GA 30307, USA.

WATKINS Gerrold. See: MALZBERG Barry Norman.

WATKINS Karen Christna, (Catrin Collier, Katherine John), b. 30 May 1948, Pontypridd, Wales. Writer. m. Trevor John Watkins, 28 Dec 1968, 2 s, 1 d. Education: Teaching Certificate, 1969, Swansea College. Publications: Without Trace, 1990; Hearts of Gold, 1992; One Blue Moon, 1993; Six Foot Under; A Silver Lining, 1994; Murder of a Dead Man, 1994. Memberships: PEN; Society of Authors; Crime Writers Association. Literary Agent: A M Heath & Co. Address: 31 Hen Parc Avenue, Upper Killay, Swansea SA2 7HA, Wales.

WATMOUGH David, b. 17 Aug 1926, London, England. Author. Education: Theology Major, King's College, University of London, 1945-49. Appointments include: War Service, Royal Naval Volunteer Reserve, 1944-45. Publications: Ashes for Easter, stories, 1972; Love and the Waiting Game, stories, 1975; From a Cornish Landscape, stories, 1975; No More into the Garden, novel, 1978; Fury, stories, 1984; The Connecticut Countess, stories, 1984; The Unlikely Pioneer, opera, 1985; Vibrations in Time, stories, 1986; The Year of Fears, novel, 1987; Thy Mother's Glass, novel, 1992; The Time of the Kingfishers, novel, 1994. Contributions to: Encounter; Spectator; New York Times Book Review; Saturday Night, Canada; Canadian Literature; Dalhousie Review; Connoisseur, New York; Malahat Review; Vancouver Step. Honours: Senior Literary Arts Award, Canada Council, 1976, 1986; Winner, Best Novel of Year Award, Giovanni's Room, Philadelphia, 1979. Memberships: The Writers Union of Canada, Chairman, Federation of British Columbia Writers. Literary

Agent: Robert Drake, Drake Literary Agency, 217 Hanover St 10, Annapolis, MD 21401, USA. Address: 3358 West First Avenue, Vancouver, British Columbia, V6R 1G4, Canada.

WATNEY John Basil, b. 1920, England. Writer. Publications: The Enemy Within, 1946; The Unexpected Angel, 1949; Common Love, 1954; Leopard with a Thin Skin, 1959; The Quarrelling Room, 1960; The Glass Facade, 1963; He Also Served, 1971; Clive of India, 1974; Beer is Best, 1974; Lady Hester Stanhope, 1975; Mervyn Peake, 1975; Mothers Ruin, 1976; The Churchills, 1977. Literary Agent: Tessa Sayle Agency, London, England. Address: Flat 36, 5 Elm Park Gardens, London SW10 9QQ, England.

WATSON John Richard, b. 15 June 1934, Ipswich, England. Professor. m. Pauline Elizabeth Roberts, 21 July 1962, 1 s, 2 d. Education: BA, MA, Magdalen College, Oxford; PhD, University of Glasgow, 1966. Publication include: Everymans Book of Victorian Verse, 1982; Wordworth is Vital Soul, 1982; The Poetry of Gerard Manley Hopkins, 1986; Wordsworth, 1983; Companion to Hymns and Psalms, 1988; A Handbook to English Romanticism, 1992. Contributions to: Essays in Critical Quarterly; Criticism; Collections of Essays. Memberships: Modern Humanities Research Association. Address: 3 Victoria Terrace, Durham DH1 4RW, England.

WATSON Lynn, b. 5 June 1948, Woodland, California, USA. Teacher; Writer. Education: University of California, Berkeley, 1966-68; BA English 1975, Sonoma State University; MFA Fiction Writing 1977, University of Iowa, Writers Workshop. Appointments: Freelance Writer for various print media and publications; Teacher, University of Iowa, College of the Desert, Sonoma State University, Santa Rosa Junior College; Artist/Facilitator, State Prison, California, 1981. Publications: Alimony or Death of the Clock, novel, 1981; Amateur Blues, poetry, 1990; Catching the Devil, poetry, 1995. Contributions to: Onthebus; Chaminade Literary Review; Cyanosis Avec; First Leaves; The Tomcat; Sonoma Review; and other literary publications. Honours: First Place, Poetry, National Poetry Association, San Francisco, 1990; Honorable Mention, World of Poetry Contest, Sacramento, 1991. Membership: California Poets in the Schools. Address: PO Box 1253, Occidental, CA 95465, USA.

WATSON Richard Allan, b. 23 Feb 1931, New Market, Iowa, USA. Professor of Philosophy. m. Patty Jo Andersen, 30 July 1955, 1 daughter. Education: BA, 1953, MA, 1957, PhD, 1961, Philosophy, University of Iowa; MS, Geology, University of Minnesota, 1959. Publications: The Downfall of Cartesianism, 1966; Man and Nature (with Patty Jo Watson), 1969; The Longest Cave (with Roger W Brucker), 1976; Under Plowman's Floor, novel, 1978; The Runner, novel, 1981; The Philosopher's Diet, 1985; The Breakdown of Cartesian Metaphysics, 1987; The Philosopher's Joke, 1990; Writing Philosophy, 1992; Niagara, novel, 1993. Contributions to: The Georgia Review; The Gettysburg Review; Numerous philosophy, anthropology and geology journals. Honours: American Health Top 10 Book Award for The Philosopher's Diet, 1985. Memberships: Honorary Life Member, National Speleological Society; Board Member, International Writers Center, Washington University. Address: Philosophy Box 1073, Washington University, St Louis, MO 63130, USA.

WATSON Will. See: FLOREN Lee.

WATT-EVANS Lawrence, b. 26 July 1954, Arlington, Massachusetts, USA. Freelance Writer. m. Julie F McKenna, 30 Aug 1977, 1 daughter, 1 son. Education: Princeton University, 1972-74, 1975-77. Publications: The Lure of the Basilisk, 1980; The Seven Altars of Düsarra, 1981. The Cyborg and the Sorcerers, 1982; The Sword of Bheleu, 1983; The Book of Silence, 1984; The Chromosomal Code, 1984; The Misenchanted Sword, 1985; Shining Steel, 1986; With a Single Spell, 1987; The Wizard and the War Machine, 1987; Denner's Wreck, 1988; Nightside City, 1989; The Unwilling Warlord, 1989; The Nightmare People, 1990; The Blood of A Dragon, 1991; The Rebirth of Wonder, 1992; Crosstime Traffic, 1992; Taking Flight, 1993; The Spell of the Black Dagger, 1993; Split Heirs (with Esther Friesner), 1993; Out of This World, 1994; In The Empire of Shadow, 1995; The Reign of the Brown Magician, 1996. Contributions to: Newer York (editor), 1991; Rayguns, Elves & Skin-Tight Suits, column for Comics Buyer's Guide, 1983-86; Comic Collector; Movie Collectors World; Starlog; Vintage Collectables; Sagebrush Journal. Honours: Isaac Asimov's Science Fiction Readers Poll Award, 1987; Nebula Award Nominee, 1987; Science Fiction Achievement Award (Hugo) for Best Short Story of 1987, 1988. Memberships: Science Fiction Writers of America; Horror

Writers Association. Literary Agent: Russell Golen, Scott Meredith Literary Agency. Address: c/o Russell Galen, Scott Meredith Literary Agency, 845 Third Ave, New York, NY 10022, USA.

WATTLES Rama Rau. See: RAMA RAU Santha.

WATTS Nigel John, b. 24 June 1957, Winchester, England. Writer. m. Sahera Chohan, 10 Aug 1991. Publications: The Life Game, 1989; Billy Bayswater, 1990; We All Live in a House Called Innocence, 1992; Twenty Twenty, 1995. Honour: Betty Trask Award, 1989. Literary Agent: Murray Pollinger. Address: 260 Ashburnham Road, Ham Richmond, Surrey, England.

WATTS Victor Ernest, b. 18 Apr 1938, Bristol, England. University Teacher. m. Mary Curtis, 4 Apr 1964, 1 s, 2 d. Education: Merton College, Oxford, 1957-61; University College, London, 1961-62; MA, Oxford, 1964; FSA. Appointments: Lecturer, 1962, Senior Lecturer, 1974, Durham University; Master of Grey College, Durham University, 1989-. Publications: Boethius the Consolation of Philosophy, 1969; The Cambridge Dictionary of English Place Names, forthcoming. Contributions to: Medium Aevum; Nomina; Journal of the English Placename Society. Memberships: English Place Name Society; Architectural & Archaeological Society of Durham & Northumberlnd. Address: The Masters House, High Close, Hollingside Lane, Durham DH1 3TN, England.

WAUGH Hillary Baldwin (Elissa Grandower, H Baldwin Taylor, Harry Walker), b. 22 June 1920. Author. m. (1) Diana Taylor, 16 June 1951, div 1980, 1 son, 2 daughters, (2) Shannon O'Cork, 11 June 1983. Education: BA, Yale University, 1942. Publications: Last Seen Wearing..., 1952; The Missing Man, 1964; Rivergate House, 1980; The Glenna Powers Case, 1981; The Doria Rafe Case, 1981; The Billy Cantrell Case, 1982; The Nerissa Claire Case, 1983; The Veronica Dean Case, 1984; The Priscilla Copperwaite Case, 1985. Honours: Grand Master, Swedish Academy of Detection, 1981; Grand Master, Mystery Writers of America, 1989. Memberships: Mystery Writers of America, Former President, Executive President, Awards Chairman, Board of Directors; Crime Writers Association, England. Address: 9 Marshall Avenue, Guilford, CT 06437, USA.

WAYMAN Tom, b. 1945, Canadian. Appointments: Writer-in-Residence, University of Windsor, 1975-76; Assistant Professor of English, Wayne State University, Detroit, 1976-77; Writer-in-Residence, University of Alberta, Edmonton, 1978-79; Instructor, Kootenay School of Writing, David Thompson University Centre, Nelson, 1980-82; Writer-in-Residence, Simon Fraser University, Burnaby, 1983; Instructor, Kootenay School of Writing, Vancouver, 1984-87; Instructor, English Department, Kwantlen College, Surrey, BC, 1988-89; College Professor, English Department, Okanagan College, Kelowna, BC, 1990-91; Instructor, Kooteray School of the Arts, 1991-92; College Professor, Okanagan University College, 1992-. Publications: Mindscapes (with others), 1971; Waiting for Wayman, 1973; Chuckles, Beaton Abbott's Got the Contract: An Anthology of Working Poems (ed), 1974; Money and Rain: Tom Wayman Live!, 1975; Routines, Transport, A Government Job at Last: An Anthology of Working Poems Mainly Canadian (ed), 1976; Kitchener/Chicago/Saskatoon, Free Time: Industrial Poems, 1977; A Planet Mostly Sea, 1979; Living on the Ground: Tom Wayman Country, Introducing Tom Wayman: Selected Poems 1973-80, 1980; Going for Coffee: Poetry on the Job (ed), 1981; The Nobel Prize Acceptance Speech, 1981; Counting the Hours: City Poems, Inside Job: Essays on the New Work Writing, 1983; The Face of Jack Munro, 1986; In a Small House on the Outskirts of Heaven, 1989; East of Main: An Anthology of Poems from East Vancouver (edited jointly with Calvin Wharton), 1989; Paperwork: Contemporary Poems from the Job, 1991; A Country Not Considered: Canada, Culture, Work, 1993; Did I Mss Anyting? Selected Poems 1973-93, 1993. Address: PO Box 163, Winlaw, BC, V0G 2J0, Canada.

WEARNE Alan Richard, b. 23 July 1948, Melbourne, Australia. Poet; Verse Novelist. Education: BA, Latrobe University, 1973; DipEd SCV Rusden, 1977. Appointments: Poetry Editor, Meanjin, 1984-87; Writer in Residence, University of Newcastle, New South Wales, 1989. Publications: Public Relations, 1972; New Devil, New Parish, 1976; The Nightmarkets, 1986; Out Here, 1987. Contributions to: Scripsi; Meanjin; Book Reviews in the Age. Honours: National Book Council Award, 1987; Gold Medal, Association for the Study of Australian Literature, 1987. Literary Agent: The Almost Managing Company, VIC 3053,

Australia. Address: 83 Edgevale Road, Kew Melbourne Vic 3101, Australia.

WEBB Bernice Larson, b. Ludell, Kansas, USA. Owner and Publisher, Spider Press; Writer; Adjunct University Professor. m. Robert MacHardy Webb, 14 July 1961, 1 son, 1 daughter. Education: BA 1956, MA 1957, PhD 1961, University of Kansas, Lawrence; Doctoral Research, University of Aberdeen, Scotland, 1959-60. Appointments: Writing Contest Judge, 1960s-; Editor, Cajun Chatter, 1964-66; Editor, The Magnolia, 1967-71; Editor, Louisiana Poets, 1970-89; Professor of Creative Writing, World Campus Afloat, 1972; Coordinator, Poetry-in-the-Schools, 1974; Consultant, Writing of Poetry, Lafayette Parish School System, Louisiana, 1970s-; Poetry Consultant, Director, Poetry Workshops, Acadiana Arts Council, 1970s-; Director, Reading-Writing Laboratories, University of Southwestern Louisiana, summers 1977-79; Book Reviewer, Journal of Popular Culture, Journal of American Culture, 1980-87. Publications: The Basketball Man, 1973, Japanese translation, 1981; Beware of Ostriches, 1978; Poetry on the Stage, 1979; George Washington Cable, commissioned essay, in Critical Survey of Long Fiction, 1983; Lady Doctor on a Homestead, 1987; Two Peach Baskets, 1991; Born to Be a Loser (co-author Johnnie Allen), 1993; Spider Webb, 1993; The Basketball Man, new revised edition, 1994. Contributions to: Many articles, short stories, 1-act plays, 100s of poems, to various publications. Honours: 28 Carruth Poetry Awards, 1946-61; Phi Beta Kappa, 1955; Fulbright Scholarship to France (alt), 1959; Foreign Exchange Scholar, Scotland, 1959-60; 3 Research Grants, 1978-86; Seaton Award, 1980; Coolidge Research Colloquium, 1985; Queen of Poetry, National Federation of State Poetry Societies, 1993. Memberships include: Past President, Past Journal Editor, Louisiana State Poetry Society; President, Southwest Branch Poetry Society; Board Member, Deep South Writers Conference; Founder, Webb's Writers; Past President, South Central College English Association; Past President, Phi Beta Kappa Association; Fellow, Society for Values in Higher Education; South Central Modern Language Association; College English Association; Conference on Christianity and Literature; American Folklore Society; National Federation of State Poetry Societies. Address: 159 Whittington Drive, Lafayette, LA 70503, USA.

WEBB Phyllis, b. 8 Apr 1927, Victoria, British Columbia, Canada. Professor; Poet; Retired. Education: BA, University of British Columbia at Vancouver, 1949; McGill University, Montreal. Appointments include: Adjunct Professor, University of Victoria, British Columbia. Publications: Trio, 1954; Even Your Right Eye, 1956; The Sea is Also a Garden, 1962; Naked Poems, 1965; Selected Poems 1954-65; Wilson's Bowl, 1980; Sunday Water: Thirteen Anti Ghazals, 1982; The Vision Tree: Selected Poems, 1982; Water and Light: Ghazals and Anti Ghazals, 1984; Hanging Fire, 1990. Honours include: Canada Council awards; Governor General's Award, 1982; Officer, The Order of Canada, 1992. Address: 128 Menhinick Drive, Salt Spring Island, British Columbia, Canada, V8K 1W7.

WEBER Eugen Joseph, b. 1925. Address: Dept of History, University of California, 405 Hilgard Avenue, Los Angeles, CA 90024-1473, USA.

WEBER George Richard, b. 7 Feb 1929, The Dalles, Oregon, USA. Certified Public Accountant. m. Nadine Hanson, 12 Oct 1957, 3 daughters. Education: BS, Oregon State University, 1950; MBA, University of Oregon, 1962. Publications: Small Business Long-Term Finance, 1962; A History of the Coroner and Medical Examiner Offices, 1963; CPA Litigation Service References, 1991. Contributions to: Cost and Management; Hyacinths & Biscuits. Honours: Bronze Star Medal with V, US Army, 1953; Selected by AICPA as one of One Hundred Future Leaders of Accounting Profession in the USA, 1963; Knightly Association of St George the Martyr, 1986. Memberships: American Institute of CPA's; Oregon Society of CPA's; Portland Committee on Foreign Relations. Address: 2603 NE 32nd Avenue, Portland, OR 97212, USA.

WEBSTER Ernest, b. 24 Oct 1923, Harbrough. Retired Director. m. 8 Oct 1942, 2 d. Education: London Matric, History & Economics. Publications: The Friulan Plot; Madonna of the Black Market; Cossack Hide Out; Red Alert; The Venetian Spy Glass; The Verratoli Inheritance; Million Dollar Stand in; The Watches. Literary Agent: Robert Hale. Address: 17 Chippendale Rise, Otley, West Yorkshire, LS21 2BL, England.

WEBSTER Jan, b. 10 Aug 1924, Blantyre, Writer. m. 10 Aug 1946, 1 s, 1 d. Education: Hamilton Academy. Publications: Trilogy: Colliers Row, 1977; Saturday City, 1978; Beggarman's Country, 1979; Due South, 1981; Muckle Annie, 1985; One Little Room, 1987; Rags of Time, 1987; A Different Woman, 1989; Abercrombie's Aunt and Other Stories, 1990; I Only Can Dance with You, 1990; Bluebell Blue, 1991; Lowland Reels, 1992; Tallies War, 1993; Makalienski's Bones, 1995. Address: c/o Robert Hale, 45-47 Clerkenwell Green, London EC1R 0HJ, England.

WEBSTER Jesse. See: **CASSILL Ronald Verlin.**

WEBSTER John (Jack) Barron, b. 8 July 1931, Maud, Aberdeenshire, Scotland. Journalist. m. Eden Keith, 17 Feb 1956, 3 sons. Education: Maud School; Peterhead Academy; Robert Gordon's College, Aberdeen. Publications: The Dons, 1978; A Grain of Truth, 1981; Gordon Strachan, 1984; Another Grain of Truth, 1988; Alistair MacLean: A Life, 1991; The Webster Trilogy, for Television, 1992; Famous Ships of the Clyde, 1993. Address: The Herald, 195 Albion Street, Glasgow G1 1QP, Scotland.

WEBSTER Noah. See: **KNOX William.**

WEBSTER Norman William, b. 21 Aug 1920, Barrow in Furness, Cumbira, England. Retired Physicist. m. Phyllis Joan Layley, 17 Feb 1945, 2 d. Education: BSc, University of London. Publications include: Joseph Locke, Railway Revolutionary, 1970; Britains First Trunk Line: The Grand Junction Railway, 1972; Horace Reactor, 1972; The Great North Road, 1974; Blanche of Lancaster, 1990. Contributions to: Cumbria; The Book Collector. Memberships: Jane Austen Society; European Movement. Address: 15 Hillcrest Drive, Slackhead, Milnthorpe, Cumbria LA7 7BB, England.

WECKMANN Luis, b. 7 Apr 1923, Durango, Mexico. Historian; Diplomat. Education: MA Hist, 1944, Phd Hist, 1949, Lic Law, 1950, National University Mexico; Dr Intl Public Law, Paris, 1951. Publications include: Las Bulas Alejandrinas de 1493, 1949, (reprinted as Constantino el Grande y Cristóbal Colón, 1993; El Pensamiento Politico Medieval, 1950, 2nd edition, 1993; Panorama de la Cultura Medieval, 1962; La Herencia Medieval de Mexico, 2 Vols, 1982, 2nd Edition, 1994; Carlota de Belgica - Archivos, 1989; La herencia medieval del Brasil, 1994. Honours: Professor Hist Emeritus, University Americas, 1990. Memberships: Amb Mexico, 1952-89; UN Assistant Secretary General, 1974-75. Address: Villa del Cardo, Cardo 4, San Miguel de Allende, Gto 37700, Mexico.

WEDDE Ian, b. 17 Oct 1946, Blenheim, New Zealand. Poet; Critic. m. Rosemary Beauchamp, 1967, 3 s. Education: MA, Auckland University, 1968. Appointments include: Writer in Residence, Victoria University, Wellington, 1984. Publications: Homage to Matisse, 1971; Made Over, 1974; Pathway to the Sea, 1974; Earthly: Sonnets for Carlos, 1975; Dont Listen, 1977; Spells for Coming Out, 1977; Castaly and Other Poems, 1980; Tales of Gotham City, 1984; Georgicon, 1984; Driving into the Storm: Selected Poems, 1987; Tendering, 1988; Novels, Dick Seddons Great Dive, 1976; Symmes Hole, 1986; Plays, Eyeball, Eyeball, 1983; Double or Quit: The Life and Times of Percy Topliss, 1984; Editor of Volumes of Poetry. Honours include: New Zealand Book Award.

WEDGEWOOD Cicely Veronica (Dame), b. 1910, England. Appointments: President, English Centre of Internationl PEN, 1950-57, English Association, 1955-56; Member, Royal Commission on Historical Manuscripts, 1952-78; Institute for Advanced Study, Princeton, 1953-68, Advisory Council, Victoria and Albert Museum, 1959-69, Arts Council Literature Panel, 1965-67; Trustee, Nationl Gallery, 1960-67, 1970-77. Publications include: The Thirty Years War, 1938; The Emperor Charles V, 1939; William the Silent, 1944; 17th Century English Literature, 1950; Poetry and Politics, 1960; Thomas Wentworth, 1961; Oliver Cronwell, 1973; Milton and His World, 1970; The Spoils of Time, 1984; History and Hope, 1987. Contributions to: Numerous. Honours: Member of Order of Merit; Dame British Empire; Officer, Order of Orange, 1958; Honorary LLD, DLitt; Honorary Fellow, Lady Margaret Hall, 1962; Honorary Fellow, UC london & London School of Economics. Memberships: English PEN; Royal Society of Literature; Royal Historical Society; Am Academy of Arts & Science; Am Philosophical Society; Am Historical Association; MA Historical Society; Society of Authors. Address: c/o Messrs W Harper Collins, Ophelia House, Fulham Palace Road, London, W6, England.

WEDGWOOD Anthony Neil. See: **BENN Tony.**

WEHRLI Peter, b. 30 July 1939, Switzerland, Writer; TV Producer. Education: University of Zurich; University of Paris. Publications include: Aukunfte, 1970; Catalogue of the 134 Most Important Observations during a Long Railway Journey, 1974; Selluloid Paradies, 1978; Tingeltangel, 1982; Alles von Allem, 1985; La Farandula, 1986; This Book is Free of Chairge; 18th Xurumbambo, 1992. Contributions to: Magazines and Journald in Switzerland, UK, USA, Italy, Albania, Malta, Argentin. Honours: Several Honours and Award including Award of the Government of Zurich; Distinguished Service Citation. Memberships: PEN; Swiss Writers Association; Gruppe Olten; International Federation of Journalists; International Association of Art Critics. Address: Schifflande 16, 8001 Zurich, Switerland.

WEIGEL George, b. 17 Apr 1951, Baltimore, Maryland, USA. Roman Catholic Theologian. m. Joan Balcombe, 21 June 1975, 1 son, 2 daughters. Education: BA Philosophy 1973, St Mary's Seminary & University, Baltimore; MA Theology 1975, University of St Michael's College, Toronto. Appointments: Fellow, Woodrow Wilson International Centre for Scholars, 1984-85; Editorial Boards of: First Things, The Washington Quarterly, and Orbis. Publications: Tranquillitas Ordinis: The Present Failure and Future Promise of American Catholic Thought on War and Peace, 1987; Catholicism and the Renewal of American Democracy, 1989; American Interests, American Purpose: Moral Reasoning and US Foreign Policy, 1989; Freedom and Its Discontents, 1991; Just War and the Gulf War, Co-Author, 1991; The Final Revolution: The Resistance Church and the Collapse of Communism, 1992; 4 other volumes edited; Idealism Without Illusions: US Foreign Policy in the 1990's, 1994. Contributions to: Numerous and ongoing. Memberships: Catholic Theological Society of America; Council on Foreign Relations. Address: Ethics & Public Policy Centre, 1015 15th Street NW, Suite 900, Washington DC 20005, USA.

WEINBERG Gerhard L, b. 1 Jan 1928, Hanover, Germany. Historian. m. Janet I White, 29 Apr 1989, 1 son. Education: BA, NY State College for Teachers, 1948; MA, University of Chicago, 1949; PhD, 1951. Publications: Germany and the Soviet Union, 1939-41, 1954; The Foreign Policy of Hitler's Germany, 1933-36, 1970; The Foreign Policy of Hitler's Germany, 1937-39, 1980; World in the Balance, Behind the Scenes of World War II, 1981; A World at Arms, A Global History of World War II, 1994; Hitlers Zweites Buch, 1961. Contributions to: Journal of Modern History; Central European History; German Studies Review; American Historical Review; Vientelyahrshefte für Zeitgenhiahte; Journal of Central European Affairs. Honours: AHA Beer Prize, 1971; GSA Halverson Prize, 1981; Hon Doctor of Humane Letters, 1989. Memberships: American Historical Association; Conference Group for Central European History; German Studies Association; World War II Studies Association. Address: Dept of History, University of North Carolina, CB 3195, Chapel Hill, NC 27599 3195, USA.

WEINBERG Steven, b. 5 Mar 1933, NY, USA. Theoretical Physicist. Education: AB, Cornell, 1954; PhD, Princeton, 1957. Literary Appointments: Past Member, Council of Scholars of Library of Congress. Publications: Dreams of a Final Theory, 1993; Discovery of Subatomic Particles, 1982; The First Three Minutes, 1977. Honours: Nobel Prize in Physics, 1979; National Medal of Science, 1991. Memberships: TX Institute of Letters; Am Academy of Arts & Science; Royal Society; National Academy of Sciences; Am Philosophical Society. Literary Agent: Morton Janklow. Address: Physics Dept, University of TX, Austin, TX 78712, USA.

WEINREICH Beatrice, (Beatrice Silverman-Weinreich), b. 14 May 1928, New York City, USA. Folklorist. m. Uriel Weinreich, 26 June 1949, dec 1967, 1 son, 1 daughter. Education: BA 1949, Brooklyn College; One year of graduate work in Folklore and Ethnography, University of Zurich, 1950; MA Anthropology 1956, Columbia University. Publications: Co-Editor, Volume II: Research Tools, The Language and Culture Atlas of Ashkenazic Jewry, 1993; Yiddish Folktales, 1988; Co-Editor, Yidisher Folklor: A Journal of Yiddish Folklore (in Yiddish), 1954; Co-Editor, Yiddish Language and Folklore: A Selective Bibliography for Research, 1959. Contributions to: Four Variants of the Yiddish Masterthief Tale, The Field of Yiddish 1, 1954; Genres and Types of the Yiddish Folktales About the Prophet Elijah, The Field of Yiddish II, 1965; The Americanization of Passover, Studies in Biblical & Jewish Folklore, 1960. Memberships: American Folklore Society; New York Folklore Society; International Society for Folk

Narrative Research. Address: c/o YIVO Institute for Jewish Research, 1048 Fifth Avenue, New York, NY 10028, USA.

WEINSTEIN Michael Alan, b. 24 Aug 1942, Brooklyn, New York, USA. Political Philosopher. m. Deena Schneiweiss, 31 May 1964. Education: BA summa cum laude 1964, New York University; MA 1965, PhD 1967, Western Reserve University. Appointments: Assistant Professor, Western Reserve University, 1967; Assistant Professor, Virginia Polytechnic Institute, 1967-68; Assistant Professor, 1972-, Purdue University; Milward Singson Distinguished Professor of Political Science, University of Wyoming, 1979. Publications: The Polarity of Mexican Thought: Instrumentalism and Finalism, 1976; The Tragic Sense of Political Life, 1977; Meaning and Appreciation: Time and Modern Political Life, 1978; The Structure of Human Life: A Vitalist Ontology, 1979; The Wilderness and the City: American Classical Philosophy as a Moral Quest, 1982; Unity and Variety is the Philosophy of Samuel Alexander, 1984; Finite Perfection: Reflections on Virtue, 1985; Culture Critique: Fernand Dumont and the New Quebec Sociology, 1985; Postmodern (Ized) Simmel, 1993. Contributions to: Photography Critic, New City (Chicago), 1990-; Over 100 articles to magazines and journals. Honours: Best Paper Prize, Midwest Political Science Association, 1969; Guggengeim Fellowship, 1974-75; Rockefeller Foundation Humanities Fellowship, 1976. Address: Department of Political Science, Purdue University, West Lafayette, IN 47907, USA.

WEINTRAUB Stanley, b. 1929, USA. Professor. Appointments: Director of Institute for the Arts and Humanities Studies, 1970-90; Research Professor to 1986; Evan Pugh Professor of Arts and Humanities, Pennsylvania State Unviersity. Publications: Private Shaw and Public Shaw: A Dual Portrait of Lawrence of Arabia and George Bernard Shaw, 1963; The Ward in the Wards: Korea's Forgotten Battle, 1964, 1977; The Art of William Golding (with B S Oldsey), 1965; Reggie: A Portrait of Reginald Turner, 1965; Beardsley: A Biography, 1967; The Last Great Cause: The Intellectuals and the Spanish Civil War, 1968; Evolution of a Revolt: Early Postwar Writings of T E Lawrence (with R Weintraub), 1968; Journey to Heartbreak: The Crucible Years of Bernard Shaw 1914-1918, 1971; Whistler: A Biography, 1974; Lawrence of Arabia: The Literary Impulse (with R Weintraub), 1975; Aubrey Beardsley: Imp of the Perverse, 1976; Four Rossettis: A Victorian Biography, 1977; The London Yankees: Portraits of American Writers and Artists in London 1894-1914, 1979; The Unexpected Shaw: Biographical Approaches to G B S and His Work, 1982; A Stillness Heard Round The World: The End of the Great War, 1985; Bernard Shaw: The Diaries 1885-1897, 1986; Victoria: A Biography, 1987; Long Day's Journey Into War, December 7, 1941, 1991; Bernard Shaw: A Guide to Research, 1992; Disraeli: A Biography, 1993; Editor: An Unfinished Novel, by George Bernard Shaw, 1958; C P Snow: A Spectrum, 1963; The Yellow Book: Quintessence of the Nineties, 1964; The Savoy: Nineties Experiment, 1966; The Court Theatre, 1966; Biography & Truth, 1968; Cashel Byron's Profession, by Shaw, 1968; The Literary Criticism of Oscar Wilde, 1968; Shaw: An Autobiography, 2 vols, 1969-70; The Green Carnation, by Robert Hichens, 1970; Saint Joan, by Shaw, 1971; Bernard Shaw's Nondramatic Literary Criticism, 1972; Directions in Literary Criticism (with Philip Young), 1973; Saint Joan Fifty Years After, 1973; The Portable Bernard Shaw, 1977; The Portable Oscar Wilde, 1981; Heartbreak House: A Facsimile of the Revised Typescript (with Ann Wright), 1981; Modern British Dramatists 1900-1945, 2 vols, 1982; The Playwright and the Pirate: Bernard Shaw and Frank Harris, a Correspondence, 1982; British Dramatists since World War II, 2 vols, 1982; Bernard Shaw: The Diaries 1885-1897, 1986; Bernard Shaw on the London Art Scene 1885-1950, 1989. Literary Agents: Michael Sissons, London; Sterling Lord, New York, USA. Address: 202 Ihlseng Cottage, University Park, PA 16802, USA.

WEISS Renee Karol, b. 11 Sept 1923, Allentown, Pennsylvania, USA. m. Theodore Weiss, 1941. Education: BA, Bard College; Connecticut Summer School of Dance, 1950; Instruction with Martha Graham and Jose Limon; Musical Education with Sascha Jacobinoff, Boris Koutzen, Emile Hauser and Ivan Galamian. Appointments: Teacher, Modern Dance to Children, Bard College; Kindergarten, Tivoli, New York Public School, 1955-58; Poetry Writing Workshop, Hofstra College, summer 1985; Princeton University Academic Year, 1985; Modern Poetry, Cooper Union, 1988; Violinist, member of Miami University Symphony Orchestra, 1941; North Carolina State Symphony, 1941-45; Oxford University Symphony and Opera Orchestras, England, 1953-54; Woodstock String Quartet, 1956-60; Bard College Ensemble, 1950-66; Hudson Valley Philharmonic,

1960-66; Touring Public Schools with Hudson Valley String Quartet, 1965; Orchestral, Chamber and Solo Work, 1966-; Princeton Chamber Orchestra, 1980-. Publications: To Win a Race, 1966; A Paper Zoo, 1968; The Bird From the Sea, 1970; David Schubert, Work and Days, biography, 1984. Contributions to: Various poems in journals; Co-editor, Quarterly Review of Literature, 1945-. Honours: A Paper Zoo listed in Best Books for Children, New York Times and Book World, 1968; New Jersey Author's Award, 1968, 1970. Address: 26 Haslet Avenue, Princeton, NJ 08540, USA.

WEISSBORT Daniel, b. 1 May 1935, London. Professor; Poet; Editor; Translator. Education: BA, Queens College, Cambridge, 1956. Appointments include: Co Founder, Ted Hughes, Modern Poetry in Translation, 1965-83; Professor, University of IA, 1980. Publications include: The Leaseholder, 1971; In An Emergency, 1972; Soundings, 1977; Leaseholder: New and Collected Poems, 1965-85, 1986; Inscription, 1990; Lake, 1993; Editor and Translator of Russian Literature. Honours include: Arts Council Literature Award, 1984. Address: Dept of English, University of IA, IA City, IA 52242, USA.

WELCH Ann Courtenay, b. 20 May 1917, London, England. Aviation Writer. m. 1) 2 daughters, (2) P P Lorne Elphinstone Welch, 24 June 1953, 1 daughter. Appointments include: Editor, Bulletin, Fédération Aéronautique Internationale, 1979-89; Editor, Royal Aero Club Gazette, 1984-; Part-time Tutor, AEI classes on Weather and Writing. Publications include: The Woolacombe Bird, 1964; Story of Gliding, 1965; New Soaring Pilot, 1970; Pilot's Weather, 1973; Gliding, 1976; Hang Glider Pilot, 1977; Book of Air Sports, 1978; Accidents Happen, 1978; Soaring Hang Gliders, 1981; Complete Microlight Guide, 1983; Happy to Fly, autobiography, 1984; Complete Soaring Guide, 1986. Contributions to: Flight International, UK; Aeroplane, UK; Royal Aero Club Gazette; Pilot; Flight Safety Bulletin. Honours: Officer, Order of the British Empire; Silver Medal, Royal Aero Club; Gold, Lilienthal and Bronze Medals, Fédération Aéronautique Internationale; Pelagia Majewska Medal, Fédération Aéronautique Internationale, 1990. Memberships: Fellow, Royal Aeronautical Society, Chairman, Light Aviation Group; Royal Meteorological Society; Royal Institute of Navigation. Address: 14 Upper Old Park Lane, Farnham, Surrey GU9 0AS, England.

WELCH Colin, (James Ross), b. 23 Apr 1924, England. Journalist. m. Sybil Russell, 1950, 1 s, 1 d. Education: Peterhouse, Cambridge. Appointments include: Glasgow Herald, 1948; Colonial Office, 1949; Leader Writer, Columnist, Parliamentary Sketch Writer, 1950-64, Deputy Editor, 1964-80, Regular Column, 1981-83, Daily Telegraph; Editor in Chief, Chief Executive Magazine, 1980-82; Columnist, Spectator, 1982-92; Columnist, Independent, 1993. Publications: Sir Frederick Ponsonby: Recollections of Three Reigns, 1951; Nestroy: Liberty Comes to Krahwinkel, 1954. Contributions to: Encounter; Spectator; New Statesman; Various Symposia. Honour: Knights Cross, Order of Polonia Restituta, 1972; Journalist of Year, 1974; Special Writer of Year, 1987. Address: 4 Goddards Lane, Aldbourne, Wilts 5N8 2DL, England.

WELCH Liliane, b. 20 Oct 1937, Luxembourg. Professor, French Literature. m. Cyril Welch, 1 daughter. Education: BA 1960, MA 1961, University of Montana; PhD, Penn State University, 1964. Appointments: Assistant Professor, French, East Carolina University, 1965-66, Antioch College, 1966-67, Mount Allison University, 1967-71; Associate Professor, 1971-72, Professor, 1977-, French, Mount Allison University. Publications: Emergence: Baudelaire, Mallarme, Rimbaud, 1973; Winter Songs, 1973; Address: Rimbaud, Mallarme, Butor, 1979; Syntax of Ferment, 1979; Assailing Beats, 1979; October Winds, 1980; Brush and Trunks, 1981; From the Songs of the Artisans, 1983; Manstorna, 1985; Rest Unbound, 1985; Word-House of a Grandchild, 1987; Seismographs: Selected Essays and Reviews, 1988; Fire to the Looms Below, 1990; Life in Another Language, 1992. Contributions to: More than 50 USA, Canadian, European, Australian Journals; Literary articles in more than 20 International Journals. Memberships: Writers Union of Canada; Federation of New Brunswick Writers; League of Canadian Poets; Association of Italian-Canadian Writers; Letzebuerger Schreftsteller Verband. Address: Box 246, Sackville, NB, E0A 3C0, Canada.

WELDON Fay, b. 22 Sept 1931, Writer. m. Ron Weldon, 12 June 1961, Alvechurch, Wocestershire, England. 4 s. Education: MA, St Andrews University, 1952. Publications include: Fat Womans Joke, 1968; down Among the Women, 1971; Female Friends, 1975; Remember Me, 1976; Praxis, 1978; Puffball, 1980; The Presidents

Child, 1982; Letters to Alice, 1984; Life and Loves of a She Devil, 1984; Rebecca West, 1985; The Sharpnel Academy, 1986; The Hearts and Lives of Men, 1987; Leader of the Band, 1988; Wolf of the Mechanical Dog, 1989; The Cloning of Joanna May, 1989; Pary Puddle, 1989; Moon Over Minneapolis or Why She Couldn't Stay, 1991; Life Force, 1992; Growing Rich, 1992; Affliction, 1994. Contributions to: Numerous Journals and Magazines. Memberships: Royal Society of Authors; Writers Guild of Great Britain. Literary Agent: Giles Gordon. Address: c/o Giles Gordon, 43 Doughty Street, London WC1N 2LF, England.

WELLINGTON Fred. See: **PURDY A F.**

WELLS Martin John, b. 24 Aug 1928, London, England. Zoologist; Educator. m. Joyce Finlay, 8 Sept 1953, 2 s. Education: BA, 1952; MA, 1956; ScD, 1966. Publications: Brain and Behaviour in Cephalopods, 1962; You, Me and the Animal World, 1964; Lower Animals, 1968; Octopus: Physiology and Behaviour of an Advanced Invertebrate, 1978. Contributions to: Several Journals. Honours: Silver Medal, Zoological Society, 1968; Fellow, Churchill College, Cambridge. Memberships: Philosophical Society; Marine Biology Association. Address: The Bury Home End, Fulbourn, Cambridge, England.

WELLS Robert, b. 17 Aug 1947, England. Teacher; Translator; Poet. Education: Kings College Cambridge, 1965-68. Appointments include: Teacher, Leicester University, 1979-82. Publications: Shae Mariners, 1970; The Winters Task, 1977; Selected Poems, 1986; Translations of the Georgics by Virgil and the Idyll by Theocritus. Address: c/o Carcanet Press, 208-212 Corn Exchange Buildings, Manchester M4 3BQ, England.

WELLS Roger, b. 30 Jan 1947, London, England. University Lecturer, div, 1 d. Education: BA, 1969, Dphil, 1978, University of York. Appointments: Lecturer, University of Wales, 1972-73; University of Exeter, 1973-75; University of York, 1975-76; Senior Lecturer, University of BRighton, 1976-. Publications include: Dearth and Distress in Yorkshire, 1793-1801, 1977; Riot an Political Disaffection in Nottinghamshire in the Age of Revolutions 1776-1803, 1983; Wretched Faces: Famine in Wartimes England, 1793-1801, 1988; Class, Conflict and Protest in the English Countryside, 1700-1880, 1990; Victorian Village, 1992. Contributions to: Social History; Rural History; Southern History; Northern History; Policing and Society; Journal of Peasant Studies; Journal of Historical Geography; Local Historian; English Historical Review; Agricultural History Review; London Journal; Labour History Bulletin; Journal of Social Policy. Memberships: Royal Historical Society. Address: School of Historical & Critical Studies, University of Brighton, Grand Parade, Brighton, BN2 1RA, England.

WELLS Rosemary, b. 1943. Author; Illustrator. Publications: A Song to Sing, O, 1968; Two Sisters & Some Hornets, 1972; Noisy Nora, 1973; Abdul, 1975; Morris' Disappearing Bag, 1975; Max's Ride, 1979; Max's Toys, 1979; Forest of Dreams, 1988; Shy Charles, 1988; Little Lame Prince, 1990; Max & Ruby's Greek Myth: Pandora's Box, 1993; Waiting for the Evening Star, 1993; Night Sounds, 1994. Honours: Boston Globe/Horn Book Award, 1989.

WELLS Tobias. See: **FORBES DeLoris Stanton.**

WELLS William K. See: **GARSIDE Jack Clifford.**

WELTON Anthony. See: **JOY David.**

WELTY Eudora, b. 13 Apr 1909, Jackson, Mississippi, USA. Education: Mississippi State College for Women; University of Wisconsin; Columbia University Graduate School of Business. Honours: National Book Award; Pulitzer Prize; National BookFoundation Medal for Distinguished Contributions to American Letters, 1991. Address: 1119 Pinehurst Street, Jackson, MS 39202, USA.

WENDT Albert, b. 27 Oct 1939, Apia, Western Samoa. Novelist. 1 son, 2 daughters. Education: MA in History at Victoria University, Wellington, 1964. Appointments: Professor of Pacific Literature, University of the South Pacific, Suva, Fiji, 1982-87; Professor of English, University of Auckland, from 1988. Publications: Sons for the Return Home, 1973; Pouliuli, 1977; Leaves of the Banyan Tree, 1979; Ola, 1990; Black Rainbow, 1992; Short stories: Flying-Fox in a Freedom Tree, 1974; The Birth and Death of the Miracle Man, 1986; Plays: Comes the Revolution, 1972; The Contract, 1972; Verse: Inside

us the Dead: Poems 1961-74; Shaman of Visions, 1984. Honours: Landfall Prize, 1963; Wattie Award, 1980. Address: Department of English, University of Auckland, Private Bag, Auckland, New Zealand.

WENTWORTH Wendy. See: **CHAPLIN Jenny.**

WERTENBAKER Timberlake. Education: Studied in France, England and the United States. Appointments include: Resident Writer at Shared Experience, London, 1983; Resident Writer at the Royal Court Theatre, London, 1985. Creative works: Productions: This Is No Place for Tallulah Bankhead, 1978; The Third, 1980; Second Sentence, 1980; Case to Answer, 1980; Breaking Through, 1980; Inside Out, 1982; Home Leave, 1982; Produced and Published: New Anatomies, 1981; False Admissions, after Marivaux, 1983; Successful Strategies, after Marivaux, 1983; The Grace of Mary Traverse, 1985; Leocadia, after Anouilh, 1985; Mephisto, after Ariane Mnouchkine, 1986; Our Country's Good, based on The Playmaker by Thomas Keneally, 1988; The Love of the Nightingale, 1988; Pelléas et Mélisande, after Maeterlinck, 1988; Three Birds Alighting On a Field, 1991; The Thebans, after Sophocles, 1992; Plays produced in London, Brighton, New York, Stoke-on-Trent, Ipswich, Los Angeles and Stratford-on-Avon; Radio and television plays. Honours include: Olivier Award, 1988; Evening Standard Award, 1988; Mrs Giles Whiting Award, 1989; London Theatre Critics Circle Award, 1992; Susan Smith Blackburn Award, 1992; Writers Guild Award, 1992. Address: c/o Michael Imison Playwrights, 28 Almeida Street, London N1 1TD, England.

WESCOTT Roger Williams, b. 28 April 1925, Philadelphia, Pennsylvania, USA. Anthropologist. m. 12 Apr 1964. Education: BA English and History 1945, MA Oriental Studies 1947, PhD Linguistic Science 1948, Princeton University; MLitt Social Anthropology 1953, Oxford University. Appointments: Director, University Playreaders, Ibadan, Nigeria, 1955-56; Assistant Professor of English, MIT, USA, 1956-57; Associate Professor of English, Michigan State University, 1957-62; Evaluator, National Endowment for Humanities, 1975-; Associate Editor, Thoughts for All Seasons, USA, 1988-. Publications: The Divine Animal, 1969; Visions: Selected Poems, 1975; Sound and Sense, 1980; Language Families, 1986; Getting it Together, 1990; Co-author, The Creative Process, 1974; Poems for Children, 1975; Literary and Linguistic Studies, 1978; Anthropological Poetics, 1990. Contributions to: Two Ibo Songs, Anthropological Linguistics, March 1962; From Proverb to Aphorism, Forum Linguisticum, 1981. Honours: Sophomore English Prize, Princeton University, 1943; Rhodes Scholar, Oxford University, 1948-50; First Holder, Endowed Chair of Excellence in Humanities, University of Tennessee, 1988-89. Memberships: President, Princeton University undergraduate Literary Society, 1944; President, International Society for the Comparative Study of Civilsations 1992-; President, Linguistic Association of Canada and the US 1976-77. Address: 16-A Heritage Crest, Southbury, CT 06488, USA.

WESLEY James. See: **RIGONI Orlando Joseph.**

WESLEY Mary. See: **SIEPMANN Mary Aline.**

WEST Anthony C(athcart Muir), b. 1 July 1910, County Down, Northern Ireland. Novelist. m. Olive Mary Burr, 1940, 11 children. Publications: The Native Moment, 1959; Rebel to Judgement, 1962; The Ferret Fancier, 1963; As Towns with Fire, 1968; River's End and Other Stories, 1958; All the King's Horses and Other Stories, 1981. Honours: Atlantic Award, 1946. Address: c/o Poolbeg Press, Knocksdean House, Forrest Great, Swords, County Dublin, Ireland.

WEST Cornell. Professor of Religion; Director of Afro-American Studies. m. 1 son. Appointments: Princeton University, 1988-94; Professor of Afro-American Studies and Philosophy of Religion, Harvard University, 1994-. Address: Dept of Religion, Princeton University, 1879 Building, Princeton, NJ 08544-1099, USA.

WEST Douglas. See: **TUBB E(dwin) C(harles).**

WEST Morris (Langlo), (Morris East, Julian Morris), b. 26 Apr 1916, Melbourne Australia. Author. m. Joyce Lawford, 1953, 3 sons, 1 daughter. Education: University of Melbourne. Publications: Gallows on the Sand, 1955; Kundu, 1956; Children of the Sun, 1957; The Crooked Road (English Title, The Big Story), 1957; The Concubine, 1958; Backlash (English Title The Second Victory), 1958; The Devil's Advocate, 1959 (filmed 1977); The Naked Country, 1960; Daughter of

Silence (novel and play), 1961; The Shoes of the Fisherman, 1963; The Ambassador, 1965; The Tower of Babel, 1968; The Heretic, a Play in Three Acts, 1970; Scandal in the Assembly, with Robert Francis, 1970; Summer of the Red Wolf, 1971; The Salamander, 1973; Harlequin, 1974; The Navigator, 1976; Proteus, 1979; The Clowns of God, 1981; The World is Made of Glass, 1983, (play 1984); Cassidy, 1986; Masterclass, 1988; Lazarus; The Lovers, 1993. Honours: National Brotherhood Award, National Council of Christians and Jews, 1960; James Tait Black Memorial Prize, 1960; Royal Society of Literature, Heinemann Award, 1960; Hon. D.Litt, Santa Clara University, 1969, Mercy College, New York, 1982; Order of Australia, 1985; Hon. D.Litt, University of Western Sydney, 1993. Memberships: Fellow, Royal Society of Literature; World Academy of Arts and Science. Address: PO Box 102, Avalon, NSW 2107, Australia.

WEST Nigel, b. 8 Nov 1951, London, England. Historian. m. 15 June 1979, 1 s, 1 d. Education: University of Grenoble; university of Lille; London University. Appointments: BBC TV, 1977-82. Publications: A Matter of Trust M15 1945-72, 1982; Unreliable Witness, 1984; Carbo M15, 1981, M16, 1983, 1985; GCHQ, 1986; Molehunt, 1986; The Friends, 1987; Games of Intelligence, 1990; Seven Spies who Changed the World, 1991; Secret War, 1992; The Illegals, 1993; Faver Book of Espionage, 1993. Contributions to: The Times; Intelligence Quarterly. Honour: The Experts Expert, 1989; The Observer. Literary Agent: Peters, Fraser and Dunlop. Address: Westintel Research Limited, PO Box 2, Goring on Thames, Berks, RG8 9SB.

WEST Sally. See: HASTREITER Marge Thielman.

WEST William Alexander, (Anthony Worth), b. 30 May 1916, Scotland. University Professor. m. (1) Kathleen Herring, 6 May 1942, (2) Marion Davies, 5 Sept 1963, 1 s, 4 d. Education: University College School; LLB, LLM, University of London. Appointments: Leader Writer, Estates Gazetee, 1965-79; Planning Correspondent, Spectator, 1975-79. Publications: Consider Your Verdict, 1950; A Number of Books on Legal Subjects. Contributions to: Times; Spectator; Economist; Daily Telegraph. Memberships: Hurlingham Club; Royal Overseas Club; Landsdowne Club. Address: 13 ST Georges Court, London SW7 4QZ, England.

WESTHEIMER David (Z Z Smith), b. 11 Apr 1917. Writer. m. Doris Rothstein Kahn, 9 Oct 1945, 2 sons. Education: BA, Rice Institute, 1937. Publications: Von Ryan's Express, 1964; My Sweet Charlie, 1965; Lighter than a Feather, 1971; The Auila Gold, 1974; The Olmec Head, 1974; Song of the Young Sentry, 1968; Summer on the Water, 1948; The Magic Fallacy, 1950; Watching Out For Dulie, 1960; This Time Next Year, 1963; Over the Edge, 1972; Von Ryan's Return, 1980; Rider on the Wind, 1984; Going Public, 1973; Sitting It Out, 1992. Memberships: Writers Guild of America West; Authors Guild; PEN; California Writers Club, Advisory Board; Retired Officers Association. Address: 11722 Darlington Avenue No 2, Los Angeles, CA 90049, USA.

WESTON Helen Gray. See: DANIELS Dorothy.

WESTRICK Elsie Margaret Beyer, b. 12 Nov 1910, Fort William, Ontario, Canada. Writer, poetry, fiction. m. Roswell G Westrick, 6 Oct 1945, 5 daughters, 2 step-sons, 1 step-daughter. Education: Diploma, Institute of Childrens Literature, 1976; Diploma, Writing for Young People, 1985; Diploma, Writing Self Fiction, 1989, Writers Digest School. Publications include: Poems, On This Holy Night, 1949; Tender Foliage of Summer, 1972; The Photograph, 1975; Beauty on a Beach, 1983; Memories of Childhood, 1983; Call of the Blue Jay, 1987; The Breath of Fall, 1986; My Last Love, 1989; The Old Lighthouse, 1990; Tender Foliage of Summer, World of Poetry's Anthology, Poems That Will Live Forever, 1991; Winter Magic, National Library of Poetry, 1992. Honours: One Hundred and One Best of Clover Publishers Award, 1970; Honorable Mention, International Poetry Competition, 1969; Golden Poet Award, World of Poetry, 1985, 1986; Award for Poetic Achievement, 1988; Silver Poet Award, World of Poetry, 1990. Memberships: Charter Member State of Liberty; Writers Digest Book Club; Center for Marine Conservation, 1991-; ITAN, 1992; PETA, 1991-92. Address: 3751 Wheeler Road, Snover, MI 48472, USA.

WEVILL David (Anthony), b. 15 Mar 1935, Yokohama, Japan. Lecturer; Poet. m. Assia Gutman, 1960. Education: BA, Caius College, Cambridge, 1957. Appointments include: Lecturer, University of TX, Austin. Publications: Penguin Modern Poets, 1963; Birth of a Spark, 1964; A Christ of the Ice Floes, 1966; Firebreak, 1971; Where the

Arrow falls, 1973; Other Names for the Heart: New and Selected Poems, 1964-84, 1985; Figures of Eight, 1987; Translator of Hungarian Poetry. Honours include: Arts Council Prize and Bursaries. Address: Dept of English, University of TX, Austin, TX 78712, USA.

WEYL Brigitte Ruth, b. Munich, Germany. Publisher. Education: MD, 1951, Freiburg; Medical State Examination, 1950; Medical Examination for Foreigners, Basel. Appointments: Medical Work, 1951-56; Editor, Die Presse, Wien, 1957-68; Publisher, Sudkurier, Konstanz, 1959-89; Publisher, Sudverlag & Universitatsverlag Konstanz, 1959-; Founder, Publisher, UVK Fachverlag fur Wissenschaft und Studium GmbH, 1993. Contributions to: Die Presse; Sudkurier; Publizistik; Within Several Books. Honours: Honorary President, Deutsch Franzosische Vereingung Konstanz, 1979-; Officer de l'Order National du Merite, 1982; Bundesverdienstkreuz 1K1, 1984; Ehrensenatorin Universitat Konstanz, 1991. Memberships: Interantional Press Institut; Gesellschaft der Freunde und Forderer der Universitat Konstanz; Stifervereinigung fur die Deutsche Wissenschaft, Landeskuratorium Baden Wurttemberg; Vereinigung Deutsch Franzosischer Gesellschaften in Deutschland und Frankreich, Kuratorium. Address: D 78420 Konstanz, PO Box 1020 51, Germany.

WHALEN Terry Anthony, b. 1 Feb 1944, Halifax, Nova Scotia, Canada. Professor of English; Editor. m. Maryann Antonia Walters, 30 Feb 1966, 2 sons, 2 daughters. Education: BA, Honours, Saint Mary's University, 1965; MA, Honours, University of Melbourne, 1968. Internatinal Graduate Seminar Certificate, Oxford University, 1970; PhD, University of Ottawa, 1980. Appointments: Tutor, University of Sydney, 1966; University of Melbourne, 1967; Lecturer, 1968-70, Assistant Professor, 1970-76, 1978-80, Associate Professor, 1981-85, Professor of English, 1985-, St Mary's University; Teaching Fellow, University of Ottawa, 1976-77; Editor, Atlantic Provinces Book Review, 1980-90. Publications: Philip Larkin and English Poetry, 1986, reprinted 1990; Bliss Carman and His Works, 1983; The Atlantic Anthology; Criticism, (Editor and Introduction), 1985; Charles G D Roberts and His Works, 1989; Contributor to: Poutledge Encyclopaedia of Post-Colonial Literature in English, 1994. Contributions to: Canadian Literature; Canadian Poetry; Critical Quarterly;Critical Review; Conradiana; Dalhousie Review; The Fiddlehead; Canadian Review of American Studies; Quarry; Sift; Thalia; The Old Northwest Times Higher Education Supplement; Modernist Studies; Australian Book Review; Contributor to books including: Canadian Poetry; New Press Canadian Classics, 1982; The New Canadian Anthology, 1988. Honours: British Commonwealth Scholarship, 1966-68; Election to Council Member Status, Writers' Federation of Nova Scotia; Grants: Canada Council; Social Sciences and Humanities Research Council of Canada; Canadian Federation for the Humanities. Memberships: Writers Federation of Nova Scotia; Association of Canadian University Teachers of English; Northeast Modern Language Association; Modern Language Association. Address: 26 Oceanview Drive, Purcells Cove, Halifax NS, B3P 2H3, Canada.

WHAM David Buffington, b. 25 May 1937, Evanston, USA. Political Writer. m. 3 Mar 1968, 1 son, 1 daughter. Education: BA, Harvard. Appointments: Co-author, Offical Report on Poor People's March for Jobs and Income, 1968; Speech Writer, Congressman James R Mann, 1970-76; Speech Writer, Adlai E Stevenson III, Democratic Candidate for Governor, Illinois, 1986. Publications: There is a Green Hill, 1967. Contributions to: December Magazine; Story Quarterly; Woodwind; The Fair Brandy, a Novella, 1966; Maelstrom; Means; Pilgrimage; etc. Honours: 1st Prize, Maelstrom Magazine, 1968. Literary Agent: Gerald McCauley, New York City. Address: 8823 Dobson Street, Evanston, IL 60202, USA.

WHEATCROFT John Stewart, b. 24 July 1925, Philadelphia, Pennsylvania, USA. College Professor; Writer. m. (1) Joan Mitchell Osborne, 10 Nov 1952, div. 1974, 2 sons, 1 daughter, (2) Katherine Whaley Warner, 14 Nov 1992. Education: BA, Bucknell University, 1949; MS, 1950, PhD, 1960, Rutgers University. Appointments: Currently Director, Stadler Center for Poetry, Bucknell University, Lewisburg, Pennsylvania. Publications: Books of poetry: Death of a Clown, 1963; Prodigal Son, 1967; A Voice from the Hump, 1977; Ordering Demons, 1981; The Stare on the Donkey's Face, 1990; Novels: Edie Tells, 1975; Catherine, Her Book, 1983; The Beholder's Eye, 1987; Killer Swan, 1992; Slow Exposures, stories, 1986; Our Other Voices (editor), interviews with poets, 1991; Mother of All Love, 1994. Contributions to: New York Times; Harper's Bazaar; Mademoiselle; Ladies' Home Journal; The Literary Review; New Letters; Criticism; Carleton Miscellany; Ohio Review; Agenda. Honours:

Alcoa Playwriting Award, 1966; National Educational Television Award, 1967; Fellowships: Yaddo, 1972, 1985; MacDowell Colony, 1973; Virginia Center for the Creative Arts, 1976, 1978, 1980, 1982. Memberships: Academy of American Poets; Poetry Society of America. Address: Stadler Center for Poetry, Bucknell University, Lewisburg, PA 17837, USA.

WHEELWRIGHT Julie Diana, b. 2 June 1960, Farnborough, Kent, England. Writer; Broadcaster. Education: BA, University of British Columbia; MA, University of Sussex. Appointments: Reporter, Vancouver Sun, 1980; President, Canadian University Press, 1981; Consultant, Open University, 1991. Publications: Amazons and Military Maids, 1989, 1994; The Fatal Lover, 1992. Contributions to include: History Today; New Statesman Society; Index on Cesorship; Middle East; New Africa; Womens Studies International Forum; Gender and History; World Magazine; The Guardian; The Times; Th TLS; The Financial Times; Queens Quarterly; Literary Review; Womans Hour. Honours: Nominated By Pandora Press for the Fawcett Award, 1989; Canada Council Non Fiction Writers Grant, 1990-91, 1994-95. Memberships: Writers Guild; Institute of Historical Research. Literary Agent: Bill Hamilton, A M Heath. Address: 5 Cleaver Street, London SE11 4DP, England.

WHELAN Peter, b. 3 Oct 1931, Newcastle-under-Lyme, England. Playwright. Education: Graduated Keele University, Staffordshire, 1955. Appointments include: Advertising Copywriter and Director, 1959-90. Publications: Lakota (co-author), 1970; Double Edge (co-author), 1975; Captain Swing, 1978; The Accrington Pals, 1981; Clay, 1982; A Cold Wind Blowing Up (co-author), 1983; Worlds Apart, 1986; The Bright and Bold Design, 1991; The School of Night, 1992 (plays produced in London, Stratford-on-Avon and Worldwide). Honours include: Two Writers Guild Best Play Nominations. Address: c/o Lemon, Unna, and Durbridge, 24 Pottery Lane, Holland Park, London W11 4LZ, England.

WHIPPLE Addison Beecher Colvin, b. 15 July 1918, Glen Falls, New York, USA. Retired Journalist. m. Jane Mulvane Banks, 27 June 1942, 1 son, 1 daughter. Education: BA 1940, Yale; MA 1941, Harvard. Publications: Yankee Whalers in the South Seas; Vintage Nantucket; The Challenge; To The Shores of Tripoli; Fighting Sail; Pirate; Tall Ships and Great Captains; The Clipper Ships; The Whalers. Contributions to: Life; Smithsonian; Readers Digest; American Heritage. Honour: John Lyman Book Award, Honorable Mention for The Challenge, 1987. Literary Award: Julian Bach, New York, USA. Address: Cove Road, Old Greenwich, CT 06870, USA.

WHISTLER (Alan Charles) Laurence, b. 21 Jan 1912, Eltham, Kent. Writer; Glass Engraver; Poet. m. Jill Furse, 1939, dec'd 1944. Education: BA, Balliol College, Oxford, 1934. Publications include: Children of Hertha and Other Poems, 1929; Armed October and Other Poems, 1932; Four Walls, 1934; The Emperor Heart, 1936; The Burning Glass, 1941; Who Live in Unity, 1944; The World's Room: The Collected poems of Laurence Whistler, 1949; The View from This Window, 1956; Audible silence, 1961; Fingals Cave, 1963; To Celebrate Her Living, 1967; For Example; Ten Sonnets in Sequence to a New Pattern, 1969; A Bridge on the Usk, 1976; Enter, 1987; Sir John Vanbrugh: Architect and Dramatist, 1664-1726, 1938; Rex Whistler, 1905-1944; His Life and His Drawings, 1948; The Initals in the Heart, 1964; The Image on the Glass, 1975; The Laughter and the Urn: The Life of Rex Whistler, 1985. Honours include: OBE, 1955; CBE, 1973; Honorary Fellow, Balliol College, Oxford, 1973. Address: c/o The College Secretary, Balliol College, Oxford, England.

WHITBY Sharon. See: **PETERS Maureen.**

WHITE Gillian Mary, b. 13 Jan 1936, Essex, England. University Professor. m. Colin A Fraser, 1 Apr 1978. Education: LLB, 1957; PhD, 1960, Barrister, Grays Inn, 1960. Publications include: The Use of Experts by International Tribunals, 1965; Principles of International Economic Law, 1988; International Economic Law and Developing States, 1992; International Law in Transition, 1992; Good Faith, 1994. Memberships include: British Institute of International And Comparative Law; International Law Association; Am Society of International Law; Royal Society of Arts. Address: c/o Faculty of Law, University of Manchester, Manchester, M13 9PL.

WHITE Jon Manchip, b. 1924, England. Author. Appointments: Story Editor, BBC London, 1950-51; Senior Executive Officer, UK Foreign Service, 1952-56; Freelance Writer, 1956-67; Professor of English, University of Texas, El Paso, 1967-77; Lindsay Young Professor of English, University of Tennessee, Knoxville, 1977-. Publications: Dragon, 1943; Salamander, 1943; The Rout of San Romano, 1952; Ancient Egypt, 1952, 1970; Mask of Dust (in USA as The Last Race), 1953; Build Us A Dam, 1954; Anthropology, 1954; The Girl from Indiana, 1955; The Glory of Egypt, editor, 1955; No Home But Heaven, 1956; The Mercenaries, 1958; Hour of the Rat, 1962; Marshal of France: The Life and Times of Maurice, Comte de Saxe, 1962; Everyday Life in Ancient Egypt, 1963; The Rose in the Brandy Glass, 1965; Nightclimber, 1968; Diego Velazquez: Painter and Courtier, 1969; The Land God Made in Anger Reflections on a Journey Through South West Africa, 1969; Cortes and the Downfall of the Aztec Empire, 1971; Life in Ancient Egypt, by Adolf Erman, Editor, 1971; Tomb of Tutankhamen, by Howard Carter, Editor, 1971; The Game of Troy, 1971; The Mountain Lion, 1971; Manners and Customs of the Modern Egyptians, by E W Lane, Editor, 1972; The Garden Game, 1973; Send for Mr Robinson, 1974; A World Elsewhere: One Man's Fascination with the American Southwest, 1975 (in UK as The Great American Desert, 1977); Everyday Life of the North American Indian, 1979; The Moscow Papers, 1979; Death by Dreaming, 1981; Chills and Fevers: Three Extravagent Tales, 1983; The Last Grand Master: A Novel of Revolution, 1985; The Journeying Boy: Scenes from a Welsh Childhood, 1991; Whistling Past The Graveyard: Strange Tales from a Superstitious Welshman, 1992. Address: Department of English, University of Tennessee, Knoxville, TN 37916, USA.

WHITE Kenneth, b. 28 Apr 1936, Glasgow, Scotland. Professor. Poet. m. Marie Claude Charlut. Education: MA, University of Glasgow, 1959; Universities of Munich & Paris. Appointments include: Professor, Sorbonne University of Paris, 1983-; Founded International Institute of Geopaetics, 1989. Publications include: Wild Coal, 1963; The Cold Wind of Dawn, 1966; The Most Difficult Area, 1968; A Walk Along the Shore, 1977; Mahamudra, 1979; Le Grand Rivage, 1980; Terre de Diamant, 1983; L'Esprit Nomade, 1987; The Bird Path: Collected Longer Poems, 1989; Handbook for the Diamond Country: Collected Shorter Poems, 1960-90; Fiction: Letters from Gourgounel, 1966; Les Limbes Incandescents, 1978; Le Visage du vent D'Est, 1980; La Route Bleue, 1983; Travels in the Drifting Dawn, 1989; Pilgrim of the Void, 1994. Honours include: French Academy Grand Prix de Rayonnement, 1985. Address: Gwenved, Chemin du Goaquer, 22 560 Trébeurden, France.

WHITE Robert Rankin, b. 8 Feb 1942, Houston, Texas, USA. Historian; Writer. Education: BA, Geology, University of Texas, Austin, 1964; MS, Hydrology, University of Arizona, 1971; PhD, American Studies, University of New Mexico, 1993. PPublications: The Taos Society of Artists, 1983; The Lithographs and Etchings of E Martin Hennings, 1978; Contributor to Pioneer Artists of Taos, revised edition 1984; Co-author, Bert Geer Phillips and the Taos Art Colony, 1994. Contributor to: Southwest Art; Print Review; El Palacio; Rio Grande History; True West; Taos County Historical Society Bulletin; Southwest Profile; New Mexico Architecture; New Mexico Historical Review; Book Talk. Memberships: President, New Mexico Book League, 1994; First Friday; President, Historical Society of New Mexico, 1991-93; Western History Association. Address: 1409 Las Lomas Road NE, Albuquerque, NM 87106, USA.

WHITE William Hollingsworth,b. Pensylvania, USA. Urban Planning Consultant; Writer. Education: Princeton University. Address: c/o Anchor Publishing Attn Martin Rowe, 1540 Broadway, NY 10036, USA.

WHITE (William) Robin(son),b. 12 July 1928, India. Author. m. Marian Biesterfeld, 3 Feb 1948, 2 sons, 1 daughter. Education: BA, Yale University, USA; Bread Loaf Fellow, Middlebury College, 1956; Stegner Creative Writing Fellow, Stanford University, 1956-57; MA, California State Polytechnic University. Appointments: Editor-in-Chief, Per-Se International Quarterly, Stanford University Press, 1965-69; Instructor, Photojournalism, 1973, Director, Creative Writing Seminar, 1984, Mendocino Art Center; Lecturer, Writing Programme, Scripps College, 1984; Fiction Editor, West-word literary magazine, 1985-; Instructor, Writer's Programme, 1985-, University of California, Los Angeles; Research Reader, The Huntington Library, 1985-; Lecturer, Writing Programme and CompuWrite, California State Polytechnic University, 1985-. Publications: House of Many Rooms, 1958; Elephant Hill, 1959; Men and Angels, 1961; Foreign Soil, 1962; All In Favor Say No, 1964; His Own Kind, 1967; Be Not Afraid, 1972; The Special Child, 1978; The Troll of Crazy Mule Camp, 1979; Moses the Man, 1981. Contributions to: Harper's; The New Yorker; New York Times; Harper's Bazaar; Prism; Saturday Evening Post; Ladies' Home Journal;

Seventeen; National Wildlife; McClean's, Canada; Mademoiselle; The Reporter; Saturday Review; Sunset Magazine; Lears; S F Focus; Camping Journal; Various learned journals and overseas periodicals; Antholgies. Honours include: Curtis Essay Prize, Yale; Harper Prize, 1959; O Henry Prize, 1960; Coordinating Council of Literary Magazines Award, 1968; Distinguished Achievement Award, Educational Press, 1974; Fulbright nomination, 1987; Spring Harvest Poetry Award, 1992, 1994. Memberships: Authors Guild. Literary Agent: Gina Maccoby, Literary Agency Inc. Address: 1940 Fletcher Avenue, South Pasadena, CA 91300, USA.

WHITEHORN Katharine (Elizabeth), b. Landon. Writer. Appointments: Staff Writer, Picture Post, London, 1956-57; Staff Writer, Womans Own, London, 1958; Editorial Staff, Spectator, 1959-61; Fasion Editor, 1960-63, Columnist, 1963-, The Observer. Publications include: Cooking ina Bedsitter, 1960; Roundabout, 1961; Only on Sundays, 1966; Whitehorns Social Survival, 1968; Observations, 1970; How To Survive in Hospital, 1972; How to Survive Children, 1975; How to Survive in the Kitchen, 1979; View from a Column, 1991; How to Survive Your Money Problems, 1983. Address: 119 Farringdon Road, London EC1R 3ER, England.

WHITEHOUSE David Bryn, b. 15 Oct 1941, Worksop, England. Education: BA 1963, MA 1965, PhD 1967, Cambridge Unversity. Appointments: Correspondent, Archeologia Medievale; Scientific Committee, Storia Della Citta; Enciclopedia dell'Arte Medievale; Arte Medievale; Editor, Journal of Glass Studies, 1988-; Advisory Editor, American Early Medieval Studies, 1991-; Advisory Board, Encyclopedia of Islamic Archaeology, 1991. Publications: Co-author: Archaeological Atlas of the World, 1975; Mohammed, Charlemagne and the Origins of Europe, 1983; Glass of the Caesars, 1987; The Portland Vase, monograph, 1990; Author: Siraf III, The Congregational Mosque, ND; Glass of the Roman Empire, 1988; Co-author: Aspects of Medieval Lazio, 1982. Author: Glass: A Pocket Dictionary, 1993; Co-author: Treasures From The Corning Museum of Glass, 1992. Contributions to: Journal of Glass Studies, Editor; Medieval Archaeology; Archeologia Medievale, Iran; Papers of the British School at Rome; Arte Medievale; Antiquity; World Archaeology; and may others. Memberships: International Association for the History of Glass, President 1991-; Unione Internazionale degli Istituti di Archeologia; Storia e Storia dell'Arte in Roma, President 1980-81; Keats-Shelley Memorial Association, Rome, President 1982-83; Society of Antiquaries of London; Royal Geographical Society; Pontificia Accademia Romana di Archeologia; Accademia Florentina Delle Arti Del Disegno. Address: The Corning Museum of Glass, One Museum Way, Corning, NY 14830, USA.

WHITFIELD Stephen Jack, b. 3 Dec 1942, Houston, Texas, USA. Teacher. m. Lee Cone Hall, 15 Dec 1984. Education: BA 1964, Tulane University; MA 1966, Yale University; Doctorate 1972, Brandeis University. Publications: Scott Nearing: Apostle of American Radicalism, 1974; Into the Dark: Hannah Arendt and Totalitarianism, 1980; A Critical American: The Politics of Dwight Macdonald, 1984; Voices of Jacob, Hands of Esau: Jews in American Life and Thought, 1984; American Space, Jewish Time, 1988; A Death in the Delta: The Story of Emmett Till, 1988; The Culture of the Cold War, 1991. Contributions to: Contributing Editor, Moment Magazine, 1980-87; Book Review Editor, American Jewish History, 1979-86. Honours: Kayden Prize for Best Book in the humanities published by an American Academic Press, 1981 for Into the Dark: Hannah Arendt and Totalitarianism; Rockefeller Foundation Fellow, Bellagio, Italy, 1991. Memberships: American Jewish Historical Society, member of Academic Council; American Studies Association; American Humour Studies Association. Literary Agent: Gerard McCauley Agency. Address: Department of American Studies, Brandeis University, Waltham, MA 02254, USA.

WHITNEY Phyllis Ayame, b. 9 September 1903, Yokohama, Japan. Writer; Adult Mystery Novel; Children's Book Editor for Newspapers; Teacher of Juvenile Writing, New York University, Northwestern University. m. (1) George A Garner, 1925, (divorced), 1 daughter; (2) Lovell F Jahnke, 1950, (deceased). Memberships: Authors League of America; Mystery Writers of America; American Crime Writers League; Society of Children's Book Writers; Children's Reading Round Table. Honours Include: Grandmaster Award, Mystery Writers of America, 1988; Edgar Allen Poe Awards, 1961, 1964; Sequoyah Children's Book Award, 1963; Spring Book Festival Award, 1947. Address: c/o McIntosh & Otis, 310 Madison Avenue, NY 10017, USA.

WHITTEN Leslie H Jr, b. 21 Feb 1928, Jacksonville, Florida, USA. Writer; Journalist. m. Phyllis Webber, 11 Nov 1951, 3 sons, 1 daughter. Education: BA, English-Journalism, Lehigh University. Publications: Progeny of the Adder, 1965; Pinion, The Golden Eagle, 1968; Moon of the Wolf, 1967; The Abyss, 1970; F Lee Bailey, 1971; The Alchemist, 1973; Conflict of Interest, 1976; Washington Cycle, poems, 1979; Sometimes a Hero, 1979; A Killing Pace, 1983; A Day Without Sunshine, 1985; The Lost Disciple, 1989. Contributions to: New York Times; Washington Post; Parade; Harper's Bazaar; Jack Anderson; The Progressive; Baltimore Sun. Honours: Doctor, Humane Letters, Lehigh University, 1989; Journalistic Awards, Edgerton Award, American Civil Liberties Union. Memberships: Former Director, Washington Independent Writers; Former Director, Investigative Reporters and Editors; Former Member, Washington Newspapers Guild; Authors Guild. Address: 114 Eastmoor Drive, Sliver Spring, MD 20901, USA.

WHITTEN Norman E Jr, b. 23 May 1937, Orange, New Jersey, USA. Professor of Anthropology and Latin America. m. Dorothea S Whitten, 4 Aug 1962. Education: BA, Colgate University, 1959; MA 1961, PhD 1964, University of North Carolina, Chapel Hill. Appointments: Editor, Boletin de Antropologia Ecuatoriana, 1973-76;Editor, Anthropology Newsletter, Latin American Anthropology Group, 1973-76; Press Board, University of Illinois Press, 1978-82; Editor, American Ethnologist, Vols 7-11, 1979-84; Member, Editorial Boards: Latin American Research Review, 1979-83; Latin American Music Review, 1979-; Journal of Anthropological Linguistics, 1979-84; Smithsonian Series in Ethnography Inquiry, 1984-; Association of Black Anthropologists, 1987-. Publications: Class Kinship and Power in an Ecuadorian Town, 1965; Afro-American Anthropology (editor), 1970; Sacha Runa: Ethnicity and Adaptation of Ecuadorian Jungle Quichua, 1976; Cultural Transformations and Ethnicity in Modern Ecuador (editor), 1981; Amazonia Ecuatoria, La Otro Cara del Progreso, 1981; BlackFrontiersmen: Afro-Hispanic Culture of Ecuador and Colombia, 1985; Sicuanga Runa: The Other Side of Development in Amazonian Ecuador, 1985; Art Knowledge and Health (with Dorothea S Whitten), 1985; From Myth to Creation: Art from Amazonian Ecuador (with Dorothea S Whitten), 1988; Pioneros Negros: La Cultura Afro-Latinoamericana del Ecuador y de Colombia, 1992; Imagery and Creativity: Ethnoaesthetics and Art Worlds in the Americas (with Dorothea S Whitten), 1993; Transformaciones Culturales y Etnicidad en la Sierra Ecuatoriana, 1993. Contributions to: American Anthropologist; Man; American Ethnologist; American Indigena; Journal of American Folklore; Journal of the Folklore Institute; Ethnology; Latin American Research Review; Journal of Ethnic Studies; Social Forces; American Sociological Review; North American Congress on Latin America. Honours: Author's Award in Anthropology, New Jersey Teachers Association, 1966; Society of Sigma Xi. Memberships: American Anthropological Association, Executive Board 1975-78, Representative to American Association for the Advancement of Science 1990-95; American Ethnological Association, Executive Board 1980-84; Latin American Studies Association, Executive Board 1983-87; Society of Cultural Anthropology; Royal Anthropological Institute. Address: 507 Harding Drive, Urbana, IL 61801, USA.

WHITTINGTON Peter. See: MACKAY James Alexander.

WICK Carter. See: WILCOX Colin.

WICKERT Erwin, b. 7 Jan 1915, Bralitz, Germany. Author; Retired Ambassador. m. Ingelborg Weides, 2 Oct 1939, 2 s, 1 d. Education: Friedrich Wilhelm University, Berlin, 1934-35; BA, Dickinson College, 1936; PhD, University of Heidelberg, 1939. Appointments: Writer, 1938; Foreign Service. Publications include: Der Auftrag des Himmels, 1961; Der Purpur, 1966; China von innen gesehen, 1982; Mut und Ubermut, 1981; Der verlassene Tempel, 1985; Der Kaiser und der Grosshistoriker, 1987; Zappas oder die Wiedeckehr des Herrn,1995. Contributions to: Frankfurter Allgemeine Zeitung; Die Welt. Honouts: Radio Play Award of WarBlinds, 1952; Grosses Bundesverdienstkreuz, 1979; State Prize of Literature. Memberships: PEN; Academy of Science & Literature; President of German Authors Council; Vice President of Free German Authors Association. Address: Rheinhöhenweg 22, Oberwinter, D 53424 Remagen, Germany.

WICKHAM Glynne, (William Gladstone), b. 1922. Writer; Broadcaster. Appointments include: Editorial Committee, Shakespeare Survey, 1974-; Chairman, Radio West, 1979-84; Culture Advisory Panel, United Kingdom; National Commission to Unesco, 1984-86. Publications include: The Relationship Between Universities and Radio, Film and Television, 1956; Early English Stges, vol 1-3; Drama in a World of Science, 1962; The Medieval Theatre, 1974; English Moral Interludes, 1975, 1985; The Theatre in Europe, 1979; A History of the Theatre, 1985, 1992. Membership: Polish Academy of Arts & Sciences. Address: 6 College Road, Bristol 8, Avon, England.

WIDDOWSON John David Allison, b. 22 June 1935, Sheffield, England, University Lecturer. m. Carolyn Lois Crawford, 1 Sept 1960, 2 s, 1 d. Education: BA, 1959, MA, 1963, Oxford; MA, Leeds, 1966; PhD, Newfoundland, 1972. Appointments: Editor, Lore and Language, 1969; Member, Editorial Advisory Board, Rural History, 1990. Publications include: Learning About Linguistics, 1974; The Linguistic Atlas of England, 1978; Dictionary of Newfoundland English, 1982; Word Maps, 1987; Language, Culture and Tradition, 1981; Studies in Linguistic Geography, 1985; Studies in Newfoundland Folklore, 1991. Contributions to: Numerous Articles and Reviews, 1962-. Honours: Certificate of Merit; Regional History Award. Memberships: The Devonshire Association; The Folklore Society; Societas Linguisticla Europaeia; The Am Folklore Society; The Oral History Society; The Canadian Oral History Society; Folklore Studies Association of Canada; Yorkshire Dialect Society. Address: The Centre for English Cultural, Tradition and Language, The University, Sheffield, S10 2TN.

WIENER Joel Howard, b. 23 Aug 1937, New York, USA. Professor of History. m. Suzanne Wolff, 4 Sept 1961, 1 son, 2 daughters. Education: BA, New York University, 1959; Research Fellow, University of Glasgow, 1961-63; PhD, Cornell University, 1965. Publications: The War of the Unstamped, 1969; A Descriptive Finding List of Unstamped Periodicals 1830-36, 1970; Great Britain: Foreign Policy and the Span of Empire, (editor), 1972; Great Britain: The Lion at Home (editor), 1974; Radicalism and Freethought in 19th Century Britain, 1983; Innovators and Preachers: The Role of the Editor in Victorian England, (editor), 1985; Papers for the Millions: The New Journalism in Britain c. 1950's-1914, editor, 1988; William Lovett, 1989. Contributions to: Labor History; Journal of Social History; New Society; Victorian Periodicals Review; Albion; Journal of Modern History; Choice; English Literature In Transition; Victorian Studies; Listener. Honours: Fellow, Royal Historical Society, 1974. Memberships: Research Society for Victorian Periodicals, President; American Historical Association; CUNY Academy for the Humanities and Sciences; American Journalism Historians Association; Conference on British Studies. Address: 267 Glen Court, Teaneck, NJ 07666, USA.

WIENERS John Joseph, b. 6 Jan 1934, Milton, Massachusetts, USA. Poet. m. Education: BA, Boston College, 1954; Black Mountain College, North Carolina, 1955-56; Teaching Fellow, State University of New York, Buffalo, 1965-67. Literary Appointments: The Roman Spring of Mrs Stone (Film). Publications: The Hotel Wentley Poems, 1958; Act of Penté, 1964; Pressed Wafer, 1967; Behind the State Capitol or Cinncinnati Pike, 1975; Selected Poems, 1958-84, 1986; She'd Turn on a Dime. Contributions to: Numerous works including: Semina Yugen; Stylus; Floating Bear; Set; Blue Grass; Granta; Joglars; Sum; The Nation; Magazine of Further Studies; Intransit; Yale Agenda; Wivenhoe Park Review; Boss; Evergreen Review; Film Culture; The World; Emerson Review; Gay Sunshine; Fag Rag; Mirage. Honours: Poet's Foundation, New York, 1961; New Hope Foundation Award, 1963; NEA, 1966, 1968; American Academy Award, 1968; Committee on Poetry Grant, 1970-72; National Endowment, Washington DC, 1984; Guggenheim Fellowship, 1985. Literary Agent: O'Khan Collan with Toag Tie, San Francisco Merchants Association. Address: 44 Joy Street 10, Boston, MA 02114, USA.

WIESEL Elie, b. 1928, Rumania. Professor; Author; Journalist. Appointments: Distinguished Professor of Judaic Studies, City College, City University of New York, 1972-76; Andrew W Mellon Professor in the Humanities, Professor of Religion, Professor of Philosophy, Boston University, Massachusetts, 1976-; Henry Luce Visiting Scholar in the Humanities and Social Thought, Whitney Humanities Centre, Yale University, 1982-83; Distinguished Visiting Professor of Literature and Philosophy, Florida International University, 1982; Journalist for Israeli, French and US Newspapers. Publications: Night, memoir, 1960; Dawn, novel, 1966; The Jews of Silence, personal testimony, 1966; Legends of Our Time, essays and stories, 1968; A Beggar in Jerusalem, novel, 1970; One Generation After, essays and stories, 1970; Souls on Fire: Portraits and Legends of the Hasidic Masters, 1972; The Oath, novel, 1973; Ani Maamin, cantata, 1973; Zalmen or the Madness of God, play, 1974; Messengers of God: Portraits and Legends of Biblical Heroes, 1976; Four Hasidic Masters, 1978; A Jew Today, essays, stories, dialogues, 1978; The Trial of God, play, 1979; The Testament, novel,

1980; Images from the Bible, 1980; Five Biblical Portraits, 1981; Somewhere a Master, Hasidic tales, 1982; Paroles d'etranger, essays, stories, dialogues, 1982; The Golem, retelling of Legend, 1983; The Fifth Son, novel, 1985; Signes d'Exode, essays, stories, dialogues, 1985; Against Silence: The Voice and Vision of Elie Wiesel, collected writings, 1985; Job ou Dieu dans la Tempete, dialogue and commentary with Josy Eisenberg, 1986; A Song For Hipe, a cantata, 1987; The Nobel Address, 1987; Twilight, novel, 1988; The Six Days of Destruction, with Albert Friedlander, 1988; Silences et memoire d'hommes, essays, 1989; L'Oublie, novel, 1989; From the Kingdom of Memory, Reminiscences, 1990; Evil and Exile, dialogues with Philippe-Michael de Saint-Cheron, 1990; Sages and Dreamers, Portraits and Legends from the Bible, the Talmud and the Hasidic Tradition, 1991; Celebration Talmudique, Portraits of Talmudic Masters, 1991; The Forgotten, 1992; A Passover Hagaddah, 1993. Honours include: Recipient, Congressional Gold Medal, 1984; Nobel Peace Prize, 1986; Grand Officer, Legion of Honour, 1990, elevated from Commander, Legion of Honour, 1984; Presidential Medal of Freedom, 1992, USA. Memberships: Various literary societies, including PEN. Literary Agent: Georges Borchardt, New York. Address: 745 Commonwealth Avenue, Boston, MA 02215, USA.

WIESENFARTH Joseph John, b. 20 Aug 1933, Brooklyn, New York, USA. Professor of English. m. Louise Halpin, 21 Aug 1971, 1 son. Education: BA, Catholic University of America, 1956; MA, University of Detroit, 1959; PhD, Catholic University of America, 1962. Appointments: Assistant Professor, La Salle College, Philadelphia, USA, 1962-64; Assistant Professor, 1964-67, Associate Professor, 1967-70, Manhatten College, New York; Associate Professor, 1970-76, Professor, 1976-, University of Wisconsin, Madison; Associate Editor, Renascence, 1972-76, 1992-; Chairman, Department of English, 1983-86, 1989-92; Chairman, Press Committee, University of Wisconsin Press, 1983-88. Publications include: Henry James and the Dramatic Analogy, 1963; The Errang of Form: An Essay of Jane Austen's Art, 1967; George Eliot's Mythmaking, 1977; George Eliot: A Writer's Notebook 1854-1879, 1981; Gothic Manners and the Classic English Novel, 1988; Ford Mador Ford and the Art, Contemprary Interature 3012, 1989. Contributions to: Numerous articles on British and American Fiction. Honours: Phi Beta Kappa, 1956; Fellow, National Endowment for the Humanities, 1967-68; Institute for Research in Humanities Fellow, 1975; Fulbright Fellow, 1981-82; Christian Gauss Prize Award Committee, 1986-88, 1989-90. Memberships: Modern Language Association; Jane Austen Society of North America; Henry James Society, Katherine Anne Porter Society. Address: Department of English, University of Wisconsin, 600 N Park Street, Madison, WI 53706, USA.

WIESENTHAL Simon, b. 31 Dec 1908, Poland. Writer. m. Cyla, 1 d. Education: Architectural Studies, Prague, Lvov. Appointments: Editor, Ausweg, 1960-. Publications include: KZ Mauthausen, 1946; Head Mufti, 1947; Agent of the Axis, 1947; The Murderes Among Us, 1967; Sunflower, 1969; Sails of Hope, 1973; The Case of Krystyna Jaworska, 1975; Every Day Remembrance Day, 1986; Justice, Not Vengeance, 1989. Honours include: Numerous Honours and Awards including, Dutch Medal for Freedom; Jean Moulin Medaille; Kaj Munk medal; Commander Oranje Nassau, Queen Juliana of the Netherlands; Justice Brandeis Award; Grand Silver Honorary Medal for Merits; Knight, Honorary Legion of France. Membership: Australian PEN. Address: Salztorgasse 6, 1010 Vienna, Austria.

WIESNER David. Children's Book Author and Illustrator. Honours: Caldecolt Medal, 1992. Address: c/o Clarion Books Publicity, 11th Floor, 215 Park Avenue South, NY 10003, USA.

WIGG T I G. See: **MCCUTCHAN Philip Donald.**

WILBUR Richard (Purdy), b. 1 Mar 1921, New York City, USA. University Professor; Poet Laureate of the USA. Education: MA, Amherst College, Harvard University. Publications include: The Beautiful Changes and Other Poems, 1947; Things of this World, 1956; Tartuffe (translated from Moliere), 1963; Loudmouse (for children), 1963; Poems of Shakespeare (with Alfred Harbage), 1966; Walking to Sleep (New Poems and Translations), 1969; School for Wives (translation), 1971; Opposites (childrens verse illustrated by the author), 1973; The Mind Reader, 1976; Responses (essays), 1976; The Learned Ladies (translated from Loliere), 1978; Seven Poems, 1981; The Whale (translation), 1982; Racines Andromache (translation), 1982; Moliere Four comedies, 1982; Racine's Phaedra (translation), 1986; New and Collected Poems, 1988; More Opposites, 1991; School for Husbands (translation from Moliere), 1992; A Game of Catch, 1994. Honours: Harriet Monroe Prize, 1948; Oscar Blumenthal Prize, 1950; Prix de Rome, American Academy of Arts & Letters, 1954-55; Edna St Vincent Millay Memorial Award, 1956; Pulitzer Prize, 1957; National Book Award, 1957; Prix Henri Desfeuilles, 1971; Brandeis Creative Arts Award, 1971; Shelley Mem Prize, 1973; Harriet Monroe Poetry Award, 1983; Drama Desk Award, 1983; Chevalier, Ordre Des Palmes Academiques, 1983; Poet Laureate Consultant in Poetry to the Library of Congress, 1987-; Aiken-Taylor Award, 1988; Los Angeles Times Book Prize (Poetry), 1988; Pulitzer Prize, 1989; St Louis Literary Award, 1989; American Academy of Arts & Letters, Gold Medal, 1991; Medal of Honour, National Arts Club, 1994. Memberships: Chancellor, Academy of American Poets; PEN; Former President, American Academy of Arts & Letters; Dramatists Guild; American Academy of Arts & Sciences. Literary Agent: Gilbert Parker, William Morris Agency. Address: 87 Dodwells Road, Cummington, MA 01026, USA.

WILBY Basil Leslie, (Gareth Knight), b. 1930, England. Appointments: University Sales Manager, 1970-76; Longman Group Publishing Manager, 1976-91; Freelance Publishing Consultant, 1991-93. Publications include: A Practical Guide to Qabalistic Symbolism, 1965; The New Dimensions Red Book, 1968; The Practice of Ritual Magic, 1969; Occult Exercises & Practices, 1969; Meeting the Occult, 1973; Experience of the Inner Worlds, 1975; The Occult: An Introduction, 1975; The Secret Tradition in Arthurian Legend, 1983; The Rose Cross and the Goddess, 1985; The Treasure House of Images, (USA Edition: Tarot & Magic), 1986; The Magic World of the Tarot, 1991; Magic and the Western Mind, (formerly A History of White Magic) 1991; Evoking the Goddess, 1993; Dion Fortune's Magical Battle of Britain, 1993.

WILCOX Collin (Carter Wick), b. 1924, American. Appointments: Teacher at the Town School, 1950-53; Partner, Amthor and Company, furniture store, 1953-55; Owner, Collin Wilcox Lamps, 1955-70; Full-time Writer, 1970-; Regional Vice-President, 1975, Member, Board of Directors, 1976, Mystery Writers of America. Publications: The Black Door, 1967; The Third Figure, 1968; The Lonely Hunter, 1969; The Disappearance, 1970; Dead Aim, 1971; Hiding Place, McCloud, 1973; Long Way Down, The New Mexico Connection, 1974; Aftershock, The Faceless Man (as Carter Wick), 1975; The Third Victim, 1976; Doctor, Lawyer..., 1977; The Watcher, Twospot (with Bill Pronzini), 1978; Power Plays, 1979; Mankiller, Spellbinder, 1980; Stalking Horse, 1981; Dark House, Dark Road, 1982; Swallow's Fall, 1983; Victims, 1985; Night Games, 1986; The Pariah, 1987; Bernhardt's Edge, 1987; A Death Before Dying, 1988; Silent Witness, 1989; Hire A Hangman, 1990; Except for the Bones, 1991; Dead Center, 1992. Address: 4174 26th Street, San Francisco, CA 94131, USA.

WILCOX James, b. 4 April 1949, Hammond, Louisiana, USA. Writer; Novelist. Education: BA, Yale University. Contributions to: New Yorker; Avenue; Louisiana Literature. Memberships: PEN; Authors Guild. Address: c/o Amanda Urban, ICM 40 W 57th Street, New York, NY 10019, USA.

WILDER Cherry. See:GRIMM Barbara Lockett.

WILDING Eric. See: TUBB E(dwin) C(harles).

WILDING Griselda. See: MCCUTCHEON Hugh.

WILDING Michael, b. 1942, England. Professor. Education: BA, 1963, MA, 1968, University of Oxford. Appointments: Lecturer, 1963-66, Senior Lecturer, 1969-72, Reader, 1972-92, Professor, 1993-, University of Sydney; Lecturer, University of Birmingham, 1967-68; Visiting Professor, University of CA, 1987. Publications include: Aspects of the Dying Process, 1972; Living Together, 1974; Short Story Embassy, 1975; Scenic Drive, 1976; The Phallic Forest, 1978; The Man of Slow Feeling, 1985; Under Saturn, 1988; Great Climate, 1990; Political Fictions, 1980; Social Visions, 1993; The Radical Tradition, Lawson, Furphy, Stead, 1993; This is for You, 1994; Book of the Reading, 1994; The Oxford Book of Australian Short Stories, 1994. Honours: Senior Fellowship, Literature Board, Australia Council, 1978; Elected Fellow, Australian Academy of the Humanities, 1988. Address: Dept of English, University of Sydney, Sydney, NSW 2006, Australia.

WILENTZ Robert Sean, b. 20 Feb 1951, NY, USA. Historian. m. Mary Christine Stansell, 30 Jan 1980, 1 son, 1 daughter. Education: BA, Columbia College, 1972; BA, University of Oxford, 1974; PhD, Yale University, 1980. Publications: Chants Democratic, 1984; Rites of Power, 1985; The Key of Liberty, 1993; The Kingdom of Matthias, 1994. Contributions to: The New Republic; Dissent. Honours: Beveridge Award, 1984; Turner Award, 1985. Memberships: Society of American Historians. Literary Agent: Thomas Wallace, Wallace Literary Agency. Address: 7 Edgehill Street, Princeton, NJ 08540, USA.

WILFORD John Noble, b. 4 Oct 1933, Kentucky, USA. Jopurnalist. m. Nancy Watts Paschall, 25 Dec 1966, 1 daughter. Education: BS, Journalism, University of Tennessee, 1955; MA, Political Science, Syracuse University, 1956; International Reporting Fellow, Columbia University, 1961-62. Appointments: Science Reporter, 1965-73, 1979-, Assistant National Editor, 1973-75, Director of Science News, 1975-79, Science Correspondent, 1979-, New York Times, New York City; Mc Graw Distinguished Lecturer in Writing, Princeton University, 1985; Professor of Science Journalism, University of Tennessee, 1989-90. Publications: We Reach The Moon, 1969; The Mapmakers, 1981; The Riddle of the Dinosaur, 1985; Mars Beckons, 1990; The Mysterious History of Columbus, 1991. Contributions to: Nature; Wilson Quarterly; New York Times Magazine; Science Digest; Popular Science. Honours: Westinghouse-American Association for the Advancement of Science Writing Award, 1983; Pulitzer Prize for National Reporting, 1984, shared 1987. Memberships: Century Club, New York City; National Association of Science Writers; American Geographical Society, Council Member, 1994-. Address: New York Times, 229 West 43rd Street, New York, NY 10036, USA.

WILFRED Leopold. See: PETERS Lenrie.

WILKERSON Cynthia. See: LEVINSON Leonard.

WILKINS Damien, b. 1963. Honours: Whiting Writers Award. Address: c/o Kelly Rosenheim Whiting, 30 Rockefeller Plaza, Room 3500, New York, NY 10112, USA.

WILKINSON Doris, b. Lexington, Kentucky, USA. University Professor. Education: BA, SocialWork & English, 1958, University of Kentucky; MA, Sociology 1960, Western Reserve University; PhD, Medical Sociology 1968, Case Western Reserve University; MPH, Public Health 1985, Johns Hopkins University; Post-doctoral Study, History of Science, Harvard University, 1991. Appointments: Executive Associate, ASA 1977-80; Professor, Howard University, 1980-84; Visiting Professor, University of Virginia, 1984-85; Professor, University of Kentucky, 1985-; Ford Fellow, Harvard University, 1989-90. Publications: 6 books, 4 edited, 1 co-edited; Over 50 articles in professional journals; Over 25 major book reviews. Honours: Ford Fellow to Harvard 1989-90; Phi Beta Kappa; Public Humanities Award, 1990; Nominated for Great Teacher, 1990; Woman's History Month Award, 1991, Midway College; Elected Vice President of American Sociological Association, 1991-92; Elected President of the Eastern Sociological Society, 1992; Great Teacher Award, 1992. Memberships: American Sociological Association, Vice President Elect, 1990-91; Eastern Sociological Society, ESS, Vice President, 1983-84, President Elect, 1990-91; Society for the Study of Social Problems, President 1987-88; District of Columbia Sociological Society, President 1982-83; President, ESS, 1992-93. Address: Department of Sociology, University of Kentucky, Lexington, KY 40506, USA.

WILKINSON Richard Herbert, b. 26 Apr 1951, Skipton, Yorks, England. Egyptologist. m. Anna Wagner, 27 Jul 1975, 2 sons. Education: PhD, University of MN, USA. Publications: Reading Egyptian Art, 1992; Symbol & Magic In Egyptian Art, 1994; Forthcoming: Complete Valley Of The Kings. Contributions to: Over forty journal and magazine articles. Honours: Numerous. Memberships: President, Arizona Chapter ARCE; International Association Egyptologists. Literary Agent: Murray Pollinger, London. Address: University of Arizona, Harvill 347, Box 10, Tucson, AZ 85721, USA.

WILL Clifford Martin, b. 13 Nov 1946, Hamilton, Canada. Physicist. m. Leslie Carol Saxe, 26 June 1970, 2 daughters. Education: BSc, Applied Mathematics, Theoretical Physics, McMaster University, 1968; PhD, Physics, California Institute of Technology, 1971. Publications: Theory and Experiment in Gravitational Physics, 1981, 2nd Edition, 1993; Was Einstein Right?, 1986, 2nd Edition, 1993. Contributions to: 6 articles on general relativity (in German) to P M Magazin, 1989; The Renaissance of General Relativity to The New Physics, 1989; Twilight Time for the Fifth Force?, to Sky and Telescope, 1990. Honours: Fellowship, Alfred P Sloan Foundation, 1975-79; Science Writing Award for Was Einstein Right?, American

Institute of Physics, 1987. Memberships: Fellow, American Institute of Physics; American Astronomical Society; International Society on General Relativity and Gravitation. Literary Agent: Gerald F McCauley Agency. Address: Department of Physics, Campus Box 1105, Washington University, St Louis, MO 63130, USA.

WILL George Frederick, b. 4 May 1941, Champaign, Illinios, USA. Author; Syndicated Columnist. 3 sons, 1 daughter. Education: BA with honours, Religion, Trinity College, Hartford, Connecticut, 1962; Magdalen College, Oxford, England; BA (Oxon), Politics, Philosophy, Economics, 1964; PhD, Politics, Princeton University, New Jersey, 1967. Appointments: Editor, The National Review, Washington DC, 1973-76; Syndicated Columnist, The Washington Post, 1974-; Contributing Editor, Newsweek Magazine, 1976-; Occasional Op-Ed Page Contributor, The London Daily Telegraph, 1987-. Publications: The Pursuit of Happiness and Other Sobering Thoughts, 1978; The Pursuit of Virtue and Other Tory Notions, 1982; Statecraft As Soulcraft: What Government Does, 1983; The Morning After: American Successes and Excesses, 1986; The New Season: A Spectator's Guide to the 1988 Election, 1987; Men at Work: The Craft of Baseball, 1990; Suddenly: The American Idea Abroad and At Home, 1990; Restoration: Congress, Term Limits and The Recovery of Deliberative Democracy, 1992; The Leveling Wind, 1994. Honours: Pulitzer Prize for Commentary, 1977; The Silurian Award, 1980; Weldon-Burckhardt Prize, Magdalen College, Oxford, 1964; Charlotte-Elizabeth Proctor Fellow, Princeton University; Honours Citation for Teaching Excellence, Michigan; Honorary Degrees: LLD, University of San Diego, 1977; DLitt, Dickinson College, Carlisle, Pennsylvania, 1978; DLitt, Georgetown University, Washington DC, 1978; University of Illinois, 1988; Doctor of Humane Letters, Duke University, 1991; The Cronkite Award, Arizona State University, 1991; Madison Medal Award, Princeton University, 1992; William Allen White Award, University of Kansas, William Allen White School of Journalism, 1993; Doctor of Humane Letters, The College of William & Mary, 1994. Memberships Include: Emil Verban Society; Trustee, Little League Foundation, 1992; Advisory Board, Institute of United States Studies University of London, 1993. Address: c/o Writers Group, The Washington Post, 1150 Fifteenth St NW, Washington DC 20071, USA.

WILLETT Frank, b. 18 Aug 1925, England. Archaeologist, Art Historian. m. M Constance Hewitt, 24 July 1950, 1 s, 3 d. Education: BA, 1947, MA, 1951, Oxford University. Appointments: Editorial Secretary, Manchestr literary And Philosophical Society, 1950-58; Member, Editorial Board, West African Journal of Archaeology, 1970-; Editorial Board, Journal of African Studies, 1973-; Curator, Royal Society of Edinburgh, 1990-. Publications: Ife in the History of West African Sculpture, 1967; African Art, 1971; The Arts of the African Peoples, 1974; Treasures of Ancient Nigeria, 1980. Contributions to: Many Articles on African Art & Archaeology. Honours: Honorary Corresponding Member, Manchester Literary and Philosophical Society, 1958; Fellow, Royal Society of Edinburgh, 1979; Commander, Order of the British Empire, 1985. Memberships: Royal Anthropological Institute. Address: The Hunterian Museum, The University of Glasgow, Glasgow, G12 8QQ, Scotland.

WILLIAMS Alberta Norine (Sonia Davis), b. 22 Apr 1904, Olds, Alberta, Canada. Writer; Author; Poet; Rancher. m. Billy D Williams, 4 Sept 1928, 1 s, 1 d. Education: ABI, Business College, Fayetteville, AR, 1921; GED, Two Spanish Courses, Creative Writing, Local History, Pueblo Community College, 1960; Writing Courses, Writer's Digest and Will Heideman. Literary Appointments: National Library of Poetry; Famous Poets Society; Mile High Poetry, Drury's Pub Co; Quill Books. Publications: Pearls Of a Lady, 1976; Potpourri of a Poet, 1992; Prairie Bird, 1994; Compiler, Rye Home Methodist Church History, 1975; Songs, limericks. plays, short stories. Contributions to: Article, Buzzard Roost Ranch, 1994. Memberships: NLAPW; Verses of the Valley, Poetry Guild, CO City, President, Poetry Society of CO; CFWC; Rye Womans Club; DAR; Cambridge, Advisory Council. Address: Lascar Rt, Box 75, Rye, CO 81069, USA.

WILLIAMS Bert Nolan, b. 19 Aug 1930, Toronto, Ontario, Canada. Writer; Teacher. m. Angela Babando, 6 Dec 1952, 1 son. Education: Self-taught. Publications: Food for the Eagle, 1970; Master of Ravenspur, 1970; The Rocky Mountain Monster, 1972; Sword of Egypt, 1977; Brumaire, play in 3 acts, 1982; Poetry, Popular Songs (music and lyrics), Short Stories, Magazine Articles. Contributions to: Well over 100 to assorted journals and magazines. Address: 10 Muirhead Road, Apt 504, North York, Ontario, M2J 4P9, Canada.

WILLIAMS Carol Elizabeth (Carol Fenner), b. 1929, USA. Children's Fiction Writer; Lecturer; Instructor. Publications: Tigers in the Cellar, 1963; Christmas Tree on the Mountain, 1966; Lagalag the Wanderer, 1968; Gorilla Gorilla, 1973; The Skates of Uncle Richard, 1978; Saving Amelia Earhart, 1982; Deer Flight, 1986; A Summer of Horses, 1989; Randall's Wall, 1991; Yolonda's Genius, 1995. Honours: Library of Congress Book of The Year, Gorilla Gorilla, 1973; Christopher Award. Address: 190 Rebecca Road, Battle Creek, MI 49015, USA.

WILLIAMS Charles Kenneth, b. 4 Nov 1936, Newark, NJ, USA. Poet. m. Chatherine Justine Mauger, 12 Apr 1975, 1 s, 1 d. Education: BA, University of PA, 1959. Appointments: Various Universities and Colleges including, George Mason University, University of CA, Boston University, Wichita State University, Brooklyn College. Publications include: Lies, 1969; I Am The Bitter Name, 1972; With Ignorance, 1977; Tar, 1983; Flesh and Blood, 1987; A Dream of Mind, 1992; Sophocles' Women of Trachis; Euripides's Bacchae. Contributions to: Am Poetry Review; Antaeus; Atlantic; Chicago Review; Grand Street; IA Review; Mademoiselle. Honours: National Book Critics Circle Award, 1983; John Simon Guggenheim Fellowship; Pushcart Press Prize, 1982, 83, 87; NEA Fellowship, 1985; Morton Dauwen Zabel Prize, 1988; Lila Wallace Writers Award, 1993. Membership: PEN. Address: 82 Rue D' Hauteville, 75010 Paris, France.

WILLIAMS David, b. 8 June 1926, Bridgend, Mid Glamorgan, Wales. Novelist. m. Brenda Yvonne Holmes, 18 Aug 1952, 1 s, 1 d. Education: Cathedral School, Hereford, 1938-43; St Johns College, Oxford, 1943-44, 1947-48. Publications include: Unholy Writ; Murder for Treasure; Wedding Treasure; Murder in Advent; Holy Treasure; Treasure by Degrees; Copper, Gold & Treasure; Treasure Preserved; Advertise for Treasure; Prescription For Murder; Divided Treasure; Treasure By Post; Planning on Murder; Banking on Murder; Last Seen Breathing; Death of a Prodigal. Contributions to: Numerous Short Stories. Memberships: Society of Authors; Crime Writers Association; Mystery Writers of Am; Carlton Club; Wentworth G C; Detection Club. Literary Agent: Curtis Brown, 28/29 Haymarket, London, SW1Y 4SP. Address: Blandings, Pinewood Road, Virginia Water, Surrey GU25 4PA, England.

WILLIAMS David Larry, b. 22 June 1945, Souris, Manitoba, Canada. University Professor. m. Darlene Olinyk, 22 July 1967, 2 sons. Education: Pastor's Diploma, Briercrest Bible Institute, Saskatchewan, 1965; BA, Honours, University of Saskatchewan, 1968; MA (AMherst), 1970, PhD, 1973, University of Massachusetts. Appointments: Lecturer, 1972-73, Assistant Professor, 1973-77, Associate Professor, 1977-83, Professor, 1983-, English, University of Manitoba, Winnipeg; Editorial Board, Canadian Review of American Studies, 1976-86; Guest Professor, Indian Association for Canadian Studies, MS University of Baroda, 1992. Publications: The Burning Wood, novel, 1975; Faulkner's Women: The Myth and the Muse, criticism, 1977; The River Horsemen, novel, 1981; Eye of the Father, novel, 1985; Chapter in Trace: Prairie Writers on Writing, 1986; To Run with Longboat: Twelve Stories of Indian Athletes in Canada (with Brenda Zeman), 1988; Confessional Fictions: A Portrait of the Artist in the Canadian Novel, 1991. Contributions to: Chapters in various books; Critical Essays on: Herman Melville, Harold Frederic, Margaret Laurence, Sinclair Ross, Rudy Wiebe, Robertson Davies, F.P. Grove, Ernest Hemingway Robert Alter, Margaret Atwood, Robert Kroetsch, Rohinton Mistry,, in CRevAS, DalRev, CanL, JCS, MSE, UTQ. Honours: Woodrow Wilson Fellow, 1968-69; Canada Council Fellow, 1969-72; Canada Council Arts Grant 'B', 1977-78, 1981-82; Manitoba Arts Council Grants, 1975, 1979; Touring Writer in Scandinavia for External Affairs, Canada, 1981; RH Institute Award for Research in Humanities, 1987; Olive Beatrice Stanton Award for Excellence in Teaching, 1992; University of Manitoba Nominee for Canadian Professor of Year, CASE (Washington DC), 1993. Memberships: Writers' Union of Canada; National Council of Prairie Region, 1978-79, 1984-85; Chairman, Search-for-a-New Manitoba-Novelist Competition, Manitoba Department of Cultural Affairs, 1981-83; PEN International. Address: Dept of English, St Paul's College, University of Manitoba, Winnipeg, R3T 2M6, Canada.

WILLIAMS Heathcote, b. 15 Nov 1941, Helsby, Cheshire, England. Playwright. Appointments include: Associate Editor for Transatlantic Review, New York and London. Publications: The Local Stigmatic, 1967; AC/DC, 1970; Remember the Truth Dentist, 1974; The Speakers, 1974; Very Tasty - a Pantomime, 1975; An Invitation to the Official Lynching of Abdul Malik, 1975; Anatomy of a Space Rat, 1976; Hancock's Last Half-Hour, 1977; Playpen, 1977; The Immortalist, 1977;

At It, 1982; Whales, 1986 (plays produced in Edinburgh, London, Boston, New York, Birmingham, Newcastle and Liverpool); Verse: Whale Nation, 1988; Falling for a Dolphin, 1988; Sacred Elephant, 1989; Autogeddon, 1991; Also: The Speakers, 1964; Manifestoes, Manifestem, 1975; Severe Joy, 1979; Elephants, 1983. Honours include: Evening Standard Award, 1970. Address: Judy Daish Associates, 83 Eastbourne Mews, London W2 6LQ, England.

WILLIAMS Herbert Lloyd, b. 8 Sept 1932, Wales. Writer. m. Dorothy Maud Edwards, 13 Nov 1954, 4 sons, 1 daughter. Publications include: The Trophy, 1967; A Lethal Kind of Love, 1968; Come Out Wherever You Are, 1976; Stage Coaches in Wales, 1977; The Welsh Quiz Book, 1978; Railways in Wales, 1981; The Pembrokeshire Coast National Park, 1987; Stories of King Arthur, 1990; Ghost Country, 1991; Davies the Ocean, 1991; The Stars in Their Courses, 1992; TV Drama and Documentaries include: Taff Acre, HTV, 1981; A Solitary Mister, BBC2, 1983; Alone In A Crowd, BBC2, 1984; Calvert In Camera, HTV, 1990; Radio Dramas: Doing The Bard, BBC Radio Wales, 1986; Bodyline, BBC Radio 4, 1991. Contributions to: New Welsh Review; The Anglo Welsh Review; Planet; The Transatlantic Review; Poetry Wales; Cambrensis; Tribune; Acumen, Western Mail. Honours: Welsh Arts Council Short Story Prize, 1972; Welsh Arts Council Writing Bursary, 1988; Aberystwyth Open Poetry Competition, 1990; Hawthornden Poetry Fellowship, 1992. Memberships: The Writers Guild of Great Britain; The Welsh Academy, Welsh Union of Writers. Literary Agent: Juri Gabriel. Address: 20 Amesbury Road, Penylan, Cardiff, CF2 5DW.

WILLIAMS Hugo Mordaunt, b. 20 Feb 1942, England. Writer; Poet. m. Hermine Demoriane, 1965, 1 d. Appointments include: Assistant Editor, London Magazine, 1961-70; Television Critic, 1983; Poetry Editor, New Statesman, 1984; Theatre Critic, Sunday Correspondent, 1990-91; Film Critic, Harpers & Queen, 1993-. Publications: Symptoms of Loss, 1965; Sugar Daddy, 1970; Some Sweet Day, 1975; Love Life, 1979; Writing Home, 1985; Travel, All the Time in the World, 1966; No Particular Place to Go, 1981; Self Portrait with a Slide, 1990. Honours: Henfield Writers Fellowship, 1981; Poetry Award, Eric Ggregory, 1965; Cholmondeley, 1970; Geoffrey Faber Memorial Prize, 1979. Address: 3 Raleigh Street, London N1, England.

WILLIAMS J R. See: WILLIAMS Jeanne.

WILLIAMS Jeanne, (Megan Castell, Jeanne Creasey, Jeanne Crecy, Jeanne Foster, Kristin Michaels, Deidre Rowan, J R Williams), b. 1930, USA. Author. Publications: To Buy a Dream, 1958; Promise of Tomorrow, 1959; Coyote Winter, 1965; Beasts with Music, 1967; Oil Patch Partners, 1968; New Medicine, 1971; Trails of Tears, 1972; Freedom Trail, 1973; Winter Wheat, 1975; A Lady Bought with Rifles, 1977; A Woman Clothed in Sun, 1978; Bridge of Thunder, 1978; Daughter of the Sword, 1979; The Queen of a Lonely Country (as Megan Castell), 1980; The Valiant Women, 1981; Harvest of Fury, 1982; The Heaven Sword, 1983; A Mating of Hawks, 1984; The Care Dreamers, 1985; So Many Kingdoms, 1986; Texas Pride, 1987; Lady of No Man's Land, 1988; No Roof but Heaven, 1990; Home Mountain, 1990; The Island Harp, 1991; The Longest Road, 1993; Daughter of the Storm, 1994; The Unplowed Sky, 1994. As J R Williams: Mission in Mexico, 1960; The Horsetalker, 1961; The Confederate Fiddle, 1962; River Guns, 1962; Oh Susanna, 1963; Tame the Wild Stallion, 1967. As Jeanne Crecy: Hands of Terror, UK Edition Lady Gift, 1972; The Lightning Tree, 1972; My Face Beneath Stone, 1975; The Winter-Keeper, 1975; The Night Hunters, 1975. As Deirdre Rowan: Dragon's Mount, 1973; Silver Wood, 1974; Shadow of the Volcano, 1975; Time of the Burning Mask, 1976; Ravensgate, 1976. As Kristin Michaels: To Begin with Love, 1976; Enchanted Journey, 1977; Song of the Heart, 1977; Make Believe Love, 1978. As Jeanne Foster: Deborah Leigh, 1981; Eden Richards, 1982; Woman of Three Worlds, 1984; The Island Harp, USA, 1991, England, 1992. Contributions to: Published over 70 stories in various magazines; Frquent reviews for Books of the Southwest, for Best West Childrens book, 1962 and 1973. Honours: Texas Institute of Letters Best Children's Book, 1958; for Best West Childrens book, 1962 and 1973; Four Western Writers of America Spur Awards; Best Novel of the West, 1981 and 1990; Lew Strauss Golden, Saddleman Award for Lifetime Achievement, 1988. Memberships: Author's Guild; Western Writers of America, Board Member, President, 1974-75. Literary Agent: Claire Smith of Harold Ober Associates. Address: Box 335, Portal, AZ 85632, USA.

WILLIAMS John Hoyt, b. 26 Oct 1940, Darien, Connecticut, USA. Professor of History. m. 27 Jan 1963, 1 son, 1 daughter.

Education: BA 1963, MA History 1965, University of Connecticut; PhD Latin American History 1969, University of Florida. Appointments: Assistant Professor of History 1969-73, Associate Professor of History 1973-78, Professor of History 1978-, Indiana State University. Publications: Rise and Fall of the Paraguayon Republic 1800-1870, 1979; A Great and Shining Road, 1988; Sam Houston, A Biography of The Father of Texas, 1993. Contributions to: Atlantic Monthly; Christian Century; Americas; National Defense; Current History; Hispanic American Historical Review; and others. Literary Agent: Robert Gottlieb, William Morris Agency. Address: History Department, Indiana State University, Terre Haute, IN 47809, USA.

WILLIAMS John Taylor, b. 19 June 1938, Cambridge, Massachusetts, USA. Attorney. m. Leonora Hall, 12 Nov 1967, 3 sons. Education: AB, Harvard College; LLB, University of Pennsylvania Law School. Appointments: National Endowment for the Arts, Literary Panel, 1989, 1990, 1991; Chief Judge Breyer, 1st Circuit, Member, US Corthouse Arts Commission; Member, US Publishing Delegation, by State Department to visit Chinese publishers, 1993. Publications: Small Voices and Great Trumpets; Minorities and the Media, Contributing Editor, 1980 (Praeger); Legal Problems in Book Publishing, Contributing Author, 1981, 1984, 1986; The Publishing Law Handbook, co-author, revised annually, Prentice Hall; Libel Defense Resource Centre: Annual 50 State Survey, LDRC, NYC Massachusetts Reporter; Rolf in the Woods, screenplay, 1987; Toussaint L'Overture, screenplay, 1989. Contributions to: The Lawyer's Role in the Acquisition and Exploitation of Life Story Rights, Boston Bar Journal, co-author, 1987. Memberships: Authors Guild; American Bar Association, Section of Patent, Trademark and Copyright Law; Chairman, Committee on Authors 1978-81; Communications and Entertainment Law Forum Committees; Massachusetts Bar Association, Business Law and Computer Law Sections. Literary Agent: The Palmer & Dodge Agency, Boston, MA. Address: Palmer & Dodge, One Beacon Street, Boston, MA 02108, USA.

WILLIAMS Malcolm David, b. 9 Apr 1939, South Wales. Author. Widower, 1 d. Education: Birmingham Univerity Institute of Education, 1951-61. Publications include: Yesterdays Secret, 1980; Poor Little Rich Girl, 1981; Debt of Friendship, 1981; Another Time, Another Place, 1982; Mr Brother's Keeper, 1982; The Stuart Affair, 1983; The Cordillera Conspiracy, 1983; The Girl from Derry's Bluff, 1983; A Corner of Eden, 1984; Sorrow's End, 1984; A Stranger on Trust, 1987; Shadows From the Past, 1989. Contributions to: Several Hundred Short Stories and serials to Various Magazines, Newspapers. Honours: 1st Prize, Short Story Competition, 1961, 1969. Memberships: Society of Authors; West Country Writers Association; Fellow World Literary Academy. Address: 40 Longlands Road, Bishops Cleeve, Cheltenham, Glos GL52 4JP, England.

WILLIAMS Miller. University Press Director. m. Education: BS Biology, Arkansas State College, 1950; MS Zoology, University of Arkansas, 1952. Literary Appointments: Founder, Editor, New Orleans Review, Loyola University, 1968-70; Advisory Editor, New Orleans Review, 1975-; Contributing Editor, Translation Review, 1976-80. Publications: Books include: A Circle of Stone, 1964; Recital, 1964; 19 Poetas De Hyo En Los Estados, 1966; Southern Writing in The Sixties: Poetry, 1966, Fiction 1966, (with J W Corrington); Poems & Antipoems (translation from Nicanor Parra), 1967; So Long at the Fair (Poems E P Dutton), 1968; Chile: An Anthology of New Writing, 1968; The Achievement of John Ciardi, 1968; The Only World There Is (Poems E P Dutton), 1968; The Poetry of John Crowe Ransom, 1971; Emergency Poems (translation from Nicanor Parra, New Directions), 1972; Contemporary Poetry in America, 1972; Halfway from Hoxie, New and Selected Poems, 1973; How Does a Poem Mean? (W John Ciardi), 1974; Railroad (with James Alan McPherson), 1976; Why God Permits Evil (poems), 1977; A Roman Collection, 1980; Sonnets of Guiseppe Belli (translation), 1981; Distration (poems), 1981; Ozark, Ozard: A Hillside Reader, 1981; The Boys on Their Bony Mules, 1983; Living On The Surface: New & Selected Poems, 1989; Adjusting to the Light (poems), 1992; Points of Departure (poems), 1995. Contributions to: Letras, Peru; Oberlin Quarterly; Saturday Review. Honours Include: Henry Bellaman Poetry Award, 1957; Bread Loaf Fellowship in Poetry, 1961; Fulbright Lecturer in US Literature, National University of Mexico, 1970-; Prix de Rome, American Academy of Arts & Letters, 1976; DHum, Lander College, 1983; National Poets Prize, 1992; Charity Randall Citation for Contribution to Poetry as a Spoken Art, International Poetry Center, Pittsburgh, 1993; John William Corrington Award for Excellence in Literature, Centenary College, Louisiana, 1994. Address: University of Arkansas Press, Fayetteville, AR 72701, USA.

WILLIAMS Nigel, b. 20 Jan 1948, Cheadle, Cheshire, England. Novelist; Playwright. Education: Oriel College, Oxford. Publications: Novels: My Life Closed Twice, 1977; Jack be Nimble, 1980; Charlie, 1984; Star Turn, 1985; Witchcraft, 1987; Breaking Up, 1988; Black Magic, 1988; The Wimbledon Poisoner, 1990; They Came from SW19, 1992; Plays: Double Talk, 1976; Snowwhite Washes Whiter, 1977; Class Enemy, 1978; Easy Street, 1979; Sugar and Spice, 1980; Line 'em, 1980; Trial Run, 1980; WCPC, 1982; The Adventures of Jasper Ridley, 1982; My Brother's Keeper, 1985; Deathwatch, after Genet, 1985; Country Dancing, 1986; As It Was, 1987; Nativity, 1989 (plays produced in London, Bristol, New York, Hull, Oxford and Stratford-on-Avon); Television plays. Honours include: Somerset Maugham Award for fiction, 1978. Address: c/o Faber and Faber, 3 Queen Square, London WC1N 3AU, England.

WILLIAMS Vera B, b. 1927. Publications: The Great Watermelon Birthday, 1980; Three Days on a River in a Red Canoe, 1981; Cherries & Cherry Pits, 1986; Stringbean's Trip to the Shining Sea, 1988; "More more more" said the Baby: 3 Love Stories, 1990; Scooter, 1993. Honours: Boston Globe/Horn Book Award, 1994.

WILLIAMSON John (Jack) Stewart, b. 29 Apr 1908, Bisbee, Arizona, USA. Writer. m. Blanche Slaten Harp, 15 Aug 1947, dec 1985, 2 step-children. Education: BA, MA 1957, Eastern New Mexico University; LHD (hon) 1981; PhD 1964, University Colorado. Appointments: Professor English, Eastern New Mexico University, Portales, 1960-77. Publications Include: Science Fiction: The Legion of Space, 1947; Darker Than You Think, 1948; The Humanoids, 1949; The Green Girl, 1950; The Cometeers, 1950; One Against the Legion, 1950; Seetee Shock, 1950; Seetee Ship, 1950; Dragon's Island, 1951; The Legion of Time, 1952; Dome Around America, 1955; The Trial of terra, 1962; Golden Blood, 1964; The Reign of Wizadry, 1965; Bright New Universe, 1967; Trapped in Space, 1968; The Pandora Effect, 1969; People Machines, 1971; The Moon Children, 1972; H G Wells: Critic of Progress, 1973; Teaching SF, 1975; The Early Williamson, 1975; The Power of Blackness, 1976; The Best of Jack Williamson, 1978; Brother to Demons, Brother to Gods, 1979; Teaching Science Fiction: Education for Tomorrow, 1980; The Alien Intelligence, 1980; The Humanoid Touch, 1980; Manseed, 1982; The Queen of a Legion, 1983; Wonder's Child: My Life in Science Fiction, 1984; Lifeburst, 1984; Firechild, 1986; Mazeway, 1990; Beachhead, 1992; Demon Moon, 1994; Co-author with Frederik Pohl: Undersea Quest, 1954; Undersea Fleet, 1955; Undersea City, 1956; The Reefs of Space, 1964; Starchild, 1965; Rogue Star, 1969; The Farthest Star, 1975; Wall Around a Star, 1983; Land's End, 1988; With James Gunn: Star Bridge, 1955; With Miles J Breuer: The Birth of a New Republic, 1931. Honours: Pilgrim Award, 1968, Science Fiction Research Association; Grand Master Nebula Award, 1976; Hugo Award for Wonder's Child: My Life in Science Fiction, 1985. Memberships: Science Fiction Writers of America, President 1978-80; Science Fiction Research Association; World Science Fiction Planetary Society. Address: PO Box 761, Portales, NM 88130, USA.

WILLIAMSON Robin, b. 24 Nov 1943, Edinburgh, Scotland. Writer; Musician; Storyteller. m. Bina Jasbinder Kaur Williamson, 2 Aug 1989, 1 s, 1 d. Publication: The Craneskin Bag, 1989; Selected Writing, 1980-83, 1984; Five Denials on Merlins Grave, 1979; Home Thoughts from Abroad, 1972; Various Music Books, Spoken Word Cassettes and Records. Contributions to: Poetry London. Literary Agent: Anthea Morton Stainer, Curtis Brown. Address: BCM 4797, London WC1N 3XX, England.

WILLINGS David Richard, b. 16 May 1932, Cambridge, England. Director, Willings Learning Clinic. Education: BA, Hons, Spanish, University of Durham, 1957; MA, Psychology, University of London, 1962; PhD, Guidance & Counselling, University of Strathclyde, 1972. Appointments: Senior Advisory Editor, STI Publishers, 1980-89; Contributing Editor, Roper Review, 1985-91; Editorial Board, Gifted Education International, 1986-; Assistant to the Editor, Gifted Education International, 1988-; Guest Editor, vol 10(3) Gifted Educational International, 1994. Publications: Pseudo-scientific thinking in modern psychology, 1962; How to use the case study, 1968; The creatively gifted (book version of PhD thesis), 1980; Operation counter attack (charts and manuals for teenage rape victims), 1990; Dahlias on the Moon, 1990, adaptation and translation of Yerma by F García Lorca, 1933, (co-author Sapphire Williamson); Minds Divorced, play on multi talented woman (co-author Dr Nicholas Chamberlain), 1992; An adventure in creative expression, 1994. Contributions to: Channel 4 TV; Roeper Review; Gifted Education International; Teaching Exceptional Children; Social Service Quarterly; International Journal for the Advancement of Counselling; Sunday Express; The Guardian. Honours: Gold Medal for outstanding services to Canadian Fencing, 1976, 1977, 1978; Sport Canada Award, services to amateur sport, 1977; New Brunswick Minister of Youth Award, services to youth, 1984; Honorary Life Member, International Federation for Popular Sport, 1993. Memberships: Fellow, World Literary Academy, 1986-; President, Atlantic Association for the Gifted, 1981-84; Coach, various hockey & fencing clubs, 1950's-92; President, World Federation of Innovators' Clubs, 1986-92. Address: Willings Learning Clinic, 116 Gaywood Road, Kings Lynn, Norfolk PE30 2PX, England.

WILLIS Meredith Sue, b. 31 May 1946, West Virginia, USA. Writer; Teacher. m. Andrew B Weinberger, 9 May 1982, 1 son. Education: BA, Barnard College, 1969; MFA, Columbia University, 1972. Publications: A Space Apart, 1979; Higher Ground, 1981; Personal Fiction Writing, 1984; Only Great Changes, 1985; Blazing Pencils, 1991; Quilt Pieces, 1990; Deep Revision, 1993; The Secret Super Powers of Mario; In the Mountains of America, 1994. Honours: Fellowship, National Endowment for the Arts, 1978; New Jersey Literary Fellowship, 1989. Memberships: PEN; Authors Guild; National Writers Union. Literary Agent: Wendy Weil. Address: 311 Prospect Street, South Orange, NJ 07079, USA.

WILLOUGHBY Cass. See: **OLSEN Theodore Victor.**

WILMER Clive, b. 10 Feb 1945, Harrogate, Yorkshire, England. Freelance Teacher, Lecturer, Writer. m. Diane Redmond, 12 Sept 1971, div 1986, 1 son, 1 daughter. Education: Kings College, Cambridge, 1964-67, 1968-71; BA 1st Class Hons, English, 1967; MA, 1970, Kings College, Cambridge. Appointments: Exhibition Committee, Pound's Artists, Tate Gallery, London and Kettle's Yard, Cambridge, 1984-85; Visiting Professor, Creative Writing, University of California, Santa Barbara, 1986; Editor: Numbers, 1986-90; Presenter of BBC Radio 3 Series, Poet of the Month, 1989-92. Publications: Poems: The Dwelling Place, 1977; Devotions, 1982; Of Earthly Paradise, 1992; Translated with G Gömöri: Miklós Radnóti, Forced March, 1979; György Petri, Night Song of the Personal Shadow, 1991; Editor of: Thom Gunn: The Occasions of Poetry, 1982; John Ruskin: Unto This Last and other writings, 1985; Dante Gabriel Rossetti: Selected Poems and Translations, 1991; William Morris: News From Nowhere and other writings, 1993; Poets Talking: The 'Poet of the Month', Interviews from BBC Radio 3, 1994. Literary Agent: A M Heath. Address: 57 Norwich Street, Cambridge CB2 1ND, England.

WILOCH Thomas, b. 3 Feb 1953, Detroit, Michigan, USA. Writer; Editor. m. Denise Gottis, 10 Oct 1981. Education: BA, Wayne State University, 1978. Appointments: Associated with Gale Research Inc, 1977-; Freelance Writing and Editing; Columnist, Retrofuturism, 1991-93; Book Reviewer, Anti-Matter Magazine, 1992-; Columnist, Photo Static, 1993-. Publications: Stigmata Junction, 1985; Paper Mask, 1988; The Mannikin Cypher, 1989; Tales of Lord Shantih, 1990; Docoded Factories of the Heart, 1991, new edition, 1994; Lyrical Brandy, 1993. Contributions to: Over 200 magazines including: Bloomsbury Review; Small Press Review; Hawaii Review; Asylum Annual 1994. Honours: Nomination, Pushcart Prize, 1988, 1990; Nomination, Rhysling Award, 1992. Memberships: Science Fiction Poetry Association; People Against Pluralities. Address: 43672 Emrick Dr, Canton, MI 48187, USA.

WILSON Alexander Galbraith, b. 19 May 1924, Cheshire, England. Writer; Composer. Education: Oxford University. Appointments: Wrote Revues for, Watergate Theatre, 1951-52; Musical, Players Club Theatre, 1953, Wyndhams Theatre, 1954, London Revival, 1984, Buccaneer, 1955, Valmouth, Lyric Hammersmith, 1958, Saville, 1959, York Playhouse, 1960, chichester, 1982; Director, London Revival, Boy Friend, 1967; composed, Music for As Dorothy Parker Once Said, 1969; Songs for BBC TV Charleys Aunt, 1969; Wrote & Performed, Sandy Wilson Thanks the Ladies, 1971; Wrote, His Monkey Wife, 1971; The Clapham Wonder, 1978. Publications: This is Sylvia, 1954; The Poodle form Rome, 1962; I Could be Happy, 1975; Ivor, 1975; The Roaring Twenties, 1977. Address: 2 Southwell Gardens, London SW7, England.

WILSON Barbara. See: **HARRIS Laurence Mark.**

WILSON Budge Marjorie, b. 2 May 1927, Halifax, Nova Scotia, Canada. Writer. m. Alan Wilson, 31 July 1953, 2 daughters. Education: BA, 1949, Diploma in Education, 1952, Dalhousie University.

Publications: The Best-Worst Christmas Present Ever, 1984; A House Far from Home, 1986; Mr John Bertrand Nijinsky and Charlie, 1986; Mystery Lights at Blue Harbour, 1987; Breakdown, 1988; Going Bananas, 1989; Thirteen Never Changes, 1989; Madame Belzile and Ramsay Hitherton-Hobbs, 1990; Lorinda's Diary, 1991; The Leaving, adult and young adult, 1990; Oliver's Wars, 1992; The Courtship (adult short fiction), 1994; Cassandra's Driftwood (juvenile), 1994; Cordelia Clark and Other Stories (adult short fiction), 1994; Many adult and children's short stories. Contributions to: University of Windsor Review, The Dress, 1993; Pottersfield Portfolio, Elliot's Daughter, 1994. Honours: CBC Literary Competition, 1981; Atlantic Writing Competition, 1986; City of Dartmouth Book Award, 1991; Young Adult Book Award, Canadian Library Association, 1991; Marianna Dempster Award, Canadian Authors Association, 1992; Ann Connor Brimer Award, 1993. Memberships: Board Member, Writers Federation of Nova Scotia; Canadian Authors Association; Writers Union of Canada; Secretary, Atlantic Representative, Canadian Society of Children's Authors, Illustrators and Performers. Address: North West Cove, RR1 Hubbards, Nova Scotia B0J 1T0, Canada.

WILSON Christopher Richard Maclean, b. 6 Jan 1934, Minehead, Somerset, England. Educator. m. Alma Louis Oliver, 5 Sept 1964, 2 sons. Education: BA 1957, MA 1961, St Catharine's College, Cambridge; Clifton Theological School, Bristol, 1960; Episcopal Theological School, Cambridge, Mass, USA; MA 1971, PhD 1977, University of Toronto. Appointments: Director, Board and Management Services, The Ontario Hospital Association, 1978-92. Publications: Hospital-wide Quality Assurance, 1987; Governing with Distinction, 1988; New on Board, 1991; Strategies in Health Care Quality, 1992; Monographs: Quality Assurance-Getting Started, 1985; Annotated Bibliography on Hospital Governance, 1989; Risk Management for Canadian Health Care Facilities, 1990. Contributions to: Canadian, American, British & Australian Journals on Management, Quality and Governance in Health Care, of over 50 articles. Honours: Writer of the Year, Canadian Association for Quality in Health Care, 1990; 1992 Honorary Fellow of University of Manchester (1992-94 tenure). Literary Agent: Sterling Lord Associates (Canada) Ltd. Address: 10 St Mary Street, Toronto, Ontario M4Y 1P9, Canada.

WILSON Colin Henry, b. 26 July 1931, Leicester, England. Author. m. (1) Dorothy Betty Troop, 1 son, (2) Joy Stewart, 2 sons, 1 daughter. Appointments: Laboratory Assistant, Gateway School, 1948-49; Civil Servant, 1949-50; National Service, RAF, AC2, 1949-50; Writer, 1954-; Visiting Professor: Hollins College, Virginia, 1966-67, University of Washington, Seattle, 1967, Dowling College, Majorca, 1969, Rutgers University, New Jersey, 1974. Publications include: The Outsider, 1956; Religion and the Rebel, 1957; The Age of Defeat, 1959; Ritual in the Dark, 1960; The Strength to Dream, 1962; Origins of the Sexual Impulse, 1963; Necessary Doubt, 1964; Eagle and the Earwig, 1965; The Glass Cage, 1966; Sex and the Intelligent Teenager, 1966; Voyage to a Beginning, 1969; Lingard, 1970; Tree by Tolkien, 1973; Hermann Hesse, 1973; Strange Powers, 1973; The Space Vampires, 1976; Mysteries, 1978; Starseekers, 1980; Access to Inner Worlds, 1982; Psychic Detectives, 1983; The Essential Colin Wilson, 1984; The Personality Surgeon, 1986; Afterlife, 1986; Jung: The Lord of the Underworld, 1984; Rudolf Steiner: The Man and His Work, 1985; An Encyclopedia of Scandal (co-author Donald Seaman), 1986; Spider World: The Tower, 1987; Aleister Crowley - The Man and the Myth, 1987; An Encyclopedia of Unsolved Mysteries (co-author Damon Wilson), 1987; Marx refuted, 1987; Written in Blood (with Donald Seaman), 1989; The Misfits - A Study of Sexual Outsiders, 1988; Beyond the Occult, 1988; The Serial Killers, 1990; Mozart's Journey to Prague (play), 1990; Spiderworld: The Magician, 1991; The Strange Life of P D Ouspensky, 1993. Contributions to: The Times; Literary Review; The Gramophone; Evening Standard Daily Mail. Membership: Society of Authors. Literary Agent: David Bolt Associates. Address: Tetherdown, Trewallock Lane, Gorran Haven, Cornwall, England.

WILSON Dave. See: FLOREN Lee.

WILSON Des, b. 1941, New Zealand. Writer. Appointments: Journalist, Broadcaster, 1957-67; Director, Shelter National Campaign for the Homeless, 1967-71; Columnist, The Guardian, 1968-70, The Observer, 1971-75; Head of Public Affairs, Royal Shakespeare Company, London, 1974-76; Editor, Social Work Today, 1976-79; Deputy Editor, Illustrated London News, 1979-81; Chairman, Campaign for Lead Free Air, 1981-85; Friends of the Earth, 1982-86; Freedom of information, 1984-91; President, Liberal Party, 1986-87; General Election Campaign Director, Liberal Democrats, 1991-92.

Publications: I know It Was The Places Fault, 1970; Des Silsons Minority Report, 1973; So You Want to be Prime Minister, 1979; The Lead Scandal, 1982; Pressure: The A to Z of Campaigning in Britain, 1984; The Enviornmental Crisis, 1984; The Secrets File, 1984; Costa del Sol, 1990; Campaign, 1992; Campaigning, The A to Z of Public Advocacy, 1994. Address: Milestone House, 39 Main Road, Long Bennington, Nr Newark, Notts, NG23 8DJ, England.

WILSON Edward Osborne, b. 10 June 1929. Professor; Author. m. Irene Kelley, 30 Oct 1955, 1 daughter. Education: BS, 1949, MS, 1950, University of Alabama; PhD, Harvard University, 1955. Publications: The Insect Societies, 1971; Sociobiology: The New Synthesis, 1975; On Human Nature, 1978; Biophilia, 1984; The Ants (with Bert Holldobler), 1990; Naturelist, 1994. Contributions to: 330 articles, mostly scientific. Honours Include: National Medal of Science, 1977; Pulitzer Prize in General Non-Fiction, 1979; Tyler Prize for Environmental Achievement, 1984; Ingersoll Prize for Scholarly Letters, 1989; Crafoord Prize, Royal Swedish Academy of Sciences, 1990; Prix, Institut de Vie, Paris, 1990; International Prize in Biology, Government of Japan, 1993; Sci Peter Kent Conservation Book Prize, Book Trust, England, 1994. Memberships Include: National Academy of Sciences; Royal Society, England; American Philosophical Scoeity; American Academy of Arts and Sciences; Royal Society of Sciences of Uppsala; Finnish Academy of Arts and Sciences. Address: Museum of Comparative Zoology, Harvard University, Cambridge, MA 02138, USA.

WILSON Edwin James (Peter), b. 27 Oct 1942, Lismore, NSW, Australia. Community Relations, Royal Botanic Gardens, Sydney. m. Cheryl Lillian Turnham, 1 Sep 1975, 2 sons, 1 daughter. Education: BSc, UNSW. Publications: Banyan, 1982; Liberty, Egality, Fraternity, 1984; THe Dragon Tree, 1985; Discovering the Domain, 1986; Wild Tamarind, 1987; Falling Up Into Verse, 1989; Songs Of The Forest, 1990; The Rose Garden, 1991; The Wishing Tree, 1992; The Botanic Verses, 1993. Memberships: NSW Poets Union. Address: PO Box 32, Lane Cove, NSW 2066, Australia.

WILSON Gina, b. 1943, Childrens Fiction Writer; Poet. Appointments: Assistant Editor, Scottish National Directory, 1967-73; Assistant Editor, Dictionary of the Older Scottish Tongue, 1972-73. Publications include: Cora Ravenwing, 1980; A Friendship of Equals, 1981; The Whisper, 1982; Just Us, 1988; Polly Pipies Up, 1989; I Hope You Know, 1989; Jim Jam Pyamas, 1990; Wompus Galumpus, 1990; Riding the Great White, 1992; Prowlpnss, 1994. Literary Agent: Gina Pollinger, London. Address: C/O Gina Pollinger, 222 Old Brompton Road, London SW5 0BZ.

WILSON Jacqueline, b. 17 Dec 1945, Bath, Somerset, England. Writer. m. William Millar Wilson, 28 Aug 1965, 1 d. Appointment: Journalist DC, 1963-65. Publications include: Nobodys Perfect, 1982; Waiting for the Sky to Fall, 1983; The Other Side, 1984; Amber, 1986; The Power of the Shade, 1987; This Girl, 1988; The School Trip, 1984; The Killer Tadpole, 1987; Stevie Day Series, 1987; Is There Anybody There, 1990; The Story of Tracy Beaker, 1991; The Mum Minder, 1993; The Suitcase Kid, 1992; Deep Blue, 1993; The Bed and Breakfast Star, 1994. Honours: Runner Up, Observer Teenage Novel Award, 1982, 1984; Shortlisted, Smarties Award, 1992; Shortlisted, Carnegie Medal, 1992; Winner, Oak Tree Award, 1992; Winner, 1993 Childrens Book Award. Literary Agent: Gina Pollinger. Address: 1B Beaufort Road, Kingston on Thames, Surrey KT1 2TH, England.

WILSON Joyce Muriel, (Joyce Stranger), b. 26 May 1921, Forest Gate, London, England. Writer; Dog Trainer. m. Dr Kenneth Bruce Wilson, 28 Feb 1944, 2 s, 1 d. Education: BSc, University College, London, 1939-42. Publications include: The Running Foxes, 1965; Rex, 1967; Flash, 1976; Walk in the Dark, 1977; Fox at Drummers Darkness, 1978; The Stallion, 1981; Never Tell A Secret; Kym; Threes A Pack; Two for Joy; A Dog in a Million; Dog Days; Double or Quit; How to Own a Sensible Dog; Midnight Magic; Animal Sanctuary Trilogy; The Hills Are Lonely; Souvenir; The Secret of Hunters Keep; Thursdays Child, 1994; House of Secrets Trilogy, 1994; Over 65 Titles. Contributions to: Serials in My Weekly & Womens Realm; Articles in Our Dogs; Off Lead; Kennel Gazette; Cat World. Honour: Shortlisted for Trento Award, 1978. Memberships: People and Dogs Society; The Humane Education Society; UK Registry for Canine Behavianists. Literary Agent: Brian Stone, Aitken & Stone Limited. Address: c/o Aitken & Stone Limited, 29 Fernshaw Road, London, SW10 0TG, England.

WILSON Keith, b. 26 Dec 1927, Clovis, New Mexico, USA. Poet; Writer. m. Helen Brigham, 15 Feb 1958, 1 son, 4 daughters. Education: BA, US Navy Academy, 1950; MA, University of New Mexico, 1956. Publications: Graves Registry and Other Poems, 1969; Homestead, 1969; While Dancing Feet Shatter The Earth, 1978; Lion's Gate, 1988; The Winds of Pentecost, 1991; Graves Registry, 1992. Honours: Creative Writing Fellowship, National Endowment for the Arts; Fulbright-Hays Fellowship to Rumania; D H Lawrence Creative Writing Fellowship. Address: 1500 South Locust, Las Cruces, NM 88001, USA.

WILSON Leslie Erica, b. 10 Aug 1952, Nottingham, England. Novelist. m. David Wilson, 20 July 1974, 2 d. Education: BA, Durham University; PGCE, Oxford. Publications: Morning is Not Permitted, 1990; Malefice, 1992; French Translation, 1994; US Publications, 1993; The Mountain of Immoderate Desires, 1994. Contributions to: Orbis; Writing Women; Guardian; Iron; Good Housekeeping Sunday Times; Independent on Sunday; London Rewiew of Books; Literary Review. Memberships: Poetry Society; Society of Authors; PEN; Royal Society of Literature. Literary Agent: A M Heath. Address: 33 Surley Road, Caversham, Reading, RG4 8ND, England.

WILSON Lorraine Margaret, b. 18 May 1939, Echuca, Victoria, Australia. Educational Consultant. Education: Trained Infant Teacher's Certificate; Certificate A, Education Department of Victoria. Publications: City Kids, series, 1978-86; Write Me A Sign, 1979; Country Kids, series, 1982-87; You Can't Make a Book in a Day (with B Scarffe, 1988); My Mum Has False Teeth and Other Stories, 1990; An Integrated Approach to Learning (with D Malmgren, S Ramage, L Schulz), 1990; Write Me A Poem, 1994. Contributions to: Curriculum and Research Bulletin; Australian Journal of Reading; Primary Education; Reading Teacher; Teaching K-8. Memberships: Australian Society of Authors; Australian Reading Association, Past President of Melbourne Council; Primary English Teaching Association; Australian Curriculum Studies Association; Australian Education Network. Address: 81 Amess St, North Carlton, Victoria 3054, Australia.

WILSON Pearl Marie, b. 26 May 1946, Pennsylvania, USA. Journalist. m. Peter Wilson, 12 Jan 1971, 1 son. Education: Journalism Cadetship, Australian Media. Publications: Mummy, Why Can't I Breathe?, 1978; Katie Goes to Hospital, 1979; If You Knew Nicky, 1983; Broadway and Beyond, 1988; Oakleigh's Golden Days. Contributions to: Gold Coast Bulletin; Press Democrat; The Sentinel; Standard News. Honours: Asthma Foundation Service Award, 1978. Memberships: Monash Medical Centre Literary Programme; National Trust of Victoria; Oakleigh Historical Society; Friends of Stonnington. Address: 7 Baker's Rd, South Oakleigh, Victoria 3167, Australia.

WILSON Shirley Cameron, b. 22 Feb 1918, Kadina, South Australia. Art Historian; Author. Education: Gold Medallist Nurse, 1937-41; Diploma In Social Science, Adelaide University, South Australia, 1952. Publications: Co-Author, The Bridge Over The Ocean, Biography of the 2nd Mayor of Adelaide, Art Collector and Connoisseur. 1973; From Shadow Into Light, South Australian Women Artist's since Colonisation, 1988. Contributions to: The British Collection At Carrick Hill; Australian Antique Collector; The Dictionary of Australian Artists; The Australian Dictionary of Biography. Memberships: Art Gallery of South Australia; South Australian State Library; Lyceum Club, South Australia. Literary Agent: Delmont Pty Ltd. Address: 51 Russell Avenue, Hazelwood Park 5066, South Australia.

WINCH Donald Norman, b. 15 Apr 1935, London, England. University Professor. m. 5 Aug 1983. Education: BSc, London School of Economics, 1956; PhD, Princeton University, 1960. Publications: Classical Political Economy & Colonies, 1965; Economics and Policy, 1969, 1972; Economic Advisory Council, 1976; Adam Smith's Politics, 1978; That Noble Science of Politics, 1983; Malthus, 1987. Contributions to: Many Learned Journals. Honours: Fellow, British Academy, 1986; Royal Historical Society, 1987. Memberships: Royal Economic Society; Economic Journal; Royal Economic Society. Address: Arts E University of Sussex, Falmer, Brighton, Sussex BN1 9QN, England.

WINCH Peter Guy, b. 14 Jan 1926, London, England. Professor of Philosophy. m. Jan 1947, 2 sons. Education: MA; BPhil, 1951, St Edmund Hall, Oxford. Publications: The Idea of a Social Science, 1951; Ethics and Action, 1972; Trying to Make Sense, 1987; Simone Weil: The Just Balance, 1989; Editor: Studies in the Philosophy of Wittgenstein, 1969; Wittgenstein: Attention to Particulars, 1990; The Political Responsibility of Intellectuals, 1990; Contributions to:

Numerous Journals and Magazines. Honours: Senior Research Fellow, Leverhulme Trust, 1976-77; Corresponding Member, Institut fur die Wissenschaften vom Menschen, Vienna, 1986-; Fellow, Kings College, London, 1985-; Honorary Fellow, University College of Swansea, 1990-. Memberships: Aristotelian Society, President 1980-81; American Philosophical Association; Association of University Teachers; American Association of University Professors. Address: 310 W Hill Street 3W, Champaign, IL 61820, USA.

WINDSOR Patricia (Colin Daniel), b. 21 Sept 1938, New York, USA. Author; Lecturer; Teacher. 1 son, 1 daughter. Appointments: Faculty Member, Institute of Children's Literature; University of Maryland Writers Institute; Editor-in-Chief, The Easterner, (Washington DC); Co-Director, Wordspring Literary Consultants; Director, Summertree Studios, Savannah, 1992-. Publications Include: The Summer Before, 1973; Diving for Roses, 1976; Mad Martin, 1976; Killing Time, 1980; The Sandman's Eyes, 1985; The Hero, 1988; Something's Waiting for You, Baker D, 1974; Home is Where your Feet are Standing, 1975; Just Like the Movies, 1990; The Christmas Killer, 1991. Contributions to: Seventeen; Family Circle; Womans Journal; Fair Lady; New Idea; Damaras World; Short Stories: "Teeth", Short Circuits (Anthology), 1992, "Toad in the Hole", On The Edge, (Anthology), "Proof of the Pudding", 1991; "A Little Taste of Death", Thirteen, 1991. Honours: Ala Best Book, 1973; Outstanding Books for Young Adults, NY Times, 1976; Edgar Allan Poe Award, Mystery Writers of America, 1986; Honor Nominee, Edgar Allan Poe Award for The Christmas Killer, 1992. Memberships: Poetry Society of Georgia; Savannah Storytellers, Secretary & Treasurer; The Authors Guild; The Childrens Book Guild; Mystery Writers of America; International Writing Guild; International Association of Business Communications. Literary Agent: Amy Berkower, USA. Address: Writers House, 21 W 26th St, NY 10010, USA.

WINE Dick. See: **POSNER Richard.**

WINEGARTEN Renee, b. 23 June 1922, London, England. Literary Critic; Author. m. Asher Winegarten, dec 1946. Education: MA, 1943, PhD, 1950, Girton College, Cambridge. Publications: The Double Life of George Sand, 1978; French Lyric Poetry in the Age of Malherbe, 1954; Writers and Revolution, 1974; Madame de Staël, 1985; Simone de Beauvoir: A Critical View, 1988. Contributions to: French Studies; Modern Language Review; Encounter; Commentary; The American Scholar; The New Criterion; And Others. Memberships: Friends of George Sand; Society of Authors; Authors Guild. Literary Agent: Georges Borchardt, NY, USA. Address: 12 Heather Walk, Edgware, Middlesex HA8 9TS, England.

WINGATE John Allan, b. 15 Mar 1920, Cornwall, England. Author. m. Marie Watts, 25 Oct 1984, 1 s, 1 d. Publications include: Submariner Sinclair Series, 1959-64; Sinclair Action Series, 1968, 69, 71; HMS Belfast, In Trust for the Nation, 1972; In The Blood, 1973; Below the Horizon, 1974; The Sea Above Them, 1975; Oil Strike, 1976; Black Tide, 1976; Avalanche, 1977; Red Mutiny, 1977; Target Risk, 1978; Seawaymen, 1979; Frigate, 1980; Carrier, 1981; Submarine, 1982; William the Conqueror, 1984; Go Deep, 1985; The Windship Race, 1987; The Fighting Tenth, 1990. Honours include: Distinguished Service Cross, 1943. Membership: Nautical Institute. Literary Agent: Ms Rosemary Bromlwy, The Rosemary Bromley Literary Agency, Hampshire. Address: c/o Lloyd Bank Plc, Waterloo Place, Pall Mall, London SW1Y 5NJ.

WINGFIELD Sheila (Claude), b. 23 May 1906, Hampshire, England. Poet. Education: Roedean School, Sussex. Publications: Poems, 1938; Beat Drum, Beat Heart, 1946; A Cloud Across the sun, 1949; A Kite's Dinner, 1938-54; The Leaves Darken, 1964; Her Storms, 1938-77; Admissions: Poems, 1974-77; Collected Poems, 1938-82; Real People, 1952. Address: c/o Rawlinson & Hunter, 1 Hanover Square, London W1 4SR, England.

WINNER Langdon, b. 7 Aug 1944, CA, USA. Teacher; Writer. m. Gail P Stuart, 10 Oct 1981, 3 s. Education: BA, 1966, MA, 1967, PhD, 1973, University of CA. Publications include: Autonomous Technology, 1977; The Whale and the Reactor, 1986. Contributions to: Technology Review; Rolling Stone. Memberships: Pres, Society for Philosophy & Technology. Address: Dept of Science & Technology Studies, Rensselaer Polytechnic Institute, Troy, NY 12180, USA.

WINSTON. See: **HEALEY Denis.**

WINSTON Sarah (Sarah E Lorenz), b. 15 Dec 1912, New York City, USA. Writer. m. Keith Winston, 11 June 1932, 2 sons. Education: New York University, 1929, 1930; Philosophy and Appreciation of Art course, The Barnes Foundation, 1966, 1967; Art Seminars (research), 1967-89. Publications: And Always Tomorrow, 1963; Everything Happens for the Best, 1969, 1970; Our Son, Ken, 1969, 1970; Not Yet Spring, (poems), 1976; V-Mail: Letters of the World War II Combat Medic, 1985; Summer Conference, 1990; Of Apples and Oranges, 1993. Contributions to: The Literary Review, Fairleigh Dickenson College; Art Journal Vista, Barnes Foundation; New England Sampler; Guideposts. Honours: 1st Prize Award, Everything Happens for the Best, 1972, 1st Prize Award, Our Son, Ken, 1974, National League of American Pen Women; Recordings of Everything Happens for the Best, V-Mail, And Always Tommorow, Library of Congress for Blind; Tape recording, Our Son, Ken, Recording for the Blind Inc. Memberships: National League of American Pen Women. Literary Agent: Dan Wright, Ann Wright Representatives Inc, New York City. Address: 1801 Morris Rd C110, Blue Bell, PA 19422, USA.

WINTER Michael John, b. 5 Aug 1964, Sydney, New South Wales, Australia. Writer; Actor; Executive Story Consultant. Education: Picton High School; N S W Police Academy. Publications: Effortless Way, rock musical, 1986; Radio Nemesis, 1990; Blue Heelers television series, 1992-95; Water Rats, 1995. Memberships: Australian Writers Guild; Australian Film Institute; Actors Equity; MEAA. Address: 22 Castlereagh Street, Tahmoor, New South Wales 2573, Australia.

WINTERSON Jeanette, b. 1959, Lancashire, England. Writer. Education: Oxford University. Appointments: Worked in Theatre & Publishing; Full Time Writer. Publications: Oranges are not the Only Fruit; Boating for Beginners; The Passion; Sexing the Cherry, 1989; Written of the Body, 1992. Honour: Whitbread First Novel Prize Winner, 1985. Address: c/o Bloomsbury, 2 Soho Square, London, W1V 5DE, England.

WISEMAN Christopher Stephen, b. 31 May 1936, Hull, England. University Teacher. Education: MA, Cambridge University; PhD, University of Strathclyde. Publications: Waiting for the Barbarians, 1971; The Barbarian File, 1975; Beyond the Labyrinth: A Study of Edwin Muir's Poetry, 1978; The Upper Hand, 1981; An Ocean of Whispers, 1982; Postcards Home, 1988; Missing Persons, 1989. Contributions to: Poetry; Times Literary Supplement; Encounter; Critical Quarterly; Malahat Review; and others; Critical articles and reviews contributed to various journals. Honours: Alberta Achievement Award for Excellence, 1988; Writers Guild of Alberta Award for Poetry, 1988; Alberta Culture Poetry Prize, 1988. Address: Dept of English, University of Calgary, Calgary, Alberta, T2N 1N4, Canada.

WISEMAN David, (Jane Julian), b. 13 Jan 1916, Manchester, England. Writer. m. Cicely Hilda Mary Richards, 2 Sept 1939, 2 s, 2 d. Education: BA, 1937, Teaching Diplom, 1938, Manchester University. Appointment: Editor, Adult Education, 1947-50. Publications: Jeremy Visick, 1981; The Fate of Jeremy Visick, 1982; Thimbles, 1982, 1983; Blodwen and the Guardians, 1983; Adams Common, 1984; Pudding and Pie, 1986; Jumping Jack, 1988; Badge of Honour, 1989; The Devils Couldron, 1989; Mums Winning Streak, 1990; Moonglow, 1990; Goliath Takes the Bait, 1993; As Jane Julian: Ellen Bray, 1985; As Wind To Fire, 1989; The Sunlit Days, 1990. Membership: Society of Authors. Address: 21 Treworder Road, Truro, Cornwall TR1 2JZ, England.

WITT Harold Vernon, b. 6 Feb 1923, Santa Ana, California, USA. Freelance Writer; Editor. m. Beth Hewitt, 8 Sept 1948, 1 son, 2 daughters. Education: BA 1943, BLS 1953, University of California, Berkeley; MA, University of Michigan, 1947. Appointments: Co-Editor, California State Poetry Quarterly, 1976; Co-Editor, Blue Unicorn, 1977-; Consulting Editor, Poet Lore, 1976-91. Publications: The Death of Venus, 1958; Beasts in Clothes, 1961; Now Swim, 1974; Suprised by Others at Fort Cronkhite, 1975; Winesburg by the Sea, 1979; The Snow Prince, 1982; Flashbacks and Reruns, 1985; The Light at Newport, 1992; American Lit, 1994. Contributions to: Poems & or Stories: New Yorker; Poetry; The Atlantic; Harper's; Poetry Northwest; Southwest Review; Prairie Schooner; Wind; Fiction 83; Plains Poetry Journal; New Letters. Honours: Hopwood Award, poetry, 1947; Phelan Award, narrative poetry, 1960; 1st Prize, San Francisco Poetry Centre poetic drama competition, 1963; Emily Dickinson Award, Poetry Society of America, 1972; Various Awards, World Order of Narrative Poets. Address: 39 Claremont Avenue, Orinda, CA 94563, USA.

WITTLIN Thaddeus (Tadeusz), b. Warsaw, Poland. Lecturer; Radio Script Writer. Education: MA, LLM, University of Warsaw. Appointments: Editor, Barber of Warsaw satirical weekly, 1931-36. Publications: Trail to Parnassus, poetry, 1929; The Dreamer and the Guests, novel, 1932; The Hasbeen, novel, 1933; The Broken Wings, novel, 1934; The Achilles Heel, short stories, 1939; Happy Days, short stories, poetry, 1946; The Island of Lovers, short stories, 1950; A Reluctant Traveller in Russia, biography, English, French, Japanese, Polish versions, 1952; Modigliani-Prince of Montparnasse, biography, English, Dutch, Polish versions, 1964; Time Stopped at 6.30, historical account, 1965; Commissar, The Life and Death of Lavrenty Pavlovich Beria, biography, English, French, Spanish, Japanese versions, 1972; The Last Bohemians, 1974; The Songstress of Warsaw, 1985; On the Banks of the Grey #Vistula River, 1990. Memberships: PEN English Centre; PEN American Centre; Societe Historique et Litteraire Polonaise, Paris. Address: 2020 F Street NW, Washington, DC 20006, USA.

WOESSNER Warren, b. 31 May 1944, Brunswick, Jew Jersey, USA. Attorney. m. Iris Freeman, 6 Jan 1990. Education: BA 1966, Cornell University; PhD 1971, University of Wisconsin-Madison; JD 1981, University of Wisconsin Law School. Appointments: Founder, Editor and Publisher, Abraxas Magazine, 1968-81, Senior Editor, 1981-; Board of Directors, Counsil of Small Magazine Editors and Publishers, 1975-77; Member Wisconsin Arts Board Creative Writing Advisory Panel, 1977-79; Board of Directors, Back Porch Radio Inc, Host Visitors From Inner Space, programme of poetry, fiction and drama performance, 1975-78; Board of Directors, Coffee House Press, 1988-92, President 1989-92. Publications: Books include: The Forest and the Trees, 1968; Landing, 1974; No Hiding Place, 1979; Storm Lines, 1987. Contributions to: Anthologies: Heartland II, 1975; Travelling America with Today's Poets, 1977; The Poets' Encyclopaedia, 1979; Anthology of Magazine Verse and Yearbook of American Poetry, 1980; the Point Riders Great Plains Poetry Anthology, 1982; The Journey Home, 1989; and others; Periodicals: Poetry, Chicago; Poetry Now; Poetry Northwest; The Nation; Ironwood; the Wormwood Review; Epoch; West Coast Poetry Review; The Beloit Poetry Journal; Prairie Schooner; Living Wilderness; Continental Drift; December; Lips; and others. Honours Include: National Endowment for the Arts Individual Fellowship for Creative Writing, 1974; Wisconsin Arts Board Individual Fellowship for Poetry, 1985; Minnesota Voices Competition, poetry, 1986. Address: 34 W Minnehaha Parkway, Minneapolis, MN 55419, USA.

WOLFE Christopher, b. 11 Mar 1949, Boston, Massachusetts, USA. College Professor; Writer. m. Anne McGowan Wolfe, 17 June 1972, 5 sons, 5 daughters. Education: BA, University of Notre Dame, 1971; PhD, Boston College (Political Science), 1978. Publications: The Rise of Modern Judicial Review, 1986; Essays on Faith and Liberal Democracy, 1987; Judicial Activism: Bulwark of Freedom or Precarious Security?, 1990. Contributions to: Various articles included in journals: A Theory of US Constitutional History, Journal of Politics, 1981; How the Constitution was Taken Out of Constitutional Law in Harvard Journal of Law and Public Policy, Summer 1987; Abortion and Morally Acceptable Political Compromise; First Things, 1992. Honour: Benchmark Book of the Year Award for The Rise of Modern Judicial Review, 1987. Memberships: American Public Philosophy Institute, President 1989-; American Political Science Association; Fellowship of Catholic Scholars; The Federalist Society. Address: Department of Political Science, Marquette University, Milwaukee, WI 53233, USA.

WOLFE Gary Kent, b. 24 Mar 1946, Sedalia, Missouri, USA. Educator; Critic. Education: Ba 1968, University of Kansas; MA 1969, PhD 1971, University of Chicago. Appointments: Editorial Board, Science-Fiction Studies, 1984-; Journal of the Fantastic in the Arts, 1988-. Publications: The Known and the Unknown: The Iconography of Science Fiction, 1979; David Lindsay, 1982; Critical Terms for Science Fiction and Fantasy, 1986; Co-author, Elements of Research, 1979; Editor, Science Fiction Dialogues, 1982. Contributions to: Over 200 Essays and Reviews in Books, Reference Works, and Journals; Currently Monthly Review Columnist for Locus Magazine. Honours: Eaton Award for Science Fiction Criticism, 1981; Pilgrim Award, Science Fiction Research Association, 1987; James Friend Memorial Award for Literary Criticism, Friends of Literature, 1992. Memberships: Committee Director, International Association for the Fantastic in the Arts, 1985-; Board of Directors, Friends of the Chicago Public Library, 1990-93. Address: 1450 E 55th Place, Apt 420 South, Chicago, IL 60637, USA.

WOLFERS Michael, b. 28 Sept 1938, London, England. Writer; Translator. Education: Wadham College, Oxford University, 1959-62; South Bank Polytechnic, 1990-91. Appointments: Journalist, The Times, London, 1965-72; Visiting Senior Lecturer, African Politics & Government, University of Juba, 1979-82. Publications include: Black Man's Burden Revisited, 1974; Politics in the Organisation of African Unity, 1976; Luandino Vierira, The Real Life of Domingos Xavier, 1978; Poems for Angola, 1979; Samir Amin, Delinking: Towards a Polycentric World, 1990; Hamlet and Cybernetics, 1991. Contributions to: Numerous Publications. Memberships: Royal Institute of International Affairs; Gyosei Institute of Management. Address: 66 Roupell Street, London SE1 8SS, England.

WOLFF Edward Nathan, b. 10 Apr 1946, Long Branch, New Jersey, USA. Professor of Economics. m. Jane Zandra Forman, 27 Nov 1977, 1 son, 1 daughter. Education: AB 1968, Harvard College; MPhil 1972, PhD 1974, Yale University. Appointments: Managing Editor, Review of Income and Walth, 1987-; Associated Editor, Structural Change and Economic Dynamics, 1989-; Journal of Population Economics, 1990-. Publications: Growth, Accumulation and Unproductive Activity: An Analysis of the Post-War US Economy, 1987; Editor, International Comparisons of the Distribution of Household Wealth, 1987; Co-author, Productivity and American Leadership: The Long View, 1989; Co-author, The Information Economy: The Implications of Unbalanced Growth, 1989; Co-Editor, International Perspectives on Profitability and Accumulation, 1992; Co-author, Competitiveness, Convergence, and International Specialization, 1993; Co-Editor, Poverty and Prosperityin the USA in the Late Twentieth Century; Editor, Research in Economic Inequality, vol 4, "Studies in the Distribution of Household Wealth". Contributions to: Over 75 articles published in professional economics journals and books. Honours: National Merit Scholarship, 1964-68; Magna Cum Laude in Economics, Harvard, 1968; Honorable Mention, Annual Awards for Excellence in Publishing, Social Sciences, 1989, by Association of American Publishers, Professional and Scholarly Publishing Division. Memberships: International Association for Research in Income and Wealth, Council Member 1987-94; American Economic Association; Conference on Research in Income and Wealth; International Institute of Public Finance. Address: 48 Morton Street, New York, NY 10014, USA.

WOLFF Tobias (Jonathan Ansell), b. 19 June 1945, Birmingham, Alabama, USA. Writer. m. Catherine Dolores Spohn, 1975, 2 sons, 1 daughter. Education: BA 1972, MA 1975, Oxford University; MA, Stanford University, 1978. Publications: In the Garden of the North American Martyrs, short stories, 1981; Editor, Matters of Life and Death: New American Stories, 1982; The Barracks Thief, 1984; Back in the World, 1985; Editor, A Doctor's Visit: The Short Stories of Anton Checkhov, 1987; This Boy's Life, a memoir, 1989; In Pharaoh's Army, Memories of the Lost War, 1994; Editor, Best American Short Stories, 1994; Editor, Picador Book of Contemporary American Stories. Contributions to: TriQuarterly; Missouri Review; Ploughshares; Atlantic Monthly; Esquire; Vanity Fair; Antaeus. Honours: Wallace Stegner Fellowship, 1975-76; NEA Fellowship, 1978, 1985; Mary Roberts Rinehart Grant, 1979; Arizona Council on the Arts and Humanities Fellowship, 1980; O Henry Short Story Prizes, 1980, 1981, 1985; Guggengeim Fellowship, 1982; St Lawrence Award for Fiction, 1982; PEN/Faulkner Award for Fiction, 1985; Rea Award for the Short Story, 1989; Whiting Foundation Award, 1989; Los Angeles Times Book Prize, 1989; Lila Wallace Foundation Award, 1994; Lyndhurst Foundation Award, 1994. Memberships: Authors Guild; PEN. Address: 214 Scott Avenue, Syracuse, NY 13224, USA.

WOLKSTEIN Diane, b. 11 Nov 1942, New Jersey, USA. Author; Storyteller. 1 daughter. Education: BA, Smith College, 1964; MA, Bank Street College of Education, 1967. Publications: The First Love Stories; The Magic Orange Tree, 1978; Inanna, Queen of Heaven and Earth, 1983; Oom Razoom, 1991; Little Mouse's Painting, 1992; The Banza; The Magic Wings; White Wave; Dream Songs; The Red Lion; Lazy Stories; Squirrel's Song; The Visit; Cool Ride in the Sky; 8,000 Stones; Step by Step, 1994. Contributions to: Many publications. Honours: Many books Notable, American Library Association; Featured on National Public Radio and on Charles Kurault, CBS Sunday Morning; Centennial Honours Award, Smith College Club, New York City. Address: 10 Patchin Pl, New York, NY 10011, USA.

WOMACK Peter, b. 27 Jan 1952, Surrey, England. Lecturer. Education: BA, Oxford University, 1973; PhD, Edinburgh University, 1984. Appointments: Lectureship, University of East Anglia, 1988-.

Publications: Ben Jonson, 1986; Improvement and Romance, 1989. Contributions to: Textual Practice, 1987; New Theatre Quarterly, 1989; Culture and History, 1350-1600; David Aers, 1992. Address: School of English & American Studies, University of East Anglia, Norwich NR4 7TJ, England.

WOOD Charles (Gerald), b. 6 Aug 1932, St Peter Port, Guernsey, Channel Islands. Playwright. Education: Birmingham College of Art, 1948-50. Publications: Prisoner and Escort, 1961; Cockade, 1963; Tie Up the Ballcock, 1964; Don't Make Me Laugh, 1965; Meals on Wheels, 1965; Fill Up the Stage with Happy Hours, 1966; Dingo, 1967; Labour, 1968; H, Being Monologues at Front of Burning Cities, 1979; Collier's Wood, 1970; Welfare, 1971; Veterans; or, Hair in the Gates of the Hellespont, 1972; The Can Opener, 1974; Jingo, 1975; The Script, 1976; Has "Washington" Legs?, 1978; The Garden, 1982; Red Star, 1984; Across for the Garden of Allah, 1986; Tumbledown, 1988; The Plantagenets after Shakespeare, 1988; Man, Beast and Virtue, after Pirandello, 1989; Screenplays: The Knack, 1965; Help (co-author), 1965; How I Won the War, 1967; The Charge of the Light Brigade (co-author), 1968; The Long Day's Dying, 1968; The Bed-Sitting Room (co-author), 1968; Fellini Satyricon, 1969; Cuba, 1980; Vile Scripts, 1981; Television scripts, including Wagner (1984) and Puccini, for Tony Palmer, and Tumbledown, 1988. Honours include: Prix Italia, RAI, 1988; BAFTA Award, 1988. Address: Long Barn, Sibford Gopwer, Near Banbury, Oxfordshire OX15 5RT, England.

WOOD David Bernard, b. 21 Feb 1944, Sutton, England. Writer; Actor; Theatre Producer; Director; Composer. m. Jacqueline Stanbury, 21 Jan 1975, 2 d. Education: BA, Worcester College, Oxford. Publications include: Musical Plays for Children, The Owl and the Pussycat Went to Sea, 1970; The Plotters of Cabbage Patch Corner, 1973; Hijack Over Hygenia, 1974; The Papertown Paperchase, 1976; Larry the Lamb in Toytown, 1976; The Gingerbread Man, 1977; Old Father Time, 1977; Mother Gooses Golden Christmas, 1978; Cinderella, 1980; Dick Whittington and Wondercat, 1982; Meg and Mog Show, 1985; The See Saw Tree, 1987; Dinosaurs and all that Rubbish, 1986; The Gingerbread Man, 1985; The Discorats, 1985; Play Theatres, 1987; Sidney the Monster, 1988; Happy Birthday Mouse, 1991; Save the Human, 1991; The BFG, 1992; The Witches, 1994; Baby Bears Buggle Ride, 1993; The BFG Plays for Children, 1993. Honour: Winner, Nottinghamshire Childrens Book of Year Award, 1989. Memberships: Society of Authors; British Actors Equity Association; Green Room Club. Literary Agent: Margaret Ramsey Limited; Tom Erhardt, Casarotto Ramsey Limited, London; Eunice McMullen, 38 Clewer Hill Road, Berks. Address: c/o Margaret Ramsey Limited, 14A Goodwins Court, St Martins Lane, London WC2, England.

WOOD Edgar Allardyce, (Kerry Wood), b. 1907, Canada. Author; Federal Migratory Bird Officer. Appointments: Correspondent and Columnist, newspapers including: Edmonton Bulletin, Edmonton Journal, Calgary Herald and Calgary Albertan, 1926-73. Publications: Robbing the Roost: The Marquis of Roostburg Rules Governing the Ancient and Dishonourable Sport, 1938; I'm a Gaggle Man Myself, 1940; Three Mile Bend, 1945; Birds and Animals in the Rockies, 1946; A Nature Guide for Farmers, 1947; The Magpie Menace, 1949; Cowboy Yarns for Young Folk, 1951; The Sanctuary, 1952; A Letter from Alberta, 1954; A Letter from Calgary, 1954; Wild Winter, autobiography, 1954; The Map-Maker: The Story of David Thompson, 1955; Willowdale, 1956; The Great Chief: Maskepetoon Warrior of the Crees, 1957; The Queen's Cowboy: Colonel Macleod of the Mounties, 1960; Great Horned MacOwl, fiction, 1961; The Boy and the Buffalo, 1963; Mickey the Beaver and Other Stories, 1964; A Lifetime of Service: George Moon, 1966; A Corner of Canada: A Personalized History of the Red Deer River Country, 1966; A Time for Fun, 1967; The Medicine Man, 1968; Samson's Long Ride, 1968; The Creek, 1970; The Icelandic-Canadian Poet Stephan G Stephansson: A Tribute, 1974; Red Deer, A Love Story, 1975; Bessie, The Coo, 1975; A Legacy of Laughter, 1986. Honours include: Governor-General's Medals, Juvenile Literature, 1955, 1957; 1st Vicky Metcalf Award, 1963; Alberta Historical Society Award, 1965; Honorary Doctorate, University of Alberta, 1969; Honorary Life Member, Alberta Federation of Naturalists, 1970; Alberta Achievement Award, 1975; Loran L Goulden Memorial Award, 1987; Order of the Bighorn, Edmonton, Alberta, 1987; Distinguished Service Award, Interpretration, Red Deer, Alberta,1988; Member of the Order of Canada, Red Deer, Alberta, 1990; Confederation Commemoration Medal, 1992. Memberships: Board Member, Alberta Natural History Society, 1936-64. Address: Site 3, RR2, Red Deer, Alberta, T4N 5E2, Canada.

WOOD John Cunningham, b. 12 July 1952, Perth, Western Australia. m. Caoline D'Cruz, 5 June 1976, 1 s, 2 d. Education: B Econ, UWA, 1973; PhD, Oxford University, 1978. Publications include: British Economists and the Empire, 1860-1914, 1983; Editor of 21 Books on Various GreatEconomists, 1983; 6 Chapters in Books; Co Author of 9 Articles; 24 Other Publications and Conference Papers. Honours: Shell Scholarship, University of Oxford, 1975-78; Nuffield College, Studentship, 1977-78; professor, University of Notre Dame; duke of Edinburghs Third Commonwealth Study Conference, 1986. Memberships: CEDA; Economic Society of Western Australia; Royal Institute of Public Administration; Helm Wood Publishers Pty Limited. Address: c/o University of Notre Dame, 19 Mouat Street, Fremantle, WA 6060, Australia.

WOOD Kerry. See: **WOOD Edgar Allardyce.**

WOOD Ronald Francis James, b. 30 Nov 1921. Ophthalmologist; Medical Practitioner. m. Mary Lynette Young, 21 Feb 1948, 3 sons, 2 daughters. Education: Bachelor of Medicine & Bachelor of Surgery, 1944; Fellow, Royal Australian College of Ophthalmologists, 1969; Fellow, Royal Australasian College of Surgeons, 1977; Foundation Fellow, Royal College of Ophthalmologists, 1987. Publications: Australia's Quest for Colonial Health, 1983; Looking Up and Looking Back at Old Brisbane, 1987; (with others) Earnest Sandford Jackson, 1987; Pioneer Medicine in Australia, 1988; Some Milestones of Australian Medicine, 1994. Contributions to: Journal of the Royal Historical Society of Queensland; Australian Journal of Ophthalmology; Australian and New Zealand Journal of Ophthalmology. Memberships: Royal Historical Society of Queensland; Queensland Club. Address: 120 Queenscroft Street, Chelmer 4068, Brisbane, Australia.

WOOD Susan, b. 1946. Publications: Bazaar, 1981; Campo Santo, 1990. Honours: Lamont Poetry Selection, 1991.

WOOD Victoria, b. 19 May 1953, Prestwich, Lancashire, England. Writer; Comedienne. m. Geoffrey Durham, 1980, 1 son, 1 daughter. Education: BA, Drama, Theatre Arts, University of Birmingham. Publications: Victoria Wood Song Book, 1984; Lucky Bag, 1985; Up to You Porky, 1986; Barmy, 1987; Mens Sana in Thingummy Doodah, 1990. Honours: Recipient, BAFTA Awards, Broadcasting Press Awards; Variety Club BBC Personality of the Year, 1987; Hon D.Litt, Lancaster, 1989; D.Litt, Sunderland, 1994. Literary Agent: Richard Stone. Address: c/o Richard Stone, 25 Whitehall, London, SW1, England.

WOODCOCK George, b. 8 May 1912, Winnipeg, Canada. Writer. m. Ingeborg Hedwig Linzer, 1949. Publications: The White Island, 1940; William Godwin, 1946; The Writer and Politics, 1948; The Anarchist Prince, 1950; Pierre Joseph Proudhon, 1956; Incas and Other Men, 1959; Anarchism, 1962; Faces of India, 1964; The Crystal Spirit, 1966; The Doukhobors, 1968; Odysseus Ever Returning, 1970; Canada and the Canadians, 1970; Herbert Read, 1972; The Rejection of Politics, 1972; Who Killed the British Empire?, 1974; Notes on Visitations, 1975; Gabrial Dumont, 1975; Peoples of the Coast, 1977; Thomas Merton, Monk and Poet, 1978; Faces from History, 1978; The Kestrel and Other Poems, 1978; The Canadians, 1979; The World of Canadian Writing, 1980; The George Woodcock Reader, 1980; The Mountain Road, poems, 1980; Taking It to the Letter, 1981; Ivan Eyre, 1985; Confederation Betrayed, 1981; The Benefactor, 1982; Letter to the Past, 1982; Collected Poems, 1983; British Columbia: A Celebration, 1983; Orwell's Message, 1984; Strange Bedfellows: The State and the Arts in Canada, 1985; Walls of India, 1985; The University of British Columbia: A Souvenir, 1986; Letters from Sooke, 1986; Northern Spring, 1987; Beyond the Blue Mountains, 1987; A Social History of Canada, 1988; Caves in the Desert, 1988; The Marvellous Century, 1988; The Century that Made Us, 1989; Powers of Observation, 1989; The Monk and His Message, 1991; Power To Us All, 1992; Letter for the Khyber Pass, 1992; George Woodcock on Canadian Poetry, 1993; George Woodcock on Canadian Fiction, 1993; Walking Through the Valley, 1994; The Cherry Tree on Cherry Street, 1994. Contributions to: Articles in many British, US and Canadian Journals; Plays, Documentaries and Talks for CBC; Film Scripts. Address: 6429 McCleery Street, Vancouver, BC V6N 1GS, Canada.

WOODCOCK Joan, b. 6 Feb 1908, Bournemouth, England. Poet. m. Alexander Neville Woodcock, 18 Sept 1937, 2 sons, 1 daughter. Appointments: Secretary and Editorial Assistant to Chief Fiction Editor of the Associated Press, London; Secretary and Assistant to a

Gaumont British film producer; Employed by Baird Television, worked with John Logie Baird on his projected biography; Extensive traveller; Exhibited Artist, and Genealogist; Published Poet. Publications: The Wandering Years, 1990; Borrowing From Time, 1992; Stabbed Awake, 1994. Contributions to: Envoi; Orbis; Iota; First Time; and others; Envoi Anthologies 1989, 90, 91; Fragments (2 anthologies for Calne Music and Arts Annual Festivals, Wiltshire); Has read her poems and been interviewed on BBC radio. Honours: Prizes: Envoi, Rhyme International (Orbis); World Order of Narrative and Formalist Poets, New York, 1991; Writers Forum. Memberships: The Poetry Society; British Haiku Society; Associate member, Peterloo Poets; Founder member, Calne Writers' Circle; Verse Writers Guild of Ohio, USA; National Federation of State Poetry Societies Inc, USA; Scottish Genealogy Society; Birmingham and Midland Society for Genealogy and Heraldry; Wiltshire and other Family History Societies. Address: 6 Hudson Road, Malmesbury, Wiltshire SN16 0BS, England.

WOODCOCK John Charles, b. 7 Aug 1926, Longparish, Hampshire, England. Cricket Writer. Education: Trinity College, Oxford; MA, Oxon. Appointments: Staff, Manchester Guardian, 1952-54; Cricket Correspondent, The Times, 1954-; Editor, Wisden Cricketer's Almanack, 1980-86. Publications: The Ashes, 1956; Barclays World of Cricket, 1980. Contributions to: Country Life; The Cricketer. Honour: Sportswriter of the Year, BR Press Awards, 1987. Address: The Curacy, Longparish, Nr Andover, Hants, SP11 6PB, England.

WOODCOTT Keith. See: **BRUNNER John Killan Houston.**

WOODEN Rodney John, b. 16 July 1945, London, England. Playwright. Publications include: Your Home in the West, 1991; Woyzeck, An Adaption from the German of Georg Buchner, Northern Stage, Newcastle Upon Tyne, 1990; Steppenwolf Theatre, Chicago, 1991; Live Theatre, Newcastle Upon Tyne, 1992; The Other Place, Stratford Upon Avon, 1992; Smoke, 1993; Moby Dick, 1993; Major Play Productions. Honours: First Prize Winner, Mobil International Playwriting Competition, 1990; Mobil Writer in Residence Bursary, 1991-92; John Whiting Award, 1991. Memberships: PEN International. Literary Agent: Micheline Steinberg. Address: c/o Micheline Steinberg Playwrights, 110 Frognal, London NW3 6XU, England.

WOODFORD Peggy, b. 19 Sept 1937, Assam, India. Writer. m. Walter Aylen, 1 Apr 1967, 3 d. Education: MA, St Annes College, Oxford. Publications: Please Don't Go, 1972; Rise of the Raj, 1978; See You Tomorrow, 1979; Misfits, 1984; Monster in our Midst, 1987; Out of the Sun, 1990; Mozart, His Life and Times, 1977; Schubert, His Life and Times, 1978; The Girl with a Voice, 1981; Love Me, Love Rome, 1984. Literary Agent: Murray Pollinger. Address: c/o Murray Pollinger, 222 Old Brompton Road, London SW5 0BZ, England.

WOODHEAD Peter Anthony, b. 11 Nov 1944, Shipley, Yorkshire, England. m. Sylvia Ann, 24 Aug 1970, 1 son, 1 daughter. Education: BA, University College, London, 1966; MA, University of Sheffield, 1969; M Phil, University of Leicester, 1985. Publications: Keyguide to Information Sources in Archaeology, 1985; Keyguide to Information Sources in Museum Studies, Co-author, 1989. Contributions to: Various articles on library topics in librarianship periodicals. Honour: The Keyguide to Information Sources in Museum Studies, selected by Choice for Outstanding Reference Book for 1990 in the USA. Membership: Library Association. Address: 81 Uppingham Road, Houghton on the Hill, Leicestershire LE7 9HL, England.

WOODS P F. See: **BAYLEY Barrington John.**

WOODWARD C(omer) Vann, b. 13 Nov 1908, AK, USA. Historian. m. Glenn McCleod, 21 Dec 1937, 1 s, dec. Education: BA, Emory University, 1930; MA, Columbia University, 1932; PhD, University of North Carolina, 1937. Literary Appointments: Guggenheim Fellow, 1946, 1960; Professor, Johns Hopkins University, 1947-61; Professor, Yale University, 1961-77. Publications: The Strange Career of Jim Crow, 1955; Origins of the New South, 1951; The Burden of Southern History, 1960; Mary Chesnut's Civil War, 1981; Thinking Back: The Perils of Writing History, 1986; Tom Watson: Agrarian Rebel, 1938; The Old World's New World, 1991. Contributions to: New York Review of Books; Harpers Magazine; New Republic; NY Times Book Review; Am Historical Review. Honours: Honorary Degrees, Cambridge; Bancroft Prize, 1952; Pulitzer Prise, 1982; Gold Medal for History by Am Academy of Art & Letters. Memberships: Am Academy of Arts & Letters; Am Academy of Arts & Sciences; Royal Historical

Society; British Academy; American Historical Association; Southern Historical Association. Address: 83 Rogers Road, Hamden, CO, USA.

WOODWORTH Steven Edward, b. 28 Jan 1961, Akron, Ohio, USA. College Professor. m. Leah Bunke, 13 Aug 1983, 3 sons. Education: BA 1982, Southern Illinois University; PhD 1987, Rice University. Publications: Jefferson Davis and His Generals, 1990. Honour: Fletcher Pratt Award, 1990. Memberships: American Historical Association; Southern Historical Association. Address: PO Box 800006, Toccoa Falls, GA 30598, USA.

WOODY Elizabeth, b. 1959. Publications: Hands into Stone: Poems, 1988; Luminaries of the Humble, 1994; Seven Hands, Seven Hearts, 1994. Honours: American Book Award, 1990.

WORSLEY Dale, b. 3 Nov 1948, Louisiana, USA. Writer. m. Elizabeth Fox, 14 July 1991. Appointments: The Writinn Programme, Columbia University, New York City, 1992. Publications: The Focus Changes of August Previco, 1980; The Art of Science Writing, 1989; Plays: Cold Harbor, 1983; The Last Living Newspaper, 1993. Honours: Fellowship in Fiction, 1986, Fellowship in Playwriting, 1989, National Endowment for the Arts. Memberships: Dramatists Guild. Literary Agents: Ellen Levine, Susan Schulman. Address: 150 Lafayette Ave 1, Brooklyn, NY 11238, USA.

WORSTHORNE Peregrine Gerard Sir, b. 22 Dec 1923, Chelsea, London, England. Journalist. m. (1) 1950, dec'd, 1 d, (2) Lucinda Lambton, 1992. Education: Peterhouse, Cambridge; BA, Cantabl Magdalen College, Oxford. Appointments: Editorial Staff, Glasgow Herald, 1946-48; Editorial Staff, WA Correspondent, 1948-50; Leader Writer, The Times, 1952-55; Leader Writer, Daily Telegraph, 1955-61; Assistant Editor, 1961-86, Editor, 1986-89, Editor, Comment Section, 1989-91, Columnist, 1991-, Sunday Telegraph. Publications: The Socialist Myth, 1972; Peregrinations, 1980; By The Right, 1987; Tricks of Memory, 1993. Contributions to: Encounter; NY Times; Foreign Affairs; 20th Century; The Spectator; WA Post; The Am Spectator; Time & Tide. Honours: Granada Columnist of Year, 1980; KBE, 1991. Memberships: Garrick Club; Beefsteak Club; Pratts Club. Address: The Old Rectory, Hedgerley, Buckinghamshire SL2 3VY, England.

WORTH Anthony. See: **WEST William Alexander.**

WOUK Herman, b. 27 May 1915, New York City, USA. Writer. m. Betty Sarah Brown, 9 Dec 1945, 3 sons (1 deceased). Education: AB, Columbia University, 1934; LHD, Honorary, Yeshiva University, 1954; LLD, Honorary, Clark University, 1960; Ltt.D, Honorary, American International College, 1979. Appointments: Visiting Professor, English, Yeshiva University, 1952-57; Scholar in Residence, Aspen Institute Humanistic Studies, 1973-74. Publications: The Caine Mutiny, 1951; The Winds of War, 1971; War and Remembrance, 1978; Marjorie Morningstar, 1955; The Caine-Mutiny Court-Martial (Play), 1953; This Is My God (non-fiction), 1959; Don't Stop the Carnival, 1965; Youngblood Hawke, 1962; City Boy, 1948; Inside, Outside, 1985; Aurora Dawn, 1947; Lomokome Papers, 1956; The Traitor (Play), 1949; Nature's Way (Play), 1957; Slattery's Hurricane, 1949; TV Screen-plays: The Winds of War, 1983; War and Remembrance, 1986; Latest novel: The Hope, 1993. Honours: Pulitzer Prize for The Caine Mutiny, 1952; Columbia University Medal for Excellence, 1952; Alexander Hamilton Medal, 1980; University of California Berkeley Medal, 1984; Washington Book Award, 1986; Golden Plate Award, American Academy of Achievement, 1986; US Naval Memorial Foundation "Lone Sailor Award", 1987. Memberships: PEN; Authors League; WGA. Literary Agent: B S W Literary Agency. Address: c/o B S W Literary Agency, 3255 N St NW, Washington, DC 20007, USA.

WRIGHT A(mos) J(asper III), b. 3 Mar 1952, Gadsded, Alabama, USA. Medical Librarian. m. Margaret Dianne Vargo, 14 June 1980, 1 son, 1 daughter. Education: BA 1973, Auburn University; MLS 1983, University of Alabama. Publications: Frozen Fruit, poetry, 1978; Right New I Feel Like Robert Johnson, poetry, 1981; Criminal Activity in the Deep South, 1800-1930, 1989. Contributions to: Anaesthesiology; Anaesthesia and Analgesia; Poem; Aura; Old West; and others. Memberships: Authors Guild; Poetry Society of America; Medical Library Association; Anaesthesia History Association. Address: 617 Valley View Drive, Pelham, AL 35124, USA.

WRIGHT Anthony David, b. 9 June 1947, Oxford, England. Historian. Education: City of London School, 1958-65; BA, Merton College, 1968; MA, British School at Rome, 1973; D Phil, Brasenose College, 1973. Appointments: General Editor, A History of the Papacy. Publications: The Counter Reformation, 1982; Catholicism and Spanish Society, 1991. Contributions to include: English Historical Review; Historical Journal; Historical Research; Northern History; Art History. Honours: Accademia Di San Carlo, 1978; Fellowship, Royal Historical Society, 1980; Visiting Fellowship, Edinburgh University, 1983. Memberships: Athenaeum, Ecclesiastical History Society. Address: School of History, University of Leeds, Leeds, LS2 9JT, England.

WRIGHT C D, b. 6 Jan 1949, Mountain Home, Arkansas, USA. Poet; Professor. m. Forrest Gander, 23 Sept 1983, 1 son. Education: BA 1971, Memphis State University; MFA 1976, University of Arkansas. Publications: Terrorism, 1979; Translations of the Gospel Back Into Tongues, 1981; Further Adventures with God, 1986; String Light, 1991; Just Whistle, 1993; The Lost Roads Project: A Walk-in Book of Arkansas, 1994; The Reader's Map of Arkansas, 1994. Contributions include: Field; Ironwood; The New Yorker; Kenyon Review; Paris Review; Conjunctions; Sulfur; Tri-Quarterly. Honours: Fellowship from National Endowment for the Arts, 1981, 1987; Witter Bynner Prize for Poetry, 1986; Guggenheim Fellowship, 1987; Mary Ingraham Bunting Fellowship, 1987; GE Award for Younger Writers, 1988; Whiting Writers Award, 1989; Rhode Island Governors Award for Arts, 1990; Lila Wallace Readers Digest Writers Award, 1992. Address: 351 Nayatt Road, Barrington, RI 02806, USA.

WRIGHT Charles Penzel Jr, b. 25 Aug 1935, Pickwick Dam, Tennessee, USA. Writer; Teacher. m. Holly McIntire, 6 Apr 1969, 1 son. Education: BA, Davidson College, 1957; MFA, University of Iowa, 1963; Postgraduate, University of Rome, Italy, 1963-64. Appointments Include: University of California, Irvine, 1966-83; University of Virginia, 1983-. Publications Include: Grave of the Right Hand, 1970; Hard Freight, 1973; Bloodlines, 1975; China Trace, 1977; Southern Cross, 1981; Country Music, selected early poems, 1982; Other Side of the River, 1984; Zone Journals, 1988; The World of the 10,000 Things, 1990. Translations: The Storm, 1978; Orphic Songs, 1984. Contributions to: Numerous magazines and journals. Honours: Edgar Allen Poe Award, Academy of American Poets, 1976; PEN Translation Award, 1979; National Book Award, poetry, 1983; Brandeis Creative Arts Award, poetry, 1987; The Ruth Lilly Poetry Prize, 1993. Memberships Include: PEN American Centre. Address: 940 Locust Avenue, Charlottesville, VA 22901, USA.

WRIGHT David, (John Murray), b. 1920, England. Writer; Poet. Appointments: Staff Member, Sunday Times, 1942-47; Editor, Nimbus, 1955-56; Editor, X Magazine, 1959-62; Gregory Fellow, University of Leeds, 1965-67. Publications include: Poems, 1949; The Forsaken Garden, 1824-1909, 1950; Moral Stories, 1952; The Faber Book of 20th Century Verse, 1953; Monologue of a Deaf Man, 1958; Roy Campbell, 1960; Seven Victorian Poets, 1964; Adam at Evening, 1965; Longer Contemporary Poems, 1966; Minho and North Prtugal: A Portrait and a Guide, 1968; Recollections of the Lakes and the Lake Poets, 1970; Lisbon: A Portrait and a Guide, 1971; A South African Album, 1975; A View of the North, 1976; The Penguin Book of Everyday Verse, 1976; Metrical Observations, 1980; Selected Poems, 1980; The Canterbury Tales, 1985; Elegies, 1990; Deafness, 1990; Poems and Versions, 1992. Honours: Honorary Fellow, Oriel, 1991; Honorary DLitt, 1993. Membership: Royal Society of Literature. Literary Agent: A D Peters Limited. Address: c/o A D Peters Limited, 10 Buckingham Street, Adelphi, London WC2N 6BU, England.

WRIGHT Derek Leslie, b. 24 Feb 1947, Wakefield, England. University Lecturer. m. Renate Lucia Mohrbach, 31 July 1981. Education: BA (1st Class), English, University of Reading, 1971; DipEd, University of Leeds, 1972; MA, American Literature, University of Keele, 1973; PhD, University of Queensland, Australia, 1986. Publications: Ayi Kwei Armah's Africa: The Sources of His Fiction, 1989; Critical Perspectives on Ayi Kwei Armah (editor), 1992; Wole Soyinka Revisited (1993); The Novels of Nuruddin Farah, 1994; New African Writing (editor), 1995. Contributions to: 70 articles on African, American and Commonwealth literatures to various journals; Poems to Westerly and Southern Review. Honours: Outstanding Academic Book Award for Ayi Kwei Armah's Africa, Choice, 1990. Memberships: Modern Languages Association of America; Association for Commonwealth Literature and Language Studies. Address: School of Humanities, Northern Territory University, Darwin, Northern Territory 0909, Australia.

WRIGHT Elinor, (Elinor Lyon), b. 17 Aug 1921, Yorkshire, England. Housewife. m. Peter Wright, 19 Apr 1944, 2 s, 2 d. Education: Lady Margaret Hall, Oxford, 1940-41. Publications include: The Golden Shore, 1957; Daughters of Aradale, 1957; Green Grow the Rushes, 1964; Echo Valley, 1965; The Dream Hunters, 1966; Strangers at the Door, 1967; Hilary's Island, 1948; Wishing Watergate, 1949; The House in Hiding, 1950; We Daren't Go a Hunting, 1951; Run Away Home, 1953; Sea Treasure, 1955; Dragon Castle, 1956; Rider's Rock, 1958; Cathie Runs Wild, 1960; Carver's Journey, 1962; The Day That Got Lost, 1968; The Wishing Pool, 1970; The King of Grey Corrie, 1975; The Floodmakers, 1976. Address: Bron Meini, Harlech, Gwynedd LL46 2YT, Wales.

WRIGHT Graeme Alexander, b. 23 Apr 1943, Wellington, New Zealand. Freelance Editor; Writer. Appointments: Managing Editor, Queen Anne Press, 1972-74; Editor, Freelance Writer, 1974-; Director, John Wisden & Co Limited, 1983-87; Editor, Wisden Cricketers Almanack, 1986-92. Publications include: Great Moments in the Olympics, 1976; Phil Read, The Real Story, 1977; Olympic Greats, 1980; Where Do I Go From Here, 1981; Test Decade, 1972-82; Botham, with Patrick Eagar, 1985; Brown Sauce, 1986; Forty Vintage Years, 1988; Betrayal, The Struggle for Crickets Soul, 1993. Address: 14 Field End Road, Eastcote Pinner, Middlesex HA5 2QL, England.

WRIGHT Judith (Arundell), b. 31 May 1915, Armidale, New South Wales, Australia. Poet; Writer; Editor. Education: University of Sydney. Appointments include: Commonwealth Literary Fund Lecturer, 1952. Publications include: The Moving Image, 1946; Woman to Man, 1949; The Gateway, 1953; The Two Fires, 1955; Australia Bird Poems, 1961; Birds, 1962; Five Senses: Selected Poems, 1963; City Sunrise, 1964; The Other Half, 1966; Poetry from Australian Pergamon Poets, 1969; Collected Poems, 1942-70; Alive: Poems, 1971-72; Fourth Quarter and Other Poems, 1976; The Double Tree: Selected Poems, 1942-76, 1978; Phantom Dwelling, 1986; Essays, Books for Children, Literary Studies and Editions of Australian Poetry. Honours include: D Litt, University of Melbourne, 1988. Address: PO Box 93, Braidwood, New South Wales 2622, Australia.

WRIGHT Kit, b. 1944, Kent, England. Lecturer; Editor; Poet. Education: New College Oxford. Appointments include: Fellow Commoner, Creative Arts, Trinity College, Cambridge, 1977-79. Publications: Treble Poets I, 1974; The Bear Looked Over the Mountain, 1977; Bump Starting the Hearse, 1983; From The Day Room, 1983; Real Rags and Red, 1988; Poems, 1974-83, 1988; Short Afternoons, 1989; Verse for Children: Arthurs Father, 1978; Rabbiting On and Other Poems, 1978; Hot Dog and Other Poems, 1981; Professor Potts Meets the Animals of Africa, 1981; Cat Among the Pigeons, 1987; Editor, Poems for Children. Honours include: Alice Hunt Bartlett Prize; Geoffrey Faber Memorial Award; Arts Council Bursary, 1985; The Hawthorn Prize; W H Heinemann Award. Address: c/o Century Hutchinson Ltd, Brookmont House, 62065 Chandos Place, London WC2N 4NW England.

WRIGHT Laurali Rose, b. 5 June 1939, Saskatoon, Canada. Writer. m. 6 Jan 1962, 2 daughters. Education: University of Calgary; Banff School of Fine Arts; University of British Columbia. Publications: The Suspect, 1985; The Favorite, 1982; Neighbours, 1979; Among Friends, 1984; Sleep While I Sing, 1986; Love in the Temperate Zone, 1988; Chill Rain in January, 1990; Prized Possessions, 1993; A Touch of Panic, 1994. Contributions to: Journalist, Western Canadian Newspapers, 1968-77; Contributor to numerous professional journals, magazines and newspapers, 1977-. Honours: Alberta First Novel Award, 1978; Edgar Allan Poe Best Novel Award, Mystery Writers of America, 1986; Arthur Ellis Award from Crime Writers of Canada, 1991. Memberships: International PEN; Writers Union of Canada; Authors Guild, USA. Literary Agent: Virginia Barber. Address: c/o Writers Union of Canada, 24 Ryerson Avenue, Toronto, Ontario, M5T 2P3, Canada.

WRIGHT Nancy Means, b. New Jersey, USA. Author. m. 2 sons, 2 daughters. Education: AB, Vassar College; MA, Middlebury College. Appointments: Instructor, English, various schools, 1960-87; Proctor Academy; Burlington College; Marist College, New York, 1990. Publications: The Losing, 1973; Down the Strings, 1982; Make Your Own Change, 1985; Vermonters At Their Craft, 1987; Tall Girls Don't Cry, 1990; Split Nipple, 1992. Contributions to: Various journals and magazines. Honours: Scholar, Bread Loaf Writers Conference, 1959; Grant for Novel in Progress Society of Children's Book Writers, 1987. Memberships: President, League of Vermont Writers, 1978-80; Poets

and Writers; Authors League; Society of Children's Book Writers. Address: Box 38, Bristol, VT 05443, USA.

WRIGHT Nicholas, b. 5 July 1940, Cape Town, South Africa (British citizen). Playwright. Education: London Academy of Music and Dramatic Art. Appointments include: Literary Manager, 1987, and Associate Director, 1992, National Theatre, London, England. Publications: Changing Lines, 1968; Treetops, 1978; The Gorky Brigade, 1979; One Fine Day, 1980; The Crimes of Vautrin, after Balzac, 1983; The Custom of the Country, 1983; The Desert Air, 1984; Six Characters in Search of an Author, after Pirandello, 1987; Mrs Klein, 1988; Thérèse Raquin, after Zola, 1990 (plays produced in London, New York, Stockton-on-Tees, Stratford-on-Avon and Washington DC); Also: 99 Plays, Essays, 1992. Honours include: Arts Council Bursary, 1981. Address: 33 Navarino Road, London E8, England.

WRIGHT Peter, b. 30 Mar 1923, Fleetwood, Lancashire, England. Forensic Linguist. m. Patricia May Wright, 3 Apr 1956, 1 s, 3 d. Education: BA, 1949, PhD, 1954, Leeds University; Advanced Diploma, London University, 1960. Appointments: Lecturer, 1965-70, Senior Lecturer, 1970-84, Honorary Senior Lecturer, Fellow in English Dialect Studies, 1984-92, Salford University; Crown of Defence, Analysing from Linguistic Angles Cases for Trial or Appeal. Publications includ: The Lanky Twang, 1974; The Yorkshire Yammer, 1976; Language at Work, 1978; Cockney Dialect and Slang, 1980; 8 Other Dialect Books. Contributions to: Various Magazines and Journals. Honours: Queens Award for Export Achievement, 1992. Memberships: Yorkshire Dialect Society; Lancashire Dialect Society; Lakeland Dialect Society. Address: 30 Broadoak Road, Stockport, Cheshire SK7 3BL, Englnd.

WRIGHT Ronald, b. 12 Sept 1948, Surrey, England. Education: MA,Archaeology and Anthropology, Cambridge University. Appointments: Snider Lecturer, University of Toronto, 1992. Publications Include: Cut Stones and Crossroads: A Journey in the TwoWorlds of Peru, 1984; On Fiji Islands, 1986; Time Among The Maya, 1989; Quechua Phrasebook, 1989; Stolen Continents, 1992; Home and Away, 1993. Contributions to: Numerous articles and book reviews in journals, including: Soho Square III, Times Literary Supplement; The Globe and Mail; New York Times Book Review; The Washington Post; Saturday Night. Honours: Honorary Fellow, Trent University; Finalist, Trillium Book Award, 1990, 1993; Winner, CBC Literary Award (essay), 1991; Gordon Montador Award, 1993. Memberships: Royal Geographical Society, Fellow; Writers Union of Canada; International PEN, Board 1989-91; Latin American Indian Literatures Association; Survival International. Literary Agents: Blake Freidmann Ltd, 37-41 Gower Street, London WC1E 6HH, England; Bella Pomer Agency, 22 Shallmar Blvd, PH2, Toronto, Ontario M5N 2Z8. Address: R.R.1, Campbellcroft, Ontario, L0A 1B0, Canada.

WRIGHT MCKINNEY Judith Arundell, b. 31 May 1915, Armidale, NSW, Australia. Writer. m. Jack Philip McKinney, 1 d. Education: University of Sydney, 1935-37; DLitt, Universities of Queensland, New England, Sydney, Monash, New South Wales. Publications include: Collected Poems, 1971; The Generations of Men, 1959; The Cry for the Dead, 1981; The Double Tree, 1985; Born of Two Conquerors, 1991; Going on Talking, 1992. Contributions to: Numerous Journals and Magazines. Honours: Grace Leven Prize, 1950; Encyclopedia Britannica Literature Prize, 1965; Robert Frost Memorial Medal, 1970; Alice Award, 1980; Queens Medal for Poetry, 1993. Memberships: Australian Society of Authors; PEN Australia. Literary Agent: Angus & Robertson Publishers. Address: PO Box 93, Braidwood, NSW 2622, Australia.

WU Duncan, b. 3 Nov 1961, Woking, Surrey, England. Academic; Writer. Education: BA, Oxford, 1984; DPhil, Oxford, 1991. Appointments: Postdoctoral Fellow, The British Academy, 1991-94. Publications: Wordsworth's Reading 1770-1799, 1993; Romanticism: An Anthology, 1994; Romanticism: A Critical Reader, 1995; William Wordsworth: A Selection, 1994; Six Contemporary Dramatists, 1994. Contributions to: The Library; Essays in Criticism; Notes & Queries; New Statesman & Society; TLS; Sight & Sound; Daily Telegraph. Memberships: Council, Charles Lamb Society; Editor, Charles Lamb Bulletin. Address: St Catherine's College, Oxford, OX1 3UJ, England.

WU William Lung-Shen, b. 1 Sept 1921, Hangchow, China. Aerospace Medical Engineering Design Specialist. 1 s, 1 d. Education: AB, Stanford University, 1943; MD, 1946; MS, Tulane University, 1955; Diploma, US Naval School Aviation Medicine, FL, 1956; USAF School

Aviation Medicine, 1961; UCLA, 1964. Appointments: Board of Directors, Emeritus Institute of Little House, Menlo Park; Member, Planning Research and Development Commission, Redwood City, CA. Publications: 8 books and 100 technical papers, including: Medical Procedures Textbook for Nuclear Operations; Project Apollo Spacecraft Technical Proposal; Applicability of Metal Coordination Principles to Metal Enzymes. Honours: Sigma Xi; J Edgar Hoover Gold Distinguished Public Service Award, American Police Hall of Fame. Memberships: AIAA; IEEE, Vice-Chairman San Diego Chapter, 1962-65; NY Academy Sciences; Institute Environmental Sciences; International University Foundation; International Academic Foundation. Address: Corinthian House 219, 250 Budd Avenue, Campbell, CA 95008, USA.

WUNSCH Josephine M, b. 1914, USA. Author. Publications: Flying Skis, 1962; Passport to Russia, 1965; Summer of Decision, 1968; Lucky in Love, 1970; The Aerie (as J Sloan McLean with Virginia Gillett), 1974; Girl in the Rough, 1981; Class Ring, 1983; Free as a Bird, 1984; Breaking Away, 1985; The Perfect Ten, 1986; Lucky in Love, 1987; Between Us, 1989. Address: 830 Bishop Road, Grosse Pointe Park, MI 48230, USA.

WYLDE. See: CARTER Martin.

WYLIE Betty Jane, b. 21 Feb 1931. Writer. m. William Tennent Wylie, 2 sons, 2 daughters. Education: BA 1950, MA 1952, University of Manitoba. Appointments: Consultant, Puppeteers of America, 1965-73; Writer-in-Library, Burlington, Ontario, 1987-88; Bunting Fellow, Radcliffe College, USA, 1989-90. Publications: Beginnings: A Book for Widows, 1977, 3rd Edition, 1985, US and UK editions; A Place on Earth, 1982; Every Woman's Money Book, 1984; The Book of Matthew, 1985; Something Might Happen, poetry, 1989; New Beginnings, 1991; 20 other books; 30 plays produced. Contributions to: Regularly, most Canadian magazines, 1973-85; Some US magazines. Honours: Education Award for Successfully Single, Ontario Psychology Foundation, 1988; Award for Radio Drama Series Victorian Spice, Canadian Nursing Federation, 1989; University of Manitoba Alumni Jubilee Award, 1990. Memberships: Founding Member, Past Vice-Chair, Treasurer, Playwrights Union of Canada; Past Chair, Writers Union of Canada; ACTRA; US Dramatists Guild; CAPAC. Literary Agent: Farber Literary Agency, New York City, New York, USA. Address: c/o Writers Union of Canada, 24 Ryerson Avenue, Toronto, Ontario, M5T 2P3, Canada.

WYLIE Laura. See: MATTHEWS Patricia Anne.

WYNDHAM Esther. See: LUTYENS Mary.

WYNN John Charles, b. 11 Apr 1920, Akron, Ohio, USA. Professor of Pastoral Theology. m. Rachel Linnell, 27 Aug 1943, 1 son, 2 daughters. Education: BA, 1941, College of Wooster; BD, 1944, Yale University; MA, 1963, EdD, 1964, Columbia University; Post doctoral fellowship, Cornell University, 1972. Appointments: Taught courses in religious journalism at Colgate Rochester Divinity School, 1959-69. Publications: How Christian Parents Face Family Problems, 1955; Sermons on Marriage and the Family, 1956; Pastoral Ministry to Families, 1957; Families in the Church: A Protestant Survey, 1961; Sex, Family & Society in Theological Focus, 1966; Sex Ethics and Christian Responsibility, 1970; Education for Liberation and other Upsetting Ideas, 1977; The Family Therapist, 1987; Family Thearpy in Pastoral Ministry, 1991. Contributions to: Over 300 articles in religious periodicals eg: Christian Century; Journal of Psychology and Theology; Ecumenische Rundschau; Presbyterian Life; The Episcopalian; Religious Education. Honours: Christian Education for Liberation and Other Upsettng Ideas judged best book of 1977 in category of religious education by Religious Media Today; Five of the listed books were bookclub selections by Religious Book Club, Pastoral Psychology Book Club and others. Memberships: The Presbyterian Writers Guild; American Association for Marriage and Family Therapy; Religious Education Association; National Council on Family Relations. Address: 717 Maiden Choice Lane 523, Catonsville, MD 21228, USA.

WYNNE-JONES Tim. Canadian. Publications: The Knot, 1982; Zoom at Sea, 1983; Odd's End, 1985; I'll Make You Small, 1986; Builder of the Moon, 1988; Fastyngange, 1988; Some of the Kinder Planets, 1993; Zoom Away, 1994; Zoom Upstream, 1994. Honours: Governor General's Award, 1993; CLA Book of the Year for Children Award, 1994.

Y

YAEGER Donald William, b. 24 Dec 1962, Hilo, Hawaii, USA. Writer. m. Denise Yaeger, 14 Feb 1994, 1 son, 1 daughter. Education: BS, Ball State University, 1984. Publications: Undue Process: The NC AA's Injustice For All, 1991; Shark Attack: Jerry Tarkanian and His Battles, 1992; Under the Tarnished Dome: How Notre Dame Betrayed Its Ideals For Football Glory, 1993; Tiger In A Lion's Den, 1994. Contributions to: Sports Illustrated; Sporting News. Literary Agent: Basil Kane. Address: PO Box 107, Tallahassee, FL 32302, USA.

YAFFE James, b. 31 Mar 1927, IL, USA. Writer; Teacher. m. Elaine Gordon, 1 Mar 1964, 1 son, 2 daughters. Education: BA, Yale, 1948. Literary Appointments: Writer in Residence, Professor, Solorado College, 1971-. Publications include: The American Jens; Nobody Does You Any Favors; Saul and Morris, Worlds Apart; Mom Meets Her Maker; Cliffhanger. Contributions to: Esquire; Atlantic Monthly; NY Times. Memberships: PEN; Writers Guild of America; History Writers of America; Authors League; American Association of University Professors. Literary Agent: Curtis Brown Ltd. Address: 1215 N Cascade, Colorado Springs, CO 80903, USA.

YANKOWITZ Susan, b. Newark, New Jersey, USA. Writer. m. Herbert Leibowitz, 3 May 1978, 1 son. Education: BA, Sarah Lawrence College; MFA, Yale Drama School. Publications: Plays: Slaughterhouse Play, 1971; Boxes, 1973; Portrait of a Scientist, screenplay, 1974; Terminal, 1975; Alarms, 1988; Night Sky, 1992; Various unpublished stage plays, screenplays, teleplyas; Silent Witness, novel, 1976-77; Taking the Fall, excerpt from novel, 1989; Night Sky, Samuel French, 1992; Night Sky, in Playwriting Women, 1993. Contributions to: Short fiction, monologues, essays in: Gnosis; Solo; Heresies; Interview with Contemporary Women Playwrights; Others. Honours: Joseph Levine Fellowship, Screenwriting, 1968; Vernon Rice Drama Desk Award, Most Promising Playwright, 1969; Grant, Rockefeller Foundation, 1973; Award, 1974; Guggenheim Fellowship, 1975; Residencies, MacDowell Colony, 1975, 1984, 1987, 1990; Creative Writing Fellowship Grant, 1979, US-Japan Fellowship Grant, 1984, National Endowment for the Arts; Grant, Playwriting, NYFA, 1989; Finalist, Best Documentary for Sylvia Path teleplay, WGA, 1989; McKnight Fellowship, Playwriting, 1990; Collaboration Grant for Night Sky, play, TCG, 1990. Memberships: New Dramatists; PEN; Dramatists Guild; Authors Guild; WGA East. Literary Agent: Mary Harden, Bret Adams Ltd, 448 W 42 Street, NY 10036, USA. Address: 205 W 89th Street, New York, NY 10024, USA.

YAOS KEST Itamar, b. 3 Aug 1934, Hungary. Poet; Author. m. Hanna Mercazy, 21 Aug 1958, 1 son, 1 daughter. Education: BA, University of Tel Aviv. Appointments: Founder, Eked Publishing House, 1958. Publications include: Nof Beashah, 1959; Eyes Heritage, 1966; Du Shoresh, 1975; Toward Germany, 1980; Leshon Hanahar Leshon Hayam, 1984; Tubes of Fire, 1986; Poems of the Prayer Book, 1991; Zimun, 1992; In The Window of the Travelling House, 1970; The Shadow of the Bird, 1971; The Hold of Sand, 1972; Anthology of Jewish Hungarian Poetry, 1960; Anthology of Hungarian Poetry, 1985; Anthology of Modern Hungarian Poetry, 1988; Jewish Fate in Hungarian Poetry, 1989. Contributions to: All Israeli Literary Magazines. Honours: Nordow Prize, 1961; Talpir Prize, 1984; Herzel Prize, 1972; Walenrode Prize, 1979; Chulon Prize, 1984; Werthime Prize, 1985; Lea Goldberg Prize, 1990; Prime Minister Prize, 1993. Membership: Association of Hebrew Writers. Literary Agent: Eked, Tel Aviv. Address: Merian Hahashunonout 25, Tel Aviv, Israel.

YARROW Chris. See: MURRAY Terry.

YEATMAN Ted P (Trezevant Player), b. 16 Dec 1951, Nashville, USA. Writer; Historical Researcher. Education: BA 1976, MLS 1977, George Peabody College for Teachers. Appointments: Senior Staff Writer, Peabody Post, 1975-76; Editorial Board, Friends of the James Farm, 1984-93; and others. Publications: Jesse James and Bill Ryan at Nashville, 1981; The Tennessee Wild West: Historical and Cultural Links with the Western Frontier, co-author, 1995; Frank and Jesse James: The Hidden Years, 1996; The Tennessee Wild West: Historical and Cultural Links with the Western Frontier, co-author, 1997. Contributions to: Potomac Magazine; Tennessee Tennesseans, 1984; The Book of Days, 1987, 1988; Read More About It,1989; Civil War Times Illustrated; North/South Trader; Show Me Libraries; James Farm

Journal; True West; Book Page; Quarterly of the National Association & Centre for Outlaw and Lawmen History. Memberships: Potomac Corral of Westerners; Friends of the James Farm, Board of Directors 1982-93, Editorial Board 1984-93; Tennessee Western History & Folklore Society, Co-Director 1981-. Address: 1302 The Terrace, Hagerston, MD 21742, USA.

YEHOSHUA Abraham B, b. 9 Dec 1936, Jerusalem, Israel. Professor. m. Rivka Kirsninski, 1960, 2 sons, 1 daughter. Education: BA, 1960; MA, 1962.Appointments: Co Editor, Keshet, 1965-72; Siman Kria, 1973-; Full Professor, University of Haifa, 1980. Publications include: Death of the Old Man, 1963; Three Days and a Child, 1970; Early in the Summer of 1970, 1973; The Lover, 1978; Between Right and Right, 1981; A Late Divorce, 1984; Possessions, 1986; Five Seasons, 1988; Mister Mani, 1990; The Wall and the Mountain, 1988; Night's Babies, 1992; The Return from India, 1994.Honours: Brener Prize; Alterman Prize; Bailik Prize; Winner of National Jewish Book Award, 1990, 93; Winner of Israeli Booker, 1992; Best Jewish Book of Year, 1993; Israel Prize for Literature, 1995. Literary Agent: Leipman Zurich, Switzerland. Address: 102A Sea Road, Haifa, Israel 34736.

YELDHAM Peter, b. Gladstone, New South Wales, Australia. Playwright; Screen-writer. m. Marjorie Crane, 27 Oct 1948, 1 son, 1 daughter. Publications: Stage Plays: Birds on the Wing, 1969-70; She Won't Lie Down, 1972; Fringe Benefits, (co-author), 1973; Away Match, (co-author), 1974; Seven Little Australians, 1988; Once A Tiger, 1994; Feature Films include: The Comedy Man, 1963; The Liquidator, 1965; Age of Consent, 1968; Touch and Go, 1979; Television Plays include: Reunion Day; Stella; Thunder on the Snowy; East of Christmas; The Cabbage Tree Hat Boys; The Battlers; Television Series include: Run From the Morning, 1977; Golden Soak, 1978; Ride On, Stranger, 1979; The Timeless Land, 1979; Also: Levkas Man, 1980; Sporting Chance, 1981; 1915, 1982; All the Rivers Run, 1983; Flight into Hell, 1984; Tusitala, The Lancaster Miller Affair, 1985; The Far Country, 1985; Captain James Cook, 1986; The Alien Years, 1987; Naked Under Capricorn, 1988; The Heroes, 1988; The Heroes, The Return, 1991; Novel: Reprisal, 1994. Honours: Sammy Award, Best Television Series in Australia, 1979; Writers Guild, Best Adaption, 1980, 1983, 1986; Penguin Award, Best Script, 1982; Writers Guild, Best Original mini-series, 1989; Order of Australia Medal, 1991. Memberships: Writers Guild, Australia; British Writers Guild. Literary Agent: Lemon, Unna & Durbridge, England; Rick Raftos Management, Sydney, Australia. Address: 21 Glover Street, Mosman, Sydney, Australia.

YGLESIAS Jose, b. 29 Nov 1919, Florida, USA. Writer. 1 son. Education: Black Mountain College, 1946-47. Appointments: Regents Lecturer, University of California at Santa Barbara, 1973. Publications: A Wake in Ybor City, 1963; The Goodbye Land, 1967; In the Fist of the Revolution, 1968; An Orderly Life, 1968; Down There, 1970; The Truth About Them, 1971; Double Double, 1976; The Kill Price, 1977; The Franco Years, 1978; Home Again, 1987; Tristan and the Hispanics, 1989; Race: (Play) Adaptation of Studs Ferkel's Book, 1993. Contributions to: The New Yorker; The Nation; New York Times Magazine; New York Review of Books; Esquire; The New Republic. Honours: Guggenheim Fellowship, 1970, 1976; National Endowment for the Arts, 1974; Honorary Doctor of Humane Letters, University of South Florida, 1990. Literary Agent: Maria Carvainis Agency. Address: 55 W 11th St, New York, NY 10011, USA.

YOFFE Elkhonon, b. 16 April 1928, Riga, Latvia. Musicologist; Librarian. m. Lydia Yoffe, 27 Feb 1955, 1 son. Education: Jazep Medin Music School, Riga, 1948; MA Percussion 1952, MA Musicology 1954, Latvian State Conservatoire, 1954. Appointments: Lecturer, Music History, Riga Ballet School, 1965-72; Lecturer, Latvian Philharmonia, 1972-78; Assistant Librarian, The Juilliard School, New York City, 1979-82; Librarian, Detroit Symphony Orchestra, 1982-. Publications: Percussion Instruments, 1962; Marger Zarius, Ignoramus Suite, 1965; Tchaikovsky in America, 1986; Ruta U God I Wanted to Live, translation, Russian, 1989; K Kondrashin, Conductors Readings of Tchaikovsky's Symphonies, translation, English, unpublished. Contributions to: Sovetskaya Muzika, Moscow; Latvieshu Muzika, Riga; Kontinent, Paris. Memberships: USSR Composers' Union, 1967-78; Major Orchestra Librarian Association (MOLA), 1982. Address: 463 Coolidge Road, Birmingham, MI 48009, USA.

YOGMAN Michael, b. 1 Mar 1947, New Jersey, USA. Physician. m. Elizabeth Ascher, 9 June 1985, 2 daughters. Education: BA 1968, Williams College; MD 1972, Yale Medical School; MSc 1978, Harvard School of Public Health. Publications: Co-Editor, In Support of Families,

1986; Affective Development in Infancy, 1986; Follow Up Management of the High-Risk Infant, 1987. Contributions to: New England Journal of Medicine; Paediatrics; Journal of Paediatrics; Paediatric Research; American Journal of Public Health; Journal of American Academy of Child Psychiatry. Memberships: Society for Paediatric Research; American Academy of Paediatrics; Society for Research in Child Development; Ambulatory Paediatric Association; World Association for Infant Psychiatry; International Conference on Infant Studies. Address: 14 Wyman Road, Cambridge, MA 02138, USA.

YOLEN Jane, b. 11 Feb 1939, USA. Author; Editor; Storyteller. m. 2 Sept 1962, 2 sons, 1 daughter. Education: BA, English Literature, Smith College, 1960; M.Ed., University of Massachustts, 1976. Appointments: Editor-in-Chief of Imprint Jane Yolen Books; Harcourt Brace Publishers, 1988. Publications: Pirates in Petticoat, 1963; The Emperor & The Kite, 1968; The Girl Who Cried Flowers, 1974; Hundredth Dove, 1976; Commander Toad in Space, 1980; Dragon's Blood, 1982; Cards of Grief, 1985; Merlin's Books, 1986; Owl Moon, 1987; Sister Light, Sister Dark, 1989; Dove Isabeau, 1989; The Devils Arithemtic, 1990; White Jenna, 1990; The Dragon's Boy, 1990; Encounter, 1991; Briar Rose, 1992; Here There Be Dragons, 1993; The Girl in The Golden Bower, 1994; Grandad Bill's Song, 1994; and 130 other books. Contributions to: New York Times Book Review; Horn Book; Washington Post; Fantasy and Science Fiction Magazine; Issac Asimov's SF Magazine; Parabola Magazine; Parent's Choice Magazine; Children's Literature in Education; New Advocate; others. Honours: National Book Award Nomination, 1974; Mythopoeic Society Award, 1986, 1993; Golden Kite Award, 1974; Christopher Medal, 1979; Daedlus Award, 1987; World Fantasy Award, 1987; Kerlan Award, 1988; Smith College Medal, 1988; Caldecott Medal Book, 1988; Regina Medal, 1992; Keene State Children's Book Award, 1995; Honorary LLD. Memberships: Children's Literature Association, Board of Directors; Science Fiction Writers of America, President, 1986-88; Society of Children's Book Writers, Board of Directors; Mystery Writers of America; Author's Guild; NAAPS. Agent: Curtis Brown Ltd, New York, USA. Address: Phoenix Farm, Box 27, Hatfield, MA 01038, USA.

YORK Alison. See: NICOLE Christopher Robin.

YORK Andrew. See: NICOLE Christopher Robin.

YORK Georgia. See: HOFFMAN Lee.

YORKE Katherine. See: ELLERBECK Rosemary Anne L'Estrange.

YORKE Margaret. See: NICHOLSON Margaret Bede.

YOUNG Allan Edward, b. 21 June 1939, New York, USA. University Professor. m. Eleanor Podheiser, 16 Sept 1962, 1 son, 2 daughters. Education: BA 1961, SUNY at Binghamton, New York; MBA 1963, PhD 1967, Columbia University. Publications: The Contribution of the New York Based Securities Industry to the Economy of the City State, 1985; The Financial Manager, 1987; Guidelines for the Financing of Industrial Investment Projects in Developing Countries, 1995. Contributions to: Over 60 articles in leading academic and professional journals in the fields of Financial Management, Securities Markets & Investments. Honours: Alexander Hamilton Chair in Entrepreneurship, Budapest, Hungary (Fulbright Lectureship and Consultancy); Trust Bank Chair in Accounting and Finance, Lincoln University, Canterbury, New Zealand. Memberships: Many economic and finance societies. Address: 27 Ely Drive, Fayetteville, NY 13066, USA.

YOUNG Axel. See: MCDOWELL Michael.

YOUNG Bertram Alfred, b. 20 Jan 1912, London, England. Freelance Writer. Appointments: Assistant Editor, 1949-62, Drama Critic, 1962-64, Punch; Drama Critic, 1964-78, Arts Editor, 1971-77, Financial Times. Publications: Bechuanaland, 1966; Cabinet Pudding, 1967; The Rattigan Version, 1986; Tooth and Claw, 1958; The Mirror up to Nature, 1982. Contributions to: Punch; Numerous Other Professional Journals and Magazines. Honour: OBE, 1980. Memberships: Critics Circle; Society of Authors; Garrick Club. Address: Clyde House, Station Street, Cheltenham, Glos GL590 3LX, England.

YOUNG Carter Travis, See: CHARBONNEAU Louis H.

YOUNG Donald, b. 29 June 1933, Indianapolis, Indiana, USA. Editor; Writer. Education: BA, Indiana University; MA, Butler University.

Appointments: Senior Editor, Encyclopedia Americana, 1967-77; Managing Editor, Aperture Foundation, 1986-87. Publications: American Roulette, 1965; Adventure in Politics (Editor), 1970; The Great American Desert (Author & Photography), 1980; The Sierra Club Guides to the National Parks, Volumes 3,4,5 (Editor), 1984-86; The Sierra Club Book of Our National Parks (co-author), 1990; Natural Mounments of America, 1990; Historic Monuments of America, 1990; Natural Parks of America, 1994. Contributions to: Numerous magazines & journals. Address: 166 East 61st Street, Apt. 3-C, New York, NY 10021, USA.

YOUNG Ed (Tse-Chun), b. 1931. Childrens Author & Illustrator. Publications: The Rooster's Horns: A Chinese Puppet Play, 1978; The Terrible Ngung Gwama: A Chinese Folktale, 1978; The Lion & the Mouse, 1979; High On a Hill: a Book of Chinese Riddles, 1980; Up a Tree, 1983; The O Bone, 1984; Lon Po Po, 1989; Seven Blind Mice, 1992; Moon Mother: a Native American Creation tale, 1993; Red Thread, 1993; Little Plum, 1994; Night Visitors, 1995. Honours: Caldecott Medal, 1990; Boston Globe/Horn Book Awards, 1990, 1992.

YOUNG Hugo John Smelter, b. 13 Oct 1938, England. Journalist. m. (1) Helen Mason, 1966, dec, 1 s, 3 d. (2) Lucy Waring, 1990. Education: BA, Balliol College, Oxford. Appointments include: Yorkshire Post, 1961; Chief Leader Writer, 1966-77, Political Editor, 1973-84, Joint Deputy Editor, 1981-84, Sunday Times; Political Columnist, The Guardian, 1984-; Director, The Tablet, 1985-; Chairman, Scott Trust, 1989. Publications: The Zinoviev Letter, 1966; Journey to Tranquility, 1969; The Crossman Affair, 1974; No Minister, 1982;But, Chancellor, 1984; The Thatcher Phenomenon, 1986; One of Us, 1989. Honours: Harkness Fellow, 1963; Congressional Fellow, 1964; Columnist of Year, 1980, 1983, 1985; What the Papers Say Award, 1985; DLitt Honor, 1993. Address: c/o The Guardian, 119 Farringdon Road, London EC1, England.

YOUNG Ian George, b. 5 Jan 1945, London, England. Writer; Editor. Appointments: Director, Catalyst Press, 1969-80; Director, TMW Communications, 1990-. Publications: Poetry: White Garland, 1969; Year of the Quiet Sun, 1969; Double Exposure, 1970, 1974; Cool Fire, 1970; Lions in the Stream, 1971; Some Green Moths, 1972; The Male Muse, 1973; Invisible Words, 1974; Common-or-Garden Gods, 1976; The Son of the Male Muse, 1983; Sex Magick, 1986; Fiction: On The Line, 1981; Non-fiction: The Male Homosexual in Literature, 1975, 1982; Overlooked & Underrated, 1981; Gay Resistance, 1985; The AIDS Dissidents, 1993; The Stonewall Experiment, 1995. Address: 2483 Gerrard Street East, Scarborough, Ontario, Canada, M1N 1W7.

YOUNG John Karl, b. 15 Aug 1951, Minneapolis, Minnesota, USA. Associate Professor of Anatomy. m. Paula Jean Spesock, 3 July 1977, 2 sons. Education: University South California, 1968-69; BS 1972, Cornell University; PhD 1977, UCLA; Postdoctoral research appointment, University Minnesota 1977-79. Publications: Cells: Amazing Forms and Functions, 1990; Plasticity in the Nervous System, by B Kotlyar, translated from Russian by J K Young, 1992; Hormones: Molecular Messengers, 1994; Development, Aging and Disease: A New Rationale for an Intervention Strategy, by V Dilman, translated by J K Young, 1994. Contributions to: 27 papers in various scientific journals including: Oestrogen and the etiology of anorexia nervosa, Neuroscience and Biobehavioural Reviews 15, 1991. Memberships: American Association of Anatomists; American Physiological Society. Address: Department of Anatomy, Howard University, 520 W Street, NW, Washington DC 20059, USA.

YOUNG Michael Dunlop, (Lord Young of Dartington), b. 9 Aug 1915, Manchester, England. Sociologist. m. (1) Joan Lawson, 1945, 2 sons, 1 daughter. (2) Sasha Moorsom, 1960, 1 son, 1 daughter. Education: BSc, London School of Economics; MA, Cambridge University; PhD, London University. Publications include: Family and Kinship in East London, 1957; Rise of the Meritocrcy, 1958; Metronomic Society, 1988; Family & Class in a London Suburb, 1960; The Symmetrical Family, 1973; Innovation and Research in Education, 1965; Learning Begins at Home, 1968; Forecasting and the Social Sciences, 1968; The Metronomic Society, 1988; Life After Work with Tom Schuller, 1990. Contributions to: New Society; New Statesman; Society; Samizdat. Honours: Honorary LittD, 1965; D Open University, 1973; Honorary DLitt, 1974; Honorary LLD, 1982; Honorary Fellow, Queen Mary College, 1983. Address: 18 Victoria Park Square, Behtnal Green, London E2 9PF, England.

YOUNG Rose. See: HARRIS Marion Rose.

YOUNG Wayland. See: **KENNET Wayland Hilton Young.**

YOUNG-BRUEHL Elisabeth, b. 3 Mar 1946, Maryland, USA. Writer; Professor. Education: BA, MA & Phd in Philosophy, New School for Social Research, New York City. Appointments: Wesleyan University 1974-91; Haverford College, 1991-. Publications: Hannah Arendt: For Love of the World, 1982; Anna Freud: A Biography, 1988; Mind and the Body Politics, 1989; Freud on Women, 1990; Creative Characters, 1991; Vigil, novel, 1983; Global Cultures, 1994. Honours: Harcornt Award for Biography, 1982; Present Tense Literary Award, 1982; National Endowment for the Humanities, 1985; Guggenheim Foundation, 1986. Memberships: Authors Guild. Literary Agent: Georges Borchardt, New York City. Address: Alden Park PH03A, 5500 Wissahickon Avenue, Philadelphia, PA 19144, USA.

YULE John, b. 11 April 1923, Melbourne, Victoria, Australia. Artist (Painter of Pictures); Writer. Education: Leaving Honours, Scotch College, Melbourne, 1940; Scholarship to Ormond College, University of Melbourne. Publication: The Living Canvas, 1986. Contributions to: Ern Malley's Journal, 1953; Several to Overland, 1982-88; Several to Melbourne Age Literary Section, 1987-88; Tucker, catalogue essay, Diggins Gallery Publication, 1990. Address: 16 Madden St, Albert Park, Victoria 3206, Australia.

Z

ZAHNISER Edward DeFrance (Ed Zahniser), b. 11 Dec 1945, Washington, District of Columbia, USA. Writer; Editor. m. Ruth Christine Hope Duewel, 13 July 1968, 2 sons. Education: AB, Greenville (Illinois) College, 1976; Officers Basic Course, Defense Information School, 1971. Appointments: Poetry Editor, The Living Wilderness Magazine, 1972-75; Founding Editor, Some Of Us Press, Washington, District of Columbia, 1972-75; Arts Editor, Good News Paper, 1981-; Editor, Arts and Kulchur, 1989-91; Curator, Public Hanging, Editor, Exhibit Catalog, 1989; Poetry Reader, Antietam Review, 1992-. Publications: The Ultimate Double Play, poems, 1974; I Live In a Small Town (with Justin Duewel-Zahniser), 1984; The Way to Heron Mountain, poems, 1986, reprint, 1989; Sheenjek and Denali, poems, 1990; Jonathan Edwards..., artist book, 1991; Howard Zahniser's Where Wilderness Preservation Began: Adirondack Wilderness Writings (editor), 1992; Shepherstown Historic Firsts, 1993; Readers Digest Book of North American Trees, (contributing editor), 1993; A Calendar of Worship & Other Poems, 1995; Several handbooks of US National Parks and portions of illustrated books on natural history topics in North America. Contributions to: Hollins Critic; Journal of Western American Literature; Carolina Quarterly; Amicus Journal; Wilderness; Antietam Review; Rolling Coulter; Riverrun; December; Backcountry; North of Upstate; Trout; Moneysworth; Mother Earth News; Snowy Egret; Hobo Jungle; Metropolitan; Throw Small Bullets; Sandscript; Oxygen 8; Psychopoetica; Others. Honours: Woodrow Wilson Fellow, 1967; 1st and 2nd Prizes in Poetry Collection, Narrative Poetry, West Virginia Writers Annual Competitions, 1989, 1991, 1992. Address: c/o Atlantis Rising, ARC Box G, Shepherdstown, WV 25443, USA.

ZAHORSKI Kenneth James, b. 23 Oct 1939, Cedarville, Indiana, USA. Professor of English; Director of Faculty Development. m. Marijean Allen, 18 Aug 1962, 2 daughters. Publications: The Fantastic Imagination, vols I&II, 1977-78; Dark Imaginings, 1978; Fantasy Literature, 1979; The Phoenix Tree, 1980; Visions of Wonder, 1981; Alexander, Walton, Morris: A Primary and Secondary Bibliography, 1981; Fantasists on Fantasy, 1984; Peter S Beagle, 1988; The Sabbatical Mentor, 1994. Contributions to: College English; CLA Journal; Wisconsin English Journal; and others. Honours: Leonard Ledvina Outstanding Teacher Award, 1974; ALA Outstanding Reference Book Award, 1979; Mythopoeic Society Special Scholarship Award, 1985; Donald B King Distinguished Scholar Award, 1987. Memberships: Professional and Organizational Development Network in Higher Education; Wisconsin Council of Teachers of English; Modern Language Association of America; National Council of Teachers of English; American Association for Higher Education. Address: 205 Arrowhead Drive, Green Bay, WI 54301, USA.

ZALBEN BRESKIN Jane, b. 21 April 1950, USA. Author; Artist; College Teacher. m. 25 Dec 1969, 2 sons. Education: BA, Art, Queen's College; Pratt Graphics Centre, 1972. Appointments: Assistant Art Director, Dial Press, 1971; Designer, TY Crowell, 1974; Art Director, Scribners, 1975; Freelance, 1976-. Publications: Cecilia's Older Brother, 1973; Lyle and Humus, 1974; Jeremiah Knucklebones by Jan Wahl, 1974; Basil and Hillary, 1975; An Invitation to the Butterfly Ball: A Counting Rhyme, by Jane Yolen, 1976; Jabberwocky, by Lewis Carroll, 1977; Penny and the Captain, 1977; Norton's Nightime, 1979; Will You Count the Stars Without Me, 1979; All in the Woodland Early: An ABC by Jane Yolen, 1979; Oliver and Alison's Week, 1980; Oh Simple!, 1981; Porcupine's Christmas Blues, 1982, Maybe it will Rain Tomorrow, 1982; Here's Looking at You, Kid, 1987; The Walrus and the Carpenter, by Lewis Carroll, 1986; Water from the Moon, 1987; Beni's First Chanukah, 1988; Earth to Andrew O Blechman, 1989; Happy Passover, Rosie, 1989; Leo and Blossom's Sukkah, 1990; Goldie's Purim, 1991; The Fortune Teller in 5B, 1991; Beni's Little Library: Jewish Holiday Boxed Set paperback, 1991; Buster Gets Braces, 1992; Inner Chimes: Poems on Poetry, 1992; Happy New Year, Beni, 1993; Papa's Latkes, 1994; Beni's First First Chanukah, 1994; Miss Violet's Shining Day, 1995; Pearl Plants a Tree, 1995; Beni's Family Cookbook, 1996; Unfinished Dreams, 1996. Contributions to: various journals and magazines including: Society of Children's Book Writers Bulletin Jewish World; Gurado IRA magazine, 1994. Honours: International Reading Association, Children's Choice Award (twice); AIGA; Art Directors Club; Judge for Golden Kite Award, 1990; Sydney Taylor Honour award, 1989; IRA, Parent's Magazine, Bank Street for Inner Chimes, 1993; Best Books New Yourk Public Library and Bank Street, 1991. Memberships: Society of Children's Book Writers. Agent: Curtis Brown Ltd, 10 Astor Place, New York, 10003. Address: 70 South Road, Sands Point, NY 11050, USA.

ZALYGIN Sergey Pavlovich, b. 6 Dec 1913, Durasovka, Russia. Writer; Ecologist. Education: Omsk Agricultural Institute. Appointments: Editor in Chief, Novy Mir Magazine, 1986-; Chairman, Nongovernmental Ecological Organization of Scientists and Publicists, Association Ecology and Peace, 1987. Publications include: Stories, 1941; Spring of 1954, 1955; Altai Paths, 1959; On the Irtich, 1964; The Saulty Revaine, 1967; My Poet, 1969; The Commission, 1975; After the Storm, 1985; New Collection of 6 Volumes of Novels, Stories and Essays, 1991-92; Many Others. Contributions to: A Series of Articles on Ecology. Honours: State Prize, 1968; Sergi Radonezhsky Orthodox Order, 1993; Various Others. Membership: Russian Academy of Sciences, 1991; Academy of Sciences, New York, 1992; Russian Union of Writers. Address: 28/3 The Lenin Prospect, Moscow, Russia.

ZAND Roxane, (Hakimzadeh), b. 21 Mar 1952, Tehran, Iran. Educator; Academic. m. Hakim Zadeh, 7 Nov 1978, 2 s. Education: B, Harvard University, 1975; DPhil, 1994. Publications: Persin Requiem. Contributions to: Jaso; Feminist Review; Nimeye Digar Feminist Quarterly. Memberships: Translators Society; Harvard Club of London. Address: 9 Templewood Avenue, London NW3 7UY, England.

ZASTROW Charles H, b. 30 July 1942, Wausau, Wisconsin, USA. Author; Professor. Education: BS Psychology 1964, MSW Social Work 1966, PhD Social Welfare 1971, University of Wisconsin-Madison. Appointments: Professor, University of Wisconsin-Whitewater 1971-; Social Work Consulting Editor, Nelson-Hall Publishers 1987-; Associate Editor, International Journal of Comparitave and Applied Criminal Justice 1976-. Publications: The Personal Problem Solver, co-author, 1977; Talk to Yourself, 1979; Social Work with Groups, 3rd ed, 1992; Introduction to Social Welfare, 4th ed, 1990; Understanding Human Behaviour and the Social Environment, co-author, 1994; The Practice of Social Work, 4th ed, 1992; Social Problems, 3rd ed, 1992; Introduction to Social Work and Social Welfare, 5th ed, 1993; You Are What You Think, 1993. Contributions to: 36 articles published in professional journals. Honour: Excellence in Teaching Award 1987 at University of Wisconsin-Whitewater. Memberships: National Association of Social Workers; Academy of Certified Social Workers; Council of Social Work Education; Register of Clinical Social Workers. Address: Social Work Depatment, University of Wisconsin-Whitewater, Whitewater, WI 53704, USA.

ZELENY Jindrich, b. 13 Nov 1922, Bitovany, Professor. m. Jirina Topicova, 21 Oct 1946, 2 d. Education: PhD, Charles University, 1948. Publications: The Logic of Marx, 1980; 5 Books on Epistemology in Czech. Contributions to: Many Magazines and Journals. Honour: State Prize for Humanities, 1988. Memberships: Steering Committee of Federation Internationale des Societes Philosophiques; Internationale Gesellschaft fur Dialektische Philiosophie; Czechoslovakia Philosophical Society. Address: Soukenicka 29, 11000 Prague 1, Czechoslovakia.

ZELLER Frederic, b. 20 May 1924, Berlin (British Subject). Writer; Sculpter. m. (2) 21 Jan 1989. Education: BA, Birbeck College, London University, England. Publications: When Time Ran Out: Coming of Age in the Third Reich, HB, US, UK, Germany, 1989, SB, US, Holland, 1989, 1990 US; (work in progress): Friendly Enemy Alien (The Fearful Forties). Honours: New American Writing Award by the National Endowment of the Arts , 1989; Selected by the US Information Agency as part of 1990 exhibit, travelling to New Delhi, Buenos Aires, Cairo, Beijing, Moscow & Zurich. Memberships: Federation of Modern Painters & Sculptors, New York; Artists' Equity Association, New York. Literary Agent: Carole Mann Agency, NYC. Address: 775 Sixth Avenue, New York City, NY 10001, USA.

ZEMANEK Alicja, b. 2 Aug 1949, Bielsko Biata, Poland. Scientist; Poetess. m. Bogdan Zemanek, 30 July 1981. Education: Doctor, Biological Science, 1977, PhD, 1977, Jagiellonian University. Publications: Egzotyczny Ogrod na Wesotej, 1986; Listopad w Bibliotece, 1988; Dzien w Którym Zniknetam, 1990; Wakacje w Krakowie, 1991; Podobni do zagajnika olch, 1993. Contributions to: Zycie Literackie; Poezja; Pismo Literacko; Artystyczne; Lektura; And Other. Memberships: Zwiazek Literatów Polskich; Polskie Towarzystowo Botaniczne. Address: ul Kopernika 27, 31 501 Cracow,

Poland.

ZEPHANIAH Benjamin, b. 1958, Birmingham, England. Poet; Performer. Education: Handsworth Green, Birmingham. Appointments include: Founding Member, Page One Book Shop, London. Publications include: Pen Rhythm, 1980; The Dread Affair: Collected Poems, 1985; Radio Play, Hurricane Dub, 1989; Television Play, The Great Picture Chase, 1990; Inna Liverpool, 1980; Rasta Time in Palestine, 1990. Honours include: Nominations for Literary Chairs, Oxford and Cambridge Universities. Address: c/o Fletcher & Boyce, 1 Kingsway House, Albion Road, London N16 0TA, England.

ZETFORD Tully. See: **BULMER Henry Kenneth.**

ZHANG Chengzhi, b. 3 Sept 1948, Beijing, China. Writer. m. 1 May 1977, 1 daughter. Education: Beijing University, 1975; Chinese Academy of Social Sciences. Appointments: Council, Chinese Writers Association, 1984; Member, Society of Beijing Moslems Culture, 1989. Publications include: Old Bridge, 1984; Zhang Chengzhi, 1986; Tours to Inner Mongolian Grassland, 1986; River of the North, 1987; Golden Farm, 1987; Yellow Mud House, 1987; Beautiful a Twinkling, 1987; The Representative Works of Zhang Cheng Zhi, 1988; The Black Steed, 1989; The Green Land, 1989. Contributions to: The Chinese Western Novel, The Novels Selected Readings. Honours: National Award, Stories, 1978; National Award, Novellas, 1981-82, 1983-84. Memberships: Chinese Writers Association; Chinese Society for Mongolian History; Chinese Society for Central Asian Culture. Address: c/o Chinese Writers Association, Sha Tan Bei Jie No. 2, 1000720 Beijing, China.

ZHANG Jie, Education: BA, 1960, China Peoples University. Publications include: Novels, Heavy Wings, 1981; Only One Sun, 1988; Collection of Short Stories and Novellas; Zhang Jies Collection of short Stories and Movie Scrips, 1980; On a Green Lawn, 1983; A Chinese Woman in Europe, 1989; You Are a Friend of My Soul, 1990; Published Abroad, As Long As Nothing Happens, Nothing Will; The Ark; Love Must Not Be Forgotten; Only One Sun; Smaraged Novella; Interior Heat, 1992; In The Twlight, 1994; Gone is the One Who Held My Dearest in the Worlds, 1994. Honours: National Short Story Awards, 1978, 79, 83; Maodun National Award for Novels, 1985; National Award for Novellas, 1985; Malaparte Literary Prize, 1989. Memberships: Chinese Association of writers; Beijing Association of Writers; International PEN; Beijing Political Conference; Am Academy and Institute of Arts & Letters. Address: International Dept, China Writers Association, 2 Shatan Beijie, Beijing 1000720, China.

ZIEGLER Philip Sandeman, b. 24 Dec 1929, Ringwood, Hampshire, England. Writer. Education: New College Oxford. Publications: The Black Death, 1968; Melbourne, 1976; Diana Cooper, 1981; Mountbatten, 1985; The Sixth Great Power Barings, 1762-1929, 1988; Duchess of Dino; Addington; William IV; Omdurman; Crown and People; King Edward VIII, 1990; Harold Wilson, 1993. Contributions to: Reviews and Articles, The Times; The Times Literary Supplement; The Daily Telegraph; The Spectator. Honours: Royal Society of Literature, Fellow, 1975; W H Heinemann Award, 1976; Fellow, Royal Historical Society, 1979; Honorary DLitt, Westminister College. Memberships: Royal Literary Fund. Literary Agent: Curtis Brown. Address: 22 Cottesmore Gardens, London, W8 5PR, England.

ZIMMERMAN Robert Allen. See: **DYLAN Bob.**

ZINDEL Bonnie, b. 3 May 1943, New York City, USA. Writer. m. Paul Zindel, 25 Oct 1973, 1 son, 1 daughter. Education: BA, Psychology, Hofstra University, 1964. Appointments include: Public Relations Director, Cleveland Playhouse, 1969-72; Producer, Intermission Feature (Boston Symphony), Station WCLVA-FM, Cleveland, 1970-72. Publications: A Star for the Latecomer, 1980; Hollywood Dream Machine, 1984. Plays: I Am A Zoo, 1976; Lemons in the Morning, 1983; The Latecomer, 1985; Adriana Earthlight, Student Shrink, 1987. Memberships: Playwrights Unit, Actors Studio; Women in Film; Authors Guild. Literary Agent: Curtis Brown. Address: c/o Curtis Brown, 10 Astor Place, New York, NY 10003, USA.

ZINN Howard, b. 24 Aug 1922, NY, USA. Historian; Writer. m. Roslyn Shechter, 30 Oct 1944, 1 s, 1 d. Education: BA, 1951, MA, 1952, PhD, 1958, Columbia University. Publications: A Peoples History of the US, 1980; Declarations of Independence, 1990; The Politics of History, 1990; Failure to Quit, 1993; Vietnam: The Logic of Withdrawal, 1967; Disobedience & Democracy, 1968. Contributions to: About 60.

Honours: Albert Beveridge Award, 1959; Thomas Merton Award, 1991. Literary Agent: Rick Balkin. Address: 29 Fern Street, Auburndale, MA 02166, USA.

ZIOLKOWSKI Theodore Joseph, b. 30 Sept 1932, USA. Professor of Comparative Literature, Princeton University; Scholar. m. Yetta B Goldstein, 26 Mar 1951, 2 sons, 1 daughter. Education: AB, 1951, AM, 1952, Duke University; University of Innsbruck, Austria, 1952-53; PhD, Yale University, USA, 1957. Publications: Novels of Hermann Hesse, 1965; Dimensions of the Modern Novel, 1969; Fictional Transfigurations of Jesus, 1972; Disenchanted Images, 1977; The Classical German Elegy, 1980; Varieties of Literary Thematics, 1983; German Romanticcism and It's Institutions, 1990; Virgil and the Moderns, 1993; Also: Der Schriftsteller Hermann Hesse, 1979; Hermann Broch, 1964. Contributions to: Numerous articles & reviews, US & European journals. Honours: James Russell Lowell Prize, criticism, Modern Language Association, 1973; Howard T Behrman Award, humanities, 1978; Wilbur Lucius Cross Medal, Yale University, 1982; Gold Medal, Goeteh Institute, Federal Republic of Germany, 1987; Henry Allen Moe Prize, American Philosophical Society, 1988. Memberships: Academy of Literary Studies; American Philosophical Society; Past President, Modern Language Association; Gottingen Academy of Sciences; American Academy of Arts & Sciences; Austrian Academy of Sciences. Address: 36 Bainbridge Street, Princeton, New Jersey 08540, USA.

ZOBEL Louise Purwin, b. 10 Jan 1922. Author; Lecturer; Teacher. m. 14 Nov 1943, Dr Jerome Freemont Zobel, 1 s, 3 d. Education: BA, Journalism, Stanford University, 1943; MA, Communication, 1976. Literary Appointments: Writer and Editor at United Press Bureau; Editor, Magazine, Association of College Unions, International, 1972-73; Cruise Enrichment Lecturer & Writing Teacher, Royal Viking Lines & Princess Cruises, 1974-83; Instructor, Writer's Digest Correspondence School, 1982-90; Keynote Speaker, Travel Lecturer, TV Personality. Publications: The Travel Writer's Handbook, 1980, revised, 1992; Let's Have Fun In Japan, 1982; Chapters in other books. Contributions to: House Beautiful; Parents Magazine; Brides Magazine; Writers Digest; The Writer; American Home; Better Homes and Gardens; New England Review; Los Angeles Times; Christian Science Monitor; San Francisco Examiner; Many others. Honours: Phi Beta Kappa, 1943; Sigma Delta Chi Award For Scholarship, 1943; Prize, Writers Digest National Article Contest, 1967, 1975, 1978, 1992, 1994; National Writers Club Contest, 1976. Memberships: AAUW, former vice-president; Women in Communication; California writers Club, Former Vice-President; ASJA; Travel Journalists Guild; International Food Wine & Travel Writers Association. Literary Agent: Michael Larsen, Elizabeth Pomada. Address: 23350 Sereno Ct, Villa #30, Cupertino, CA 95014, USA.

ZUROWSKI Andrzej, b. 24 Sept 1944, Poland. Essayist; Theatre Critic. m. Magda Oller, 23 Aug 1988, 1 s, 3 d. Education: MA, 1967; phD, 1973. Appointments: Chief Artistic Programmes, Polish TV, 1967-90;Commentator, 1990-; Lecturer, Gdansk University, 1975-77, 1986-. Publications include: Spotkaine z Mitem, 1976; Teatr Wybrzeze, 1946-76, 1976; Ludzie w Reflektorach, 1982; Zza Kulis Szeptem, 1982; Zasoby i Sposoby, 1988; Czytajac Szekspira, 1994. Contributions to: Dialog; Kultura; Literatura; Zycle; Literackie; Shakespeare Quarterly; Contemporary Review; New Theatre Quarterly; Teatr; Sipario; International Theatre Year Book. Honours: Polish Theatre Critics Club Award, 1970, 77, 88; Gdansk Voivode Award, 1981, 84; Edward Csato Award, 1984; Fakty Award, 1984; Gdansks Lord Mayor Award, 1988; Gdansks Patron of Art Society, Artistic Prize, 1988; Medals. Memberships: Union of Polish Writers; Theatre Critics Club; IATC; International Association of Theatre Critics. Address: Glogwoa 21, 81 589 Gydnia, Poland.

ZWICKY (Julia) Fay, b. 4 July 1933, Melbourne, Australia. Poet. m. (1) Karl Zwicky, 1957, (2) James Mackie, 1990. Education: BA, University of Melbourne, 1954. Appointments include: Senior Lecturer, University of Western Australia, 1972-87. Publications: Isaac Babel's Fiddle, 1975; Kaddish and Other Poems, 1982; Ask Me, 1990; Story, Hostages, 1983; The Lyre in the Pawnshop: Essays on Literature and Survival, 1974-84, 1986; Editor, Australian Poetry. Honours include: New South Wales Premier's Award, 1982; Western Australian Premier's Award, 1991. Address: 30 Goldsmith Road, Claremont, Western Australia 6010, Australia

Appendices

APPENDIX A

LITERARY AGENTS

The following list of agents does not claim to be exhaustive although every effort has been made to make it as comprehensive as possible. In all instances, authors are advised to send preliminary letters to agents before submitting manuscripts.

ARGENTINA

The Lawrence Smith Literary Agency
Aveni da de los Incas 3110
Buenos Aires 1426
Contact: *Lawrence Smith, Mrs Nancy H Smith*
Literary works accepted for translation into Spanish & Portuguese. Publications in volume or serial for representation in theatre, film, television or radio.

AUSTRALIA

Australian Literary Management
2A Armstrong Street
Middlepark, Vic 3206
Contact: *Caroline Lurie*
Represents Australian writers in fields of fiction, non-fiction, children's books, theatre and film. Handles Australian/New Zealand rights only for a small number of American writers in conjunction with other literary agents.

Curtis Brown (Aust) Pty Ltd
27 Union Street, Paddington
Sydney, NSW 2021
Contact: *Tim Curnow*
Fiction, Non-Fiction, Children's Writers, television, screen, radio & stage, also represents Directors.

Rick Raftos Pty Ltd
PO Box 445, Paddington
Sydney, NSW 2021
Contact: *Rick Raftos, Jane Rose*
Represents Performing Arts Writers, television, screen, radio & stage, also represents Directors.

BRAZIL

Karin Schindler
Caixa Postal 19051
04599 Sao Paulo SP
Contact: *Karin Schindler*
Handles everything for the sale of Portuguese language rights in Brazil

BULGARIA

The Bulgarian Copyright Agency JUSAUTOR
17 Ernst Telman Blvd
1463 Sofia
Contact: *Mrs Yana Markova, Director General*
Representative of Bulgarian authors, promoting work for publication & performance abroad.

CANADA

Acacia House Publishing Services Ltd
51 Acacia Road
Toronto, Ontario M4S 2K6
Managing Director: *Frances Hanna*

Authors' Marketing Services Ltd
217 Degrassi Street
Toronto, Ontario M4M 2K8
Contact: *Larry Hoffman*
Adult fiction and non-fiction, parental self-help, business and biography.

Bella Pomer Agency Inc
22 Shallmar Blvd, PH2
Toronto, Ontario M5N 2Z8
Contact: *Bella Pomer*
International representation for full-length fiction & non-fiction. No cook books, how-to books or unsolicited manuscripts.

The Bukowski Agency
182 Avenue Road, Suite 3
Toronto, Ontario M5R 2J1
President: *Denise Bukowski*

Kellock & Associates Ltd
11017 - 80 Avenue
Edmonton, Alberta T6G OR2
Contact: *Joanne Kellock*
Handles all non-fiction for trade market, all fiction, literary, commercial, genre, all works for children. Also acts for illustrators of books for children.

MGA/Sterling Lord Association Canada
10 St Mary Street, Suite 510
Toronto, Ontario M4Y 1P9
Contact: *Linda McKnight*

Lucinda Vardley Agency Ltd
297 Seaton Street
Toronto, Ontario M5A 2T6
Manager: *Anne Gilbert*

CZECH REPUBLIC

Slovak Literary Agency, LITA
Zamocnicka 9
815 30 Bratislava
Contact: *JUDr Matej Andras, Director*
Protects rights of Slovak authors abroad, foreign authors in Slovakia.

DENMARK

Leonhardt Literary Agency Aps
35 Studiestraede
DK-1455 Copenhagan K
Handles all kinds of bookrights.

FRANCE

Agence Strassova
4 Rue Git-le-Coeur
75006 Paris
Contact: *Mrs Greta Strassova, Mme Monique Marie*
Handles general literature.

European American Information Services Inc
10 Rue de l'Abreuvoir

92400 Courbevoie, Paris
USA address: 110 East 59th St
New York, NY 10022
Contact: *Vera le Marie*
Representing author Catherine Nay and French publishers in North America & North American publishers and agents in France.

Francoise Germain
8 Rue de la Paix
75002 Paris
Contact: *Madame Francoise Germain*
Representation of French and foreign authors.

La Nouvelle Agence
7 Rue Corneille
75006 Paris
Contact: *Ms Mary Kling*
Representation in France for US, English, Italian & German agents and publishers as well as French authors.

Michelle Lapautre Literary Agency
6 rue Jean Carries
75007 Paris
Contact: *Michelle Lapautre*
Representing English-language publishers, agents and authors for the sale of French translation rights.

Promotion Litteraire
26 Rue Chalgrin
75116 Paris
Contact: *M Giannetti*
Publishers' consultants representing leading American, French and Italian publishers, International authors, scout service, general fiction and non-fiction books, film and TV scripts, movie rights and properties.

GERMANY

Buro für Urheberrechte, Copyright Office, Copyright Information Center
Clara-Zetkin-Str 105
1080 Berlin
Contact: *Dr Andreas Henselmann*

Corry Theegarten-Schlotterer Verlags-und Autoren-Agentur
Kulmer Str 3
8 Munchen 81
Contact: *Ms C Theegarten-Schlotterer*
Co-production of books of international interest, fiction and non-fiction, biographies. No childrens' books.

Frallt Medium Agency
Brahmsallee 29
D-2000 Hamburg 13
Contact: *Prof Fritz Kurt Albrecht*
Manuscripts for newspapers and bookpublishers, plays and features for theatre, broadcasting, television and film.

Geisenheyner & Crone International Literary Agents
Gymnasiumstrasse 31B
D-7000 Stuttgart 1
Contact: *Mr Ernst W Geisenheyner*
Representing German & foreign authors and publishers especially in the Socialist countries.

GPA Gerd Plesel Agentur & Veriags GmbH
Linprunstrasse 38
D-8000 Munchen 2
Contact: *Gerd J Plesel*
Represents publishers and literary agencies from the English language world in general and selected ones from French and German. Also major American and British Studios for ancilliary rights.

Hans Hermann Hagedorn
Erikastr 142
2000 Hamburg 20
Contact: *Hans Hermann Hagedorn.*

Literarische Agentur Brigitte Axster
Dreieichstr 43
D-6000 Frankfurt
Contacts: *Brigitte Axster, Dr Petra Christina Hardt, Uta Angerer*
Authors agent representing English, Dutch, French and Italian publishers in German speaking countries.

Skandinavia Verlag, Marianne Weno - Michael Gunther
Ithweg 31
D-1000 Berlin 37
Contact: *Michael Gunther*
Handles plays for radio, stage and television. Represents contemporary Scandinavian playwrights.

INDIA

Ajanta Books International
IUB Jawahar Nagar
Bungalow Road, Delhi 110007
Contact: *S Balwant*
Research work on Social Science & Humanity especially on Indian themes, oriental or modern.

ISRAEL

Rogan-Pikarski Literary Agency
200 Hayarkon Street
PO Box 4006, 61 040 Tel Aviv
Contact: *Ilana Pikarski*
Represents major US and European publishers and agents for Hebrew volume, serial and performance and merchandising rights, also has New York agency.

ITALY

Agenzia Letteraria Internazionale
3 Via Fratelli Gabba
Milano
Contact: *Donatella Barbiere*
Represents exclusively in Italy American, English and German publishers and agencies.

Natoli & Stefan
Galleria Buenos Aires 14
I-20124 Milano
Contact: *Dott Gianni Natoli*
Represents fiction and non-fiction authors rights, co-editions, translations.

JAPAN

Tuttle-Mori Agency
Fuji Bldg 8th Floor
2-15 Kanda Jimbocho, Chiyoda-ku
Tokyo 101
Contact: *Mr Takeshi Mori*
Largest literary agency for foreign rights in Japan.

THE NETHERLANDS

Auteursbureau Greta Baars Jelgersma
Bovensteweg 46
NL-6585 KD Mook
Contact: *Greta Baars Jelgersma*
Represents authors and publishers, translations from the Scandinavian and modern languages. International co-printing of illustrated books and arranging profitable offers for book production. Oldest international literary agency in The Netherlands.

Prins & Prins Literary Agency
Postbus 5400
1007 AK Amsterdam
Contact: *Henk Prins*
Representation in The Netherlands of foreign publishers.

NORWAY

Hanna-Kirsti Koch Literary Agency
PO Box 3043/Elisenberg
0207 Oslo 2
Contact: *Mr Eilif Koch*
Representing foreign authors in Norway.

Ulla Lohren Literary Agency
PO Box 150
Tasen, 0801 Oslo 8
Contact: *Ulla Lohren*
Represents agents and publishers from Canada, UK, USA and others for Scandinavian rights in fiction, non-fiction and children's books.

POLAND

Authors' Agency
ul Hipoteczna 2
00-950 Warszawa
Contact: *Wladyslaw Jakubowski*
Handles Polish copyrights, foreign contracts, information.

PORTUGAL

Ilidio da Fonseca Matos Literary Agency
Rua de S Bernardo
68-30, 1200 Lisboa
Contact: *Ilidio da Fonseca Matos*
Represents in Portugal: Curtis Brown Ltd; Laurence Pollinger Ltd; The New American Library; Doubleday and Company Inc; Rowohlt Verla - Diogenes Verlag.

SPAIN

Andres de Kramer
Castello 30
28001 Madrid
Handles only foreign writers and foreign rights of theatrical plays and production in Spain.

Bookbank S A
Rafael Calvo 13
28010 Madrid
Contact: *Angela Gonzalez*
Represents foreign publishers and/or agents and/or writers for the sale of Spanish language and Portuguese rights. Also Spanish language authors.

Julio Fyanez Literary Agency
Via Augusta 139
08021 Barcelona
Contact: *Mr Julio Fyanez*
Represents publishers, agencies and independent authors from all countries and Spanish authors abroad. Covers Spain, Latin America, Portugal and Brazil.

Ute Korner de Moya Literary Agency
Ronda Guinardo 32-5-5
08025 Barcelona
Contact: *Ute Korner*
Represents foreign publishers, agents and authors in the Spanish and Portuguese speaking countries.

SWEDEN

D Richard Bowen
Post Box 30037
S-200 61 Malmo 30
Contact: *D Richard Bowen*
Publishers' literary and sales agent, translation rights, etc., negotiated.

Lennart Sane Agency AB
Hollandareplan
537434 Karlshamn
Contact: *Lennart Sane*
Representing US, British and Scandinavian authors, publishers and agencies for translation rights in Europe and Latin America.

Monica Heyum Literary Agency
PO Box 3300 Vendelso
S-13603 Haninge
Contact: *Monica Heyum*
Handles fiction, non-fiction and children's books.

SWITZERLAND

Dieter Breitsohl AG Literary Agency
PO Box 245
CH 8034 Zurich
or: Heimatstr 25
CH 8008 Zurich
Contact: *Dr Jutta Motz*
Handles non-fiction, psychology, psychosomatic, religion, theology, mythology.

Liepman AG
Maienburgweg 23, Postfach 572
CH-8044 Zurich
Contact: *Dr Ruth Liepman, Eva Koralnik, Ruth Weibel*
Represents American, British, Canadian, French, Dutch and Israeli publishers and agents for the German language rights, and authors from the manuscript on worldwide.

New Press Agency Society
Haus am Herterberg, Haldenstr 5
CH-8500 Frauenfeld, Herten
Contact: *Rene Marti.*

Paul & Peter Fritz AG Literary Agency
Jupiterstrasse 1
Postfach 8032 Zurich
Contact: *Peter S Fritz*
Represents English language authors for the
German language rights and authors for worldwide.
No unsolicited manuscripts.

UNITED KINGDOM

Jacintha Alexander Associates
47 Emperor's Gate
London SW7 4HJ
Contact: *Jacintha Alexander, Julian Alexander*
Handles full-length general and literary fiction and
non-fiction of all kinds. No plays, poetry, textbooks
or science fiction. Film and TV scripts handled for
established clients only.

Blake Friedman Literary Agency Ltd
37-41 Gower Street
London WC1E 6HH
Contact: *Carol Blake (books), Julian Friedman
(film/TV), Conrad Williams (original scripts/radio)*
Worldwide representation of fiction and non-fiction,
television and film rights and scripts. No juvenile
projects or poetry.

Carnell Literary Agency
Danescroft, Goose Lane, Little Hallingbury
Bishop's Stortford, Herts CM22 7RG
Contact: *Mrs Pamela Buckmaster*
Specializes in science fiction and fantasy, also
handles general fiction, non-fiction and children's
fantasy.

Casarotto Ramsay Ltd
National House, 60-66 Wardoir Street
London W1V 3HP
Contacts: *Jenne Casarotto, Greg Hunt, Tracey
Smith (Film/TV/Radio), Tom Erhardt, Mel Kenyan
(Stage), Maggie Hanbury (Books)*
Handles scripts for TV, theatre, film and radio,
general fiction and non-fiction.

Rosica Colin Limited
1 Clareville Grove Mews
London SW7 5AH
Contact: *Joanna Marston*
All full length manuscripts including theatre, films,
television and sound broadcasting works in the
USA, European countries and overseas.

Rupert Crew Limited
1A King's Mews
London WC1N 2JA
Contact: *Doreen Montgomery, Shirley Russell*
Representation offered to limited clientele,
specialising in promoting major book projects: non-
fiction, general and women' fiction.

Curtis Brown Ltd (London)
Haymarket House, 28-29 Haymarket
London SW1Y 4SP
Contact: *Address material to company.*

Handles a wide range of subjects including fiction,
general non-fiction, children's and specialist, scripts
for film, TV, theatre and radio.

Campbell Thomson and McLaughlin Ltd
1 King's Mews
London WC1N 2JA
Contact: *John McLaughlin, Charlotte Bruton*
Handles book-length manuscripts excluding
children's, science fiction and fantasy. No plays, film
scripts, articles or poetry. Short stories from existing
clients only.

Jonathan Clowes Ltd
10 Iron Bridge House
Bridge Approach
London NW1 8BD
Contact: *Brie Burkeman*
Fiction and non-fiction plus scripts. No textbooks or
children's.

Elspeth Cochrane Agency
11-13 Orlando Road
London SW4 0LE
Contact: *Donald Baker, Elspeth Cochrane*
Authors handled for theatre, films, television. Books
for all types of publication.

Felix de Wolfe
Manfield House, 376-378 The Strand
London WC2R 0LR
Contact: *Felix de Wolfe*
Handles quality fiction and scripts only. No non-
fiction or children's. No unsolicited manuscripts.

Eric Glass Ltd
28 Berkeley Square
London W1X 6HD
Contact: *Eric Glass, Janet Crowley*
Books, plays, screenplays and television plays. Sole
agents for the Société des Auteurs et Compositeurs
Dramatiques of Paris for the English speaking
countries.

Elaine Green Ltd
37 Goldhawk Road
London W12 8QQ
Contact: *Elaine Green, Carol Heaton*
Handles novels, quality non-fiction and journalist's
books. No original scripts for theatre, film or TV.

David Grossman Literary Agency Ltd
110-114 Clerkenwell Road
London EC1M 5SA
Contact: *Address material to the company*
Fiction and general non-fiction. No verse or
technical books for students. No original
screenplays or teleplays.

A M Heath & Co Ltd
79 St Martin's Lane
London WC2N 4AA
Contact: *Sara Fisher, Bill Hamilton, Michael
Thomas.*
Handles fiction and general non-fiction. No scripts
or poetry.

David Higham Associates Ltd
5-8 Lower John Street
Golden Square
London W1R 4H4

Contact: *Anthony Goff, John Rushi (Scripts), Elizabeth Cree (Books)*
Representing professional authors and writers in all fields throughout the world.

International Copyright Bureau Ltd
22A Aubrey House
Maida Avenue
London W2 1TQ
Contact: *Joy Westendarp*
Handles scripts for TV/theatre/film and radio. No books.

M B A Literary Agents Ltd
45 Fitzroy Street
London W1P 5HR
Contact: *Diana Tyler, John Richard Parker, Meg Davis, Ruth Needham*
Represent writers in all mediums: books, television, radio. Handles fiction and non-fiction. No poetry or children's fiction. Also scripts for film, TV, radio and theatre.

William Morris Agency UK Ltd
31-32 Soho Square
London W1V 5DG
Contact: *Stephen M Kenis (films), Jane Annakin (TV/Theatre), Lavinia Trevor (Books).*
Scripts handled for theatre, film, TV and radio. Also fiction and general non-fiction.

The Penman Literary Agency
175 Pall Mall
Leigh-on-Sea
Essex SS9 1RE
Contact: *Leonard G Stubbs*
Full length novel manuscripts. Also theatre, films, television, sound broadcasting.

Peters Fraser and Dunlop Group Ltd
503/4 The Chambers
Chelsea Harbour, Lots Road
London SW10 0XF
Contact: *Kenneth Ewing, Tim Corrie*
Agents for stage drama, TV plays and series, radio drama, fiction and non-fiction and children's books, representation for producers and directors of stage, TV and film.

Laurence Pollinger Limited
18 Maddox Street
London W1R 0EU
Contact: *Gerald J Pollinger, Margaret Pepper, Romany van Bosch.*
Author's agents for all material with the exception of original film stories, poetry and freelance journalistic articles.

Murray Pollinger
222 Old Brompton Road
London SW5 0BZ
Contact: *Murray Pollinger, Gina Pollinger, Sara Menguc*
Agents for all types of general fiction and non-fiction with the exception of plays, poetry and travel.

Shelley Power Literary Agency Ltd
Le Montaud
24220 Berbigières, France
Contact: *Shelley Power*

General fiction and non-fiction. No poetry, plays or short pieces. Offers worldwide representation.

Rogers Coleridge and White Ltd
20 Powis Mews
London W11 1JN
Contact: *Deborah Rogers, Gill Coleridge, Patricia White, Ann Warnford Davis*
Handles fiction, non-fiction and children's books. No plays or poetry.

Tessa Sayle Agency
11 Jubilee Place
London SW3 3TE
Contact: *Rachel Calder (Books), Penny Tackaberry (Drama)*
Full length manuscripts, plays, films, television, sound broadcasting. Represented in all foreign countries.

Vincent Shaw Associates
20 Jay Mews
Kensington Gore
London SW7 2EP
Contact: *Vincent Shaw, Lester McGrath*
Handles film, TV, theatre and radio only. Unsolicited manuscripts read.

Shiel Land Associates Ltd
43 Doughty Street
London WC1N 2LF
Contact: *Anthony Shiel*
Represents literary authors. Represents worldwide including translation, film, television and theatre.

Solo Syndication and Literary Agency Ltd
49-53 Kensington High Street
London W8 5ED
Contact: *Don Short*
Specialising in celebrity autobiographies and biographies. Non-fiction only except for established authors.

Peter Tauber Press Agency
94 East End Road
London N3 2SX
Contact: *Peter Tauber, Robert Tauber*
Full representation, specialising in well-researched epic women's saga fiction.

Ed Victor Ltd
162 Wardour Street
London W1V 3At
Contact: *Ed Victor, Maggie Phillips, Sophie Hicks, Graham Greene*
Commercial fiction and non-fiction. No scripts or academic books.

Watson Little Ltd
12 Egbert Street
London NW1 8LJ
Contact: *Mandy Little, Sheila Watson*
Represents wide range of fiction and non-fiction. No poetry, short stories or articles, or books for very young children.

A P Watt Ltd
20 John Street
London WC1N 2DR
Contact: *Caradoc King, Linda Shaughnessy, Rod Hall, Lisa Eveleigh, Nick Marston, Derek Johns*

Full length works for all media including plays and telescripts. No poetry. Representation throughout the world.

UNITED STATES OF AMERICA

California

The Artists Agency
10000 Santa Monica Blvd, Suite 305
Los Angeles, CA 90067
Contact: *Merrily Kane*
Representation of novels and screenplays for motion pictures.

The Sandra Dijkstra Literary Agency
1155 Camino Del Mar
Del Mar, CA 92014
Contact: *Sandra Dijkstra, Katherine Goodwin*
Handles quality and commercial adult fiction and non-fiction. Representation to major publishers in USA. British rights. Translations.

Renee Wayne Golden APLC
8983 Norma Place
West Hollywood
CA 90069
Contact: *Renee Wayne Golden*
Representation of selected authors.

Paul Kohner Inc
9169 Sunset Boulevard
Los Angeles, CA 90069
Contact: *Gary Salt, Neal Stevens*
Non-fiction preferred to fiction. No short stories, poetry, science fiction or gothic.

Michael Larsen/Elizabeth Pomada Literary Agency
1029 Jones Street
San Francisco, CA 94109
Contact: *Elizabeth Pomada*
Handles general fiction and non-fiction for adults, self help, popular psychology.

Singer Media Corp
Seaview Business Park
1030 Calle Cordillera, Unit 106
San Clemente, CA 92673
Contact: *Dr Kurt Singer*
Newspaper syndicate and literary agency, also photo bank. Handles sophisticated modern romance novels, biographies, mysteries, horror books.

Jack Scagnetti Talent & Literary Agency
5330 Lankershim Blvd, No 210
North Hollywood, CA 91601
Contact: *Jack Scagnetti*
Handles screenplays, television scripts, treatments, books, major magazine articles. Franchised signatory to Writers Guild of America-West.

H N Swanson Inc
8523 Sunset Blvd
Los Angeles, CA 90069
Contact: *Thomas Shanks, N V Swanson*
Represents writers for novels, screenplays, television and theatre. Worldwide representation.

Connecticut

Sidney B Kramer
Mews Books Ltd
20 Bluewater Hill
Westport, CT 06880
Contact: *Sidney B Kramer, Fran Pollack*
Specializes in juvenile (pre-school - young adult), cookery, adult non-fiction and fiction, technical and medical software, film and TV rights etc. Prefers work of published/established authors, will accept small number of new/unpublished authors.

New England Publishing Associates Inc
PO Box 5
Chester, CT 06412
Contact: *Elizabeth Frost Knappman, Edward W Knappman*
Editorial assistance and representation for non-fiction books for the adult market.

Van der Leun & Associates
464 Mill Hill Drive
Southport, CT 06490
Contact: *Patricia Van der Leun*
Handles fiction and non-fiction, specializes in illustrated books, art and science. No unsolicited manuscripts. Representation in all foreign countries.

Colorado

Flannery, White & Stone, A Writer's Agency
180 Cook, Suite 404
Denver, CO 80206
Contact: *Connie Solowiej*

District of Columbia

Ronald L Goldfarb & Assocs
918 16th Street, NW, Suite 400
Washington, DC 20006
Contact: *Joshua J Kaufman*

Florida

Lighthouse Literary Agency
PO Box 2105, Winter Park, FL 32790
Director: *Sandra Kangas*

Georgia

Deering Literary Agency
1507 Oakmonth Drive
Acworth, GA 30101
Directors: *Charles and Dorothy Deering*

Hawaii

Rhodes Literary Agency
Box 89133
Honolulu, HI 96830
Contact: *Fred C Pugarelli*
Handles novels, non-fiction books, magazines, poetry books, single poems, religious materials, motion picture and television scripts, stage plays, juvenile books, syndicated materials, radio scripts, textbooks, photos, books of cartoons etc.

Illinois

Austin Wahl Agency Ltd
53 West Jackson Boulevard, Suite 342
Chicago, IL 60604
Contact: *Thomas Wahl*

Handles motion picture and TV scripts, novels and non-fiction books.

Maryland

Columbia Literary Associates Inc
7902 Nottingham Way
Ellicott City, MD 21043
Contact: *Kathryn Jensen*

Massachusetts

The Otte Company
9 Goden Street
Belmont, MA 02178
Contact: *Jane H Otte*
Handles adult fiction and non-fiction full length books. Representation in all major markets and Hollywood.

Michael Snell Literary Agency
Box 655
Truro, MA 02666
Contact: *Patricia Smith*
Development and sale of adult non-fiction, primarily in business, computers, science, psychology and law.

Gunther Stuhlmann, Author's Representative
PO Box 276
Becket, MA 01223
Contact: *Barbara Ward, Gunther Stuhlmann*
Representation world wide of quality literature and non-fiction.

Michigan

Creative Concepts Literary Agency
5538 Herford
Troy, MI 48098
Director: *Michele Glance Serwach*

Minnesota

The Lazear Agency Inc
430 First Avenue North, Suite 416
Minneapolis, MN 55401
Contact: *Jonathon Lazear*

Missouri

Joyce A Flaherty, Literary Agent
816 Lynda Court
St Louis, MO 63122

Montana

Phoenix Literary Agency
PO Box 669, Livingston, MT 59047
President: *Robert Latilla*

New Hampshire

Northeast Literary Agency
69 Broadway, Concord, NH 03301
Editor: *Mary Hill*

New Jersey

Barbara Bauer Literary Agency
179 Washington Ave
Matawan, NJ 07747
Contact: *Barbara Bauer*
Specialize in new and unpublished authors, quality fiction and non-fiction for children and adults.

Rosalie Siegel, International Literary Agent Inc
1 Abey Drive
Pennington, NJ 08534
Contact: *Rosalie Siegel, Pamela Walker*
Adult fiction and non-fiction particularly quality fiction. Also French fiction and non-fiction.

New Mexico

The Rydal Agency
PO Box 2247, Santa Fe, NM 87504
Director: *Clark Kimball*

New York

Carole Abel Literary Agent
160 West 87th Street
New York, NY 10024
Contact: *Carole Abel*
Handles trade and mass market fiction and non-fiction books. No unsolicited manuscripts, query first. Agents in Hollywood and most foreign countries.

Dominick Abel Literary Agency Inc
146 W 82 St, Suite 1B
New York, NY 10024
Contact: *Dominick Abel.*

Acton, Dystel, Leone & Jaffe
928 Broadway, Suite 303
New York, NY 10010
Contact: *Jane Dystel*
Non-fiction and novels.

Marcia Amsterdam Agency
41 West 82nd Street
New York, NY 10024
Contact: *Marcia Amsterdam*
Handles adult and young adult fiction, movie and TV rights, screenplays, teleplays.

Julian Bach Literary Agency Inc
22 East 71st Street
New York, NY 10021
Contact: *Julian Bach, Emma Sweeney, Susan Merritt, Ann Rittenberg*
Agents for fiction and non-fiction. No science fiction or fantasy, poetry or photography.

The Bethel Agency
641 West 59th Street
New York, NY 10019
Contact: *Lewis R Chambers*
Handles fiction and non-fiction, plays for theatre, film and television, sub-division handles children's books.

Brandt & Brandt Literary Agency Inc
1501 Broadway
New York, NY 10036
Contact: *Carl D Brandt, Gail Hochman*
Handles fiction and non-fiction. No unsolicited manuscripts, query first, no reading fee. Agents in most foreign countries.

Connor Literary Agency
640 West 153rd Street
New York, NY 10031
Contact: *Marlene K Connor*
Handles commercial fiction and non-fiction, illustrated books, cookbooks, self-help, ethnic subjects, how-to. Foreign agents in major countries.

Curtis Brown Ltd
10 Astor Place, 3rd Floor
New York, NY 10003
Contact: *Perry Knowlton, Peter Ginsberg*
Handles fiction, non-fiction, science fiction, mystery, romance. Also children's fiction, non-fiction and theatrical, film and television. Handles general trade fiction, non-fiction, juvenile and film and TV rights. Representatives in all major countries. No unsolicited manuscripts. Query first.

Anita Diamant Literary Agency
310 Madison Ave
New York, NY 10017
Contact: *Anita Diamant, Robin Rae*
Handles book manuscripts, fiction, non-fiction, foreign film rights.

The Jonathan Dolger Agency
49 East 96th Street, Suite 9B
New York, NY 10128
Contact: *Jonathan Dolger*
Handles adult fiction and non-fiction, illustrated books. No unsolicited material, query letter & SASE first.

Donadio & Ashworth Inc,
Literary Representatives
231 West 22nd Street
New York, NY 10011
Contact: *Neil Olson*

Ethan Ellenberg Literary Agency
548 Broadway, No 5-E
New York, NY 10012
Contact: *Ethan Ellenberg*
Handles quality fiction and non-fiction, first novels, commercial fiction, military, history, sci-fi. Query before submission of manuscripts.

Ann Elmo Agency Inc
60 East 42nd Street
New York, NY 10165
Contact: *Ann Elmo, Lettie Lee*
Handles all types of fiction, non-fiction, juveniles, plays for book and magazine publication, as well as for film, TV and stage use.

Freida Fishbein Ltd
2556 Hubbard Street
Brooklyn, NY 11235
Contact: *Janice Fishbein*
Handles plays, books, motion picture and television scripts. No short stories, poetry or young children's books.

Samuel French Inc
45 West 25th Street
New York, NY 10010
Contact: *Lawrence Harbison*
Specializing in plays.

Jay Garon-Brooke Associates Inc
101 West 55th Street, Suite 5K
New York, NY 10019
Fiction and non-fiction. No category romance, western or mysteries.

Max Gartenberg Literary Agent
521 5th Avenue, Suite 1700
New York, NY 10175
Contact: *Max Gartenberg*

Handles book-length manuscripts of non-fiction and fiction including all rights therein.

Gelles-Cole Literary Enterprises
320 E 42 St, Suite 411
New York, NY 10017
Contact: *Sandi Gelles-Cole*
Handles commercial fiction and non-fiction.

The Jeff Herman Agency
500 Greenwich Street, Suite 501-C
New York, NY 10013
President: *Jeffrey H Herman*

John Hawkins & Associates Inc
71 West 23rd Street, Suite 1600
New York, NY 10010
Contact: *J Hawkins, W Reiss*
Provides all services of representation & limit works to book-length manuscripts in prose. No theatrical, film or TV scripts.

International Creative Management
40 West 57th Street
New York, NY 10019
Contact: *Gordon Kato*

Janklow & Nesbit Associates
598 Madison Avenue
New York, NY 10022
Contact: *Lynn Nesbit*

JCA Literary Agency Inc
27 West 20th Street, Suite 1103
New York, NY 10011
Contact: *Jane C Cushman*
Handles general fiction, non-fiction. No screen plays. Query first with SASE.

JET Literary Associates Inc
124E 84th Street, Suite 4A
New York, NY 10028
Contact: *James E Trupin*
Handles book length fiction and non-fiction only.

Asher D Jason Enterprises Inc
111 Barrow Street
New York, NY 10014
·**Contact:** *Asher D Jason*
Handles non-fiction and fiction. Representation to all American publishers.

Lucy Kroll Agency
390 West End Avenue
New York, NY 10024
Contact: *Lucy Kroll, Barbara Hogenson*
Handles fiction and non-fiction including scripts for film, TV and radio.

Peter Livingston Associates Inc
465 Park Avenue
New York, NY 10022
Contact: *Peter W Livingston, David C Johnston*
Handles serious non-fiction, business, politics, popular science etc. Literary and commercial fiction, film and TV. No poetry or children's books. Foreign rights.

Elaine Markson Literary Agency Inc
44 Greenwich Avenue
New York, NY 10011
Contact: *Elaine Markson*

McIntosh and Otis Inc
310 Madison Avenue
New York, NY 10017
Contact: *Julie Fallowfield, Dorothy Markinko*
Adult and juvenile fiction and non-fiction. No textbooks or scripts.

Scott Meredith Literary Agency Inc
845 Third Avenue
New York, NY 10022
Contact: *Jack Scovil, Scott Meredith*
Handles general fiction and non-fiction, books and magazines, juveniles, plays, TV scripts, motion picture rights and properties. Accept unsolicited manuscripts, reading fee. Agents in all principal countries.

William Morris Agency
1350 Avenue of the Americas
New York, NY 10019
Contact: *Mel Berger*

Jean V Naggar Literary Agency
216 E 75th Street
New York, NY 10021
Contact: *Jean Naggar*
Complete representation in all areas of general fiction and non-fiction.

Pickering Associates Inc
432 Hudson Street
New York, NY 10014
Contact: *John Pickering*
Full service literary agency with co-agents in Hollywood and all principal translation markets.

Susan Ann Protter Literary Agent
110 West 40th Street, Suite 1408
New York, NY 10018
Contact: *Susan Protter*
Principally hard and soft cover books and the various rights involved. Fiction, non-fiction, health, science, biography, history, science fiction etc.

Rosenstone/Wender
3 East 48th Street, 4th Floor
New York, NY 10017
Contact: *Susan Perlman Cohen, Phyllis Wender.*

Russell and Volkening Inc
50 West 29th Street, No 7E
New York, NY 10001
Contact: *Miriam Altshuler, Timothy Seldes*
Literary fiction and non-fiction.

Charlotte Sheedy Literary Agency Inc
611 Broadway, Suite 428
New York, NY 10012
Contact: *Charlotte Sheedy*

The Shukat Company Ltd
340 West 55th Street, Ste 1-A
New York, NY 10019
Contact: *Scott Shukat, Larry Weiss*
Handles theatre musicals, plays, books (fiction and non-fiction), TV and MP.

Evelyn Singer Literary Agency Inc
PO Box 594
White Plains, NY 10602
Contact: *Evelyn Singer*

Exclusive representation. Handles fiction, non-fiction, for adults, young adults, children, first serial rights, foreign rights, movie and TV rights with sub-agents.

Philip G Spitzer Literary Agency
50 Talmadge Farm Lane
East Hampton, NY 11937
Contact: *Philip G Spitzer*
Handles general fiction and non-fiction, also screenplays.

Renee Spodheim
698 West End Avenue, No 5-B
New York, NY 10025
Contact: *Renee Spodheim*
All trade. Fiction and non-fiction. No juveniles.

Sterling Lord Literistic Inc
One Madison Avenue
New York, NY 10010
Contact: *Peter Matson*
Handles full length and short manuscripts, theatre, films, TV, radio. Represented in Europe by Intercontinental Literary Agency.

2M Communications Ltd
121 West 27 Street, 601
New York, NY 10001
Contact: *Madeleine Morel*
Handles contemporary non-fiction, popular culture, celebrity biographies.

Wieser & Wieser Inc
118 East 25th Street
New York, NY 10010
Contact: *Olga Wieser*
Handles literary & commercial fiction, general non-fiction including all rights, film and TV rights.

Writers House Inc
21 West 26th Street
New York, NY 10010
Represents popular and literary fiction, mainstream and genre, including thrillers, science fiction, fantasy and romance. Also juvenile and young adult.

Pennsylvania

James Allen Literary Agent (in Association with Virginia Kidd Literary Agents)
PO Box 278, 538 East Harford Street
Milford, PA 18337
Contact: *Virginia Kidd*
Handles fiction, specializing in science fiction, submit to magazines & book publishers. Representation in foreign countries & Hollywood.

Ray Peekner Literary Agency Inc
Box 3308
Bethlehem, PA 18017
Contact: *Barbara Puechner*
Handles general fiction, particularly mystery suspense. Quality YA.

Rhode Island

Rock Literary Agency
Box 625, Newport, RI 02840
Contact: *Andrew Rock*

Texas

The Blake Group Literary Agency
One Turtle Creek Village, Suite 600
3878 Oaklawn, Dallas, TX 75219
Contact: *Lee B Halff*
Represents limited number of published &
unpublished authors. Handles fiction, non-fiction,
plays & poetry, periodicals, publishers & producers.
No reading fee. SASE essential.

Gloria Stern Literary Agency
2929 Buffalo Speedway, Lamar Tower 2111
Houston, TX 77098
Contact: *Gloria Stern*
Represent 90% trade, non-fiction, mostly biography,
education and women's and social issues. Also
health, some self-help and serious fiction.

Utah

Bess Wallace Associates Literary Agency
Box 972
Duchesne, UT 84021
Contact: *Bess D Wallace*
Manuscripts sold, edited, typed, ghost-writing,
typesetting for self publishers, writers for writing
assignments, copy-editing for publishers. Query
first.

Washington

The Catalog (TM) Literary Agency
Box 2964
Vancouver, WA 98668
Literary Agent: *Douglas Storey*

Wisconsin

Lee Allan Agency
PO Box 18617
Milwaukee, WI 53218
Contact: *Lee A Matthias*
Handles book length novels, mysteries, thrillers,
westerns, science fiction, horror, romance & young
adult fiction. No TV material, non-fiction, poetry,
magazine articles or short stories.

APPENDIX B

LITERARY ORGANIZATIONS

Please note that while every effort has been made to include as many societies and organizations as possible, the editors acknowledge that the following list is by no means exhaustive. Many societies are organized and administered by unpaid individuals from their own homes, not only do the addresses of secretaries change frequently, therefore, but these are difficult to trace. Secretaries of societies which have yet to be listed are consequently urged to send details for publication in future editions of the **INTERNATIONAL AUTHORS AND WRITERS WHO'S WHO** to the editors at the following address:

The International Authors and Writers Who's Who
International Biographical Centre
Cambridge CB2 3QP, England

The friendly co-operation of the listed societies is gratefully acknowledged, the future assistance of others is cordially invited.

AUSTRALIA

Australian Writers' Guild Ltd
60 Kellett Street
Kings Cross, Sydney, NSW 2011
Professional association for writers in areas of television, radio, screen & stage to promote and protect the professional interests.
Approx 1800 members.
Executive Officer: Angela Wales.

Bibliographical Society of Australia and New Zealand
c/o Secretary, Miss R T Smith
76 Warners Ave, Bondi Beach, NSW 2026
To encourage and promote research in all aspects of physical bibliography.
Approx 300 members.
President: Mr Trevor Mills; Vice President: Mr John E Fletcher; Secretary: Miss R T Smith.

Children's Book Council of Australia
PO Box 420
Dickson, ACT 2602
President: Laurie Copping; Secretary: Lynn Fletcher.

The Dickens Fellowship
29 Henley Beach Road
Henley Beach, Adelaide, SA 5022
Literary society devoted to study & appreciation of the life and works of Charles Dickens.
Approx 120 members.
Hon Sec: Dr A F Dilnot, Mrs G M Taylor, Mrs Barbara Barrett.

Poetry Society of Australia
PO Box N110, Grosvenor Street
Sydney, NSW 2000
Publications: New Poetry (quarterly); also poems, articles, reviews, notes and comments, interviews.
Joint Secretaries: Robert Adamson; Debra Adamson.

The Society of Editors
PO Box 176
Carlton South, Vic 3053
Professional association of book editors, regular training seminars, monthly meetings & newsletter.
Approx 300 members.

President: Colin Jevons; Secretary: Susannah McFarlane.

BELGIUM

International PEN Club, Belgian French Speaking Centre
76 Avenue de 11 Novembre, BP7
B-1040 Brussels
Receptions of foreign writers, defense of the liberty of thought of all writers, participation at the world-wide congresses of PEN.
Approx 230 members.
President: Mr Georges Sion; General Secretary: Mr Raymond Quinot.

Koninklijke Academie voor Wetenschappen
Letteren en Schone Kunsten van Belgie
Paleis der Academien, Hertogsstr 1
B-1000 Brussels.
Permanent Secretary: Gerard Verbeke.

Societe de Langue et de Litterature Wallonnes
Universite de Liege, Place du XX Aout
B-4000 Liege
Holds meetings, lecturers, exhibitions, library, media, archives, publications.
Approx 300 members.
President: Jean Brumioul; Vice Presidents: Albert Maquet and Andre Goosse; Secretary: Victor George.

Societe Royale des Bibliophiles et Iconophiles de Belgique
4 Boulevard de l'Empereur
B-1000 Brussels
Publication of "Le Livre et l'Estampe" (Semestrial), Expositions.
Approx 150 members.
President: Baron de Sadeleer; Vice President: Michel Wittock; Secretary: Auguste Grisay.

BRAZIL

Academia Cearense di Letras
Palacio Senador Alencar, Rua Sao Paulo 51
60000 Fortaleza CE
To cultivate and develop literature and scientific achievement. Meets monthly, annual publication.

Approx 40 active members, unknown number of correspondent & honorary members.
Secretary General: J Denizard Macedo de Alcantara.

Associacao Brasileira de Imprensa (Brazilian Press Association)
Rua Araujo Porto Alegre
71-Centro-Rio de Janeiro-RJ.

Brazilian Translators Union (SINTRA)
Rua de Quitanda
194-sala 1005-Centro
CEP-20091-Rio de Janeiro-RJ

Companhia Editora Nacional
Rua Joli
294-Sao Paulo-SP

Sindicato de Escritores of Rio de Janeiro
Av Heitor Beltrao
353-Rio de Janeiro-RJ
CEP 20550

CANADA

Association des Editurers Anglophones du Quebec
c/o Black Rose Books, 3981 St Laurent Blvd
Montreal, Quebec H2W 1YS
An association of book publishers in Quebec.
Approx 8 members.
President: Simon Dardick; Secretary: Pamela Chichinskas.

The Association of Canadian Publishers
2 Gloucester Street, Suite 301
Toronto, Ontario M4X 1L5
Trade association representing the interest of the Canadian-owned and operated publishing industry.
Approx 150 members.
President: Philip Cercone; Executive Director: Wayne Gilpin; Vice President: Diana Douglas; Director of Member Services: Joshua Samuel.

The Canada Council
350 Albert Street, PO Box 1047
Ottawa, Ontario K1P 5V8
Head, Writing & Pubn Section: Naim Kattan.

Canadian Authors Association
275 Slater Street, Suite 500
Ottawa, Ontario K1P 5H9
18 branches across Canada. Annual national conference, work to protect Canadian writers, spokesman to govt, sponsors awards programme, publishes periodicals.
President: Mary E Dawe; National Vice President: Gail Corbett; Secretary: Fred Kerner; Treasurer: David Chilton.

The Canadian Centre (English-speaking) PEN
24 Ryerson Avenue
Toronto, Ontario M5T 2P3
Fosters understanding among writers of all nations, fights for freedom of expression, to work for the preservation of the world's literature.
President: Graeme Gibson; Executive Director: Jan Bauer.

Canadian Copyright Institute
35 Spadina Road

Toronto, Ontario M5R 2S9
Established to promote the use of copyright in the public interest.
Membership: 12 organizations, 50 individuals.
Chairman: John Irwin; Vice President: Fred Kerner; Secretary: Barry Reese.

Federation Professionnelle des Journalistes du Quebec
2083 Beaudry Street, Rm 302
Montreal, Quebec H2L 3G4
Representation and defense of journalists professional interest, freedom of the press, public's right to quality information etc.
Approx 1000 members.
President: R Barnaby.

Freelance Editors' Association of Canada (FEAC)
35 Spadina Road
Toronto, Ontario M5R 2S9
Professional development seminars held twice yearly, Tom Fairly Award - award for editorial excellence by editor working on a freelance basis.
Approx 150 members.
President: Peter Colenbrander

La Societé des Écrivains Canadiens de la Langue Française
1195 rue Sherbrooke Ouest
Montreal, Quebec H3A 1H9
Contact: Jacques Constantin

League of Canadian Poets
24 Ryerson Avenue
Toronto, Ontario M5T 2P3
Executive Director: Angela T V Ribiero

Literary Press Group
Subs of Association of Canadian Publishers
260 Kings St E
Toronto, Ontario M5A 1K3
Promote Canadian fiction, poetry, drama & literary criticism. Sales representation across Canada.
Approx 45 members.
Director: John Ball; Sales Rep Mgr: Lisa Alward.

Literary Translators Association
3492 rue Laval
Montreal, Quebec H2X 3C8
Advice to members, legal services, link between authors and translators, John Glasso Translation Prize, International Translators Conferences.
Approx 110 members.
President: Michael Buttiens; Co Presidents: Marie C Brasseur and Sherry Simon.

Periodical Writers' Association of Canada
24 Ryerson Avenue
Toronto, Ontario M5T 2P3
To promote and protect the interests of Canadian periodical writers.
Approx 360 members.
Director: Paulette Pelletier-Kelly.

Playwrights Union of Canada
54 Wolseley St, 2nd Floor
Toronto, Ontario M5T 1AS

Writers' Union of Canada
24 Ryerson Avenue

Toronto, Ontario M5T 2P3
Professional association of published trade book writers.
Approx 700 members.
Executive Director: Penny Dickens.

CHINA

China Pen Centre
2 Shatan Beijie
Beijing, China.

DENMARK

The Danish Society of Language and Literature
Frederiksholms Kanal 18A
DK-1220 Kobenhavn K
Scholarly editing in Danish language, literature & history, dictionaries *c.* 150 titles, 750 volumes.
Approx 62 members.
President: Iver Kjaer; Secretary: Dr Erik Dal.

Danish Writers' Association
Strandgade 6, St
DK-1401 Kobenhavn K
Attending to social, artistic, professional & economic interests of Danish authors in Denmark & abroad.
Approx 1600 members.
President: D Trier Morch.

Dansk Litteraturinformationscenter
Ameliegade 38
DK-1256 Kobenhavn K

Danske Sprog-og Litteraturselskab
Frederiksholms Kanal 18A
DK-1220 Copenhagen
Publications: Standard editions of literary, linguistic and historical texts, including diaries and correspondence.
Administrator: Dr Erik Dal.

Nyt Dansk Litteraturselskab
Bibliotekscentralen, Tempovej 7-11
DK-2750 Ballerup
Works for re-publishing of titles missing in public libraries in co-operation with publishers.
Approx 276 members.
Manager: Jorgen Rishoj

FINLAND

Kirjallisuudentutkijain Seura
Fabianinkatu 33
SF-00170 Helsinki
Publications: Kirjallisuudentutkijain Seuran Vousikirja (The Yearbook of the Literary Research Society).
Secretary: Paivi Karttunen.

Suomalaisen Kirjallisuuden Seura
PO Box 259
SF-00170 Helsinki
(Located at: Hallituskatu 1, Helsinki)
Secretary-General: Urpo Vento; Librarian: Henni Ilomaki; Dir, Folklore Archive: Pekka Laaksonen; Dir, Literature Archive: Kaarina Sala.

Svenska Litteratursallskapet i Finland
Mariegatan 8
SF-00170 Helsinki

Publications: Skrifter (Writings).

Svenska Osterbottens Litteraturforening
Auroravagen 10
SF-65610 Smedsby
Co-owner of the publishers in Scriptum, publishing the journal Horisont, organizes writers' seminars, program evenings: lyrics, prose, music.
Approx 170 members.
President: Torbjorn Ehrman; Vice President: Helge Englund; Secretary: Yvonne Hoffman.

FRANCE

Centre National des Lettres
53 rue de Verneuil
F-75007 Paris
To uphold and encourage the work of French writers, give financial help to writers, translators, publishers & public libraries, promote translation into French.
President: Jean Gattegno; Secretary-General: Veronique Chatenay-Dolto.

Societe des Gens de Lettres
Hotel de Massa, 38 rue du Faubourg Saint-Jacques
F-75014 Paris
Approx 11,000 members.
President: Didier Decoin; Vice President: Michele Kahn; Secretary General: Jacques Bens.

Societe des Poetes Francais
Hotel de Messa, 38 rue de Faubourg Saint-Jacques
F-75014 Paris
Lectures, prizes, defending interests of members, loans to distinguished members in distress, quarterly bulleting.
Approx 1200 members.
Honorary Presidents: Pascal Bonetti, Marthe-Claire Fleury-Bonetti, Pierre Orsenat; Honorary Vice President: Roland Le Cordier; Presidents: Brigitte Level and Jacques Raphael-Leygues; Vice Presidents: Jean Bancal, Magdelein Labour and Francoise des Varennes.

GERMANY

Arbeitskreis fur Jugenditeratur e V
Elisabeth Str 15
D-8000, Munich 40
Encourages and coordinates all efforts to support literature for children and young people.
Approx 45 member organizations, 175 individual members.
Managing Director: F Meyer.

Deutsche Akademie fur Sprache und Dichtung
Alexandrakeg 23
6100 Darmstadt
Approx 144 members.
President: Professor Dr Herbert Heckmann; General Secretary: Dr Gerhard Dette.

Deutsche Schillergesellschaft e V
7142 Marbach am Neckar
Schillerhohe 8-10
Approx 3600 members.
President: Professor Dr Eberhard Lammert.

Deutsche Shakespeare-Gesellschaft West
Rathaus
D-4630 Bochum 1
Publication of a yearbook, Shakespeare Jahrbuch, yearly conferences.
Approx 1850 members.
President: Professor Dr Werner Habicht; Vice President: Professor Dr Ulrich Suerbaum; Chairman: Professor Dr Raimund Borgmeier; Treasurer: Claus Schmidt.

Deutsche Thomas-Mann-Gesellschaft
Sitz Lubeck, Konigstr 67a
D-2400 Lubeck
Chairman: Professor Dr Eckhard Heftrich.

Literarischer Verein in Stuttgart e V
Postfach 102251
D-7000 Stuttgart 1
(Located at: Rosenbergstr 113, Stuttgart)
Publications: Bibliothek des Literarischen Vereins in Stuttgart Vol 1 (1842) - Vol 311 (1987).
President: Karl G Hiersemann.

Maximilian-Gesellschaft e V
Postfach 102251
D-7000 Stuttgart 1
Approx 1200 members.
President: Professor Dr Horst Gronemeyer; Vice President: Professor Dr Paul Raabe.

PEN Zentrum
Friedrichstrasse 194. 199
Berlin 1080
Lectures, symposia, literary sessions.
Approx 86 members.
President: Professor Dr Heinz Kamnitzer; Vice President: Walter Kaufmann.

GREECE

The Circle of the Greek Children's Books
Zalongou 7
GR-10678, Athens
Promoting children's literature in Greece, seminars, information material, national contests for the writing of children's books etc.
Approx 180 members.
President: Constantinos P Demertzis; Vice President: Vito Angelopulu; Secretary: Loty Petrovits-Andrutsopulu.

HUNGARY

Artisjus
Agency for Literature and Theatre
POB 67, V, Vorosmarty ter 1
H-1364 Budapest

Institute of Literary Studies of the Hungarian Academy of Sciences
Menesi ut 11-13
H-1118 Budapest
Research of history of Hungarian literature, also research in literary theory, literary critisism to influence contemporary literature, source publications on the history of Hungarian literature, editing of reference books and bibliographies.
Approx 57 research professionals.
Director: Professor Tibor Klaniczay; Deputy

Director: Professor Gyorgy Bodnar.

ICELAND

Rithofundasambund Islands, The Writers' Union of Iceland
PO Box 949
IS-121 Rejkjavik
Union of Icelandic writers that guards copyrights, protects interests in field of literature & book-publishing, drama, textbooks, radio & television scripts etc.
Approx 265 members.
Chairman: Einar Karason; Managing Director: Rannveig G Agustsdottir.

INDIA

Indian Folklore Society
3 Abdul Hamid
Calcutta 700 069
To organize seminars, meetings, conference study groups & publish journals & books on Indian folklore & its allied disciplines in collaboration of Indian publications.
Approx 218 members.
President: Madame Sophia Wadia; Vice President: Mr Sankar Sen Gupta.

The PEN All India Centre
Theosophy Hall, 40 New Marine Lines
Bombay 400 020
National centre of The International PEN, publishes The Indian PEN quarterly.
Approx 116 members.
President: Annada Sankar Ray; Vice Presidents: Dr K R Srinivasa Iyengar and M R Masani; Secretary: Nissim Ezekiel.

The Poetry Society of India
L-67A Malaviya Nagar
New Delhi 110 017

Sahitya Akademi
Rabindrar Bhavan, 35 Ferozeshah Road
New Delhi 110 001
National organization to work for the development of Indian letters, to set high literary standards, foster & co-ordinate literary activities in the Indian languages & promote through them all the cultural unity of the country.
Secretary: Professor Indra Nath Choudhuri.

INDONESIA

PEN Centre
c/o Jl Cemara 6, Jakarta Pusat
Secretary: Dr Toeti Heraty Noerhadi

IRELAND

Irish Academy of Letters
School of Irish Studies, Thomas Prior House
Merrion Road, Dublin 4
Secretary: Evan Boland.

Irish Book Marketing GP
Book House Ireland, 165 Mid Abbey Street
Dublin 1
National association of book publishers, trade representation, training courses, national &

international book fairs & promotions.
Approx 56 members.
Chairman: Michael Gill.

Irish PEN
26 Rosslyn, Killarney Road
Bray, Co Wicklow
President: Francis Stuart; Secretary: Arthur Flynn.

Society of Irish Playwrights
Room 804, Liberty Hall
Dublin 1
To foster interest in & promote contemporary Irish drama. To guard the rights of Irish playwrights.
Approx 120 members.
Chairman: John Synch; Secretary: Patricia Martin.

ISRAEL

ACUM Ltd (Society of Authors, Composers and Music Publishers in Israel)
PO Box 14220
61140 Tel Aviv
Approx 1300 members.
Chairman: Shlomo Tanny; Director General: Ran Kedar; Secretary General: Jochanan Ben-David.

The PEN Centre Israel
19 Shmaryahu Lewin St
Jerusalem 96664
Publishes a bulletin of information and translation of literature in European languages, meetings with members & receptions for guest writers.
Approx 70 members.
President: Aharon Megged; Secretary Treasurer: Haim Toren.

ITALY

Istituto Lombardo Accademia di Scienze e Lettere
Via Brera 28
I-20121 Milan
Organization of conferences, meetings etc. Publications of literature and sciences, exchanged with similar associations all over the world.
Approx 80 science, 80 literary members.
President: Professor Giancarlo Bolognesi.

Societa Italiana Autori Drammatici (SIAD) (Enter Morale)
Via PO 10
00198 Roma

JAPAN

The Dickens Fellowship
Bungei-Gakubu, Seijo University
6-1-20 Seijo, Setagaya, Tokyo
Lectures, symposia, reading circles, publishing bulletins.
President: Koichi Miyazaki; Vice Presidents: Shigerk Koike, Kazuhika Yoneda and Masaie V Matsumara; Hon Secretary: Professor Koichi Miyazaki.

The English Literary Society of Japan
501 Kenkyusha Bldg, 9 Surugadai 2-Chome
Kanda, Chiyoda-ku, Tokyo 101
An association of scholars in the fields of English and American literature and the English language. The society's journal "Studies in English Literature" is published thrice yearly.
Approx 3800 members.
President: Professor Yasunari Takahashi; Secretary: Professor Kenji Nakamura.

Japan Poets Association
c/o Eiji Kikai, 3-16-1, Minami
Azabu, Minato-ku, Tokyo 105
To cultivate the mutual friendship among poets. To award H's Prize and Modern Poet Prize.
Approx 500 members.

KOREA

The Korean PEN Centre
186-210 Jangchung-dong 2-ka
Jung-gu, Seoul 100
Bi-annual seminars. Annual literary prize awards, publication of quarterly bulletin. Takes part in annual International PEN Congress.
Approx 800 members.
President: Mme Sook-Hee Chun; Vice Presidents: Chong-hyuk Yun, Eul-byung Chung and Geun-sam Lee; Secretary: Hyun-bok Lee.

MALAWI

The Writers's Group
PO Box 280
Zomba
Publications: Odi The Muse.
Secretary: Dr A J M Nazombe.

MOROCCO

L'Union des Ecrivains du Maroc
5 rue Ab Bakr Seddik
Rabat

NETHERLANDS

The Dickens Fellowship, Haarlem Branch
26-28 Markstr
1411 EA Naarden
Branch of The Dickens Fellowship, London. Organizes lectures, editing "The Dutch Dickensian".
Approx 80 members.
President: Professor Dr J H A Lukin; Vice President: Dr J J C Kabel; Hon Secretary: Mr J C Van Kessel.

Nederlandse Taalunie
Stadhoudersplantsoen 2
2517 JL Den Haag

Netherlands Centre of the International PEN
Meeweg 25
1405 BC Bussum
Dutch branch of a world association of writers, poets, essayists, novelists, editors & playwrights.
Approx 350 members.
President: Joost de Wit; Secretary: Rudolf Geel.

NEW ZEALAND

Arts Council of New Zealand
Old Public Trust Building, 131-135 Lambton Quay
Wellington PO Box 3806, Wellington

Christchurch Dickens Fellowship
PO Box 6126
Christchurch
Study works of Dickens at regular monthly

meetings.
Approx 50 members.
President: Gary Fox; Vice Presidents: Hubert Cocks and Thelma Conroy; Secretary: Peter Oakley.

International Writers' Workshop NZ (Inc)
57 Baddeley Avenue
Kohimarama, Auckland
Tutored workshops, group evaluation of work. Workshops designed to interest & encourage writers.
Approx 150 members.
President: Mrs Joyce Beumelburg; Vice President: Mrs Joyce Irving; Secretary: Alison Tye.

New Zealand Women Writers' Society Inc
PO Box 11-352
Wellington
Stimulates & encourages creative work in literature, foster comradeship among members.
Approx 280 members.
President: Joy Tonks; Vice President: Betty Bremner; Secretary: Barbara Wilkinson.

PEN (New Zealand Centre) Inc
PO Box 2283
Wellington
Promotion of cooperation & mutual support among writers in all countries & encourage creative writing in NZ.
Approx 600 members.
President: Kevin Ireland; Vice Presidents: Maurice Gee and Lynley Hood; Executive Secretary: Jenny Jones.

NORWAY

Det Norske Videnskaps-Akademi
Drammensveien 78
Oslo 2
Publications: Skrifter Avhandlinger Arbok
Secretary-General: Professor Dr A Semb-Johansson; Executive Secretary: Kjell Herlofsen.

NORLA - Norwegian Literature Abroad
PO Box 239, Sentrum
N-0103 Oslo 1
Information office for Norwegian literature.
Managing Director: Kristin Brudevoll.

PANAMA

Instituto Nacional de Cultura
Apartado 662
Panama 1.

POLAND

Instytut Badan Literackich
Nowy Swiat 72, Palac Staszica
00-330 Warsaw
Publications: Pamietnik Literacki (Literary Journal, quarterly), Biuletyn Polonistyczny (Bulletin of Polish Literary Scholarship).
Acting Directors: Professor Alina Witkowska, Dr Ryszard Gorski and Dr Zbigniew Jaronsinski.

Zwiazek Literatow Polskich (Union of Polish Writers)
Krakoweskie Przedmiescie 87
00-950 Warszawa.

SOUTH AFRICA

English Academy of Southern Africa
PO Box 124
Witwatersrand 2050

Institute for the Study of English in Africa
Rhodes University, PO Box 94
Grahamston 6140
Publishes English in Africa and New Coin Poetry. Conducts research into needs of black pupils learning English.
Director: Professor L S Wright; National Director, Molteno Project: Professor P S Walters; Secretary: Mrs C M A Brown.

Nasionale Afrikaanse Letterkundige Museum en Navorsingsentrum
Private Bag X20543
Bloemfontein 9300

National English Literary Museum
Private Bag 1019
Grahamstown 6140.

SWEDEN

Kungl Vitterhets Historie och Antikvitets Akademien
Villagatan 3
S-114 32 Stockholm
Publications: Fornvannen (journal), Handlingar (memoirs), Arkiv (archives), Arsbok (Yearbook), Monografier (monographs).
Secretary: Professor Erik Frykman.

Svenska Osterbottens Litteraturforening
c/o Sven-Erik Klinkmann, Henriksgatan 7-9 4N
SF-65320 Vasa, Finland
Publications: Horisont

SWITZERLAND

PEN Club Centre
Postfach 1383
CH-3001 Bon
Approx 200 members.
President: Ernst Reinhardt; Secretary General: Hans Erpf.

PEN Internazionale-Centro della Svizzera Italiana e Romancia
PO Box 2126
CH-6901 Lugano 1
Organizes the Congresses etc. Organized the 50th Congress of PEN in Lugano.
Approx 110 members.
President: Mr Grytzko Mascioni; Vice President: Mrs Magda Kerenyi; Secretary General: Mrs Attilia Fiorenza Venturini.

Schweizer Autoren Gruppe Olten
Sekretariat, Siedlung Halen 43
CH-3047 Herrenschwanden
Author's society.
Approx 220 members.
President: Lukas Hartmann; Secretary: Hans Muhlethaler.

Schweizerischer Bund fur Jugendliteratur
Gewerbestr 8
CH-6330 Cham

Promotion and diffusion of literature for children & young adults, distribution of specially developed material, further education.
Approx 5000 members.
Secretary: Ursula Merz.

Schweizerischer Schriftsteller-verband
Kirchgasse 25
CH-8022 Zurich
Professional organization, founded in 1912, for the protection of writers' interests. Publications: FORUM der Schriftsteller, Dictionary of Swiss authors.
Approx 630 members.
President: Ernst Nef; Vice President: Janine Massard; Secretary: Hans Muhlethaler.

THAILAND

The Siam Society
PO Box 65
Bangkok
Society promotes & tries to preserve artistic, scientific and other cultural affairs of Thailand & neighbouring countries. Publishes Journal of the Siam Society & The Siam Society Newsletter.
Approx 1250 members.
President: Mr Patanachai Jayant; Hon Secretary: Mrs Virginia M Crocco.

UNITED KINGDOM

Arvon Foundation
Totleigh Barton, Sheepwash
Beaworthy, Devon EX21 5NS
(Also at: Lumb Bank, Heptonstall
Hebden Bridge, W Yorks HX7 6DF)
Offers residential writing courses.
Chairman: Lawrence Sail; Co-Presidents: Terry Hands and Ted Hughes, OBE.

Association of British Science Writers (ABSW)
c/o British Association for the Advancement of Science
Fortress House, 23 Savile Row, London W1X 1AB
Administrator: Barbara Dills; Secretary: Peter Briggs.

Association for Scottish Literary Studies
Department of English, University of Aberdeen
Aberdeen AB9 2UB
Publications: Scottish Library Journal; Scottish Literary Journal Supplement (both twice yearly).
Secretary: Dr D S Robb.

The Authors' Club
40 Dover Street
London W1X 3RB
Club for Writers.
Approx 75 members.
Secretary: Mrs Ann Carter.

Birmingham & Midland Institute
9 Margaret Street
Cultural institute & library sponsoring musical, literary, poetical, art activities.
Approx 1200 members.
President: The Viscountess Cobham; Senior Vice President: Nathan Myers; Junior Vice President: W Jarvis; Administrator: Mr J Hunt.

Book Trust
Book House, 45 East Hill
London SW18 2QZ
An independent charitable trust whose task is to promote reading & the using of books.
Approx 3000 members.
Chief Executive: Beverly Anderson.

Books across the Sea
The English-Speaking Union, Dartmouth House
37 Charles St, London W1X 8AB
Publications: Ambassador Booklist (quarterly)
Librarian: Jean Huse.

British Science Fiction Association
29 Thornville Road, Hartlepool
Cleveland TS26 8EW
Literary criticism, news, reviews, serious articles, meetings, writers workshop, lending library & magazine chain.
Approx 1000 members.
Membership Secretary: Jo Raine.

Cambridge Bibliographical Society
University Library
Cambridge CB3 9DR
Publications: Transactions (annually); Monographs (irregular).
Honorary Secretary: F R Collieson.

The Charles Lamb Society
1A Royston Road, Richmond
Surrey TW10 6LT
To study the life, works & times of Charles Lamb & his circle, to stimulate the Elian spirit of friendliness & humour, form a collection of Eliana.
Approx 350 members.
President: Professor John Beer; Chairman: Dr D G Wilson OBE; Secretary: Mrs M R Huxstep.

Crime Writers' Association (CWA)
PO Box 172, Tring
Hertfordshire HP23 5LP
Secretary: Anthea Fraser

The Dickens Fellowship
The Dickens House, 48 Doughty Street
London WC1N 2LF
HQ in London, over 60 branches worldwide, of Dickens enthusiasts. Organises talks, conferences, publishes "The Dickensian", concerned with preservation of buildings associated with Dickens.
Approx 4000 members.
Contact: Edward G Preston

Early English Text Society
Christ Church
Oxford OX1 1DP
Publish 1 or more volumes per year of English texts earlier than 1558.
Approx 1050 members.
Executive Secretary: R F S Hamer; Editorial Secretary: Dr H L Spencer.

Edinburgh Bibliographical Society
New College Library, Mound Place
Edinburgh EH1 2LU
Lectures & publications (Transaction, irregular, issued only to members) on all bibliographical matters.

Approx 200 members.
Honorary Secretary: Dr M Simpson.

The English Association
The Vicarage, Priory Gardens
Bedford Park, London W4 1TT
To promote the understanding & appreciation of English language & literature.
Approx 900 members.
Secretary: Ruth Fairbanks-Joseph.

Francis Bacon Society Inc
Canonbury Tower, Islington
London N1
Publications: Baconiana (periodically), Jottings (periodically), booklets, pamphlets (list on request).
Chairman: Noel Fermor.

H G Wells Society
English Department, Nene College
Moulton Park, Northamption NN2 7AL
Circulates newsletter & journal, Wellsian, & organizes lectures & conferences to promote an active interest in the life & work of H G Wells.
Approx 300 members.
Honorary Secretary: Dr Sylvia Hardy.

The Incorporated Bronte Society
Bronte Parsonage, Haworth
Keighley, West Yorkshire BD22 8DR
The preservation of the literary works of the Bronte family & of manuscripts and other objects related to the family.
Approx 3200 members worldwide.
President: Lord Briggs of Lewes; Director: Ms Jane Sellars; Secretary: Mrs Eunice Skirrow.

Institute of Contemporary Arts
The Mall
London SW1
Galleries, performance, music, cinema, talks, conferences, restaurant, bar, 'Bookshop'.
Approx 6500 members.
Director: Mik Flood; Director Talks: Linda Brandon.

The Johnson Society of London
255 Baring Road, Grove Park
London SE12 0BQ
To study the works of Dr Samuel Johnson, his circle, his contempories & his times through lectures & articles in 'The New Rambler'.
Approx 110 members.
Honorary Secretary: Mrs Z E O'Donnell

The Keats/Shelley Memorial Association
10 Landsdowne Road
Tunbridge Wells, Kent TN1 2NJ
To promote the works of Keats, Shelley, Byron & Leigh Hunt & maintain the house in Rome where Keats died.
Approx 250 members.
Contact: Honorary Secretary

Kent & Sussex Poetry Society
Castens, Carpenters Lane
Hadlow, Kent TN11 0EY
Readings, workshops, discussions to promote love & understandings of poetry.
Approx 50 members.
Contact: Doriel Hulse

The Kipling Society

2nd Floor, Schomberg House, 80-82 Pall Mall
London SW1Y 5HG
Promotion of Kipling studies, discussion meetings, annual luncheon, quarterly journal.
Approx 900 members.
Secretary: Norman Entract

Lancashire Authors' Association
Heatherslade, 5 Quakerfields
Westhoughton, Bolton, Lancashire BL5 2BJ
Publications: The Record (quarterly)
General Secretary: Eric Holt

London Writer Circle
c/o Cathy Smith, 23 Prospect Road
London NW2 2JU
Lectures and criticisms of manuscripts.
Approx 150 members.
President: Gordon Wells; Vice President; Rosemary Wells; Secretary: Cathy Smith.

National Union of Journalists
Acorn House, 314 Grays Inn Road
London WC1X 8DP
General Secretary: John Foster

Northern Arts Poetry Library
The Willows, Morpeth
Northumberland NE61 1TA
Aims to collect all contemporary poetry in English published in Great Britain. Includes works by individual poets and has a huge range of anthologies. Also has a wide range of poetry magazines.

Oxford Bibliographical Society
Bodleian Library
Oxford OX1 3BG
Publications: First Series, vols I-VII, 1923-46; New Series, vol 1, 1948-.
Secretary: Dr P Bulloch.

PEN English Centre
7 Dilke Street, Chelsea
London SW3 4JE
Publications: The Pen (broadsheet, twice a year)
General Secretary: Josephine Pullein-Thompson

PEN Scottish Centre
c/o Scott, 33 Drumsheugh Gardens
Edinburgh EH3 7RN
National Centre of the World Association of Writers PEN International, to promote friendly co-operation of writers in all countries through literary gatherings.
Approx 145 members.
President: Professor A N Jeffares; Vice Presidents: Paul H Scott and Mary Baxter; Honorary Secretary: Laura Fiorentini.

The Poetry Library
South Bank Centre
London SE1 8XX
Includes all 20th-Century poetry in English and a collection of all poetry magazines published in the UK. Also arranges functions and provides an information service.

The Poetry Society
22 Betterton Street
London WC2H 9BU
Operates as a book club, quarterly members receive a new book of poetry, an annual anthology

also part of membership.
Approx 1700 members.
General Secretary: Paul Ralph.

Romantic Novelists' Association
35 Ruddlesway, Windsor
Berkshire SL4 5SF
Aims to raise the prestige of romantic authorship. Open to published romantic & historical authors & probationers entering work for the Netta Muskett Award.
Approx 560 members.
Secretary: Joyce Bell

Royal Society of Literature of the United Kingdom
1 Hyde Park Gardens
London W2 2LT
Lectures, publications & awards.
Approx 750 members.
President: Lord Jenkins of Hillhead

Shakespearean Authorship Trust
11 Old Square, Lincoln's Inn
London WC2A 3TS
Object of Trust is "The advancement of learning with particular reference to the social, political & literary history of England in the 16th century & authorship of the literary works commonly attributed to William Shakespeare".
Trustees: Dr L L Ware, Dr D W T Vessey, Mr J H W Siberrad and Lord Vere of Hanworth.

Sherlock Holmes Society of London
3 Outram Road, Southsea
Hampshire PO5 1QP
Study of the life & works of Sherlock Holmes & Dr Watson.
Approx 1000 members.
Honorary Secretary: G S Stavert.

Society of Civil Service Authors
8 Bawtree Close, Sutton
Surrey SM2 5LQ
Encourages authorship by past and present members of the Civil Service.
Honorary Secretary: Mrs Joan Hykin

Surrey Poetry Centre, (Guildford & Wey Poets)
15 Woodside Road, Purley
Surrey CR8 4LQ
A poetry group that meets twice monthly for workshop, reading of members' works, discussion, poetry competition adjudication etc.
Approx 28 members.
Honorary General Secretary: Stella Stocker.

Swansea & District Writers' Circle
932 Carmathen Road, Fforestfach
Swansea SA5 4AB
To encourage 'writers' in an exchange of ideas & experience, & possibly help with problems encountered in creative writing.
Approx 40 members.
President: Edith Courtney; Secretary: Beth Quinn.

The Thomas Hardy Society
PO Box 1438, Dorchester
Dorset DT1 1YH
Promotion & appreciation of works of T Hardy, summer conference, lectures, walks in Wessex.

Approx 900 members.
Honorary Secretary: Mrs Helen Gibson

The Tolkien Society
35 Amesbury Crescent, Hove
East Sussex BN3 5RD
Furthering interest in the life & works of Professor J R R Tolkien. Newsletter.
Approx 700 members.
Honorary President: Professor J R R Tolkien CBE 'in pertetuo'; Chairman: Brin Dunsire; Secretary: Anne Haward.

Ver Poets
Haycroft, 61/63 Chiswell Green Lane
St Albans, Herts AL2 3AL
Aim to promote poetry & help poets. Holds 6 competitions for members every year, 1 open international competition.
Approx 200 members.
Chairman: Ray Badman

Welsh Academy (Yr Academi Gymreig)
3rd Floor, Mount Stuart House
Mount Stuart Square, Cardiff CF1 6DQ
Aims to promote Anglo-Welsh literature through readings, conferences, workshops, schools, projects. Organizes Cardiff Literature Festival.
Approx 95 members.
Director: Kevin Thomas; Co-ordinator: Dafydd Rogers

Women Writers Network (WWN)
23 Prospect Road
London NW2 2JU
Provides and exchanges information, support and opportunities for working writers. Also arranges functions and provides a newsletter.
Membership Secretary: Cathy Smith

The Writer's Guild of Great Britain
430 Edgware Road
London W2 1EH
Represents professional writers in film, radio, televsion, theatre and publishing. Regularly provides assistance to members on items such as contracts and conditions of work.
General Secretary: Alison Grey

UNITED STATES OF AMERICA

Arizona

The Authors Resource Centre (TARC Inc)
PO Box 64785
Tucson, AZ 85728-4785
Serves writers etc, writers' research library, literary agency, sponsors 40 workshops & seminars, publishes TARC Report for writers.
Approx 300 members.
President/Excutive Director: Martha R Gore; Secretary/Treasurer/Educational Director: Victor M Gore.

The Society of Southwestern Authors
Box 30355, Tucson, AZ 85751-0355
Organization of pro writers for supportive fellowship, recognition of member writers' professional achievement, & encouragement & assistance for persons striving to become writers.
Approx 125 members.

President: John Stickler; Corres Secretary: Susy Smith.

California

San Diego Novel Writers Workshop
8431 Beaver Lake Drive
San Diego, CA 92119
For professional novel writers. Read & critique members' writing. Offer encouragement, aid & comfort. Semimonthly meetings.
Approx 20 members.
Director: Chet Cunningham.

Society of Children's Book Writers
22736 Vanowen Street, Suite 106
West Hills, CA 91307
Offers bi-monthly 'Bulletin' MSS exchange, meetings, conferences, Golden Kite awards, insurance, grants, advise.
Approx 5000 members.
President: Stephen Mooser; Executive Director: Lin Oliver (Ms).

Writers Guild of America, West, Inc
8955 Beverly Blvd
West Hollywood, CA 90048
Represents its membership in contract negotiation and compliance with the film and television industry.
Approx 7500 members
Executive Director: Brian Walton; President: George Kirgo; Vice President: Del Reisman; Secretary/Treasurer: Adam Rodman.

Colorado

The Associated Business Writers of America
1450 S Havana Ste 620
Aurora, CO 80012
Association for business writers.
Approx 150 members.
Executive Director: James Lee Young.

The National Writers Club
1450 S Havana Ste 620
Aurora, CO 80012
Association for freelance writers.
Approx 5000 members.
Executive Director: James Lee Young.

Delaware

International Reading Association
800 Barksdale Road, PO Box 8139
Newark, DE 19714
Professional education association dedicated to the improvement of reading ability & development of the reading habit worldwide through publications, research, meetings, conferences & international congresses.
Approx 85,000 members.
President: Patricia S Koppman; Executive Director: Ronald W Mitchell.

District of Columbia

National Endowment for the Humanities
Public Information Office
1100 Pennsylvania Avenue, NW, Room 406
Washington, DC 20506
Attention: Joy Evans

National League of American Pen Women
Pen Arts Building
1300 17th Street NW
Washington, DC 20036
President: Muriel C Freeman

National Press Club
529 14th Street, NW
Washington, DC 20045
General Manager: William Vose

PEN Syndicated Fiction Project
PO Box 15650
Washington, DC 20003
Director: Caroline Marshall

Washington Independent Writers
733 15th Street, NW, Suite 220
Washington, DC 20005
Director: Isolde Chapin

Florida

International Society of Dramatists
Box 1310
Miami, FL 33153
Information clearinghouse for dramatists in all media: stage, screen, TV, radio, provides continually updated lists of script opportunities in English worldwide. Monthly publications. Annual playwriting award.
Approx 10,550 members.
President: Andrew Delaplane.

Illinois

American Library Association
50 East Huron
Chicago, IL 60611
Provides leadership for the development, promotion, improvement of library & information services to enhance learning.
Approx 44,000 menbers.
Director: Linda Chrismond; Editor: Arthur Plotnik.

Illinois Writers Inc
c/o English Dept, Illinois State University
Normal, IL 61761-6901
To promote the literary arts of Illinois poets, fiction writers, & small press publishers. Publish bi-annual review & bi-monthly newsletter.
Approx 5000 members.
Chairperson: Deborah Bosley; Newsletter Editor: Mary Maddox.

Independents Writers of Chicago
7855 Gross Point Road, Suite G-4
Skokie, IL 60077
Monthly meetings & four workshops per year dealing with the business aspects of independent writing. Writers' line job referral; insurance.
Approx 350 members.
President: M A Porucznik.

International Black Writers & Artists Inc
Box 1030
Chicago, IL 60690
Poetry readings, contests, pot lucks, workshops, annual conferences, writers picnic.
Approx 250 members.
President: Edna Crutchfield; Chairman: Hazel Harrison; Vice Presidents: Donald Bakeer and Gene Williams; Secretary: Carl Crutchfield.

Society of Midland Authors
29 East Division Street
Chicago, IL 60610
To promote friendly contact & professional interchange among authors of the Midland, to explore topics of literary & professional interest in open monthly programmes, honour the best of Midland writing with cash awards annually. Approx 180 members.
President: Dempsey J Travis; Vice President: Rick Kogan.

Maryland

The Lewis Carroll Society of North America
617 Rockford Road
Silver Spring, MD 20902
To promote interests in & be a centre for Lewis Carroll studies.
Approx 300 members.
President: Charles Lovett; Vice President: Alan Tannenbaum; Secretary: Maxine Schaefer.

Minnesota

Catholic Library Association
St Mary's College, Campus 26
700 Terrace Heights, Winoma, MN 55987
An organization of professional librarians interested in providing service according to the Catholic philosophy.
Approx 3000 members.
President: Emmertt Corry; Executive Director: Natalie A Logan.

New Hampshire

The MacDowell Colony Inc
100 High Street
Peterborough, NH 03458
Retreat for writers, composers, visual artists & filmmakers with professional standing in field. Board of Directors: 39; Staff: 10; Colony Fellows approx: 2000.
Chairman: Vartan Gregorian; President: David W Helenaik; Executive Director: Mary Carswell.

New York

The Academy of American Poets
177 E 87 St
New York, NY 10128
Sponsor The Lamont Poetry Selection, The Walt Whitman Award, The Harold Morton Landon Translation Award, The Lavan Younger Poets Award & annual college poetry prizes; workshops, classes & literary historical walking tours; award fellowships to American poets for distinguished poetic achievement.
Approx 2000 members.
President: Mrs Edward T Chase; Executive Director: William Wadsworth.

American Society of Journalists and Authors Inc
1501 Broadway, Suite 302
New York, Ny 10036
Service organization providing exchange of ideas, market information. Regular meetings with speakers from the industry, annual writers conference; medical plans available. professional referral service, annual membership directory; first amendment advocacy group.

Approx 750 members.
President: Thomas Bedell; Executive Vice President: Katharine Davis Fishman; Secretary: Eleanor Dienstag.

Brooklyn Writers' Network (BWN)
2509 Avenue K
Brooklyn, NY 11210
Seeks to improve contact between professional writers & publishing industry; newsletter; directory; conferences; workshops.
Approx 500 members
Director: Ruth Schwartz.

International Association of Crime Writers Inc
JAF Box 1500
New York, NY 10116
President: Roger L Simon; Executive Director: Mary A Frisque; Sec-Treas: Thomas Adcock; Secretary: Jerome Charyn.

Mystery Writers of America Inc
17 East 47th Street, 6th Floor
New York, NY 10017
To support & promote the mystery. Chapters around country hold monthly meetings with speakers, sponsors the Edgar Allan Poe Awards.
Approx 2500 members.
Executive Secretary: Priscilla Ridgway.

The International Women's Writing Guild (IWWG)
Box 810, Gracie Sta
new York, NY 10028
A network for the empowerment of women through writing. Services include manuscript referral & exchange, writing conferences & retreats, group rates for health & life insurance, legal aid, regional clusters & job referrals.
Approx 5000 members.
Executive Director: Hannelore Hahn.

PEN American Center
568 Broadway
New York, NY 10012
An international organization of writers, poets, playwrights, essayists, editors, novelists & translators whose purpose is to bring about better understanding among writers of all nations.
Approx 2100 members.
President: Larry McMurty; International President: Rene Tavernier; Executive Director: Karen Kennerly.

Poetry Society of America
15 Gramercy Park
New York, NY 10003
A service organization dedicated to the promotion of poets and poetry. Sponsors readings, lectures, contests/houses the Van Voorhis Library.
Approx 1700 members.
President: Molly Peacock; Director: Elise Paschen.

Poets & Writers Inc
72 Spring Street
New York, NY 10012
National nonprofit information center for those interested in contemporary American literature. Publish a directory of American poets & fiction writers; sponsor readings & workshops program.
Excutive Director: Elliot Figman.

Pushcart Press
PO Box 380
Wainscott, NY 11975
Literary publishers.
President: Bill Henderson.

Science Fiction and Fantasy Writers of America Inc
5 Winding Brook Drive, Suite 1B
Guilderland, NY 12084
Professional association of SF/Fantasy writers, editors, agents, anthologists; presenters of the SFWA Nebula Awards.
Approx 1100 members.
President: Greg Bear; Vice President: Michael Cassott; Secretary: Frank Catalano.

Teachers & Writers Collaborative
5 Union Square West
New York, NY 10003
Teachers & Writers sends professional artists into public schools to teach their art forms. Also publish books & a magazine about how to teach creative writing.
Approx 350 members.
Executive Director: Nancy Larson Shapiro; Chairman of the Board: Steven Schrader; Assoicate Directors: Pat Padgett and Gary Lenhart; Publications Director: Ron Padgett; Programme Director: Elizabeth Fox.

Translation Center
412 Dodge Hall, Columbia University
New York, NY 10027
Publish a magazine bi-annually. Dedicated to finding and publishing the best translations of significant works of foreign contemporary literature.
Director: Frank MacShane; Secretary: Elizabeth Koyama.

Writers Guild of America (WGA) East Inc
555 W 57 St
New York, Ny 10019
Labor union representing professional writers in motion pictures, TV & radio. Membership available only through the sale of literary material or employment for writing services in one of these areas.
Executive Director: Mona Mangan; President: Edward Adler; Vice President: Adrian j Meppen; Sec-Treas: Jane Bollinger.

Ohio

Ohioana Library Association
65 S Front St, 1105 Ohio Depts Bldg
Columbus, OH 43215
Gives annual awards for books by Ohioans & about Ohio. Publishes 'Ohioana Quarterly'.
Approx 1000 members.
President: Ruth Mount; Director: Linda Hengst; Vice President: Ann Bowers; Secretary: Kenneth Warren; Office Manager: Sandra Reed.

Pennsylvania

Association of Professional Translators
Three Mellon Bank Centre - 2623
Pittsburgh, PA 15259
Holds bi-monthly meetings, members teach professional translation courses at University of Pittsburgh.
Approx 125 members.
Presidents: Tom Clark, Marcella Martin and Mary Jo Bensasi; Secretary: Mary Jeanne Fredley; Permanent Officer: Josephine Thornton.

National Book Critics Circle
400 North Broad Street
Philadelphia, PA 19103
Gives annual awards for fiction, poetry, biography/autobiography, general non fiction, criticism. Purpose: to raise the standards of book criticism & enhance public appreciation of literature.
Approx 500 members.
President: Nina King; Vice President & Treasurer: Eliot Fremont-Smith; Vice President & Secretary: Alida Becker.

Outdoor Writers' Association of America
2017 Cato Avenue, Suite 101
State College, PA 16801
Professional authors, journalists, broadcasters, photographers & artists who cover hunting, fishing, camping, canoeing & · similar outdoor sports; workshops held at annual conference.
Approx 1900 members.
President: Joel Vance; Vice Presidents: Thomas Huggler, Lonnie Williamson and William Hilts; Executive Director: Sylvia G Bashline.

The Philomathean Society of the University of Pennsylvania
Philmathean Halls, Box H, College Hall,
Univ of Pennsylvania, Philadelphia, PA 19104
Translate Rosetta Stone, offered first lectures in US history. Aim: to increase the knowledge of the members and to increase the academic prestige of the University.
Approx 2200 members.
Moderator: Darren Rosenblum; First Censor: Jessica Cooperman; Secretary: James Bessin; Senior Member: Eugene A Bolt Jr.

South Dakota

South Dakota State Poetry Society Inc
909 E 34th Street
Sioux Falls, SD 57105
Poetry magazine 10 times a year, 'Pasque Petals'. Newsletter 'Serendipity'. Meetings, workshops, yearly contests.
Approx 250 members.
President: Verlyss V jacobson; Vice President; Myra Osterberg; Treasurer: Emma Dinut.

Texas

American Literary Translators Association (ALTA)
Box 830688, University of Texas
Richardson, TX 75083
Sponsor the Gregory Rabassa Prize for the translation of fiction from any language into English & the Richard Wilbur Prize for the translation of poetry from any language into English. Awards, which consist of the publication of the winning poems are awarded biannually.
Approx 1000 members.
Executive Secretary: Sheryl St Germain

Science Fiction Research Association Inc
6021 Grassmere
Corpus Christi, TX 78415
Professional study of science fiction & fantasy; annual scholar award. Archives maintained at University of Kansas, Lawrence. Sponsor workshop awards & prizes.
President: Elizabeth Anne Hull; Vice President: Neil Barron; Secretary: David Mead; Treasurer: Thomas Remington.

Western Writers of America
2800 N Campbell
El Paso, TX 79902
An organization of professionals dedicated to the spirit & reality of the West, past & present.
Approx 600 members.
President: David Dary; Vice President: Nancy Hamilton; Secretary: Barbara Ketcham.

Virginia

Associated Writing Programs (AWP)
Old Dominion University
Norfolk, VA 23529-0079
National, non-profit organization of writers & writers who teach.
Approx 4000 members.
President: Joe David Bellamy; Vice President: Kate Daniels; Secretary: Alberto Rios.

APPENDIX C

LITERARY AWARDS AND PRIZES

The following list of Literary Awards and Prizes does not claim to be exhaustive although every effort has been made to make it as comprehensive as possible.

AT & T Non-Fiction Award
206 Marylebone Road
London NW1 6LY, England
The winner is chosen from entries submitted by publishers. Awarded to the best work of general non-fiction published by a British publisher for the first time in the 12 months between 1 April and 31 March. Entries must be written in English by living writers from the British Commonwealth or the Republic of Ireland.
Annual prize of £25,000 (first prize) - each shortlisted author receives an AT & T computer worth £1500
Publicity Contact: Colman Getty; Administration: Booksellers Association
1988   Nairn in Darkness and Light by David Thomson
1989   Touching the Void by Joe Simpson
1990   Citizens: A Chronicle of the French Revolution by Simon Schama
1991   Invisible Woman by Claire Tomalin
1992   Wild Swans by Jung Chang
1993   Never Again: Britain 1945-51 by Peter Hennessy
1994   Edward Heath: A Biography by John Campbell

The J R Ackerley Prize for Autobiography
English Pen, 7, Dilke Street
Chelsea, London SW3 4JE, England
Prize is awarded for Literary Autobiography, written in English and published in the year preceeding the Award.
Annual prize of £2000
Contact: Tom Aitken, Awards Secretary
1982   Shaky Relations by Edward Blishen
1983   Her People by Kathleen Dayus
        The High Path by Ted Walker
1984   Still Life by Richard Cobb
1985   Deceived with Kindness by Angelica Garnett
1986   Time and Time Again by Dan Jacobson
1987   After The Funeral by Diana Athill
1988   Little Wilson & Big God by Anthony Burgess
1989   The Grass Arena by John Healy
1990   Daddy, We Hardly Knew You by Germaine Greer
1991   St Martin's Ride by Paul Binding
1992   Almost a Gentleman: An Autobiography by John Osborne
1993   More Please by Barry Humphries
1994   And When Did You Last See Your Father? by Blake Morrison

Jane Addams Children's Book Award
Jane Addams Peace Association
777 United Nations Plaza
New York, NY 10017, USA
Prize awarded for a book that best combines literary merit with themes stressing peace, social justice, world community & the equality of the sexes & all races.
Award: Certificate presented annually.
Contact: Andrea Spencer-Linzie
1980   The Road From Home by David Kherdian
1981   First Woman in Congress: Jeannette Rankin by Florence White
1982   A Spirit to Ride the Whirlwind by Athena V Lord
1983   Hiroshima No Pika by Toshi Maruki
1984   Rain of Fire by Marion Dane Bauer
1985   The Short Life of Sophie Scholl by Hermann Vink
1986   Ain't Gonna Study War No More: The Story of American Peace Seekers by Milton Meltzer.
1987   Nobody Wants a Nuclear War, written and illustrated by Judith Vigna
1988   Waiting For The Rain: A Novel of South Africa by Sheila Gordon
1989   Anthony Burns: The Defeat and Triumph of a Fugitive Slave by Virginia Hamilton
1990   Long Hard Journey by Patricia McKissak & Frederick McKissak
1991   The Book of Peace by (ed) Ann Durell & Marilyn Sachs
1992   Journey of the Sparrows by Fran Leeper Bluff
1993   A Taste of Salt by Frances Temple

The Age Concern Book of the Year Award
c/o The Literary Editor, The Age
250 Spencer Street, Melbourne, Vic 3000 Australia
Prize is awarded to a published book of literary merit, written by living Australians.
Award of $3000 to the author of a non-fiction book and $3000 to a work of imaginative writing.
Contact: Literary Editor
1981   A Million Wild Acres by Eric Rolls
        Turtle Beach by Blanche d'Alpuget
1982   Fly Away Peter by David Malouf
        John Monash by Geoffrey Serle
1983   Mr Scobie's Riddle by Elizabeth Jolley
        A History of Tasmania, Vol 1 by Lloyd Robson
1984   The Bellarmine Jug by Nicholas Hasluck
        H B Higgins: The Rebel as Judge by John Rickard
1985   Illywhacker by Peter Carey
        Mapping the Paddocks by Chester Eagle
        Vietnam: A Reporter's War by Hugh Lunn
1986   Sister Ships by Joan London
        George Johnston: A Biography of Garry

Kinnane
1987 Stories from the Warm Zone by Jessica Anderson
The Fatal Shore by Robert Hughes
1988 Forty-Seventeen by Frank Moorhouse
Big-Noting by Robin Gerster
1989 Mariners Are Warned! by Marsden Hordern
My Father's Moon by Elizabeth Jolley
1990 Blessed City by Gwen Harwood
Longleg by Glenda Adams

The Alice Literary Award
c/o Federal President
Society of Women Writers (Australia)
GPO Box 2621, Sydney, NSW 2001, Australia
Presented by the Society of Women Writers (Australia) biennially for a distinguished and long term contribution to literature by an Australian women.
Contact: Majorie Wilke, Federal President
1980 Dame Judith Wright
1982 Dame Mary Durack
1984 Kylie Tennant
1986 Ruth Park
1988 Nancy Cato

American Book Award
Before Columbus Foundation
660 13th Street, Suite 203
Oakland, CA 94612, USA
Recognises outstanding literary achievement by contemporary American authors without restriction for race, sex, ethnic background, or genre. The purpose to acknowledge the excellence & multicultural diversity of American writing.
The awards are non-profit. There are no categories & all winners are accorded equal status.
Contact: Gundars Strads
1980 Tortuga by Rudolfo Anaya
Random Possession by Mei-Mei Berssenbrugge
Mouth on Paper by Jayne Cortez
Hello, La Jolla by Ed Dorn
All I Asking to Is My Body by Milton Murayama
Ceremony by Leslie Silko
Snake-Back Solos by Quincy Troupe
Future Preconditional by Douglas Woolf
1981 Turn Again to mer & Other Poems by Helen Adam
On Call by Miguel Algarin
The Shameless Hussy by the American Library Trustee Association
The Salt Eaters by Toni Cade Bambara
Back Then Tomorrow by Peter Blue Cloud
The Choice by Rose Drachler
The Liberties by Susan Howe
In Time by Robert Kelly
Songs for Jadina by Alan Lau
Travelling Light by Lionel Mitchell
Felita by Nicholasa Mohr
A Scent of Apples by Ben Santos
Lifetime Achievement Awards for Frank Stanford & Larry Neal
1982 The Book of Jamaica by Russell Banks
Emplumada by Lorna Dee Cervantes
Chickencoop Chinaman and Year of the

Dragon by Frank Chin
Enclave by Tato Laviera
Collected Poems by E L Mayo
Songs for the Harvester of Dreams by Duane Niatum
This Passover or Next I Will Never Be in Jerusalem by Hilton Obenzinger
Sangre by Leroy Quintana
Pre-Faces & Other Writings by Jerome Rothenberg
Shino Suite by Ronald Tanaka
Marked by Fire by Joyce Carol Thomas
Bodies & Soul by Al Young
Island: Poetry and History of Chinese Immigrants on Angle Island 1910-1949 by Him Mark Lai, Genny Lim and Judy Yung (editors)

Lifetime Achievement Award for Kay Boyle
1984 Confirmation: An Anthology of African-American Women by Amiri Baraka and Amina Baraka
The Heat Bird by Mei-Mei Berssenbrugge
Days Without Weather by Cecil Brown
Breaking Silence: An Anthology of Contemporary Asian American Poets by Joseph Bruchac
A Puerto Rican in New York and Other Sketches by Jesus Colon
O Albany by William Kennedy
The Mama Poems by Maurice Kenny
Naked in Deccan by Venkatesh Kulkarni
Praisesong for the Widow by Paule Marshall
Pre-Biter by Ruthanne Lum McCunn (author), You-shan Tang (illustrator), and Ellen Lai-shan Yeung (trans)
Echoes Inside the Labyrinth by Thomas McGrath
Citizen 13660 by Mine Okubo
The Captive Soul of the Messiah: New Tales About Reb Nachman by Howard Schwartz
Axe Handles by Gary Snyder
Lifetime Achievement Award for Josephine Miles
1985 The House on Mango Street by Sandra Cisneros
Ground Work: Before the War by Robert Duncan
Love Medicine by Louise Erdrich
Justice at War by Peter Irons
Solo in the Box Car, Third Floor E by Angela Jackson
Say Ray by Ron Jones
Queen of the Ebony Isles by Collen J McElroy
Poets Behind Barbed Wire by Jiro Nakano and Kay Nakano
Round Valley Songs by William Oandasan
Amelia Earhart by Maureen Owen
Homegirls and handgrenades by Sonia Sanchez
At Seventy: A Journal by May Sarton
Living Up the Street by Gary Soto
Genthe's Photographs of San Francisco's

Old Chinatown by John Kuo Wei Tchen

The Book of Jerusalem by Julia Vinograd

Lifetime Achievement Award for Joe Flaherty

1986 Time's Now by Miguel Algarin

The Dream Book: An Anthology of Writing by Italian American Women by Helen Barolini (editor)

A Daughter of the Nobility by Natasha Borovsky

Smiles on Washington Square by Raymond Federman

I Hear You Knockin by Jeff Hannusch

Seeing Through the Sun by Linda Hogan

My Emily Dickinson by Susan Howe

This Bridge Called My Back: Writings by Radical Women of Color by Cherrie Moraga and Gloria Anzaldua

Yokohama, Calfornia by Toshio Mori

The Sun Is Not Merciful by Ann Lee Walters

Irish Musicians/American Friends by Terence Winch

Close Your Eyes and Think of England by Michael Feingold

Lifetime Achievement Award for Hisaye Yamamoto

1987 Sin by Ai

liberazione della donna: feminism in Italy by Lucia Chiavola Birnbaum

Confessions of Madame Psyche by Dorothy Bryant

The Mixquiabuala Letters by Ana Castillo

Ready From Within by Septima Clark and Cynthia Stokes Brown (editor)

Celebrating Bird: The Triumph of Charlie Parker by Gary Giddins

Face Games by Juan Felipe Herrera

The Essential Etheridge Knight by Etheridge Knight

Practising Angels, A Contemporary Anthology of San Francisco Bay Area Poetry by Michael Mayo

Portrait of a Little Boy in Darkness by Daniel McGuire

Mama by Terry McMillan

American Splendor by Harvey Pekar

Selected Poems, 1958-1984 by John Wieners

Fools Crow by James Welch

Circumnavigation by Cyn Zarco

Lifetime Achievement Awards for Charles Blockson and Dennis Clark

1989 Eva Luna by Isabel Allende

Chinaman Pacific and Frisco R R Co by Frank Chin

Homemade Love by J California Cooper

Columbia Literary History of the United States by Emory Elliott (ed)

The Exiles of Erin: 19th Century Irish American Fiction by Charles Fanning

Memory of Fire by Eduardo Galeano

The Signifying Monkey: A Theory of Afro-American Literary Critism by Henry L Gates Jr

The Right Thing To Do by Josephine

Gattuso Hendin

Repairing America by William Hohri

Wode Shuofa (My Way of Speaking) by Carolyn Lau

A Burst of Light by Andre Lorde

Way by Leslie Scalapino

Stones's Throw by Jennifer Stone

Floating the River in Melancholy by Shuntaro Tanikawa

From the Pyramids to the Projects: Poems of Genocide and Resistance by Askia Muhammed Touré

The Ultraviolet Sky by Alma Luz Villanueva

Lifetime Achievement Award for Amiri Baraka and Ed Dorn

Editor/Publis' ~r Award for Nicolás Kannellos

1990 Spider Woman's Grandaughters by Paula Gunn Allen

Black Athena, Vol I by Martin Bernal

Urban Multicultural Poetry by Michelle T Clinton, Sesshu Foster, Naomi Quinonez, eds

Miles: The Autobiography by Miles Davis with Quincy Troupe

Hearts of Sorrow by James M Freeman

Women on War by Daniela Gioseffi

Vivar a Hostos by Jose Emilio Gonzalez

Italian Days by Barbara Grizzuti Harrison

Symbolic Immortality by Sergei Kan

People Who Led to My Plays by Adrienne Kennedy

The Forbidden Stitch by Shirley Geok-lin Lim, Mayumi Tsutakawa, Margarita Donnelly, eds

Mulberry and Peach by Hualing Nieh

For Every Goodbye Ain't Gone by Itabari Njeri

The Light at the End of the Bog by John Norton

Romans and Blacks by Lloyd A Thompson

The Harlem Fox by John C Walter

Hand into Stone by Elizabeth Woody

American Academy and Institute of Arts and Letters - Gold Medal

633 West 155 St

New York, NY 10032-5699, USA

Gold Medals are awarded each year for distinguished achievement in two of the following categories: belles letters & painting; biography & music; fiction & sculpture; history & architecture; poetry & music; drama & graphic art. Not awarded every year to a writer.

Award: Two medals

Contact: Betsey Feeley

1980	Edward Albee
	Peggy Bacon
1981	Malcolm Cowley
	Raphael Soyer
1982	William Schuman
	Francis Steegmuller
1983	Bernard Malamud
	Louise Nevelson
1984	Gordon Bunshart
	George F Kennan
1985	Leonard Bernstein

Robert Penn Warren
1986 Edward Albee
Jasper Johns
1987 Jacques Barzun
Isabel Bishop
1990 C Vann Woodward
1991 Richard Wilbur

1993 Elizabeth Hardwick
1994 Walter Jackson Bate

American Academy and Institute of Arts and Letters - Literature
33 West 155 St
New York, NY 10032-6599, USA
1980 Anne Beattie
William Dickey
Paul Fussell
Maxine Kumin
George Oppen
Robert Pinsky
Lewis Thomas
Larry Woiwode
1981 Louise Gluck
Gail Godwin
Howard Frank Mosher
James Salter
Elizabeth Sewell
William Stafford
Hilma Wolitzer
Jay Wright
1982 David H Bradley Jr
Frederick Buechner
MacDonald Harris
Daryl Hine
Josephine Jacobson
Donald Keene
Berton Roueche
Robert Stone
1983 Alfred Corn
Stephen Dixon
Robert Mezey
Mary Oliver
David Plante
George Starbuck
Leo Steinberg
Edmund White
1984 Amy Clampitt
Don De Lillo
Sanford Friedman
Robert Hass
Lincoln Kirstein
Romulus Linney
Bobbie Ann Mason
Craig Nova
1985 Alan Dugan
Maria Irene Fornes
George Garrett
Carolyn Kizer
Gilbert Sorrentino
Paul West
John Williams
Paul Zimmer
1986 Russell Banks
Frederick Busch
Robert A Caro
Robert Kelly

Barry Lopez
David Mamet
Marsha Norma
Lore Segal
1987 Evan S Connell
Ernest J Gaines
Ralph Manheim
Sandra McPherson
Steven Millhauser
Robert Phillips
Roger Shattuck
1988 William Barrett
David Bottoms
Rosellen Brown
David Cope
John Clellon Holmes
John McCormick
James Seay
William Weaver
Norman Williams
1989 Richard Ford
Martin Greenberg
Ron Hansen
Herbert Morris
Gregory Rabassa
David R Slavitt
Arturo Vivante
Joy Williams
1990 M H Abrams
Rick De Marinis
Debora Greger
Rachel Hadas
Shelby Hearon
Maxine Hong Kingston
David Lehman
Edmund S Morgan
1991 Edgar Bowers
Christopher Davis
Jaimy Gordon
Rachel Ingalls
Harry Matthews
J D McClatchy
Albert F Moritz
James Schevill
1992 Alice Adams
John Crowley
Richard Foreman
Vicki Hearne
Ruth Prawer Jhabvala
Tim O'Brien
Simon Schama
August Wilson
1993 Ellen Atkins
Richard Bausch
Vance Bourjaily
Deborah Eisenberg
Rolf Fjelde
Tina Howe
Denis Johnson
A G Mojtabai
1994 Jon Robin Baitz
Marvin Bell
Stuart Dybeck
Adrienne Kennedy
Tony Kushner
Mary Lee Settle
Chase Twitchell

Geoffrey Wolff

Hans Christian Andersen Awards
International Board on Books for Young People
Nonnenweg 12 Postfach
CH-4003 Basel, Switzerland
The winner is selected by an international jury and announced during the IBBY Congress.
Awarded biennially to the author and illustrator (since 1966) whose work has made a lasting contribution to children's literature.
Executive Director: Leena Maissen.

1956	Eleanor Farjeon
1958	Astrid Lindfren
1960	Erich Kastner
1962	Meinder Dejong
1964	Rene Guillot
1966	Alois Carigiet
	Tove jansson
1968	James Kriiss
	Jose Maria Sanchez Silva
	Jiri Trnka
1970	Gianni Rodari
	Maurice Sendak
1972	Scott O'Dell
	Ib Spang Olsen
1974	Maria Grip
	Farshide Mesghall
1976	Cecil Bodker
	Tatjana Mawrina
1978	Paula Fox
	Otto Svend
1980	Bohumil Riha
	Suekichi Akaba
1982	Lygya Bojunga Nunez
	Zbigniew Rychlicki
1984	Mitsumasa Anno
	Christine Nostlinger
1986	Patricia Wrightson
	Robert Ingpen
1988	Annie M G Schmiot
	Dusan Kalli
1990	Tormod Haugen (Norway)
	Lisbeth Zwerger (Austria)
1992	Virginia Hamilton (USA)
	Kveta Pacaovska (Czecholslovakia)

Arvon International Poetry Competition
Kilnhurst, Kilnhurst Road
Todmorden, Lancashire OL14 6AX, England
Poetry competition open to anyone in the world for poems of any length written in the English language.
Biennial, first prize of £5000 with at least 15 other prizes.
Contact: David Pease

1980	The Letter by Andrew Motion
1982	Ephraim Destiny's Perfectly Utter Darkness by John Hartley Williams
1985	Rorschach Writing by Oliver Reynolds
1987	The Notebook by Selima Hill
1989	Halfway Pond by Sheldon Flory

Australian Literature Society Gold Medal
Association for the Study of Australian Literature Ltd
c/o English Department, University College, ADFA
Campbell, ACT 2600, Australia

Awarded annually for the most outstanding Australian literary work, or (occasionally), for outstanding services to Australian literature.
Contact: Susan McKernan, Secretary

1983	Child's Play; Fly Away Peter by David Malouf
1984	The People's Other World by Les Murray
1985	Archimedes and the Seagle by David Ireland
1986	Beachmasters by Thea Astley
1987	The Nightmarkets by Alan Wearne
1988	Louisa by Brian Matthews
1989	Forty-Seventeen by Frank Moorhouse
1990	Possible Worlds and Collected Poems by Peter Porter

Authors Club First Novel Award
Author Club
40 Dover Street, London, W1X 3RB
The winner is selected from entries submitted by publishers and awarded to the most promising first novel of the year published in the UK by a British author.
Prize: £750

1980	The Good Morrow by Dawn Lowe-Watson
1981	The Magic Glass by Dr Anne Smith
1982	The Privileged Children by Frances Vernon
1983	Summer at the Haven by Katherine Moore
1984	Lama, A Novel of Tibet by Frederick Hyde-Chambers
1985	Eightsome by Magda Sweetland
1986	Playing Fields by Helen Harris
1987	The Levels by Peter Benson
1988	The Holy Innocents by Gilbert Adair
1989	The Silver Pigs by Lindsey Davis
1990	The Way You Tell Them by Alan Brownjohn
1991	The Book of Wishes and Complaints by Zina Rohan
1992	The Healing Cape by David Park
1993	Season of the Rainbirds by Nadeem Aslam

Bancroft Prizes
Columbia University, 202A Low Library,
New York, NY 10027, USA
Contact: V R Gallagher

James Tait Black Memorial Prize
Dept of English Literature, David Hume Tower
George Square, Edinburgh EH8 9JX, Scotland
Eligible works of fiction and biographies are those written in English, originating with a British publisher, and first published in Britain in the year of the award. The nationality of the writer is irrelevant.
Two prizes of £1500 each are awarded annually; one for the best biography or work of that nature, the other for the best work of fiction, published during the calendar year.
Contact: Dept of English Literature
Biography

1980	Tennyson: The Unquiet Heart by Robert B Martin
1981	Edith Sitwell: Unicorn among Lions by Victoria Glendinning
1982	James Joyce by Richard Ellmann
1983	Franz Liszt: The Virtuoso Years by Alan Walker
1984	Virginia Woolf: A Writer's Life by Lyndall

Gordon
1985   Jonathan Swift: A Hypocrate Reversed by David Noakes
1986   Helen Waddell by D Felicitas Corrigan
1987   Victor Gollancz: A Biography by Ruth Dudley Edwards
1988   Wittgenstein: A Life: Young Ludwig (1889-1921) by Brian McGuinness
1989   Federico Garcia Lorca: A Life by Ian Gibson
1990   The Invisible Woman: The Story of Nelly Ternan and Charles Dickens by Claire Tomalin
1991   Darwin by James Moore and Adrian Desmond
1992   The Reckoning: The Murder of Christopher Marlowe by Charles Nicholl
1993   Dr Johnson & Mr Savage by Richard Holmes

Fiction
1980   Waiting for the Barbarians by J M Coetzee
1981   Midnight's Children by Salman Rusdie
        The Mosquito Coast by Paul Theroux
1982   On the Black Hill by Bruce Chatwin
1983   Allegro Postillions by Jonathan Keates
1984   Empire of the Sun by J G Ballard
        Nights at the Circus by Angela Carter
1985   Winter Garden by Robert Edric
1986   Persephone by Jenny Joseph
1987   The Golden Bird: Two Orkney Stories by George Mackay Brown
1988   A Season in the West by Piers Paul Read
1989   A Disaffection by James Kelman
1990   Brazzaville Beach by William Boyd
1991   Downriver by Iain Sinclair
1992   Sacred Country by Rose Tremain
1993   Crossing the River by Caryl Phillips

Bollingen Prize in Poetry
Yale University, Beinecke Library
Box 1603A, New Haven, CT 06520, USA
Prize is awarded for the best book of poetry by an American author during the preceeding two years.
Biennial prize of $10,000
1981   Howard Nemerov and May Swenson
1983   Anthony E Hecht and John Hollander
1985   John Ashbury and Fred Chappell
1987   Stanley Kunitz
1989   Edgar Bowers
1991   Laura (Riding) Jackson and Donald Justice
1993   Mark Strand

Booker Prize
Book Trust, Book House
45 East Hill, London SW18 2QZ, England
Awarded for the best full-length novel published between 1 October and 30 September in UK. Novel must be written in English and written by a citizen of Britain, the Commonwealth, Republic of Ireland or South Africa.
Annual prize of £20,000
Contact: Christine Shaw, Head of Publicity
1980   Rites of Passage by William Golding
1981   Midnight's Children by Salman Rushdie
1982   Schlindler's Ark by Thomas Keneally
1983   Life & Times of Michael K by J M Coetzee
1984   Hotel du Lac by Anita Brookner
1985   The Bone People by Keri Hulme

1986   The Old Devils by Kingsley Amis
1987   Moon Tiger by Penelope Lively
1988   Oscar and Lucinda by Peter Carey
1989   The Remains of the Day by Kazuo Ishiguro
1990   Possession by A S Byatt
1991   The Famished Road by Ben Okri
1992   The English Patient by Michael Ondaatje
        Sacred Hunger by Barry Unsworth
1993   Paddy Clarke Ha Ha Ha by Roddy Doyle
1994   How Late It Was, How Late by James Kelman

The W H Smith/Books in Canada First Novel Award
130 Spadina Avenue, Suite 603
Toronto, Ontario M5V 2M3, Canada
Prize is awarded for the best Canadian first novel published in English during the calendar year.
Annual prize of $1000
Contact: Christopher Noxon, Editorial Assistant
1980   Gentle Sinners by W D Valgardson
1981   Obasan by Joy Kogawa
1982   Shoeless Joe by W P Kinsella
1983   Willie: A Romance by Heather Robertson
1984   Perdue: Or How The West Was Lost by Geoffrey Ursell
1985   The Story of Booby O'Malley by Wayne Johnston
1986   The Life of Helen Alone by Karen Lawrence
1987   The Butterfly Chair by Marion Quednau
1988   A Man of Little Faith by Rick Salutin
1989   The Missing Child by Sandra Birdsall
1991   Lives of the Saints by Nino Ricci
1992   Such a Long Journey by Rohinton Mistry
1993   The Afterlife of George Cartwright by John Steffler
1994   Losing Eddie by Deborah Joy Corey

The Buckland Award
Trustees Executors and Agency Company of New Zealand Ltd
24 Water St, PO Box 760
Dunedin, New Zealand
Prize is awarded annually for work of the highest literary merit by a New Zealand writer.
1980   Living in the Maniototo by Janet Frame
1981   Various Poems by Elizabeth Smither
1982   Meg by Maurice Gee
1983   To the Island by Janet Frame
1984   The Bone People by Keri A Hulme
1985   Wednesday to Come by Renne G Taylor
1986   The Loop in Lone Kauri Road: Poems 1983-85 by Allen Curnow
1987   Symmes Hole by Ian Wedde
1988   Dirty Work by Nigel Cox
1989   The Rock Garden by Fiona Farrell Poole

CNA Literary Award
The Director, Book Trade Assn of South Africa
PO Box 326
Howard Place 7450, South Africa
Established in 1961 for the best original works, one in English and one in Afrikaans, published for the first time during the calendar year of the competition. Awarded annually.
7500 rand each for the winner and 2500 rand for the runners-up in both the English and Afrikaans

categoeis, with an additional prize of 3000 rand for the best designed book.

1980	Waiting for the Barbarians by J M Coetzee
1981	July's People by Nadine Gordimer
1982	A Chain of Voices by André P Brink
1983	The Life & Times of Michael K by J M Coetzee
1984	Selected Poems by Douglas Livingstone
1985	Call me Woman by Ellen Kuzwayo
1986	The 29th Parallel by David Robbins
1987	Phoebe & Nio by E M McPhail

Randolph Caldecott Medal

Association for Library Service to Children
50 E Huron St, Chicago
IL 70711-2795, USA
Prize is awarded to an ullustrator of the most distinguished American picture book for children published in the preceding year.
Annual prize of bronze medal.
Contact: Susan Roman, Executive Director

1980	Ox-Cart Man by Donald Hall
1981	Fables by Arnold Lobel
1982	Jumanji by Chris Van Allsburg
1983	Shadow by Blaise Cendrars
1984	The Glorious Flight: Across the Channel with Louis Bleriot by Alice Provensen and Martin Provensen.
1985	Saint George and the Dragon Retold by Margaret Hodges
1986	The Polar Express by Chris Van Allsburg
1987	Hey, Al by Arthur Yorinks
1988	Owl Moon by Jane Yolen
1989	The Boy of the Three-Year Nap by Allen Say
1990	Lon Po Po: A Red-Riding Hood Story from China by Ed Young
1991	Black and White by David Macaulay
1992	Tuesday by David Weisner
1993	Mirette on the High Wire by Emily Arnold McCully
1994	Grandfather's Journey by Allen Say

The CLA Book of the Year for Children Award

Canadian Library Association, 200 Elgin St, Ste 206, Ottawa, Ontario K2P 1L5, Canada
The award is presented to an author of an outstanding Childrens book published during previous calendar year. Suitable for children up to 14 years of age and published in Canada.
Annual award
Contact: Brenda Shields

1980	River Runners by James Houston
1981	The Violin-Maker's Gift by Donn Kushner
1982	The Root Cellar by Janest Lunn
1983	Up to Low by Brian Doyle
1984	Sweetgrass by Jan Hudson
1985	Mama's Going to Buy You a Mockingbird by Jean Little
1986	Julie by Cora Taylor
1987	Shadow in Hawthorn Bay by Janet Lunn
1988	A Handful of Time by Kit Pearson
1989	Easy Avenue by Brian Doyle
1990	The Sky is Falling by Kit Pearson
1991	Redword by Michael Bedard
1992	Eating Between the Lines by Kevin Major
1993	Ticket to Curlew by Celia Barker Lottridge

1994	Some of the Kinder Planets by Tim Wynne-Jones

Canada - Australia Literary Award

350 Albert Street, PO Box 1047
Ottawa, Ontario K1P 5V8, Canada
Prize is awarded alternately to an English-language Canadian writer or an Australian writer for his/her complete works.
Annual prize of $3000 and a journey to the hosting country where the prize is being awarded.
Contact: Josianne Polidori

1980	Roger McDonald
1981	Leon Rooke
1982	Barry Oakley
1983	Mavis Gallant
1984	Les A Murray
1985	Jack Hodgins
1986	Rodney Hall
1987	Sharon Pollock
1988	Elizabeth Jolley
1989	Audrey Thomas
1991	Georgia Savage
1992	David Adams Richards
1993	Louis Nowra

Canadian Authors Association Literary Awards

CAA, 275 Slater Street, Suite 500
Ottawa, Ontario K1P 5H9, Canada
Four categories: fiction, non-fiction, poetry; and drama. Nominations apply to book length works by Canadian writers published or produced during the previous calendar year.
One award per year in each category, $5000 cash prize plus silver medal in each category.
Contact: Awards Chairman
Poetry

1980	There's A Trick With A Knife That I'm Learning To Do by Michael Ondaatje
1981	Land of the Peace by Leona Gom
1982	The Acid Test by Gary Geddes
1983	The Presence of Fire by George Amabile
1984	Birding, or Desire by Don McKay
1985	Book of Mercy by Leonard Cohen
1986	The Glass Air by P K Page
1987	The Collected Poems, 1956-86 by Purdy
1988	Selected Poems by Pat Lane
1989	Daniel by Bruce Rice
1990	Homeless Heart by Don Bailey
1991	Prelude to the Bacchanal by Richard Lemm
1992	Miner's Pond by Anne Michaels
1993	Inventing the Hawk by Lorna Crozier
1994	Selected Poems by George Bowering

Drama

1980	Ned and Jack by Sheldon Rosen
1981	After Baba's Funeral and Sweet & Sour Pickles by Ted Galay
1982	Rexyl by Allan Stratton
1983	Back To Beulah by W O Mitchell
1984	Granite Point by W D Valgardson
1985	Gone The Burning Sun by Ken Mitchell
1986	Salt-Water Moon by David French
1987	Farther West by John Murrell
1988	Rock and Roll by John Gray
1989	Nothing Sacred by George F Walker
1990	Bordertown Cafe by Kelly Rebar

1991 Goodnight Desdemona (Goodmorning Juliet) by Anne-Marie MacDonald
1992 Bootlegger Blues by Drew Taylor
1993 I Had a Job I Liked, Once by Guy Vanderhaeghe
1994 The Stillborn Lover by Timothy Findley

Fiction
1980 No award
1981 Voices in Time by Hugh MacLennan
1982 Obasan by Joy Kogawa
1983 Shoeless Joe by W P Kinsella
1984 Willie: A Romance by Heather Robertson
1985 Not Wanted On the Voyage by Timothy Findley
1986 What's Bred in the Bone by Robertson Davies
1987 No award
1988 The Color of Blood by Brian Moore
1989 The Victory of Geraldine Gull by Joan Clark
1990 Running West by James Houston
1991 Evening Snow Will Bring Such Peace by David Adams Richards
1992 News From a Foreign Country Came by Alberto Manguel
1993 The Innocence of Age by Neil Bisoondath
1994 The Robber Bride by Margaret Atwood

Non-fiction
1980 A Bloody War by Hal Lawrence
1981 The Invasion of Canada - 1812-13 by Pierre Berton
1982 The Young Vincent Massey by Claude Bissell
1983 Grits by Christina McCall-Newman
1984 The Ghost Walker by R D Lawrence
1985 The Private Capital by Sandra Gwyn
1986 Company of Adventurers by Peter C Newman
1987 Meeting of Generals by Tony Foster
1988 My Father's House by Sylvia Fraser
1989 Caves in the Desert by George Woodcock
1990 Shadow of Heaven by John English
1991 Inside Memory by Timothy Findley
1992 The Dange Tree by David Macfarlane
1993 Welcome Home by Stuart McLean
1994 People of Terra Nullius: Betrayal and Rebirth in Aboriginal Canada by Boyce Richardson

Melville Cane Award
Poetry Society of America, 15 Gramercy Park
New York, NY 10003, USA
For a published book on poetry (in even-numbered years) alternating (in odd-numbered years) with a book of poems published within the award year.
Annual award $500.
Contact: Susan Sully
1980 Selected Poems by Richard Hugo
1981 The Poet's Calling in the English ode by Paul Fry
1982 The Red Coal by Gerald Stern
1983 Robert Lowell by Ian Hamilton
1984 New and Collected Poems by Alan Dugan
1985 Kenneth Patchen and American Mysticism by Raymond Nelson
1986 Triumph of Archilles by Louis Gluck
1987 Visions and Revisions of American Poetry by Lewis Turco

1988 Cemetery Nights by Steven Dobyns
Memories of the Future: The Daybooks of Tina Modotti by Margaret Gibson
1989 Conrad Aiken: Poet of the White Horse Vale by Edward Butscher
1990 Harp Lake by John Hollander
1991 White Paper by J D McClatchy
1992 The 6-Cornered Snowflake by John Frederick Nims
1993 An Essay on French Verse for Readers of English Poetry by Jacques Barzan
1994 Year of the Comet by Nicholas Christopher

Carnegie Medal
The Library Association, 7 Ridgmount St
London WC1E 7AE, England
Carnegie Medal is awarded annually for an outstanding book for children written in English and receiving its first publication in the United Kingdom during the preceding year.
1980 City of Gold by Peter Dickinson
1981 The Scarecrows by Robert Westall
1982 The Haunting by Margaret Mahy
1983 Handles by Jan Mark
1984 The Changeover by Margaret Mahy
1985 Storm by Kevin Crossley-Holland
1986 Granny was a Buffer Girl by Berlie Doherty
1987 The Ghost Drum by Susan Price
1988 A Pack of Lies by Geraldine McCaughrean
1989 Goggle-Eyes by Anne Fine
1990 Wolf by Gilliam Cross
1991 Dear Nobody by Berlie Doherty
1992 Flour Babies by Anne Fine
1993 Stone Cold by Robert Swindells

Children's Book Circle Eleanor Farjeon Award
c/o Orchard Books, 96 Leonard Street
London EC2A 4RH, England
Prize awarded for distinguished service to children's books both in the UK and overseas.
Prize: £500
Contact: Francesca Dow
1981 Margaret Marshall
Virginia Jensen
1982 Aiden & Nancy Chambers
1983 Jean Russell
1984 Shirley Hughes
1985 Bob Leeson
1986 Judith Elkin
1987 Valerie Bierman
1988 National Library for the Handicapped Children
1989 Anna Home
1990 Jill Bennett
1991 Patricia Crampton
1992 Stephanie Nettell
1993 Susan Belgrave
1994 Eileen Colwell

Cholmondeley Award for Poets
Society of Authors, 84 Drayton Gardens
London SW10 9SB, England
The non-competitive award is for work generally, not for a specific book and submissions are not required.
Annual prize of £8000 (shared).
1980 George Barker

Terence Tiller
Roy Fuller
1981 Roy Fisher
Robert Garioch
Charles Boyle
1982 Basil Bunting
Herbert Lomas
William Scammell
1983 John Fuller
Craig Raine
Anthony Thwaite
1984 Michael Baldwin
Michale Hoffmann
Carol Raine
1985 Dannie Abse
Peter Redgrove
Brian Taylor
1986 Lawrence Durrell
James Fenton
Selima Hill
1987 Wendy Cope
Matthew Sweeney
George Szirtes
1988 John Heath-Stubbs
Sean O'Brien
John Whitworth
1989 Peter Didsbury
Douglas Dunn
E J Scovell
1990 Kingsley Amis
Elaine Feinstein
Michael O'Neill
1991 James Berry
Sujata Bhatt
Michael Hulse
Derek Mahon
1992 Allen Curnow
Donald Davie
Carol Ann Duffy
Roger Woddis
1993 Patricia Beer
George Mackay Brown
P J Kavanagh
Michael Longley
1994 Ruth Fainlight
Gwen Harwood
Elizabeth Jennings
John Mole

Arthur C Clarke Award
23 Oakfield Road
Croydon, Surrey CR0 2UD, England
Prize is given to best science fiction novel of the year.
Annual prize of £1000.
Contact: David V Barrett
1987 The Handmaid's Tale by Margaret Atwood
1988 The Sea and Summer by George Turner
1989 Unquenchable Fire by Rachel Pollock
1990 The Child Garden by Geoff Ryman
1991 Take Back Plenty by Colin Greenland
1992 Synners by Pat Cadigan
1993 Body of Glass by Marge Piercy
1994 Vurt by Jeff Noon

Commonwealth Writers' Prize
Commonwealth Foundation, Marlborough House

Pall Mall, London SW1Y 5HY, England
Prize is awarded annually for a work of fiction, novel or collection of short stories - written in English by a citizen of the commonwealth and published in the preceding year. Sponsored by the Commonwealth Foundation.
Prize of £10,000 for best book, £3000 for best first published book, eight regional prizes of £1000.
Contact: Professor Kirpal Singh
1987 Summer Lightning and Other Stories by Olive Senior
1988 Heroes by Festus Iyayi
1989 The Carpathians by Janet Frame
Women of Influence by Bonnie Burnard
1990 Solomon Gursky Was Here by Mordechai Richler
Visitors by John Cranna
1991 The Great World by David Malouf
Shape-Shifter by Pauline Melville
1992 Such a Long Journey by Rohinton Mistry
Divina Trace by Robert Antoni
1993 The Ancestor Game by Alex Miller
The Thousand Faces of Night by Githa Hariharan
1994 A Suitable Boy by Vikram Seth
The Case of Emily V by Keith Oatley

Thomas Cook Travel Book Awards
Thomas Cook Group, 45 Berkeley Street
London W1A 1EB, England
Three awards for best travel book, best guide book and best illustrated travel book, published in the current year.
Annual awards of £7500 - best travel book, £2500 - best guide book.
Contact: Edmund Swinglehurst
Travel
1980 Tracks by Robyn Davidson
1981 Old Glory by Jonathan Raban
1982 The Sinbad Voyage by Tim Severin
1983 From Heaven Lake by Vikram Seth
1984 To The Frontier by Geoffrey Moorhouse
1985 So Far From God by Patrick Marnham
86/87 Between the Woods and the Water by Patrick Leigh Fermor
1988 Behind the Wall by Colin Thubron
1989 Riding the Iron Rooster by Paul Theroux
1990 Our Grandmothers' Drums by Mark Hudson
1991 Hunting Mister Heartbreak by Jonathan Raban
1992 A Goddess in the Stones by Norman Lewis
In Search of Conrad by Gavin Young
1993 The Heart of the World by Nik Cohn
1994 City of Djinns by William Dalrymple
Guide
1980 The 1980 South American Handbook by John Brooks (ed)
1981 China Companion by Evelyn Garside
1982 India by G Crowther, P A Raj, T Wheeler
1983 Companion Guide to New York by Michael Leapman
1984 Cruising French Waterways by Hugh McKnight
1985 Shell Guide to Nottinghamshire by Henry Thorold
86/87 Fontana/Hatchette Guide to France 1986
1988 The Tibet Guide by Stephen Batchelor

1989	Landscapes of Madeira by John and Pat Underwood
1990	Blue Guide Turkey by Bernard McDonagh
1991	Caribbean Islands Handbook by Ben Box & Sarah Camer
1992	London's American Past by Fran Hazelton
1993	Thailand by Lucy Ridout and Paul Gray
1994	New York : Eyewitness Travel Guide by Eleanor Berman

Illustrated Guide

1988	Languedoc by Charlie Waite/James Bentley
1989	The Marco Polo Expedition by Richard B Fisher and Tom Ang
1990	What the Traveller Saw by Eric Newby
1992	Eyes To The Hills by Gordon Stainforth

The Duff Cooper Memorial Prize
54 St Maur Road
London SW6 4DP, England
Prize is awarded annually in memory of Alfred Duff Cooper, 1st Viscount Norwich (1890-1954). It consists of a specially bound and inscribed copy of his autobiography, Old Men Forget, together with a small cheque representing the interest on the money subscribed for the purpose by his friends after his death.
Prize: £500
Contact: Artemis Cooper

1980	Tennyson: The Unquiet Heart by Robert Bernard Martin
1981	Edith Sitwell: A Unicorn Among Lions by Victoria Glendinning
1982	James Joyce by Richard Ellmann
1983	Collected Poems by Peter Porter
1984	Ivy Compton-Burnett by Hilary Spurling
1985	Edmund Goose: A Literary Landscape by Ann Thwaite
1986	C R Ashbee: Architect, Designer and Romantic Socialist by Alan Crawford
1987	The Fatal Shore: History of the Transporation of Convicts to Australia, 1987-1868 by Robert Hughes
1988	Serious Character: Life of Ezra Pound by Humphrey Carpenter
1989	Federico Garcia Lorca: A Life by Ian Gibson
1990	Clever Hearts: Desmond and Molly McCarthy: A Biography by Hugh & Mirabel Cecil
1991	Wittgenstein: The Duty of Genius by Ray Monk
1992	Never Again: Post-war Britain 1946-51 by Peter Hennessy
1993	A History of Warfare by John Keegan

Crime Writers' Association Awards
PO Box 172, Tring
Herts HP23 5LP, England
CWA - Gold Dagger
Best crime novel of the year nominations by publishers only.
Annual prize of Gold plated dagger and cheque (amount varies).
Contact: The Secretary

1980	The Murder of the Maharajah by H R F Keating
1981	Gorky Park by Martin Cruz Smith
1982	The False Inspector Dew by Peter Lovesey
1983	Accidental Crimes by John Hutton
1984	The Twelfth Juror by B M Gill
1985	Monkey Puzzle by Paula Gosing
1986	Live Flesh by Ruth Rendell
1987	A Fatal Inversion by Barbara Vine (Ruth Rendell)
1988	Ratking by Michael Dibdin
1989	The Wench is Dead by Colin Dexter
1990	Bones and Silence by Reginald Hill
1991	King Solomon's Carpet by Barbara Vine
1992	The Way Through the Woods by Colin Dexter
1993	Cruel and Unusual by Patricia Cornwell
1994	The Scold's Bride by Minette Walters

CWA - Gold Dagger Non-Fiction
Gold plated dagger and cheque (amount varies)

1980	Conspiracy by Anthony Summers
1981	Prisoner With a Name, Cell Without a Number by Jacobo Timerman
1982	Earth to Earth by John Cornwell
1983	Dougie Dealer by Petr Watson
1984	In God's Name by David Yallop
1985	Killing for Company by Brian Masters
1986	Evil Angels by John Bryson
1987	Perfect Murder by Bernard Taylor and Stephen Knight
1988	The Secret Lives of Trebitsch Lincoln by Bernard Wasserstein
1989	A Gathering of Saints by Robert Lindsey
1990	The Passing of Starr by Jonathan Goodman
1991	Giordano Bruno and the Embassy Affair by John Bossy
1992	The Reckoning by Charles Nicholl
1993	Murder in the Heart by Alexandra Artley
1994	Criminal Shadows by David Canter

CWA - Silver Dagger
Silver Dagger plus cheque (amount varies)
Contact: The Secretary

1980	Monk's Hood by Ellis Peters
1981	The Dead of Jericho by Colin Dexter
1982	Ritual Murder by S T Harmon
1983	The Papers of Tony Veitch by William McIlvanney
1984	The Tree of Hands by Ruth Rendell
1985	Last Seen Alive by Dorothy Simpson
1986	A Taste for Death by P D James
1987	Presumed Innocent by Scott Turow
1988	Toxic Shock by Sarah Paretsky
1989	The Shadow Run by Desmonde Lowden
1990	The Late Candidate by Mike Phillips
1991	Deep Sleep by Frances Fyfield
1992	Bucket Nut by Liza Cody
1993	Fatlands by Sarah Dunant
1994	Miss Smilla's Feeling for Snow by Peter Hoeg

CWA - Silver Dagger Non-Fiction
Silver Dagger plus cheque (amount varies)

1978	The Capture of the Black Panther by Harry Hawkes
1979	Fraud by Jon Connell and Douglas Sutherland

CWA - Cartier Diamond Dagger
Prize is awarded by Chairman and Committee for outstanding contribution to the genre.
Annual prize of Diamond Dagger

Contact: The Secretary

1986 Eric Ambler
1987 P D James
1988 John le Carré
1989 Dick Francis
1990 Julian Symons
1991 Ruth Rendell
1992 Lesley Charteris
1993 Edith Pargeter
1994 Reginald Hill

CWA John Creasey Memorial Award
Presented for the best crime novel by a previously unpublished author.
Cash Prize (under review), plus magnifying glass.
Contact: The Secretary

1980 Dupe by Liza Cody
1981 The Ludi Victor by James Leigh
1982 Caroline Miniscule by Andrew Taylor
1983 The Ariadne Clue by Carol Clemeau
     The Night the Gods Smiled by Eric Wright
1984 A Very Private Enterprise by Elizabeth Ironside
1985 The Latimer Mercy by Robert Richards
1986 Tinplate by Neville Steed
1987 Dark Apostle by Denis Kilcommons
1988 Death's Bright Angel by Janet Neel
1989 A Real Shot in the Arm by Annette Roome
1990 Postmorten by Patricia Daniels Cornwell
1991 Deep Sleep by Frances Fyfield
1992 The Ice House by Minette Walters
1993 No award
1994 Big Town by Doug J Swanson

Danish Academy Prize for Literature
Rungstedlund, 109 Rungsted Strandvej
DK-2960 Rungsted Kyst, Denmark
Prize is awarded bi-annually for an outstanding work of literature.
Prize of DKr 100,000 awarded.
Contact: Alan Philip

1980 Henrik Nordbrandt
1981 Dorrit Willumsen
1982 Per Højholt
1984 Jess Ornsbo
1986 Henrik Stangerup
1988 Halfdan Rasmussen
1990 Jens Smærup Sørensen

The Encore Award
The Society of Authors
84 Drayton Gardens, London SW10 9SB, England
The Prize is awarded for a second published novel.
Annual Prize: £7500

1990 A Lesser Dependency by Peter Benson
     Calm at Sunset, Calm at Dawn by Paul Watkins
1991 Richard's Feet by Carey Harrison
1992 Downriver by Iain Sinclair
1993 The Heather Blazing by Colm Toibin
1994 Afternoon Raag by Amit Chaudhuri

The English Academy of Southern Africa
PO Box 124
Witwatersrand 2050, South Africa
Thomas Pringle Awards
1985 Robert Greig
     Karen Learmont-Batley

Patrick Cullinan
1986 Gus Silber
     Jan Gorek
     Njabulo Ndebele
1987 David Williams
     Lionel Abrahams
     Mark Swift
1988 John M Coetzee
     Rosie Zwi
1989 Stephen Gray
     Binkie Marwick
     Douglas Livingstone
1990 Dorothy Driver
     Patrick Cullinan
1991 Charlotte Bauer
     Gregory Cunningham
     Tatumkulu Afrika

Oliver Schreiner Prize
1985 A State of Fear by Menan du Plessis
1986 Journal of a New Man by Lionel Abrahams
1987 No award
1988 The Arrowing of the Cane by John Conyngham
1989 Blood of Our Silence by Kelwyn Sole
1990 A Snake in the Garden by Norman Coombe
1991 Missing Persons by Ivan Vladislavic

The Geoffrey Faber Memorial Prize
Faber and Faber Ltd, 3 Queen Square
London WC1N 3AU, England
Awarded annually, alternate years prose and fiction. Given to a volume of verse or prose fiction first published originally in UK during 2 years preceding year of award. Eligible writers must be under 40 at time of publication, citizen of UK, Ireland, Commonwealth, or South Africa.
Prize: £1000
Contact: Sarah Gleadell/Belinda Matthews

1980 The Slant Door by George Szirtes
     Love Life by Hugo Williams
1981 Waiting for the Barbarians by J M Coetzee
1982 Why Brownlee Left by Paul Muldoon
     The Strange Museum by Tom Paulin
1983 Shuttlecock by Graham Swift
1984 In Memory of War by James Fenton
1985 Flaubert's Parrot by Julian Barnes
1986 A Quiet Gathering by David Scott
1987 Man Descending by Guy Vanderhaeghe
1988 Agrimony by Michael Hofmann
1989 Sea Music by David Profumo
1990 Shibboleth by Michael Donaghy
1991 The Fog Line by Carol Birch
1992 Madoc by Paul Muldoon
1993 The Quantity Theory by Will Self
1994 Myth of the Twin by John Burnside

Fawcett Society Book Prize
New Light of Women's Lives
46 Harleyford Road, London SE11 5AY, England
Prize is given to a fiction, non-fiction book in alternate years. Must offer enlightenment on women's position. Must have first been published in Britain, Commonwealth, Ireland.
Annual prize of £500.
Contact: Charlotte Burt

1982 Women, Power and Politics by Margaret Stacey and Marion Price

1983	Union Street by Pat Barker
	Beka Lamb by Zee Edgell
1984	The Tidy House by Caroline Steedman
1985	Here Today by Zoe Fairbairns
1986	Monuments and Maidens by Marina Warner
1987	Redhill Rococo by Sheena MacKay
1988	Iron Ladies: Why Do Women Vote Tory by Beatrix Campbell
1989	Boy Blue by Stevie Davies
1990	The Long Road to Greenham by Jill Liddington
1991	Judasland by Jennifer Dawson
1992	Cleopatra: Histories, Dreams and Distortions by Lucy Hughes-Hallett
	The Haunting of Sylvia Plath by Jacqueline Rose
1993	Wild Swans by Jung Chang
1994	Daphne du Maurier by Margaret Forster

Fellowship of the Academy of American Poets
584 Broadway, Suite 1208
New York, NY 10012, USA
Contact: Siobahn Reagan

1980	Mona Van Duyn
1981	Richard Hugo
1982	John Ashbery
1983	Philip Booth
	James Schuyler
1984	Robert Francis
	Richmond Lattimore
1985	Amy Clampitt
	Maxine Kumin
1986	Irving Feldman
	Josephine Jacobsen
	Howard Moss
1987	Alfred Corn
	Josephine Jacobsen
1988	Donald Justice
1989	Richard Howard
1990	William Meredith
1991	J D McClatchy
1992	Adrienne Rich
1993	Gerald Stern

The Kathleen Fidler Award
c/o Book Trust Scotland, The Scottish Book Centre
Fountainbridge Library, 137 Dundee Street
Edinburgh EH11 1BG, Scotland
A novel of not less than 20,000 words for children aged 8-12. Author must not have had a novel published previously for this age group. Entries typewritten, double-spaced on one side of paper. Annual prize of £1000, entry published by Blackie Children's Imprint, now owned by Penguin - to be held for one year.
Contact: Administrative Officer

1983	Adrift by Alan Baillie
1984	Barty by Janet Collins
1985	No Shelter by Elizabeth Lutzeir
1986	Diamond by Caroline Pitcher
1987	Simon's Challenge by Theresa Breslin
1988	The Flight of the Solar Duck by Charles Morgan
1989	Mightier than the Sword by Clare Bevan
1990	Magic With Everything by Roger Burt
1991	Greg's Revenge by George Hendry
1992	Richard's Castle by Susan Coon

1993	48 Hours with Franklin by Mij Kelly
1994	Run, Zan, Run by Catherine Macphail

Forward Poetry Prize
Foward Publishing, Carrington House
126-130 Regent Street, London W1R 5FE, England
Awarded to three catagories of poetry, the best poetry collection of the year, the best first collection and the best single published poem in English and by a citizen of the UK or the Republic of Ireland.
Prize £10,000 (best collection), £5000 (best first collection) and £1000 (best single poem).
Contact: Christine Shaw
Best Collection
1992	The Man With Night Sweats by Thom Gunn
1993	Mean Time by Carol Ann Duffy
1994	Harm by Alan Jenkins

Best First Collection
1993	Nil Nil by Don Paterson
1994	Progeny of Air by Kwame Dawes

Best Single Poem
1993	Judith by Vicki Feaver
1994	Autumn by Iain Crichton

Goodman Fielder Wattie Book Award
PO Box 44-146
Auckland 2, New Zealand
Book published in New Zealand in the previous year by a New Zealand author (includes New Zealand residents and Pacific Island countries).
Annual - 1st prize of NZ $20,000, 2nd prize of NZ $10,000, 3rd prize of NZ $5000, Food Industry Book Award NZ $6000
Contact: Gerard Reid

1980	Leaves of the Banyan Tree by Albert Wendt
	New Zealand Adrift by Dr Graeme Stevens
	Indirections by Charles Brasch
1981	Eruera by Eruera Stirling and Anne Salmond
	Te Rauparaha by Patricia Burns
	The Lovelock Version by Maurice Shadbolt
1982	Craft New Zealand by Doreen Blumhardt and Brian Brake Reeds
	Other Halves by Sue McCauley
	The South Island of new Zealand from the Road by Robin Morrison and Alister Taylor
1983	To the Is-Land by Janet Frame
	Eagle's Trees & Shrubs of New Zealand - 2nd series by Audrey Eagle
	Historic Buildings of New Zealand: South Island
1984	Maori: A Photographic & Social History by Michael King
	The New Zealand House by Michael Fowler
	An Angel at My Table by Janet Frame
1985	The Envoy from Mirror City by Janet Frame
	Bread & Roses by Sonja Davies
	The Natural World of the Maori by Margaret Orbell
1986	The Matriarch by Witi Ihimaera
	From the Cradle to the Grave by Barry Gustafson
	Potiki by Patricia Grace
	Te Kaihau/The Windeater by Keri Hulme
1987	Season of the Jew by Maurice Shadbolt
	Head and Shoulders by Virginia Myers

Nga Morehu: The Survivors by Judith Binney and Gillian Chaplin
1988 The Treaty of Waitangi by Claudia Orange
Oracles & Miracles by Stevan Eldred-Grigg
A Man's Country by Jock Phillips
1989 Sylvia by Lynley Hood
Wines & Vineyards of New Zealand by Michael Cooper
The Unfortunate Experiment by Sandra Coney
1990 Moriori by Michael King
Hanly: A New Zealand Artist by Russell Haley
The Forest Carpet by Bill & Nancy Malcolm

Governor General's Literary Awards

The Canada Council, 350 Albert St, PO Box 1047 Ottawa, Ontario K1P 5V8, Canada
Awarded to Canadian authors of the best books in the English & French languages in six categories: poetry, drama, fiction, non-fiction, translation & children's literature (text & illustration).
Annual prize of $10,000
Contact: Josianne Polidori

Fiction
1980 Burning Water by George Bowering
1981 Home Truths: Selected Canadian Stories by Mavis Gallant
1982 Man Descending by Guy Vanderhaegh
1983 Shakespeare's Dog by Leon Rooke
1984 The Engineer of Human Souls by Josef Skvorecky
1985 The Handmaid's Tale by Margaret Atwood
1986 The Progress of Love by Alice Munro
1987 A Dream Like Mine by M T Kelly
1988 Nights Below Station Street by David Adams Richards
1989 Whale Music by Paul Quarrington
1990 Lives of the Saints by Nino Ricci
1991 Such a Long Journey by Rohinton Mistry
1992 The English Patient by Michael Ondaatje
1993 The Stone Diaries by Carol Shields

Poetry
1980 McAlmon's Chinese Opera by Stephen Scobie
1981 The Collected Poems of F R Scott by F R Scott
1982 The Vision Tree: Selected Poems by Phyllis Webb
1983 Settlements by David Donnell
1984 Celestial Navigation by Paulette Jiles
1985 Waiting for Saskatchewan by Fred Wah
1986 The Collected Poems of Al Purdy by Al Purdy
1987 Afterworlds by Gwendolyn MacEwen
1988 Furious by Erin Mouré
1989 The Word for Sand by Heather Spears
1990 No Time by Margaret Avison
1991 Night Field by Don McKay
1992 Inventing the Hawk by Lorna Crozier
1993 Forests of the Medieval World by Don Coles

Drama
1980 McAlmon's Chinese Opera by Stephen Scobie
1981 Blood Relations by Sharon Pollock
1982 Billy Bishop Goes To War by John Gray
1983 Quiet in the Land by Anne Chislett

1984 White Biting Dog by Judith Thompson
1985 Criminals in Love by George F Walker
1986 Doc by Sharon Pollock
1987 Prague by John Krizanc
1988 Nothing Sacred by George F Walker
1989 The Other Side of the Dark by Judith Thompson
1990 Goodnight Desdemona (Good Morning Juliet) by Ann-Marie MacDonald
1991 Amigo's Blue Guitar by Joan MacLeod
1992 Possible Worlds & A Short History of the Night by John Mighton
1993 Fronteras Americanas by Guillermo Verdecchia

Non-fiction
1980 Discipline of Power: The Conservative Interlude and the Liberal Restoration by Jeffrey Simpson
1981 Caribou and the Barren-lands by George Calef
1982 Louisbourg Portraits: Life in an Eighteenth-Century Garrison Town by Christopher Moore
1983 Byng of Vimy: General and Governor General by Jeffery Williams
1984 The Private Capital: Ambition and Love in the Age of Macdonald and Laurier by Sandra Gwyn
1985 The Regenerators: Social Criticism in Late Victorian English Canada by Ramsay Cook
1986 Northrop Frye on Shakespeare by Northrop Frye
1987 The Russian Album by Michael Ignatieff
1988 In the Sleep Room by Anne Collins
1989 Willie: The Life of W Somerset Maugham
1990 Trudeau and Out Times by Stephen Clarkson and Christina McCall
1991 Occupied Canada: A Young White Man Discovers His Unsuspected Past by Robert Hunter and Robert Calihoo
1992 Revenge of the Land by Maggie Siggins
1993 Touch the Dragon by Karen Connelly

Children's Literature
1980 Petrouchka by Elizabeth Cleaver
Hebert Luee by Bertrand Gauthier
The Trouble with Princesses by Christie Harris
Les Gens de mon pays by Miyuki Tanobe
1981 The Gardian of Isis by Monica Hughes
Nos amis robots by Suzanne Martel
Les Papinachois by Joanne Quellet
Ytek and the Arctic Orchid by Heather Woodall
1982 Fabien 1 and Fabien 2 by Ginette Anfousse
Hunter in the Dark by Monica Hughes
Agnes et le singulier bestiaire by Darcia Labrosse
ABC, 123, The Canadian Alphabet and Counting Book by Vlasta Van Kampen
1983 Petit Ours by Philippe Beha
Hockeyeurs Cybernetiques by Denis Cote
Hans Christian Andersen's The Little Mermaid re-told by Margaret Crawford
Maloney by Laszlo Gal

The Ghost of the Mounties by Sean O'Huigin
1984 Drole D'ecole by Marie-Louise Gay
Lizzy's Lion by Marie-Louise Gay
Sweetgrass by Jan Hudson
Le Cercle Violet by Daniel Sernine
1985 Murdo's Story: A Legend from Northern Manitoba by Terry Gallagher
L'Alphabet by Roger Pare
Casse-tete chinois by Robert Soulieres
Julie by Cora Taylor
1986 Shadow in Hawthorn Bay by Janet Lunn
Le Dernier des raisins by Raymond Plante
Album de famille by Stephane Poulin
Have You Seen Birds by Barbara Reid
1987 Rainy Day Magic by Marie-Louise Gay
Venir au Monde by Darcia Labrosse
Gallahad Schwartz and the Cockroach Army by Morgan Nyberg
Le Don by David Schinkel and Yves Beauchesne
1988 Amos's Sweater by Kim LeFave
The Third Magic by Welwyn Wilton Katz
Le Jeux de Pic-mots by Phillippe Beha
Cassiopee ou L'Ete polonais by Michele Marineau
1989 The Magic Paintbrush by Robin Miller
Bad Boy by Diana Weiler
Benjamin et la saga des oreillers by Stephane Poulin
Temps mort by Charles Montpetit
1990 The Orphan Boy by Paul Morin
Redwork by Michael Bedard
Les Fantaisies de l'Oncle Henri by Pierre Pratt
Le Vraie Histoire du Chien de Clara Vic by Christiane Duchesne
1991 Doctor Kiss Says Yes by Joanne Fitzgerald
Pick-Up Sticks by Sarah Ellis
Un Champion by Sheldon Cohen
Deux Heures et Demi avant Jasmine
1992 Hero of Lesser Causes by Julie Johnston
1993 Some of the Kinder Planets by Tim Wynne-Jones

Eric Gregory Trust Fund Award
The Society of Authors
84 Drayton Gardens
London SW10 9SB, England
For poets aged under 30 who are likely to benefit from more time given to writing.
Prize: £27,000 (shared)
1986 Mick North
Lachlan Mackinnon
Oliver Reynolds
Stephen Romer
1987 Peter McDonald
Maura Dooley
Stephen Knight
Steve Anthony
Jill Maughan
Paul Munden
1988 Michael Symmons Robert
Gwyneth Lewis
Adrian Blackledge
Simon Armitage
Robert Crawford

1989 Gerard Woodward
David Morley
Katrina Porteus
Paul Henry
1990 Nicholas Drake
Maggie Hannon
William Park
Jonathan Davidson
Lavinia Greenlaw
Don Paterson
John Wells
1991 Roddy Lumsden
Glyn Maxwell
Stephen Smith
Wayne Burrows
Jackie Kay
1992 Jill Dawson
Hugh Dunkerly
Christopher Greenhaigh
Marita Maddah
Stuart Paterson
Stuart Pickford
1993 Eleanor Brown
Joel Lane
Deryn Rees-Jones
1994 Julia Copus
Alice Oswald
Steven Blyth
Kate Clanchy
Giles Goodland

Guardian Fiction Prize
The Guardian, 119 Farringdon Road
London EC1R 3ER, England
The winner is chosen by a panel of five judges. Submissions are not requested. Awarded to: a work of fiction by British or Commonwealth writer and published in the UK.
Prize: £2000
1980 A Month in the Country by J L Carr
1981 Kepler by John Banville
1982 Where I Used to Play on the Green by Glyn Hughes
1983 Empire of the Sun by J G Ballard
1985 Hawksmoor by Peter Ackroyd
1986 Continent by Jim Crace
1987 The Levels by Peter Benson
1988 Sweet Desserts by Lucy Ellman
1989 Rosehill: Portraits from a Midlands City by Carol Lake
1990 Shape-Shifter by Pauline Melville
1991 The Devil's Own Work by Alan Judd
1992 Poor Things by Alasdair Gray
1993 The Eye in the Door by Pat Barker
1994 Debatable Land by Candia McWilliam

Guardian Children's Fiction Award
The Guardian, 119 Faringdon Road
London EC1R 3ER, England
Work of fiction by a Commonwealth or British author, published in Britain in previous year, excluding picture books and previous winners.
Annual prize of £1000.
Contact: Children's Book Editor, Joanna Carey
1980 The Vandal by Ann Schlee
1981 The Sentinels by Peter Carter
1982 Goodnight Mister Tom by Michelle

Magorian
1983 The Village by the Sea by Anita Desai
1984 The Sheep-Pig by Dick King-Smith
1985 What is the Truth? by Ted Hughes
1986 Henry's Leg by Ann Pilling
1987 The True Story of Spit MacPhee by James Aldridge
1988 The Runaways by Ruth Thomas
1989 A Pack of Lies by Geraldine McCaughrean
1990 Goggle-Eyes by Anne Fine
1991 The Kingdom by the Sea by Robert Westall
1992 Paper Faces by Rachel Anderson
       The Exiles by Hilary McKay
1993 Low Tide by William Mayne
1994 The Mennyms by Sylvia Waugh

The Hawthornden Prize

42A Hays Mews, Berkeley Square
London W1X 7RU, England
For imaginative literature by a British subject under the age of 41 published during the previous year.
Annual prize of £5000
Contact: Mrs Judy Mooney
1980 Arcadia by Christopher Reid
1981 St Kilda's Parliament by Douglas Dunn
1982 Sour Sweet by Timothy Mo
1983 Allegro Postillion by Jonathan Keats
84-87 No awards
1988 Behind the Wall by Colin Thubron
1989 Talking Heads by Alan Bennett
1990 Short Afternoons by Kit Wright
1991 The Invisible Woman by Claire Tomalin
1992 Of Love and Asthma by Ferdinand Mount
1993 The Tap Dancer by Andrew Barrow
1994 In the Place of Fallen Leaves by Tim Pears

Ernest Hemingway Foundation Award

PEN American Center, 568 Broadway
New York, NY 10012, USA
Prize is awarded for a distinguished first published book of fiction by an American author.
Annual prize of $7500
Contact: John Morrone
1980 Mom Kills Kids and Self by Alan Saperstein
1981 Household Words by Joan Silber
1982 Housekeeping by Marilynne Robinson
1983 Shiloh and Other Stories by Bobbie Ann Mason
1984 During the Reign of the Queen of Persia by Joan Chase
1985 Dreams of Sleep by Josephine Humphreys
1986 Lady's Time by Alan V Hewat
1987 Tongues of Flame by Mary Ward Brown
1988 Imagining Argentina by Lawrence Thornton
1989 The Book by Ruth by Jane Hamilton
1990 The Ice at the Bottom of the World by Mark Richard
1991 Maps to Anywhere by Bernard Cooper
1992 Wartime Lies by Louis Begley
1993 Lost in the City by Edward P Jones
1994 The Magic of Blood by Dagoberto Gilb

O Henry Award

Texas Institute of Letters, Box 9032
Wichita Falls, TX 76308-9032, USA
Contact: James Hoggard, The Secretary

David Higham Prize for Fiction

Book Trust, Book House, 45 East Hill
London SW18 2QZ, England
Award for first novel or book of short stories published in the UK in year of the award. Author must be citizen of Britain, Commonwealth, Republic of Ireland or South Africa.
Annual prize of £1000
Contact: Caroline Sanderson
1980 Keep on Running by Ted Harriot
1981 A Separate Development by Christopher Hope
1982 Where I Used to Play on the Green by Glyn Hughes
1983 The Notebook of Gismondo Cavalletti by R M Lamming
1984 A Parish of Rich Women by James Buchan
1985 Family Myths and Legends by Patricia Ferguson
1986 Continent by Jim Crace
1987 The 13th House by Adam Zameenzad
1988 Life in the Palace by Carol Birchg
1989 Motherland by Timothy O'Grady
1990 Soldiers and Innocents by Russell Celyn Jones
1991 O Caledonia by Elspeth Barker
1992 Halo by John Loveday
1993 Love Your Enemies by Nicola Barker
1994 The Longest Memory by Fred D'Aguiar

Historical Novel Prize in Memory of Georgette Heyer

The Bodley Head, Random Century
20 Vauxhall Bridge Road
London SW1V 2SA, England
Awarded for full length previously unpublished historical novel set before 1939.
Annual prize of £5000.
Contact: Mrs J Black
1980 Children of Hachiman by Lynn Guest
1981 Zemindar by Valerie Fitzgerald
1982 No prize awarded
1983 Queen of the Lightning by Kathleen Herbert
1984 The Terioki Crossing by Alan Fisher
1985 Legacy by Susan Kay
1986 I Am England by Patricia Wright
1987 No prize awarded
1988 Trust and Treason by Margaret Birkhead
1989 A Fallen Land by Janet Broomfield

Boston Globe - Horn Book Award

Box 5378, Boston Globe, Boston
MA 02107-5378, USA
Prize is awarded for books published within the previous year. Three categories: fiction, non-fiction, and picture book.
Annual prize of $500.
Contact: Stephanie Loer
1980 Conrad's War by Andrew Davies
       Building: The Fight Against Gravity by Marion Salvador
       The Garden of Abdul Gasazi by Chris Van Allsburg
1981 The Leaving by Lynn Hall
       The Weaver's Gift by Kathryn Lasky
       Outside Over There by Maurice Sendak
1982 Playing Beatie Bow by Ruth Park

Upon the Head of the Goat: A Childhood in Hungary 1939-44 by Aranka Siegal

A Visit ot William Blake's Inn: Poems for Innocent and Experienced Travellers by Nancy Willard

1983 Sweet Whispers, Brother Rush by Virginia Hamilton

Behind Barbed Wire: The Imprisonment of Japanese Americans During World War II by Daniel S Davis

A Chair for My Mother by Vera B Williams

1984 A Little Fear by Patricia Wrightson

The Double Life of Pochahontas by Jean Fritz

Jonah and the Great Fish by Warwick Hutton

1985 The Moves Make the Man by Bruce Brooks

Commodore Perry in the Land of the Shogun by Rhonda Blumberg

Mama Don't Allow by Thacher Hurd

1986 In Summer Light by Zibby Oneal

Auks, Rocks and the Odd Dinosaur: Tales from the Smithsonian's Museum of Natural History by Peggy Thomson

The Paper Crane by Molly Bang

1987 Rabble Starkey by Lois Lowry

The Pilgrims of Plimothi by Marcia Sewall

Mufaro's Beautiful Daughters: An African Tale by John Steptoe

1988 The Friendship by Mildred D Taylor

Anthony Burns by Virginia Hamilton

The Boy of the Tree-Year Nap by Dianne Snyder

1989 The Village by the Sea by Paula Fox

The Way Things Work by David Macauley

Shy Charles by Rosemary Wells

1990 Maniac Magee by Jerry Spinelli

The Great Little Madison by Jean Fritz

Lon Po Po by Ed Young

1991 The True Confessions of Charlotte Doyle by Avi Appalachia & Cynthia Rylant

The Tale of the Mandarin Ducks by Katherine Paterson

1992 Missing May by Cynthia Rylant

Talking with Artists by Pat Cummings

Seven Blind Mice by Ed Young

1993 Ajeemah and His Son by James Berry

The Fortune Tellers by Lloyd Alexander

Sojourner Truth by Patricia C & Frederick McKissack

1994 Scooter by Vera B Williams

Eleanor Roosevelt by Russell Freedman

Grandfather's Journey by Allen Say

The Hugo Awards

World Science Fiction Society, PO Box 1270 Kendall Sq Station, Cambridge, MA 02142, USA Established 1953 as Science Fiction Achievement Awards for the best science fiction writing in several categories.

Annual prize of chrome-plated rocket ship model.
Contact: Donald E Eastlake III

Novels

1980 The Fountains of Paradise by Arthur C Clarke

1981 The Snow Queen by Joan D Vinge

1982 Downbelow Station by C J Cherryh

1983 Foundation's Edge by Isaac Asimov
1984 Startide Rising by David Brin
1985 Neuromancer by William Gibson
1986 Ender's Game by Orson Scott Card
1987 Speaker for the Dead by Orson Scott Card

Novella

1980 Enemy Mine by Barry B Longyear
1981 Lost Dorsai by Gordon R Dickson
1982 The Saturn Game by Paul Anderson
1983 Souls by Joanna Russ
1984 Cascade Point by Timothy Zahn
1985 Press Enter by John Varley
1986 Twenty-four Views of Mount Fuji by Hokusai by Roger Zelazny
1987 Gilgamesh in the Outback by Robert Silverberg

Novelette

1980 Sandkings by George R R Martin
1981 The Cloak and the Staff by Gordon R Dickson
1982 Unicorn Variation by Roger Zelazny
1983 Fire Watch by Connie Willis
1984 Blood Music by Greg Bear
1985 Bloodchild by Octavia Butler
1986 Paladin of the Lost Hour by Harlan Ellison
1987 Permafrost by Roger Zelazny

Short Story

1980 The Way of Cross and Dragon by George R Martin
1981 Grotto of the Dancing Deer by Clifford D Simak
1982 The Pusher by John Varley
1983 Melancholy Elephants by Spider Robinson
1984 Speech Sound by Octavia Butler
1985 The Crystal Spheres by David Brin
1986 Fermi and Frost by Frederik Pohl
1987 Tangents by Greg Bear

Non-fiction book

1980 The Science Fiction Encyclopedia by Peter Nicholls (ed)
1981 Cosmos by Carl Sagan
1982 Danse Macabre by Stephen King
1983 Isaac Asimov: The Foundations of Science Fiction by James Gunn
1984 Encyclopedia of Science Fiction and Fantasy, vol III by Donald Tuck
1985 Wonder's Child: My Life in Science Fiction by Jack Williamson
1986 Science Made Stupid by Tom Weller
1987 Trillion Year Spree by Brian Aldiss with David Wingrove

Alice Hunt Bartlett Prize

The Poetry Society, 21 Earls Court Sq London SW5 9DE, England Established in 1966 and awarded annually. Prize is awarded for a published collection of poetry, not less than 20 poems or 400 lines. Special consideration is given to younger or newly emerging poets.

Annual prize of £500. Prize last awarded in 1988. Subsequently funding for the prize has run out.
Contact: Awards Administrator

1980 Unhistorical Fragments by John Whitworth
1981 The Sorrow Garden by Thomas McCarthy
Unplayed Music by Carol Rumens
1982 The Flower Master by Medbh McGuckian

1983 Watching for Dolphins by David Constantine
1984 Kisses for Mayakovsky by Alison Fell
     The Stubborn Forest by Paul Hyland
1985 The Humble Administrator's Garden by
     Vikram Seth
     The Visitor's Book by John Davies
1986 The Sea Skater by Helen Dunmore
1987 Brunizem by Sujata Bhatt

Ian St James Awards

c/o The New Writer's Club, PO Box 101
Tunbridge Wells, Kent TN4 8YD, England
Presented to previously unpublished authors for
fictional short stories of between 5-10,000 words.
Prize: (Total) £32,000. Sixty-four runners-up are
published in Acclaim Magazine.

1990 Mothering Sunday by Annie Hedley
     A Seeing Lesson by William Walker
     A Whore's Vengeance by Louise Doughty
1991 Small Beginnings by Faith Addis
     French Kisses by Alan Dunn
     Me and Renate by Stephanie Ellyne
1992 Black Sky at Night by Jeremy Cain
     Good at Things by Francesca Clementis
     Me and the Stars by Peter Naylor
1993 Berlin Story by Philip Sealey
     The Olive Tree by Hilary Waters
     Figure of Eight by Min Dinning
     Karmic Mothers by Kate Atkinson
     Moira Flaherty by Juliet McCarthy
     Black Lizzie Black by James Maguire

The Independent Award for Foreign Fiction

The Independent, 1 Canada Square
Canary Wharf, London E14 5DL, England
Prize awarded for full length novel or a collection of
short stories, translated into English and published
in the preceding year.
Prize: £10,000.
Contact: John Walsh

1991 Immortality by Milan Kundera (trans by
     Peter Kussi)
     Rain In The Wind by Saiich Maruya (trans
     by Dennis Keene)
1992 The Death of Napoleon by Simon Leys
     (trans by Patricia Clancy)
1993 The Year of the Death of Ricardo Reis by
     Jose Saramago
1994 The Sorrow of War by Bao Ninh (trans by
     Frank Palmos and Phan Thanh
     Hao)

The Ingersoll Prizes
T S Elliot Award for Creative Writing
Ingersoll Foundation, 934 N Main St
Rockford, IL 61103, USA
For works in literature, including fiction, drama,
poetry, essays & literary criticism.
Annual prize of $15,000
Contact: Thomas J Fleming, Exec Secretary

1983 Jorge Luis Borges
1984 Anthony Powell
1985 Eugene Ionesco
1986 V S Naipaul
1987 Octavio Paz
1988 Walker Percy
1989 George Garrett

1991 Mario Vargas Llosa
1992 Muriel Spark
1993 Fred Chapell

Richard M Weaver Award for Scholarly Letters
Ingersoll Foundation, 934 N Main St
Rockford, IL 61103, USA
For a lifetime of distinguished achievements in the
humanities, including philosophy, history, ethics &
social & political science.
Annual award of $15,000.
Contact: Thomas J Fleming, Secretary

1983 James Burnham
1984 Russell Kirk
1985 Robert Nisbet
1986 Andrew Lytle
1987 Josef Pieper
1988 Edward Shils
1989 Edward O Wilson
1990 Forrest McDonald
1991 John Lukacs
1992 Walter Burkert
1993 Eugene Genovese

The Irish Times International Fiction Prize
Irish Times Ltd
11-15 D'Olier Street, Dublin 2, Republic of Ireland
The winners are chosen from nomination.
Submissions are not required. Awarded annually to:
international fiction and poetry, written in English or
Irish.
Prize: IR£7500 (non-fiction); IR£7500 (first book
award; IR£10,000 (International Fiction).
Contact: Gerard Cavanagh.

International Fiction Prize
1989 Libra by Don DeLillo
1990 Possession by A S Byatt
1991 Wartime Lies by Louis Begley
1992 Mating by Norman Rush
1993 The Shipping News by Annie Proulx

Irish Literature Prize
1989 The Men Who Loved Evelyn Cotton by
     Frank Ronan
1990 Amongst Women by John McGahern
     (fiction)
     Belfast Confetti by Ciaran Carson
1991 Ireland 1912-1985 by J J Lee (non-fiction)
     The South by Colm Toibin (first book)
1992 The Butcher Boy by Patrick McCabe
     (fiction)
     Selected Poems by Derek Mahon (poetry)
1993 An Evil Cradling by Brian Keenan (non-
     fiction)
     The Fallen and Other Stories by John
     MacKenna (first book)

The Jerusalem Prize
Binyaney Ha'ooma, POB 6001
Jerusalem 91060, Israel
The prestigious prize is awarded to a writer whose
work expresses the idea of "the freedom of the
individual in society".
Prize of US $5000 every two years
Contact: Zev Birger, Chairman & Managing Director

1981 Graham Greene
1983 V S Naipaul
1985 Milan Kundera
1987 J M Coetzee

The Kalinga Prize
UNESCO, 7 Place de Fontenoy
75700 Paris, France
Annual prize of £1000
Contact: The Assistant Director-General for Science
1980 Aristide Bastidas
1981 David F Attenborough
Dennis Flanagan
1982 Oswaldo Frota-Pessoa
1983 Abdullah Al Muti Sharafuddin
1984 yves Coppens
Igor Petryanov
1985 Sir Peter Medawar
1986 Nikolai G Basov
David Suzuki
1987 Marcel Roche
1988 Björn Kurtén
1989 Saad Ahmed Shabaan

Lamont Poetry Selection
Academy of American Poets,
584 Broadway, Suite 1208
New York, NY 10012, USA
Supports the publication of an American poet's
second volume of poetry. Publishers in the United
States are invited to submit to the Academy
manuscripts by American poets who have already
published one book of poems in a standard edition.
Annual prize of $1000
Contact: Siobahn Reagan
1980 More Trouble with the Obvious by Michael
Van Walleghen
1981 The Country Between Us by Carolyn
Forche
1982 Long Walks in the Afternoon by Margaret
Gibson
1983 The Dead and the Living by Sharon Olds
1984 Deep Within the Ravine by Philip Schultz
1985 Victims of the Latest Dance Craze by
Cornelius Eady
1986 The Minute Hand by Jane Shore
1987 The River of Heaven by Garret Kaoru
Hongo
1988 Unfinished Painting by Mary Jo Salter
1989 Crime Against Nature by Minnie Jo Pratt
1990 The City in Which I Love You by Li-Young
Lee
1991 Campo Santo by Susan Wood
1992 Wildwood Flower by Kathleen Stripling
Bryer
1993 Stained Glass by Rosanna Warren
1994 Song by Brigit Pegeen Kelly

Gerald Lampert Award
League of Canadian Poets, 24 Ryerson Avenue
Toronto, Ontario N5T 2P3, Canada
Contact: Edita Pegrauskaige, Executive Director

The Peter I B Lavan Younger Poet Awards
The Academy of American Poets
584 Broadway, Suite 1208
New York, NY 10012, USA
Awarded to three poets under forty annually. Poets
must be American citizens and have published at
least one full length collection of poetry.
Annual prize of $1000
Contact: Siobahn Reagan

1983 Edward Hirsch
Brad Leithauser
Gjertrud Schnackenberg
1984 Vicki Hearne
Cleopatra mathis
Katha Politt
1985 Diane Ackerman
Michael Blumenthal
Richard Kenney
1986 Rita Dove
Rodney Jones
Timothy Steele
1987 Jon Davis
Debora Gregor
Norman Williams
1988 Marie Howe
Naomi Shihab Nye
John Yau
1989 Melissa Green
Jeffrey Harrison
William Logan
1990 George Bradley
Jorie Graham
Mary Jo Salter
1991 Nicholas Christopher
J Allyn Rosser
Peter Schmitt
1992 Cyrus Cassells
Richard Lyons
Rosanna Warren
1993 Thomas Bolt
David Clewell
Christopher Merrill

Grace Leven Prize for Poetry
c/o Perpetual Trustee Company Ltd
39 Hunter St, Sydney, NSW 2000, Australia
For recognition of the best volume of poetry
published during the twelve months immediately
preceding the year in which the award is made.
Writers must be Australian-born and writing as
Australians, or naturalised in Australia and resident
in Australia for not less than ten years.
Annual prize of Australian $200.
Contact: M J O'Donnell, Charitable Trusts Manager.
1980 The Boys Who Stole the Funeral by Leslie
Allan Murray
1981 Nero's Poems by Geoffrey Lehmann
1982 Tide Country by Vivian Smith
1983 Collected Poems by Peter Porter
1984 The Three Gates and Other Poems by
Rosemary Dobson
1985 Selected Poems by Robert Gray
The Amorous Cannibal by Chris Wallace
Crabbe
1986 Washing the Money by Ryhil McMaster
1987 Occasions of Birds and other Poems by
Elizabeth Riddell
1988 Under Berlin by John Tranter
1989 A Tremendous World in Her Head: Selected
Poems by Dorothy Hewett
1990 Dog Fox Field by Les A Murray
1991 The Empire of Grass by Gary Catalano
Penial by Doctor Kevin Hart

Los Angeles Times Book Prizes
Los Angeles Times, Times Mirror Square

Los Angeles, CA 90053, USA
Contact: Laura Morgan, P R Supervisor

McColvin Medal
c/o Library Association
7 Ridgmount Street, London WC1E 7AE, England
The winner is chosen from nominations made by Library Association members.
A medal is awarded to: an outstanding reference book first published in the UK during the preceding year.
Prize: A medal
Contact: The Library Association
1980 Guide to the Local Administrative Units of England Volume I: Southern England by Frederic A Youngs
1981 The New Grove Dictionary of Music and Musicians by Stanley Sadie (editor)
1982 The Dictionary of Blue and White Printed Pottery 1780-1880 by A W Coysh & R K Henrywood
1983 Dictionary of British Book Illustrators: The Twentieth Century by Brigid Peppin & Lucy Micklethwait
1984 The History of Glass by D Klein & W Lloyd (general editors)
1985 The Artist's Craft: A History of Tools, Techniques and Material by James Ayres
1986 The British Musical Theatre Volume I: 1865-1914 Volume II: 1915-1984 by Kurt Ganzl
1987 Fermented Foods of the World: A Dictionary & Guide by Geoffrey Campbell-Platt
1988 The Encyclopaedia of Oxford by Christopher Hibbert (editor)
1989 The Oxford English Dictionary 2nd Edition by John Simpson & Edmund Weiner (editors)
1990 William Walton: A Catalogue 2nd edition by Stewart Craggs
1991 The Cambridge Encyclopaedia of Ornithology by Michael Brooke & Tim Birkhead
1992 The New Grove Dictionary of Opera by Stanley Sadie (editor)
1993 The Illustrated History of Canal and River Navigation by Edward Peget-Tomlinson

McKitterick Prize
Society of Authors
84 Drayton Gardens, London SW10 9SB, England
Annual award for a work first published in the UK or previously unpublished. Open to writers over 40 who have had no previous work published other than that submitted.
Prize: £5000.
Contact: Award Secretary
1990 Chimera by Simon Mawer
1991 A Summer to Halo by John Loveday
1992 News From a Foreign Country Came by Alberto Manguel
1993 The Tap Dancer by Andrew Barrow
1994 Zennor in Darkness by Helen Dunmore

The Mail on Sunday John Llewellyn Rhys Prize
Book Trust, Book House
45 East Hill, London SW18 2QZ, England
Awarded for a work - fiction, non-fiction, poetry or drama - by an author under 35 at time of publication. Books must have been published in the UK in year of award in English by a citizen of Britain or the Commonwealth. Sponsored by the Mail on Sunday.
Annual 1st prize of £5000; £500 for shortlisted entries.
Contact: Caroline Sanderson
1980 The Diamonds at the Bottom of the Sea by Desmond Hogan
1981 The Laird of Abbotsford by A N Wilson
1982 An Ice-Cream War by William Boyd
1983 The Slow Train to Milan by Lisa St Aubin de Teran
1984 Dangerous Play by Andrew Motion
1985 Out of the Blue by John Milne
1986 Loving Roger by Tim Parks
1987 The Passion by Jeanette Winterson
1988 The March Fence by Matthew Yorke
1989 Sylvia Townsend Warner by Claire Harman
1990 Wittgenstein: The Duty of Genius by Ray Monk
1991 Night Geometry and the Garscadden Trains by A L Kennedy
1992 Sweet Thames by Matthew Kneale
1993 On Foot to the Golden Horn: A Walk to Istanbul by Jason Goodwin

Somerset Maugham Awards
Somerset Maugham Trust Fund
The Society of Authors, 84 Drayton Gardens
London SW10 9SB, England
Awarded to a writer on the strength of a published work.
Prize: Three awards of £5000 each to be used for foreign travel.
Contact: The Secretary
1980 The Inklings by Humphrey Carpenter
      Bomer Command by Max Hastings
      Arcadia by Christopher Reid
1981 Metroland by Julian Barnes
      The Healing Art by A N Wilson
      Hearts of Gold by Clive Sinclair
1982 Lantern Lecture & Other Stories by Adam Mars-Jones
      A Good Man in Africa by William Boyd
1983 Keepers of the House by Lisa St Aubin de Teran
1984 The Last Testament of Oscar Wilde by Peter Ackroyd
      The Polish Revolution: Solidarity by Timothy Garton Ash
      The Indoor Park by Sean O'Brien
1985 Dark Glasses by Blake Morrison
      By the Fisheries by Jeremy Reed
      Her Living Image by Jane Rogers
1986 Family Myths and Legends by Patricia Ferguson
      Frontiers by Adam Nicolson
      Tongues of Flame by Tim Parks
1987 The Cormorant by Stephen Gregory
      Issac Campion by Janni Howker
      The Lamberts by Andrew Motion

1988	The Land that Lost its Heroes by Jimmy Burns
	Selling Manhattan by Carol Ann Duffy
	Whore Banquets by Matthew Kneale
1989	Romantic Affinities by Rupert Christiansen
	The Swimming Pool Library by Alan Hollinghurst
	The Birds of the Innocent Wood by Deirdre Madden
1990	Our Grandmothers' Drums by Mark Hudson
	The Automatic Man by Sam North
	The Vision of Elena Silves by Nicholas Shakespeare
1991	The Other Occupant by Peter Benson
	Honour Thy Father by Lesley Glaister
	Four Bare Legs in a Bed by Helen Simpson
1992	But Beautiful by Geoff Dyer
	Lempriere's Dictionary by Lawrence Norfolk
	Householder by Gerard Woodward
1993	Jella by Dea Birkett
	Bucket of Tongues by Duncan McLean
	Out of the Rain by Glyn Maxwell
1994	Other Lovers by Jackie Kay
	Looking for the Impossible Dance by A L Kennedy
	The Crossing Place by Philip Marsden

The Milner Award
The Friends of the Atlanta Fulton Public Library
One Margaret Mitchell Square
Atlanta, GA 30303, USA
Award to a living American author of children's books.
The winning author is awarded a specially commissioned work of the internationally famous glass sculptor, Hans Frabel, and a $1000 honorarium.

1983	Judy Blume
1984	Peggy Parish
1985	Paula Danziger
1986	Barbara Park
1987	Lois Lowry
1988	Francine Pascal
1989	John Steptoe
1990	Louis Sachar
1991	Marc Brown
1992	Barthe DeClements
1993	Matt Christopher
1994	Joanna Cole

National Book Awards
NBA Foundation
260 Fifth Avenue, 4th Fl
New York, NY 10001, USA
Award given to living American authors for books published in the USA; one fiction & one non-fiction. Annual first prize of $10,000 and $1000 for short-listed works.
Contact: Executive Director, Neil Baldwin

1980	By Myself by Lauren Bacall
	Max Perkins: Editor of Genius by A Scott Berg
	A Gathering of Days: A New England Girl's Journal 1830-32 by Joan W Blos
	The Complete Directory to Prime Network TV Shows by Tim Brooks and Earle Marsh

Stained Glass by William F Buckley Jr
Julia Child and More Company by Julia Child
And I Worked at the Writer's Trade by Malcolm Cowley
Mandelstam's The Complete Critical Prose and Letters by Jane Gary Harris and Constance Link
Godel, Escher, Bach: An Eternal Golden Braid by Douglas Hofstadter
The World According to Garp by John Irving
White House Years by Henry Kissinger
Bendigo Shafter by Louis L'Amour
A Swiftly Tilting Planet by Madeleine L'Engle
The Culture of Narcissism by Christopher Lasch
Ashes by Philip Levine
The Green Ripper by John D MacDonald
The Rise of Theodore Roosevelt by Edmund Morris
The Gnostic Gospels by Elaine Pagels
Jem by Frederick Pohl
Sophie's Choice by William Styron
A Distant Mirror: The Calamitous 14th Century by Barbara W Tuchman
A Severe Mercy by Sheldon Vanauken
The Book of the Dun Cow by Walter Wangerin
Birdy by William Wharton
The Right Stuff by Tom Wolfe
The Dancing Wu Li Masters: An Overview of the New Physics by Gary Zukav

1981	Sister Wolf by Ann Arensberg
	Samuel Beckett by Diedre Bair
	Christianity, Social Tolerance and Homosexuality by John Boswell
	The Night Swimmers by Betsy Byars
	Ramona and Her Mother by Beverly Cleary
	The Panda's Thumb by Stephen Jay Gould
	Oh, Boy! Babies! by Alison Cragin Herzig and Jane Lawrence Mali
	China Men by Maxine Hong Kingston
	The Last Cowboy by Jane Kramer
	Been in the Storm so Long: Aftermath of Slavery by Leon F Litwick
	Plains Song by Wright Morris
	The Need to Hold Still by Lisel Mueller
	The Medusa and the Snail by Lewis Thomas
	Evening Edged in Gold by John E Woods

1982	A Penguin Year by Susan Bonners
	Life Supports by William Bronk
	In the Shade of Spring Leaves by Robert Lyons Danly
	Dale Loves Sophie to Death by Robb Forman Dew
	Lucy: The Beginnings of Humankind by Donald C Johanson and A Maitland Edey
	The Soul of a New Machine by Tracy Kidder
	Ten Thousand Leaves by Ian Hildeo Levy
	So Long, See You Tomorrow by William Maxwell
	Mornings on Horseback by David McCullough
	Naming Names by Victor Navasky

People of the Sacred Mountain: A History of the Northern Cheyenne Chief and Warrior Societies by Father Peter John Powell

Words by Heart by Ouida Sebestyen

Outside Over There by Maurice Sendak

Noah's Ark by Peter Spier

Walter Lippman and the American Century by Ronald Steel

Rabbit is Rich by John Updike

The Generation of 1914 by Robert Wohl

Taking the Quantum Leap: The New Physics for Nonscientists by Fred Alan Wolf

1983 Voices of Protest: Huey Long, Father Coughlin and The Great Depression by Alan Brinkley

China: Alive in the Bitter Sea by Fox Butterfield

Miss Rumphius by Barbara Cooney

The Mathematical Experience by Philipp P Davis

National Defense by James Fallows

A Place Apart by Paula Fox

Homesick by Jean Fritz

Chimney Sweeps by James Cross Giblin

The Red Magician by Lisa Goldstein

A House is a House for Me by Mary Ann Hoberman

Baudelaire's Les Fleurs du Mal by Richard Howard

Selected Poems by Galway Kinnell

Utopian Thought in the Western World by Frank E Manuel and P Fritzie Manuel

Nathaniel Hawthorne in His Time by James Mellow

The Women of Brewster Place by Gloria Naylor

"Subtle is the Lord. . ." The Science and the life of Albert Einstein by Abraham Pais

Doctor De Soto by William Steig

Marked By Fire by Joyce Carol Thomas

Isaak Dinesen by Judith Thurman

The Color Purple by Alice Walker

The Collected Stories by Eudora Welty

Country Music by Charles Wright

1984 Stones for Ibarra by Harriet Doerr

Victory Over Japan by Ellen Gilchrist

Andrew Jackson and the Course of American Democracy 1833-1945 vol III by Robert V Remini

1985 White Noise by Don Delillo

Common Ground: A Turbulent Decade in the Lives of Three American Families by J Anthony Lukas

Easy in the Islands by Bob Shacochis

1986 Arctic Dreams by Barry Lopez

World's Fair by E L Doctorow

1987 Paco's Story by Larry Heinemann

The Making of the Atomic Bomb by Richard Rhodes

1988 Paris Trout by Pete Dexter

A Bright and Shining Lie: John Paul Vann America in Vietnam by Neil Sheehan

1989 Spartina by John Casey

From Beirut to Jerusalem by Thomas L Friedman

1990 Middle Passage by Charles Johnson

The House of Morgan by Ron Chernow

1991 Mating by Norman Rush

Freedom by Orlando Patterson

What Work is by Philip Levine

1992 All the Pretty Horses by Cormac McCarthy

Becoming A Man by Paul Monette

New and Selected Poems by Mary Oliver

1993 The Shipping News by E Annie Proulx

United States: Essays 1952-1992 by Gore Vidal

Garbage by A R Ammons

1994 A Frolic of His Own by William Gaddis

Worshipful Company of Fletchers by James Tate

How We Die by Sherwin B Nuland

National Book Critics Circle Awards

400 North Broad Street
Philadelphia, PA 19103, USA
For excellence in biography/autobiography, criticism, fiction, general nonfiction & poetry published for the first time during the previous year by American writers.
Annual scroll & citations.
Contact: Carun Romano

1980 The Transit of Venus by Shirley Hazzard

Sunrise by Frederick Seidel

Walter Lippmann and the American Century by Ronald Steel

Part of Nature, Part of Us: Modern American Poets by Helen Vendler

1981 Rabbit is Rich by John Updike

A Coast of Trees by A R Ammons

The Mismeasure of Man of Stephan Jay Gould

A Virgil Thomson Reader by Virgil Thomson

1982 George Mills by Stanley Elkin

Antarctic Traveller by Katha Pollitt

The Path to Power: The Years of Lyndon Johnson by Robert A Caro

The Second American Revolution and Other Essays 1976-82 by Gore Vidal

12-volume edition of Byron's Letters and Journals by Leslie A Marchand

1983 Ironweed by William Kennedy

The Price of Power: Kissinger in the Nixon White House by Seymour M Hersh

Minor Characters by Joyce Johnson

The Changing Light at Sandover by James Merrill

Hugging the Shore: Essays and Criticism by John Updike

1984 Love Medicine by Louise Erdrich

Dostoevsky: The Years of Ordeal 1850-1859 by Joseph Frank

Twentieth Century Pleasures by Robert Hass

Weapons and Hope by Freeman Dyson

The Dead and the Living by Sharon Olds

1985 The Accidental Tourist by Anne Tyler

The Triumph of Achilles by Louise Gluck

Henry James: A Life by Leon Edel

Common Ground by J Anthony Lukas

Habitations of the Word by William Gass
1986   Tombee: Portrait of a Cotton Planter by
        Theodore Rosengarten
        Less Than One: Selected Essays by Joseph
        Brodsky
        Kate Vaiden by Reynolds Price
        War Without Mercy: Race and Power in the
        Pacific War by John W Dower
        Wild Gratitude by Edward Hirsch
1987   Chaucer: His Life, His Works, His World by
        Donald Howard
        Dance Writings by Edwin Denby
        The Making of the Atomic Bomb by Richard
        Rhodes
        The Counterlife by Philip Roth
        Flesh and Blood by C K Williams
1988   The Middleman and Other Stories by
        Bharati Mukherjee
        The One Day by Donald Hall
        Oscar Wilde by Richard Ellmann
        Parting the Waters by Taylor Branch
        Work and Lives by Clifford Geertz
1989   Billy Bathgate by E L Doctorow
        The Broken Cord by Michael Dorris
        A First-Class Temperament by Geoffrey C
        Ward
        Not by Fact Alone by John Clive
1990   Bitter Angel by Amy Gerstler
        The Content of Our Character by Shelby
        Steele
        Encounters and Reflections by Arthur Danto
        Means of Ascent by Robert Caro
        Rabbit at Rest by John Updike
        Transparent Gestures by Rodney Jones
1993   All the Pretty Horses by Cormack McCarthy
        Young Men and Fire by Norman Maclean
        Collected Poems, 1946-91 by Hayden
        Carruth
        Lincoln at Gettysburg by Gary Wills
        Writing Dangerously: Mary McCarthy &
        Carol Brightman
1994   Opera in America by John Dizikes
        Genet by Edmund White
        My Alexandria by Mark Doty
        A Lesson Before Dying by Ernest J Gaines
        The Land Where the Blues Began by Alan
        Lomax

National Poetry Competition
The Poetry Society, 22 Betterton Street,
London WC2H 9BU, England
Prizes awarded for an unpublished poem of less
than 40 lines by anyone over the age of 16.
Prizes: £3000 (1st); £500 (2nd); £250 (3rd); plus
smaller prizes.
Contact: Competition Organizer, Betty Redpath.
1985   Jo Shapcott
        Ian Keenan
        William Palmer
1986   Carole Satyamuri
        Adam Thorpe
        Bill Turner
1987   Ian Duhig
        Michael Donaghy
        Harry Smart
1988   Martin Reed
        Ian Caws

        Rodney Pybus
1989   William Scammell
        Patricia Pogson
        Glyn Maxwell
1990   Nicky Rice
        Frances Wilson
        Geoffrey Constable
1991   John Levett
        Jo Shapcott
        Don Paterson

SFWA Nebula Awards
Science Fiction and Fantasy Writers of America Inc
5 Winding Brook Drive, Suite 1B
Guilderland, New York, NY 12084, USA
Publication during the previous calendar year, and
nomination by SFWA President.
Annual trophy.
Contact: Peter Dennis Pautz
Grand Master
1984   Andre Norton
1986   Arthur C Clarke
1987   Isaac Asimov
1988   Alfred Bester
1989   Ray Bradbury
1990   Not Awarded
Novel
1980   The Fountains of Paradise by Arthur C
        Clarke
1981   Timescape by Gregory Benford
1982   The Claw of the Conciliator by Gene Wolfe
1983   No Enemy But Time by Michael Bishop
1984   Startide Rising by David Brin
1985   Neuromancer by William Gibson
1986   Ender's Game by Orson Scott Card
1987   Speaker for the Dead by Orson Scott Card
1988   The Falling Woman by Pat Murphy
1989   Falling Free by Lois McMaster Bujold
1990   The Healer's War by Elizabeth Ann
        Scarborough
Novelette
1980   Sandkings by George R R Martin
1981   The Ugly Chickens by Howard Waldrop
1982   The Quickening by Michal Bishop
1983   Fire Watch by Connie Willis
1984   Blood Music by Greg Bear
1985   Bloodchild by Octavia E Butler
1986   Portraits of His Children by George R R
        Martin
1987   The Girl Who Fell into the Sky by Kate
        Wilhelm
1988   Rachael in Love by Pat Murphy
1989   Schrodinger's Kitten by George Alec
        Effinger
1990   At the Rialto by Connie Willis
Novella
1980   Enemy Mine by Barry Longyear
1981   The Unicorn Tapestry by Suzy Mckee
        Charnas
1982   The Saturn Game by Poul Anderson
1983   Another Orphan by John Kessel
1984   Hardfought by Greg Bear
1985   Press Enter by John Varley
1986   Sailing by Byzantium by Robert Silverberg
1987   R & R by Lucius Shepard
1988   The Blind Geometer by Kim Stanley
        Robinson

1989 The Last of the Winnebagos by Connie Willis
1990 The Mountains of Mourning by Lois McMaster Bujold

Short Story
1980 Giants by Edward Bryant
1981 Grotto of the Dancing Deer by Clifford D Simak
1982 The Bone Flute by Lisa Tuttle (declined)
1983 A Letter From the Clearys by Connie Willis
1984 The Peacemaker by Gardner Dozois
1985 Morning Child by Gardner Dozois
1986 Out of All Them Bright Stars by Nancy Kress
1987 Tangents by Greg Bear
1988 Forever Yours, Anna by Kate Wilhelm
1989 Bible Stories for Adults, No 17: The Deluge by James Morrow
1990 Ripples in the Dirac Sea by Geoffrey A Landis

Neustadt International Prize for Literature
World Literature Today, 110 Monnet Hall
Univ of OK, Norman, OK 73019-0375, USA
The prize honours distinguished and outstanding achievement in fiction, poetry, or drama written in any language. Awarded only to living writers, and at least a representative sampling of the writer's work must be available in English or French. Nominations are made only by members of the international jury and the prize is not open to application.
Biennial, awarded in even-numbered years, US $25,000 plus an eagle's feather in silver and a special certificate.
Contact: Dr Djelal Kabir
1980 Josef Skvorecký
1982 Octavio Paz
1984 Paavo Haavikko
1986 Max Frisch
1988 Raja Rao
1990 Tomas Tranströmer
1992 Joao Cabral de Melo Neto
1994 Kamau Brathwaite

John Newbery Medal
American Library Association, 50 E Huron St
Chicago, IL 70711-2795, USA
To the author of the most distinguished contribution to American literature for children published during the preceding year.
Annual award: bronze medal
Contact: The Administrator
1980 A Gathering of Days by Joan W Blos
1981 Jacob Have I Loved by Katherine Paterson
1982 A Visit to William Blake's Inn: Poems for Innocent and Experienced Travellers by Nancy Willard
1983 Dicey's Song by Cynthia Voight
1984 Dear Mr Henshaw by Beverly Cleary
1985 Hero and the Crown by Robin McKinley
1986 Sarah, Plain and Tall by Patricia MacLachlan
1987 The Whipping Boy by Sid Fleischman
1988 Lincoln: A Photobiography by Russell Freedman
1989 Joyful Noise: Poems for Two Voice by Paul Fleischman

1990 Number the Stars by Lois Lowry
1991 Maniac Magee by Terry Spinelli
1992 Shiloh by Phyllis Reynolds Naylor
1993 Missing May by Cynthia Rylant
1994 The Giver by Lois Lowry

New Zealand Book Awards
Advisorcorp House, 131-135 Lambton Quay
Wellington, New Zealand
Contact: Rosemary Wildblood, Programme Manager
1988 Fiona Kidman
1989 Benzina by Cilla McQueen
Tarawera by Ronald Keam
The Carpathians by Janet Frame
The Fold of the Land by Bridget Williams

Nobel Prize for Literature
The Swedish Academy, Box 5232,
Sturegatan 14, S-10245, Stockholm, Sweden
Based on the principle of competence and universality, in the field of literature the most outstanding work of an idealistic tendency.
Prize in the region of SEKr 6,500,000 (around $1 million) - increasing each year to cover inflation.
Contact: Information Section
1980 Czeslaw Milosz
1981 Elias Canetti
1982 Gabriel Garcia Marquez
1983 William Golding
1984 Jaroslav Seifert
1985 Claude Simon
1986 Wole Soyinka
1987 Joseph Brodsky
1988 Naguib Mahfouz
1989 Camilo José Cela
1990 Octavio Paz
1991 Nadine Gordimer
1992 Derek Walcott
1993 Toni Morrison
1994 Kenzaburo Oe

Francis Parkman Prize
Society of American Historians Inc
Affiliate of Columbia University
603 Fayerweather Hall
New York, NY 10027, USA
Contact: Mark Carnes, Executive Secretary

PEN/Faulkner Award for Fiction
Folger Shakespeare Library
201 East Capitol Street, SE
Washington, DC 20003, USA
Contact: Janice Delaney, Executive Director

Edgar Allan Poe Awards
236 West 27 Street, New York
NY 10001, USA
Contact: Priscilla Ridgeway, Executive Director
Best Novel
1980 Whip Hand by Dick Francis
1981 Peregrine by William Bayer
1982 Billingsgate Shoal by Rick Boyer
1983 La Brava by Elmore Leonard
1984 Briar Patch by Ross Thomas
1985 The Suspect by L R Wright
The Day the Senior Class Got Married by

Charles Purpura (Children's live action)

1986	A Dark-Adapted Eye by Barbara Vine
1988	Old Bones by Aaron Elkins
1989	A Cold Red Sunrise by Stuart M Kaminsky
1990	Black Cherry Blues by James Lee Burke
1991	New Orleans Mourning by Julie Smith
1992	A Dance at the Slaughterhouse by Lawrance Block
1993	Bootlegger's Daughter by Margaret Maron
1994	The Sculptress by Minette Walters

Grand Master

1980	Stanley Ellin
1981	Julian Symons
1982	Margaret Millar
1983	John Le Carre
1984	Dorothy Salisbury Davis
1985	Ed McBain
1986	Michael Gilbert
1987	Phyliss A Whitney
1988	Hillary Waugh
1990	Helen McCloy
1991	Tony Hillerman
1992	Elmore Leonard
1993	Donald E Westlake
1994	Lawrence Block

Prijs Der Nederlandse Letteren (Prize for Dutch Literature)
Nederlandse Taalunie, Stadhoudersplantsoen 2
2517 JL Den Haag, Nederland
A literary prize to celebrate the entire oeuvre of a particular literary writer who writes in the Dutch language in the categories prose, poetry, essays and/or drama.
Prize of f 30,000 every three years.
Contact: Oscar de Wandel, De Algemeen Secretaris

1980	Maurice Gilliams
1983	Lucebert
1986	Hugo Claus
1989	Gerrit Kouwenaar

Prix Goncourt
Restaurant Drouant
18 Place Gaillon, 75002 Paris, France
Contact: Francois Nourissier

1980	Le Jardin d'Acclimatation by Yves Navarre
1981	Anne Marie by Lucien Bodard
1982	Dans la Main de l'Ange by Dominique Fernandez
1983	Les Egares by Frederick Tristan
1984	L'Amant by Marguerite Duras
1985	Les Noces Barbares by Yann Queffelec
1986	Valet de Nuit by Michel Host
1987	La Nuit sacrée Seuil by Tahar Ben Jelloun
1988	L'Exposition coloniale Seuil by Erik Orsenna
1989	Un grand pas vers le bon Dieu Grasset by Jean Vautrin
1990	Les Champs d'honneur by Jean Rouaud
1991	Les Filles du Calvaire by Pierre Combescot
1992	Texaco by Patrick Chamoiseau
1993	Le Rocher de Tanios by Amin Maalouf
1994	Un Aller Simple by Didier Van Caulwelaert

The Pulitzer Prizes
Columbia University
New York, NY 10027, USA

21 prizes in newspaper journalism, letters, music and drama - for some of the prizes entrants must be American citizen.
Annual prize of $3000.
Contact: The Administrator

Fiction

1980	The Executioner's Song by Norman Mailer
1981	A Confederacy of Dunces by the late John Kennedy Toole
1982	Rabbit is Rich by John Updike
1983	The Color Purple by Alice Walker
1984	Ironweed by William Kennedy
1985	Foreign Affairs by Alison Lurie
1986	Lonesome Dove by Larry McMurtry
1987	A Summons to Memphis by Peter Taylor
1988	Beloved by Toni Morrison
1989	Breathing Lessons by Anne Tyler
1990	The Mambo Kings Play Songs of Love by Oscar Hijuelos
1991	Rabbit at Rest by John Updike
1992	A Thousand Acres by Jane Smiley
1993	A Good Scent From a Strange Mountain by Robert Olen Butler
1994	The Shipping News by E Annie Proulx

Drama

1980	Talley's Folly by Lanford Wilson
1981	Crimes of the Heat by Beth Henley
1982	A Soldier's Play by Charles Fuller
1983	Night, Mother by Marsha Norman
1984	Glengarry Glen Ross by David Mamet
1985	Sunday in the Park with George by James Lapine
1986	No award
1987	Fences by August Wilson
1988	Driving Miss Daisy by Alfred Uhry
1989	The Heidi Chronicles by Wendy Wasserstein
1990	The Piano Lesson by August Wilson
1991	Lost in Yonkers by Neil Simon
1992	The Kentucky Cycle by Robert Schenkkan
1993	Angels in America by Tony Kushner
1994	Three Tall Women by Edward Albee

History

1980	Been in the Storm So Long by Leon F Litwack
1981	American Education: The National Experience, 1783-1876 by Lawrence A Cremin
1982	Mary Chesnut's Civil War by C Vann Woodward (editor)
1983	The Transformation of Virginia, 1740-1790 by Rhys L Isaac
1984	No award
1985	Prophets of Regulation by Thomas K McCraw
1986	...The Heavens and the Earth: A Political History of the Space Age by Walter A McDougall
1987	Voyagers to the West: A Passage in the Peopling of America on the Eve of the Revolution by Bernard Bailyn
1988	The Launching of Modern American Science 1849-1876 by Robert V Bruce
1989	Parting the Waters: America in the King Years 1954-63 by Taylor Branch
1990	In Our Image: America's Empire in the

Philippines by Stanley Karnow
1991 A Midwife's Tale: The Life of Martha Ballard, Based on Her Diary, 1785-1812 by Laurel Thatcher Urich
1992 The Fate of Liberty: Abraham Lincoln and Civil Rights by Mark E Neely Jr
1993 The Radicalism of the American Revolution by Gordon S Wood

Biography
1980 The Rise of Theodore Roosevelt by Edmund Morris
1981 Peter the Great: His Life and World by Robert K Massie
1982 Grant: A Biography by William S McFeely
1983 Growing Up by Russell Baker
1984 Booker T Washington: The Wizard of Tuskegee, 1901-1915 by Louis R Harlan
1985 The Life and Times of Cotton Mather by Kenneth Silverman
1986 Louise Bogan: A Portrait by Elizabeth Frank
1987 Bearing the Cross: Martin Luther King Jr and the Southern Christian Leadership Conference by David J Garrow
1988 Look Homeward: A Life of Thomas Wolfe by David Herbert Donald
1989 Oscar Wilde by the late Richard Ellmann
1990 Machiavelli in Hell by Sebastian de Grazia
1991 Jackson Pollock: An American Saga by Steven Naifeh and Gregory White Smith
1992 Fortunate Son: The Healing of a Vietnam Vet by Lewis B Puller Jr
1993 Truman by David McCullough
1994 W E B Dubois: Biography of a Race, 1868-1919 by David Levering Lewis

Poetry
1980 Selected Poems by Donald Justice
1981 The Morning of the Poem by James Schuyler
1982 The Collected Poems by the late Sylvia Plath
1983 Selected Poems by Galway Kinnell
1984 American Primitive by Mary Oliver
1985 Yin by Carolyn Kizer
1986 The Flying Change by Henry Taylor
1987 Thomas and Beulah by Rita Dove
1988 Partial Accounts: New and Selected Poems by William Meredith
1989 New and Collected Poems by Richard Wilbur
1990 The World Doesn't End by Charles Simic
1991 Near Changes by Mona Van Duyn
1992 Selected Poems by James Tate
1993 The Wild Iris by Louise Gluck
1994 Neon Vernacular by Yusef Komungakaa

General Non-fiction
1980 Gödel, Escher, Bach: an Eternal Golden Braid by Douglas R Hofstadter
1981 Fin-de-Siècle Vienna: Politics and Culture by Carl E Schorske
1982 The Soul of A New Machine by Tracy Kidder
1983 Is There No Place on Earth for Me by Susan Sheehan
1984 The Social Transformation of American

Medicine by Paul Starr
1985 The Good War: An Oral History of World War Two by Stods Terkel
1986 Move Your Shadow: South Africa, Black and White by Joseph Lelyveld
Common Ground: A Turbulent Decade in the Lives of Three American Families by J Anthony Lukas
1987 Arab and Jew: Wounded Spirits in a Promised Land by David K Shipler
1988 The Making of the Atomic Bomb by Richard Rhodes
1989 A Bright Shining Lie: John Paul Vann America in Vietnam by Neil Sheehan
1990 And Their Children After Them by Dale Maharidge
1991 The Ants by Bert Holldobler and Edward O Wilson
1992 The Prize: The Epic Quest for Oil, Money and Power by Daniel Yergin
1993 Lincoln at Gettysburg by Gary Wills
1994 Lenin's Tomb: Last Days of the Soviet Empire by David Remnick

Pushcart Prize: Best of the Small Presses
Pushcart Press, Box 380
Wainscott, NY 11975, USA
Contact: Bill Henderson, President

The Queen's Presentation Medals - Poetry
Buckingham Palace
London, England
The Medal is given for a book of verse published in the English Language, but translations of exceptional merit may be considered. It was originally awarded only to British citizens but the scope was widened in 1985 to make Her Majesty's subjects in Commonwealth Monarchies eligible for consideration.
Awarded Gold Medal.
1981 Dennis Joseph Enwright
1985 Norman MacCaig
1988 Derek Walcott
1989 Allen Curnow
1990 Sorley Maclean

The Rhea Award for the Short Story
Dungannon Foundation, 131 East 66th Street
New York, NY 10021, USA
Contact: Lisl Cade

The Romantic Novelists' Association
RNA, 35 Ruddlesway, Windsor
Berks SL4 5SF, England
Prize of £5000
Contact: Dorothy Entwistle, Secretary
1982 Zemindar by Valerie Fitzgerald
Flint and Roses by Brenda Jagger
The Unreasoning Earth by Jean Chapman
A Countess Below Stairs by Eva Ibbotson
Emma Sparrow by Marie Joseph
Mango Walk by Rhona Martin
The Black Mountains by Janet Tanner
The Avonhurst Inheritance by Sylvia Thorpe
1983 Magic Flutes by Eva Ibbotson
Gemini Girls by Marie Joseph
Antigua Kiss by Anne Weale

Celebration by Rosie Thomas
Rose Domino by Sheila Walsh
The Ravensley Touch by Constance Heaven

1984 A Highly Respectable Marriage
Margaret Normanby by Josephine Edgar
Copper Kingdom by Iris Gower
A London Season by Anthea Bell
A Heritage of Shadows by Madeleine Brent
The Silver Falcon by Sarah Hylton
The Listening Silence by Marie Joseph

1985 Sunrise by Rosie Thomas
A Winter's Child by Brenda Jagger
Silk for a Lady by Rosina Pyatt
A Fragile Peace by Teresa Crane
The Merry Maid by Mollie Hardwick
What the Heart Keeps by Rosalind Laker
At the Going Down of the Sun by Elizabeth Darrell

1986 A Song Twice Over by Brenda Jagger
Kessie by Joyce Marlow
This Side of Christmas by Louise Elliott
Company of Swans by Eva Ibbotson
Here I Stay by Barbara Michaels
Silver Shadows, Golden Dreams by Margaret Pemberton
Rachael and the Viscount by Alanna Wilson

1987 A Better World Than This by Marie Joseph
Just You Wait and See by Stan Barstow
And in the Morning by Elizabeth Darrell
Lady of Hay by Barbara Erskine
The Lushai Girl by Roberta Forrest
Tree of Gold by Rosalind Laker
Jessica by Connie Monk

1988 The Juniper Bush by Audrey Howard
Destiny by Sally Beauman
The Lodestar by Pamela Belle
Distinctions of Class by Anita Burgh
The Raging Fire by Constance Heaven
The Silver Touch by Rosalind Laker
As It Was In the Beginning by Madeleine Pollard

1989 The Peacock's Feather by Sarah Woodhouse
Daughters of the Storm by Elizabeth Buchan
Dance of the Peacocks by Elizabeth de Guise
Spring Imperial by Evelyn Hart
The Shell Seekers by Rosamund Pilcher
The Pink Stallion by Lucy Pinney

1990 Passing Glory by Reay Tannahill
1991 Phantom by Susan Kay
1992 Sandstorm by June Knox-Mawer
1993 Emily by Cynthia Harrod-Eagles
1994 Consider the Lily by Elizabeth Buchan

Royal Society of Literature Award Under the W H Heinemann Bequest
Royal Society of Literature
1 Hyde Park Gardens, London W2 2LT, England
Awards given for any kind of literature by living authors
Prize: £5000 (under review)
Contact: The Secretary
1979   The Older Hardy by Robert Gittings
Live Bait by Frank Tuohy

1980 Beckford of Fonthill by Brian Fothergill
Moortown by Ted Hughes
1981 The Unquiet Heart by Robert Martin Tennyson
Seeing the World by Dick Davis
1982 Harold Nicolson: A Biography by James Leigh Milne
Old Glory by Jonathan Raban
1983 The Fortunate Traveller by Derek Walcott
1984 Eleeni by Nicholas Gage
1985 Secrets of a Woman's Life: The Latter Life of Ivy Compton-Burnett by Hilary Spurling
T S Eliot by Peter Ackroyd
1986 The Black Robe by Brian Moore
1987 The Blind Watchmaker by Richard Dawkins
1988 The Russian Album by Michael Ignatieff
1989 Elizabeth Barrett Browning by Margaret Forster
1990 Ford Madox by Alan Judd
1991 Available for Dreams by Roy Fuller
Short Afternoons by Kit Wright
1992 Goethe: The Spirit and the Age by Nicholas Boyle
1993 Shylock by John Gross
1994 The Civilisation of Europe in the Renaissance by John Hale

Sagittarius Prize
Society of Authors
84 Drayton Gardens, London SW10 9SB, England
Awarded for first published novels by authors over the age of 60.
Prize: £2000.
Contact: The Administrator.
1991 The Sea Has Many Voices by Judith Hubback
1992 Parnell and the English by Hugh Leonard
1993 The Strange Case of Mademoiselle P by Brian O'Doherty
1994 Red Branch by G B Hummer

Science Book Prizes
COPUS, c/o The Royal Society
6 Carlton House Terrace, London SW1Y 5AG, England
Awarded to the authors of the popular non-fiction, science and technology books, written in English and published during 1990, which are judged to contribute most to the public understanding of science.
Prize: Rhône-Poulence Prize £10,000; Science Book Junior Prize £10,000 (shared)
Contact: Jill A Nelson.
1988 Living With Risk by the British Medical Association Board of Science
1989 Bones of Contention by Roger Lewin
1990 The Emperor's New Mind by Roger Penrose
1991 Wonderful Life by Stephen Jay Gould
Cells are Us by Fran Balkwill & Mic Rolph
Cell Wars by Fran Balkwill & Mic Rolph
1992 The Rise and Fall of the Third Chimpanzee by Jared Diamond
The Amazing Voyage of the Cucumber Sandwich by Peter Rowan
How Nature Works by David Burnie

1993 The Making of Memory by Steven Rose
Mighty Microbes by Thompson Yardley
1994 The Language of the Genes by Steve Jones
Eyewitness Guide: Evolution by Linda
Gamlin
Science with Weather by Rebecca Heddle
& Paul Shipton
The Ultimate Dinosaur Book by David
Lambert

Smarties Prize for Children's Books
Book Trust, Book House
45 East Hill, London Sw18 2QZ, England
Award given for a children's book written in English
by a citizen of the UK, or an author resident in the
UK, and published in the UK in the year ending 31
October.
Annual prize for overall winner, £8000; £2000 other
catagories.
Contact: Caroline Sanderson
1985 *Over 7's category winner*
Gaffer Samson's Luck by Jill Paton Walsh
Under 7's category
It's Your Turn Roger! by Susanna Gretz
Innovation category
Watch It Work! The Plane by Ray Marshall
and John Bradley
1986 *7-11 years category and overall winner*
The Snow Spider by Jenny Nimmo
6 years and under category
The Goose That Laid the Golden Egg by
Geoffrey Patterson
Innovation category
The Mirrorstone by Michael Palin, Alan Lee
and Richard Seymour
Village Heritage by Miss Pinnell and the
children of Sapperton School
1987 *9-11 years category and overall winner*
A Thief in the Village by James Berry
6-8 years category
Tangle and the Firesticks by Benedict
Blathwayt
Under 5 years category
The Angel and the Soldier Boy by Peter
Collington
1988 *0-5 years category and overall winner*
Can't You Sleep, Little Bear? by Martin
Waddell
6-8 years category
Can It Be True? by Susan Hill
9-11 category
Rushavenn Time by Theresa Whistler &
Brixworth Primary School
1989 *0-5 years category and overall winner*
We're Going on a Bear Hunt by Michael
Rosen
6-8 years category
Bill's New Frock by Anne Fine
9-11 years category
Blitzcat by Robert Westall
1990 *9-11 years category and overall winner*
Midnight Blue by Pauline Fisk
6-8 years category
Esio Trot by Roald Dahl
0-5 years category

Six Dinner Sid by Inga Moore
1991 *0-5 years category and overall winner*
Farmer Duck by Martin Waddell and Helen
Oxonbury
9-11 years category
Krindle Krax by Philip Ridley
6-8 years category
Josie Smith and Eileen by Magdaline Nabb
1992 *9-11 years category and overall winner*
The Great Elephant Chase by Gillian Cross
6-8 years category
The Story of Creation by Jane Ray
0-5 years category
Nice Work Little Wolf by Hilda Offen
1993 *6-8 years category and overall winner*
War Game by Michael Foreman
9-11 years category
Listen to the Dark by Maeve Henry
0-5 years category
Hue Boy by Rita Phillips Mitchell
1994 *9-11 years category and overall winner*
The Exiles at Home by Hilary McKay
6-8 years category
Dimanche Diller by Henrietta Branford
0-5 years category
So Much by Trish Cooke and Helen
Oxonbury

W H Smith Literary Award
Strand House, 7 Holbein Place
London SW1W 8NR, England
Presented for outstanding contribution to English
literature in the year under review, to the author of
a book written originally in English and published in
the UK. Authors considered will be from the
Commonwealth and Republic of Ireland.
Annual award £10,000
Contact: Michale MacKenzie.
1980 Selected Poems 1950-1975 by Thom Gunn
1981 The Shooting Party by Isabel Colegate
1982 Last Waltz in Vienna by George Clare
1983 Wise Virgin by A N Wilson
1984 Required Writing (Miscellaneous Pieces
1955-62) by Philip Larkin
1985 The Pork Butcher by David Hughes
1986 The Good Terrorist by Doris Lessing
1987 Collected Poems 1953-85 by Elizabeth
Jennings
1988 The Fatal Shore by Robert Hughes
1989 A Turbulent, Seditious and Factious People:
John Bunyan and his Church (A
Biography) by Christopher Hill
1990 A Careless Widow and Other Stories by Sir
Victor Pritchett
1991 Omeros by Derek Walcott
1992 The Scramble for Africa by Thomas
Pakenham
1993 Daughters of the House by Michèle Roberts
1994 A Suitable Boy by Vikram Seth

South African Sunday Times Alan Paton Award
1992 The Scramble for Africa by Thomas
Pakenham

Sunday Express Book of the Year Award
Ludgate House, 245 Blackfriars Road
London SE1 9UX

Prize awarded annually for the most stylish, literate and also the most readable work of fiction first published in Britain.
Prize: £20,000
1987   The Colour of Blood by Brian Moore
1988   Nice Work by David Lodge
1989   Restoration by Rose Tremain
1990   Age of Iron by J M Coetzee
1991   Landing on the Sun by Michael Frayn
1992   A Place of Greater Safety by Hilary Mantel
1993   The Blue Afternoon by William Boyd
1994   Felicia's Journey by William Trevor

Tom-Gallon Award
Society of Authors
84 Drayton Gardens, London SW10 9SB, England
A biennial award for writers of limited means who have had at least one short story published.
Prize: £500.
1984   The Egg Man by Janni Howker
1986   The House of Funerals by Laurence Scott
1988   Taking Doreen Out of the Sky by Alan Beard
1990   Sister Monica's Last Journey by Richard Austin
1992   Reading the Signals by David Callard

Translators Association Translation Prizes
The Translator's Association
84 Drayton Gardens, London SW10 9SB, England
The John Florio Prize (Italian-English)
1989   Patrick Creagh for his translation fo Danube by Claudio Magris
The Scott Moncrieff Prize (French-English)
1989   Derek Mahon for his translation of The Selected Poems of Phillippe Jacottet
1990   John and Beryl Fletcher for their translation of The Georgics by Claude Simon
1991   Brian Pearce for his translation of Bread and Circuses by Paul Veyne
1992   Barbara Wright for her translation of The Midnight Love Feast by Michel Tournier
        James Kirkup for his translation of Painted Shadows by Jean-Baptiste Niel
The Portuguese Translation Prize (Portuguese-English)
1992   (Inaugral Year) Margaret Jull Costa for her translation of The Book of Disquiet by Fernando Pesoa
        Nicholas Round for his translation of Frei Luis de Sousa by Almeida Garrett
The Schlegel-Tieck Prize (German-English)
Prize: £2200.
Contact: Kate Pool
1989   Peter Tegel for his translation of The Snake Tree by Uwe Timm
        Quintin Hoare for his translation of The Town Park and Other Stories by Herman Grab
1990   David McLintock for his translation of Women in a River Landscape by Heinrich Böll
1991   John Woods for his translation of The Last World by Christoph Ransmayr
        Hugh Young for his translation of The Story

of the Last Thought by Edgar Hilsenrath
1992   Geoffrey Skelton for his translation of Training Ground by Seigfried Lenz
1993   Michael Hofman for his translation of Death in Rome by Wolfgang Koeppen
        John Brownjohn for his translation of The Swedish Cavlier by Leo Perutz
1994   Krishna Winston for his translation of Goebbels by Ralf Georg Reuth
The Bernard Shaw Translation Prize (Swedish-English)
Contact: Kate Pool
1991   (Inaugral Year) Tom Geddes for his translation of The Way of a Serpent by Torgny Lindgren

Betty Trask Awards
The Society of Authors, 84 Drayton Gardens London SW10 9SB, England
Awards are for authors under 35 and commonwealth citizens for a first novel of a traditional or romantic nature.
Annual prize of £25,000 (shared)
1984   Winter Journey by Ronald Frame
        Cold Showers by Clare Nonhebel
        A Parish of Rich Women by James Buchan
        Playing Fields in Winter by Helen Harris
        The Disinherited by Gareth Jones
        The Devil's Looking Glass by Simon Rees
1985   Legacy by Susan Kay
        A Season of Peace by Gary Armitage
        A Very Private Enterprise by Elizabeth Ironside
        Instead of Eden by Alice Mitchell
        The Standing Hills by Caroline Stickland
        The Earth Abides Forever by George Schweiz
1986   Tongues of Flame by Tim Parks
        Family Myths and Legends by Patricia Ferguson
        Mzungu's Wife by Philippa Blake
        Whore Banquets by Matthew Kneale
        The Road to Dilmun by J F McLaughlin
        The Prodigal Father by Kate Saunders
1987   Hard Luck by James Maw
        The Levels by Peter Benson
        Return Journey by Helen Flint
        Lost Time by Catherine Arnold
        Gestures by H S Bhabra
        The Pink Stallion by Lucy Pinney
1988   The General Interruptor by Alex Martin
        A Case of Knives by Candia McWilliam
        Behind the Waterfall by Georgina Andrewes
        Left of North by James Friel
        Burning Your Own by Glenn Patterson
        Small Tales of a Town by Susan Webster
1989   The Life Game by Nigel Watts
        Watercolour Sky by William Riviere
        Harry's Last Wedding by Paul Houghton
        Uncle Harry's Last Stand by Alasdair McKee
1990   Ripley Bogle by Robert McLiam Wilson
        The Wild Hunt by Elizabeth Chadwick
        No Strange Land by Rosemary Cohen
        The Vision of Elena Silves by Nicholas Shakespeare

1991	A Strange and Sublime Address by Amit Chaudhuri
	Teaching Little Fang by Mark Swallow
	Quite Contrary by Suzannah Dunn
	Honour Thy Father by Lesley Glaister
	Lives of the Saints by Nino Ricci
1992	The Dream Stone by Liane Jones
	Kissing Through a Pane of Glass by Peter M Rosenberg
	Under the Frog by Tibor Fisher
	The Last of His Line by Eugene Mullen
	Never Mind by Edward St Aubyn
1993	You'll Never Be Here Again by Mark Blackaby
	Pig Unpublished by Andres Cowan
	Tommy Was Here by Simon Corrigan
	Mothers and Other Lovers by Joanna Briscoe

The Travelling Scholarship Fund
The Society of Authors
84 Drayton Gardens, London SW10 9SB, England
Non-competitive awards enabling British writers to travel abroad

1988	Sybille Bedford
	David Harsent
	Barry Hines
	Nicholas Wollaston
1989	Roy Heath
	Adrian Mitchell
	Elizabeth North
1990	David Caute
	Roy Fisher
	David Hughes
	Robert Nye
1991	Anne Devlin
	Elaine Feinstein
	Iain Sinclair
	Emma Tennant

Whitbread Book of the Year
Booksellers Association, Minster House,
272 Vauxhall Bridge Road
London SW1V 1BA, England
To promote and increase good English literature in each of the separate categories.
Prize: £20,500 (Book of the Year); £2000 (all nominees).
Contact: Corinne Gotch.

Novels

1980	How Far Can You Go? by David Lodge
1981	Silver's City by Maurice Leitch
1982	Young Shoulders by John Wain
1983	Fools of Fortune by William Trevor
1984	Kruger's Alp by Christopher Hope
1985	Hawksmoor by Peter Ackroyd
1986	An Artist of the Floating World by Kazuo Ishiguro
1987	The Child in Time by Ian McEwan
1988	The Satanic Verses by Salman Rushdie
1989	The Chymical Wedding by Lindsay Clarke
1990	Hopeful Monsters by Nicholas Mosley (and Book of the Year)
1991	The Queen of Tambourine by Jane Gardam
1992	Poor Things by Alisdair Gray
1993	Theory of War by Joan Brady (and Book of the Year)

1994	Felicia's Journey by William Trevor (and Book of the Year)

Biography

1980	On the Edge of Paradise: A C Benson the Diarist by David Newsome
1981	Monty: The Making of a General by Nigel Hamilton
1982	Bismarck by Edward Crankshaw
1983	Vita by Victoria Glendinning
	King George V by Kenneth Rose
1984	T S Eliot by Peter Ackroyd
1985	Hugh Dalton by Pen Pimlott
1986	Gilbert White by Richard Mabey
1987	Under the Eye of the Clock by Christopher Nolan (and Book of the Year)
1988	Tolstoy by A N Wilson
1989	Coleridge: Early Visions by Richard Holmes (and Book of the Year)
1990	A A Milne: His Life by Ann Thwaite
1991	A Life of Picasso by John Richardson (and Book of the Year)
1992	Trollope by Victoria Glendinning
1993	Philip Larkin by Andrew Motion
1994	The Married Man: A Life of D H Lawrence by Brenda Maddox

Children's Novel

1980	John Diamond by Leon Garfield
1981	The Hollow Land by Jane Gardam
1982	The Song of Pentecost by W J Corbett
1983	The Witches by Roald Dahl
1984	The Queen of the Pharisees' Children by Barbara Willard
1985	The Nature of the Beast by Janni Howker
1986	The Coal House by Andrew Taylor
1987	A Little Lower Than the Angels by Geraldine McCaughrean
1988	Awaiting Developments by Judy Allen
1989	Why Weeps the Brogan? by Hugh Scott
1990	AK by Peter Dickinson
1991	Harvey Angell by Diana Hendry
1992	The Great Elephant Chase by Gillian Cross (and Book of the Year)
1993	Flour babies by Anne Fine
1994	Gold Dust by Geraldine McCaughrean

First Novel

1981	A Good Man In Africa by William Boyd
1982	On the Black Hill by Bruce Chatwin
1983	Flying to Nowhere by John Fuller
1984	A Parish of Rich Women by James Buchan
1985	Oranges Are Not The Only Fruit by Jeanette Winterson
1986	Continent by Jim Crace
1987	The Other Garden by Francis Wyndham
1988	The Comforts of Madness by Paul Sayer (and Book of the Year)
1989	Gerontius by James Hamilton Paterson
1990	The Buddha of Suburbia by Hanif Kureishi
1991	Alma Cogan by Gordon Burn
1992	Swing Hammer Swing! by Jeff Torrington
1993	Saving Agnes by Rachel Cusk
1994	The Longest Memory by Fred D'Aguiar

Short Story

1984	Tomorrow is our Permanent Address by Diane Rowe

Poetry

1985	Elegies by Douglas Dunn (and Book of the Year)

1986	Stet by Peter Reading
1987	The Haw Lantern by Seamus Heaney
1988	The Automatic Oracle by Peter Porter
1989	Shibboleth by Michael Donaghy
1990	Daddy, Daddy by Paul Durcan
1991	Gorse Fires by Michael Longley
1992	The Gaze of the Gorgon by Tony Harrison
1993	Mean Time by Carol Ann Duffy
1994	Out of Danger by James Fenton

Whiting Writers' Awards
Mrs Giles Whiting Foundation
1133 Avenue of the Americas
New York, NY 10003, USA
Award to emergent writers in recognition of their writing achievement as well as promise for producing outstanding future work.
Annual award of $30,000
Contact: Mrs Kellye Rosenheim, Assistant Director
Fiction

1985	Raymond Abbott
	Stuart Dybeck
	Wright Morris
	Howard Norman
	James Robison
	Austin Wright
1986	Kent Haruf
	Denis Johnson
	Darryl Pinckney
	Padgett Powell
	Mona Simpson
1987	Joan Chase
	Pam Durban
	Deborah Eisenberg
	Alice McDermott
	David Foster Wallace
1988	Lydia Davis
	Bruce Duffy
	Jonathan Franzen
	Mary La Chapelle
	William T Vollmann
1989	Ellen Akins
	Marianne Wiggins
	Tobias Wolff
1990	Yannick Murphy
	Lawrence Naumoff
	Mark Richard
	Christopher Tilghman
	Stephen Wright
1991	Rebecca Goldstein
	Allegra Goodman
	John Holman
	Cynthia Kadohata
	Rick Rofihe
	Anton Shammas
1992	R S Jones
	J S Marcus
	Damien Wilkins
1993	Jeffrey Eugenides
	Dagoberto Gilb
	Sigrid Nunez
	Janest Peery
	Lisa Shea
1994	Louise Edwards
	Randall Kenan
	Kate Wheeler

Poetry

1985	Douglas Crase
	Jorie Graham
	Linda Gregg
	James Schuyler
1986	John Ash
	Hayden Carruth
	Frank Stewart
	Ruth Stone
1987	Mark Cox
	Michael Ryan
1988	Michale Burkard
	Sylvia Moss
1989	Russell Edson
	Mary Karr
	C D Wright
1990	Emily Hiestand
	Dennis Nurkse
1991	Thylias Moss
	Franz Wright
1992	Jane Mead
	Roger Fanning
1993	Mark Levine
	Nathaniel Mackey
	Dionisio D Martinez
	Kathleen Pierce
1994	Mark Doty
	Wayne Koestenbaum
	Mary Swander

Non-fiction

1985	Wright Morris
	Austin Wright
1986	Darryl Pinckney
1987	Mindy Aloff
	Gretel Ehrlich
1988	Gerald Early
	Geoffrey O'Brien
1989	Ian Frazier
	Natalie Kusz
	Luc Sante
1990	Harriet Ritvo
	Amy Wilentz
1991	Stanley Crouch
	Anton Shammas
1992	Eva Hoffman
	Katha Pollitt
1993	No Award
1994	Kennedy Fraser
	Rosemary Mahoney
	Claudia Roth Pierpont

Plays

1986	August Wilson
1987	Reinaldo Povod
1989	Timberlake Wertenbaker
1990	Tony Kushner
1991	Scott McPherson
1992	Suzan-Lori Parks
	Keith Reddin
	Jose Rivera
1993	Kevin Kling

Writer's Guild/McCallan Awards
The Writers Guild of Great Britain
430 Edgware Road, London W2 1EH, England
Contact: Alison Gray, General Secretary
Fiction

1991	The Inn at the Edge of the World by Alice Thomas Ellis

1992	Persistent Rumours by Lee Langley
1993	Time and Tide by Edna O'Brien
1994	How Late It Was, How Late by James Kelman

Non-fiction
1991	Jean Rhys: Life and Work by Carole Angier
1992	Wild Swans by Jung Chang
1993	Daphne du Maurier by Margaret Forster
1994	Genet by Edmund White

Children's Book
1991	Haroun and the Sea of Stories by Salman Rushdie
1992	The Secret Summer of Daniel Lyons by Roy Apps
1993	Johnny and the Dead by Terry Pratchett
1994	The Frozen Waterfall by Gayle Hicyilmaz

Yorkshire Post Awards
Yorkshire Post Newspapers Ltd, PO Box 168, Wellington St, Leeds LS1 1RF, England
Awarded to a work of fiction of non-fiction published in the UK in the year preceding the prize by a British of UK resident writer. Publisher entry only - up to four books may be submitted by any one publisher. Prize: £1000.

Book of the Year
1980	George Orwell - A Life by Bernard Crick
1981	Venice: The Greatness and the Fall by J J Norwich
1982	Clinging to the Wreckage by John Mortimer
1983	Battle for the Falklands by Max Hastings & Simon Jenkins
1984	Overlord: The Battle for Normandy by Max Hastings
1985	The Right of the Line by John Terraine
1986	James Anthony Eden by Robert Rhodes
1987	1914 by Lyn Macdonald
1988	The Silence in the Garden by William Trevor
1989	Citizens by Simon Schama
1990	Anthony Trollope: A Victorian in his World by Richard Mullen
1991	Engage the Enemy More Closely by Corelli Barnett
1992	Shylock by John Gross
1993	Franco by Paul Preston

Finest Fiction Work
1980	Earthly Powers by Anthony Burgess
1981	The Mosquito Coast by Paul Theroux
1982	Getting it Right by Elizabeth Jane Howard
1983	Act of Darkness by Francis King
1984	Stanley and the Women by Kingsley Amis
1985	Unexplained Laughter by Alice Thomas

Best First Work
1980	The Victorians and Ancient Greece by Richard Jenkyns
1981	Churchill and De Gaulle by Francois Kersaudy
1982	Alanbrooke by David Fraser
1983	Montgomery in Europe 1943-45 by Richard Lamb
1984	Eric Linklater: A Critical Biography by Michael Parnell
1985	Pictures From The Water Trade by John David Morley
1986	Duff Cooper by John Charmley
1987	The Cartomancer by Anne Spillard

1988	The Blindfold Horse by Susha Guppy
1989	In Xanadu by William Dalrymple
1990	Epics of Everyday Life by Susan Richards
1991	Forgotten Land by Harriet O'Brien
1992	Stalin's Nose by Rory McLean
1993	The Language of the Genes by Dr Steve Jones